O9-CFT-232

A SUPPLEMENT TO THE

OXFORD ENGLISH DICTIONARY

A SUPPLEMENT TO THE
OXFORD ENGLISH DICTIONARY

EDITED BY
R. W. BURCHFIELD

VOLUME IV · Se–Z

OXFORD
AT THE CLARENDON PRESS
1986

Oxford University Press, Walton Street, Oxford OX2 6DP
Oxford New York Toronto
Delhi Bombay Calcutta Madras Karachi
Kuala Lumpur Singapore Hong Kong Tokyo
Nairobi Dar es Salaam Cape Town
Melbourne Auckland
and associated companies in
Beirut Berlin Ibadan Nicosia

Oxford is a trade mark of Oxford University Press

Published in the United States
by Oxford University Press, New York

British Library Cataloguing in Publication Data
A supplement to the Oxford English dictionary.
Vol. 4: Se–Z
1. English language—Dictionaries
I. Burchfield, Robert W. II. Oxford English Dictionary
423 PE1625
ISBN 0–19–861136–6

Library of Congress Cataloging in Publication Data
(Revised for vol. 2)
Main entry under title:
A Supplement to the Oxford English dictionary.
1. English language—Dictionaries. I. Burchfield, R. W.
II. Oxford English dictionary.
PE1625.N53 1933 Suppl. 423 82–6411
ISBN 0–19–861115–3 (v. 1)

Typesetting by Latimer Trend & Company Ltd.
Printed in Great Britain by
Thomson Litho Ltd., East Kilbride
and bound at the University Press, Oxford

This Supplement to the Oxford English Dictionary

is respectfully dedicated to

HER MAJESTY THE QUEEN

by her gracious permission

PREFACE

1. *Volume 4* (OEDS 4)

WHEN Miss Marghanita Laski read the galley-proofs of the entry for *off* in Volume 3 of this Supplement she remarked, 'I am almost completely flummoxed by this, and must ask your indulgence on it'. Professor Audrey Duckert, another of our regular contributors, independently remarked, 'I'm glad I didn't have to write *off* for OED, but I'll never write OED *off*'. *Off* was a complex entry, or set of entries, both in the *OED* and in OEDS 3, and the same is necessarily true of a good many entries in this final volume—those for *un-* (prefix) and *up* (various parts of speech), for example. Our language is a complicated mechanism at the best of times, and sometimes almost frighteningly so when presented in its largest dimension as in the following pages.

But not all of the elements of the English language are complex. Many of the expressions that appear in this final volume merely illustrate the concepts, inventions, and movements of our generation—words of very recent origin (1984) like *yumpie* and *yuppie*, and somewhat older expressions like *self-fulfilling prophecy*, *sputnik*, and *test-tube baby*. We are all in an electronic environment, and the entries for such words as *SNOBOL*, *transputer*, and *wysiwyg* draw attention both to the ingenuity of the world of the green screen and to the manner in which its practitioners embrace the techniques of present-day word-formation.

Every effort has been made to keep up with the language as it developed even while the final volume of the Supplement was being prepared. *The Growing Pains of Adrian Mole* (1984) is quoted under *yoyo*, for example, and there are numerous examples from 1985 sources in the later letters of the alphabet in this volume.

As in earlier volumes no effort has been spared to verify details of the coinage, meaning, or other aspects of each word entered in the Supplement. The Bodleian Library, the British Library, and the Library of Congress, in particular, have probably never experienced such a systematic combing of their resources as has been necessary for the preparation of the four volumes of OEDS. We owe an incalculable debt to the custodians of these libraries, and also to many other specialized libraries in Britain and abroad, for their cooperation. We are also deeply indebted to numerous scholars and men of letters who have over the years assisted us with the definition or the circumstances of origin of expressions they have coined themselves, e.g. *acceptance world* (Anthony Powell), *drogulus* (A. J. Ayer), *dymaxion* (Buckminster Fuller), *hobbit* (J. R. R. Tolkien), *jog* sb.[2] sense 3 (N. F. Mott), *non-event* (I. Gilmour MP), *psephology* (R. B. McCallum), *quark* (M. Gell-Mann), *tracklement* (D. Hartley), and *tribology* (C. G. Hardie). Part of the pleasure and the value of historical lexicography lies in the establishing of the circumstances of a coinage from the coiner himself.

* * *

Sadly the need arises once more to set down the names of people associated with the Supplement who have not survived to see the publication of this final volume: Professor A. J. Bliss, Professor S. Deas, Dr N. R. Ker, John Lyman, Professor Raven I. McDavid Jr., Professor Mitford M. Mathews, Peter Opie, Professor Dr László Országh (Hungary), Professor Dr. I. Poldauf (Czechoslovakia), Professor I. Willis Russell, and Peter Tamony.

Major contributors of quotations in the period 1982–5 included the following: G. Charters (Australia), G. Chowdharay-Best, G. A. Coulson, F. D. Hayes, Miss M. Laski, Sir E. Playfair, and F. R. Shapiro. The product of their work is to be seen on virtually every page of this volume.

The outside proof-readers, who systematically scrutinized sets of galley-proofs and submitted their comments and criticisms during the preparation of Volume IV, were Professor A. R. Duckert, M. W. Grose, T. F. Hoad, Mrs D. D. Honoré, Miss M. Laski, Professor E. G. Stanley, and Mrs H. C. Wright. The volume would have been much the poorer without their expert attention.

The outside consultants to whom we have turned for advice on particular words while the volume was being prepared were: Dr G. E. H. Abraham, Dr G. C. Ainsworth, Professor A. J. Aitken, A. D. Alderson, R. E. Allen, Dr P. W. Atkins, A. J. Augarde, Professor J. R. Baines, †Professor A. J. Bliss, Dr. S. Bradbury, Dr J. Branford, Dr W. H. Brock, Sir A. K. Cairncross, Dr B. G. Campbell, Professor F. G. Cassidy, Dr P. A. Charles, M. J. E. Coode, Dr J. Cortés, Professor G. N. C. Crawford, Mrs U. Dronke, †Professor S. Deas, Dr B. J. Freedman, R. B. Freeman, W. K. V. Gale, P. G. W. Glare, Dr I. Goddard, Dr G. H. Gonnet, P. S. Green, R. Hall, R. E. Hawkins, M. T. Heydeman, Dr D. M. Jackson, P. Jarrett, Dr Russell Jones, Dr D. Julier, Dr W. J. Kirwin, Professor K. Koike, Professor J. D. Latham, Professor J. Leech, Professor B. Lennox, Dr G. Lewis, R. P. W. Lewis, Dr A. Loveless, Dr D. J. Mabberley, Dr R. S. McGregor, Professor J. B. McMillan, Dr T. Magay, Dr L. V. Malakhovski, Dr F. H. C. Marriott, R. D. Meikle, Professor G. Milner, D. D. Murison, Mrs I. Opie, M. B. Parkes, Miss V. Richardson, Professor R. H. Robins, Dr H. M. Rosenberg, Professor J. M. Rosenberg, Professor N. G. Sabbagha, R. Scruton, A. J. Stevens, Dr I. N. Stewart, Dr J. B. Sykes, Associate Professor Tao Jie, Miss D. J. Thompson, Professor G. Treitel, G. W. Turner, J. O. Urmson, Professor T. G. Vallance, Professor R. L. Venezky, Dr M. Weitzman, the Revd Canon Professor M. F. Wiles, and Dr D. Zorc.

This fourth volume contains about 13,500 Main Words divided into some 25,000 senses. There are about 11,000 defined Combinations within the articles and a similar number of undefined Combinations. The illustrative quotations are estimated to number 130,000.

It is appropriate to mention here that the printing of this final volume marks the end of an era in the printing trade. I believe that it may be the last major book to be set up in type by the hot-metal process. The printing house concerned, Latimer Trend of Plymouth, nobly retained its hot-metal department until the entry for *Zyrian* was safely in type.

I should like to take this last opportunity to thank various people: first and foremost, the Delegates of The Oxford University Press, and their senior officers, for allowing this ambitious and very costly project to take its course; all members of my staff since 1957 for their skilled and determined assistance as a seemingly endless procession of problems presented themselves for solution; Miss Marghanita Laski, surely one of the most prolific contributors of illustrative quotations—some 250,000—to any dictionary in history; Clarence L. Barnhart (and more recently his son Robert K. Barnhart) who opened his valuable quotation files to us from the beginning of the preparation of OEDS; and Professor E. G. Stanley, the Rawlinson and Bosworth Professor of Anglo-Saxon in the University of Oxford, a personal friend for nearly forty years, who was among the first to help me build up a team of source-readers for the Supplement and and who has subsequently given close critical attention to sets of galley-proofs in every letter of the alphabet.

2. *A Supplement to the OED* (OEDS)

It is natural when a task of some magnitude has been completed to give some account, however inadequate, of the manner in which the project evolved.[1]

In 1957, when I began, I was both encouraged and worried by the first sentence in the General Explanations of the *OED:* 'The vocabulary of a widely-diffused and highly-cultivated

[1] A fuller account of the evolution of OEDS is given in my article 'The End of an Innings but not the End of the Game', Threlford Memorial Lecture, *The Incorporated Linguist* Volume 23, Number 3, Summer 1984, pp. 114–119.

living language is not a fixed quantity circumscribed by definite limits.' I was also much taken by Dr Murray's employment of the phrase *Lexicon totius Anglicitatis*. 'Limits' and 'totality' plainly suggested that boundaries would need to be set at many stages along the journey.

At the outset I was invited by the Delegates of the Oxford University Press to prepare a new *Supplement to the OED* in a single volume of about 1,275 pages, and to aim at completion within seven years. Both figures seemed reasonable at the time, as far as I can recall. The only significant model before me was that of the *OED* itself. James Murray had been instructed by the Delegates to complete the Dictionary within ten years. But the ten years, I reasoned, had turned into forty-four partly because Murray was a pioneer in the field of historical lexicography,[1] and partly because he and his co-editors had to deal with the language from the time of the first records (eighth century) of English till the late nineteenth century. I had rather less than a century's worth of language to consider.

In the event OEDS has taken nearly twenty-nine years to complete, and one volume has turned into four. By 1957 the language had proliferated at a much greater rate since the beginning of the century than I had at first judged. This dramatic increase was underlined by the publication in 1961 (i.e. not long after I had established my editorial policy and at a point when I thought the main collecting of evidence had been completed) of *Webster's Third New International Dictionary*. The sheer quantity of words in this majestic and influential work made it obvious that I had underestimated the problems confronting me. The whole editorial process, and particularly the extension of the 'definite limits' of inclusion, had to be reconsidered. The mine-shafts into the seams of words needed to be dug much more deeply.

A second circumstance leading to delay was my acceptance of responsibility for the governance of the smaller Oxford dictionaries. In 1957 there were only four Oxford English dictionaries for native speakers apart from the *OED* itself: in chronological order of first publication, the *Concise Oxford Dictionary* (first published in 1911), the *Pocket Oxford Dictionary* (1924), the *Little Oxford Dictionary* (1930), and the *Shorter Oxford English Dictionary* (1933). Now this small flotilla of scattered ships—scattered because in 1957 they had no base to operate from—has turned into an invincible fleet of more than twenty dictionaries and lexical guides, all flying the Oxford flag from their base at 37a St. Giles', Oxford. The editors of all these smaller works, and many of their editorial assistants, first cut their lexicographical teeth on OEDS.

* * *

When I look back at the work of Murray, I cannot but marvel at the permanent value of so much of his editorial policy, and even of his clerical procedures. Like Murray and his editorial colleagues we have worked by hand on dictionary slips, the only difference being that our slips are standardized in size (6 in. × 4 in.). They filed bundles of slips in wooden pigeon-holes after tying them with string or tape. We have placed our slips in an upright manner in strict alphabetical order in the trays of fire-proof cabinets. One procedure of Murray's has been abandoned: as often as not his readers cut up books, including many valuable ones from earlier centuries, in the process of collecting quotations. This would today be regarded as vandalism. We were able to hasten the process of preparing slips containing evidence from much-cited sources (e.g. the technical glossaries of the British Standards Institution), by mass-producing them with typed titles and with the help of a photo-copier and paper guillotine, rather than, as in Murray's day, by the use of hand-setting composition in a printing house. I am sure too that our standards of research and verification of the printed evidence have been consistently higher than those of our predecessors. Victorian standards were lower in such matters; ours is a more pedantic age. The

[1] The *OED* was not in fact the first historical dictionary. Jacob Grimm and Wilhelm Grimm started their *Deutsches Wörterbuch* at an earlier date, and their first volume (*A–Biermolke*) was published in 1854.

resources of even the greatest libraries then were also much more limited than they are now. Many quotations in the *OED* were taken from secondary sources like, for example, C. Pettman's *Africanderisms* (1913) and J. Redding Ware's *Passing English of the Victorian Era* (1909): we have tried always to verify such quotations in the original source. We have also tried always to verify quotations from poems and short stories in their first place of publication and not merely in collected editions.

In matters of editorial policy, except for the abandonment of the once obligatory initial capital in the headwords, we have endeavoured in OEDS to display the entries in the manner of the parent work, even to the extent of retaining Murray's old-fashioned (though very convenient) pronunciation system. If a word has developed new senses we have placed these in their logical place in the numerical sequences first devised nearly a century ago, sometimes needing to make use of strings of asterisks, as explained on p. xxi. We have given the same attention to every department of modern English vocabulary—etymologies, definitions, illustrative examples, combinations, proverbs, idiomatic phrases, and all the rest—as did the lexicographers who preceded us, except that the entries for words entering the language in the twentieth century are more generously illustrated by examples than was judged necessary in the past.

* * *

One unforeseeable circumstance that has had an intangible and yet curiously potent effect on present-day attitudes to historical lexicography is that the period of preparation of OEDS has coincided with the arrival of new linguistic (and especially structuralist) attitudes. What I have elsewhere called 'linguistic burial parties' have appeared, that is scholars with shovels intent on burying the linguistic past and most of the literary past and present. I refer to those who believe that synchronic means 'theoretically sound' and diachronic 'theoretically suspect'. It is theoretically sound, the argument of the synchronicists runs, to construct contrastive sentences or other laboratory-invented examples which draw attention to this or that element of grammar or lexis, and to do *only* that. I profoundly believe that such procedures, leading descriptive scholars never to quote from the written language of even our greatest modern writers, leave one looking at a language with one's eyes partly blindfolded.

I want to dwell on these matters a moment longer because the editorial policy adopted in the four volumes of OEDS was formed in all its essentials between 1957 and 1960, when the new linguistic attitudes were at an embryonic stage. A small measure of autobiography is necessary. Between 1951 and 1957 I had retranscribed the text of the late-twelfth-century set of versified homilies called the *Ormulum*. I had also compiled an *index verborum* to it, and had given lectures to Oxford undergraduates on the language of the *Ormulum* and on the language of other medieval works like the *Peterborough Chronicle*, the *Ancrene Wisse*, and the *Ayenbite of Inwyt*. For such work, indispensable prerequisites included a knowledge of the linguistic monuments of Old English, Old Norse, Gothic, and other Germanic languages, also of Old French, and a professional knowledge of all the elements of comparative Indo-European philology that had a bearing on the vocabulary and grammar of medieval English. I also conducted tutorials and seminars on the language of writers like Spenser, Shakespeare, Milton, Dickens, and many others. In that context the grammaticality of 'Colourless green ideas sleep furiously', and the contrast between *langue* and *parole*, had no relevance at all. Above all else it became clear to me that the entire vocabulary of all the main literary, philosophical, religious, etc., works that had survived from the period since 1100, as well as that part of pre-Conquest English that remained in the language after 1066, had been included in the *OED*. Any omissions were attributable to human frailty not to deliberate design. There were no exclusion zones, no censorings, no blindfoldings, except for the absence of two famous four-letter (sexual) words. Dr Murray, his colleagues, and his contributors had dredged up the whole of the accessible vocabulary of English (the sexual words apart) and had done their best to record them systematically in the *OED*. I concluded that if the Dictionary had room for the word *thester* as adjective ('dark') and noun ('darkness'), and Orm's *þeossterrleȝȝc* 'darkness', it could, and must, admit the vocabulary of Edith Sitwell and Wystan Auden. Of course the structuralists and other scholars at one or more remove from the primary work of Ferdinand de Saussure could not see this, and they probably never will. It seems that they would prefer to bury Orm's vocabulary along with that of the best writers of the present day. But OEDS, like its parent work, has been hospitable, almost from the beginning, to the special vocabulary, including the once-only uses, of writers like T. S. Eliot, Virginia Woolf, D. H. Lawrence, and others. It must be emphasized that in practice these uses form only a tiny fraction of the vocabulary presented here; in other words the balance of the volumes has not been disturbed by them nor has the publication of the dictionary been delayed by their presence.

Perhaps the main departure from the policy of Murray was my decision to try to locate and list the vocabulary of all English-speaking countries, and not merely that of the United Kingdom. For the most part Murray preferred to fend off overseas words until they had become firmly entrenched in British use. Words more or less restricted to North America, Australia, New Zealand, South Africa, the West Indies, and so on, were treated almost like illegal immigrants. All that has been changed and, as far as possible, equality of attention has been given to the sprawling vocabulary of all English-speaking countries. At a time when the English language seems to be breaking up into innumerable clearly distinguishable varieties, it seemed to me important to abandon Murray's insular policy and go out and find what was happening to the language elsewhere.

* * *

As work on the Supplement proceeded, the number of scientific, technical, and specialized academic words and senses that needed to be included multiplied spectacularly. The astonishing growth in academic and scientific research and in industrial and technological achievements, especially since the 1939–45 war, is plainly reflected in the text of OEDS. The first sputnik was launched in 1957 just as work on OEDS was beginning. As we proceeded with the dictionary, visits to the moon by astronauts and the exploration of outer space by far-travelling rockets became routine features of our age. Nuclear power stations came into being along with quantities of nuclear weapons and other weapons of war, and all the attendant vocabulary. Nobel prize-winners, playwrights, philosophers, and writers of every kind wrote their books and articles. The *New York Times* and other newspapers increased hideously in size, as did the regular issues of learned journals in chemistry, medicine, and all the other academic subjects. New vocabulary reached our language from the wars and revolutions of the twentieth century, and from the considerable extension of leisure travel. A curious by-product of the scholarship of our age is that the metalanguages of linguisticians and philosophers have now reached a point where writers of monographs cannot even reach the starting line without regularly defining exactly what they mean by such ordinary (and certainly not new) expressions as *accent*, *sentence*, *utterance*, and *word*, not to go further afield. Some linguistic scholars can now express themselves only in a manner which is 'as inviting as a tall wall bottle-spiked' (to use Professor Ricks's memorable phrase),[1] others only in tree-diagrams, others again by ritual exercises like distinguishing 'the cat sat on the mat' from 'the mat sat on the cat'. I cannot believe that historical lexicography will crumble or be damaged in any permanent way by these transient schools of thought, but the danger exists.

* * *

[1] *London Review of Books* 6 June 1985, p. 9.

In his famous Dictionary, Dr Johnson expressed his indebtedness to Junius and Skinner in the following manner: 'the only names which I have forborn to quote when I copied their books; not that I might appropriate their labours or usurp their honours, but that I might spare a perpetual repetition by one general acknowledgement'. It is appropriate that I should acknowledge in similar terms our frequent indebtedness to several major works of reference and learned journals throughout the preparation of OEDS: the great regional historical dictionaries, especially *A Dictionary of American English*, *A Dictionary of Americanisms*, and *A Dictionary of Canadianisms*; the slang dictionaries of Eric Partridge; *The Barnhart Dictionary of New English since 1963* and its successor *The Second Barnhart Dictionary of New English*; the multifarious glossaries of the British Standards Institution; innumerable specialized glossaries and textbooks in every subject, as well as the *Encyclopaedia Britannica* and other encyclopaedias and yearbooks; and the learned journals *American Speech* and *Notes and Queries*.

The passage of time has almost made it seem as if the editing of the *OED* and of OEDS has been part of a continuous process. My own work on the final pages of OEDS has also overlapped with the beginning of a new and very ambitious project—the merging in electronic form of the twelve volumes of the *OED* and the four volumes of the Supplement. This imaginative project, the computerization of the *OED*,[1] should ensure that the Oxford tradition—indeed its pre-eminence—in historical lexicography will be maintained into the twenty-first century and beyond.

* * *

It has given me boundless pleasure to 'ascertain the significance' of so many modern English words, and 'to perform all the parts of a faithful lexicographer'. The performance of the task has also taken me to lecture platforms and broadcasting houses in most major countries in the world. In this country I have had the special privilege of advising the BBC on the standards of spoken English presented by them,[2] and the opportunity to discuss the issues with some of the famous broadcasters of our time. I have also participated in many programmes, on both radio and television, in which the English language has been the main topic of discussion or of entertainment, from the studios of Radio 3 and of the external services to the more relaxed ones broadcasting programmes like 'Call My Bluff' and 'Desert Island Discs'. I have tried throughout to insist on the permanent value of the primary canons of my trade: the necessity of recording the indelicate as well as the delicate or neutral works of our century, demotic vocabulary as well as that which is taken to be elegant, words that offend ethnic sensibilities as well as those that cause no offence, overseas English vocabulary as well as that used in the United Kingdom, and the literary language as well as the ordinary printed word.

Now time has moved on. Volumes I and II of OEDS have already been reprinted twice and Volume III once. This Supplement, begun in a small house in a back street in Oxford and finished nearly three decades later in a Georgian mansion in one of Oxford's noblest streets, will surely stand as a lasting testament to the fruitfulness and inventiveness of the language of our age.

In a recent visit to Washington I came across the following statement on a plaque in the Capitol:

> After the departure of British Forces from New York, American Independence was close at hand. George Washington resigned his military commission at the State House in Annapolis before the Continental Congress. 'Having now finished the work assigned to me, I retire from the great theatre of action.' 23 Dec. 1783.

[1] A convenient description of the project by its Editor, E. S. C. Weiner, can be found in the *Journal of English Linguistics* (April 1985), pp. 1–13.

[2] *The Quality of Spoken English on BBC Radio* (BBC, 1979); *The Spoken Word* (BBC, 1981).

With the completion of a task assigned to me in 1957, I now retire from the 'great theatre' of lexicography, and will devote myself in the years ahead to a reconsideration of English grammar.

R.W.B.

Oxford
June 1985

CONTENTS

VOLUME IV

EDITORIAL STAFF

The dates given after the names indicate when each person joined the editorial staff of this dictionary. The letter P precedes the names of those who worked as part-timers.

Senior Editors (General):	LESLEY S. BURNETT	1974–80, 1982–4
	J. A. SIMPSON	1976–85
	E. S. C. WEINER	1977–84
Senior Editor (Science):	A. M. HUGHES	1968–85
Senior Editor (Natural History):	SANDRA RAPHAEL	1969–83
Assistant Editor (Bibliographical Collation):	J. PATERSON	1975–85

Editorial Assistants

E. C. DANN	1963–83	AMANDA J. BURRELL	1979–83
ADRIANA P. ORR	1966–83	DELLA J. THOMPSON	1980–2
DEBORAH D. HONORÉ	1970–80, P1980–3	D. B. W. BIRK	1980–2
EDITH BONNER	1976–83	M. A. MABE	1980–3
A. HODGSON	1976–82	R. C. PALMER	1981–2
YVONNE L. WARBURTON	1976–84	KATHERINE H. EMMS	1981–3
JULIA C. SWANNELL	1976–83	ALANA G. DICKINSON	1981–3
ELIZABETH M. KNOWLES	1977–83	R. C. BEATTY	1981–3

Several of the above assisted with parts of the final stages of work on Volume IV, either part-time or on a free-lance basis.

Members of the editorial staff received valuable part-time assistance from the following library researchers: Grace M. Briggs (1959–85), M. Yvonne Offord (1982–5), Rita G. Keckeissen (1968–85), Daphne Gilbert-Carter (1975–85), Sally Hinkle (1977–85), and G. Chowdharay-Best (1984–5), the first two in Oxford, Mr Chowdharay-Best in London, and the others in New York, Washington, and Boston respectively. Mr F. D. Hayes also continued his work on the reading of sources.

Miss Knowles, Mrs Burrell, and Ms Emms were mainly concerned with research (especially for 'first uses') and with the verification of quotations. Mrs Honoré dealt with terms in the Social Sciences, and Mr Mabe, Mr Beatty, and Mrs Dickinson with scientific terms. All other Editorial Assistants named above undertook general editorial work.

Some other members of the Department and some free-lance readers have assisted with the reading of proofs, especially Dr Margaret A. Cooper, D. J. Edmonds, M. Harrington, Miss Freda J. Thornton, and Dr W. R. Trumble.

Secretarial: Karin C. E. Vines (1981–6).

KEY TO THE PRONUNCIATION

THE pronunciations given are those in use in the educated speech of southern England (the so-called 'Received Standard'), and the keywords given are to be understood as pronounced in such speech.

I. *Consonants and Semi-Consonants*

b, d, f, k, l, m, n, p, t, v, z *have their usual English values*

g as in *go* (gō^{u}).
h ... *ho*! (hō^{u}).
r ... *r*un (rɒn), te*rr*ier (te·riəɹ).
ɹ ... he*r* (hə̄ɹ), fa*r*the*r* (fā·ɹðəɹ).
s ... *s*ee (sī), *s*ucce*ss* (sŏkse·s).
w ... *w*ear (wē^{ə}ɹ).
hw... *wh*en (hwen).
y ... *y*es (yes).

þ as in *th*in (þin), ba*th* (bɑþ).
ð ... *th*en (ðen), ba*th*e (bē^{i}ð).
ʃ ... *sh*op (ʃǫp), di*sh* (diʃ).
tʃ ... *ch*op (tʃǫp), di*tch* (ditʃ).
ʒ ... vi*s*ion (vi·ʒən), dé*j*euner (deʒōne).
dʒ ... *j*u*dg*e (dʒɒdʒ).
ŋ ... si*ng*i*ng* (si·ŋiŋ), thi*n*k (þiŋk).
ŋg ... fi*ng*er (fi·ŋgəɹ).

(FOREIGN AND NON-SOUTHERN)

ṅ as in French nasal, e*n*viro*n* (aṅviroṅ).
l^{y} ... It. serra*gli*o (serā·l^{y}o).
n^{y} ... It. si*gn*ore (sin^{y}ō·re).
χ ... Ger. a*ch* (aχ), Sc. lo*ch* (lǫχ), Sp. fri*j*oles (frī·χoles).
χ^{y} ... Ger. i*ch* (iχ^{y}), Sc. ni*ch*t (niχ^{y}t).
γ ... North Ger. sa*g*en (zā·γĕn).
γ^{y} ... Ger. le*g*en, re*g*nen (lē·γ^{y}ĕn, rē·γ^{y}nĕn).
k^{y} ... Afrikaans baardmanne*tj*ie (bā·rtmanək^{y}i).

The reversed r (ɹ) and small 'superior' letters (pe·rĕm^{p}təri) are used to denote elements that may be omitted either by individual speakers or in particular phonetic contexts.

II. *Vowels*

The symbol ¯ placed over a vowel-letter denotes length.

The incidence of main stress is shown by a raised point (·) after the vowel-symbol, and a secondary stress by a double point (:) as in *callithumpian* (kæ:lĭþɒ·mpiăn).

The stressed vowels a, æ, e, i, o, u become obscured with loss of stress, and the indeterminate sounds thus arising, and approximating to the 'neutral' vowel ə, are normally printed ă, æ̆, ĕ, ĭ, ŏ, ŭ.

A break ˌ is used to indicate syllable-division when necessary to avoid ambiguity.

ORDINARY		LONG		OBSCURE	
a as in	Fr. *à la* mode (a la mod').	ā as in	*a*lms (āmz), b*ar* (bāɹ).	ă as in	*a*mœb*a* (ămī·bă).
ai ...	*aye*=yes (ai), Is*ai*ah (əizai·ă).				
æ ...	m*a*n (mæn).			æ̆ ...	*a*ccept (æ̆kse·pt), mani*a*c (mē^{i}·niæ̆k).
ɑ ...	p*a*ss (pɑs), ch*a*nt (tʃɑnt).				
ɑu ...	l*ou*d (lɑud), n*ow* (nɑu).				
ɒ ...	c*u*t (kɒt), s*o*n (sɒn).	ɒ̄ ...	c*u*rl (kɒ̄ɹl), f*u*r (fɒ̄ɹ).	ɒ̆ ...	dat*u*m (dē^{i}·tɒ̆m).
e ...	y*e*t (yet), t*e*n (ten).	ē (ē^{ə}) ...	th*e*re (ðē^{ə}ɹ), p*ea*r, p*a*re (pē ɹ).	ĕ ...	mom*e*nt (mō^{u}·mĕnt), sev*e*ral (se·vĕrăl).
‖e ...	Fr. attach*é* (ataʃe).	ē(ē^{i}) ...	r*ei*n, r*ai*n (rē^{i}n), th*ey* (ðē^{i}).	ĕ ...	separ*a*te (*adj.*) (se·părĕt).
‖ę ...	Fr. ch*e*f (ʃęf).	‖ę̄ ...	Fr. f*ai*re (fę̄r').		
ə ...	ev*e*r (e·vəɹ), nat*io*n (nē^{i}·ʃən).	ə̄ ...	f*i*r (fə̄ɹ), f*e*rn (fə̄ɹn), *ea*rth (ə̄ɹþ).	ė ...	add*e*d (æ·dėd), *e*state (ėstē^{i}·t).
əi ...	*I*, *eye* (əi), b*i*nd (bəind).				
‖ə ...	Fr. tour d*e* force (tūrdəfors).				
i ...	s*i*t (sit), m*y*st*i*c (mistik).	ī (ī^{ə}) ...	b*ie*r (bī^{ə}ɹ), cl*ea*r (klī^{ə}ɹ).	ĭ ...	van*i*ty (væ·nĭti).
i ...	Psych*e* (səi·ki), r*e*act (riˌæ·kt).	ī ...	th*ie*f (þīf), s*ee* (sī).	ĭ ...	r*e*main (rĭmē^{i}·n), b*e*lieve (bĭlī·v).
o ...	ach*o*r (ē^{i}·koɹ), m*o*rality (moræ·lĭti).	ō (ō^{ə}) ...	b*oa*r, b*o*re (bō^{ə}ɹ), gl*o*ry (glō^{ə}·ri).	ŏ ...	the*o*ry (þī·ŏri).
oi ...	*oi*l (oil), b*oy* (boi).				
o ...	her*o* (hī^{ə}·ro), z*o*ology (zoˌǫ·lŏdʒi).	ō (ō^{u}) ...	s*o*, s*ow* (sō^{u}), s*ou*l (sō^{u}l).	ŏ ...	vi*o*let (vəi·ŏlėt), par*o*dy (pæ·rŏdi).
ǫ ...	wh*a*t (hwǫt), w*a*tch (wǫtʃ).	ǭ ...	w*a*lk (wǭk), w*a*rt (wǭɹt).	ǫ̆ ...	*au*thority (ǫ̆þǫ·rĭti).
ǫ,ǫ̇* ...	g*o*t (gǫt), s*o*ft (sǫ̇ft)*.	ǭ ...	sh*o*rt (ʃǭɹt), th*o*rn (þǭɹn).	ǫ̆ ...	c*o*nnect (kǫ̆ne·kt), amaz*o*n (æ·măzǫ̆n).
‖ö ...	Ger. K*ö*ln (köln).	‖ȫ ...	Fr. c*œu*r (kȫr).		
‖ö ...	Fr. p*eu* (pö).	‖ȫ ...	Ger. G*oe*the (gȫtĕ), Fr. j*eû*ne (ʒȫn).		
u ...	f*u*ll (ful), b*oo*k (buk).	ū (ū^{ə}) ...	p*oo*r (pū^{ə}ɹ), m*oo*rish (mū^{ə}·riʃ).		
iu ...	d*u*ration (diurē^{i}·ʃən).	iū, ^{i}ū ...	p*u*re (piū^{ə}ɹ), l*u*re (l^{i}ū^{ə}ɹ).	iŭ, ^{i}ŭ	verd*u*re (və̄·ɹdiŭɹ), meas*u*re (me·ʒ^{i}ŭɹ).
u ...	unt*o* (ɒ·ntu), fr*u*gality (fru-).	ū ...	tw*o* m*oo*ns (tū mūnz).	ŭ ...	alt*o*gether (ǭltŭge·ðəɹ).
i*u* ...	Matth*ew* (mæ·þiu), virt*ue* (və̄·ɹtiu).	iū, ^{i}ū ...	f*ew* (fiū), l*u*te (l^{i}ūt).	iŭ ...	circ*u*lar (sə̄·ɹkiŭlăɹ).
‖ü ...	Ger. M*ü*ller (mü·lĕr).				
‖ü ...	Fr. d*u*ne (dün).	‖ǖ ...	Ger. gr*ü*n (grǖn), Fr. j*u*s (ʒǖ).		

^{ə} (see ī^{ə}, ē^{ə}, ō^{ə}, ū^{ə}) } see Vol. I of Dict., p.
$^{i, u}$ (see ē^{i}, ō^{u}) } xxxiv, note 3.
' as in able (ē^{i}·b'l), eaten (ī·t'n) = voice-glide.

* Words such as *soft, cloth, cross* are often still pronounced with (ǭ) by Southern speakers in England but the pronunciation with ǫ is now more usual.

‖ Only in foreign (or earlier English) words.

LIST OF ABBREVIATIONS, SIGNS, ETC.

Some abbreviations here listed in italics are occasionally, for the sake of clarity, printed in roman type, and vice versa.

a. (in Etym.)	adoption of, adopted from
a (as *a* 1850)	*ante*, 'before', 'not later than'
a.	adjective
abbrev.	abbreviation (of)
abl.	ablative
absol.	absolute, -ly
Abstr.	Abstract(s)
acc.	accusative
ad. (in Etym.)	adaptation of
Add.	Addenda
adj.	adjective
adv.	adverb
advb.	adverbial, -ly
(Advt.),	advertisement
Aeronaut.	in Aeronautics
AF., AFr.	Anglo-French
Afr.	Africa, -n
Agric.	in Agriculture
Alb.	Albanian
Amer.	American
Amer. Ind.	American Indian
Anat.	in Anatomy
Anglo-Ind.	Anglo-Indian
Anglo-Ir.	Anglo-Irish
Anthrop., *Anthropol.*	in Anthropology
Antiq.	in Antiquities
aphet.	aphetic, aphetized
app.	apparently
Arab.	Arabic
Aram.	Aramaic
Arch., *Archit.*	in Architecture
arch.	archaic
Archæol.	in Archæology
Arm.	Armenian
assoc.	association
Astr.	in Astronomy
Astrol.	in Astrology
attrib.	attributive, -ly
Austral.	Australian
A.V.	Authorized Version
bef.	before
Bibliogr.	in Bibliography
Biochem.	in Biochemistry
Biol.	in Biology
Bot.	in Botany
Bulg.	Bulgarian
c (as *c* 1700)	*circa*, 'about'
c. (as 19th c.)	century
Canad.	Canadian
Cat.	Catalan
catachr.	catachrestically
Celt.	Celtic
Cent. Dict.	*Century Dictionary*
Cf., cf.	*confer*, 'compare'
Ch.	Church
Chem.	in Chemistry
Cinemat., *Cinematogr.*	in Cinematography
cl. L.	classical Latin
cogn. w.	cognate with
collect.	collective, -ly
colloq.	colloquial, -ly
comb.	combined, -ing
Comb.	Combinations
Comm.	in Commercial usage
Communic.	in Communications
comp.	compound, composition
compar.	comparative
compl.	complement
Conch.	in Conchology
concr.	concrete, -ly
conj.	conjunction
cons.	consonant
const.	construction, construed with
corresp.	corresponding (to)
cpd.	compound

Cryst.	in Crystallography
Da.	Danish
D.A.	*Dictionary of Americanisms*
D.A.E.	*Dictionary of American English*
dat.	dative
def.	definite, -ition
deriv.	derivative, -ation
derog.	derogatory
dial.	dialect, -al
Dict.	Dictionary; *spec.*, the *Oxford English Dictionary*
dim.	diminutive
D.O.S.T.	*Dictionary of the Older Scottish Tongue*
Du.	Dutch
E.	East
Eccl.	in Ecclesiastical usage
Ecol.	in Ecology
Econ.	in Economics
ed.	edition
E.D.D.	*English Dialect Dictionary*
Educ.	in Education
e.g.	*exempli gratia*, 'for example'
Electr.	in Electricity
ellipt.	elliptical, -ly
Embryol.	in Embryology
e.midl.	east midland (dialect)
Eng.	English
Engin.	in Engineering
Ent.	in Entomology
erron.	erroneous, -ly
esp.	especially
et al.	*et alii*, 'and others'
etc.	et cetera
Ethnol.	in Ethnology
etym.	etymology
euphem.	euphemistically
exc.	except
f. (in Etym.)	formed on
f. (in subordinate entries)	form of
F.	French
fem. (*rarely* f.)	feminine
fig.	figurative, -ly
Finn.	Finnish
fl.	*floruit*, 'flourished'
Fr.	French
freq.	frequent, -ly
Fris.	Frisian
Funk's Stand. Dict.	*Funk and Wagnalls Standard Dictionary*
G.	German
Gael.	Gaelic
Gaz.	Gazette (in names of newspapers)
gen.	genitive
gen.	general, -ly
Geogr.	in Geography
Geol.	in Geology
Geom.	in Geometry
Geomorphol.	in Geomorphology
Ger.	German
Gmc.	Germanic
Goth.	Gothic
Gr.	Greek
Gram.	in Grammar
Heb.	Hebrew
Her.	in Heraldry
Herb.	among herbalists
Hind.	Hindustani
Hist.	in History
hist.	historical
Hort.	in Horticulture
Ibid.	*Ibidem*, 'in the same book or passage'
Icel.	Icelandic
Ichthyol.	in Ichthyology

id.	*idem*, 'the same'
i.e.	*id est*, 'that is'
IE.	Indo-European
imit.	imitative
Immunol.	in Immunology
imp.	imperative
impers.	impersonal
impf.	imperfect
ind.	indicative
indef.	indefinite
inf.	infinitive
infl.	influenced
int.	interjection
intr.	intransitive
Introd.	Introduction
Ir.	Irish
irreg.	irregular, -ly
It.	Italian
J., (J.)	Johnson's *Dictionary* (quoted from)
(Jam.)	Jamieson, *Scottish Dict.*
Jap.	Japanese
joc.	jocular, -ly
l.	line
L.	Latin
lang.	language
Let., *Lett.*	letter, letters
LG.	Low German
lit.	literal, -ly
Lit.	Literary
Lith.	Lithuanian
LXX	Septuagint
Mal.	Malay, Malayan
Manuf.	in Manufacture, -ing
masc. (*rarely* m.)	masculine
Math.	in Mathematics
MDu.	Middle Dutch
ME.	Middle English
Mech.	in Mechanics
Med.	in Medicine
med.L.	medieval Latin
Metaph.	in Metaphysics
Meteorol.	in Meteorology
MHG.	Middle High German
midl.	midland (dialect)
Mil.	in military usage
Min.	in Mineralogy
MLG.	Middle Low German
mod.	modern
mod.L.	modern Latin
(Morris),	E. E. Morris's *Austral English* (quoted from)
Mus.	in Music
Mythol.	in Mythology
N.	North
N. Amer.	North America, -n
N. & Q.	*Notes and Queries*
Nat. Hist.	in Natural History
Naut.	in Nautical language
Neurol.	in Neurology
neut. (*rarely* n.)	neuter
NF., NFr.	Northern French
nom.	nominative
north.	northern (dialect)
Norw.	Norwegian
N.T.	New Testament
Nucl.	Nuclear
Numism.	in Numismatics
N.Z.	New Zealand
obj.	object
obl.	oblique
Obs., *obs.*	obsolete
occas.	occasional, -ly
Oceanogr.	in Oceanography
OE.	Old English (= Anglo-Saxon)
OF., OFr.	Old French
OFris.	Old Frisian
OHG.	Old High German

OIr.	Old Irish
ON.	Old Norse (Old Icelandic)
ONF.	Old Northern French
Ophthalm.	in Ophthalmology
opp.	opposed (to), the opposite (of)
Opt.	in Optics
orig.	origin, -al, -ally
Ornith.	in Ornithology
OS.	Old Saxon
OSl.	Old (Church) Slavonic
O.T.	Old Testament
p.	page
Palæogr.	in Palæography
Palæont.	in Palæontology
pa. pple.	passive or past participle
(Partridge),	E. Partridge's *Dictionary of Slang and Unconventional English* (quoted from)
pass.	passive, -ly
pa. t.	past tense
Path.	in Pathology
perh.	perhaps
Pers.	Persian
pers.	person, -al
Petrogr.	in Petrography
Petrol.	in Petrology
(Pettman),	C. Pettman's *Africanderisms* (quoted from)
pf.	perfect
Pg.	Portuguese
Pharm.	in Pharmacology
Philol.	in Philology
Philos.	in Philosophy
phonet.	phonetic, -ally
Photogr.	in Photography
phr.	phrase
Phys.	in Physics, physical; (*rarely*) in Physiology
Physiol.	in Physiology
pl.	plural; plate
poet.	poetic, -al
Pol.	Polish
Pol.	in Politics
Pol. Econ.	in Political Economy
pop.	popular, -ly
poss.	possessive
ppl. a., ppl. adj.	participial adjective
pple.	participle
Pr.	Provençal
prec.	preceding (word or article)
pred.	predicative
pref.	prefix
pref., Pref.	preface
prep.	preposition
pres.	present
priv.	privative
prob.	probably
pron.	pronoun
pronunc.	pronunciation
prop.	properly
Pros.	in Prosody
Prov.	Provençal
pr. pple.	present participle
Psych., *Psychol.*	in Psychology
Q.	Quarterly (in names of periodicals)
quot(s).	quotation(s)
q.v.	*quod vide*, 'which see'
R.	Royal (in names of periodicals, etc.)
Radiol.	in Radiology
R. C. Ch.	Roman Catholic Church
redupl.	reduplicating
refash.	refashioned, -ing
refl., refl.	reflexive
reg.	regular
rel.	related (to)
repr.	representative, representing
Rhet.	in Rhetoric
Rom.	Roman, Romance, Romanic
Rum.	Rumanian
Russ.	Russian
S.	South
S. Afr.	South Africa, -n
sb.	substantive
sc.	*scilicet*, 'understand' or 'supply'
Sc., *Scot.*	Scotch, Scottish
Sci.	(in) Science, scientific
Sc. Nat. Dict.	*Scottish National Dictionary*
Ser.	series
sing.	singular
Skr.	Sanskrit
Slav.	Slavonic
S.N.D.	*Scottish National Dictionary*
Sociol.	in Sociology
Sp.	Spanish
sp.	spelling
spec.	specific, -ally
(Stanf.),	*Stanford Dictionary of Anglicised Words and Phrases* (quoted from)
subj.	subject, subjunctive
subord. cl.	subordinate clause
subseq.	subsequent, -ly
subst.	substantively
suff.	suffix
superl.	superlative
Suppl.	Supplement
Surg.	in Surgery
s.v.	*sub voce*, 'under the word'
Sw.	Swedish
s.w.	south-western (dialect)
syll.	syllable
Syr.	Syrian
techn.	technical, -ly
Tel.	Telegraph (in names of newspapers)
Telegr.	in Telegraphy
Teleph.	in Telephony
(Th.),	Thornton's *American Glossary* (quoted from)
Theatr.	in the Theatre, theatrical
Theol.	in Theology
Tokh.	Tokharian
tr., transl.	translation (of)
trans.	transitive
transf.	transferred sense
Trig.	in Trigonometry
Turk.	Turkish
Typog., *Typogr.*	in Typography
ult.	ultimate, -ly
unkn.	unknown
U.S.	United States
usu.	usual, -ly
v., vb.	verb
var(r)., vars.	variant(s) of
vbl. sb.	verbal substantive
Vet., *Vet. Sci.*	in Veterinary Science
viz.	*videlicet*, 'namely'
v. str., or *w.*	verb strong, or weak
vulg.	vulgar
W.	Welsh; West
wd.	word
Webster	*Webster's (New International) Dictionary*
WGmc.	West Germanic
w.midl.	west midland (dialect)
WS.	West Saxon
(Y.),	Yule & Burnell's *Hobson-Jobson* (quoted from)
Zoogeogr.	in Zoogeography
Zool.	in Zoology

Signs and Other Conventions

Before a word or sense

† = obsolete
‖ = not naturalized, alien
¶ = catachrestic and erroneous uses (see Dict., Vol. I, p. xxi)

In the listing of Forms

1 = before 1100
2 = 12th c. (1100 to 1200)
3 = 13th c. (1200 to 1300), etc.
5–7 = 15th to 17th century. (See General Explanations, Dict., Vol. I, p. xxx)

In the etymologies

* indicates a word or form not actually found, but of which the existence is inferred
:– = normal development of

The printing of a word in SMALL CAPITALS indicates that further information will be found under the word so referred to.

In cross-references * indicates that the word or sense referred to is in the Supplement.

After the number of a sense * and ** (etc.) indicate new senses which are not directly related to the senses so numbered in the main body of the Dictionary, but which have to be inserted within the existing numerical sequence because of the custom in the Dictionary of placing the Combinations at the conclusion of each article.

.. indicates an omitted part of a quotation.

PROPRIETARY NAMES

THIS Supplement includes some words which are or are asserted to be proprietary names or trade marks. Their inclusion does not imply that they have acquired for legal purposes a non-proprietary or general significance nor any other judgement concerning their legal status. In cases where the editorial staff have established in the records of the Patent Offices of the United Kingdom and of the United States that a word is registered as a proprietary name or trade mark this is indicated, but no judgement concerning the legal status of such words is made or implied thereby.

TRANSLITERATION OF FOREIGN SCRIPTS

The lists below show the schemes of transliteration used in this Supplement for the most commonly occurring languages that have not adopted the Roman alphabet.

Arabic: (omitted), ب b, ت t, ث ṯ, ج j, ح ḥ, خ ḵ, د d, ذ ḏ, ر r, ز z, س s, ش š, ص ṣ, ض ḍ, ط ṭ, ظ ẓ, ع ʻ, غ ġ, ف f, ق ḳ, ك k, ل l, م m, ن n, ه h, ة (omitted), و w, ي y; ʻ ʼ; vowels a, i, u, ā, ī, ū.

Chinese: Wade–Giles system without tone-numbers; in Volumes III and IV Pinyin.

Hebrew: א ʼ, ב b, ג g, ד d, ה h, ו w, ז z, ח ḥ, ט ṭ, י y, כ k, ל l, מ m, נ n, ס s, ע ʻ, פ p, צ ṣ, ק q or ḳ, ר r, שׂ ś, שׁ sh or š, ת t;

spirant consonants underlined or with added h; doubled consonant for *daghesh forte*;

vowels a, e, i, o, u; long vowels with macron or circumflex according as written defective or *plene*; shva and reduced vowels superscript or omitted.

Japanese: 'Modified Hepburn' system, British Standard 4812: 1972.

Russian: А а a, Б б b, В в v, Г г g, Д д d, Е е e, Ж ж zh, З з z, И и i, Й й ĭ, К к k, Л л l, М м m, Н н n, О о o, П п p, Р р r, С с s, Т т t, У у u, Ф ф f, Х х kh, Ц ц ts, Ч ч ch, Ш ш sh, Щ щ shch, Ъ ъ ″, Ы ы ȳ, Ь ь ʹ, Э э ė, Ю ю yu, Я я ya.

Sanskrit: अ a, आ ā, इ i, ई ī, उ u, ऊ ū, ऋ ṛ, ॠ ṝ, ऌ ḷ, ए e, ऐ ai, ओ o, औ au, ं ṃ, ः ḥ, क k, ख kh, ग g, घ gh, ङ ṅ, च c, छ ch, ज j, झ jh, ञ ñ, ट ṭ, ठ ṭh, ड ḍ, ढ ḍh, ण ṇ, त t, थ th, द d, ध dh, न n, प p, फ ph, ब b, भ bh, म m, य y, र r, ल l, व v, श ś, ष ṣ, स s, ह h; post-consonantal vowels ा -ā, ि -i, ी -ī, ु -u, ू -ū, ृ -ṛ, ॄ -ṝ, ॢ -ḷ, े -e, ै -ai, ो -o, ौ -au.

NOTES

Arabic: ْ (sukūn) omitted
ّ (šadda) doubled consonant
Assimilate l of definite article.
Hyphenate article to noun.
Diphthongs aw, ay; nunation an, in, un.
Extra letters in Persian p, ch, zh, g; s, t, z, ṣ, ẓ, ż replace ṣ, ṭ, ẓ, ṯ, ḏ, ḍ; vowels include e, o.
Extra letters in Urdu ṭ, ḍ, ṛ.
This is for classical Arabic; colloquial forms may include further letters, e.g. ə at *FELLAGHA.

Hebrew: also for Aramaic and Yiddish.

Japanese: n is assimilated before b, m, p (*kombu*, not *konbu*).

Russian: stress generally marked by acute accent on vowel; stressed ȳ written ý.

Sanskrit: bare stem used (dictionary form); -a is not written in devanagari.
Also for Hindi.

S

(continued)

|| **se** (se). *Chinese Mus.* Also **che, she, tche.** [a. Chinese *sê*.] A twenty-five-stringed plucked musical instrument, somewhat similar to the zither.

This ancient instrument was already widely used during the Spring and Warring States period (770–476 B.C.). The number of strings was not fixed in ancient times. In quot. 1955, wrongly described as a lute.

1874 C. ENGEL *Catal. Mus. Instruments in S. Kensington Mus.* 53 The ancient stringed instruments, the *kin* and *chê*, were of the dulcimer kind. *Ibid.* 182 *Tche.* Wood, mounted with bone. Sixteen thin brass wires. The movable bridges belonging to the instrument are wanting. **1884** J. A. VAN AALST *Chinese Mus.* 62 The Sê..is said to have been invented by P'ao Hsi.., and to have had originally 50 strings... But the sê now in use has 25 strings..elevated on a movable bridge. **1908** A. C. MOULE in *Jrnl. N. China Branch R. Asiatic Soc.* XXXIX. 108 Shê (Che)... A horizontal psaltery, curved above and flat below... There are twenty-five silk strings..stretched along the body. **1955** A. FANG in E. Pound *Classic Anthol.* p. xi, Of the two kinds of lute, the *k' in* has seven strings and the *se* twenty-five. **1977** KWANG-CHIH CHANG *Archaeol. Anc. China* (ed. 2) ix. 402 Remains of wooden bases for the musical instrument *se* have been collected from the tombs.

sea, *sb.* Add: **I. 2. c.** [tr. L. *mare* (see *MARE[4]).] (Earlier and later examples.)

1667 R. HOOKE *Micrographia* I. lx. 245 Those mountains, which are by Hevelius call'd the Apennine Mountains, and some other, which seem to border on the Seas of the Moon. **1698** C. HUYGENS *Celestial Worlds Discover'd* II. 130 Those vast countries which appear darker than the other, commonly taken for and call'd by the name seas, are discover'd with a good long telescope, to be full of little round cavities. **1833** J. F. W. HERSCHEL *Treat. Astron.* vi. 229 What is, moreover, extremely singular in the geology of the moon is, that although nothing having the character of seas can be traced, (for the dusky spots which are commonly called seas, when closely examined, present appearances incompatible with the supposition of deep water,) yet there are large regions perfectly level, and apparently of a decided alluvial character. **1907** G. P. SERVISS *Moon* iii. 146 This..does not invalidate what I have said about the lunar 'seas', or plains, darkening near sunset more rapidly than we should expect them to do, as a simple result of the low angle at which the sunlight strikes them. **1949** *Jrnl. Brit. Interplanetary Soc.* VIII. 185 The origin of the characteristic features of the lunar surface, craters, mountain ranges and 'seas', is far from being understood. **1974** *Times* 17 Apr. 16/3 It seems that the maria and the basins of the lunar 'seas' are of volcanic origin.

5. d. Roughness of the sea brought about by wind blowing at the time.

1927 G. BRADFORD *Gloss. Sea Terms* 152/1 The waves prevailing at any time are spoken of collectively as the sea, but they must be due to the wind then blowing. **1970** J. VERHOOGEN et al. *Earth* vii. 341/1 In the presence of the generating wind, waves have steep, sharp, asymmetric crests, and broad troughs, and the whole water surface is irregularly choppy. This condition is known as sea. **1977** *Offshore Engineer* July 35/1 In August 1975, the LWC began by using graphical methods to produce sea-swell forecast charts, combining 'sea', or wind-driven waves and 'swell', which is persistent wave movement continuing after the wind has dropped.

8. c. *Physics.* A (physical or mathematical) space filled with particles of a certain kind, *esp.* one in which only the particles near the boundary or surface are significant.

1955 [see *FERMI 1]. **1965** PHILLIPS & WILLIAMS *Inorg. Chem.* I. vi. 207 Because there are electron energy levels lying only very little above the surface of the calm Fermi sea, electrons can take up energy at normal temperatures in a metal and so make a contribution to the specific heat. **1972** *Sci. Amer.* Apr. 26/3 Once an atom has lost an electron it becomes a positive ion that finds itself in a deep electrostatic potential well created by the surrounding sea of negative electrons. **1979** *Ibid.* Sept. 76/3 These events are explained by interactions involving a 'sea' of quarks and anti-quarks that have a virtual existence in the vicinity of a proton.

II. 10. c. *worse things happen at sea* and varr.: a consolatory catch-phrase.

1829 P. EGAN *Boxiana* 2nd Ser. II. 346 The Fancy were too game to complain.., contenting themselves with the old saying, 'that worse accidents occur at sea!' **1869** C. H. SPURGEON *John Ploughman's Talk* v. 41 To be poor is not always pleasant, but worse things than that happen at sea. **1948** 'N. SHUTE' *No Highway* xii. 297 Oh well, worse things happen at sea. I expect we shall get over it. **1978** M. KENYON *Deep Pocket* viii. 97 Worse things 'ave 'appened at sea, he told himself, if 'e shoots..you'll 'ardly feel a thing.

16. b. In the Naut. proverbial phr. *he that would go to sea for pleasure, would go to hell for a pastime* and varr.

1899 A. J. BOYD *Shellback* viii. 110 Shentlemens vot goes to sea for pleasure vould go to hell for pastime. **1910** D. W. BONE *Brassbounder* xxvi. 289 He gave a half-laugh, and muttered the old formula about 'the man who would go to sea for pleasure, going to hell for a pastime!' **1924** R. CLEMENTS *Gipsy of Horn* iii. 50 'He who would go to sea for pleasure would go to hell for a pastime' is an attempt at heavy satire. **1933** M. LOWRY *Ultramarine* i. 50 Well, a man who'd go to sea for fun'd go to hell for a pastime.

III. 18. Simple attributive: **a.** Of or belonging to the sea or a sea: *sea-bed* (later examples), *-marge* (later examples), *-romp*, *-surge*, *-swell*, *-swill.*

1937 *Discovery* Sept. 279/2 The sea-bed gave out a bluish light. **1975** *Offshore* Sept. 49-04/1 Other firms in this business include Heerema, with three special ships designed to drill seabed holes up to 1,200 ft in 700 ft of water. **1923** H. BELLOC *Sonnets & Verse* 159 The rank sea-marge. **1976** *New Yorker* 8 Mar. 122/3 The bird has been watched on the sea-marge of Jamaica Bay. **1876** G. M. HOPKINS *Wr. Deutschland* xvii, in *Poems* (1967) 57 They..rolled With the sea-romp over the wreck. **1912** E. POUND *Ripostes* 25 Known on my keel many a care's hold, And dire sea-surge. **1930** —— *XXX Cantos* vii. 25 Ear, ear for the sea-surge. **1880** W. WHITMAN *Daybks. & Notebks.* (1978) III. 628 A little sea-swell on the water. **1927** H. CRANE *Let.* 12 Sept. (1965) 306 The movement of the verse..of the 'Ave Maria', with its sea-swell crescendo. **1878** G. M. HOPKINS *Poems* (1967) 74 Till a lifebelt and God's will Lend him a lift from the sea-swill.

b. That is an attribute or quality of the sea: *sea-beat*, *-sound*, *-voice* (later examples), *-wash.*

a **1953** DYLAN THOMAS *Quite Early One Morning* (1954) 16 Sea captains..going down into a..cabin of sleep, rocked to the sea-beat of their ears. **1961** Sea-sound [see *HIGHVELD]. **1974** *BP Shield Internat.* Oct. 18/2 All sea-sounds were eclipsed by the noise of the drilling operation. **1930** T. S. ELIOT *Ash Wednesday* 20 The lost lilac and the lost sea voices. **1955** C. TOMLINSON *Necklace* 9 The sea-voice Tearing the silence from the silence. **1930** W. DE LA MARE *On Edge* 297 With the sea-wash in her ears. **1965** E. RICHARDSON *Living Island* 123 There is no sigh of wind and scarcely a whisper of seawash.

c. Consisting of sea: *sea-approach.*

1913 J. MASEFIELD *Mainsail Haul* (ed. 2) 139 The defences to the sea-approach were powerful. **1940** E. COLSTON SHEPHERD *Britain's Air Power* 9 The more usual work of these [coastal reconnaissance] aircraft is that of continuous patrol over all the sea approaches to Germany.

d. Phenomena occurring at sea: *sea-dusk*, *-gust*; also designating actions or events which take place at sea, as *sea-burial*, *-death*, *-rescue.*

1838 POE *Narr. A. G. Pym of Nantucket* vii. 74 The mate..ordered the men to..allow it [*sc.* the body] the usual rites of sea-burial. **1922** JOYCE *Ulysses* 51 Seadeath, mildest of all deaths known to man. **1916** —— *Portrait of Artist as Young Man* (1969) v. 226 Swallows flying through the seadusk over the flowing waters. **1970** T. HUGHES *Crow* 31 The curlew trawled in seadusk through a chime of wineglasses. *c* **1866** G. M. HOPKINS *Poems* (1930) 138 She listened how the sea-gust shook. **1874** *Trans. Highland Soc.* 245 Great loss and much misery is often caused by these destructive 'sea-gusts'. **1959** *Listener* 6 Aug. 217/3 A British sea-rescue plane. **1976** *Morecambe Guardian* 7 Dec. 25/6 A dramatic sea rescue during the early hours of July 5.

e. (*a*) Deposited by or in the sea: *sea-stone*; (*c*) proceeding from the sea: *sea-fog* (later examples), *-fret* (earlier and later examples), *-mist.*

1834 J. J. AUDUBON *Ornith. Biogr.* II. 201 The sea-fog began to approach the land so swiftly, that..we judged it prudent to return to our vessel. **1893** KIPLING in *Pall Mall Budget* 14 Dec. 1950/2 West you'll turn and south again beyond the sea-fog's rim. **1972** *Gloss. Aeronaut. & Astronaut. Terms* (*B.S.I.*) xv. 6 *Sea fog*, fog formed at sea, usually by condensation of moisture in the lower layers of a warm air current passing over a relatively cold sea surface. **1842** C. RIDLEY *Let.* Feb. in *Cecilia* (1958) vii. 86 This evening everything was thawing but I imagine it was only what they call a sea fret. **1963** *Times* 13 June 4/6 Those who came yesterday out of the heat in the surrounding country were surprised to find Brighton enveloped in a sea fret, which..reduced visibility to a furlong or two. **1893** KIPLING in *Pall Mall Budget* 14 Dec. 1947/2 The *Northern Light* drove into the bay and the sea-mist drove with her. **1974** L. DEIGHTON *Spy Story* i. 11 A flurry of sea mist that rolled in upon us. **1918** D. H. LAWRENCE *New Poems* 27 Sad he sits on the white sea-stone. **1922** JOYCE *Ulysses* 291 From his girdle hung a row of sea-stones. **1936** *Geogr. Jrnl.* LXXXVIII. 105 Bib Nambas..are very Melanesian,..with a frequent pigmoid strain, often with white seastones through their noses.

f. Situated in or by the sea: *sea-cave* (later examples), *garden*, *marsh* (later examples), *pen*, *-track.*

1917 D. H. LAWRENCE *Look! We have come Through!* 26 They dwelt in a huge, hoarse sea-cave. **1979** *Amer. Poetry Rev.* Mar.–Apr. 45/2 Three craft..negotiate intricate sharp turns and arcs through..narrow canals into sea-caves. **1881** W. D. HAY *Three Hundred Years Hence* vii. 135 With..sea-garden food, life in these deep-down Harbours is by no means unenjoyable. **1947** I. L. IDRIESS *Isles of Despair* xxxvii. 246 The sea gardens of the lagoons. **1977** *Times* 14 May 12/7 Snorkelling among the magnificent sea gardens which eddy among the rocks. **1835** J. J. AUDUBON *Ornith. Biogr.* III. 241 The Long-billed Curlew spends the day in the sea-marshes. **1982** 'J. GASH' *Firefly Gadroon* vi. 65 The sea marshes show between the long runs of banks and dykes. **1976** *Daily Colonist* (Victoria, B.C.) 3 Oct. 32/3 They [*sc.* salmon fry] were transferred to sea pens on barges.. and continued rapid growth in salt water. **1890** KIPLING *Gipsy Trail* in *Poems 1886–1929* (1929) III. 284 Out on a clean sea-track. **1949** E. MUIR *Coll. Poems* (1960) 164 The smooth sea-tracks that open and close again.

h. *sea-battle* (later example).

1940 N. LAST *Diary* 9 Apr. in *Nella Last's War* (1981) 47, I kept..wondering if our sailors were winning in the reported sea battle.

j. Pertaining to life at sea: *sea-boot* (later examples; also in Naut. slang phr. *a face like a sea-boot*, a dejected or wry expression), *-booted* (later example); *-bread* (earlier example), *-clothes* (later example), *-language* (later example), *-rig*, *-stock* (later example).

1916 'TAFFRAIL' *Pincher Martin* viii. 150 Wot's up wi' yer? You've got a face on yer like a sea-boot. **1946** *Nature* 14 Sept. 386/2 Land Army hose, sea-boot stockings,..and jungle-green pullovers also came under the scheme. **1971** G. M. BROWN *Fishermen with Ploughs* 47 His sea boots filled, and Willag said no more. **1933** L. LUARD *All Hands* 44 The decks..were alive with jovial sea-booted men. **1834** A. UNDERWOOD *Jrnl.* Dec. in *Southwestern Hist. Q.* (1928) Oct. 131, I in company with two of my fellow passengers started taking with us some sea bread water &c. determined to camp out that night. **1933** W. DE LA MARE *Fleeting* 45 His stiffening sea-clothes grey with salt. **1928** L. P. SMITH *Words & Idioms* 20 The sea-languages of the world. **1840** R. H. DANA *Two Years before Mast* 4, I made my appearance on board at twelve o'clock, in full sea-rig. **1892** C. H. FRETWELL *Anc. Mariner* 38, I..purchased my sea-stock of warm clothing, intending to join on the following day.

n. By sea; also, pertaining to navigation: *sea-crossing*, *-trader*, *-trading.*

1936 *British Birds* XXIX. 367 They undertake a 1,200 mile sea-crossing from Greenland to Ireland. **1962** H. R. LOYN *Anglo-Saxon England* i. 24 A sea-crossing is perilous to tribal institutions. **1899** C. J. CUTCLIFFE HYNE *Further Adv. Capt. Kettle* i. 4 Kettle had come across many types of sea-trader in his time. **1921** *Nineteenth Cent.* July 150 She failed..to become a great sea-trading nation.

o. In designations of persons: *sea-fellow.*

1909 E. POUND *Personae* 37 As Glaucus tasting the grass that made him sea-fellow with the other gods. **1918** D. H. LAWRENCE *New Poems* 27, I wish a wild sea-fellow would come down the glittering shingle.

p. In appellations of imaginary beings: *sea-girl.*

1917 T. S. ELIOT *Prufrock* 16 Sea-girls wreathed with seaweed red and brown. **1923** E. P. MATHERS tr. *J. C. Mardrus's Bk. of Thousand Nights & One Night* VII. 80 Suddenly they saw twelve sea girls..come up out of the water and dance a round upon the sand. **1939** DYLAN THOMAS *Map of Love* 5 The sea-girls' lineaments Glint in the staved and siren-printed caverns.

q. That lives or is found in the sea: *sea-gem*, *-harvest*, *-spawn*, *-vegetable* (later example).

1922 JOYCE *Ulysses* 289 Golden ingots, silvery fishes,..purple seagems and playful insects. **1888** L. A. SMITH *Music of Waters* 341 The herring fishery in the Isle of Man is the staple industry of the place—the Manx sea-harvest it is called. **1916** JOYCE *Portrait of Artist as Young Man* (1969) iv. 171 The sea harvest of shells and tangle. **1922** —— *Ulysses* 38 Signatures of all things I am here to read, seaspawn and seawrack. **1979** *Dallas* (Texas) *Times Herald* 30 May 8-E/1 Fans of the delicacy [*sc.* seaweed] believe that the term 'sea vegetables' would..enhance the image of native dishes.

19. Objective: *sea-rider.*

1939 W. B. YEATS *Last Poems* 29 That sea-rider Oisin led by the nose Through three enchanted islands.

20. Similative: *sea-cold* (hence *sea-coldly* adv.), *-grey* (later example), *-shot*, *-smiling* adjs.

1921 W. DE LA MARE *Veil* 78 In sea-cold Lyonesse. **1931** A. HUXLEY *Cicadas* 57, I reach for grapes, but from an inward vine Pluck sea-cold nipples, still bedewed with brine. **1955** E. BOWEN *World of Love* vi. 105 'You mean, you were late at the sea?' 'Not at all,' said Antonia sea-coldly. **1970** T. HUGHES *Crow* 34 Seeing sea-grey mash a mountain of itself. **1874** G. M. HOPKINS *Jrnls. & Papers* (1959) 248 The sea-shot blue-and-green woollen gown our Lady wears. **1922** JOYCE *Ulysses* 277 Charming, seasmiling and unanswering Lydia on Lidwell smiled.

21. Instrumental: *sea-blown*, *-fed*, *-lulled*, *-strewn*, *-sucked* adjs.

1857 J. G. WHITTIER in *National Era* 22 Oct. 170/5 So to us who walk in summer through the cool and sea-blown town. **1945** J. BETJEMAN *New Bats in Old Belfries* 27 Whose fantastic mausoleum Sings its own seablown Te Deum. **1922** JOYCE *Ulysses* 238 A sailorman, rustbearded, ..eyes her. A long and seafed silent rut. **1847** J. R. LOWELL *Poet. Wks.* (1912) 121 Fair Beatrice's spirit wandering now In some sea-lulled Hesperides. **1921** W. DE LA MARE *Veil* 85 The mild noon air of Spring again Lapped shimmering in that sea-lulled lane. **1892** W. B. YEATS *Countess Kathleen* 125 When fades the sea-strewn rose of day. **1934** T. S. ELIOT *Rock* ii. 56 Many left their bodies to the kites of Syria Or sea-strewn along the routes. **1934** Dylan Thomas *18 Poems* 33 Half of the fellow father as he doubles His sea-sucked Adam in the hollow hulk. **1966** *New Statesman* 11 Feb. 196/1, I used To think of the soul As round and smooth Like a sea-sucked pebble.

23. a. Special combinations: **a. sea-affairs:** delete † and add further examples; **sea-air** *attrib.*, pertaining to or involving both the sea and the air; **sea-bag** *U.S.*, a seaman's travelling bag or trunk; also *transf.*, a heavy artillery shell; **sea bed,** † (*a*) a bed for use on board ship (*obs.*); (*b*) the floor of the sea: see sense 18 a in Dict.; **sea-beggar** (later examples); **sea-blessing** *Naut. slang* = *sailor's blessing* s.v. *SAILOR 5 c; **Sea Cadet,** a member of the Sea Cadet Association (see quot. 1976), a voluntary youth organization which seeks to foster and develop for public benefit a sea cadet corps and to provide sea training and promote education in maritime affairs; **sea-change** (later examples); now freq. *transf.* with or without allusion to Shakespeare's use (quot. 1610 in Dict.), an alteration or metamorphosis, a radical change; **sea chest,** (*b*) (see quot. 1909); **sea-cloth,** (*a*) (earlier example); (*b*) cloth used for making sailors' clothing; **sea clutter** = *sea return*(*s*) below; **sea-cook** (earlier and later examples of phr. *son of a sea-cook*); **sea-corpse** *poet.*, the corpse of a person drowned at sea; **sea-dingle** (later *arch.* example); **Sea Dyak:** see *DYAK; **sea-farm:** also **sea-farmer; sea-farming** *vbl. sb.*, mariculture; also as *ppl. a.*; **sea-fever,** longing or desire for the sea or sailing on it; **sea-fire** (later examples); **sea ivory** (earlier and later examples) (see also sense 23 f below); **sea-jockey** *N. Amer.*, a nimble sailor; the sailor of a small craft; occas. *derog.* (cf. *JOCKEY 5 b); **sea-keeping,** of a ship, hovercraft, etc.: the endurance of (rough) conditions at sea; **sea-kindly** *a.* (later examples); **sea-kindliness** (later examples); **sea-lane,** a route at sea for shipping; **sea-lift** *N. Amer.*, a large-scale transportation of troops, supplies, etc., by sea (cf. *AIRLIFT 2); hence as *v. trans.*, to transport by sea; **sea-loch** (later examples); **sea-lock** (later example); **sea-log** (earlier example); **sea-longing,** a yearning for the sea, sea-fever; **sea-mail,** mail conveyed by sea; a service for conveying letters, parcels, etc., by sea (not an official term); so as *v. trans.* (*rare*), to send by sea; cf. *AIRMAIL; **sea marker,** a device which can be dropped from an aircraft to produce a distinctive patch on water below it; **sea-mount,** a large natural elevation rising abruptly from the ocean floor, usu. entirely underwater; an underwater mountain; **Sea People(s)** = *Peoples of the Sea* s.v. *PEOPLE *sb.* 1 c; **sea-price** *Naut. colloq.*, an inflated price; **sea return(s),** unwanted radar images due to reflection from a rough sea; **sea-road** *rare*, a route by sea; **sea scout,** a member of the (Boy) Scout movement engaged in activities pertaining to the sea and seamanship; **sea seiche,** a seiche occurring in the open sea; **Sea Sled** (see quot. 1948) (a proprietary name in the U.S.); **sea-speed** (earlier example); **sea-stack** = STACK *sb.* 7; **sea-state,** the degree of turbulence at sea, esp. as measured according to a scale of average wave height; **sea-time,** (*a*) (later examples); (*c*) the duration of a journey at sea; **sea-toss** (example); **sea-train,** (*a*) a ship used for the transportation of railway cars; (*b*) a group of ships carrying supplies or equipment; **sea-valve** (examples); **sea-wise** *a.*, versed in the ways of the sea; also *absol.* as *sb.*; **sea-woman,** (*b*) a female sailor; a woman working at sea.

1726 Swift *Gulliver* III. i. 2 Having experienced my knowledge in sea-affairs to be at least equal to his, he would enter into any engagement to follow my advice. **1939** J. Masefield *Live & Kicking Ned* 29 He told me something of sea-affairs. **1945** L. E. O. Charlton *Roy. Air Force* 266 A strong Japanese battle fleet..delivered an attack..reminiscent of the sea-air battles of Midway and the Coral Sea. **1959** H. Barnes *Oceanogr. & Marine Biol.* iii. 106 Information about temperature and salinity conditions and their variation enables deductions to be made about physical processes taking place in the sea-air interface. **1918** M. Denig *Let.* July in K. Cowing *Dear Folks at Home* (1919) 250 A few big 'sea-bags' had hit near by. **1919** *Sea-Bag* 9 Feb. 3 Down in the bottom of a sea bag you may find the suit that a German Sub would have fired at if we had been lucky enough to really see a Fritz. **1926** J. W. Thomason *Fix Bayonets!* 148 If Brother Boche had kept flingin' them seabags around here, he'd a-hurt somebody. **1958** J. Kerouac *On Road* II. ii. 187 He grabbed his seabag and threw things into that. **1977** *N.Y. Rev. Bks.* 23 June 6/2 How easy it would have been at that point, one thinks, for the Marine Corps to have packed up its sea bags and departed. **1637** in *Archives of Maryland* (1887) IV. 76 The Inventary of the goods & chattells of mr John Baxter... 1. rugg & an old sea-bed. **1722** Defoe *Moll Flanders* 381 My Governess.. came down herself..bringing me in the first Place, a Sea Bed, as they call it, and all its Furniture. **1774** N. Cresswell *Jrnl.* 8 Apr. (1925) 9 Bought a Sea Bed; paid Captn. Parry my passage. **1922** P. S. Allen *Let.* 30 Mar. (1939) xvi. 183 We are now on our way to Rotterdam..to attend..the 350th anniversary of the recapture of Brill by the 'Sea-beggars' from the Spaniards on 1 April 1572. **1963** *Times* 22 Feb. 17/3 He spoke for an hour to a packed audience of intent undergraduates and history dons about ..the 'invasion' of the Netherlands by Prince William of Orange's sea beggars. **1883** W. C. Russell *Round Galley Fire* 109 The sea-blessings showered out by the cook as he chases his dishes and pans and burns his fingers. **1912** W. I. Downie *Reminisc. Blackwall Midshipman* ii. 19 Sea blessings galore descended on my unfortunate head. **1933** S. Bradford *Shell-Backs & Beachcombers* viii. 181 The mate..gave me his sea-blessing for having recommended such a man to him. **1976** *Times* 13 May 5/8 The Navy League, formed 81 years ago to press for more naval power for Britain, announced yesterday that it is changing its name to the Sea Cadet Association. **1977** *Navy News* June 32/5 Members are grateful to the Leicester Unit, Sea Cadet Corps, for the use of their H.Q. for branch meetings. **1917** E. Pound *Lustra* 193 Full many a fathomed sea-change in the eyes That sought with him the salt sea victories. **1923** J. M. Murry *Pencillings* 164 The characters which have suffered this sea-change, 'of whose bones are coral made', are the only unpleasant characters we remember. **1948** A. C. Baugh *Lit. Hist. England* II. IX. 173 An interesting paper suggesting that romance is transplanted epic, which has undergone a kind of sea-change in the passage. **1974** R. Helms *Tolkien's World* ii. 32 Even before *The Hobbit* was published he was at work on its sequel, a work in which Middle-earth has undergone a wondrous sea change. **1976** *Listener* 8 Apr. 450/3 The Messianic vision..has undergone some strange sea-changes outside Judaism. **1977** 'E. Crispin' *Glimpses of Moon* vii. 117 He..could, moreover..bring about a sea-change in the image of even the most bumbling police officers going about their duties, so that they emerged as prodigies of intelligence, zeal and kindness. **1909** *Cent. Dict.* Suppl., *Sea-chest,* in ship-building, a short open pipe extending from the outside plating to the interior just inside the inner bottom, the inner end of which is closed by a sea-valve placed in a position accessible from the interior of the vessel. **1942** G. C. Manning *Man. Ship Construction* (1943) iii. 76 Sea valves must be so placed as to be easily worked from the engine-room platforms. When they make connection with the sea through the double bottom or otherwise so that they would require a long neck if fastened directly to the shell they are attached to sea chests which are secured on the inside of the shell plating. **1972** L. M. Harris *Introd. Deepwater Floating Drilling Operations* 248 All sea chest strainers were removed. The sea valves were opened and examined. The sea chests were thoroughly examined. **1883** Stevenson *Treas. Isl.* VI. xxxi. 263 'He was a seaman,' said George Merry, who..was examining the rags of clothing. 'Leastways, this is good sea-cloth.' **1890** 'Biff' Hall *Turnover Club* xviii. 172 The wings are removed, and what is technically known as a 'sea cloth' takes their place. **1905** 'Q' *Shining Ferry* III. xviii. 218 A bustious, big fellow, with a round hat like a missionary's, and all the rest of him in sea-cloth. **1946** Sea clutter [see *CLUTTER *sb.* 2 c]. **1970** P. Clissold *Radar in Small Craft* ii. 26 Sea clutter is not likely to be of any consequence beyond three or four miles, but at short range it can obscure stronger targets. **1806** J. Davis *Post-Captain* v. 27 'A precious husband!' exclaimed captain Brilliant... 'A son of a sea-cook! If he was to fall overboard, I would not heave him a rope.' **1922** Joyce *Ulysses* 624 Boisterously trolling, like a veritable son of a seacook. **1977** A. Hunter *Gently Instrumental* iv. 59 You're a right son of a seacook, aren't you? **1878** G. M. Hopkins *Poems* (1967) 74 They say who saw one sea-corpse cold He was all of lovely manly mould. *c* **1931** Auden in M. Roberts *New Signatures* (1932) 30 Doom is dark and deeper than any sea-dingle. **1968** E. S. Iversen *Farming Edge of Sea* ii. 31 The most important group of animals to sea farmers are mollusks (clams, oysters, and mussels), crustaceans (shrimps, crabs, and lobsters), and fishes. **1962** *New Scientist* 18 Oct. 129 Sir Alister Hardy, of Oxford, the leading prophet of sea-farming. **1972** *Aquaculture* I. 232 Seafarming is feasible and it can be carried out with profit. **1975** *Times* 24 Apr. 3/2 By next year the group of sea-farmers expect to have 1,250,000 Pacific oysters..ready for the market. A company, Western Aquaculture, is one of the sea-farming organizations. **1902** J. Masefield (*title of poem*) Sea-fever. **1931** *Daily Express* 23 Sept. 9/4 Men with the sea-fever on them pottered about among the debris of the docks. **1980** P. Moyes *Angel Death* i. 9 The much smaller island..has been infected by the current sea-fever to the point of constructing a small yacht basin. **1903** Kipling *Five Nations* 74 Flying-fish about our bows, Flying sea-fires in our wake. **1947** K. Tennant *Lost Haven* ii. 30 About her the impersonal sea-fire broke and the strange lights vibrated and shone. **1851** H. Melville *Moby Dick* I. xvi. 111 Those thews ran not through base blocks of land wood, but deftly travelled through sheaves of sea-ivory. **1968** G. Jones *Hist. Vikings* I. i. 23 Southwards.. went skins and furs, amber, sea-ivory, and slaves. **1847** H. Melville *Omoo* xvi. 58 Jermin, sea-jockey that he was, sometimes stood in the fore-chains. **1897** *Outing* Dec. 234/1 Aboard one of these well-balanced and swift little vessels the sea jockey's art can easily be acquired. **1971** D. Conover *One Man's Island* 67 The sea jockeys have taken over the waterways... Outboard cruiser owners—sea jockeys, as we call them. **1963** *Times* 2 Mar. 8/4 Their employment in certain roles will depend largely on their sea-keeping qualities. **1972** C. Mudie *Motor Boats & Boating* 144 Maximum speeds have crept up from some forty knots to eighty knots in ten years and seakeeping has improved out of all recognition with rough water speeds nearly doubled. **1936** C. Winchester *Shipping Wonders of World* I. 690/3 The Livonia..proved her 'sea-kindliness' by crossing the Atlantic in the worst of weather. **1976** *Yachting World* Oct. 110/2 Of course, the boat doesn't usually match true wind speed in open sea conditions, but it does exhibit truly phenomenal sea-kindliness with the hydrofoils set in moderate and heavy conditions. **1958** J. L. Kent *Ships in Rough Water* xi. 157 A seakindly ship is one which rides the seas in rough weather without shipping green water and with little spray blown inboard. **1981** *Times* 2 Feb. 22 There is a possibility of building hulls which can achieve speeds in excess of 30 knots on a waterline length of only 75 metres. These..should be extremely sea-kindly. **1878** Sea-lane [in Dict., sense 18 c]. **1948** *British Birds* XLI. Suppl. 1 After some months on its sea-lanes one could not but feel that the true answer to any one question could only be known if it were possible to cover the whole area in a matter of a few days. **1978** J. A. Michener *Chesapeake* 346 Can we keep the sea lanes open? **1956** *Sun* (Baltimore) 19 Dec. 2/1 The General Eltinge will sail..tomorrow with the first of 5,500 Hungarian refugees to head toward the United States by sea... The sealift complements commercial air services and the airlift inaugurated by United States military planes. **1967** *Economist* 4 Mar. 802/2 [The United States] has the air-lift and sea-lift capacity to be on hand whenever a power vacuum develops. **1972** S. Burnford *One Woman's Arctic* i. 15 It had been brought in by the annual sea-lift the year before. **1974** *Greenville* (S. Carolina) *News* 23 Apr. 14/3 The Middle East fighting proved, he says, our capacity to airlift and sealift needed munitions and equipment over long distances. **1980** *N.Y. News* 11 May 14/2 Officials put at 30,598 the total number of Cubans sealifted to freedom across the Florida strait. **1934** Sea loch [see *FIARD, FJARD]. **1975** J. G. Evans *Environment Early Man Brit. Isles* iii. 67 The various long bays of south-west Ireland, some of which, like the sea lochs of western Scotland, have been glacially deepened as well. **1959** *Times* 8 Dec. 13/6 Down at the sea-locks..the tugs would be worrying like strange small sea animals. **1853** D. G. Rossetti *Let.* 16 Apr. (1965) I. 131 Your 'sea-log' gave me the greatest pleasure. **1955** J. R. R. Tolkien *Return of King* 149 Deep in the hearts of all my kindred lies the sea-longing. *a* **1973** —— *Silmarillion* (1977) xxiii. 244 The sea-longing woke in his heart. **1951** R. Macaulay *Let.* 12 Aug. in *Lett. to Friend* (1961) 173, I think I shall airmail this [letter]... But I really will seamail the next. **1971** *New Society* 14 Jan. 47/1 This [order coupon] gives inland and overseas rates (airmail and seamail). **1933** *Gloss. Aeronaut. Terms* (*B.S.I.*) 64 *Sea marker,* a device dropped from an aircraft on to water, providing a distinguishable patch for determining the drift-angle. **1944** 'N. Shute' *Pastoral* iii. 43 He began a chat with the Equipment Officer about sea-markers that did not mark. **1941** *Bull. Geol. Soc. Amer.* LII. 338 A number of remarkable submarine mountains, termed 'seamount' by the United States Board on Geographic Names, rise sharply to heights of 1 to more than 2 miles above the gulf floor. **1959** *New Scientist* 1 Jan. 14/1 The few Pacific seamounts whose summits do form islands are mostly coral atolls. **1962** [see *GUYOT]. **1977** *Dædalus* Summer 118 Both noticed that the magnetic field over some seamounts could be explained only if the seamount was reversely magnetized. **1928** C. Dawson *Age of Gods* xv. 358 It is extremely improbable that the Sea Peoples actually penetrated into the Hittite homelands. **1957** *Antiquity & Survival* II. 145/1 Sisera stood at the head of the Canaanite coalition, and perhaps belonged to the Sea People who invaded Palestine in the 12th century B.C. and gained control of the sea-coast. **1978** N. K. Sandars *Sea Peoples* iv. 83 Wild northerners..took ship to arrive on the borders of Egypt as those mysterious 'Sea Peoples' who so terrified Rameses III. **1910** D. W. Bone *Brassbounder* 64 'Good ol' "sea price",' said Martin. 'Many an 'appy 'ome, an' garden wit' a flagstaff, is built o' "sea price".' **1924** R. Clements *Gipsy of Horn* iv. 71 Sea-price is often a figure which a Maltee Jew would hesitate to ask. **1972** N. Ayland *Schooner Captain* xv. 134 All the bread he would let them have was a two pound loaf, for which he charged sea price. **1945** E. W. Cowan *Sea-Return Effects & their Elimination in AN/APS-6* (M.I.T. Radiation Lab. Rep. No. 707) 1 An airplane flying very close to the sea may be hidden by sea return. **1959** *Listener* 12 Feb. 277/1 It is almost impossible to pick up that iceberg with the radar equipment, because of what we call 'sea return' or 'sea clutter'. **1966** D. Taylor *Introd. Radar & Radar Techniques* iii. 40 The actual performance obtained with this form of A.S.V. equipment depended on aircraft height, state of sea (because of sea returns), operator's experience, etc. **1893** *Columbus* (Ohio) *Dispatch* 9 Nov., If fish disappeared from the sea-roads and fiords. **1906** *Outlook* 19 May 677/1 We hold the great sea-roads to the East. **1907** T. C. Middleton *Geogr. Knowl. Discov. Amer.* 25 The Vivaldi brothers of Genoa..in 1291 essayed a sea-road to India. **1911** R. S. S. Baden-Powell *Sea Scouting for Boys* 8 Sea Scouts are of two kinds, viz. (1) Coastguard Scouts; (2) Seamen Scouts. **1912** C. Beresford in W. Baden-Powell *Sea Scouting & Seamanship for Boys* p. vi, The Sea Scouts were formed as an auxiliary to..the Boy Scouts. The object of the Sea Scouts is to teach lads at or near the sea seamanship, navigation, pilotage, knotting and splicing, how to handle boats under oars and sail, [etc.]. **1950** *Oxf. Jun. Encycl.* IX. 87/1 The boy who is fond of the sea can become a Sea Scout... There are Sea Scout Troops on rivers and inland waterways as well as on the sea. **1977** *Listener* 24 Mar. 382/3, I was a sea scout and sailed and rowed boats. **1925** J. Proudman in *Monthly Notices R. Astron. Soc.* (*Geophysical Suppl.*) I. 247 By 'sea-seiches' we mean those oscillations of fairly definite period but of irregular amplitude and phase which are frequently observed on the sea coast. **1967** *Oceanogr. & Marine Biol.* V. 42 These modes have been called sea seiches..and are basically similar to the transient oscillations or seiches set up by wind and atmospheric pressure in closed basins. **1916** *Rudder* Apr. 175 One noticeable thing about the sea sled..is the absence of bow-wave. **1948** R. de Kerchove *Internat. Maritime Dict.* 639/2 *Sea sled,* a type of construction adopted for small craft of high speed in which the ordinary V bottom is inverted in order to collect a layer of air under the bows of the boat. **1957** *Official Gaz.* (U.S. Patent Office) TM-10/2 Norman A. McDonald, Skokie, Ill. Filed Jan. 24, 1957. Sea Sled.. For Boats. First use Mar. 15, 1953. **1887** W. H. White *Mod. War Ships* 94 The 'sea-speeds' of all war-ships are always estimated on different assumptions. **1899** *Geogr. Jrnl.* Mar. 288 The isolated rock-masses and sea-stacks, which we are enabled to trace by means of the soundings. **1973** C. BONINGTON *Next Horizon* xxi. 292 A sea-stack on the north coast of Scotland. [**1963** *Meteorol. Gloss.* (Met. Office) (ed. 4) 222 The degree of sea disturbance is reported in a 'state of sea' code in which the scale number increases from 0 to 9 according to the average wave height.] **1967** *Jane's Surface Skimmer Systems 1967–68* 85/1 The journey has been covered successfully in Sea States 2–4, with wave heights up to 5 ft 0 in (1·5 m). **1977** *Offshore Engineer* Apr. 74/1 The calculator multiplies measured value of the load by a factor determined by sea-state, and compares result with safe-load for the particular crane luff angle specified in manufacturer's table. **1933** J. MASEFIELD *Bird of Dawning* 16, I wished to get sea-time, sir, so as to be able to pass for master. **1930** *Times* 26 Mar. 17/4 Her sea-time beat the Bremen's best..by eighteen minutes. **1977** *Navy News* Aug. 22 (Advt.), Service includes normal roster sea-time in Leander and Type 12 frigates and small ships. **1847** H. MELVILLE *Omoo* xxiv. 92 'Give him a sea-toss!' 'Overboard with him!' **1933** *Nat. Geogr. Mag.* May 581/1 Freight-car contents are transferred here into the holds of liners, and recently a terminal was established which places loaded cars themselves within huge vessels called 'seatrains'. **1942** W. S. CHURCHILL *Second World War* (1951) IV. I. xxii. 349 These equipments will sail for Suez..in two sea-trains taken from the Havana sugar traffic, doing 15 and 13 knots respectively. **1947** *Sun* (Baltimore) 14 July 7/3 The ships which..should be started this year..are..two for Alaskan trade specifically, two sea trains and two 'mystery'. **1895** KIPLING *Day's Work* (1898) 81 A sea-valve that communicated directly with the water outside. **1915** CHESTERTON *Poems* 16 On them the sea-valves cluster and the grey sea-forests curl. **1934** *Sun* (Baltimore) 17 Sept. 12/1 The sea-wise reason that in a strong breeze and an attendant unruly sea that elongated prow will come down and pound against the chop or plunge into a heavy swell. **1966** T. H. RADDALL *Hangman's Beach* I. ii. 29 The sea-wise folk of Halifax awaited word from Europe. **1939** *Sun* (Baltimore) 1 July 20/2 Twenty-three seawomen sailed into Baltimore harbor yesterday afternoon aboard the ship William J. Stanford. **1963** *Punch* 21 Aug. 288/3 The endless queue of frustrated seawomen.

d. sea-attorney (examples); **sea-biscuit** = *sand dollar* s.v. SAND *sb.*[2] 10 b in Dict. and Suppl.; **sea butterfly** (examples); **sea-clam,** substitute for def.: one of several species of clam found on the Atlantic coast of North America, esp. the surf clam, *Spisula solidissima*; cf. HEN-CLAM; (earlier and later examples); **sea-moth,** a small fish of the family Pegasidæ, found in Indo-Pacific waters and having bony plates covering the body and enlarged pectoral fins; **sea-poacher** (later examples); **sea tiger** = BARRACUDA; **sea wasp,** a poisonous jellyfish belonging to the order Cubomedusæ, found in Indo-Pacific waters.

1849 H. MELVILLE *Mardi* I. 55 There is the ordinary Brown Shark, or sea-attorney, so called by sailors. **1854** *Putnam's Mag.* Apr. 362/2 The dippers dip carefully, lest they get a stroke from the ray..or a rip from his cousin the 'sea-attorney'. **1949** G. E. & N. MACGINITIE *Nat. Hist. Marine Anim.* xxvi. 236 The sand dollars, sea biscuits, or cake urchins..resemble very much flattened sea urchins. **1972** *Islander* (Victoria, B.C.) 12 Mar. 16/4 White people call them [*sc.* sea-urchins] sea-biscuits or sand-dollars. **1932** BORRADAILE & POTTS *Invertebrata* 494 The Pteropoda (sea butterflies)..are modified for pelagic life. **1972** M. S. GARDINER *Biol. Invertebrates* v. 161/1 Planktonic 'pteropods'..or 'sea butterflies'. **1765** J. BARTRAM *Jrnl.* 29 July in *Trans. Amer. Philos. Soc.* (1942) XXXIII. 16/2 There is many clam shels of different sises..y[e] very same with our sea clams. **1782** [see *HARD-SHELLED *a.* 1]. **1935** J. C. LINCOLN *Cape Cod Yesterdays* 49 Along the outer bar, almost two miles from shore..were the large 'sea clams'. **1960** J. J. ROWLANDS *Spindrift* 83 Sea clams are from four to six inches long and about four inches wide. **1905** D. S. JORDAN *Guide to Study of Fishes* II. xiii. 239 These 'sea-moths' are fantastic little fishes. **1947** K. H. BARNARD *Pict. Guide S.Afr. Fishes* III. 76 The Dragon-fish or sea-moth..is also encased in bony plates like the sea-horses... It derives its name of sea-moth from its habit of skimming over the surface of the water. **1978** *Nature* 26 Oct. 693/1 The sea moths are a small family (Pegasidae) of marine fishes found only in the Indian and Western Pacific oceans, from East Africa to Hawaii. **1836** W. YARRELL *Hist. Brit. Fishes* I. 70 The Armed Bullhead, Pogge. Lyrie, Sea-poacher, Pluck, Noble. **1905** D. S. JORDAN *Guide to Study of Fishes* II. xxv. 449 The sea-poachers or alligator-fishes, *Agonidæ*, are sculpins enclosed in a coat of mail. [**1924** L. L. MOWBRAY in J. O. La Gorce *Bk. Fishes* 143 Well deserving its nickname of 'The Tiger of the Sea', the carnivorous Barracuda..darts at its prey on sight.] **1937** M. N. KAPLAN *Big Game Anglers' Paradise* iv. 180 Although ichthyologists gave the great barracuda the euphonious name *Sphyraena barracuda*, in common parlance it bears the *nom-de-guerre*, 'Sea-tiger'. **1963** Sea tiger [see *PICUDA]. **1910** A. G. MAYER *Medusæ of World* III. 504 The flexible part of the tentacles are [*sic*] armed with nematocysts, the stinging power of which is so great that the name 'Sea Wasp' is commonly given to these medusæ. **1966** J. H. BARNES in W. J. Rees *Cnidaria & their Evolution* 332 The origin of such stings was not known, but..it must have been a sea wasp. **1977** C. MCCULLOUGH *Thorn Birds* xiii. 301 We're too far south here for sea wasps.

e. sea-bamboo *S. Afr.*, a large kelp, *Ecklonia maxima*; = SEA-TRUMPET 3.

1798 S. H. WILCOCKE tr. *Stavorinus' Voy. East Indies* I. I. i. 25 On the 10th of November, we saw for the first time trumpets, or sea-bamboo, floating on the ocean. **1822** W. BURCHELL *Trav. Interior S. Afr.* I. ii. 28 The Dutch call this plant *Zee bambos* (sea-bamboo), and boys after cutting its stem to a convenient length when dry, sometimes amuse themselves in blowing it as a horn or trumpet. **1946** L. G. GREEN *So Few are Free* viii. 116 The place is called Bamboes Bay, because the sea bamboo is piled high on the beach after heavy gales. **1973** *Stand. Encycl. S. Afr.* IX. 562/2 The largest kelp of Southern Africa is the sea-trumpet or sea-bamboo..which commonly reaches lengths of over 6 metres.

f. sea arrow-grass, a marsh plant, *Triglochin maritima*, with fleshy grass-like leaves and spikes of green flowers; **sea-aster** (later examples); **sea convolvulus** = SEA-BELL I, *sea-bindweed*; **sea ivory,** a pale greyish lichen, *Ramalina siliquosa*, growing in flattened branches on sea-shore rocks; see also sense 23 a in Dict. and Suppl.; **sea lungwort** (later examples); **sea myrtle** = *groundsel-tree* s.v. GROUNDSEL *sb.*[1] 2.

1770 J. HILL *Herbarium Britannicum* II. 215 (*heading*) Sea Arrow Grass. **1851** C. A. JOHNS *Flowers of Field* II. 245 Sea Arrow-grass... Salt marshes, common. **1975** J. G. EVANS *Environment Early Man Brit. Isles* ii. 37 A number of species..today confined to coastal or estuarine situations, such as sea arrow grass..and sea thrift. **1925** G. BONNIER *Brit. Flora* 96 Sea Aster. Salt marshes: July–Sept. **1960** *Oxf. Bk. Wild Flowers* 136/2 Sea Aster.. is common in salt-marshes and on cliffs and rocks round the coasts. **1921** 'K. MANSFIELD' *Let.* 8 Aug. (1977) 227 Bathing dresses hanging over verandas, and sandshoes on window sills, and little pink 'sea' convolvulus. **1966** *Oxf. Bk. Flowerless Plants* p. viii/1 'Sea Ivory'..grows abundantly wherever there are rocks exposed at high-water mark. **1797** J. E. SMITH *Eng. Bot.* VI. 368 (*heading*) Sea lungwort. **1960** Sea lungwort [see *oyster-plant* s.v. *OYSTER 5d]. **1883** G. O. SHIELDS *Rustlings in Rockies* xxi. 195 Within the space of this five acres may be found.. sea myrtle, grape vine and ivy of several varieties. **1938** M. K. RAWLINGS *Yearling* xxiii. 279 The October blooming of dog-fennel and sea-myrtle had turned to a feathery fluff.

sea-bass. Restrict *U.S.* to senses in Dict. and substitute for defs. of senses a and c: **a.** A marine food fish of the family Serranidæ; cf. JEW-FISH. **c.** The black sea-bass, *Centropristis striatus*, found along the Atlantic coast of North America (earlier and further examples). Add: **e.** = BASS *sb.*[1] 2; *LOUP *sb.*[4]

1765, 1888 [see *BLACK FISH 1]. **1900** F. NORRIS *Blix* 129 There were..sheaves of fishing-rods, from the four-ounce wisp of the brook-trout up to the rigid eighteen-ounce lance of the king-salmon and sea-bass. **1961** E. S. HERALD *Living Fishes of World* 177/2 The giant sea basses, sometimes called jewfishes,..are the largest American serranids. *Ibid.* 192/1 The genus *Cynoscion* includes..the California white seabass, *C. nobilis*. **1966, 1969** [see *LOUP *sb.*[4]]. **1973** J. GRIGSON *Fish Cookery* 104 To walk into a fishmonger's and see a tray of sea bass is a beautiful sight.

sea-bathe, *v.* Delete *rare* and add earlier and later examples. Hence **sea-·bathing** *ppl. a.*

1792 LADY TEMPLETOWN *Let.* 11 June in A. E. Newdigate-Newdegate *Cheverels* (1898) vii. 104 Eliza is sea-bathing at Ramsgate. *a***1930** D. H. LAWRENCE *Last Poems* (1932) 156 These all-but-naked sea-bathing city people. **1951** N. M. GUNN *Well at World's End* xviii. 141 We did nothing but sun-bathe and sea-bathe.

sea-bathing. (Earlier examples.)

1749 S. RICHARDSON *Let.* ?Nov.–Dec. (1964) 133 The sea-bathing I have not tried.

attrib. **1781** J. HARE *Let.* 13 Feb. in *15th Rep. R. Comm. Hist. MSS.* (1897) App. VI. 457 We are to go in about six weeks' time to some sea-bathing place.

sea beach. (Earlier example.)

1742 *Rep. Comm. Houses Assembly S.-Carolina Exped. against St. Augustine* 21 He encamped that Night at Lacenela (the first Palmeta Hut on the Sea-Beach).

Seabees (sī·bīz), *sb. pl.* Also with small initial. [f. representation of initial letters of *construction battalion* + pl. *-s*.] **a.** (Members of) the Construction Battalions formed as a volunteer branch of the Civil Engineer Corps of the U.S. Navy.

1942 *Army & Navy Jrnl.* 21 Mar. 790/2 'Seabees' is the new name chosen to designate the new Naval Construction Regiments... With the name an insignia has been adopted —a flying bee, fighting mad. On its head it sports a sailor hat. In its fore hand or leg it clutches a spitting 'Tommy Gun'; in its amidship hand, a wrench, and in its aft hand, a carpenter's hammer. **1945** D. DEMPSEY in *Best One-Act Plays of 1944* 21 I'm in the Seabees, which means I'm in the Navy. **1950** 'D. DIVINE' *King of Fassarai* xi. 90 'The Seabees are starting in here—' he placed his pencil on the chart. **1960** S. W. ROSKILL *War at Sea* III. I. 339 The 'Seabees' also proved themselves first-class fighting troops when the need arose. **1980** G. V. HIGGINS *Kennedy for Defense* xix. 174 Some cops were in the Seabees, lotta cops was in the Army.

b. *attrib.* or as *adj.* (Sometimes in *sing.* form.)

1942 *Sun* (Baltimore) 17 Nov. 13/3 Brief ceremonies attended by naval officers marked the placing in operation of the third 'seabees' center constructed in Virginia. **1977** *Hongkong Standard* 12 Apr. 8/4 Of the 1,400 navy men here, more than 800 are seabee construction workers who will leave when the facility is completed. **1981** G. V. HIGGINS *Rat on Fire* v. 35 You were running that Seabees reunion.

seaboard, *sb.* **4.** (Earlier example.)

1788 F. ASBURY *Jrnl.* 10 July (1821) II. 36 The Gnats are almost as troublesome here, as the moschetoes in the low-lands of the sea-board.

sea-boat. 1. a. Delete † *Obs.* and add later examples. **c.** *spec.* A small, manœuvrable craft sent out from a larger vessel, as in cases of emergency at sea.

1856 RUSKIN *Harbours of England* 1 One object there is still, which I never pass without the renewed wonder of childhood; and that is the bow of a Boat... The blunt head of a common bluff undecked sea-boat. **1892** R. C. LESLIE *Sea-Boat* 4 The building of a bluff-bowed, flat-floored sea-boat, is a much greater test of a boat-builder's skill than the construction of any form of longer and sharper craft. **1909** *Man. Seamanship* (Admiralty) II. viii. 142 Never call away a 'lifeboat' at sea except for the purpose of saving life; on all other occasions call away the 'sea boat'. **1914** 'BARTIMEUS' *Naval Occasions* xx. 179 The seaboat's crew had gone through an undress rehearsal of 'Man overboard!' **1963** H. C. DE MIERRE *Long Voyage* ix. 148 Port and starboard sea-boats had been put in the water. **1972** C. MUDIE *Motor Boats & Boating* 76 Over twelve feet in length..the types of boat begin to diverge from the general purpose dinghy..into seaboats for family use and for fishing.

Seabright (sī·brəit). Also with small initial. The name of a small town on the coast of New Jersey, used *attrib.* and *absol.* to designate a variety of flat-keeled fishing-boat from the region, esp. adapted for landing on beaches in heavy seas.

1911 *Rudder* XXV. 83 (*caption*) Jersey Coast fishermen getting one of their power Seabright skiffs off and on the beach. **1930** G. PINCHOT *To South Seas* i. 7 The bronze and mahogany launch was replaced by a Seabright dory twenty-two feet long by seven feet wide. *Ibid.* xii. 237 In the Seabright again I put it on the floor. **1971** P. J. GUTHORN *Sea Bright Skiff* v. 74 The Sea Bright skiff rum boats were progressively, but never completely, replaced by boats of V-bottom design.

sea-cat. 2. Restrict † to sense in Dict. and add: **b.** *S. Afr.* One of several species of octopus, esp. *Octopus vulgaris*.

1785 G. FORSTER tr. *Sparrman's Voy. Cape of Good Hope* I. ii. 26 The *sepia loligo*, and the *sepia octopodia*,..are known to our sailors by the name of black-fish and sea-cats. **1882** *Cape Q. Rev.* Oct. 36 Even the sea cat responded to the hook. **1913** W. W. THOMPSON *Sea Fisheries Cape Colony* ii. 51 The octopus or sea-cat..appears to find a more congenial habitat on the rocky stretches of sea-board. **1957** S. SCHOEMAN *Strike!* iii. 38 If seacat is used, a baby octopus put on whole will be most acceptable.

5. *Mil.* (In form *Seacat* or *Sea Cat.*) The name of a short-range, ship-to-air, guided missile (system).

1959 *Times* 5 Feb. 7/3 By early next year a considerable number of Britain's warships will be equipped with surface-to-air missiles, and these weapons..will almost certainly include the Short SX-A5 which was named the Seacat by the Admiralty and the Ministry of Supply yesterday. **1969** B. B. SCHOFIELD in P. Kemp *Hist. Royal Navy* xxvii. 294/1 In April 1958 a contract was awarded for the development of a close-range ship-to-air guided weapon to replace the 40-mm Bofors A/A guns in H.M. ships... This was achieved by the production of the Seacat missile. **1977** *Navy News* June 6 The 2,500 ton warship is armed with an automatic rapid fire 4·5 in. gun, Sea Cat and Exocet missile systems, and she operates a Wasp helicopter.

sea-conny. Add: Also **secunnie.** (Further examples.)

1810 M. GRAHAM *Jrnl. Residence India* (1812) 85 The gunners and quarter-masters..are Indian-Portuguese; they are called *secunnies*. **1929** D. J. MUNRO *Roaring Forties* xxxii. 160 With a crash and lurch that sent the secunnie (helmsman), at the wheel flying over the top of it the ship struck.

sea-craft. Add: **3.** Sea-going craft; sea-vessels considered collectively.

1919 *Q. Rev.* Jan. 184 Vessels, whether sea-craft or air-craft. **1928** *Daily Express* 18 Jan. 1 Our oldest craft, seacraft.

sea-crafty, *a.* (Later example.)

1955 J. R. R. TOLKIEN *Return of King* v. ix. 153 Sea-crafty men of the Ethir gazing southward spoke of a change coming with a fresh wind from the sea.

sea-dog. Add: **5.** (Earlier U.S. example.)

1823 J. F. COOPER *Pilot* II. xi. 187 Ahead, heave ahead, sea-dogs!

Hence **sea-·doggery,** behaviour or practice characteristic of a sea-dog or sea-dogs (sense 5); sailors collectively.

1928 *Daily Express* 9 Oct. 3/3 A little grey Dover full of small, sturdy ships..and a general air—assisted by a strong smell of oil, pea soup and roasting mutton—of waggish sea doggery. **1961** *John o' London's* 20 July 111/3 A background of adventure and sea-doggery.

seadrome (sī·drōᵘm). [f. SEA *sb.* + *-DROME, after *AERODROME.] A floating aerodrome, an offshore airport; *spec.* (in early use) one of a series of constructions on or at which a (sea) plane could alight (for refuelling) during a journey.

The *seadrome* exists solely as a concept. None has yet been built.

1923 *Daily Mail* 17 July 10 The feature of the project is that there should be eight 'seadromes'..moored permanently on the Atlantic air route. **1936** J. Grierson *High Failure* xiv. 293 A series of floating platforms (colloquially called 'sea-dromes') on which planes could alight, spaced at intervals of 5–600 miles across the Atlantic. **1947** *Jrnl. R. Aeronaut. Soc.* LI. 143/2 If alighting places for flying boats were more easy to provide than aerodromes, could Mr. Lipscomb offer any reason why they..suffered from lack of 'sea-dromes', whereas there were plenty of very costly aerodromes for landplanes? **1948** *Trinidad Guardian* 18 June 2/1 (*heading*) Seadrome site inspected. **1969** *Daily Tel.* 4 Sept. 24/2 The seadrome scheme for Foulness plans a floating airport complex measuring five million square yards. **1970** *New Scientist* 22 Jan. 156/1 The two firms of engineers..are already discussing their plans for a 'Seadrome' with one of the Thames estuary development companies.

sea-fishing. (Earlier example.)
1745 Ellis *Mod. Husbandman* VI. ii. 66 Sea-fishing is the..healthiest Fishing of all others.

sea-floor. **1.** The floor of the sea.
1855 [in Dict. s.v. Sea *sb.* 18 a]. **1922** [see *outwander *v.*]. **1946** *Proc. Prehist. Soc.* XII. 24 The seal must have sunk in deep water and come to rest on the sea-floor. **1967** *Oceanogr. & Marine Biol.* V. 317 Two principal dispersal mechanisms affect shelf benthos; these are, (1) shallow seafloor connections and, (2) surface currents. **1981** *London Mag.* July 9 A door slams, a heavy wave, a door, the sea-floor shudders.

2. **sea-floor spreading** *Geol.*, (the hypothesis of) the formation of fresh areas of oceanic crust, occurring through the upwelling of magma at mid-ocean ridges and its subsequent outward movement on either side.
1961 R. S. Dietz in *Nature* 3 June 854/1 [The concept proposed here, which can be termed the 'spreading sea-floor theory', is largely intuitive, having been derived through an attempt to interpret sea-floor bathymetry.] *Ibid.* 856/2 Sea floor spreading obviates this difficulty: continents never move through the sima. **1971** *Nature* 1 Jan. 9/2 The whole of geophysics has been transformed within a few years by the discovery of seafloor spreading. **1977** A. Hallam *Planet Earth* 42/3 If its magnetic signature allowed an age to be assigned to each piece of ocean floor, it was possible to calculate a velocity for sea-floor spreading.

sea·food. orig. and chiefly *U.S.* Food obtained from the sea; fish, crustacea, etc., used as food. Freq. *attrib.*
1836 *Knickerbocker* VIII. 423 She said that she had come to Screamy Point to get 'sea-food'. **1906** *N.Y. Even. Post* 10 Mar. 5 Up State residents are among the best customers of the sea food, fruit and produce dealers. **1927** *Weekly Dispatch* 1 May 1/2 The correct name of the Poydras levee [at New Orleans] is the Carnavon levee, so named by the Carnavon family in England, who built it in 1870 to protect the plantation and seafood packing plant they then owned. **1935** A. Baugh *Hist. Eng. Lang.* xi. 462 A writer in the London *Daily Mail* recently complained that an Englishman would find 'positively incomprehensible' the American words..*sea-food*,..and *hired-girl*. **1944** T. Barbour *That Vanishing Eden* 166, I was dining with some friends at a popular seafood restaurant in Miami. **1953** J. Hilton *Time & Time Again* i. 6 'I hope you like sea-food.'.. 'Sea-food?.. Fish, that is? Oh yes, I do, indeed.' (..True enough, though this 'sea-food' set Charles thinking that he also enjoyed 'land-food'.) **1965** H. Gold *Man who was not with It* iii. xxv. 234 Grack's contact man cooked in a diner on the seafood coast of Baltimore. **1978** K. Hudson *Jargon of Professions* iii. 82 Twenty or thirty years ago..fish was upgraded to seafood.

sea-god. (Later examples.)
1900 A. Nutt *Fairy Mythol. Shakes.* 31 Mongan, son of the Irish sea-god Manannan mac Lir. **1950** 'D. Divine' *King of Fassarai* xiii. 100 To-day the fish had been wary and the sea god not kind. **1978** R. Mitchison *Life in Scotland* iii. 60 The islanders of north Lewis sacrificed to a sea god at Hallowtide.

sea-going, *a.* Add: **1. b.** Capable of being used or suitable for use on a sea-going vessel; carried or conducted by sea.
1895 [see Sea-going *sb.*]. **1928** C. Dawson *Age of Gods* viii. 182 The sea-going trade of the Ægean world. **1962** *Listener* 29 Mar. 540/1 Land-base missiles and sea-going missiles.

sea-grass. Add: **2.** (*b*) (Later examples.) Also, the dried stems of this plant, used in ropes, chair-seats, etc.
1900 *Jrnl. Soc. Arts* 12 Jan. 170/1 Sea grass is a long thin grass that grows on the protected flats of the Lower St. Lawrence River. *Ibid.* (*heading*) Canadian sea grass for upholstering. **1911** [see *porch chair* s.v. *porch 7]. **1933** P. T. Tucker *Riding High Country* ii. 31 His las' rope was sea grass. **1979** *Dictionaries* I. 64 Sea grass is..a derived product with a local name.

4. *attrib.* (Later examples.)
1911 *Daily Colonist* (Victoria, B.C.) 11 Apr. 7/1 (Advt.), Special sale of sea grass chairs. **1967** *Southerly* XXVII. 152 Immemorial deck-chairs and seagrass tables.

sea-green, *a.* and *sb.* Add: **A.** *adj.* **2.** In phr. *sea-green incorruptible*, applied to Robespierre by Carlyle (see quot. 1837 in Dict.) and now commonly used allusively (often followed by some other word) to designate a person of rigid honesty or uncompromising idealism. Also in extended use and *absol.*, impervious to moral corruption.
1931 *Economist* 7 Mar. 492/1 Although Mr. Hu Han-min at Manking may be a 'sea-green incorruptible' of as pure a dye as Robespierre, the local representatives of the Party in the country districts are often oppressors of the poor. **1936** H. G. Wells *Anat. Frustration* ix. 94 His [*sc.* Philip Snowden's] early appearance as the 'sea green incorruptible' of the British Labour revolution. **1958** *Spectator* 1 Aug. 157/1 Utopia is to be attained only by sea-green incorruptibility. **1960** C. P. Snow *Affair* xl. 372 'I shall have to,' Skeffington replied, obdurate and sea-green. **1976** *Listener* 5 Aug. 143/3 He is, for all that, a man of sea-green integrity. **1977** *New Society* 17 Feb. 328/1 A former Chief Constable from the north west..a man of cast-iron integrity from a religious background and ..a sea-green incorruptible.

sea-gull. Add: **2.** A casual, non-Union, dock labourer. *N.Z. slang.*
c **1926** 'Mixer' *Transport Workers' Songbk.* 46 What a study! Let us paint it As the sea-gulls fly about, While the stringer birds are anxious For the meeting to come out. **1943** 2 *N.Z.E.F. Times* 20 Sept. 5 As a result of a survey of non-Union labour on the wharves..500 out of 800 'sea-gulls' were interviewed at the Auckland District Manpower Office. **1959** G. Slatter *Gun in my Hand* xvii. 225 Ended up as a sea-gull on the Wellington wharves loading up the Home boats. **1966** G. W. Turner *Eng. Lang. Austral. & N.Z.* vii. 150 The watersiders have their own special language, but the only term I know from experience is *seagull*, the casual non-union labourer who picks up a job during busy times on the waterfront.

sea-island, *a.* Add to def.: *Gossypium barbadense*, distinguished by long silky fibres. (Earlier and later examples.)
1803 J. Davis *Travels in U.S.A.* 78 Of cotton there are two kinds; the sea-island and the island. The first is the most valuable. **1807** *Salmagundi* 15 Oct. 327 The lady of a Southern planter will..trail a bale of sea-island cotton at her heels. **1934** *Nat. Geogr. Mag.* Feb. 260/2 At Hampton Point and Retreat the first sea-island cotton was grown from seeds introduced from the island of Anguilla, in the West Indies. **1970** *Observer* 15 Mar. 48/6 (Advt.), Shirts and pyjamas made to measure, sea island poplins ..pure silk. **1977** P. Moyes *To kill Coconut* xiii. 180 Sea Island isn't grown only in the Caribbean.

B. *sb.* An offshore mooring station where oil tankers can discharge their cargo and from which the oil can be pumped ashore.
1975 *Offshore Engineer* Sept. 17 (*caption*) When linked to the 'sea islands' already installed, it will be more than 1 km long. **1979** F. Forsyth *Devil's Alternative* ix. 218 They berthed at 'sea islands', networks of pipes on stilts, well out to sea, from which their oil could be pumped ashore.

seal, *sb.*[1] Add: **4. a.** *seal-oil* (earlier and later examples).
1732 in *Calendar State Papers, Amer. & W. Indies* (1939) 227 Value of seal oil made last winter, £2478 10s. **1973** L. Russell *Everyday Life Colonial Canada* xii. 155 Until the 1860s, seal oil was an important lamp fuel in the eastern colonies, and was also used in food and as a lubricant.

c. *seal-brown* (earlier and later examples).
1881 [see *fawn *sb.*[1] 3]. **1963** B. Vesey-Fitzgerald *Cat Owner's Encycl.* 36 The body should be a solid colour of rich dark seal-brown shading.

5. **seal-hole,** substitute for def.: a hole in ice kept open by seals coming to it for air and getting out of the water through it; (further example); **seal rookery** = Rookery 2 b.
1974 R. Adams *Shardik* iii. 22 He crouched and watched, vigilant as an Eskimo at a seal-hole. **1901** *Daily Colonist* (Victoria, B.C.) 9 Oct. 8/3 That the contention.. that the seal herds in the Behring Sea are decreasing is not being borne out by fact, is shown by recent advices from the seal rookeries in the Pribyloffs. **1974** G. Jenkins *Bridge of Magpies* iii. 46 Possession [Island] was as inviting as a seal rookery—and as smelly.

seal, *sb.*[2] Add: **7. d.** *gen.* Any means of preventing the passage of gas or liquid into or out of something, esp. at a place where two surfaces meet.
a **1884** Knight *Dict. Mech.* Suppl., *Seal*, an automatic valve closing a pipe. **1938** J. Strong *Mod. Physical Lab. Practice* iv. 152 A method of making a vacuum-tight seal between metal and porcelain. **1970** K. Ball *Fiat 600, 600D Autobook* x. 118/2 The seal..is compressed on the forward stroke to prevent leakage past the plunger. **1974** *Encycl. Brit. Macropædia* XIII. 857/2 Metal-can closures operate by..vacuum seals (which rely on atmospheric pressure on the lid).

8. a. *seal-engraver* (earlier example), *-engraving*.
1786 J. Wedgwood *Let.* 24 June (1965) 295 The material..is..nearly as hard as agate... It will bear to be cut..at the seal-engraver's lathe. **1948** D. Diringer *Alphabet* 73 From E. M. I. (thirtieth century B.C.) onwards, seal-engraving was practised.

seal, *v.*[1] Add: **II. 8. c.** To render (a surface of wood, etc.) impervious by the application of a special coating.
1940 H. T. Davey *Wood Finishing* xvii. 202 When dealing with inlays it is best to seal them with shellac before attempting to spray. **1958** *Listener* 18 Dec. 1055/2 If you still want a glossy finish, you must seal the hardboard first, and the easiest way of doing that is to apply a thin coat of plastic emulsion paint. **1977** *Reader's Digest Bk. Do-It-Yourself Skills & Techniques* iv. 140/3 Some porous timbers may require two light coats, but do not apply any more than is needed to seal the surface.

d. To prevent access to and egress from (an area or space); to close (entrances) for this purpose. Usu. with *off*.
1931 *Industr. & Engin. Chem.* (Analytical Ed.) 15 Oct. 349/2 The tube is immersed in liquid air, and when the gasoline is frozen, the area *B* is sealed off. **1946** A. Vagts *Landing Operations* iv. lix. 775 The Germans..concluded that they must try to seal off the Cotentin at its base. **1948** *Sci. News* VII. 44 For the moment, treated areas are being 'sealed' by the total removal of all bush within a two-miles belt, and a watch is being kept to see what happens to the small remaining fly population. **1974** 'M. Innes' *Mysterious Commission* xi. 99 This cellarage had..been boarded over and sealed off from the studio. **1981** E. Clark *Send in Lions* v. 53 The search..began immediately. Air and sea ports were sealed.

11. Also, to confine so as to prevent access or egress. Also with *off*.
1926 R. W. Lawson tr. *Hevesy & Paneth's Man. Radioactivity* i. 2 If we seal off 1·3138 gm. $RACl_2$..in an evacuated tube. **1940** W. Faulkner *Hamlet* ii. i. 140 We sealed it up in a asbestos matchbox. **1946** A. Vagts *Landing Operations* iv. lix. 774 The choice facing Rundstedt and Rommel was between an attempt to throw the Allies back into the sea.., or sealing them off in the Cotentin.

sealable, *a.* (Later example.)
1979 *Nature* 19 Apr. p. xiv/2 The processing of liquids in sealable glass containers.

sealant (sī·lănt). [f. Seal *v.*[1] + -ant[1].] A substance designed to seal a surface or container against the passage of a gas or liquid; a material used to fill up cracks.
1945 *Materials & Methods* XXII. 1750 (*caption*) A bronze flame thrower part which required pressure tightness and chemical resistance on the part of the sealant. **1954** *Wall St. Jrnl.* 13 July 8/2 Goodrich tires have a further sealant—an extra layer of butyl in a gummy form which flows into and seals a puncture after the puncturing object is removed. **1966** T. Pynchon *Crying of Lot 49* ii. 26 Barbed wire again gave way to the familiar parade of.. sealant makers, bottled gas works,..and whatever. **1971** *Good Motoring* Sept. 4/2 The Beetle, a 'standard' model which has done about 100,000 miles on the road, was fitted with..a magneto and sealant round doors and body. **1978** S. S. Peng *Coal Mine Ground Control* xii. 417 Mine sealant sprayed in a thin coating on the roof and rib not only strengthens..but also seals the surface from the wet-dry cycles of the ventilated air.

sealapack, var. *sillapack.

sea-lawyer. **2.** (Earlier and later examples.)
1829 W. N. Glascock *Sailors & Saints* I. ii. 31 What tack are we on now?—got hold of a sea-lawyer it seems. **1873** [see *pleasure-navy* s.v. *pleasure *sb.* 6 a]. **1953** Dylan Thomas *Under Milk Wood* (1954) 4 Alfred Pomeroy Jones, sealawyer, born in Mumbles. **1967** A. Dubus *Lieutenant* iii. 78 Forget about this sea lawyer business and face your Goddamn punishment like a man.

sealchie, -kie. Add: Also **silkie, silky.** Also, in folklore, a creature or spirit having the appearance of a seal; *spec.* one able to assume human form. (Further examples.)
1852 in *Proc. Soc. Antiquaries Scotl.* I. 88, I am a man, upo' the lan' An' I am a Silkie in the sea. **1856** E. Edmondston *Sk. & Tales Shetland Islands* vii. 80 The seal ..retired to the neighbourhood..where a mermaid had her abode. The latter..asked if she could help him. *Selkie* imagined she might, but only by regaining for him..the covering of which he had been so ruthlessly bereft. **1899** J. Spence *Shetland Folk-lore* 24 In old times there was an aversion to and superstitious dread of killing a *selkie* lest it should be a metamorphic Finn. **1933** J. Buchan *Prince of Captivity* 28 He has heard the silkies singing at dawn on farther islets than St. Kilda. **1976** K. Briggs *Dict. Fairies* 354 In Orkney..the great seal, the grey seal, the crested seal and others, are called 'the selkie folk' because it is believed that their natural form is human, that they live in an underwater world..and put on seal-skins and the appearance of seals to enable them to pass through the waters from one region of air to another.

sealed, *ppl. a.* Add: **1. h.** (Earlier example.)
1850 [see *bull's wool, bullswool* s.v. *bull *sb.*[1] 11].

i. *Sealed Knot*, the name of an organization which re-enacts battles of the English Civil War for pleasure and charitable purposes.
The name is taken from a secret Royalist organization of the mid-seventeenth-century dedicated to the Restoration of the Stuart line.
1971 *Certificate of Incorporation* No. 1014700, I hereby certify that *The Sealed Knot* Limited is this day incorporated under the Companies Acts 1948 to 1967 and that the Company is limited. Given under my hand at London the 17th June 1971. **1976** A. Price *War Game* i. iii. 71 There are a number of these Civil War groups—the Sealed Knot was the first one. **1978** R. Westall *Devil on Road* ii. 7 I'd heard about the Sealed Knot. Guys..poncing around in Cavalier gear, losing the Civil War all over again.

2. a. Also of a railway train or carriage: closed to entry or exit, or admitting restricted movement, during its journey.
Freq. with allusion to Lenin's passage from Finland to Russia in 1917 in a train 'sealed' to prevent contact with German citizens.
1949 *Radio Times* 15 July 3/1 We took a sealed train to Avonmouth, a crowded troopship out into the Atlantic. **1975** M. Pearson *Sealed Train* vi. 90 The sealed carriage

and its baggage wagon were..drawn backward toward Switzerland. *Ibid.* 94 As the Sealed Train steamed north, the Kaiser's troops were striving..to check the new Allied offensive. **1979** O. Sela *Petrograd Consignment* 159 Zinoviev..has suggested that they travel through Germany in a sealed carriage, without stops.

b. Also with *up*. *a sealed book* (earlier example).

[**1611** Bible *Isaiah* xxix. 11 And the vision of all is become vnto you, as the wordes of a booke that is sealed.] **1814** Lamb *Let.* 29 Aug. (1888) 278 My left arm reposes on the *Excursion*. I feel what it would be in quiet. It is now a sealed book. **1884** W. James in *Mind* IX. 201 No impression penetrates to the sealed-up sensibility. **1943** C. Day Lewis *Word over All* 17 Or a heightening At most of the sealed-up hour wherein we awaited What?

d. *sealed-off*: closed so that neither access nor egress is possible.

1926 R. W. Lawson tr. *Hevesy & Paneth's Man. Radioactivity* ii. 19 A wider evacuated tube with sealed-off ends and thick walls. **1938** *New Statesman* 19 Feb. 277/2 One is left wondering whether the town hall has sealed-off rooms, and whether the chief officials enter by different doors. **1963** B. Fozard *Instrumentation Nucl. Reactors* iv. 42 For beta-particle measurements sealed-off tubes with thin end-windows can be used. **1978** R. Ludlum *Holcroft Covenant* iii. 40 Are you telling me that two people got off that plane, walked through sealed-off corridors into the sealed-off, guarded customs area, and *vanished?*

e. *sealed room* = *locked room* s.v. *Locked *ppl. a.* e. Also *absol.* in related use. (Freq. used in detective novels.)

1939 'M. Innes' *Stop Press* II. v. 286 Mr. Eliot's was distinctly not a mystery of the sealed-room type. **1944** J. D. Carr *Till Death do us Part* v. 52 If we have any clue to these sealed-room affairs, my guess is that there's the clue. **1971** A. Morice *Death of Gay Dog* xii. 135 One victim and five suspects, all together in a sealed room, as the saying goes.

f. *sealed-beam*: applied (usu. *attrib.*) to a motor-vehicle headlamp in which light source, reflector, and lens form a sealed, self-contained unit.

1939 *Daily Progress* (Charlottesville, Va.) 19 Aug. 4/1 The result of three years of cooperative effort by engineers.., the invention is described in a special story to The New York Times as a "sealed beam", which at once provides greatly increased range and breadth of light with stronger intensity through its high, or "country", beam and reduction of glare with increased illumination of the right side of the road with its low or "traffic" beam'. **1954** [see *prefocused *ppl. a.*]. **1965** *Economist* 23 Oct. p. x/1, Lucas did not adopt sealed-beam headlights..until well after the Americans. **1972** 'S. Abbey' *Bk. of Marina* xi. 97 Sealed-beam units form, in effect, large bulbs, each with either one or two filaments, an integral reflector and a front lens.

g. *sealed source*: a pellet of radioactive material in a sealed capsule, used in radiotherapy and radiography.

1962 *B.S.I. News* Mar. 17/2 Radiography sealed-sources —pellets of radioactive material contained in sealed capsules. **1971** *New Scientist* 1 Apr. 26/2 The US market is estimated to be worth over $80 million a year with some..$20 million on basic radioisotopes and sealed sources.

h. Of a road: surfaced with tar macadam, etc. Cf. *tar-sealed *ppl. a.* Chiefly *Austral.* and *N.Z.*

1938 *Ann. Rep. Dept. Main Roads New South Wales 1937* 4 Generally, for country roads in New South Wales the sealed gravelled pavement has proved to be quite adequate. **1966** *Weekly News* (N.Z.) 5 Dec. 47/6 It was good to be back on the sealed highway. **1969** *Northern Territory News* (Darwin) *Focus '69* 11 (Advt.), Contractors for bitumen sealed surfaces across the Territory. **1977** *Weekly Times* (Melbourne) 19 Jan. 63/7 (Advt.), Situated on sealed road handy Frankston and Dandenong. **1979** B. L. C. Johnson *Pakistan* xii. 184/1 Roads of a high standard (sealed)..now total 27,152 km.

sea legs, *pl.* Add: Also *fig.*

1895 Lloyd George *Let.* 27 Mar. (1973) 83, I have got my sea legs in the House. They now listen to me with deference. **1977** *Rolling Stone* 7 Apr. 78/3 *Sailin'*, then, is a solid album by a promising singer/songwriter who is still finding her sea legs.

Hence **sea-legged** *a.*

1913 W. de la Mare *Peacock Pie* 109 Here is a sea-legged sailor. **1946** Dylan Thomas *Deaths & Entrances* 55 Goodbye to the man on the sea-legged deck.

sealer, *sb.*¹ Add: **5.** One who or that which seals (Seal *v.*¹ 8 in Dict. and Suppl.).

1881 *Instructions to Census Clerks* (1885) 58 Blacking Manufacture: Liquid:..Sealer. **1921** *Dict. Occup. Terms* (1927) §159 *Sealer, ink bottle;* seals filled bottles of ink with sealing wax or with paper seals. **1928** *Daily Express* 6 July 5/5 The machine seals the lids of special cans... Mr. A. Appleyard..and Mr. Hirst..have tested this British hand sealer scientifically. **1940** H. T. Davey *Wood Finishing* xvii. 199 The object of a sealer is to block the pores of the wood so as to stop the succeeding coats of lacquer sinking in. **1958** *Listener* 4 Sept. 359/2 Mix yourself some sanding sealer from starch and cellulose lacquer. **1971** *Home Preserv. Fruit & Veg.* (Min. Agric.) (ed. 13) 63 The can sealer must be cleaned thoroughly after use. **1977** *Reader's Digest Bk. Do-It-Yourself Skills & Techniques* iv. 140/2 Apply a light coat of the sealer by brush or cloth direct to the unfilled timber, working it well in.

6. *Canad.* A glass jar designed to preserve fruit, vegetables, etc.

1932 N. M. Jamieson *Cattle in Stall* 12 Just take in a great half-gallon sealer and get it filled—for about half a dollar! **1959** *Weekend Mag.* (Montreal) 15 Aug. 39/2, I went into the fruit cellar, turned on the light and was actually picking up two quart sealers of icicle pickles. **1970** *Canad. Antiques Collector* July–Aug. 23/2 The demand for these preserving jars dwindled with the beginning of the cheap production of glass 'sealers' and the discovery of the method of canning in tins.

sealer, *sb.*² **2.** (Earlier examples.)

1770 G. Cartwright *Jrnl.* 31 Dec. (1792) I. 76 After breakfast we set off homewards, being accompanied by two of the sealers. **1825** J. F. Cooper *Lionel Lincoln* II. vi. 138 The sealers of New-England have been able to discover Terra Australis.

sealing, *vbl. sb.*¹ Add: **5. b.** The action or process of rendering impervious; also *concr.*, material used for this.

1955 C. Jasper *Handbk. Decorating & Painting* ii. 51 Sealing. The best form of treatment..for making the plaster suitable to receive oil paint, is to apply..alkali resisting primer. **1960** *McGraw-Hill Encycl. Sci. & Technol.* XIV. 532/2 Sealing..prevents penetration of or redissolution in subsequent finish coats. **1962** *Which? Car Suppl.* Oct. 139/2 The rubber sealing round the ventilating panes was not effective.

sealing, *vbl. sb.*² (Earlier and later examples.)

1839 *Southern Lit. Messenger* V. 3/1 In a few years [they] made Stonington famed for sealing.

attrib. **1786** G. Cartwright *Jrnl.* (1792) III. 237 All the sealing-posts now exhibit a very different appearance from what they originally did. **1911** *Daily Colonist* (Victoria, B.C.) 26 Apr. 14/2 The United States expressed a willingness to compensate the owners of the sealing fleet for the loss of the industry. **1933** J. Buchan *Prince of Captivity* I. iii. 91 A sealing sloop had crawled up the coast as soon as spring opened the shore waters. **1977** *Time* 10 Oct. 62/1 Before he was out of his teens he had.. shipped on a sealing expedition to the Bering Sea.

sealing-wax. Add: **b.** Used *attrib.*, esp. as **sealing-wax red,** to designate a bright red colour, vermilion.

1907 *Yesterday's Shopping* (1969) 156/2 These Colours Kept in Stock..Sealing wax red..Sky..Stone. **1912** Mrs. P. Campbell *Let.* Aug. in *B. Shaw & Mrs. Campbell* (1952) 35 The scullery maids..with their bloody nails and sealing-wax lips make my hair stand on end. **1930** [see *post-office red* s.v. *Post Office 3]. **1930** A. P. Herbert *Water Gipsies* xxv. 380 Her lips were the hot sealing-wax lips which she knew he hated. **1939** *Burlington Mag.* Oct. 162/2 About 1550 the famous 'sealing-wax red' first appears on Turkish pottery. **1957** [see *Isnik].

sea-lion. Add: **3. b.** [tr. G. *seelöwe.*] In full, *Operation Sea-lion*, the code name for the German plan to invade the United Kingdom after the fall of France in the war of 1939–45. (Announced by Hitler in July 1940 and cancelled in October of that year.)

1949 W. S. Churchill *Their Finest Hour* xiv. 261 Our excellent Intelligence confirmed that the operation 'Sea Lion' had been definitely ordered by Hitler. **1951** F. H. Hinsley *Hitler's Strategy* iv. 83 In his [*sc.* Hitler's] mind 'Sea Lion' was never more than a colossal bluff. *Ibid.* x. 191 The final cancellation of operation 'Sea Lion'..was less important for itself than as an indication of the state of mind to which Hitler had already been reduced. **1978** D. Kyle *Black Camelot* xi. 178 Heydrich..must have obtained Raeder's copy after Sea Lion was cancelled.

seal point. [f. Seal *sb.*¹ + *point *sb.*¹ A. 26 c.] One of the dark brown markings on the buff fur of one type of Siamese cat; also, a Siamese cat with markings of this colour. Hence **seal-pointed** *a.*

1934 P. Wade *Siamese Cat* xv. 101 Even the best Blue Pointed cannot..equal in beauty our Seal Pointed cats. *Ibid.* 102 Let us concentrate on breeding perfect Siamese with deep seal points. **1939** I. M. Mellen *Pract. Cat Bk.* i. 35 The adult body color of the Siamese is pale fawn.. and the seal brown, almost black ears, muzzle, tail and feet are called collectively 'points', the color described being known as seal point. *Ibid.* 39 (*heading*) Qualities of a good seal point Siamese. **1958** *Listener* 18 Sept. 410/2 The first Siamese to become a champion arrived in 1896. He was a seal point. **1966** 'K. A. Saddler' *Gilt Edge* vi. 91 A seal point Siamese cat sneaked in. **1980** A. Scholefield *Berlin Blind* iii. 106 He..saw a cat. It was a beautiful sealpoint Siamese.

sealskin, *sb.* **2.** (Earlier example.)

1858 Queen Victoria *Let.* 27 Feb. in R. Fulford *Dearest Child* (1964) 62, I am so glad you find the sealskin comfortable; it is a nice warm thing.

Sealyham (sī·liˌăm). [The name of *Sealy Ham* (House) near Haverfordwest, the home of the Edwardes family which developed the breed in the 19th cent.] A small stocky white terrier, sometimes with markings of other colours, distinguished by a thick, rough coat, drooping ears, a small, erect tail, and a square, bearded muzzle. Also *attrib.*

1894 R. B. Lee *Hist. & Descr. Mod. Dogs: Terriers* xvi. 386 There is a strain of terrier much talked about of late known as the Sealy Ham. **1907** [see *Jack Russell* (*terrier*) s.v. *Jack *sb.*¹ 37]. **1917** W. J. Locke *Red Planet* xix. 250 You remember Jingo, the Sealyham. **1924** [see *cairn 2]. **1930** R. H. Mottram *Europa's Beast* x. 241 The Sealyham ..merely slept. **1954** M. K. Wilson tr. *Lorenz's Man meets Dog* viii. 79 A Sealyham's love of fun, and his fidelity to his master can prove a real moral support to a melancholy type of person. **1966** J. Betjeman *High & Low* 12 Where's Kathleen Stokes with her Sealyhams? **1979** R. Rendell *Means of Evil* 153 He emerged from the front door with two Sealyhams on a lead.

seam, *sb.*¹ Add: **I. 1. d.** Also in colloq. phrases, as *to burst* (*fall apart*, etc.) *at the seams*.

1962 Ross & Singer *Guilty Party* in *Plays of Year* XXIV. 74 You were bursting at the seams a little. Can we ease the strain for you? **1965** J. Von Sternberg *Fun in Chinese Laundry* (1966) ii. 43 In a few instances when I thought that I would come apart at the seams..I managed to make the director listen. **1969** 'V. Packer' *Don't rely on Gemini* (1970) xv. 131 He had begun to fall apart at the seams—to imagine..that the stars..were conspiring against him. **1977** *Times* 30 Apr. 9/6 My marriage..came apart at the seams.

f. *Cricket.* The raised band of stitching around the centre of a ball. Cf. *seam bowler*, sense 10 below.

1888 Steel & Lyttelton *Cricket* iii. 119 The ball is usually, by a slow bowler, grasped firmly with all the fingers resting on the seam, as this gives more purchase and resistance for the fingers to operate. **1906** F. R. Spofforth in Beldam & Fry *Great Bowlers & Fielders* 10 It is almost impossible to swerve unless the seam of the ball is up and down. **1948** C. Sly *How to bowl them Out* x. 75 The ball..resembles the planet Saturn in that it has a ring or projecting ridge round its waist..known as the seam. **1972** R. Illingworth *Young Cricketer* iii. 50 Grip the ball with the seam upright... Angle the seam to fine leg and not to third man.

g. *French seam* (Needlework), a double-stitched seam that is folded and sewn to resemble a plain seam on the right side.

1903 *Home Fashions* 12 Sept. 18/3 The sleeve is joined by French seam. **1964** *McCall's Sewing* 276/1 After cutting the panels, join them with tiny French seams.

6. b. *Metallurgy.* A superficial linear defect on worked metal usu. caused by closure of a blow hole.

c **1840** B. Legge *Guide to Iron Trade* 36 Having sems [*sic*] in a longitudinal direction. **1923** Glazebrook *Dict. Appl. Physics* V. 362/2 These surfaces become oxidised both during cooling of the ingot and during reheating for forging or rolling, and give rise to rokes or seams. **1924** Greaves & Wrighton *Pract. Microsc. Metallogr.* ix. 78 Seams show a similar microscopical appearance to rokes and are caused in rolling billets or bars by one portion of the metal folding over another. **1967** A. K. Osborne *Encycl. Iron & Steel Industry* (ed. 2) 373/2 Seams may also be caused by rippled surfaces or by recurrent teeming laps.

10. seam allowance, the amount of material in sewing which is calculated to be taken in by a seam; **seam bowler** *Cricket*, a medium og fast bowler who uses the seam to make the ball deviate in the air or off the pitch durinr delivery; hence **seam-bowling; seam-squirrel** *U.S. slang* (chiefly *Mil.*), a louse; **seam welding,** a form of resistance welding in which a linear weld is obtained by means of rolling disc-shaped electrodes which produce a line of overlapping welds (see also quot. 1964); so **seam-weld** *v. trans.*; also **seam weld** *sb.*; **seam welder,** a machine for **seam welding.**

1949 I. R. Duncan *Compl. Sewing Book* xv. 301 Plain seams may be used for every type of garment... The amount of seam allowance depends upon the material; generally from ⅜ to ½ an inch is required. **1964** *McCall's Sewing* 277/1 Press fold formed along edge of seam allowance. **1977** R. Richardson *Discovering Patchwork* 63/2 Window templates made of clear plastic with a shaded area round the edge... The shaded area is the seam allowance. **1948** J. Arlott *How to watch Cricket* iii. 14 The term 'seam-bowler' is almost identical [with 'pace bowler'] since it refers to those bowlers who use the seam to swing, or cut the ball. **1978** R. V. Jones *Most Secret War* xliv. 414, I had previously not believed such tales as the swinging of cricket balls by seam bowlers. **1956** R. Alston *Test Commentary* 136 Johnson persisted in a seam-bowling attack. **1976** Dexter & Makins *Testkill* 174 The steady England pressure which was now resting on the excellent seam bowling of Kirkstead. **1899** J. R. Skinner *Hist. Fourth Illinois Volunteers* 129 When it was first rumored that the old confederate seam squirrel had invaded our quarters, a small panic seized many. **1929** L. Thomas *Woodfill of Regulars* 240 The rest of the boys.. stopped chasin' seam-squirrels in their undershirts. *a* **1956** C. J. Post *Little War of Private Post* (1960) 255 There is the gray-back, or seam-squirrel, from the days of our Civil War. **1920** *Whittaker's Electr. Engineer's Pocket-bk.* (ed. 4) 646 On light work, about 3 ft. of seam weld can be made per min. **1980** L. M. Gowd *Princ. Welding Technol.* xi. 164 After the first weld has been made,..the current must be raised to maintain the size of the welds. Accepting this limitation, satisfactory continuous seam welds can be made. **1921** Seam welder [see *seam welding* below]. **1959** Neumann & Bockhoff *Welding of Plastics* vii. 126 In using high-frequency seam welders, the breakdown strength of the plastic must be considered. **1976** *Western Mail* (Cardiff) 27 Nov. 6/5 Spot-welders, seam-welders and projection welding machines up to 20 KVA are also among the factory's equipment. **1917** Oberg & Jones *Machinery's Encycl.* VI. 496/2 By the seam-welding process, two sheets of wrought iron or steel are welded together along the edge by a continuous lap-weld... Plates can be successfully seam-welded at a rate of about one foot per minute. **1921** *Automobile Engineer* XI. 108/1 Seam welding..can be adopted with advantage when a tight joint is required.., a seam welder differing from a spot welder mainly in that roller electrodes are used instead of the pointed electrodes. **1964** Wordingham &

REBOUL *Dict. Plastics* 158 *Seam welding*, with thermoplastic materials, the method of forming a welded seam, either by the use of welding rollers..for continuous welding, or by jig welding. **1975** BRAM & DOWNS *Manuf. Technol.* ii. 62 Seam welding is similar to spot welding, the difference being that the spots overlap each other, making a continuous weld seam.

seam, *v.*[2] Add: **5.** *Cricket.* **a.** *intr.* Of a pitch: to aid a seam bowler; of a ball: to swing during delivery on account of the seam.

1960 E. W. SWANTON *West Indies Revisited* 118 According to the players, the pitch was still 'seaming' a bit. **1974** *Reading Evening Post* 3 Sept. 14/7 Both opening bowlers made the ball seam considerably and Fletcher was next to go. **1976** *Liverpool Echo* 23 Nov. 18/7 The pitches out there have been known to seam.

b. *trans.* Of a bowler: to cause (a ball) to seam.

1963 T. BAILEY *Improve Your Cricket* ii. 81 At medium pace it is possible to seam the ball..and naturally to vary pace, length and angle of flight. **1976** J. SNOW *Cricket Rebel* 21 Thomson..and..Pascoe..taking seven of the first eight wickets between them on a damp wicket which helped them seam the ball about.

seamanite (sī·mănəit). *Min.* [See quot. 1930 and -ITE[1].] A rare hydrated phosphate and borate of manganese,

$Mn_3^{2+}(OH)_2[B(OH)_4][PO_4]$,

occurring as transparent, yellow, orthorhombic crystals.

1930 E. H. KRAUS et al. in *Amer. Mineralogist* XV. 220 In recognition of Professor [A. E.] Seaman's long and influential service as Professor of Geology and Mineralogy at the Michigan College of Mining and Technology, and his valuable contributions to the geology and mineralogy of the Upper Peninsula of Michigan, the authors propose the name of seamanite for this new mineral. **1971** *Ibid.* LVI. 1531 Seamanite is certainly a candidate for one of the most exotic of mineral structures. The Mn-O octahedral arrangement is one of the most peculiar and unexpected on record.

sea-mark. 2. b. (Later examples with allusion to SHAKES. *Oth.* v. ii. 271.)

1932 *Proc. Brit. Acad.* XVII. 57 He [*sc.* Virgil] fixed for the imagination of the Roman race..the limit of its aspiration and achievement, the very sea-mark of its utmost sail. **1955** *Times* 11 May 11/4 Often they even marked, though not the very butt and seamark of his utmost sail, at least his objective for the time being.

seamer. Add: **2.** *Cricket.* A seam bowler; also, a delivery by a seam bowler.

1952 *Observer* 25 May 10/1 R. Smith, with his medium-paced 'seamers'—to use a modern and not too unmeaning term—and Bailey..began almost to persuade us that their names might be G. Lohmann and S. F. Barnes. **1955** *Times* 5 July 4/1 Silk was probably right in thinking that his seamers would get more out of it than his spinners. **1963** *Times* 13 June 3/1 It indicated that the intention of both captains was to rely entirely upon their seamers, which they duly did. **1976** DEXTER & MAKINS *Testkill* 140 With the new ball due well before lunch he sensibly switched to Flinders' leg-spin and Lytton's seamers.

seamfree (sī·mfrī), *a.* (and *sb.*) [f. SEAM *sb.*[1] + FREE *a.*] Of stockings: = SEAMLESS *a.* in Dict. and Suppl. Also *absol.* as *sb.*

1959 *Manch. Guardian* 27 July 4/2 Plaza..have a seamfree called 'Riviera' which wears well. **1960** *Sunday Express* 14 Feb. 14/4 The percentage of seam-free stockings sold today is steadily rising. **1976** *Leicester Trader* 24 Nov. 2/4 There are several styles [of stockings] to choose from at Plants including Wolsey Monte Carlo seamfree 15 denier at 59p a pair.

seaming, *vbl. sb.* **b.** *seaming machine* (earlier U.S. example).

1847 *Rep. Comm. Patents 1846* (U.S.) 214 My improved seaming machine for turning down and forming a seam of the flange surrounding the bottoms of the buckets.

seamless, *a.* Add: **1.** (Further examples.) Now *esp.* of tubing and women's stockings or tights.

1876 *Encycl. Brit.* IV. 218/2 Solid or seamless brass tubes..are made by drawing down short thick cast cylinders of brass till they reach the desired gauge or thinness. **1904** GOODCHILD & TWENEY *Technol. & Sci. Dict.* 146/1 The [cycle] frame is generally formed of thin seamless steel tubing. **1921** *Daily Colonist* (Victoria, B.C.) 4 Oct. 5/1 Seamless (fashioned without seams). The women's hose knit to fit without a seam. **1959** *Observer* 22 Mar. 3/8 The seamless stocking, or 'circular' as the trade calls it, has always been made, but used to be thought of as an inferior thing. **1968** *Economist* 9 Nov. 94/1 Tubes is commissioning a new seamless tube mill, where profits ought to start this autumn. **1969** A. J. HALL *Stand. Handbk. Textiles* (ed. 7) iii. 154 The seamless hose are knitted on circular machines.

2. fig. *spec.* as *seamless web*, orig. with reference to the concept of history as an integral whole (see quot. 1898).

1862 E. DICKINSON *Poems* (1955) I. 246 As if some Caravan of Sound Had parted Rank, Then knit, and swept—In Seamless Company. **1898** POLLOCK & MAITLAND *Hist. Eng. Law bef. Edw. I* (ed. 2) I. I. i. 1 Such is the unity of all history that any one who endeavours to tell a piece of it must feel that his first sentence tears a seamless web. **1929** *Oxf. Poetry* 12 A small patch of light on the seamless blank. **1952** AUDEN *Nones* 39 The three wise Maries come Sossing through seamless waters. **1964** [see *INTEGRALISM]. **1976** T. EAGLETON *Crit. & Ideology* iii. 94 *The Prelude* is *formally* fissured by its ideological contradictions, unable to rise to the seamless impersonal epic it would wish itself to be. **1977** *Time* 10 Oct. 10/3 'Many of us find it intellectually difficult', he said, 'to penetrate the seamless web of the Japanese politico-economic system.'

sea monkey. 1. A heraldic animal which is part monkey, part fish.

1909 A. C. FOX-DAVIES *Compl. Guide Heraldry* xiii. 230 It may be as well to allude to the asserted heraldic existence of the sea-monkey, though I am not aware of any instance in which it is borne.

2. A brine shrimp, *Artemia salina*, often used as food for fish in aquaria.

1973 *Sunday Mail* (Brisbane) 3 June 6/2 'Sea monkeys' ..are currently booming in the United States. They come as a parcel of eggs that look like dried crystal. But..after the eggs are dropped into water they grow into what looks like sea shrimp. **1976** 'D. HALLIDAY' *Dolly & Nanny Bird* ii. 29 'They're Sea Monkeys.'.. 'Brine shrimps... Fish eat them.'

sea-monster. 2. (Later examples.)

1917 E. POUND *Lustra* .86 The sea-monster Bulges the squarish bronzes. **1952** C. DAY LEWIS tr. *Virgil's Aeneid* III. 65 Below, she is a weird sea-monster With dolphin's tail and a belly of wolverine sort.

Seanad Eireann (ʃæ·năd ēə·răn). [Ir. *Seanad Éireann* the senate of Ireland.] The upper house of the parliament of the Republic of Ireland. Freq. *ellipt.* as **Seanad**.

1922 [see *OIREACHTAS 2]. **1923** W. B. YEATS in *Senate Speeches* (1961) 36, I hope I have the leave of the Seanad to use a different form of words. **1937** *Bunreacht na hÉireann* (*Constitution of Ireland*) 48 Article 18. 1. Seanad Eireann shall be composed of sixty members, of whom eleven shall be nominated members and forty-nine shall be elected members. **1962** M. AMELLER *Parliaments* I. ii. 10 While the method of appointment of members of the Second Chamber is not altogether in keeping with ordinary democratic principles, that is offset by the fact that the powers of the Seanad are considerably curtailed. **1974** *Encycl. Brit. Macropædia* IX. 886/2 There are..60 members of the Seanad... The Seanad may delay..bills passed by the Dáil.

séance. Add: **1.** Also *séance royale*, a royal audience. (Earlier and later examples.) Also *loosely* (chiefly *U.S.*), a meeting or discussion.

1789 A. YOUNG *Jrnl.* 20 June in *Trav. France* (1792) I. 115 A message from the King.., that he should meet them on Monday; and, under pretence of preparing the hall for the seance royale, the French guards were placed..to prevent any of the deputies entering the room. **1922** JOYCE *Ulysses* 644 Come, he counselled, to close the *séance*. **1934** E. POUND *Eleven New Cantos* xxxiv. 16 At the Seance Royale last Thursday he had talked of His death in defence of the country. **1962** W. SCHIRRA in *Into Orbit* 32 We would lock ourselves up in our office at Langley until we had a solution that satisfied us all... We called a session like this a 'seance'. **1977** *Time* 17 Jan. 41/1 For an hour most nights, he conducts a long-distance séance (at $3 a minute) with..his Australian proconsul, from the..desk in his study.

3. b. A 'sitting' for a portrait.

1877 DISRAELI *Let.* 14 Apr. (1929) viii. 117 Now I am going to the Palace for my 3rd Seance [to Von Angeli]. **1919** R. FRY *Let.* 21 Oct. (1972) II. 460 All wanted me to draw their portraits so that every evening in the café I had to have a *séance*.

sea-otter. Add: **2.** The thick dark fur of *Enhydra lutris*.

1813 A. HENRY *Jrnl.* 19 Nov. in E. Coues *New Light Early Hist. Greater Northwest* (1897) II. 753 His son had a robe of two sea otters, for which he demanded 48 beavers. **1915** *Chambers's Jrnl.* Jan. 48/2 Of sea-otter, too, perhaps one of the loveliest furs of all, the supply is failing. **1956** J. G. LINKS *Bk. Fur* III. 139 A sea otter collar to his coat was to the great industrialist of the last century what a private stratocruiser is to his successor.

seaplane (sī·plēⁱn). [f. SEA *sb.* + *PLANE *sb.*[5]] An aeroplane designed to be able to operate from water; *spec.* one with floats, in contrast to a flying boat.

1913 [see *HYDROPLANE *sb.* 3]. **1914** *Daily Express* 2 Nov. 5/2 The old cruiser Hermes..had been recently used as a seaplane-carrying ship. **1921** *Daily Colonist* (Victoria, B.C.) 5 Oct. 12/3 Seaplane stations have been established by the Air Board of Canada. **1938** *Sun* (Baltimore) 21 July 1/8 Hooked together—the seaplane Mercury above and the flying boat Maia below—the two planes rose from the river Shannon this evening. **1954** P. K. KEMP *Fleet Air Arm* 87 Three cross-Channel steamers were taken up to be transformed into seaplane carriers. **1973** [see *REFUEL *v.* 2].

sea-purse. Add: **4. a.** [ad. the Algonquian language Munsee (Delaware) *sepoûs*, brook, small river: see Mathews *Dict. Americanisms* (1951).] (Earlier and later examples.)

1842 W. P. HAWES *Sporting Scenes* I. 102, I kept watch of him—when I came to a sea poose—I went in and to the east of it. **1904** *N.Y. Tribune* 29 May II. 7/1 McDonald was a good swimmer, but, getting caught in a sea puss, was shot out to the deep sea with great velocity. **1932** *Sun* (Baltimore) 5 Sept. 6/3 The sea-purse swooped in and picked up a girl bather, who was suddenly seen to whirl about on the surface of the water like a cork.

seaquarium (sīkwēə·riəm). Pl. **seaqua·ria.** [f. SEA *sb.* + A)QUARIUM.] An aquarium for large marine animals.

1955 *Travel* Dec. 54/2 On the other side of the Sunshine State, at Miami Beach, a new $2,000,000 Seaquarium features giant fishbowls of what is probably the largest collection of tropical marine life in the world. **1959** *Listener* 30 July 186/1 A diver feeding dolphins in the Miami Seaquarium, Florida. **1962** *New Scientist* 15 Mar. 607/2 The great natural aquaria (or seaquaria or oceanaria) in Florida and California. **1969** *Daily Tel.* 24 Apr. 16/3 The seaquarium's Manatee tank is only five feet deep. **1978** *New York* 3 Apr. 74 Come bask in the warmth of exotic..Sonesta Beach Hotel & Tennis Club... Room with private balcony. Admission to the Seaquarium and Crandon Park Zoo. **1982** *Times* 21 Jan. 4/5 The three Clacton whales were kept in Iceland in a 'seaquarium'.

search, *sb.* Add: **2. d.** (Earlier U.S. example.)

1798 *Deb. Congress U.S.* 12 June (1851) 1907 Gentlemen appeared to confound the right of search with the right of capture.

6. *search area, -party* (later examples), *plane, team*; **search coil** *Electr.* = *exploring coil* s.v. *EXPLORING *vbl. sb.*; **search-warrant** (earlier examples).

1973 H. NIELSEN *Severed Key* i. 13 Word of the airline crash had spread rapidly... Only the hardiest of the amateur sailors would be able to reach the search area. **1977** *New Yorker* 27 June 62/3 The search area could not be reduced much below forty thousand square miles. **1897** *Electrician* 30 July 439/2 You travel along the line of the main, carefully tracking the cable with the search coil, and listening intently at the telephone receiver. **1933** [see *fluxmeter, flux meter* s.v. *FLUX *sb.* 13]. **1953** R. J. C. ATKINSON *Field Archaeol.* (ed. 2) i. 39 The soil is usually removed in a series of shallow layers, and the surface of each layer can be swept with the search-coil. **1978** J. IRVING *World according to Garp* ii. 30 She quickly organized a search party among the healthier and more mobile patients. **1981** A. MORICE *Men in her Death* viii. 91 I'll be on my way. Robin will be sending out search parties if I'm not home soon. **1966** M. WOODHOUSE *Tree Frog* xxvi. 195 They would send out a search plane as soon as it got light. **1978** R. LUDLUM *Holcroft Covenant* xxx. 348 A capsized craft fitting the description of the small boat was sighted by low-flying coastal search planes. **1976** L. SANDERS *Hamlet Warning* xxvii. 239 Organize your men into search teams for the sectors they hold. **1739** W. STEPHENS *Jrnl.* 26 Mar. in *Colonial Rec. Georgia* (1906) IV. 306 It was thought proper to send out several Officers with a search Warrant. **1752** FIELDING *Amelia* I. III. xi. 269, I believe I should have applied to a Magistrate for a Search-warrant for that Picture.

search, *v.* Add: **I. 3. c.** *search me*: used (chiefly *imp.* in response to a question) to imply that the speaker has no knowledge of some fact or no idea what course to take. *colloq.* (orig. *N. Amer.*).

1901 MERWIN & WEBSTER *Calumet 'K'* iii. 37 'Search me,' said Denis. 'They've tied us up for these two weeks.' **1907** F. H. BURNETT *Shuttle* xxvi. 262 If this ain't the limit! You may search *me*! **1916** 'B. M. BOWER' *Phantom Herd* xi. 191 What ails that darned thing?.. You can search me. **1920** 'SAPPER' *Bull-Dog Drummond* ii. 60 'Why did he send his confidential secretary..to Belfast?' 'Search me,' said Hugh. **1930** E. WAUGH *Vile Bodies* i. 9 Word of eighteen letters meaning carnivorous mammal. Search me if I know how they do think of these things. **1949** G. DAVENPORT *Family Fortunes* III. i. 189 'How could the road be washed out—I went over it yesterday morning and it hasn't rained since!' 'Search me.' **1959** J. THURBER *Years with Ross* iv. 61 Faced with these formidable questions, any of his intimates..might easily murmur..'God Knows' or 'Search me'. **1965** D. FRANCIS *For Kicks* viii. 110 'Where did he go for the summer?' I asked... 'Search me.' **1980** B. BAINBRIDGE *Winter Garden* xiii. 102 'But where am I going?' asked Ashburner... 'Search me,' said Bernard. 'It's supposed to be a surprise.'

4. (Later example.)

1963 in H. W. Baade *Jurimetrics* 13 Western Reserve University established a Center..which has been engaged ..in the investigation of methods of searching literature by electronic machines.

IV. 14. In special combs. with other vbs. forming verbal and substantival phrases (freq. used *attrib.*), as *search and destroy* (orig. *U.S.*), designating an uncompromising military strategy effected by the advance of troops through a given territory (first employed in the war in Vietnam); also *ellipt.*; *search and rescue* (orig. *U.S.*), designating a (chiefly *Mil.*) land or sea rescue service.

1966 *Economist* 22 Oct. 369/3 This is a different use of men from the highly mobile 'search and destroy' operations in which the American forces have been engaged up to now. **1970** [see *Green Beret* s.v. *GREEN *a.* 12]. **1973** D. LEES *Rape of Quiet Town* iv. 57 Sarrat's unit conducted search-and-destroy missions. **1977** 'E. MCBAIN' *Long Time no See* xiii. 222, I was out there on a search-and-destroy. **1944** *Yank* 2 June 3/2 At last somebody thought of the Siberian Huskies assigned to a nearby Army search and rescue outfit. **1950** *Jrnl. R. United Service Inst.* XCV. 158 (*heading*) 'Search and rescue' radio watch. **1972** *Gloss. Aeronaut. & Astronaut. Terms* (*B.S.I.*) XIII. 3 *Search and rescue*, a service provided to notify the appropriate organizations of aircraft in need of search-and-rescue aid and to assist such organizations. **1977** *R.A.F. News* 11–24 May 9 (Advt.), Winching a capsized yachtsman to safety on board a Royal Air Force search-and-rescue Wessex.

searcher. Add: **3. d.** (Earlier example.)
1706 *Albany Fort Jrnl.* 1 July in G. Williams *Hudson's Bay Miscellany* (1975) 72/2 State of stores... 1 pair seachers for great guns.

4. b. A penetrating or embarrassing question. *colloq.*
1923 J. MANCHON *Le Slang* 260 *Searcher*,..une question (ou un problème) embarrassante. **1951** N. M. GUNN *Well at World's End* xi. 81 He..asked me some questions, and searchers they were.

search-light. Add: **1.** Also, the beam of light thrown by such a lamp.
1919 KIPLING in *Hutchinson's Story Mag.* July 12 And the crazy skies are lit By the searchlights of the Pit. **1929** S. LESLIE *Anglo-Catholic* xvi. 225 He pointed..to the Northern sky, across which dropped a silver ribbon of attenuated search-light. **1943** L. B. LYON *Evening in Stepney* 12 Across and across it move The search-lights, reckoning hate on a hidden clock.

Hence as *v. trans.*, to illuminate with a search-light; also *fig.*
1914 W. DE MORGAN *When Ghost meets Ghost* I. xxix. 344 That officer..was searchlighting areas for want of something to do. **1966** *Prison Service Jrnl.* VI. 21/2 We find our own failings..are searchlighted.

searlesite (sɜ̄·ɹlzəit). *Min.* [f. the name of John W. *Searles*, who put down the well in California from which the first specimen came: see -ITE[1].] A hydrated borosilicate of sodium, $NaBSi_2O_6.H_2O$, occurring as white monoclinic crystals.
1914 LARSEN & HICKS in *Jrnl. Washington Acad. Sci.* IV. 397 The mineral for which the name searlesite is proposed was found in samples from the deep well in Searles Lake, San Bernardino County, California. **1950** *Amer. Mineralogist* XXXV. 1017 In the stratum of trona 10 feet thick that is reached by the shaft at a depth of 1500 feet, subhedral crystals of searlesite up to 7 inches long, 4 inches wide, and one inch thick are not uncommon. **1974** *Mineral. Abstr.* XXV. 303/1 The phyllosilicate searlesite, $Na_2B_2(OH)_4Si_4O_{10}$, has been made from mixtures of Na_2O, B_2O_3, SiO_2 and excess H_2O heated under steam pressure at 250°C for up to 8 days.

sea-robin. 1. (Earlier example.)
1814 S. L. MITCHILL *Fishes N.Y.* 430 Gurnard, or Sea Robin, *Trigla lineata.*

Sears–Roebuck (sɪ̄ᵊɹz rōᵘ·bɒk), *a. U.S. slang.* Also **Sears and Roebuck.** The name of the American merchandising firm of *Sears, Roebuck* and Co., used allusively of an inexperienced, 'green', or amateurish person, or of something cheap or of little value.
1917 R. LORD *Captain Boyd's Battery, A.E.F.* (1919) ii. 23 Two tents of Shavetails (i.e. Reverse Officers, Ninety-Day Wonders, Sears & Roebuck Specials,..etc.) have been attached to us for instruction purposes. **1930** *Our Army* Jan. 4 He's a regular Sears-Roebuck product; three months of training, three tons of dignity and three ounces of horse sense. **1932** *Amer. Speech* VII. 270 *Sears-Roebuck driller*, an inexperienced and incapable driller. **1942** BERREY & VAN DEN BARK *Amer. Thes. Slang* §21/14 Cheap; paltry... *Sears-Roebuck.* **1971** M. TAK *Truck Talk* 137 *Sears-Roebuck license*, the license said to be held by an inferior driver.

sea-salt, *sb.* Add: Hence **sea-·salted** *a.*, impregnated or seasoned with sea-salt.
1925 V. WOOLF *Mrs. Dalloway* 70 The brisk sea-salted air of their intimacy. *a* **1941** —— *Captain's Death Bed* (1950) 31 This gnarled and sea-salted man was no smug clergyman underneath.

sea-shell. 1. a. (Earlier *attrib.* example.)
1871 MRS. STOWE *Pink & White Tyranny* i. 4 He saw this distant vision of airy gauzes, of pearly whiteness, of sea-shell pink.

sea-sick, *a.* Add: **1. b.** *sea-sick medicine, pill, tablet*, a preparation taken to counter seasickness.
1925 E. H. YOUNG *William* iii. 29 Mother's going to give us some sea-sick medicine before we start. **1951** N. MITFORD *Blessing* II. xii. 268 The stewardess..stood over her with a bottle of sea-sick tablets. **1959** 'M. M. KAYE' *House of Shade* iii. 38 He..had made her take several seasick pills. **1969** G. M. BROWN *Orkney Tapestry* i. 17 In Scrabster they sip brandy or swallow sea-sick tablets. **1972** W. ELLIS *Knife Edge* ii. 20 Seasick pills. We must get some before we set off.

sea-sickness. (Later *attrib.* examples.)
1955 E. BLISHEN *Roaring Boys* III. 151 His sea-sickness pills he carried in a little phial. **1973** H. NIELSEN *Severed Key* i. 12 Find the seasickness pills in the first aid kit in the forward locker.

sea-side, seaside. Add: **2.** (Earlier example.)
1782 W. COWPER *Let.* Nov. (1904) II. 20 Mr. Bull..is gone to the seaside with Mrs. Wilberforce, and will be absent six weeks.

4. a. (Earlier and later examples.) Freq. in *seaside café, holiday, resort, villa.*
1781 W. COWPER *Let.* 26 Sept. (1904) I. 358 The modern passion for seaside entertainments. **1873** *Young Englishwoman* June 281/1 The collars can be procured..of chemists at seaside resorts. **1909** *Sat. Even. Post* 5 June 17/2 As soon as the theaters or 'hall-shows', as the circus men call them, close, the summer-garden or seaside parks open. **1939** F. THOMPSON *Lark Rise* ii. 36 Children..went to parties and for sea-side holidays. **1967** N. FREELING *Strike out where not Applicable* 39 A messy, ugly building..that..had climbed beyond modest seaside-café beginnings. **1973** 'B. MATHER' *Snowline* xix. 228 Looking like a seaside landlady who has just caught her daughter in bed with the star lodger. **1974** *Listener* 3 Jan. 27/1 The opera..went on, with success, at the seaside resort. **1976** P. R. WHITE *Planning for Public Transport* vii. 141 The traditional seaside excursion demand has fallen, most weekend leisure trips now being made by car. **1981** 'W. HAGGARD' *Money Men* xi. 117 Dame Molly has rented a seaside villa.

b. seaside finch *U.S.*, a small sparrow, *Ammospiza maritima*, found on the Atlantic coast of North America; **seaside grape,** add: = SEA-GRAPE 4; (further examples); **seaside sparrow** = *seaside finch* above.
1811 A. WILSON *Amer. Ornithol.* IV. 68 Sea-side Finch ..derives its whole subsistence from the sea. **1872** E. COUES *Key to N. Amer. Birds* 137 Sea-side Finch. Olive-gray, obscurely streaked on the back and crown. **1756, 1792** Sea-side grape [see GRAPE *sb.*[1] 3 b]. **1837** J. L. WILLIAMS *Territory of Florida* 37 The seaside grape..and custard apples are frequently found in the hummocks. **1929** R. HUGHES *High Wind in Jamaica* i. 16 The lane, or drive, was gorgeous: for the first few hundred yards it was entirely hedged with 'seaside grapes'. **1978** T. J. WRIGHT in V. H. Heywood *Flowering Plants of World* 78/2 The purple berries of the West Indian seaside grape.. are eaten. **1886** *Code Nomencl. & Check-list N. Amer. Birds* (Amer. Ornithologists' Union) 269 Seaside Sparrow ..Salt marshes of the Atlantic coast. **1937** T. G. PEARSON in Grosvenor & Wetmore *Bk. Birds* II. 272/2 The northern seaside sparrow inhabits..the vicinity of the ocean beaches. **1978** C. HARRISON *Field Guide Nests, Eggs & Nestlings N. Amer. Birds* 394 Seaside Sparrow..breeds on salt marshes.

c. Special Combs., as **seaside (picture-)postcard,** a postcard of a type commonly sold at the sea-side, *spec.* one depicting a caricature of lewd or vulgar humour; **seaside rock (candy),** rock-candy in the form of a cylindrical stick, usu. with a cross-section displaying the name of a resort in coloured lettering, commonly sold at the seaside.
1955 M. ALLINGHAM *Beckoning Lady* ii. 22 They looked like a seaside picture-postcard..wedged in the tub cart together, with the donkey in front. **1957** R. HOGGART *Uses of Literacy* I. ii. 31 The fifty-year-old formality of seaside postcards: most of the year 'decent' working-class people would hardly approve of them, but on holiday they are likely to 'let up a bit' and send a few to friends—cards showing fat mothers-in-law and fat policemen, weedy little men with huge-bottomed wives, ubiquitous bottles of beer and chamber-pots. **1979** J. WAINWRIGHT *Duty Elsewhere* xv. 45 The exaggerated bawdiness of seaside postcards. **1963** *Listener* 3 Jan. 40/2 Seaside rock and candy-floss. **1968** W. GARNER *Deep, Deep Freeze* vii. 96 Carnality ran through her like the letters through seaside rock candy. **1978** R. HILL *Pinch of Snuff* xxv. 262 He left them in a three-cornered trap..with a four-letter word burned on the lawn. Perhaps like sea-side rock it went all the way through.

sea·sider. [f. SEA-SIDE + -ER[2].] A frequenter of the seaside. (In quot. 1976 used as the nickname of an Association football team.)
1870 *Amer. Naturalist* III. 230 The Savannah Sparrow, though only occasionally found breeding so far south as Massachusetts, is evidently a sea-sider. **1892** *Pall Mall Gaz.* 23 June 1/3 The average lady seasider in this country frugally wears out her summer finery by the 'sad sea waves'. **1976** *West Lancs. Evening Gaz.* 15 Dec. 1. 18/7 Alan Ball comes to Blackpool tomorrow to talk terms with the Seasiders when he will be offered some of the most attractive terms ever offered by Blackpool.

season, *sb.* Add: **II. 13. c.** (*a man*, etc.) *for all seasons*: (one) ready for any situation or contingency, adaptable to any circumstance.
Orig. used with reference to Sir Thomas More (1478–1535); cf. ERASMUS *Encomium Moriae* (1509) Pref., *omnium horarum hominem.*
1520 R. WHITTINTON *Vulgaria* fol. 14[r] And as tyme requireth, [Thomas More is] a man of merueylous myrth & pastymes: and somtyme of sad grauite: as who say a man for all seasons. **1960** R. BOLT (*title*) A man for all seasons. **1968** *Listener* 26 Dec. 842/3 If there can really be no simple account of Mr Powell's general political position save that he is a man for all seasons, the same is true of his position on immigration. **1972** A. PRICE *Col. Butler's Wolf* xii. 131 She's a nice sort of girl... A girl for all seasons. **1973** *Listener* 29 Nov. 745/1 He [*sc.* John Kennedy] was a man for all seasons, a man for all people. **1976** M. BIRMINGHAM *Heat of Sun* viii. 114 The vulture.. a bird for all seasons, I decided, ready to match one's every mood. **1981** M. WARNER *Joan of Arc* xiii. 263 Joan, a heroine for all seasons.

III. 16. b. (Later examples.)
1781 H. NEWDIGATE *Let.* 15 Oct. in A. E. Newdigate-Newdegate *Cheverels* (1898) iii. 46 A Hamper of good things,.. Pears & Pines in perfection, *Rouleaux* never out of season. **1847** A. BRONTË *Agnes Grey* xviii. 282, I pretended to want to save it [*sc.* a hare]..as it was so glaringly out of season. **1960** *Mrs. Beeton's Bk. Househ. Managem.* vii. 93 When a fruit is out of season in one part of the globe it is usually in season in another.

VI. 21. *season-cracked* adj.; **season-check** *U.S.* (see quot. 1905); **season cracking,** the occurrence of longitudinal cracks in cold-worked brass or bronze; so **season crack** *sb.* and *v. intr.*; **season ticket** (earlier and later examples); **season-ticket holder** (earlier example).
1887 J. KIRKLAND *Zury* 32 Ye see that season-check in the butt-end [of a black-walnut log]. **1905** *Bull. Bureau of Forestry* (U.S. Dept. Agric.) No. 61. 33 *Check*, a longitudinal crack in timber caused by too rapid seasoning... Syn.: season check. **1909** WEBSTER, Season cracks. **1915** *Trans. Amer. Inst. Metals* VIII. 322 It was found that all those cartridge cases which had season cracked had primers on. **1957** R. A. HIGGINS *Engin. Metall.* I. v. 87 A controlled low-temperature anneal..applied to hard-drawn 70/30 brass tube will effectively reduce its tendency to 'season-crack'..without reducing strength or hardness. *Ibid.* II. xiv. 292 Residual..stresses in cold-worked alloys often manifest themselves during service in the form of 'season cracks'. **1938** M. K. RAWLINGS *Yearling* xxvi. 347, I got a old dug-out right above here, is mighty sorry and season-cracked, but hit'd carry you acrost the creek. **1910** *Brass World* VI. 269/1 One of the most annoying things that happens to brass while in use is its season cracking. **1923** GLAZEBROOK *Dict. Appl. Physics* V. 410/2 The essential condition for 'season cracking' is the presence in the finished article of internal stresses of considerable magnitude. **1967** A. H. COTTRELL *Introd. Metall.* xxiii. 467 The season cracking of α-brass in ammoniacal environments may be due to local dezincification along the grain boundaries. **1820** *Columbian Centinel* (Boston, Mass.) 2 Dec. 1/1 For sale, a Boston Theatre Season Ticket, at a fair price. **1869** W. JAMES *Coll. Ess. & Rev.* (1920) 1 People who are comfortably in possession of a season-ticket over the Stygian ferry. **1953** C. DAY LEWIS *Italian Visit* i. 14 The season tickets that rattle us back and forth in a groove from Centre to circumference. **1862** J. SIMMONDS *Railway Travellers Handy Bk.* 48 We may here remind season-ticket holders to renew their privilege.

seasonable, *a.* Add: ¶**4.** *erron.* used for SEASONAL *a.* 2.
1923 *Glasgow Herald* 20 Mar. 9 Persons engaged in seasonable trades in which the duration of seasonable employment is too short to enable them to qualify for benefit. [**1980** *Listener* 10 Jan. 51/3 Will the BBC please note that the word they want is 'seasonable', not 'seasonal'. One has seasonable items like mince pies and carols; 'seasonal' is applied to rainfall and fluctuations in car sales, i.e., things that happen with the changing seasons.]

seasonably, *adv.* Add: ¶**2.** *erron.* used for SEASONALLY *adv.*
1928 *Britain's Industr. Future* (Liberal Industr. Inquiry) IV. xxvii. § 7. 388 The hours worked in all the jobs concerned (omitting those in which hours varied weekly or seasonably).

seasonality (sīz'næ·lĭti). orig. *U.S.* [f. SEASONAL *a.* + -ITY.] **1.** The condition of being dependent on the seasons or other temporal cycle; the state of recurring at regular intervals.
1934 in WEBSTER. **1936** *S.P.E. Tract* XLV. 191 University professors and other persons of literary or academic reputation have been responsible for such coinages as..*seasonality.* **1959** *Economist* 18 Apr. 218/2 The common seasonality of the tourist trade, horticulture and fishing makes these occupations awkward neighbours for year-round industrial enterprise. **1971** *Nature* 5 Feb. 406/2 The relatively sharp seasonality of fruiting and leaf formation would have effectively restricted exclusive arboreal feeding for an animal as large as a chimpanzee. **1976** J. S. FLEMMING *Inflation* xi. 109 Moreover baskets including foodstuffs will display seasonality which one would probably not want to reflect in the adjusted payments.

2. The degree to which a climate has distinct seasons.
1968 R. W. FAIRBRIDGE *Encycl. Geomorphol.* 721/2 No consideration has been given to seasonality of climate. **1972** *Sci. Amer.* June 64/1 A sharp reduction in coral diversity that began in late Eocene times and lasted throughout the Oligocene epoch seems to reflect a continued increase in seasonality of climate and a substantial lowering of mean temperatures.

seasonally, *adv.* Add: **2.** According to the season.
1937 DAVIES & YODER *Business Statistics* v. 239 In January..the unadjusted index was 88 and in February it was 91. This was a rise, but not so much as would be seasonally expected, as is shown by adjusted figures for the same months, which are 91 and 89. **1942** CROXTON & COWDEN *Appl. Gen. Statistics* xviii. 524 There will be an enormous drop in the seasonally adjusted data between December and January. **1971** *Daily Tel.* 17 Dec. 15 Seasonally adjusted..the figures show an increase in borrowing by industry of about £50 million over the previous quarter. **1974** *Nature* 1 Feb. 269/2 Both parameters depend on the mesospheric circulation, whose main features at a particular latitude vary seasonally. **1982** *Guardian* 15 Apr. 14/2 The seasonally adjusted level of unemployment..remained at 11·8 per cent.

sea-song. Add: Also *fig.*
1944 BLUNDEN *Shells by Stream* 31 The wind may sing his sea-song later In your review as he will in mine.

seasoning, *vbl. sb.* Add: **1. d.** (Earlier example.)
1807 *Salmagundi* 16 May 198 Strangers always.. undergo a *seasoning* as europeans do in the West-Indies.

g. The process whereby a transported slave becomes inured to the conditions of slavery. *Obs.* exc. *Hist.*
1771 A. BENEZIT *Some Hist. Acct. Guinea* xiii. 130 At a moderate computation of the slaves who are purchased

by our African merchants in a year, near thirty thousand die upon the voyage and in the seasoning. **1786** T. Clarkson *Ess. Slavery & Commerce Human Species* III. iv. 139 This seasoning is said to expire, when the two first years of their servitude are completed; It is the time which an African must take to be so accustomed to the colony, as to be able to endure the common labour of a plantation, and to be put into the *gang*. **1804** R. Bisset *Defence of Slave Trade* 88 Instead of *thirty-three* in the hundred dying, as asserted by the author of the 'Concise Statement', *not three* in the hundred die of the seasoning. **1977** *Time* 7 Feb. 59/3 The passage took longer, with 'seasoning' camps at the beginning, usually on an island off the African coast.

h. The application of one of various finishes to leather after tanning.

1897 C. T. Davis *Manuf. Leather* (ed. 2) 358 A seasoning mixture is applied to the surface after tanning and before coloring. **1974** *Encycl. Brit. Macropædia* X. 763/2 In unpigmented seasoning [of leather], a simple glazing finish or seasoning may contain egg albumin, water, and glycerin.

sea-swallow. Add: **2. c.** An edible swiftlet of the genus *Collocalia*, found in south-east Asia.

1902 [in Dict., sense 3].

seat, *sb.* Add: **II. 6. d.** *U.S.* A place in the membership of the New York Stock Exchange.

1820 *Constitution N.Y. Stock & Exchange Board* in E. C. Stedman *N.Y. Stock Exchange* (1905) iv. 68 If two-thirds of the members present are for reinstating him, he shall again be entitled to his seat at the Board. **1882** J. D. McCabe *N.Y. by Sunlight & Gaslight* xxi. 337 A seat in the Board costs about $6000, and is the absolute personal property of its owner. **1948** *Time* 14 June 90/2 All who buy and sell on the floor must own Stock Exchange seats, which are currently worth about $65,000 apiece (1929 price: $625,000). **1972** *Times* 16 May (Wall Street Suppl.) p. viii/5 Among the brokers the numbers of 'seats' on the exchange remained unchanged at 1,366 (as it has done since December 1953).

7. *spec.* in a coach, train, aeroplane, etc.

1810 E. Weeton *Let.* 28 Dec. (1969) I. 318 Perhaps when Mr. and Mrs. P. go to Preston..I may get a seat with them..if they go in the chaise. **1976** *Daily Mirror* 16 July 9/6 The bosses are taking up too many first-class seats on main line commuter services. **1977** C. Forbes *Avalanche Express* vi. 68 Harry Wargrave occupied his normal seat..the gangway seat [in the aircraft].

b. Also *spec.* of a lavatory.

1907 *Yesterday's Shopping* (1969) 518/2 Seat Covers.. for use on 'w.c.'s'. **1938** E. Bowen *Death of Heart* I. iv. 81 Portia..re-wound the gramophone on the shut seat, and Stravinsky filled the bathroom. **1979** M. Hastings *Bomber Command* vi. 155 The Elsan toilet which most crews had used with acute caution since a 50 Squadron gunner left most of the skin of his backside attached to the frozen seat one icy night over Germany.

10. Delete ? *Obs.* and add later *dial.* examples.

1962 *Sunday Express* 1 Apr. 21/5 These lairs [of hares] are usually called 'forms',..though in..Kent, the cosier word 'seats' is preferred. **1972** Evans & Thomson *Leaping Hare* iv. 52 They'll dig a little hole so they can cover, so they're level with the top of the land... A *seat* we call it.

IV. 22. b. The position of a horseshoe with respect to the hoof. Cf. *seated *ppl. a.* 7.

1851 H. Stephens *Bk. Farm* (ed. 2) I. 338/1 The transparent shoe, showing the usual seat given to the shoe upon the forefoot.

23. b. The surface on which the head of a poppet-valve rests when the valve is closed.

1841 Valve-seat [see Valve *sb.*[1] 7 a]. **1916**, etc. [see *Grind v.[1] 5 b]. **1936** E. A. Phillipson *Steam Locomotive Design* x. 353 The springs provided to assist the valves to return to their seats are located in the steam spaces. **1963** R. F. Webb *Motorists' Dict.* 220 It is essential that the valve is accurately ground to match the seat so as to form an effective gas seal. **1970** K. Ball *Fiat 600, 600D Autobk.* i. 13 Refacing of the valve head seating area must be done on a special universal grinder enabling the angle of the seat to be accurately set.

V. 27. d. *the seat of one's pants*: see *pants *sb. pl.* 1 e.

e. *to be on seat*: to be present in one's office. *W. Afr. pidgin.*

1971 J. Spencer *Eng. Lang. W. Afr.* 29 A very useful one which might be recommended to English-speaking communities elsewhere is the expression (to be) *on seat*, as in a sentence such as 'The Deputy Secretary is back on seat today'; meaning he is in the office, or generally available, as opposed to being absent. **1976** *Listener* 17 June 773/1 If you ask his servant where the district commissioner has gone, the servant tells you he is at the office with the impressive phrase: 'Master's on seat.'

VI. 28. *seat-back, -cover, reservation.*

1872 'Mark Twain' *Roughing It* iii. 30 The conductor bent all the seat-backs down. **1976** M. Birmingham *Heat of Sun* ii. 21, I..turned my head, half expecting to be able to see over the seat-back. **1881** C. C. Harrison *Woman's Handiwork* III. 193 A seat-cover of slate-green plush. **1970** *Washington Post* 30 Sept. B13/4 (Advt.), Morris Katz & Sons Car Radio & Seatcover Center, Inc. **1973** W. McCarthy *Detail* iii. 181 He checked in for his seat reservation.

29. seat belt, a safety belt for a person in a moving conveyance, *spec.* one worn in an aircraft, esp. at take-off or landing, or one worn in a motor vehicle as a protection in an accident or in an emergency stop; also *fig.*; hence **seat-belted** *a.*, wearing a seat belt; **seat-board,** (*d*) a board forming a seat in a vehicle; **seat-mate:** for *U.S.* read *N. Amer.* and add earlier and later examples; **seat-mile,** a statistical unit denoting one mile travelled by one passenger, *spec.* in travel by air; **seat-pack,** a parachute carried in a pack worn over the posterior.

1932 *Luftfahrt* (Illustrierte technische Wörterbücher XVII) 128/3 Seat belt. **1933** *Aeroplane* 27 Dec. 1101/2 'Please fix seat-belts.' (Note! not *safety* belts.) **1959** *B.S.I. News* Apr. 18/2 Arising from the interest now being displayed in seat belts for motorists, a new technical committee of the B.S.I. recently held its first meeting, at which it was decided that a British Standard for these articles would serve a useful purpose. **1966** T. Pynchon *Crying of Lot 49* vi. 150 You're chicken, she told herself, snapping her seat belt... She drove savagely along the freeway. **1970** C. Hampton *Philanthropist* iii. 32 He.. came and sat next to me on the sofa, and I thought this is it, fasten your seat belts. **1977** B. Freemantle *Charlie Muffin* xix. 192 They had cleared the airport and the seat-belt sign had been turned off. **1967** J. Redgate *Killing Season* (1968) I. xv. 65 The redhead sat, seat-belted, talking. **1873** J. H. Beadle *Undevel. West* iii. 70 The wagon made fearful lurches, and our seatboard rattled over it in every direction. **1859** *Ladies' Repository* Nov. 645/1 She will tickle the neck of her seat-mate with a bit of grass. **1968** *Globe & Mail* (Toronto) 17 Feb. 7/1 A television interview by my hon. friend's seatmate. **1976** L. Sanders *Hamlet Warning* (1977) xv. 124 On the night flight to Lisbon..his seatmate was a German auto parts specialist. **1953** *Wall St. Jrnl.* 24 Mar. 22/2 Mr. Cole predicted the combined airlines would have an annual capacity of 1,470,000,000 seat miles..by June of next year. **1961** P. W. Brooks *Mod. Airliner* i. 26 The most important non-stop stage lengths have been achieved—notably London–New York, 3,500 seat-miles. **1977** *Guernsey Weekly Press* 21 July 1/4 The 'plane is claimed to be economical with a fuel consumption per seat-mile lower than that of any other modern commercial transport aircraft. **1930** O. H. Kneen *Everyman's Bk. of Flying* xii. 217 For use in airplanes, the *seat pack* is generally used. **1946** W. F. Burbidge *From Balloon to Bomber* iii. 45 The 'seat pack' forms a cushion during the plane journey.

seat, *v.* Add: **4. a.** Delete † and add later examples of *intr.* for *refl.* use with other consts.

1916 Hirshfeld & Ulbricht *Steam Power* xi. 207 The valves are all double-seated.., that is, they seat at both ends. **1963** C. R. Cowell et al. *Inlays, Crowns, & Bridges* iv. 41 This must be done quickly otherwise the cement will begin to set and the restoration will not seat accurately. **1972** L. M. Harris *Introd. Deepwater Floating Drilling Operations* ix. 93 As the well-head seats on the previously set permanent guide structure and foundation-pile housing, it is latched and rigidly attached to the housing.

Seatainer (sī·tē^{i}nəɹ). *Austral.* Also **seatainer.** [f. Sea *sb.* + Con)tainer.] A container for the transportation of freight by sea.

1964 *Economist* 25 July 361/1 (Advt.), Carriage of all cargo in 'Seatainers'. **1965** S. J. Baker *Ampol Bk. Australiana* (ed. 2) 112 World's first ship designed solely to carry 'seatainers'—large aluminium containers of uniform size inside which up to 17 tons of cargo may be packed. **1969** *Jane's Freight Containers 1968–69* 332/1 A new 'Seatainer' terminal will soon be brought into operation. **1974** *Australian* 12 Aug. 12/8 (*heading*) Seatainer important facility to Melbourne.

seated, *ppl. a.* Add: **7.** Of a horseshoe: hollowed out so that the bearing surface rests on the wall of the hoof.

1831 W. Youatt *Horse* xvii. 311 (*heading*) The concave-seated shoe. **1908** *Animal Managem.* (War Office) 227 Seating is the hollowing out of the bearing surface, opposed to the sole, so that a seated shoe bears on the wall alone.

seater. Restrict *rare* to sense 1 in Dict. and add: **2.** Substitute for entry: As second element, designating a vehicle or article of furniture having a specified seating capacity, as *two-* (*three-*, etc.) *seater*.

1906 [in Dict.]. **1916** H. Barber *Aeroplane Speaks* Pl. xvi, The familiar biplanes with 80 h.p. Gnomes, and 5-seater with 100 h.p. Anzani. **1923** Galsworthy *Captures* 217 Hubert Marsland..had occasion to stay the progress of his two-seater about ten miles from London for a minor repair. **1941** J. D. Carr *Case of Constant Suicides* iii. 44 A..five-seater car was drawn up before the tourist-office. **1966** 'A. Hall' *9th Directive* xx. 184 It was a massive black Lincoln sedan; a seven-seater executive-style transport. **1978** R. V. Jones *Most Secret War* iv. 39 It seemed that, if we developed the detector to the operational stage, it would have to be mounted in single seater fighters.

seater, var. *saeter, setter.

sea-thistle. 1. Delete ? *Obs.* and add later example.

1979 *Bull. Yorks. Dial. Soc.* Summer 7 The only kind of flowers were the dark blue sea thistle with very strong prickly leaves but no smell.

seating, *vbl. sb.* Add: **3.** (Earlier U.S. example.)

1790 *Pennsylvania Packet* 11 Dec. 1/2 A very choice Parcel of Hair Seatings, of various widths and patterns.

5. b. The raised outer part of a horseshoe which rests on the wall of the hoof; also, the hollowing out of a horseshoe so that the outer part rests on the wall of the hoof.

1831 W. Youatt *Horse* xvii. 319 A strip of felt or leather is sometimes placed between the seating of the shoe and the crust. **1908** *Animal Managem.* (War Office) 228 The object of seating is to take pressure off the sole.

5*. Of garments: the process of going out of shape at the seat.

1960 *Sunday Express* 11 Sept. 15/4 *Never* wear a slick, straight skirt without a tight-fitting slip beneath... That way there'll be no 'seating'. **1974** Lippman & Erskine *Dressmaking made Simple* iii. 53 Linings are essential in straight skirts to prevent seating.

6. a. *seating-face.*

1925 *Morris Owner's Man.* 77 These two photographs show a valve before..and after grinding-in. Note the different appearance of their seating faces.

b. *seating plan.*

1929 'E. Queen' *Roman Hat Mystery* xxii. 303 We had already borrowed a seating-plan. **1949** M. Mead *Male & Female* 406 Men holding the highest titles from each village were combined in a formal seating-plan. **1974** O. Manning *Rain Forest* I. vi. 75 Millman, seating-plan in hand, put Murodi at Lady Urquhart's right and Ogden on her left.

Seato (sī·to, siē^{i}·to). Also **S.E.A.T.O., SEATO.** [Acronym f. the initial letters of *S*outh *E*ast *A*sia *T*reaty *O*rganization (after N.A.T.O.), set up in 1954.] A military alliance, lasting from 1954 to 1977, of Australia, New Zealand, France, Pakistan, the Philippines, Thailand, the United Kingdom, and the United States.

Pakistan withdrew from the alliance in 1972.

1954 *N.Y. Times* 23 July 16/1 Preparations are under way to call an international conference in August or September..to devise a SEATO for the East to match NATO in the West. **1955** *Times* 31 May 6/7 The programme proposes the strengthening of the links of friendship with France, and membership of the S.E.A.T.O. pact. **1957** *Observer* 6 Oct. 10/6 Pakistan has openly shown that she would expect Seato to assist her in the event of an attack from India. **1966** 'A. Hall' *9th Directive* i. 14 We have the SEATO headquarters here... Bangkok is a key city in the South-east Asian complex. **1970** *Ann. Reg. 1969* 149 The fourteenth Seato Council met in Bangkok on 20–21 May. **1977** *Times* 30 June 6/4 The South-East Asian Treaty (Seato) Organization..will fade into history tomorrow [*sc.* 30 June]..when the flags of its six remaining members, the United States, Britain, the Philippines, Thailand, Australia and New Zealand, are lowered from the organization's deserted headquarters in Bangkok for the last time.

Seatonian (sītō^{u}·niăn), *a.* [f. the name of the Eng. divine Thomas *Seaton* (1684–1741), the founder of the prize + -ian.] *Seatonian prize*: a prize awarded (since 1750) for religious poetry at the University of Cambridge. Also *ellipt.* (in quot., a poem to be submitted for this).

[**1773** (*title*) Musæ Seatonianæ. A complete collection of the Cambridge prize poems, from their first institution.. to the present time.] **1795** A. W. Trollope (*title*) The destruction of Babylon, a Seatonian prize poem. **1864** A. J. Munby *Diary* 27 Sept. in D. Hudson *Munby* (1972) 203 Finished my first Seatonian; hurriedly, and with brain throbbing. **1908** H. Pentin *Judith* iv. 68 In the year 1865 'Judith' was the subject set for the Seatonian Prize Poem at Cambridge. **1961** *Listener* 31 Aug. 323/3 Very occasionally in the blank-verse wastes of the Seatonian prize-poems one comes across a single line..that adumbrates the future author of *A Song to David*. **1972** *Cambr. Univ. Reporter* 6 Dec. 391 The Examiners for the Seatonian Prize for the best English Poem on a sacred subject give notice that the subject for the year 1973 is '*Apocalypse*'.

sea-turtle[2]. Substitute for def.: A marine turtle belonging to the families Cheloniidæ or Dermochelyidæ. (Earlier and later examples.)

1612 W. Strachey *Trav. Virginia* (1849) 195/1 A sea turtle, tuwcuppewk. **1888** H. C. Bumpus in J. S. Kingsley *Riverside Nat. Hist.* III. 444 Sea-turtles are of considerable value as food. **1958** J. Carew *Black Midas* iii. 35 Mendoza had trapped a sea turtle and four men had to lift it into his donkey cart.

seau (sō^{u}). *Ceramics.* Also *erron.* † **sceau.** Pl. **seaux.** [Fr., lit. 'bucket'.] A vessel in the shape of a pail or bucket used for cooling wine, etc. (freq. forming part of dinner services of the eighteenth century).

1784 H. Walpole *Descr. Strawberry-Hill* 82 A sceau for liquors, of Seve. **1851** *Illustr. Catal. Gt. Exhib.* III. 710/1 Porcelain Inkstands, Seaux, Card Trays. **1869** C. Schreiber *Jrnl.* (1911) I. 37 Some Bleu du Roy vases, small,..a pair of sceaux of the same colour. *Ibid.* 53 Picked up..a marked St. Claud sceau at Bencoux's. **1875** E. Meteyard *Wedgwood Handbk.* Gloss. 409 Seaux formed a part of all costly dinners and dessert services, particularly if intended for foreign countries... A choice pair of seaux in sea-green jasper is in the Marjoribanks Collection. **1974** Savage & Newman *Illustr. Dict. Ceramics* 259 *Seau à bouteille*,..a bucket-shaped receptacle for holding ice to chill a single bottle of wine.

sea-view. **2.** (Earlier examples.)
1790 J. WOODFORDE *Diary* 10 May (1927) III. 188 My Brother and Wife..very highly pleased with Yarmouth and the Sea View. **1844** A. W. KINGLAKE *Eothen* iv. 63 The reality of that very sea-view, which had bounded the sight of the Greeks.

sea-washed, *a.* Add: **b.** *sea-washed turf*, a dense turf found in coastal regions of northern England.
1931 R. BEALE *Bk. Lawn* vi. 56 Turf can roughly be divided into three categories—Cumberland, Sea-washed or Marsh; Down, Heath or Moorland; and Meadow Turf. **1954** A. G. L. HELLYER *Encycl. Garden Work* 137/1 Sea-washed turf or Cumberland turf..owes its fineness to the fact that it is washed by salt water at high tides. **1962** I. GREENFIELD *Turf Culture* ii. 73 One [variety of creeping bent]..is a common constituent of the sea-washed turf used for bowling greens. **1977** *Lancs. Life* Nov. 82/4 Lancashire's only herd of wintering wild Bewick swans from Siberia..crop the sea-washed turf.

sea-way, seaway. Add: The form *seaway* (no hyphen) is now the more usual. **1. b.** An artificial or natural channel connecting two tracts of sea.
1866 [see sense 1 a in Dict.]. **1977** A. HALLAM *Planet Earth* 222/1 Towards the close of the period the old seaway of Tethys was progressively eliminated as the African plate moved northwards to impinge upon the Asian plate.

c. An inland waterway with passage to the sea, esp. one capable of accommodating large ocean-going vessels. *N. Amer.* (chiefly in phr. *St. Lawrence Seaway*).
1921 A. M. EVANS in *Chicago Daily Tribune* 4 Aug. 21/7 Coastwise trade between Chicago and Atlantic ports.. stands second only to the foreign commerce possibilities offered by the St. Lawrence seaway project. **1933** *Sun* (Baltimore) 23 June 3/1 (*heading*) Lakes-to-the-Gulf seaway dedicated... The joining of the Great Lakes with the Gulf of Mexico..by a $102,000,000 inland waterway was completed officially today. **1941** F. D. ROOSEVELT in *Great Lakes-St. Lawrence Basin: Hearings* (1942) I. 2, I recommend authorization of construction of the St. Lawrence seaway and power project, pursuant to the agreement of March 19, 1941, with Canada, as an integral part of the joint defense of the North American continent. **1959** *Times* 27 June 6/5 The royal yacht Britannia.. entered the 2,300-mile St. Lawrence Seaway to mark the ceremonial opening of that great engineering project. **1968** *Encycl. Brit.* XIX. 910/2 The broader concept of the 'seaway', and one which is in general usage, includes the entire system of lakes, locks, canals, and rivers which have converted over 6,600 mi. (10,621 km.) of mainland Great Lakes shore line of the United States and Canada into another seacoast. **1976** *Leader-Post* (Regina, Saskatchewan) 24 June 1. 1/2 An oil spill that stretched 15 miles along the St. Lawrence Seaway.

seaweed. Add: **3.** *seaweed-green* sb. and adj.; **seaweed-marquetry** (see quot. 1975).
1937 *Burlington Mag.* Oct. p.xxiii/1 A wine-ewer of translucent seaweed green jade. **1965** [see *KAWA-KAWA[1] 2]. **1976** J. WILSON *Let's Pretend* i. 7 The bunches of seaweed green ribbon. **1979** *Guardian* 28 Feb. 13/2 The skirt is a seaweed green verging on khaki. **1935** *Burlington Mag.* May 233/2 King William's writing-table in seaweed marquetry, with his cypher. **1967** G. SIMS *Last Best Friend* xiv. 120 The carpet was a spinach-green Gobelin and there were Cromwellian chairs and a seaweed marquetry desk. **1975** *Oxf. Compan. Decorative Arts* 699/1 *Seaweed marquetry*, marquetry patterns composed of very fine elements resembling seaweed or endive leaves.

Sebago. Add to def.: *Salmo sebago*, native to lakes of eastern North America. (Earlier example.)
1873 C. HALLOCK *Fishing Tourist* i. 31 The Sebago Trout..is a monster trout.

Sebastianism (sebæstiă·niz'm). Chiefly *Hist.* [f. the name of Dom *Sebastian* (1554–78), King of Portugal + -ISM; cf. Portuguese *Sebastianismo.*] (See quot. 1980.) Also **Sebastia·nist** (also *attrib.* or as *adj.*), ‖ **-a**, an adherent or supporter of Sebastianism.
1881 R. F. BURTON *Camoens* I. 363 The 'Sebastianistas', as they were called, looked forward to a manner of Messiah. *Ibid.*, The Braganza House used the Sebastianist legend to strengthen Portuguese nationality. **1907** R. B. CUNNINGHAME GRAHAM in G. C. Graham *Santa Teresa* p. vii, The few Sebastianists who, it is said, lingered in Portugal almost down to the present century. **1911** *Encycl. Brit.* XXIV. 566/2 'Sebastianism' became a religion. **1944** S. PUTNAM tr. *E. da Cunha's Rebellion in Backlands* ii. 112 The political mysticism of Sebastianism. Extinct in Portugal, it persists unimpaired today..in our [Brazilian] northern back-country. **1974** *Encycl. Brit. Micropædia* IX. 14/1 Sebastianistas believed that the King had not died during the battle. **1976** H. V. LIVERMORE *New Hist. Portugal* 165 The national rumour of Sebastianism had now taken firm root. **1980** *Times Lit. Suppl.* 4 July 764/2 Sebastianism takes its name from the myth current during the period of Spanish rule, that Portugal's King Sebastian, in fact killed in Morocco, would one day return to lead the nation to greatness and glory.

Sebei (səbē^i^·). Also **Sabei, Sapei, Savei.** [Native name.] A people inhabiting parts of eastern Uganda and western Kenya; a member of this people; also, their Nilo-Hamitic language. Also *attrib.* or as *adj.*
1902 H. JOHNSTON *Uganda Protectorate* II. xix. 868 The Sabei men also hang to their locks of hair and to their ear-lobes rather striking ornaments. *Ibid.*, The dwellings of the Sabei are like those of the Masaba Bantu tribes. **1935** THOMAS & SCOTT *Uganda* v. 86 Half-Hamitic languages are spoken by the Teso..and by the Sebei. **1953** TROWELL & WACHSMANN *Tribal Crafts of Uganda* i. 50 The Sebei are members of another branch of the Nilo-Hamites, being very closely related to the Suk-Nandi group in Kenya. *Ibid.* 51 Both Karamaja and Sebei fit their gourds with leather thongs for carrying. **1963** M. DE K. HEMPHILL in Oliver & Mathew *Hist. E. Afr.* I. xi. 419 The Sapei were moving to the west, and the Kony to the north. **1967** W. GOLDSCHMIDT *Sebei Law* p. vii, The first and outstanding debt is owed to the Sebei themselves, the officials, the informants, and the many citizens who helped to shape my image of Sebei customs. **1968** P. LADEFOGED et al. *Lang. in Uganda* II. 81 Kupsabiny, the language spoken by the Sebei, has some likeness to its neighbour, Suk (or Pokot), but is otherwise distinct from any other members of the group. **1973** *Sci. Amer.* July 77/1 Brideprice is the largest single outlay of goods that an ordinary Sebei makes in his lifetime. **1976** *Drum* (E. Afr. ed.) Nov. 18/2 All the Kenya tribes of the Luo, Masai, Kisii, Baluhya, Turkana, Sebei, Teso, Suk, Pokot, Nandi, Marakwet, Samburu, and Elgeyo are my grandchildren. **1977** Savei [see *SAPINY].

Sebilian (sĭbi·liăn), *a.* (and *sb.*) *Archæol.* [ad. F. *Sébilien* (E. Vignard 1923, in *Bull. de l'Institut Franç. d'Archéol. Orientale* XXII. 3), f. the name of *Sebil*, a village in Upper Egypt: see -IAN.] Of or pertaining to an Upper Palæolithic and Mesolithic culture of Upper Egypt; also *ellipt.* as *sb.*
1932 *Antiquity* VI. 193 In the Nile Valley some rather peculiar industries, probably allied to the Aurignacian, are called Sébilian. **1936** L. S. B. LEAKEY *Stone Age Afr.* x. 193 In North Africa at Sebil, the Early Sebilian gradually evolves by way of a Middle Sebilian into a true Microlithic stage known as the Upper Sebilian. **1952** V. G. CHILDE *New Light Most Anc. East* iii. 32 The stage intermediate between the food-gathering culture of Sebilian hunters and the settled agriculture of the oldest sedentary inhabitants of Egypt. **1969** COLES & HIGGS *Archaeol. Early Man* II. xiii. 196 The later stages of the Sebilian material contain microlithic forms, and one associated with aurochs, buffalo and shell middens. Suggested dates for the Sebilian industries range from c. 16,000 to 11,000 B.P. **1976** *Sci. Amer.* Aug. 34/1 A fourth industry, the Sebilian..is found at Kom Ombo.

sebk(h)a, varr. *SABKHA.

seborrhœa. Add: Also (chiefly *U.S.*) **seborrhea.** (Further examples.)
1940 BECKER & OBERMAYER *Mod. Dermatol. & Syphilol.* v. 56/2 It is advisable to assume that seborrhea and the diseases to which it predisposes, namely acne vulgaris, seborrheic dermatitis and rosacea, do not appear before puberty. **1973** *Nature* 8 June 350/1 In Parkinsonism the associated seborrhoea is induced by excessive secretion of a pituitary sebotrophic hormone. **1978** J. KILMARTIN tr. *R. Aron-Brunetière's Beauty & Medicine* ii. 22 Even people with fairly mild seborrhea or acne are self-conscious about it.

seborrhœic *a.* (also **-rrheic**) (further examples).
1955 *Sci. News Let.* 12 Feb. 104/3 The scientists have reported using the glands in cases of..seborrheic dermatitis. **1971** [see *liver spot* s.v. *LIVER *sb.*[1] 7]. **1977** *Lancet* 27 Aug. 440/2 One troublesome feature.., the seborrhœic scalp rash, responds excellently to application of a tar shampoo.

sebotrophic (sebotrō^u^·fik), *a.* *Physiol.* Also **-tropic** (-trō^u^·pik, -trǫ·pik). [f. SEB(UM + -O + *-TROPHIC, *-TROPIC.] Tending to stimulate sebaceous activity.
1957 LORINCZ & LANCASTER in *Science* 19 July 124/1 Methods of preparation and assay of a crude extract of anterior pituitary glands of hogs showing tropic effects on sebaceous, preputial, and Harderian glands in the rat are described. These effects can be called sebotropic because the ectodermal glands affected produce secretions rich in lipids. **1968** EBLING & ROOK in A. Rook et al. *Textbk. Dermatol.* II. xlv. 1335/2 Biological tests for sebotrophic activity..were carried out..on the preputial gland. **1973** [see *SEBORRHŒA].

sec. Add: Later examples as abbrev. of SECRETARY *sb.*[1] and (in colloq. phrases) of SECOND *sb.*[1]
1869 *Bradshaw's Railway Man.* XXI. 48 *Officers.*—Gen. Man., James Smithells; Sec., Archibald Gibson. **1953** WODEHOUSE *Performing Flea* 130 One of those tall, statuesque, frozen-faced secs who took his dictation in an aloof, revolted sort of way. **1956** A. WILSON *Anglo-Saxon Attitudes* II. ii. 319 'I'm afraid I can't stop now. I'm late for an appointment.' 'It won't take a sec,' said Vin. *a* **1960** E. M. FORSTER *Maurice* (1971) vi. 37 Wait a sec, and I'll come too. **1962** A. LURIE *Love & Friendship* x. 199, I wonder if you could hold the baby for me, Missus Turner, please, just for a sec. **1979** M. BOYCE *I was There!* 14/2 The Rugby Club's General Committee Banned 'Sine Die' their ticket Sec, my Uncle Will.

sec (sek), *a.* [Fr.] Of champagne and other wines: = DRY *a.* 8. Also *fig.* Cf. *extra sec* s.v. *EXTRA *adv.* a.
1863 T. G. SHAW *Wine, Vine & Cellar* xviii. 334 It is evident that the word 'sack' cannot be understood to have denoted sec (dry). **1899** *Judge* (N.Y.) XVI. 419/2 Berton 'sec' Champagne. **1891**, etc. [see *EXTRA *adv.* a]. **1931** *Morning Post* 10 Aug. 4/3 The Bayreuth Festival... Wagner sec. **1960** WODEHOUSE *Jeeves in Offing* xvi. 165, I was in my room, having shed the moistened outer crust and substituted something a bit more *sec* in pale flannel.

sécateur. Delete ‖ and add: Now usu. in pl. form *secateurs* and with anglicized pronunc. (sekătə̄ɹz) or (se·kătə̄ɹz). Further examples.
1924 H. H. THOMAS *Compl. Amateur Gardener* vii. 67 The pruning outfit should consist of..a hone or sharpening stone,..and sécateurs. **1937** *Carter's Blue Bk. Gardening 1937* 365 (Advt.), The amazing manner in which this Secateur quickly and cleanly cuts off the thickest of branches, very soon becomes a fascination to the user. **1967** E. MAVOR *Redoubt* x. 172 She dressed her enormous bulk in..a baize gardening apron with capacious pockets for her bass and secateurs. **1968** R. H. W. BROWN *Gardening Complete* ii. 27 The tools which the gardener must have for a start are two spades, a fork, a rake, three hoes, a trowel, a dibber, a pair of secateurs, [etc.]. **1977** P. THROWER *Every Day Gardening* i. 16/1 (*caption*) If the garden includes numerous trees, shrubs and fruit trees a pair of long-handled secateurs is especially useful.

Secchi (se·ki). Also **secchi.** [The name of Angelo *Secchi* (1818–78), Italian astronomer.] *Secchi('s) disc*: a type of opaque white disc which is used in determining the transparency of water; the disc, maintained in a horizontal attitude, is allowed to sink and the depth at which it ceases to be visible from the surface is recorded.
Secchi and Cialdi first described the use of discs of this kind in 1865 (*Compt. Rend.* LXI. 101).
1913 *Science* 14 Nov. 703/1 The inland lakes of Wisconsin are not very transparent; the transparency, as shown by Secchi's disk, varying from less than 1 m. to about 7 m. **1931** *Trans. Wisconsin Acad.* XXVI. 337 The transparency as determined by the Secchi disc shows some correlation with the amount of organisms present in the water. *Ibid.* 419 Transparency..is measured by the visibility of Secchi's disc. **1963** G. L. PICKARD *Descriptive Physical Oceanogr.* iii. 23 The colour of sea-water can be judged most conveniently against the white Secchi disc.. as it is lowered to determine the transparency of the water. **1975** *New Yorker* 12 May 80/3 They threw a secchi disc into the ocean to measure turbidity.

secco, *sb.* Add: **2.** Ellipt. for 'secco recitative'.
1960 *Times* 2 July 12/2 There are three tenor recitatives accompanied by piano in a modern equivalent of the old *secco*. **1969** *Daily Tel.* 18 Jan. 17/5 The beloved melody contains no fewer than 18 appoggiaturas actually written out by Mozart (he never does in seccos).

secede, *v.* Add: **3.** *trans.* To withdraw (a component territory) from a federal union or the like; to detach or cede (a piece of land). *rare.*
1946 W. FAULKNER *Portable Faulkner* 739 A plot to secede the whole Mississippi Valley from the United States and join it to Spain. **1963** A. SMITH *Throw out Two Hands* xv. 156 Many people feel it was wrong..for any park to secede part of itself for any reason.

secentismo, secentist, varr. *SEICENTISMO, *SEICENTIST.

secesh, *sb.* **b.** Delete ¶ *nonce-use* and add earlier example.
1863 TROLLOPE in *Good Words* Dec. 858/2, I won't talk secesh to you out here in the cold.

secession. Add: **3. d.** Also with capital initial. [tr. G. *Sezession.*] A radical movement in art that began in Vienna and was contemporaneous with, and related to, art nouveau; the style of this movement. Freq. with *the*. Cf. *SEZESSIONSTIL, SECESSIONIST b (quot. 1901).
[**1890** *Art Jrnl.* July 221/1 The important secession which..followed upon the recent retirement of M. Meissonier from all connection with the great annual exhibition of Paris. **1894** *Mag. of Art* XVII. 416/1 The secession of Munich is only one of the effects of the painter's shyness of regulation.] **1896** *Amer. Architect & Building News* 8 Feb. 63/1 'Secession' is a *nom de guerre* of the 'Verein Bildener Kuenstler Muenchens (A.V.)'. *a* **1935** F. PONSONBY *Recollections of Three Reigns* (1951) ix. 123 Inside it was composed of every style of mural decoration, but predominantly what was called 'art nouveau' or 'secession'. **1972** T. WALTERS *Art Nouveau* 6 The Secessionists..were determined to carefully build up a whole revolutionary way of life in which every object..whether a lavatory seat or an underground station, was designed to meet the ideals of the Secession.

5. c. In sense *3 d, as *secession exhibition, school, style* [tr. G. *Sezessionstil*].
1911 R. FRY *Let.* 13 Apr. (1972) I. 345, I thought that the Grafton might be used for a general secession exhibition of all non-academy art of any importance. **1949** *New Yorker* 5 Feb. 78/2 De Chirico..declares that the École de Paris..was really founded on the Munich Secession School. **1973** *Times* 18 Dec. (Hungary Today Suppl.) p. i/3 The *Vigszinhaz*..is in the turn of the century *Secession* style, the Vienna version of *art nouveau.*

secessionist. Add: **c.** (Further examples.) Also *pred.* (quasi-*adj.*).
1894 *Mag. of Art* XVII. 379 Salon of the Champ de Mars..the secessionist Salon. **1954** B. & R. NORTH tr. *M. Duverger's Pol. Parties* II. i. 294 If a party is clearly in a minority in the country as a whole but in a majority in

certain districts its attitude becomes autonomist or even secessionist. **1962** *Daily Tel.* 9 Feb. 19/1 Mr. Gizenga, arrested and accused of 'secessionist activities'. **1978** *Detroit Free Press* 2 Apr. 16c/3, I learned of the secessionist movement in the Upper Peninsula.

Sechuana (setʃuā·nā). Also **Sechoana, Sechwana, Secuana, Setswana,** † **Sichuana.** [a. Tswana *se-*, prefix meaning 'language' + *-chuana* *TSWANA.] = *TSWANA *sb.* b. Also *attrib.* or as *adj.*

Setswana is now the preferred term for the language.

1811 [see *KORI[1]]. **1815** A. PLUMPTRE tr. *H. Lichtenstein's Trav. S. Afr.* II. li. 407 Under the name of *Beetjuana, Sihtjuana,* or *Muhtjuana* are to be included all the tribes that inhabit the country which extends from the river Kurahman. **1824** W. J. BURCHELL *Trav. S. Afr.* II. xi. 295 The Bachapins call this language the Sichuána. **1839** W. C. HARRIS *Wild Sports S. Afr.* ii. 11 This.. individual..possessed a fair smattering of the English and Sichuana languages. **1850** [see *BECHUANA]. **1905** G. W. STOW *Native Races S. Afr.* xxi. 407 The Bachoana proper, including the Batlapin, Barolong, etc., speaking the Sechoana and Serolong. **1916** S. T. PLAATJE *Sechuana Proverbs* 15/1 The present confusion..is apt to hamper missionary enterprise among Sechuana-speaking Natives. **1919** H. H. JOHNSTON *Bantu & Semi-Bantu Langs.* iii. 317 *Secuana* dialects are spoken in Bechuanaland, north of the 28th degree of South latitude. **1935** A. L. JAMES *Broadcast Word* i. 10 There is a story told of the Bechuana that..the early missionaries taught them the Lord's Prayer in the native language, Sechuana. **1961** L. VAN DER POST *Heart of Hunter* I. vii. 110 A language they had evolved in the course of the journey out of a little Swahili, some Sechuana and a lot of onomatopœia. **1964** D. VARADAY *Gara-Yaka* xii. 108 When at a loss for a word he helped himself in Afrikaans, Chivenda, Sechwana, Zulu, and Shangaan. **1977** 'J. MCVEAN' *Bloodspoor* iii. 22 *Morena.* 'Chief.' The Setswana term for any white man of authority.

secko (se·ko). *Austral. slang.* [Shortened form of SEX *sb.* + *-O[2].] A sexual pervert; a sex offender.

1949 R. PARK *Poor Man's Orange* v. 38 'Just look at that dirty ole secko, will you?' he said disgustedly. **1969** W. DICK *Naked Prodigal* i. 13 You look like you'd be the sorta bloke who'd take little kids down a lane and give 'em two bob, yuh bloody secko. **1974** *Bulletin* (Sydney) 6 Apr. 45/2 'I noticed Australians use a lot of diminutives, like Chrissie, pressie and journo.' 'In jails sex offenders are called seckos,' I told him.

sec-mod (sek mǫd), colloq. abbrev. of *secondary modern* s.v. *SECONDARY *a.* 5 f.

1968 *Listener* 28 Mar. 421/2 The wretched life-style on offer to most sec-mod school-leavers. **1973** *Times* 31 May 10/7 Black and white kids, in their sec-mod school uniform.

seco- (se·ko). *Chem.* [f. L. *sec-āre* to cut + -o.] A formative element used in naming derivatives, esp. of steroids, in which fission of a ring has occurred (see quot. 1951). Hence also as quasi-*adj.*

1951 R. S. CAHN et al. in *Jrnl. Chem. Soc.* 3535 Ring fission, with addition of a hydrogen atom at each terminal group thus created, shall be indicated by the prefix *seco*, the original steroid numbering being retained. **1959** L. F. & M. FIESER *Steroids* iv. 156 This was identified as the 2,3-secodicarboxylic acid..by saponification, oxidation to the 7-ketone, and Wolff-Kishner reduction to the known 2,3-secocholestane-2,3-dicarboxylic acid. **1961** I. E. BUSH *Chromatogr. Steroids* ii. 102 The opening of rings to form seco-dicarboxylic acids. *Ibid.* vi. 342 The C_{19} triols..are oxidized to the D-seco-16,17-dialdehydes. **1977** *Lancet* 16 Apr. 841/1 The physiological regulation of secretion of this *seco*-steroid by the kidney.

secobarbital (sekobā·ɹbitǎl). *Pharm.* Chiefly *U.S.* [f. SECO(NDARY *a.* + *BARBITAL.] = *QUINALBARBITONE.

1952 *Analytical Chem.* XXIV. 1605/1 Considerable differences in the [optical density] ratios at various wave lengths are found with these barbiturates. For example, at 270 mμ butylallylonal has the highest ratio, +0·81, followed by secobarbital +0·69. **1962** *New Scientist* 22 Feb. 426/1 Some results obtained with secobarbital.. and other drugs are also mentioned. **1974** M. C. GERALD *Pharmacol.* xi. 205 Short-acting barbiturates such as.. secobarbital ('red devils'). **1976** *Billings* (Montana) *Gaz.* 11 July 9-A/1 In order on DAWN's list of drugs most frequently recorded in crisis situations..were heroin, marijuana, aspirin, LSD, secobarbital (..known as 'red devils').

secodont (se·kodǫnt), *a. Zool.* [f. L. *sec-āre* to cut + Gr. ὀδοντ-, ὀδούς tooth.] Of a tooth: adapted or suited for cutting. Of an animal: having such teeth.

1891 FLOWER & LYDEKKER *Introd. Mammals* 32 Trituberculism differentiating into a secodont and a bunodont series, according as to whether the dentition becomes of a cutting or a crushing type. **1968** R. ZANGERL tr. *Peyer's Compar. Odontol.* 244 Both upper and lower carnassials [in modern carnivores] are secodont; that is, they have sharp cutting edges that run parallel to the edge of the jaw.

secohm (se·kōᵘm). *Electr. Obs.* exc. *Hist.* [f. SEC(OND *sb.*[1] + OHM[2].] A name proposed for a unit of inductance.

1887 AYRTON & PERRY in *Nature* 9 June 131/2 Hence we are driven to suggesting a temporary name for the unit, and as the first three letters in 'second' are common to the name in English, French, German, Italian, &c., and ohm is also common, we venture to suggest 'secohm' as a provisional name. **1948** *Atlantic Monthly* May 613/2 The motion to adopt 'henry' as the name of this unit.. was seconded by..Professor Ayrton, who had himself, a few years ago, proposed the word 'sec-ohm' as being a proper name for the unit of induction. **1963** JERRARD & MCNEILL *Dict. Sci. Units* 127 The secohm was equal to the product of one legal ohm and one second and its magnitude was about the same as a henry.

Seconal (se·kŏnæl, -ǎl). *Pharm.* Also **seconal.** [f. SECON(DARY *a.* + AL(LYL.] A proprietary term for *SECOBARBITAL. Also, a tablet of this.

1935 *Official Gaz.* (U.S. Patent Office) 23 July 727/2 Eli Lilly and Company, Indianapolis... *Seconal.* For products of secondary amyl allyl barbituric acid and the sodium salts thereof..useful as hypnotics. Claims use since Apr. 11, 1935. **1937** *Jrnl. Amer. Pharmaceut. Assoc.* XXVI. 1248 It was concluded that 'Seconal' had a shorter duration of action and that its minimal anesthetic dose and minimal lethal dose were smaller than those of 'Sodium Amytal'. **1938** *Trade Marks Jrnl.* 23 Feb. 218/1 Seconal. **1950** E. HEMINGWAY *Across River & into Trees* ii. 11 He was also anxious to lie down and take a seconal. **1958** 'A. BRIDGE' *Portuguese Escape* xiii. 217 She swallowed some Seconal with a gulp of water. **1959** N. MAILER *Advts. for Myself* (1961) 214 Drugging myself into sleep with an overload of seconal. **1965** G. MARX *Let.* 12 Oct. (1967) 68 At 8 we take two Seconals, three aspirin and a shot of LSD. **1973** M. AMIS *Rachel Papers* 176 'What did you give him?' 'Half a Mandie, a Seconal—I can't remember—and two Mogadon, I think.'

second, *sb.*[1] Add: **2.** Now one of the base units of the International System of Units, and redefined in terms of the frequency of a spectral transition of an isotope of cæsium (see quot. 1968). (Further examples.)

1955 *Sci. Amer.* Mar. 52/2 Accordingly the International Committee is to define the second as: 1/31,556,925·975 of the tropical year 1900. **1968** *Nature* 16 Nov. 651/1 The basic unit of time in the International System of Units, formerly identical with the astronomical second of ephemeris time, is now based on a natural periodicity of the caesium atom and is defined in the following terms: 'the second is the duration of 9 192 631 770 periods of the radiation corresponding to the transition between the two hyperfine levels of the ground state of the caesium-133 atom'. **1975** *Oxf. Compan. Sports & Games* 975/1 This reduced the previous world records by half a second, the biggest single advance in the history of the events.

3. second-foot, a unit of the rate of flow of water, equal to one cubic foot per second.

1898 *U.S. Dept. Agric. Yearbk. 1897* 640 Where water is abundant, the duty has been known to be as low as 50 acres..to the second-foot. **1914** RIES & WATSON *Engin. Geol.* v. 250 The height of the black lines illustrates the relative quantity of water expressed in cubic feet per second, or second feet, occurring throughout the year. **1928** *Manch. Guardian Weekly* 31 Aug. 178/3 The assumption is that the main river, suitably fortified with levees, can carry rather less than 2,000,000 cubic feet of water per second (or 2,000,000 second feet as it is briefly described).

second, *a.* and *sb.*[2] Add: **A.** *adj.* **2. a.** (Later examples of phr. *second to none.*)

1861 GEO. ELIOT *Let.* 17 May (1954) III. 414, I doing little else but feel eminently uncomfortable, for which..I have a faculty 'second to none'. **1961** J. HELLER *Catch-22* (1962) xi. 112 He would stand second to none in his devotion to country.

b. (Later examples.)

1880, etc. Second last [see *LAST *a.* 1 b]. **1910** W. M. RAINE *Bucky O'Connor* (1920) xx. 226 I'll agree to the second dearest in the world. **1959** J. KIRKUP tr. *S. de Beauvoir's Memoirs of Dutiful Daughter* II. 116 She was.. the second eldest daughter. **1977** *Word 1972* XXVIII. 104 The second-youngest of the fluent speakers. **1979** *Nature* 15 Feb. 561/2 *Secernosaurus* is the second most primitive hadrosaur known.

c. *second master* (examples); similarly *second mistress*; *second mate* (examples in naut. slang phrases referring to measures of liquor).

1843 J. F. COOPER *Ned Myers* II. ii. 61 Putting a second-mate's nip of brandy into my glass. **1853** 'C. BEDE' *Adv. Mr. Verdant Green* i. 6 The second master..'licked a feller' for a false quantity. **1866** *School Life at Winchester Coll.* xiv. 177 The *Roll* which was published every November, giving a list of the entire establishment of the College, commencing with the Warden, Head master, (Informator,) Second master, (Hostiarius,) the ten fellows, three chaplains; the under masters [etc.]. **1923** L. MAGNUS *Jubilee Bk. Girls' Public Day School Trust* iv. 58 Her retirement coincided with that of her Second Mistress, Mrs Withiel. **1933** P. A. EADDY *Hull Down* 99 He pulls a pint bottle out of the case, and drawing the cork pulls out a good Second Mate's four fingers. **1952** V. NOAKE *Hist. Alice Ottley School Worcester* xiii. 140 Miss Spurling's successor..was Miss Hilda M. Roden, second mistress of the Stamford High School, Stamford, Lincs. **1967** S. WATERS *Indentures Indorsed* xxxv. 232 A couple of second mate's pegs was usually enough to set us all singing. **1976** C. DEXTER *Last seen Wearing* xxx. 211 School masters, even experienced second masters, aren't all that highly recompensed.

d. (Earlier and later examples.)

1776 W. HOWE *Let.* 7 June in *9th Rep. R. Comm. Hist. MSS.* App. III. (rev. ed.) 35 in *Parl. Papers 1910* (Cd. 5038) XXXV. 675 The seniority of his rank..would have placed him second in command in Canada had he not been previously employed to the southward. **1939** C. S. FORESTER *Captain Hornblower, R.N.* xvi. 173 On his first commission his second-in-command had taken advantages of lapses on his part. **1982** *Observer* 16 Apr. 14/6 His second-in-command is a Sierra Leonean major.

4. b. Hence (without allusion to the proverb) *to be* (*come as*, etc.) *second nature* (*to* one): to be as if natural or instinctive. Occas. in ellipt. constructions without a vb.

1910 S. E. WHITE in *Sunset* Apr. 421/1 Bob..rolled over twice with the rapid, vigorous twist second-nature to a seasoned half-back. **1944** *Sun* (Baltimore) 28 Nov. 8/2 Civilian air defense comes as second nature to them. **1954** T. S. ELIOT *Confidential Clerk* III. 96, I do feel more at ease when I'm behind a desk: It's second nature. **1967** SINGHA & MASSEY *Indian Dances* xviii. 159 They become second nature to her when she is dancing.

6. b. ellipt. for *second class* (in travelling by rail, etc.).

1912 R. BROOKE *Let.* Jan. (1968) 334 The maids of the Ordinary Rich go second, with you and the normal me. **1937** W. H. SAUMAREZ SMITH *Let.* 10 July in *Young Man's Country* (1977) ii. 80 As I'm not getting Travel Allowance for this trip, I'd decided to travel 2nd. *a* **1976** A. CHRISTIE *Autobiogr.* (1977) VI. i. 289 Ladies travelling alone would never have travelled third class... Even ladies' maids always travelled second.

7. a. Further syntactical combs., as *second empire, generation, house, language, opinion, reading, secretary, sex, slip, string, subject* (see these words); **second Adam** (earlier examples); **second ballot,** a deciding ballot taken between the candidate who won a previous ballot without securing an absolute majority and the candidate with the next highest number of votes; also *attrib.* of an electoral system using this; **second banana** *slang* (orig. *U.S.*), a supporting comedian (cf. *top banana* s.v. *TOP *sb.*[1] 32); **second base** (see *BASE *sb.*[1] 15 c); **second blessing** orig. *U.S.*, an experience of God's grace subsequent to conversion, believed by some Christian groups to be the means of receiving the power to live a sanctified life; **second bottom,** (*a*) *U.S.*, the first terrace above the normal flood plain of a stream; (*b*) *Austral.*, a second stratum of gold-bearing material found by sinking below the bottom (*BOTTOM *sb.* 4 c); **second breakfast,** a light meal taken late in the morning or early in the afternoon; **second car,** an additional family car; **second chamber** (earlier example); **second channel** *Radio* = *IMAGE *sb.* 7**; usu. *attrib.*; **second cut,** (*b*) *Austral.* and *N.Z.* (the mark of) a blow made to remove badly-cut fleece; a piece of short or inferior wool produced by this; † **second day,** in Quaker usage, Monday; **second-degree** *Med.*, used to designate burns that are sufficiently severe to cause blistering but not permanent scarring (see quot. 1972); see also DEGREE *sb.* 6 d; **second feature,** the supporting feature in a cinema programme; also *fig.* and *attrib.*; **second finger,** the finger next to the forefinger, the middle finger; **second front,** in the war of 1939–45, a front in Nazi-occupied Europe in addition to the Russian sector of fighting; also *fig.* and *attrib.*; **second fronting** *Philol.* [tr. G. *zweite Aufhellung* (K. Luick *Historische Grammatik der englischen Sprache* (1914) 164)], a sound-change in varieties of Old English by which the vowels *æ* (produced by an earlier fronting) and *a* became *e* and *æ* respectively; **second gear,** the gear next above the lowest or bottom gear on a motor vehicle or bicycle; **second greaser** *Naut. slang*, a second mate; **second growth,** (*a*) (earlier example); (*b*) the second category of growths (see *GROWTH[1] 1 d) or qualities into which wines are divided; also *attrib.*; **second home,** a second dwelling-place owned or supported in addition to the principal home; a home from home; also *fig.* and *attrib.*; hence **second homer,** the owner of a second home; **Second Isaiah** = *Deutero-Isaiah* s.v. DEUTERO-; **second line,** also *gen.*: any second row or series; freq. *attrib.* or as *adj.*, esp. designating persons or things that rank second in ability, value, etc.; hence **second-liner, -lining** *vbl. sb.*; **secondman,** an assistant driver on a diesel or electric train, replacing the fireman on a steam train; **second messenger** *Physiol.*, a substance whose release within a cell is promoted by a hormone or 'first messenger', and which brings about a response by the cell; **second mortgage,** a supplementary or puisne mortgage; † **second (motion) shaft** = *LAYSHAFT; **second ranker,** a member of the second rank, a second-liner;

second row *Rugby Football,* the middle row of a team's pack; also *attrib.*; hence **second rower** *Austral.*, a second-row forward; **second service,** delete † and add later examples; (see also quot. 1844); **second shaft:** see *second (motion) shaft* above; **second sound** *Physics,* a form of longitudinal wave which has many properties in common with sound and is observed in superfluid helium (see quots. and cf. *SOUND *sb.*[3]); **second speed** = **second gear*; † **second stop** *Cricket* = *long-stop* s.v. LONG *a.*[1] A. 18 d; **second-stor(e)y man** *N. Amer. Criminals' slang,* a cat-burglar; **second strike,** a second, retaliatory attack conducted with weapons designed to withstand an initial nuclear attack or first strike; freq. *attrib.*; **second table,** the servants' table at a meal; also *spec.* the senior of two servants' tables; **second tap** *Engin.* (see quot. 1888); **second thigh,** the part of the rear leg of a quadruped that corresponds to the human calf; **Second War,** short for **Second World War*; **Second World** [after *THIRD WORLD], (*a*) (following the outlook of the Chinese leadership) the developed countries apart from the two 'superpowers'; (*b*) (poss. reflecting the orig. implication of the term *Third World*) the Communist bloc; **Second World War,** the war which began with the German invasion of Poland on 1 Sept. 1939 and ultimately involved the majority of the nations of the world; hostilities ceased in Europe on 7 May 1945 and in the Far East on 12 Sept. 1945.

1587 BIBLE (Genevan) 1 Cor. xv. 45 (*marginal gloss*), To wit, with the Spirit of God, which descendeth from Christ the second Adam, into us. **1655** J. TAYLOR *Unum Necessarium* vi. 362 Receiving more by the second Adam than we did lose by the first. **1667** MILTON *Paradise Lost* x. 383 The Tempter set Our second Adam in the Wilderness, To shew him all Earths Kingdomes and thir Glory. **1910** *Rep. R. Comm. Electoral Syst.* 3 in *Parl. Papers* (Cd. 5163) XXVI. 295 The Second Ballot.—A candidate, to be returned at the first election must receive an absolute majority of the valid votes cast. If no candidate obtains such a majority, a second election is held, at which (in the most usual form of the system) only the two candidates compete who received most votes at the first election. **1932** *News Chron.* 15 Mar. 9/1 The electorate, at the second ballot, were left to choose between Hindenburg, Marx and Thaelmann. **1954** B. & R. NORTH tr. *M. Duverger's Pol. Parties* II. i. 239 There were variations of procedure in the simple-majority second-ballot system. **1976** Second ballot [see *PREFERENTIAL *a.* c]. **1953** *N.Y. Times* 24 May II. 11/2 In television and radio, Mr. Carney has played second banana to many star comedy performers. **1974** *Ibid.* 28 Dec. 26/1 He [*sc.* Jack Benny] was often the butt of his second bananas, who devastated him with their barbs. **1977** *Time* 13 June 42/2 Their Yank allies, doubtless because they had second-banana roles in the original production 33 years ago, have dim, brief lives on the screen. **1891** B. CARRADINE *Sanctification* ii. 14 My soul was reaching out..for..what is properly called the *second* blessing. *Ibid.* iv. 33 This definition and explanation of entire sanctification, or the second blessing. **1940** *Amer. Sociol. Rev.* Oct. 741 The Pentecostal groups..believe further in the gift of tongues as an additional evidence of God's grace, awakened..by the 'second blessing'. **1977** *Christian* IV. 204 The call to Community has something of the aura of the conversion experience, or perhaps even more of the so called 'second blessing'. **1787** J. MATHEWS *Jrnl.* 23 Aug. in S. P. Hildreth *Pioneer Hist.* (1848) vii. 184 Went to view the Indian works, which are about a mile from the fort. They extend for about half a mile on the second bottom. **1788** *Massachusetts Spy* 19 June 3/2 Next to these are what is called second bottoms, which are elevated plains, and gentle risings of the richest uplands. **1855** R. CALDWELL *Gold Era of Victoria* x. 116 As regards the question of 'second bottoms', which has excited considerable discussion,..all such attempts must..end in disappointment and loss to those engaged in them. **1863** J. C. PATERSON *Gold Fields of Victoria 1862* vii. 80 There is no known reason why there should not be a second bottom on Bendigo Flat. **1905** CHAMBERLIN & SALISBURY *Geol.* iii. 195 (*caption*) Diagram illustrating a distinct terrace and a 'second bottom'.., which may be regarded as a low terrace. **1924** *Prof. Papers U.S. Geol. Survey* No. 126. 14/1 Bluffs 30 to 50 feet in height separate the flats of the gravel-covered terraces from the second bottoms. **1775** J. WOODFORDE *Diary* 2 Jan. (1924) I. 144 We stayed at Whitney and made a second breakfast, we treated the maid at Whitney. **1802** M. NUGENT *Jrnl.* 15 Jan. (1907) ii. 72 Had fruit for the children at 10; then second breakfast a little after 11.—Dined at 3. **1967** O. HESKY *Time for Treason* xi. 83 Barzilai..was regretting that he hadn't utilised this period..by having a 'second breakfast', a habit dear to the stomachs of those raised in certain parts of Europe. **1966** *Guardian* 16 May 5/3 We had been trying to choose an inexpensive 'second car' for my wife. **1981** L. STEPHAN *Murder or Not* xi. 87 The Subaru was a second car, used by Mr Cook to commute to his job. **1828** J. S. MILL in *Westm. Rev.* Apr. 282 In whichever way selected, this second chamber would have been..inveterately hostile to nearly every necessary reform. **1932** C. L. BOLTZ *Everyman's Wireless* xv. 309 If the tuning circuit..is not sufficiently selective it is possible to receive..a signal whose frequency differs from that of the oscillator by the fixed intermediate frequency, but in the opposite direction... Such interference..is sometimes called 'second channel' interference. **1940, 1962** [see *IMAGE *sb.* 7**]. **1975** G. N. PATCHETT *Radio Servicing* III. ii. 11 It is essential to remove the second channel station before it reaches the frequency-changer or mixer. **1882** ARMSTRONG & CAMPBELL *Austral. Sheep Husbandry* xiv. 168 In shearing the first side of the sheep, each blow should be continued round until the back-bone is passed; this avoids the second cut caused by the blow up the back which should not be allowed, as the 'cutting through' which results considerably depreciates the value of the wool. **1897** D. McK. WRIGHT *Station Ballads* 34 Mighty lot of wool you've lost! Second cuts? Well, that ain't my fault, you've his wrinkled hide to thank. **1900, 1929** [see *FRIBBY *a.* (*sb.*)]. **1950** *N.Z. Jrnl. Agric.* Oct. 311 An efficient shearer will not make many 'second cuts', but the presence of them among the fleeces in a bale will antagonize the wool buyer. **1691** G. FOX *Jrnl.* (1911) II. 367 For the yearly second days Meeting in London. **1705** S. SEWALL *Jrnl.* 7 Dec. in *Mass. Hist. Soc. Coll.* (1879) VI. 147, I refer'd them to second-day Morning Decr 10. to meet at the Secretary's Office. [**1807** MORRIS & KENDRICK *Edin. Med. Dict.* s.v. *Burn*, Burns are attended with a degree of inflammation, greater or less, according to the violence of the injury; and, according to the different appearances they put on, they may be divided into four different classes, 1. When the burnt part is affected only with a sense of heat and inflammation; 2. When it is also accompanied with intense pain and vesication; 3. When the integuments are converted into an eschar; and, 4. When all the soft parts are scorched to the very bone.] **1930** PACK & DAVIS *Burns* iv. 20 Second Degree. Degree two is one of vesication. **1972** MILLER & KEANE *Encycl. & Dict. Med. & Nursing* 155/1 First-degree burns damage the epidermis; second-degree burns damage both epidermis and dermis; third-degree burns damage the epidermis, dermis and subcutaneous tissue. **1927** *Melody Maker* May 515/1 It was quite an ordinary film. I should have only booked it as a second feature, and then only if there was nothing else available. **1959** C. MACINNES *Absolute Beginners* 61 'You're a romantic!' she said. 'A second feature Romeo!' **1970** J. HANSEN *Fadeout* vi. 49 He..would sit up half the night..enchanted by the tired wisecracks..in forgotten RKO second features of the thirties. **1860** *Man. Artillery Exercises* (Army) 241 The cock resting against the knuckle-joint of the first finger; this and the second finger only resting on the small of the stock. **1932** *News Chron.* 15 Mar. 8/6 Making the tips of his first and little fingers touch; then bringing the second finger smoothly under the arch thus formed. **1941** W. S. CHURCHILL *Let.* 4 Sept. in *Second World War* (1950) III. xxv. 407 There is no chance..of a second front being formed in the Balkans without the help of Turkey. **1942** *New Statesman* 3 Jan. 3/2 The key to victory is to open..that 'second front in continental Europe' for which Stalin has publicly called. **1944** M. LASKI *Love on Supertax* ii. 24 He said he'd..make sure there were enough helpers handing out the Second Front leaflets. **1946** *Life* 11 Mar. 63/1 The Russians facetiously called Spam 'the second front'. **1961** E. WAUGH *Unconditional Surrender* I. i. 21 A scarred brick wall, on which..a zealous, arthritic communist had emblazoned the words, *Second Front Now.* **1963** A. HOWARD in Sissons & French *Age of Austerity* 30 The conservatives were waging what turned out to be a decisive second front. **1939** *PMLA* LIV. 19 The second raising and fronting of West Germanic *a*, which changed *dæg* to *deg* and *dagas* to *dægas*, must..have occurred, not during the fifth century, but during the eighth and early ninth. **1959** A. CAMPBELL *Old Eng. Gram.* v. 64 Second fronting is not a general Merc[ian] change, for it is practically absent in *Ru.*[1], and ME sources show that it was limited to a small part of the vast Midland area. **1972** E. J. DOBSON *Eng. Text of Ancrene Riwle* p. lxxvi, The normal Mercian *ē* produced by indirect *i*-mutation followed by second fronting. **1902** Second gear [see *GEAR *sb.* 7 b]. **1976** T. HEALD *Let Sleeping Dogs Die* iii. 62 He..kept the car at fifteen miles an hour in second gear. **1888** Second greaser [see *GREASER 1 b]. **1916** F. W. WALLACE *Shack Locker* 145 The second greaser paused and added 'I didn't stop, sir.' **1934** C. MOORE *Twilight of Jibs & Topsails* xiv. 227 It started in the mate's watch, and I was in that of the—called in nautical parlance—'second greaser', meaning, of course, the second mate. [**1824** A. HENDERSON *Hist. Anc. & Mod. Wines* II. ii. 155 Among the secondary growths, those of Cramant, Avise, Oger, and Menil, are the most deserving of mention.] **1829** J. F. COOPER *Wept of Wish-ton-wish* I. ii. 26 Much of the surface of this opening ..was now concealed by bushes of what is termed the second growth. **1883** C. REDDING *Hist. Mod. Wines* v. 110 The best wines are from the *noirien* grape, and the best of the first growths fetch sixty-six francs, and of the second growths forty-four francs. **1920** [see *GROWTH[1] 1 d]. **1980** P. ABLEMAN *Shoestring's Finest Hour* ii. 31 An admirable roast beef en croute..cheered down by a second-growth Pomerol of an excellent year. **1883** QUEEN VICTORIA *Let.* 12 Dec. in R. Fulford *Beloved Mama* (1981) 153 Italy seems to be a second home. I expect you will settle there some day. **1915** F. HARDY *Let.* 17 July in R. Gittings *Older Hardy* (1978) xiii. 167 A second home for the people I like, and who have been good to me. **1937** W. H. SAUMAREZ SMITH *Let.* 10 July in *Young Man's Country* (1977) ii. 79 The Saturday Club, which, since his wife's departure for England, is practically a second home to him. **1959** M. GILBERT *Blood & Judgement* xiii. 142 He was away from home a lot and..she began to think he'd set up a second home of his own somewhere. **1970** 'E. LATHEN' *Pick up Sticks* x. 85 All this second-home building helps. **1980** *Times* 1 Aug. 13/7 Roll on the revolution when.. we shall be entitled to substantial state pensions, preferential housing and second homes. **1976** *Local Council Rev.* Summer 48 Bit by bit, house by house, the indigenous population is replaced by commuters or second-homers. The village becomes a suburb in the fields. **1881** T. K. CHEYNE *Prophecies of Isaiah* II. 201 The present essay..relates exclusively to the last twenty-seven chapters: not as if chaps. i.–xxxix. constituted 'the First Isaiah', and chaps. xl.–lxvi. 'the Second'. **1881** —— in *Encycl. Brit.* XIII. 380/2 The honied rhetoric of him whom we are accustomed to call the Second Isaiah. **1888** M. ROSENTHAL *Isaiah & Unity of his Prophecy* II. 57 Canon Cheyne..breaks up the so-called second Isaiah into several personages and various authorship... He thinks that second Isaiah was originally much shorter. **1977** G. W. H. LAMPE *God as Spirit* i. 31 It was now, in his own time, and not in some remote future, that Second Isaiah believed that the herald was coming. **1912** C. MACKENZIE *Carnival* (ed. 5) iv. 43 Lilli Vergoe, a second-line girl in the Corps de Ballet of the Orient Palace of Varieties. **1939** RUSSELL & SMITH in Ramsey & Smith *Jazzmen* 27 The funerals and parades always had a 'second line' which consisted of the kids who danced along behind. **1955** SHAPIRO & HENTOFF *Hear Me talkin' to Ya* iii. 39, I was a 'second-line' kid. That meant I'd follow the big bands down the streets, and..carry their cases while they played. **1969** *Daily Tel.* 6 Mar. 2 Numerous bright features also developed in the so-called second-line issues [of stock]. **1972** *Jazz & Blues* Sept. 10/1 The second line beat is the funky, calypso-like 2/4 cadence struck up by the bass drummer in a New Orleans funeral parade. **1975** *Cricketer* May 17/3 The Robins were still operating with their second-line bowlers. **1980** J. MELVILLE *Chrysanthemum Chain* 142 Those guys [*sc.* politicians] on your list are essentially second-line. **1958** C. WILFORD in P. Gammond *Decca Bk. of Jazz* ii. 40 The improvisations of master executants ..preserved on record, for ready imitation by a host of second-liners. **1972** *Jazz & Blues* Sept. 10/1 These 'second liners' wave handkerchiefs and umbrellas and..break into a dipping, funky-butt step—half shimmy, half strut—that is known as 'second lining'. **1981** *Times* 24 Apr. 18/2 Other companies reporting provided some good rises, particularly among second-liners. [**1963** *Railway Gaz.* 15 Mar. 289 If such a method of operation can be agreed the many problems of providing a second man when moving locomotives light over running lines, terminal movements, and tripping will be simplified.] **1964** *Locomotive Jrnl.* LXXVII. 205/2 Scores of Trainmen (Drivers, Firemen/2nd Men, and Guards) in the Sheffield Area have their normal diagrammed turns tampered with in an effort by the B.R.B. to scratch a few complete crews together. **1977** *Modern Railways* Dec. 461/1, 12 years' haggling from which the one significant gain was agreement to phase out the secondmen in freight and shunting locomotive cabs by attrition. **1965** E. W. SUTHERLAND et al. in *Rec. Progress Hormone Res.* XXI. 640 The hormone (the first messenger) interacts with a component of the cell membrane to initiate increased accumulation of a mediator (the second messenger), which then acts upon components of the effector cell. **1968** *Circulation* XXXVII. 300/1 Although cyclic AMP stands as the only well-established second messenger to date, data supporting such a role for cyclic GMP have been obtained. **1979** *Sci. Amer.* Sept. 127/1 The methylxanthine drugs, such as caffeine and theophylline, are thought to exert their effects by acting through the second-messenger system. **1959** M. SHADBOLT *New Zealanders* 13 Finally, in desperation, he took out a second mortgage on the farm to pay Mother's fare to New Zealand. **1974** *Guardian* 23 Jan. 11/6 Taking out a crippling second mortgage on their own house. **1977** M. ALLEN *Spence in Petal Park* xii. 56 One of the lines he offered was loans secured by a second mortgage. **1902** A. C. HARMSWORTH *Motors & Motor-Driving* x. 202 Immediately above this shaft is a second shaft arranged parallel to it. **1904** A. B. F. YOUNG *Compl. Motorist* (ed. 2) iv. 116 On the top speed the drive is direct, the second motion shaft then lying idle. *Ibid.* 132 With their well-cut and thoroughly hardened gear-teeth the second shaft runs noiselessly. **1912** *Motor Manual* (ed. 14) v. 165 The two shafts in the gearbox are called respectively the first motion shaft and the second motion shaft. **1959** *Times* 20 Oct. 19/3 Substantial two-way business in industrial shares partly reflected switching out of low-yield shares into higher yielding second rankers. **1977** *Belfast Tel.* 17 Jan. 4/1 A new account opened on an indecisive note with leaders keeping largely to Friday's levels. Among second-rankers Campari, 37p, Rotaprint, 24p. **1892** A. BUDD in F. Marshall *Football: Rugby Union Game* ix. 124 Having obtained it [*sc.* the ball], the practice is to deposit it behind the first or second row of forwards. **1918** V. H. CARTWRIGHT in J. E. Raphael *Mod. Rugby Football* ix. 133 The two second row men..should be the strongest forwards on the side. **1960** E. S. & W. J. HIGHAM *High Speed Rugby* iv. 186 The 3-2-3 formation requires two second-row forwards with very strong backs. **1969** *Australian* 24 May 36/7 Owen Butler and Dick Millard, the two towering NSW Country second rowers, are specialist lineout jumpers. **1844** J. C. ROBERTSON *How shall we conform to Liturgy of Church of England?* (ed. 2) xii. 168 That part of the communion-office which is appointed to be used when there is no administration of the sacrament, and which..I shall, according to the custom of the seventeenth century, speak of as the 'Second Service'. **1920** M. WEBB *House in Dormer Forest* v. 56 On Sundays Solomon went once to church. Once a month he attended 'the second service'. **1964** C. MACKENZIE *Life & Times* III. 33 Glorified morning prayer would have to be endured before the bisected so called second service was reached. **1944** F. LEIB tr. E. Lifshitz in *Jrnl. Physics* (Moscow) VIII. 111/1 We look for the velocity v_2..in the 'first' and 'second' sound waves. **1944** J. SMORODINSKY tr. V. Peshkov in *Ibid.* 381/1 There must be in this liquid [*sc.* helium] two kinds of periodic motions: the ordinary sound..and the so-called 'second sound'. **1964** *New Scientist* 18 June 744/2 Second sound..is not really sound at all, but a heat wave that combines two potentially useful properties of sound and heat. **1975** *Nature* 2 Oct. 359/3 M. B. Robin..has..detected the heat pulse from a non-radiative transition by means of the 'second sound' pulse propagated in super-fluid helium and recorded by a superconducting lead bolometer. [**1902** A. C. HARMSWORTH *Motors & Motor-Driving* x. 205 To obtain the second of the three speeds provided.] **1912** *Motor Manual* (ed. 14) iii. 74 Second speed position. **1925** *Morris Owner's Manual* 10 When it has gained some headway, change into second speed. **1970** K. BALL *Fiat 600, 600D Autobook* vi. 57/1 Remove the second-speed driving gear, ballbearing and shaft retaining plate and slide out the reverse shaft and gear. **1773** in H. T. Waghorn *Cricket Scores* (1899) 97 Lear (2nd stop). **1847** W. DENISON *Cricketer's Companion* p. xv, The whole of this enormous quantity of 'byes' would seem to have been the result of inferior men having been appointed to the 'second or long-stop' situation. **1886** T. F. BYRNES *Professional Criminals of Amer.* 182 Pickpocket, burglar and second-story man. **1916** [see *porch-climber* s.v. *PORCH 7]. **1965** 'MALCOLM X' *Autobiogr.* 46 Hustlers..

sold 'reefers', or had just come out of prison, or were 'second-story men'. **1978** J. CARROLL *Mortal Friends* II. iii. 169 You're nothing but a pack of second-story workers, milkbottle robbers, and doormat thieves! **1960** *Manch. Guardian* 27 July 16/3 Rockefeller's plea for 'all the money it takes' to ensure the United States 'the deterrent capability of a massive and superior second strike'. **1960** *Ibid.* 12 Sept. 9/1 We would need superior reconnaissance and target acquisition systems... These would need to be supported by a secure second-strike capability to reduce the risk of being outflanked. **1963** *Listener* 31 Jan. 194/1 The Soviet Union almost certainly has a 'second strike' capacity too. **1976** LD. HOME *Way Wind Blows* x. 152 As a second-strike weapon it [*sc.* the Polaris submarine] was a real deterrent. **1814** JANE AUSTEN *Mansfield Park* I. x. 220 She was quite shocked when I asked her whether wine was allowed at the second table. **1857** C. M. YONGE *Dynevor Terrace* I. xiv. 227 Their servants gave themselves airs..especially the butler, who played the guitar, and insisted on a second table. *a* **1911** D. G. PHILLIPS *Susan Lenox* (1917) II. xiii. 311 A man..can go on up and up. But not for girls. Nothing doing but charity and pity and the second table and the back door. **1953** G. E. & K. R. FUSSELL *English Countrywoman* v. 133 The new cook expected to dine in the housekeeper's room, at a second table set up there. **1888** *Lockwood's Dict. Mech. Engin.* 309 *Second tap*, a tap intermediate in size between a taper and a plug tap. **1964** S. CRAWFORD *Basic Engin. Processes* i. 24 If the hole being tapped is an open or through hole the second tap is quite suitable for finishing the thread. **1893** M. H. HAYES *Points of Horse* iv. 40 The hock is extended, for the most part, by muscles which form the rear-most portion of the gaskin ('second thigh'). **1933** L. E. NAYLOR *Mod. Fox Terrier* vi. 62 The worst possible form of hind-quarters consists of a short second-thigh and a straight stifle. **1972** *Country Life* 10 Feb. 332/1 He [*sc.* a foxhound] was first-rate in every requisite of the chase, remarkable for his muscular back and loins, buttocks and second thighs. **1964** M. MCLUHAN *Understanding Media* xxiii. 353 Multi-nationalisms had long deprived Europe of its economic unity. The Common Market came to it only with the Second War. **1975** P. FUSSELL *Great War & Mod. Memory* vii. 247 The same principle of literary selection..is visible in a poem of the Second War by Herbert Corby. **1974** *Times* 13 Apr. 5/7 Mr Teng announced that the 'socialist camp' no longer existed, and that the planet was divided into the First World, consisting of the two superpowers, the Second World, consisting of the other developed countries, and the Third World, which included the developing countries. **1974** *Economist* 18 May 66/1 The conventional image of recent years has been of a first world of developed market economies, a second world of 'socialist' states, and the 'third world' of the developing nations. **1975** *Time* 8 Sept. (Canada ed.) 20/2 The 'Second World' of the Socialist countries will make a show of complete support. **1978** *Church Times* 25 Aug. 4/2 The scene was dominated by the post-war tension between the First and Second Worlds. **1979** *Dædalus* Spring 124 In this approach, Europe would be seen as playing the role of what Chinese diplomacy likes to refer to as 'the second world'. **1980** *Sci. Amer.* Sept. 107/2 The already industrialized countries of the capitalist and communist blocs (respectively the 'first world' and 'second world'). [**1930** H. G. WELLS *Autocracy of Mr. Parham* 257 (*heading*) Book the Fourth: The Second World War.] **1942** *Polit. Sci. Q.* Sept. 321 The economic developments associated with the second World War have restored to American railroads a volume of traffic comparable to that which they handled before the great depression. **1949** *Radio Times* 15 July 35/1 Professor W. K. Hancock..describes the plan for the series of Civil Histories of the United Kingdom during the Second World War. **1978** J. N. WARD *Following Plough* i. 17 My generation of theological students had to come to some sense of certainty about our vocation with minds much occupied by the imminence of the Second World War.

b. *second-ranking.*

1966 N. NICOLSON in H. Nicolson *Diaries & Lett.* (1966) 29 In 1927 he joined the Embassy in Berlin as its second-ranking official.

B. *sb.*² **I. 1. e.** Chiefly *Baseball*. Used *ellipt.* for *second base* (see sense A. 7 a above).

1861 *Sunday Mercury* (N.Y.) 20 Oct. 5/5 'Dicky' safely reached the second. **1900** ADE *Fables in Slang* 34 She believed that she could get away with any Topic that was batted up to her and then slam it over to Second in time to head off the Runner. **1976** *Billings* (Montana) *Gaz.* 6 July 1-c/5 Miquel Rodriquez was hurt while sliding into second on a wild pitch. **1977** *New Yorker* 19 Sept. 40/1 When he had fielded the soft-ball and his daughter was racing from first to second, he couldn't think what else to do.

f. Phr. *to deal seconds* (see quot. 1951). *U.S.*

1951 *Amer. Speech* XXVI. 101/1 *Seconds, to deal*, to deal cards other than the top card on the deck. It is practically impossible to detect this if the dealer is clever enough. **1978** M. PUZO *Fools Die* xviii. 194 Not a top-notch mechanic but one who could easily deal seconds. That is, Cully could keep the top card for himself and deal the second card from the top.

2. b. (Later example.)

1954 W. FAULKNER *Fable* 240 Company commanders and battalion seconds stained with the filth of front lines.

d. = *second gear* (see sense A. 7 a above).

1907 M. PEMBERTON *Amateur Motorist* vi. 45, I got the 'second' in that time with a clash as of subterranean wheels. **1925** A. HUXLEY *Along Road* I. 19 The Citroën went into second and remained there; slowly we puffed up the long ascent. **1940** R. STOUT in *Mystery Book* 400 The roadster whirred by in second. **1973** M. WOODHOUSE *Blue Bone* xii. 140, I slipped the transmission up into second and poured on the power.

e. *Mountaineering.* The second climber of a team.

1907 G. D. ABRAHAM *Compl. Mountaineer* v. 67 A difficult overhanging pitch refused to yield to ordinary tactics; so I mounted on my second's shoulders. **1920** G. W. YOUNG *Mountain Craft* v. 230 The leader or last man will not, by the nature of the case, require the support of a good second. **1951** E. COXHEAD *One Green Bottle* i. 27 I'd planned to lead in rubbers. Seeing that my second's a beginner, and to be quite on the safe side. **1976** G. MOFFAT *Over Sea to Death* v. 53 She placed her slings, clipped in her rope and, watching it fall, caught her second's eye.

f. The second in command of a six or patrol in the Scouting and Guiding movement.

1917 R. E. PHILIPPS *Patrol System & Lett. to Patrol Leader* ii. 14 The Second is a boy selected by the Patrol Leader to be his assistant. **1949** W. HILLCOURT *Baden-Powell's Aids to Scoutmastership* I. 41 In this council it is often found convenient to admit the Seconds (Assistant Patrol Leaders) also as members. **1958** R. HAZLEWOOD *Scoutmaster's Guide from A to Z* 213 Originally called a 'corporal' the Second (No. 2 in the Patrol) is the P.L.'s assistant. **1969** *Policy, Organisation & Rules of Girl Guides Assoc.* (rev. ed.) 42 The Patrol is the group for work and play. It consists of not more than eight girls, including the Patrol Leader and Second.

5. (Further examples.)

1908 *Sears, Roebuck Catal.* 349/2 We could sell seconds for less money than any of our competitors if we dealt in that class of merchandise. **1942** E. PAUL *Narrow St.* iii. 20 This friend was able to sequester from the large department-store stock 'seconds' which had no detectable imperfections. **1952** [see *IMPERFECT *sb.* 3]. **1972** *Accountant* 17 Aug. 195/2 Garages could fit 'seconds' without being spotted, or even swop old tyres. **1976** E. WARD *Hanged Man* ii. 9 They listened to the patter act of a Manchester huckster selling tea-set seconds.

7*. *pl.* A second helping of food at a meal; occas. the second or sweet course. *colloq.*

1792 D. O'CONNELL *Let.* 14 Sept. (1972) I. 4 We get very small portions at dinner; most of the lads..get what they call *seconds*, that is, a second portion every day. **1918** L. E. RUGGLES *Navy Explained* 124 When there is not enough of the first issue of rations the mess cook is requested to go to the galley and get 'seconds'. **1942** *Yank* 28 Oct. 8 We were more delighted than we can say to get a hamburger in a foreign land and went for seconds. **1960** 'R. EAST' *Kingston Black* xiv. 139 Kitty had served tinned fruit and farm cream for seconds. **1974** P. GZOWSKI *Bk. about this Country* 59/1 This dish has been served to hundreds of people over the years and requests for seconds (or even thirds) are usual. **1981** A. PRICE *Soldier no More* 121 Lexy scraped the frying pan... Would you like seconds, David darling?

II. 8. b. (Earlier pugilistic examples.)

1743 J. BROUGHTON in P. Egan *Boxiana* (1818) I. 51 In every main battle, no person whatever shall be upon the stage, except the principals and their seconds. **1841** *Fistiana* 63 That each man shall be attended to the ring by a second and a bottle-holder, the former provided with a sponge, and the latter with a bottle of water.

second, *v.*¹ Add: **1. e.** *Mountaineering.* To act as a second (*SECOND *sb.*² 2 e) to (the leader of a climb) or on (a climb). Also *absol.*

1951 E. COXHEAD *One Green Bottle* ii. 49 He wants someone to second him up the north wall. **1968** P. CREW *Encycl. Dict. Mountaineering* 106/1 To second a climb is to do a climb as the second man on the rope. **1972** D. HASTON *In High Places* i. 8 It's not hard to see why leading [on a rock climb] is that much more exciting than seconding.

second, *v.*² Add: Also *transf.* of officials in other occupations and employments. Hence **seco·nded,** *ppl. a.*

1920 *Westm. Gaz.* 22 May 10/1 It was finally agreed that Lord Moulton should be seconded to the service of the Corporation and of the dye industry for..one year. **1928** *Times* 21 July 13/3 They established an elaborate organization, under an important Minister, and manned by specially seconded Civil servants of high standing. **1955** *Times* 23 June 13/4 Mr. Mayne was seconded for special frontier duties, in the course of which he made many acquaintances and friends among the Pathans. **1977** *News of World* 17 Apr. 1/1 The Commission consisted of the chairman, deputy chairman, and 30 seconded civil servants.

secondary, *a.* and *sb.* **A.** *adj.* **1. c.** Delete † *Obs.* and add: *secondary wife* (*a*) (later example); (*b*) a socially or legally recognized inferior wife in some societies; similarly *secondary consort.* Also *secondary marriage,* (*a*) concubinage; (*b*) marriage to a secondary wife (sense *(*b*)); similarly *secondary union.*

1788 Secondary marriage [in Dict.]. **1847** A. STRICKLAND *Lives Queens of England* X. ii. 328 He likewise obliged the princess to receive at her court, and to countenance the duke of Monmouth's mistress, or secondary wife, Lady Harriet Wentworth. **1924** D. HOSIE *Two Gentl. China* (ed. 2) ix. 91 The ladies of the household.. often wield a power that must be reckoned with, if they are fond of intrigue, like a certain secondary wife of an official of our acquaintance. **1931** W. F. SANDS *Undiplomatic Mem.* 69 From kitchenmaid she was raised to the first rank of secondary consorts..and in due course became the mother of the monarch's third son. **1950** *Jrnl. R. Anthrop. Inst.* LXXX. 101/2 In view of the difficulty of establishing the exact nature of the forms of 'secondary marriage', 'the doctrine of presumption of marriage now applies to the Chinese'. *Ibid.* 103/1 A.. significant shift of a class of women from the status of kept mistresses to that of secondary wives. **1950** I. SCHAPERA in A. Radcliffe-Brown *Afr. Systems Kinship* 149 A 'secondary union'..is merely an extension of an existing marriage. Its essential character is that, for the purposes of child-bearing, one of the original parties..is replaced by another person of the same sex, who is regarded as a bodily substitute, and not as an independent spouse. **1970** J. M. MESKILL in M. Freedman *Family & Kinship in China* 148 In the Wu-feng Lin genealogy.. secondary wives..are recorded as well as main wives.

h. *secondary evidence* (Law): (see quots. 1921, 1976).

1810 in E. H. East *Rep. Cases King's Bench* VIII. 289 The fact of its loss being proved, so as to let in the secondary evidence of its contents; that matter was sufficiently established by parol. **1885** *Law. Rep. Chanc. Div.* XXIX. 290 A probate was not even secondary evidence of a lost will until the statute 20 & 21 Vict. **1921** S. L. PHIPSON *Law of Evidence* (ed. 6) i. 7 The term *secondary evidence*, on the other hand, is by common usage confined to documents; it deals only with the means of proving their *contents*; and it is in general admissible whenever the absence of the primary source has been satisfactorily explained. **1976** *Halsbury's Laws of England* (ed. 4) XVII. 9 In the unavoidable absence of the best or primary evidence of documents, the court will accept secondary evidence. This is evidence which suggests, on the face of it, that other and better evidence exists.

i. *secondary association* (Cytology): (see quot. 1931).

1931 W. J. C. LAWRENCE in *Cytologia* II. 353 It is now possible to demonstrate the occurrence of two different types of chromosome association in polyploids. We may define these two modes of association as follows: Primary association 1) arises from prophase pairing and 2) determines segregation. Secondary association 1) is a post-synaptic phenomenon and 2) does not affect segregation. It is a differential approximation of the bivalents in the equatorial plane. **1959** [see *MULTIVALENT *sb.*].

3. a. (Further examples.)

1790 *Phil. Trans. R. Soc.* LXXX. 247 (*heading*) Secondary triangles, subdivided into two sets, for the improvement of the maps of the country, and the plan of the City of London. **1908** BREED & HOSMER *Princ. & Pract. Surveying* II. i. 5 From the sides of the primary triangles as bases a secondary system of triangles is laid out, the sides being shorter than those of the primary system. **1975** J. B. HARLEY *O.S. Maps* i. 7 This primary network is broken down successively into a secondary triangulation (giving a continuous network of stations between 8 km and 12 km apart), a tertiary triangulation (with a density of control points 4 to 7 km apart), and other lower orders of control.

h. *Electr.* (i) Delete *secondary battery* and its def. (see next sense) and add: With reference to any device utilizing electromagnetic induction, esp. a transformer: of, pertaining to, or carrying the output electrical power. (Earlier and further examples.)

1832 *Phil. Mag.* XI. 300 Although the principal current in A be continued, still the secondary current in B is not found to accompany it, for it ceases after the first moment. **1847** *Patent Jrnl.* 16 Oct. 476/1 Upon the primary circuit being completed through the primary coils, a secondary circuit is induced through the secondary coils, but in an opposite direction. **1881** S. P. THOMPSON *Elem. Lessons Electr. & Magn.* 365 Causing the inductive action in the secondary circuit at 'make' to be comparatively feeble. **1931** *B.B.C. Year-bk.* (1932) 436/2 The output of the secondary winding of the output transformer. **1947** R. LEE *Electronic Transformers & Circuits* iii. 58 Single-phase full-wave rectifiers with two anodes have higher secondary volt-amperes for a given primary v-a rating than a filament transformer. **1962** *Newnes Conc. Encycl. Electr. Engin.* 810/2 The induced secondary voltage E_s lags ϕ by 90° and the secondary current I_s lags behind E_s by an angle which depends upon the impedance of the secondary circuit. **1969** J. J. SPARKES *Transistor Switching* vi. 146 They are called secondary circuits to contrast them with the input circuits.

(ii) Of a cell or battery: in which the chemical reaction that generates the current is reversible and which therefore can store electrical energy supplied to it.

1872 *Jrnl. Chem. Soc.* XXV. 589 The author has investigated what proportion of the energy is lost whilst the secondary battery receives its charge. **1881** *Electrician* 3 Sept. 249/2 No one is inclined to underrate the claims of M. Planté in connection with this form of secondary battery. **1902** [in Dict.]. **1922** GLAZEBROOK *Dict. Appl. Physics* II. 72/2 There is no essential electro-chemical difference between the secondary cell and the primary cell when either is used as a generator of electrical energy. **1962** *Newnes Conc. Encycl. Electr. Engin.* 9/1 Also known as the storage cell or secondary cell, the accumulator is reversible, i.e. it can, after discharging, be brought back to a full state of charge by passing a reverse current through it. **1979** *Nature* 22 Mar. 335/2 (*caption*) Schematic for repeating cell in a forced ionisation secondary battery using a bipolar ion exchange membrane.

i. Substitute for entry: (i) Applied to compounds regarded as being derived from ammonia († or water) by replacement of two hydrogen atoms by organic radicals (cf. *PRIMARY *a.* 6 f (i)); also extended to analogous derivatives of other elements, esp. phosphorus. [The sense is due to Gerhardt & Chiozza, who used F. *secondaire* (*Compt. Rend.* (1853) XXXVII. 88).]

1854 *Q. Jrnl. Chem. Soc.* VI. 195 To convert the preceding compounds [*sc.* primary amides] into secondary amides, or amides representing a molecule of ammonia in which 2 atoms of hydrogen are replaced by the negative radicals, we heat these primary amides with an equivalent quantity of chloride of benzoyl, of cumyl, sulphophenyl, &c. **1888, 1889** [see *PRIMARY *a.* 6 f (i)]. **1932** I. D. GARARD *Introd. Org. Chem.* xi. 154 Dimethylamine is a typical secondary amine. **1962, 1965** [see *PRIMARY *a.* 6 f (i)]. **1974** *Encycl. Brit. Macropædia* XIII. 697/1 The reaction of amines with nitrous acid is an old and important reaction... From secondary amines, nitrosamines precipitate as non-basic, yellowish oils.

(ii) Applied to organic compounds other than amines, etc. (see prec. sense) in which the characteristic functional group is located on a saturated carbon atom which is itself bonded to two other carbon atoms. [Applied orig. to alcohols by H. Kolbe, who used G. *secundär* (*Ann. der Chem. und Pharm.* (1864) CXXXII. 102).]

1864 *Chem. News* 26 Nov. 260/1 By a secondary alcohol the author [*sc.* Kolbe] means a body in which two of the typical hydrogen atoms in a typical alcohol are substituted by two atoms of some other alcohol radicals. **1876** *Phil. Mag.* II. 162 To so-called normal butylic alcohol is generally assigned the structural formula $CH_2(C_3H_7)OH$; to secondary butylic alcohol the formula $CH(CH_3)(C_2H_5)$-OH; [etc.]. **1876** [in Dict.]. **1900** PERKIN & KIPPING *Org. Chem.* vi. 107 Tertiary alcohols are, as a rule, more difficult to obtain than the primary or secondary compounds. **1932** I. D. GARARD *Introd. Org. Chem.* iii. 34 Secondary butyl alcohol..is made from butylene..just as isopropyl alcohol is made from propylene. **1972** R. A. JACKSON *Mechanism* v. 88 In general, primary compounds undergo S_N2 substitution more readily than do secondary compounds, and S_N2 reactions on tertiary compounds go with great difficulty if at all.

(iii) Applied to a saturated carbon atom which is bonded to two other carbon atoms; also, bonded to or involving such an atom. Of an ion or free radical: having (respectively) the electric charge or the unpaired electron located on a secondary carbon atom.

1903 A. J. WALKER tr. *Holleman's Text-bk. Org. Chem.* I. 46 If it [*sc.* a carbon atom] is linked to two carbon atoms it is named secondary; if to three, tertiary; if to four, quaternary. **1926** H. G. RULE tr. *J. Schmidt's Text-bk. Org. Chem.* 70 If two, three or all four valencies are linked to carbon, the atom under consideration is termed secondary, tertiary or quaternary respectively. **1950** E. R. ALEXANDER *Princ. Ionic Org. Reactions* iii. 42 We find..that a primary or secondary carbonium ion extracts a hydrogen atom with a pair of electrons from an alkane so as to form a secondary or tertiary carbonium ion. **1972** [see *PRIMARY *a.* 6 f (iii)]. **1972** NORMAN & WADDINGTON *Mod. Org. Chem.* vi. 82 The order of stability of carbonium ions is tertiary > secondary > primary.

k. Applied to bodily characteristics which are peculiar to one sex but are not essential to reproduction; sometimes the sexual ducts and organs are also included. Cf. *PRIMARY *a.* 6 h.

1780 J. HUNTER in *Phil. Trans. R. Soc.* LXX. 529 It is my intention at present to extend my inquiry on this subject no farther than as to what relates to that resemblance which one sex bears to that of another in those distinguishing properties which I term secondary... There is often a change of the secondary properties of one sex into another. *Ibid.* 530 The male..loses that resemblance which he before bore to the female in various secondary properties, exclusive of what relates to the organs of generation. *Ibid.* 531 A change of those secondary characters. **1859** C. DARWIN *Orig. Species* v. 156, I think it will be admitted..that secondary sexual characters are very variable. **1871**, etc. [see *PRIMARY *a.* 6 h]. **1926** H. M. KYLE *Biol. Fishes* xii. 290 It is amongst the freshwater Teleosts..that the secondary sexual characters are most developed... Usually it is the pectoral fins that are longer in the male. **1977** STEEN & PRICE *Human Sex & Sexuality* iv. 59 Androgens, of which testosterone is the principle one, control the development of secondary sex characteristics (distribution of hair, quality of voice, skeletal form, sebaceous gland activity).

l. *Geol.* Of a mineral: that is not an original constituent of the rock; formed by the alteration or replacement of primary constituents of the rock.

1886 [see *PRIMARY *a.* 6 i]. **1897** G. P. MERRILL *Treat. Rocks* III. iii. 249 Those dikes containing so large a proportion of secondary epidote as to be of a dull greenish hue are almost invariably more enduring than the granites. **1931** A. JOHANNSEN *Descr. Petrogr. Igneous Rocks* I. ii. 28 Secondary minerals may be introduced by the addition of material such as boron, fluorine, etc., to form tourmaline, topaz, fluorite, etc. **1974** FLINT & SKINNER *Physical Geol.* vi. 94/2 Water combines with the remaining aluminum silicate radical to create the clay mineral kaolinite... The resulting kaolinite we call a secondary mineral, because it was not present in the original rock.

m. *secondary shaft* = *LAYSHAFT.

1888 [see *LAYSHAFT]. **1902** A. C. HARMSWORTH et al. *Motors* x. 205 Causing the secondary shaft..to be rotated. **1926** H. T. RUTTER *Mod. Motors* II. vii. 261 Parallel to the gear-shaft in the gear box is another shaft, which is called the 'lay' shaft, 'secondary', or countershaft.

n. *secondary spectrum*: a fringe of colours bordering an image formed by a lens corrected for two wavelengths and due to the non-coincidence of the foci of other wavelengths.

1893 W. E. BAXTER tr. *H. van Heurck's Microscope* 370 The final upper lens, which is also a triplet, is used to destroy the secondary spectrum. **1932** HARDY & PERRIN *Princ. Optics* vi. 115 This residual chromatism gives rise to a fringe of color surrounding the image of an extended object, which is known as the secondary spectrum. **1978** R. KINGSLAKE *Lens Design Fund.* iv. 75 The fact that achromatizing a lens for two colors fails to unite the other colors is known as secondary spectrum; it should not be confused with the secondary chromatic aberration.

o. *Physics* and *Astr.* Of, pertaining to, or designating radiation that has been produced by the interaction of other (primary) radiation with matter. Of cosmic rays: produced in the earth's atmosphere by the impact of primary rays.

1898 *Sci. Abstr.* I. 128 The secondary rays emitted by the metal..pass some centimetres through the air. **1921** J. SCOTT-TAGGART *Thermionic Tubes* i. 11 Under some conditions the electron bombardment liberates a number of secondary electrons attached to the atoms of the plate. **1938** [see *PRIMARY *a.* 6 k]. **1944** *Electronic Engin.* XVI. 372/1 In order to avoid or minimise secondary emission it is necessary that grid structures shall be maintained reasonably cool during the operating life of a valve. **1959** [see *PRIMARY *a.* 6 k]. **1964** M. GOWING *Britain & Atomic Energy 1939–1945* i. 39 When the uranium oxide was bombarded with fast neutrons the initial fission did not propagate itself because the secondary neutrons lost energy. **1974** *Encycl. Brit. Macropædia* V. 200/1 Secondary cosmic rays consist mainly of subatomic particles that are short-lived..; they cannot have come far and are thus known to have been produced within the atmosphere.

p. *secondary poverty*: effective poverty due to waste, inefficiency, or some other drain on resources, rather than to insufficiency of means.

1901 B. S. ROWNTREE *Poverty* p. viii, Families whose total earnings would be sufficient for merely physical efficiency were it not that some portion of it is absorbed by other expenditure... Poverty falling under this head is described as 'secondary' poverty. **1909** M. F. DAVIES *Life in Eng. Village* xii. 146 These people..appear to have a struggle to keep going, and their incomes do not probably exceed the limit of secondary poverty. **1970** M. REIN in P. Townsend *Concept of Poverty* ii. 60 If the diet is to..avoid building into its definition a confusion between primary and secondary poverty, then the standards of economy must be relaxed and a more realistic assumption of human error accepted.

q. Designating action taken by workers on strike to prevent other firms from doing business with the strikers' employers; *esp.* applied to a boycott or the picketing of the premises of firms not otherwise involved in the dispute. orig. *U.S.*

1909 *Pacific Reporter* XCVIII. 1083/1 This is the argument commonly advanced to establish the illegality of what has been called..a 'secondary' rather than a 'primary' boycott. **1916** L. WOLMAN *Boycott in Amer. Trade Unions* i. 142 The secondary boycott is distinctly different in effect from the simple strike; since..it inflicts injury upon an innocent third party. **1938** *Atlantic Reporter* CXCV. 379/2 The Legislature..never contemplated..'secondary picketing'. *Ibid.* 378/1 Secondary picketing is illegal. **1942** *Yale Law Jrnl.* May 1209 Secondary picketing against the employer's vendee, is the only effective means of publicizing the facts of a labor contest. **1979** *Daily Tel.* 13 Jan. 1/2 The Freight Transport Association said secondary picketing had been reduced in some areas, but expressed concern about the position in [the] Midlands where the dispute was unofficial. **1980** *Illustr. London News* Mar. 19/1 The Law Lords referred to their judgment in the case of McShane v Express Newspapers, in which they had decided that secondary blacking on the part of journalists, on the instruction of their union, fell within the immunity granted under section 13 of the 1974 Act.

r. Designating an earthquake S wave (see *S 6).

1919, etc. [see *PRIMARY *a.* 4 h].

s. *secondary industry*: industry that converts the materials provided by primary industry (see *PRIMARY *a.* 6 n) into commodities and products for the consumer.

1930 *Economist* 19 July 107/2 The design behind the former movement is clearly to enable nascent secondary industries to compete in the home market. **1944** [see *LIGHT *a.*[1] 4 c]. **1950** *N.Z. Jrnl. Agric.* Aug. 127/3 The tending of land, livestock, and crops has figured so prominently in the lives of New Zealanders—and will continue to do so despite the growth of secondary industries. **1977** D. M. SMITH *Human Geogr.* viii. 232 The mineral or crop may be exported in its raw state for processing in Europe or North America, thus depriving the producing country of a possible basis for building up secondary industry.

t. *secondary air*: air supplied to a combustion zone where combustion with primary air is occurring.

1931 *Engineering* 9 Jan. 40/2 Complete combustion to CO_2 takes place at the end of the chamber, when an enveloping stream of secondary air meets the first stream. **1951** COHEN & ROGERS *Gas Turbine Theory* vii. 195 If devices are used to increase the turbulence and so distribute the secondary air more uniformly throughout the burning gases, the combustion efficiency will be improved but at the expense of increased pressure loss.

u. Of radar: relying on signals transmitted automatically by aircraft in response to signals reaching it from the radar.

1945 R. WATSON-WATT in *Nature* 15 Sept. 323 Radar in war fell into three convenient categories, each of which has come to stay in the peace... Secondary radar requires that small measure of co-operation which is involved in the fitting and switching on of an otherwise automatic responder. **1961** *Engineering* 6 Jan. 1/2 What secondary radar does for the controller on the ground is to give him identification of aircraft as they come within range. **1967** *New Scientist* 19 Oct. 151/2 Air traffic control is increasingly making use of secondary radar.

v. *secondary structure* (Biochem.), the three-dimensional form that the chain of a polynucleotide or polypeptide molecule assumes as a result of non-covalent bonds between neighbouring amino-acid residues.

1952 [see *PRIMARY *a.* 6 v]. **1960** *Nature* 8 Oct. 99/2 Ribonucleic acid is a single-stranded molecule the secondary structure of which arises from intramolecular interactions. **1974** [see *PRIMARY *a.* 6 v]. **1977** D. E. METZLER *Biochemistry* ii. 102/2 The value of β is always positive but that of τ can be negative, the secondary structure (Watson–Crick helix) being fully formed but with left-handed superhelical turns present.

4. a. (Further examples in *Bot.*)

1861 R. BENTLEY *Man. Bot.* 122 Adventitious or Secondary Root.—This name is applied to all roots which are not produced by the direct elongation of the radicle of the embryo. **1880** C. E. BESSEY *Botany* 147 Where the secondary leaves (leaflets) grow from an extremely short axis. **1973** H. C. BOLD *Morphol. Plants* (ed. 3) xxx. 570/2 Branches of the radicle are secondary roots; all other roots are adventitious.

c. *secondary road*: a road of a class lower than that of a main road; a minor road.

1903 in *Parl. Papers 1904* XXIV. 279 (Cd. 1793) p. vi, Roads of this class are known in different parts of the country as Secondary Roads, Contribution or Contributory Roads, 'Grant in aid' Roads, &c. **1929** A. HUXLEY *Let.* 1 Dec. (1969) 321 Even the secondary roads were tolerable. **1938** E. AMBLER *Cause for Alarm* xiv. 228 The only roads we'll have to worry about are..secondary roads. **1959** T. S. ELIOT *Elder Statesman* III. 88 It was late at night. A secondary road. I ran over an old man lying in the road. **1974** J. THOMSON *Long Revenge* iv. 45 He turned off into the network of secondary roads.

5. f. *secondary instruction* (earlier example); *secondary school* (earlier and further examples); also *attrib.*; *secondary modern school*: a secondary school of a kind established by the Education Act of 1944, offering a general education to children not selected for grammar or technical schools (cf. *central school* s.v. *CENTRAL *a.* 4 and *modern school* s.v. *MODERN *a.* 2 e); also (in colloq. use) *ellipt.* as *secondary modern* (freq. *attrib.*).

1809 R. L. EDGEWORTH *Ess. on Professional Educ.* i. 41 In the secondary schools for boys of nine or ten.., the principles of general grammar should be explained. **1835** *Southern Lit. Messenger* I. 275 Others classify them into 1st *primary* schools..2nd *secondary* schools, for the rudiments of Arithmetic, Geography, English Grammar, and further progress in reading and writing. **1863** M. ARNOLD in *Macm. Mag.* VIII. 355/1 The Royal Commissioners have thought themselves precluded..from making a thorough inquiry into the system of secondary instruction on the Continent. **1892** in *Parl. Papers* IX. 373 This Act may be cited as the Secondary School Teachers Registration Act, 1892. **1926** W. H. HADOW et al. *Rep. Consult. Comm. Educ. Adolescent* (Board of Educ.) 266 The expression 'secondary school' was borrowed from the French '*école secondaire*', which was used apparently for the first time in the *Rapport et projet de décret sur l'organisation générale de l'instruction publique*, submitted to the Legislative Assembly by Condorcet in April, 1792. **1937** *Burlington Mag.* Sept. 107/2 No student..can possibly acquire more than a secondary-school smattering in the subject. **1943** C. NORWOOD et al. *Curriculum & Examinations in Secondary Schools* (Board of Educ.) I. iii. 15 At the age of 11+, or earlier in some cases, a child would pass into one of the three types of secondary education which we have postulated, secondary Grammar School, secondary Technical School, secondary Modern School. **1955** *Punch* 30 Mar. 404/2 'The thing that makes me nervous,' I said tentatively, 'is if they fail their 11-plus and land up in a Secondary Modern.' **1956** H. LOUKES *Secondary Modern* i. 45 They are not to be regarded, these secondary modern children, as a backward group. **1961** M. KELLY *Spoilt Kill* II. 103 He taught maths in a secondary modern somewhere down south. **1976** *Yorkshire Evening Press* 9 Dec. 13/6 Derwent Secondary Modern School, York, was entered and £6.50 stolen. **1976** *Evening Post* (Nottingham) 14 Dec. 6/2 His early education finished at 14 when he left the Player Secondary School. **1982** *Guardian* 26 Apr. 3/2 Critics say it is a back door way of re-introducing grammar and secondary modern schools.

g. Archæol. *secondary burial* or *interment*: a burial of human remains in a site used for burial at an earlier time (see also quot. 1960); *Secondary Neolithic*: (of or pertaining to) that part of the Neolithic period in Britain marked by the fusion of native Mesolithic cultural elements with those of immigrant European agricultural peoples.

1865 J. LUBBOCK *Pre-Historic Times* iv. 110 It appears reasonable to conclude that these interments belong to the ante-metallic period; especially when..we find several secondary interments, plainly belonging to a later age. **1877** W. GREENWELL *Brit. Barrows* 13 These secondary interments have been made either by placing the body on the surface of an existing barrow..or by making an excavation into it. Secondary burials occur in all parts of a barrow. **1954** S. PIGGOTT *Neolithic Cultures* i. 15 These Secondary Neolithic cultures, as I have called them, were to form the basis of the ensuing British Bronze Age. **1960** K. M. KENYON *Archæol. in Holy Land* iv. 86 The burials as we find them were secondary. That is to say, the bones were only placed in their present position after the flesh had largely decayed. **1963** E. S. WOOD *Collins Field Guide Archaeol.* I. iv. 60 The secondary Neolithic is now appearing more complicated than it looked a few years ago. **1963** H. N. SAVORY in Foster & Alcock *Culture & Environment* iii. 26 It is therefore no longer necessary to envisage a narrow horizon on which Primary and Secondary Neolithic and 'Beaker' elements can scarcely be disentangled. **1977** KWANG-CHIH CHANG *Archaeol. Anc. China* (ed. 3) viii. 406 Three ways to dispose of the dead were distinguished..: cremation and ash urns;

interment of the dorsal and stretched type; and probably secondary burials.

h. *secondary succession* (Ecol.): (see quot. 1905).

1905 F. E. CLEMENTS *Research Methods in Ecol.* iv. 247 Generally speaking, all successions on denuded soils are secondary... The great majority of secondary successions owe their origin to floods, animals, or the activities of man, and they agree in occurring upon decomposed soils of medium water-content. **1932** FULLER & CONARD tr. *Braun-Blanquet's Plant Sociol.* xi. 279 Fires are always followed..by a secondary succession, which tends anew towards the climax. **1973** P. A. COLINVAUX *Introd. Ecol.* vi. 77 Secondary succession is best understood by considering what happens to a farm when it is abandoned.

i. *secondary hardening* (Metallurgy): a further hardening which occurs in some previously hardened steels when they are tempered; so *secondary hardness*.

1915 EDWARDS & KIKKAWA in *Jrnl. Iron & Steel Inst.* XCII. 12 The temperature at which this secondary hardening begins is progressively raised with increasing percentages of tungsten. *Ibid.*, As regards the temperature at which the maximum secondary hardness is obtained..for the steel with no tungsten this is 494°. **1937** *Discovery* May 155/2 The tempering of high speed steel is primarily undertaken to give maximum secondary hardness. **1949** P. C. CARMAN *Chem. Constitution & Properties of Engin. Materials* v. 192 On tempering, the hardness decreases slightly between 300° and 500°C., and then secondary hardening takes place between 500° and 600°C. **1967** A. H. COTTRELL *Introd. Metall.* xxv. 517 The steel is tempered at 650°C to produce secondary hardening by precipitation of alloy carbides.

j. *Psychol.* In various phrases. *secondary conditioned reflex*: a reflex transferred from the original stimulus to one associated with it; similarly *secondary conditioned stimulus*; *secondary conditioning*: conditioning in which the response is transferred to a subsequent, associated stimulus; similarly *secondary reinforcement, reinforcer, reward*.

1927 G. V. ANREP tr. *Pavlov's Conditioned Reflexes* iii. 34 The appearance of a black square in the dog's line of vision is now used as yet a further stimulus, which is to be given the character of a secondary conditioned stimulus. **1938** B. F. SKINNER *Behav. Organisms* ix. 245, I am inclined to doubt the reality of secondary conditioning of a respondent in general. **1940** HILGARD & MARQUIS *Conditioning & Learning* iii. 63 Secondary rewards such as approval, money, prestige and so forth. **1944** B. MALINOWSKI *Sci. Theory of Culture* xii. 138 The secondary reinforcement becomes attached to the instrumental performance as a whole, and to all its component parts. **1957** E. R. HILGARD *Introd. Psychol.* (ed. 2) x. 242/1 A feature of secondary reinforcement that is very important for human social behavior is its wide application. *Ibid.*, There is also experimental evidence in support of the principle that secondary reinforcers have wide generality. **1976** *Howard Jrnl.* XV. I. 12 The relics of past experiences, surviving through the mechanism of secondary reinforcement. **1977** R. A. RESCORLA in Davis & Hurwitz *Operant-Pavlovian Interactions* vi. 155 No increase in response rate was produced by this supposed secondary reinforcer.

k. *secondary recovery*, the recovery of oil by means of special techniques from reservoirs which have been substantially depleted; freq. *attrib.*

1940 P. D. TORREY in E. DeGolyer *Elements Petroleum Industry* xiii. 289 The two most commonly employed secondary recovery methods are water-flooding and gas-repressuring. **1945** L. M. FANNING *Our Oil Resources* iv. 96 In most instances secondary-recovery operations are more costly than primary operations. **1971** I. G. GASS et al. *Understanding Earth* xxiii. 330/2 Oil is obtained at this site by a technique of secondary recovery which involves the injection of water under pressure. **1973** C. J. MAY in Hobson & Pohl *Mod. Petroleum Technol.* (ed. 4) v. 174 Of perhaps more general interest is the application of secondary recovery methods to reservoirs which have been largely depleted by natural forces.

6. b. *secondary constriction* (Cytology): a chromosomal constriction not associated with the centromere.

1932 C. D. DARLINGTON *Recent Adv. Cytol.* ii. 34 There are also found in many chromosomes 'secondary' constrictions which have no relationship with any present spindle attachment. **1957** C. P. SWANSON *Cytol. & Cytogenetics* v. 131 The secondary constrictions seen in somatic metaphase chromosomes generally arise as the result of nucleolar formation. **1975** [see *SATELLITE *sb.* 9].

B. *sb.* **9.** Also, a secondary circuit, current, etc. (Earlier and further examples.)

1837 M. FARADAY in *Ann. Electr., Magnetism, & Chem.* I. 199 Why do secondaries almost annihilate the terminal effects of primitives? **1896** [see *PRIMARY *sb.* 5]. **1923** E. W. MARCHANT *Radio Telegr. & Teleph.* v. 67 If the ratio of transformation is made too great, the primary circuit may be tuned for quite a different wave-length from the secondary. **1947** R. LEE *Electronic Transformers & Circuits* i. 5 The right-hand winding is connected to a load and is called the secondary. **1967** [see *PRIMARY *sb.* 5].

11. *Physics* and *Astr.* A secondary ray or particle, esp. a secondary cosmic ray.

1921 *Proc. Nat. Acad. Sci.* VII. 17 Practically no secondaries have a velocity of more than 5 volts, even when the exciting primary electrons have velocities of 300 volts. **1932, 1942** [see *PRIMARY *sb.* 8]. **1964** *Cambr. Rev.* 24 Oct. 48/2 A shower of secondaries of total energy $\geqslant \epsilon$. **1975** D. G. FINK *Electronics Engineers' Handbk.* vi. 113 The yield..drops at higher energies, since high-energy electrons penetrate deeper in the material and the secondaries generated there are unable to reach the material surface with enough energy to be emitted.

12. *Gram.* = *ADJUNCT *sb.* 5 b.

[**1914**: see *ADJUNCT *sb.* 5 b.] **1924** JESPERSEN *Philos. Gram.* xviii. 252 (*heading*) Secondaries and tertiaries. **1928** —— *Internat. Lang.* II. 97 The definite article is a secondary and therefore uninflected in number or gender. **1940** —— *S.P.E. Tract* LIV. 157 We thus distinguish between clause primaries, clause secondaries, and clause tertiaries. **1959** M. SCHLAUCH *Eng. Lang. in Mod. Times* viii. 221 In this system a leading term..is a primary; its direct modifier (e.g. an adjective) is a secondary.

13. *Path.* An additional tumour arising from cells carried to the site from the initial tumour.

1952 RAVEN & HANCOCK *Cancer in Gen. Practice* xxii. 153 No treatment is effective except in the case of prostatic, and occasionally breast, secondaries which may respond to androgens or oestrogens. **1969** BETHELL & BURG tr. *Solzhenitsyn's Cancer Ward* II. ii. 12 She could not come to terms with the possibility that radioactive gold might exist somewhere while her son's secondaries were penetrating his groin. **1977** *Proc. R. Soc. Med.* LXX. 199/2 Patients with hypercalcaemia and breast cancer usually have widespread osteolytic bone secondaries.

14. *U.S. Football.* The defensive backfield.

[**1912** *Collier's* 23 Nov. 11/2 He hears people about him rattling away about 'Minnesota shifts', 'secondary defense', and so on.] **1955** *Sports Illustr.* 12 Sept. 31/2 Four of them are ready to leap back into the secondary as line-backers. **1972** J. MOSEDALE *Football* ii. 18 Dutch is like a rabbit in a brush heap when he gets into the secondary. **1980** *Washington Star* 13 Aug. 65 The Redskins are confident their secondary is in fine shape without White... 'We're going to be fine in the secondary,' Beathard said. 'To hell with him.'

15. Short for *secondary school* or *secondary modern school. colloq.*

1962 L. DAVIDSON *Rose of Tibet* 7 'Where does he teach?' 'He used to at the Edith Road Girls' Secondary in Fulham.' **1975** 'J. BELL' *Victim* xiv. 148 The passenger was a girl of twelve from a local comprehensive. Which led back to a London secondary in a northern suburb.

second class, *sb. phr.* [Cf. SECOND-CLASS *a.* in Dict. and Suppl.] The second of a ranked series of classes in which things are grouped; esp. of university degrees, railway carriages, and mail.

1810 *Oxf. Univ. Calendar* 57 The second class is subdivided into two parts, according to the different degrees of merit. **1844** *Punch* VII. 258/2 In travelling by the second class, you will..be choked with dust and ashes from the engine. **1852** [see CLASS *sb.* 5]. **1863** *Statutes at Large U.S.A.* XII. 705 The second class embraces all mailable matter exclusively in print, and regularly issued at stated periods. **1883** *U.S. Official Postal Guide* Jan. 733 'Nixes' is a term used..to denote matter of domestic origin, chiefly of the first and second class, which is unmailable. **1931** H. CRANE *Let.* 20 June (1965) 373 The post (for books, etc. 2nd class) is apt to be very slow to Mexico.

second-class, *a.* Add: **1. a.** *absol.*, also a second-class railway ticket or compartment.

1863 A. H. CLOUGH *Poems* (ed. 2) 300 Punctual they met, a second-class he took. **1888** KIPLING *Wee Willie Winkie* (1907) 205 There was only one Second-class on the train. **1901** ——*Kim* vii. 166 Father Victor..put him into an empty second-class next to Colonel Creighton's first. **1956** *Times* 4 June 10/7 In 1875 one of the railway companies abolished 'second class', and called it 'third'.

b. *second-class matter* (earlier example); now replaced by *second-class mail*: mail sent at the lower of two rates; so *second-class letter*, etc.

1873 *U.S. Postal Laws* II. viii. 176 Postage on second-class matter must be prepaid *in money*. **1968** *Times* 19 Mar. 2/1 Principal recommendations are: a two-tier system providing a first class letter service..and a slower second class service. *Ibid.* 9/1 The proposal for a first and second class mail service is a confession of failure. **1972** R. HILL *Fairly Dangerous Thing* I. i. 11 A confirmation had been sent off the previous day, second-class mail. **1976** *Cumberland & Westmorland Herald* 4 Dec. 9/6 A second-class letter posted after the last collection on a Friday night would not be dealt with until the following Monday. **1981** G. HAMMOND *Revenge Game* xiv. 155 Put a second-class stamp on it and it may *never* get there.

c. *second-class road*: a road of a second class; a B-road (see *B 2 (ii)).

1906 *Min. Evidence R. Comm. Motor Cars* 191/2 in *Parl. Papers* (Cd. 3081) XLVIII. 89 The roads within the country used for heavy traffic may be divided into three classes: first-class roads,..second-class roads, which require strengthening only, [etc.]. **1914** in *5th Ann. Rep. Road Board* 77 in *Parl. Papers 1914–16* XXXV. 127 The roads are to be divided into three classes—1. First Class; 2. Second Class; 3. All other roads. **1922** *Michelin Guide Gt. Brit.* (ed. 6) (Atlas) 31 Second-class roads are designated 'B' with its [*sic*] number. **1975** 'G. BLACK' *Big Wind for Summer* ii. 29, I drove..into a second-class road that became acutely third class.

d. *second-class citizen*: a person assigned to an inferior class of citizenship; one deprived of normal civic and legal rights; also in extended and *fig.* uses. Hence *second-class citizenship*. orig. *U.S.*

1942 *Time* 6 July 16/3 Finerty..argued that destitute 'second-class citizens' like Waller were barred from serving on Virginia juries. **1948** G. ORWELL *Let.* 4 Jan. in *Coll. Ess.* (1968) IV. 401 Zilliacus wrote in demanding what amounts to Fascist legislation and creation of 2nd-class citizens. **1951** I. SHAW *Troubled Air* xv. 217 Cohen.. can't get into an hotel. He tells Levy, '..we're second-class citizens in this country.' **1958** J. K. GALBRAITH *Affluent Soc.* ix. 107 We relegate one important class of production to a second-class citizenship. **1965** *Austral. Encycl.* I. 322/1 These people [*sc.* convicts] were second-class citizens, well versed in the routines of unorthodox speech. **1972** D. LESSING *Golden Notebook* (ed. 2) p. viii, Women are second-class citizens, as they are saying energetically and competently in many countries. **1974** *Listener* 17 Jan. 95/3 To show what the graphic artist (a second-class citizen in the art world) is capable of. **1975** S. LAUDER *Killing Time on Corvo* xvii. 160 Brazil.. offered more opportunities to an educated girl than the restrictions, the second-class citizenship, of old-fashioned Portugal.

2. (Earlier and later examples.)

1863 MRS. GASKELL *Let.* 1 June (1966) 702 We shall have..to return—I was going to say 2nd class. **1877** TROLLOPE *Amer. Senator* II. xxv. 268 Why could she not go by herself, second class, like any other young woman? **1974** *Times* 22 Oct. 14/4 I'll pay rail fares, of course. Second class. I always travel second class.

secondee (sekǫ:ndī·). [f. SECOND *v.*[2] + -EE[1].] A person temporarily transferred to a new unit, department, etc.

1980 *Old Lady of Threadneedle St.* 16 June 56/2 As a Bank secondee I found no difficulty in being accepted in the Treasury. **1981** *Times* 10 Mar. 2/5 He was described as a 'secondee' or trainee in the Prime Minister's press office. **1982** *Ann. Rep. Nat. Westminster Bank 1981* 23 Feb. 15/1 Following their period of secondment, the Bank will benefit on their return from the wide experience that has been gained by the secondees.

second-guess (se:kənd ge·s, se·kənd ges), *v. colloq.* (orig. and chiefly *N. Amer.*). [Prob. back-formation from next.] **1.** *trans.* To anticipate the action of (a person), to outguess; to predict or foresee (an event), to apprehend (simultaneously or beforehand) by guess-work.

1941 *Broadcasting* 22 Dec. 11/2 *Do not* try to second-guess or master-mind our military officials. Leave this for established military analysts and experts, who are experienced enough to await the facts before drawing conclusions. **1942** BERREY & VAN DEN BARK *Amer. Thes. Slang* §646/2 Predict the outcome [of a sporting event].., *second-guess*. *Ibid.* §733/7 'Dope the races.' (To figure out or prophesy probable results from past performances &c.).., *second-guess*. **1963** 'R. L. PIKE' *Mute Witness* viii. 137 Desperate people get panicky, and I never try to second-guess panicky people. **1974** *Globe & Mail* (Toronto) 22 Oct. 7/5 Any attempt to second-guess the economics of the situation to the end of the decade and beyond is a hazardous and probably futile task. **1976** *Publishers Weekly* 29 Mar. 49/2 Just when you think you've second-guessed [the author] WS, he turns the tables on you. **1980** *Sci. Amer.* Feb. 68/3 A mechanism by which his world-class backgammon program will develop a profile of an opponent's over-all playing style so that it can second-guess his moves and play accordingly.

2. To subject (a person or his action, esp. a decision) to criticism after the result of the action is known; to judge, question, or reconsider by hindsight. Also *refl.* and *absol.* or *intr.*

1946 [implied in *second-guessing* vbl. sb. below]. **1950** *Sun* (Baltimore) 27 Jan. 2/8 Second-guessing the conduct of Pacific war, Admiral Frederick C. Sherman points..to a whole series of lost chances. **1951** *Ibid.* 28 Sept. (B ed.) 17/7 We lost 11 in a row and I still get nightmares thinking about some of those games. I'm still second guessing myself on some of them. **1955** *Galaxy Sci. Fiction* Apr. 86/2 They say that a century or so ago..there were only about five billion [people]. But anyone can second-guess that. **1965** H. WAUGH *End of Party* x. 72 'They should have called the police,' Avery growled... Fellows said with a shrug, 'It's always easy to second-guess.' **1974** M. HOYT *Thirty Miles for Ice Cream* x. 126 We second-guessed that the spot where I went through [the ice] had been sheltered. **1978** J. KRANTZ *Scruples* viii. 223 Even Billy's New York lawyers approved, because Josh Hillman was an exceedingly brilliant lawyer... He protected Billy's interests without trying to second-guess their own, far more informed, decisions. **1980** *Daily Tel.* 4 Jan. 3/3 He had pointed out the defect [in the manufacture of a car] to Sir Michael, who had replied in a cavalier manner, saying it was not his job to 'second-guess' his designers.

Hence **se:cond-gue·ssing** *vbl. sb.* (usu. in sense 2).

1946 *Richmond* (Va.) *Times-Dispatch* 26 Dec. 12/1 Pate, in naming Jake Kramer and Ted Schroeder as the entire United States Davis Cup team,..left himself wide-open to what could be the greatest second-guessing attack of many years. **1963** *Life* 9 Aug. 44/3 The besetting sin of the theater is second-guessing, trying to anticipate what the public wants and what will be commercially sound. **1981** *Washington Post* 25 Feb. E 7/3 As Dennie walked back to the jocks' room, the Instructor couldn't resist a bit of second-guessing. 'I told you to stay on the rail,' he said.

second-guesser (se:kənd ge·səɹ). *colloq.* (orig. and chiefly *U.S.*). Also as two words. [f. SECOND *a.* + GUESSER, poss. in slang sense 'umpire (in baseball)', the orig. meaning being 'one who acts as if he is a second umpire': cf. also prec.] **a.** In *Baseball*, a spectator who criticizes the playing of a team or the decisions of the umpire, usu. with the benefit of hindsight; hence *gen.*, one who criticizes (the actions or decisions of) another person after the event. **b.** One who predicts the result of a horse-race. *rare.*

1937 *Sporting News Record Bk.* 65 [Guesser, an umpire.] *Ibid.* 66 Secondguesser, one who is continually criticizing moves of players and manager. **1939** *New Yorker* 13 May 80/2 He may not be quite the wonder horse the flushed and eager second-guessers insist he is. **1941** B. SCHULBERG *What makes Sammy Run?* xi. 192 After *Deadline* the second-guessers were saying I could only make mellers [*sc.* melodramas]. **1942** BERREY & VAN DEN BARK *Amer. Thes. Slang* §637/3 *Second guesser*, a 'fan' who criticizes the umpire. **1950** R. CHANDLER *Let.* 9 Oct. (1966) 80, I suppose these primping second-guessers who call themselves critics think he shouldn't have written the book at all. **1953** BERREY & VAN DEN BARK *Amer. Thes. Slang* (1954) §671/5 *Second guesser*, a fan ready with advice on how the game should be played—after it is over. *Ibid.* §730/7 *Second guesser*, the pest who always knew what horse would win—after it has won. **1972** R. K. SMITH *Ransom* IV. 154 You're a professional second guesser, Stuart. Why didn't you speak up when we were discussing the question? **1978** *Times* 18 Apr. 16/5 President Johnson recognized the value of opposition and even appointed George Ball as his in-house second-guesser.

second hand, second-hand. Add: **B.** *adj.* **2. c.** *absol.* or quasi-*sb.* A second-hand book.

1905 *Westm. Gaz.* 21 Oct. 18/2 If a book..doesn't get a good sale within the first two months, it is no good as a second-hand. **1966** J. B. PRIESTLEY *Salt is Leaving* i. 6 He might be going off to some auction sale—y'know, to buy some more secondhands.

3. *second-hand shop* (examples). Also *second-hand bookstall, store.*

1795 J.-B. LECHEVALIER *Let.* in W. B. Stevens *Jrnl.* 24 Sept. (1965) III. 306 The old Plates, Plaisters, Sermons, Pieces of Iron, Brass and Copper that you purchased lately in that second hand Shop. **1875** L. TROUBRIDGE *Life amongst Troubridges* (1966) 115 Here there were all sorts of things..old iron stalls, second-hand book stalls. **1904** *Dialect Notes* II. 421 You can get most anything at the second-hand store. **1942** *Tee Emm* (Air Ministry) II. (recto rear cover), They may even end up on a second-hand bookstall. **1981** *Country Life* 16 July 205/1 A book very well worth looking out for in second-hand shops.

second-ha·ndedness. [f. SECOND-HANDED *a.* + -NESS.] The quality or condition of being second-hand or hackneyed; secondhandness.

1905 G. B. SHAW *Let. c* Aug. (1972) II. 551, I have striven hard to open English eyes to the emptiness of Shakespeare's philosophy, to the superficiality and second-handedness of his morality. **1920** R. MACAULAY *Potterism* II. iii. 90 Once you are tied up with a party, you can only avoid second-handedness, taking over views ready made. **1929** A. N. WHITEHEAD *Aims Educ.* iv. 79 The second-handedness of the learned world is the secret of its mediocrity.

second-ha·nder. *colloq.* Also **secondhander.** [f. SECOND-HAND *a.* + -ER[1].] **a.** A second-hand commodity. **b.** A second-hand shop.

1896 'MARK TWAIN' in *Harper's Mag.* Aug. 350/2, I.. see him buy a red flannel shirt and some old ragged clothes... I seen our other pal lay in *his* stock of old rusty second-handers. **1969** *Daily Tel.* (Colour Suppl.) 12 Dec. 27/4, I went to the secondhander and got some little nylon dresses, and bows for her hair. **1977** *Drive* Mar.–Apr. 40/3 Beware these secondhanders—they were made for fleet-buyers only.

seconding (se·kəndiŋ), *ppl. a.* *rare*$^{-1}$. [f. SECOND *v.*[1] + -ING[2].] That acts as a second or supporter.

1748 RICHARDSON *Clarissa* VII. xlix. 191 Curse upon my contriving genius! Curse upon my intriguing head, and upon my seconding heart!

secondment[2]. Add: Also in *transf.* sense (see *SECOND *v.*[2]); freq. in phr. *on secondment.*

1955 *Times* 25 July 7/5 It should be possible for oversea universities to defray such losses..if they wish to attract teachers on secondment. **1964** M. GOWING *Britain & Atomic Energy 1939–1945* x. 288 Ways would have to be found of overcoming the staffing difficulty by various kinds of secondment. **1966** C. SWEENEY *Scurrying Bush* i. 14 From East Africa.. I went to the Sudan on secondment to the Sudan Government. **1976** *Milton Keynes Express* 30 July 33/3 (Advt.), An experienced teacher required..to cover the secondment of the permanent teacher. **1982** *Guardian* 20 Apr. 1/4 Sir Michael was on secondment from Chloride, for which they received an undisclosed payment from BL.

secondness (se·kəndnės). [f. SECOND *a.* + -NESS.] The quality or fact of being second; *spec.*, in the philosophy of C. S. Peirce (see *PEIRCE), the category of fact or reaction that gives to the category of idea or quality ('firstness') its actual existence or form.

c **1890** C. S. PEIRCE *Coll. Papers* (1931) I. §358. 184 When the second suffers some change from the action of the first, and is dependent upon it, the secondness is more genuine. **1903** —— *Ibid.* §24. 7, I think we have here a mode of being of one thing which consists in how a second object is. I call that Secondness. **1934** *Mind* XLIII. 490 Secondness comprises the actual facts of the world—the *hic et nunc* of things. **1966** F. J. COPLESTON *Hist. Philos.* VIII. xiv. 312 The meaning of an intellectual concept can be explicated in terms of the ideas of necessary relations between ideas of secondness and ideas of firstness, between..ideas of volition or action and ideas of perception. *Ibid.* 322 From one point of view secondness can be called 'fact', while from another..it is existence or actuality.

1979 *Trans. Philol. Soc.* 177 The affixation of *me* will in El[amitic] terms have turned the '2nd' which *II-um* represents into '2nd-ness' for the mere purpose of rendering meaningful the addition to it of the locatival affix *ma*, 'in secondness' amounting in effect to an adverbial 'secondly'.

secondo (sėkǫ·ndo). *Mus.* [It., = second.] In a pianoforte duet, the lower part; the pianist who plays this part.

1792 J. A. K. COLIZZI *Three Duets for Two Performers on Harpsichord or Piano Forté* 2 Secondo. **1883** GROVE *Dict. Mus.* III. 30/2 In pianoforte duets..*Secondo* or 2 *do* is put over that [*sc.* the part] for the 'bass' [player]. **1954, 1965** [see *PRIMO *sb.* 1]. **1976** *Gramophone* Jan. 1218/1 The technical level of accomplishment, particularly on the part of the *secondo* player, is not all it should be.

second-rateness. Add: (Further examples.) Now the usual form.

1905 G. B. SHAW *Irrational Knot* p. xiii, This consoles us for the undeniable secondrateness of the people we do know. **1945** R. KNOX *God & Atom* vi. 84 We tacitly acknowledged in ourselves a kind of moral second-rateness which served as an excuse for low standards. **1976** *Times Lit. Suppl.* 17 Dec. 1576/4 The second-rateness of Douglas (but to be second-rate is to be next to first-rate).

second-rater. (Later examples.)

1916 E. POUND *Lett.* (1971) 87 Virgil is a second-rater, a Tennysonianized version of Homer. **1955** [see *BEACHED *ppl. a.* 3]. **1977** *Times Lit. Suppl.* 22 Apr. 481/2 His adamant opposition to American participation in Hitler's war damned him conclusively, for me, as a mean-minded second-rater or worse.

second sight. 3. (Earlier example.)

1859 L. WRAXALL tr. *Robert-Houdin's Mem.* II. i. 4 Chance led me straight to the invention of *second sight.*

secos, var. *SEKOS.

secousse. Add: **b.** *gen.* in Fr. sense. *poet. rare.*

1945 AUDEN *Coll. Poetry* 130 Blows a wind that whispers..Of hopes that will not survive the *secousse* of this spring Of blood and flames.

secrecy. Add: **5.** Special Comb.: **secrecy system,** a system for ensuring the secrecy of transmitted speech by scrambling it at the transmitter.

1940 [see *PRIVACY 1 b]. **1949** [see *communication theory* s.v. *COMMUNICATION 12].

secret, *a.* and *sb.* Add: **A.** *adj.* **1. h.** Also *secret session,* a meeting of a legislative or deliberative body, conducted in secret. orig. *U.S.*

1872 W. BAGEHOT *Eng. Const.* (ed. 2) p. xlvii, This objection might be easily avoided by requiring that the discussion upon treaties in Parliament like that discussion in the American Senate should be 'in secret session', and that no report should be published of it. **1916** H. H. ASQUITH in *Hansard Commons* 27 Nov. 37, I think it would be premature to consider this question till it has been decided whether a Secret Session should be held. **1940** W. S. CHURCHILL *Secret Session Speeches* (1946) 17 The reason why I asked the House to go into Secret Session was not because I had anything particularly secret or momentous to say. **1946** G. B. SHAW *Geneva* (ed. 2) 4 All threatening news was mentioned only in secret sessions of parliament, hidden under heavy penalties.

i. Also *secret dovetail* (Joinery): (see quot. 1972).

1882 W. J. CHRISTY *Joints* 168 Mitred Dovetail Joint... It is also designated secret dovetail. **1963** F. HILTON *Adv. Carpentry & Joinery* x. 180/2 Two members are jointed using a secret dovetail and the third stub-tenoned, with the surfaces mitred. **1972** *Gloss. Terms Timber* (*B.S.I.*) 52 *Secret dovetail*, a dovetailed angle in which dovetails are used but do not show on the face of either member.

n. Also *secret-dimpling, -smiling.*

1925 BLUNDEN *Eng. Poems* 83 Black was the secret-dimpling stream. **1928** —— *Retreat* 33 Thus the bright-templed rhyme Before the secret-smiling author came.

p. *secret life*: a private life of a nature concealed from the common observer; *spec.* one consisting of covert sexual dealings.

1880 (*title*) My secret life. **1927** E. M. FORSTER *Aspects of Novel* v. 113 Happiness and misery exist in the secret life, which each of us lives privately. **1928** GALSWORTHY *Swan Song* III. vii. 272 A secret life and Lippinghall! Long, long might that conjunction be deferred! **1973** L. COOPER *Tea on Sunday* xxvii. 207 Did you know that Holdsworth has a secret life?.. Lisa..saw him just going out of the bar with a glamour girl. **1976** C. BERMANT *Coming Home* I. vii. 107 My secret life was now revealed to my parents.

4. c. (*a*) **secret service.** Also, an organization which performs this function; *spec.* (*U.S.*) a government department concerned with national security.

1859 *Atlantic Monthly* Feb. 163/2 The Secret Service was doubled..while half Paris must have been under arrest. **1867** L. C. BAKER *Hist. U.S. Secret Service* 34 There is nothing in the Secret Service that demands a violation of honor, or a sacrifice of principle, beyond the ordinary rules of warfare. **1939** T. S. ELIOT *Old Possum's Bk. Pract. Cats* 34 And when the loss has been disclosed, the Secret Service say: 'It *must* have been Macavity!' **1972** *Police Rev.* 10 Nov. 1445/1 The principal mission of the United States Secret Service today is safeguarding the lives of the President of the United States, the Vice-President, and many other important personalities in public life. **1981** A. PRICE *Soldier no More* vii. 93 I've got it... You're in the Secret Service.

(*b*) **secret agent,** a person engaged on secret service, esp. espionage.

a **1715** [see GUARD *sb.* 7a]. **1837** J. P. HENDERSON *Let.* 5 Nov. in *Diplomatic Corresp. Texas* (Amer. Hist. Assoc.) (1911) III. 827 The Government of the United States.. [sent] a secret agent to Texas to enquire into her situation, power etc. **1893** S. WEYMAN *Gentleman of France* II. xviii. 136 You are here as the secret agent of the King of Navarre. **1907** CONRAD (*title*) The secret agent. **1939** G. GREENE *Confidential Agent* I. ii. 67 In melodrama a secret agent was never tired. **1973** W. FAIRCHILD *Swiss Arrangement* ix. 114 Lisa laughed suddenly. 'I never thought I'd be going to bed with a secret agent,' she said.

(*c*) **secret police,** a police organization operating in secret, *spec.* one owing allegiance to the state or government and used for political purposes. Also *secret policeman.*

1823 F. BURNEY *Waterloo Jrnl.* in *Jrnls. & Lett.* (1980) VIII. 394 Buonaparte..trusted in the address of that mental diving machine, his secret police, for warding off any hazard. **1863** 'OUIDA' *Held in Bondage* I. x. 233 The world has a trick of serving, like the Swiss Guard and the secret police, whichever side is uppermost and pays them best. **1910** A. BENNETT *Clayhanger* II. xiv. 257 Some concealed emissary of the Russian secret police. **1938** E. AMBLER *Cause for Alarm* vii. 119 The Ovra..has become a regularly constituted secret police force. **1973** D. MILLER *Chinese Jade Affair* xviii. 176 The woes of being a secret policeman during the visits of V.I.P. personalities. **1981** G. PRIESTLAND *Priestland's Progress* ii. 38 Paul..had begun life as a religious secret policeman commissioned to stamp out the Church.

e. secret list chiefly *Mil.*, a register of research work or developments about which information may not be disclosed. Also *transf.*

1933 *Meccano Mag.* Feb. 109/1 As the aeroplane is on the Air Ministry Secret List, performance figures are not yet available for publication. **1949** KOESTLER *Promise & Fulfilment* II. v. 269 The war research which they are doing..is still on the secret list. **1955** E. WAUGH *Officers & Gentlemen* I. x. 129 There's an agitation..to take you off the secret list. Heroes are urgently required to boost civilian morale. **1977** 'J. D. WHITE' *Salzburg Affair* vii. 63 A missile projector, brand new..and still on the secret list.

f. secret weapon, a weapon (often of potentially decisive force) classified as secret. Also *fig.* and *transf.*

1936 E. AMBLER *Dark Frontier* I. vi. 91 He once told me that in these days there was no such thing as a secret weapon. **1939** W. S. CHURCHILL *Into Battle* (1941) 150 The magnetic mine..may perhaps be Herr Hitler's much vaunted secret weapon. **1953** E. SIMON *Past Masters* II. 78 See the candid camera at work, that misnamed secret weapon. **1962** *Listener* 2 Aug. 160/2 The formidable Signor Mattei, who is Italy's anything but secret weapon. **1980** A. SCHOLEFIELD *Berlin Blind* II. 75 Ah, the secret weapons... They are going to bring England to her knees.

B. *sb.* **I. 3. c.** (Earlier example.) Also *secret of Polichinelle* = *SECRET DE POLICHINELLE.

1828 CARLYLE in *Foreign Rev.* II. III. 101 The 'open secret' is no longer a secret to him, and he knows that the Universe is *full* of goodness; that whatever has being has beauty. **1853** C. BRONTË *Villette* III. xxiii. 336, I wanted to prove to Miss Lucy that I *could* keep a secret... How many times has she saucily insinuated that all my affairs are the secret of Polichinelle!

secretagogue (sĭkrī·tăgǫg), *sb.* and *a. Physiol.* Also (*erron.*) **secreto-.** [f. SECRET(E *v.*[1] + Gr. ἀγωγός drawing forth.] **A.** *sb.* A substance which promotes secretion. **B.** *adj.* Tending to promote secretion.

1924 *Amer. Jrnl. Physiol.* LXVIII. 143 Secretin solutions prepared from different duodena..showed variations in their efficacy as pancreatic secretagogues. **1926** *Jrnl. Amer. Med. Assoc.* 28 Aug. 641/1 The acid washings of the upper portion of the small intestine collected from a living dog possess marked secretagogue action on the pancreas when intravenously injected. **1935** *Amer. Jrnl. Physiol.* CXII. 512 An extract of the duodenal mucosa which would possess certain properties, namely, that the intravenous injection of it would cause no secretion of pancreatic juice until acidified or that the secretagogue potency already present would be greatly increased by acidification. **1971** *Nature* 15 Oct. 497/1 We have tested this possibility in rats treated with a combination of two gastric secretogogues (substances which stimulate secretion of gastric juice), pentagastrin and carbachol.

secretaire[2]. Add: Also 8 **secretare. a.** (Earlier examples.)

1771 in *Maryland Hist. Mag.* (1919) XIV. 136 If you have moved it thence it may be in the old secretare in the Chappell. **1792** T. BLAIKIE *Diary Scotch Gardener* (1931) 235 He was forced by them to come to force or break open the Secretaire and drawers.

b. ‖ **secrétaire à abattant** (a abatañ), a variety of fall-front writing cabinet (see quot. 1977).

1920 F. M. ATKINSON tr. *R. de Félice's French Furnit. under Louis XVI & Empire* II. ii. 56 The *secrétaire à abattant* is one of the favourite pieces of this epoch... That is the large drop-front escritoire, a serious, rather masculine piece. **1936** *Burlington Mag.* May p. xvii/1 A magnificent upright Louis Quinze *secrétaire à abattant*, by B.V.R.B. (Boucher, already mentioned). **1967** *Times*

14 Mar. 21/6 Today,..at 11 a.m. at Blenstock House... Bureau Bookcase.., a Dutch Marquetry Secretaire a abattant. **1977** FLEMING & HONOUR *Penguin Dict. Decorative Arts* 718/1 A *secrétaire à abattant*..was first made in the C17 and was very popular in late-C18 France. It stands against a wall and looks like a cabinet or cupboard with the fall-front flap closed vertically.

secretarial, *a.* Add: **a.** (Later examples.) Also *spec.* designed for the training of office secretaries, as *secretarial college, course, school.*

1922 A. L. CHURCH *Training of Secretary* 193 (Index) Secretarial schools. **1935** R. STRACHEY *Careers & Openings for Women* II. iv. 140 Short six or seven months' secretarial courses to make sure of an early start. **1935** L. H. TURNER *Dict. Careers* 73 A few [scholarships are] given by the leading secretarial colleges. **1941** A. HUXLEY *Let.* 27 Nov. (1969) 473 Sophie has deserted acting for a secretarial school. **1953** B. GORDON-CUMMING *Gentle Rain* 119, I went through secretarial courses and things like that. **1967** K. GILES *Death in Diamonds* i. 7, I finished secretarial school and I speak four languages. **1976** M. MAGUIRE *Scratchproof* vii. 107 She'd left secretarial college bubbling with big job enthusiasm.

secretariat(e. Add: The form **secretariat** (also with initial capital) is now usual. Also, the administrative and executive department of a government or similar organization (as the United Nations), usu. directed by a Secretary(-General). Freq. in Communist use [cf. Russ. *sekretariát*].

1926 *Encycl. Brit.* III. 428/1 This 'plenum' elects..the Secretariat of the Central Committee of five members with two deputies. **1934** B. MAXWELL *Soviet State* iii. 42 The Central Committee of the Union..is divided into three sections: (1) a Secretariat, which performs the current work of organization and execution. **1934** WEBSTER, *Secretariat*,..the permanent organ of the League of Nations, comprising the Secretary-General, with officials and secretaries appointed by him. **1949** T. LIE *Road to Peace* 1 Next, I want to thank my staff, the members of the Secretariat. **1955** *Bull. Atomic Sci.* Mar. 85/2 The movement works through its secretariat in Amsterdam where the activities of its national groups are coordinated. **1965** A. NOVE in B. Pearce tr. *Preobrazhensky's New Economics* p. viii, The party secretariat did not yet have the importance it acquired under Stalin. **1977** *Whitaker's Almanack 1978* 957 The real power in the Party [Communist] is vested..in the Politbureau, the Secretariat and the permanent Departments of the Central Committee.

secretary, *sb.*[1] (and *a.*). Add: **A.** *sb.* **2.** Also *spec.* in various civil service and parliamentary sub-ministerial posts: *parliamentary private secretary*: see *PARLIAMENTARY *a.* 1; *permanent secretary*: see *PERMANENT *a.* 1 d; *second* (or *third*) *secretary*: a senior civil servant in the Treasury immediately subordinate to the permanent (or second) secretary.

1932 *Whitaker's Almanack 1933* 329/1 Treasury... Permanent Secretary and Head of H.M. Civil Service, Sir Warren Fisher... Second Secretary, Sir Richard V.N. Hopkins. **1939** *Whitaker's Almanack 1940* 433/1 Second Sec., Sir Richard V. N. Hopkins... Joint Third Secretaries, Sir Frederick Phillips..; Sir Alan Barlow. **1964** LD. BRIDGES *Treasury* xv. 145 The next rank in the Treasury is known as Second Secretary, which is the equivalent of a Permanent Secretary in other major departments. *Ibid.* 146 The next rank in the Treasury is Third Secretary which is the equivalent of a Deputy Secretary in a major department. **1976** in R. Crossman *Diaries* II. 200 Philip Allen (K.C.B. 1964) was Second Secretary to the Treasury 1963–6.

3. (Later examples in British and examples in U.S. use.)

In the United Kingdom, there have been numerous changes (too complex to set down here) in the nomenclature and duties of Secretaries of State since the nineteenth century. Since 1945, principal Secretaries of State have included the Secretary of State for the Home Department (Home Secretary), Foreign and Commonwealth Affairs (Foreign Secretary), Industry, Defence, Employment, and Northern Ireland. The title Chief Secretary (to the Treasury) was introduced in 1961: it is a ministerial appointment as opposed to the various civil servant Treasury Secretaries. The principal Secretary of State (usu. the Home Secretary) is sometimes referred to as the 'First Secretary'.

The nomenclature of senior U.S. cabinet ministers has also been subject to many changes.

1789 *Deb. Congr. U.S.* 26 Sept. (1834) 90, I likewise nominate Thomas Jefferson, for Secretary of State. **1846** J. K. POLK *Diary* 20 Mar. (1910) I. 293 Forty or fifty persons..called; among them the Russian Minister, the Secretary of State, [etc.]. **1906** 'MARK TWAIN' *Autobiogr.* (1924) I. 236 He had been ambassador, brilliant orator,.. admirable Secretary of State. **1940** W. FAULKNER *Hamlet* I. iii. 74 A gold-filled diploma from the Secretary of State at Jackson saying for all men to know by these presents, greeting, that them twenty thousand goats..is goats. **1961** *Times* 10 Oct. 12/1 As Chief Secretary (a title used for the first time) Mr. Brooke will come under the general policy direction of the Chancellor. **1962** *Hansard Commons* 19 July 632 The Prime Minister: My right hon. Friend the First Secretary of State will act as Deputy Prime Minister. *a* **1974** R. CROSSMAN *Diaries* (1975) I. 610 Oh dear, it is a panjandrum committee—the Prime Minister, First Secretary, Foreign Secretary, the Minister of Defence, the Minister of Labour for some reason, myself. **1976** *Billings* (Montana) *Gaz.* 20 June 8-A/4 Nixon, whom Bill Rogers (secretary of state from 1969 to 1973) referred to as the world's youngest elder statesman, had acquired enormous stature in world affairs.

4. (Later examples shortened from *secretary hand.*)

1969 M. B. PARKES *Eng. Cursive Book Hands 1250–1500* p. xx, One of the outstanding features of the history of English handwriting in the fifteenth century is the gradual infiltration of this new script, which in its English form we now call 'secretary', into all classes of books and documents, until by the sixteenth century it had become the principal script in use in this country. **1978** *Bodl. Libr. Rec.* IX. 324 The writing exercises..are confined to the rectos of the pages, except for practice alphabets in secretary and in a text hand on ff. 30b and 57b respectively.

5. (Earlier and further examples.) Now chiefly *U.S.*

1803 T. SHERATON *Cabinet Dict.* 303 *Secretary.* This term..among cabinet makers..is applied to certain pieces of furniture to write at. **1805** *Times* 7 Nov. 4/4 Genuine household furniture, and valuable Effects..consisting of..Excellent mahogany secretary and bookcase. **1819** A. CONSTABLE *Let.* 21 Mar. in J. Constable *Corr.* (1962) I. 178 The secretary in the White Room sold for 9 pounds or guineas, I forget which. **1865** G. W. BAGBY *Writings* (1885) II. 27 When you come to open his 'secretary'..you will find his bonds, accounts..lying about loose. **1975** D. RAMSAY *Descent into Dark* ii. 68 Anita.. was..stripping the finish from a maple secretary with a blowtorch. **1980** A. N. WILSON *Healing Art* xi. 129 There was a grandfather clock, and a roll-top secretary.

7. *secretary desk* (later example: for † read † exc. *U.S.*); (appositively) *secretary-treasurer, -typist*; **secretary-bird,** (*b*) [*BIRD *sb.* 1 d], a punning term for a young woman employed as a secretary; **secretary-general**: also *spec.* the title of the principal official of a Communist party or of some international organizations (as the United Nations); hence **secretary-generalship.**

1969 W. DOUGLAS-HOME (*title*) The secretary bird. **1974** I. MURDOCH *Sacred & Profane Love Machine* 50 Since Pinn had become what she called a 'secretary bird' she had become much smarter. **1976** DEAKIN & WILLIS *Johnny go Home* xvi. 184 Even London's 'Secretary Birds'..have problems finding somewhere to live. **1967** MRS. L. B. JOHNSON *White House Diary* 23 Apr. (1970) 509 Mr. Hoes showed me a secret drawer in the secretary desk. **1934** B. MAXWELL *Soviet State* iii. 42 In theory the Political Bureau is appointed by the Central Committee; in reality the Secretary-General of the Party, if he is powerful enough, makes the selection. This is the case at present, since Stalin is the Secretary-General. **1949** T. LIE *Road to Peace* 1 (*heading*) Secretary-General of the United Nations. **1954** E. H. CARR *Interregnum* 336 Speculating what the secretary-general would report at the next party congress. **1968** *U.N. Security Council Proc.* 10 in *Parl. Papers 1967–8* (Cmnd. 3757) XLII. 229 The Secretary-General deplores any resort to force to settle international problems, wherever it may occur, in contravention of the Charter of the United Nations. **1959** *Economist* 9 May 506/1 According to one view of secretary-generalship. **1977** *Westindian World* 3–9 June 10/1 The whole trend of his Secretary-Generalship so far..is to place the Commonwealth firmly in its global setting. **1920** *Constitution of Santa Barbara Club* (Santa Barbara, Calif.), Officers..Secretary-Treasurer William Wyles. **1979** *Yale Alumni Mag.* Apr. (Suppl.) cn 11/2 He is a past president and secretary-treasurer of the American Association of Law Schools. [**1939** *Daily Tel.* 18 Dec. 13/2 (Advt.), Secretary-shorthand-typist, good correspondent, required immediately for engineer.] **1957** S. SMITH *Not waving but Drowning* 34 Dark was the day for Childe Rolandine the artist When she went to work as a secretary-typist. **1976** *Milton Keynes Express* 2 July 4/4 His wife, a secretary-typist, had left for work.

se·cretary, *v.* [f. SECRETARY *sb.*[1]] **a.** *trans.* To assist (someone) secretarially. *nonce-use.* **b.** *intr.* To work as a secretary (esp. an office secretary). Also const. *to. colloq.* Hence **se·cretarying** *vbl. sb.*

1927 *Punch* 26 Oct. 450/1 Poor old Henry..is in the soup again... He secretaries my uncle,..and as a rule we lunch together. **1933** WODEHOUSE *Heavy Weather* v. 73 Fellow named Carmody, who has been secretarying there. **1958** *Times Lit. Suppl.* 26 Dec. 749/4 Dish-washing here, secretarying there, finally helping out as Bursar in a school dominated by the headmaster's demented wife. **1971** K. DICK *Ivy & Stevie* 55 Stevie..secretaried..to Sir Neville Pearson and Sir Frank Newnes. **1975** P. G. WINSLOW *Death of Angel* vi. 142 She got fed up with secretarying.

‖ **secret de Polichinelle** (səkre də poliʃinel). [Fr., secret of Polichinelle: see PUNCHINELLO.] A supposed secret which is generally known; an open secret.

1857 *Sat. Rev.* 14 Nov. 435/1 The accredited phrase in certain circles about the Court of Spain is, that there is a mystery about it; but the mystery is like the *secret de Polichinelle*. **1908** G. K. CHESTERTON *All Things Considered* 117 There is a..class of things which humanity does agree to hide... But..though they are, in one sense, a secret, they are also always a 'sécret [*sic*] de Polichinelle'. **1952** A. CHRISTIE *Mrs McGinty's Dead* xxiv. 171 A *secret de Polichinelle* is a secret that everyone can know. **1979** A. BUCHAN *Scrap Screen* vii. 103 It was a *secret de Polichinelle* in the Grosvenor family that the boy..was not the Dean's.

secretin (sĭkrī·tin). *Physiol.* [a. G. *secretin* (Bayliss & Starling 1902, in *Centralbl. f. Physiol.* XV. 682); cf. SECRETION and -IN[1].] A hormone that is released into the bloodstream from the gut, esp. in response to acidity, and stimulates pancreatic secretion.

1902 BAYLISS & STARLING in *Jrnl. Physiol.* XXVIII. 331 We have already suggested the name 'secretin' for this body, and as it has been accepted and made use of by subsequent workers it is as well to adhere to it. **1927** HALDANE & HUXLEY *Animal Biol.* i. 18 Food..stimulates the intestine chemically, causing it to secrete a special substance from its lining; this passes into the blood, circulates through the whole body, but, though it exerts no effect on most organs, it stimulates the pancreas..to activity. This substance is called secretin. **1962** [see *prosecretin* s.v. *PRO-[2] 1]. **1965** LEE & KNOWLES *Animal Hormones* viii. 121 Hydrochloric acid is not the only substance which induces the secretion of secretin; both digesting fat and bile salts are effective.

secretive, *a.* Add: Now usu. with pronunc. (sī·krĕtiv).

secretor (sĭkrī·tǫɹ). *Physiol.* [f. SECRET(E *v.*[1] + -OR, originally to render G. *ausscheider* (Schiff & Sasaki 1932, in *Klin. Wochenschr.* 20 Aug. 1428/2).] **a.** One who secretes appreciable amounts of blood-group antigens with his or her bodily fluids.

1941 *Amer. Jrnl. Obstetrics & Gynecol.* XLII. 933 This applies to about 80 per cent of all individuals (secretors) and if a fetus of Group A belongs to the class of non-secretors (20 per cent)..the maternal iso-agglutinin anti-A may serve as the source of the intrauterine hemolytic process. **1950** *Sci. News* XV. 111 Most people secrete the appropriate blood group substances (antigens) in bodily secretions such as saliva and tears. About one-seventh of the population, however, do not do this, and are called 'non-secretors'... Some cysts, in 'secretors', contain the A and B substances in very high concentration. **1962** R. JEFFRIES *Exhibit No. Thirteen* xi. 112 An examination of the semen enabled a typing to be made... The murderer is from group B and is what is known as a secretor. **1971** J. Z. YOUNG *Introd. Study Man* xl. 585 The secretor genes are quite independent of the ABO genes.

b. *gen.* One who or that which secretes.

1972 *Sci. Amer.* Aug. 46/2 Recently Everitt and his colleagues have learned that when the female monkey's adrenals—the principal secretors of the male hormone androstenedione—are removed, her sexual receptivity is greatly reduced. **1977** *Lancet* 22 Oct. 841/2 Of these secretors, 50% secreted 50 μl of fluid and 10% secreted as much as 400 μl of fluid.

2. *attrib.* **secretor character, status,** the state of being or not being a secretor (sense a).

1956 *Brit. Med. Jrnl.* 29 Sept. 728/1 We have obtained a series of unrelated duodenal ulcer cases and compared their secretor character with controls taken from the general population. **1970** GERSHOWITZ & NEEL in D. Aminoff *Blood & Tissue Antigens* 39 The secretor status of stomach cancer patients should be investigated. **1976** *Proc. R. Soc. Med.* LXIX. 36/2 Attempts have been made to discover whether individuals are carrying the dystrophia myotonica gene by examining their secretor status.

sect, *v.*[2] (Later example.)

1882 G. A. SALA *Amer. Revisited* II. ii. 19 Almost every thoroughfare in the city being sected and intersected by lines for horse-cars.

-sect [ad. L. *sect-*, pa. ppl. stem of *secāre* to cut: cf. SECT *v.*[2]], a formative element of vbs. (as *hemisect, transect, trisect*) and adjs. (as *multisect*); *spec.* in *Bot.* in adjs. denoting forms of leaves (as *palmatisect, pedatisect, pennatisect*).

sectarianism. (Earlier example.)

1817 COLERIDGE *Biogr. Lit.* I. xii. 249 The spirit of sectarianism has been..the cause of our failures. We have imprisoned our own conceptions by the lines, which we have drawn, in order to exclude the conceptions of others.

section, *sb.* Add: **2. e.** (*b*) (Examples.) (*d*) *Austral.* and *N.Z.* An area of undeveloped land, variable in size. (*e*) *Austral.* and *N.Z.* A plot of land suitable for building on. (*f*) In various African countries, an administrative district (see quot. 1951).

(*b*) **1785** *Jrnls. Continental Congr. U.S.* (1933) XXVIII. 299 The plats of the townships..shall be marked by subdivisions into sections of 1 mile square. **1809** F. CUMING *Sk. Tour Western Country* (1810) 197 This Crouse is a wealthy man, having..a farm of two sections, containing thirteen hundred acres. **1849** E. CHAMBERLAIN *Indiana Gazetteer* (ed. 3) 420 North of Eel river are about 40 sections of barrens intermixed with small prairies. **1890** *Stock Grower & Farmer* 8 Mar. 5/3 The intervening sections of the Atlantic and Pacific railroad land grant [in Arizona] are owned by the cattle men and are not fenced. **1924** H. CROY *R.F.D. No. 3* 3 He had only one hundred and twenty acres of land, while most of the farmers had a quarter, or a half section, even a section. **1975** *New Yorker* 27 Oct. 114/2 We have six hundred and forty acres—what you call a section—and they wish to flood it to make recreation.

(*d*) **1836** *S. Austral. Gaz. & Colonial Register* 18 June 4/2 Surveyed land shall be divided, as nearly as may be, into sections of eighty acres each, with the exception of the site of the first town, which shall be divided into acre sections. **1841** W. DEANS *Let.* 25 Mar. in J. Deans *Pioneers of Canterbury* (1937) i. 31 Some part of the rural sections may not just be what could have been wished. **1923** in J. Reid *Kiwi Laughs* (1961) His idea was that he and I should get the firewood rights on a thousand-acre section, up under the mountain reserve. **1950** *N.Z. Jrnl. Agric.* Jan. 26/2 Ten 10-acre sections have been allocated to returned servicemen.

(*e*) **1836** [see (*d*) above]. **1851** *Lyttelton* (N.Z.) *Times* 11 Jan. 5 The immediate choosing of the town acre sections has been a most important and useful measure. **1886** F. Hume *Myst. Hansom Cab* (1887) v. 19 She.. purchased a small section at St. Kilda, and built a house on it. **1935** J. Guthrie *Little Country* ii. 43 They would much rather have had an eighth-acre section. **1961** B. Crump *Hang on Minute Mate* 97 Tony..was paying off a section in Tokoroa and talking about putting in for one of them Government loans to build a house with. **1977** *N.Z. Herald* 8 Jan. 4–6/2 (Advt.), Waiheke Island, sections and batches urgently wanted.

(*f*) **1951** K. L. Little *Mende of Sierra Leone* v. 104 The overall picture..is one of small towns around each of which is spread a number of component villages. This combination of town and villages constitutes a social and political entity which, in the older sense, corresponds to what is officially termed, nowadays, the 'section' of a chiefdom. **1957** M. Banton *W. Afr. City* viii. 151 He is assisted by seven section chiefs and certain tribal officials. **1977** *Times of Zambia* 7 Sept. 7/7 He has received the reports from all governors in the province on the recent village and section elections.

g. (Later examples.) Also, the fourth part of a platoon; now used of various small tactical units.

1913 *Army Order 323* 1 Oct. 4 The non-commissioned officers and men of the machine-gun section..will be distributed for discipline and administration in peace amongst the four companies. **1915** D. O. Barnett *Let.* 24 Mar. in *Denis Oliver Barnett* (1915) 100 At first I thought the whole section was done in, as rifles and equipment flew in the air. **1939** J. T. Gorman *Army of To-Day* iii. 69 All the men in a section or platoon are taught to use the light (Bren) machine-gun *individually*. **1943** *Britain's Mod. Army* ix. 192/2 Columns of threes are now used, each column in a platoon representing a section with the commander at its head. Thus a section can 'peel off' quickly to a threatened flank, without leaving a gap in the column as used to occur when a section left the old column of fours. **1968** R. M. Barnes *Brit. Army of 1914* i. 35 The infantry advanced in small parties—probably sections in fours, spaced out at fairly wide intervals, or in a 'diamond formation' of sections or platoons.

n. *U.S. Railways.* (See quot. 1890.)

1872 *Newton Kansan* 3 Oct. 3/2 The caboose and the next three cars to it of the 1st section was badly smashed up. **1890** *Railways of Amer.* 162 But the more usual way of handling extra trains, when circumstances will permit, is to let them precede or follow a regular train upon the same schedule. The train is then said to be run in 'sections', and a ten minutes' interval is allowed between them. **1948** *Chicago Tribune* 11 Apr. 1 Ho! the second section! And no flagman out from the train we stopped.

o. *Mus.* A group of similar instruments forming part of a band or orchestra; also the players of such instruments. See also *rhythm section* s.v. *rhythm *sb.* 9 a.

1880 Grove *Dict. Mus.* II. 569/2 The Instrumental Band, as now constituted, naturally divides itself into certain sections, as distinct from each other as the Manuals of an Organ. **1944** W. Apel *Harvard Dict. Mus.* 520/1 It is only in the use of a relatively strong string section that Monteverdi's orchestra is progressive. **1955** Keepnews & Grauer *Pictorial Hist. Jazz* 103/2 Those two men added were both saxophone players; the total of three, instead of a single clarinetist, made a 'section'. That of course is one of the key words, one of the fundamentals of big-band music. **1977** J. Wainwright *Do Nothin'* viii. 124 The sax section—Ric..fills it out, with the tenor.

p. A metal bar, esp. one with a cross-section that is not a simple shape (see quots.).

1881 *Jrnl. Iron & Steel Inst.* 703 A book containing rules and measurements for the construction of various forms of sections of rolled iron, has been drawn up... It is full of formulae applicable to different sizes and forms of sections. **1902** *Ibid.* LXII. 499 Vollkommer suggests an arrangement of plant for the continuous casting and rolling of light sections from fluid metal. **1924** H. J. Skelton *Econ. Iron & Steel* 278 In Great Britain the product in bars or rods shaped in a rolling mill, when not round or square or flat in cross section, is called a 'section' or sectional material. **1956** A. K. Osborne *Encycl. Iron & Steel Industry* 412/2 Structural shapes. (Sections.) Hot rolled steel bars of various cross-sectional contours such as channels, angles, bulb angles, I and H beams, T and Z bars, joists and other complicated contours. **1965** M. H. T. Alford tr. *Tselikov & Smirnov's Rolling Mills* ii. 28/2 The second type [of mill] is used for lighter sections nearer in size to the products of medium section mills. **1971** W. K. V. Gale *Iron & Steel Industry* 181 *Section (shape) (profile)*, any rolled product which is not a round, square, or flat. This is British usage. In USA the term is often shape and in Europe, profile.

q. *Austral.* and *N.Z.* A fare stage on a bus or tram route.

1931 V. Palmer *Separate Lives* 285 He had travelled out the two sections to Aunt Rachel's dingy little house in the suburbs. **1948** *Landfall* June 112 He fingered the two pennies that remained from the half-crown... He'd have to walk to the end of the first section, catch the tram there.

7. a. (sense 2 e (*b*)) *section corner*; (sense 2 k) *section boss, crew, hand, man* (earlier and later examples), *master* (earlier example), *work*; (sense *2 o) *section man, work*.

1870 *Daily Territorial Enterprise* (Virginia City, Nevada) 22 Oct. 3/1 The clothes of the section boss caught upon the brake..as he was in the act of jumping off. **1947** K. D. Lumpkin *Making of Southerner* 163 The deacon was section boss on the railroad. **1817** *Niles' Weekly Reg.* XII. 97/2 At the distance of every mile..section corners are established. **1947** *Mich. Hist.* Sept. 319 He traced it up to the section corner and discovered that the cruiser had signed his name on the tree. **1884** Section-crew [see *push-car* s.v. *push-]. **1962** W. Stegner *Wolf Willow* i. ii. 33 Anonymously denounced in the *Leader* for nearly derailing the speeder of a section crew. **1976** *Columbus* (Montana) *News* 1 July 8/4 My sister and her friend thought I should go on the hand-car with the section crew. **1873** *Newton Kansan* 27 Feb. 3/2 A drunken section hand..laid down upon the railroad track to take a nap. **1904** F. Lynde *Grafters* xxiii. 284 When the section hands pelt stray dogs with new spikes from the stock keg. **1969** *Islander* (Victoria, B.C.) 2 Nov. 5/2 There are no sectionhands in the pass these days, nature finally triumphed in the thirties, closing the line. **1869** W. H. Jackson *Jrnl.* 1 Aug. in *Time Exposure* (1940) xi. 182 Got the section men to take us aboard their handcar. **1921** *Daily Colonist* (Victoria, B.C.) 23 Oct. 27/5 A section man..was killed last night while jumping from a moving train. **1936** D. McCowan *Animals Canad. Rockies* viii. 73 In spring..the section men burn the grass along the right-of-way of the railroad. **1955** L. Feather *Encycl. Jazz* vii. 194 Reluctant soloist but excellent sectionman. **1872** W. S. Huntington *Road-Master's Asst.* p. iii, The enormous expense of track repairs..may be greatly reduced by a reform in the every-day practice of the track-layer and section-master. **1891** C. Roberts *Adrift in Amer.* 71 Section work is track repairing. **1958** C. Fox in P. Gammond *Decca Bk. Jazz* vii. 91 Its attack and vitality ..made up for any roughness in the section-work. **1977** J. Wainwright *Do Nothin'* v. 66 Miller's secret? Size, tight section work and damn good arrangers.

b. Section Eight (also **8**) *U.S. Mil. slang*, discharge from the Army under section eight of Army Regulations 615–360 on the grounds of insanity or inability to adjust to Army life; hence **section-eight** *v.*, (usu. in *pass.*) to discharge from the Army on such grounds; **section head,** (*a*) the person in charge of a section of an organization; (*b*) the heading of a section of a newspaper or periodical; **section house,** (*b*) *U.S.* a house occupied by the men responsible for the maintenance of a section of a railway; **section-line,** (*a*) delete † and add later examples; now only *U.S.*; **section sergeant**, a police sergeant in charge of a section.

1943 *Yank* 23 July 15/2 If it weren't for Yank and its puzzles I'm sure there would be plenty of Section 8s in places like this. **1945** *Yank* 7 Dec. 8/1 Nobody knew whether he was getting section-eighted out of the Army. **1950** E. Hemingway *Across River & into Trees* xxxiii. 207 You stay in until you are hit badly or killed or go crazy and get section-eighted. **1971** J. Aiken *Nightly Deadshade* iii. 31 The place..becomes a reservoir of feebles, bullied by the section heads. **1973** W. H. Hallahan *Ross Forgery* ii. 14 Redhaired man with a Sandhurst accent..a former section head of British Military Intelligence. **1977** *Time* 15 Aug. 5/2 The new format includes different section heads, a new type face for headlines, hairline rules to set off columns. **1869** W. H. Jackson *Jrnl.* 24 Aug. in *Time Exposure* (1940) xi. 183 Decided to board at the section house rather than cook ourselves. **1903** *N.Y. Even. Post* 29 Aug. 1/2 Crowbars and tools.. were identified as having been taken from the railroad section house. **1976** *Columbus* (Montana) *News* 1 July 8/4, I accompanied my sister and her beau to a dance at a section house near the railroad. **1872** *Newton Kansan* 12 Sept. 2/4 The farmers..are leaving space for a road along the section lines. **1948** H. A. Jacobs *We chose Country* 24 We bowled along, climbing past snatches of woods and the straight section-line roads to a high plateau. **1956** *Police Jrnl.* XXIX. 1. 52 Sergeants are 'right in the picture'. Supervising each man on his patrol is still an important part of his duties but he is now the head of a team whose job is to police the section. **1964** M. Banton *Policeman in Community* ii. 15 The division is divided into four sections, each of which is in the charge of a sergeant. .. Their section sergeants use the station as their headquarters and go out from there to supervise their constables. **1973** J. Wainwright *Pride of Pigs* 12 Sergeant Crawley took some backhanders... Are you in favour of section sergeants taking nawpings?

section, *v.* Add: **1. c.** With *off*: to make (an area, part of a structure, etc.) into a separate section.

1960 'E. McBain' *Give Boys Great Big Hand* xiii. 156 The Carellas had sectioned off one corner of the house and disconnected the heating to it. **1976** J. Snow *Cricket Rebel* 72 The authorities sectioned off the stand next to the dressing room for Army marksmen.

sectional, *a.* Add: **1. a.** (Earlier U.S. example.)

1806 *Deb. Congr. U.S.* (1852) 15 Apr. 1042 Let a narrow, selfish, local, sectional policy prevail and struggles will commence.

3. (Examples.)

1901 *Furniture Rec.* 15 June Suppl. 4 The Gunn K.D. Sectional Book Cases. **1909** 'O. Henry' *Roads of Destiny* v. 74 A word from me was more to them than a whole deckle-edged library from East Aurora in sectional bookcases was from anybody else. **1937** *Discovery* Feb. 35/1 They had hoped to use a very light sectional building. **1957** *Times* 2 July (Agric. Suppl.) p. vi/2 A typical old barn now houses the grain intake pit, cleaner, pre-dry bin, continuous dryer, and sectional storage bins. **1960** *Which?* Jan. 5 Sectional boiler, coke-fired.

4. Of steel: rolled in the form of sections (sense *2 p).

1881 *Jrnl. Iron & Steel Inst.* 703 The sectional forms given..are intended to supply the requirements of engineers engaged in the construction of railways, warehouses, public buildings, and similar work. **1916** *Ibid.* XCIII. 354 All the sectional material rolled differs from the ideal by not giving equal distribution of stress in the material. **1924** H. J. Skelton *Econ. Iron & Steel* 279 Wherever practicable, it is desirable that rolled shapes or sectional material in mild steel should be ordered from the list of British Standard Sections.

B. *ellipt.* as *sb.* A piece of furniture composed of sections which can be used separately; *spec.* one which can be used either as a sofa or as a set of chairs. *U.S.*

1961 in Webster. **1972** *Village Voice* (N.Y.) 1 June 3/1 (Advt.), Top quality convertible sofas & sectionals. **1977** *Time* 28 Mar. 50/2 One day Lily and Richard decided that the living-room sofa would look better as a sectional. Practical kids, they picked up a saw and divided it into three pieces. **1980** *Redbook* Oct. 86 (Advt.), Display the sectionals alone or group them with matching modular pieces.

sectionalization (se:kʃənăləizē̆i·ʃən). [f. Sectionalize *v.* + -ation.] The action or result of dividing into sections.

1904 in Webster. **1920** *Public Opinion* 17 Sept. 268/1 The very formula of 'nationalisation' was a sham, sectionalisation was the object. **1933** *Archit. Rev.* LXXIII. 110/2 What gives interest to London is the diversity of its quarters without extreme sectionalization. **1966** *McGraw-Hill Encycl. Sci. & Technol.* VIII. 490/1 Sectionalization is a method of distributing mine power so that power cables can be isolated..without shutting off the mains supply to several working sections.

sectionalize, *v.* Add: **1.** Chiefly as **se·ctionalized** *pa. pple.* and *ppl. a.* (Further examples.) Hence **se·ctionalizing** *vbl. sb.*

1937 *Discovery* Nov. 360/1 A sectionalised enquiry into the bases of photographic construction. **1957** *Practical Wireless* XXXIII. 357/3 (Advt.), Sectionalised windings ensure low leakage inductance and brilliant top note response. **1965** J. Bingham *Fragment of Fear* iv. 67 Luckily I have a sectionalised mind, and my thoughts were now on Juliet. **1971** *Nature* 7 May 2/1 In the event.. the foundation may have been lumbered with a number of vested interests which will sectionalize its proceedings. **1976** *Gramophone* Sept. 506/1 It will be seen from the accompanying sectionalized photo..that there are two magnetic gaps. **1977** *Ibid.* Feb. 1343/3 By intelligent sectionalizing, it has been possible to produce modules which can be tested and proved individually before incorporation.

sectionist. Add: † **2.** *N.Z.* The owner or occupier of a section (sense *2 e (*d*)) of land. *Obs.*

1841 W. Deans *Let.* 25 Mar. in J. Deans *Pioneers of Canterbury* (1937) i. 32 The secondary sectionists are to choose their land at Wanganui.

sectionize, *v.* Add: **a.** (Later U.S. examples.) Also *absol.*

1872 *Rep. Indian Affairs 1871* (U.S.) 185 [Various tribes] were induced either to sectionize, or in some way to admit white settlers. **1873** J. H. Beadle *Undeveloped West* 399 He is the only Choctaw in the district who is in favor of sectionizing and admitting white immigration. **1949** *Surveying & Mapping* Jan.–Mar. 31/2 Long before Florida was sectionized by ranges and townships, rulers of the Old World bestowed favors on a selected few supporters by granting them titles to vast parcels of land in America.

sector, *sb.* Add: **I. 2.** Further extended or specific senses.

g. (*a*) *Mil.* A part or section of a front, corresponding generally to a sector of a circle the centre of which is a headquarters.

1916 'Boyd Cable' *Action Front* 237 The Colonel was.. vainly trying to recall any sap-head within his sector of line. **1917** W. J. Locke *Red Planet* xiv. 161 Somewhere in this region—or sector, as we call it nowadays—there was a certain bit of ground that had been taken and retaken over and over again. **1930** S. Sassoon *Mem. Infantry Officer* iv. 61 Rose Trench..and Willow Avenue, were among the first objectives in our sector [of the Somme attack].

(*b*) A part or branch of an economy, or of a particular industry or activity. Freq. in phrases *private sector* (see *private *a.* 7 j), *public sector* (see *public *a.* 2 j).

1937 A. Huxley *Ends & Means* xii. 196 The accomplished intellectual understands the relations subsisting between many sectors of apprehended reality. **1950** *Hansard Commons* 7 Mar. 183 Every Member of this House ..could point to examples of gross feather bedding both in Government Service, in the socialised sector of the economy and in private industry. **1959** *Listener* 5 Nov. 767/2 Problems of a comparable nature in other sectors of industry. **1964** *Ann. Reg. 1963* 195 The Government's failure to carry out its declared aims—land reform..and planned development in all sectors of the economy—was to some extent caused by the President's readiness to yield too easily to pressure. **1980** *Sci. Amer.* Sept. 134/1 This development is the outcome of an explicit long-term policy to establish an adequate indigenous capacity in all the basic sectors, particularly metals and machinery, heavy chemicals.

(*c*) *gen.* One of the regions or districts into which a geographical area has been divided.

1943 H. A. Wallace *Century of Common Man* (1944) 82 The ignorance that clouds many communities in many sectors of our own nation. **1958** *Listener* 9 Oct. 547/1 It has recently become fashionable to divide the Middle East into two major entities: the Arab sector and the non-Arab sector. **1971** *Daily Tel.* 12 Apr. 2/1 Experts believe nearly half of the country's daily oil consumption will be produced from the British sector of the sea by 1976.

h. *Computers.* A subdivision of a track on a magnetic drum or disc, or the block of data stored on it.

1958 *Computer Jrnl.* I. 128/1 Information is stored on 'sectors', each capable of containing 32 numbers... There are 1,024 such sectors, two to each track on a drum. **1962** *Gloss. Terms Automatic Data Processing (B.S.I.)* 68 *Sector*, a specified part of a track or band on a magnetic disc or drum store: hence, in programming, a deprecated alternative name for a block applied to the group of words stored on a sector. **1976** G. WIEDERHOLD *Database Design* ii. 40 If tracks cannot be divided by hardware into sectors, system software may divide a track into smaller units.

i. *Gram.* The position in a sentence normally occupied by any one of the basic units of which the sentence is composed. Cf. *sector analysis*, sense 3 below.

[**1955** E. H. JORDEN *Syntax Colloq. Jap.* v. 13 Evidence furnished by focus-classes indicates that minor sector boundaries should be observed even here—that the IC division should occur between the gerund of the copula and the following verb, where the sector boundary occurs.] **1966** R. L. ALLEN *Verb Syst. Present-Day Amer. Eng.* iii. 88 An examination of a large number of sequences suggests that in most non-literary sentences there is a kind of 'spectrum' of basic positions, which may be called 'sectors'. **1968** R. CRYMES *Some Syst. Substitution Correlations in Mod. Amer. Eng.* ii. 36 The major positions in the major English sentence, which is a sentence having time orientation [,]..exist in fixed sequence, and they are called sectors. **1974** CHISHOLM & MILIC *Eng. Lang.* VII. lii. 424 According to the grammatical description called Sector Analysis, the English sentence consists of ten sectors.

3. sector analysis *Gram.*, the analysis of sentences in terms of the positions occupied by the basic units of which they are composed (cf. sense 2 i above); **sector scanning**, scanning with radar, sonar, or the like in which the detector rotates to and fro through a fixed angle; so **sector scan** *sb.* (freq. *attrib.*, with hyphen).

1966 R. L. ALLEN *Verb Syst. Present-Day Amer. Eng.* iii. 88 The order..of the occupied sectors remains constant... Many of the details of this 'sector' analysis lie beyond the scope of the present study. **1971** D. T. BÌNH *Tagmemic Comparison of Structure of Eng. & Vietnamese Sentences* iii. 66 Sector analysis..primarily emphasizes the positions of units on the sentence, trunk, and predicate.. levels. **1977** *Amer. Speech 1975* L. 127 Only the concluding chapters give any attention to the problems of composition, and much of this is a discussion of sector analysis. **1946** *Radar: Summary Rep. & Harp Project* (U.S. Nat. Defense Res. Comm.) 143/2 *Sector scan*, motion of the scanner reflector back and forth through a limited angle, instead of through 360°. **1969** R. P. SELBY in C. J. Richards *Mech. Engin. in Radar & Communications* ix. 387 Radar installations used for air-traffic control are sometimes required to operate on demand in sector-scan mode, the area of scan usually not exceeding 20° and the rate of scan approximately 20 scans per minute. **1978** *Nature* 9 Nov. 174/1 A simple sector scan mode is used, at a frequency of 1 Hz, with the target coupled acoustically to the transducer with water. **1946** *Princ. & Applic. of Underwater Sound* (U.S. Nat. Defense Res. Comm.) (1968) xi. 213/1 A plan position indicator is..required for sector scanning, the CRO spot..tracing a synchronous map of the motion of the active region. **1969** R. P. SELBY in C. J. Richards *Mech. Engin. in Radar & Communications* ix. 386 It is sometimes required to move an antenna system about a vertical axis in an oscillatory mode (sector-scanning), thereby turning the antenna through a limited arc in either direction. **1974** Y. KIKUCHI in G. W. Stroke et al. *Ultrasonic Imaging & Holography* 267 Asberg has been proposing a high speed sector scanning of a focusing mirror system receiver for obtaining an ultrasonic cinematogram of the living heart. **1977** *Navy News* July 18/2 Because the number of wrecks on our continental shelf is so high..modern equipment such as Hydrosearch—the British sector-scanning surveying sonar—is particularly needed.

sectoral, *a.* Add: **b.** (See *SECTOR *sb.* 2 g.)

1969 P. ANDERSON in Cockburn & Blackburn *Student Power* 223 There were various sectoral attacks and refutations of Marx by marginalist economists like Böhm-Bawerk. **1971** *Seminar* Nov. 12/2 The second..category of English dailies in India is of the more 'professional' dailies... Lumped together, they certainly represent what may be called 'a sectoral monopoly'. **1981** *Times* 13 Aug. 16/4 In the sectoral breakdown, the statistics show that the banks have increased their support to manufacturing industry.

2. *sectoral horn* (Radio), a horn antenna having a rectangular cross-section and plane sides flared in one dimension only.

1939 W. L. BARROW in *Proc. IRE* XXVII. 41 A horn whose cross section is rectangular and whose sides flare in one direction only..will be termed a sectoral horn. **1959** K. HENNEY *Radio Engin. Handbk.* (ed. 5) xx. 88 The sectoral horn is flared in one dimension only, either in the plane parallel to the electric vector (*E* plane) or in the plane parallel to the magnetic vector (*H* plane).

sectored (se·ktəɪd), *a.* [f. SECTOR *sb.* + -ED[2], or SECTOR *v.* + -ED[1].] Divided into sectors; applied *spec.* to a disc divided into alternate black and white sectors of equal size.

1900 W. M. STINE *Photometrical Measurements* i. 21 Illumination..viewed through a sectored disk, rotating at a critical speed. **1972** *Nature* 13 Oct. 407/1 He demonstrated this phenomenon by using a black-and-white sectored disk rotated on a phonographic turntable.

sectorial, *a.*[1] Add: **c.** *Bot.* Applied to a type of chimæra (see quot. 1968). Also as *sb.* [ad. G. *sektorialchimäre* (E. Baur 1909, in *Zeitschr. f. induktive Abstammungs- u. Vererbungslehre* I. 342).]

1927 *Jrnl. Genetics* XVIII. 257 In a sectorial plant a sector (of the stem) is formed of tissue of another species or type. *Ibid.*, Sectorials of the type to which the term is restricted in this paper are of very rare occurrence. **1934** W. NEILSON JONES *Plant Chimaeras & Graft Hybrids* ii. 18 True sectorial chimaeras are relatively uncommon; most of the plants recorded as 'sectorials' were probably mericlinal in structure. **1959** *New Biol.* XXX. 38 The first composite branch to arise had one side producing tomato leaves and the other producing nightshade leaves, and it was, therefore, concluded that the branch was composed half of tomato tissue and half of nightshade tissue. This type of structure is known as a Sectorial chimera. **1968** [see *PERICLINAL *a.* 2 b].

Hence **secto·rially** *adv.*, in or into sectors.

1963 *Heredity* XVIII. 266 These plants have..a sectorially divided growing point.

sectorization (se:ktəraizē[i]·ʃən). *rare.* [f. SECTOR *sb.* + -IZE + -ATION.] Division into sectors; administration or operation on the basis of sectors or local divisions.

1962 *Flight International* LXXXII. 479/1 Traffic growth in recent years has increased the pressure on both pilots and controllers, especially in the sphere of voice communications, so that means have had to be found to reduce their workload. Various alleviating possibilities have been tested, such as 'sectorization', but they in turn usually introduce new difficulties. **1976** *Social Psychiatry* XI. 27 Sectorization of the psychiatric care, which means that all psychiatric care within a geographical area should be under a common management.

Secuana, var. *SECHUANA.

secular, *a.* Add: **I. 3. b.** Also *secular-minded* adj.

1899 T. VEBLEN *Theory of Leisure Class* xii. 314 The sacerdotal scheme of life..does not hold good for the clergy of those denominations which have..diverged from the old established schedule of beliefs or observances... Their manner of life..does not differ in an extreme degree from that of secular-minded persons. **1930** A. BIRRELL *Et Cetera* 159 An equally veracious, though most secular-minded Presbyterian divine. **1957** N. FRYE *Anat. Criticism* 265 In the Anglo-Saxon congregation of Wulfstan there must have been a few secular-minded highbrows who were thinking..of the preacher's mastery of alliterative rhythm.

II. 7. a. *secular equation*, also more widely, any equation of the form $| a_{ij} - b_{ij}\lambda | = 0$ $(i, j = 1, 2, \ldots, n)$, in which the left-hand side is a determinant and which arises in quantum mechanics; (further examples).

1937 E. C. KEMBLE *Fund. Princ. Quantum Mech.* x. 361 Its components must yield a nontrivial (*i.e.*, nonvanishing) solution of the set of *g* equations $\Sigma_n(A_{mn} - a\delta_{mn})x_n = 0$... Such a solution exists only if the determinant of the coefficients vanishes, *i.e.*, if *a* is a root of the so-called 'secular' equation det $(\mathbf{A} - a\mathbf{I}) = ..0$. **1974** GILL & WILLIS *Pericyclic Reactions* i. 21 To obtain the wave functions corresponding to these energies it is necessary to solve the secular equations using the appropriate values of *E*.

8. *Econ.* and *Statistics.* Of a fluctuation or trend: occurring or persisting over an unlimited period; not periodic or short-term.

1895 A. MARSHALL *Princ. Econ.* (ed. 3) I. v. v. 470 There are secular movements of normal price, caused by the gradual growth of knowledge, of population and of capital, and the changing conditions of demand and supply from one generation to another. **1926** L. D. EDIE *Econ.* II. iv. 49 Economic fluctuations fall into four major types: seasonal, secular, cyclical, and residual. **1971** H. S. SHRYOCK et al. *Methods & Materials Demography* II. xiii. 377/2 If the observations are made at different times of the year, seasonal movements may also be apparent. When we are trying to describe the growth of a population over a relatively longer period of time (for example, India from 1872 to 1961) we are generally interested in the secular trend only. **1973** *Daily Tel.* 15 Jan. 17/6 This is the first time the Government has had to pay so much for money but the secular trend of interest rates will stop rising only if the rate of inflation is brought down. **1976** *Sci. Amer.* Sept. 107/1 The secular trend of workers migrating out of agricultural jobs as a result of technological change in agriculture has recently slackened.

secularist, *sb.* (and *a.*) **4.** (Earlier example.)

1888 MRS. H. WARD *R. Elsmere* III. VI. xxxviii. 166 The most notorious secularist lecturers held forth.

secularly, *adv.* Add: **3.** *Astr.* Over a long period of time.

1971 *Nature* 24 Dec. 453/1 We might expect δf to be secularly dependent in the same way as H_e ($\propto P^{-2}$). **1979** *Ibid.* 20 Sept. 200/1 Even in the worst case of deviation from thermal equilibrium, that is when the fully convective star expands adiabatically,..the system would still be secularly stable against mass exchange.

secule (se·kiul). *Geol. Obsolescent.* [f. L. *sæculum* age, generation.] A period of geological time corresponding to a stratigraphical zone; = *MOMENT *sb.* 2 d.

1903 A. J. JUKES-BROWNE in *Geol. Mag.* X. 37 The term hemera may, however, be occasionally convenient to signify the duration of a subzone, as age signifies the duration of a stage, but if we want to avoid confusion we must not speak of the hemera of a zone. For this another word should be coined..I would suggest that the Latin word *seculum* will furnish us with 'secule' which finds an actual French equivalent in *siècle*. **1933** W. J. ARKELL *Jurassic Syst. Gt. Brit.* i. 21 Several hemeræ may be contained in one secule or zone-moment. **1956** *Amer. Jrnl. Sci.* CCLIV. 459 Schindewolf reasserts..his extreme view ..that the zone as conceived by Oppel was a purely chronological notion and that the term zone should be used only as a time term (= secule). **1969** [see *MOMENT *sb.* 2 d].

secundigravida (sĭkʊndigræ·vidă). *Obstetrics.* Pl. **idas-, -idæ.** Also **secundagravida.** [mod.L., f. as next + *gravida*, fem. of *gravidus* GRAVID *a.*] A woman pregnant for the second time.

1904 in STEDMAN *Dunglison's Dict. Med. Sci.* (ed. 23) 1007/1. **1940** *Amer. Jrnl. Obstetr. & Gynecol.* XL. 988 Eighty-seven examinations were upon primigravidas, 61 upon secundigravidas, and 114 upon patients of greater parity. **1977** *Lancet* 22 Jan. 195/2 This policy should be restricted to secundigravidæ and those who have had two babies.

secundipara (sĭkʊndi·pără). *Obstetrics.* Pl. **-paras,-paræ** [mod. L., f. *secundus, secundi-* second + *-para*, fem. of *-parus*, from *parere* to bring forth.] A woman who has twice been delivered of children.

1897 *Lippincott's Med. Dict.* 918/2 *Secundipara*, a woman bearing a child for the second time. **1938** *Nature* 24 Dec. 1121/2 Cases with metastatic tumours were associated with a significant increase in the amount of trimethylamine... In primiparæ, the average amount was 0·30 and in secundiparæ 0·29. **1972** E. C. HUGHES *Obstetr.-Gynecol. Terminol.* vii. 332 A secundipara is a woman who has given birth for the second time to an infant or infants, alive or dead, weighing 500 gm or more.

secundum. Add: *secundum idem*, 'according to the same argument, calculation, etc.', in the same manner or respect.

1696 J. SERGEANT *Method to Sci.* 390 To Affirm that the Atome is Chang'd according to One of those Different Regards or Notions, *viz* the Form, and Not-chang'd according to the Other, viz the Matter, has not the least show of Affirming and Denying *secundum idem*; nor, consequently, the least show of a Contradiction. **1865** S. HODGSON *Time & Space* ii. 140 The two objects are then not limited and unlimited secundum idem. **1882** W. JAMES in *Mind* Apr. 187 The union and the division are not *secundum idem*: it divides them by keeping them out of the space between, it unites them by keeping them out of the space beyond.

secure, *a.* Add: **II. 3. f.** Of a telephone (line): free from the risk of being tapped (*TAP *v.*[1] 2 c).

1961 in WEBSTER. **1975** B. MEGGS *Matter of Paradise* (1976) v. i. 106, I don't want to say anything more right now; this telephone isn't secure.

secure, *v.* Add: **7.** *Hort.* (See quot. 1928.)

1928 *Daily Express* 11 Aug. 4/2 The Japanese varieties of the chrysanthemum are now beginning to show their flower buds, and these should be 'secured', as it is called, at the earliest possible moment. This is done by pinching out with the thumb and finger the incipient side shoots or laterals that will be found in process of formation immediately beneath the buds and in the axils of the leaves. **1951** *Dict. Gardening* (R. Hort. Soc.) I. 476/1 It should be possible to secure the first crown bud of many varieties during the last week in July.

Securicor (sĭkiū[ə]·rikǫɪ). [Invented name f. SECURI(TY + COR(PS.] A private security organization employed in the guarding and safe transport of money, goods, and property. Freq. *attrib.*, esp. as *Securicor man, van.* Also *fig.* (with small initial).

There is a large number of firms bearing this name owned by Security Group Ltd. (formerly Associated Hotels).

1953 *Change of Name Certificate* 3 Jan. in Dept. of Trade file (354883) Night Guards Limited... Securicor Ltd. **1961** *Security Gaz.* Feb. 64/3 (*caption*) Securicor guards are responsible for the safety of Ireland's greatest art treasure, the 1,000 year old 'Book of Kells'. **1962** *Daily Tel.* 6 Sept. 13/1 An executive of Securicor, the security organization, said..'They were stupid to try to change vehicles.' *Ibid.*, Mr. Norman Negus, 54, a Securicor guard, walked out of the bank..carrying the cash box chained to him. As he approached the armoured Securicor van the ambush was sprung. *Ibid.*, Another Securicor man, locked inside the armoured van, sounded the alarm siren. **1968** *Listener* 12 Dec. 804/3 Unless future student audiences can be screened in advance by the BBC's own securicor, one sees small hope for this series. **1970** *Guardian Weekly* 14 Mar. 9/1 Securicor, Security Express, and Factoryguards—the three main companies which account for about 90 per cent of the manned protection in Britain. **1977** D. BAGLEY *Enemy* xxx. 239 The auctioneer has Securicor men all over the place.

security. Add: **I. 1. b.** The safety or safeguarding of (the interests of) a state, organization, person, etc., against danger, esp. from espionage or theft; the exercise of measures to this end; (the maintenance of) secrecy about military movements or diplomatic negotiations; in espionage, the maintenance of cover. Hence (with capital initial), a department (in government service, etc.) charged with ensuring this. (This sense tends towards 'the condition of making secure'.)

1941 *Times* 16 July 3/1 In order to ensure public security, the occupation of the principal localities in Syria and the Lebanon will be undertaken in accordance with the programme which will allow immediate replacement of French by the occupying forces. **1941** E. John *Lofoten Let.* 34 Major Talbot..prides himself..on the 'security' of this expedition... [*note*] That is the Army term for what normal people call 'secrecy'. **1945** [see *leakage 2]. **1955** *Bull. Atomic Sci.* Apr. 165/3 'Security', as it relates to the continuing struggle between the free world and the Soviet bloc, is an abundantly common yet widely misunderstood word. **1959** *Listener* 8 Oct. 558/1 You can call at offices, clubs, studios, and institutions—anywhere that does not verge on security—and usually they will tell you, foreigner though you are, the telephone numbers of their staff. **1961** R. Seth *Anat. Spying* v. 83 In the spy's vocabulary, Security means doing nothing that is likely to reveal his clandestine rôle... Each separate aspect of Security may be small..but any one aspect neglected is sufficient to cause the spy's downfall. **1965** M. Allingham *Mind Readers* vi. 59, I thought that might have been what Security told you when they sent for you. **1976** M. Delving *China Expert* iv. 44 Security persuaded him to leave the army, and a place was found for him in..MI5. **1976** *Daily Tel.* 20 July 2/3 Security at places like the airport is always under review. **1982** *Observer* 6 June 1/7 While Israeli reaction has been to praise the British police..there is some evidence that security outside the hotel was lax.

3. Delete *arch.* and add further examples.

1977 *Monitor* (McAllen, Texas) 7 June 16A, A feeling of security comes with owning your own home. **1979** R. Jaffe *Class Reunion* (1980) III. i. 305 She knew now it was one of her weaknesses to look for total security.

10. (Further examples.) Also, in the U.S., such a document issued to investors to finance a business venture.

1848 [see Negotiable *a.* 1]. **1899** *Ann. Amer. Acad. Pol. & Soc. Sci.* XIV. 181 The term 'negotiable securities' is applicable in a general sense to many forms of commercial paper, including drafts and bills of exchange, but it is usually employed for the share-capital of corporations and for the bonds of such corporations and of local and state governments. **1925** R. H. Montgomery *Financial Handbk.* VII. 526 The financial executive..will naturally adapt the securities offered by his company so as best to fit in with the market he is trying to reach. **1937** J. I. Bogen *Corporation Finance* xiii. 223 Most..successful enterprises can raise funds..through the sale of securities... So broad has the ownership of stocks and bonds become that the United States has been described as a 'nation of investors'. **1962** *2001 Business Terms* (Alexander Hamilton Inst.) 246 *Securities*, stocks and bonds of business firms used to raise long-term capital. **1970** M. Greener *Penguin Dict. Commerce* 296 *Security*, a misused term often applied indiscriminately to shares, debentures, etc. In fact a security is something given or guaranteed by the borrower as a safeguard for a loan. The term is often applied to debentures and similar loan stock, and to negotiable instruments. Certificates of liability are known as securities, so sometimes are government stocks or any loans whose repayment is guaranteed. The term should not be applied to shares.

III. 11. security (also **securities**) **analyst** *U.S.*, a person who analyses the worth of securities, as by measuring the ratio of their cost to their dividends and earnings; **security blanket** orig. *U.S.* [idea popularized by the American cartoonist Charles M. Schulz (b. 1922) in the comic strip 'Peanuts' in which a boy named Linus carries a cot blanket for comfort], an object (esp. a blanket) given to a child to afford reassurance by its familiarity; also *fig.*

1934 Graham & Dodd *Security Analysis* VII. l. 586 There is a fundamental cleavage of viewpoint between the speculator and the securities analyst. **1937** *N.Y. Times* 18 May 40/4 Plans for the organization of the New York Society of Security Analysts. **1961** 'E. Lathen' *Banking on Death* iii. 22 One of Robichaux and Devane's security analysts was leaving the firm. **1979** A. Maling *Koberg Link* (1980) xx. 109 I'm a securities analyst. [**1956** C. M. Schulz *Good Grief, More Peanuts* 25 (*caption*) This is a 'security and happiness' blanket... *All* little kids carry them.] **1971** *Newsweek* 19 July 48/1 Deferred-admissions plans—a sort of security blanket that prospective students can carry with them during a year's sabbatical. **1973** *Ladies' Home Jrnl.* Dec. 102 A worn, torn, one-eyed teddy bear about a foot long was my 'security blanket'. **1975** *New Yorker* 21 Apr. 99/1 There's a security-blanket comfort in thinking you have something there in actuarial terms that you can rely on. **1976** *New Society* 28 Oct. 179/2 This [book], to give well deserved recognition to its usefulness..is already as dog-eared as a security blanket. **1978** *Maledicta* II. 81 The subjunctive mood is his security blanket.

12. *attrib.* with reference to (the maintenance of) security in military, penal, civil, and commercial contexts (see sense 1 b above).

a. Of devices which assist security, as *security fence, gate, lock*, etc. Also, of areas so protected, as *security wing*.

1904 Security-door [in Dict., sense 11]. **1963** *Security Gaz.* V. 187/2 The main innovation at Blundeston is the 12 ft. high security fence. **1968** *Rep. Work Prison Dept.* 6 in *Parl. Papers 1967–68* (Cmnd. 3774) XXXI. 57 The use of special security wings to house prisoners who require the strictest security is an expedient which poses severe problems. **1971** *Country Life* 10 June 1439/3, I gathered that they [*sc.* four stone figures] once guarded the four corners of Aldgate, one of London's well-known security gates. **1976** 'M. Albrand' *Taste of Terror* xviii. 107 I'm going to..put security locks on every door in the house. **1976** *Washington Post* 19 Apr. c21/2 (Advt.), Will throw in bumper rack, tie downs, security chain & lock. **1976** *Evening Times* (Glasgow) 1 Dec. 3/6 A key that was missing would let anyone escape from the block into the grounds—but it wouldn't let them out of the security gates.

b. Of measures, etc., intended to ensure security, as *security clearance, measure, pact, rating*, etc.

1925 *Times* 2 Sept. 11/4 The jurists..are discussing the technical details of the proposed Security Pact at the Foreign Office. **1945** *News Rev.* 10 May 9 The security black-out will be lifted to enable us to print some details about the nation's war effort. **1952** *Ann. Reg. 1951* 424 There were renewed expressions of disquiet from scientists about the encroachment of security measures on personal freedom of speech and action. **1955** M. Reifer *Dict. New Words* 185/1 *Security clearance*, the establishment, by means of investigation and executive determination, that a prospective federal employee or consultant is not a security risk, and may be hired. **1958** *New Statesman* 20 Sept. 365/2 With the off-shore islands and Formosa blanketed by a security screen, it is difficult to know exactly what is happening there. **1963** Mrs. L. B. Johnson *White House Diary* 2 Dec. (1970) 13 Dr. Henry Smyth, the lone dissenter in the 4-to-1 Commission decision when Dr. Oppenheimer lost his security clearance. **1963** L. Deighton *Horse under Water* xxi. 94 Act grown-up or I'll cut your security rating back. **1976** H. Tracy *Death in Reserve* xv. 118 It's your red area security pass. **1978** R. Ludlum *Holcroft Covenant* xxxi. 363 Suppose the guards were more alert, security measures more effective.

c. Of persons or organizations charged with the maintenance of security, as *security guard, man, officer, police, service*, etc. Also *security van*.

1940 *Hutchinson's Pictorial Hist. War* 4 Feb.–9 Apr. 180 It was quiet on the island at first, the Nazis believing the raiders to be just another security patrol. **1944** P. Gibbs *Battle Within* 135 If one of our Security Police had been in the church to-day he might have tapped you on the shoulder after the service and led you off to Brixton Gaol. **1945** *Daily Express* 4 June 1/1 A double check is being made by security officers on the three Belfast–Dublin trains that stop at Goraghwood daily for Customs examination. **1948** *Straits Times* 20 July 6/2 It is still true that 'the estates, mines and kampongs'—to echo Mr. MacDonald's broadcast again—do not feel that the security forces are doing enough for them. **1951** N. Brook in *Ld. Denning's Rep.* 79 in *Parl. Papers 1962–3* (Cmnd. 2152) XXIV. 349, I recommend that the Security Service should in future be responsible to the Home Secretary. **1955** Earl Winterton *Fifty Tumultuous Years* 74 He had no aide-de-camp with him, no 'security guard' and no police escort, not even a groom. **1958** *New Statesman* 7 June 716/2 But the Socialist Deputies of Nord and Pas de Calais..replied to these fears by saying openly to Guy Mollet: 'If you're afraid of the paratroops and you can't depend on the security police, arm the miners.' **1959** *Times Lit. Suppl.* 27 Mar. 182/2 Ministers, Civil servants and security men buzzing round the graceless tycoon who is producing a new bomber. **1963** A. Douglas-Home in *Hansard Commons* DCLXXXVI. 859 If we were to set up a Standing Security Commission, I think, first, that it should have a judicial chairman. **1963** D. Francis *Odds Against* ix. 135 [We] could arrange for some sort of guard on the course. Security patrols, that kind of thing. **1966** M. Woodhouse *Tree Frog* xxi. 153 There were no security guards..there wasn't anywhere to run to. **1970** G. F. Newman *Sir, You Bastard* vii. 198 An attack on a security van. **1973** *Times* 15 May 12/6 Britain's involvement in Northern Ireland was real and earnest, as the security forces knew. **1975** D. Lodge *Changing Places* v. 165 A solitary security man in his shelter lifted a lazy hand in salute. **1975** A. A. Thompson *Message from Absalom* iii. 17 Security police carrying rifles. **1976** H. Wilson *Governance of Britain* ix. 167 Until 1952 the Prime Minister was directly responsible for the security service. **1978** R. V. Jones *Most Secret War* liii. 520 One morning just before a weekend, the Security Officer rushed round the M.I.6 offices telling everyone to take down all maps off their walls. **1981** 'W. Haggard' *Money Men* xiii. 144 A security van drove up... It contained his loot.

d. With adjs. to form adjs., as *security-conscious, -minded* (hence *-mindedness*).

1943 J. H. Fullarton *Troop Target* 26 'If you ask me,' said Quigg, 'this Fifth Column palaver is mostly propaganda to make us security-minded.' **1955** I. Fleming *Moonraker* xv. 149 Drax..seemed to be meticulously security-conscious. **1955** M. Gilbert *Sky High* v. 69 The Inspector's tone implied exactly what he thought about the security-mindedness of County Councillors. **1960** 'R. East' *Kingston Black* xx. 185 In military intelligence it's second nature to be security-minded about public telephones. **1968** M. Jones *Survivor* i. 22 I've always heard they're madly careless in the Air Force. Not security-conscious like the Navy. **1972** M. Gilbert *Body of Girl* xxiii. 200 He decided to test the security-mindedness of the person chiefly concerned. **1976** 'M. Barak' *Secret List Heinrich Roehm* I. iv. 46 The Israelis are going to be much more security-minded now.

e. Special Combs.: **security blanket**, an official sanction introduced in order to maintain complete secrecy or safety from danger; **security check**, (*a*) a verification of identity or reliability, *spec.* of the loyalty of an official employee, for the purposes of security; (*b*) a phrase incorporated in a broadcast message from a spy to confirm his identity or to indicate that he is not operating under duress; hence **security-check** *v. trans.*, to subject to a security check; **Security Council**, a principal council of the United Nations consisting permanently of the Great Powers of 1945 and temporarily of certain others, charged with the settlement of disputes (and orig. with the threat of military action against aggressors); **security risk**, a person whose tenure of an official position constitutes a possible danger to the security of the state, etc.; also, a situation endangering security.

1955 *New Yorker* 5 Feb. 88/2 The size of the Regular Army is under a security blanket at present. **1972** *Times* 13 Sept. 8/8 At Heathrow..there was a tight security blanket. **1945** *Daily Express* 4 June 1/1 A security check on their identity cards and permits on the Ulster–Eire border showed that they were apparently in order. **1961** R. Seth *Anat. Spying* vi. 98 The operator is instructed to insert in all his messages what is known as a Security-check. **1966** 'A. Hall' *9th Directive* iii. 31 With the flap on..they were probably security-checking the Ambassador himself. **1978** R. Ludlum *Holcroft Covenant* xxxii. 374 Security check requested. **1979** F. Forsyth *Devil's Alternative* x. 232 The cipher clerks are..security-checked to the highest level. **1944** *Times* 10 Oct. 5/6 Tentative proposals have been made for the establishment of a general international organization under the title of The United Nations. The proposals..deal with..its principal organs, including a General Assembly, a Security Council, and an International Court of Justice. **1968** *Security Council Proc. Czechoslovakia* 3 in *Parl. Papers 1967–8* (Cmnd. 3757) XLII. 229 The Security Council met at 6.30 p.m. (New York Time) on 21st August. After protracted debate, the Council agreed to the inscription of the item on Czechoslovakia on its agenda. **1977** *Whitaker's Almanack 1978* 806/2 The Security Council consists of fifteen Members, each of which has one representative and one vote. **1948** Security risk [see *clearance 5 c]. **1951** *Ann. Reg. 1950* 186 Mr. Acheson was..asked whether he himself, in view of his friendship for Hiss, could be considered a security risk. **1965** M. Spark *Mandelbaum Gate* vii. 216 He disapproved of letting young chaps into the Foreign Service who openly professed to have no religion at all. A security risk, Freddy felt decidedly. **1975** *Radio Times* 2–8 Aug. 43/3 He was accused of being a 'security risk' because of his early Communist associations.

sedan. Add: **1. c.** = *saloon 4 c. Chiefly *N. Amer.* (Not used in the U.K.)

1912 *Motor World* 14 Nov. 18/1 In the new [Studebaker] cars, there is another coupe, and a 'Sedan', both mounted on a new four-cylinder chassis. **1915** *Literary Digest* (N.Y.) 21 Aug. (cover advt.), A touring car when the windows are down... With the windows raised, a luxurious sedan. **1922** *Short Stories* Feb. 98/1 The sedan had been equipped with an exhaust foot warmer or heater. **1935** M. M. Atwater *Murder in Midsummer* i. 6 A black sedan was drawn up on the shoulder of the road. **1966** 'A. Hall' *9th Directive* xx. 184 It was a massive black Lincoln sedan; a seven-seater executive-style transport. **1977** *Time* 8 Aug. 23/1 The two were surrounded by four pistol-carrying men and ordered into a nearby Peugeot sedan.

3. *sedan car, model*; **sedan clock** *Hist.* = *sedan-chair clock* s.v. *sedan chair c.

1931 M. de la Roche *Finch's Fortune* xxv. 325 A sedan car stopped before the door. **1957** *N.Z. Listener* 22 Nov. 4/4 New Zealand English has diverged from the English of England more than is generally realised owing to the influence of American usage. 'Sedan' car often appears in the advertisements, where an English advertisement would print 'saloon'. **1950** D. de Carle *Watchmakers' & Clockmakers' Encycl. Dict.* 129/1 *Sedan clock*, a small hanging clock usually associated with the period of the Sedan Chair. **1968** —— *Clocks & their Value* 93 The value of a sedan clock depends on the case but can be anything from about £15 to £35. **1948** *Herald-Press* (St. Joseph, Mich.) 14 Aug. 5/1 Besides making some substantial changes in its present sedan models it plans to put a hard top convertible into production.

sedanca (sĕdæ·nkă). Also **Sedanca.** [f. Sedan + the name of Count Carlos de *Salaman)ca*, Spanish nobleman and Rolls-Royce agent, by whom the word was apparently coined.] In full, *Sedanca de Ville*. A sumptuously appointed cabriolet de ville mounted on a Rolls-Royce chassis. Cf. (U.S.) *town car* s.v. *town *sb.* 10.

1926 *Motor* 26 Oct. 615/3 The other body shown on a Rolls-Royce chassis is styled a Sedanca limousine. It can also be used as a cabriolet, inasmuch as the Barker patent de ville extension over the front seat can be removed completely. **1929** *Motor* 2 July (Suppl.) p. xl/1, 1927 (October) 40–50 hp Phantom Rolls-Royce enclosed-drive Sedanca de Ville. **1937** *Times* 20 Oct. 20/1 The Rolls-Royce Company show a..Phantom III sedanca at £3,040. **1963** D. Scott-Moncrieff *Thoroughbred Motor Car 1930–40* ii. 121 (*caption*) Rolls-Royce 20/25 with French-built sedanca-de-ville coachwork, 1935. **1978** *Times* 8 June 28 (Advt.), This magnificent Brewster Salamanca is one of 2 mint Silver Ghosts entered, along with..Rolls, 220/25 Sedanca, Alvises, Lagondas, [etc.].

sedan chair. Add: **c. sedan-chair clock, watch** *Hist.*, a large travelling watch of a type supposed to have been hung in sedan chairs.

1904 F. J. BRITTEN *Old Clocks & Watches* (ed. 2) iv. 244 During the eighteenth century watch movements having plain silver dials from three inches to four inches in diameter were fixed in circular frames of wood, polished and with a moulded edge. They were called 'Sedan Chair Watches', though I cannot aver that they were as a rule carried in those useful, but obsolete conveyances. **1951** E. WENHAM *Old Clocks for Mod. Use* vii. 47 It is still possible to obtain one of these..portable timepieces generally referred to as 'Sedan chair clocks' or, to give them another earlier name, 'post-chaise clocks'. **1960** *House & Garden* Apr. 99/3 Sedan-chair clocks..reproductions and an antique.

sedate, *a.* Add: **1. e.** Of inanimate objects: not unduly striking in colour or design; quiet and restful in tone.

1924 A. D. SEDGWICK *Little French Girl* I. vi. 48 Sedate chairs with backs and seats embroidered in green and dove-colour were ranged along the wall. **1978** J. CARROLL *Mortal Friends* III. v. 310 Brady stood in the bridge of the window, looking out on the sedate front lawn.

3. *Comb.*, as *sedate-looking* adj.

1925 T. DREISER *Amer. Tragedy* I. II. xxxvii. 411 So clean, modest and sedate-looking a girl. **1977** *Rolling Stone* 19 May 90/5 The sedate-looking trio sings R and B with fervor.

sedate, *v.* Restrict † *Obs.* to sense in Dict. and add: **b.** *Med.* To make (a patient) sleepy or quiet by means of drugs; to administer a sedative to.

1945 *Richmond* (Va.) *Times-Dispatch* 21 Sept. 1/1 Two capsules are ordinarily considered enough to sedate a person—that is, produce a tendency to sleep. **1961** *Amer. Speech* XXXVI. 145 The informal speech of physicians embodies a great many technical colloquialisms that may be called the argot of medicine... 'He was very apprehensive, so I sedated him heavily.' **1977** *Proc. R. Soc. Med.* LXX. 549/1 He was sedated, intubated and ventilated and full supportive therapy was given with further blood transfusions.

Hence **seda·ted** *ppl. a.*, under the influence of a sedative drug.

1953 R. LEHMANN *Echoing Grove* 129 'How is she?'.. 'Expecting you. Be careful, won't you? She's still sedated—mildly, of course.' **1974** L. DEIGHTON *Spy Story* xi. 107, I was half inclined to give the sedated Miss Shaw a miss. **1976** J. PHILIPS *Backlash* (1977) III. i. 125 Elliot wasn't going to come to. He was heavily sedated.

sedation. Add: **1. a.** (Further example.) Now esp. with reference to the use of sedative drugs.

1979 *Guardian* 19 Feb. 22/6 The dead youth's parents were under sedation yesterday at their home in Dan-y-Cribyn. **1982** J. PENN *Notice of Death* vii. 65 We may get more in the morning from Mrs H., but at the moment she's under sedation.

‖ **sedekah** (sedekă·). [Malay, f. Arab. *ṣadaqa*.] In Malaysia: alms; a voluntary offering.

1839 T. J. NEWBOLD *Straits of Malacca* I. ii. 88 When a boy has gone through the Koran..his parents give *Sedekah*, or alms. **1900** W. W. SKEAT *Malay Magic* vi. 403 In the case of a Sultan as many as possible bear a hand in sending him to the grave..partly for the sake of the *sĕdĕkah* or alms given to the bearers. **1972** A. AMIN tr. *Shahnon Ahmad's No Harvest but Thorn* ix. 96 Lahuma need not worry any more, thought Jeha. The feast would be a *sedekah* to all.

sedentarization (se:dentărəizē·ʃən). [f. SEDENTAR(Y *a.* + -IZE: see -ATION.] The settlement of a nomadic people in a permanent homeland or place of habitation.

1960 F. BARTH in *Problems of Arid Zone* (UNESCO) 342 The solution..favoured by the state authorities..has been the simple and radical one of sedentarization: the total elimination of nomads by settling them on the land as agriculturalists. **1969** *Times Lit. Suppl.* 21 Aug. 929/2 Both the sedentarization of the tribes and the redistribution of land were thought..politically desirable. **1979** *West Africa* 13 Aug. 1459/2 Nor, they concluded..would the pastoralists themselves regret such a social and economic transformation once they realised that sedentarisation was good for them.

sedentary, *a.* and *sb.* Add: **A.** *adj.* **5.** *Geol.* Of a soil or sediment: = *RESIDUAL *a.* 2 f.

1870 S. W. JOHNSON *How Crops Feed* II. iii. 143 Sedentary soils, or Soils in place, are those which have not been transported by geological agencies. **1906** [see *RESIDUAL *a.* 2 f]. **1929** *Daily Tel.* 22 Jan. 4/7 The soil being considered 'sedentary' in character. **1943** MILLAR & TURK *Soil Sci.* i. 4 Since they have not suffered the mixing that accompanies transportation by ice and water there are many variations in the characteristics, both physical and chemical, of sedentary materials. **1975** FLEGMANN & GEORGE *Soils* iv. 103 This visual gradation is particularly obvious when a soil has been formed *in situ* by the gradual weathering of parent rock, such soils being referred to as sedentary.

6. *Comb.*, as *sedentary-looking* adj.

1937 W. B. YEATS *Vision* (rev. ed.) 37 Aherne..was stout and sedentary-looking.

‖ **Seder** (sē^i·dəɹ). Also with small initial. [Heb. *sēdher* order, procedure.] A Jewish ritual service and ceremonial dinner held on the first evening of the Passover and repeated on the second evening by Orthodox Jews outside Israel. Freq. *attrib.*

1865 *Chambers's Encycl.* VII. 312/1 At a later period, a certain number of cups of red wine were superadded to this meal, to which, as its special ceremonies and the order of its benedictions were fixed, the name *Seder* (arrangement) was given. **1891** [see *HAGGADAH 2]. **1892** I. ZANGWILL *Childr. Ghetto* II. xxii. 166 She would have to.. see the sour faces of her little ones round a barren *Seder* table. *Ibid.* xxv. 205 Seder Night was a charmed time. The strange symbolic dishes..the special Hebrew melodies. **1909** *Cent. Dict.* Suppl. s.v., The celebrant, generally the head of the family, begins with the first of the thirteen functions in the seder service. **1932** C. ROTH *Hist. Marranos* vii. 185 The traditional *Seder*-service. **1958** C. P. SNOW *Conscience of Rich* I. iii. 24 We were as good as engaged after seder night in '96. **1970** I. SIEFF *Memoirs* vi. 95 Herbert Samuel..spoke the holy words, the traditional conclusion to the *Seder* service on the eve of the Passover: 'Next year in Jerusalem.' **1978** J. SACKS in P. Moore *Man, Woman, & Priesthood* iii. 39 The best known of these events is the *Seder* on the first nights of Passover. **1982** *Listener* 7 Jan. 13/1, I sat round the Seder table during Passover.

sedge, *sb.*[1] Add: **1. f.** The characteristic greenish- (or reddish-)brown shade of sedge.

1927 *Daily Express* 12 Mar. 3/5 Sedge, a bright shade similar to the always popular almond, but with a tendency towards jade. **1938** J. W. DAY *Dog in Sport* iv. 66 By 1885 the present type had largely evolved, the main differences being that the breed then possessed one colour only, a dark brown shading into a reddish sedge.

5. a. *sedge-ground, -peat.* **b.** *sedge-choked, -embattled* adjs.

1942 W. FAULKNER *Go down, Moses* 92 The old worn-out brier- and sedge-choked fields spreading away. **1934** E. BLUNDEN *Mind's Eye* 138 We shall see..the gilt-leaved beechwood and the sedge-embattled lake. **1667** in *Rec. Town Plymouth* (Mass.) (1889) I. 95 All that pte of the pond or sedge ground which lyeth between a place there called the Gurnett and the bounds of Samuell Ryders land. **1910** C. HARRIS *Eve's Husband* 30 The poor brown sedge-ground of an old field. **1943** G. ERDTMAN *Introd. Pollen Analysis* i. 6 The comparatively low pine pollen frequency of a sedge-peat was considered to be due to the fact that the pine sheds its pollen at a time when the sedges have attained full growth. **1952** *Chambers's Jrnl.* Jan. 61/2 We propose to..fork in ample horticultural sedge-peat in the spring. **1977** R. DAVIES *Pract. Gardening Encycl.* ii. 21/1 Sedge (or fen) peats are the remains of reeds and sedges and are dark coloured and well decayed.

6. sedge-cock *dial.* = MISSEL-THRUSH.

1886 R. HOLLAND *Gloss. Words County Chester* 305 Sedcock,..the missel thrush... Sedgecock. **1955** E. POUND *Classic Anthol.* I. 75 June's green hopper moves a thigh, 'Sedge-cock' wings it in July. **1965** *Jrnl. Lancs. Dial. Soc.* Jan. 9 Mistle thrush... Sedgecock, Setcock, Sedcock: Oldham; nr. Stockport.

sediment, *sb.* Add: **4. sediment ring** *Astr.*, a ring of rock masses orbiting a planet, regarded as debris from the time of its formation.

1955 *Sci. News Let.* 22 Jan. 53/1 Dr. Kuiper said that the moon, as it sped away from the earth, plowed through a 'sediment ring', a swarm of small satellites moving around the earth. **1970** [see *PLANETISMAL *a.* and *sb.*].

sediment, *v.* Delete *rare* and add: **1.** (Later examples.)

1908 *Chambers's Jrnl.* May 396/1 Chemical precipitation was found essential to coagulate the suspended matter and thus enable the greater proportion of it to be sedimented in subsidence basins. **1976** *Nature* 19 Aug. 662/1 We then sedimented the eggs rapidly..in a hand centrifuge.

2. *intr.* **a.** To settle as sediment.

1927 *Brit. Jrnl. Exper. Path.* VIII. 122 In a typical rough culture of *enteritidis*..the bacteria rapidly sediment to the bottom. **1961** *Lancet* 5 Aug. 322/1 The erythrocytes being allowed to sediment within the syringe. **1971** *Nature* 25 June 527/2 Each preparation sedimented in the analytical ultracentrifuge as a single component with a sedimentation coefficient..of about 9·5S.

b. Of a liquid: to deposit a sediment.

1934 in WEBSTER. **1962** LUNTZ & WRIGHT in A. Pirie *Lens Metabolism Rel. Cataract* 319 Blood was collected..in a mixture of 1% sodium ethylenediamine tetra-acetic acid and 5% dextran..and allowed to sediment. **1978** *Nature* 10 Aug. 611/1 (*caption*) Heparinated blood was allowed to sediment at room temperature to separate red cells from plasma.

sedimented *ppl. a.* (*fig.* example); **sedimenting** *ppl. a.* (later example).

1962 H. BLOEMENDAL et al. in A. Pirie *Lens Metabolism Rel. Cataract* 303 More rapidly sedimenting material is observed, but the shape of the corresponding boundary does not allow calculation of the sedimentation coefficient. **1977** D. L. ALTHEIDE in D. E. Johnson *Existential Sociol.* iv. 149 These tasks become taken for granted as sedimented knowledge for the members.

sedimentable (se·dimentăb'l), *a.* [f. prec. + -ABLE.] That may be deposited or obtained as sediment. Hence **se:dimentabi·lity.**

1943 *Jrnl. Gen. Physiol.* XXVI. 352 As an elemental volume within the ascending layer is partially or completely cleared of sedimentable material, it has to move only a relatively short distance..before it reaches a region of comparable concentration. **1971** *Jrnl. Insect Physiol.* XVII. 865 Additions of 0·1% Triton..increase..enzymatic activity..without markedly altering the sedimentability of the enzyme. **1978** *Nature* 2 Mar. 55/2 After storing for 1 week at room temperature, at least 50% of the antimony was retained within sedimentable liposomes, the remainder having escaped into solution.

sedimentation. Add: **2.** *Comb.*, as **sedimentation coefficient, constant,** a measure of the size of a microscopic particle, equal to the terminal outward velocity of the particle when centrifuged in a fluid medium divided by the centrifugal force acting on it; (expressed in units of time: cf. *SVEDBERG); **sedimentation rate,** the rate of descent of particles suspended in a fluid; *spec.* in *Med.*, of the red cells in drawn blood; **sedimentation tank,** a tank in which sewage is allowed to stand so that the solid matter in suspension may have time to settle.

1962 H. BLOEMENDAL et al. in A. Pirie *Lens Metabolism Rel. Cataract* 300, α-Crystallin, prepared by vertical starch block electrophoresis, has a sedimentation coefficient of 19 S (molecular weight 810,000). **1978** *Nature* 12 Jan. 170/2 Nervous tissue and muscle in rat and chicken contain several molecular forms of acetylcholinesterase.., distinguishable by their sedimentation coefficient in sucrose gradient. **1929** SVEDBERG & KATSURAI in *Jrnl. Amer. Chem. Soc.* LI. 3577 The term 'Sedimentation Constant' has been adopted as a simplified means of expressing the old term 'Specific Sedimentation Velocity'. **1966** B. POLLARA et al. in R. T. Smith et al. *Phylogeny of Immunity* ix. 94/2 The antibody produced by this animal is different from that of the other lower vertebrates, having a sedimentation constant of approximately 9S. **1946** *Nature* 30 Nov. 794/2 In accordance with Stokes's law, sedimentation-rates of such red-cell aggregates will be greater than those of single non-polarized blood cells. **1978** *Ibid.* 12 Oct. 532/1 To predict long-range trends in marsh stability, accurate measurements are needed of both subsidence and sedimentation rates. **1920** *Glasgow Herald* 3 Nov. 13 The sewage passes into a sedimentation tank designed so as to bring down in the form of sludge as much of the suspended solids as possible. **1966** *McGraw-Hill Encycl. Sci. & Technol.* XII. 221/2 In some [sewage] treatment plants screenings are passed through a grinder and returned to the flow so that they will settle out in the sedimentation tank.

sedimentology (se:dimĕntǫ·lŏdʒi). [f. SEDIMENT *sb.* + -OLOGY.] The branch of geology which deals with the nature and properties of sediments and sedimentary rocks. So **se:dimentolo·gical** *a.*, of or pertaining to sedimentology; **se:dimentolo·gically** *adv.*, by means of sedimentology; from the point of view of sedimentology; **se:dimento·logist,** an expert in sedimentology.

1932 H. WADELL in *Science* 1 Jan. 20/2 Sedimentology is here suggested as a term for the subject taught, retaining sedimentation for the act or process of deposition. The new term and its derivatives sedimentologist, sedimentologic and sedimentological will tend towards clearness. **1957** *Jrnl. Geol.* LXV. 485/1 It might be possible to subdivide further the material in this core from a sedimentological point of view into two components: (1) material of sand size.., and (2) lutite. **1958** *Times* 22 Mar. 8/3 Mr R. J. L. Allen..has been appointed George Martin Lees Research Fellow in Sedimentology. **1961** *Jrnl. Sedimentary Petrol.* XXXI. 207/1 The expression of kurtosis has not been used extensively by sedimentologists. **1966** *Palaeogeogr., Palaeoclimatol., Palaeoecol.* II. 113 The ironstones..mark, sedimentologically, a complete reversal of the trend towards increasing oxygenation. **1967** *New Scientist* 20 July 146/1 A number of grants for further research into sedimentology have been made to the University of Reading. **1970** *Nature* 2 May 425 Sedimentological studies of depositional environments of the modern Omo River delta and floodplain. **1973** *Ibid.* 8 June 342/1 Their [*sc.* marine grasses'] former presence can nevertheless be deduced by sedimentology and palaeontology. **1977** A. HALLAM *Planet Earth* 245/1 The paleoecologist has to be paleobiologist, sedimentologist and biologist.

seditty, var. *SADITTY *a.*

Sedobrol (se·dobrǫl). A proprietary name for a medicinal preparation.

1913 *Trade Marks Jrnl.* 22 Jan. 105 *Sedobrol*... Chemical substances prepared for use in medicine and pharmacy. John Henry Land.., 10, Market Place, Coalville, Leicestershire; Chemist. **1921** R. MACAULAY *Dangerous Ages* v. 102 There have been wonderful cures for insomnia lately... Which new thing? Sedobrol? Paraldehyd? **1934** E. WAUGH *Handful of Dust* iii. 129 They had boiled water in an electric kettle and were drinking Sedobrol together. **1939–40** *Army & Navy Stores Catal.* 406/3 Sedobrol Tablets 10's 2/–, 30's 5/–.

sedoheptulose (sīdohe·ptiŭlōᵘz, -s). *Chem.* [f. SED(UM + -O + *hept*)*ose* s.v. *HEPTA- + *-ULOSE[2].] A heptose that is found in the leaves of certain plants of the genus *Sedum* (notably *S. spectabile*), a phosphate of which is involved as an intermediate in carbohydrate metabolism in animals. Formerly called † **sedoheptose.**

1917 LA FORGE & HUDSON in *Jrnl. Biol. Chem.* XXX. 68 Since the analyses of the three crystalline derivatives that have been described show conclusively that the sugar of *Sedum spectabile* contains seven carbon atoms, it will be named, with reference to its origin, sedoheptose. **1938** *Thorpe's Dict. Appl. Chem.* (ed. 4) II. 286/2 The natural ketoheptoses are *d*-mannoketoheptose..; perseulose.., and sedoheptose obtained from *Sedum spectabile.* **1939** *Jrnl. Amer. Chem. Soc.* LXI. 343/2 In the presence of mineral acids, sedoheptulose is transformed to a crystalline anhydride. **1959** [see *RIBULOSE]. **1970** R. W. McGILVERY *Biochem.* xvi. 325 The only known function for the 7-carbon sedoheptulose-7-phosphate in animals is its participation as an intermediate in the pentose phosphate pathway.

Sedormid (sĭdǭ·ɹmid). *Pharm.* A proprietary term for *N*-(2-isopropylpent-4-enoyl)urea, $C_9H_{16}N_2O_2$, a white crystalline solid employed as a sedative and hypnotic.

1928 *Trade Marks Jrnl.* 9 May 736/2 *Sedormid*... The Hoffman–La Roche Chemical Works Limited..London. **1929** *Official Gaz.* (U.S. Patent Office) 14 May 299/2 *Sedormid.* For sedative and hypnotic. Claims use since Mar. 14, 1929. **1934** *Lancet* 21 Apr. 845/1 Two..cases of thrombopenic purpura were due to prolonged administration of the new hypnotic Sedormid (allylisopropyl-acetyl-urea). **1964** M. HYNES *Med. Bacteriol.* (ed. 8) vii. 79 In some patients the hypnotic Sedormid combines with the platelets and thrombocytopenic purpura follows. **1974** M. C. GERALD *Pharmacol.* iv. 80 Compare the ease in saying and remembering..allylisopropylacetylcarbamide vs. Sedormid.

Sedra (se·dră). Also **Sedrah, Sidra(h,** and with small initial. [Aram. (via Yiddish *sedre*): cf. *SEDER.] In Jewish sabbatical liturgy, one of the fifty-four sections of the Pentateuch read in the Synagogue at the Sabbath morning service. Cf. PARASHAH.

Quot. 1909 does not accord with modern usage.

1907 I. ZANGWILL *Ghetto Comedies* 128 We are reading the *Sedrah* (weekly portion) about Joseph. **1909** *Cent. Dict.* Suppl., The Pentateuch is divided into fifty-four sedras or sections, which are subdivided into parashoth. The sedras must be read at the morning Sabbath services during the year, but as a year has only 52 weeks, in order to finish the sedras two of them are read on two special Sabbaths. **1962** *New Jewish Encycl.* 370/2 In common usage, the word 'Parashah' also refers to the entire *Sidrah* (or Sedrah), or to any of the various sections or paragraphs in the scroll of the Torah. The Torah is subdivided into *Sidrot* (sections), the reading of which is completed in a one year cycle; and each Sidrah is further subdivided into Parashiyot (sing. Parashah). **1973** *Jewish Chron.* 19 Jan. 18/2 Nehama Leibowitz's studies in the weekly *sidra* have justifiably become renowned as a key for the unlocking of the treasures found among the Jewish Biblical exegetes.

seducee. (Later example.)

1962 GREGOR & NICHOLAS *Moral & Story* iv. 120 The 'innocent' seducee dies a depraved alcoholic, while her seducer is redeemed.

see, *sb.*[1] Add: **3.** (sense 2) *see-city.*

1937 *Daily Tel.* 28 Aug. 13/3 On this day, very nearly 1,500 years ago, Augustine lay dying in his see-city of Hippo. **1956** D. E. W. HARRISON in D. L. Linton *Sheffield* 199 Meanwhile Sheffield became in 1914 the see-city of a diocese stretching to Goole on the Ouse.

see, *sb.*[2] Restrict *rare*, etc., to sense b in Dict. and add: **a.** (Later examples.) Used as a colloq. replacement for LOOK *sb.* (cf. also *LOOK-SEE).

1927 J. MASEFIELD *Midnight Folk* 251 The son took out a pocket telescope..and handed it to his father. 'Take a see for yourself, pop.' **1938** E. WILLIAMS *Corn is Green* I. i. 10 Ought to be 'ere by now, I'll 'ave a see.

see, *v.* Add: **A. 3. a.** *β.* (Earlier and U.S. examples of *seed.*)

1746 G. MURRAY *Let.* 17 Apr. in C. Petrie *Jacobite Movement: Last Phase* (1950) v. 113, I never seed him in time of action, neither at Gledsmoor, Falkirk, nor this last. **1777** P. THICKNESSE *Year's Journey* II. xlix. 134 An English servant..told me..that he *seed* her very plain. **1833** J. NEAL *Down-Easters* I. i. 14 Never seed sich a fellow since I breathed the breath of life. **1893** H. A. SHANDS *Some Peculiarities of Speech in Mississippi* 55 *Seed*, Negro and illiterate white for *saw*. **1945** in B. A. Botkin *Lay my Burden Down* 18 He was the ugliest man I ever seed.

d. *colloq.* and *dial.* **seen** (chiefly *1st pers. sing.*: see also *Eng. Dial. Dict.*).

1796 *Aurora* (Philadelphia) 30 Sept. 3/3 So fine a sight (says Yankee to his friend) I swear I never seen—you may depend. **1850** *Knickerbocker* July 87 We spoke of Major Andre. 'Oh,' said the old lady, 'I seen him more'n fifty times.' **1861** T. HUGHES *Tom Brown at Oxf.* II. vii. 114 'Hev'ee seed aught o' my bees?'.. 'E'es, I seen 'em.' *c* **1915** in N. I. White *Amer. Negro Folk-Songs* (1928) iii. 146, I seen King Pharoe's daughter seeking Moses on the water. **1976** *Alyn & Deeside Observer* 10 Dec. 12/6 Richardson told Detective Constable Mahoney: 'I seen this Irish bloke and followed him to the Hawarden Castle.'

8. *γ.* (U.S. examples.)

1845 *Great Kalamazoo Hunt* in *Big Bear of Arkansas* 49 Well, after I had looked out for about fifteen minutes or so, and seed the boss begin to get desperately frightened, [etc.]. **1938** M. K. RAWLINGS *Yearling* xvi. 188 Seems to me I've seed it before.

δ. 9— *U.S. colloq.* and *dial.* **saw.**

1867 C. F. BROWNE *A. Ward in London* II. vii. 123 We have saw a entertainment as we never saw before. **1941** J. FAULKNER *Men Working* ii. 33 How-some-ever, I've saw them.

B. I. 1. a. *Proverb.* (Later examples.)

1560 T. BECON *Catechism* in *Works* I. sig. Bbb2, This also must honest maids provide, that they be not full of tongue... A maid should be seen, and not heard. **1773** R. GRAVES *Spiritual Quix.* I. III. xviii. 179 It is a vulgar maxim, 'that a pretty woman should rather be seen than heard'. **1858** GEO. ELIOT *Janet's Repentance* viii, in *Sc. Cler. Life* II. 167 Little gells must be seen and not heard. **1908** L. M. MONTGOMERY *Anne of Green Gables* ii. 22 It's such a relief to talk..and not be told that children should be seen and not heard. **1980** L. LEWIS *Private Life of Country House* v. 63 Two or three children..supposed to be seen and not heard and not to speak unless spoken to.

d. Also in phr. *to see things,* to suffer hallucinations or false imaginings. (Usu. *colloq.* as pres. pple.)

1922 M. A. VON ARNIM *Enchanted April* iii. 48 Mrs. Fisher..had no wish to find herself shut up..with somebody who saw things... It would be disagreeable..if Mrs. Wilkins were suddenly to assert that she saw Mr. Fisher. Mr. Fisher was dead; let him remain so. **1928** KIPLING *Woman in his Life* in *Limits & Renewals* (1932) 47 After a drink or two..he told the tale of a friend who 'saw things'. **1935** A. CHRISTIE *Three Act Tragedy* III. vii. 180 Says I imagined it. Says I was 'seeing things'. **1953** B. GLEMSER *Dove on his Shoulder* ii. 13 'I must be seeing things', the major said... 'You alcoholic bastard.' **1977** 'D RUTHERFORD' *Return Load* ii. 31 Was I seeing things or was that Sally driving your truck?

i. *to see* (a person) *coming,* to make out one who can be fooled or deceived. Also in proverbial phrase *when you've seen one, you've seen them all*; a conjuror's phrase *now you see him, now you don't,* and varr. Also, *to see red*: see *RED *sb.*[1] 1 f.

c **1811** BLAKE *Public Address* in *Writings* (1978) II. 1046 When you have seen one of their Pictures you have seen all. **1869** 'MARK TWAIN' *Innocents Abr.* xxiii. 177 To me it seemed that when I had seen one of these martyrs I had seen them all. **1931** T. R. G. LYELL *Slang, Phrase & Idiom* 671 D'you mean to say you paid £100 for that car? My dear fellow, they must have seen you coming! As scrap iron, it's worth perhaps £10—not a penny more!! **1949** G. DAVENPORT *Family Fortunes* II. iv. 145 'If you've seen one you've seen them all,' said Sam. **1967** T. STOPPARD *Rosencrantz & Guildenstern are Dead* II. 62 It's just a man failing to reappear, that's all—now you see him, now you don't. **1973** *Illustr. London News* May 100/4, I know many people who feel that once you've seen one Jancso film, you've seen them all. **1980** G. M. FRASER *Mr American* xix. 370 If the American..had subsequently proved to be of moderate means, would he have been quite so welcome?.. Old Man Clayton had seen him coming. **1980** P. G. WINSLOW *Counsellor Heart* xx. 221 The only way is to..have them think it's something else. Now you see it, now you don't.

j. *transf.* or *fig.* of radar equipment, cameras, artificial satellites, etc.

1923 E. W. MARCHANT *Radio Telegr. & Teleph.* iv. 36 The method that was described by Hertz for detecting or 'seeing' radio waves was to use a spark gap in a circuit which was tuned to the frequency of the waves. **1945** *Rev. Sci. Instruments* XVI. 46/1 The photo-tube camera is mounted beneath the photofluorograph hood and 'sees' the object image on the screen which is 'seen' by the photographic camera at the apex of the hood. **1952** E. LARSEN *Radar works like This* 9 Thus the picture of what the waves 'see' is built up from glowing blobs on the screen. **1957** T. ADLER *Seeing Earth from Space* v. 126 The earth satellite Vanguard II..looks down on the earth from a much greater height than 86 miles. So it can see more of the earth than the camera that took this picture did. **1975** D. G. FINK *Electronics Engineers' Handbk.* xxv. 4 When connected to the antenna, the receiver sees a low-noise background of empty space, modified by surrounding terrain or sea surfaces and atmosphere, [etc.].

2. a. *Proverb.* (Later examples.)

1718 MRS. CENTLIVRE *Bold Stroke for Wife* II. 31, I am sorry such a well-invented Tale should do you no more Service. We old Fellows can see as far into a Mill-stone, as him that picks it. **1862** H. KINGSLEY *Ravenshoe* II. ix. 80 He could see through a brick wall as well as most men. **1885** C. M. YONGE *Two Sides of Shield* II. i. 16 He should defer his letter till he had..talked to his sister Jane, who could see through a milestone any day. **1920** 'SAPPER' *Bull-Dog Drummond* v. 127 He could see farther into a brick wall than most of the people who called him a fool. **1978** A. PRICE *'44 Vintage* xviii. 204 I had a grandma could see clear through me and a brick wall both, so it's no surprise you can figure us.

3. a. Also, to foresee or forecast (an event, trend, etc.) (later examples); *U.S.*, to understand (a person). Also, *to see* (something) *coming*: to foresee or anticipate.

1872 E. EGGLESTON *End of World* xxiii. 158 '[I] see yer,' said Bill, trying in vain to draw his coat. **1873** J. H. BEADLE *Undevel. West* xx. 369 'Marshal's got a good thing, though.' I see you; best place to make money in the United States. **1946** G. B. SHAW *Geneva* Pref. 7 Historians and newspaper editors can see revolutions three centuries off but not three years off. **1966** M. WOODHOUSE *Tree Frog* xxii. 161 'Let me guess... I know radar and guidance.'.. I nodded. I could see it coming a mile off. **1971** *Times* 16 June 21/5 Boost in gas reserves seen... The Soviet Union will expand production of oil.. and of natural gas..over 'the coming years'. **1974** 'E. LATHEN' *Sweet & Low* xv. 149 Thatcher sympathized with him. This was one he had not seen coming, either.

f. Also *colloq.* with omission of the second person subj. pronoun, appended parenthetically to a statement, freq. implying refusal to tolerate dissent, or as a mere filler; also standing alone (= 'do you see?') as an interrogative, with similar force.

1952 J. BINGHAM *My Name is Michael Sibley* xv. 183 You and me have got to understand each other right, see? **1959** N. MAILER *Advts. for Myself* (1961) 39 Listen, bud, you ain't talkin' to Joe Crap, see; you watch what you say with me. **1968** *Listener* 19 Dec. 810/3, I believe in having a go, see, so long as there's some fun in it, see. **1976** T. SHARPE *Wilt* v. 45 There was this student all dressed up like a waiter see.

g. (Later examples.)

1892 KIPLING in *Sun* (N.Y.) 28 Aug. II. 6/2 Each, in his separate star, Shall draw the Thing as he sees It for the God of Things as they are! **1934** E. O'NEILL *Days without End* III. ii. 113 He sees it clearly as a throwback to boyhood experiences. **1976** M. MACHLIN *Pipeline* xi. 135 Dad's idea of an oil man is a financier in a starched collar... I see it more like the way you did things Gramps.

h. To perceive (good or attractive qualities) *in* a person or thing, often in an interrogative clause; to perceive (a certain characteristic or type) *in* a person or thing.

1832 SCOTT *Ct. Robert* in *Tales of my Landlord* 4th Ser. I. iv. 113 Hereward, though flattered by the unusual degree of attention which the Princess bestowed upon him, saw in her only the daughter of his Emperor. **1835** BROWNING *Paracelsus* III. 419 A professorship At Basil! Since you see so much in it. **1863** 'OUIDA' *Held in Bondage* I. viii. 193 What could De Vigne possibly see in that woman? **1864** J. BRYCE *Holy Rom. Emp.* 62 He put to death the rebel Crescentius, in whom modern enthusiasm has seen a patriotic republican. **1916** 'TAFFRAIL' *Pincher Martin* vii. 114 Can't think what he sees in her. **1927** A. P. HERBERT *Plain Jane* 95 I'm not a jealous woman, But I *can't* see what he sees in her. **1971** P. O'DONNELL *Impossible Virgin* v. 107 She said quietly, 'Don't ask me what I see in him, please... Don't make judgments.'

i. To recognize the rightness or desirability of (an idea or thing); to give credence to, believe, accept; to consent to (a proposal). Usu. with *it. colloq.* (orig. *U.S.*).

1850 *California Courier* (San Francisco) 14 Nov. 2/2 This may be all right—but if it is, we cannot see it. **1860** R. NICHOLSON *Autobiogr.* 67 'Get up, my man, and let us go on,' said the stranger, almost throttling Cracroft. That worthy gentleman, however, 'could not see it', as we now say in modern slang. With a struggle he stammered that he had lost the wager. **1864** HOTTEN *Slang Dict.* 223 In street parlance, 'to see' is to know or believe; 'I don't see that,' i.e., 'I don't put faith in what you offer, or I know what you say to be untrue.' **1877** H. RUEDE *Sod-House Days* (1937) 8 The hack driver wanted us to go with him to Osborne, but the fare was $3.50 (trunks extra) and we 'could not see it'. **1890** KIPLING in *United Service Mag.* June 236, I said..'I don't keep a canteen up my sleeve.' They couldn't see it. **1934** G. B. SHAW *Too True to be Good* II. 60 But the old man never could be brought to see it. He said the proper profession for me was the bar. **1945** J. L. MARSHALL *Santa Fe* vii. 98 Fred then tried to interest the Burlington in his idea... But the Burlington couldn't see it. **1971** 'E. LATHEN' *Longer the Thread* (1972) vi. 65, I know that's what it looks like... But, for the life of me, I can't see it.

j. Usu. in negative or interrogative context with personal obj. (esp. *refl.*) and compl. (pple. or phrase): to perceive in one's mind's eye; to envisage as possible or acceptable.

1875 L. TROUBRIDGE *Jrnl.* 2 June in J. Hope-Nicholson *Life amongst Troubridges* (1966) x. 117 My dreadful yellow that I don't see myself wearing at all. **1915** R. BROOKE *Let.* 26 Jan. (1968) 657, I don't 'see' Viola [Tree] as the Lithuanian. **1926** CHESTERTON in W. R. Titterton *G. K. Chesterton* (1936) II. vii. 169, I do not quite see myself as the President of the League of Little People. **1955** R. BANNISTER *First Four Minutes* 16, I could not see myself in the winning place. **1962** M. TREVOR *Newman* 441 He stuck to his opinion that Bayswater was not the place for them; he could not see Faber going there. **1976** M. MACHLIN *Pipeline* iv. 45, I can't see dying because of your feelings about conservation.

4. d. *intr.* To read music. *colloq.*

1955 L. FEATHER *Encycl. Jazz* 347 *See*, read (music). 'He doesn't see too well' refers to a performer who reads music slowly. **1970** C. MAJOR *Dict. Afro-Amer. Slang* 101 *See*,..to read music.

5. a. Also *to see and* (*to*) *be seen* (later examples); hence *see-and-be-seen* attrib. phr.

1738 SWIFT *Polite Conv.* 41 Her Ladyship went to see, and to be seen. **1828** W. SCOTT *Jrnl.* 3 May (1972) 468 After the dinner I went to Mrs. Scott of Harden to see and be seen by her nieces. *a* **1911** W. S. GILBERT *Lost Bab Ballads* (1932) 31 To see and be seen is for what we pay At Islington on the half-crown day. **1960** *Times* 3 June 6/5 London audiences to which the social see-and-be-seen set attaches itself. **1961** *Economist* 25 Nov. 770/1 This mixing of 'blind' traffic with see-and-be-seen aircraft is particularly dangerous in overcrowded terminal areas.

f. Also *see here,* a brusque form of address used to preface an order, expostulation, reprimand, etc. Cf. *look here* s.v. LOOK *v.* 4 a.

1898 G. B. SHAW *Mrs. Warren's Profession* II. 185 Now see here, George: what are you up to about that girl? **1925** F. SCOTT FITZGERALD *Great Gatsby* vii. 152 'Now see here, Tom,' said Daisy, turning around from the mirror. **1941** J. D. CARR *Case of Constant Suicides* ii. 29 'See here,' pursued Alan... 'Let us get this straight.' **1974** G. JENKINS *Bridge of Magpies* ix. 148 'See here,' I said. 'There's been another death. I want you to signal the fisheries frigate.'

6. b. (Later examples in sense 'to ascertain by consideration'. Sometimes used as a formula for not giving a direct answer on the spot.)

1851 I. SPENCER *Let.* 11 Jan. in U. Young *Life I. Spencer* (1933) III. iii. 181 About going to France, we shall see. **1898** G. B. SHAW *Arms & Man* III. 62 We shall see. And you shall wait my pleasure. **1925** F. SCOTT FITZGERALD *Great Gatsby* vii. 137 What he really said was: 'Yes... Yes... I'll see.' **1959** R. MATTHEWS tr. *J. Steinmann's Saint Jerome* I. xi. 49 He would tell his friend about it, and later they would see.

7. b. *to see* (a person) *home* (earlier example); *to see* (a person) (*all*) *right*: to ensure (his) well-being or safety; *to see* (a person) *over, through*: of a thing, to be sufficient for (his) needs; also with prep. *over* or *through* (a period of time or difficulty).

1819 Keats *Let.* 16 Apr. (1958) II. 92 Do you..get groggy..so as to be obliged to be seen home with a Lantern. **1894** 'Mark Twain' in *St. Nicholas* Mar. 393/1 Thirty camel-loads of treasures was enough to see a dervish through, because they live very simple. *a* **1914** 'Saki' *Beasts & Super-Beasts* (1914) 217 If you'll lend me three pounds that ought to see me through comfortably. **1959** *Times* 19 Mar. 5/5 He said he would see me all right if I said I saw the two police strike the boy. **1965** *Listener* 25 Nov. 865/1 Although Louis MacNeice was a fluent and sometimes facile poet, his sense of fact generally saw him through. *a* **1966** 'M. na Gopaleen' *Best of Myles* (1968) 87 To be saddled with the task of 'seeing' an inebriated friend 'right'. **1966** M. Steen *Looking Glass* iii. 52 He.. wrote me a cheque for twenty pounds—'to see me over'. **1971** *N.Z. Listener* 22 Mar. 13/1 Tell yer, I'll see you right at a boardin' place until you get jacked up. **1974** S. B. Hough *Fear Fortune, Father* i. 15, I could remember Lawson saying to me, 'I'll see you all right.' **1976** M. Butterworth *Remains to be Seen* vi. 89, I stopped the milk till Monday... But if you want a couple of pints to see you over the weekend.

10. a. Also, to experience (a specific age in life): usu. in negative context; *to have seen better days* (examples of things); *to have seen everything, it all*: to have experienced all the possible events and situations of life (often used as an expression of resignation or boredom); *to see the New* (*Old*) *Year in* (*out*): see *year 7.

1806 To have seen better days [see Day *sb.* 13 a]. **1899** H. James *Awkward Age* I. i. 3 He had..doubled the Cape of the years—he would never again see fifty-five. **1925** F. Scott Fitzgerald *Great Gatsby* i. 21 I've been everywhere and seen everything and done everything. **1930** W. S. Maugham *Cakes & Ale* v. 72 'But she's not as old as you are,' I said... 'She'll never see thirty again.' **1941** F. Thompson *Over to Candleford* x. 144 Laura [wore] a green smock which had seen better days. **1957** 'M. M. Kaye' *Shadow of Moon* xiv. 216 'I escorted her out from England.' '*What!*.. Now I have seen everything!' **1959** N. Mailer *Advts. for Myself* (1961) 209 Pot gave me a sense of something new about the time I was convinced I had seen it all. **1973** G. Greene *Honorary Consul* ii. iii. 80 She's not twenty, and, you know, I won't see sixty again. **1973** 'E. McBain' *Hail to Chief* i. 6 Men..with..eyes that had seen it all, seen it all: Monoghan and Monroe from Homicide. **1977** G. Tindall *Fields Beneath* vi. 90 The workhouse itself was a 'handsome brick edifice' that had seen better days. **1978** T. Willis *Buckingham Palace Connection* viii. 161 'A boat race,' said Tremayne... 'Now I've seen everything!' said Story.

12. a. Also, *to see a man* (*about a dog*) and varr.: a joc. form of excuse or explanation used to avoid giving the real reason for one's absence or departure; *spec.* (*euphem.*) to obtain an alcoholic drink; to go to the lavatory. orig. *U.S.*

1867 *Ball Players' Chron.* 12 Sept. 3/1 The rest of our nine having gone to see a man there was nobody to take the bat. **1890** Barrère & Leland *Dict. Slang* II. 216 *To see a man* (American), to go and have a drink at the bar. **1927** *Amer. Speech* III. 221 *See a man about a dog*, to go out and buy liquor. **1931** T. R. G. Lyell *Slang, Phrase & Idiom* 670 Excuse me a moment,—I shan't be long; I just have to go and see a man about something! **1945** *Richmond* (Va.) *Times-Dispatch* 25 Oct. 14/5 Greet the homecoming hero with a load of this and he will immediately find that he has to go somewhere else and see a man about a dog. **1969** *Private Eye* 28 Mar. 14, I got to see a man about a dog! **1977** A. C. H. Smith *Jericho Gun* v. 63 I've got to dash. Must see a man about a horse.

b. (Earlier example of U.S. colloq. sense 'to interview in order to bribe'.)

1867 *Ball Players' Chron.* 12 Dec. 4/2 This, that or the other 'professional' is 'seen'—that is the professional term for the act of bribery—and lo and behold! the second game between the rival clubs is marked by a signal defeat.

e. *see you*: colloq. formula of farewell, often in weakened sense without reference to an anticipated meeting (in full *I'll see you*). Also with advbs. and other extensions, as *around*, *soon*, etc. Also, (*I'll*) *be seeing you*. Cf. F. *au revoir*, G. *auf Wiedersehen*.

1891 S. Weyman *New Rector* II. i. 25 He waved an awkward farewell to Jack, muttered 'See you soon!' and went off. **1906** 'O. Henry' in *McClure's Mag.* Aug. 392/1 Now lift your hat and come away, while you receive Lou's cheery 'See you again'. **1932** J. W. Harris *Days of Endeavour* xiii. 228 The boys..follow it with no more than a cheery, 'So-long, old son; see you in Liverpool!' **1937** D. & H. Teilhet *Feather Cloak Murders* ii. 33 He waved cheerfully to the Baron, said, 'I'll be seeing you.' **1945**, etc. [see *hooray *int.*]. **1951** M. Kennedy *Lucy Carmichael* v. i. 239 'Well..be seeing you.'.. 'Be seeing you,' agreed Owen without enthusiasm. **1959** I. Fleming *Goldfinger* xix. 264 'See you around.' He grinned at Bond and moved off down the room. **1962** L. Deighton *Ipcress File* xi. 71 Thanks, chief. See you. **1970** J. Porter *Rather Common Sort of Crime* ii. 24 Well, ta ever so! Be seeing you! **1975** I. McEwan *First Love, Last Rites* 96 'See you tomorrow, then.'.. 'Yes, tomorrow.' **1978** J. Irving *World according to Garp* xiii. 253 'See ya,' she called, and drove off... 'See ya,' Garp mumbled after her.

13. a. (Earlier example in *Poker*.)

1880 [see *bet *sb.* 1 b].

15. c. (Later example.)

1921 G. B. Shaw *Back to Methuselah* ii. 83 That would be—let me see—five times three hundred and sixty-five is—um.

II. Phraseological combinations.

17. see about—. (Earlier example.)

1839 Dickens *Let.* Feb. (1965) I. 510 Will you dine with us at 5 — and see about a box without loss of time?

22. see over—. (Earlier and later examples with reference to buildings.)

1793 J. Woodforde *Diary* 23 June (1929) IV. 36 We took a walk to Weston House and saw it all over. *c* **1869** Taylor & Dubourg in M. R. Booth *Eng. Plays of 19th Cent.* (1973) III. 245 Mr. Secker's card for a friend of his to see over the ruins. **1909** M. Beerbohm *Yet Again* (ed. 5) 3 If I were 'seeing over' a house. **1920** 'O. Douglas' *Penny Plain* v. 62, I was going to ask if I might see over the house. **1977** 'M. Yorke' *Cost of Silence* i. 9 The house ..was..up for sale... People saw over it and were dashed by the need to replumb and repair.

26*. a. see off. To put to flight, chase off (esp. of a dog). Also *trans.* and *fig.*, to get the better of, defeat, put down. *colloq.* (orig. *Mil.*). Cf. sense 7 b in Dict.

1915 H. Bruckshaw *Diary* Aug. in *Times* (1976) 7 Feb. 12/6 We had at last cleared the place except for sundry stragglers who would no doubt be seen off later. **1919** W. Lang *Sea Lawyer's Log* xi. 137 You may 'see off' a messmate by overwhelming him with violence, outpointing him in cunning or overcoming him with policy. **1929** *Times* 21 Feb. 11 When he and another detective went to arrest the men Hughes called to the Alsatian. 'See 'em off.' **1944** R. P. Fleming *Jrnl.* in D. Hart-Davis *Peter Fleming* (1974) xii. 293 An unusually well-found fighting patrol..perfectly capable of seeing-off the small parties from L. of C. **1961** *Sunday Express* 10 Dec. 5/2 (*caption*) Fast as I tell him to 'See 'em off' they tell him to 'Sit'. **1969** Y. Carter *Mr. Campion's Farthing* ix. 86, I know an audience of stuffed shirts when I see one. Besides—I just had to see that pompous bastard off. **1981** 'M. Yorke' *Hand of Death* x. 90 He'd..been rebuffed... She'd seen him off good and proper.

b. Cricket. *to see off the new ball*: to bat until the shine has been removed from the ball (esp. at the start of an innings).

1969 J. Arlott *Cricket: Great All-Rounders* vii. 108 Bailey was the intractable substance which..made a good innings better by seeing off a new ball down the order to give the tail-enders a chance. **1977** *Observer* 20 Mar. 1/4 The openers had batted for a while and had seen a lot of the new ball off.

27. see out. c. (Earlier example.)

1756 *Connoisseur* II. 555 Tom Buck..can *see out* the stoutest freeholder in England.

d. (Earlier examples.)

1782 *Let.* 12 Feb. in *Essex Inst. Hist. Coll.* (1859) I. 13/2, I am Detarmend as I have beene so long in the servis to se it out. **1783** H. Newdigate *Let.* 23 Mar in A. E. Newdigate-Newdegate *Cheverels* (1898) iv. 50 Ye Opera.. is to be wonderfully shewy & the last Dance ye best, so we must see it out.

e. Of a thing (esp. one's personal property): to last (at least) as long as (a person or his lifetime); to outlast or suffice to the end.

1969 M. Pugh *Last Place Left* xix. 143 The suits I have will see me out. **1976** *Guardian* 10 Apr. 10/8, I imported a German car, a convertible Beetle... No more of these are being imported, but I expect it to see me out.

28. see through. (Earlier and later examples.)

1828 L. Hunt in *Companion* 6 Feb. 48 *William III.* The Dutchman, call'd to see our vessel through. **1913** J. Vaizey *College Girl* xviii. 250 Her thoughts flew off to Ralph Percival..recalling with pleasure his promise to 'see her through'. **1916** H. G. Wells (*title*) Mr. Britling sees it through. **1939** *War Illustr.* 14 Oct. 147 (*heading*) Mr. Briton'll see it through. **1977** G. Butler *Brides of Friedberg* v. 129 Don't worry..I'll see you through.

Seebeck (zēi·bek). *Physics.* [The name of Thomas Johann *Seebeck* (1770–1831), Russian-born German physicist, who discovered the effect (*Abhandl. der K. Akad. der Wissensch. zu Berlin: Phys. Klasse* (1822–23) 265).] **Seebeck effect,** the phenomenon whereby an e.m.f. is generated in a circuit containing junctions between dissimilar metals if these junctions are at different temperatures; the phenomenon of thermoelectricity.

1903 *Whittaker's Electr. Engineer's Pocket Bk.* 99 If a junction between two dissimilar metals be heated or cooled, a flow of electricity will take place across the junction. If a current be passed through such a junction, a change of temperature will be produced. The former phenomenon is known as the Seebeck effect, the latter as the Peltier effect. **1906** *Sci. Abstr.* A. IX. 481 The Thomson-, Peltier-, and Seebeck-effects may be combined in one diagram, and the author does this for the case of iron and silver. **1964** S. H. Avner *Introd. Physical Metall.* i. 6 The total emf in a thermoelectric pyrometer, sometimes called the Seebeck effect, is therefore the algebraic sum of four emf's, two Peltier emf's at the hot and cold junctions and two Thomson emf's along each of the wires. **1973** J. G. Tweeddale *Materials Technol.* I. iv. 97 If an electric circuit is suitably completed a current will flow between the materials (the Seebeck effect).

seed, *sb.* Add: **1. a.** Also, *to go to seed* (Go *v.* 44 b): to cease flowering as seeds develop; *fig.*, to become habitually unkempt, ineffective, etc.; to deteriorate.

1817 J. K. Paulding *Lett. fr. South* I. xvii. 188 His white dimity could not last for ever, and he gradually went to seed. **1859** [see Go *v.* 44 b]. **1929** G. Ade *Let.* 8 Feb. (1973) 139 We have ridden for miles and miles [in Peking], visiting temples and palaces of incredible size and beauty, some of them slightly gone to seed and others filled with the most wonderful museum displays of Chinese art. **1951** E. Paul *Springtime in Paris* ii. 33 Clients, mostly young and disreputable, or old and gone to seed. **1967** G. F. Fiennes *I tried to run Railway* iv. 42 He seemed to be going to seed a bit; to be a bit slow.

d. Cf. *bird-seed* s.v. *bird *sb.* 9.

2. b. *Chem.* A small crystal of the desired substance introduced into a liquid in order to promote crystallization and to provide a nucleus for crystal growth. Orig. *spec.* in sugar manufacture. Also *fig.*

1909 in *Cent. Dict.* Suppl. **1915** H. C. Prinsen-Geerligs *Pract. White Sugar Manuf.* ii. i. 80 White sugar destined for direct consumption should not only be white and brilliant, but should also possess a regular form and a rather large size; this latter desideratum makes it preferable to start the building up of the grain from a well-developed seed. **1959** *Engineering* 13 Feb. 219/2 Seeds can be cut to provide grown crystals that can be sawn in the most efficient manner. **1966** *McGraw-Hill Encycl. Sci. & Technol.* III. 601/1 A small crystal of the desired substance is added to the solution as a 'seed' to induce the formation of the first crystals. **1973** *Nature* 12 Oct. 294/1 Some cardinal topics in evolutionary biology were adopted as 'seeds' on which other constituents of the programme might crystallise: protein polymorphism, for example.

2*. *Sport*, esp. *Lawn Tennis.* [f. sense *11 of the vb.] One of a number of seeded players in a tournament.

1933 M. D. Lyon in *Aldin Bk. Outdoor Games* 509 'But why put my beloved lawners last?' waits the Thibetan 'seed'. **1954** *Sun* (Baltimore) 22 June 17/3 The remaining four men's seeds won just the way they were supposed to due to the sudden decision by Wimbledon to seed 12 instead of the traditional eight. **1958** *Times* 20 Mar. 16/5 (*heading*) Badminton seeds dislodged. **1963** *Times* 12 June 5/6 Mr. McKinley, the United States number one and runner-up at Wimbledon in 1961, is top seed in the men's event. **1977** *Western Morning News* 30 Aug. 12/8 Fiona Moffitt, the number five seed from Dawlish, is Devon's main hope for the title.

3. (Later examples.)

1914 J. London *Let.* 24 Feb. (1966) 415, I have never wantonly scattered my seed. **1973** K. A. Sey *Ghanaian English* vii. 84 *To take seed*, to become pregnant.

6. b. *Med.* A small container for holding a radioactive material such as radon when it is placed in body tissue in radiotherapy. Cf. *radon seed* s.v. *radon 2.

1925 *Glasgow Herald* 26 Mar. 9 To capture the gas emanating from radium, purify it, and bottle it in tiny tubes called from their shape seeds. **1974** R. M. Kirk et al. *Surgery* iv. 66 The gas radon ^{222}Rn, a product of radium decay, with a half-life of four days, can be sealed in gold tubes or 'seeds' and implanted into the tissues. **1980** *Daily Tel.* 4 Dec. 6/8 It can implant radioactive seeds by needle when surgery has failed to remove malignancy or patients can no longer sustain external radiation therapy.

7. a. Simple attrib. (*a*) *seed catalogue, -fall, -house, packet, rate, set, tray, weight*; (*b*) *seed-ball, -speck, -stalk* (earlier example); (*c*) *seed-potato(es)* (examples); (*d*) *seed drill* (earlier and later examples).

1917 D. H. Lawrence *Look! We have come Through!* 119 The seed-ball of the sun Is broken at last. [**1760** J. Webb (*title*) A catalogue of seeds and hardy plants.] **1901** L. H. Bailey *Princ. Veg. Gardening* v. 168 The differences..might be of such a character that they could not be definitely described in a seed catalogue. **1938** N. Marsh *Death in White Tie* xxv. 266 He hastily gathered up..parish magazines, *Church Times*, and seed catalogues. **1973** K. Giles *File on Death* v. 138 Do you get much mail?'.. 'Today there were three letters and a seed catalogue.' **1792** W. Rutherford *Let.* 28 Feb. in *Trans. Soc. Promotion of Useful Arts* (N.Y.) I. 121 Some years ago a farmer in Somerset county, in New Jersey, first introduced a seed-drill of his invention. **1850** *Mary Wedlake's Priced List Farming Implements* 14 (*heading*) Improved corn and seed drill. **1941** [see *combine *sb.* c]. **1973** L. Russell *Colonial Canada* iii. 38 The seed drill was invented in the 1850s; in this the seeds were not just dropped into the furrows, but were inserted into the soil through flexible tubes with a cutting edge in front. **1968** *Jrnl. Forestry* LXVI. 422/2 The estimated seedfall.. averaged..almost 1 pound per acre. **1981** *Country Life* 16 July 184/1 My fear of the allium menace..prompts me to dead-head every species before seed-fall. **1912** 'C. F. Benton' *Fairs & Fetes* 116 Give to every purchaser a catalogue, which will be donated by any seed-house on request. **1941** *Sun* (Baltimore) 6 Aug. 16/7 Gray's standard manual apparently *versus* a Philadelphia seed-house. **1935** A. G. L. Hellyer *Pract. Gardening* v. 43 Beginners are safe in following the directions printed on the seed packet. **1981** 'M. Yorke' *Hand of Death* xvi. 143 Ronald ..sorted through old seed packets. **1742** J. Savage in *New Hampshire Probate Rec.* (1916) III. 115, I Give to my Dear and Loving Wife..Ground..for to plant one bushel of Seed pertators. **1901** L. H. Bailey *Cycl. Amer. Hort.* III. 1419/2 The seed Potatoes are cut to one eye, and dropped about 12 to 15 in. apart. **1977** *Belfast Tel.* 22 Feb. 22/4 (Advt.), Foundation stock seed potatoes for sale. **1960** *Times* 28 Nov. 16/5 The recommended seed-rate [for maize] is 30 to 35 lb. an acre. **1977** J. L. Harper *Population Biol. Plants* viii. 250 Seed of *T*[*rifolium*] *repens* was sown together with varying seed rates of *Lolium perenne*. **1946** *Nature* 12 Oct. 519/2 The reactions based on pollen-tube growth and seed-set determinations of these two groups of plants are given in the accompany-ng table. **1978** *Ibid.* 7 Sept. 54/2 In artificial field bean pollination, manual stripping of open flowers is a recommended practice for increasing seed set in autosterile lines. **1917** D. H. LAWRENCE *Look! We have come Through!* 59 Rose-leaves that whirl in colour round a core Of seed-specks kindled lately. **1744** W. ELLIS *Mod. Husbandman* Jan. ii. 32 A Turnep runs up a Seed-stalk sometimes near seven Feet high. **1953** E. R. JANES *Sweet Peas* vii. 53 Standard seed trays give little trouble. **1971** P. D. JAMES *Shroud for Nightingale* vi. 183 A small stack of seed trays, pruning shears, a trowel and small fork. **1927** HALDANE & HUXLEY *Animal Biol.* x. 219 They will produce plants each of which will have the same range of seed-weight as did its parent. **1977** J. L. HARPER *Population Biol. Plants* vii. 203 The year to year variation in seed weight is quite large.

b. Objective and objective genitive. *seed planter, sower, -sowing* (example), *-testing*; *seed-eating* adj.

1927 HALDANE & HUXLEY *Animal Biol.* x. 205 If..a tame sea-gull is fed on corn instead of fish, the whole lining of its stomach alters, becoming thicker and more like that of seed-eating birds. **1977** J. L. HARPER *Population Biol. Plants* xx. 629 A plague of seed-eating mammals, birds or insects may prevent regeneration. **1850** *Rep. Comm. Patents 1849* (U.S.) I. 151 Having thus fully described my improved grain and seed planter. **1848** *Commerc. Rev.* VI. 133 Seed-Sowers, &c.—These machines are quite ingenious and labor-saving in their contrivance, [etc.]. **1977** *Young's Sporting Appliances* (S. Young & Sons Ltd.) 5 Seed sower. **1865** *Rep. Maine Board Agric.* X. 65 The use of the drill for general seed-sowing is at present considered too expensive. **1896** *U.S. Dept. Agric. Yearbk. 1895* 175 The importance of seed testing is recognized not only by professional seedmen, but also by intelligent farmers. **1910** *Chambers's Jrnl.* Oct. 685/1 Next comes seed-testing under the microscope, which shows the weed, seeds, and rubbish amongst them. **1950** *N.Z. Jrnl. Agric.* Mar. 243/1 Some 80 years ago the first seed-testing station was established in Saxony by Professor Nobbe. **1973** *Country Life* 15 Mar. 714/2 Work on onions at the Cambridge Official Seed Testing Station.

d. Instrumental, as *seed-borne* adj.

1931 *Bull. W. Virginia Agric. Exper. Station* No. 245. 5 The economic losses occasioned by these few seed-borne parasites..are enormous. **1968** *Times* 16 Dec. 7/1 A seed-borne fungus disease.

8. seed bank, (*a*) a place where seeds of different plant varieties and species are stored as a safeguard against their possible extinction; (*b*) the seeds that have accumulated naturally in a given area of ground; **seed bull,** a bull kept to serve cows; **seed-cotton** (earlier example); **seed crystal** = sense 2 b above; **seed dressing,** a preparation applied to seed in order to protect it against pests; the practice or an instance of employing this; **seed fat,** a fat obtained from seeds; **seed-leaf,** (*b*) used *attrib.* and *absol.* to designate a kind of tobacco grown in the northern United States and used chiefly for wrapping cigars (so called because it was first grown from imported seed); **seed metering,** automatic control of the numbers of seeds sown or planted by a machine; **seed money** *U.S.*, money allocated (esp. from public funds) for the initiation of a project and designed to stimulate the independent economic expansion of the project; **seed orchard,** a group of trees cultivated for the production of seed; **seed parent,** in hybridization, a plant whose seed is fertilized by pollen from a different plant; **seed stitch** *Needlework* = *SEEDING *vbl. sb.* 3*; **seed year,** one of the years in which a particular tree produces a good crop of seeds.

1958 *Economist* 25 Oct. 328/2 In America's first central seed bank, which has recently been opened at Colorado State University, there is space to store supplies of several hundred thousand basic seed stocks. **1974** *Nature* 24 May 303/2 As part of a worldwide effort to conserve this fast disappearing genetic resource, a seed bank had already been set up. **1977** J. L. HARPER *Population Biol. Plants* iv. 83 The store of seeds buried in soil (the seed bank) is composed in part of seeds produced on the area and partly of seeds blown in from elsewhere. **1932** E. HEMINGWAY *Death in Afternoon* xi. 118 The usual ranch has two hundred cows and four seed bulls. **1797** F. BAILY *Jrnl. Tour N. Amer.* 285 The seed-cotton loses three-fourths of its weight by jenning. **1934** *Industr. & Engin. Chem.* Nov. 1201/1 The initial formation of crystal nuclei is profoundly influenced by the chance presence of very small seed crystals of the solute. **1962** [see *MELT *sb.*[3] 2]. **1974** *Encycl. Brit. Macropædia* V. 337/1 If the structure and interatomic spacing of the surface..approximate that of the crystal, growth on the surface can resemble growth on a normal seed crystal. **1926–7** *Army & Navy Stores Catal.* p. lxxi/2 Seed Dressings, Liquid. **1955** E. HOLMES *Pract. Plant Protection* iv. 31 By far the most important fungicidal seed-dressings are those based on chemicals known as the organo-mercury products. **1977** M. B. GREEN et al. *Chemicals for Crop Protection & Pest Control* xii. 103 The convenience and economy of seed-dressing makes it..a clear choice when the disease can be controlled this way. **1940** T. P. HILDITCH *Chem. Constitution of Natural Fats* i. 18 However varied the fatty acids in seed fats may be, the resulting triglycerides are..fundamentally similar in type. **1949** *Thorpe's Dict. Appl. Chem.* (ed. 4) IX. 8/2 In many seed fats..the main component acids are confined to palmitic, oleic, and linoleic in varying proportions. **1963** *Times* 22 May (Suppl.) p. iv/2 The main sources of edible oils and fats are vegetable fats—particularly palm oil; seed fats, notably those of groundnut, coconut, soya bean, palm kernel and cotton seed; [etc.]. **1852** *Hunt's Merch. Mag.* XXVII. 555 The 'seed leaf' is raised on the Miami River. **1888** *Encycl. Brit.* XXIII. 425/2 The 'seed-leaf' tobacco of Pennsylvania, Connecticut, and Ohio, grown from Havana seed, is devoted to cigar-making in the United States. **1910** 'MARK TWAIN' *Speeches* 267, I bought what was called a seed-leaf cigar with a Connecticut wrapper. **1946** W. W. GARNER *Production of Tobacco* ii. 35 The process of fermenting the leaf in cases in preparation for manufacture..began about 1845 and gave great impetus to the manufacture of the 'Seed and Havana' cigar, composed of Cuban filler and Connecticut Seedleaf wrapper. **1968** B. C. AKEHURST *Tobacco* xi. 266 The current U.S. Department of Agriculture classification is as follows: Class 4..Type 41 Pennsylvania Seed Leaf. **1955** R. BAINER et al. *Princ. Farm Machinery* xi. 225 Most seed-metering devices may be classified as: (*a*) those having cells on a moving member, the cells being sized to accommodate single seeds or groups of a few seeds each, (*b*) the so-called 'force-feed' devices.., (*c*) stationary-opening units. **1971** *Power Farming* Mar. 29/4 The gearing..has been improved to give greater precision in seed metering. **1966** *N.Y. Times* 21 Aug. F15/2 The bonds would have enabled the state to gain $17-million, to be used as seed money to set up the loan guarantee rotary fund. **1970** *Sat. Rev.* (U.S.) 10 Jan. 27/1 This has been seed money in the best sense of the term. As President Nixon pointed out to Congress last month, every dollar of Foundation money has stimulated the donation of three dollars from other sources. **1977** *Time* 12 Dec. 33/2 It calls for $120 million in federal seed money to create 14,000 new jobs and rehabilitate four neighborhoods. **1951** H. MCKUSICK in *Tree Planters' Notes* VIII. 8 It..seems logical that we should explore the possibility of establishing seed orchards. **1979** *Beautiful British Columbia* Fall 40 Others are from seed orchards maintained by the province and the forest companies. **1902** *Jrnl. R. Hort. Soc.* XXVII. 209 We suggested..crossing our common Wood Anemone..with the scarlet *Anemone fulgens*, making the Wood Anemone the seed parent. **1970** R. GORER *Devel. Garden Flowers* 19, I have tried to follow the convention in which the seed parent is the first named and the pollen parent the second. **1934** M. THOMAS *Dict. Embroidery Stitches* 182 Tiny stitches taken at all angles and in any direction but of more or less even length produce a surprisingly effective filling, as the diagram of Seed Stitch shows. **1964** *McCall's Sewing* xiii. 246/2 *Seed stitch*,..a very tiny chain stitch tightly drawn and scattered in all directions to fill an open area. **1889** W. SCHLICH *Man. Forestry* I. II. ii. 173 The quantity of seed is governed by two things:—(1.) The average yield of each seed-year; and (2.) The frequency of seed-years. **1979** H. W. HOCKER *Introd. Forest Biol.* ii. 55 Heavy seed years do not occur at frequent intervals, but are usually offset by succeeding years of light to very light crops.

seed, *v.* Add: **II. 6. a.** Also *absol.*

1888 *Vermont Agric. Rep.* X. 48, I..then seed broadcast with grass-seed. **1979** [see *PLANT *v.* 1].

b. *spec.* (i) To introduce a crystal or small particle into (a liquid or apparatus) so as to induce crystallization. Cf. *SEED *sb.* 2 b.

1909 in *Cent. Dict.* Suppl. **1921** *Jrnl. Physical Chem.* XXV. 534 Points on the stable curve..were then easily determined by seeding the proper mixtures..with small crystals from this lot of hydrate. **1930** *Amer. Speech* VI. 14 Sometimes a crystallizer is seeded with a nest egg of sugar. **1936** H. L. ALLING *Interpretative Petrol. Igneous Rocks* iv. 41 Supercooled water, left undisturbed, is stable if not in contact with ice. 'Seeding' it with the solid phase produces crystallization. **1964** G. H. HAGGIS et al. *Introd. Molecular Biol.* iv. 94 It has further been possible recently to study this process *in vitro* by 'seeding' near-saturated solutions of calcium phosphate with collagen fibres.

(ii) To introduce crystals of a substance such as silver iodide into (a cloud, etc.) in order to cause precipitation.

1947 *Sun* (Baltimore) 9 Sept. 3/3 Today's storm developed too close to the Florida West Coast to be seeded with dry ice or other crystals by Army and Navy planes. **1958** *Observer* 12 Jan. 6/3 The nearest thing to weather control so far is 'seeding' clouds with ice or silver iodide to persuade them to give up their rain. **1974** *Nature* 11 Oct. 461/3 Potential hail clouds are observed by radar, and then seeded by lead iodide from a rocket fired into the cloud's centre. **1975** *Daily Colonist* (Victoria, B.C.) 16 July 3/3 The United States government did not seed hurricane Fifi, nor was it ever contemplated.

(iii) *Biol.* To inoculate (a culture vessel) *with* cells from a culture which is to be propagated.

1960 *Virology* X. 387 One hundred-millimeter petri dishes were seeded with cells from primary cultures of normal mouse. **1978** *Nature* 23 Mar. 372/2 The procedure was repeated using cultures of Wi-38 cells prepared in..eight-compartment chamber slides..that had been seeded three days earlier with 15,000 cells in each compartment.

7. a. (Earlier modern examples.)

1814 J. TAYLOR *Arator* (ed. 2) 154 When the wheat was seeded on high and narrow ridges. **1851** C. CIST *Cincinnati* xv. 317 The cotton crop is seeded in the spring.

d. *Biol.* To inoculate (cells from a culture) *into* a culture vessel or medium.

1965 *Proc. Nat. Acad. Sci.* LIV. 1585 The cells were..seeded into 60-mm plastic dishes at a density of $2{\cdot}5 \times 10^6$ cells per dish. **1973** *Nature* 22 June 450/1 Cells (10^7) were seeded into each 100-mm Petri dish (Falcon Co.) and incubated at 37°C in a humidified incubator with 5% CO_2 in air.

11. *Sport*, esp. *Lawn Tennis.* To assign (to several of the better competitors) a position in an ordered list, so that those most highly ranked do not meet until the later stages of an elimination competition; to arrange (a draw or event) to this end. Cf. *SEED *sb.* 2*. orig. *U.S.*

1898 *Amer. Lawn Tennis* 13 Jan. 4/2 Several years ago, it was decided to 'seed' the best players through the championship draw, and this was done for two or three years. **1900** *Spalding's Lawn Tennis Ann.* 78 It is generally advisable to 'seed' the draw in handicap tournaments so that the players in each class shall be separated as far as possible one from another. **1911** *Spalding's Off. Lawn Tennis Guide* 55 Unlike many big events, Longwood is never seeded, and in consequence the possibility of an uneven draw materialized. **1924** *Times* 23 June 4/4 This year, for the first time, the draw has been 'seeded'; how little seeding accords with British notions may be gathered from there being no reference in the Oxford Dictionary—at any rate in the smaller one... In some countries the seeding is designed to keep the better players apart until the final stages. **1929** *Times* 29 June 4/4 Three of the women who had been 'seeded' for the draw were defeated during the day. **1953** *Sunday Graphic* 7 June 22/4 Rose, likely to be seeded in the first four at Wimbledon, did not play up to his reputation. **1955** *N.Y. Times* 10 May 33/5 Joe Burk's Red and Blue eight, which beat Navy and Harvard Saturday for the Adams Cup, was seeded first in the draw for the tenth annual regatta. **1972** D. DELMAN *Sudden Death* (1973) i. 17 Timmy was up against a big Australian kid who'd given me fits at Wimbledon... Timmy..would probably go into the tournament seeded second behind Cole. **1982** *Guardian* 8 June 22/8 She is seeded 14th and is not particularly worried that a seeding at Wimbledon is unlikely.

seed-corn. Add: **1.** (Later *fig.* examples.)

1962 *Economist* 19 May 688/1 The loans and grants from his agency are 'seed corn'; they stimulate local initiative and self-help. **1977** *Times* 20 Dec. 10/8 The IBA should be prepared to use the secondary rental income from these established stations which are already well into profit, as seedcorn money to help establish and run independent stations in smaller townships.

2. seed-corn maggot *U.S.*, the yellowish-white larva of a fly, *Hylemya platura*, which infests the seed of many vegetables and other crop plants, preventing sprouting or causing the seedlings to be weak and sickly; also, the adult fly.

1869 C. V. RILEY *First Ann. Rep. Noxious Insects Missouri* 154 (*heading*) The seed-corn maggot. **1902** *Bull. Div. Entomol. U.S. Dept. Agric.* XXXIII. 84 The Seed-Corn Maggot..has received no less than seven Latin names. **1949** *Jrnl. Econ. Entomol.* XLII. 77/1 The seed corn maggot..injures bean, pea and corn seedlings before the plants emerge. **1975** *Nature* 7 Aug. 487/1 Larvae of the seedcorn maggot..may damage or kill young plants of many crop species by feeding on the cotyledons and plumules.

seeded, *ppl. a.* Add: **5.** Of fruit, esp. dried fruit: having the seeds removed.

1921 *Daily Colonist* (Victoria, B.C.) 1 Apr. 6/1 (Advt.), Sun-Maid seeded raisins, bulk, packets of 15 oz.

6. *Sport*, esp. *Lawn Tennis.* Of a competitor: assigned a position in a list of seeds (*SEED *sb.* 2*) in an elimination competition. Also of a draw arranged in such a manner. Also *transf.*

1922 *Spalding's Tennis Ann.* 30 Commencing in 1922, all championships and other sanctioned tournaments except handicap events shall have a seeded draw. *Ibid.* 31 Seeded men in the top half of the draw. **1954** *New Yorker* 28 Aug. 57/1 The semifinals had the No. 1 and No. 2 seeded teams in each division. **1961** *Listener* 21 Sept. 437/1 One more look at the seeded players, a convincing warts-and-all likeness of Wingate, Stilwell an 'unmitigated disaster', and some memorable marginalia to the saga of Slim.

seeder. Add: **2.** (Earlier U.S. example.)

1868 *Rep. Iowa Agric. Soc. 1867* 226 The seeder can be adjusted in five minutes.

3. *cloud seeder*: one who or that which seeds clouds.

1953 *Jrnl. Amer. Water Works Assoc.* XLV. 1144/1 The skilled commercial cloud seeder is qualified by training and experience to undertake the large-scale operations that make cloud seeding economically worthwhile. **1958** *Ann. Reg. 1957* 485 Experiments with an electrostatic cloud seeder consisting of an aircraft trailing two 300 ft. cables carrying a 50,000 volt charge of electricity. **1975** *Nature* 28 Aug. 690/3 The responsibility..rests as much with the policy makers as it does with the plant breeders, the climatologists and the cloud seeders. **1981** *Economist* 20 June 55/1 Utilities that hire cloud-seeders, hoping to increase water-flow into their reservoirs, may cause the heavens to fall on the tourist industry.

seeding, *vbl. sb.* Add: **2. c.** *transf.* (Cf. *SEED *v.* 6 b.)

1926 *Jrnl. Chem. Soc.* II. 2774 Crystallisation could be easily induced by 'seeding'. **1935** J. N. FRIEND *Physical Chem.* II. v. 128 This cannot be done even by careful seeding as the hydrate is too soluble to be reached in this way. **1939** E. LILJENCRANTZ *Cancer Handbk. of Tumor Clinic* xi. 94 Medulloblastoma is distinguished by its tendency toward subarachnoid dissemination or 'seeding' along the entire cerebrospinal axis. **1947** *Sun* (Baltimore) 8 Sept. 3/2 The Miami plane will fly above the storm to photograph the effects of 'seeding' by the weather-science plane. **1958** S. M. BROOKS *Basic Facts Med. Microbiol.* i. 29 Inoculation means the seeding of a culture medium with an organism..using a sterile platinum wire (straight or looped) or a sterile glass pipette. **1966** WRIGHT & SYMMERS *Systemic Path.* II. xxxiv. 1248/1 The ability of a glioma to spread by seeding is of considerable practical importance. **1972** *Materials & Technol.* V. xx. 713 This process may be induced by the introduction of a few crystals of ephedrine oxalate—a process known as 'seeding'. **1977** *Jrnl. R. Soc. Arts* CXXV. 160/1 By far the largest and most sustained effort to modify weather deliberately has involved the artificial seeding of clouds in an attempt to increase the rainfall or suppress damaging hailstorms.

3*. A stitch in embroidery (see quot. 1960). Cf. SEED *v.* 9; *seed-stitch* s.v. *SEED *sb.* 8.

c **1840** LADY WILTON *Art of Needlework* xx. 317 There is slabbing—veining—and button stitch; seeding—roping—and open stitch. **1960** B. DEAN in G. Lewis *Handbk. Crafts* 24 Stem stitch..and seeding.., which consists of a small back stitch with another worked over it, to form an irregular filling, are also useful.

3.** *Sport*, esp. *Lawn Tennis*. The placing of competitors in a list of seeds (*SEED *sb.* 2*); (also *pl.*) the order or ranking so produced.

1912 A. F. WILDING *On Court & Off* 140 Arranging or 'seeding' is a distinction without any material difference. **1937** P. B. HAWK *Off Racket* i. 13 'Seeding' was believed to be unfair to certain contestants and to make for a less interesting tournament by eliminating..the probability of thrilling matches in the early rounds. **1955** *N.Y. Times* 10 May 33/5 (*heading*) Penn crew tops sprint seedings. **1958** *Oxford Mail* 15 Jan. 8/1 For the first time, seeding is to be introduced into the Amateur Golf Championship being played at St. Andrews in the week beginning June 2. **1978** *Times* 4 July 19/3 Another clay court specialist, Miss Jausovec, upset the seedings by beating Wendy Turnbull.

4. (sense 2) *seeding rate*; (sense *3**) *seeding(s)-committee, system*; **seeding felling** (see quot. 1928).

1936 *Times* 22 June 7/4 If six of the chosen eight come through the seeding committee will have guessed well. **1960** *Times* 4 July 15/6 In spite of the skilful pruning of the seedings committee. **1976** *Liverpool Echo* 7 Dec. 17/7 Mrs. Marshall had a tough fight in her semi-final..as the girls battled to give the seeding committee for the finals an idea of current form. **1928** R. S. TROUP *Silvicultural Systems* iv. 32 The seeding felling, under which the canopy is opened out in order to afford sufficient light to ensure the survival for a short time of seedlings springing from seed shed by the overhead trees. **1968** CHAMPION & SETH *Gen. Silviculture for India* v. 269 The overwood may be removed in only two fellings, first the main seeding felling. **1930** L. S. DICKINSON *Lawn* iv. 34 The seeding rate 3½ pounds per 1,000 square feet of lawn. **1949** G. H. ALGREN *Forage Crops* xxiv. 241 The seeding rates shown for certain crops..are too high. **1929** *Times* 24 June 7/1 The 'seeding' system undoubtedly has its merits.

seedling, *sb.* and *a.* Add: **A.** *sb.* **4.** **seedling blight,** a disease of seedlings, esp. a seed-borne, sometimes fatal disease of flax that affects esp. seedlings and is caused by the fungus *Colletotrichum lini*.

1919 PETHYBRIDGE & LAFFERTY in *Jrnl. Dept. Agric. & Technical Instr. Ireland* XX. 327 It is usually not recognised in the brairding crop until the seedlings are one or two inches high... It is during these early stages that the disease causes most damage, and it is for this reason that we have proposed the name 'Seedling-blight' for it, although the trouble is not entirely confined to plants in the seedling stage. **1980** F. HOPE *Recognition & Control of Pests & Dis. Farm Crops* (ed. 2) 159/1 Seedling Blight *Colletotrichum lini* can be a destructive disease of flax seedlings.

seedy, *a.* Add: **2. b.** Also *spec.* as a result of excessive eating or drinking; = CROP-SICK *a.* (Earlier examples.)

1729 R. SAVAGE *Author to be Lett* 7 After an Evening's hard boozing, my brother Bards..have been what we call Seedy or Crop-sick. **1845** *Punch* IX. 40/2 Young Oxford eats a wondrous meal, And drinks a lot of beer, And in the morning oftentimes, Full seedy does appear.

seegar. Delete *obs.* and add: Representing a U.S. colloq. or dial. pronunciation, with stress on the first syllable. (Later examples.)

1935 Z. N. HURSTON *Mules & Men* (1970) I. v. 119 Settin' by de fire smokin' uh seegar. **1976** W. GOLDMAN *Magic* III. viii. 171 'Got any of them jazzy see-gars?' Fats wondered. **1976** *Time* 27 Sept. 46/1 Carter does not fit many Southern stereotypes. He is not a hard drinker, poker player, or profane and garrulous see-gar-chomping raconteur.

seeing, *vbl. sb.* Add: **1. a.** *seeing is believing* (later examples).

1712 J. ARBUTHNOT *Lewis Baboon* iv. 21 There's nothing like Matter of Fact; Seeing is Believing. **1848** J. C. & A. W. HARE *Guesses at Truth* 2nd Ser. 497 *Seeing is believing*, says the proverb... Though, of all our senses, the eyes are the most easily deceived, we believe them in preference to any other evidence. **1909** *Times Lit. Suppl.* 28 May 198/2 Seeing is believing;..only art can make history really credible, or a great name more than a label to an abstraction. **1975** A. PRICE *Our Man in Camelot* v. 84 'Show him the stuff.'.. 'Okay. Maybe you're right... Seeing is believing, I guess.'

2*. *Astr.* The quality of telescopic observation; the extent to which a stellar image remains steady and free from twinkling, or a planetary image sharp.

In modern usage seeing is quantified as the apparent angular diameter of a point source as seen in a powerful telescope.

1903 *Phil. Mag.* V. 674 Observatories are put even on high mountains to get rid of the disturbances in this atmosphere, which tend to make the image of every object tremulous.., and to prevent what the astronomer terms 'good seeing'. **1969** N. CALDER *Violent Universe* 21 The best 'seeing' at any working observatory is said to be that at Cerro Tololo, in Chile. **1977** *Nature* 21 Apr. 693/2 The seeing during the observations was generally between 1" and 2".

seeing, *ppl. a.* Add: **2.** *seeing eye*: in various senses of the vb. SEE, the faculty of seeing; *seeing-eye dog* (U.S.): a guide-dog trained to lead the blind.

Seeing eye is registered in the U.S. as a proprietary name for guide-dogs trained to lead the blind.

1921 P. LUBBOCK *Craft of Fiction* x. 146 The 'seeing eye' to which it is presented is not his, but the reader's own. **1930** *Official Gaz.* (U.S. Patent Off.) 26 Aug. 553/2 The Seeing Eye, Nashville, Tenn... *The Seeing Eye* for trained dogs. Claims use since Mar. 30, 1929. **1938** *Sun* (Baltimore) 18 May 8/7 Many people..will be much moved by the story of how the first of the now famous 'seeing-eye' dogs has been carried by plane back to the Seeing Eye School at Morristown, N.J., there to spend its last days quietly. **1948** J. CANNAN *Little I Understood* viii. 101, I don't pretend to be able to draw. I've just got the seeing eye. **1950** P. BOTTOME *Under Skin* xvi. 137 He had bought her [*sc.* a blind woman] a 'Seeing Eye' dog, who took her wherever she wished. **1969** K. M. WELLS *Owl Pen Reader* II. 210 You see, Grandpa had the seeing eye and grandma hadn't. **1979** 'A. HAILEY' *Overload* III. xiii. 267 The interior [of the bar] was dark and smelled of mildew. 'Christ!' Nancy said. 'We need a seeing-eye dog.'

seeing, quasi-*conj.* Add: Also (*colloq.*) with *as* (*how*).

1833 DICKENS *Let.* 18 Mar. (1965) I. 17 Seeing as I cannot fail to do that I have engaged in a pursuit. **1895** *Dialect Notes* I. 399 Seein' as how it's you, I'll do so-and-so. **1952** M. LASKI *Village* vii. 121, I suppose—seeing as how we've both been let down—you wouldn't care to come in with me? **1974** S. GULLIVER *Vulcan Bulletins* 29 Seeing as how you're always short of £sd, I thought you could maybe earn a bit.

seek, *sb.* Restrict † *Obs.* to sense in Dict. and add: **2.** *Computers.* The movement of a read/write head to a new position on a storage device; **seek-time,** the time taken by this, as part of the total access time.

1965 *IEEE Trans. Computers* XIV. 580/2 No more than three concurrent seek operations per data channel are justified for System I. **1967** *AFIPS Conf. Proc.* XXX. 11/1 Suppose that secondary memory is a disk... The operation of moving the arm is known as a seek; but the policy shortest seek time first..is unsatisfactory. **1974** *Communications Assoc. Computing Machinery* XVII. 139/2 The objective of optimally scheduling a sequence of requests on the DASD to minimize seektime or rotational delays. **1980** *Sci. Amer.* Aug. 118/3 First the head must be positioned over the proper track. This requires a 'seek time'.

seek, *v.* Add: **I. 12. b.** (Later examples.) Cf. SICK *v.*[2]

1928 KIPLING *Limits & Renewals* (1932) 64 Go seek, boy! It's Dinah! Seek! **1968** P. N. WALKER *Carnaby & Gaolbreakers* xix. 178 'Seek,' and the two police dogs were cast about the mini car.

seeker. Add: **1. a.** Also in phr. *seeker after truth*.

1840 [see SCIENTIST]. *a* **1968** A. FARRER *Interpret. & Belief* (1976) 138 Madame Blavatsky, than whom few women have been more remarkable for the power of making solid objects fade into thin air among the mountains of India, and crystallize back to physical solidity in the middle of English drawing-room cushions, thence to be hacked out with scissors by delighted seekers after truth.

seelapak, var. *SILLAPAK.

seem, *sb.* For † *Obs.* read ? *Obs.* or *dial.* (chiefly *Sc.*) and add later examples.

1730 A. RAMSAY *Tea-Table Miscellany* (ed. 5) 213 His seim in Thrang of fiercest Stryfe, When Winner ay the same. **1812** JANE AUSTEN *Let.* 29 Nov. (1952) 499 It [*sc.* a cloak] is to be Grey Woollen & cost ten shillings. I hope you like the *sim* of it. **1837** J. M. WILSON *Tales of Borders* III. 131/1 There comes slowly, as if frae the womb o' a cloud o' mountain mist, the seim o' a turreted abbey. **1913** H. P. CAMERON tr. *T. à Kempis's Imit. Christ* II. vii. 63 Ye'se sune be begunkit, gin ye regaird allenarlie the ootrin seim o' men.

seem, *v.*[2] Add: **II. 4. a.** Also in weakened sense (chiefly interrogative).

1901 A. K. MCCLURE '*Abe' Lincoln's Yarns & Stories* 65 'What seems to be the matter?' inquired Lincoln with all the calmness and self-possession he could muster. **1958** B. W. ALDISS *Non-Stop* IV. iii. 219 'What seems to be the trouble?' he asked. **1974** WODEHOUSE *Aunts aren't Gentlemen* xvi. 134 My voice shook a bit as I applied for further details. 'What seems to be the trouble?' I asked. **1977** G. MARKSTEIN *Chance Awakening* xix. 55 He dialled 100..'What seems to be the trouble?' asked the operator.

e. Also, in negative contexts (preceded by *can*): to seem unable. *colloq.*

1874 HARDY *Far from Madding Crowd* II. xiii. 168 Troy could hardly seem to believe her to be his proud wife Bathsheba. **1898** G. GISSING *Human Odds & Ends* 57 As a lad, I couldn't stick to anything—couldn't seem to put my heart into any sort of work. **1937** I. BAIRD *John* xix. 229 He couldn't seem to get the boy out of his head. **1969** M. PUGH *Last Place Left* vii. 44 Somehow I can't seem to get warm.

seep, *sb.* Restrict *dial.* to senses 1 and 3 in Dict. and add: **2.** (Later examples.)

1902 *Nature* 4 Dec. 113/1 At Comanche Spring, a small 'seep',..the limestone bluffs have been covered in a number of places with rude paintings of characteristic Indian design. **1903** *Bull. U.S. Geol. Survey* No. 212. 97 In this well small seeps or pockets of petroleum were found at several depths. **1966** *McGraw-Hill Encycl. Sci. & Technol.* X. 60/2 Almost without exception, seeps are at topographically low spots where water has accumulated. Oil..rises to the surface of the water, covering it with an iridescent film. **1972** *Science* 16 June 1257/2 The existence of submarine seeps is often mentioned in discussions of oil pollution.

seep, *v.* For *dial.* and *U.S.* read formerly *dial.* and *U.S.* and add: Also *fig.*

1922 H. CRANE *Let.* 6 May (1965) 85 A new literary magazine.., *Secession*, which is (first number) just seeping into this country. **1931** W. G. MCADOO *Crowded Years* xviii. 284 The..emotions generated by the European struggle seeped into American thought. **1942** *R.A.F. Jrnl.* 13 June 13 The Commandos had been part of the British Army for about eight months before they seeped into print. **1955** A. L. ROWSE *Expansion Elizabethan England* iv. 141 In 1585 a plan for peopling Munster was drawn up... Meanwhile the Irish came seeping back. *a* **1974** R. CROSSMAN *Diaries* (1976) II. 453 One thing I learnt from my brief visit was how well-informed the Transport House staff are about internal Cabinet affairs and how they seep with anti-Government gossip.

Hence **see·ping** *ppl. a.*

1927 M. EIKER *Over Boat-Side* xi. 161 The nagging, monotonous, unessential, seeping harassments that sap a man of achievement.

seepage. For *Sc.* and *U.S.* read orig. *Sc.* and *U.S.* and add: **1.** *spec.* the slow movement of water into or out of the ground (as distinct from percolation through it); also, the slow movement of water through the ground under the action of gravity. (Further examples.)

1913 V. B. LEWES *Oil Fuel* 61 The surface indications, apart from seepages of oil, escape of natural gas from the soil, [etc.]..are practically nil. **1923** *U.S. Geol. Survey Water-Supply Paper* No. 494. 43 Seepage may be divided ..into influent seepage..and effluent seepage. **1950** *N.Z. Jrnl. Agric.* June 559/2 Placing concrete 'seep collars' round the pipe reduces the possibility of seepage. **1967** R. C. WARD *Princ. Hydrol.* viii. 311 Most of the rainfall which percolates through the soil layer to the underlying groundwater will eventually reach the main stream channels as groundwater runoff (sometimes referred to as ..effluent seepage). **1974** *Daily Tel.* 4 Apr. 17 An extensive seepage of fuel oil from a fractured feed pipe. **1976** RAUDKIVI & CALLANDER *Analysis Groundwater Flow* i. 1 The motion of groundwater can be subdivided as follows: seepage; capillary rise and capillary flow; percolation, which occurs..under the action of a hydraulic gradient; turbulent groundwater flow.

fig. **1952** *Time* 14 Apr. 17/2 *Seepage* (n.), small net decrease in circulation, resulting from temporary suspension of subscriptions. (Opposite of *creepage.*) **1961** L. MUMFORD *City in History* x. 285 The 'law of cultural seepage': the making of innovations by a favored minority and their slow infiltration..into the lower economic ranks. **1976** *National Observer* (U.S.) 17 July 3/1 So far the seepage has had minimal effect on the multibillion-dollar Social Security system.

2. *attrib.*, as *seepage flow, loss, spring, water, well*; **seepage lake,** a lake that loses water chiefly by seepage into the ground containing it.

1939 A. K. LOBECK *Geomorphology* v. 159 Run-off.. occurs in two ways: (*a*) as surface run-off..; and (*b*) as ground-water run-off,..often called seepage flow. **1976** RAUDKIVI & CALLANDER *Analysis Groundwater Flow* i. 2 This movement is complicated by the presence of ground air, most of which is expelled from the ground or dissolved in the seepage flow. **1934** *Ecol. Monogr.* IV. 441 These lakes may be classified into..those with outlets and those without them... The movement of water through lakes of the second type is entirely under ground and they are named seepage lakes. **1975** R. G. WETZEL *Limnology* iv. 40 In seepage lakes the lake seal is..likely to be effective over much of the deeper portions of the basin. **1902** *U.S. Geol. Survey Water-Supply & Irrigation Paper* No. 67. 42 C. E. Grunsky has measured the seepage loss in King River and the Fresno canal. **1937** C. F. TOLMAN *Ground Water* vii. 169 Seepage loss from this river is less than 5 per cent of the total flow. **1908** T. C. HOPKINS *Elem. Physical Geogr.* ii. 60 Sometimes..the water..seeps or trickles out along the line of outcrop of the layer in sufficient quantities to keep the surface wet,..forming a swamp or bog on the hillside. This is called a seepage spring. **1964** G. B. SCHALLER *Year of Gorilla* (1965) x. 264 We came upon six elephants pawing the soil of a seepage spring. **1883** Seepage water [in Dict.]. **1876** RAUDKIVI & CALLANDER *Analysis Groundwater Flow* i. 1 The capacity of the soil to hold suspended capillary water and water in the attached films is called field capacity and it is the excess over the field capacity which is free to travel downwards as gravity or seepage water. **1969** N. W. PARSONS *Upon Sagebrush Harp* xviii. 103 Later that winter the farm papers began to tell of farm dugouts and seepage wells for the well-less prairie.

seer[1]**.** Add: **5.** Comb. *seerlike* adj.; **seercraft,** the prophetic art.

1883 R. C. JEBB *Sophocles* I. 139 Thus did the messages of seer-craft [*Oedipus Tyrannus* 723 φῆμαι μαντικαί] map out the future. **1913** G. MURRAY tr. *Euripides' Rhesus* 6 Sage and prophet, learned in the way of seercraft. **1849** J. G. WHITTIER *Proem* in *Poems* p. iv, Nor mine the seer-like power to show The secrets of the heart and mind. **1975** *New Yorker* 21 Apr. 96/2 One indication of the seer-like quality of these underwriting judgments can be glimpsed in the Continental Insurance underwriters' manual concerning the accident probabilities of drivers.

seer: see also SEIR-FISH, SEER-FISH in Dict. and Suppl.

seersucker. Add: Also 8 **sea sucker, see-sucker.** Also *attrib.* or as *adj.* (Earlier Amer. and later examples.) Also, a garment made of seersucker.

No longer restricted to the U.S. and India.

1722 C. CARROLL in *Maryland Hist. Mag.* (1925) XX. 64 To Corded Dimothy..To I Sea Sucker D°. **1736** *Virginia Gaz.* 15 Oct. 4/2 Ran away..a Servant Woman..took..a Seersucker Gown. **1958** B. MALAMUD *Magic Barrel* 124 He dried himself and dressed. When he came forth in his seersucker, she offered salami. **1964** *Punch* 29 Apr. p. xiv/2 For men, striped cotton seersucker jackets. **1975** B. GARFIELD *Hopscotch* vii. 77 A trim sandy man..in the regulation seersucker. **1981** L. STEPHAN *Murder or Not* vi. 40 Her seersucker shift..with its thin blue and white stripes.

see-safe, *a.* and *adv.* [f. SEE *v.* + SAFE *a.*] (See quot. 1960.)

1926 S. UNWIN *Truth about Publishing* vi. 180 Some firms occasionally seek to protect themselves when buying books of doubtful saleability by marking their order.. 'see safe'. If this condition is passed..the publisher can be called upon..to exchange any surplus copies. *Ibid.*, If the firm has bought fifty-two copies of a new novel and marked the order 'twenty-six see safe', the publisher.. may find himself obliged to take twenty-six back and to supply some more saleable work in their place. **1939** F. D. SANDERS *Brit. Bk. Trade Organisation* 42 The Committee recommended..that books ordered as a result of such information be treated on the 'see safe' principle. **1959** *Bookseller* 24 Oct. 728/3 After say, 20 evening class students have called at a bookshop, all asking for the same title, the bookseller may be moved to telephone an order, three copies firm and three see-safe. **1960** G. A. GLAISTER *Gloss. Book* 372/2 *See safe*, said of books bought by a bookseller from a publisher..with the understanding that at some future date the publisher may be asked to exchange the bookseller's surplus for copies of another title. **1974** I. NORRIE in Mumby & Norrie *Publishing & Bookselling* (ed. 5) II. 423 As the paperback boom gathered force it was increasingly difficult to sell new novels..by unknown writers... What was known as the 'see safe' system (titles which did not sell could be swopped for those which did) was adopted.

see-saw, *v.* **2.** (Earlier example.)

1754 RICHARDSON *Grandison* VI. 285 Your nurse, in your infancy, *see-sawed* you.

seesee (sī·si). Also **see-see, sisi.** [Echoic: see quot. 1969.] In full, *seesee partridge.* A small sand partridge, *Ammoperdix griseogularis*, found in parts of western Asia.

1851 J. GOULD *Birds of Asia* VII. Pl. I Sportsmen reckon it very easy to kill, and it is said to be delicious eating: the name Seesee expresses its call. **1858** *Proc. Zool. Soc.* XXVI. 503 It [sc. *Ammoperdix bonhami*] is known by the name of 'Sisi' in the Punjab. **1864** T. C. JERDON *Birds of India* III. 567 (*heading*) The Seesee partridge. *Ibid.* 568 The Seesee is only found in the Punjab. **1923** *Blackw. Mag.* July 125/2 Game abounded—black partridge and sisi, hare and pigeon. **1928** *Ibid.* Apr. 544/2 We had an exciting and noisy hunt after a see-see partridge. **1969** ALI & RIPLEY *Handbk. Birds India & Pakistan* II. 8 Seesee Partridge... A small sandy grey-brown, concealingly desert-coloured partridge... When flushed on a hillside the birds invariably fly downhill, the wings producing the characteristic high-pitched squeaking *see-see* noise..which has given the bird its name.

see-through (sī·þru), *a.* and *sb.* Also (chiefly *U.S.*) **see-thru.** [f. vbl. phr. *to see through*: SEE *v.* 24 a.] **A.** *adj.* That can be seen through; transparent, diaphanous; having spaces allowing the passage of light. **a.** Of a fabric or (usu. woman's) garment.

1950 *Life* 10 Apr. 100 (*heading*) See-through fabrics bring undercovering to the surface. **1951** *Sunday Pictorial* 21 Jan. 2/1 'See-through' nighties..may be heavenly for women, but they have many disadvantages. **1960** J. IRONSIDE *Fashion Alphabet* 30 The present trend towards see-through dresses and no-bras indicates that it [*sc.* the bare breast] is only one step away. **1968** B. NORMAN *Hounds of Sparta* xix. 143 Some slinky girl spy in a see-through nightdress. **1979** M. HEBDEN *Death set to Music* iii. 24 You don't normally come down dressed in a see-through robe to answer the door. **1980** *Quilt World* Sept./Oct. 63/1 'Mirror' or 'See-Thru' quilt, make in one day, instructions 50c.

b. in other contexts.

1956 *Sun* (Baltimore) 5 Sept. 19/3 The 40 by 80-foot building at the northwest corner of Light and Cross streets is of the 'open' or 'see-through' style of architecture that reveals the revolution that banking in all its phases has been undergoing. **1966** *Punch* 5 Oct. 506/2 Each resident is given a few square feet of privacy, enclosed by see-through fencing. **1967** 'G. BAGBY' *Corpse Candle* (1968) ix. 122 'With a glass house..there's no place a man could go there to take his pants off.' 'It's not all that see-through,' I assured him. **1975** G. SEYMOUR *Harry's Game* ii. 22 The troops..with..the medieval Macron see-through shields. **1978** J. IRVING *World according to Garp* xv. 314 He cleared a see-through spot on the dusted and caked rear window.

B. *sb.* **1.** The quality of allowing the passage of light; the extent to which it is possible to see clearly through something; unimpeded vision.

1954 *Sun* (Baltimore) 21 Dec. 5/6 (Advt.), In opaque nylon tricot for less see thru. **1957** *Jrnl. Optical Soc. Amer.* XLVII. 785/2 A material with good 'see-through' qualities may, in fact, be quite hazy. **1959** *Motor Man.* (ed. 36) xiii. 273 The driver has a clear 'see-through' if the towing angle is correct. **1969** C. O. RASPOR in W. R. R. Park *Plastics Film Technol.* iv. 97 Transparency or 'see through' refers to the capability of seeing objects through a film without loss of detail caused by blurring or distortion. **1974** E. CASTAGNA in P. F. Bruins *Packaging with Plastics* 126 Contact clarity, i.e., see-through to contained liquids, is excellent for copolymers.

2. A see-through fabric or garment.

1962 G. CALLINGFORD *Third Party Risk* iii. 42 Might buy 'erself..brushed nylon if she don't fancy the see-through. **1971** *Guardian* 1 June 9/2 Conditioned as we are to seeing hot pants and cool see-throughs worn in city streets. **1974** P. HAINES *Tea at Gunter's* xiv. 149 You know—a rented place, Lu; and me in one of those flimsy see-throughs, lying about on the settee.

‖ **Sefer Torah** (sēⁱ·fəɹ tōᵊ·ro). Also **Sepher Torah;** *pl.* **Sifrei Torah** (sifrēⁱ·). [ad. Heb. *sēp̄er tōrā* book of (the) Law; cf. TORAH.] = *Scroll of the Law* s.v. *SCROLL *sb.* 1 e.

1650 E. CHILMEAD tr. *L. Modena's Hist. Rites, Customes, & Manners of Jews* x. 29 And there are in this Ark, or Chest, sometimes Two, sometimes Four..of these Books: and they are called..Sepher torah, The Book of the Law. **1893** I. ZANGWILL *Ghetto Tragedies* 9 The *Sepher Torah* is to the Jew at once the most precious and the most sacred of possessions. **1936** S. M. LEHRMAN *Jewish Festivals* 139 The Megillah is completely unrolled..to distinguish it from the 'Sefer Torah'. **1960** *Commentary* June 495/2 Anyone who inscribes even one letter on a Sefer Torah earns a *mitzvah*. **1973** *Jewish Chron.* 18 May 39/1 (Advt.), Wanted for immediate purchase..two Sifrei Torah. Must be first-class condition. **1976** B. WILLIAMS *Making of Manch. Jewry* x. 242 The warden.. encouraged them to purchase a *Sepher Torah*.

seg (seg), *sb.*³ [Abbrev. of SEGMENT *sb.*] A metal stud attached to the toe or heel of a shoe (or boot) to strengthen or protect from wear.

1958 *Shoe & Leather Trades Buyers Reg., Brands Directory & Diary* 100/1 Blakey's Boot Protectors Ltd.,... Boot protectors..all sorts and sizes, malleable cast hob nails, segs & studs, cricket spikes. **1970** *Guardian* 24 Dec. 9/3 The boys made indoor slides across the hall.. scoring great weals in the polish with their segs and blakeys. **1976** A. HILL *Summer's End* viii. 123 Might be metal segs, them half-moons of metal you hammered into the heels and sole-tips of your boots to stop 'em wearing out quick.

seg (seg), *sb.*⁴ **a.** Also **seggie.** U.S. colloq. abbrev. of *SEGREGATIONIST *sb.* Cf. *OUTSEG *v.* **b.** Slang (chiefly *U.S.*) abbrev. of *SEGREGATION 1 g.

1965 *Britannica Bk. of Year* 869/2 *Seg*,..a segregationist. Also *seggie.* **1970** *New Yorker* 12 Dec. 107 Fulbright for the first time openly appealed for black votes, because he believed that he couldn't win without them and that the 'seggies'..would vote against him no matter what he did. **1971** *Harper's Mag.* Jan. 35 When people wore the American flag then it was to show that they were not segs, because the segs of course wore the Confederate flag. **1974** *Guidelines to Volunteer Services* (N.Y. State Dept. Correctional Services) 43 *Seg*, segregation unit. **1977** *New Society* 23 June 616/2 He went straight into the segregation unit [at Wormwood Scrubs]... He continued his [hunger] strike simply in order to prevent an early return to 'seg'.

segashuate, var. *SAGACIATE.

Seger (zēⁱ·gəɹ). [The name of Hermann August *Seger* (1839–93), German ceramics technologist.] *Seger* (also *seger*) *cone*: each of a series of small numbered cones or pyramids made of different mixtures of refractory material and flux so that they melt at different known temperatures, used to indicate the temperature inside kilns, etc.

[**1890** *Jrnl. Iron & Steel Inst.* II. 680 Professor Seger's 'normal' clay pyramids..should find extended application. **1894** *Ibid.* XLV. 432 Le Chatelier's pyrometer was used.., as Seger's cones did not appear to exactly meet all requirements.] **1895** *Ibid.* XLVII. 304 These Seger cones give the temperatures with quite sufficient accuracy. **1931** G. W. TYRRELL *Volcanoes* iv. 115 He used a stout iron pipe within which seger cones were fastened at regular intervals, and thrust it into the lava as far as he could. **1964** H. HODGES *Artifacts* i. 40 There are several series of pyrometric cones of which the Seger cones are, perhaps, the most commonly used. **1971** *Materials & Technol.* II. v. 271 The plaque..is heated above 1000°C at about 10°C per minute, and the end point is taken as the temperature (as indicated by the condition of the Seger cones) at which the tip of the test cone is on a level with the base.

seggie: see *SEG *sb.*⁴

segment, *sb.* Add: **4. b.** *Anthrop.* An autonomous sub-branch of a lineage group which remains within the larger tribal or clan structure.

1940 M. FORTES in Fortes & Evans-Pritchard *Afr. Polit. Systems* 243 A maximal lineage has an hierarchical structure. It consists of two or more major segments, each of a lesser span than the (inclusive) maximal lineage... Each major segment comprises lesser segments constituted on the same principle. **1950** M. GLUCKMAN in A. R. Radcliffe-Brown *Afr. Systems of Kinship* 169 The lineages within the clan are usually residential units. Their segments are cores of villages. **1977** HUNTER & WHITTEN *Stud. Cultural Anthrop.* xviii. 397/1 A hierarchical type of authority structure that rests on levels of increasingly inclusive tribal segments.

c. *Linguistics.* A unit forming part of a continuum of speech or (less commonly) text; an isolable unit in a phonological or syntactic system.

1943 K. L. PIKE *Phonetics* vii. 107 A *segment* is a sound (or lack of sound) having indefinite borders but with a center that is produced by a crest or trough of stricture during the even motion or pressure of an initiator. **1946** B. BLOCH in *Language* XXII. 237 A segment is a word or a sequence of words that does not occur alone as a pause-group in a major sentence. **1953** C. E. BAZELL *Linguistic Form* 7 Morphemic segments may frequently be classed together under one morpheme in the American sense, and considered from this standpoint are regarded as allomorphs. **1960** E. SIVERTSEN *Cockney Phonol.* iv. 122 /ð/ may be manifested, not as a separate segment, but in the dental quality of a preceding apical segment whose phonemic norm is otherwise alveolar. **1964** E. PALMER tr. *Martinet's Elem. Gen. Linguistics* i. 26 The word *puerum*, adequately characterized by the segment *-um* as the object of the verb. **1972** W. LABOV *Language in Inner City* iii. 99 As a rule the ordering of variable constraints within a segment is more regular than ordering across segments.

d. *Computers.* (See quot. 1954.)

1954 *Computers & Automation* May 18/2 *Segment*, a part of a complete specific routine, which can be entirely stored in the internal storage and contains the coding necessary to automatically call in and transfer control to other segments. **1963** *Communications ACM* VI. 391/2 Segments of a program could not be treated as independent entities. In general, a symbol name, if used in one segment, could not be used in another segment with a different meaning. **1969** [see *OVERLAY *sb.* 6]. **1977** HUGHES & MICHTOM *Structured Approach to Programming* v. 107 A segment is both a logical and physical subdivision of a module. Logically, it is a subfunction of the module's function. Physically, it is limited to the number of source-code lines that will fit on one printer page of source output (50 to 60 lines).

9. c. In *Linguistics* (see sense 4 c above).

1961 F. W. HOUSEHOLDER in Saporta & Bastian *Psycholinguistics* 20/2 Exact boundaries were not as important as some early workers thought; location of segment-centers is in general adequate. **1969** *Language* XLV. 303 They would be stated in terms of component-sized entities (hypophonemes), however, not in terms of segment-sized entities (classical phonemes). **1971** *Archivum Linguisticum* II. 135 The features of articles and the features of suffixes are extracted from this complex and distributed in their proper places by 'segment transformations' or 'segmentalization'. **1978** *Language* LIV. 47 Cf. Eng. *svelte, sphere* etc., whose initial clusters violate the segment-sequence constraints of English.

segment, *v.* Add: Now usu. with pronunc. (segme·nt). **2. b.** *Anthrop.* Of a lineage group or clan: to divide into smaller autonomous branches within the larger social structure. Cf. sense *4 b of the sb.

1940 E. E. EVANS-PRITCHARD in Fortes & Evans-Pritchard *Afr. Polit. Systems* 284 In the diagram below, A is a clan which is segmented into maximal lineages B and C. **1965** P. C. LLOYD in M. Banton *Polit. Systems & Distrib. Power* 66 The Ngoni have a lineage structure which continually segments. **1974** L. MAIR *Afr. Societies* x. 127 All lineages segment in the course of generations.

3. (Examples in *Computing* and *Linguistics.*) Cf. senses *4 c, d of the sb.

1959 E. M. GRABBE et al. *Handbk. Automation, Computation, & Control* II. ii. 130 A discussion of an automatic system which faces the problem of segmenting a program, either data or instructions, into pieces is given by this group. **1962** C. O. FRAKE in Gladwin & Sturtevant *Anthrop. & Human Behavior* 75 How do we segment the stream of speech into category-designating units? **1969** P. B. JORDAIN *Condensed Computer Encycl.* 202 No matter how much central memory is provided for a computer, it will always be possible to write a program too large to fit. The most common way to handle this situation is to segment the program into overlays. **1972** W. LABOV *Language in Inner City* ii. 50 Young black children frequently find it difficult to segment *I'm* into *I am.* **1977** HUGHES & MICHTOM *Structured Approach to Programming* vi. 122 A module..is segmented in the same hierarchical fashion that a system or program is developed.

Hence **segme·nting** *ppl. a.* and *vbl. sb.*

1912 J. S. HUXLEY *Individual in Animal Kingdom* vi. 149 The blastomeres or separate cells of the segmenting egg. **1959** E. M. GRABBE et al. *Handbk. Automation, Computation, & Control* II. ii. 130 It is imperative that a programmer be allowed to override any automatic segmenting and allocation system in order to provide increased efficiency. **1977** HUGHES & MICHTOM *Structured Approach to Programming* vi. 122 Segmenting is best handled at the stepwise refinement stage.

segmentable (segme·ntăb'l), *a.* [f. SEGMENT *v.* + -ABLE.] Capable of being divided into segments (*Linguistics* in quots.). Hence **segmentabi·lity.**

1957 TRAGER & SMITH *Outl. Eng. Structure* 52 The phenomena that are segmentable were analyzed as phonemes of one kind or another. **1962** H. C. CONKLIN in Householder & Saporta *Probl. Lexicogr.* 122 Unitary lexemes may be either *simple* (unsegmentable) or *complex* (segmentable). **1964** *Language* XL. 207 The 'segmentability' and the quantum mechanics available to linguists strikes these other workers as very rigorous. **1979** *Trans. Philol. Soc.* 82 The 'weak' adjective endings are clearly segmentable suffixed formatives.

segmental, *a.* Add: **2. a.** *segmental apparatus*, the brain-stem of a vertebrate.

1917 [see *PALÆENCEPHALON]. **1974** D. & M. WEBSTER *Compar. Vertebr. Morphol.* xi. 240 Segmentation in the developing brain is neither as regular nor as apparent as it is in the spinal cord. However, during early development (at least), segmentation can be determined in the basal portion, which is, therefore, known as the 'segmental apparatus'.

c. *Linguistics.* Of, pertaining to, or designating the division of speech or (less commonly) text into segments (cf. *SEGMENT *sb.* 4 c). Freq. in phr. *segmental phoneme*, a consonant or vowel phoneme, which can occur as one of the units in a sequence of such phonemes.

1938 B. L. WHORF *Lang., Thought, & Reality* (1964) 126 Timbre phonemics (segmental): Table of phonemes. Pattern congruity. Allophones or probitional variants. Allophonic constellation. **1942** C. F. HOCKETT in *Language* XVIII. 8 Features..which clearly extend over a series of several segmental groupings are suprasegmental. **1950** R. A. HALL in *Ibid.* XXVI. 12 Forty-seven segmental phonemes is not an excessive number to posit for a language. **1958** *English Studies* XXXIX. 104 The segmental sounds are almost exclusively transferred from indigenous languages of the area. **1966** *Amer. Speech* XLI. 225 Pitch levels are not always suprasegmental features. When they are short enough, they can be considered one of the distinctive features of a segmental phoneme. **1976** *Word 1971* XXVII. 57 The speech rhythms and patterns and intonations of the pregnant mother will [not] generate..'segmental phonemes', or anything so phonetically sophisticated relatedly. **1981** *Canad. Jrnl. Linguistics* XXVI. 74 The initial portions of the word have the same segmental values and the same relative prominence as the base word.

segmentalization (segme:ntălaizēi·ʃən). [f. next + -ATION.] Division into segments; *spec.* in *Linguistics*, transformation of a grammatical feature into a distinct segment of speech or text. Cf. *SEGMENT *sb.* 4 c.

1964 E. BECKER in I. L. Horowitz *New Sociology* 115 There is another kind of confusion..in complex society, which Mills called attention to as a 'segmentalization of conduct'. **1969** *Language* XLV. 718 The auxiliary *be* is introduced by a segmentalization transformation from features of the following element. **1970** *Canad. Jrnl. Linguistics* XVI. 17 Their [*sc.* linguistic features'] eventual extraposition (or 'segmentalization') is blocked in the case of participles.

segme·ntalize, *v.* [f. SEGMENTAL *a.* + -IZE.] *trans.* To divide into segments. Hence **segme·ntalized, segme·ntalizing** *ppl. adjs.*; **segme·ntalizer.**

1956 H. WHITEHALL et al. in *Kenyon Rev.* XVIII. 413 The constructive features must necessarily serve a descriptive grammar as *segmentalizers*—they are our chief scissors of linguistic perception. **1956** *Ibid.* 417 Both the rhythm-pointing and the segmentalizing functions of the three interrelated configurational features are of basic prosodic importance. **1968** *Language* XLIV. 774 Even when the feature is segmentalized, like *should* in Modern English, it remains an 'auxiliary' of the main verb. **1976** *Brit. Jrnl. Sociol.* XXVII. 317/1 The teaching practice of academic sociology..presents its subject matter in segmentalized courses on stratification, organization, politics, religion, etc.

segmentally, *adv.* Add: (Examples in *Linguistics.*) Cf. *SEGMENT *sb.* 4 c.

1957 S. POTTER *Mod. Linguistics* v. 105 Sentences may be analyzed *segmentally* into phonological units called *phonemes* and *syllables*; into morphological units called *morphemes* and *words*; and into syntactic units called *phrases* and *clauses*. **1964** R. H. ROBINS *Gen. Linguistics* vi. 262 Stress and pitch are just as fit to serve as the markers or exponents of grammatical categories and of syntactic relations as are segmentally represented morphemes.

segmentary, *a.* Add: **2.** (Examples in *Anthrop.* use.) Cf. *SEGMENT *sb.* 4 b.

1940 E. E. EVANS-PRITCHARD in Fortes & Evans-Pritchard *Afr. Polit. Systems* 284 Fission and fusion are two aspects of the same segmentary principle. **1957** V. W. TURNER *Schism & Continuity in Afr. Soc.* x. 291 Overlapping of territorial and kinship groupings such as one finds in segmentary societies. **1977** HUNTER & WHITTEN *Stud. Cultural Anthrop.* xviii. 396/1 Like other Bedouin tribes, Mutayr have what is called a segmentary tribal structure.

segmentation. Add: **2. a.** (Later examples in *Anthrop.* and examples in *Linguistics* and *Computing.*) Cf. *SEGMENT *sb.* 4.

1943 M. SCHLAUCH *Gift of Tongues* 254 French has its own formulas of segmentation like *quant à*. **1950** A. R. RADCLIFFE-BROWN *Afr. Systems Kinship* 40 For structures having successive segmentations the term 'polysegmentary' has been suggested. **1953** C. E. BAZELL *Linguistic Form* p. i, Space has been found to touch on several aspects of linguistic form which pass unnoticed in more extensive treatments of the subject... The problem of segmentation..has for this reason been left in the background. **1962** C. O. FRAKE in Gladwin & Sturtevant *Anthrop. & Human Behavior* 76 The segmentation of speech into the grammatically functioning units revealed by linguistic analysis is a necessary, but not sufficient, condition for terminological analysis. **1962** *Spring Joint Computer Conf.* 307/1 Segmentation is the process of dividing a single program into pieces. This is done to permit the operation of programs that are too large to completely fit into memory. **1971** W. WILDER in R. Needham *Rethinking Kinship & Marriage* 213 It might well be possible to decide whether local segmentation among the Purum appeared to lead to the formation of alliance groups. **1973** C. W. GEAR *Introd. Computer Sci.* vi. 243 The process of breaking a program into a number of smaller segments is called *segmentation.*

segmentative (segme·ntătiv), *a. Linguistics.* [f. SEGMENT *sb.* + -ATIVE.] = *SEGMENTAL *a.* 2 c (see also quot. 1936).

1936 *Language* XII. 127 Punctual and segmentative aspects of verbs in Hopi... The segmentative aspect is formed by final reduplication of this root plus the durative suffix *-ta*. **1961** *Amer. Speech* XXXVI. 159 This and other such 'segmentative' analyses fail to explain a number of other grammatical facts about nominals.

segmented, *ppl. a.* Add: **3.** *Archæol.* Of a prehistoric gallery (grave): divided into sections or segments; having compartments.

1920 *Glasgow Herald* 9 Mar. 9 Vestiges of a segmented central gallery were disclosed. **1939** V. G. CHILDE *Dawn Europ. Civilization* (ed. 3) xii. 206 On the slopes of the Pyrenees, [etc.]..gallery graves are divided into a series of intercommunicating compartments by low, transverse slabs... Such tombs are known as *segmented cists.* **1954** S. PIGGOTT *Neolithic Cultures* vi. 160 In the typical form of 'segmented gallery' a number of such slabs divide the chamber into a series of compartments.

4. *gen.*

1950 *Sci. News* XV. Pl. 5 (*caption*) The segmented appearance of the flame is due to the shock wave which is formed in the jet as it leaves the nozzle. **1967** *Jane's Surface Skimmer Systems 1967–68* 59/2 The pockets, based on the segmented skirts of a hovercraft, form a seal around the body.

segmenter (segme·ntəɹ). *Zool.* [f. SEGMENT *v.* + -ER^1.] A fully developed sporozoan schizont ready to divide into a number of merozoites.

1929 R. W. HEGNER et al. *Animal Parasitol.* xi. 144 (*caption*) *Plasmodium vivax.* 1, Ring stage; 2, schizont; 3, segmenter; 4, gametocyte. **1946** P. F. RUSSELL et al. *Practical Malariol.* ii. 31 (*caption*) A large segmenter in an endothelial cell in the brain. **1978** *Jrnl. Protozool.* XXV. 449/1 In schizonts and segmenters knobs often obscure the unit membrane structure.

sego. Add: In full, *sego lily.* (Earlier and later examples.)

1851 H. HOWE *Hist. Coll. Gt. West* 432 Hogs fatten on a succulent bulb or tuber, called the Seacoe, or Seegose Root, which is highly esteemed as a table vegetable by the Mormons. **1852** H. STANSBURY *Expl. & Survey Gt. Salt Lake* 160 Sego..is much used by the Indian tribes as an article of food. **1875** *Amer. Naturalist* IX. 18 The general Indian name of 'Sego' is applied indiscriminately to all the edible bulbs of this region [*sc.* Utah]. **1915** ARMSTRONG & THORNBER *Western Wild Flowers* 64 [The mariposa] is called Sego Lily..in Utah and is the 'State flower'. **1963** J. J. CRAIGHEAD et al. *Field Guide to Rocky Mt. Wildflowers* 18 Sego Lily... A white tuliplike flower with a triangular cup-shaped appearance.

segregable, *a.* Delete *rare* $^{-1}$ and add earlier and later examples.

1905 *Rep. Evol. Comm. R. Soc.* II. 124 An extracted type..may carry on segregable determinants, whereby the individuals may, in reality, differ from each other, though outwardly alike. **1978** P. SUTCLIFFE *Oxf. Univ. Press* vi. 241 Milford tried to divide his business into 'segregable categories'.

segregant (se·grĭgănt), *a.* Restrict † *Obs. rare* $^{-1}$ to *gen.* sense in Dict. and add: **2.** *Genetics.* Having or being a genotype derived by segregation; usu., one different from that of either parent.

1936 *Discovery* May 161/1 The earlier investigators of heredity emphasised the discontinuous nature of inheritance... This is understandable when it is remembered that the segregant types, with which the earlier work was done, were of a very sharply contrasted nature. **1971** *New Scientist* 8 July 92/1 When certain chromosomes were eliminated, the malignant phenotype reappeared and the segregant cells were again able to produce tumours. **1974** *Nature* 27 Sept. 322/1 So called 'tritypes' involving any three of the four segregant genotypes should also be recovered frequently.

B. *sb. Genetics.* A segregant organism.

1955 *Genetics* XL. 894 No instances of adenineless segregants were obtained. **1976** *Nature* 29 Apr. 785/1 All 28 haploid segregants of strain DP62..were indistinguishable from strain NP73.

segregate, *v.* Add: **1. b.** To subject (people) to racial segregation; to enforce racial segregation in (a community, institution, etc.). Cf. *DESEGREGATE *v.*, *INTEGRATE *v.* 2 b.

1908 R. S. BAKER *Following Color Line* III. xiv. 299 All through my former chapters I have been showing how the Negroes are being segregated. So are the Chinese segregated, and the blacks in South Africa. **1930** *Economist* 27 Sept. 563/1 It is not surprising that a South African Nationalist politician should..proclaim his preference for his own party's policy of 'segregating' the natives and safeguarding 'the natural superiority' of the whites. **1948** *Rep. Native Laws Commission 1946–48* (Dept. Native Affairs, South Africa) 33/1 This effect was accentuated by the policy which sought to segregate the Africans as far as possible in specially demarcated 'Reserves'. **1958** *N.Y. Post* 20 Apr. II. 7/3, I guess the DAR is not so much for segregating the colored as it is against doing you-know-what with them.

3. b. *Genetics.* To undergo or display segregation (sense *1 e).

1904 W. BATESON et al. in *Rep. Evol. Comm. R. Soc.* II. 120 The fern-leaved type is recessive to the palm-leaved, segregating from it perfectly. **1930** R. A. FISHER *Genetical Theory Nat. Selection* i. 9 Mendel also demonstrated what a theorist could scarcely have ventured to postulate, that the different factors examined by him in combination, segregated in the simplest possible manner, namely independently. **1974** *Encycl. Brit. Macropædia* XIV. 775/1 The once-separate genes have been brought together..to produce a tightly packed unit of several genes sufficiently near each other on the chromosome that they segregate together.

segregated, *ppl. a.* Add: Also *spec.* of institutions, groups, etc.: divided or separated on the basis of race. Cf. *SEGREGATE *v.* 1 b.

1948, 1956 [see *INTEGRATED *ppl. a.* c]. **1958** *Listener* 11 Dec. 982/1 Nine-tenths of the Negro children in the whole Southern region still go to segregated schools. **1960** *Guardian* 22 Mar. 13/7 San Antonio, Texas, iaunched its campaign against segregated lunch-counters. **1971** *Graphic* (Durban) 7 May 4/5 You are the future Black citizens of this segregated Republic.

segregation. Add: **1. e.** *Genetics.* The separation of pairs of homologous alleles or chromosomes, esp. as occurs at meiosis in the formation of gametes by a heterozygous organism, to whose progeny different traits may consequently be transmitted.

1902 W. F. R. WELDON in *Biometrika* I. 229 If the hybrids of the first generations [of two races of peas]..be allowed to fertilise themselves, all possible combinations of the ancestral race-characters will appear in the second generation with equal frequency... Characters intermediate between those of the ancestral races will not occur... This may be called the Law of Segregation. **1904** *Rep. Evol. Comm. R. Soc.* II. 128 The balance of evidence is in favour of the belief that gametic segregation takes place at the reduction-division. **1930** R. A. FISHER *Genetical Theory Nat. Selection* i. 8 The segregation of single pairs of genes, that is of single factors, was demonstrated by Mendel in his paper of 1865. **1954** *Genetics* XXXIX. 432 The..abnormal segregation of *s* has been observed whenever C 602/λ has been used as the *F*-parent in cross. **1970** *Watsonia* VIII. 48 We hope that the present investigation will show clearly that the concept of segregation following allopolyploidy (intergenomic segregation, Jones 1967) can offer another possible explanation of this phenomenon.

f. The enforced separation of different racial groups in a country, community, or institution. Cf. *APARTHEID.

1903 T. T. FORTUNE in B. T. Washington et al. *Negro Problem* vii. 215 The Afro-American people have been held together rather by the segregation decreed by law.. than by ties of consanguinity. **1916** *Virginia Rep.* CXVII. 692 The cities and towns of this State have the power..to pass segregation ordinances separating the places of residence of white and colored citizens, respectively. **1927** [see *EURAFRICAN *a.* and *sb.* 3]. **1947** *Forum* (Johannesburg) 17 May 29/1 Political segregation is only possible where territorial segregation is in force. **1952** [see *DESEGREGATE *v.*]. **1957** *Times* 18 May 6/3 The ruling of the Supreme Court that racial segregation in public schools [in South Africa] was unconstitutional. **1974** *Spartanburg* (S. Carolina) *Herald* 25 Apr. A1/6 The black majority has the franchise in tribal homelands under South Africa's race segregation policy.

g. The isolation or separate confinement of dangerous or troublesome prisoners. Hence *concr.* (also *segregation unit*) a part of a prison designated for this purpose. Chiefly *U.S.*

1952 K. J. SCUDDER *Prisoners are People* 82 We set aside a few cells at Chino for segregation... If some man at Chino becomes defiant or refuses to work, he is placed in segregation. **1955** T. E. GADDIS *Birdman of Alcatraz* x. 91 The rear half of the structure held eighteen segregation cells... It was a prison within a prison. **1964** D. GLASER *Effectiveness of Prison & Parole System* viii. 174 The duration of disciplinary segregation is much briefer in federal prisons than in most state prisons... Men in segregation now receive the regular inmate food. *Ibid.* 175 Such units, usually called 'administrative segregation' in federal prisons, resemble the regular disciplinary section of a prison... The inmate may be restricted to quarters temporarily without being transferred to the segregation unit. **1974** P. W. KEVE *Prison Life & Human Worth* ix. 158 The segregation unit needs intensive service. *Ibid.* 162 A man..cannot get out of segregation unless he meets certain good behavior standards. **1977** *New Yorker* 24 Oct. 114/3 Such sentences often included a certain number of days in segregation.

segregationist (segrĭgēi·ʃənist), *a.* and *sb.* [f. SEGREGATION + -IST.] **A.** *adj.* Of, pertaining to, or designating persons or policies advocating or supporting political or racial segregation. Cf. *INTEGRATIONIST *a.*

1954 W. K. HANCOCK *Country & Calling* vi. 171 Segregationist theory had partial relevance in that it emphasized South Africa's diversity of cultural inheritance. **1957** *Economist* 30 Nov. 774/2 One has to go as far to the right as Senator Ellender, the segregationist Democrat from Louisiana. **1961** *Encounter* XVI. 7/1 There is no segregationist legislation in Algeria. **1976** *National Observer* (U.S.) 21 Feb. 6/1 He could not accept its [*sc.* a club's] 'segregationist policy prohibiting any black guest'.

B. *sb.* An adherent or advocate of segregation. Cf. *INTEGRATIONIST *sb.* and *SEG *sb.*[4] a.

1955 [see *INTEGRATIONIST *sb.*]. **1957** P. WORSLEY *Trumpet shall Sound* x. 206 One of their spokesmen.. posed the 'sixty-four dollar' question of the segregationist 'Would you let a native marry your daughter or sister?' **1962** *Daily Tel.* 2 Apr. 12/2 This is because Southern segregationists are yielding to the inevitable, or at least refraining from militant resistance. **1977** *Time* 24 Jan. 27/1 Joseph Rauh..charged that Bell had given 'aid and comfort to segregationists' while an Atlanta attorney.

† **segregator** (se·grĭgēⁱtəɹ). *Med. Obs.* [f. SEGREGATE *v.* + -OR.] An instrument for obtaining the urine from one kidney unmixed with that from the other.

1903 *Ann. Surg.* XXXVII. 30 The segregator could not possibly have attained the results given thus by catheterism and the strong aspiration. **1919** W. C. PEDERSEN *Urology* xiii. 704 The development of segregators corresponds with that of catheterization cystoscopes.

segue (se·gwēⁱ), *v. Mus.* [a. It. *segue*, 3rd pers. sing. pres. of *seguire* to follow.] *intr.* ‖ **1.** (See quot. 1959.)

1740 J. GRASSINEAU *Mus. Dict.* 214 *Segue*, it follows, or comes after; this word is often found before *aria, alleluja, amen.* **1801** T. BUSBY *Compl. Dict. Mus.* p. xxxii, The Italian word *Segue*, set against any of these abbreviations, signifies a repetition of the same notes, or passage. *Ibid. s.v. Segue,* (Ital.) it follows: as *Segue Coro*, the chorus follows. **1876** STAINER & BARRETT *Dict. Mus. Terms* 390/1 *Segue* (It.), follows, succeeds, comes after; as, *segue il coro*, the chorus follows; *segue l'aria*, the aria follows. **1959** *Collins Mus. Encycl.* 592/2 *Segue*,.. 'Follows'. Used as a direction (1) to proceed to the following movement without a break, and (2) to continue a formula which has been indicated, such as arpeggiating of chords or doubling in octaves.

2. *slang.* Of a person or music: to move without interruption from one song or melody to another. Freq. const. *into*. Also *transf.* and *fig.*

1958 D. HALPERIN in P. Gammond *Decca Bk. of Jazz* xx. 250 Then, without stopping, the guitarist and Ellington segued into *Body and soul*. **1962** 'K. ORVIS' *Damned & Destroyed* (1966) iii. 26 The Haydn selection reached the oboe part—melody segued and started to build. **1967** A. ARENT *Gravedigger's Funeral* (1968) xii. 190 Just then the orchestra segued into something I recognised. **1970** *New Yorker* 12 Sept. 32/2 The first started off with some flourishes from a Bach organ toccata and segued into 'She Comes in Colors'. **1976** C. LARSON *Muir's Blood* (1978) xxv. 135 The organist..*segued* resonantly from 'In the Garden' to 'Rock of Ages'.

transf. and *fig.* **1972** G. BAXT *Burning Sappho* v. 78 The crowds..let up a roar which soon segued into a mixture of cheers, jeers, jests, gibes. **1977** *Time* (Chicago) 17 Oct. 79/3 Bertolucci abruptly and wisely segues from the festivities to an epilogue, set in the present, that brings the enormous film full circle. **1978** LOGAN & WOFFINDEN *Illustr. New Musical Express Encycl. Rock* 199/1 How do the world's most celebrated adolescents [*sc.* the Rolling Stones] segue into middle age?

segue (se·gwēⁱ), *sb. Mus. slang.* [f. prec.] An uninterrupted transition from one song or melody to another. (Used of both live and pre-recorded music.)

1937 *Printers' Ink Monthly* May 42/1 *Segue*, the transition from one musical number to another without break or announcements. **1952** B. ULANOV *Hist. Jazz in Amer.* (1958) xix. 240 We could be doing 'Limehouse Blues' way up in tempo, look at the clock, and do a direct segue into the theme. **1977** *Rolling Stone* 13 Jan. 19/1 The band plays an hour straight, moving fluidly from one number to another; indeed, Parker calls Edwards the 'King of Segue'. **1980** S. BRETT *Dead Side of Mike* xv. 162 'He just does a long sequence of slow, sexy numbers, so they can dance real close... Straight *segue*.' 'What's a *segue?*' 'Record to record, no chat.'

‖ **seguiriyas** (sēⁱgirī·as). Also **seguiriya**, etc. [Andalusian-Gypsy var. of Sp. *seguidilla* SEGUIDILLA.] In full, *seguiriyas gitana* [Sp. *gitano*, fem. *gitana* gypsy]: a regional variety of flamenco music; the song or dance which accompanies this.

1922 I. BROWN *Nights & Days on Gypsy Trail* iv. 86 Silverio asked the guitar player to strike up a Gypsy seguirya, and throwing back his head..he sang..the very song that one of the cantadores present had improvised years before. **1926** J. B. TREND *Mus. Sp. Hist. to 1600* 7 The more modern forms (*flamenco*) often sound more 'oriental' than the older, traditional *Cante hondo*; and the oldest, the *Siguiriya gitana*, seems..less tinged with superficial orientalism than any. **1936** W. STARKIE *Don Gypsy* xix. 289 The *siguiriya gitana*..is full of tears and tragedy and for that reason is often called *playera* (the weeping poem). **1948** 'LA MERI' *Sp. Dancing* vii. 92 Of the flamenco estilos which are more distinctly song than dance, the *Seguidillas Gitano* (seguiriyas gitana) is the most typical. It is composed of four lines as against the seven which go to make up the Spanish Seguidillas. **1967** CHUJOY & MANCHESTER *Dance Encycl.* (rev. ed.) 856/1 Rhythm-forms of flamenco dances are: Alegrias, Soleares, Bulerias, Farruca, Zapateado, Tango, Zambra, and Seguiriyas. **1972** H. MACINNES *Message from Malaga* ii. 40 Once, she too had danced the *seguiriyas*.

‖ **Seguridad** (segū·riðað). [Sp., security.] The Spanish security service.

1937 F. BORKENAU *Sp. Cockpit* ii. 120, I soon found out that these people belonged to the Seguridad, in other words the ordinary police of the old régime. **1938** E. HEMINGWAY *Fifth Column* (1939) II. i. 47 A room in Seguridad headquarters. **1977** *Guardian Weekly* 3 Apr. 13/1 From time to time it's learned that this or that army officer has been replaced by a liberal, or that new police and Seguridad chiefs have been appointed.

Sehna (se·nă). Also **Sena, Senne**, etc. The name of a town (now Sanandaj) in Kurdistan, used *attrib.* and *absol.* to designate a variety of finely-woven Persian rug or a knot used in weaving some oriental carpets (see quot. 1910). Also *Comb.*, as **Sehna-Kurd** (see quot. 1931²).

1901 J. K. MUMFORD *Oriental Rugs* xi. 183 In most of the Sehnas the diaper of small patterns covers the entire field. *Ibid.*, A few Sehna rugs have the pear pattern wrought upon a large scale. *Ibid.* 198 The genuine Mir Sarabands are tied in the Sehna knot. **1910** *Encycl. Brit.* V. 393/2 The second traditional knot is the Persian or Sehna knot, which..is tied so that from every space between the warp-threads one end of the knot protrudes. **1931** A. U. DILLEY *Oriental Rugs & Carpets* iv. 102 Sehna (Senneh or Senna) rugs..are distinguished by masterful accomplishment in small pattern. *Ibid.* 103 Sehna-Kurd is the name applied to rugs woven by the Kurds in emulation of the Sehnas. **1957** [see *GHIORDES]. **1962** C. W. JACOBSEN *Oriental Rugs* 289 The finest old Sena with silk warp will often have 500 to 600 knots to the square inch. A good average new Sena with cotton warp will have from 150 to 250 knots to the inch. *Ibid.* 291 We class many of the better rugs from Hamadan district (woven in small villages) and superior to the usual Hamadan, Sena-Kurds. **1975** 'E. LATHEN' *By Hook or by Crook* xviii. 167 A very nice, versatile Sena... This Sena is..twenty-six hundred dollars. **1975** *Oxf. Compan. Decorative Arts* 612/1 The Ghiordes knot is quite commonly used in western districts [of Persia] but a fine Sena knotting predominates. **1978** *Times* 13 Oct. 19/4 One expensive carpet, an unsold Senna at £40,000.

‖ **Sehnsucht** (zē·nzuχt). [Ger.] Yearning, wistful longing.

[**1847** THACKERAY *Van. Fair* (1848) iv. 28 It is no blame to them that after marriage this *Sehnsucht nach der Liebe* subsides.] *a* **1861** A. H. CLOUGH *Poems* (1869) II. 193 (*title*) Sehnsucht. **1862** J. A. SYMONDS *Let.* 9 Dec. (1967) I. 372 Today I had a wondrous Sehnsucht to hear our choir once more. **1902** W. JAMES *Varieties Relig. Exper.* xvi. 383 An excellent old German Lady..used to describe to me her *Sehnsucht* that she might yet visit 'Philadelphia', whose wondrous name had always haunted her imagination. **1911** G. BELL *Let.* 6 May (1927) I. xii. 303 When the 1st of May came I had a great 'Sehnsucht' for the daffodils and the opening beech leaves at Rounton. **1941** [see *RADIO *sb.* 3]. **1955** C. S. LEWIS *Surprised by Joy* i. 14 The Castlereagh Hills..taught me longing—*Sehnsucht*; made me..a votary of the Blue Flower. **1972** J. I. M. STEWART *Palace of Art* xiv. 141 The stickiest romance of all attends, of course, upon gondolas by moonlight, and Gloria felt she must by no means counter or abridge this small enclave of adolescent *Sehnsucht* in her almost undeviatingly rational friend.

‖ **Seicentismo** (sēitʃenti·zmo). Also **Secentismo**. [It., f. *seicento* SEICENTO.] = SEICENTO; also, the character or quality of works produced during this period.

1881 *Encycl. Brit.* XIII. 511/1 This period [*sc.* the hundred and forty years from the treaty of Cateau Cambresis to the war of the Spanish succession] is known in the history of Italian literature as the Secentismo. Its writers..tried to produce effect with every kind of affectation, with bombast, with the strangest metaphors, in fact, with what in art is called mannerism, 'barocchism'. **1923** *Oxf. Broom* Apr. 17 Timid critics..excusing themselves on the ground that Seicentismo is analogous to the modern spirit, Fascismo, nay—Futurism even. **1926** R. FRY *Transformations* 95 A more guarded enthusiasm for these works than altogether suits recent converts to Seicentismo.

Seicentist. Add: Also *pl.* ‖ **Se(i)centisti.** Also *attrib.* or as *adj.*

1841 W. SPALDING *Italy & Ital. Islands* II. III. iv. 414 The *seicentisti*, or artists of the seventeenth century. **1881** *Encycl. Brit.* XIII. 511/2 The 'Secentisti' erred by an overweening desire for novelty, which made them always go beyond the truth. **1931** A. HUXLEY *Music at Night* I. 38 The bright reassuring Heaven,..the stage immensities and stage mysteries, all the stock-in-trade of the *seicentisti*, are absent from his [*sc.* El Greco's] pictures. **1938** L. MACNEICE *Mod. Poetry* i. 7 Theocritus is more escapist than Euripides..the Seicentist poets than Dante.

Seicento. Add: Also **seicento.** (Later examples.) Also *attrib.*

1926 E. HUTTON tr. *A. Venturi's Short Hist. Ital. Art* vii. 339 The glory of the *Seicento* at Milan is summed up in the names of Ceraro and Cairo. **1938** *Burlington Mag.* Aug. 82/2 To pass from the seicento to the settecento is inevitably to experience a slackening of tension which the impressive body of Solimenas..do little to check. **1947** D. MAHON *Studies in Seicento Art & Theory* 1 The writer was primarily interested in discovering why this occurred, and became involved..with certain aspects of Seicento art theory. **1972** *Listener* 7 Sept. 317/2 Festive scraps from the Seicento. **1979** *Now!* 21–27 Sept. 116/1 Two outstanding *seicento* marble busts..remind the viewer of J. Pierpont Morgan's greater collection of sculpture formed in America with the help of Henry Duveen.

seiche. Add: A short-lived standing oscillation of a lake or other body of water (as a bay or basin of the sea), somewhat resembling a tide, which may be caused by abrupt changes in atmospheric conditions or by small earth tremors. (Later examples.)

1905 *Geogr. Jrnl.* XXVI. 46 A seiche was observed.. within the shelter of the pier at the east end of Loch a' Chroisg... The amplitude was a quarter of an inch, and the period about 11½ minutes. **1932** *Geogr. Rev.* XXII. 476 The strongest current caused by the seiches was found in the south-east corner of Great Bear Lake. **1957** G. E. HUTCHINSON *Treat. Limnol.* I. v. 299 The phenomenon has long been recognized locally in the Lake of Geneva, and the term seiche was recorded by Fatio de Duillier (1730) as applied to the oscillation in that lake. **1962** *New Scientist* 13 Sept. 560/1 Wind can also cause whole lakes and bays to oscillate..and these movements, called 'seiches', can communicate energy to the ground. **1971** *Nature* 4 June 306/2 The dominant internal seiche has a wavelength twice the length of the Loch, and a marked asymmetry.

Hence **sei·ching**, the occurrence of a seiche; the motion occurring in a seiche.

1955 *Sci. Amer.* Jan. 2/2 The extreme heights reached by the water in specific locations is due to another phenomenon known to oceanographers as 'seiching', which is similar to the sloshing of water in a bathtub. **1967** *Oceanogr. & Marine Biol.* V. 27 In contrast, Corkan..and Rossiter..found..little evidence of North Sea seiching. **1971** *Nature* 4 June 308/1 It is likely that the effect of the Earth's rotation is principally to cause a small alternating transverse tilt of the isotherms across the Loch during the seiching motion.

Seidel[1] (zəi·d'l). *Ophthalm.* [The name of Erich *Seidel* (1882–1946), German ophthalmologist, who described the sign (see below) in 1914 (*Archiv f. Ophthalm.* LXXXVIII. 102).] Used in the possessive, as **Seidel's sign**, the occurrence of one or two hooked scotomata extending from the blind spot.

1918 R. H. ELLIOT *Glaucoma* iv. 220 Should the condition of increased intra-ocular pressure continue, Seidel's sign will pass on into Bjerrum's sign. **1932** *Optician* LXXXIII. 398/1 With 2/1,000 white definite Seidel's signs were evident as horns extending about 1⅜ in. both above and below the projected blind-spot. **1964** S. DUKE-ELDER *Parsons' Dis. Eye* (ed. 14) xxi. 305 Occasionally there is a sickle-shaped extension of the blind-spot above or below, or both, with the concavity of the sickle directed towards the fixation point (Seidel's sign); this is of more doubtful significance [as a symptom of glaucoma].

‖ **seidel**[2] (zəi·d'l). [Ger., orig. a liquid measure varying locally between about a third and a half litre.] A beer mug or glass (in quot. 1930 used *loosely*); the quantity that such a vessel will contain.

1922 E. E. CUMMINGS *Enormous Room* iv. 92 Such.. hands as might have grasped six seidels..on 13th street. **1930** D. RUNYON in *Collier's* 1 Feb. 12/1 Wilbur Willard all mulled up to a million, what with him having been sitting out a few seidels of Scotch with a friend. **1957** M. SWAN *British Guiana* xi. 180, I was welcomed with a seidel of Pilsener. **1980** G. V. HIGGINS *Kennedy for Defense* ii. 14 Knackwurst, German potato salad, couple seidels of Jake's Special Dark.

seif (sīf, sēⁱf). *Physical Geogr.* Also **sif.** [ad. Arab. *saif*, lit. 'sword'.] A sand dune having the form of a narrow ridge elongated in a direction parallel to that of the prevailing wind. Also *seif dune*.

1925 W. J. H. KING *Myst. Libyan Desert* xxiii. 221 In front of us..was a high three-headed *sif*, or longitudinal sand dune. **1931** *Geogr. Jrnl.* LXXVIII. 16 In form it is a typical *sif* dune, a long straight ridge of sand with a single longitudinal chain of crests rising to billowy pyramids set at regular intervals, in silhouette something like huge saw-teeth. **1933** *Ibid.* LXXXII. 107 The Prince's map of this area shows a sudden change in the direction of the straight parallel lines of *seif* dunes which cross the country. **1941** R. A. BAGNOLD *Physics of Blown Sand & Desert Dunes* xv. 234 The early observers..held that it blew at right angles to the dune direction, whereas later observations over a longer period show that it blows parallel to the dunes... Both are right, since cross-winds are essential for seif formation. **1953** *Sci. News* XXVII. 16 The greatest height recorded for a *seif* dune is 210 metres... Their lengths vary from about 60 to 120 kilometres. **1975** *Nature* 20 Feb. 617/2 Until the recent drought, seif dunes were mainly active in this region north of the 150-mm isohyet. **1976** *Ibid.* 26 Feb. 654/1 Nearby, near the oasis of Bilma, a small dune field of seifs and barchans again indicates that the wind at right angles to the barchans would be to the left of the main trend.

Seigneur. Add: **a.** Also *transf.* in extended use.

1924 WODEHOUSE *Ukridge* vii. 156 'Yes, yes, yes,' said Ukridge, with testy impatience, quite the seigneur resenting interference from an underling. **1978** A. MORICE *Murder by Proxy* i. 20 They used to own all the land... He still sees himself as the Seigneur of the neighbourhood.

c. In the Channel Islands, the lord of the manor; *spec.* the overlord of Sark.

1694 P. FALLE *Acct. Isle of Jersey* iv. 114 The place of Bailly being lately become vacant by the..death of Sir Philip de Carteret,..Seigneur of St. Ouen,..the States of the Island..have..chosen for Judge Delegate Philip le Geyt. **1815** T. QUAYLE *Agric. Islands on Coast of Normandy* 298 Some small specimens of copper ore are said to have been discovered... Little hope is entertained by the Seigneur of the fief [*sc.* Sark], that the quantity of ore will be found considerable. **1835** H. D. Inglis *Channel Islands* 313 The lord of Serk is the sole lay impropriator of tithes. The tithe paid to the seigneur is the tenth sheaf of wheat, barley, oats, beans, &c. **1856** C. Le Quesne *Constitut. Hist. Jersey* ii. 31 At the Assize d'Héritage, or first day of sitting, the principal feudal seigneurs, or lords holding *in capite* from the Crown, are bound to appear. **1885** A. Edwardes *Girton Girl* I. v. 118 He had come to be Seigneur of Tintajeux through the inheritance of his Guernsey wife. **1935** E. Platt *Sark as I found It* ix. 67 Mr. Collings, the late Seigneur, had more than one offer during his lifetime to restart the mines. **1957** *Encycl. Brit.* V. 231/1 In Jersey, if a land-owner dies without a direct heir, the *seigneur* claims for a year and a day the income of his estate; the *seigneurs* of St. Ouen's and La Motte still license taverners. **1976** *Times* 10 Mar. (Channel Islands Suppl.) p. ii/3 You can cross to Sark where buying a freehold property depends simply on availability and the consent of the island's Seigneur.

seigneurial, *a.* Add: Also *fig.*, lordly; authoritative.

1970 *Times Lit. Suppl.* 23 July 787/2 In the United States, Linguistics has long derived authority from the presence there of the two most seigneurial of living linguists, Roman Jakobson and Noam Chomsky. **1972** A. Friedman in Cox & Dyson *20th-Cent. Mind* I. xii. 428 Conrad's irony is heavy and fuming, his seigneurial distance from his madmen..woefully great.

Seigneurie. Add: **2. b.** In the Channel Islands, the residence of a Seigneur (sense *c).

1935 E. Platt *Sark as I found It* ix. 65 The Seigneurie must always be the centre of entertaining in Sark. **1978** *Times Lit. Suppl.* 26 May 572/5 There is a nice photograph of him in a group of them outside the Seigneurie, looking as if there is a nasty smell under his nose.

‖ **Seilbahn** (zəi·lbān). [Ger., f. *seil* cable, rope + *bahn* way, road.] A cable railway; an aerial cableway.

1963 I. Fleming *On Her Majesty's Secret Service* ix. 99 Together with the Gemeinde, the local authorities, he constructed the Seilbahn. **1972** *Daily Tel.* 12 Feb. 14/7 Sonntag, a delightful old village clustered round a tall-spired church has a *seilbahn* from which the venturesome may 'sail' across the deep ravine in a cable cab to Stein.

seine, *sb.*[1] Add: **c.** *seine twine* (earlier example); **seine-net:** also as *v. intr.*, to fish with a seine; hence **seine-netter, seine-netting** *vbl. sb.*

1961 Seine-net *v.* [see *Nephrops]. **1947** A. C. Hardy *Seafood Ships* vii. 99 The seine netter..is invariably under 100 ft. long and of wooden construction. **1970** *Cape Times* 28 Oct. (S.A. Fishing Rev.) 1/2 The days when trawlers and seine-netters could make maximum hauls virtually on their doorsteps are over. **1905** J. Johnstone *Brit. Fisheries* p. xxviii, This latter method of seine-netting brings us to the consideration of the methods of the in-shore or longshore man. **1977** *Grimsby Even. Tel.* 14 May 7/7 A list of..stretches of water to be closed to trawling and seine netting. **1770** *Boston Gaz.* 12 Mar. 4/2 (Advt.), The right sort of three-threaded Sein Twine.

‖ **se ipse** (se ipse). [Eng. adaptation of L. *se ipsum*; cf. Ipse *pron.*] Himself: used emphatically with preceding sb.

1853 W. Jerdan *Autobiogr.* IV. xiii. 238 It was Wordsworth *se ipse*... The ideal was complete. **1943** G. Cope *Democracy within Church* 8 The then Archbishop of Canterbury did not hesitate to rebuke his sovereign..and so demonstrated that the clerical oath of allegiance is not to the monarch *se ipse*.

seir-fish, seer-fish. Add: Also *ellipt.* as **seer.**

1913 C. F. Holder *Game Fishes of World* viii. 83 The Seer..leaps eight feet and has a fighting weight of fifteen pounds. **1971** *Fashion Panorama* (Ceylon) Apr.–June (Advt., verso front cover), 12 lbs. comprising Seer, Crabs or Prawns.

‖ **seises** (se·isez), *sb. pl.* [Sp., (*los*: also used) *seises* (the) sixes, pl. of *seis* six.] The choristers (formerly six, now usu. ten) in certain Spanish cathedrals, esp. Seville, who perform a ritual dance with castanets before the altar during the octave of Corpus Christi and certain other festivals.

1845 R. Ford *Hand-bk. for Travellers Spain* I. ii. 255/2 At this Octave and at Corpus, the Quiresters or *Seises* (formerly they were six in number) dance before the high altar [of Seville Cathedral] with castanets and with plumed hats on their heads... They are dressed as pages of the time of Philip III. They wear blue and white for the Virgin, red and white for Corpus. **1885** E. de Amicis *Spain & Spaniards* ix. 324 The most curious privilege..of the Seville Cathedral, is the..dance of *los seises*, which takes place every evening.., for eight consecutive days, after the festival of *Corpus Domini*. **1903** A. Symons *Cities* 128, I returned to the Cathedral to see the dance of the Seises... The sixteen boys..came forward and knelt before the altar. **1926** J. B. Trend *Mus. Sp. Hist. to 1600* v. 85 The ten little *Seises* who dance, sing, and clack their castanets before the high altar of Seville Cathedral for the festivals of Corpus Christi and the Immaculate Conception. **1938** B. Schönberg tr. *C. Sachs's World Hist. Dance* vii. 337 The classical number of participants in the *Morris Dance*, six, was once the same for the Spanish cathedral dance..—and even today, although there are ten performers, they are still known as *los seises*, 'the sixes'. **1941** G. Chase *Music of Spain* xvi. 256 The *seises* (choirboys) of Seville Cathedral, who every year, during the octave of Corpus Christi, dressed in quaint costumes of the time of Carlos III.., dance before a special altar to the sound of their own castanets and the accompaniment of an orchestra. **1969** S. Sitwell *Gothic Europe* xii. 132 Dancing with castanets before the high altar..is performed by the *seises* or choristers.

seismal, *a.* (Example.)

1977 A. Hallam *Planet Earth* 78/3 Gravimetric, seismal and geothermal investigations of several rift zones.

seismic, *a.* Add: **1. a.** Also, pertaining to or involving earth vibrations produced artificially by explosions. *seismic survey*, † (*a*) a survey of an area in connection with its liability to earthquakes; (*b*) a survey (for oil and gas) employing seismic methods.

1887 *Trans. Seismol. Soc Japan* X. 36 The first method of avoiding earthquake motion in a given district is to make a seismic survey of that area. **1935** *Geol. Natural Gas* (Amer. Assoc. Petroleum Geologists) 664 Seismic surveys isolated a relatively small area with structural closure on the upthrown side of the fault. **1941** *Bull. Amer. Assoc. Petroleum Geologists* XXV. 1261 The unsolved problems in the field of seismic surveying require for their solution a more complete understanding of the properties of the earth strata. **1944** A. Holmes *Princ. Physical Geol.* xii. 206 Near the middle of the sheet the ice has been shown by seismic methods..to be over 8,000 feet thick. **1969** *Times* 16 July 4/2 The scientific equipment bay where the seismic experiment and the laser rangefinding device are stowed. **1972** *Daily Tel.* 1 May 2/7 Seismic studies show these areas could be almost as rich in oil and gas as the North Sea. **1979** *Jrnl. R. Soc. Arts* CXXVII. 405/1 The first stage in oil and gas exploration is usually in the form of seismic surveys.

b. *fig.*

1962 S. E. Finer *Man on Horseback* xii. 222 These bands of successor-states form so many seismic zones of preternatural military eruption. **1979** A. Draper *Fish 10* Churchill's seismic decision to empty the national coffers in one bold operation..was only taken when the Germans were hammering at the door.

2. Special collocations: **seismic prospecting,** prospecting by investigating the propagation in rock of artificially created elastic waves; **seismic reflection,** the reflection of elastic waves at boundaries between different rock formations; usu. *attrib.*; **seismic refraction,** the refraction of elastic waves on passing between formations of rock having different seismic velocities; usu. *attrib.*; **seismic sea-wave** = *Tsunami; **seismic velocity,** the velocity of propagation of elastic waves in a particular rock; **seismic wave,** an elastic wave in the earth produced by an earthquake or by artificial means.

1929 *Trans. Amer. Inst. Mining & Metall. Engineers* LXXXI. 626 In seismic prospecting in general, fewer data are employed than in pure seismology. **1963** C. A. Heiland *Geophysical Exploration* ix. 439 Uses of seismic prospecting in mining have been few. **1932** *Trans. Amer. Inst. Mining & Metall. Engineers* XCVII. 469 A second application of the method of least squares is the outlining of a buried structure by seismic reflections. **1940** *Bull. Amer. Assoc. Petroleum Geologists* XXIV. 1391 The sequence of methods of examination..is likely to be that of reconnaisance geology, detailed geologic mapping,.. and core-drilling or seismic reflection examination. **1977** A. Hallam *Planet Earth* 29/2 In the search for oil-bearing strata, geophysicists make use of the seismic-reflection technique to the virtual exclusion of all other exploration methods. **1934** *Trans. Amer. Inst. Mining & Metall. Engineers* CX. 473 (*heading*) Seismic refraction methods as applied to shallow overburdens. **1979** *Nature* 3 May 56/2 In 1977 an 800-km long seismic refraction profile was shot across Iceland and along the south-eastern flank of the Reykjanes Ridge. **1905** C. Davison *Study of Recent Earthquakes* vi. 163 (*heading*) Seismic sea-waves. **1944** A. Holmes *Princ. Physical Geol.* xvii. 362 Strong submarine earthquakes are followed by seismic sea waves. **1966** *McGraw-Hill Encycl. Sci. & Technol.* XIV. 355/1 Explosions or collapses taking place under water may cause water waves, sometimes of great size. These fall within the class of tsunamis (seismic sea waves). **1935** *Bull. Amer. Assoc. Petroleum Geologists* XIX. 1 The idea that the longitudinal seismic velocity of sediments increases with the age of the sediments has been held rather generally for some time. **1977** A. Hallam *Planet Earth* 11/1 Observed seismic velocities..allow the variation of density with depth in the Earth to be determined. **1900** H. Nagaoka *Elastic Constants of Rocks & Velocity of Seismic Waves* (Publ. Earthquake Investigation Comm. in Foreign Languages No. 4) 65 The investigation of the seismic waves affords the best means of feeling the pulse of the interior of the earth. **1925** M. Mühlberg in I. A. Stigand *Outl. Occurrence & Geol. of Petroleum* 217 The transmissive velocity for seismic (as also acoustic) waves is different in various media. **1966** *McGraw-Hill Encycl. Sci. & Technol.* XII. 147/1 Seismic waves from explosions and earthquakes occur in the frequency range from about 100 to 1/3000 cps.

seismically *adv.*: also, by seismic methods.

1941 *Bull. Amer. Assoc. Petroleum Geologists* XXV. 1258 The average depth to which the Gulf Coast has been seismically surveyed. **1978** *Nature* 27 Apr. 791/2 The absence of a seismically detectable Tertiary–Quaternary sediment cover.

seismics (səi·zmiks), *sb. pl.* [f. Seismic *a.*: see -ic 2.] Seismic exploration techniques, esp. such techniques considered as a whole.

1934 *Trans. Amer. Inst. Mining & Metall. Engineers* CX. 462 Roman has developed the application of the method to seismics very satisfactorily. **1976** D. McLeod tr. *Beckmann's Geol. Petroleum* II. iv. 64 Reflexion seismics are the most frequently-used, but also the most expensive of all methods used in petroleum exploration.

seismocardiography (səi:zmokāɹdiǫ·grăfi). [f. Seismo- + Cardiography.] The analysis of movements of the chest as a means of studying those of the heart. So **seismoca·rdiogram,** the record made by this process; **sei·smocardiographic** *a.*, of or pertaining to seismocardiography.

1962 *Probl. Space Biol.* I. 461 The constructional details of a seismocardiographic transducer on dogs are given. *Ibid.* 463 Seismocardiography is a form of ballistocardiography. *Ibid.*, The recording of the seismocardiograms is impossible during movements. **1965** *Proc. 14th Internat. Astronaut. Congr., 1963* III. 38 During weightlessness the animal showed an absolute and relative increase of the first cycle of the seismocardiogram. **1970** L. I. Kakurin et al. in D. E. Busby *Rec. Adv. Aerospace Med.* 43 Biomedical monitoring was carried out by means of a unified sensor system. It comprised seismocardiographic (SCG) and pneumographic (PG) sensors. **1979** *Human Physiol.* V. 542 The use of seismocardiography in clinical, athletic, and space medicine,..and for mass examinations of the population is..a promising development.

seismograph. Add: Also as *v. trans.* and *intr.*, to study (a region) by means of seismography; to prospect for oil by seismic methods; **seismogra·phically** *adv.* (*fig.* in quot. 1964).

1925 M. Mühlberg in I. A. Stigand *Outl. Occurrence & Geol. of Petroleum* 218 The times of arrival are recorded seismographically. **1940** *Trans. Amer. Inst. Mining & Metall. Engineers* CXXXVIII. 305 (*heading*) Continuous profiling method of seismographing for oil structures. **1964** *New Statesman* 10 Apr. 577/1 In the quintessential Hanley lodging-house, every creak or whisper registered seismographically. **1968** C. Helmericks *Down Wild River North* xxvi. 423 They go 'seismographing' right overland through the wilderness. **1969** J. Mavor *Voyage to Atlantis* ix. 203 Dr Marinatos suggested we seismograph the whole field in order to determine whether the Minoan layer was relatively level and therefore a logical town site.

seismologically, *adv.* Add: (Examples.) Also *fig.*

1955 *Sci. Amer.* Sept. 59/1 Seismologically speaking, the crust differs from the underlying part of the mantle in the fact that P and S waves travel in it more slowly and with more variable speed. **1970** *Nature* 15 Aug. 649/2 This earthquake was a nice reminder that Britain is not as seismologically quiet as people believe. **1977** H. Greene *FSO—1* xix. 171 In an arm of government as seismologically sensitive as the Foreign Service,..Friburn's sudden resignation was a shock on the level of six or seven on the diplomatic Richter scale.

seismologist. (Earlier and later examples.)

1859 R. Mallet in *Rep. Brit. Assoc. 1858* 133 The subject appears to me worthy of more examination at the hands of Vulcanologists and Seismologists. **1955** *Sci. Amer.* Sept. 168/2 Our values agree well with those obtained by seismologists, who measure the thickness of the crust by the travel time of earthquake waves. **1973** *Nature* 27 July 195/2 This region of northern California, highly populated with seismologists and seismometers, is proving to be quite a testing ground for prediction.

seismonasty (səi·zmonæsti). *Bot.* [f. Seismo- + *nasty *sb.*[2]] A nastic movement made in response to a mechanical shock. Hence **seismona·stic** *a.*, of or pertaining to a movement of this kind.

1912 W. H. Lang tr. *Strasburger's Text-bk. Bot.* I. 323 (*heading*) Seismonasty. *Ibid.*, Every disturbance resulting from a mechanical shock acts as a stimulus... These movements are termed seismonastic. **1951** [see *nastic *a.*]. **1965** Bell & Coombe tr. *Strasburger's Textbk. Bot.* (new ed.) 382 A whole series of plants displays movements of this kind after touching, a phenomenon termed seismonasty. *Ibid.* 383 Many petals, stamens and stigmata show seismonastic reactions.

seismotectonic (səi:zmotektǫ·nik), *a.* [f. Seismo- + Tectonic *a.*] Of, pertaining to, or designating features of the earth's crust, such as faults, which are associated with or revealed by earthquakes; † *seismotectonic line* (see quots. 1907, 1924).

1907 W. H. Hobbs in *Beiträge zur Geophysik* VIII. 224 A tendency of the damaged communes to be arranged in essentially right lines (seismotectonic lines) is noteworthy. **1907** —— *Earthquakes* ii. 32 Buried planes may, however, often be traced as lines of destruction especially marked out upon the surface of the ground. Such straight lanes of special damage from earthquake have been called seismotectonic lines, or structure lines revealed by earthquakes. **1924** *Bull. Seismol. Soc. Amer.* XIV. 31 Hobbs, 1907, describes as seismotectonic lines certain structure-lines which he believes to be revealed by earthquakes. **1974** *Nature* 19 Apr. 661/2 Here, we describe three additional earthquake faults found during recent seismotectonic field studies in Iran. **1980** *Ibid.* 19 June 529/2 An aftershock study was begun..in an effort to examine seismotectonic processes near Mt. St. Helens.

Seistan (sī·stān). Also **seistan.** [The name of a low-lying region of eastern Iran and south-western Afghanistan.] A strong northwesterly wind prevalent in this region in the summer months. Also *attrib.*, as *Seistan wind.*

1906 *Geogr. Jrnl.* XXVIII. 224 The extraordinary frequency and violence of the Seistan wind, and the regularity with which it blows from the same quarter, are very remarkable. **1940** *Chambers's Techn. Dict.* 754/1 *Seistan*, the 120-day summer north wind in E. Persia. **1959** R. E. HUSCHKE *Gloss. Meteorol.* 503 The seistan is associated.. with the deep summer-time low over northwest India. **1967** R. W. FAIRBRIDGE *Encycl. Atmospheric Sci. & Astrogeology* 1155/2 The 'seistan' or 'Wind of 120 days' is the characteristic wind of Seistan in eastern Iran, which blows from late May till the end of September, from north-northwest, sometimes with velocities from 70–120 mph.

Seitz (zəits). [See quot. 1944: a proprietary term in the U.S.] Used *attrib.* and in *Comb.* with reference to filtration, as **Seitz disc**, a small disc of compressed asbestos fibres, used for filtration; **Seitz filter**, a type of filter in which liquids are purified by passage through a readily replaceable Seitz disc; so as *v. trans.*; **Seitz-filtered** *ppl. a.*, **Seitz filtration; Seitz pad**, a Seitz disc.

1925 *1st Progress Rep. Foot-&-Mouth Dis. Res. Comm.* (Min. of Agric. & Fisheries) App. II. 20 A routine form of asbestos filter of German manufacture, the Seitz filter, has been employed with success. **1928** T. M. RIVERS *Filterable Viruses* ii. 59 Smaller filters with Seitz discs have been made for use in experimental work. [**1944** *Official Gaz.* (U.S. Patent Office) 4 Apr. 12/2 Republic Filters, Inc., Paterson, N.J... *Seitz.* The trade-mark is a facsimile of the signature of Mr. Seitz, the late inventor of the basic construction of the filtering apparatus manufactured and sold by applicant.] **1946** *Nature* 31 Aug. 293/2 After the fungus has grown in the liquid medium for about two weeks, the culture medium is Seitz-filtered and collected in autoclaved tubes and ampoules. **1947** *Ann. Rev. Microbiol.* I. 378 The second experiment.. involved thirty-six men who were divided into three groups of twelve each and sprayed, respectively, with untreated sputum and throat washings, with the material filtered through sintered glass or Seitz pads, or with the same material autoclaved. **1956** *Nature* 21 Jan. 134/1 Another 2 ml. of the same medium, containing 0·05 per cent aesculin sterilized by Seitz-filtration, [was] added. *Ibid.* 10 Mar. 481/2 (*caption*) Curve *B* shows the results in Seitz-filtered artificial duodenal contents alone. **1961** *Lancet* 29 July 227/2 The pH was adjusted to 7·4 and the medium sterilised by Seitz filtration. **1964** M. HYNES *Med. Bacteriol.* (ed. 8) ii. 25 The Seitz filter has almost entirely replaced all other types of filter... Filtration is carried out through an asbestos pad clamped to the bottom of a metal container.

sei whale (sēi wēil). Also **sejhval**; (*erron.*) **seivhal.** [Anglicization of Norw. *sejhval*, f. *sei* coal-fish + *hval* WHALE *sb.*] A blue-grey rorqual, *Balænoptera borealis.*

1912 *Rep. Brit. Assoc.* 158 The Right whales and Sejhvals are said to appear only during the earlier part of the season. **1916** R. S. ANDREWS in *Mem. Amer. Mus. Nat. Hist.* I. 295 The vernacular term Sei Whale (*Sejhval*), adopted in this memoir, is the name by which *Balænoptera borealis* is known to the Norwegians. **1919** R. W. CLARK in E. Shackleton *South* I. 364 The sperm-whale and the sei-whale have shown a good deal of seasonal variation. **1923** *Chambers's Jrnl.* Jan. 112/1 The lesser rorqual, the seivhal, and the humpback, another whalebone whale, take some small fish. **1939** *Nature* 16 Dec. 999/2 (*caption*) Species..Sei, Right, Sperm. **1958** *Times* 12 Nov. 11/6 A unit is defined as equalling one blue whale..or six sei whales. **1974** *Country Life* 11 Apr. 866/1 With the cessation of whaling in the Faeroes and Norway the numbers of fin and sei whales in those areas..will..increase.

seize, *v.* Add: **III. 11.** Also with *up.* Of a machine or mechanism: to stick, jam, or lock fast; to become unworkable, as by reason of undue heat or friction. Also *fig.*

1917 *Blackw. Mag.* May 807/1 Our engine recovered slightly now that its recovery was not so important, and it behaved well until it seized up for better or worse when we had landed. **1963** *Listener* 31 Jan. 198/2 As for the camera itself, at 40 below zero the wind-on mechanism jammed and the range-finder seized up. **1981** P. AUDEMARS *Gone to her Death* ii. 44 Better we should find the trouble on our hoist rather than having something seize up on the main road.

fig. **1955** CORMACK & MCDOUGALL in C. Morris *Social Case-Work in Gt. Britain* (ed. 2) i. 35 When the social service system was primitive it could do without case-work: the more elaborate modern machine would seize up. **1960** C. DAY LEWIS *Buried Day* ix. 182, I read the book; then, for hour after hour, I sat trying to think of something to say about it. I could not... My brain had seized up. **1976** DEXTER & MAKINS *Testkill* 100 Any exercise.. might make me seize up.

Hence **seize-up** *Mech.*, the action or state of seizure (cf. sense *11 of the vb.).

1912 *Motor Man.* (ed. 14) vi. 232 Unless one makes quite certain that every bearing and cylinder be properly relubricated before starting up again, a 'seize-up'..is not improbable.

seized, *ppl. a.* (Later examples.)

1911 E. W. WALFORD *Maintenance of Motor Cars* ii. 30 The procedure is to allow the parts to cool down..and to inject a copious supply of oil to the seized part. **1977** F. DURBRIDGE *Passenger* iii. 154 He walked the six miles into Reading..told a story about a seized engine.

seizing, *vbl. sb.* **1.** (Later examples in sense 11 of the vb.)

1911 E. W. WALFORD *Maintenance of Motor Cars* ii. 30 An engine may suddenly pull up, and it be found impossible to turn the crankshaft with the starting handle. The popular expression for this is 'seizing'. **1925** *Morris Owner's Man.* 29 Neglect of this results in harsh running and an overheated engine, loss of power, and finally 'seizing-up' of pistons or connecting rods.

‖ **Sejm** (sēim). Also **Seym.** [Pol.] In Poland: a general assembly or diet; a parliament; *spec.* (since 1921) the lower house of the Polish parliament.

[**1698** B. CONNOR *Hist. Poland* II. II. iii. 83 The Grand Diet or Parliament of Poland, by the Natives call'd Seym Walny.] **1893** W. R. MORFILL *Poland* v. 40 Ladislaus had assembled the first known *Seym*, or Diet, at Checiny... It consisted of the princes..prelates, barons and knights. **1916** G. E. SLOCOMBE *Poland* ix. 85 Their [*sc.* the nobles'] first step was to obtain a revival of the *sejm* or general Diet of Poland. **1924** A. E. TENNANT *Studies in Polish Life & Hist.* ix. 162 The new Sejm is a democratic assembly in which all classes are represented. **1934** E. J. PATTERSON *Poland* iii. 83 Under the constitution the powers of the Seym were very great...In case of a disagreement between the two houses the Senate could be over-ridden by a majority of 11/20 in the Seym, in ordinary session. **1959** Z. PELCZYNSKI in D. E. Butler et al. *Elections Abroad* ii. 125 The Sejm had been evolving and adapting itself to the policy of 'democratisation'. **1981** *Financial Times* 13 Jan. 1/3 It will be discussed at a special Polish Communist Party congress this spring, then go for approval to the Sejm (Parliament).

sejunct, *a.* For *rare*$^{-2}$ read *rare* and add later nonce-use.

1922 JOYCE *Ulysses* 378 Images, divine and human, the cogitation of which by sejunct females is to tumescence conducive.

‖ **sekere** (sekere·). Also **shekere.** [Yoruba.] A Yoruba gourd-rattle.

1921 S. & O. JOHNSON *Hist. Yorubas* I. viii. 121 The Calabash drum—ornamental with strings of cowries—is called *Sèkèrè.* **1937** I. O. DELANO *Soul of Nigeria* xiii. 160 The acrobatic dancers..tour the Yoruba land... They have their beaters, and what they beat is called 'Sekere'. These are not drums, but gourds to which a number of cowries have been attached, so that they make a noise when shaken. **1963** W. SOYINKA *Lion & Jewel* 61 Distant music. Light drums, flutes, box-guitars, 'sekere'. **1975** *New Yorker* 29 Sept. 41/2 The other instruments are.. and two shekeres—large West African calabashes strung with beads.

‖ **sekos** (sī·kǫs). *Egyptology.* Also **secos.** [a. Gr. σηκός pen, enclosure.] A sacred enclosure in an ancient Egyptian temple.

1820 G. BELZONI *Narr. Egypt & Nubia* III. 291 Having observed, that the part where the sekos and cella must be was not touched, I set the men to work there. **1837** *Penny Cycl.* IX. 316/2 Facing its entrance was that leading into the *sekos* or shrine containing the figure of the deity. **1887** *Dict. Architecture* (Architectural Publ. Soc.) VII. 45/1 In the Egyptian temples the *secos* was the same as the *adytum* of the Greeks and Romans.

‖ **Sekt** (zekt). [Ger.; cf. SACK *sb.*[3]] A German sparkling white wine or champagne.

1920 G. SAINTSBURY *Notes on Cellar-bk.* vi. 84 The 'Cabinet *Sekt*'..was 'a very *German*' champagne. **1924** [see *FLUTE *sb.*[1] 3 a]. **1951** R. POSTGATE *Plain Man's Guide to Wine* v. 96 A horrible German imitation [of champagne] called Sekt. **1962** P. PURSER *Peregrination 22* xvi. 72 Do you remember the time in Berlin you were so sick after drinking too much sekt? **1971** 'M. SINCLAIR' *Sonntag* xxii. 129 The bottle of *Sekt* in front of them was good though.

selachyl (sĭlēi·kəil, -kil). *Chem.* [a. G. *selachyl* (Tsujimoto & Toyama 1922, in *Chem. Umschau auf dem Gebiete der Fette*, etc. XXIX. 36): see SELACHIAN *a.* and *sb.* and -YL.] *selachyl alcohol*: an oily liquid, α-glyceryl *cis*-9-octadecenyl ether, $C_{21}H_{42}O_3$, found in the liver oils of elasmobranch fishes.

1922 *Chem. Abstr.* XVI. 1513 The formula $C_{20}H_{40}O_3$ [*sic*] was selected to represent this unsatd. alc. and the name selachyl alcohol given to it. **1944** *Jrnl. Biol. Chem.* CLV. 448 Selachyl alcohol has been isolated from natural sources so far only as an oil. **1964** *Oceanogr. & Marine Biol.* II. 177 The most abundant alcoholic component of the alkoxydiglycerides is invariably selachyl alcohol, followed by chimyl alcohol and then by batyl alcohol.

seladang (sĕlā·dæŋ). Also **saladang, salandang, sladang.** [Malay, in Borneo *seladang*, in Sumatra *saladang.*] = GAUR; also, formerly, the Malayan tapir, *Tapirus indicus.*

1821 T. S. RAFFLES in *Trans. Linnean Soc.* XIII. 270 It [*sc. Tapirus Malayanus*] is known by different names in different parts of the country [*sc.* Sumatra]. By the people of Limun it is called Saladang. **1839** T. J. NEWBOLD *Straits of Malacca* I. vii. 435 The Seladang is supposed by some zoologists to be identical with the Tapir. **1868** *Proc. Asiatic Soc. Bengal* 194 The Malayan bison, an animal well known to the Malays under the name of *Sladang*..[is] more formidable when wounded than the tiger. **1875** E. BLYTH *Cat. Mammals & Birds of Burma* 47 In the Malayan peninsula, where it is known as the *Salandang*, this animal [*sc.* the Gaur] would appear to be becoming extremely rare. **1905** T. R. HUBBACK *Elephant & Seladang Hunting* 44 The seladang has no dewlap and no hump. *Ibid.* 47 Seladang are only found in little-inhabited districts. **1927** H. M. TOMLINSON *Gallions Reach* xxxv. 263 A likely corner for sladang, the instantaneous bull which does not wait for trouble but makes it when you are not looking. **1933** L. AINSWORTH *Confess. Planter in Malaya* 219 The Seladang or Malayan Bison is diminishing in numbers, and is now found almost exclusively in Negri Sembilan and Pahang. **1965** R. MCKIE *Company of Animals* viii. 130 Seladang (this spelling will be used for both singular and plural) are among the largest of the ox tribe and are remote relatives of domestic cattle. **1974** R. BUTLER *Buffalo Hook* iv. 28 The seladang is the wild buffalo of Malaysia.

Selah. (Later allusive examples.)

1906 J. LONDON *Let.* 1 Dec. (1966) 229, I want an answer... I want it to the point... Selah. **1924** E. E. CUMMINGS *Let.* 13 May (1969) 107 The Independants found me not incapable of a 40′ × 50′ '*abstract*' canvas which..hung very well (by itself)—this lidel effut cost me 9 days work and was dry on time, selah-sounds. **1947** W. STEVENS in *Q. Rev. Lit.* III. 110 The dove in the belly builds his nest and coos, Selah, tempestuous bird. **1975** *New Yorker* 26 May 33/3 Then I can go back to doing what every really dedicated writer wants to do. Nothing. Selah, Phil.

‖ **selamlik** (selā·mlik). Also with capital initial. [Turk., lit. 'place of greeting', f. *selâm* a. Arab. *salām* SALAAM *sb.*) + *-lik* place.]

1. A room in a Muslim house set aside for business or the reception of male friends; the part of such a house reserved for men. Cf. *HAREMLIK.

1838 D. URQUHART *Spirit of East* I. xxi. 392 The European arrives... Some of the attendants, in reply to his inquiries, point to the door of the Selamlik. **1854** R. CURZON *Armenia* 79 We went into the selamlik (or reception room) together. **1888** K. BEY *Evil of East* vii. 127 Every Turkish house is divided into two distinct parts:—the *selamlik* for men, and the *haremlik* for women. **1900** 'ODYSSEUS' *Turkey in Europe* vii. 331 One feels that.. their existence is really divided into the departments of Selamlik and Harem, which means the difference, not only between the men's and the women's part of the house, but between formal and domestic life. **1936, 1941** [see *HAREMLIK]. **1965** J. FLEMING *Nothing is Number* I. i. 15 The *selamlik*, or male reception room, is inviolate.

2. The public procession of the Sultan to a mosque on Friday at noon. Now *Hist.*

1888 'BEY KESNIN' *Evil of East* vi. 125 On Fridays, for Selamlik, the soldier makes himself as smart as possible to escort his sovereign to the mosque. **1905** *Globe* (N.Y.) 21 July 1/2 It is reported here officially from Constantinople that during to-day's selamlik an attempt was made to assassinate the sultan. **1935** H. EDIB *Clown & his Daughter* ix. 45 Selim Pasha decided to speak about Rabia's musical training to the Imam after the Selamlik—the Friday ceremony of His Majesty's going to the mosque. **1955** H. LUKE *Old Turkey & New* (rev. ed.) vii. 166 On Friday, the 10th November, 1922 Vahid ed-Din attended his last selamlik. **1980** J. LEES-MILNE *Harold Nicolson* 56 The First Balkan War had begun. That day [*sc.* 17 Oct. 1912] Harold witnessed the ceremony of the Selamlik.

Selbornian (selbǭ·ɹniăn), *a.* Also **Selburnian.** [f. *Selborne*, the name of a village in Hampshire + -IAN.] **1.** Of, pertaining to, or connected with Selborne, the parish described in *The Natural History and Antiquities of Selborne* (1789) by Gilbert White (1720–93). Also as *sb.*, an inhabitant of Selborne or an admirer of the writings of Gilbert White.

1869 J. R. LOWELL in *Atlantic Almanac* 32/1 How pleasant is his innocent vanity in adding to the list of the British, and still more of the Selbornian, *fauna!* **1928** *Observer* 26 Feb. 8/5 Another book about 'Gilbert White', ..a book full of pleasures for all Selbornians. **1938** H. J. MASSINGHAM *Writings of Gilbert White* I. p. x, He writes of the Selburnian echo. *Ibid.* p. xxii, How absorbed the greatest and most typical of Selburnians was with gardening. **1954** R. M. LOCKLEY *Gilbert White* i. 9 Already he was able to convey his love of the Selbornian scene.

2. *Geol.* A name given by A. J. Jukes-Brown (see quot. 1900) to the Upper Greensand and Gault beds in the Albian stage of the Cretaceous in Southern England, from the prominent occurrence of these deposits near Selborne. Also *absol.* Now *rare* or *Obs.*

1900 A. J. JUKES-BROWN *Cretaceous Rocks Brit.* I. 1 The Selbornian comprises the beds which are generally known as the Gault and the upper Greensand. *Ibid.* 31 Gault clay and greensand are only two of the different kinds of deposits that make up the group for which the name Selbornian is now proposed. **1910** [see *ALBIAN *a.* and *sb.*]. **1922** J. C. HUGHES *Geol. Story of Isle of Wight* vi. 37 Some prefer to call the Lower Greensand Vectian, from Vectis, the old name of the Isle of Wight, and the Upper Greensand Selbornian, a name generally adopted, because it forms a marked feature of the country about Selborne.

seldom, *a.* For '*Obs.*..action' read 'Now chiefly *U.S.*' and add further examples.

1883 'MARK TWAIN' *Life on Mississippi* xxi. 222 The seldomest spectacle on the Mississippi to-day is a wood-pile. **1959** W. GOLDING *Free Fall* i. 26 My seldom night terrors. **1961** E. WILSON in WEBSTER s.v., With her small seldom smile.

seldomly, *adv.* (Later example.)

c **1864** E. DICKINSON *Poems* (1955) II. 610 The ships.. That touch how seldomly Thy Shore?

seldseen, *a.* (Later *poet.* example.)
1916 E. Blunden *Pastorals* 30 Even as she flung the seld-seen gaud away.

select, *sb.* (Later N. Amer. examples.)
1961 S. Taylor in Webster s.v., It is possible to buy ware that is composed wholly of selects. **1968** *Globe & Mail* (Toronto) 15 Jan. 17/6 The All-Star game tomorrow night with the selects meeting the Stanley Cup defending champions from Toronto.

selectable, *a.* Delete *rare* and add later example in sense 'capable of being selected'.
1975 *Gramophone* Nov. 950/3 Low and high pass filters..with two selectable cut-off points for bass and treble are also featured.

Selectasine (sĭle·ktăsīn). The proprietary name of a colour-printing process which uses a single silk screen for each of the colours (see quot. 1934).
1918 *Official Gaz.* (U.S. Patent Office) 29 Jan. 1075/1 Method of delineating or reproducing pictures and designs... Assignors to Selectasine System, San Francisco, Cal., a Corporation of California. Filed Dec. 1, 1915. **1926** H. L. Hiett *Man. Stencil Screen Process Work* 79 Invented by Edward A. Owens, San Francisco, Cal., assignor to Selectasine System, Inc., San Francisco. **1934** H. Curwen *Processes of Graphic Reproduction in Printing* 1. 40 Selectasine is best suited to showcards of very bold design... A sheet of fabric ready impregnated with wax is the basis, and one sheet is used for each colour of the design. The wax filling is removed from the fabric following the shape of the colour to be worked, and a stencil is thus formed. **1948** H. Missingham *Student's Guide in Commercial Art* ii. 137 (*heading*) Silk screen or Selectasine process.

selectee (sĭlektī·). *U.S.* [f. Select *v.* + -ee.] A person selected for military service under the Selective Service system; a draftee. Now chiefly *transf.*
1940 *Army & Navy Register* (U.S.) 30 Nov. 7/2 The public considers the percentage of rejections of selectees high. **1942** *Newsweek* 27 Apr. 41/3 The Selectee is to be given a furlough up to ten days to arrange his personal affairs. **1958** *Optima* Mar. 47/2 The suspicion remains that the selectee is being favoured because he is regarded as the 'comer'—the man most likely to succeed in the immediately foreseeable future. **1979** *Tucson* (Arizona) *Citizen* 20 Sept. 10a/3 Most of Carter's selectees ..passed in a breeze.

selection. Add: **2. a.** Also, a musical passage or a sequence of selected musical extracts.
1857 W. Acton *Prostitution* vii. 103 [We]..enjoyed in a grim kind of way the 'selection' from some favourite opera. **1899** *Observer* 1 Oct. 5/3 The 'selection', which always begins the second part of the concert, was the familiar fantasia on English airs. **1929** *Radio Times* 8 Nov. 411/1 Selection of Songs by T. C. Sterndale Bennett. **1945** S. Hughes in C. Madge *Pilot Papers* I. 94 The brass band repertoire..consists principally of marches.. waltzes and light opera selections. **1968** M. Ball (*title*) Selections from the classics for chime bar music making.

5. a. (sense 1) *selection board, committee, panel, test*; **selection pressure** *Biol.*, differential mortality or fertility such as tends to make a population adapt genetically; **selection restriction** *Linguistics*, a syntactic or semantic restraint on the concurrence of dependent lexical items; **selection rule** *Physics*, any of a number of rules which describe, within certain limits, which particular quantum transitions can occur in an atom, molecule, etc., and which are 'forbidden'.
1940 R. S. Lambert *Ariel & all his Quality* xi. 302 Methods of appointing new staff..by advertising vacancies and setting up selection boards. **1976** L. Deighton *Twinkle, twinkle, Little Spy* xvi. 162 Douglas was sent to a swanky private school..but was still unable to pass the U.S. Army officers' selection board. **1909** *Daily Graphic* 26 July 6/3 It is safe to believe that the Selection Committee has done its best, the players will do their best, Australia will do its best. **1932** Q. D. Leavis *Fiction & Reading Public* i. ii. 22 The Book Society...was started..in 1927 ..with a Selection Committee of five novelists and journalists. **1978** J. Pudney *Thank Goodness for Cake* 97, I was short-listed and looked over by a selection committee. **1974** *BP Shield Internat.* Oct. 8/1 Conference members..were screened by a selection panel. **1944** J. S. Huxley *On living in Revolution* 79 [In the Australian area] there is less scope for variation,..so that general selection-pressure never became so intense. **1977** J. L. Harper *Population Biol. of Plants* ii. 46 Groups of species caught in different evolutionary pathways may face the same selective forces, e.g. a selection pressure to disperse. **1964** Katz & Postal *Integrated Theory of Linguistic Descriptions* ii. 15 Each reading in the dictionary entry for a lexical item must contain a *selection restriction*, i.e., a formally expressed necessary and sufficient condition for that reading to combine with others. **1976** *Word 1971* XXVII. 133 One reason is that the selection restrictions of the verb *throw* require an animate subject. **1931** H. P. Robertson tr. *H. Weyl's Theory of Groups & Quantum Mech.* iv. 198 The selection rule for the inner quantum number *j* is obtained in an analogous manner. **1977** I. M. Campbell *Energy & Atmosphere* viii. 218 The origin of the selection rules for radiative transitions between electronically excited states and the ground state lies in fundamental quantum theory. **1935** *Discovery* Jan. 17/2 The most anxious moment in the design of a selection test now comes. If we take a group of workers..can the new test sort them into their correct relative order? **1967** Wills & Yearsley *Handbk. Managem. Technol.* xi. 202 Are we right to ignore *selection tests*?

b. *Forestry.* Used *attrib.* with reference to a system of forest management under which there is a continuing selection of individual trees for felling over the whole area, on the basis of their saleability.
1891 W. Schlich *Man. Forestry* II. 133 The term *selection system* was introduced into India; it is perhaps not an ideal term, since a certain amount of selection is practised in all systems; it has been retained, as none better is at present available. **1911** H. S. Graves *Princ. handling Woodlands* ii. 72 The development of the individual trees in a selection stand is somewhat different than in an even-aged stand. **1935** N. C. Brown *Gen. Introd. Forestry U.S.* viii. 105 The selection method is likely to be best adapted to general silvicultural and economic conditions found in this country. **1950** *Q. Jrnl. Forestry* XLIV. 15 Rabbits are probably the greatest drawback to the selection system or any irregular system in this country. **1979** O. Kuthanová tr. *Jeník's Pict. Encycl. Forests* 451 (*caption*) Diagram showing selection felling in a high forest; four stages of forest with alternating generations of trees in man-made clearings.

selectional (sĭle·kʃənăl), *a.* [f. Selection + -al.] Of or pertaining to selection. Freq. in *Linguistics*; *selectional restriction* = *selection restriction* s.v. *selection 5 a.
1961 R. B. Long *Sentence & its Parts* ii. 40 Predeterminer modifiers generally are adverbial in function, and mensurant, selectional..or adjunct-like in force. **1964** *Language* XL. 38 There are, then, selectional restrictions between determiners and relative clauses. **1968** *Ibid.* XLIV. 579 On the other hand, there are cogent observations about the role of 'suffixoids' such as *-er* of *hammer* as selectional factors favoring the development of homophonous derivational affixes. **1971** *Nature* 9 Apr. 410/2, I identified all the maxima and minima of PDS for a given population and summed the successive absolute differences to give me an index that combined both selectional and random factors. **1977** *Word 1972* XXVIII. 89 The NP analysis of copular predicates can be retained for comparatives if *nios* is viewed as some sort of denominalizing particle which makes a comparative adjective compatible with the selectional restrictions of *tá*.
So **sele·ctionally** *adv.*
1958 P. Maas *Textual Crit.* 13 The task of proving the existence of the conjecturally (or 'selectionally'..) presupposed errors plays a considerable..role in textual criticism. **1965** N. Chomsky *Aspects of Theory of Syntax* ii. 116 We label as Noun the one that is selectionally dominant.

selectionism (sĭle·kʃəniz'm). [f. Selection + -ism.] The belief that evolution proceeds by natural selection; opp. to Lamarckism.
1912 A. Tridon tr. *Delage & Goldsmith's Theories Evol.* xi. 163 (*heading*) A discussion of Roux's theory; its merits. —Its relation to selectionism and Lamarckism. **1944** J. S. Huxley *On Living in Revolution* vi. 70 In the last twenty-five years..an enormous amount of new facts about evolution have been discovered, and the balance has now swung over heavily, and, I think, permanently, in favour of Darwinism or selectionism. **1982** *New Scientist* 15 Apr. 162/1 Neutralism never seriously claimed to do more than ride piggyback on selectionism.

selectionist, *sb.* and *a.* For **a, b** read **A, B** and add: **A.** *sb.* **a.** (Later example.) † **b.** One who believes that evolution proceeds primarily by natural selection for small differences (*Obs.*); opp. *mutationist; **c.** One who holds a selectionist view of genetic variation (cf. sense B. b below).
1909 W. Bateson *Mendel's Princ. Heredity* i. 3 If species had really arisen by the natural selection for impalpable differences,..the limits between species should be..indefinite... The selectionists believe..that it represents the facts of nature. **1911** [see *mutationist]. **1959** *Encounter* Sept. 62/2 The selectionist must assume..that consciousness is *useful*. **1979** *Sci. Amer.* Nov. 96/3 Selectionists maintain that for a mutant allele to spread through a species it must have some selective advantage.
B. *adj.* **a.** (Later example.) **b.** Of or pertaining to the belief that the majority of observed genetic variation is maintained by natural selection rather than by random effects.
1944 J. S. Huxley *On Living in Revolution* vi. 69 By Darwinism..was meant the selectionist theory of the method of evolution. **1971** *Nature* 13 Aug. 487/1 They maintain that a selectionist hypothesis would predict radical changes to be favoured over conservative changes. **1974** *Ibid.* 1 Nov. 62/2 A selectionist interpretation of the more rapid rate of molecular evolution in a living fossil is possible. **1978** *Sci. Amer.* Sept. 45/1 Selectionist evolution..is neither a chance phenomenon nor a deterministic phenomenon but a two-step tandem process combining the advantages of both.

selective, *a.* Add: **1. d.** *Psychol.* Applied to the capacity for, or process of, selection manifested by the mind or senses in reacting to certain stimuli and not to others, esp. *selective attention*.
1875 W. James in R. B. Perry *Thought & Char. W. James* (1935) I. 528 The *whole* mass of impressions falling on any individual are chaotic, and become orderly only by selective attention and recognition. **1935** G. Murphy *Briefer Gen. Psychol.* xii. 210 From the point of view..of what takes the most prominent place in consciousness, there is a further selective function to be considered. **1958** D. E. Broadbent *Perception & Communication* ii. 15 The performance of selective listeners seems to vary with information as defined by communication theory, rather than with amount of stimulation in the conventional sense. **1968** Trabasso & Bower *Attention in Learning* i. 18 Our primary goal is to offer new theory and new results regarding selective attention in discrimination learning. **1978** G. Underwood *Strategies of Inform. Processing* vii. 237 The selective rehearsal of some members of the memory set in preference to others.., the selective 'forgetting' of some items previously encoded.

e. *Educ.* (See quot. 1960–1.) Also applied to any school within the selective (as opposed to the comprehensive) system. Cf. *comprehensive *a.* 1 d.
1926 *Educ. of Adolescent* (Board of Educ. Consult. Comm.) iii. 79 As post-primary education develops, the schools dealing with the post-primary or secondary stage of education should include..schools of the type of the existing selective Central Schools, which give at least a four years' course from the age of 11+. **1955** O. Banks *Parity & Prestige in Eng. Secondary Educ.* viii. 97 Both the selective central school and the junior technical school originated in the period before the first world war. **1960–1** *Where?* Winter 17/1 *Selective school*, a school for which the pupils have been selected (usually at 11 plus) on the grounds that they can benefit from a more academic education. **1974** *Times* 17 Apr. 1/5 Over half of our secondary school pupils are still in selective schools. **1978** *Jrnl. R. Soc. Arts* CXXVI. 335/1 The decision to change our schooling from a selective to a comprehensive system.

f. *Philos.* Applied to a doctrine of realism put forward in the early 20th century which maintained that sense-data exist in material objects and that the senses of the perceiver select those which are appropriate to be registered.
1932 H. H. Price *Perception* ii. 40 Now let us turn to the *selective* interpretation. According to this, the somatic data..merely..enable us to be conscious of environmental data. **1944** W. T. Stace in P. A. Schilpp *Philos. B. Russell* 365 The view of selective realism is quite different... The sense-qualities actually exist in the object, whether it is perceived or unperceived, just as common sense supposes. What the sense-organ does is to *select* which of the sense-qualities we shall perceive. **1967** *Encycl. Philos.* VII. 78/2 Their..attempt..to deal with illusions..is a version of what is often called the selective theory.

2. Special collocations: *selective breeding*; *selective employment tax* (also with capital initials), a tax levied by the British Government between 3 May 1966 and 1 Apr. 1973, payable on all employees at varying rates and refunded to employers in selected branches of manufacturing industry; cf. S.E.T. s.v. *S 4 a; *selective service* (U.S.), a system of military service (from 1917 to 1973) under which draftees were selected from those persons required to enrol; *selective strike*, a form of industrial action in which union labour is not totally withdrawn but withheld in chosen sectors; *selective weedkiller*, a substance which kills some plant species without harming others.
1931 J. S. Huxley *What dare I Think?* i. 40 Selective breeding I have just touched upon. **1971** F. Hamilton *World Encycl. Dogs* 354 Selective breeding down through the last 150 years has produced the Foxhound of today. **1966** *Times* 4 May 1/1 A selective employment tax payable by employers only is to be introduced by the Government from September 5 to divert manpower from the service industry into manufacturing. **1973** *Guardian* 13 Apr. 13/5 Selective Employment Tax ended on 1 April 1973. As an employer, you may be eligible for a refund of S.E.T. **1978** *Jrnl. R. Soc. Arts* CXXVI. 405/1 The next phase was the indictment of the so-called 'candyfloss industries' and their punishment through the Selective Employment Tax. **1917** *New Republic* 9 June 148/2 The New Republic advocated the principle of selective service for this emergency. **1920** E. H. Crowder *Spirit of Selective Service* v. 119 There were to be two phases to Selective Service, the one, enrollment, the other selection. **1969** G. L. Wamsley *Selective Service & Changing Amer.* i. 1 A step can be taken toward understanding why Selective Service has come under attack after years of anonymity. **1976** N. Thornburg *Cutter & Bone* vii. 157 Nor did he meekly submit to his Selective Service draft notice. **1959** *Wall St. Jrnl.* 29 Dec. 2/2 Selective strikes would be expedient to the union, since they would concentrate pressure on individual companies. **1979** *Arizona Daily Star* 1 Apr. a1/5 The powerful Teamsters union early today called 'selective strikes' against a portion of the trucking industry. **1928** H. Martin *Sci. Princ. Plant Protection* ix. 170 The peculiar virtues of the metallic sulphates as selective weedkillers. **1965** *Listener* 22 July 142/1 Historically, selective weedkillers have been used since 1895 when solutions of copper sulphate were used to destroy charlock in cereal crops. **1976** *Field* 18 Nov. 1040/2 Base fertilizer for lawns should be applied in March or early April..and the selective weedkiller a week or two later.

selectivist (sĭle·ktivist). [f. Selective *a.* + -ist.] One who supports a selective theory or policy. Hence **sele·ctivism.**
1932 H. H. Price *Perception* ii. 44 The Selectivist is asked to say *which* colour belongs to the rose when nobody

is looking at it. **1944** W. T. STACE in P. A. Schilpp *Philos. B. Russell* 365 There are grave objections to selectivism, but that is not the present point. **1967** *Guardian* 4 Sept. 14/8 The selectivists are right in saying that much more should be done to channel social benefits to the people who need them most. **1969** *Physics Bull.* Mar. 108/1 They are apt to ignore work not published in their country's journals, a selectivism matched by the singlemindedness of the articles.

selectivity (se:lekti·vĭti). [f. SELECTIVE *a.* + -ITY.] **1.** *Radio.* The ability of a receiver to tune separately to signals of adjacent frequencies, measured by the frequency difference between the half-power points of the pass-band of the receiver.

1903 *Electr. World & Engin.* 1 Aug. 173/2 The system of selectivity devised by Sir Oliver [Lodge] was the outcome of a series of classical experiments based upon his syntonic Leyden jars in which one jar is caused to discharge through a circuit by the sparks of another jar, provided the two circuits are of equal electrical dimensions. **1930** *Manch. Guardian* 20 Sept. 15/7 It is no exaggeration to say that..four-valve sets are more than equal in power and selectivity to a six or seven-valve set of the old type. **1943** C. L. BOLTZ *Basic Radio* viii. 131 The sharper is the resonance curve the better it will select, for supplies at frequencies quite near the resonant one will have very much less effect. The sharpness of the curve is therefore a measure of the selectivity. **1976** *Which?* Sept. 203/2 If you want to receive particularly weak signals, you need a set which has good selectivity.

2. *gen.* The quality of being selective.

1948 E. G. BORING et al. *Found. Psychol.* x. 218/1 This selectivity of perception amounts to giving one sense impression a clear track. **1951** RUESCH & BATESON *Communication* iii. 84 An alternate solution of the psychiatrist is to abstract and condense his observations before writing them down; selectivity, therefore, becomes an unavoidable issue. **1969** *Computers & Humanities* III. 278 The main program was the Formatting Program in which the two files were used as input to produce six indexes, four of which were selective. A 'selectivity module' had been introduced to make the selections possible. *a* **1974** R. CROSSMAN *Diaries* (1976) II. 471 We were able to discuss one of the minor sensations of the recess—Ray Gunter's speech in August, in which he said we must be realistic and brave and face up to the need for selectivity and the means test. **1978** G. UNDERWOOD *Strategies of Information Processing* vii. 235 To information processing theory..attention and selectivity are central features.

selector. Add: **c.** (Further examples.) *spec.* (*a*) in a gearbox, the part that moves the gearwheels into and out of engagement; (*b*) *Teleph.*, a mechanism which automatically establishes electrical connection with one of a group of available contacts according to the number of impulses in the incoming signal; (*c*) in a motor vehicle with automatic transmission, the control by which the driver selects the mode of operation of the transmission.

1903 *Electr. Rev.* (Chicago) XLIII. 583/1 Each subscriber is connected to the exchange by two lines which end in what is called a first selector switch... The first selector consists of a couple of relays. **1926** H. T. RUTTER *Mod. Motors* II. vii. 262 By moving the gear lever by hand it actuates what are termed selector rods, which are forked rods that slide the gear wheels on the gear-shaft one at a time into a position to mesh with the respective gear wheels on the lay-shaft. **1930** *Bell System Tech. Jrnl.* IX. 22 By placing several selectors in series a network of central offices may be built up, each office serving 10,000 telephones. **1961** *Listener* 16 Nov. 832/1, I would have been waiting, like some predetermined selector, for the necessary keys to fall into position. **1967** K. H. BRINKMANN tr. *K. Trautman's Design of Automatic Telephone Exchanges* 16 Each selector has a relay set which controls the switching functions... Ten final selectors would suffice to serve 100 subscribers since each switch interconnects two subscribers. **1967** *Times* 31 Mar. 3/7 The coroner said the selector lever must have been in 'drive'. **1973** D. BARNES *See the Woman* (1974) I. 9 Conrad stopped, pushed the selector to park..and opened the car door. **1973** H. FANTEL *True Sound of Music* (1974) vii. 105 To start with, any amplifier has a selector switch. As its name implies, it lets you pick the program source you want to hear: radio, record player, or tape. **1976** L. THOMAS *Dangerous Davies* ii. 13 The record..swooped again onto the turntable at her touch of the selector button.

d. *Sport.* One of a number of officials appointed to select a team.

1928 *Daily Mail* 2 Apr. 14/1 The selectors could not find in England a team good enough to stop this very perfect Scottish machine. **1934** F. J. C. GUSTARD *Eng. v. Austral.* 9 His action may have saved the selectors a certain amount of embarrassment. **1953** B. HARRIS *Cricket Triumph* i. 19 Laker did not come into the side until the third test match, for in the selectors' minds he and Roy Tattersall..were of equal talent. **1976** J. SNOW *Cricket Rebel* 138, I said somewhere in a newspaper article that 1974 summer that the selectors would have to be shot before I made a Test comeback. I think my assessment was right.

Hence **selecto·rial** *a.*, of or pertaining to a team selector (sense d above).

1959 *Times* 12 Oct. 15/4 The manner of its achievement cannot but raise some doubts in selectorial minds. **1963** A. ROSS *Australia 63* 13 Selectorial opinion, for one reason or another, was hardening against Sheppard. **1975** *Cricketer* May 37/1 Mr Holloway..seems to feel (as indeed I do) that selectorial bias in favour of the southern and more particularly Home counties is an inescapable fact.

selectorate (sĭle·ktŏrėt). [Blend of SELECTOR and ELECTORATE.] That section of a political party which has the effective power to choose a representative.

1967 P. PATERSON *Selectorate* i. 27 Within the Conservative selectorate there are almost as many grades and ranks and classifications as in a masonic order. **1969** *Daily Tel.* 10 Dec. 14 Most [primaries], while broadening the selectorate, are still open to the criticism that the many are brought in only at the final stage, to exercise a choice over a few candidates chosen by a committee. **1980** *Times* 20 June 14/4, I favour confining the selectorate to MPs.

Selectric (sĭle·ktrik). Also **selectric.** [Blend of SELECT *v.* and ELECTRIC *a.* and *sb.*] A proprietary name for a kind of electric typewriter.

1964 *Official Gaz.* (U.S. Patent Office) 29 Sept. TM 211/2 International Business Machines Corporation, Armonk, N.Y. Filed May 15, 1964. *Selectric* for typewriters. First use July 21, 1961. **1967** *Trade Marks Jrnl.* 8 Nov. 1716/2 *Selectric*... Electrically operated typewriting machines; electrically operated machines... International Business Machines Corp... New York... 23rd February 1967. **1970** [see *golf ball* s.v. *GOLF *sb.* b]. **1971** *Computers & Humanities* V. 2/3 If a magnetic tape selectric typewriter (MT/ST) or a keypunch is used, the sorting and page-entering processes can be eliminated. **1977** J. WAMBAUGH *Black Marble* vi. 76 They can also..start operating *your* Selectric.

selectron (sĭle·ktrǫn). Also **Selectron.** [f. SELECT *v.* + *-T)RON.] A kind of cathode-ray tube formerly used in computers as a means of storing digital information.

1947 *Math. Tables & Other Aids to Computation* II. 229 'The selectron—a tube for selective electrostatic storage' by Dr. Jan Rajchman. **1947** [see *INSTRUCTION 4 c]. **1950** W. W. STIFLER *High-Speed Computing Devices* xiv. 370 The Selectron utilizes the fact that an insulated secondary-electron emitter can be made to 'float' at either of two stable potentials. **1957** R. K. RICHARDS *Digital Computer Components & Circuits* vi. 265 Among the more important forms of electrostatic storage are the 'Williams tube', the 'barrier-grid tube', the 'holding-gun tube', and the Selectron, each of which has at one time or another been successfully used in a digital computer.

selen-. 1. selensulphur, delete † and substitute for def.: a native variety of elemental sulphur containing a small proportion of selenium; (later examples).

1882 [see *HIERATITE]. **1944** C. PALACHE et al. *Dana's Syst. Min.* (ed. 7) I. 142 Old specimens of reddish brown selensulfur from Vulcano gave *n* [*sc.* refractive index] 2·544–2.675 indicating 83–90·5 per cent Se; but this high Se content lacks confirmation.

selendang, var. *SLENDANG.

selenious, *a.* (Earlier example.)

1827 MITSCHERLICH & NITZSCH in *Q. Jrnl. Sci., Lit. & Art* II. 471 The acid is isomorphous with the sulphuric acid, and may with propriety be called selenic acid, that described by M. Berzelius being considered as the selenious acid.

selenium. a. For 'increased' read 'decreased' in small-type note.

b. selenium cell, a photoconductive or photovoltaic cell containing selenium (later examples).

1929 [see *PHOTOCONDUCTIVE *a.*]. **1946** *Nature* 20 July 88/1 In the early days of his training he [*sc.* J. L. Baird] devised an improved pattern of selenium cell, which led him to develop a crude form of television. **1977** J. HEDGECOE *Photographer's Handbk.* 32 Your meter may use a selenium cell which generates a minute current of electricity, measured on a galvanometer.

seleniuretted, *a.* (Later example.)

1947 *Electronic Engin.* XIX. 363/1 On exposure to a moist atmosphere, sulphuretted, seleniuretted and telluretted hydrogen can be detected.

selenocentric, *a.* (Examples.)

1970 N. ARMSTRONG et al. *First on Moon* v. 118 On July 17 at 1300 Moscow time the probe was placed in a selenocentric orbit. **1973** *Nature* 2 Nov. 7/2 [They] have detected increases of up to 100% in the density of picogram particles, in this case in selenocentric space, by using microphone sensors on board the satellites.

selenodesy (selinǫ·dėsi). *Astr.* [f. Gr. σελήν-η moon + -O, after GEODESY.] The study of the shape and features of the moon. Hence **selenode·tic** *a.*, of or pertaining to selenodesy.

1962 Z. KOPAL *Moon* p. ix, The contents of the present volume..have been divided into five parts: I. Rocket exploration of the moon... II. Selenodesy and mapping of the moon. **1962** D. W. G. ARTHUR in *Ibid.* 102 The simplest of the two major selenodetic problems is the determination of the Moon's geometrical figure. **1962** *Flight International* LXXXII. 251/1 Selenodetic measurements of the Earth-Moon distance. **1967** J. RÖSCH in Kopal & Goudas *Measure of Moon* 71 Our task in starting up Selenodesy is not to determine the shape of a fictitious surface, but simply to establish reference points on the surface of the Moon to which we can refer the positions of other points. **1977** R. W. KING et al. in J. D. Mulholland *Sci. Applications Lunar Laser Ranging* 51 (*heading*) Lunar dynamics and selenodesy.

self, *pron., a.,* and *sb.* Add: **A.** *pronoun* and *pronominal adj.* **7.** *spec.* written on a cheque or counterfoil.

1866 [in Dict.]. **1873** D. G. ROSSETTI *Let.* 14 July (1967) III. 1192 If however you would prefer the cheque made out to *Self* as usual..I will send you another. **1935** G. HEYER *Death in Stocks* vi. 74 He drew a cheque for a hundred pounds to self on Friday. **1967** C. WATSON *Lonely Heart 4122* ii. 23 He turned back the counterfoils... The uppermost..was marked 'Self', a withdrawal of four hundred pounds.

B. *adj.* **I. 3. b.** Also in wider application.

1930 R. A. FISHER *Genet. Theory Nat. Selection* vii. 165 In rats, the hooded (black and white) pattern is a simple recessive to the 'self' or 'solid' coloration. **1950** *Sun* (Baltimore) 7 Jan. 22/7 The 'self' pigeon..has a solid color while the 'barred' has a blue background with black bars across the wing.

II. 5. b. (Later examples.) *spec.* in *self belt, -fabric.*

1960 *Times* 21 Jan. 14/4 Jackets had either let-in or low-placed self belts. **1961** *Guardian* 28 Feb. 7/4 Jacket caught at the hips by a self-fabric belt. **1969** *Sears Catal.* Spring/Summer 10 Shower-resistant coat features self-fabric yoke for added protection. **1979** *Daily Tel.* 13 Feb. 15/1 (Advt.), Soft shirt dress..—no waist seams and self belt.

C. *sb.* **I. 4. a.** (*one's*) *old self*: (examples).

1841 C. FOX *Jrnl.* 30 Sept. (1972) 115 Dr. Calvert..was quite his old self, talking on his old subjects in his old way. **1975** H. FLEETWOOD *Picture of Innocence* x. 177 You seem quite like your old self again.

II. 6. b. Something (as an animal or garment) of a single colour. Cf. sense 3 b of the adj. in Dict. and Suppl.

1930 R. A. FISHER *Genet. Theory Nat. Selection* vii. 165 Rats of both selected lines were bred back to unselected selfs. **1978** *Lochaber News* 31 Mar. 2/1 (Advt.), 'Dereta' coats, superb collection of tweeds and selfs in a variety of fabrics, designs and colours.

self (self), *v.* [f. SELF *pron., a.,* and *sb.*] *trans.* To fertilize by means of pollen from the same plant; = SELF-FERTILIZE *v.*

1905 R. C. PUNNETT *Mendelism* 61 When this, the normal mode of fertilisation, takes place, the flower is said to be selfed. **1924** E. W. MACBRIDE *Study of Heredity* vi. 143 When the recessive green peas are sown they give rise to plants which, when 'selfed', bear only green peas. **1949** H. L. MENCKEN in Kirby & Woolf *Philologica* 316 So far I have heard of no verb made of what appears to be a pronoun save *to self*. **1970** *Watsonia* VIII. 142 Rousi selfed a number of plants.

Hence **selfed** (selft) *ppl. a.*; **se·lfing** *vbl. sb.*, fertilization in this manner (in quot. 1924: a plant grown from seed so derived).

1924 *Genetics* IX. 30 Two such selfings of plants in family J were grown. **1927** *Technical Bull. N.Y. State Agric. Exper. Station, Geneva* No. 127. 4 Four selfed varieties of *P*[*runus*] *salicina* gave no seed. **1942** *Jrnl. Genetics* XLIII. 312 Their doubly heterozygous progeny will on selfing produce a range of genotypes with phenotypic differences. **1953** *Heredity* VII. 185 This mating system occurs in plants which have an imperfect selfing mechanism. **1977** M. ALLAN *Darwin & his Flowers* xv. 256 Nine of the original selfed plants had died. **1978** *Nature* 2 Feb. 441/1 Experimental selfings and crossings each lead to similar and relatively high levels of fruit set.

self-. Add: **1. a.** With nouns of action. *self-abandon, -abandonment* (later example), *-acquittal, -adjustment, -advertisement* (earlier example), *-affirmation, -aggrandisement* (later example), *-betterment, -castration, -censorship, -commiseration, -comprehension, -concealment, -confession, -confrontation, -constraint, -correction* (later example), *-critique, -crucifixion, -dedication* (later example), *-definition, -deification, -demolition, -deprecation, -description, -desertion* (earlier example), *-development, -discipline* (earlier and later examples), *-discovery, -display* (earlier example), *-disposal* (later example), *-dramatization, -duplication, -education* (earlier example), *-employment* (later example), *-enjoyment* (later examples), *-enrichment, -exhibition, -expansion, -exposure* (later examples), *-fulfilment, -generation, -immolation* (later examples), *-incrimination, -ingratiation, -interrogation* (earlier example), *-invitation, -laceration, -linkage, -management, -manipulation, -mockery, -mortification* (later example), *-mutilation, -objectification, -organization, -parody, -perception, -perpetuation, -portrayal, -prostration, -protection* (earlier example), *-punishment* (later example), *-purification, -rebuke, -recognition, -recrimination, -regeneration, -renewal, -repetition, -replication, -reproduction, -rule* (*Pol.* examples), *-scrutiny* (later examples), *-starvation, -stultification, -therapy, -transformation, -valuation* (later example), *-verification.*

1901 'L. MALET' *Hist. Sir R. Calmady* I. ix. 74 Her mother love..had none of the sweet self-abandon..which that earlier passion had. **1958** R. KNOX *Priestly Life* ix. 96 Self-abandonment has been preached by writers of undoubted orthodoxy. **1750** RICHARDSON

Let. 29 Mar. (1964) 157 The place allows the latter [*sc.* conversationalists] to sit far enough from the [card-] tables not to be interrupted with remarks, blames, self-acquittals, of the engaged. **1892** 'Mark Twain' *Amer. Claimant* xiv. 132 You can't get the best of all verdicts, self-acquittal. **1848** J. S. Mill *Pol. Econ.* I. II. xi. 406 Population had exercised its power of self-adjustment. **1962** A. Battersby *Guide to Stock Control* v. 51 This capacity for self-adjustment is a necessary part of *any* practical control system. **1840** J. S. Mill in *Edin. Rev.* LXXII. 27 What is saved in the workmanship may be more profitably expended in self-advertisement. **1854** Geo. Eliot tr. *Feuerbach's Essence Christianity* iii. 45 The exclusive self-affirmation of the human nature. **1924** W. B. Selbie *Psychol. Relig.* 53 That desire for..self-affirmation..is so characteristic of man at all stages of his development. **1979** *Dædalus* Summer 92 We are thrown back on our own truth and to the act of self-affirmation that constitutes our personal identity. **1937** *Discovery* July 225/2 A Board of Directors seeking only self-aggrandisement. **1931** G. F. Stout *Mind & Matter* 174 Each blindly strives towards its own self-maintenance and self-betterment. **1977** A. Giddens *Stud. in Social & Polit. Theory* i. 39 He criticizes Comte along with Spencer for..treating the impulse to self-betterment as if it were a general cause of the evolution of society. **1934** R. Campbell *Broken Record* vii. 161 Amongst the average English literary men, it is usual for them to go soft at thirty (the moral self-castration of the exoletus). **1950** R. Ames in *Science & Society* XIV. 195 The obvious need of the oppressed..for self-censorship of his social ideas. **1904** K. C. Thurston *John Chilcote* xi. 119 He had..a feeling of bitter self-commiseration that for the moment outweighed all other considerations. **1909** W. James *Pluralistic Universe* i. 36 It may be a supreme reaction of the universe upon itself by which it rises to self-comprehension. **1935** *Mind* XLIV. 94 The Delphic *Γνῶθι σεαυτὸν*..counsels self-knowledge *versus* his [*sc.* Nietzsche's] and every Power-Man's need for self-concealment. **1963** Auden *Dyer's Hand* 109 A capacity for self-disclosure implies an equal capacity for self-concealment. **1885** W. James *Lit. Remains H. James* 19 Society is the same Creator, with the nothingness saved, determined to transparency and self-confession. **1923** F. G. Ellerton *Let.* 4 Nov. in *John Bailey* (1935) 236, I take it that the *pargoletta* passage is of the nature of a self-confession on Dante's part. **1961** *New Statesman* 23 June 1010/3 'Mellowness' becomes a means of avoiding the self-confrontations he says he has funked all his life. **1883** F. H. Bradley *Logic* III. I. vi. 450 Synthesis..would not force its parts into violent conjunctions, but, itself in each, by the loss of self-constraint would embrace its own fulfilment. **1953** D. F. Pocock tr. *Durkheim's Sociol. & Philos.* ii. 36 The act..cannot be accomplished without effort and self-constraint. **1965** *Math. in Biol. & Med.* (Med. Res. Council) III. 85 The use of computers in diagnosis will need provision for..self-correction by new data, and for questioning unusual or missed signs. **1959** E. Pulgram *Introd. Spectrogr. Speech* 7 Switching from one linguistic code to another is conducive to self-critique. **1897** W. J. Locke *Derelicts* II. xxiii. 413 The tragic futility of such self-crucifixion. **1943** J. S. Huxley *Evolutionary Ethics* 67 The desire for self-dedication..should be available to society's common pool. **1957** M. J. Huntingdon in R. K. Merton *Student-Physician* 181 First-year students ..think of each other primarily as students. This is reflected in their self-definitions. **1980** S. Brett *Dead Side of Mike* ii. 19 Definition, and particularly self-definition is very important to me as an artist. **1903** 'Mark Twain' in *N. Amer. Rev.* Apr. 510 She..has carried self-deification to a length which has not before been ventured in ages. **1962** E. Snow *Other Side of River* xvii. 122 Chiang made a fair start toward self-deification. **1935** T. S. Eliot *Murder in Cathedral* ii. 66 Dominated by the lust of self-demolition. **1924** W. Holtby *Crowded Street* xxxv. 260 Don't you think that this self-deprecation of yours was a little like cowardice? **1977** A. Giddens *Stud. in Social & Polit. Theory* ix. 307 Suicide represents an extreme on a range of possible forms of self-aggression, which extends from relatively minor forms such as verbal self-deprecation to actual self-destruction. **1902** W. James *Var. Relig. Exper.* xvi. 415 In spite of their repudiation of articulate self-description, mystical states in general assert a pretty distinct theoretic drift. **1978** J. Dunn in Hookway & Pettit *Action & Interpretation* 157 Two main difficulties follow from this centrality of the human capacity for self-description in specifying the field of the sciences of man. **1796** F. Burney *Camilla* V. 454 Thy afflicting, however blamable self-desertion. **1817** Coleridge *Biog. Lit.* I. xii. 275 Intelligence is a self-development. **1895** W. J. Locke *At Gate of Samaria* i. 7 She read books with the eagerness only exhibited by the young girl craving for self-development. **1977** Warren & Ponse in Douglas & Johnson *Existential Sociol.* x. 285 The Goffmanic masked self..comes into play when the audience is..to be manipulated rather than for such motives as self-development, [etc.]. **1796** Ld. Glenbervie *Diary* 15 Oct. (1928) I. 87 Every young person..should be conducted to form himself to such habits of self-discipline. **1946** *Nature* 27 July 113/1 The man who pursues truth for its own sake and studies science in an impersonal way, with rigorous self-discipline, is really showing his belief in a religion and is taking up a religious attitude. **1965** J. A. Michener *Source* 532 The Arabs arrived when they were strongest, in the throbbing flush of self-discovery and unification. **1838** J. S. Mill in *Westm. Rev.* Apr. 7 M. de Vigny,..a man..of a rare simplicity of heart, and freedom from egotism and self-display. *a* **1885** G. M. Hopkins *Poems* (1918) 78 One part, Reason, selfdisposal, choice of better or worse way, Is corpse now, cannot change. **1933** *Week-end Rev.* 11 Feb. 151/1 Like Hamlet, he had an incurable habit of self-dramatization. **1959** *Encounter* July 66/2 It was not so much insincerity as self-dramatisation. **1817** Coleridge *Biog. Lit.* I. xii. 268 A perpetual self-duplication of one and the same power into object and subject. **1953** J. S. Huxley *Evol. in Action* i. 16 They [*sc.* the chromosomes] have divided longitudinally after self-duplication. **1831** J. S. Mill *Let.* 22 Oct. (1910) I. 8 The only thing which I can usefully do at present,..is to work out.. principles of morals, government, law, education, above all self-education. **1976** *Times* 13 Aug. 13/7 In the poorest parts of the country..self employment is frequently the only manner in which a living income can be put together. **1870** D. G. Rossetti *Let.* 7 Nov. (1965) II. 914 That sense of the poet's self-enjoyment which is indispensable to the enjoyment of the reader. **1960** H. Read *Forms of Things Unknown* III. ix. 149 No explanation of art as 'objectified self-enjoyment'..can account for the facts of art history. **1920** B. Russell *Pract. & Theory Bolshevism* II. i. 127 Self-enrichment seemed the natural aim of a man's political actions. **1939** A. Huxley *After Many a Summer* I. ii. 24 Jeremy made his mannequin's gesture of apologetic self-exhibition. **1939** *Mind* XLVIII. 238 He sees that the root motive of mysticism is self-expansion—though he does not use this expression. **1921** D. H. Lawrence *Tortoises* 40 Doomed to partiality,.. Want, Self-exposure, hard humiliation, need to add himself on to her. **1979** J. Rathbone *Euro-Killers* ii. 22 Neither man was prepared to risk possible self-exposure by offering his ideas. **1936** *Mind* XLV. 242 He affirms the awareness of God to be 'rooted in' the human interest of self-fulfilment. **1981** R. Barnard *Sheer Torture* x. 109 Cultivating your ego, aiming at total self-fulfilment, doing your own thing. **1950** *Essays & Studies* III. 37 Everything in his poetry goes to suggest that it was created..by a largely spontaneous..process of self-generation. **1898** G. B. Shaw *Perfect Wagnerite* 95 Her self immolation on the pyre. **1961** D. G. James *Matt. Arnold* iii. 57 The omission of it [*sc. Empedocles*] from the 1853 volume..was a fine piece of self-immolation. **1911** *U.S. Reports* (U.S. Supreme Court) CCXXI. 388 The clear and simple directness of the privilege against self-incrimination. **1977** 'E. McBain' *Long Time no See* xv. 267 You are warned of your right to counsel and your privilege against self-incrimination. **1948** *Commentary* Nov. 417/2 Intelligence, humor, and charm is often humiliatingly exploited..as entertainment and self-ingratiation. **1963** *Times* 9 Feb. 4/2 The pallid self-ingratiation of Sally Logan's performance. *a* **1854** J. S. Mill *Draft Autobiogr.* (1961) 122 Let..your scrutiny, your self interrogation exhaust themselves on that. **1754** Richardson *Grandison* VI. 68 We then endeavoured to recollect the words of his self-invitation hither. **1805** Jane Austen *Let.* 24 Aug. (1952) 162, I defy her to accept this self-invitation of mine, unless it be really what perfectly suits her. **1963** *English Studies* XLIV. 144 Here, however, he will not allow himself to feel the self-laceration in the final stanzas of that canto. **1977** *Jrnl. Protozool.* XXIV. 9/2 Pattern formation by self-linkage. *a* **1866** J. Grote *Exam. Utilitarian Philos.* (1870) vi. 116 Good self-management his highest aim. **1977** Warren & Ponse in Douglas & Johnson *Existential Sociol.* x. 277 There is a difference in degree between the problems and self-management of gays and most other people. **1949** M. Mead *Male & Female* x. 216 The female child's genitals are less exposed..to self-manipulation. **1964** E. H. Mizruchi in I. L. Horowitz *New Sociol.* 257 Mental self-manipulation appears to be characteristic of the assembly-line work process. **1954** Koestler *Invisible Writing* iii. 40 Amiable Hans was a bald, moon-faced little man with a wealth of humour and self-mockery. **1931** J. S. Huxley *What dare I Think?* v. 169 He [*sc.* the humanist] finds the desire for a sacrifice and self-mortification just as natural..as the desire for achievement and self-assertion. **1864** G. O. Trevelyan *Compet. Wallah* 380 What is there in common between the faith of Heber and Swartz and a creed which enjoins suicide and self-mutilation. **1980** *Jrnl. R Soc. Arts* Feb. 137/2 It represents self-mutilation, it can only lead to genocide and biocide. **1933** *Times Lit. Suppl.* 16 Mar. 174/1 His book is one long and infinitely various act of self-discovery, self-objectification, made possible only by self-forgetfulness. **1969** T. F. Torrance *Theol. Sci.* i. 42 We are frequently engaged in mythological self-objectifications of this sort. **1898** G. B. Shaw *Perfect Wagnerite* 11 The..self-organization of life. **1967** *Oceanogr. & Marine Biol.* V. 274 Ecological succession is a process of self-organization. **1958** S. Spender *Engaged in Writing* 89 He [spoke]..in the comic manner which was half-serious self-parody. **1978** *New York* 3 Apr. 64/3 The majesty of our landscape has its own built-in note of self-parody, and it has eluded these artists. **1678** Cudworth *Intell. Syst.* I. iii. 160 If the souls of Men and Animals be at any time without Consciousness and Self-perception, then..Clear and Express Consciousness is not Essential to Life. **1972** M. Argyle *Social Psychol. of Work* iv. 60 The self-image also includes self-perceptions such as being 'intelligent' or 'lively'. **1843** J. S. Mill *Logic* II. III. xv. 32 A permanent effect..possessing the property of self-perpetuation. **1906** W. G. Sumner *Folkways* 473 They show how deep is the interest of human beings in the sex taboo, and in the self-perpetuation of society. **1962** F. I. Ordway et al. *Basic Astronautics* vi. 247 We think of life as a system or aggregate of chemical reactions that possess the inherent capability of self-perpetuation. **1914** G. B. Shaw *Dark Lady of Sonnets* 121 Self-betrayal is one thing; and self-portrayal, as in Hamlet and Mercutio, is another. **1872** Geo. Eliot *Middlem.* III. li. 354 The divine tribunal had changed its aspect for him; self-prostration was no longer enough. **1834** J. S. Mill in *Monthly Repos.* VIII. 838 This is.. the best sort of self-protection. **1974** R. H. S. Crossman *Diaries* (1975) I. 14 My own generalizations and predictions..sometimes provide an exercise in self-punishment since some of them read very foolishly today. **1924** W. B. Selbie *Psychol. Relig.* x. 202 A longing for self-purification. **1871** Geo. Eliot *Middlem.* I. iii. 41 Dorothea checked herself suddenly with self-rebuke for the presumptuous way in which she was reckoning on uncertain events. **1927** T. Wilder *Bridge of San Luis Rey* II. 15 Each..was on the point of losing her mind under the alternations of self-rebuke and the outbursts of passion. **1955** *Essays & Studies* VIII. 75 Emma is shown as incapable of self-recognition. **1961** Webster, Self-recrimination. **1965** J. A. Michener *Source* 700 He was thrown into a world of self-recrimination and remorse. **1918** W. S. Churchill in M. Gilbert *Winston S. Churchill* (1977) IV. Compan. I. 366 They should by.. a real act of self-regeneration make a definite break with the system. **1962** E. Snow *Red China Today* (1963) xlviii. 373 In prison there is the omnipresent *threat* of force and humilitation, combined with the demand for self-regeneration. **1959** B. & R. North tr. *Duverger's Pol. Parties* I. ii. 87 One of the constant features of the French Communist party is its perpetual self-renewal. **1971** J. Z. Young *Introd. Study Man* xi. 147 They [*sc.* 'post-mitotic' cells] are provided with especially active mechanisms for self-renewal. **1848** Poe in *Graham's Mag.* Feb. 131/1 Apparent plagiarisms ..arise from an author's self-repetition. **1959** *New Biol.* XXVIII. 93 The most characteristic property [of life], that of self-replication, has been studied theoretically by certain mathematicians. **1926** J. S. Huxley *Essays of Biologist* vii. 256 The attributes of living matter which mark it off from inorganic matter become dominant—its capacity for self-reproduction, [etc.]. **1964** *Sci. Amer.* Sept. 154/2 Seen in this light, crystal growth is self-reproduction. **1900** G. B. Shaw *Let.* 14 Mar. (1972) II. 156 The definite intention to clear out of India as soon as the natives are capable of self rule is the most pious of superfluities. **1978** *Times* 5 May 6/8 There is apprehension..that Israel will impose its own peace plan which offers a measure of self-rule for the West Bank. **1865** D. G. Rossetti *Let.* 21 Nov. (1965) II. 581 This [feeling of rage]..leads not to envy in the least, but to self-scrutiny. **1979** *Dædalus* Summer 3 Genuine charity and a constant and severe self-scrutiny are psychologically unthinkable without the moral pride that is all but inseparable from spiritual energy. **1947** C. Gray *Contingencies* 37 The voluntary self-starvation of the rich. **1904** W. James in *Mind* XIII. 466 Can there be self-stultification in urging any account whatever of truth? Can the definition ever contradict the deed? **1959** *Spectator* 11 Sept. 336/3 He came to each [session] with notes on the successive steps in his 'self-therapy'. **1949** Koestler *Promise & Fulfilment* II. iv. 253 This difference..was demonstrated by Irgun's..self-transformation into a *bona fide* democratic party. **1946** P. Bottome *Lifeline* xxxix. 297 Their self-valuation was threatened. **1854** Geo. Eliot tr. *Feuerbach's Essence Christianity* i. 6 Consciousness is self-verification. **1975** T. P. Whitney tr. *Solzhenitsyn's Gulag Archipelago* II. III. i. 11 Prisoners, wherever possible, were to be brought into self-verification and self-supervision.

b. With vbl. sbs. *self-advertising* (earlier example), *-compounding, -doctoring, -doubting, -loathing* (later example), *-poisoning, -policing, -questioning* (earlier example), *-scourging* (later example), *-searching* (later example), *-teaching, -understanding.*

1762 Goldsmith *Life of Richard Nash* 13 Little Things..without merit..by self-advertizing, attract the attention of the day. **1890** W. James *Princ. Psychol.* I. vi. 158 Self-compounding of mental facts is inadmissible. **1817** Jane Austen *Sanditon* v, in *Minor Wks.* (1954) 388, I can be no Judge of what the habit of self-doctoring may do. **1951** C. R. Acton *Dog Annual* 143 The all-important power of..self-doctoring. **1754** Richardson *Grandison* VI. 115 She embraced me,..and cleared up all my self-doubtings. **1971** P. O'Donnell *Impossible Virgin* ix. 176 She..was filled with self-loathing because it was she who had trapped him. **1907** W. James in *McClure's Mag.* (1908) Feb. 420/2 Democracy as a whole may undergo self-poisoning. **1968** *Times* 28 Oct. 3/1 Professor Kessel..has found that 34 per cent of 511 patients admitted for self-poisoning gave warning. **1960** *Times* 13 May 18/5 Unless some self-policing is done in the American film industry. **1977** *Jrnl. R. Soc. Arts* CXXV. 450/1 Self-policing by the data storage industry is simply not an adequate safeguard. **1856** Bagehot in *National Rev.* Apr. 370 He has no passionate self-questionings, no indomitable fears, no asking perplexities. **1916** G. B. Shaw *Androcles & Lion* p. xx, Saints amazed the world with their austerities and self-scourgings. **1978** J. Sacks in P. Moore *Man, Woman, & Priesthood* iii. 28 It has led to considerable self-searching in the Jewish community in recent years. **1891** Self-teaching [see *nursery school* s.v. *nursery 8 c]. **1967** G. Jackson *Let.* 31 Jan. in *Soledad Brother* (1971) 107 A good self-teaching book on Arabic. **1903** G. B. Shaw *Man & Superman* III. 129 Life's incessant aspiration to higher organization, wider, deeper, intenser, self-consciousness, and clearer self-understanding. **1977** A. Giddens *Stud. in Social & Polit. Theory* i. 57 In the philosophy of science, as contrasted to the methodological self-understanding of the social sciences, the 'orthodox model' has long since become subject to broad-ranging attack.

c. With agent-nouns. *self-dramatizer, -educator, -seeder.*

1936 A. Thirkell *August Folly* viii. 247 'She is a self-dramatiser,' said Charles. **1948** *Medium Ævum* XVII. I (*title*) A medieval self-educator. **1970** P. Dickinson *Seals* ii. 35 Great self-educators, these Pibbles. **1966** 'J. Berrisford' *Wild Garden* viii. 99 One of the most..accommodating self-seeders is a biennial evening primrose—*Oenothera lamarckiana*.

d. With nouns of state or condition. *self-disgust, -disrespect, -doubt* (later examples), *-hero-worship, -infatuation, -mastery* (later examples), *-mistrust* (later example), *-picture, -scorn, -tolerance* (Immunol.).

1921 E. M. Hull *Sheik* v. 160 A self-disgust seized him. He had been within an ace of betraying the man. **1977** *Listener* 28 Apr. 552/4 George Grosz..the master of self-disgust. **1853** J. Brown *Let.* (1912) 132 Dr. Scott's illness and death, and my own profound self-disrespect and indifferent health and overwork,—altogether I was in a sorry condition. **1938** Ld. Lymington *Famine in Eng.* 74 They are waiting to be led to salvation, and out of the slough of self-disrespect into which they have been driven. **1930** E. Waugh *Vile Bodies* vi. 106 Magically, self-doubt began to spread in the audience. **1980** J. McClure *Blood of Englishman* xv. 142 His hunch..drifted dangerously towards the jagged reef of self-doubt. **1927** J. S. Huxley *Relig. without Revelation* iv. 130 'My country, right or wrong'..

words which are immortal as the fittest inscription on the pedestal of the golden calf of self-hero-worship. **1948** L. Spitzer *Linguistics & Lit. Hist.* iv. 156 An enthusiasm inspired by self-infatuation. **1973** M. Amis *Rachel Papers* 16 Thinking back, actually, 'self-infatuation' strikes me as a rather ill-chosen word. It isn't so much that I like or love myself. Rather, I'm sentimental about myself. **1933** *Burlington Mag.* Dec. 260/1 The art of self-mastery, the grand style. **1979** *Dædalus* Summer 90 One must be..forever inaccessible to the seductions that distract or subtract from the forces necessary for self-mastery and self-defense. **1977** R. Holland *Self & Social Context* i. 20 From Freud they need clinical methods which give such primacy to the individual case but they dislike the 'pathological' self-picture. **1946** Dylan Thomas *Let.* 30 May (1966) 288 Inevitable moments of depression and self-mistrust. **1861** E. B. Browning *Mother & Poet* in *Last Poems* (1862) 95 Some women bear children in strength, And bite back the cry of their pain in self-scorn. **1964** M. Hynes *Med. Bacteriol.* (ed. 8) vii. 74 An animal will not normally form antibodies to its own tissues, even though these may be powerfully antigenic to a litter-mate. The mechanism of this self-tolerance and the consequences of its breakdown are discussed later. **1977** I. M. Roitt *Essent. Immunol.* iv. 109 Although we are uncertain of the mechanism, the idea that deletion of specific clones is responsible for tolerance induction is attractive. For example, it can account for the development of self-tolerance.

e. With adjs. *self-analytical, -aware, -corrective, -corroborative, -critical, -derisive, -expressive, -incriminatory, -infirmative, -mistrustful, -protective, -reproductive, -submersive, -sure.*

1943 H. Read *Educ. through Art* iii. 42 It may be that such eidetic individuals are more self-analytical than an eidetic person without creative gifts would be. **1924** R. Graves *Mock Beggar Hall* 28 Alert, with both eyes open, self-aware. **1979** A. Chisholm *Nancy Cunard* viii. 75 An intelligent, imaginative, self-aware young man. **1909** Webster, Self-corrective. **1934** *Mind* XLIII. 506 The inductive method is self-corrective. *a* **1812** J. Bentham *Rationale Judicial Evid.* (1827) III. v. xv. 224 We must..express the distinction between the two opposite kinds of evidentiary chains: styling the one, for example, the *self-infirmative* chain, we may style the other the *self-corroborative.* **1909** W. James *Meaning of Truth* xiii. 267 The hypothesis will, in short, have worked successfully all round the circle and proved self-corroborative. **1936** *Mind* XLV. 98 This suggestion that art, like religion, is self-critical in its activity. **1979** B. Malamud *Dubin's Lives* ix. 346 The tone of the book was self-critical. **1867** J. R. Lowell *Fitz Adam's Story* in *Poems* (1912) 575 He went on with a self-derisive sneer. **1928** D. H. Lawrence *Woman who rode Away* 172 His rather hooked nose self-derisive. **1934** *Essays & Studies* XIX. 28 The most seemingly self-expressive 'human document'. **1977** R. Holland *Self & Social Context* v. 102 He must develop an autonomous aspect of self to account for the more self-expressive or impulsive actions. **1949** Koestler *Promise & Fulfilment* i. xiii. 149 [He]..refused to testify..on the grounds that his testimony would be self-incriminatory. *a* **1812** Self-infirmative [see *self-corroborative* above]. **1875** A. Swinbourne *Picture Logic* (ed. 2) xxii. 142 Self-infirmative inference is where each fresh fact weakens the conclusion. **1897** G. B. Shaw *Let.* 10 Aug. (1965) I. 795 It is sheer want of practice that makes actors self-mistrustful when they are asked to..tell a story on the stage. **1890** W. James *Princ. Psychol.* II. xxiii. 381 The tendency to contract is the source of all the self-protective impulses and reactions which are later developed. **1979** B. Malamud *Dubin's Lives* ix. 337 Some people complicate their feelings in self-protective ways. **1943** J. S. Huxley *Evolutionary Ethics* v. 34 The capacity for self-reproduction, or better self-reproductive evolution. *a* **1914** Joyce *Stephen Hero* (1944) xvi. 36 Stephen, as he looked contemptuously at the laughing faces, thought of a self-submersive reptile. **1918** G. Frankau *One of Them* in *Poet. Works* (1923) II. 75 Goddess indeed! A self-sure, jade-eyed, slim puss, of life's each latest luxury impassioned. **1954** *Numbers* (N.Z.) July 1/5 Paul was lying on his bed, reading. Twenty-five; good-looker; self-sure.

f. With ppl. adjs. in *-ing. self-abbreviating, -adjusting* (earlier example), *-analysing, authenticating, -blanching, -correcting, -defeating, -defining, -delighting, -deprecating, -describing, -developing, -distributing, -doubting, -dramatizing, -enduring, -enhancing, -enjoying, -equilibrating, -executing, -explaining, -generating, -guaranteeing, -hating, -humbling* (later example), *-hurting, -immolating, -incriminating, -ingratiating, -interpreting* (later example), *-mocking, -negating, -observing, -optimizing, -ordering, -organizing, -parodying, -perpetuating* (later examples), *-policing, -prolonging, -propagating* (earlier example), *-punishing* (later example), *-recognizing, -reflecting, -reinforcing, -renewing, -replicating, -reproducing, -searching, -serving, -stultifying, -supplying, -teaching, -validating.*

1922 Joyce *Ulysses* 718 The selfprolonging tension of the thing proposed to be done and the selfabbreviating relaxation of the thing done. **1848** J. S. Mill *Pol. Econ.* II. iii. xx. 154 There is a self-adjusting power in the variations of the exchange itself. **1922** W. B. Yeats *Trembling of Veil* iii. 144 The subtle torture of self-analysing passion. **1980** A. Wilson *Setting World on Fire* iii. i. 264 Find a play..which has a thoughtful, self-analysing part for an old actor like me. **1935** H. H. Farmer *World & God* i. ix. 158 Our interest is in the Christian experience of God as personal, which in the nature of the case must be self-authenticating. **1976** H. Montefiore in *Christian Believing* 151 His character is to me self-authenticating. **1907** A. French *Bk. Vegetables* 78 Varieties [of celery] are many, and classify chiefly as to height, color (red tint), and 'self-blanching' properties. **1976** 'D. Halliday' *Dolly & Nanny Bird* xi. 138 Simon had turned the colour of self-blanching celery. **1944** *Mind* LIII. 212 The last topic with which Hr. von Wright deals is Reichenbach's contention that induction is a self-correcting process. **1979** *Dædalus* Summer 150 The idea of a developing and self-correcting body of scientific inquirers offered what seemed to him a more satisfactory model. **1909** W. M. Urban *Valuation* xiv. 413 In this concept of the self-defeating process we have a negative test of validity. **1949** M. Mead *Male & Female* ix. 196 The Weimar Republic's self-defeating practice of giving..jobs..to older men. **1979** B. Malamud *Dubin's Lives* ix. 336 Their talk was self-defeating. **1968** Self-defining [see *literal *sb.* 3]. **1908** W. B. Yeats *Poetry & Ireland* 10 None other has a continual deliberate self-delighting happiness. **1958** *Times Lit. Suppl.* 17 Jan. 30/1 Mr Amis, seen by himself in a way in which ironical, self-deprecating people do see themselves. **1971** S. Hill *Strange Meeting* ii. 111 Barton turned his head and smiled, and then his face changed again, the old, self-deprecating expression over it. **1864** Bagehot in *National Rev.* Nov. 34 Such self-describing poets describe what is *in* them, but not *peculiar* to them. **1978** J. Dunn in Hookway & Pettit *Action & Interpretation* 156 Between a describer and a self-describing object there exist relations which are peculiar. **1865** Self-developing [see *self-changing* in Dict.]. **1980** N. Marsh *Photo-Finish* iii. 79 The lens cap..produced instant self-developing results. **1945** Koestler *Yogi & Commissar* iii. iv. 242 Koehler assumes that there are self-distributing electromagnetic currents between the cortical projections of retinal points. **1966** *English Studies* XLVII. 201 Only the second look of recent criticism has shown how homosexual were those claims, and how self-doubting and despairing. *a* **1974** R. Crossman *Diaries* (1975) I. 339, I had noticed already that Ray Gunter was a dramatic, self-dramatizing kind of chairman. **1945** Auden *Coll. Poetry* 120 That through his self-annulment the real world Of self-enduring instants may endure Its final metamorphosis. **1965** F. Sargeson *Memoirs of Peon* viii. 265 The self-enhancing aim of endeavouring to ameliorate the lot of the family. **1854** Geo. Eliot tr. *Feuerbach's Essence Christianity* ii. 40 The understanding alone..is the self-enjoying, self-sufficing existence. **1951** Auden *Enchafèd Flood* iii. 102 All it desires is to be in equilibrium, a self-enjoying, self-sufficient self. **1947** *Mind* LVI. 58 The problem of a self-equilibrating physical system can now be attacked with both vigor and generality. **1974** W. Rees-Mogg *Reigning Error* iv. 81 A gold system is a self-equilibrating system operating on a constant world money supply. **1962** *Listener* 15 Mar. 455/1 Not all the provisions of the treaty [*sc.* Treaty of Rome] are of this so-called 'self-executing' character. **1903** J. Joyce *Let.* 9 Mar. (1966) II. 35, I enclose you self-explaining documents. **1865** H. Maudsley *Meth. of Study of Mind* 18 It is ridiculous to suppose that the man of genius is ever a fountain of self-generating energy. **1968** H. Harris *Nucleus & Cytoplasm* vi. 122 On any model..we are forced to consider how a set of conditions, initially produced in a cell by external stimuli, can become self-generating. **1887** A. Seth *Hegelianism* vi. 205 Hegel, like Plato, seeks reality not in the actual world, but in the eternal realm of an absolute and self-guaranteeing thought. **1961** J. Wilson *Reason & Morals* iii. 164 What is irrational is that such people take their feelings as self-guaranteeing, that they treat them as carrying their own justification with them. **1977** *New Yorker* 29 Aug. 82/3 Perhaps there was the same sort of self-hating or fearful motive behind Hitler's orders to murder the most helpless patients in the hospitals of the Third Reich. **1938** R. Graves *Coll. Poems* p. xiii, It is an exorcism of physical pretensions by self-humbling honesties. **1915** D. H. Lawrence *Rainbow* ii. 52 A burst of religious, self-hurting fervour had passed over the country. **1939** R. Campbell *Flowering Rifle* vi. 150 And better maimed Of a self-hurting member so inflamed. *a* **1922** T. S. Eliot *Waste Land Drafts* (1971) 101 line 26 One soul,..Self-immolating on the Mound. **1925** T. Dreiser *Amer. Tragedy* I. i. iii. 16 Any self-abnegating and self-immolating religious theory. *Ibid.* ii. xxi. 303 He was not without the self-incriminating thought that in seeking this..he was driving toward a relationship which was not legitimate. **1964** *Harvard Law Rev.* Nov. 219 Implicit..is the proposition that in a pretrial police interrogation the accused has a right to remain silent, which he must waive intelligently before any self-incriminating statements will be admissible at trial. **1925** T. Dreiser *Amer. Tragedy* I. ii. xxiii. 313 Clyde..now approached, his manner the epitome almost of a self-ingratiating..dog of high breeding and fine temperament. **1935** A. C. Baugh *Hist. Eng. Lang.* vii. 266 One further habit which was somewhat weakened [in Middle English], although by no means broken, was that of combining native words into self-interpreting compounds. **1966** *English Studies* XLVII. 204 The self-mocking,..witty, ironical, comic Whitman. **1963** L. Trilling in N. Frye *Romanticism Reconsidered* 83 One of Keats's boldest expressions of his sense that there is something perverse and self-negating in the erotic life. **1960** Koestler *Lotus & Robot* ii. xi. 243 The split between the acting self and the self-observing self disappears. **1961** *Times* 23 Mar. 17/2 The anti-hero, oddly likable and self-observing. **1961** D. Gabor et al. in C. Cherry *Information Theory* xxvii. 348 (*heading*) A self-optimizing nonlinear filter, predictor and simulator. **1968** *Brit. Med. Bull.* XXIV. 251/1 Priban and Fincham..have been examining the adjustment of the rate and depth of breathing and the generation of individual breaths, using a 'self-optimizing' model. **1923** J. S. Huxley *Essays of Biologist* vi. 217 A universe which the march of knowledge is showing us ever more clearly as self-ordered and self-ordering. **1958** R. Williams *Culture & Society* iii. 298 The development of an organized and self-organizing working class. **1946** P. Larkin *Jill* 13 Never having heard before this self-parodying Southern coo. **1958** S. Spender *Engaged in Writing* 14 Asphalt's ..blotched face with its self-parodying leer. **1938** Huxley & Haddon *We Europeans* iii. 8 The gene is then as self-perpetuating in its new type as it was in its old. **1971** N. Stacey *Who Cares?* viii. 139 It was quite obvious that few of our efforts looked like being self-generating and self-perpetuating. **1955** G. Gorer *Exploring Eng. Character* xv. 296 The English character became, to a very marked degree, 'self-policing'. **1922** Self-prolonging [see *self-abbreviating* above]. **1843** J. S. Mill *Logic* I. iii. xiii. 565 It is..upon such substances that the self-propagating power of chemical action is likely to exert itself in the most marked manner. **1978** H. McLeave *Borderline Case* (1979) i. 14 A bloody-minded, self-punishing type. **1964** *Punch* 20 May 760/3 His.. reaction..is bitterly self-recognising. **1921** J. McTaggart *Nature of Existence* I. iv. xxxi. 299 Every substance which is a self-reflecting unity possesses two sorts of unity—organic unity and unity of self-reflection. **1953** J. S. Huxley *Evolution in Action* iv. 91 The organization..of large groups of nerve-cells and their connecting outgrowths into self-reinforcing circuits of excitation. **1875** J. R. Lowell in *Cambridge in Centennial Proc.* 30 The wingèd years, that winnow praise and blame, Blow many names out: they but fan to flame The self-renewing splendors of thy fame. **1977** J. L. Harper *Population Biol. Plants* 306 The food of an animal is self-renewing. **1946** *Nature* 21 Sept. 406/1 Alternatively ..some self-replicating cytoplasmic constituent of a complex cell, such as a plasmagene, may become capable of multiplying when transferred to a new environment. **1926** J. S. Huxley *Ess. Pop. Sci.* 230 The chromosomes are self-reproducing. **1964** *Sci. Amer.* Sept. 149 (*caption*) The little red and blue 'creatures' in the photograph.. are the two kinds of part of an elementary self-reproducing machine designed by..L. S. Penrose. **1838** W. E. Channing *Self-Culture* 12 There are two powers of the human soul which make self-culture possible, the self-searching and the self-forming power. **1978** P. Griffiths *Conc. Hist. Mod. Music* iii. 34 Both have a public rhetoric which was..foreign to Schoenberg in his profoundly self-searching form of Expressionism. **1827** J. Bentham *Rationale Judicial Evid.* III. vi. ii. 415 The probability, of mendacity, self-serving mendacity, and consequent deception, attached to the admission of the testimony of the party in his own behalf. **1896** *Southwestern Reporter* XXXIII. 791/1 On a criminal trial, self-serving acts of the defendants are properly excluded. **1904** J. H. Wigmore *Treat. Syst. Evidence* III. lvii. 2273 There is no principle of evidence especially excluding 'self-serving' statements by an accused or by any one else. **1958** *Listener* 18 Sept. 412/2 How far would the majority go in applying the general rule excluding what are sometimes called self-serving statements to conduct? **1972** J. Philips *Vanishing Senator* (1973) ii. iii. 76, I always thought he was a kind of cheap, self-serving jerk. **1904** W. James in *Mind* XIII. 474 It seems to me to illustrate beautifully how self-stultifying the conception of a truth that shall merely register a standing fixture may become. **1955** J. L. Austin *How to do Things with Words* (1962) iv. 51 This commits you to it and refuses to commit you to it. It is a self-stultifying procedure. **1842** E. FitzGerald *Let.* 16 Aug. (1960) 37 When I read of your..riding into Naples with huge self-supplying beakers full of the warm South I am sure you had best stay where you are. **1946** *Nature* 2 Nov. 606/1 A permanent self-supplying community of professional miners. **1964** J. Z. Young *Model of Brain* v. 69 In particular we are interested in a self-teaching homeostat, that is to say, one whose information and instructions are not entirely built in by heredity. **1945** *Mind* LIV. 46 These beliefs were after all cases of immediate knowledge which would therefore be self-validating and so require no further explanation.

i. With advs. *self-deprecatingly, -organizingly, -understandingly.*

1924 W. Holtby *Crowded Street* xxxv. 259 She laughed self-deprecatingly. **1966** S. Beer *Decision & Control* xiv. 346 More typically, and more 'self-organizingly', we say that energy evens out. **1933** Auden *Dance of Death* 32 Self-understandingly I come.

2. a. With pa. pples. and ppl. adjs. in which *self-* denotes the agent or what is conceived as the agent. *self-acquitted* (earlier example), *-adjusted, -bound, -built, -caused* (earlier example), *-chosen* (later examples), *-compelled, -confessed, -constituted* (earlier example), *-defined, -developed, -educated* (later examples), *-employed, -fancied, -fed* (later examples), *-generated, -indexed, -instressed, -invited* (earlier and later examples), *-observed, -ordered, -organized, -outwitted, -paced, -paid* (earlier example), *-proclaimed, -produced* (later example), *-seeded, -selected, -sentenced, -set* (later example), *-sold, -tinted*; *self-clinging, -pronouncing.* Also with related advs., as *self-confessedly,* and occas. with other adjs., as *self-adhesive.*

1814 F. Burney *Wanderer* III. xlv. 107 Their honour was self-acquitted and their generosity was self-applauded. **1958** *Engineers' Digest* XIX. 244/1 (*heading*) Self-adhesive nameplates. **1977** *Lancashire Life* Dec. 80/1 Products range from a reproduction of a timbered English pub for a Paris shoe exhibition to self-adhesive stickers for confectionery packets. **1924** W. B. Selbie *Psychol. Relig.* 55 They [*sc.* primitive religions]..become self-adjusted to man's growing intellectual capacity and needs. **1838** E. B. Browning *Seraphim* 50 The winding, wandering music that returns Upon itself in starry course, self-bound To praise, and praise, and praise. **1935** T. S. Eliot *Murder in Cathedral* i. 29 Cabined in Canterbury, realmless ruler, Self-bound servant of a powerless Pope. **1845** J. R. Lowell in *Broadway Jrnl.* 8 Mar. 154/2 A guess At the spirit's deathlessness, Which ye entertain with fear In your self-built dungeon here. **1970** A. G. Frank in I. L. Horowitz *Masses in Lat. Amer.* vi. 220 In Mexico City 30 per cent of the population lives in self-built housing. **1748** Richardson *Clarissa* IV. 347 Evils self-caused..admit not of palliation. **1856** Bagehot *Coll. Works* (1965) I. 408 Anything free refers to the people; anything elected seems self-chosen. **1972** *Guardian* 19 Jan. 2/7 Vienna's self-chosen image of 'Schlamperei', roughly translated as carefree sloppiness. **1952** A. G. L. Hellyer *Sanders' Encycl. Gardening* (ed. 22) 240 *H[ydrangea] petiolaris*, self-clinging climbing species, white. **1922** Joyce *Ulysses* 712 Ever would he wander, selfcompelled, to the extreme limit of his cometary orbit. *c* **1900** H. A. Jones *Mrs. Dane's Defence* iv. 83, I intend that Mrs. Bulsom-Porter shall stay..as a self-confessed scandal-monger. **1981** M. Underwood *Hand of Fate* ii. 91 Even a self-confessed liar is capable of telling the truth. **1977** A. Giddens *Stud. in Social & Polit. Theory* i. 72 Lakatos's sophisticated methodological falsificationism is self-confessedly an attempt to reconcile a version of Popper's philosophy of science with some of the major difficulties created for the latter by the works of Kuhn and others. **1809** J. Orrok *Let.* 28 Sept. (1927) 110 Here, and at every other Station, they had self-constituted Committees and carried everything their own way. **1856** E. B. Browning *Aurora Leigh* i. 28 Books, that prove God's being so definitely, that man's doubt Grows self-defined the other side the line, Made atheist by suggestion. **1977** R. Holland *Self & Social Context* v. 95 There is a strong sense of tension between socially given role demands and self-defined role demands. **1846** J. D. Morell *Hist. Philos.* II. v. 117 We..come, at length, at the end of the process, to a self-produced, or rather a self-developed, *subject-object*. **1898** 'Mark Twain' in *Harper's Mag.* Mar. 533/2 When an Austrian is called Doctor it means that he is either a lawyer or a physician, and that he is not a self-educated man. **1977** *Listener* 15 Dec. 783/1 From his self-educated mother, Trilling inherited a love of English literature. **1947** *Hansard Commons* 15 Dec. 1441 Mr. Amory asked the Minister of Food why persons who would qualify otherwise for the extra cheese are ineligible if they are self-employed. **1978** *Jrnl. R. Soc. Med.* LXXI. 768 'Persons' include both salaried and self-employed, including those self-employed persons established in one country who provide services in another. **1859** J. S. Mill in *Fraser's Mag.* LX. 767/1 An enemy, or a self-fancied rival. **1881** O. Wilde *Poems* 123 That holocaust, That self-fed flame. **1960** *Farmer & Stockbreeder* 1 Mar. 72/2 He had heard a lot of farmers expressing disappointment in the..meat yield from self-fed silage. **1935** M. Lowenfeld *Play in Childhood* i. 37 Play ..is taken as applying to all activities in children that are spontaneous and self-generated. **1965** J. D. Chambers in Glass & Eversley *Population in Hist.* xiii. 333 The increase in the industrial population was partly self-generated. **1938** (*title*) The Oxford companion to music: self-indexed and with a pronouncing glossary. **1978** *Canad. N. & Q.* Dec. 1/2, I am in the process of preparing a bibliography of Canadian periodicals that are self-indexed, or which have been indexed externally. **1879** G. M. Hopkins *Poems* (1967) 81 What the heart is! which, like carriers let fly..To its own fine function, wild and self-instressed. **1748** Richardson *Clarissa* VII. 288 Some other more distant relations.., self-invited..attended. **1979** C. MacLeod *Family Vault* (1980) xviii. 162 The first of the self-invited guests slumped into a wooden chair. **1955** S. Spender *Making of Poem* i. iv. 67 The observer is self-observed. **1923** Self-ordered [see *self-ordering*, sense 1 f above]. **1959** I. & P. Opie *Lore & Lang. Schoolch.* xii. 252 A contributor..gives a vivid description of a particular party of self-organized jollyboys. *c* **1865** G. M. Hopkins *Poems* (1967) 120, I storm and shock you. So I fail. And like a self-outwitted blast Fling to the convent wicket fast. **1962** H. C. Weston *Sight, Light & Work* (ed. 2) iii. 76 Persons of average vision are able to perform self-paced tasks requiring the perception of detail. **1835** J. S. Mill in *Lond. Rev.* I. ii. iv. 360 The unpaid is apt to become the self-paid. **1943** A. V. Barber *Let.* 8 Feb. in W. Temple *Lett.* (1963) 58 Their arguments reveal elementary, and sometimes even self-proclaimed, ignorance of the monetary mechanism. **1979** A. Chisholm *Nancy Cunard* xi. 103 John Banting..was to become England's sole self-proclaimed Surrealist painter. **1977** *Lancet* 30 July 207/2 A large proportion of the food consumed is self-produced. **1851** *Illustr. Catal. Gt. Exhib.* iii. 542/1 Complete phonological English alphabet constructing self-pronouncing words with the proper orthography. **1931** (*title*) The Royal Webster dictionary for home and school, self-pronouncing. **1970** P. Y. Carter *Mr Campion's Falcon* ix. 68 A belt of self-seeded larches. **1924** G. B. Shaw *St. Joan* Pref. p. xlii, The saints and prophets..are always really self-selected, like Joan. **1977** J. D. Douglas in Douglas & Johnson *Existential Sociol.* i. 17 At first the recruits to this rationalized segment of society were self-selected. **1865** G. M. Hopkins *Poems* (1967) 169 Will no one show I argued ill? Because, although Self-sentenced, still I keep my trust. *a* **1957** R. Campbell tr. *Camões's Lusiads* in *Coll. Poems* (1960) III. 129 Like Canace, self-sentenced and undone. **1956** *Nature* 10 Mar. 490/1 The distribution of this self-set seed mainly on the more heterozygous members of the population restricts the rate of fixation of genetic variability under these conditions. **1977** *Times Lit. Suppl.* 28 Jan. 94/2 Downright despair over his herculean, self-set task. **1856** J. G. Whittier *Panorama* 23 The self-sold knaves of gain and place. **1924** G. B. Shaw *Saint Joan* Pref. p. lii, We do not..rush to the opposite extreme in a recoil from her as from a witch self-sold to the devil. **1922** Joyce *Ulysses* 344 A neat blouse of electric blue, self-tinted by dolly dyes.

b. With nouns of action, as *self-selection* (see also *self-assembly 1, etc.). Similarly with verbs (usu. forming adjs., occas. sbs.), as *self-build, -erect, -feed* (see also *self-drive *a.*).

1952 *Times* 5 Mar. 5/6 The first self-build society put up its first houses over three years ago. There are now several scores of societies with hundreds of houses built or building. **1976** *Eastern Even. News* (Norwich) 13 Dec. 13 (Advt.), Renta-tower lightweight self-build staging. **1924** *Motor* 28 Oct. 697/1 The open tourer, with its self-erect transparent side screens. **1960** *Farmer & Stockbreeder* 16 Feb. 20/2 (Advt.), Self-erect cattle shelter. **1897** *Sears, Roebuck Catal.* 127/1 Self-feed Base Burner... A neat, attractive stove. **1951** *Sun* (Baltimore) 31 May 9/5 Mixing salt with cottonseed meal enables livestock growers to self-feed controlled amounts of protein supplement to their beef cattle. **1958** *Times* 1 July (Suppl.) p. viii/7 For up to 20 cows the trailer can be a home-made self-feed rack standing on an ordinary farm trailer. **1969** *Times* 24 Feb. 12/2 Larger farmers have taken advantage of improvement grants to erect concrete-and-asbestos covered yards and silos, generally using a combination of self-feed and easy-feed. **1975** *N.Z. Jrnl. Agric.* Sept. 63/1 We self-fed our grass silage. **1962** E. Godfrey *Retail Selling & Organization* i. 7 Members..can..obtain.. financial assistance in the conversion of their shops to self-service or self-selection. **1979** *Guardian* 5 Nov. 22/2 A half of all Jobcentre placements are made as a result of the self-selection of a job by a job-seeker.

3. a. With adjs. and ppl. adjs. *self-absorbed* (later examples), *-addressed* (later examples), *-conflicting* (earlier example), *-embedded, -enclosed* (earlier example), *-grounded, -imprisoned, -nodding* (pres. pple.). With sbs. and vbl. sbs. *self-aggression, -communing, -communion, -discontent, -dissatisfaction* (later examples), *-embedding, -preoccupation, -relation.*

1903 Somerville & 'Ross' *All on Irish Shore* 132 His face was pale and strange and entirely self-absorbed. **1980** D. Newsome *On Edge of Paradise* 8 One can admit to being self-absorbed... Arthur was genuinely self-critical. **1904** *Delineator* Dec. 1084 If you will send a stamped self-addressed envelope, we will tell you where you can take a course. **1976** *Oxford Consumer* Mar. 11/1 Sending a stamped self-addressed envelope ($6 \times 3\frac{1}{2}$) to the Chief Superintendent, St Aldate's Police Station. **1964** M. Argyle *Psychol. & Social Probl.* iv. 55 There is some evidence that self-aggression is a result of displaced aggression. **1927** E. M. Forster *Aspects of Novel* iii. 67 The..self-communings which politeness and shame prevent him from mentioning. **1963** *Times Lit. Suppl.* 11 Jan. 21/3 A seven-year-old girl's self-communings. **1818** Byron *Don Juan* i. xci. 48 His self-communion with his own high soul. **1916** Joyce *Portrait of Artist* (1969) 160 The impression which effaced his troubled selfcommunion was that of a mirthless mask reflecting a sunken day from the threshold of the college. **1819** Shelley *Prometheus Unbound* iv. 259 Its intense yet self-conflicting speed. **1872** Geo. Eliot *Middlem.* III. lviii. 290 His endurance was mingled with a self-discontent. **1891** W. James *Let.* 6 July (1920) I. 310 You've been saved many forms of self-dissatisfaction and misery. **1981** V. Canning *Boy on Platform One* ii. 30 She felt a rare mood of self-dissatisfaction. **1964** *Language* XL. 226 Syntactically complex self-embedded constructions in English. **1963** Self-embedding [see *push-down *a.* 1]. **1978** *Language* LIV. 171 Yngve is probably best known as the man who erroneously attributed to left-branching the effects of self-embedding. **1814** F. Burney *Wanderer* IV. lxxi. 240 Juliet passed three days, self-inclosed. **1817** Coleridge *Biog. Lit.* I. xii. 265 We are to seek..for some absolute truth..a truth self-grounded, unconditional and known by its own light. **1940** *Mind* XLIX. 171 All demonstration leads back to indemonstrable bases, and grounds must themselves be grounded on what is self-grounded. **1920** 'K. Mansfield' *Let.* 27 Oct. (1977) 190 Don't you feel that what English writers lack today is experience of Life. I don't mean that superficially. But they are self-imprisoned. **1922** Joyce *Ulysses* 212 Amused Buck Mulligan mused in pleasant murmur with himself, self-nodding. **1959** 'M. Ainsworth' *Murder is Catching* xv. 173 The sublime self-preoccupation of so many actors. **1883** F. H. Bradley *Logic* III. i. vi. 448 The analysis in the end is hence *not* synthesis, if that means self-relation. **1906** D. H. MacGregor in *Hibbert Jrnl.* July 800 The fact of self-distinction from the world is as ultimate as that of self-relation to it.

b. With adjs. and related sbs., vbs., pples. *self-complete* (earlier example), *-significant, -sterile* (also as *sb.*).

1857 E. B. Browning *Aurora Leigh* vii. 289 Both faces leaned together like a pair Of folded innocences, self-complete. **1882** G. M. Hopkins *Lett. to R. Bridges* (1955) 165 This seems in English a point..insisted on, that words shall be single and specific marks for things, whether self-significant or not. **1913** Self-sterile [see *incompatibility 4 b].

4. With pples. *self-actuating, -closing* (later examples), *-defrosting, -hardening, -igniting* (also *fig.*), *-levelling, -loading, -locking, -lubricating, -operating, -propelling* (earlier example), *-recording* (earlier example), *-setting, -stabilizing, -threading, -tuning, -unloading, -winding* (earlier example); *self-powered, -propelled* (later examples). With sbs. *self-demagnetization, -ignition, -registration, -stabilization.* With vbs. (forming adjs., sbs., and vbs.): *self-lock, -register.*

1959 H. Barnes *Oceanogr. & Marine Biol.* 168 Our attention will, therefore, be focussed on remotely controlled or self-actuating underwater cameras. **1931** *Times Educ. Suppl.* 27 June 249/4 Noise is minimized by the use of self-closing double doors. **1971** *Oxf. Univ. Gaz.* 18 Feb. 671/1 The barrier must be self-closing after a car has passed through. **1960** *Times* 7 Mar. 13/5 Refrigerators.. self defrosting. **1912** *Proc. Physical Soc.* XXIV. 342 (*heading*) The self-demagnetisation of annealed steel rods. **1906** Self-hardening [see *air-hardening a.* s.v. *air $sb.^1$ B. II]. **1865** *Naval & Mil. Gaz.* 16 Sept. 589/2 Self-igniting cartridges. **1948** L. Spitzer *Linguistics & Lit. Hist.* iv. 167 Diderot has experienced to the bitter end the self-annihilation of the self-igniting mind. **1927** *Automobile Engineer* XVII. 500/1 Compression ignition stands out clearly as the one factor controlling the onset of detonation in engine practice, this simultaneous activation of compressed combustion being what is understood by the 'self-ignition temperature' of a combustible. **1969** *Gloss. Terms assoc. with Fire* (*B.S.I.*) i. 7 *Self-ignition temperature*, the temperature at which a flammable gas/air mixture will ignite without an external source of ignition. **1960** *Farmer & Stockbreeder* 16 Feb. 47/3 (Advt.), Patent self-levelling linkage ensures uniform depth of cultivation despite ground variations. **1965** *Sun* 28 Sept. 6/2 Citroen..continue their anti-flash campaign. They are fitting 'self-levelling' headlights to a new..version of their Drophead Coupe. **1977** *Observer* 8 May 33/3 Low-roll cornering and self-levelling rear suspension keep the handling predictable under all loads. **1899** *Kynoch Jrnl.* Oct.–Nov. 2/2 Jones's self-loading cartridge case. **1973** *Country Life* 28 June 1907 Self-loading forage machines, used primarily for handling loose hay. **1977** *R.A.F. News* 8–21 June 5/3 Their equipment includes..self-loading rifles and Sterling sub-machine guns. **1976** V. Canning *Doomsday Carrier* i. 6 The door swung back to self-lock. *a* **1884** E. H. Knight *Pract. Dict. Mech.* Suppl. 795/2 *Self locking hook*, one which automatically closes. **1938** *Archit. Rev.* LXXXIII. p. lx/3 The glass is held by a continuous self-locking spring aluminium cover strip. **1980** D. Bloodworth *Trapdoor* xxx. 185 The door was self-locking and he could not force his way in. **1967** M. Chandler *Ceramics in Mod. World* v. 154 Among the many highly-specialized uses of graphite refractories is the making of self-lubricating piston rings. **1947** M. M. Lewis *Language in Society* 136 The machines of war are its self-operating weapons. **1962** A. Nisbett *Technique Sound Studio* 260 '*Midget*' *recorder*,..a self-powered recorder which is light enough to be carried about without too much difficulty. **1928** C. F. S. Gamble *Story N. Sea Air Station* xxii. 428 To clear out the stores and take them by sea to other stations,..a large, self-propelled concrete lighter (*R.A.F. 110*) was used. **1945** *Finito! Po Valley Campaign* 31 Tanks and self-propelled guns were captured intact. **1977** J. Stern in *Winter's Tales 23* 178 Of his last years several were spent..in a self-propelled wheelchair on the roads..of Dorset. **1862** *Times* 7 Apr. 9/4 A self-propelling bathing-machine. **1866** *Trans. Brit. Assoc. 1865* 20 (*heading*) Description of the magnetic storm of the beginning of August 1865, as recorded by the self-recording magnetographs at the Kew and Lisbon observatories. **1847** *Phil. Trans. R. Soc.* CXXXVII. 111 It would be superfluous to speak of those proposals..for self-registering, photographically, the variation of the declination magnet. **1885** *Arch. Ophthalmol.* XIV. 54 The advantages offered by a perimeter with self-register are too evident to be overlooked. **1847** *Rep. Brit. Assoc. Adv. Sci. 1846* ii. 11 In order to adapt it for self-registration, a light conical brass tube..was affixed to the lower side. **1908** *Sears, Roebuck Catal.* 37/2 The shuttle is the most perfect self threading cylindrical shuttle... The needle is self setting. **1948** W. E. Stephens et al. *Nuclear Fission & Atomic Energy* ix. 128 An interesting possible mechanism for self-stabilization of a chain reaction in the presence of a cadmium absorber was suggested by Adler and von Halban. **1953** *Jrnl. Inst. Electr. Engineers* C. i. 101/1 The self-stabilizing effect is so important in establishing an inherently safe and stable plant [*sc.* nuclear reactor]..that it should always be carefully studied. **1908** Self-threading [see *self-setting* above]. **1964** *Discovery* Oct. 67/2 The Rank Organisation has recently marketed a 16 mm projector which is self-threading. **1956** R. Sheckley in Aldiss & Harrison *Decade 1950s* (1976) 189 The portable sub-space set was self-tuning. **1960** *Farmer & Stockbreeder* 16 Feb. 72/3 He could load five tons of chopped silage from the barn silo into two self-unloading trailers to feed 180 cows in three-quarters of an hour. **1964** *New Scientist* 4 June 596/2 The self-unloading ship is not new but economic factors have until recently restricted its operation. **1825** *Mechanics' Mag.* III. 293/2 M. Recordon.. proceeded to England, where he obtained a patent for his invention of self-winding watches, which were then in great request.

5. b. Delete ? *Obs.* and add: *self-power, -value, -worth; selftaste, -yeast* (nonce-wds.).

a **1688** R. Cudworth *Treat. Freewill* (1838) 62 God Almighty could not make such a rational creature as this is..which had no self-power, no hegemonic or ruling principle. **1896** W. James *Let.* 24 July (1920) II. 41 Full of swelling and bursting *Weltschmerz* and religious melancholy, yet no more flexibility or self-power in his mind than in a boot-jack. **1964** E. Becker in I. L. Horowitz *New Sociol.* 123 This is the basic phenomenology of alienations: the failure to develop self-powers by transacting with the world of things. **1880** G. M. Hopkins *Sermons & Devotional Writings* (1959) 125 Above all my shame, my guilt, my fate are the very things in feeling, in tasting, which I most taste that selftaste which nothing in the world can match. **1959** *Guardian* 28 Aug. 4/3, I did meet Colin Wilson, and..I found that with him I received my sense of my self-value in its fullness. **1944** *Horizon* Feb. 104 The feeling of self-worth experienced by contented individualists. **1978** M. Puzo *Fools Die* xlvii. 501 The lack of self-worth, the desire to please someone that they thought really cared about them. *a* **1889** G. M. Hopkins *Poems* (1967) 101 Selfyeast of spirit a dull dough sours.

self-abnegation. Add: Also **self-a·bnegator** (*rare*).

1907 G. B. Shaw *John Bull's Other Island* p. xix, The Catholic is theoretically a Collectivist, a self-abnegator, a Tory.

self-abso·rption. 1. [Self- 3 a.] Absorption in one's own emotions, interests, or situation; self-preoccupation.

1862 [in Dict. s.v. Self- 3 a]. *a* **1930** D. H. Lawrence *Last Poems* (1932) 94 The lovely and self-absorbed girl Looked back at the handsome and self-absorbed young man And thrilled. And in that thrill he felt: Her self-absorption is even as strong as mine. **1979** V. S. Naipaul *Bend in River* xi. 188, I did not wish to lose myself in the ..self-absorption of that fantasy.

2. *Physics.* [*self- 2 b.] Absorption of radiation by the material emitting it. Cf. *self-shielding *vbl. sb.*

1938 *Proc. Cambr. Philos. Soc.* XXXIV. 600 With radium E, strong sources may be obtained showing negligible self-absorption. **1950** *Atomics* Nov. 334/2 The self-absorption of β-rays in radioactive films..has been investigated. **1978** H. H. Bauer et al. *Instrumental Analysis* x. 265 At too high a current, Doppler broadening and self-absorption (absorption of part of the emitted radiation by the dense cloud of atoms in the source itself) will occur.

self-abuse. **3.** For 'self-pollution' read 'masturbation'.

self-active, *a.* (Later examples.)

1906 G. H. Howison *Let.* 9 Feb. in R. B. Perry *Tht. & Char. W. James* (1935) I. 776 The self-active unity of consciousness. **1936** Allport & Odbert in *Psychol. Monogr.* XLVII. I. 17 It was customary for psychologists to conceive some 'power of the mind'..and by naming it to regard the power as fixed and self-active.

self-activity. (Later *Psychol.* examples.)

1932 C. S. Myers *Absurdity of Mind–Body Rel.* 4 All conscious mental activity is self-activity; only the self is conscious—conscious, at first, solely of self-activity (conation) and of modifications of that self-activity (affects). **1961** R. C. Tucker *Philos. & Myth in Marx* viii. 134 'Self-activity'.., by which Marx means free creativity in which a person feels thoroughly at home with himself..and experiences his energies as his own.

self-actualiza·tion. Chiefly *Psychol.* [Self- 1 a.] Realization or fulfilment of oneself, esp. considered as a drive or need.

1939 H. Ansbacher tr. *Goldstein's Organism* v. 197 Experiences..teach us that we have to assume only one drive, the drive of self-actualization. **1943** A. H. Maslow in *Psychol. Rev.* L. 382 What a man *can* be, he *must* be. This need we may call self-actualization. **1957** C. Argyris *Personality & Organization* vii. 181 The degree of self-actualization increases sharply for individuals as their dependence..and submissiveness are decreased. **1975** *Ecologist* V. 123/1 The evolving form of marriage seems to aim at what might be called 'self-actualization' of the persons.

Also **self-a·ctualize** *v. intr.*; **self-ac·tualized** *ppl. a.*, **-a·ctualizing** *ppl. a.* and *vbl. sb.*; **self-a·ctualizer.**

1874 Self-actualizing *ppl. a.* [in Dict. s.v. Self- 1 f]. **1943** A. M. Farrer *Finite & Infinite* xi. 119 Will is the self-actualising potency of (the process of) a project. **1954** A. H. Maslow *Motivation & Personality* xii. 223 The creativeness of the self-actualized man. *Ibid.* 230 A firm foundation for a value system is automatically furnished to the self-actualizer. **1959** H. B. Anderson *Creativity* xv. 242 To do this much would..appear to be a step toward self-actualizing. **1961** H. C. Smith *Personality Adjustment* xiv. 381 Somerset Maugham shows..the qualities of spontaneity..and self-acceptance that are found in self-actualizers. **1977** R. Holland *Self & Social Context* iv. 61 Arguing that there is a given 'instinctoid' tendency for the human being to self-actualise, that is to go beyond the satisfaction of the more basic needs to seek satisfaction of the higher needs. **1980** *Redbook* Oct. 58/1 Once I had seen close up what Friedan labeled the 'self-actualized woman', I was damned if I would take a chance with anything else.

self-admiring, *ppl. a.* (In Dict. s.v. Self-admiration.) (Later examples.)

1871 Geo. Eliot *Middlem.* (1872) I. I. i. 7 Dorothea.. was open, ardent, and not in the least self-admiring. **1951** M. McLuhan *Mech. Bride* (1967) 141/1 Is this little tough the twin brother of any self-patting, self-admiring deb? **1981** J. Carey *John Donne* iv. 99 His poems..though self-absorbed..are not self-admiring.

self-aliena·tion. *Philos.* and *Social Sci.* [Self- 1 a.] Alienation that takes place within the self, esp. in *Marxism.* Cf. *alienation 1 c.

1906 J. B. Baillie *Outl. to Idealistic Construct. Exper.* vii. 242 For this Self-alienation is itself regarded as necessary, as the very expression of free self-consciousness. **1926** H. J. Stenning tr. *Marx's Sel. Ess.* 13 The immediate task of philosophy, when enlisted in the service of history, is to unmask human self-alienation in its unholy shape. **1938** K. Korsch *Marx* II. xi. 158 The actual 'self-alienation' of the wage-labourer. **1964** S. M. Jourard *Transparent Self* ii. 11 It often comes to pass..that our public selves become so estranged from our real selves that the net consequence is self-alienation. **1977** A. Giddens *Stud. in Social & Polit. Theory* v. 199 For Marx ..money is the epitome of human self-alienation under capitalism, since it reduces all human qualities to quantitative values of exchange.

self-ali·gning, *ppl. a.* *Mech.* [Self- 4.] Capable of aligning itself automatically. Of a bearing or the like: having a degree of flexibility as regards alignment. Hence **self-ali·gnment.**

1904 *Science* 29 Jan. 164/1 Where the ends of the polar axis are supported on separate piers the bearings can be made self-aligning. **1905** [in Dict. s.v. Self- 4]. **1930** *Engineering* 26 Sept. 394/3 A self-aligning double roller feed for vertical double-spindle moulders. **1960** *Farmer & Stockbreeder* 15 Mar. 148/1 All-steel welded construction with self-aligning ball bearings throughout. **1962** G. A. T. Burdett *Automatic Control Handbk.* iv. 9 A method of maintaining self-alignment.

self-ana·lysis. [Self- 1 a.] Analysis by or of oneself; *spec.* Psychol., psychoanalysis of oneself undertaken by oneself.

1860 A. J. Munby *Diary* 12 Mar. in D. Hudson *Munby* (1972) 54 Self analysis helps one... I am sensible of a feeling of placid halfcontemptuous indifference. **1862** [in Dict. s.v. Self- 1 a]. **1911** E. Jones in *Amer. Jrnl. Psychol.* XXII. 520 The greatest value is to be attached to self-analysis, a fact to which attention cannot too often be called. *a* **1930** D. H. Lawrence *Last Poems* (1932) 28 Self-analysis Which goes further and further, and yet never finds an end. **1958** K. Menninger *Theory of Psychoanal. Technique* vii. 159 The process of self-analysis continues automatically..with increasing freeing and expanding of ego functions. **1977** M. Jahoda *Freud & Dilemmas of Psychol.* iii. 52 The self-analysis is important beyond this and..stakes the claim for psychoanalysis to be a reflexive psychology. **1981** B. Masters *Georgiana* viii. 204 With time on her hands, Georgiana gave way to self-analysis, introspection, regret.

Hence **self-a·nalyst.**

1929 Sheehan & Gaffney *Tristram Lloyd* III. i. 187 He was a self-analyst, and he carried the principle into every-day life, sorting, sifting, examining motives and principles. **1958** B. W. Aldiss *Non-Stop* III. iv. 184 He was not enough of a self-analyst to see it was a quality he had..himself.

self-asse·mbly. **1.** [*self- 2 b.] Subsequent assembly of something bought in the form of a kit; usu. *attrib.*, denoting items (e.g. furniture) sold in this form.

a **1966** in G. N. Leech *Eng. in Advertising* (1966) xv. 137 Peerless brings within your reach..the luxury of a Built-in Bedroom at a price you can really afford With Dovetail Self-assembly Units. **1978** *Dumfries Courier* 20 Oct. 27/1 (Advt.), Broom unit for self assembly £10. **1980** *Daily Tel.* 9 July 2/1 A subsidiary..which makes self-assembly garages and prefabricated home extensions.

2. *Biol.* [Self- 1 a.] The spontaneous formation of a sub-cellular particle from its components, e.g. that of a ribosome or of a virus in a medium containing the appropriate RNA and proteins. Hence **self-asse·mble** *v. intr.*

1969 *Jrnl. Molecular Biol.* XL. 412 We feel that the general principle of self-assembly revealed in the present *in vitro* system also operates *in vivo*. **1977** *Jrnl. Protozool.* XXIV. 9/1 Self-assembly of a restricted number of different macromolecular subunits to form comparatively simple structures such as a rhizoplast, a pelta, or a trichocyst. **1978** *Sci. Amer.* Nov. 53 (*caption*) The virus 'self-assembles' spontaneously in the test tube from its constituent RNA molecule and protein subunits, giving rise to infective virus particles indistinguishable from those found in nature.

self-asserting, *a.* (In Dict. s.v. Self-assertion.) (Earlier example.)

1837 J. S. Mill in *Westm. Rev.* XXVIII. 98 Carrel's manner was not of the self-asserting kind.

self-asse·ssment. [Self- 1 a.] Assessment or evaluation of oneself, one's actions or attitudes by oneself; an instance of this; *spec.* calculation of taxable liability by oneself.

1954 *Brit. Jrnl. Med. Psychol.* XXVII. 142/1 The psychiatric inventory described here (to be known as the Tavistock Self-assessment Inventory) is one which has been developed over the past few years in the Tavistock Clinic. **1960** *Spectator* 1 July 34 In the study of myth, Professor Kerényi explained in a 'self-assessment' written ten years ago, one must accept the 'axiom' of depth psychology. **1972** *Accountant* 12 Oct. 441/2 Special arrangements will secure for them the equivalent of tax credits, and self-assessment is waiting in the wings. **1979** *Internat. Rehabilit. Med.* I. 53/1 They were asked to assess the ability with which they performed a variety of activities during the preceding few weeks..self-assessments.

self-ba·lancing, *ppl. a.* [Self- 1 f, 4.] **1.** In technical use: capable of balancing itself automatically; automatically producing balance.

1912 *Chambers's Jrnl.* Sept. 638/1 An upright position is always assured when the car is stationary, a continuous self-balancing motion being given to the vehicle. **1954** D. E. Carritt in Isaacs & Iselin *Oceanogr. Instrumentation* 182 Snodgrass et al. have constructed a self-balancing photoelectric filter photometer.

2. *Accounting.* Designating that in which the debit side of the accountable items is equal to the credit side; *self-balancing ledger* (see quot. 1970).

1898 S. S. Dawson *Accountant's Compendium* 350/2 The Customers' Ledger .. is self-balancing because of the operation of the Controlling Account. **1931** *Economist* 3 Jan. 7/2 The gross figures, including self-balancing revenue, show receipts from all sources amounting to £486·5 millions. **1953** *Chambers's Jrnl.* June 343/1 Catering generally is a profitable or at least self-balancing item in the seaside resort budget. **1964** R. B. Notestein in I. L. Horowitz *New Sociology* 52 The economy was self-balancing, with authority exerted by impersonal regional markets. **1970** M. Greener *Penguin Dict. Commerce* 297 *Self-balancing ledger*, an accounting term for a personal ledger containing a control account.

self-being. Restrict † *Obs.* to *concr.* use and add: (Later examples.) Now *rare.*

1880 G. M. Hopkins *Sermons & Devotional Writings* (1959) 122 And this whether I speak of human nature or of my individuality, my selfbeing. **1915** A. Vonier *Personality of Christ* v. 31 The scholastic maintains that self-being underlies self-consciousness, as the cause underlies the effect. **1977** R. Holland *Self & Social Context* ii. 41 He attributes the non-disclosure to role-playing, which is placed in sharp contrast with real self-being.

self-bi·as. *Electronics.* [Self- 1 d.] Bias applied to the grid of a valve by means of a resistor in the cathode circuit or the grid circuit. So **self-bi·ased** *ppl. a.*, **self-bi·asing** *vbl. sb.*

1931 Moyer & Wostrel *Radio Handbk.* xiii. 708 (*heading*) Self-biasing grid-glow tube. **1932** F. E. Terman *Radio Engin.* xi. 389 (*caption*) Self-bias circuits for obtaining a negative grid bias..by utilizing the voltage drop across a resistance in series with the cathode. *Ibid.*, When an anode detector is self-biased by the arrangement shown.., the detector characteristics are quite different from those obtained with a bias derived from a battery. **1939** H. J. Reich *Theory & Application Electron Tubes* vi. 161 (*caption*) Impedance-capacitance–coupled amplifier, showing the use of self-biasing resistors. **1945** [see *push-pull *a.* 2]. **1960** *Practical Wireless* XXXVI. 319/1 This condenser discharges through the grid leak.., building up the self bias for the valve.

self-binder. Add: **2.** (See quot.)

1950 *Times* 26 July 6/5 A self-binder for *The Times*, which takes one month's issues on sprung cords, is now available.

self-bio·graphy. *rare* or *Obs.* [Self- 1 d.] = Autobiography.

1796 I. D'Israeli *Miscellanies or Lit. Recreations* 95 (*heading*) Some observations on diaries, self-biography and self-characters. **1813** J. F. Stanfield *Essay on Study & Composition of Biography* I. i. 2 Our supply of genuine self-biography is but scanty.

self-bli·mped, *a.* [Self- 4; cf. *blimp 1 b.] Of a ciné camera: fitted with a sound-proof cover; insulated from sound by its own housing.

1961 in Webster. **1965** R. Fielding *Technique Special-Effects Photogr.* x. 269 The projector must be somehow silenced... Either the machine must be self-blimped or installed within a sound-proof projection room. **1969** *Focal Encycl. Film & Television* 74/2 Sound cameras of recent design are..self-blimped..so that mechanical noise is reduced to an absolute minimum. **1979** D. Cheshire *Bk. Movie Photogr.* 174 The camera must run as silently as possible to avoid disturbing the animals. You may need a 'self-blimped' camera.

self-ca·ncelling, *ppl. a.* [Self- 1 f, 4.] That cancels itself; that negate each other. **1.** In technical use: designed to stop working automatically when no longer required; applied esp. to traffic indicators of motor vehicles.

1935 [see *dipper 8]. **1945** *Autocar Handbk.* (Autocar Techn. Staff) (ed. 18) x. 196 Some form of 'self-cancelling' arrangement is..fitted, to avoid drivers unknowingly going along with an indicator extended. **1960** *News Chron.* 6 May 8/8 They have omitted..to make the traffic indicators self-cancelling. **1963** *Times* 15 Jan. 12/1 By flicking in the self-cancelling overdrive in third and top the motorway cruising speed went up to about 80. **1972** *Daily Tel.* 12 July 10/5 Not only is the stalk on the column very flimsy and mounted on the wrong side..but the indicators are not self-cancelling.

2. *gen.*

1943 *Mind* LII. 295 It has been made a *self-cancelling* expression like the expression 'ride a motor cycle' as used by someone who is determined to use 'ride' only where what you ride is something living. **1965** *Spectator* 15 Jan. 60/1 The concept of fighting for export orders has become largely self-cancelling.

self-capa·citance. *Electr.* [Self- 5 b.] The inherent capacitance of a circuit or component. Also **self-capa·city.**

1923 E. W. Marchant *Radio Telegr. & Teleph.* v. 66 Such coils have a considerable inductance, and 'self-capacity'. **1937** L. D. Weld *Gloss. Physics* 207/2 *Self-capacitance*, distributed capacitance of an electric circuit due to its containing closely wound coils of insulated wire, the adjacent turns of which have a condenser effect. **1958** *Practical Wireless* XXXIV. 22/2 This was found to be essential since the timebase was affecting the appearance of the trace due to the self-capacity of the X switch. **1960** *Ibid.* XXXVI. 397/2 A small capacitance which is in fact the self-capacitance of the crystal.

self-care (stress variable). [Self- 1 a, *2 b, 3 a.] Care for oneself; self-interested behaviour; freq. used *attrib.* to denote an institution in which patients and convalescents attend to many of their own needs.

1904 in Webster. **1932** Auden *Orators* II. 41 The second law of thermodynamics—self-care or minding one's own business. **1962** *Punch* 7 Nov. 658/1 Recovering your strength you're passed to the Self-Care Unit. **1979** *Internat. Rehabilit. Med.* I. 59/1 Assessment of the competence of patients in essential activities of daily living (A.D.L.), such as mobility, self care, and domestic activities.

self-ca·tering, *vbl. sb.* [Self- 3 a.] Catering for oneself; *spec.* providing one's own domestic services (as meals and cleaning) in rented holiday accommodation. Chiefly *attrib.* of holidays and vacation accommodation.

1970 *Country Life* 1 Oct. 802/1 There has also been a discernible movement towards self-catering holidays, in farmhouses, chalets, caravans and cottages. **1972** *Guardian* 9 Dec. 13/2 Holiday camps are increasingly turning to self-catering. **1973** *Times* 25 Jan. (Channel Islands Suppl.) p. v/3 Self-catering accommodation is.. increasing rapidly. **1977** *Western Morning News* 1 Sept. 6/5 (Advt.), Comfortable all-electric self-catering Farmhouse; 2 double bedrooms week 3/10 September. **1981** *Daily Tel.* 27 Jan. 12/5 Two redundant stone-built barns ..have been converted into self-catering bunkhouses for walkers.

self-ce·ntring, *ppl. a.* Add: **2. b.** Of the steering of a motor vehicle: tending to return automatically to a central alignment. Also as *vbl. sb.*

1926 H. T. Rutter *Mod. Motors* II. ix. 331 The steering gear is arranged to be self-centring, so that little pressure is required to maintain the car in a straight line. **1963** *Times* 5 Feb. 7/5 At first, the powerful self-centring action of the steering makes the car feel heavy and slightly unstable. **1975** *Drive* New Year 102/3 The tail certainly wags the Beetle, especially in the wet when even the responsive, self-centring steering won't help to avoid trouble. **1977** *Times* 18 Aug. 23/3 The main criticisms of steering were..stiffness of operation, and lack of self-centring.

self-cha·nging, *ppl. a.* **1.** (In Dict. s.v. Self- 1 f.)

2. [Self- 4.] Of a gearbox: preselective.

1930 [see *fluid flywheel* s.v. *fluid *sb.* 3]. **1939** *Country Life* 11 Feb. p. xxx/3 The self-changing gear box and the special anti-snatch Armstrong Siddeley transmission.

self-clea·ning, *ppl. a.* (*vbl. sb.*) [Self- 1 b, f, 4.] Designed to keep itself clean automatically. Also as *vbl. sb.*, the action or capability of doing this.

1898 L. S. Robertson tr. *Bertin's Marine Boilers* iv. 91 Self-cleaning grates with movable bars have been used in America. **1930** *Daily Express* 6 Oct. 7/5 (Advt.), The Ewbank Success sweeper is fitted with ball bearings, a self-cleaning brush and rubber protectors. **1960** *Farmer & Stockbreeder* 15 Mar. 119/2 The self-cleaning action of the slats has not been particularly evident. **1971** *Engineering* Apr. 31/1 So far, cost and complexity have ruled out self-cleaning [for vending machines]. **1979** *Arizona Daily Star* 5 Aug. (Advt. Section) 17/7 Self-cleaning patio pool, landscaped, block wall.

self-clea·nsing, *ppl. a.* (*vbl. sb.*) [Self- 1 b, f, 4.] Tending automatically to keep itself clean. Also as *vbl. sb.*

1911 H. S. Watson *Sewerage Systems* iii. 41 All sewers should be self-cleansing. **1921** T. Goodhugh *Operative Dental Surg.* xviii. 262 Food in mastication cleans the teeth on the exposed surfaces, which are called 'self-cleansing surfaces'. **1963** J. Osborne *Dental Mech.* (ed. 5) viii. 147 The resin..may then be lightly polished to give a surface that is readily self-cleansing. **1978** *Jrnl. R. Soc. Med.* LXXI. 718 In these situations, self-cleansing is less common and keratin may accumulate.

self-co·cking, *ppl. a.* (*vbl. sb.*) [Self- 4.] Of a firearm: cocked and fired by pulling the trigger; double-action. Also *fig.*, and as *vbl. sb.*

1862 [see *back-action]. **1880** *News & Press* (Cimarron, New Mexico) 23 Dec. 3/1 Mr. T. O. Boggs of Tramperos, while in the act of drawing a self-cocking pistol from his pocket, accidentally discharged it. **1892** [in Dict. s.v. Self- 4]. **1902** W. D. Hulbert *Forest Neighbors* 161 Four shots, as fast as the self-cocking revolver could pour the lead into his body. **1964** H. L. Peterson *Encycl. Firearms* 17/1 The revolver patented by Robert Adams in 1851 was the English challenge to the Colt revolver, but unlike the latter it was made with a solid frame and a self-cocking action.

Hence **self-co·cker**, a firearm thus cocked and fired.

1863 [in Dict. s.v. Self- 4]. **1902** S. E. White in *McClure's Mag.* Apr. 552/2 It was wonderful work, rattling fire, quicker than a self-cocker even.

self-coi·ncidence. [Self- 3 a.] The fact or state of coinciding with its former position following a displacement.

1904 *Knowledge* June 110/1 Every molecule of the medium..is brought by certain so-called 'movements' into the position previously occupied by some other molecule of the medium (the medium is said to be 'brought to self-coincidence' by such a movement). **1966** [see *isometric *a.* 7].

self-colour. **1.** (Later examples of clothing and embroidery.)

1927 T. Woodhouse *Artificial Silk* ix. 86 Knitted garment of a self-colour are made, in this simplest form, by the manipulation of a single continuous thread. **1950** *Sun* (Baltimore) 9 May 18 (Advt.), Barbara Lee leg-contour proportioned-fit sheer nylons with contrast or self-color seams. **1964** A. Butler *Teaching Children Embroidery* ii. iv. 35 Free experimenting, with stitches used in some areas, in which self-colour is worked as a texture. **1976** *Morecambe Guardian* 7 Dec. 1/1 (Advt.), 100% wool skirt suit with self-colour embroidery.

self-compa·tible, *a.* and *sb. Bot.* [Self- 3 b.] **A.** *adj.* Able to be fertilized by means of its own pollen. **B.** *sb.* A self-compatible plant or species. Opp. *self-incompatible *a.* and *sb.*

1922 *Bot. Gaz.* LXXIII. 111 There are in the feebly self-compatible plants of these species no specially marked tendencies to self-compatibility at any definite phase of the blooming period. **1938** [see *self-incompatible *a.* and *sb.*]. **1955** *Heredity* IX. 70 The trees he tested could be divided on their setting capacity into those which were self-compatible and those which were self-incompatible. **1969** *Ibid.* XXIV. 165 We may suppose that dioecy here evolved recently from hermaphroditism in a *self-compatible* ancestor. **1979** *Nature* 20–27 Dec. 837/2 The usual explanation that dioecy arises in a self-compatible taxon as a way of ensuring outcrossing is certainly possible.

So **self-compatabi·lity**, the state of being self-compatible.

1917 *Jrnl. Genetics* VII. 78 The behaviour of the various series indicates an irregular inheritance of the characteristics of self-compatibility. **1969** *Heredity* XXIV. 613 Different self-compatibility alleles may occur localised in different habitats.

self-co·ncept. *Soc. Psychol.* [Self- 1 d.] A person's concept or idea of himself. Also **self-conce·ption.**

1934 in Webster. **1938** *Psychol. Abstr.* XII. 770/1 (Index) Self-concept, adolescence. **1947** *Amer. Psychologist* Sept. 365/2 Our observations of psychotherapeutic experience would seem to indicate that absence of any threat to the self-concept is an important item in the problem. **1957** *Amer. Sociol. Rev.* XXII. 218/2 The following analysis is limited to the executives' and the supervisors' self-conceptions and conceptions of each other. **1968** *Internat. Encycl. Social Sci.* XIV. 150/1 Since the 1940s, problems related to self concept have surged forth as indispensable..topics for scientific study in psychology and sociology. **1977** M. Edelman *Polit. Lang.* ii. 29 The self-conceptions that are a part of these contradictory cognitive structures.

self-concern, -concerned. Delete † *Obs.* and add later examples.

1941 *Mind* L. 179 The self is part 'psyche' and part 'spirit': the psyche or animal soul self-concerned and partial, the spirit disinterested and catholic. **1972** P. D. James *Unsuitable Job for a Woman* iv. 148 Even their compassion had been overlaid with self concern. **1982** J. O'Faolain *Obedient Wife* i. 23 It says something about the way you see me. Forgive my self-concern.

self-condensa·tion. *Chem.* [Self- 1 a.] A condensation reaction between two molecules of the same compound. Also **self-conde·nse** *v. intr.*, to undergo such a reaction.

1946 *Nature* 12 Oct. 514/1 The highly reactive bifunctional compound, γ-bromopropylamine,..would immediately undergo self-condensation. **1959** A. Albert *Heterocyclic Chem.* vii. 269 β-Keto-esters..self-condense to pyrones, e.g. ethyl acetoacetate gives 2-methyl-5-acetyl-6-hydroxy-γ-pyrone. **1964** N. G. Clark *Mod. Organic Chem.* xxiii. 478 The self-condensation of acetophenone provides one of the rare examples of the carbonyl group of an aromatic ketone participating in a condensation reaction. **1976** *Austral. Jrnl. Chem.* XXIX. 1039 Self-condensation of cyanoacetamides under the influence of phosphorus oxychloride leads to pyridines and pyridinium salts in high yield.

self-confident, *a.* (Earlier and later examples.)

a **1617** P. Baynes *Christian Lett.* (1620) sig. C5, O Lord..thou hast promised that thou wilt circumcise our selfe-confident hearts, so that we shal haue no trust in the flesh, but haue all our reioycing in thee. **1921** E. O'Neill *Diff'rent* I, in *Emperor Jones* 221 Her face..attracts the eye by a certain boldly-appealing vitality of self-confident youth. **1951** in M. McLuhan *Mech. Bride* (1967) 72/1 It's a self-confident look.

self-co·njugate, *a.* Add: **b.** *Math.* Of a subgroup: having the property that for any elements h in the subgroup and g in the group, the product ghg^{-1} is in the subgroup.

1888 G. G. Morrice tr. *Klein's Lectures on Ikosahedron* i. i. 7 Every group contains..two self-conjugate subgroups: viz., in the first place, the totality of all its operations, *i.e.*, the group itself, and, in the second place, that simplest group which consists of the identical operation alone. **1937** A. A. Albert *Mod. Higher Algebra* vi. 131 We call $\mathfrak{A}$ a normal divisor (or invariant subgroup, or self-conjugate subgroup) of $\mathfrak{G}$. **1979** Page & Wilson *Introd. Computational Combinatorics* iv. 74 A partition whose Ferrers graph reads the same by rows and by columns is called self-conjugate.

Hence **self-co·njugately** *adv.*, as a self-conjugate subgroup.

1897 W. Burnside *Theory of Groups* x. 208 If two of these sub-groups have a common subgroup of order 4, it must be contained self-conjugately..in a sub-group of order 24 or 56. **1901** L. E. Dickson *Linear Groups* p. vii, Largest subgroup containing the Abelian group self-conjugately.

self-conscious, *a.* Add: **1 a.** (Earlier example.)

a **1688** Cudworth *Treatise of Freewill* (1838) 71 We are certain by inward sense that we can reflect upon ourselves and consider ourselves, which is a reduplication of life in a higher degree; for all cogitative beings as such are self-conscious.

2. (Earlier and later examples.)

1834 J. S. Mill *Let.* 12 Jan. in *Wks.* (1963) XII. 208, I begin to think that instead of being, as I once thought I was, the most self-conscious person living, I am much less self-conscious *now*..than almost anybody. **1937** 'G. Orwell' *Road to Wigan Pier* xiii. 255 Self-conscious Socialists dutifully addressing one another as 'Comrade'. **1974** J. Irving *158-Pound Marriage* ii. 42 She had never been self-conscious about what she wore.

self-consciousness. **4.** (Earlier and later examples.)

1833 J. S. Mill *Let.* 25 Nov. in *Wks.* (1963) XII. 195 A man singularly free, if we may trust appearances, from self-consciousness. **1932** G. Greene *Stamboul Train* i. i. 5 Her body..even while stumbling..retained its self-consciousness.

self-consistent, *a.* Add: **b.** *Physics.* Of a trial solution of Schrödinger's equation for a nucleus with more than one electron: consistent with its own postulates (see quots.).

1928 D. R. Hartree in *Proc. Cambr. Philos. Soc.* XXIV. 113 If the final field is the same as the initial field, the field will be called 'self-consistent'. **1958** Sykes & Bell tr. *Landau & Lifshitz' Quantum Mechanics* x. 232 Schrödinger's equation for atoms containing more than one electron cannot be directly solved in practice, even by numerical methods. Approximate methods of calculating the energies and wave functions of the stationary states of the atoms are therefore important. The most important of these methods is what is called the self-consistent field method. The idea of this method consists in regarding each electron in the atom as being in motion in the 'self-consistent field' due to the nucleus together with all the other electrons. **1974** Eisberg & Resnick *Quantum Physics* ix. 347 It might seem that there is no way to find the net potential of an atom at intermediate distances from its center... But it can be taken care of by demanding that the net potential be self-consistent.

Hence **self-consi·stently** *adv.*

1953 F. J. Whitfield tr. *L. Hjelmslev's Prolegomena to Theory of Lang.* 9 We require of linguistic theory that it enable us to describe self-consistently and exhaustively all conceivable or possible Danish texts. **1973** *Physical Rev.* B. VII. 674 Energy bands, Fermi surfaces, and densities of states of calcium as a function of lattice constant have been calculated self-consistently by the augmented-plane-wave method.

self-contained, *a.* Add: **b.** Now more usually of a flat, or suite of rooms, within a house.

1910 *Bradshaw's Railway Guide* Apr. 1174 The only Hotel in the Town having self-contained Suites. **1928** E. A. Robertson *Cullum* xi. 206 We came back in the evening to what was practically a self-contained flat—no one else slept on that landing. **1977** *Wandsworth Borough News* 16 Sept. 15/1 Planning Proposals..7 Eckstein-road, Clapham Junction—conversion to form two self-contained flats.

self-contented, *ppl. a.* (Earlier example.)

1819 Shelley *Rosalind & Helen* 29 Men, women, children, slunk away, Whispering with self-contented pride.

self-contradiction. Add: Also **self-contra·di·ctorily** *adv.*

1943 *Mind* LII. 313 We remember the man who never said, 'To see an event we should have to see it in an instant', thus self-contradictorily misdescribing our use of 'see an event'. **1959** P. F. Strawson *Individuals* i. 34 The standard..is set self-contradictorily high. **1981** G. MacBeth *Kind of Treason* ii. 17 The Clapham Center, as it was rather self-contradictorily called.

self-cri·ticism. [Self- 1 a.] **1.** Criticism of oneself.

1857 [in Dict. s.v. Self- 1 a]. **1926** J. S. Huxley *Essays in Popular Science* 162 The normal tendency of strongly-felt religious emotion to..set itself up as an absolute standard untempered by tolerance or by the self-criticism of reason. **1937** O. Jespersen in *S. P. E. Tract* XLVIII. 269 While one pronounces the beginning of an utterance the mind is busy preparing the rest, not only what to say, but how to say it. But most of this linguistic self-criticism is..lost to the world. **1956** H. Kurnitz *Invasion of Privacy* ii. 20 In this last phrase of good-natured self-criticism, Stradling's voice shifted into a glacial gear. **1977** *Lancet* 13 Aug. 357/1 Dr Bartsch reiterates our self-criticism that the two groups of patients were not comparable in all respects.

2. *Pol.* Criticism undertaken publicly by oneself of one's actions, attitudes, or policies, considered as a duty in order to ensure conformity with communist party doctrine. Also *transf.*

1933 E. & C. Paul tr. *Stalin's Leninism* II. 122 An abyss divides the self-criticism of the opposition..from Bolshevik self-criticism, the purpose of which is to *strengthen* the Party spirit. **1966** J. Bingham *Double Agent* vii. 101 Colonel Golchenko has performed an act of self-criticism in accordance with the principles of our party. **1976** M. Machlin *Pipeline* x. 116 Finally, after a scathing self-criticism session in the collective's skid row tenement in Seattle, Sonia decided she had had enough. **1978** D. Bloodworth *Crosstalk* x. 84 She was in trouble —public accusations that she was a counterrevolutionary, self-criticism sessions, denunciations,..the works.

self-cultiva·tion. [Self- 1 a.] = Self-culture.

1873 J. S. Mill *Autobiogr.* iv. 119, I did not neglect other modes of self-cultivation. **1964** R. Miliband in I. L. Horowitz *New Sociology* 80 A society..where man's social..setting would encourage self-cultivation and craftsmanship.

self-culture. (Earlier and later examples.)

1829 J. Sterling *Let.* 10 Nov. in Carlyle *Life John Sterling* (1851) i. vii. 56, I have no doubt that, by practice and self-culture, she will be a far finer actress. **1926** B. WEBB *My Apprenticeship* ii. 60 A device of my own for self-culture—reading the books of my free choice.

self-deli·verance. [SELF- 1 a.] Suicide by an incurable patient who finds his suffering intolerable.

This euphemism is not yet (1982) in wide currency. The related expression *self-deliveration* has also been used.

1975 M. R. BARRINGTON in M. Kohl *Beneficent Euthanasia* 214 Taking one's own life..would be more readily comprehended as responsible behavior if it were expressed as 'self-deliveration'. *Ibid.* 245 *Self-deliverance*, accession to deliverance. *Self-deliveration*, suicide where deliveration has or might have been given. **1975** *Hansard Lords* 4 Dec. 47/2 Self-deliverance to be regarded as death by misadventure. **1980** *Daily Tel.* 12 Aug. 6/2 The decision not to publish [a guide to suicide] would mean 'tragedy and continued distress..for many who wish to bring about their own self-deliverance'.

self-deluded, *ppl. a.* Add: **self-deluder** (earlier example), **-deluding** *ppl. a.* (later examples).

1748 RICHARDSON *Clarissa* VII. xv. 61 Poor mistaken creature!—Unhappy self-deluder! **1955** *Bull. Atomic Sci.* Apr. 168/1 It is shortsighted and self-deluding to ascribe more than a small part of Russian success to efficient espionage. **1980** D. FRANCIS *Reflex* xii. 142 He was a pernicious self-deluding little egotist.

self-denying, *vbl. sb.* (Later example.)

1878 TROLLOPE *Is he Popenjoy?* I. xiii. 174, I hate all kind of strictness and duty and self-denying.

self-destru·ct, *v.* orig. *N. Amer.* [f. SELF- 1 a, h: cf. DESTRUCT *v.* in Dict. & Suppl.]

1. *intr.* Of a thing: to destroy itself automatically. Also *fig.*

1969 *Daily Colonist* (Victoria, B.C.) 30 Mar. 43/4 This message will self-destruct in 10 seconds but the printed message is the one that lives on. **1970** *New Yorker* 28 Nov. 58 Our definition of 'history' is going to change as we raise our consciousness. Our definition's going to—it's going to self-destruct. **1973** *Guardian* 18 June 4/6 Watergate came from within. The system itself has begun to self-destruct. **1977** D. FRANCIS *Risk* xiv. 188 He's programmed to self-destruct before the end of the season... He'll go bust to the bookies. **1979** R. PERRY *Bishop's Pawn* i. 14 The tape would automatically self-destruct after twenty minutes.

Hence as *sb.*; **self-destructing** *ppl. a.*

1970 *New Scientist* 27 Aug. 406 (*title*) Self-destructing proteins may tick away our years. **1972** *Village Voice* 1 June 25/3 These are finally not poems or plays or stories, but self-destructs. **1977** *Daily Tel.* 21 May 12/4 Built into the whole modernist adventure was a kind of self-destruct. **1978** J. MCNEIL *Consultant* xxxvi. 295 Alloway's program has done a convenient self-destruct.

2. *attrib.* as *adj. phr.*

1966 R. W. TAYLOR *Doomsday Sq.* iii. 36 There's a double safeguard in a self-destruct system that would operate automatically in case of navigational error. **1969** M. CRICHTON *Andromeda Strain* x. 108 At the lowest level of this laboratory is an automatic self-destruct device. **1975** J. GRADY *Shadow of Condor* xvi. 250 He flicked the last strap holding him to the machine. He also punched the delayed self-destruct switch.

self-destructive, *a.* Add: **self-destru·ctiveness.**

1733 A. BAXTER *Enq. Human Soul* VI. xlv. 267 Nothing s a mark of impossibility, but a self-destructiveness in the idea. **1977** J. D. DOUGLAS in Douglas & Johnson *Existential Sociol.* i. 46 Self-hatred and the resulting self-destructiveness pervades the lives of the poor.

self-determination. Add: **2.** *Pol.* The action of a people in deciding its own form of government; free determination of statehood, postulated as a right (see quot. 1929).

1911 *Encycl. Brit.* XXIII. 653/1 The more enlightened of the emperors..made a genuine endeavour to give a due share in the work of government to the various subject races. But nothing could compensate for the lack of self-determination. **1917** *Times* 28 Dec. 8/1 According to the declarations of..the quadruple alliance, protection of the right of minorities forms an essential component part of the constitutional right of peoples to self-determination. **1918** WOODROW WILSON in *N.Y. Times* 12 Feb. 1/5 National aspirations must be respected; peoples may now be dominated and governed only by their own consent. 'Self-determination' is not a mere phrase. It is an imperative principle of action, which statesmen will henceforth ignore at their peril. **1929** W. S. CHURCHILL *World Crisis* V. xi. 203 Although the expression 'Self-determination' will rightly be forever connected with the name of President Wilson, the idea was neither original nor new. The phrase itself is Fichte's 'Selbst bestimmung'. **1946** D. L. SAYERS *Unpopular Opinions* 100 Eire demanded self-determination... Northern Ireland also wanted self-determination, and was determined to remain with England. **1959** E. H. CARR *Socialism in One Country* II. IV. xxi. 278 It was not only in Soviet Russia that a potential clash could be discerned between the claims of national self-determination and the claims of economic progress. **1968** 'J. LE CARRE' *Small Town in Germany* x. 162 The Yanks are going crazy about self-determination. Why don't they try it in East Germany? **1976** LD. HOME *Way Wind Blows* xii. 168 'Self-determination' was a slogan to which the Soviet leaders paid lip-service.

self-differentia·tion. [SELF- 1 a.] Differentiation arising from within oneself or itself; *spec.* in *Biol.*, that of embryonic tissue occurring more or less independently of other parts of the embryo.

1891 W. J. GREENSTREET tr. *Guyau's Educ. & Heredity* ix. 288 We are capable of self-imitation, self-differentiation, or self-modification. **1902** *Encycl. Brit.* XXVIII. 150/2 This partial independence has been called self-differentiation (*Selbstdifferenzierung*) by Roux, and is entirely a characteristic feature of ontogeny. **1926** [see *DIFFERENTIATION 1 a]. **1972** *Jrnl. Embryol. & Exper. Morphol.* XXVIII. 547 The capacity of Henson's node for self-differentiation and induction.

self-diffu·sion. *Chem.* [SELF- 3 a.] Migration of constituent atoms or molecules within the bulk of a substance, esp. in a crystalline solid.

1924 *Chem. Abstr.* XVIII. 2632 By mixing such comps. with AgI interchange of ions (self-diffusion) can be effected. **1938** R. W. LAWSON tr. *Hevesy & Paneth's Man. Radioactivity* (ed. 2) xviii. 173 Not until the introduction of radioactive indicators was it possible to open up to observational study the phenomenon of self-diffusion. **1958** *New Scientist* 2 Jan. 24/2 Autoradiograph (*a*) shows the self-diffusion after treatment at 800°C—this has occurred mainly along the boundaries of the grains or crystals of metal that make up bulk iron. **1974** D. M. ADAMS *Inorg. Solids* ix. 286 Self-diffusion work with silver isotopes confirms that these ions move freely between the available sites in the iodine lattice.

self-dissocia·tion. *Chem.* [SELF- 1 a, d.] = *SELF-IONIZATION. So **self-disso·ciated** *a.*, that undergoes self-ionization.

1905 *Jrnl. Physical Chem.* IX. 178 The conductivity of the pure solvents is explained by assuming 'self-dissociation' and considerable space is devoted to mere speculation as to what the composition of the ions might be in the various individual cases. **1973** SCHMIDT & SIEBERT in J. C. Bailar et al. *Comprehensive Inorg. Chem.* II. xxiii. 873 Sulphuric acid is also slightly self-dissociated into sulphur trioxide and water. *Ibid.*, The complete self-dissociation reaction in the sulphuric acid solvent system can be described..by the above equation.

se·lf-drive, *a.* [*SELF- 2 b.] Designating a motor vehicle hired to be driven by oneself, not by a chauffeur, or an agency which supplies such vehicles. Also *ellipt.* as *sb.*, a self-drive car or van, and **se·lf-driven** *ppl. a.*

1929 *Star* 21 Aug. 13/3 (Advt.), Motor-cars for hire. Self-drive Sal[oon]s, tourers fr. 17/6 day. **1932** KIPLING *Limits & Renewals* 80 A natty little grey and black self-driven coupé came from Brighton way. **1953** R. MACAULAY *Last Lett. to Friend* (1962) 97, I have hired a self-drive car, as there seems no other way of getting about Cyprus. **1969** J. LEASOR *They don't make them like that any More* vi. 194 We could hire a self-drive from somewhere. **1972** L. P. BACHMANN *Ultimate Act* xvi. 125 At the international self-drive agency I handed over my credit card. **1978** N. FREELING *Night Lords* ii. 14 French show-offs in Jaguars..Americans in self-drives. **1982** 'W. HAGGARD' *Mischief Makers* xi. 132, I have hired a self-drive removal van... We will load those crates.

self-effacement. Add: Also **self-effa·cingness.**

1951 S. SPENDER *World within World* 167 Forster's strange mixture of qualities—his self-effacingness combined with a positive assertion of his views.

self-election. Add: Also **self-ele·cting** *ppl. a.*

1855 BAGEHOT in *National Rev.* Oct. 271 In the towns, the franchise belonged to a close and self-electing corporation. **1980** D. FRANCIS *Reflex* vii. 76 That they [*sc.* the Jockey Club] were also self-electing meant in practice that the members were almost all..upper-class.

self-e·nergy. *Physics.* [SELF- 5 b.] The energy possessed by a particle in isolation from other particles and fields; the energy of interaction of a particle, quasi-particle, or current with its own field.

1883 O. HEAVISIDE in *Electrician* 10 Mar. 390/1 We have next..to consider the potential energy of a current system on itself, as distinguished from its energy with respect to another system. The last being called the mutual energy, we may for brevity term the former the self-energy. **1933** *Nature* 30 Dec. 1004/2 The use of the classical function *L* gives infinite values of self energy and other physical quantities which are, in fact, certainly finite. **1956** E. H. HUTTEN *Lang. Mod. Physics* iii. 97 The electron as a point-particle would possess infinite self-energy: this must occur when a finite charge is concentrated into a point—thus making the charge density, or charge per unit volume, infinite. **1962** CORSON & LORRAIN *Introd. Electromagn. Fields* vi. 243 The first two terms on the right are self-energies arising from the interaction of each current with its own field. **1977** *Dædalus* Fall 25 Just as the exchange of virtual photons between two electrons produces an energy of interaction between them, so also in quantum field theory the emission of virtual photons and their reabsorption by the same electron produces a self-energy.

self-estra·ngement. *Social Psychol.* [SELF- 1 a; cf. G. *selbstentfremdung*.] Estrangement from one's natural self, esp. such as is thought to result from the alienating development of consciousness or from involvement in a complex industrialized culture. Hence **self-estra·nged** *ppl. a.*

1878 A. C. BRACKETT *Science of Educ.* 43 [The mind's] first stage of development is self-estrangement—it is absorbed in the observation of objects around it... This process of self-estrangement and its removal belongs to all culture. **1910** J. B. BAILLIE tr. *Hegel's Phenomenol.* II. vi. 488 (*heading*) Spirit in self-estrangement—the discipline of culture. *Ibid.* 490 The equilibrium of the whole ..rests on the alienation of its opposite. The whole is, therefore, like each particular moment, a self-estranged reality. **1951** P. TILLICH *Systematic Theol.* I. ii. 74 A second part of the system must give an analysis of man's existential self-estrangement..and the question implied in this situation. **1972** M. ARGYLE *Social Psychol. of Work* ix. 226 Self-estrangement—failure to regard the work as a central life interest or means of self-expression, experiencing a depersonalized detachment while at work. **1978** J. UPDIKE *Coup* (1979) iv. 138 You can't talk about that without talking about the self-estrangement induced by forced labor.

self-evalua·tion. *Psychol.* [SELF- 1 a.] Appraisal of one's actions or attitudes, esp. in relation to an objective standard. Hence **self-eva·luative, -eva·luatory** *adjs.*

1933 *Psychol. Abstr.* VII. 473/2 To attain self-evaluation, psycho-physiological and psychotechnical methods must be supplemented by introspection. **1957** N. FRYE *Anat. Criticism* 179 The hero Denis comes to a point of self-evaluation. **1957** R. B. CATTELL *Personality & Motivation* vi. 220 Self-evaluatory methods of gathering personality data include questionnaires, biographical inventories, [etc.]. **1966** J. FLESCHER *Dual Therapy* vii. 154 The self-evaluative recording seems to promote the therapist's training as well as the patient's progress. **1979** A. CHISHOLM *Nancy Cunard* xxx. 315 A nightmare crisis of self-evaluation.

self-exciting, *ppl. a.* Add: **a.** (Later examples.) Also *transf.*, with reference to the hypothesis that the earth's magnetic field is generated in the earth's core by a mechanism analogous to that of a dynamo.

1922 GLAZEBROOK *Dict. Appl. Physics* II. 195/1 The great advantage of direct-current machines is that: (i) They can be made self-exciting. **1954** E. BULLARD in G. P. Kuiper *Earth as Planet* iii. 129 The possibility that the motion of the material of the core could cause it to act as a self-exciting dynamo. **1971** *Sci. Amer.* Dec. 80/1 The influence of the Coriolis force on the motions of the outer core is thought to be critical to the operation of the self-exciting dynamo that generates the main magnetic field of the earth.

b. *Radio.* Self-oscillating; (see quot. 1943).

1922 *Proc. IRE* X. 251 The basis of super-regeneration was the discovery that a variation in the relation between the negative and positive resistances prevented a system which would normally oscillate violently from becoming self-exciting. **1943** *Gloss. Terms Telecomm.* (*B.S.I.*) 69 *Self-exciting sender*, a radio sender in which the oscillator determining the frequency also generates the radio-frequency power.

self-excitation (later examples); **self-exci·te** *v. intr.* and *trans.*; **self-exci·ted** *ppl. a.*, self-exciting.

1921 J. H. MORECROFT *Princ. Radio Communication* vi. 562 A possible arrangement of self-excitation, in which the phase of the voltage impressed on the grid is adjustable. *Ibid.* 563 (*caption*) Conditions occurring in the self-excited tube. **1922** GLAZEBROOK *Dict. Appl. Physics* II. 196/2 It is also necessary that the winding should have a sufficiently low resistance, otherwise self-excitation will not occur. *Ibid.*, At this speed..the machine will not self-excite. **1940** *Amateur Radio Handbk.* (ed. 2) xvii. 245/1 Developments during the few years prior to the war tended to relegate self-excited transmitters into the background. **1962** *Newnes Conc. Encycl. Electr. Engin.* 672/2 An induction generator can be self-excited by means of a capacitor. *Ibid.* 673/1 Unwanted self-excitation with dangerously-high voltages may occur in induction generators. **1977** *Jrnl. R. Soc. Arts* CXXV. 764/1 Before the appearance of the self-excited dynamo in 1867 it was by no means obvious that magneto-electric induction would power the world's industries.

self-fertile, *a.* Add: Also **self-ferti·lity.**

1917 *Genetics* II. 525 That some of his families arising from selfed seed behaved exactly as the families arising from crossed seed shows that he is often (at least) dealing with a pseudo self-fertility. **1924** *Ibid.* IX. 16 The self-fertile plants differed among themselves in the expression of their self-fertility. **1956** *Nature* 10 Mar. 490/1 On hybridization, spontaneous self-fertility was restored. **1970** *Bot. Gaz.* CXXXI. 139/2 Species were rated for self-fertility by their ability to set seed under isolated conditions.

se·lf-field. *Physics.* [SELF- 5 b.] A field intrinsically associated with a charged particle, particle beam, or current, esp. as contrasted with any externally applied field that may be present.

1934 *Proc. R. Soc.* A. CXLIII. 437 The usual quantum mechanics is the limiting case in which the self-field is regarded as rigidly bound to the centre. **1970** *Particle Accelerators* I. 1/1 If the self-fields are large enough to trap the ions,..the cluster can be accelerated. **1976** *Nature* 19 Aug. 651/1 In the vicinity of the disk there is a small toroidal self-field $B\phi$ from the proton beams.

self-fina·ncing, *ppl. a.* [SELF- 1 f.] That finances itself; *spec.* (of a programme of development, etc) that pays for its own implementation or continuation. Also as *vbl. sb.* and (as a back-formation) **self-fina·nce** *v. trans.*

1957 A. C. L. DAY *Outl. Monetary Econ.* xxiii. 312 Such self-financing by large-scale industry has been very important in recent years. **1962** H. E. BEECHENO *Introd. Bus. Stud.* xvi. 150 The whole body of these policies must therefore be set on a self-financing basis. **1962** E. SNOW *Other Side of River* (1963) lix. 448 Cadres working in the brigade..'penetratingly explained' the necessity to 'self-finance' next year's development program. **1964** *Financial Times* 12 Mar. 5/8 It is becoming harder to rely principally on self-financing in order to raise capital for expansion. **1972** *Accountant* 19 Oct. 489/2 The Canadian company has maintained its contribution to group earnings and at the same time is self-financing its own expansion. **1979** *Jrnl. R. Soc. Arts* CXXVII. 656/1 They discuss the Society's miscellaneous activities, such as.. the establishment in 1851–2 of self-financing public lavatories. **1980** I. ST. JAMES *Money Stories* II. i. 42 Can't you sell some diamonds and plough the cash back into fresh equipment? Make the project self-financing?

self-flu·xing, *ppl. a.* [SELF- 4.] Of iron ore: capable of being smelted without the addition of a flux, usu. because it contains a high proportion of lime. Also as *vbl. sb.*

1884 [in Dict. s.v. SELF- 4]. **1923** HARBORD & HALL *Metall. of Steel* (ed. 7) II. xxvi. 504 A few ores have an excess of lime, and if unable to secure self-fluxing ores the blast furnace manager endeavours to mix siliceous and calcareous ores when obtainable to form a self-fluxing mixture. **1973** *Times* 12 Feb. (Anchor Project Suppl.) p. ii/5 To have constructed an integrated plant.. near the ore terminal would have entailed..the transport of a considerable amount of local ore in the reverse direction (or the loss of 'selffluxing' economies).

self-forgetful, *a.* Add: (Earlier and later examples.)

1848 J. G. WHITTIER *Pæan* in *Poet. Works* (1898) 336/1 They died, their brave hearts breaking slow, But self-forgetful to the last..Their breath upon the darkness passed. **1981** F. INGLIS *Promise of Happiness* I. ii. 37 Many arts and crafts..offer an occasion for self-forgetful joy and peace.

self-forgetfulness (earlier and later examples).

1805–6 WORDSWORTH *Prelude* (1959) IV. 294 The quiet stream Of self-forgetfulness. **1942** C. S. LEWIS *Screwtape Lett.* xiv. 72 Let him think of it not as self-forgetfulness but as a certain kind of opinion..of his own talents and character.

self-fulfi·lling, *ppl. a.* orig. *Social Sci.* [SELF- 1 f.] In phr. *self-fulfilling prophecy*: a prophecy or prediction which gives rise to actions that bring about its fulfilment (see quot. 1949).

1949 R. K. MERTON *Soc. Theory & Soc. Structure* vii. 181 The self-fulfilling prophecy is, in the beginning, a *false* definition of the situation evoking a new behavior which makes the originally false conception come *true*. **1962** BLAKE & MOUTON in M. Sherif *Intergroup Rel.* v. 113 Another dynamic, the self-fulfilling prophecy, also operates to cause one to misplace motivation. **1973** *Times* 7 Dec. 18/8 Panic buying of spirits..caused largely by forecasts of the shortage—a self-fulfilling prophecy. **1979** D. GURR *Troika* ix. 60 '*Wonderful*..to meet again. Didn't I tell you that we should? *Vodka!*'.. 'A self-fulfilling prophecy, Alexey Ilyich.'

self-given, *a.* For † *Obs.* read *rare* and add later examples.

1909 R. KANE *Sermon of Sea* viii. 120 This object of intuitive consciousness must have its moral kind, its spiritual character, its self-given growth in evil or in good. **1934** T. S. ELIOT *Rock* ii. 84 Those who prize the serpent's golden eyes, The worshippers, self-given sacrifice of the snake.

self-glorification. (Earlier and later examples.)

1838 J. S. MILL in *Westm. Rev.* Apr. 37 Those antique characters which, without self-glorification or hope of being appreciated, 'carry out..the sentiment of duty to its extremest consequences'. **1953** *Encounter* Oct. 49/1 It was..only Stalin who was thus hymned in the inevitable major key of Soviet self-glorification.

self-governed, *ppl. a.* Add: **2.** (Earlier and further examples.)

1709 SHAFTESBURY *Moralists* II. 150, I suppose you will send your Disciple to seek for Deity in Mechanism; that is to say, in some exquisite System of self-govern'd Matter. **1848** J. S. MILL *Pol. Econ.* II. IV. vii. 320 They will require that their conduct and condition shall be essentially self-governed. **1859** J. BROWN *Let.* 19 Aug. (1912) 171 Frankfort is a little Republic, self-governed, and a thriving, handsome, well-conditioned town.

self-governing *ppl. a.* (earlier and later examples).

1845 J. S. MILL in *Edin. Rev.* LXXXI. 511 For two centuries, the Scottish peasant..has been a reflecting, an observing, and therefore naturally a self-governing, a moral and a successful human being. **1933** *Discovery* Feb. 68/1 The greatest problem facing British Statesmen of modern times—the problem of transforming that India, in which society is organized on a religious basis, into a self-governing community on modern democratic lines. **1976** *Glasgow Herald* 26 Nov. 6/6 What business man in his right mind would prefer minimum lending rate of 14½% to one in the 5–7% range which a self-governing Scotland would..achieve.

self-gravita·tion. *Astr.* [SELF- 3 a.] The gravitational forces acting among the components of a massive body.

1962 K. H. PRENDERGAST in L. Woltjer *Distribution & Motion Interstellar Matter* 233 In our own galaxy, if you consider the terms in the equations of motion, other than the gravitational field of all the matter, then there are three: the random velocities, some sort of ordered magnetic field, and the self-gravitation of the gas. **1968** R. A. LYTTLETON *Mysteries Solar Syst.* i. 36 Self-gravitation within the disk can far exceed the solar disruptive effect. **1977** *Dædalus* Summer 36 Roughly speaking we can attribute this change from Newtonian theory to the greater self-gravitation which matter possesses according to general relativity.

Hence **self-gravita·tional** *a.*; **self-gra·vitating** *ppl. a.*, influenced by self-gravitation; **self-gra·vity**, self-gravitation.

1962 P. O. LINDBLAD in L. Woltjer *Distribution & Motion Interstellar Matter* 223 A massive ring in a central force field..can carry two different kinds of bisymmetrical waves by self-gravitational action. **1962** G. B. FIELD in *Ibid.* 318 Is the system a self-gravitating one in the sense that the gas acts on the gas, or is it not? **1972** *Sci. Amer.* Apr. 43/2 The restoring forces that limit the height of the tides are due to the planet's elasticity and self-gravity. **1976** *Nature* 11 Nov. 114/1 Ultimately, self-gravity must drive the enormous contractions which convert diffuse gas into new stars. **1979** *New Scientist* 3 May 424/2 A self-gravitating mass of gas, cohering under its self-attraction, would adopt spherical symmetry.

self-hate. [SELF- 1 d.] = next.

1947 F. FRENAYE tr. *C. Levi's Christ stopped at Eboli* (1948) iv. 28 To the hates of the gentry he added self-hate. **1951** K. HORNEY *Neurosis & Human Growth* v. 110 Pride and self-hate are actually one entity. **1979** R. BLYTHE *View in Winter* ix. 289 Creeping indifference is a large factor in the self-hate of the aged.

self-ha·tred. [SELF- 1 d.] Hatred of oneself, esp. of one's actual self when contrasted with one's imagined self. Cf. prec.

1865 D. G. ROSSETTI *Let.* 21 Nov. (1965) II. 581 Ambition, i.e. the feeling of pure rage and self-hatred when any one else does better than you do. **1896** A. THOROLD tr. *Dialogue of St. Catherine of Siena* lxiii. 134 Digging up the root of self-love, with the knife of self-hatred and the love of virtue. **1942** C. S. LEWIS *Screwtape Lett.* xiv. 72 All the abjection and self-hatred are designed, in the long run, solely for this end. **1975** G. ST. GEORGE *Proteus Pact* (1976) iii. 95 He descended vertiginously into utter self-loathing..paralyzed by..self-hatred.

self-hea·ting, *vbl. sb.* (*ppl. a.*) [SELF- 1 b, f, 4.] The action of becoming heated spontaneously or automatically. Also as *ppl. a.*, that is designed to heat itself automatically; (of food) held in a self-heating container.

1929 *Chem. Abstr.* XXIII. 1561 The effect..of self-heating of metals after previous chilling is attributed here to establishment of equil[ibrium] in a metastable system. **1952** KOESTLER *Arrow in Blue* v. xxxii. 272 Some new 'colossal' project like the radioactive soap or the self-heating bricks. **1959** P. CAPON *Amongst Those Missing* 23 They found several battered cans of self-heating soup. *Ibid.* 24 The fuses on the self-heating cans did not burn too well. **1961** *Guardian* 29 May 2/3 Tins of self-heating cocoa fell from their appointed places into the bilges. **1965** PHILLIPS & WILLIAMS *Inorg. Chem.* I. xvi. 576 As a result of self-heating effects, polonium and polonium compounds are always at temperatures markedly above their surroundings. **1981** J. R. L. ANDERSON *Death at High Latitude* ix. 135, I opened three more cans of our self-heating soup, the only means we had of getting a hot drink.

self-help. Add: Also **self-he·lper.**

1891 G. B. SHAW *Quintessence of Ibsenism* ii. 34 No one ever feels helpless by the side of the self-helper. **1976** W. GOLDMAN *Magic* III. vii. 165 'How come you have all these same kind of books?'.. 'That's my self-help collection. I'm an addict.'.. 'Why're you such a self-helper?'

self-he·terodyne, *a. Radio.* [SELF- 1 e.] Being or employing a heterodyne receiver in which the same valve is used for the generation and rectification of local oscillations. Hence **self-he·terodyning** *ppl. a.* and *vbl. sb.*

1918 [see *AUTODYNE]. **1922** *Proc. IRE* X. 245 In the various forms of self-heterodyne circuits a free oscillation of constant amplitude is maintained in the system and the circuit may be considered as having zero resistance, but only for that particular amplitude of current. **1929** DUNCAN & DREW *Radio Telegr. & Teleph.* xii. 344 The circuit is commonly known as a self-heterodyning detector because the tube functions both as an oscillator and detector. *Ibid.* 351 (*heading*) The phenomenon of self-heterodyning.

self-hypno·sis. *Psychol.* [SELF- 1 a, d.] = *autohypnosis* s.v. *AUTO-[1] a. Also **self-hy·pnotism, -hypnotiza·tion, -hy·pnotized** *ppl. a.*, **-hy·pnotizer.**

1852 J. BRAID *Magic* 20, I stated that I had found in the writings.., 'many statements corroborative of the fact, that the eastern saints are all self-hypnotizers.' *Ibid.* 108 Special gifts imparted to them in token of the great superiority of their religious system, of inducing a state of self-hypnotism, or ecstatic trance. **1891** G. C. KINGSBURY *Practice Hypnotic Suggestion* vi. 91 It would be.. interesting..to try if suggestions written out by ourselves, and used as the object of our fixed gaze for the purpose of self-hypnotization, would have any after influence. **1902** H. B. WOOLSTON in *Amer. Jrnl. Psychol* XIII. 71 This sort of self-hypnosis may lead even to an identification of the individual with the ideal form that absorbs his mind. **1925** A. S. M. HUTCHINSON *One Increasing Purpose* III. xvi. 333 He..gazed up, up, into cloudless perfect blue until, selfhypnotised, he seemed to himself to be rising up there. **1939** G. GREENE *Lawless Roads* x. 252 He had listened to the pilgrims' tales. It couldn't be self-hypnotism. **1959** *House & Garden* July 32/1 The wondrous and covetable gift of self-hypnotism. **1960** *Times* 11 Feb. 13/2 He [*sc.* McCarthy] was not a self-hypnotized genius of hate like Hitler. **1976** M. V. KLINE in E. Dengrove *Hypnosis & Behav. Therapy* x. 139 The use of self hypnosis and..of audio tape recordings.

self-identifica·tion. [SELF- 1 a.] Identification with something outside oneself.

1941 *Manch. Guardian Weekly* 14 Mar. 214/3 Are we to sympathise with the young? Certainly... But need this be called 'Self-identification with the experience, interests, and problems of other young people?' **1959** *Twentieth Cent.* June 629 The great admiration which James.. felt for the work of Sainte-Beuve..in many ways a matter of self-identification. **1973** C. SAGAN *Cosmic Connection* (1975) i. 6 There is a serious question whether such a global self-identification of mankind can be achieved before we destroy ourselves with the technological forces our intelligence has unleashed.

Hence **self-ide·ntifying** *ppl. a.*

1963 N. FRYE *Romanticism Reconsidered* 14 The self-identifying admiration which so many Romantics expressed for Napoleon. **1976** H. WILSON *Governance of Britain* iv. 92 His post-box will include hundreds of letters a week from self-identifying officials or members of local organizations of his party.

self-i·mage. [SELF- 1 d.] An image or conception of oneself, esp. considered in relation to others.

1939 S. SPENDER *Still Centre* 101 The self-image Lifted in light against the lens Stares back with my dumb wall of eyes. **1951** M. MCLUHAN *Mech. Bride* (1967) 66/1 She embodies that self-image of a knight in shining armor. **1969** C. FREMLIN *Possession* xiv. 117 The way into these cloying, stagnant emotional pools is smooth... You come out..with your self-image in shreds. **1977** *Church Times* 14 Jan. 10 It stresses..the Vatican's self-image as the centre of Christian prayer and charity and of work for justice and peace.

self-important, *a.* Add: So **self-impor·tantly** *adv.*

1961 in WEBSTER. **1977** T. HEALD *Just Desserts* vi. 134 A police sergeant who arrived self-importantly. **1981** *London Rev. Bks.* 19 Nov.–2 Dec. 7/1 Marilyn Butler..is importantly and not self-importantly a citizen of the world.

self-incompa·tible, *a.* and *sb. Bot.* [SELF- 3 b.] **A.** *adj.* Unable to be fertilized by means of its own pollen. **B.** *sb.* A self-incompatible plant or species. Opp. *SELF-COMPATIBLE *a.* and *sb.*

1922 *Bot. Gaz.* LXXIII. 119 Plants may be completely self-incompatible throughout. **1938** CRANE & LAWRENCE *Genetics of Garden Plants* ix. 188 Self-compatibles crossed with self-incompatibles will give both self-compatibles and self-incompatibles in the proportion 1:1 or 2:1 according to the constitution of the self-incompatible plants used. **1944** *Nature* 5 Aug. 164/2 The nuclear and cytoplasmic systems of self-incompatible plants are mutually and constructively related. **1968** *Times* 23 May 17/5 In some species more individuals are self-incompatible than in others. **1979** *Nature* 25 Oct. 671/2 This species is self-incompatible.

So **self-incompatibi·lity.**

1917 *Genetics* II. 506 The words self-incompatibility and self-impotence have been substituted for self-sterility by various writers. **1952** *Heredity* VI. 286 The primary function of self-incompatibility is the avoidance of self-fertilisation. **1970** *Watsonia* VIII. 142 The failure of fruit production following self-pollination results from self-incompatibility rather than sterility.

self-induced, *pa. pple.* and *ppl. a.* Add: **2.** *gen.* Induced by oneself or itself.

1949 WELLEK & WARREN *Theory of Lit.* iii. 21 What it articulates is superior to their own self-induced reverie or reflection. **1954** G. I. M. SWYER *Reprod. & Sex* 246 This often happens in clumsy attempts at self-induced criminal abortion. **1981** J. BRABAZON *Dorothy L. Sayers* xx. 267 The pressures on Patrick McLaughlin, some of them self-induced.

self-induction. Add: (Earlier and later examples.) Also, the coefficient of self-induction.

1865 J. C. MAXWELL in *Phil. Trans. R. Soc.* CLV. 472 The equation of the current x in a circuit whose resistance is R, and whose coefficient of self-induction is L, acted on by an external electromotive force ξ, is $\xi - Rx = d(Lx)/dt$. *Ibid.* 475 Hence the effect..is to increase the apparent resistance and diminish the apparent self-induction of the circuit. **1902** *Encycl. Brit.* XXVIII. 56/1 The circuit in the jar C is provided with a sliding piece, F, by means of which the self-induction of the discharging circuit..can be adjusted. **1958** CONDON & ODISHAW *Handbk. Physics* IV. i. 17/1 If the current in the circuit increases for any reason, the flux through the circuit must also increase, and this gives rise to an emf of self-induction which acts to oppose the increase in the current by Lenz's law.

self-instructed, *ppl. a.* (Example.)

1833 J. S. MILL in *Tait's Mag.* III. 348 Narrowness and self-conceit..are the..failings of the self-instructed.

self-insu·rance. [SELF- 1 a.] Insurance of oneself or one's interests by maintaining a fund to cover possible losses. Hence **self-insu·rer, -insu·ring; self-insu·red.**

1905 *Ann. Amer. Acad. Polit. & Social Sci.* XXVI. 452, I am informed by the managers and officers of the largest steamship lines that self-insurance is practiced extensively by their companies in one form or another. **1909** WEBSTER, Self-insurer. **1932** *Sun* (Baltimore) 8 Sept. 4/4 Self-insuring might be permitted to employers or industrial groups who can guarantee maintenance of a benefit system equal or superior to the standards of the State system. **1934** WEBSTER, Self-insured. **1972** *Accountant* 5 Oct. 422/1 Premiums..are tax-deductible... This is an important advantage for the self-insurer... The company with a poor loss record has most to gain from self-insurance.

self-ioniza·tion. *Chem.* [SELF- 1 a, d.] Spontaneous dissociation of a proportion of the molecules of a liquid into ions.

1931 *Chem. Rev.* VIII. 201 Bishop..used the hydrogen electrode for titrations in ethanol and emphasized the effect of the low self-ionization of the solvent on the titration curves. **1972** COTTON & WILKINSON *Adv. Inorg. Chem.* (ed. 3) v. 181 Pure H_2SO_4 shows extensive self-ionization resulting in high conductivity.

selfish, *a.* Add: **1. c.** *Genetics.* Of a gene or genetic material: tending to be perpetuated or to spread although of no effect on the phenotype.

1976 R. DAWKINS *Selfish Gene* i. 3 Let us understand what our own selfish genes are up to, because we may then at least have the chance to upset their designs. **1979** *Human Genetics* (Ciba Symp.) 41 It seems to me that repetitive DNA is the only true selfish gene. **1981** *Nature* 13 Aug. 648/1 Selfish DNA, which contains no genetic information but which is perpetuated in eukaryote genomes, has attracted a lot of attention recently.

self-limitation. 1. (Earlier example).

1847 J. D. MORELL *Hist. View Philos.* (ed. 2) II. v. 105 The idea of the objective arises from the self-limitation of our own free activity.

self-limiting, *ppl. a.* Add: *spec.* in *Med.* = SELF-LIMITED *ppl. a.* 2.

1954 S. DUKE-ELDER *Parsons' Dis. Eye* (ed. 12) x. 125 The factor dominating the prognosis..is the recurrence of relapses on its cessation unless the malady is eradicable or self-limiting. **1965** J. POLLITT *Depression & its Treatment* v. 71 Premenstrual depression is a short-lived, self-limiting depressive illness. **1977** *Lancet* 19 Mar. 648/2 Whooping-cough is a self-limiting infection which should never be fatal with proper medical care.

self-li·quidating, *ppl. a. Comm.* (orig. *U.S.*). [SELF- 1 f.] Of, pertaining to, or designating credit, or a loan, that repays itself with the money accruing within a certain period after its investment. Also of a premium similarly offered.

1915 *U.S. Fed. Reserve Board 1st Ann. Rep. 1914* 9 It is recommended that the Federal Reserve Banks confine themselves strictly to dealing in short-term, self-liquidating paper growing out of commercial, industrial, and agricultural operations. **1928** *Burroughs Clearing House* May 32/3 If the purpose is a constructive one, stimulating production and of a self-liquidating character..then the loan should be made. **1939** *Construction & Financing of Self-Liquidating Projects* (U.S. Congr. House Comm. on Banking & Currency) 2 In view of this splendid repayment record there can be little doubt that the tenancy program has been established on a sound, self-liquidating basis. **1942** W. B. TAYLOR *Financial Policies of Bus. Enterprise* IV. xiii. 288 Short-term loans, commonly made for less than a year, are usually self-liquidating and hence not adapted to the raising of fixed capital. **1967** *Economist* 10 June p. xxxi/2 The traditional role of providing short term, self-liquidating trade finance to a nation of shopkeepers is too narrow. **1971** R. L. WILLSMER *Directing Marketing Effort* II. xviii. 292 A self-liquidating premium looks good because it theoretically costs nothing.

Also **self-li·quidator,** a self-liquidating premium.

1944 *Premium Practice* Mar. 8/2 Mr. Cahill mentioned the following: (a) self-liquidators. **1948** *Ibid.* Oct. 30/1 The juvenile field was once the objective of the self-liquidator. Now it is the adult thing. **1962** G. MEREDITH *Effective Merchandising with Premiums* II. iv. 37 It would be impossible to identify one promotion as the beginning of modern self-liquidator practice. **1970** R. WILLSMER in G. Wills *New Ideas in Retail Managem.* xii. 170 Self-liquidating premium offers continue to lead the field... Only eight store-promoted self-liquidators were recorded.

self-liquida·tion. [SELF- 1 a.] **1.** *Comm.* (orig. *U.S.*). The action or process of repaying a self-liquidating loan. Cf. *SELF-LIQUIDATING *ppl. a.*

1932 *Burroughs Clearing House* Mar. 23/1 The idea of self-liquidation, of having a definite source of repayment in sight, of inquiring into the purpose of the loan with a view to finding out how far the money is to be sunk in fixed assets, all these relate to the liquidity of loans. **1949** H. V. PROCHNOW *Term Loans & Theories of Bank Liquidity* i. 5 The belief that commercial banks..should extend credit only for short periods and for purposes which result in the self-liquidation of the credit. **1951** *Banco Nazionale del Lavoro Q. Rev.* July–Sept. 135/2 In the last few decades the theory of 'self-liquidation' has been gradually set aside and replaced by the 'shiftability theory'.

2. The destruction or elimination of oneself by oneself. Also *fig.* Cf. *LIQUIDATION 3 b.

1949 KOESTLER *Promise & Fulfilment* II. iv. 253 This difference..was demonstrated by Irgun's voluntary self-liquidation..as opposed to the Stern Group's persistence in terrorism. **1964** I. L. HOROWITZ *New Sociology* 17 The recent work in some quarters..seems to point precisely in the direction of the self-liquidation of sociology. **1977** *Canadian Jrnl. Sociology* II. 106 The inevitable self-liquidation of science is another way of speaking of science's tie to life.

se·lf-loop. [SELF- 3 a.] In a graph or network, a line that returns to the node it leaves.

1964 S. E. SALMAGHRABY in *Managem. Sci.* X. 499 We shall reserve the terms 'self-loop' to designate a branch that leads from a node to itself. **1980** *Sci. Amer.* Mar. 18/1 In graph theory a graph is defined as any set of points joined by lines, and a simple graph is defined as one that has no self-loops (lines that join a point to itself) and no parallel lines (two or more lines joining the same pair of points).

self-made, *ppl. a.* Add: *self-made man* (earlier examples).

1832 *Reg. Deb. Congr. U.S.* 2 Feb. 277 In Kentucky,.. every manufactory..is in the hands of enterprising self-made men. **1854** DICKENS *Hard Times* I. iv. 18 Mr. Bounderby..could never sufficiently vaunt himself a self-made man.

self-mai·ling, *a. U.S.* [SELF- 1 f.] Designating postal matter that may be folded or otherwise secured, and sent by post without enclosure in an envelope. Also **self-mai·ler.**

1950 *Self-mailer, -mailing* in WEBSTER Add. **1963** *Publishers' Weekly* 2 Sept. 28/1 Two types of mailing pieces have been prepared for the book trade: a self-mailer and a statement enclosure. For the self-mailer, which is a full-color, four-piece unit, the print order is 650,000.

self-maintai·ning, *ppl. a.* [SELF- 1 f.] That maintains or sustains itself or (oneself); *spec.* = *HOMŒOSTATIC *a.*

1879 [see *race-maintaining* s.v. RACE *sb.*[2] 11]. **1890** W. JAMES *Princ. Psychol.* II. xxvi. 582 If this were the entire nervous mechanism, the movement, once begun, would be self-maintaining. **1933** *Mind* XLII. 146 Immortality demands self-maintaining effort and formed character. **1959** G. D. MITCHELL *Sociol.* vi. 101 It can thus be seen that witchcraft as a system of beliefs and practices is self-maintaining. **1971** J. Z. YOUNG *Introd. Study Man* viii. 115 The whole mass constitutes one single self-maintaining system.

Also **self-mai·ntenance.**

1867 H. SPENCER *Princ. Biol.* II. VI. ix. 454 Increased cost of self-maintenance entailed decreased power of propagation. **1909** W. JAMES *Pluralistic Universe* iii. 121 The problem of understanding how the complete coherence of all things in the absolute should involve as a necessary moment in its self-maintenance the self-assertion of the finite minds. **1942** *R.A.F. Jrnl.* 13 June 18 Every man has to know something about cooking as a part of his self-maintenance in the field. **1971** J. Z. YOUNG *Introd. Study Man* xi. 143 Continuous replacement is the absolutely necessary condition of self-maintenance.

self-ma·ss. *Physics.* [SELF- 5 b.] The mass of a particle arising relativistically from its self-energy.

1955 O. KLEIN in W. Pauli *Niels Bohr* 112 Since we are neglecting the interaction between electrons and electromagnetic fields the question of the self-mass does not appear. **1977** *Dædalus* Fall 27 Thus the electron mass found in tables of physical data..would have to be identified with the bare mass *plus* the infinite 'self mass', produced by the interaction of the electron with its own virtual photon cloud.

self-mate, *sb.* (Earlier example.)

1867 *Chess Player's Mag.* III. 45 The self-mate, though not difficult, is very prettily conceived.

self-medica·tion. [SELF- 1 a.] Medication carried out on oneself.

1942 *Horizon* June 371 *Le vice anglais* is most certainly and typically self-medication. **1961** *New Scientist* 5 Jan. 16/3 In spite of the National Health Service British pharmacists continue to sell large quantities of preparations for self-medication.

self-mo·tivated, *ppl. a.* [SELF- 2.] Motivated by oneself; *spec.* stimulated to work by one's own enthusiasm and ambition. Also **self-mo·tivating** *ppl. a.*; **self-motiva·tion.**

1973 *Daily Tel.* 27 July 13 (Advt.), Applicants should be..self-motivating, enthusiastic and determined to succeed. **1974** *Spartanburg* (S. Carolina) *Herald Jrnl.* 20 Apr. B5/1 Secretary. Must be good typist, have good personality and be self-motivated. **1978** *Detroit Free Press* 16 Apr. F6/6 (Advt.), Nationwide meat wholesaler looking for self-motivated people. **1980** *West Lancs. Evening Gaz.* 6 Nov. 15 (Advt.), If you're over 21 with a car and possess the self-motivation and determination to succeed [etc.].

self-movement. (Earlier example.)

1883 F. H. BRADLEY *Princ. Logic* 448 Want of individuality in the *datum* that we began with, absence of self-movement and impossibility of self-development, this is the first defect.

self-no·ise. [SELF- 5 b.] Noise generated directly by a particular object.

1953 *Jrnl. Acoustical Soc. Amer.* XXV. 314/2 The self-noise characteristics of this [wind]screen were measured at two wind speeds as a function of the frequency. **1954** L. L. BERANEK *Acoustics* vi. 174 The self-noise produced by an electrostatic microphone is that produced by the d-c resistance of the crystal or dielectric shunted by the capacitance. **1960** *McGraw-Hill Encycl. Sci. & Technol.* XII. 504/1 Self-noise increases rapidly with the speed of the ship. **1975** D. G. FINK *Electronics Engineers' Handbk.* xxv. 125 Self-noise has many directional characteristics..; ambient noise generally has an omni-directional distribution.

self-noughting. Also **-naughting.** [SELF- 1 b.] Depreciation or effacement of oneself, as manifested in the lives of saints and mystics. (Probably derived by E. Underhill from Hilton's *Scale of Perfection*: see quot. *a* 1400 s.v. NOUGHTING *vbl. sb.*)

1911 E. UNDERHILL *Mysticism* ix. 477 The 'self-naughting' or 'purification of the will', which here takes place, is the struggle to resolve that disharmony. **1937** *Mind* XLVI. 91 We remember what has been written by writers such as those cited above about self-surrender, submission and self-noughting or annihilation. **1959** *Month* Dec. 331 This is the true self-noughting, to know meself incapable of any good. **1976** H. A. WILLIAMS *Tensions* v. 89 Through this discovery of our true identity in God and the self-naughting which inevitably accompanies it, we become truly ourselves.

self-observation. [SELF- 1 a.] Objective observation of one's attitudes, reactions, or thought processes.

1832 J. S. MILL in *Monthly Repos.* VI. 652 The knowledge of supersensual things, of man's mental and moral nature, where the appeal is to internal consciousness and self-observation. **1865** —— *Comte* 63 It is clear to him that we can learn very little about the feelings, and nothing at all about the intellect, by self-observation. **1948** *Mind* LVII. 511 [Social scientists]..making use of ..official statistics.., interviews of various types.., and new techniques of self-observation. **1977** METTEE & SMITH in Suls & Miller *Social Comparison Processes* iv. 98 A theory..based on self-observation of one's own behavior rather than on observation and comparison with.. others.

self-orienta·tion. [SELF- 1 a.] **1.** The orientation or directing of one's actions or attitudes for oneself or by oneself.

a **1896** G. DU MAURIER *Martian* (1897) vi. 250 The feeling of self-orientation which was so necessary to him. **1936** WIRTH & SHILS tr. *Mannheim's Ideol. & Utopia* i. 22 To the extent that mechanistic psychology and..the social impulsion towards all-embracing mechanization, negated these values, they destroyed an important element in the self-orientation of human beings in their everyday life.

2. *Social Psychol.* Underlying motivation that orients one's behaviour primarily towards what concerns oneself.

1951 PARSONS & SHILS *Toward Gen. Theory of Action* i. 77 We maintain that there are only five basic pattern variables... They are..2. Self-orientation—Collective orientation. **1964** GOULD & KOLB *Dict. Soc. Sci.* 489/1 In applying the moral mode of value-orientation, the actor must choose between action for private goals (self-orientation) and action on behalf of collective goals (collectivity-orientation).

Also **self-o·riented** *ppl. a.*

1936 *Mind* XLV. 72 Mr Leon holds, with Butler if not with Plato, that all the natural appetites, though self-oriented, are in themselves innocent. **1975** R. H. RIMMER *Premar Experiments* (1976) i. 49 At first the child is completely self-oriented, autistic, hedonistic.

self-oscilla·tion. *Electronics.* [SELF- 3 b.] The generation of continuous oscillations in a circuit, amplifier, etc., in circumstances of excessive positive feedback.

1921 J. SCOTT-TAGGART *Thermionic Tubes* vi. 204 The potentiometer..if suitably adjusted, will effectually prevent self-oscillation. **1943** K. R. STURLEY *Radio Receiver Design* I. viii. 394 As the coupling between anode circuit and input is increased a point is reached where self-oscillation occurs. **1963** B. FOZARD *Instrumentation Nuclear Reactors* x. 118 Feedback may be defined as positive, in which case it produces an increase in gain and may lead to instability and self-oscillation.

Hence **self-o·scillate** *v. intr.*, to display self-oscillation; **self-o·scillating** *ppl. a.*

1928 L. S. PALMER *Wireless Princ. & Pract.* ix. 328 Similar trouble arises when unstable receiving circuits self-oscillate accidentally. **1962** SIMPSON & RICHARDS *Physical Princ. Junction Transistors* xviii. 459 Such a circuit..is called a self-oscillating mixer or a frequency converter stage.

self-pity. Add: Also **self-pi·tying** *ppl. a.*

1754 RICHARDSON *Grandison* V. xxxiv. 217, I should have thought myself concerned,..to have expatiated on the self-pitying reflexion conveyed in these words. **1927** C. CONNOLLY *Let.* 1 Jan. in *Romantic Friendship* (1975) 205 Propertius too self-pitying and conceited really to suffer. *a* **1974** R. CROSSMAN *Diaries* (1976) II. 266 Over the weekend I'd been a bit self-pitying and not merely defeatist but defeated.

self-pleased, *ppl. a.* (Earlier example.)

1748 RICHARDSON *Clarissa* VI. lxxxvi. 311 How, self-pleased, she could smile round.

self-pollina·tion. [SELF- 1 a.] The deposi-

tion on a stigma of pollen from stamens within the same flower or another flower on the same plant.
1872 *Jrnl. Bot.* X. 25 Hildebrand has shown that sometimes, where at first sight self-pollenation [*sic*] (a better word, I think for '*Bestäubung*', than 'pollenization', suggested by Mr. Bennett) seems to be the intention of Nature, this is not followed by fertilization. **1876** [in Dict. s.v. SELF- 1 a]. **1974** A. HUXLEY *Plant & Planet* xiii. 124 A fail-safe device, such as..self-pollination as a last resort.

Hence **self-po·llinate** *v. trans.*; **self-po·llinated** *ppl. a.*, **-po·llinating** *vbl. sb.* and *ppl. a*; **self-po·llinator**, a species which commonly shows self-pollination.
1890 J. R. A. DAVIS *Flowering Plant* ix. 130 Regularly self-pollinated flowers are characterized by inconspicuousness. *Ibid.*, All this [*sc.* absence of scent and nectar, inconspicuousness, etc.] is carried to the extreme in cleistogamous flowers, i.e., minute self-pollinating ones, which never open. **1933** *Jrnl. R. Hort. Soc.* LVIII. 283 At first the trees were too young to yield reliable results by crossing and self-pollinating. *Ibid.* 358 Hips developed freely, but even in those which were self-pollinated rarely more than one achene was formed. **1960** *McGraw-Hill Encycl. Sci. & Technol.* VIII. 223/1 A second generation, bred by self-pollinating the hybrid. **1961** WEBSTER, Self-pollinator. **1977** *Nature* 2 June 402/2 It was suggested that some of the Mediterranean floras..evolved..from cross- into self-pollinators because insects could not have followed the new hardy plants into the hot dry environment. **1979** *Ibid.* 25 Oct. 671/2 This species is self-incompatible (1978 seed sets of self-pollinated flowers on five bagged plants compared with those of open-pollinated flowers on eight unbagged plants were 0.3 ± 0.08 (*n* = 256) compared with 7.1 ± 0.71 (*n* = 43)).

self-po·rtrait. [tr. G. *selbstbildnis, selbstporträt*; cf. SELF- 1 d.] A self-made portrait of oneself. Cf. PORTRAIT *sb.* 1 b and 3 b.
1831 *Fraser's Mag.* Mar. 129/1 The two self-portraits, so far as they are filled up, may be looked upon as real likenesses. **1896** *Academy* 25 Apr. 350/3 A self-portrait of the artist in the act of drawing. **1919** *Q. Rev.* Oct. 322 The high society of the 17th century had shown their taste for an analysis of this kind in their self-portraits. **1975** *Amer. N. & Q.* XIV. 58/2 G. C. Williamson, *English Conversation Pictures of the Eighteenth and Early Nineteenth Centuries*..provides a self-portrait of an era. **1977** R. L. WOLFF *Gains & Losses* vii. 413 As an authentic portrait (and self-portrait) of the late 1840's..*Oakfield* has no equal.

Also **self-po·rtraiture.**
1847 BAGEHOT in *Prospective Rev.* III. 532 Nor without the will can the self-scrutinizing power show to men those startling self-portraitures. **1979** *Dædalus* Summer 89 The self-portraiture is but the further elaboration of a thought that was from the outset oriented toward personal life.

self-possessed, *ppl. a.* (Earlier example.)
1818 SCOTT *Heart Midl.* I. vii. 228 He..came forward to meet him, with a self-possessed, and even dignified air.

selfquai·ned, *ppl. a. nonce-wd.* [SELF- 2; cf. *QUAIN *v.*²] Having natural angles or corners.
1888 G. M. HOPKINS *Poems* (1967) 199 A coffer, burly all of blocks Built of chancequarrièd, selfquainèd, hoarhuskèd rocks.

self-que·nching, *ppl. a.* (*vbl. sb.*) [SELF- 1 f, b.] Having within itself a cause of quenching. Also as *vbl. sb.*, quenching that occurs spontaneously. Also **self-que·nched** *ppl. a.*, self-quenching.
1936 *Rev. Sci. Instruments* VII. 31/1 When the discharge is self-quenched, the total charge passed through the counter is directly proportional to the primary ionization. **1940** *Physical Rev.* LVII. 1035/2 All counters are self-quenching if they overshoot, and if they do not, the inherent instability of the discharge will cause the discharge to be extinguished. **1946** *Ibid.* LXIX. 689/2 A study was made of the characteristics of self-quenched G-M counters filled with mixtures of argon and 28 different organic vapors. **1959** F. W. WILSON *Tool Engineer's Handbk.* (ed. 2) xv. 27 With extremely rapid heating rates and shallow heating, the mass of the part may conduct heat away fast enough to quench the part suitably. This is termed 'self-quenching'. **1963** B. FOZARD *Instrumentation Nuclear Reactors* v. 51 If bromine..is added to the neon–argon mixture, satisfactory operation as a self-quenching counter is achieved. **1970** D. L. HORROCKS in E. D. Bransome *Liquid Scintillation Counting* 36/2 Self-quenching seems to occur in molecules that have unprotected, coplanar chromophores so that there can be a complete mirror image overlap of the chromophores of the excited and unexcited solute molecules. **1971** *Gloss. Electrotechnical, Power Terms* (*B.S.I.*) III. i. 32 *Self-quenching oscillator*, a generator of short trains of oscillations, the trains being separated by intervals of quiescence caused by the accumulation of electric charge in a capacitor in the circuit.

self-raising, *ppl. a.* (Earlier example.)
1854 *Daily Placer Times & Transcript* (San Francisco) 7 Mar. 1/4 Among the advantages of the Self-Raising Flour, are: The saving of time in preparing it for the oven, [etc.].

self-ra·ting, *vbl. sb. Psychol.* [SELF- 1 b.] Rating of one's own attributes, feelings, or behaviour; an instance of this.
1938 G. W. ALLPORT *Personality* xvi. 444 In self-rating there is a tendency to overestimate those qualities considered desirable and to underestimate those considered undesirable. **1945** *Jrnl. Clin. Psychol.* I. 297/1 The second approach to verbal self-ratings..consists simply in the.. assertion that a 'self-rating' constitutes an intrinsically interesting and significant bit of verbal behavior. **1958** M. ARGYLE *Relig. Behaviour* x. 124–5 Several investigators have examined the factors associated with marital happiness or 'adjustment'—this being measured by means of self-ratings. **1972** *Jrnl. Social Psychol.* LXXXVI. 121 Some researchers have gone beyond this correlational approach to include self-ratings and peer ratings.

self-realization. (Earlier example.)
1874 W. WALLACE *Logic of Hegel* xxi. p. clx, This process..may be called self-realisation (or development).

self-re·ference. [SELF- 3 a.] Reference to oneself or itself; the direction of one's attention at oneself, esp. in forming a comparative assessment of one's characteristics or experience; *spec.* in *Philos.*, the characteristic or quality of referring to itself contained in certain paradoxes, propositions, or statements.
1910 WHITEHEAD & RUSSELL *Principia Math.* I. ii. 64 In all the above contradictions..there is a common characteristic, which we may describe as self-reference or reflexiveness. **1943** *Mind* LII. 20 Man is a microcosm of *Natura*, and his self-reference involves him therefore only in partial impotence. **1952** *Psychol. Abstr.* XXVI. 31/2 (*title*) The use of a new experimental autokinetic situation in the evaluation of self reference. **1960** E. H. GOMBRICH *Art & Illusion* vii. 239 The perplexing effect of this self-reference is very similar to the paradoxes beloved of philosophers. **1966** G. N. LEECH *Eng. in Advertising* viii. 81 Only in a few stereotyped contexts..is third person address and self-reference still used. **1978** M. HESSE in Hookway & Pettit *Action & Interpretation* 7 Self-reference of social theorising as part of its own subject matter. **1981** *Sci. Amer.* Apr. 6/2 One has only to watch the Muppets or Monty Python on television to see dense and intricate webs of self-reference.

Also **self-re·ferent, -refere·ntial (-ially** *adv.*) *adjs.*; **self-refe·rring.**
1943 *Mind* LII. 20 Man's power over..himself as he appears in the self-referent perspective. **1946** *Mind* LV. 65 If a theory is included in its own subject-matter, we say that it is a *self-referential* theory. *Ibid.* 67 Complete doubt of everything led to a self-referentially inconsistent view and so had to be abandoned. **1958** A. PAP *Semantics & Necessary Truth* ix. 263 The kind of self-referential proposition forbidden by the theory of types. **1969** *Mind* LXXVIII. 9 A partly self-referring sentence, such as art. 88 of the Danish constitution. **1979** *Sci. Amer.* Nov. 29/3 These irreducible questions tend, however, to be rather artificial and self-referent. **1980** *Times Lit. Suppl.* 5 Sept. 957/2 The self-referential and profoundly paradoxical late novels.

self-refe·rral. [SELF- 1 a.] The referring of oneself to an expert or (esp. medical) specialist for advice or treatment. Cf. *REFERRAL b.
1971 *New Society* 14 Jan. 65/1 Fewer of its clients died in the high-risk first year after self-referral. **1975** *Language for Life* (Dept. Educ. & Sci.) xix. 281 There was an immediate and large increase in the number of self-referrals. **1979** *Internat. Rehabilit. Med.* I. 75/2 Some of the outcome measures to which numbers can be applied are..responses to stress (e.g. self-referral to social services).

Also **self-refe·rred** *ppl. a.*
1960 *Cambr. Rev.* 7 May 506/2 'Self-referred' patients generally turn out to be at least as ill as those who are referred by their tutors or general practitioners.

self-reflexive, *a.* Delete † and add: Also, characterized by reflexive action on itself; containing a reflection or image of itself. (Later examples.)
1933 A. KORZYBSKI *Science & Sanity* xx. 323 All human 'knowledge' is structurally circular and self-reflexive, and so depends on some conscious or unconscious theory of knowledge and undefined terms. **1957** *Essays in Criticism* VII. 46 When everything is worked in to comprise part of a highly involute and self-reflexive symbolic pattern, there is just too much of it for poetry; it becomes mainly a complex intellectual parlour game. **1977** *Dædalus* Fall 105 The best way to illustrate the complex and self-reflexive progress of a semiotic enterprise is to consider what semiotics has done and promised to do for the study of the most complex of sign systems, literature. **1980** *San Francisco Bay Guardian* 16–23 Oct. 17/3 We all know about Vladimir Nabokov and self-reflexive writing.

So **self-refle·xiveness,** the quality or condition of being self-reflexive.
1933 A. KORZYBSKI *Science & Sanity* iv. 58 A word *is not* the object it represents; and languages exhibit also this peculiar self-reflexiveness, that we can analyse languages by linguistic means.

self-regulating, *ppl. a.* (Examples in non-technical use.)
1846 J. D. MORELL *Hist. Philos.* I. iv. 323 The human mind..is a spontaneous, self-regulating existence. **1975** *Listener* 11 Sept. 328/3 This new ideal of the self-regulating individual.

self-regulation. Add: *spec.* in *Biol.* = *HOMŒOSTASIS.
1912 J. S. HUXLEY *Individual in Animal Kingdom* i. 18 Protoplasm has primitively a great power of self-regulation. **1957** —— *Relig. without Revelation* (rev. ed.) ix. 215 There has been an enormous rise in level of harmonious organisation—think of a bird or a mammal as against a flatworm or a jellyfish; inflexibility and the capacity for self-regulation.

self-reinfo·rcement. *Psychol.* [SELF- 1 a.] The reinforcement or strengthening of one's own response to a stimulus or situation. Also *transf.* Also **self-reinfo·rcer; self-reinfo·rcing** *ppl. a.* Cf. *REINFORCEMENT 3 c.
1963 *Jrnl. Experim. Psychol.* LXVI. 245/1 This procedure [*sc.* switching on a light for oneself] was called self-reinforcement. *Ibid.*, The frequency and accuracy of self-reinforcing responses..increased with more learning. **1973** *Jrnl. Genet. Psychol.* Sept. 86 Generally self-reinforcement studies have not attempted to deal with the classroom learning situation. **1977** P. F. SECORD in T. Mischel *Self* ix. 261 Positive self-reinforcers are seen as increasing the frequency of desirable behavior, and aversive self-reinforcers are thought to reduce undesirable behavior. **1979** *Sci. Amer.* Sept. 52/1 The process is self-reinforcing: the flow of sodium ions through the membrane opens more channels and makes it easier for other ions to follow.

self-reliance. (Earlier example.)
1833 J. S. MILL *Let.* 25 Nov. in *Works* (1963) XII. 195 Combining perfect self-reliance with the most unaffected modesty.

self-repo·rt. *Psychol.* [SELF- 3 a.] A report about oneself or aspects of one's behaviour made by oneself. Freq. *attrib.*
1970 *Jrnl. Gen. Psychol.* Oct. 169 Self-report statements of awareness are influenced by the same independent variables as other verbal behaviors. **1972** *Jrnl. Social Psychol.* LXXXVI. 124 The LSQ was designed to elicit a self-report of actual behaviour. **1977** J. D. DOUGLAS in Douglas & Johnson *Existential Sociol.* 305 My theoretical variables..could not be directly related to the experience of the people killing themselves by anything except my own imagination and a few snatches of self-report data.

self-reproach. (Earlier example.)
1754 RICHARDSON *Grandison* III. 3 Dear Miss Grandison, don't give me cause for self-reproach.

self-rescuer. *Coal-mining.* [SELF- 1 c.] A safety device carried by coal-miners to give protection against noxious gases (see quot. 1977).
1961 in WEBSTER. **1962** *Guardian* 31 Oct. 5/5 A new safety apparatus known as a 'self-rescuer', which gives a miner 30 minutes to reach a fresh-air area. **1977** *Guardian Weekly* 4 Dec. 19/3 Both the lamp..and the self-rescuer (a steel box containing a mask to refine dangerous gases, also hung from the waist) were heavy. **1979** *Daily Tel.* 13 July 6/8 The miners also carry safety equipment called a 'self-rescuer' and have automatic gas detectors.

self-revealed, *ppl. a.* (Examples.)
1923 J. W. HARVEY tr. *Otto's Idea of Holy* xx. 175 For the abyss between creature and Creator.., sin and holiness, is..increased by that deeper knowledge that comes from the Gospel of Christ: and, as a result of the emotion ..stirred in the recognition of it, that in which 'the holy' stands self-revealed is taken here..both as the refuge from, and the means by which to approach, Holiness. **1978** *Church Times* 11 Aug. 6/3 Barth's God is God self-revealed not as a doormat but as Father, Son and Spirit.

self-reve·rsal. [SELF- 3 b.] **1.** Reversal (of motion) by agency of the mover itself.
1886 R. WORMELL *Electr. in Service of Man* 61 This [induction] machine is exceedingly powerful in favourable weather, but has an important defect, in a tendency to self-reversal, which is apt to occur at a stoppage.

2. *Physics.* The darkening of the middle of a bright spectral line as a result of radiation emitted by a hot gas being partly reabsorbed as it passes through parts of the gas that are cooler.
1905 E. C. C. BALY *Spectroscopy* xii. 384 The lines generally were sharper than in the case of the arc in air,.. and there were fewer self-reversals. **1934** H. E. WHITE *Introd. Atomic Spectra* xiv. 250 The centers of the potassium-doublet, the calcium-singlet, and the copper-doublet lines show self-reversal due to absorption. **1977** A. CORNEY *Atomic & Laser Spectrosc.* x. 313 Systematic errors are difficult to avoid in these experiments since the profile..is usually considerably distorted by self absorption or even self reversal.

3. *Geol.* The postulated reversal of the magnetization of some rocks by intrinsic means, rather than by reversal of the Earth's magnetic field (see quot. 1971).
1952 T. NAGATA et al. in *Jrnl. Geomagnetism & Geoelectr.* IV. 22 An experimental proof of self-reversal of thermo-remanent magnetism of igneous rocks is obtained. **1971** *Nature* 5 Feb. 378/1 At this point [*sc.* the early 1950s] an alternative to field reversal began to receive serious consideration. This was self-reversal, the possibility that some rocks possessed an intrinsic property whereby they could acquire a magnetization antiparallel to the ambient field, or whereby an originally parallel magnetization could reverse spontaneously.

self-rising, *ppl. a. U.S.* [SELF- 3 b.] = SELF-RAISING *ppl. a.*
1865 *Chicago Tribune* 10 Apr. 1/6 Rogers' Self Rising Flour. The best, cheapest and most convenient Flour. **1930** *Randolph* (W. Va.) *Enterprise* 20 Nov. 4/3 Girls love

to make 'skillet biscuits' with a self-rising flour when out camping. **1976** *Encycl. Brit. Micropædia* IV. 195/1 The wide variety of wheat flours generally available includes.. self-rising flour, refined and bleached with added leavening and salt.

self-satisfaction. (Earlier example.)
1739 Hume *Treat. Hum. Nature* II. I. 32 We are not much satisfy'd with the thing itself; and are still less apt to feel any new degrees of self-satisfaction upon its account.

self-sea·ling, *ppl. a.* [Self- 4.] Becoming gas- or liquid-tight automatically; used esp. of a type of fuel tank.
1895 *Montgomery Ward Catal.* Spring & Summer 545/3 Owing to frequent inquiries for a self-sealing jar..we decided to purchase the Globe Glass Top Jar. **1920** *Flight* XII. 605/2 A tank of his design was dropped from a height of approximately 400 ft... Although badly battered and bent, it is stated that no leakage of petrol occurred. The tank is a metal one and designed to be self-sealing. **1978** R. V. Jones *Most Secret War* x. 78 The single bomber that we had shot down was found to have self-sealing tanks.

self-seeker. Add: **2.** A push-button device on a radio for automatic tuning to the desired station. Cf. *self-seeking *ppl. a.* 2.
1960 *News Chron.* 22 Apr. 11/3 If the programme displeases you, press the button again and the self-seeker will move on to the next station.

self-seeking, *ppl. a.* Add: **2.** Of a radio: fitted with a self-seeker (sense *2).
1972 *Times* 14 Sept. 31/8 At 90 mph it is still quiet enough to enjoy the self-seeking radio. **1976** *Drive* Jan.–Feb. 82/2 Electric quarter lights, self-seeking radio with automatic electric aerial, two cigarette lighters.

self-se·rvice. [Self- 1 a.] **1.** A system whereby customers in a shop, restaurant, etc., serve themselves instead of being attended to or waited on by the staff, usu. paying for all purchases in one place. Also, an establishment or department where this system obtains.
1919 *Ladies' Home Jrnl.* Jan. 65/2 The Duffy-Powers Company, operating a full-fledged department store in Rochester, New York, inaugurated self-service—that is, the customers, not the store, provide the service—in its grocery department. **1928** *Daily Mail* 7 Aug. 3/3 This same principle of self-service has..been successfully applied to food shops. **1944** M. Paneth *Branch Street* 6 The outing ended in a 'Lyons' with 'self service'. **1952** *Economist* 29 Nov. 636/1 Food shops..may soon be turning over to self-service. **1961** *Listener* 7 Dec. 983/1 Big stores, self-services, cinemas losing business. **1962** H. O. Beecheno *Introd. Bus. Stud.* xi. 101 Self-service is..a very suitable form of retailing for pre-weighed or measured, pre-packed goods which the customer can select for himself and pay for at a cash-taking position as he leaves the shop. **1972** J. Mann *Mrs Knox's Profession* v. 31 She had pulled into the motorway café..and had gone into the self-service to buy a cup of tea.
2. *attrib.* or as *adj.* Designating: **a.** A place where customers may serve themselves.
1919 *Ladies' Home Jrnl.* Jan. 65/3 After several months .., not only are all the self-service departments reported on a self-supporting basis, but with sales increasing. **1950** 'N. Shute' *Town like Alice* xi. 330, I sat on the veranda with Jean, studying her drawing of the layout of the self-service grocery. **1952** D. Riesman in *Antioch Rev.* Dec. 430 The self-service supermarket, with its abundance of foods capably displayed. **1967** *Times* 16 May 21/1 The situation with self-service filling stations is a classic case. **1977** B. Pym *Quartet in Autumn* ii. 24 Letty did her shopping..at a small self-service store run by Uganda Asians that stayed open till eight o'clock in the evening.
b. A system of this nature.
1919 *Ladies' Home Jrnl.* Jan. 65/2 It [*sc.* a department store] followed this with an even greater inauguration—the self-service system in the sale of shoes..and women's wearing apparel. **1969** *Which?* Nov. 338/2 For clothes, some people liked self-service arrangements... Older women preferred the help..of an assistant.
c. A facility operated by the customer or user.
1952 S. Kauffmann *Philanderer* (1953) xiv. 240 Then he walked back into the house and went up in the self-service elevator. **1960** [see **coin-operated* adj. s.v. *coin *sb.* 8].
d. Merchandise bought by self-service.
1958 *Spectator* 18 July 118/1 Packaging for 'self-service' retailed goods. **1967** M. Drabble *Jerusalem the Golden* viii. 194 They..collected themselves a large self-service meal.
Also **self-se·rve** *attrib.* (chiefly *N. Amer.*).
[**1916** *Amer. Mag.* Oct. 69/1 'We told the customers to make their own selection, which they did.' 'It was a sort of serve-self arrangement, like a restaurant,' I said. '*Serve self*..,' repeated Garner. '*Serve-Self Sale.* I have it.'] **1931** W. Faulkner *Sanctuary* xxxi. 305 A self-serve place, where the customers moved slowly along a railing in single file. **1981** *Univ. Coll. London Bull.* Dec. 4/2 Self-serve counters would replace the current type.

self-shie·lding, *vbl. sb.* Chiefly *Nucl. Physics.* [Self- 1 b.] Shielding of the interior of a body as a result of the outer parts' absorbing radiation coming from the exterior; also = *self-absorption 2.
1958 *Proc. 2nd U.N. Internat. Conf. Peaceful Uses Atomic Energy* XIII. 435/1 As the poison becomes depleted, its self-shielding decreases and the poison burns out faster than the fuel, causing a reactivity rise. **1963** B. Fozard *Instrumentation Nucl. Reactors* i. 3 In many practical cases difficulties [in measuring the radioactivity of a source] arise due to such phenomena as self-shielding. **1977** J. Moteff in J. Weisman *Elem. Nucl. Reactor Design* v. 143 The receptor is shielded from each point source not only by interposed shielding material but also by materials within the source itself. This second contribution to the total shielding is called self-shielding or self-absorption.
So **self-shie·lded** *ppl. a.* (quot. 1964 refers to shielding from electromagnetic fields).
1958 *Proc. 2nd U.N. Internat. Conf. Peaceful Uses Atomic Energy* XIII. 433/2 The analytical treatment of self-shielded or lumped poisons. **1964** R. F. Ficchi *Electr. Interference* vii. 119 A self-shielded distributor cap is available commercially that makes use of the same physical configuration as a nonshielded cap. **1973** P. F. Zweifel *Reactor Physics* ix. 248 The center of the resonance line is strongly self-shielded.

self-si·milar, *a.* [Self- 3 a.] Similar to itself; having no variety within itself, uniform; *spec.* in *Math.* similar to itself at a different time, or to a copy of itself on a different scale.
1867 R. W. Emerson *May-Day* 48 Stumbling on through vast self-similar woods. **1956** A. A. Townsend *Struct. Turbulent Shear Flow* v. 101 The rate of strain in shear flow is self-similar everywhere. **1967** *Science* 5 May 636 Many [geographical curves] are statistically 'self-similar', meaning that each portion can be considered a reduced-scale image of the whole. **1978** *Sci. Amer.* Apr. 22/3 A coastline, for example, may be self-similar when viewed from a height of several miles down to several feet, but below that the fractal property is lost. **1978** *Amer. Scientist* LXVI. 713/1 The flow tends toward a self-similar solution, i.e. a flow in which the profiles of the physical quantities behind the shock wave remain constant in time.
Hence **self-simila·rity.**
1967 *Science* 5 May 636/1 Seacoast shapes are examples of highly involved curves such that each of their portion can—in a statistical sense—be considered as a reduced scale image of the whole. This property will be referred to as 'statistical self-similarity'. **1978** *Sci. Amer.* Apr. 22/2 Unlike these striking artificial curves the fractals that occur in nature—coastlines, rivers, trees, star clustering, clouds and so on—are so irregular that their self-similarity (scaling) must be treated statistically.

self-sown, *pa. pple.* and *ppl. a.* Add: Hence **self-sow** *v. intr.*, to propagate itself by seed.
1909 *Country Life in Amer.* Aug. 394/1 Annuals that 'self-sow' are welcome. **1980** *Country Life* 3 July 52/2 The milk thistle..might self-sow over-exuberantly.

self-sta·rter. [f. next.] **1.** An electrical device for starting the engine of a motor vehicle without the need to crank it. Also *fig.*
1894 *Work* 17 Feb. 73/3 The many improvements made in recent years in the use of ignition tubes, self-starters. **1902** A. C. Hawksworth *Motors & Motor-Driving* vii. 137 In the case of cars with two or more cylinders various self-starters have also been introduced. **1927** *Sat. Even. Post* (N.Y.) 24 Dec. 15/3 Conversation with him was never a self-starter; you had to crank it. **1973** M. Russell *Double Hit* xxv. 190 There was the squawk of a self-starter, a roar, a piping of tyres.
2. A person who acts on his own initiative (*spec.* at work). *colloq.*
1960 *Times* 1 Feb. 2/4 (Advt.), The Man: Must be a self-starter yet able to work within references given to him. **1964** Mrs. L. B. Johnson *White House Diary* 15 Nov. (1970) 203 Luci describes herself as a 'self-starter'. **1971** *Sunday Times* (Johannesburg) 28 Mar. 30/4 (Advt.), Suitable applicants will be self-starters in the 25–35 year age group. **1979** *Arizona Daily Star* 5 Aug. (Advt. Section) 4/2 Must be self-starter with project management experience.

self-starting, *ppl. a.* [Self- 4.] That comes into operation automatically or semi-automatically. Of a motor vehicle: fitted with a self-starter. Also *fig.*
1866 *Proc. Inst. Mech. Engineers* 268 An arrangement for rendering the self-adjusting injector also self-starting has been contrived at the writer's works. **1887** [in Dict. s.v. Self- 4]. **1910** *Daily Mail Year Bk.* 157/1 A few non-dazzling headlights, and one or two dual ignition and self-starting devices. **1912** *Chambers's Jrnl.* Aug. 556/2 Self-starting motor-cars. **1927** M. Asquith *Lay Sermons* i. 22 After making elaborate notes on all his self-starting symptoms, he wrote a long prescription. **1965** *Wireless World* July 56/1 (Advt.), Synchronous electric clock movements... Self-starting.

self-stee·ring, *vbl. sb. Naut.* [Self- 4.] The steering or directing of a vessel on a predetermined course by automatic means; **self-steering gear** (also **sails**), apparatus by which this is achieved; also *absol.*
1950 E. C. Hiscock *Cruising under Sail* II. xix. 363 For a single-handed or short-handed ocean passage I consider that self-steering sails are most necessary. **1956** P. Johnson in J. Morwood *Sail Evolution* (A.Y.R.S. Publ. No. 3) 22 It is not only to the single-handed ocean voyager that self steering is useful. **1957** T. Herbert *Self Steering* (A.Y.R.S. Publ. No. 13) 6 *Self Steering* may be defined as the ability of a sailing boat to stay on a set course relative to the wind... The various types of self steering gears fall into two broad categories: 1. Those gears which convert variations in wind pressure on the sails into rudder movements [etc.]. **1971** J. R. L. Anderson *Reckoning in Ice* viii. 153, I had no self-steering on Gudrid, but she was a beautifully balanced boat. **1976** *Southern Even. Echo* (Southampton) 1 Nov. 3/6 The 29-year-old blonde Lymington girl..expressed her admiration for..the winner—'one of the greatest sailors who have ever been, because he sailed without self-steering gear.'

self-stimula·tion. *Psychol.* [Self- 1 a.] Stimulation of oneself for pleasure or excitement; *spec.* masturbation. Also, stimulation of its own pleasure centres effected in an animal by means of implanted electrodes (see quot. 1956).
1947 M. M. Lewis *Lang. in Society* i. 18 There, at that level [*sc.* babbling]—as a form of play, of self-stimulation, of narcissism—it [*sc.* language] might remain. **1951** Ford & Beach *Patterns of Sexual Behav.* ix. 155 American men who begin to masturbate..discontinue the practice.. because self-stimulation is replaced by heterosexual intercourse. **1956** J. Olds in *Sci. Amer.* Oct. 114/3 In the rhinencephalon the effects were milder, producing self-stimulation at rates around 200 times per hour. **1964** J. Z. Young *Model of Brain* xiv. 234 With stimulating electrodes implanted in them animals can be made either to seek self-stimulation from one centre or to avoid it if the electrode is in..one nearby. **1977** R. Holland *Self & Social Context* iv. 62 Olds' study of self-stimulation by rats with implanted electrodes.

self-stu·dy. [Self- 1 a, *2 b.] **1.** Study or contemplation of oneself.
1683 [in Dict. s.v. Self- 1 a]. **1936** L. Pearsall Smith *Reperusals & Re-Collections* i. 6 He found moral profit also in the self-study, for how, he asked, can we correct our vices if we do not know them.
2. Study by oneself; private study.
1958 *Practical Wireless* XXXIV. 1 (Advt.), Designed and arranged for self-study at home. **1962** E. Snow *Other Side of River* (1963) xviii. 130 Mao had already made wide-ranging contacts and done omnivorous reading in the Changsha library. In his self-study he was guided by his favorite professor. **1977** P. Strevens *New Orientations Teaching of English* ii. 13 The adult who works on his own with a self-study course is still, though in an extended way, learning with a teacher.

self-sufficiency. Add: **1. a.** Now freq. used in sense *1 b of the adj.
1932 *World Agriculture* (R. Inst. Internat. Affairs Study Group) viii. 133 A measure of self-sufficiency in food is regarded as one of the primary elements in natural defence. **1953** G. E. & K. R. Fussell *Eng. Countrywoman* iii. 90 The canopy of self-sufficiency that covered all the needs of the manor house. **1973** J. & S. Seymour *Self-Sufficiency* i. 9 What I am interested in is *post*-industrial self-sufficiency: that of the person who has gone through the big-city-industrial way of life..and wants to go on to something better. **1974** *News & Courier* (Charleston, S. Carolina) 7 Apr. A-12/2 They argue that the 1985 target date for self-sufficiency is unrealistic, and that..some oil and gas still must be imported. **1980** 'M. Innes' *Going it Alone* iv. 31 She had persuaded herself..that self-sufficiency must now be the prime concern of the small rural gentry.

self-sufficient, *a.* Add: **1. b.** *spec.* Of persons, groups, or nations: able to provide enough of a commodity (as food, oil) to supply one's own needs, without obtaining goods from elsewhere; self-reliant, self-supporting, independent. Freq. const. *in.*
1932 [implied at *self-sufficiency 1 a]. **1955** K. A. H. Murray *Agriculture* iii. 40 For countries that are practically self-sufficient in their food requirements.., war or the threat of war may necessitate little or no change in agricultural effort or output. **1973** J. & S. Seymour *Self-Sufficiency* i. 10 More and more people, in all the highly industrial societies, are trying partially to opt out of the big-industry set-up and become less specialized and more self-sufficient. **1977** *Undercurrents* June–July 11/2 If we are to become self-sufficient in food production in Britain we are told that we must eat more grain and less meat. **1978** *Lancs. Life* July 54/2 He was soon back in the Lake District.., becoming self-sufficient through selling his paintings and wood sculptures, doing odd jobs and growing his own food.
Hence as *sb.* (*rare*), one that is sufficient in itself (oneself).
1909 W. James *Meaning of Truth* xiv. 276 Mr. Russell, and also Mr. Hawtrey..seem to think that in our mouth also such terms..are self-sufficients with no context of varying relation that might be further asked about. **1926** I. Brown *H. G. Wells* iii. 43 They have the Cockney's superb self-mastery, his power to rise to an occasion... Bert Smallways in *The War in the Air* is another of these admirable self-sufficients.

self-suggestion. 2. (Earlier example.)
1893 A. Lang in *Folk-Lore* IV. 433 But I am not my own dupe. Others may be more fortunate or more amenable to self-suggestion.

self-supporting, *ppl. a.* (Earlier and further examples.)
1829 *Lond. Med. & Surg. Jrnl.* II. 341 (*heading*) Atherstone self-supporting dispensary. **1845** J. S. Mill in *Edin. Rev.* LXXXI. 521 It is an indispensable condition that there be a reasonable prospect of their being at some future time self-supporting. **1893** G. B. Shaw *Widowers' Houses* II. 52 *Trench*: We must do the best we can with seven hundred. I think we ought to be self-supporting.

1936 N. STREATFEILD *Ballet Shoes* iii. 46 You will at least have taken a step towards trying to make them self-supporting. **1972** *Guardian* 1 Sept. 1/1 Britain took a giant stride towards becoming self-supporting in oil yesterday.

self-surrendering, *ppl. a.* (Earlier example.)

1878 J. G. WHITTIER *Vision Echard* 12 Its [*sc.* love's] self-surrendering freedom, Its loss that gaineth all.

self-sy·stem. *Psychol.* [SELF- 5 b.] The organized complex of drives and responses pertaining to (an aspect of) the self; the final choice of potentialities which the individual seeks to develop.

1897 W. JAMES *Let.* 1 Feb. (1920) II. 57 It is a case of the conflict of two *self-systems* in a personality up to that time heterogeneously divided, but in which..the higher loves and powers come definitively to gain the upper-hand. **1940** H. S. SULLIVAN *Psychiatry* III. 9/1 Along with the learning of language, the child is experiencing many restraints on the freedom which it had enjoyed.. and from these restraints there comes the evolution of the self system. **1977** R. HOLLAND *Self & Social Context* ii. 31 Anxiety is the special 'dynamism' that attaches to the development of a 'self-system'.

self-ta·pping, *ppl. a. Mech.* [SELF- 4.] Designating a hardened screw that will cut its own thread in a hole in metal that would otherwise need tapping. Also **self-ta·pper** (*colloq.*).

1936 R. T. KENT *Mech. Engineers' Handbk.* (ed. 11) III. ix. 36 Self-tapping screws are screws that may be driven into an untapped hole, forming the thread in the hole as they are driven. **1955** *Archit. Rev.* CXVII. 213/1 From the point of view of large-scale production of sheet metal components, the greatest design change has been brought about by the Parker-Kalon or self-tapping screw. **1970** K. BALL *Fiat 600, 600D Autobook* viii. 99/1 Slightly tighten the self-tapping bushes. **1978** *Hot Car* June 98 (Advt.), A spoiler which needs only six self tappers to secure it to withstand heavy impact.

self-ti·mer. *Photogr.* [SELF- 1 c or 4.] A mechanism that introduces a delay between the operation of the shutter release and the opening of the shutter, so that the photographer can photograph himself.

1951 L. A. MANNHEIM et al. *Rollei Way* 53 To make exposures with the self-timer..pull the button outwards. **1968** M. WOODHOUSE *Rock Baby* xvii. 173 He had..a self-timer on the camera and there were pictures of the two of us together. **1978** *Detroit Free Press* 5 Mar. A14 (Advt.), The Polaroid Prontol RF Land Camera..comes with self timer and tripod.

self-transce·ndence. [SELF- 1 a, d.] Transcendence or surpassing of oneself or one's limitations; the achievement of or capacity to achieve a higher level of awareness, compassion, etc. Also **self-transce·ndency.**

1885 W. JAMES in *Mind* X. 27 We are not to ask, 'How is self-transcendence possible?' **1895** —— in *Psychol. Rev.* II. 110 Those mysterious notions of self-transcendency and presence in absence which are such essential parts of the ideas of knowledge, both of common men and of philosophers. **1946** J. S. HUXLEY *Unesco* ii. 62 Individuals..can only achieve fullest self-development by self-transcendence. **1956** *Essays in Criticism* VI. 17 An irony of a more darkly moral colouring, a sardonic self-transcendence, was known to Friedrich Schlegel. **1975** P. BAELZ *Forgotten Dream* iii. 46 To place such emphasis on the possibility of creative self-transcendence..at once suggests that we have escaped from sober reality into a world of our own make-believe.

So **self-transce·ndent** *a.*, **self-transce·nding** *ppl. a.*

1884 W. JAMES in R. B. Perry *Tht. & Char. of W. James* (1935) I. xxxvi. 579 A consciousness not self-transcendent in form is inconceivable. **1904** —— in *Jrnl. Philos.* I. 538 Common-sense theories left the gap untouched, declaring our mind able to clear it by a self-transcending leap. **1948** J. L. ADAMS tr. *Tillich's Protestant Era* v. 67 Self-transcending realism is a universal attitude toward reality..combines two elements, the emphasis on the real and the transcending power of faith. **1975** P. BAELZ *Forgotten Dream* ii. 25 Man also has the ability to distance himself from what is immediately presented to him as himself... He is self-transcending.

self twist. [SELF- 4.] A method of spinning in which the yarn is twisted by the lateral movement of a roller. Usu. (with hyphen) *attrib.*

1970 SELLING & LORD in P. R. Lord *Spinning in '70s* vii. 96 The second section deals with the so-called *self-twist yarns* such as those produced experimentally in Australia. **1972** *Sci. Amer.* Dec. 55/1 Self-twist spinning was developed in Australia, where a great deal of research is done on wools. **1974** [see *open end* adj. s.v. *OPEN *a.* 22 c]. **1980** *Jrnl. R. Soc. Arts* May 364/1 Perhaps our most notable success has been the development of the wool spinning method called 'Self-twist'.

selham, var. *SULHAM.

‖ **selicha** (sèlī·χă, sèliχā·). Also **seliha**; pl. **selichot, -oth,** etc. [a. Heb. *səlīḥā*, pl. *səlīḥōṯ* penitential prayer.] A Hebrew liturgical poem recited in penance on fast days, before Rosh Hashanah, and before and on Yom Kippur.

1864 *Chambers's Encycl.* VI. 155/1 The *Selichoth*, or Penitential Prayers. **1909** *Cent. Dict.* Suppl. 1194/2 The selihot are acrostically arranged, many containing not only the alphabet but also the names of the composer and his father. **1925** W. O. E. OESTERLEY *Jewish Background Christ. Liturgy* ii. 76 What are called the *Selichôth* (i.e. prayers for forgiveness; the word comes from the root *salach* 'to forgive') form an important element in the Jewish liturgy. **1960** S. BECKER tr. *A. Schwarz-Bart's Last of Just* (1961) I. 9 He is the author of the famous Seliha, Oh God, cover not our blood with thy silence. **1974** *Jewish Chron.* 13 Sept. 34/3, I was at selichot the other morning (none of your midnight revels for me) with my soul on high. **1976** B. WILLIAMS *Making of Manch. Jewry* xii. 304 In October 1870 the congregation agreed on minor ritual changes—including the abbreviation of the *Piyyutim* and *Selicoth.*

seligmannite (se·ligmănəit). *Min.* [ad. G. *seligmannit* (H. Baumhauer 1901, in *Sitzungsber. d. K. Preuss. Akad. d. Wissensch. zu Berlin* 110), f. the name of Gustav *Seligmann* (1849–1920), German mineral collector: see -ITE[1].] An arsenic sulphide of lead and copper, $PbCuAsS_3$, occurring as brittle, dark grey to black, orthorhombic crystals having a metallic lustre.

1902 *Mineral Mag.* XIII. 205 Seligmannite... Of this mineral,..only five crystals, varying in size from ½ to 4 mm., have been found. **1969** *Zeitschr. für Krist.* CXXX. 224 The structure of seligmannite is built up essentially of a framework of CuS_4 tetrahedra and AsS_3 pyramids, with lead atoms inserted in the large holes.

selion. Add: **2.** A furrow turned over by the plough. *nonce-use.*

1877 G. M. HOPKINS *Poems* (1967) 69 No wonder of it: shéer plód makes plough down sillion Shine.

Selish, var. *SALISH.

Seljuk, *a.* and *sb.* Add: **A.** *adj.* **2.** Designating a style of oriental carpet.

1931 A. U. DILLEY *Oriental Rugs & Carpets* xiii. 267 Seljuk, lifted out of Turkish history, and Dinar..are the names of oriental rugs produced in Greece. **1952** B. MIALL tr. *H. Jacoby's How to know Oriental Carpets & Rugs* 13 The oldest known Oriental carpets, the so-called Seljuk carpets of the thirteenth century, which came originally from the Ala-eddin Mosque at Konia, are now preserved, with other magnificent examples, in the Evkaf Museum at Istanbul. **1963** I. SCHLOSSER *European & Oriental Rugs & Carpets* 118 The Seljuk carpets..in the Evkaf Museum..have small but very interesting geometric patterns.

Selkup (selkŭ·p). Also **Sel'kup·** [Native name.] A member of a Samoyedic people of northern Siberia; the language of this people belonging to the Uralic family of languages. (Formerly known as 'Ostyak Samoyed': cf. *OSTYAK; SAMOYED *sb.* and *a.* in Dict. and Suppl.)

1962 [see *NENETS]. **1964** in S. P. Dunn *Levin & Potapov's Peoples of Siberia* 597 The summer dwelling of the Northern Sel'kups was the birchbark tent. **1967** D. S. PARLETT *Short Dict. Languages* 107 The Southern languages include Ostyak Samoyed (Sel'kup), and Kamassian. **1972** *Language* XLVIII. 206 Of the southern group, only Sel'kup ('Ostyak Samoyed') can be considered a living language. **1974** *Encycl. Brit. Macropædia* XVIII. 1022/2 The fourth language, Selkup, lies to the south in a region between the central Ob and central Yenisey. **1975** G. F. CUSHING tr. *Hajdu's Finno-Ugrian Languages & Peoples* iii. 215 The only representatives of the southern group of Samoyeds still extant are the Selkups.

sell, *sb.*[2] Add: **2. a.** (Earlier example.)

1838 *Actors by Daylight* 4 Aug. 179 (*heading*) Editorial consequence—Specimens of wit—A decided sell.

b. The technique of selling by advertising or persuasive salesmanship; the practice or fact of this. Usu. with qualifying word: cf. *hard sell* s.v. *HARD *a.* 22 a; *soft sell* s.v. *SOFT *a.* 27.

1952, etc. [see *hard sell* s.v. *HARD *a.* 22 a]. **1970** G. GREER *Female Eunuch* 11 The main force of their energy filtered away..through the sexual sell of the fifties. **1976** SCOTT & KOSKI *Walk-In* (1977) xiii. 81 He was like an encyclopedia salesman moving into the soft, memorized sell.

3. Delete ? *U.S.* and add later examples.

1981 *Times* 20 July 20/1 Cooke, Lumsden waver between a hold and sell recommendation for Dowty Group. *Ibid.* 27 July 20/1 Woodside Petroleum is a sell. **1981** *Sunday Times* 2 Aug. 43/6 We rated them a sell ahead of the disappointing figures last month.

4. For *U.S.* read orig. *U.S.* and add: **a.** (Earlier and later examples.) Also *gen.*, (one who makes) a sacrifice of principle or betrayal.

1862 M. B. CHESNUT *Diary* 6 May in C. V. Woodward *M. Chesnut's Civil War* (1981) 336 Another sellout to the devil. It is this giving up that kills me. **1883** J. HAY *Bread-Winners* 151 How much did the Captain give you for that sell-out? **1940** 'G. ORWELL' *Jrnl.* 24 June in *Coll. Essays* (1968) II. 354 High-up influences in England are preparing for a similar sell-out [to Pétain's]. **1953** *Landfall* (N.Z.) Dec. 283 This film could have ended with a punch; but this would have been running counter to the sacrosanct Hollywood tradition of the inevitable happy ending. So there is a sell-out. **1959** *Economist* 11 Apr. 134/2 Specially elected members (reference to whom the wilder parts of the audience had greeted with familiar African cries of 'stooges', 'sell-outs'). **1960** J. LEHMANN *I am My Brother* 4 A gigantic sell-out to the Nazis. *a* **1974** R. CROSSMAN *Diaries* (1975) I. 182 Then Maurice Edelman made an inflammatory half-hour attack on the Government, charging me and Frank Cousins with every kind of crime, including a sell-out to the Americans. **1980** *Times* 19 Feb. 6 Mr. Robert Mugabe's Zanla guerrillas infiltrated the region..maiming or murdering those who were considered sell-outs.

c. The disposal of a commodity because of great demand; also, a completely disposable commodity. Also *transf.*, an event for which all tickets have been sold; the occasion of such an event.

1859 *N.Y. Herald* 11 July 6/5 (Advt.), Our goods shall be sold cheap!! In this great sellout. **1923** *Variety* 11 Oct. 17/4 Business at 'Give and Take' at the Adelphi was generally big last week... Wednesday..was a virtual sell-out. **1933** *Sun* (Baltimore) 29 Aug. 8/3 The [actor's] interpretation may not be art, and it may not even be O'Neill, but it may easily be a sellout and it will almost assuredly be entertaining. **1945** *Ibid.* 27 Apr. 10-0/1 On a sharp sell-out of rails and steels after the opening, dealings were relatively heavy. **1945** S. LEWIS *C. Timberlane* (1947) xliii. 289, I have four tickets... They're absolutely impossible to get, show is a sell-out, but the agent is a friend of mine. **1950** *Sport* 22–28 Sept. 2/1 The Cup Final..is always a sell-out but crowds at other games are always below maximum. **1962** *Listener* 27 Dec. 1095/1 The shortage of shopping times for working people ..causes overcrowding, queuing, poor service and sell-outs on Saturday. **1968** *Globe & Mail* (Toronto) 15 Jan. 17/2 A sellout crowd of 75,546 watched..Vince Lombardi's National Football League champions. **1977** *Time* 19 Dec. 41/2 Such delicacies are instant sellouts.

5. sell-off. *Stock Exchange* (orig. and chiefly *U.S.*). A sale or disposal of bonds, shares, or commodities, usu. causing a fall in price.

1937 *Sun* (Baltimore) 6 Feb. 19/1 The sell-off was less pronounced than that of the share market and was slower in developing. **1941** *Ibid.* 16 Oct. 21/1 Adverse war news was blamed in most quarters for the selloff in stocks and commodities. **1958** *Time* 8 Dec. 98/3 The sell-off did not alarm most market experts. **1981** *Times* 21 May 24/1 The recent sell-off by a major institution has done much to cloud market sentiment.

sell, *v.* Add: **3. g.** *to sell down the river*: see *RIVER *sb.*[1] 3* a.

h. To advertise or publish the merits of (a commodity, idea, etc.); to persuade (a person) to accept or buy. Also, to convince (someone) of the worth of (something). (Variously with direct and indirect object.) *colloq.* (orig. *U.S.*).

1916 *Amer. Mag.* Mar. 50/1 I'd make my readers want to enlist. I'd 'sell' them the army. **1925** *Publishers' Weekly* 5 Dec. 1863 An advertising campaign to sell New York as the printing center of the world. **1931** W. G. MCADOO *Crowded Years* iii. 41, I had to 'sell' the idea to men like the elder J. P. Morgan. **1938** E. BOWEN *Death of Heart* III. iii. 362 They forget Major Brutt has come here to get a job... Oh dear, oh dear, I shall never sell him at all. **1942** *R.A.F. Jrnl.* 2 May 30 My work—in horrid modern commercial terms—is to 'sell' the R.A.F. to the Army. **1951** H. MACINNES *Neither Five nor Three* I. v. 77 The people of France were sold such ideas as.. 'Patriotism is for the rich'. **1956** B. HOLIDAY *Lady sings Blues* (1973) xix. 158 It seemed like a crazy idea, but he sold me. And what's more important, he sold a lot of other people. **1960** *Guardian* 9 Nov. 6/4 We have to sell to the public the idea that being a foster mother is a service..to the community. **1976** J. I. M. STEWART *Memorial Service* iv. 60 It's just no good your trying to sell me those rotten dons.

i. Const. *on.* To make (someone) enthusiastic about, or convinced of the worth of, something. Freq. *pass. colloq.* (orig. *U.S.*).

1918 *Maclean's Mag.* Mar. 52/2 The writer believes it is possible to finally 'sell' the Teutons on the advantages of peace as compared with war. **1928** WODEHOUSE *Money for Nothing* vii. 133 Come to think of it. I'm not too sold on this thing, anyway. **1932** E. WILSON *Devil take Hindmost* x. 112 He rarely mentions Communism, but..he is as much sold on it as any..party member. **1948** *Manch. Guardian Weekly* 9 Dec. 8 He is not selling anybody on America. **1950** *Newsweek* 1 May 45/1, I am going to..sell her on the idea of picking up the option for another 25 years. **1969** L. HELLMAN *Unfinished Woman* xii. 177 He had been doing his thesis on modern American novelists... I tried hard to sell him on Faulkner and Fitzgerald. **1970** J. EARL *Tuners & Amplifiers* iii. 72 If you are sold on a medium price ceramic cartridge it would pay to look for an amplifier with a 2MΩ ceramic (piezo) input of around 50mV sensitivity. **1978** A. PRICE *'44 Vintage* iv. 46 I've never been absolutely sold on the classics.

j. *refl.* use of sense 3 h above.

1938 L. BEMELMANS *Life Class* I. v. 73 He told me that what was most important in life was..the ability to 'sell' oneself, to call [hotel] guests by their correct names and to remember their faces. **1968** *Globe & Mail* (Toronto) 3 Feb. 11/3 Supersalesmanship is used to sell to adolescents, who must also learn to sell themselves. **1978** H. JOBSON *To die a Little* ii. 36 Sales gimmicks are out. We don't need them. The scheme sells itself.

4. b. *to sell short*: see SHORT *adv.* 11.

6. † **a.** Phr. *made to sell*: manufactured or contrived to secure a ready sale without regard to quality. *Obs.*

1827 P. CUNNINGHAM *Two Yrs. New South Wales* (ed. 2)

I. xvii. 297, I..seized a musket 'made to sell', and sallied out. **1855** P. H. DELAMOTTE *Pract. Photogr.* (ed. 2) 42 In some cameras, 'made to sell', no care is taken to adjust this plane. **1860** *Cassell's Illustr. Family Paper* Apr. 300/3 We shall hear fewer complaints of seed, unless it be from those who obtain packets which are only 'made to sell'.

b. *transf.* with personal subj.

1915 R. FRY *Let.* 21 Nov. (1972) II. 391 My show is turning out a great success..as far as attendance goes... Of course I don't sell—I never expected to. **1966** C. ACHEBE in *Black Orpheus* Mar. 45, I had a Raleigh bicycle, brand new, and everybody called me Jolly Ben. I was selling like hot bread.

12. sell out. d. Also *intr.* for *pass.*

1914 *Daily Mail* 31 Jan. 1/2 My first parcel from you sold out very quickly. **1974** M. BIRMINGHAM *You can help Me* ii. 39 The Friday flower stall was rapidly selling out.

e. For *U.S.* read orig. *U.S.* and add: To betray a person or cause for gain (cf. *sell-out* s.v. SELL *sb.*² in Dict. and Suppl.): (*a*) *intr.* (Later examples.)

1903 G. B. SHAW *Man & Superman* III. 78 He has sold out to the parliamentary humbugs and the bourgeoisie. **1946** KOESTLER *Thieves in Night* 112 The English are going to sell out on us. **1976** *Survey* Winter 86 Barbé called for tactics of disobedience to the colonial administrators and to the traditional chiefs who had 'sold out' to the French government.

(*b*) *trans.* (Examples.)

1857 *Lawrence* (Kansas) *Republican* 2 July 1 If the *Times* has not been 'sold out' to the Border Ruffian party, it looks very much as if it had been 'chartered'. **1867** *Oregon State Jrnl.* 19 Jan. 3/1 The writer thinks the officers were 'badly sold out'. **1936** M. MITCHELL *Gone with Wind* ix. 189 Why quibble about the Yankees earning an honest penny selling out the Union? **1940** J. B. PRIESTLEY *Postscripts* 45 It let the old hands, the experts,..speak for it, and they sold it out. **1967** *Times* 17 Nov. 8/6 With shouts of 'They sold us out, the bastards', the meeting moved to 'the moment of truth'. **1976** 'J. CHARLTON' *Remington Set* xxviii. 141 What happened is, Rog sold us out.

14. sell up. c. *intr.* To dispose of (a house, business, etc.) by sale.

1862 *Manch. Examiner & Times* 8 July 6/2 We hed a varra good heawse i' Stanley-street, once; but we hed to sell up an' creep hitherto. **1977** E. DEWHURST *Curtain Fall* xviii. 216 She would be coming home only in order to sell up.

sellaite (se·lăˌəit). *Min.* [a. It. *sellaite* (Strüver 1868, in *Atti d. R. Accad. d. Sci. di Torino: Classe di Sci. fis.*, etc. IV. 35), f. the name of Q. *Sella* (1827–84), Italian mining engineer and mineralogist: see -ITE¹.] Native magnesium fluoride, MgF_2, occurring as fibrous aggregates of colourless tetragonal crystals.

1872 G. J. BRUSH *Dana's Syst. Min.* (ed. 5) App. I. 14 Sellaite... Found with anhydrite at Geibroula in Piedmont. **1923** J. W. MELLOR *Comprehensive Treat. Inorg. & Theoret. Chem.* IV. xxix. 296 Warm crystals of sellaïte show a faint violet luminescence with cleavage. **1933** *Mineral. Abstr.* V. 238 Microscopical examination of the dolomite of bore-cores from the southern Harz showed the presence of sellaite as minute (0·04–0·075 mm.) tetragonal prisms. **1968** I. KOSTOV *Mineralogy* 189 Sellaite is isostructural with rutile.., the chain type of structure explaining its perfect {110} cleavage, prismatic to acicular habit, and optically positive character.

seller¹. Add: **1. c.** *Business.* In various phrases, as: (*a*) *seller four* (*ten, twenty, the year*, etc.): a form of contract in which the seller has the right to effect delivery within the specified number of days (four, ten, etc.); *seller's option*: the right of the seller to specify the number of days after which a sale is effected.

1849 *Merchants' Mag.* (U.S.) XX. 670 Fifty-six, buyer 20; 3rd broker—55⅞, seller 10. **1857** *Ibid.* XXXVII. 134 Sales at seller's option are generally a fraction below the current cash price. **1869** 'MARK TWAIN' *Innocents Abr.* xxxiv. 369 Sales of one lot Circassians, prime to good, 1852–1854..; one forty-niner—damaged—at £23, seller ten, no deposit.

(*b*) *seller's market*: a market in which there is excess demand at the going rate so that it is easy to effect additional sales. Also *fig.*

1934 in WEBSTER. **1948** G. CROWTHER *Outl. Money* (ed. 2) v. 163 The raw material markets may be transformed overnight from 'seller's markets' (i.e. where buying is insistent and the seller is in the strategic position) into 'buyer's markets', while the opposite movement is much slower. **1965** ZIGROSSER & GAEHDE *Guide to Collecting Orig. Prints* vi. 91 In boom times and a seller's market, almost anyone can set up as a dealer and make a success of it. **1979** R. JAFFE *Class Reunion* III. vii. 275 Everybody..here seems to be going to some shrink. They're all into self-help,..or screaming sessions, or group therapy... It's a seller's market.

3. Also used of other commodities. (Earlier and later examples.)

1895 *Montgomery Ward Catal.* Spring & Summer 6/2 Brocaded Brilliantines... This line we expect will be one of the greatest sellers of the season. **1925** *Daily Tel.* 13 May 20/7 (Advt.), Traveller Wanted.—We offer the latest new line. Big seller. Live men can earn £10 week. **1976** *Times* 1 May (Food Suppl.) p. ii/6 On tinned meat he said: 'My advice is to stock the major sellers, such as stewed steak.'

4. A selling race. *colloq.*

1922 *N. & Q.* 12th Ser. XI. 207/1 *Seller*,..a selling race —one in which the winner is bound to be offered by public auction. **1927** *Daily Express* 23 June 12/2 The game little Congou colt took another seller. **1928** *Daily Sketch* 7 Aug. 22/4 Another interesting proposition at the Midland meeting is the Loud Report filly in the juvenile seller.

selling, *vbl. sb.* Add: **c.** *selling job, -power*; **selling-point,** a place at which sales may be effected (cf. *point-of-sale* s.v. *POINT *sb.*¹ D.12*****), a retail outlet; **selling price** (earlier example); **selling race**: also *selling chase.*

1965 D. FRANCIS *For Kicks* iii. 44 The horses had all won selling chases—races where the winner was subsequently put up to auction. **1963** MRS. L. B. JOHNSON *White House Diary* 23 Nov. (1970) 8, I will have to..see about getting Lynda Bird to come back and live in Washington with us and go to school somewhere up here (and that will be a selling job!). **1976** I. LEVIN *Boys from Brazil* iii. 77 He's never been as sure as the rest of us that the project will work... The selling job we had to do! **1953** *Chambers's Jrnl.* June 343/1 In recent years some seaside resorts have entered the catering business... Margate, starting with nothing in 1946, now has fifty-two selling-points. **1960** R. WILLIAMS *Border Country* 158 Within a month..he would have all the selling-points he needed. **1904** J. LONDON *Let.* 11 July (1966) 161 My selling-power has increased. **1960** C. S. LEWIS *Studies in Words* 104 The literary innovators want to retain the prestige, almost the 'selling-power', of the consecrated word. **1815** Selling price [see *PRICE-CURRENT].

selling, *ppl. a.* **3.** That helps to effect a sale; esp. in phrr. *selling point, title.*

1875 TROLLOPE *Way We live Now* II. lxxxix. 248, I don't believe that anything like real selling praise is ever given to anybody, except to friends. **1959** *Times* 4 Mar. 11/7 The educational usefulness of television in backward areas depends on a firm grasp of the staffing problem. Otherwise it will be a selling-point, not a reality. **1963** P. PHILLIPS in Sissons & French *Age of Austerity* 148 The old selling phrase 'pre-war value' lost some of its attraction. **1965** W. HAGGARD *Hard Sell* ii. 12 'A delightful name for an aeroplane, isn't it?'.. 'I'd call it a selling title.' **1978** *Times* 27 Jan. 13/7 A French name is still a selling point for clothes.

sell-off: see *SELL *sb.*² 5.

Sellotape (se·lotēⁱp), *sb.* Also **sellotape, cello-tape.** [f. CELL(ULOSE *sb.* + -O + TAPE *sb.*¹] The proprietary name of a cellulose or plastic self-adhesive tape, freq. dispensed from reels for domestic use. Also *gen.*

1949 *Trade Marks Jrnl.* 9 Nov. 1002/2 Sellotape... Adhesive tape (stationery). Adhesive Tapes Limited, 8, Brunel Road, Acton, London, W.3; Manufacturers and Merchants. **1957** *Landfall* (N.Z.) XI. II. 169 Does she want to come a cropper, dashed earthward by wings casually fastened with sellotape? **1960** P. A. BENNETT in J. Pudney *Pick of Today's Short Stories* XI. 16 A wind.. blew down all the pictures stuck with cellotape to the wall. **1960** H. PINTER *Birthday Party* 76 There's some Sellotape somewhere. We can stick them together. **1971** *Petticoat* 24 July 3/1 It's certainly a lot less painful than ordinary cellotape which we've been using up till now. **1974** J. COOPER *Women & Super Women* 19 They always talk about having 'stuck together because of the children', as though the little blighters have been using glue and sellotape on them. **1980** *Guardian Weekly* 3 Feb. 20/5 So far he has largely run on string and Sellotape.

Hence as *v. trans.*, to fasten with Sellotape; **se·llotaped** *ppl. a.*, **se·llotaping** *vbl. sb.*

1960 P. A. BENNETT in J. Pudney *Pick of Today's Short Stories* XI. 16 She..cellotaped them [*sc.* pictures] to the wall. **1964** A. WILSON *Late Call* iii. 113 He continued to sellotape Beth's caricatures to the walls. **1965** M. DRABBLE *Millstone* 178 Lydia really did have to rewrite two whole chapters as well as doing a lot of boring sellotaping. **1969** E. MCGIRR *Entry of Death* iii. 56 An assortment of cellotaped cartons. **1976** *Daily Tel.* (Colour Suppl.) 14 May 36/3 There are four pictures (one bought in Piccadilly, the others from *Elvis Monthly*) Sellotaped to the wall.

sell-out: see SELL *sb.*² 4 in Dict. and Suppl.

‖ **selon les règles** (sĕloṅ lĕ regl'), *phr.* [Fr.] According to the rules (of polite society). Also *fig.*

Victorian writers frequently wrote the third word with an acute accent.

1825 H. WILSON *Mem.* IV. 30 Our's bid fair to grow into a strong mutual fancy, if not to real true love, selon les régles. **1837** G. H. LEWES *Let.* in A. T. Kitchel *G. Lewes & G. Eliot* (1933) i. 12 In spite of its not being *selon les régles* of this most artificial of worlds..I take the shortest and easiest way I can think of for our better acquaintance. **1864** C. M. YONGE *Trial* II. iv. 74 He thinks he is proceeding *selon les régles.* **1893** —— & COLERIDGE *Strolling Players* xxv. 225 There was so much laughter around that George thought a jest quite *selon les règles.* **1921** L. STRACHEY *Q. Victoria* iii. 73 Was not such a course of conduct..simply *selon les règles?*

Selsdon man (se·lzdən). *Pol.* [The name of the *Selsdon* Park Hotel near Croydon, Surrey (see below) + MAN *sb.*¹: after *Piltdown man*, etc.] Used orig. and chiefly by political opponents to denote an imagined person or persons believed to be pursuing the policies outlined at a conference of Conservative Party leaders held at the Selsdon Park Hotel 30 Jan.–1 Feb. 1970.

1970 H. WILSON in *Labour Govt.* (1971) xxxvii. 759 Selsdon Man is designing a system of society for the ruthless and the pushing. **1971** BUTLER & PINTO-DUSCHINSKY *Brit. General Election of 1970* vi. 131 To Mr. Wilson, these were demonstrations of atavistic Conservative instincts, which he summed up in a phrase he repeated time and again: 'Selsdon man'. **1974** *Times* 31 Dec. 12/4 Selsdon man went wrong because it appeared to make the Conservative Party into a set of decimalized economic liberals. **1979** *Internat. Jrnl. Sociol. of Law* Feb. 102 'Selsdon Man' climbed into office..by exploiting the traditional staple stuff of postwar British electoral politics—prices, unemployment and speculation about the 'economy'.

selsyn (se·lsin). Also **Selsyn.** [f. SEL(F- + SYN(CHRONOUS *a.*] A kind of electric motor closely resembling a magslip and employed similarly in pairs in order esp. to transmit and receive information about the position or motion of mechanical equipment. Also *selsyn motor.*

Formerly a proprietary term in the U.S.

1926 *Official Gaz.* (U.S. Patent Office) 27 Apr. 802/1 General Electric Company, Shenectady, N.Y... *Selsyn*... Electrical apparatus for transmitting and receiving motion. Claims use since April, 1921. **1930** *Gen. Electr. Rev.* July 378/2 A distinct possibility exists in the application of Selsyn motors to remote control. **1945** *Rev. Sci. Instruments* XVI. 132/2 The Central Scientific Company announces the availability of a limited supply of a.c. Selsyn motors. **1948** *Electronic Engin.* XX. 17 A recorder ..was modified..by removing the motor and replacing it by a gear train driven by a selsyn. **1962** J. BELL in G. A. T. Burdett *Automatic Control Handbk.* iv. 11 In the German Navy of the 1914–18 war an early form of a.c. synchronous transmission was used; this was copied by U.S.A. in the G.E. 'Selsyns', the forerunners of the present U.S.A. synchros. **1967** [see *MAGSLIP].

selvatic: see *SYLVATIC, SILVATIC *a.* 2.

selvage, selvedge, *sb.* Add: **5. b.** *Geol.* An alteration zone at the edge of a rock mass.

1934 [see *PARAGENESIS 2]. **1958** *Econ. Geol.* LIII. 292 Selvages of hydrothermal alteration of quartz monzonite along the contacts of some larger aplite-pegmatite bodies. **1979** *Nature* 5 Apr. 511/2 That some basic dykes have conspicuous charnockite selvedges might indicate metasomatic interchange between acid and basic rocks as a primary cause of the conversion, except that many dykes ..have no such marginal alteration. **1981** *Cambr. Encycl. Earth Sci.* 211/1 The majority of M[id-]O[cean]R[idge] B[asalt] lavas have a pillow form..and glass selvages—characteristics of rapid cooling in seawater.

selve (selv), *v. rare.* [f. SELF *sb.*] *intr.* (only G. M. Hopkins) and *trans.* (To cause) to become and act as a unique self. Hence **selved** *ppl. a.*, **se·lving** *vbl. sb.* Also *Comb.*, as *selved-up.*

1880 G. M. HOPKINS *Sermons & Devotional Writings* (1959) 122 Human nature, being more highly pitched, selved, and distinctive than anything in the world. *Ibid.* 123 Nothing else in nature comes near this unspeakable stress of pitch, distinctiveness, and selving, this selfbeing of my own. *Ibid.* 125 Nothing can..exercise function and determination before it has a nature to 'function' and determine, to selve and instress, with. *Ibid.*, I may treat the question from the side of my being, which is said to be compounded, selved-up, or identified with this universal mind. **1953** K. RAINE *Coll. Poems* (1956) 166 Ceasing to trouble the flowing of things with the fleeting Dream and hope and despair of this transient perilous selving. **1976** H. A. WILLIAMS *Tensions* v. 87 Around that dim and dull awareness of our identity with God we begin, gradually and instinctively, to centre and selve the rest of what we are. That centring and selving takes the whole of our life.

Sem (sem). *Egyptology.* Also **sam.** [Egyptian.] An Egyptian officiating priest who wore a distinctive robe made from a leopard's skin. Also *attrib.*, as *sem priest.* Cf. *SETEM.

1882 G. RAWLINSON *Hist. Anc. Egypt* I. xi. 438 The 'Sem',..or officiating high-priest, wore, as his costume of office, a complete leopard-skin, with head, claws, and tail. **1898** E. A. W. BUDGE tr. *Bk. Dead* cxvi. 181 The goddess Maāt is carried by the arm of him who eateth the Eye, and who is its divine judge, and the Sem priest carrieth me over upon it. **1910** *Hastings's Encycl. Relig. & Ethics* III. 538/1 Canonical part of the dress of the *sam* priest. **1927** H. CARTER *Tomb of Tut-ankh-amen* II. 28 Ay as king with royal insignia, clad in a leopard's skin of the *Sem* priest.

sema (sī·mă, sē·-). *Linguistics.* Pl. **se·mas, se·mata.** [a. G. *sema* (V. Skalička *Zur ungarischen Grammatik* (1935) 13), f. Gr. σῆμα sign.] = *SEME. Also *transf.*

1938 C. E. BAZELL in *Trans. Philol. Soc.* 112 It is only from the standpoint of their formatives that these morphemes behave like the 'cellules' (we should say the semata) of a single morpheme. *Ibid.* 113 There seems no reason to doubt that the smallest element in grammar, as Skalička holds, is the sema. **1973** D. OSMOND-SMITH tr. *Bettetini's Lang. & Technique of Film* i. 4 One must take into account..the so-called 'semas'—that is, signs whose signifieds correspond to a verbal proposition.

Semainean (sĕmai·niăn), *a. Archæol.* Also **Semainian.** [f. the name of *Semaine(h*, a village in Upper Egypt + -AN.] A term used by W. M. F. Petrie to designate the last period of predynastic culture in Egypt. Also *absol.* as *sb.*

? **1925** *Catal. Egyptian Antiquities found at Badari in 1925* 3 Approximate dates..9,000 B.C....Gerzean Age... 7,000 B.C. ... Semainean Age ... 5,500 B.C. ... First Dynasty. **1928** [see *GERZEAN *a.*]. **1939** W. M. F. PETRIE *Making of Egypt* vii. 55 We now reach the last of the ages, the Semainean, best represented at Semaineh, 17 miles west of Qena. **1958** V. G. CHILDE *New Light on Most Anc. East* v. 99 Petrie..postulated a 'dynastic race' and interpolated a Semainian period to contain the conquest and a Semainian culture to result from it. **1964** *Jrnl. Near Eastern Studies* XXIII. 274 Sir Flinders Petrie.. divided the Naqadian into three principal phases, named, with reference to the sites of El Amrah, Gerzeh, and Semaineh, the 'Amratian', the 'Gerzean', and the 'Semainean' and otherwise known as Naqada I, Naqada II, and Naqada III.

semal, semul, var. of SIMOOL in Dict. and Suppl.

‖ **Semana Santa** (semā·na sa·nta). [Sp.] In Spain: = HOLY WEEK.

1910 S. L. BENSUSAN *Home Life in Spain* vi. 73 The *feria* persists for a full fifteen days, starting on the Sunday before Easter and only beginning to pass when the last day of Semana Santa is a week old. **1966** E. McGIRR *Funeral was in Spain* 56 That's Semana Santa in Spain. The week before Easter Sunday. **1979** A. SCHOLEFIELD *Point of Honour* 73 The flames and the smoke reminded me of a *semana santa* procession.

Semang (sĕma·ŋ), *sb.* and *a.* Also **Samang.** [Mal.] **A.** *sb.* (A member of) a Negrito people inhabiting the interior of the Malay peninsula. **B.** *adj.* Of or pertaining to this people.

1812 [see *POLYNESIAN *a.*]. **1814** [see *PAPUAN *sb.* 1]. **1839** T. J. NEWBOLD *Brit. Settlements in Straits of Malacca* II. xv. 377 It would appear that the Semang does not differ much in personal appearance from the Jakun. *Ibid.* 379 The Semang women..are said to be in common. **1860** MAYNE REID *Odd People* 415 The Samangs—a tribe inhabiting the mountainous parts of the Malayan peninsula —are also a negro or negrillo race. **1902** *Encycl. Brit.* XXVI. 485/2 The Vaalpens represent..a state of arrested development analogous to that of the Samangs and other Negritoes of the Malay Peninsula. **1920** R. J. WILKINSON *Hist. Peninsular Malays* (ed. 2) i. 2 The word Semang.. has come to be regarded as contemptuous. No negrito will answer to it. *Ibid.* i. 3 For practical purposes a Semang is a nomadic primitive Peninsular negrito whose numeral system stops at two. **1948** A. L. KROEBER *Anthropol.* (ed. 2) x. 424 Asia is particularly rich in tribal societies with 'internally marginal' cultures. Examples are..Palaung, Kachin, Moi, Semang, Sakai, and many others in the states of Farther India and Malaya. **1974** *Encycl. Brit. Micropædia* IX. 46/2 *Semang*, Negrito people of the Malay Peninsula... In the 1970s their population was estimated to be less than 3,000, with only about 100 in Thailand (where they are known as Ngok, or Ngo).

semanteme (sĭmæ·ntīm). *Linguistics.* [a. F. *sémantème*, f. Gr. σημαντικός significant, after *morphème* *MORPHEME, *phonème* PHONEME.] A unit of meaning; a linguistic element which expresses a concept; = *SEMEME. Hence **semante·mic** *a.*

1925, etc. [see *MORPHEME]. **1933** *S.P.E. Tract* XXXVIII. 596 We already have plenty of synonyms for rumour, news, report, &c., to which semantemes the word *khubber* does not add any new shade of meaning. **1938** I. GOLDBERG *Wonder of Words* xvi. 324 If, in addition to its phonemic and semantemic elements, a word has another element, that element is morphemic. **1949** C. E. BAZELL in E. P. Hamp et al. *Readings in Linguistics II* (1966) 213 The inflections of tense..are naturally always determinants of the verbal semanteme. **1960** G. THOMSON *Greek Lang.* 1 The words composing a sentence may be divided into two kinds: those which express concepts ('full words' or semantemes) and those which express relationships between concepts ('empty words' or morphemes). **1977** A. SHERIDAN tr. *J. Lacan's Ecrits* iii. 63 The effects would no longer be produced, thus revealing that they do not depend even conditionally on the semanteme.

semantic, *a.* and *sb.* Add: **A.** *adj.* **2. a.** (Earlier and later examples.)

1894 E. W. FAY in *Amer. Jrnl. Philol.* XV. 433 Freedom of interchange between *r* and *l* is limited by semantic considerations. **1901** H. OERTEL *Lectures on Study of Lang.* i. 72 He was the first to distinguish clearly between the *formal* and the *semantic* side of a word. *Ibid.* v. 297 In the discussion of all semantic changes the logical aspect must be carefully kept separate from the psychological aspect. **1920** B. MALINOWSKI in *Bull. School Oriental Studies London Inst.* I. IV. 62 Sound semantic definitions valid for a wide range of linguistic types are needed before any grammatical analysis of native languages is possible. **1943** *Time* 22 Nov. 99/3 U.S. intellectuals in 1943 went out and ratified the Constitution all over again. But some of them had semantic reservations. **1968** *N.Y. Post* 15 Jan. 45/3 Each day passes with some new semantic quibble emanating from Washington. **1976** J. S. GRUBER *Lexical Structures in Syntax & Semantics* 1 We would acknowledge the necessity for interpretive semantics of some sort (e.g. a semantic calculus), but not one based on the interpretation of words and phrases.

b. In weakened uses.

1959 W. R. FISHEL in *New Leader* 2 Nov. 13/1 We do ourselves and our Asian neighbors a distinct disservice when we insist on stretching them or shrinking them to fit our particular semantic bed. **1971** L. KOPPETT *N.Y. Times Guide Spectator Sports* ii. 41 Lesson No. 1 must be clung to through all the semantic storms.

B. *sb. pl.* **1. a.** Also, (the study or analysis of) the relationships between linguistic symbols and their meanings. Const. as *sing.* and *pl.* (Earlier and further examples.)

Now the usual word in this sense.

[**1883** M. BRÉAL in *Études Grecques en France* XVII. 133 Cette étude..nous l'appellerons la *Sémantique*..c'est-à-dire la science des significations.] **1893** E. WILLIAMS tr. M. Bréal in *Trans. Amer. Philol. Assoc.* XXIV. 27 All, or almost all, the chapter of linguistics treating of Semantics, or the science of meanings, has yet to be written. **1895** C. R. LANMAN in *Ibid.* XXVI. p. xi, The doctrine of the principles that underlie the processes of the development of the meanings of words may be called semantics or semasiology. **1912** E. WEEKLEY *Romance of Words* 79 The convenient name semantics has been applied of late to the science of meanings, as distinguished from phonetics, the science of sound. **1920** B. MALINOWSKI in *Bull. School of Oriental Studies London Inst.* I. iv. 35 All these works..are résumés of the present state of linguistics, and they reflect the insufficient attention hitherto given to Semantics. **1933** L. BLOOMFIELD *Language* viii. 138 When the phonology of a language has been established, there remains the task of telling what meanings are attached to the several phonetic forms. This phase of the description is *semantics*. It is ordinarily divided into two parts, *grammar* and *lexicon*. **1941** J. RANSOM *New Criticism* i. 5 *The Meaning of Meaning* is in terms of the new philosophy of language; the authors refer to the latter as Symbolism, but since their book the name of it appears to have become standardized as Semantics. **1952** *Economist* 21 June 813/2 Professor Hayakawa says nothing about..the importance of semantics in the determination of word-origins and word-history. **1964** E. A. NIDA *Toward Sci. Transl.* iii. 35 While semantics deals with the relationship of symbols to referents, syntactics is concerned with the relationship of symbol to symbol. **1972** HARTMANN & STORK *Dict. Lang. & Linguistics* 204/2 *Linguistic semantics* has studied meaning more in terms of the connexions between speech acts and the physical and intellectual environment of the speaker. **1980** *Times Lit. Suppl.* 7 Mar. 268/1 Frege's goal was not to provide a semantics for natural language as he found it.

b. In weakened uses.

1944 M. RYSKIND in *Sat. Rev. Lit.* 23 Dec. 4/1 The technique of character-assassination instead of arguments is..standard totalitarian semantics. **1966** *N.Y. Post* 3 Aug. 6/4 Sen. Pastore said that everybody was engaged in semantics. 'It comes down to a very fine point,' he said, stating the obvious in a nutshell. **1978** K. HUDSON *Jargon of Professions* 16 Almost daily in the press briefing, whenever a newsman raises his hand to ask for clarification of some mealy-mouthed statement: 'I am not going to debate semantics with you,' the spokesman replies.

2. *transf.* The interpretation of signs in general.

1946 C. MORRIS *Signs, Lang. & Behavior* viii. 219 *Semantics* deals with the signification of signs in all modes of signifying... When so conceived, pragmatics, semantics, and syntactics are all interpretable within a behaviorally oriented semiotic. **1962** *Listener* 11 Jan. 70/2 Exposure to art, erroneous notions mixed with some accurate ones of history, the private struggle with semantics and meaning. **1970** G. GREER *Female Eunuch* 33 The notion of a curve is so closely connected to sexual semantics that some people cannot resist sniggering at road signs.

C. Special collocations. **semantic aphasia** *Path.*, disturbance in understanding the significance of any but the simplest forms of words or speech caused by disorder in the cerebral cortex; **semantic differential** *Psychol.*, a technique devised to measure the distribution of meaning that a person attaches to a concept, by rating descriptive words selected by him from an evaluated list; a scale or test to achieve this; **semantic paradox** *Logic*, a paradox caused by ambiguity of meaning in the language of a statement, rather than by its logical reasoning; **semantic poetry** (see quot. 1969).

1926 H. HEAD *Aphasia* II. 259 A case of Semantic Aphasia. **1958** *Lang. & Speech* I. 26 This symptom, appearing distinctly in cases where the affection damages the most complex and most recently formed zones of the parieto-occipital region at its border with the temporal region, constitutes a basic symptom of so-called 'semantic aphasia'. **1974** L. F. SIES *Aphasia Theory & Therapy* i. 51 Semantic aphasia produces an inability to perceive the complex relationships by which language classifies separate concepts. **1953** C. E. OSGOOD *Method & Theory in Exper. Psychol.* xvi. 713 The distribution of his [*sc.* the subject's] judgments on a standardized series of such scales serves to differentiate the meaning of this concept from others; for this reason this measuring instrument has been called a 'semantic differential'. **1962** *Listener* 11 Jan. 62/1 Identification with parents was measured by the similarity of children's description of their parents, and of the kind of person they would most like to be themselves, on a series of seven-point rating scales known as the 'semantic differential'. **1962** U. WEINREICH in Householder & Saporta *Probl. Lexicogr.* 26 Semantic-differential tests. **1979** T. SHAPIRO *Clinical Psycholinguistics* iii. 26 Procedures such as the semantic differential offer valid and important experimental properties to understand meaning. [**1939** *Mind* XLVIII. 358 This semantico-empirical paradox can easily be solved by the ramified theory of types without using the simple theory of types. **1948** H. C. BRODIE tr. *Chwistek's Limits of Sci.* ii. 40 Logical paradoxes must be distinguished from semantical paradoxes.] **1960** P. ZIFF *Semantic Anal.* iv. 134 The fact that the semantic paradoxes can be formulated in English has led some philosophers, primarily logicians, to the conclusion that English is in a muddled state. **1978** T. J. SMILEY in F. P. Ramsey *Foundations* 8 Ramsey transforms the problem by drawing the now standard distinction between the logical and the semantic paradoxes. **1949** S. THEMERSON (*title*) Bayamus and the Theatre of Semantic Poetry. **1951** *Times* 5 Apr. 5/1 Nothing could prevent Mr. Vyshinsky or Mr. Acheson from discussing Etruscan pottery or semantic poetry if they really wished to do so. **1969** *Poetry Rev.* LX. 274 Semantic Poetry is based on the idea that words such as *moon, night, heart, flower*, etc., having become clichés have become devalued and devoid of affective effect. SP avoids all form of rhetorical device and relies upon a text derived from traditional language by replacing each word by its dictionary definition... Semantic Poetry does not rarefy the verbal material to condense the meaning.

Hence **sema·ntical** (also **-ly** *adv.*) *a.*; **semanti·cian, sema·nticist,** a student of semantics; **semanti·city,** the quality of being semantic or possessing meaning derived from signs.

1895 M. BLOOMFIELD in *Amer. Jrnl. Philol.* XVI. 409 Every word, in so far as it is semantically expressive, may establish, by hap-hazard favoritism, a union between its meaning and any of its sounds. **1917** *Jrnl. Eng. & Gmc. Philol.* XVI. 472 The professional semanticist is visualized in his work-shop,..feverishly fingering the leaves of a host of lexical tomes, standard and dialect, old, middle and new. **1921** H. E. PALMER *Princ. Lang.-Study* 62 The lexicologist or semantician will study the meanings. **1926** C. M. DOKE *Phonetics of Zulu Lang.* 217 (*caption*) Words semantically alike but differing in tone. **1936** *Mind* XLV. 272 Chwistek, a semanticist and metamathematician noted for his work on the theory of types. **1941** J. RANSOM *New Criticism* iv. 282 All discourse consists in signs.., there is the *semantical* dimension proper, involving the reference of a sign to an object. **1960** *Sci. Amer.* Sept. 90/2 The dog's panting [does not] exhibit the design-feature of 'semanticity'... The calls of gibbons.. possess semanticity. **1960** *Economist* 15 Oct. 251/1 In Natal..there has been some talk of secession—semantically disguised because secession today bears a stigma it did not carry ten years ago. **1973** J. M. ANDERSON *Structural Aspects Lang. Change* 186 Many of the outstanding semanticists have been optimistic about finding some kind of regularity behind semantic processes. **1975** *Language* LI. 207 This distinction [between competence and performance]..is constantly attacked..by the 'semanticians'. **1975** I. ROBINSON *New Grammarians' Funeral* viii. 165 He says that music hasn't semanticity because 'Vivaldi's *Four Seasons* is stylized away from the reality it pretends to imitate'. **1978** C. HOOKWAY in Hookway & Pettit *Action & Interpretation* 26 The semantical and intentional discourse of the subjects provides an additional control.

semanticize (sĭmæ·ntisəiz), *v. Linguistics.* [f. SEMANTIC *a.* + -IZE.] *trans.* To invest (something) with meaning; also, to analyse semantically. So **sema·nticized** *ppl. a.*, **sema·nticizing** *vbl. sb.*

1942 *Sat. Rev. Lit.* 10 Jan. 14 (*heading*) Semanticizing. **1961** WEBSTER, Semanticize. **1964** P. MEADOWS in I. L. Horowitz *New Sociol.* 450 The straitlaced purity of semanticized communication-theory. **1976** *Times Lit. Suppl.* 31 Dec. 1631/2 Lotman appears to be over-eager to semanticize, in his own words, 'any element on the parole level'.

semantico- (sĭmæ·ntiko), also **sema·nto-,** combining form f. Gr. σημαντικός of SEMANTIC *a.*, used with adjs. and advbs. in sense 'semantic(ally) and..'.

1932 W. L. GRAFF *Lang. & Languages* 277 All linguistic change is a process pertaining to..semanto-phonetic expression. *Ibid.* 420 Archaic Chinese seems to have had a system of..semanto-phonetically changeable radicals. **1939** Semantico-empirical [see *semantic paradox* s.v. *SEMANTIC *a.* C.]. **1971** *Language* XLVII. 80 These structures are semanto-syntactic, which means that the semantic properties or bundles of properties are arranged not in a linear order but in a hierarchical one. **1976** *Word 1971* XXVII. 268 Semantico-intentionally there are two stages of development. **1977** P. STREVENS *New Orientations Teaching of English* ii. 25 *Semantico-grammatical categories*—expressing universal concepts of time, quantity, space and matter, as well as expressing grammatical concepts of *case* ('who did it, who it happened to, and what got changed').

semantron (sĭmæ·ntrǫn). *Gr. Orthodox Ch.* Also **simandro, simantron;** pl. **semantra.** [med. Gr. use of Gr. σήμαντρον sign, mark.] A wooden or metal bar struck by a mallet used to summon worshippers to service.

1849 R. CURZON *Visits to Monasteries of Levant* p. i, Interior of the Court of a Greek Monastery. A monk is calling the congregation to prayer, by beating a board called the simandro..which is generally used instead of bells. **1850** J. M. NEALE *Hist. Holy Eastern Ch.* I. II. ii. 217 The word *semantra*..properly signifies..the instruments ..by which the people were called together before bells were introduced into the east... They are of two kinds, wooden and iron. The wooden semantron is generally a long, well planed piece of timber. **1912** W. G. HOLMES *Age Justinian & Theodora* I. i. 110 At the boom of the great *semantron*..the various congregations issue forth to attend their respective places of worship. **1939** *Archit. Rev.* LXXXV. 289/1 Round the church..is a broad path along which a monk walks summoning the faithful to prayer by hammering on a simantron, a long piece of wood which he balances in one hand. **1958** *Times Lit.*

Suppl. 10 Oct. 581/5 The simantron..which summons the monks of Athos to prayer is a wooden not a brass instrument.

semaphore, *sb.* Add: **2.** This method of signalling; *spec.* a system for conveying messages by a code whereby the arms are moved through certain positions in a vertical plane relative to the body.

1904 [in Dict., sense 1 b]. **1918** E. S. FARROW *Dict. Mil. Terms* 544 *Semaphore*, a method of signalling in which the letters depend on the position of one or both arms in relation to the body. When sending semaphore, the signaller always faces the distant station. **1975** *Scout Handbk.* (1976) 124/1 Semaphore uses a different position of the arms for each letter.

semaphore *v.*: also *fig.*

1957 R. CAMPBELL *Coll. Poems* II. 32 The lonely hamlets semaphore their loss. **1981** *Economist* 24 Jan. 88/1 American firms are nervously semaphoring price rises after a strong recovery at the end of 1980.

semasiology. (Earlier example.)

[*a* **1829** C. K. REISIG *Vorlesungen über Lateinische Sprachwissenschaft* (1839) II. 286 (*heading*) Semasiologie oder Bedeutungslehre.] **1847** J. W. GIBBS *Philol. Studies* (1857) 18 The development of intellectual and moral ideas from physical, constitutes an important part of *semasiology*, or that branch of grammar which treats of the development of the meanings of words.

semasiolo·gic *a.* = SEMASIOLOGICAL *a. rare.*

1909 L. BLOOMFIELD in *Mod. Philol.* VII. 248 A number of examples are here given of secondary Germanic ablaut forms exhibiting a..feature of semasiologic differentiation.

sematic, *a.* Restrict *Biol.* to sense in Dict. and add: † **2.** = SEMANTIC *a. Obs. rare*$^{-1}$.

1855 J. W. POWELL in *Trans. Anthropol. Soc. Washington* III. 189 While in the present state of knowledge it is perhaps not possible to set forth clearly the resultant sematic and structural effects upon any language, in linguistic arts important effects are discovered.

sematology. Add: Hence **sematolo·gical** *a. rare.*

1882 J. A. H. MURRAY *Let.* 27 Mar. in K. M. E. Murray *Caught in Web of Words* (1977) x. 190 All that you urge against phonetic statements, can be urged with far greater force against sematological ones.

semblable, *sb.* **2.** Delete † *Obs.* and add later examples in revived use.

1922 JOYCE *Ulysses* 377 It behoves every most just citizen to become the exhortator and admonisher of his semblables. [**1923** T. S. ELIOT *Waste Land* i. 8 You! hypocrite lecteur!—mon semblable,—mon frère!] **1941** V. WOOLF *Between Acts* 242 There was Dodge, the lip-reader, her semblable, her conspirator. **1979** *Dædalus* Summer 30 These thoughts picture Othello as, in various ways, a semblable of yours.

semble, *a.* For † *Obs.* read *Obs.* (exc. *arch. poet.*) and add later example.

1965 AUDEN *About House* (1966) 40 Six lenient semble sieges, None of them perilous, Is now a Perfect Social Number.

sembling (se·mbliŋ), *vbl. sb. Ent.* Also **symbolling.** [See SEMBLE *v.*[1]] The coming together of a male and a female moth; *spec.* a method of trapping male moths by using a captive female to attract them.

1748 J. DUTFIELD *New Nat. Hist. Engl. Moths & Butterflies* s.v. Emperor Moth. What is called Symbolling, or, the Coming together, is particularly observable of this Species. **1870** [see SEMBLE *v.*[1] 1 b]. **1894** *Science* 23 Mar. 156/2 The sembling of a large native moth. **1924** *Contemp. Rev.* Sept. 364 Collectors of lepidoptera have long known the trick of 'sembling' to obtain a large series of males of certain moths.

seme (sīm). *Linguistics.* [ad. Gr. σῆμα sign: cf. *SEMA.] **a.** A sign. **b.** A unit of meaning; *spec.* the smallest unit of meaning. Cf. *PHEME, *RHEME.

a **1866** J. GROTE in *Jrnl. Philol.* (1872) IV. 158 The noematism of it [*sc.* a language] might be..written..by symbols naturally suggesting themselves for the visual percepts, and by others agreed upon for abstract terms and those related to other senses than the eye. It might be well to call such quasi-writing or exhibition to the eye by other than vocal elements, *sematism*, and the symbols *semes*. **1906** C. S. S. PEIRCE in *Monist* XVI. 506 By a *Seme*, I shall mean anything which serves for any purpose as a substitute for an object of which it is, in some sense, a representative or Sign... The term 'The mortality of man' is a Seme. **1923, 1931** [see *PHEME]. **1951** E. A. NIDA in *Word* VII. 5 The simple term *seme* identifies any minimal feature of meaning. **1966** D. G. HAYS in *Automatic Transl. of Lang.* (NATO Summer School, Venice, 1962) 163 These semes are more nearly the units wanted in translation than the morphs or morphemes that comprise them. **1973** *Screen* Spring/Summer 18 [Eric Buyssens]..established a certain number of notions and distinctions (*seme* and *semic act, intrinsic* and *extrinsic semes, direct* and *substitutive semes*).

semeiological, *a.* (Later examples in sense 3 of *SEMEIOLOGY.)

1932 W. L. GRAFF *Lang. & Languages* 303 What is called change of meaning is essentially a semeiological phenomenon. **1968** JACOBSON & SCHOEPF tr. *Levi-Strauss's Structural Anthrop.* xvii. 364 Anthropology aims to be a semeiological science, and takes as a guiding principle that of 'meaning'. **1968** *Listener* 25 Jan. 122/1 The wide-awake analogue to this use of television is the employment of the medium for basic communication—infralinguistic and, if semiological at all, concerned with the most primitive human signals. **1973** D. OSMOND-SMITH tr. *Bettelini's Lang. & Technique of Film* i. 1 The basic material that the Barthes group take as a starting-point for their semiological and aesthetical observations is not their own. **1978** *Guardian Weekly* 5 Feb. 21/4 In semiological parlance, the film's lacunae often seem rather more important than what's actually happening on screen.

semeiology. Add: Sense 1 is now *obs.* The form **semiology** (sīmi,ǫ·lŏdʒi) is now usual. **3.** The branch of science concerned with the study of linguistic signs and symbols. Also in extended use.

[**1916** F. DE SAUSSURE *Cours de Linguistique Générale* iii. 34 On peut donc concevoir une science qui étudie la vie des signes au sein de la vie sociale; elle formerait une partie de la psychologie sociale, et par conséquent de la psychologie générale; nous le nommerons *sémiologie* (du grec *sēmeîon* 'signe').] **1923** OGDEN & RICHARDS *Meaning of Meaning* i. 8 The initial recognition of a general science of signs, 'semiology', of which linguistic would be a branch, was a very notable attempt in the right direction. **1932** W. L. GRAFF *Lang. & Languages* 72 Semeiology, the science of signs and symbols, is only in its infancy. **1947** *Word* III. 29 [According to de Saussure] there is a science of semiology, hitherto unrecognized... This semiology is differentiated by definition from semantics. **1959** *Times Lit. Suppl.* 20 Nov. 669/2 Joyce has become an inexhaustible hunting ground for hermeneutical exegesists to whom semeiology..is a science beside which plain criticism offers no excitements. **1967** *Economist* 14 Oct. 156/2 The tired businessman who refreshes himself with courses like 'Structural Linguistics, Semiology and Criticism'. **1972** *Times Lit. Suppl.* 21 July 833/1 He has written..about literature and about the semiology of the cinema. **1976** T. EAGLETON *Crit. & Ideology* v. 166 Literature must indeed be re-situated within the field of general cultural production; but each mode of such production demands a semiology of its own.

Hence **sem(e)io·logist.**

1973 D. OSMOND-SMITH tr. *Bettelini's Lang. & Technique of Film* i. 3 There exists a certain confusion in the use of terms recently coined by semiologists. **1975** *Listener* 20 Mar. 367/3 Though the 'synchronic' approach of the semiologists is for the moment more fashionable, it is impossible not to be interested in the history of social myths. **1979** *Dædalus* Summer 111 It has proved much more elusive to disclose the overall intention underlying their visual assembly in any way that an anthropologist or semiologist would recognize as coherent.

semeiosis, var. *SEMIOSIS.

semeiotic, *a.* Add: The form **semiotic** (sīmi,ǫ·tik) is now usual. **3.** Of or pertaining to semiotics or the use of signs. Cf. *SEMEIOTICS 2.

1923 H. G. BAYNES tr. *Jung's Psychol. Types* i. 82, I say 'semiotic' in contradistinction to 'symbolic'. What Freud terms symbols are no more than *signs* for elementary instinctive processes. **1957** *Publ. Amer. Dial. Soc.* XXVIII. 4 It is an utterance that 'craves' a verbal or other semiotic (e.g., a nod) response. **1973** AKHMANOVA & MARČENKO *Meaning Equivalence & Linguistic Expression* 7 The Morse code is a semiotic system *par excellence*, for in it every unit of content and every unit of expression are in regular one-to-one correspondence... The same applies..to all the other semiotic systems such as, for instance, notation in music, or chemical formulae, or mathematical signs. **1974** S. MORAWSKI *Inquiries into Fundament. of Aesthetics* viii. 302 The fourth approach..considers the artistic communication itself and its semiotic connections. **1978** J. UPDIKE *Coup* (1979) vii. 257 No doubt this semeiotic treasure-lode [*sc.* a wallet] enriches the arcana of some light-fingered ex-nomad.

B. *absol.* as *sb.* = *SEMEIOTICS 2.

[**1690** LOCKE *Hum. Und.* IV. xx. 361 The third Branch may be called σημιωτική, or *the Doctrine of Signs*, the most usual whereof being words, it is aptly enough termed also λογική, Logick.] *c* **1897** C. S. PEIRCE *Coll. Papers* (1932) II. II. ii. 134 Logic, in its general sense, is..only another name for *semiotic* (σημειωτική), the quasi-necessary, or formal, doctrine of signs. **1937** C. MORRIS *Logical Positivism, Pragmatism, & Sci. Empiricism* 4 Semiotic being the general science which includes all of these [dimensions] and their interrelations. **1953** F. J. WHITFIELD tr. *Hjelmslev's Prolegomena to Theory of Lang.* 76 The so-called metalanguage (or, we should say, *metasemiotic*), by which is meant a semiotic that treats of a semiotic. **1973** R. JAKOBSON *Sci. of Lang.* ii. 32 The subject matter of semiotic is the communication of any messages whatever, whereas the field of linguistics is confined to the communication of verbal messages.

Hence **sem(e)ioti·cian.**

1946 C. MORRIS *Signs, Lang., & Behavior* I. i. 4 At some point the semiotician must say: 'Henceforth we will recognize that anything which fulfills certain conditions is a sign.' **1946** *Mind* LV. 46 Other groups of workers in the same field, as, for example..the Semioticians (*e.g.* Carnap, Morris). **1960** H. READ *Form of Things Unknown* I. ii. 34 In general, semioticians have confined themselves to the study of the various types of discourse which make use of language. **1976** *Visible Language* X. 68 It is possible, in the case of some 'auto-illustrations', to follow those semioticians who prefer to view iconic motivation as a special case of metonymic *pars pro toto*.

semeiotical, *a.* Add: **2.** = *SEMEIOTIC *a.* 3.

1938 C. MORRIS in *Internat. Encycl. Unified Sci.* I. II. 29 'Rules of sign usage', like 'sign' itself, is a semiotical term and cannot be stated syntactically or semantically. **1946** *Mind* LX. 146 As a semiotical psychiatrist, a Therapeutic Positivist has to hand a technique for the resolution of philosophical problems and disputes.

Hence **sem(e)io·tically** *adv.*

1916 C. E. LONG tr. *Jung's Analytical Psychol.* p. vii, The Vienna School interprets the psychological symbol semiotically, as a sign or token of certain primitive psychosexual processes. **1972** W. C. STOKOE *Semiotics & Human Sign Lang.* i. 15 Semiotically considered the difference between fingerspelling and a sign language could hardly be greater.

semeiotics. Add: The form **semiotics** (sīmi,ǫ·tiks) is now usual. **2.** The science of communication studied through the interpretation of signs and symbols as they operate in various fields, esp. language (see *SEMEIOTIC *sb.* for parallel form). Cf. *SEMEIOLOGY.

1880 G. MALLERY *Introd. Study Sign Lang. among N. Amer. Indians* 4 Our native semiotics will surely help the archæologist in his study of native picture-writing. **1911** A. M. LUDOVICI tr. *F. Nietzsche's Antichrist* in *Twilight of Idols* xxxii. 169 One should guard against seeing anything more than a language of signs, semeiotics, an opportunity for parables in all this. **1955** A. HUXLEY *Genius & Goddess* 42 He kissed her—kissed her with an intensity of passion..for which the semiotics and the absent-mindedness had left her entirely unprepared. **1964** T. SEBEOK et al. *Approaches to Semiotics* 5 Margaret Mead proposed semiotics..as a term which might aptly cover 'patterned communication in all modalities'. **1973** D. OSMOND-SMITH tr. *Bettelini's Lang. & Technique of Film* i. 2 Some talk of a universal semiotics, capable of including within itself all aspects of the film as sign-system. **1980** *Semiotica* XXIX. 185 (*heading*) A firework for the semiotics of visible human action.

sememe (sī·mīm). *Linguistics.* [f. Gr. σῆμ-α sign + *-EME.] A unit of meaning; *spec.* the smallest unit of meaning. Cf. *SEME.

[**1904** A. NOREEN *Vårt Språk* V. III. 6 Detta sålunda definierade abstrakta begrepp 'betydelse' uppträder in concreto alltid i någon viss språklig dräkt, som ofta kan efter omständigheterna vara mycket varierande, och det kallas då semem, hvilken term alltså kan definieras som: ett visst bestämdt idéinnehåll, uttryckt i någon språklig form, likgiltigt hvilken. **1911** A. L. ELMQUIST in *Jrnl. Eng. & Gmc. Philol.* X. 321 Semology [in Noreen's *Vårt Språk*] deals with the 'semem' and Morphology with the 'morfem'.] **1913** *Jrnl. Eng. & Gmc. Philol.* XII. 87 This need not have been the only or even perhaps the usual sememe associated with the morpheme *flik* in O. Scand. **1926** L. BLOOMFIELD in *Language* II. 157 The sememes..which stand in one-to-one correspondence with the morphemes, cannot be further analyzed by linguistic methods. **1933** —— *Language* x. 162 The meaning of a morpheme is a *sememe*. The linguist assumes that each sememe is a constant and definite unit of meaning, different from all other meanings, including all other sememes, in the language. **1949** [see *CONTRASTIVENESS]. **1954** C. E. BAZELL in E. P. Hamp et al. *Readings in Linguistics II* (1966) 329 At the European Semantic Conference, held at Nice in March, 1951..it was agreed to call the fundamental unit of content (in the linguistic norm) the *sememe*. **1965** N. CHOMSKY *Aspects of Theory of Syntax* 230 We could perfectly well state the facts..in terms of such new notions as 'semantic subject', 'semantic object', various kinds of 'sememes', etc., but such proliferation of terminology contributes nothing toward clarifying the..issues. **1973** *Screen* Spring/Summer 234 Greimas analyses the units of content (lexemes) into constant minimal semantic nuclei (semes) and contextual semantic units (sememes).

Hence **seme·mic** *a.*, **seme·mically** *adv.*

1953 C. E. BAZELL *Linguistic Form* 81 The sememic level is approached when several congruent morphemes of this type are regarded as a single unit, for commutation is then usually possible. *Ibid.*, Sememically the unit may normally be taken as zero. **1968** P. M. POSTAL *Aspects Phonol. Theory* viii. 198 The four current properly linguistic strata are, in hierarchical order from 'top' to 'bottom', the sememic, the lexemic, the morphemic, and the phonemic. **1973** *Archivum Linguisticum* IV. 119 By a 'semantic base' Hutchins means a set of 'sememic graphs'.

semen. Add: **2.** *attrib.*, as **semen bank**, a store of semen which is kept available for artificial insemination.

1954 *Fertility & Sterility* V. 28 A semen bank could be organized and maintained, with the same scientific attitude and spirit of research as is found in all other therapies for helping the infertile. **1972** *Sat. Rev.* (U.S.) 10 June 40/3 Semen banks..are gaining popularity among vasectomy candidates as a solution to the irreversibility problem.

semi[2] (se·mi). Colloq. abbrev. of: **1.** SEMI-DETACHED house.

1912 R. MACAULAY *Views & Vagabonds* xvi. 292 To settle down in the new semi and 'do for' her Ben,..what had heaven to offer more than that? **1939** R. FERGUSON in *Queen's Bk. of Red Cross* 234, I wish my girl could see it, but..it might spoil her for a little semi on a housing estate. **1958** J. SYMONS *Gigantic Shadow* ii. 8 These were the moments when the watchers in their suburban semis wriggled most deliciously in their overstuffed armchairs. **1977** B. PYM *Quartet in Autumn* iii. 28 That house which, in the estate agents' language, was on its way to becoming a 'twenty thousand semi'.

2. *semi-evening dress* s.v. *SEMI- 8. Now *rare.*

1927 N. COWARD *Sirocco* II. i. 38 Miss Johnson is wearing what might technically be described as a 'semi'. Mrs Breeze is in a tea-gown. **1934** C. L. ANTHONY *Touch Wood* II. ii. 57 Mrs McCrossan and Mr Berridge enter. Mrs McCrossan is in her semi.

3. *semifinished* (steel): see *semi- 8. Usu. in *pl. Industry.*

1931 *Economist* 5 Dec. 1054/2 If Continental exporters of 'semis'..feel that a high tariff is likely to be imposed in the..Budget, steel imports..are likely to increase. 1950 *Engineering* 21 July 59/2 Home produced steel semies are reaching the re-rolling mills in very large quantities. 1975 'D. Jordan' *Black Account* xii. 62 Have you ever thought that the next stage would be a semis plant?

4. *semi-final* s.v. Semi- 8.

1942 Berrey & Van den Bark *Amer. Thes. Slang* § 643/6 Next to last event... *semi.* 1976 *Star* (Sheffield) 29 Oct. 2/5 Last heat of the TV sheepdog trials and it's no secret that Scotland meet England West in the first semi.

5. *semi-trailer; *semi-truck* s.v. *semi- 8. *U.S.* (with pronunc. se·məi) and *Austral.*

1942 Berrey & Van den Bark *Amer. Thes. Slang* § 81/16 *Semi*,..a two-wheeled truck. 1961 *Amer. Speech* XXXVI. 272 It is common to call..a trailer a *semi.* 1968 J. M. Ullman *Lady on Fire* (1969) viii. 102 They..rolled past a row of semis lined up at an unloading dock. 1969 *Northern Territory News* (Darwin) *Focus '69* 97/2 The Stuart Highway..has become increasingly busy with road trains and semis to meet the needs of the increased population. 1976 B. Bova *Multiple Man* (1977) iv. 49 The Beltway..was almost always jammed with..heavy semis delivering the daily bread.

6. *semi-submersible* (rig, barge, etc.): see *semi- 8. *Oil Industry.*

1975 *Offshore* Aug. 19/1 We will operate three semis of the Aker H-3... These rigs are well published in various publications. 1977 *Offshore Engineer* Apr. 51 (*caption*) Drillships closely follow semis in the oversupply stakes.

semi-, *prefix.* Add: The pronunc. (se·məi) is common in the U.S. **I. 1. a.** Compounded with adjs. and pples.: (further examples, including some used *ellipt.* as *sbs.*); *semi-rural* (earlier example), *-servile* (earlier example), *-social* (later example).

1871 Bagehot in *Fortn. Rev.* 1 Aug. 158 A semi-abstract discussion of practical topics. 1974 K. Clark *Another Part of Wood* ii. 52 From behind the semi-abstract clouds there appeared the same sexy girls. 1963 W. R. Rose in Wyndham Lewis *Lett.* 558 René Harding, the uncompromising, semi-autobiographical hero of *Self Condemned.* 1926 J. M. Keynes *End of Laissez-Faire* iv. 41, I suggest, therefore, that progress lies in the growth and the recognition of semi-autonomous bodies within the State. 1974 tr. *Wertheim's Evolution & Revolution* 371 This semi-autonomous activity by living beings..is increasingly determining the course of nature on earth. 1952 C. P. Blacker *Eugenics: Galton & After* 178 The countries of Asia are rapidly emerging from their colonial or semi-colonial status. 1974 tr. *Wertheim's Evolution & Revolution* 67 The colonial or semi-colonial backyards which capitalism..was exploiting in such a way as to provoke strong popular counter-forces. 1965 *Math. in Biol. & Med.* (Med. Res. Council) i. 7 A service for the collection and recording of this information is also being made available on a semi-commercial basis to any hospital in the United States. 1839 De Quincey in *Tait's Edin. Mag.* Sept. 573/2 This..semi-conscious feeling..taught them to feel the extremity of their danger. 1977 J. D. Douglas in Douglas & Johnson *Existential Sociol.* i. 22 Most of our experiences in everyday life are only semiconscious. 1937 *Discovery* Sept. 277/2 The comfort and interest with which the [television] pictures may be viewed in a semi-darkened room. 1680 T. Browne *Let.* 6 Sept. (1946) 181 Esquire Mildmay..a melancholy & semi-delirious person, yet fayre condition'd. 1975 M. Amis *Dead Babies* xiii. 67 His strangled shout had been a semi-delirious reply to Quentin's courtly knock. 1942 E. Partridge *Usage & Abusage* 91/2 *Conditional clauses* have always caused trouble to the semi-educated and the demi-reflective. 1954 Koestler *Invisible Writing* iv. xxxiv. 371 There is a character in *The Magic Mountain*, the semi-educated Frau Stoehr, who is always trying to be refined. 1920 T. S. Eliot *Sacred Wood* 49 You see..how completely any semi-ethical criterion of 'sublimity' misses the mark. 1943 V. Sackville-West *Eagle & Dove* ii. ix. 138 A semi-experimental perception of God, in very varying degrees of intensity and clarity. 1938 H. Nicolson *Diary* 22 Aug. (1966) 356 Russia has no sympathy for the semi-fascist systems established in the Balkans. *a* 1974 R. Crossman *Diaries* (1977) III. 299 This semi-fascist reaction has been accompanied by a general lack of credibility in the whole establishment. 1956 *Railway Mag.* Feb. 113/2 When travelling from Cologne to Wiesbaden in a semi-fast, we left Cologne 20 min. late. 1937 Koestler *Spanish Testament* iii. 63 Spain was still, when the People's Front came into power in 1936, a semi-feudal country, with sharp social contrasts. 1970 C. Furtado in I. L. Horowitz *Masses in Lat. Amer.* ii. 31 As an instrument for domination over a society where some forms of semi-feudal decentralization prevailed, the State emerged in colonial times as a strong bureaucracy. 1960 *Farmer & Stockbreeder* 26 Jan. 66/2 Any kind of fixed or semi-fixed equipment .. will be considered. 1906 E. Johnston *Writing & Illuminat. & Lettering* xv. 317 The writing approaches the *stylographic*... It may conveniently be termed *Semi-formal.* 1977 *Stornoway Gaz.* 27 Aug. 1/7 The possibility of formal or semi-formal competitions could not be discounted. 1947 A. Koestler in *Partisan Rev.* XIV. 144 The unions become more and more absorbed into semigovernmental, managerial functions. 1950 B. Russell *Unpopular Essays* iv. 64 A rare moment of self-knowledge must have inspired the initial aphorism, which was made bearable to its author by its semi-humorous form. 1851 Mill *Logic* (ed. 3) II. v. v. 352 As the former is the error of sheer ignorance, so the latter is especially that of semi-instructed minds. 1955 J. Burnaby *Christian Words & Christian Meanings* iii. 62 The same tendency in modernised form is to be observed in much semi-instructed Christian thinking of our own time. 1921 F. Scott Fitzgerald *Let.* 25 Aug. (1964) 148 I'm sick of the flabby semi-intellectual softness in which I flounder with my generation. 1957 J. Kerouac *On Road* (1958) ii. 176 In Frisco eager crowds of young semi-intellectuals sat at his feet and listened to him. 1851 H. Melville *Moby Dick* III. xl. 230 Most mariners cherish a very superstitious feeling about seals, arising..from..the human look of their round heads and semi-intelligent faces. 1949 Koestler *Promise & Fulfilment* i. viii. 90 Haganah had a kind of semi-legal status which varied according to the political constellation. 1979 *Dædalus* Winter 157 The strength of the 'second' or 'parallel' market within the economy—in reality an entire spectrum of legal, semilegal, and illegal markets. 1909 O. Lodge *Survival of Man* vi. 86 Public performances..often tend to obscure a phenomenon by covering it with semi-legitimate contempt. 1927 *Mod. Philol.* Nov. 221 Even the semi-literate speaker actually obtains some of his speech material by linguistic borrowing from written records. 1957 E. Partridge *English gone Wrong* i. 5 The best English of the semi-literate. 1976 P. Cave *High Flying Birds* i. 10 Those who have perused my semi-literate journals masquerading as novels in the past may be familiar with some of my previous exploits. 1924 W. B. Selbie *Psychol. Relig.* 269 The persistence of the belief in such a semi-material ghost soul is a most interesting fact. 1924 *Econ. Jrnl.* XXXIV. 346 Meanwhile I got a good deal interested in the semi-mathematical side of pure Economics. 1902 W. James *Var. Relig. Exper.* iii. 69 Here is the abridged record of another mystical or semi-mystical experience. 1951 S. Ullmann *Princ. Semantics* iii. 158 The somewhat abstruse and occasionally semi-mystical jargon in which his views are often couched has given rise to a number of misinterpretations. 1962 H. R. Loyn *Anglo-Saxon England* i. 26 The semi-mythical island of Brittia, to which..the souls of the dead were ferried. 1962 Y. Malkiel in Householder & Saporta *Probl. Lexicogr.* 5 Perspective essentially involves the deliberate or semi-naïve attitude of the collector toward the chosen slice of material. 1890 W. James *Princ. Psychol.* II. xxiv. 420 In ordinary fear, one may either run, or remain semi-paralyzed. 1922 Joyce *Ulysses* 302 The semiparalysed *doyen* of the party..had to be assisted to his seat by the aid of a powerful steam crane. 1973 *Morning Star* 16 Jan. 5/3 There [is] a much better and wider distribution of shops selling semi-prepared foods [in Moscow now]. 1931 E. H. Morris *Temple of Warriors* i. 5 A more than life-size sculpture of a semireclining human figure. *a* 1974 R. Crossman *Diaries* (1976) II. 742, I am semi-retired. 1835 Dickens *Let.* (1965) I. 56 You would prefer living in Chambers to remaining in your present semi-rural tranquility. 1930 Auden *Poems* 75 And I, stung by the sun, Think, semi-satisfied That, 'ere the smile is done, The eye deliberate May qualify the joy. 1954 S. Duke-Elder *Parsons' Dis. Eye* (ed. 12) vi. 86 (*caption*) Semi-schematic diagram showing the correspondence of the structures seen in the normal eye by gonioscopy with those of a microscopic section. 1955 D. W. Maurer in *Publ. Amer. Dial. Soc.* xxiv. 4 The language [of criminal subcultures] is usually secret or semisecret. 1939 *Daily Tel.* 18 Dec. 12/8 (Advt.), Audit clerk, semi-senior, able to work without supervision. 1951 *Sport* 16–22 Mar. 9/2 Alec Talbot..finished his career with another semi-senior club, Stourbridge. 1976 *Eastern Daily Press* (Norwich) 16 Dec. 5/4 (Advt.), Applicants from ambitious semi-seniors would be welcome. 1840 Poe *Autobiogr.* in *Graham's Mag.* Nov. 225/1 The design was never more than semi-serious. 1977 J. F. Fixx *Compl. Bk. Running* xiv. 167, I don't know of a single even semiserious runner who smokes. 1848 Mill *Pol. Econ.* 22 The immediate cultivators of the soil..ceased to be in a servile or semi-servile state. 1896 T. W. Sanders *Encycl. Gardening* (ed. 2) 35 Place plants in semi-shady position outdoors June to Aug. 1973 M. Amis *Rachel Papers* 67 Semi-shaven, dishcloth hair, *duffle*-coat, baggy brown Farmer-Giles corduroys. 1927 Carr-Saunders & Jones *Soc. Struct. Eng. & Wales* v. 50 It is not usual to think of those occupied in retail dealing as divided into skilled, semi-skilled, and unskilled. 1940 W. S. Churchill *Into Battle* (1941) 166 We have to make a huge expansion of our labour force, and especially of those capable of performing skilled or semi-skilled operations. 1976 E. Stewart *Launch!* (1977) 16 In 810—semiskilled—they were playing Tensor beams across eight-by-five-inch printed circuits. 1925 T. Dreiser *Amer. Trag.* (1926) I. ii. viii. 206 They were in the midst of one of those semi-religious, semi-social and semi-emotional church affairs, the object of which was to raise money for the church. 1922 Joyce *Ulysses* 659 A noggin and a quarter of soured adulterated milk, converted by heat into water, acidulous serum and semi-solidified curds. *Ibid.* 680 A series of static, semistatic and peripatetic intellectual dialogues. 1962 J. T. Marsh *Self-Smoothing Fabrics* xxiii. 382 Variations of the crumpling method have produced a few semi-subjective tests. 1943 *List Retail Controlled Prices* (Ministry of Food) (ed. 3) 6 Biscuits, sweet or semi-sweet. 1972 *Times* 15 Nov. (Ital. Wine Suppl.) iv./3 Est! Est!! Est!!!..comes in both dry and semi-sweet. 1954 W. K. Hancock *Country & Calling* viii. 227 There are..many words of technical or semi-technical origin which have lodged themselves..firmly in everyday speech. 1976 *Classical Q.* XXVI. 216 Both lines, as Nicolaus notes..allude to a semi-technical legal term. *a* 1974 R. Crossman *Diaries* (1976) II. 27 It was a reasoned, semi-theoretical speech and it produced an amazingly good response. 1851 H. Melville *Moby Dick* II. xliii. 294, I am convinced that from the heads of all ponderous profound beings, such as Plato,..Dante, and so on, there always goes up a certain semi-visible steam, while in the act of thinking deep thoughts.

b. Compounded with a sb. to form an adj. phr.: (further examples).

1955 Keepnews & Grauer *Pict. Hist. Jazz* xi. 117 They made much use of jazz and semi-jazz conceptions in their dance music. 1938 *New Statesman & Nation* 23 July 143/2 What is needed is an extended application of the Trade Board method over a wide range of growing trades which mass-produce luxury or semi-luxury goods. 1962 H. E. Beecheno *Introd. Bus. Stud.* xi. 98 The more expensive type of goods..which are not the subject of so much branding and national advertising—the luxury and semi-luxury goods. 1935 *Discovery* Aug. 220/1 Subsistence or semi-subsistence farming was the rule, the settlers eked out a bare existence from such poor land. 1975 *Sci. Amer.* May 76/3 Most of them work as semi-subsistence farmers and live according to Mayan cultural patterns.

2. Compounded with sbs.: (further examples).

1948 D. Diringer *Alphabet* ii. iv. 286 Groups of 'Assyrians'..developed a semi-autonomy, owing allegiance only to their *maliks.* 1874 J. S. Mill *Ess. Relig.* 70 An argument for the utility of religion is an appeal..to semi-believers to make them avert their eyes from what might possibly shake their unstable belief. 1964 L. MacNeice *Astrol.* vii. 230 The semi-charlatan who may not subscribe to any code of ethics. 1962 E. Snow *Other Side of River* iv. 36 China's major ocean and river ports fell under foreign control and she became a semicolony not of one nation but of all the major industrial and naval powers. 1865 J. S. Mill *Exam. Hamilton's Philos.* vii. 104 But such a semi-concession..cannot save him. 1929 *Evening News* 18 Nov. 4/5 His weariness was so heavy that it bore him into a state of semi-consciousness. 1958 T. Stanwell-Fletcher *Clear Lands* 89 That cold, beautiful semidark of the Arctic night. 1914 W. S. Churchill *Let.* 8 Oct. in M. Gilbert *W. S. Churchill* (1972) III. *Compan.* i. 182 We must not be led into frittering away resources by keeping half a dozen anchorages in a state of semi-defence. 1977 *Financial Times* 7 Oct. 23/3 Mr Wedgwood Benn's silky semi-defence of Government strategy from the platform. 1963 *Times* 7 Feb. 4/4 A Prime Minister with the support of the House of Commons may be in a stronger position than a President who has not got the support of Congress, but he is not the sole executive officer as a President is, or a dictator such as Khrushchev, or a semidictator such as de Gaulle. 1938 *New Statesman & Nation* 20 Aug. 288/2 They operated in a twilight of semi-illegality. 1949 Koestler *Insight & Outlook* vi. 84 The comic effects of *misspelling* in the letters of children or semi-illiterates. 1952 E. Grierson *Reputation for Song* vii. 58 She lived with an aunt, a semi-invalid. 1974 *Howard Jrnl.* XIV. 78 Sir Cyril Burt defined semi-literates as those 'who cannot make effective use of reading or writing'. 1920 J. M. Keynes *Econ. Consequences Peace* 95 Germany is threatened with a deluge of luxuries and semi-luxuries from abroad. 1961 tr. Zhou Enlai in *Look* 31 Jan. 104/2 A considerable period is needed before China can surpass the norm with regard to mechanization and semimechanization. 1906 E. Dyson *Fact'ry 'Ands* xiii. 169 He smote himself on the breast..leaving the packer in a condition of semi-paralysis. 1958 F. Newton in P. Gammond *Decca Bk. Jazz* v. 65 Variety songs, effect-catching numbers and calculated semi-pornography. *a* 1930 D. H. Lawrence *Phoenix* (1936) v. 597 Some sort of semi-profession, such as school-teaching. 1805–6 Wordsw. *Prelude* (1850) v. 113 This Arab phantom, which my Friend beheld, This semi-Quixote. 1835 J. S. Mill in *London Rev.* II. 272 A last desperate attempt of the Tories to creep back into power as semi-reformers. 1935 *Mind* XLIV. 524 Retirement (or shall we say semi-retirement) has given Dr. Schiller increased leisure. 1971 D. J. Smith *Discovering Railwayana* viii. 47 After the grouping..many of the relics were consigned to semi-retirement in backyard and basement. 1952 A. G. L. Hellyer *Sanders' Encycl. Gardening* (ed. 22) 40 Position, semi-shade or north aspect. 1900 W. S. Churchill in *Morning Post* 20 July 5/7 It was not possible for the conquering army to allow the capital..to be in a state of semi-siege. 1929 *New Yorker* 12 Oct. 25/3 It is like the semi-stupor of an habitual intoxication. 1977 *Proc. R. Soc. Med.* LXX. 689/1 High alcohol intake probably meets this need as well as providing them with an intermittent refuge in sedation and semistupor. 1863 J. S. Mill *Let.* 7 Jan. (1910) I. 273 He has triumphed wonderfully over the difficulty of rendering the thoughts or semi-thoughts of Plato. 1867 —— *Let.* 19 Oct. (1910) II. 90 Parliamentary semi-work or idleness.

3. Compounded with vbs.: (further examples).

1973 M. Amis *Rachel Papers* 102 Kiss and semi-lick throat and neck. 1962 *Times* 9 Apr. (Suppl.) p. iii/3 The dispensation of powdered lime with oxygen is used to semi-refine molten iron before final treatment.

4. Compounded with advs.: (further example).

1945 *Plastics* IX. 143/1 Practical mechanical [safety] devices capable of functioning either fully or semi-automatically.

4*. The prefix used *absol.* as an advb., in sense 'partly, to some extent'. *colloq.*

1979 K. M. Peyton *Marion's Angels* vi. 102 'I thought you were on holiday.' 'Semi.'

II. 5. a. semi-interquartile range *Statistics*, half of the interquartile range.

1911 G. U. Yule *Introd. Theory Statistics* viii. 134 There are three such measures in common use—the standard deviation, the mean deviation, and the quartile deviation or semi-interquartile range. 1971 T. R. Harshbarger *Introd. Statistics* v. 91 The semi-interquartile range is half the quartile range: $Q = \frac{1}{2}(Q_3 - Q_1)$. Q is also called the quartile deviation.

b. semi-monthly (earlier examples); **semi-weekly** (earlier and later examples).

1851 C. Cist *Sk. & Statistics Cincinnati* 75 These are semi-monthlies. 1860 *Ex. Doc. 36th U.S. Congr. 2 Sess. Senate* No. 1. 435 The present contract..provides for an additional monthly trip between New York and San Francisco, making the service tri-monthly instead of semi-monthly as heretofore. 1791 T. Jefferson *Let.* 21 July in A. A. Lipscomb *Writings T. Jefferson* (1903) XIX. 79 Besides this, Fenno's being the only weekly or semi-weekly newspaper. 1833 A. H. Tracy *Let.* 10 June in T. W. Barnes *Mem. T. Weed* (1884) iv. 49 Put Millard Fillmore on your list for the Semi-Weekly. 1926 *Jrnl. Biol. Chem.* LXIX. 92 The weights of the rats and of their food intake were recorded semiweekly.

6. b. *Math.* **semi-convergent** *a.*, applied to a series the sum of whose terms converges while the sum of the moduli of its terms diverges; hence **semi-convergence; semi-major (-minor) axis,** half of the length of the longest (shortest) diameter of an ellipse.

1902 E. T. WHITTAKER *Mod. Anal.* 12 Absolute convergence and semi-convergence. **1872** *Monthly Notices R. Astron. Soc.* XXXII. 262 Most functions are expansible in an ascending (convergent) series of the form $A_0 + A_1x + A_2x^2 + \ldots$, and a descending (semi-convergent) series of the form $B_1/x - B_2/x^2 + B_3/x^3 - \ldots$ **1959** A. ZYGMUND *Trigonometric Series* (ed. 2) II. iv. 175 If *f* is continuous, and S[*f*] is uniformly semi-convergent to *f* from below, then S[*f*] converges uniformly. [**1850** J. HAAN *Analytical Geom. & Conic Sections* v. 45 The equation to the ellipse [is]..$y^2/b^2 + x^2/a^2 = 1$.., *a* and *b* being termed respectively the semi-axis major and the semi-axis minor.] **1899** GRACE & ROSENBERG *Coordinate Geom.* iv. 50 Find the length of the ordinates of each of the curves in Ex. 3 corresponding to the middle points of the semi-major axis. **1977** *Whitaker's Almanack 1978* 156/1 The squares of the periodic times vary as the cubes of the semi-major axes. **1909** C. N. SCHMALL *First Course in Analytical Geom.* viii. 191 Prove that the semi-minor axis is a mean proportional between the parts of tangent cut off. **1962** CORSON & LORRAIN *Introd. Electromagn. Fields* iv. 175 A charge *Q* is uniformly distributed throughout the volume of an ellipsoid of revolution whose semi-major axis is *a* and whose semi-minor axes are *b*.

7. a. *semi-liquid* (later example), *-lucent* (later example), *-matt, -moist.*

1963 D. W. & E. E. HUMPHRIES tr. *Termier's Erosion & Sedimentation* x. 193 Some marly deposits still contain 41·3% of water, which results in numerous landslips in this plastic, semi-liquid material. **1919** V. WOOLF *Night & Day* xi. 138 Rodney's windows..were a semilucent red colour. **1967** Semi-matt [see *MATT *a.*]. **1967** E. CHAMBERS *Photolitho-Offset* xvii. 259 The soft, tacky gelatinous Everdamp paper makes for easier working, being semi-moist and ready for use.

b. *semi-Christianity, -socialism* (later example), *-socialist.*

1882 J. SNODGRASS tr. *H. Heine's Relig. & Philos. in Germany* II. 67 Leibnitz..was well able to defend Christianity in its integrity. I say, in its integrity, for he defended it against semi-Christianity. **1961** C. S. LEWIS *Let.* Feb. (1966) 297 For some people at some moments what I call semi-Christianity may be useful. **1930** W. K. HANCOCK *Australia* xi. 225 The Liberal party still continued to tread..the familiar path of semi-socialism. **1939** N. & S. WEYL *Reconq. Mexico* iv. 110 Mexico's long indoctrination with semisocialist theory..made leftist political candidates almost a political inevitability. **1976** N. O'SULLIVAN *Conservatism* i. 30 A great body of conservative thought..has itself tended to move in a semi-socialist or collectivist direction.

c. Gram. *semi-compound* (also as *sb.*), *-grammatical, -phonetic* adjs.; **semi-consonant** (earlier example); **semi-predicative** *a.*, quasi-predicative; forming part of a predicate; **semi-sentence,** a statement or utterance which possesses some of the features of a sentence.

1963 F. T. VISSER *Hist. Syntax* I. iv. 389 An older semi-compound verb of the type *overpass.* **1964** *English Studies* XLV. 50 Some combinations..can therefore be considered as compounds or semi-compounds. **1820** F. BOPP in *Ann. Oriental Lit.* I. 6 The letter *y*..in Sanskrit or Gothic words..is always to be considered as a semi-consonant. **1964** P. STREVENS *Papers in Lang. & Lang. Teaching* (1965) iv. 61 The body of data..includes grammatical, semi-grammatical and non-grammatical features. **1933** L. BLOOMFIELD *Language* xvii. 290 Semi-phonetic devices, such as rising combinations of letters for a single phoneme. **1964** *Language* XL. 302 He had to depend mainly on the semiphonetic materials recorded by H. Paasonen. **1914** O. JESPERSEN *Mod. Eng. Gram.* II. 386 It is used in that sense as a semi-predicative post-adjunct. **1933** L. BLOOMFIELD *Language* xii. 206 Some numeratives are used also in other syntactic positions, as..*all, both* as semi-predicative attributes (*the boys were both there*). **1954** *Acta Universitatis Carolinae* VII. 35 In the present article, the term 'semi-sentence' constructions covers both participial and infinitive phrases as well as those having neither of these, but which, owing to their binary character, have a distinct predicational form (e.g. *If lawful.*). **1969** *Word* XXV. 195 A sentence which contains no predicate is a semi-sentence. **1975** N. CHOMSKY *Logical Struct. Linguistic Theory* viii. 244 We are building a system of phrase structure only for first-order grammatical sentences, a category that presumably excludes such semisentences as 'sincerity appointed the table'.

d. Nat. Hist. *semi-erect, -sessile, -social, -terrestrial*; **semi-evergreen,** normally evergreen but shedding some leaves if conditions become severe.

1894 R. B. LEE *Hist. & Descr. Mod. Dogs of Gr. Brit. & Ireland (Terriers)* xv. 353 Ears..if not cut, to be small V-shaped and carried semi-erect. **1931** A. G. L. HELLYER *Sander's Encycl. Gardening* (ed. 21) 409 S[*milax*] *herbacea*, greenish, bluish-black fruits, twining or semi-erect, N. America. **1952** *Ibid.* (ed. 22) 10 Adenocarpus... Deciduous or semi-evergreen shrubs or small trees. **1978** *Detroit Free Press* 16 Apr. (Parade Suppl.) 32/2 (Advt.), The lush, semi-evergreen foliage erupts in massive clusters of star-shaped, fiery red blooms. **1962** D. NICHOLS *Echinoderms* xii. 156 These facts suggest that the animal remained semi-sessile on the sea-bottom and searched the surrounding area with its tentacles. **1962** *Sci. Survey* XVII. 285 Numbers of insects are affected [by sounds].. which are related, not to sexual activity, but to social or semi-social activities. **1932** J. S. HUXLEY *Probl. Relative Growth* i. 33 Twenty-four grams is a very small weight for many crabs, including forms of semi-terrestrial and burrowing habits. **1964** *Oceanogr. & Marine Biol.* II. 302 The semi-terrestrial hermit crab, *Coenobita perlatus*,.. varies the frequency with which it visits water of different salinities.

e. *semi-ape* (example), *-dwarf* (also as *adj.*).

1886 KIPLING *General Summary* in *Departmental Ditties*, We are very slightly changed From the semi-apes who ranged Pre-historic India. **1931** Semi-dwarf [see *PETER PAN 2]. **1959** *Sci. News Let.* 22 Aug. 120/3 Stiff-stemmed semidwarf wheat may be the answer for Pacific Northwest growers whose wheat suffers extensively from lodging. **1979** *Nature* 3 May 7/1 In India..rice research has tended to focus on light-yielding semi-dwarfs for irrigated land.

g. Path. *semi-narcosis.*

1937 KOESTLER *Spanish Testament* ii. 235 That merciful state of semi-narcosis induced by..spinning illusions. **1965** J. POLLITT *Depression & its Treatment* v. 67 In very severe cases, continuous sleep (continuous narcosis) or continuous semi-narcosis with chlorpromazine and small amounts of Sodium Amytal must be given.

h. Chem. *semi-reduced*; **semialdehyde,** a derivative of a compound containing two identical functional groups (e.g. a dicarboxylic acid) in which one of the groups has been converted into an aldehyde group; **semi-covalent** *a.*, having some covalent character.

1942 *Jrnl. Biol. Chem.* CXLV. 69 In the presence of this enzyme..α-ketoglutaric acid formed succinic semialdehyde and CO_2. **1976** *Nature* 16 Dec. 652/2 GABA concentrations were measured using GABA transferose and succinic semialdehyde dehydrogenase to generate NADH, which was measured spectrofluorometrically. **1965** PHILLIPS & WILLIAMS *Inorg. Chem.* I. v. 156 Semi-covalent bonding involving *d* orbitals may also be expected to lead to high coordination numbers for early members of the transition series. *Ibid.* x. 386 The anaerobic system..tends to yield acetic acid, alcohol, and similar semi-oxidized and semi-reduced compounds.

j. semi-coke, a smokeless fuel that leaves little ash, made from coal by carbonization at a low temperature (usu. 500–600°C); **semi-coking** *a.*, designating a coal that is intermediate between a good coking coal and one that does not produce coke; **semi-steel,** substitute for def.: a low-carbon cast iron produced by melting mild steel with pig iron in a furnace (earlier and later examples).

1918 *Chem. & Metallurgical Engin.* XIX. 580/1 Charles Howard Smith..proposed to get an intermediate soft 16 to 20 per cent volatile semi-coke. **1972** HARKER & ALLEN *Fuel Sci.* v. 70 The tar and most of the volatile matter are driven off leaving a material known as 'semi-coke'. **1915** *Iron & Coal Trades Rev.* XCI. 421/2 No serious attempts have hitherto been made to utilise in the low-temperature system non-coking and semi-coking coals for the production of oils. **1977** *Jrnl. R. Soc. Arts* CXXV. 64/2 High grade coke can be made from a coal mixture including a proportion of only semi-coking coal. **1858** *Q. Jrnl. Chem. Soc.* X. 145 Mr. Bessemer claims the production..of a particular product called semi-steel. **1929** *Iron & Steel Industry* III. 35 The metallurgist has long regarded the term 'semi-steel' as a misnomer, although the use of the term within the foundry business is harmless when it is simply made to imply the use of steel in a cast iron mixture... Instead, we have at present the innuendo that 'semi-steel' is more or less a definite iron-carbon alloy of superior properties compared to cast iron, whereas it is in reality an 'unknown quantity'. **1958** *Engineering* 21 Mar. 384/2 The bottom grate is of heat resistant 30 per cent chrome semi-steel and is reversible for burning coal or coke.

k. Archit. *semi-Gothic* (examples).

1768 *Acct. Denmark* 94 The royal palace of Rosenburg ..is a handsome structure in the semi Gothic taste. **1925** F. MADAN *Oxf. outside Guide-Books* (ed. 2) 186 The Firm's premises..were entirely rebuilt and included the present 'semi-Gothic' elevation.

8. semi-active *a.*, designating a method of missile guidance in which the missile responds to a signal transmitted from elsewhere and reflected by the target; **semi-antique** *a.*, of a rug or carpet: between fifty and one hundred years old; also *absol.* as *sb.*; **semi-Bantu** *a.*, of or pertaining to a number of languages in Central and West Africa closely related to the Bantu family; also as *sb.*; **semi-basement,** a basement room or rooms set only partially below ground level; **semi-broch** *Archæol.*, in the Hebrides and western mainland of Scotland: a hollow-walled fort-like structure representing a stage of development between the galleried dun and the broch; **semi-cell** *Bot.*, each of the two parts of a cell which is constricted in the middle, as in desmids; **semi-chemical** *a.*, applied to (wood pulp made by) a pulping process in which wood chips are subjected to mild chemical delignification followed by mechanical processing; **semi-classical** *a.*, (*a*) *gen.*, esp. in *Music*; (*b*) *Physics*, designating a theory that is intermediate in its assumptions and methods between the classical, or Newtonian, description and that of modern physics, esp. in quantum mechanics and relativity; hence **semi-classically** *adv.*; **semi-closed** *a.*, (*b*) *Med.*, applied to methods of administering anæsthetics employing a gas supply that is closed from the atmosphere and in excess of the patient's needs, the excess being vented to the atmosphere; (cf. *OPEN *a.* 11 h, *SEMI-OPEN *a.*); **semi-cursive** *a. Palæogr.*, of or pertaining to one of various scripts combining cursive features with elements of a more formal style; also *absol.* as *sb.*; **semi-diesel, -Diesel** *a.*, of an engine: (see quot. 1974); also as *sb.*, an engine of this type; **semi-display** *Typogr.*, a lay-out (for advertisements, etc.) intermediate between the run-on and displayed styles; hence **semi-displayed** *a.*; **semi-documentary** *a.*, of or pertaining to a film that presents factual or semi-factual material in fictional form; also as *sb.*; **semi-empirical** *a.*, that derives in part from theoretical considerations and in part from the results of experiment; so **semi-empirically** *adv.*; **semi-evening dress** (also **gown,** etc.), (a) fashionable dress (gown, etc.) of less than fully formal design suitable for both afternoon and evening wear; also *ellipt.* as **semi-evening** *sb.*; **semi-fabricated** *a.*, (of a material) formed into some standard shape for use in the making of finished articles; so **semifabricator,** a manufacturer of semifabricated goods; **semi-finalist,** a competitor in a semi-final; **semifinished** *a.*, (of a material, esp. steel) manufactured or treated for use in the making of finished articles; **semi-fitting** *a.*, designating clothing that partly fits the figure; **semi-gloss** *a.*, designating a finish intermediate between matt and glossy; **semi-intensive** *a. Agric.*, of or pertaining to a method of rearing livestock that includes features of intensive farming; **semileptonic** *a. Particle Physics*, involving both leptons and hadrons; hence **semileptonically** *adv.*; **semi-main** *U.S.* = *REPÊCHAGE; **semi-manufacture,** a product made from raw materials and used in the manufacture of finished goods; **semi-portal** *a.*, applied to a crane mounted on a frame consisting essentially of a horizontal member supported at one end by an upright; **semi-proletariat** *Communism* [tr. Chinese *bànwú-chǎnjiējí* (1926 Mao Zedong)], the class of poor peasants and others intermediate between the proletariat and the petty bourgeoisie; **semi-psychic** *adv.* and *a. Bridge*, (see quot. 1964); **semi-quantitative** *a.*, partly quantitative; approximate; based on or yielding approximate figures; hence **semi-quantitatively** *adv.*; **semi-reflecting** *a.*, designating a material of low reflectivity (usu. a film deposited on a transparent base) which permits partial reflection and partial transmission; hence **semi-reflection; semi-reflector; semi-reflective** *a.*; **semi-scale,** half or some fraction of full-scale; usu. *attrib.*; [**semi-sequitur** [after *non sequitur*], an inference or conclusion which is related only indirectly to the premisses; **semi-sub,** short for **semi-submersible* sb.; **semi-submersible** *a.* and *sb.*, (applied to) an offshore drilling platform or barge equipped with submerged hollow pontoons that can be flooded with water when the vessel is anchored on site in order to give it stability against waves and wind; **semi-synthetic** *a.*, that is a mixture of synthetic and natural materials, or has been prepared by artificial modification of a natural material; that is a combination of synthetic and natural processes; **semi-tropical** *a.* (earlier example); **semi-truck** *U.S.*, = *SEMI-TRAILER; **semi-variable** *a. Econ.*, of a cost (see quot. 1965); **semi-works** *U.S.*, a manufacturing plant used to develop and perfect a new product or process after testing in a pilot plant and before full-scale production; usu. *attrib.*

1954 K. W. GATLAND *Devel. Guided Missile* (ed. 2) iii. 83 Final guidance is obtained by the technique known as 'semi-active homing', the missile responding to target reflection from the ground radar. **1945** G. G. LEWIS *Pract. Bk. Oriental Rugs* (ed. 6) v. ii. 304 Antique or semi-antique Chinese rugs are as scarce as hen's teeth. **1970** J. FRANSES *European & Oriental Rugs* 3 Its wool is handspun on all the early carpets and semi-antiques. **1979** *Tucson Mag.* Apr. 23/1 The semi-antique Iranian prize rug was rolled up. **1919** H. H. JOHNSTON *Compar. Study Bantu & Semi-Bantu Languages* ii. 17 The semi-Bantu languages on this north-west borderland have a vocabulary which contains a greater or smaller amount of Bantu roots. *Ibid.* 814 The Indiki language of the southern Maneñguba country [is an]..interesting form of Semi-Bantu. **1977** *Language* LIII. 291 Bantu and Semi-Bantu classifiers do have meaning. **1934** Semi-basement in WEBSTER. **1963** *Punch* 20 Nov. 729/1 Desks crowded among filing cabinets in semi-basement. **1974** *Country Life* 7 Mar. (Suppl.) 321/1 Semi-basement boiler/drying room, playroom. **1903** E. BEVERIDGE *Coll & Tiree* x. 73

The Semi-broch type. It may be bold to introduce a new name in our description of the Tiree Duns, but a type seems to occur here which is..distinct from the ruder Hill-Forts. **1963** *Times* 16 Feb. 10/4 Tiree has some 20 dun sites, of which four appear to be hollow-walled semi-brochs. **1980** *Glasgow Archaeol. Jrnl.* VII. 73/1 There are only three semibrochs on the whole of the NW coast of Scotland. **1872** H. C. Wood *Contrib. Hist. Fresh-Water Algæ N. Amer.* 101 Divided into two symmetrical semi-cells. **1927** West & Fritsch *Treat. Brit. Freshwater Algæ* 259 The young semicells are clearly recognisable and nuclear division is complete before any change takes place in the chloroplasts of the parent. **1969** F. E. Round *Introd. Lower Plants* ii. 27 Each mature semicell is ornamented or produced into spines and looked at from the apices is constructed on a bilateral..or triangular basis. **1925** *Paper Trade Jrnl.* 15 Oct. 57/1 The various processes ..for the production of semi-cellulose as above defined may conveniently be termed semi-chemical inking processes, as they consist essentially of some chemical treatment combined with a mechanical disintegration of the partially cooked wood. **1961** *Times* 2 June 26/2 A new semi-chemical pulp mill to use indigenous woods. **1974** *Sci. Amer.* Apr. 56/3 Semichemical processes are applied mainly to hardwoods because of the lower content of lignin in such wood. **1949** *Billboard* 2 Apr. 34/3 Albums listed are those classical and semi-classical albums selling best in the nation's retail record stores. **1964** J. W. Linnett *Electronic Struct. Molecules* i. 6 In quantum mechanics the orbits of the Bohr-Sommerfeld semi-classical methods are replaced by orbitals. **1970** G. K. Woodgate *Elem. Atomic Struct.* i. 4 Another important quantity corresponds semi-classically to the speed of the electron in the first Bohr orbit as a fraction of the speed of light. **1914** J. T. Gwathmey *Anesthesia* vi. 272 Semi-Closed method.—Martin Ware has reported one or two thousand cases without a fatality. **1977** *Proc. R. Soc. Med.* LXX. 784/2 Anaesthesia with spontaneous breathing usually employs a semi-closed circuit. **1927** *Bull. Bezan Club* IV. 11 These lines, on both the Greek and Latin sides, are written not in a stiff, formal book-script, but in an easy-going semi-cursive. **1948** D. Diringer *Alphabet* II. x. 545 The Italian semi-cursive minuscule..developed from the Roman minuscule, was employed throughout Italy from the seventh to the ninth century, and continued to be used in Tuscany until the twelfth century. **1968** *PMLA* LXXXIII. 23/1 The script..may be described as an upright, bold but somewhat ungainly *cursiva* (*anglicana*) *formata*, or semi-cursive in older and looser nomenclature. **1911** *Engineer* 7 June 27/1 (*caption*) Semi-Diesel oil engine. **1920** R. A. McMillan *Guide to B.O.T. Exam. for Extra First-Class Engineers* xv. 396 A common type of Semi-Diesel is the Bolinder engine. **1960** G. Blanchet *Search in North* i. 19 From the engine exhaust came the hollow staccato of the semi-diesel. **1974** *McGraw-Hill Dict. Sci. & Techn. Terms* 1323/2 *Semidiesel engine.* 1. An internal combustion engine of a type resembling the diesel engine in using heavy oil as fuel but employing a lower compression pressure and spraying it under pressure, against a hot (uncooled) surface or spot, or igniting it by the precombustion or supercompression of a portion of the charge in a separate member or uncooled portion of the combustion chamber. 2. A true diesel engine that uses a means other than compressed air for fuel injection. **1971** *Cabinet Maker & Retail Furnisher* 24 Sept. 537 Run-on and Semi-display Announcements are set only in Times Bold and Times Roman. **1976** *Horse & Hound* 10 Dec. 65/1 (Advt.), Advertisers wishing to take a smaller space may use semi display with a minimum size of 2 cms but no blocks or illustrations are permissible in this style. **1972** *Daily Tel.* 5 July 6 *Run-on* (minimum setting) and *semi-displayed* (with lines of white space, indents, or double-line capitals)—£1.40 per line. **1939** L. Jacobs *Rise of Amer. Film* 413 Allied in spirit to the semi-documentary films were the realistic regional dramas. **1948** L. Levy *Music for Movies* xiii. 131 (*heading*) The semi-documentary. **1958** *New Statesman* 3 May 567/3 Granada's main achievement is to prove that serious semi-documentary or discussion programmes (*Under Fire*, *Youth wants to Know*, *What the Papers Say*) can be successful entertainment. **1935** Condon & Shortley *Theory of Atomic Spectra* i. 9 The results..were obtained in semi-empirical ways from consideration of a formulation of the theory that was only true in the limit of large quantum numbers. **1970** Semi-empirical [see *pre-exponential* s.v. *pre- B. 1 d]. **1976** *Physical Rev. Lett.* XXXVI. 375/1 We may now semiempirically incorporate the major factor neglected so far. **1917** *Vogue* Early Apr. 3/1 Semi-evening or Afternoon Gown in best quality Chiffon Taffetas and Ninon de Soie. **1923** A. Huxley *Antic Hay* x. 156 For semi-evening dress, shell rims with gold earpieces. **1923** B. Ruck *Dancing Star* i. vi. 117 Ripple's frock was the kind of garment dear to the compromise-loving British heart. It was '*a semi-evening*', which, to a purist, means that the dress is appropriate neither to evening or afternoon. **1938** E. Bowen *Death of Heart* i. ix. 155 She asked me to come to Peter Jones's with her to help her choose a semi-evening dress. *a* **1976** A. Christie *Autobiogr.* (1977) iii. iv. 155, I had a pale grey *crêpe de Chine* semi-evening dress. **1947** J. Newton *Introd. Metallurgy* (ed. 2) v. 238 Rolling not only produces finished shapes such as plates, sheets,..and rails, but many semifabricated shapes such as steel, copper, and brass rod for wire drawing; steel billets for forging and piercing. **1976** *Scotsman* 24 Dec. 4/5 Alcan (US), are also to raise prices for their semifabricated aluminium products. **1967** *Economist* 29 July 425/3 Hitherto most of this east European aluminium has been bought by the giant non-American producers... It has then either been passed on to their own semi-fabricators or sold to the independent semi-fabricators at the official producers' price. **1898** Semi-finalist [see -ist 4 b]. **1922** *Daily Mail* 24 Nov. 11 Beaten semi-finalists. **1972** D. Delman *Sudden Death* (1973) ii. 39 The year before he'd been champion at Wimbledon and a semi-finalist at Forest Hills. **1942** *R.A.F. Jrnl.* 16 May (*verso rear cover*), Germany would have to supply raw materials and semi-finished products. **1959** [see *forge-master* s.v. *forge *sb.* 6 b]. **1972** *Daily Tel.* 9 Feb. 2/4 The plastics industry expects that about 50 per cent. of finished and semi-finished products will be wholly or partially metricated by mid-1971. **1897** Semi-fitting [in Dict., sense 1 a]. **1930** *Daily Express* 8 Sept. 7/5 (Advt.), Semi-fitting bodice, with belt forming waist-line. **1963** *Times* 8 Jan. 11/2 A mid-tone matt or semi-gloss single colour. **1935** J. S. Hicks *Encycl. Poultry* II. 509 A semi-intensive house may be of any size from one, say, 6 ft. by 6 ft. by 6 ft., capable of housing ten or a dozen birds, to a mammoth affair for the accommodation of 500 or more layers. **1966** *Economist* 1 Oct. 72/2 Beef growers are turning to what is termed 'semi-intensive' beef rearing instead. This combines intensive grazing with fattening on high protein compounds to produce a 15- to 18-month-old beast for market. **1965** *Physical Rev. Lett.* XIV. 51 (*heading*) SU(6) and semileptonic interactions. **1979** *Nature* 14 June 588/2 If the D decays semi-leptonically some of its energy is taken by the unobserved neutrino. **1968** *Surfer Mag.* Jan. 48/1 Overland finally got into the finals by winning the men's semi-main. **1979** *Tucson* (Arizona) *Citizen* 28 Apr. 2B/5 The top two finishers in the consolation and 25-lap semi-main will qualify for the final run for the lion's share of the $12,000 purse. **1935** *Economist* 16 Feb. 353/1 Japan is exporting more finished goods and manufactured foodstuffs, importing more raw materials and semi-manufactures. **1979** *Shell Trade in Eastern Europe* (Shell Internat. Petroleum Co.) 3 Historically, Eastern European exports to the West have been principally raw materials, semi-manufactures, fuels and agricultural produce. **1908** A. Tolhausen tr. *Böttcher's Cranes* vi. 256 (*heading*) Semi-portal travelling crane, with central steam supply station. **1958** *Times Rev. Industry* Oct. 20/3 Electric semi-portal cranes serving three transit sheds. **1951** tr. M. Litvinoff in J. Degras *Soviet Documents on Foreign Policy* I. 136 This new apparatus of power should embody the dictatorship of the working class (and in some places also the rural semi-proletariat, i.e. the poor peasants). **1965** J. Ch'ên *Mao & Chinese Revolution* (1967) i. v. 110 The semi-proletariat, according to Mao, consisted of the overwhelming majority of the semi-tenant peasants, poor peasants, handicraftsmen, shop assistants and pedlars. **1975** J. De Bres tr. *Mandel's Late Capitalism* xi. 362 Many of the producers in the export branch are recruited from the stratum of the semi-proletariat who engage in wage labour only to obtain a supplementary income to eke out their means of subsistence in agriculture. **1960** T. Reese *Play Bridge with Reese* 118 Unless he has opened semi-psychic he should have both the minor suit Queens. **1962** *Listener* 3 May 790/3 North opened with a semi-psychic One Club. **1964** *Official Encycl. Bridge* 493/2 *Semi-psychic*, a departure from normal bidding methods which is not a complete bluff but is still intended to deceive the opponents. The term usually refers to an opening bid well below minimum values, but lead-inhibiting bids belong in the same category. **1929** Parker & Crozier in C. Murchison *Found. Exper. Psychol.* viii. 362 The comparison of odors is possible, in an empirically semi-quantitative way, by the use of several such instruments. **1977** *Sci. Amer.* May 39/2 The first semiquantitative step in generalizing the theory of crystalline semiconductors to amorphous materials was taken by Sir Nevill Mott of the University of Cambridge. **1956** *Nature* 21 Jan. 127/1 The intermediate products formed in the hydrolysis of the cyclic oligomers of ϵ-caprolactam..have been identified and semi-quantitatively determined. **1927** *Jrnl. Sci. Instruments* IV. 491 (*heading*) Semi-reflecting surfaces. **1946** *Nature* 20 July 101/2 For glass surfaces that have not been made semi-reflecting these [interference patterns] do not have the contrast of reflected interference patterns. **1976** Z. Knittl *Optics of Thin Films* ix. 374 A common feature of many synthesis problems is the condition for $1(\omega^2)$ to be flat in a certain range about $\omega = 0$ and at a certain level. Depending on this level we have the anti-reflection or the semireflection problem. **1973** *Sci. Amer.* June 69/1 The devices can be made transmissive for rear-lighting applications,..or semireflective for both kinds of operation. **1945** *Jrnl. Sci. Instruments* XXII. 103/1 Before 1936, the majority of semi-reflectors were made by chemical deposition of silver. **1976** Z. Knittl *Optics of Thin Films* ix. 397 Chebyshev-type semireflectors..may be only one of the ways of achieving a broad-band maximum. **1946** *Nature* 7 Sept. 337/2 It is impossible in chemical engineering and many other branches of applied science to conduct research entirely in the laboratory; full-scale or semi-scale plant must be used. **1973** *Ibid.* 2 Feb. 319/1 In 'semi-scale' tests (about a tenth the size of a real reactor) water failed..to stay in the test vessel. **1965** *Punch* 24 Nov. 779/1 The discords between received Edwardian fiction and child-observed fact work as poignantly as ever, as do the semi-sequiturs: 'He was broad and stout and had a manful way of carelessly swinging his arms that gave him many friends.' **1975** *Offshore Engineer* Sept. 55/1 *Staflo*..and *Sea Quest*..along with the ill-fated *Ocean Prince*, are the only semi-subs built in the UK. **1962** *World Oil* Sept. 96/3 The rig is an all weather, semi-submersible which is submerged to the 40 foot level in normal drilling operations. **1963** *World Petroleum* Aug. 47/1 The semi-submersible vessels give a desired balance between cost, safety and performance. **1975** *North Sea Background Notes* (Brit. Petroleum Co.) 11 Semi-submersibles can be used for drilling when resting on the sea bottom, but they are generally employed in the floating position. **1980** *Christian Sci. Monitor* (Mid-western ed.) 4 Dec. 11/1 A third delineation well..was spudded on Nov. 14 five miles west of P-15 by the newly arrived semi-submersible drilling rig. **1946** *Nature* 7 Sept. 350/2 The method may give still better results if..semi-synthetic mediums are used for the toxin production. **1974** *Ibid.* 19 Apr. 706/2 Rats..were fed a semisynthetic diet for 3 months. **1856** J. C. Patteson *Let.* 18 June in C. M. Yonge *Life J. C. Patteson* (1874) I. 258 Many New Zealand and many semi-tropical plants. **1975** J. Grady *Shadow of Condor* viii. 130 The bus parked between two idling semi-trucks. **1965** H. K. Compton *Gloss. Purchasing & Supply Managem. Terms.* 123 *Semi-variable cost*, a cost which is partly fixed and partly variable, such as the cost of placing orders, carrying stock, etc., each of which has a fixed cost content, and a variable cost proportional to the volume of throughput. **1971** D. C. Hague *Managerial Econ.* ii. v. 104 Depreciation is a semi-variable cost. **1935** *Industr. & Eng. Chem.* XXVII. 863/2 The main purpose of the semi-works is the development to a financially profitable stage of those processes which have been initiated in the laboratory. **1945** H. D. Smyth *Gen. Acct. Devel. Atomic Energy Mil. Purposes* vii. 74 These include all aspects of the research, development and semi-works studies necessary for the design, construction, and operation of chain-reacting piles. **1956** A. H. Compton *Atomic Quest* 152 A 'semi-works' installation where they could train the men needed for the final operation and where they could make preliminary tests of their equipment and processes.

semi-a·rid, *a.* [Semi- 7 i.] Having slightly more precipitation than an arid climate, grasses being the characteristic vegetation.

1898 [in Dict., s.v. Semi- 7 i]. **1916** *Daily Colonist* (Victoria, B.C.) 22 July 4/2 Irrigation is being more and more applied to cultivated lands that are neither arid nor semi-arid. **1941** J. S. Huxley *Uniqueness of Man* ii. 61 The semi-arid bush country provides but scanty nutriment. **1976** *Sci. Amer.* Sept. 99/2 The wheat plant, which dominates the semiarid croplands of the world, fills the need in this area for a cultivated crop with a lower demand for water and a great tolerance of drought.

semi-automa·tic, *a.* and *sb.* [Semi- 1 a, 7 l.]

A. *adj.* Partially automatic; *spec.* designating a system, device, or machine whose function is not completely automatic.

1890 W. James *Princ. Psychol.* I. 5 The performances of animal *instinct* seem semi-automatic, and the ***reflex acts*** of self-preservation certainly are so. **1937** [see *chrome *sb.* 1 b]. **1970** *Computers & Humanities* IV. 351 *Scope:* To make more specific and semiautomatic the testing technique of scientific works, intensive critique of books and other lengthy works.

2. Specialized uses. **a.** Of a type of lathe: that can perform a number of distinct operations on a given work-piece without intervention from an operator.

1903 T. R. Shaw *Lathes, Screw Machines, Boring & Turning Mills* xii. 505 A semi-automatic lathe, having four spindles, is illustrated. **1950** S. J. Gibson in A. W. Judge *Centre, Capstan & Automatic Lathes* II. iv. 181 The 'Maximatic'..is semi-automatic only in the sense that the loading is done by hand.

b. *Mil.* Of a firearm: that loads itself or performs part of the loading operation automatically, but does not fire continuously.

1911 H. A. Bethell *Mod. Artillery in Field* i. 15 Semi-Automatic Actions.—In these the breech opens automatically during the run up, and ejects the cartridge case. **1945** C. E. Balleisen *Princ. Firearms* i. 2 Most 'automatic' pistols are only *semiautomatic.* **1976** J. Wainwright *Walther P.38* 7 The Luger..was a *semi*-automatic pistol... Its trigger had to be squeezed for each shot.

c. Applied to a telephone system of which the operation is automatic except that dialling of the required number is done by an operator (see quots.).

1912 J. Poole *Pract. Telephone Handbk.* (ed. 5) xxxii. 536 Semi-automatic systems are in use on the Continent, and also in some towns in America, but not to any great extent. **1927** C. W. Wilman *Man. Automatic Telephony* xxii. 219 It is claimed for semi-automatic systems that many of the advantages of automatic systems, such as the rapidity of connection and instantaneous clearing, are retained, while the subscribers are relieved of the duty of dialling. **1976** T. H. Flowers *Introd. Exchange Systems* iii. 65 It was asserted that if a subscriber paid for service as he did, it was not right and was even dishonest to make him do his own operating, so semi-automatic exchanges with operators to do the dialling was the right thing.

B. *sb.* **1.** A semi-automatic lathe.

1902 *Lockwood's Dict. Mech. Engin.* (ed. 3) 444 *Semi-automatics*, these constitute a large class of machines which occupy a middle position between the..'full' automatic machines and those which involve the constant attendance of an operator. **1963** N. Weinstein tr. *Boguslavsky's Automatic & Semi-Automatic Lathes* i. 32 If internal surfaces are to be machined in addition to external surfaces, semi-automatics having a central end-working toolslide, or a turret are employed.

2. A semi-automatic firearm.

1964 H. L. Peterson *Encycl. Firearms* 31/2 In 1916, the Germans introduced a limited number of Mauser semi-automatic rifles. The French followed in 1917, with the Saint-Étienne gas-operated semi-automatic. **1978** S. Brill *Teamsters* vi. 239 The gunman reached down, held the High Standard semiautomatic against Mrs. Rand's chin and fired three more shots.

semi-barbarous, *a.* (Earlier example.)

1798 A. F. M. Willich *Elements Crit. Philos.* p. cxxii, The ancient Britons were as little acquainted with the art of writing, as any of the rude and semi-barbarous nations of those times.

se:mibrachia·tion. *Zool.* [Semi- 2 a.] A mode of progression exhibited by certain monkeys in which the forelimbs may be used both as legs in a quadrupedal gait and as arms by which to grasp and swing.

1961 J. R. Napier in *Symp. Zool. Soc. Lond.* V. 127 The twist [of the head] is generally seen in Primates that combine a quadrupedal gait with the specialized arboreal locomotor patterns of brachiation and semi-brachiation. [*Note*] The term semibrachiation has been devised by the author in association with Dr E. H. Ashton to describe the highly arboreal and acrobatic activities of certain of New and Old World monkeys. **1972** W. C. O. Hill *Evolutionary Biol. Primates* ix. 65 Old World exponents of semibrachiation include the six or more genera of the family Colobidae (the Asiatic leaf monkeys and the African *Colobus*).

Hence **semibra·chiating** *ppl. a.*; **semibra·chiator,** an animal that exhibits semibrachiation.

1963 J. R. NAPIER in *Symp. Zool. Soc. Lond.* X. 186 The mode of locomotion of semibrachiators is basically that of an arboreal quadruped but, in addition, a variable amount of time is spent in swinging by the arms and leaping with the forelimbs outstretched to grasp a handhold. *Ibid.* 188 The African semibrachiating *Colobus* shows a decided preference for the higher strata of the forest canopy. **1973** *Nature* 10 Aug. 373/2 With respect to locomotion, the first component separates quadrupedal cercopithecoids from both knuckle-walkers..and the quadrupedal arm-swinger (so-called 'semi-brachiator') *Ateles.*

semicarbazide (semikā·ɹbăzəid). *Chem.* [f. SEMI- 7 h + CARB- + Az(o- + -IDE.] A colourless, crystalline, basic solid, $NH_2 \cdot CO \cdot NH \cdot NH_2$, derived from urea by substitution of a hydrazino group for one of the amino groups, which reacts with carbonyl compounds to form semicarbazones. Also, a derivative of this.

1892 *Jrnl. Chem. Soc.* LXII. II. 1297 When amidoguanidine is treated with dilute acids, or with caustic alkalis, it is first converted into semicarbazide with liberation of ammonia. **1938** G. H. RICHTER *Textbk. Org. Chem.* xiii. 224 Semicarbazide is a valuable reagent for.. the Wolff-Kishner reduction of the carbonyl group. **1968** R. O. C. NORMAN *Princ. Org. Synthesis* x. 315 In order to obtain derivatives for the characterization of the carbonyl compound it is more satisfactory to use a monosubstituted hydrazine; semicarbazide, phenylhydrazine, and 2,4-dinitrophenylhydrazine are commonly chosen.

semicarbazone (semikā·ɹbăzōᵘn). *Chem.* [f. prec. + -ONE.] Any of a class of (usu. crystalline) compounds of general formula $RR'C:N \cdot NH \cdot CO \cdot NH_2$ which are prepared by the condensation of semicarbazide with carbonyl compounds, in order to characterize the parent carbonyl or to protect the carbonyl group in synthesis.

1896 *Jrnl. Chem. Soc.* LXX. I. 343 Mesityl oxide semicarbazone melts at 156°. **1938** G. H. RICHTER *Textbk. Org. Chem.* vii. 102 The semicarbazones may be converted into hydrazones by the action of sodium ethylate. **1973** H. J. E. LOEWENTHAL in J. F. W. McOmie *Protective Groups in Org. Chem.* ix. 340 In general, and in the steroid field in particular, ease of semicarbazone formation from different types of carbonyl groups follows the order observed with other protecting groups.

semicha (semī·χă). *Judaism.* Also **semichah, semikhah,** and with capital initial. [Heb. *sᵉmīkhāh*, lit. leaning.] The laying-on of hands by which a rabbi is ordained; the ordination of a rabbi. Also, a diploma of rabbinical ordination.

The laying-on of hands, practised only in antiquity, was later replaced by a proclamation (also called *semicha*).

1866 *Chambers's Encycl.* VIII. 70/1 Out of the number of the regular disciples (Talmidim) were chosen the Chaberim (Colleagues), who, again, were elected to the dignity of a rabbi by the 'Semichah', or imposition of hands by three members of the Sanhedrim. **1914** J. HASTINGS *Encycl. Relig. & Ethics* VII. 604/2 Among these Rabbis there grew up the desire to re-establish the old Rabbinic supremacy of Palestine. They desired to institute once more the *sᵉmîkhāh*, or ordination, and thus ordain a Sanhedrin which would be recognized throughout the world. **1962** *New Jewish Encycl.* 438/2 Technically, Semikhah ceased some two thousand years ago, and was not established anew until the 14th or 15th century. In modern times rabbinical students are granted Semikhah, that is, they receive a rabbinical diploma and become ordained as rabbis upon graduation from a rabbinical school or *Yeshivah*. **1973** *Jewish Chron.* 9 Feb. 22/1 The principal..accepts the fact that some of his best students go on to Gateshead for their semicha, not merely with resignation, but with positive approval. **1976** B. WILLIAMS *Making of Manch. Jewry* vii. 184 The possession of Rabbinical *semikhah* endorsed by European rabbis of unquestioned repute.

semicondu·cting, *a.* *Physics.* [SEMI- 7 a.] Having the properties of a semiconductor.

1782 tr. A. Volta in *Phil. Trans. R. Soc.* LXXII. p. xii, The surface of those bodies does not contract any electricity, or if any electricity adheres to them, it vanishes soon, on account of their semi-conducting nature. **1787** [in Dict. s.v. SEMI- *prefix* 8]. **1884** J. T. SPRAGUE *Electricity* (ed. 2) xiii. 573 A semi-conducting incandescent material compounded of infusible earths and carbon or metals. **1975** D. G. FINK *Electronics Engineers' Handbk.* VII. 31 By far the most widely used semiconducting materials are germanium and silicon.

Also **semicondu·ctive** *a.*, in the same sense; **semicondu·ction, se:miconducti·vity.**

1931 *Proc. R. Soc.* A. CXXXIII. 469 To explain the general outlines of semi-conduction. **1953** *Jrnl. Inst. Electr. Engineers* C. I. 76/2 The value of semiconductive glaze lies in its use in situations where trouble is expected due to flashover of insulators under adverse weather..conditions. **1954** R. P. TURNER *Transistors* i. 8 Many..elements and compounds have been found to possess semiconductivity in varying amounts. **1960** *Cambr. Rev.* 27 Feb. 394/1 Although a Cambridge physicist, A. H. Wilson, put forward the basic theory of their behaviour in 1931, it is really only in the last ten years that the phenomena of semiconductivity have been clearly understood. **1973** K. SEEGER *Semiconductor Physics* i. 2 Semiconduction is specified by the following properties:[etc.].

semicondu·ctor. *Physics.* [SEMI- 7 a.] **1. a.** A material whose capacity to conduct electricity is intermediate between that of a good conductor and an insulator. *Obs.* exc. as in next sense.

1838 *Ann. Electr., Magn., & Chem.* III. 316 Lichtenberg ..observes..'it is deserving of a trial also whether phosphorus would not become ignited at points whence a stream [of electricity] is issuing, on a semi-conductor being inserted between them'. **1863** E. ATKINSON tr. *Ganot's Elem. Treat. Physics* IX. iv. 592 The retardation which electricity experiences in traversing a semi-conductor, such as a wet string. **1879** [in Dict. s.v. SEMI- 8]. **1900** *Engineering* 28 Sept. 412/3 Semi-conductors like iron filings.

b. *spec.* Such a material in which there is a narrow gap between permitted energy bands, so that the only current carriers are electrons thermally excited from the valence band into the conduction band (*intrinsic semiconductor*: see *INTRINSIC *a.* 3 e) or into intermediate energy levels provided by impurity ions (*extrinsic semiconductor*).

1931 *Proc. R. Soc.* A. CXXXIII. 459 It is not possible to maintain that the difference between good and bad conductors is one of degree only... There is an essential difference between a semi-conductor, such as germanium, and a good conductor, such as silver, which must be accounted for by any theory which attempts to deal with semi-conductors. **1946** *Electronic Engin.* XVIII. 66/2 It is well known that 'semi-conductors', such as carbon, silicon.., etc., possess negative temperature coefficients of resistance at ordinary temperatures. **1961** G. R. CHOPPIN *Exper. Nuclear Chem.* iii. 41 The semiconductor detectors..are made from thin (approximately 1mm) wafers of semiconductor silicon. **1970** J. SHEPHERD et al. *Higher Electrical Engin.* (ed. 2) xx. 623 In an extrinsic or doped semiconductor, impurities are added to the intrinsic material to give a predominance of either electrons (in *n*-type material) or holes (in *p*-type material) as charge carriers. **1979** *Jrnl. R. Soc. Arts* Oct. 692/2 Sometimes a significant advance in technology may itself create a new market, as did the advent of the semiconductors to the small 'transistor radio' market.

2. Special Combs.: **semiconductor diode,** a diode whose rectifying action depends on the properties of a junction between a semiconductor and either a metal or another type ef semiconductor; cf. *junction diode* (s.v. *JUNCTION *sb.* 4); **semiconductor junction** = *JUNCTION *sb.* 2 b; **semiconductor rectifier,** a semiconductor diode, usu. one intended for large currents; **semiconductor triode,** a junction transistor having two junctions.

1954 *Trans. IRE Prof. Group Broadcast & Television Receivers* July 34 (*heading*) Semiconductor diodes for TV receivers. **1975** FINK & MCKENZIE *Electronics Engineers' Handbk.* VII. 34 One of the highest-volume uses of the semiconductor diode is in computers. *Ibid.* 35 When a semiconductor junction is exposed to light, photons generate hole-electron pairs. **1946** *Physical Rev.* LXIX. 42/2 This effective contact e.m.f. is one important parameter in the theory and practice of semi-conductor rectifiers. **1962** *Times* 14 May 14/7 Semiconductor rectifiers on heavy-duty electric railway locomotives. **1948** *Physical Rev.* LXXIV. 230/1 (*heading*) A semi-conductor triode. **1970** D. F. SHAW *Introd. Electronics* (ed. 2) xii. 262 The transistor is a semiconductor triode possessing characteristics which are similar in many respects to those of thermionic triodes.

se:mi-conse·rvative, *a.* *Biochem.* [SEMI- 1.] Of the replication of nucleic acid: such that one complete strand of each double helix is directly derived from its parent.

The term was originally proposed (see quot. 1957) to designate a class of models of the replication of DNA; it is now accepted that its true mechanism of replication falls in this class.

1957 DELBRUCK & STENT in McElroy & Glass *Chem. Basis of Heredity* 707 The considerable number of proposed schemes may be divided into three general classes as conservative, semi-conservative, and dispersive. *Ibid.* 709 Semi-conservative mechanisms are those which conserve the atomic identity of single chains of the parental DNA duplex, although effecting a permanent separation of the two chains from each other in the course of replication. **1970** *Nature* 7 Nov. 522/1 There is good evidence that DNA replication is semi-conservative and involves separation of the two strands which then act as templates. **1976** P. COLLARD *Devel. Microbiol.* viii. 106 Semi-conservative replication thus provided a possible answer to the riddle of the stability of the genome from generation to generation.

Hence **se:miconse·rvatively** *adv.*

1966 *Jrnl. Molecular Biol.* XV. 372 Since all the DNA is replicated semiconservatively..such a segregation pattern could arise most simply if every chromosome contained all its DNA within a single molecule. **1979** *Nature* 3 May 75/2, pBR322 DNA replicates semiconservatively and completely in a crude lysate of *E. coli*.

semi-cry·stalline, *a.* [SEMI- 7 a.] Having or being a structure of crystals embedded in an amorphous groundmass; having or being a structure possessing crystalline character to some extent.

1816, etc. [in Dict., s.v. SEMI- 7 a]. **1871** *Phil. Mag.* XLII. 404 This silica forms a series of semi-crystalline bands parallel with the walls of the fissure. **1927** *Proc. Physical Soc.* XXXIX. 370 In 1924 I [*sc.* Rutherford] put forward a suggestion that the central nucleus was a closely ordered arrangement of α particles and electrons in a semi-crystalline formation. **1975** *Sci. Amer.* Dec. 99/2 Representative values for the percentage by volume of crystals in a number of semicrystalline polymers are high-density polyethylene, 75 percent; low-density polyethylene, polypropylene and nylon, 50 percent.

semi-demi-. (Earlier examples in both senses.)

a **1661** FULLER *Worthies* (1662) II. 246 [Rabbits'] wool is..used in making of hats, commonly..called half-beavers, though many of them hardly amount to the proportion of semi-demi-castors. **1826** J. F. DANNELEY *Mus. Gram.* 4 The Semidemisemiquaver has four hooks.

semi-det (semi,de·t), *sb.* Short for SEMI-DETACHED house.

1960 J. STROUD *Shorn Lamb* x. 110 An unexpected footpath in between a couple of semi-dets. **1978** J. MCNEIL *Consultant* xx. 174 A neat semidet with a bay window.

semi-detached, *a.* Add: **B.** *absol.* as *sb.* A semi-detached house. *colloq.*

1928 D. H. LAWRENCE *Lady Chatterley's Lover* xi. 188 New little streets of semi-detacheds were run up. **1957** M. & A. POTTER *Interiors* 43/2 The garden city notions.. blotting the green countryside everywhere with varieties of the popular 'semi-detached'. **1979** C. DEXTER *Service of All Dead* iii. 23 He'd found a quiet little semi-detached to rent.

semidine (se·midīn). *Chem.* [ad. G. *semidin* (P. Jacobson 1893, in *Ber. d. Deut. Chem. Ges.* XXVI. 700), f. *semi-* SEMI- + *benzi-din* benzidine (s.v. BENZO-).] Any compound which is either (*a*) an *ortho-* anilino-derivative, or (*b*) an *N-para*-aminophenyl derivative, of a *para*-substituted aniline (distinguished as *ortho-* and *para*-semidines respectively); also *semidine base*; *semidine reaction, transformation*, etc., the rearrangement of *para*-substituted hydrazobenzenes in the presence of acid to yield *ortho-* and *para*-semidines (in proportions governed by the nature of the substituents).

1893 *Jrnl. Chem. Soc.* LXIV. I. 330 The hydrazo-compound..undergoes molecular change yielding two compounds, derivatives of ortho- and of para-amido-diphenylamine. It is proposed to call this reaction the semidine reaction, and to designate the orthamido-diphenylamine bases thus obtained by the name ortho-semidines; the paramidodiphenylamine bases by the name parasemidines. **1898** *Ibid.* LXXIV. I. 441 Only 50 per cent. of the total semidines obtained. **1938** A. J. MEE tr. *P. Karrer's Org. Chem.* xxxiv. 498 If a *para*-position in hydrazobenzene is already occupied by a substituent, there are still further possibilities of isomerization. In addition to a diphenyline base and benzidine compounds .., two diphenylamine derivatives are formed in which only one of the benzene nuclei has rotated, the so-called *p*-semidine and *o*-semidine bases. The transformation is known as the semidine transformation. **1959** E. S. GOULD *Mech. & Structure in Org. Chem.* xv. 658 The re-arrangements of hydrazobenzenes to benzidines, to di-phenylenes, and to *o*-semidines are third-order reactions, first order in substrate and second order in hydrogen ion. **1975** R. F. BROWN *Org. Chem.* xxii. 772 A small amount of *o* shift occurs anyway, as well as a halfway shift to give semidines.

semi-dire·ct, *a.* [SEMI- 1 a.] Not wholly direct; *spec.* (of lighting) so disposed that most but not all of the light reaches the illuminated area without first being reflected.

1914 S. C. BATSTONE *Electr. Light Fitting* viii. 166 If a frosted glass bowl or something of a similar nature be placed between the lamps and the surface or space to be illuminated, the result is 'semi-direct lighting'. **1926** J. S. HUXLEY *Essays of Biologist* i. 15 We can learn a great deal from the semi-direct methods of paleontology. **1957** *Encycl. Brit.* XIV. 107/2 Semidirect [lighting equipment] .. 10–40 [% upward]. .. 60–90 [% downward]. **1971** POWELL & HIGMAN *Finite Simple Groups* viii. 294 We form the semi-direct product *GI*.

se·mi-field. *Math.* [SEMI- 7 a.] Used variously to denote a set, together with operations answering to addition and multiplication, that has certain specified properties of a field but not all of them.

1923 *Ann. Math.* XXIV. 240 A set *D* which satisfies these postulates will be called a semi-field. **1966** *Math. Rev.* XXXI. 39/2 A semifield is essentially an algebraic structure which satisfies all field axioms except perhaps associativity and commutativity of multiplication; the more customary terminologies are 'division ring' (not necessarily associative) and 'distributive quasifield'.

se·mi-group. *Math.* [ad. F. *semi-groupe* (J.-A. de Séguier *Élem. de la Théorie des Groupes Abstraits* (1904), i. 8); cf. SEMI- 7.] A set together with an associative binary operation under which it is closed.

1904 *Bull. Amer. Math. Soc.* XI. 160 The author [*sc.* de Séguier] introduces..a semigroup *G* in connection with any subset *S* containing a system of generators of *G*. The postulates defining *G* are: (1) associativity; (2) for any *a* in *S* and *b* in *G*, there is at most one solution (*n* in *G*) of *an* = *b*; (3) similarity for *na* = *b*. **1905** *Trans. Amer. Math. Soc.* VI. 205 The correct theorem involves the concept semi-group, which reduces to a group when there is a finite number of elements, but not in general for an infinitude of elements. **1968** P. A. P. MORAN *Introd. Probability Theory* ii. 66 The convolution operation..has some of the properties of multiplication in that it is associative..and commutative,..but division is not in general possible. With this operation the set of all discrete distributions on (0, 1, ...) is therefore said to form a 'semi-group'. **1972** A. G. HOWSOW *Handbk. Terms Algebra & Anal.* v. 25 A semigroup..possessing..an identity element..is called a monoid. **1979** *Proc. London Math. Soc.* XXXVIII. 335 First we find exactly when the resolvent operators and the semigroup operators are strong Feller operators.

se:mi-indire·ct, *a.* [SEMI- 1 a.] Of lighting: so disposed that most but not all of the light reaches the illuminated area indirectly, after having been reflected or scattered by some surface. Cf. *SEMI-DIRECT *a.*

1914 J. ECK tr. *Högner's Light, Radiation & Illumination* (*table facing p.* 44), Ordinary direct-current arc lamp with standard arrangement of carbons and opal glass bowl below the arc producing semi-indirect illumination. **1964** S. DUKE-ELDER *Parsons' Dis. of Eye* (ed. 14) xxxvii. 559 In semi-indirect lighting the use of opalescent bowls permits a certain amount of direct illumination.

semi-invariant: see SEMINVARIANT in Dict. and Suppl.

semikhah, var. *SEMICHA.

semi-le·thal, *a.* and *sb. Genetics.* [SEMI- 7 a.] **A.** *adj.* Of an allele or a chromosomal abnormality: causing impaired viability of most of the individuals homozygous for it.

1917 *Proc. Nat. Acad. Sci.* III. 621 The viability of the three sex-linked dominants was .. already known; the remaining six dominants were tested. In all, it was found that three of the nine are not lethal, one..is semi-lethal, and five..are completely lethal when homozygous. **1927** *Brit. Jrnl. Exper. Biol.* V. 124 This mutation appears to be semi-lethal, as the animals homozygous for it are delicate and difficult to rear. **1937** *Genetics* XXII. 471 A group of nine changes obtained from male 8..proved to be semilethal. **1962, 1973** [see *LETHAL *a.* 1 d].

B. *sb.* A semi-lethal gene.

1919 *Proc. Soc. Exper. Biol. & Med.* XVII. 12 Four of the lethals (perhaps five) are more strictly speaking 'semi-lethals', as they occasionally allow the male possessing them to live. **1944** *Proc. Nat. Acad. Sci.* XXX. 174 *Fu* is a tail mutation closely resembling *Ki*. It acts as a semi-lethal, some *Fu Fu* being viable. **1974** *Nature* 2 Aug. 451/3 Most of such populations in North America and Europe proved to be polymorphic for variant genes, usually embryonic lethals or semilethals, belonging to the T series.

Sémillon (semiyoṅ). Also **Semillon** and with small initial. [Fr. dial. (Midi), ult. ad. L. *semen* seed.] A white grape of France; also a similar one grown abroad; the white wine made from this grape.

1875, etc. [see *SAUVIGNON a]. **1926** [see *MONBAZILLAC]. **1963** *Times* 12 Mar. (Austral. Suppl.) p. xv/7 The best dry whites are made from the riesling and the semillon. **1978** *Courier-Mail* (Brisbane) 16 Nov. 20/5 If you think you know semillon, you may be surprised by the flavour of Huntington Estate's Mudgee semillon, 1978.

semi-log (stress variable), *a.* [Shortened f. next: cf. *LOG *sb.*[3] and *a.*] = next.

1921 W. C. MARSHALL *Graphical Methods* ii. 16 It often happens that log-log or semi-log paper would be preferable to rectangular ruled paper. **1941** *Trans. Amer. Soc. Mech. Engineers* LXIII. 539/2 We may expect..information on just why actual log curves do not plot straight on semilog paper. **1978** *Sci. Amer.* Mar. 150/3 A plot of the data on a semilog graph is shown.

se:mi-logari·thmic, *a.* Also **semilogarithmic.** [SEMI- 8.] Having or being a scale that is linear in one direction and logarithmic in the other. Cf. prec.

1919 A. C. HASKELL *How to make & use Graphic Charts* iv. 20 The semi-logarithmic chart has a wide use for the plotting of comparative statistics of similar kind but dissimilar magnitude. **1930** R. PEARL *Med. Biometry & Statistics* (ed. 2) vi. 183 The scale of the ordinates is divided not in arithmetic progression but in proportion to the logarithms of numbers in arithmetic progression. Such a ruling is called an arithlog or semi-logarithmic grid. **1977** J. L. HARPER *Population Biol. of Plants* xv. 458 Some of these are redrawn in Fig. 15/1 on a semi-logarithmic scale to show the change in range of dispersal if the seed crop is halved.

Hence **se:mi-logari·thmically** *adv.*

1919 A. C. HASKELL *How to make & use Graphic Charts* iv. 18 This is shown very clearly by charting the same data on both arithmetically and semi-logarithmically ruled paper. **1976** *Nature* 11 Mar. 153/2 Figure 1 is an action spectrum obtained by plotting semi-logarithmically the reciprocal of retinal irradiance ($1/W\ cm^{-2}$) against wavelength (nm) for each exposure duration.

semi-mature, *a.* Restrict † *Obs. rare*$^{-1}$ to sense in Dict. and add: **b.** [SEMI- 7 a.] Partially mature. (Examples in senses 1 b and *d of MATURE *a.*)

1928 *Bull. Amer. Soil Survey Assoc.* IX. 39 Semimature soil. **1976** *Southern Even. Echo* (Southampton) 16 Nov. 2/8 Semi-mature trees are to be planted in Station Road.

semi-metal. Delete *Old Chem.* and add: Now usu. signifying incomplete metallic character in other physical properties, esp. electrical conductivity; *spec.* an element (as arsenic, antimony, bismuth) or other substance having properties intermediate between those of true metals and those of semiconductors. (Later examples.)

1912 W. E. FORD *Dana's Man. Mineral.* (ed. 13) iv. 115 The semimetals—tellurium, arsenic, antimony and bismuth—belong together in a crystal group, all of them showing rhombohedral crystals with closely agreeing fundamental angles. **1952** *Chem. Abstr.* XLVI. 1187 Semimetals with continuous properties between metals and ceramics. **1972** *Science* 19 May 753/1 There is a clear trend both with increasing pressure and with atomic number from a semiconductor to a semimetal with a distorted simple cubic structure to a metallic, simple cubic phase.

semi-metallic, *a.* Add: (Later example.) Cf. *SEMI-METAL.

1974 D. M. ADAMS *Inorg. Solids* v. 88 In contrast, the heaviest elements of the same groups (Pb, Bi, Po) are metallic or semimetallic as revealed by a progressive change down the group in properties such as electrical conductivity and optical behaviour, as well as by changes of structure type.

semimicro- (semimǝi·kro), *prefix* and quasi-*adj. Chem.* [f. SEMI- 1 a + MICRO- 2 a, *8 b.]

a. Formative element denoting a scale of quantitative analysis between micro-scale and macro-scale (commonly 0·01–0·1 gramme), as in *semimicroanalysis, -analytical* adj., *-determination, -method.*

1951 A. I. VOGEL *Text-Bk. Quantitative Inorg. Analysis* (ed. 2) xi. 814 Semi-micro-analysis is concerned with the manipulation of 10–100 mg. of material, whilst micro-analysis deals with 1–10 mg. of material. **1938** *Jrnl. Soc. Chem. Industry* Dec. 464/1 (*heading*) The determination of free and saline ammonia using a semi-microanalytical method. **1937** *Industr. & Engin. Chem.* (*Analytical Ed.*) 15 June 296 (*heading*) Micro-, semimicro-, and macro-determination of halogens in organic compounds. **1933** *Ibid.* Nov. 402/1 Northrop..has used a semi-micromethod with an accuracy of 0·2 per cent. **1963** tr. *Alexeyev's Quantitative Analysis* i. 16 The main advantages of the micro- and semimicromethods are their high speed and the need for only very small amounts of material.

b. Used without hyphen as an independent word.

1935 *Industr. & Engin. Chem.* (*Analytical Ed.*) Nov. 432/1 Semi-micro adaptations of the classical Kjeldahl method..have been reported. **1946** F. SCHNEIDER *Qualitative Organic Microanalysis* ii. 39 Bernhauer describes several types of micro or semi-micro receivers for vacuum distillations. *Ibid.* vii. 195 A test for the nitro group carried out on a semi-micro scale. **1974** [see *MICRO- 8 b]. **1976** *Lancet* 13 Nov. 1091/2 Plasma creatinine (semi-micro alkaline-picrate method) and urea (diacetyl-monoxime method) concentrations were measured.

semi-mo·nocoque. [SEMI- 7 a.] **a.** *Aeronaut.* A fuselage or other structure having a rigid outer skin and a framework of longerons or stringers, so that stresses are shared between the skin and the framework. Usu. *attrib.*

1918 *Flight* 28 Feb. 224/2 This semi-*monocoque* structure would retain its strength even after damaging some of the longitudinal members. **1931** WARNER & JOHNSTON *Aviation Handbk.* 653 The semimonocoque has the skin reinforced by longerons and vertical bulkheads but has no diagonal web members. *Ibid.*, For the semimonocoque type the verticals should be designed as for the true monocoque designs. **1948** [see *MONOCOQUE a]. **1960** C. H. GIBBS-SMITH *Aeroplane* xii. 93 As many of the so-called 'monocoque' structures came to include internal stiffening members—the skin bearing most but not all of the loads —the term 'stressed-skin' is better, implying a 'semi-monocoque' rather than a wholly unaided 'shell' structure. **1980** R. C. MIKESH *Albatros D.Va* i. 13 Their semi-monocoque, smoothly contoured plywood fuselage was a radical change from the boxy, fabric-covered structures then in general use.

b. In a motor vehicle, a body or chassis combining features of the monocoque and space-frame types. Usu. *attrib.*

1966 *Publ. Amer. Dial. Soc.* 1964 XLII. 8 *Semi-monocoque, adj.*, applied to a chassis which combines constructions of both monocoque and space frame, such as that of the Jaguar. **1973** C. CAMPBELL *Design Racing Sports Cars* viii. 134 The Formula 1 solution is usually called 'semi-monocoque' since the typical design has a centre section that is more like a bath-tub than an egg.

seminal, *a.* and *sb.* Add: **A.** *adj.* **4. a.** Also, freq. used of books, work, etc., which are highly original and influential; more loosely: important, central to the development or understanding of a subject.

1947 *Partisan Rev.* XIV. 409 To be sure, Engels' more specialized *Anti-Dühring* and *Feuerbach*, if less seminal are more systematized, more apposite to Lenin's immediate purposes. **1957** D. J. ENRIGHT *Apothecary's Shop* 233 The seminal works of modern literary criticism (such as Eliot's earlier essays and Leavis's *Revaluation*). **1960** *Guardian* 14 Oct. 8/6 Everything he says is of real value... This is what academics call a seminal book. **1960** *Twentieth Century* Nov. 438 Since the war there has been..no seminal poet in the younger generation. **1977** *New Yorker* 6 June 122/2 That the two pianists, each seminal, agreed to play together at all was startling.

seminar[2]**.** Delete ||, transfer stress-dot to first syllable, and add: **b.** A conference of specialists; also, more generally, a course of instruction for managers, etc. orig. *U.S.*

1944 *Sun* (Baltimore) 21 Sept. 6/2 Problems of condemnation for the temporary war use of property will be featured at a seminar conducted by the American Institute of Real Estate Appraisers. **1969** *Listener* 10 Apr. 482/2 For the first time in its history, the Conservative Party has held a one-day seminar, not on Exports, or on Trade Unions, or on Defence, but on the Arts. **1982** *REMARC Database News* July 1 Key members of the Scottish Library Network..attended a REMARC seminar at the Carrollton Press data-entry facility at Irvine, Scotland.

2. *attrib.*

1948 *Sun* (Baltimore) 12 May 12/3 Two years ago he started the personal campaign that took him into large communities and small, and he developed a sort of '*seminar*' method of question-and-answer discussion at luncheons, meetings of students and similar gatherings. **1959** Seminar-paper [see *fence-sitting* s.v. *FENCE *sb.* 11]. **1977** J. D. DOUGLAS in Douglas & Johnson *Existential Sociol.* i. 27 One can even see the feelings leading to important actions, such as separating from a lover or starting a seminar workshop to deal with the feelings. **1981** *Times Lit. Suppl.* 6 Feb. 136/4 The names of these daunting authors..make an occasional modest appearance on reading-lists and in seminar-rooms.

seminarist. 3. (Later example.)

1972 *Daily Tel.* 14 Jan. 17 For a fee of £60, seminarists will be impressed with the need for strategic plans for growth..over the next decade, fed but not accommodated.

Seminole (se·minōᵘl), *sb.* and *a.* Also 8 **Seminollie,** 8–9 **Siminole,** etc. [ad. Creek *simanó:li* wild, runaway, earlier and dial. *simaló:ni*, f. Amer. Sp. *cimarrón* (cf. *CIMARRON).] **A.** *sb.* **1.** A member of any of several groupings of North American Indians that comprise or comprised Creek Confederacy emigrants in Florida, or their descendants now resident in Florida and Oklahoma, esp. the present-day Florida Indians, who speak the Muskogee and Mikasuki languages of the Muskogean family. Also as *collect. sing.*

1763 W. G. DE BRAHM in *Amer. Indian Ethnohist.: S. & S.E. Indians: Florida Indians* (1974) I. 244 The Surveyor General..must have fallen in with many Hunting Ganges of Semiolilies. **1771** in *Ibid.* III. 17 The Seminolies or East Florida Creeks had frequent intercourse with Spaniards..by means of Fishing vessels. **1789** *Amer. State Papers: Indian Affairs* (1832) I. 15 Some of the most southern towns of the Lower Creeks, or Seminoles, are within the territory of Spain. **1866** 'F. KIRKLAND' *Pict. Bk. Anecdotes* 318/2 He fainted at the spectacle, and was soon after butchered by a Seminole. **1910** F. W. HODGE *Handbk. Amer. Indians* II. 500/2 While still under Spanish rule the Seminole became involved in hostility with the United States. **1946** *Nat. Geogr. Mag.* Jan. 53/2 The later Seminole, who were primarily an offshoot of the Creeks and Hitchiti, were also a Muskhogean people. **1972** *Listener* 28 Dec. 904/3 Hidden here in the Everglades..a race of forgotten, proud but degenerate Seminoles.

2. An Eastern Muskogean language of the Seminoles.

1848 *Southern Lit. Messenger* XIV. 482/2, I concluded at the time [that the opera] was written in Seminole, as the only word which I distinctly heard was *en ca.* **1933** [see *CREEK *sb.*[3]]. **1972** J. L. DILLARD *Black Eng.* iv. 153 The sentence is in fact Pidgin English with some re-lexification by Seminole.

B. *adj.* **1.** Of, pertaining to, or designating any of the Seminole groupings, or these peoples collectively.

[**1774**: see sense 2 below.] **1775** W. BARTRAM in *Trans. Amer. Philos. Soc.* (1943) XXXIII. 160 These were Seven likely Young Siminole Fellows all elligantly drest & painted after the Indian fashions. **1797** J. MORSE *Amer. Gazetteer* s.v. *Calos*, Not far from this is a considerable town of Seminole Indians. **1837** H. MARTINEAU *Society in Amer.* II. 71 The Seminole fathers would not deliver them up. **1881** *Rep. Indian Affairs* (U.S.) p. lv, [They] were willing to incorporate the whole Seminole tribe into their nation. **1945** L. R. TRYON *Poor Man's Doctor* 3 The belt-like stone-crop, symbol of fertility to the original Seminole inhabitants of this paradise. **1973** A. H. WHITEFORD *North Amer. Indian Arts* 96 Seminole patchwork is unique among Indians of North America.

2. Special collocations: **Seminole horse,** a small horse belonging to a feral stock once found in south-eastern North America and locally domesticated by Indians and others; **Seminole war,** any of three wars waged by the U.S. against the Seminole Indians in 1817–18, 1835–42, and 1855–58.

1774 W. BARTRAM in *Trans. Amer. Philos. Soc.* (1943) XXXIII. 148 Here we saw herds of deer bounding before the chace of the naked active Floridian mounted on his fleet Siminole horse. **1806** P. WAKEFIELD *Excursions N. Amer.* xvi. 107 Extensive savannahs..maintain innumerable herds of deer, cattle, and Siminole horses, which are of a small breed. **1931** F. HARRISON *John's Island Stud (South Carolina) 1750–1788* 170 The Seminole (or Creek) horse, small in size and capricious in nature, having its origin in Florida. **1818** *Repub. Constellation* (Winchester, Va.) 11 July 2/1 Gen. Jackson..obtained full proof that the Spanish authorities at Pensacola had been active in fomenting the Seminole war. **1837** H. MARTINEAU *Society in Amer.* II. II. i. 71 Probably few of the United States troops who fell in the late Seminole war knew how the strife arose. **1948** *Florida Hist. Q.* July 35 Had not the Seminole war intervened, there is little question that the settlement of the present Taylor county would have begun ten years earlier than it did. **1973** D. AARON *Unwritten War* IV. xi. 171 Sergeant Weber.. veteran of the Seminole War.

seminoma (seminōᵘ·mă). *Path.* [mod.L., ad. F. *seminome* (M. Chevassu *Tumeurs du Testicule* (1906) i. 15), f. L. *sēmin-*, *sēmen* SEMEN: see *-OMA.] A malignant tumour of the testis, now acknowledged to derive from spermatogenic tissue.

[**1919** J. EWING *Neoplastic Dis.* xl. 773 (*caption*) Embryonal carcinoma of testis. ('Seminome of Chevassu').] **1931** *Amer. Jrnl. Obstetrics & Gynecol.* XXII. 697 The term seminoma was chosen because this testicular new-growth in parts of its structure resembles seminal tubules. **1966** WRIGHT & SYMMERS *Systemic Path.* I. xxvi. 820/1 Between 40 and 50 per cent of all testicular tumours are seminomas. **1974** J. D. MAYNARD in R. M. Kirk et al. *Surgery* viii. 190 The seminoma is a firm uniform mass of sheets of polyhedral cells with a tendency to undergo central necrosis.

semi-noma·dic, *a.* *Anthrop.* [SEMI- I a.] Of a people, way of life, etc.: partially nomadic and partially settled. Freq. applied to a social group that depends largely on seasonal pasturing.

1843 J. C. PRICHARD *Nat. Hist. Man* xxx. 316 The Kafirs are associated together in large communities under chiefs, or kings... They are semi-nomadic, although living in towns of considerable size..which they occasionally move. **1918** G. BELL *Let.* 17 Mar. (1927) II. xvii. 450 They were men of the Ghazzi, a semi-nomadic tribe near Nasiriyeh. **1954** KOESTLER *Invisible Writing* x. 110 The natives were left to their semi-nomadic existence. **1960** J. BRIGHT *Hist. Israel* ii. 73 The patriarchs..were semi-nomadic stockbreeders such as we know from the Tale of Sinuhe (twentieth century) or the Mari texts.

Hence **semi-no·mad** *a.* and *sb.*

1948 in D. Diringer *Alphabet* II. iv. 277 Semi-nomad Arabs may have had their settlements round the natural wells from time immemorial. **1960** J. BRIGHT *Hist. Israel* ii. 72 The patriarchs are portrayed as seminomads living in tents. **1972** *Catholic Bibl. Q.* Apr. 231 A seminomad sheep-farmer.

seminvariant. Add: **2.** *Statistics.* Any of a set of functions of a statistical distribution, each expressible as a polynomial in the moments.

Now usually spelt *semi-invariant.*

[**1903** T. N. THIELE *Theory of Observations* vi. 24 From the sums of powers we can easily compute also another serviceable collection of symmetrical functions, which for brevity we shall call the half-invariants.] **1922** A. FISHER *Math. Theory Probabilities* (ed. 2) xiv. 191 (*heading*) Semi-invariants of Thiele. **1930** *Biometrika* XXII. 225 Thiele, in 1889, after defining the semi-invariants, used symmetric functions of the observations of a sample which are the same functions of the sample moment coefficients as the population semi-invariants are of the population moment coefficients. He supplied an expression covering all the semi-invariants of the mean. **1968** P. A. P. MORAN *Introd. Probability Theory* vi. 267 The κ_n ($n \geqslant 2$) are dependent only on $\mu_2, \mu_3, ..$ and are the same for all distributions of the form $F(x + d)$ ($-\infty < d < \infty$). They are therefore sometimes known as 'semi-invariants' since they are invariant under translation.

semi-official, *a.* (Earlier example.)

1806 *Deb. Congr. U.S.* 6 Mar. (1852) 597 Must we have semi-official authority, even for a title-page?

semiology. The usual spelling is now *semi-* not *semei-*: see SEMEIOLOGY and derivs. in Dict. and Suppl.

semi-opacous, *a.* For '= next' read = SEMI-OPAQUE *a.*

semi-o·pen, *a.* [SEMI- I a, 7 a.] Partially open; *spec.* in *Med.*, applied to methods of administering anæsthetics in which the inspired gas is atmospheric air partially restricted or controlled by some device. Cf. *OPEN *a.* 11 h, *semi-closed* adj. (*b*) s.v. *SEMI- 8.

1914 J. T. GWATHMEY *Anesthesia* vi. 276 If ethyl chlorid [*sic*] is administered to adults from an open or semi-open inhaler large quantities of the drug will be needed to bring about even partial anesthesia. **1972** [see *OPEN *a.* 11 h].

semiosis (sīmi,ōᵘ·sis). Also **semeiosis.** [a. Gr. σημείωσις sign, inference from a sign.] The process whereby something functions as a sign (see also quots. 1971 and 1981).

c **1907** C. S. PEIRCE *Coll. Papers* (1934) V. III. i. 332 It is important to understand what I mean by *semiosis*. All dynamical action..either takes place between two subjects..or..is a resultant of such actions between pairs. But by 'semiosis' I mean, on the contrary, an action, or influence, which is, or involves, a coöperation of *three* subjects, such as a sign, its object, and its interpretant. **1938** A. HUXLEY *Let.* 18 Nov. (1969) 438 It interests me a lot and has set me reading along a number of interesting lines—Carnap, Neurath, Morris and Korzybski on the problems of semiosis. **1963** J. WIESENFARTH *H. James* v. 97 The novel..is, rather, a study in logic and semiosis. **1971** HEATH & PRENDERGAST tr. J. Kristeva in *Signs of Times* 3 What we call semeiosis is not the signifying activity in all its complexity, but only one of the signifying acts such as the structure of judgement allows it to filter through. **1981** M. WARNER *Joan of Arc* I. i. 28 Elements of mimesis..cling to..accounts of her..death, while..an accretion of semiosis, the search for inner meaning, covers their story.

semiotic, semiotics: see SEMEIOTIC *a.*, SEMEIOTICS in Dict. and Suppl.

semipe·rmeable, *a.* [tr. G. *halbdurchlässig* (J. H. van't Hoff 1887, in *Zeitschr. für physik. Chem.* I. 482), f. *halb-* HALF, semi- + *durchlässig* pervious, permeable.] Of a membrane or other structure: selectively permeable to certain atoms and molecules; *spec.* permeable to molecules of water but not to those of any dissolved substance. Also in extended use.

1888 W. RAMSAY tr. J. van't Hoff in *Phil. Mag.* XXVI. 82 The porous membrane..will be termed in the following pages a 'semipermeable membrane'. **1895** W. C. D. WHETHAM *Solution & Electrolysis* iv. 34 These semipermeable membranes are made by filling a porous pot with the solution of a salt such as potassium ferrocyanide, and surrounding the outside with another solution..which gives an insoluble precipitate when in contact with the first. **1930** *Engineering* 28 Nov. 670/1 Each droplet [of sap] being subject to forces equivalent to the osmotic pressure acting on a plant cell within a semipermeable membrane. **1974** L. THOMAS *Lives of Cell* (1975) 162, I am glad to have a semipermeable memory after getting into this. **1978** P. W. ATKINS *Physical Chem.* viii. 222 The chemical potential of the solvent on both sides of the semipermeable membrane must be equal.

Hence **se:mipermeabi·lity,** the property or condition of being semipermeable.

1900 W. H. HOWELL *Text-bk. Physiol.* (ed. 2) I. ii. 66 The semi-permeability is only approximately complete. **1974** L. THOMAS *Lives of Cell* (1975) 173 Oxygen filters out the very bands of ultraviolet light that are most devastating for nucleic acids and proteins, while allowing full penetration of the visible light needed for photosynthesis. If it had not been for this semipermeability, we could never have come along.

semi-pro·, *a.* and *sb.* *colloq.* (orig. and chiefly *U.S.*). **A.** *adj.* **a.** = *SEMI-PROFESSIONAL *a.* 1 b. *spec.* of sports.

1908 *Spalding's Official Base Ball Guide* 368 (Advt.), The 'Semi-Pro' League Ball; regulation size and weight.. Price, $1.00. **1910** *Baseball Mag.* Apr. 4/2 The semi-pro league flourishes. **1969** *Wall St. Jrnl.* 30 Sept. 28/2 Sam turned to umpiring..working in semipro and minor leagues. **1972** J. MOSEDALE *Football* viii. 116 He was playing semi-pro ball on Sundays. **1980** *Washington Post* 15 Aug. D2/1 The Metro Buccaneers, a first-year semipro football team, will play an exhibition game..Sunday.

b. = *SEMI-PROFESSIONAL *a.* 1 a. Chiefly in *Music* and *Photography*.

1927 *Melody Maker* Aug. 757/3 This competition will be open to amateur, semi-pro. or full pro. combinations. **1934** S. R. NELSON *All about Jazz* iv. 82 There are thousands of 'semi-pro' dance bands, the members of which work at their ordinary occupations during the day and play in their leisure. **1965** *Melody Maker* 17 July 15, I am forming a semi-pro trio to play at weddings. **1977** *Time* 26 Sept. 43/1 She is a semipro photographer.

B. *sb.* = *SEMI-PROFESSIONAL *sb.*

1910 *Baseball Mag.* Apr. 4/2 The despised semi-pros were drawing big crowds. **1912** *N.Y. Tribune* 7 Oct. 8/5 Enste, of the semi-pros, connected with his slow ball.. for a home run wallop. **1966** *Melody Maker* 15 Oct. 6 Semi-pros have always played an important role on the jazz scene.

semi-profe·ssional, *sb.* and *a.* [SEMI- I a, 2 b.] **A.** *sb.* One who receives payment for an occupation or activity but does not rely on it for subsistence.

1897 *Sporting News* (St. Louis, Missouri) 27 Mar. 1 Doheny was only a semi-professional before he joined the New Yorks. **1971** *Daily Tel.* 4 Oct. 11/2 From the beginning..semi-professionals and professionals swooped down on the city's many basements..where they offered new drama.

B. *adj.* **1. a.** Designating a person or group receiving payment for an occupation or activity but not relying on it for subsistence.

1900 G. BELL *Let.* 21 Mar. (1927) I. v. 70 He is a photographer, semi-professional. **1951** KOESTLER *Age of Longing* i. 8 Gaston..had become a semiprofessional dancer and near-gigolo. **1972** *Daily Tel.* 22 May 1/8 The Storm are a semi-professional group formed about nine months ago.

b. Applied to an organization, activity, etc., involving semi-professionals.

1976 *Eastern Even. News* (Norwich) 9 Dec. 19/5 They would have to take drastic measures to keep the club within the semi-professional Magnet League any longer. **1978** *Homes & Gardens* Oct. 166 As each new instrument is made..it is tested in one of the semi-professional concerts given by the group.

2. Of or pertaining to an occupation considered intermediate in standing between a learned or skilled profession and a trade or handicraft.

1950 T. H. MARSHALL *Citizenship & Social Class* 150 They [*sc.* techniques] lend themselves in the same way to the establishment of semi-professional associations. **1965** *Word Study* Oct. 3/1, I wonder, however, if most of us have not observed an equally wanton use of the word *type* among various professional and semiprofessional groups in our country.

3. Of equipment: of a kind or quality close to that appropriate for professional use.

1953 E. T. CANBY *Home Music Systems* xiii. 229 The semi-professional machines come with two or three speeds. **1975** *Gramophone* Sept. 531/2, 3M announced a new line..called the CTR series, featuring..a semi-professional 8-track recorder-player.

semiquinone (semikwi·nōᵘn). *Chem.* [SEMI- 7 h.] A molecule or ion derived from a quinone and having one of the two oxygen atoms ionized or bonded to a hydrogen atom.

1931 L. MICHAELIS in *Jrnl. Biol. Chem.* XCII. 213 The difference between 1 molecule of each of the two successive steps will be proved to be only 1 electron (*i.e.* hydrogen atom) without any change in molecular size. The intermediary form will in this case be designated as a semiquinone. **1956** *Nature* 10 Mar. 483/1 Alcohols are attacked by photo-excited anthraquinones A^* with the production of semiquinones AH. **1973** B. J. HAZZARD tr. *Organicum* vi. 380 Since..the semiquinone and *p*-benzoquinone are not resistant to alkali, the oxidation is carried out in acid solution and then takes place via quinhydrones.

Hence **semiqui·(no)noid** *a.*, having or being a structure resembling that of a semiquinone; also *absol.* as *sb.*

1932 *Jrnl. Biol. Chem.* XCVI. 704 Let us designate the three forms of the substance as *R* (the reduced form), *S* (the semiquinoid or intermediary form), and *T* (the totally oxidized, or quinoid, or holoquinoid form). **1935** *Chem. Rev.* XVI. 265 Among the three constituents of a two-step system it is not always the semiquinoid that exhibits the greatest instability. **1964** J. W. LINNETT *Electronic Struct. Molecules* vii. 110 The two members are such that the transfer of one electron from one of the molecules to the other (e.g. from diamine to chloranil) will produce two semiquinonoid-type radicals.

semi-ri·gid, *a.* and *sb.* [SEMI- I, 7 l.] **A.** *adj.* **a.** Of an airship: having a flexible gas container to which is attached a stiffened keel or framework.

1908 [in Dict., s.v. SEMI- 7 l]. **1919** H. SHAW *Text-bk. Aeronautics* xvii. 200 The semi-rigid type includes the Forlanini, Lebaudy, etc., of which the envelopes are not rigid, but are stiffened longitudinally by a framework, running the whole length of the envelope. **1935** C. G. BURGE *Compl. Bk. Aviation* 148/2 As with non-rigid and semi-rigid airships, a rigid at the start of a journey has its gas space about 90–95 per cent full of hydrogen. **1955, 1974** [see *KEEL *sb.*[1] 3 b].

b. *gen.* Somewhat rigid; having a certain amount of rigidity; *semi-rigid theory* (see quot. 1959).

1929 *Rep. & Mem. Aeronaut. Res. Comm.* No. 1155. 19 (*heading*) Specification of a simple type of semi-rigid wing. **1937** *Jrnl. R. Aeronaut. Soc.* XLI. 723 It was..possible to deduce from the semi-rigid theory design recommendations. **1946** *Nature* 30 Nov. 798/2 Rigid frames of triangular and square shapes, and semi-rigid frames. **1959** J. L. NAYLER *Dict. Aeronaut. Engin.* 234 *Semi-rigid theory*, an approximate theory of elastic structure in which the theoretical infinite number of degrees of freedom is represented by a finite number, each being associated with an invariable mode. **1963** C. R. COWELL et al. *Inlays, Crowns, & Bridges* xi. 118 The retainer which is united to a pontic by a semi-rigid joint is called the 'minor' retainer.

B. *sb.* A semi-rigid airship.

1920 [see *RIGID *sb.* 2]. **1925** E. H. LEWITT *Rigid Airship* i. 1 The airship may be divided into three classes: non-rigids, semi-rigids, and rigids. **1935** C. G. BURGE *Compl. Bk. Aviation* 148/2 The semi-rigid is very similar in operation to the non-rigid.

‖ **semis**[1] (sē·mis). *Rom. Antiq.* [L., app. reduced f. *semi-* SEMI- + *as* AS *sb.*] A Roman coin, equivalent under the Republic and the early Empire to half an as, and under the later Empire to half a solidus. Cf. TREMIS.

1853 H. N. HUMPHREYS *Coin Collector's Man.* I. xxi. 260 The *Semis*, *Semisis*, or *Semi-as*, has an S upon it to denote its weight, as half that of the 'as'; it represented six ounces, and the type most usual in the Roman *series* is the head of Jupiter. **1949** *Oxf. Class. Dict.* 210/2 The coinage [of the early Empire] comprised *aureus* and half-piece in gold, *denarius* and half-piece in silver, *sestertius*, *dupondius*, and *semis* in orichalcum (brass), *as* and *quadrans* in copper. **1962** R. A. G. CARSON *Coins* 180 Gold solidi were issued with some frequency, the semis or half-piece only rarely in the reign of the three brothers. *Ibid.* 197 In keeping with the earlier fifth-century tradition the obverse of the semis and the tremissis showed the diademed and cuirassed bust of the emperor in profile. **1979** *Nature* 5 July 46/2 The magnetisation of an orichalcum semis of the Roman Emperor Tiberius remained below the noise level up to the maximum fields available.

‖ **semis**[2] (sĕmī·). [F., lit. 'sowing'; cf. SEMÉE *a.* and *sb.*] A form of decoration used in bookbinding, in which small ornaments are repeated regularly.

1926 R. GLAZIER *Man. Historic Ornament* 155 Some French bindings for Henry IV. are tooled with a *semis* of monograms on flowers. **1960** G. A. GLAISTER *Gloss. Book* 323/2 *Powdered*, the effect obtained on a book cover when small flower ornaments are repeated regularly in rows over it. Early examples date from 1560 on books bound for Charles IX of France. Also known as *semis* or *semé*. **1960** H. HAYWARD *Antique Coll.* 253/1 *Semis*,.. a repeating pattern of small ornaments used by bookbinders, 'sown' over the covers of books. **1977** FLEMING & HONOUR *Penguin Dict. Decorative Arts* 719/1 *Semis*, an heraldic term also used in bookbinding for a diaper design made by the repetition of one or more small tooled ornaments.

se·mispecies. *Biol.* [SEMI- 7 e.] A subdivision of a species regarded as having more individuality than does a subspecies.

1940 E. MAYR in *Amer. Naturalist* LXXIV. 256 The taxonomist finds it sometimes useful for practical purposes to treat as full species what should be regarded as subspecies on the basis of the definition. Groups of such 'semi-species' are called superspecies in the subsequent discussion. **1953** J. S. HUXLEY *Evolution in Action* iii. 71 The borderline of incipient species or semi-species. **1978** *Sci. Amer.* Sept. 60/1 Semispecies from the same locality will not crossbreed in the laboratory but semispecies from different localities will.

semi-spo·rts. [SEMI- 1 b.] Used *attrib.*: **1.** Of articles of attire: somewhat informal or casual.

1929 *Footwear Organiser* July 25/1 There is no doubt that semi-sports shoes in two-colour effects will be largely worn. **1973** SCHOEFFLER & GALE *Esquire's Encycl. 20th Cent. Men's Fashions* 194 By the early forties not only was a semisports outfit acceptable for town wear but, according to *Esquire*, it was 'smart to be sporty'.

2. Of a motor car: possessing some of the characteristics of a sports car.

1933 *Motor* 10 Oct. 513/1 The 20 h.p. Daimler semi-sports saloon. **1966** 'E. PETERS' *Piper on Mountain* iii. 56 Half the world buys British when it comes to cars, especially semi-sports jobs like this.

semi-ste·rile, *a. Biol.* [SEMI- 7 d.] Reduced in fertility by approximately 50 per cent.

1914 J. BELLING in *Jrnl. Heredity* V. 71/1 The plants with perfect pollen have also perfect ovules; the plants with semi-sterile pollen have also half their ovules sterile. **1927** *Ibid.* XVIII. 267/1 Ears produced on semi-sterile individuals bear only 50 per cent of the normal number of seeds irrespective of the source of the pollen used, since the lethal operates prior to fertilization. **1956** *Nature* 10 Mar. 452/2 The cytological properties of a series of semi-sterile stocks. **1978** *Ibid.* 20 July 253/1 Using this method, dieldrin-resistant sterile or semisterile males would be released into the field.

Hence **semi-steri·lity.**

1914 J. BELLING in *Jrnl. Heredity* V. 73/1 These plants are favorable for an investigation of semi-sterility since no complications arise from self-sterility, incompatibility, or intercrossing by insects. **1978** *Nature* 20 July 253/1 A release programme involving..males carrying genetic aberrations that give high semisterility.

Semite. (Earlier example.)

1848 C. BUNSEN in *Rep. Brit. Assoc. Advancem. Sci. 1847* XVII. 266 The country which, according to the most ancient traditions of the Semites, was the cradle of mankind.

Semi:to-Hami·tic, *a.* and *sb.* = *HAMITO-SEMITIC *a.* and *sb.* Also **Semitic-Hamitic** *a.* and *sb.*

1879 E. S. ROBERTS tr. *D. Pezzi's Aryan Philol.* I. i. 46 Hence the Southern and Central African dialects, the Erythræan (Semito-Hamitic) and the Aryan. **1910** *Encycl. Brit.* XII. 894 The development of a grammatical gender, this principal characteristic of Semito-Hamitic, in Bari and Masai, may be rather accidental than borrowed. **1928** *Language* IV. 129 If there is a Semitic-Hamitic language-group, then not primitive Semitic, but primitive Semitic-Hamitic must be correlated with primitive Indo-European. **1949** W. F. ALBRIGHT *Archaeol. Palestine* iii. 61 Since very similar human skeletons have been found in the Badarian of Egypt as well as in late chalcolithic Gezer and Byblus, it seems to follow that these folk belonged to the ancestral Semito-Hamitic stock. **1964** *Jrnl. Semitic Studies* IX. 137 The Semito-Hamitic family, for which the very apt term Erythraic has been recently proposed by A. N. Tucker and M. A. Bryan. **1974** *Encycl. Brit. Macropædia* VIII. 589/2 Also known as the Semito-Hamitic, Erythraean, Afro-Asiatic, and Afrasian language group, it [*sc.* Hamito-Semitic] is the main language family of northern Africa.

semitone. 3. (Earlier example.)

1818 'T. BROWN' *Brighton* I. i. 39 'Yes, my lord,' said Zephyr, and, in a semi-tone, muttered, 'he'll overlook many things.'

semi-trai·ler. [SEMI- 7 a.] A road trailer that has a wheel system at the rear only and is coupled to a suitable tractor to form an articulated lorry. Freq. *transf.*, an articulated lorry made up in this way.

1919 *Engineering* 28 Nov. 718/2 With the semi-trailer the tractor partly carries and partly hauls the load, the front end of the two-wheeled vehicle being carried on a platform directly over the rear or driving wheels. **1926** *Encycl. Brit.* II. 987/2 This semi-trailer was a two-wheeled construction, the forward end of which was supported on the tractor frame by means of a swivelling fifth wheel. This end of the semi-trailer could be supported by means of jacks. **1949** *Automobile & Carriage Builders' Jrnl.* CIII. III. 38/1 Probably the world's most curvaceous semi-trailer. **1956** 'N. SHUTE' *Beyond Black Stump* 44 The diesel semi-trailer..ground to a standstill in a swirl of red dust. **1962** *Coast to Coast 1961–62* 141 A loaded semi-trailer stood beside the kerb in front of the hotel.. and Keppler started towards it, hoping for a lift. **1978** O. WHITE *Silent Reach* xv. 154 His car collided with a semi-trailer.

semi-transparency. (Earlier example.)

1787 J. WEDGWOOD *Let.* 16 June (1965) 308 The original artist availed himself of the semitransparency of the white glass.

semi-uncial, *a.*: Add: Cf. *half-uncial* s.v. *HALF- II. n.

semo- (sī·mo), combining form of Gr. σῆμα sign, used as the first element in **semolexe·mic** *a.*, of linguistic rules: governing the conversion of units of meaning into lexical items; **semolo·gical** *a.*, of or pertaining to semology; hence **semolo·gically** *adv.*; **semo·logy**, the study of meaning as an aspect of language; = SEMANTIC *sb.* 1 a in Dict. and Suppl.; **semota·ctic** *a.*, of or pertaining to the ordering of units of meaning; hence **semota·ctically** *adv.* Cf. *SEMANTICO-.

1968 *Language* XLIV. 578 The last four pages of chapter 6 are devoted to a discussion of 'semolexemic rules', which map sememic networks onto lexemic trees. **1913** *Jrnl. Eng. & Gmc. Philol.* XII. 78 The change may be purely semological. **1928** C. BERGENER *Contribution to Study of Conversion of Adjectives into Nouns* iv. 170 *Light*, *dark*, and *dusk* form a semological association-group. **1975** M. A. K. HALLIDAY in S. Rogers *Children & Lang.* IV. 225 This is an analysis at the semological level in which the elements of structure are functional in character. **1913** *Jrnl. Eng. & Gmc. Philol.* XII. 78 Morphologically and semologically the stem *flik* exhibits types of word-formation and meaning development that are representative. **1911** A. L. ELMQUIST in *Ibid.* X. 318 The grammar [of Noreen's *Vårt Språk*] is in four parts.. (3), Semology, a new term for semasiology. *Ibid.*, The grammar offers a large number of new features, the Semology, perhaps, most of all. **1928** C. BERGENER *Contribution to Study of Conversion of Adjectives into Nouns* i. 7 We are not only concerned with the semology but also with the morphology of converted adjectives. **1958** G. L. TRAGER in *Studies in Linguistics* XIII. 8 There seems to be no subdivision of either kinesics or paralinguistics exactly analogous to the phonology–morphology–semology of language. **1970** *Canadian Jrnl. Linguistics* XVI. 22 Below each disjunction each wire leads (though not necessarily immediately) to an inverse conjunction, the other wire of which leads up to the semology. **1966** S. M. LAMB *Outl. Stratif. Gram.* 14 Semotactic patterns differ from tactic patterns for lower strata in having considerable numbers of upwards ANDS. **1967** D. G. HAYS *Introd. Computational Linguistics* xiii. 215 If parsing is performed after this dictionary lookup, its object is to determine semotactic well-formedness. **1969** *Language* XLV. 491 The principal area of stylistic concern is the discourse, not primarily the pleasing sound patterns or the juxtaposition of semotactically felicitous phrases.

semon (sī·mǫn). *Linguistics.* [Irreg. f. Gr. σῆμα: cf. -ON[1].] In stratificational grammar: an element of meaning or one which combines with others to make up a sememe.

1965 S. M. LAMB in *Amer. Anthropol.* LXVII. II. 46 Turning now to semology, the elementary unit is the semon, and a sememe is a unit composed of one or more semons. In a clause such as *he found his brace and bit* all the sememes are simple, but the following expressions contain or are complex sememes, i.e. sememes composed of multiple semons: *she put all her eggs in one basket.., don't give up the ship.* **1968** *Language* XLIV. 576 Hockett divides the 'semons' (the labels on the nodes in the sememic networks) into three classes, called 'links', 'kernels', and 'modifiers'. **1973** *Archivum Linguisticum* IV. 119 Within his general model the speaker makes a selection of 'semons' (elementary semantic features) on the basis of his 'awareness of a "cognitive experience" '.

sempervirent, *a.* Add: Also *absol.* as *sb.*, an evergreen plant (*rare*).

1957 J. D. SALINGER in *New Yorker* 4 May 42/1 She nudged an unopened box of Sal Hepatica..to align it with the other sempervirents in its row.

sempiternity. Delete † *Obs.* and add later examples.

1933 *Mind* XLII. 309 Spinoza did not mean by 'eternity' either endless future duration or endless past and future duration ('sempiternity'). **1980** *Dædalus* Spring 255 The fraternal impulse of the heroic youth in the barque unsettles the moral ground of Hell's sempiternity.

Semple (semp'l). *Med.* The name of Lt.-Col. Sir David *Semple* (1856–1937), English bacteriologist, used *attrib.*, *absol.*, in *Comb.*, and in the possessive to designate a vaccine against rabies described by him in 1911 (*Sci. Mem. by Officers of Med. & Sanitary Depts. of Govt. of India* No. 44), and the techniques of preparing and administering it.

1934 *Q. Bull. Health Organisation* III. 615 Killed phenol vaccines... 4000 mg. Semple. *Ibid.* 618 Semple's modification of Fermi's original method (*i.e.*, the phenol vaccine is incubated at 37°C. for twenty-four hours) is employed. **1938** *Jrnl. Amer. Med. Assoc.* 20 Aug. 690/2 The Semple modification of the Pasteur treatment is commercially available and should be given twice daily. **1939** *Ibid.* 29 July 392/1 The Alabama State Health Department distributes Semple vaccine without charge to physicians for the treatment of those exposed to rabid animals. **1949** *New Gould Med. Dict.* 920/2 The vaccine used is made from 4% inoculated rabbit brain attenuated with 0·5% phenol; called *Semple's vaccine.* **1971** E. S. TIERKEL in Nagano & Davenport *Rabies* 3 The Semple vaccine eventually became the biologic of choice in many countries. **1977** C. KAPLAN *Rabies* vii. 108 A Semple-type vaccine was first used in 1921 for the successful mass vaccination of dogs in Japan.

‖ **semplice** (se·mplitʃe), *a.* and *adv. Mus.* [It., simple.] **A.** *adj.* Simple. **B.** *adv.* Simply. (Chiefly as a direction.)

1740 GRASSINEAU *Mus. Dict.* 218 *Semplice*, simple, not doubled, compounded, or composed of any thing else, as *cadenza simplice*, is a cadence in which all the notes are equal in all the parts. **1801** BUSBY *Dict. Mus.* s.v., *Semplice*, (Ital.), a word implying that the movement before which it is placed is to be performed with chasteness and simplicity. **1883** GROVE *Dict. Mus.* III. 461/1 *Semplice*, 'simple'; a direction denoting that the passage so marked is to be performed without any adornment or deviation from the time, used particularly in passages of which the character might possibly be misunderstood. **1976** *Gramophone* Nov. 786/2 The moment I suggest as a prime sample of Zukerman's profound insight is the third theme in that same movement with its rising phrases marked *pianissimo* and *semplice*.

‖ **sempre** (se·mpre), *adv. Mus.* [It.] Always, still: used to qualify an adj. or advb. Also *transf.*

1801 BUSBY *Dict. Mus.* s.v., *Sempre*, (Ital.), always, or throughout: as *sempre piano*, soft throughout. **1816** in G. Thomson *Sel. Collection Irish Melodies* 139 Judy Lovely Matchless Creature *Sempre dolce.* **1883** GROVE *Dict. Mus.* III. 461/2 *Sempre*, 'always'; a word used in conjunction with some other mark of time or expression to signify that such mark is to remain in force until a new direction appears. **1959** *Collins' Mus. Encycl.* 594/1 *Sempre*, 'always, still', as in *sempre piano*, still softly. **1959** E. POUND *Thrones* xcvii. 29 Earth under Fortuna, each sphere hath its Lord, with ever-shifting change, sempre biasmata.

semseyite (se·msi,əit). *Min.* [ad. Hung. *semseyit* (J. S. Krenner 1881, in *Magyar tudományos Akad. Értes.* XV. 113), f. the name of Andor *Semsey* (1833–1923), Hung. nobleman and amateur mineralogist: see -ITE[1].] A monoclinic sulphide of lead and antimony, $Pb_9Sb_8S_{21}$, found usu. as grey or black tabular or prismatic crystals with a metallic lustre.

1886 *Jrnl. Chem. Soc.* L. 313 Semseyite from Felsöbánya; small, grey tabular crystals. **1920** *Brit. Mus. Return* 142 in *Parl. Papers* XXXVI. 673 Semseyite from Dumfriesshire. **1955** [see *ROSETTED *a.* 1 a]. **1976** *Mineral. Abstr.* XXVII. 306/2 Genetic antagonism between semseyite..and boulangerite..may have been caused by variation in oxidizing power of sulphur between the two media.

sen, *sb.* (Earlier example.)

1727 J. SCHEUCHZER tr. *Kæmpfer's Hist. Japan* I. 17 The use of silver Money was forbid, and in its stead brass Sennis coin'd.

‖ **sen** (sen), *sb.*[2] [Indonesian, etc., repr. CENT[1].] In Indonesia, Malaysia, and other countries of the Far East: a coin or unit of currency valued at one hundredth of the principal measure.

1957 *Whitaker's Almanack 1958* 965 Indonesia... *Rupiah* of 100 *Sen.* **1959** *Ibid. 1960* 961 Cambodia... *Riel* of 100 *Sen.* **1962** R. A. G. CARSON *Coins* 557 The islands became the independent republic of Indonesia in 1950. The unit of the new coinage is the rupiah of 100 sen.

Sen., sen., abbrev. of SENIOR *a.* 1 a. Cf. JUN. in Dict. and Suppl.

1676, etc. [see SENIOR *a.* 1 a]. **1837** [see *JUN.]. **1955** *Times* 8 July 6/7 In two suits in another bedroom was found £115 10s., which Thomas Foote, sen., said was his. **1960** *Bedside 'Guardian'* IX. 140 It was an old tradition, Professor Arthur M. Schlesinger, sen., has said, [etc.].

Sen., abbrev. of SENATOR 1 f. *U.S.*

1857 WEBSTER & GOODRICH *N. Webster's Explanatory & Pronouncing Dict. Eng. Lang.* App. 462/1 *Sen.*, Senator. **1972** *Guardian* 3 July 1/2 (*heading*) Sen McGovern fights on. **1974** *Sumter* (S. Carolina) *Daily Item* 23 Apr. 1B/1 She has written Sen. Thomas O. Bowen..several times.

Sena, var. *SEHNA; **Senacar,** var. *SENECA.

senaite (sē[i]-, se·nā,əit). *Min.* [f. the name of Joachim da Costa *Sena*, 19th-cent. Brazilian mineralogist + -ITE[1].] A rhombohedral titanate of iron, lead, and manganese, found

as rough black crystals and rounded fragments in diamond-bearing sands in Brazil.
1898 Hussak & Prior in *Mineral. Mag.* XII. 30 (*heading*) Senaite, a new mineral belonging to the ilmenite group, from Brazil. **1976** *Acta Crystallographica* XXXII. B. 1509/1 Senaite, crichtonite, and davidite form a closely related series of minerals with similar morphologies and chemical compositions.

senate. Add: **1. f.** (Earlier U.S. example.)
1776 A. Adams *Let.* 15 Sept. (1875) 227 Whether you are in the American Senate or on board the British fleet, is a matter of uncertainty.

senatorial, *a.* **3.** (Examples.)
1785 T. Jefferson *Notes Virginia* App. 2 Let each county at the time of electing its delegates, chuse senatorial electors... Let the senatorial districts be divided into two classes. **1864** *Harper's Mag.* Mar. 568/2 Mrs X—..resides in our senatorial district. **1948** *Daily Ardmoreite* (Ardmore, Oklahoma) 23 July 14/6 This Senatorial district of Carter county is the birthplace and home of Joe.

send, *v.*[1] Add: **I. 2. c.** *slang* (orig. *U.S.*). To transport or arouse emotions in (a person); to enthral, delight (esp. of popular music). Also *absol.* Hence **se·nding** *ppl. a.*
1932 *Melody Maker* Oct. 836/1, I enclose the following wire which Louis (Musicmouth) Armstrong sent to Big John... 'My boy Earl was marvellous as ever yessir he sent me.' **1935** *Vanity Fair* (N.Y.) Nov. 71/3 Hot artists or bands that can put across their licks successfully are '*senders*'; they '*send*'. **1937** *Amer. Speech* XII. 47/1 The action of this trumpet really sends me and that's no jive. **1943** *N.Y. Times* 9 May II. 5/4 There has [*sic*] been some really solid trumpet players who can really send; some like Louis Armstrong who had a trumpet like heaven. *Ibid.*, Jimmy has a sending band and when he plays, brother, even the seats jump. **1955** V. Nabokov *Lolita* I. xxiv. 138, I do not know if in these tragic notes, I have sufficiently stressed the peculiar 'sending' effect that the writer's good looks.. had on women of every age and environment. **1956** B. Holiday *Lady sings Blues* (1973) ix. 86 Meade Lux Lewis knocked them out; Ammons and Johnson flipped them..Newton's band sent them. **1959** C. MacInnes *Absolute Beginners* 16 A film we went to ages ago that rather sent us. **1975** N. Mitchison *All change Here* iv. 39 So much modern poetry is ironic or deliberately held on a low note; that may be artistically admirable, but it doesn't send the reader.

8. a. (Examples of messages sent mechanically or electrically.)
1873 *Independent Defender* (San Francisco) 15 Nov. 3/1 The operator..excitedly telegraphed back, don't send so d—d fast. **1924** *Radio Times* 19 Dec. 585/3 This is only a receiving station. We can't send. We can only listen. **1929** *Amer. Speech* IV. 288 The sender's task is to 'move it',..—or simply 'send'. **1974** W. Garner *Big Enough Wreath* xi. 140 What if he'd asked to see the print-out? What if he'd gone over to see you send?

c. Of a shop: to deliver goods ordered.
1871 G. H. Lewes *Let.* 27 Aug. in *Geo. Eliot Lett.* (1956) V. 181 Take care the Stores people send on Thursday. **1968** *Observer* (Colour Suppl.) 22 Dec. 17/4 The shops won't send and now they've stopped the bus.

III. 23. send back. (Earlier example.)
1870 *Baily's Mag.* Aug. 359 A good catch..sent him back when only a few runs were wanted.

25. send down. c. (Earlier example.)
1871 *Baily's Mag.* Oct. 415 At times, no bowler in England sends down such utterly unplayable balls.

d. To dispatch or commit to prison by sentence. Freq. *pass.* *slang* (orig. *U.S.*).
1840 *Picayune* (New Orleans) 2 Aug. 2/5 She scorned to find surety in $500 to keep the peace, so she was sent down. **1880** G. A. Sala *Amer. Revisited* (1882) I. v. 85 They were 'sent down' for ten days. **1941** 'R. West' *Black Lamb* II. 315 We caught the murderer..and he was sent down for a long sentence. **1960** G. Butler *Death lives Next Door* vi. 118 I'm Ted Springer's missus. Sent him down for three years, you did. **1976** 'P. B. Yuill' *Hazell & Menacing Jester* iii. 39 'Is there any chance he *could* go to gaol?' 'You'd like him sent down, would you?'

e. To cause to accompany someone (to dinner).
1888 Mrs. H. Ward *R. Elsmere* II. II. xvii. 74 They would be sent down to dinner together to a certainty. **1892** 'A. Hope' *Mr. Witt's Widow* viii. 98 That lady.. sent Laura down to dinner with him.

f. *send her down, Davy* (also *Hughie,* etc.) and varr.: phr. expressing a wish for rain to fall. Cf. *Hughie. *slang* (chiefly *Austral.* and *N.Z.*).
1919 W. H. Downing *Digger Dial.* 44 *Send her down, Steve!*, let it rain on. **1925** Fraser & Gibbons *Soldier & Sailor Words & Phrases* 72 *David* (or *Davy*), *send it down*, a soldier's greeting to a shower of rain likely to postpone a parade. **1928** L. H. Nason *Sergeant Eadie* xi. 321 Hurray! Send her down, Davie; no drill today! **1937, 1958** [see *Hughie]. **1975** *Panorama* (Austral.) Nov. 2/5 '*Send 'er down, Hughie!*' An expression in nationwide use since the turn of the century, which is..an invocation to Heaven..to send rain.

27. send in. c. Also, to send (the opposing side) in to bat first.
1912 P. F. Warner *England v. Australia* vi. 48 Trumper beat Douglas in the toss, and sent us in. **1930** C. G. Macartney *My Cricketing Days* iii. 18 They might have given us a good game had not our captain..won the toss and sent them in on a bad wicket. **1969** *Wisden Cricketers' Almanack* 478 Although Lancashire were without..their opening bowlers, Leicestershire sent them in on winning the toss.

28. send off. † **b.** = sense 25 b. *Obs.*
1843 [see *faculty 9 b].

c. *Sport.* To order (a player) to leave the pitch as a punishment.
1906 W. Pickford in Gibson & Pickford *Association Football* III. xvi. 6 A referee may send a player off at once and without any previous caution, if he is guilty of violent conduct. **1976** *Milton Keynes Express* 2 July 43/4 Newton..suffered a severe setback in the first half when they had a player sent off.

29. send on. c. To dispatch (a letter, etc.) forward from the place to which it was addressed.
1833 S. Smith *Life & Writings J. Downing* liii. 183 Dear sir, I want you to send this on to cousin Jack. **1879** Geo. Eliot *Let.* 7 July (1956) VII. 179, I have had 2 letters from him which Miss Gibson sent on. **1895** 'G Mortimer' *Like Stars that Fall* xiv. 198 Didn't you get the letter sent on?

33. send up. d. (Earlier example.)
1821 *Salt-Bearer* (Eton Coll.) 129 He more than once had the honour of being 'sent up for good', *i.e.* having his verses read over by the head master as particularly worthy of commendation.

f. To mock, make fun of (a person or thing); to parody.
1931 T. R. G. Lyell *Slang, Phrase & Idiom in Colloq. Eng.* 673 The last time he came in, he was sent up unmercifully by half the room. **1957** 'N. Blake' *End of Chapter* 68 Who's Johnnie Ray? He's—go on! you're sending me up! **1962** *John o' London's* 29 Nov. 506/3 The effect..is as if he is attempting to 'send up' the whole picture. **1969** *Times* 13 Dec. p. v/2 These represented the British sense of humour, our genius for sending ourselves up, but they seem to me rather to be reinforcements of such attitudes. **1977** P. G. Winslow *Witch Hill Murder* II. xvii. 220, I wasn't sending you up the other night. I was *afraid*.

IV. 34. The infin. used: **a.** to describe the position of a switch for transmission.
1876 *Jrnl. Soc. Telegr. Engineers* V. 494 The switch has been put on 'send'. **1976** C. Egleton *State Visit* ix. 88 Because he kept the switch on 'send', they could just hear the band.

b. *attrib.* in the sense 'sending', as the name of a part.
1973 C. Bonington *Next Horizon* xiii. 194 He ended up by telling me to press the send switch of the radio three times as affirmative and twice for negative, in reply to his questions. **1976** K. Thackeray *Crownbird* ix. 198 He pulled his microphone towards him..and depressed the send button.

sendable, *a.* (Later examples.)
1901 *Chambers's Jrnl.* July 464/1 We have become so used to connecting the convenient little slips of sendable money with the Post-Office. **1965** P. Wylie *They both were Naked* I. iii. 150 She had been sendable because she wanted to be sent.

Sendai (se·ndəi). *Biol.* and *Med.* The name of a city in northern Honshu, Japan, used attrib. as **Sendai virus,** a paramyxovirus (first identified in Sendai) which causes disease of the upper respiratory tract in mammals, and is used in the laboratory to produce cell fusion.
[**1953** T. Sano et al. in *Yokohama Med. Bull.* IV. 215 We consider this disease a new form of virus pneumonitis and have termed it 'Newborn Virus Pneumonitis (Type Sendai)'.] **1958** *Ann. Rev. Microbiol.* XII. 66 Similar to the influenza virus, one of the new agents, Sendai virus, propagates sufficiently well in eggs to permit primary isolation by amniotic inoculation. **1970** *Nature* 25 July 339/2 The possibility of introducing alien genetic material into mammalian eggs by fusion with somatic cells using Sendai virus. **1976** *Ann. Rev. Microbiol.* XXX. 29 The transcriptive complex of a representative paramyxovirus, Sendai virus, contains a major structural polypeptide, NP..a less abundant polypeptide, P..and a high-molecular-weight polypeptide that is present in minute amounts.

sender. Add: **d.** One who or that which moves or enthrals, esp. a popular musician. Also in phr. *solid sender* (cf. *solid *a.* 18**). Cf. *send *v.*[1] 2 c. *slang* (orig. and chiefly *U.S.*).
1935 *Vanity Fair* (N.Y.) Nov. 38/1 None of these plates will be senders. *Ibid.* 71/3 Hot artists or bands that can put across their licks successfully are '*senders*'. **1938** *Metronome* Apr. 26/2 A really solid sender is the third record from the right in my collection. **1938** *Amer. Speech* XIII. 314/2 *Sender*, one who is extremely well-dressed or witty. **1954** [see *drag *sb.* 3 d]. **1960** *Spectator* 7 Oct. 523 Fabian, the teenagers' sender, indistinguishable from Cliff Richards. **1978** G. Vidal *Kalki* vi. 147 Arlene was addicted to the slang of her youth. 'A solid sender!' she added, nicely dating herself to World War II during which she entertained the troops.

sending, *vbl. sb.* Add: **1. b.** (Later examples.)
1938 *Times* 17 Feb. 15/6 The great expense of the traditional sending-off parties for soldiers called to the colours. **1978** *Rugby World* Apr. 7/3 The laws..make no provision for a foul committed *before* a try—unless it be sending off. **1982** 'W. Haggard' *Mischief-Makers* vi. 65 The referee, white, had sent off a black... There was a code which governed sendings-off, particularly in amateur [football] matches.

4. [ON., in same sense.] An unpleasant or evil thing supposed to be sent by a wizard, or through a wizard at the request of another party, as a punishment or act of revenge.
1864 Powell & Magnusson *Icel. Legends* 238 If he did not return to them by Christmas-day next, they would despatch a Sending to him who should kill him. **1888** Kipling *In Black & White* 68 A Sending..is a Thing sent by a wizard. **1915** *Hastings's Encycl. Relig. & Ethics* VIII. 218 A phenomenon analogous to that of the werwolf is that of the 'sending'—a thing or animal, sometimes animated or even created by the sorcerer, or some part of the sorcerer himself (his soul, etc.) and sent out by him to annoy or injure people. **1980** G. Household *Sending* v. 68 What your Norse shamans and the sagas called a 'sending'..a sort of portable ghost.

send-off. Add: **1.** (Earlier examples.) Also *transf.* and *fig.*
The earliest sense of the word appears to be 'a sending off or starting of contestants in a race'.
1841 *Spirit of Times* 18 Dec. 499/2 Sleepy John was the favorite against the field; by bad management of the groom John got a miserable send off and lost at least fifty yards. **1867** *Harper's Mag.* Dec. 135/1 As they say at Jerome Park, a 'good send off' at life's outset is, four to one, better than a 'false start'. **1875** *Chicago Tribune* 15 July 1/3 There was considerable jockeying, and..an even send-off [in the boat-race] was not obtained. **1908** G. G. Greenwood *Shakespeare Problem Restated* xv. 483 If we could only get to the back of his [*sc.* Jonson's] mind, we should find that there was some efficient cause operating to induce him to give the best possible send-off to that celebrated venture. **1934** [see *cash *v.*[2] 2 c]. **1977** J. McClure *Sunday Hangman* ii. 19 Every warder has to witness at least one little send-off.

se·nd-up. *colloq.* [f. vbl. phr. *to send up*: see *send *v.*[1] 33 f.] An act of mocking or teasing; a parody, a satire.
1958 A. Wilson *Middle Age of Mrs. Eliot* 355 If she teased him a bit maliciously, it was with such caressing malice that the ragging was more like a flirtation than a 'send up'. **1962** *Guardian* 24 Dec. 4/6 'Merry Christmas You Suckers'.., according to the record company, is 'a send-up of the whole commercialised business'. **1970** G. F. Newman *Sir, You Bastard* iii. 108 Gordon moved away, accepting his opinion as infallible, and never suspecting the blatant send-up. **1976** J. I. M. Stewart *Young Patullo* xi. 256 What had taken place would have been describable a decade later as a send-up.

Sendzimir (se·ndzimiᵊɹ). The name of Tadeusz or Thaddeus K. *Sendzimir* (b. 1894), Polish-born American engineer, used *attrib.* with reference to a type of rolling mill developed by him for cold rolling of steel, in which each of two working rolls is supported by two larger rolls, which are themselves backed by three still larger rolls (a further tier of four larger rolls is sometimes used).
1936 *Jrnl. Iron & Steel Inst.* CXXXIV. 166P, In the case of cold rolling mills for wide strip, simpler designs could be developed, like those described by Mr. Nöll. In these forms, however—as in the Sendzimir mill which he described—it was essential to avoid at all costs friction on the pulling drum, which might entail damage to the upper surface of the strip. **1956** W. D. Hargreaves in D. L. Linton *Sheffield* 294 A Sendzimir mill, which uses work rolls of only 2¼ inches diameter in conjunction with a cluster of backing rolls, operates for the production of thin gauges without intermediate annealing. **1967** A. H. Cottrell *Introd. Metallurgy* xxii. 442 Long slender rolls are too elastically flexible to compress the metal unless they are supported by heavy backing rolls... This principle has been particularly developed in Rohn and Sendzimir mills for rolling thin foil. **1975** C. M. Black tr. *Thelning's Steel & its Heat Treatment* vi. 290 To a large extent the steels are used for tools for shaping and forming. The so-called Sendzimir rolls, i.e. rolls forming a cluster-roll mill, constitute an example of such use.

Seneca. Add: Also † **Senacar, Senecke, Sineque,** etc. Substitute for etym.: [ad. N. Amer. Du. *Sennecas, Sennecaas,* collect. name for the Upper Iroquois tribes, perh. orig. a Mahican name for the Oneida or their village.] **A.** *sb.* (A member of) one of the five (later, six) tribes of the Iroquois Confederacy of North American Indians; their language. **B.** *adj.* Of or pertaining to this tribe.
Formerly used also to designate the four Upper Iroquois tribes, and the Iroquois collectively.
[*c* **1616** in *Documents Colonial Hist. N.Y.* (1856) I. *facing* p. 11 Sennecas.] **1664** J. Winthrop *Let.* 6 Feb. in *Mass. Hist. Soc. Coll.* (1863) 4th Ser. VI. 531, 3000 of the Seneckes, a people in league with the Mohawkes beyond them, are gathered together. **1684** *New-Hampshire Hist. Soc. Coll.* (1827) II. 199 The sd Mohauck, Senacar, or other Indians, [shall] be paid out of such monies as shall be raised in the sd Province. **1684** [see *Onondaga]. **1709** S. Sewall *Jrnl.* 12 Aug. in *Mass. Hist. Soc. Coll.* (1879) 5th Ser. VI. 262, 300 Eastern Indians..were gon to the 5 Nations to pray leave to dwell with them; and..others refusing them, they were gon to the Senecas. **1724** H. Jones *Pres. State Va.* I. i. 5 The Senecaa Indians in their War Dress may appear as terrible as any of the Sons of Anak. **1775** J. Adair *Hist. Amer. Indians* 393 A party of the Senekah Indians came to war against the Katahba. **1823** [see *cayuga]. **1874** [see *Onondaga]. **1895** [see Six *a.* 1 d]. **1900** *Congress. Record* (U.S.) 26 Jan. 1232/2 Among the Seneca Indians a singularly beautiful belief prevailed. **1910** Kipling *Rewards & Fairies* 187 Senecas aren't Hurons, they're Iroquois, of course, and Toby told him so. **1933** L. Bloomfield *Language* iv. 72 The languages of the Iroquois type..*Seneca.* **1969** *Observer*

(Colour Suppl.) 25 May 61/1 The Iroquois leader Sagoyewatha, known as Red Jacket, was one of the Seneca tribe who fought alongside the British during the American War of Independence. **1976** T. A. SEBEOK *Native Lang. Americas* I. 537 Wright at one time devised a unique set of letters to be used in printing Seneca, but they were never adopted.

C. *attrib.* **Seneca grass** (earlier example); **Seneca oil,** delete † and add: now only *Hist.* (earlier and later examples).

1814 J. BIGELOW *Florula Bostoniensis* 245 Seneca grass... An erect, early grass, with a small panicle of short flowers. **1795** J. SCOTT *U.S. Gazetteer* s.v. *Allegany*, In this county is Oil creek: It flows from a spring much celebrated for a bitumen resembling Barbadoes tar, and is known by the name of Seneca Oil. **1910** KIPLING *Rewards & Fairies* 161 He took orders for that famous Seneca Oil which he had the secret of from Red Jacket's Indians. **1959** *Chambers's Encycl.* X. 619/1 In North America crude oil was undoubtedly used by the Indians, and Seneca oil skimmed from the surface of water near Lake Seneca..utilized for rheumatism, coughs, burns, sprains etc.

Senecal, *a.* For † *Obs.* read *Obs.* exc. in allusion to Chapman's use (see quot. 1612) and add later examples. Also as *sb.*: a writer of drama in the Senecan manner; *spec.*, one of a group of early seventeenth-century playwrights (see quot. 1926).

1926 T. S. ELIOT in *Times Lit. Suppl.* 9 Dec. 906/3 In the effort to 'place' Davies, who appears anomalous, critics have compared him..to the Senecals, to Chapman and Daniel and Greville... The type of his thought.. separates him from the Senecals. **1934** H. ELLIS *Chapman* 62 Chapman often refers to Seneca and the 'Senecal men', and he was also influenced by Epictetus. **1954** E. REES *Tragedies of George Chapman* iv. 114 Chapman was too much of a humanist to forget that even a 'Senecal man' is human.

Senecan, *a.* Add: Hence **Se·necanism.**

1934 T. S. ELIOT *Elizabethan Essays* 40 Much of Chapman's Senecanism has lately been shown..to be directly borrowed from Erasmus. **1978** *Studies in Eng. Lit.: Eng. Number* (Tokyo) 173 Jonson's use of Hoskyns' essay as a foundation for his own brand of Senecanism looks back to the past as well as to the future in the development of English prose.

senecio (senī·ʃio, -sio, -e·kio). [L. *senecio* old man, groundsel, in reference to the hairy pappus of the plant: adopted by Linnæus (*Hortus Cliffortianus* (1737) 406) as the name of a genus: cf. SENCION.] An annual or perennial herb or shrub of the large genus so called, which belongs to the family Compositæ and includes many cultivated plants and a few poisonous ones. Cf. GROUNDSEL *sb.*[1] 1, *JACOBÆA 1, RAGWORT[1] 1.

1562, 1657 [see GROUNDSEL *sb.*[1] 1]. **1784** J. ABERCROMBIE *Propagation & Botanical Arrangement Plants & Trees* II. 678 (*heading*) *Senecio longifolius.* Long-leaved Cape Senecio. **1859** D. BUNCE *Travels with Dr. Leichhardt* ix. 105, I obtained specimens of..a..new species of *Stackhousia*, and a yellow, flowering *Senecio.* **1896** E. J. VON DADELSZEN *N.Z. Year-Bk.* 470 There are several kinds of ranunculus, and a bewildering variety of celmesias..and senecios also flourish. **1902** L. H. BAILEY *Cycl. Amer. Hort.* IV. 1656/1 A distinguishing mark of the Senecios lies in the character of the involucre. **1920** *Lancet* 23 Oct. 848/2 Senecio disease, or cirrhosis of the liver due to senecio poisoning... We have called the condition about to be described 'senecio disease' for want of a more appropriate name. **1954** *New Biol.* XVII. 14 The unique African alpine flora of giant Senecios (members of the same genus as common groundsel). **1975** P. LIVELY *Going Back* i. 4, I came out..past the buddleias and senecios past the iris garden hedge.

Senegal (se·nĕgǭl). [The name of a river and a republic, formerly a French overseas territory, in western Africa.] **1.** Used *attrib.* in names of local animals and plants.

1783 J. LATHAM *Gen. Synopsis Birds* IV. 456 Senegal Warbler, *Motacilla Senegalensis.* Length five inches and a quarter... Inhabits Senegal. **1781** T. PENNANT *Hist. Quadrupeds* I. 91 Antelope..Senegal. *Antilope Bubalis*.. with horns almost close at the base, a little above bending out greatly... Inhabits Senegal. **1833** *Penny Cycl.* I. 187/1 The Senegal custard apple (*Anona Senegalensis*). **1896** H. A. BRYDEN *Tales S. Afr.* 60 Great spur-heeled Senegal cuckoos flapped heavily from one reed-bed to another. **1952** MACKWORTH-PRAED & GRANT *Birds E. & N.-E. Afr.* I. 516 Senegal Coucal. *Centropus senegalensis.* **1966** C. SWEENEY *Scurrying Bush* xi. 158 The Senegal galago is one of the commonest mammals in the Nuba Mountains in southern Kordofan.

2. Special Comb. *Senegal gum* = *gum-senegal* s.v. GUM *sb.*[2] 3 a.

1867 P. L. SIMMONDS *Dict. Trade* (rev. ed.) Suppl. 454/1 *Senegal gum*, an African gum obtained from *Acacia Senegalensis.* **1951** KIRK & OTHMER *Encycl. Chem. Technol.* VII. 332 Kordofan gum is the finest gum obtainable... Senegal gum ranks second in importance and is much used for technical purposes although some of the better grades are used in pharmaceutical work.

Senegalese (se:nĕgǭlī·z), *sb.* and *a.* [f. prec. + -ESE.] **A.** *sb.* A native or inhabitant of Senegal. **B.** *adj.* Of or pertaining to Senegal.

Formerly applied loosely to an inhabitant of any French colony in West or Central Africa.

1917 *19th Cent.* Feb. 313 The Senegalese were in the fight with us. **1919** H. H. JOHNSTON *Compar. Stud. Bantu & Semi-Bantu Langs.* p. vi The facilities accorded to me in 1915 to visit the camps and hospitals of the 'Senegalese' soldiers in France. This assemblage of negroes from all parts of French West and West-Central Africa was a singularly fortunate circumstance. **1926** *Blackw. Mag.* Oct. 501/1 His French was fluent,..the French of the Senegalese troops. **1938** L. BEMELMANS *Life Class* II. ii. 131 In the Ballroom kitchen, Kalakobé the Senegalese is dragging the huge casseroles up out of the elevator. **1978** *Black World* May 93/1 The struggle of the Senegalese against the invading French forces nearly a century ago. **1980** *Times Lit. Suppl.* 24 Oct. 1200/2 The belligerent exchange between the Senegalese writers at Frankfurt was symbolic of larger antagonisms.

Senegambian (senĕgæ·mbian), *sb.* and *a.* [f. *Senegambia* (see below) + -AN.] **A.** *sb.* A native or inhabitant of Senegambia, former name of the region surrounding the Senegal and Gambia rivers in West Africa (cf. *SENEGAL, *GAMBIA); *U.S. colloq.*, applied to a Black American. **B.** *adj.* Of or pertaining to Senegambia; also used of Black Americans.

Senegambia is the name of a confederation of Senegal and Gambia, formed for military and trade purposes in February 1982; both countries retain their sovereignty; the president of Senegal is president of the confederation.

1900 *Dialect Notes* II. 58 *Senegambian*, a negro or negress. **1902** *Encycl. Dict.* Suppl. 646/3 Senegambian. **1911** *Encycl. Brit.* XXIV. 642/2 The conquest of the Senegambian region by the French followed. **1920** H. C. WITWER in *Collier's* 11 Dec. 21/1 A little bimbo.. is struttin' around and bellerin' about the undaunted white race to a big fat grinnin' Senegambian porter. **1942** W. FAULKNER *Go down, Moses* 49 What the hell kind of Senegambian Montague and Capulet is this anyhow? **1943** G. S. SCHUYLER in *Pittsburgh Courier* 11 Sept. 13/7 There are thousands of Negroes living in similar or better houses, despite the race hustling talk about the 'horrible houses' of Harlem. All the civilized Senegambians live in good homes. **1947** *Publ. Amer. Dial. Soc.* VIII. 36 *Senegambian.* I am acquainted with this word as meaning a Negro from Senegambia—whether ten, fifteen, or fifty years old. Used as a term of contempt. **1970** P. OLIVER *Savannah Syncopators* 70 The importance of the Senegambian slave trade lies in the accessibility of these parts to the Sudan savannah interior.

senesce, *v.* Delete *rare* and add later examples.

1909 G. B. SHAW *Let.* 22 June (1972) II. 847, I am not adolescing but senescing. **1955** *New Biology* XVIII. 12 If they [*sc.* experimental animals] do not senesce, they will tend to decrease in number exponentially. **1965** J. D. SALINGER in *New Yorker* 19 June 34/1 Few of these.. boys will mature. The majority..will merely senesce. **1979** *Nature* 5 July 55/2 The secondary compounds that deter grazers while the plants are alive do not disappear immediately when plants senesce and die.

‖ **senex** (se·neks). Pl. **senes.** [L., old man.] In literary contexts, the stock figure of an old man. Also in various L. phrases. Cf. *OLD MAN 1 f.

1898 E. P. MORRIS *Captives & Trinummus of Plautus* p. xxxvi, Hegio becomes in part the *comicus stultus senex*, chiefly concerned with the humiliation of having been deceived. **1923** G. NORWOOD *Art of Terence* v. 76 How much better to collect the necessary funds permanently and elegantly from the *senes*! *Ibid.* vii. 128 Micio has gone back to his normal position of a *lepidus senex.* **1957** N. FRYE *Anat. Criticism* 172 Central to the *alazon* [*sc.* imposter] group is the *senex iratus* or heavy father. **1957** F. N. ROBINSON *Wks. Chaucer* (ed. 2) 684/1 The Oxford carpenter is an example of the familiar figure of the 'senex amans'. **1968** E. SEGAL *Roman Laughter* iv. 119 Plautus makes the inversion of status still more meaningful for his countrymen by presenting as comic butts *senes* who are also *senatores.* **1975** H. A. KELLY *Love & Marriage in Age of Chaucer* xi. 271 William Langland, writing when he himself was admittedly a *senex non potens*, shows that the sentiment could be held seriously in a less absurd match than that between January and May. **1977** *Times Lit. Suppl.* 20 May 623/3 An archetypal comedy plot, deprecating December/May marriages and involving the victory of the young man over the *senex*... The emotions of a comic *senex.*

Senhouse (se·nhaus). *Naut.* [Origin unknown.] In full, *Senhouse slip.* A slip (SLIP *sb.*[3] 3 e) designed to secure the end of a cable.

1923 *Man. Seamanship* (Admiralty) II. ix. 163 The special towing Senhouse slip is inserted between the first and second shackle of the cable. **1948** R. DE KERCHOVE *Internat. Maritime Dict.* 648/2 *Senhouse slip*, a short length of chain of the same strength as the anchor cable, with a slip hook at one end and a shackle at the other. It is shackled to the cable clench, its purpose being to allow the bitter end of the cable to be easily slipped in case of emergency. **1961** F. H. BURGESS *Dict. Sailing* 183 *Senhouse*, a large slip in the cable locker near the clench bolt for holding the cable should it have to be unbolted and slipped. **1963** P. J. ABRAHAM *Last Hours* 135 He remembered knocking the Senhouse slip on one of the gripes away. **1976** *Oxf. Compan. Ships & Sea* 126/2 *Senhouse slip*... Its normal place in a ship used to be in the cable lockers where the inboard end of the cable is secured, but in several modern ships the end of the cable is shackled on to a deck bolt in the locker, no Senhouse slip being used. Smaller Senhouse slips are used in many smaller vessels and yachts to hold the ends of the guard-rails to the stanchions.

senicide. For *rare* [−1] read *rare* and add later example.

1931 R. R. MARETT in W. Rose *Outl. Mod. Knowledge* 419 One must not make too much of the occasional cases of..senicide, namely, the putting away of the old.

senile, *a.* Add: **1. b.** *Path.* **senile dementia,** a severe form of senile deterioration, in which loss of memory, disorientation in time and space, and inability to cope with everyday life are strongly marked. Hence **senile dement,** one who suffers from this. Cf. DEMENTIA.

1851 R. DUNGLISON *Dict. Med. Sci.* (ed. 8) 276/1 *Senile dementia, Insanity of the aged*, a form of moral insanity, in which the whole moral character of the individual is changed. **1902** A. R. DEFENDORF *Kraepelin's Clin. Psychiatry* viii. 273 Senile dementia includes those forms of mental disease appearing in the period of involution. **1948** W. A. O'CONNOR *Psychiatry* xii. 269 The senile dement exhibits to a profound degree the characteristic failings of the deteriorated senile person. **1954** W. MAYER-GROSS et al. *Clin. Psychiatry* xi. 482 The two pictures of senile dementia and normal ageing are qualitatively different and must be distinguished. **1976** *Scotsman* 20 Nov. (Weekend Suppl.) 3/4 Laing comments on this: 'I am sure he was not suffering from senile dementia, nor was it a slip of the pen.'

senile (sī·nəil), *sb.* [f. the adj.] An aged person; one who exhibits the weakness or diseases of old age.

1938 N. CAMERON in *Amer. Jrnl. Psychol.* LI. 664 The seniles..exhibited..the loose cluster-form of organization (*asyndesis*). **1962** *Lancet* 8 Dec. 1212/2 Of every 100 potential long-stay male patients, 30 were schizophrenics, 21 seniles, and 12 manic-depressives. **1981** J. B. HILTON *Playground of Death* v. 67 The old girl was well into her eighties... You never know where you stand with these so-called seniles.

senior, *a.* and *sb.* Add: **A.** *adj.* **1. c.** *senior citizen*, a term for an elderly person, esp. one who is past the age of retirement. orig. *U.S.*

Freq. used in official communications and by the media as a euphemism for 'old-age pensioner'.

1938 *Time* 24 Oct. 12/2 Mr. Downey had an inspiration to do something on behalf of what he calls, for campaign purposes, 'our senior citizens'. **1956** *School & Society* (U.S.) 12 May 169 As a basis for their education, it [*sc.* pragmatism] is good for the young, the middle-aged, and our senior citizens. **1962** *British Advent Messenger* 28 Sept. 30/2 Owing to the extensive alterations to be done it was October 27, 1958, before we could welcome any of those dear senior citizens who were so anxiously waiting to enter the Home. **1966** T. PYNCHON *Crying of Lot 49* iv. 90 Vesperhaven House, a home for senior citizens that Inverarity had put up. **1969** *Listener* 23 Jan. 101/2 More organised resistance came from the 'senior citizen'—or old age pensioners'—lobby. **1974** H. MACINNES *Climb to Lost World* iv. 56 We staggered up the bank to the village like senior citizens en route to the post office to collect their pensions. **1977** B. PYM *Quartet in Autumn* xxi. 192 She *is* a retired person, a senior citizen, you might say.

2. e. *Stock Exch.* Applied to securities the owners of which have first claim to be repaid by the issuing company. Cf. *junior stock* s.v. *JUNIOR *a.* (*sb.*) 5.

1914 H. HALFORD *Dict. Stock Market Terms* (ed. 2) 79 Senior stocks. Debentures and Preference Stocks carrying a fixed rate of interest and ranking for dividend in priority to the Ordinary and Deferred Stocks. **1925** H. PARKINSON *ABC of Stocks & Shares* 63 Among the 'senior' securities of the large railway companies the investor may roam at will. **1939** MEAD & GRODINSKY *Ebb & Flow of Investment Values* i. 5 Granted these formal requirements in ratios, priorities, and margins of safety, the senior securities of certain industries secured by certain forms of property,..are recommended. **1964** P. WYCKOFF *Dict. Stock Market Terms* 238 Senior Securities. Bonds and preferred stock which receive prior consideration when a corporation fails or is being dissolved.

4. *senior common-room* (examples).

1774 J. WOODFORDE *Diary* 14 Jan. (1924) I. 122 We all went into the Sen[r] Common Room. **1959** M. BRADBURY *Eating People is Wrong* i. 28 As Treece was leaving the Senior Common Room..the Vice-Chancellor appeared in the doorway. **1981** E. NORTH *Dames* iii. 41 They were in the Senior Common Room standing by the first school photograph.

5. Special collocations: **senior class** *U.S.*, a class in college or high school made up of students in their fourth year of academic study; **senior college** *U.S.*, a college in which the last two years' work for the bachelor's degree is done; **senior high (school)** *N. Amer.*, a secondary school comprising the three (or four) upper high school grades (cf. *junior high (school)* s.v. *JUNIOR *a.* (*sb.*) 5); **senior school,** a school, or part of a school, for older children; **senior year** *U.S.*, the fourth and last year of a high school or college course.

1766 T. CLAP *Ann. or Hist. Yale College* 14 The Senior Class were removed to Milford. **1837** [in Dict., sense 2 b]. **1900** C. W. WINCHESTER *Victories of Wesley Castle* 25 Wesley and Chester went to the city of Dorchester on some business for the senior class. **1980** *Redbook* Oct. 231/2, I couldn't go on the senior-class trip to Washington. **1899** *Univ. of Chicago Reg.* 37/1 The Faculties of the Schools of Arts, Literature, and Science have been organized as follows:..(2) The Faculty of the Senior Colleges [etc.]. **1942** *Bull. Vanderbilt Univ.* 15 May 69 The

College is divided, for certain purposes, into the Junior College and the Senior College. **1977** *Information Please Almanac for 1978* 826 (*heading*) Accredited U.S. Senior Colleges and Universities. **1909** *Ann. Rep. Bd. Educ.* (Columbus, Ohio) 29 You have established a Junior High School..leaving the tenth, eleventh and twelfth grades for the Senior High Schools. **1949** *Los Angeles Times* 23 June II. 5/1 Then they enter senior high school, and become 'juniors' and then seniors. **1955** [see *COMPOSITE *a.* 6 c]. **1974** *Encycl. Brit. Macropædia* VI. 422/1 The elementary–secondary sequence overall is 12 years in length.., but the subdivisions of these years are various: ..six-three-three (elementary school, junior high school, and senior high school), [etc.]. **1871** Senior school [see *junior school* s.v. *JUNIOR *a.* 5]. **1930** *Times* 26 Mar. 12/1 The first step in reorganization is to group all the senior children from 11 upwards in separate senior schools or departments or 'senior tops'. **1963** [see *DJEBBA, DJIBBAH]. **1963** BARNARD & LAUWERYS *Handbk. Brit. Educ. Terms* 175 *Senior School*, (1) An obsolete term used to describe the free non-selective post-primary schools (age-group 11–14) established under the pre-1944 elementary code. They provided a course of general studies with some vocational bias... (2) A term sometimes used to describe the top classes/forms of a grammar or public school. **1796** J. MORSE *Amer. Univ. Geogr.* (ed. 3) I. 420 The undergraduates are not permitted to attend them [*sc.* medical lectures] till their senior year. **1924** S. S. COLVIN *Introd. High School Teaching* 12 A number of high schools offer in their senior year a vocational course.

B. *sb.* **3*.** With *the.* The familiar name of the United Service and Royal Aero Club.

1906 G. W. E. RUSSELL *Social Silhouettes* xxviii. 195 If he is an old soldier, he is eligible for 'The Senior', and may make free with the Duke of Wellington's dry sherry and Dugald Stewart's still drier library. **1974** *Financial Times* 29 June 15/3 Commander James Allen, secretary of the United Services and Royal Aero (which is widely known in club circles as the Senior), [etc.]. **1974** R. MCDOUALL *Clubland Cooking* 11 Going west from Trafalgar Square we come first to the United Service Club, known as 'The Senior', because it was for senior officers of the Army and Navy. **1975** *Sunday Times* 25 May 24/1 The closure of the Senior will shake all the generals and admirals who have taken it for granted since 1815.

senium (sī·niŭm). *Med.* [a. L. *senium* debility of age, f. *senēre* to be feeble, f. *senex* old.] The period of old age. Usu. with *the.*

1911 STEDMAN *Med. Dict.* 786/1 *Senium*, old age, especially the debility of the aged. **1932** F. M. LIPSCOMB *Dis. Old Age* p. v, I have included only..those maladies which have a high incidence in the senium. **1968** J. G. HOWELLS *Family Psychiatry* ii. 23 Individual members of the family..may be of any age, from infancy to senium. **1977** T. R. HARRISON *Princ. Internal Med.* (ed. 8) 8/2 In the absence of disease there is a steady falloff [of nerve and muscle cells] which begins at about the end of the growth period and continues at an accelerated pace into the senium.

Senna, etc., varr. *SEHNA.

sennegrass (se·nĕgrɑs). [a. Norw. *senegras*: cf. ON. *sina*, Sw. dial. *sena* withered grass.] An Arctic sedge, *Carex vesicaria*.

1897 tr. *Nansen's Farthest North* II. 95 Turn them [*sc.* Finn shoes] inside out, fill them with sennegraes [*sic*] or sedge,..and creep into the sleeping bag. **1919** E. SHACKLETON *South* xii. 229 Oil mixed with reindeer hair, bits of meat, sennegrass, and penguin feathers form a conglomeration which cements the stones together.

sennet[1]. For † *Obs.* read *Obs.* exc. *Hist.* and add later examples.

1922 JOYCE *Ulysses* 471 Four buglers on foot blow a sennet. **1942** E. BLOM *Music in Eng.* iii. 49 Shakespeare was much attached to music, and it would be rash to conclude from the mere evidence of printed texts that he contented himself in his plays with a few songs and an occasional tucket (*toccata*) or sennet (*sonata*) for trumpets behind the scenes.

Senni (se·ni). The name of a tributary of the River Usk, Powys, S. Wales, used *attrib.* as **Senni Bed**, any of a series of fossiliferous sandstones in the Lower Old Red Sandstone of S. Wales, well seen in the valley of the Senni. Usu. *pl.*

1904 A. STRAHAN *Geol. S. Wales Coalfield* V. i. 3 Nearly all the remainder of the Old Red [Sandstone] tract is occupied by the red sandstones of the Brownstone division, but a thick and persistent group of sandstones and marls with cornstones, generally characterised by a green colour, appears in some of the deeper valleys, among others that of the Senni, from which fact the name of Senni Beds has been applied to them. **1927** *Q. Jrnl. Geol. Soc.* LXXXIII. 197 The plant-remains are entombed in sage-green arenaceous shales, which are intercalated among the typical sage-green sandstones of the Senni Beds of this locality. **1970** R. M. BLACK *Elements Palaeont.* xix. 302 (*caption*) A psilophyte; a primitive vascular plant from the Lower Old Red Sandstone (Senni Beds), South Wales.

‖ **sennin** (se·n,nin). Also **sennen** [Jap., wizard, recluse, f. Chinese *hsien-jên* an immortal man.] In Oriental mythology: originally in Taoism, an elderly recluse who has acquired immortality through meditation and self-discipline; hence, a human being with supernatural powers, a recluse embodying the spirit of nature.

1875 AUDSLEY & BOWES *Keramic Art of Japan* II (caption to plate X, division 1), Figure of a Buddhist Sennen, playing the *Koto*, and seated on the back of a fish. **1908** [see *KIRIN]. **1912** F. H. DAVIS *Myths & Legends of Japan* xxix. 356 The *Sennin* are mountain recluses, and many are the legends told in connection with them. Though they have human form, they are, at the same time, immortal, and adepts in the magical arts. **1915** E. POUND *Cathay* 19 In the storied houses of San-Ko they gave us more Sennin music. **1930** —— *XXX Cantos* iv. 17 Père Henri Jacques would speak with the Sennin, on Rokku.

Senoi (senoi·). [Native name, meaning 'man'.] **A.** *sb.* The name of a people inhabiting the provinces of Perak, Kelantan, and Pahang in West Malaysia; the language of this people. **B.** *adj.* Of or pertaining to this people. Cf. *SAKAI *sb.* (and *a.*).

1891 *Jrnl. Straits Branch R. Asiatic Soc.* Dec. 14, I shall deal chiefly with the Sĕn-oi dialect. *Ibid.* 16 The country South of this line being inhabited by Sĕn-oi, and the northern division by Tĕm-be. *Ibid.* 22 There are two distinct *r*'s in Sĕn-oi. **1910** R. J. WILKINSON *Papers on Malay Subjects: Aboriginal Tribes* 21 The Northern Sakai of the Plus valley, a different race, also speak of themselves as *Senoi* and *Mai Darat*. *Ibid.* 23 The true 'Senoi' quiver is plain. **1923** I. H. N. EVANS *Studies in Religion, Folk-Lore & Custom in Brit. N. Borneo & Malay Peninsula* II. 202 A Senoi man told me the following legend. **1958** J. SLIMMING *Temiar Jungle* 3 The largest of the three racial divisions, the Senoi, is divided linguistically into..the Semai-Senoi who are scattered across southern Perak & North Pahang and the Temiar-Senoi living to the north of the Semai. **1972** E. A. NIDA *Bk. of Thousand Tongues* 386/2 Senoi is spoken by 15,000 to 20,000 people in the South Perak, Ipoh, Tanjong Malim, and Central Pahang states of Malaya. *Ibid.*, The Senoi moved into the higher inland areas during the early 19th century. *Ibid.*, Now speakers of different Senoi dialects can understand one another only with great difficulty.

señorita. 1. b. (Earlier example.)

1823 J. A. QUITMAN *Let.* 23 Aug. in J. F. H. Claiborne *Life & Corr. J. A. Quitman* (1860) I. iv. 85 The belles.. 'tote' their fans with the air of Spanish señoritas.

Senousian, Senoussi, etc., see *SENUSSI.

senr., abbrev. of SENIOR *a.* 1 a. Cf. *SEN., SEN.

1763 J. BELL *Trav. from St. Petersburg* p. v/1 Peter Bell, senr. Esq. **1885** T. HARDY *Let.* 18 Mar. (1978) I. 131 The arrangement I made with Mr Macmillan Senr & Mr Craik. **1932** BLUNDEN *Face of England* 73 John Bowers, senr., came through the clap-gate.

‖ **senryu** (se·nrī,u). The name of Karai *Senryu* (1718–90), a Japanese poet, used to denote a type of Japanese verse, similar in form to *HAIKU but more intentionally humorous or satirical in content and usually without seasonal references.

1938 T. KUNITOMO *Jap. Lit. since 1868* II. i. 156 His submissive attitude which he likened to the spirit of *senryû* increased in his later writings. **1958** *Japan: its Land, People & Culture* xiii. 665/2 By applying the rule of 5.7.5. but disregarding other rigid rules *senryu* (satirical poems) were written in a freer spirit and with humour. **1977** G. GRIGSON *Faber Bk. Epigrams & Epitaphs* p. viii, Both *haiku* and *senryu* are epigrams—if epigram is taken to mean brevity; but a *haiku* has been defined as expressing a moment of vision into the nature of the world and a *senryu* as expressing a moment of satirical insight into the nature of ourselves... With us, rather unfortunately, 'epigram' has come only to suggest something like *senryu*, short and sharp.

sensal (se·nsăl), *a. Philos. rare.* [f. SENSE *sb.* + -AL.] Of or pertaining to sense or meaning (opp. *verbal*), or to the senses.

a **1866** J. GROTE *Treat. Moral Ideals* (1876) xxi. 518 Part of our sensal organization. **1896** V. WELBY in *Mind* V. 29 We might be allowed to coin a new derivative and speak of 'sensal' where we often now speak of 'verbal' questions. **1927** J. M. E. MCTAGGART *Nature of Existence* II. v. xxxviii. 116 We rejected the existence of matter and of sensa, because material and sensal qualities, as ordinarily defined, would not permit the determination, within the substances possessing them, of an infinite series of parts within parts. **1938** C. D. BROAD *Exam. McTaggart's Philos.* II. VII. xxxiii. 249, I conclude then that McTaggart's argument against the possibility of extended particulars, whether material or sensal, breaks down at the fourth step in my synopsis of it.

sensate, *a.* Add: **5.** *Sociol.* In the theory of P. A. Sorokin, a type of culture in which the satisfaction of material needs and desires is the main objective. Cf. *IDEALISTIC *a.* 2 and *IDEATIONAL *a.* 2.

1937 [see *IDEATIONAL *a.* 2]. **1959** C. C. ZIMMERMAN in J. S. Roucek *Contemp. Sociol.* 18 In sensate culture the main outlook for the individual is for extra-person stimuli, for articles which appeal to the ordinary untrained tastes, such as is seen in a quantity consumption culture. **1967** T. PARSONS *Sociological Theory & Mod. Society* IV. xii. 388 The idealistic synthesis has then proceeded to break down into an increasingly sensate phase. **1977** J. D. DOUGLAS in Douglas & Johnson *Existential Sociol.* i. 69 Most men have distinguished between such sacred thought and everyday, practical thought. (It is important, however, to note that rarely has this distinction been as sharp and important as in our increasingly sensate or secular culture.)

sensation. Add: **5. a.** *sensation drama* (earlier example), *novel* (earlier example), *novelist, scene* (earlier example), *story*; **b.** *sensation-mongering, -seeker, -seeking; sensation-giving, -hungry, -mongering* adjs.; **c.** Special comb.: † **sensation cell,** a sense-cell (*obs.*).

1892 LIEW & BEYER tr. *Ziehen's Introd. Physiol. Psychol.* 160 He has lost the acoustic memory-cells, but retained the acoustic sensation-cells. **1904** E. B. TITCHENER tr. *Wundt's Physiol. Psychol.* I. 289 It thus becomes necessary to posit the existence of two sorts of cortical cells: sensation cells and idea cells. **1860** MRS. S. COWELL *Jrnl.* 13 Mar. in M. Willson Disher *Cowells in Amer.* (1934) 36 We..saw Matilda Heron..in a 'new sensation Drama' called 'Mathilde'. **1865** MILL *Exam. Hamilton's Philos.* xxvii. 526 The knowledge-giving and the sensation-giving properties of an impression of sense. **1951** KOESTLER *Age of Longing* v. 86 She was sorry to disappoint the expectations of sensation-hungry journalists. **1925** W. DEEPING *Sorrell & Son* xvi. 147 It wasn't..our hard work, Stephen, that saved us, but luck, and the noise made by a section of a sensation-mongering press. **1937** *Downside Rev.* LV. 402 The idea of his indulging in 'sensation-mongering' of any sort or kind was ridiculous. **1980** *Times Lit. Suppl.* 24 Oct. 1210/5 They have given a..sober account of..the trial, leaving all the sensation-mongering to frequent interspersions from newspaper headlines. **1863** *Q. Rev.* Apr. 486 A sensation novel, as a matter of course, abounds in incident. **1863** Sensation novelist [see *PURPOSE *sb.* 3]. **1932** Q. D. LEAVIS *Fiction & Reading Public* II. iv. 154 Mrs. Radcliffe makes an appeal less to the nerves than to the imagination... The sensation novelists make a brute assault on the feelings and nerves in quite another way. **1861** H. MORLEY *Jrnl. London Play-goer* (1866) 282 Mr. Falconer's 'Peep o' Day'..deserves full houses..for what is called, according to the new term in theatrical slang, which Mr. Boucicault imported for us from the other side of the Atlantic, its 'sensation' scene. **1976** D. FRANCIS *In France* i. 21 All day..cars..disgorged crowds of reporters, photographers and plain sensation-seekers. **1923** R. MACAULAY *Told by Idiot* IV. 296 It was a queer affair, born of the emotionalism and sensation-seeking that beset many people at that time. **1869** L. M. ALCOTT *Little Women* II. xi. 157 She took to writing sensation stories—for..even all-perfect America read rubbish.

d. *Audiometry.* **sensation level,** the number of sensation units by which the loudness of a sound (supposedly proportional to its pressure amplitude) exceeds the loudness at which it would be barely perceptible; **sensation unit,** the unit of loudness by which two sounds differ if one is louder by a factor $10^{0.05}$. (Both terms are disused.)

If loudness were truly proportional to pressure (or displacement) amplitude, and hence to the square root of power, a sensation unit would be equal to a decibel.

1925 J. C. STEINBERG in *Physical Rev.* XXVI. 508 By sensation level is meant the number of units that the amplitude of any sound wave must be reduced in order to reach the threshold. **1927** *Ibid.* XXIX. 597 A unit of loudness somewhat better for our purpose would have been the least perceptible increment of loudness of a 700 cycle tone compared with its sensation level. **1929** H. FLETCHER *Speech & Hearing* iii. 68 A change of the power level of a sound by one decibel is approximately the smallest that the ear can detect. When this unit is used in this connection the term 'sensation unit' has come into use. The sensation level of any sound reaching the ears is the number of sensation units it is above the threshold level for audition. **1931** STEWART & LINDSAY *Acoustics* ix. 224 For the sake of convenience several authors are using the terms sensation unit and sensation level.

sensational, *a.* **2.** (Earlier example.)

1854 A. G. HENDERSON tr. *Cousin's Philos. of Kant* iii. 32 The sensational philosophy..pretends to deduce all knowledge from experience.

sensationalism. 1. (Earlier example.)

1846 J. D. MORELL *Hist. Philos.* I. p. x, There are four expressions which occupy a very prominent place throughout the whole work, and those are—sensationalism, idealism, scepticism, and mysticism. Now of these four, the first, I believe, is a word entirely new, and, therefore, demands some apology for its introduction.

sensationalist. Add: **1.** (Earlier example.)

1847 J. D. MORELL *Hist. Philos.* (ed. 2) I. i. 118 Sensationalists have attempted to contravene this view.

2. Also *attrib.* or as *adj.*

1979 *Guardian* 24 Aug. 8/6 A sensationalist and grossly misrepresentative newspaper story. **1980** *Times Lit. Suppl.* 18 Apr. 443/5 Compared with the style of Lady Falkender, Joe Haines *et toute cette galère*, so effectively convicted by their own sensationalist memoirs, the Garden Suburb was distinctly civilized in tone.

sensationalize, *v.* Add: Hence **sensa:tionaliza·tion.**

1955 *Times* 15 Aug. 7/5 By silence, and by mistrust of any publicity save that in the jargon of scientific journals, science has succeeded (in the words of Rutherford) in its own 'sensationalization'. **1977** *Lancet* 27 Aug. 449/1 It fell into disuse with..the sensationalisation of the 'opium vice' by writers such as De Quincey.

sensationism. Add: **2.** = SENSATIONALISM 1.

1846 J. D. MORELL *Hist. Philos.* I. p. xi, Next, I thought of sensism and sensationism, as being terms well adapted to describe the philosophy which builds itself up upon sense, or sensation; but these seemed to fail in respect to taste and euphony. **1936** *Brit. Jrnl. Psychol.* July 96 Stout saw the futility of associationism and sensationism forty years ago. **1948** W. McDougall *Social Psychol.* (ed. 29) 427 The essential novelty (for German psychology) of the teaching of this [sc. *Gestalt*] school is the repudiation of atomistic sensationism.

sensationist. Add: **2.** = Sensationalist 1. Also *attrib.*

1890 W. James *Princ. Psychol.* I. ix. 277 Now most believers in the ego make the same mistake as the associationists and sensationists whom they oppose. **1942** E. G. Boring *Sensation & Perception* i. 4 An empiricist is apt to be a sensationist, because it is by way of the senses that the mind has experience of the external world. **1953** K. Britton *J. S. Mill* vi. 192 From Locke to James Mill, there continued a complicated debate about the way in which we know physical objects; Reid and Hamilton providing an intelligent opposition to the sensationist school.

Hence **sensationi·stic** *a.*

1936 *Brit. Jrnl. Psychol.* July 97 The agreement, in principle, to discard the sensationistic hypothesis.

sense, *sb.* Add: **I. 1. f.** With defining word: the intuitive knowledge or appreciation of what action or judgement is appropriate to a given situation or sphere of activity. (Closely related to sense 1 d.)

1879, 1880 [see *colour-sense* s.v. Colour, colour *sb.* 18]. **1923** G. Atherton *Black Oxen* vii. 23 The reportorial news-sense died painlessly. **1926,** etc. [see *dress sense* s.v. *Dress *sb.* 4 a]. **1932,** etc. [see *clothes-sense* s.v. *Clothes *sb. pl.* 4]. **1932** E. V. Lucas *Reading, Writing & Remembering* i. 29 Had he [*sc.* Dickens] been possessed of more prudence or money-sense..his last years would have been more leisurely and peaceful. **1957** H. Read *Tenth Muse* xxii. 182 The producer, and the actor, are firmly convinced that there is some sixth sense, a feeling for what is possible in the theatre, a 'stage-sense'.

9. (Further examples.)

1962 A. Nisbett *Technique Sound Studio* vi. 106 The live broadcast seems to have a greater sense of occasion. **1974** R. Adams *Shardik* lvi. 472 From natural awe and sense of occasion, they did not press forward.

III. 27. *to make sense*: also in extended use (freq. in neg. contexts).

1921 G. B. Shaw *Back to Methuselah* iv. 148 She spoke to me without any introduction, like any improper female... Improper female doesnt make sense. **1936** *Punch* 12 Feb. 170/2 It can't be right, it can't be. Spats and a bowler-hat, but no umbrella—it doesn't make sense.

29. b. Chiefly *Math.* That which distinguishes a pair of entities which differ only in that each is the reverse of the other.

1894 H. W. L. Hime *Outl. Quaternions* i. i. 2 No two vectors are equal unless they have, first, equal lengths, and, secondly, similar directions—the phrase 'similar directions' meaning 'parallel directions with the same sense'. **1947** Courant & Robbins *What is Math.?* (ed. 4) iii. 159 Although inversion preserves the *magnitude* of angles, it reverses their *sense*; i.e. if a ray through *P* sweeps out the angle *x*. in a counterclockwise direction, its image will sweep out angle *y*. in a clockwise direction. **1950** [see *oriented *ppl. a.* 1]. **1962** A. Nisbett *Technique Sound Studio* 251 The doublet [microphone] can become bi-directional, cardioid or omnidirectional, simply by varying the size and sense of the potential on one of the diaphragms. **1977** Holland & Treeby *Vectors* i. 10 The vector (1/*a*)a is a unit vector in the direction and sense of a.

IV. 30. *sense-appearance, -apprehension, -awareness, -cell, -consciousness* (earlier example), *-element, -feeling, -idea, -impulse, -life, -material, -modality, -object, -observation, -percept, -perception* (earlier and later examples), *-phenomenon, -picture, -presentation, -symbolism, -verification*; (senses 19 and 20) *sense-assimilation, -change, -development, -group, -link, -linkage, -loan, -unit, -word*; (instrumental) *sense-given* adj.; **sense aerial** = *sense-finder* below; **sense-content,** (*a*) *Philos.*, whatever is present to one of the senses; a sense-datum; (*b*) the sense or meaning contained in an idea or literary passage; **sense-experience,** experience that is derived from the senses; **sense-field** *Philos.* (see quot. 1925); **sense-finder,** an aerial designed for sense-finding; **sense-finding,** with some radio direction-finders: the operation of determining which of two indicated directions 180° apart is correct; **sense history,** (*a*) *Philos.* (see quot. 1923); (*b*) the history of the development of meaning attached to a word; **sense-quality** *Philos.* and *Psychol.*, the quality of the sensory properties inherent in an object; **sense-withdrawal** *Yoga* = *pratyahara; **sense-world,** the external world as it is known through the senses; the 'world' of experience that is derived from one of the senses.

1941 W. J. D. Allan *Radio Navigation* ii. 42 The third method of finding sense is by means of a sense aerial. **1970** Taylor & Parmar *Ground Studies for Pilots* vii. 245 By adjusting the phasing of the loop and sense aerials, the cardioid and its image are produced in rapid alterations. **1894** A. C. Fraser in *Locke's Essay Hum. Und.* II. iv. xi. 328 When ideas, or qualities of things, are..not merely revived in memory or imagination, in the absence of the actual sense-appearances. **1947** *Mind* LVI. 300 A chief begetter of the sense-datum theory was the problem set by illusory sense-appearances. *a* **1902** R. Adamson *Devel. Mod. Philos.* (1903) II. ii. i. 229 Leibniz..maintains that our sense-apprehension of the colour green is a confused sense-apprehension of the two colours blue and yellow. **1921** Hannay & Collingwood tr. *Ruggiero's Mod. Philos.* 206 The first 'something' is mere sense-apprehension. **1935** M. E. Houtzager *Unconscious Sound- & Sense-Assimilations* i. 26 Place-names..change according to sound-laws, but also..through unconscious sound- and sense-assimilations. **1922** A. N. Whitehead *Princ. Relativity* ii. 20 Divest consciousness of its ideality, such as its logical, emotional, aesthetic and moral apprehensions, and what is left is sense-awareness. **1978** *English Jrnl.* Dec. 57/2 The second group of students did get to try to drink from a water fountain which was truly a unique experience in sense-awareness. **1908** *Practitioner* Oct. 548 In the case of all our senses, the effects are produced by reponsive protoplasmic movements of the specially adapted sense-cells. **1953** N. Tinbergen *Herring Gull's World* iii. 19 The sense-cells in the retina are the units of vision. **1976** H. R. Schiffman *Sensation & Perception* ix. 125/2 (*caption*) The tips of the sense cells extend into a pit. **1931** G. Stern *Meaning & Change of Meaning* x. 261 Clippings seldom give rise to sense-changes. **1951** W. Empson *Structure Complex Words* 26 The cause of a sense-change need have nothing to do with the use made of it after it has been pushed through. **1858** A. C. Fraser *Rational Philos.* 94 So-called *sense*-consciousness can be analysed. **1896** L. T. Hobhouse *Theory of Knowl.* ii. 42 It is quite enough for our purpose that *some* sense-contents should be complex. **1902** W. James *Varieties Relig. Experience* iii. 55 The words 'soul', 'God', 'immortality', cover no distinctive sense-content. **1962** W. Nowottny *Lang. Poets Use* v. 111 The action of the poem..is not something agglomerated out of the successive sense-contents of each line. **1975** W. S. Robinson in H. N. Castaneda *Stud. in Sellars' Philos.* 105 An analogue..designed to apply specifically to sensing sense contents, is presupposed. **1882** J. A. H. Murray *Let.* in K. M. E. Murray *Caught in Web of Words* (1977) x. 190 Nobody exc[ept] my predecessors in specimens of the Dicty has yet *tried* to trace out historically the sense-development of English words. **1960** C. S. Lewis *Studies in Words* 29 Indeed the sense-development of the word *proper* itself..is a striking instance. **1889** J. Venn *Empirical Logic* vi. 150 The adhesive power between the sense-element and the notion is particularly strong in the case of..smell. **1862** A. C. Fraser in *Macm. Mag.* VI. 194/2 The steady reference to sense-experience ..distinguished Locke. **1871** Sense-experience [see Pre-perception]. **1923** T. P. Nunn *Educ.* xiii. 171 All that constitutes..the quantitative as distinguished from the qualitative aspects of sense-experience. **1968** *Listener* 30 May 685 Principles native to the mind which we utilise in grasping sense-experience. **1890** W. James *Princ. Psychol.* II. xx. 268 The *education* of our space-perception consists largely of two processes—reducing the various sense-feelings to a common *measure*, and *adding them together* into the single all-including space of the real world. **1925** C. D. Broad *Mind & its Place* iv. 195 A sensum is not something that exists in isolation; it is a differentiated part of a bigger and more enduring whole, viz., of a sense-*field*. **1971** A. J. Ayer *Russell & Moore* iii. 65 To obtain the equivalent of sensibilia, on the basis of our primitive percepts, all that is needed, I believe, is the projection of spatial and temporal relations beyond the sense-fields in which they are originally given. **1934** Webster, Sense finder. **1953** C. H. Cotter *Elem. Navigation* xlvii. 485 The principle of the sense finder is as follows. Depending on whether the transmitting station lies in a certain direction or the opposite direction, the e.m.f. in the loop aerial will be altered in phase by 180°. **1937** D. C. T. Bennett *Compl. Air Navigator* iv. 134 A sense-finding arrangement is usually incorporated in Fixed Loop Direction Finders. **1957** R. Watson-Watt *Three Steps to Victory* lviii. 361 Our Radio Research Station work..had included 'sense-finding', the removal of the direction-finding ambiguity between one compass bearing and its exact opposite. **1871** A. C. Fraser *Life of Berkeley* x. 369 We may even, with Berkeley, call these sense-given phenomena 'sensations'. **1933** *Mind* XLII. 292 A great variety of sense-given shapes—squares, parallelograms, trapezia, etc.—would then..all be either portions or distortions of the surface of this cube. **1928** C. Bergener *Contrib. to Study of Conversion of Adjectives into Nouns* 1, I have..made an attempt.., after arranging the material in sense-groups, to ascertain the productivity of this mode of word-formation during the different periods of the language. **1966** G. N. Leech *Eng. in Advertising* viii. 89 One of the skills of writing formal English consists in..arranging one's ideas so as to make the end of each sense-group..as far as possible the appropriate place for emphasis. **1923** C. D. Broad *Sci. Thought* x. 362 Let us call the whole series of sensible fields which an observer O senses in the course of his life, O's *sense-history*. **1933** *Oxf. Eng. Dict.* I. p. v, The aim of this Dictionary is to present..the words that have formed the English vocabulary..with all the relevant facts concerning their form, sense-history, pronunciation, and etymology. **1954** A. J. Ayer *Philos. Ess.* iv. 95 The occurrence, within a given sense-history, of a series of sense-fields. **1871** A. C. Fraser *Life of Berkeley* iii. 75 Sense-ideas are with Berkeley real and presentative; not representative images. **1900** B. Russell *Philos. Leibniz* xiv. 161 Sense-ideas must..be distinguished by their own nature. **1896** L. T. Hobhouse *Theory of Knowl.* ii. 56 A felt total impression resulting from the forty separate sense-impulses. **1894** A. C. Fraser in *Locke's Essay Hum. Und.* II. iv. xi. 332 For it is not metaphysically impossible that there may be a *dream*, continuous and orderly, like the actual sense-life of a man. **1964** M. McLuhan *Understanding Media* i. i. 19 Money has reorganized the sense life of peoples just because it is an *extension* of our sense lives. **1957** N. Frye *Anat. Criticism* iv. 272 The poetic creation..is an associative rhetorical process, most of it below the threshold of consciousness, a chaos of paronomasia, sound-links, ambiguous sense-links, and memory-links very like that of the dream. **1962** W. Nowottny *Lang. Poets Use* i. 15 The sense-linkage effected by rhyme is an effect of which Arnold was well aware. **1931** Sense-loan [see *cross-influence* s.v. *cross-B.]. *a* **1902** R. Adamson *Devel. Mod. Philos.* (1903) II. 68 Nor does inner sense-material lend itself even to the less complete theoretical form of natural science. **1894** Creighton & Titchener tr. *Wundt's Hum. & Anim. Psychol.* vii. 119 The individual sensation is estimated by the relation in which it stands to other sensations of the same sense-modality. **1977** P. Strevens *New Orientations Teaching of Eng.* ix. 115 The sense-modalities of vision and hearing. **1908** W. James *Meaning of Truth* (1909) xii. 239 Our private concepts represent the sense-objects to which they lead us, these being public realities independent of the individual. **1920** A. N. Whitehead *Concept Nat.* viii. 170 The appearance of sense-objects is conditioned by the adventures of material objects. **1949** *Mind* LVIII. 58 The position will be, as Mr. Russell in fact saw, that the constituents of physical constructs are not simply sense-*objects* but sensations or sense-experiences. **1909** W. James *Pluralistic Universe* iv. 145 Hypotheses, and deductions from these, controlled by sense-observations and analogies with what we know elsewhere, are to be thanked for all of science's results. **1956** E. L. Mascall *Christian Theol. & Nat. Sci.* ii. 48 Scientific theories need for their expression technical terms..whose definition in terms of sense-observations is extremely complicated and remote. **1907** W. James *Pragmatism* vi. 218 Some part of a system that dips at numerous points into sense-percepts. **1846** J. D. Morell *Hist. Philos.* I. ii. 205 In doing this, Kant took it for granted, as a thing lying altogether beyond the region of proof, the reality of our sense-perceptions. **1971** R. I. Aaron *Knowing & Function of Reason* iv. 79 This conclusion is reinforced by arguments from the change induced in sense-perception by drugs, such as mescaline. **1871** A. C. Fraser *Life of Berkeley* x. 371 There is no evidence that an unperceived sensation or sense-phenomenon exists. **1971** R. I. Aaron *Knowing & Function of Reason* iv. 79 What is sensed has been variously described as idea, impression,..sense-phenomenon, sensum, and so on. **1920** A. S. Eddington *Space, Time & Gravit.* ii. 32 It would be unreasonable to limit our thought of nature to what can be comprised in sense-pictures. **1884** S. H. Hodgson *Let.* 14 Feb. in R. B. Perry *Thought & Char. W. James* (1935) I. 625 The answer must, for me, be given by a 'what' which is at least a *possibility* of sense presentation. **1932** W. T. Stace *Theory of Knowl.* iii. 34 The images of hallucination and dream are just as much part of the given as are sense presentations. **1896** L. T. Hobhouse *Theory of Knowl.* ii. 38 The idea of sensation as giving these simple sense-qualities and nothing else. **1954** R. Wells in Saporta & Bastian *Psycholinguistics* (1961) 280/2, I refer to the fact that they are all names of sense-qualities. **1871** A. C. Fraser *Life of Berkeley* x. 375 The substantiality and causality of matter thus resolve into a Universal Sense-symbolism, the interpretation of which is the office of physical science. **1892** H. Sweet *New Eng. Gram.* i. 20 A word may be defined as an ultimate independent sense-unit. **1974** R. Quirk *Linguist & Eng. Lang.* vi. 97 We are dealing with languages whose structures differ so much that..translation..is possible only if we deal in large sense-units. **1907** W. James *Pragmatism* vi. 209 Their relations are perceptually obvious at a glance, and no sense-verification is necessary. **1937** K. T. Behanan *Yoga* xiii. 215 In *pratyahara* or the sense-withdrawal stage, a deliberate effort is made to diminish the impulses streaming in through the sense organs. **1960** J. Hewitt *Yoga* viii. 116 Sense-Withdrawal is something which you must do for yourself, your 'I' must be in complete control. *c* **1874** Sense-word [see *rhythm-word* s.v. *rhythm 9 a]. **1911** W. James *Some Probl. Philos.* viii. 139 Monism usually treats the sense-world as a mirage or illusion. **1932** W. T. Stace *Theory of Knowl.* ix. 212 Those characters of the 'thing'..are in different sense-worlds.

sense, *v.* Add: **4.** (Earlier examples.)

1841 A. M. Maxwell *Run through U.S.* I. 102 The noun *sense* they convert into a most comical verb—'I sense', or 'She sensed him to do it'. **1849** *Knickerbocker* XXXIII. 201 'Do you sense what you are doing, Jack?' said she. 'Sense it, Suzy?' replied B.,—'I do, to the letter.'

6. Of a machine, instrument, etc.: to detect (some circumstance or entity).

1946 *Ann. Computation Lab. Harvard Univ.* I. 22 In the event that one or both of the factors involved in a multiplication are negative numbers, this fact is sensed and stored by the multiply unit. **1962** F. I. Ordway et al. *Basic Astronomics* v. 197 After arrival on the Moon the fluid is vented, an operation sensed by a pressure switch. **1978** *Sci. Amer.* June 54/3 In general particle detectors operate by sensing the ionization of atoms caused by the passage of a charged particle.

sense-datum (se·ns,dēⁱ:tɒ̆m). *Philos.* Pl. **-data.** [f. Sense *sb.* 1 + Datum.] Whatever is the immediate object of any of the senses, usually, but not always, with the implication that it is not a material object.

1882 J. Royce in *Mind* VII. 44 What relation does the external reality bear to the sense-datum? **1890** W. James *Princ. Psychol.* II. xx. 146 It is no wonder if some authors have gone so far as to think that the sense-data have no spatial worth at all. **1912** B. Russell *Probl. Philos.* i. 12 Let us give the name of 'sense-data' to the things that are immediately known in sensation: such things as colours, sounds, smells, hardnesses, roughnesses, and so on. **1938** W. S. Maugham *Summing Up* 260 The sense-datum, on which I thought all knowledge was based, seemed to me something given, which had to be accepted whether it suited the convenience or not. **1956** A. J. Ayer *Probl. Knowl.* 85 What..is immediately given in perception is an evanescent object called an idea, or an impression, or a presentation, or a sense-datum, which is not only private to a single observer but private to a single sense. **1980** *Dædalus* Spring 11 From the point of view of strict empiricism, the attempt to go beyond sense data..seems to fail.

‖ **sensei** (sensēⁱ). [Jap.] In Japan: a teacher or instructor; a professor; a respectful title, occasionally with ironic connotations, for one skilled in an art. Also *transf.*

1884 tr. *J. J. Rein's Japan* II. i. 378 The Ban-i (foreign barbarian) of yesterday was the Ijin-san (foreign gentleman) of to-day, and in the mode of address even a sen-sei (worthy scholar). **1934** E. BLUNDEN *Mind's Eye* 93 A copy of some newly acquired book, or a Japanese clay figure for the sensei's table. **1959** *Times Lit. Suppl.* 10 July 411/1 The ordinary reader begins to feel that he cannot get very far in poetry without a *sensei* or a *guru*. **1972** J. BALL *Five Pieces of Jade* iii. 35 My karate sensei tells me that I should learn Japanese. **1981** J. MELVILLE *Sort of Samurai* i. 7 I'm afraid your colleague my father never really forgave me, Horiguchi-sensei.

Sen-Sen (se·nsen). *N. Amer.* Also **sen-sen.** The proprietary name of a breath-sweetener, freq. used to disguise the smell of drink or cigarettes.

1911 *Official Gaz.* (U.S. Patent Office) 30 May 1273/2 Sen-Sen Chiclet Company, New York, N.Y. Filed Mar. 23, 1911... Chewing-Gum and Cachous. Claims use since on or about the month of March, 1894. **1936** J. Dos PASSOS *Big Money* 497 He was waiting..in the lobby.. chewing sensen to take the smell of three whiskeys..off his breath. **1947** J. STEINBECK *Wayward Bus* vii. 98 He took a few grains of sen-sen out of his inner shirt pocket and threw them in his mouth. **1951** P. BRANCH *Lion in Cellar* i. 8 He was eating sen-sen cachous. **1972** *Even. Telegram* (St. John's, Newfoundland) 28 June 12/1 Imbibers chewed Sen Sen to take the odor of liquor off their breath.

‖ **sensibile** (sensi·bile). *Philos.* Usu. in pl. **sensibilia** (sensibi·liă). [L., neut. of *sensibilis* SENSIBLE.] A term popularized by Bertrand Russell to denote the kind of thing which, if sensed, is a sense-datum.

1856 J. HINTON *Sel. from MSS.* (1871) II. 159 The matter of the schools, the substratum that underlies and is to be distinguished from the 'properties' or 'sensibilia', must be the 'actualistic', eternal (or spiritual.) That is, it is the eternal *not seen*..i.e. it is the hypothesis. **1906** J. A. STEWART in *Mind* Oct. 521 The Ideas [of Plato].. are 'known'..only as performing their function of making *sensibilia* intelligible. **1918** B. RUSSELL *Mysticism & Logic* viii. 148, I shall give the name *sensibilia* to those objects which have the same metaphysical and physical status as sense-data, without necessarily being data to any mind. Thus the relation of a *sensibile* to a sense-datum is like that of a man to a husband: a man becomes a husband by entering into the relation of marriage, and..a *sensibile* becomes a sense-datum by entering into the relation of acquaintance. **1921** tr. *Ruggiero's Mod. Philos.* 324 On this basic duality Varisco builds his theory. On the one side there exists the reality of sensibilia. **1940** A. J. AYER *Found. Emp. Knowl.* ii. 71 We shall have to take as a criterion for the existence of a sensibile the truth of a single hypothetical proposition. **1962** J. L. AUSTIN (*title*) Sense and sensibilia.

‖ **sensibilité** (sańsibilite). *rare.* [Fr.] = SENSIBILITY.

1926 D. H. LAWRENCE *Plumed Serpent* v. 90 And in all the crowd, a sense of guardedness..a curious soft *sensibilité*. **1960** *Encounter* XV. II. 64 It was a matter of being formed alike, of having the same *sensibilité*.

sensibility. Add: **2. c.** *dissociation of sensibility*: T. S. Eliot's term for a separation of thought from feeling which he held to be first manifested in poetry of the later seventeenth century.

1921 T. S. ELIOT in *Times Lit. Suppl.* 20 Oct. 669/4 The poets of the seventeenth century..possessed a mechanism of sensibility which could devour any kind of experience...In the seventeenth century a dissociation of sensibility set in, from which we have never recovered. **1930** E. M. W. TILLYARD *Milton* 356 Some sort of dissociation of sensibility in Milton, not necessarily undesirable, has to be admitted; but that he was responsible for any such dissociation in others (at least till this general dissociation had inevitably set in) is untrue. **1943** L. C. KNIGHTS *Explorations* (1963) 93 It is as a contribution to our understanding of the seventeenth century 'dissociation of sensibility'—from which, as Mr. Eliot remarked,.. 'we have never recovered'—that I wish to consider some of the work of Francis Bacon. **1947** T. S. ELIOT *Milton* 7, I wish first to mention another reproach against Milton, that represented by the phrase 'dissociation of sensibility'...I believe that the general affirmation represented by the phrase 'dissociation of sensibility'.. retains some validity, but I now incline to agree with Dr. Tillyard that to lay the burden on the shoulders of Milton and Dryden was a mistake. **1957** F. KERMODE *Romantic Image* viii. 143 The theory of the dissociation of sensibility is, in fact, the most successful version of a Symbolist attempt to explain why the modern world resists works of art that testify to the poet's special, anti-intellectual way of knowing truth.

sensible, *a.* (and *sb.*). Add: **IV. 14. c.** Of clothing, footwear, etc.: practical rather than attractive or fashionable.

1855 MRS. GASKELL *North & South* xii. 146 Margaret was busy embroidering a small piece of cambric... Mrs. Thornton..liked Mrs. Dale's double knitting far better; that was sensible of its kind. **1888** KIPLING *Under Deodars* 8 Nice, large, sensible shoes for all couples to stumble over as they go into the verandah! **1907** *Yesterday's Shopping* (1969) 339/3 The 'Sensible' carrier bag.. is the only paper Bag with a firm bottom. **1924** A. CHRISTIE *Man in Brown Suit* xx. 169 Forty, if she's a day, wears pince-nez and sensible boots and an air of brisk efficiency that will be the death of me. **1944** AUDEN *For Time Being* ii. 36 The river on this side of which initiative and honesty stroll arm in arm wearing sensible clothes. **1959** *Observer* 22 Mar. 1/1 Chintz curtains and no-nonsense bundles of flowers in sensible pots. **1978** R. HILL *Pinch of Snuff* x. 100 Genuine English county..unobtrusively elegant..in simple twinset and sensible shoes.

‖ **sensiblerie** (sańsiblěri). [Fr.] = SENTIMENTALITY a.

1931 *Times Lit. Suppl.* 7 May 559/1 The sentiment is obviously genuine, and never falls into excesses of *sensiblerie*. **1960** *Twentieth Cent.* Aug. 169 A piece of long-drawn-out, commercial *sensiblerie*, with no real tragic bite. **1974** *Financial Times* 4 Apr. 32/1 A brotherhood utterly devoid of sentimentality or *sensiblerie*.

sensibly, *adv.* **4.** (Earlier and later examples.)

1898 G. B. SHAW *Candida* I. 103 Do you think that the things people make fools of themselves about are any less real and true than the things they behave sensibly about? **1932** D. L. SAYERS *Have his Carcase* i. 9 She was dressed sensibly in a short skirt and thin sweater. **1970** N. MARSH *When in Rome* iii. 51 They wore sensibly shady hats.

sensillum (sensi·lŏm). *Zool.* Pl. **sensilla.** Also **sensilla** (pl. **-æ**), **sensillium** (*rare*). [mod.L. (coined in Ger. by E. Haeckel in *Systematische Phylogenie* (1895) III. ii. 119), dim. of L. *sensus* perception.] A simple sensory receptor in invertebrates, esp. arthropods, consisting of a cell or small group of cells that is a modification of the cuticle or epidermis and is often hair- or rod-shaped.

1925 A. D. IMMS *Gen. Textbk. Entomol.* 65 The tactile sensillæ of insects are often distributed over the entire integument. **1935** R. E. SNODGRASS *Princ. Insect Morphol.* xvii. 525 The scolopophorous organs are usually compound sense organs, each consisting of a bundle of simple sensilla having a common point of attachment on the body wall. **1962** GORDON & LAVOIPIERRE *Entomol. for Students of Med.* xxxiv. 211 On the 9th tergite of both the male and female flea, there is a small pincushion-like structure (the pygidium or sensillium) which is believed to have a sensory function. **1962** *Science Survey* III. 281 The last main class of hearing organs in insects comprises the various hair sensillae, scattered all over the body. **1963** R. P. DALES *Annelids* vii. 143 The sense cells on these tentacles or cirri are commonly fusiform in shape with a sensilla or sensillae projecting through the cuticle. **1971** *Nature* 24 Dec. 477/1 Each campaniform sensillum [on a cockroach leg] functions through a single primary sense cell. **1973** *Jrnl. Invertebrate Path.* XXII. 409 (*caption*) Portion of another integumentary growth with apparent sensillium.

sensing, *vbl. sb.* (in Dict. s.v. SENSE *v.*). Add: *spec.* **a.** *U.S. Mil.* An observation of the point of impact of a shot with respect to the target.

1937 *Sun* (Baltimore) 16 Aug. 16/2 Transfers to the targets will be made by means of a high burst with shrapnel, the bursts being brought to a check point at a particular elevation and range by means of sensings from lateral observation points. **1944** H. F. GREGORY *Anything Horse can Do* vii. 74 Conducting an artillery adjustment by communicating 'sensings' by changing the line of flight of the Autogiro. **1962** *Ordnance Techn. Terminol.* (U.S. Army Ordnance School, AD 660 112) 269/2 *Sensing*, the direction of a point of burst or impact, or centers of burst or impact with respect to the target; such as over, short, air or graze.

b. The action of an automatic device in detecting, observing, or measuring something. Freq. *attrib.*

1950 *Jrnl. Res. Nat. Bureau of Standards* (U.S.) XLV. 295/1 A sensing element in the gas stream normally attains a steady temperature below that of the gas itself, because of radiation and conduction from the sensing element. **1955** *Flight Test Man.* (Advisory Group on Aeronaut. Res. & Devel., NATO) I. IIA. x. 15/1 The collection methods of determining liquid water content below freezing..are essentially based upon the sensing of icing. **1962** F. I. ORDWAY et al. *Basic Astronautics* v. 185 (*caption*) Infrared vidicon tube...It could also be employed for horizon sensing. **1967** *Electronics* 6 Mar. 127/1 An infrared scanner will compete in the fast-developing market for thermal sensing and display devices. **1977** *Dædalus* Fall 38 All the rest of the electromagnetic spectrum became available to astronomers only when the development of sounding rockets and artificial satellites made it possible to send their sensing instruments above the atmosphere.

c. = *sense-finding* s.v. *SENSE *sb.* 30.

1961 C. H. COTTER *Princ. & Pract. Radio Direction Finding* ii. 36 The device provided to resolve the 180° ambiguity is known as a sensefinder, and the process of doing so is known as sensing. **1976** W. H. P. CANNER *Air Navigation* vi. 139 Sensing refers to the resolution of the ambiguity in bearings.

sensism. b. (Earlier example.)

1846 [see *SENSATIONISM 2].

sensitive, *a.* and *sb.* Add: **A.** *adj.* **3.** *sensitive plant* (earlier and later *fig.* examples: now freq. of persons).

1821 P. EGAN *Boxiana* 1st Ser. III. 236 Martin went to work with both his hands so quickly, that his opponent's sensitive plant rolled about like a humming top, and he fell out of the ring covered with crimson. **1907** J. LONDON *Let.* 27 Sept. (1966) 251 All 'sensitive plants' are egomaniacs; they are colossally stuck upon themselves. **1926** GALSWORTHY *Silver Spoon* I. vi. 41 Well, sir, the Press is a sensitive plant. I'm afraid you might make it curl up. **1974** 'S. WOODS' *Done to Death* 190 'So nice to be considered a sensitive plant,' said Emma.

5. e. Of a drilling machine: designed to give the operator continuous and sensitive control over the pressure and rate of drilling.

1895 C. J. APPLEBY *Illustr. Handbk. Machinery* IV. 53 Six speed sensitive drilling machine..is capable of drilling holes up to ⅜ in. diameter, and will swing 18 inches. **1942** [see *pillar drill* s.v. *PILLAR *sb.* 12]. **1971** C. R. HINE *Machine Tools & Processes for Engineers* xi. 261 This machine is slightly heavier than the sensitive drill press.

f. Involved with or likely to affect national security. Also with reference to other issues: that must be treated with care; likely to give offence if mishandled.

1953 *Manch. Guardian Weekly* 7 May 2 People in 'sensitive' jobs or departments—that is in positions having access to top secret or policy information. **1968** *Globe & Mail* (Toronto) 17 Feb. 7/1 Under the policies of the Government of Canada no one can buy arms and ship them from Canada to any sensitive area, whether that be Vietnam or anywhere else. **1973** P. GEDDES *Ottawa Allegation* x. 138, I realise it's from a sensitive source, but could I see it for myself? **1977** T. HEALD *Just Desserts* iv. 68 Probe gently. We are in what is known as a sensitive area.

g. Of a mathematical, statistical, or physical quantity: largely or appreciably influenced by changes in some other quantity, the choice of method or model, etc. Const. *to*.

1955 [see *ROBUST *a.* 4]. **1966** A. BATTERSBY *Math. in Managem.* ix. 231 The cost is not 'sensitive' to the batch size. **1968** FOX & MAYERS *Computing Methods for Scientists & Engineers* iii. 31 The results show that y_r is extremely sensitive, for large r, to small changes in the initial condition. **1979** G. E. P. BOX in Launer & Wilkinson *Robustness in Statistics* 211 How sensitive are inferences made about θ to these contemplated misspecifications of the model?

sensitivity. Add: **3. a.** The degree to which a device, test, or procedure responds to small amounts of or slight changes in that to which it is designed to respond; the ratio of the response of a device to the stimulus causing it; = SENSITIVENESS 3.

1918 E. S. FERRY *Handbk. Physics Measurements* II. iv. 179 (*heading*) Determination of the sensitivity of a galvanometer. **1937** H. EAGLE *Lab. Diagnosis of Syphilis* vi. 117 The longer the incubation period, the greater was the sensitivity of the test. **1944** E. S. SMITH *Automatic Control Engin.* iii. 17 Sensitivity is merely the ratio effect/cause. The over-all sensitivity is equal to the product of all the component sensitivities of the instrument. **1955** *Sci. Amer.* Mar. 68/2 The three procedures represent an ascending scale of sensitivity, and a descending scale of specificity. **1973** *Nature* 7 Dec. 343/2 An unsuccessful search for gravitational radiation was reported about a year ago by Braginskii *et al.*, with detectors of comparable sensitivity to those of Weber.

b. *spec.* in *Radio*, (a measure of) the ability of a receiver or other part of a radio system to pick up or respond to weak radio signals.

1928 L. S. PALMER *Wireless Princ. & Pract.* ix. 305 Most poor rectifying contacts can be improved by either the application of a small potential difference or by the application of heat, but with some of these contacts the increased sensitivity persists after the removal of the potential difference or heat. **1931** MOYER & WOSTREL *Radio Handbk.* iii. 124 Many crystals do not have a uniform sensitivity over the entire surface. **1962** *Which?* Feb. 40/1 We tested the radios to see how well they would receive weak stations. Their ability to do this is called sensitivity. **1965** *Wireless World* Sept. 457/1 The sensitivity of an audio amplifier is nowadays (following the British Standard) often specified in terms of a 'sensitivity voltage', i.e. the e.m.f. applied in series with the stated source resistance, to the input terminals in order to obtain the rated output power or voltage. **1975** G. J. KING *Audio Handbk.* v. 111 Each channel of a two- or four-channel amplifier should be measured for sensitivity independently.

4. *Psychol.* Used *attrib.*, esp. in *sensitivity group*, *training*, to denote training in small groups aimed at increasing a person's awareness of the behaviour, feelings, and motives of others and of himself. Cf. *T-group* s.v. *T 6*.

1954 *Personnel* XXX. 256/1 The suggested approach to leadership training combines these two features in order to focus sensitivity training on those interpersonal problems which intimately involve the members of the training group. **1964** M. ARGYLE *Psychol. & Social Probl.* x. 133 Many students could..benefit from sensitivity training, aimed at increasing the accuracy of perception of social situations. **1969** *Listener* 26 June 881/1 A sensitivity group of persons gets together in order to cultivate a heightened awareness of themselves and each other, in a sort of group therapy. **1971** *Harvest Years* Mar. 8/2 (*caption*) A few scenes from a sensitivity session. **1977** E. G. & N. C. BORMANN *Speech Communication* (ed. 2) i. 12 Sensitivity groups have been used to train management personnel..and to institute individual and organizational change.

sensitization. Add: **1.** (Later examples in *Physiol.*)

1916 [see *SENSITIZIN]. **1947** *Ann. Rev. Microbiol.* I. 298 Very striking is the effect of mycobacteria on sensitization to some simple compounds such as picryl chloride and 2:4 dinitrochlorobenzene... When these are injected intraperitoneally a state of anaphylaxis alone ensues, while the use of mycobacteria produces in addition sensitization of the contact dermatitis type. **1969** *Daily Progress* (Charlottesville, Va.) 12 Jan. A2/4 It also brings its own problems of sensitization to the horse serum from which it is made.

2. *Psychol.* The fact or condition of responding in a sensitized or sensitive (as opp. to a repressed) manner, esp. to an emotional stimulus; the process of being sensitized to a particular stimulus.

1947 *Jrnl. Personality* XVI. 75 Such sensitization represents..the obverse of defense...We now find sensitization in the presence of 'dangerous' stimulus objects. **1959** *Ibid.* XXVII. 364 The opposite syndrome, composed of high Admission, low Denial, and high Anxiety scores describes the other end of the repression continuum, which has been labeled 'sensitization'. **1967** *Psychol. Reports* XX. 459 The word 'sensitization' is used because the purpose of the procedure is to build up an avoidance response to the undesirable stimulus. **1976** *Jrnl. Clin. Psychol.* XXXII. 321 Results were interpreted according to an approach-avoidance model of repression-sensitization.

sensitize, *v.* **2.** Transfer quot. 1904 to sense 3 below and add later example.

1978 *Dædalus* Spring 228 It is..reasonable to hope that the fraction of abuses, mistakes, surprises, and other alarming problems will drop as the professionals involved become more and more sensitized to the possibility of such problems.

3. *Physiol.* To render (an organ or organism) sensitive *to* the presence of some agent; *esp.* to render (the immune system) sensitive *to* the presence of antibody. Also *absol.*

1904 [in Dict., sense 2]. **1909** *Jrnl. Amer. Med. Assoc.* 30 Oct. 1473/1 The substance which is produced in the corpus luteum and which sensitizes the mucosa of the uterus has a specific affinity to the uterine tissue. **1922** *Jrnl. Physiol.* LVI. 143 The presence of free CO_2 'sensitises' the nerve cells to H ions. **1947** *Ann. Rev. Microbiol.* I. 305 It would be of great interest to identify the fraction or fractions which exert the adjuvant effect of mycobacteria and to know whether the effect could be produced without sensitizing to tuberculin. **1970** Passmore & Robson *Compan. Med. Stud.* II. xxii. 12/1 IgM antibodies are unable to sensitize tissues for anaphylactic reactions.. although IgG and IgA molecules, are able to do so.

sensitized *ppl. a.*, **sensitizing** *vbl. sb.* and *ppl. a.* (later examples in *Physiol.*).

1909 *Jrnl. Amer. Med. Assoc.* 30 Oct. 1471/2, I have.. been able to ascribe a definite function to the corpus luteum, namely, that of supplying a sensitizing substance to the uterus which prepares the latter to respond with the production of the maternal placenta, if an external stimulus of a mechanical nature is added. *Ibid.* 1472/1 We wished..to select the safest period for the egg to attach itself to a sensitized uterine mucosa. *Ibid.* 1473/1 This process of sensitizing enables the connective tissue of the uterine mucosa to proliferate periodically. **1941** *Nature* 26 July 116/1 The small, often-repeated doses of these drugs..provide a chance for the patient to become sensitized to the drug. **1947** *Ann. Rev. Microbiol.* I. 299 For the rapid production of allergic encephalitis in both the monkey and the guinea pig the presence of mycobacteria in the sensitizing injection seems to be essential. **1978** *Price's Textbk. Practice of Med.* (ed. 12) IV. 381/1 The signs and symptoms of generalized anaphylaxis that may follow..the parenteral injection of foreign serum, protein, or drugs, or sometimes even insect bites or stings in a sensitized individual, include a marked fall in blood pressure [etc.].

sensitizer. Restrict *Photogr.* to sense in Dict. and add: † **2.** *Immunol.* = *sensitizin. *Obs.*

1903 *Nature* 13 Aug. 360/2 The sensitizers of the tubercle bacillus. **1935** N. P. Sherwood *Immunol.* vi. 112 Anaphylactic sensitizers.—Many persons have considered these interesting antibodies as identical with the precipitins but more recently some doubt has been cast on this hypothesis.

3. *Psychol.* A person or thing that has a sensitizing effect; one who reacts by being sensitive to a stimulus (rather than repressing it).

1948 *Jrnl. Abnormal & Soc. Psychol.* XLIII. 151/2 Nature orientation acts as a sensitizer, lowering thresholds for acceptable stimulus objects. Let us call this mechanism selective sensitization. **1951** *Ibid.* XLVI. 557/1 Needs could act as sensitizers, lowering the recognition thresholds for need-related stimuli. **1972** S. R. Maddi *Personality Theories* v. 207 Psychiatric outpatients were.. classified on the basis of their therapeutic interviews and other clinical tests as either sensitizers or repressers. **1976** *Psychol. Rep.* XXXIX. 189 The death message resulted in significantly more..anxiety than the neutral message for repressors as well as for sensitizers.

† **sensitizin** (se·nsitəizin). *Immunol. Obs.* [f. Sensitize *v.* + -in[1].] A substance which confers sensitivity on a species of antibody.

1916 R. Weil in *Jrnl. Immunol.* I. 1 In the following papers the term 'Anaphylactic antibody' has been replaced by the word 'Sensitizen'. This has the advantage of brevity. The word is formed on the analogy of the words precipitin and agglutinin, and carries its own significance —namely that substance which confers sensitization. **1920** *Ibid.* V. 319 The experiments furnish further evidence that precipitin and 'sensitizin' are identical.

sensitometric (se:nsĭtome·trik), *a.* *Photogr.* [f. Sensitometry: cf. *-metric.] Of or pertaining to sensitometry.

1881 *Brit. Jrnl. Photogr.* 25 Feb. 97/1 A committee was formed..to decide, if possible, the sensitometric question. **1949** *Electronic Engin.* XXI. 118/3 In such cases as motion picture processing where it is desirable to develop to constant gamma in the face of increasing exhaustion of developer, sensitometric strips are frequently included every few hundred feet so that the development may constantly be checked. **1967** E. Chambers *Photolitho-Offset* vii. 85 The starting point of sensitometry requires an understanding of sensitometric principles, involving the sensitometric curve.

Hence **sensitome·trically** *adv.*

1891 *Photographic Jrnl.* XVI. 65 The raw emulsion was mixed with the silver salts of various dyes dissolved in alcoholic solution of ammonia and tested sensitometrically, as well as spectroscopically. **1969** *Amat. Photographer* 9 Apr. 67/1 The integrating method of enlarging photometry is perhaps more difficult to explain sensitometrically.

sensitometry. (Earlier example.)

1881 *Brit. Jrnl. Photogr.* 25 Feb. 97/1 Photographic literature during the last six months has contained very numerous articles on the question of sensitometry.

sensize, *v.* Add: So **se·nsized** *ppl. a.*

This happens to pre-date the finite verb (in Dict.).

1846 J. D. Morell *Hist. View Philos.* II. v. 86 'The world,' says Fichte, 'is the sensized material of our practical life.'

sensor (se·nsəɪ, -ǒɪ). [f. the adj. or f. Sense *v.* + -or.] A device giving a signal for the detection or measurement of a physical property to which it responds.

1958 *New Scientist* 10 Apr. 22/2 The 'sensor' is a small cylinder enclosed in a bigger cylinder full of silicone fluid and set on bearings which allow it to turn. **1958** *Guided Missiles* (U.S. Dept. of the Air Force) vi. 273/1 Pickoffs include any of the devices that are used to transfer the energy received at the sensor to the following detecting and amplifying stage. **1963** *Ann. Reg. 1962* 401 Infra-red sensors designed to detect rocket launchings. **1969** *New Yorker* 12 Apr. 104/2 Inside his space suit, the astronaut has a number of sensors that report on the state of his health. **1975** *Sci. Amer.* July 108/2 A repellent acts in one way on the carbon dioxide sensor and in a different way on the moisture sensor. **1976** *Early Music* July 351/3 Its sensor passes over the object to be copied thousands of times in different directions, and passes this information to cutting heads. **1977** *Navy News* Aug. 32/1 Vast improvements in propulsion, sensor systems and weapons.. have placed great demands on training facilities. **1980** *Sunday Express* 19 Oct. 27 Every Metro has brake pad wear sensors to tell you when to change the brake pads.

sensori-. Add: **sensori-motor** (later examples); also, that relates to activity involving both sensory and motor pathways; **sensorineu·ral** *a.*, applied to defective hearing that is due to a lesion of the inner ear or auditory nerve.

1908 W. McDougall *Introd. Soc. Psychol.* ii. 29 An innate or inherited psycho-physical disposition, which.. probably has the form of a compound system of sensori-motor arcs. **1932** S. Zuckerman *Soc. Life Monkeys & Apes* ix. 147 The sensori-motor mechanisms of the primates differ from those of the lower mammals. **1977** *Language* LIII. 153 Piaget 1952 and Piaget and Inhelder 1971 view representation as an internalization of active sensori-motor imitation. [**1960** *Laryngoscope* LXX. 885 A sudden unilateral or bilateral sensory-neural (perceptive) hearing loss.] **1964** *Arch. Otolaryngol.* LXXX. 382/1 In this type of slowly progressive sensorineural hearing loss the only finding is atrophy of the stria vascularis, the functional manifestation of which is hearing loss showing a flat audiometric curve. **1977** *Lancet* 12 Nov. 1003/2 Perforation of the round-window membrane was found in three children with severe sensorineural deafness.

sensorial, *a.* Add: Hence **senso·rially** *adv.*

1890 W. James *Princ. Psychol.* I. ii. 42 All of Munk's *birds* seemed totally blind (blind sensorially) after removal of the hemispheres by his operation. **1935** *Jrnl. Compar. Psychol.* XX. 10 A stimulus, a..property of which was its membership in a series which was only in part sensorially present on any one trial. **1962** Y. Malkiel in Householder & Saporta *Probl. Lexicogr.* 22 Multicolored plates..might be useful, especially to the sensorially perceptive etymologist.

sensory, *sb.* Add: **3.** *Psychol.* A person in whom sensation supposedly dominates over action. *rare.*

1902, 1929 [see *motor *sb.* 2 c].

sensory, *a.* Add: **2.** Special collocations: **sensory aphasia** *Path.*, aphasia evidenced by impaired speech, memory, writing, or reading which is due to cerebral defect or injury affecting comprehension or the ability to integrate incoming acoustic information, and freq. differentiated from incapacities deriving from motor defects; **sensory deprivation** *Psychol.*, the act or process whereby an organism is deprived of stimulation affecting one or more of the sense organs; the state or condition produced by such deprivation; **sensory-motor** *a.* = *sensori-motor a.* s.v. Sensori- in Dict. and Suppl.

1884 *Brain* VI. 401 The author [*sc.* Wernicke] also makes good use of the phenomena of the different forms of aphasia, which he divides into motor, conductive, sensory, and total aphasia. **1926** H. Head *Aphasia* I. ii. iii. 202 'Sensory' aphasia, or amnesia, was divided into 'visual' and 'auditory'. **1959** *Psychol. Rev.* LXVI. 46/2 It is significant that with careful study of even a small number of patients, the traditional dichotomy between motor and sensory aphasia began to disappear. **1976** E. D. Mysak *Path. Speech Syst.* iii. 85 Sensory aphasia [is reported] with tumors in the left parietal region. **1948** D. Bakan *Investig. Effect of Sensory Deprivation on Stall Perception* i. 4 What is the effect of sensory deprivation on the accuracy with which the pilot can detect the edge of the stall proper. **1961** S. Cobb in P. Solomon et al. *Sensory Deprivation* p. xviii, The symptoms of the deprived child with 'atypical' and 'autistic' reactions are without doubt related to the phenomena seen in adults after experimental sensory deprivation. **1978** O'Connor & Hermelin *Seeing & Hearing & Space & Time* v. 65 Sensory deprivation, especially of audition, appears to decrease duration. **1957** Menon & Patel *Teaching of Eng. as Foreign Lang.* xi. 125 Spelling is a sensory-motor habit acquired by motor responses to certain sensory stimuli.

Hence **se·nsorily** *adv.*

1925 E. Sitwell *Poetry & Criticism* 20 Though it seems to us as though we heard them sensorily, yet the sound is unheard in reality. **1949** M. Mead *Male & Female* i. 17 Needs..for continuous contact with one sensorily identifiable human being throughout the first two years of life. **1954** *Essays in Criticism* IV. 313 Mill's attempt to define poetry as something not heard but *overheard*..is successful..in so far as it removes the sensorily ascertainable audience and replaces it with a mysterious audience.

sensual, *a.* Add: **4. a.** For Now *rare* or *Obs.* read Now only in phr. *the average sensual man* (see *average *a.* 2 b).

sensualization. (Earlier example.)

1798 A. F. M. Willich *Elem. Crit. Philos.* 141 The sensualization of an idea of reason.

sensu lato: see *sensu stricto.

sensum (se·nsɒ̆m). *Philos.* Pl. **sensa.** [L., sensed, that which is sensed, neut. pa. pple. of *sentīre* to discern by the senses, to perceive.] = *sense-datum.

1868 A. Bain *Senses & Intellect* (ed. 3) 376 In Sensation, we seem to have the sentient mind, and the thing felt—*sentiens* and *sensum*. **1920** S. Alexander *Space, Time, & Deity* II. iii. ii. 58 The non-mental external object which in this case is the *sensum* or *sensibile*. **1923** C. D. Broad *Sci. Thought* viii. 240 Such objects as *y* I am going to call Sensa. **1937** L. S. Stebbing *Philos. & Physicists* vi. 130 It is only because Russell and Joad *first* know that there are external objects that they are able to *infer* that there are private sensa. **1949** G. Ryle *Concept of Mind* vii. 213 The theory says that when a person has a visual sensation ..his having this sensation consists in his finding or intuiting a sensum. **1967** *Encycl. Philos.* VII. 80/2 The essential point is that perceiving proper is the direct awareness of sensa. **1974** R. M. Yost in Carterette & Friedman *Handbk. Perception* I. ii. 33 One cannot locate a visual sensum in empty physical space without presupposing the Absolute Theory of Space.

Sensurround (se·nsɒ̆raund). Also **sensurround.** [Blend of Sense *sb.* and Surround *v.*] The proprietary name of a special-effect technique whereby a cinema audience is apparently surrounded by low-frequency sound and air vibrations generated from the soundtrack of a film. Also *attrib.* and *transf.*

1974 *Newsweek* 2 Dec. 104/2 The quake under your seat is created by 'Sensurround', a system that hooks into the film's soundtrack and sets off low-level tremors at a cost of $500 a week to the theater owners. **1975** *New Yorker* 26 May 81/1 'But my dear,' said Mrs. Vreeland, her voice achieving in the small room much of the effect that Sensurround does in movie theaters, 'those wrapped heads are my *greatest achievement.*' *Ibid.* 82/2 'My *God*, Ferle,' said Mrs. Vreeland, employing her Sensurround voice. **1976** *Official Gaz.* (U.S. Patent Office) 6 Apr. 22/1 MCA Systems, Inc., Universal City, Calif.... *Sensurround* for electronic apparatus for generating special effects, including simulated earthquake effects, in motion picture theaters... First use Sept. 3, 1974. **1977** *Time* 11 July 51/3 *Rollercoaster* is the latest—and so far least—excuse to trot out Sensurround, that technology that is still in search of a character and, for that matter, a plot worthy of its woofers. **1980** *Spectator* 31 May 24/1 Every corner of the theatre is used to produce a sensurround, stereophonic effect, the noise and flashing all around us.

‖ **sensu stricto** (se·nsu stri·kto). [L., lit. 'in the restricted meaning'.] Strictly speaking; in the narrow sense (of a term, esp. in the natural sciences). Opp. to **sensu lato** (lā·to) [L. *lātus* broad], in the broad sense. Cf. *stricto sensu.

1941 J. S. Huxley *Uniqueness of Man* xi. 240 Human biology is but an extension of biology *sensu stricto.* **1942** W. B. Turnbull in *Bot. Rev.* VIII. 656 (*heading*) Algae (sensu lato). **1952** Sensu stricto [see *isochemical* adj. s.v. *iso- a]. **1954** [see *neocerebellum]. **1959** A. R. Clapham et al. *Excursion Flora Brit. Isles* 569 Sensu lato. In the broad sense. **1963** D. W. & E. E. Humphries tr. *Termier's Erosion & Sedimentation* xiv. 299 Griottes 'sensu stricto' composed of alternate beds of shale and limestones, irregularly corrugated. **1973** B. J. Williams *Evolution & Human Origins* xi. 176 In the material that follows I shall use the term Neandertal *sensu lato*, that is, in the broad sense. **1977** *Verbatim* Sept. 4/1 The trouble is caused not by length *sensu stricto* but by complexity.

sent, *ppl. a.* (Later examples.)

1825 H. C. ROBINSON *Diary* Dec. (1967) 86 *Irving.* He is a highly gifted man; he is a sent man, but they who are sent sometimes go further than they ought. **1940** *Amer. Speech* Oct. 337/1 *To be sent*, to be completely satisfied and in a stupor from the drug. **1951** *Manch. Guardian* 21 June 5/1 The slang of jazz addicts, which is full of phrases like 'hepsters', getting 'high', being 'sent' and other euphemisms for the delirium induced by improvised solos on the cornet and slide trombone. **1958** *Spectator* 25 July 133/3 The girls wore thick eye-makeup and 'sent' expressions.

sentence, *sb.* **4. a.** For † *Obs.* read *Obs.* exc. *Hist.* and add later example.

1962 T. P. DUNNING in Davis & Wrenn *English & Medieval Studies* 178 That element of the *sentence* expressed by Pandarus in Book 1—Fortune as the way of the world—is here stated at some length by Criseyde.

b. For † *Obs.* read *Obs.* exc. *poet.* and add later example.

1917 T. S. ELIOT *Prufrock & Other Observations* 15 Politic, cautious, and meticulous; Full of high sentence, but a bit obtuse.

6. c. *Logic.* A correctly ordered series of signs or symbols that expresses a proposition in an artificial or logical language.

1937 A. SMEATON tr. *Carnap's Logical Syntax Lang.* I. 26 We have already surveyed all the possible ways of constructing sentences and numerical expressions in Language I. **1957** P. SUPPES *Introd. Logic* (1959) iii. 54 A sentence is a formula which has no free variables. **1976** EVANS & MCDOWELL *Truth & Meaning* p. viii, Conditions (1), (2), and (3) require that *L* be a logically perfect language, with sentences free from structural or lexical ambiguity.

9. (sense 6) *sentence-building, -completion, -construction, -form, -formation, -forming, -formula, -frame, -intonation, -meaning, -melody, -modifier, -pattern, -rhythm, -type*; *sentence-final, -forming, -initial* (also *-initially* adv.), *-modifying, -opening* adjs.; **sentence adverb** *Gram.*, an adverb used to qualify a complete sentence (see also quot. 1892); also **sentence adverbial; sentence diagram,** a schematic representation of the relationships between the constituent parts of a sentence; so **sentence diagramming; sentence-particle** *Gram.* (see quot. 1953); **sentence-token** *Logic* (see quot. 1936); **sentence-word** (earlier example).

1892 H. SWEET *New Eng. Gram.* I. 127 Sentence-adverbs. The answer to the question *is he here?* can be either the affirmative *yes* or the negative *no.* It is evident that *yes* and *no* are sentence-modifying adverbs and at the same time sentence-words like come! John!, alas! **1916** E. A. SONNENSCHEIN *New Eng. Gram.* 33 Several..adverbs.. may be used to qualify the sentence as a whole; when so used they are called sentence-adverbs. *Ibid.*, Some sentence-adverbs (especially 'too', 'else', 'only', 'even') may be used in such a way as to emphasize the word which stands next to them in the sentence. **1980** *Amer. Speech 1976* LI. 168 Among the adverbs were some that are often classed together as sentence adverbs: *luckily, wisely, foolishly, rightly.* **1964** KATZ & POSTAL *Integrated Theory of Linguistics Descriptions* iv. 95 The answers to yes–no questions are in fact sentence adverbials, i.e., *yes, no,* and perhaps by extension *maybe, of course, certainly,* etc. **1921** H. E. PALMER *Princ. Lang.-Study* 22 Exercises exist which ensure accuracy in..sentence-building. **1966** J. DERRICK *Teaching Eng. to Immigrants* v. 205 Other sentence-completion exercises, in which there can be slightly more freedom of choice, can consist of 'half sentences' in which part or whole of the subject or predicate is missing and has to be filled in by the pupil. **1921** H. E. PALMER *Princ. Lang.-Study* iii. 58 The learner need know little about the sciences dealing with inflexions, sentence-construction, or meanings. **1937** MOFFETT & JOHNSON *Basic Writing* 509 A sentence diagram is merely a device by which the structure of a sentence can be..shown. *Ibid.* 632 (Index) Sentence diagramming. **1977** *Language* LIII. 493/1 The syntax section is fully and competently developed...L compares phrase-structure trees to traditional sentence diagrams, with which many students will be familiar. **1959** *College Composition & Communication* May 91 The question of just what ends we hope to attain by the use of any system of sentence diagraming. **1949** Sentence-final [see *intonationally* adv. s.v. *INTONATION[1]]. **1978** *Language* LIV. 79 Lehmann observes that the interrogative in Japanese is marked by placing *ka* after verbs in sentence-final position. **1930** T. SASAKI *On Lang. of R. Bridges' Poetry* 92 The language of poetry is in not a few points similar to primitive language, which usually favours 'gegenständliches Denken', and therefore prefers attributive sentence-form. **1965** *Language* XLI. 372 A form that differs from any elementary sentence-form of the language. **1935** G. K. ZIPF *Psycho-Biol. of Lang.* v. 185 They [*sc.* substantive and verb] are not a *sine qua non* of sentence-formation. **1921** H. E. PALMER *Princ. Lang.-Study* 25 In choosing the units of our vocabulary we may be guided by..sentence-forming utility. **1936** J. KANTOR *Objective Psychol. Gram.* III. xvii. 241 Those grammarians who call the verb a sentence-forming word, a phenomenon word, or an *Aussagewort*, also pay tribute to its action-referring character and save themselves from a too great stress of time. **1932** W. L. GRAFF *Lang.* I. iii. 132 Because it [*sc.* How do you do?] is itself a sentence, not merely sentence material, it may be termed a sentence formula or a formular sentence. **1962** G. A. MILLER in *Amer. Psychologist* XVII. 756/1 One opinion is that we learn 'sentence frames' that we keep filed away in a sort of sentence-frame dictionary. The declarative, interrogative, affirmative, negative, active, passive, compound, complex, etc., sentence frames are all supposed to be learned separately and to have no intrinsic relation to one another. **1964** *Language* XL. 6 Mere sentence-initial position of *Wh* does not suffice to differentiate between inversion and noninversion. **1978** *Ibid.* LIV. 85 Sentence initial subjects in Japanese and English may be viewed as most distant from the verb. **1976** *Word 1971* XXVII. 302 This word is then placed sentence-initially. **1934** J. J. HOGAN *Outl. Eng. Philol.* I. iv. 25 It [*sc.* the sentence] has a musical tune, Sentence-Intonation. **1945** *Mind* LIV. 366 The vital question 'how separate words..can combine to yield sentence-meanings' is dealt with very summarily. **1922** O. JESPERSEN *Language* I. iv. 97 The heightened interest in everything concerning 'accent' (stress and pitch) has also led to investigations of sentence-stress and sentence-melody. **1928** H. POUTSMA *Gram. Late Mod. Eng.* (ed. 2) I. I. v. 320 The question whether an adverbial adjunct is a sentence-modifier or a word-modifier, is of considerable importance. *Ibid.* i. 101 Weak *do* is used in connexion with sentence-modifying *not.* **1962** J. SÖDERLIND in F. Behre *Contrib. Eng. Syntax* 117 This is a bold type, found in sentence-opening subject position. **1934** PRIEBSCH & COLLINSON *German Lang.* II. xi. 445 German has one Greek characteristic which makes it neater and fuller of expressive shades than English, viz. the use of sentence-particles (*ja, doch*..etc.) and their cumulations (*ja doch*..etc.). **1953** *Trans. Philol. Soc. 1952* 6 The name 'sentence particle' (*satzpartikel*) was given by Kuhn to all unstressed and weak-stressed words which modify not one part of the sentence but the whole of it, and are therefore syntactically independent parts of the sentence. **1935** G. K. ZIPF *Psycho-Biol. of Lang.* v. 201 The question of equilibrium which lies at the root of the development of all sentence-patterns. **1926** FOWLER *Mod. Eng. Usage* 560/1 The separating adverb could have been placed outside the infinitive with little or in most cases no damage to the sentence-rhythm. **1957** R. W. ZANDVOORT *Handbk. Eng. Gram.* VI. 239 The different word order.. may be due to a desire for variety, as much as to the requirements of sentence-rhythm. **1936** *Jrnl. Philos.* XXXIII. 703 A *sentence-token* is a particular set of particular symbolic marks (of a sort, let us say, to represent a complete assertion). **1976** A. N. PRIOR *Doctrine of Propositions* i. 35 We may say at once that the dominant tendency in Logic is for the term 'proposition' to be used not for a 'sentence-token' but for a 'sentence-type'. **1933** L. BLOOMFIELD *Language* x. 169 The use of the secondary phoneme [!] gives us the sentence-type of exclamation. **1848** C. BUNSEN in *Rep. Brit. Assoc. Advancem. Sci.* 282 The Egyptian root is not the unalterable particle, or rather sentence-word, of the Chinese.

Hence **se·ntencehood** [-HOOD], the condition of constituting a grammatically complete sentence.

1961 *Language Learning* XI. 175 These..are some of the requirements which one might reasonably set for an adequate theory of English 'sentencehood'. **1967** *Philos. Rev.* LXXVI. 151 In many sentences 'probable' can replace 'possible' without destroying sentencehood.

‖ **sententia** (sente·nʃiă). Pl. **-æ** (erron. **-a**). [L.] = SENTENCE *sb.* 4 a. Also in mod. use, a thought or reflection.

1917 E. E. CUMMINGS *Let.* 5 May (1969) 19 The immemorially delightful sententia of a pocket-size sailor.. i.e. 'submarines pooh-pooh'. **1926** C. CONNOLLY *Let.* 25 Dec. in *Romantic Friendship* (1975) 199, I sent you one diary for quotations and the other was for sententiae. **1933** R. TUVE *Seasons & Months* i. 43 The Seasons motif found new uses... It became a vehicle for 'sententia', folk proverbs which appealed to generations fed upon Hending and Alfred. **1960** *Times* 29 Sept. 15/5 Those platitudinous *sententiae* that pass for conversational small change. **1964** C. S. LEWIS *Discarded Image* vii. 191 Chaucer begins with a *Sententia* or maxim in the *Parlement.* **1971** *English Studies* LII. 456 An attempt is made to trace the process by which the popular proverb attained equal status with the literary *sententia.*

sentential, *a.* Restrict Now *rare* to other senses and add: **2. a.** (Later examples in mod. Linguistics.)

1956 J. H. GREENBERG in Saporta & Bastian *Psycholinguistics* (1961) 471/2 *Sentential meaning.* The meaning of a maximal linguistic structure (i.e., of a sentence). **1965** N. CHOMSKY *Aspects of Theory of Syntax* ii. 100 Nouns with sentential Complements (such as 'the *idea* that he might succeed'). **1978** *Studies in Eng. Lit.: Eng. Number* (Tokyo) 96 They are excluded either by Ross's 'rightward bounding constraint' and 'sentential subject constraint', or by Chomsky's 'subjacency condition'.

b. *Logic.* In collocations denoting logical operations relating to sentences or propositions; esp. as *sentential calculus, connective, function.* Cf. *PROPOSITIONAL *a.* b.

1937 A. SMEATON tr. *Carnap's Logical Syntax of Lang.* III. 91 Primitive sentences of the sentential calculus. *Ibid.* 138 Frege himself had already made a similar classification of all sentential functions into levels and kinds which also were arranged according to the kinds of their arguments. **1957** P. SUPPES *Introd. Logic* iii. 43 We have developed the logic of the sentential connectives. **1966** *Math. Reviews* Jan. 7/1 The author presents a set of nine axiom schemes and two rules for the predicate calculus based on the infinite-valued sentential calculus of Łukasiewicz. **1976** G. EVANS in Evans & McDowell *Truth & Meaning* viii. 215 Intuitionistic sentential connectives cannot be regarded as representing truth functions in any finite many-valued logic. **1976** A. R. LACEY *Dict. Philos.* 75 *x is red* can be called a propositional, statemental (rare) or sentential function, according as *blood is red* is regarded as a proposition, statement or sentence. Sentential functions are often called open sentences. The term *closed sentential function* is occasionally used of ordinary sentences.

sentiment. Add: **6. d.** *them's my sentiments*: a colloq. expression of agreement or approval. (In quot. 1847, a declaration of belief.)

1847 THACKERAY *Van. Fair* (1848) xxi. 179 The sooner it is done the better, Mr. Osborne; them's my sentiments! **1886** J. BAILEY *Let.* 28 Nov. (1935) 26, I was delighted, as I could have said to every word: 'Them's my sentiments!' **1937** A. HUXLEY *Let.* 16 Feb. (1969) 414, I ought to have written long since to thank you for your Sunrise Poem, about which I felt strongly that them was my sentiments. **1940** 'B. M. BOWER' *Spirit of Range* xiv. 162 'I'm willing to be just a boneheaded cow-puncher.' 'Accent on the bone,' Pink murmured. 'Them's my sentiments, old socks.'

sentimentalist. (Earlier examples.)

1783 *Scots Trimmer* III. 27 Dean Milles, who is ravished with the beauties of Sterne, would, in all probability, have given the admirers of this charming sentimentalist a huge quarto, price only one guinea. **1784** R. BELL (*title*) Illuminations for legislators and for sentimentalists.

sentimentali·stic, *a. rare.* [f. SENTIMENTAL *a.* + -ISTIC.] Possessing sentimental characteristics; characterized by an exaggerated sentimentality.

1904 M. BEERBOHM *Let.* 13 Apr. (1964) 161 All this sounds very 'literary' and sentimentalistic, but it is real enough to me. **1912** E. POUND *Prolegomena* in *Poetry Rev.* Feb. 75 As for the nineteenth century,.. I think we shall look back upon it as..a rather sentimentalistic, mannerish sort of a period.

sentimentalize, *v.* Add: **1. a.** (Earlier example.)

1788 W. COMBE *Orig. Lett. Sterne* 14 In the mean time we will philosophize and sentimentalize;—the last word is a bright invention of the moment in which it was written, for yours or Dr. Johnson's service.

sentimentalizing *vbl. sb.* (earlier example).

1789 E. SHERIDAN *Jrnl.* 20 Aug. (1960) viii. 184 Tickell marries Miss Lee next week and so ends his sentimentalising.

sentinel, *sb.* Add: **6. a. sentinel pile** *Path.*, an external hæmorrhoid situated at the lower end of an anal fissure.

1910 *Practitioner* Apr. 520 It is probable that the fissure results from the tearing down of one of the anal valves, the free border of which eventually appears at the anus as a rounded œdematous tag—the so-called sentinel pile. **1974** R. M. KIRK et al. *Surgery* vi. 132 The oedematous skin at the lower end of the fissure protrudes as a 'sentinel' pile.

sentoku (se·nt*oku*). [Jap.] Originally, a Chinese bronze produced during the era (1426–35) of Emperor Hsüan of the Ming Dynasty; later, a golden-yellow Japanese bronze vessel made after the Chinese fashion; the bronze itself.

1902 *Encycl. Brit.* XXIX. 722/2 A golden yellow bronze, called *sentoku.* **1904** E. DILLON *Porcelain* vi. 92 Hsuan-te (1425–35)...This period gave its name to the famous pale bronze so admired in later days by the Japanese...The name *Sentoku* that they give to it is the Japanese reading of the characters forming this emperor's name. **1931** *Illustr. London News* 15 Aug. 268/3 That..characteristic Japanese alloy, *sentoku,* a sort of yellow bronze which is very soft and resembles brass rather than bronze. **1968** G. SAVAGE *Conc. Hist. Bronzes* iv. 128 *Sentoku,* containing up to thirteen per cent of zinc, may have been used in the fifteenth century, and legend has it that vessels of this kind also contained gold.

sentry, *sb.*[1] Add: **6.** *sentry duty.*

1917 W. OWEN *Let.* 16 Jan. (1967) 428 Servants don't do Sentry Duty. **1977** *Belfast Tel.* 28 Feb. 4/3 A soldier who shot dead a Derry man and injured two other people while on sentry duty in the city last May was jailed for five years.

sentry, *v.* Add: **a.** (Earlier example.) **c.** *intr.* and *refl.* To place as a sentry; also *fig.*

1820 J. S. KNOWLES *Virginius* v. II. 78 Though a legion Sentried that brothel, which he calls his palace, I'd tear her from him! **1922** JOYCE *Ulysses* 221 Corny Kelleher..glanced..at a pine coffinlid sentried in a corner. **1979** G. SWARTHOUT *Skeletons* 155 John and Paul had sentried themselves before the bank door, barring my re-entry.

sentry-go. Add: **b.** Also *transf.*

1922 [see *CAVE *int.*]. **1938** G. GREENE *Brighton Rock* I. i. 4 This was Hale's job to do sentry go, until a challenger released him, in every seaside town in turn.

Senufo (sənū·fo). Also **Senoufo, Senufu.** [Akan.] A people of the Ivory Coast in western Africa; any of the sub-group of Gur (Niger–Congo) languages (or dialects) spoken by them. Also *attrib.* or as *adj.*

1911 F. W. H. MIGEOD *Languages of W. Afr.* I. i. 34 The Senufu..inhabit a big area of territory in the Ivory Coast hinterland. **1913** *Ibid.* II. xx. 317 Primeval languages not elsewhere classed:—*Berber,*.. *Bisogo,*.. *Senufo. Ibid.* xxi. 324 The Senufo group,.. in the Ivory Coast lagoons. **1928** *Africa* I. 220 The best examples of this Western Sudanese art, in the work of the Bammana, Senoufo, Itabe and Mossi, show a strong preponderance of the tendency to cover with ornament. **1935** *Chambers's Encycl.* VIII. 609/1 The Siena or Senufo hold that a man's soul passes into the body of his totem-animal, and conversely the spirit of the dead animal enters a new-born child of the clan. **1969** MORGAN & PUGH *W. Afr.* I. i. 24 The Senoufo are a Voltaic community who have adopted many Manding and Akan customs. They live well to the south, in sub-Sudanic and sub-Guinean environments. **1972** *Times* 28 Nov. 24/5 (Advt.), A Senufo carved-wood mask. **1972** *Language* XLVIII. 848, 7a is given by..Sedlak for..Baule, Gbeya, Senufo-Senadi.

Senussi (sênū·si). Also **Sanusi, Senoussi,** etc. [Arab. *sanūsī*, the name *Senussi* (see below).] (A member of) a Muslim religious fraternity founded in 1837 by Sidi Muhammad ibn Ali es-Senussi. Also *attrib.* or as *adj.*

1891 F. R. Wingate *Mahdiism of Egyptian Sudan* i. 2 The Senussi branch of the Shadli school, so called from the Senus mountain in Algiers, dates its inception about 1837. **1899** A. S. White *From Sphinx to Oracle* xii. 118 A man may become a Senussi without abandoning his Order. **1906** *Daily Chron.* 24 Apr. 7/6 The mysterious influence of the Senoussi. **1915** T. E. Lawrence *Let.* 22 Mar. (1938) 195 The Idrisi family, who are the Senussi and Assyr together. **1942** *R.A.F. Jrnl.* 27 June 15 The Senussi Arabs have a legend about the creation of the desert. **1949** E. E. Evans-Pritchard *Sanusi of Cyrenaica* i. 8 The Sanusi have never shown themselves more hostile than other Muslims to Christians and Jews. **1959** *Listener* 15 Jan. 100/2 The Sanusi religious family, settled among the Bedouin tribes of Cyrenaica. **1978** A. Melville-Ross *Blindfold* xxi. 123 King Idris, with his strong pro-British leanings and strict Senussi code of honour.

Also **Senu·ssian** *sb.* and *a.*; **Senu·ss(i)ism, Senu·ssist** *a.* and *sb.*; **Senu·ss(i)ite** *sb.* and *a.*

1884 *Science* 14 Nov. 457 A Mussulman confraternity known as the Senousians. *Ibid.* 459 Five hundred camels ..ready at a moment's notice to convey to the interior the persons and property of the Senousian authorities. **1899** A. S. White *From Sphinx to Oracle* xii. 114 Absolutism and occultness are the two most potent powers in Senussi-ism. **1900** *Daily News* 15 Jan. 6/4 The only great religious organization of Moslem Protestants in Northern Africa are the Senoussi-ites, and they are harmless. *Ibid.*, So far, owing to the secrecy observed by Senoussist emissaries, no direct evidence regarding the movement is obtainable. **1934** Webster, Senusi...Also Senousi, Senussite. **1957** *Encycl. Brit.* XX. 331/2 The Darfur revolt of 1888–89..was nevertheless carried out in the name of the Senussites. *Ibid.* 332/2 In Cyrenaica Senussite resistance to the Italians was organized by Sheikh Rida. **1977** B. Lucas tr. *De Foucauld's Lett. from Desert* vii. 139 Our Tuaregs remain calm despite the capture of Djanet by the Senoussists.

Senussia (sênusī·ă). Also **Senusiya,** etc. [Arab. *sanūsīya.*] The fraternity founded by es-Senussi.

1888 *Encycl. Brit.* XXIII. 575/2 The sectaries of Senûsíya are found in all parts of North Africa. **1891** F. R. Wingate *Mahdiism Egyptian Sudan* i. 4 The Senussiyeh attacked the robbers. **1911** *Encycl. Brit.* XXIV. 649/1 Considerable diversity of opinion has prevailed among writers and travellers claiming knowledge of the *Senussia.* **1949** E. E. Evans-Pritchard *Sanusi of Cyrenaica* i. 8 The Grand Sanusi had himself been a member of a succession of orders before he started his own and he allowed..members of other Orders to belong to the Sanusiya at the same time. **1974** *Encycl. Brit. Micropædia* VIII. 888/1 *Sanūsīyah,* also spelled *Sennusiya,* in a strict sense, a Muslim Ṣūfī (mystic) brotherhood established in 1837 by Sīdī Muḥammad ibn 'Alī as-Sanūsī.

‖ **senza** (se·ntsă), *prep. Mus.* [It.: see note s.v. Sans prep.] Without; in various phrases, as *senza bassi* without the basses, *senza tempo* in no definite time, etc.

1724 *Short Explic. Foreign Wds. in Mus. Bks., Senza,* without. This word is used in the following Manner. *Senza d'aria,* without the Air...*Senza Violino,* without the Violins [etc.]. **1740** Grassineau *Mus. Dict., Senza,* signifies without, as *senza stromenti*—without instruments. **1762** Sterne *Tr. Shandy* VI. xi. 50 *Con l'arco* upon this;—*senza l'arco* upon that.—All I know is, that they are musical terms. **1945** A. Huxley *Time must have a Stop* ii. 16 Forbidden themes, repulsively fascinating, disgustingly attractive! Sebastian would embark on them with a quiet casualness—*pianissimo,* so to speak, and *senza espressione.* **1959** *Listener* 4 June 1001/3 Aubrey Brain played this *senza sord.*

separate, *pa. pple., a.,* and *sb.* Add: **B.** *adj.* **2. b.** In a hotel or boarding-house: *separate table.* Also *spec.* of rooms, etc., to which each of a married couple retires separately.

1756 *Old Maid* 21 Feb. 86, I have proposed separate beds, but he will never hear of it. **1817** Jane Austen *Let.* 20 Feb. (1952) 480, I w^d^ recommend to her & Mr. D. the simple regimen of separate rooms. **1838** H. Martineau *Retrospect* I. 236 We..had..a separate table, at Mrs. Peyton's boarding-house. **1910** *Bradshaw's Railway Guide* 1008 (Advt.), *White Lion*...Coffee Room (separate tables), Billiard Room. **1971** J. Fleming *Grim Death & Barrow Boys* xi. 161 A Private Hotel on the sea-front where they had dinner at night and separate tables. **1977** C. Storr *Tales from Psychiatrist's Couch* 36 She sleeps in a twin bed in London, but in the cottage we have separate rooms.

e. Phr. *separate but equal,* asserting the equality of races under racial segregation. *U.S.*

[**1776** T. Jefferson in *Dunlop's Pennsylvania Packet* 8 July 1/1 When in the course of human events, it becomes necessary for one People..to assume among the powers of the earth, the separate and equal station to which the laws of Nature and of Nature's God entitle them. **1890** *Louisiana Acts* CXI. 152 An Act..requiring all railway companies..to provide equal but separate accommodations for the white and colored races.] **1892** F. W. Gage *Negro Problem in U.S.* iii. 92 If railroad companies care to furnish separate but equal accommodations on equal terms to each race, no objection need be made. **1914** *U.S. Reports* (1915) CCXXXV. 160 It was not an infraction of the Fourteenth Amendment for a State to require separate, but equal, accommodations for the two races. **1948** *Time* 9 Feb. 75/1 In Missouri, where a 'separate but equal' law school has had its longest test. **1954** E. Warren in *U.S. Reports* CCCXLVII. 495 We conclude that in the field of public education the doctrine of 'separate but equal' has no place.

f. *separate school* Canad., a school receiving pupils from a racial or religious minority.

For detailed evidence and comment see *Dict. Canadianisms.*

1852 *Dundas Warden* (Canada West) 28 May 2/7 The law makes provision for Separate Schools, to meet an exigency—namely, the anticipated intrusion of the religious dogmas of a majority upon a minority. **1857** H. F. Douglass in *Ontario Hist.* (1963) June 88 Separate schools and churches are nuisances that should be abated as soon as possible, they are dark and hateful relics of Yankee Negrophobia. **1872** *Canadian Monthly* July 64/1 The Roman Catholics spoke frankly and sincerely for their separate schools, the New Brunswickers for their local liberties. **1911** *Daily Colonist* (Victoria, B.C.) 14 Apr. 5/2 Steps are being taken by the Roman Catholic authorities towards the establishment of separate schools in and near Vancouver. **1968** [see *junior high (school)* s.v. *junior *a.* (*sb.*) 5]. **1976** *Globe & Mail* (Toronto) 16 Jan. 29/8 That meant I was Roman Catholic,.. that my oppressed and persecuted parents had to pay for my separate school education as well as the education of all the heathens in the public schools.

g. *separate development,* the systematic development or regulation of a group or race by itself independently of other groups or races in a society; orig. and chiefly *S. Afr.,* = *apartheid.

1955 *Summary Rep. Comm. Socio-Econ. Devel. Bantu Areas S.Afr.* iii. xxv. 105/1 (*heading*) Objections to the policy of separate development. **1962** [see *parallelism 2]. **1968** *Economist* 12 Oct. 17/1 A rigid, and openly acknowledged, form of 'separate development' operates there [*sc.* in Londonderry]. The most populous ward..is wholly Catholic..but skilful use of the 'property qualification' for local government elections [etc.]..ensure that these 12 councillors are Protestant Unionists. **1977** [see *plural democracy* s.v. *plural *a.* (*sb.*) 2]. **1979** E. Norman *Christianity & World Order* v. 61 The Dutch Reformed Church does not teach white racial superiority, nor is Separate Development an attempt to institutionalize *racial discrimination.*

C. *sb.* **5.** (Earlier example.)

1862 *Cornh. Mag.* Nov. 640 Professional thieves..form a net-work..by..which all criminal knowledge circulates. In prison and out of it, in the lowly village lodging-house and..'doing their separates' at Pentonville..they..spread criminal knowledge.

6. *Geol.* Any of the fractions into which constituents of a soil or other material can be separated according to a property such as particle size or mineral composition. Cf. *soil separate* s.v. *soil *sb.*[1] 10.

1909 A. G. McCall *Physical Properties of Soils* 84 The separates to be determined are as follows: Fine gravel 2·0–1·0 mm, Coarse sand 1·0–0·5,..Clay 0·005. **1924** F. E. Bear *Soil Managem.* vii. 56 In the Illinois soil survey, silt is defined as a separate the particles in which may vary from 0·03 to 0·001 millimeter in diameter. **1952** L. M. Thompson *Soils & Soil Fertility* ii. 10 The sand separate which occurs in an amount greater than any other separate is used to indicate the name; for example, fine sandy loam indicates a predominance of fine sand. **1977** *New Scientist* 21 Apr. 120/1 Isotopic abundance anomalies in mineral separates from meteorites.

7. *pl.* Articles of (esp. women's) dress which may be worn in various combinations and not only as parts of a matching outfit.

1945 *Britannica Bk. of Year* 276/2 These 'separates' were outfits of which the several parts could be interchanged to form many combinations. **1948** *Sun* (Baltimore) 3 Apr. 3/7 (Advt.), Tropical separates... Of crisp tropical rayon suiting nicely tailored... You can either 'mix 'em or match 'em'. **1958** *TV Times* 20 June 15/2 She finds 'separates' ideal for her type of performance. **1964** *McCall's Sewing* i. 13/1 Separates are the answer to the schoolgirl's needs. Skirts, sweaters, jackets and blouses that can mix and match are perfect. **1979** *Sunday Star* (Toronto) 30 Sept. D2/2 She's learned the knack of putting her own looks together with separates. She's off to school one day in gray dress pants, hot pink sweater and pale pink tam.

8. A self-contained, free-standing component of a sound reproduction system. Usu. *pl.*

1974 *Times* 8 Apr. 12/1 Demand for all kinds of audio systems—'separates' and otherwise. **1977** *Gramophone* Apr. 1625/2 Akai showed, along with five new receivers, that it too was getting into a wide line of separates and speakers.

separate, *v.* Add: **I. 1. a.** Also with *out.*

1962 H. E. Beecheno *Introd. Bus. Stud.* xi. 93 For the mass of smaller businesses these functions must be separated out. **1980** V. Cunningham *Sp. Civil War Verse* 64 The various elements of his poetry can't be separated out like this.

d. To discharge (a person) *from* the armed forces (*U.S. Mil.*); † to remove from employment.

1859 R. Thornton *Jrnl.* 25 June in E. C. Tabler *Zambezi Papers of Richard Thornton* (1963) I. 103 About 3 p.m. Dr. L. gave me an official letter separating me from the Expedition. **1888** *Civil Service* (U.S.) *Comm. 4th Rep.* 51 A statement of the number of persons who have been 'separated' from the classified service by removal, resignation, and death cannot be made. **1946** *Britannica Bk. of Year* 833/1 *Separate,* to discharge or release from active duty in the armed services. **1971** *Reader's Digest* (U.S. ed.) Oct. 13/1 This year one million veterans will be separated from the service.

separated, *ppl. a.* Add: **1.** (Further examples); also, *absol.* examples in sense 'one who has withdrawn from a conjugal relationship but is not divorced' (chiefly *pl.*). *U.S.*

1951 N. Mitford *Blessing* ii. v. 192 It's always like that with separated couples... Each one is trying to give the child a better time than the other. **1960** *Time* 17 Oct. 112/2 A collection of psychologizing short stories about young separateds. **1975** *Observer* (Colour Suppl.) 5 Jan. 7/2 Feiffer is 45, separated, has a daughter, lives in New York. **1975** *Publishers Weekly* 27 Jan. 234/3 Explores the bisexual lifestyle through in-depth interviews with marrieds, singles and 'separateds'.

2. *Math.* (See quot. 1968.)

1956 J. M. H. Olmstead *Intermediate Analysis* iii. 77 The set of rational numbers and the set of irrational numbers are disjoint, but are about as far from being separated as two disjoint sets of real numbers can be. **1964** T. O. Moore *Elem. Gen. Topology* ii. 40 A space X is connected iff X is not the union of two separated sets. **1968** E. T. Copson *Metric Spaces* v. 62 Two sets A and B in a metric space M are said to be separated if neither has a point in common with the closure of the other.

separation. Add: **1. b.** *U.S.* Resignation or dismissal from employment, a university, etc.; discharge from the armed forces.

1779 T. Jefferson *Let.* 27 Mar. in *Writings* (1893) II. 179 The separation of these troops would be a breach of public faith. **1897** C. M. Flandrau *Harvard Episodes* 229 He would feel [sorrow] at what the official college gracefully terms the 'separation' of Billy from the University. **1923** J. D. Hackett *Labor Terms* in *Managem. Engin.* May, *Separation,* the termination of employment, either voluntary or involuntary, at the instance of the employer or worker. **1955** *Univ. of Va. News Letter* 15 June 1/2 Just as births exceed deaths to yield an expanding population, so new entrants exceed separations through deaths and retirements to yield an expanding labor force. **1976** *Washington Post* 19 Apr. C15/10 (Advt.), Excellent opportunity in proposal writing for former surface Naval officer who completed 1 or 2 tours prior to separation.

c. *separation of powers* Pol.: the vesting of the legislative, executive, and judiciary powers of government in separate bodies.

[**1748** Montesquieu *De l'Esprit des Loix* I. xi. vi. 245 Il n'ya a point encore de Liberté, si la puissance de juger n'est pas séparée de la puissance législative & de l'exécutrice. **1788** A. Hamilton et al. *Federalist* II. xlvii. 92 The Meaning of the Maxim, which requires a Separation of the Departments of Power, examined and ascertained.] **1896** A. L. Lowell *Govts. & Parties in Continental Europe* I. i. 55 The Declaration of The Rights of Man proclaimed in 1789 that a community in which the separation of powers was not established had no constitution. **1921** J. Bryce *Mod. Democracies* II. ii. xxxix. 23 No official of the Federal Government is eligible to sit in Congress, no official of the Government of a State to sit in its legislature. This provision, a tribute to the famous doctrine of the Separation of Powers, was meant to prevent the Executive from controlling the Legislature. **1973** *N.Y. Times* 15 Aug. 36/1 President Nixon's attorneys..asserted that the constitutional separation of powers precluded the courts from commanding him to make those tapes available to a grand jury.

13*. *Photogr.* and *Printing.* **a.** Each of three or more monochrome reproductions of a coloured picture, made in different colours in such a way that they combine to reproduce the full colour of the original.

1922 [see *colour separation* s.v. *colour *sb.*[1] 18]. **1933** T. S. Barber *Art & Pract. Printing* IV. xiv. 163 The Three-colour Process requires three half-tones, made from photographic colour separations. **1967** Karch & Buber *Offset Processes* v. 170 In making the separation from a colored original or transparency, the circular glass halftone screen..is used. **1972** *Physics Bull.* Sept. 533/3 An original colour picture must first be processed to obtain four continuous tone 'separations', that is images on film which present the red, green and blue content of the original together with a 'key'.

b. The process of obtaining a set of monochrome reproductions of a coloured picture in each of which the tones correspond to the proportions of a particular colour in the original.

1924, 1930 [see *colour separation* s.v. *colour *sb.*[1] 18]. **1931** F. R. Newens *Technique Colour Photogr.* iii. 25 This tri-pack gives extremely good colour separation. **1949** Melcher & Larrick *Printing & Promotion Handbk.* 48/2 Color separation is the technique by which the colors of the original art work..are sorted out so that all the reds appear in the red plate, the blue and the shades of blue in the blue plate, etc. *Ibid.* 49/1 Flat-color jobs present no problem... Full-color originals are more difficult. Here the printer may do his separations by the fake process method or by the process-color method. **1974** *Encycl. Brit. Macropædia* XIV. 304/2 In the direct method [of making colourplates], screen negatives are prepared directly from the copy through the colour-separation filters and a halftone screen.

13.** *Physics* and *Aeronaut.* The separation of the boundary layer from the surface of a body moving relative to the surrounding fluid.

1926 H. GLAUERT *Elem. Aerofoil & Airscrew Theory* viii. 100 When two parallel layers of fluid are moving in the same direction with different velocities, the surface of separation is a vortex sheet. **1935** K. D. WOOD *Techn. Aerodynamics* ii. 46 At zero lift, there is commonly a certain amount of separation under the nose of the airfoil. **1949** O. G. SUTTON *Sci. of Flight* ii. 40 The air stream has found it difficult to turn the corner... In technical language the flow separates. We shall see later that separation is of immense importance in all problems of aerodynamics. **1978** D. KÜCHEMANN *Aerodynamic Design of Aircraft* ii. 37 The most important boundary-layer phenomenon is flow separation.

13*.** Distinction or difference between the signals carried by the two channels of a stereophonic system; a measure of this.

1960 MARKELL & STANTON *Installing Hi-Fi Systems* i. 11 The portion of the room in which the maximum stereo effect is heard is fairly limited, and complete separation between the sound signals at the ears of the listener is impossible in a practical situation. **1962** *Times* 5 July 15/6 In general quality the discs were still preferable although on the tapes the stereo 'separation' was more marked. **1974** HARVEY & BOHLMAN *Stereo F.M. Radio Handbk.* vi. 129 Some adjustment over the degree of cross-coupling may be provided by a preset control.. labelled separation. **1975** G. J. KING *Audio Handbk.* viii. 185 For good stereo image placement the separation should not be less than 20 dB over the important part of the spectrum.

14. **separation anxiety** *Psychol.*, anxiety provoked in a child by the threat or actuality of separation from its mother or mother substitute; also *transf.*; **separation factor** *Nucl. Engin.*, the ratio of the concentration of a particular isotope after a process of enrichment to the concentration before; also, the ratio of the concentrations in the two mixtures produced by the process; **separation negative,** a separation (sense 13* a above) in the form of a photographic negative; **separation plant**, an installation for the separation of isotopes of a chemical element; **separation point** *Physics* and *Aeronaut.*, a point on a surface at which boundary-layer separation begins.

1943 W. R. D. FAIRBAIRN in *Brit. Jrnl. Med. Psychol.* XIX. 340/2 The problem of separation-anxiety in the soldier is anticipated under a totalitarian regime by a previous exploitation of infantile dependence. **1973** J. BOWLBY *Attachment & Loss* II. vi. 95 Despite Freud's increasing insistence on the key role of separation anxiety in neurosis, there has been marked reluctance to adopt his ideas. **1977** *Sunday Mail* (Brisbane) 23 Oct. 24/7 *Separation Anxiety:* The child fears the parent will abandon him. Newson and Newson showed that very many parents used this as a threat. **1945** H. D. SMYTH *Gen. Acct. Devel. Atomic Energy Mil. Purposes* ix. 94 In nearly every process a high separation factor means a low yield, a fact that calls for continual compromise. **1978** *Sci. Amer.* Aug. 31/3 A typical separation factor for an early machine was 1·25, which means that if the fraction of uranium 235 in the feed gas is 0·71 percent, as it is in natural uranium, the product contains ·794 uranium 235 and the waste contains ·635 percent. **1931** F. R. NEWENS *Techniques Colour Photogr.* iii. 25 Although it is possible to produce the three-colour separation negatives by a single exposure, either in a one-exposure tricolour camera, or by means of a film tri-pack.., neither method is at present readily available. **1957** P. JENKINS *Colour Separation Negatives* 30 A fundamental rule in separation-negative making is that any neutral (grey, white, or black) should be reproduced as an equal density on each of the three negatives. **1974** A. SUSSMAN *Amateur Photographer's Handbk.* (ed. 8) xviii. 478 The problem of separation negatives, so far as the amateur is concerned, was overcome in 1935 when Eastman Kodak introduced Kodachrome film. **1945** H. D. SMYTH *Gen. Acct. Devel. Atomic Energy Mil. Purposes* viii. 84 The principal installations constructed at the Clinton Laboratory site were the pile and the separation plant. **1974** *Encycl. Brit. Macropædia* XIII. 325/1 Groves arranged contracts for a gaseous diffusion separation plant, a plutonium production facility and a calutron pilot plant. **1946** A. W. SHERWOOD *Aerodynamics* vii. 101 If the velocity of flow over the sphere is increased, the local Reynolds number *Rl* for any point in the boundary layer is proportionally increased, with a maximum value at the separation points. **1978** D. KÜCHEMANN *Aerodynamic Design of Aircraft* ii. 37 The flow lifts off the wall at a separation point where the skin friction becomes zero and the air flows backwards behind it.

separationist. (Earlier example.)

1831 LD. HOLLAND *Let.* 3 Jan. in R. B. McDowell *Public Opinion in Ireland 1801–1846* (1952) vi. 143 Withdrawing from O'Connell and the separationists.

separatism. (Further examples.)

1957 P. KEMP *Mine were of Trouble* x. 190 Separatism and Anarchism were the strongest political forces in Catalonia. **1962** *Globe & Mail* (Toronto) 30 Jan. 4/1 Whoever is responsible..has done more for the advancement of separatism in this province [*sc.* Quebec] in 60 minutes than Dr. Chaput could in 60 years. **1971** *Daily Tel.* 19 July 7/4 The background that gave rise to Moslem separatism in British India, the emergence of the State of Pakistan, and the subsequent history. **1978** *Encounter* Feb. 12/2 Separatism is a problem in Quebec as well as in Scotland.

separatist, *sb.* and *a.* Add: **A.** *sb.* **1. f.** A critic who ascribes the *Iliad* and the *Odyssey* or any portions of them to separate authors. Cf. SEPARATOR 1.

1903 A. PLATT *Iliad Bk. XVIII* p. xiv, Even among the ancients..there was a set of people called χωρίζοντες or Separatists, who held that the *Iliad* and *Odyssey* were by different authors. **1976** W. R. JOHNSON *Darkness Visible* 159 If I speak of things Homeric now as a separatist, now as a literal or oral unitarian, [etc.].

separatrix. Add: Pl. **separatrices** (-trisīz). **4.** *Physics.* A boundary between regions having differing configurations of magnetic lines of force.

1956 *Proc. CERN Symp. High Energy Accelerators* I. 50/1 We see in fig. 3 the region of stability or 'bucket' within which particles execute stable phase oscillations... The bucket boundary, or separatrix is given by eq. (43). *Ibid.* 54/2 The region between the two separatrices. **1979** *Sci. Amer.* Aug. 44 (*caption*) The tokamak..is equipped with a magnetic divertor, an arrangement in which a magnetic-field separatrix is employed to prevent impurity ions from entering the main plasma column.

sepetir (sepətī·ɹ). Also **sapetir.** [Mal.] A forest tree of the genus *Sindora* or *Pseudosindora,* belonging to the family Leguminosæ and native to south-east Asia; also, the hardwood timber produced by a tree of this kind.

[**1897** G. KING in *Jrnl. Asiatic Soc. Bengal* LXVI. II. 205 Mr. Curtis gives the Malay name of this [Sindora intermedia Baker] in Pangkor as '*Sapetir*'.] **1927** F. W. FOXWORTHY *Common Forest Trees Malay Peninsula* 91 It is doubtful if Sepetir produces more than one per cent of the timber in the forest. **1934** A. L. HOWARD *Man. Timbers of World* (ed. 2) 480 Sepetir...The colour of the wood is yellow-brown, with dark streaks. **1956** *Handbk. of Hardwoods* (Forest Prod. Res. Lab.) 210 Sepetir is the British Standard name for the timber of *Sindora* spp. and *Pseudosindora palustris.* **1971** *Country Life* 1 Apr. App. 42/2 A very rare..occasional table..the surfaces veneered in burnt walnut, rosewood, plane and sepetir (Malaya).

Sephadex (se·fădeks). *Chem.* A proprietary term for a preparation of dextran used for the separation and purification of chemicals on the basis of molecular size.

1959 *Trade Marks Jrnl.* 16 Sept. 827/1 *Sephadex*... Polymers being chemical compounds for industrial use in the purification of chemical substances. Aktiebelaget Pharmacia..Sweden..11th March 1959. **1970** [see *DEXTRAN]. **1975** WILLIAMS & WILSON *Biologist's Guide to Princ. & Techniques Pract. Biochem.* iii. 79 Cellulose derivatives (and Sephadex materials) have been used successfully in this way. **1978** *Nature* 12 Oct. 565/2 It was reduced with sodium dithionite and then isolated in 0·01 M phosphate buffer (*p*H 7) by Sephadex chromatography.

Sepher Torah, var. *SEFER TORAH.

sepia. Add: **4. a.** Also **sepia print** (see quot. 1940).

1892 W. E. WOODBURY *Encycl. Photogr.* 556 Black and sepia prints must not be washed together in the same dish. **1940** *Chamber's Techn. Dict.* 758/2 *Sepia print*.., a release print in which the image is dyed sepia instead of being left black. **1977** *Spare Rib* July 62/4 A marvellous collection of sepia prints showed women at work in the hospital's wards.

b. Of American Blacks: *euphem.* for 'black'. *U.S.*

1942 BERREY & VAN DEN BARK *Amer. Thes. Slang* §32/8 Negro color distinctions... *sepia.* **1944** H. L. MENCKEN in *Amer. Speech* XIX. 166 Some of them also use such terms as..*sepia* to get away from the..inaccurate *black,* and in 1944 there was a *Sepia* Miss America contest. **1947** S. LEWIS *Kingsblood Royal* xxiii. 138 A certain number of sepia merchants get rich on the rest of us chosen people.

Sepik (se·pik). [Native name.] The name of a river and district in Papua New Guinea, used *attrib.* of the peoples of the district and of their languages and artefacts.

1949 M. MEAD *Male & Female* viii. 178 The Sepik peoples—Iatmul, Tchambuk, and Mundugumor—make little of menstruation ceremonies. **1966** E. LINDALL *Time too Soon* (1967) xii. 120 We've got two Sepik policemen here. **1971** *Current Trends in Linguistics* VIII. 516 The first modern study of Sepik languages was that undertaken by Laycock. **1973** *Sunday Times* 10 June (Colour Suppl.) 42/1 Certain Protestants were notorious for destroying all native works of art, especially Sepik sculptures.

‖ **seppuku** (sepū·ku). Also **Seppuku,** etc. [Jap., colloq. pronunc. of *setsu fuku,* f. Chinese *qiē* to cut (with a sword or knife) + *fù* belly.] = HARA-KIRI.

1871 A. B. MITFORD *Tales Old Japan* II. 193 Seppuku (*hara-kiri*) is the mode of suicide adopted amongst Samurai when they have no alternative but to die. **1890** B. H. CHAMBERLAIN *Things Japanese* 141 The Japanese word *harakiri,* so well-known all over the world, is but little used by the Japanese themselves. The Japanese almost always prefer to employ the synonym *seppuku,* which they consider more elegant because it is derived from the Chinese. **1923** J. STREET *Mysterious Japan* xvi. 198 At the sound of the guns he took his short sword and committed seppuku. **1947** R. BENEDICT *Chrysanthemum & Sword* x. 200 He could only come to terms with chu by killing himself according to the rules of seppuku. **1973** A. BROINOWSKI *Take one Ambassador* xi. 178 You would at once..kill yourself. By *seppuku,* slitting of the stomach.

septal, *a.*[1] Add: **2.** *Bot.* Growing in hedges.

1847 H. C. WATSON *Cybele Brit.* I. 66 The proposed series of terms run thus:—..Septal.—Plants of hedge-banks and hedge-rows. **1926** J. J. WALKER *Nat. Hist. Oxford Distr.* 114 *Cuscuta europæa* L. is very rare..; in Oxford it was associated with another septal species, *Humulus Lupulus* L.

3. *Archæol.* Designating a stone or slab forming a barrier between compartments in a burial chamber.

1910 T. H. BRUCE in J. A. Balfour *Book of Arran* 61 The chamber is divided by two septal slabs into three compartments. **1937** *Proc. Prehist. Soc.* New Ser. III. 167 The segmentation of the gallery is achieved by means of septal slabs, rather lower than the side slabs, and in the Irish cairns these septal slabs are set between pairs of vertical jamb stones. **1958** G. DANIEL *Megalith Builders Western Europe* ii. 44 This segmentation or septalisation may be done by jambs projecting from each side, or by transverse stones or septal stones... Septal stones sometimes reach..half-way up the height of a chamber.

septanose (se·ptănōᵘz, -s). *Chem.* [a. G. *septanose* (Micheel & Suckfüll 1933, in *Ann. d. Chem.* DII. 89), f. L. *sept-em* seven + *-anose* after *FURANOSE, *PYRANOSE.] A structure containing a seven-membered ring, adopted by some sugars; a sugar having this structure. Freq. *attrib.* Hence **se·ptanoside,** a glycoside in septanose form.

[**1933** *Chem. Abstr.* XXVII. 3453 An equil. mixt. of α- and β-2,3,4,5-tetraacetylgalactoseptanoses.] **1934** *Ibid.* XXVIII. 1025 For an approx. 1% soln. in 0·01 *N* HCl of the septanoside..the half-time value of hydrolysis at 95° is about 28 min. *Ibid.*, The 7-membered septanose ring is not strained. *Ibid.*, Some indication of a parallelism between the instability of the free sugars (furanoses, septanoses) and the ease of hydrolysis of their glucosides. **1948** R. J. MCILROY *Chem. of Polysaccharides* i. 4 A third type of ring, the seven membered or septanose structure has been prepared. This ring is comparable to the furanose ring in stability. It has not been obtained from natural sources. **1973** *Carbohydrate Res.* XXVIII. 75 It is found that the pseudorotation of the septanose ring and the dioxolane rings are correlated to the position of attachment of the latter rings to the central septanose ring. **1974** *Jrnl. Chem. Soc.: Chem. Commun.* 1010/1 Nitroethane condensed smoothly..with the hydrated dialdehyde (I) to give..the crystalline septanoside..in 38% yield.

septate, *a.* (Example other than in *Nat. Hist.*: cf. *SEPTUM f.)

1947 L. G. H. HUXLEY *Survey Princ. & Practice Wave Guides* ii. 39 The field configuration in the septate coaxial system is very similar..to the pattern of the principal wave on a coaxial transmission line.

septcentenary (septsentī·nări). [f. L. *sept(em* seven + CENTENARY *sb.*, after *bicentenary,* etc.] A seven-hundredth anniversary.

1924 *Glasgow Herald* 21 Aug. 5/2 The present condition of Dornoch Cathedral, the septcentenary of which is to be celebrated on the 27th inst., presents a striking contrast to that of Elgin Cathedral. **1978** *Church Times* 29 Sept. 5/1 Septcentenary.—A programme of celebrations to mark the 700th anniversary of the establishment of a Christian church in Macclesfield is about to begin.

septectomy (septe·ktǫmi). *Surg.* [f. SEPT(UM + *-ECTOMY.] **a.** Resection of the nasal septum. *rare*—⁰.

1949 in *New Gould Med. Dict.* 922/2. **1961** in A. S. MACNALTY *Brit. Med. Dict.* 1292/1.

b. Resection of the atrial septum; septostomy.

1972 *Lancet* 27 May 1140/1 Previous atrial septectomy or septostomy had been performed. **1977** *Ibid.* 18 June 1275/2 At the age of 4 weeks the pulmonary artery was banded,.. and atrial septectomy was performed.

September. Add: **c.** **September massacres** *Fr. Hist.*, a mass killing of political prisoners in Paris on 2–6 September 1792.

1805–6 WORDSWORTH *Prelude* (1959) x. 370, I thought of those September Massacres, Divided from me by a little month. **1905** BARONESS ORCZY *Scarlet Pimpernel* xi. 109 The news of the awful September massacres, and of the Reign of Terror and Anarchy. **1976** *Listener* 23–30 Dec. 817/1 There began to seem a fatal unsteadiness in the Revolution... There had been the atrocity of the September massacres.

septet(t, -ette. a. (Earlier example.)

1828 E. HOLMES *Ramble among Musicians of Germany* 263 He [*sc.* Hummel] was pleased to hear that a lady..had repeatedly played in public his septett for the pianoforte.

septic, *a.* and *sb.* Add: **A.** *adj.* **2.** *septic tank,* a tank (associated either with a sewage works or with a residence that is not connected to a main sewer) in which the solid portions of sewage are allowed to settle and accumulate and are purified by the action of anaerobic bacteria.

1902 *Encycl. Brit.* XXIX. 379/1 The 'septic tank-system' was devised by Cameron of Exeter in 1896.

Ibid. XXXII. 526/1 At the present time the common cesspool is being resuscitated and improved under the name of a septic tank. **1909** *Chambers's Jrnl.* Feb. 87/1 The sewage system is of the latest character, with a septic tank. **1939** *Archit. Rev.* LXXXVI. 11/2 Bathrooms are installed on both ground and first floors, while other equipment includes an electric generating plant, a deep well with electric pump and septic tank. **1951** *Good Housek. Encycl.* 315/1 An adequate supply of good water at a safe distance from the septic tank. **1976** *Eastern Even. News* (Norwich) 13 Dec. 7/2 His septic tank did not work, and nor did most others in the village.

3. In trivial use: unpleasant, nasty, 'rotten'. *slang.*

1914 'I. Hay' *Knight on Wheels* xviii. 172 Philip enquired after Mr. Brett, and learned that that 'septic blighter' (Timothy's description) had retired from the position of Housemaster. **1932** S. Gibbons *Cold Comfort Farm* xviii. 248 Rennett had had a pretty septic life. **1958** L. Durrell *Balthazar* 248 What septic weather to-day! **1974** G. Mitchell *Winking at Brim* vii. 62 Mummy and Daddy have had a row. Isn't it septic of them?

B. *sb.* Restrict † *Obs.* to sense in Dict. and add: **2.** *ellipt.* A septic tank. *Austral. colloq.*

1961 P. White *Riders in Chariot* iii. viii. 231 Rosetrees lived..in a texture-brick home—city water, no sewerage, but their own septic. **1977** *Weekly Times* (Melbourne) 19 Jan. 65/2 (Advt.), Lovely new home.., 2 bathrooms, 2 septics and large living area.

septo-[2]. Add: **septo·stomy** *Surg.* [*-stomy], the surgical creation of a hole through the atrial septum; **septo·tomy** *Surg.* [-tomy] = prec.

1967 *Circulation* XXXVI. Suppl. 217/1 At the time of the diagnostic catheterization, atrial septostomy is performed by the balloon-catheter technique. **1977** *Lancet* 18 June 1276/1 The arterial oxygen saturation was 34% and did not improve after balloon septostomy. **1966** *Jrnl. Amer. Med. Assoc.* 13 June 992/2 Early clinical trials on infants with TGV [i.e. transposition of the great vessels] indicate that the procedure is as effective in prolonging life as surgical septotomy.

Septoria (septǭ·riă). Also **septoria.** [mod.L. (E. M. Fries *Novitiæ Floræ Suecicæ* (1819) v. 78, as *Septaria*; *Systema Orbis Vegetabilis* (1825) I. 119, as *Septoria*), f. L. *sept-um* Septum + *-āria, -ōria.*] **a.** An imperfect fungus of the genus *Septoria*, which includes forms having spores borne in dark pycnidia and many of which cause disease in plants.

1891 *Bull. Torrey Bot. Club* XVIII. 372 The *Septoria* on celery is to all appearance non-septate. **1932** *Phytopathology* XXII. 795 Both Septorias were collected on celery from the Kalamazoo marshes. **1946** K. S. Chester *Nature & Prevention Cereal Rusts* x. 139 Later in the spring, when abundant foliage is available to both fungi, *Septoria* sometimes destroys the lower leaves while the leaf rust attacks the upper ones. **1972** R. Gair et al. *Cereal Pests & Dis.* v. 128 In Scotland the common *Septoria* on barley is *S. avenae* f. sp. *triticea*.

b. One of several leaf spot diseases caused by a fungus of this kind. Also *attrib.*

1916 *Special Bull. Michigan Agric. Exper. Station* No. 77. 2 (*title*) The Septoria leaf spot disease of celery, or celery blight. **1920** *Bull. W. Australia Dept. Agric.* No. 69. 11 Septoria, or Dry Blight, is a fungus disease caused by one of three species of fungus. **1926** Fawcett & Lee *Citrus Diseases & their Control* xviii. 478 (*caption*) Septoria spots on California lemon fruits. **1947** J. G. Dickinson *Dis. Field Crops* xi. 217 Two Septoria blotches occur on wheat throughout the world. **1968** *Times* 16 Dec. 7/1 One disease, of which we had heard relatively little up to this year, seems to have had marked effects on the wheat crop. This was septoria, commonly known as glume blotch, although it also attacks seedlings and leaves earlier in the season. **1972** R. Gair et al. *Cereal Pests & Dis.* vii. 154 Like other *Septoria* diseases, speckled blotch is favoured by wet and humid weather. **1976** E. Scarrow *N.Z. Vegetable Gardening Guide* 36 Brown spots appearing on the leaves of celery are due to a fungus disease called septoria, which is seed-borne.

septum. Add: **b.** (Further examples.) *septum lucidum* or *pellucidum*, a thin double layer of tissue forming a partition between the two lateral ventricles of the brain.

1698 W. Cowper *Anat. Humane Bodies* App., 7th Table, fig. 30, That part of the corpus callosum by Vieussens, call'd fornix vera, between which, and the fornix..is plac'd the septum lucidum. **1713** W. Cheselden *Anat. Human Body* iii. xii. 135 Under the corpus callosum appear the two lateral or superior ventricles, which are divided into right and left by a very thin membrane named septum lucidum, which is extended between the corpus callosum and fornix. **1803** C. Bell *Anat. Human Body* III. i. i. 15 Those septa, or, as they are called, processes of the dura mater, being extended across from the internal surface of the cranium, support the brain in the sudden motions of the body. **1807** R. Morris et al. *Edin. Med. & Physical Dict.* II, Septum lucidum, or Septum pellucidum. **1899** F. H. Gerrish *Text-bk. Anat.* 362 The fascia sends inward to the femur two intermuscular septa, which partition the thigh into an anterior compartment and a posterior. **1942** F. A. Mettler *Neuroanatomy* iv. 97 Stretched between the copula, rostrum, genu and anterior half of the corpus callosum is a thin, vertically arranged membrane, the translucent septum (s. pellucidum). **1978** *Nature* 19 Jan. 209/1 Whether this input results in cellular discharge depends..on input through the second major afferent pathway to the hippocampus from the septum.

f. *Electronics.* A metal plate placed transversely across a waveguide and attached to the walls by conducting joints.

1947 L. G. H. Huxley *Survey Princ. & Practice of Wave Guides* ii. 39 The original electromagnetic field.. transforms to that shown..where the magnetic loops are bent over so that their longitudinal portions run in opposite senses, one on each side of the septum. **1964** J. L. Altman *Microwave Circuits* iii. 87 Symmetrical obstacles, such as irises, septa, and posts of various cross-sections and positions within the waveguide, are of great practical importance as matching elements..or as elements of waveguide filters and periodic structures.

Sequanian (sekwā·niăn), *a. Geol.* Also ‖ **Sequanien.** [ad. F. *Séquanien*, f. L. *Sēquani* an ancient Celtic people of eastern Gaul: see -ian.] Name of a substage of the Upper Jurassic in north-western Europe, below the Kimmeridgian; of or pertaining to this substage and the rocks that characterize it, and the geological age during which they were deposited.

1851 [see *Kimmeridgian *a.*]. **1881** *Q. Jrnl. Geol. Soc.* XXXVII. ii. 571 De Loriol..wishes to call the Astartian and Corallian by one name, Sequanian. **1882** A. Geikie *Text-bk. Geol.* 797 *Corallien.* Some authors take the upper part of this group into a separate section under the name of Sequanien, largely developed in the east of France, where it consists of massive limestones sometimes 400 feet thick. **1903** *Ibid.* (ed. 4) II. 1156 The Oxfordian and Corallian divisions of the Jurassic system, or Callovian, Oxfordian, and Sequanian formations, are in general feebly represented in the Alpine region. **1970** R. J. Small *Study of Landforms* iv. 145 The widely out-cropping Bathonian dolomite has been carved into a multitude of minor karstic forms which are overlooked by gently rounded hills of Sequanian limestone.

‖ **sequelula** (sĭkwe·liŭlă). *nonce-wd.* [mod.L. dim. of *sequēla* Sequela.] A little sequel (sense 7) or continuation of a literary work.

1912 M. Beerbohm *Christmas Garland* 61 (*title*) A sequelula to 'The Dynasts'. **1941** E. Blunden *Thomas Hardy* 237 Soon after the completed publication of *The Dynasts*, a 'Sequelula' to it was delivered to the world.

sequenator (sī·kwĕnēⁱtəɹ). *Biochem.* [Irreg. f. *sequen(ce *v.* + *-ator.] = *sequencer[2] 2.

1967 Edman & Begg in *European Jrnl. Biochem.* I. 81/1 We propose the term 'sequenator' for an instrument which determines the sequence of an ordered linear polymer by repeating a chemical process. **1973** *MTP Internat. Rev. Sci., Org. Chem.* VI. 48 The operation of the sequenator relies on the insolubility of the protein during the extraction procedure and short peptide chains are too soluble to be successfully degraded. **1978** *Nature* 19 Jan. 281/2 The sequence of the first 44 residues of this peptide has been determined on a protein sequenator (unpublished results).

sequence, *sb.* Add: **I. 2. c.** *Biochem.* The order of the constituent nucleotides in a nucleic acid molecule or of the amino-acids in a polypeptide or protein molecule.

1959 *Arch. Biochem. & Biophysics* LXXXV. 290 The sequence of these trinucleotides was determined by digestion with semen monoesterase followed by snake venom diesterase with the resulting formation of a purine nucleoside, a purine nucletide (Pu), and a pyrimidine nucleotide (Py). **1965** *Science* 19 Mar. 1462/1 During protein synthesis, the amino acid sequence of the polypeptide chain is determined by the interaction of a messenger RNA with transfer RNA's specific for a given amino acid. **1970** *Biochem. Jrnl.* CXVIII. 831/1 The recent determination of partial sequences at the cohesive ends of DNA from bacteriophage λ..is an excellent example of the application of repair reactions with DNA polymerase..to nucleotide sequence studies. **1977** *Sci. Amer.* Dec. 55/1 The complete nucleotide sequence of the DNA of a small bacterial virus, φX174, has been established.

3. d. *Cinematogr.* and *Television.* A passage consisting of several shots unified about a single theme or event.

1929 *Morning Post* 24 May 12/7 Until recently, in all talking sequences, the actor has been compelled to be static. **1934** C. Lambert *Music Ho!* iv. 262 A famous sequence in the silent film *Mother*. **1941** B. Schulberg *What makes Sammy Run?* vi. 125 He stayed up..reading one screen play after another... The plan was for him and Sammy to write alternate sequences. **1958** *Daily Mail* 19 July 8/8 Parody of a French film sequence set in a sleezy bistro. **1976** D. Clark *Dread & Water* v. 105 He's got a movie shot of Silk climbing that mountain... The sequence is just one of Silk climbing.

e. *Geol.* (*a*) An ordered succession, esp. of strata in conformity.

1931 Gregory & Barrett *General Stratigr.* vi. 96 The fullest Russian sequence is in the Urals, where the Lower Devonian consists of marine slates, quartzites, and occasional limestones. **1975** A. E. Ringwood *Composition & Petrology of Earth's Mantle* vii. 243 In estimating the abundance of andesitic volcanism in Precambrian shield sequences, allowance should be made for the andesitic component of associated geosynclinal sediments.

(*b*) In various specific usages (see quots.).

1933 R. C. Moore *Hist. Geol.* v. 54 No designation for the rocks of an era is in common use. The term 'sequence' will be used in this book. **1949** L. L. Sloss et al. in *Mem. Geol. Soc. Amer.* No. 39. 110 The writers term the assemblages of strata separated by the above-described objective horizons 'sequences'. Sequences should be considered as rock units, assemblages of formations and groups. **1962** Silberling & Roberts in *Geol. Soc. Amer. Special Paper* No. 72. 6 A different kind of subdivision..is required in northwestern Nevada for the upper Paleozoic and lower Mesozoic rocks. The subdivisions adopted are lithologically and geographically discrete units of major rank termed 'sequences' that are set apart from underlying or overlying sequences by unconformities.

III. 8. *attrib.* and *Comb.*, as **sequence control** *Computing*, a method of controlling the execution of distinct operations in a defined order; so **sequence-controlled** *ppl. a.*; **sequence dancing** (see quot. 1949); also **sequence dance; sequence date** *Archæol.*, a relative chronological date based upon comparison of a series of objects from an archæological site; hence **sequence dating; sequence shot** *Cinematogr.* (see quot. 1973); **sequence space** *Math.*, a space whose points are sequences.

1946 *Electr. Engin.* LXV. 387 (*caption*) Front view of calculator showing sequence control mechanism.., which tells machine what to do and when to do it. **1962** Sequence control [see *control register* s.v. *control *sb.* 5]. **1964** C. Dent *Quantity Surveying by Computer* iii. 24 Control is ..directed to address No. 2 in the memory store for its next instruction, and so on, in numerical sequence. This mode of operation is called 'Automatic Sequence Control'. **1946** *Ann. Computation Lab. Harvard Univ.* I. p. ix, In May 1944, the Staff of the Computation Project began operations with the Automatic Sequence Controlled Calculator as an activity of the Bureau of Ships. **1950** W. W. Stiffler *High-Speed Computing Devices* v. 63 An automatic sequence-controlled calculator is a computing machine into which such a [sequencing] mechanism is built. **1927** *Melody Maker* Sept. 865/2 They are to a great extent sequence dances and based on what many consider to be old-fashioned steps and movements. **1978** *Abingdon Herald* 12 Jan. 1/9 The Wootton and Dry Sandford Sequence Dance Club. **1940** A. H. Franks *Ballroom Dancer's Handbk.* 109 Sequence dancing really has no place in the art of modern ballroom dancing and such dances are regarded as novelties. **1949** A. Chujoy *Dance Encycl.* 424/2 *Sequence Dancing*, a term used in England to describe those ballroom dances in which the steps have to be taken in a certain definite order, as a consequence of which all couples are always making the same movement at one time. **1980** *Radio Times* 29 Nov.–5 Dec. 86/3 This is Sequence Dancing... When one lady twirls 200 other ladies twirl. **1901** Sequence date [see S.D. s.v. *S 4 a]. **1920** W. M. F. Petrie *Prehist. Egypt* ii. 4 For permanent reference the whole 900 graves, when placed in their most probable order or sequence, were divided in 51 equal sections, and these were numbered 30 to 80, and such numbers termed Sequence Dates, marked as S.D. **1923** T. E. Peet in *Cambr. Anc. Hist.* I. vi. 247 Petrie, at Diospolis Parva, invented the now famous system of 'Sequence Dating'. **1958** L. Cottrell *Anvil of Civilisation* ii. 39 He [*sc.* Petrie] invented the system which we call 'sequence dating' which..enables archaeologists to establish the *comparative* age of a site by the type of pottery found on it, even when it lies below the 'historical horizon'. **1973** S. Heath in *Screen* Spring/Summer 114 A *sequence-shot*, a whole scene in one shot (e.g. *autonomous segment* 17 of *Adieu Philippine* showing Michel, the hero, and his friend Daniel working in the TV studio). **1974** M. Taylor tr. *Metz's Film Lang.* iii. 42 There was Jean Renoir with his many statements in favor of the sequence shot. **1940** H. S. Allen in *Proc. London Math. Soc.* XLVIII. 310 A set *S* of sequences containing the origin and such that for every *x* and *y* in *S* and every number *r*, *x*+*y* and *rx* are in *S* is called a sequence space. **1968** G. Ludwig *Wave Mech.* i. iii. 37 The formulation of a matrix in diagonal form and the solution of the eigenvalue problem are therefore equivalent problems, the first being defined only in the sequence space.

sequence (sī·kwĕns), *v.* [f. the sb.] **1.** *trans.* To arrange in a definite sequence or order.

1954 *Computers & Automation* Dec. 20/2 *Sequence*,..to select A if A is greater than or equal to B, and select B if A is less than B, or some variation of this operation. **1965** J. S. Bruner in *Beyond Information Given* (1974) xxv. 442 We..closed our eyes to the pedagogic problem of how to represent knowledge, how to sequence it in a form appropriate to young learners. **1974** M. B. Brown *Economics of Imperialism* ix. 226 Countries can be sequenced as markets for different products according to their standards of consumption. **1976** *Daily Tel.* 12 Aug. 2/3 To get the maximum use out of Heathrow's two main runways aircraft are carefully 'sequenced' from the four reporting points that serve the airport.

2. *Biochem.* To ascertain the sequence of monomers in (a biological polymer such as a polypeptide or a nucleic acid).

1970 S. Blackburn *Protein Sequence Determination* xx. 274 The future should see the increasing use of methods able to sequence very large molecules. **1977** *Sci. Amer.* Dec. 67/2 Now that DNA can be sequenced readily and rapidly we can expect that in the next few years the precise composition of many DNA's will be established.

Hence **se·quenced** *ppl. a.*, **se·quencing** *vbl. sb.*

1961 P. Siegel *Understanding Digital Computers* xv. 329 A sequencing unit to be used with a drum memory and a two-address instruction is shown. **1970** *Nature* 14 Mar. 1026/2 Data..on the patterns of change in amino-acid substitutions in all the completely sequenced proteins show anything but a random pattern of substitution. **1971** *Archivum Linguisticum* II. 139 The realization rules accept as input specific pairs of such feature-sets and render them as sequenced strings of morphemes which are, in surface structure, simple *NPs*. **1977** *Sci. Amer.* Dec. 56/2 The smallest DNA molecules, those of certain viruses, are perhaps 70 times longer than the 75-nucleotide transfer-RNA molecules that were the subject of early RNA sequencing.

sequencer[2] (sī·kwĕnsəɹ). [f. Sequence *sb.* + -er[1].] **1. a.** (See quot.)

1954 *Computers & Automation* Dec. 21/1 *Sequencer*, i n punch card machinery, a mechanism which will put items of information in sequence.

b. An apparatus for performing or initiating operations in the correct sequence; *spec.* one forming part of the control system of a computer.

1964 *New Scientist* 6 Feb. 319/1 A late decision to photograph the Moon in passing was defeated by a malfunction in the so-called central computer and sequencer. **1977** N. FREELING *Gadget* v. 222 We..make an automatic sequencer which takes over the work of sending the signals. **1978** D. J. KUCK *Struct. Computers & Computations* I. iv. 282 The sequencer drives the entire machine through a specified sequence of events which carry out (indeed are) whatever the instruction is defined to do.

2. *Biochem.* An apparatus for determining the sequence of monomers in a biological polymer.

1971 *European Jrnl. Biochem.* XX. 89 Using the sequencer and unpurified reagents, it was possible to degrade entirely a 0·24 μmole sample of the 21 amino acid insulin A-chain (oxidized) and to analyze the products. **1977** *Sci. Amer.* Oct. 103/1 The exact positions at which the labeled amino acid appears are determined with the aid of an automatic machine called a sequencer, which chemically removes one amino acid at a time from the polypeptide chain beginning at the amino terminal (NH_2) end.

sequential, *a.* Add: **1. d.** *sequential induction* (Biochem.): the formation in sequence of a group of related enzymes, consequent upon the induction of the first enzyme of the series (see quot. 1953).

1953 M. COHN et al. in *Nature* 12 Dec. 1096/2 We.. propose the following terms and designations... The exposure of an organism to a single inducer which is also a substrate may result in the induction of a sequence of enzymes, since the metabolism of the primary, exogenous inducer gives rise to the formation of a succession of intermediary metabolites each of which in turn serves as an inducer for the enzyme which converts it into the next member of the metabolic chain. This phenomenon is termed 'sequential induction' (simultaneous or successive adaptation). **1968** H. HARRIS *Nucleus & Cytoplasm* vi. 118 We have glimpses of this kind of organization in the phenomenon of 'sequential induction' (induction *en chaîne*) of enzymes in bacteria. **1971** *Bacteriol. Rev.* XXXV. 89/2 A sequential induction is characterized by a shift in the chemical nature of the inducer.

2. b. *Computers.* Of, pertaining to, or designating various aspects of a computer system and its control programming that operate or are utilized serially; *sequential search*, a search through a data list or file that is carried out serially.

1951 *Proc. IRE* XXXIX. 276/2 *Sequential control*, the manner in which instructions to a digital computer are set up in sequence and are fed consecutively to the computer during the solution of a problem. **1964** T. W. MCRAE *Impact of Computers on Accounting* iii. 53 A computer..carries out each of these operations in automatic sequence under the control of the computer programme. This particular characteristic is known as 'sequential processing'. **1965** *Information & Control* VIII. 159 (*heading*) Discrete sequential search. **1969** P. B. JORDAIN *Condensed Computer Encycl.* 447 Once written, a sequential file has to be read in the same order (or sometimes in the inverse order) in which it has been written. **1970** O. DOPPING *Computers & Data Processing* x. 133 The magnetic tape can be called a sequential access memory, or serial access memory, because the records must be written and read in sequence. **1973** C. W. GEAR *Introd. Computer Sci.* ii. 44 We refer to the set of input cards as a sequential data set because it is possible to read a card only after the preceding card has been read. **1979** J. E. ROWLEY *Mechanised In-House Information Syst.* i. 26 Any search must process the complete tape, from start to end, seeking matches between terms, i.e. a sequential search.

5. *Television.* **a.** Of or pertaining to the normal method of scanning a television image, in which all the lines are traversed in the same direction, with a rapid, blanked fly-back after each.

1940 *Chambers's Techn. Dict.* 759/1 *Sequential scanning*, scanning in which the spot traverses each line in the same direction, returning rapidly from the end of one line to the beginning of the next. **1942** *Electronics* Apr. 164/1 System 2 employs sequential scanning in order to eliminate interline flicker. **1966** G. H. HOTSON *Television Receiver Theory* i. 5 A sequential raster..would be set up by drawing 625 lines one under the other. **1967** H. A. COLE *Basic Television* iii. 26 Provided that the rate of sequential scanning is high enough, the eye can be successfully 'tricked', by reason of the persistence of its vision, into believing that a very rapidly renewed image on the viewing screen has in fact been there all the time.

b. Of, pertaining to, or designating various systems of colour television in which picture information for the primary colours is transmitted successively in quantities corresponding to a dot, line, or field. Cf. *dot-* (also *field-*, *line-*) *sequential system* s.v. *DOT *sb.*[1] 5 f, *FIELD *sb.* 21, *LINE *sb.*[2] 32.

1947 *Electronics* Jan. 72/2 The sequential system is characterized by the fact that the transmitted signal contains information about one primary color only at any instant of time. **1951** *Proc. IRE* XXXIX. 1195/1 In the case of field-sequential or line-sequential presentation, step-wise switching from color to color is desired. In the case of dot-sequential presentation, sine-wave switching by circular deflection with uniform angular velocity is preferred. **1975** D. G. FINK *Electronics Engineers' Handbk.* xx. 12 The field sequential system employs a monochrome television camera, with a color-scanning disk mounting near the focal plane... The video signal derived from the camera tube thus consists of sequential color fields in the order that the primary light filters appear in front of the camera tube.

6. *sequential circuit* (Electronics), a logic circuit whose output depends on the order or timing of the inputs.

1954 D. A. HUFFMAN in *Jrnl. Franklin Inst.* CCLVII. 165 In a circuit having secondary relays, the possibility of a 'memory' exists since the states of operation may not uniquely determine the output transmissions. A circuit having secondary relays will be called a sequential circuit. **1969** J. J. SPARKES *Transistor Switching* iv. 93 In combinational and sequential circuit diagrams it is usual to use special symbols. **1975** D. G. FINK *Electronics Engineers' Handbk.* XXIII. 41 In some cases problems exist in sequential circuits when a circuit action depends critically on which relay or logic element completes its operations first.

sequester, *v.* Add: **5.** *Chem.* To form a stable complex, esp. a chelate, with (an ion) so as effectively or actually to remove it from solution; to form a stable complex with (a biochemical molecule).

1934 R. E. HALL *U.S. Patent 1,956,515* 5/2 The water softening action of the sodium metaphosphate..is rather to sequester or lock up the calcium in a but extremely slightly [*sic*] ionizable condition in a soluble sodium-calcium-metaphosphate complex molecule. **1953** *Sci. Amer.* June 70/2 The iron..is tightly imprisoned and hidden away—'sequestered', in the poetic language of chelation technology—by EDTA's chelate rings. **1962** *Which?* Oct. 297/2 Instead of softening water by replacing the calcium and magnesium in hard water by sodium..you can 'wrap up' the calcium and magnesium—sequester them—and so isolate them from the soap during washing. **1973** *Nature* 13 July 103/2 Insect yolk proteins ..are synthesized and secreted by the fat body, and are sequestered from the haemolymph by the developing oocytes. **1977** *Sci. Amer.* July 92/1 When the cations are sequestered in an organic cage molecule, the resulting complex is so stable that the 'backsliding' reaction is prevented.

sequestering *vbl. sb.* (later examples).

1949 *Thorpe's Dict. Appl. Chem.* (ed. 4) IX. 512/2 The term 'sequestering' introduced by Hall Laboratories to designate the virtually complete elimination of Ca^{++} ions whilst retaining the calcium in solution in the form of a soluble complex. **1962** *Which?* Oct. 297/2 The best known sequestering agents for softening water in this way are the sodium metaphosphates. **1973** P. A. ALLUM *Politics & Society in Post-War Naples* ix. 316 Antonio Gava's manoeuvres to try to become Campanian Regional Chairman..included the sequestering of a DC regional councillor in a trunk.

sequestrant (sĭkwe·strănt), *sb.* (*a.*) *Chem.* [ad. L. *sequestrānt-em*, pr. pple. of *sequestrāre* (see SEQUESTER *v.*).] A sequestering agent. Also *attrib.* or as *adj.*

1951 *Chem. Abstr.* XLV. 3756 (*heading*) Analytical applications of complexones (sequestrants). **1967** [see *lactobionic* adj. s.v. *LACTO- 2]. **1972** *Sci. Amer.* Mar. 19/3 Sequestrants are added to food to bind trace metals and thus prevent any oxidative activity the metals in an ionized state might have on the food.

sequestrate, *v.* Add: **1. b.** *Physiol.* To render (a biochemical compound) metabolically unavailable without destroying it; to remove from the circulation.

1961 *Lancet* 29 July 258/1 The placenta, like the liver, can sequestrate and degrade insulin. **1977** *Proc. R. Soc. Med.* LXX. 521/1 They suggested that the increased titres might be due to failure of the cirrhotic liver to sequestrate gut-derived antigens, which then reached immunologically competent areas of the body.

sequestration. Add: **5*.** *Chem.* The action or state of being sequestered (sense *5).

1948 *Jrnl. Chem. Education* XXV. 483/1 In sequestration, the multivalent positive ion has practically disappeared from the solution without being evolved as a gas, removed as a precipitate or deposited as an element. **1959** R. L. SMITH *Sequestration of Metals* iii. 26 Sequestration is most usually achieved by chelation, even although chelation itself covers many phenomena which would not be considered sequestration. **1973** D. F. LONG tr. *Degrémont's Water Treatm. Handbk.* (ed. 4) ix. 293 The total sequestration of calcium requires about 50g of polyphosphate per degree TH.

sequestrectomy (sĭkwestre·ktŏmi). *Surg.* [f. SEQUESTR(UM + *-ECTOMY.] The surgical excision of a sequestrum or sequestra; = SEQUESTROTOMY.

1940 in *Chambers's Techn. Dict.* 759/1. **1954** E. L. FARQUHARSON *Textbk. Operative Surg.* v. 136 Sequestrectomy.—Small loose sequestra may be discovered only during an operation to improve drainage, and are then removed as part of the operation. **1963** R. WARREN *Surgery* xxxi. 1071/2 Sequestrectomy. Removal of sequestrum (or dead bone) is done primarily for osteomyelitis.

Sequestrene (sĭkwe·strīn). Also **sequestrene.** [f. SEQUESTR(ATION + -ENE.] A proprietary term for preparations of ethylenediamine tetra-acetic acid and its salts used as sequestering agents; *spec.* one containing sequestered iron for use on iron-deficient soils.

1949 *Official Gaz.* (U.S. Patent Office) 8 Feb. 320/2 Alrose Chemical Co., Inc., Cranston, R.I... *Alro Sequestrene*... Claims use since Jan. 16, 1948. **1949** *Agric. Chemicals* IV. iv. 73/2 'Sequestrene', unlike the polyphospates, is compatible with cationic surface-active agents. **1951** *Proc. Soc. Exper. Biol. & Med.* LXXVI. 619/1 Four Sequestrenes are available at present, Sequestrene AA (the free acid), SNA 2 (di-sodium salt), SNA 3 (trisodium salt) and SNA 4 (tetrasodium salt). **1958** *Times* 4 Oct. 9/5 The green leaves become pale and chlorotic. There may be several reasons for this condition but nearly always application of sequestrene compound.. will effect a quick..cure. **1965** *Listener* 1 July 25/3 Sequestrenes..are now widely sold for application to plants suffering from an iron deficiency. **1977** *Vole* No. 1. 34/3 Rugosas..may need sequestrene if there is an excess of lime.

sequined, *ppl. a.* Add: Also *fig.*

1918 E. SITWELL *Clown's Houses* 8 Beside the sea, metallic-bright And sequined with the noisy light. **1969** 'E. LATHEN' *When in Greece* xiii. 140 The sea spread a sequined carpet..below.

‖**serab** (serā·b). Also **sirab.** [ad. Arab. *sarāb*.] A mirage.

a **1835** F. D. HEMANS *Wks.* (1844) III. 87 Suns of blasting light perchance illume The glistening Serab which illudes his eye. **1839** *Penny Cycl.* XV. 261/2 This kind of mirage is not peculiar to Egypt; it is known in Persia also, where it is called *Serab* or *Sir-ab* (miraculous water). **1883** *Encycl. Brit.* XVI. 50/2 When the soil is parched up the appearance of the mirage (seráb) is very common.

Serabend, var. *SARABAND[2].

serac. Add: ‖ **sérac.** (Later examples.)

1900 *Proc. Boston Soc. Nat. Hist.* XXIX. 295 Weathering occurs where variations of external temperature penetrate to the bed-rock, as is particularly the case between the séracs of glacial cascades. **1933** J. BUCHAN *Prince of Captivity* I. iii. 92 They came on ice-fields..and mountainous seracs which would have puzzled an Alpine climber. **1936** M. ROBERTS *Poems* 36 The snow falls, and the séracs; and the green glacier-ice Moves down. **1963** G. CARR *Lewker in Norway* vi. 124 On the further side of the right-hand ridge he could just see the upper *séracs* of the Bojumsbre. **1979** C. KILIAN *Icequake* vi. 86 Huge fields of seracs—the topographical nightmare caused by intersecting crevasses.

seradeh, obs. var. SHRADDHA, SRADDHA.

seral (sɪ̈ə·răl), *a.*[2] *Ecol.* [f. *SERE *sb.*[2] + -AL.] Of or pertaining to a sere; being a member of a sere other than its climax.

1916 F. E. CLEMENTS *Plant Succession* ix. 184 In lowland and montane regions examples of priseres are often more numerous than those of subseres, and such regions are of the first importance for seral investigations. **1926** TANSLEY & CHIPP *Study of Vegetation* ii. 18 We have a special technical term for the developmental series of communities... We apply the adjective *seral*, as opposed to *climax*, to such communities. **1932** *Forestry* VI. 190 The principal seral stages in natural succession from grassland or heath to beechwood are shortly described for certain soil types. **1955** P. A. BUXTON *Nat. Hist. Tsetse Flies* ix. 278 It appears to be generally true that the grassland is seral and that it is prevented from developing into bush or woodland by annual fires. **1973** P. A. COLINVAUX *Introd. Ecol.* vi. 77 The communities are.. classified into a number of subordinate communities, the seral stages, and the generic taxon, the *Beech-maple climax community*.

serape. Delete ‖ and add: Also † **zarape.** Now in wider use. (Earlier and later examples.)

1834 A. PIKE *Prose Sk. & Poems* 138 The men with.. the zarape or blanket of striped red and white. **1836** [see *RANCHERO]. **1892** *Dial. Notes* I. 194 *Serápe*, a Mexican blanket, generally woven by hand by Indian women, with stripes of variegated colors. The *serape* has no opening or slit for the head, like the *poncho*, but is worn by men only, thrown across the shoulders. **1916** 'B. M. BOWER' *Phantom Herd* 68 He had finished with an old Mexican serape draped around his person for warmth. **1950** *Chicago Tribune* 1 Mar. 20/3 The feminine counterpart of the serape is the rebozo. **1979** *United States 1980/81* (Penguin Travel Guides) 49 Mexican, Indian, and 'Old West' items are especially good buys. Serapes..and wool rebozos.. make nice gifts.

Serapeum (serăpī·ŏm). *Egyptology* and *Anc. Hist.* Also **Serapeion** (-əi·ǫn), **Serapeium**; pl. **Serapeia.** [a. late L., ad. Gr. Σεραπεῖον, f. Σέραπις Serapis.] A temple of Serapis; *spec.* the great precinct near Memphis, where the sacred Apis bulls were buried, and a temple in Alexandria.

1841 *Penny Cycl.* XXI. 260/2 He had temples (Serapeia) in several parts of Egypt. **1847** J. LEITCH tr. *Müller's Anc. Art* 243 The Serapeum was at the same time a sanatory institution. **1877** A. B. EDWARDS *Thousand Miles up Nile* iv. 86 According to one of these precious Serapeum tablets, the wounded bull did not die till the fourth year of the reign of Darius. **1927** TARN & GRIFFITH *Hellenistic Civiliz.* x. 294 The Serapeum at Delos has revealed that the triad who were so to influence Hellenism were..Isis, Sarapis, and Anubis. **1928** *Daily Tel.* 11 Dec.

13/4 It was suggested that the so-called Greek Serapeum was in truth nothing but the resting-place of the mother cows of Egyptian Apis. **1961** A. GARDINER *Egypt of Pharaohs* xii. 326 Not a single inscription of Dyn. XXI was found in the Serapeum [at Memphis]. **1972** P. M. FRASER *Ptolemaic Alexandria* I. v. 271 The Serapeum on Rhacotis Hill [in Alexandria] was within the Ptolemaic and Roman city-walls.

seraph[1]. Add: **3.** *seraph-arrival, -cloud, -sense; seraph-bright, -haunted, -sent* adjs.

1876 G. M. HOPKINS *Wr. Deutschland* xxiii, in *Poems* (1967) 59 With the gnarl of the nails in thee,..his Lovescape crucified And seal of his seraph-arrival. **1949** BLUNDEN *After Bombing* 49 Marbles, mosaics, carvings, seraph-bright Paintings of wall and window. **1928**—— *Japanese Garland* 30 Their mysteries luring that young seraph-cloud Swan-like between the mountain and the moon. **1958** G. BARKER *Two Plays* 52 Lie dreaming on that seraph-haunted shore. **1928** BLUNDEN *Retreat* 65 Her touch is seraph sense. **1932**——*Face of England* 126 They sparkled free In seraph-sent lucidity.

seraphim. Add: **2. c.** *β* (Later example.)

1924 E. SITWELL *Sleeping Beauty* iv. 23 From flowers as white as seraphims' breath.

d. Delete † *Obs.* and add later examples of *β*.

1920 'K. MANSFIELD' *Let.* Nov. (1928) II. 80 A cherubim and a seraphim come winging their way towards me. **1974** *Times Lit. Suppl.* 29 Mar. 314/3 Lamartine is content to be a seraphim.

Serax (se·ræks). *Pharm.* A proprietary name in Canada and the U.S. for *OXAZEPAM.

1957 *Official Gaz.* (U.S. Patent Office) 27 Aug. TM 148/2 American Home Products Corporation... *Serax.* For ataractic. First use Feb. 4, 1957. **1968** *Jrnl. Pharmaceut. Sci.* LVII. 312/2 Oxazepam is a psychotropic agent. [*Note*] Marketed as Serax by Wyeth Laboratories, Philadelphia, Pa. **1974** M. C. GERALD *Pharmacol.* xvi. 309 The benzodiazepine derivatives include..oxazepam (Serax). **1977** *Rolling Stone* 30 June 81/3, I..reached into my shirt pocket, removed two ·30 mg. Serax capsules, popped them into my mouth, and washed them down with the drink.

seraya (serai·ă). [Mal.] A forest tree of the genus *Shorea* or *Parashorea*, belonging to the family Dipterocarpaceæ and native to south-east Asia; also, the hardwood timber produced by a tree of this kind. Cf. *LAUAN, *MERANTI.

1893 G. KING in *Jrnl. Asiatic Soc. Bengal* LXII. II. 112 Its vernacular name in Penang is *Seraya.* **1916** *Bull. Dept. Forestry Brit. N. Borneo* No. 1. 19 The better coloured and figured pieces of Seriah make very acceptable substitutes for Mahogany, in panels, veneers, etc. **1920** A. L. HOWARD *Man. Timbers World* 256 The wood has been called by a variety of names such as East Indian mahogany and East Indian cedar, as well as by its proper name of serayah. **1940** E. J. H. CORNER *Wayside Trees Malaya* I. 213 The *Seraya*..is perhaps the only forest-tree that can be identified from afar by its pale, outstanding crown. **1956** *Handbk. of Hardwoods* (Forest Prod. Res. Lab.) 153 Red seraya or light red seraya..may be described as the North Borneo equivalent of light red meranti. *Ibid.* 212 White seraya grows to an average height of 120 ft. **1962** J. C. S. BROUGH *Timbers for Woodwork* (rev. ed.) xvi. 174 Seraya..ranges from straw to reddish-brown. **1965** R. MCKIE *Company of Animals* i. 36 We stopped high on the ridge in light jungle topped by seraya trees. **1971** [see *LAUAN].

Serb, *sb.* **1. b.** (Earlier example.)

1861 MILL *Repr. Govt.* xvi. 292 The population of Hungary is composed of Magyars, Slovacks, Croats, Serbs, Roumans, and in some districts, Germans.

Serbian, *sb.* (Earlier example.)

1848 C. BUNSEN in *Rep. Brit. Assoc. Advancem. Sci. 1847* 267 The sixth family is that of the Slavonic nations in their two great branches;..the western, the languages of the Tschechs (Bohemians), Slovaks, Poles, and Serbians.

Serbo-. Add: *Serbo-Croat; Serbo-Bulgarian, -Greek* adjs.

1923 G. BUCHANAN *My Mission to Russia* I. vi. 69 The so-called Serbo-Bulgarian Customs Union Treaty, negotiated in 1905, was never ratified by the Skuptschina. **1905** Serbo-Croat [in Dict.]. **1931** *Times Lit. Suppl.* 29 Jan. 82/3 Translations..from the Russian,..Judaeo-Spanish and Serbo-Croat. **1976** W. H. CANAWAY *Willow-Pattern War* vii. 78 Petar was bilingual in Serbo-Croat and Albanian. **1958** *Everyman's Encycl.* XI. 234/1 Later there were attempts to replace the decaying Byzantine empire by a Serbo-Greek empire. **1972** D. DAKIN *Unification of Greece* ix. 126 The Serbo-Greek alliance of 1867.

sere (sī͡ᵊɪ), *sb.*[2] *Ecol.* [f. L. *serĕ-re* to join in a series.] A series of plant communities, each naturally succeeding the previous one.

1916 F. E. CLEMENTS *Plant Succession* i. 4 A sere is a unit succession. It comprises the development of a formation from the appearance of the first pioneers through the final or climax stage. **1940** *Geogr. Jrnl.* XCVI. 8 The seres which follow the destruction of climax vegetation in the alpine region [of the Himalayas] vary. **1960** N. POLUNIN *Introd. Plant Geogr.* xi. 323 Such is succession, the developmental series of communities constituting a sere and leading up to a state of relative stability and permanence known as the climax.

sere, sear, *a.*[1] Add: **3. c. sereward** *adv.*, towards decay (*rare*$^{-1}$).

1902 T. HARDY *Poems of Past & Present* 142 The sun and shadows wheel, Season and season sereward steal.

serein. Delete 'after sunset'.

serendibite (sĕre·ndibəit, sĕrendi·bəit). *Min.* [f. *Serendib, Serendip*, a former name for Sri Lanka + -ITE[1].] A borosilicate of aluminium, calcium, and magnesium, $(Ca,Mg)_5Al_5BSi_3O_{20}$, found as bluish triclinic crystals in which iron often replaces some of the aluminium and magnesium.

1902 *Nature* 20 Feb. 383/2 Messrs. G. T. Prior and A. K. Coomára-Swámy gave an account of the mode of occurrence and characters of 'serendibite', a new boro-silicate from Ceylon. **1978** W. A. DEER et al. *Rock-Forming Minerals* (ed. 2) IIA. 661 A number of serendibite.. occurrences in spinel-diopside skarns have been described from the Tayezhnoye iron ore localities of southern Yakutia... Serendibite is also found with sinhalite, warwickite and tourmaline..in the skarns of Handemi district, Tanzania.

serendipitous (serendi·pitəs), *a.* [f. SERENDIPIT(Y + -OUS.] **a.** Of persons: having the faculty of making happy and unexpected discoveries by accident.

1958 *Times Lit. Suppl.* 22 Aug. 468/4 In the matter of adventure Miss de Banke was serendipitous to the *n*th degree. **1968** 'E. MCBAIN' *Fuzz* ix. 146 La Brisca seemed to be a serendipitous type who led them on a jolly excursion halfway across the city. **1975** *Reader's Digest* Oct. 150/2 And all for the best, too, as serendipitous San Diegans gladly tell you.

b. (The more usual sense.) Applied to discoveries, meetings, etc., of this kind.

1965 J. WAKEFIELD *Death the Sure Physician* 50 It's rather fortunate that I should come across a chap with similar interests...distinctly serendipitous, in fact. **1971** *Nature* 20 Aug. 538/2 This suggestion was confirmed by the isolation of a stable tricarbonyliron complex of tetraphenylbutadiene by a serendipitous method (many of the best discoveries in the field have been made by chance). **1979** *Amer. Speech 1978* LIII. 272 As among these three systems, the girls couldn't have cared less, Yerke's suggestion was serendipitous.

Hence **serendi·pitously** *adv.*

1969 C. C. WINTER *Pract. Urol.* vii. 211 Prostatitis is one of the most common of urologic disorders. It may be symptomless and discovered serendipitously in a routine, two glass urinalysis in which the first specimen shows some white blood cells or a few more than in the second glass. **1974** *Daily Tel.* (Colour Suppl.) 29 Nov. 16/3 We can imagine Hodder meeting Stoughton..and their discovering, serendipitously, a mutual interest in books. **1980** *Times Lit. Suppl.* 14 Nov. 1275/4 He had the knack of always being serendipitously on hand when a tenement caught fire.

serendipity. Add: (Later examples.) Also, the fact or an instance of such a discovery.

Formerly rare, this word and its derivatives have had wide currency in the 20th century.

1926 E. MEYNELL *Life of Francis Thompson* xiii. 221 To the Serendipity Shop—the venture of a friend in Westbourne Grove—he would often go. **1955** *Sci. Amer.* Apr. 92/1 Our story has as its critical episode one of those coincidences that show how discovery often depends on chance, or rather on what has been called 'serendipity' —the chance observation falling on a receptive eye. **1971** S. E. MORISON *European Discovery Amer.: Northern Voy.* i. 3 Columbus and Cabot..(by the greatest serendipity of history) discovered America instead of reaching the Indies. **1980** *TWA Ambassador* Oct. 47/2 It becomes a glum bureaucracy, instead of the serendipity of 30 people putting out a magazine.

Hence **serendi·pitist.**

1939 JOYCE *Finnegans Wake* 191 You..semisemitic serendipitist, you (thanks, I think that describes you) Europasianised Afferyank! **1968** *Punch* 13 Nov. 684/1 There are the financial serendipitists, the men blessed monetarily by a fortunate law.

serg, var. *SARGE[2].

sergeant, serjeant, *sb.* Add: **9. b.** *sergeant-pilot.*

1919 J. T. B. MCCUDDEN *Five Years in R.F.C.* III. iii. 86 About the end of August, 1915, a Serjeant-Pilot named Watts arrived for duty. *a* **1963** J. LUSBY in 'B. James' *Austral. Short Stories* (1963) 221 The new boys comprised Australians, Englishmen, and Canadians... Most were sergeant-pilots, and in age retired school-boys.

11. sergeant-fish, delete *U.S.*, for Latin name substitute *Rachycentron canadum* and add: the cobia, a large game fish found in tropical and subtropical seas (earlier and later examples).

1873 *Forest & Stream* I. 258/1 Sergeant Fish..derives its trivial name from a black stripe running along its silvery sides..like that on the trowsers of a sergeant. **1947** K. H. BARNARD *Dict. Guide S.Afr. Fishes* 112 Sergeant-fish... A somewhat rare fish, of elongate shape,..occasionally caught at Port Elizabeth and Natal. **1958** *Washington Post* 24 Sept. 1/2 An unusually fine run of cobia (the sergeant fish)..has caused big game fishermen to toss caution to the gods of Izaak Walton.

sergeant-major. Add: **4.** *Mil. slang.* Used *attrib.* to designate: (*a*) coffee with cream or milk and sugar (*U.S.*); (*b*) strong sweet tea; tea with rum; also in the possessive and *ellipt.*

1923 T. BOYD *Through Wheat* viii. 131 'Bring your canteen cups. Sergeant-major coffee.'..'Coffee, hot! And milk and sugar in it!' **1925** FRASER & GIBBONS *Soldier & Sailor Words* 254 *Sergeant Major's Tea*, tea with sugar and milk, or a dash of rum, in it. **1929** J. L. HODSON *Grey Dawn—Red Night* II. v. 210 Two of them got up before the rest and made a fire and produced 'sergeant-major's tea' and bacon done to a turn. **1929** J. B. PRIESTLEY *Good Compan.* I. iv. 115 I'd like a drop o' tea with some rum in it, good old sergeant-major's. **1939** JOYCE *Finnegans Wake* 331 Pointing up to skyless heaven like the spoon out of sergeantmajor's tay. **1948** PARTRIDGE *Dict. Forces' Slang 1939–1945* 164 *Sergeant-major's*, a Samson-strong, love-sweet brew of tea, popularly supposed to be the perquisite of holders of that rank. **1981** J. WAINWRIGHT *Urge for Justice* I. v. 30 This tea..it damn near dissolved the spoon. A real 'sergeant major' brew. The way tea *should* be made.

Hence as *v. trans.*, to order or shout in a brusque and stentorian manner; **sergeant-majorish, -majorly** *adjs.*, characteristic of or resembling a sergeant-major.

1925 G. W. DEEPING *Sorrell & Son* viii. 77 Moreover, he might pocket a sergeant-majorly share of the tips. **1926** A. BENNETT *Lord Raingo* xxxvi. 168 'Bow,' said the sergeant-majorish official behind him, in a no-nonsense voice. **1931** E. A. ROBERTSON *Four Frightened People* ii. 77 Then we heard the voice of Mrs. Mardick sergeant-majoring the truant few. *a* **1935** T. E. LAWRENCE *Mint* (1955) II. iii. 108 Cursing fellows forbidden to look resentful..is a sergeant-majorish trick which good corporals would not allow themselves. **1962** M. DUFFY *That's how It Was* iv. 43 'She'll soon learn,' the voice sergeant-majored high above me.

serial, *a.* and *sb.* Add: **A.** *adj.* **a.** (Earlier example.)

1840 A. BRISBANE tr. *Fourier's Social Destiny* xxiv. 344 Industry was developed sufficiently..to admit of the application of the Serial mechanism to it.

b. Also of a radio play: broadcast in (usu. weekly) episodes. *serial rights* (later examples).

1890 [see *RIGHT *sb.*[1] 9 f]. **1903** J. LONDON *Let.* 10 Mar. (1966) 150 The serial right has passed out of my hands. **1933** *B.B.C. Year-Bk. 1934* 213 Serial plays were a popular innovation: and their exciting episodes seemed to have appealed to..as many grown-ups as youngsters. **1944** *R.A.F. Jrnl.* Aug. 290 The American market..still offers big money for serial rights. **1955** *Radio Times* 22 Apr. 42/1 A new serial play in six parts written for broadcasting. **1960** *B.B.C. Handbk.* 68 An increased output of serial plays and characterized documentaries. **1970** [see *film rights* s.v. *FILM *sb.* 7 c].

c. (Further examples.) *serial section*, each of a series of sections through tissue made in successive parallel planes; hence *serial-section* vb. trans., *serial sectioning* vbl. sb. In Computing = *SEQUENTIAL *a.* 2 b.

1885 A. B. LEE *Microtomist's Vade-Mecum* xxiv. 203 (*heading*) Serial section mounting. **1908** *Q. Jrnl. Exper. Physiol.* I. 129 Where the epithelium persists..serial sections show that the cleft is completely closed by it. **1948** *Gloss. Computer Terms* (U.S. Office of Naval Res. Special Devices Center: M.I.T. Servomechanisms Lab. Rep. R-138) 10 *Serial programming*, execution of complete arithmetic operations one at a time. Coding is simpler and easier to organize where simultaneous arithmetic operations are avoided. Serial programming is possible with either parallel or serial digit transmission. **1960** GREGORY & VAN HORN *Automatic Data-Processing Systems* viii. 248 Latency time for instructions stored in serial-access memories can increase program running time enough to warrant using other arrangements for storing instructions. **1961** *Lancet* 2 Sept. 523/1 The hypothalami ..were embedded in celloidin and serial-sectioned. **1964** G. H. HAGGIS et al. *Introd. Molecular Biol.* v. 113 Consideration of the confusion which would result from the examination of fifty serial-section electron microscope pictures placed on top of each other. **1969** P. B. JORDAIN *Condensed Computer Encycl.* 449 In character-oriented memory computers, serial addition permits forming sums with inexpensive hardware... In faster, word-organized computers, parallel addition is used. **1977** *Sci. Amer.* Sept. 130/1 Serial-access and block-access memories have access times that depend on the storage location selected. **1979** *Nature* 22 Feb. 596/2 Here was a man who had pioneered..the technique of serial sectioning, which enabled palaeontologists to examine the internal structures of fossils that would never have been accessible for study.

d. *Biol.* Involving or produced by the propagation of a micro-organism or tissue by means of a series of cultures, each grown from material derived from the previous one.

1904 *Proc. Amer. Acad. Arts & Sci.* XL. 277 In investigating the persistence of the (+) and (−) characters in the individual strains, the writer has begun a number of serial cultures. **1947** *Ann. Rev. Microbiol.* I. 26 During the early period of study the original culture on serial plating continued to produce colonies about 5 per cent of which contained only z_{30} and 95 per cent contained $z_{30}z_{31}$. **1970** L. T. MORTON *Med. Bibliogr.* (ed. 3) 609 Laveran and Mesnil discovered that trypanosomes could be maintained indefinitely in rats and mice by serial passage.

e. *Educ.* and *Psychol.*: *serial learning*, the learning of words, numbers, etc., as a series so that each item acts as a stimulus for the next; *serial position*, the position of items in a serial test studied for its effect on learning; hence *attrib.* as *serial-position curve, effect*; *serial test*, a test of ability that makes use of

items in serial arrangement; hence *serial testing*. Also *serial reproduction*.
1926 H. HEAD *Aphasia* I. II. i. 149 The order in which these serial tests are applied must be varied to suit the circumstances of the case. **1926** *Jrnl. Exper. Psychol.* IX. 195 (*title*) Specific serial learning; a study of backward association. **1926** *Amer. Jrnl. Psychol.* XXXVII. 538 It is apparent..that the effects of serial position upon memorization still constitute something of an issue. **1932** F. C. BARTLETT *Remembering* vii. 173 There is some suggestion that material treated by way of serial reproduction may gain a kind of group stamp or character. **1948** E. R. HILGARD *Theories of Learning* iv. 97 (*caption*) Serial position effect in the memorization of a list of 15 nonsense syllables. **1952** MCGEOCH & IRION *Psychol. Hum. Learning* iv. 115 (*heading*) Learning as a function of serial position. *Ibid.* x. 369 The results of one series of experiments by the method of serial reproduction..are important for their bearing upon the social diffusion of information. **1962** E. R. HILGARD *Introd. Psychol.* (ed. 3) ix. 273/2 Serial learning is easier than paired-associates learning. **1971** *Jrnl. Gen. Psychol.* LXXXV. 100 RFT performance was not found to be stable..but rather changed in the direction of greater field dependence on serial testing. **1972** *Jrnl. Social Psychol.* LXXXVI. 106 For both liked and disliked names the typical serial position curve was noted with most errors occurring in the middle of the lists. **1979** A. C. CATANIA *Learning* x. 243 Another variety of intraverbal relation occurs in serial learning, the learning of a list of items in a particular order.

f. In grammatical terminology; *spec.* in certain West African languages, designating a construction consisting of a series of verbs.
1933 L. BLOOMFIELD *Language* xii. 195 Endocentric constructions are of two kinds, *co-ordinative* (or *serial*) and *subordinative* (or *attributive*). **1957** S. POTTER *Mod. Linguistics* v. 114 It [*sc.* the phrase *good men*] is a subordinate or attributive construction as opposed to such a phrase as *men and women*, which is said to be co-ordinate or serial. **1963** *Jrnl. Afr. Languages* II. II. 145 One..feature of the syntax of Twi and many other West African languages which seems to have escaped the notice of the grammar-writers is that the only possible position for an object pronoun is immediately after a verb... It is necessary to introduce an extra verb to take the extra object pronoun... This introduction of an extra verb in this way results in a *serial verbal construction*. **1971** G. ANSRE in J. Spencer *Eng. Lang. W. Afr.* 157 Many of them [*sc.* the languages of West Africa] exhibit similarities in their grammatical patterning, such as the occurrence of a sequence of verbal forms within the same sentence which has come to be known as 'serial verbal construction'. **1977** E. A. GREGERSEN *Lang. in Afr.* v. 49 A distinctive feature of many West African languages is a multiple verb construction, known in the literature as serial verbs.

g. *serial number*, a number assigned to a person, item, etc., indicating position in a series; *spec.* a number printed on a banknote or manufactured article by which it can be identified.
1935 F. W. CROFT *Crime at Guildford* xiv. 201 All these high-class cameras bore a serial number. **1938** L. M. HARROD *Librarians' Gloss.* 135 *Serial Number*, the number indicating the order of publication in a series. **1959** *Ibid.* (ed. 2) 246 *Serial Number*... 2. One of the consecutive numbers appearing in front of an entry in a bibliography or catalogue. **1960** *Bedside 'Guardian'* IX. 135 It shows a willingness to surrender but a refusal to reveal one's serial number. **1962** L. DEIGHTON *Ipcress File* i. 11 People posted to him..were..given a new serial number from the batch..reserved for Civil Servants seconded to military duties. **1968** 'R. SIMONS' *Death on Display* iv. 55 Crow..took himself off to check on the serial numbers of the five-pound notes. **1971** R. K. SMITH *Ransom* (1972) III. 121 Very good field glasses for a kid... Probably stolen. He typed the serial number on the form. **1976** J. CROSBY *Snake* (1977) xxiv. 129 She paid cash with bills that had been carefully laundered... Elf doubted whether the Feds had the serial numbers on her bills but she was taking no chances.

h. *Mus.* Applied to a type of composition which takes as its starting-point an arrangement of the twelve tones of the chromatic scale. Cf. *DODECAPHONIC *a.*, *SERIES 20; *twelve-note*, *-tone* s.v. *TWELVE *numeral a.* and *sb.* III. c.
1947 H. SEARLE in *Penguin Music Mag.* Dec. 22 Fartein Valen, whose *Sonetto di Michelangelo*..uses a serial technique derived from Berg. **1958** *Times* 6 June 4/4 Reti considers a number of alternatives to serial tonality, which is what dodecaphonists now practise in default of the milk of the word of Schönberg. **1963** *Times Lit. Suppl.* 3 May 320/4 Most of us reserve the term 'series' for an ordered succession of notes, as in the works of Schoenberg, but do not apply it to a collection of pitches such as are found in the works of Scriabine or Debussy Mr. Perle extends 'serial composition' to both classes of music. **1978** P. GRIFFITHS *Conc. Hist. Mod. Music* vii. 88 The plate opposite shows the opening of his [*sc.* Webern's] Symphony (1928), arranged to display the serial structure. **1982** *Sunday Times* 25 July 41/6 In his [*sc.* Eisler's] film music he made bold use of the technique of montage, juxtaposing elements from jazz, cabaret and serial polyphony.

B. *sb.* **b.** A film shown in a number of episodes; a radio or television play broadcast in (usu.) weekly episodes.
1914 R. GRAU *Theatre of Science* xi. 245 The latter arranged with the late Thomas W. Hanshew..to prepare a serial. **1939** *BBC Handbk.* 20 An interesting aspect of the year's radio-dramatic work was the development of serial plays. The serial feature, which is the backbone of American radio, had made comparatively few appearances here before 1938... Publishers..found that the 'Monte Cristo' serial caused a great demand for the novel. **1950** G. WEBB *Inside Story of Dick Barton* i. 13 One certain way of arousing interest and gaining an audience was through the medium of the radio serial. **1955** *Radio Times* 22 Apr. 21/1 *Counterspy*, the six-part serial which begins in Children's Hour on Friday. **1964** K. C. LAHUE (*title*) Continued next week: a history of the moving picture serial. **1974** *Broadcast* 22 July 14/1 There is abundant evidence that the serial, or its twin brother the series, is a popular form of TV programming. People seem to like stories in which the same characters appear and reappear.

serialism (sī^ə·riăliz'm). [f. SERIAL *a.* + -ISM: cf. next.] **1.** The name given by J. W. Dunne (1875–1949) to a theory of the serial nature of time, which he evolved to account for the phenomenon of precognition, esp. in dreams (see quots.).
1927 J. W. DUNNE *Exper. with Time* xxi. 153 The serialism of the fields of presentation. *Ibid.* xxvi. 206 Serialism as a theory of the Universe. **1934** *Discovery* Aug. 239/1 His theory that in dreams the dreamer appears sometimes to move out of one dimension of time into another. Serialism, as Mr Dunne terms his main principle, is a fascinating idea. **1937** *Mind* XLVI. 165 The novelty of Serialism lies in this: in a Serial Universe it is permissible to rotate the geometrically mapped-out axis of a time-dimension (T_2) until its divisions coincide with those of a time (T_1) one dimension lower. **1974** *Country Life* 7 Feb. 233/1 J. W. Dunne's theory of Serialism..that we may discover the future in our dreams.

2. A belief or assumption that every process takes place in a regular succession.
1943 C. S. LEWIS *Abolition of Man* iii. 39 Such a reply springs from the fatal serialism of the modern imagination—the image of infinite unilinear progression which so haunts our minds... We tend to think of every process as if it must be like the numeral series.

3. *Mus.* The practice or principles of serial composition.
1958 [see *ATONAL *a.*]. **1967** *Spectator* 18 Aug. 200/1 If we are to assume that atonality refers to the idiom characterising Schoenberg's works prior to his adoption of serialism..then Penderecki's Passion..does not come in .o this category. **1977** P. JOHNSON *Enemies of Society* xvii. 228 Serialism does not provide a workable order, at least for most listeners, because the structure is mathematical rather than aural.

serialist (in Dict. s.v. SERIAL *a.* and *sb.*). Add: **1.** (Later example.)
1902 A. BENNETT *Truth about Author* xii, in *Academy* 5 July 44/2, I found an outlet..more remunerative than the concoction of serials; and I am a serialist no longer.

2. One who holds views that accord with a serial theory; *spec.* one who learns by studying items arranged in a series.
1936 *Mind* XLV. 31 The controversy between substrativists and serialists is one of long standing. **1975** G. PASK *Conversation, Cognition & Learning* 561 Serialists learn, remember and recapitulate a body of information in small, well-defined and sequentially-ordered segments.

3. *Mus.* A composer or advocate of serial music.
1959 *Atlantic Monthly* Feb. 88/2, I do believe, however, that success will not wholly pass by the rhythmic experimenters and the 100 per cent serialists. **1962** *Times* 26 Feb. 14/7 The two pieces..illustrated the difference of outlook between the newest generation of English serialists and their predecessors. **1980** *Early Music* Apr. 253/3 Many of these works are characterized by a degree of formal organization which would delight serialists.

4. *attrib.* or as *adj.*
1936 *Mind* XLV. 31 The serialist hypothesis..seems to me beset with difficulties and obscurities. **1959** *Times* 13 Feb. 13/4 The Institute of Contemporary Arts is presenting a whole serialist programme. **1975** G. PASK *Conversation, Cognition & Learning* iv. 108 The respondent is free to learn in any way and is found to adopt a holist or serialist approach.

serialization (in Dict. s.v. SERIAL *a.* and *sb.*). Add: **1.** Also, the broadcasting of a radio or television play in serial form.
1965 *Radio Times* 18 Feb. 15/1 *The Mill on the Floss*, of which a four-part serialisation..begins tonight. **1972** *Daily Tel.* 31 Jan. 7/2 This serialisation may well prove such compulsive viewing as to create new interest in this neglected German liberal.

2. *gen.* The action or state of forming a series.
1857 H. CLAPP tr. *Fourier's Social Destiny* I. iv. 37 The Administrative unity of the Globe is nothing more nor less than the Serialization of the general interests, operations and relations of the Human Race. **1962** *Listener* 22 Mar. 513/1 The fate of man is now 'serialization'. We lose our individuality and our capacity for action by being turned into merely one term in a series which could equally well be replaced by any other term. **1966** A. MANSER *Sartre* xiii. 214 Sartre, in demanding the abolition of serialisation, seems to be asking for an impossible Utopia.

3. *Mus.* The composition of serial music.
1959 *Observer* 23. Aug 7/3 This group [of composers] practices a technique of *total serialisation*, whereby not merely notes but all elements of music (pitch, instrumentation, rhythm, volume, etc.) are used in row formation, i.e., in regular patterns. **1966** F. HOYLE *October First is too Late* xi. 126 The style of this Greek music was more akin to the key system than to the modern serialization. **1976** P. STADLEN in D. Villiers *Next Year in Jerusalem* 328 Stravinsky..turned into a serial convert in his old age... In total serialization, the individual note no longer functions as part of a musical thought.

serialize, *v.* (in Dict. s.v. SERIAL *a.* and *sb.*). Add: **a.** (Later examples.) Also, to broadcast serially; to publish the work of (an author) in serial form.
1923 S. HOCKING *My Book of Memory* xiii. 186, I submitted it to other editors who had serialized my stories, but with the same result. *a* **1965** A. CHRISTIE *Autobiogr.* (1977) VIII. 414, I was beginning to be serialised in America... The money..[was] far larger than anything I ever made from serial rights in Britain. **1971** *Guardian* 2 Mar. 9/3 The paperback sales of Compton Mackenzie's 'Sinister Street' jumped from a steady annual 2,000 to 16,000 when BBC-2 serialised the book.

b. (Earlier example.)
1857 H. CLAPP tr. *Fourier's Social Destiny* I. i. 8 These three Faculties or Forces serialize the play and action of the other Motors of the Soul.

c. *Mus.* To compose according to a serial technique.
1959 *Listener* 8 Oct. 564/1 The fashionable Webernites went on to serialize not only the notes themselves, but the silences, the durations, the dynamic indications..all by the number twelve. **1960** *Twentieth Century* Nov. 460 A note was said..to exist in a *field* determined by the possible error of the performer. This element was immediately serialized.

Hence **se·rialized, se·rializing** *ppl. adjs.*
1857 H. CLAPP tr. *Fourier's Social Destiny* I. iv. 32 The primary functions of the three Regulative or Serializing Faculties. **1921** *Public Opinion* 26 Aug. 204/2 Take the average short story, or serialised novel, and test it for the real wisdom involved. **1976** A. SHERIDAN-SMITH tr. *Sartre's Critique of Dialectical Reason* I. iv. 312 This serialised antagonism..constitutes an initial structure of alterity. **1976** M. SPARK *Takeover* xi. 154 The theme of Hubert had become one of Mary's favourite serialized entertainments.

seriate (sī^ə·ri$\bar{e}^i$t), *v.* [Back-formation from SERIATION.] *trans.* To arrange (items) in a sequence according to prescribed criteria.
1944 *Genetics* XXIX. 526 We shall refer to these and other genes in the series, requiring testers to distinguish them and to seriate them, as iso-alleles. **1968** D. L. CLARKE *Analytical Archæol.* II. xi. 453 Initially, the matrix technique was devised for seriating assemblages in terms of their proportions of component types. **1972** *Computers & Humanities* VI. 179 The program constructs a classification of objects and seriates the classes by minimizing the distance according to the Brainerd Robinson model of seriation.

seriation. Add: (Later examples.) In mod. use, esp. in *Archæol.*, the action or result of arranging items in a sequence according to prescribed criteria.
1917 *Anthrop. Papers Amer. Mus. Nat. Hist.* XVIII. 283 We have found that another seriation based on the percentages of redware yields a cheaper result. **1944** *Genetics* XXIX. 534 The test indicated that the males carried bobbed alleles capable of seriation when in combination with the testes. But in homozygous condition several of these seriated alleles produced identical maximum bristle types. **1951** G. W. BRAINERD in *Amer. Antiq.* XVI. 304/1 If a series of collections comes from a culture changing through time, their placement on the time axis is a function of their similarity... This..allows a 'seriation' or ordering of collections to be formed which, if time be the only factor involved, must truly represent the temporal placing of the collections. *Ibid.* 311/2, I believe that..seriations formed by this technique will allow refinements in chronology greater than those currently possible. **1966** *Amer. Anthropologist* LXVIII. 1449 When the data are very reliable.., then both ordering criteria produce the same seriation of collections. Confidence in the resulting seriation is therefore high. **1971** *World Archaeol.* III. 197 The established sequence of changing settlements also corresponded with that reached by seriation of the pottery collections from the relevant sites.

sericitization. Substitute for def.: Conversion into, or replacement by, sericite. (Later examples.)
1908 *Trans. N.Z. Inst.* XLI. 69 These figures show..that the type of rock-alteration may be regarded as partial sericitization. **1962** W. A. DEER et al. *Rock-Forming Minerals* III. 24 This sericitization may begin, and be complete, at an early stage of the metamorphism.

Hence **se·ricitized** *ppl. a.*, converted into (a form containing) sericite.
1935 *Geol. Mag.* LXXII. 276 Plagioclase..occurs as large sericitized laths. **1965** G. J. WILLIAMS *Econ. Geol. N.Z.* xiii. 195/2 The wall-rocks are sericitized and chloritized.

series. Add: **II. 9. b.** A set of radio or television programmes concerned with the same theme or having the same range of characters and broadcast in sequence.
1949 *Radio Times* 15 July 15/1 Fifth talk in the series devoted to English and French writings on art. **1962** *Listener* 11 Oct. 581/2 A series, *Zero One*, opened with an episode called *Stone Face*. **1974** *Radio Times* 14 Mar. 18/1 Series consultant Charlie Gillett.

11. a. (i) Also used for any assemblage of successive, usu. conformable, strata (without regard to the rank of the assemblage: cf. next sense). (Further examples.) Now *Obs.*
1827 *Trans. Geol. Soc.* II. 293 The strata..were in fact

the equivalent of the oolitic series. **1836** W. Buckland *Geol. & Mineral.* I. ix. 76 The Tertiary Series introduces a system of new phenomena, presenting formations in which the remains of animal and vegetable life approach gradually nearer to species of our own epoch. **1882** A. Geikie *Text-bk. Geol.* 648 The rocks of the Cambrian series present great uniformity of lithological character over the globe.

(ii) *Stratigraphy.* The primary subdivision of a system, composed of a number of stages and corresponding to an epoch in time; the rocks deposited during any specific epoch.

At the 1881 meeting of the International Geological Congress, a scheme of nomenclature was adopted in which the stratigraphical terms *group, system, series, stage* in decreasing order of comprehensiveness correspond to the terms *era, period, epoch, age* for time intervals. The *system* and its subdivisions are now regarded as the primary time-stratigraphical terms, and the use of *group* in this sense is deprecated.

1881 *Geol. Mag.* Decade II. VIII. 558 The final result of the discussions was the adoption of terms in the following order, the most comprehensive being placed first:..Series..Epoch... As equivalents of *Series*, the terms *Section* or *Abtheilung* may be used... According to this scheme, we would speak of the Palæozoic Group or Era, the Silurian System or Period, the Ludlow Series or Epoch, and the Aymestry Stage or Age. **1898** *Jrnl. Geol.* VI. 355 The faunas of the Trenton limestone, the Utica and Hudson River shales are very intimately related, and that relation should be indicated by grouping the three together as stages of a single series. **1931** *Bull. Geol. Soc. Amer.* XLII. 426 The Pleistocene or Glacial Period will be divided into epochs and ages, and the Pleistocene or Glacial system into corresponding rock terms, series and stages. **1931** Gregory & Barrett *General Stratigr.* x. 155 In Scotland the Upper Estuarine Series includes the Brora Coal seam, of which the roof is Callovian. **1961** *Bull. Amer. Assoc. Petroleum Geologists* XLV. 658 The term 'series' is not restricted to stratified rocks, but may be applied to intrusive rocks in the same time-stratigraphic sense. **1976** H. D. Hedberg *Internat. Stratigr. Guide* vii. 72 The series is a unit in the conventional chrono-stratigraphic hierarchy, ranking above a stage and below a system. The geochronologic equivalent of a series is an epoch. A series is always a subdivision of a system; it is usually but not always broken up into stages.

b. Any group of (usu. igneous) rocks having similar forms of occurrence and petrographical characteristics.

1844 C. Darwin *Volcanic Islands* vi. 123 Is it not more probable, that these dikes have been formed by fissures penetrating into partially cooled rocks of the granitic and metamorphic series, and by their more fluid parts,.. oozing out, and being sucked into such fissures? **1892–94** *Bull. Philos. Soc. Washington* XII. 178 Since neighboring centers may be erupting different phases of the rock series at one and the same time,..the same kinds of rock may occur in different parts of the whole complex series representing the order of eruption of the rocks in one region. **1909** J. P. Iddings *Igneous Rocks* I. ii. iii. 408 The term series should be applied to groups of rocks characterized by similarity of certain chemical or mineral constituents and by variations in others; the rocks being members of one family. Series may traverse the general system of classification in various directions. **1975** A. E. Kingwood *Composition & Petrology of Earth's Mantle* vii. 243 The behaviour of the orogenic series is fundamentally different from that of the tholeiitic and alkalic series.

12. a. *in series* (earlier and later examples): in *Electr.* also said of circuit components connected together so as to form a single electrical path between two points (also *transf.*); const. *with.*

1884 *Jrnl. Soc. Telegr.-Engineers* XIII. 498 If you couple two such alternate-current machines in series, they will so control each others phase as to nullify each other. **1922** *Proc. IRE* X. 249 It was necessary to use a two-electrode tube in series with the auxiliary emf. **1943** C. L. Boltz *Basic Radio* viii. 132 When a condenser and resistor are in series in a circuit, the charging current when a D.C. supply is switched on causes a p.d. across the resistor for a fraction of a second. **1960** *Practical Wireless* XXXVI. 412/1 In series with the key jack is filled a potentiometer VR1 which provides a useful variation of the oscillator tone. **1968** *Brit. Med. Bull.* XXIV. 250/1 Each tissue consists of two compartments connected in series. **1975** G. J. King *Audio Handbk.* iv. 84 The two transistors are connected in series across the supply.

b. (Later examples.) Also more generally, pertaining to or involving connection in series. Also *Comb.*

1920 *Whittaker's Electr. Engineer's Pocket-bk.* (ed. 4) 227 A motor has a series characteristic when the exciting or main flux is produced by the load current (or by part of it). **1926** R. W. Hutchinson *Wireless* vi. 101 In the above example of resonance the capacity and inductance were in series and such a case is often referred to as series resonance. **1950** *Engineering* 6 Jan. 8/2 The noise limiter ..employs a series-diode circuit. **1957** *Practical Wireless* XXXII. 379/1 (Advt.), It is essential to use mains primary types with T.V. receivers having series-connected heaters. **1961** *Amateur Radio Handbk.* (ed. 3) ix. 257/2 Valves such as the 807 can be used in both positions in a series-modulation system from a 1000 volts supply. **1962** G. A. T. Burdett *Automatic Control Handbk.* i. 26 The outstanding characteristic of the d.c. series motor is powerful torque at starting and also at low speeds. **1970** J. Shepherd et al. *Higher Electr. Engin.* (ed. 2) ix. 265 In Fig. 9.5(*a*) two mutually coupled coils are connected in series. The connexion is called series aiding, since current enters the dotted ends of the coils, which thus produce aiding fluxes. **1974** Harvey & Bohlman *Stereo F.M. Radio Handbk.* iii. 51 The attenuation produced by the series insertion of a crystal into a circuit operating at a variable frequency. **1975** D. G. Fink *Electronics Engineers' Handbk.* xiii. 80 The two series-connected windings in series with the load are called gate windings.

13. b. *Phonology.* (See quot. 1952.)

1952 A. Martinet in *Word* VIII. 13 A number of consonantal phonemes characterized by one and the same articulation will be said to form a 'series' if their other characteristic articulations can be located at different points along the air channel. Thus in English /p/, /t/, /č/, /k/,..will form a series, and so will /b/, /d/, /ǧ/, /g/. **1956** E. Stankiewicz *Phonemic Patterns of Polish Dialects* in *For Roman Jakobson* 521 This reduction resulted in the fusion of alveolars and palatals into a single series (š, ž, č, ǯ). **1969** C. A. M. Baltaxe tr. *Trubetzkoy's Princ. Phonol.* i. iv. 125 Many languages have two apical series, one characterized by the tip of the tongue pointed upward, the other by the tip of the tongue pointed downward, instead of a single series characterized by the participation of the tip of the tongue.

15. a. *Chem.* A set of related elements or compounds, esp. a group or period of the periodic table, or a number of compounds differing successively in composition by a fixed amount; a set of elements or compounds arranged in order of magnitude of some property.

1849 *Q. Jrnl. Chem. Soc.* II. 297 (*heading*) On a new series of organic bodies containing metals and phosphorus. **1869, 1876** [see Homologous *a.* 3]. **1922** [see *group *sb.* 3 c (ii)]. **1943** [see *electro-chemical* adj. s.v. *electro-]. **1958**, etc. [see *nephelauxetic *a.*]. **1962** Cotton & Wilkinson *Adv. Inorg. Chem.* xxiv. 495 For practical purposes..the third transition series begins with hafnium ..and embraces the elements Ta, W, Re, Os, Ir, Pt and Au. **1964** N. G. Clark *Mod. Org. Chem.* ii. 12 Members of the series may be represented by a general molecular formula, and each member differs from the next by CH_2; the paraffins have the general formula C_nH_{2n+2}. **1972** Cotton & Wilkinson *Adv. Inorg. Chem.* (ed. 3) xiii. 373 The stability of these hydrides falls rapidly along the series, so that SbH_3 and BiH_3 are very unstable thermally.

b. = *radioactive series* s.v. *radioactive *a.* 4.

1904 [see *disintegration a]. **1926** R. W. Lawson tr. *Hevesy & Paneth's Man. Radioactivity* xxiv. 180 The resulting end-product of the uranium-radium series does not emit rays, and is hence stable. **1949** F. Soddy *Story of Atomic Energy* v. 50/2 The RaE changes to Radium F,..the last radio-element in the main uranium series. **1974** *Encycl. Brit. Macropædia* I. 67/2 The mass numbers of all isotopes of the so-called thorium series..turn out to be multiples of four, and the series is known as the 4*n* series.

16. A set of alloys or minerals having the same chemical composition except for the relative proportions of two elements that can replace one another.

1855 *Phil. Mag.* X. 249 We..prepared a series of alloys in which copper predominated. **1859** *Phil. Trans. R. Soc.* CXLVIII. 357 The alloys of a series such as those of 2 equivalents of bismuth and 1 of lead, 3 Bi and 1 Pb, 4 Bi and 1 Pb, 5 Bi and 1 Pb, all conduct the same, viz. about 1·9, the various increasing quantities of lead exercising no influence on the conductibility of the alloys. **1911** *Encycl. Brit.* XVIII. 512/2 In other groups [of minerals] the replacement may be indefinite in extent, and between the ends of the series the different members may vary indefinitely in composition. **1914** C. H. Desch *Intermediate Compounds* vi. 50 The compound Mg_3Bi_2 has a conductivity very near that of bismuth, and the two series $Mg–Mg_3Bi_2$ and $Mg_3Bi_2–Bi$ are simple conglomerates. **1971** I. G. Gass et al. *Understanding Earth* i. 17/1 The plagioclase feldspars show a slightly more complex type of ionic replacement and form the series $NaAlSi_3O_8$ (albite)–$CaAl_2Si_2O_8$ (anorthite).

17. a. *Baseball.* A set of games played on successive days between two teams. Also *World Series*: see *world *sb.*

1862 *Sunday Mercury* (N.Y.) 13 July 6/3 This last game ended the series, and the players were to return this.. morning. **1906** *World* (N.Y.) 26 July 8/4 To wind up their series with the Western teams, the hilltop boys gave the Michiganders a double drubbing. **1960** *Time* 3 Oct. 67/2 The Yankees have..individual stars who can rouse themselves to greatness and win a short series by themselves. **1973** *Internat. Herald Tribune* 15 June 15/4 It was the first time in almost a month that the Mets had won two straight. And it was the first time in exactly a month that they had captured a series.

b. *Cricket.* A set of Test matches between two sides on any one tour.

1912 A. A. Lilley *Twenty-Four Years Cricket* xiv. 195 The only Test match of the tour that had a definite conclusion was the second of the series. **1935** *Wisden* ii. 1 The Australian team of 1934 arrived in this country with the knowledge that during the previous series of Test Matches in Australia they had been beaten four times. **1966** J. Arlott in B. Johnston *Armchair Cricket 1966* 12 The fifth—Oval—Test of that series was the first scheduled for regular eye-witness accounts on each day. **1976** *0–10 Cricket Scene* (Austral.) 5/2 Ian Chappell and Ian Redpath both gave away Test cricket, and with Edwards leaving the scene on a series before, Australia had lost their three most consistent, fighting batsmen.

18. *Physics.* A set of lines in a spectrum whose frequencies are mathematically related in a fairly simple way.

1890 *Jrnl. Chem. Soc.* LVIII. ii. 674 The corresponding components of the pairs form series whose wave-numbers are functions of the successive natural numbers. **1922** [see *Lyman]. **1952** R. W. Ditchburn *Light* xvii. 543 These formulæ suggest that the wave numbers of all these series may be expressed as differences of a set of wave numbers which are known as spectroscopic 'terms'. **1966** Williams & Fleming *Spectrosc. Methods in Org. Chem.* ii. 21 When more than two triple bonds are conjugated, the spectrum shows a characteristic series of low intensity bands..at intervals of 2300 cm^{-1}..and high intensity bands..at intervals of 2600 cm^{-1}. **1978** E. P. Bertin *Introd. X-Ray Spectrometric Analysis* i. 37 X-ray spectral lines are grouped in series *K, L, M, N*; all lines in a series result from electron transitions from various higher orbitals to the indicated shell.

19. *Soil Sci.* A group of soils which are derived from the same parent material and are similar in profile, though not necessarily in the texture of the surface horizon; = *soil series* s.v. *soil *sb.*[1] 10.

1904 *Ann. Rep. U.S. Dept. Agric. 1903–4* 269 These types have been arranged in 31 series, in which the soils are related in point of origin. **1913** *U.S. Bureau of Soils Bull.* No. 96. 8 A soil series is named from some town, village, county, or natural feature existing in the area when it was first encountered. **1917** Mosier & Gustafson *Soil Physics & Management* viii. 79 The Cecil series include the most important and widely distributed soils of the Piedmont Plateau. **1952** L. M. Thompson *Soils & Soil Fertility* vi. 86 Several of the great soil groups of the United States include hundreds of series. **1970** E. M. Bridges *World Soils* v. 34/2 The Ettrick Association derived from Silurian greywackes and shales has six component series in the Jedburgh and Morebattle district.

20. *Mus.* The arrangement of the twelve-tone chromatic scale which is used as the starting-point of a piece of *serial music; = *tone-row* s.v. *tone *sb.* 11.

1930 *Mod. Music* VII. iv. 5 The tonal material of a composition [by Schönberg] is a *series* of Twelve tones, borrowed from the chromatic scale and grouped in a special arrangement... The word 'series' is by no means identical with the idea of 'theme'... The series is to be considered rather as a tone-complex, whose successions and intervalic relations always recur. **1940** E. Křenek *Studies in Counterpoint* p. viii, The primary function of the series is that of a sort of 'store of motifs' out of which all the individual elements of the composition are to be developed. **1959** *Observer* 23 Aug. 7/3 According to this new system [of musical composition], a fixed *series* or succession of the twelve notes of the chromatic scale forms a framework which is the basis of the composition. **1978** P. Griffiths *Conc. Hist. Mod. Music* vii. 88 The music is ..constructed as a four-part canon, each part of which begins with a statement of the series in a different form.

21. *Eccl.* With a specifying number: a designation of one of the alternative experimental forms of service used within the Church of England since 1965.

These rites were replaced in 1980 by those printed in the *Alternative Service Book.*

1965 (*title*) Alternative Services: First Series. **1965** (*title*) Alternative Services: Second Series. **1967** *Church Quarterly Rev.* CLXVIII. 442 It is undoubtedly the rite of Series 2 which points the way forward. *Ibid.* 449 It is appropriate here to look at the third form of Series 1 in which the self-oblation is omitted from the Canon. **1971** *Churchman* LXXXV. 212 The amended text..has now been published as *Holy Communion: Series 3.* **1973** *Franciscan* XV. 169 In our worship at S. Bene't's we have moved..from Series II to Series III, using John Rutter's setting. **1977** B. Pym *Quartet in Autumn* i. 15 What would be the reaction of the congregation if Father G. tried to introduce Series Three? **1981** Barton & Halliburton in *Believing in Church* iv. 107 The Durham book, which had in fact proposed that form of invitation which became the invitation to confession in Series 2 Communion.

22. Special Comb. **series-parallel** *Electr.*, used *attrib.* with reference to combinations of series and parallel connection, esp. to denote a method of control of sets of electric traction motors in which the motors work in series on starting and are switched to parallel working when a certain speed is reached; **series spectrum**, a spectrum consisting of a series (sense *18) of lines.

1894 K. Hedges *Amer. Electr. Street Railways* vi. 68 In the series parallel method of control, the motors are first connected in 'series'. **1903** *Trans. Inst. Naval Archit.* XLV. 182 A voltage of 220, the motors to have series parallel control. **1957** *Railway Mag.* June 427/2 The operating voltage is 500 volts d.c., with orthodox series-parallel control for the four-motor equipments. **1968** *Radio Communications Handbk.* (ed. 4) i. 13/2 This is the value of the equivalent inductance of the four coils in this series-parallel arrangement. **1922** A. D. Udden tr. *Bohr's Theory of Spectra* ii. ii. 29 Although the series spectra of the elements of higher atomic number have a more complicated structure than the hydrogen spectrum, simple laws have been discovered showing a remarkable analogy to the Balmer formula. **1974** G. Reece tr. *Hund's Hist. Quantum Theory* vii. 100 With the aid of the *n, l, j* scheme it was possible to understand the multiplicity of the terms in the optical series spectra for atoms with one, two or three external electrons.

serif. Add: Hence **se·rifed, seriffed** *a.*

1936 *Geogr. Jrnl.* LXXXVII. 571 Any criticism.. should be directed towards the lettering, particularly to the large serifed capitals indicating principal settlements. **1957** S. Morison *Aspects of Authority & Freedom* 12 It is not impossible that seriffed letters were considered more suitable for a revered text than unseriffed ones. **1980** B. Crutchley *To be Printer* 134 Hence the danger that seriffed forms will be passed over when they could do a job as well or better and at the same time enhance our aesthetic enjoyment.

serigala (sĕri·gală). [Mal.] The Malaysian

wild dog, *Cuon alpinus*. Cf. *red dog* s.v. *RED *a.* 17 a; DHOLE.

1903 J. L. BONHOTE in Annandale & Robinson *Fasciculi Malayenses: Zool.* I. 12 There are two species of *srigâla* not uncommon in the Jarum district. **1945** C. L. B. HUBBARD *Observer's Bk. Dogs* 212 Serigala. The larger variety of Malayan Wild Dog... Long-coated, red-and-tan, with thick tail. **1965** C. SHUTTLEWORTH *Malayan Safari* v. 70 The serigala is related to the dhole of India. **1978** LD. MEDWAY *Wild Mammals Malaysia* (ed. 2) 84/1 Serigala..occurring on the mainland wherever extensive tracts of tall forest remain, though nowhere abundant.

serigraph. Add: **2.** An original print produced by serigraphy. orig. *U.S.*

1941 C. ZIGROSSER in *Print Collector's Q.* XXVIII. 455 A number of leading practitioners of the art..have adopted the word 'Serigraph' for silk screen stencil prints. **1959** *Information Bull. Libr. Congr.* 25 May 284 Henry Miller..has presented 7 rare ephemera to the Library. Two of them are promotional pamphlets for his *Into the Night Life* (1947), a serigraph or silk-screen creation. **1961** C. ZIGROSSER in *What is Original Print?* (Print Council of Amer.) 24 A number of artists who make original prints in the medium [*sc.* silk-screen printing] have decided to call them *serigraphs* to distinguish them from commercial silk screen reproductions. **1971** M. TURK *Buried Life* vi. 90 Sister Corita, I.H.M., one of the great contemporary printmakers whose own 'blabs & scrawls & squiggles' (otherwise known as serigraphs) hang in over forty museums. **1978** *New York* 3 Apr. 30/3 Pure color and shape in serigraphs.

serigraphy (seri·grafi). orig. *U.S.* Also **Serigraphy.** [Irreg. f. L. *sēricum* silk (see SERIC *a.*) + -GRAPHY; cf. F. *sérigraphie*, G. *serigraphie*.] The art or process of printing original designs by means of the silk-screen method.

1940 *Parnassus* Dec. 31 Serigraphy, or the silk screen process, is a comparative newcomer among the graphic arts. **1946** H. SHOKLER *Artists Man. Silk Screen Print Making* iv. 68 The explorations in Serigraphy have comprehended much more than simply textures and color. **1952** *Print* (N.Y.) VII. 4/2 In serigraphy there is no need to reverse the image. The artist draws directly on the silk. **1965** ZIGROSSER & GAEHDE *Guide Coll. Orig. Prints* iv. 55 Serigraphy is specially adapted for color work, although Ben Shahn has used it effectively just with black lines... Serigraphy is part of the general method of silk-screen printing.., but the name serves to differentiate original artists' prints from commercial productions. **1977** *Crafts* Nov./Dec. 67/3 Serigraphy—The art of silk screen printing. Summer courses in West Cornwall.

Hence **seri·grapher,** one who practises serigraphy; **serigra·phic** *a.*, of or pertaining to serigraphy.

1944 *Canadian Art* Oct.–Nov. 8/2 Only the most experienced serigrapher can do this without the danger of muddling up his original artistic conception. **1946** H. SHOKLER *Artists Man. Silk Screen Print Making* i. 25 Paper is to the serigrapher what canvas is to the painter. **1957** *Screen Printer & Display Producer* July 12 (*caption*) A general view of the serigraphic exhibition. *Ibid.* 16/1 Any screen process stencil which is the result of writing, drawing or painting directly upon the screen is now generally known as a 'serigraphic' stencil.

serine[2] (se·rīn). *Chem.* Formerly also **-in.** [ad. G. *serin* (E. Cramer 1865, in *Jrnl. für prakt. Chem.* XCVI. 93), f. L. *sēr-icum* silk: see -INE[5].] **a.** A colourless, crystalline amino-acid, $CH_2OH{\cdot}CHNH_2{\cdot}COOH$, which is widely distributed in animal proteins.

1880 *Jrnl. Chem. Soc.* XXXVIII. 713 Cramer's..serine is isomeric with amidohydroxypropionic acid. **1882** *Ibid.* XLII. 38 It..agrees in all its properties with Cramer's serin from silk, except that it is less soluble in water. **1908** HALL & DEFREN tr. *Abderhalden's Text-bk. Physiol. Chem.* viii. 149 Serine as it occurs in nature is lævo-rotatory. **1957** FOX & FOSTER *Introd. Protein Chem.* vii. 122 Serine is convertible to glycine in mammals, a capability that explains also its convertibility to heme. **1975** D. A. BENDER *Amino Acid Metabolism* (1978) iii. 59 Both serine and threonine have hydrophilic side-chains and therefore contribute to the hydrophilicity of proteins when they are in exposed regions of the chain.

b. *Comb.* In names of various enzymes which catalyse reactions of serine or serine residues, or reactions yielding serine.

1938 *Biochem. Jrnl.* XXXII. 403 The decay of *dl*-serine deaminase appears to be due to a loss from the cell by diffusion of some substance or substances acting as coenzyme. **1943** *Jrnl. Biol. Chem.* CL. 262 The desulfurase and serine dehydrase of mammalian tissue were found to be similar to those of the microorganisms. **1956** *Ibid.* CCXX. 775 Since the reaction we have studied mainly is the formation of serine, and because of the similarity to aldol type reactions, we propose the name serine aldolase for this enzyme system. **1967** *New Scientist* 17 Aug. 353/1 Organophosphorus pesticides..are known to act as competitive inhibitors of the 'serine esterase' group of enzymes. **1974** *Sci. Amer.* July 74/2 Serine proteases participate in digestion, in the formation and dissolution of blood clots, in the immune reaction to foreign cells and organisms, in the fertilization of the ovum by the spermatozoon.

‖ **seringueiro** (seriŋgē·ru). Also (*erron.*) **seringero.** [Pg., f. SERINGA.] In Brazil: a person employed to gather rubber.

1860 MAYNE REID *Odd People* 82 The 'seringero' has provided a large quantity of palm-nuts, with which he intends to make a fire for smoking the caoutchouc. **1880** [see SERINGA 2]. **1913** [see *ESTRADA]. **1934** *Times Lit. Suppl.* 15 Nov. 797/1 A Portuguese novelist, perhaps the only literary man who has ever actually worked as a *seringueiro*. **1968** R. E. POPPINO *Brazil* iv. 141 The rubber worker—known as a *seringueiro*—..also prepared his own crude shelter. **1970** E. B. BURNS *Hist. Brazil* v. 240 The dwindling number of Indians was pressed into service as *seringueiros*... The isolated, difficult life of the exploited *seringueiro* explained the recruitment problem.

serio-comedy. Add: Also *transf.*

1929 BLUNDEN *Nature in Eng. Lit.* v. 125 From this serio-comedy of the strawyard the [farmer's] boy raises his face to the setting Sun and..gets to bed. **1936** H. A. L. FISHER *Hist. Europe* II. xviii. 634 The fashionable ladies who played so active a part in this serio-comedy.

serio-comic, *a.* Add: **b.** as *sb.* (Earlier example.)

1895 [see *male impersonator* s.v. *MALE *sb.* 4].

serious, *a.* Add: **3.** Also *spec.* of music and literature (in contrast with 'light').

1901 G. B. SHAW *Three Plays for Puritans* p. xxiv, The Diabolonian position is new to the London playgoer of today, but not to lovers of serious literature. **1934** S. R. NELSON *All about Jazz* i. 14 To compare modern syncopation with serious music as an art form is manifestly ridiculous. **1942** H. HAYCRAFT *Murder for Pleasure* xii. 265 Many 'serious' writers manage to support their solider endeavours by turning their talents to occasional short magazine fiction. **1960** L. P. HARTLEY *Facial Justice* xxiii. 200 But to return to classical, or 'serious' music. **1971** 'E. CANDY' *Words for Murder Perhaps* ii. 25 You open a detective story in the mood in which you might attend a sherry party... But you approach a serious novel as you go to meet someone you greatly care for. **1974** *Country Life* 26 Dec. 1989/1 The BBC's serious and light music departments function as separate..entities.

8. *serious-minded* adj. (later examples), *-mindedly* adv.

1921 A. HUXLEY *Crome Yellow* vii. 71, I sometimes wonder whether Denis is altogether serious-minded, whether he isn't rather a dilettante. **1965** H. GOLD *Man who was not with It* xxxii. 310, I had a serious-minded mother. **1966** 'W. COOPER' *Memoirs of New Man* I. v. 64, I heard two people serious-mindedly handing them to and fro.

serir (sĕrīᵊ·ɹ). *Physical Geogr.* Pl. **serir, serirs.** [Arab. *serir* dry.] In Libya and Egypt: a flat area of desert strewn with rounded pebbles and boulders. Cf. *REG[2].

1886 *Encycl. Brit.* XXI. 149/2 Nearly all the rest of the Sahara consists in the main of undulating surfaces of rock.., vast tracts of water-worn pebbles (*serir*), and regions of sandy dunes. **1925** W. F. HUME *Geol. Egypt* I. iv. 88 The same undulating 'serir' pebble-strewn country extends to the west of the Nile Valley, forming low undulations which are nevertheless sufficiently developed for whole camel parties to become rapidly lost to sight. **1942** O. D. VON ENGELN *Geomorphol.* xviii. 411 In the Libyan Sahara similar surface sheets, there composed of coarse rounded pebbles, a pebble armor, are known as serir; in the western Sahara smaller rounded pebbles, tightly packed, constitute the reg. **1974** *Encycl. Brit. Micropædia* III. 486/2 Evaporation of capillary water may cause the precipitation of calcium carbonate, gypsum, and other salts that cement the pebbles together to form a desert conglomerate. In the western Sahara such a surface is known as a reg.., whereas in the eastern Sahara it is called a serir.

sermonette. Add: Also *transf.* and *fig.*

1943 E. GILLETT *Lit. of Eng.* xiv. 223 The tendency to allow digressions and sermonettes to swamp the main purpose of the novel. **1975** *Publishers Weekly* 23 June 72/3 Gavin is sincere and interesting, but too often he digresses into sermonettes that sound like echoes of the *National Review*. **1978** *Listener* 26 Jan. 110/2, I feel I should be issuing at least a sermonette from the mount.

Sernyl (sə̄·ɹnil). *Pharm.* Also **sernyl.** A proprietary name for *PHENCYCLIDENE.

1958 *Official Gaz.* (U.S. Patent Office) 9 Sept. TM 52/1 Parke, Davis & Company... *Sernyl*... For psychopharmacologic agents with anesthetic and analgesic properties. First use Nov. 22, 1957. **1959** *Antibiotic Med. & Clin. Therapy* VI. 79 Recently, laboratory observations indicated that phencyclidine (Sernyl) possessed central nervous system depressant properties associated with improvement in mood. **1964** C. WILLOCK *Enormous Zoo* vi. 107 Drugs so far used include..Sernyl. **1970** PASSMORE & ROBSON *Compan. Med. Stud.* II. v. 28/2 Phencyclidene (sernyl) was introduced as an analgesic agent, but has been found to produce psychotomimetic effects. **1974** [see *PHENCYCLIDENE].

sero-. Add: *sero-hepatitis* (earlier example); **se:roagglutina·tion,** agglutination of the cultured cells of a micro-organism by an antiserum, as showing the serological identity of the micro-organism with the one that gave rise to the antiserum; **se:ro-amnio·tic** *a.*, pertaining to the serosa and the amnion; **se·rodeme** *Biol.* [DEME *sb.*[2] in Dict. and Suppl.], an immunologically distinct strain of organisms; **se:rodifferentia·tion,** differentiation between micro-organisms by serological means; **se:roepidemio·logy,** the serological study of the prevalence and distribution of a pathogen in a population; so **se:roepidemiolo·gic, -lo·gical** *adjs.*; **se·rogroup,** a group of serotypes with similar but distinguishable serological reactions; hence as *v. trans.*, to assign to a particular serogroup; **se·rogrouping** *vbl. sb.*; **se·ro-immunity,** immunity conferred by the administration of antiserum; **seromu·coid** *Physiol.* [ad. It. *sieromucoide* (C. U. Zanetti 1903, in *Gazz. chim. ital.* XXXIII. I. 160)], a mucoprotein found in blood serum; **serone·gative** *a.*, opp. next; **seropo·sitive** *a.*, showing or accompanied by the presence of a characteristic serological reaction; hence **se:ro-positi·vity; se:rotaxo·nomy,** the use of the serological reactions and structural similarities of proteins from different animals to provide information about their taxonomic relationship; hence **se:rotaxono·mic** *a.*

1910 *Jrnl. Amer. Med. Assoc.* 12 Feb. 573/2 (*heading*) Seroagglutination of *Sporothrix schenkii*. **1975** *Jrnl. Clin. Microbiol.* II. 268 (*heading*) Seroagglutination test for identification of *Mycobacterium paratuberculosis*. **1890** K. MITSUKURI in *Anatomischer Anzeiger* V. 512 A connection—quite elongated and definite in later stages—between the amnion and the serous envelope separates them [*sc.* the extra-embryonic coelomic cavities of the two moieties of the amnion] to the very end of the development... This connection I propose to call the sero-amniotic connection. **1958** B. M. PATTEN *Found. Embryol.* xi. 183 The cavity between serosa and amnion (sero-amniotic cavity) is part of the extra-embryonic coelom. **1966** C. A. HOARE in *Ergebnisse der Mikrobiol. und Immunitätsforsch.* XXXIX. 55 A more suitable term [than 'type'] is 'deme'.., which denotes a population.. within a specified taxon.., and may be combined with an appropriate prefix... *T. evansi*..contains immunologically distinct strains, which..represent serodemes. **1978** *Nature* 25 May 300/2 We have transmitted through *Glossina morsitans morsitans* trypanosomes of the AnTat serodeme. **1960** *Virology* X. 376 (*heading*) A simple test for serodifferentiation of poliovirus strains within the same type. **1974** *Bull. World Health Organization* L. 479 This heterogeneous immune response permits the preparation of specific antisera for intratypic serodifferentiation. **1958** *Jrnl. Amer. Med. Assoc.* 31 May 541/1 This paper will report seroepidemiologic results associating the increase in influenza-pneumonia mortality..with the influenza virus. **1978** *Ibid.* 16 Jan. 210/1 To define the epidemiologic features of occupationally acquired hepatitis B infection among physicians, we conducted a sero-epidemiologic survey of physicians attending three American Medical Association conventions. **1959** *Amer. Jrnl. Public Health* XLIX. 847 (*heading*) A laboratory analysis of the 1957–1958 influenza outbreak in New York City. II. A seroepidemiological study. **1975** *Nature* 1 May 12/2 Limited seroepidemiological studies have shown that most individuals of a low socio-economic level had hepatitis antibodies. **1967** *Bull. World Health Organization* XXXVII. 79 (*heading*) WHO collaborative study on the sero-epidemiology of Rubella. **1977** *Lancet* 12 Nov. 1038/2 The seroepidemiology of herpes simplex virus (H.S.V.) type 2 infection in man has been hampered by difficulties in demonstrating antibodies specific for H.S.V. type 2 in sera with cross-reacting H.S.V. type 1 antibodies. **1954** WOLFF & BROOM in *Documenta Med. Geogr. & Tropica* VI. 92 When two or more serotypes show marked similarities in their serological reactions..it is convenient to assemble them into groups, which we suggest should be known as 'serogroups' (serological groups). **1962** *Austral. Jrnl. Exper. Biol. & Med. Sci.* XL. 84 We..propose that strain 'Robinson' be recognized as a new serotype in the *pyrogenes* serogroup with the designation *Leptospira robinsoni*. **1963** *Jrnl. Clin. Investigation* XLII. 989/2 Serogrouping of *E. coli* permitted the recognition of 25 instances of recurrent infection with a different serogroup ..and 24 instances of recurrence with the same serogroup. **1977** *Lancet* 29 Jan. 257/1 None of the other serogroups of streptococci (A, C, D, G and F) produce any pigment. **1977** *Jrnl. Clinical Path.* XXX. 834 (*heading*) Use of antiserum agar plates for serogrouping of meningococci. *Ibid.* 836 The meningococcal strains were serogrouped by slide-agglutination. **1839** *Lond. Med. Gaz.* XXIII. 570/1 By sero-hepatitis is meant inflammation of the serous or peritoneal tunic of the liver. **1907** *Jrnl. Amer. Med. Assoc.* 6 Apr. 1219/1 Sero-immunity to bile salts. **1975** *Amer. Jrnl. Epidemiol.* CI. 333/1 Most reports on sero-immunity have dealt with small children, following vaccine programs with very little information on maintenance of artificially induced antibody. **1931** *Biochem. Jrnl.* XXV. 1064 It is considered unlikely that the carbohydrate isolated from serum-albumin and globulin preparations was in reality derived from admixed seromucoid. **1955** *Methods Biochem. Anal.* II. 281 It is appropriate to replace the term plasma mucoprotein with the established term seromucoid. **1932** SCHAMBER & WRIGHT *Treatm. Syphilis* xxv. 404 (*table*) Two to 3 courses of combined therapy usually suffice for seronegative primary syphilis. **1977** *Lancet* 9 Apr. 811/2 A seronegative donor showed no response at any concentration of antigen. **1932** SCHAMBER & WRIGHT *Treatm. Syphilis* xxv. 417 The treatment of seronegative primary syphilis should continue for two years and for seropositive primary syphilis..for from two to three years. **1975** *Nature* 12 June 546/1 Seronegative and seropositive squirrels were housed in an isolated room in different cages, usually in groups of six. **1969** *Acta Path. & Microbiol. Scandinavica* LXXVII. 278 The numbers of sero-positive experimental mice are expressed as ratios of the numbers surviving because this gives a more accurate impression of the sero-positivity of each group. **1967** *Nature* 9 Sept. 1213/1 Systematics Association... Symposium on 'Chemotaxonomy and Serotaxonomy'. **1968** P. G. H. GELL in J. G. Hawkes *Chemotaxonomy & Serotaxonomy* vii. 74 The evidence that the heavy chains of other immunoglobulins were involved in the same evolutionary process comes from work on the allotypes. Here we return to studies rather closer to serotaxonomy. **1968** HAWKES & TUCKER in *Ibid.* viii. 77 The first stage of a serotaxonomic revision of the family Solanaceae is described in which seeds have been used as the source of saline soluble protein. **1971** *Nature* 9 Apr. 412/2 He is rather cautiously optimistic about the future possibilities of protein and DNA studies and of serotaxonomy.

seroconversion (sɪᵊrokǫnvɜ·ɹʃən). *Biol.* and *Med.* [f. SERO- + CONVERSION.] A change from a seronegative to a seropositive state.

1964 *Jrnl. Amer. Med. Assoc.* 18 May 639 (*heading*) Poliovirus shedding and seroconversion. **1968** *New Scientist* 28 Nov. 500/2 Successive tests then showed that there were nine seroconversions... Illnesses that suggested viral infection preceded seroconversion in four of the children. **1977** *Lancet* 15 Oct. 811/1 Vaccination of children in the first 6 months of life was unsuccessful—only 1 seroconversion in 58.

Hence **seroconve·rt** *v. intr.*, to acquire such sensitivity.

1969 *Amer. Jrnl. Dis. Children* CXVIII. 331/1 Antibody was slower to appear, titers were lower, one of the animals failed to seroconvert, and SN antibody was not detected. **1977** *Lancet* 18 June 1314/2 Of these [patients],..1 seroconverted to positive anti-HBs.

serologic (sɪᵊrǫlǫ·dʒɪk), *a.* [f. *SEROLOG(Y + -IC.] = next.

1910 *Jrnl. Amer. Med. Assoc.* 2 July 94/1 (*heading*) Vacuum bottles as aid in bacteriologic and serologic work. **1978** *Jrnl. R. Soc. Med.* LXXI. 362 By retrospective diagnosis on clinical and serologic grounds other episodes of LD have come to light.

serological, *a.* Substitute for def.: Pertaining to, by means of, or involving serology; (of strains of micro-organism) distinguishable by serology. (Later examples.)

1917 *Lancet* 8 Dec. 847/1 Arkwright..was unable by serological methods to establish any specific differences between epidemic and sporadic strains of the meningococcus. **1931** *Times Lit. Suppl.* 31 Dec. 1054/4 Serological diagnosis of cancer. **1946** *Nature* 14 Dec. 879/2 The very similar chemical and physical properties and behaviour of the specific blood-group factors..forced one to rely on serological techniques for their differentiation. **1955** *New Biol.* XIX. 9 Pneumococci are classified into various serological types on the basis of the polysaccharides which form their capsules. **1966** *Punch* 7 Dec. 863/2 Recently the British Veterinary Association were given figures which showed how much sub-clinical ill-health may perhaps be due to *brucella.* Of three hundred and nine vets examined sixty-three per cent had serological evidence of infection. **1977** *Dædalus* Summer 165 It took a great deal of time, and work, before it could be understood that.. there were more than forty different serological types of the principal streptococcal species responsible for human disease.

Hence **serolo·gically** *adv.*

1913 *Jrnl. Amer. Med. Assoc.* 6 Sept. 808/2 Serologically all nervous diseases are divided into two general and easily distinguishable classes, the negative and positive types. **1976** *Ann. Rev. Microbiol.* XXX. 107 Each fungus contains two serologically unrelated and electrophoretically distinguishable viruses.

serologist (sɪᵊrǫ·lŏdʒɪst). [f. next + -IST.] A student or practitioner of serology.

1914 *Lancet* 25 Apr. 1216/2 (*heading*) Appointment of serologist in Calcutta. **1939** *Jrnl. Amer. Med. Assoc.* 1 Apr. 1245/1 The physical condition of the patient was not known to the serologist at the time the blood studies were made. **1959** M. BURNET *Clonal Selection Theory of Acquired Immunity* iii. 30 As every serologist knows, absorption of the serum with a series of more or less closely related bacterial suspensions will leave behind antibody solutions of quite distinct functional character. **1976** 'J. Ross' *I know what it's like to Die* xxx. 199 'Is there any news about the blood in the Ford?'.. 'Sorry... The serologist was out.'

serology (sɪᵊrǫ·lŏdʒɪ). [f. SERO- + -LOGY.] The study of blood serum; *spec.* the study of pathogens and other potential antigens by means of the immune responses which they induce as evidenced in blood serum; also, the serological characteristics *of* a disease or individual.

1909 *Jrnl. Amer. Med. Assoc.* 11 Sept. 891/2 (*heading*) Serology of syphilis. **1921** *Glasgow Herald* 22 Feb. 7 Medicine, surgery, and prevention of infectious diseases had been utterly revolutionised since bacteriology and serology were developed. **1948** *Nature* 20 Mar. 428/1 The studies in systematic serology which have been conducted at Rutgers University since 1925. **1956** *Jrnl. Mammalogy* XXXVII. 11 (*heading*) Comparative serology of carnivores. **1977** *Blut* XXXV. 165 (*heading*) Erythrocyte serology of some malignant diseases.

serosa (sɪ̆rō̆ᵘ·sǎ). *Anat.* and *Med.* [f. mod.L. *membrāna serōsa* serous membrane.] A serous membrane; *spec.* (*a*) those lining the peritoneal, pleural, and pericardial sacs; † (*b*) the chorion of a bird embryo.

1890 BILLINGS *Med. Dict., Serosa.* 1. The membrane of the bird embryo corresponding to the mammalian chorion. 2. Serous membrane. **1898** A. S. PACKARD *Text-bk. Entomol.* 533 The *serosa*..forms a closed sac which covers the whole surface of the egg. **1921** B. M. PATTEN *Early Embryol. of Chick* xi. 87 The albumen-sac..is surrounded by folds of serosa, and the allantois after its establishment develops within the serosa, between it and the amnion. Thus the serosa eventually encompasses the embryo itself and all the other extra-embryonic members. **1964** *Urologia Internationalis* XVII. 14 Reconstruction of the urinary bladder was done after subtotal vesicosectomy. One method employed Teflon lined by serosa.

serosal (sɪ̆rō̆ᵘ·sǎl), *a. Anat.* and *Med.* [f. L. *serōs-us*, f. *ser-um* SERUM + -AL.] Of or pertaining to serosa or serum.

1949 *Jrnl. Physiol.* CX. 40 The serosal surface of the intestine. **1958** B. M. PATTEN *Found. Embryol.* xi. 187 There is thus formed a double layer of mesoderm, the serosal component of which is somatic mesoderm and the allantoic component of which is splanchnic mesoderm. **1968** [see *MESOTHELIAL *a.*]. **1976** *Path. Ann.* XI. 4 (*caption*) Colonic wall with full-thickness ischemic necrosis. The inflammatory infiltrate is situated in the serosal region.

serositis (sɪᵊrosəɪ·tɪs). *Path.* [f. L. *serōs-us* serous + -ITIS.] Inflammation of serous membrane.

1892 F. P. FOSTER *Illustr. Encycl. Med. Dict.* IV. 2788/1 Serositis. *Ibid.*, *Multiple serositis*, simultaneous inflammatory effusion into several serous sacs. **1905** H. A. HARE *Text-bk. Pract. of Med.* 465 The pericardium suffers from a chronic hyperplastic or fibroid inflammatory process, which likewise affects the serous membranes elsewhere, whence the name 'multiple serositis'. **1926** *Jrnl. Amer. Med. Assoc.* 24 Apr. 1323/2 (*heading*) Lipiodol in diagnosis and treatment of tuberculous serositis. **1961** R. D. BAKER *Essent. Path.* v. 92 Wherever an infarct extends to a serous surface it produces serositis.

serotinal (sɪ̆rō̆ᵘ·tɪnǎl), *a. Biol.* [f. as SEROTINE *a.* and *sb.*[2] + -AL.] Autumnal, serotine.

1898 *Minnesota Bot. Stud.* II. 19 The psoraleas, prairie clovers and blazing stars would probably occur to all as among the most abundant of the secondary species in the vernal, estival and serotinal aspects of the prairies respectively. **1959** *Insectes Sociaux* I. 103 Serotinal workers showed least success, callow workers produced an intermediate group of larvae, and vernal workers produced the best growth and development.

serotine, *sb.*[1] Substitute for def.: A small brown bat belonging to the genus Eptesicus, esp. the European *E. serotinus.* Also *attrib.*, as *serotine bat.* (Later examples.)

1903 H. JOHNSTON *Brit. Mammals* 86 It has been named the 'serotine' bat from its habit of only making its appearance late in the evening. **1910** G. H. BARRETT-HAMILTON *Hist. Brit. Mammals* 131 In the British Isles the Serotine is entirely confined to the south of England. **1934** G. C. SHORTRIDGE *Mammals S.W. Afr.* I. 62 On first appearing Serotine Bats usually fly backwards and forwards with comparative regularity. **1965** D. R. ROSEVERE *Bats W. Afr.* 246 The Serotine Bats are widespread throughout Africa, Europe, Asia, America and Australia. **1971** L. H. MATTHEWS *Life Mammals* II. iii. 104 The most familiar members of it [*sc.* the genus *Eptesicus*] are the big brown bat..of North America, and the Serotine..of Europe and Asia..and west Africa.

serotinous, *a.* Add: **2.** *Bot.* Of a cone: remaining long unopened, slow to release seed.

1880 *Bot. Gaz.* V. 54 How long pine seeds retain their vitality when enclosed in serotinous cones which sometimes occur on certain species has probably never been very carefully noted. **1911** *Forestry Q.* IX. 9 Cones may persist on the branches from 10 to 25 years, or even longer, and are serotinous. **1942** H. I. BALDWIN *Forest Tree Seed* vi. 83 McIntyre suggests that the seed is well preserved in the cones of the so-called serotinous pines because fungi are excluded. **1970** *Canad. Jrnl. Bot.* XLVIII. 1805/2 Genetic control of cone serotiny has been demonstrated in jack pine..where the serotinous cone class was suggested to be homozygous recessive.

Hence **sero·tiny,** the property or state of being serotinous.

1960 *Forest Sci.* VI. 194 Jack pine is one of the ten North American pines whose cones exhibit some measure of serotiny. **1970** [see above]. **1977** J. L. HARPER *Population Biol. of Plants* xx. 629 The evolution of serotiny in pines ensures that seed is stored in cones on the tree and only released to germinate after a fire.

serotonergic (sɪᵊrŏtonɜ·ɹdʒɪk), *a. Physiol.* [f. next + Gr. ἔργ-ον work + -IC: cf. *ADRENERGIC, *CHOLINERGIC *adjs.*] Of a nerve ending: that liberates, and is stimulated by, serotonin. Also **se:rotonine·rgic** *a.* in the same sense.

1957 *Ann. N.Y. Acad. Sci.* LXVI. 598 They see mental disturbance as an imbalance between adrenergic or 'serotonergic' inhibition and cholinergic excitation in the more susceptible cerebral synapses. **1967** *Activitas Nervosa Superior* IX. 207 (*heading*) Integrated effect of psychotropic drugs on the balance of cholino-, adreno-, and serotoninergic processes in the brain. **1974** *Sci. Amer.* Feb. 84/2 There is no escaping the conclusion that nutrient intake does alter the amount of serotonin present in the serotoninergic neurons of the brain. **1977** *Lancet* 9 Apr. 812/2 The results suggest that in the first period of head injury, patients with a frontotemporal-lobe contusion show a decreased cerebral dopaminergic activity as well as a decreased serotonergic activity.

serotonin (sɪᵊrŏtō̆ᵘ·nɪn). *Biochem.* [f. SERO- + TON(IC *a.* and *sb.* + -IN[1].] 5-Hydroxytryptamine; a monoamine neurotransmitter, $C_{10}H_{12}N_2O$, active in the production of vasoconstriction and anaphylactic shock, and in the regulation of cycles of body temperature and sleep.

1948 M. M. RAPPORT et al. in *Science* 24 Sept. 329 The general behaviour of the crystalline substance is suggestive of its homogeneity. We would like provisionally to name it *serotonin*, which indicates that its source is serum and its activity is one of causing constriction. **1949** *Jrnl. Biol. Chem.* CLXXX. 969 A recommendation has been made to reserve the name serotonin for the indole amine rather than the previously isolated complex. **1955** *Sci. News Let.* 19 Mar. 179/3 Serotonin has a chemical structure something like LSD-25. **1970** *Times* 4 May 11/8 The profound changes exerted by PCPA [*sc.* parachlorophenylalanine] on the cats' activities indicate the pervasive role played by serotonin in regulating the animals' drive and behaviour. **1974** M. C. GERALD *Pharmacol.* xvii. 324 There is a large body of evidence that links LSD's actions to its effects at serotonin receptor sites in the central nervous system. **1980** *Brit. Med. Jrnl.* 29 Mar. 939/3 There is also the question whether all the serotonin taken up by platelets in such an experiment is.. incorporated into the same pool as endogenous serotonin.

serotype (sɪᵊ·rotəɪp), *sb. Microbiol.* [f. SERO- + TYPE *sb.*[1]] A serologically distinguishable strain of a micro-organism.

1954 WOLFF & BROOM in *Documenta de Medicina Geographica et Tropica* VI. 82 They differed from authentic strains of *L*[*eptospira*] *icterohaemorrhagiae* and from all the other serotypes. *Ibid.* 85 We suggest the term 'serotype' (serological type)..should be adopted to designate the basic taxon of a serological classification based on the agglutinogens of the leptospires. **1963** *Lancet* 12 Jan. 92/2 Antibodies against all three serotypes are found in many samples of human and animal serum. **1976** *Ann. Rev. Microbiol.* XXX. 160 The serotypes of the sweet potato pathogens were similar but quantitatively distinct from the stone fruit tree pathogens.

So **seroty·pic** *a.*, of or pertaining to serotypes.

1953 *Jrnl. Immunol.* LXXI. 232 (*heading*) Serotypic recombination in *Salmonella.* **1973** *Infection & Immunity* VII. 499 Some recent isolates had different serotypic behaviour before and after purification, and..the widely distributed prototype strain T960 was composed of at least two different serotypes.

serotype (sɪᵊ·rotəɪp), *v. Microbiol.* [f. prec.] *trans.* To assign to a particular serotype. So **se·rotyping** *vbl. sb.*

1968 *Manch. Guardian Weekly* 29 Aug. 9 In recent years Portsmouth has seen 331 cases of a particular Salmonella infection: of these 271 have been traced by serotyping through the abattoir and back to the farm. **1970** *Nature* 28 Nov. 827/1 The serotyping of histocompatibility antigens relies heavily on complement-dependent serologic reactions. **1975** *Jrnl. Clinical Microbiol.* I. 469 A rapid and economical micromethod for serotyping strains of *Mycobacterium avium* is described. **1976** *Ann. Rev. Microbiol.* XXX. 183 Most investigators involved in the investigation of the role of T-strain mycoplasmas in nongonococcal urethritis..have ..made no attempt to serotype the ureaplasmas isolated. **1977** *Lancet* 8 Oct. 774/1 Serotyping and biotyping indicated that all 8 isolates were unrelated.

serozem, var. *SIEROZEM. **Serpa,** obs. var. *SHERPA.

Serpasil (sɜ̄·ɹpǎsɪl). *Pharm.* [f. *RE)SERP(INE.] A proprietary name for reserpine.

1953 *Trade Marks Jrnl.* 29 Apr. 358/2 *Serpasil*... Ciba Limited... Switzerland. **1953** *Official Gaz.* (U.S. Patent Office) 20 Oct. 564/2 Ciba Pharmaceutical Products, Inc... *Serpasil.* For sedative, hypotensive, and spasmolytic agent... Claims use since Mar. 17, 1953. **1954** *Jrnl. Pharmacol. & Exper. Therapeutics* CX. 205 This alkaloid, Serpasil (formerly known as Reserpine), produces a prolonged central nervous system depression in laboratory animals. **1963** *Times* 31 May 19/5 Among the antihypertensives doctors showed great interest in Serpasil. **1967** H. BECKMAN *Dilemmas in Drug Therapy* 175/1 Usual dosages of the Rauwolfia preparations employed in treating hypertension are as follows:..reserpine (Reserpoid, Serpasil, etc.), orally, 0·25–1·0 mg. daily in two or three divided doses.

serpent, *sb.* Add: **1. e.** A pale green fashion shade.

1895 *Montgomery Ward Catal.* Spring & Summer 12/1 Plain colored Gros Grain Silk... Colors: Green, prune,.. mode, serpent, tan. **1927** *Daily Express* 5 Apr. 6 Navy, Ash, Serpent, Pink.

7. The instrument is now enjoying revived use in the performance of early music. (Later examples.)

1928 *Punch* 2 May 485/1 The Serpent is a bass wind-instrument of wood, so-called from its shape. **1976** *Early Music* Oct. 477/2 We learn how Boosey and Hawkes bend brass tubes, but not why, or how, the cornett and serpent are bent.

10. c. *serpent-wise* adj.

1933 W. DE LA MARE *Fleeting* 144 Her eyes Stirred not a hair's breadth, serpent-wise.

f. *serpent-wise* adv.

1927 E. SITWELL *Rustic Elegies* 40 The wicked knife flashed serpent-wise.

serpenticone (sɜɹpe·ntɪkō̆ᵘn). *Palæont.* [f. *serpenti-*, comb. form of SERPENT *sb.* (see -I-) + CONE *sb.*[1]] An ammonoid in which the whorls are slender and overlap very little, so that the shell resembles a coiled snake.

1923 H. H. SWINNERTON *Outl. Palæont.* x. 214 The forms assumed by these derivatives [of cadicones] were determined mainly by modification of the whorl shape in two directions. In the one the venter and dorsum became arched; the outer consequently embraced the inner whorls and the umbilicus became narrower and even disappeared. The shell thus produced was globose in shape and is described as a sphærocone... In the other modification the whorl increased in height..; the effect of this was to produce a shell with a widely open umbilicus and having the appearance of a coiled snake. The descriptive term serpenticone is therefore applied to this type of shell. **1970** R. M. BLACK *Elements Palaeont.* viii. 87 *Dactylioceras*..has an evolute shell with a wide, shallow umbilicus; the whorl section is oval. It is a typical serpenticone.

serpentine, *sb.* Add: **10. c.** A lake or canal of a winding shape, esp. the one constructed in Hyde Park in 1730.

1837 W. TAYLER *Jrnl.* 2 Jan. in J. Burnett *Useful Toil* (1974) II. 176 Went round Hyde Park, saw some thousands of people sliding and skaiting on the Serpentine. **1853** GEO. ELIOT *Let.* 22 Oct. (1954) II. 120, I am hoping for a row..on the Serpentine, which is really almost as good as a lake. **1885** C. M. YONGE *Nuttie's Father* II. xiii. 157 He said he'd take him to the Serpentine to sail his ship. **1971** *Country Life* 2 Sept. 546/2 By 1747 he [*sc.* George Anson of Shugborough] had erected a Chinese house on a little island formed by a new canal or serpentine. **1977** P. WILLIS *Charles Bridgeman* iv. 96 When Bridgeman's widow in her Petition to the Lords of the Treasury asks for money for making 'the lake in Hyde Park' she is obviously referring to the Serpentine.

serpentine, *a.* Add: **3.** Also, esp. in reference to canals or lakes.

1730 *London Jrnl.* 26 Sept. 2/3 Next Monday they begin upon the Serpentine River and Royal Mansion in Hyde-Park. **1824** J. C. LOUDON *Encycl. Gardening* (ed. 2) III. iv. 1011 Those wavy serpentine canals..are never mistaken for natural scenes. **1948** C. HUSSEY in M. Jourdain *Work of William Kent* 23 The most famous Serpentine Lake, that in Hyde Park, was ordered by Queen Caroline and is probably due to Bridgeman.

11. a. serpentine superphosphate *N.Z.*, a mixture of superphosphate and crushed serpentinite, used as a fertilizer.

1941 ELLIOTT & LYNCH in *N.Z. Jrnl. Agric.* 15 Sept. 179/1 The name serpentine superphosphate will be used in future in place of 'silico superphosphate', as it is a more accurate description of the material. It is made by mixing three parts of hot, newly-made superphosphate with one part of ground serpentine and allowing the mixture to 'mature' in heaps for several days. **1965** G. J. WILLIAMS *Econ. Geol. N.Z.* x. 143/1 Serpentinite is quarried in considerable quantity in New Zealand for the manufacture of 'serpentine-superphosphate'.

serpentinite (sɜ̄·ɹpĕntinəit). *Petrogr.* [f. SERPENTINE *sb.* + -ITE[1].] A rock consisting largely of serpentine or related minerals.

1936 G. C. SELFRIDGE in *Amer. Mineralogist* XXI. 463 The term serpentinite is suggested for rocks composed of serpentine or antigorite or a mixture of both. **1956** *Amer. Jrnl. Sci.* CCLIV. 201 Bare *roches moutonées* of serpentinite stand out from the heather. **1965** [see *serpentine superphosphate* s.v. *SERPENTINE *a.* 11 a]. **1977** A. HALLAM *Planet Earth* 137 Serpentinites are rocks originally very rich in olivine that has been entirely converted to serpentine.

Hence **serpentini·tic** *a.*

1975 *Nature* 25 Dec. 701/2 The ubiquitous association of ultrabasic (mostly serpentinitic) rocks with glaucophane-schists may be represented here by the serpentinite-dunite of Gibbs Island and the glaucophane-schists of Smith Island.

serpentinize, *v.* **2.** (Earlier example.)

1886 [see *PERIDOTITIC *a.*].

serpierite (sɜ̄·ɹpīᵊrəit). *Min.* [a. F. *serpierite* (A. des Cloizeaux 1881, in *Bull. de la Soc. min. de France* IV. 92), f. the name of J. B. *Serpieri,* 19th-cent. Italian engineer: see -ITE[1].] A hydrated basic sulphate of copper, zinc, and calcium found as crusts or aggregates of small pale blue orthorhombic crystals.

1892 E. S. DANA *Dana's Syst. Min.* (ed. 6) 963 Serpierite... Crystals minute... Occurs on smithsonite at the zinc mines of Laurium, Greece. **1927** *Mineral. Mag.* XXI. 387 Smithsonite ($ZnCO_3$) is also tolerably abundant ..and it is in cavities of this smithsonite that the serpierite occurs. **1964** *Amer. Mineralogist* XLIX. 1145 Devillite and serpierite were identified on the basis of morphology, optics, and microchemical tests.

serpulid. Add: Also *attrib.* or as *adj.*

1935 *Discovery* Apr. 98/2 The only growths..are..two species of serpulid worms. **1963** R. P. DALES *Annelids* 15 The most specialized tube-dwellers are the sabellid and serpulid fan-worms. **1980** *Nature* 29 May 323/1 The coarse and medium sand fractions consist of rock and pelecypod fragments, aragonitic and calcitic algae, serpulid tubes and peneroplid Foraminifera.

Serrano (serā·no). Also **serrano; † Serano.** [a. Sp. *serrano* of the mountains; a highlander.] (A member of) an Indian people of southern California; the Uzo-Aztecan language of these Indians, a component of the Takic branch.

1858 *San Francisco Bull.* 5 Nov., The true native Americans of the wild forests—such as the Yumas,.. Mohaves and Serranos—predominate. **1876** *Ann. Rep. U.S. Geogr. Surveys West of 100th Meridian* III. 553 Case-inflection is formed here..by adding to nouns post-positions as suffixes:..tumuet, in Serrano, mountain. **1896** F. BOAS in *Proc. Amer. Assoc. Advancem. Sci.* 1895 XLIV. 261 The Serano call themselves Mā'ringayam. *Ibid.* 262 The Serano is less closely related to the other Shoshonean dialects than these are among themselves. **1907** A. L. KROEBER *Shoshonean Dialects Calif.* I. 69 The Gitanemuk..vocabulary was..obtained at Tule river reservation... The vocabulary is the first that has been printed of this dialect, although it differs but little from Serrano, which has been known for years. **1921** *Glasgow Herald* 17 May 3/8 In due time he will become a 'Serrano' as the inhabitants of the highland regions are contemptuously styled by the dwellers in the cities of the coast. **1927** D. H. LAWRENCE *Mornings in Mexico* 84 The serranos, the Indians from the hills, wearing their little conical black felt hats. **1946** C. MCWILLIAMS *Southern Calif. Country* 26 The Serranos and the Gabrieleno were associated with the Mission San Gabriel. **1969** J. MANDER *Static Soc.* vi. 158 The *serranos* are pure Indian. They are the direct descendants of the Incas, and of the tribes subjugated by the Incas; and they speak Quechua in preference to Spanish. **1974** *Encycl. Brit. Micropædia* IX. 73/2 In the early 1970s, there were fewer than 400 Serrano proper remaining. **1977** *Language* LIII. 459 The Serrano element which L gives as *-nuk,* base /-nowk(ɨ-)/, shows up as *-nuk* only in 3sg. *pɨ-nuk.*

‖ **serré** (sere), *a.* [Fr., pa. pple. of *serrer* to close together.] Compact, logical; constricted by grief or emotion.

a **1854** J. S. MILL *Early Draft Autobiogr.* (1961) 115 Our debates..habitually consisted of the strongest arguments & most philosophic principles which either side was able to produce, thrown often into close & *serré* confutations of one another. **1908** D. H. LAWRENCE *Let.* 9 Oct. (1962) I. 28 My heart is '*serré*'—I shall soon have nothing inside my chest but the spent fragments of my organ of affection. **1931** T. S. ELIOT *Sel. Essays* (1932) VII. 448 Whether the transition is cogent or not, is merely a question of whether the mind is *serré* or *dolié.*

‖ **sertão** (ser·tauŋ). *Geogr.* Also † **Sertam; sertao, Sertão.** Pl. **sertãos, sertões** (se·rtoiŋʃ). [Pg.] The name of an arid, barren region, characterized by caatinga, in the interior of Pernambuco and neighbouring states in NE Brazil; also applied to other areas in Brazil of similar character. Also, more widely, the remote interior or outback of Brazil.

1816 H. KOSTER *Trav. in Brazil* vi. 77 The trees had mostly lost their leaves. I had now entered upon the Sertam, and surely it deserves the name. **1851** *Illustr. Catal. Gt. Exhib.* v. 1429/2 The cap is made in the Sertaô (the interior) of the province of Pernambuco. **1876** *Encycl. Brit.* IV. 226/1 Except on the loftiest mountains, and on the wide *sertãos,* the vegetation of Brazil is luxuriant beyond description. **1903** W. R. FISHER tr. *A. F. W. Schimper's Plant-Geogr.* III. iii. 275 In contrast with its southern portion, the middle part of Central Brazil, the so-called Sertão district, possesses a xerophilous woodland climate. **1926** R. NASH *Conquest of Brazil* iv. 144 This Negro-Indian cross was considerable only in the lawless sertões of Matto Grosso. **1930** C. F. JONES *S. Amer.* xxxiii. 471 The physical landscape of Northeast Brazil consists of three major divisions: marginal lowlands; *sertão,* parched uplands of brushwood and grasses..; *serra,* elevated mountain zones. **1950** E. G. ASHTON *S. Amer.* iv. 51 With a rather more generous rainfall on the *sertãos*..the characteristic vegetation resembles the savanna of the Matto Grosso. **1961** *Times* 8 Aug. 9/7 President Kubitschek's decision to move the capital from Rio to the heart of the undeveloped *sertao.* **1966** K. WEBB tr. *Pohl & Zepp's Latin Amer.* ii. 43 A particular vegetation type of these drier lands is the *caatinga* of the north-east, the *sertão.* This region of semi-desert has a vegetation cover made up of sparse thorn forest... *Sertão* in this sense means a particular place—the dry interior of north-east Brazil; in a more general usage *Sertão* means the sparsely inhabited backlands of the interior of Brazil. It is the equivalent of the Australian 'outback'. **1971** P. C. C. GARNHAM *Progress in Parasitology* ix. 191 The scene is laid in the sertão and its wide empty spaces in northern Minas Gerais.

Hence **sertanista** (-ani·sta), one engaged in activity in the *sertão*; one knowledgeable about the *sertão* and its inhabitants.

1944 S. PUTNAM tr. *E. da Cunha's Rebellion in Backlands* i. 45 The northern *sertanistas*..were fully a match for the bandeirantes of the south. **1973** *Daily Colonist* (Victoria, B.C.) 22 June 5/2 Francisco Meireles and the two other sertanistas (Indian experts),..flew from Belem.

Sertoli (sɜɹtōᵘ·li). *Anat.* The name of Enrico *Sertoli* (1842–1910), Italian histologist, used *attrib.*, with *of,* and in the possessive, to designate a type of somatic cell described by him, found in the walls of the seminiferous tubules.

1880 E. KLEIN *Atlas of Histol.* xxxi. 270 Inside this *membrana propria* are several layers of epithelial cells, the seminal cells... They correspond to the germ-cells of Sertoli. **1888** *Buck's Handbk. Med. Sci.* VI. 522/2 Next to the tunica comes a layer... This layer contains two kinds of cells: First, the large Sertoli's cells, as they may be called after their discoverer. **1901** *Gray's Anat.* (ed. 15) 1004 The supporting cells, or cells of Sertoli. **1930** W. BLOOM *A. A. Maximow's Text-bk. Histol.* xxxi. 595 The Sertoli cells in a seminiferous tubule with active spermatogenesis are very infrequent in comparison with the number of spermatogenic cells. *Ibid.,* The sustentacular cells or the cells of Sertoli. **1965** LEE & KNOWLES *Animal Hormones* iii. 65 In many vertebrates oestrogens are secreted by the testis, probably by the Sertoli cells, but whether this hormone has a physiological action is still in doubt.

serum. Add: **2. b.** *serum jaundice, rash, urticaria*; **serum broth** *Bacteriology,* a broth (*BROTH *sb.* 1 b) containing added serum.

1934 L. E. H. WHITBY *Med. Bacteriol.* (ed. 2) ix. 109 Salicin serum broth..is an excellent selective medium for *Streptococcus pyogenes.* **1979** H. MCLEAVE *Borderline Case* v. 53 The tubes of serum broth and tissue culture supplied by WHO. **1945** *Jrnl. Amer. Med. Assoc.* 28 July 911/1 (*heading*) Transmission experiments in serum jaundice and infectious hepatitis. **1908** *Glasgow Med. Jrnl.* LXIX. 277 The most obvious and constant features of the symptom-complex are the skin eruptions, or serum rash. **1905** *Practitioner* May 665 The duration of serum urticaria varies within somewhat wide limits.

c. Used *attrib.* (with or without a following hyphen) to denote (the concentration of) substances in the serum.

1958 J. B. MIALE *Lab. Med.—Hematol.* viii. 372 When the iron deficiency is caused by inadequate utilization of iron a *decreased* serum iron concentration and *increased* storage of iron in the tissues are usually seen. **1959** *Jrnl Physiol.* CXLVI. 353 All the serum proteins are capable of binding thyroxine to some extent. **1960** LEAVELL & THORUP *Clin. Hematol.* iv. 187 The normal level of serum bilirubin on cord blood is considered to be from 0·8 to 2·6 mg. per 100 ml. **1961** *Lancet* 26 Aug. 492/2 Treatment of atherosclerosis..may best be directed towards improving fat tolerance as well as reducing specific serum-lipid fractions. *Ibid.* 2 Sept. 499/1 The associations of high serum-cholesterol levels with coronary heart-disease do not necessarily indicate any *causal* relationship. **1962** *Ibid.* 22 Dec. 1293/1 There was no correlation on admission between the degree of weight deficit and the serum-transaminase levels. **1977** J. F. FIXX *Compl. Bk. Running* i. 5 In Southern California not long ago, fifty-eight doctors were given physical exams... More than half had high serum lipid levels.

d. Special Combs.: **serum agglutination,** agglutination of antigens by components of serum; **serum disease,** serum sickness; **serum hepatitis,** a viral hepatitis transmitted by injections of blood serum; **serum reaction,** serum sickness; **serum sickness** [tr. G. *serumkrankheit* (C. von Pirquet 1903, in *Wiener klin. Wochenschr.* XVI. 1244/2)], anaphylactic reaction to injected foreign serum.

1914 *Jrnl. Hygiene* XIV. 264 In order to be able to observe serum agglutination and acid agglutination with the same bacterial extract the bacilli from a 24 to 48 hrs. agar slope were washed off with 10 c.c. of distilled water and the resulting emulsion was centrifuged. **1970** W. H. PARKER *Health & Dis. in Farm Animals* xii. 161 An infected cow will give a positive reaction to the serum agglutination test. **1908** *Glasgow Med. Jrnl.* LXIX. 277 (*heading*) The serum disease in man after single and repeated doses. **1951** Serum disease [see *serum sickness* below]. **1943** *Lancet* 16 Jan. 83/1 (*heading*) Measles serum hepatitis. **1946** *Med. Clinics N. Amer.* XXX. 1408 'Virus hepatitis'..includes both infectious hepatitis..and homologous serum hepatitis. **1971** *New Scientist* 25 Mar. 676/1 This work promises a screening method which should help eliminate the danger of serum hepatitis developing after blood transfusions. **1905** *Practitioner* May 664 In cases of relapse, or of a second attack of diphtheria, the serum reaction may be very marked. **1916** *Arch. Internal Med.* XVIII. 497 Most of the cases of serum sickness occurred during convalescence from pneumonia. **1951** B. SCHICK tr. *von Pirquet & Schick's Serum Sickness* i. 5 We have abandoned the expression 'serum exanthema'... In its place we have proposed the name 'serum disease' or 'serum sickness'. **1970** W. H. PARKER *Health & Dis. in Farm Animals* xxi. 289 The most important practical significance of anaphylaxis in farm animals is that in the treatment of disease 'serum sickness' may follow the repeated use of serum from another species.

servagerous, var. *SAVAGEROUS *a.*

serval. Add: Also *serval cat.*

1919 F. W. FITZSIMONS *Nat. Hist. S. Afr.: Mammals* I. 142 These Serval Cats often break cover. **1933** N. DOUGLAS *Looking Back* II. 340 Somebody shot a serval cat.

servaline, *a.* Substitute for etym.: [a. mod.L. specific name of *Felis servalina* (W. Ogilby 1839, in *Proc. Zool. Soc.* 94), f. SERVAL + -INE[1].] and add: used to designate a serval in a darker colour phase than usual, with less obvious markings, once considered a separate species. Also as *sb.* (Later examples.)

1915 G. AYLMER in *Proc. Zool. Soc.* 154 The differences between the Servals and the Servaline Cats are of no systematic importance. **1964** L. S. CRANDALL *Managem. Wild Mammals in Captivity* 364 Specimens with markings reduced almost to dots were once distinguished under the name of servaline cat. **1970** DORST & DANDELOT *Field Guide Larger Mammals Afr.* 138 The servaline is a mere colour phase.

servant, *sb.* Add: **1.** *servant of all work* (earlier example); *servants' hall* (earlier examples).

c **1702** C. FIENNES, *Journeys* (1947) I. 55 Just behind the hall is the Servants hall. **1785** G. WASHINGTON *Diaries* 12 Mar. (1925) II. 349 In a line with the East end of my Kitchen, and Servants' Hall. **1819** *Morning Post* 14 Jan. 1 (Advt.), Wanted immediately, a servant of all-work, where others are kept for the children.

5. *servant-class, -problem, -trouble, -wife.*

1876 C. M. YONGE *Womankind* xxvii. 236 To raise the notions of the servant and factory-classes about marriage.

1920 'O. DOUGLAS' *Penny Plain* xiii. 134 Mawson..belonged to that fast disappearing body, the real servant class. **1916** A. BENNETT *These Twain* III. xvii. 361 The servant problem had been growing acute. **1973** R. LEWIS *Blood Money* viii. 117, I suppose you see it as somewhat anachronistic—a young girl 'in service'... But you won't be here to discuss the servant problem, Inspector Crow. **1859** GEO. ELIOT *Let.* 26 Feb. (1954) III. 26 The servant-trouble seems less mountainous to me than it did the other day. **1977** A. WILSON *Strange Ride of Rudyard Kipling* vi. 272 Carrie Kipling['s]..diaries are entirely mundane..financial transactions..servant troubles. **1906** J. JOYCE *Let.* 3 Dec. (1966) II. 199 Servant-wife blows her nose in the letter and lawyer confronts the mistress.

serve, *sb.*² Add: **3.** In fig. phr. *to give* (someone) *a serve*: to deal roughly with; to criticize or reprimand sharply. *Austral. slang.*

1974 STACKPOLE & TRENGROVE *Not just for Openers* 104, I continued to give Snow a bit of a serve. **1977** *Australian* 1 June 3 He was glad to be leaving and he would be giving the country a serve in an unnamed English newspaper if it was willing to pay enough for his views. **1980** *Daily Tel.* 25 June 17/3 He debunks the fashionable diets but also criticises doctors for not speaking out about bad eating habits. 'I give them a little serve,' he said, using an Australian expression.

serve, *v.*¹ Add: **III. 33.** (Later *fig.* examples.)

1884 L. A. TOLLEMACHE *Safe Studies* 359 The violent recoil against materialism which..has induced many good..persons to sell their scientific birthright and to serve tables. **1906** F. POLLOCK *Let.* 28 Dec. in *Pollock-Holmes Lett.* (1942) I. 136 Such men should not be put to serve the tables of university routine.

35. d. Phr. *serve-yourself*, used *attrib.* of a shop, restaurant, etc., where the customer serves himself.

1937 M. HILLIS *Orchids on your Budget* iii. 50 Those serve-yourself emporiums..often have simple ones [*sc.* evening wraps]..which..won't look very different from the costly one on your neighbor. **1949** E. S. GARDNER *Reluctant Witness* in *Case of Crying Swallow* (1974) 166 Mugs handed him a photograph. It showed a young woman standing in a serve-yourself grocery store. **1971** *Guardian* 2 Jan. 8/5 There are plans for..bold new excursions into what some experts see as the coming serve-yourself hotel era.

IV. 42. b. Also in phr. *serve-yourself*, used *attrib.* of foods or meals which one serves to oneself.

1971 M. LEE *Dying for Fun* ii. 19 His host, left to himself, would have taken him to a little piece of America in London, with serve-yourself fried chicken. **1976** *Newmarket Jrnl.* 16 Dec., A serve-yourself buffet with a choice of several hot and cold dishes is the ideal solution to entertaining over the festive season.

43. c. (Earlier example.)

1793 J. MACDONELL *Jrnl.* 15 Aug. in *Five Fur-Traders of Northw.* (1933) 101 Our Bourgeois came up with us and ordered each man a dram, which I served out to them.

V. 47. b. *serve(s)* (you, etc.) *right*: also as *attrib. phr.*

1935 H. STRAUMANN *Newspaper Headlines* i. 29 Lastly there is the *Daily Worker*, the Communist paper, with its serve-him-right attitude. **1946** N. E. ORCHARD in W. S. Knickerbocker *Twentieth Cent. Eng.* 164 Another little girl was sent off by herself when she needed punishment and made to read the family genealogy. Today when she visits the cemetery where her forebears lie,..she walks between the tombstones, a 'serves-you-right' expression on her face. **1977** *New Yorker* 15 Aug. 66/2 The widespread serves-them-right judgment that greeted New York's misfortune.

servery. Add: (Later examples.) Also, = *serving-hatch* s.v. SERVING *vbl. sb.* 3.

1942 G. MITCHELL *Laurels are Poison* vi. 54 Kitty returned..to get her own tea from the Servery. **1960** E. W. HILDICK *Jim Starling & Colonel* ix. 75 They finally lined up in front of the servery. **1974** *Times* 3 May 11/3 The dividing unit acts as a servery, with drawers on the dining side for cutlery and linen.

Servian, *sb.* Add: **b.** The Serbian language.

1808 C. STOWER *Printer's Gram.* 287 (*heading above the alphabet*) Servian. **1842** *Penny Cycl.* XXII. 127/2 The Servian was employed as a written language for the first time by Dositheus Obradovich. **1885** [see *CROATIAN *sb.* and *a.*]. **1900** H. H. CHADWICK in *Indogerman. Forsch.* XI. 168 The -*ā*- was probably accented, as in Servian.

Servian, *a.*² (Earlier example.)

1839 *Dublin Rev.* Aug. 87 This method of election was a manifest reaction and encroachment upon the Servian constitution.

service, *sb.*¹ Add: **I. 5. b.** Also, the Air Force and intelligence departments.

II. 12. a. *active service* (earlier example).

1799 *Times* 1 June 3/2 General Moreau..caused the administrations that were unfit for the active service of the war..to be removed back towards France.

IV. 19. b. Also in phr. *for services rendered* (orig. *Mil.*).

[**1916** *Times* 24 July 9/4 The King has approved the issue of a silver badge to..men..who on account of age or..wounds or sickness caused by military service have..been discharged from the Army... The badge is in the form of a circle... The circle bears the words 'For King and Empire—Services rendered', and circumscribes the Imperial cipher.] **1933** *Radio Times* 14 Apr. 75/2 The war was newly over... Everywhere you saw the little silver badge 'For Services Rendered'. **1938** M. ALLINGHAM *Fashion in Shrouds* xx. 378 That's where Mazarini used to pay his thugs for services rendered on the racecourse. **1976** W. H. CANAWAY *Willow-Pattern War* xviii. 189 As a *quid pro quo* for services rendered in another context, the Americans made their information available to Bonn.

V. 27. d. In the restaurant-car of a railway train, on a ship, etc.: the serving of a meal at one of a number of separate sittings, as *first service*, etc.

1914 KIPLING in *Nash's Mag.* July 484/1 Here is a fragment from the restaurant-car... 'I will give you the number, sar, at the time—for places at the first service.' **1926** E. HEMINGWAY *Sun also Rises* 86 Leaving the dining-car I asked the conductor for tickets for the first service. **1932** G. GREENE *Stamboul Train* III. ii. 140 Late for the last service Dr. Czinner came down the restaurant-car.

30. a. Also applied to other facilities, such as electricity, waste disposal, etc., esp. provided for domestic use. Freq. *pl.*

1963 *Ann. Reg. 1962* 450 Both make use of clusters of towers, mostly containing services, to give vertical emphasis and to free interior space. **1963** *Gloss. Gen. Building Terms* (*B.S.I.*) 24 *Services*, installations for (1) the introduction into and distribution within a building or structure of water, air, gas, liquid fuel, electricity, heat or other source of energy (2) the disposal of waste from a building or structure or (3) fire-fighting within a building or structure. **1979** *Nature* 1 Feb. p. xiii/2 The overhead service booms may provide such services as gas/electricity/water/vacuum/lighting.

31. b. Expert advice or assistance given by manufacturers and dealers to secure satisfactory results from goods made or supplied by them; *spec.*, the provision of maintenance or repair work to ensure the efficient running of a motor vehicle, etc.; a routine operation of examination and maintenance performed on a motor vehicle, etc.

1919 W. H. BERRY *New Motoring* xxiv. 183 The need of a better service system for motorists has often been emphasised... There is ample room for a big development of a scheme for rendering practical car service. **1925** *Morris Owner's Man.* 93 (*caption*) Whenever you see this hanging sign you know that it denotes an establishment where Morris Service can be obtained. **1930** *Economist* 6 Sept. 454/2 There are obviously wide undeveloped markets, of which Britain should be able to secure at least a proportion..if English manufacturers can compete with those of America in the matter of 'service'. **1947** *E. African Ann. 1946–7* 24 'Service After Sales' is as much a Ford feature here as it is in other parts of the world. **1960** I. JEFFERIES *Dignity & Purity* iii. 44 The flat was paid up and the car never needed any service at all. **1974** 'J. LE CARRÉ' *Tinker, Tailor, Soldier, Spy* xx. 168 Take your car in for a service at your local garage. **1977** *Western Morning News* 30 Aug. 10/4 (Advt.), Backed by our largest combine stores and skilled after-sales service.

c. *Broadcasting.* The supply of programmes by a particular broadcasting station.

1927 *B.B.C. Handbk. 1928* 32 Broadcasting Service. By 'service' is meant providing this public..with at least one programme a day. **1933** *B.B.C. Year-bk. 1934* 167 In August last the West Regional, the fourth of the new Regional Stations, began radiating a full programme service. **1949** *Radio Times* 15 July 9/1 *Variety Fanfare* returns to the air... Bowker Andrews first introduced this show in the North of England Home Service. **1957** [see *CARRY *v.* 40 b]. **1977** *Church Times* 9 Dec. 8/3 Now that the 7.30 half-hour on Radio Four has been taken over for other things, there is a gap from 10.15 a.m. until 11 p.m. on Sunday on this service without a word being said about religion.

d. pl. *Econ.* The section of the economy that supplies needs of the consumer but produces no tangible goods.

1936 *Discovery* Nov. 355/2 The distinction between capital goods and current goods is, of course, one of the most important in the whole of economics, but the remarkable growth in the number of those engaged in 'services', now estimated at 40 per cent. of the working population, is not so generally realised. **1941** *Economist* 22 Feb. 235/1 The British public spent almost £900 millions in 1937 on services, excluding entertainments, rent, rates and taxes. The largest constituents of the total were travel, domestic service, public utilities, hotels and restaurants. **1948** [see *current goods*]. **1965** *McGraw-Hill Dict. Mod. Econ.* 466 *Services*, the component of the gross national product that measures the output of intangible items. Services include such items as telephone service, railway, bus, and air transportation, private education, and radio and television repair. **1972** *Accountant* 17 Aug. 211/2 Manufacturing costs are of diminishing importance in an economy in which services are a major part of the whole.

e. *pl.* The provision of petrol, refreshments, etc., for motorists in buildings constructed near to or beside a motorway or other major road; the group of buildings themselves.

1967 *Autocar* 28 Dec. 6/2 It was a relief to see the 'Services 1 mile' sign. **1968** *Listener* 1 Aug. 134/3 We drove back on Sunday night along the endless M1, punctuated only by almost identical airport-international-style 'Services'. **1975** C. STORR *Chinese Egg* xxix. 193 She was passing the Heston Services, she'd be at the Henley exit in another quarter of an hour.

VI. 34. b. *service-side* (later examples).

1898 [see *half-court* s.v. *HALF- II. i]. **1963** *Times* 13 May 3/5 Lawrence's policy of holding the service-side at all costs, often using the side galleries to achieve the change of ends.

36. (Earlier example.)

1822 M. MCSWINEY *Let.* 6 Jan. (1972) II. 348 This debt I understand was due for the service of a *bull*.

VII. 37. a. (Further examples.) Also, belonging to the Air Force; military (opp. civilian). (ii) in *pl.*

1917 *Times* 1 Nov. 3/5 The Services Club, 19, Stratford-place, W., have just acquired an adjoining house. **1926** E. HEMINGWAY *Sun also Rises* xvii. 212 Always slept with a loaded service revolver. **1929** *Star* 21 Aug. 9/1 Private and even Service pilots have appeared near to the station at prohibited times. **1933** *Radio Times* 14 Apr. 75/2 The slang of the hour was Service slang. **1937** A. CHRISTIE *Dumb Witness* i. 13 Emily Arundell's people ..were what is known as 'all service people'. **1945** *Manch. Guardian Weekly* 21 Dec. 323/3 There was an all-night Services canteen at Victoria station. **1945** *Tee Emm* (Air Ministry) V. 35 The Service scale of Tropical Kit, issued to airmen. **1954** *Economist* 11 Sept. 3/1 A trained test pilot is less likely to come to harm in a new and temperamental machine than an enthusiastic service flyer. **1958** *Listener* 6 Nov. 719/2 In 1947 Montgomery became Chief of the Imperial General Staff... He had to co-operate on equal terms with the Service Chiefs of the other two fighting services. **1973** J. ROSSITER *Manipulators* iv. 48, I was so horribly humiliated—my service career finished. **1977** *R.A.F. News* 22 June–5 July 18 (*caption*) Alan won trophies for both rapid and snap shooting using the service-issue self-loading rifle. **1980** C. SMITH *Cut-Out* xiii. 92 Photographs of her husband in service dress and holding a swagger cane.

b. (Further examples.)

1902 A. BENNETT *Grand Babylon Hotel* i. 13 Jules walked to the service-door. **1909** H. G. WELLS *Tono-Bungay* I. i. 28 One came down the main service stairs.. and..one went through a red baize door. **1919** *Chambers's Jrnl.* Jan. 57/2 What is known as the 'service' door..is likely to become popular for hotels, if not for private houses, all over the world. **1933** *Archit. Rev.* LXXIII. 24/2 (*caption*) The service-bay between the kitchen and the restaurant. **1950** T. S. ELIOT *Cocktail Party* I. iii. 65, I shall take the precaution Of leaving by the service staircase. **1955** W. GADDIS *Recognitions* II. viii. 653 A transmitter? Mr. Inononu demanded at the head of the service stairs. **1956** H. KURNITZ *Invasion of Privacy* xiv. 92 She went out the back, through the service entrance. **1961** M. W. BARLEY *Eng. Farmhouse & Cottage* II. i. 64 His home consisted of a hall with a chamber over it, a ground floor chamber in which he slept, and four service-rooms, kitchen, buttery, milkhouse and cheese-house. **1976** H. NIELSEN *Brink of Murder* xii. 106 The manager conceded that there was a service door and.. accompanied them upstairs on the service stairway. **1976** *Washington Post* 19 Apr. C20/1 (Advt.), Eat in kitchen with service bar. **1978** R. LUDLUM *Holcroft Covenant* xxxix. 452, I could say that someone fitting his description was seen leaving by the service entrance. **1979** M. SOAMES *Clementine Churchill* xxiv. 395 A service-lift to the floor below.

c. Of or pertaining to services (sense *31 d), as *service industry, occupation, sector, trade.*

1941 *Economist* 18 Jan. 65/2 The very considerable increase in the standard of living..explains the growth of the 'service', as distinct from the 'productive' industries since the last war. **1959** *Times* 5 Sept. 10/3 The rapid expansion of service occupations—administration, the professions, retailing, entertainment and numerous health and welfare services. **1966** *Listener* 5 May 642/2 There is to be a selective employments tax to help get workers out of service industries into the factories. **1970** S. L. BARRACLOUGH in I. L. Horowitz *Masses in Lat. Amer.* iv. 150 This is reflected in the rapid increase of employment in the 'service' sector. **1970** G. JACKSON *Let.* 17 Apr. in *Soledad Brother* (1971) 221 The new slavery..places the victim..in the case of most blacks in support roles inside and around the factory system (service trades), working for a wage. **1979** G. WAGNER *Barnado* ii. 18 All the service industries took on extra labour at the beginning of the season.

38. service alley, a road or passage giving access to the back of a row of houses; **service area,** (*a*) the area in which broadcast transmissions can be received distinctly; (*b*) a space adjoining a house for the accommodation of dustbins, etc.; (*c*) an area providing petrol, refreshments, etc., for motorists; **service car** *Austral.* and *N.Z.*, a small motor-coach for public transport; **service ceiling** *Aeronaut.* (see *CEILING *vbl. sb.* 6 b); **service charge,** a charge made (additional to that for the food, etc.) for services rendered, esp. for service in a hotel or restaurant; **service club** *N. Amer.*, an association of business or professional people which seeks to promote community welfare and goodwill; **service contract,** a contract of employment; a business agreement between contractor and customer, normally one guaranteeing the maintenance and servicing of equipment; **service engineer,** an engineer engaged on the maintenance and servicing of equipment; **service flat,** a flat in which domestic service and other facilities are provided at a charge included in the rent; hence **service flatlet; service mark** orig. *U.S.*, a name or designation, protected by law, used by a commercial undertaking to distinguish a service offered by it from the services of competitors; **service module** *Astronautics*, a separable section of a spacecraft, esp. one in the U.S. Apollo series, containing the main engine and other supporting equipment; **service plate** *U.S.*, a large ornate plate which marks a place at table and on which dining plates, etc., are set during the first courses; **service record,** the record of service of a soldier, employee, etc.; **service reservoir,** a (usu. small) reservoir filled from an impounding reservoir at times of low demand to supplement the supply to the local area at time of high demand, so as to reduce the necessary capacity of the conduits from the impounding reservoir; **service road,** a subsidiary road giving access to houses, shops, etc., away from a main road; **service routine** *Computers*, = *utility routine* s.v. *UTILITY *sb.*; **service station,** an establishment providing service and maintenance for motor vehicles; more recently, merely = *filling-station* s.v. *FILLING *vbl. sb.* 4.

1922 J. HERGESHEIMER *Bright Shawl* 11 The street outside was narrow..once no more than a service alley for the larger dwellings back of which it ran. **1974** P. MCCUTCHAN *Call for Simon Shard* xi. 98 You take the back, Alan. There'll be a service alley. **1927** *B.B.C. Handbk. 1928* 62 Rival schemes can be compared as between those which base themselves upon very high power and believe that service areas can be over 100 miles radius, and those which cover the country from more centres and with therefore somewhat less power. **1956** *Good Housek. Home Encyl.* (ed. 4) 327/2 The service area behind or at the side of the house. **1958** *News Chron.* 25 Nov. 7/4 The great London–Birmingham Motorway... A road remarkably straight, soaring over 150 specially built bridges; with flyovers, flyunders; with service and eating areas every 12 miles. **1970** J. EARL *Tuners & Amplifiers* iii. 74 If you have in mind trying for more distant stations..outside the normal service area, then you will certainly need a tuner of top sensitivity. **1971** M. MCCARTHY *Birds of Amer.* 76 The yard in back of their house was all flagged, with..a 'service area' containing garbage cans. **1980** J. MCNEIL *Spy Game* xiv. 141 They careered into the narrow, curving entrance to a service area... He cruised the crowded car park. **1924** R. REES *April's Sowing* ii. 19 I'd have gone in the service car. **1933** *Bulletin* (Sydney) 26 July 20/1 The drivers of service cars Outback. **1948** V. PALMER *Golconda* xxi. 173 He piled his traps into the dusty service-car and climbed up beside the driver. **1965** S. T. OLLIVIER *Petticoat Farm* xii. 166 The road was open, they knew, because the service cars were running through. **1920** *Flight* XII. 980/2 Principal characteristics of the Martin torpedo 'plane are:—Service ceiling..12,000 ft. **1944** H. F. BROWNE *Aeroplane Flight* vi. 97 At the service ceiling the aeroplane can fly only at speeds between 180 m.p.h. and 240 m.p.h. **1978** J. D. ANDERSON *Introd. to Flight* vi. 237 The service ceiling represents the practical upper limit of steady, level flight. **1929** *Post Office Guide* July 157 Any sum not exceeding £10 may be withdrawn by telegraph if the depositor pays the cost of the telegrams and a service charge of one shilling. **1955** R. CHANDLER *Let.* 7 Feb. (1981) 382, I paid a service charge on the bill... This service charge is supposed to take the place of tipping. **1977** B. BAINBRIDGE *Injury Time* ii. 23 She looked at the bill and was astonished at the service charge. **1926** *Daily Colonist* (Victoria, B.C.) 16 July 2/5 He intended this time to take a party of executive officers of service clubs. **1978** J. L. HENSLEY *Killing in Gold* (1979) v. 65 He'd joined.. one of the service clubs, Lions, Rotary, or Kiwanis. **1948** *Rep. Native Laws Commission 1946–48* (Dept. Native Affairs, S. Afr.) 26/1 The service contract duplicate, which is issued to a Native in urban areas where registration of service contracts in terms of the Natives (Urban Areas) Consolidation Act is in force, is likewise regarded by them as a pass. **1958** *Listener* 20 Nov. 824/1 It would be wrong to abandon altogether the distinction between service contracts and other types of contract. **1975** *Petroleum Economist* Aug. 299/2 In 1968, a service contract was agreed with Elf/ERAP by which the French company would have a share of any production which resulted. **1958** *Practical Wireless* XXXIV. 67/1, I do feel pity for the poor service engineer. **1980** *West Lancs. Even. Gaz.* 28 Nov. 25 Sweda International..has vacancies for Service Engineers to service and maintain their range of electro-mechanical and electronic machines. **1922** W. J. LOCKE *Tale of Triona* iv. 38 She found herself the lucky tenant of a little suite in a set of service flats in Victoria Street. **1973** 'E. FERRARS' *Foot in Grave* iv. 70 Being solitary in my service flat suits me, and that's how I'm going on. **1960** M. SPARK *Bachelors* x. 141 Those who were conducting love affairs in service flatlets found it convenient that the maids did not come in with their vacuum cleaners on Sundays. **1945** *Business Week* 30 June 86/2 A separate register would be authorized for 'service' marks to identify services rather than merchandise. This register would include 'names, symbols, titles, designations, slogans, character names, and distinctive features of radio or other advertising used in commerce'. **1949** H. BENNETT *Trade-Marks* 130 Under the Lanham act service marks will be registrable for the first time. The new law thus gives great protection to a category of names and designations whose trade importance was not recognized under the old law. **1959** *Listener* 31 Dec. 1147/1 Trade marks, trade names, the so-called 'service-marks' of organizations such as transport undertakings and radio stations. **1973** S. A. DIAMOND *Trademark Problems & how to avoid Them* i. 2 Trademarks are not limited to goods; they may be used for services, like transportation, insurance, entertainments and advertising. Strictly speaking, they are then called 'service marks'. **1961** *Space Technol.* Oct. 41 (*caption*) Service module. **1962** *Manned Space Flight Program of N.A.S.A.* (U.S. Congress Senate Comm. on Aeronaut. & Space Sci.) 131 The service module..will contain the propulsion used for midcourse guidance corrections, for emergency abort situations, and for lunar takeoff. **1968** *Times* 16 Dec. 7/4 Before reentry, the command module holding the astronauts will separate from what is called the service module, the section of the spacecraft containing the main engine and power supplies. **1974** Service module [see *RETRO-FIRE *sb.*]. **1929** *Woman's Home Compan.* Apr. 67/2 The service plate has been removed and a..fish plate has taken its place. (The individual place..is never left without a plate before it.) **1934** J. B. PRIESTLEY *Eng. Journey* vii. 223 A very queer American custom, that of having what are known as 'service plates', which are never loaded with food but are placed before guests between courses, to be looked at and admired... These luxury plates were usually very ornate and would be specially made, here in the Potteries, for each customer. Some Americans liked to have a picture of their college on their plates. **1977** H. FAST *Immigrants* I. 49 A maid placed a plate of crab meat and mayonnaise on his service plate. **1918** E. S. FARROW *Dict. Mil. Terms* s.v., When an enlisted man is detached from his company, his service record will be forwarded by endorsement to his new commanding officer. **1923** J. D. HACKETT *Labor Terms* in *Managem. Engin.* May, *Service Record*, a summary of all the facts necessary for appraising the worth of an individual to an employer. **1981** J. B. HILTON *Playground of Death* x. 123 There's his service record... He was a brave man. **1869** *Bradshaw's Railway Man.* XXI. 266 The service reservoir of the Ashton waterworks. **1967** J. H. STEPHENS *Water & Waste* iii. 49 The purpose of the service reservoir, and its close relative, the water tower, is to allow for the peaks in demand. **1921** H. FOSTON *At Front* 16 Unmetalled portions of the 'service' road. **1935** *Times* 30 Dec. 13/6 There are signs in this neighbourhood that the future development will be the right one of groups of houses set back and approached by service roads. **1976** *Southern Even. Echo* (Southampton) 12 Nov. (Advt. Suppl.) 7/6 In quiet and well screened service road, a most attractive and compact 3-bedroom bungalow. **1954** *Computers & Automation* Dec. 21/1 *Service routine*,..a routine designed to assist in the actual operation of the computer. **1969** P. B. JORDAIN *Condensed Computer Encycl.* 451 The most common service routines are the input/output programs... Other service routines perform such services as program loading, common calculations.., tracing, memory dumps, tape dumps, and the like. **1921** *Sci. Amer.* Dec. 135/3 Each..pipe at the service station is provided with a plug... Each automobile comes into the service station charged with static. **1925** *Morris Owner's Man.* 61 Do not forget that Messrs. Lucas have for your benefit, Service Stations in the following towns. **1935** *Economist* 7 Dec. 1132/2 The tendency..for manufacturing companies to transfer their service stations away from the centre of London..has.. lessened the convenience to the..motorist of running his car direct to the maker's service station for minor repairs. **1940** R. CHANDLER *Farewell, my Lovely* vii. 52 He gassed up there and the service station kid recognized him. **1977** *Lubricants Business* (Shell Internat. Petroleum Co.) 7 Supermarkets are increasingly competing with service stations for motor oil sales.

service, *sb.*[2] **4. service-berry,** (*b*) substitute for def.: a N. American tree or shrub of the genus *Amelanchier*, belonging to the family Rosaceæ and bearing clusters of white flowers followed by small, dark-coloured berries; also, the fruit of this tree or shrub; (earlier example).

1784 F. ASBURY *Jrnl.* 31 July (1821) I. 370 The child he fed with..sawice berries.

service (sɜ̄·ɹvis), *v.* [f. SERVICE *sb.*[1]] **1.** *trans.* To be of service to; to serve; to provide with a service.

1893 R. L. STEVENSON *Catriona* I. xvi. 178 If I am to service ye the way that you propose, I'll lose my lifelihood. **1948** J. STEINBECK *Russian Jrnl.* (1949) 15 Airports are so far from the cities they supposedly service. **1955** *News of North* (Yellowknife, N.W.T.) 18 Nov. 1/5 A new town house, available to water and sewer service, would be assessed at a much higher rate than duplicate property in a part of the town not serviced this way. **1969** D. WIDGERY in Cockburn & Blackburn *Student Power* 139 It is unlikely that a radical Executive would be able to.. service the entirely different attitude of the apolitical small colleges. **1974** R. ADAMS *Shardik* lviii. 518 How many permanent camps or staging-forts would be needed to service a regular trade-route?

2. To perform routine maintenance or repair work on (a motor vehicle or other piece of equipment). orig. *U.S.*

1926 *Amer. Speech* II. 112/2 The automobile dealer says: 'Run the new car five hundred miles at twenty or less an hour, then have it thoroughly serviced with grease and oil.' **1930** *Bookman* Dec. 398 Probably the greatest cost in Television will be that expended for servicing the equipment. **1935** A. P. HERBERT in *Punch* 27 Feb. 236/1, I denounce, Comrades, the foul new verb 'to service', an invention, I believe, of someone in the motor-trade. **1949** 'G. ORWELL' *Nineteen Eighty-Four* II. 131 She enjoyed her work, which consisted chiefly in running and servicing a powerful but tricky electric motor. **1958** *Listener* 23 Oct. 655/2 Vehicles—whether moving, parked, unloading or being serviced—have already taken charge of the present ground level. **1978** R. LEWIS *Uncertain Sound* vi. 154 Your car was serviced on the Thursday.

3. To pay interest on (a debt).

1942 *Sun* (Baltimore) 15 Jan. 2/1 Secretary of Interior Ickes announced today that interest payments on outstanding bonds of the Philippine Government would continue to be met and serviced through the United States Treasury. **1952** *Times* 1 Aug. 9/2 Nobody oversea will ever accept the idea that a company which has all the pesetas it could want should be bankrupted in Spain.. because the Spanish Government has not allowed it to buy sterling to service a sterling debt. **1975** *Daily Tel.* 21 Oct. 17/7 Unless there is a huge Federal loan guarantee by the end of next month the city will not be able to meet its payroll, let alone service its debts.

4. = SERVE *v.*[1] 52; also of a man, to have sexual intercourse with (a woman).

1961 in WEBSTER. **1966** [see *post coitum* s.v. *POST *Latin preposition*]. **1973** W. H. CANAWAY *Harry doing Good* II. v. 188, I knew a feller that married a twin. Identical. He was getting worn out..till he found out he was servicing both of these twins. **1976** T. HEALD *Let Sleeping Dogs Die* iv. 78 One dog could presumably service several bitches in a day.

5. a. To supply (a person) *with* something. **b.** To process.

1969 *Daily Tel.* 6 Oct. 9/6 It is a proper function of local theatres to service their audiences with the latest in world taste. **1971** *Ibid.* 27 May 14/8 We'll be able to service the retailer with merchandise much faster than it can possibly be shipped in from overseas. **1971** D. POTTER *Brit. Eliz. Stamps* vi. 70 A Post Office First-Day Cover service was available, and no charge was made if the envelope carried sufficient postage. The complete set was serviced for the cost of the envelope and the stamps. **1973** *Daily Tel.* 16 Apr. 2/2 This year building societies have been without funds to service all the mortgages required, and sales are being cancelled.

Hence **se·rviced** *ppl. a.*, provided with service or services; maintained.

1938 C. HIMES *Headwaiter* in *Black on Black* (1973) 150 Over by the elevator where the room service was stationed, a waiter lounged indolently by a serviced table. **1968** *Globe & Mail* (Toronto) 13 Feb. 31/6 (Advt.), Serviced industrial land Northwest Metro bargain price. **1978** R. V. JONES *Most Secret War* xliv. 419 Each pilot could draw a serviced aircraft, probably a different one from that which he last flew, for each new operation.

serviceability. Add: (Later examples.) Also of machinery: the capacity to be maintained or repaired; reliability.

1913 *Chambers's Jrnl.* June 478/1 The claims of reliability, serviceability, and efficiency have been established. **1942** *R.A.F. Jrnl.* 3 Oct. 25 He looks at the Situation Map, the serviceability blackboard, and other items of visual intelligence. **1946** *Happy Landings* July 3/3 Drills connected with the serviceability of the engine ..are clearing the supercharger gears and exercising propellers in flight. **1961** B. FERGUSSON *Watery Maze* xiii. 319 It had been calculated at Quadrant that the 'serviceability rate'—that is, the number which one could actually count on for use on D-Day—would be 90 per cent for LSTs and 85 per cent for the rest. **1981** S. DUNMORE *Ace* II. ii. 162 The shortages affected serviceability.. damaged aircraft had to be cannibalized to provide spares.

se·rviceman. Also with capital initial, hyphened, and as two words. [SERVICE *sb.*[1]]

1. A man who serves, or has served, in the armed forces.

1899 (*title*) Constitution of the Service men of the Spanish war (Columbus, Ga.). **1917** *Hansard Commons* 4 May 608 (*heading*) Disabled service men. **1918** *Sheffield Daily Tel.* 18 Sept. 2/6 Discharged soldiers should be represented on all committees that have to deal with the training of discharged service men. **1945** *Daily Express* 14 Aug. 3/7 Duty-Free cigarettes sent to Service men in Europe may be officially rationed soon. **1959** *Listener* 23 July 119/2, I go about a good deal, talking to trade unionists and to work-people generally, to managers, to civil servants, to servicemen, and to students and teachers of all kinds. **1976** M. GREEN *Children of Sun* (1977) viii. 366 Only 750 Old Etonian servicemen died in this war... In the first one..1,150 died.

2. A man who maintains and repairs equipment (*SERVICE *sb.*[1] 31 b).

1961 in WEBSTER. **1969** D. E. WESTLAKE *Up your Banners* xxviii. 195 Our serviceman wouldn't make the installation at night, sir. **1970** *Which?* May 143/2 All except the Bendix needed at least one visit from a serviceman before they were working properly. **1974** *Sci. Amer.* Jan. 120/3 Beginners will find that neighboring radio hams and television servicemen can pass along useful construction tips.

Similarly **se·rvicewoman.**

1945 *Observer* 21 Oct. 6/1 (Advt.), For thousands of Service men and women the order is 'carry on'. **1972** J. WILLIAMS *Home Fronts* v. xv. 255 The historic Norfolk House in St James's Square was given over to servicewomen from overseas.

servicer (sɜ̄·ɹvisəɹ). [f. *SERVICE *v.* + -ER[1].] One who services.

1973 *Houston* (Texas) *Chron.* (Suppl.) 14 Oct. 8/2 A better way to collect the oil from driveway auto servicers is being sought. *a* **1974** R. CROSSMAN *Diaries* (1976) II. 406 Many of the owners are people of substance who have servicers for their vehicles, chauffeurs so to speak, who look after them as a whole-time occupation.

servicing (sɜ̄·ɹvisiŋ), *vbl. sb.* [-ING[1].] **1.** The action of maintaining or repairing a motor vehicle, etc. Also *fig.*

1935 *Economist* 7 Dec. 1131/2 Recognised dealers with facilities for the..'servicing' of the vehicles sold. **1956** *Good Housek. Home Encycl.* (ed. 4) 143/2 Servicing and repairs which can be carried out by the handyman of the house. **1959** I. JEFFERIES *Thirteen Days* x. 156 'Where's the bint, John?'.. 'I left her at the hospital for servicing and overhaul.' **1970** *Motoring Which?* July 91/1 All three needed routine servicing every 3,000 miles. **1978** D. DEVINE *Sunk without Trace* 253 There was the car... Why did she put it in for servicing that particular week?

2. The action of paying interest on a debt.

1939 *Times* 2 Mar. 13/2 Financial circles hope that an arrangement will be reached in the meantime for the continued servicing of foreign loans. **1946** *Sun* (Baltimore) 7 Oct. 5/2 Servicing of these two issues has required $647,507.50 a year.

3. The action of providing a service.
1944 *Ann. Reg. 1943* 90 Most of their reciprocal aid.. had therefore been 'servicing', taking the form of providing transportation, accommodation, airfields,..local supplies to American forces. **1946** J. S. Huxley *Unesco* ii. 58 The general educational servicing of the public in the fields of science and culture.

4. *attrib.* and *Comb.*
1930 *Economist* 31 May 1207/1 The unclassified group of trades—which includes road transport and most of what Americans term 'servicing' industries—contributed 20.08 per cent. **1944** *R.A.F. Jrnl.* Aug. 256, I joined the Servicing Commando unit at the Transit Camp. **1955** *Univ. of Virginia News Let.* 15 June 1/5 Growth of the servicing-type industries, such as retail and wholesale trade, utilities, business and repair services. **1968** [see *Poisson 1). **1978** R. V. Jones *Most Secret War* xxxix. 360 At Zempin we hoped to have the aircraft and its servicing installations isolated.

servigrous (sɜɪvəi·grəs), *a.* *U.S. dial.* Also **savigrous, sevigrous, survigrous.** [Orig. unknown: freq. associated with a dial. pronunc. of *vigorous*, and cf. *savagerous *a.*] Fierce, severe, tough, vigorous. Hence **servi·grously** *adv.*
1835 A. B. Longstreet *Georgia Scenes* 227 'Pretty *sevigrous*, but nothing killing yet,' said Billy Curlew, as he learned the place of Spivey's ball. **1888** 'C. E. Craddock' *Keedon Bluffs* 88 He's a servigrous jumper, sure! *Ibid.* 215 The mos' servigrous singer they hed. **1890** T. N. Page in *Harper's New Monthly Mag.* Dec. 114/1 She so savigrous I tolt her I 'ain' nuver had nobody to prevaricate nuttin' 'bout me. **1901** *Nashville* (Tenn.) *Banner* 28 Oct. 4/3 The New York Sun..employs that expressive provincialism of the Southern mountaineer, 'servigrous'... The Sun says Mr. William Travis Jerome is 'servigrous' in the kind of oratory he uses. **1913** H. Kephart *Our Southern Highlanders* xiii. 294 Survigrous (ser-*vi*-grus) is a superlative of vigorous (here pronounced *vi*-grus, with long *i*): as 'a survigrous baby', 'a most survigrous cusser'. **1928** M. Chapman *Happy Mountain* vii. 70 The Preacher must have been a rip-snorting and most survigrous young-un before he caught religion. **1938** C. H. Matschat *Suwannee River* 81 Ary fowkses knows as how onion juice, rubbed in servigerously, sprouts hair like weeds after a rain, iffen so be ye stand in the sun.

serving, *vbl. sb.* **3.** *serving-mallet* (earlier *transf.* example), *spoon*; **serving cart** *U.S.*, a small trolley from which food and drink may be served.
1969 *Sears Catal.* Spring/Summer 9/2 Serving cart... Removable tray. **1978** *Neiman Marcus Christmas Bk.* 98 'Le Gourmand' is a serving cart and more. Made of solid maple with butcher block top that slides back to reveal a stainless well for ice or storage. **1850** H. Melville *White Jacket* II. xliv. 296 Ten of us Waisters mean to club together, and buy a serving-mallet boat. **1960** M. Spark *Bachelors* x. 155 'What!' said Marlene, holding the cold peas in the serving-spoon suspended. **1978** M. Russell *Daylight Robbery* xix. 184 Mrs Braithwaite dropped the serving spoon upon her plate with a clatter.

servo (sɜ̄·ɪvo), *sb.* [The first element of Servo-motor (and *servo-mechanism) used substantively.] **1. a.** A servo-mechanism or servo-motor.
1910 *Engineering* 14 Jan. 56/2 A patent 'Servo' regulator valve is fitted in the dome [of the boiler]. **1924** *Motor* 7 Oct. 448/3 The servo actually trebles the braking effect usually obtainable for a given pedal pressure. **1948** I. A. Greenwood in I. A. Greenwood et al. *Electronic Instruments* viii. 220 A convenient classification of servos may be made in accordance with their uses, the principal examples of which are 'position servos' and 'velocity servos'. **1959** *Times* 1 Sept. 12/2 The..company have now introduced a vacuum-hydraulic brake servo which can be fitted easily to cars and light motor vehicles and is claimed to make a vast improvement in braking. **1966** *Electronics* 17 Oct. 108 To test a servo that controls a radar antenna, the antenna must be moved. **1971** *Sci. Amer.* July 120/3 The first truly automatic servo..was the fantail, a small windwheel mounted at right angles to the main sails and geared to turn the entire top of the windmill. **1976** B. Jackson *Flameout* (1977) iv. 28, I put electronic sensors on the wing tips and tail to respond to phugoid oscillations and dampen yaw. The control servos respond to the input from the sensors.

b. *transf.* = *servo-mechanism b.
1953 P. A. Merton in G. E. W. Wolstenholme *Spinal Cord* (Ciba Foundation Symp.) 249 The stretch reflex servo, which is so obviously concerned with maintaining length and not tension, must necessarily have receptors which record length. **1969** *Proc. Roy. Soc.* B. CLXXIII. 156 Voluntary movement could be initiated by the α route without sacrificing the advantages of a servo.

2. *attrib.* and *Comb.*, as *servo actuation, -actuator, assistance, loop*; *servo-actuated, -assisted, -driven, -operated* adjs.; **servo-a·mplifier,** the part of a servo-mechanism that responds to the small error signal and delivers a corresponding large signal to drive the servo-motor; **servo brake,** (*a*) a vehicle brake whose application is assisted by the momentum of the vehicle; (*b*) a brake that is operated by a servo-mechanism; hence **servo-braking** *vbl. sb.*; **servo flap** *Aeronaut.* = *servo tab* below; **servohydrau·lic** *a.*, both servo-controlled and hydraulic; **servo-mu·ltiplier,** a device for separately multiplying each of several voltages by a single voltage, the former being applied to a set of potentiometers on the same shaft as a potentiometer controlled by a servomotor receiving the latter voltage; **servo system** = *servo-mechanism a; also *transf.*; **servo tab** *Aeronaut.*, a tab, operated directly by the pilot, which gives rise to aerodynamic forces that assist in moving the main flap.
1961 *Hovering Craft & Hydrofoil* Oct. 18/2 The ultimate servo-actuated mechanical device may take ten years. **1959** K. Henney *Radio Engin. Handbk.* (ed. 5) xxv. 9 Deviations of the airplane about the yaw axis result in rotation of the heading stator with respect to the rotor and a signal to the rudder servoamplifier, causing servo-actuation of the rudder surface and the servo loop action described above. **1970** *Times* 4 Sept. (Aviation Suppl.) p. iv/4 Savings will also accrue from the replacement of the common mechanically coupled control systems in the aircraft by electronic systems with electro-hydraulic servo-actuators operating various aircraft control surfaces. **1946** *Radar: Summary Rep. & Harp Project* (U.S. Nat. Defense Res. Comm., Div. 14) 143/2 *Servo-amplifier*, the amplifier of power impulses in a servo system. **1947** *Electronic Engin.* July 215/1 In a characteristic arrangement, a valve circuit, known as the 'servo amplifier', controls the rotation of an electric motor. **1959** K. Henney *Radio Engin. Handbk.* (ed. 5) xxv. 8 The signal from the servoamplifier is applied to the elevator servomotor which actuates and drives the elevator surface. **1966** *McGraw-Hill Encycl. Sci. & Technol.* XII. 199/2 The servoamplifier is often electronic but may be a magnetic amplifier, a relay type of amplifier, or any combination of these types. **1929** *Times* 2 Nov. 4/7 A pedal applies the rearmost Euro [brakes] with vacuum servo assistance. **1972** *Guardian* 28 Jan. 3/4 (Advt.), To stop, there's a dual circuit four-disc system with servo assistance. **1951** *Automobile Engineer* May 199/1 (*heading*) Servo-assisted hydraulic brakes. **1976** *Field* 18 Nov. 1021 (Advt.), All four alloy wheels enjoy servo-assisted disc brakes. **1924** A. W. Judge et al. *Mod. Motor Cars* II. vii. 118 The Hispano-Suiza servo-brake controls are shown in perspective arrangement. **1926** *Encycl. Brit.* II. 980/2 This led to the development of so-called servo brakes, in which the momentum of the car was utilised to reinforce the effort of the driver in applying the brake. **1951** *Automobile Engineer* Feb. 60/1 (*heading*) Duo servo brakes. **1924** *Motor* 28 Oct. 707/1 We are now able..to give the first complete description of the servo-braking system adopted. **1947** *Proc. IRE* XXXV. 450/2 It is possible to divide one voltage by another using a servodriven potentiometer. **1966** M. Woodhouse *Tree Frog* xxi. 153 One small directional dish [antenna] which..I guessed was servo-driven. **1929** *Rep. & Mem. Aeronaut. Res. Comm.* No. 1262. 2 The control column is attached directly to the servo flap by means of wires. **1935** *Aircraft Engin.* VII. 303/1 During the past year or so there has been a growing tendency towards the use of small servo flaps on elevators and rudders either for trimming or for balancing. **1972** *Physics Bull.* Aug. 492/2 Fulmer Research Institute has recently installed a Mand servohydraulic testing facility to meet the increasing demand for testing larger specimens under widely varying rates of loading. **1980** *Jrnl. R. Soc. Arts* May 319/2 Facilities include a £350,000 Schenk servo hydraulic rig for testing structural fabrications to destruction. **1946** *Radar: Summary Rep. & Harp Project* (U.S. Nat. Defense Res. Comm., Div. 14) 143/2 *Servo loop*, that collection of elements in a servomechanism which measures the error in the quantity to be controlled and applies a correction tending to reduce that error to zero. **1953** P. A. Merton in G. E. W. Wolstenholme *Spinal Cord* (Ciba Foundation Symp.) 247 The stretch reflex is a feedback or servo loop, the feedback being negative. **1978** R. Jansson *News Caper* 10 Even with all the damping in the servo loops the controls leaped out of my hands... We flopped around the sky. **1952** G. A. & T. M. Korn *Electronic Analog Computers* vi. 245 In the case of servomultipliers, probably the best solution..is to make sure that the follow-up and multiplying potentiometers are all loaded by equal resistances. **1965** A. W. Langill *Automatic Control Systems Engin.* II. xviii. 503 Although the servomultiplier is normally employed to form the product of two analog voltages, the system is also used extensively in the generation of arbitrary functions. **1928** *Rep. & Mem. Aeronaut. Res. Comm.* No. 1171. 9 (*heading*) Theory for aerofoil R.A.F. 28 with servo operated flap. **1947** *Proc. IRE* XXXV. 444/1 Servo-operated torque amplifier. **1946** *Radar: Summary Rep. & Harp Project* (U.S. Nat. Defense Res. Comm., Div. 14) 143/2 *Servo system*, a mechanical, frequently electromechanical, system for transmitting accurate mechanical position from one point to another by electrical or other means. The position is corrected by feeding back an error signal. **1947** *Electronic Engin.* July 215/2 All quantities may be converted to a consistent electrical basis by employing a servo system. **1964** *Language* XL. 219 The fact that some sort of neurological servosystem does monitor encoding cannot be doubted. **1971** *Engineering* Apr. 45/2 A servo-system can be used to restore the balance after change of displacement. **1939** F. K. Teichmann *Airplane Design Man.* xiii. 207 If the tab can be controlled from the cockpit, it may be used to operate the larger surface and is then called a control-tab or a servo-tab. **1975** L. J. Clancy *Aerodynamics* xvi. 551 Another related device is the so-called servo-tab, which is designed to provide all the hinge movement required to deflect the control.

Hence as *v. trans.*, to control or operate by a servo-mechanism; **se·rvoed** *ppl. a.*
1971 *New Scientist* 12 Aug. 359/2 Ferguson solved this problem with their ingenious double-sided vacuum servo, which servos the brakes on and servos them (and the driver's foot) off. **1978** *Nature* 20 Apr. 704/2 The mapping operation was achieved by driving the telescope in declination at the maximum servoed rate of 130′ min^{-1} back and forth across the galactic plane.

Servo-. Add: Also *Servo-Turkish* adj.
1897 E. A. Bartlett *Battlefields of Thessaly* iii. 72 The last Servo-Turkish campaign, that of 1876. **1914** W. G. Lawrence in *Home Lett. T. E. Lawrence* (1954) 509 The Servo-Turkish war.

servo control. [f. *servo *sb.*] **1.** † **a.** *Aeronaut.* An aircraft control using a servo tab (see *servo *sb.* 2). *Obs.* **b.** *gen.* = *servo-mechanism a.
1928 *Rep. & Mem. Advisory Comm. Aeronaut.* No. 1187.4 There is no spring force on the servo control. **1934** *Jrnl. Aeronaut. Sci.* I. 155/1 The device now known as the servo control flap is a development of the 'Flettner Rudder' which was invented by the designer of the rotor ships. **1947** *Jrnl. Inst. Electr. Engineers* XCIV. iia. 184/2 No output is produced in the bearing channel, and the feed to the corresponding servo control is consequently zero. **1951** *Instruments* XXIV. 650/1 Servocontrols for the steel industry require..relatively high power level. **1977** *Proc. R. Soc. Med.* LXX. 208/2 As with all tools, the servo-control incubator is only as good as the persons who use it.

2. The use of a servo-mechanism to assist with the control of a system; the action or practice of controlling a system by means of a servo-mechanism.
1929 *Rep. & Mem. Aeronaut. Res. Comm.* No. 1262. 1 If no limit be set to the force which a pilot can exert then the maximum rolling moment possible with servo control is always less than that without it. **1953** P. A. Merton in G. E. W. Wolstenholme *Spinal Cord* (Ciba Foundation Symp.) 247 (*heading*) Speculations on the servo-control of movement. **1977** *Proc. R. Soc. Med.* LXX. 207/1 The principle of servo-control is that the instrument senses the baby's temperature and adjusts the thermal environment automatically.

Hence **se·rvo-control** *v. trans.*, **se·rvo-controlled** *ppl. a.*
1935 *Rep. & Mem. Aeronaut. Res. Comm.* No. 1652. 1 There have been several occurrences of flutter of servo-controlled rudders. **1948** I. A. Greenwood in I. A. Greenwood et al. *Electronic Instruments* viii. 217 Practically all heavy antiaircraft artillery..is servo-controlled by the output of some type of computer. **1972** *Physics Bull.* Apr. 232/2 The gratings are ruled in a very uniform layer of aluminium deposited on to an optically flat substrate.. using a large precision ruling engine servocontrolled by laser interferometers. **1977** *Proc. R. Soc. Med.* LXX. 207/2 The disadvantage of a servo-controlled incubator is that the temperature of the baby as a clinical guide to serious conditions..is lost.

se·rvo-me:chanism. Also without hyphen and as two words. [f. *servo *sb.* + Mechanism.] **a.** A powered mechanism in which a controlled motion is produced at a high energy or power level in response to an input motion at a lower energy level; *esp.* one in which feedback is employed to make the control automatic, and generally comprising a measuring device, a servo-amplifier, and a servo-motor.
1926 *Encycl. Brit.* II. 980/2 Some cars..were fitted with an hydraulic servo mechanism. **1935** *Jrnl. R. Aeronaut. Soc.* XXXIX. 794 The [de-icing] device..comprises two essentials, the ice detector and the servo-mechanism which controls the supply of alcohol. **1959** *Times Lit. Suppl.* 24 Apr. 245/2 All self-regulating machines are servo-mechanisms, in which one part of the machine regulates the operation of the other. **1960** *Times* 29 Jan. 3/1 (Advt.), The applicant should have a good knowledge of servomechanism theory. **1973** *Sci. Amer.* Nov. 129/1 Our seismographs and tiltmeters operate in tunnels several hundred feet underground and are provided with servomechanisms that automatically compensate for temperature changes. **1977** D. Fry *Homo Loquens* vii. 91 For centuries firearms..operated on the ballistic principle of the boy who throws the ball; in the last decades, feedback control has been introduced into this area by the employment of servo-mechanisms.

b. *transf.* A non-mechanical system that is characterized by self-regulating feedback, esp. in *Genetics* and *Physiol.* Also *fig.*
1953 J. S. Huxley *Evolution in Action* ii. 46 Natural selection..provided a genetic servo-mechanism to regulate the mutant back towards normality in its effects. **1958** *Times Lit. Suppl.* 17 Jan. 34/3 The human or animal body is a remarkable example of servo-mechanisms, in which the expenditure of a small amount of energy is used to release a large amount of energy, and in which a balance..is maintained by 'feed-back' processes. **1964** M. McLuhan *Understanding Media* I. iv. 41 This extension of himself by mirror numbed his perceptions until he became the servomechanism of his own extended or repeated image. **1971** *Nature* 10 Dec. 325/1 Natural selection is not a chance process but a feedback servo-mechanism between the gene pool and the environment. **1976** *New Yorker* 15 Nov. 157/1 Their basic assumption is that speech can best be understood as the output of a servomechanism—that is, a device with built-in feedback loops which continuously monitors its own performance and modifies its activity accordingly.

Hence **servo-mecha·nical** *a.*
1947 *Proc. IRE* XXXV. 770/2 The..servomechanical type of control may be preferable where slow drifts over long periods of time are encountered. **1966** S. Beer *Decision & Control* xvi. 418 In this servomechanical model there is a special facility for identifying precisely what is self-regulating about the system. **1977** *Lancet* 5 Nov. 955/2 The finding of only partial suppression of A.C.T.H. with normal levels of cortisol is difficult to understand in conventional servomechanical concepts.

servo-motor. Add: Also **servomotor, servo motor.** More widely, any device used as the motive element in a servo-mechanism. (Later examples.)

1932 *Jrnl. Iron & Steel Inst.* CXXV. 642 The apparatus ..makes use of the dilatations of the test bar to regulate the temperature of the furnace by means of a servo-motor. **1933** *Electrician* 16 June 796/2 The servo-motor for controlling the vanes is located between the turbine and generator shafts, so that the coupling flanges of the respective machines form the lower and upper servo-motor covers. **1951** *Automobile Engineer* May 199/1 A mechanically operated transmission brake functions as a servo-motor to apply pressure to the master cylinder of a hydraulic braking system. **1976** *Gramophone* Sept. 510/1 A DC servo motor powers the movement of the arm.

‖ **servus** (ze·rvus), *int.* [Ger., a. L. *servus* servant.] An informal greeting or farewell used in Austria and southern Germany.

1893 E. R. PENNELL *To Gipsyland* ii. 33 All..drank to me in the wine of their country, and cried aloud their '*Servus! Viva! Eljeu!*' **1966** R. E. PICKERING *Himself Again* iv. 33 'Servus,' he said shortly. I ordered a coffee. **1978** H. MCINNES *Prelude to Terror* viii. 89 As for her hotel in Vienna..the Sacher..everyone tugging a forelock and saying '*Servus!*'

sesame. Add: **c.** *sesame-seed* (later examples).

1972 *House & Garden* Feb. 98/2 Swiss fondue.. Sesame seed sticks..make a happy accompaniment. **1973** *Time Out* 2–8 Mar. 27/4 They also have..sesame seed rolls with really thick fillings for around 13p. **1978** *Nagel's Encycl.-Guide: China* 380 Rolls covered with sesame seeds are eaten at the same time.

Sesotho (sesū·tu). Also **Sesuto, Sesutu.** [Bantu, = 'language of the Sotho'.] A south-eastern Bantu language spoken by members of the *SOTHO people. Also *attrib.* or as *adj.*

1846 J. C. BROWN tr. *Arbousset & Daumas's Narr. Tour N.-E. of Cape of Good Hope* xxiii. 251, I spoke Sesuto, a dialect which the chief of the place.., also understood. **1871** J. MACKENZIE *Ten Years North of Orange River* 492 They [*sc.* clicks] are found in other African languages, as in Zulu and Kaffir, and a few words in Sesuto. **1894**, etc. [see *kitchen Dutch* s.v. *KITCHEN *sb.* 7]. **1916** J. BUCHAN *Greenmantle* ix. 120, I spoke rapidly in Sesutu, for I was afraid the captain might know Dutch. **1939** tr. *E. N. Marais's My Friends the Baboons* vii. 81 From the struggling mass there arose constant laughter, mingled with Sesutu curses of the grossest kind. **1953** P. LANHAM *Blanket Boy's Moon* IV. iii. 208, I am a Mosotho; I love Lesotho; I love my language Sesotho. **1975** J. MCCLURE *Snake* x. 138 Marais made a point of thanking her in Sesotho, the only Bantu language he spoke. **1980** —— *Blood of Englishman* ix. 86 Zondi was fluent in Afrikaans ..and Sesuto.

Sesquesahamock, obs. var. *SUSQUEHANNOCK.

sesqui-. Add: **1. b. sesquite·rpene, -te·rpenoid,** any terpene having the formula $C_{15}H_{24}$; any simple derivative of such a compound.

1888 Sesquiterpene [in Dict.]. **1922** *Nature* 16 Feb. 226/2 The principal constituents identified are safral, camphor, pinene, sesquiterpenes, eugenol, and alcoholic bodies. **1966** *New Scientist* 8 Dec. 576/2 The substance.. is derived from farnesol, one of the basic sesquiterpenes, vegetable substances..which imitate the function of the juvenile hormone. **1976** *Nature* 5 Aug. 487/2 The essential oils D-bornyl acetate, α- and β-santalol and several plant sesquiterpene hydrocarbons have been shown to induce sexual excitement in male American cockroaches. **1951** *Jrnl. Chem. Soc.* 2988 (*heading*) Sesquiterpenoids... Evidence for a nine-membered ring in caryophyllene. **1976** *Nature* 5 Aug. 488/2 Cadinol, a sesquiterpenoid biogenetically related to germacrene D, has been isolated from a plant and shown to be a stimulant for both male and female cockroaches.

sesquicentenary (se:skwisentī·nări). [f. SESQUI- + CENTENARY *sb.*] A one-hundred-and-fiftieth anniversary; a festival celebrating this; = SESQUICENTENNIAL *sb.*

1961 in WEBSTER. **1969** *New Scientist* 20 Nov. 389/1 The Cambridge Philosophical Society has just celebrated its sesquicentenary. **1978** *Times* 9 Jan. 9/7 This weekend's two 'Mainly Schubert' concerts..were of a kind to make one wish that his centenary celebrations, this year is the sesquicentenary of his death, came around more often.

sesquicentennial, *a.* and *sb.* For *U.S.* read chiefly *U.S.* and add: **B.** *sb.* (Later examples.)

1931 [see *RED *sb.*[1] 1 g]. **1976** *Times Lit. Suppl.* 12 Mar. 278/2 In 1926 the sesquicentennial [of Adam Smith's *Wealth of Nations*] was celebrated more modestly with a series of lectures given in the new home of economic orthodoxy, the London School of Economics. **1978** *Nature* 8 June 421/2 This year is the sesquicentennial of the announcement by Wöhler that marked the birth of synthetic organic chemistry.

sesquioxide. Add: Hence **se:squioxi·dic** *a.*

1906 *Proc. R. Inst.* XVII. 102 Sesquioxydic mordants. **1932** [see *red loam* s.v. *RED *a.* 17 e].

sesquiplane (se·skwĭplēⁱn). Now *Hist.* Also ‖ **sesquiplan.** [ad. F. *sesquiplan*, f. *sesqui-* SESQUI- + *plan* PLANE *sb.*[3]] A biplane having one wing of surface area not more than half that of the other.

1921 *Flight* 29 Sept. 650/2 The Nieuport-Delage 'Sesquiplans' are to all intents and purposes monoplanes, but with a small plane covering-in the wheel axle as in some of the German Fokkers. **1921** *Aeroplane* 5 Oct. 293/2 Why the machine is called the 'Sesquiplan' is even a greater mystery than the name of the 'Bamel'. *Ibid.* 19 Oct. 348/2 (*heading*) What is a sesquiplane? **1930** *Flight* 17 Jan. 115/2 Its most unusual feature was that, although a *sesquiplane*, its top wing was smaller in span and chord than the lower wing. **1939** C. H. L. NEEDHAM *Aircraft Design* I. vi. 74 The sesquiplane arrangement, in which one wing, generally the top, has roughly twice the area of the lower wing, is a compromise which enables the advantages of the biplane structure to be combined with somewhat improved aerodynamic characteristics. **1960** C. H. GIBBS-SMITH *Aeroplane* II. 220 The Coanda sesquiplane of 1910. There has recently arisen some controversy about this machine... Until recently it has been accepted as an all-wood sesquiplane, with cantilever wings, powered by a 50-h.p. Clerget engine driving a 'turbo-propulseur' in the form of a large but simple ducted air-fan. **1981** ANDREWS & MORGAN *Supermarine Aircraft since 1914* 174 The superstructure was of sesquiplane form, that is with the lower wing only one third the area of the top wing.

sessile, *a.* Add: **2.** Also in extended use.

1917 M. WEBB *Gone to Earth* xiii. 118 People remained in a sessile state over tea for a long time. **1926** T. E. LAWRENCE *Seven Pillars* (1935) 7 The current of tribal movements..sessile or nomad. **1930** AUDEN *Poems* 56 No chattering valves of laughter emphasised Nor the swept gown ends of a gesture stirred The sessile hush. **1971** *Guinness Bk. Records* (ed. 18) 169/2 The longest recorded push of a normally sessile object is of 411 miles in the case of a wheeled hospital bed.

2*. *Cryst.* Of a dislocation in a crystal: unable to migrate through the lattice; fixed.

1949 F. C. FRANK in *Proc. Physical Soc.* A. LXII. 202 Glide is prevented by a large restoring force... Such a dislocation will be called 'sessile', in contrast with 'glissile' dislocations—those which are capable of glide. **1966** C. R. TOTTLE *Sci. Engin. Materials* iv. 101 Frank described one form of sessile dislocation, in which an aggregate of vacant lattice sites collapses to form a loop of dislocation surrounding a disk of stacking fault. **1973** J. G. TWEEDDALE *Materials Technol.* I. v. 111 In the latter case they lock together (forming a sessile dislocation) and become very difficult to separate.

3. sessile oak, *Quercus petræa*, which has stalkless acorns; = DURMAST.

[**1838** J. C. LOUDON *Arboretum et Fruticetum Britannicum* III. 1736 (*heading*) The sessile-flowered Oak.] **1906** ELWES & HENRY *Trees Gt. Brit.* II. 291 Sessile or Durmast Oak... More regular branching, resulting in a denser crown of foliage. **1971** *Country Life* 23 Dec. 1772/1 The lighter soils and hills were covered by the sessile oak, with acorns pressed against the twigs, and leaves on long stalks.

session, *sb.* Add: **2. a.** Also, a business period on the Stock Exchange and other commercial markets.

1928 *Daily Mail* 25 July 19/3 At second session Tin cash £217 15*s.* to £217 17*s.* 6*d.* **1981** *Times* 1 May 20/2 Leading industrials enjoyed one of the best sessions for some time.

3. d. (Earlier and later examples.) Now in general use, of both the school and the university year. Also, a portion of the day during which classes are given.

1714 J. MORICE *Let.* 2 Aug. in W. C. Dickinson *Two Students at St. Andrews* (1952) 53 Alexander Sharp..being a Double Bajan with Mr Pringle last Session. **1862** G. MEREDITH *Let.* 23 Dec. (1970) I. 180, I presume that if I send to Bankers at Norwich, according to direction, before the next session, it will do. **1911** *Rep. Labour & Soc. Cond. Germany* (Tariff Reform League) III. VI. 126 Children go to school at seven o'clock in the morning and stay until eleven; then there is a break, the next session commencing at two and going on till five. **1932** *Leader* 9 July 1 The college is recognised and aided by the Government Board of Indian Medicine. The next session begins from 1st August, 1932. **1976** *Billings* (Montana) *Gaz.* 27 June 2-D/6 Temporary shelter became a problem... Ricks College in Rexburg, a junior college on high ground, has opened its doors until its summer session starts.

4. b. Cf. *QUARTER-SESSIONS 1.

6*. *transf.* [Senses not necessarily dependent upon the notion of 'sitting'.] A period of time given to or set aside for the pursuit of a particular activity. **a.** *gen.*

1920, etc. [see *BULL *sb.*[4] 3 b]. **1970** [see *rap session* s.v. *RAP *sb.*[1] 7]. **1976** *Cumberland News* 3 Dec. 24/5 A short session of dominoes followed.

b. in which musicians perform music, esp. for recording. Also, the music so recorded. Cf. *jam session* s.v. *JAM *sb.*[1] 3; *recording session* s.v. *RECORDING *vbl. sb.* 5.

1927 [see *recording session* s.v. *RECORDING *vbl. sb.* 5]. **1929** *Melody Maker* Apr. 381/1 The trouble is due to inferior musicians being engaged for this session. **1947** G. BEALL in R. de Toledano *Frontiers of Jazz* vii. 87 He is present on most of the records, however, taking part in the recording session although the men know his part would not be directly apparent. **1962** *Radio Times* 17 May 43 The jazz musician..is merely inviting himself back to his friend's place for a beer after their session. **1969** R. A. NOBLETT *Stavin' Chain* 7 This version has not been released on record... The session is, however, interesting.

c. A disturbance or argument. *colloq.* (chiefly *Austral.* and *N.Z.*).

1919 H. L. WILSON *Ma Pettengill* iv. 130 Then Ben came down and had a wholehearted session with me. He said I ought to have a talk with Ed and reason him out of his folly. **1930** L. W. LOWER *Here's Luck* i. 5 We had a bit of a session—a 'go in' as they call it. I tried to reason with him. **1949** J. R. COLE *It was so Late* 10 'Don't shoot the barman, he's half shot already.'.. 'Bit of a session, eh?'

7. (sense 6) *session clerk* (later example); (sense 6*) *session fee, man, work*; **session musician,** one who is engaged to play music, usu. accompaniments, at a recording session.

1876 Session clerk [see *PAROCHIAL *a.* (*sb.*) 1 a]. **1977** *Times* 1 Nov. 14/5 The orchestra had a choice: either to take a share of the royalties or settle for what the trade calls a session fee—a once-and-for-all payment. **1958** J. ASMAN in P. Gammond *Decca Bk. Jazz* xiv. 170 Men who worked in a number of musical fields, providing the recording studios with a reliable nucleus of session-men for every kind of date. **1980** *Oxford Times* 20 June 18 She is expertly backed by..fine sessionmen. **1968** *Guardian* 23 Feb. 10/6 The vast majority of pop records made rely to some extent on session musicians. **1980** P. GOSLING *Loser's Blues* ii. 12 Separately as session musicians on other pop discs they were occasionally..in the charts. **1976** J. WAINWRIGHT *Walther P. 38* 82, I moved around from band to band..and sat in on my share of session work at the recording studios.

sessional, *a.* Add: **c.** Also Canad., *sessional indemnity*, the remuneration received by a member of a legislative assembly.

1900 E. B. OSBORN *Greater Canada* 105 The average partisan gets to Ottawa for the sake of his sessional indemnity and what he can make by means of his position. **1963** *Globe & Mail* (Toronto) 12 July 8/2 Increases in sessional indemnities and expenses that the Quebec Legislature has just approved put it in a class by itself.

d. Pertaining to, or lasting a session (sense 3 d) in an educational institution.

1965 *Listener* 28 Jan. 137/2 Each student has to pursue two sessional courses, which last the whole year, designed to give an introduction to some subject not studied at sixth-form level. **1978** *Sci. Amer.* Jan. 12/2 Geesey is a sessional lecturer in the department of biochemistry and microbiology at the University of Victoria in British Columbia.

e. Pertaining to any period of activity of limited duration. Cf. *SESSION *sb.* 6*.

1973 *Scotsman* 12 Jan. 17/4 (Advt.), Part-time medical officers for sessional work. **1977** *Times* 29 Aug. 6/2 Members of mixed card clubs paid a sessional fee according to the stake at their table.

sessioneer (seʃənīᵊ·ɹ). [f. SESSION *sb.* + -EER.] = *session musician* s.v. *SESSION *sb.* 7.

1958 T. HALL in P. Gammond *Decca Bk. Jazz* xix. 235 Joe Muddel is one of the busiest 'sessioneers' in Britain's radio, film and TV studios. **1977** *Sounds* 9 July 34/3 He's marshalled such star sessioneers as Richie Albright..and the Memphis Horns into fine order.

‖ **sestiere** (sestiẹ̄·re). Pl. **-ieri.** [It., f. L. *sextārius* the sixth part of a measure.] In Italy: one of six districts or areas of a city. Cf. *QUARTIERE.

1599 L. LEWKENOR tr. *Contarini's Commonwealth & Govt. Venice* 185 The Citie of Venice is divided into sixe parts, which they call Sestieri. **1673** J. RAY *Observations Journey Low-Countries* 151 This City [*sc.* Venice] is.. divided into six parts or regions, called thence *Sestieri.* **1832** S. DE SISMONDI *Hist. Ital. Republics* iv. 84 The town [of Florence] was divided into six parts, each *sestier*, as it was called, named two *anziani.* **1893** J. A. SYMONDS tr. A. Condivi in *Life of Michelangelo* I. i. 2 He was appointed captain of a Sestiere; for Florence in those days was divided into Sestieri, instead of Quartieri. **1934** *Burlington Mag.* Sept. 100/1 St. Peter, the patron of the *sestiere* of the town which he represented. **1980** *Times* 8 Dec. (Winter Holidays Suppl.) p. v/4 The most satisfactory way of tackling the surface of [Venetian] sights is to concentrate on one of the city's six *sestieri* (districts) at a time.

seston (se·stǫn). *Biol.* and *Oceanogr.* [a. G. *seston* (R. Kolkwitz 1912, in *Ber. Deut. Bot. Ges.* XXX. 341), ad. Gr. σηστόν, neut. of σηστός that which is filtered, f. σήθειν to strain, filter; cf. PLANKTON.] Fine particulate matter suspended in water, esp. that which is organic or living.

1916 B. D. JACKSON *Gloss. Bot. Terms* (ed. 3) 344/2 *Seston*, plankton material retained by very fine meshed sieves. **1941** *Ecol. Monogr.* XI. 58/1 The varieties in sestonic phosphorus are correlated with both the mass of organic seston and the quantity of phytoplankton, as measured by its chlorophyll content. **1957** G. E. HUTCHINSON *Treat. Limnol.* I. vi. 417 Seston color of this sort is often observed in highly productive lakes. **1967** *Ibid.* II. xix. 235 The seston consists of bioseston, or plankton and nekton, which latter is ordinarily quantitatively negligible, and of abioseston or tripton. *Ibid.* 243 The entire mass of suspended matter in a volume of free water is called seston, the nonliving part, tripton. **1971** *New Scientist* 15 July 145/2 The evidence suggests that the amount of chlorophyll from phytoplankton..is diminishing.., while the amount of seston (oxygen consumers) is increasing.

Hence **sesto·nic** *a.*, of, pertaining to, or being seston.

1941 [see above]. **1967** *Oceanogr. & Marine Biol.* V. 221 At a glance these ribbons appeared to be sestonic debris from coastal algae of phanerogams.

Sesuto, Sesutu, varr. *SESOTHO.

set, *sb.*[1] Add: **I. 7. b.** A grudge. Chiefly in phr. *to have* (or *take*) *a set on* (a person), to have a grudge against. *Austral.* and *N.Z. colloq.* Cf. *SET *v.* 125 b.

1903 'T. COLLINS' *Such is Life* (1937) i. 36 'Hasn't Warrigal Alf got a set on you, too?' asked Thompson coldly. **1941** BAKER *Dict. Austral. Slang* 64 *Set*, a grudge against (someone), e.g., 'have a set on someone'. **1946** K. TENNANT *Lost Haven* (1947) xiv. 228 If the Old Man hadn't tried to give Mark Thorne such particular hell when he was starting his shop, perhaps Thorne wouldn't have taken a set on all the Sudermans... If he hadn't the set on the Sudermans..he wouldn't have wanted to cut off his nose to spite his face. **1948** D. BALLANTYNE *Cunninghams* (1963) II. vi. 155 He had a bit of a set on Frank and Sydney and was always pinching their cheeks and telling them they were young roughnecks.

9. (Later examples.)

1923 *Rep. Progr. Appl. Chem.* VIII. 231 The time of set has been found to depend upon the proportion of combined water..in the hydrated calcium aluminate. *Ibid.*, Removal of water..results in the time of set being reduced. **1957** V. J. KEHOE *Technique Film & Telev. Make-Up* xii. 149 Warm weather hastens the set of the material, so chilling the bowl is advisable to slow down the set. **1963** D. SETON *Essent. Mod. Cookery* 156 The use of lemon juice or citric or tartaric acid is essential to ensure a good set [in marmalade].

b. *initial set* (Building), a condition attained by cement when it begins to stiffen, but before hardening commences.

1891 T. POTTER *Concrete* (ed. 2) I. iii. 104 If a plasterer finds his mortar for stucco is becoming too stiff..the initial set has commenced. **1927** *Engineer* 5 Aug. 143/2 At the completion of the operation the concrete has taken an initial set. **1953** VAN DEN BRANDEN & KNOWLES *Plastering* iv. 98 The initial set of Portland cement mortar occurs about two to three hours after the dry materials have been wetted.

II. 12. Also *spec.* in *Psychol.*, a predisposition or expectation that influences the response of a person or animal: used variously of conscious or unconscious, or of mental or physical, states. Cf. *SET *v.* 93 c.

1890 W. JAMES *Princ. Psychol.* I. iv. 124 It is not in the moment of their forming, but in the moment of their producing *motor effects*, that resolves and aspirations communicate the new 'set' to the brain. **1911** E. L. THORNDIKE *Animal Intell.* vi. 249 If a cat pushes a button around with its nose, while..the act to which its general 'set' impels it..is that of clawing at an opening, it will be less aided in the formation of the habit than if it had been chiefly concerned in what its nose was doing. **1918** R. S. WOODWORTH *Dynamic Psychol.* iii. 56 Danger arouses a 'set' of the nervous system towards escape. **1931** *Brit. Jrnl. Psychol.* Apr. 379 The theory..that ability in proof-reading is largely a matter of attitude or mental 'set'. **1953** J. B. CARROLL *Study of Lang.* iii. 77 There are actually prelinguistic organismic events (sets, attitudes, etc.) which can be identified with what expression theorists regard as 'thoughts' and 'ideas'. **1968** *Science* 13 Dec. 1236/1 'Set' refers to the subject's psychological expectations of what a drug will do to him in relation to his general personality structure. **1979** FORGUS & SHULMAN *Personality* i. 9 We can measure the dominant perceptual sets..and..these sets, in fact, direct perceptual selectivity.

18. b. The action or result of fixing the hair when damp so that it dries in the required style. Also with reference to fixing the hair by other means (with heat, a setting lotion, etc.). Also *hair-set*. Cf. *SET *v.*[1] 81 b.

1933 G. A. FOAN *Art & Craft Hairdressing Spec. Suppl.* iv. 23/2 The procedure here outlined in reference to the final touch must be followed exactly as indicated in order to prevent entirely spoiling the set. **1938** H. GOODMAN *Princ. Professional Beauty Culture* v. 90 After permanent set the intramolecular breakdown and rebuilding processes have effectively evolved a new..conformation. **1940** W. PECK *Bewildering Cares* iv. 110, I met her once at the hairdresser's bewailing that she couldn't afford a nice steak for Herbert on their income, and she had obviously spent the price of it on a 'set'. **1946** K. TENNANT *Lost Haven* (1947) xiii. 204 You can't get a hairset here and I have to do my own. **1975** *Country Life* 27 Mar. 806/1 Many women disliked wearing a hat because it squashed their 'set'.

19. d. *Bell-ringing.* The inverted position of a bell when it is set. Cf. SET *v.* 66.

1677 F. STEDMAN *Campanalogia* 23 A prospect of true ringing at any certain compass under the Sett, may thus be taken. *Ibid.* 39 The reason why one of them is said to move up, is, because he that rings that bell, in the making of the change must hold it up at the Sett a little longer than ordinary, to delay its striking, whereby 'tis made to follow the other note which before it preceded. **1901** H. E. BULWER *Gloss. Techn. Terms Bells* (1904) 33 *Set*, the position of a bell after being 'raised', when it rests mouth upward a little beyond the balancing point [etc.].

e. *Carpentry.* The amount that the blade of a plane projects below the sole.

1898 F. & H. P. FLETCHER *Carpentry & Joinery* xxvi. 281 The set of the plane may be adjusted during use by tapping the iron of the nose. **1950** M. T. TELLING *Carpentry & Joinery* II. 116 All [planes] will do specially true work if properly set and sharpened and many of them have mechanical means of adjusting the cutting iron to a fine set.

III. 23. d. An undeveloped or rudimentary fruit; *collect.*, flowers that have been fertilized and should develop into fruit. Also, the development of fruit following fertilization. Cf. SET *v.* 98.

1888 C. M. DOUGHTY *Trav. in Arabia Deserta* II. xv. 436 Every cluster, which had inclosed in it a spray of the male blossom, was lapped about with a wisp of dry forage; and this defended the sets from early flights of locusts. **1928** *Daily Tel.* 12 June 5/2 Of culinary apples the set appears good on the whole... Dessert cherries have had a fair set. **1929** AUCTER & KNAPP *Orchard & Small Fruit Culture* viii. 369 In such orchards, if the blossoms are properly pollinated, much better sets occur. **1964** H. B. TUKEY *Dwarfed Fruit Trees* xxiii. 422 Bee flight is noticeably reduced at 60 degrees F. or below, and pollination, fertilization, and fruit set are accordingly reduced. **1973** H. G. KINGHAM *U.K. Tomato Man.* xvi. 126 For all crops overhead damping with a course spray helps to improve set.

26. *Lawn Tennis* (always spelt *set*). **a.** A group of games counting as a unit towards a match for the person or pair of persons who win the greater number of games in it.

1949 *Lawn Tennis* ('Know the Game' Ser.) 15 The first player or pair to win six games wins the set, except that should the score become five games each—'Five All'—one player or pair must become two games ahead to win the set. **1980** *Guardian* 14 July 18/5 Miss Jevans..had a bad patch in the second set before winning 6–1, 7–5.

b. *Comb.*, as **set point**, the state of a set when one side or player needs only one point to win the set; also, the point itself (cf. *match-point* (*a*) s.v. *MATCH *sb.*[1]).

1928 *Observer* 1 July 29/3 When that cunning player.. would, at set-point, send one as hard as he could hit it straight down the centre line. **1946** *Times* 26 June 2/3 The Dutch pair, after missing a set point when leading by six games to five, finally secured the first set at 9–7. **1972** D. DELMAN *Sudden Death* vi. 152 Set point. I crouch, racket twirling.

28. (Earlier and later examples.) Also, more widely, the setting, stage furniture, etc., used on stage in a theatre. In *Film-making* and *Television*, the scenery (usu. built up rather than painted) and other properties used in the filming of an individual scene; the place or area in which filming takes place. Freq. in phr. *on* or *off* (*the*) *set*. Also *attrib.* and *Comb.* Cf. *film set* s.v. *FILM *sb.* 7 c.

1859 E. FITZBALL *Thirty-Five Years of Dramatic Author's Life* I. vi. 91 The vast scenes were pushed into sets, imperfectly painted. **1894** MRS. H. WARD *Marcella* I. i. 5 The complete disappearance of this earliest 'set', to use a theatrical phrase, from the scenery of her childhood. **1912** F. A. TALBOT *Moving Pictures: How they are made & Worked* x. (caption facing p. 109), Building a solid set for 'The Two Orphans'. **1918** H. CROY *How Motion Pictures are Made* 107 With the sets determined upon, preparation for the taking of the picture is begun. **1936** WODEHOUSE *Laughing Gas* iv. 51 She was supposed to be on the set, made up, at six on the following a.m. for some retakes. **1947** A. HUXLEY *Let.* 27 July (1969) 573 The ticklish situation on the set made it impossible to come to New York for Claire's wedding. **1953** K. REISZ *Technique Film Editing* i. 60 Dialogue-writing, set-design and acting all become subjugated to this central purpose. **1956** C. McCULLERS in *Mademoiselle* Sept. 174/2 Mabel Goodley, the painter and set-designer. **1961** G. MILLERSON *Telev. Production* i. 15 The set designer, responsible for the scenic treatment. **1973** *Listener* 22 Nov. 727/3 The same people are very much less agreeable in *Meet Pamela* than they are 'off-set' in *Day for Night*. **1977** M. BABSON *Murder, Murder, Little Star* xviii. 154 Had there been a further scene..in the dressing-room? Twinkle was being too good on set.

30. h. A trap or snare; a series of traps. *N. Amer. Trapping.*

1912 V. E. ROE *Maid of Whispering Hills* 74 What is all this beside that which waits the runner of the trail at every 'set' in those many miles? **1942** *Sun* (Baltimore) 2 Feb. 4/3 Each morning the trapper makes the rounds of his 'set'. He strips the skin from the animals..and takes the pelts to market. **1977** *Globe & Mail* (Toronto) 30 Mar. 33/3 We were still within 20 yards of the trap's position, when a 55-pound beaver, swimming unseen under the ice, hit the set.

33. (Later examples.) *esp.* a heavy punch or chisel for use on metal or stone. Cf. *SATE *sb.*

1905 P. N. HASLUCK *Handyman's Bk.* 134/1 For punching the nail head below the surface of the work, the steel set is used. **1920** A. H. FAY *Gloss. Mining & Mineral Industry* 605/1 *Sett*, a quarryman's term for a square-faced steel tool which is held in position and struck with a sledge to cause a fracture in a rock mass. **1924** [see *BOLSTER *sb.*[1]]. **1942** W. H. ATHERTON *Workshop Pract.* (ed. 2) V. 176 The Hot Sate or Sett..is in constant use for cutting away extraneous metal while hot. **1962** J. G. ROBERTSON *Metalwork* viii. 95 The Hot Set (Sett or Sate)..is used for cutting off on the cutting face of the anvil. A smith holds the work and hot set whilst a striker wields the sledge hammer. The hot set is designed to cut hot metal. **1964** H. HODGES *Artifacts* iv. 77 The heads were either cast, or formed as the rivets were closed using sets (setts) or snaps.

set, *sb.*[2] **I. 2. d.** Substitute for def.: a subdivision of pupils or students (esp. in a single year) for instruction on a particular subject: usu. one of a number of such groupings and often constituted according to ability. (Earlier and later examples.)

1882 in R. S. Churchill *Winston S. Churchill* (1967) I. Compan. I. iii. 90 Place in 3rd Set of 14 boys for ½ Term—14th. **1914** 'I. HAY' *Lighter Side School Life* i. 15 He must know whether Mr. A. in the Senior Science Set is expounding theories of inorganic chemistry which have been obsolete for ten years. **1963** M. BEADLE *These Ruins are Inhabited* vi. 86 Sets are ability groups. In each subject the boys had been divided into fast, average and slower-moving sections; each of these sets met as a class. **1971** P. D. JAMES *Shroud for Nightingale* ii. 41 We haven't used the demonstration room since Nurse Pearce's death but otherwise the set is continuing to work according to plan.

3. a. (Later examples.) Freq. with qualifying adj. or sb. indicating the location, affiliation, or characteristic activities of the group, as *the Bloomsbury* (*Chelsea, Cliveden*, etc.) *set*. Cf. *jet set* s.v. *JET *sb.*[3] 11.

1914 [see *BLOOMSBURY]. **1922** M. COWLEY in *Dial* LXXIII. 231 She [*sc.* K. Mansfield] has three backgrounds only: continental hotels, New Zealand upper-class society, and a certain artistic set in London. **1938** H. NICOLSON *Diary* 19 Sept. (1966) 361 We talk of..how terrible has been the influence of the Cliveden set. **1944** N. COWARD *Middle East Diary* 49 This place is the last refuge of the soi-disant 'International Set'. **1960** J. BETJEMAN *Summoned by Bells* ix. 107, I climbed,.. Until I reached what seemed to me the peak—The leisured set in Canterbury Quad. **1977** *News of World* 17 Apr. 5/5 The Prince of the Beatniks abdicated... He said goodbye to the Chelsea Set.

b. A meeting of a street gang or group of street people', esp. a party; the place where such a group meets. Also, the group itself. *U.S. colloq.*

Freq. in Black English.

1959 *Esquire* Nov. 70 *Set*, a party. **1967** *Trans-Action* Apr. 5/2 The more or less organized center of street life is the 'set'—meaning both the peer group and the places where it hangs out. **1969** R. L. KEISER *Vice Lords* iv. 40 A set had been planned... Throughout the prior week, the set was a constant topic of conversation. The clothes that were going to be worn and the girls that were going to be present were repeatedly discussed. **1970** E. BULLINS *Theme is Blackness* (1973) 178 What's happenin'? What'cha doin' tonight, baby? Why don't we make the set? **1972** J. MILLS *Report to Commissioner* 100 When junkies and pushers on a particular set learn or suspect an agent's identity, he has 'taken a burn'. **1975** *Amer. Speech 1972* XLVII. 152 Blue eyes, you are not in my set.

II. 5. b. = *pump-set, pumpset* s.v. *PUMP *sb.*[1] 6 b.

c **1889** W. TATE *Princ. Mining* xxi. 157 The lifting set delivers into a cistern from which the forcing set pumps the water to bank. **1950** *Water Power* II. 219 The installation comprises two vertical sets consisting of motor and pump only. **1977** *Pump Costs* (5th Techn. Conf. of Brit. Pump Manuf. Assoc.) 231 The circuits were modified to give a signal 'pump unprimed' but not to shut down the set.

c. A piece of electrical or electronic apparatus, as a telephone, a telegraph receiver or transmitter, a radio or television receiver, etc. Also, a radar transmitter and receiver. Cf. *HANDSET.

1891 *Man. Instruct. Army Telegr. Field Telegraphs* Plate II (*caption*) Two single current sets. **1898** *Electrician* 4 Mar. 625/2 A diminutive telephone set..is now being put on the market. **1903** *Science Siftings* XXV. 49/1 The instruments of the portable military outfits are similar to those of the permanent station sets. **1915** A. FAGE *Aeroplane* iv. 42 A wireless set driven by a motor-cycle engine is mounted in front of the passenger's seat. **1923** *Radio Broadcast* Jan. 181/2 Drug stores, music stores, cigar stores, even men's furnishing stores have radio sets for sale. **1931** B. BROWNE *Talking Pictures* vi. 146 Wherever one looked there seemed space and wide, flat walls. One of the larger-sized sets should have been required to fill such an amount of enclosing surfaces. **1936** W. H. S. SMITH *Let.* 13 Dec. in *Young Man's Country* (1977) ii. 46, I dropped in on Stansbury..to hear his wireless which is a very good set. **1948** J. L. HORNUNG *Radar Primer* v. 123 The electrical features of radar sets for use in airplanes are similar to those of sets used on ships. **1955** *Radio Times* 22 Apr. 30/1 (Advt.), Here is a.. table radiogram... Fine sets these Ferguson's. **1961** L. MUMFORD *City in Hist.* xvi. 496 Reality has been progressively reduced to what filters through the screen of the television set. **1972** *Works Engineer* June 12 (*heading*) Standby electric generator sets. **1974** P. N. WILSON *Water Turbines* 17 (*caption*) Model of 83,000 HP Francis turbine hydro-electric set at Eildon Power Station, Australia. **1976** M. GILBERT *Night of Twelfth* ix. 88 He used to have that old set going all day. You'll be just in time for the six o'clock news.

8. f. A number of pieces of Jazz or popular music performed in sequence by a musician or group. Cf. sense 8 b.

1946 B. TREADWELL *Big Bk. Swing* 125/2 *Set*, group of musical selections. **1955** S. WHITMORE *Solo* II. v. 159 Between sets at Fack's Jaeger found himself alone. **1967** *New Yorker* 21 Jan. 52, I played two sets and Marsala asked me to join the band. **1977** *Sounds* 1 Jan., We all write lyrics but they're too disgusting to be included in the set.

10. † **b.** *Math.* Used variously, as defined by the individual author. *Obs.*

1837 W. R. HAMILTON in *Trans. R. Irish Acad.* (Sci.) XVII. 422 The author hopes to publish hereafter..a Theory of Triplets and Sets of Moments. **1848** —— in *Ibid.* XXI. 201 When we have in any manner been led to form successively the separate conceptions of any number of moments of time, we may afterwards form the *new* conception of a system, or momental set, to which all these separate moments belong. **1886** *Phil. Trans. R. Soc.* CLXXVII. 23 If the collection be such that whatever undistinguished components *abcd*..., *pqrs*...we select, and whatever other component *lmno*... we select, *w, x, y, z*... can always be selected from the collection, then the collection will be termed a set.

c. *Math.* and *Logic.* An assemblage of distinct entities, either individually specified or which satisfy certain specified conditions. Cf. *ELEMENT *sb.* 5 d.

1857 *Phil. Trans. R. Soc.* CXLVII. 717 Any values (x_1, y_1, z_1,...) satisfying the equations, are said to constitute a set of roots of the system. **1897** W. BURNSIDE *Theory of Groups* i. 1 Let a_1, a_2, ..., a_n be a set of *n* distinct letters. **1903** *Trans. Amer. Math. Soc.* IV. 27 A set of elements in which a rule of combination O is so defined as to satisfy the following three postulates shall be called an Abelian group with respect to O. **1937** *Jrnl. Symbolic Logic* II. 66 According to the leading idea of the von Neumann set theory we have to deal with two kinds of individuals, which we may distinguish as sets and classes. The distinction may be thought of in this way, that a set is a multitude forming a proper thing, whereas a class is a predicate regarded only with respect to its extension. **1965** PATTERSON & RUTHERFORD *Elem. Abstr. Algebra* i. 3 If *x* is an element of a set *S*, we write $x \in S$. **1972** A. G. HOWSON *Handbk. Terms Algebra & Anal.* ii. 8 A set is a totality of certain definite, distinguishable objects of our intuition or thought—called the elements of the set. This classic definition of a set was given by Georg Cantor in 1874. Such attempts to give elementary definitions of a set are, however, doomed to failure, their being in the main based on the use of undefined synonyms, such as 'collection', and leading to logical inconsistencies (see *Russell paradox*..). For this reason, mathematicians now regard the notion of a set as an undefined, primitive concept. **1975** I. STEWART *Concepts Mod. Math.* iv. 47 There is only one empty set. All empty sets are equal.

d. *transf.* Used variously in *Linguistics* (see quots.).

1935 W. F. TWADDELL *On Defining Phoneme* 60 A modification occurs only in phonetic fractions corresponding to forms, the relations of which constitute relations of sets of micro-phonemes. **1942** BLOCH & TRAGER *Outl. Linguistic Anal.* iii. 45 A structural set is a group of all the phonemes which occur in a given phonetic environment and hence, in that position, directly contrast with each other. **1964** M. A. K. HALLIDAY et al. *Linguistic Sci.* ii. 22 The range of possibilities in a closed choice is called technically a system, that in an open choice a set... We often talk of 'closed system' and 'open set'.

14. *running set*: see *RUNNING *ppl. a.* 17 f.

III. 15. Special Comb.: **set theory**, the branch of mathematics which deals with sets without regard to the nature of their individual constituents; an axiomatization which allows of the discussion of sets; **set-theoretic, -theoretical** *adjs.*, of or pertaining to set theory; hence **set-theoretically** *adv.*

1964 E. MENDELSON *Introd. Math. Logic* p. vii, In the belief that beginners should be exposed to the most natural and easiest proofs, free-swinging set-theoretic methods have been used. **1957** P. SUPPES *Introd. Logic* xi. 232 A function is a set-theoretical, not a linguistic, entity. **1952** S. C. KLEENE *Introd. Metamath.* xiv. 424 B is a 'theorem' set-theoretically. **1936** W. V. QUINE in *Jrnl. Symbolic Logic* June 45 Set-theoretic Foundations for Logic... In his set theory Zermelo uses the variables 'x', 'y', etc. for the representation of 'things' generally. **1937** *Jrnl. Symbolic Logic* II. 65 The system of axioms for set theory to be exhibited in this paper is a modification of the axiom system due to von Neumann. **1971** *Where* Nov. 332/1 Many would probably 'solve' it by using set theory and drawing a Venn diagram. **1975** N. CHOMSKY *Logical Struct. Linguistic Theory* iii. 107 We will assume ..that each level includes a full set theory, so that we can also form sets of strings, sequences of strings, etc.

set, *v.*[1] Add: **I. 5. a.** (Later U.S. examples.)

1884 C. H. SMITH *Bill Arp's Scrap Bk.* vi. 74 Lawyers and doctors have to set about town. **1913** H. KEPHART *Our Southern Highlanders* xiii. 298 'Come in and set.' 'Cain't stop long.' **1938** M. K. RAWLINGS *Yearling* i. 12 'If a feller'd light me a candle,' she said, 'I'd git shut o' the dishwashin' and mebbe have time to set and enjoy myself.' **1974** P. DE VRIES *Glory of Hummingbird* (1975) iii. 37 Lolly came almost every evening to set a spell.

III. 14. c. (Earlier example.)

1844 W. J. PELL *Treat. Game of Dominoes* 22 The largest count that can be made..is 129. To effect this, the winning hand must set.

IV. 25. a. Also, *to set afoot* or *on foot* (see AFOOT 3, FOOT *sb.* 32 c).

1615 R. COCKS *Jrnl.* 30 July (1883) I. 28 An other matter is now set on foote, which I never did heare of till this instant. **1638** [see AFOOT 3]. **1736** T. LEDIARD *Life Marlborough* III. 364 A Treaty of Peace was again set on foot. **1829** SCOTT *Anne of Geierstein* III. ix. 263 He..has in a right godly manner tried to set afoot a treaty of peace with my own father. **1890** *Sunday Mag.* Aug. 531/2 Enquiries were at once set on foot.

34. Also *to set a fire* (without prepositional complement): to kindle or start a fire. *U.S.*

1906 *N.Y. Even. Post* 15 Nov. 3 Two fires in tenement house letter boxes were set to-day at an early hour. **1976** *Washington Post* 19 Apr. B1/7 The school had been broken into and the fire had been set.

VI. 65. b. *Computers.* To cause (a binary storage unit) to enter a prescribed state, *spec.* that representing 1. Also *intr.*, to enter a prescribed state.

1948 *Electronics* Apr. 127/1 The initial values can be set into the computer without too much time lag. **1957** R. K. RICHARDS *Digital Computer Components & Circuits* vi. 263 The real problem in devising a large-capacity storage system is not so much in the storage elements themselves as in providing means to gain access to any specified individual storage element for the purpose of sensing..or setting its status. **1968** MALEY & HEILWEIL *Introd. Digital Computers* vi. 82 The latch is simply a circuit whose output can be set to 1, or reset to 0, and it will remain at either one of these two values until another set or reset operation changes its value. **1971** J. H. SMITH *Digital Logic* i. 12 A binary divider is a modified toggle which has only one input. If electrical pulses are applied to this input the unit will 'set'. The second pulse will 'reset' the circuit.

72. Delete † and add later *absol.* example.

1964 F. BOWERS *Bibliogr. & Textual Criticism* VI. i. 161 The sole purpose of saving the printer the labour of setting from a difficult manuscript.

73. to put (words) *to* music (examples); to put (music) *to* words: no longer *Obs.*

1965 *Listener* 3 June 836/2 One does not make music 'colloquial' by using it to set colloquial words. **1966** BENNETT & SMITHERS *Early M.E. Verse & Prose* 108 The music to which it [*sc.* a lyric] is set clearly shows that the words were composed to fit the tune. **1970** *Oxf. Compan. Music* (ed. 10) 498/1 The tunes set to these hymns were partly adaptations of the ancient plainsong, partly arrangements of folk song and partly original. **1979** *N.Y. Rev. Bks.* 17 May 32/4 Byrd set this notorious poem to music, and the setting certainly did not escape notice.

74. *to set the stage* (*for*): also *fig.*, to prepare the way or conditions for (an event, etc.).

1937 *Discovery* June 175/1 Given suitable conditions, the stage is always set for the transformation. **1972** *Review & Herald* 7 Dec. 12/2 However, it is first necessary to 'set the stage'. **1980** *Sci. Amer.* Jan. 122/1, I can best set the stage for describing Morelli's instrument by reviewing the two basic types of spectroscope and spectrophotometer.

76. b. To adjust (the blade of a plane in relation to the sole) in order to vary the depth of cut.

1677 J. MOXON *Mech. Exerc.* IV. 63 When you set the Iron of the Fore-Plain, consider the Stuff you are to work upon. **1857–9** E. L. TARBUCK *Encycl. Pract. Carpentry & Joinery* I. iii. 26 The projection of the plane iron may be very nicely regulated, or set, rank, or fine, that is projecting from the face in a greater or less degree. **1938** C. H. HAYWARD *Carpentry Bk.* i. 27 When a piece of wood with a difficult grain has to be planed, the back-iron is advanced and the plane set as fine as possible.

81. Restrict † *Obs.* to sense in Dict. and add: **b.** To arrange and fix (the hair) when damp so that it dries in the desired style; *occas.*, to fix a hair-style by other means.

1926 *Hairdressing* 10 Sept. 241/1 This can only be done by superior work; namely, excellent setting of the finished permanent. **1932** *Mod. Woman* Feb. 72/1 A perfectly easy method of keeping your hair perfectly waved, set and curled at home. **1957** V. J. KEHOE *Technique Film & Telev. Make-Up* xv. 214 Hair lacquer or spray..is used for setting the hair in place after it has been dressed. **1967** N. FREELING *Strike out where not Applicable* 10 Ash-blonde hair cut fairly short and set every week in Leiden. **1976** C. BERMANT *Coming Home* I. vii. 105 Her hair was always smartly set.

86. Delete *Obs.* or *arch.*

1980 M. BODDY *Building Societies* iv. 46 The composite rate [of tax paid by building societies] was set at 79·3 per cent of the basic rate (then 35 per cent), i.e. 27·75 per cent.

VIII. 92. Delete 'Now *dial.*' Now usu. in sense 'likely, about (to)'. Also, in *Journalese*, const. *for* followed by *sb.*

1976 *Daily Tel.* 30 Nov. 1/6 Electricity prices are set to go up again on New Year's Day. **1978** *Sunday Tel.* 10 Dec. 1 (*heading*) Callaghan set for showdown with Benn. **1979** *Daily Tel.* 28 Feb. 2/6 The Inner City partnerships outside London seem set for increases above the average. **1982** *Times* 16 Oct. 9/6 The armchair moralists of Academe..are now set to carp about the sinking of the Belgrano.

93. c. *Psychol.* To predispose (a person or other organism) to a given response; usu. *pass.* Also *intr.* for *pass.* Cf. *SET *sb.*[1] 12.

1909 *Amer. Jrnl. Psychol.* XX. 569 The psychophysical organism 'sets' to meet an imminent situation; and on the conscious side, this 'set' is expectation. **1938** *Mind* XLVII. 88 An observer in an experiment is said to be *set* towards an aspect of a situation if he is directed to it by the instructions. **1961** LINDGREN & BYRNE *Psychol.* vi. 143/2 Alterations in our familiar surroundings are often missed because we are 'set' to perceive certain stimuli.

95. c. Also *spec.* of an athlete poised to start a race (further *pass.* examples). In wider use: to be prepared for action; to be ready (*to* do something). Freq. in phr. (*to be*) *all set.* Cf. *on your mark*(*s*), (*get set, go*) s.v. *MARK *sb.*[1] 12 e.

1844 J. GREGG *Commerce of Prairies* I. 51 Each teamster vies with his fellow..and it is a matter of boastful pride to be the first to cry out—'All's set!' **1882** W. A. BAILLIE-GROHMAN *Camps in Rockies* i. 3 'All set!' echoes from each of the horsemen in front. **1913** [see *CROUCH *sb.*[2] b]. **1930** *Amer. Speech* VI. 120 Set for big bout. **1935** *Encycl. Sports* 580/1 At the words 'Get set' you should let the weight come forward on to the finger tips and the leading foot, raising the left knee but lowering the back and head. **1949** N. MARSH *Swing, Brother, Swing* v. 84 All set, boys? Let's go. **1956** A. H. COMPTON *Atomic Quest* iii. 162 The du Pont Company was getting set to build the plutonium production plant. **1957** DUNCAN & BONE *Oxf. Pocket Bk. Athletic Training* (ed. 2) v. 62 On the command 'set' the body rises up smoothly with the body-weight on the hands and front foot. **1962** J. HELLER *Catch-22* vi. 51 Just when I was all set to really start stashing it away, they had to manufacture fascism and start a war. **1979** *Daily Tel.* 26 Feb. 21/4 National Westminster is set to produce full year figures tomorrow.

97. a. (Later example.)

1974 M. LINDLAW *Super Sweets & Puddings* 9 *To set jelly quickly.* Dissolve the jelly tablet in ½ pint (1½dl) hot water, then make up to 1 pint (6dl) with cold water or ice cubes. Stir until on the point of setting.

c. (Later examples.)

1963 D. SETON *Essent. Mod. Cookery* 151 The sugar is very important in jam-making. If too much or too little is used, the jam will not set. **1973** *Cooking for Today* (Good Housekeeping) 264/4 Pour one third of this jelly into a picnic jelly mould and put in a cool place to set.

X. 125. b. Phr. *to have* or *get* (a person) *set*: to have a score to settle with, 'have it in for' (that person). *Austral.* and *N.Z. slang.* Cf. *SET *sb.*[1] 7 b.

1916 C. J. DENNIS *Songs Sentimental Bloke* 40 This Romeo 'e's lurkin' wiv a crew—A dead tough crowd o' crooks—called Montague. 'Is cliner's push—wot's nicknamed Capulet—They 'as 'em set. *c* **1926** 'MIXER' *Transport Workers' Song Bk*, 17 You growl and swear you can't get work Or the boss has got you set. **1945** BAKER *Austral. Lang.* vi. 121 A man who has acquired a strong dislike of another person... He *gets someone set* and *words him*, rebukes him. **1959** —— *Drum* 112 *Get someone set*, to have a grudge against a person; to prepare to pay someone out.

XII. 141. set back. a. (Later examples.) Hence, with a sum of money as compl.: to cost (a person so much). Also *fig.*, to take aback, to disconcert.

1847 *Spirit of Times* 31 May 159/1 The captain used to boast that he could pack a gallon without its setting him back any. **1884** 'MARK TWAIN' *Huck. Finn* viii. 66 The nigger was set back considerable, because he reckoned it was all done with witchcraft. **1900** ADE *Fables in Slang* 131 Daughter was..seated under a Canopy that had set Father back thirty-two Dollars. **1922** S. LEWIS *Babbitt* x. 142 How much'll it set me back? **1937** J. STEINBECK *Of Mice & Men* 79 'What's it set you back?' George asked. 'Two and a half [dollars].' **1940** H. L. ICKES *Secret Diary* (1954) III. 183 This set him back on his heels. **1966** 'J. HACKSTON' *Father clears Out* 53 'Goin' t' leave it?' the prince asked, a bit set back. **1974** *Country Life* 14 Nov. 1445/1 Even a moderately-sized piece of cheesecake sets you back 20p.

146. set in. d. Also *pass.*

1837 DICKENS *Let.* ? Dec. (1965) I. 346, I was in the humour for writing last night—..was regularly set in—when there came a double knock.

149. set out. a*. To spread (leather) on a flat surface while wet, in order that it may dry free from wrinkles.

1885 C. T. DAVIS *Manuf. Leather* xxiii. 423 The side having been stuffed, and next 'set out'..the next step in the process of manufacturing upper leather is that of whitening. **1909** H. G. BENNETT *Manuf. Leather* xxi. 261 The butts are now struck out, 'set out' or 'pinned'. **1946** J. W. WATERER *Leather in Life, Art & Industry* II. ii. 147 The butts are piled up to drain... They are 'set out' to remove wrinkles and smooth the grain. **1969** T. C. THORSTENSEN *Pract. Leather Technol.* v. 70 After bleaching, the bends are wrung and sent to an oil wheel... This process usually takes about one hour. The leather is 'set out' to smooth and dry.

150. set over. g. To kill or murder. *U.S. Criminals' slang.*

1931 G. IRWIN *Amer. Tramp & Underworld Slang* 166 *Set over*, to kill, probably since the victim is set over or apart. **1944** W. R. BURNETT *Nobody lives Forever* xxii. 159 I've been trying to find you ever since you set Doc over. **1949** —— *Asphalt Jungle* xxxiii. 211 They have to set a guy over.

154. set up. m. (*f*) (Earlier and later examples.) Also in phr. *to set them up*, to provide free drinks.

1880 A. A. HAYES in *Harper's New Monthly Mag.* Jan. 209/1 You bet he lived high; always set up the drinks. **1883** SWEET & KNOX *On Mexican Mustang* iii. 47 Then he swore, and cussed the 'demmed country, you know', but finally got into good humor, and set 'em up all round. **1906** C. DE L. CANFIELD *Forty-Niner* ix. 83 Of course, it was drinks all around; you can't do anything in this country without setting 'em up first. **1949** [see *rock candy* s.v. *ROCK *sb.*[1] 9 a]. **1965** G. MELLY *Owning Up* vi. 64 In exchange for a song or two from me, he was prepared to set them up all night.

p. (*c*) To make the necessary interconnections and initial settings in (a computer) for the performance of a particular calculation; to do this so that the computer will solve (an equation), perform (a calculation), etc.

1931 *Jrnl. Franklin Inst.* CCXII. 459 A bus shaft is assigned to each significant quantity appearing in the equation. The several relations existing between these are then set up by means of connections to the operating units. **1948** *Electronics* Apr. 124/1 When combining circuit elements to form an analog computer, the first step is to set up the differential equations to be solved. *Ibid.* 126/3 Consider setting up the computer for solving the differential equation $p^2y - 0{\cdot}2py - y = 0$. **1962** MACKAY & FISHER *Analogue Computing at Ultra-High Speed* xiii. 171 The procedure for setting up a given equation on an analyser is not difficult. **1964** G. A. & T. M. KORN *Electronic Analog & Hybrid Computers* ii. 37 The computer is 'set up' for the given problem when a suitable arrangement of computing elements establishes the correct relationships between computer voltages.

aa. (*c*) To prepare, set in readiness (apparatus, machinery, etc.). (A more generalized application of prec. sense.)

1922 H. D. BURGHARDT *Machine Tool Operations* II.

viii. 157 Sometimes an unskilled man or boy can operate several machines after they have been 'set up' by a skilled mechanic. **1962** A. NISBETT *Technique Sound Studio* viii. 142 To be able to put the disc on the turntable, locate the right groove, . . and set the record up ready for playing in. **1977** P. DICKINSON *Walking Dead* I. iii. 39 Foxe felt most fully alive. . when he was setting up a new experiment.

(*d*) *gen.* To make preparations or arrangements for; to contrive, plot (a move, trick, etc.); to arrange (a social engagement).

1965 P. O'DONNELL *Modesty Blaise* vii. 83 If Gabriel or anyone else has been setting up a job from here, Paco will know about it. **1968** [see *NIM *sb.*[2]]. **1971** *Daily Tel.* 28 Oct. 3 (*heading*) Boy, 12, set up cripple's death jury is told. **1973** R. BUSBY *Pattern of Violence* vi. 104 Let's set this thing up. I'll get onto the divisional commander. **1973** *Houston* (Texas) *Chron.* (Suppl.) 14 Oct. 8/4 We set up a date and a couple of weeks later Agnew and I sat down in his suite in a Chicago hotel. **1978** R. THOMAS *Chinaman's Chance* xxii. 228 'Could you set it up?' 'No problem.'

cc. (*c*) To bring (someone) to a position from which he may be knocked down, to make vulnerable (*lit.*, as in *Pugilism*); *fig.* (*colloq.* and *slang*), to lead on in order to fool, cheat, or incriminate (a person); to 'frame'. orig. *U.S.*

1950 J. DEMPSEY *Championship Fighting* x. 49 If you can land solidly with a straight left or with a left hook, you'll generally knock your opponent off balance, at least, and 'set him up' for a pot-shot with your right. **1956** B. HOLIDAY *Lady sings Blues* xxi. 168 When I saw them running across the rooftops with my money, I knew I'd been had. Somebody had set me up. **1963** L. DEIGHTON *Horse under Water* xxxi. 127 Either Mr Ivor Batcher was double-crossing his boss or I was being set up. **1964** S. BELLOW *Herzog* 109 Of course he understood that Tennie was setting him up, and that he was a sucker for just the sort of appeal she made. **1979** A. PRICE *Tomorrow's Ghost* ii. 23 'You're deliberately using them for bait, for God's sake.' 'Oh no we're not... We didn't set them up.' **1981** 'E. V. CUNNINGHAM' *Case of Sliding Pool* ix. 101 He had a partner, whom he set up from the very beginning for the kill.

kk. (Later examples.)

1935 R. BASS in *Scribner's Mag.* Feb. 122/1 The body must never be left alone for an instant until it is left in the grave. It must be 'set up' with. **1968** E. R. BUCKLER *Ox Bells & Fireflies* ix. 127 Neighbors took turns 'setting up' with the patient night after night.

set, *v.*[2] [f. SET *sb.*[2]] *trans.* To group (pupils) into sets (see SET *sb.*[2] 2 d in Dict. and Suppl.); also *absol.* Hence **se·tting** *vbl. sb.*[2]

1953 *Organ. Comprehensive Secondary Schools* (London County Council) 14 A practicable arrangement would be to re-set only across three adjacent forms. 'Setting' in this way would not determine the rate at which each set would work. **1957** B. SIMON *New Trends in Eng. Educ.* II. 46, I will not ask the reader to follow me in the intricacies of fifth-year setting. **1962** J. VAIZEY *Britain in Sixties* v. 56 Some. . feel that. . children should be 'setted' for each subject. **1965** *Observer* 7 Nov. 4/8 Mathematics teachers consider it necessary to set after two terms. **1973** MORRISON & MCINTYRE *Teachers & Teaching* (ed. 2) iii. 126 There is reason to believe that the practise of 'setting'—different streaming for each of several subjects—reduces these effects. **1975** *Language for Life* (Dept. Educ. & Sci.) xv. 224 Speaking purely for English, most of us have reservations about arrangements by which pupils are streamed or setted according to ability.

set, *ppl. a.* Add: **I. 1. a.** (Later examples of *set book*. Also *set text*.)

1966 N. NICOLSON in H. Nicolson *Diaries & Lett.* (1966) 28 He read. . the whole of Aeschylus' *Seven Against Thebes* because it was my set-book at school. **1968** *Listener* 22 Aug. 244/3 By the end of 1967, however, it had sold more than 15,000 copies, mainly because a few enterprising examining bodies had chosen it as a set book for A-level GCE. **1982** *Times* 12 Aug. 8/3 Mrs Thatcher's Family Policy Committee has been given a set text in the form of a paper by the recently appointed head of the Downing Street Policy Unit.

i. Of jelly: that has become firm. Cf. SET *v.*[1] 97 a, c

1973 *Cooking for Today* (Good Housekeeping) 264/4 Pour half this vanilla jelly on to the set coffee jelly. **1974** M. LINDLAW *Super Sweets & Puddings* 58 Make up the Angel Delight. . and pipe or swirl on to the set jelly.

2. e. Of a meal in a hotel, etc.: consisting of a predetermined collection of dishes or items of food at a fixed price.

1914 'SAKI' *Beasts & Super-Beasts* 308 The one-and sixpenny set dinner receded. . to a Sunday extravagance. **1923** C. STONE *Let.* 30 June in C. Mackenzie *My Life & Times* (1966) V. 250, I fancy F. will get herself set teas, and other meals out. **1938** D. DU MAURIER *Rebecca* xxvi. 423 Colonel Julyan waded through the whole set lunch. **1957** W. CAMP *Prospects of Love* III. i. 148 She promptly chose the five shilling set meal. **1973** J. PATTINSON *Search Warrant* vii. 105 If you have the set lunch, it comes cheaper. **1978** *Times* 3 June 11/4 There was an advertised set lunch at £5.50 plus VAT.

6. c. *set fair*: also *fig.* and in extended use.

1873 BROWNING *Red Cotton Night-Cap Country* ii. 108 Like some kindly weathercock. . stuck fast at Set Fair. **1921** W. DE LA MARE *Mem. Midget* xxix. 197 Her mood, like our weather that April, was almost always 'set fair'. **1978** J. PEARSON *Façades* xxiii. 399 Everything appeared set fair for the happiest of stays.

II. 8. set copper, a form of metallic copper containing about 6 per cent of cuprous oxide, produced by oxidation during refining; **set joint** *U.S. slang* (see quots. and *flat joint* (*b*) s.v. *FLAT *a.* 15); **set point,** the value of a physical quantity that an automatic controller or regulator is set to maintain; also *transf.*; **set scene** (earlier example); **set scrum(mage),** *Rugby Football*, an organized scrummage ordered by the referee during the course of play; opp. *loose scrum*(*mage*) s.v. *LOOSE *a.* 9; **set shot** *Basketball* a shot at the basket made from a still position; **set stocking** *Agric.* (orig. *N.Z.*), the grazing of animals, esp. sheep, in the same pasture for a considerable period; so **set-stock** *v. trans.*

1904 *Trans. Amer. Inst. Mining Engineers* XXXIV. 671 Some of the copper is oxidized to cuprous oxide and dissolved by the metal bath. When the quantity of dissolved cuprous oxide has reached about 6 per cent, the metal is said to have been brought to 'set-copper'. **1959** J. NEWTON *Extractive Metallurgy* vi. 376 Usually it is not possible to take any short-cuts in refining copper—the metal must be carried to the set-copper stage and then poled. **1926** MAINES & GRANT *Wise-Crack Dict.* 14/1 *Set joint*, unbeatable game. **1931** *Amer. Speech* VI. 335 *Set-joint*, . . a gambling device operated with a numbered wheel and arrow-spindle. These are always fitted with a *gimmick* which prevents the customer from winning too often, or which may be used by the operator to lead the customer on until he will place a large bet, when the operator applies the gimmick and the customer loses. **1941** T. J. RHODES *Industr. Instruments for Measurem. & Control* ix. 419 Where it is not permissible for the process temperature to deviate for any appreciable period from the original set point, it is necessary to use a mode of control previously described as proportional and floating. **1972** *Science* 9 June 1125/1 One of the principal homeostatic 'set points', that for body temperature, seems to depend on the constant ratio of Na^+ to Ca^{2+} in the caudal hypothalamus. **1975** D. G. FINK *Electronics Engineers' Handbk.* xxiv. 14 Display of the measurement, set point, and output levels is normally provided. **1866** 'OLD STAGER' *Stage Reminisc.* ix. 122 The sizes and sets of yarns occupied his thoughts much less than theatrical 'lengths' and 'set scenes'. **1938** MACDONALD & REES *Rugger Practice & Tactics* ii. 34 Few tries are scored in good football by movements that start from a set scrum. **1960** E. S. & W. J. HIGHAM *High Speed Rugby* xiv. 185 We deal with the set scrum first, because it forms the basis of loose scrums and loose rucks. **1977** *S. Wales Guardian* 27 Oct. 16/3 By this stage Llandovery's forwards were dominating the set scrums. **1925** R. M. RAYNER *Man. Rugby Football for Public Schools* viii. 47 (*heading*) On getting possession in 'set' scrummages. **1971** *Times* 15 Feb. 9/4 Bryce, Miller and Moroney are an experienced front row and rubbed in the fact. . at the set scrummages. **1940** *N.Y. Times* 21 Jan. v-1/3 The cadets, their set shots hitting the mark with a remarkable degree of accuracy, gained the upper hand at the outset. **1976** *Milton Keynes Express* 9 July 42/3 Wickham, Wynn and Waller were all desperately unlucky with set shots. **1956** *N.Z. Jrnl. Sci. & Technol.* A. XXXVII. 555 Most New Zealand farmers producing fat lambs. . generally prefer to set-stock the ewes and lambs from lambing time onwards. **1964** *Weekly News* (Auckland) 21 Oct. 54/4 Under New Zealand conditions, ewes and lambs are usually set-stocked from lambing until weaning, although rotational grazing is practised on some farms. **1981–2** *Deer Farmer* (N.Z.) Summer 8/3 Hinds are set-stocked or mob-stocked over winter at about 10 to the acre. **1950** *N.Z. Jrnl. Agric.* Feb. 100/2 Make sure that the calves are rotated through the paddocks at intervals of a few days. Set stocking at this time of the year is bound to result in. . some deaths. **1975** *Country Life* 26 June 1702/1 In the last 35 years we would seem to have gone full circle—from set-stocking, strip-grazing, paddock-grazing. . and now the so called 'intensive' set-stocking.

10. set-in, (*a*) (later examples, of clothing).

1895 *Montgomery Ward Catal.* Spring & Summer 280/2 Men's overshirts... Set in bosom, yoke back, [etc.]. **1969** *Sears Catal.* Spring/Summer 37/3 Wing collar, set-in sleeves.

set-. Add: **set-ope** *dial.* [OPE *a.* and *sb.*], a device for holding open a gate, window, etc. (? *obs.*); **set-screw,** add: a screw that enables two contiguous parts to be brought into and held in their correct relative position, and is usually threaded the full length of the shank (earlier and later examples).

1823 E. MOOR *Suffolk Words* 336 The gate oont keep back; the *set-ope* is gone. **1912** *Civ. Serv. Supply Assoc. Catal.* 1351 Melon frames. . glazed with 21 oz. sheet glass, and fitted with improved set-opes. **1850** T. TREDGOLD *Steam Engine* (ed. 3) I. IV. 19 When the piston is taken to pieces. . , the two set-screws *h* are taken out of the holes into which they are screwed in the piston cover, and two handles screwed into them. **1947** J. C. RICH *Materials & Methods of Sculpture* ix. 277 A setscrew is used [in proportional dividers] to hold the two arms together and to adjust the dividers. **1970** K. BALL *Fiat 600, 600D Autobook* vi. 69/1 Undo the setscrew securing the angled extension piece to the gear-rod.

setar, var. SITAR in Dict. and Suppl.

set-aside, *sb.* and *adj. phr.* *U.S.* [f. vbl. phr. *set aside*: cf. SET *v.* 139 a, ASIDE *adv.*] **A.** *sb. phr.* Something set aside; *spec.* a quantity of commodities, agricultural produce, etc., reserved by governmental order for a special purpose (*orig.* for supplying the military forces). Also, the action of securing thus.

1943 *Sun* (Baltimore) 16 June 28/8 'Set asides' for the armed forces have increased measurably. **1954** *Ibid.* 21 July B-12/3 One of the foggier sections of the pending overall farm bills would provide for 'set-asides' of surplus commodities now held by the Government. The purpose of the set-aside is clear enough, if the method of effecting it is not. **1966** *Wall St. Jrnl.* (Eastern ed.) 5 Dec. 12/2 The Government ordered drastic increases in defense set-asides on copper during the first half of 1967. **1975** *New Yorker* 26 May 66/2 A visitor asked Butz, who had become Secretary of Agriculture late in 1971, if as Secretary he would have preferred to limit the 'set-aside' of cropland withheld from production in 1972. **1980** *Outdoor Life* (U.S.) (Northeast ed.) Oct. 47/1 Another may be squeaky clean on wilderness set-aside, for example, but falter badly when it comes down to a sensible attitude on gun control.

B. *adj. phr.*

1943 *Daily Progress* (Charlottesville, Va.) 6 Oct. 3/5 A protest. . to the War Food Administration against inclusion of smaller sizes of certain varieties of fruit in the government's 'set-aside' order to protect needs for the armed services. **1979** *Financial Times* 19 Jan. 37/7 There is in addition a 'set-aside' programme in the U.S. for both wheat and maize to restrict plantings.

set-back. Add: **2. b.** *N. Amer.* The setting back or recessing of a building from the edge of a roadway (as an element of environmental planning); the limit of this withdrawal or the open area created.

1916 *Ann. Rep. Planning Board of Brookline, Mass., 1915* 5 Disregard of the customary setback which has hitherto maintained a margin of cheerful green. **1923** *Stud. Building Height Limitations* (Zoning Comm. Chicago Real Estate Board) 163, I would like to ask in the case of a narrow street whether it would be automatically widened by the establishment of a fixed set-back. **1937** *Sun* (Baltimore) 30 Sept. 24/2 Claiming the building of a stone wall along a lot boundary on Wendover road 'is in total disregard of the theory of setbacks and open spaces in Guildford'. **1947** *Daily Progress* (Charlottesville, Va.) 13 Sept. 2/1 (*heading*) Staples approves rural setbacks. **1961** L. MUMFORD *City in Hist.* Note to plate 51, The architect is freed from arbitrarily uniform prescriptions as to garden allotments, setbacks from roads and obsolete street patterns. **1975** *Canadian Antiques Collector* Mar.—Apr. 27/1 One fence encloses a typical store and defines a deep setback for a distinctive house.

c. *N. Amer.* A feature of the design of a skyscraper by which higher storeys are successively set back a certain distance behind the line of lower storeys, leaving a horizontal area in front; the horizontal area so formed.

1923 *Stud. Building Height Limitations* (Zoning Comm. Chicago Real Estate Board) 23 Additional Heights of Buildings should be allowed, provided proper set-backs are required for such additional stories. **1926** *Daily Colonist* (Victoria, B.C.) 12 Jan. 3/6 It [*sc.* a proposed skyscraper] is to be of the type recently developed. . with a reduction of area, or a 'set back' from the street line above the tenth floor and similar reductions taking place at intervals thereafter. **1934** *Sun* (Baltimore) 16 May 2/1 Former Governor Alfred E. Smith. . announced that on June 1 the club would open a new terrace cafe on one of the setbacks of the Empire State Building. **1945** *Washington Post* 17 Aug. 1/8 His body cleared more than 100 feet of building setbacks in the seven tiers of parapets designed as obstacles to suicide plunges. **1964** 'J. H. ROBERTS' *Q Document* i. 12 The façade of the building was deceptive, with sculpted indentations and setbacks. **1977** *Guardian Weekly* 6 Nov. 18/4 One of the victims is hurled through a closed window, his body coming to rest on a setback seven floors below.

5. (sense *2 b) *setback line, space.*

1917 *Establishment of Setbacks* (City of N.Y. Comm. on City Plan) 4 The set-back line secures on certain streets a uniform set-back of buildings from the street line. **1948** *Daily Progress* (Charlottesville, Va.) 4 Nov. 1/4 An agreement. . to permit the super market. . to stay four feet inside the prescribed ten-foot setback line. *Ibid.*, If and when the city needs the full ten-foot setback space to widen Preston Avenue, [etc.].

set-down. Add: **1. b.** (Earlier example.)

1727 SWIFT *Let.* 29 Feb. in *Corr.* (1963) III. 268 Mr Schutz's coach that usd to give you so many a Set-down, is wheeled off to St. James's.

2. (Earlier example.)

1780 T. PASLEY *Jrnl.* 1 Aug. in *Private Sea Jrnls.* (1931) 105 Gave John a set-down for impertinence.

3. (Earlier and later examples.)

1824 J. R. ANTHONY *Diary* 3 Feb. in Z. Pease *Life in New Bedford 100 Yrs. Ago* (1922) 76 After we had got our fill, returned back to our house with a bowl full [of fried oysters] for the girls. Had a good set down and parted at 12 o'clock. **1858** *Harvard Mag.* Sept. 281 We Americans think that we cannot live unless we have our three 'set-downs'. . each day, which is absurd. **1907** J. LONDON *Road* 28 At the very next house I was given a 'set-down'. Now a 'set-down' is the height of bliss. **1914** *Sat. Even. Post* 4 Apr. 10/2 That kid don't want no handouts. He gets setdowns. Yes, siree, bo; every time. Setdowns in the kitchen. **1941** J. SMILEY *Hash House Lingo* 48 *Set down*, good meal.

4. The action or an instance of landing in or from an aircraft.

1951 *Sun* (Baltimore) (B ed.) 28 May 28/4 The pilot had called in to report his 'set down'. **1968** O. WYND *Sumatra Seven Zero* xii. 183 Would it surprise him to know. . that he had been under observation from the moment of set down?

‖ **setem** (se·tem). *Egyptology.* Also **Setem.** [ad. Egyptian *sm, stm.*] = *SEM.

1963 C. M. FORDE tr. *Desroches-Noblecourt's Tutankha-*

men vi. 181 He officiated as the last scion of the royal family in the role of the *Setem* priest at the funeral of his predecessor. **1972** I. E. S. Edwards *Treasures of Tutankhamun* 43 (*caption*) King Ay, wearing the leopard skin of a *setem*-priest performs the Opening of the Mouth ceremony.

‖ **se-tenant** (sə͵tənaṅ) *a.* *Philately.* [Fr., 'holding together'.] Of postage stamps: joined together as when printed; usu. applied to two or more stamps of different denominations or designs. Also as quasi-*adv.*

1911 F. J. Melville *Chats on Postage Stamps* 49 Se tenant.—A French expression signifying that the stamps referred to have not been separated: usually employed in reference to an error, or variety, when still forming a pair with a normal stamp. **1938** D. B. Armstrong *Key to Stamp Collecting* s.v., *Se Tenant.*—French phrase meaning 'joined together', and applied to a pair of stamps, one of which differs from the other. **1957** *Encycl. Brit.* XVII. 715A/1 *Se-tenant* stamps are two or more unsevered from each other. The term is usually applied to unusual pairs or larger pieces in which one or more of the stamps differs from the other. Sometimes two denominations of stamps will be printed in one sheet and a pair of stamps of the different denominations would be described as 'a *se-tenant* pair'. **1971** [see *funny *a.* 1 b]. **1980** *Jrnl. R. Soc. Arts* July 535/2 The stamps have been printed as four se-tenant designs of one value, that is four different designs joined together on one sheet.

seter, var. *saeter, setter.

Seto (se·to). The name of a city 12 miles north-east of Nagoya in Japan used *attrib.* and *absol.* to designate the pottery and porcelain produced from the kilns established there in the 13th cent.

1881 Audsley & Bowes *Keramic Art of Japan* 125 The specimens..cost about four times as much as corresponding articles of Arita or Seto make. *Ibid.* 226 Other descriptions are called..Seto-Suke, Seko-Kuro, and..Ki-Seto, or yellow Seto after the colour of the glaze used. **1925** W. Weston *Wayfarer in Unfamiliar Japan* xii. 127 The region whose chief and oldest settlement, Seto, gives its name to the Japanese term *Seto-mono* (lit. 'Seto ware'), porcelain, just as we ourselves employ the word 'china' to connote articles of a similar nature. **1945** W. B. Honey *Ceramic Art of China & Other Countries of Far East* v. 181 The 'yellow Seto' (*ki-seto*) was possibly suggested by a variety of the *temmoku*, but more probably by late Corean ware. **1959** R. Kirkbride *Tamiko* ix. 67 The tea arrived in small porcelain cups which Ivan recognized as Seto, very old and rare, from the kiln at Nagoya. **1972** P. Murray tr. *Shoya Yoshida's Folk-Art* (ed. 2) 52 (*caption*) Seto water dropper with peony relief.

set-out. Add: **1. g.** (Earlier and later examples.)

1833 Dickens *Let.* ? Jan. (1965) I. 14, I am consequently unable to tell the story and to deliver a plain unvarnish'd tale of the set out. **1903** Somerville & 'Ross' *All on Irish Shore* i. 15 'I'm sure Fennessy wishes to hear no more of it,' said Barnet acridly to Mrs. Griffen, when Mrs. Alexander had passed swiftly out of hearing, 'after the way those girls have been worryin' on at him about it all the morning. Such a set out!' **1933** D. L. Sayers *Murder must Advertise* x. 166 'Coo! that was a set-out, that was.'

set piece. Also **set-piece, setpiece.** [Set *ppl. a.*] **1. a, b.** See Set *ppl. a.* 8.

c. A (passage of) formal composition in prose or verse; a discourse, narrative, etc., composed according to a set pattern.

1932 C. Brown *Eng. Lyrics of 13th Cent.* p. xiv, In the English romance *Arthour and Merlin* a series of lyrics on the various months—May, June, February, &c.—are introduced as set pieces to divide the romance into Fitts. **1954** *Essays in Criticism* IV. 1 Little reason to suppose that Menenius is as impartial or as wise as his famous set-piece, the fable of the belly and the members, might at first sight suggest. **1959** I. & P. Opie *Lore & Lang. Schoolch.* ix. 156 And there is the recurrent set-piece: 'What's your name?' 'Sarah Jane.' 'Where do you live?' 'Down the lane' [etc.]. **1968** *Listener* 10 Oct. 475/3 Amis's prose is very good, and some of his little set-pieces are brilliant, as well as modish. Thus, the American road-scene. **1977** *Broadcast* 7 Nov. 13/3 'Hard Times'..as a novel..has a few splendid set pieces and many incidental pleasures. **1980** *Times Lit. Suppl.* 19 Sept. 1012/1 The ceremony of the Holy Fire in the Holy Sepulchre in Jerusalem—the major set-piece of the novel.

2. *Theatr.* A piece of scenery, either flat or three-dimensional and usu. free-standing, that represents a single feature such as a tree, a gate, or the like.

1859 E. Fitzball *Thirty-Five Years of Dramatic Author's Life* I. vi. 140 His long costly robes, becoming entangled with a set piece, pulled down with it, the orange tree excepted, every morsel of scenery on the stage. **1884** [see *cloth *sb.* 7]. **1930** Selden & Sellman *Stage Scenery & Lighting* i. vi. 163 The character of an outdoor setting is better suggested by a few plastic 'set' and 'built' pieces, such as ground rows, silhouette hills, rocks, trees, and fences placed in front of the sky than by anything placed on the drop. **1970** H. Nelms *Scene Design* ii. 19/1 Except for the cyc and the ground row needed to mask its lower edge, the whole setting..consists of a single set piece. This is a flat piece of scenery placed by itself somewhere in the playing space.

3. An organized movement, action, or manœuvre; *spec.* in *Sport,* a prescribed (and usu. rehearsed) movement or feature of the game by which the ball is returned to play, as at a scrummage in Rugby or a free kick in Football.

1938 D. S. Milford *Hockey* vi. 122 We have now finished our survey of the full-back positions for what may be called 'set pieces'. **1947** *Jrnl. R. Aeronaut. Soc.* LI. 840/1 The fourth and last type of operation is the raid against an enemy shore base, usually referred to as a 'set-piece'. This is really rather similar to a Bomber Command operation at shorter range and with smaller aircraft. **1960** E. S. & W. J. Higham *High Speed Rugby* xx. 314 Set-piece Rugby. This is not a game in the strict sense, but a series of set pieces, following rapidly, one on another, at a word from the coach or referee. **1977** *Western Mail* (Cardiff) 5 Mar. 18/5 Modern rugby is a game of pressure and most of this is upon the halves, from set pieces and loose play.

4. (with hyphen) *attrib.* passing into *adj.* Having the attributes of a set-piece; formally or elaborately planned or composed; set (cf. Set *ppl. a.*).

1947 *Jrnl. R. Aeronaut. Soc.* LI. 840/1 (*heading*) The 'set-piece' attack. **1962** E. Godfrey *Retail Selling & Organization* ii. 11 The windows themselves may be enclosed, providing a background for set-piece displays. **1968** *Economist* 17 Feb. 43/1 The not quite universal tendency of reporters to compare the setpiece battle situation that has been building up at Khe Sanh, close to the boundary between South and North Vietnam, to Dienbienphu. **1976** H. Wilson *Governance of Britain* 9 The prime minister is not only required to make a set-piece ministerial or other broadcast on major occasions; he is constantly in the news.

Setswana, var. *Sechuana.

settable, *a.* Delete *rare* and add later examples.

1967 *Electronics* 6 Mar. 6/2 The synthesized center-frequency marker and side markers are accurate, stable, and precisely settable. **1981** *Times Lit. Suppl.* 22 May 573/2 So much of modern poetry has no sense of rhythm or rhyme, and therefore is neither memorable nor settable to music.

‖ **settecento** (setetʃe·nto). [It.: short for *mil settecento* one thousand seven hundred.] The eighteenth century considered as a period of Italian art, architecture, music, etc.

1926 E. Hutton tr. *A. Venturi's Short Hist. Ital. Art* vi. 286 The secret of the fascination Corregio exercised on the art of the *Seicento* and *Settecento*..must be sought in the extraordinary sensibility of his nature. **1936** A. Huxley *Olive Tree* 151 It is a scene from a *settecento* Earthly Paradise—before the Fall of 1789. **1941** *Burlington Mag.* Aug. 38/2 With our last selection, we pass from the Cinquecento to the Settecento. **1966** T. Pynchon *Crying of Lot 49* i. 10 The Fort Wayne Settecento Ensemble's variorum recording of the Vivaldi Kazoo Concerto.

setter, *sb.*[1] Add: **I. 1. a.** (Further examples.)

1964 *New Statesman* 20 Mar. 455/1 Mr Holloway is severe on other people's abuses of English—particularly the setters of examination questions. **1976** *Listener* 23 & 30 Dec. 820/3 The *Listener* setter [of crossword puzzles] caters..for the cognoscente.

11. a. *Irish setter* = *red setter* s.v. *red *a.* 17 a (examples). *English, Gordon setter*: see under first element in Suppl.

1866 J. Walker in *Field* 6 Jan. 3/2, I should feel obliged by your allowing me to say a word or two..on the colour and general characteristics of the Irish setter. **1912** A. Huxley *Let.* 13 May (1969) 42 He, the dog, is a beautiful Irish setter, the only one of his kind within a radius of miles, as the beast has only just been introduced into Germany. **1975** J. M. Brearley (*title*) This is the Irish Setter.

setter: see *saeter, setter.

setting, *vbl. sb.*[1] Add: **I. 1. a.** (Further examples.)

1921 H. G. Crockett *Pract. Leather Manuf.* ii. x. 141 When the goods have become sufficiently dry for setting, and in a fairly stiff condition, they are taken down and brushed over with water. **1953** D. Woodroffe *Leather Dressing* xiv. 144 Sometimes the setting is done by striking out a second time on the same machine. **1965** M. McIntyre *Place of Quiet Waters* ii. 23 There was a..bucksaw, badly in need of setting.

2. a. (Later examples in contexts other than Croquet.)

1948 'Duplex' *Sharpening Small Tools* iv. 71 To adjust the setting of the plane..the tension screw is slightly slackened and the set adjustment lever is moved upwards or downwards. **1979** *Homes & Gardens* June 154/1 Some recent models also have a thermometer and control dial so you are able to alter the setting.

e. A set of cutlery or crockery, or of both, sufficient for one place at table. Cf. *place-setting* s.v. *place *sb.*[1] 29.

1952 A. Vanderbilt *Compl. Bk. Etiquette* ix. 98 A young bride can do very well with four- or six-place settings consisting of dinner knife, dinner fork, salad fork, butter knife, teaspoon, and dessert spoon. **1961** *Times* 30 May 15/6 Veneered oak canteen containing settings for 8 people, including fish knives and forks, in Mappin Plate. **1975** M. Orr *Rich Girl, Poor Girl* xxi. 278 Maggie..was given..a twelve-piece setting of Danish flatware.

6. c. *Psychol.* and *Sociol.* A person's disposition or cast of mind formed by experience and colouring his behaviour. Also, the immediate environment considered as an influence upon behaviour; *spec.* an environment designed to create a particular atmosphere, esp. for experiments with mind-affecting drugs.

1914 M. Prince *Unconscious* x. 311 Antecedent experiences of life..conserved in the unconscious formed a setting that gave the point of view and attitude of mind. **1954** Barker & Wright *Midwest & its Children* iii. 45 A behavior setting has been defined as a standing pattern of behavior and as part of the milieu which are synomorphic and in which the milieu is circumjacent to the behavior. *Ibid.* vi. 223 A day from the life of a child in the settings of a community gives a sample of behavior and habitat that is..limited. **1963** E. Goffman *Behav. in Public Places* ii. 21 The same physical space can come to be used as a setting for more than one social occasion, and hence as a locus for more than one set of expectations. **1968** *Science* 13 Dec. 1236/1 It is necessary to control set and setting... The total environment in which the drug is taken is the setting. **1974** M. C. Gerald *Pharmacol.* xviii. 341 Among the variables that modify the marijuana response are dosage, route of administration, set, and setting.

7. (Earlier example.)

1871 D. G. Rossetti *Lett.* (1967) III. 923 Dr. Bennett..can publish his setting if he makes no alteration in the words.

9. b. A clutch (of eggs).

1902 E. Nesbit *Five Children & It* iii. 85 A setting of Buff Orpington eggs that had not turned out well. **1938** M. K. Rawlings *Yearling* xiv. 140 The setting was hatched. The young quail, each no bigger than the end of his thumb, scattered like small windblown leaves.

11. (Further examples.)

1963 D. Seton *Essent. Mod. Cookery* 150 The setting property of jam is due to the presence of pectin in the fruit. *Ibid.* 151 Setting-point is reached when the jam forms a flake and drops off the spoon cleanly or sharply when shaken. **1969** *Jams, Preserves & Homemade Sweets* (Good Housekeeping Libr. Cooking) i. 10 Lemon juice..aids the setting. *Ibid.* 11 After the sugar has been added, the jam should be watched carefully and tested for setting without undue delay.

III. 13. a. (Further examples.)

1894 J. E. Davis *Elem. Mod. Dressmaking* (1895) 46 The setting-in of the second sleeve [is] proceeded with. **1942** P. I. Smith *Princ. & Processes Light-Leather Manuf.* v. 161 After dyeing and fat-liquoring the next process is setting-out or striking out, which today is usually done by hand. **1942** W. S. Churchill *End of Beginning* (1943) 27 It was agreed that I should propose to those concerned the setting-up of a Pacific Council in London. **1953** D. Woodroffe *Leather Dressing* xiv. 144 Striking out forms an excellent treatment prior to the setting out process. **1959** *20th Cent.* Nov. 345 The setting-up of an alternative..television service. **1962** A. Nisbett *Technique Sound Studio* viii. 146 If wear is noticeably accelerated,..rather complicated ways of setting up have to be devised. **1975** Bram & Downs *Manuf. Technol.* vi. 168 To assist 'setting up', tenon blocks are provided to engage in table slots. **1979** A. B. Emary *Woodworking* viii. 37 The steps..are setting out, which means making certain full-size drawings—in the trade this is called making a workshop rod, compiling a list of timber required for the job, and placing the necessary marks on the timber from the information on the rod.

b. setting-out, (*b*) *U.S.* = Set-out 3; **setting-up** *U.S. dial.,* an all-night vigil, esp. one kept by relatives beside the body of a dead person (cf. Set *v.*[1] 154 kk in Dict. and Suppl.).

1848 *Ladies' Repository* VIII. 337, I think you can afford to give that to Hen and Kate as part of their 'setting-out'. **1900** J. de F. Shelton *Salt-Box House* xxi. 169 Despite the high prices caused by the war, her [bridal] setting-out was not inferior, having its full complement of silver, china..Irish-stitch (damask), [etc.]. **1835** C. Gilman *Recoll. Southern Matron* in *Southern Rose* 14 Nov. 41/2 This solemnity is usually styled by the negroes 'a setting up'. **1905** 'P. Pennington' *Jrnl.* 25 Dec. in *Woman Rice Planter* (1913) viii. 272 All the grown servants have gone to the 'setting up', which is one of the strongest articles of their creed..the feeling that they must not be found in their beds on this mysterious night when the King of the world was born. **1949** 'J. Nelson' *Backwoods Teacher* xv. 160 Most of them stayed a few minutes and departed, perhaps leaving one member of the family for the 'settin'-up'.

d. Phr. *setting-to-rights,* the action of putting things in their correct places (on a shelf, etc.). Cf. Set *v.*[1] 25 a.

1847 C. M. Yonge *Scenes & Characters* xxiii. 284 That wearisome operation, a complete setting-to-rights; Eleanor..extended her cares from the stores to every other household matter. **1911** K. D. Wiggin *Mother Carey's Chickens* xiv. 124 Dozens of shelves in odd spaces helped much in the tidy stowing away of household articles... In the midst of all this delightful and cheery setting-to-rights a letter arrived.

14. setting-board, (*b*) (later examples); **setting coat** (later examples); **setting lotion,** lotion that is applied to the hair in order to assist the process of setting; **setting-room** *N. Amer. dial.* = Sitting-room 1; **setting stuff,** the fine plaster from which a setting coat is made; **setting-up exercise** (examples).

1894 W. Furneaux *Butterflies & Moths* ix. 122 The most important requirement is the setting boards, of which several are necessary. **1976** V. Nabokov *Details of Sunset* 158 He would first pin the carefully killed insect in the cork-bottomed groove of the setting board. **1916** E. A. Doncaster *Limes & Cements* xiii. 144 The setting coat..is made of the pure lime as it runs from the basin.

1927 A. H. Telling *ABC of Plastering* 206 The setting coat should be about one-eighth of an inch thick. **1926** *Hairdressing* 27 Aug. 181/1 No setting lotion nor dressing of any kind was used. **1941** N. Marsh *Death & Dancing Footman* (1942) ii. 42 She was met by the..familiar smells of hot hair, setting lotion, and the sachets used in permanent waving. **1977** J. Wilson *Making Hate* xiii. 157 That thick sweetish smell you always get in ladies' hairdressers..setting lotion or hairspray. **1741** *Probate Rec. New Hampshire* (1915) III. 30, I give to my Beloved Wife ..ye furniture of ye Chamber over our Setting room. **1832** W. D. Williamson *Hist. Maine* II. xxviii. 703 Our indigenous cherry, black-birch, and curl maple,..were shoved from the parlour and setting-room, to admit articles of foreign mahogany. **1908** J. C. Lincoln *Cy Whittaker's Place* iii. 38 It's your dad's house come back alive, it is so! Look at this settin' room. **1911** *Encycl. Brit.* XXI. 785/1 Setting stuff should not be applied until the floating is quite firm and nearly dry, but it must not be too dry or the moisture will be drawn from the setting stuff. **1927** A. H. Telling *ABC of Plastering* 187 Setting or fine stuff consists of one part of plasterer's putty to two or three parts of sand. **1939** W. Verrall *Solid & Fibrous Plastering* v. 64 Setting or skimming stuff can be applied in its raw state or an addition of 10 to 15 per cent. of plaster of Paris added. **1935** O. Nash *Primrose Path* 37 A few setting-up exercises. **1970** *Soviet Weekly* 25 Apr. 2 He gets up at half past five, does a few setting-up exercises, takes a bath, has breakfast, goes for a walk before starting work.

setting, *vbl. sb.*²: see *set *v.*²

setting, *ppl. a.* (Later examples.)

1969 *Jams, Preserves & Homemade Sweets* (Good Housekeeping Libr. Cooking) ii. 38 Poor setting fruits can be combined with the better ones to give added colour or flavour. **1974** M. Lindlaw *Super Sweets & Puddings* 53 Make up the Dream Topping..or whisk the cream until it begins to thicken. Whisk into the setting jelly.

setting-pole. Add: Chiefly *N. Amer.* (Earlier and later examples.)

1763 J. Bell *Trav. from St. Petersburg* II. xiii. 140 The barques..run often a-ground..and the people were obliged to..heave them off..with levers and setting poles. **1931** G. L. Nute *Voyageur* 40 Up to this point they had used 'setting poles' as well as paddles whenever the current was too swift for the ordinary method of propelling the canoe. **1959** *Moosehead Gaz.* (Dexter, Maine) Feb. 18/3 Junior eased the canoe down through the rocky rips with a setting pole.

settle, *v.* Add: **I. 3. b.** Also, *rarely*, in *active*: to install (someone) in a residence.

1853 Geo. Eliot *Lett.* (1954) II. 97 What do you think of my going to Australia with Chrissey and all her family? —to settle them, and then come back.

4. g. *U.S. slang.* To sentence (a person) to imprisonment, put in prison.

1899 'J. Flynt' *Tramping with Tramps* 396 *Settled*, in prison. **1914** Jackson & Hellyer *Vocab. Criminal Slang* 75 *Settled*,..convicted of misdemeanor or statutory offence. Example: 'He's settled for a two spot.' **1916** *Literary Digest* 19 Aug. 425/1 Foley was 'pinched' and 'settled' in San Quentin. **1930** *Amer. Mercury* Dec. 457/2 He goes to the counter and gets settled for a nickel. **1955** D. W. Maurer in *Publ. Amer. Dial. Soc.* xxiv. 151 Maybe he will get *settled*, or sent to prison; among pickpockets this term does not carry the implication of a long sentence or a life-term..; it usually means two years.

II. 11. a. Also with *in*, to become established in a new home. Hence, to become accustomed to a new abode or to new surroundings.

1929 *Star* 21 Aug. 15/1 The Jellicoes..are 'settling in' at their new London home this autumn. **1951** M. McLuhan *Mech. Bride* (1967) 67/2 It will want to 'settle in, and enjoy the sense of belonging in America. **1960** J. Stroud *Shorn Lamb* xiii. 151 He'll settle in, I feel sure. It'll be a long job though. **1977** 'A. York' *Tallant for Trouble* iii. 48 We met the Brices after we came. We threw a party, to settle in, and the Brices were top of the list.

IV. 18. b. Of food or a meal: to be digested.

1944 L. P. Hartley *Shrimp & Anemone* iv. 44 What about these toboggans? We've given our tea time to settle.

19. b. Also *spec.* of an infant or a child.

1972 P. D. James *Unsuitable Job* iii. 88 The Webbers couldn't bear the boy to go to hospital; they'd tried it once and he didn't settle. **1976** 'D. Halliday' *Dolly & Nanny Bird* viii. 106 You can let go now, he won't settle.

21. c. (Later example.)

1900 H. A. Jones *Mrs. Dane's Defence* ii. 39 We will very soon settle Mrs. Bulsom-Porter.

23. b. Also *to settle down* or *in*, of the weather, a season, etc.: to set in.

1889 J. K. Jerome *Three Men in Boat* v. 70 'Going to clear up, d'ye think?'.. 'Well, no, sir; I'm afraid it's settled down for the day.' **1939** K. Pinkerton *Wilderness Wife* x. 110 By the first week in December the winter began to 'settle in', as they say in the North.

V. 26. b. Also without prepositional compl.

1976 *Cambridge Independent Press* 16 Dec. 1. 10/5 But Felixstowe settled and after 25 minutes they took the lead when Bailey touched home Goffin's cross.

28. b. Also *to settle down.*

1869 J. Greenwood *Seven Curses London* ii. 19 At sixteen..the pair embark in housekeeping and 'settle down'. **1891** G. Chamier *Philosopher Dick* v. 120 'Didn't I tell you he was a looking hout for some crib to settle down.' 'Settle down, indeed! What do you mean?' 'Why, he's about to get spliced.' **1911** G. B. Shaw *Getting Married* 118 They had all, as they called it, settled down, like balloons that had lost their lifting margin of gas. **1928** E. O'Neill *Strange Interlude* vi. 230 He looks pretty dissipated..too many women..ought to get married and settle down.

VI. 32. e. *to settle for*, to decide or agree on, to content oneself with.

1959 P. Bull *I know Face* i. 11 My father wanted me to be a chartered accountant, a profession which seemed to me to lack glamour. However, in order to show willing, I did settle for 'journalism'. **1963** H. Garner in R. Weaver *Canad. Short Stories* (1968) 2nd Ser. 27 There were plates of doughnuts..but I settled for a mug of coffee. **1972** C. Fremlin *Appointment with Yesterday* xi. 82 'You couldn't start straight away, could you?.. Or would you rather have some coffee?'.. Milly found the courage to settle for the coffee.

settleable, *a.* Restrict *nonce-wd.* to sense in Dict. and add: **2.** Having the property of settling or sinking to the bottom of a liquid.

1940 Imhoff & Fair *Sewage Treatment* ii. 30 It is important to know how much of the solid matter is in suspension, how much is settleable, and how much is in solution. **1947** [see *floc]. **1969** *Sci. Jrnl.* Mar. 81/2 In the activated sludge process the ability of the organisms to flocculate into settleable clumps is automatically inbred.

settlement. Add: **III. 11. c.** The sinking of floc and other solid particles in liquid sewage. Also *attrib.*, as *settlement tank*.

1912 H. Lemmoin-Cannon *Textbk. Sewage Disposal in U.K.* xviii. 62 Tanks of the same kind..are used for the purpose of attaining the settlement of the suspended organic solids by sedimentation. **1927** T. H. P. Veal *Disposal of Sewage* v. 54 Quiescent settlement tanks are operated on what is known as the fill-and-draw principle. *Ibid.* 55 The amount of clarification effected in a given time by quiescent settlement is greater than that effected by the continuous flow method. **1977** C. B. Capper in A. G. Callely et al. *Treatment Industrial Effluents* vi. 90 Probably the oldest method of removing suspended solids was by the use of horizontal-flow settlement tanks.

17. *attrib.* and *Comb.*, as (senses 6, 14) *settlement area, pattern*; (sense 9 b) *settlement price, terms*; **settlement day** = *settling day* s.v. Settling *vbl. sb.* 3 b; **settlement house** *U.S.*, an institution in an inner city area, usu. sponsored by a church or college, that gives educational, recreational, and other social services to the community (cf. sense 16).

1963 H. N. Savory in Foster & Alcock *Culture & Environment* iii. 31 The south Wales seaboard was a primary settlement-area of the continental colonists. **1977** *Word 1972* XXVIII. 72 Brittany is a dispersed settlement area, and farms are either isolated or in small clusters. **1896** W. H. S. Aubrey *Stock Exch. Investm.* 314/2 (Index), Settlement days. **1901** C. Duguid *How to read Money Article* xvii. 75 Directly one account is ended by the fortnightly settlement, another account begins. It commences at noon on the first settlement day. **1907** J. Strong *Challenge of City* 307 Your letter..was duly received and reply thereto delayed awaiting report from the inspection districts wherein are located the Settlement houses you mentioned. **1959** *New Statesman* 24 Oct. 534/2 In relation to the street gangs, most of these disquisitions regard the conventional 'agencies'—boys' clubs, mixed clubs, settlement houses, community centres—as ineffectual. **1978** G. Vidal *Kalki* v. 114 Of course, Amelia did work in settlement houses, helping the poor. **1958** G. Lienhardt *Tribes without Rulers* 98 Dinka settlement-patterns differ from each other according to the two broadly different kinds of country. **1928** *Daily Mail* 25 July 19/3 Tin: Standard cash quoted £217 10s. to £217 12s. 6d.; three months, £214 10s. to £214 12s. 6d.; settlement price, £217 10s. **1931** C. Maughan *Markets of London* 122 Rubber is also sold on 'settlement terms', which means that a buyer receives a profit or pays a loss every fortnight, in a similar way to settlements on the Stock Exchange.

settler. Add: **1. c.** A clerk in a betting shop who calculates the winnings.

1963 L. Meynell *Virgin Luck* vii. 172 'But what do you do..?' 'Settle. I'm a settler. I work out a bet. It goes down on a slip and after the race the settlers go through the slips and work them out.' **1966** P. Willmott *Adolescent Boys of East London* vi. 102 Non-manual jobs of a more 'routine' kind, mainly clerks and shop assistants, draughtsmen and betting-shop 'settlers'. **1977** *Evening Post* (Nottingham) 27 Jan. 14/1 (Advt.), Saturday settler required by independent licensed Betting Office.

2. a. (Earlier Amer. examples.) *old settler*: see *old *a.* D 4.

1696 *Rec. Early Hist. Boston* (1881) VI. 51 The first goers or first setlers of Woodstock. **1739** W. Stephens *Jrnl.* 15 Dec. in *Colonial Records State of Georgia* (1906) IV. 469 One Bunyon, a Builder of Boats and a Settler there.

5. settler's clock (earlier example); **settler's effects** *Canad.*, goods brought into the country by an immigrant for his personal use that are exempt from import duty; also *transf.*; **settler's matches** (earlier example).

1827 P. Cunningham *Two Years in N.S.W.* I. 232 The loud and discordant noise of the laughing jackass (or settler's clock, as he is called)..acquaints us that the sun has just dipped behind the hills. **1911** *Daily Colonist* (Victoria, B.C.) 2 Apr. 14/3 She landed 150 tons of cargo here, including three boilers..settler's effects, and general freight. **1939** K. Pinkerton *Wilderness Wife* i. 13 Beside us on the station platform that morning were our canoe, camp outfit and a few 'settler's effects'. **1965** I. Reekie *Along Old Melita Trail* ii. 12 Coming to Manitoba with two cars of settlers' effects. **1891** H. Lawson in *Bulletin* (Sydney) 19 Dec. 21/2 And we walked so very silent—being lost in reverie—that we heard the 'settlers'-matches' gently rustle on the tree.

settling, *vbl. sb.* Add: **5. a.** Also *settling down.*

1911 G. B. Shaw *Getting Married* 118 The process of settling down would go on until they settled into their graves.

b. *settling in*, the action of establishing one's residence in a new place or of becoming accustomed to new surroundings. Chiefly *attrib.*, as *settling-in allowance, grant.*

1955 *Times* 16 July 2/4 Generous settling-in allowance during first month, and housing assistance can be afforded to selected applicants. **1965** *Wireless World* Aug. 120 (Advt.), Free air travel will be provided for a successful applicant..and a 'settling in' allowance will also be paid on arrival in Salisbury. **1973** *Soviet Weekly* 17 Feb. 11/3 Some redundant teachers were willing to be sent to localities where there was a shortage of teachers. They were given settling in grants totalling two or three months average earnings, plus a quarter of that sum for each member of their family. **1974** *Economist* 31 Aug. 83/1 (Advt.), A settling-in allowance of up to £400 is payable in approved circumstances and assistance with housing for a short time is a possibility.

c. Special Comb.: **settling time**, the time taken for a measuring or control instrument to get within a certain distance of a new equilibrium value without subsequently deviating from it by that amount.

1951 Chestnut & Mayer *Servomechanisms & Regulating System Design* I. xiv. 410 (*heading*) Settling time t_s to reach 5 per cent of final value. **1974** J. W. Brewer *Control Systems* x. 285 Rise time is a measure of the speed of response, and the ratio of settling time to rise time is a measure of damping.

6. a. (Further *attrib.* examples.)

1867 J. A. Phillips *Mining & Metallurgy of Gold & Silver* ix. 183 When settling pits are used for the purpose of collecting the tailings for subsequent treatment, it is necessary that at least two of them should be provided, so that whilst one is being filled the other may be cleaned up. **1868** *Times* 4 Aug. 4/3 A complete churning and intimate union are effected by the sewage passing through a number of small apertures into cells, in each of which revolves a stirrer, and thence out of the cells into two very spacious settling tanks. **1894** G. E. Waring *Mod. Meth. Sewage Disposal* xvii. 234 The flocculent matter passing the screen clogged the 4-inch absorption-tiles after a time. This was obviated by constructing a settling-chamber. **1899** *Rep. Dept. Mines on Goldfields N.Z. 1898–99* 45 The crushed ore passes over amalgamated copper-plates, 12 ft. long, into four sets of spitzlutten or settling-boxes. **1915** G. B. Kershaw *Sewage Purification & Disposal* iv. 117 In most settling towers the bottom of the tank is formed in the shape of a cone, the sludge drain being placed at the apex. **1928** W. A. Mitchell *Civil Engineering* v. 572 The term settling basin is ordinarily applied to a reservoir which contains from one to four days' supply of water. **1940** Imhoff & Fair *Sewage Treatment* iv. 72 In these tanks, the lower story serves as a sludge chamber and the upper one as a settling chamber. **1941** C. A. Ward *Those Raw Materials* vi. 272 The separation of sludge [from oil] may take place in settling tanks or may be brought about by centrifugal means. **1955** Linsley & Franzini *Elements Hydraulic Engin.* x. 249 Settling basins..just below the point of diversion so that sediment can be collected and sluiced back into the river. **1964** *Grouts & Drilling Muds in Engin. Pract.* 29/2 Retention [of the mud] in settling pits should be not less than 12 min. **1978** *Sci. Amer.* July 99/1 Conventional sewage treatment employs a combination of large settling tanks, bacterial cultures and sludge-thickening devices to decontaminate waste water and to concentrate the solid residue.

set-to. Add: **2. b.** Also, in weakened sense: an argument, a heated debate.

1898 Lloyd George *Let.* 25 Dec. (1973) 116 We have had several sets to over church matters & female suffrage & we hit without sparing. **1912** Ld. Fisher *Let.* 2 Aug. in R. H. Bacon *Life Ld. Fisher* (1929) II. xvi. 155 At the Defence Committee yesterday.. we had a regular set-to with Lloyd George. **1976** Nichols & Armstrong *Workers Divided* ii. 135, I like nothing better than a good set-to with a good shop steward.

c. (Earlier example in the sense 'a drinking-bout'.)

1813 W. Dunlap *Mem. G. F. Cooke* I. iv. 63, I doubt not that his dinner with the Irish manager was a roaring set-to, a full and convincing proof of what is called Irish hospitality.

3. (Earlier U.S. example.)

1840 *Spirit of Times* 9 May 115 For two miles he trailed, keeping his horse in position for a set-to in the last mile.

se·t-up, *sb.* [f. vbl. phr. *to set up*: cf. Set *v.* 154 in Dict. and Suppl.] **1.** See *set-up* (a) s.v. Set-. Also *spec.* a stand or display at a carnival, etc.

1841, etc. [see *set-up* (a) s.v. Set-]. **1925** C. R. Cooper *Lions 'n' Tigers* v. 135 Mike..responded almost immediately,..returning to his various 'stands' and 'set-ups' as though he had never been away. Mike is still on the job with the circus. **1938** E. Caldwell *Southways* 53 'You win the set-up!' Bess cried, ducking under the railing. 'It's all yours! Go on in there and take it!'

2. a. The way in which something is organized, arranged, or constituted; an organization, arrangement, system, or situation. See also *set-up* (b) s.v. Set-.

Set-up occurs in a vague and indefinite sense in a large number of contexts, but several reasonably distinct areas of use can be isolated: (*a*) a business or administrative structure or organization; also, an economic, social, or political system (both with reference to the system or the persons involved); (*b*) a domestic situation, as determined either by lifestyle or personal relationships; (*c*) a team (esp. in *Sport*); (*d*) the layout of some mechanical apparatus or equipment.

1890 [see *set-up* (*b*) s.v. SET-]. **1922** *Proc. IRE* X. 249 Oscillograms of the essential current and voltage relations existing in the systems of the type illustrated by Figures 1 and 2 were obtained with the set up of apparatus illustrated in Figures 5 and 6, respectively. **1928** *Daily Express* 12 Mar. 13/2 The national set-up of motion picture chairmen. **1932** *Sun* (Baltimore) 31 Oct. 8/2 It develops that this Princeton 'set-up' actually outrushed Michigan, to produce what..ought to be classed..as at least a Class B 'upset'. **1932** D. FROME *By-Pass Murder* v. 39 Servants..belong to that..class of people whose public and private lives have no connection with each other... Publicly and privately their set-ups are as different as Fulham Road and Grosvenor Square. **1933** *Sun* (Baltimore) 29 July 1/1 They provided the set-up for the conspiracy. They helped organize the groups responsible for bombings, sluggings and strikes. **1939** [see *AMPUTEE]. **1942** *Archit. Rev.* XCII. 52/2 The reason for this must be found in the general economic set-up of these countries. **1943** F. L. WRIGHT *Autobiogr.* (rev. ed.) v. 403 Other workmen.., learning of our set-up, asked us to take them on. **1946** E. G. WEBBER *Johnny Enzed in Italy* 9 Nice set up you've got here, Dig. **1949** E. L. MASCALL *Existence & Analogy* iii. 48 Before we know where we are we shall have the best possible world and the whole Leibnitian set-up. **1951** *Sport* 27 Jan.–2 Feb. 7/1 The transfer had had full notice in the Press and yet he was shown included in the home set-up. **1952** H. READ *Philos. Mod. Art.* xiii. 233 What the work of art 'expresses', in an emotional sense, depends very largely on what the spectator brings, in the way of an emotional set-up, to the work of art. **1953** W. BURROUGHS *Junkie* 7 But these people were jerks for the most part and, after an initial period of fascination, I cooled off on the setup. **1958** *Times* 19 May 11/2 At the time of the battle of Marathon the Athenians had..a rather inefficient command set-up. **1962** A. NISBETT *Technique Sound Studio* xi. 191 In a full-scale studio 'telephone conversation' set-up it is usual to have two microphones, one normal and the other with a filter in the circuit. **1962** J. LUDWIG in R. Weaver *Canad. Short Stories* (1968) 2nd Ser. 254 What a set-up for those two kids! Jimmy would spend a fortune on Shirley, but Maxie would spend the night. **1971** *Physics Bull.* Sept. 513/1 Multinational Data, a joint setup linking ICL with the French Compagnie International pour l'Informatique and the American Control Data Corporation. **1973** B. BROADFOOT *Ten Lost Years* xi. 122 A fellow..offered us a job. This was the set-up and..we jumped at it. *a* **1974** R. CROSSMAN *Diaries* (1976) II. 295 Burke is now far the most powerful of the Prime Minister's confidants, and has got Harold tightly integrated into the Whitehall set-up. **1977** *Western Morning News* 30 Aug. 3/5 The family atmosphere certainly grips those who come from abroad, many of whom can find nothing to compare with the set-up in their own countries.

b. *Computers.* The arrangement of interconnections and setting of parameters in a computer, esp. an analogue one, necessary for the performance of a particular calculation.

1935 *Mem. & Proc. Manchester Lit. & Philos. Soc.* LXXIX. 67 A second diagram is then drawn up showing the various gear ratios, positive directions of rotation of the various shafts, [etc.].., and from this second diagram the actual set-up of the machine is made. **1945** *Jrnl. Franklin Inst.* CCXL. 277 After a few days of operation the 'set-up' time per solution became tolerably small. **1952** G. A. & T. M. KORN *Electronic Analog Computers* ii. 32 A number of computer laboratories have successfully used so-called setup sheets as an intermediate step between the preparation of the block diagram and the actual computer setup. **1970** D. E. HYNDMAN *Analog & Hybrid Computing* iv. 82 A considerable amount of time is generally required to patch and check out a problem set-up.

c. The arrangement of guns, decoys, etc., for shooting wildfowl.

1939 *Sun* (Baltimore) 6 Nov. 7/4 Mr. Leichhardt has directed them to..examine the shooting 'set-ups' at the various lodges. **1957** R. SCHARFF *Compl. Duck Shooter's Handbk.* iv. 105 You'll get more ducks if you have some goose decoys in your setup. **1973** G. GRESHAM *Compl. Wildfowler* x. 150 Some days the birds just won't decoy properly. They..pitch in before they reach your setup.

d. *Cinematogr.* (See quot. 1959.)

1941 B. SCHULBERG *What makes Sammy Run?* xi. 284 A director..worrying..about the camera set-ups. **1957** V. J. KEHOE *Technique Film & Telev. Make-Up* i. 17 In motion pictures, where the scene is shot from each angle separately in different lighting set-ups and schemes, the lighting effect can be designed to be complementary to the make-up. **1959** W. S. SHARPS *Dict. Cinematogr. & Sound Recording* 128/1 *Set-up*, the arrangement of the scenery, props, performers, lights, microphones and cameras for a particular shot. **1963** *Movie* Feb. 31/1 The open court scenes are presented within a framework of two medium close camera set-ups. **1976** C. LARSON *Muir's Blood* xviii. 101 He got here at a quarter after nine. We won't get our first setup before noon.

e. The difference between the maximum and minimum heights of a water surface tilted by wind action.

1951 *Jrnl. Res. Nat. Bureau of Standards* (U.S.) XLVI. 373/1 An attempt was made to establish the relationship between set-up and the depth of water for the case where waves were present. **1968** R. W. FAIRBRIDGE *Encycl. Geomorphol.* 235/1 The intertidal zone is not a simple transition but rather a zone of maximum energy, whose peak level ranges through the tide cycle (plus storm-wave 'setup').

3. *colloq.* (orig. and chiefly *U.S.*). In *Boxing*, a fighter who can be easily defeated by his opponent (with the implication that he has been deliberately chosen on these grounds); *gen.*, an opponent who is easy to defeat; a thing that is easily overcome or accomplished, a 'push-over'. *spec.* in *Lawn Tennis*, a ball that is easy to hit or smash.

1926 R. HUGHES in *Hearst's Internat.* Feb. 44/2 A guy was tellin' me that set-ups are has-beens or never-wases who get paid to stand up just long enough to be knocked out. **1926** *Clues* Nov. 162/2 *Set-up*, something easy; soft. **1932** *Sun* (Baltimore) 23 Sept. 1/2 Blaine himself did not take him [*sc.* Chapple] seriously, considered his opposition a 'set-up'. **1946** *College Topics* (Univ. of Va.) 7 Dec. 3/1 It must not be forgotten that Georgia had pretty much of a set-up as far as the schedule was concerned and it would have been a real surprise if Georgia had been beaten. **1950** *Sun* (Baltimore) 24 Mar. B 22/4 Marciano has fought a string of set-ups, and there are few known boxers on La Starza's list. **1957** M. MILLAR *Soft Talkers* vi. 63, I went after him anyway, tooth and nail. It was easy. Ron was a perfect set-up. **1961** *Times* 18 May 5/2 He is well aware that the best players never miss a 'set-up'. **1969** *New Yorker* 14 June 44/3 Graebner could now probably explode one. He has what is almost a set up on his power side.

4. *U.S. colloq.* The glass, ice, soda, etc., required for mixing a drink, which is served to customers, who supply their own spirits, in unlicensed premises.

1930 *Sun* (Baltimore) 24 Dec. 11/1 If the club did not ban liquor drinking on the premises and cease serving 'set-ups' its lease would be in danger. **1944** C. HIMES *Cotton gonna kill me Yet* in *Black on Black* (1973) 197 You pays two bucks to get in this joint, fo' bucks for a half-pint grog, two bucks for a coke setup. **1954** F. P. KEYES *Royal Box* xiii. 186 But Herb asked did I want to turn him into a lone drinker, and where was the icebox, he could make his own setups, and the first thing I knew we were sitting at the table drinking ice-cold highballs. **1964** *Listener* 19 Nov. 803/3 The head waiter will probably relieve him of the bottle, place it on his table, and then serve him unlimited quantities of what are called 'set-ups' to make it palatable. These are the tonic-water, the ice, the soda, or whatever it is. **1973** W. MCCARTHY *Detail* i. 65 He looked over to the sideboard and saw a complete assortment of liquors, rums and set-ups.

5. *U.S. colloq.* A place- or table setting at a restaurant; the dishes, cutlery, etc., which make up this.

1934 in WEBSTER. **1941** J. SMILEY *Hash House Lingo* 48 *Set up*, table eating utensils. **1978** J. D. MACDONALD *Empty Copper Sea* iii. 34 He led us to a corner booth set up for four, whipped away the extra setups.

6. *colloq.* (orig. *U.S.*), A scheme or trick whereby an innocent person is caused to incriminate himself or a criminal is caught red-handed; a 'frame-up'.

1968 *Sun Mag.* (Baltimore) 13 Oct. 28/3 That's how the narcs get most guys on possession of narcotics—through set-ups. **1970** W. BURROUGHS JR. *Speed* iv. 78 A set-up crossed my mind, but Jesus, who cared if it was a set-up or not, we were still busted. **1973** *Black Panther* 7 Apr. 8/2 As he was bringing the food inside he noticed the driver of the truck had turned and was running away. Grady immediately realized it was all a set-up. **1978** J. GARDNER *Dancing Dodo* xxix. 236 Arthur's clean... It was a set-up... I had him checked like you'd check a dodgy engine.

7. Special Comb.: **set-up man**, (*a*) *U.S.* (see quot. 1953); (*b*) *N. Amer.* a man who sets up machinery or equipment.

1953 W. BURROUGHS *Junkie* i. 18 They are always looking for a 'setup man', someone to plan jobs and tell them exactly what to do. **1954** [see *job enlargement* s.v. *JOB *sb.*[2] 7]. **1968** *Globe & Mail* (Toronto) 13 Jan. 48/2 (Advt.), Foreman and set-up man, polyethylene film extrusion, for afternoon shift. **1978** *Detroit Free Press* 16 Apr. F1/3 (Advt.), Willing to train experienced set-up man who has leadership potential.

sevagerous, var. *SAVAGEROUS *a.*

seven, *a.* and *sb.* Add: **A.** *adj.* **1. e.** In *Naut.* slang phrs. *to knock seven bells out of* (someone): to beat (someone) severely; similarly, *to scare seven bells out of*: to terrify. Cf. BELL *sb.*[1] 3 b.

1929 F. C. BOWEN *Sea Slang* 121 *To knock seven bells out of a man*, to give him a hiding or knock him out. **1932** J. W. HARRIS *Days of Endeavour* ix. 158 Three angry Norwegians..knocked seven bells out of him. **1933** M. LOWRY *Ultramarine* iv. 206 Yis. He's knocked seven bells out of harder cases than you in his time. **1943** F. C. HENDRY *True Tales of Sail & Steam* i. 11 She [*sc.* a ship] scared seven bells out of us and gave us the worst month I have ever known at sea.

2. g. *seven-a-side(s*, a form of Rugby Union football played with only seven men on each side; hence, a rugby match or tournament played with teams of this size. Cf. sense *2 e of the sb.

1900 *Scottish Sport* 13 Apr. 6/1 Melrose..will to-morrow resound with a Babel of tongues..eager and excited over the first of the Border seven-a-side tournaments. *a* **1917** E. C. SMITH *Braid Haaick* (1927) 24 The 'Greens' hev wun the seevin-a-sides at their ain spoarts. **1935** *Encycl. Sports* 529/1 *Seven-a-Side.* This variant of the Rugby Union game is much played by the better clubs towards the end of the season... There are, usually, three forwards and four backs on either side. **1961** *Times* 5 May 11/1 We would much rather have seen the seven-a-sides at Twickenham.

B. *sb.* **2. e.** Short for *seven-a-side(s* (see sense *2 g of the adj.).

1926 *Times* 26 Apr. 5/5 Cussen showed in the semi-final what pace means in the game of Sevens. **1977** *Daily Mirror* 15 Mar. 30/1 Rosslyn Park are angry that they cannot call their famous schools sevens tournament by the names of their sponsors.

3. c. Phr. *to throw a* (or *the*) *seven* and varr., to die; also, to faint or vomit. *Austral. slang.*

1894 H. LAWSON *Martin Farrell* in *Coll. Verse* (1967) I. 269, I am pretty cronk and shaky—too far gone for hell or heaven, An' the chances are I'm goin'—that I'm goin' to 'do the seven'. **1899** W. T. GOODGE *Hits! Skits! & Jingles!* 17 You could bet on me chuckin' the seven If she slung me for some other bloke! **1908** [see *MARBLE *sb.* 4 b]. **1932** A. UPFIELD *Royal Abduction* xxvi. 201 If she sees the thing she won't scream and throw a seven. She'll shoot. **1966** T. RONAN *Once there was Bagman* x. 217 The partially digested fruit must have swollen inside me, for before long I was chucking sevens around the flat as I had done a few years before when I had that touch of ptomaine poisoning.

d. *seven-and-a-half*, a round game of cards in which the object is to make the number seven-and-a-half without exceeding it, by counting the pips on the cards.

Court cards (except for the King of Diamonds) are counted as worth half a point.

1937 *Sun* (Baltimore) 26 Jan. 5/5 All other games and machines—..twenty-one, blackjack, seven-and-a-half, big Injun, Klondyke and craps are mentioned specifically—require a $50-per-month license. **1964** A. WYKES *Gambling* vii. 178 Blackjack and seven-and-a-half are found more rarely in the casinos of Europe than those of America.

C. 1. a. *seven-maned, -stringed, -tongued, -towered.*

1949 S. SPENDER *Edge of Being* 29 The seven-maned Golden lions. **1965** J. A. MICHENER *Source* (1966) 251 He carried a small seven-stringed lyre made of fir wood trimmed with antique bronze and strung with twisted sheep's gut. **1913** E. STOCK *Heroic Bishop* ii. 12 In later days he became known in India as 'the seven-tongued man'. **1959** E. POUND *Thrones* xcvi. 19 From the Palace, half-circle that street is, ending near the seven-towered castello.

b. *seven-leaved* (later example).

1927 E. SITWELL *Rustic Elegies* 81 The seven-leaved man-plant.

2. *seven-course, -cubit, -eighths, -feet* (earlier example), *-figure, -foot* (examples), *-octave* (earlier example), *-point, -sacrament.*

1933 C. DAY LEWIS *Magnetic Mountain* 12 The penny-a-liner, the seven-course diner. **1858** M. ARNOLD *Merope* 28 Agamemnon's unhappy,..world-fam'd, Seven-cubit-statur'd son. **1881** O. WILDE *Poems* 117 The seven-cubit spear. **1939** M. B. PICKEN *Lang. Fashion* 123/1 *Seven-eighths length*, length of coat that is shorter than dress or skirt by a little less than one-eighth of the length from shoulder to hem. **1963** BIRD & HUTTON-STOTT *Veteran Motor Car* 186 A patent plate clutch, a new form of universal joint and seven-eighths-elliptic back springs of which the upper portions were cantilevered. **1979** *Tucson* (Arizona) *Citizen* 20 Sept. 2B/1, I was told that nothing will make my fall wardrobe look more up-to-date than a seven-eighths-length coat. **1782** 'J. H. ST. JOHN DE CRÈVECŒUR' *Lett. from Amer. Farmer* vi. 169 The right whale, or seven feet bone..about sixty feet long. **1842** *Penny Cycl.* XXIII. 498/1 Seven-figure numbers to 100 thousand. **1933** *Brit. Jrnl. Psychol.* XXIII. 358 Seven-figure logarithms were used in all calculational work. **1972** *Daily Tel.* 10 Apr. 3/8 Lord Salisbury..died before the Budget so his family cannot benefit from the top duty scale reduction..for seven-figure fortunes. **1935** *Discovery* Feb. 62/1 We read on p. 42 that Watt's 'Old Bess' had a single cylinder of 33 inches diameter—usually termed bore—and a 7 foot stroke. **1950** *Amer. Speech* XXV. 237/2 *Seven-foot line*, a line of sight seven feet off the property line from one seven-foot point to another. **1869** 'MARK TWAIN' *Innoc. Abr.* lix. 580 Any one can see a part of the unquestioned and undisputed Temple of Solomon, the same consisting of three or four stones lying one upon the other, each of which is about twice as long as a seven-octave piano. **1889** *Cent. Dict.*, *Seven-point..*, *a.*, related to seven points, as, the seven-point circle. **1939** A. RODGER in F. C. Bartlett et al. *Study of Society* II. xi. 259 Causes of occupational failure..are..classifiable under seven headings. [*Note*] This seven-point plan, has, of course, other uses. **1977** *Word 1972* XXVIII. 310 A seven-point scale. **1935** *Burlington Mag.* Feb. 81/1 The well-known series of Seven Sacrament fonts, nearly all confined to..Norfolk and Suffolk. **1955** M. D. ANDERSON *Imagery Brit. Churches* III. i. 54 There are about forty Seven Sacrament fonts... The bowls are carved with panels of figure sculpture, each representing one of the Sacraments.

3. *seven-shooter* (earlier examples).

1860 *Charleston* (S. Carolina) *Mercury* 6 Nov. 3/5 (Advt.), Allen & Wheelock's seven shooters. **1872** 'MARK TWAIN' *Roughing It* ii. 23, I was armed to the teeth with a pitiful little Smith & Wesson's seven-shooter..and it took the whole seven to make a dose for an adult.

seven-league(d, *a.* (Earlier example.)

1793 W. B. STEVENS *Jrnl.* 27 Feb. (1966) I. 70 Wrote to Dewe that I would put on my seven league boots next weekend and stretch my course to Appleby.

sevenpence. Add: Also *transf.*, † transportation for seven years (earlier example).

1821 P. EGAN *Life in London* II. iii. 230 My Lord, if I am to stand *seven-pence*, my Lord, I hope you'll take it into your consideration.

seven sisters. Add. **5.** The seven inter-

national oil companies noted for their dominant influence on the production and marketing of petroleum (see quot. 1976).
1962 *Times* 29 Oct. 11/2 Mattei..liked to take the view that the 'Seven sisters'—as he called the majors—were making excessive profits out of both Governments and consumers. **1966** J. ALDRIDGE *Statesman's Game* xviii. 137 Was this..a challenge to the Seven Sisters of the oil world? **1976** *N.Y. Rev. Bks.* 15 Apr. 20/1 The group of international oil companies often referred to as 'the Seven Sisters'—Exxon, Mobil, Gulf, Standard Oil of California, Texaco, British Petroleum, and Royal Dutch Shell.

6. The group of long-established colleges (originally for women only) which were formerly regarded as the most prestigious women's colleges in the U.S. Cf. *IVY LEAGUE.
1962 *Changing Times* Apr. 37/2 The most difficult women's colleges to get into are the so-called 'Seven Sisters'—Barnard, Bryn Mawr, Mount Holyoke, Radcliffe, Smith, Vassar and Wellesley. **1979** *N.Y. Rev. Bks.* 17 May 43/2 (Advt.), Yale grad..would like to meet a 'seven sisters' graduate. **1980** L. BIRNBACH et al. *Official Preppy Handbk.* 86/2 The feminine equivalent of the Ivy League is the group of colleges known as 'The Seven Sisters'.

seventeen, *a.* Add: **4. seventeen-year cicada** = next; **seventeen-year(s') locust** (earlier and later examples).
1870 *Amer. Naturalist* III. 106 The eggs and young of the seventeen-year Cicada. **1950** *Chicago Daily News* 13 Jan. 42 The periodic or 17-year cicada lives the longest of any known insect. **1817** *Columbian Centinel* (Boston) 14 May 1/4 The southern papers have announced that the present is the year for the appearance of what is called.. the Seventeen Years Locust... The insect lives above ground about two months, and 17 years in it. **1843** H. D. THOREAU *Let.* 7 July (1958) 121 Have you seen the Seventeen year locust in Concord? **1975** *Islander* (Victoria, B.C.) 3 Aug. 3/1 The juice-sucking 17-year locusts—which are really cicadas—were also around.

seventh, *a.* Add: **2. c.** *seventh wave*, the wave traditionally thought to be the biggest in an increasing swell of the sea; also *fig.*, a culminating act or experience.
1891 KIPLING *City of Dreadful Night* i. 3 Six moderately pure mouthfuls of [Calcutta] air may be drawn without offence. Then comes the seventh wave and the queaziness of an uncultured stomach. **1908** G. MEREDITH *Let.* 24 Jan. (1970) III. 1623 You know the seventh wave. There must be a gathering of the waters before a big surge is thrown on shore. **1940** L. MACNEICE *Poems 1925–1940* 251 The Northern Lights and the Seventh Wave. **1976** E. WARD *Hanged Man* i. 3 A seventh wave pulled him backwards into undertow.

seventh-day. 1. b. *Seventh-day Adventist*: (earlier and later examples.)
1860 *Advent Rev. & Sabbath Herald* (Washington) 23 Oct. 179/2 *Resolved*, that we take the name of Seventh-day Adventists. **1931** *Times Lit. Suppl.* 19 Feb. 139/2 Seventh Day Adventist missions. **1956** R. MACAULAY *Towers of Trebizond* v. 49 The local Anglican priest.. would give him news of the Seventh-Day Adventist Mission. **1977** *Hongkong Standard* 12 Apr. 5/1 Seventh Day Adventist Church Conference.

seventy, *a.* and *sb.* Add: **A.** *adj.* **2. b.** *seventy-eight*, a gramophone record designed to be played at a speed of seventy-eight revolutions per minute (a speed that was standard until the introduction of the long-playing record); also written *78*; *seventy-five*, (*b*) a gun of 75 mm. calibre formerly used in the armies of the French Republic and the U.S.A.; also written *75*; *seventy-three(s* (U.S. slang), best wishes, good-bye; also written *73*.
1951 SACKVILLE-WEST & SHAWE-TAYLOR *Record Guide* 720 The wise collector will retain his 78 gramophone and the pick of his 78 recordings, continuing to buy good new 78s (especially single discs). **1967** R. PETRIE *Foreign Bodies* xi. 156 Stina looked out her two old seventy-eight records and the four tunes on them sounded through the villa all day. **1971** G. STEINER *In Bluebeard's Castle* iv. 92 There is a science and market..in worn 'seventy-eights'. **1977** *Gramophone* Apr. 1527/1 The LP, at 33⅓ revolutions per minute, and the single, at 45 rpm, have retained their popularity with record-buyers, at the same time sounding the death-knell of the 78, which was finally abandoned in 1958. **1915** E. WHARTON *Fighting France* 56 We begin to come more and more frequently on big colonies of 'Seventy-fives'. **1969** A. HORNE *To lose a Battle* xxi. 510 Amongst the guns taken were some 7,000 French '75s' of First War vintage. **1941** *Traffic World* LXVIII. 198/1 Morse code operators..used many arbitrary numbers to shorten their work..4 meaning 'where', ..73 'best regards' and 22 'kisses'. **1976** *S9* (N.Y.) May/June 31/2 Seventy-threes, and 'bye.

B. *sb.* **2.** (Earlier and later examples of a decade in a particular century.)
1887 W. E. S. FALES *Brooklyn's Guardians* iv. 57 Before the 'Seventies', Brooklyn was essentially a city of homes. **1922** JOYCE *Ulysses* 630 The tattoo..was all the go in the seventies or thereabouts, even in the House of Lords. **1977** *Rolling Stone* 21 Apr. 66/1, I was fascinated with the notion that Mike was what I might have become had I been a man, the lastborn instead of the first—, a child of the Seventies rather than the Sixties.

seven-up. Add: **1.** (Earlier example.)
1830 *N.Y. Constellation* 11 Sept. 2/5 Some tugged at the bottle,..and some played seven-up.

2. Seven up. Also **Seven-Up,** etc., and as **7-Up.** The proprietary name of a popular carbonated soft drink.
1928 *Official Gaz.* (U.S. Patent Office) 13 Nov. 304/2 'Seven Up.' For carbonated, nonalcoholic, noncereal, maltless beverages sold as soft drinks and syrups, extracts, and flavors used in making the same. **1953** *Trade Marks Jrnl.* 24 June 555/2 Seven-up... Non-alcoholic drinks and preparations for making such drinks, all included in Class 32. **1968** N. FLEMING *Counter Paradise* v. 78 Crystal ordered a coffee for herself and a Seven-Up for Jake. **1978** *Washington Post* 5 Sept. 10A/1 Bottles of 7-Up, suddenly the hottest commodity in Egypt.

seven year(s, -years', *attrib. phr.* Add: *seven year(s' itch* (orig. *U.S.*), used to designate conditions supposed to last for, appear, or recur after, seven years; freq. applied *joc.* to an urge towards infidelity after seven years of marriage.
1854 H. D. THOREAU *Walden* 355 These may be but the spring months in the life of the race. If we have had the seven-years' itch, we have not seen the seventeen-year locust yet in Concord. **1899** C. W. CHESNUTT *Conjure Woman* 154 Lawsuits wuz slow ez de seben-yeah eetch. **1936** C. SANDBURG *People, Yes* 112 'May you have the sevenyear itch,' was answered, 'I hope your wife eats crackers in bed.' **1955** *Sun* (Baltimore) 16 May 12/7 When I was a boy we called the skin rash from poison ivy..'the seven-year-itch' and firmly believed that it would reappear every year for seven years. **1959** 'O. MILLS' *Stairway to Murder* xiv. 149 Lapse understood and sympathised with. It's so common they've even got a name for it. It's the seven-year itch. **1980** P. MOYES *Angel Death* x. 132 There's something called the seven-year itch..middle-aged men quite suddenly cutting loose.

severalth, *a.* *U.S. dial.* Also **severaleth.** [f. SEVERAL *a.* + -TH².] The ordinal form of SEVERAL *a.* 4 as an indefinite number.
1902 A. H. LEWIS *Wolfville Days* xvi. 238 Re-fillin' his glass for the severaleth time. **1949** 'J. NELSON' *Backwoods Teacher* ii. 23 But presently, apologizing for the 'severalth' time—to use a good word we learned at Big Piney—..Mrs Helms did sit down.

several-fold, *a., adv.*, and *sb.* Delete *rare* and add later examples.
1945 *Times* 7 Aug. 4/2 The Secretary of War..said later that an improved bomb would be forthcoming soon. It would increase by 'severalfold' the present effectiveness of the new weapon. **1979** *Nature* 29 Mar. 468/1 The rate of protein synthesis increases severalfold during the early cleavage stages. **1981** *Spectator* 7 Nov. 29 The reasons were severalfold.

severance. Add: **2. d.** Discharge from contractual employment. Also *ellipt.* = *severance pay* below.
1941 *North Western Reporter* CCXCVII. 652/1 There was a complete 'severance of employment' and compensation would be calculated on basis of $2.50 per day. **1945** *Monthly Labor Rev.* Jan. 48 The American Newspaper Guild..regards dismissal pay as an equity which the individual builds up on his job and for which he should be compensated regardless of the reason of severance. **1965** *Bull. U.S. Dept. Labor* No. 1425-2. ii. 9 Some agreements gave no details of the plan's characteristics—i.e., when severance would be paid, [etc.]. **1977** *Time* 5 Dec. 72/2 When CBS decided that Schorr must go, its lawyers in February 1976 agreed to pay Schorr more than two years' salary, and severance besides.

3. *attrib.* and *Comb.*, as (sense 2 d) *severance arrangement, money, payment*; **severance cutting** (see quot. 1928); **severance felling** = prec.; **severance pay,** money paid in compensation to one whose contractual employment is terminated; cf. *redundancy pay* s.v. *REDUNDANCY 3.
1971 *Guardian* 14 Jan. 13/3 Some kind of compulsory severance arrangement..will have to be negotiated. **1905** *Terms Forestry & Logging* (U.S. Dept. Agric.) 20 Severance cuttings are made to strengthen the trees on the edge of a stand. **1928** R. S. TROUP *Silvicultural Systems* ii. 8 'Severance cuttings'..are cleared lines of varying breadth, usually 30–50 feet, cut through the wood while it is still comparatively young in order to induce low branching by the border trees. **1895** W. R. FISHER tr. *Schlich's Man. Forestry* 469 Severance-fellings should be forty to fifty feet broad. **1951** W. L. TAYLOR *Estate Forestry* xiv. 131 Gale and flood are countered by.. correct orientation of forest rides and severance fellings. **1975** *N.Y. Times* 5 Nov. 23/3 The parent company closed down the edition [*sc.* the Scottish Daily Express] 18 months ago.., and the employees decided to keep it going as a cooperative. They put severance money of $1.3 million into the venture. **1953** P. C. BERG *Dict. New Words* 143/1 Severance pay. **1956** *Economist* 7 July 12/2 The unions now appear to be ready to lay rather more emphasis on bargaining for higher severance pay. **1979** *Now!* 21–27 Sept. 95/1 The £1,750 tax-free severance pay provides a cushion for defeated MPs. **1962** *Listener* 19 July 86/1, I believe a compensation scheme—severance payment—is important.

severe, *a.* Add: **III. 9. b.** Substitute for def.: *transf.* Of geographical terrain etc.: causing exertion or making great demands of endurance or skill; taxing, hard to 'negotiate'. Also *spec.* of a rock or mountain or the route by which it may be climbed. Hence as *sb.* (usu. with capital initial).
1881 *Sportsman's Year-bk.* 49 Twenty miles a day is often the work of a crack greyhound intended to run in a severe country. **1897** [in Dict.]. **1897** O. G. JONES *Rock-Climbing in Engl. Lake District* p. xxiii, Exceptionally Severe Courses: Screes Great Gully. **1935** D. PILLEY *Climbing Days* iv. 66 It was bizarre that a *severe* should sometimes seem simple, when a *moderate* caused nerve storms of impotent despair. **1951** C. COXHEAD *One Green Bottle* iii. 86 'Ah yes, the Amphitheatre Buttress... An easy Difficult, isn't it?' She..herself led Very Difficults, and occasionally..an easy Severe. **1958** E. NEWBY *Short Walk in Hindu Kush* iii. 34 Easy, moderate, difficult, very difficult, severe, very severe, exceptionally severe, and excessively severe. **1970** *Guardian* 28 Aug. 18/6 The Wen Slab, a broad expanse of smooth, sheer rock classed as 'very severe'. **1975** G. MOFFAT *Miss Pink* iii. 43 It's the big stack off the north headland: a hundred and fifty feet high... A good Severe, we thought. **1976** H. MACINNES *Death Reel* iii. 23 'Is there any climbing on Bidean?' 'I reckon Lilly's route is the best line on this side. About 600 feet, Severe.'

11. (Earlier example.)
1805 T. E. WHITE *Jrnl.* (1904) 32, I got up this morning with the determination to have a severe nap before night.

13. (Later example.)
1802 J. WOODFORDE *Diary* 13 July (1931) V. 401 It was like to be a severe contested Election.

IV. *Comb.*, as *severe-faced, -looking* adjs.
1939 W. FORTESCUE *There's Rosemary* xxxv. 220 Together we hurried down the garden path—to meet Queen Alexandra, Princess Victoria, and a severe-faced lady coming out of the garden door. *a* **1957** J. CARY *Captive & Free* (1959) xliii. 186 A very severe-looking young woman.

severization. For *rare*⁻¹ read *Obs. rare* and add earlier example.
1849 *Theatrical Programme* 20 Aug. 84 Brilliant Feats of Swordsmanship, including the Severisation of a Leg of Mutton.

Sévigné, sevigné. Add: Also, a jewel or ornament of the kind used to decorate a head-dress. Also *attrib.* Now *Hist.*
1826 M. WILMOT *Let.* 29 Feb. (1935) 239 Black velvet stomacher..fastened to the top with a sevigné, garnett and pearl..and another garnett sevigné on her forehead. **1840** M. EDGEWORTH *Let.* 30 Dec. (1971) 574 Sevigné headdress of black velvet with Sevigné jewels in front.

Sevillan, *a.* (Examples.) Also as *sb.*
1883 G. MEREDITH *Let.* 16 Mar. (1970) II. 690 We have just produced pots [of marmalade], which are Sevillan. **1930** H. BAERLEIN *Spain* x. 138 Three hundred Murillos of the best period used to be the quota of a Sevillan gentleman when Théophile Gautier travelled in these parts, and the Sevillan was willing to sell one or two of his treasures. **1971** D. CORY *Sunburst* iv. 50 The Sevillan summer was getting into its blazing stride.

Sevillano (sevilʸā·no), *sb.* and *a.* Also fem. **-a** and erron. **Sevilliana.** [Sp.] = SEVILLIAN *a.* and *sb.*
1884 O. PATCH *Sunny Spain* i. 14 The Sevillanas, as the ladies of Seville are called, are remarkable for their beauty. **1897** H. C. CHATFIELD-TAYLOR *Land of Castanet* iv. 93 The fair Sevilliana sits in her darkened chamber. **1904** B. KENNEDY *Tramp in Spain* iv. 25, I like the Sevillanos. They are a fine, free and easy people. **1932** E. HEMINGWAY *Death in Afternoon* 324 Now Ronda means sober and tragic in the Plaza with a limited repertoire and sevillano means light-hearted..with flowery style and a lengthy repertoire. **1970** R. A. H. ROBINSON *Origins of Franco's Spain* 325 Protest of 2,000 Sevillano farmers to Alcalá-Zamora. **1976** E. P. BENSON *Bulls of Ronda* iii. 14, I see..that you are a Sevillano.

Sevillian, *a.* and *sb.* Add: (Earlier and later examples.) Also **Sevilian.**
1830 DISRAELI *Let.* 26 July (1885) 30 The Sevillians say that *Cadiz es toda facada. Ibid.* 32 You see what a Sevillian écritoire is by this despatch. **1926** E. A. PEERS *Royal Seville* i. 18 The ceramic art which is so noted a Sevilian industry. *Ibid.* ii. 29 The Sevilians like to say that the Guadalquivir salts the sea. **1957** A. MACNAB *Bulls of Iberia* xv. 170 A Sevillian from the classic San Bernardo quarter. **1967** A. ROSIN tr. *G. Pillement's Unknown Spain* 55 The charm of the Sevillians, who are known for their laughter.

sevruga. Add: **1.** (Later examples.)
1940 A. SIMON *Conc. Encycl. Gastron.* II. 14/2 The Ship caviar is light in colour and small; that from the Sevruga is smaller still. **1964** A. LAUNAY *Caviare & After* i. 18 There are three varieties of acipenser used in the production of caviare, the Beluga, the Ocietrova or sturgeon and the Sevruga.

2. Caviare made from the roe of this fish.
1959 W. HEPTINSTALL *Hors d'Œuvre & Cold Table* 29 Beluga Malossol caviar..has..the largest grain and..the highest price. Next comes Sevruga Malossol at about two-thirds of the price of the Beluga caviar. **1977** *Times* 16 Nov. 18/5, I have never been able to say 'when', whether it be a second helping of Sevruga or just another wee drop of the hard stuff.

sew, *v.*¹ Add: **1. e.** (Later examples.)
1880 J. W. ZAEHNSDORF *Art of Bookbinding* v. 21 A third sheet having been sewn.., the needle brought out at the kettle-stitch, must be thrust between the two sheets first sewn. **1929** A. J. VAUGHAN *Mod. Bookbinding* I. 24 Before a book is sewn by hand the back is required to be marked..as a guide for the needle. **1968** I. ROBINSON *Introd. Bookbinding* 27 When the second section has been sewn the long and short ends of thread are drawn taut.

4. c. (*b*) Also, to bring about the conviction of (a person).

1927 *Dialect Notes* V. 462 *Sew up*, v., to convict on overwhelming evidence. **1929** D. HAMMETT *Red Harvest* vii. 80, I expected something like that. That's why I sewed you up. And you are sewed up. **1945** E. S. GARDNER *Case of Gold-Digger's Purse* xv. 159 The police have sewed him up on a written statement.

d. *colloq.* To bring (something) to a desired conclusion or condition; to complete satisfactorily; to organize or gain control of (a person or thing); *spec.* to ensure the favourable outcome of a game or match. Freq. in phr. *all sewn* (or *sewed*) *up*.

1904 ADE *True Bills* 136 The Man with the Megaphone Voice cut no Ice whatsoever, for they had him sewed up. **1915** *Dialect Notes* IV. 235 *Sew up, v. phr.*, to make certain of (a place on a team, in a club, etc.). **1933** E. E. CUMMINGS *eimi* 245 We glide to marriage 'they've got that all sewed up' blonde's mari affirms. **1936** 'P. QUENTIN' *Puzzle for Fools* xxi. 198 He said that..he had Broadway sewed up—him and a few other fellows. **1942** E. S. GARDNER *Case of Careless Kitten* (1944) xii. 100 By the time you get there, Lieutenant Tragg will have things sewed up so tight you'll have to pay admission to get within a block of the place. **1945** —— *Case of Gold-Digger's Purse* xv. 165 The police have all the witnesses sewed up tight. **1953** A. UPFIELD *Murder must Wait* xxi. 191 A Chinese I..played draughts with..let me win a man..and I'd think I had him well sewn up..and then he'd clean the board. **1960** T. MCLEAN *Kings of Rugby* xi. 163 It was Henderson who sewed up the match a moment later. **1977** *News of World* 17 Apr. 23/3 Charlton appeared to have the game sewn up. **1979** *Quarto* Oct. 3/1 During this period the novelists had it all sewn up.

e. To enclose or seal off. *colloq.*

1962 *New Statesman* 21 Dec. 899/1 Knowing that it's only a matter of minutes before the Law would sew up the district with a cordon, we drop one of the team at the local railway station.

5. sew-on *a.*, attached by sewing.

1905–6 *T. Eaton & Co. Catal.* Fall & Winter 158/4 Sew-on Hose Supporters, which are stitched on to corset. **1977** *Evening Post* (Nottingham) 24 Jan. 8/1 (Advt.), Sew on Patches By Leomotif. Fantastic range of over 300 designs.

sewage, *sb.* Add: **3.** *sewage disposal*; **sewage lagoon** *N. Amer.* = *LAGOON[1] 2**.

1873 *Practitioner* XI. 381 The health-aspect of sewage disposal. **1939** *Country Life* 11 Feb. p. xxi/1 (Advt.), Sewage disposal for country houses, factories, farms, etc. **1978** J. WAINWRIGHT *Thief of Time* 29 The septic tank..forms part of the sewage-disposal system of the bungalow. **1930** S. H. ADAMS *Mod. Sewage Disposal & Hygienics* 472/2 (Index), Sewage lagoon. **1958** *Progress* (Preeceville, Sask.) 28 May 1/6 Northwest of town the earthwork for the sewage lagoon has been completed. **1976** *Billings* (Montana) *Gaz.* 30 June 4-D/3 Froid's water, sewer and sewage-lagoon systems.

sewelling, var. SHEWELLING *sb.*

sewer, *sb.*[1] Add: **2. b.** (Later example.)

1945 N. MITFORD *Pursuit of Love* vii. 56 Who is that sewer with Linda?

5. *sewer-scent, -stench*; **sewer-gas** (earlier example); **sewer lagoon** *U.S.* = *sewage lagoon* s.v. *SEWAGE *sb.* 3; **sewer line** *U.S.*, a pipeline that is a sewer.

1849 in E. R. Pike *Human Docs. Victorian Golden Age* (1967) 276 These gases, which so many people are daily inhaling..are identically the same in nature with..sewer-gas. **1959** *Washington Post* 31 Oct. B1/5 To construct the outfall line to the location of the sewer lagoons would require trenches in excess of 25 feet. **1977** *It* May 6/3 (*caption*) Rosselli and his back-up man went down a manhole behind the fence..and followed the sewer-line away from Dealey Plaza. **1929** D. H. LAWRENCE *Pansies* 54 And it's funny my dear young men, that you in your twenties should love the sewer scent Of obscenity. *Ibid.*, A vapour of rottenness out of their mouths, like sewer-stench wreathing.

sewing, *vbl. sb.*[1] Add: **1. a.** (Earlier and later examples in *Bookbinding*.)

1835 J. A. ARNETT *Bibliopegia* 20 There are various ways of sewing, according to the size and thickness of the sheets of a book. **1880** J. W. ZAEHNSDORF *Art of Bookbinding* v. 22 This is the strongest sewing executed at the present day. **1951** L. TOWN *Bookbinding by Hand* v. 99 If the sewing is done too tightly the book will be 'nipped in' at the kettle-stitches.

4. *sewing card, chair, -room*; *sewing girl*; *sewing-bird* (examples), *table* (examples); of a gathering for the purpose of sewing, as *sewing bee, circle*.

1862 M. COLT *Went to Kansas* 23 Have had two sewing bees; one for the old ladies, and one for the young. **1936** F. CLUNE *Roaming round Darling* xxi. 209 Funds are raised in various ways, such as dances, sewing-bees, jam and wood days. **1976** R. BARNARD *Little Local Murder* iii. 35 Mrs Smith, a woman of no importance who had had a forlorn hope of starting a sewing-bee. **1857** *Spirit of Times* (N.Y.) 21 Nov. 192/3 (Advt.), Gold bracelets, gold pencils, sewing-birds. **1949** R. J. SIM *Pages from Past* 10 Who can say when the ancestor of the sewing bird made its appearance on the edge of the table? **1887** A. M. SULLIVAN *Let.* 20 Mar. in H. Keller *Story of my Life* (1903) III. iii. 312 Her father..sees her contentedly stringing her beads or making horizontal lines on her sewing-card. **1961** M. K. ASHBY *Joseph Ashby* vii. 87 Tripping round in action songs..and the sewing cards..certainly made them [*sc.* the children] happier. **1868** *Ann. Rep. Secretary Michigan State Board Agric.* VII. 354 A. Dondero, Detroit..[exhibited] 1 willow ladies' sewing chair. **1978** D. CLARK *Liberties* v. 99 He looked at Mrs Middleton on the sewing chair. **1846** *Knickerbocker* XXVII. 373 As if I too belonged to a sewing-circle, and read charity sermons. **1912** L. M. MONTGOMERY *Chron. Avonlea* ii. 50 The minister's wife..asked her if she wouldn't come to their Sewing Circle. **1979** B. PARVIN *Deadly Dyke* ix. 47 Find out if there's a local sewing circle..in the village. **1848** 'N. BUNTLINE' *Mysteries & Miseries N.Y.* II What, a little sewing girl, eh? **1870** O. LOGAN *Before Footlights* 576 Among the same number of sewing-girls of our great cities. **1852** E. E. HALE *If, Yes & Perhaps* (1868) 56, I always offered my services in the Sunday-schools and sewing-rooms. **1978** R. HILL *Pinch of Snuff* v. 50 We use this as a sewing-room... Alice..makes all our clothes in here. **1863** A. D. WHITNEY *Faith Gartney's Girlhood* xxi. 199 In her low chair by her sewing-table, sat the young sister. **1924** H. T. LOWE-PORTER tr. *T. Mann's Buddenbrooks* I. i. 6 There was a sewing-table by the window. **1979** *Country Life* 27 Sept. Suppl. 59/3 Faded mahogany sewing table.

sewing-machine. Add: **1.** (Earlier and later *attrib.* examples.) Freq. as *sewing-machine oil*.

1863 in *Rebellion Rec.* V. I. 70 Elias Howe, Jr., the inventor of the sewing-machine needle, was a private in this regiment. **1895** *Montgomery Ward Catal.* 262/3 See Index for Sewing Machine Oil. **1977** A. SCHOLEFIELD *Venom* v. 205 He found a can of..sewing-machine oil and squirted it into the lock.

3. *attrib.* **a.** Designating a musical instrument whose operation resembles the action of a sewing-machine. **b.** *fig.* Of rhythm: precise, regular, inexpressive.

1874 J. CODMAN *Mormon Country* viii. 80, I found the solitary musician seated at one of those sewing-machine 'melodeons', and grinding out the Missionary hymn. **1934** C. LAMBERT *Music Ho!* IV. 247 Bach's sewing-machine counterpoint. **1974** *Early Music* Apr. 119/2 His purpose is to counter the 'sewing-machine' style of playing Bach by the 'purists'.

sewn, *ppl. a.* Add: **b.** With advbs. forming adjs., as *sewn-in, -on*.

1961 *Guardian* 15 Sept. 10/1 Garments..will have sewn-in labels giving simple washing instructions. **1965** E. C. HISCOCK *Cruising under Sail* (ed. 2) I. vii. 136 In way of the grommet the boltrope is usually protected against chafe by sewn-on leather or plastic. **1977** *Guardian* 10 Jan. 8/1 The pallid youth in the tie-die shirt with a sewn-on picture of Marx.

sex, *sb.* Add: **1. c.** *the weaker sex* (later example); *the second sex* (further examples); *the sterner sex* (example).

1849 C. BRONTË *Shirley* III. xiv. 312 'Mama' is rather a misanthropist, is she not? Not the best opinion of the sterner sex? **1928** D. K. PARKER tr. *Schopenhauer: Selections* 443 Women..form the *sexus sequior*—the second sex. **1953** H. M. PARSHLEY tr. S. de Beauvoir (*title*) The second sex. **1961** 'F. O'BRIEN' *Hard Life* v. 42 Decent people should look after women—isn't that right? The weaker sex. **1974** J. MITCHELL *Psychoanalysis & Feminism* II. ii. 306 Woman is the archetype of the oppressed consciousness: the second sex.

e. Delete 'Now *rare*' and add further examples.

1892 'MARK TWAIN' *Amer. Claim.* xvii. 160 The customers applauded, the sex began to flock in. **1920** D. LINDSAY *Voyage to Arcturus* i. 2 He was used to such receptions at the hands of the sex.

3. b. Sexual intercourse. Freq. in phr. *to have sex* (*with*).

1929 D. H. LAWRENCE *Pansies* 57 If you want to have sex, you've got to trust At the core of your heart, the other creature. **1952** S. KAUFFMANN *Philanderer* (1953) x. 174 Her arms went around his neck and his hand rested on her waist, and they had a brief moment of friendship before the sex began. **1960** R. EAST *Kingston Black* viii. 82 She refused to have sex with him. **1962** *Listener* 7 June 1006/2 Why wasn't Bond 'more tender' in his love-making? Why did he just 'have sex' and disappear? **1962** *Woman's Own* 18 Aug. 29/3 Those trends in our society that make sex before marriage so easy. **1971** *Petticoat* 17 July 6/2 The most conspicuous consequence of sex before marriage is the possibility of pregnancy. **1980** *Times* 6 Sept. 2/2 Michael was alongside me, and in due course, on top of me. We had not had sex, but we were contemplating it.

c. Genitalia; a penis. *slang.*

1938 D. GASCOYNE *Hölderlin's Madness* 18 And the black cypresses strained upwards like the sex of a hanged man. **1956** H. GOLD *Man who was not with It* (1965) xviii. 162 His eyes turned to his pants, gaping open, and his sex sick as an overhandled rattler gaping through. **1977** T. ALLBEURY *Man with President's Mind* i. 9 The narrow white briefs that barely captured her sex.

5. (Many combs. are paralleled by a collocation with SEXUAL *a.* 3.) *sex activity, affair* [AFFAIR 3], *aid, -anger, antagonism, awareness, behaviour, circuit* [CIRCUIT 7], *clinic, complex* [*COMPLEX *sb.* 3], *-compulsion, -consciousness, -contrast, -craving, difference, distribution, education, emotion, equality, -excitement, -experience, -exploitation, -feeling, fiend* [FIEND 4 a], *film, -flow, game, -hate, -hatred, hygiene, -inertia, -instruction, joke, life, -longing, -love, -machine* [MACHINE *sb.* 4 d], *magazine, mania, maniac, manifestation, manual* [MANUAL *sb.* 1 b], *-morality, novel, obsession, organ* [ORGAN *sb.*[1] 5], *orgy, partner, -party* [PARTY *sb.* 9], *-power, problem, question, repression, show, -specificity, starvation, stereotype, -stereotyping, story, -talk, -thrill, -union, war, warfare*; *sex-alive, -angry, -conscious* [*CONSCIOUS *a.* 12], *-crazed, -emancipated, -influenced, -mad* [MAD *a.* 4 c], *-obsessed, -segregated, -smelling, -specific, -starved* adjs.; **sex act,** the (or an) act of sexual intercourse; **sex-appeal,** sexual attractiveness; qualities which attract members of the opposite sex; also *fig.*; hence **sex-appeal** *v. trans.* and *intr.*, to attract sexually; **sex-appealing** *ppl. a.*, having or exerting sex appeal; **sex attractant,** a substance produced by one sex of a species that attracts members of the opposite sex, or a synthetic substance with the same property; also *attrib.* or as *adj.*; **sex-blind** *a.*, not discriminating between the sexes; **sexboat** *U.S. slang*, **sex-bomb** *slang* = *sexpot* below; **sex change,** a change of sex; *spec.* an apparent change of sex brought about by surgical means, treatment with hormones, etc.; also *attrib.*; **sex chromatin,** the material of a small heterochromatic body (believed to be an inactivated X chromosome) of which there is one in a normal (XX) female cell and in general one less than the number of X (or Z) chromosomes in a cell; also *attrib.*; **sex chromosome,** each of the chromosomes (normally two in number) in a cell's chromosomal complement the particular combination of which (as XX or XY) determines an individual's sex; opp. *AUTOSOME; hence *sex-chromosomal* adj.; **sex crime,** a crime involving sexual assault or with a sexual motive; a sexual act regarded as a crime; hence *sex criminal*; **sex-determinant,** that which determines an individual's sex; **sex determination,** the biological process that settles the sex of an individual; **sex determiner,** a gene which determines the sex of the individual bearing it; **sex-determining** *ppl. a.*, determining an individual's sex; **sex discrimination** orig. *U.S.*, unfavourable treatment motivated by prejudice against members of a particular sex; hence *sex-discriminating* ppl. adj., *sex-discriminatory* adj.; **sex drive,** the principle which motivates satisfaction of sexual needs; **sex factor,** (*a*) a sex-determining chromosome or gene; (*b*) [tr. F. *facteur sexuel* (Jacob & Wollman 1957, in *Compt. Rend.* CCXLV. 1840)], a bacterial plasmid which can promote the transfer of genetic material from its ('male') host to another ('female') bacterium in which recombination then takes place; **sex-free** *a.*, (*a*) having a liberated attitude towards sex; (*b*) not involving sex; **sex hormone,** any of the (natural or synthetic) hormones that affect sexual development or behaviour, esp. those produced by the gonads; **sex impulse,** the impulse towards satisfaction of sexual needs; **sex instinct,** the behaviour and feelings associated with sexual reproduction considered as an instinct for the survival of the species; **sex-interest,** concern with a sexual relationship, esp. as a theme or episode in a story, film, etc.; **sex-intergrade,** an intersex; **sex-killer,** a murderer who sexually assaults his victim; hence *sex-killing* vbl. sb.; **sex kitten** *colloq.*, a young woman who exploits her sex appeal; hence *sex-kittenish* adj.; **sex-mosaic** *Biol.*, an individual some of whose cells are of one sex and the rest of the other; **sex object,** a person towards whom or thing towards which the sexual impulse is directed; a person regarded only as the object of sexual desire; **sex offence,** (*U.S.*) **offense,** a breach of law or etiquette involving sex; **sex-offender,** a person guilty of a sex offence; **sex play,** (*a*) a play about sex or with sexual content; (*b*) sexual activity stopping short of intercourse; **sexpot, sex-pot** *colloq.*, a sexually exciting person, esp. a woman; also, a sexually very active or sex-obsessed person; also *attrib.* or as *adj.*; **sex ratio,** the ratio of the numbers of individuals of each sex; **sex relation,** (*a*) sexual relationship; (*b*) *pl.* sexual intercourse; also *sex relationship*; *sex-related* adj.; **sex-reversal,** adoption of a form or role characteristic of the opposite sex; hence **sex-reversed, -reversing** *ppl. adjs.*; **sex role** *Social Psychol.*, the culturally determined role or behaviour which a person learns as appropriate to his or her sex; **sex shop,** a shop selling sex magazines, aids, etc.; **sex surrogate,** a person employed as a sexual partner for a person undergoing therapy for sexual problems; **sex symbol,** (*a*) a person who is for many the epitome of sexual attraction and glamour; (*b*) a symbol with a sexual signification; **sex therapy,** therapy that deals with a person's psychological impediments to sexual intercourse or with other sexual problems; so *sex therapist*; **sex-typed** *ppl. a. Sociol.* and *Psychol.*, typified as being characteristic of either the male or the female sex; so *sex-typing* ppl. adj. and vbl. sb.; **sex urge** = *sex drive* above.

1918 M. STOPES *Married Love* vi. 62 What must be taking place in the female system as a result of the completed sex act? **1958** *Listener* 21 Aug. 263/1 A consciousness of guilt in the sex act. **1972** J. SYMONS *Bloody Murder* xii. 160 Detailed accounts of sex acts is [*sic*] still less frequent in the crime story than in ordinary novels. **1898** C. P. STETSON *Women & Econ.* iii. 44 Woman..has developed in the lines of action to which she was confined; and those were always lines of sex-activity. **1949** M. MEAD *Male & Female* x. 208 The burden of choosing between sex activity and other activities has been taken off the individual. **1933** DYLAN THOMAS *Let.* Nov. (1966) 51 She who lives serene..And drags her tea-time sex affair all fresh To the dinner table. **1949** M. MEAD *Male & Female* v. 118 Two inexperienced adolescents had a first sex-affair. **1977** *Gay News* 7–20 Apr. 14/3, I should like to dismiss this neat little toy as a sex-aid for sadomasochists. **1923** Sex-alive [see *ranch dog* s.v. *RANCH *sb.*[2] 3 a]. **1923** D. H. LAWRENCE *Kangaroo* xiii. 294 And if for a time you *do* overcome her with reason, the sex-anger only arises more hideously. *Ibid.*, You can reason with a sex-angry woman till you are black in the face. **1909** E. ROBINS *Votes for Women* I. 44 This ferment of feminism..[is] likely to bring a very terrible thing in its train... Sex antagonism. **1952** A. CHRISTIE *Mrs McGinty's Dead* xii. 93 We really get a feeling of sex antagonism between the chap and the girl. **1924** *Amer. Mercury* II. 318/1 An actress with sex appeal is four times out of five a more effective actress. **1924** G. R. CHESTER *On Lot & Off* 25 She'd sex appeal me all right! **1937** G. FRANKAU *More of Us* v. 61 'Ergo et propter hoc festina lente', Remarked Athene from that smoke-blue ceiling. But Innocent continued sex-appealing. **1953** *Encounter* Nov. 32/2 For the frustrated and starved, it [*sc.* Communism] has all the sex-appeal of a strong, monolithic creed. **1979** *Guardian* 30 Mar. 9/6 Two conflicting general [education] policies have been put forwards by the Conservatives... Both have political sex appeal. **1980** N. FREELING *Castang's City* xi. 68 A very feminine charm, next door to sex appeal. **1928** *Daily Express* 24 Nov. 4/1 Sex-appealing women should cut out the hurt feelings, the dewy eyes, trembling lips, the 'Please, I'm just a woman' stuff. **1932** *News Chron.* 20 June 4/1 Both [stories] are glittering, glamorous, sex-appealing. **1964** *Listener* 27 Aug. 291/2 The study of sex-attractant odours in insects has shown that these may be so highly specific that a very slight change in their chemical structure may make them less effective or even quite ineffective. **1976** *Globe & Mail* (Toronto) 13 Sept. 5/1 Many species manufacture and use chemicals as sex attractants. **1925** *John o' London's Weekly* 5 Dec. 360/1 In many fishes..there seems little hint of sex-awareness. **1949** M. MEAD *Male & Female* xiv. 284 The period between childhood sexuality focussed on the parent and the stirring of adolescent sex awareness. **1923** J. S. HUXLEY *Ess. of Biologist* IV. 144 Castrated animals fail to realize either possibility of normal sex-behaviour. **1949** M. MEAD *Male & Female* xvii. 354 The exaggerated over-concern with the other..puts an extraordinary strain on sex behaviour. **1975** *New Yorker* 29 Sept. 29/1 Even in an ideal sex-blind situation you are going to encounter different kinds of blocksmanship between you and your goals. **1977** *N.Y. Post* 30 Mar. 3 Spokesmen for several liberal groups..declared yesterday that totally sex-blind job assignments are a violation of prisoners' rights. **1962** E. LACY *Freeloaders* ii. 22, I don't buy the bit that every mademoiselle is automatically a sexboat because she's French. **1963** L. DEIGHTON *Horse under Water* xxii. 98 I've got the photo of your secretarial sex-bomb. **1976** P. CAVE *High Flying Birds* iii. 42 Sex-bomb, Sonya Stelling might be. Oscar contender she was not. **1946** *Nature* 3 Aug. 173/2 These results.., while providing virtual proof of sex-change from male to female in a section of the male population, point also to the probable occurrence of two types of males in *P*[*atella*] *vulgata*. **1960** *Twentieth Century* Mar. 258 Sex-change may well seem, as *The Times* said, 'unprepossessing' as a subject for comedy. **1970** *Daily Tel.* 21 Dec. 2/6 More people with transsexual problems are seeking National Health sex-change operations. **1952** GRAHAM & BARR in *Anat. Rec.* CXII. 709 The term 'sex influenced chromatin', or simply 'sex chromatin', will be used in the description to follow for the nuclear structure characterized by a size relation to sex. **1962** *Lancet* 27 Jan. 216/2 In all cases the sex-chromatin pattern was shown to be consistent with the morphological sex. **1913** *Jrnl. Exper. Zool.* XV. 593 The two white females..came from the union of the two-X egg with the no-X sperm of the vermillion pink male, and should be entirely maternal and entirely non-paternal in sex chromosomal composition, i.e., they should be exact counterparts..of their mother. **1906** E. B. WILSON in *Jrnl. Exper. Zool.* III. 28 These chromosomes are the bearers of the male and female qualities (or the factors essential to the production of these qualities) respectively. They may also be designated (whenever it is desirable to avoid circumlocution) as sex-chromosomes. **1926** J. S. HUXLEY *Ess. Pop. Sci.* 46 From all the facts, we can, I think, be sure that all the higher animals possess special X or sex-chromosomes, two in one sex, one in the other, by whose agency sex is determined. **1974** GOODENOUGH & LEVINE *Genetics* x. 466 The sex of a fly is determined, in part, by the number of euchromatic sex chromosomes, called X chromosomes, possessed by an individual. **1920** D. H. LAWRENCE *Women in Love* xvi. 221 Each acknowledges the perfection of the polarised sex-circuit. **1951** R. CAMPBELL *Light on Dark Horse* 319 These Germans had money from the Komintern and they set up sex-clinics and communist-cells. **1972** *Newsweek* 27 Nov. 65 The sex clinic is fast becoming as vital a part of the modern hospital as the emergency room. **1921** R. MACAULAY *Dangerous Ages* vi. 111 You prefer to avoid discussing certain aspects of your life. You obviously have a sex complex. **1928** D. H. LAWRENCE *Lady Chatterley's Lover* vi. 64 Be damned to the artificial sex-compulsion! refuse it! **1912** T. DREISER *Financier* xx. 222 From the first she was somewhat sex-conscious. **1952** S. KAUFFMANN *Philanderer* (1953) ii. 30 But she's certainly a sex-conscious girl. It's in her voice, in the way she sits, the way she drinks. **1911** *Freewoman* 7 Dec. 56/1 The impression given..is that the editors and most of the contributors picture the average woman as an individual wallowing in sex-consciousness. **1953** D. A. BANNERMAN *Birds Brit. Isles* II. 193 'Sex consciousness'..remains for a long time, the male continuing to feed the female..even after the young are hatched. **1911** J. A. THOMSON *Biol. Seasons* iii. 263 The male 'ends' are salmon red or dull pink; the female 'ends' are greenish-grey or drab—the sex-contrast eking itself out in colour. **1949** M. MEAD *Male & Female* v. 110 The little boys will feel..the potential sex-contrast with the mother. **1921** D. H. LAWRENCE *Psychoanal. & Unconscious* i. 20 The incest-craving is not the result of inhibition of normal sex-craving. **1954** R. BISSELL *High Water* xx. 218 Well I'm reading this here story about a sex-crazed maniac. **1925** *Amer. Mercury* Feb. 196 Sex crimes, which are commonly regarded as a natural result of drug taking, actually never occur among addicts. **1965** G. MCINNES *Road to Gundagai* vi. 99 The murder of Alma Tirtschke by Colin Ross..was a sex crime which gripped Melbourne for weeks. **1977** *Gay News* 7–20 Apr. 10/1 Three gay people locked away in a private house constitutes a public meeting, and sexual acts that take place between any or all of them are sex crimes. **1972** J. SYMONS *Players & Game* xv. 100 Inadequacy. That's the mark of sex criminals. **1902** *Biol. Bull.* III. 73 If we accept the theory that chromatin is the bearer of hereditary qualities, there could be little doubt regarding the necessary chromosomic character of a sex determinant. **1889** GEDDES & THOMSON *Evolution of Sex* iii. 49 The temperature of the time, not of birth but of sex determination, must of course be noted. **1977** *Dædalus* CVI. IV. 137 Primitive wasps.. evolved the sex determination mechanism of haplodiploidy, whereby unfertilized eggs yield males and fertilized eggs yield females. **1912** *Jrnl. Exper. Zool.* XII. 509 Bateson and Punnett ('11) describe certain exceptions occurring in their sex-linkage experiment with fowls, which they suggest may be due to a failure of the usual association between the sex-linked factor and the sex-determiner, i.e., to 'crossing over' in the female. **1960** E. J. GARDNER *Princ. Genetics* vii. 123/2 When the parallelism was discovered between the chromosome cycle and gene behaviour it was generally assumed that genes other than sex determiners were also located in the sex chromosomes. **1901** GEDDES & THOMSON *Evol. Sex* (ed. 2) 51 In regard to rotifers (*Hydatina*), Maupas maintains that temperature is the sex-determining factor. **1966** *Lancet* 24 Dec. 1397/1 This discrepancy between mammals and birds..might reflect different evolutionary origins of chromosomal sex-determining mechanisms in the two classes. **1918** M. STOPES *Married Love* iii. 19 Vaguely, perhaps, men have realised that much of the charm of life lies in the sex-*differences* between men and women. **1979** *Bull. Amer. Acad. Arts & Sci.* Feb. 25 Clear sex differences in the probability of labor force participation and in the kinds of jobs held. **1964** C. BARBER *Ling. Change in Present-Day Eng.* iv. 105 The sex-discriminating word used to indicate that the member of some profession or the holder of some office is a woman. **1976** *Listener* 4 Mar. 264/3, I do not care if it is unfair, or sex-discriminating, for a woman to get an old age pension five years before a man. **1916** *Campaign Text-Bk.* (National Woman's Party) 62 Enfranchised women in the United States regard the removal of sex discrimination from our national constitution as a political need of primary importance. **1965** *Financial Times* 24 Nov. 3/3 New guideline interpretations on sex discrimination have just been issued by the Commission... So far the Commission has received over 400 complaints of sex discrimination. **1976** *Times* 6 Jan. 2/3 Employers who have cheated women of equal pay by job-grading schemes..may be taken to court for sex discrimination. **1976** A. OAKLEY in Mitchell & Oakley *Rights & Wrongs of Women* i. 27 This practical equality challenged the law which was sex-discriminatory. **1949** M. MEAD *Male & Female* xiii. 266 The very simple accidents of sex distribution inside any family give a structure within which a child can feel unwanted. **1918** R. S. WOODWORTH *Dynamic Psychol.* vii. 173 The association is not entirely a spreading of the sex drive into the esthetic sphere. **1963** A. HERON *Towards Quaker View of Sex* 54 There may be a period..when the sex-drive is latent. **1979** J. SHERWOOD *Hour of Hyenas* ii. 23 You are very striking-looking, but..my power drive is far stronger nowadays than my sex drive. **1920** *Jrnl. Amer. Med. Assoc.* 25 Sept. 884/2 The conference will..consider the topic of venereal disease from these..aspects: (1) medical measures; (2) enforcement of repression and protection laws; and (3) sex education. **1969** *Guardian* 7 Aug. 7/6 A series of sex-education talks I'd been giving at a North-east London youth club. **1936** D. H. LAWRENCE *Pornography & So On* 46 The most high-flown sex-emancipated young people. **1911** O. SCHREINER *Women & Labour* 232 The ignorant savage,..who violates and then clubs a female into submission, may be dominated, and is, by sex emotions of a certain class. **1967** A. MARSHALL in *Coast to Coast 1965–6* 108 He was sure the men he knew were incapable of any sex emotion other than an animal lust. **1907** E. DENSMORE (*title*) Sex equality. **1921** *Daily Mail Year Bk.* 42/1 The organization of the League of Nations has from the outset been founded on the principle of sex equality. **1977** 'J. GASH' *Judas Pair* i. 14 She settled weeping while I found a coat. I'm all for sex equality. **1922** LD. DAWSON OF PENN *Love–Marriage–Birth Control* 23 If this harmful restraint succeeds in preventing conception there eventuates the inevitable prevalence of sex excitement. **1936** D. H. LAWRENCE *Pornography & So On* 30 Sex-excitement of a secretive, furtive sort. **1919** M. STOPES *Married Love* (ed. 7) ix. 141 Women so harried by the undue drains of unregulated sex-experience. **1953** Sex experience [see *sex play* below]. **1914** J. LONDON *Let.* 26 Mar. (1966) 419 The recent sex-exploitation in our magazines and books. **1911** R. C. PUNNETT *Mendelism* (ed. 3) xi. 107 The factor which repels the red-eye factor is in this case to be found in the male, and here consequently it is the male which must be regarded as heterozygous for a sex factor that is lacking in the female. **1931** E. B. FORD *Mendelism & Evolution* i. 14 Two doses of the sex factors carried by the X-chromosomes evoking the development of one of the sexes. **1955** *Science* 25 Feb. 305/1 The sex alleles of monosporoidal lines from a cross can be determined by matings in corn seedlings with lines representing each of the four haploid combinations of the parental sex factors. **1959** *Genetics* XLIV. 497 (*heading*) A variant sex factor in *Escherichia coli*. *Ibid.*, The wild type sex factor (F') of strain K-12 is characterized by its low affinity for the chromosome and its lack of any preferential site of attachment. **1968** W. HAYES *Genetics of Bacteria & their Viruses* (ed. 2) xiv. 799 If the sex factor happens to be inserted into the chromosome.., the replication initiated in the sex factor proceeds around the complete, integrated structure so that the chromosome is transferred as well. **1973** R. G. KRUEGER et al. *Introd. Microbiol.* xv. 423/2 The spread of a sex factor like △ through successive populations of cells carrying different resistance genes on nontransmissible plasmids could result at each step in a strain carrying more and more genes for antibiotic resistance. **1918** M. STOPES *Married Love* v. 50 Even after a woman's dormant sex-feeling is aroused..it may even take as much as from ten to twenty minutes of actual physical union to consummate her feeling. **1937** *Discovery* May 162/2 Conjugal affection, as distinct from sex-feeling. **1970** *Women Speaking* Apr. 4/2 The nearest man ever comes to this reduction to a word is when he offends society sexually: he *is a sex fiend*. **1976** T. HEALD *Let Sleeping Dogs Die* vi. 111 She was picked up by a sex fiend..and raped. **1970** Sex film [see *sex-instruction* below]. **1936** D. H. LAWRENCE *Pornography & So On* 44 The sex-flow is dying out of the young. **1929** —— *Pornography & Obscenity* 24 But the bohemian is 'sex free'. **1960** *Encounter* Sept. 72/1 Gerda is one of those sex-free affairs between tormented men and life-accepting women. *a* **1911** D. G. PHILLIPS *Susan Lenox* (1917) II. x. 244 The favorite children's games, often played in the open street ..were sex games. **1976** J. CROSBY *Nightfall* xxvi. 148 'Don't you like sex games?' she said. *a* **1930** D. H. LAWRENCE *Last Poems* (1932) 140 All this talk of equality between the sexes is merely an expression of sex-hate. **1913** J. LONDON *Let.* 11 Oct. (1966) 408 She cherishes a sex hatred for a woman who was bigger than she. **1917** *Jrnl. Exper. Zool.* XXIII. 371 (*heading*) The free-martin; a study of the action of sex hormones in the foetal life of cattle. **1965** *New Scientist* 22 Apr. 218/3 The materials contained in the various forms of The Pill are synthetic sex hormones. **1951** M. MCLUHAN *Mech. Bride* (1967) 23/2 The reader is treated as the sluggish male is treated by the sex-hungry cave woman in the shirt ads. **1912** G. F. LYDSTON (*title*) Sex hygiene for the male and what to say to the boy. **1949** M. MEAD *Male & Female* i. 17 Proper diet, rest, and sex hygiene have taken care of that. *a* **1911** D. G. PHILLIPS *Susan Lenox* (1917) II. xi. 281 In the streets the sex impulse shows stripped of all disguise. **1957** J. S. HUXLEY *Relig. without Revelation* ix. 223 The powerful emergence of the sex-impulse in adolescence. **1936** D. H. LAWRENCE *Pornography & So On* 45 You may even bring about a state of utter indifference and sex-inertia. **1951** H. A. LINDSAY et al. in *Jrnl. Nat. Cancer Inst.* XII. 244 During accelerated synthesis of Nissl material the sex-influenced chromatin moves from its usual position, next to the nucleolus, toward the nuclear membrane. **1898** C. P. STETSON *Women & Econ.* iii. 56 What business has a little girl with the instincts of maternity?.. They are sex-instincts, and should not appear till the period of adolescence. **1976** A. MONTAGU *Nature of Human Aggression* (1978) iv. 64 Everyone 'knows' from his or her own experience that there is such a thing as a sex instinct. **1935** E. BOWEN *House in Paris* I. iii. 42 We do not consider him ripe for direct sex-instruction yet, though my husband is working towards this through botany. **1970** *Guardian* 10 Dec. 10/4 From time to time we have to see, not sex films, but sex-instruction films. **1911** *Maclean's Mag.* Apr. 139/2 There is scarcely any 'sex interest' in it at all. **1940** 'G. ORWELL' in *Horizon* Mar. 189 Both of these papers admit a certain amount of sex-interest into their stories. **1917** Sex-intergrade [see *INTERSEX]. **1962** *Lancet* 27 Jan. 216/2 The hypothesis, advanced by Lang, that some male homosexuals are sex intergrades—i.e., morphologically male but genotypically female. **1941** 'G. ORWELL' in *Horizon* IV. 155 More than half, perhaps three-quarters, of the jokes are sex jokes. **1959** M. GILBERT *Blood & Judgement* ii. 26 You'd be surprised.. how many sex-killers turn out to be their mothers' favourite sons. **1972** J. MCCLURE *Caterpillar Cop* ii. 15 Murders..kept things going... But wanton sex killings involving the young were quite another matter. **1958** *Daily Sketch* 2 June 11/4 Clever film men have moulded her sex-kitten type. **1966** *Guardian* 7 Jan. 9/2 Brigitte Bardot..the original sex kitten with the French charm. **1977** D. MORRIS *Manwatching* 256 This is why we like 'sex kittens' more than females who are 'catty'. **1963** J. FOWLES *Collector* II. 166 Antoinette was almost parodying herself, she was so sex-kittenish. **1898** C. P. STETSON *Women & Econ.* vii. 143 It should be..understood..that the higher development of social life following the economic independence of women makes possible a higher sex-life than has ever yet been known. **1922** S. PATON *Signs of Sanity* vi. 205 Some phases of our instinctive activities..we discuss frankly..; others, notably the sex-life, we treat in a..furtive manner. **1936** 'P. QUENTIN' *Puzzle for Fools* xx. 181, I get no kick out of the sex-life of the white-tailed baboon. **1976** *Vogue* 15 Mar. 13/2 *He* is being reviled for apparently having absolutely no sex life, none at all. **1979** R. JAFFE *Class Reunion* I. v. 47 Richard was the only boy..who had a regular sex life with a girl, and so he was a celebrity. **1925** T. DREISER *Amer. Tragedy* (1926) II. III. xiv. 183 All those..sex-longings

..had long since been covered with an easy manner. **1898** C. P. Stetson *Women & Econ.* xii. 260 The generous giving impulse of sex-love. **1976** R. Delmar in Mitchell & Oakley *Rights & Wrongs of Women* ix. 281 There are several conditions which, in Engels..make sex love the rule within the proletariat. **1935** H. Edib *Clown & his Daughter* viii. 43 Now she wants to burden me with another sex-machine. **1970** *Times* 9 Dec. 16/4 Lulu herself, from her first days as an insatiably successful sex-machine to her last days as an amateur prostitute, has no existence outside her appetite. **1943, 1974** Sex-mad [see *mad *a.* 4 c]. **1931** Sex magazine [see **confession magazine*]. **1980** P. Kinsley *Vatchman Smith* vii. 66 The customs officer..sold any sex-magazines he could confiscate from foreign tourists. **1895** *Fortn. Rev.* 1 Apr. 592 Sex mania in art and literature can be but a passing phase. **1895** H. Garland *Rose of Dutcher's Coolly* viii. 90 The brakeman came through and eyed her with the glare of a sex-maniac. **1971** *Daily Tel.* 14 Dec. 3 The Jersey sex maniac..was jailed for 30 years yesterday for 13 indecent and sexual offences against young girls and boys. **1975** 'D. Rutherford' *Mystery Tour* i. 8 Wasn't that [*sc.* the murder] the work of some sadistic sex maniac? **1911** O. Schreiner *Women & Labour* v. 187 It is among certain orders of birds that sex manifestations appear to assume their most harmonious and poetical forms on earth. **1949** M. Mead *Male & Female* viii. 167 These [*sc.* seizures] are extremely violent, but without specific sex manifestations. **1975** H. McCloy *Minotaur Country* iii. 21 He would be a sober, industrious lover. He would read all the sex manuals. **1926** W. R. Inge *Lay Thoughts* iii. 254 The pleasantest side of our civilization—the ease with which innocent friendships are made between men and women—stands or falls with that Christian sex-morality which is now being openly flouted. **1958** *Listener* 4 Dec. 933/2 Queen Victoria..instituted a new reign of sex-morality. **1903** *Bull. Museum Compar. Zool. Harvard Coll.* XL. 197 Unilateral and mixed hermaphrodites are an exceptional form of sex-mosaic. **1926** J. S. Huxley *Ess. Pop. Sci.* 296 It is possible in the case of abnormal distribution of the sex-chromosomes during development to obtain some parts of the body with the male-determining, others with the female-determining complement of chromosomes, with the result that a sex-mosaic or gynandromorph is the result [*sic*]. **1955** *Japanese Jrnl. Zool.* XI. 350 The 1st gynandromorph is a simple bilateral sex mosaic showing yellow Ww gene in the left male wings and white Ww gene in the right female wings. **1923** in C. D. Stelling *Yea & Nay* 33 (*heading*) Is there any alternative to the sex novel? **1951** M. McLuhan *Mech. Bride* (1967) 23/2 Amid the unmitigated torrent of sadistic sex novels works of reflection are tolerated only if they are.. 'warmly human'. **1911** *Amer. Jrnl. Psychol.* XXII. 423 Instead of sublimating the sex impulse, he [*sc.* Leonardo da Vinci] directed it towards the physical Jesus *in toto*. It was simply the substitution of one sex object for another. **1963** B. Friedan *Feminine Mystique* (1965) xi. 266 For the woman who lives according to the feminine mystique, there is no road to achievement, or status, or identity, except the sexual one: the achievement of sexual conquest, status as a desirable sex object, identity as a sexually successful wife and mother. **1980** G. Greene *Doctor Fischer of Geneva* ix. 59 Deane is not an actor: he is a sex object. Teenage girls worship him. **1914** *New Republic* 26 Dec. 27/1 An almost lyrical open-airness.. saved 'The Garden Without Walls,'..from being sex-obsessed. **1979** *London Rev. Bks.* 25 Oct. 13/1 Civilised human beings are remarkable among animal species for being sex-obsessed. **1920** F. M. Ford *Let.* 19 Sept. (1965) 127 The end would be the most horribly costive neurastheniac you can imagine, with incredible sex obsessions sedulously concealed. **1911** J. London *Let.* 8 Jan. (1966) 330 You are suffering from what you deem a sex-offence. **1977** J. Thomson *Case Closed* vii. 85 The offences..included fraud, burglary,..assault, sex offences of various sorts. **1939** *Columbia Law Rev.* Mar. 535 Prior to the enactment of this statute in Illinois, a criminal sex offender received no special treatment. **1976** K. Bonfiglioli *Something Nasty* iii. 33 We 'ave only two known sex-offenders worth the name in this Parish. **1902** W. James *Var. Relig. Exper.* i. 12 That without the chemical contributions which the sex-organs make to the blood, the brain would not be nourished so as to carry on religious activities..may be true or not true. **1978** *Times* 15 Mar. 6/3 Old symbols like mutilation of sex organs.. are passé. **1962** J. Heller *Catch-22* xxi. 208 Officers' clubs everywhere pulsated with blurred but knowing accounts of lavish, hushed-up drinking and sex orgies there. **1949** M. Mead *Male & Female* ix. 195 But patterns that regulate competition in the choice of sex partners are learned patterns. **1970** Sex partner [see *sex therapy* below]. **1958** J. Kerouac *On Road* i. i. 8 He told him of..his innumerable girls and sex-parties and pornographic pictures. **1916** G. B. Shaw *Overruled* 63 Plays occupied wholly with the conventional results are..unsatisfying as sex plays. **1932** Wodehouse *Louder & Funnier* 270 When I write my daring sex-play, I have to submit it to Lord Cromer, who starts licking his blue pencil the moment he has opened the envelope. **1953** H. M. Parshley tr. *De Beauvoir's Second Sex* II. vii. 682 The excessive sentimentality,..and platonic crushes of adolescent girls,..are much more injurious than a little childish sex play and a few definite sex experiences. **1961** W. Brown *Bedeviled* 17 Gradually, however, the fondling developed into open sex play which frightened her. **1957** F. Morton *Art of Courtship* 156 How pitiful the American who cannot command the smile of a sexpot. **1961** *Harper's Bazaar* May 57/2 Ovid..the dirty old sexpot. **1963** J. T. Story *Something for Nothing* i. 17 'I like the hockey type,' Albert said. 'I can't stand these sex-pots.' **1975** *New Yorker* 5 May 115/1 Graham Chapman, John Cleese..with Connie Booth and Carol Cleveland as their sexpot aides. **1981** *London Mag.* July 89/2 Tough Games Mistress. Rebellious sexpot pupil (pregnant again). **1918** M. Stopes *Married Love* viii. 76 The periods of complete abstinence should be opportunities for transmuting the healthy sex-power into work of every sort. **1977** *London's Outrage* i. 7 The bully-boy sex-power of Nazism/fascism is very attractive and an easy solution to our complex moral and social dilemmas. **1900** J. X. Merriman *Let.* 1 July (1966) 222 The shrieking sisterhood who write on sex problems and scream out for votes. **1979** *Guardian* 10 July 9/1 Professional partners used in the treatment of sex problems. **1902** G. B. Shaw *Mrs. Warren's Profession* p. xx, Plays which treat sex questions as problems for thought instead of as aphrodisiacs will be freely performed. **1917** F. W. S. Browne in *Proc. Brit. Soc. for Study Sex Psychol.* 7 General early marriage, even if possible under present conditions, does not solve the sex question. **1906** *Biometrika* V. 79 The sex-ratio for the family of each individual is directly calculated and tabled. **1974** J. Burnett *Useful Toil* i. 48 Because of the unequal sex ratio one in three [Victorian] women were 'doomed' to spinsterhood. **1977** *Detroit Free Press* 11 Dec. 9-c/1 A high-ranking official of Planned Parenthood says television's standards on sex-related programming should be as much a public issue as its standards on televised violence. **1898** C. P. Stetson *Women & Econ.* i. 5 The economic status of the human female is relative to the sex-relation. **1911** O. Schreiner *Let.* in First & Scott *Olive Schreiner* (1980) vii. 291 [She] thinks it's wrong for people, even if married, to have sex relations with each other except just when they want to make a child. **1949** M. Mead *Male & Female* i. 14 The infant..before he can toddle has absorbed a particular style of sex relations. **1980** First & Scott *Olive Schreiner* viii. 307 A cutting about sex relations between Indians and white women. **1898** C. P. Stetson *Women & Econ.* iv. 74 Let us bear in mind that all the tender ties of family are ties of blood, of sex-relationship. **1963** A. Heron *Towards Quaker View of Sex* i. 8 There are certain historical characteristics of the Society of Friends that ought specially to lead to..understanding of the significance of the sex relationship. **1926** M. Leinster *Dew on Leaf* v. 29 He talked..about health, climate, and sex-repression. **1958** J. Cannan *And be Villain* i. 27 Richard used to treat me as a case of sex repression. **1916** *Amer. Naturalist* L. 388 In the generic crosses which give all, or nearly all, males at the beginning of the season and all, or nearly all, females in the autumn what is happening?—true sex reversal? or is it selective fertilization, differential maturation or a selective elimination of ova in the ovary? **1926** J. S. Huxley *Ess. Pop. Sci.* iv. 53 Hens which had undergone sex-reversal to cocks. **1949** M. Mead *Male & Female* vi. 129 Peoples may provide sex-reversal rôles for both sexes. **1926** J. S. Huxley *Ess. Pop. Sci.* iv. 53 Similar results have now been obtained..by breeding from sex-reversed moths. *Ibid.* 52 Some sexually abnormal human beings are the victims of this sex-reversing power. **1959** Sex-reversed [see *feminization 2]. **1927** W. B. Wolfe tr. *Adler's Understanding Human Nature* i. vii. 135 There are only *two* sex rôles possible. One must orient oneself according to one of two models, either that of an ideal woman, or according to that of an ideal man. **1969** W. H. Sewell in E. F. Borgatta *Social Psychol.* 218/1 The sex-role concepts of children and..sex-role pressure in the socialization of the male child. **1977** *China Now* July/Aug. 3/3 The sex-roles are traditionally presented and the girl who helps Mummy to hang out the washing is rewarded. **1955** T. H. Pear *English Social Differences* 200 This class-segregated, sex-segregated regime. **1970** *Guardian* 26 Nov. 4/2 'Sex-shops'..are now established in many West German cities. **1974** K. Millett *Flying* (1975) iii. 307 Sarah stops by and gives us an account of the new sex shop in Tottenham Court Road. **1981** *Observer* 4 Jan. 3/2 How do you designate a sex shop anyway? Does selling contraceptives make Boots a sex shop? **1959** P. Bull *I know Face* x. 187 A city almost entirely devoted to sex-shows. **1922** Joyce *Ulysses* 535 The dark sexsmelling theatre unbridles vice. **1961** *Giornale di Microbiologia* IX. 149 Two phages have been isolated which are sex-specific on *E[scherichia] coli* K 12. **1976** P. Marks in Mitchell & Oakley *Rights & Wrongs of Women* v. 179 They may differ among themselves about how far vocations, and thus education, should be sex-specific. **1961** *Giornale di Microbiologia* IX. 147 The same strains used to test the sex-specificity of phages μ_2 and ϕ_1 were challenged with phages T_1, .., T_7. **1912** M. Hastings *New Sin* ii. 57 Sex-starvation, they call it. It's awful, but it can be done because it must be done. **1977** 'D. Rutherford' *Return Load* i. 12 He wondered whether sex starvation had..started to provoke hallucinations... He had seen..a gorgeous red-head. **1927** A. Huxley *Proper Studies* 292 St. Anthony and the unwashed, underfed, sex-starved monks of the Thebaid. **1978** M. Birmingham *Sleep in Ditch* 164 Their first guess is that I'm a sex-starved grass-widow, glimpsing seducers behind every door. **1949** M. Mead *Male & Female* vi. 137 A sex stereotype that decries the interests..of each sex is usually not completely without a basis. **1977** *N.Z. Herald* 8 Jan. 2-2/7 The society has new projects planned for its second decade, including a survey into sex-stereotyping. **1936** Sex-story [see **crime-story*]. **1979** *Guardian* 10 July 9/1 Dr. Martin Cole's Institute for Sex Education and Research..has been supplying sex surrogate therapy for ten years. *a* **1911** D. G. Phillips *Susan Lenox* (1917) II. xx. 442 Men..might regard her as nothing but sex symbol; she regarded herself as an intelligence. **1951** M. McLuhan *Mech. Bride* (1967) 94/2 The 'line' [of chorus girls] itself..is even more basic than the sex symbol of the flower. **1976** Botham & Donnelly *Valentino* i. 12 The olive skin of the man who would.. become the world's first and most enduring sex symbol. **1931** G. T. Renier *English: Are they Human?* iv. 85 The wide-spread ignorance of the technique of love among average Englishmen..results from the taboo on direct sex-talk. **1977** C. Fremlin *Spider-Orchid* xiii. 94 They have these sex talks..at school from the age of nine. **1978** J. Pudney *Thank Goodness for Cake* 80 At the football club sex talk proliferated, constantly spiced with dirty stories. **1976** *National Observer* (U.S.) 13 Mar. 6/3 American life-styles: a TV anchorman,..a rock star,..a groupie, a sex therapist. **1977** DeLora & Warren *Understanding Sexual Interaction* iv. 90 Sex therapists, who direct their creative energy toward the specifically sexual difficulties of individuals or couples. **1961** R. A. & F. R. Harper in *Encycl. Sexual Behaviour* I. 348/2 Individuals and groups vary..in the quality and quantity of sex therapy they need. **1970** Belliveau & Richter *Understanding Human Sexual Inadequacy* (1971) iii. vii. 77 Success in sex therapy is dependent upon communication between the sex-partners. **1928** D. H. Lawrence *Lady Chatterley's Lover* i. 6 In the actual sex-thrill within the body, the sisters nearly succumbed to the strange male power. **1941** Miller & Dollard *Social Learning & Imitation* xii. 198 By the time a child reaches his second year sex-typing has already begun. *Ibid.*, The punishments meted out to adults who actually exhibit such tendencies tend to maintain and strengthen the sex-typed habits acquired. **1979** *Bull. Amer. Acad. Arts & Sci.* Feb. 31 The modal pattern for each sex is, nonetheless, conventionally sex-typed. **1976** *New Society* 4 Mar. 509/1 The 'blue/gun for a boy: pink/dolly for a girl', sex-typing syndrome. **1898** C. P. Stetson *Women & Econ.* x. 213 We confuse the natural result of marriage in children, common to all forms of sex-union, with the family,—a purely social phenomenon. **1923** M. Stopes *Contraception* iii. 39 The type of woman who..has acquired the view that all sex union after the procreation of the desired number of children has been accomplished, is wrong. **1920** M. Sanger *Woman & New Race* ix. 111 This man is not concerned with his wife's sex urge, save as it responds to his own at times of his choosing. **1966** D. Francis *Flying Finish* vi. 74 Bravery is built in... You can't stamp it out any more than the sex urge. **1912** L. Housman (*title*) Sex-war and woman's suffrage. **1978** J. Irving *World according to Garp* xvii. 362 'Fucking *women*,' the cabby said. 'Fucking *men*,' said Garp, feeling..that he had done his duty to ensure that the sex war went on. **1911** 'I. Hay' *Safety Match* i. i. 4 The sides of the house are equally balanced both for purposes of companionship and in the event of sex-warfare.

sex, *v.* Add: **2.** *to sex up* (slang), to give a sexual flavour to, to increase the sexual content of.

Examples of the adj. or quasi-adj. *sexed-up* 'sexually aroused' are included here for convenience.

1942 Berrey & Van den Bark *Amer. Thes. Slang* § 361/5 *Make sexy, sex it up*, to introduce sex into, as a story. *Ibid.* § 361/9 Passionate; amative; lustful..(*all*) *sexed up*. **1958** *Observer* 24 Aug. 5/7 The business of 'sexing up' the titles of foreign films is..a trick well known in both France and Britain. **1959** *Ibid.* 11 Oct. 21/4 Reads rather like an old-time boy's book sexed up and sadistified for the 1950s. **1969** J. Gardner *Compl. State of Death* vi. 97 What do you do when you get sexed up? Mortify the flesh? **1976** *Nature* 15 July 177/3 Erickson and Zenone tested the reaction of 35 males to two groups of females... The males..showed more aggression and less courtship towards the 'sexed up' females.

3. *intr.* To have sexual intercourse. *slang.*

1966 'G. Black' *You want to die, Johnny?* ix. 172 The surprising thing isn't the number of teenagers who sex and dope, but rather..that there are so many that don't. **1980** J. Barnett *Palmprint* i. 6 Maybe we sex together at yo' place.

sexational (seksē^i·ʃənăl), *a. slang* (orig. *U.S.*). Also **sexsational.** [Blend of Sex *sb.* and Sensational *a.*] Sexually sensational. So **sexa·tionalism.**

1927 *Time* 16 May 39 Newspaper sensationalism has developed into sex-ationalism. **1928** *Daily Express* 30 July 3/3 You send us films of sexational novels and pornographic plays, which our censors cut to pieces. **1937** *Time* 27 Dec. 30/2 Sexational, robustious Cinemactress Mae West appeared on a commercial broadcast for the first time in four years. **1957** R. Hoggart *Uses of Literacy* viii. 213 Their authors' favourite descriptive epithet for them is 'sexational'. **1968** *Punch* 29 May 789/3 These are the qualities that save the film from being what *Variety* often calls 'sexsational'. **1976** *West Lancs. Evening Gaz.* 8 Dec. 3/2 (Advt.), 1st Blackpool showing of the Sexsational *Highway through the Bedroom* (X).

sexcapade (se·kskăpē^i d). *colloq.* [Blend of Sex *sb.* and Escapade.] A sexual escapade.

1965 F. Raphael *Darling* xxvii. 134 We are not complicating our holiday with disgusting sexcapades. **1976** *Honolulu Star-Bull.* 21 Dec. a-11/1 A generally less swinging group than the lone men off on sexcapades who helped give tourism a bad name.

sexduction (seksdɒ·kʃən). *Microbiology.* Also **sex-duction.** [Blend of Sex *sb.* and Transduction.] The transfer of part of a bacterial genome from one bacterium to another by a sex factor.

1960 [see *F III. 1 l]. **1964** G. H. Haggis et al. *Introd. Molecular Biol.* x. 277 It is possible by exploiting a special phenomenon, known as sex-duction, to bring about a stable state of diploidy for a short length of the chromosome containing all the genes involved in the lactose system. **1974** *Molecular & Gen. Genetics* CXXX. 99 The number of sexductants in a λ-immune recipient is not significantly affected while sexduction into a non-immune recipient is increased by a factor 10–20.

sexed, *a.* Add: **3.** With prefixed adv.: having the sexual desires, emotions, or functions developed in a specified way.

1898, etc. [see *over-sexed *a.*]. **1921** *Outward Bound* Mar. 13/2 Had Elizabeth been as strongly sexed as she. **1949** M. Mead *Male & Female* vi. 139 The tall, fiery, infinitely proud, specifically nervously sexed man and woman. **1974** M. Taylor tr. *Metz's Film Lang.* i. 9 Each one is disguised by a whole rigorously sexed body.

4. Of poultry: divided into the two sexes.

1960 *Farmer & Stockbreeder* 1 Mar. 148/3 (Advt.), Day old sexed pullets. **1971** *Farmers Weekly* 19 Mar. 92/2 (Advt.), Sexed poults.

sexennium (sekse·niə̆m). [L.: see Sexennarian.] A period of six years.

1959 *Amer. Jrnl. Phys. Anthropol.* XVII. 132/1 Over the sexennium from age 5 years to age 11 years, some children augment their skeletal face depth more than twice as much as other children. **1970** D. M. WALKER *Princ. Scottish Private Law* I. ii. 882 When the sexennium has run the constitution and resting—owing of the debt must be proved by the writ or oath of the debtor.

sexful (se·ksfŭl), *a. rare.* Also **sexfull.** [f. SEX *sb.* + -FUL.] Conveying sexual emotions; sexy.
1898 G. MOORE *Evelyn Innes* xvii. 232 Soprano voices of a rarer and more radiant timbre than any woman's sexful voice. **1959** D. BARTON *Loving Cup* 144 A sexless voice..was singing a sexfull dance lyric.

sexi-. Add: **sexivalent** *a.* (earlier example).
1872 *Phil. Mag.* XLIII. 260 Carbon is quadrivalent; two carbon atoms may unite by mutually saturating 1, 2, or 3 pairs of affinities, thus giving rise to a radical C^2, which may be sexi-, quadri-, or bivalent accordingly: thus, C^2H^6, C^2H^4, C^2H^2.

sexing, *vbl. sb.* Add: **1.** Delete *rare* and add later examples.
1970 *Nature* 11 July 190/1 None of these specimens was sufficiently mature to allow accurate sexing. **1973** *Ibid.* 14 Dec. 423/2 Final proof of an increase in frequency of Y sperm must await sexing of offspring conceived of spermatozoa exposed to the isolation process.
2. With *up*: see *SEX *v.* 2.
1954 KOESTLER *Invisible Writing* xxxi. 330 [Otto] thought that a little sexing-up of the war could do no harm.

sexism (se·ksiz'm). [f. SEX *sb.* + -ISM after *RACISM.] The assumption that one sex is superior to the other and the resultant discrimination practised against members of the supposed inferior sex, esp. by men against women; also conformity with the traditional stereotyping of social roles on the basis of sex.
1968 C. BIRD in *Vital Speeches* (U.S.) 15 Nov. 90 Sexism is judging people by their sex where sex doesn't matter. **1968** S. VANAUKEN *Freedom for Movement Girls—Now* 7 The parallels between *sexism* and *racism* are sharp and clear. Each embodies false assumption in a myth. **1971** *Guardian* 15 Jan. 11/4 The concept of a 'woman's page'.. perpetuates sexism by stressing the 'special' domestic interests supposedly adhering to women. **1971** *Publishers' Weekly* 22 Mar. 14 The Women's National Book Association panel during NBA Week on 'sexism' in children's books. **1973** *Ms.* Nov. 39/2 An insidious form of sexism pervades most biographies of famous women, a tendency to treat women's work as peripheral to their lives. **1981** *Amer. Speech* LVI. 84 Although they recognize the inherent sexism of the generic masculine, the Fowlers see no real alternative.

sexist (se·ksist), *sb.* and *a.* [f. SEX *sb.* + -IST after *RACIST *sb.* and *a.*] **A.** *sb.* One who advocates, practises, or conforms to sexism. **B.** *adj.* Of, pertaining to, or characteristic of sexism or sexists.
1965 P. M. LEET *Speech* 18 Nov. (mimeographed), When you argue..that since fewer women write good poetry this justifies their total exclusion, you are taking a position analogous to that of the racist—I might call you in this case a 'sexist'—who says that since so few Negroes have held positions of importance..their exclusion from history books is a matter of good judgment rather than discrimination. **1968** C. BIRD in *Vital Speeches* (U.S.) 15 Nov. 90 There is recognition abroad that we are in many ways a sexist country. *Ibid.*, Women are sexists as often as men. **1968** S. VANAUKEN *Freedom for Movement Girls—Now* 2 The sexist myth is the greatest and most pervasive myth the world has ever told itself. *Ibid.* 7 A *sexist* is one who proclaims or justifies or assumes the supremacy of one sex (guess which) over the other. **1971** *Publishers' Weekly* 22 Mar. 20/2 We live in a sexist society. By sexist we mean predetermining social roles on the basis of sex alone. **1976** *New Yorker* 5 Apr. 57/1 He was very stern and disagreeable and a gross sexist. **1977** MILLER & SWIFT *Words & Women* ix. 143 The language of American school books mirrors the sexist assumptions of society. **1978** J. IRVING *World according to Garp* xvi. 344 The sexist notion that women are..the acceptable prey of predatory males.

sexlessly, *adv.* (Later examples.)
1965 F. RAPHAEL *Darling* ix. 38 The West End was sexlessly bent on commerce. **1978** *Daily Tel.* 6 July 13/1 He is frequently bidden to the neat little house..where Leonora flirts with him, mothers him, indeed sexlessly gobbles him up.

sex-limited (stress variable), *a.* [f. SEX *sb.* + LIMITED *ppl. a.*] †**1.** = *SEX-LINKED *a.* 1. *Obs.*
1909 W. BATESON in A. C. Seward *Darwin & Mod. Science* v. 94 A study of the sex-limited descent of certain features in other animals. **1919** R. C. PUNNETT *Mendelism* (ed. 5) 95 Sex-limited inheritance..has been demonstrated in other birds besides poultry.
2. Of a genetic character or a phenotype: capable of occurring only in individuals of one sex. Of an individual: having such a character or phenotype.
[**1871** C. R. DARWIN *Descent of Man* viii. 282 (*heading*) Inheritance as limited by sex. *Ibid.* 285 If any variation appeared in a female pigeon, which was from the first sexually limited in its development to the females, it would be easy to make a breed with the females alone thus characterized. **1905** *Brit. Med. Jrnl.* 28 Oct. 1094/1 The abnormality, though affecting both boys and girls, is mainly limited to one sex in each family.] **1923** *Jrnl. Genetics* XIII. 215 As a contribution towards the adoption..of uniform terminology for the various modes of inheritance (at present, such terms as 'sex-limited' and 'sex-linked' are often used at random), I would point out that the denomination '*sex-linked*' (geschlechtsgebunden) ought to be applied only to conditions of inheritance explainable by the presence of the factor in question in those sex-chromosomes which are normally found in individuals of both sexes. *Ibid.* 216 The expression 'sex-limited inheritance' is not very judicious... 'Sex-limited manifestation' would be better. **1944** *Genetics* XXIX. 520 The mutant is strongly sex-limited in phenotypic expression. **1975** *Jrnl. Zool.* CLXXVII. 330 In butterflies, most sex-limited morphs are controlled by autosomal genes, their expression being dependent on the sex of the developing individual.
3. *transf.* Occurring only in one sex.
1949 M. MEAD *Male & Female* xi. 237 To the phrasing of any piece of human behaviour, however sex-limited it may seem to be, both sexes contribute their imaginations.
Hence **sex-limita·tion.**
1911 *Jrnl. Genetics* I. 189 The operation of the system of sex-limitation is similar in all these examples, the only difference being that in the one group the repulsion is from the factor *F*, in the other from the factor *M.* **1922** *Encycl. Brit.* XXXII. 419/2 (*heading*) Sex-limitation and sex-linkage. **1975** *Jrnl. Zool.* CLXXVII. 329 Polymorphism in butterflies is complicated by various factors, notably sexual dimorphism and sex-limitation.

sex-linked (stress variable), *a.* [f. as prec. + LINKED *ppl. a.*] **1.** Being or determined by a gene that is carried on a sex chromosome.
[**1905** *Brit. Med. Jrnl.* 28 Oct. 1095/1 Thus, in haemophilia, the abnormality is habitually linked with one sex.] **1912** *Jrnl. Exper. Zool.* XIII. 80 In the male-producing sperm, where no X is present, the sex-linked characters are always absent. **1923** [see *SEX-LIMITED *a.* 2]. **1974** *Encycl. Brit. Micropædia* III. 23/2 Colour blindness, which affects about 20 times as many males as females, is a sex-linked recessive character.
2. Occurring only or characteristically in one sex.
1932 AUDEN *Orators* II. 42 Self-regard, in origin a mere accident of overcrowding, like haemophilia is a sex-linked disease. **1956** H. W. PAPASHVILY *All Happy Endings* v. 75 In the writing of *Uncle Tom's Cabin*, Mrs. Stowe had exhibited many of those qualities considered by her contemporaries to be sex-linked to females—sympathy, tact, sensitivity, sensibility.
So **sex-linkage,** the state or condition of being sex-linked.
1912 *Jrnl. Exper. Zool.* XII. 512 In this case it would seem that complete sex-linkage, such as that found..in barred fowls, would not occur at all. **1975** *Zool. Jrnl.* CLXXVII. 330 Such sex-linkage..may give rise to a situation where a morph is common in one sex, and very rare in the other.

sexly, *a.* Delete † *Obs.*, for *rare*$^{-1}$ read *arch. rare*, and add later example.
a **1945** E. R. EDDISON *Mezentian Gate* (1958) xxxviii. 203 You [*sc.* a woman] are hampered by no sexly weakness: as fit as any man living to undertake it.

sexology (seksǫ·lŏdʒi). orig. *U.S.* [f. SEX *sb.* + -OLOGY.] The scientific study of sex and of the relations between the sexes.
1902 W. H. WALLING (*title*) Sexology. **1912** *Amer. Jrnl. Urology* VIII. 441 The author believes that..there is practically no individual who can claim to have entirely avoided sexual activities of any kind, an opinion in which Lowenfeld, whose experience in sexology is so extensive, concurs. **1936** C. S. LEWIS *Allegory of Love* I. 13 The second factor is the medieval theory of marriage—what may be called, by a convenient modern barbarism, the 'sexology' of the medieval church. **1977** E. J. TRIMMER et al. *Visual Dict. Sex* (1978) i. 18 Reich is..in all the history of sexology, perhaps the most single-minded believer in the centrality of sex to human lives.
Hence **sexolo·gical** *a.*, of or pertaining to sexology; **sexo·logist,** one who studies sexology.
1914 *Amer. Jrnl. Clinical Med.* Aug. 687/1 There may be some homosexuals who are reconciled to or even proud of their abnormality, as some sexologists claim, but I must confess that I have not met such types. **1920** *Contemp. Rev.* July 93 A point of some sexological interest. **1949** KOESTLER *Insight & Outlook* xiv. 196 The distinction made by some sexologists between the detumescent and contractile components of the sexual drive. **1973** I. ROBINSON *Survival of English* v. 178 The only happy aspect of the sexological misapplication of the jargon of science is that the common language is strong enough to make it appear at times what it is, howlingly funny. **1980** *Times Lit. Suppl.* 28 Nov. 1355/1 The sexual inclinations of a sexologist presumably have to be investigated in some detail, even if the whole truth is not intrinsically interesting.

sexophone (se·ksŏfōᵘn). *rare.* [Blend of SEX *sb.* + SAXOPHONE.] An imaginary musical instrument resembling a saxophone and producing sexual sensations. Also *attrib.* So **sexo·phonist.**
1932 A. HUXLEY *Brave New World* v. 88 The Sixteen Sexophonists were playing an old favourite. *Ibid.* 89 The sexophones wailed like melodious cats under the moon. **1945** V. NABOKOV *Real Life Sebastian Knight* xi. 93 Physical love is but another way of saying the same thing and not a special sexophone note, which once heard is echoed in every other region of the soul.

sexpert (se·kspɜ̄ɹt). *slang* (orig. *U.S.*). [Blend of SEX *sb.* and EXPERT *sb.*] An expert on sexual matters.
1924 [see *DIM *a.* 4 b]. **1979** *Radio Times* 9–15 June 78/1 Every other interviewed sexpert seemed to come from California where..you can graduate in any old spurious subject.

sexploitation (seksploitēⁱ·ʃən). [Blend of SEX *sb.* and EXPLOITATION.] The exploitation of sex, esp. in films. Also *attrib.*
1942 in Berrey & Van den Bark *Amer. Thes. Slang* § 361/1. **1948** G. V. DESANI *All about Mr. Hatterr* ii. 73 Damme, make the eternal triangle pay out a dividend! First that Portuguese feller victimised, then self! Damme, sexploitation! **1967** *Time* 17 Feb. 99 Jack Smith's four-year-old *Flaming Creatures*, an incredible tedious parody of a sexploitation picture, demonstrates how easy it is to fall asleep in the steamy midst of an hour-long transvestite orgy. **1977** E. J. TRIMMER et al. *Visual Dict. Sex* (1978) xxiv. 272 Sexploitation in advertisements seeks to tell the public that the problems of human sexuality are easily solved by the purchase of manufactured goods. **1981** *Times* 29 Jan. 4/4 It will become the 164th 'sexploitation' establishment in an area of less than one square mile.
So **sexploi·t** *v. trans.* to exploit sexually; **sexploi·tative** *a.*
1970 M. PEI *Words in Sheep's Clothing* App. A 218 Lastly, there is the entrancing possibility of a vast extension of *sex*-portmanteau forms, for which a precedent already exists in 'sexploit' and 'sexploitation'. **1977** *Gay News* 24 Mar. 29/2 *Inserts* advertises itself as..simultaneously serious and sexploitative. **1977** M. SOKOLINSKY tr. *Merle's Virility Factor* ix. 180 That sociologist broad.. she never stopped telling me: 'Bess, you've been sexploited by men.'

sexsational, var. *SEXATIONAL *a.*

sextal (se·kstăl), *a.* [f. L. *sext-us* sixth + -AL.] Pertaining to a system of numerical notation with 6 as base.
1943 *Trans. Philol. Soc. 1941* 10 A purely native six-system; that is what we have in Finno-Ugrian... The sextal system, though not common among the languages of the world, is quite well-attested. **1962** *Punch* 4 Apr. 554/3 Age-grouping would be standardised (on the sextal scale, of course). **1971** *Nature* 12 Mar. 133/3 Like the SI prefixes, it perpetuates the sextal (and ternary) system for counting indices, while the rest of our number system is decimal.

sextary. **2.** For 'sixth' read 'sixteenth'.

sextuplicate, *a.* Restrict *Obs. rare*$^{-1}$ to sense in Dict. and add: **B.** *sb.* (See quot. 1934.) Also in phr. *in sextuplicate*, in sixfold quantity, in six copies.
1934 WEBSTER, *Sextuplicate, n.*, a sixth thing corresponding to five others of the same kind; an exact copy of something of which five other exact copies exist. **1975** *Daily Tel.* 1 Aug. 12 Contestants..have been asked to submit their entries in sextuplicate. **1978** *Nature* 31 Aug. 897/2 (*caption*) Each column represents the result for one patient, averaging 4 to 10 separate assays (in sextuplicate) per tissue. **1979** *Ibid.* 29 Mar. 465/1 After preincubation, the tubes were returned to ice and ^{3}H-5-HT was added in sextuplicate.

sextuplication. (Later example.)
1935 *Antiquity* IX. 298 The sextuplication of the King's Chamber roof.

sextupole (se·kstiupōᵘl), *a.* and *sb. Physics.* [f. *sextu-*, in SEXTUPLE *a.* and *sb.* and related words + POLE *sb.*^{2}] **A.** *adj.* Having six magnetic (or electric) poles, three of each polarity. **B.** *sb.* A sextupole device.
1961 in *Progr. Nucl. Physics* (1964) IX. 114 A Sextupole Magnet Design. **1969** [see *QUADRUPOLE *sb.* b]. **1976** *Physics Bull.* Nov. 499/2 Extra dipoles, sextupoles and octupoles act as correcting magnets in case of defects in the magnet lattice and for superfine control. **1979** *Sci. Amer.* May 64/1 The atoms emerge from a nozzle as a low-energy beam, then pass into the strongly nonuniform field of a sextupole, or six-pole, magnet... It discriminates strongly between spin-up and spin-down electrons.

sexual, *a.* Add: Many collocations are paralleled by and equivalent to combs. with *sex* (see *SEX *sb.* 5). These are not individually listed or defined below.
The division of senses in the Dict. was satisfactory at the time of publication of this part (1913). In the sections below, our aim has been to compress as best we could into the original framework selected examples from our large collection of printed evidence.—Ed.
1. (Further examples.) *sexual politics*, the principles determining the relationship of the sexes; so *sexual-political* adj., *sexual politician.*
1968 S. HYNES *Edwardian Turn of Mind* vi. 201 It was an easy grammatical step..to shift the blame from sexual discrimination to sex itself. **1970** K. MILLETT *Sexual Politics* p. xii, The prospect of radical change in sexual politics. *Ibid.* II. iii. 110 The sexual-political predilections of each faction. *Ibid.* iv. 233 So we proceed to the counter-revolutionary sexual politicians themselves—Lawrence, Miller and Mailer. **1981** N. TUCKER *Child & Book* vii. 212 Children's perceptions of their sexual roles are built up from many different sources.

2. (Further examples.) *sexual dimorphism*, the condition in which there exist marked differences in form or appearance between the sexes of a species in addition to differences in the sexual organs themselves; *sexual interference* (euphem.), sexual assault or molestation; *sexual selection*: see SELECTION 3 b.

1800 WORDSWORTH *Lyrical Ballads* I. p. xxxii, From this principle the direction of the sexual appetite, and all the passions connected with it take their origin. **1849** W. M. THACKERAY *Pendennis* I. xxv. 239 That anxiety with which brooding women watch over their sons' affections... I have no doubt there is a sexual jealousy on the mother's part, and a secret pang. **1868** H. MAUDSLEY *Physiol. & Pathol. of Mind* (ed. 2) II. iii. 405 Acute dementia..connected, he believes, with the effect produced on the nervous system by sexual intercourse. **1888** Sexual dimorphism [see DIMORPHISM b]. **1898** *Alienist & Neurologist* Oct. 613 From whatever side and from whatever symptoms we start, we always unfailingly reach the region of the sexual life. **1898** 'S. GRAND' *Beth Bk.* xliv. 417 The sex question..is the stock-in-trade of every author, as if there were nothing..in the lives of men and women but their sexual relations. **1902** *Encycl. Brit.* XXVII. 625/2 *Bonellia* and *Hamingia* are very interesting examples of sexual dimorphism... The male is reduced to a minute..organism, which passes its life..in a special recess of the nephridia of the female. **1903** G. B. SHAW *Man & Superman* p. xvi, The Don Juan play..is to deal with sexual attraction. **1928** W. S. MAUGHAM *Sacred Flame* III. 142 You can't go without food... But you can go without the satisfaction of your sexual appetites. **1929** D. H. LAWRENCE *Pornography & Obscenity* 18 The young man and the young woman went and had sexual intercourse together. **1932** S. ZUCKERMAN *Soc. Life Monkeys & Apes* xiii. 212 It is possible that sexual dimorphism plays some part in determining the monogamy or polygyny of a species. **1934** BLUNDEN *Choice or Chance* 58 You saw the mystical idea of course—..roughly, my Tristram is the Sexual Force. **1951** N. MITFORD *Blessing* xi. 118 If you don't empty your mind and heart of sexual jealousy..you will never be happy with me. **1957** R. CHANDLER *Let.* 28 Apr. (1981) 441, I had not filled myself with sexual fantasies. **1960** C. DAY LEWIS *Buried Day* vi. 107 The conflict and guilt set up by masturbation.. and the sexual fantasies attached to it. **1968** S. HYNES *Edwardian Turn of Mind* vi. 195 The biological facts of sexual attraction and the urge to reproduce. **1968** 'A. GILBERT' *Night Encounter* iv. 45 Quite a young girl... No attempt at sexual interference, no signs of pregnancy. **1970** *Cambr. Anc. Hist.* (ed. 3) I. I. v. 156 Even allowing for marked sexual dimorphism, it is still obvious that more than one species [of Australopithecine] demands recognition. **1971** P. D. JAMES *Shroud for Nightingale* vii. 246 The late Mr. Dettinger hadn't understood [many things], his wife's sexual needs among them. **1973** B. A. TONKIN tr. *Lorenz & Leyhausen's Motivation Human & Animal Behaviour* iii. 53 The sexual drives bring forces of a new kind pulling in a new direction. **1974** H. R. F. KEATING *Underside* xi. 108 She must know..that men had sexual urges, that they could not live without any sexual experience of any sort. **1978** P. G. WINSLOW *Coppergold* 163 Post-mortem had shown that the girl had had sexual relations with a man just before her death. **1979** *Times Lit. Suppl.* 23 Nov. 20/1 Edel..suggests.. that after it was clear that a sexual relationship with Virginia was impossible he [*sc.* Leonard Woolf] sublimated his sexual drives in work. **1980** D. NEWSOME *On Edge of Paradise* 382 He had no sexual life; all his sexual instincts had to be sublimated. **1981** A. EDWARDS *Sonya* xix. 321 Her diary..is filled with musings on her sexual needs, frustrations, and fantasies. **1981** G. MARKSTEIN *Ultimate Issue* 261 'And at these places sexual intimacy took place—' Christ almighty..how many more times is he going to say it. Sexual misconduct. Sexual intercourse.

3. (Earlier and further examples.) *sexual athlete*, a sexually vigorous person, a skilled performer in sexual intercourse; so *sexual athleticism, athletics*; *sexual inversion*: see *INVERSION 10; *sexual psychopathy*: see PSYCHOPATHY 1; hence *sexual psychopath, psychopathic* adj.; *sexual revolution*, the liberalization of established sexual and moral attitudes to sex.

1792 M. WOLLSTONECRAFT *Rights of Woman* vii. 273 (*heading*) Modesty.—comprehensively considered, and not as a sexual virtue. **1888** K. PEARSON *Ethics of Freethought* v. 120 Another good example is that of sexual morality; here the most difficult questions arise. **1897** C. LOMBROSO in T. L. Stedman *Twentieth Century Practice* XII. 402 We have seen that in the most extraordinary tendencies of sexual psychopathy..the somatic and hereditary signs are epileptoid in character. **1908** G. B. SHAW *Getting Married* 182 Whilst the subject is considered shameful..we shall have no systematic instruction in sexual hygiene. **1910** tr. *Freud's Lectures* in *Amer. Jrnl. Psychol.* XXI. 218 The claims of our civilization make life too hard for the greater part of humanity..without producing an excess of cultural gain by this excess of sexual repression. **1924** *Internat. Jrnl. Psycho-analysis* V. 95 (*heading*) The sexual offender. **1934** A. HUXLEY *Beyond Mexique Bay* 44 Places where people..obey other sexual taboos. **1936** 'R. WEST' *Thinking Reed* viii. 265 It sounded insincere, as if she were merely obeying a sexual convention. **1938** *John Marshall Law Q.* III. 407 The proposed law is as follows: An Act to Provide for the Commitment and Detention of Criminal Sexual Psychopathic Persons. **1939** R. PEARL *Nat. Hist. Population* 293 Some present-day examples of sexual athletes who make Casanova, the traditional star, seem a somewhat puny performer. *Ibid.*, I thought you might be interested in some cases of—as it seems to me—prodigious sexual athleticism. **1941** *Horizon* Sept. 161 All societies, as the price of survival, have to insist on a fairly high standard of sexual morality. **1945** T. P. WOLFE tr. *Reich's Sexual Revolution* ix. 64 Soviet sexual legislation was the clearest expression of the first attack of the sexual revolution on the reactionary sexual order. **1950** *Amer. Jrnl. Sociol.* LVI. 142/1 Since 1937 twelve states and the District of Columbia have enacted sexual psychopath laws. *Ibid.* 142/2 The concept of the 'sexual psychopath' is so vague that it cannot be used for judicial and administrative purposes. **1954** B. KARPMAN *Sexual Offender* xii. 224 Determination of the question of sexual psychopathy is by a superior court and commitment is for an indefinite period. **1957** H. M. HACKER in *Marriage & Family Living* XIX. 232/1 In societies which differentiate strongly between masculine and feminine social roles, individuals who manifest personality traits ascribed to the opposite sex or who feel inadequate in fulfilling their part of the sexual division of labor may become confused in their sexual identification, and feel that they must also change their sexual object. **1958** J. BYROM *Or be He Dead* iii. 37 Essays about sexual perverts. **1961** R. F. C. HULL tr. *Jung's Freud & Psychoanal.* in *Coll. Works* IV. IV. 321 As soon as we enter the field of neurosis, this antithesis is stretched to the limit. God becomes the symbol of the most complete sexual repression. **1963** B. FRIEDAN *Feminine Mystique* (1965) xi. 266 A woman who is herself only a sexual object, lives finally in a world of objects, unable to touch in others the individual identity she lacks herself. **1967** B. W. TUCHMAN in *Sat. Rev.* (U.S.) 25 Feb. 28/3 Sexual perversion and hallucinatory drugs..'are not what human history is about.' **1968** S. HYNES *Edwardian Turn of Mind* vi. 201 The [suffrage] movement never made sexual freedom a goal. **1968** A. DIMENT *Bang Bang Birds* II. vi. 81 You'd think his life work was spreading American sexual mores around the world. **1969** *Daily Tel.* (Colour Suppl.) 24 Oct. 35/2 The family is not composed of sexual athletes and cannot make love 20 times a day and so cannot try everything. **1970** *Guardian* 12 Nov. 10/3 Would he have to do anything awful in the way of sexual athleticism? **1970** K. MILLETT *Sexual Politics* iii. 62 A sexual revolution would require.. an end of traditional sexual inhibitions and taboos. **1971** G. STEINER *In Bluebeard's Castle* I. 15 Bourgeois sexual ethics were a veneer, masking a great area of turbulent hypocrisy. **1971** H. LEE *Surrogate Wife* (1972) 27 Nice girls..were less likely to be able to copulate with strangers, even if those strangers were sexual therapists. **1972** P. D. JAMES *Unsuitable Job* iv. 144 One of the more innocuous of sexual deviations. **1972** P. COUSINS (*title*) Christianity and sexual liberation. **1975** G. HOWELL *In Vogue* 62 Sexual deviation was becoming respectable. *Ibid.*, The sexual education of the jazz age. **1975** L. FARLEY in *N.Y. Times* 19 Aug. 38/1 Sexual harassment of women in their place of employment is extremely widespread. **1976** *Globe & Mail* (Toronto) 16 Feb. 1/6 Police said the report of a pathologist who examined the bodies makes no mention of a sexual assault. **1976** *Jrnl. R. Soc. Arts* June 351/2 The 4,500 magazines dealing in specialized trades or tastes from ironmongery to sexual athletics. **1977** *Evening Gaz.* (Middlesbrough) 11 Jan. 3/4 Sexual offences, mainly indecent assault on females, increased by 17. **1977** R. GREEN in W. H. Masters et al. *Ethical Issues in Sex Therapy & Research* vii. 198 There are clinicians of considerable sophistication utilizing sexual surrogates. **1978** *Times* 7 Aug. 2/4 Contraception..is producing..a profound alteration in sexual behaviour. **1979** J. CROSBY *Party of Year* xvi. 99 Decadent bourgeois sexual perversions. **1977** C. FREMLIN *Spider-Orchid* viii. 61 In spite of Permissiveness and the Sexual Revolution..nothing had changed! **1981** J. B. HILTON *Surrender Value* xiv. 104 He was a mild man... There was no record..of sexual aberration. **1982** R. GRAYSON *Montmartre Murders* xi. 91, I have been told that Suji's sexual appetite is formidable.

sexualization (se:ksiuălaizēⁱ·ʃən). [f. SEXUALIZE *v.* + -ATION.] The act or process of sexualizing; the state of being sexualized; adaptation to a sexual role.

1889 *Classical Rev.* III. 391 We are inclined to doubt Pott's confident assumption that sexualization is a necessary consequence of personification. **1977** A. H. WILLIAMS in A. W. Franklin *Challenge of Child Abuse* xii. 168 In sadism, it is important to recognize the sexualization of the pleasure in the cruel transaction. **1979** *Country Life* 29 Mar. 947/4 The lives available to a woman..education, sexualisation, part-time prostitution, suburbanisation.

sexy (se·ksi), *a.* [f. SEX *sb.* + -Y[1].] **a.** Concerned with or engrossed in sex. **b.** Sexually attractive or provocative, sexually exciting; also *fig.* Also *Comb.*, as *sexy-looking* adj.

[**1925** *La Nouvelle Revue Française* Jan. 313 Depuis que Joyce a publié un livre qu'ils croient 'sexy'—cet état d'esprit n'a pas d'équivalent français—on s'en empare.. que sa méthode sert de modèle à des gens qui..se disent surréalistes.] **1928** *Sunday Dispatch* 2 Dec. 19/2 Australian audiences..like sex plays, but they mustn't be too sexy. **1934** DYLAN THOMAS *Let.* 9 May (1966) 120, I shall now attempt to..look all sexy at the mantel-piece. **1935** J. T. FARRELL *Judgment Day* ii. 22 He watched the dark sexy-looking waitress scurry with a large tray of food. **1940** N. MITFORD *Pigeon Pie* ii. 29 He had been most famous as a singer of those sexy ballads which were adored by our grandparents. **1942** [see *GLAMORIZE *v.*]. **1947** J. STEINBECK *Wayward Bus* 84 Her voice was throaty and sexy. **1959** *Housewife* Oct. 131/2 Did she keep her figure beautiful and wear sexy nightgowns? **1963** A. ROSS *Australia 63* 23 A sexy-looking torch singer breathed huskily into her microphone. **1970** *Wall St. Jrnl.* (Eastern ed.) 22 Sept. 1/6 Corn and soybeans may not sound as sexy as electronics or aerospace. **1975** R. PLAYER *Let's talk of Graves* iii. 80 The seminarists were..casting perplexed eyes to Heaven, the Immaculate Conception being far too sexy to explain to adolescents. **1977** *New Scientist* 17 Mar. 638/1 Expensive, high-technology, politically sexy.. small wonder the big dam is popular all round. **1978** *Rolling Stone* 12 Jan. 44 A 'sexy' (TV for a good story) news idea. **1981** V. GLENDINNING *Edith Sitwell* iv. 57 Nancy Cunard—sexy, vital, unpredictable.

Hence **se·xily** *adv.*, **se·xiness**.

1925 *Glasgow Herald* 28 May 4/2 The stallion seems to vanish altogether near the end of the story, and the Welsh groom is put into prominence, with mere 'sexiness' thus supplanting magnificent vitality. **1947** J. STEINBECK *Wayward Bus* 83 Wide-set eyes meant sexiness. **1953** R. LEHMANN *Echoing Grove* 240 Late party, the latest place, place of lugubrious eroticism, sexily spot-lit. **1971** *Ink* 12 June 6/3 So-called permissiveness, sexiness, moral relaxation have gone as far as they can without beginning to alter *radically* our civilization. **1978** P. BRYERS *Cat Trapper* ix. 61 She curled sexily on a cushion.

Seychellois (sēⁱʃelwa·), *sb.* and *a.* Fem. **Seychelloise** (-wa·z). Pl. **Seychellois,** fem. **-oises** (-wa·z). [Fr.] **A.** *sb.* A native or inhabitant of the Seychelles, a group of islands in the Indian Ocean. **B.** *adj.* Of or pertaining to the Seychelles or their inhabitants.

1898 F. A. BARKLY *From Tropics to North Sea* viii. 34 The Seychellois have a method of walling houses with the bark of the lathe palm. **1936** J. A. F. OZANNE *Coconuts & Créoles* xii. 184 The young Seychellois is quite safe from European competition. *Ibid.* 186 Most of these young Seychellois boys are very keen sportsmen. **1960** I. FLEMING *For Your Eyes Only* 207 The only conceivable security hazard in the Seychelles lay in the beauty and ready availability of the Seychelloises. **1971** *Vogue* Dec. 73, I took passage on the launch with a crew of Seychellois police. **1978** T. ALLBEURY *Lantern Network* iii. 34 She was a Seychelloise from Mahé. **1980** *Illustr. London News* Mar. 67/2 As a tourist you will find both English and French spoken and understood; the Seychellois speak their own patois.

Seyfert (sēⁱ·fəɹt). *Astr.* The name of Carl K. *Seyfert* (1911–60), U.S. astronomer, who first described such galaxies in 1943 (*Astrophysical Jrnl.* XCVII. 28), used *attrib.* with reference to a class of galaxies characterized by bright compact cores that show strong infra-red emission.

1959 *Astrophysical Jrnl.* CXXX. 26 Another characteristic feature of many of the Seyfert galaxies is the apparently small size of their nuclei in which the broad emission features arise. **1963** *Ibid.* CXXXVII. 1032 It is possible that an event of the Seyfert type is experienced by all spiral galaxies and not only by the Sa and Sb systems. We believe this to be a reasonable assumption, but it has the effect only of reducing the frequency of Seyfert objects among spirals by a factor of 2 or less. **1969** *Ibid.* CLVIII. 859 The detection of such [nonstellar] absorption features in Seyfert spectra is rather difficult. **1970** *Nature* 31 Jan. 410/2 Seyfert galaxies with their extraordinarily bright and unusual nuclei could easily be intermediaries between quasars and normal galaxies. **1970** *Sci. Jrnl.* Feb. 57/1 Many of the phenomena observed in Seyfert galaxies are similar to those seen in quasistellar objects. **1971** *New Scientist* 17 June 695/1 A compact infrared source with a spectrum similar to that of the Seyfert nuclei, but with a smaller energy output.., appears to be located at the centre of our Galaxy.

b. *absol.* A Seyfert galaxy.

1968 *Physical Rev. Lett.* XXI. 1540/1 NGC1275 and 3C120..are a hundred times more luminous in the radio than most of the Seyferts. **1977** *Dædalus* Fall 56 The association of X-ray emitters with active compact galaxies..has been confirmed by the discovery of an X-ray emission by the Seyfert galaxy 3C120..and of a dozen more Seyferts by Pounds and his associates working with Ariel-5.

Seym, var. *SEJM.

seymouriamorph (sīmōᵊ·riămǭɹf). [a. mod.L. name of suborder *Seymouriamorpha*, f. generic name *Seymouria* (F. Broili 1904, in *Palæontographica* LI. 81), f. *Seymour* name of a town in Baylor County, Texas + -IA[1].] A fossil tetrapod belonging to the suborder Seymouriamorpha, considered to include transitional forms between amphibians and reptiles.

1945 A. S. ROMER *Vertebr. Paleontol.* (ed. 2) xxvii. 527 The degenerate genus *Kotlassia* represented the seymouriamorphs in the late Permian. **1977** A. HALLAM *Planet Earth* 269 The terrestrial anthracosaurs, known as seymouriamorphs, include the only large terrestrial amphibians known.

Seyssel (sēⁱ·sel). The name of two villages on the upper Rhône, used *attrib.* or *absol.* to designate various white wines made there.

1926 P. M. SHAND *Book of Wine* v. 171 The best-known Savoy wine is Seyssel... Much of the wine sold as Seyssel only enjoys the type-name by courtesy. **1968** V. & M. PETTITT *Len Deighton's Travel Dossier* 46 *Savoy*... Seyssel wines (much is made into 'vin mousseux'). **1968** [see *ROUSSETTE 3].

sez (sez). ¶. Jocular spelling of *says*, 3rd person sing. pres. of SAY *v.*[1], esp. in representations of uneducated speech, and in phrase *sez you* (see *SAY *v.*[1] 3 b).

1844 'J. SLICK' *High Life in N.Y.* I. i. 8 Cousin John took out his watch..and, sez he,—'Come, Mr. Slick.' **1886** F. H. BURNETT *Little Lord Fauntleroy* i. 9 Sez he to me: 'Mary,' sez he, 'I'm very much int'rusted in the 'lection,' sez he. **1904** WODEHOUSE *William Tell* vii. 45 'What I sez,' said Friesshardt, 'is, wot's the use of us wasting our time here?' **1930** *Outlook* (N.Y.) 12 Nov. 417/3, I am so tired of hearing sap, oh boy, and how, sez you, guts and dirty bum, that I could almost leave for the Fiji Islands to escape them. **1931** *Week-end Rev.* 24 Oct. 513/1 Mr. Lowe is well known for his invention of the famous catch-phrase 'Sez you!' **1933** Dylan Thomas *Let.* Nov. (1966) 53 May I borrow that foul expression of yours—it isn't yours, really—and whisper Sez You into his ear. **1940** H. G. Wells *Babes in Darkling Wood* II. i. 125 They must not attempt either to monopolise or possess. (Sez we.) **1960** J. Stroud *Shorn Lamb* xi. 128 If I make a movement, he sez: 'Oh, don't be disgusting!' he sez. **1973** B. Graeme *Two & Two make Five* xiii. 123 'He's..not nearly so useful in a rough house.' 'Sez you!' Sanders growled. **1977** [see *say *v.*[1] 3 b].

‖ **Sezession** (zetsesiō·n). *Art.* Pl. **Sezessionen.** [G.] = *secession 3 d.

1905 *Burlington Mag.* VI. 422/2 The Austrian Government..did not look with a favourable eye upon this 'Sezession', and withheld all support which the 'Sezession' claimed as well as other societies of artists. **1959** P. & L. Murray *Dict. Art & Artists* 296 The *Sezessionen* were groups of artists in Germany and Austria who re-signed from established academic bodies and exhibiting societies in order to forward the aims of various modern (usually Impressionist) movements. **1962** *Listener* 1 Mar. 384/3, I said nothing about..the artists of the *Sezession.* **1970** *Oxf. Compan. Art* 106/1 When in 1910 a number of young painters were rejected by the Sezession—among them members of Die Brücke—they started the *Neue Sezession.*

Also **Sezessioni·st**, an artist belonging to the *Sezession*; **Sezessionstil** (-ʃtī·l) [G. *stil* style], the style of the *Sezession.*

1958 M. L. Wolf *Dict. Painting* 264 *Sezessionists*, an art group in Vienna associated with the *art nouveau* movement, popular between 1890 and 1905. **1967** J. N. Barron *Lang. of Painting* 19 In Belgium, it [sc. *Art Nouveau*] was associated with *Les Vingt* (The XX); in Vienna, with the Sezessionists. **1970** *Oxf. Compan. Art* 80/1 In Germany the style was called *Jugendstil*..; in Austria it was called *Sezessionstil.* **1978** *Country Life* 10 Aug. 394/1 (*caption*) The Bull Inn, Paisley. Built in 1900–1901..it combines Scottish Baronial features with a curved gable akin to the contemporary Viennese *Sezessionstil.*

sferics (sfe·riks), *sb. pl.* orig. *U.S.* Also with capital initial; (*rarely*) **spherics.** [Contraction and respelling of *atmospherics *sb. pl.*] Atmospherics; sometimes used to denote a radio direction-finding system used to locate storms by means of the atmospherics they produce. Hence **sfe·ric** *a.*, of or pertaining to sferics.

1945 in *U.S. Army Signal Res. & Development Lab., Techn. Rep. 2199* (AD 266–795) (1961) 97 (*heading*) Military characteristics for automatic atmospherics (sferics) equipment. **1949** *Marine Observer* XIX. 199 'Sferic' is the code word which has been used for some years now to designate reports of positions of areas in which thunderstorms are taking place. **1951** R. C. Wanta in T. F. Malone *Compendium Meteorol.* 1297/1 Sferics (less commonly spherics) is a contraction of the word atmospherics meaning natural electrical phenomena detected by radio methods. **1963** T. Pynchon *V.* ix. 230 As it turned out, the whistler was only the first of a family of sferics whose taxonomy was to include clicks, hooks, risers, nose-whistlers and one like a warbling of birds called the dawn chorus. **1968** B. W. Atkinson *Weather Business* ii. 41 Sferic fixes depend on the radiation of electromagnetic waves caused by lightning flashes in the clouds. **1974** *Nature* 10 May 134/2 Observers under the balloon reported no thunder or lightning; thus we attribute the spherics to an intense thunderstorm system that was over the eastern United States at the time. *Ibid.*, Our local v.l.f. monitor recorded strong spheric activity.

sforzando. Delete sense b and substitute: **b.** As *sb.* Pl. **sforzandi, sforzandos.** A note or group of notes specially emphasized or rendered louder than the rest; an increase in loudness and emphasis; also *transf.* Also *attrib.* or as *adj.*

1849 *Belfast News-Letter* 6 Feb. 4/4 Prima donna instrumentalists of the sforzando order. **1890** G. B. Shaw in *Scots Observer* 28 June 143/2 The smoothing-out of all the old jerks and jigs and *sforzandos* from the surface of the stream of melody. **1902** [in Dict., sense b]. **1947** Auden in *Amer. Scholar* Autumn 405 Fill a Dwarf's ears with sforzandos and the dwarf will Believe he's a giant. **1956** T. Beecham 26 Apr. in H. Procter Gregg *Beecham Remembered* (1976) II. 180 Well, you know what dramatic effects are in my experience? It's making loud thumps on a percussion instrument, *sforzandi* in the strings—constant *sforzandi*—a few pathetic whinings on the wind, and sudden blasts on trumpets..and trombones. **1965** *New Statesman* 7 May 736/3 The woodwind skirls and *sforzando* brass exclamations still evoke the native dance-song. **1976** *Gramophone* Mar. 1463/1 He is meticulous in observing the jab of sudden sforzandos.

sforzato. Add: (Later examples.) Pl. **sforzati, sforzatos.**

1969 *Listener* 17 July 89/2 The hard sound of the first 'g' in the word is reflected in *sforzato* harp notes. **1976** *Daily Tel.* 8 Mar. 8/3 Presumably, if the lost autograph of the 32 in C minor had meanwhile surfaced,..with all *sforzatos* abolished, this fact would have been mentioned. **1977** 'E. Crispin' *Glimpses of Moon* iii. 41 '*Dernghl*' he exclaimed in his nose, imitating sforzato stopped horns. **1977** *Gramophone* Dec. 1098/2 No. 2 in E minor has as its first movement a funeral march that alternates between minor and major and is full of suspensions and *sforzati.* **1978** *Jrnl. R. Soc. Arts* CXXVI. 354/1 It is impossible for us to say definitely how soft is soft, or how loud is loud or how much emphasis to put on a sforzato.

sfumato, *a.* Add: Also as *sb.*, the technique of softening outlines and allowing tones and colours to shade gradually into one another; a softened outline or hazy form produced in this way.

1909 R. Fry *Let.* 16 Feb. (1972) I. 312 The black is a wonderful *sfumato* with scarcely any modelling. **1935** *Burlington Mag.* Feb. 72/2 The fine 'sfumato' and the delicacy of the surface. **1936** *Ibid.* Oct. 192/1 The influence of Venice is said to have succeeded the abandonment of Leonardo's *sfumato.* **1965** *New Statesman* 7 May 732/2 In all encounters with Leonardo there is never a definite answer to any of the artistic, aesthetic, historical or psychological questions which he raises. The *sfumato*—the suggestive smoke-like contour—is as much a characteristic of his personality as it is a feature of his drawing.

‖ **sgraffiato** (sgrafˌfiā·to). *Pottery.* Pl. **sgraffiati** (-tī). [It., pa. pple. of *sgraffiare* to scratch, to produce sgraffito: see Sgraffito.] = Sgraffito b.

1862 J. C. Robinson in *Catal. Special Exhibition Wks. of Art S. Kensington Mus.* (1863, rev. ed.) Section xxi. 400 (*heading*) Sgraffiato or Incised Wares. **1900** F. Litchfield *Pott. & Porc.* ii. 13 This ware has been termed *sgraffiati, sgraffiato*, or incised ware. **1957** Mankowitz & Haggar *Conc. Encycl. Eng. Pott. & Porc.* 71/2 Several important slipware potteries existed in North Devon... Jugs and other presentation wares decorated in *sgraffiato* style with mariner's compasses, Royal arms, country scenes, or birds and foliage are typical. **1973** *Times Lit. Suppl.* 28 Dec. 1590/3 The medieval sgraffiato pottery of north and north-west Iran was based on Sasanian metalwork. **1980** *Catal. Fine Chinese Ceramics* (Sotheby, Hong Kong) 24 A large sgraffiato jar with shouldered ovoid body.

sgraffito. b. (Earlier example.)

1878 [see *Doulton].

Sgt., abbrev. of Sergeant *sb.*

1899 *Morning Post* 6 Dec. 5/2 No. 3732 Squad.-Sgt.-Maj. should be Shoeing-Smith John Hobbs. **1909** *Army & Navy Gaz.* 10 Apr. 342/2 Sgt. Huntley beat Sgt. Kilvert. **1948** *R.A.F. Rev.* June 22/3 Sgt. A. Roff, R.A.F., Selitar, Singapore. **1977** *Belfast Tel.* 28 Feb. 1/7 'Sgt. Joe', as he was affectionately known, was considered to be the model village policeman.

sh (ʃ), *v.* Also **sh-sh-sh.** [f. Sh *int.*; cf. Shshsh, *shush *v.*] **a.** *trans.* To reduce to silence or tranquillity with the sound of 'sh!', or attempt to do so.

1887 A. J. Evans *At Mercy of Tiberius* vii. 125, I patted and, 'she-e-d' her [*sc.* a baby], but she got her head above cover..and..set up a squall. **1916** 'B. Cable' *Action Front* 62 Ainsley 'sh-sh-sh-ed' him to silence.

b. *intr.* To become quiet in response to an order 'sh!'.

1925 'R. Crompton' *Still—William* iii. 53 'Sh!' William said fiercely. Violet Elizabeth 'Sh'd' obediently. **1972** Wodehouse *Pearls, Girls, & Monty Bodkin* ix. 136 She uttered a 'Sh!' of such significance that Grayce instinctively lowered her voice. 'Mrs. Molloy!' 'Sh!' Grayce might have retorted that she *had* sh-ed and that if she sh-ed any further she could become inaudible.

Shabas, var. *Shabbos.

‖ **shabash** (ʃaba·ʃ), *int.* [Hindi or Urdu.] Well done! Also as *sb.*, an exclamation of *Shabash!*

1843 C. I. C. Davidson *Travels in Upper India* I. 209, I was awakened at night from a sound sleep by the repeated *savâshes! wâh! wâhs!* from the residence of the thannadar. **1886** Yule & Burnell *Hobson-Jobson* 618/1 *Shabash!* interj. 'Well done!' 'Bravo!' Pers. *Shāh-bāsh.* 'Rex fias!' **1901** Kipling *Kim* iv. 105 'Oh, *shabash!*' murmured Kim..'Well done, indeed?' **1907** P. S. Allen *Let.* 8 Mar. (1939) 58 However in 10 days I shall be clear for Erasmus for the rest of the year. Shabash! **1974** H. R. F. Keating *Bats fly up for Inspector Ghote* iii. 24 Cries of 'Jolly good show' and 'Shabash, Inspector, shabash.'

‖ **Shabbat** (ʃaba·t). Also **Shabat, Shabbath.** [Heb. *šabbāṯ* Sabbath. Cf. *Shabbos.] Among Sephardic Jews and in the State of Israel: the Sabbath. Also in phr. *Shabbat shalom* [*shalom *int.* and *sb.*], 'peaceful Sabbath', a form of salutation used on the Sabbath.

1934 Webster, Shabbath. **1965** J. A. Michener *Source* 42 After we see it, why don't we go on to Zefat? It'll be Shabbat and we can attend the Vodzher Rebbe's synagogue. **1966** L. Davidson *Long Way to Shiloh* viii. 116 'All right. Thanks. Shalom.' 'Shabat Shalom.' **1971** D. Meiring *Wall of Glass* ii. 21 What would Arabs be doing on Tel Aviv beach?.. Above all on a Shabat? *Ibid.* v. 40 I'd been waiting for the sound of the ram's horn, to light my Shabat candles. **1976** C. Bermant *Coming Home* I. iii. 47 There is a traditional Jewish dish called *cholent*.. normally eaten for Shabbat lunch. **1980** *Encounter* Oct. 56/2 We bade each other *shabbat shalom.*

b. *Comb.*, as **Shabbat-goy** = *Sabbath goy* s.v. *Sabbath 4.

1859 [see *remnant *sb.* 2 b].

shabbify, *v.* Delete *nonce-wd.* and add later *fig.* example.

1961 E. Williams *George* xi. 149 Thomas became, for life, Tom,..and Biblical Job..was overnight shabbified into Joe.

‖ **Shabbos** (ʃa·bəs). Also **Shabas, Shabbes, Shabbuss, Shabes, Shabus.** Pl. **-im.** [Yiddish *shabes* ad. Heb. *šabbāṯ* Sabbath. See also *Shabbat.] Among Ashkenazi Jews: the Sabbath. Also *attrib.* Phr. to *make Shabbos*, to prepare for the Sabbath.

1876 Geo. Eliot *Dan. Der.* II. iv. xxxiii. 348 'Shlav'm Shabbes fyock on,' said Adelaide Rebekah. 'Her Sabbath frock... She'll have her Sabbath frock on this evening.' **1892** I. Zangwill *Childr. Ghetto* I. 151, I shall have no fish for Shabbos. **1959** H. Pinter *Birthday Party* I. 14 After lunch on Shabbuss we'd go and sit in a couple of deck-chairs. **1960** F. Raphael *Limits of Love* III. iv. 317 The chauffeur always carried a box of good things..which the inmates came to enjoy on the following *shabas* eve. **1968** M. Richler in R. Weaver *Canad. Short Stories* 2nd Ser. 150 We're orthodox here. Today is *shabus.* **1968** L. Rosten *Joys of Yiddish* 318 *Shabbes* begins just before sunset on Friday. The wife and mother, dressed in her very best, lights the *Shabbes* candles and offers a benediction. **1975** C. Potok *In Beginning* ii. 126 Yesterday was such a nice day. It was a pleasure to make Shabbos yesterday. *Ibid.* iii. 185 I'll read it [*sc.* the Torah]..in the synagogue, for Shabbosim and holidays. **1979** H. Howard *Sealed Envelope* xiv. 181 Every week she expects you for shabbos dinner but always you have excuses.

b. *Comb.*, as **Shabbos-goy** [*goy] = *Sabbath goy* s.v. *Sabbath 4; also fem. **Shabbos-goya(h**; also *fig.*

1892 I. Zangwill *Childr. Ghetto* I. 158 Poor women, frequently Irish, known as *Shabbos-goyahs* or *fire-goyahs*, acted as stokers to the Ghetto at twopence a hearth. **1959** M. Wilson *They came as Strangers* III. iii. 194 Victor Gollancz's parents were strictly orthodox,..never took a bus on the Sabbath and had a *Shabbes goy* to light the fires on that day. **1962** B. Abrahams tr. *Life of Glückel of Hameln* IV. 102 Send the *shabbos-goya* to me. I want to send her somewhere. **1969** A. Laski *Dominant Fifth* v. 187 Perhaps..we..have deliberately assimilated him, made him a tame cat, or *Shabbos-goy.* **1978** *Maledicta 1977* I. 323 Reinhold Aman, president, director, chief-lucubrator and *shabes-goy* of Maledicta, edits, typesets and publishes this journal considered by the repressed as a Gross Encounter of the Worst Kind.

shabby, *a.* Add: **1. c.** (Earlier example.)

1805 T. F. Fremantle *Let.* 1 Aug. in P. Fremantle *Wynne Diaries* (1940) III. vii. 195, I shall not apologise.. for the very shabby letters I have been..writing to you.

3. b. For *dial.* read '*dial.* and *colloq.*' and add earlier and later examples.

1853 D. G. Rossetti *Let.* 12 July (1965) I. 148 The weather had been generally very shabby. **1950** W. Stevens *Let.* 1 Feb. (1967) 663 While we have had an occasional day of proper winter, mostly it has been pretty shabby.

shabby (ʃæ·bi), *v.* [f. the adj.] **1.** *intr.* To act shabbily. *rare.*

1898 M. Deland *Old Chester Tales* 213 'They'll be shabbying on me,' said Katy.

2. *trans.* and *intr.* To make or become shabby.

1912 *Daily Chron.* 5 Mar. 9/2 She will probably find that a good deal of the..'shabbying' of her clothes is caused by..throwing her dresses carelessly down on chairs. **1920** H. Begbie *Life of W. Booth* I. iii. 56 The shadow of poverty deepening every day upon the shabbying walls of his unhappy home. **1962** D. Lessing *Golden Notebk.* IV. 536 You'll be one of those tough, square, solid middle-aged men, like a shabbying brown bear, your golden crew-cut greying judiciously at the temples.

shabby-gentility. (Earlier and later examples.)

1829 Carlyle *German Playwrights* in *Foreign Rev.* III. 115 Old threadbare material, scoured up into a state of shabby-gentility. **1898** G. B. Shaw *Plays Pleasant & Unpleasant* II. 156 The shifts of impecunious shabby-gentility.

Shabes, var. *Shabbos.

‖ **shabti** (ʃa·bti). *Egyptology.* [a. Egyptian *šbty.*] = *ushabti. Cf. *shawabti.

1864 *Zeitschrift für Ägyptische Sprache und Alterhumskunde* Oct./Nov. 90 The principal variants of the names of these figures have been given by M. Chabas as..*šuabti*, ..*šabt*,..*šabti* and..*šebti*; to these..may be added many additional forms. **1935** W. M. F. Petrie (*title*) Shabtis. **1936** *Times Lit. Suppl.* 18 July 601/1 Next to the scarab the *shabti* is perhaps the object most readily acquired by visitors to Egypt... This book is of first importance for the study of *shabti*-figures. **1953** *Flinders Petrie Centenary Exhib.* 21 The *shabti* is a figure placed in tombs to answer by magic for the deceased when called to labour in the Fields of the Blessed. **1964** I. E. S. Edwards et al. *Introd. Guide Egyptian Collections in Brit. Mus.* vi. 155 *Shabti*-figures are exhibited in the Third Egyptian Room. The name *shabti* is of uncertain meaning. The same figures were called *shawabtis* in the New Kingdom and *ushabtis* in the Late Period.

shabunder. Add: Also **shahbandar** (now the usual spelling), **shahbender.** Also, the title of an officer with wider responsibilities; *spec.* one of three chief local officials who administered Sarawak under the Sultan of Brunei.

1922 O. Rutter *Brit. North Borneo* v. 135 The Padas Damit district..was taken over..as a result of the operations against Pengiran Shabandar Hassan. **1960** S. Runciman *White Rajahs* III. ii. 93 It [*sc.* the land] belonged to a Brunei Princess, whose brother, the Pangiran Shabandar, administered it. **1964** D. K. Bassett in Wang Gungwu *Malaysia* II. vii. 122 The chief *shahbandar* of Kedah. **1969** J. M. Gullick *Malaysia* ii. 40 Control of the port, supervision of the merchants and collection of customs duties were divided among four harbour-masters, called *shahbandars*, who looked after the traders in one region. **1971** N. Tarling *Britain, Brookes & Brunei* I. i. 4 The system of offices, of a mixed Hindu-Muslim character, included..men of noble blood or *pengirans*, the most important being the *shahbandar*. **1974** S. E. Morison *European Discovery of America: Southern Voyages* xviii. 443 The Shahbender (title of the ruler of Brunei) sent out..a beautiful prao with gilt work on bow and stern.

Shabus, var. *Shabbos.

‖ **shabu-shabu** (ʃa·buʃa·bu). [Jap.] A Japanese dish of thinly sliced beef or pork cooked with vegetables in boiling soup.

1970 T. Egami *Oriental Cookery* 130 Shabu-Shabu. The word *shabu-shabu* derives from the sound of thin slices of succulent beef being gently swirled with chopsticks..in hot broth. **1973** *Times* 9 June 11/2 The speciality dish shabu-shabu (£1.80); raw beef and geometrically cut vegetables, briefly cooked by the waitress in a pagoda-shaped pot of broth, and served with rice and savoury dip. **1979** *United States 1980/81* (Penguin Travel Guides) 179 You can sample delicious shabu-shabu, Japan's answer to Swiss fondue.

Shabzieger, var. *Schabzieger.

shack, *sb.*[3] Add: **1.** (Earlier and later examples.) Also applied to other similar structures, and used outside U.S. and Canada.

1878 *Rep. Indian Affairs* (U.S.) 42 Too much praise cannot be given to these homesteaders for..the erection of this building, while they, themselves, were living in shacks. **1932** A. Christie *Peril at End House* v. 70 We saw a lot of messy-looking shacks, and then by good luck we found this. **1936** D. Glover *Home Thoughts* 18 A mountain shack Where blankets, candles, frying-pan Bespeak the only needs of man. **1939** *Denver Post* 2 Jan. 16-B/6 Other work will include the building of a ski shack. **1950** J. Baxter in *Landfall* (N.Z.) XIII. 10 There in a corrugated iron shack Behind a brushwood fence, he lives alone. **1960** *Daily Mail* 11 Apr. 4/4 In Durban..Bren guns and heavy machine-guns covered the hillsides spotted with native shacks.

b. *shack town.*

1923 H. Steele *Spirit-of-Iron* 105 Where little shack-towns rose, it knew there should be cities. **1962** G. MacEwan *Blazing Old Cattle Trail* i. 4 The residents of what had been an unprepossessing shack-town found their community overrun with rip-roaring cowboys, gamblers, gunmen, even women.

2. *U.S. slang.* A house.

1910 C. E. Mulford *Hopalong Cassidy* xiii. 128 You stay in that shack. Don't leave it for a second, understand? **1930** *Living Age* 1 Apr. 188 I've gotta tote this outfit of waffles and candy to grandmomma's shack.

3. *U.S. slang.* = *radio shack* s.v. *Radio *sb.* 7.

1929 *Amer. Speech* V. 49 *Shack*, wireless room or office. **1947** *Christian Science Monitor* 15 Jan. 9/1 Al's [ham radio] station, like most of the other 75,000 American amateurs, is a bedroom converted into what they call a 'shack'. **1960** [see *Rig *sb.*[4] 3 d].

shack (ʃæk), *sb.*[5] *U.S.* [prob. f. Shack *sb.*[2] or Shack *v.*[2]] A slow trot. Also *attrib.*

1881 *Harper's Mag.* Feb. 375/2 [He] walked with a peculiar shack gait. **1900** H. Garland *Eagle's Heart* 144 He continued his steady onward 'shack' toward the West. **1938** G. Butler *Running & Runners* iii. 85 Probably the best exercise of the whole lot is the 'shack' a word derived from the ponderous movement of a cart-horse. This is a movement mid-way between running and walking.

shack (ʃæk), *sb.*[6] *N. Amer. slang.* Also **shacks.** [Origin obscure.] The brakeman or guard on a train.

1899 'J. Flynt' *Tramping with Tramps* 397 *Shack*, a brakeman. **1907** J. London *Road* 213 As the freight got out of Philadelphia she began to hit up speed. Then I understood what the shack had meant by suicide. **1926** *Amer. Speech* I. 652/2 *Shacks*, brakeman on train. **1931** 'D. Stiff' *Milk & Honey Route* ii. 27 A great many hobo writers..are full ready to tell the novice how to outwit the brakemen, or shacks. **1947** L. M. Beebe *Mixed Train Daily* 313 The stock was valuable and a roundup was imperative, but, as the shacks and hoggers of the S.V. were unaccustomed to the saddle, a score of professional cowpokes were engaged for the task. **1976** Lieberman & Rhodes *Compl. CB Handbk.* vi. 136 *Shack*, railroad conductor.

shack, *v.*[2] Add: **1. b.** To move with a slow ambling gait, to go at a slow trot. *U.S.*

1833 in B. F. Hallett *Full Rep. Trial E. K. Avery* 61, I *shacked* down some of the hills, (partly run). **1916** H. Titus *I Conquered* ii. 31 Yonder [was] a man shacking along on a rough little horse, head down, listless. **1947** *Sat. Even. Post* 8 Mar. 53/1 Each winter Steve shacked in to Barry's camp a couple of times, sat in the log office a day and shacked out.

shack (ʃæk), *v.*[4] *slang* (orig. *N. Amer.*). [f. Shack *sb.*[3]; cf. Shack *v.*[2] 2.] **1.** *intr.* To live in a shack.

1895 *Dialect Notes* I. 393 *Shack*..(v.) to live in a *shack* or keep a bachelor's hall in general. 'They sent away their wives and *shacked* for a time.' **1935** Z. N. Hurston *Mules & Men* I. vi. 127 You ain't de Everglades Cypress Lumber Comp'ny sho nuff. Youse just shacking in one of their shanties. **1954** C. Bruce *Channel Shore* 16 Men had sailed east from here to the Cape Breton coast, to shack on the beaches and fish the waters off Petit de Grat. **1975** *Maclean's Mag.* (Toronto) May 43/3 We used to shack there, camp ourselves where the mine was.

2. a. *intr.* Usu. with *up.* To obtain temporary accommodation, to shelter for the night; to lodge *with* (esp. as a sexual partner), to set up house *with*, to cohabit (*with*); hence, to have sexual intercourse *with*.

1935 Z. N. Hurston *Mules & Men* I. vii. 161 Ah..was doin' fine till Ah shacked up with a woman dat had a great big ole black cat. **1942** Berrey & Van den Bark *Amer. Thes. Slang* § 62/9 *Shack up*, to stay in a camp for the night. **1945** *Sun* (Baltimore) 1 Mar. 6/6 More wanderlust grips the sow and she shacks up with half a dozen families before the original owner gets wind of her again. **1946** *Time* 14 Oct. 40/3 The medicine man..had shacked up with a halfbreed cook. **1947** L. Waller *Show me Way* III. xxii. 191 She wanted me to shack with her tonight. **1949** R. Chandler *Little Sister* xviii. 120 I'm not talking about her love life... She doesn't have to shack up with a red-hot. **1951** J. D. Salinger *Catcher in Rye* ix. 73, I was going to shack up in a hotel for a couple of days and not go home till vacation started. **1959** H. Hobson *Mission House Murder* iii. 22 Besides appearing at performances she has to shack up with Johnny. **1965** S. T. Ollivier *Petticoat Farm* ix. 128 A man's got to have something to offer a girl before he asks her to shack up with him. **1968** *Listener* 15 Feb. 210/1 Some [trusted prisoners] even had their own cars to go up town and shack in some motel with a woman. **1972** P. Lively *Driftway* x. 136 We'll shack up for the night. There's a field farther on where the farmer's not one of those choosy fellows as'll turn me off after half an hour. **1976** W. Greatorex *Crossover* 193 Galina's not my wife... We shack up, that's all. **1981** A. Morice *Men in her Death* viii. 80 This must have been..before they become friendly enough to shack up together.

b. *trans.* Usu. with *up.* To provide with accommodation or lodging, esp. as a sexual partner. Chiefly in pass. *to be shacked* (*up*), to be staying or lodging, to be cohabiting (*with*).

1927 *Dialect Notes* V. 462 *Shack up*, v., to put up for the night. **1946** *Amer. Speech* XXI. 252 'I'm shacked up around here' means that the speaker has found a friendly *fräulein* who in substance maintains a home for him. The *fräulein* herself is a 'shack job'. **1953** P. Frankau *Winged Horse* IV. 242 He's shacked up with Celia. **1957** *Economist* 30 Nov. 787/1 Private Girard's marriage to the Japanese girl with whom he had been 'shacked up'. **1958** 'E. McBain' *Killer's Payoff* (1960) ii. 19 'Where is this Newton?' 'He's shacked in a hotel..downtown.' **1967** [see *Girl *sb.* 2 g]. **1973** *Globe & Mail* (Toronto) 29 Sept. 1/2 Even the mayor was shacked up and everybody knew. **1975** D. Lodge *Changing Places* iii. 125 Philip Swallow is shacked up with Melanie at that address.

So **sha·cking** *vbl. sb.*

1884 *Prince Albert* (Saskatchewan) *Times* 13 June 3/2 Of all the enjoyments Prince Albert can number, there's none equals shacking on a *pre-emption* claim. **1945** *Yank* 8 June 14 Must be. I'm sure not crackin' up from shackin' up. **1980** M. Underwood *Clear Case of Suicide* xiii. 96 Casual shacking up was quite different from holy matrimony.

shack-job (ʃæ·kdʒɒb). *U.S. slang.* Also **shack job.** [f. *Shack *v.*[4] + *Job *sb.*[2] 4 f.] = *Shack-up 2.

1946 [see *Shack *v.*[4] 2 b]. **1951** *New Yorker* 10 Mar. 112/2 Allowing him to sleep with their daughter (this was an early shack-job, not the girl mentioned above). **1955** W. Gaddis *Recognitions* I. iv. 158 Look, rabbit, I'm looking for a shack-job, see? **1966** *Sunday Times* (Colour Suppl.) 4 Dec. 73/3 *Shack job*, easy-woman.

shackle, *sb.*[3] Delete *U.S.* and add earlier example.

1835 D. Webster *Original Scottish Rhymes* 194 There'll be gude tents an' shachels For drinkers to roar an' to rift.

shackles (ʃæk'lz). *dial.* and *slang.* [Prob. f. Shackle-bone.] Broth, soup, or stew.

1886 F. T. Elworthy *West Somerset Word-Bk.* 658 *Shackles*.., broth. Every mornin' my old 'ummun makth me a basin o' *shackles*, and her knowth how to make 'em too, mind, way a plenty o' liks (leeks) in 'em. **1909** W. H. Davies *Beggars* xiii. 104 The following are a few slang words used by beggars... soup—shackles. **1931** 'G. Orwell' *Coll. Essays* (1968) I. 70 New words (i.e. words new to me)... *Shackles*, broth or gravy. **1969** *Tel.* (Brisbane) 29 July 2/4 Mr. Coppard records how one night he stumbled on a field kitchen and enjoyed a wonderful meal of schackels, a soup made up from leftovers.

shackle-up (ʃæ·k'lɒp). *slang.* Also **shackle up.** [Origin uncertain: cf. prec.] An act of preparing food in a pot.

1935 H. Neville *Sneak Thief on Road* 347 Shackle-up —a great cooking of food in a pot. **1936** J. Curtis *Gilt Kid* xx. 202 A spare shirt and a couple o' tins in case they want to have a shackle up.

shackling, *ppl. a.* **2.** (Earlier examples.)

1790 W. Maclay *Jrnl.* 24 May (1890) vii. 272 His whole figure has a loose, shackling air. **1793** J. Lindley in *Friends' Misc.* (1836) (ed. 2) II. 63 And the wagon very shackling, made the tour very disagreeable. **1846** J. K. Polk *Diary* 9 June (1929) iii. 114 Mr. Bancroft reminded Mr. Buchanan of a remark which he had made in the Cabinet some months ago, that the title of the United States north of 49° was a shackling one.

shackly, *a.* Add: (Earlier examples.) Also **shackley.**

1843 *Indiana Q. Mag. Hist.* III. 121, I stopped at a small poverty-stricken little town called Mt Meridian; shackly houses, huts and hovels..gave no great expectation of refinements. **1843** *New Mirror* 18 Nov. 116/2 Hitched with oakum before a shackley go-cart, the rocking evolution of whose wheels showed that it was long since they had firmly revolved in their own proper axis.

shack-shack, shac-shac (ʃæ·kʃæk), vars. Chac-chac. Cf. Shak-shak.

1848 in *Caribbean Q.* (1956) IV. III & IV. 184 Bands of music (soi-disant) including those inelegant instruments, the tin kettle and salt box, the bangee and shack shack. **1953** P. L. Fermor *Violins of Saint-Jacques* 58 The leaders wielded shackshacks: cylinders of bamboo filled with rattling seeds. **1955** *Caribbean Q.* IV. II. 101 The band includes..a cuatro..a set of home-made drums with cymbal and triangle, and shac-shacs. **1959** P. Capon *Amongst Those Missing* 243 The music..was strongly rhythmic and the rhythm was marked by the rattling of shack-shacks and maracas.

shack-up (ʃæ·kɒp). *slang* (chiefly *U.S.*). Also **shack up, shackup.** [f. *Shack *v.*[4] 2.] **1.** Cohabitation. Also *attrib.*

1935 Z. N. Hurston *Mules & Men* I. ii. 54 'Oh, you kin be had,' Gold retorted... 'Yeah? But not wid de trace chains. Never no shack up. Ah want dis tip-in love and tip yo' hat and walk out.' **1974** *Times Lit. Suppl.* 18 Oct. 1155/2 An affair with David,..a shack-up with Colin. **1977** *Toronto Star* 21 May B5 One down-to-earth mother referred to 'my child's shack-up partner'.

2. A partner in cohabitation or sexual intercourse.

1969 E. R. Johnson *Mongo's back in Town* ii. 20 That's not like Angel. She was still Mike's shackup. **1972** J. Gores *Dead Skip* (1973) xxiii. 163 He didn't even know if the guy was married or single. He might have a shack-up there for the night.

shac-shac: see *Shack-shack.

shad, *sb.* Add: **3.** For † *Obs. rare* [−1] read *rare* and add later example.

1894 'Mark Twain' in *St. Nicholas* Jan. 252/2 Spiders in a desert, you shad?.. You don't ever reflect, Huck Finn, and I reckon you really haven't got anything to reflect with.

4. a. *shadbone, -fisher* (earlier example), *roe.*

1962 Auden *Dyer's Hand* (1963) 303 Thus, she describes a tomcat's face: the shadbones regularly set about the mouth. **1860** *Harper's Mag.* Nov. 795/1 A party of shad-fishers, pulling in their seine. **1888** *All about Alaska* (Pacific Coast Steamship Co.) 54 Herring roe is to the native Sitkans what the shad roe is to the dwellers on the Susquehanna and the Potomac. **1976** *National Observer* (U.S.) 23 Oct. 19/4 And, this is the place for exotic fish eating, with surprises like..shad roe, wolf fish.

b. shad-blow = *shad-bush*; **shad-bush** (earlier example); **shad-flower,** (*a*) (earlier example); **shad-fly** (earlier example); **shad-worm** (earlier example).

1846 D. J. Browne *Trees Amer.* 282 The Canadian Amelanchier..[also called] June Berry, Shad-blow, Shad-flower. **1890** *Harper's Mag.* Apr. 710/2 Shadblow, with leaves of bluish green, white flowers or green berries waiting for the sun to make them red. **1960** *Washington Post* 25 Jan. B1/4 Trees considered to be worth only 60 per cent..are..common horse-chestnut, shadblow serviceberry, [etc.]. **1818** A. Eaton *Man. Bot. N. & Middle States* 145 *Aronia..botryapium* (shad-bush). **1817** —— *Man. Bot. Northern States* 55 *Aronia..botryapium*, (shad-flower). **1825** *Canad. Mag.* IV. 474 The ephemeral Spring Fly, called..by the English the Shad Fly, as they are supposed to indicate the approach of the fish. **1851** M. H. Perley *Rep. Fisheries Bay of Fundy* 88 At Windsor, the 'Shad-worm' is found upon the mud flats.

shad-bellied, *a.* **a, b.** (Earlier examples.)

1832 J. P. Kennedy *Swallow Barn* III. i. 3 A shad-bellied blue bobtail coat. **1847** [see *Night-owl 2].

‖ **shadchan** (ʃa·dχăn). Also **schadchen, schatchen, shadchen, shadkhan, shadkin, shatchen.** [Yiddish *shadkhn*, ad. Heb. *šaddᵊkān*, f. *šiddēk* to arrange a marriage; cf. *Shiddüch.] A Jewish professional matchmaker or marriage-broker. Also *fig.*

a **1890** in Barrère & Leland *Dict. Slang* (1890) II. 219/2 Ten per cent of the dowry goes to the shadkin when the others become kin. **1892** I. Zangwill *Childr. Ghetto* I. 60 He sent a *Shadchan* to propose to her, and they were affianced, Chayah's father undertaking to give a dowry of two hundred gulden. **1897** F. Moss *Amer. Metropolis* iii. 216 A man named J— H—..acted as schatchen (match-maker). **1950** D. Riesman in *Psychiatry* May 177/1 The lies and sales talk of the schadchen, the Jewish marriage brokers. **1957** L. Stern *Midas Touch* I. viii. 68 'Shatchen,' Israel muttered into his beard, 'Matchmaker.' **1959** 'W. Haggard' *Venetian Blind* vii. 98, I married her..because my parents, on the advice of a reliable *shadchan*..considered the match suitable. **1968** [see *marriage broker* s.v. *Marriage 8]. **1976** *Publishers Weekly* 11 Oct. 94/2 Taking the role of *shadkhan*, the authors bring together seeker and supplier.

‖ **shadda** (ʃa·dda). *Gram.* Also **šèdda, shaddah.** [a. Arab. *šadda*, lit. strengthening.] In Arabic, a sign, also called *tašdīd*, written or printed above a consonant to indicate that it is doubled.

1896 W. Wright tr. *Caspari's Gram. Arabic Lang.* (ed. 3) I. I. iii. 14 In African Mss. the vowel is not always written with the šědda. **1925** W. H. T. Gairdner *Phonetics of Arabic* ix. 58 The sign written over the consonant-letter in Arabic writing is called aʃ ʃadda ('force'). **1958** D. Cowan *Introd. Mod. Literary Arabic* 5 If two identical consonants come together and are not separated by a vowel only one is written with the mark ّ above it. This mark is called..*shadda* or 'strengthening'. **1962** Haywood & Nahmad *New Arabic Gram.* i. 10 A doubled letter is not written twice, unless separated by an intermediate vowel. Instead, the sign ّ (called..tashdīd or..shadda) is written over the letter. **1969** A. G. Chesne *Arabic Lang.* ii. 28 Other diacritical marks were..introduced. Among these are..the *shaddah* for doubling a consonant. **1971** R. A. Wisbey *Computer in Lit. & Ling. Research* 228 Though the vowels are not to be included, as they are usually omitted in the script, shadda, the sign which denotes the doubling of a letter, and the various combinations with hamza are to be plotted.

‖ **Shaddai.** (ʃa·dəi). *Judaism.* Also **Shadai.** [Heb., of uncertain meaning; in the English versions of the Bible usu. translated 'Almighty'.] One of the names of God in the Bible and cabbala, inscribed on certain ritual objects and on talismans.

1620 J. Donne *Sermon* (1957) III. 191 Shaddai is the name of God, and yet Shaddai is spoyle, violence and depredation. **1881** *Encycl. Brit.* XIII. 812/1 The angel Metatron inhabits this world. He alone constitutes the world of pure spirit, and is the garment of Shaddai, *i.e.*, the visible manifestation of the Deity. **1892** I. Zangwill *Childr. Ghetto* I. v. 133 The doorposts twinkled with *Mezuzahs*—cases or cylinders containing sacred script, with the word *Shaddai* (Almighty) peering out of a little glass eye at the centre. **1926** W. & E. Muir tr. *Feuchtwanger's Jew Süss* I. 37 Three furrows, sharp, deep, short and almost vertical above his nose cleft his forehead; and they formed the sacred letter Shin, the first letter of God's name, Shaddai. **1962** I. B. Singer *Slave* ii. 219 The incantation a scribe had written out for her:.. *Yuhah* will guard me! *Shaddai* will save me! *Taftifiah* will be a wall for me. **1969** E. Stewart *Heads* 91 There was an amulet..the little golden heart with the letters that spelled *Shadai..Shadai*, he thought: *eternal.*

shaddup (ʃɒdɒ·p), repr. a colloq. or vulg. pronunc. of imper. *shut up!* (see Shut *v.* 19 m).

1959 R. Condon *Manchurian Candidate* iv. 78 Shaddup! You hear? Shaddup! **1977** *Daily News* (Perth, Austral.) 19 Jan. 3 (*caption*) 'Forget it, mother it doesn't bother me.' 'It bothers me! People'll think I'm gettin' old!' 'Shaddup.' **1977** *Daily Mirror* 6 Apr. 24 (*caption*) 'Snooker isn't a trifle!' 'Aw, Shaddup!!'

shade, *sb.* Add: **II. 6. c.** (Further examples.) Now usu. in *pl.* and no longer exclusively in humorous use. Also *loosely*, with reference to some person or thing in the past of which a present event is reminiscent.

1899 R. Whiteing *No. 5 John Street* xviii. 183 Shade of Tilda! not a bud but would outvalue your entire stock. **1928** H. Crane *Let.* 22 Feb. (1965) 317 A paean from Venusberg! Oy-oy-oy! I have just had my ninth snifter of Scotch. O shades of Bert Savoy! **1968** *Listener* 25 July 98/2 The persistent..demand..for a major change in the relationship between a free people and the state, for an end to arbitrary, secretive and alien government and for the restoration and maintenance of free institutions. Shades of Disraeli, maybe. **1977** *Times* 26 Nov. 4/3 Colleges..were..conducting campaigns to ban Jewish societies... Shades of Nazi Germany (he said). **1978** H. Wouk *War & Remembrance* xxiv. 238 There's a fridge, but it doesn't work. Shades of Singapore.

7. For † *Obs.* read 'Now chiefly *Hist.*' and add later examples.

1960 H. Hayward *Antique Coll.* 255/1 Edward Foster of Derby often painted faces in brown, blue or some other colour, and unless details are shown in the faces, such may also be termed shades. **1970** *Oxf. Compan. Art* 1065/1 The great vogue of silhouette portraits (more often known in England as 'shades') came between 1750 and 1850. **1979** *Jrnl. R. Soc. Arts* July 513/1 Anything but an average shade, it is, none-the-less, a competent head-and-shoulders in strict profile.

III. 11. e. Also (*pl.*), sunglasses, tinted glasses. *colloq.* (chiefly *U.S.*).

1958 *Amer. Speech* XXXIII. 225 Less frequently used among nonmusicians (primarily for lack of an occasion) are *shades* (dark glasses). **1965** *N.Y. Times* 11 Apr. E14/6 Your teen-age daughter asks what you think of her 'shades', which you are canny enough to know are her sunglasses. **1976** *National Observer* (U.S.) 10 Apr. 1/4 'Hiya, Rog,' says somebody else, popping up clip-on shades. **1980** G. V. Higgins *Kennedy for Defense* vii. 68, I looked at Emerson, hiding behind his shades and his imported-cigarette smoke.

h. (See quot. 1894.)

1894 T. Elliston *Organs & Tuning* 127 *Shade*, a flap of metal at the top of a reed pipe to regulate the power, at the top of a flue pipe to tune by—also applied when the tone, pitch, or power of a pipe is affected through being shaded or shadowed by an obstruction. **1925** H. F. Milne *How to build Small Two-Manual Chamber Pipe Organ* 127 The pipes in many reed stops are of an inverted conical shape, and the regulating device may take the form of either a cap or shade. **1951** R. Whitworth *Organ Stops & their Uses* i. 13 The pipe represented at letter L is the much over-used swell oboe for 4 ft C. The bell and its shade on the top should be noticed.

IV. 12. c. Instrumental, as *shade-softened* adj.

1866 G. M. Hopkins *Jrnls. & Papers* (1959) 138 Very level clouds, long pelletted sticks of shade-softened grey in the West.

13. shade-bearer, a plant which is shade-tolerant; **shade-bearing** *a.*, = *shade-tolerant* adj. below; **shade-card,** a card illustrating the range of colours in which goods are supplied; also *fig.*; **shade-lover, plant,** a plant which thrives in shady conditions; **shadepull** *U.S.*, a cord for pulling down a window-shade; **shade-tolerant** *a.*, able to grow normally in the shade of taller plants.

1891 Shade-bearer [see *light-demander* s.v. *Light *sb.* 16]. **1959** *Times* 7 Dec. (Agric. Suppl.) p. viii/4 Beech can be the underplant used for amenity work, because it is a shade-bearer. **1889** W. Schlich *Man. Forestry* I. ii. 117 Certain species cannot thrive unless they enjoy a large measure of light throughout life, while others will bear a certain amount of shade. Accordingly, the former are called 'light demanding', and the latter shade bearing species. **1975** T. C. Whitmore *Tropical Rain Forests of Far East* vi. 71/2 The population structure of light-demanding and shade-bearing species in a stand of high forest is markedly different. **1895** *British Warehouseman* Feb. 38/2 A new and very attractive shade-card, comprising all the newest tints. **1955** *Radio Times* 22 Apr. 22/2 A free illustrated colour booklet about Snowcem and a shade card. **1961** P. Mason *Common Sense about Race* iv. i. 120 There are words conveying ..subtle nuances of skin-colour..a kind of verbal shade-card. **1960** *Farmer & Stockbreeder* 9 Feb. (Suppl.) 4/2 Other worthwhile shade-lovers—the climbing fig..and the sweetheart plant. **1926** H. A. Spoehr *Photosynthesis* ii. 103 It would be interesting to determine whether shade plants such as the *Oxalis*..do not utilize a greater proportion of the light absorbed than plants growing in the direct sunlight. **1974** Shade plant [see *Solarization 1 c]. **1955** W. Gaddis *Recognitions* I. vi. 202 The housefly..drawn to a new destination the instant it halted, from the shade-pull to the floor, from there to the lampshade. **1973** *Philadelphia Inquirer* (Today Suppl.) 7 Oct. 41/3 Meg is replacing such geegaws with tasteful black shadepulls. **1952** J. D. U. Ward *Woodman's Diary* 310 Some other species, mostly in the shade-tolerant category..allow a wide latitude for neglect and error. **1964** V. J. Chapman *Coastal Veg.* ix. 214 On Fair Isle, Red campion (*Melandrium rubrum*) grows well in the fescue swards, probably because being a woodland species it is shade-tolerant.

shade, *v.*[1] Add: **5. a.** Delete '(now *dial.*)' and add further examples.

1928 S. Lewis *Man who knew Coolidge* I. 45 And I got to admit that Walt's radio shades mine just the least little bit. **1972** *Sydney Morning Herald* 26 Aug. 31/7 University slightly shade Gordon in points scored for and against. **1973** *Observer* 3 June 28/7 Denness, whose 534 runs in first-class matches this season have him shading even Boycott. **1975** *Cork Examiner* 30 May 15/1 Womble survived a bad last hurdle mistake to shade strongly challenging Glenicmurrin by a short head.

9. c. *trans.* To make a slight or gradual reduction in (a price, value, etc.). Also *intr.* of shares, prices, etc.: to decline slightly in value, cost, etc.

1875 *Chicago Tribune* 27 Oct. 6/4 Prices are not strong, the quotations being shaded on fair orders. **1899** *Pitman's Commercial Correspondence & Commercial English* xii. 119 Please, therefore, do your best to deliver the finest quality you possibly can at the figure named, or, if you can shade the price a little, it would be advisable to do so. **1903** *Boston Transcript* 24 Oct. 22 To spur his freight traffic manager to get business without shading rates. **1928** *New Statesman* 28 July (Finance Suppl.) p. x, The newsprint and pulp industry..has..been developed rather faster than the demand, with the result that prices have been shaded. **1966** *Times* 17 June 16/4 If a favourite or near-favourite was being quoted at two-to-one as its price in the ring and on the rails, and if a certain bookie had not got it in his book, far from 'shading the odds', he had to increase them to attract money on that horse for his book. **1973** 'R. MacLeod' *Burial in Portugal* iv. 90 When he'd bought, Consolidated had already been shading at 130 and Maltsters had been on the upswing at 146. **1978** *Daily Tel.* 29 Mar. 21 Banks may be invited..to shade the margin over base rate which they charge private customers and small businesses. **1981** *Times* 7 May 24 General Accident..shaded 10p to 334p.

d. *trans.* To modify the pitch of (an open organ stop) by placing something near the top of the pipe. *rare.*

1876 Stainer & Barrett *Dict. Mus. Terms* 395/1 *Shading of pipes*, the placing of anything so near the top of an organ pipe as to affect the vibrating column of air which it contains. **1894** [see *Shade *sb.* 11 h].

shaded, *ppl. a.* Add: **1. b.** (Earlier and later examples.) Also as second element with a specifying colour.

1836 Dickens *Sk. Boz* (1837) 2nd Ser. 352 A shaded lamp by the bed-side. **1903** H. James *Ambassadors* xvi. 222 His dinner with Maria Gostrey, between the pink-shaded candles. **1956** E. Grierson *Second Man* i. 32 The secluded corner table with the shaded lights. **1973** I. Drummond *Jaws of Watchdog* xii. 157 A red-shaded lamp.

6. Of prices, values, etc.: see *Shade *v.*[1] 9 c.

1960 *Farmer & Stockbroker* 26 Jan. 4/1 Oilcakes in limited demand at shaded rates. **1976** *Birmingham Post* 16 Dec. 9/11 R. and A. G. Crossland at 16½p and Moss Engineering 44p shaded, brighter contrasts being provided by Willmot Breeden at 49p.

‖ **shadi** (ʃā·dī). [Hind. *shādī*.] In the Indian subcontinent: a wedding, marriage.

1893 Kipling *Many Inventions* 223 Make the *shadi* swiftly, and the girl will make him a Mussalman. **1897** F. A. Steel *Potter's Thumb* 299 There's going to be a big shâdi (wedding)..to-morrow morning. **1978** 'M. M. Kaye' *Far Pavilions* xxx. 443 A canopy..beneath which the sacred fire would be lighted and the officiating priests perform the *shadi*, the marriage ceremony.

shading, *vbl. sb.* Add: **4. c.** A spurious variation in brightness over parts of a televised image. Freq. *attrib.*

1940 D. G. Fink *Princ. Television Engin.* ix. 414 The remaining item of equipment necessary to produce a composite video signal of adequate quality is the shading correction generator required with camera tubes of the iconoscope (storage-mosaic) type. **1961** G. Millerson *Technique Television Production* iii. 50 Shading is reduced manually, by adjusting electronic correction circuits. **1969** G. L. Hansen *Introd. Solid-State Television Systems* xi. 269 If the red, green, and blue channels were called upon to reproduce a white scene, the unbalance caused by the corner shading in the red channel would produce a red hue in the corner. *Ibid.*, Shading generators..supply waveforms to the cathodes of the camera tubes to offset the variations that are present because of shading irregularities.

shadkhan, shadkin, vars. *Shadchan.

shadoof. Add: Also **schaduf, shaduf.**

1937 *Times Lit. Suppl.* 10 Apr. 268/2 The sounds which run as an undercurrent beneath the activities of Egyptian life..are the creak of the water-wheel and of the *shaduf.* **1961** G. Clark *World Prehist.* v. 109 For any great extension of the fertile zone it was necessary to cut channels and lift the Nile waters into them by some such device as the *schaduf.* **1974** *Encycl. Brit. Micropaedia* IX. 100/3 (*caption*) Villagers in the state of Tamil Nadu, India, using a shaduf to raise water from a stream into irrigation channels.

shadow, *sb.* Add: **I. 1. d.** *Psychol.* In the theory of C. G. Jung (1875–1961), the dark aspect of personality formed by those fears and unpleasant emotions which, being rejected by the self or persona of which an individual is conscious, exist in the personal unconscious; an archetype in which this aspect is concentrated.

1923 H. G. Baynes tr. *Jung's Psychological Types* iv. 203 For the sake of understanding, it is, I think, a good thing to detach the man from his shadow, the unconscious... One sees much in another man which does not belong to his conscious psychology, but which gleams out from his unconscious. **1940** S. Dell tr. *Jung's Integration of Personality* (1941) iii. 70 To take his [*sc.* the devil's] place there are human beings to whom we gratefully resign our shadows. With what pleasure..we read newspaper reports of crime. *Ibid.* 88 The three archetypes so far mentioned—the shadow, the anima, and the wise old man—are of the kind immediately experienced in personified form. **1959** *Listener* 29 Oct. 723/2 Jung defined an archetypal image which he called the shadow... The shadow actually became, in his designation, a term which covered a wide variety of impulses and wishes, most of which were felt to be evil or at least inadmissible. **1973** *Jrnl. Genetic Psychol.* Mar. 165 The shadow is described as the dark side of the personality or representing the original conception of evil in the world. The latter conception places the shadow in the collective unconscious.

3. b. = *eye-shadow* s.v. *Eye *sb.*[1] 28.

1936 *Time* 26 Oct. 39/2 Make-up Man Senz 'deepened' Miss Phillips' bulgy eyes with dark brown 'shadow'. **1966** *Vogue* Dec. 84/3 Soft liquid shadows in browns, greys and seaweed greens to put near the curve. **1976** 'E. McBain' *Guns* vii. 198 She wears orange lipstick... There is green shadow on her eyelids.

II. 4. a. Phr. *under* or *in the shadow of*: within the purlieus of, close up against, in proximity to.

1853 C. Brontë *Villette* I. v. 85, I lie in the shadow of St. Paul's. **1931** *Times Lit. Suppl.* 20 Aug. 625/4 The gradual rise of Innsbruck from a little village lying under the shadow of the great castle of the Dukes of Andechs to the..capital city of Tyrol.

e. (Earlier example.)

1873 *Proc. London Math. Soc.* IV. 271 Immediately in the rear of a sufficiently large sphere there will be a sound shadow.

f. A dark area in a (positive) radiograph (appearing as a light area in a negative).

1903 Pusey & Caldwell *Practical Application Röntgen Rays* I. v. 120 (*caption*) Apparatus for orthographic projection of *x*-ray shadows on fluorescent screen. **1928** A. Turnbull tr. *Köhler's Röntgenol.* 187 Dense bean-like shadows lateral to the upper opening of the hip-joint.. have been observed. **1964** le Roux & Dodds *Portfolio Chest Radiographs* i. 17 (*caption*) A normal P.A. chest radiograph of a young adult female with dense mammary shadows.

6. e. *spec.* The Opposition counterpart of a cabinet minister; a member of the shadow cabinet (see sense 16 b below).

1912 Ld. Lansdowne *Let.* 23 Feb. in R. Blake *Unknown Prime Minister* (1955) v. 103 But if the House of Commons 'shadows' are to number 11, I don't see how I can leave out Londonderry. **1961** *Daily Tel.* 1 Dec. 14 The five members of the Labour front bench who have exchanged 'shadows'. **1975** R. Lewis *Margaret Thatcher* i. 4 When he resigned from the leadership, out of all the Shadows, only Lord Carrington, one of nature's gentlemen, went round to his old chief to express his consolation and regrets. **1980** *Times* 8 Dec. 2/4 Mr Denis Healey..has continued as shadow on Treasury affairs.

f. Freq. in phr. *to wear* (oneself or another) *to a shadow*.

1840 DICKENS *Lett.* (1969) II. 51 Commend me to him though he *does* wear me to a shadow. **1847** C. M. YONGE *Scenes & Characters* xviii. 236 And poor Lily wearing herself to a shadow, in vain attempts to mend matters. **1887** [in Dict.]. **1977** *Grimsby Even. Tel.* 14 May 1/6 He was wearing himself to a shadow touring the country and Holland and Sweden trying to get new contracts.

8. d. *Football.* A player who marks (MARK *v.* 15 c) another player in the opposing team.

1976 *Southern Even. Echo* (Southampton) 15 Nov. 13/7 The rare occasions he outwitted his experienced close-marking shadow, Billy Tucker. **1976** *Times* 2 Dec. 12/2 The ability of Everton's forwards to escape from their marking shadows had been apparent throughout.

IV. 15. a. *shadow-leaf, -pattern, -tackle, -train, -wife, -word, -world* (earlier and later examples).

1957 C. DAY LEWIS *Pegasus* 55 Frecklings of sunlight and flickerings of shadowleaf. **1943** KOESTLER *Arrival & Departure* III. 86 He stared at the ceiling of the dim room on which the shutters projected a streaky shadow-pattern of grey and white ribs. **1967** E. SHORT *Embroidery & Fabric Collage* i. 32 *Shadow patterns.* If any three-dimensional object is suspended between a bright light and a sheet of white card or paper, and the object revolved, a series of patterns will be made by the shadow of the object on the card. **1888** G. M. HOPKINS *Poems* (1967) 72 Shivelights and shadowtackle in long lashes lace, lance, and pair. **1932** AUDEN in *Rev. Eng. Stud.* (1978) Aug. 282 A shadow-train flitted foreshortened through fields. **1939** —— & ISHERWOOD *Journey to War* 279 Loss is their shadow-wife. **1932** D. H. LAWRENCE *Etruscan Places* ii. 42 Pelasgian is but a shadow-word. **1957** E. PARTRIDGE *English gone Wrong* II. 38 In the U.S.S.R., *right* is a shadow-word; and rights, something one possesses only theoretically. **1853** Shadow-world [see *LIVE *v.*[1] 5]. **1953** S. SPENDER *Creative Element* 93 What Lawrence protested against was not intellect but the kind of intellectualization whereby men create a shadow-world for themselves.

b. *shadow-coloured, -hung, -stroked* adjs.; also similative, as *shadow-white* adj.

1947 K. TENNANT *Lost Haven* x. 147 In these sweeps of land were shadow-coloured birds and the beautiful midnight blue of the wild pigeons. **1952** R. CAMPBELL tr. *Baudelaire's Poems* 43 When you're asleep, dear shadow-coloured wench. **1913** 'SAKI' *When William Came* (1914) xviii. 288 A grey shadow-hung land which seemed to have been emptied of all things that belonged to the daytime. **1866** G. M. HOPKINS *Jrnls. & Papers* (1959) 144 Prettily shadow-stroked spikes of pale green grain. **1918** D. H. LAWRENCE *New Poems* 54 Into the shadow-white chamber silts the white Flux of another dawn.

16. shadow box, a case with a protective transparent front in which is displayed a painting, jewel, etc.; also *attrib.*; **shadow-box** *v. intr.* and *trans.*, to box (against) an imaginary opponent, as a form of training; also *fig.*; so **shadow-boxing** *vbl. sb.*; **shadow-check** (see quot. 1957); chiefly *attrib.*; **shadow cretonne, -print, -tissue,** a reversible material having a woven-in pattern which gives a shadowy, blurred effect; **shadow embroidery** = *shadow work* below; **shadow figure** = *shadow puppet* below; **shadow-grey** *a.* and *sb.*, (a) dark grey; **shadow lace,** a lace with an indistinct pattern; **shadow mask** *Television*, a perforated metal screen situated directly behind the phosphor screen in certain types of colour television tube, and having a pattern of precisely located holes through which the electron beams pass so as to strike the correct dots on the phosphor screen; freq. *attrib.*, as *shadow-mask tube*; **shadow-picture,** (*b*) a picture formed by a shadow (usu. of a person's hand or hands) thrown upon a screen or other surface (cf. SHADOWGRAPH 1); **shadow-play** (earlier and later examples); also, a puppet play of the shadow theatre; also *attrib.* and *fig.*; **shadow-price** (see quot. 1965); also *transf.*; hence **shadow-pricing** *vbl. sb.*; **shadow print:** see *shadow cretonne* above; **shadow puppet,** a puppet used in a shadow play; **shadow-site,** an archaeological site revealed by shadowing on the ground; **shadow-stitch,** (*b*) a criss-cross embroidery stitch used on sheer materials for filling in spaces, and which, being worked on the wrong side, shows through on the right side in a shadowy way with an outline resembling a back-stitch; **shadow stripe** (see quots. 1940, 1947); so **shadow-striped** *a.*; **shadow tag** *N. Amer.* (see quot. 1977); **shadow test** (examples of sense (*a*)); **shadow theatre,** a form of puppetry in which flat figures are passed between a strong light and a translucent screen, the audience watching on the other side of the screen; also, a place where such puppet shows are performed; **shadow tissue:** see *shadow cretonne* above; **shadow work,** embroidery done in shadow-stitch; also *attrib.* and *fig.*

1909 *Cent. Dict.* Suppl., Shadow-box..*n.* **1969** [see *OPTICAL *a.* 2 c]. **1973** *Houston Chron.* 21 Oct. 18 (Advt.), Giant hutch mirror with shadow-box frame and shelves. **1976** *National Observer* (U.S.) 17 Jan. 14/1 (Advt.), This stunning golden shadow box pendant. **1924** S. LEWIS *Free Air* i. 8 She fought the steering-wheel as though she were shadow-boxing. **1927** [see *punch-bag* s.v. *PUNCH *sb.*[2] 3]. **1932** H. S. DRAGO *Champ* i. 15 Andy protested that it wasn't necessary as he shadow-boxed an imaginary opponent. **1951** *Scott. Jrnl. Theol.* IV. 321 Unlike many Fundamentalists he is aware that the battle has passed into new phases and he is not satisfied to shadow box on deserted fields. **1971** *Nature* 22 Oct. 510/1 These representatives of European governments are still shadow-boxing with each other. **1977** *Time* 19 Dec. 68/2 It was O.K. to shadowbox at a professional gym. **1919** E. CORRI *Refereeing 1,000 Fights* 69 The mascot stripped to the waist to do some shadow boxing. **1939** *Sun* (Baltimore) 17 Feb. 10/1 Shadow boxing over the selection of a site for the Leakin Memorial Park will continue next week. **1966** *Illustr. London News* 10 Sept. 10/3 But in any case, the gnomes know that a good deal of what is going on is 'shadow-boxing'. **1978** A. GARVE *Counterstroke* I. 60 He did a little shadow boxing and some skipping. **1908** *Sears, Roebuck Catal.* 1058/2 The background is a fairly dark shadow check effect. **1957** *Terms & Definitions* (Textile Inst.) (ed. 3) 89 *Shadow stripe*.., an effect, due to different reflections of light, produced in woven fabrics by employing yarns of different physical properties, usually of 'S' and 'Z' twist, in warp or weft (or in both, when it becomes a shadow check). **1960** *Woman* 23 Apr. 9/1 Dainty shadow-check shirt-waisters. **1932** *Sale Catal.*, Made of good quality Shadow Cretonne. **1943** E. BOWEN *Seven Winters* 48 Pink-and-cream 'shadow' cretonne. **1973** 'D. HALLIDAY' *Dolly & Starry Bird* xviii. 284 His bruises stood out like shadow cretonne on a chesterfield. **1920** J. HERGESHEIMER *Linda Condon* ii. 11 Shadow embroidery and fine shell edges. **1935** H. EDIB *Clown & his Daughter* xliii. 240 It meant that she could easily buy a leather set of shadow figures for Tewfik. **1976** *Jrnl. R. Soc. Arts* Apr. 254/2 Flat Figures and Shadow Figures are a distinct type of puppet... In the Shadow Theatre the figures are placed between a light and a translucent screen. **1918** W. BEEBE *Jungle Peace* (1919) ii. 26 The shadow-grey sea. **1932** *Sale Catal.*, A beautiful quality plain silk... Shades:..shadow grey and gunmetal. **1914–15** *T. Eaton Catal.* Fall & Winter 32 All White Evening Dress of Paillette Silk and Allover Shadow Lace. **1977** C. McCULLOUGH *Thorn Birds* iii. 61 His mother clad in a long bustled gown of palest pink shadow lace. **1951** *Proc. IRE* XXXIX. 1187/1 The first public demonstration of.. shadow-mask color tubes..was made in March, 1950. *Ibid.* 1188/2 The triangular pattern [of holes] was chosen for the shadow mask in experimental tubes primarily because of its mechanical properties. **1965** *Wireless World* July 354/2 The Mullard colour-selection shadow mask with graded holes. **1975** K. WICKS *Television* 54 The most common type of picture tube in use today is the shadow-mask tube. **1889** J. POLLARD *Plays & Games for Little Folks* 32 *Shadow Pictures.* In order to make these pictures show well on the wall, there must be but one lamp in the room, and that must stand back of the performer. **1977** O. SCHELL *China* (1978) III. 244 At break we sit on the freshly turned earth and make shadow pictures with our hands. **1890** CHAMPLIN & BOSTICK *Young Folks' Cycl. Games & Sports* 625/2 *Shadow plays*, plays in which not the actors, but their shadows, are seen by the audience. **1900** W. W. SKEAT *Malay Magic* vi. 514 Another very characteristic performance is the Shadow-Play. **1932** E. WAUGH *Black Mischief* iii. 92 He liked..to appear in society..to survey the shadow-play of fashion. **1938** *Burlington Mag.* Aug. 87/2 Shadow-play puppets. **1964** *Catal. National Mus. Kuala Lumpur* 3/1 The shadow play exhibit is arranged so that the visitor can see backstage and learn how the figures are manipulated during the drama. **1971** *Country Life* 17 June 1544/1 A shadow play, the Wayang Kulit of parchment puppet figures manipulated from behind a lamplit screen. **1965** A. WATERSTON *Development Planning* ix. 322 If the true economic cost of a project is to be determined in situations where market prices are out of line..it may be necessary to 'adjust' the prevailing prices by estimating the extent to which they deviate from 'equilibrium' prices. The adjusted prices, variously known as 'shadow' or 'accounting' prices, are then substituted for prevailing prices and used to determine real costs and benefits to an economy and to compare the project under consideration with other projects on a comparable basis. **1970** S. L. BARRACLOUGH in I. L. Horowitz *Masses in Lat. Amer.* iv. 157 Should labor be counted as a cost valued at current wage rates when there are no alternative job opportunities? If not, what 'shadow prices' should be used? **1981** *Sci. Amer.* June 116/3 Marginal values are sometimes called shadow prices or imputed prices. **1965** A. WATERSTON *Development Planning* ix. 323 Shadow-pricing can also permit valid comparisons to be made of a public sector project with a private sector project. **1976** *Nature* 8 July 84/1 Does this justify the attachment of a money-tag to all values, even though this means what economists call 'shadow pricing' (for example, the 'value' of a view of the South Downs is the extra cost of not defacing the view if a road or a line of electric pylons has to be built in the neighbourhood)? **1926** G. G. DENNY *Fabrics* (ed. 2) I. 111 *Warp print or shadow print.* Silks, ribbons and cretonnes woven with plain filling on a printed warp which gives a faint and shadowy design. **1968** J. IRONSIDE *Fashion Alphabet* 246 *Shadow print*, the warp yarns are printed with the design before weaving, giving a shadowy print effect. **1923** H. W. WHANSLOW *Everybody's Theatre, & How to make It* iv. 42 A fine collection of these Javanese shadow puppets. **1971** H. TREVELYAN *Worlds Apart* iii. 43 There were the ingenious hand-made toys, the shadow-puppets manipulated on sticks. **1929** O. G. S. CRAWFORD *Air-Photography for Archaeologists* 3/1 Inequalities in the surface of the ground produce shadows. All sites where remains are visible on the ground fall into this class. They may be called *shadow-sites*. **1946** R. J. C. ATKINSON *Field Archaeol.* I. 47 Shadow-sites are those whose surface is irregular, consisting of banks, mounds, ditches and terraces whose presence is revealed by the shadows they cast when seen in the low light of the rising or setting sun. **1932** *Mod. Woman* Feb. 56/1 This shadow stitch is just like herring-boning worked rather closely together... It gives you the shape of the leaf outlined in back-stitch on the right side and padded with long, crossed stitches on the wrong. **1932** *Pontings Whitsun Sales Catal.* 11 Morning Washing Frock for the larger than stock size in shadow stripe art. silk. **1940** *Chambers's Techn. Dict.* 762/2 *Shadow stripes*,..cotton cloths, of plain or satin weave, in which stripes are produced by using warp yarns of different directions of twist. The shadow effect is due to light being reflected in different directions by the different twists. **1947** J. STEVENSON-HAMILTON *Wild Life S. Afr.* vi. 52 Burchell's zebra.. 'Shadow stripes', that is to say light brown bands impinged upon the white ground which separates the black markings. **1930** *Economist* 18 Oct. 713/1 As a result a substantial amount of business was booked, principally in shadow striped poplins. **1969** I. & P. OPIE *Children's Games* ii. 86 The game [*sc.* Shadow Touch] is also played in Canada and the United States ('Shadow Tag'). **1977** *Hartford* (Conn.) *Courant* 6 June 15/3 There was 'Shadow Tag' on sunny days—the 'It' player ran after the others, trying to jump on a shadow with a foot. **1884** H. E. JULER *Ophthalmic Sci. & Pract.* xiv. 363 The two following [methods] are very useful in estimating refraction; in both the ophthalmoscopic mirror alone is employed, and is held at a considerable distance from the eye. The first of these may be called the 'Fundus-Image' test; the other has been called 'Retinoscopy', but would be more appropriately designated by some such term as 'Shadow Test'. **1889** G. A. BERRY *Dis. of Eye* xiv. 462 It has been called the shadow test because attention is directed perhaps more to the dark shadow which borders the illuminated area than to the area itself. **1964** S. DUKE-ELDER *Parsons' Dis. of Eye* (ed. 14) vii. 69 Retinoscopy, or, more correctly, skiascopy or the shadow test, is the most practicable method of estimating the conditions of the refraction objectively. **1923** H. W. WHANSLOW *Everybody's Theatre, & How to make It* iv. 41 China.. has had its shadow-theatres for many centuries. **1932** J. NICOLL tr. *Van Boehn's Dolls & Puppets* viii. 35 The Chinese shadow theatre..has no public, and the educated classes pay no attention to it now. **1970** *Guardian* 22 July 20 Mr P. L. Amin Sweeney, who has just gained a Ph.D. for a thesis on the Malay shadow theatre, yesterday demonstrated the art with a lamp, a screen, and 40 flat hide puppets. **1920** *Queen* 3 Apr. 17 (Advt.), Shadow Tissue. **1939–40** *Army & Navy Stores Catal.* 1073/2 Shadow tissues at 1/3 per yard. **1919** 'C. DANE' *Legend* 94, I possess that underlying shadow-work (I admit it's no more) of fact to guide me in deciphering her method in the first book. **1932** D. C. MINTER *Mod. Needlecraft* 25/1 If the material is very transparent, a white thread on a white ground is..effective. This 'shadow work', as it is called.., can be prettily used on collars and cuffs and small articles. **1932** *Mod. Woman* Feb. 56 The shadow work tea cloth and cosy. **1967** Shadow work [see *pattern darning* s.v. *PATTERN *sb.* 13 b].

b. Designating members of an opposition party nominated as counterparts of members of the government in power holding cabinet or other offices, or the offices held, as *shadow cabinet, minister, ministry*, etc.

1906 A. J. BALFOUR *Let.* in Ld. Newton *Ld. Lansdowne* (1929) 354 If we are to have, as you suggest, a Committee consisting of members selected from the Front Bench in both Houses,..what we should really have would be a shadow Cabinet once a week. **1925** J. O'CONNOR *Hist. Ireland 1798–1924* II. xxiii. 302 The Dail might go on to the crack of doom passing secret resolutions, appointing shadow ministers, [etc.]. **1953** EARL WINTERTON *Orders of Day* p. xi, I was in Mr. Churchill's 'Shadow Cabinet' from 1945 to 1950. **1958** *Spectator* 20 June 799/2 The Chancellors and Shadow-Chancellors. **1965** *New Statesman* 19 Mar. 436/2 Mr Ernest Marples, 'Shadow' Minister of Technology, will start work today at the English Electric Leo-Marconi works at Kidsgrove, Staffs. **1970** C. HAMPTON *Philanthropist* ii. 18 The Shadow Minister of Health..was hit in the ankle by a ricochet. **1973** *Ottawa Jrnl.* 21 Feb. 29/2 Opposition Leader Stanfield and his shadow cabinet have been using it to try and discredit Liberal economic policies in advance of the budget. **1976** H. WILSON *Governance of Britain* vii. 150 As shadow chancellor, I had..made some strong comments on some of the projects. *Ibid.* viii. 158 The Conservative leader.. also nominates the members of the so-called Shadow Cabinet and allocates the shadow 'portfolios'. **1977** M. WALKER *National Front* iii. 57 The Shadow Home Secretary..supported the motion. **1980** *Austral. Financial Rev.* 11 Apr. 15/2 Labor's energy policy for the next Federal election, which was unveiled..by the Leader of the Opposition..and the Shadow Minister for Minerals and Energy.

c. Designating organizations, structures, etc., built or instituted to substitute for or duplicate those existing in an emergency or to fulfil special needs, esp. before and during the war of 1939–45. Also as *adj.*

1936 *Economist* 31 Oct. 195/2 There was the scheme for the 'shadow' industry... This..was to consist of a set of new factories built at the expense of the Government, but supplied with skilled labour and management by the private companies. **1937** *Sunday Express* 24 Jan. 14/2 Experts other than Lord Nuffield have doubts whether the Government's shadow factory system for air-craft production is wise or workable in war time. **1938** *Times* 16 Mar. 7/2 Both in the regular industry..and in the shadow scheme, which was designed as a reinforcement and an insurance, engines were somewhat ahead of air-frames. **1939** *Sun* (Baltimore) 6 July 1/5 The factories themselves, conventional and 'shadow', are turning out a certain number of aircraft and engines each month—the actual number could not be learned. **1939** *Air Ann. Brit. Empire* 3 The Standard Motor Company is also concerned in shadow manufacture of new engine components. **1940** *Ann. Reg. 1939* 20 The whole 'shadow' organisation should be in a position to function as soon as an emergency arose. **1944** *Jrnl. R. Aeronaut. Soc.* XLVIII. 370 Considerable experience had been gained by the Bristol Co., in their licence manufacture all over the world, which had already taught them the method of laying out drawings and preparing data remote from the parent factory, and this was of the utmost help in getting going on the 'shadow' production. **1946** *R.A.F. Jrnl.* May 160 He may have spent his last few years before donning a uniform on a war job in a shadow factory—a shadow factory which, with the coming of peace, has now closed. **1980** J. DITTON *Copley's Hunch* II. iv. 178 The war came.. then they put up one of those shadow factories at—well, I'd best not say where.

shadow, *v.* Add: **12. b.** *Speech Therapy. trans.* and *intr.* To repeat (another's words) with the minimum of delay, as a treatment for stuttering.

1955 *Nature* 5 Nov. 874/2 The subject 'shadows' an unseen message read by the operator steadily and continuously. *Ibid.*, It now seems that stammerers..find little difficulty and can be induced to 'shadow' fluently. **1973** C. VAN RIPER *Treatment of Stuttering* iii. 80/2 When stutterers 'shadowed' the speech of a model speaker almost complete 'suppression' of stuttering occurred. **1977** D. FRY *Homo Loquens* x. 149 A stammerer who is shadowing will hear the appropriate sequence of sounds in advance and this should cancel out any built-in delay in his system.

c. *trans.* To act as a shadow (see *SHADOW *sb.* 6 e) in respect to (a parliamentary minister, ministry, etc.). Also *absol.*

1969 *Daily Tel.* 28 Oct. 16 An unusual trio of Tory political partners is associated with the..gallery... One is Geoffrey Rippon, who 'shadows' Defence. **1971** F. R. LEAVIS in *Human World* Aug. 8 The politician..was at that time 'shadowing' Education. **1974** *Times* 12 Mar. 1/1 Mr Carr shadows Mr Healey at the Treasury. Sir Alec Douglas Home maintains..foreign affairs and Mr Rippon will shadow on Europe. **1977** *Times* 5 Nov. 1/5 The new spokesman on Treasury and economic affairs..will be Mr Peter Tapsell, who formerly helped to 'shadow' the Foreign Office.

13. *Microscopy.* To subject (a specimen) to the process of *SHADOW-CASTING *vbl. sb.* 1.

1945 *Proc. Soc. Exper. Biol. & Med.* LVIII. 267 (*caption*) A micrograph of a similar preparation after it has been shadowed by the oblique deposition upon it of a thin layer of chromium. **1966** D. G. BRANDON *Mod. Techniques Metallogr.* 48 By shadowing the surface of the replica with a heavy metal from a carefully collimated source at a known angle, the intensity differences from point to point on the surface can be related directly to the surface topography of the specimen. **1978** *Nature* 19 Jan. 231/2 Increased ammoniation is indicated principally by the change in morphology of particles collected (during ascent) on a carbon surface and 'shadowed' with silicon oxide later in the laboratory.

shadow-casting, *ppl. a.* and *vbl. sb.* **A.** *ppl. a.* That casts a shadow or shadows.

1859, 1882 [in Dict. s.v. SHADOW *sb.* 15 c]. **1904** W. DE LA MARE *Henry Brocken* 145 Laid embraced in the shadow-casting moonlight. **1953** *Jrnl. Exper. Psychol.* XLV. 206/1 The shadow-casting object is placed as close to the screen as possible, whereas the distance between the light source and the object is made large.

B. *vbl. sb.* **1.** *Microscopy.* A technique for enhancing an electron-microscope image by projecting a beam of small particles or atoms (usu. of a heavy metal) on to the sample at a small angle to the horizontal, so as to form a deposit giving the appearance of shadows cast by sideways illumination.

1944 WILLIAMS & WYCKOFF in *Jrnl. Appl. Physics* XV. 712/2 Information was needed in our work other than that provided by stereoscopic photography. A procedure for measuring heights based on shadow-casting was accordingly developed to meet this need. **1947** *Ann. Rev. Microbiol.* I. 11 With the addition of the shadow casting technique, about eleven fibrils were clearly seen to compose the cilium of *Paramecium*. **1971** V. A. PHILLIPS *Mod. Metallogr. Techniques & Applications* v. 183 It is customary to enhance the contrast of replicas by shadow casting, that is, by evaporating a heavy metal from an angle to give shadow effects in the final electron micrograph, equivalent to oblique light illumination.

2. *lit.* The casting of shadows, esp. in *Psychol.* as a technique of perceptual research. Also *attrib.*

1957 *Psychol. Rev.* LXIV. 291/2 Previous shadow-casting devices..have not been constructed for this systematic purpose. **1971** *Nature* 3 Sept. 55/2 The geometric principles of shadow casting and the use of chromatic filters for dichoptic stimulation are established techniques.

Hence (as a back-formation) **sha·dow-cast** *v. trans.*, to enhance (a microscopic image) by shadow-casting; to subject (a microscopic specimen) to shadow-casting; also as *ppl. a.*; **shadow caster,** a device employed in perceptual research in order to cast shadows, esp. one for producing seemingly three-dimensional shadows.

1944 *Jrnl. Appl. Physics* XV. 715/2 (*caption*) Example of a shadow-cast electron micrograph for the determination of the heights of objects. **1957** *Psychol. Rev.* LXIV. 291/2 Considering the mount and the screen as two geometrical planes, changes in the position of the mount will yield all possible perspective transformations of the shadow relative to the shadow caster. **1969** *Vision Res.* IX. 154 The principal advantage of the stereoscopic shadow-caster over other stereoscopic projection methods lies in its versatility in the study of binocular kinetic space perception. **1971** V. A. PHILLIPS *Mod. Metallogr. Techniques & Applications* v. 187 After being allowed to harden, it is dry-stripped and shadow cast. **1971** *Nature* 3 Sept. 55/2 To produce this effect, a stereoscopic shadow caster was used, in which two point sources slightly separated horizontally cast the shadows of three vertical rods on a rear-projection screen. **1979** *Ibid.* 27 Sept. 287/2 Film samples were transferred to..electron microscope grids... Transferred films were shadowcast in the direction of compression with platinum–palladium at an angle of 10° before examination in a Siemens Elmiskop.

shadowed, *ppl. a.* Add: **10.** *Microscopy.* Subjected to the process of *SHADOW-CASTING *vbl. sb.* 1.

1944 *Jrnl. Appl. Physics* XV. 714/2 Photographing and measuring the lengths of the shadowed areas thus formed on the preparation. **1949** *Proc. Soc. Exper. Biol. & Med.* LXXI. 80/1 (*caption*) Chromium shadowed preparation of the same slide. **1973** P. J. GOODHEW *Specimen Preparation in Materials Sci.* v. 151 If a high resolution is required then the grain size of the shadowed replica is important.

shadowgraph, *sb.* Add: **1. a.** Also *fig.* Also, = SHADOWGRAPHIST.

1886 *St. Stephen's Rev.* 27 Mar. 5/2 At the New Club.. on Saturday next..Mason and Titus, the American shadowgraphs, who nightly provoke so much laughter at the Oxford, will appear at 11.30 p.m. **1928** A. S. EDDINGTON *Nature of Physical World* p. xvi, In the world of physics we watch a shadowgraph performance of the drama of familiar life. **1965** J. VON STERNBERG *Fun in Chinese Laundry* i. 2 To disembody human beings into shadowgraphs of my concepts of them is no labor of love.

b. An image formed by light which has passed through a fluid and been refracted differently by regions of different density (used esp. in the study of fluid flow).

1926 *Proc. R. Soc.* A. CXI. 336 Shadowgraphs of the jets emerging into the atmosphere from nozzles of different forms and at different initial pressures were obtained by the method described above. **1945** *Jrnl. Optical Soc. Amer.* XXXV. 505/2 If one places a viewing screen between the jet..and the second mirror, the image of the jet as seen on the screen will show what is commonly referred to as a shadowgraph. **1955** F. J. WEYL in *High Speed Aerodynamics & Jet Propulsion* IX. 21 By far the most extensive use of shadowgraph techniques..concerns the recording of shock waves and slip discontinuities. **1974** W. MERZKIRCH *Flow Visualization* iii. 85 Shadowgraphs made with short-duration light pulses display a scale of details much finer than that which the hot-wire technique can resolve. **1978** *Nature* 5 Jan. 47/1 (*caption*) Shadowgraph photograph showing the tilted layers and interfaces produced by inserting a block of ice into salt-stratified water at room temperature.

2. (Further examples.)

1975 *Nature* 25 Sept. 276/2 The X-ray shadowgraph image is converted into a charge image on a dielectric by the ionisation of a gas or liquid in a chamber. **1978** *Sci. Amer.* Nov. 62/1 The simplest and most successful way to produce an image with X rays is with contact X-ray microscopy. This technique, which achieves a resolution substantially better than that of the light microscope, creates a shadowgraph of the specimen.

shadowing, *vbl. sb.* Add: **2.** Also *transf.* (cf. *SHADOW *sb.* 4 f).

1977 *Lancet* 3 Sept. 512/1 A chest radiograph showed slight inflammatory shadowing in the right upper zone.

4. For †*Obs.* read *rare* and add later example.

1827 J. F. COOPER *Prairie* I. 17 The martin's fur.. was of a fineness and shadowing that a queen might covet.

6. b. *Speech Therapy.* Repetition of another's words with the minimum of delay, as a treatment for stuttering.

1955 *Nature* 5 Nov. 874/2 'Shadowing' means repeating concurrently. **1975** in J. Eisenson *Stuttering: 2nd Symposium* 347 It would appear that speech behavior during shadowing shares something in common with singing.

6*. *Microscopy.* = *SHADOW-CASTING *vbl. sb.* 1.

1945 *Science* 8 June 596/1 Their orientation with respect to the direction of shadowing. **1973** P. J. GOODHEW *Specimen Preparation in Materials Sci.* v. 148 Much shadowing is performed with heavy elements, a wide variety of which have been used.

shadow-land. Add: **2.** A place in shadow; a gloomy, unhappy place; an indeterminate border-land between other places, states, etc.

1923 *Daily Mail* 13 July 13 To lead Ireland out of the shadow-land of much unnecessary suffering and turmoil into a brighter and happier state. **1949** BROOKS & WARREN *Fundamentals of Good Writing* vi. 241 If we understand the extremes..we can use common sense to discriminate among the examples of the shadowland in between. **1960** AUDEN *Homage to Clio* 18 Within a shadowland of trees. **1966** *New Statesman* 27 May 775/3 Malcolm X the Harlem hustler had gloried in the sexual power-game of the race war's shadowlands.

Shadrach. Add: **2.** (See quots.) *local.*

1827 in S. Holland *Mem. Sydney Smith* (1855) I. 259 His fires are blown into brightness by *Shadrachs*, tubes furnished with air from without, opening into the centre of the fire. **1954** D. HARTLEY *Food in England* iv. 46 In some places, a draught is obtained by shadrack, an underground arrangement like a small blast furnace through which the blast of a rotary fan is carried under the [peat] fire.

shaduf, var. SHADOOF in Dict. and Suppl.

SHAEF (ʃēɪf). Also **S.H.A.E.F., Shaef.** [Acronym f. the initials of *S*upreme *H*eadquarters *A*llied *E*xpeditionary *F*orce.] The operational headquarters of the allied expeditionary force that invaded occupied Europe in 1944–5.

1944 *N.Y. Times* 21 May IV. 8/2 'SHAEF' stands for Supreme Headquarters Allied Expeditionary Force. **1944** C. MILBURN *Diary* 6 June (1979) 215 The great assault is known as S.H.A.E.F., pronounced 'shafe'—Supreme Headquarters Allied Expeditionary Force. **1945** *Times* 28 May 3/3 Shaef announced yesterday that it is expected that the port of Hamburg will be open on June 1 to allied shipping and supplies for our armies in the liberated countries. **1958** *Listener* 21 Aug. 272/3 The Cossac spirit carried on into Shaef and through to triumph. **1977** P. USTINOV *Dear Me* xi. 145 SHAEF, the Allied Supreme Headquarters, wished an official film to be made about the war in the West.

shaft, *sb.*[2] Add: **9*.** In various slang uses. **a.** The penis. Also † *shaft of delight.*

[**1719** T. D'URFEY *Wit & Mirth* IV. 72 It is a Shaft of Cupid's cut, 'Twill serve to Rove, to Prick, to Butt.] **1772** G. A. STEVENS *Songs, Comic, & Satyrical* 11 For Cupid's Pantheon, the Shaft of Delight Must spring from the Masculine Base. **1971** B. W. ALDISS *Soldier Erect* 45 It was never enough merely to lower your trousers—they had to come off,..so that you could crouch there naked but for your shirt, frantically rubbing your shaft.

b. A human leg. *U.S.*

1935 A. J. POLLOCK *Underworld Speaks* 103/2 *Shaft*, a woman's leg. **1939** C. MORLEY *Kitty Foyle* 95 If anyone showed a good shaft Pop would wink at me.

c. *U.S.* An act or instance of unfair or harsh treatment; slighting, rejection, 'the push'; esp. in *to give* or *get the shaft.*

1959 *Amer. Speech* XXXIV. 155 A girl or boy who makes a play for another's date is *snaking*... If he succeeds, the loser gets the *shaft* (sometimes *with barbs*), *the purple shaft*, or *the maroon harpoon*, depending upon the degree of injury to his pride. **1960** WENTWORTH & FLEXNER *Dict. Amer. Slang* 461/1 *Shaft*.., an act or an instance of being taken advantage of, unfairly treated, deceived, tricked, cheated, or victimized; a raw deal. Usu. in 'to get the (*or* a) shaft'. Fig., the image is the taboo one of the final insult, having someone insert something, as a barbed shaft, up one's rectum. **1964** *Mad Mag.* July 14 Looks like somebody gave him the shaft! **1977** *Amer. Speech* 1975 L. 65 She gave him the shaft after he broke their date last weekend. **1979** *Mod. Photography* Dec. 86/2, I would give more of my business to Minolta but for the company's uncooperative, anti-consumer thinking. Doubtless there are many such as myself who have gotten the shaft.

10. c. shaft-hole (*attrib.* examples).

1928 [see *core-casting* s.v. *CORE *sb.*[1] 15]. **1958** W. WILLETTS *Chinese Art* I. ii. 75 (*heading*) Objects derived from the shaft-hole adze. **1971** *Listener* 7 Jan. 14/1 (*caption*) Copper shaft-hole tools of the Balkan late neolithic.

e. shaft-tailed whidah, widow bird, a dark-coloured African weaver-bird, *Vidua regia*, having long tail-feathers with bare shafts.

1881 F. & C. G. OATES *Matabele Land & Victoria Falls* facing p. 220 (*caption*) Shaft-tailed Whydah Bird. **1900** A. C. STARK *Birds S. Afr.* I. 148 Shaft-tailed Widow Bird... The four central, elongated tail-feathers are webbed at their ends.., the rest of them consists of bare shaft. **1948** C. D. PRIEST *Eggs of Birds breeding S. Afr.* 135 Shaft-tailed Whydah..undoubtedly parasitic. **1974** *Sci. Amer.* Oct. 96/2 The shaft-tailed widow bird of South Africa..mimics the repertory of its host, the violet-eared waxbill.

f. shaft-alley *Naut.* (see quot. 1884); also used *attrib.* to designate unofficial or unreliable information or its source, attributed to gossip in shaft-alley; **shaft horsepower,** brake horsepower, *spec.* power delivered to a propeller shaft or the shaft of a turbine; **shaft turbine** (see quot. 1958).

1884 *Naval Encycl.* 732/1 *Shaft-alley*, a passage extending from the engine-room to the stern..in which is contained the propeller-shaft and its bearings. **1922** L. HISEY *Sea Grist* 155 It was rumored by shaft alley wireless that we would reach Antwerp, Belgium, in two days. **1941** R. G. M. EHLERS *Diary of Ship's Surgeon* (1944) 67 A 'shaft alley' rumor brought word that all ships had been ordered out of Hong Kong. **1945** *Sun* (Baltimore) 30 Aug. 7–0/5 It's the job of these six men to go down to the nethermost portion of this ship in 'Shaft Alley', where the big propeller shafts whirl. **1908** A. E. TOMPKINS *Marine Engin.* (ed. 3) v. 61 The torsion-meter is used to measure this angular twist between two points of a shaft, and from this angle the shaft horse-power is calculated. **1974** *Petroleum Rev.* XXVIII. 490/1 The high shaft horsepower was the conditioning factor for this proportion of pilot fuel. **1958** *Chambers's Techn. Dict.* Add. 1013/1 *Shaft turbine*, any gas turbine aero-engine wherein the major part of the energy in the combustion gases is extracted by a turbine and delivered, through appropriate gearing, to a shaft. **1970** LAMBERMONT & PIRIE *Helicopters & Autogyros of World* (ed. 2) 147 It had two shaft-turbine engines mounted on the cabin top instead of two Pratt and Whitney piston engines.

shaft, *sb.*[3] Add: **4. a.** Also objective, as *shaft-sinker.*

1922 D. H. LAWRENCE *Aaron's Rod* vii. 70 His father had been a shaft-sinker.

b. shaft-house (earlier example); **shaft pillar**

Mining, a body of coal or rock unworked in order to provide support for an adjacent shaft.

1872 *Statistics of Mines & Mining 1870* (U.S. Treasury Dept.) 344 The quartz is brought from the mine, unless the mill is in or near the shaft-house, in wagons. **1855** G. C. Greenwell *Pract. Treat. Mine Engin.* vi. 155 The situation of coal pits varies so much, together with the position of the seams of coal, dykes and slips, that no rule can be laid down for the form of the pillars of coal, left near the shaft, which are called the shaft pillars. **1929** I. C. F. Statham *Winning & Working* xxx. 499 This subsidence was not..wholly due to the removal of the shaft pillar, but was partly accounted for by crushing of the shaft pillar in an upper seam. **1977** *Irish Press* 29 Sept. 8/4 A third semipermanent pillar, known as the shaft pillar, cuts across the orebody from north to south.

shaft, *v.*[2] Add: **4.** *trans.* To treat unfairly or harshly; to cheat, deceive; to take advantage of; to slight, reject. *slang* (orig. and chiefly *N. Amer.*).

1959 *Amer. Speech* XXXIV. 155 A raw deal from any other source may also be referred to in this way; for example, one may be *shafted* or *jabbed* by the opposite sex, a professor, a policeman, parents, or anyone else for any real or imagined injury. **1966** 'E. Lathen' *Murder makes Wheels go Round* xiii. 108 He was a menace to Wahl... He'd railroaded Orin Dunn into jail... He was shafting Buck Holsinger! **1970** *Deb. Senate Canada* 1 June 755/2 As I have told my constituents in Hamilton, Ontario, which seems to have been continually shafted by this government. **1971** B. Malamud *Tenants* 19 Rent control..is an immoral situation. The innocent landlord gets shafted. **1976** M. Machlin *Pipeline* xxxv. 397, I think how they're shafting us with this whole deal.

5. = *fuck *v.* 1 *trans. coarse slang.*

1970 G. Lord *Marshmallow Pie* xxi. 185 There was this young girl among them, not even sixteen yet..like as not being shafted by every dirty long-haired crud in town. **1971** B. W. Aldiss *Soldier Erect* 82 How sinful he looked, squatting there by the water while his wife was being shafted by some dirty big Mendip only a few feet away! **1971** J. Wainwright *Last Buccaneer* ii. 228 He was Jimmy Needler—that's all...and the rest of the world could go shaft itself.

Hence **sha·fting** *vbl. sb.*

1971 B. W. Aldiss *Soldier Erect* 124 Hello there, gran! What do you do? Gobble? Where are the birds? We want three as are fit enough to stand a gude shafting. **1972** J. Wainwright *Requiem for Loser* iii. 50 What a monumental shafting he'd deliver to some lucky bint. **1973** *Farm & Country* 20 Nov. 23/3 Hugh Blaine charged that farmers 'suffered a shafting at the hands of feed dealers last year'. **1975** R. H. Rimmer *Premar Experiments* i. 94 After double-dealing with his own people and selling them to the slavers, some slaver gave the king and his family a shafting and enslaved them too.

shag, *sb.*[1] Add: **3. c.** *ellipt.* A shag carpet or rug; shag pile. See sense 6 c below.

1951 K. R. Gillespie *Home Furnishings* v. 164 A few cotton floor coverings woven on standard carpet backs have come into the market, in addition to the bouclé weaves, shags, [etc.]. **1974** *Anderson* (S. Carolina) *Independent* 18 Apr. (Sears Advts. Suppl.) 5 Nylon pile shag. Long shag that's slow to show soil! **1976** H. Nielsen *Brink of Murder* xii. 108 The floor was carpeted with soft yellow shag.

6. a. shag end *N. Amer. colloq.* = Fag-end 2.

1972 J. Mosher *Adultery* iv. xxi. 176 It was the shag end of winter and there were scarcely any victuals to be had. **1977** G. V. Higgins *Dreamland* i. 13 The years that came between that night..and the shag end of 1971.

c. Of carpets, rugs, etc.: having a long, rough, pile. Also *shag pile*. Cf. Shaggy *a.* 1 c.

1946 *House Beautiful* Oct. 199 (Advt.), Charm Tred Shag Cotton Rugs. **1947** *Sun* (Baltimore) 1 Dec. 13/4 (Advt.), Heavy Loop Pile Shag Rugs. **1969** D. E. Westlake *Up your Banners* (1970) xlii. 309 The silence had the texture of a shag rug. **1974** *Times* 3 May 11/4 Kosset Panorama, the cheapest shag carpet I have seen. *Ibid.* 12 Aug. 22/8 (Advt.), *Carpets*..Shag Piles and Berber Weaves.

shag, *sb*[2]. Add: **b.** Also *a shag on a rock*: used in various Austral. colloq. phrases as a type of the isolated or exposed.

1845 R. Howitt *Impressions of Australia Felix* 233 'Poor as a bandicoot', 'miserable as a shag on a rock', &c.; these and others I very frequently heard them make. **1929** J. Raeside *Golden Days* 16 The flood waters did not subside, and we were there like three shags on a rock. **1971** D. Ireland *Unknown Industrial Prisoner* 275 It's easy enough to curse England. Leaving us out here like a shag on a rock.

shag, *sb.*[6] *coarse slang.* [f. *shag *v.*[3]] **a.** An act of copulation.

1937 Partridge *Dict. Slang* 748/2 *Shag*, a copulation; also, copulation generically. **1971** B. W. Aldiss *Soldier Erect* 114 It was not just a good shag I needed. It was romance.

b. One who copulates. *rare.*

1971 K. Amis *Girl, 20* ii. 76 Ageing shag tries to stimulate jaded appetite by re-creating situation of days of first discovery of sex. **1978** —— *Jake's Thing* ix. 94 The moustached shag and the flat-chested bint..had moved away from the bar with their drinks.

shag, *sb.*[7] [Perh. f. Shag *v.*[2] or **v.*[3]] A dance popular esp. in the U.S. in the 1930s and 1940s, and characterized by vigorous hopping from one foot to the other. Hence as *v. intr.*, to dance the shag; **sha·gger**[1], one who dances the shag.

1932 (*title of jazz tune*) Shag. **1937** [see *Big Apple* s.v. *big *a.* B. 2]. **1938** *Sun* (Baltimore) 24 June 4/3 The Virginia reel, the shag, the sugarfoot and truck-ing predominate on the dance program. **1939** Ramsey & Smith *Jazzmen* xiii. 271 The Crescent Billiard Hall.. frequented by the best shaggers in town. *Ibid.*, Usually when Brunions reaches the third chorus..the kids have stopped shagging. **1940** *Time* 29 Jan. 17/1 A citizenry shagging to the tune of *Oh Johnny!* refused to take the 1940 Campaign seriously. **1954** S. G. L. Dannett et al. *Down Memory Lane* 131 The shag is a fast, nervous, hopping dance, performed in time to a strongly accentuated rhythm. **1963** *N.Y. Times Mag.* 27 Oct. 104/2 [The Negroes'] body rhythm and frank sensuality turned the formal European waltz into..the shag, the Susie Q. and the big Apple.

shag, *a.* **2.** For † *Obs.* read 'Now *rare*' and add later example.

1975 R. L. Duncan *Dragons at Gate* (1976) i. 12 Jenkins feigned the appearance of his early thirties..sandy-colored shag hair.

shag (ʃæg), *v.*[3] *coarse slang.* [Origin unknown, perh. f. Shag *v.*[1]] **1.** *trans.* and *intr.* To copulate (with).

1788 Grose *Dict. Vulgar Tongue* (ed. 2), *Shag*, to copulate. **1879–80** *Pearl* (1970) 258 A fellow who's had the mishap, To forget, when he shagged her, to button his flap. **1958** N. Levine *Canada made Me* iv. 102 You know what they're talking about? If they got shagged last night. **1969** J. Wood *Three Blind Mice* iii. 32 We..go and shag ourselves half-stupid all night..and *pay* them for it in the morning! **1973** *Nation Rev.* (Melbourne) 24–30 Aug. 1417/4 The credo of the new fashioned mammy is if you shag, I shag. **1977** C. McCullough *Thorn Birds* xvii. 413 There are plenty of men who will shag anything if it's a virgin. **1980** R. Adams *Girl in Swing* xxi. 279 'He's never absent.' And the corporal next to Jack muttered, 'Well, I 'ope 'e ain't 'angin' around when I'm shaggin' my missus.'

2. Used profanely in imprecations and exclamations. Cf. *fuck *v.* 2 and sense 1 of next.

1933 M. Lowry *Ultramarine* ii. 88 'Paddy—give us Paddy McGulligan's daughter, Mary Ann.' 'Oh shag off!' **1971** R. Ludlum *Scarlatti Inheritance* iv. 43 'Get four men and get out there.' 'Go *shag*, Captain.' 'Are you disobeying your superior officer?' **1973** G. Pinsent *Rowdyman* 135 'Then shag you!' I shouted, as he swaggered away.

Hence **sha·gger**[2]; **sha·gging** *vbl. sb.*[2] and *ppl. a.*

1970 G. Greer *Female Eunuch* 41 All the vulgar linguistic emphasis is placed upon the *poking* element;.. *rooting*, *shagging* are..acts performed upon the passive female. **1971** B. W. Aldiss *Soldier Erect* 9 God, what sodding, shagging, scab-devouring misery it all was! *Ibid.* 12, I could watch my reflection in the mirror of the wardrobe... Now *there* was a born shagger, if ever I saw one, given the chance. **1977** *Zigzag* Aug. 4/3 Plus the fact it gets hotter than shagging in the back of a car during the summer of '76.

shag (ʃæg), *v.*[4] [Origin unknown. Possibly connected with Shag *v.*[1] or (esp. in sense 1) **v.*[3]; but it is not even certain that senses 1 and 2 belong to the same verb.] **1.** *intr.* To make off; to wander aimlessly; to traipse. Freq. with advbs. *slang.*

When followed by *off* there is some overlap with sense 2 of *shag *v.*[3]

1851 *Gloss. Provinc. Words Gloucs.* 11 *Shag*, to steal away. **1932** J. T. Farrell *Young Lonigan* iv. 192 He watched a familiar looking airedale dog shag about. **1938** D. Runyon *Furthermore* xiv. 278 The Princess is getting too grown-up to be shagging around Broadway, and.. she is now going to public school. **1968** 'B. Mather' *Springers* xv. 162 I'll take you into Russia with me—or you can shag off on your own. **1976** W. H. Canaway *Willow-Pattern War* xiv. 140 We'd been shagging around over these mountains for four days now, and we hadn't seen one single musk deer.

2. *trans.* To chase. Also const. *up*. *spec.* in *Baseball*, to go for or catch (fly balls). *U.S. colloq.*

1913 C. H. Claudy *Battle of Baseball* 318, I was allowed to 'shag' foul balls. **1932** J. T. Farrell *Young Lonigan* ii. 66 Demons..would come and lean over his bed..until his old man came and shagged them away. **1955** *Sun* (Baltimore) 3 Mar. 19/8 Coan..shagged flies under the tutelage of Coach Tom Oliver. **1979** *Navajo Times* (Window Rock, Arizona) 24 May 15/1, I was originally picked as an outfielder, so I played two years shagging balls in the outfield. **1981** G. V. Higgins *Rat on Fire* v. 37 Every so often..I got to shag up a couple of guys who haven't told a clean joke in years and give the guy free entertainment.

shaganappi, *sb.* and *a.* For *U.S.* read *N. Amer.* and add: **a.** *sb.* (Earlier examples in both senses.) **b.** *adj.* Also, cheap, inferior, makeshift.

1743 J. Isham *Obs. Hudsons Bay* (1949) 46 Shag, a nap, pee or a string of Leather tauk' a miss. **1820** G. Simpson *Jrnl.* 10 Sept. (1938) 58 Any dressed skins, sinews, and Shaganapy lines that can be spared, you will send here for New Caledonia. **1895** W. Elkington *Five Years in Canada* xi. 101 A few years ago the only horses in the country were bronchos and Indian 'shaganappies' as they are called. **1900** W. A. Fraser *Mooswa* 35 Have patience, little shaganappi (cheap) Bird. **1961** W. O. Mitchell *Jake & Kid* i. 2 At the Rabbit Hill school concert last night, folks heard a shaganappy speech. *Ibid.* viii. 106 Thinka anybuddy havin' a shaganappy thing like that in their house!

shagged, *a.*[1] **2. b.** (Earlier and later examples.)

1784 J. Byng *Jrnl.* 11 July in *Torrington Diaries* (1934) I. 161 A most fearful mountain, call'd Drwsycood, of awful, and shagged front. **1927** F. B. Young *Portrait of Clare* iii. viii. 350 The twisted apple-trees stood shagged with a silvery blight.

shagged (ʃægd), *a.*[2] *slang.* [Origin uncertain: perh. rel. to Shagged *a.* or *shag *v.*[3] Cf. also Fagged *ppl. a.*] Weary, exhausted. Also with *out*.

1932 Auden *Orators* iii. 99 Wakeful at night, in the morning fagged; They feel like angels, but they look just shagged. **1947** D. M. Davin *Gorse blooms Pale* 178 They're all in pretty good nick, considering. Shagged, of course. **1950** Dylan Thomas in *Circus* Apr. 8/2 He is..thin, not to say of a shagged-out appearance. **1960** *Observer* 20 Mar. 10/3 Oh cut it out, Sarge—let up! I'm shagged. **1971** *Peace News* 10 Sept. 8/2 The haggard and shagged-out end products of a lifetime spent in the pursuit of materialism. **1975** G. W. Target *Strike Strikers* iii. 51 The two other-rankers were now sitting in the back of the jeep, with all of 'em looking shagged out.

shaggery (ʃæ·gəri). *N.Z.* [f. Shag *sb.*[2] + -ery.] A breeding colony of shags.

1882 W. D. Hay *Brighter Britain!* II. vi. 222 They [*sc.* Kawau] build in trees, in large 'shaggeries'. **1921** H. Guthrie-Smith *Tutira* xxii. 207 Fish are attracted to the vicinity of shaggeries.

shaggily, *adv.* (Examples.)

1859 Geo. Eliot *Adam Bede* I. x. 196 His hair was tossed shaggily about his forehead. **1921** D. H. Lawrence *Birds, Beasts & Flowers* (1923) 82 It was a fiery fortress frowning shaggily on the world. **1977** T. Heald *Just Deserts* i. 11 A dark, shaggily suave person.

shaggy, *a.* Add: **3.** *shaggy-chested*, *-haired* (later examples), *-legged*, *-throated*; **shaggy dog story**, a lengthy tediously detailed story of an inconsequential series of events, more amusing to the teller than to his audience, or amusing only by its pointlessness; also *shaggy dog yarn*, etc.; **shaggy (ink-)cap** = next; **shaggy mane** (examples).

1894 M. C. Cooke *Edible & Poisonous Mushrooms* 57 Shaggy Caps... This is one of the best of edibles, and common enough everywhere. **1979** *Guardian* 31 Oct. 14/1 The delightful pleasures of Shaggy Cap soup or Lawyer's Wig stew. **1922** Joyce *Ulysses* 510 Ben Jumbo Dollard, rubicund,..shaggychested, shockmaned,..stands forth. [**1945** D. Low in *N.Y. Times Mag.* 4 Feb. 40/1 The logical lunacy of 'Shaggy Dog'.] **1946** *Coll. Shaggy Dog Stories* facing p. 1 Stories of the Shaggy Dog variety are essentially tales to be told rather than read. **1947** *Beat* Apr. 6/3 Here's one of my favourite 'shaggy dog' stories. **1952** A. R. K. Barnard in A. Redman *Somewhat 'Shaggy'* 4 The comparatively recent type of story—the 'Shaggy Dog' yarn. **1952** Koestler *Arrow in Blue* i. viii. 68 The people of Budapest have a peculiar shaggy-dog kind of humour. **1958** *Listener* 16 Oct. 623/1 It was a shaggy-dog story about a small-town worthy who shams madness to avoid paying bills. **1972** P. Ruell *Red Christmas* xi. 102 He seemed to be in the middle of an autobiographical shaggy-dog story. **1866** Geo. Eliot *Felix Holt* II. xvi. 15 The shaggy-haired, cravatless image of Felix Holt. **1974** L. Deighton *Spy Story* i. 14 A shaggy-haired giant, complete with kilt. **1953** J. Ramsbottom *Mushrooms & Toadstools* Pl. 22 (*caption*) Shaggy Ink-Cap..often in enormous numbers on made-up ground. **1970** J. Webster *Introd. Fungi* ii. iv. 311 *Coprinus comatus* is a large terrestrial species (the shaggy ink-cap or lawyer's wig) which is edible. **1927** D. H. Lawrence *Etruscan Places* (1932) i. 16 He grins and drinks wine, and immediately one sees again the shaggy-legged faun. [**1885** J. A. Palmer *Mushrooms Amer.* Pl. II (*caption*) Shaggy-Maned Mushroom.] **1895** W. H. Gibson *Our Edible Toadstools & Mushrooms* 28 The Shaggy-mane..is conspicuously even-gilled, and is a decided delicacy. **1976** *National Observer* (U.S.) 13 Mar. 19/2 Now is the time of the shaggy manes and field mushrooms. **1946** R. S. Thomas *Stones of Field* 17 Thunder-browed and shaggy-throated All the men were there.

shagroon (ʃăgrū·n). *N.Z. slang* (now *Hist.*). [Perh. ad. Ir. *seachrán* wandering.] An early settler in Canterbury, New Zealand, from anywhere except Britain, esp. one from Australia.

1851 W. Lyon (*title*) Dream of a shagroon. **1851** E. Ward *Jrnl.* 20 Feb. (1951) 132 Started with Henry and a 'shagroon' cattle-driver. **1898** E. E. Morris *Austral English* 410/2 The men who came from England were called *Pilgrims*, all others *Shagroons*; probably a modification of the Irish word *Shaughraun*. **1930** L. G. D. Acland *Early Canterbury Runs* 1st Ser. i. 3 The Australians were known as 'Prophets' or 'Shagroons'. **1966** G. W. Turner *Eng. Lang. Austral. & N.Z.* i. 16 In Canterbury, immigrants from Victoria, locally called *shagroons*, set up sheep stations on the plains and were contemptuous of the agricultural enterprises of the *pilgrims* as the Canterbury Association's settlers were called.

Shah Abbas (ʃā æ·bās). The name of a Shah of Persia (1558–1628) used *attrib.* and *absol.* to designate Persian rugs and carpets like those made for him or their characteristic design.

1901 J. K. MUMFORD *Oriental Rugs* vi. 74, I have known a Persian who paid thirty dollars..for a fragment of one of these old Shah Abbas rugs. *Ibid.*, The Shah Abbas pattern is still made in rug factories. **1913** W. A. HAWLEY *Oriental Rugs* ix. 105 Only a few Persian rugs have the formal repetitive patterns, such as the Herati, Guli Hinnai, Mina Khani, and Shah Abbas. **1973** P. O'DONNELL *Silver Mistress* i. 16 The sumptuous silken glow of the Shah Abbas carpet.

‖ **shahāda** (ʃahā·da). Also **shahādah.** [Arab. *šahāda* testimony, evidence.] The Muslim profession of faith, 'Lā ilāha illā Allāh, Muḥammad rasūl Allāh' ('there is only one God, and Muḥammad is his prophet').

1885 T. P. HUGHES *Dict. Islam* 571/1 *Shahādah*.., 'evidence'. **1929** E. D. ROSS tr. *Lammens's Islam* iii. 56 The customary offering of prayer, of which the *shahāda* forms an integral part, takes the place of this obligation. **1970** *New Yorker* 29 Aug. 45/1 A European who repented the error of his faith and proclaimed the *shahada*—'There is but one God and Mohammed is His Prophet'—before dying would always go directly to Heaven. **1981** *Daily Tel.* 19 June 15/8 Everything in Islamic art and thought should be seen in the light of the *shahada*, or profession of faith.

‖ **Shahanshah** (ʃā·ənʃā·). Also **Shahenshah, Shahinshah, Shah-in-Shah,** etc. [Pers. *šāhanšāh* king of kings: see SHAH.] 'King of kings': a title given to the Shah of Iran (Persia).

1815 J. MALCOLM *Hist. Persia* I. vi. 92 The son of Babek was hailed..with the proud title of Shahan Shah, or King of Kings. **1824** J. MORIER *Hajji Baba* II. iii. 63 The *Shah-in-Shah* speaks like an angel. **1877** E. S. DALLAS *Kettner's Bk. of Table* 478 It is to be hoped that the land of vegetable marrows sometimes makes a dish of them for the Shah en Shah—king of kings. **1892** LD. CURZON *Persia & Persian Question* I. xiv. 434 He remains the Shahinshah, or King of Kings. **1938** 'M. ESSAD-BEY' et al. *Reza Shah* iii. 44 The trim appearance of the Cossacks..impressed the Shahanshah tremendously. **1953** J. H. ILIFFE in A. J. Arberry *Legacy of Persia* i. 31 The Shāhanshāh (King of kings) is..always aloof from his subjects. **1972** N. GORDIMER *Livingstone's Companions* 5 He had been sent to Iran for the coronation of the Shahanshah. **1980** *Listener* 14 Feb. 199/3 The set book was the historic speeches of the Shahenshah published in English translation.

Shahaptan, var. *SAHAPTIN. **shahbandar,** now the usual spelling of SHABUNDER in Dict. and Suppl.

‖ **Shahbanu** (ʃā·bānu). Also **Shahbanou, Shahr-banu.** [Pers., f. *šāh* SHAH + *bānū* lady.] The title of the wife of the Shah of Iran (Persia).

1915 P. M. SYKES *Hist. Persia* II. xlvii. 44 It is universally believed by Persians, that Husayn married the daughter of Yezdigird, who is known throughout Persia as 'Shahr-bánu' or the 'Queen'. **1975** *Vogue* Dec. 149 The Shahanshah and Shahbanou and the Imperial Family. **1976** *Times* 6 Apr. 9/1 (*caption*) H. I. M. Farah Pahlavi, Shahbanu of Iran. **1980** J. CARTWRIGHT *Horse of Darius* xi. 155 A stiff family group..with the Shah.., the Shahbanu and the younger children.

shaheed, var. *SHAHID. **Shahenshah,** var. *SHAHANSHAH.

‖ **shahid** (ʃā·īd). Also **shaheed.** [Arab. *šahīd* witness, martyr.] A Muslim martyr.

1881 *Calcutta Rev.* LXXVII. 74 The martyrs of the new Indian religion, known by the Musalman name *shahid*, were to have their exceeding great reward in a future state. **1934** *Encycl. Islam* IV. 259/1 The Muslim who falls on the battlefield is called *Shahīd*..'witness, martyr'. **1967** P. M. HUBBARD *Custom of Country* (1969) vii. 87 All Pakistanis killed fighting the Indians were *shaheeds*, martyrs of Islam. **1977** *Bangladesh Times* 20 Jan. 8/3 Shaheed Asaduzzaman, a student of Dacca University, was one of the many shaheeds who laid down their lives during the mass movement of 1969.

Shahinshah, Shah-in-Shah, vars. *SHAHANSHAH.

‖ **shahnai** (ʃa·nai). Also **shannai, shehnai.** Pl. same. [ad. Hindi and Urdu *śahnāī*, f. Pers. *šāhnāy*.] An Indian wind instrument of the oboe class.

1914 A. H. FOX STRANGWAYS *Music of Hindostan* i. 46 In the temple at Madura I heard the *nāgasāram* (N. India *shahnai*), a kind of oboe with a very loud tone. **1957** *New Oxf. Hist. Music* I. iv. 223 Among the imported wind-instruments we may count the different varieties of the oboe class, such as *shannai* (*surnahi*) which spread from the Near East across continents and to the far islands of the Indonesian archipelago. **1967** *Evening Standard* 20 Sept. 10/2 There has also been this extraordinary blossoming of Indian music... You are now expected to know about Bismillah Khan and his shehnai. **1969** R. SHANKAR *My Music* i. 40/2 The oboelike *shahnai* ..is thought to be an auspicious instrument and is often played..to celebrate..marriage. **1971** *Illustr. Weekly India* 18 Apr. 27 No Mendelssohn's Wedding March for her. She must have *shehnai* and Gujarati songs! **1981** LD. HAREWOOD *Tongs & Bones* xii. 195 The two greatest woodwind players I ever heard—Heinz Holliger, the Swiss oboist, and Bismillah Khan, the Indian *shahnai* player.

Shahr-banu, var. *SHAHBANU. **shaikh,** var. SHEIKH. **shaikha(h,** var. *SHEIKHAH. **shaikhdom,** var. SHEIKHDOM. **shaitel,** var. *SHEITEL. **Shaivism, Shaivite,** vars. *SAIVISM, *SAIVITE.

shake, *sb.*[1] Add: **II. 2. h.** (Later examples.) Also, *in three* (or *two*) *shakes of a sheep's* (or *lamb's*) *tail*, (*in*) *half a shake.*

1858 S. A. HAMMETT *Piney Woods Tavern* xxiv. 260 Out come my mare, and in a couple of shakes of a sheep's tail we was a doin' our three minits jest as fine as silk. *Ibid.* xxvi. 283 In hafe a shake Bingham broke through 'em. **1867** G. W. HARRIS *Sut Lovingood* 113 Pat tuck me at my word, an' wer outen site in the shake ove a lamb's tail. **1884** 'MARK TWAIN' *Huck. Finn* xli. 414, I says to myself spos'n he can't fix that leg just in three shakes of a sheep's tail, as the saying is? spos'n it takes him three or four days? **1902** E. NESBIT *Five Children & It* ii. 51 He'll be ready in a brace of shakes, he says. **1934** N. SCANLAN *Tides of Youth* 117 Half a shake—any more beer? **1936** W. GREENE *Death in Deep South* ii. 93 If you boys will just hold your horses, I'll have a statement for you. Harmon's typing it now. It'll be ready in a shake. **1958** J. WAIN *Contenders* xii. 265 In two shakes he's solved the problem. Or shaken it anyway. **1966** *Guardian* 29 July 8/7 Then they are off again... I nearly wrote 'in two shakes of a lamb's tail'. **1973** E. LEMARCHAND *Let or Hindrance* xii. 140 I'll knock you up bacon and eggs in a brace of shakes.

i. *a fair shake*: a fair deal. Also, *an even shake, a good shake*, and opp., *an unfair shake.* U.S. slang.

1830 *Central Watchtower & Farmer's Jrnl.* (Harrodsburg, Kentucky) 22 May 1/3 Says I, any way that will be a fair shake. **1902** S. E. WHITE *Blazed Trail* xxxi. 218 'That ain't a fair shake,' cried the man excitedly. **1949** E. B. WHITE *Let.* 20 Nov. (1976) 315 *The New Yorker* disagrees with practically everything Boyer believes in... Nevertheless, it has given Boyer a fair shake. **1969** L. G. ARTHUR in A. E. Wilkerson *Rights of Children* (1973) x. 124 What does the child receive in return:..just psychiatric screen, shiny tiled walls, and electronic listening. It doesn't seem an even shake! **1972** *Time* 17 Apr. 33/1 The Administration took office..expecting an unfair shake. **1976** M. MACHLIN *Pipeline* xix. 243 What about the natives? They're not getting such a good shake. **1980** in S. Terkel *Amer. Dreams* 341 I'd like to see an America where so much power was not in the hands of the few. Where everybody'd get a fair shake.

j. orig. *Naut.* An act of shaking a sleeper to rouse him. Also *fig.*, a morning call.

1933 P. A. EADDY *Hull Down* 49 If I'm asleep give me a shake at eight bells. **1945** 'TACKLINE' *Holiday Sailor* iv. 47 A shake. Another shake. I peer muzzily down at Gordon's upturned face. 'Quarter to four, Smiler, if you want any tea.' 'Uh? Oh, righto—thanks. I'll be up.' **1979** D. GURR *Troika* vii. 43 The knocking intruded slowly into consciousness. The room was dark, although my shake was for six-thirty.

k. A party, *esp.* a rent party. *U.S. slang.*

1946 [see *PERCOLATOR c]. **1956** S. LONGSTREET *Real Jazz Old & New* xvi. 126 Depression came... You could always wrassel up a piano and get together to listen and charge a few coins and have a skiffle. Or, as some said, a rent party, or a shake. **1977** *Amer. Speech 1975* L. 65 *Shake*.., party. 'There's a shake at Jim's house.'

3. b. For 'only *U.S.*' read '*U.S.* and *N.Z.*' and add further examples.

1845 E. J. WAKEFIELD *Adventure in N.Z.* II. xv. 368 The most severe earthquake occurred that I had yet felt... The natives..acknowledged that they had never experienced so bad a *ru*, or 'shake'. **1929** 'E. MILTON' *Love & Chiffon* 219 In good old New Zealand, you'd realize these shakes are mere nothings. **1948** J. COURAGE in *Landfall* II. 298 The earthquake happened late..but the shake woke Mr Blakiston immediately. **1949** *Los Angeles Times* 14 May 1/4 Newspaper and police switchboards were flooded immediately with requests for information on the shake.

4. a. *the shakes* (later examples).

1966 M. WOODHOUSE *Tree Frog* xii. 93 It was like getting the shakes on an exposed pitch of rock. **1976** B. BOVA *Multiple Man* xiii. 135 The sliding glass doors.. were locked...So I sat around and waited, trying not to get the shakes.

b. *the shakes* (further examples of sense 'delirium tremens').

1927 *New Republic* 9 Mar. 72/1 The following is a partial list of words denoting drunkenness now in common use in the United States..to have the shakes. **1947** A. MARSHALL in *Coast to Coast 1946* 177 The longest bender I ever had was eight months. It took me three years to get over the shakes it gave me. **1977** *New Yorker* 3 Oct. 40/1 Have you ever had the D.T.s? The shakes?

d. A shaking movement in a dance; *the Shake*, a dance characterized by such movements.

1946 [see *BUMP *sb.*[1] 1 f]. **1956** B. HOLIDAY *Lady sings Blues* (1973) iv. 41 The Cotton Club—a place Negroes never saw inside unless they played music or did the shakes or shimmies. **1962** *Guardian* 31 Dec. 5/1 The Madison threatens to become compulsory dancing; creeping up behind it come the Slop, the Shake, the Waddle,.. the Bossa Nova. **1966** [see *JERK *sb.*[1] 2 f].

6. b. *to give* (someone) *a* or *the shake* or *the cold shake*: to cold-shoulder, rebuff; evade, escape. *U.S.*

1875 E. EDDY *Let.* 29 Oct. in J. F. Daly *Life A. Daly* (1917) xxv. 215, I desire to give the 'Two Orphans' a shake. **1883** 'MARK TWAIN' *Life on Miss.* iii. 33 None of them herded with Dick Allbright. They all give him the cold shake. **1930** D. RUNYON in *Collier's* 1 Feb. 13/3 Although I give her..all my affection, she will probably give me the shake. **1970** N. FLEMING *Czech Point* (1971) viii. 106 If these jokers want to tail us, they've damn well got to do it properly from behind. Overtake and give them the shake.

7. (Later examples.)

1913 D. H. LAWRENCE *Sons & Lovers* x. 266 You think you're terrific great shakes, and that you live under the eternal insult of working in a factory. **1939** *Sun* (Baltimore) 8 Nov. 6/8 Women feel..that, no matter what poor shakes of wives they are, their husbands are blessed beyond their deserts in getting them. **1948** G. H. JOHNSTON *Death takes small Bites* vii. 159 He couldn't have been any great shakes as a driver because he didn't beat you by much. **1970** H. MCLEAVE *Question of Negligence* xxiii. 191 I'm no great shakes at this modern dancing. **1976** *Daily Mirror* 18 Mar. 2/3 Sir Richard may not have been particularly great shakes. But he was never given much chance to show his paces.

III. 10. b. Also *sing.* when *attrib.* or *comb.* (see sense 13 below). Occas. also used outside the U.S. (Earlier and later examples.)

1772 TILLINGHAST & HOLROYD *Let.* 23 Nov. in *Commerce of Rhode Island* (1914) I. 420 We herewith send you all the Shakes we can yet get in. **1939** I. BAIRD *Waste Heritage* xviii. 240 Weathered barns with the lichen growing on the shakes. **1964** L. LINTON *Of Days & Driftwood* ix. 51 The first place of worship was a very small building of shakes. **1977** *Tel.* (Brisbane) 20 Dec. 36/5 Shakes are hand split and have a rustic appearance. **1982** *Times* 26 Jan. 11/3 The design of these shakes was identical to that of the traditional oak shakes used in England for many centuries.

12. (Examples.)

1948 D. BALLANTYNE *Cunninghams* I. xxix. 146 You sat..sucking raspberry shakes through straws. **1953** [see *PARFAIT]. **1966** B. H. DEAL *Fancy's Knell* iii. 44 'I'll have a burger too,' the redhaired boy said. 'And a shake.' **1981** J. D. MACDONALD *Free Fall in Crimson* x. 114 She sucked up the shake.

IV. 13. (sense 10 b) *shake cabin, house, roof, shanty*; *shake-maker*; *shake-sided* adj.; **shake dancer** *slang* (see quot. 1968); so (as a back-formation) **shake dance**; **shake music** (see quot. 1942); **shake wave** = *S wave* s.v. *S 6.

1885 L. W. SPRING *Kansas* v. 64 Big Springs in the autumn of 1855 was a place of four or five shake-cabins and log-huts. **1967** M. CRAVEN *I heard Owl* (1968) v. 36 Old Marta was there and the girl called Keetah, and the two small children.., come from the shake cabins to pick blueberries. **1956** B. HOLIDAY *Lady sings Blues* (1973) x. 98 A shake dancer with her pimp. **1968** J. LOCK *Lady Policeman* xi. 102, I was..assigned..to the women entertainers. They were known as 'shake dancers'... The art consisted of shaking bare or almost bare breasts to music. *Ibid.*, Her daughter..did bare-breasted shake dances. **1976** *National Observer* (U.S.) 2 Oct. 21/5 She becomes a shake-dancer and B-girl. **1857** *Lawrence* (Kansas) *Republican* 9 July 3 You are always welcome to his log or shake house. **1901** J. MUIR *Our National Parks* ix. 298, I found many shake-makers at work in it, access to these magnificent woods having been made easy by the old mill wagon road. **1935** Shake music [see *JUNGLE *sb.* 3 c]. **1942** BERREY & VAN DEN BARK *Amer. Thes. Slang* § 579/1 *Syncopated music; jazz*... Shake music, a savage style similar to 'jungle music'. **1947** *Michigan Hist.* June 178 It was a small log cabin with a shake roof. **1978** J. HYAMS *Pool* vi. 68 It had..a steep moss-covered shake roof that turned green in the rain. **1879** *Atlantic Monthly* Aug. 154/1 Every one of the frail shake shanties is a centre of destruction. **1970** J. HANSEN *Fadeout* i. 8 The overhang of a shake-sided cabana. [**1929** H. JEFFREYS *Earth* (ed. 2) vi. 86 The type (9) are called the longitudinal, irrotational, condensational, primary, or *P* waves; (10) and (11) the transverse, distortional, equivoluminal, secondary, or *S* waves. Prof. H. H. Turner has very appropriately called them the 'push' and the 'shake'.] **1944** A. HOLMES *Princ. Physical Geol.* xvii. 369 The S or 'shake' waves are distortional waves, in which each particle vibrates at right angles to the direction of propagation. **1969** *Daily Tel.* 2 Sept. 12 Seismic records obtained so far from the landing site show the absence of the so-called 'shake-waves'.

shake, *sb.*[2] (Earlier example.)

1846 *Swell's Night Guide* 36 Many of the Haymarket shakes frequent this lumber.

shake, *v.* Add: **III. 5. b.** *more than you can shake a stick at* (and vars.): more than one can count, a considerable amount or number. *colloq.* (orig. and chiefly *U.S.*).

1818 *Lancaster* (Pa.) *Jrnl.* 5 Aug. 3/1 We have in Lancaster as many Taverns as you can shake a stick at. **1843** R. CARLTON *New Purchase* I. xii. 86 Our queen snake was..retiring, attended by more of her subjects than we even dared to shake a stick at. **1904** J. C. LINCOLN *Cap'n Eri* iv. 56 There's more Snows in Nantucket than you can shake a stick at. **1939** L. M. MONTGOMERY *Anne of Ingleside* xxi. 137, I had more beaux than you could shake a stick at. **1960** 'E. MCBAIN' *Give Boys* (1962) iv. 32 We get more damn cancellations than you can shake a stick at. **1982** *Folio* Spring 4 More consuls and dictators hanging from her family tree than a prudent man would shake a bundle of twigs at.

6. f. *to shake a foot* (earlier example), *hoof* (U.S.), *leg* (*b*) to hurry; *to shake it*: for † read *obs.* exc. *U.S. Blacks*'; also, *to shake that thing.*

1848 *Buffalo Gals* (song) 3, I ax'd her would she hab a dance... I taught dat I might get a chance, To shake a foot wid her. **1904** *N.Y. World Mag.* 1 May 6/3 Shake a leg..meaning to 'hurry up'. **1927** *Jrnl. Abnormal & Social Psychol.* XXII. 16 'Shake it', 'shake that thing', etc. Such expressions are very frequent in the blues.

Ostensibly they refer to dancing, but they are really Negro vulgar expressions relating to coitus. **1927** S. Lewis *Elmer Gantry* xxv. 333 Come on, Reverend. I bet you can shake a hoof as good as anybody! The wife says she's gotta dance with you! **1935** F. M. Davis *Black Man's Verse* 34 Strut it in Harlem, let Fifth Avenue shake it slow Plink plank plink a plink. **1952** Wodehouse *Barmy in Wonderland* viii. 82 'Clean this place up.'.. 'Yes, sir.' 'And shake a leg.' **1967** M. C. Melnick in A. Dundes *Mother Wit* (1973) 273/1 If you shake it, I'll buy you a diamond ring.

9. a. (*a*) fig. *to shake hands with an old friend, the wife's best friend* (colloq.), of men: to urinate.

1952 M. Tripp *Faith is Windsock* iii. 44 'I'm going out for a crafty smoke; anyone coming?' 'Sure, I'll come... I want to shake hands with an old friend, anyway.' **1965** *Times Lit. Suppl.* 16 Sept. 812/2 Expressive Australianisms to describe this prosaic function;..pointing Percy at the porcelain, shaking hands with the wife's best friend, [etc.].

c. For 'Now only *U.S. slang*' read 'Now chiefly *U.S.*' and add further examples.

1911 M. Beerbohm *Zuleika Dobson* xv. 228 'Are you going to die to-day, or not?' 'As a matter of fact, I am, but—' 'Shake!'..Oover wrung the Duke's hand. **1927** *Punch* 20 Apr. 444/3 'Long may it flourish!' said Roger, shaking vigorously. **1938** M. K. Rawlings *Yearling* vii. 61 'You got to promise..not to beat the very puddin' outen me after you've hunted him.' 'Shake.' A hairy paw closed over Penny's hand. **1966** 'J. Hackston' *Father clears Out* 199 Tom..said, almost benignly, 'Now shake!' and they shook,..in the true spirit of eternal friendship. **1972** J. Gores *Dead Skip* viii. 55 He stood up, stuck out his hand... They shook.

11. b. Also, to upset the composure or complacency of (someone). *colloq.*

1943 C. H. Ward-Jackson *It's a Piece of Cake* 54 'That'll shake him,' as the transport officer said when he refused to provide a vehicle for the Group Captain without written authority. **1966** *New Yorker* 25 June 52 It shook me some when I looked at the label.

d. (Further examples.) Also *N.Z.* Also, less strongly, to be keen on, to be impressed by, to admire, and const. *after*.

1907 H. Lawson in *Austral. Short Stories* (1951) 84 The trouble is that I'm so long, and I always seem to get shook after little girls. **1926** K. S. Prichard *Working Bullocks* 301 Didn't know she was so shook on Mark Smith. **1934** L. G. D. Acland in *Press* (Christchurch) 27 Jan. 15/7 *Shook on, to be*, to admire; to be keen on; e.g., 'I'm not s.o. his horse.' **1940** F. Sargeson *Man & his Wife* (1944) 22 Mother wasn't too shook on our doing it at first, but afterwards she didn't mind. **1947** D. M. Davin *Gorse blooms Pale* 78, I wasn't as shook on Phyllis as all that. **1965** M. Shadbolt *Among Cinders* xxii. 209 The bush. Still not too bloody shook on it, are you? **1975** *Sunday Tel.* (Sydney) 29 June 49 I'm not all that shook on cocktail parties myself.

12. c. *to shake down* intr. and refl., to settle down, to accommodate oneself to circumstances, a condition, position, etc.

1864 C. M. Yonge *Trial* II. x. 178 Mr. Cheviot, as the family shook down together, became less afraid of Ethel. **1875** Trollope *Prime Minister* (1876) I. vii. 109 You'll find they'll shake down after the usual amount of resistance and compliance. **1916** 'Taffrail' *Pincher Martin* i. 4 You needn't look so scared. You'll soon shake down. Is this your first ship? **1959** *Times* 31 May 11/2 By the time a new American President has..shaken himself down in the White House, the West German federal elections..will be approaching. **1973** *Times* 26 Apr. 17/1 Agricultural prices..produced..several sharp clashes of interest. This is an integral part of the process of shaking down. **1980** R. Adams *Girl in Swing* (1981) xxii. 307 And how is the beautiful Karin? Is she shaking down nicely in England?

13. b. (Later example.)

1921 Galsworthy *To Let* vii. 181 Impressions of the United States, whose dust he had just shaken from off his feet—a country..so barbarous in every way.

c. For *U.S.* read 'orig. *U.S.*' and add to def.: Also, to give (a person) the slip; to jilt; occas. to abandon (a place); to shake off (an illness, feeling, etc.). (Earlier and further examples.)

1872 'Mark Twain' *Roughing It* xlvii. 336 He never shook his mother... No indeedy..he looked after her and took care of her. **1874** (song) *I'll Never Get Drunk Any More*, Chorus: The pledge I will take, the whisky I'll shake, Oh I'll never get drunk any more. **1884** 'Mark Twain' *Huck. Finn* xxxi. 323 That little rascal has stole our raft and shook us, and run off. **1893** Kipling *Seven Seas* 96 We've shaken the Clubs and the Messes To go and find out and be damned. **1907** R. W. Service *Songs of Sourdough* 13, I was all caked in on a dance-hall jade, but she shook me in the end. **1934** in J. A. & A. Lomax *Amer. Ballads & Folk Songs* xx. 459 She shook me for the driver. **1935** M. de la Roche *Young Renny* iv. 28 'He was paying us a visit and the time went on and—he just came with us.' 'You mean you couldn't shake him?' **1949** R. Chandler *Let.* 21 Mar. (1981) 157 I'm going down to Palm Springs for a week to try to shake this cough. **1953** 'S. Ransome' *Drag Dark* (1954) xiii. 131 We deliberately shook you that night, then tailed you back here. **1958** J. Kerouac *On Road* v. 34 'I have a date with my boy friend.' 'Can't you shake him?' **1965** V. Canning *Whip Hand* v. 51 If anyone was following you must have shaken them. **1972** 'T. Coe' *Don't lie to Me* (1974) vii. 75 The picture of the murderer stayed in my head... Trying to shake it, trying to shake the mood it was giving me, I searched for other things to think about. **1974** 'J. Ross' *Burning of Billy Toober* x. 97 If you don't shake it [*sc.* heroin], it'll kill you in the end. **1977** *Rolling Stone* 16 June 34/4 Blauer had admitted himself to a New York state hospital hoping to shake a debilitating depression. **1979** 'S. Woods' *This Fatal Writ* 129 If you know you're being followed, it isn't too difficult to shake a tail.

16. c. *to shake down*, to extort money from, to blackmail or otherwise pressurize (a person) *for* (occas. *of*) money, etc. *slang* (orig. and chiefly *U.S.*).

1872 G. P. Burnham *Mem. U.S. Secret Service* p. viii, *Shake, out* to 'shake down'; to extort money from individuals. **1916** J. London *Let.* 12 Oct. (1966) 473 'Uncle Charley'..then proceeded to shake you down in proper money-lender..fashion. **1927** J. Barbican *Confess. Rum-Runner* xiv. 148 For only last week they were shook down for five hundred by a stray fellow from the Department. **1949** *Los Angeles Times* 5 May 1/3 Ferguson.. accused them of trying to 'shakedown' Mickey Cohen of $5000. **1956** H. Kurnitz *Invasion of Privacy* vii. 54 'You weren't by any chance trying to shake him down?'..'No, sir. Not a penny.' **1966** T. Pynchon *Crying of Lot 49* ii. 28 He left after shaking her down for four bits for carrying the bags. **1976** 'J. Ross' '*I know what it's like to Die*' xxii. 144 Sickert had been shaken down for protection money.

d. *to shake down*, (esp. of police, etc.) to search (a person or place). *slang* (orig. and chiefly *U.S.*).

1915 *N.Y. World* 9 May (Suppl.) 14/1 *Frisk*, to shake down or search. **1955** D. W. Maurer in *Publ. Amer. Dialect Soc.* xxiv. 46 They..shook down my hotel. **1968** *Listener* 15 Feb. 210/1 Inmate guards have been in complete control of the prison. They..shook down incoming prisoners to take radios and watches and so on. **1977** D. Bagley *Enemy* xvii. 141 Once Mayberry had been shaken down the guards were taken from Penny and Gillian. **1979** D. Anthony *Long Hard Cure* xxv. 198 The Sony had been in plain sight... Billy Combs was shaking down the rest of the house.

21. g. (Earlier example.)

1884 'Mark Twain' *Huck. Finn* vi. 40 People allowed there'd be another trial to..give me to the widow for my guardian... This shook me up considerable, because I didn't want to go back to the widow's.

IV. 22. shake-hands (earlier example).

1800 F. Burney *Let.* 18 July (1973) IV. 436 William will be much pleased by a private congratulatory *shake hands* from you in his own Apartment.

shake-down. Add: **2. b.** A forced contribution; an instance of extortion. Cf. *Shake *v.* 16 c. orig. and chiefly *U.S.*

1902 in *Dict. Americanisms* (1951) s.v. *shake*, To the historic phrase 'blackmail'..have been added, as words of similar evil omen, the new and expressive terms shake-down and rake-off. **1903** A. H. Hodder *Fight for City* 219 He [*sc.* a New York policeman] was fined 30 days' pay because he would not stand for a 'shake-down', which means that he had refused to give from time to time upon demand 5 or 10 dollars..to his superiors to be used for purposes unknown. **1916** J. London *Let.* 12 Oct. (1966) 473 A usurer..slunk out because..he saw the shake-down of me would not go through. **1941** *Sun* (Baltimore) 31 Mar. 1/7 Jack Pollack ..was named..as the man behind a demand for a $2,500 'shakedown' to kill a liquor license bill in the Legislature. **1978** S. Brill *Teamsters* ix. 329 While the shakedown was proved, it was never shown that the money went to Presser personally.

c. A search of a person or a place. Cf. *Shake *v.* 16 d. orig. and chiefly *U.S.*

1914 Jackson & Hellyer *Vocab. Criminal Slang* 75 *Shake down*, noun. General currency. A personal search; a deprivation of one's personal belongings... Example: 'If this dick nails you you'll have to stand a shake down.' **1936** *Sun* (Baltimore) 31 Jan. 3/5 A sudden 'shakedown' of the Stateville Penitentiary resulted in the seizure of several knives. **1958** *Landfall* (N.Z.) XII. 11. 123 But about nine o'clock, without any warning, there was a shake-down [of prisoners]. **1977** D. Bagley *Enemy* viii. 53, I really wanted..to give Ashton's study a good shake-down. But..it's bad form..to be found searching through your host's private papers.

3. *attrib.* (sense 2 a) *shakedown test*; (sense *2 b), as *shake-down dodge, scheme*; (sense *2 c), as *shake-down party*; **shake-down cruise** *Naut.* (orig. *U.S.*), a cruise designed to test a newly-launched ship and its equipment and to train its crew; also *fig.*; similarly **shake-down flight** *Aeronaut.*

1927 G. Bradford *Gloss. Sea Terms* 156/1 *Shakedown cruise*, one for the purpose of adjusting machinery and instruments, and familiarizing a crew with a new vessel. **1933** *Sun* (Baltimore) 21 Jan. 16/7 The newest addition to the navy..is on its 'shake-down' cruise. **1968** *Wall St. Jrnl.* (Eastern ed.) 12 Sept. 1/1 The first week on the road..has been a shakedown cruise for the Senator and his staff—enabling the candidate to test stump themes,.. giving aides experience at writing speeches and organizing motorcades, [etc.]. **1978** P. O'Donnell *Dragon's Claw* ii. 27 The boat's 'ad a shakedown cruise and..it 'andles beautifully. **1934** D. Runyon in *Collier's* 24 Nov. 52/2 He is only going back to his old shake-down dodge, so all you have to do is to buy him off. **1939** *Sun* (Baltimore) 25 Mar. 20/3 The 10,000-mile shakedown flight will require about two weeks. **1952** *Here & Now* (N.Z.) II. iv. 32 The shake-down parties have been through the cells pretty often. **1976** *Honolulu Star-Bull.* 21 Dec. A-2/4 The mayor's own press secretary was convicted in a shake-down scheme. **1942** *R.A.F. Jrnl.* 2 May (recto rear cover), To send them into actual service..without modification or further shakedown test.

sha·ke-out. [f. vbl. phr. *to shake out*: see Shake *v.* 20.] **1.** *Stock Exch.* (See Shake *sb.*[1] 8 a.) Also, a sudden fall in prices, a sudden general disposal of particular stocks, etc.

1928 *Sun* (Baltimore) 7 Dec. 1/3 Measured by the Associated Press averages of twenty leading industrials and twenty leading rails, which dropped $9.45 and $4.38, respectively, it was one of the quickest and most drastic shakeouts in recent market history. **1981** *Times* 14 Aug. 18/3 Properties came in for a small shakeout with Stock Conversion a weak market 10p lower at 370p.

2. An upheaval or reorganization, esp. one involving contraction, streamlining, shedding of personnel, closure of some businesses, etc.

1939 *Times* 9 Mar. 8/1 There had been what was sometimes called a 'shake-out' in the film industry during the past year. A number of those elements which did not raise the repute of the film industry had been removed. **1956** *Sun* (Baltimore) 20 Jan. 13/1 New claims for jobless pay increased about 20 per cent in Maryland last week under the impetus of the usual year-end economic 'shake out'. **1957** *Time* 2 Sept. 59/1 In downtown Washington, D.C., eight, or about half, of the city's big discount houses went out of business in the past year. The shake-out is almost as severe in Los Angeles, Boston and Dallas. **1963** *Listener* 21 Feb. 319/2 Public-house gossip is perhaps most busy about the need for a shake-out of the party system. **1964** *Financial Times* 3 Mar. 12/7 A shake-out in the business world, with pressure on profits and profit margins forcing the inefficient producer, or..retailer, out of business or into efficiency. **1967** *Listener* 19 Jan. 80/3 A nation-wide witch-hunt and counterbalancing resistance movement which could well make the upheaval of the past year [in China] seem like the mildest of shake-outs. **1974** *Howard Jrnl.* XIV. 39 Successive recessions and mechanization have meant a 'shake-out' of labour in traditionally labour-intensive industries. **1981** *Economist* 28 Nov. 26/1 Workers left in droves, because they were laid off. The worst of that shake-out is over.

shaker. Add: **1. a.** *mover and shaker, shaker and mover* (U.S.), a person who influences events, a person who gets things done.

1874 A. O'Shaughnessy *Music & Moonlight* 1 Yet we are the movers and shakers Of the world for ever, it seems. **1972** F. Knebel *Dark Horse* (1973) ix. 124 The rich movers and shakers..always manage to manipulate the Congress for their own benefit and screw the rest of us. **1975** J. F. Burke *Death Trick* iv. 61 Beniamino Tucci was..known as the Little Godfather of the Upper West Side. A mover and shaker with many interests. **1977** *Time* 10 Oct. 1/2 Perish the thought that a shaker and mover should work for the Government.

2. b. A simple percussion instrument that is shaken; *spec.* = Chac-chac. Cf. *Shack-shack, etc.

[**1837** I. M. Belisario *Sk. Negro Pop. in Jamaica* (caption to Plate 7), Shaka, a rattle used by the French Set Dancers.] **1943** *Penguin New Writing* XVIII. 96 He finished with a flourish of the shakers and threw his drumstick into the air. **1958** E. Borneman in P. Gammond *Decca Bk. Jazz* xxi. 275 A male leader and a small group..who accompanied themselves on..shakers and gong-gong. **1965** E. M. Matterson *Play with Purpose for Under-Sevens* ix. 145 Shakers can be made from a wide variety of empty containers to make a number of sounds. **1972** S. Dickinson *Mother's Help* iii. 45 Shakers or rattles, are probably the easiest instrument of all to make.

4. b. *attrib.* (Earlier and further examples, esp. of artefacts produced by or of a type produced by Shakers.)

1817 *Niles' Reg.* XII. 371/1 At Enfield, Vermont, he visited the '*Habitation of the Shaken* [sic] *community*', to use their own phraseology, or in more familiar language the Shaking Quakers. **1856** in C. C. Richards *Village Life in Amer.* (1912) 77 We went down town this morning and bought us some shaker bonnets to wear to school. **1863** *Trans Illinois Agric. Soc.* (1865) V. 256 Your committee would..suggest that they put on their..shaker bonnet, [etc.]. **1864** T. Norris *Amer. Angler's Bk.* xiii. 371 Two or three pairs of stout yarn socks ('Shaker' socks are best). **1866** A. D. Whitney *Summer in Leslie Goldthwaite's Life* vi. 92 On this little green stood her Shaker rocking-chair. **1895** *Montgomery Ward Catal.* 561/3 Baby Carriage Robes..Shaker flannel, pinked edge and embroidered center. **1928** *Antiques* XIV. 134 A study of the characteristic forms of Shaker furniture suggests the hypothesis that the early craftsmen adapted to their own designs existing Colonial models. **1967** D. Skirrow *I was following this Girl* iii. 20 Early American Engraving up this way. Early Shaker Woodwork in the Brook Street Foyer. **1975** J. Gores *Hammett* i. 11 He wore a maroon worsted Shaker coat over a wool shirt. **1978** *Jrnl. R. Soc. Arts* CXXVI. 305/2 The Fraktur and Shaker artists, many of whose works..seem to have anticipated Paul Klee.

8. d. Substitute for def.: A container in which cocktails or other mixed drinks are blended by shaking. Freq. as the second element of a comb. (Earlier and later examples.)

1868 [see **cocktail shaker*]. **1895** *Montgomery Ward Catal.* 435/1 Liquor Mixers or Lemonade Shakers of tin. **1922** S. Lewis *Babbitt* viii. 110 He did not possess a cocktail-shaker. A shaker was proof of dissipation. **1929** E. Linklater *Poet's Pub* ii. 39 Holly poured his chosen liquors into a long silver shaker, added broken fragments of ice, screwed down the top, and, like a man with the palsy, shook. **1946** 'P. Quentin' *Puzzle for Fiends* v. 35 She carried a small shaker of Manhattans. **1959** A. W. Sherring *Tip Off* xiii. 135 Big Boy Gale watched them in the bar mirror as he poured drinks from a shaker. **1971** *Scope* (S.Afr.) 19 Mar. 77/2 Many people consider the shaker and mixer as being the same thing, but there is a considerable difference: cocktails with clear ingredients are prepared by stirring in a mixer, cloudy liquids are agitated in a shaker.

f. *U.S.* = Castor[2] 1.

1910 J. W. Tompkins *Mothers & Fathers* 29 Miss Elsie would be terribly shocked at this shaker. **1969** J. A. McPherson in A. Chapman *New Black Voices* (1972) 153

Shouldn't you polish the shakers or clean out the Pantry or squeeze oranges? **1978** S. BRILL *Teamsters* vii. 284 The small formica booth table with the mini-juke box built into the wall just above the salt and pepper shakers.

9. Short for *Shaker bonnet*: see sense 4 b above. *U.S. local.*

1858 M. D. COLT *Let.* in *Went to Kansas* (1862) xiii. 238, I did not wear the green silk calash, but a shaker, made of brown muslin smoothed over a pasteboard frame; it was very fashionable; besides it kept the sun out of my face, and was very genteel for a school-ma'am. **1881** *Harper's Mag.* May 854/2 The bonnet is far too fine. I will buy you a shaker at the store. **1905** K. D. WIGGIN *Rose o' River* 9 Rose had tried on..children's gingham 'Shakers', mourning bonnets for aged dames, [etc.]. **1909** *Dialect Notes* III. 415 *Shaker*, a palm leaf sunbonnet.

shakerism (earlier example).

1818 *Catholic Vindicator* 5 Dec. 41 Anabaptism or independentism, quakerism or shakerism.

shakerful (ʃē^{i}·kəɹful). [f. SHAKER 8 d + -FUL.] The contents of a (cocktail) shaker; the amount that a shaker will hold.

1946 E. HODGINS *Mr Blandings builds his Dream House* vii. 95 A second shakerful of still paler Martinis. **1966** T. PYNCHON *Crying of Lot 49* i. 15 Gliding like a large bird in an updraft toward the sweating shakerful of booze. **1977** [see *SCREWDRIVER 3].

Shakespeare (ʃē^{i}·kspī^{ə}ɹ). [The name of William *Shakespeare*: see SHAKSPERIAN *a.* (and *sb.*).] **1.** A person (occas. a thing) comparable to Shakespeare, esp. as being pre-eminent in a particular sphere.

1821 M. EDGEWORTH *Let.* 23 Oct. (1971) 243 Humboldt is the Shakespear of travellers—as much superior in genius to other travellers as Shakespear to other poets. **1859** A. J. MUNBY *Diary* 17 Mar. (1972) 28 When..the poetic soul..has learnt..to see the poetic side of all such things, *then* we may have a Homer of the railway and a Shakespeare of the Ballot. **1905** 'MARK TWAIN' in *N. Amer. Rev.* Jan. 3 The telegraph, the telephone..the Pullman car..the Shakespeares of the inventor-tribe, so to speak. **1931** R. CAMPBELL *Georgiad* ii. 36 A Fabian Shakespeare of the Summer Schools To other poets laying down my rules.

2. *attrib.*, as **Shakespeare collar,** (*a*) = *polo collar* s.v. *POLO[1] 3; (*b*) (see quot. 1960); **Shakespeare country,** the part of Warwickshire around Stratford-on-Avon, birthplace of Shakespeare; **Shakespeare industry,** the large-scale production of writings about Shakespeare, items commemorating Shakespeare, etc.; the commercial exploitation of objects, places, etc., associated with Shakespeare.

1907 *Yesterday's Shopping* (1969) 873/1 Cotton Football Shirts..Shakespeare collar, and three buttons. **1913** [see *polo collar* s.v. *POLO *sb.*[1] 3]. **1960** C. W. CUNNINGTON et al. *Dict. Eng. Costume* 192/1 *Shakespeare collar.* 1860's on. A shallow turn-over collar, the points projecting downwards onto the shirt-front. **1900** J. LEYLAND *Shakespeare Country* 92 This survey of Shakespeare Country has traversed a rich district of middle England that was familiar to the great poet in his boyhood. **1966** J. WAINWRIGHT *Crystallised Carbon Pig* iv. 20 The plan worked..as smoothly..as an American tourist's trip through the Shakespeare country. **1972** *Times* 4 Aug. 4/2 The 'Shakespeare country' around Stratford-upon-Avon, Oxford and Cambridge are the main non-metropolitan attractions. **1939** BROWN & FEARON (*title*) Amazing monument: a short history of the Shakespeare industry. **1958** *Listener* 2 Oct. 523/1 Is not much of this book-making on the Bard another branch of the Shakespeare industry? **1962** *Observer* 4 Mar. 13/6 The 1864 affair.. marked the dawn of the Shakespeare industry. At Stratford..'streets were adorned with flags and banners; the townsfolk and visitors wore the..Shakespeare badge', [etc.].

Hence **Sha·kespeare** *v. intr.* (*nonce-wd.*), to act in a Shakespeare play.

1896 G. B. SHAW *Our Theatres in Nineties* (1932) II. 90 Madame de Navarro has declaimed, spouted, statuesqued, Shakespeared, and all the rest of it.

Shakespearian, *a.* (and *sb.*) Now the usual form of SHAKSPERIAN *a.* (and *sb.*). Add: **a.** *adj.* (Earlier examples.)

1755 H. FIELDING *Voy. to Lisbon* 100 A poetic, if not a Shakespearian genius. **1805** C. WILMOT *Let.* 4 Aug. in *Russ. Jrnls.* (1934) II. 164, I rooted out Hamlet's Garden ..& got into a *Shakespearian tantrum* at finding myself in the place.

b. *sb.* (Further examples.) Also, one who believes that Shakespeare wrote the plays usually attributed to him; an imitator of Shakespeare's style, one of his school; an admirer of Shakespeare's works.

1874 [see *BACONIAN *a.* and *sb.* 2]. **1912** E. NESBIT *Let.* in D. L. Moore *E. Nesbit* (1933) xv. 268 Are you a Baconian or a Shakespearean? **1930** N. STREATFEILD *Ballet Shoes* iii. 38 We'll read some more one day. I'll make a Shakespearean of you. **1964** *English Studies* XLV. 353 It also establishes the negative method of praising Heywood, as a minor Shakespearian. **1971** *Daily Tel.* 8 Mar. 10/4 One of those devoted Shakespeareans who knows his author backwards. **1979** F. KERMODE *Genesis of Secrecy* iv. 79 Shakespearians may find explanations of the mysteriousness..of *Hamlet*, by considering instead the *ur-Hamlet*.

Shakespeariana (further examples); **Shakespea·rianizing** *vbl. sb.*, the action or instances of imitating passages from the works of Shakespeare; **Shakespea·rianly** *adv.*, in a Shakespearian manner; **Shakespearism** (further example); **Sha·kespearite,** one who believes that Shakespeare wrote the plays traditionally attributed to him.

1861 *Sat. Rev.* 30 Nov. 557/2 'The national pulse beats Shaksperianly.' So at least says Mr. James Orchard Halliwell in one of two circulars..which have lately reached us about 'the National Shaksperian Fund'. **1865** F. THIMM (*title*) Shakespeariana from 1564 to 1864. **1890** *Merry England* July 242 A fine, Shakespearianly virile bit of poetry. **1903** G. B. SHAW *Let.* 12 Jan. (1972) II. 303 Ben Jonson never could quite get over the absurdity of the Shakespearisms which he knew so well at the Mermaid passing off in cold ink as literature. **1909** 'MARK TWAIN' *Is Shakespeare Dead?* v. 50 Two of these cults are known as the Shakespearites and the Baconians... The Shakespearite knows that Shakespeare wrote Shakespeare's Works. **1921** G. B. SHAW in *John Keats Memorial Volume* 176 The lines beginning (Shakespearianly) with How fever'd is the man who cannot look Upon his mortal days with temperate blood! **1936** F. R. LEAVIS *Revaluation* vi. 223 *The Cenci*..is full of particular echoes of Shakespeare... This Shakespearianizing..is..quite damning. **1953** *John o' London's* 12 June 520/4 A musical piece, with Arthur Askey..Shakespeareanly disguised. It was called *The Kid from Stratford.* **1955** *Times* 3 Aug. 9/5 One such foundation has for many years placed a standing order for the purchase of Shakespeariana offered at our leading sale rooms. **1964** *Economist* 11 Apr. 144/3 The appetite for Shakespeareana.

sha·ke-up. (In Dict. s.v. SHAKE *sb.*[1] 8 b.) Substitute for def.: An act of shaking up or being shaken up, or the result of this; a thorough or drastic change or rearrangement; a disturbing or unsettling experience. (Earlier and further examples.)

1847 J. S. MILL *Lett.* (1910) I. 131 To give that general shake-up to the torpid mind of the nation which the French Revolution gave to Continental Europe. **1880** 'MARK TWAIN' *Tramp Abr.* xxxviii. 438 My nerves had hardly grown quiet after this affair when they got another shake-up,—one which utterly unmanned me for a moment. **1882** *National Police Gaz.* 18 Nov. 7/2 (*heading*) The Union Square Company has a matrimonial shake-up all around. **1899** R. H. BARBOUR *Half-back* vi. 59 There'll be a shake-up to-morrow... He's going to put Greer on the scrub to-morrow. **1916** 'TAFFRAIL' *Pincher Martin* xvi. 312 But, orl the same, Tubby boy, I reckons it's done us orl good ter 'ave a bit of a shake up like this 'ere [*sc.* a naval engagement]. **1938** E. BOWEN *Death of Heart* III. i. 325, I can't see that this change has done you harm. Nor the shake-up either; you were getting too quiet. **1962** E. SNOW *Red China Today* (1963) xxii. 165 'Rectification', self-criticism, retraining and restudy among party and nonparty cadres are followed by shake-ups which affect millions. **1967** D. PINNER *Ritual* viii. 85 You didn't half give me a shake-up. **1969** *Listener* 27 Mar. 410/2, I read that BBC radio is due for a programme shake-up. **1970** 'D. HALLIDAY' *Dolly & Cookie Bird* iii. 35 It was sporting of your father to ask me. I can imagine what a shake-up it must have been, without taking me on as well. **1980** *Christian Sci. Monitor* (Midwestern ed.) 4 Dec. 4/1 As a result of the latest shake-up, which occurred at the party meeting, the political balance has shifted away from the conservatives.

shaking, *vbl. sb.* **1. c.** (Further examples.)

1926 J. S. HUXLEY *Ess. in Pop. Sci.* ix. 118 Taking them [*sc.* Infusoria] on a railway journey to give them a good shaking-up. **1928** *Daily Mail* 9 Aug. 12/4 The best opinion is that a thorough shaking-out will do much good, but there is no need for alarm. **1958** L. DURRELL *Mountolive* vi. 134 Only Pursewarden had not put in an appearance... Mountolive planned to give him a shaking-up at the first opportunity.

shaking, *ppl. a.* **b.** (Further examples.)

1888, 1955 [see *PARKINSON[1]].

Shaksperian, etc.: see also *SHAKESPEARIAN *a.* (and *sb.*).

Shakti, var. *SAKTI.

‖ **shaku** (ʃa·*ku*). Also 8 **sackf, sak, saku.** Pl. same. [Jap., ad. Chinese *chǐ* a foot.] **1.** A Japanese measure of length, equal to 11·9 inches (30·3 cm.); (see also quot. 1974).

1727 J. G. SCHEUCHZER tr. *Kæmpfer's Hist. Japan* I. xi. 136 One *Sackf* and a half long. *Ibid.* II. iv. 180 Snow.. to the height of four *Sak* and five Suns, that is about four foot and a half. *Ibid.* III. vi. 246 His Stature..of nine *Saku*, and nine *Suns*, proportionable to the greatness of his Genius. **1878** *Trans. Asiatic Soc. Japan* VI. II. 249 The seismograph consisted of a copper vessel, whose diameter was 8 *shaku* or feet. **1884** tr. *J. J. Rein's Japan* ii. 415 The interval of three shaku (1 metre). **1893** E. ARNOLD *Adzuma* I. i. 2 He could..run so fleetly that a cord of thirty *shaku*, tied to his waist, would stream in a straight line behind him. **1974** *Encycl. Brit. Micropædia* IX. 106/3 *Shaku*, a unit of length, area, and volume in Japan, equivalent to 10/33 metre, 3·306 square decimetres, and 18·039 cubic centimetres.

2. A flat baton made of wood or horn, a little over a foot in length, upon which a Japanese court noble formerly would note memoranda, but later carried as a mark of honour in the presence of the emperor, or by the emperor himself.

1875 F. V. DICKINS tr. *Chiushingura* (1876) 208 'Twas the Emperor's whim That the tree should from him Have a *shaku* with Ta-iu writ on. **1880** *Trans. Asiatic Soc. Japan* VIII. 351 A short staff called the *Shaku*, which was generally held vertical in the right hand. **1894** C. M. SALWEY *Fans of Japan* 6 The *shaku*..was a stick in the shape of the outside frame of a folding fan, about two feet in length, about an inch and a half to two inches at the top, decreasing at the base to about one inch. **1928** *Daily Express* 12 Nov. 3/7 The Emperor, after seating himself on the throne, was presented with the small wooden baton (shaku) which is a traditional symbol of authority found in many Shinto rites.

shakudo. Add: (Earlier example.) Also *attrib.*

1860 S. B. KEMISH *Jap. Empire* 114 The beautiful work called *syakfdo*, in which various metals are partly blended, partly combined, producing an effect much resembling fine enamel. **1911** *Encycl. Brit.* XV. 179/2 To apply a lining of silver to a shakudo box. **1981** G. MACBETH *Kind of Treason* ix. 91 The little black cups of the *nanako* on the *shakudo* grounds.

‖ **shakuhachi** (ʃa:*ku*ha·tʃ*i*). [Jap., f. *SHAKU + *hachi* eight (tenths).] An end-blown Japanese flute, made of bamboo.

1893 F. T. PIGGOTT *Music & Musical Instruments of Japan* I. 43 The Shakuhachi, introduced into Japan from China by Prince Tsuneyoshi as far back as..1335, seems to have been treated from the first as a solo instrument. **1949** *Western Folklore* July 202 Their melodies are found to be very pleasing, especially if the *shakuhachi*, or bamboo flute, is used as accompaniment. **1965** W. SWAAN *Jap. Lantern* ii. 22 Two itinerant beggar-priests playing the shakuhachi, an archaic type of bamboo flute. **1981** *Daily Tel.* 17 Mar. 11/7 The first half was devoted to traditional pieces, performed on the shakuhachi, a simple bamboo flute.

shaky, *a.* Add: **2. b.** *the Shaky Isles* (colloq.), New Zealand (from the frequency of earthquakes).

1933 *Bulletin* (Sydney) 2 Aug. 20/2 The widespread notion that they're peculiar to the Shaky Isles. **1941** S. J. BAKER *N.Z. Slang* vi. 49 New Zealand was no longer merely a colony; it became *the Dominion, the Shakey Isles*, ..and so on. **1971** *Sunday Tel.* (Sydney) 16 May 37/2 He came over from the Shaky Isles in his early 30s.

5. e. *shaky do* [*DO *sb.*[1] 2 b], a difficult or risky situation, a close shave. *slang* (orig. *R.A.F.*).

1942 T. RATTIGAN *Flare Path* III. 150 They had rather a shaky do last night. **1943** C. H. WARD-JACKSON *It's a Piece of Cake* 54 *A shaky-do*, any occurrence that has serious consequences or just escapes them. This may vary from a pilot temporarily losing control of his Whitley as a result of being hit by flak, to an erk who is out of station bounds without a pass and only just avoids a Service policeman. **1944** T. H. WISDOM *Triumph over Tunisia* ix. 79 No. 18 Squadron, which had been involved in many similar 'Shaky do's', was asked to lay on the raid. **1949** F. MACLEAN *Eastern Approaches* II. vi. 244 The earth all round was kicked up by a burst from the plane's tail-gunner... 'This,' said the Australian, 'is going to be a shaky do.'

shale, *sb.*[2] Add: **2. b. shale oil** (further examples); **shale shaker,** a vibrating screen used in oil and gas drilling to remove drill cuttings from the circulating drilling mud that is passed through it.

1945 HEALD & AYRES in L. M. Fanning *Our Oil Resources* vi. 185 Crude shale oil is produced from oil shale by retorting. **1976** *Time* 20 Dec. 41/1 Prices for getting shale oil or using wet-steam deposits in the earth to generate electricity are also far from commercially acceptable. **1959** *Petroleum Handbk.* (Shell) (ed. 4) 85 On reaching the well head it is diverted via a horizontal flow line to a vibrating screen or 'shale shaker'. **1974** G. S. ORMSBY in P. L. Moore et al. *Drilling Practices Manual* vi. 152 The term 'shale shaker' is used in drilling mud work to cover all the devices that in another industry might be differentiated as 'shaking' screen, 'vibrating screens', and 'oscillating screens'.

shaler, var. *SHEILA.

shall, *v.* Add: **II.** ***The past tense* should *with temporal function.*

14. d. Also in noun-clause dependent on expressions of willing, etc., (esp. the verb *want*) in the pres. tense. *colloq.* (orig. and chiefly *U.S.* and in representations of Jewish speech).

1852, 1903 [see WANT *v.* 5 b]. **1920** W. D. HOWELLS *Vacation of Kelwyns* 188 Want I should drive ye home? **1960** F. RAPHAEL *Limits of Love* 3 You want we should go bankrupt? **1970** R. MILLAR *Abelard & Heloise* I. iii. 11 He asks you should go to him. **1978** J. ROSENTHAL *Evacuees* iv. 89 They want they should take you away.

17. (Later example).

1945 R. GIBBINGS *Lovely is Lee* xxvii. 133 On the 23rd of March 1889 who should be born in Cork but myself?

****The past tense* should *with modal function.*

18. a. Also, in statements of expectation, likelihood, prediction, etc.

1922 GALSWORTHY *Loyalties* III. i. 82 'Mr. Twisden's not in, then?'..'No. He's at the Courts. They're just up; he should be in directly.' **1954** WODEHOUSE & BOLTON *Bring on Girls* viii. 101 'It will run a bit short, I suppose, but it should have a wide appeal.' 'Very wide,' said Guy. 'You've got a winner.' **1961** E. F. SCHUMACHER in *Small* *is Beautiful* (1973) II. iii. 117 Proved oil reserves should be enough for forty years. **1963** 'J. LE CARRÉ' *Spy who came in from Cold* x. 94 A couple of weeks should see you through. **1966** T. FRISBY *There's a Girl in my Soup* I. 2 That blanket should be warm by now. **1970** R. MILLAR *Abelard & Heloise* I. ii. 27 A makeshift effort, but it should serve. *Ibid.* xiv. 35 Master Simon says he should be up in a week.

Phrase. *this is as it should be.*

1829 CARLYLE in *Edin. Rev.* June 458 This is as it should be; for not in turning back,..but only in resolutely struggling forward, does our life consist. **1860** J. W. PALMER tr. *M. J. Michelet's Love* IV. i. 184 The mother lives entirely in that cradle; the world is as nothing to her. This is as it should be, for it is the saving of the babe.

b. Delete ? *Obs.* and add further examples. Also, ought according to expectation to be, presumably will be (cf. sense *18 a).

1821 BYRON *Cain* I. i. 365, I have heard it said, That seraphs *love most*—cherubim *know most*—And this should be a cherub—since he loves not. **1855** KINGSLEY *Westw. Ho!* II. ix. 249 That should be Barbados..unless my reckoning is far out.

c. (Earlier and later examples.)

1811 LADY GRANVILLE *Let.* 6 Oct. (1894) I. 21 You should have heard the shout when he said by mistake, [etc.]. **1908** BELLOC *Cautionary Tales for Children* 26 That Night a Fire *did* break out—You should have heard Matilda Shout! **1971** S. GRAY *Butley* II. 58 But you should see our flat. Even Joey's room is like a pigsty.

d. Used ironically, expressing the inappropriateness or unlikeliness of the action advocated or state envisaged, as *I should worry*, there is no reason for me to worry, I am not worried. *colloq.* (orig. a Yiddishism).

1892 KIPLING *Naulakha* xiii. 154 [Amer. loq.] I should murmur!.. It makes me feel good all over. **1906** F. H. BURNETT *Shuttle* (1907) xxxviii. 381 'Hope you had a fine time, Mr. Selden?' 'Fine! I should smile! Fine wasn't in it.' **1914** 'HIGH JINKS JR.' *Choice Slang* 13 *I should worry*, I do not care. **1929** 'E. QUEEN' *Roman Hat Myst.* vi. 80 'Well,' grinned the District Attorney, 'I carry a lot of insurance, so I should worry.' **1937** D. L. SAYERS *Busman's Honeymoon* x. 224 'You watch your step, Polly. Maybe 'e's married three times a'ready.' 'I *should* worry,' said the girl, with a toss of the head. **1945** A. KOBER *Parm Me* 155 'The cilling you think he's going to fix?' 'You should live so long!' he'll say. **1957** *N.Y. World-Telegram* 13 Sept. 22/5 All I ask of these scientists is that they put in writing their guarantee that insects will get us yet. We should be so lucky. **1967** V. C. WELBURN *Johnny So Long* II. iii. 76 Don't try to digest everything at once. Hell, I should talk. **1970** M. O'BRINE *Crambo* lxiii. 170 If that's the best their gunners can do, we should worry. *Ibid.* lvii. 230 'It's your life,' said Waterhouse. 'I should live that long,' said Gesing. **1975** R. RENDELL *Shake Hands for Ever* iii. 29 They both came in at about ten—my God, I should be so lucky!

shallot, shalot. **2.** Delete † *Obs.* and add later examples.

1938 *Oxf. Compan. Mus.* 658/1 A certain number [*sc.* of organ pipes] have a tongue of metal like that of a toy trumpet, vibrating against the open (or partially open) side of a little brass tube (called *eschallot* or *shallot*) at the bottom of the pipe.., and these are called *Reed Stops*. **1969** J. CURNUTT tr. *Andersen's Organ Building & Design* iii. 51 The *shallot*..consists of a tube which is closed at the lower end and planed flat on one side so that a throat-shaped opening is produced.

shallow, *a.*[1] and *sb.*[3] Add: **A.** *adj.* **1. a.** *shallow end*, spec. of a swimming-pool; also *fig.*; *shallow well*, a well that is not deep; *spec.* (see quot. 1972[2]).

1877 J. T. FANNING *Practical Treat. Water Supply Engin.* I. vii. 104 Shallow well and spring supplies are, usually, yields of water from the drift formation alone. **1924** 'I. HAY' (*title*) The shallow end. **1929** R. HUGHES *High Wind in Jamaica* i. 9 The little ones, of course, only splashed about the shallow end: but John and Emily dived. **1943** *Bull. Amer. Assoc. Petroleum Geologists* XXVII. 838 Of the shallow wells drilled for gas, 80 per cent were producers and 20 per cent were dry. **1959** ACKERMAN & LÖF *Technol. in Amer. Water Development* x. 281 The first irrigation was from shallow wells within the suction lift of centrifugal and piston pumps. **1972** J. ROSSITER *Rope for General Dietz* vi. 78 She broke away, swimming to the shallow end and climbing out. **1972** *Gloss. Geol.* (Amer. Geol. Inst.) 650/2 *Shallow well.* (a) A water well..that taps the shallowest aquifer in the vicinity. The water is generally unconfined ground water. (b) A well whose water level is shallow enough to permit use of a shallow-well (suction) pump, the practical lift of which is taken as 22 ft.

shallow, *a.*[2] (Earlier example.)

1839 H. BRANDON in W. A. Miles *Poverty, Mendicity & Crime* 165/1 *Shallow Coves*, or *Shallow Fellows*,—fellows who go about the country, half-naked, with a Guernsey jacket, but no hat, shoes, nor stockings.

shalloway (ʃæ·lowē[i]). *Canad. Obs.* exc. *Hist.* [Origin unknown.] A small coastal sailing craft.

1676 in D. W. Prowse *Hist. Newfoundland from Eng., Colonial, & Foreign Rec.* (1895) viii. 206 No Indians come [to Placentia] but some Canida Indians from forts of Canida in french shalloways. **1774** G. CARTWRIGHT *Jrnl. Residence Coast of Labrador* (1792) II. 14 Hooper's shalloway having sprung her foremast,..I sent the boat-builder to make her a new one. **1971** E. R. SEARY *Place Names* v. 86 The fishing boats in the cod and seal fishery were formerly called shallops and shalloways... The shalloways were open boats, what are now called punts.

shallow-pate. Add: Now *arch.* (Further examples.)

1930 [see *DOWD *sb.*[1]]. **1964** *Listener* 24 Dec. 1002/1 That complicated shallow-pate, Jean-Paul Sartre,.. makes of his subjective and personal passions a sort of objective truth.

‖ **shalom** (ʃalǫ·m), *int.* and *sb.* [Heb., lit. 'peace'.] In Jewish society, a word used as a salutation at meeting or parting. See also *Shabbat shalom* s.v. *SHABBAT. So **shalom aleichem** (alē[i]χe·m) *int.* [Heb. *'[a]lêkem*], peace be with you.

1881 E. B. TYLOR *Anthropology* i. 11 The Arab still salutes the stranger with *salâm alaikum*, 'peace upon you', nearly as the ancient Hebrew would have said shâlôm lâchem, that is, 'peace to you'. **1898** I. ZANGWILL *Dreamers of Ghetto* p. vi, I saw two Jews that met by chance... *Shalom Aleichem*, mournfully each said. **1959** I. JEFFERIES *Thirteen Days* iv. 49 Shalom. Cigarette, Sarge? **1962** L. R. BANKS *End to Running* II. xiii. 265 There would be cries of 'Shalom, Shalom! Come in! Have a drink!' **1972** O. SELA *Bearer Plot* xxxix. 219 With a whispered '*Shalom*' she was gone. **1977** *Rolling Stone* 19 May 6/4, I was ready to say goodbye America, shalom Israel.

‖ **shalwar** (ʃɒ·lvār). Also **salvar, salwar, shalvar.** [Urdu *šalwār*, Hindi *salvār*, ad. Pers. *šalwār* SHULWAR.] **a.** Loose trousers worn by both sexes in some South Asian countries, esp. those worn by women together with a *kameez*.

1951 P. MILES *They came to Mountain* ix. 91 Over her *salvar* she wore stockings tied up with bootlaces. **1955** R. PRAWER JHABVALA *To whom she Will* xv. 102 She was very fine now in a pink silk kamiz with blue roses on it and a pink salwar. *Ibid.* 295 The salwar is 104 inches wide at the waist and tied with a cord: when the cord is pulled the material falls in a bunch of folds over the stomach. The legs taper towards the ankles. **1957** *Geogr. Mag.* Aug. 198/1 A sophisticated taste will prefer the fashions of Paris and Bombay to the unbecoming *qamis* and *shalwar* of the North. **1967** *Times* 28 Sept. 2 (*caption*) Muslim children wearing their traditional baggy trousers outside Moat Girls' School, Leicester, yesterday. The shalwars will be allowed by the education authority on religious grounds. **1972** H. R. F. KEATING *Inspector Ghote trusts Heart* iii. 34 She was wearing not a sari but a bright, cherry-red kameez and salwar. **1973** *Observer* (Colour Suppl.) 28 Oct. 72/1 Semi-transparent trousers (shalvar) approx £30.

b. *Comb.*, as **shalwar-, salwar-kameez(e** [see *KAMEEZ(E], a woman's outfit consisting of *shalwar* and *kameez* or loose tunic.

1955 R. PRAWER JHABVALA *To whom she Will* xxx. 222 A lively sturdy girl in coloured salwar-kamiz. **1966** J. & R. GODDEN *Two under Indian Sun* iv. 104 She in salwar-kameeze, the loose tunic and trousers..worn by Muslim and up-country girls. **1977** A. DESAI *Fire on Mountain* III. xi. 136 A bunch of schoolgirls in bright indigo *salwar-kameez*.

sham, *sb.*[1] and *a.* Add: **A.** *sb.* **3. c.** (Earlier example.)

1884 *Cottage Hearth* (Boston) Aug. 254/1 Large shams made of four very small handkerchiefs..are elegant in appearance over blue or pink under covers.

B. *adj.* **1. b.** *sham operation* (Biol.), an operation in which an incision is made but nothing is removed, performed on animals of an experimental control group so that they suffer the same incidental effects of the operation as the animals on which a true operation is performed. Hence *sham-o·perate* vb. trans., to perform a sham operation on; *sham-o·perated* ppl. adj.

1963 *Life Sci.* II. 475 Rats..were thymectomized within the first eighteen hours after birth. Approximately half of the litters were sham-operated. The polyoma virus was injected subcutaneously either immediately after thymectomy or sham-operation or two to three weeks afterwards. *Ibid.* 477 Rats thymectomized at birth seem to be much more sensitive to the oncogenic action of the polyoma virus than are normal or sham-operated rats. **1970** *Physiol. Zool.* XLIII. 91/1 Matched animals in an approximately 1:1 ratio were 'parietalectomized'..or sham-operated according to standard procedures. **1975** *Nature* 27 Mar. 349/1 Pinealectomy and sham operation were performed as described previously, and 10 d later a 2-mm semicircular wound was made in the right ear of each animal, including the controls. *Ibid.* 349/2 The result indicated that control, sham-operated, and melatonin-treated animals form one group.

5. *sham-dead, -Tudor.*

1934 *Discovery* Oct. 304/1 It cannot be long before the incongruity of the sham-Tudor house with the 1934 interior is generally recognised. **1945** [see *JACOBETHAN *a.*]. **1970** T. HUGHES *Crow* 53 So in one hand he held a sham-dead spider.

shama, var. *SHAMMA.

shamal. Add: Also **shamaal, shemmal.**

1900 S. M. ZWEMER *Arabia* x. 107 The prevailing wind at Bahrein..is the *shemmāl* or Northwester. **1980** D. CREED *Scarab* xiii. 129 The Shamaal blows strong from the north.

shaman, *sb.* (and *a.*) Add: **A.** *sb.* Delete † from sense 'an adherent of Shamanism' and add later example. Also more recently, with recognition of the widespread similarity of primitive beliefs, the term denotes esp. a man or woman who is regarded as having direct access to, and influence in, the spirit world which is usu. manifested during a trance and empowers them to guide souls, cure illnesses, etc. Also *fig.* Hence **sha·manka, sha·maness, sha·manin,** terms sometimes applied to a female shaman.

1921 R. H. LOWIE *Primitive Society* xii. 328 It was indeed through the shaman, who revealed the will of the spirits, that the chief was chosen. **1925** G. RÓHEIM *Austral. Totemism* vii. 350 This rite..is based on the scheme of death and rebirth and..the vocation of a shaman is often chosen at puberty. **1936** *Jrnl. R. Anthropol. Inst.* LXVI. 80 The term *shamanka* is used by travellers and anthropologists for all female shamans. This usage is unscientific and misleading... For the sake of convenience, however, I shall follow current usage. **1938** in F. Boas *Gen. Anthropol.* ix. 469 Because the North Californian woman happens to be a shaman does not mean that she treats her family and friends differently. **1952** KOESTLER *Arrow in Blue* xiii. 106 Vladimir Jabotinsky..became the first political shaman in my life. **1955** H. V. ELWIN *Relig. Indian Tribe* v. 146 A shamanin who has done the wrong things is regarded rather as a nun who has broken her vows. **1964** W. R. TRASK tr. *Eliade's Shamanism* i. 4 The shaman is also a magician and medicine man... But beyond this, he is a psychopomp, and he may also be priest, mystic, and poet. *Ibid.*, Through this whole region in which the ecstatic experience is considered the religious experience par excellence, the shaman, and he alone, is the great master of ecstasy. *Ibid.* vii. 241 A shamaness..resolves to bring back his soul and goes down to the 'world of the dead'. **1968** N. K. SANDARS *Prehist. Art of Europe* i. 26 In Siberia there were also women who were shamankas. **1971** I. M. LEWIS *Ecstatic Relig.* ii. 56 We are perfectly justified in applying the term shaman to mean..a 'master of spirits'. **1971** *Times Lit. Suppl.* 19 Nov. 1453/3 The Maori shaman clasps in his arms the tree on which his people rely for food, clothing, shelter and transport. **1972** P. M. BARTZ *South Korea* 42/1 Primitive spirit worship (shamanism) was followed by Buddhism... Today, there are said to be 27,000 shamans, 10,000 of them women. **1977** D. R. McCANN *Black Crane* p. i, These oracles to *Chesŏk*..were recited by a *mudang*, or shamaness. **1979** *London Rev. Bks.* 25 Oct. 1/1 America lacks this type of magician—the shamans there are grander, more worldly, more pretentious.

shamanic, *a.* Add: Also, of or connected with a shaman.

1964 *Listener* 29 Oct. 677/2 The initiation dreams, the general schema of shamanic flight..are not a shaman monopoly.

shamanism. Add: Also the beliefs, rituals, techniques, etc., associated with a shaman, the general pattern of which is found almost universally in primitive cultures at the food-gathering stage of social development.

1930 G. RÓHEIM *Animism, Magic, & Divine King* III. iv. 166 The sexual organs play a large part in Chukchee shamanism. **1947** H. C. E. ZACHARIAS *Protohistory* iv. 109 Shamanism..by which term I mean not merely the forms of hysteria and of falling into a trance. **1963** in H. N. Michael *Stud. in Siberian Shamanism* 120 Evenk shamanism was characterized by such phenomena as..a special shamanistic language, numerous and extremely effective pieces of equipment, [etc.]. **1964** W. R. TRASK tr. *Eliade's Shamanism* i. 4 A first definition of this complex phenomenon, and perhaps the least hazardous, will be: shamanism = *technique of ecstasy*. **1972** G. JONES *Kings, Beasts, & Heroes* III. i. 129 They nourished him with foaming hornfuls drawn from the deep casks of wonder, myth, shamanism, make-believe, wish-fulfilment, unreason.

shamanize *v.*, *intr.*: hence **sha·manizing** *vbl. sb.* and *ppl. a.*

1949 W. HOWELLS *Heathens* viii. 126 Evans-Pritchard has the same thing to say about Zande witch doctors, who do shamanizing of a less distinct type. **1963** in H. N. Michael *Stud. in Siberian Shamanism* 8 The people were beating the drum ('shamanizing'). **1964** *Listener* 29 Oct. 677/2 The vital function shamanizing can take on..may be seen in the *Bardo Thodol*, the Tibetan 'Book of the Dead'. *Ibid.*, In a shamanizing society, 'Venus and Adonis'.., 'The Wanderings of Oisin', 'Ash Wednesday', would all qualify their authors for the magic drum.

shamas(h (ʃa·məs). Also **shammas(h, shammes, shammos,** etc. Pl. **-im.** [Yiddish *shames*, Heb. *šammāš* attendant, f. *šimmēš* to serve.] **1.** A beadle or sexton in a Jewish synagogue.

1650 [see *CHAZZAN]. **1675** L. ADDISON *Present State of Jews* xi. 90 First the Summas, or Sacristan. **1862** *Once a Week* VII. 191/2 The shamas, a kind of curate and clerk combined, brings a glass of wine. **1892** I. ZANGWILL *Childr. Ghetto* I. 6 Many of the worshippers were tempted to give beyond their means for fear of losing the esteem of the *Shammos*, or beadle, a potent personage only next in influence to the President. **1896** I. ABRAHAMS *Jewish Life Mid. Ages* 8 It was an ancient custom in several places for the Shamash or verger to announce every Saturday the result of law-suits, and to inform the congregation that certain properties were on the market. **1903** *Standard* 27 Apr., There is a 'shammas' acting as beadle, door-keeper, collector, cook, and utility-man in emergencies. **1909** *Cent. Dict.* Suppl., Shammash. **1946** KOESTLER *Thieves in Night* 288 It was opened by the *shamash* or door-keeper. **1960** L. P. GARTNER *Jewish Immigrant in England 1870–1914* vii. 189 The observant immigrant in the East End..could not look to..the rabbi nor to the more commonplace *shammash* (sexton) for edification. **1967** C. POTOK *Chosen* i. 27 You should see his father. He's one of Reb Saunders' shamashim. **1968** L. ROSTEN *Joys of Yiddish* 329 The visiting rabbi stopped in the middle of his sermon and signaled to the *shammes.* **1973** *Jewish Chron.* 2 Feb. 26/2 The death of Mr Harry Goldman in his 74th year has cast a shadow over the members of the Singers Hill Synagogue, where he served as shammas for 40 years. **1976** *New Yorker* 29 Mar. 64/2 The divinely inspired shammes, or custodian, of the synagogue.

2. An extra candle used for lighting the Chanukah candles.

1961 in WEBSTER. **1976** Y. L. BIALER *Jewish Life* 161 The Hanukkah lights are..not to be used for ordinary purposes... Alongside each Hanukkah lamp the sages instituted the use of a special candle for normal household purposes, calling it the 'caretaker' (*shamash*).

shamateur (ʃæ·mătəɹ, ʃæmătə̄·ɹ). [f. SHAM *a.* + AM)ATEUR.] A sportsman who is classed as an amateur but behaves like a professional, esp. one who makes money out of his performances.

1896 *Badminton Mag.* II. 533 For frank and open professionalism there may be a good deal to be said, but nothing can make the 'promateur' and the 'shamateur' attractive. **1928** *Sunday Dispatch* 8 July 22/3 The Football Association do not regard their clean-up of non-professional Soccer as completed by the sensational exposure and punishment of four hundred 'shamateurs' and their accomplices in the North. **1955** T. H. PEAR *Eng. Social Differences* 247 An Oxbridge college which trained its 'eight' so rigidly that they did not take a reasonable part in university life, was criticised as exposing the University to the suspicion of encouraging 'shamateurs'. **1962** *Punch* 18 Apr. 627/2 The bitchery of high shamateur tennis. **1973** RIESSEN & EVANS *Match Point* I. x. facing p. 92 (*caption*) It was hard work being a 'shamateur'—lugging all that booty around.

Hence **sha·mateurism.**

1928 *Sat. Rev.* 4 Feb. 126 Where the interests of amphitheatre and arena come first, 'shamateurism' must pass eventually into an honest professionalism. **1964** *Punch* 6 May 668/1 Shamateurism has grown steadily in lawn tennis. **1979** *Financial Rev.* (Sydney) 27 Aug. 25/2 Shamateurism is common enough and their activities probably do not inflict any real damage.

shamba. Add: Also, a farm or plantation.

1942 *E. Afr. Ann. 1941–2* 17/2 They are to be found in every kind of work..from shamba labourer to school teacher. **1952** *Chambers's Jrnl.* Apr. 247/1 There would be rain soon and the ground must be ready for planting before it came. There were two shambas to be cultivated, one for millet and one for beans. **1973** *Reader's Digest* Feb. 200/1 Most Kenyans, for example, have *shambas* (small farms) back in their tribal homelands. **1980** *Times* 23 Feb. 6/2 Jos had pegged out several acres to turn into a coffee shamba.

shamble, *sb.*[1] Add: **5. b.** *pl.* In more general use, a scene of disorder or devastation; a ruin; a mess. orig. *U.S.*

1926 P. H. DE KRUIF *Microbe Hunters* III. iv. 83 Once more his laboratory became a shambles of cluttered flasks and hurrying assistants. **1942** E. WAUGH *Put out More Flags* ii. 150 Alastair learned, too, that all schemes ended in a 'shambles' which did not mean, as he feared, a slaughter, but a brief restoration of individual freedom of movement. **1966** M. R. D. FOOT *SOE in France* viii. 184 Helped the commandos to make a thorough shambles of the main dockyard. **1979** *Daily Tel.* 5 Sept. 6/6 Haiti remains a dictatorship, its economy in a shambles.

shambled, *ppl. a.* Add: **2.** *U.S.* Wrecked, ruined. Cf. *SHAMBLE *sb.*[1] 5 b.

1940 *Newsweek* 17 June 21/2 (*caption*) Nazis photographed the shambled Dunkerque's water front. **1952** *Time* 11 Aug. 25/1 (*caption*) Reconstruction of the shambled town..is expected to take at least five years.

shambolic (ʃæmbǫ·lik), *a. colloq.* [f. *SHAMBLE *sb.*[1] 5 b, perh. after SYMBOLIC *a.*] Chaotic, disorderly, undisciplined.

Reported to be 'in common use' in 1958.—Ed.

1970 *Times* 18 June 9 His office in Printing House Square is so impeccably tidy that it is..a standing reproach to the standard image of shambolic newspaper offices. **1975** *Times* 14 June 8/5 The average listener is in the position of anybody who encounters an organization at work for the first time. It may appear shambolic but how much is that because he hasn't yet made sense of it. **1978** R. JANSSON *News Caper* xiii. 110 We may have a shambolic landing, Jean. I want you to go right through the aircraft reminding people about the emergency drill. **1980** *Jrnl. R. Soc. Arts* July 509/1 It will continue in a much more shambolic manner than the urbanization that has occurred in the Western World.

shame, *sb.* Add: **I. 7.** (Later example.)

1922 JOYCE *Ulysses* 533 And with loving pencil you shaded my eyes, my bosom and my shame.

II. 16. a. (*d*) Also, in S. Afr., as an expression of sympathy or pleasure.

1932 *Grocott's Mail* (Grahamstown, S. Afr.) 9 Jan. 3 During the address of our local dairy representatives..I heard several murmurs of Oh! and Shame! and grant the statements were given in a manner that commanded much sympathy. **1952** N. GORDIMER *Soft Voice of Serpent* (1953) i. 6 'Shame, isn't he a funny old man,' she said. **1976** *Sunday Times* (Johannesburg) 14 Nov., Oh, look, look!..those foals. Oh, shame, aren't they sweet.

III. 17. (sense 7) *shame-cloth, -rag; shame-closing, -making, -wounded* adjs.; **shame culture,** a culture in which conformity of behaviour is maintained through the individual's fear of being shamed.

1922 JOYCE *Ulysses* 55 She blinked up out of her avid shameclosing eyes. **1963** M. LAURENCE *Tomorrow-Tamer* 226 Not yet five years old, she wore only a shamecloth, a mere flutter of red and beaded rag around her middle and between her legs. **1947** R. BENEDICT *Chrysanthemum & Sword* x. 223 True shame cultures rely on external sanctions for good behaviour. **1953** M. B. SINGER in Piers & Singer *Shame & Guilt* II. iii. 56, I shall consider whether the test data support the conclusion that American Indian cultures are predominantly shame cultures. **1977** A. GIDDENS *Stud. in Social & Polit. Theory* 393 Some anthropologists have sought to contrast the 'guilt cultures' of Western Europe with 'shame cultures'. **1934** R. MACAULAY *Going Abroad* xxxv. 297 He adoring some one else, that was shame-making and humbling too. **1977** D. RAMSAY *You can't call it Murder* I. 26 Nothing to do with her, thank God. Offering such thanks was shame-making. **1938** R. GRAVES *Coll. Poems* 166 Those froward hermits..Wore but a shame-rag, dusk or dawn, And rolled in thorny places. **1922** JOYCE *Ulysses* 49 Our souls, shamewounded by our sins, cling to us yet more.

shamedly, *adv.* For *nonce-wd.* read *rare* and add later example.

1913 D. H. LAWRENCE *Sons & Lovers* x. 260 Then she herself took her place on the sofa, shamedly.

shaming, *ppl. a.* Add: Hence **sha·mingly** *adv.*

1970 D. NEVILLE-ROLFE *Power without Glory* II. 247 Shorthand and typing... I originally took a shamingly long time to learn both. **1979** *Homes & Gardens* June 169/1 Eventually my bus arrived; a collection of shamingly healthy-looking people in breeches and clumpy boots gathered round.

shamisen, var. SAMISEN in Dict. and Suppl.

‖**shamma** (ʃæ·mă). Also **chamma, shama.** [Amharic.] A long loose robe resembling a toga, worn by both men and women in Ethiopia.

1862 H. A. STERN *Wanderings among Falashas in Abyssinia* xxi. 311 The costume of the Abyssinian is exceedingly simple. Men of all ranks..wear a *shama,* or loose dress of white cotton. **1893** J. T. BENT *Sacred City of Ethiopians* ii. 35 A young stripling in cotton drawers and the red-striped *shamma* of everyday wear. **1930** H. NORDEN *Africa's Last Empire* iii. 62 She was swathed in the usual *chamma.* **1969** *Daily Tel.* 18 Oct. 10/8 The streets are full of the gentle flutter of the white muslin *shammas* worn by the shy, slim Ethiopian women.

Shammar (ʃæ·māɹ). [Native name.] (A member of) a bedouin tribe originating in the Nafud desert of Saudi Arabia. Also *attrib.* or as *adj.*

1911 G. BELL *Let.* 14 Apr. (1927) I. xii. 300 Now the Shammar are *Beda*; only the Shammar and the Anazeh are real Bedawin, the others are just Arabs. **1916** T. E. LAWRENCE *Home Lett.* (1954) 311 There is a very heady old Shammar, and an Aneyze. **1929** F. STARK *Let.* 24 Nov. (1974) I. 215 He..has now suggested a visit to one of the Shammar chiefs up the Tigris. **1959** W. THESIGER *Arabian Sands* iii. 54 In Syria I had seen the Shammar migrating, a whole people on the move, covering the desert with their herds.

shammas(h, shammes, -os, vars. *SHAMAS(H.

shampoo, *sb.* Add: **1.** (Later examples in sense *2 b of the vb.)

1951 *Good Housek. Home Encycl.* 172/1 Soiled silk lampshades can be given a soap-and-water shampoo. **1970** *Which?* Aug. 251/2 Which carpet shampoo you choose depends on how much carpet you have to clean and how often you want to clean it.

2. *shampoo and set* (cf. *SET *sb.*[1] 18 b).

1935 A. CHRISTIE *Death in Clouds* xiii. 136 Is it a shampoo and set, or are you having a tint to-day? **1977** *Belfast Tel.* 22 Feb. 1/4 Customers will have to shell out an extra 10–15 pc for a snip of the scissors or a shampoo and set in many cases.

3. *slang.* Arbitrary alteration of CHAMPAGNE. Cf. SHAM *sb.*[2]

1957 R. LONGRIGG *Switchboard* 192 'You'd better have some shampoo, darling.'..'Shampoo?' 'Champagne.' **1959** A. SINCLAIR *Breaking of Bumbo* ii. 31 The waiter brings a bottle of champagne... Shampoo, Sheila dear?

shampoo, *v.* Add: **2. a.** Also *absol.*

1976 *Glasgow Herald* 26 Nov. 17/4 This conditioning treatment is used before you shampoo, and so resembles the sort of reconditioning treatments available at a salon.

b. *transf.* To wash (a carpet, upholstery, etc.) with a cleansing agent. Also *absol.*

1954 A. C. MOORE *How to clean Everything* I. 138/1 Synthetic (soapless) detergents..are available in liquid, paste and powder form to shampoo hair, rugs and upholstery. **1969** *Sears Catal.* Spring/Summer 1359 Outdoor carpets... They'll take whatever comes in stride..resist spots, stains..just vacuum or shampoo clean. **1970** *Which?* Aug. 252/1 If you are going to shampoo your carpet only now and then..a cheap aerosol would be most economical.

shampooer. Add: **b.** A device for applying carpet shampoo.

1960 *Farmer & Stockbreeder* 22 Mar. (Suppl.) 11/2 The new mechanical shampooers simplify the job greatly. **1974** *Spartanburg* (S. Carolina) *Herald* 25 Apr. A5 (Advt.), Rent a twin brush carpet shampooer.

shamshin, var. SAMISEN in Dict. and Suppl.

shamus (ʃā·mǝ̆s, ʃēⁱ·mǝ̆s). *U.S. slang.* Also **sharmus, shommus.** [Orig. uncertain: perh. f. *SHAMAS(H or the Irish proper name *Seamus.*] A police officer; a private detective.

1925 H. LEVERAGE *Dict. Underworld* in *Flynn's Mag.* 28 Mar. 660 *Sharmus,* a detective; a cop. **1928** J. O'CONNOR *Broadway Racketeers* xvii. 186 Every Shommus on the beat knew we were going South with the stuff, but they couldn't prove it. **1930** [see *KOSHER *a.* (*sb.*) c]. **1950** 'S. RANSOME' *Deadly Miss Ashley* ii. 19 Men in my profession don't call each other shamuses... We private operatives call ourselves private operatives. **1960** WODEHOUSE *Jeeves in Offing* iv. 49 You mean that I'm to be a sort of private eye or shamus, tailing them up? **1977** *New Yorker* 2 May 38/3, I think my wife is having me tailed by a private shamus.

Shamvaian (ʃæmvai·ăn), *a. Geol.* [f. *Shamva* + -IAN.] Of or pertaining to rocks in the vicinity of Shamva, a town in northern Zimbabwe; *spec.* the epithet of a Pre-Cambrian mountain-building episode in southern Africa when these were affected.

1947 A. M. MACGREGOR in *Bull. S. Rhodesian Geol. Surv.* No. 38. 8 Although the Shamva Grits of the Mazoe Valley were not the first to be described they occupy the largest continuous area... The name 'Shamvaian' is proposed. *Ibid.* 15 The Shamvaian rocks of the Bembesi valley are generally similar to the upper series at Que Que. **1951** *Trans. Geol. Soc. S. Afr.* LIV. p. xxix, The largest area of these rocks..is that of the Shamva grits in the Mazoe Valley which is selected as the type area of the Shamvaian system. **1964** A. E. PHAUP in S. H. Haughton *Geol. Ore Deposits S. Afr.* II. 2 Some reefs may be pre-Bulawayan and pre-Shamvaian in age, but the majority are post-Shamvaian. **1971** I. G. GASS et al. *Understanding Earth* xxii. 317/1 At least seven major mountain-building events (periods of orogenesis) are recorded in Africa and are..(ii) 2500–2800 million years ago (Shamvaian orogeny); [etc.].

Shan (ʃān), *sb.*[4] and *a.*[2] Also **Sciam, Shaan.** [Burmese.] **A.** *sb.* (A member of) a group of Mongoloid peoples of the Tai family, inhabiting parts of Burma, south China, and Indo-China. Also, the Tai language spoken by these peoples. **B.** *adj.* Of or pertaining to the Shan or their language.

1800 M. SYMES *Acc. Embassy Ava* xi. 274 An intelligent man..informed him, that..the first Shaan town was called Thangdat. *Ibid.*, Shaan, or Shan, is a very comprehensive term given to different nations, some independent, others the subjects of the greater states. **1833** W. TANDY tr. *Sangermano's Descr. Burmese Empire* ix. 57 The zaboà or petty princes of the Sciam, subject to the Burmese. **1898** [see *LOLO]. **1920** *Blackw. Mag.* June 839/1 You sell liquor and opium to Burmans and Shans. **1927** *Ibid.* June 819/1 Men armed with..long Shan knives were patrolling the approaches. **1951** R. FIRTH *Elem. Social Organiz.* iv. 145 The Pai of the Chinese Shans; the *anga* of the Tikopia..are..examples of the allocation of large-scale resources in goods and labour with primary reference to status yields. **1968** O. WYND *Sumatra Seven Zero* ii. 25 Your companion knows Shan. She learned it to pass the time. **1977** *Whitaker's Almanack 1978* 828 Burmese is the official language, but minority languages include Shan, Karen, Chin, and the various Kachin dialects.

shananacking, var. *SHENANIGAN.

shandite (ʃæ·ndəit). *Min.* [ad. G. *shandit* (P. Ramdohr in *Sitzungsber. d. Deutsch. Akad. d. Wissensch. zu Berlin* (*Math.-naturwissensch. Kl.*) *1949* (1950) VI. 26), f. the name of S. J. Shand (1882–1957), Scottish geologist: see -ITE[1].] A sulphide of nickel and lead, $Ni_3Pb_2S_2$, found as yellow rhombohedral crystals.

1950 *Amer. Mineralogist* XXXV. 450 On receiving this result Dr. Ramdohr intimated in a private communication (Nov., 1949) that he proposed to name the new mineral shandite, after Professor S. J. Shand,..who had suggested..the study of the Insizwa nickel ores which led to the discovery of parkerite. *Ibid.*, Two lots of artificial shandite were prepared by fusing charges of 1 gm. and 2 gm. of the powdered elements in the proportions 3Ni:2Bi:2S. **1968** I. KOSTOV *Mineralogy* 117 Shandite has a distorted spinel structure, the nickel atoms being arranged along the pseudocubic diagonals; this explains its ferromagnetic properties.

shandy, *sb.* Add: (Later examples.) Also, a mixture of beer and fizzy lemonade.

1919 *Chambers's Jrnl.* Sept. 593/1 Staff-Sergeant Jack Dorley, R.E., finished off his shandy with a long draught. **1947** K. TENNANT *Lost Haven* xvii. 267 Miss O'Shea was drinking ginger-beer and her escort had a shandy. **1969** A. CHRISTIE *Hallowe'en Party* v. 39 For me, I think a shandy. The ginger beer and the beer? **1976** *Milton Keynes Express* 30 July 2/7 He said Mr Westley had drunk four pints of shandy during the evening but his driving had not appeared to be affected.

Shang (ʃæŋ). Also **Chang, Xanga.** [Chinese *shāng*.] The name of a dynasty which ruled China during part of the second millennium B.C., probably from the 16th to the 11th century B.C. Also *attrib.* or as *adj.* Also called **Shang-Yin** [f. the place-name *Yin* in Honan Province, the dynasty's final capital].

1669 J. OGILBY tr. *Nieuhoff's Embassy Grand Tartar Cham* xviii. 281 [Then] arose the family of Xanga, whereof the Emperor Tangus, in the year before Christ's Birth 1766, was the first who called it Xanga, from a Lordship of the same name he possessed. **1736** R. BROOKES tr. *Du Halde's Gen. Hist. China* I. 298 (*heading*) The Second Dynasty, called *Chang*, which comprehends the Lives of Twenty Eight Emperors in the Space of 644 Years. **1797** *Encycl. Brit.* IV. 653/1 The whole of their [*sc.* of the Chinese] emperors..are comprehended in 22 dynasties, mentioned in the following table... 2. Shang, or Ing. **1877** *Ibid.* VI. 259/2 Confucius's own ancestry is traced up, through the sovereigns of the previous dynasty of Shang, to Hwang-ti. **1933** R. FRY *Let.* 15 Dec. (1972) II. 686 Some..accomplished pre-Cheou bronzes: Shang they say but anyhow earlier than anything I knew. **1939** *Burlington Mag.* Feb. 85/2 Practically everything is problematical... This applies to the use of Shang weapons, though their date seems fairly safe. **1958** W. WILLETTS *Chinese Art* I. 108 Writing in Shang-Yin times may have been more widespread through society than was at first believed. **1972** S. H. HANSFORD *Gloss. Chinese Art & Archaeol.*, *Ku*..is applied especially to objects attributed to the..Hsia, Shang-Yin and Chou, and the Han Dynasty. **1978** *New Archaeol. Finds in China* II. 2 Shang relics have been newly discovered in regions other than the Central Plains.

Shangaan (ʃaŋgā·n). [Native name.] (A member of) a Bantu people inhabiting Zimbabwe, Mozambique, and South Africa; the language of the south-east Bantu group spoken by this people. Also *attrib.* or as *adj.*

1887 J. W. MATTHEWS *Incwadi Yami* 183 The native labour of the diamond fields..includes nearly twenty different tribes such as Zulus, Swazees, Basutos, Shangaans, [etc.]. **1911** *Encycl. Brit.* XXVII. 189/2 The Shangaan are members of a Bantu tribe from the Delagoa Bay region who took refuge in the Transvaal between 1860 and 1862 to escape Zulu raids. **1932** C. FULLER *Louis Trigardt's Trek* 39 Trigardt adopted a version from other than local natives, probably his Shangaan guides. **1948** *Rep. Native Laws Comm. 1946–48* (Dept. Native Affairs, S. Afr.) 38/1, I have had in hand a most valuable document, prepared by a young Shangaan. **1968** C. BURKE *Elephant across Border* iv. 118 An elderly man..got out, speaking quietly in Shangaan to an African. *Ibid.* 128 They suddenly saw Murray and his Shangaan tracker. **1973** *Standard Encycl. S. Afr.* IX. 601/1 The Transvaal Tsonga—called Machangana (Shangaans),..—have been recognised as one of the eight Bantu peoples living in the Republic of South Africa.

shanghai, *sb.* Add: **2.** Also in *N.Z.* and as **shangeye.**

1940 F. SARGESON *Man & Wife* (1944) 7, I was out in the backyard with my shanghai, and..I took a shot at a thrush. **1947** D. M. DAVIN *Gorse blooms Pale* 57 Bits of shangeye as they called their catapults. **1972** M. GEE *In my Father's Den* 44 He made me shanghais and bows and arrows.

shanghai, *v.* Add: **1. b.** *transf.* To transfer forcibly or abduct; to constrain or compel. *colloq.* (orig. *U.S. Mil. slang*).

1919 in *Amer. Speech 1972* (1975) XLVII. 97 The second third has been 'shanghaied' for garrison duty. **1934** *Sun* (Baltimore) 21 May 7/5 Arguments will be heard..on Insuli's plea that that court has no jurisdiction over him because he was 'shanghaied' from Istanbul. **1958** *People* 4 May 15/6 We began to wonder if she'd got herself shanghaied. **1974** *Sunday Times* 15 Dec. 3/1 Hunt..thought he was being 'Shanghai-ed'—prison jargon for a transfer to another prison as a punishment. **1976** J. GIBSON *As I saw It* xxviii. 491 Most of my guests get shanghaied into giving a general knowledge talk to the boys.

Hence **shanghai·er,** one who shanghais.

1917 *Chambers's Jrnl.* Jan. 19/1 Once..a shanghaier had been shanghaied by a rival shanghaier. **1926** J. BLACK *You can't Win* xii. 152 Here I learned to beware the crafty shanghaier with his knockout drops.

Shanghailander (ʃæŋhəi·lændəɹ). [f. SHANGHAI, after HIGHLANDER, ISLANDER, etc.] A native or inhabitant of Shanghai.

1917 *China Press* (Shanghai) 20 June 6/3 The Shanghailanders are still working to get a pipe band together and yesterday there were two leathery-lunged Scots extracting sounds from their machines in the Town Hall. **1937** E. LINKLATER *Juan in China* vii. 123 They were Shanghailanders. **1959** *Time* 8 June 36/3 The impertinent, self-assured Shanghailander of the past has disappeared.

Shanghainese (ʃæŋhəinī·z). [f. SHANGHAI + -*n*- + -ESE, after CHINESE, etc.] The Chinese dialect of the Wu group spoken in Shanghai; a native or inhabitant of Shanghai (also *collect.*). Also *attrib.* or as *adj.*

1964 *Asia Mag.* 12 July 22/3 The Chinese [in Hong Kong]..speak no less than seven tongues—Cantonese, Hoklo,..Shanghainese, Chiuchow and Fukienese. **1965** M. WEST *Ambassador* vi. 116 He looked more like a Shanghainese than a Viet. **1970** T. LILLY *Projects Section* iv. 36 The Shanghainese must surely be among the most handsome people in the world. **1971** K. HOPKINS *Hong Kong* 225 Shanghainese firms were mainly established in Hong Kong, in the late 1940s and early 1950s, by capitalists from Shanghai who fled from Communism. **1977** H. FAST *Immigrants* II. 114 'You see, my mother is Shanghainese—.' 'Not really,' Feng Wo interrupted. 'She comes from a tiny village to the south of the city.' *Ibid.* 115, I was speaking Shanghainese and Mandarin before I ever knew a word of English.

Shango (ʃæ·ŋgo). Also **shango.** [f. the name *Shango* of the god of thunder and lightning in the Yoruba religion of W. Nigeria.] **1.** A syncretistic cult practised in the Caribbean. Freq. *attrib.*

1953 *Caribbean Q.* III. I. 16 In 1916 I had the first experience of the Shango. **1958** J. CAREW *Wild Coast* xi. 155 The shango gods, Dumbhalla, Legba, Moko. **1963** G. J. McCALL *Social Problems* x. 364/2 'Hoodoo'..corresponding to..*shango* in Trinidad. **1974** *Trinidad Guardian* 2 Nov. 7/6 Sometimes they used the heady chants heard at 'wakes', shango meetings, and other such ceremonies.

2. A dance associated with the Shango cult.

1948 E. LEAF *Isles of Rhythm* vi. 142 It had a more pronounced sex base than the Afro-Caribbean religious dances such as *Voodoo, Shango* and *Obeah*. **1971** *Advocate-News* (Barbados) 17 Sept. (Guyana Suppl.) p. i/1 *Cumfa*, a spirit dance like the Trinidad 'Shango'.

Shangri-La (ʃæ:ŋgrilā·). Also **Shangrila, shangri-la,** etc. The name of *Shangri-La* [f. Tibetan *la* mountain pass], a Tibetan utopia in *Lost Horizon* (1933), a novel by James Hilton, used *transf.* to designate an earthly paradise, a place of retreat from the worries of modern civilization. (In quot. 1945 as quasi-*adj.*)

[**1933** J. HILTON *Lost Horizon* ix. 212 When the High Lama asked him whether Shangri-La was not unique in his experience..he answered..'To be quite frank, it reminds me very slightly of Oxford, where I used to lecture.' **1938** 'E. QUEEN' *Four of Hearts* xv. 197 'It's a simply hideous place.'..'It's not exactly another Shangri-La.'] **1941** *Time* 23 June 53/1 The Captain operates an insular Shangri-La in the South Pacific. **1945** L. DURRELL *Let.* 15 Dec. in *Spirit of Place* (1969) 81, I was afraid I would sound so heartlessly healthy and the country so Shangri la that you would write me a stinker. **1960** D. LESSING *In Pursuit of English* i. 15 Their Shangri-La would be populated..with nice professional people. **1971** *Sat. Rev.* (U.S.) 11 Dec. 53/1 The Windward Islands..excel any of the shangri-las of the South Pacific. **1977** *China Now* July/Aug. 19/1 The lamasery, for all its association with the Shangrila myth of eternal youth and joy, brought misery.

shank, *sb.* Add: **5. w.** Substitute for def.: A straight piece of metal tubing fitted to a brass instrument to lower its pitch. (Examples.)

1885 G. B. SHAW in *Our Corner* Nov. 313 Brass instruments have resources in shanks and tuning-slides for flattening. **1938** *Oxf. Compan. Mus.* 114/1 By the addition [to a horn or trumpet] of a crook (a curved additional length of tubing) or a shank (a straight additional length), the fundamental note could be altered. **1977** *Early Music* V. 221/2 Every hand horn that we found..had a C alto shank among the set of crooks.

6. a. (Later examples.)

1873 *Catal. Loan Exhib. Anc. & Mod. Jewellery* (South Kensington Museum) 72 Gold ring, the shank formed of leaves; in centre a transparent stone. **1928** *Daily Express* 18 June 5/2 The middle stone may be placed into a knife-edged shank with a 'coronet' setting, producing a solitaire ring. **1978** *Morecambe Guardian* 14 Mar. 16/5 Mrs Tyson was fined a further £20 for stating orally..that a ring was solid gold when it had a hollow shank filled with wax.

7. e. *Fishing.* (*a*) A line of pots attached to a rope, used to catch crabs, whelks, etc. (*b*) = *shank-net* (see sense 11 in Dict.).

1962 *Listener* 28 June 1105/2 Not far short of 600 fathoms of rope go to one shank of pots (a shank holds thirty-six pots). **1971** *Country Life* 29 Apr. 1000 (*caption*) Fishermen shooting out their shank of pots. Between 24 and 70 pots are attached at intervals along the rope to form the shank. **1973** W. ELMER *Terminol. Fishing* ii. 72 Shanks are designed to be dragged in shallow waters.

9. Esp. in phr. *shank of the evening* (earlier and later U.S. examples).

1829 *Virginia Lit. Museum* I. 418/2 'Won't you spend the *balance* of the evening with me?' In some places, shank is quaintly used with the same signification. **1856** P. THOMPSON *Hist. Boston* 722 *Shank of the evening*, the twilight or dusk of the evening, and in some cases the latter part of it. **1972** WODEHOUSE *Pearls, Girls, & Monty Bodkin* vii. 97 'It's very late.' 'Shank of the evening.' **1973** *Publishers Weekly* 19 Nov. 56/2 The stuff that makes the antennae of music pros and music-lovers twitch during cultural quarrels in the shank of a Lincoln Center evening.

10*. *Golf.* An act of striking the ball with the heel of the club.

1942 *Sun* (Baltimore) 8 July 12/7 It should be stated here that a slice isn't a shank. **1960** *Times* 31 May 4/1 Miss Price had a shank at the 13th.

shank, *v.* Add: **4.** *Golf.* To strike (the ball) with the heel of the club.

1927 *Daily Express* 26 Oct. 3/4 Of all the awful things a man may do to a golf ball the most demoralising and the most mystifying is to 'shank' it. **1942** *Sun* (Baltimore) 8 July 12/7 Try to shank one. That's about the best cure I know after thirty years of golf. **1976** *Par Golf* Aug. 39/2 He had shanked his second and bunkered his third.

shanking, *vbl. sb.* Add: **4.** *Golf.* The action of striking (the ball) with the heel of the club.

1924 C. J. H. TOLLEY *Mod. Golfer* 247 Shanking is a fault which is frequently occurring. **1942** *Sun* (Baltimore) 8 July 12/6 Shanking, in golf, is hitting the ball deep in the heel of the club, thereby causing the ball to fly away at a right angle. **1976** *Sunday Mail* (Glasgow) 26 Dec. 34/2 Norman..had a comparatively poor season last year..(mainly due to a bout of shanking which he is convinced has cleared).

shannai, var. *SHAHNAI.

Shannon[2] (ʃæ·nən). *Information Theory.* The name of Claude Elwood *Shannon* (b. 1916), U.S. mathematician, used *attrib.* and in the possessive to designate various concepts arising from his work, esp. *Shannon's* (*second* or *capacity*) *theorem*, a theorem regarding the ability of a noisy channel to carry information with no more than an arbitrarily small frequency of errors (see quot. 1970).

1956 L. BRILLOUIN *Sci. & Information Theory* i. 7 This is exactly Shannon's formula..for a problem with just two signals. **1956** *IRE Trans. Information Theory* II. 102/1 In the discrete case this quantity [of information] is evaluated correctly according to the well-known Shannon formula. **1963** N. ABRAMSON *Information Theory & Coding* vi. 173 Shannon's second theorem can..be characterized as a little more than an existence proof. **1970** H. A. RODGERS *Dict. Data Processing Terms* 98/1 *Shannon's capacity theorem*, in information theory, a theorem stating that it is possible to encode a source of messages having an information rate *H* bits/sec so that its information can be transmitted through a noisy channel with an arbitrarily small frequency of errors, provided that $H \leqslant C$ bits/sec, where *C* is called the limiting capacity of the channel. **1972** L. L. GATLIN *Information Theory & Living System* iv. 98 A fundamental condition under which the Shannon theorem is valid is that the rate of emission from the source..must not exceed the channel capacity.

shant. Add: Hence *loosely*, a drink.

1960 *News Chron.* 5 Aug. 7/8 We did not want to roll anybody but we had a few shants and I always get a bit garritty then. *Ibid.*, We all like a fight when we have had a few shants. **1970** A. DRAPER *Swansong for Rare Bird* vii. 52 'So I had a few shants,' I said.

shanty, *sb.*[1] Add: Also **chanty. 1. c.** (Earlier examples.)

1824 *Canadian Mag.* III. 201 They commence by building a log cabin called a *Chanty* to shelter them from the weather, and hence another appellation they are known by, namely *Chanty Men.* **1829** J. MACTAGGART *Three Years in Canada* I. 242 In these shanties they pass the time pretty well, considering them to be made up of Highlandmen, Irishmen, and Yankees.

2. Also in *N.Z.* (Earlier and further examples.)

1862 *Otago Goldfields & Resources* 28 These accommodation houses are not mere 'shanties' and the traveller, with ordinary precautions, is always safe. **1880** H. LAPHAM in D. M. Davin *N.Z. Short Stories* (1953) 57 When I first saw it..nearly every second house was a 'shanty' or a store.

3. (sense 1) *shanty-dweller, home, shop, slum*; (sense 2) *shanty-keeper* (earlier example); **shanty Irish** *a. U.S.*, belonging to the Irish lower-classes; also *ellipt.*; so **shanty Irish** *sb. pl.*, **shanty Irishman; shantyman** (earlier example); **shanty town,** a suburb consisting of shanties, *spec.* a poor or depressed area of a city or town.

1970 *E. Afr. Standard* (Nairobi) 23 Jan. 1/3 Rich-quick land racketeers who leased small plots to shanty-dwellers in return for 'rent'. *Ibid.* 2 Jan. 15/4 The fire..destroyed some 98 shanty homes. **1928** J. TULLY *Shanty Irish* xi. 117 I'm just plain Shanty Irish an' I'll go to hell when I die. **1966** [see *RESIDENCY 1 a]. **1975** J. F. BURKE *Death Trick* (1976) v. 79 That shanty Irish bitch!..She hit me..and got away. **1934** J. T. FARRELL *Young Manhood Studs Lonigan* xx. 334 The Irish made a shanty Irishman out of Christ. **1874** V. PYKE *Adventures G. W. Pratt* I. iii. 6 The shanty-keeper interposed. **1824** Shanty man [see sense 1 c above]. **1891** H. MELVILLE *Timoleon* 63 And here and there a shanty-shop Where Fez-caps, swords, tobacco, shawls Lay orderless. **1969** *Cultural News from India* Nov. 20 Shanty shops on pavements, packed buses and tram cars..mark the biggest annual festival of Bengal. **1969** A. G. FRANK *Latin Amer.* (1970) xix. 300 The wealth and elegance of downtown Mexico City dazzle the visitor..but equally do the miles of Mexico City's shanty slums depress. **1876** *Potter's American Monthly* Oct. 400/2 (*caption*) Shanty town. **1880** *New York Daily Graphic* 4 Mar. 38 (*caption*) A scene in shantytown, New York. **1917** U. SINCLAIR *King Coal* 36 There's lots of people have boarders in shanty-town. **1946** [see *HOOVERVILLE]. **1954** H. GIBBS *Background to Bitterness* II. vii. 121 By the end of 1871 over 10,000 diggers occupied the hot, corrugated iron shanty-town of Kimberley. **1980** *Times* 4 Jan. 6/5 The overpopulated [Turkish] cities are girdled with slummy shanty towns.

shanty, *sb.*[2] (Earlier examples.)

1856, 1867 [see *CHANTEY, CHANTY].

shantying, *vbl. sb.* (Earlier and later examples.)

1824 *Canadian Mag.* III. 202 Such is the usual routine of what is called *Shantying* in Canada. **1926** F. RICKABY *Ballads & Songs of Shanty-Boy* 47 Shantying I'll give o'er when I'm landed safe on shore, And I'll lead a different life.

Shaoshing (ʃauʃi·ŋ). Also shao hsing, shao-hsing, shao shing. The name of a town (Pinyin *Shaoxing*) in the Zhejiang province of China, used *attrib.* to designate the rice wine produced there. Also *ellipt.*

1961 *Sunday Express* 26 Nov. 19/4 Everything I wanted to cook called for 'shao shing' or yellow rice wine. **1965** O. A. Mendelsohn *Dict. Drink & Drinking* 306 There are three types of shaohsing: Shan Niang is full-bodied [etc.]. **1969** *Times* 9 Dec. (Taiwan Suppl.) p. viii/7 I would praise Shanghai because the best *Shaoshing* wine once came from spring-water on a hill on the outskirts. **1980** E. Behr *Getting Even* vii. 90 They drank the ritual toast, in hot shao hsing wine.

shape, *sb.* Add: **I. 9. c.** Phr. *in all shapes and sizes*: in a great variety of forms.

1958 J. Townsend *Young Devils* xxi. 196 Parents come in all shapes and sizes. **1967** 'A. Cordell' *Bright Cantonese* xvii. 189 You've got competition..in all shapes and sizes. **1980** P. Moyes *Angel Death* v. 60 Tourists come in all shapes and sizes.

10. a. (Later examples.)

1968 *Listener* 28 Mar. 400/3 The BBC in the shape of Harman Grisewood referred him to the government. **1976** *Eastern Even. News* (Norwich) 22 Dec. 14/4 Gothic had mixed luck, falling foul of County Council in the shape of David Simpson.

11. *to take shape* (later examples).

1939 *Daily Tel.* 18 Dec. 1/2 The great grey hulk of Germany's pocket-battleship..began to take shape. **1982** *New Scientist* 2 Sept. 609/1 The idea that nuclear armaments could be used..had taken firm shape in the minds of the technical people.

13. Delete *Sporting* and substitute for def.: Condition, state of health, repair, or fitness. orig. *U.S.*

1865 O. W. Norton *Army Lett.* (1903) 249, I got through it all in good shape. **1901** [in Dict.]. **1924** J. Galsworthy *Forest* II. ii. 52 With only nine Soudanese ..and less than thirty carriers—all in bad shape; it's precious long odds against our getting through. **1976** *National Observer* (U.S.) 24 July 3/5 Most of the corn-growing areas..were in pretty good shape for moisture.

14. b. (Earlier example.)

1880 *Girl's Own Paper* 20 Mar. 191/3 You might also buy a shape, and make a little hat to match.

e. pl. *Gambling.* (See quot. 1936.) *U.S. slang.*

1928 [see *miss-out]. **1936** *Flynn's Mag.* 21 Mar. 139/2 'Shapes' are dice which have beveled faces on some sides of the cube. These cause the dice to trip faster when these surfaces strike the playing table.

f. *Bridge.* The distribution of suits in a hand of cards.

1954 G. S. Coffin *Bridge Play from A–Z* i. 17 There are in bridge three dominant Playing Shapes: I. No-trump Shape. II. Trump/No-trump Shape. III. Ruff Shape. **1958** *Listener* 27 Nov. 901/3 The shape is unsuitable for a double—the bidding might go too high. **1961** A. Truscott *Bridge* ii. 22 The shape of a hand is the way the cards are divided between the four suits.

IV. 17. *shape-shifting* sb. (earlier example), *-changer, -changing* vbl. sb.; **shape elastic** *adj. phr. Physics*, pertaining to or designating a component of the scattering cross-section of an atomic nucleus that is regarded as independent of the formation of a compound nucleus; **shape factor** *Physics*, an algebraic factor in the expression predicting the profile of a spectral line; **shape memory**, a property exhibited by certain alloys of recovering their initial shape when they are heated after having been plastically deformed; **shape-note** (chiefly *U.S.*), one of a series of notes having heads of different shapes, used to represent the degrees of a scale.

1906 W. B. Yeats *Poems, 1899–1905* 63 Shadows, illusions, That the shape-changers..have cast into his mind. **1978** H. R. E. Davidson in Porter & Russell *Animals in Folklore* 141 The tales of shape-changers in the Sagas are not told 'for true'. *Ibid.* 127 (*heading*) Shape-changing in the Old Norse Sagas. **1954** H. Feshbach et al. in *Physical Rev.* XCVI. 449/2 It will be practical..to subdivide the elastic cross section into two parts... We call the second part..the 'compound elastic' cross section... The first part we call 'shape elastic' cross section; this is the part of the elastic scattering which occurs without the formation of a compound [nucleus]. **1971** P. E. Hodgson *Nuclear Reactions & Nuclear Structure* vii. 142 The method of analysis described..applies only to the shape elastic part of elastic-scattering cross-sections. **1955** E. Konopinski in K. Siegbahn *Beta- & Gamma-Ray Spectrosc.* x. 301, S_n will be called the 'shape factor'... Whenever S_n happens to be independent of the energy W,..the spectrum has the 'statistical shape' $\sim pW(W_0-W)^2$, modified only by the Coulomb effect. **1970** *Physical Rev.: C* I. 644/1 It is important that the correlation coefficients and the energy dependence of the shape factor be known to an accuracy of a few percent to provide a meaningful test of nuclear models. **1968** de Lange & Zijderveld in *Jrnl. Appl. Physics* XXXIX. 2195/1 On heating above 90°C the reverse transformation takes place. The sudden change of configuration into the original shape, which occurs then, is called here the shape-memory effect. **1975** *Nature* 22 May 281/2 The spring has to be made of one of the alloys—a select band—which exhibit shape-memory. **1932** V. Randolph *Ozark Mountain Folks* 248 Right hyar is whar I get in some good licks for shape-notes, too. **1980** P. M. Young *George Grove* vii. 146 The congregational singing in the enthusiastic manner derived from *Sacred Harp*,..and the 'shape-note' books. **1884** A. Lang in M. Hunt *Grimm's Household Tales* I. p. lxvii, He escapes with her..by her magical gift of shape-shifting.

shape, *v.* Add: **I. 11. c.** *intr.* To assume a shape or form; to develop or progress. Freq. const. *up*.

1865 O. W. Norton *Army Lett.* (1903) 278 As things are shaping I do not much think I shall try till after Congress meets. **1903** *N.Y. Times* 10 Sept. 6/3 Matters are shaping for an effort on the part of the organized teamsters to reproduce in this city the..conditions which exist in Chicago. **1921** R. D. Paine *Comr. Rolling Ocean* xvii. 293 Here is how it shapes up to me. **1941** B. Schulberg *What makes Sammy Run?* vii. 153 It's shaping up something terrific... It looks like the biggest opening this town ever had. **1951** *Sport* 27 Apr.–3 May 12/1 How will Yorkshire shape up this summer? **1965** *Listener* 25 Nov. 871/1 The autumn output has shaped up most satisfactorily, far better than its schedules might suggest. **1980** N. Marsh *Photo-Finish* vi. 156 He pulled out... He didn't fancy the way things shaped up.

II. 16. d. Also *absol.* or *intr. rare.*

1848 J. F. Cooper *Oak Openings* I. iv. 49 Perhaps it would be best for me to shape at once for Ohio.

19. b. Also in *Golf*: to get into the proper attitude or stance for a stroke.

1930 Wodehouse *Very Good, Jeeves!* vi. 160 It was while I was shaping for a rather tricky shot that the front-door bell went.

d. *to shape up*: to pull oneself together or meet a required standard; to show one's capabilities. Also, to get oneself into good physical condition.

1938 E. Bowen *Death of Heart* I. v. 98 There seemed no reason why he should not shape up. **1951** *Chambers's Jrnl.* Nov. 645/1 He shaped up awkwardly against a man who was not only champion but twelve years his junior. **1963** *Time* 8 Nov. 10/3 You stated that an icosahedron is a two-sided solid figure... Shape up, sir! It's really a 20-sided solid figure. **1976** *National Observer* (U.S.) 10 July 8/2 After that [*sc.* adolescence] one is expected to shape up, get a job, get married. *Ibid.* 14 Aug. 11/1, I have gained 5 more pounds, and so once again am embarked on a semiserious effort to shape up. **1977** N. Marsh *Last Ditch* vi. 154 He taught her to ride and was uncommon proud of the way she shaped up.

e. Phr. *to shape up or ship out*: used as a threat of transference or dismissal if a satisfactory performance is not achieved. *slang* (orig. *U.S. Mil.*).

1956 *Amer. Speech* XXXI. 108 *Shape up or ship out!*, start soldiering or be sent to a combat zone. **1968** *Review & Herald* 19 Sept. 24/2 We ought to tell them to 'shape up or ship out'. **1977** *Guardian Weekly* 30 Oct. 15/1 If the International Labor Organization didn't shape up within two years, the U.S. government would ship out.

20. (Earlier example.) Also with *out* or *up*.

1855 R. Carboni *Eureka Stockade* 9 By this time two covies..had stripped to their middle, and were 'shaping' for a round or two. **1899** S. MacManus *In Chimney Corners* 12 'I'll fight you,' says Billy, shaping out and winding the bit of stick three times over his head. **1927** *Daily Express* 31 May 7 He shaped up to Murphy, when he punched the watchman on the jaw with his fist and knocked him insensible. **1977** N. Marsh *Last Ditch* ii. 47 If you feel like a fight you've only to say so and we'll shape up and make fools of ourselves.

SHAPE (ʃeⁱp). Also S.H.A.P.E., Shape. [Acronym f. the initials of *S*upreme *H*eadquarters *A*llied *P*owers in *E*urope, set up in 1951.] An organization established by the N.A.T.O. Council embodying a structure of command for the defence of western Europe.

1950 *Sun* (Baltimore) 20 Dec. 4/3 The 60-year-old five-star general..will create another international staff at SHAPE (Supreme Headquarters, Allied Powers in Europe). **1951** *N.Y. Times* 3 Apr. 8/3 General of the Army Dwight D. Eisenhower formally assumed command and activated the Supreme Headquarters of the Allied Powers in Europe (Shape) into an operational headquarters this morning [2 Apr.]. **1955** *Times* 20 July 8/2 He had accepted the leadership of the Supreme Headquarters in Europe (S.H.A.P.E.) as being a true agency for peace. **1958** *Listener* 25 Sept. 453/1 The signatures of the four Shape Supreme Commanders. **1976** H. Wilson *Governance of Britain* vii. 136 On 8 March the list concludes with southern Africa, Staffordshire, the United Nations and SHAPE.

shaped, *ppl. a.* Add: **3.** Special collocations: **shaped charge**, an explosive charge having a cavity which causes the blast to be concentrated into a small area; **shaped note** = *shape note* s.v. *shape *sb.* 17.

1889 F. H. Gilson *Hist. Shaped or Character Notes* 4 The great variety of systems embodying the same idea, —that is, a separate shape for each syllable,—came to be so confusing that the majority of the advocates of shaped notes finally agreed to adopt one system. **1945** *Chicago Tribune* 18 Nov. vii. 1/5 We sang from song books printed with old time shaped notes. **1948** *Sun* (Baltimore) 2 Jan. 1/3 A light but potent recoilless gun of the new type, using a 'shaped charge' like that of the bazooka. **1979** A. Hailey *Overload* I. ii. 14 What the saboteur used, they decided, was a 'shaped charge'—a cone of dynamite which, when detonated, had a forward velocity similar to that of a bullet.

shaper. Add: **5.** *Electronics.* A device which modifies an input to produce an output having a specific waveform.

1967 [see *keyer]. **1971** J. H. Smith *Digital Logic* vi. 109 When the count of ten is reached..a gate will produce a signal which is shaped by the shaper unit.

sha·pe-up. *U.S.* Also shapeup. [f. vbl. phr. *to shape up*: see Shape *v.* in Dict. and Suppl.]

1. A system of hiring dock workers for the day or half-day by arbitrary selection from a gathering of men on site. Also *transf.*

1940 *Sun* (Baltimore) 8 Nov. 22/7 Under the shape-up system..longshoremen are forced to gather on the docks ..every morning from 5 o'clock on..for the sake of a half day's pay. **1948** *Ibid.* 26 Nov. 2/2 Retention of the traditional twice-a-day 'shapeup' or work call, with the guarantee of four hours work for men called to work only once in a single day. **1954** *Ibid.* 9 Apr. 20/4 There are now from 22 to 24 cities being considered for the major leagues... This is the opinion of Ford Frick, baseball's high commissioner... 'Of course,' Frick said, 'I don't know when their shape-up will take place.' **1967** *Boston Sunday Herald* 30 Apr. I. 7/1 Boston's union longshoremen have sounded the death knell of their traditional but unwieldy dock shape-up. **1977** *Time* 17 Oct. 57/2 When Marlon Brando starred in *On the Waterfront* (1954), the morning shape-ups of New York Dock workers were pretty much as the movie portrayed them—noisy, brawling scenes of men fighting for the jobs available.

2. The action or an instance of shaping up.

1963 *Washington Post* 2 Oct. D2 The United States Olympic track and field team will have a final 'shapeup' meet in the Los Angeles Coliseum. **1977** *Time* 7 Feb. 20/2 He [*sc.* Lipshutz] presides at the daily 8 a.m. staff meetings... She is the only..outspoken liberal at Lipshutz's daily shape-ups. *Ibid.* 4 Apr. 60/2 Then, as the Central Intelligence Agency became mired in inefficiency, Schlesinger was tapped for the shape-up operation. As CIA director he immediately began to demythologize the agency.

shaping, *vbl. sb.* Add: **1. b.** *Electronics.* The process of modifying the waveform of an electrical signal.

[**1902** *Electr. Rev.* 10 Oct. 641/2 On adjusting the inductance and resistance of the shunt, along with the receiving condenser and its shunt, the signals are effectively curbed and shaped at the receiving end without reference to the sending station.] **1924** *Jrnl. Inst. Electr. Engineers* LXII. 192/1 The relation of damping to the reception of wireless signals, viz. its relation to the 'shaping' of the received dots and dashes. **1949** H. E. Penrose *Princ. & Pract. Radar* x. 152 A diode may..be employed with the primary object of exercising amplitude control, or..with the primary object of shaping. **1971** J. H. Smith *Digital Logic* iv. 68 The output of the shaping circuit is fed to the S_p trigger pulse input and a 20 μF capacitor is used to control the pulse length.

c. *Radar.* Modification of a radar beam so as to obtain a desired spatial configuration.

1945 C. S. Pao *Shaping Primary Pattern of Horn Feed* (M. I. T. Radiation Lab. Rep. No. 655) 2 Such beam shaping cannot usually be achieved by merely changing the geometrical dimensions of the horn. **1975** D. G. Fink *Electronics Engineers' Handbk.* xxv. 66 In the horn-fed reflector the shaping can be achieved by either the reflector or the feed.

‖ **shapka** (ʃæ·pka). [Russ., = hat.] A brimless Russian hat of fur or sheepskin. (See also quot. 1945.)

1945 *Richmond* (Va.) *News-Leader* 2 Aug. 14/3 Newest thing in casual headgear is called a 'shapka' (meaning a small informal hat in Hungarian)... This headpiece is a cross between a 'babushka' and a snood, and can be worn over any kind of coiffure. **1958** *Philadelphia Sunday Bull.* 30 Mar. v. 1/3 Wearing one of those 'shapka', or tall Russian hats, the wisecracking Hope descended on a Moscow shivering in six-degree-below-zero temperature. **1963** V. Nabokov *Gift* iv. 271 He never removed either his fur-lined dressing gown or his lambskin shapka. **1977** *Time* 14 Feb. 33/2 Every [Russian] man wears a *shapka*, a fur..hat with ear flaps.

sharable, var. *shareable *a.* **Shararat,** var. *Sherarat.

‖ **sharav** (ʃara·v). Also **Sharav.** [ad. Heb. *šārāḇ* parching heat.] A hot desert wind occurring in the Middle East in April and May; = Khamsin.

1968 *Listener* 27 June 827/2 In Crete they really cannot help it if the killingly hot *sharav* has blown across from the Levant. **1969** O. Hesky *Sequin Syndicate* ix. 96 Mornings when the *sharav* would blow. **1973** *New Scientist* 14 June 670 Ill winds such as the Föhn in Germany and the Sharav in the Near East can produce a malaise in humans. **1980** *Times* 4 Sept. 2/6 Seasonal 'ill-winds' such as the Mediterranean föhn and sirocco and the Middle Eastern sharav.

Sharawaggi. Delete ‖ and *Obs.* and add: (ʃæ:rawæ·dʒi). Also with small initial. Revived in the twentieth century with particular application to landscape gardening and architecture.

For a discussion of etymological hypotheses see 1949 *Archit. Rev.* CVI. 391/2.

1933 *Times Lit. Suppl.* 28 Dec. 913/4 Gothicism, *Chinoiserie*, all that may be summed up in the magic word

Sharawadgi that was imposed by ignorance or mystification upon the connoisseurs of the time as a genuine Oriental art term. **1937** A. R. Humphreys *William Shenstone* ii. 41 Sharawadgi, as understood in England, has three main ingredients... It has no faith in mathematics and deifies irregularity... It finds beauty in infinite variety... It treats natural material according to that material's own potential organic pattern. **1944** *Archit. Rev.* XCV. 3 (*heading*) Exterior furnishing or sharawaggi: the art of making urban landscape. **1965** Nairn & Pevsner *Buildings of England: Sussex* 294 What Petworth shows more than anything else is Sharawaggi..: good buildings of all dates mixing perfectly at least up to 1920.

shard, sherd, *sb.*[1] Add: **II. 4. a.** *spec. Archæol.*, a piece of broken pottery. (Later examples.)

Sherd is now established as the normal *Archaeol.* spelling.

1937 *Jrnl. R. Anthrop. Inst.* LXVII. 233, I could find no bronze-age sherds. **1955** *Sci. Amer.* July 46/3 We came upon a few fragmentary sherds of Aegean painted pottery. **1971** *World Archaeol.* III. 203 Many historic Amphlett sherds were recovered.

Shardana, Sherden (ʃɑɹdā·nă, ʃə·ɹdĕn), *collect. pl.* [ad. Egyptian *Šrdn.*] One of the Sea Peoples, tentatively identified with the later Sardinians, who fought against the Egyptians in the 13th century B.C. and afterwards served them as mercenaries. Hence **Sha·rdan,** a member of this people. Also *attrib.*

1877 *Encycl. Brit.* VII. 739/2 The king of the Rebu (Libyans), with the warriors of several tribes joined the Shardana (Sardones), the Shakalasha (Sikels), [etc.]. **1910** *Ibid.* IX. 85/2 The Sherden had been in the armies of Rameses II., and are distinguished by their remarkable helmets and apparently body armour of metal. **1928** C. Dawson *Age of Gods* xiii. 300 The Shardana..were especially important and formed the royal bodyguard. **1952** O. R. Gurney *Hittites* i. 35 The Sherden..appear frequently in Egyptian inscriptions. **1960** K. M. Kenyon *Archæol. in Holy Land* ix. 224 For centuries Shardans.. had been in the habit of serving the Egyptians as mercenaries. *Ibid.* 227 It is known on literary evidence that Shardan mercenaries were employed by the Egyptians.

share, *sb.*[3] Add: **5. d.** Also, *upon shares, on the shares.*

1817 *Massachusetts Spy* 29 Jan. 1/2 To be let, upon Shares or *Hire*, a *Farm.* **1882** [see *renter *sb.*[1] 4 b].

6. *share bonus, broker* (earlier example), *capital, -dealing, index, -mart, -owner(ship), premium, price*; **share-farmer** chiefly *Austral.*, one who works on a farm for an agreed portion of the profits; so **share-farming** *vbl. sb.*; **share-hand** *U.S.*, a farm-worker or tenant who raises crops on shares; **shareman** (earlier and later N. Amer. examples); **share-milker** *N.Z.*, one who works on a dairy farm for an agreed portion of the profits (cf. *share-farmer* above); hence **share-milk** *v. trans.*, **share-milking** *vbl. sb.*; **share-pusher** (see quot. 1914); hence **share-pushing** *vbl. sb.* and *ppl. a.*; **sharesman,** (*b*) (earlier and later examples).

1928 *Daily Chron.* 9 Aug. 8/4 A share bonus of 50 per cent. was provided on account of the year 1917–18. **1845** (*title*) Railway Maria; or, The Irish sharebroker. **1848** *Bradshaw's Railway Almanack* 57 Guaranteed 5 per cent. in perpetuity upon £3,000,000 (the authorized Share Capital). **1974** *Terminol. Managem. & Financial Accountancy* (Inst. Cost & Managem. Accountants) 62 *Equity share capital*, the issued share capital of a company which carries an unrestricted right to participate beyond a specified amount in a distribution. **1955** *Times* 17 May 18/4 Not inconsiderable profits have been made from time to time in sharedealing. **1969** *Times* 2 May (Suppl.) p. viii/4 The finance houses do not distribute as dividend the profits made on the realization of investments, colloquially known as share-dealing profits. **1928** R. G. Stapledon *Tour in Austral. & N.Z.* iv. 28 Many successful men have started as share-farmers. **1966** *Southerly* XXVI. 203 *Sharemilker*..is a New Zealand term, which is certainly not in use in New South Wales, where the popular term is *sharefarmer.* **1927** *Austral. Encycl.* I. 46 The details of 'share-farming' contracts varied with the district: thus in some cases the landowner provided everything but the labour and took two-thirds of the crop in return, in others the farmer provided plant, labour, and half the bags required and took half the crop. **1932** A. Jose *Australia Human & Economic* 262 Thus there came into favour a system of 'share-farming' (in Europe better known as metayage), which gave the actual cultivators an interest in good tillage while retaining in the owner's hands full control of his property. **1960** *Farmer & Stockbreeder* 12 Jan. 51/1 Several new variations of the old share-farming system were propounded. **1911** Jenks & Lauck *Immigration Problem* 83 How much value careful cultivation, kitchen gardens and small store accounts may be to the cotton 'share hand' and tenant. **1930** *Financial News* 13 Aug. 1/5 (*heading*) Industrial Share Index. **1982** *Financial Times* 1 May 24/2 The FT-Actuaries 500 share index eased only 0.9 per cent from Thursday's record high. **1687** *Connecticut Colony Public Rec.* (1859) III. 425 Fishermen..shall not presume to break off their voyage..without the consent of the owner, master and share-men. **1820** in C. R. Fay *Life & Labour in Newfoundland* (1956) viii. 139 Sharemen are frequently indigent planters who have fallen into debt with their merchant and who cannot afford to use their own boats. **1966** A. R. Scammell *My Newfoundland* 26, I was shareman with his father..three summers on the lower Labrador. **1870** J. K. Medbery *Men & Mysteries Wall St.* 19 In all the great European share-marts there is a general executive organization. **1937** Gordon & Bennett *Gentlemen of Jury* ii. 67 Two months later the mother is 'out in the sheds' helping to share-milk 100 cows. **1935** J. Guthrie *Little Country* xii. 203 Advertisements..for a farm-hand or a share-milker. **1977** *N.Z. Herald* 8 Jan. 4–7/2 (Advt.), A position has become available for a 50–50 sharemilker on a 130-acre dairy farm. The present sharemilker has purchased his own farm property. **1937** H. G. Philpott *Hist. N.Z. Dairy Industry* i. iii. 65 [He] adopted the system of farm labour now commonly known as 'share milking'. **1958** *Times* 16 June 12/7 In New Zealand 'share milking', as it is called, is controlled by a wages board award. **1973** *Massey Ferguson Rev.* (N.Z.) Mar.–Apr. 5/3 Sharemilking is an important cornerstone of the dairy industry in New Zealand. **1968** *Sci. Jrnl.* Nov. 89/1 Competitors, suppliers, customers, shareowners, bankers and the government. **1978** *Detroit Free Press* 5 Mar. B 13/3 [They] have made lifetime careers of trying to give shareowners a voice in the running of publicly held companies. **1962** *Economist* 24 Mar. 1149/2 (*heading*) Wider shareownership. **1930** *Daily Express* 6 Oct. 14/2 The discount on this issue has been entirely written off from share premium and capital reserve accounts. **1930** *Economist* 19 Apr. 896/2 Rayon share prices were found to have fully discounted in advance the retention of the duties. **1980** W. Ash *Incorporated* xiii. 156 You can imagine what could've happened to share prices if..that got out beforehand. **1914** H. Halford *Dict. Stock Market Terms* 79 *Share pusher*, one who endeavours to dispose of Shares to the public by circular or advertisement, instead of selling them on the market. **1938** 'N. Shute' *Ruined City* xii. 247 We're a precious pair... Couple of bloody share-pushers, if you ask me. **1965** B. Sweet-Escott *Baker Street Irregular* i. 34 A look which suggested that I must be a cross between a share-pusher and a black marketeer. **1928** *Daily Mail* 3 Aug. 19/3 The day on which the sections penalising share-pushing shall come into force. **1928** *Evening News* 18 Aug. 11/3 Shares of this sort are among those that figure prominently in the share-pushing circulars of the 'bucket-shop' brigade. **1972** *Times* 28 Dec. 17/4 The City section..has developed considerable expertise in cases involving prospectuses, sharepushing and market rigging operations. **1977** N. Faulks *No Mitigating Circumstances* xi. 152 A number of other persons were charged with having taken part in share-pushing transactions. **1867** G. E. Clark *Seven Years of Sailor's Life* xxvii. 272 The sharesmen were all looking at the steamer that lay just ahead. **1912** *Oysterman & Fisherman* Mar. 14/1 The crew wage and crew feeding system practiced by the 'sharesmen'-outfitters.

share, *v.*[2] Add: **4. f.** *Chem.* Of an atom, orbital, etc.: to hold (one or more electrons) in common with another atom or orbital, so as to form a covalent bond. (See also *shared *ppl. a.*)

1919 *Jrnl. Amer. Chem. Soc.* XLI. 888 An octet may share an even number of its electrons with 1, 2, 3, or 4 other octets. **1923** *Trans. Faraday Soc.* XIX. 461 In chemically stable molecules we have only to consider atoms sharing pairs of electrons. It is well known that such structures do not exhibit any signs of electrical polarity. One must therefore suppose that the net charge on both atoms is zero, *i.e.* that the two shared electrons are in general so distributed that when one is in one atom the other is in the other. **1964** J. W. Linnett *Electronic Structure of Molecules* ii. 29 The two electrons may be regarded as being shared between the 1*s* orbital of the hydrogen and one of the 2*p* orbitals of the fluorine.

6*. *intr.* and *trans.* In the language of Moral Rearmament: to confess one's sins openly; to impart to others one's spiritual experiences. Also const. *with.* Also in wider use.

1932 [implied at *sharing *vbl. sb.*[2] 2]. **1933** S. A. King *Challenge to Oxford Groups* v. 48 What does the Bishop think a man feels when he has 'shared' for 'witness' and finds that God has used that 'sharing' to bring a brother out of..bondage? **1934** R. Macaulay *Going Abroad* xiv. 111 She would, thought he, be able to share with another girl in a way she could not with him. *Ibid.* xvii. 135, I must say, I did annoy my father a bit by sharing with him a few things I'd thought about him. **1940** Graves & Hodge *Long Week-End* xii. 205 One of their practices was to 'share' confessions of their sins. **1949** A. Wilson *Wrong Set* 19, I do believe you're trying to get me to 'share'. And I never even guessed that you were a Grouper. **1981** B. Paul *Your Eyelids are growing Heavy* (1982) ix. 121 She 'shared' with the group the fact that she'd begun to have severe bouts of depression.

7. share-out: for 'Chiefly' in Dict. read 'occas.' Also that which is distributed; a portion or share (of profits, interest, etc.), a 'cut'. (Later examples.)

1941 *Sun* (Baltimore) 27 Jan. 4/1 It could be 'well in at the head of the table for the shareout' when the war ended. **1951** A. L. Rowse *England of Elizabeth* viii. 325 The new nobility around the young king helped themselves to a vast share-out of Crown and Church lands. **1963** *Times* 7 May 18/2 No, a share-out it may be—and each shareholder may have his own private, affectionate name for it—but in..the businesslike print of The Birmingham Post, 'dividend' is the better term. **1976** *Scottish Daily Express* 23 Dec. 6/2 Kilkerr was forced to accept his share-out from Soho vice bosses on Friday nights.

shared *ppl. a.* (later examples in *Chem.*).

1923 [see sense 4 f above]. **1939** L. Pauling *Nature Chem. Bond* i. 6 In methane the carbon atom, with its two inner electrons and its outer shell of eight shared electrons, has assumed the stable ten-electron configuration of neon. **1977** H. S. Pickering *Covalent Bond* ii. 17 A variant of the covalent bond occurs in which the two shared electrons of the bond come originally from one of the two atoms.

shareable (ʃɛ̄ə·răb'l), *a.* Also **sharable.** [f. Share *v.*[2] + -able.] That may be shared. Hence **shareabi·lity.**

1920 *Q. Rev.* July 161 It must be shared or at least must be shareable; otherwise it were nothing at all. **1932** W. T. Stace *Theory of Knowl. & Existence* 332 Shareability of perception is what distinguishes the real from the unreal. **1935** W. de la Mare *Early One Morning* i. 19 In the telling of these vividly sharable experiences no direct hint is given that the author is actually seeing himself..as a child. **1977** Fontana & Van de Water in Douglas & Johnson *Existential Sociol.* iii. 102 The potential shareability of human understanding..is so great that complex systems of exchange can be constructed by groups who share no language. **1980** *Dædalus* Spring 20 Scientific understanding is essentially and eminently shareable.

share-crop (ʃɛ̄ə·ɹkrǫp), *v.* Chiefly *U.S.* Also **sharecrop, share crop.** [f. Share *sb.*[3] + Crop *v.*] **a.** *intr.* To farm on shares (see Share *sb.*[3] 5 d). **b.** *trans.* To grow (a crop) on this system; also *transf.* So **sha·re-crop** *sb.*, a crop raised on shares; also *attrib.*; **sha·re-cropper,** one who share-crops; also *attrib.*; and hence **sha·re-cropped** *ppl. a.*; **sha·re-cropping** *vbl. sb.* and *ppl. a.*

[**1867** in J. H. Easterby *S. Carolina Rice Plantation* (1945) 231 This will be cheaper in the end than the contract or share of the crop system.] **1907** *Springfield* (Mass.) *Weekly Republ.* 25 Apr. 1 The 'share crops' system is what its name implies, the immigrant being housed and fitted with all the necessaries and then sharing the proceeds of the harvest with the landowner. **1925** *Annals Amer. Acad.* Jan. 61/1 Number of farmers operated by tenants of various kinds (cash, share and share-cash 'croppers', standing tenants, etc.) increased about 100,000. **1928** J. Peterkin *Scarlet Sister Mary* xxi. 235 The..thing would cost as much as his whole share-crop of cotton would make in five years. **1929** L. R. Gottschalk *Era French Revolution* 33 Most of them had become métayers, who, like our share-croppers, farmed a piece of land for a stipulated portion..of the harvest. **1930** *Dialect Notes* VI. ii. 83 *Share-crop*, v., to farm 'on shares'... The word, like the practice, is very common. **1936** *Daily Progress* (Charlottesville, Va.) 3 Nov. 1/5 Bridges, who sharecrops for W. G. Gray, Senath attorney, sat in a big chair and poked wood in the fire. **1944** *Chicago Daily News* 2 Dec. 4/6 The Capone gang owned several locals of the hotel and restaurant workers in Chicago, and had Lou Romano share-cropping them. **1945** *Reader's Digest* Nov. 26/1 He found hundreds of blacks who share-cropped cotton. **1945** B. A. Botkin *Lay My Burden Down* 225 That was the beginning of the sharecropping system. **1947** *Social Forces* Dec. 202/1 One hundred Negro sharecropper families on the King and Anderson plantation. **1960** H. E. Bates *Aspidistra in Babylon* 215 A toothless Chinaman..share-cropped vanilla farther up the hill. **1962** E. Snow *Red China Today* (1963) lvi. 427 The 'well-to-do' peasants (living at a prosperous share-crop level) resented anything that looked like loss of control over their savings, homes and land. **1970** S. L. Barraclough in I. L. Horowitz *Masses in Lat. Amer.* iv. 104 When legalized slavery and forced labor were abolished.. various forms of share-cropping took their place. **1973** W. McCarthy *Detail* i. 62 Paul..came from a large, poor, sharecropper family, in the heart of the delta land of Mississippi. **1973** *Advocate-News* (Barbados) 17 Feb. 8/2 A depression time share-cropping family. **1974** *Evening Herald* (Rock Hill, S. Carolina) 18 Apr. 13/2 He was born in Greenville County, S. C., and spent his youth helping his father sharecrop. **1976** *Jrnl. Devel. Econ.* III. 345 In this exercise, we limit ourselves in focus to a single sharecropped plot on the fazenda.

Sharia (ʃărī·ă). Also **Shariah, Shariat,** † **Sharieh,** † **Sheriat,** and with small initial. [Arab. *šarī'a.*] The Islamic religious law, including the teachings of the Koran and the traditional sayings of Muhammad.

1855 R. F. Burton *Personal Narr. Pilgrimage to El-Medinah* II. xxi. 281 In fact, justice at El Medinah is administered in perfect conformity with the Shariat or Holy Law. **1877** *Encycl. Brit.* VII. 113/2 Shi'at or Sher'iat, *i.e.* legal religion under the supervision of a murshid. **1920** *19th Cent.* Sept. 500 Questions of divorce and inheritance are decided by the religious or Sharieh judge, from whom there is an appeal to the Sharieh Court of Appeal in Jerusalem. **1921** *Glasgow Herald* 16 July 7 A code based on the Shariat and prepared upon his orders would come into force. **1927** *Ibid.* 21 Oct. 11 The Sheriat (Moslem) canonical law has practically been abolished, a civil code borrowed from Switzerland being substituted for all questions of marriage and inheritance. **1936** F. Stark *Southern Gates Arabia* iii. 39 The law is the Muhammedan shari'a. **1965** *Mod. Law Rev.* XXVIII. v. 543 The marriage was dissolved, according to Mohammedan law by the unilateral declaration of *talak* divorce in the appropriate Sharia Court. **1971** *Illustr. Weekly India* 4 Apr. 47/1 For long *Sharia* has not been administered by a Caliph or Imam. **1979** *Guardian* 28 Mar. 18/4 At the basis of a way of life which was remarkable for its homogeneity, is the Shariah—meaning simply the way or path.

sharif, Sharifian, varr. Shereef, Shereefian *a.* in Dict. and Suppl.

sharing, *vbl. sb.*[2] Add: **2.** *spec.* The action of *share *v.*[2] 6*.

1932 A. J. Russell *For Sinners Only* ii. 25 They [*sc.* The Oxford Group] defined Sharing as meaning two distinct things—further definable as Confession and

Witness. **1945** N. L. McClung *Stream runs Fast* xxx. 298 They have class meetings, too, but they call them 'quiet times', and they tell their spiritual experiences, but they call that 'sharing', and they care nothing about money. **1964** T. Driberg *Mystery of Moral Re-Armament* ii. 38 An ill-judged attempt by Buchman to promote, if only vicariously, the practice of Sharing.

shark, *sb.*[1] Add: **1. d.** *transf. Naut. slang.* A sardine.

1916 'Taffrail' *Pincher Martin* viii. 144 There was a peculiar tang in the air... He found out afterwards that it emanated from various sardine-preserving factories, and the discovery put him off canteen 'sharks' for quite a week.

2. c. (Further example of sense 'the press-gang'.)

1866 'Mark Twain' *Lett. from Hawaii* (1967) 81 The professional 'sharks' in New Bedford and New London who furnish crews to ships.

d. (Earlier example.)

1806 *Port Folio* 17 May 304/1, I got plenty of promises, Latin, and jaw, And who ever got more from a lawyer? Of the sport I got sick, so threw up the game, For my cash by the sharks had got eaten.

e. *U.S. College slang.* A highly intelligent or able student. ? *Obs.*

1895 W. C. Gore in *Inlander* Dec. 111 *Shark*,..a person who is very bright either in a general way or (more often) in some particular line of work. **1903** *Williams College Class Book* 29 'Dido' is a Math. shark of the first water. **1909** *Springfield* (Mass.) *Weekly Republ.* 8 July 12 The 'shark' does well in his lessons, but recognizes that study is the first thing in college. 'Sharks' play games. **1920** [see *elocute *v.*].

4. a. *shark-fisher, -steak* (earlier example); *shark-fishing* (later examples); *shark-infested, -proof* adjs.

1897 'Mark Twain' *Following Equator* xiii. 142 He was passing by a nodding shark-fisher. **1914** *Chambers's Jrnl.* Feb. 89/1 Shark-fishing is regarded as being as much a trade as a sport. **1976** L. Deighton *Twinkle, twinkle, Little Spy* xi. 117 Is she interested in stud farms or shark fishing? **1978** *Detroit Free Press* 5 Mar. a 17/1 Rescue crews Saturday searched shark-infested waters for the bodies of..crewmen killed in the crash of a..domestic airliner. **1923** 'R. Daly' *Enchanted Isl.* x. 92 She had been bathing in the shark-proof palisade below. **1967** *Coast to Coast 1965–66* 162 Some evenings the Roebourne mob..would..swim in..our shark-proof pool beside the wharf. **1847** H. Melville *Omoo* xiv. 65 A shark-steak and be hanged to you!

b. shark-bait, *Austral. colloq.*, a lone or daring swimmer well out from shore; hence **shark-baiter, -baiting; shark net** *S. Afr. local*, a length of netting positioned off-shore to protect bathers from sharks; also *shark netting*; **shark's fin** = *shark-fin*; also in **shark's fin soup; sharkskin,** (*a*) also *attrib.*; (*b*) (i) a woven or warp-knitted fabric of wool, silk, or rayon with a smooth, slightly lustrous, finish; freq. *attrib.*; (ii) an outfit made of this fabric; **shark-toothed** *a.* (earlier and later examples).

1920 A. H. Adams *Australians* 177 Farther out in the deep water swam the venturous line of experts, technically known as 'shark-bait'. **1937** K. S. Prichard *Intimate Stranger* i. 16 'Shark-bait', boys and girls on the beaches called her, she was so daring. Always swimming out there beyond the reef. **1924** A. Wright *Rung In* iii. 31 It might be only some foolhardy 'shark baiter', as he heard the more venturesome of the bathers termed. **1965** *Austral. Encycl.* VIII. 82/2 Solitary bathers are more often attacked than groups, but the 'shark-baiter' farthest off shore is not necessarily the victim. **1951** Cusack & James *Come in Spinner* 221 I've given up shark-baiting. Mug's game. **1967** K. S. Prichard *Subtle Flame* 99 I'm no good at shark baiting. **1970** *Studies in English* (Univ. Cape Town) I. 33 These bracelets were originally made out of shark netting. The surfer would dig his way out to the shark nets, cut himself a piece and tie it around his wrist. **1977** J. McClure *Sunday Hangman* ix. 95 The shark nets protecting the bathers off its [*sc.* Durban's] beaches. **1933** *Gourmet's Bk. Food & Drink* iii. 49 In his own country the Chinaman's evening meal is a somewhat variegated affair..and includes..shark's fins, cucumber, fish brawn. *c* **1938** *Fortnum & Mason Price List* 58/1 Soups..Sharks' Fins per bot. 7/6. **1966** *Guardian* 30 July 7/3 In the heart of Chinatown, shark's fin soup with crab sauce. **1978** *Nagel's Encycl.-Guide: China* 379 Sharks' fins need lengthy preparation, because they are bought dried. **1851** H. Melville *Moby Dick* III. xxvii. 174 With matted beard, and swathed in a bristling shark-skin apron..Perth was standing between his forge and anvil. **1932** C. Beaton *Diary* Mar. in *Wandering Years* (1961) xiii. 255, I bought vast quantities, at almost negligible cost, of football vests, exotic footgear, the scantiest shorts in all colours and in white sharkskin. **1944** R. Chandler *Lady in Lake* ii. 11 The man wore trunks and the woman what looked like a very daring white sharkskin bathing suit. **1957** L. Durrell *Justine* iii. 183 Now in his ice-smooth sharkskin with the scarlet cummerbund he seemed..the richest and most handsome of the city's bankers. **1974** D. Ramsay *No Cause to Kill* ii. 110 Ivy Eastbrook..in silk shirt and sharkskin trousers. **1979** E. Koch *Goodnight, Little Spy* ii. 6 During the winter he wore..five serge suits and two sharkskins. **1794** T. Dwight *Greenfield Hill* 79 What stretches Avarice's gulphy maw, And opens wide her shark-tooth'd jaw. **1935** C. Day Lewis *Time to Dance* 42 Over the shark-toothed Timor sea Lost their bearings.

shark, *v.*[3] Delete *U.S. local.* and add: Only as sha·rking [formed after *fishing*, etc.], shark-fishing; also *attrib.*

1881 A. J. Northrup *'Sconset Cottage Life* xi. 100 No summer experience at 'Sconset is complete without..one 'sharking' expedition. **1882** E. K. Godfrey *Island of Nantucket* 329 A visit can be made to the 'sharking grounds'. **1937** J. W. Day *Sporting Adventure* 219 The Isle of Arran, off the Scottish coast, is the centre from which the new sport is being followed. A fishing-smack has been fitted out specially there for parties who wish to go out 'sharking'. **1960** *Sunday Express* 24 July 13/5 Good sharking!

sharka (ʃā·ɹkă). Also (*rare*) **sarka.** [f. Bulg. *sharka na slivite* pox of plums.] = *plum pox* s.v. *plum *sb.* 6 d.

1961 *Tidsskrift for Planteavl* LXV. Saernummer 138 The sarka virus disease (plum pox) is the most significant virus of fruit trees in Yugoslavia. **1973** *Plant Virol.* 167 Sharka has become one of the very serious problems for the plum production in Europe. **1974** K. M. Smith *Plant Viruses* (ed. 5) ii. 13 In the parenchyma cells of fruit from plum trees infected with the 'Sharka' virus, 'plum-pox', cytoplasmic and intranuclear inclusion bodies have been observed. **1976** [see *plum pox* s.v. *plum *sb.* 6 d].

sharp, *a.* and *sb.*[1] Add: **A.** *adj.* **1. d.** (Further N. Amer. examples.)

1836 *Col. Crockett's Exploits in Texas* i. 20 A fellow.. who in those parts was considered as sharp as a steel trap. **1912** *Dialect Notes* III. 589 They won't fool him; he's a *sharp as tacks*. **1976** *National Observer* (U.S.) 10 Apr. 13/4 Mrs. Owen..is not only as sharp as a tack but is perhaps the best-looking school principal in Texas or elsewhere.

3. b. Substitute for def.: Of reasoning or discourse: acute, sagacious. Also, of remarks: pointed, apt, witty. (Later example.)

1968 *Observer* 14 Apr. 24/7 It was a sharp idea of the BBC's Religious Department, letting Malcolm Muggeridge wander round the Holy Land.

f. In colloq. phr. *you're so sharp you'll cut yourself* and varr.: variously used as an observation, reproof, or warning implying over-cleverness.

[**1903** 'T. Collins' *Such is Life* (1944) 278 Gosh! you've been on the turkey; you'll be cutting yourself some of these times.] **1910** 'H. H. Richardson' *Getting of Wisdom* xiv. 142 If you're so sharp, you'll cut yourself! **1930** W. S. Maugham *Cakes & Ale* x. 116 You're so sharp you'll cut yourself if you don't look out. **1968** J. Fleming *Kill or Cure* xiv. 189 He was as sharp as a bag of monkeys, that sharp he'd cut himself.

4. k. Of vehicular transport: ahead of schedule, early; hence of a time-table, etc.: tight, demanding. *colloq.*

1942 Berrey & Van den Bark *Amer. Thes. Slang* § 768 *Hot, sharp*, ahead of schedule. **1945** *Transit News* (Capital Transit Co., Washington, D.C.) 15 June, When a car or bus is ahead of schedule, it's 'Hot or Sharp', while when late it's 'Dragging'. **1977** *Modern Railways* Dec. 480/2 Certain of the intermediate schedules are quite sharp.

6*. As a general term of approbation. orig. *U.S. slang.* **a.** Excellent, fine.

1940 J. O'Hara *Pal Joey* 97, I sound like everything was sharp. **1963** in C. Booker *Neophiliacs* (1969) viii. 186 WIP'S opens late february london's sharpest nightclub. **1979** *Arizona Daily Star* 5 Aug. (Advt. Section) 20/4 The home is sharp with four bedrooms. *Ibid.* 20/3 Sharp and roomy 4 bdrm split plan with spacious modern kitchen.

b. Of clothes: stylish, fashionable, smart, 'snappy'. Hence of the wearer: well-dressed, attractive.

1944 C. Calloway *Hepsters Dict.*, *Sharp*.., neat, smart, tricky. Ex., 'That hat is sharp as a tack.' **1956** B. Holiday *Lady sings Blues* i. 20, I was always the sharpest kid in the block when I was dressed up. **1962** *Observer* 18 Feb. 23/2 It's more a desire for things you haven't got but feel you've a right to, because other people have them—a sharp suit, good things, neat things, flashy things. **1969** W. Ash *Take-off* iv. 57 When Jacques turned up, he was looking pretty sharp..in the sort of dark suit which..looks expensive. **1977** N. Marsh *Last Ditch* iii. 55 Louis..looked almost embarrassingly smooth in breeches, boots, sharp hacking-jacket and gloves.

c. Of a motor vehicle: smart, well-equipped; in good condition. Cf. *sharp *sb.*[1] 13.

1970 *Globe & Mail* (Toronto) 28 Sept. 27/4 (Advt.), Chevrolet convertible, fully equipped, a real sharp car. **1974** *Anderson* (S. Carolina) *Independent* 19 Apr. 10B/6 (Advt.), V-8, automatic power steering, electric seats.. one of the sharpest around. **1977** *Drive* Sept.–Oct. 16/1 The Saab interior, however, is drab—not sharp at all.

11. a. *spec.* of the definition of a photographic image; also *transf.* of a lens producing a sharp image. (Further examples.)

1883 J. H. T. Ellerbeck *Amateur's First Handbk.* iv. 22 Screw out the whole until, having taken the cap off the lens, you find the image, upside down, coming up sharp, then take a magnifier and see that it is perfectly sharp. **1921** *Daily Colonist* (Victoria, B.C.) 6 Apr. 5/1 (Advt.), Negatives which are exceptionally clear and 'sharp' make splendid enlargements. **1961** G. Millerson *Technique Television Production* iii. 34 Many simple photographic and motion-picture cameras have no focusing mechanism. And yet, at the push of a button, they produce acceptably sharp pictures. **1979** *SLR Camera* Jan. 42/3 Although we did not shoot our optical test target we can say that this is a very sharp lens.

b. *Physical Sci.* Of a phenomenon, condition, or state, esp. resonance: having, or occurring over, a narrow range of values of energy; capable of graphical representation by a curve showing a sharp peak; clearly defined.

1906 G. Eichhorn *Wireless Telegr.* vi. 40 The slighter the damping, the sharper the resonance. **1936** R. S. Glasgow *Princ. Radio Engin.* ix. 248 The effect of resistance predominates and the tuning is sharpest at the low-frequency end. **1960** Dicke & Wittke *Introd. Quantum Mech.* xvi. 308 The longer a particle can stay trapped before escaping, the sharper the energy level is. **1971** P. E. Hodgson *Nuclear Reactions & Nuclear Structure* xiv. 414 If the resonance is sharp..the cross-section due to the resonating partial waves greatly exceeds that due to all the other partial waves.

B. *sb.* **8. b.** (Earlier example.)

1840 *Spirit of Times* 12 Sept. 330/2 This race completely took in the 'sharps', who brought the bay filly as a 'bite' on purpose to beat the chesnut, who won the race.

10. (Earlier example.)

1834 *Chambers's Edin. Jrnl.* III. 129/2 The traveller, knowing the fondness of the Africans for needles, had brought..a great quantity of *Whitechapel sharps*.

12. *Diamond-cutting.* **b.** A sharp piece of diamond used to mark the point of intended cleavage; a pencil-like tool to which such a diamond is attached.

1903 W. R. Cattelle *Precious Stones* 67 To cleave, the crystal is fastened to the end of a stick and a V-shaped incision made in the grain with a sharp piece of diamond, called a 'sharp'. **1973** G. Jenkins *Cleft of Stars* iii. 36 Called technically a 'sharp', my diamond pencil looked like an ordinary pencil made of metal.

13. *N. Amer. slang.* A second-hand car in excellent condition (see quot.). Cf. sense 6* c of the adj. above.

1960 Wentworth & Flexner *Dict. Amer. Slang* 463/2 *Sharp*,..a used but well-cared-for automobile having extra accessories.

C. *Comb.* **1.** *sharp-bladed, -boned, -bowed, -ribbed, -scented, -textured, -thorned.*

1913 J. London *Let.* 5 Sept. (1966) 397 You must in your dealings be..as straight as the edge of the sharpest-bladed sword. **1933** W. de la Mare *Fleeting* 119 A homelier music than this bleaching wind's In these sharp-bladed grasses. **1794** T. Dwight *Greenfield Hill* 44 His sharp-bon'd horse..Tied, many an hour, in yonder tavern-shed. **1976** W. Trevor *Children of Dynmouth* i. 14 Timothy Gedge was..a boy with a sharp-boned face and wide, thin shoulders. **1865** W. Whitman *Drum-Taps* 41 O the beautiful, sharp bow'd steam-ships. **1946** I. Irving *Royal Navalese* 155 *Sharp-bowed*, the description of a man who has had a very close-cropped hair-cut. **1844** J. R. Lowell *Poems* 220 Grim Boaz, who, sharp-ribbed and gaunt, yet feared A thing more wild and starving than himself. **1910** W. de la Mare *Three Mulla-Mulgars* xvii. 224 Thimble lay in a sleep so quiet..it seemed to Nod the heart beneath the sharp-ribbed chest was scarcely stirring. **1927** E. Sitwell *Rustic Elegies* 81 The sharp-scented rose-boughs. **1864** G. M. Hopkins *Let.* 20 July (1956) 213 *Roughed it*; I believe it means irritating the skin on sharp-textured blankets. **1967** *Coast to Coast 1965–66* 195 You lie down in the sharp-textured air of the desert night. **1912** W. de la Mare *Listeners* 92 Wreathed shall with incense be Thy sharp-thorned may. **1965** J. A. Michener *Source* (1966) 76 Sharp-thorned vines clutched at them and sucking mud tried to grasp their ankles.

2. sharp end *Naut. slang*, the bows of a ship; also *transf.*, the front line, the centre of activity; esp. in phr. *at the sharp end*; **sharp eye-spot,** a fungal disease of cereals similar to eyespot but caused by *Corticium solani* (*Thanetophorus cucumeris*) and characterized by more clearly defined markings; **sharpshins** *dial.*, (*a*) a fleet-footed person; (*b*) a sharp-witted person; an intelligent child; **sharp-toothed** *a.* (later examples).

1948 Partridge *Dict. Forces' Slang* 166 *Sharp end, the*, the bows of the ship... (Navy.) (2) Hence, *at the sharp end*..at the front, well forward. **1973** D. Francis *Slay-Ride* i. 9 Arne pointed the sharp end back... The dinghy slapped busily through the little waves. **1976** *New Scientist* 28 Oct. 230/2 Within a few months I was appointed financial controller... But I still wasn't at the sharp end. **1980** A. Price *Hour of Donkey* ii. 36 The distant sound of bombing indicated that he was very close to the sharp end of the war. **1943** *Nature* 7 Aug. 161/1 In the first wheat crop after grass, eyespot is generally absent or rare, but sharp eyespot is found just as commonly as on old arable land. **1980** F. Hope in E. Gram et al. *Recognition & Control of Pests & Dis. Farm Crops* (ed. 2) 136/1 Sharp Eyespot (*Rhizoctonia cerealis*/*Corticium solani*) is similar in appearance to Eyespot, the main difference being that the lesions are more defined and angular, whilst the dark borders are easily distinguished from the linear areas. **1883–6** C. S. Burne *Shropshire Folk-Lore* xxxv. 581 'Sharpshins' is still applied in Shropshire, 1st, to light heels, 2nd, to sharp wits, *e.g.* 'Be off, sharpshins!' = run away, make haste... 'Now then, sharpshins! taking me up as usual!'..said in rebuke to some smart speech, display of cleverness, or captious criticism. **1915** D. H. Lawrence *Rainbow* iii. 76 'What does she say, that I'm a fawce little thing?' the small girl asked afterwards. 'She means you're a sharp-shins.' **1855** W. Whitman *Leaves of Grass* 62 Blind loving wrestling touch! Sheathed hooded sharptoothed touch! **1938** M. K. Rawlings *Yearling* xxi. 270 They had found..the weak and the strong brought together to earth, the sharp-toothed and the dull.

sharp, *adv.* Add: **1. a.** Also, smartly, nattily (after *sharp *a.* 6* b).

1951 J. H. Smyth *I, Mobster* xiii. 142 He was dressed sharp, like the wise guys on Broadway. **1981** 'D. Shannon' *Murder most Strange* i. 15 He was..dressed real sharp, a gray suit, not just sports clothes.

sharp, *v.* **1. a.** For 'Now only *dial.*' read 'Now *dial.* or *arch.*' and add later example.

a **1945** E. R. EDDISON *Mezentian Gate* (1972) xxviii. 137 A ready means lay to hand in converse with brother: a merry war, sharping and training up the claws of her wit.

5. c. (Later example used *intr.* with personal subject.)

1895 [see *FLAT *v.*[2] 7].

f. *intr.* for *refl.* To dress *up*, to dress smartly. *U.S. colloq.* Cf. *SHARP *a.* 6* b.

1957 J. KEROUAC *On Road* (1958) I. ix. 53 Tim, Rawlins, and I decided to sharp up for the big night.

Sharpa, obs. var. *SHERPA.

sharpen, *v.* Add: **1. c.** In fig. phr. *to sharpen one's pencil*: to prepare to work; to revise or improve one's work.

1957 *Times Lit. Suppl.* 15 Nov. 689/3 This is where the post-historic Ph.D. men will sharpen their pencils. **1965** *Daily Progress* (Charlottesville, Va.) 17 June 33/5 He suggested that Stahr and Hovde go home and suggest to local power officials that they 'sharpen their pencils' and figure out lower rates. **1969** *Listener* 2 Jan. 10/2 We.. published our findings. Radio telescopes all over the world were trained on the sources, while theoreticians sharpened their pencils.

2. Now freq. const. *up.* **a.** (Later examples.)

1947 'L. STARR' *Corrie* xii. 161 Just a little cocktail..to sharpen up our appetites for lunch. **1953** S. PLATH *Let.* 15 May (1978) I. 114 Sharpening up writing again, once it's rusty, is very painful.

c. Also, of a political measure.

1962 *Listener* 2 Aug. 160/1 French anti-cartel policy was sharpened up by the act of 1958.

g. *refl.* To improve one's appearance; to smarten oneself up.

1952 S. SELVON *Brighter Sun* ii. 24 Since the Americans came the girls sharpened themselves up and wouldn't be had for less than five Yankee dollars.

Sharpey's fibre (ʃā·ɹpi). *Anat.* [Named after William *Sharpey* (1802–80), Scottish anatomist, who described such fibres in 1856 (J. Quain *Anat.* (ed. 6) I. p. cxx).] A fibre of connective tissue passing from the periosteum through the lamellæ of a bone or tooth.

[**1878** *Q. Jrnl. Microsc. Sci.* XVIII. 132 The lamellæ when stripped off from a bone that has been softened in acid but subsequently freed from all traces of the acid by long steeping in water or spirit exhibit under the microscope the appearance of intercrossing fibres (the reticulating fibres of Sharpey).] **1890** G. M. GOULD *New Med. Dict.* 400/2 *Sharpey's fibers*, calcified fibers of white, fibrous tissue bolting together the peripheric lamellæ of bone. **1896** A. CLARKSON *Text-bk. Histol.* vi. 151 In addition to fibres forming the lamellæ themselves, there are others—perforating, or Sharpey's fibres—to be found in bone. **1946** *Nature* 24 Aug. 269/1 Superficially placed osteocytes with their processes, and Sharpey's fibres, stand out black against the colourless matrix. **1962** BLAKE & TROTT *Periodontology* ii. 12 The parts of the fibres which lie embedded within cementum or bone are known as Sharpey's fibres.

sharpie. Restrict *U.S.* to sense in Dict. and add: **1.** (Earlier example.)

1860 *Diary* 10 Dec. in *Outing* (1913) Mar. 688/2, I took some of the skiffs and sharpies behind the Emma S...and we went down to Whig inlet.

2. *colloq.* (orig. *U.S.*). **a.** = SHARPER[1] 2; **b.** = SHARP *sb.*[1] 8 b.

1942 BERREY & VAN DEN BARK *Amer. Thes. Slang* §461 *Clever Crook*,..sharper, sharpie, sharpshooter, slicker. *Ibid.* §637 *Sports predictor*,..dopester, sharp, sharpie. **1944** *Chicago Daily News* 4 Nov. 6/1 Central characters of both plays are engaging highbinders and sharpies who are not exactly thieves, but more than slightly overoptimistic in their use of..other people's money. **1949** W. R. BURNETT *Asphalt Jungle* xiv. 92 He..couldn't make up his mind whether he'd been a chump or a sharpie. **1964** S. BELLOW *Herzog* 3 He had chosen to be dreamy..and the sharpies cleaned him out. **1974** *Times Lit. Suppl.* 3 May 465/4 The same wise-cracking, classless sharpie..can make throwaway remarks about Ingrid Haebler in his own tatty old flat. **1979** T. GIFFORD *Hollywood Gothic* vi. 71, I had drunks.. directors, producers, New York sharpies of every kind.

3. *Austral. colloq.* A young person who adopts certain extreme or provocative styles of hair, dress, etc. (see quot. 1975); the Australian counterpart of the *SKINHEAD.

1965 W. DICK *Bunch of Ratbags* 202 The more a sharpie protested he was not a bodgie, the more they [*sc.* the police] laughed and belted him. **1972** *Sydney Morning Herald* 20 Jan. 2 It was alleged in evidence that Still died during an incident involving 'sharpies' and 'long-hairs' outside Greystanes Progress Hall. **1975** *Sun-Herald* (Sydney) 13 Apr. 7 A sharpie is usually aged between 14 and 19 years. The boys wear their hair cropped short on the top and sides and longer at the back. The girls often wear 'dolly' makeup and have their ears pierced. Tattoos are often worn by both sexes. The sharpies wear blue jeans or high-waisted slacks supported by old-fashioned braces, matched with a tee shirt and sometimes a woollen cardigan. **1977** *Sunday Mail* (Brisbane) 21 Aug. 37/3 Carmel says her mother accepted her being a sharpie—even a punk—till she shaved her hair off.

4. *N. Amer. colloq.* That which is smart or in good condition. Used esp. of cars. Cf. *SHARP *a.* 6* a, c; *SHARP *sb.*[1] 13.

1970 *Globe & Mail* (Toronto) 26 Sept. 47/7 (Advt.), Chevrolet Malibu 2-door hardtop, fully equipped, a real sharpie. **1979** *Tucson* (Arizona) *Citizen* (Advt. Suppl.) 28 Apr. 17/1 Starter home..carpeting, drapes and remodeled kitchen. Call..to see this little sharpie.

5. *attrib.* or as *adj.* in above senses.

1961 W. BROWN *Bedeviled* 19 He was a tall, slender youth with the sharpie clothes and the long sideburns of the juvenile delinquent. **1975** *Sunday Mail* (Brisbane) 13 Apr. 30/1 Police will mount an all-out campaign against Sydney's sharpie gangs. **1980** *Times Lit. Suppl.* 7 Nov. 1270/4 Higgins..tells his latest story from the point of view of a hustling Irish-American sharpy lawyer.

sharping, *vbl. sb.* **1. a.** (*U.S.* and *transf.* examples of *SHARP *v.* 5 c.)

1895, 1956 [see *FLATTING *vbl. sb.* 3].

sharpish, *a.* Add: **2.** quasi-*adv.* = SHARPLY *adv.* (esp. sense 4); somewhat sharply. *colloq.*

1886 BAUMANN *Londinismen* 174/1 He looks sharpish for his rents. **1899** *Longman's Mag.* July 273 When a barge does come, Dorcas 'bustles her about sharpish', and there is a great to-do. **1952** *Chambers's Jrnl.* Feb. 119/1 We're late ourselves. Better be off sharpish if we're going to be home for tea. **1975** T. ALLBEURY *Special Collection* viii. 54 They shuffled him back to Moscow pretty sharpish.

sharpite (ʃā·ɹpəit). *Min.* [a. F. *sharpite* (J. Mélon 1938, in *Bull. Séances Inst. R. Colonial Belge* IX. 333), f. the name of Major R. R. *Sharp*, who discovered the uranium deposit where it was first found: see -ITE[1].] A hydrated carbonate of uranium found as greenish yellow crusts of thin radiating fibres.

1939 *Mineral. Abstr.* VII. 225 Sharpite forms yellowish-green, radially fibrous crusts on curite and becquerelite from Shinkolobwe, Katanga. **1971** *Ibid.* XXII. 92/1 Secondary uranium mineralization occurs among secondary Fe, Cu, and Pb minerals in Kletno; it is represented by nasturan, uranium black, gummite, fourmarierite, and traces of sharpite.

sharply, *adv.* Add: **7*.** Smartly, fashionably.

1965 V. CANNING *Whip Hand* ii. 15, I was sharply dressed for the part, young man on holiday, well-heeled. **1981** P. INCHBALD *Tondo for Short* vii. 73 He was dressed as sharply as he could manage.

sharpness. Add: **9. b.** *Physical Sci.* The extent to which a phenomenon, condition, etc., is sharp (sense *11 b).

1906 G. EICHHORN *Wireless Telegr.* vi. 40 Wien clearly demonstrated the greater sharpness of resonance in loosely-coupled systems than in the simple system. **1921** [see *PEAKINESS]. **1966** COTTON & WILKINSON *Adv. Inorg. Chem.* (ed. 2) xxvii. 733 (*caption*) Note the greater sharpness of the solution spectra.

sharp practice. Add: **2. a.** (Earlier example.) **b.** (Earlier and later examples.)

The second instance in quot. 1836 may also belong with 2 b.

1836 DICKENS *Pickw.* (1837) xx. 209 'Dodson and Fogg—sharp practice their's—capital men of business is Dodson and Fogg, Sir.' Mr. Pickwick admitted the sharp practice of Dodson and Fogg. **1845** C. M. KIRKLAND *Western Clearings* 42 His 'law studies'..were comprised in six months' 'sharp practice', as clerk to a gentleman who had quitted the shoe-maker's bench for the law. **1914** WODEHOUSE *Man Upstairs* 182 He could not say exactly that it was sharp practice on Owen's part. **1944** 'BRAHMS' & 'SIMON' *Titania has Mother* ix. 95 'Sharp practice?' said the Fairy Peaseblossom. 'Oh no, ma'am. Just diplomacy.'

Sharps (ʃāɹps). *U.S.* Also with small initial. The name of Christian *Sharps* (1811–74), American gunsmith, applied *absol.* to any of a number of firearms invented and manufactured by him; esp. a celebrated variety of breech-loading, single-shot rifle. Also in the possessive and *attrib.*

1850 *Sci. Amer.* 9 Mar. 193/2 (*heading*) Sharps' breech-loading patent rifle. **1873** *Forest & Stream* XXIX. 2 As long as the Indian agents send cases of breech-loading Sharps marked 'hardware'..as Government annuity, we must expect these murders, robberies, etc., on the part of the Indians. **1929** B. DAVIS *Truth about Geronimo* 161 His gun, an antiquated Sharps rifle, had gone off accidentally. **1958** 'W. HENRY' *Seven Men at Mimbres Springs* xv. 176 Doc Harnaday and his old Sharps could..'hit a yearling bull..at 900 yards'.

sharp-set, *a.* **1. b.** (Later example.)

1918 V. WOOLF *Diary* 5 Feb. (1977) I. 119 She [*sc.* a dog]..wags her tail as hard as she can, & snatches at any scrap of talk as if she were sharp set.

sharp-shin. Add: **2.** The small North American sharp-shinned hawk, *Accipiter striatus*; cf. *sharp-shinned* s.v. SHARP *a.* C. 2.

1912 W. B. BARROWS *Michigan Bird Life* 264 There were Sharp-shins everywhere—sweeping about through the woods. **1937** *Nat. Geogr. Mag.* July 132/2 We have watched the sharp-shin dodge through the thickest brush after its quarry. **1960** R. T. PETERSON *Field Guide Birds Texas* 58 Sharp-shin's square-tipped tail can look slightly rounded when spread.

sharp-shod, *a.* Chiefly *N. Amer.* [f. SHARP *adv.* + SHOD *ppl. a.*] Of a horse: provided with caulked shoes; rough-shod. Also [as a back-formation] **sharp-shoe** *v. trans. rare.*

1889 *Cent. Dict.*, Sharp-shod. **1904** in *Eng. Dial. Dict.* **1906** *Daily Colonist* (Victoria, B.C.) 20 Jan. 8/2 It was quite apparent from the horses' tracks in the snow that one saddle horse was sharp shod. **1935** H. DAVIS *Honey in Horn* xviii. 305 A man run down by a bunch of sharp-shod horses has a tendency to scatter around badly. **1962** J. ONSLOW *Bowler-Hatted Cowboy* xi. 100 We sharp-shod our horses in front with shoes that had sharp calkins at the heels and one on each toe.

sharpshooter. Add: **1. b.** Restrict to *fig.* and add later examples.

1933 *Sun* (Baltimore) 26 May 1/3 They were set apart as a shining target upon which all political sharpshooters practiced. **1960** *Twentieth Cent.* May 447 Sociology is not at present and is not likely to become in the near future a subject for intellectual sharpshooters.

c. *U.S. Mil.* A rifleman of a particular grade; *spec.* one who has attained the level of proficiency between that of marksman and expert.

1889 *N.Y. Times* 15 Sept. 13/2 Until within a comparatively recent period all officers and members of organizations armed with the Remington rifle scoring 25 points or better at 200 and 500 yards, 6 shots at each distance..were accounted 'marksmen'... Later on a distinction was made in respect of men making 42 points or better, by classing them as 'sharpshooters'. **1918** E. S. FARROW *Dict. Mil. Terms* 551 *Sharpshooter*,..in small-arms firing, a grade of rifleman just below that of expert rifleman. **1974** M. ALLEN *Super Tour* i. 6 The entrance was guarded..by the chief gatekeeper or one of his three sons, all armed with rifles and all rating as sharpshooters when they had done their military service. **1977** *Time* 22 Aug. 34/3 He flunked his first rifle-shooting test but eventually qualified as an infantry sharpshooter (the middle ranking between marksman and expert) with the M-16 rifle.

2. Transferred senses. † **a.** *Cricket.* = SHOOTER 9. *Obs.*

1863 *Boy's Own Vol.* Christmas 218 Among the best men with sharpshooters were Wenman, among the old players, Carpenter and Daft, and last, not least, Mr. E. Grace.

b. *Sport.* A player whose aim is particularly accurate. *U.S.*

1912 *N.Y. Tribune* 21 Sept. 12/1 Devore..was the principal sharpshooter of the second encounter, as he answered for all four runs. **1974** *State* (Columbia, S. Carolina) 27 Feb. 3-B/1 Virginia Military..builds its offense around freshman sharpshooter John Krovic.

c. *U.S. colloq.* = SHARP *sb.*[1] 8 b.

1942 *Sun* (Baltimore) 7 Mar. 10/5 The sharpshooters have been saying that Market Wise should romp in. **1944** *Ibid.* 21 Sept. 17/5 The real romance of the race track..is the betting crowd. First you get the experts or the sharpshooters.

3. One of several leafhoppers of the family Cicadellidæ, feeding on grasses, grape-vines, and other plants.

1902 *Yearbk. U.S. Dept. Agric. 1901* 377 Early cotton.. avoids to a great extent damage to the plant by the boll-worm, cotton worm, and sharp-shooter. **1959** *Washington Post* 23 July A20/2 Priesendorfer identified them as leafhoppers, commonly called sharpshooters.

sharpshooting *vbl. sb.* and *ppl. a.* (later *transf.* examples).

1948 *Sporting Mirror* 19 Nov. 5/1 First Division clubs are queuing up to bid for Vic Lambden, Bristol Rovers' sharpshooting centre forward. **1976** *Norwich Mercury* 10 Dec., It was the same Carrow player who had scored the first goal, and he was certainly giving Old Boys a lesson in sharpshooting. **1978** M. PUZO *Fools Die* xvi. 172 The client was a sharpshooting Wasp Wall Street broker named Buddy Stove.

sharpster (ʃā·ɹpstəɹ). *colloq.* (chiefly *U.S.*). [f. SHARP *sb.*[1] + -STER.] **1.** = SHARPER[1] 2.

1942 BERREY & VAN DEN BARK *Amer. Thes. Slang* §436 *Cheat*,..sharpster, shaver, shyster. **1955** *Archivum Linguisticum* VII. 153 An adjectival derivative..with the pejorative sense of 'sharpster'. **1965** *English Studies* XLVI. 465 A boxer, among scores of other appellations, may be a *fightster*..; a dishonest gambler, a *sharpster*.

2. A 'sharp' or stylish dresser. (In quot. *attrib.*)

1957 J. KEROUAC *On Road* (1958) II. vi. 144 Once I knocked on his door..and he opened it wearing..a vest with nothing underneath, and long striped sharpster pants.

sharrer (ʃæ·ră). *colloq.* Also **sharra.** Short for CHAR-À-BANC. Cf. *CHARA[2].

1934 D. L. SAYERS *Nine Tailors* 114 There's a regular party comin'..in Jack Brownlow's sharrer. **1966** 'L. LANE' *ABZ of Scouse* 102 She fell outer ther sharrer. **1977** *Listener* 15 Dec. 801/2 And charabanc: it went from bang to bong and back again to bang... 'Meanwhile,' says Mr Ferris, 'the nation went about its business and called it either a coach or a sharra.'

sharry (ʃæ·ri). *colloq.* Also **sharrie.** As prec. Cf. *CHARRY.

1923 *Chambers's Jrnl.* Dec. 7/1 Many who travel by 'sharry' do so because they want the pleasures of the road. **1974** P. WRIGHT *Lang. Brit. Industry* ix. 79 Part of many a market square..was daily reserved as a parking area for motor-coaches (then called *sharries* or *charry-bangs*).

‖ **shashlik** (ʃæ·ʃlik). [ad. Russ. *shashlýk*, ult. f. Turk. *šiš* a spit, skewer; cf. *SHISH KEBAB.] An Eastern European and Asian kebab of mutton and garnishings often served on a skewer. Also *attrib.*

1925 R. F. WILSON *Paris on Parade* vi. 163 He gives them..*shashlik*, alternately spitted morsels of mutton and bacon grilled over charcoal. **1951** 'A. GARVE' *Murder in Moscow* xv. 144, I was giving Watson luncheon.. and he had to dash away with his *shashlik* almost untouched. **1960** *Guardian* 29 Aug. 5/6, I ate..shashlik with retsina. **1977** *N.Y. Times* 9 May L2/2 An outdoor shashlik stand just off Ashkhabad's Marx Prospekt was pulling in passers-by.

Shasta (ʃæ·stă, *locally* ʃæ·sti), *a.* and *sb.* Also **Saste, Shaste, Shasty.** [Native name.] **A.** *adj.* **1.** Designating a tribe of American Indians living in the highlands of northern California or the language of the Hokan group spoken by this people.

1843 T. J. FARNHAM *Trav. Gt. Western Prairies* II. 208 The doctor..had his face very much slashed in a contest with the Shasty Indians near the southern border of Oregon. **1851** G. GIBBS *Jrnl.* in H. R. Schoolcraft *Indian Tribes* (1853) III. iv. 161 This man was afterwards dispatched..to make another attempt to assemble the Shasté tribes. **1963** *Language* XXXIX. 40 The Shasta language of northern California and southern Oregon has a long history of relevance for Hokan studies.

2. Special collocations in *Nat. Hist.*: **Shasta cypress,** the Macnab cypress, *Cupressus macnabiana*, a small tree native to California; **Shasta daisy,** a perennial herb, *Chrysanthemum* × *superbum*, of the family Compositæ, a hybrid developed by Luther Burbank (1849–1926) and bearing large white flowers; **Shasta (red) fir,** a large red fir, *Abies magnifica* var. *shastensis*, native to western North America; **Shasta lily,** a yellow-flowered fragrant lily, *Lilium kelleyanum*, native to the mountains of central and northern California.

1897 G. B. SUDWORTH *Nomencl. Arborescent Flora U.S.* 76 *Cupressus macnabiana*. Macnab Cypress..[also called] Shasta Cypress. **1908** N. L. BRITTON *N. Amer. Trees* 101 The tree..is also called Fragrant cypress, Shasta cypress, Macnab's cypress. **1901** L. BURBANK *New Creations* (Suppl.) 8 When 'Shasta Daisies' were being bred and educated up to their present state more admiration has been bestowed upon them by visitors than upon any other flowering plant growing on my grounds. **1977** *Monitor* (McAllen, Texas) 26 June 1C/7 The church was decorated with pedestal urns of white Shasta daisies. **1897** G. B. SUDWORTH *Nomencl. Arborescent Flora U.S.* 58 *Abies magnifica* Shasta Fir..[also called] Shasta Red Fir. **1949** COLLINGWOOD & BRUSH *Knowing your Trees* 106 Red Fir, also known as red-barked fir, Shasta fir and golden fir, is found on high mountain slopes and meadows. **1915** ARMSTRONG & THORNBER *Western Wild Flowers* 34 Shasta Lily is a variety with a small bulb. **1937** J. H. MCFARLAND et al. *Garden Bulbs in Color* 155 There are several varieties of this Washington or Shasta Lily.

B. *sb.* **1.** (A member of) the Shasta people.

1843 T. J. FARNHAM *Trav. Gt. Western Prairies* II. 311 (*population table*) Shastys 500. **1846** H. HALE *Ethnogr. & Philol.* (U.S. Exploring Exped.) 218 The women of the Saste..are tattooed in lines from the mouth to the chin. **1855** *Crescent City* (California) *Herald* 27 Oct., Some of the Shastas..are represented as having been the last to retreat. **1903** G. W. JAMES *Indian Basketry* 79 The fine white grass, used by the Shastas in the maufacture of their baskets is gained from great elevations in the mountains. **1935** R. BENEDICT *Patterns of Culture* ii. 42 Among the Shasta it was the convention that only women were so blessed. **1973** A. H. WHITEFORD *N. Amer. Indian Arts* 47 The..Shasta..had..food baskets.

2. Their language. Also *Comb.*, as **Shasta-Achomawi.**

1851 G. GIBBS *Jrnl.* 12 Oct. in H. R. Schoolcraft *Indian Tribes* (1853) III. iv. 151 Higher on the main river, the prevailing language is the Shasté. **1905** *Amer. Anthropologist* VII. 213 (*heading*) The Shasta-Achomawi: a new linguistic stock, with four new dialects. **1913** [see *HOKAN]. **1965** *Language* XLI. 175 Dixon's Shasta-Achomawi group..was placed in Dixon and Kroeber's Hokan stock.

Hence **Sha·stan** *a.* and *sb.* [-AN], (designating) a linguistic grouping of the Shasta and certain other peoples (formerly including the Achomawi-Atsugewi), or the peoples so comprised.

1910 *Bull. U.S. Bureau Amer. Ethnol.* XXX. II. 528/2 Shastan Family..a linguistic stock comprising two principal groups, the Sastean and the Palaihnihan of Powell. **1963** *Language* XXXIX. 43 This neatly validates the theory of contraction with the Shastan subfamily. *Ibid.*, There may have been as many as five such families a little over a century ago, viz. *Shastan*..; *Palaihnihan*..; *Pomoan*..; *Chumashan*..; and *Yuman*. **1974** *Encycl. Brit. Micropædia* IX. 118/2 *Shastan Indians*, a group of Indian peoples speaking related languages of the Shastan family of Hokan stock... The culture of the Shastans was imitative of the Yurok and Karok.

Shaster, Shastra. Add: The form *sastra* (or the scholarly transliteration *śāstra*) is now freq. used. (Further examples.) Also, a body of teaching, a science; a treatise. Hence **Shastra·ic, Sastra·ic** *a.*

1845 *Encycl. Metrop.* XXI. 673/1 Those who study the Védas..are styled *Waïdik*,..when learned in the six Sástras they are called *Sástri*. **1932** S. DASGUPTA *Hist. Indian Philos.* II. xiv. 445 At the first stage a man performs his duties in accordance with the injunctions of the *śāstras*. **1956** V. RAGHAVAN *Indian Heritage* p. lvii, These systems later came to be called *Sastras*, meaning thereby merely that they are authoritative and systematic schools of thought. **1960** KOESTLER *Lotus & Robot* i. 59 It is significant that every science in India is called a Sastra—a system of thought with a spiritual purpose. **1961** WEBSTER, Shastraic. **1967** SINGHA & MASSEY *Indian Dances* i. 33 The shastraic literature which kept it alive. **1968** *Indian Mus. Jrnl.* V. 46 Its gigantic volume, comprehensive subject-matter, *śāstraic* treatment of the subject-matter. **1974** *Encycl. Brit. Macropædia* III. 433/1 From the 2nd century AD onward, Mahāyāna authors wrote 'treatises' (*śāstras*) in their own names.

shat, *pa. pple.* of SHIT *v.* in Dict. and Suppl.; also var. SHOTT in Dict. and Suppl.

shatchen, var. *SHADCHAN. **shatranji,** var. *SITRINGEE.

shatter, *sb.* **1.** (Further example.)

1872 *Argosy* XIII. 199 It's a sad thing..for men like you to be obliged to work yourselves to shatters to keep them.

shatter, *v.* Add: **7. shatter belt** *Geol.*, a belt of fractured or brecciated rock formed as a result of faulting; **shatter cone** *Geol.*, a fluted conical structure produced in rock by intense mechanical shock, esp. by that associated with meteoritic impact; hence **shatter-coned** *a.*, characterized by the presence of shatter cones; **shatter-coning** *vbl. sb.*, the formation or presence of shatter cones; **shatter crack** *Metallurgy* (see quot. 1958); **shatter-pate** (later example); **shatter-pated** *a.* (later examples); **shatter-proof** *a.*, proof against shattering; also *fig.*

1910 PEACH & HORNE in Murray & Pullar *Bathymetr. Survey Scottish Fresh-Water Lochs* I. 459 Shatter belts situated along lines of fault or dislocations of the strata have exercised a considerable influence in producing the isolation of these individual masses. **1970** R. J. SMALL *Study of Landforms* iii. 102 Where crustal movement leads to the creation of crushed or brecciated zones ('shatter-belts')..., the development of river valleys may be closely guided. **1933** W. H. BUCHER in *Rep. 16th Internat. Geol. Congr.* 1070 In the same vicinity more convincing evidence of the action of an explosive force is seen in the local development of 'shatter cones', innumerable incipient cracks traversing beds of rather coarsely crystalline dolomite in the shape of interpenetrating cones, not unlike cone-in-cone. **1979** *Sci. Amer.* Mar. 43/3 Macroscopic evidence includes 'shatter cones', structures of quartzite that flare outward and downward, away from the direction of impact. **1967** *McGraw-Hill Yearbk. Sci. & Technol.* 110 The Steinheim Basin..is the prototype shatter-coned structure. **1968** *New Scientist* 28 Nov. 501/2 A really definitive theory of shatter coning is still lacking. **1975** *Nature* 29 May 394/1 Shatter coning and intense microtwinning of calcite..are indicators of shock metamorphism. **1930** *Jrnl. Iron & Steel Inst.* CXXI. 703 Rapid cooling through the secondary brittle range is believed to cause the formation of shatter cracks in rails showing secondary brittleness. **1958** A. D. MERRIMAN *Dict. Metallurgy* 315/2 *Shatter cracks*, a name used in reference to fine internal fissures, particularly when found in the heads of steel rails. The cracks lie at random in all directions and occur most frequently in large steel forgings. **1976** *Times* 7 Dec. 14/5 This poor shatterpate's condition. **1917** J. B. CABELL *Cream of Jest* (1927) xxi. 115 Everywhere, in every age,..men stumbled amiable and shatter-pated through a jungle of miracles, blind to its wonderfulness. **1938** *Sun* (Baltimore) 18 Feb. 12/2 Ah reckon yo're a mite shatter-pated in yore wit-box. **1936** *Ibid.* 6 Feb. 6/2 Two men who locked the doors of their automobile from the inside..watched State police vainly try to break through shatterproof glass. **1953** M. MCCARTHY in *Reporter* 3 Mar. 38/2 These people live in shatterproof hierarchical structures. **1978** M. DEWIS *Law Health & Safety at Work* v. 245 The plaintiff relied on a statement that the windscreens were shatterproof and bought one of their cars.

shattered, *ppl. a.* Add: **c.** *colloq.* Extremely distressed or exhausted; upset, overcome.

1930 A. CHRISTIE *Murder at Vicarage* ii. 14 How tiresome everyone is. I feel shattered... If only I had some money I'd go away. **1968** *Listener* 12 Sept. 337/2, I came in at tea-time, I sat down and I was absolutely shattered. **1978** S. RADLEY *Death & Maiden* viii. 75, I honestly can't tell you anything about Mary. I'm shattered, that's all I know.

shatterer. (Later example.)

1923 *Weekly Dispatch* 25 Feb. 2 Stravinsky..is a disturber of our peace, a shatterer of illusions.

shattering, *vbl. sb.* (Examples in sense 3 of the vb.)

1960 *Farmer & Stockbreeder* 16 Feb. 77/1 Some plants produced seed heads which were less susceptible to shattering than others. **1974** E. STACEY *Peace Country* ii. 112 The report said that he lost considerable of the crop from shattering.

shattering, *ppl. a.* Add: **2. c.** In trivial use, astounding, upsetting; tiresome.

1924 WODEHOUSE *Bill the Conqueror* v. 97 Any ordinary disaster she might have coped with, but this was too shattering. **1948** R. LEHMANN *Note in Music* (ed. 2) 114 We don't converse much. But now and then she lets fall a shattering remark. **1958** [see *LAVATORIAL *a.* 2]. **1967** *Listener* 16 Nov. 637/3 The hundreds of quotations.. about..murders, the savage punishments, and slave life in the New World, are shattering.

shatteringly *adv.* (later examples).

1911 G. K. CHESTERTON *Ballad White Horse* v. 112 On the helm of a high chief Fell shatteringly his brand. **1939** H. J. MASSINGHAM *Countryman's Jrnl.* xxx. 132 The argument applies far more shatteringly to the Purbeck limestone.

shattuckite (ʃæ·tŏkəit). *Min.* [f. the name *Shattuck* (see quot. 1915) + -ITE[1].] A hydrated silicate of copper found as pale blue orthorhombic crystals.

1915 W. T. SCHALLER in *Jrnl. Washington Acad. Sci.* V. 7 Shattuckite is a blue hydrous copper silicate from the Shattuck Arizona Copper Company's mine at Bisbee, Arizona... Shattuckite forms pseudomorphs after malachite and also occurs as small spherulites. **1928** *Mineral. Abstr.* III. 485 Scalenohedra..of calcite from Tantara mine, Katanga, are completely changed to dioptase or to a mixture of deep-blue pleochroic shattuckite and pale-blue non-pleochroic plancheite. **1977** *Amer. Mineralogist* LXII. 491 The crystal structure of shattuckite, $Cu_5 (SiO_3)_4(OH)_2$ has been refined in the orthorhombic space group *Pcab*.

shaughraun (ʃɑ·xrā, ʃaxrā·n). *Anglo-Ir.* and *Newfoundland.* Also **shaughran,** (Newfoundland) **shaugraun** (-g-). [ad. Ir. *seachrán* a wandering, a straying, an error.] **a.** In phrs. *to go a shaughraun*: to go wrong; *on* (or *in*) *a* (or *the*) *shaughraun*: in a vagrant or drifting state. **b.** A vagabond.

1843 W. CARLETON *Traits & Stories Irish Peasantry* I. 5 His speculation was gone a shaughran, as he termed it. *c* **1874** D. BOUCICAULT in M. R. Booth *Eng. Plays of 19th Cent.* (1969) II. 165 (*title*) The Shaughraun. *Ibid.*, Conn, the shaughraun, the soul of every fair, the life of every funeral, the first fiddle at all weddings and patterns. **1892** E. LAWLESS *Grania* I. II. ii. 153 'Tis eight days in the week she'll find herself working..yes, and going a shaughraun most like at the tail of it all. **1922** JOYCE *Ulysses* 134 We'll paralyse Europe as Ignatius Gallaher used to say when he was on the shaughraun, doing billiardmarking in the Clarence. **1955** L. E. F. ENGLISH *Historic Newfoundland* (St John's Newfoundland Tourist Devel. Div.) 36 *Shaugraun*, a vagabond state. **1961** 'F. O'BRIEN' *Hard Life* v. 34 Well the dear knows I think you are trying to destroy my temper, Father, and put me out of my wits and make an unfortunate shaughraun out of me. **1963** *Amer. Speech* XXXVIII. 300 *Shaugraun*,..(1) A vagabond state, (2) a person in a vagabond state, a bum. 'He spent his youth in a shaugraun.' 'He was a shaugraun.' [Newfoundland].

‖ **shauri** (ʃɑu·ri). Pl. **shauries, shauris.** [a. Swahili, f. Arab. *šūrā.*] Counsel, debate, problem.

1925 N. K. STRANGE *Wife in Kenya* xvii. 123 Sometimes such strangers came on business intent, to have a grand shauri, or a remunerative deal in posho. **1938** E. HEMINGWAY *Fifth Column* (1939) 121 The gun-bearers..go with us. It's their *shauri*. You see, they signed on for it. **1970** *Kenya Farmer* Feb. 8/5 Often he can solve a problem by calling a meeting of the staff and obtaining their views and suggestions, not only on their personal *shauris*, but also on improvements in sales and service. **1975** T. DINESEN *My Sister, Isak Dinesen* vi. 79 Sometime in the future, in which we shall remember all the shauries (especially difficult and unpleasant things) as shadows and smile at them.

shave, *sb.*[2] **3. a.** (Earlier examples.)

1834 C. A. DAVIS *Lett. J. Downing* 39 I've got some real shaves myself in that way. **1855** J. R. PLANCHÉ *Discreet Princess* in *Extravaganzas of Planché* (1879) V. 130, I much suspect this is some barbarous 'shave'.

shave, *v.* Add: **12. a.** To cut down in amount, to reduce. orig. and chiefly *U.S.*

1898 *Boston Herald* 23 Jan. 14/3 There are indications that tariff sheets are being secretly shaved. **1941** B. SCHULBERG *What makes Sammy Run?* vii. 141 The studio was having one of its periodic drives to cut overheads—which seemed to mean shaving stenographers' wages first. **1962** WODEHOUSE *Service with Smile* xi. 180 In the hope of making him shave his price a bit? **1972** *Times* 16 Feb. 13/8 This coin enables traders to shave their prices and if it did not exist there would be a considerable rounding up.

b. To deduct (a small amount) *from* or *off* (a quantity, time, etc.).

a **1961** in *Webster* (1961) s.v., New procedures shave minutes from the unloading process. **1982** *Times* 26 Aug. 15/2 The Bank shaved another 1/8 of a percentage point off the rate at which it buys bills from the discount houses.

13. *Comb.*, as **shavecoat,** a man's casual garment resembling a housecoat; **shavetail** orig. *U.S. Mil. slang*, (*a*) an untrained pack animal, identified by a shaven tail; also *attrib.*; (*b*) *fig.* a newly commissioned officer, *spec.* a second lieutenant; also gen., an inexperienced person; also *attrib.*

1964 *N.Y. Times Mag.* 29 Nov. 73 Weldon makes something like a shavecoat. It's extra comfortable and convenient for shaving. **1970** *Sunday Mail* (Brisbane)

27 Dec. 6D The bridegroom wore a mustard colored shavecoat. But it was a very nice shavecoat. **1846** *New Orleans Delta* 31 Aug. 366/2 [This mule] was followed by Shavetail Kicky, Esq., who, in a few pertinent remarks, expressed his ass-ent to the proceedings. **1891** J. G. Bourke *On Border with Crook* 153 Officers..are known as 'bell-sharps' and 'shave-tails'..the former being the old captain..and the latter the youngster fresh from his studies. **1908** R. E. Beach *Barrier* 283 The first shave-tail desperado that meets him will spit in his eye. **1948** F. Blake *Johnny Christmas* I. 26 He had..six shavetail Indian ponies packed with articles he had brought down to sell. **1976** L. Deighton *Twinkle, Twinkle, Little Spy* vii. 70, I was a shavetail, just out of pilot training. **1980** *Blair & Ketchum's Country Jrnl.* Oct. 43/1 That last practice started in the mines, where a 'shavetail' was a snaky mule, not to be trusted.

shaved, *ppl. a.* Add: **1. a.** *spec.* of ice cut in thin slices or shavings for chilling drinks.

1927 E. Hemingway *Fiesta* III. xix. 272, I..had a glass of lemon juice and shaved ice. **1962** *Listener* 16 Aug. 248/2 Snowball, which consists of shaved ice covered with scarlet syrup. **1971** J. Philips *Escape a Killer* (1972) I. ii. 20 The martini shaker in its bed of shaved ice.

shaver. 5. a. Delete † *Obs.* and add later examples. Now esp. a small electrical appliance with a set of blades working against a perforated guard.

1897 *Sears, Roebuck Catal.* 111/3 A little gem and a dandy shaver, no better steel put in a razor. **1924** *Punch's Almanack for 1925* 3 Nov. p. xxviii/1 (Advt.), The Wilkinson safety shaver with hollow-ground blades is the ideal..gift for men. **1960** N. Mitford *Don't tell Alfred* xviii. 193 'What do you pack?' 'Shavers—you know, razors.' **1980** R. Moody *Devil you Don't* iii. 33 He..took out his shaver and toothbrush.

6. *colloq.* = *shavecoat* s.v. *Shave *v.* 13.

1926 H. Pearson *Whispering Gallery* vii. 106 At a big meeting of hospital directors he turned up..in..unbusiness-like colours. One of the directors whispered to another: 'He'll be coming in his 'shaver' next.'

7. *attrib.*, as **shaver point, socket,** a power point for an electric shaver.

1971 *Fremdsprachen* XV. 145/1 *Shaver point,* Trockenrasiersteckdose. **1977** *Western Morning News* 30 Aug. 10/4 (Advt.), Good-sized kitchen; radios, shaver points, &c. all bedrooms. **1965** *Newnes Practical Householder Encycl.* III. 1329/1 The shaver is operated from a special shaver socket unit. **1978** *Cornish Guardian* 27 Apr. 19/2 (Advt.), Strip lights with shaver sockets.

Shavian (ʃēi·viăn), *a.* and *sb.* [f. *Shavi(us,* the latinized surname of George Bernard Shaw (1856–1950), playwright and critic + -AN.] **A.** *adj.* Pertaining to, characteristic of, or resembling G. B. Shaw or his works or opinions.

1904 *Times* 2 Nov. 6/2 Not a play but a thoroughly characteristic 'Shavian' farago. **1935** G. K. Chesterton *G. B. Shaw* 292 The Shavian evolutionist does really want to cast the whole body of man into Chaos. **1960** [see *metabiological* adj. s.v. *metabiology]. **1977** M. T. Bloom *13th Man* vi. 101 Your mother..named you for a Shavian heroine and..you've turned into one.

B. *sb.* An admirer or follower of G. B. Shaw. (In quot. 1921, a character of Shaw's.)

1905 G. B. Shaw *Let.* 10 Feb. (1972) II. 512 Though he is an admirer of Shaw, he is no Shavian. *Ibid.* 18 Feb. 515 Are you going to write a natural history, like a true Shavian? **1921** *Spectator* 28 May 680/2 The poet Eugene Marchbanks is perhaps as near to primary emotion as any Shavian. **1967** O. Lancaster *Eye to Future* I. 8 My mother..always remained a devoted Shavian. **1978** P. Boardman *Worlds of Patrick Geddes* xi. 405 P. G. uses modern socialism as his next example... He names Marx ..the Fabians..and the Shavians with income-equalisations.

Hence **Shavia·na,** objects or texts relating to G. B. Shaw; **Sha·vianism,** the tenets or a characteristic saying of G. B. Shaw; also *nonce-wds.* in Shaw's writings, as **Shaviani·smus** = prec.; **Shavia·nity,** the quality or state of being Shavian; **Sha·vianized** *a.*, that has been rendered Shavian in character.

1903 G. B. Shaw *Let.* 2 Sept. (1972) II. 357 Your theme ..is that the book is a mere rechauffée of stale Shavianized Nietzsche. **1905** —— *Let.* 3 Jan. (1972) II. 496 The dawning of Ibsenism & Nietzscheanism & 'Shavianism' seemed to him the coming of chaos. **1920** —— *Shaw on Theatre* (1958) 133 The younger generation, Shavians to a man, demonstrated their Shavianity by scoffing at me as a Back Number. **1927** *Observer* 12 June 15/1 It [*sc.* a foreword to a volume of plays] will be prized by collectors of Shaviana for its friendly and human qualities. **1927** G. B. Shaw *Pen Portraits & Reviews* (1932) 2 The Shavianismus tickled him enormously; and he was never tired of quoting..my jokes. **1958** *Sunday Times* 27 Apr. 8/2 This slender item of Shaviana. **1975** *Listener* 14 Aug. 218/4 A revival of Shavianism.

shaving, *vbl. sb.* Add: **4. b.** (Earlier example.)

1813 T. Eaton *Rev. N.Y.* 127 Again the broker claims per cent. For he on shaving is attent.

5. *shaving cream, -cup* (earlier example), *dish, foam, -glass* (earlier and later examples), *mirror,* † *rag, soap* (earlier example), *-tackle* (earlier and later examples), *water* (earlier example); **shaving box** (earlier example); **shaving brush** (earlier example); **shaving horse** (earlier and later examples); **shaving-knife,** (*a*) (later example); **shaving stick,** a stick of shaving soap.

1774 J. Woodforde *Diary* 14 Jan. (1924) I. 122 For a Shaving Box of one Darcy..pd 0.1.0. **1792** —— *Diary* 26 July (1927) III. 364 At D[itt]o for Shaving Brush and Powder. **1851** C. Cist *Sk. Cincinnati in 1851* 226 A. E. Wetherill, manufacturer of..soaps and shaving creams. **1922** S. Lewis *Babbitt* i. 5 He snatched up his tube of shaving-cream, furiously he lathered. **1976** 'Z. Stone' *Modigliani Scandal* III. iv. 136 Peter Usher put down his safety razor..and washed the remains of the shaving cream off his face. **1871** 'Mark Twain' *Sketches* 258 Noted the numbers on the private shaving-cups in the pigeon-holes. **1879** C. Schreiber *Jrnl.* 17 Sept. (1911) II. 205 An Oriental shaving dish with the arms of Groningen. **1961** L. G. G. Ramsey *Connoisseur New Guide Antique Eng. Pott. Porc. & Glass* 28 One-handled bleeding bowls, and shaving-dishes with a segment out of the rim. **1974** *Harrod's Christmas Catal.* 11 'His' contains..deodorant, shaving foam, soap and talc. **1979** M. Page *Pilate Plot* i. 10 A can of aerosol shaving foam. *a* **1817** Jane Austen *Persuasion* (1818) IV. i. 18 Now I am quite snug, with my little shaving glass in one corner. **1967** S. Beckett *Stories & Texts for Nothing* VI. 99 The glass, a round shaving-glass, double-faced. **1841** *Southern Lit. Messenger* VII. 527/2 A receptacle for spinning-wheels, wash-tubs, pitchforks, shaving horses, and sundry other implements of domestic industry. **1930** *Times Educ. Suppl.* 18 Oct. p. iv/1 A few tools for the lathe..a saw, a shaving-horse. **1974** P. Blandford *Country Craft Tools* ix. 128 Most shaving horses still in existence show that all sizes were made. **1843** *Knickerbocker* XXII. 386 The rub-a-dub of the cooper's mallet, the creak of his shaving-knife were still. **1911** *Daily Colonist* (Victoria, B.C.) 30 Apr. 10/2 In the surrounding staterooms, the rest began to hang up shaving mirrors and get into deck shoes. **1958** 'R. Crompton' *William's Television Show* vii. 187 The double reflection of the dressing-table mirror and the shaving mirror over the hand basin gave her a perfect view of her profile. **1796** T. Wale in H. J. Wale *My Grandfather's Pocket-Bk.* (1883) xvii. 341 Wash given out to Mrs. Wheeler... 1 pair under stockings, thread. 3 shaving wrages. **1814** Jane Austen *Let.* 18 Nov. (1952) 412 The dirty Shaving Rag was exquisite! **1790** *Pennsylvania Packet* 19 Apr. 4/2 He has likewise for Sale..Shaving soap. **1886** Kipling *Departmental Ditties* (ed. 2) 14 Pears's shaving-sticks will give you little taste and lots of lather. **1915** S. Lewis *Trail of Hawk* 328, I must go in and get a shaving-stick. **1978** D. Bagley *Flyaway* xxviii. 268 I'm old-fashioned enough to use a soap shaving-stick. **1842** Dickens *Let.* 3 Apr. (1974) III. 181 My shaving tackle, dressing case, brushes, books, and papers. **1980** *Daily Tel.* 16 Feb. 3/1 In some units..patients are expected to share toothbrushes and shaving tackle. **1837** Dickens *Pickw.* xxxix. 426 'Shaving water, Sam,' said Mr. Pickwick.

shaving, *ppl. a.* (Further examples.)

1789 E. Butler *Diary* 12 Jan. in G. H. Bell *Hamwood Papers Ladies Llangollen* (1930) 169 The most bitter Cold I ever remember, cutting shaving wind. **1810** B. Hunt *Diary* 20 Jan. in *Chester County* (Pennsylvania) *Hist. Soc. Bull.* (1898) 17/2 Most shaveing Cold weather.

Shavuoth (ʃăvū̆·əs, ʃavuo·t). Also **Shavuot, Shevuos, Shevuoth.** [a. Heb. *šābûʿōṯ*, pl. of *šābûaʿ* week.] = Pentecost 1. Cf. *Feast of weeks* s.v. Week *sb.* 2 e.

1892 I. Zangwill *Childr. Ghetto* III. xii. 194 He died four years ago come next *Shevuos.* **1941** G. G. Scholem *Major Trends Jewish Mysticism* viii. 297 An incident during the night before the feast of *Shevuoth* in 1665. **1944** M. Samuel in M. W. Weisgal *Chaim Weizmann* I. 88 The Jews were more transfigured by *their* celebration of Shavuoth and Sukkoth than the Russian peasants by *their* thanksgiving celebrations. **1962** *New Jewish Encycl.* 442/2 Since the early 1800's Shavuot has been generally the time when annual confirmation exercises are held. **1968** L. Rosten *Joys of Yiddish* 338 Synagogues are decorated with greens on *Shevuoth.* **1975** C. Potok *In the Beginning* i. 63 The last time I had been in the synagogue was about a week ago during the Festival of Shavuoth. **1981** *Amer. Speech* LVI. 13 The word spelled *Shavuot* 'Pentecost' will almost always be read..with the traditional Yiddish or Ashkenazic pronunciation as if it were spelled *Shevuos.*

‖ **shawabti** (ʃawæ·bti). *Egyptology.* Pl. **shawabtiu,** (anglicized) **shawabtis.** [ad. Egyptian *šwʒbt(y)*, prob. f. *šwʒb* persea-wood, from which the figurines may originally have been made. In later Egyptian this was replaced by *wšbty* *ushabti.] = *ushabti. Cf. *shabti.

1922 Ld. Carnarvon in *Daily Mail* 18 Dec. 10 Propped against the wall is a most beautiful portrait shawabti of the King. **1923** Carter & Mace *Tomb of Tut. Ankh. Amen* I. 120 Beside this shrine. there was a large *shawabti* statuette of the king. **1960** *Oxf. Univ. Gaz.* 4 Mar. 805/2 A XXth Dynasty polychrome terracotta shawabti figure of the chantress of Amun, Inhay. **1961** *Ibid.* 10 Mar. 832/1 Eight fragments of royal shawabtiu in various stones inscribed with cartouches of King Akhnaten. **1970** P. R. S. Moorey *Anc. Egypt* iii. 68 Among a wide variety of other funerary equipment the magical servant figures or *shawabtis* are the most common.

Shawanese, *a.* Substitute for entry: Obs. var. *Shawnee *a.* and *sb.*

Shawian (ʃǭ·iăn), *a. nonce-wd.* [f. the name of George Bernard *Shaw* (1856–1950), playwright and critic, + -IAN.] = *Shavian *a.* Also in other *rare* or *nonce* formations, esp. in Shaw's correspondence, as **Sha·wism, Sha·wite: Sha·wesque, Sha·wist** adjs., etc.

1894 G. B. Shaw *Let.* 2 Dec. (1965) I. 466 He resolved to follow up the vein of comedy opened by Henry Arthur Jones..before venturing upon the Shawian quicksand. **1895** —— *Let.* 27 Aug. (1965) I. 551, I have finished the draft of a one act piece about Napoleon, a very Shawesque curtain raiser. *Ibid.*, I want to write a big book of devotion for modern people..—a gospel of Shawianity. **1897** E. Terry *Let.* 9 Jan. in *Ellen Terry & Shaw* (1931) 144 His are my sentiments, but how comes it it's all put in a Shawesque manner? **1897** G. B. Shaw *Let.* 14 July (1965) I. 782 If I steal the plot my version will be so Shawified that nobody will recognize it. **1898** *Westm. Gaz.* 15 Jan. 8/1 Mr. Raymond Blathwayt's 'Talk' with Mr. George Bernard Shaw..is full of characteristic Shawisms. **1899** G. B. Shaw *Let. c* 26–30 Dec. (1972) II. 125, I again urge you to make that Marxian column of yours an intelligently Socialist (that is, Shawist) one. **1900** —— *Let.* 27 Jan. (1972) II. 142 The Shawish quality of my characters. **1903** —— *Let.* 26 Jan. (1972) II. 305 [Dr. L. Kellner]..was one of the first German Shawites. **1904** *Times* 2 Nov. 6/2 A rivulet of 'story' meanders through a meadow of 'Shawisms'. **1928** *Weekly Dispatch* 13 May 12/7 Here was a golden opportunity for an exhibition of Shawishness that was instantly forthcoming.

shawl, *sb.* Add: **2*.** [Anglo-Irish.] A common prostitute. Cf. *shawlie. *slang.*

1922 Joyce *Ulysses* 308 Blind to the world up in a shebeen in Bride street after closing time, fornicating with two shawls.

3. b. shawl collar (see quot. 1960); also **shawl-collared** *a.*

1913 *T. Eaton & Co. Catal.* Spring & Summer 4/3 The graceful shawl collar is edged with whipcord silk. **1960** C. W. Cunnington et al. *Dict. Eng. Costume* 192/2 *Shawl collar,* 1820's on..a term denoting a broad turn-over collar of a coat or waistcoat, continuous with the lapels, i.e. without a notch between. **1974** *Country Life* 17 Jan. 106/3 Shawl-collar cardigans are the thing to look for. *Ibid.* 107/1 Shawl-collared, kimono-style cardigan.

shawl, *v.* Add: Also *absol.* Hence **shaw·ling** *ppl. a.* (In quots. *fig.*, of snow.)

1930 R. Campbell *Adamastor* 72 Around your rocks you furl the shawling snow. *a* **1953** Dylan Thomas *Prospect of Sea* (1955) 97 Our snow was not only shaken in whitewash buckets down the sky, I think it came shawling out of the ground.

shawlie (ʃǭ·li). *colloq.* (chiefly *Irish* and *northern*). Also **shawly.** [f. Shawl *sb.* + -IE.] A woman (usu. poor or working-class) who wears a shawl over her head.

1914 F. Niven *Justice of Peace* II. iii. 258 'Shawlies'—as the girls who are to be seen in the neighbourhood of the Trongate of Glasgow, wearing shawls over their heads, are locally called. **1928** F. T. Jesse *Many Latitudes* 233, I will put a shawl over my head. I will go along the way I was one of them Shawlies from the quays. **1934** S. Beckett *More Pricks than Kicks* 63 A lowly house dear to shawlies. **1947** P. Doncaster *Sigh for Drum Beat* ii. 12 He knew they were the footsteps of a woman. A shawly, with her shawl wound about her body and a baby snuggled into it. **1966** 'L. Lane' *ABZ of Scouse* II. 72 A working-class Liverpool woman usually elderly and of scruffy appearance. Once known as a *shawlie* from the local habit of wearing a shawl. **1980** J. Masters *Heart of War* v. 68 She had been transformed into a typical Dublin shawlie, only more ragged and dirtier than most.

shawmist (ʃǭ·mist). [f. Shawm *sb.* + -IST.] One who plays the shawm. (In earlier centuries called a *shawmer* or *shawm-player.*)

1961 A. Baines *Musical Instr. through Ages* ix. 233 The European shawmist presses the lips to a wooden 'pirouette'. **1977** *Early Music* July 333/1 The shawmist, perhaps accompanied by the tambourine player, can only have performed monophonic melodies.

Shawnee. Substitute for entry: (ʃǭnī·), *a.* and *sb.* Also † **Savan(n)a, Shawanee, Shaweno, Shawnese, Shonee,** etc. [ad. Munsee *šá:wano:w*, f. Shawnee *ša:wano:ki* people of the south. Early forms in *-ese* prob. represent a hybrid formation with -ESE, later interpreted as the pl. of a stem in *-ee.*] **A.** *adj.* **1.** Of or pertaining to a tribe of Algonquian Indians, formerly resident in the eastern U.S. and now in Oklahoma; designating a member of this tribe or its language.

1674 H. Woodward *Let.* 31 Dec. in *S. Carolina Hist. Soc. Coll.* (1897) V. 460 Two days before my departure arrived two Savana Indians. **1714** J. Lawson *Hist. Carolina* 171 The Savanna Indians, who formerly lived on the Banks of the Messiasippi, and remov'd thence to the Head of one of the Rivers of South-Carolina. **1728** in C. S. R. Hildeburn *Century of Printing* (1885) 94 Two Indian Treaties..Between the Honourable..Lieut. Governour of the Province of Pennsylvania..And The Chiefs of the Conestogoe, Delaware, Shawanese and Canawese Indians. **1737** *Documents Colonial Hist. New-York* (1855) VI. 106, I am very Sorry that there has been any Misunderstanding betwixt Governour Pen & the Shaweno Indians. **1748** C. Weiser *Jrnl.* 10 Sept. in R. G. Thwaites *Early Western Travels* (1904) I. 31, I made a Present to the old Shawonese Chief. **1788** [see Mohican, Mohegan *a.*]. **1817** *State Papers & Publick Documents U.S.* (1819) (ed. 3) XII. 450 The balance of our men (except five Shonee Indians who had left us several days before),..came on this side of the first chain of mountains. **1821** T. NUTTALL *Jrnl. Trav. Arkansa* 54 We stopped awhile at a Shawnee camp. **1826** T. FLINT *Recoll.* 231 A rich commandant..married a Shawnee wife. **1855** A. W. WHIPPLE *Explor. Railway Route* III. 51 [Figure D illustrates] one of a pair of Shawnee ear-drops..made by a native artist. **1949** *Democrat* 30 June 7/4 Several Shawnee towns were set up in various places over the state [of Alabama]. **1973** A. H. WHITEFORD *N. Amer. Indian Arts* 17 Creek and Shawnee bowls have designs incised around the rims.

2. Shawnee salad, a perennial herb, *Hydrophyllum virginianum*, native to eastern North America and bearing clusters of white or purple flowers; **Shawnee wood** (examples).

1780 J. DONELSON *Jrnl.* 29 Mar. in *Three Pioneer Tennessee Documents* (1964) 9 Gathered some herbs in the bottoms of Cumberland, which some of the Company called Shawanee Sallad. **1822** *Trans. Hort. Soc. Lond.* 1st Ser. IV. 445 The *Hydrophyllum Virginicum* is called by the Americans of the Western States, Indian Sallad, or Shawanee Sallad, because these Indians eat it as such, when tender. **1829, 1866** [see SHAWANESE *a.*]. **1931** W. N. CLUTE *Common Names Plants* 31 At least three plants commemorate them: the Shawnee Law.., the Shawnee salad.., and the Shawnee tree, also called Shawnee wood. **1818** W. P. C. BARTON *Compendium Floræ Philadelphicæ* I. 9 Catalpa-Tree, Catawba-Tree, Schawnes-wood. **1931** Shawnee wood [see *shawnee salad* above].

B. *sb.* **1.** The name of a tribe of Algonquian Indians; a member of this tribe.

1693 *Documents Colonial Hist. New-York* (1854) IV. 43 Wee are glad that the Showannoes..did make their application to you last fall for protection. **1737** *Ibid.* (1855) VI. 107, I Recommend to you to keep the Shawenoes among your Selves as you have Done the Tuskierores to prevent their Going to the French. **1755** R. DINWIDDIE *Let.* 14 Dec. in S. M. Hamilton *Lett. to Washington* (1898) I. 149 The Cherokees have taken up the Hatchet against the French & Shawnese. **1786** [see *HURON]. **1828** M. NEVILLE *Last of Boatmen* in *Western Souvenir 1829* 118 The scout thought it as praiseworthy to bring in the scalp of a Shawnee, as the skin of a panther. **1837** R. M. BIRD *Nick of Woods* I. 15 The Shawanee and the Wyandot still hunted the bear and buffalo in the cane-brake. **1854** *Southern Lit. Messenger* XX. 401 The Shawnese still deserved their chastisement. **1891** H. F. O'BEIRNE *Leaders Indian Territory* p. viii/1 The Shawnees awaited their opportunity until the Tonkaway braves had departed on a big hunt. **1964** B. G. HOFFMAN *Anthrop. Papers of Smithsonian Inst. No. 70* 223 The Shawnee have what may be considered the best claim to having resided in..the Fort Ancient territory.

2. The language of this tribe.

1792 H. H. BRACKENRIDGE *Mod. Chivalry* I. v. iii. 61 It would be necessary for him only to talk Irish, which he might pass for the Shawanee. **1940** [see *LEXEME]. **1972** *Language* XLVIII. 846 [It] is supposed to be found in..Tacana, Shawnee..and Wichita.

Shay[2] (ʃēⁱ). *N. Amer.* The name of Ephraim *Shay* (1813–1916), Amer. engineer, applied to a geared locomotive designed by him in 1874 for hauling timber.

1894 J. DREDGE *Transportation Exhibits at World's Columbian Exposition of 1893* 308/1 (*heading*) The Shay Locomotive. *Ibid.* 308/2 The Shay Locomotive Engine No. 75, on the Montana Union Railway, on December 6th, 1890, hauled a train of fifteen loaded cars up the Anaconda high line, a distance of 1½ mile on a 3½ per cent. grade..at a rate of speed equal to 4 miles per hour. **1936** *ABC Brit. Columbia Lumber Trade Directory* 74 Elk River Timber Co., Ltd...75 Miles of Track; 5 Locos; 4 Shays. **1942** R. L. HAIG-BROWN *Timber* 253 *Shay*, a geared locomotive, slow but powerful and adapted to heavy hauling. Shays of about 70 tons are commonly used in hauling logs from the landing to the mainline. **1953** *Harmac News* (Vancouver, B.C.) Oct. 8/1 A 42-ton Shay was hauling logs for Wiest logging in 1914. **1962** *Amer. Speech* XXXVII. 135 *Shay*, the most popular of the geared locomotives used in the woods. The several cylinders are upright on the engineer's side of the frame, and the boiler is offset to balance them. A propeller shaft driven by cranks runs along one side of the engine and is geared to the axles. **1974** *Islander* (Victoria, B.C.) 7 July 3/1 The 45-ton Shay (named for designer Ephraim Shay) will be replaced by a 120-ton Baldwin diesel-electric locomotive.

shazam (ʃăzæ·m), *int. Children's slang.* [Invented word: see quots. 1940 and 1976.] A 'magic' word used like 'abracadabra' or 'presto' to introduce an extraordinary deed or story.

1940 *Whiz Comics No. 2* 5 'Speak my name!' 'Shazam!' ..As Billy speaks the magic word he becomes Captain Marvel. **1964** *Playboy* May 63 Shazam! **1976** in M. Horn *World Encycl. Comics* 157/1 Captain Marvel was really a homeless orphan named Billy Batson who was taken to see the old wizard Shazam. When Billy spoke his name, he was magically transformed... The lure of simply yelling 'Shazam'—which stood for Solomon's wisdom, Hercules' strength, Atlas' stamina, Zeus' power, Achilles' courage, and Mercury's speed. **1978** *Amer. Poetry Rev.* July/Aug. 44/4 Incantatory rituals are often marked by the repetition of magic formulas. Abbra Cadabra. Enny Meeny Minny Mo. Shazam. A Tisket a Tasket or Hi do Hi do hi de ho.

shcherbakovite (ʃəɪbăkǫ·vəit). *Min.* [ad. Russ. *shcherbakovit* (Es'kova & Kazakova 1954, in *Doklady Akad. Nauk SSSR* XCIX. 837), f. the name of D. I. *Shcherbakov* (1893–1966), Russian mineralogist: see -ITE[1].] A silicate of potassium, sodium, barium, titanium, and niobium, $(K,Na,Ba)_2(Ti,Nb)_2(Si_2O_7)_2$, found as brittle, brown, orthorhombic crystals.

1955 *Mineral. Abstr.* XII. 569 (*heading*) Shcherbakovite—a new mineral. **1964** *Doklady Acad. Sci. U.S.S.R.: Earth Sci. Sect.* CLI. 129/1 The goniometric measurements were made on small long prismatic crystals of shcherbakovite from an arfvedsonite-feldspar vein in the Khibiny alkalic massif.

shchi, var. STCHI in Dict. and Suppl.

shd, shd., abbrev. or contraction of *should* s.v. SHALL *v.*

1780 J. WOODFORDE *Diary* 9 Dec. (1924) I. 297 Edm[d] also mentions..that his Father shd say that he had left some shirts behind. **1811** SHELLEY *Let.* 12 Jan. (1964) I. 45, I see no reason why they shd. always continue so. **1885** HARDY *Let.* 13 Mar. (1978) I. 131, I shd say that a married daughter..who is here, strikes me as a particularly sensible woman. **1930** E. POUND *XXX Cantos* viii. 29 And I shd. like to be party to it, as was promised me. **1962** L. DAVIDSON *Rose of Tibet* 6, I feel strongly we shd go out for a fictional kind of title. **1973** *Black World* Sept. 84 Ever get tired of other people telling you what you shd be doing for yr self?

she, *pers. pron.* Add: **I. 2. e.** Applied *colloq.* to things (both material and immaterial) to which the female sex is not conventionally attributed (esp. in *Austral.* and *N.Z.*). Freq. in idiomatic phrases *she's jake* (or *right*): see *JAKE *a.*, *RIGHT *a.* 15 d.

1903 'T. COLLINS' *Such is Life* (1944) i. 5 You dunno what you're doin' when you're foolin' with this run. She's hair-trigger at the best o' times, an' she's on full cock this year. **1938** N. MARSH *Artists in Crime* vi. 81, I went down to the studio... She was locked, but the key's left on a nail. **1941** J. STREET *Father's House* x. 190 A wet spell would ruin us and she was coming rain before long. **1958** *N.Z. Listener* 18 July 6/2 If you tear the hamstring, in the back of the leg just above the knee, you're gone a million—she's nasty. **1969** *Private Eye* 25 Apr. 12 She's apples Eric—I don't reckon I feel like brekkie! **1973** P. WILSON *N.Z. Jack* xxi. 187 'Fix it all right?' I asked. 'She's jake now, mate,' he said. 'There she is, good as new'.

V. 9. *she-wolf* (examples); also *fig.*; **she-stock, -stuff** *U.S.*, female cattle.

1868 J. S. NORTHCOTE *Celebrated Sanctuaries of Madonna* v. 297 The marriage, doomed to so unhappy an issue, between Edward II. of England, and Isabella, the she-wolf of France. **1923** H. G. EVARTS *Tumbleweeds* 87 The herd would have been worked on the spot,..the she-stuff ..being allowed to scatter. *Ibid.* 88 There were..no she-stock on the range. **1936** *Discovery* Nov. 333/2 A figure of the Roman she-wolf is being erected in Addis Ababa. **1937** *Sun* (Baltimore) 15 Nov. 14/6 She stock gathered enough strength to finish around 25c. higher than a week earlier. **1961** *Wranglin' Notes* (Eaton's Ranch, Wyoming) Nov., Our hay crop was cut, baled and stacked early this year. It is fed to the 200 'she stuff' and calves that winter on the lower ranch.

10. a. *she-being.*

1881 G. M. HOPKINS *Sermons & Spiritual Writings* (1959) 170 The woman, that is she-being, not she-man, of the Apocalypse.

b. *she-fiend, -goblin, -guardian, -man* (later example).

1846 DICKENS *Pictures fr. Italy* 25 A gate, which this She-Goblin unlocked. **1881** She-man [see *she-being*, sense 10a above]. **1922** JOYCE *Ulysses* 48 A shefiend's whiteness under her rancid rags. **1937** E. POUND *Fifth Decad Cantos* xlii. 12 By Della Rena and M. Magdalene the She Guardian, *tutrice.*

d. *she-woman.*

1931 *Sunday Dispatch* 31 May 12/4, I am one hundred per cent. SHE-woman. **1951** B. RUSSELL *New Hopes for changing World* 162 Correlative to the he-man is the she-woman, who is equally undesirable.

12. *she-tragedy* (later example).

1978 *N. & Q.* Feb. 85/1 As a 'she-tragedy' and a history play (of sorts), the choice of Banks's play is an interesting move.

13. *she-male* (*U.S. colloq.* and *dial.*) = FEMALE *sb.*

18.. in B. A. Botkin *Treas. Amer. Folklore* (1944) I. 8 Davy Crockett's hand would be sure to shake if his iron was pointed within a hundred mile of a shemale. **1917** S. LEWIS *Job* xv. 246 Course you high-strung virgin kind of shemales take some time to learn to get over your choosey, finicky ways. **1941** E. P. O'DONNELL *Great Big Doorstep* 125 How can that one inside be cruel to dogs like that? If they were she-males always dropping pups, I wouldn't say.

e. In catch-phr. *who's she—the cat's mother?* and varr., said to one (esp. a child) who uses the pronoun of the third person singular impolitely or with inadequate reference.

1897 'S. GRAND' *Beth Bk.* xx. 204 Don't call your mamma 'she'. 'She' is the cat. **1913** C. MACKENZIE *Sinister St.* I. i. 9 'Who's She?' demanded Nurse. 'She's the cat's mother.' **1949** N. STREATFEILD *Painted Garden* ix. 105 'She said so.' Jane looked superior. 'She, my boy, is the cat's mother.' **1959** I. & P. OPIE *Lore & Lang. Schoolch.* iii. 52 To one who keeps saying 'she' in an impolite manner the reproof is: 'Who's *she*, the cat's mother?' **1972** CASSON & GRENFELL *Nanny Says* 21 Who's she? The cat's grandmother?

she, var. *SE.

s/he, written representation of 'he or she', used as nom. sing. third person pron. to include both genders.

1977 *Gay News* 24 Mar. 6/3 The questionnaire asks congregations whether they would call a minister to their pulpit if s/he were gay. **1978** *Amer. Educator* Winter 65 A child's sexual orientation is determined before s/he enters school. **1982** *Benedicta!* Fall 13 Can s/he figure out your address?

sheaf, *sb.* Add: **6. b.** *Math.* A topological space each point of which is associated with a structure having all the properties of an Abelian group (e.g. a vector space or a ring) in such a way that there is an isomorphism between the structures on neighbouring points. [The sense is due to J. Leray, who used F. *faisceau* (*Jrnl. de Math.* (1950) XXIX. 5).]

1955 *Ann. Math.* LXII. 56 The French word 'faisceau' has been translated into English as 'sheaf' or 'stack'. In this paper we use the word 'stack', since 'sheaf' has been used before in mathematics. **1958** R. G. SWAN *Theory of Sheaves* 1 Sheaves are very useful in proving theorems. **1973** R. O. WELLS *Differential Anal. Complex Manifolds* ii. 43 A sheaf..on a space X is a carrier of localized information about the space.

7. sheaf catalogue *Librarianship* (see quot. 1976); **sheaf oats** *U.S.* (now *rare*), oats bound in sheaves.

1902 *Library World* V. 129 Some librarians I know..are hesitating in their adoption of a ms. catalogue between the card and a new rival—the sheaf catalogue. **1913** J. H. QUINN *Library Cataloguing* iv. 33 The book-form of catalogues with separate leaves, known as 'sheaf-catalogues'. **1976** *Gloss. Documentation Terms* (*B.S.I.*) 60 *Sheaf catalogue*, a catalogue recorded on slips of paper of uniform size filed in loose-leaf binders. **1765** G. CROGHAN *Jrnl.* 10 June in R. G. Thwaites *Early Western Travels* (1904) I. II. 140 The young reeds being preferable to sheaf oats. **1894** *Outing* XXIV. 337/1 Ten minutes later the horses were quietly eating their corn and sheaf oats.

shear, *sb.*[1] Add: **1. j.** In phr. *off* (*the*) *shears*: of sheep, just shorn. *Austral.* and *N.Z.*

1888 J. BRADSHAW *N.Z. of Today* vi. 110 The hoggett.. in 1882 could be readily sold 'off the shears' at twelve shillings. **1896** T. W. HENEY *Girl at Birrell's* 69 Now and again a buyer visited the stations to get cheap sheep 'off shears'. **1930** L. G. D. ACLAND *Early Canterbury Runs* 1st Ser. viii. 216 He drove them over Porter's Pass off the shears. **1964** T. RONAN *Packhorse & Pearling Boat* 147 The sheep had arrived off-shears.

6. *shear-blade* (earlier example), *-mark.*

1812 *Niles' Weekly Reg.* 25 Jan. 390/1 The subscriber at short notice can furnish clothier's shear blades. **1934** DYLAN THOMAS *Let.* 25 Apr. (1966) 111 There were no shear-marks visible in my last letter for the reason that I had cut out nothing.

shear, *sb.*[2] Add: **II. 8. shear centre,** the point in the plane of a section of a structural member through which a shear force can be applied without producing torsion; **shear flow,** flow which is accompanied by or occurs under the influence of a shearing force: **shear modulus** = *modulus of rigidity* s.v. *RIGIDITY 1 b; **shear plane** *Geol.*, a boundary surface between bodies of rock or ice which have experienced relative motion parallel to the surface; **shear strength** = *shearing strength* s.v. SHEARING *vbl. sb.* 8 b; **shear stress,** stress tending to produce shear; **shear-thickening** *sb.* and *a.*, (the property of) becoming more viscous when subjected to shear; similarly, **shear-thinning** *sb.* and *a.*; **shear wave,** an elastic wave which vibrates transversely to the direction of propagation; an S-wave.

1937 A. P. POORMAN *Strength of Materials* (ed. 3) vii. 142 This point of application of the load, in order that there shall be no twist of the beam as it deflects, is called the shear centre. **1972** T. H. G. MEGSON *Aircraft Struct.* vii. 247 For cruciform or angle sections..the shear centre is located at the intersection of the sides. **1950** *Phil. Mag.* XLI. 890 (*heading*) The eddy viscosity in turbulent shear flow. **1975** RAUDKIVI & CALLANDER *Adv. Fluid Mech.* iv. 155 A shear flow has non-zero gradients of mean velocity and the fluid is being sheared by the mean motion. **1937** DODGE & THOMPSON *Fluid Mech.* viii. 165 An analogy is often drawn between the coefficient μ and the shear modulus of elastic materials. **1973** J. G. TWEEDDALE *Materials Technol.* I. iv. 86 The shear modulus may be obtained from experimental values of torsional load and torsional strain measured on a cylindrical test segment. **1888, 1903** Shear plane [in Dict., sense 7]. **1969** BENNISON & WRIGHT *Geol. Hist. Brit. Isles* xvi. 356 Recent work on the mechanism of ice flow shows that shear planes occur and that these carry material from the sole of the ice sheet to the surface. **1931** LAURSON & COX *Properties & Mechanics of Materials* i. 13 For most brittle materials..the tensile strength is least, the shear strength next, and the compressive strength greatest. **1978** *Sci. Amer.* Apr. 122/3 Under some circumstances molten silicates may not behave like ordinary fluids; they may have a shear strength greater than zero. **1937** DODGE & THOMPSON *Fluid Mech.* viii. 165 There is..an important distinction between the effects of shear stress on solids and on liquids. **1971** J. W. IRELAND *Mech. Fluids* viii. 242 Determine the shear stress at the pipe walls when water flows at the rate of 300 litres/min. through a 7·5 cm diameter pipe 150 m long. **1963** A. J. de Vries in P. Sherman *Rheol. Emulsions* 146 (Index), Shear thickening, activation energy. **1966** *Jrnl. Colloid & Interface Sci.* XXII. 554/1 This shear thickening leads to a maximum viscosity beyond which shear thinning occurs as the shear rate is increased. **1978** *Sci. Amer.* Nov. 143/2 The easiest example of a shear-thickening fluid that you can whip up in the kitchen is a simple mixture of water and cornstarch (or any common starch). **1966** Shear-thinning [see *shear-thickening* above]. **1974** P. L. Moore et al. *Drilling Practices Manual* ii. 25 Most [drilling] muds are shear thinning. **1978** *Sci. Amer.* Nov. 142/3 The advantage of shear-thinning is perhaps most apparent in ink. You want the ink in your ball-point to flow freely (by being sheared) as you write, but you do not want it to flow when the pen is in your pocket. **1936** J. B. Macelwane *Introd. Theoret. Seismol.* vii. 147 An isotropic elastic solid can transmit two types of waves, compressional and shear waves. **1977** A. Hallam *Planet Earth* 12 The outer core does not transmit shear waves and so must be liquid.

shear, *v.* Add: **5. d.** (Earlier example in mod. sense.) Now *rare.*

1852 *Trans. Mich. Agric. Soc.* III. 139 An article upon Sheep, describing bucks that shear the big fleeces.

e. *Austral.* and *N.Z.* To own or keep (sheep).

1930 L. G. D. Acland *Early Canterbury Runs* 1st Ser. ii. 35 The homestead..belongs to J. E. Scott who still shears about 3000 sheep there. **1965** J. S. Gunn *Terminol. Shearing Industry* ii. 18 *Shear*,..this word is..used by woolgrowers to indicate the size of their flocks, for example, 'I shear about 5000'.

sheared, *ppl. a.* Add: **2.** Subjected to shear; strained or distorted by shearing stress.

1930 J. S. Flett in Peach & Horne *Geol. Scotl.* ii. 56 Sheared Granite-Gneiss. This rock belongs to the group of muscovite-biotite-granites, and is rich in alkali felspar.

shearer. Add: **6. b.** A coal-cutting machine that cuts in a vertical plane parallel to the coal face.

1956 E. Mason *Deputy's Man.* I. xviii. 258 Most of the cutter-loading machines use vertical shearers which make a cut perpendicular to the plane of the seam... Disc shearers have picks attached to a vertical wheel rotating on a horizontal shaft. **1971** *New Scientist* 29 July 260/1 As the shearer cuts its way along the face, coal was automatically loaded on to a conveyor. **1979** *Jrnl. R. Soc. Arts* Jan. 90/1 By far the most common coal-getting machine in use to-day is known as the shearer.., which removes a slice of coal of about two-thirds of a metre in depth from the face by a revolving drum fitted with tungsten carbide tipped picks.

shearing, *vbl. sb.* Add: **1.** (Later *concr.* examples.)

1848 J. R. Lowell *Poet. Works* (1896) 136/2 Your goddess of freedom, a tight, buxom girl..who can sing at a husking or romp at shearing. **1901** M. Franklin *My Brilliant Career* xvi. 136, I was looking forward to the shearing.

7. *shearing time* (delete † and add later examples); *shearing-floor, paddock, -shed* (earlier example); *shearing-machine* (later example).

1863 R. Henning *Let.* 26 Nov. (1966) 146 The shearing floor is made to accommodate twelve shearers. *a* **1914** A. B. Paterson in *Penguin Bk. Austral. Ballads* (1964) 178 Round the shearing-floor the listening shearers gape. **1977** Yin Ming *United & Equal* 70 The commune has gradually mechanized its operations. It now has over 80 items of mechanized equipment—trucks, tractors, diesel engines, fodder-processors, mowers and shearing machines. **1933** L. G. D. Acland in *Press* (Christchurch, N.Z.) 25 Nov., *Shearing paddock*, handy paddock to hold sheep during shearing. **1857** H. W. Harper *Let.* 1 Sept. in *Lett. from N.Z.* (1914) 19 He took me to his shearing shed. **1862** *Rep. Comm. Patents 1861: Agric.* (U.S.) 137 Shearing time..is the month of June. **1953** O. E. Middleton in C. K. Stead *N.Z. Short Stories* (1966) 188 Shearing-time was always a worry for Charlie.

shearling. 2. Delete † *Obs.* and add: In recent use, *spec.* the woollen lining or body of a coat, etc. Chiefly *U.S.*

1971 *New Yorker* 16 Oct. 143/2 (Advt.), Suede on the outside, the white shearling on the inside. **1977** L. O'Donnell *Aftershock* (1979) ii. 31 She shrugged out of her shearling-lined coat and hung it on the rack.

sheat-fish: see Sheath-fish, sheat-fish in Dict. and Suppl.

sheath^1. Add: **2. k.** A contraceptive made of thin rubber worn on the penis; a condom.

1861 G. Drysdale *Elem. Soc. Science* (ed. 4) ii. 349 The accessory and sensational part of the venereal act is obtained..by the use of the sheath (which is..very frequent, but more so on the continent than in this country). **1897** *Science of Generation* xx. 235 The use of various mechanical contrivances, such as French Safes, Condom Sheaths, etc. **1919** M. C. Stopes *Let. to Working Mothers* 14 Some men like to use a sheath, and this is quite a safe method. **1962** *Lancet* 2 June 1194/1 The survey shows that the sheath and coitus interruptus are still the methods most commonly used for contraception in this country. **1977** E. J. Trimmer et al. *Visual Dict. Sex* (1978) xiv. 134 Careful attention must be taken in the rolling on of the sheath so as not to damage it.

l. A long close-fitting dress or skirt, usu. with a slit or pleat on one side. Cf. *sheath dress, gown*, etc., sense 7 a in Dict. and Suppl.

1904 H. O. Sturgis *Belchamber* xx. 273 A sinuous young lady, clad in a sheath of some glittering, shimmering blackness. **1932** in C. W. Cunnington *Eng. Women's Clothes in Present Cent.* (1952) vii. 222 The moulded sheath glorifies the body beautifully. **1958** *Observer* 20 July 9/5 Dresses for day and evening are cut as figure-gripping sheaths to which are added built-out and stiffened hip-pockets of a vast size. **1976** G. Moffat *Over Sea to Death* ii. 24 She wore a bright green jersey sheath which emphasised her sharp angles.

3. b. *Electronics.* The anode of a thermionic valve. (Disused.)

1919 R. D. Bangay *Oscillation Valve* 57 It [*sc.* the Fleming Valve] consists of a metal or carbon filament (F) and a metal cylinder (S) (usually called the sheath) surrounding the filament..the sheath [thus forming] the anode of the valve. **1922** Glazebrook *Dict. Appl. Physics* II. 880/2 A battery..has its positive terminal connected to the sheath.., and its negative one to the filament.

c. *Physics.* A region of charged particles or plasma surrounding an object.

1923 *Science* 12 Oct. 290/1 Around each negative electrode there is thus a sheath of definite thickness containing only positive ions and neutral atoms. **1955** A. von Engel *Ionized Gases* viii. 194 The anode is therefore covered with a luminous sheath—the anode glow which is sometimes divided into several luminous spots. **1973** Krall & Trivelpiece *Princ. Plasma Physics* i. 46 If the potential of the probe is much larger than the local potential of the plasma, the probe attracts electrons and repels ions, forming a sheath region around the probe, which is electron-rich.

7. a. *sheath dress.*

1925 in C. W. Cunnington *Eng. Women's Clothes in Present Cent.* (1952) vi. 184 The beltless sheath dress. **1945** N. L. McClung *Stream runs Fast* xv. 132 She was a sweet-faced little violet of a woman, in a sheath dress of silver cloth. **1980** 'M. Hebden' *Pel under Pressure* xiii. 129 She had one of those sheath dresses on. Fitted like a skin.

b. sheath cell *Anat.*, a Schwann cell (*Schwann b).

1906 Sheath cell [see *Schwann b]. **1967** D. Bodian in G. C. Quarton et al. *Neurosciences* 13/1 Axons that are enclosed by a single fold of a sheath cell are referred to as unmyelinated axons.

sheath-fish, sheat-fish. Add: The latter spelling is now usual.

sheave, *sb.^{1}* Add: **2. c.** *sheave-wheel.*

1939 C. W. Towne *Her Majesty Montana* 118 A Butte miner..is lowered to his labors in a steel cage suspended from a heavy wire cable passing over sheave-wheels on a head-frame. **1971** *Financial Mail* (Johannesburg) 26 Feb. 648/1 They depend upon our equipment—like high speed man cage and skip guide rollers, sheave wheels.

sheave, *sb.^{2}* Add: **3.** *Paper-making* = *shive *sb.^{2}* 2. ? *Obs.*

1880 J. Dunbar *Pract. Papermaker* 15 All rags.. contain sheive, which nothing but judicious boiling will remove. **1888** Cross & Bevan *Text-bk. Paper-Making* vi. 90 Such impurities as weeds..if not removed would be liable to appear in the finished paper as dark-coloured specks, technically known as 'sheave'. **1894** G. Clapperton *Pract. Paper-Making* xi. 135 The pressure applied in the super-calender is often such as to cause all the sheave and gritty matters to show up.

shebang. Also † **chebang, shee-bang.** For *U.S.* read *N. Amer.* and add: **1. a.** (Earlier examples.)

1862 W. Whitman *Jrnl.* 23–31 Dec. in *Specimen Days & Collect* (1882–3) 27 Their shebang enclosures of bushes. **1863** —— *Jrnl.* Jan. in *Ibid.*, The soldiers guarding the road came out from their tents or shebangs of bushes.

b. (Example in phr. *the whole shebang.*)

1877 B. Harte *Story of Mine* 85 That..don't fetch me even of he'd chartered the whole shebang.

c. A low drinking establishment, a tavern.

[**1878** C. Hallock *Hallock's Amer. Club List & Sportsman's Gloss.* p. x, *Shebang*, any sort of structure from a shanty to a hotel.] **1901** H. G. Parker *Right of Way* viii. 49 There were people who called the tavern a 'shebang'. **1908** B. W. Sinclair *Raw Gold* vi. 68 There was a sort of sheebang—you couldn't call it a hotel if you had any regard for the truth—on the outskirts of Walsh for the accommodation of wayfarers without a camp-outfit. **1963** E. C. Guillet *Pioneer Farmer & Backwoodsman* I. xix. 314 Less picturesque were the *shebangs* dotted along the rivers, where squaws and whiskey awaited the shanty boys and their winter pay.

2. (Examples.) Freq. in phr. *the whole shebang.*

1869 'Mark Twain' *Lett. to Publishers* (1967) 26, I like the book, I like you and your style and your business vim, and believe the chebang will be a success. **1904** W. N. Harben *Georgians* ix. 88, I sold out my shebang, put the money in my pocket. **1924** H. Crane *Let.* 5 Dec. (1965) 196, I am growing more and more sick of factions, gossip, jealousies, recriminations, excoriations and the whole literary shee-bang. **1933** E. E. Cummings *Let.* 13 Sept. (1969) 124 Camels placidly nibble the whole shebang, not merely the smallish but the spike thorns. **1948** V. Palmer *Golconda* xiv. 109 I've..seen him standing up there on one of those outcrops overlooking the company's buildings as if he'd like to call down fire from heaven on the whole shebang. **1967** *Boston Sunday Herald* 7 May iv. 5/2 You can't get rid of the feeling..that the people in charge of the shebang are far more pessimistic and confused than they were the last time you were here. **1977** R. E. Megill *Introd. Risk Analysis* iii. 28 The standard deviation is then calculated by dividing the total number of wells, *N*, into the sum of all the group deviations..and then taking the square root of the whole shebang.

shebeen. Add: **a.** Also in South Africa, a (usu. Black) illicit establishment where liquor is sold or consumed. In extended sense: a drinking-party, esp. among West Indians.

1900 *Kruger's Secret Service* vi. 135 In Fordsburg there was a shebeen kept by a certain Pulinski... Pulinski took me inside, where I found the place to be full of Kaffirs. **1931** J. Mockford *Khama* x. 77 So zealous was Khama in enforcing his ban on beer, that he afterwards led raids on shebeens himself and fired the huts of the brewers with his own hand. **1943** *Cape Argus* 13 Jan. 3 Carousals that cannot be described as shebeens, but that are almost as mischievous. **1944** I. D. du Plessis *Cape Malays* v. 81 Shebeens have sprung up in clusters, wine is brought in from Monday to Saturday by 'runners'. **1958** *Times Lit. Suppl.* 22 Aug. 472/5 The flashy, teeming, squalid world of the urban localities..laughter, gramophones, shebeens, and 'tsotsi' thugs making night excursions dangerous for Africans and police alike. **1962** D. Lessing *Golden Notebk.* i. 57 Peter..spends his last night in the Colony drunk, and by chance encounters his dark love in some shabby Shebeen. **1975** *New Society* 10 July 71/1 The West Indians [in Southampton], who are more free and easy, and tend to have noisy all night parties and shebeens. **1980** *Times* 31 May 5/1 The South African Government, after years of battling to control illicit drinking dens, known as shebeens, in black townships, has conceded defeat and legalized them.

b. *shebeen-keeper*; **shebeen queen** *S. Afr.*, a woman who runs a shebeen.

1922 Joyce *Ulysses* 443 In the shadow a shebeenkeeper haggles with the navvy and the two redcoats. **1954** R. St. John *Through Malan's Afr.* xxx. 236 Shebeen queens were warned to stop their liquor selling. **1977** *Time* 10 Jan. 24/1 After the fire-bombing of a few that stayed open, the shebeen queens (women that operate most speakeasies) duly shut up shop, and Sowetoans did their Christmas drinking quietly at home.

shebeener (later S. Afr. examples).

1942 [see *beer-hall* s.v. *beer *sb.^{1}* 4]. **1950** [see *dop *sb.^{3}* 2].

shebo, var. *shiveau.

‖ **shechita** (ʃĕ·χītă). Also **shecheta, shechitah, shehita(h.** [Heb. *šeḥīṭâ*, f. *šāḥaṭ* to slaughter.] The Jewish method of slaughtering animals. Cf. Shochet.

1875 J. Picciotto *Sk. Anglo-Jewish Hist.* xxvii. 217 The Portuguese would willingly join in the formation of a general body for the management of the Shechita (arrangements for slaughtering and preparing cattle for food *more Judaico*). **1891** M. Friedländer *Jewish Relig.* 463 Any deviation from these rules in the act of killing the animal renders the *shechitah* unlawful. **1910** *Jewish Chron.* 14 Jan. 34/1 (*heading*) The Shecheta Board, the Public, and the Butchers. *Ibid.* 1 Apr. 13/2 Fröken von Konow..constantly describes Shechita as a religious observance, but when it suits her purpose she speaks of it as an act 'practised under the cloak of religion'. **1921** *Dict. Occup. Terms* (1927) § 448 *Slaughterer, Jewish*;.. *shecheta*,..is employed by Jewish Board of Shecheta. **1939** *Contemp. Jewish Record* II. iii. 32 Charges of alleged brutality have been made the basis for the prohibition of *Shehitah* in several European countries. **1941** *Ibid.* IV. 539 The Iron Guards..bestially murdered them in parody of *shehita*. **1964** E. Huxley *Back Street New Worlds* ii. 25 Animals must be killed by a method known as *shechita*, the severing of all veins and arteries in the neck with a single knife-stroke. **1976** C. Bermant *Coming Home* i. i. 18 Insofar as slaughter can be humane, *shechita* is humane—to the animal. It is, however, inhumane to the *shochet*, for..he has to face the..almost pleading eyes of the animal.

shed, *sb.^{1}* Add: **6. b.** *Comb.*, as **shed-rod, -stick**, a device by which the warp is opened.

1968 W. Bray *Everyday Life of Aztecs* vii. 144 This passage is easy to achieve by means of a roller or shed-rod inserted across the warp under every alternate thread. **1910** L. Hooper *Hand-Loom Weaving* i. vii. 84 After the weft has been drawn straight, the shed-stick being again in a flat position, its edge may be brought down smartly upon the whole weft in order to beat it together. **1960** G. Lewis *Handbk. Crafts* 98 Shed sticks, which hold the cross..in place.

shed, *sb.^{2}* Add: **1. b.** For *Austral.* read *Austral.* and *N.Z.* and add examples.

1857 F. Cooper *Wild Adventures in Austral.* 105 He was bound for the shearing through New England. By this time, most likely, he has set in at some of the sheds on the Namoi. **1893** H. Lawson *Coll. Prose* (1972) II. 24 Men tramping in search of a 'shed' are not called 'sundowners' or 'swaggies'; they are 'trav'lers'. **1911** C. E. W. Bean *'Dreadnought' of Darling* v. 50 They were rich men—shearers—probably making from one big shed to another. **1940** F. Sargeson *Man & his Wife* (1944) 47 We got a job picking up fleeces in a big shed. **1955** G. Bowen *Wool Away!* (1956) 2 Good weather, good shed, good sheep, good boss, and a good gang create an atmosphere of work and action.

c. = *hangar b. ? *Obs.*

1909 *Daily Chron.* 3 Nov. 1/6 They have been watching the great shed gradually nearing completion..., and have been eagerly awaiting the advent of the airship. **1916** H. Barber *Aeroplane Speaks* 27 The Aeroplane is wheeled out of its shed on to the greensward of the Military Aerodrome.

3*. [By analogy with *barn *sb.* 1 d.] In nuclear physics, a proposed unit of area of nuclear cross-section equal to 10^{-24} barn (10^{-48} cm.^{2}).

The unit is impracticably small and appears to have had minimal use.

1956 W. C. MICHELS et al. *Internat. Dict. Physics & Electronics* 820/2 *Shed*, a unit of nuclear cross section equal to 10^{-24} barn or 10^{-48} square centimetre. **1965** *Guinness Bk. Records* (ed. 12) 80 The smallest unit of area is a 'shed', used in sub-atomic physics. **1968** F. KERTESZ *Lang. Nuclear Sci.* (Oak Ridge Nat. Lab. TM 2367) 20 During the study of the neutrino, a much smaller surface was used in theoretical studies and the area 10^{-44} cm^2 [*sic*] was quite logically named the shed; however, this latter name did not receive general acceptance. **1979** *New Scientist* 12 July 168/2 The Shed..seems to me to be less witty [than the barn].

4. (sense 1 b) *shed-boss, -hand*; *shed-shaped* adj.; **shed master,** one in charge of a locomotive shed (see quot. 1921); **shed roof** (earlier and later Amer. examples); **shed-room** *U.S.*, a shed attached to a house and serving as a room.

1892 W. E. SWANTON *Notes on N.Z.* ii. 97 Then there is the 'shed boss', who looks after everything, sees the sheep are shorn properly, takes the tally, looks after pressing etc. **1940** E. C. STUDHOLME *Te Waimate* 110 In the early days the manager acted as shed-boss. **1905** W. BAUCKE *Where White Man Treads* 229 The shed-hands and shearers were mostly Maoris. **1961** *N.Z. Listener* 26 May 8/1 The two shedhands played their unending game of poker. **1921** *Dict. Occup. Terms* (1927) § 700 *Shed master*, in charge of smaller locomotive shed than that supervised by shed superintendent. **1960** *Times* 2 Sept. 6/6 He should have sent a message to the shed-master. **1978** J. BLACKBURN *Dead Man's Handle* 8 How the shed-master had cursed when he heard the old steamer come clanking home with a fractured bearing. **1736** in *Maryland Hist. Mag.* (1908) III. 45 The Shead Ruff of Capt Cressap's house. **1817** in *Essex Inst. Hist. Coll.* (1866) VIII. 235 These [carriages] are..built like our mud-scows, with a shed roof over your head, looking like a floating ropewalk. **1976** 'O. BLEECK' *No Questions Asked* xii. 130 Above the wall I caught a glimpse of a white-graveled, sloping shed roof. **1843** *Knickerbocker* XXI. 304, I had in the morning secured a bed in a shed-room. **1932** H. CRANE *Let.* ? Jan. (1965) 395 We've relegated him to the shed-room in back of the kitchen. **1857** THOREAU *Maine Woods* (1864) 246 A shed-shaped tent will catch and reflect the heat like a Yankee-baker.

shed, *v.*[1] Add: **1. a.** (Further examples.)

1921 *Kelso Chron.* 26 Aug. 2 A better never lifted paw, To shed or wear off a stell. **1942** R. B. KELLEY *Animal Breeding* xv. 140 The shepherd has to shed or separate these [marked sheep] from the flock of 20. **1949** *Scots Mag.* Sept. 463 Wicket-gates for 'shedding' the sheep into various pens. **1951** N. M. GUNN *Well at World's End* xvii. 131 Some evenings ago, I fell in with a shepherd. I had shed one of his ewes and ultimately run her into a corner. **1977** *Field* 13 Jan. 55/2 The shepherd guided the dog to cut out, or 'shed' the marked sheep. **1981** I. A. GORDON in *N.Z. Listener* 27 June 86 When you shed sheep they are out in the open.

10. a. Also *absol.*

1879 *St. Nicholas* Nov. 84/2 He still grows till he is called a 'Buster', and then sheds. Then he is called a 'Soft Crab'. **1974** M. G. EBERHART *Danger Money* (1975) xiii. 139 Her jacket still bore some stray beige hairs from Toby [*sc.* a cat]; doesn't he ever stop shedding? she thought.

f. *transf.* To take off (a garment); to doff, divest oneself of. Also *fig.*

1858 *Lawrence* (Kansas) *Republican* 28 Oct. 1/6 She was compelled to 'shed' her woman's 'fixin's', and put on a man's breeches and hickory shirt. **1884** 'MARK TWAIN' *Huck. Finn* xx. 196 The duke shed his coat and said he was all right, now. **1922** JOYCE *Ulysses* 523 You will shed your male garments, you understand, Ruby Cohen? **1976** *Times* 18 Mar. 1 Cabinet members had been allowed to shed their ministerial cloaks and campaign for their own beliefs.

g. Of a share: to fall in price by (an amount). *Financial colloq.*

1947 *Financial Times* 29 Jan. 1/7 Preferences remained comparatively steady, although B.A.G.S. Sixes shed ½ to 22½. **1981** *Times* 11 Apr. 19/5 Hawker Siddeley added 2p to 266p and Glaxo shed a similar figure at 322p.

h. *to shed* (*a, the,* etc.) *load*: temporarily to curtail the electricity supply to an area in order to prevent excessive demand on the generating plant. Cf. *load-shedding* s.v. *LOAD *sb.* 8.

1947 *Times* 27 Feb. 7/3 The alternative was to go on running every day, and to shed the load because they could not carry the peak load. **1952** *Blackw. Mag.* Dec. 483/1 And if the local electrician chose the middle of your party to shed a load—well, where were you then? **1975** *IEEE Trans. Power Apparatus & Systems* XCIV. 360/1, 65% of the companies shed 25% or 30% of their load on underfrequency. *Ibid.* 360/2 Most companies shed load in two or three steps.

shed, *v.*[2] Add: **b.** Also with *up* (*N.Z. colloq.*).

1950 *N.Z. Jrnl. Agric.* Oct. 310 Sheep brought in for shearing should be spelled before shedding up, otherwise the pens in the shed get very dirty and much wool is stained. **1981** I. A. GORDON in *N.Z. Listener* 27 June 86 When you shed-up sheep you put them under cover to prevent their fleeces from getting wet before shearing.

shed: see *SHET.

shedding, *vbl. sb.* Add: **1.** (Examples spec. with reference to sheep.)

1832 *Trans. Highl. Soc.* 295 When gathered to the same fold or shedding-place together. **1921** *Kelso Chron.* 26 Aug. 2 Test—Hauld between two poles, drive round trainer, and proceed between two other sets of poles before penning, shedding, and wearing. **1942** R. B. KELLEY *Animal Breeding* xv. 140 In Scotland 'shedding' is a special feature of the dog's training. **1956** J. MURRAY *Rural Rhymes* 27 An' them they had a sheep tae pairt Frae a' the rest—ca'ed sheddin'. **1957** *Dumfries & Galloway Standard* 19 Oct. 5/6 Midge had a good run out and the most perfect lift in the competition, perfect fetch, driving and shedding but lost one mark in the penning to total 49 points. **1959** *Times* 18 Sept. 7/5 He appeared to be well in the lead when he reached the shedding ring. **1977** *Field* 13 Jan. 55/2 Each dog guided a bunch of sheep round the formalized trial course and finished by bringing them to his master in the 'shedding' ring.

3. d. The premature falling of the young bolls of cotton plants.

1899 *Yearbk. U.S. Dept. Agric.* 728 Over the eastern portion shedding was reported, with complaints of drought in portions of the Carolinas. **1974** J. W. PURSEGLOVE *Trop. Crops* 348 The first flowering period requires relative dryness, otherwise excessive boll shedding ensues.

4. *Electr.* = *load-shedding* s.v. *LOAD *sb.* 8. Also *fig.*

1945 *Electrician* 25 May 457/1 Some shedding of the load may still be unavoidable during next winter. **1958** *Listener* 12 June 990/3 In June there is a shedding of the load of serious drama. **1971** *IEEE Trans. Power Apparatus & Systems* XC. 1460/2 The load selected for shedding will be different for various systems because of geographical, historical, political and reliability factors.

Sheehan (ʃī·ăn). *Path.* [The name of H. L. *Sheehan* (b. 1900), English pathologist.] *Sheehan's syndrome*: pituitary insufficiency (cf. **Simmonds' disease*) caused by necrosis of the gland as a result of post-partum hæmorrhage and shock.

1950 R. F. ESCAMILLA in S. Soskin *Progr. Clinical Endocrinol.* x. 529 Case II represents an instance of onset of the disease following a complicated delivery, and is therefore an example of the subclassification of Simmonds' disease described by Sheehan, and called 'Sheehan's syndrome' by some authors. **1973** *Daily Colonist* (Victoria, B.C.) 18 July 2/3 Since the pituitary controls other endocrine glands, Sheehan's syndrome produces symptoms resulting from failure of other glands.

sheelah, var. *SHEILA.

‖ **sheela-na-gig** (ʃī·lă,nă,gi:g). Also **shela-, sheila-, shiela-**; **-gigg.** [ad. Ir. *Síle na gcíoch* Julia of the breasts.] A medieval carved stone female figure sometimes found on churches or castles in Britain and Ireland (see quot. 1934[1]). Also *ellipt.*, as **sheela, sheila.**

1846 *Proc. R. Irish Acad. 1843–4* II. viii. 575 In the church at Dowth there is a shela-na-gig, carved in stone quite different to that which composes the walls of the church. **1861** *Jrnl. Kilkenny Archæol. Soc. 1860–61* VI. 69 This effigy..belongs to that class of sculpturings which in Ireland have extended down to the middle of the sixteenth century... They are known amongst the peasantry of the southern counties by the name of 'Sheela-ni-giggs'. **1882** *Jrnl. R. Hist & Archæol. Soc. Irel. 1879–82* XV. II. 283 The name by which works of this class are generally known is '*Sheelanagigg*'. Our 'Sheela' here measures two feet in length. **1929** *Man* XXIX. 134 A stone..hollowed out to form in relief the rudely carved figure of a woman of the kind known in Ireland as Sheela-na-gig. **1934** *Jrnl. R. Anthropol. Inst.* XXXVII. 97 The more modern examples..are known as the Sheila-na-gig. These are always nude and are represented in the frontal aspect, the legs usually wide apart, and the hands so posed as to call attention to the genitalia. *Ibid.* 98 The Sheila from Blackhall Castle..is represented with breasts and long hair. **1977** *Times* 14 Sept. 5/1 The figures, called Sheela-na-Gig, are not found only in Ireland,..one of the best preserved is on the corbel of a church in Kilpeck [Hereford and Worcester]. *Ibid.* 5/2 The British Sheelas are slightly older than the Irish.

sheen, *sb.*[1] Add: **3.** A very thin film or slick of oil (esp. on water).

1970 *Daily Colonist* (Victoria, B.C.) 29 Apr. 1/1 Investigators reported four light sheens—the term being used instead of [oil] slicks because the material appears to be spread quite lightly on the water—were sighted from aircraft. **1978** *Daily Tel.* 28 Mar. 1/4 There was 'an extremely thin sheen of oil six to seven miles off Jersey' which was of no danger to marine life or holidaymakers.

sheen, *sb.*[2] (Earlier example.)

1839 H. BRANDON in W. A. Miles *Poverty, Mendicity & Crime* 165/1 *Sheen*, bad money.

sheen (ʃīn), *sb.*[3] *U.S. slang.* [Prob. abbrev. of *MACHINE *sb.* 1 e.] A car; an automobile.

1968–70 *Current Slang* (Univ. S. Dakota) III–IV. 107 *Sheen*, car. **1975** *Amer. Speech* 1972 XLVII. 153 Hey, look down the street pas' that sheen double-parked. **1980** in S. Terkel *Amer. Dreams* 125 My friends are always talkin' about havin' a nice sheen. That's a nice car or van, something set up real nice on the inside.

sheened, (ʃīnd), *ppl. a.* [f. SHEEN *v.* + -ED[1].] Having a sheen, shining. Freq. in predic. use const. with *with.*

1920 E. SITWELL *Wooden Pegasus* 100 Beneath umbrellas I can see Pink faces sheened with stupidity. **1942** [see *KNOLE SOFA]. **1955** *Times* 19 May 12/5 The lady-smocks, 'all silver white', or sheened with lilac.

sheeny, *sb.*[1] Add: (Earlier and later examples.) Now only as a term of vulgar abuse.

1816 J. H. LEWIS *Lectures on Art of Writing* (ed. 7) vi. 84 A motley-fool the *thing* I mean is, One of the common puffing sheenies. **1918** G. FRANKAU *One of Them* x. 75 What cared Jill for Grand Dukes, *Principini*,.. For Russ, Yank, Dago, Teuton, Gaul, or Sheeney? **1946** [see *LID *sb.* 1 f]. **1976** *Honolulu Star-Bull.* 21 Dec. E-3/3 Hey mom, there's a couple of sheenies at our door with a turkey. **1977** H. FAST *Immigrants* II. 88 Maybe we didn't do so bad for a Dago fisherman and a sheeny storekeeper.

sheep, *sb.* Add: **2. a.** (*c*) (Later examples.) Also *attrib.*, as *sheep-and-goat.*

1923 [see *one-nighter* s.v. *ONE B. 33]. **1943** J. S. HUXLEY *Evolutionary Ethics* iii. 19 Our ethics will be unrealistic if, after dividing our impulses into sheep and goats, we..transform the goats into scapegoats. **1954** N. COWARD *Future Indefinite* III. ii. 138, I..tried repeatedly to analyse my emotions coldly and clearly; to still my anxieties by segregating them, by separating the sheep from the goats. **1962** *Listener* 15 Mar. 469/2 This 'sheep and goats' view, though it may appear plausible, is not to be taken for granted. **1978** K. HUDSON *Jargon of Professions* 13 Is the author using it [*sc.* jargon or propaganda] deliberately as a means of sorting out the sheep from the goats?

c. (Later examples.)

1922 JOYCE *Ulysses* 453 He was down and out but, though branded as a black sheep,..he meant to reform. **1932** R. ALDINGTON *Soft Answers* 76 Every privileged class tries at first to whitewash its black sheep. **1944** W. S. MAUGHAM *Razor's Edge* v. 176 There was a time when the black sheep of the family was sent from my country to America. **1958** 'J. BYROM' *Or be he Dead* viii. 115 I'm the Black Sheep of the family, so if you ever meet any of my relatives, you'll be wise not to mention me. **1979** *Jrnl. R. Soc. Arts* CXXVII. 650/1, I should like to think that they would do this for any black sheep among the countries who tried to defy all reasonable precautions.

3. a. Also, *one might as well be hanged for a sheep as a lamb* and varr. (earlier and later examples).

1678 J. RAY *Eng. Proverbs* (ed. 2) 350 As good be hang'd for an old sheep as a young lamb. **1836** F. MARRYAT *Mr. Midshipman Easy* II. ii. 58 We may as well be hanged for a sheep as a lamb,..I vote that we do not go on board. **1913** D. H. LAWRENCE *Sons & Lovers* x. 259 It seemed as if she did not like being discovered in her home circumstances... But she might as well be hung for a sheep as for a lamb. She invited him out of the mausoleum of a parlour into the kitchen. **1977** B. PYM *Quartet in Autumn* xv. 133 Letty..decided that she might as well be hung for a sheep as a lamb and make the most of her meal.

d. *to count sheep*: as a soporific, to count imaginary sheep jumping over an obstacle one by one.

[**1854** S. SMITH *'Way down East* xi. 273 He shut his eyes with all his might, and tried to think of sheep jumping over a wall.] **1920** E. O'NEILL *Beyond Horizon* III. i. 128, I couldn't get to sleep to save my soul. I counted ten million sheep if I counted one. *a* **1922** T. S. ELIOT *Waste Land Drafts* (1971) 27 When restless nights distract her brain from sleep She may as well write poetry, as count sheep. **1977** H. PITCHER *When Miss Emmie was in Russia* x. 75 Nanny..was trying her hardest to persuade Irina to go to sleep. Did you know that if you count sheep, it is watching the sheep *jump* that sends you off?

5. a. (Later examples.)

1914 G. B. SHAW *Misalliance* Pref. p. lxxiii, Bullied and ordered about, the Englishman obeys like a sheep. **1930** —— *Apple Cart* II. 72 The way you fellows scuttle backward and forward from one mind to another whenever Joe holds up his finger is disgusting. This is a Cabinet of sheep. **1948** WODEHOUSE *Uncle Dynamite* xiii. 226 She looks on you as a..poor, spineless sheep who can't say boo to a goose.

7. b. *sheep-flock* (later *attrib.* example).

1876 G. M. HOPKINS *Poems* (1967) 65 And sheep-flock clouds like worlds of wool.

c. *sheep crib, down* (earlier example), *paddock, ranch, shed, station* (later examples), *wagon.*

1921 K. S. WOODS *Rural Industries round Oxf.* II. i. 80 Hazel..is made into wattle or 'flake' hurdles and sheep cribs. **1946** N. WYMER *Eng. County Crafts* vii. 77 These bands..also undertake the making of such articles as hen-coops, pump-buckets, sheep-cribs. **1789** G. WHITE *Selborne* i. 2 A vast hill of chalk..divided into a sheep down, the high wood, and a long hanging wood. **1930** L. G. D. ACLAND *Early Canterbury Runs* 1st Ser. v. 103 This part of the station is still called the 'sheep paddocks'. **1874** J. G. McCOY *Hist. Sk. Cattle Trade* i. 1 Thus it is common to hear of a corn ranch, a wheat ranch, a sheep ranch. **1981** G. McDONALD *Fletch & Widow Bradley* xviii. 72 She worked six months on a sheep ranch. **1946** J. W. DAY *Harvest Adventure* vii. 110 Allus came up to my sheep-shed, an' if I 'ad people a-watchin' me at work—tourists an' loike—would say, 'Ah! company I zee.' **1911** C. E. W. BEAN '*Dreadnought' of Darling* i. 8 The long blue-grey galvanised-iron wool-shed of some sheep station. **1944** F. CLUNE *Red Heart* 59 They came to the last outpost of civilisation, at Mount Abundance sheep station. **1909** E. RUPERT *Let.* 24 May in *Atlantic Monthly* (1913) Oct. 434/2 About noon the first day out we came near a sheep-wagon. **1962** G. MACEWAN *Blazing Old Cattle Trail* xx. 134 The canvas-roofed sheep wagon was the ultimate in household compaction, combining the essentials of kitchen, dining-room, bedroom and sheep dog quarters.

d. *sheep-rancher.*

1904 *Country Life* July 287/1 The Montana sheep-rancher figures that the wool will pay all expenses, leaving the increase for his profit. **1976** A. J. RUSSELL *Pour*

Hemlock (1979) vii. 61 A sheep rancher who owned vast lands on the Colorado Plateau, in northeastern Arizona.

e. *sheep-bitten, -grazed, -proof, -scattered, -white* (later example).

1917 J. MASEFIELD *Lollingdon Downs* 31 Night is on the downland, on the lonely moorland, On the hills where the wind goes over sheep-bitten turf. **1925** W. DE LA MARE *Three Sleeping Boys* in *Broomsticks* 256 The bird-haunted, sheep-grazed meadows. **1976** *Southern Even. Echo* (Southampton) 2 Nov. (Advts. Suppl.) 3/8 Turfs, good quality, sheep grazed and weed treated, machine cut 3ft. × 1ft. **1882** ARMSTRONG & CAMPBELL *Austral. Sheep Husbandry* xvii. 186 This fence can be made still more sheep-proof..by leaving out the bottom wire, and having..a light embankment thrown up. **1903** 'T. COLLINS' *Such is Life* iv. 134 The fence, much damaged by floods, was repaired merely to the sheep-proof standard. **1950** *N.Z. Jrnl. Agric.* July 74/2, 20 paddocks, all sheep-proof fenced. **1978** I. MURDOCH *Sea* 401 After the bog there was ordinary farm land, sheep-scattered hillsides. **1945** DYLAN THOMAS in *Poetry* (Chicago) July 175 The frozen hold Flocked with the sheep white smoke of the farm house cowl.

8. sheep blowfly, a large greenish blowfly belonging to the genus *Lucilia*, esp. *L. coprina*, the larva of which is a pest of sheep in Australia; **sheep-bush** *Austral.*, either of two species of *Geijera*, *G. parviflora* or *G. linearifolia*, of the family Rutaceæ, a small evergreen tree sometimes used as fodder for sheep; **sheep-camp,** (*a*) *N. Amer.*, a camp for sheep herders; (*b*) *Austral.* and *N.Z.*, a resting or assembly place of sheep (cf. *CAMP *sb.*[2] 4 c); (*c*) *S. Afr.*, a fenced-in enclosure for sheep (cf. *CAMP *sb.*[2] 15); **sheep cocky** *Austral.* and *N.Z. colloq.*, a sheep-farmer on a small scale (cf. COCKY *sb.*[2] 2); **sheep-crook** (later example); **sheep-dip,** (*a*) (later examples); also *fig.* (see quots. 1945, 1976); **sheep-dipping** (later examples); **sheep-dog:** also as *v. trans.*, to urge (someone) on in the manner of a sheep-dog; to direct or 'herd'; also **sheep-dogging** *vbl. sb.*; **sheep-farm** (earlier example); **sheep-kill** = *sheep-laurel;* **sheep-laurel** (earlier and later examples); **sheep-meat,** (*b*) in mod. trading use: meat obtained from sheep; mutton and lamb; (also written as one word); **sheepnose,** a small cider apple (see quots.); **sheep-poison,** (*a*) (earlier examples); **sheep-run** (further examples); **sheep-sick** *a.* (later example); **sheep-sorrel** (earlier U.S. example); **sheep trot** *nonce-wd.*, a dance as of satyrs.

1932 *Discovery* July 210/2 The sheep blowfly..is reliably estimated to do £4,000,000 worth of damage every year [in Australia]. **1974** R. D. HUGHES *Living Insects* v. 128 Cool temperatures in autumn can induce a pause in the development of the prepupal larva of the sheep blowfly. **1889** Sheep-bush [see WILGA]. **1933** *Bulletin* (Sydney) 7 June 25/2 Sheep bush..is tall and ornamental. It has long narrow leaves. **1965** *Austral. Encycl.* IX. 310/2 The smaller related G[*eijera*] *linearifolia*, which extends into Western Australia, is called sheep-bush. **1869** J. MUIR *Jrnl.* 25 June in *My First Summer in Sierra* (1911) 85 Though only a sheep camp, this grand mountain hollow is home. **1921** H. GUTHRIE-SMITH *Tutira* xx. 180 Before the establishment of sheep-camps growing grass and clover, there was nothing to tempt pig from the low grounds. **1931** *Amer. Speech* VII. 120 A *sheep camp*, or the migratory home of a pair of shepherders, consists of a canvas-topped wagon with a stove in it and a *bunk* or bed at the back. **1939** P. A. ROLLINS *Gone Haywire* v. 114 He had stopped at a sheep camp and played casino. **1947** [see *CAMP *sb.*[2] 15]. **1950** *N.Z. Jrnl. Agric.* May 463/1 The paddock was a sheep-camp paddock or similar place where considerable numbers of sheep were frequently concentrated. **1973** *Kingston* (Ontario) *Whig-Standard* 11 Aug. 7/2 A few miles down-river there was a sheep-camp. **1949** F. SARGESON *I saw in My Dream* II. xiv. 206, I never can teach my wife that a sheep-cocky's dogs aren't pets. ? **1873** HARDY *Lett.* (1978) I. 25, I have sketched in my note-book during the past summer a few correct outlines of smockfrocks, gaiters, sheep-crooks, rick-'staddles'..and some other out-of-the-way things that might have to be shown. **1911** W. H. KOEBEL *In Maoriland Bush* v. 93 He was selling a new species of sheep-dip. **1915** *N.Z. Jrnl. Agric.* 20 Nov. 411 Do not economize in the purchase of sheep-dip. **1945** MENCKEN *Amer. Lang.* Suppl. I. 262 Many generic names for alcoholic stimulants..*sheep-dip*, [etc.]. **1968** K. WEATHERLY *Roo Shooter* 118 His seat was an old five-gallon drum that had once held sheep dip. **1976** *New Yorker* 3 May 65/1 'Sheep dip' was what the lumberjacks called their tea. **1915** J. R. MACDONALD *N.Z. Sheepfarming* xxvii. 71 It is needless to set forth all the conditions for complete success in sheep dipping, seeing that..it is the custom to attach directions for use on every packet or drum. **1968** J. ARNOLD *Shell Bk. Country Crafts* 228 The primary use, for a coracle, now, is for fly-fishing and sheep-dipping. **1973** *Times Lit. Suppl.* 13 Apr. 418/4 Working with Thomas Jones and sheep-dogged by vigilant helpers, I entered a new dimension of scholarship. **1981** S. JACKMAN *Game of Soldiers* I. 15 The Group Senior Signals Officer..has done his time..on Coastal Command Sunderlands, sheep-dogging convoys in the Western Approaches. **1969** E. BLISHEN *This Right Soft Lot* I. ii. 40 A surprising number of boys seemed never to have seen the Thames before... So I did a little quick sheep-dogging, and at last we reached the gallery. **1776** T. PENNANT *Tour Scotl.* II. 400 A letter from Mr. George Malcolm, concerning Sheep-farms, &c. **1968** E. R. BUCKLER *Ox Bells & Fireflies* vii. 106 The purple loops of the sheepkill. **1810** F. A. MICHAUX *Hist. Arbres Forestiers Amér. Sept.* I. 35 Mountain laurel..sheep laurel,..nom secondaire. **1954** Sheep laurel [see *LAMBKILL]. **1975** *Austral. Outlook* XXIX. 298 New Zealand supplies 80 per cent of EEC sheepmeat imports. **1978** *Times* 19 June 17/3 The word 'sheepmeat' with which Brussels refers to mutton and lamb, is translated from the official French term, *Viande ovine*. **1979** *Times* 13 Nov. 17/6 The recent use of the term 'sheepmeat' in place of mutton and lamb is depressing in the extreme and will, I should think, put many people off buying what is one of our most important farm products. **1817** W. COXE *View Cultivation of Fruit Trees* 125 Bullocks Pippin..is more generally distinguished by the vulgar name of Sheep-nose, from a supposed resemblance between the form of the apple and that part of a sheep. **1925** C. MORLEY *Safety Pins* 178 We have seen apples of strange shapes, something like a pear (sheepnoses, they call them). **1943** B. DAMON *Sense of Humus* 234 The Sheepnose, for example, had an interesting shape and a name just right. **1790, 1814** Sheep poison [see *LAMBKILL]. **1851** W. FOX *Six Colonies of New Zealand* i. 27 The..plain...is surrounded by hills which afford excellent sheep-runs. **1911** C. E. W. BEAN *'Dreadnought' of Darling* i. 8 The names painted on so many of the railway stations were merely the names of large sheep runs. **1936** A. RUSSELL *Gone Nomad* iv. 23, I even learnt to operate on the lambs myself, and to perform the many other jobs that combine to make up the yard work on a sheep run. **1962** *Times* 6 June 15/6 Most of it poor land and sheep-sick at that. **1806** P. GASS *Jrnl.* 14 Mar. (1807) xviii. 188 A great quantity of sheep-sorrel growing in the woods. **1926** E. SITWELL *Elegy on Dead Fashion* 10 The satyrs danced the sheep-trot all the day.

9. *sheep's trotters* (later *sing.* example); **sheep's foot,** (*c*) *sheep's foot roller*, a kind of tamping roller consisting of a steel drum studded with projecting feet; **sheep's grey,** material composed of a mixture of black and white wool; also *attrib.* or as *adj.*; **sheep's nose** = *sheepnose* sense 8 above; **sheep's wool,** (*a*) (later example).

1934 J. H. BATEMAN *Highway Engin.* (ed. 2) xiii. 224 Various types of tamping rollers have been developed.. and include sheep's-foot and sectional rollers. **1973** G. E. BERTRAM in Hirschfeld & Poulos *Embankment-Dam Engin.* 1/1 The recent development of heavy vibratory rollers capable of compacting rockfill has produced the most significant change in placement procedures in the construction of earth and rockfill dams since the introduction of the sheepsfoot roller for the compaction of earthen core materials. **1852** *Trans. Mich. Agric. Soc.* III. 483 Ten yards or over of sheep's gray cloth. **1877** *Rep. Vermont Board Agric.* IV. 92 The men and boys' garments of the sheep's grey. **1976** *National Observer* (U.S.) 28 Aug. 13/4 (Advt.), Pullover or Cardigan. Colors: Blue Heather, Natural White, Sheeps Grey. **1936** *N. & Q.* CLXX. 183/2 Sheep's Nose, an old-time variety of apple whose name is almost forgotten. **1967** Sheep's nose [see *HANG-DOWN *sb.* and *a.*]. **1922** JOYCE *Ulysses* 427 A cold sheep's trotter, sprinkled with whole pepper. **1978** S. SHELDON *Bloodline* viii. 105 Samuel huddled into his threadbare sheep's-wool coat.

sheep-hook. Add: Also *fig.*

1866 G. M. HOPKINS *Jrnls. & Papers* (1959) 143 Beeches..scatter their tops in charming tufted sheep-hooks drooping towards each other and every way.

sheepman. 1. For *U.S.* and 'in Canada' read orig. *N. Amer.* and add later examples.

1924 W. M. RAINE *Troubled Waters* xi. 114 If one sheepman were permitted to invade the range, dozens of others would drive across into the forbidden territory. **1930** L. G. D. ACLAND *Early Canterbury Runs* 1st Ser. v. 106 D. Oliver, the head shepherd, became manager. He was a very good sheepman from Australia. **1937** *Times Lit. Suppl.* 6 Feb. 86/3 There has never been in Britain the hostility between the cattlemen and the sheepmen. **1950** H. J. MASSINGHAM *Curious Traveller* ix. 168 The communal sheep-men of the mountain parishes only pay half a crown a year to the Lady Marcher if they enclose a mountain pasture. **1966** 'J. HACKSTON' *Father clears Out* 37 A new volume on sheep-raising,..proclaiming to the world that Father was a sheep-man. **1977** F. ORMSBY *Store of Candles* 15 Even the barflies move to corner tables, Mouthing 'Sheepman'.

sheep-o(h (ʃī·pōu), *int.* and *sb. Austral.* and *N.Z.* [f. SHEEP *sb.* + *-O[2].] **A.** *int.* A shearer's call for a sheep to shear. **B.** *sb.* (Chiefly *N.Z.*) = *penner-up* s.v. *PENNER[4].

1900 H. LAWSON *On the Track* 132 'Go it, you—tigers!' yells a tarboy. 'Wool away!' 'Tar!' 'Sheep Ho!' We rush through with a whirring noise till breakfast time. **1911** W. H. KOEBEL *In Maoriland Bush* viii. 124 The 'sheep-oh' sets to work to fill the nearly emptied pens. **1925** R. REES *Lake of Enchantment* vii. 111 The [shearing] gang [included]..some boys to act as 'sheep-os'—that is to keep the pens in the shed filled up from the yards outside. **1940,** etc. [see *PENNER[4]]. **1949** P. NEWTON *High Country Days* 5 The cry of 'Sheepo!' would rouse the 'penner-up'. **1955** G. BOWEN *Wool Away!* (1956) vii. 96 The 'sheepo' is the man who fills the catching pens. He gets this title from the fact that when a shearer catches the last sheep in his pen, he gives the call of 'sheepo'.

sheep's head. Add: **2. b.** *Cards.* A simple form of skat.

1886 E. E. LEMCKE *Skat* 4 Skat is of quite recent origin. .. It bears a great resemblance to the Wendish game of '*Schafskopf*' (Sheepshead) and '*Dreiben*' (three legs). **1913** *Off. Rules Card Games* (U.S. Playing Card Co.) (ed. 17) 205 Schafkopf..(Sheepshead)... Object of the Game—To win in tricks certain cards of counting value as follows: A's, 11, 10, K's 4, Q's 3, and J's 2. **1939** C. ISHERWOOD *Goodbye to Berlin* 186 A group of youths.. were playing Sheep's Head. **1951** F. BROWN *Murder can be Fun* iv. 57, I knew he played schaffskopf—sheepshead. ..It's a three-handed game. **1976** *National Skat & Sheepshead Q.* Dec. 21 Fred Suter always wanted to prove that Sheepshead players will back a Classic Tournament.

3. a. Also applied to similar fishes, esp. the marine *Archosargus rhomboidalis* of Florida and the fresh-water drumfish, *Aplodinatus grunniens*.

1924 J. O. LA GORCE *Bk. Fishes* 71/2 The Sheepshead belongs to the Porgy family. **1962** K. F. LAGLER et al. *Ichthyol.* v. 147 In some fishes such as the sheepshead and the sea bream (*Archosargus*) they [*sc.* the cutting teeth] look almost human. **1979** *South Padre Parade* (South Padre Island, Texas) Dec. 6/3 These visiting fishermen caught their limit while fishing locally for speckled trout and sheepshead.

sheepskin. Add: **1. c.** A coat made of sheepskin.

1917 W. J. LOCKE *Red Planet* xxi. 270 From the shapeless tam-o'-shanter to the huge boots..[he] was caked in mud. Over a filthy sheepskin were slung all kinds of paraphernalia. **1977** A. SCHOLEFIELD *Venom* II. 83 The policeman made no reply, hunching down again in his sheepskin.

3. a. *sheepskin-lined* adj.

1950 C. EDWARDS in *McCall's Mag.* Mar. 68/3 A pair of sheepskin-lined slippers. **1980** *Country Life* 3 July 56/1 The *del* is the colourful Mongolian dress... Winter *dels* are sheepskin-lined (a man's *del* can require up to 40 lambskins).

b. *sheepskin rug.*

1917 *Harrods Catal.* 763/1 Sheepskin rugs 35/0 to 120/0. **1936** 'J. TEY' *Shilling for Candles* xxvi. 278 An atmosphere of marble mantlepieces and sheepskin rugs. **1976** J. BINGHAM *God's Defector* vi. 73 In front of the dressing-table was a white sheepskin rug.

sheepy, *a.* Add: **b.** Full of sheep.

1934 DYLAN THOMAS *Let.* 25 Apr. (1966) 110, I even go without a coat (sometimes) in this cold weather, & tread be-jumpered over the sheepy fields. **1979** R. BARNARD *Posthumous Papers* viii. 73 The lonely, sheepy expanses of her native land.

sheer, *a.* and *adv.* **A.** *adj.* **6. a.** For Now *U.S.* read Chiefly *U.S.* (exc. of stockings) and add later examples.

1911 E. M. CLOWES *On Wallaby* viii. 225 America seems to have taken to fashioning her literature with a crimping-iron and 'sheer-lawn', while Australia hacks hers out with a billyhook from back-block and Bush. **1934** A. WOOLLCOTT *While Rome Burns* 284 Ravishing French peasant girls with high heels, sheer stockings, and a disposition to say 'Ooh, la la' at appropriate intervals. **1951** in M. McLuhan *Mech. Bride* (1967) 95 Ivory Flakes care helps safeguard sheerest nylons. **1977** D. CLARKE *Gimmel Flask* iii. 56 She was..dressed in a tan moygashel suit, sheer nylons on excellent legs.

b. *absol.* as *sb.*

1934 in WEBSTER. **1937** *Jrnl.* (Lincoln, Nebraska) 25 Apr. (Advt.), Saucy sheers for budgeteers. **1943** *Amer. Speech* XVIII. 94 [New Zealand] words like *bobby-pin* (English 'kirby-grip'), *sheer* (dress material), *tubables* (washable frocks), are taken from American, not English, advertisements. **1952** C. W. CUNNINGTON *Eng. Women's Clothes in Present Cent.* vii. 257 Stockings..in service sheers, 4/11 to 6/11. **1966** *Daily Tel.* 26 Oct. 13/3 His curtain sheers.. are better than the German Dralon sheers we saw in the shops last winter. **1978** *Lancs. Life* Apr. 85/1 There is..a new range of Swiss sheers and prints with louvred blinds to match.

sheerly, *adv.* **4.** (Later examples.)

1920 C. M. GRIEVE *Northern Numbers* 69 The barrier.. Lifts sheerly..To the unknowledgeable skies. **1947** E. MEYNELL *Sussex* i. 15 Across the road,..the chalk drops again almost as sheerly, down to the water-levels and the Ouse valley. **1964** G. B. SCHALLER *Year of Gorilla* (1965) vii. 184 We followed a buffalo trail upward to the base of the huge rock wall that rose sheerly to the peaked summit.

sheesh kabab, var. *SHISH KEBAB.

sheet, *sb.*[1] Add: **3. c.** In proverbial phr. *as white* (or *pale*) *as a sheet*. Cf. WHITE *a.* 5 b.

1751 FIELDING *Amelia* III. VII. viii. 84 He entered.. with a face as white as a sheet. **1839** W. T. THOMPSON *Chron. Pineville* (1845) 142 He turned pale as a sheet. **1872** HARDY *Under Greenwood Tree* I. I. viii. 125 You'll be white as a sheet to-morrow. **1929** E. RICE *Street Scene* I. 72 Well, there was the three o' them—Mr. Maurrant lookin' at Sankey as if he was ready to kill him, an' Mrs. Maurrant as white as a sheet, an' Sankey as innocent as the babe unborn. **1952** A. J. CRONIN *Adv. in Two Worlds* xxxix. 276 Sitting on a high stool, he seemed little larger than a shrimp, pale as a sheet, with..big dark eyes.

5. e. A dollar bill (*U.S.*) or pound note; the monetary value of this. *slang.*

1937 *Research Stud. State Coll. Washington* V. 19 What a fellow gets for one sheet from an officer he can sell to the boys..for five and ten sheets. **1958** F. NORMAN *Bang to Rights* I. 48 Which if it did happen would cost some one half a sheet. **1969** M. PUGH *Last Place Left* xxvi. 191 A sheet the night. Five quid if you last a week. **1978** *Hot Car* June 94 Maserati air horns [have]..a howling, double high-pitched, screaming noise... This cacophony can be yours, whatever car you drive, for less than ten sheets.

f. *U.S. slang.* = *rap sheet* s.v. *RAP *sb.*[1] 7.

1958 *N.Y. Times Mag.* 16 Mar. 88/3 *Sheet*, a criminal

record. **1976** C. Weston *Rouse Demon* (1977) xxvi. 125 Somebody scared him into it. Let's take a look at his sheet, I want to know who.

6. b. (Later examples.)

1880 J. W. Zaehnsdorf *Art of Bookbinding* i. 1 Should the amateur wish to have his books in sheets, he may get them by asking his bookseller for them. **1972** P. Gaskell *New Introd. Bibliogr.* 144 Long books were divided in quires of 12–24 sheets before this folding took place; hence 'books in quires' as a synonym for books in sheets.

e. For *rare* read chiefly *U.S.* and add later examples.

1926 R. Hughes in *Hearst's Internat.* Feb. 44/1 'How come the newspapers keep saying your fights are all fixed?'.. 'Ah, who cares what the doity sheets say!' **1958** *Spectator* 20 June 807/2 A mass-circulation London Sunday sheet. **1977** R. M. Ours in Bond & McLeod *Newslett. to Newspapers* III. 220 Rivington made it clear that he intended no partisan sheet.

12. a. *sheet-whiteness*; *sheet-pale* adj.

1906 Hardy *Dynasts* II. III. v. 225 Sir David Baird, still helpless from his wound, was carried in a cot, sheet-pale and thin. **1956** H. Gold *Man who was not with It* xxvii. 250 This..creature who was Pauline's dark daughter; but now ice-whiteness, sheet-whiteness,..in her still and scared face.

b. sheet band *Printing* (see quot.); **sheet erosion,** the erosion of soil by rain-water acting more or less uniformly over a wide area; **sheet-fed** *a. Printing,* using paper in the form of cut sheets; **sheet-flood,** a short-lived expanse of running water that spreads as a continuous film over a large area following sudden heavy rain; **sheet-flow** *Geomorphol.,* a flow that covers a wide expanse of a surface instead of being confined in a channel; **sheet glass,** add: (*a*) in mod. use, a kind of flat glass made by a vertical drawing process (cf. *Fourcault); **sheet ice,** ice formed in a thin, smooth layer on water; **sheet lightning** (earlier example); **Sheetrock,** the proprietary name of a plaster-board made of gypsum between heavy paper (also with small initial); **sheet-wash,** sheet erosion; (erosion caused by) a sheet-flood.

1946 V. S. Ganderton in H. Whetton *Pract. Printing & Binding* x. 120/2 Carefully set, the sheet bands hold the sheet up to the cylinder and help to expel air from between the sheet and the cylinder, and thus minimize buckles. **1917** Mosier & Gustafson *Soil Physics & Management* xxvii. 361 Sheet erosion is the source of far greater loss than gullying. **1978** W. W. Emmett in M. J. Kirkby *Hillside Hydrol.* v. 171 Rilling is generally considered to be evidence of more accelerated erosion than sheet erosion. **1926** Sheet-fed [see *rotary *a.* 2 b]. **1973** W. H. Hallahan *Ross Forgery* iv. 52 The paper salesman..sold these people paper in sheets for sheet-fed presses. **1897** W. J. McGee in *Bull. Geol. Soc. Amer.* VIII. 88 Colloquially a moving water-body of this type is sometimes known as a 'wash'; but since the term is commonly applied primarily to the product and only secondarily to the agency, and since it is usually restricted to limited, though broad channels.., it seems desirable to use some other designation for the water-body; and the term *sheetflood* has come into use in notes and in conversation. **1938** *Bull. Geol. Soc. Amer.* XLIX. 1344 One of the most striking peculiarities of sheetfloods is the shortness of their flow in distance as well as in time. **1977** A. Hallam *Planet Earth* 49 After storms, flow is in the form of sheet-floods, comparatively shallow floods running over a broad area. **1928** *Bull Geol. Soc. Amer.* XXXIX. 481 The deposit was obviously not a sheet-flow; it was a stream [of detrital material] of unknown length. **1977** A. Hallam *Planet Earth* 85/2 This leads to preferential weathering at the break in slope, the weathering products being removed by sheetflow, wind and other processes. **1974** *Encycl. Brit. Macropædia* VIII. 202/1 Sheet glass of admirable flatness for many common purposes, unmarred by glass-to-metal contact, is produced by the continuous vertical draw process. *c* **1900** in *Regional Lang. Stud.—Newfoundland* (1978) VIII. 24 *Sheet ice,* thin ice of one or two nights frost. **1964** H. H. Smith *Shelter Bay* 123 But even thin ice—what we call sheet ice, could cause us plenty of trouble. **1794** J. B. S. Morritt *Let.* 24 June (1914) ii. 50 We have beautiful sheet lighting every evening, and have had for above a week. **1921** *Official Gaz.* (U.S. Patent Office) 29 Nov. 1065/2 *Sheetrock*... Plaster Wall-Board. Claims use since Aug. 28, 1917. U.S. Gypsum Co., Chicago. **1924** *Trade Marks Jrnl.* 5 Nov. 2475 *Sheetrock*... Plaster in sheets, for use as wall boards in building or decoration. U.S. Gypsum Co..., Chicago. **1973** R. B. Parker *Godwulf Manuscript* (1974) ix. 71 It was a tiny office... No windows, sheetrock partitions painted green. **1936** Finch & Trewartha *Elem. Geogr.* xxv. 559 One of the most widespread and least noticed kinds of erosion on tilled land is sheet wash. **1939** *Geogr. Jrnl.* XCIII. 305 If Tibu accounts of the nature of the rainfall are even partially credited, some form of sheet-wash can readily be imagined covering the whole floor of even a broad wadi, and undercutting its sides. **1964** A. Holmes *Princ. Physical Geol.* (ed. 2) xx. 613 A sudden change of slope seems to be favoured by torrential seasonal rainfalls and by the liberation of only minute amounts of fine debris which can be readily swept away by sheet-wash over the pediment. **1972** J. G. Cruickshank *Soil Geogr.* ii. 39 Fluvial erosion by rivers or sheet wash is the most important present form of transportation of material.

13. a. *sheet metal.*

1933 *Rep. & Mem. Aeronaut. Res. Comm.* No. 1553. 18 Constructions in thin sheet metal (*e.g.* monocoque fuselage) normally consist of a large area of sheet divided into a number of small panels by a system of stiffeners. **1959** *Motor Man.* (ed. 36) i. 3 The sheet metal forming the front wings and the sides of the bonnet. **1976** Lieberman & Rhodes *Compl. CB Handbk.* v. 97 It is fastened securely by two sheet-metal screws that actually screw into the rain-gutter groove of the trunk.

d. sheet music, music published in sheet form (as opp. to book form).

1857 *Lawrence* (Kansas) *Republican* 11 June 3 (Advt.), City drug store... Periodicals, lithographs, sheet music, etc. **1881** [in Dict.]. **1929** J. B. Priestley *Good Companions* III. iii. 534 Performing rights, sheet music, gramophone records. **1981** J. Wainwright *Urge for Justice* I. xii. 84 The window of the shop was crammed with sheet music.

sheet, *v.*[1] Add: **5.** Also of rain: to fall in a sheet or sheets (sense 7 b). Freq. with *down.*

1971 D. Beaty *Temple Tree* 9 The monsoon rain was still sheeting down. **1978** *Detroit Free Press* 16 Apr. 2B/1 Bumping over the high noon thunderheads, with rain sheeting across the little round windows, the air passenger over the South Pacific grips the seat arms.

sheeted, *ppl. a.* Add: **5.** *Geol.* Of rock (esp. granite) or a rock formation: having been divided into thin laminæ; *sheeted zone,* a belt of highly fissured rock associated with a fault, the fissures freq. being occupied by veins of minerals.

1903 *Bull. U.S. Geol. Survey* No. 213. 99 The granite is sheeted near the veins, the planes of sheeting being parallel to the veins themselves. **1905** H. Ries *Econ. Geol.* xvii. 339 (*caption*) Ore along sheeted zone. *Ibid.* 340 Composite veins in sheeted basalt dikes. **1939** W. H. Emmons et al. *Geol.* (ed. 2) xvii. 425 Some veins fill single openings..others fill closely spaced parallel openings, which are sheeted zones. **1943** *Jrnl. Geol.* LI. 82/1 During the glacial epoch these sheeted granites..must have been easily plucked and quarried by the advancing ice. **1974** *Nature* 29 Nov. 375/2 Shattered pebbles and sheeted bedrock are common weathering phenomena in most modern deserts.

sheeting, *vbl. sb.* Add: **3*.** *Geol.* The occurrence or development of closely spaced, approximately parallel fractures or joints in rock. Freq. *attrib.*

1899 *Trans. Inst. Mining & Metallurgy* VIII. 67 The multiple fracturing, parallel to the walls of the dyke, is a characteristic feature of such lodes... This feature can be described as a sheeting of the rock. **1903** [see *sheeted *ppl. a.* 5]. **1912** E. C. Eckel *Building Stones & Clays* iii. 39 Geologists..ascribe some or all sheeting structure to strains induced during the original cooling of the mass, or to the effects of later external stresses. **1934** O. Bowles *Stone Industries* viii. 108 Widely separated sheeting planes occur at a depth of 250 feet at Quincy, Mass. **1965** A. Holmes *Princ. Physical Geol.* (ed. 2) ix. 217 The sheeting or sheet structure that is often seen in exposures of granitic and other plutonic intrusions.

sheetlet (ʃī·tlėt). [f. Sheet *sb.*[1] + -let.] A small sheet; *spec.* in *Philately* (cf. Sheet *sb.*[1] 5 d).

1934 in Webster. **1971** D. Potter *Brit. Eliz. Stamps* xi. 123 Three separate editions, 2s, 4s and 6s, contained sheetlets of one stamp. **1978** *Sunday Telegraph* (Colour Suppl.) 29 Jan. 39 (Advt.), A beautifully designed pack containing the unique series of stamps (in sheetlets) to be issued by the Crown Agents.

sheevo, var. *shiveau.

Sheffer (ʃe·fəɹ). *Logic.* [The name of Henry M. *Sheffer* (1883–1964), U.S. philosopher.] *Sheffer('s) stroke*: the symbol |; also, the logical function of non-conjunction (and sometimes non-disjunction) that it represents, described by Sheffer in 1913 (*Trans. Amer. Math. Soc.* XIV. 481–8) (so *Sheffer stroke function*).

1932 Lewis & Langford *Symbolic Logic* ix. 306 The prefixes are analogues of Sheffer's stroke-function $p|q$ in its two interpretations. **1950** L. M. Hammond et al. tr. *Hilbert & Ackermann's Princ. Math. Logic* i. 11 Since ∨ and — can be expressed by Sheffer's stroke, the same holds for the other fundamental connectives. **1957** [see *non-conjunction 2]. **1960** N. R. Scott *Analog & Digital Computer Technol.* x. 392 If the low-potential and high-potential signal levels are identified respectively with binary 0 and 1, this circuit performs the Sheffer stroke function. **1972** A. G. Howson *Handbk. Terms Algebra & Anal.* i. 2 More basic still are the Sheffer stroke | and the connective ↓..since all the other connectives can be defined in terms of | (or ↓) alone.

Sheffield. Add: **2.** The name of Henry North Holroyd, third Earl of *Sheffield* (1832–1909), used *attrib.* in **Sheffield Shield,** a trophy presented by him in 1892 and contested annually by Australian state cricket teams (freq. *attrib.*).

1901 *Wisden's Cricketers' Almanack* (ed. 38) 462 The result determined the possession of the Sheffield Shield for the season. **1912** *Dict. National Biogr.* 2nd Suppl. II. 290/2 In 1891–2 Lord Sheffield, at his sole expense, took to Australia a team..under the management of Alfred Shaw. This enterprise greatly stimulated Australian cricket; the earl presented the Sheffield Shield, a trophy to be competed for annually by cricketers of Victoria, New South Wales, and South Australia. **1930** C. G. Macartney *My Cricketing Days* iii. 20 My first season with the new club turned out to be my first in inter-state and Sheffield Shield cricket. **1977** *World of Cricket Monthly* June 19/1 The Australian cricketers we have signed are available to play Test, Sheffield Shield and club cricket when they are not playing in the super Test and other series.

‖ **shefstvo** (ʃe·fstvə). Also **chefstvo.** [Russ.] Patronage, sponsorship: variously used (see quots.).

1937 S. N. Harper *Govt. Soviet Union* viii. 134 The institution of so-called 'patronage' (*chefstvo*) is extended also to the Red Army and aims to keep those in military service in the everyday life of the community. **1948** J. Towster *Political Power in U.S.S.R.* xiii. 322 Another form of tutelage was the so-called *shefstvo* or patronage by industrial regions over agricultural regions. **1950** B. Moore *Soviet Politics* viii. 173 Another method, which evidently sprang up in the early thirties and then was permitted to die a natural death, was called 'patronage' (*shefstvo*), usually the patronage of a specific factory or of a specific group of workers over some section of the administration. **1955** H. Hodgkinson *Doubletalk* 120 *Shefstvo,* patronage exercised by a *shef* or 'chief' is the Soviet equivalent of 'empire building' in Western business and service jargon.

‖ **shehecheyanu** (ʃeheχeyā·nu). Also **shehechyoni,** etc. [Heb., lit. 'that has sustained us'.] A Jewish benediction pronounced on the evening of a principal holy day and on new occasions of thanksgiving.

1892 I. Zangwill *Childr. Ghetto* II. xvi. 53 He was wondering whether he ought to say *Shehechyoni*—the prayer over a new pleasure. **1959** R. S. Brookes *Dict. Judaism* 213 *She'hechiyanu,* a blessing recited on the first evening of festivals, on eating the first fruits of the season and on donning a new raiment [*sic*] for the first time. **1966** L. Davidson *Long Way to Shiloh* xv. 227 When they.. told me that the possibility existed, that by some miracle of God's grace, the holy Menorah was still in Eretz Yisroel ..I said a *shechayanu.* **1972** C. Raphael *Feast of History* i. 23 The Seder ceremony was an occasion for joy... We thanked God—in the famous *She'heheyanu* prayer—that he had 'kept us alive and sustained us and brought us to this moment'. **1980** *Jewish Chron.* 28 Mar. (Passover Suppl.) p. iii/1 He'd done the kiddush and the *shehecheyanu.*

shehita(h, var. *shechita. **shehnai,** var. *shahnai.

sheikh. Delete ‖ and add: **1. b.** (Chiefly in spelling *sheik.*) A type of a strong, romantic lover; a lady-killer. [after *The Sheik,* a novel by E. M. Hull (1919), and its cinematic adaptation *The Sheikh,* 1921, starring Rudolph Valentino.]

1925 *Lit. Digest* 14 Feb. 28/2 We hear almost nothing more of the matinée idol any more... The 'sheik' has taken his place. **1927** *Amer. Speech* II. 202/2 The girl calls the young man..'my sheik'. **1932** S. Gibbons *Cold Comfort Farm* xviii. 245 The mask smiled..from a great silver screen: 'Seth Starkadder in "Small-Town Sheik".' **1939** 'G. Orwell' *Coming up for Air* I. i. 10 When your last natural tooth goes, the time when you can kid yourself that you're a Hollywood sheik is definitely at an end. **1956** S. Longstreet *Real Jazz Old & New* xii. 95 John Held Jr. drew the jazz-flapper and her sheik best... The lad was apple-headed, his hair buttered tight down. He wore bell-bottomed trousers, a racoon coat, drove a Stutz Bearcat and played or danced to jazz a lot. **1980** 'L. Egan' *Motive in Shadow* v. 87 He's sure a handsome sheik, kid.

shei·khling, a petty sheikh.

1914 G. Bell *Let.* 19 Jan. (1927) I. xiii. 326 A young sheikhling of the Sikhur joined us..and spent the night with us as guests. **1974** W. Garner *Big enough Wreath* iv. 40 Mini-presidents and rich sheiklings seeking advice.

‖ **Sheikha** (ʃēⁱ·kă, ʃī·kă). Also **Shaikha(h, Sheika,** and with small initial. [Arab *šaiḵa.*] An Arab lady or matron of good family; hence, the (chief) wife of a sheikh. (Also as a title of respect.) Also *transf.,* the consort of a 'sheikh' (cf. *sheikh 1 b) (*slang*).

1853 J. Richardson *Narr. Mission Cent. Afr.* II. xiv. 247, I had a visit from a great sister of the Sarkee, a woman who is a Sheikha (female Sheikh), and receives the revenues of fifty villages for her own private use. **1926** Maines & Grant *Wise-Crack Dict.* 13/2 *Sheika,* Sheik's sweetie. **1949** H. R. P. Dickson *Arab of Desert* viii. 144 Al Jazi, sister of Khalid al Hithlain..had a will of her own, and was a veritable 'Shaikhah'. **1967** M. Childs *Taint of Innocence* iii. 189 The Emir, the Sheika, and a party..had left the palace. **1976** *Times* 22 Sept. 2/3 Shaikha ——, a Saudi Arabian noblewoman, who bought 50 Chepstow Villas, Notting Hill. **1976** L. Blandford *Oil Sheikhs* 256 Sheikha Osheh is..married to Sheikh Mubarak. **1980** D. Creed *Scarab* xiv. 134 They *are* Arabs—and so are you, sheikha.

sheila (ʃī·lă). Now *Austral.* and *N.Z. colloq.* Also 9 **shaler; shelah,** etc. [Orig. uncertain. Early *shaler* is not formally explained. It may represent a generic use of the (originally Irish) personal name *Sheila,* the counterpart of Paddy *sb.*[2] 1 a (see quot. 1828); in any case, it became assimilated to this at some later stage.] A girl or young woman; a girlfriend. (Playfully affectionate and predominantly in male use.)

[**1828** *Monitor* (Sydney) 22 Mar. 1053/2 Many a piteous Shela stood wiping the gory locks of her Paddy, until released from that duty by the officious interference of the knight of the baton.] **1839** H. Brandon in W. A. Miles *Poverty, Mendicity & Crime* 165/1 *Shalers*, girls (country phrase). **1847** G. W. M. Reynolds *Myst. London* III. xxv. 71/1 Cop that young shaler unto thee. **1864** Hotten *Slang Dict.* 225 *Shaler*, a girl. Corrupt form of *Gaelic, caille*, a young woman. **1895** C. Crowe *Austral. Slang Dict.* 72 *Shaler*, a girl. **1918** *N.Z.E.F. Chrons.* 5 July 252/2, I goes and stays out at Ngaire with my shieler's people. **1919** W. H. Downing *Digger Dialects* 44 *Sheila*, a girl. **1928** A. Wright *Good Recovery* 117 Leave the sheilas alone, they're sure to pool a man sooner or later. **1930** V. Palmer *Men are Human* xxvii. 251 There was a sheelah he had working for him once, a lively piece with black eyes. **1940** F. Sargeson *Man & his Wife* (1944) 66 I've got a job in a grocer's shop and I'm trotting a sheila. She's a pearl of a sheila too. **1951** F. Hardy *Power without Glory* (ed. 5) i. 21 'What d'yer expect us to do, just sit around and starve ourselves?'..'Please yer bloody self, but you've got to think of yer mother, and that sheila of yours.' **1959** *Woman's Own* 4 July 11/3 They have a daughter—a nice-looking sheila, too. **1962** *Coast to Coast 1961–62* 21 'I know a sheila,' Sonny began. 'A real trimmer.' **1969** *Private Eye* 21 Nov. 14 Don't be shit-scared of these sheilahs who work for me. **1976** *Times Lit. Suppl.* 9 Apr. 418/3 His past would be remythologized by a host of pre-war radio announcers, sepia footballers and nude sheilahs from the master brush of Norman Lindsay. **1977** D. Seaman *Committee* 63 They made the usual jokes about the local Sheilas.

sheila-na-gig, var. *sheela-na-gig. **sheirut,** var. *sherut.

‖ **sheitel** (ʃē^i·t'l). Also **shaitel.** [ad. Yiddish *sheytl*, f. MHG. *scheitel* crown of the head.] Among strictly Orthodox Ashkenazi Jews: a wig worn by a married woman.

1892 I. Zangwill *Childr. Ghetto* I. ii. 41 A small, sickly-looking woman, with..the wig without which no virtuous wife is complete... A lower stratum of unmatched brown peeped out in front of the *Shaitel*. **1957** L. Stern *Midas Touch* i. vii. 63 His mother..no longer wore her sheitel, or traditional wig. **1973** *Jewish Chron.* 19 Jan. 22/3 A comely young rebbetzin in a glamorous sheitel and eyelashes long enough to brush dandruff from lapels has been touring American universities to attract straying Jewish youths back to their faith.

shekel. Add: **1. c.** An Israeli unit of currency introduced in February 1980, equivalent to ten former Israeli pounds; a note of this value.

1980 *Times* 23 Feb. 1/2 From next week the Israeli pound is to be replaced by a new currency named after the Biblical shekel... Each shekel will be purchased with 10 present Israeli pounds. **1980** *Whitaker's Almanack 1981* 979 Israel..Israeli Shekel of 100 New Agora..[Notes] Shekels 50, 10, 5, 1.

2. Also in phr. *to rake in the shekels*, to make money rapidly or 'hand over fist' (from a venture). Cf. *rake *sb.*[1] 2 a (*a*).

1887 [see *high *a.* 10 h]. **1915** J. Buchan *39 Steps* i. 18 The capitalists would rake in the shekels, and make fortunes by buying up wreckage.

shekere, var. *sekere. **shekest(h)eh,** obs. vars. *shikasta.

sheld-duck. Add: Now usu. **shelduck.**

1925 C. W. R. Knight *Aristocrats of Air* x. 124, I did not succeed in locating a Shelduck's nest. **1939** J. Fisher *Birds as Animals* xi. 190 In..black skimmer and shelduck, both birds incubate. **1966** E. Palmer *Plains of Camdeboo* xi. 190 Shelduck, well-known for making their nests in holes, often choose ant-bear burrows. **1972** *Country Life* 3 Feb. 274/1 The shelduck is the largest and most striking bird of the English shores.

shelf, *sb.*[1] Add: **I. 1. e.** *off the shelf*: from a supply of ready-made goods. Also (with hyphens) as *adj. phr.*

1936 *Industr. & Engin. Chem.* Feb. 150/2 The individual customer must generally have his material fabricated to his order and cannot obtain material [aluminium] 'off the shelf'. **1958** *Engineering* 11 Apr. 455/2 Using sets built to a standard pattern which would be available 'off the shelf' and made up of interchangeable parts. **1962** J. Glenn in *Into Orbit* 37 They had to use 'off-the-shelf' items in order to save time. **1978** *Nature* 26 Oct. 784/1 As CAMAC equipment is often sold as individual products to system builders, items are often available either 'off the shelf'.

3*. A police informer. *Austral. slang.*

1926 J. Doone *Timely Tips for New Australians* (Gloss.), *Shelf*, a slang word denoting an informer. **1952** *People* (Austral.) 3 Dec. 8/2 The jail authorities knew such trafficking went on and often set traps for the warders through the good offices of *shelfs* or *trusties* (prisoners who were informers).

II. 4. b. Also unqualified (freq. *attrib.*).

1913 *Jrnl. Geol.* XXI. 525 The mode of formation keeps the face of the shelf within a certain distance from the sea-surface. *Ibid.*, The shelf zone is..a biologic horizon of the first importance. **1934** C. R. Longwell et al. *Outl. Physical Geol.* vii. 125 The shelf beyond the long-quiescent Atlantic coast of North America is 60 to 80 miles wide off the Carolinas. **1964** *Oceanogr. & Marine Biol.* II. 61 The temperature minimum at 150m may be formed, in part, by mixing of winter Bering Sea water with shelf water. **1978** Friedman & Sanders *Princ. Sedimentol.* xii. 360/2 (*caption*) Shelf lagoon between margin of a continental block and a reef tract that is situated at the edge of the continental mass.

III. 6. *shelf-load, -space*; *shelf-like* adj.; **shelf appeal,** the attractiveness to a customer of packaged goods displayed in a shop; **shelf back** *U.S.*, the spine of a book; **shelf cod,** cod found in inshore waters above the continental shelf; **shelf ice** [tr. G. *schelfeis* (O. Nordenskjöld 1908, in *Zeitschr. der Ges. für Erdkunde zu Berlin* XLIII. 618, following suggestion of A. Penck)], ice which forms a thick level layer on water (usu. the sea) but is attached to land; **shelf life,** the length of time that a commodity may be stored without becoming unfit for use or consumption; **shelf-list** (examples); so **shelf-lister,** one who compiles shelf-lists; **shelf paper,** paper used for lining shelves; **shelf sea,** an expanse of sea overlying continental shelf.

1933 *Shelf Appeal* July 3 (*heading*) Shelf Appeal. A monthly publication devoted to the planning, designing, manufacturing & display of the package. **1963** *B.S.I. News* Apr. 20/1 The 'shelf-appeal' pack designed to catch the eye of the ordinary shopper. **1964** *Times Rev. Industry* Feb. 23/1 With the post-war swing to more branded goods, self-service, enhanced hygiene and the need for 'shelf-appeal', the demand for more and better packaging has expanded fast. **1925** J. A. Holden *Bookman's Gloss.* 97 *Shelf-back*, the back of a book, on which the title is lettered. **1931** *Publishers' Weekly* 9 May 2322 It..is strongly bound and has the name of the periodical stamped in gold on cover and shelfback. **1960** G. A. Glaister *Gloss. Book* 375/1 *Shelf back*, the spine of a book. **1935** L. Luard *Conquering Seas* 37 Cod... Shelf Cod. **1976** *Eastern Even. News* (Norwich) 9 Dec. 12/5 Grimsby fish. Poor supply, good demand; six boats landed 1917 kit. Shelf cod £4 to £5. **1910** *Geogr. Jrnl.* XXXV. 726 To this ice formed *in situ* out of snow accumulations in the sea Nordenskiöld gives the name 'shelf-ice'. **1938** *Ibid.* XCI. 511 Of all the glacial features in this region, perhaps the greatest interest attaches to the shelf-ice filling King George VI Sound. **1977** *New Yorker* 20 June 55/1 The river's edges are lined with ice that is stationary—'shelf ice', 'shore ice', the first to freeze at the start of winter and the last to go in spring. **1927** *Manufacturing Confectioner* Jan. 12 (*heading*) What is the shelf life of your hard candy? **1933** R. A. Watson Watt et al. *Applications of Cathode Ray Oscillograph in Radio Res.* i. 27 The batteries may..be of very small size; 'shelf-life' and loss through casual leakage..are more important than their actual load current. **1940** *Austral. Jrnl. Dentistry* XLIV. 39 Either copper or copper and zinc must be present in the alloy if it is to possess a reasonable 'shelf life'. **1956** *Visible Packaging of Flour Confectionery* (British Cellophane Ltd.) 3 For small fancy cakes a moistureproof heat-sealing wrap..should give a shelf-life of several days. **1969** *Observer* 26 Jan. 5/5 The shelf-life of donated blood is about 21 days. **1980** D. Francis *Reflex* viii. 99 Some photographic chemicals lose their power with age. Shelf life, and so on. **1851** H. Melville *Moby Dick* I. iii. 18 On one side stood a long, low, shelf-like table covered with cracked glass cases, filled with dusty rarities. **1962** *Science Survey* XI. 178 The inner membrane whose shelf-like folds protrude into the interior of the organelle. **1910** A. E. Bostwick *Amer. Public Library* 171 The name 'shelf list' is sometimes improperly given to a class list. **1979** *Amer. N. & Q.* June 166/2 Each volume of the shelflist is in four parts, viz., the classification schedule, the shelflist proper (showing shelf mark, author, title, place of publication, and date), the same items (excluding serials) in chronological order, and an author and title index. **1927** W. W. Bishop *Pract. Handbk. Mod. Libr. Catal.* 21 The catalog room..should be..on the same floor with the order clerks, classifiers and shelf-listers. **1950** G. Greene in *Dickens's Oliver Twist* p. vii, We must forget that long shelf-load of books. **1980** *Jrnl. R. Soc. Arts* Mar. 177/2 Spend how much money you will, apply ten shelf loads of regulations, there is no way of promising that there is no risk of failure. **1895** *Montgomery Ward Catal.* 113/3 Shelf Paper, pinked in fancy designs, each sheet 8½ inches wide, 33 inches long. **1968** *Listener* 27 June 841/1 Kerouac types *On the Road* on a 120-foot roll of shelf paper but cannot get it published. **1913** T. C. Chamberlin in *Jrnl. Geol.* XXI. 523 The waters that rest upon these sea-shelves may be known conveniently as shelf-seas. **1969** Bennison & Wright *Geol. Hist. Brit. Isles* ii. 21 Sediments laid down in deeper water..have a quite different faunal content from the shelf-sea deposits. **1954** W. K. Hancock *Country & Calling* iii. 95 It became my fate to struggle with a brute documentary mass that has to be measured in miles of shelf-space. **1978** J. Irving *World according to Garp* ii. 28 Her books...outgrew the shelf space.

shelf, *v.*[3] Add: **2.** *Austral. slang.* To inform upon. Cf. *shelf *sb.*[1] 3*.

1953 K. Tennant *Joyful Condemned* xi. 96 Central has only to lamp you coming in here, and we all go up. Jimmy here shelfed me before. **1958** V. Kelly *Greedy Ones* 104 We were mates in this affair and you don't shelf your mates. And anyone who does shelf a mate has got to take what's coming to him.

shell, *sb.* Add: **I. 8. b.** The empty case of a fruit.

1902 H. L. Wilson *Spenders* xxvii. 313 Mr. Milbrey glanced at the two shells of the orange which the butler was then removing. **1974** *Times* 20 Apr. 10/8 Grapefruit mixes well with cottage cheese, and you can use the shell to hold the salad.

9. b. (Earlier example.)

1815 C'tess Granville *Lett.* (1894) I. 73 Madame de Coigny has difficulty in re-uniting people *chez elle*, and if one meets a Frenchman there, he draws into his shell and sits in gloomy silence.

II. 12. b. A thin body bounded by two closely spaced curved surfaces: (*a*) as a concept in *Statics*; (*b*) in *Civil Engin.*, a structural member of this form that has strength by virtue of its shape.

1877 G. M. Minchin *Treat. Statics* xiv. 432 Hence.. every shell of uniform density and small thickness, bounded by similar, similarly situated, and concentric surfaces produces a constant potential at all points in its interior. **1892** A. E. H. Love *Treat. Math. Theory Elasticity* I. vii. 221 Consider the case of a spherical shell, whose outer and inner surfaces are subjected to hydrostatic pressure. **1952** O. Faber *Reinforced Concrete* xiii. 192 For clear widths of about 150 ft. and over it is found to be economical to provide arched shells spanning direct, with stiffening ribs at about 25 ft. to 35 ft. centres. **1967** H. Kraus *Thin Elastic Shells* p. vii, Sophisticated uses of shells are currently being made in missiles and space vehicles, submarines, nuclear reactor vessels, refinery equipment, and the like. **1972** R. E. Owen *Roofs* vi. 81 A cylindrical shell transmits direct load to its columns.

c. *U.S.* A concave structure designed to accommodate a band or orchestra.

1938 D. Baker *Young Man with Horn* i. vi. 71 At the rear of the room was the orchestra shell, very shell-like, fluted along the upper edge. **1978** *Chicago* June 22/2 Each concert will be given on two evenings, and performances will take place..in the new James C. Petrillo Music Shell at Jackson and Columbus.

18. a. (Earlier example.)

1867 *Harper's Mag.* Oct. 654/2 Look at these beautiful 'shells', resting one above the other on the brackets on either wall.

19. b. *Physics.* (A set of electrons forming) one of a number of concentric structures around the nucleus of an atom; *spec.* a set of electrons each having the same principal quantum number. Also, (a set of nucleons forming) a corresponding structure within a nucleus.

1904 J. J. Thomson in *Phil. Mag.* VII. 255 When the corpuscles [*sc.* electrons] are not constrained to one plane, but can move about in all directions, they will arrange themselves in a series of concentric shells. **1919** *Proc. Nat. Acad. Sci.* V. 252 The electrons in any given atom are distributed through a series of concentric (nearly) spherical shells, all of equal thickness. **1932** *Physical Rev.* XLI. 370/1 For some time, there has been speculation as to whether or not the atomic nucleus can be regarded as consisting of shells of protons, just as the external structure is known to consist of shells of electrons. **1952** *Sci. News* XXIII. 36 Neon has 10 electrons in two complete shells. **1961** G. R. Choppin *Exper. Nuclear Chem.* iii. 30 Frequently, rather than emit a gamma ray, a nucleus will interact with its external electronic shells and cause emission of an electron. **1972** *Sci. Amer.* Oct. 101/1 In nuclei there also is a periodic recurrence of certain properties as nucleons are added to fill successive shells of quantum states. **1974** G. Reece tr. *Hund's Hist. Quantum Theory* viii. 106 The formation of molecules was thus a problem of atomic structure, namely the tendency of atoms to form ions with complete shells.

23. b. Also *N. Amer.*, the unlined body of a coat; *U.S.*, an article of clothing for the upper body, *spec.* a woman's (usu. sleeveless) over-blouse or a light all-weather jacket.

1913 *T. Eaton & Co. Catal.* Semi-Annual Sale 17/3 Men's muskrat-lined coat..Collar is genuine Canadian otter; the shell is cut from standard quality black beaver cloth. **1962** *Mademoiselle* Aug. 276/2 A white cardigan.. to show a matching sleeveless shell. **1967** *Boston Sunday Globe* 23 Apr. 5/2 (Advt.), 3-pc. acetate double knit suit with rayon metallic shell. **1976** *National Observer* (U.S.) 1 May 7/4 (Advt.), Nylon shell for men and women. Ultra light, all weather sports jacket of tough two-ply coated nylon. **1976** U. Curtiss *Dig Little Deeper* x. 89 Paula came in, wearing a topaz-colored pants suit over a ribbed cream shell.

e. The body of a car.

1937 *Times* 13 Apr. (Brit. Motor Suppl.) p. xiii/1 The various stages through which the car body shell can pass, therefore, are as follows. **1972** *Oxford Mail* 13 Oct. 1/5 Output of body shells for the Marina range was halted for a time.

IV. 25. b. A company which has ceased to trade but which is still quoted on the stock exchange.

1964 *Economist* 19 Dec. 1378/2 A company had ceased normal trading and was a pure shell. **1969** 'D. Rutherford' *Gilt-Edged Cockpit* iv. 68 It's called buying a shell. A tax loss company. When you set the Hackforth loss against our profit we're left with practically no tax to pay. **1981** *Times* 27 May 20/6 Mr Alastair Milne..headed a consortium bidding for former cash shell Phoenix Mining two years ago.

VI. 34. d. *shell-grey, -pink* (later examples).

1963 *Times* 8 June 12/3 Short dresses of shell-grey silk with flared skirts. **1932** J. C. Powys *Glastonbury Romance* ii. xxi. 701 The new silk lining of her ottoman had dyed itself..into an incredible shell-pink. **1951** E. Paul *Springtime in Paris* xii. 229 Anatole turned shell pink, then a kind of raspberry shade. **1977** 'E. Anthony' *Silver Falcon* (1978) 133 The house was..painted shell-pink.

35. b. *shell-gravel, -grit, -sand* (later examples).

1882 W. D. Hay *Brighter Britain!* I. xi. 307 A straight, broad path, smooth and white with shell-gravel. **1923**

JOYCE *Ulysses* 48 Loose sand and shellgrit crusted her bare feet. **1938** Shell-grit [see *ROULETTED *pa. pple.* b]. **1964** *Oceanogr. & Marine Biol.* II. 418 *Spatangus purpureus*..lives in shell-gravel. **1977** *Stornoway Gaz.* 27 Aug. 4/9 These are well worth looking for in June or July in the grassland behind our many shell-sand beaches.

c. *shell-box, -road* (earlier example).

1836 T. POWER *Impressions of Amer.* II. 99 We soon gained the shell road however, and found it as good as the streets of Mobile. **1853** C. BRONTË *Villette* III. xxxi. 35 Slipping into his hand the ruddy little shell box. **1976** J. FLEMING *To make Underworld* ii. 21 She makes these shell boxes, y'know..all stuck over with shells.

e. *shell-pattern* (earlier and later examples).

1780 J. WEDGWOOD *Let.* 21 Oct. (1965) 260, I now expect to sell a good deal of his green shell pattern. **1897** *Private Life of Queen* xxii. 180 The enormous 'shell pattern' service of knives, forks and spoons. **1967** E. SHORT *Embroidery & Fabric Collage* iii. 68 Aluminium templates can be bought in a number of geometric shapes and also a shell pattern.

36. a. *shell-burst, crater, -fire* (examples), *-gun* (later example), *-hole, -madness, -splinter, -storm, -trap*; **b.** *shell-dodging*; *shell-firing* adj.; **c.** *shell-pitted, -pocked, -smitten, -torn* adjs.

1917 W. OWEN *Let.* 2 Mar. (1967) 440 Did you see any shell-bursts? **1980** G. M. FRASER *Mr American* xxvi. 556 It wis a shell-burst that Ah stopped. **1916** 'BOYD CABLE' *Action Front* 49 The neutral ground..was a sea of mud, broken by heaped earth and yawning shell craters. **1977** J. CLEARY *High Road to China* i. 32, I..was trapped in a shell crater with three dead men. **1917** 'CONTACT' *Airman's Outings* 241 Freed from the immediate necessity of shell-dodging. **1900** W. S. CHURCHILL in *Morning Post* 25 June 5/7 In spite of an accurate shellfire they continued to advance boldly against the highest part of the hill. **1977** *Listener* 28 Apr. 559/2 They had had built a reinforced concrete pillbox—a shelter against the shrapnel and the unceasing shellfire. **1900** W. S. CHURCHILL in *Morning Post* 1 Jan. 6/1 The shell-firing Maxim continued its work. **1942** *R.A.F. Jrnl.* 16 May 15 These include.. constant-speed 3-blade propeller; shell-firing guns; wireless and oxygen equipment. **1940** *Flight* 12 Dec. 522/2 The shell-gun or 'cannon' has been in action mounted in the machines of Fighter Command. **1916** 'BOYD CABLE' *Action Front* 141 The stretcher-bearers who lifted him from the shell-hole. **1971** S. HILL *Strange Meeting* iii. 203 Then suddenly they came between the stumps of some trees, dropped down into a shell hole. **1923** KIPLING *Irish Guards in Gt. War* I. 329 A dazed day of 'shell-madness', when all ears and eyes were intolerably overburdened with echoes and pictures. **1918** W. S. CHURCHILL *Let.* 12 Sept. in M. Gilbert *W. S. Churchill* (1975) IV. I. vii. 147 For an hour we ran through devastated, shell pitted facias—scraggy shreds of woods. **1925** *Scribner's Mag.* Sept. 234/2 Only the 49th lay perforce in the open, on a bleak, shell-pocked slope. **1917** J. MASEFIELD *Old Front Line* 71 It has been more burnt and shell-smitten than most parts of the lines. **1910** W. S. CHURCHILL in R. S. Churchill *W. S. Churchill* (1967) I. Compan. II. 1071 The driver..was wounded severely in the scalp by a shell-splinter almost immediately. **1974** N. FREELING *Dressing of Diamond* 137 He had been ripped by a shell splinter and sewn up casually. **1903, 1914** Shell-storm [see *RAFALE]. **1918** W. OWEN *Let.* 4 Jan. (1967) 525 He was badly wounded, and..still wears the shell-torn boots. **1949** S. SPENDER *Edge of Being* 24 Moving in death through shell-torn tenements. **1879** *Encycl. Brit.* IX. 461/2 Such shell-traps..are scrupulously avoided by modern [military] engineers. **1923** KIPLING *Irish Guards in Gt. War* I. 97 Annequin..had become more than ever a shell-trap.

38*. In sense *25 b: *shell company, corporation, game, operation, transaction.*

1958 *Economist* 15 Mar. 957/1 Shell companies have nothing to do with oil. They are corporate entities empty of their trading assets; they hold only cash or near cash assets in their balance sheets and otherwise have nothing but a stock exchange quotation—which is essential. **1977** *Irish Press* 29 Sept. 7/7 It was in April 1972 that Fitzwilliam Resources, of the same stock that formed Fitzwilliam Securities and Fitzwilton Ltd., (the Irish 'shell' company, which is now a shadow of its former self), took a 6 per cent stake in Tara. **1969** *Wall St. Jrnl.* 3 July 4/2 The Securities and Exchange Commission said it's disturbed by the increasing use of inactive 'shell' corporations as vehicles for distributing unregistered stock to the public. **1974** A. A. THOMPSON *Swiss Legacy* xx. 204 They are shell corporations... They have no assets, no activities, nothing. They are merely conduits for money going elsewhere. **1969** *N.Y. Rev. Books* 2 Jan. 42/3 What becomes almost obscene about such a reactionary shell game..is that these very same corporate chiefs are right now planning an increase in unemployment. **1977** F. BRANSTON *Up & Coming Man* xi. 108 A shell operation, where you buy a dormant or nearly defunct company and inject assets into it. **1958** *Spectator* 11 July 68/3 This should put a stop to 'shell' transactions.

39. shell-back, (*a*) (earlier U.S. example); also *transf.*; hence **shell-backed** *a.*; **shell beach,** a beach composed wholly or predominantly of sea-shells; *spec.* the name of one such on the Channel Island of Herm; **shell-bird,** (*a*) *Canada*, the red-breasted merganser, *Mergus serrator*; (*b*) *nonce-use*, a tortoise; **shell-briar** *a.*, designating a type of tobacco-pipe with a rough, dark-stained stem and bowl; **shell button** (earlier U.S. example); **shell cocoa,** the husks of cocoa-beans or the drink made from an infusion of these; **shell concrete** *Building*, concrete used in shell construction; **shell construction** *Building*, the use of thin curved shells (sense 12 b above) to roof areas having wide spans; **shell egg,** an egg in its natural state in the shell (opp. to *dried egg*: cf. *DRIED *ppl. a.* 1); **shell-game** (earlier and later examples); also *fig.*; **shell-gritted** *a.* *Archæol.*, denoting a ware made of a paste mixed with particles of shell; **shell ice** *Canad.* = *cat-ice* s.v. CAT *sb.*[1] 18; **shell midden** *Archæol.* = *shell-heap*; **shell model** *Nuclear Physics*, a theoretical description of nuclear structure in which the nucleus is considered to consist of nucleons arranged in shells (sense *19 b); **shell-moulding** *vbl. sb.*, in *Founding*, a method of making moulds and cores in which a shell of resin-bonded sand is formed in parts around a heated metal pattern, the parts being joined together after removal of the pattern; so **shell-mould,** a mould made in this way; **shell rock** *N. Amer.*, hard rock consisting largely of compacted sea-shells; **shell roof,** a roof consisting of a shell (sense 12 b above); **shell shock,** (*a*) a name given, esp. during the war of 1914–18, to certain psychological disturbances occurring in conditions of active warfare and supposed to result primarily from exposure to shell-fire; also *fig.*; (*b*) *slang*, cocoa; hence **shell-shock** *v. trans.*, to affect with shell shock; **shell-shocked** *a.*, suffering from shell shock; **shell-shocker,** a sufferer from shell shock; **shell steak,** a steak cut from the short loin; **shell-stitch,** one of various knitting or sewing stitches producing shell-like patterns; **shell structure** *Physics*, the structure of the atom envisaged as consisting of a number of electron shells (sense 19 b above); **shell transformer,** a shell-type transformer (see below); **shell-type** *sb.* and *a.*, (applied to) something having or resembling a shell in any sense; *shell-type transformer*, a transformer having its windings wholly or largely enclosed within the metal 'core'.

1853 J. T. DOWNEY *Filings from Old Saw* (1956) vi. 30 Both the nerve of 14 strong armed shell-backs, and the occasional disbursement of an extra *tot* of whiskey, kept her going. **1943** A. RANSOME *Picts & Martyrs* xi. 103 He felt as if he was going to sit for an examination and he wanted to make no mistakes with those two old shellbacks, Nancy and Peggy, as examiners. **1959** J. CARY *Captive & Free* 207 The old hulk was full of crabs—there doesn't seem to be anything else in the sub-editor's room. Old shellbacks that have been chewing on Fowler for forty years. **1963** *Listener* 21 Feb. 350/3, I have no doubt a lot of right-wing shell-backs are now conceding, with blimpish magnanimity, that there's really something to be said for these young fellows after all. **1974** *Times* 9 Dec. 13/3 In both division lobbies right-wingers rubbed shoulders with left-wingers, shellbacks with parliamentary apprentices. **1930** R. CAMPBELL *Adamastor* 30 A shell-backed saint, whom time maroons. **1972** *Daily Tel.* 29 Dec. 7/8 Mr Marcus is always eloquent when he is contrasting innocence with shell-backed experience. **1835** H. D. INGLIS *Channel Islands* 323 Herm possesses another attraction,..its shell beach. **1915** E. R. LANKESTER *Diversions of Naturalist* 144 The shells which are accumulated as shell-beaches have come from animals which lived in quantity at depths of ten or twenty fathoms. **1964** H. MYHILL *Introducing Channel Islands* v. 114 It is possibly the situation of this beach..which has led to the accumulation there of countless thousands of shells of great variety. There are said to be over five hundred distinct species represented, and they have given it the name of the Shell Beach. **1770** G. CARTWRIGHT *Jrnl.* 2 Oct. (1792) I. 40 They returned with three shellbirds and a saddleback. **1973** E. GOUDIE *Woman of Labrador* II. iv. 102 Shell birds are not very good eating because they taste very fishy. **1921** D. H. LAWRENCE *Tortoises* 12 Nay, tiny shell-bird, What a huge vast inanimate it is, that you must row against. **1972** M. J. BOSSE *Incident at Naha* i. 17 He..lit a pipe, his largest shell-briar Apple. **1977** A. SCHOLEFIELD *Venom* v. 203 The chubby face, from which the fragrant bowl of a shell-briar emerged. **1789** *Deb. Congr. U.S.* 29 Aug. (1834) 796 An exclusive patent..for manufacturing shell buttons of different dimensions. **1902** J. T. LAW *Law's Grocer's Man.* (ed. 2) 1170/2 Shell cocoa. **1909** J. JOYCE *Let.* 21 Aug. (1966) II. 238, I sent Nora a stone of shell cocoa. Pay the duty on it which cannot be high and see that Nora takes it *every morning* and *evening*. **1922** W. B. YEATS *Trembling of Veil* II. xiii. 119 She had lived for many weeks upon bread and shell-cocoa, so that her food never cost her more than a penny a day. **1949** *Archit. Rev.* CVI. 302/2 The boiler house, which has a shell-concrete roof. **1958** *Times* 23 Sept. 16/3 The structures he [*sc.* Candela] has designed there—mostly in shell-concrete—have begun to attract attention far outside Mexico. **1946** *Archit. Rev.* C. 8 The roofs of the canteen and the concert studio are of shell construction, 4·8 in. thickness. **1974** *Encycl. Brit. Macropædia* IV. 1078/1 Shell construction, where the strength of a thin curved concrete membrane is used advantageously to produce a light and aesthetic roof capable of bridging wide spaces without appreciable bending. [**1942** *Sun* (Baltimore) 18 Feb. 24/7 There are, according to experts, three kinds of markets for eggs—shell (direct-to-consumer variety), frozen and dried.] **1943** E. OLIVER *Night Thoughts of Country Landlady* viii. 60 Before buying the very small but essential allowance of grain required to make these hens lay, you must hand over your coupons for 'Shell Eggs'. **1949** S. GIBBONS *Matchmaker* i. 11 On Tuesday we have bacon and egg pie, Father, and on Wednesday boiled shell eggs. **1972** *Guardian* 24 Mar. 10/8 Present minimum import prices for shell eggs and for..dried whole egg are to continue unchanged. **1890** B. HALL *Turnover Club* 169 Would endeavour to make a collection of Japanese coins, with their cards and a shell game. **1942** *Sun* (Baltimore) 19 Mar. 19/6 The defendant pleaded innocent to charges of operating a shell game. **1972** *Times Lit. Suppl.* 29 Dec. 1570/1 Both memory and history are shell games. **1977** *Rolling Stone* 21 Apr. 88/2 Both of them create with the sleight of hand of a shell-game swindler. **1954** S. PIGGOTT *Neolithic Cultures* iii. 108 A bowl of typically 'Abingdon' shell-gritted ware from Great Ponton in south Lincolnshire. **1965** I. F. SMITH *Windmill Hill & Avebury* v. 50 The heavier rims are decorated more often than the simple and rolled rims, and shell-gritted ware more often than flint-gritted. **1875** *United Service Mag.* CXXXIX. 42 [It] is brittle and bad for skating, 'shell-ice' as it is called. **1977** *Globe & Mail* (Toronto) 9 Mar. 36/7 Travel isn't too good. There's shell ice with pockets of water underneath and flooding around the cracks and heaves, but no actual danger yet. **1924** *Proc. Prehist. Soc. 1923–24* IV. II. 206 Directly resting upon the brickearth was a shell midden. **1971** *Nature* 11 June 397/2 Between 1881 and 1913 three Mesolithic 'shell midden' sites were excavated on the Island of Oronsay in the Inner Hebrides. **1946** *Physical Rev.* LXIX. 538 On the shell model the radius should be equal to Gamow's radius plus the radius of the alpha-particle. **1970** I. E. MCCARTHY *Nuclear Reactions* I. iv. 83 The independent particle model for finite nuclei is the shell model. [**1947** *F.I.A.T. Final Rep. No. 1168* (Brit. Intelligence Objectives Sub-Comm.) 2 Such a bed helps the thin mold shell resist the hydrostatic pressure of the influent liquid metal.] **1950** *Materials & Methods* Aug. 45/3 For the investigation of the metallurgical characteristics of the tin bronze alloys as affected by plastic bonded shell molds, a master pattern plate is being utilized. **1973** J. G. TWEEDDALE *Materials Technol.* II. ii. 39 Since, for simplicity, a shell mould is made up from two, outer shell parts, it is not always possible to build in the best pouring channel system. **1951** *Iron Age* 15 Nov. 111/1 The Builders Iron Foundry has been working with the Croning Process, or shell molding method of producing castings. **1979** J. NEELY *Pract. Metall. & Materials of Industry* xxiv. 325/2 The advantages of shell molding over other forms of sand casting are that high precision, good finishes, and more complex shapes are possible, and less machining is needed. **1807** J. BARLOW *Columbiad* IX. 321 And mark thy native orb!..What an age her shell-rock ribs attest! **1837** J. L. WILLIAMS *Territory of Florida* 56 The bank is formed of concrete shell rock. **1935** H. DAVIS *Honey in Horn* xvi. 261 The road under the horses' feet was black shellrock. **1954** G. MAGNEL *Prestressed Concrete* (ed. 3) x. 303 (*caption*) Prestressed beams for shell roof. **1972** R. E. OWEN *Roofs* vi. 91 Most shell roofs are easy to drain to their edges or ends. **1915** *Brit. Med. Jrnl.* 11 Dec. 848/2 The necessity of investigating cases of 'shell shock' very carefully in order to differentiate those that are functional from those that are due to organic lesions. **1918** E. A. MACKINTOSH *War, the Liberator* 148 The Corporal..collapsed suddenly with twitching hands and staring, frightened eyes, proclaiming the shell-shock he had held off while the work was to be done. **1925** FRASER & GIBBONS *Sailor & Soldier Words* 255 *Shell shock*... Since the war, the term has been officially abolished, in favour of the technical term 'Psycho-neurosis'. **1933** J. F. C. FULLER *Generalship* 20 The most rapid way to shell-shock an army is to shell-proof its generals; for once the heart of an army is severed from its head the result is paralysis. **1935** M. HARRISON *Spring in Tartarus* III. 300 The cocoa which Jim sold at a penny the cup, was called 'shell-shock'. **1943** G. GREENE *Ministry of Fear* II. i. 111 There's not a finer shell-shock clinic in the country. **1952** S. KAUFFMANN *Philanderer* (1953) vii. 108 An unfortunate rambling man, supposed to have been shell-shocked in the war. **1959** *Listener* 5 Mar. 406/1 A mug of 'shell-shock'—that is what we call cocoa. **1978** *Ibid.* 9 Feb. 168/2 Seeking relief from this shell-shock, I phone a screenwriter friend. **1978** *Maledicta 1977* I. 121 The student was shell-shocked by the letter. **1918** E. A. MACKINTOSH *War, the Liberator* 146 The man rejected the offer with scorn, as badly shell-shocked men will. **1973** P. DICKINSON *Green Gene* ix. 180 'How are you?' he said. 'Burnt out,' said Mr. Leary. 'Shell-shocked.' **1918** KIPLING *Debits & Credits* (1926) 65 It appeared that the silent Brother was a 'shell-shocker'. **1968** *Funk & Wagnalls Cook's & Diner's Dict.* 213/2 *Shell steak*, another name for club steak. **1969** R. LOCKRIDGE *Murder in False Face* v. 67 You can watch a tall stranger cutting fat from a shell steak. **1973** *Listener* 19 Apr. 501/1 A landscape of luscious rib roasts, lamb chops, shell steaks, T-bone steaks, sirloin steaks, fillet mignon,..and so on. **1895** *Montgomery Ward Catal.* 291/1 Fascinators, hand made, shell stitch, made of Shetland floss. **1976** *Woman's Day* (U.S.) Nov. 128/1 Crocheted rainbow afghan in shell-stitch pattern fairly glows with its twelve different colors. **1955** FRIEDMAN & WEISSKOPF in W. Pauli *Niels Bohr* 146 Some years ago when the evidence for the shell structure was accumulating and some of the inadequacies of the compound nucleus picture were becoming more apparent. **1974** G. REECE tr. *Hund's Hist. Quantum Theory* vii. 92 During this period new facts were discovered which made it possible to understand..the shell structure. **1888** G. KAPP in *Jrnl. Soc. Telegr.-Engineers & Electricians* XVII. 96 We may divide transformers broadly into two classes—one in which the copper coils are spread over the surface of the iron core, enveloping the latter more or less completely; and the other in which the core is spread over the surface of the copper coils, forming a shell over the winding. I propose to call the former 'core transformers', and the latter 'shell transformers'. **1902** *Encycl. Brit.* XXXIII. 418/1 Shell transformers have the disadvantage generally of poor ventilation for the copper circuits. **1888** *Jrnl. Soc. Telegr.-Engineers & Electricians* XVII. 113 These figures show that even in stout rings..the core type [of transformer] is better than the shell type. **1922** GLAZEBROOK *Dict. Appl. Physics* II. 911/2 The three-phase shell-type transformer is a development of the single phase, having three individual sets of coils and the three cores arranged to form one composite core. **1935** *Discovery* Nov. 333/2 The early pottery lamps of the Ægean, Phœnicia, etc. (known to the British Museum as the 'cocked-hat' type, though 'shell-type' seems much more expressive, both as to shape and origin). **1947** R. LEE *Electronic Transformers & Circuits* ix. 239 Lower capacitance obtains with two coils than with a shell-type transformer of the same interleaving. **1964** W. L. GOODMAN *Hist. Woodworking Tools* 179 In 1864 the first shell-type chuck with adjustable jaws was patented by Barber.

b. shell-bark, for Latin names substitute *Carya ovata* or *C. laciniosa*; also, the nut produced by one of these trees; (earlier and later examples); **shell-cracker** *U.S.*, the red-ear sunfish, *Lepomis megalotis*; **shell parrot** = *BUDGERIGAR.

1769 R. SMITH *Jrnl.* 11 May in F. W. Halsey *Tour of Four Great Rivers* (1906) 21 The Timber in these Parts.. consists of..red Oak Hazel Bushes, Ash and Gum together with Butternut and Shellbark, Hiccory in plenty. **1785** G. WASHINGTON *Jrnl.* 15 Apr. (1925) II. 362, I planted..a row of the Shell bark hickory Nutt from New York. **1885** *Harper's Mag.* Dec. 78/2 The chipmunk..[has] his hoard of hazel-nuts and shell-barks. **1948** *N.W. Ohio Q.* Winter 13 Two or three did not get in until dark bearing the big loads of fine shellbarks. **1969** T. H. EVERETT *Living Trees of World* xii. 98/2 The big shellbark hickory..chiefly inhabits rich, deep, fairly moist soils. **1889** Shell-cracker in *Cent. Dict.* **1947** B. W. DALRYMPLE *Panfish* 180 The name 'Shellcracker' comes from his habit of feeding on small crustaceans. **1975** *Southern Living* Aug. 18/3 Fishing is good for bass, crappie, bream, bluegill and shellcracker. **1890** 'LYTH' *Golden South* xiv. 127 The tiny budgerigar, sometimes called the shell parrot. **1954** *Coast to Coast 1953–4* 88 The shell-parrots, in glittering, swerving flights, were shrill over the reaches of the river.

shellac. Add: **1.** (Earlier *attrib.* example and later examples in the manufacture of gramophone records.)

1913 *Jrnl. Franklin Inst.* CLXXVI. 192 These modern composition disk records are in reality seals of the human voice, because the substance they are made of is a modified sealing wax,..containing shellac as a basic substance. *Ibid.*, Shellac is much adulterated, and the mineral and fibrous substances which are added require careful selection. **1933** *Amer. Speech* VIII. 13/1 Professor Jones.. has them [*sc.* cardinal vowels] recorded on shellac. **1962** A. NISBETT *Technique Sound Studio* 266 Formerly, shellac was used for pressing records, and having much greater elasticity was suitable for record materials when only very heavy..pick-up heads were available.

attrib. **1765** T. H. CROKER et al. *Compl. Dict. Arts & Sciences* II. s.v. *Japanning*, The proper japan ground..is much the best formed of shell-lac varnish.

2. A gramophone record made of shellac.

1954 *Billboard* 21 Aug. 18/2 Unless a publisher could get hold of an acetate of his song, he had to wait until the shellacs were ready. **1977** G. V. HIGGINS *Dreamland* xvi. 180, I remember the phonograph playing... There was one tune... He played it all the time, scratchy and noisy as the old shellacs were.

shellac (ʃelæ·k), *v.* orig. and chiefly *U.S.* Also **shellack**; *pa. pple.* **shellacked.** [f. the sb.]

1. *trans.* To coat or varnish with shellac.

1876 *Scribner's Monthly* Feb. 488/1 It is made of plain white pine, brought to a good surface and shellacked. **1917** C. MATHEWSON *Second Base Sloan* 90 Wayne threatened to varnish or shellac the paper so that it would turn the rain. **1969** *Sunday Times* 9 Feb. 58/1 They tend to wear dark blue silken suits or little black dresses and look as if they had been shellacked or sprayed with fixative just before they left home.

2. *slang.* To beat, thrash, punish.

1930 C. F. COE *Gunman* iv. 53 These two bums that Lefty shellacked were members of Red Karfola's gang. **1935** J. HARGAN *Gloss. Prison Lang.* 7 Shellack, to punish or beat. **1977** *Time* 8 Aug. 28/2 Pitcher McArdle was shellacked for..six runs in the first inning.

Hence **shella·c(k)ed** *ppl. a.*, (*a*) coated, varnished, or fastened with shellac; (*b*) *U.S. slang*, intoxicated, 'plastered'.

1881 C. C. HARRISON *Woman's Handiwork* III. 139 Book-shelves have been made of pine, painted in flat color or stained and shellacked. **1884, 1902** [see SHELLACKED *pa. pple.*]. **1922** *Dialect Notes* V. 148 *Shellacked*, stewed, bunned, etc. **1935** J. T. FARRELL *Judgment Day* I. iv. 85 You know, when I first found out about how you'd get shellacked, I thought it was pretty terrible. **1941** WYNDHAM LEWIS *Let.* 17 Oct. (1963) 300 The silly 'toughness' of the Irish immigrant mass, shellacked into a sly, bluff, servility. **1948** H. L. MENCKEN *Amer. Lang.* Suppl. II. 644 When a novelty is obvious it seldom lasts very long, *e.g.*, *shellacked* for drunk.

shella·c(k)ing, *vbl. sb.* Chiefly *U.S.* [f. *SHELLAC *v.* + ING[1].] **1.** In Dict.

2. A beating or thrashing, a 'pasting'; a defeat. *slang.*

1931 E. H. LAVINE *Third Degree* x. 121 When this method failed, as it invariably did, he would leave the room and the *shellacking* continued. **1941** *Sun* (Baltimore) 18 Sept. 13/1 The main bulk of the Twenty-ninth Division handed the One Hundred and Fifteenth Regimental Combat Team a shellacking on the combat range today. **1956** W. H. WHYTE *Organisation Man* ii. 22 By the time of the First World War the Protestant Ethic had taken a shellacking from which it would not recover. **1960** T. MCLEAN *Kings of Rugby* 56 'Ronnie' left the field to run into the greatest shellacking he had ever had. **1978** H. WOUK *War & Remembrance* xxxiii. 351 The Japs can't recover from the shellacking they took at Midway.

shelled, *ppl. a.* Add: *shelled corn*: Indian corn removed from the cob. *U.S.*

1676 in *Maryland Archives* (1884) II. 560 A Peck of Indian, shell'd Corn or Oates. **1714** J. GREEN *Diary* in *Essex Inst. Hist. Coll.* (1869) X. 104, I agreed to give Mr. Ganson five bushels of shelled corn at harvest, for ye damage my oxen did ye last night. **1828** W. COBBETT *Treat. Cobbett's Corn* § 136 The Americans call it, and.. we must call it, 'shelled corn'. **1950** *Chicago Tribune* 20 Mar. IV. 1/3 The class of Illinois shippers primarily affected would be those who consign shelled corn to far western states.

sheller. 1. b. (Earlier U.S. example.)

1859 *Rep. Comm. Patents 1858* (U.S.) I. 361 The nature of this invention relates..to the form and arrangements of the shellers.

Shelleyan, *a.* (and *sb.*) Add: (Examples of variant form *Shelleian.*)

a **1907** F. THOMPSON in *Dublin Rev.* (1908) July 36 Perhaps none of his poems is more purely and typically Shelleian than *The Cloud.* **1930** BLUNDEN *De Bello Germanico* 26 Such a bed is not surpassed by the Shelleian shakedown of roses.

Hence **Shelleya·na** [ANA *suff.*], books or items relating to Shelley; **She·lleyist** = SHELLEYITE.

1886 *Academy* Mar. 218/2 'Shelleyana' of all kinds. **1924** P. CRESWICK *Beaten Path* xxxvii. 203 'Had I any books about Shelley?'..'We have considerable Shelleyana,' said I. 'Here is the special shelf.' **1934** G. B. SHAW *Prefaces* 506/1 They were Shelleyists, but not atheists.

shell-fishing. (Earlier example.)

1868 *Harper's Mag.* Dec. 12/2 Our men, some of whom were practiced in the business of shell-fishing,..very soon dug up a very fine feast of clams.

Shelluh, Shelook, obs. varr. *SHILLUK.

shelt (ʃelt). *Sc.* Also **shalt, shilt, sholt.** [Abbrev. of SHELTIE.] A Shetland pony.

1774 *Aberdeen Jrnl.* 27 June 4/2 (Advt.), There are Three Shalts, and several Year-olds of very fine Kinds. **1777** J. DUFF *Let.* 1 May in A. & H. Tayler *Lord Fife & his Factor* (1925) iv. 103, I would wish my Horses, My black Shelt, the roan Poney and Smith..to be at Mar Lodge. **1817** J. CHRISTIE *Instructions* 29 We on with our sholts, a jogging and budging. **1880** J. WATT *Poet. Sk.* 59 To wirk some orra beast, or drive a milk shilt. **1920** *Glasgow Herald* 21 Oct. 8 It was the custom of the priest to go about his pastoral duties on a favourite pony..; indeed, he and the 'shelt' were inseparable. **1951** *Scots Mag.* July 278 They have their work cut out for them, those sturdy shelts. **1980** D. K. CAMERON *Willie Gavin* xx. 199 Mettlesome black *shelts* they had been, high-stepping, jingling their bright harness.

shelter, *sb.* Add: **1. b.** Also, an enclosed shelter from air-raids, nuclear fall-out, etc., usu. underground. Cf. *ANDERSON, *MORRISON.

1918 *Ann Reg. 1917* I. 175 Much greater public attention was paid to the question of air-raids... Arrangements were made to provide shelters throughout London. **1938** *Times* (Weekly ed.) 29 Dec. 3/1 Sir John Anderson outlined his plans for the provision of shelters against high explosive bombs. **1943** G. GREENE *Ministry of Fear* I. i. 17 The sirens began their nightly wail... She was making for her favourite shelter down the street. **1961** E. S. TURNER *Phoney War* v. 50 The authorities had no intention of allowing the Underground to be used as a shelter.., but when the bombing began the people simply bought tickets and took possession of it. **1961** [see *FALL-OUT *sb.*]. **1978** L. DEIGHTON *SS-GB* ii. 18 She was killed..during the air attacks... He was in the shelter that day.

f. (Earlier and later examples.)

1890 W. BOOTH *In Darkest Eng.* II. ii. 97 You come along to one of our Shelters. On entering you pay fourpence, and are free of the establishment for the night. **1934** *Changing Men* 25 There has been no homelier, happier place than the Woman's Shelter in High Street. **1976** *New Society* 17 June 633/2 All lodging houses, hostels and night shelters in Glasgow were visited on two nights last winter.

g. A (temporary) home for animals. *U.S.*

1971 *New Yorker* 30 Oct. 41/1 The Bide-A-Wee animal shelter in Westhampton. **1979** *Arizona Daily Star* 22 July J 4/4 Lillian Schaaf willed her $1 million estate for a new animal shelter to be built on land she owned outside Worthington, Ohio.

3. (sense 1 b) *shelter-life, marshal, warden*; designating conditions and ailments attributed to time spent in air-raid shelters, as *shelter cough, paralysis, rash, throat* (all *temporary*); **shelter foot, leg,** a painful, swollen foot or leg after a person has slept in a sitting position (*temporary*); **shelter half,** one half of a shelter tent; **shelter tent** (earlier example); **shelter tree,** also, any tree grown to provide shelter; **shelter wood,** trees left standing to provide shelter in which saplings can grow; freq. *attrib.*

1940 *New Statesman* 19 Oct. 372/1 In every shelter I have been in during the past six weeks I have heard that hacking 'shelter cough' and the wheezy sleep of the bronchial cases. **1941** *Lancet* 6 Dec. 690/1 In shelter-foot the most potent causative factors are venous stagnation and increased capillary permeability. **1942** *Sun* (Baltimore) 23 Apr. 22/2 When the Doaks family goes into a bomb shelter.., Mr. Doaks is likely to say, '..I'll just doze off here in this deck chair'. Next morning Mr. Doaks has a pair of painfully swollen legs and feet—shelter foot. **1911** F. FUNSTON *Mem. Two Wars* 354 Not even shelter-halves, popularly known as 'dog tents', were carried, and many..a night we stretched out in the rain. **1966** *Sunday Times* (Colour Suppl.) 4 Dec. 73/3 *Shelter half*, half a pup tent, and carried by every GI. **1940** *Lancet* 7 Dec. 722/1 (*heading*) Shelter legs. *Ibid.* 722/2 The elderly and obese are loth to make use of bunks in the shelters..and since they are apt to sit about all day as well as all night they readily acquire shelter leg. **1944** *Newsweek* 20 Mar. 97/1 Renewed Nazi raids brought an old ailment back to London—'shelter legs'. **1943** WYNDHAM LEWIS *Let.* 26 Jan. (1963) 342 A sculptor of course cannot exactly be commissioned to do marbles of shelter-life. **1974** *Times* 21 Jan. 4/3 The Medical Officer of Health reported in 1940 that the increase in deaths from respiratory diseases was at least partially due to shelter life. **1940** *New Statesman* 19 Oct. 372/2 Lord Horder's Committee attaches much importance to the shelter marshals, who should be paid, whole-time officials, chosen from the wardens' service for their proper human understanding and given a status which would entitle them to the help of the police and authority over the shelterers. **1942** *Sun* (Baltimore) 23 Apr. 22/2 A similar ailment is called 'shelter paralysis'. **1943** *Our Towns* (Women's Group on Public Welfare) iii. 78 *Scabies* or 'the Itch' has now almost achieved respectability under the name of 'Shelter Rash'. **1862** O. W. NORTON *Let.* 16 June in *Army Lett.* (1903) 88 Anyone who has lived in these shelter tents any length of time can appreciate the difficulties of writing in a heavy shower. **1940** *New Statesman* 19 Oct. 372/1 Equally common are the complaints of 'shelter throats', which may mean anything from tonsilitis to diphtheria. **1891** W. SCHLICH *Man. Forestry* II. ii. 133 They in their turn become mother and shelter trees. **1980** *Garden* CV. 106/1 The Corot-like view of immense weeping willows forming the lake's head must surely have gained by the recent deaths of elms and other shelter trees, though the garden is now more exposed to north-east winds. **1974** C. FREMLIN *By Horror Haunted* 12 The kids larking about..the Shelter Wardens shouting at them. **1889** W. SCHLICH *Man. Forestry* I. ii. 208 The wood is created, or regenerated, under the shelter of the whole or part of the old crop, which forms the shelter-wood. **1928** R. S. TROUP *Silvicultural Systems* vii. 82 The original idea underlying the adoption of the shelter-wood strip system was the necessity for working against the prevailing westerly wind, so that the newly exposed edges of mature woods should always be protected from it. **1979** *Sci. Amer.* Feb. 71/3 The final system is called shelterwood cutting, because the mature stand is removed in two or more partial cuts so that the new stand can become established under the shelter of a partial canopy of remaining trees.

shelter, *v.* Add: **1. e.** To protect (invested income) from taxation; to invest with this purpose.

1963 *Vital Speeches* XXIX. 357/2 A tightening of the personal holding company rules, to end the escapes from individual taxation now available through the use of these devices to shelter investment income. **1972** P. C. REID *Corporate & Executive Tax, Sheltered Investments* ix. 125 The prospective investor should always keep in mind that the major objective is to shelter his income. **1973** *Times* 10 Dec. 7/5 False rumours..that I sheltered the income on which my daughter, Tricia, should have paid taxes. **1975** *Tax Shelter Investments* (U.S. Congress Jt. Comm. on Internal Revenue Taxation) III. 22 He sheltered $13,000 with a cattle feeding operation.

sheltered, *ppl. a.* Add: **b.** *sheltered life,* a life protected from the ordinary hazards and hardships of living. Also *sheltered existence.*

1888 KIPLING *Plain Tales* 14 There was a Boy once who had been brought up under the 'sheltered life' theory; and the theory killed him dead. **1920** *Ladies' Home Jrnl.* Feb. 185/1 Three thousand dollars and no business experience, thirty-three years of sheltered life, and two children under ten years of age—this was my problem when I was left a widow. **1937** WODEHOUSE *Summer Moonshine* (1938) xix. 221 Hers had been a sheltered life... She had never been brought face to face with tragedy. **1959** J. KIRKUP tr. *S. de Beauvoir's Mem. Dutiful Daughter* II. 117 She led a very sheltered existence in the Basque country, where there were not many eligible young men. **1977** W. H. SAUMAREZ SMITH *Young Man's Country* ii. 35, I had lived a fairly sheltered life in England... Now for the first time in a position of responsibility and power, I was learning how people behave.

c. *Econ.* Designating trades, industries, etc., which are not exposed to competition, and the commodities in which they deal.

1924 *Westm. Gaz.* 18 Aug. 4/5 In the so-called sheltered trades real weekly wages have generally been maintained at at least their pre-war level. **1930** *Economist* 4 Jan. 24/1 The higher Japanese price-level is accounted for largely by such 'sheltered' goods as red beans, miso. **1972** *Wall Street Jrnl.* 9 Aug. 1/5 A number of tax shelter plans are designed to allow investments in sheltered industries like oil.

d. Affording relief or exemption from tax; untaxed. *U.S.*

1955 W. J. CASEY *Tax Sheltered Investments* (ed. 2) xix. 205 Partnership operation allows you a write off of losses, a sheltered return on a quick success by sale of your partnership interest. **1970** *Tax Sheltered Investments* (A. Anderson & Co.) i. 1 All sheltered investments generate one or more of these advantages. **1974** *Los Angeles Times* 13 Oct. III. 9/2 The second $50,000, which was to be 'sheltered income', was to be sent..directly to an insurance company as a payment for an annuity purchased by Hunter.

e. Designating places for living or working (or suitable work) provided for the mentally or physically infirm, where special assistance and facilities are available.

1961 *Oxford Mail* 16 Mar. 4/6 The three-storey house [for patients of a mental hospital in the final stages of readjustment to community life]..was opened last month and is known officially as a 'sheltered hostel'. **1971** *Rand Daily Mail* 3 Apr. 11/4 One of these tenants is a humble man who earns R14 a week in a sheltered employment factory. **1973** *Howard Jrnl.* XIII. 276 Sheltered workshop facilities, industrial training or punitive labour. **1976** *Ilkeston Advertiser* 10 D c. 16/2 The county council had already decided to stop the grants—towards general improvement areas,..council house adaptation for the handicapped a d sheltered housing. **1977** *New Society* 3 ar. 441/2 Patients leaving Herrison [Mental Hospital] have been 'graded' according to the kind of home they can cope with outside. Those least able to run their own lives are in sheltered accommodation. **1980** *Times* 23 July 12/2 If you are still undecided about sheltered housing or a home, you might investigate the various facilities.

shelterer. Add: **1. b.** One who takes shelter from an air-raid.

1940 R. Macaulay *Lett. to Sister* (1964) 116 The Central London tube was so crammed with thousands of shelterers that I couldn't get near the platform. **1944** *Ourselves in Wartime* v. 71 Tiers of bunks, canteens, adequate sanitation and first-aid posts were provided. These amenities helped the shelterers to make the best of a bad job. **1957** R. W. Zandvoort in *Wiener Beiträge zur englischen Philologie* LXV. 270 Air raid shelters were a necessary refuge... Books..were the best means to divert the attention of *shelterers* (as they were called) and others from the pressures and anxieties of life in wartime. **1980** P. Fitzgerald *Human Voices* xi. 163 The LPTB's bunks occupied the walls... Other shelterers had arrived.

Sheltie, shelty. 2. For *nonce-use* read *rare* and add later example.

1967 H. W. Sutherland *Magnie* vii. 94 They were queer, the Shelties, came from nothing... England was heaven to them.

3. = *Shetland sheep-dog* s.v. *Shetland 1 d. Also *attrib.*

1911 *Our Dogs* 27 Oct. 984/3 (Advt.), Two promising Sheltie pups for sale. **1916** B. Thynne *Shetl. Sheep-Dog* 5 The origin of the Sheltie is 'wrapt in mystery'. **1950** A. C. Smith *Dogs since 1900* xii. 248 After the interruption caused by the first war, the Shelties began to assert their charms. **1972** *Times* 19 Sept. 24/6 (Advt.), King Charles and Sheltie Collie, both 2 years old..free to loving family. **1980** 'T. Hinde' *Daymare* iv. 26 He had been council dust-cart driver till he ran down one Sheltie too many.

shelving, *vbl. sb.*[1] **2.** (Earlier example.)

1817 M. Austin *Let.* 30 June in E. C. Barker *Austin Papers* (1924) I. 316 He has the Plank..selected,..as many as is wanted for shelving.

shelvy, *a.*[2] (Earlier example.)

1811 D. Buchan in J. Barrow *Chron. Hist. Voyages* (1818) App. I. 8 At noon several difficulties presented themselves in crossing a tract of shelvy ice, intersected with deep and wide rents.

Shema (ʃemaˑ). Also **Shemah, Shemang.** [Heb. *šemaʿ* hear, imper. of *šāmaʿ* to hear.] The first word of the verse Deut. vi. 4 used as a name for three portions of the Scriptures, Deut. vi. 4–9, xi. 13–21, Numbers xv. 37–41, to be repeated twice daily by all adult Jewish males, and used as a Jewish confession of faith.

1706 I. Abendana *Discourse Eccl. & Civil Polity of Jews* iv. 106 Every day we use an office containing three sections of the law, commonly styled *Shemang*, i.e. *Hear*. **1816** J. Allen *Mod. Judaism* xix. 331 Another essential part of the daily service..is the reading of three portions of scripture. The first of these portions beginning with the word *Shema*... This term is applied to all the portions taken together, and the recital of them is called *Kiriath Shema*, the *Reading of the Shema*. To recite these passages twice every day they maintain to be expressly enjoined. **1864** *Chambers's Encycl.* VI. 155/1 The first additions to the *Shemah* formed the introductory thanksgiving for the renewed day. **1876** Geo. Eliot *Daniel Deronda* IV. vii. lxi. 221 The *Shemah*, wherein we briefly confess the divine Unity, is the chief devotional exercise of the Hebrew. **1926** *Brit. Weekly* 5 Aug. 367/3 Esther.. joins in that immemorial declaration of her people the Shemang or Confession of Unity. **1936** E. Underhill *Worship* (ed. 2) I. ii. 28 The Jews' daily repetition of the *Shema*, the Christians' ritual use of the Lord's Prayer, and the Moslems' of the First *Sura*, are all justified by psychology no less than by religion. **1949** W. F. Albright *Archaeol. of Palestine* x. 221 In 1902 the Nash fragment containing the Ten Commandments and the Shema ('Hear, O Israel..') was discovered in the Faiyum. **1972** J. Caine *Hamlet, my Boy* vi. 86 He reminded himself that a Jew was supposed to say the *Shema* in the hour of death. **1977** H. Kaplan *Damascus Cover* (1978) xii. 123 'Don't you know the Shema?' She was either a Jewess or a highly trained agent.

Shemite, *a.* Add: (Earlier example.)

1791 *Gentl. Mag.* Feb. 107/1 Arabic..contains a good deal of Persian and Gothic and other Shemite dialects.

Shemitic *a.* (earlier example); **Shemitish** *a.* (earlier example).

1822 *Malte-Brun's Universal Geogr.* I. xxiii. 570 As most of the nations that speak these languages descend, according to Moses, from Shem, this stock has been distinguished under the general name of the Shemitic languages. **1838** W. B. Winning *Man. Compar. Philol.* 277 The assumptions..that the Hebrew tongue must necessarily be of Shemitish derivation.

shemmal, var. Shamal in Dict. and Suppl.
shemmi, var. *shimmy *v.*[1]

shemozzle (ʃėmǫ·z'l). *slang.* Also † **chimozzle; s(c)h(e)-, s(c)hi-, s(c)hlemozzle.** [Of uncertain origin. In early use (*shlemozzle*, etc.) apparently East End slang: perh. ad. Yiddish *shlimazl* misfortune, unlucky person (see *schlimazel), with subsequent reduction of *schle-* to *sche-*.] A muddle or complication; a quarrel, row, rumpus, mêlée.

1899 A. M. Binstead *Houndsditch Day by Day* 23 It was through no recklessness or extravagance that he was in this shlemozzle. **1900** *From Front* xiv. 183 We might look upon this little chimozzle as a kind o' misunderstanding. **1901** J. M. Cobban *Golden Tooth* xvii. 170 If Will comes out of this shemozzle. **1916** 'Peter' *Trench Yarns* ii. 16 In the ensuing shemmozle Samuel got laid out with the butt-end of a rifle. **1916** 'Taffrail' *Pincher Martin* vii. 120 'We ain't the best o' friends, 'cos me an' 'im 'ad a bit o' a shimozzle—' 'Shimozzle!..What on earth's that?' 'Bit o' a dust-up, sir.' **1928** *Sunday Dispatch* 29 July 15/2 Those..who saw so little of war that they still think it to be a gloriously romatic shlemozzle. **1930** S. Sassoon *Mem. Infantry Officer* vi. 156 When I showed the battle-plan to the Sergeant-Major, all he said was 'We'll have a rough house from Ale Alley.' But no one had any idea it was going to be such a schimozzle as it was! **1936** J. G. Brandon *Pawnshop Murder* i. 9 Has a *schlemozzle*, and takes 'is stuff over to Paris. **1937** G. Frankau *More of Us* xv. 160 Then Sophie called; and, brooding, 'Nice schemozzle If that lot stays to feed as well as sozzle.' **1943** T. Worling *White Ensigns* viii. 146 'How many more shimozzles like yesterday are we going to get?' Mr. Hebard queried. **1949** 'N. Blake' *Head of Traveller* xi. 191 Even if it turns out that none of us is implicated in the murder, there's still going to be a shocking shemozzle, I'm afraid, about his original disappearance. **1951** S. Kaye-Smith *Mrs. Gailey* v. 292 It was in the papers. What a schemozzle! **1955** E. Waugh *Officers & Gentlemen* 276 There was something of a schemozzle last night but we weren't in that. **1960** I. Cross *Backward Sex* 167 The whole schmozzle is over. **1966** *Telegraph* (Austral.) 27 Dec. 8/4 The next day saw one of the greatest shemozzles in Australian sport. **1978** L. Meynell *Papersnake* ii. 22 There was going to be one hell of an uncomfortable shemozzle in his life if he didn't get his priorities right.

Hence **shemo·zzle** *v. intr.*, to decamp, make off, 'scarper'.

1903 Farmer & Henley *Slang* VI. 172/2 *Shemozzle*.. Verb (East End). To be off; to decamp. **1925** Fraser & Gibbons *Soldier & Sailor Words* 256 *Shemozzle, to*, to make off: to get out of the way—e.g., 'We saw the M.P.'s (Military Police) coming, so we shemozzled.' **1944** Auden *For Time Being* (1945) 118 He was caught by a common cold and condemned to the whiskey mines, But schemozzled back to the Army.

‖ **shen** (ʃən). Also **Shen, Shin,** etc. [Chinese *shén*.] In Chinese philosphy: a god, person of supernatural power, or the spirit of a dead person.

1847 W. H. Medhurst *Dissert. Theol. Chinese* 5 It would appear, that..Shîn and..Kweî, are terms equivalent to spirit and anima, in the human system. **1901** J. J. M. de Groot *Relig. Syst. China* IV. ii. 4 Confucius means to say, the shen manifests itself in its full development in man by his khi or 'breath'; indeed, only animated man lives and breathes. **1905** E. H. Parker *China & Religion* i. 21 The spirits of men were called *kwei*, and those of Heaven and Nature *shên*. **1934** A. D. Waley *Way & its Power* 29 'If the monarch loses his *shên*,' says *Han Fei Tzŭ*, 'the tigers will soon be on his tracks.' **1955** E. Herbert *Taoist Notebk.* 43 Thus Mencius in his moral hierarchy posited two grades—the 'spirit-like' (*Shên*), the saint beyond man's power of comprehension. **1978** F. Mann *Acupuncture* (ed. 3) iv. 32 Shen is usually translated as 'spirit', a word which to the Western mind more often than not suggests the supernatural. But Shen..is a down-to-earth word.

shenanigan (ʃėnæ·nigăn). orig. *U.S.* Also **shenan(n)egan, -igan, -gin; shin-; -(c)kin;** and other vars. [Origin obscure.] Trickery, skulduggery, machination, intrigue; teasing, 'kidding', nonsense; (usu. *pl.*) a plot, a trick, a prank, an exhibition of high spirits, a carry-on. Hence **shena·niganning, shena·nigin(g),** *pres. pple.* and *vbl. sb.*

1855 *Town Talk* (San Francisco) 25 Apr. 2 Are you quite sure? No shenanigan? **1856** *Spirit of Age* (Sacramento) 30 Apr. 2 These facts indicate that there is some *shenanegan* going on. **1857** C. E. De Long *Jrnl.* 15 Aug. in *Calif. Hist. Soc. Q.* (1930) IX. 156 Race came off Whiskey Bill winner, the Mare's rider held in, and Smith pronouncing it shenanigan. **1862** 'Mark Twain' *Let.* May (1917) I. iii. 77 Consider them all..guilty (of 'shenanigan') until they are proved innocent. **1894** M. J. Jaques *Texan Ranch Life* xiii. 115 He assured me that he was not 'shenan-neganning' me, and that the dish would prove a delicacy. **1897** *Outing* (U.S.) XXIX. 483/1 A man who is firmly kind, but who will stand no shinanigan. **1901** W. S. Walker *In Blood* xxxi. 332 We're mates all round, an' no more shenannikin. **1902** R. Barr *Victors* v. 81 If I were to pay them they might think there was some shenanigan about it. **1924** J. Masefield *Lord Harker* iii. 146 Now, brother, answer me and no damned shinanniking. **1926** E. Ferber *Show Boat* xiv. 305 I'd never had a fight on my boat and wasn't going to begin any such low life shenanigans now. **1928** *Saturday Even. Post* 10 Mar. 11/2 The renunciation of Mr Coolidge was a distinct disappointment to the great mass of the Republican Party,..and this left the way open for some astute shenanigan in various states. **1930** 'S. S. Van Dine' *Scarab Murder Case* xv. 212 There's too much shenanigan going on around here to suit me. I want action. **1935** S. O'Casey *Let.* c 10 Feb. (1975) I. 540 It is really hateful that I should be compelled to turn my thoughts to the pious shinanachin of a few Jesuits & a group of Methodist Preachers. **1936** 'R. Hyde' *Passport to Hell* x. 152 Two more followed him to take care of him and see he didn't lose his pay-roll shenannigin in his Irish way with the mademoiselles. **1938** J. I. Rodale *King's English on Horseback* 137/1 *Mischief*,..Shenanigins. **1940** Dylan Thomas *Portrait of Artist as Young Dog* 122 No shananacking in the old moonlight. **1947** W. Greenwood *Cure for Love* i. 23 'Here, listen, you two. No shinanigin'.'.. 'Shinanigin'? What's that?'..'Shinanigin'? Well-er-it's. ..Well-er-just shinanigin'... Messing about.' **1948** D. Ballantyne *Cunninghams* i. vi. 34 You see you go tomorrow, then... No shinnanicking now. **1960** T. Griffith *Waist-High Culture* ii. 81 Readers [of newspapers] do not recognize every shenanigan inflicted upon them. **1969** in Halpert & Story *Christmas Mumming in Newfoundland* 90 The entire household looks on, laughing at the girls' shenanigans. **1973** B. Bainbridge *Dressmaker* 11 They'd all catch their death of cold shenanniging about in the middle of the night. **1973** *Nation Rev.* (Melbourne) 31 Aug. 1448/2 (*heading*) Shennanigans behind the silver screen. **1974** *Ridge Citizen* (Johnston, S. Carolina) 18 Apr. 2/1 We don't condone whatever wrongdoing or shenanigans that may have taken place at Watergate or elsewhere. **1976** R. Lewis *Witness my Death* ii. 56 There might have been a certain amount of shenanigans going on behind the scenes. **1978** *New York* 3 Apr. 16/2 House Calls—Glenda Jackson, Art Carney, Richard Benjamin, and Charlie Matthau in a film directed by Howard Zieff, about medical shenanigans in and out of a hospital. **1980** *Times* 3 Jan. 10/4 Doubtful political shenanigans..in the Central Pacific.

shending, *vbl. sb.* For † *Obs.* read *Obs.* exc. *arch.* and add later example.

1935 J. D. Wilson *What happens in Hamlet* vi. 203 The King at his prayers, the shending of Gertrude, the slaying of Polonius, Hamlet's departure to England.

‖ **sheng**[1] (ʃɒŋ). *Mus.* Also 8– **cheng;** 9 **sang, sing.** [Chinese *shēng*.] A Chinese wind instrument consisting of a set of reed pipes.

1795 W. Winterbotham *Hist., Geogr., & Philos. View Chinese Empire* ix. 428 The ancient *cheng* differed in the number of their pipes; those used at present have only thirteen: this instrument appears to have some affinity with our organs. **1839** *Chinese Repository* VIII. 52 The *săng*..is a collection of tubes varying in length so as to utter sounds at harmonic intervals from each other. **1845** *Encycl. Metropol.* XVI. 579/2 The *Sheng* or *Sing*; the lower half of a gourd, in which a row of pipes is fixed, with a curved and lateral one on which the performer blows. **1937** *Times Lit. Suppl.* 16 Jan. 41/3 The *sheng* is assigned by the notation to a certain level of the voice. **1961** J. Howarth in A. Baines *Musical Instruments through Ages* xiii. 321 In 1777,..Père Amiot..sent the present of a sheng from China to Paris. **1972** Liu Jung-en *Six Yüan Plays* 15 The *shêng*, consisting of thirteen pipes of different lengths forming a circle each with a finger hole and having a mouthpiece through which the musician blows and sucks. **1973** *Times* 11 June 14/2 The concertina was inspired by the Cheng (Chinese mouth organ). **1980** *Early Music* July 355/1 These, the sho of Japan and the sheng of China, are forms of free-reed mouth organ with a rigid wind chest held in the hands, the fingers remaining free to open and close the reeds in the cane pipes.

‖ **sheng**[2] (ʃɒŋ). [Chinese *shēng*.] The principal male character in a Chinese opera. Also *attrib.*

1886 *Jrnl. R. Asiatic Soc.* (*North-China Branch*) XX. 208 The characters in Chinese plays are arranged under five denominations... The hero is *shêng*. He wears a black beard, but his face is not concealed. **1937** Arlington & Acton *Famous Chinese Plays* p. xxiii, *Shêng* are divided into *Wên*, Civil, and *Wu*, Military. These are the leading actors. **1972** C. P. Mackerras *Rise of Peking Opera* i. 2 There were seven types of actors in the *nan-hsi*... Some of these terms can still be found..in Peking Opera today. For example, the *sheng* and *tan* were—and still are—the principal male and female characters respectively. **1973** R. F. S. Yang in Yuan-li Wu *China* 74/1 Yen was the founder of the Yen school of the 'bearded *sheng*' voice.

shenzi (ʃeˑnzi). [Swahili.] In East Africa, an uncivilized tribesman. In extended sense, a barbarian, a person outside the person's cultural group.

1910 T. Roosevelt *Afr. Game Trails* x. 258 The 'shenzis'—wild natives called in Swahili..'wa-shenzi'. **1921** *Blackw. Mag.* Jan. 121/2 He, an askari of G company, ran away from a lot of miserable shouting shenzis! **1926** *Spectator* 3 July 10/2 Local *shenzis*..had gathered round the gramophone. **1976** K. Thackeray *Crownbird* vi. 111 The Chinese face was impassive... That he should be..involved with this bunch of shenzis..was very confusing.

she-oak. Add: **2.** (Earlier example.)

1873 J. C. F. Johnson *Christmas on Carringa* 1 Able to put away at a sitting a larger quantity of colonial 'sheoak' than any man of his inches.

b. *attrib.* and *Comb.*, as *she-oak beer*; **she-oak net**, a safety net for sailors boarding ship (see quot. 1898).

1927 F. H. SHAW *Knocking Around* 106 She-oak beer, the common Australian beverage, was a potent tipple. **1898** MORRIS *Austral Eng.* 415/1 *She-oak nets*, nets placed on each side of a gangway from a ship to the pier, to prevent sailors who have been indulging in *she-oak* (beer) falling into the water. **1925** R. CLEMENTS *Gipsy of Horn* 111 Old Australian traders used to spread a net under the gangway, called therefrom the sheoke net, whose office it was to save mariners who 'missed stays' when coming aboard from falling into the dock. **1938** W. E. DEXTER *Rope Yarns* 234 A dog..followed every drunken sailor—never by any chance a sober one—down the pier to his ship. If he managed to get on board safely the dog returned, but if he fell into the she-oak net it would howl until the man was rescued.

sheogue (ʃī·ōg). Also **shee-og.** [ad. Ir. *sióg* fairy.] In Ireland: a fairy.

1852 W. WILDE *Irish Pop. Superstitions* 14 The sheeogue [*sic*] is the true fairy. *Ibid.* 52 The mystic pipers of the sheogues..are said..to favour mortals with their melodies. **1892** W. B. YEATS *Countess Kathleen* 26 You poured out wine as the wood sheogues do When they'd entice a soul out of the world. *Ibid.* 50 Brother, where wander all these dwarfish folk, Hostile to men, the sheogues of the tides? **1893** —— *Celtic Twilight* 117 He would not hear of ghosts or sheogues. **1959** D. A. MAC MANUS *Middle Kingdom* i. 20 There are the stories of human encounters with the small spirits, the 'wee folk' of Ulster, the 'little people' of the South, the 'Shee-og' of Gaeldom.

sheol. (Examples of *slang* use.)

1889 [see *RAH *int.* and *sb.*]. **1903** A. M. BINSTEAD *Pitcher in Paradise* v. 117 Briefly, Dickie, I have been out all night and there's sheol to pay. **1920** B. CRONIN *Timber Wolves* vii. 116 Them big bugs are the meanest things this side sheol.

shepherd, *sb.* Add: **4.** (Earlier example.)

1855 R. CARBONI *Eureka Stockade* 9 The faithful shepherds..were sure to snore in peace a foot and a half under ground from the surface and six score feet from 'bang on the gutter'.

5*. = *German shepherd* (*dog*) s.v. *GERMAN *a.*[2] and *sb.*[2] 4 a.

1938 J. STEINBECK *Long Valley* 13 The rangy dog darted from between the wheels and ran ahead. Instantly the two ranch shepherds flew out at him. **1978** R. LUDLUM *Holcroft Covenant* ix. 104 Suddenly, the menacing faces of enormous long-haired black shepherds lunged at the windows on both sides of the car.

6. d. shepherd plaid = *shepherd's plaid* (SHEPHERD *sb.* 7 c).

1940 [see *KILLER 7]. **1970** *Globe & Mail* (Toronto) 25 Sept. 3/1 (Advt.), New multiple colored striped worsteds, shepherd plaids and a host of plains are now ready for your inspection.

7. b. shepherd's crook arm, a chair-arm shaped somewhat like a shepherd's crook; **shepherd's pie** (earlier and later examples).

1960 H. HAYWARD *Antique Coll.* 256/2 *Shepherd's crook arm*, chair or settee arm of elegantly curving shape, the end in the form of a shepherd's crook, fashionable during the first three decades of the 18th cent. **1973** *Country Life* 30 Aug. (Suppl.) 74/2 Walnut Queen Anne armchair..has a spoon-back, shepherds' crook arms and graceful cabriole legs. **1877** E. S. DALLAS *Kettner's Bk. of Table* 256 In Scotland they produce..such a stew, cover it over with a crust, and call it shepherd's pie... The shepherd's pie of Scotland is..too farinaceous—potatoes within and paste without. **1969** R. WOLLHEIM *Family Romance* 228 What I couldn't face was ordering shepherd's pie. **1977** B. PYM *Quartet in Autumn* xviii. 164 Put a shepherd's pie in the oven.

shepherd, *v.* Add: **3.** (Earlier example.) Also *N.Z.*

1855 R. CARBONI *Eureka Stockade* 8 Here begins as a profession the precious game of 'shepherding', or keeping claims in reserve; that is the digger turned squatter. **1864** *Append. Jrnls. House Reps. N.Z.* C. IV. 8 Shepherding forbidden.

Sherarat (ʃerərā·t). Also **Shararat, Shererat.** [Arab.] (A member of) a nomadic tribe of northern Saudi Arabia. Also *attrib.*

1830 J. L. BURCKHARDT *Notes on Bedouins & Wahábys* 17 *El Sherárát*, in the sandy plain S. of the Akabe el Shamye and eastward of the Hadj route. Their numbers are considerable, and all are Wahabys. *Ibid.*, South of the Sherárát on the E. of the Hadj road, as far as the vicinity of Mekka, the whole country is inhabited by Aenezes. **1875** *Encycl. Brit.* II. 247/2 Thirdly, in the northern desert, the Howeytat and Sherarat, comparatively small and savage tribes. **1888** C. M. DOUGHTY *Travels in Arabia Deserta* I. iii. 57 Upon the other hand are..low heights much more distant, in the Sherarát nomad country. **1917** T. E. LAWRENCE *Lett.* (1938) 234 The Arab losses in the fight came to two killed (a Rualla and a Sherarat) and several wounded. **1955** H. ST. J. PHILBY *Sa'udi Arabia* iii. 90 'Abdul-'Aziz now [in 1798] switched his offensive to the north: sending..the Amin of Buraida, to raid the Shararat on the Syrian border with telling effect.

sherardize. Substitute for entry:

sherardize (ʃe·rāɹdəiz), *v.* Formerly also **Sherardize.** [f. the name of *Sherard* O. Cowper-Coles (1867–1936), English chemist + -IZE.] *trans.* To coat (iron or steel articles) with zinc by heating in contact with zinc dust at a temperature below the melting point of zinc. So **she·rardized** *ppl. a.*, **she·rardizing** *vbl. sb.*

1901 *Brit. Pat.* 9927 1 By our process, which we name 'Sherardizing' to distinguish it from galvanizing, the thickness and evenness of the deposit can be regulated..and any description or shape of iron or steel can be..dealt with. **1904** [in Dict.]. **1904** *Engin. Rev.* XI. 107/2 In practice Sherardised iron and steel are found to withstand the ordinary corrosive agents galvanised iron is exposed to, to a remarkable degree. *Ibid.*, Bolts which had not been Sherardised. **1935** H. R. SIMONDS *Finishing Metal Products* ii. 12 It is possible to sherardize sash of large size only before it is assembled, as sherardizing is destroyed by welding. **1963** *Times* 22 Apr. (Zinc Suppl.) p. v/1 Sherardizing is excellent for small things like screws, for which only regular and small changes in dimensions can be tolerated. **1977** *Offshore Engineer* June 67 (Advt.), We still sherardize every nut, washer and bolt to cut maintenance to virtually zero.

Sherari (ʃerā·ri), *a.* and *sb.* Also **Sherary.** [Arab.] **A.** *adj.* Of or pertaining to the Sherarat. **B.** *sb.* A member of the Sherarat; also, a dromedary bred by the Sherarat.

1888 C. M. DOUGHTY *Travels in Arabia Deserta* II. ii. 32 'It is he,' said the Emir, 'Sheráry hound! how durst thou do this violence?' Metaab bade the stranger take the Sheráry's lance. *Ibid.* ix. 239 The thelûls [riding camels] of the Sherarát..are praised above other in Western Arabia: Ibn Rashid's armed band are mounted upon the light and fleet *Sheráries*. **1926** T. E. LAWRENCE *Seven Pillars* IV. lii. 273 At last the Sherari boy said if we gave him scope he would settle his account and leave him living. *Ibid.* liv. 284 My camel, the sherari racer, Naama, stretched herself out. **1927** —— *Revolt in Desert* xi. 154 It had killed only two of us, one Rueli and one Sherari.

sherbet. Add: **3. b.** (Later Austral. examples.)

1917 H. LAWSON *Coll. Verse* (1969) III. 214 Beer that *we* called 'sherbet'. **1974** F. ARCHER *Treasure House* i. 18 He had a strident voice and with a few sherbets under his belt you knew he was about.

4. *sherbet cup* (later examples); **sherbet dabs** (see quot. 1957); **sherbet fountain,** a confection consisting of a bag of sherbet with a liquorice 'straw' through which it is sucked up.

1805 M. WILMOT *Jrnl.* 9 Apr. in Londonderry & Hyde *Russian Jrnls.* (1934) I. 140 Some Sherbet Cups in silver stands. **1966** MRS L. B. JOHNSON *White House Diary* 2 Aug. (1970) 403 My brother Tony Taylor had sent a set of sherbet cups that had belonged to my mother. **1957** J. KIRKUP *Only Child* 118 Another treat was Sherbet Dabs: we got a caramel-flavoured lollipop which we dipped into a bag of sherbet. **1958** *Listener* 23 Oct. 649/2 The Bonds' shop was not the place for liquorice root, tiger nuts, or sherbet dabs. **1957** R. HOGGART *Uses of Literacy* I. ii. 57 The boy's odder pleasures of taste, not so much..the sherbet-fountains, monkey nuts and aniseed balls, but..a penny stick of licorice or some cinnamon root from the chemist.

Sherbro (ʃɜ̄·ɹbro). [ad. a native name.] (A member of) a people of the southern coast of Sierra Leone; also, their language. Also *attrib.* or as *adj.*

1836 F. H. RANKIN *White Man's Grave* I. ii. 33 The Bulloms of Sherbro, or the Sherbros, pronounced 'Saybras', are to the south of the colony. **1887** *Encycl. Brit.* XXII. 44/2 The following are the more important races that can be distinctly classified:—Mandingos, 1190;..Sherbros, 2882 [; etc.]. **1944** M. GORVIE *Our People of Sierra Leone Protectorate* iii. 20 There is today to be found in the Temne language a large number of Sherbro words. **1957** M. BANTON *W. Afr. City* v. 95 The Sherbro specialize in fishing and water-front work. **1970** J. R. CARTWRIGHT *Politics in Sierra Leone 1947–67* i. 13 It is likely that all these tribes with the possible exception of the Limbas and the Sherbros along the coast, entered Sierra Leone within the past 600 years.

Sherden: see *SHARDANA.

shereef. Add: Forms: **sharif** (later examples).

1959 *Economist* 3 July 11/2 Even the assorted amirs, sultans and sharifs of south Arabia. **1974** C. MAJUL in Gowing & McAmis *Muslim Filipinos* I. 4 The sultans of Sulu have all claimed descent from this *sharif*.

Hence **Sheree·fate,** the office of Shereef; **Sheree·fial** *a.* = SHEREEFIAN *a.* in Dict. and Suppl.

1917 R. STORRS *Orientations* (1937) x. 244 He [*sc.* the Sultan of Muscat] professes entire satisfaction..with the Sharifial movement. **1920** *19th Cent.* Aug. 233 It was to the British Government..that the Sherifial family of Mecca addressed their communications during the war. **1924** *Glasgow Herald* 8 Mar. 9 He began his official career by assisting successive Sherifs, and in 1908..was appointed to the Sherifate by the Porte.

Shereefian, *a.* Add: **2.** Of or pertaining to the Shereef of Mecca. Also as *sb.*, a supporter of the Shereef.

1921 G. BELL *Let.* 17 Apr. (1927) II. xx. 590, I am therefore identified as a Sharifian. **1926** T. E. LAWRENCE *Seven Pillars* I. xvi. 82 Blood feuds were nominally healed, and really suspended in the Sherifian area. *Ibid.* II. xviii. 93 Garland single-handed was teaching the Sherifians how to blow up railways with dynamite. **1929** W. S. CHURCHILL *World Crisis* V. 462 He came of the Sherifian family which, as guardians of the Holy Places at Mecca, commanded wide veneration throughout the Islamic world. **1935** R. H. KIERNAN *Lawrence of Arabia* viii. 174 He was defeated by the fanatical Wahabis in a fight which resulted in the destruction of a Sherifian force of four thousand men. **1976** *Times Lit. Suppl.* 30 Apr. 519/2 Correspondence which on the Sharifian side was a continuation of the attempts made before the outbreak of the 1914–18 War to enlist the services of Great Britain in Sharif Husayn's resistance to the centralizing policy of the Turkish government. *Ibid.*, To these proposals the Sharifians demanded an answer within thirty days.

3. Of, pertaining to, or designating descent from Muhammad.

1936 E. WAUGH *Waugh in Abyssinia* 86 The Emir's family claimed high, Sheriffian descent. **1976** *Times Lit. Suppl.* 13 Feb. 164/2 No doubt sultans did issue certificates of 'sherifian' descent. *Ibid.* 164/3 The conversion to the specifically 'sherifian' idiom of prestigious ancestry. **1977** P. RAYMOND *Matter of Assassination* vii. 75 His Sharifian Majesty, exalted of God, received us in his audience chamber.

Shererat, var. *SHERARAT. **Sheriat,** var. *SHARIA.

Sheridanesque (ʃe:ridăn·esk), *a.* [f. the name of Richard Brinsley *Sheridan* (1751–1816), British dramatist + -ESQUE.] Of, pertaining to, or characteristic of Sheridan or his plays.

1931 [see *RACINIAN *a.* and *sb.*]. **1933** BLUNDEN *Charles Lamb* ii. 61 He [*sc.* Lamb] ventured to show what he could do independent of the Sheridanesque cleverness around him.

So **She·ridania:na** [*-IANA], anecdotes about Sheridan.

1826 F. REYNOLDS *Sheridaniana* p. iii, The..volume..is intended to comprehend all that is most interesting..about..Sheridan—a person so eminently qualified to form the subject of such a work, that it seems somewhat singular that the *present* should be the first collection of Sheridaniana. **1931** *Times Lit. Suppl.* 16 Apr. 303/3 Sheridaniana? There is 'at the bottom of this stagnant well' some trace of truth, the misery of a reputation for wit.

sheridanite (ʃe·ridănəit). *Min.* [See quot. 1912 and -ITE[1].] A chlorite, $(Mg,Al,Fe^{2+})_6$-$(Si,Al)_4O_{10}(OH)_8$, chemically similar to clinochlore but containing less silicon.

1912 J. E. WOLFF in *Amer. Jrnl. Sci.* CCXXXIV. 476 Although it seems hardly permissible to add a new name to the forty or fifty now found under the chlorite group, yet the purity of this material, its peculiar chemical composition and the certainty that it will be available in large quantity, perhaps justifies the name of 'Sheridanite', from the county [in Wyoming] in which it occurs. **1967** *Canad. Mineralogist* IX. 30 The fine white material in the core of the specimen from Zlatoust, Russia... This material gave an extremely sharp chlorite *x*-ray pattern. The structural formula..classes it as a sheridanite, as defined by Foster (1962).

sheriff. Add: **1. a.** (*a*). (Later examples.) The boroughs and cities which had their own sheriffs are no longer styled 'counties of themselves', but many of them, e.g. Canterbury, Chester, Gloucester, still have sheriffs. The Sheriffs of the City of London ceased to be also Sheriffs of Middlesex in 1888.

1888 *Act* 51 & 52 *Vict.* c. 41 s. 41(8) The sheriffs of the city of London shall not have any authority except in the city. *Ibid.* s. 46(6) The right of the mayor, commonalty, and citizens of the city of London to elect the sheriff of Middlesex shall cease, and it shall be lawful for Her Majesty the Queen to appoint a sheriff of the county of Middlesex. **1972** *Local Govt. Act* c. 70 s. 219(1) Sheriffs appointed for a county or Greater London shall be known as high sheriffs. **1974** C. A. CROSS *Principles Local Govt. Law* (ed. 5) xxvii. 488 The Queen in granting a charter to preserve the privileges of a city or borough existing prior to April 1, 1974, may confer on the city or borough the power to appoint a sheriff, as opposed to a high sheriff.

(*b*). Short for *sheriff's officer* (sense 4 a in Dict.); = BAILIFF 2.

1928 *Daily Mail* 30 July 7/1 You have had the sheriff in your house? *Ibid.*, Who put the sheriff into your house?

4. a. sheriff court (later examples); **sheriff officer** (later example); **sheriff's sale** *N. Amer.*, a public sale conducted by a sheriff following a court order for seizure and sale of property to satisfy a judgment.

1894 *Scots Law Times* I. 701 Except in Sheriff Court Cases, the figures refer to the number of the Case, and not to the number of the Page. **1962** T. B. SMITH *Scotland* iv. 102 The sheriff court has jurisdiction to try all crimes committed within the sheriffdom, except treason, murder, attempt to murder, rape, incest, certain offences against the Official Secrets Acts, deforcement of messengers, and breach of duty by magistrates. **1978** *Dumfries Courier* 13 Oct. 2/5 The sequel took place at Dumfries Sheriff Court on Friday when Savage pleaded guilty to the offence. **1932** *Encycl. Laws Scotland* XIII. 527 Sheriff Officers are the persons by whom writs are served and executions carried out in the Sheriff Courts. **1798** *Pittsburgh Gaz.* 6 Oct. 1/2 (Advt.), Sheriff's Sales. **1883** *Brandon* (Manitoba) *Daily Mail* 9 Jan. 4/1 There will be a sheriff's sale of goods and chattels belonging to the late firm of Hambly & Miller, barbers, etc., on Saturday next. **1947** *Steamboat* (Colorado) *Pilot* 30 Jan. 2/8 The electric light plant..was sold at sheriff's sale. **1966**

Globe & Mail (Toronto) 6 Sept. 30/1 Sheriff's Sale of Lands—Under and by Virtue of an Execution issued out of the Ninth Division Court of the County of York to me directed against the lands and tenements of [etc.].

Sherlock (ʃɛ̄·ɹlǫk), *sb.* [See *HOLMESIAN *a.* and *sb.*, and next.] A person who investigates mysteries or shows great perceptiveness; a private detective.

1903 G. V. HOBART *Back to Woods* iii. 57 'Down there, eh?' snorted the country Sherlock. **1928** D. L. SAYERS *Ld. Peter views Body* 42 I'm riding with Freddy Arbuthnot,..as you might see by my legs, if you were really as big a Sherlock as you make out. **1932** KIPLING *Limits & Renewals* 178 We aren't exactly first-class Sherlocks. **1967** N. FREELING *Strike out where not Applicable* 27 Mr. van der Valk, my dear, our police Sherlock. **1972** 'L. EGAN' *Paper Chase* xii. 191 You'll have to turn Sherlock and solve the case yourself.

So **She·rlock** *v. intr.* and *trans.*, to engage in detective work; to investigate (something), to make deductions about; **She·rlockian,** *sb.* and *a.* (*a*) *sb.* = *SHERLOCK *sb.*; (*b*) *adj.* pertaining to or characteristic of Sherlock Holmes; = *HOLMESIAN *a.*; **She·rlockia:na** [*-IANA], things connected with Sherlock Holmes, writings about Sherlock Holmes; **She·rlocking** *vbl. sb.*, detective work.

1903 *Bookman* XVII. 5/2 If you decipher this you are a real Sherlockian. **1913** *Manch. Guardian* 15 Jan., Any man with a bundle or package was suspicious, so we 'sherlocked' around for a bit and watched him go into a barber's shop to get disguised by having his hair cut. There we 'pinched' him. **1920** J. GALSWORTHY *Foundations* I, in *Plays* (1929) 468 Don't call in the police!..Let me do the Sherlocking for you. **1934** *Discovery* Sept. 273/2 It is now close on four hundred years since that door was used and sandals trod those steps, but we are able to 'Sherlock' this detail of old times. **1937** STEVENS & SHORTEN *How to watch Football Game* vi. 51 No use in trying to Sherlock the next play. Anything can happen. **1942** H. HAYCRAFT *Murder for Pleasure* xiii. 276 Vincent Starrett's *Private Life of Sherlock Holmes* with its valuable appended bibliography of Sherlockiana. **1957** J. KEROUAC *On Road* (1958) 135 They tried some amateur Sherlocking by asking the same questions twice. **1959** *Listener* 3 Dec. 993/1 A startling piece of detective work, followed up with exact, devoted, Sherlockian tenacity. **1962** W. S. BARING-GOULD *Sherlock Holmes* 263 Late 1895–late 1896 called by many Sherlockian commentators 'The Missing Year', and the subject of much learned speculation. **1963** 'G. CARR' *Lewker in Norway* i. 25 You're really disappointed because you can't go Sherlocking after that young man. **1972** E. ROUTLEY *Puritan Pleasures of Detective Story* ii. 27 This is not a contribution to Sherlockiana, but the..cult of Sherlock Holmes is itself..in the field of our enquiry. **1975** *Daily Tel.* 27 May 14/3 He..had built up an outstanding collection of Sherlockiana, including such rarities as a copy of the Beeton's Christmas Annual of 1887 in which the first Holmes adventure.. was originally published. **1977** *New Yorker* 20 June 71/1 He lights his pipe. It is long and low and looks somewhat Sherlockian.

Sherlock Holmes (ʃɔ̄·ɹlǫk hōᵘmz). [See *HOLMESIAN *a.* and *sb.*] A person resembling Sherlock Holmes; = *SHERLOCK *sb.*

1896 E. TURNER *Little Larrikin* x. 108 It took her nearly five minutes to wonder sufficiently at him..and call him a Sherlock Holmes. **1914** T. A. BAGGS *Back from Front* xxiv. 118 It needed no Sherlock Holmes to discover where English cavalry had bivouacked for the night. **1957** A. MACNAB *Bulls of Iberia* xvi. 237 The press critics kept very quiet about it, and one need not be a Sherlock Holmes to guess why. **1981** *Times* 22 Apr. 6/5 The doctor becomes a medical Sherlock Holmes.

So **Sherlock Holmes** *v. trans.*, to make deductions about, to assess, to deduce (cf. *SHERLOCK *v.*); **Sherlock Ho·lmesian** *a.* = *SHERLOCKIAN *a.*; **Sherlock Ho·lmesing** *vbl. sb.* = *SHERLOCKING *vbl. sb.*

1922 JOYCE *Ulysses* 620 He had been meantime taking stock of the individual in front of him and Sherlockholmesing him up. **1929** C. I. LEWIS *Mind & World-Order* ix. 287 All the Sherlock Holmesing in the world would not help him a bit because he would not be able to recognize evidence when he found it. **1954** E. EAGER *Half Magic* iii. 35 'She just as good as said so,' said Jane, 'and I Sherlock Holmesed the rest.' **1958** *Observer* 16 Mar. 14/3 The stern Sherlock Holmesian K.C. **1958** A. WILSON *Middle Age of Mrs. Eliot* I. 89 All this woman's intuition is just a lot of Sherlock Holmesing. **1972** *Sci. Amer.* Mar. 106/3 He proceeded indeed by a kind of Sherlock Holmesian logic, which presumes that in eliminating the impossible and the more implausible it has arrived at the true.

Sherman[1] (ʃɔ̄·ɹmăn). The name of John *Sherman* (1823–1900), U.S. senator, used *attrib.* to designate either of two acts passed by Congress in 1890, one to prohibit combinations in restraint of inter-state or foreign trade, the other to maintain the price of silver by government purchase of silver bullion; also, to designate treasury notes issued under the provisions of the latter act.

1892 *Dem. Platform* in K. Porter *Nat. Party Platforms* (1924) 162 We denounce the Republican legislation known as the Sherman Act of 1890. **1894** *Harper's Mag.* Jan. 318/1 Mr. Voorhees's substitute repealing the Sherman law was passed by a vote of 43 to 32. **1897** *Money* May 23 Government notes called Treasury notes of 1890, sometimes *Sherman notes*, sometimes *Coin notes*..were issued in payment of purchases of silver bullion from 1890–93. **1947** *Atlantic Monthly* June 73/1 In 1890 the Sherman Act was passed to 'appease the restive masses', but it would be fifty years before Thurman Arnold would demonstrate, briefly, that the Act could be made to work. **1948** *Duncan* (Oklahoma) *Daily Banner* 1 July 1/3 The U.S. Supreme Court..held that officers of the company and the firm itself had violated the Sherman anti-trust law. **1974** *Encycl. Brit. Micropædia* IV. 303/1 The Bland-Allison Act was superseded in 1890 by the Sherman Silver Purchase Act, which increased the government's monthly silver purchases by 50 percent. Fear that the U.S. was about to abandon the gold standard precipitated the Panic of 1893, causing the Sherman Act to be hastily repealed the same year.

Sherman[2] (ʃɔ̄·ɹmăn). The name of W. T. *Sherman* (1820–91), U.S. general, used *attrib.* and *absol.* to designate an American type of medium tank, much used during the war of 1939–45. Also *General Sherman* (*tank*).

1942 *Times* 6 Nov. 6/3 (*caption*) A picture just received from America of General Sherman tanks. **1942** W. S. CHURCHILL *End of Beginning* (1943) 229 This very powerful force.., including all the best tanks, the Grants and the Shermans, was withdrawn from the battle front. **1944** *Sun* (Baltimore) 15 Nov. 11/2 The Sherman tanks jumped off with orders to cross the river. **1965** A. J. P. TAYLOR *Eng. Hist. 1914–45* xv. 554 To aid Auchinleck, the Americans diverted 300 Sherman tanks to Suez. **1969** STUBBS & CONNOR *Armor-Cavalry* I. 64 A much improved M3 medium was standardized in 1941 as the M4, better known throughout the war by its British designation, the General Sherman. **1971** E. LUTTWAK *Dict. Mod. War* 176/1 The Israeli army uses a large number of converted Shermans fitted with a new 105-mm gun.

Sherpa (ʃɔ̄·ɹpă). Also 9 Serpa, Sharpa. [ad. Tibetan *sharpa*, inhabitant of an eastern country.] **1.** (A member of) a Tibetan people living on the southern slopes of the Himalayas. Also *attrib.* or as *adj.*

1847 B. H. HODGSON in *Jrnl. Asiatic Soc. Bengal* XVI. 1237 Cis-Himálayan Bhotias vel Tibetans, called.. Serpa, &c. *Ibid.* 1238 The sub-Himálayan races..inhabit all the central and temperate parts of these mountains, the juxta nivean or nethermost tracts being left to the Rongbo vel Sérpá. **1874** —— *Ess. on Nepál & Tibet* II. ii. 30 Cis-Himálayan Bhotias vel Tibetans, called Rongbo, ..Sérpa or Sharpa etc. **1922** G. H. LEIGH-MALLORY in C. K. Howard-Bury *Mount Everest* xiv. 224 The Tibetan coolies..were notably less strong than our Sherpas. **1924** *Glasgow Herald* 16 Apr. 10/6 Two of them after a merry-making battered each other in a terrific manner, but the following morning..they were nursing each other with the greatest care and mutual pity. Such is a Sherpa porter. **1950** T. LONGSTAFF *This my Voyage* iv. 67 He.. had not yet shown us that Sherpas could be the mainstay of any Himalayan expedition. **1970** *Daily Colonist* (Victoria, B.C.) 11 Nov. 38/4 Sen Tensing, the sherpa bearer, shuddered in fright. **1979** *Daily Tel.* 17 May 1/4 One of mountaineering's best known Sherpas, Ang Phu, was feared killed yesterday in a fall on Everest after helping a Yugoslav expedition put a second team on the summit.

2. *transf.* and *fig.* A mountain guide or porter; a guide; an official who makes the preparations for a summit conference.

1959 M. PUGH *Chancer* 137 What was the idea of trying that cliff? Did you fancy your chance as a sherpa? **1976** P. CAVE *High Flying Birds* iii. 35 'O.K.,' I said. 'Lead the way, sherpa.' **1980** *Times* 23 June 1/2 The seven leaders inevitably based much of their comment on the draft communique drawn up for publication after the meeting by the seven government officials—known as the 'sherpas' —who have been charged with preparing this summit.

sherri-varrie: see *SHIVAREE.

sherry, *sb.*[1] Add: **1. a.** Now a fortified wine. (Further examples.)

1958 A. L. SIMON *Dict. Wines, Spirits & Liqueurs* 146/1 Sherry is made from the best wine of each vintage, to which some Brandy is added, after which it is kept for many years with the best wine of other vintages. **1967** *Times* 1 Aug. 6/5 'Sherry' means a wine coming from the Jerez district of Spain. The Court, giving judgment,.. decided that it would be unjust now to restrain Vine Products Ltd...from using the expressions 'British sherry', 'English sherry', 'Cyprus sherry', 'South African sherry', and 'Australian sherry', used for certain wines in England.

c. A glass or drink of sherry.

1924 GALSWORTHY *White Monkey* II. ix. 192 Will you have a sherry? **1979** M. MCCARTHY *Cannibals & Missionaries* i. 19 He had been counting on picking Gus's brains..over a sherry or a bourbon.

2. (Examples.)

1907 [see *PORT *sb.*[7] c]. **1925** [see *LIQUEUR *sb.* 2]. **1974** [see *PORT *sb.*[7] c].

3. a. *sherry decanter, trifle* [TRIFLE *sb.* 6 b]; *sherry-style, -type* adjs.; **sherry-bar,** a bar at which sherry is the principal drink sold; **sherry morning,** a morning sherry party; **sherry party,** a party at which sherry is the principal drink served.

1951 G. GREENE *End of Affair* v. ii. 181 Waterbury was waiting in a sherry-bar off Tottenham Court Road. **1950** J. CANNAN *Murder Included* vii. 164 A tray with two glasses and a sherry decanter. **1977** G. MCDONALD *Confess, Fletch* xxiii. 104 There were Scotch bottles, bourbon bottles, gin bottles, sherry and port decanters. **1976** *Milton Keynes Express* 16 July 2/3 A sherry morning on Sunday brought in £98.32 for Olney Town Cricket Club funds. **1936** *Cherwell* 7 Mar. 158/2 A tendency to throw sherry parties and get a little drunk. **1977** 'J. LE CARRÉ' *Honourable Schoolboy* xi. 239 Christmas was hardly noticed apart from a rather battered sherry party. **1960** *Times* 3 Oct. (Wine Trade Suppl.) p. iv/5 In the United States there is a domestic wine business which last year turned out..20 million gallons of sherry-style wine. **1951** H. SMITH *Master Bk. Dessert Pies & Sweets* viii. 279 *Sherry Trifle*, arrange slices of Swiss roll at the bottom of a round glass dish and sprinkle liberally with sherry. **1979** K. BONFIGLIOLI *After you with Pistol* xxii. 176 Two helpings of sherry-trifle. **1962** *Times* 3 Feb. 9/4 A glass of sherry-type wine.

c. sherry-negus (earlier example).

c **1863** T. TAYLOR *Ticket-of-Leave Man* I. 7 Two sherry negus, two shillings.

sherry, *v.*[2] Restrict *nonce-wd.* to sense in Dict. and add: **2.** To add sherry to. Chiefly as **she·rried** *ppl. a.*

1970 *Guardian* 15 Apr. 10/2 A heavily sherried trifle. **1977** D. J. ELLIOTT in D. Marcus *Best Irish Short Stories 2* 156 They ate prawns in aspic, sherried.

‖ **sherut** (ʃɛ̄ɪrū·t). Also **sheirut.** [Heb., lit. 'service'.] In Israel, a large taxi shared by several passengers.

1950 G. MIKES *Milk & Honey* 91 Between the two [bus and taxi] there is the communal taxi, the *sherut*. **1968** P. DURST *Badge of Infamy* xiv. 133 He flagged down a *sherut*, one of the ramshackle taxi-cum-buses which plied between Haifa and Tel Aviv. **1977** H. KAPLAN *Damascus Cover* (1978) iii. 21 The *sheirut* drivers, loudly beckoning arriving passengers to share a taxi to Tel Aviv or Jerusalem. **1981** *Daily Tel.* 24 June 11 Jitneys and sheruts should be introduced on the roads to make public transport more efficient.

‖ **sherwani** (ʃɔɪwā·ni). [Hindi.] In the Indian sub-continent, a knee-length coat, buttoning to the neck, worn by men.

1911 [see *ACHKAN]. **1964** D. N. WILBUR *Pakistan* viii. 168 Among well-to-do Moslems generally, a long coat known as a *sherwani* is worn. **1971** R. RUSSELL tr. *A. Ahmad's Shore & Wave* vi. 54 He gravely took off his *sherwani* and hung it on the coat-hanger.

sheshbesh (ʃe·ʃbeʃ). Also **shesh-besh.** [Turk., f. Pers. *shash* six + Turk. *beş* five.] A variety of backgammon played in the Middle East. Also *attrib.*

1971 L. DAVIDSON *Smith's Gazelle* ii. 37 The sheshbesh players pressed his arm in sympathy. **1975** C. A. HADDAD *Moroccan* (1977) iv. 44 My friends would come over..to play sheshbesh. **1977** H. KAPLAN *Damascus Cover* (1978) vii. 67 In this part of the world we have been playing sheshbesh, what you call backgammon, for nearly three thousand years.

shet (ʃet), **shed** (ʃed), repr. a U.S. dial. and colloq. pronunc. of SHUT *v.* and *ppl. a.*, esp. in phrase *to get* (*be, stay*) *shet of* (see SHUT *v.* 11 a).

1837 A. SHERWOOD *Gazetteer of State of Georgia* (ed. 3) 70/1 *Get shet of*, for get rid of. **1848,** etc. [see *open-and-shut* s.v. *OPEN *a.* 22 c]. **1871** E. EGGLESTON *Hoosier School-Master* (1872) xxxii. 162 I'm glad to be shed of you! **1930** G. B. JOHNSON in B. A. Botkin *Folk-Say* vii. 357 The Negro raises..'great big' hogs, and tries to 'get shet of' his enemies, just as poor white folk have done for hundreds of years. **1935** Z. N. HURSTON *Mules & Men* I. iii. 77 Throw mah trunk out befo' you shet up dat place! **1943** E. CALDWELL *Georgia Boy* 80, I thought you was trying to get shed of it. **1974** *State* (Columbia, S. Carolina) 15 Feb. 1–B/1 A gentleman at the coffee counter began munching his hamburger a whole lot slower yesterday when the waitress admitted she just couldn't 'get shet' of her strep throat. **1976** *Verbatim* Sept. 8/1 The range of his scholarship and the deftness of his intuition..are bound in an engaging prose style that makes a reader grateful to be shet for a while of the orthodox taxonomist. **1978** J. A. MICHENER *Chesapeake* 726 'Turlocks hate us colored,' he warned his daughters, 'so the smart thing, stay shed of 'em... Just you stay clear, like me, an' you find no trouble.'

Shetland. Add: **1. c.** Also with small initial. (Earlier and later examples of things made of this wool.) *Shetland floss*, Shetland wool. *Shetland knitting*, a traditional style of knitting characterized by a distinctive technique and by the following of Scandinavian patterns in 'natural' colours.

1854 *Morning Post* 7 July 1/5 (Advt.), Shetland shawls and veils in great variety. **1895** Shetland floss [see *double-knit* adj. s.v. *DOUBLE *a.* A. 6]. **1934** W. MOFFATT *Shetland: Isles of Nightless Summer* i. 23 The wool is invariably short, curly and silky... This wool is famous all over the world, and is so valued that unscrupulous people in other lands sell wool called 'Shetland Floss' that was never within a thousand miles of Shetland. **1935** in *Scottish Woollens* (Nat. Assoc. Sc. Woollen Manufacturers) (1956) 55 Shetlanders..still knit a great variety of articles, and the finest Shetland knitting is still unrivalled. **1966** N. FREELING *Dresden Green* I. 17 A beige shetland pullover. **1974** *People's Jrnl.* (Inverness & Northern Counties ed.) 7 Sept. 9/1 They studied island crafts such as silverwork, handloom weaving, carding and spinning, and Shetland knitting. **1979** R. JAFFE *Class Reunion* 5 Plain dark shetland cardigans. **1980** L. BIRNBACH et al. *Official Preppy Handbk.* 107/1 You should be comfortable with a turtleneck,..a button-down shirt and a Shetland sweater.

d. *Shetland sheep-dog*, a small long-coated collie belonging to the breed so called; also *Shetland collie*.

1908 *Our Dogs* 27 Mar. 681/2 Shetland Collies.—This variety is at present in the hands of a few fanciers only. **1909** *Ibid.* 15 Oct. 937/1 Shetland Collies or Sheepdogs, the original type and colour. **1960** E. MILLER *Shetland Sheepdog* 5 So much experimenting has gone on with this breed, that the Shetland Sheepdog is still far from being 'typed' like a Poodle or Boxer. **1971** F. HAMILTON *World Encycl. Dogs* 97 The name Shetland Collie was the first choice but the Collie Clubs objected so strongly that the Kennel Club would not allow it. **1977** *Belfast Tel.* 14 Feb. 12/9 (Advt.), Shetland sheepdog puppies.

2. *absol.* **a.** A shetland pony.

1836 S. C. STEVENSON *Let.* Sept. in E. Boykin *Victoria, Albert, & Mrs. Stevenson* (1957) 30, I cannot tell you how I covet one of these little shetlands for my little nephews. **1975** *Country Life* 6 Feb. 327/1 The ponies shown included Connemaras,..Shetlands and Welsh.

b. A Shetland shawl, sweater, etc.

1870 CROWN PRINCESS OF PRUSSIA *Let.* 18 Mar. in R. Fulford *Your Dear Letter* (1971) 207 In my condition.. I..never am in my own room without a lace shawl or a shetland or black mantilla. **1972** *Vogue* 1 Mar. 57/1 Classic Shetland and cashmere sweaters... Shetlands in 79 colours. **1979** A. V. BADGLEY *Rembrandt Decisions* xi. 156 Stout oxfords, ribbed wool stockings, itchy shetlands.

c. A Shetland sheep-dog.

1945 C. L. B. HUBBARD *Observer's Bk. Dogs* 143 A perfect Collie in miniature, the Shetland is efficient and nimble. **1958** O. GWYNNE-JONES *Shetland Sheepdog Handbk.* i. 8 By 1912 Shetlands were classified at..sixteen shows.

‖ **sheva.** Add: Also **shewa** (ʃəwā·), **shva.**

1. (Earlier and later examples.)

1582 MULCASTER *Elementarie* xvii. 113 Like to a silent Hebrew Scheua. **1818** P. S. DUPONCEAU in *Trans. Amer. Philos. Soc.* I. 241 A small vacant space, as it were, between the consonants, like the *Sheva* of the Hebrews. **1914** DAVIDSON & MCFADYEN *Introd. Hebrew Gram.* (ed. 19) 23 The place of shᵉwa vocal, simple or composite, is under the first of two consonants that begin a syllable. **1939** J. WEINGREEN *Pract. Gram. for Classical Hebrew* 9 The shewa is not a vowel. The quick vowel-like sound is like the 'e' in 'because'. **1965** *Language* XLI. 543 The shva is a masoretic grapheme.

2. (Earlier and later examples.) See also *SCHWA.

1818 [see *phonologist* s.v. *PHONOLOGY]. **1939** E. PROKOSCH *Compar. Germanic Gram.* 94 IE ə and ь are distinguished as 'shva primum' and 'shva secundum', but the term 'shva' alone always refers to ə.

Shevuos, Shevuoth, varr. *SHAVUOTH.

Shiah. (Later examples of form *Shia.*)

1926 T. E. LAWRENCE *Seven Pillars* II. xxvii. 140 They were Shias, and had been since the days of Kerbela. **1955** *Times* 31 Aug. 6/6 The Shia mourning day, Ashura, commemorating the death of Imam Hussein, grandson of the prophet, passed off without incident. **1969** *Pioneer* (Lucknow) 13 Aug. 4/8 Syeds are mostly Shias in Lucknow. **1974** *Educ. & Community Relations* Jan. 5 Celebrated with processions mostly by the Shia sect.

shiatsu (ʃi,æ·tsu). Also **Shiatsu, shiatzu.** [Jap., lit. finger-pressure.] A kind of therapy, of Japanese origin, in which pressure is applied with the thumbs and palms to certain points on the body. Also *attrib.*

1967 *Tel.* (Brisbane) 4 Dec. 12 A Japanese physiotherapist..believes that his shiatsu finger massage is good for treating high blood pressure, insomnia and hernia. **1969** T. NAMIKOSHI *Shiatsu: Health & Vitality at your Fingertips* i. 10 Widely practiced in Japan today, shiatsu is described by the Ministry of Welfare as follows: Shiatsu is a treatment in which the thumbs and palms of the hands are used to apply pressure to certain points in order to correct irregularities of the living body. *Ibid.* 13 The thumbs are often used in shiatsu treatment. *Ibid.* iv. 81 Apply strong shiatsu pressure to the eight points on the calf. **1975** *Publishers Weekly* 18 Aug. 29 (Advt.), Shiatzu was developed centuries ago in Japan as a refinement of the acupuncture treatment from China. **1980** *Daily Tel.* 21 June 12/4 There are 13 pressure-points in *shia-tsu*.

Shibayama (ʃibāyā·mă). Also **shibayama.** The name of a Japanese family of carvers, used *absol.* and *attrib.* to denote a distinctive style of inlay work which they originated.

1928 F. M. JONAS *Netsukė* 174 Shibayama is the name by which all encrusted work is known. **1956** F. MEINERTZHAGEN *Art of Netsuke Carver* III. 45 'Shibayama' work, mostly of poor quality, in the form of vases, jars, trays, etc., was made from the late 19th century up to recent times. **1971** *Country Life* 22 Apr. 941/1 The design is composed of gold lacquer and *shibayama*, that is pieces of ivory, tortoiseshell, mother-of-pearl used to build up the picture. **1982** 'J. GASH' *Firefly Gadroon* iv. 36 A set of Shibayama knife-handles.

‖ **shibui** (ʃi·bu,i), *a.* and *sb.* Also **shibu.** [Jap., f. *shibu* an astringent substance.] **A.** *adj.* Tasteful in a quiet, profound, or unostentatious way. **B.** *sb.* Tastefulness, refinement, appreciation of elegant simplicity.

In Japanese the substantival form is *shibu* (the substance) or *shibumi* (its quality); the adj. is *shibui.*

1947 J. MORRIS *Phoenix Cup* II. 28 A picture, a piece of pottery, a kimono, or what you will, may be, from the Japanese point of view, in exquisite taste, and yet not *shibui*; to be thus described there must be also some invocation of quietude and austerity. **1958** *Japan: its Land, People & Culture* xxix. 1019/2 As beauty approaches the highest level it becomes a subtle beauty represented by what is known as the *shibu* taste. **1960** E. MANNIN *Flowery Sword* x. 166 Vulgarity and *shibui* side by side. **1965** *This is Japan 1966* 121/2 The sense of appreciation known as *shibui*, which enables Japanese to derive such satisfaction from the drinking of the tea, might seem to the foreigner a type of high, super-refined, even affected taste. **1970** J. KIRKUP *Japan behind Fan* 27 That ghastly good taste, common to all modern hotels, that turns the most *shibui* atmosphere into something expensive and pretentious.

‖ **shibuichi** (ʃibui·tʃi). [Jap., f. *shi* four + *bu* part(s) + *ichi* one.] An alloy consisting of three parts of copper to one of silver, extensively used by the Japanese on account of its beautiful silver-grey patina. Also *attrib.*

1880 T. W. CUTLER *Gram. Jap. Ornament* 19 The *shibu-ichi* is inlaid with gold and *shakudo.* **1902** *Encycl. Brit.* XXIX. 720/1 Neither metal, when it emerges from the furnace, has any beauty, *shakudo* being simply dark-coloured, and *shibuichi* pale gun-metal. **1911** *Ibid.* XV. 179 On the surface of a shibuichi box-lid we see the backs of a flock of geese. **1977** *Times* 14 Oct. 17/5 The top priced *tsuba*..is..made from a Japanese alloy called shibuichi.

shice (ʃəis), *sb.* and *a.* Also **shise.** *slang* (? *Obs.*). [G. *scheiss*; cf. SHICER.] **A.** *sb.* Nothing; base money; something worthless. **B.** *adj.* Worthless, counterfeit, spurious.

1859 HOTTEN *Dict. Slang* 91 *Shice*, nothing; 'to do anything for *shice*', to get no payment. **1877** *Five Years' Penal Servitude* iii. 240, I ascertained while at Dartmoor that a very large 'business' is done in 'shise'. *c* **1890** *Five Years of Prison Life* ii. 62 Seeing how the fellow was acting he sent him two 'shise' notes, which gave him a dose that 'corked him'. **1939** J. B. PRIESTLEY *Let People Sing* x. 256 'I keep tellin' Knocker it's a shice,' said Micky earnestly.

shicer. Add: **1.** (Earlier example.) Also, something worthless, a failure.

1846 *Swell's Night Guide* 61 The shiser thinks to bounce us by flashing a shofel quid. **1874** A. BATHGATE *Colonial Experiences* viii. 97 There are, of course, many what may be called technical terms in connection with the pursuit of mining... Such, for example, as 'duffer' or 'shiser', anything that is useless. **1916** J. B. COOPER *Coo-oo-ee* xiv. 203 'The case is a "shicer" already,' replied Jack. 'Hawley has given it up.'

shick (ʃik), Austral. and N.Z. abbrev. of *SHICKER *a.*, *sb.* 1.

1916 C. J DENNIS *Moods of Ginger Mick* 19 The toff's too shick or silly fer to 'eave 'is carkis out. **1941** BAKER *Dict. Austral. Slang* 65 *Shick*, drunk. Also (n.) a drunken person. **1966** B. BEAVER *You can't come Back* 144 The wonder was we got that far without falling over and breaking them, because we were both pretty shick by then.

shicker (ʃi·kəɹ), *a.* and *sb.* *Austral.* and *N.Z. colloq.* and in Jewish speech. Also **shiker, shikker, shikkur.** [ad. Yiddish *shiker* ad. Heb. *šikkôr*, f. *šākar* to be drunk. Perh. infl. by *SHICKERY *a.* and *adv.*] **A.** *adj.* Drunk, intoxicated.

1892 I. ZANGWILL *Childr. Ghetto* I. ii. 53 'But I'll get drunk on gingerbeer,' Pesach laughed back. 'You can't,' Fanny said... 'Ha! ha! ha! Can't even get *shikkur* on it. What a liquor!' **1898** *Bulletin* (Sydney) 17 Dec. Red Page, *Shiker*, drunk. **1899** A. BINSTEAD *Houndsditch Day by Day* 46 She comes over shikkur an vants to go to shleeb. **1916** J. B. COOPER *Coo-oo-ee* v. 60 Hickford said the deceased was 'shicker' on the night before his death. **1949** *Hilltop* (N.Z.) I. II. 20 Sid should have some chance to get shicker as everybody else. **1963** 'M. CORRIGAN' *Why do Women —?* xv. 106 She was shikker and she took it into her head to come here. **1970** *N.Z. Listener* 12 Oct. 12/5 After midnight, Jerry got so shicker that he was quarrelling with everyone.

B. *sb.* **1.** A drunk.

1906 [see *on one's ear* s.v. *EAR *sb.*[1] 1 c]. **1938** X. HERBERT *Capricornia* xviii. 234 He's the biggest shikker in Town. Now nick off, you old sponge. **1945** A. KOBER *Parm Me* 156 Right away they are coming here, the whole bunch!.. Will be Uncle Henry and Uncle Philip—two foist-class *shikkers*! **1949** D. M. DAVIN *Roads from Home* I. iii. 41 A shicker. Broke too, by the sound of it. **1964** S. BELLOW *Herzog* 135 He drank his pay—a *shicker*. **1970** S. ELLIN *Bind* xlvii. 234, I was hunting in the swamps with my *shikker* friend... I dumped my *shikker* off at Flagler Street.

2. Liquor; esp. in phr. *on the shicker.* (Only *Austral.* and *N.Z.*)

1916 C. J. DENNIS *Moods of Ginger Mick* 154 *Shicker*, intoxicating liquor. **1918** *N.Z.E.F. Chron.* 27 Feb. 33/1 He saved his strength for shicker. **1928** A. WRIGHT *Good Recovery* 85 'Yes, I've been on the shicker,' he answered huskily. **1945** R. RENE *Mo's Memoirs* 49 One night the magician had been on the shicker, and with a fine disregard for life and limb he let the lion out. **1958** H. D. WILLIAMSON *Sunlit Plain* 58 He was on the shicker when I was there last week.

shicker (ʃi·kəɹ), *v.* *Austral.* and *N.Z. colloq.* [f. as prec.] *intr.* To take alcoholic drink, to get drunk.

a **1922** H. LAWSON *Benno & his Old 'Uns* in *Prose* (1964) III. 230 Her Old 'Un 'shickered' till he got 'mucked' every pay day. **1951** CUSACK & JAMES *Come in Spinner* 33 He'd gamble his shirt off on any damn thing that's got a leg to run on, but he doesn't shicker.

shickered (ʃi·kəɹd), *a.* *Austral.* and *N.Z. colloq.* Also **shikkered.** [f. *SHICKER *a.* and *sb.*, or *v.*] Drunk, intoxicated.

1911 L. STONE *Jonah* I. ix. 124 'E's bin shickered since last We'n'sday. **1911** H. FOSTON *In Bellbird's Lair* vii. 34 He thinks we're 'shickered'. **1916** C. J. DENNIS *Moods of Ginger Mick* 19 There's a shickered toff slings Rosie googoo eyes. **1930** A. W. GROOM *Merry Christmas* xvi. 123 Every time I get shikkered I sober up after an' say 'Never again, Sandy'. **1934** T. WOOD *Cobbers* xvi. 209 He *tole* me he was goin' to get sh-shickered, an' he has... He'sh as drank'sh forty catsh! **1947** D. M. DAVIN *Gorse blooms Pale* 212 When you're shickered you know..things aren't really as good as they seem. **1952** J. CLEARY *Sundowners* i. 42 He's drunk! Shickered to the eyeballs! **1961** P. WHITE *Riders in Chariot* 261 'I'm gunna get out of this!' he announced at last. 'I'm gunna get shickered stiff!' **1972** C. DRUMMOND *Death at Bar* v. 114 'You look half shickered, love,' said Charlie. 'I'll be right when I've been sick,' said Mrs. Gaukroger.

shickery (ʃi·kəri), *a.* and *adv.* *slang* (? *obs.*). [Origin unknown.] **A.** *adj.* Shabby, rickety, shaky; also, drunk. **B.** *adv.* Shabbily, badly.

1851 H. MAYHEW *London Labour* I. 424/1 There's another sort who carry on the crocussing business, but on a small scale; they..are called hedge crocusses... But as the hedge crocus is shickery togged, he makes poorly out. **1859** HOTTEN *Dict. Slang* 91 *Shickery*, shabby, badly. **1878** 'R. BOLDREWOOD' in *Town & Country Jrnl.* 26 Jan. 170/1 Old Tom had a goodish cheque this time, and was at it a week afore I come in. He *was* rayther shickerry. **1888** —— *Robbery under Arms* III. xv. 220 Four panels of shickery two-rail fence.

shicksa, var. *SHIKSA.

shickster (ʃi·kstəɹ). *slang* (? *obs.*). [f. *SHIKSA: see -STER.] (See quots. 1937, 1965.)

1839 H. BRANDON in W. A. Miles *Poverty, Mendicity & Crime* 165/1 *Shickster*, a lady. **1846** *Swell's Night Guide* p. iii, The..bully, or cracksman, who would screw a drum,..collar the shiksters denarly, or paste a greenhorn. **1882** *Sydney Slang Dict.* 10/2 He got the cant of togs from a *shickster* whose husband's in a bone-box. **1937** PARTRIDGE *Dict. Slang* 755/2 *Shickster*, any (Gentile) woman or girl..a none too respectable girl or woman. **1965** *English Studies* XLVI. 454 The way for *shyster* in American English is paved by *shickster*..of Yiddish origin; in criminals' cant it designated a respectable girl or lady..but it soon deteriorated to 'prostitute'.

‖ **shidduch** (ʃi·dəχ). Also **shiddach.** [Yiddish, ad. Heb. *šiddūḵ* courtship, arranged marriage.] An arranged marriage, a (good) match. See also *SHADCHAN.

1892 I. ZANGWILL *Childr. Ghetto* I. 108 Every match is a grand *Shidduch* before the marriage; after, we hear another tale. **1968** L. ROSTEN *Joys of Yiddish* 339, I am considering getting married. But I warn you I'll accept nothing but a remarkable *shiddach*! **1976** C. BERMANT *Coming Home* I. i. 16 A *shidduch* was arranged for him and he married the pretty..daughter of a Vitebsk.. merchant.

shiela-na-gig, var. *SHEELA-NA-GIG.

shield, *sb.* Add: **I. 1. d.** *two sides of a shield*: two ways of looking at something, two sides to a question; *the other side* (or *reverse*) *of the shield*: the other side of a question or consideration, the side which is less obvious or which has not been presented (cf. *the reverse of the medal* s.v. MEDAL *sb.* 3 b, Fr. *le revers de la médaille*).

? **1855** A. W. CHAPMAN *Let.* in R. K. Webb *Harriet Martineau* (1960) i. 27, I consider it a great misfortune, in one sense,..a blessing, often times, in another. There are two sides to every shield. **1885** C. M. YONGE (*title*) The two sides of the shield. **1909** P. COLLIER *England & English* i. 16 These beef-eating, port-drinking fellows in Piccadilly..are well enough..but this other side of the shield is distressing to look at. Poor, stunted..denizens of the East End. **1911** H. S. WALPOLE *Mr. Perrin & Mr. Traill* ii. 24 The reverse of the shield is..given in that first letter to his mother.

II. 8. b. A protective device in clothing, as a *dress-shield*.

1884, etc. [see *dress-shield* s.v. *DRESS *sb.* 4 a]. **1897** *Sears, Roebuck Catal.* 321/3 Kleinert pays for the dress if it is ruined by perspiration, if his shields are used in it.

c. *Mech.* (See quots.)

1888 *Lockwood's Dict. Mech. Engin.* 316 *Shield.* (1) A covering employed to protect the bearings and spindles of emery-grinding machines from the action of the gritty dust. (2) A guard placed over or in front of band and circular saws and portions of machinery to protect the workmen from accidents. **1967** J. L. & G. H. F. NAYLER *Dict. Mech. Engin.* 323 *Shield*, a contrivance or covering, protective plate, or screen, to protect machinery or the operator, from damage or accident.

d. *Physics.* An electrically conducting cover of a device or apparatus intended to protect it from external electric or magnetic fields or to reduce or eliminate interference radiated by the device or apparatus itself. Cf. SCREEN *sb.*[1] 6.

1919 J. A. FLEMING *Thermionic Valve* ii. 66 (*caption*) Fig. 34 shows the valve..with copper-gauze shield for protecting from external electric fields. **1947** R. LEE *Electronic Transformers & Circuits* vi. 174 Multiple shields increase the action..because eddy currents induced in the shields set up fluxes opposing the stray field. **1975** D. G. FINK *Electronics Engineers' Handbk.* VI. 32 It is often desirable to shield part of the circuit from electromagnetic fields. The shields can absorb, reflect, or degrade (by multiple internal reflections) the electromagnetic energy. The most commonly used shields are braided copper.

e. *Physics.* A mass of material, usu. lead or concrete, intended to absorb neutrons and other ionizing radiation emitted by a reactor or accelerator. See also *biological shield* s.v. *BIOLOGICAL *a.*

1933 *Proc. R. Soc.* A. CXLI. 262 The steel shield S prevents the impact of secondary electrons upon the glass walls. **1947** M. D. KAMEN *Radioactive Tracers in Biol.* iv. 93 Protection against γ radiation is best afforded by working with remote control devices behind heavy lead shields at least 2–3 inches thick. **1962** *Newnes Conc. Encycl. Nuclear Energy* 756/2 Such a shield is an iron or barium loaded concrete. The main part of the shield in most reactors, called the bulk or biological shield, is made of such material. **1974** *Encycl. Brit. Macropædia* XIII. 319/1 Typically, a 'core barrel'..is enclosed in a thermal shield, a pressure vessel, a water shield against neutrons, and a blanket of reinforced concrete for gamma-ray absorption.

III. 15. d. A policeman's badge of office. *U.S.*

1903 *N.Y. Evening Post* 29 Oct. 3 The ex-policeman who turned in his shield in September. **1956** 'E. MCBAIN' *87th Precinct* (1959) 19 Why don't you turn in your shield? Become a hackie or something? **1970** E. R. JOHNSON *God Keepers* xv. 167 Nobody said that a detective rating..and a shield provided detectives with all the right answers.

16. b. A shield-shaped centre of a chair-back.

1897 [see *shield-back* adj., sense 19a below].

17. (Earlier example.)

1855 *Poultry Chron.* III. 140/1 (*table*) Toys, or any other Variety [of pigeon] not mentioned above; such as Suabians.., Shields, Swiss, &c.

17*. *Physical Geogr.* **a.** A large, seismically stable mass of Archaean basement rock having the form of a flat or gently convex peneplained platform and usu. forming the nucleus of a continent. Freq. with capital initial in proper names, as *Baltic, Canadian Shield.* [tr. G. *schild* (introduced in this sense by E. Suess *Das Antlitz der Erde* (1888) II. III. ii. 42).]

In quot. 1968 *ellipt.* for *Canadian Shield.*

1906 H. B. C. SOLLAS tr. *Suess's Face of Earth* II. III. ii. 30 The whole of the north-east of America, from the mouth of the St. Lawrence to that of the Mackenzie.. belongs to a broad table-land of horizontal Palaeozoic beds, from beneath which the Archaean foundation crops out in the middle of the table-land not unlike a flat shield. This Archaean shield is thus surrounded by a ring of horizontally stratified sediments... It is to the exposed Archaean surface that we give the name of the Canadian shield. **1906** [see *BALTIC *a.* 3]. **1915** C. SCHUCHERT *Text-bk. Geol.* II. xxi. 461 Most of the present continents have been formed around ancient protuberances of the lithosphere, the nuclear lands or shields. **1939** A. K. LOBECK *Geomorphol.* i. 4 Suess showed that certain substantial areas of the earth have always been rigid and unyielding, as, for example, the Canadian and Baltic Shields of America and Europe, the eastern Siberia Shield of Asia, [etc.]. **1963** D. W. & E. E. HUMPHRIES tr. *Termier's Erosion & Sedimentation* ii. 40 The ancient shields, which are also called 'old platforms', are none other than peneplains which have almost attained a final form. **1968** *Beaver* Autumn 14/1 He was with the voyageurs somewhere out in the bush covering some historic route over the Shield. **1969** BENNISON & WRIGHT *Geol. Hist. Brit. Isles* iii. 41 Before the break up of the continents the Lewisian rocks were probably contiguous with the Canadian-Greenland shield, one of the original continental cores. **1971** I. G. GASS et al. *Understanding Earth* iii. 55/1 The oldest continental regions, the Precambrian Shields, are often dominated by igneous rocks such as granite or by highly metamorphosed rocks such as gneiss.

b. The dome of a shield volcano.

1937 *Bull. Volcanologique* I. 94 Composite structures resulting from the accumulations of a series of shifting vents of shield type. **1943** *Amer. Jrnl. Sci.* CCXLI. 241 On the north and northwest its great lava shield abuts against the dormant or extinct volcanoes of Mauna Kea and Hualalai, and on its southeastern slope rests the smaller, younger shield of Kilauea volcano. **1976** *Sci. Amer.* Jan. 33/2 Olympus Mons is enormous by terrestrial standards. Its shield is between 500 and 600 kilometers across, some five times larger than the largest shield on the earth.

IV. 18. a. (sense 15 d) *shield number.*

1972 J. GORES *Dead Skip* i. 8 The policeman..repeated his name, adding his shield number.

c. *shield-backed* adj. (earlier example).

1880 [see *REGENCY 7 b].

19. shield-back *a.*, having a shield-shaped back; **shield volcano** [tr. G. *schildvulkan* (H. Reck 1910, in *Geol. und palæont. Abhandl.* IX. 84)], a volcano having the form of a very broad dome with gently sloping sides, characteristic of the eruption of basic lavas of low viscosity.

1897 K. W. CLOUSTON *Chippendale Period Eng. Furnit.* 65 In the 'shield back' chair, which is Hepplewhite's favourite shape, the shield and its interior ornament making the splat never touch the seat of the chair at all. **1939** *Country Life* 11 Feb. p. xxvii (Advt.), Fine Antique Hepplewhite Mahogany Shield-back Arm Chair with attractively carved splats. **1978** *Morecambe Guardian* 14 Mar. 9/7 Other new items are shield-back dining chairs and matching carver chairs with loose drop-in seat. [**1911** *Geol. Mag.* VIII. 59 The so-called 'Schild' volcanoes in Iceland.] **1911** *Geogr. Jrnl.* XXXVII. 666 These shield-volcanoes rise from a roundish base, with a gently convex surface surmounted by an elevated ring surrounding the crater. **1944** A. HOLMES *Princ. Physical Geol.* xx. 457 Hawaii..has been built up from the sea floor by the coalescence of several shield volcanoes. **1977** *Whitaker's Almanack 1978* 1037/1 The Isla Fernandina is the summit of a very large shield volcano rising from the sea floor to 1,495 metres above sea-level.

b. shield snake, a venomous southern African snake, *Aspidelaps scutatus*, distinguished by a large scale on its head.

1910 F. W. FITZSIMONS *Snakes S. Afr.* iv. 84 This snake is known as the Shield Snake, because it has a large scale on its nose which is partly detached at the sides. **1973** *Stand. Encycl. S. Afr.* IX. 613/1 The shield-snake is egg-laying.

shield, *v.* Add: **1. b.** *Electr.* = *SCREEN *v.* 1 c. Const. *from, against.* Also *absol.*

1922 *Wireless World* 1 July 416/1 The high amplifications possible with multi-stage valve receivers..lead to unexpected results when endeavouring to shield instruments from radio frequency fields. **1935** F. E. TERMAN *Measurements in Radio Engin.* xiv. 342 There are circumstances when it is desirable to shield against electrostatic fields without interfering in any way with the magnetic fields which are present. **1970** J. SHEPHERD et al. *Higher Electr. Engin.* (ed. 2) vii. 226 Sometimes sufficient shielding can be obtained by a few short-circuited copper turns, placed round the object to be shielded in such a direction that the axis of the turns is in the direction of the magnetic field.

shielded, *ppl. a.* **4.** (Further examples.)

1927 *Morning Post* 8 Sept. 10/1 The high frequency stage should be screened, and if one of the new shielded valves is used the circuit will be a simple one, easily handled, and cheaply built. **1970** J. SHEPHERD et al. *Higher Electr. Engin.* (ed. 2) vii. 225 For steady (or static) fields, the only method of achieving shielding is to provide a low-reluctance magnetic path for the stray flux, in such a way that this flux bypasses the shielded point.

shielding, *vbl. sb.* Add: **2.** *Physics.* Material which protects or shields: **a.** against electric and magnetic fields (cf. *SHIELD *sb.* 8 d); also, a shield.

1930 *Proc. IRE* XVIII. 435 The complete exciter unit is enclosed with a metal grill in addition to the individual shielding compartment for the various stages. **1933** *Practical Wireless* 4 Feb. 962/2 A heavy flexible metal shielding fits tightly over these bakelite shells, and through the shells ordinary rubber-covered lead-in wire is threaded. **1975** D. G. FINK *Electronics Engineers' Handbk.* XVII. 31 The Wagner ground connection..can be used in place of shielding at lower frequencies if the utmost precision is not required.

b. against radiation (cf. *SHIELD *sb.* 8 e).

1945 HAWLEY & LEIFSON *Atomic Energy* 185 There was not sufficient radioactive emanation to be dangerous within a radius of fifty feet of the pile; notwithstanding this, precautionary shielding would be necessary in a locomotive unit. **1950** *Chemical Engin. Progress* XLVI. 109/1 To critical size must be added enough shielding to make reactors safe, and the amount of shielding required ..is of considerable volume and weight. **1958** W. K. MANSFIELD *Elem. Nucl. Physics* v. 45 The shielding of a reactor will be designed to absorb the γ-rays rather than α and β-rays. **1974** *Encycl. Brit. Macropædia* XIII. 319/1 The shielding of the reactor must keep heat losses and radiation levels external to the reactor down to acceptable levels.

shift, *sb.* Add: **IV. 10. a.** For 'Now *rare*' read 'Now chiefly *N. Amer.*' and add further examples.

1927 M. DE LA ROCHE *Jalna* xix. 250 He pictured her in a fine embroidered shift, curled softly beneath the silk eiderdown. **1929** W. FAULKNER *Sartoris* 177 The flowers you know are all there, in their shifts and with their hair combed out for the night. **1936** M. DE LA ROCHE *Whiteoak Harvest* xxii. 301 She is such a slack creature that I dare say the poor child doesn't own a clean shift.

b. A straight loose dress.

1957 M. B. PICKEN *Fashion Dict.* 293/1 *Shift*,..loose dress hanging straight from shoulders, with fulness closely belted at waistline. **1965** H. L. BROCKMAN *Theory of Fashion Design* v. 95/2 The shift automatically lengthens the figure at the expense of widening it at the waistline. **1975** D. LODGE *Changing Places* v. 177 Girls in kaftans, saris, skinny sweaters, bloomers, shifts, muu-muus.

V. 14. a. *to get a shift on* (colloq.), to get a move on (see MOVE *sb.* 6 in Dict. and Suppl.).

1906 [see *POLE *v.*[1] 8]. **1977** *Times Educ. Suppl.* 21 Oct. 9/2 We could have started certainly a year earlier, even two years earlier if we had got a shift on.

c. *Physics.* A displacement of a spectral line from the expected position or from some reference position; hence, a change of an energy level in an atom, molecule, etc.; *chemical shift*, in nuclear magnetic resonance or Mössbauer spectroscopy, the position of a resonance in the spectrum measured relative to some standard signal, the separation being characteristic of the chemical environment of the resonating nucleus. See also *RED SHIFT.

1884 *Phil. Mag.* XVIII. 161 A shift of the lines towards the more refrangible side of the spectrum. **1897** *Astrophysical Jrnl.* V. 210 Here is certainly a *vera causa* for some shift towards the red in molecules causing light. **1932** *Physical Rev.* XLII. 350 The direction of the shift is again such that Hg^{204} has the highest energy. **1945** R. A. SAWYER *Exper. Spectroscopy* v. 118 Changes in temperature and pressure may lead to serious difficulties in prism spectrographs through broadening and shifts of spectral lines. **1952** *Physical Rev.* LXXXVIII. 1070/1 A shift in the nuclear resonance, known as the chemical shift, is due to the effects of diamagnetism and induced paramagnetism in a molecule. **1961** A. D. THACKERAY *Astron. Spectroscopy* xiii. 186 Interpreted as a radial velocity this shift implies that the nebula in question is running away from us at a speed of slightly over 60,000 km/sec. **1966** *McGraw-Hill Encycl. Sci. & Technol.* VIII. 600a/1 Chemists have become interested in using the Mössbauer effect because of the isomer shift (also called isomeric or chemical shift); this results from the interaction of the electron density..at the nucleus with the nuclear charge. **1970** G. K. WOODGATE *Elem. Atomic Struct.* viii. 154 Since the perturbing states of opposite parity lie a long way away,..one expects the Stark shift of the ground state to be small. **1978** P. W. ATKINS *Physical Chem.* xix. 625 The two methylene protons are in a different part of the molecule; they therefore have a different chemical shift, and come into resonance at another magnetic field.

d. *Philol.* A phonetic change. See also **accent-shift, *consonant-shift, *sound-shift, *stress-shift, *vowel-shift.*

[**1875**: in Dict., sense 14 b.] **1894** O. F. EMERSON *Hist. Eng. Lang.* xiv. 241 § 271 The shift from voiceless to voiced in certain positions has taken place since Teutonic times. **1909** O. JESPERSEN *Mod. Eng. Gram.* (1949) I. viii. 231 In most cases the spelling had become fixed before the shift, which..is one of the chief reasons of the divergence between spelling and sound in English... The shift may be represented graphically. **1934** PRIEBSCH & COLLINSON *German Lang.* II. i. 86 A clean cut was made between those dialects which underwent the shift and those which remained unaffected. *Ibid.* 88 The shift from stop to spirant was carried out over the whole High German area.

e. A change of gear in a motor vehicle. *N. Amer.*

1915 V. W. PAGÉ *Questions & Answers* (rev. ed.) xxvii. 446 The clutch must be disengaged before a shift can be made. **1947** R. F. KUNS in Kuns & Plumridge *Automotive Fundamentals: Chassis & Power Transmission* 164 The overdrive shift is made automatically, by simply lifting the foot from the accelerator for about 1½ seconds.

f. *Chem.* A migration of an atom or group, or of electrons, from one point in a molecule to another, or occas. between molecules, in a chemical reaction.

1932 *Jrnl. Amer. Chem. Soc.* LIV. 3278 The shift of the electron pair includes the atom or group which it holds. **1947** *Ibid.* LXIX. 290/2 On the other hand, the hydrogen atom with its pair of electrons might be transferred by an *inter* rather than an *intra* molecular shift. **1953** C. K. INGOLD *Structure & Mechanism in Org. Chem.* ix. 482 Other rearrangements involve only the shift of a methyl group to an adjoining position. **1968** R. O. C. NORMAN *Princ. Org. Synthesis* xiv. 435 A typical example of a hydride shift occurs in the reaction of a primary aliphatic amine with nitrous acid; e.g. n-propylamine gives isopropanol, together with propylene, and only a trace of n-propanol. **1975** C. J. COLLINS in R. F. Brown *Org. Chem.* xvi. 535*b* Prior to our explanation it was commonly held that all 1,2-shifts—for example, of hydrogen, alkyl, or aryl during Wagner–Meerwein, pinacol, Demjanov rearrangements and the like—took place with inversion of configuration at the migration terminus.

g. *Computers.* The movement of the digits of a word in a register one or more places to left or right, equivalent to multiplying or dividing the corresponding number by a power of whatever number is the base.

1946 *Ann. Computation Lab. Harvard Univ.* I. 73 The first molding is..used for reset and the second to read out the tens digit of the amount of shift in conjunction with the proper molding of the first column... The shift is counted to the right. **1966** *IFIP–ICC Vocab. of Information Processing* 70 Digits shifted beyond the end of the word or register may simply be dropped, or in a cyclic shift (or end-around shift) they may be returned to the opposite end of the word or register in a circular fashion. **1970** O. DOPPING *Computers & Data Processing* v. 80 Sometimes it is necessary to analyze the individual characters of a word. The computer can do this by means of shift instructions. These are instructions for left shift and right shift.

15. b. *Pianoforte.* The mechanism for or act of shifting the keyboard action by means of the soft pedal.

1896 A. J. HIPKINS *Pianoforte* 41 Unless these are directly opposite the strings by a decided shift or return, a snarling quality of tone will be heard. *Ibid.* Up to about 1830 there was a further shift permissible to one string only, the *Una Corda* of Beethoven. **1944** W. APEL

Harvard Dict. Mus. 778/2 Beethoven..not only calls for a gradation in three steps..but even for a gradual execution of the shift: *poco a poco due corde.*

17*. Something which effects a shift. **a.** A mechanism for changing gear in a motor vehicle; a gear-lever. Cf. *gear-shift* s.v. *GEAR *sb.* IV. *N. Amer.*

1914 *Automobile* 9 Apr. 771/2 (Advt.), New electric shift. 1926 F. Scott Fitzgerald *Great Gatsby* vii. 144 'Shall we all go in my car?' suggested Gatsby... 'Is it standard shift?' demanded Tom. 1968 *Globe & Mail* (Toronto) 13 Jan. 26/1 (Advt.), Mercury Parklane Marauder...radio, bucket seats, floor shift. 1978 J. Irving *World according to Garp* xii. 224 The gear knob of the Volvo's stick shift came off in her hand.

b. = *shift key*, sense 18 below.

1919 H. Etheridge *Dict. Typewriting* 208 It is usual to provide duplicate keys on each side of the keyboard, so that the shift may be operated with either hand. 1936 A. Dvorak et al. *Typewriting Behavior* x. 260 Really you strike the shift just a tiny fraction of a second before you strike the capital letter. 1957 A. C. Lloyd et al. *Gregg Typewriting for Colleges* 10 A-finger reaches over, to Shift.

c. = *shift code*, sense 18 below.

1957 *Encycl. Brit.* XXI. 886/2 With such a code [as the Baudot code] it is possible to obtain 32 different combinations, 26 of which are assigned to letters of the alphabet, leaving 1 for the idle condition, and 5 for functions such as space, figure shift, letter shift, etc. 1972 *Computers & Humanities* VI. 149 The tape punch would consequently have fewer possibilities than the card punch, if this numer of 44 were not doubled by a shift giving an extra punch code to change from lower to upper case, or from upper to lower case. 1980 L. Moore *Foundations Programming with Pascal* ii. 38 The 5-bit code commonly used by Creed teleprinters had two shift-codes, a 'letter shift' and a 'figure shift'. Each of the remaining thirty codes was mapped to two characters, one belonging to the 'letter' set and the other to the 'figure' set.

17.** *Telegr.* and *Computers.* A change from one set of characters to another; also, a set of characters indicated by any particular shift code.

1913 H. W. Pendry *Baudôt Printing Telegraph System* 2 He adapts therein several elements of the earlier Hughes system—namely, the type-wheel and printing arrangement as well as a similar figure shift device. 1928 A. Williams *Telegr. & Teleph.* ii. 33 The possible number of permutations is thirty-one, but each of these can be made to signify either of two characters by a 'shift' at the receiving end corresponding to the shift key of an ordinary typewriter. 1960 M. G. Say et al. *Analogue & Digital Computers* ix. 265 Such an arrangement is very appropriate in telegraphy, where changes from one shift to the other are not common. 1967 D. G. Hays *Introd. Computational Linguistics* iv. 75 Some of the shifts are capitalization, boldface, superscript, and large. Most alphabets require shifts and diacritics. 1970 O. Dopping *Computers & Data Processing* ii. 41 We say that the characters are in two shifts, a letter shift and digit shift, in the same way as the characters on a typewriter are in two shifts or cases. 1971 T. C. Collocott *Dict. Sci. & Technol.* 1064/1 In teleprinters, one shift is capital letters, the other figures and special signs.

VI. 18. *shift-worker, -working* (sense 12); *shift-strap* (sense 10); **shift character, code,** *Telegr.* and *Computers*, a character in a code that indicates that subsequent characters are to be interpreted in terms of a different fount or coding scheme; **shift dress** = sense *10 b; **shift-key,** a key for adjusting the mechanism in a typewriter when characters in a different position on the keys, such as capitals, are to be used; **shift lever** *N. Amer.*, a gear-lever in a motor vehicle; **shift-lock,** a device for holding the shift-key of a typewriter continuously depressed; also *attrib.*; **shift register** *Computers*, a register specifically intended for subjecting data to a shift (sense 14 g above); **shift-round** *colloq.*, reallocation of positions, a move to another position; **shift-sign** *Phonetics* (see quot. 1939); **shiftsman** (see quot. 1921); **shift-stick** *colloq.*, a gear-lever in a motor vehicle; **shift terminator** *Computers*, a character introduced into a string of text to cancel the effect of a preceding shift code; **shift valve,** a valve that moves to produce automatic gear-changes in a motor vehicle.

1967 D. G. Hays *Introd. Computational Linguistics* iv. 75 But there are also 8 shift characters, that influence the style or position of following graphic characters, and a shift terminator. 1970 O. Dopping *Computers & Data Processing* ii. 41 After the letter shift character in the teleprinter code, all the following characters are interpreted as belonging to the letter case until there is a digit shift character, and vice versa. 1967 D. G. Hays *Introd. Computational Linguistics* iv. 70 When we read a shift code, we must remember what shift we are in until receiving another. 1972 *Computers & Humanities* VI. 149 We get 44 characters which may be preceded by either the upper-case or the lower-case shift code. 1980 Shift code [see sense 17* c above]. 1966 Shift-dress [see *Ming sb.² c]. 1970 'D. Halliday' *Dolly & Cookie Bird* iii. 30, I was wearing a high-necked shift dress. 1893 *Manual of Typewriter* 1. 15 When the machine in use is one with a single keyboard,—that is to say, one with a shift-key by the depression of which the upper-case characters are brought into play,—the shift-key should be governed by the little finger. 1940 M. Crooks *Home Instruction Course in Touch Typewriting* 56 You may like to note, whilst on the subject of the shift key, that there is an additional key—usually above one of the shift keys—called the 'Shift Lock'. 1980 *Daily Tel.* 4 Nov. 13/4 Beth Porter as mehitabel (archie couldn't work the shift key) in *the roach and the pussycat.* 1920 F. B. Scholl *Automobile Owner's Guide* 7 Place the shift-lever into the first-speed slot and let up on the clutch pedal. 1973 R. Hayes *Hungarian Game* xlvii. 286 When the engine turned over he jammed the shift lever into reverse and pressed the accelerator. 1899 J. Wardle *Universal Typewriter Man.* 21 Shift lock.—When it is desired to write a large number of capital letters or signs, the Cylinder may be brought forward by means of the Lock Handle, and this action will fasten the Cylinder in that position. 1936 M. Crooks *Bk. of Remington Typewriter* iii. 27 The action of the shift lock key is quite simple. 1977 E. Mackay *Typewriting Dict.* 195 The shift key should be depressed by the little finger... If a whole word, heading, sentence, etc., is required in capital letters, the typist should depress the shift lock, which 'locks' the typewriter mechanism. 1950 W. W. Stifler *High-Speed Computing Devices* xiii. 299 A multiplier might be devised using the parallel adder and the shift register... The product accumulator is twice the length of the operand registers and is also a shift register. 1975 *Nature* 27 Mar. 366/3 A bubble device consists simply of an assembly of a number of integrated circuits each of which carries magnetically activated tracks, that is, shift registers, along which are driven patterns of bubbles and gaps representing binary data. 1940 J. Reith *Diary* 3 Apr. (1975) v. 244 Cabinet changes tonight..a weird shift-round. *a* 1974 R. Crossman *Diaries* (1975) I. 611 Thursday, the day of my shift-round. 1939 B. Bloch in H. Kurath et al. *Handbk. Linguistic Geogr. New England* iv. 129 *Shift Signs*..In order to avoid the necessity of using special symbols for the innumerable shades of sound intermediate between any two of the vowels shown in the diagram.., the phonetic alphabet of the Linguistic Atlas provides shift signs in the form of small arrowheads, which are placed after a vowel symbol to indicate varieties heard as articulated in a higher, a lower, a more advanced or a more retracted position than the vowel denoted by the unmodified letter. 1970 *Publ. Amer. Dial. Soc. 1968* L. 5 Shift signs, ʌ raised, v lowered,..are used to show modification of the vowels. 1921 *Dict. Occup. Terms* (1927) § 044 *Shifter, shiftman, shiftsman*..; general terms for labourers assisting repairers, timberers, etc., in building stoppings and clearing falls of stone. *Ibid.* § 054 *Shifter, shiftman, shiftsman*,..works at night, when mine workers are absent, repairing road-ways, etc. 1924 *Public Opinion* 8 Feb. 127/1 Machinery shall be in charge of a competent shiftsman. 1968 *Autocar* 14 Mar. 25/1 (Advt.), Aussies have better things to do with their arms than glue them to a shift-stick. 1975 *Publishers Weekly* 17 Mar. 53/1 Even readers who don't know a shiftstick from a lollipop may find themselves caught up in the pace of this exciting inside-story of a veteran Indy 500 racing-car mechanic. 1922 Joyce *Ulysses* 222 A white petticoatbodice and taut shiftstraps. 1967 Shift terminator [see **shift character*]. 1967 D. G. Hays *Introd. Computational Linguistics* iv. 76 If a whole sentence is in italics, the italic-shift character occurs just once in continuous mode, with a shift terminator at the end. 1949 *Automotive Industries* 1 May 68/3 The mechanism contains other forms of valves designed to perform automatic control functions. Among these are:..shift valve for direct drive, having a modulator valve at one end. 1955 W. H. Crouse *Automotive Transmission & Power Trains* vii. 223 The throttle pressure is applied to the spring end of the shift valve. 1970 *AA Bk. Car* 110/3 A system of brake bands and clutches selected by hydraulic shift valves. 1942 T. K. Djang *Factory Inspection in Gt. Brit.* vii. 142 The Home Secretary may require certain conditions for the safe-guarding of shift workers. 1977 *Rep. Comm. Future of Broadcasting* (Cmnd. 6753) iii. 23 Shift workers wanting more entertainment during off-peak hours. 1937 M. L. Yates *Wages & Labour Conditions in Brit. Engineering* iv. 54 Shift-working was the subject of a separate Agreement between the Employers' Federation and the Amalgamated Engineering Union in 1920. 1963 *Times* 6 May (Suppl. Electr. Power Brit.) p. iii/7 Because our tempo of life is geared to what we regard as orthodox hours, shift working is a burden and now disrupts family life.

shift, *v.* Add: **III. 12. e.** To change (gear), move (a gear lever). Also *intr.*, to change *from* one gear *into* another; *to shift up* or *down*, to engage a higher or a lower gear. Also *fig.*

1910 J. E. Homans *Self-Propelled Vehicles* (ed. 7) xxix. 381 In shifting from high to low gears, all intermediate speeds were engaged. *Ibid.* xlv. 625 On shifting the transmission lever for the speed changes, if the transmission be of the selective type, the two movements ..may offer some difficulty to the beginner. 1946 W. H. Crouse *Automotive Mech.* xvii. 388 Let us shift into second and note the actions that take place. *Ibid.* 389 Synchromesh devices come into use when gears are shifted into second and high. 1961 Webster, *Shift gears*, to make a change from one method, tempo, or approach to another. 1962 J. D. MacDonald *Girl* viii. 99 She drove with her brown hands high on the wheel... She shifted up and shifted down. 1965 A. Miller *Incident at Vichy* 32 For some of us it's difficult to shift gears and go into reverse. 1969 *New Yorker* 6 Sept. 105/2 The Rumanians, having barely paused to shift their ideological gears, began holding the..congress. 1970 D. MacKenzie *Kyle Contract* (1971) 13 He drove out of Palamos... He shifted into drive and settled back. 1973 R. Hayes *Hungarian Game* liii. 319, I..shifted from second to third and..let my hand linger a while on the gear lever's mahogany knob. 1973 *Sci. Amer.* Apr. 11/2 (Advt.), Once on the valley floor I shifted up into fourth. 1973 *Time* 16 Apr. 53/1 'We're shifting gears,' says Vail, 'and hiring guys with a track record of seven, eight, nine years' experience.' 1976 H. Nielsen *Brink of Murder* xv. 132 Simon switched on the ignition and shifted into reverse.

f. *Computers.* To move (data) to right or left in a register. Also *absol.*

1946 *Ann. Computation Lab. Harvard Univ.* I. 72 The quotient shift counter..is used to calculate the number of columns the quotient must be shifted to the right upon reading out to the buss in order to conform with the operating decimal position. 1947 A. W. Burks et al. in *Coll. Wks. J. von Neumann* (1963) V. 44 We do not consider multiplication by 2 as a true product since we will have a facility for shifting right or left in one or two pulse times. 1966 *IFIP–ICC Vocab. of Information Processing* 70 Digits shifted beyond the end of the word or register may simply be dropped. 1968 Fox & Mayers *Computing Methods for Scientists & Engineers* ii. 21 The first operation 'shifts' a_2 to the right by $b_1–b_2$ places.

16. b. Also, to spend (money).

1923 E. P. Oppenheim *Inevitable Millionaires* xiv. 148, I should trip it to Monte. That's the place to shift the shekels.

23. To move, to travel, esp. quickly; to get a move on. Cf. *SHIFT *sb.* 14 a.

1922 M. Arlen *'Piracy'* I. i. 21, I am..going to leap on my motor-bike and shift like hell to London. 1968 A. Diment *Bang Bang Birds* ix. 170 The speedo needle clawed its way up..to finally flicker over the 180 mark. Kilometres an hour of course but we were still shifting. 1970 M. Kenyon *100,000 Welcomes* v. 37 You'll have time for a bite at Murphy's if you shift.

shifta (ʃi·ftă). Pl. **shifta, shiftas.** Also with capital initial. [Somali *shúfto* bandit, ad. Amharic.] A Somali bandit or guerrilla, operating mainly in northern Kenya. Also *attrib.*

1950 *Times* 18 Feb. 5/3 Mr. H. V. Rose, who is in charge of the anti-Shifta operations, has reported a steady decline in the number of incidents this month, as the number of contacts made by 'ferret' forces with the Shifta bands has increased. 1959 *Times* 29 June 11/7 The *shiftas*, although they may relieve the traveller of his goods, seldom harm his person. 1967 *Economist* 27 May 900/3 The Kenyan government warned its Somali neighbour that if they went on supporting the ethnic Somali *shifta* terrorists (freedom-fighters, the Somalis say) in Kenya's north-eastern province, Kenya might hit back. 1972 'I. Drummond' *Frog in Moonflower* v. 81 Somali *shifta*..were tough and greedy and they had a perverted sense of political mission. 1977 *Time* 23 May 20/2 About 1,000 *shiftas*—armed nomads of the Western Somali Liberation Front—periodically mount hit-and-run attacks along the Somali frontier. 1980 *Daily Tel.* 8 Jan. 1/8 She might have been killed by marauding Somali bandits called 'Shifta', who are blamed for much of the game poaching in Northern Kenya.

shiftable, *a.* **2.** Delete *? nonce-use* and add earlier example.

1832 *Let.* 17 Apr. in *J. Constable's Corr.* (1962) I. 269 Abram would have accompanied her on Monday, but as business required *his* going *this day*, we thought it quite unnecessary to alter his plans for so *shiftable a young lady.*

Hence **shiftabi·lity,** the ability to be shifted.

1951 [see *SELF-LIQUIDATION 1]. 1972 *Linguistic Inquiry* III. 377 (*heading*) On the shiftability of past participles. 1976 *Language* LII. 39 The shiftability of the NP has nothing to do with whether the containing prepositional phrase has or has not originated in a relative clause.

shifter. Add: **6. b.** The gear-change mechanism or control in a motor vehicle. Freq. *attrib.* *N. Amer.*

1910 J. E. Homans *Self-Propelled Vehicles* (ed. 7) xxix. 378 The arm of the sliding gear shifter meets a raised portion of the reverse shaft. 1915 Hobbs & Elliott *Gasoline Automobile* iii. 67 These two sets [of sliding gears] are operated by two shifter yokes which lead to the gear control lever in the car. 1920 V. W. Pagé *Model T Ford Car* (new ed.) vii. 341 To stop the motor close the throttle and turn shifter to the horizontal position. 1946 W. H. Crouse *Automotive Mech.* xvii. 390 A close-up view of the gear selector and shifter rods. 1972 G. V. Higgins *Friends of Eddie Coyle* xiii. 78 'How come you got the automatic?.. I'd want the Hurst shifter in it.' 'You wouldn't want it once you started buying clutches for it.'

shifting, *vbl. sb.* Add: **2. c.** (Earlier example.)

1793 *Sporting Mag.* I. 198/2 Shifting is running from your adversary, whenever he attempts to strike you, or to come near you, or when you have struck him, and is done with a view of tiring him out.

e. *Philol.* The process of regular phonological change. Cf. *SHIFT *sb.* 14 d. See also *sound-shifting* s.v. *SOUND *sb.*³

1888 J. Wright *Old High-German Primer* vi. 27 The most striking feature in which High German differs from the other West Germanic languages is the general shifting which certain consonants underwent. 1905 O. F. Emerson *Hist. Eng. Lang.* 238 There has been no consistent shifting of a considerable number of consonants as in High German. 1938 *Language* XIV. 112 (*heading*) Phonological shifting in American Norwegian. 1954 F. G. Cassidy in Robertson & Cassidy *Devel. Mod. Eng.* v. 100 Note that though some shifting begins before Chaucer's day, the shift as a whole is subsequent.

4. shifting-boards (earlier example); **shifting clothes, trousers** *dial.*, clothes, trousers, into which a person changes, esp. after work.

1833 Poe in *Southern Lit. Messenger* (1835) Dec. 35/2, I therefore thought proper to contrive a hiding-place in the hold. This I did by removing a small portion of the shifting boards. 1885 F. Gordon *Pyotshaw* 51 Ma guid shiftin' claes clean spilt. 1957 *Scotland's Mag.* June

46 The first of the noisy band of workers came 'skailing' out of the pithead baths, in their shifting clothes. **1913** D. H. LAWRENCE *Sons & Lovers* viii. 199 She wiped him in a desultory fashion, and went upstairs, returning immediately with his shifting-trousers. When he was dried he struggled into his shirt.

shifting, *ppl. a.* Add: **1. b. shifting agriculture** = **shifting cultivation*; **shifting cultivation,** any of several forms of agriculture in which an area of ground is cleared of vegetation and cultivated for a (usu. small) number of years and then abandoned because of nomadic habits or deliberate fallowing or because the yield of crop has become uneconomic, when cultivation is begun elsewhere; hence **shifting cultivator; shifting keyboard** *Pianoforte*, a keyboard action of a grand piano, etc., which is moved by the use of the soft pedal; so **shifting pedal; shifting spanner,** an adjustable spanner.

1934 W. FITZGERALD *Africa* III. v. 354 Cocoa-planting necessitated the abandonment of the old system of shifting agriculture. **1973** W. T. W. MORGAN *E. Africa* iv. 92 In the general absence of fertilisers and lacking any complete rotation system, a system of fallowing was necessary. In the tropics this system has come to be referred to as 'shifting agriculture'. **1922** Shifting cultivation [see *CHENA]. **1952** P. W. RICHARDS *Tropical Rain Forest* xvii. 378 The destruction of the primary forest which gives rise to secondary successions may take place in different ways and for various reasons. By far the most important cause of destruction up to the present has been the system of shifting cultivation (the ladang system of Malaysia and the taunggya system of Burma) which is practised by nearly all the native peoples of the tropics. **1971** J. H. GALLOWAY in Blakemore & Smith *Latin America* viii. 382 Much of the agriculture of Mato Grosso and Goiás is still primitive, unproductive shifting cultivation. **1945** K. J. PELZAR *Pioneer Settlement in Asiatic Tropics* ii. 16 The shifting cultivator does not use the same piece of land every year; instead, he kills or cuts down at regular intervals—every year, every other year, or every third year—the trees of a small forest patch. **1979** *Nature* 16 Aug. 533/1 Shifting cultivators fell and burn forest land, then plant food crops and raise animals and later move on when soil fertility drops. **1896** A. J. HIPKINS *Pianoforte* 40 In many upright pianos, however, although some are made with shifting keyboards..a soft pedal is contrived by mechanically dropping a strip of cloth..between the hammers and the strings. **1922** A. H. LINDO *Pedalling in Pianoforte Music* II. x. 143 The mechanism of the shifting keyboard, which is fitted to many Uprights and to nearly all Grands, is preferable. **1880** GROVE *Dict. Mus.* II. 682/2 The shifting pedal, first introduced by Stein in his Saitenharmonica. **1962** K. DALE tr. *Riefling's Piano Pedalling* 28 As regards the grand piano at any rate, it is correct to speak of the shifting pedal (*Verschiebung*) because the whole mechanism, keyboard and hammer, is shifted slightly to the right when the left pedal is pressed down. **1829** *Mechanics' Mag.* 31 Jan. 423/2, I send you..a plan of a new shifting-spanner, which answers better than the wedge-spanner. **1935** J. GUTHRIE *Little Country* ii. 38 I'll let you have my shifting spanner.

shifty, *a.* Add: **1.** (Earlier U.S. examples.)

1783 *Maryland Jrnl.* 18 Feb. 3/3 Ran away,..a Negro Man, named Pompey,..very artful and shifty. **1838** 'TEXAN' *Mexico v. Texas* 217 Flambeau, who was extremely shifty, soon built up a nice little booth.

2. b. Also *Comb.*, as *shifty-eyed* adj.

1922 H. JENKINS *John Dene of Toronto* i. 11 A shifty-eyed little man. **1977** M. BABSON *Lord Mayor of Death* xiv. 92 He must have looked a right shifty-eyed bastard.

4. Delete *rare* and add further examples.

1907 J. G. MILLAIS *Newfoundland* xii. 244 The wind had dropped, and showed signs of being shifty. **1976** *Yachts & Yachting* 20 Aug. 377/1 Weatherwise the 116-strong fleet had mostly light and shifty winds.

Shiga. (ʃi·ga). *Bacteriol.* The name of Kiyoshi *Shiga* (1870–1957), Japanese bacteriologist, who discovered this bacterium in 1898, used *attrib.* and in the possessive to denote the Gram-negative bacterium *Shigella dysenteriæ*, which causes dysentery in man, and the toxin produced by it.

1900 *Philad. Med. Jrnl.* VI. 423/1 They proceeded upon the false assumption that Shiga's microorganism was a variety of B[acillus] coli communis. *Ibid.*, Comparison of the Eberth–Gaffky and Shiga bacilli show the criterions of difference are by no means numerous. **1946** *Nature* 10 Aug. 207/2 It supervised the production of typhus vaccine and Shiga toxoid, and made suitable recommendations to the Department of National Defence concerning their use. **1947** *Ann. Rev. Microbiol.* I. 313 The Shiga bacillus is rare except in the Middle East and in India. *Ibid.* 316 There is no evidence that the Shiga toxin plays a significant part in producing the pathology of dysentery. **1976** EDINGTON & GILLES *Path. in Tropics* (ed. 2) vi. 328 *Shigella... Subgroup A:* Ten antigenically distinct serotypes, including Shiga's bacillus.

Shigella (ʃige·lă). *Bacteriol.* Also **shigella.** Pl. **-ellæ, -ellas.** [mod.L., f. *SHIG(A + L. *-ella* (see -EL[2]).] **1.** A member of the genus of Gram-negative, rod-shaped bacteria so called, which includes some causing dysentery in man and other animals.

[**1919** CASTELLANI & CHALMERS *Man. Trop. Med.* (ed. 3) xxxvi. 934 Non-motile—Genus 3, *Shigella* Castellani and Chalmers, 1918.] **1937** M. FROBISHER *Fund. Bacteriol.* xxx. 316 A number of the shigellas..(also commonly known as dysentery bacilli) cause intestinal disturbances. **1969** *New Yorker* 11 Oct. 123/3 A shigella infection produces a rather distinctive kind of damage that can be detected by microscopic examination. **1977** *Lancet* 19 Feb. 409/2 Fæces from 11 children and 3 adults who were ill were examined for salmonellæ, shigellæ, and *Staphylococcus aureus* with negative results.

2. = *SHIGELLOSIS. Also *Shigella dysentery.*

1963 G. MAXWELL *Rocks Remain* ii. 21 Immediate veterinary tests showed the presence of liver fluke... When further tests showed the presence of Shigella dysentry [*sic*], we decided to abandon interest in the flukes altogether. **1973** *Daily Colonist* (Victoria, B.C.) 10 May 25/1 Belinda Manybears, three months old, was suffering from shigella, a type of dysentery, at the time of her death. *Ibid.* 1 July 32/2 An intestinal disease doctors have tentatively diagnosed as Shigella swept through the luxury ship. **1977** Shigella dysentery [see *SHIGELLOSIS].

shigellosis (ʃigelōᵘ·sis). *Path.* [f. prec. + -OSIS.] Infection with or a disease caused by shigellæ.

1944 HARDY & WATT in *Jrnl. Amer. Med. Assoc.* 22 Apr. 1179/1 In line with the accepted use of 'brucellosis' for all Brucella infections, we recommend the adoption of 'shigellosis' for all infections due to pathogenic varieties of shigella. **1977** *Proc. R. Soc. Med.* LXX. 374/1 Shigellosis in monkeys closely resembles Shigella dysentery in humans.

Shiho, var. *SAHO *sb.* and *a.*

shih-tzu (ʃī·tsu). Also **shitzu.** [ad. Chin. *shīzigǒu* f. *shī* lion + *zǐ* son + *gǒu* dog, formerly transliterated *shih-tzu kou.*] A small long-coated dog of the breed so called, originally developed in China, often tan or grey and white in colour, with long ears and a tail curling over the back. Also *attrib.*

1921 V. W. F. COLLIER *Dogs China & Japan* iii. 52 These books [*sc.* the imperial dog-books]..portray dogs closely resembling the 'Pekingese' type, as also the 'Shih-tzu' dog and the 'Pug'. **1934** *Kennel Gaz.* May 385/3 It was decided that dogs might be registered under the heading of A.O.V. Shih-Tzu, and that those now registered as Apsos could be altered without charge. **1948** C. L. B. HUBBARD *Dogs in Britain* xx. 328 The Shih Tzu ..is a close relative of the Lhasa Apso with which it has often been confused. **1961** *Guardian* 9 Nov. 10/6 Who,.. apart from dog-fanciers, has ever heard of a shih-tzu? **1969** *Queen* 17 Sept. 56/1 She sits..softly scratching the tummy of one of her Shitzu dogs. **1979** A. CHISHOLM *Nancy Cunard* xxxii. 332 Perhaps she had tripped..trying to avoid one of the Shih Tzu puppies.

Shiism. (Further examples.)

1915 P. M. SYKES *Hist. Persia* II. xlvii. 43 Persia, where Shiism is the official religion. **1964** W. THESIGER *Marsh Arabs* v. 43 Shiism had started as a political movement among Arabs to advance the claims of Ali and his descendants to the Caliphate... In time, Shiism split Islam as decisively as the Reformation divided the Catholic Church. **1982** *Times* 31 May 6/1 From the Gulf to the Levant, there are 2,000 miles of Shiism, broken only by the irritation of Iraq's survival.

shiitake (ʃi,ita·ke). [Jap., f. *shii* a name used for several evergreen trees + *take* mushroom.] A mushroom, *Lentinus edodes*, of the family Agaricaceæ, cultivated in Japan and China on logs from various trees of the family Fagaceæ, esp. *Castanopsis cuspidata* or *Quercus* species. Also *attrib.*

1877 *Grevillea* V. 103 The Shii-take species..have this peculiar excellence, that though they are all but tasteless in their raw state, when they are dried they have an extremely fine flavour. **1925** *Bot. Mag. Tokyo* XXXIX. 319 The best and most common mushrooms in Japan are Shii-take and Matsu-take. **1936** *Nature* 31 Oct. 746/2 Production of the shiitake has little horticultural similarity to mushroom growing. **1953** J. RAMSBOTTOM *Mushrooms & Toadstools* vii. 74 The cultivation of shiitake in Japan is believed to date back over two thousand years. **1961** R. SINGER *Mushrooms & Truffles* v. 139 Logs with Shiitake mycelium were dragged to a suitable site. **1975** J. GRIGSON *Mushroom Feast* 262 On account of the prolonged and laborious method of cultivation, shiitake are more expensive even on their home ground.

Shijō (ʃi·dʒōᵘ). [The name of the street in Kyōto, Japan, where the founder lived.] Used *attrib.* to designate a school of Japanese painting.

1884 SATOW & HAWES *Murray's Handbk. Japan* (ed. 2) 97 The Shijō art was a compromise, retaining Chinese perspective and ignoring the laws of chiaroscuro, but copying details of form in flowers and animals with remarkable fidelity. **1902** *Encycl. Brit.* XXIX. 717/1 Amongst the associates of the Shijô master was the celebrated Ganku. **1970** *Oxf. Compan. Art* 696/2 A subdivision of the Maruyama School called the Shijo School.

shikar, *sb.* Add: Phr. *on shikar*, on a hunting expedition, out hunting.

1944 J. CORBETT *Man-Eaters of Kumaon* 186 Of all the men I have been on shikar with Ibbotson is by far and away the best. **1955** *Times* 14 May 10/5 His service in the Indian Army and his periods of leave, which were almost invariably spent on *shikar*, developed his eye for country and his taste for natural history.

‖ **shikara** (ʃikā·rā). Also **shikarah, shikari.** [Hind.] A long, swift boat used in Kashmir. Also *attrib.*

1875 F. DREW *Jummoo & Kashmir Territories* viii. 181 A *shikāri* is the sort of boat that is in daily use with the English visitors; a light boat, manned..by six men, it goes at a fast pace. **1893** E. F. KNIGHT *Where Three Empires Meet* iii. 35 Leaving our slow doongahs to follow us, we hailed some of the gondolas of Srinagur; long, swift canoes known as *shikarahs*, in which we reclined luxuriously on soft cushions. **1933** *Discovery* Nov. 348/2 A *shikara* or river taxi. **1964** V. S. NAIPAUL *Area of Darkness* iv. 103 Their *shikara* boats were a cluster of red and orange awnings and cushions; and in *shikaras* we were ferried over to the houseboats. **1981** S. RUSHDIE *Midnight's Children* I. 14 The thaw had come rapidly... Many of the small boats, the shikaras, had been caught napping. *Ibid.* 16 He floated past the shikara moorings.

shikara, var. *SHIKHARA.

shikari. Now the usual form of SHIKAREE.

1881 *Encycl. Brit.* XII. 741/1 Rewards are given by government to native *shikàris* for the heads of tigers. **1885** [see SHIKAREE a]. **1907** [see SHIKAREE b]. **1936** W. H. SAUMAREZ SMITH *Let.* 21 Nov. in *Young Man's Country* (1977) ii. 43 When they find that I am neither a Blue, nor a brilliant horseman, nor an experienced shikari, nor a bridge-player, they may think twice about offering the appointment to me. **1964** R. PERRY *World of Tiger* i. 8 Peacocks and tigers live together, say Indian shikaris, because the peacock is a thirsty bird and the tiger is a thirsty animal. **1971** *Illustr. Weekly India* 11 Apr. 45/1, I had become a keen shikari; there were few better areas than the country 80 miles round Delhi for small game. **1977** *New Yorker* 27 June 28/2 We're going to use you for bait, as a decoy. The way shikaris stake out a goat in India.

‖ **shikasta** (ʃikæ·stā). Also † **shekest(h)eh, shikast, shikasteh,** etc. [Pers., lit. 'broken'.] A late cursive Persian script.

1771 W. JONES *Gram. Persian Lang.* 15 As to the Shekesteh, it is very irregular and inelegant, and is chiefly used by the idle Indians, who will not take time to form their letters perfectly. **1849** F. MADDEN tr. *Silvestre's Universal Palæogr.* I. 52 For private affairs and official papers, the writing is generally careless and inelegant, destitute of its diacritical marks, and thence named *shekestheh*, or broken. **1889** SACHAU & ETHÉ *Catal. Persian Manuscripts in Bodl. Libr.* 186 Ff. 51–67 is partly written in Shikasta.., partly in Nastaʻlīk. **1901** KIPLING *Kim* xiv. 364 He..tore a leaf from a note-book, and.. wrote in gross Shikast—the script that bad little boys use when they write dirt on walls. **1954** A. F. L. BEESTON *Catal. Additional Persian Manuscripts in Bodl. Libr.* 4/2 Ff. 604–5 are pieces of a letter in shikasta. **1966** HOSKING & MEREDITH-OWENS *Handbk. Asian Scripts* ii. 20 The last phase in Persian writing was the evolution of the *Shikasteh* (literally 'broken') script from Nastaʻlīk. **1970** G. UNWIN tr. *Jensen's Sign, Symbol & Script* xi. 331 For correspondence the Persians invariably employ the Sikästä script.

shikepoke, var. SHITEPOKE in Dict. and Suppl. **shiker,** var. *SHICKER *a.* and *sb.*

‖ **shikhara** (ʃi·khără). Also **shikara, śikhara, sikr(a).** [Skr. *śikhara*, point, peak, spire.] A pyramidal tower on a Hindu temple, sometimes having convexly curved sides.

1829 J. TOD *Ann. & Antiquities Rajast'han* I. 670 The pinnacle or *sikra* rises, like the crown of the Hindú Cybele. **1838** *Penny Cycl.* XII. 238/1 The body of the temple, or sanctuary,..over which rises a pyramidical *sikr*, or roof. **1891** J. FERGUSSON *Hist. Indian & Eastern Archit.* II. ii. 221 The towers or spires called Sikras.., which invariably surmount the cells in which the images are placed. **1927** A. COOMARASWAMY *Hist. Indian & Indonesian Art* III. 80 In more characteristic examples in the Ganges valley the *sikhara* and cella together form a tower. **1930** K. T. SHAH *Splendour that was 'Ind* viii. 151 Prof. Macdonell is of the view that the *Shikhara* is a natural evolution of the Buddhist Stupa. Later critics of India's art treasures are inclined, however, to hold that the *Shikhara*, with all the symbolism of which it was the concrete and complex expression, was introduced in India by the Vedic Aryans. **1959** HOOYKAAS & CHRISTIE tr. *Frederic's Indian Temples & Sculpture* 297 The temple itself has a *sikhara* of Khajuraho type. **1972** 'E. PETERS' *Death to Landlords* xi. 158 On the outermost platform of rock, its *shikhara* tapering into the air..stood the modern white memorial. **1974** *Daily Colonist* (Victoria, B.C.) 8 Sept. 13/6 But the most noteworthy aspect of the Khajuraho temple is the shikara, or spire. **1977** *Jrnl. R. Soc. Arts* CXXV. 579/1 In the larger temples the *śikhara* tends to be..surrounded by smaller subsidiary *śikharas.*

shikimi (ʃikī·mi). Also **skim(m)i.** [Jap.] A small evergreen tree, *Illicium anisatum*, the Japanese anise, belonging to the family Illiciaceæ, native to Japan and Korea, and bearing aromatic leaves and fragrant white or yellow flowers followed by star-shaped fruits; often associated with funeral rites. Also *attrib.*

1727 J. G. SCHEUCHZER tr. *Kæmpfer's Hist. Japan* v. xv. 598 He had..a large tub of water standing by him..and some skimmi branches lying by it. **1881** *Jrnl. Chem. Soc.* XL. 918 To this substance..the author [*sc.*

J. F. Eijkman] gives the name of 'shikimine', from the Japanese name of the fruit 'shikimi'. **1889** J. J. Rein *Industries Japan* 136 The fruits of the Skimi, which is consecrated to Buddha and therefore much grown about Buddhist temples and cloisters, made a great stir some time ago. They came to market as a spice, instead of the Star anis, which they closely resemble, and turned out to be poisonous. **1896** L. Hearn *Kokoro* iii. 43 A vase containing *shikimi*—that sacred plant used in the Buddhist ceremony of making offerings to the dead. **1976** E. H. Walker *Flora of Okinawa & Southern Ryukyu Islands* 472 Shikimi, a variant of *ashiki-mi*, bad (i.e. poisonous) fruits. In Buddhist ceremonies the leaves are burned as incense.

shikimic (ʃiki·mik), *a. Biochem.* [ad. F. *shikimique* (J. F. Eijkman 1885, in *Recueil des Travaux chim. des Pays-Bas* IV. 49), f. Jap. *shikimi* Japanese anise (from which it was first isolated): see prec., -ic.] *shikimic acid*: a hydro-aromatic acid, $C_6H_6(OH)_3(COOH)$, which is formed in many bacteria and higher plants as an intermediate in the synthesis of phenylalanine, tyrosine, and other aromatic compounds from aliphatic precursors.

1886 *Jrnl. Chem. Soc.* L. 95 Shikimic acid, $C_7H_{10}O_5$, ..is a white, crystalline compound, insoluble in alcohol, ether, and chloroform, but readily soluble in water. **1953** Fruton & Simmonds *Gen. Biochem.* xxxi. 742 It would appear..that at least four aromatic compounds can be formed from carbohydrate by mechanisms that involve shikimic acid as an intermediate. **1978** *Nature* 20 July 216/2 The exact nature of the bracken fern 'carcinogen' remains elusive and although various chemicals, such as shikimic acid, which have been extracted from bracken show some oncogenic activity, the major compound responsible has not yet been identified.

shikker, -ur, varr. *shicker *a.* and *sb.*

shikkered, var. *shickered *a.*

‖ **shiksa** (ʃi·ksă). Also **shicksa, shiksah, shikse(h).** [Yiddish *shikse*, ad. Heb. *šiqṣâ*, f. *šeqeṣ* a detested thing + *-â* fem. suff.] In Jewish speech, a gentile girl. Also *attrib.* or as *adj.* Cf. *shickster.

1892 I. Zangwill *Childr. Ghetto* I. i. vi. 158 We must keep a *Shiksah* to attend to the Shabbos fire. **1928** *Daily Express* 21 Feb. 9/2 There is a suggestion that he has fallen in love with a 'shiksa' (a Christian girl), played by May McAvoy, the 'Ben Hur' star. **1930** E. Ferber *Cimarron* xi. 183 His deep-sunk eyes looked at them. *Shicksas.* **1959** M. Levin *Eva* 11 How often as children had we..watched our *shikseh* maids at their prayers, or in moments of closeness with the *shiksehs*..fingered their crosses. **1963** M. McCarthy *Group* xiv. 318 An Orthodox Jew can't marry a shiksah... They frown on exogamy. **1964** D. Gray *Devil wore Scarlet* iii. 26 Daisy isn't Jewish, of course. She's a Shicksa. **1969** L. Michaels *Going Places* 87 Shikse blonde or purple eggplant, she was his wife. **1978** J. Krantz *Scruples* viii. 226 His mother, a lady of the old school, had repeatedly and solemnly warned him that there is a yellow-haired, blue-eyed shiksa lying in wait for every good Jewish boy. **1979** R. Jaffe *Class Reunion* ii. iv. 156 She had heard stories that young doctors had affairs with shiksa nurses.

shilajatu, var. *silajit.

Shilha (ʃi·lhă). Also **Shilh, Shilhah, Shleuh, Shluh.** [Native name.] (A member of) a Berber people of southern Morocco; also, the language of this people. Also *attrib.* or as *adj.*

1713 S. Ockley *Acct. S. W. Barbary* i. 28 It is about 30 days journey distant from Macquanes... They also differ from the other Moors in their language, and have a peculiar dialect to themselves, which they call *Shilhah.* **1841** G. Borrow *Zincali* I. i. vii. 113 The tribes who speak the Shilha language, and who are the descendants of the ancient Numidians. *Ibid.* 118 The sect of Sidi Hamed au Muza... Their language is the Shilhah, or a dialect thereof. *Ibid.* II. iii. 117 The coast of Northern Africa, where only Arabic and Shilhah are spoken. **1882** [see *Kabyle]. **1921** E. Sapir *Language* 73 The Hamitic languages of Northern Africa, e.g. Shilh. **1951** W. Blunt *Black Sunrise* iv. 42 The Berber-speaking inhabitants can be further subdivided into Berbers proper, Shluhs, etc. **1972** E. A. Nida *Bk. Thousand Tongues* (ed. 2) 389/2 Shilha is a Berber language spoken in several dialects throughout southern Morocco. Most Shilha men are bilingual in Arabic and their mother tongue. **1973** A. Adam in Gellner & Micaud *Arabs & Berbers* iii. xvii. 325 *Tachelhit*, the language of the Shleuh, who inhabit the western High Atlas, the Anti-Atlas and the plains or valleys of southwestern Morocco. **1976** K. L. Brown *People of Salé* iii. viii. 153 Generally the term used in Salé for those speakers of Berber languages, whether they came from the Rif, Middle Atlas, High Atlas, Anti-Atlas or the valleys of southern Morocco, was Shluh.

shill (ʃil), *sb. slang* (chiefly *N. Amer.*). [Perh. abbrev. of *shillaber.] A decoy or accomplice, esp. one posing as an enthusiastic or successful customer to encourage other buyers, gamblers, etc.

1916 *Editor* 2 Dec. 518/2 *Shill, copper*:—One who leads the others by patronizing a show or game. **1926** *Amer. Mercury* Dec. 466/1 A wrestler..offered to throw anyone for 500 smacks and a couple of shills accepted his defy. **1935** H. Davis *Honey in Horn* xv. 231 She had often thought of renting him out as a shill for some tent-show evangelist. **1955** T. Sterling *Evil of Day* xxi. 208, I used to be a shill in a Reno gambling club. **1971** J. Gray *Red Lights* vi. 136 The commonest trap was for a shill to haunt Ninth Avenue disguised as a farm hand. **1978** M. Puzo *Fools Die* ii. 19 As a shill she played with casino money... She was subject not to fate but to the fixed weekly salary she received from the casino.

shill (ʃil), *v.*[3] *slang* (chiefly *N. Amer.*). [f. *shill *sb.*] **1.** *intr.* To act as a shill.

1914 L. E. Jackson *Vocab. Criminal Slang* 75 To 'shill' is to act in the capacity of a hired criminal. **1928** *Amer. Speech* III. 376 *Shill*, to boost for the auctioneer. **1948** F. Brown *Dead Ringer* 156 She was going to shill on Walter's wheel. **1965** H. Gold *Man who was not with It* xxv. 236 It's how to get the audience... I shilled for my wife. **1975** *Weekend Mag.* (Montreal) 11 Jan. 9 Canadian advertisers are confined mainly to hockey players when they're looking for an athlete to shill for them.

2. *trans.* To entice (a person) as a shill; to act as a shill for (a gambling game, etc.).

1974 R. B. Parker *God save Child* xxii. 150 Doctor Croft was the one who shilled old Fraser Robinson onto Vicki's scam. **1978** M. Puzo *Fools Die* x. 96 Diane, the blonde that shills baccarat.

shillaber (ʃi·lăbəɹ). *slang* (chiefly *N. Amer.*). [Origin unknown.] = *shill *sb.*

1913 *Collier's* 6 Dec. 29/2 The business men turned out to be 'shillabers', if you know what 'shillabers' are. **1924** G. Bronson-Howard *Devil's Chaplain* vii. 111 One time 'ballyhoo' and 'shillaber', proprietor of 'Chief Bigspoon's..' medicine show. **1940** *Amer. Speech* XV. 122/1 *Shill* or *shillaber*, an accomplice who plays a confidence game so that the *mark* sees him win.

shilling. Add: **1. a, 2. a.** No longer in official use after the introduction of decimal coinage in 1971, but still occas. used to denote five new pence or the five-pence piece.

The coin itself was allowed to circulate for some time after decimalization, alongside the new (and equivalent) five-pence piece, which it resembled in shape, size, weight, and composition.

1974 'J. le Carré' *Tinker, Tailor, Soldier, Spy* i. 18 Spikely discovered..a draft of the next day's examination paper, and rented it to candidates at five new pence a time. Several boys paid their shilling.

b. Also used as a unit of currency (representing variously 12 pence and 100 cents) in other countries, as Kenya, Uganda, Malta, etc.; *freq.* preceded by the name of the issuing country; also, the coin itself.

1921 W. S. Churchill in *Hansard Commons* 30 May 596 As recommended by the Currency Committee appointed in Kenya in February, 1921, the standard coin will be, not a florin, but a shilling... Rupee contracts.. will be construed at the rate of two shillings to one rupee. **1927** W. McG. Ross *Kenya from Within* xii. 208 The new scheme..was that both florin and rupee should disappear, the shilling be introduced and all existing cental coins be degraded, by edict, to half their value. **1969** *Times* 16 Sept. (Somali Republic Suppl.) p. v/3 The internal value of the Somali shilling has..been relatively stable. **1977** *Times* 24 June 14/8 On the free market in Kenya.. 100 Uganda shillings usually bring no more than 20 Kenya shillings.

6. (sense 1 b) *shilling bill*; *shilling gallery* (earlier example); **shilling mark** *Typogr.* = Solidus[1] 2.

1976 K. Thackeray *Crownbird* viii. 161 Priest..tucked some hundred shilling bills into his pocket. **1801** *Monthly Mirror* June 421 He grins and looks broad nonsense with a stare, to the vast delight of the shilling gallery. **1888** C. T. Jacobi *Printers' Vocabulary* 123 *Shilling mark*, the sign thus / which was used in old books as a 'scratch comma'. **1904** Murray & Bradley *Hart's Rules for Compositors* (ed. 15) 29 The diagonal sign / or 'shilling-mark'.

Shilluk (ʃilu·k). Also † **Chillouk,** † **Shelluh,** † **Shelook, Shillook.** [Native name.] The name of a Sudanese people dwelling mainly on the west bank of the Nile: a member of this people; also the Nilotic language of this people. Also *attrib.* or as *adj.*

1790 J. Bruce *Travels to discover Source of Nile* IV. viii. ix. 458 This race of negroes is, in their own country, called Shillook. They founded Sennaar. **1799** W. G. Browne *Travels in Africa, Egypt, & Syria* App. ii. 453 Shillûk is a town of idolaters... The name *Shillûk* is not Arabic, and its meaning is unknown.— When asked concerning their name or country, the people reply *Shillûk.* **1832** W. M. Leake in *Jrnl. R. Geogr. Soc.* II. 26 On the twelfth day they reached the first island of the Shillúks. **1835** *Jrnl. R. Geogr. Soc.* V. 42 Twelve hours farther brought them to the first island of the Shelooks. **1840** *Penny Cycl.* XVI. 232/1 The first island of the Shilluks.. is not far from Aleis. **1873** E. E. Frewer tr. *Schweinfurth's Hrt. Africa* I. 261 The jet-black Shillooks, Nueir, and Dinka, native of the dark alluvial flats, stand out in marked distinction to the dwellers upon the iron-red rocks. **1894** [see *Nuer]. **1913** *Rep. Brit. Assoc.* 633 Dr. Seligmann's discoveries among the Shilluks of the Nile Valley. **1921** E. Sapir *Language* 80 *Shilluk*, one of the languages of the headwaters of the Nile. **1927** *World Domin.* Oct. 319 All travellers note the Shilluk style of hairdressing. **1927** *Times* (Weekly ed.) 29 Dec. 30/1 Across on the east bank you will see the Shilluk. **1949** [see *Nuba]. **1964** E. A. Nida *Toward Sci. Transl.* iii. 51 Shilluk uses 'break' only with objects such as wood. **1973** *Times* 27 Mar. (Sudan Suppl.) p. viii/3 (*caption*) A Shilluk tribesman with a traditional musical instrument in the Southern Sudan. **1976** D. Topolski *Muzungu* iv. 56 The Shilluk repeat the cutting process from quite an early age.

shim, *sb.*[2] Restrict *local* to senses 1–4 in Dict. and add: **5. a.** (Earlier and later examples.)

1860 Clark & Colburn *Recent Practice Locomotive Engine* 62/2 Where no gibs are employed in the cross-head blocks, 'shims' or thickness pieces of sheet-tin or copper are interposed under the ends of the guide-bars. **1916** R. T. Nicholson *Bk. of Ford* viii. 118 Paper 'shims' —that is, slips of paper shaped to the flats—between cap and socket. These 'shims' will prevent your tightening the nuts up too far. **1953** J. Lawrence *Questions & Answers on Automobile Transmission & Steering* iv. 90 To rectify the pre-load, adjust the shim pack between the outer bearing cone and the pinion shank or spacer. **1977** *New Yorker* 4 July 33/2 He took out the shims and adjusted them for proper clearance.

b. *Criminals' slang* (chiefly *U.S.*). = *loid.

1968 L. O'Donnell *Face of Crime* i. 12 The lock was of the deadbolt type that doesn't yield to the opportunist's plastic shim. **1973** R. Parkes *Guardians* i. 8 Had the door fitted flush to the frame, the old perspex shim wouldn't have slipped in. **1977** 'L. Egan' *Blind Search* x. 172 Denny and I went to Nonie's place, and he used a shim to get us in.

shim, *v.*[2] Add: **2. a.** *N. Amer.* Also const. *out.* (Examples.)

1937 H. E. Stafford *Troubles of Electr. Equip.* iii. 46 The only permanent way is..by decreasing the air gap by shimming the pole shoes. **1967** E. B. Nickerson *Kayaks to Arctic* xiv. 126 Each cabin had a single door, well shimmed but still hanging out of plumb. **1974** R. M. Pirsig *Zen & Art of Motorcycle Maintenance* v. 57 You're going to have to shim those out.

b. *Criminals' slang* (chiefly *U.S.*). To open (a lock or door) with a shim. Cf. *shim *sb.*[2] 5 b.

1972 J. Wambaugh *Blue Knight* (1973) ii. 25 The burglar..would shim doors which isn't too hard to do in any hotel.

‖ **shimada** (ʃimā·dă). The name of a town in Honshu, central Japan, applied *absol.* and *attrib.* to a young unmarried ladies' formal hairstyle in which the hair is drawn into a queue and fastened at the top of the head.

1910 Jukichi Inouye *Home Life in Tokyo* ix. 113 Both the *shimada* and the *marumage* are heavy as they require false hair. **1936** K. Nohara *True Face of Japan* v. 173 The unmarried girl wears the *shimada* coiffure. **1959** R. Kirkbride *Tamiko* vii. 53 A Geisha girl, gorgeous in kimono and shimada hairstyle.

‖ **shime-waza** (ʃī·meˌwā·ză). *Judo.* Also **shime waza.** [Jap., f. *shimeru* to tighten, constrict + *waza* art, deed, work.] The art of strangulation; a strangle-hold. Also *attrib.*

1954 E. Dominy *Teach Yourself Judo* 191 *Shime Waza*, the art of Strangulation. **1956** K. Tomiki *Judo* iii. 92 There are two methods of strangling, namely necklock and cheeklock. But the latter is excluded from the practice in *judo*, only the former being referred to as *shime-waza.* **1957** *Judo* (Know the Game Series) 26/2 Lastly there is the shimewaza group (strangling and choking techniques)... The definition is as follows: the strangle aims at compressing the common carotid artery just behind the sternomastoid muscle which runs up both sides of the neck... If this pressure is maintained it is only a matter of a few seconds before the man becomes unconscious. **1978** D. Starbrook *Judo Starbrook Style* vi. 98 A shimewaza is a stranglehold.

shimiyana (ʃimiyā·nă). *S. Afr.* Also **shimiaan, shimiyane, shimya(a)n.** [ad. Zulu *isi)shimeyana.*] An intoxicating home-brewed drink made from treacle or sugar and water.

1870 A. F. Lindley *After Ophir* xix. 306 *Shimyan* and *jwarlar* were produced for our consumption, and we were invited to witness the usual dancing performances at the *kraal* after dark. **1900** J. Robinson *Lifetime S. Afr.* 307 'Shimyaan', a concoction of treacle and water allowed to ferment in the sun. This beverage was maddening in its effects, and the parent of much crime. **1934** R. Campbell *Broken Record* 68 You loaf, you drink *shimiaan.* **1946** *Cape Times* 29 Oct. 5 The presiding magistrate called in a number of native spectators to decide whether a drum of brew before the court was shimiyana. **1949** *Cape Argus* 6 Aug. 1/4 Malinga pleaded guilty to being in possession of three gallons of shimiyane which, he said, he brewed for his own consumption. **1961** T. Matshikiza *Chocolates for My Wife* 76 They plug you cockfull of Shimiyana. Some randy home brew.

shimmer, *v.*[1] Add: **2.** *intr.* To move effortlessly; to glide, drift (*by, off*, etc.).

1904 in *Eng. Dial. Dict.* V. 385 [Yorks.] He shimmered by, a piece o' way off. **1923** Wodehouse *Inimitable Jeeves* x. 102 Jeeves shimmered off, and Cyril blew in, full of good cheer and blitheringness. **1930** C. Williams *War in Heaven* xi. 176 'I just want to shimmer up, like Jeeves, not walk,' she said. **1973** M. Amis *Rachel Papers* 151 Move my hand over her bronze tights, tracing her hip-bone, circling beneath the overhang of her buttock, shimmer flat-palmed down the back of her legs.

shimmeriness (ʃi·mərinės). [f. Shimmery *a.*[1] + -ness.] The condition of being shimmery; a flickering or insubstantial quality.

1913 D. H. Lawrence *Sons & Lovers* ii. vii. 153 Only this shimmeriness is the real living. The shape is a dead crust. **1948** M. Schorer in *Hudson Rev.* I. 76 His [*sc.* Lawrence's] belief in a..poetry in which nothing is fixed, static, or final, where all is shimmeriness and impermanence.

shimmy, *sb.*[1] (Earlier and later examples.)
1837 F. Marryat *Snarleyyow* xliii. 267 We have nothing but petticoats here and shimmeys. **1889** *Macmillan's Mag.* Sept. 360, I did count on gettin' myself a new shimmy. **1952** *New Yorker* 20 Sept. 35/1 To persuade the young matron to doff her wet shimmy.

shimmy (ʃi·mi), *sb.*[2] Also **shimi.** [App. a use of Shimmy *sb.*[1]] **1.** A lively modern dance resembling a foxtrot accompanied by simulated quivering or shaking of the body which first achieved wide popularity in the early nineteen-twenties; a performance of this dance. Also in phr. *to shake a shimmy.* orig. *U.S.*
[**1917** *Variety* 30 Nov. 19/1 The opening number was programed as a combination of 'Strutter's Ball', 'Shimme-Sha-Wabble' and 'Walking the Dog'.] **1918** *Dancing Times* Nov. 35 It is still very, very crude—and it is called 'Shaking the Shimmy'... It's a nigger dance, of course, and it appears to be a slow walk with a frequent twitching of the shoulders. **1920** C. Sandburg *Smoke & Steel* 223 Shimmying the fast shimmy to the Livery Stable Blues. **1922** *Weekly Dispatch* 31 Dec. 9 'Shimmy' banned in New York... The Chicago camel-walk, scandal, balconnades, and shimmy dances must cease. **1924** P. Marks *Plastic Age* 275 That music was enough to make a saint shed his halo and shake a shimmy. **1935** J. T. Farrell *Judgment Day* I. xvi. 387 The building began to waver and dance before his eyes. Funny. The building was doing the shimmy. **1947** M. Berger in R. de Toledano *Frontiers of Jazz* viii. 96 They did the Virginia reel, slow and fast quadrilles and the shimmy. **1956** B. Holiday *Lady sings Blues* (1973) iv. 41 White people.. came to the Cotton Club—a place Negroes never saw inside unless they played music or did the shakes or shimmies. **1975** P. G. Winslow *Death of Angel* xii. 232 Frayne..held the towel behind his hips and did what.. used to be called the shimmy. **1977** *New Hampshire Times* 27 July 12/2 Glasses in New Hampshire cupboards began to rattle as houses started modest shimmies.
2. *transf.* An oscillation or vibration of the wheels, etc., of a motor vehicle or of an aircraft undercarriage; *spec.* = **wheel wobble.*
1925 *Proc. Inst. Automobile Engineers* XIX. 822 This phenomenon..is variously termed 'wheel flap', 'shimmy', 'goldfishing', 'tramping', 'wobble', according to the nationality and imagination of the writers. **1936** *Aircraft Engin.* July 199/1 With the use of the front castorable wheel another difficulty develops..in the form of wheel shimmy. **1940** G. Frankau *Self-Portrait* lxii. 385 'Frankie'..developed a shimmy in her full elliptic springing that made her solid steering column feel like india-rubber. **1943** F. L. Wright *Autobiogr.* (rev. ed.) v. 411 At high speed it would settle down and shake itself almost to pieces in a perfect frenzy (the garage-doctors called it a shimmy). **1958** H. G. Conway *Landing Gear Design* viii. 150 Shimmy can be divided into two basic types: large angle and small angle (or kinematic) shimmy. **1968** K. J. Bunker in J. G. Giles *Steering, Suspension & Tyres* vii. 132 Shimmy..is usually started by road irregularities. **1977** *Grimsby Even. Tel.* 5 May 5/1 (Advt.), Terrific tyre bargains!.. Wheel balancing. Got the 'shimmy'—Got the 'shakes'? Expert correction.
3. *attrib.* and *Comb.*, as (sense 1) *shimmy dance, dancer, dress;* **shimmy damper,** a device fitted to aircraft undercarriages and motor vehicles in order to prevent or reduce shimmy; **shimmy-fox(trot)** = next; also, (a piece of) music to accompany this dance; **shimmy shake, shiver** = *shimmy *sb.*[2] 1; hence *shimmy shaker.*
1928 *Proc. Inst. Automobile Engineers* XXII. 741 It is important when using a shimmy damper to avoid the use of spring connections..in the steerage linkage. **1946** *Jrnl. R. Aeronaut. Soc.* L. 533/2 In only one aircraft had a hydraulic shimmy damper been used, and that was a direct copy of the damper used in Douglas aircraft. **1958** H. G. Conway *Landing Gear Design* viii. 153 (*caption*) A well-known type of American shimmy damper on the rotating vane principle. **1919** *N.Y. World* 17 Jan. 7/5 (*heading*) Shimmy dance is banned in greater New York. **1922** Joyce *Ulysses* 533 You found me in evil company, highkickers, coster picnic makers, pugilists..and the nifty shimmy dancers. **1967** *Boston Globe* 5 Apr. 59/3 A largely nude shimmy dancer put in all the bumps and grinds with a gyrating G.I. **1919** *Honey Pot* I. I. 8 The Eton collar which, in addition to her plain blue 'shimmy' dress.. made her resemble a school-girl of sweet sixteen. **1968** P. Oliver *Screening Blues* vi. 206 The women dressed exotically and were supported by scantily clad chorus girls wearing the shimmy dresses of the period. **1934** C. Lambert *Music Ho!* III. 224 Jannings going to the dogs is not a more melancholy spectacle than some worthy Teutonic fiddler putting a little pep into a 'shimmy-fox'. **1926–7** *T. Eaton & Co. Catal.* 305/1 *Collegiate*—Shimmy Fox Trot. **1928** *Observer* 15 Apr. 12 Instead of a scherzo she has written a shimmy-foxtrot. **1925** Infanta Eulalia of Spain *Courts & Countries after War* i. 18 The history of dancing during the Revolution repeated itself, with the differences that the Carmagnole of '93 was the Shimmy Shake or the Bunny Hug of 1914. **1920** *Sat. Even. Post* 27 Nov. 42/4 Then they was a pair of young shimmy shakers. **1919** *N.Y. Sun* 16 Jan. 14/4, I was dancing the shimi shiver.

shimmy, *v.*[1] orig. *U.S.* Also **shemmi.** [f. prec.] **1. a.** *intr.* To dance the shimmy.
1919 J. R. Pickell *Twenty-Four Days on Troopship* xiv. 74 O, boys, we don't care, If we never get home, If mother will shimmy So long as we roam. **1919** A. J. Piron (*song-title*), I wish I could shemmi like my sister Kate. **1932** J. Laver *Nymph Errant* viii. 199 Constantine shimmied until beads of perspiration gathered on his shiny forehead. **1977** *Zigzag* Apr. 28/1 He gyrates, shimmies, shakes his ass.
b. *trans.* To dance (the shimmy); to shake (part of the body) as in the shimmy.
1920 [see *shimmy *sb.*[2] 1]. **1956** H. Gold *Man who was not with It* xi. 85 Pauline used to tell me..shimmying her loose bare arms of which she was so proud for their milky flesh, 'like this, like that, and ziggety-zaggety'. **1974** J. Irving *158-Pound Marriage* vii. 148 She shimmied her fingers the way Tyrone Williams did before the whistle.
2. *intr. fig.* and *transf.* To shake, quiver, vibrate; to progress hastily or irregularly.
1925 C. R. Cooper *Lions 'n' Tigers* ix. 235 Leader Mary was beginning to shimmy slightly with increased flight. **1941** *Picture Post* 3 May 9/2 The gunfire came surging back... The floor of the basement shimmied underneath me and the whole house shook like a Chinese lantern in a breeze. **1942** *Jrnl. Aeronaut. Sci.* IX. 400/1 It is impossible for any side force to build up on the tire to cause it to shimmy. **1958** H. G. Conway *Landing Gear Design* viii. 152 Aircraft..with less than a certain amount of castoring friction shimmied and those with more did not. **1969** L. Michaels *Going Places* 135 She..shimmied up my arm and hung from my shoulder like a bunch of bananas. **1976** *Times Lit. Suppl.* 2 July 814/3 When his wife was asleep, he would shimmy down a pillar to the ground floor. **1980** *Daily Tel.* 29 Nov. 17/3 Palm, shimmying in the warm breezes all along the coasts.
Hence **shi·mmying** *vbl. sb.* and *ppl. a.*
1919 J. R. Pickell *Twenty-Four Days on Troopship* 73 The star in the heavens, Looked down with a frown, To see mother so shimmied In her shimmeying gown. **1928** Galsworthy *Swan Song* II. xiii. 217 He..watched the dancing on deck—funny business nowadays, shimmying, bunnyhugging, didn't they call it. **1942** R. H. Bound in R. A. Beaumont *Aeronaut. Engin.* xv. 412/2 Main tail wheels have been subject to one very serious defect, namely, shimmying; this consists of violent oscillations of the tail-wheel from side to side when the aircraft is running over the ground. **1972** *Sci. Amer.* Oct. 100/3 Most of the behavior of a nucleus undergoing nuclear fission can be understood as the splitting of a shimmying electrically charged drop. **1977** *Gay News* 24 Mar. 23/1 A mere suggestion of a shimmying hip and you were lectured by a bartender.

shimmy (ʃi·mi), *v.*[2] [Alteration of Shimmer *v.*[1] under infl. of *shimmy *v.*[1]] *intr.* and *trans.* To 'dance' *in;* to transport (a person) quickly.
1923 Wodehouse *Inimitable Jeeves* vii. 76, I bounded into the sitting-room, but it was empty. Jeeves shimmied in. **1930** G. MacMunn *Behind Scenes in Many Wars* x. 187 A small destroyer..would shimmy us over to the beaches from Imbros. **1980** G. V. Higgins *Kennedy for Defense* x. 104, I just love seeing fat fees shimmy out the door to go elsewhere.

† **shimose** (ʃimō^u·se). *Mil. Obs.* [The name of Masachika *Shimose* (1859–1911), Japanese engineer.] A form of lyddite made in Japan. Also † **shi·mosite.**
1904 *Amer. Inventor* 1 June 256/2 An explosive used by the Japanese, and called Shimose, after its inventor,.. is said to be more powerful than either dynamite or guncotton, and to possess features found in no other high-power explosive. **1915** A. Marshall *Explosives* 322 The first satisfactory solution of the problem was the adoption of picric acid by France. This was quickly followed by similar measures taken by practically all the other Powers, each of whom, however, gave the substance a different name; France..Mélinite, England..Lyddite,.. Japan..Shimosite. **1917** *Chambers's Jrnl.* Apr. 258/2 The picric acid compound known as lyddite in England, melinite in France, and *shimose* in Japan.

shimozzle, var. *shemozzle. **shimya(a)n,** vars. *shimiyana.

shin, *sb.*[1] Add: **5.** *shin-guard* (earlier example); **shin-cracker** *Austral.* (see quots.); **shin-oak** (earlier example); **shin-plaster:** for *U.S.* read *Hist.* (orig. *U.S.*) and add: (*b*) (further examples); (*c*) *Canad.*, a twenty-five dollar bill; **shin-splint,** (*a*) (*dial.* (see quot. 1893–4); (*b*) *pl.* (const. as *sing.* and *pl.*), any of a number of painful conditions of the lower leg that may be caused by running on hard surfaces; **shin-tangle** *Canad.* (see quot. 1905).
1928 *Wentworth Mag.* (Sydney) June 33 'Shin-crakers', that is, blows on the shin owing to the rock suddenly breaking off. **1945** S. J. Baker *Austral. Lang.* 99 *Shin-cracker*, a subsoil of close-grained, brittle sandstone where the potch or silica runs. **1969** E. Waller *There's Opal out There* 20 Ailments common to the Lightning Ridge, such as shincracker shin. **1971** J. S. Gunn *Opal Terminol.* 42 *Shin cracker.* Also *shincracker*, common name for the fine-grained Coocoran claystone which on exposure at the surface becomes a hard, brittle, siliceous rock that usually has to be dug through to get to the opal ground. Its name is appropriate because, when worked with a sinking pick or jack hammer, pieces shatter or fly off to strike the digger's shins, hence the injury called 'shin-cracker shin'. **1884–5** *Derbyshire Football Guide* 97 (Advt.), *Shin-guards* ..2s. 6d. **1844** J. Gregg *Commerce of Prairies* II. 200 Black-jacks..[are] intermixed with a very diminutive dwarf oak, called by the hunters 'shin-oak'. **1887** *Grip* (Toronto) 2 Apr. 10/2, I will give further particulars on receipt of a shin-plaister. **1929** H. Colebatch *Story of Hundred Years* xxxvii. 458 The 'shin-plasters' of Connor, Doherty, and Durack, and of many hotel and store keepers, form the regularly accepted currency. **1936** M. Mitchell *Gone with Wind* xvii. 308, I haven't a cent. Rhett, give me a few shin plasters. Here, Big Sam, buy some tobacco for yourself. **1962** H. Green *Time to pass Over* v. 77 Old Josh felt disposed to part with a few of his mouldy shinplasters. **1972** *Tel.* (Brisbane) 10 Nov. 40/1 Some years ago I was working in Boulia, where there wasn't a bank. Shin plasters were issued by Mr. J. P. Howard who owned the hotel at Boulia. **1812** in J. Bell *Rhymes of Northern Bards* 35, I lost a' my shin-splints among the great stanes. **1893–4** R. O. Heslop *Northumberland Words* II. 632 *Shin-splints*, a kind of greave or leg armour worn on the shins by trimmers, etc., to protect the legs in working. **1930** Stedman *Med. Dict.* (ed. 11) 951/1 *Shin splints*, myositis and periostitis affecting chiefly the extensor muscles of the lower lateral aspect of the legs. **1938** A. Thorndike *Athletic Injuries* xxi. 180 Shin splints in track, cross country and other sports are a very definite injury—a tearing of the origin of the tibialis posticus muscle from the tibia in its lower third. **1977** J. F. Fixx *Compl. Bk. Running* v. 71 Shin splints—pains in the front of the leg that are common in beginning runners. **1905** J. Outram *In Heart Canad. Rockies* 176 A dense undergrowth..is often designated by the expressive term 'shin-tangle'. **1973** P. Geddes *Ottawa Allegation* xiv. 181 Nothing else was about except for the birds, making for cover under the shintangle.

Shin (ʃīn), *sb.*[2] [Native name.] One of the Dardic peoples inhabiting the Gilgit agency of Kashmir; a member of this people.
1875 F. Drew *Jummoo & Kashmir Territories* xviii. 428 The table..shows in what countries the Shīn caste is found... The Shīn occur, mixed with Yashkun, along the Indus Valley. **1879** *Encycl. Brit.* X. 598/1 The middle castes, Shin and Yashkun, form the body of the Dard people. The pure Shin looks more like a European than any high-caste Brahman of India. **1910** *Ibid.* XII. 20/1 The dominant race is that of the Shins, whose language is universally spoken. **1913** A. Neve *Thirty Years in Kashmir* ix. 84 My own impression is that the Rajah families were originally Shins... The Shin races (*i.e.*, the Dards) first occupied the eastern Hindu Kush. **1938** R. C. F. Schomberg *Kafirs & Glaciers* xii. 206 The people of Ashret are not Chitralis but Dangariks who speak Palula, a language allied to the Shina spoken at Gilgit... They are probably Shins who came from Chilas.

Shin (ʃin), *sb.*[3] [Jap., = genuine, authentic.] The name of a major Japanese Buddhist sect which teaches salvation by faith in the Buddha Amida and emphasizes morality rather than orthodoxy. Usu. *attrib.* or as *adj.*
1877 W. E. Griffis *Mikado's Empire* (ed. 2) I. xvi. 173 The Shin sect hold a form of the Protestant doctrine of justification by faith, believing in Buddha instead of Jesus. **1904** L. Hearn *Japan: Attempt at Interpretation* xiii. 302 Nobunaga agreed to spare the lives of the Shin priests. **1960** B. Leach *Potter in Japan* ii. 49 Dr. Suzuki is the leading writer on both Zen and Shin Buddhism, both in English and Japanese. **1976** *Education & Community Relations* July/Aug. 8/1 Talks by the Chief Abbot of the Nishi Hongwanji (Shin Sect) of Japan.

shin, *v.* Add: **2.** (Earlier examples.)
1838 J. C. Neal *Charcoal Sketches* 106 Shin it, good man..shin it as well as you know how! **1840** G. T. Strong *Diary* 8 May (1952) 138 One banner in particular —representing Matty shinning away from the White House.
3. Also, to shoot in the shins.
1819 E. Evans *Pedestrious Tour* 214 Soldiers are apt to fire too high. He was often heard to say to his troops in battle: 'Shin them, my brave boys!'

Shina (ʃī·na). [Native name: cf. *Shin *sb.*[2]] The Indo-Aryan language spoken by the Shin. Also *attrib.*
1854 A. Cunningham *Ladák* ii. 37 The Persian character, which all the Dards make use of in writing their own language, of which there are three distinct dialects,— the Shiná, the Khajunah, and the Arniya. The *Shiná* dialect is spoken by the people of Astor, Gilgit, Chelas, Darél, Kohli, and Pálas. **1903** Risley & Gait *Census India 1901* I. I. 310 Shina, one of the non-Sanskrit Indo-Aryan forms of speech. **1936** R. C. F. Schomberg *Unknown Karakoram* I. iii. 39 Shum, which means dog in the Shina tongue. **1977** D. Murphy *Where Indus is Young* vii. 147 Talking rapidly in Shina, the Gilgit language.

shinanigan, -gin, etc., vars. *shenanigan.

Shin Bet (ʃin bet). Also **Shin Beth** and as one word. [mod.Heb., f. *šīn* + *bēṯ*, the names of the initial letters of *šērûṯ biṭaḥôn kᵉlālî* (general) security service.] The principal security service of Israel. Also *attrib.*
1964 L. Deighton *Funeral in Berlin* xlii. 264 Samantha was a Shinbet agent after him for war crimes. **1968** C. Leader *Angry Darkness* xii. 111 Schererzade was now in the hands of the Shinbeth, the coldly efficient and unemotional Israeli Intelligence Service. **1969** A. Marin *Rise with Wind* vi. 76 The statement..went directly to the Shin Beth. **1972** *Guardian* 27 Jan. 3/4 The street always becomes stiff with Shin Bet (Secret Service) men looking studiously unobtrusive. **1981** A. Winch *Blood Money* xiii. 134 A man..who has been positively identified by the Israeli Shin Beth.

shindig. Substitute for entry:
shindig (ʃi·ndig). Also **shin-dig.** [Of uncertain origin: perh. f. Shin *sb.* + Dig *sb.*[1], but infl. by Shindy in later senses.] † **1.** *U.S.* (See quot. 1859.) *obs.*
[**1849**: see *hoe-down.] **1859** [in Dict.].

2. A country dance; a party, ball, 'knees-up'; a lively gathering of any kind. Also *fig.* orig. *U.S.*

1871 B. HARTE in *Atlantic Monthly* Sept. 373/1 'Is this a dashed Puritan meeting?'.. 'It's no Pike County shindig.' **1892, 1899** [in Dict.]. **1935** C. W. PARMENTER *Kings of Beacon Hill* I. xv. 98 Does everyone attend those shindigs, Sandy, or is a girl invited by some special boy? **1946** [see *FURORE 2]. **1956** WALLIS & BLAIR *Thunder Above* (1959) ix. 98 He was killed in an air defence exercise. One of those NATO shindigs. **1959** *New Statesman* 27 June 883/2 The competition among the 'old nobility' to attend what they termed 'Aspers' little shindig' was so fierce that five private detectives were hired to keep out the unwelcome. **1962** E. LUCIA *Klondike Kate* viii. 172 Kate never lacked a date for such shindigs. **1977** C. McCULLOUGH *Thorn Birds* xi. 267 'What's a ceilidh anyway?'..'It's Gaelic for a gathering, a shindig.'

3. = SHINDY 3.

1961 PARTRIDGE *Dict. Slang* Suppl. 1268/2 *Shindig*, an altercation, a violent quarrel, a tremendous fuss. **1966** *Listener* 17 Feb. 255/1 A classic row developed over the half birth of Peter Watkins's film *The War Game*, and this did not wholly distract from the shindig on the other side of the fence about a programme on the police. **1977** 'E. CRISPIN' *Glimpses of Moon* vi. 87 They'd kick up a shindig, naturally, but it was always their husbands they were furious with.

shindy. **3.** (Earlier and later examples.)

1829 B. HALL *Trav. N. Amer.* III. 325, I never saw a more complete row, or as a fellow near me called it, 'a more regular shindy'. **1841** *Sporting Rev.* July 52 The docket of bankruptcy..created, as our polite continental neighbours call it, 'a sensation', or, in downright English, 'a shindy'. **1916** 'TAFFRAIL' *Pincher Martin* vii. 115 If you want to kick up a shindy, Mister Parkin, you'd best do it ourside. **1903** SOMERVILLE & 'ROSS' *All on Irish Shore* vii. 177 There was a frightful shindy, Carew wanting to have his blood, and all the rest of us trying to prevent a row. **1962** L. DEIGHTON *Ipcress File* x. 61 We're not having another Burgess and Maclean shindy, questions in the House and all that. **1976** J. I. M. STEWART *Memorial Service* iv. 53 There was quite a shindy, and there might have been more of it.

shine, *sb.*[1] Add: **2. f.** *spec.* The shiny surface of a new cricket ball.

1950 [see *OPENER 1 e]. **1976** J. SNOW *Cricket Rebel* 30 Mike Smith didn't call upon me until Fred Trueman and Rumsey had seen the shine off the new ball.

3. a. (Further examples opposed to *rain.*) Also fig. phr. (*come*) *rain or shine*, in any circumstances, come what may.

1905 H. A. VACHELL *Hill* vi. 138 With me you're first, rain or shine. **1908** *Sears, Roebuck & Co. Catal.* 1076/2 These overcoats do double service, being adapted for all kinds of chilly weather, rain or shine. **1952** M. R. RINEHART *Pool* vii. 54 She walks everywhere here in the city, rain or shine. **1978** M. BIRMINGHAM *Sleep in Ditch* 115 He said..we'd got to put up with each other for ten years, 'come rain or shine'.

b. Abbrev. of *MOONSHINE 4.

1933 *Sun* (Baltimore) 22 July 8/7 You should take a julep made from the wonderful 'shine' made in the hills of Western Maryland. **1938** M. K. RAWLINGS *Yearling* i. 12 'Goin' to Grahamsville allus do make me hongry.' 'You git a snort o' 'shine there, is the reason,' she said. **1969** P. KAVANAGH *Such Men are Dangerous* (1971) iii. 42 Whiskey? A quart of shine, which the Lord loves, it being a natural product. **1977** E. LEONARD *Hunted* (1978) ix. 90 'Hundred-proof pure Kentucky bourbon. How about that.' Like it was a treat and all Davis drank was some kind of piss-poor shine.

5. An abusive term for a Black. Also *attrib.* *U.S. slang.*

1908 J. M. SULLIVAN *Criminal Slang* 24 *Shine*, a colored person. **1929** D. HAMMETT *Dain Curse* iv. 34 How'd you make out with the shine? **1934** J. T. FARRELL *Young Manhood* III. xv. 227 They saw one beautiful blonde girl with a coal-black, sweating nigger, and they said nothing, only because there were too many shines in the place. **1940** R. CHANDLER *Farewell, My Lovely* iii. 13 His voice said bitterly: 'Shines. Another shine killing. That's what I rate after eighteen years in this man's police department.' **1953** W. BURROUGHS *Junkie* v. 51 A Negro sitting opposite us smiled. 'The shine is wise,' said Roy in my ear. 'He is O.K.' **1969** S. GREENLEE *Spook who sat by Door* xiii. 116 He's a shine detective lieutenant.

shine, *sb.*[2] **4.** For U.S. read *colloq.*, orig. *U.S.* and add earlier and later examples.

1839 *Crockett Almanac 1840* 14, I wonst had an old flame I took sumthin of a shine to. **1934** F. H. BUSHICK *Glamorous Days* xxiii. 278 Nobody wanted the old corn cutter except this Irishman, who took a shine to it. **1956** P. SCOTT *Male Child* II. iv. 152, I suppose I oughtn't to blame you if Marion's taken a shine to you... You must have a way with women. **1961** *Guardian* 23 Mar. 10/6 Shaw evidently took a shine to the young hero-worshipping woman. **1978** L. MEYNELL *Papersnake* x. 132 He took to you... He took a shine to you. **1980** *Times Lit. Suppl.* 18 July 799/1 If her [*sc.* Barbara Pym's] heroines were married, they were not unfaithful to their husbands, although they might take a shine to the curate.

shine, *v.* Add: Forms: *Pa. t.* and *pa. pple.* **shined** (further U.S. examples).

1929 [see *CONCORDANCY]. **1929** W. FAULKNER *Sound & Fury* 105 He wore a derby and shined shoes. **1948** *Sun* (Baltimore) 18 Oct. 12/5 It was full of adept and memorable phrases... It shined with wit and humor. **1950**, etc. [see sense 9 c below]. **1974** *Black World* Jan. 57/1 Her shiny black paint shined in the sun. **1982** *Chicago Sun-Times* 12 July 65 But Red Smith was a beacon who shined for half a century.

9. c. To direct the rays of (a light) *on, on to, under*, etc.

1889 *Cent. Dict.* 5573/3 The policeman *shone* his lantern up the alley. **1950** *Sun* (Baltimore) 14 July 8/4 Two men in the office shined a flashlight under the platform. **1967** P. SHAFFER *Black Comedy* 48 The Colonel takes the torch from Harold and shines it pitilessly in Schuppanzigh's face. **1978** J. IRVING *World according to Garp* xi. 210 The policeman shined his light over Garp. **1979** *Sci. Amer.* Mar. 85/2 The intense light from this source was shined on a crystal that served as a frequency doubler.

10. c. *to shine up to*: to try to please; to make oneself pleasant to. *U.S.*

1882 *Century Mag.* Oct. 827 It was then that David first set out to shine up to her. **1902** S. E. WHITE *Blazed Trail* xlii. 204 You might shine up to Hilda Farrand and join the rest of the fortune-hunters. **1971** C. FICK *Danziger Transcript* (1973) 143, I never saw him sell a single secret..or shine up to a Kraut PW.

shiner. Add: **1. f.** A diamond or other jewel. Usu. *pl. slang.*

1884 *Queenstown Free Press* 15 Jan. (Pettman), When they dug it up they at once came to the conclusion it was a real shiner. **1928** M. C. SHARPE *Chicago May* 287 *Sparklers, sparks, shiners*.., etc.—diamonds. **1934** D. L. SAYERS *Nine Tailors* 274, I never had those shiners. **1959** [see *ICE *sb.* 4 c].

g. A black eye. *slang.*

1904 'No. 1500' *Life in Sing Sing* 253/1 *Shiner*, a discolored eye. **1932** [see *HECK *sb.* and *int.*]. **1934** A. MERRITT *Burn Witch Burn!* vii. 89 All I can do is..be dignified an' maybe hand out a shiner or two if they get too rough. **1943** C. S. FORESTER *Ship* xviii. 114 That's a rare shiner you've got there, Grant. **1958** C. WILLIAMS *Man in Motion* (1959) iii. 29 At first I thought it was because of the shiner and the bruises on my face, but then I began to wonder. **1967** [see *LEFT *sb.* 2 a]. **1977** *Daily Mirror* 16 Mar. 3/5 Annie Walker, Coronation Street's snooty landlady, is about to show up in the snug.. sporting a real shiner. But her black eye is not the result of a well-rehearsed punch-up in the taproom.

h. *Paper-making.* A glistening particle of a mineral impurity on the surface of finished paper.

1922 *Manufacture of Pulp & Paper* III. VIII. 3 In colored papers, shiners will not take the dye. **1963** R. A. HIGHAM *Handbk. Papermaking* vii. 197 When supercalendering papers with a high percentage of straw in the furnish, there is a tendency towards shiners and windows.

2. d. A window-cleaner. *slang.*

1958 *Listener* 20 Nov. 818/2 His fellow shiners disregarded the L.C.C. by-law, because very few windows are equipped with metal hooks for holding on a safety belt. **1967** *Sunday Times* 8 Jan. 3/7 Len is widely regarded as London's top 'shiner' (window cleaner). **1977** *Centuryan* (Office Cleaning Services) Christmas 1/1 There we were, shiners and cleaning ladies, surrounding Fred and Dora on the float by London Wall.

shingle, *sb.*[1] Add: **1. b.** (Further examples.)

1957 J. FRAME *Owls do Cry* 26 Francie Withers has a brother who's a shingle short. **1966** P. WHITE *Solid Mandala* 82 He accepted Arthur his twin brother, who was, as they put it, a shingle short. **1968** *Southerly* XXVIII. 3 Royal said: 'I reckon we're a shingle short to 'uv ended up on the Parramatta Road.'

d. *to hang out* (or *set up*) *one's shingle*, to begin to practise a profession.

1879 [in Dict.]. **1944** V. W. BROOKS *World of Washington Irving* xvi. 308 Catlin hung out his shingle as a portrait-painter and made a little money for his next trip. **1963** J. N. HARRIS *Weird World Wes Beattie* i. 8 He had hung up his shingle and commenced the practice of criminal law in the lower courts. **1977** *Time* 22 Aug. 48/2 Any academic can set up his shingle and be a literary critic.

e. A style of cutting women's hair short, as in the bob, but with the back hair shingled (cf. SHINGLE *v.*[1] 2 a). Also, hair cut in this way.

1924 *Hairdressing* Feb. (*caption*), Based on the 'shingle'. **1927** F. E. BAILY *Golden Vanity* xvii. 265 Doris powdered her face, combed her dark shingle, lit a cigarette, and picked up her beef cubes. **1945** N. MITFORD *Pursuit of Love* xx. 172 She had a short canary-coloured shingle (windswept) and wore trousers. **1975** G. HOWELL *In Vogue* 13/1 The small pitted cloche brought in the bob, which became the 'shingle' or the 'bingle' of the twenties.

2. a. *shingle effect* (sense 1 e); **shingle cap, net**, a cap-shaped hair-net for preserving the hair-style in bed; **shingle wig**, a short-haired wig cut in a shingle.

1926 *Vogue* Late Nov. 85 A charming little shingle cap for night wear. **1934** A. CHRISTIE *Murder on Orient Express* II. xi. 146 She had on a shingle cap and I only saw the back of her head. **1977** 'E. MCBAIN' *Long Time no See* x. 152 Her blond hair was cut in..bangs on the forehead, a shingle effect at the back of her head. **1928** R. MACAULAY *Keeping up Appearances* ix. 89 She had bought..three shingle nets. **1928** *Times* 19 Dec. 15/7 After bathing the shingle-wig was slipped over the dishevelled head.

b. (*b*) *shingle saw.*

1882 R. GRIMSHAW *Suppl. Grimshaw on Saws* 235 One we know of is running a 42-inch shingle saw in heading 1500 revolutions per minute. **1974** D. SEARS *Lark in Clear Air* i. 19 Snoring with a shrill gutter like a shingle-saw slicing knotty cedar.

shingle, *sb.*[2] Add: **1.** In New Zealand also loose angular stones in mountain country.

1900, etc. [see *shingle-slip* below]. **1944**, etc. [see *shingle-slide* below]. **1959** *Tararua* XIII. 46 The word *shingle* itself is given an unusual meaning in New Zealand. In standard usage it refers only to the small roundish water-worn stones of the seashore or rivers. We use it also of moderately-sized, angular stones, such as in fact are found in shingle slides.

3. *shingle-bed* (earlier example); **shingle slide** *N.Z.* (see quot. 1944); **shingle-slip** = **shingle slide*.

1861 C. C. BOWEN *Poems* 76 Ghastly white beneath, Lay stretched the rough, drear shingle-bed. **1944** *Mod. Junior Dict.* (Whitcombe & Tombs) (ed. 7) 365 *Shingle-slide* or *-slip*,..a term used in New Zealand for (steep) mountain-sides covered with loose, sliding stones, in England called 'screes'. **1959** A. McLINTOCK *Descr. Atlas N.Z.* 32 With the baring of the ground between the tussocks, sheet and wind erosion have taken place and there has been a speeding up of the creep of the mantle of rock waste, resulting in the formation of new shingle slides and an increase in area of old ones. **1900** *Canterbury Old & New* 190 One of the most characteristic features of our Canterbury Alps is afforded by the numerous 'shingle-slips' formed by the weathering of rocks. **1971** *N.Z. Listener* 19 Apr. 56/4 The creek beside the shingle slip just below the confluence.

shingle, *v.*[1] **2.** Restrict *U.S.* to senses in Dict. and add: **a.** Also, to cut (women's hair) so that it tapers from the back of the head to the nape of the neck; also *absol.*, to have the hair so cut.

1924 *Punch* 17 Sept. 319 It moves me not if Araminta shingles Her locks, or Evelina has them bobbed. **1926** GALSWORTHY *Silver Spoon* iv. 25 Fully dressed for the evening, she had but little on, and her hair was shingled. *Ibid.*, She had been one of the first twelve to shingle. **1976** M. GREEN *Children of Sun* (1977) v. 207 Women began to bob their hair immediately after the war, were shingling it by 1925.

shingled, *ppl. a.*[1] Add: **3.** Of hair: cut with the ends exposed all over the head or in a shingle. Of persons: having hair so cut.

1889 KIPLING *From Sea to Sea* (1899) I. xxi. 414 The American missionary teaches the Japanese girl to wear bangs—'shingled bangs'—on her forehead. **1924** M. ARLEN *Green Hat* i. 42 Iris Storm was the first English-woman I ever saw with 'shingled hair'. This was in 1922. **1926** R. MACAULAY *Crewe Train* I. iii. 19 She looked..like a Beardsley woman shingled. **1930** W. S. MAUGHAM *Cakes & Ale* xxiii. 231 'Very quiet,' I said to the shingled barmaid. **1953** 'N. SHUTE' *In Wet* vii. 210 He stroked the soft, shingled hair at the back of her head. **1978** *Church Times* 1 Sept. 5/4 Their hair is shingled and rigidly marcel-waved. They stand in Junoesque poses like over-blown flappers.

shingler[1]. Add: **2.** A woman who has her hair shingled. *transitory.*

1926 *Glasgow Herald* 11 Nov. 3/4 Was the first shingler a suffragette? **1929** D. MACKAIL *How Amusing!* 337 Though..Duval has done a certain amount of shingling,.. his shop..has no separate entrance for shinglers.

shingling, *vbl. sb.*[1] Add: **2.** (See *SHINGLE *v.*[1] 2 a.)

1924 *Chambers's Jrnl.* June 483/2 You do not care for the shingling and bobbed hair styles? **1926** GALSWORTHY *Silver Spoon* iv. 25 'My dear girl,' Michael had said, when shingling came in, 'to please me, don't! Your *nuque* will be too bristly for kisses.' **1939–40** *Army & Navy Stores Catal.* 901 Hair Clipper... Specially designed for Shingling, Bobbing, and for removing any superfluous hair.

shingly, *a.*[2] Add: (Austral. and N.Z. examples: see *SHINGLE *sb.*[2] 1.)

1857 J. T. THOMSON in N. M. Taylor *Early Travellers in N.Z.* (1959) 336 The plains are alluvial and shingly. **1878** E. S. ELWELL *Boy Colonists* 182 After a long.. climb, they reached the top. It was bare and shingly. **1926** K. S. PRITCHARD *Working Bullocks* v. 52 They rode for hours..along the shingly ledges of steep hill-sides. **1949** A. E. WOODHOUSE in A. E. Currie *Centennial Treasury Otago Verse* 87 The shingly rivers seaward swirling.

Shingon (ʃi·ŋgǭn). Also 9 Singon. [Jap., = true word, mantra, f. *shin* true + *gon* word.] The name of a Buddhist sect founded in Japan in the eighth century and devoted to esoteric Buddhism. Also *attrib.*

1727 J. G. SCHEUCHZER tr. *Kæmpfer's Hist. Japan* I. II. v. 199 In the 1850 streets of this city, there were ..10 070 of the sect *Singon*. **1834** *Chinese Repository* Nov. 323 There are now in Japan the following sects which are tolerated by government. 1. Zen... 5. Singon... *Singon* means to repeat true psalms. **1880** E. J. REED *Japan* I. iv. 81 The learned Kobo Daishi..was likewise the founder of the *Shingon* ('True Words') sect of Buddhists in Japan. **1894** *Trans. Asiatic Soc. Japan* XXII. 382 (*heading*) The history of the Shingon sect. **1908** A. LLOYD *Wheat among Tares* iv. 40 Kōbō's faith—the so-called Mantra or Shingon Buddhism—so much resembles Manichaeism that it may be said to be practically the same system. **1931** G. B. SANSOM *Japan* III. xii. 222 The Shingon doctrines are mystical, and not to be explained in words. **1961** *Listener* 31 Aug. 316/1 A Buddhist sect, called Shingon,..is one of the most flourishing sects in Japan today. **1977** T. KASHIMA *Buddhism in America* i. 4 Shingon Buddhism..is based on the *Dainichi* Sutra (the Great Sun Sutra).

shining, *ppl. a.* Add: **1. d. shining cuckoo**, a

copper-coloured cuckoo, *Chalcites lucidus*, found in New Zealand and other parts of the Pacific.

1782 J. LATHAM *Gen. Synopsis Birds* I. II. 528 Shining C[uckow]..Size of a small Thrush..inhabits New Zealand. **1888** W. BULLER *Birds N.Z.* (ed. 2) I. 133 A peculiar whistling cry..announces the arrival in our country of the shining cuckoo. **1965** F. SARGESON *Memoirs of Peon* vi. 155 It was..something like the call of the shining cuckoo, a sound just in the air.

2. c. *shining armour* (see quot. 1533 in Dict. under 1 a, and *knight in shining armour* s.v. *KNIGHT *sb.* 4 e) (freq. ironic): a sign of preparedness to fight nobly in a good cause, esp. in defence of the weak.

1910 *Times* 22 Sept. 5/1 The action of an ally in taking his stand in shining armour at a grave moment by the side of your most gracious Sovereign. **1913** S. SHAW *William of Germany* xi. 249 The Emperor's soldiers and his Dreadnoughts, his mailed fist and shining armour, are built and put on in the spirit of precaution and defence. **1919** G. B. SHAW *Inca of Perusalem* 220 What other defence have we poor common people against your shining armor, your mailed fist, your pomp and parade? **1940** E. F. BENSON *Final Edition* xiii. 268 His Field Marshalls took his sabre-rattlings and his stupendous announcements that he was the chosen instrument of the Lord of Hosts at their face value,..and made him keep polishing up the shining armour which he had donned for his secret reassurance. **1960** J. STROUD *Shorn Lamb* xxii. 242 When I first came galloping out of the University, in shining armour..it was To the Rescue of the Deprived Child. **1968** 'M. UNDERWOOD' *Man who killed too Soon* vi. 61, I could tempt him to don his shining armour and try a rescue operation.

5. (Further examples.)

1887 G. M. HOPKINS *Poems* (1967) 71 Raced With, along them, cragiron under and cold furls—With-a-fountain's shining-shot furls. **1915** D. H. LAWRENCE *Rainbow* ii. 52 Sometimes, all shining-eyed, she was back at her own home. **1923** KIPLING *Irish Guards in Great War* I. 289 Everything was as shining-new as death.

shinnanicking, var. *SHENANIGAN.

Shinner² (ʃi·nəɹ). Colloq. abbrev. of *SINN FEINER (ʃin fēⁱ·nəɹ).

1921 *Glasgow Herald* 9 Apr. 12 The sands are running out as Ireland will shortly be ruined. 'Shinners' may be killed daily. **1974** J. JOHNSTON *How Many Miles to Babylon?* 51, I thought I'd heard it about that you were with the Shinners.

shinnery (ʃi·nəri). *U.S.* [f. SHIN *sb.*¹ + -ERY.] An area of scrub in which shin-oak predominates.

1901 *Rev. Reviews* XXIV. 310/1 It [*sc.* 'creeps'] is due mainly to an insufficiency of nourishment in the grass, particularly in pastures where 'shinnery' or dwarf oak trees abound. **1913** W. C. BARNES *Western Grazing Grounds* 268 The scrub oak of the western ranges..forms ..great areas called 'shinneries'. **1946** *Oklahoma Game & Fish News* Mar. 4/1 The located crow roosts in the shinnery motts west of Elk City.

shinning, *vbl. sb.* **2.** (Earlier example.)

1834 A. GREENE *Perils of Pearl Street* i. 16 The exercise of *shinning*.

shinny (ʃi·ni), *sb.*² *Southern U.S.* [Alteration of *SHINE *sb.*¹ 3 b: see -Y⁶.] = *MOONSHINE 4.

1934 in WEBSTER. **1944** D. VAN DE VOORT in B. A. Botkin *Treas. Amer. Folklore* v. 686 Wiley went over to the safe and got out his pappy's jug of shinny. **1960** H. LEE *To kill Mockingbird* xiii. 139 Miss Maudie Atkinson baked a Lane cake so loaded with shinny it made me tight. **1972** J. CARR *Second Oldest Profession* xi. 166 There are often regional names by which the illicit distillate is recognized. Some of these are 'cannonball swig'.. 'preacher's lye'..'shinny'..'kickapoo joy juice'.

shinny, *v.* Add: (Later examples.) Also with *down, absol.*, and with advb. acc., as *to shinny one's way*.

1936 J. STEINBECK *In Dubious Battle* vi. 86 Jim shinnied down the tree. **1937** *Sun* (Baltimore) 23 Oct. 12/7 It is difficult to imagine a man over 60 shinnying up a porch post. **1967** 'E. QUEEN' *Face to Face* xiii. 61 Somehow he's managed to shinny his way back into her good graces. **1976** *Daily Tel.* 29 Sept. 15/2 They must.. shinny up ropes, and slide down vines. **1977** *Time* 4 Apr. 42/2 Coming on fast is Robert Shaw, Israeli counter-terrorist, who must shinny down a rope from a helicopter.

Hence **shi·nnying** *vbl. sb.*

1906 *Washington Post* 22 May 2 As its girth precluded 'shinnying', Gladden procured a ladder.

Shinshū (ʃi·nʃū). [Jap., f. *shin* *SHIN *sb.*³ + *shū* sect = *SHIN *sb.*³

1727 J. G. SCHEUCHZER tr. *Kæmpfer's Hist. Jap.* I. IV. i. 264 The monks of the Chinese and other *Sensju* monasteries send also some of the fraternity to go a begging six times a month. **1896** L. HEARN *Kokoro* x. 193 Wealthier sects had established Buddhist schools on the Western plan: and the Shinshū could already boast of its scholars.

Shinwari (ʃinwā·rī). [Native name.] (A member of) a nomadic people inhabiting areas of Afghanistan around the Khyber Pass. Also *attrib.*

1875 *Encycl. Brit.* I. 232/1 Lead is found..in the Shinwari country. **1888** KIPLING *Phantom 'Rickshaw* 85 Would they could have foretold that my *kafila* would have been cut up by the Shinwaris almost within shadow of the Pass! **1958** O. CAROE *Pathans* xv. 234 The Mohmands and Safis formed a tribal confederacy with large numbers of Afridis and Shinwaris to oppose the passage of the royal troops. **1978** 'M. M. KAYE' *Far Pavilions* v. 87 We have a proverb in the country beyond the Khyber, that says 'A snake, a scorpion and a Shinwari have no heart to tame.'

shiny, *a.* Add: **A.** *adj.* **b.** Also, apparently excellent.

1915 KIPLING *Fringes of Fleet* 40 'Why didn't you then?' I asked. There were loads of shiny reasons. **1970** *Guardian* 14 Dec. 4/1 The Andean Pact is Latin America's ..shiniest attempt at creating a regional common market, but its gleaming paintwork is likely to take some hard knocks.

ship, *sb.*¹ Add: **2.** *ship in a bottle*, a model ship inside a bottle the neck of which is smaller than the ship.

1949 N. MITFORD *Love in Cold Climate* I. xii. 128 The safes..were full of treasures..a carved nut; a ship in a bottle; [etc.]. **1976** *Times* 2 Feb. 16/4 Construction kits are popular..including a ship-in-a-bottle outfit.

3. a. *to burn one's ships* (earlier example).

1871 HARDY *Desperate Remedies* II. i. 39 He saw the strokes plainly, instantly resolving to burn his ships and hazard all on an advance.

b. *ship of fools* [after the title of Sebastian Brant's satirical work *Das Narrenschiff* (1494), translated into English by Alexander Barclay as *The shyp of folys of the worlde* (1509)], a ship whose passengers represent various types of vice or folly.

1609 DEKKER *Guls Horne-Booke* 3 Any person aforesaid, longing to make a voyage in the Ship of Fools. **1807** W. H. IRELAND (*title*) Stultifera navis; qua omnium mortalium narratur stultia. The modern ship of fools. **1864** TENNYSON *Voyage* x, in *Enoch Arden* 149 'A ship of fools' he shriek'd in spite. **1919** KIPLING *Debits & Credits* (1926) 358 He Who launched our Ship of Fools many anchors gave us. **1975** *Times Lit. Suppl.* 7 Feb. 126/4 The Apocalypse as depicted by Bosch, the upside-down world of Goya, the Ship of Fools having landed its cargo.

c. *ships that pass in the night* [after the phrase by Longfellow: see quot. 1873], used of people whose acquaintance is necessarily transitory.

1873 LONGFELLOW *Aftermath in Tales of Wayside Inn* III. iv. 59 Ships that pass in the night, and speak each other in passing... So on the ocean of life we pass and speak one another, Only a look and a voice, then darkness again. **1893** B. HARRADEN (*title*) Ships that pass in the night. **1939** WODEHOUSE *Uncle Fred in Springtime* xiv. 198 The thought that they had met and parted like ships that pass in the night was very bitter to him. **1978** D. BAGLEY *Flyaway* xxv. 235 'Inquisitive, isn't he?' 'Not abnormally so. Chit-chat between ships that pass in the night.'

d. *a tight ship*, a ship in which ropes, etc., are tight; hence a strictly run ship; usu. *transf.* and *fig.*

1971 'H. CALVIN' *Poison Chasers* i. 6 Dai liked a tight mainsheet... 'Pull in tighter, boy... I want a tight ship.' **1972** *Sat. Rev.* (U.S.) 24 June 42/1 The two student judges ..ran a tight ship. Firm commands—'There will be no knitting in my courtroom.' **1977** *Times Lit. Suppl.* 13 May 593/3 Dr Kelly runs a tighter ship altogether than Dr Sheeran: her bibliography is a model of both inclusion and exclusion.

4. b. Substitute for def.: A balloon, aircraft, or powered spacecraft. (Examples.)

1679 R. HOOKE *Philos. Collections* No. 1. 18 A demonstration, how it is practicably possible to make a ship which shall be sustained by the air, and may be moved either by sails or oars. **1709** *Evening Post* 20–22 Dec. 2 The description of a flying ship, lately invented. **1784,** etc. [see *aerial ship* s.v. *AERIAL *a.* 5]. **1860** *Brit. Patent 1598* 1 An improved navigable balloon or aerostatic ship. **1908** H. G. WELLS *War in Air* v. 151 The ships of the German air-fleet rising one by one. **1930** *Sci. Wonder Q.* Spring 352 Both men ran toward the ship..for if the rocket were destroyed, they would be lost in the icy wastes of Venus. **1980** J. CARTWRIGHT *Horse of Darius* xvi. 251 'O.K. Let's get in the ship.'.. As soon as they were airborne, Teymour told him what had happened.

5. d. (Later example.) Now *Hist.*

1981 *Times* 14 July 3/2 Two hollow log 'ships' for boiling brine were found, dating to the sixteenth century.

8. a. *ship-canal* (earlier and later examples), *-channel* (earlier example), *-crane, -pump* (earlier example).

1798 I. ALLEN *Hist. Vermont* 268 A ship canal would be the means of importing salt, and exporting the preceding articles cheap. **1959** *Chambers's Encycl.* III. 38/1 The great ship canals of modern times have been built to carry large ocean-going vessels; but the earlier ship canals..can take only small ships and barges. **1775** J. QUINCY *Let.* 31 Oct. in J. Sparks *Corr. Amer. Revolution* (1853) I. 73 The ship-channel..runs between the east head of Long Island and the south point of Deer Island. **1932** AUDEN *Orators* I. 16 Like those ship-cranes along Clydebank. **1742** W. ELLIS *Timber-Tree Improved* II. xxxvii. 181 The Timber is..of especial Use..for Ship-pumps.

b. For 'Scandinavian' read 'Scandinavian and Anglo-Saxon'. (Later examples.)

1907 H. M. CHADWICK *Origin Eng. Nation* xi. 288 The launching of the funeral ship really was an ancient custom ..from which both ship-cremation (on land) and ship-burial were derived. **1940** *Burlington Mag.* Dec. 174/1 The great Anglo-Saxon ship-burial at Sutton Hoo..was excavated in the summer of 1939. **1963** C. GREEN *Sutton Hoo* ii. 33 (*heading*) The ship-barrow excavation.

c. *ship-jumper, -jumping.*

1964 *Punch* 4 Mar. 336/3 Except for a few ship-jumpers, most come by air. **1959** P. McCUTCHAN *Storm South* xv. 213 Genuine cases of ship-jumping by men who had had enough of sail.

d. *ship-based, -borne* (later examples) adjs.

1973 J. D. R. RAWLINGS *Pictorial Hist. Fleet Air Arm* vi. 69 The Navy..could see a use for the helicopter as a ship-based submarine spotter. **1932** *19th Cent.* Feb. 206 The second [method] is the limitation by agreement of numbers of ship-borne aircraft. **1978** *Navy News* May 5/2 The Phoebe..came out of her two-and-a-half-year refit with..shipborne torpedoes fitted.

9. a. ship('s) biscuit (earlier example with the possessive); **ship-broking** *vbl. sb.* = *shipbrokerage* in Dict.; **ship('s) company** (later examples); **ship('s) decanter,** a decanter with a base of greater width than the shoulder; **ship-lap,** (*b*) boards interlocked by rebates, used esp. for cladding; **ship-lap** *v.*: hence **ship-lapped** *ppl. a.*; **ship-mate**: also in phr. *to be ship-mates with*, to sail in the same vessel with; hence *transf.*, to be acquainted with, to have knowledge of (*colloq.*); **ship plane,** an aeroplane specially adapted for operating from an aircraft carrier; **shipside,** (*a*) (see sense 8 a in Dict.); also *spec.*, the outside of the hull of a ship; (*b*) the dock adjacent to a moored ship; **ship('s) stores,** (*a*) (earlier example); (*b*) sing. (*U.S.*) a shop on board ship; **ship('s) time,** (*a*) (earlier example); (*b*) *Canad. local*, (the time of) the arrival of an annual supply ship; **ship-to-air,** used *attrib.* to designate a missile fired from a ship at an aerial target; **ship-to-ship,** used *attrib.* to designate communications, missiles, etc., directed from one ship to another; **ship-to-shore,** used *attrib.* to designate communications, missiles, etc., directed from a ship to land; also *ellipt.* as *sb.*, a radio-telephone operating in this manner.

1855 E. ACTON *Mod. Cookery* (rev. ed.) xxxi. 603 The residents are then compelled to have recourse..to ship's biscuit. **1955** *Times* 29 June 14/5 Our shipbroking department had an active 12 months and profited during the latter part of the year from the substantial rise in tramp freights. **1969** *Daily Tel.* 24 Jan. 5/3 Wigham-Richardson is largely concerned with marine insurance, shipbroking and chartering. **1891** Ship's company [see *ship's writer*, sense 9 c in Dict.]. **1978** *Cornish Guardian* 27 Apr. 13/5 Shore-based organisations..will be involved..as well as 25 to 35 members of the ship's company. **1929** W. A. THORPE *Hist. Eng. & Irish Glass* II. Plate cxxix (*caption*), Ship's decanter, four angular rings round the neck. **1976** J. CARROLL *Madonna Red* (1977) iii. 93 The ambassador was holding a crystal ship's decanter. **1979** P. ALEXANDER *Show me Hero* vii. 90 A ship decanter and two wine glasses. **1939** W. FAULKNER *Wild Palms* 15 The flimsy walls (they were not even tongue-and-groove..but were of ship-lap). **1977** *Cornish Times* 19 Aug. 13/2 (Advt.), Our..plumbing, shiplap claddings and drainage systems are always in stock. **1958** *Archit. Rev.* CXXIII. 327 (*caption*) Northern elevation with ship-lapped pine used as facing for the first floor. **1876** W. LAMONT *Yachting in Arctic Seas* 13 These six Tromsönians were, in seagoing phrase, the *hardest bargains* I was ever shipmates with. **1880** W. CLARK RUSSELL *Sailor's Sweetheart* III. ii. 60, I had never been shipmates with an island of this kind before. **1961** G. FOULSER *Seaman's Voice* i. 13, I was never shipmates with a boom mainsail. **1919** in C. G. Grey *All World's Aircraft* I. 96A The *Beardmore* W.B. III. was evolved from the *Sopwith* 'Pup' in an effort to turn this machine into a ship-plane. **1922** *Flight* XIV. 126/2 Landplanes designed so as to facilitate thei r landing on a ship's deck will ordinarily be known as Ship Planes. **1942** *Ark Royal* Aug. 13/2 A ship-plane represents certain constructional problems which entail a sacrifice of speed. **1439–1887** Shipside [in Dict., sense 8 a]. **1937** *Sun* (Baltimore) 26 Mar. 26/3 He parked his car in a garage, left orders with an automobile company to have a new machine at shipside [etc.]. **1969** *Jane's Freight Containers 1968–69* 83/3 General cargo facilities..have two shipside tracks. **1972** C. MUDIE *Motor Boats & Boating* 93 Most sports fishermen therefore incorporate a section of the cockpit coamings, shipside, or transom which can be removed to help loading. **1785** *Daily Universal Register* 1 Jan. 4/3 Sundry ships stores, consisting of sails, cables, anchors. **1943** *U.S. Navy Bluejacket's Man.* (ed. 11) 1143 The ship's store, perhaps better known as the 'Canteen', is also under the jurisdiction of the supply officer. **1969** A. R. BOSWORTH *My Love Affair with Navy* ii. 44 He had been to the ship's store, and he came into the ward with several candy bars. **1771** A GRAHAM *Observations on Hudson's Bay* (1969) ix. 282 How affairs went on last shiptime I know not. **1869** 'MARK TWAIN' *Innoc. Abr.* v. 47 Young Mr. Blucher..was a good deal worried by the constantly changing 'ship time'. **1956** *Beaver* Winter 52/1 Time to plan the spring work—but why do that; shiptime is far away and now is really the time for that rest. **1957** *Times Survey Brit. Aviation* Sept. 2/4 A ship-to-air weapon. **1972** *Times* 29 Sept. 4/8 The through-deck carriers will carry..the ship-to-air missile, Sea Dart. **1904** H. W. WILSON in *Cambr. Mod. Hist.* VIII. xv. 482 The battle of Camperdown..was not, as had been planned, a mere ship-to-ship encounter. **1944** *Proc. IRE* XXXII. 326/2 Ship-to-ship telephone communication. **1977** *Navy News* Aug. 19 (*caption*) H.M.S. Fife, one of four guided missile destroyers in Portsmouth Navy Days, with her new Exocet ship-to-ship missiles mounted just below her bridge. **1923** *Monthly Weather Rev.* LI. 5/1 The cost of radio ship-to-shore tolls. **1962** K. C. HUTCHIN *How not to kill your Husband* xlvii. 221 The worst invention of recent years connected with sailing is 'ship-to-shore' radio-telephone. **1971** N. FREELING *Over High Side* III. 197 We've got the ship-to-shore. Couldn't we phone someone? **1977** B. GARFIELD *Recoil* xiv. 148 'Why the hell don't you ever turn on your ship-to-shore?'..'I go on this boat to get away from telephones.' **1979** *Daily Tel.* 22 Sept. 36/3 Makers of ship-to-shore oil pipes.

c. *ship's doctor* (later example); **ship's writer** (earlier and later examples); **ship's yeoman** (earlier example).

1974 L. DEIGHTON *Spy Story* xviii. 190 There was the ship's doctor. **1881** *Naval Encycl.* 745/2 *Ship's writer*, a petty officer who, under the directions of the executive-officer, does the writing and keeps the watch-, muster-, conduct-, and other books of the ship. **1969** T. PARKER *Twisting Lane* 43 He wasn't a sailor, he was a kind of a clerk on board ship... I believe he was called a ship's writer. **1850** Ship's yeoman [see YEOMAN 2 c].

ship, *v.* **6. a.** Delete † *Obs.* and add later *U.S.* examples. Cf. sense 6 c below.

1904 H. JAMES *Golden Bowl* II. xxxvii. 279 You regularly make me wish that I had shipped back to American City. **1978** M. PUZO *Fools Die* xvi. 171 By the time Frank and his units left the armory and shipped to Fort Lee there was a lot of bad blood.

c. U.S. Mil. slang. *to ship out*: to depart, to be transported; also *fig.* (cf. *shape up or ship out* s.v. *SHAPE *v.* 19 e); *to ship over*: to re-enlist, to volunteer for a tour of duty.

1908 L. G. TISDALE *Three Years behind Guns* xxiii. 259 Do you want to ship over? **1924** ANDERSON & STALLINGS *What Price Glory?* I. i. 7 When I left China the Yangtse was full of the bodies of virgins that drowned their beautiful selves because I was shipping over. **1948** [see *CASH *v.*[2] 2 b]. **1953** *CEC Bull.* Jan. 31/1 This outfit shipped out of Davisville 12 September 1943. **1964** G. L. COON *Short End* 223, I wouldn't ship over in Korea, and especially in Pankari. **1978** M. PUZO *Fools Die* xvi. 171 At the end of the month, when everybody shipped out, I bought Frank a present.

7. c. (Earlier example.)

1857 *Harper's Mag.* Sept. 459/2 A few of the more enterprising operators..thought nothing of shipping two or three thousand tons per annum.

e. *intr.* Of perishable goods: to admit of being transported.

1867 *Trans. Illinois State Agric. Soc.* VII. 510 It ships well, and is a very good peach. **1927** *Daily Express* 9 Nov. 5/5 Persimmons..will probably be as plentiful and popular as the banana, because it ships well and grows.. freely.

10. b. (Earlier U.S. example.)

1833 B. SILLIMAN *Man. Sugar Cane* 80 [The pan] is made to ship and unship.

11. a. (Further example.)

1851 H. MELVILLE *Moby Dick* I. xxxiii. 236 He pauses, ships a new face altogether.

b. *to ship a stripe*: to gain promotion in the navy or air-force. *colloq.*

1915 H. ROSHER *In R.N.A.S.* (1916) 38, I see in this morning's paper that I have shipped another stripe (Flight Lieutenant). **1924** *Blackw. Mag.* Mar. 333/2 For once his clothes were more interesting than mine for he had 'shipped' his half-stripe, and was a whole degree more important in the world!

shipboard. Add: **3.** Esp. in phrs. *shipboard acquaintance, romance*, etc., to denote casual or ephemeral relationships.

1916 G. B. SHAW *Overruled* 78 Was it the usual aimless man's lark: a mere shipboard flirtation? **1933** F. BALDWIN *Innocent Bystander* vi. 107 A shipboard romance will do a lot for his ego. **1963** 'W. HAGGARD' *High Wire* iv. 37 I'm a casual pick-up in the snow, a sort of shipboard acquaintance. **1978** 'M. M. KAYE' *Far Pavilions* ix. 148 It had been possible for Mrs Harlowe to introduce both young men as shipboard acquaintances. **1980** J. GARDNER *Garden of Weapons* II. viii. 194 He should be able to treat the business with Miriam like some shipboard romance. But his growing bewitchment would not allow that.

ship-breaker. Add: Also, a firm or company engaged in the business of breaking up old vessels.

1935 *Sun* (Baltimore) 21 May 12/6 The sale of some of the big outdated ocean liners to shipbreakers (that's the name for companies that take old ships apart with hammers and acetylene torches).

ship-breaking, *vbl. sb.* **2.** (Later examples.)

1931 A. HUXLEY *Let.* 6 Aug. (1969) 351 There are bits of Toulon harbour—ship-building and ship-breaking yards..I have always longed to paint. **1976** *S. Wales Echo* 26 Nov. 38/8 The Welshman..has business interests which include farming..and ship-breaking.

ship-load. (Earlier Amer. example.)

1639 *Portsmouth* (Rhode Island) *Rec.* (1910) 10 For men to gett a shipp lood of..pipe stauffes.

shipoo, var. *SHYPOO.

shippable, *a.* Restrict *rare*⁻⁰ to sense in Dict. and add: **2.** That can be shipped.

1920 *Glasgow Herald* 17 Nov. 11 The Southern Hemisphere promises for 1921 a shippable surplus of 40,000,000 qr. **1979** *Sci. Amer.* Apr. 31/1 This magazine page is a coated stock, several layers of clay filler and white pigment having been rolled onto the moving web during its passage from a wet slurry to a shippable roll.

shipper. 3. b. For *U.S.* read orig. *U.S.* and add earlier and later examples.

1840 *Niles' Register* 4 Apr. 80/2 Principal transportation lines have resolved to give the shipper or owner the full advantage of the reduction of twenty cents per barrel. **1950** *Times* 28 Feb. 4/5 Charter aircraft have been carrying bulk cargoes... By carrying full loads in each direction low rates have been available to shippers.

4. (Earlier example.)

1852 *Trans. Michigan State Agric. Soc.* III. 160 By the shipper the logs may be geared deeper or shallower.

shipping, *vbl. sb.* Add: **6. a.** *shipping company, house, lane, line.*

1897 *Whitaker's Almanack* 709/1 The New Zealand Shipping Company was established to run steamers direct to New Zealand, Tasmania, and Australia. **1924** *Times Trade & Engin. Suppl.* 29 Nov. 239/1 Shipping companies are complaining that apple shipments are not as heavy as they desire. **1919** *Brit. Manuf.* Nov. 40/2 The attempt to do away with the shipping house. **1931** W. G. CARR *By Guess & by God* xii. 194 German submarines which.. lurked about the shipping lanes waiting to attack the Allied merchantmen. **1974** L. DEIGHTON *Spy Story* xii. 122 Ice-breakers keeping two shipping lanes clear all through the winter. **1908** J. R. SMITH *Ocean Carrier* II. iii. 275 The starting of rival shipping lines is deterred by the certainty of fierce competition. **1981** A. GRAHAM-YOOLL *Forgotten Colony* xviii. 244 The Houlder Brothers shipping line..had been prominent in the meat trade for almost one century.

b. shipping fever *Vet. Sci.* (orig. *U.S.*), any of several diseases typically contracted by cattle while being shipped from place to place, esp. one caused by bacteria of the genus *Pasteurella.*

1932 *Jrnl. Amer. Vet. Med. Assoc.* LXXX. 165 The incidence of shipping fever was greatest during wet, cold weather. **1955** *Sci. News Let.* 15 Oct. 249/3 Shipping fever, the costly cattle disease that strikes like human influenza, makes the movement of cattle from range to feedlot one of the most dangerous activities in the livestock industry. **1970** T. G. HUNGERFORD *Dis. Livestock* (ed. 7) 332/1 Smeal recorded a case which clinically suggested shipping fever.

ship-repair (ʃipˌrīpēᵊ·ɹ). [f. SHIP *sb.*[1] + REPAIR *v.*[2]] The business or craft of restoring a ship to a sound condition. Usu. *attrib.* So **shi·p-repairing** *vbl. sb.*; hence **shi·p-repairer,** a firm engaged in the business of repairing ships.

1941 W. S. CHURCHILL *Secret Session Speeches* (1946) 32 At least another 40,000 men must be drawn into ship-repairing. **1969** *Jane's Freight Containers 1968–69* 198/2 An adjacent yard also provides a ship-repair service. **1976** *Eastern Evening Press* (Norwich) 19 Nov. 1 The Government continued on a collision course..after winning a Commons vote..to retain ship-repairing yards. **1976** *Western Mail* (Cardiff) 22 Nov. 5/2 The ship-repairers don't want to be nationalised. **1976** *Jrnl.* (Newcastle) 26 Nov., The House of Lords refused to back down over 12 ship-repair firms in the old session of Parliament.

shipwreck, *v.* **2.** (Later *fig.* example.)

1932 J. BUCHAN *Gap in Curtain* iii. 153 His only success was with me, for I..could talk to him about..the inaccuracies of the Greville Memoirs. But the real rock on which the thing shipwrecked was Protection.

shipyard. Add: **2.** *attrib.* as **shipyard eye,** an epidemic form of keratoconjunctivitis caused by a virus.

1943 *Sun* (Baltimore) 17 June 13/6 The Health Department mentioned the new eye infection, shipyard eye, which appeared last winter. **1974** *Jrnl. Hygiene* LXXIII. 158 Because of this frequent occurrence of the disease among workers in shipyards, the term 'shipyard eye' was coined.

shiralee (ʃirălī·). *Austral. slang.* Also **shirallee.** [Origin unknown.] A bundle of blankets or personal belongings, a swag (sense 10).

1892 G. PARKER *Round Compass in Australia* 49 Let him down easy and slow... Drop in his shirallee and water-bag by him. **1945** BAKER *Austral. Lang.* v. 102 A drum..is the equivalent of *swag,..shiralee,..*or *bluey* as the tramp's rolled blanket is variously called. **1955** D. NILAND (*title*) The shiralee. **1955** *Times* 4 Aug. 9/2 The shiralee is the swag, the burden, the Australian swagman carries. **1974** *Sunday Sun* (Brisbane) 5 May 4/2 The fences, the barns, the houses—they're all gone and I'm out on the road with my shiralee.

Shiraz. Add: **1. b.** (Earlier example.) **d.** Denoting a rug or carpet made in the district of Shiraz; also *ellipt.*

b. 1840 N. P. WILLIS *Loiterings of Trav.* II. 224 He politely begged pardon for smoking in the Countess's presence, and filled the enamelled bowl with Shiraz tobacco.

d. 1900 J. K. MUMFORD *Oriental Rugs* xi. 213 The Shiraz displays unusual features of finish. *Ibid.* 214 The true Shiraz rugs may be known almost invariably by the small checked selvage. **1920** T. E. LAWRENCE *Let.* 16 Feb. (1938) 299 As for the rugs, please take any that seem worthy to you. There were two Afghans in the Arab Bureau, & a big (and not bad but thin) Shiraz, in the Savoy. **1932** P. SELVER tr. *Čapek's Tales from Two Pockets* 189 I've got piles and piles of Shiraz, Shirvan.. and other common-or-garden carpets. **1968** L. DURRELL *Tunc* III. 153 A small and lovely carpet—an authentic Shiraz according to the label. **1980** G. THOMPSON *Murder Mystery* (1981) xxviii. 215 A large brandy snifter now lay on the floor on the Shiraz rug.

2. The name of a variety of grape from which red wine is made, grown orig. in the Rhône valley of France; the wine made from this grape.

The French name for the grape is *syrah* (*scyras, sirrah* are also found). The Eng. form is app. an alteration of this, influenced by the belief that the vine was brought (by Crusaders) from Iran and is therefore to be identified with that from which *Shiraz* (sense a in Dict.) is made.

[**1908** E. & A. VIZETELLY *Wines of France* 140 For red Hermitage the vine..is the Ciras, Scyras, or Sirrah, a corruption, it is alleged, of Shiraz, the tradition being that the hermit of the mount brought some vine cuttings with him from the East. The Ciras is, at any rate, a distinct variety.] **1927** A. I. PEROLD *Treat. Viticulture* v. 271 Shiraz, the grape of Hermitage,..produces a fine, famous red wine. **1966** *Courier-Mail* (Brisbane) 25 Oct. 2/10 He thought his 1952 shiraz was of such vast quality there was no bottle in a restaurant cellar to equal it. **1973** 'E. FERRARS' *Small World Murder* viii. 102 They drank one of the Lyndon's own wines, a Shiraz. **1977** A. SCHOLEFIELD *Venom* I. 38 Replanting areas with *shiraz* vines.

shire, *sb.* Add: **3. f.** A rural administrative district in some states of Australia. Freq. *attrib.*

1909 BRIERLEY & IRISH *Crown Lands Acts New South Wales* (ed. 2) (Advt.), Ordinances for Municipalities or Shires. **1947** K. TENNANT *Lost Haven* iii. 58 A man with any push would form a progress association and devil the shire council about the roads. **1977** *Bulletin* (Sydney) 22 Jan. 46/2 The town also has a shire community centre.

6. a. Also = *shire counties* (see sense 8 b below).

1977 *Daily Tel.* 14 Mar. 2/7 In the shires Labour are defending a rump of seven non-Metropolitan counties they still hold out of 39: Cleveland, Derbyshire, Durham, [etc.].

8. b. shire county, a non-metropolitan county of the U.K., as instituted by the local government reorganization of 1974; **shire-town,** (*b*) *U.S.* = *county seat* s.v. COUNTY[1] 8 b.

1972 *Times* 21 Sept. 4/2 The AMC received no guidance whether metropolitan county councils would want to be grouped with 'shire' counties or with district councils. **1977** *Daily Tel.* 25 Apr. 6/8 Britain's great conurbations and the shire counties are preparing for a..tussle. **1648** *New Hampshire Provincial & State Papers* (1867) I. 189 The Court doth think fitt that the shire town of Norfolke be referred to further consideration. **1717** S. SEWALL *Diary* 13 Jan. (1882) III. 132 Cambridge is the Shire-Town for Middlesex. **1881** *Century Mag.* Dec. 251/1 It was the central town in the county, and yet not the shire-town. **1969** *Bangor* (Maine) *Daily News* 10 July 1/5 (*caption*) This particular sign in Whiting..has omitted an 'a' from the shiretown of Washington County.

shirk, *sb.*[2] **2.** (Earlier example.)

1863 *Sat. Rev.* 29 Aug. 278/1 Small shirks may be apples of Sodom, but they clearly constitute with some people one of the main pleasures of life.

shirk, *v.* Add: **1. c.** *intr.* To shift or fend *for* oneself. *U.S.*

1843 C. MATHEWS *Various Writings* 71/1 As for Harvest, let him shirk for himself. **1874** *Rep. Vermont Board Agric.* II. 422 They are then turned into the pasture to shirk for themselves.

Shirley[2] (ʃɔ̄·ɹli). The name of a district of Croydon, Surrey, used *attrib.* in **Shirley poppy** to designate an annual poppy bearing single or double flowers, usu. red, pink, or white, and belonging to a variety of *Papaver rhœas* developed by William Wilks (1843–1923), vicar of Shirley and secretary of the Royal Horticultural Society. Also *absol.*

1886 W. WILKS in *Jrnl. Hort.* 21 Oct. 367/1, I call them 'Shirley Poppies', as there seems so much doubt as to their specific name. **1889** *Ibid.* 15 Aug. 126/2, I sent a pinch of seed to a leading firm of London nurserymen last spring for comparison with the Shirley. **1904** *Nature* 25 Aug. 408/1 Many a white-edged poppy may have germinated and perished before Mr. Wilks saved the individual which in a few generations gave rise to the Shirleys. **1932** E. G. WHEELWRIGHT *Garden of Pleasant Flowers* iii. 82 Other common annuals easily raised are godetias,..Shirley poppies, and love-in-a-mist. **1978** R. GORER *Growing Plants from Seed* iv. 53 Shirley and opium poppies transplant very badly.

shirred, *a.* Add: **2.** Also *fig.*

1929 S. JAMESON in *Legion Bk.* 105 The waters..in sunshine ruffled and shirred with living light. **1946** C. MCCULLERS *Member of Wedding* I. 29 The March winds banged on the window-panes, and clouds were shirred and white on the blue sky. **1973** P. WHITE *Eye of Storm* viii. 363 A brisk day: the harbour waters slightly shirred, newspaper rising and flapping in gutters.

shirt, *sb.* Add: **1. h.** A shirt of a particular colour worn as the emblem or uniform of a political party or movement. Also *transf.*, the wearer of such a shirt. Cf. *BLACKSHIRT, *RED SHIRT.

1864 [see *RED SHIRT, REDSHIRT]. **1922** [see *BLACK-SHIRT, BLACK SHIRT]. **1934** *Times* 28 Feb. 15/5, I beg leave to point out that our election law requires to be brought up to date, since it was framed at a time when the political 'shirt' parties were undreamt of. **1939** H. G. WELLS *Holy Terror* II. i. 114 Two purple shirts who had visited his rooms in his second year. **1940** E. A. WALKER *South Africa* 23 Latterly more than one anti-Semitic 'shirt' movement has arisen owing a good deal to German encouragement and example. **1975** *Times Lit. Suppl.* 11 Apr. 392/1 *Antifalange*, a commentary on an apologia for the old shirts of the Spanish fascist movement.

2. d. (Later examples of *the shirt off one's back.*)

1925 W. N. BURNS *Saga Billy the Kid* 67 He was a free-hearted, generous boy. He'd give a friend the shirt off his back. **1980** *Times* 7 Oct. 10/5 One day this industry will have the shirt off my back.

f. *to put one's shirt on* (a horse, etc.) (examples); *to get* (a person's) *shirt out* (later example); *to keep one's shirt on*: to remain calm (orig. *U.S.*); *to lose one's shirt*: to lose all one's possessions.

1854 *Spirit of Times* (N.Y.) 4 Nov. 447/3, I say, you durned ash cats, just keep yer shirts on, will ye? **1904** W. H. SMITH *Promoters* i. 15 I'll tell you how, if you'll keep your shirt on. **1932** WODEHOUSE *Louder & Funnier* 113 Sure he knows you know, Bill... Don't get your shirt out. **1935** E. B. MANN *Thirsty Range* xi. 144 He hit the market..about the time the bottom dropped out of it. He lost his shirt! **1938** E. BOWEN *Death of Heart* I. i. 25 He had not foreseen ever having to put his shirt on either [woman]. **1945** *Chambers's Jrnl.* Oct. 554/1 Okay, okay—keep your shirt on. Let's see what can be done. **1954** T. S. ELIOT *Confidential Clerk* II. 63 Marriage is a gamble. But I'm a born gambler And I've put my shirt—no, not quite the right expression—Lucasta's the most exciting speculation I've ever thought of investing in. **1981** P. THEROUX *Mosquito Coast* xi. 131 'Keep your shirt on,' Father shouted.

5. a. *shirt pocket, -tail* (earlier example).

1962 L. DEIGHTON *Ipcress File* xxiii. 150 The very young soldier reached into his shirt pocket. **1977** D. AITKIN *Second Chair* i. 3 My hand in my shirt pocket, tugging at the little diary. **1846** J. W. WEBB *Altowan* I. vi. 174 He..leaped into the river,..and made a shirt-tail across the prairie on the other side.

c. shirt-bosom (earlier example); **shirt-button** (earlier and later examples); **shirt-dress**, a dress having a bodice styled like a shirt; **shirt front**: also *transf.* of the breasts of other animals; also *attrib.* of a cricket pitch: very smooth and even (*colloq.*); **shirt-jac(ket)** chiefly *U.S.*, a garment resembling a shirt but worn as a jacket; **shirtlifter** *Austral. slang*, a male homosexual; **shirtmaker** = *shirt-waist dress* below; freq. *attrib.* (a proprietary term in the U.S.); **shirt-tail,** (*a*) see sense 5 a in Dict.; (*b*) *U.S.*, used *attrib.* or as *adj.* to designate something small and insignificant, or a remote relationship; freq. as **shirt-tail boy**, a very young boy; **shirt-waist**: for *U.S.* read 'orig. *U.S.*' and add earlier example; also formerly a garment worn by men and boys; freq. *attrib.* as **shirt-waist dress,** a dress having a shirt-waist bodice; **shirtwaister** = prec.

1833 J. NEAL *Down-Easters* I. 3 His collar turned back, and his shirt-bosom all open to the waist. **1651** R. VERNEY in M. M. Verney *Memoirs* (1894) III. ii. 38 Blew Thread, Shirt Buttons and old White..Buttons. **1742** C. CARROLL *Let.* 24 Nov. in *Maryland Hist. Mag.* (1925) XX. 178 Three or four Papers good shirt Buttons but not made on Wire. **1978** P. NIESEWAND *Underground Connection* 123 He undid his shirt buttons and stripped to the waist. **1943** in C. W. Cunnington *Eng. Women's Clothing Present Cent.* (1952) viii. 273 Necklines avoid the shirt-dress look which has been so widespread in recent years. **1973** *Country Life* 22 Feb. 492/1 If ever there was a right season to wear a shirt-dress, this is it. **1978** *Detroit Free Press* 5 Mar. D 12/1 A delicate mini-floral two-piece shirtdress. **1877** E. S. DALLAS *Kettner's Bk. of Table* 104 The carp is to be stuffed... The skin may be left on his shirtfront. **1920** P. F. WARNER *Cricket* 212 The result of all this work is that the pitch literally shines—and looks as if it had been ironed. 'Shirt-front wickets' they call them. **1963** *Times* 18 May 4/5 By merely bowling accurately, with seam upright, they presented problems which West Indian batsmen, reared on the shirt-front surfaces of their own grounds, found too complicated. **1967** L. EGAN *Nameless Ones* xiii. 158 He [*sc.* the cat] was a handsome sight, his gray tiger stripes smooth and his white shirt front immaculate. **1964** *Playboy* Nov. 173 The cool, crisp and comfortable shirt-jac which looks like a shirt, but is worn outside the trousers. **1977** *Guardian Weekly* 10 July 9/1 'Shirt-jacs', as they call tropical suits in Trinidad. **1975** *Daily News* (N.Y.) 26 July 12 Many leisure suits have shirt-jackets rather than the traditional jacket. **1966** BAKER *Austral. Lang.* (ed. 2) x. 216 *Shirt lifter*, a sodomite. **1974** B. HUMPHRIES in *Bulletin* (Sydney) 19 Jan. 13 When I first seen them photos of him in his 'Riverina Rig' I took him for an out-of-work ballet dancer or some kind of shirtlifter. **1926** *Official Gaz.* (U.S. Patent Office) 15 June 584/2 Best & Co... Shirtmaker frock..women's and children's dresses. **1960** *Guardian* 27 July 7/3 For this summer they have chosen a shirtmaker in drip-dry cotton. **1976** 'R. ROYLE' *Cry Rape* xx. 91, I chose a simple navy shirtmaker dress. **1845** J. HOOPER *Adventures Capt. Simon Suggs* 13 From the time he was a 'shirt-tail boy', [his wits] were always too sharp for his father's. **1846, 1873** Shirt-tail [in Dict. and Suppl., sense 5 a]. **1878** J. C. GUILD *Old Times in Tennessee* 411, I traversed these granite hills and beautiful vales as a shirt-tail boy. **1929** W. FAULKNER *Sound & Fury* 256 My people owned slaves here when you all were running little shirt tail country stores. **1938** M. K. RAWLINGS *Yearling* xxxiii. 421 Nobody but your folks'll bother with a little ol' shirt-tail boy like you. **1941** *Amer. Speech* XVI. 24/2 *Shirt-tail kin*, a remote relationship. **1975** *Publishers Weekly* 8 Sept. 57/2 A shirttail relation of the hotel-owning branch of the family. **1879** *Harper's Bazaar* 14 June 377 Kilt suits made here have the pleats stitched to a belt at the waist, and are then buttoned to a white shirt waist. **1902** *Sears Catal.* 819/3 Three hundred dozen men's regular $1·50 shirtwaists to go at 50 cents. **1957** *Observer* 1 Dec. 11/2 This gives the many lovely, tight-belted shirt-waist dresses a heavy look. **1980** *Times* 2 Sept. 10/1 The shirt-waist dress..is still a basic article of apparel. **1957** *Observer* 1 Dec. 11/2 These shirt-waisters are lovely, bodices luxuriously bloused [etc.]. **1973** *Country Life* 8 Mar. 633/2 The longer cardigan jacket..is worn in the daytime over shirtwaisters.

shirtless, *a.* (Later examples.)

1962 J. F. POWERS *Morte d'Urban* 218 Some shirtless youths in an old car rolled up from behind him. **1971** *Daily Tel.* (Colour Suppl.) 16 July 36/1 It had been a long slog up, shirtless, sweating, rucksacks bumping.

shirtsleeve. Add: **1. a.** (Earlier example of *in one's shirtsleeves.*) Also used *loosely* in pl. with reference to the absence of a coat.

1789 J. WOODFORDE *Diary* 30 July (1927) III. 126 The latter was..working in his garden in his Shirt Sleeves. **1832** F. TROLLOPE *Dom. Manners Amer.* II. xxv. 56, I saw one man..take off his coat that he might enjoy the refreshing coolness of shirt sleeves. **1942** D. M. CROOK *Spitfire Pilot* 45 We were flying in shirt sleeves. **1977** *Times* 29 Oct. 5 (*caption*) A Panama hat and shirtsleeves for the Duke of Edinburgh in the tropical sun.

2. *attrib.* (in sing. or pl.) **a.** That is in shirt-sleeves; usu. *fig.*, hard-working, workman-like; down-to-earth, informal; (see also quot. 1959).

1864, 1908 [in Dict.]. **1924** LAWRENCE & SKINNER *Boy in Bush* 11 The shirt-sleeves familiarity, the shabby clothes. **1959** *Times* 7 Sept. 16/1 Shirtsleeves weather. **1967** *Boston Sunday Herald* 26 Mar. I. 44/2 (Advt.), A 'self-starter' and a guy who will fit into a small shirtsleeve agency. **1979** G. SEYMOUR *Red Fox* iii. 44 [He] would have given much to have exchanged the brilliance of the surroundings for a shirtsleeves working area.

b. *shirtsleeve(s) diplomacy*, management of political affairs which is characterized by lack of formality or sophistication; *shirtsleeve order* (Mil.), the wearing of uniform without a jacket.

1931 W. F. SANDS *Undiplomatic Mem.* 22, I admit some pride in believing that they acted like gentlemen in the matter, though perhaps it was only shirt-sleeves diplomacy. **1959** *Times* 22 Aug. 9/5 Maximum cartridges are an asset for long-range shots, but perhaps hardly ideal for shirt-sleeve order. **1977** *Listener* 11 Aug. 164/3 Accessibility ..and, in the best sense, shirtsleeve diplomacy are on. **1979** 'J. D. WHITE' *Brandenburg Affair* iv. 37 Colonel Petrov..was another huge man... Even in shirt-sleeve order..his massive arms..gave him an air of permanence.

shirty, *a.* Restrict *slang* to sense in Dict. and add: **1.** (Earlier and later examples.)

1846 *Swell's Night Guide* 54 'I am exceedingly obliged,' grunted Tomkins, in rather a shirty tone, and continued reading. **1856** H. PHILLIPS *Jrnl.* 18 Apr. (typescript) 30 Jem and Mrs R. Shirty. **1911** [see *ROUSE *v.*[4]]. **1916** *Chambers's Jrnl.* June 404/2 Please don't get shirty, old chap. **1927** [see *RAG *sb.*[1] 3 c]. **1934** WODEHOUSE *Right Ho, Jeeves* vii. 73 But don't tell me that when he saw how shirty she was about it, the chump didn't back down? **1960** J. RAE *Custard Boys* I. v. 54 All right; all right; there's no need to get shirty about it.

2. [f. SHIRT *sb.* 1.] Resembling or modelled on a shirt.

1958 J. KEROUAC *On Road* IV. 288 A sixteen-year-old colored girl..in her short shirty dress. **1973** *Guardian* 10 Apr. 13/2 Fox-trimmed parka with shirred waist, shirty cuffs.

Hence **shi·rtily** *adv.*

1974 P. CAVE *Mama* (new ed.) xiv. 113 'Seems a bloody con to me,' he mumbled shirtily. **1978** D. FRANCIS *Trial Run* vii. 105 They told us pretty shirtily just now not to bother them.

Shirvan (ʃɜɪvā·n). The name of a region in the Soviet republic of Azerbaijan, used *attrib.* or *ellipt.* to denote a short-napped rug or carpet made in that area and similar to those of Daghestan.

1892 CARDINAL & HARFORD *Oriental Carpets & Rugs* 21 Daghestan. This title includes those kinds known as Kazaos, Karabaghs, Cubas, Shirvans, &c. **1913** [see *KABISTAN]. **1931** [see *DAGHESTAN, DAGESTAN]. **1970** L. DEIGHTON *Bomber* xxiii. 350 Modern Shirvans. They won't interest you, you know too much about carpets.

shise, var. *SHICE *sb.* and *a.*

‖ **shishi** (ʃī·ʃi). [Jap.] A lion, *spec.* as a decorative motif on Japanese porcelain.

1970 *Ashmolean Mus. Rep. Visitors 1969* 48 Saucer, with two *shishi* in Kakiemon enamels. **1976** *Daily Tel.* 20 July 12/3 The interior is enamelled in iron-red, blue, turquoise and yellow with a shishi beneath a spray of peony.

shish kebab (ʃi·ʃ kĭbæb). Also **sheesh kabab, shish-kebab, shishkebab, shushkabab.** [a. Turkish *şişkebap*, f. *şiş* skewer + *kebap* roast meat.] **1.** A dish consisting of pieces of meat (usu. lamb) grilled on skewers. Cf. CABOB 1, *KEBAB.

1914 S. LEWIS *Our Mr. Wrenn* ii. 26 I'm sure you'll like shish kebab. **1921** A. C. TRAIN *By Advice of Counsel* 73 Sardi had ordered *sheesh kabab*. **1951** KOESTLER *Age of Longing* I. vii. 153 'What kind of dishes do you really like?' ..'Shashlik. And shushkabab.' **1960** *Times* 4 June 7/6 Stands of appetizing *shish-kebab* on bamboo skewers. **1976** *Outdoor Living* (N.Z.). I. II. 63 Perfectly suited to barbecue cooking are shishkebabs and the variations are infinite. **1980** P. WAY *Icarus* xli. 180 The cluster of shish kebab stalls.

2. *Physical Chem.* A fibrous crystalline structure formed in some flowing or agitated polymer solutions, consisting of many plate-like crystallites (*kebabs*) growing outwards from a long ribbon or rod (a *shish*).

1966 A. J. PENNINGS in H. S. Peiser *Crystal Growth* 391/2 Most of the fibres exhibit lamellar overgrowth..and helical structures can also be observed. These structures will be referred to as Shish-kebabs. **1974** J. SCHULTZ *Polymer Materials Sci.* ii. 111 Electron and x-ray diffraction experiments have shown that the polymer chains in both shish and kebab are aligned parallel to the fiber axis. **1975** *Nature* 15 May 195/3 The shish kebab, of overall diameter about 1 μm and length up to several mm, apparently has a central core, the 'shish', about 20 nm diameter skewering lamellar crystals, the 'kebabs'. **1979** *Ibid.* 29 Mar. 440/1 The formation of fibrous precipitates, almost entirely of the shish kebab structure, on the stirrer by stirring supercooled solutions of polyethylene and isotactic polystyrene respectively.

shit, *sb.* Add: The form **shite** now chiefly occurs as an occasional jocular or quasi-euphemistic variant.

1971 B. W. ALDISS *Soldier Erect* 137 Do you think Churchill gives a shite for the Fourteenth Army? **1976** *New Musical Express* 17 Apr. 11/4 If you have to spend a lot of time with people who are interested in their chess boards and little card games and shite like that, it can drive you *nuts*.

1. a. (Later examples.)

1961 F. KING *Custom House* xix. 275 Leave that shit alone! Filthy dog. **1967** P. ROTH *Portnoy's Complaint* (1969) 47 Trying to clear my feet of my undershorts before anybody can peek inside, where..I always discover in the bottommost seam a pale and wispy brushstroke of my shit. **1973** E. JONG *Fear of Flying* (1974) ii. 25 In general the toilets run swift here and the shit disappears long before you can leap up and turn around to admire it. **1980** K. DOVER *Greeks* ii. 38 We might pick on his revelation of what Greek warfare was like... Blood and shit and pus are the same..in all ages.

b. (Later examples.)

1921 D. H. LAWRENCE *Let.* 10 Nov. (1962) II. 673 They are both such abject shits it is a pity they can't be flushed down a sewer. **1922** E. M. FORSTER *Let.* 27 Sept. in P. N. Furbank *E. M. Forster* (1978) II. v. 106, I think that most Indians, like most English people, are shits. **1926** C. CONNOLLY *Let.* 3 Aug. in *Romantic Friendship* (1975) 157 Her son is a complete little shit though.. witty and humorous beyond his years. **1941** J. REITH *Diary* 20 Oct. (1975) v. 281 Beaverbrook—to no one is the vulgar designation shit more appropriately applied—telephoned about park railings. **1956** I. MURDOCH *Flight from Enchanter* xii. 176 'You beastly contemptible shit of a crook,' said Hunter. **1968** *Observer* 29 Sept. (Colour Suppl.) 25/3 We hate the staff here. Keep away from them as much as possible. The shits. **1975** D. LODGE *Changing Places* ii. 67 Is that little shit still shooting his mouth off in there? **1976** J. I. M. STEWART *Young Patullo* viii. 165 She was a third-class harlot who made up for it by being a first-class shit. **1978** J. IRVING *World according to Garp* xii. 217 Oh, I never knew what *shits* men were until I became a woman.

c. In negative contexts: Anything. Phr. *not to give a shit*: not to care at all.

1922 JOYCE *Ulysses* II. 587 He's a whitearsed bugger. I don't give a shit for him. **1969** W. LABOV in J. E. Alatis *Teaching Standard Eng. to Speakers of Other Languages* (1970) 15 The average whitey out here got everything, you dig? And the nigger ain't got shit, y'know. **1970** *Landfall* (N.Z.) Sept. 218 Nobody gives a shit for nobody. **1973** D. BARNES *See Woman* (1974) I. 19 Don't tell them shit. The skipper is on his way, and he'll decide what to tell them. **1978** K. AMIS *Jake's Thing* iii. 30 An interviewer..being very rude to a politician..and the politician not giving a shit.

d. *transf.* Rubbish, trash.

1930 A. HUXLEY *Let.* 7 Jan. (1969) 326 In every case something precious and lovely had been taken away and replaced by a mound of shit. **1957** I. CROSS *God Boy* (1958) xxii. 192 They just tell me she's in a hospital and that God knows best and all that shit. **1966** L. COHEN *Beautiful Losers* I. 8 Listen, F., don't give me any of your mystical shit. **1976** M. SPARK *Takeover* x. 149 Even if it's shit it gets people thinking about religion. **1977** *Rolling Stone* 5 May 6/2, I enjoyed Simmons' logic that Shakespeare is 'shit' simply because he can't understand it.

e. *fig.* Misfortune, unpleasantness. Esp. in phr. *to be in the shit*: to be in trouble or difficulty.

1937 PARTRIDGE *Dict. Slang* 758/2 *sh**, in the*, in trouble. **1958** S. BECKETT *Malone Dies* 98 In any case, here I am back in the shit. **1971** B. W. ALDISS *Soldier Erect* 162 We were all in the shit together and it was madness to try and escape it. **1977** *Rolling Stone* 24 Mar. 55/5, I feel really lucky that I've had the opportunity to go through some of the heartaches and shit we've been through the past year.

f. An intoxicating or euphoriant drug, *spec.* cannabis, heroin, or marijuana.

1950 L. Rivers in *Neurotica* Autumn 45 Senor! You want some shit? How much? Senor, I have great stuff. **1960** J. Gelber *Connection* II. 88 At that time shit was relatively scarce and I had to go out of the city to score. **1972** *Daily Tel.* 3 Apr. 8 Acid (LSD) and 'shit' (cannabis), were on open sale, and..a notice was pinned to a tent stating: 'Anybody with some black shit for sale, ask for Irish Mick.' **1980** S. Wilson *Dealer's War* III. ix. 229 'Hope it's good shit,' I whispered as he swabbed my arm.

g. In phrases *up shit creek*: in an unpleasant situation or awkward predicament (cf. *up the creek* s.v. *Creek *sb.*[1] 5); *shit out of luck*: (see quot. 1942); (*when*) *the shit flies* or *hits the fan*: alluding to a moment of crisis or its disastrous consequences; *to beat, kick,* or *knock the shit out of* (someone): to thrash or beat severely; *to get one's shit together* (U.S.): to collect oneself, to manage one's affairs.

1937 J. Dos Passos *U.S.A.* I. 70 We're up shit creek now for fair. **1942** Berrey & Van den Bark *Amer. Thes. Slang* § 219/10 Unlucky..shit out of luck, (all) washed up. **1966** P. O'Donnell *Sabre-Tooth* iv. 62 We're all going to be there, where the shit's flying. **1966** L. Cohen *Beautiful Losers* I. 122 Let's beat the shit out of him. **1967** Partridge *Dict. Slang* Suppl. 1355/2 Wait till the major hears that! Then the shit'll hit the fan! **1968** A. Diment *Bang bang Birds* ix. 172 Should the shit hit the fan and the Swedes come over stroppy, he could say..'weren't nothing to do with us, son!' **1969** *Win* 15 May 31/2 We sense the government and its agents daily becoming more ineffective as we get our own shit together. **1971** B. W. Aldiss *Soldier Erect* 260 The Japs..were meek and respectful... The shit had been knocked out of them. **1973** *Black World* June 62 He sure didn't want a family.. to support..just when he was '..gettin' my shit together to finish school'. **1977** H. Fast *Immigrants* III. 171 It's been too quiet. Tomorrow, the shit hits the fan. **1978** M. Puzo *Fools Die* i. 10, I will show you the artist getting the shit kicked out of him for the sake of his art. *Ibid.* xl. 450 So you see, my dear, you're shit out of luck. **1981** *Private Eye* 31 July 11/2 If they'd followed her this far up shit creek it's a long way to walk back.

2. b. *the shits*, diarrhœa (in persons). Also *fig.*

1947 *Amer. Speech* XXII. 305 I'd rather die with the screaming shits. **1967** *Coast to Coast 1965–6* 200 Women have always given me the shits. **1977** *Zigzag* Mar. 8/1 'I've had the shits,' he cried. 'You want to avoid the food.'

3. a. In terms of abuse, as *shit-ass, -bag, -breeches, -face, -head, -heel, -pot*; **b. shit-hole** (see quot. 1937); usu. *fig.*; **shit-hot** *a.* (see quot. 1961); also used *loosely* as a term of approbation; **shit-house** (later examples); also in *gen.* use as a term of disgust or contempt (freq. *attrib.*); **shit-kicker** *U.S.*, a rustic; **shit-list** (see quots. 1942, 1945); **shit-scared** *a.*, extremely frightened; **shitwork**, (esp. in the language of feminists) work considered to be menial or routine, esp. housework.

1942 Berrey & Van den Bark *Amer. Thes. Slang* § 396 Terms of disparagement..shit-ass. **1971** B. Malamud *Tenants* 165 He then cried out, 'Oh what a hypocrite shitass I am to ask a Jew ofay for advice how to express my soul work.' **1937** Partridge *Dict. Slang* 758/2 *Sh**-bag*, the belly; in pl., the guts. **1961** *Ibid.* Suppl. II. 1269/1 *Shit-bag*,..an unpleasant person. **1968** Bethell & Burg tr. *Solzhenitsyn's Cancer Ward* I. viii. 121 All he could see was this shitbag wolfing a chicken bone. **1973** Shit-bag [see *mental *a.*[1] 1 c]. **1922** Joyce *Ulysses* 428 Hey, shitbreeches, are you doing the hattrick? **1937** W. L. G. Cowan *Loud Report* II. 97 'Hallo, s— face.' **1973** M. Amis *Rachel Papers* 115 'Why,' I wondered, 'did old shitface come round? What was he after?' **1961** Partridge *Dict. Slang* Suppl. 1269/2 *Shit-head*, an objectionable person. **1971** J. Michener in *Reader's Digest* Apr. 240 Again the girls were particularly abusive, taunting the guards, calling them 'shit-heads', 'half-ass pigs'. **1979** P. Niesewand *Member of Club* viii. 56 You lying shithead! **1935** J. Hargan *Gloss. Prison Lang.* 7 *Shitheel*, an inmate who considers himself superior to all the others. **1939** J. Steinbeck *Grapes of Wrath* 212 And Mae, when she is alone with Al, has a name for them. She calls them shitheels. **1977** H. Fast *Immigrants* VI. 359 You could have sent a registered letter, or that little shitheel of an errand boy, Clancy? **1937** Partridge *Dict. Slang* 758/2 *Sh**-hole*, the rectum. **1969** A. Cornelisen *Torregreca* v. 176, I made up my mind early I wasn't going to..spend my life..in one of those shit-holes. **1977** *Zigzag* June 28/3 John went to a Catholic school in Caledonian Road—'a right shit-hole'. **1961** Partridge *Dict. Slang* Suppl. 1269/2 *Shit-hot*, unpleasantly enthusiastic,..very skilful, cunning, knowledgeable. **1973** M. Amis *Rachel Papers* 199 They've elected a new guy... I don't know anything about him. Except that he's shit-hot. **1976** *Sounds* 11 Dec. 29/2 Chuck Leavell's pretty damn good all the time, and the rhythm section's still shit-hot. **1922** Joyce *Ulysses* 335 Cute as a shithouse rat. **1972** G. Morley *Jockey rides Honest Race* 173 You're probably right..but I still feel shithouse about it. **1973** J. Wainwright *Devil you Don't* 46 Have you explained all this shithouse philosophy to the rate-payers? **1976** P. Cave *High flying Birds* ii. 19 'Nothing wrong with it—safe as a brick-built shithouse,' I assured her. **1977** *Zigzag* Aug. 5/2 If you're banned in town A and then banned in town B, well then town C has just got to ban you or it's, 'well what kind of shithouse place are you running there, councillor?' **1966** *Publ. Amer. Dial. Soc.* 1964 XLII. 29 The commonplace generic term for any rustic, *shit kicker*. **1969** L. Michaels *Going Places* 23, I was a city boy. No innocent shitkicker from Jersey. **1969** *Rolling Stone* 28 June 14/1 Saturday nights the avid shitkicker can whoop it up. **1942** Berrey & Van den Bark *Amer. Thes. Slang* §336/2 *Blacklist*,..shit or stink list. **1945** *Amer. Speech* XX. 263 In the vulgar talk of the barracks, soldiers uninhibitedly use the phrase *shit list*, for a list of men whom one dislikes and is anxious to see embarrassed or inconvenienced. **1965** *Liberator* Aug. 23/1 Sweet Mac is on my shit list. **1970** R. D. Abrahams *Positively Black* i. 8 Moynihan had made it onto the black shit-list in spite of his obvious sympathies. **1937** Partridge *Dict. Slang* 758/2 *Sh**-pot*, a thorough or worthless humbug (person); a sneak. **1971** B. Malamud *Tenants* 132 Lesser, don't think you so hot, You got the look of a shit-pot. **1958** P. Scott *Mark of Warrior* 169 I'm shit-scared stuck up there with all my men gone. **1977** *Rolling Stone* 13 Jan. 12/4 Stewart was 'shit scared' about opening night. **1968** *No More Fun & Games* Oct. 43 Along with their equal integrated position they can equally misuse their less political sophisticated sisters to do their shitwork. **1972** *Guardian* 30 Mar. 13/3 They call it..'shit work' and they equate it with emptying dustbins and crawling on your belly in a coal mine... The resentment against housework came up like a great surging wave. **1980** D. Spender *Man Made Lang.* i. 48 Because of its parallels with housework, Fishman argues that women do the shitwork in conversation.

c. *attrib.* or as *adj.*

1968 H. Davies *Beatles* ix. 66, I think it [*sc.* jazz] is shit music, even more stupid than rock and roll. **1971** B. Malamud *Tenants* 104 He sat on the bed with a shit smile on his mouth. **1973** Boyd & Parkes *Dark Number* v. 55 'Look, so you've got a crippled leg.'.. He winced at that and turned away. 'That was a shit thing to say.'

shit, *v.* Add: *Pa. t.* and *pa. pple* **shat.** Forms: *Pa. t.* 7—**shit; shat, shitted.** *Pa. pple* **shat, shit. 1.** (Further examples.)

c **1784** W. Blake *Island in Moon* in *Compl. Writings* (1966) 46 'The trumpeter shit in his hat,' said the Epicurean. **1929** C. Connolly *Let.* Nov. in *Romantic Friendship* (1975) 329 It [*sc.* a kinkajou]..had a genius for sitting where it shat. **1952** M. Lowry *Let.* 24 Nov. (1967) 323 A seagull has shat on the roof of the convent. **1975** R. Hoban *Turtle Diary* xlix. 199 Their dogs shitted on the paths. **1976** *Listener* 22 Jan. 92/1 The titillation of finally finding out that great men and women spat and shat and had piles. **1979** *Guardian Weekly* 4 Nov. 21/2 Shat in his pants with fear.

2. (Later example.)

1978 T. L. Smith *Money War* (1979) I. 149 The planes.. had shit a neat stream of Day-Glo orange bricks.

3. a. Esp. in phr. *to shit oneself*: (*a*) to defile oneself with excrement; (*b*) *fig.*, to be afraid.

1914 Ld. Fisher *Let.* 14 Aug. in M. Gilbert *Winston S. Churchill* (1972) III. *Compan.* I. 35 The French Admiral shot himself. The English Admiral 'shit' himself. **1968** A. Diment *Bang Bang Birds* iv. 51 You can shit yourself. I'm not working for you. **1977** *Spare Rib* May 8/3, I was shitting myself before I came, looking for all kinds of excuses. **1980** *Sunday Times* 27 Apr. 42/3, I can easily arrange not to be diverted by knowing when a sorry old man shat himself.

b. In slang phrases *to shit* (*someone*): to tease or attempt to deceive; *to shit a brick*: (see quot. 1961); also as *int.*

1934 H. Miller *Tropic of Cancer* 61 Carl looks at me in despair. 'Is he shitting me, that bastard?' **1961** Partridge *Dict. Slang* Suppl. 1269/1 *Shit*, esp. *be shitting, bricks*, to be really worried,..to be thoroughly frightened. **1965** M. Shadbolt *Among Cinders* x. 83 'A queer thing. Something psychological.' 'Shit a brick,' he said. **1971** B. W. Aldiss *Soldier Erect* 187 You're shitting me, Jock! You never did it! **1976** H. Ferguson *Confessions Long Distance Acid Head* 48 By the time I got back to the hospital they were all shitting bricks. **1978** J. Krantz *Scruples* vii. 216 'Prince will shit a brick,' Billy said with a giggle. **1979** C. Kilian *Icequake* iii. 47 Didja see the wave comin' across the Shelf?.. There was a wave. I'm not shittin' you.

shitting *ppl. a.* (later *fig.* examples); **shitter,** (*a*) (later example); (*b*) a privy; a lavatory pan.

1952 *Amer. Speech* XXXIII. 270 Here I bring together all the current terms [for 'horse']. The most common are *pony, cayuse, shitter,* and *scate.* **1967** M. Shulman *Kill 3* II. iv. 77 You bastard! You shitting little bastard! **1969** R. Fernandez in A. Chapman *New Black Voices* (1972) 380 Markings on a shitter wall. **1971** B. W. Aldiss *Soldier Erect* 168 The blokes say Calcutta's got more whore-houses than it has shitters. **1971** *Black Scholar* Sept. 46/2 He lit a square and sat down on the shitter and tried to collect his thoughts. **1980** L. Cooper *Desirable Residence* xliii. 160 That shitting girl looks at me as if I was dirt.

shit (ʃit), *int.* Also **shee-y-it, she-it** (emphatic forms), **shite.** [f. the sb. and vb.] **1.** A coarse exclamation of annoyance or disgust.

1920 Joyce *Let.* 3 Jan. (1957) I. 134 O shite and onions! When is this bloody state of affairs going to end? **1922** E. E. Cummings *Enormous Room* xi. 219 My father is dead! Shit! Oh, well. The war is over. Good. **1925** D. H. Lawrence *Let.* 7 Nov. (1962) II. 865 Why doesn't somebody finally and loudly say Shit! to it all! **1959** 'E. McBain' *87th Precinct* xix. 138 'When I came back, he was gone.' 'Shit,' Willis said. **1969** 'J. Morris' *Fever Grass* xvii. 150 'Shit!' Scully said disgustedly. 'Oh, shee-y-it!' **1977** *Time* 14 Nov. 66/3 Aw, she-it, as the street kids say.

2. In trivial use.

1937 J. Dos Passos *U.S.A.* I. 73 Shit, let's try pick 'em up. **1969** *Private Eye* 23 May 14 Shit! What a lovely scene. **1976** P. Cave *High flying Birds* iii. 42 'Aw, shit. It was nothing,' she muttered, writing the matter off casually.

shite-hawk (ʃəi·thǭk). [f. Shit(e) *sb.* + Hawk *sb.*[1]] **1.** In India, a name used for a kite of the genus *Milvus.* (This sense probably much earlier in oral use.)

1967 Partridge *Dict. Slang.* Suppl. 1356/2 Shite-hawk... A vulture: British Army in India: ca. 1870–1947. **1971** B. W. Aldiss *Soldier Erect* 75 The universal kite-hawks—universally known as 'shite-hawks'—had been plentiful in Kanchapur; in Vadikhasundi, they were two a penny. Like the fly, the shite-hawk was one of India's essential scavengers.

2. *transf.* = Shit *sb.* 1 b.

1958 M. K. Joseph *I'll soldier no More* iv. 95 That shitehawk... Why can't a man like that be shot like a sick horse. **1981** J. B. Hilton *Playground of Death* v. 64, I liked the man... And yet he was a shite-hawk. He was a journalist.

shitepoke. Also **shikepoke. 1.** Add: also, the black-crowned night heron, *Nycticorax nycticorax*, or the bittern, *Botaurus lentiginosus.* (Earlier and later examples.)

1775 *First Bk. Amer. Chron.* ii. 19 They drummed with their drums,..running too and fro like shite-pokes on the muddy shore. **1913** [see *hop-toad]. **1942** W. Faulkner in *Sat. Even. Post* 28 Mar. 11/3, I..went to the barn and got the slingshot and the shikepoke egg. **1966** *Publ. Amer. Dial. Soc.* XLII. 17 The green heron... Another widely-used name is shitepoke (or shikepoke). **1972** G. Beine *Land of Coyote* 88 A shitepoke waded about searching for frogs.

2. (See quot. 1926.)

1926 in H. Wentworth *Amer. Dial. Dict.* (1944) 550/2 *Shitepoke*,..applied opprobriously to a person. **1936** D. Lutes *Country Kitchen* 19 I'll return it—when they've returned all the molasses and sugar and eggs and everything else they've borrowed in the last year—the old shitepoke.

shitless (ʃi·tlės), *a. coarse slang.* Alluding to a state of extreme fear or physical distress. Esp. in phr. *to be scared shitless.*

1936 L. Durrell *Spirit of Place* (1969) 42 We're scared shitless because if there's any place Benito wants more than Ethiopia it's Corfu. **1964** L. Auchincloss *Rector of Justin* x. 158 You're scared shitless this little affair will do you out of old Tanager's dough, aren't you? **1971** B. Malamud *Tenants* 62 On my first solo gig I was.. beaten shitless, and dumped in jail. **1976** *New Musical Express* 12 Feb. 24/1 The self-appointed custodians of public morality who campaign against pornography because they're simply scared shitless by it.

shitten, *a.* **b.** (Later examples.)

1846 *Swell's Night Guide* 49 Which of us had hold of the crappy (sh-ten) end of the stick? **1931** [see *lord *sb.* 12 d].

shitticism (ʃi·tisiz'm). *joc.* [f. *shitty *a.*, after *witticism.*] A scatological figure of speech.

1936 R. Frost *Let.* 9 May (1964) 277 My contribution was the witticisms: yours the shitticisms. **1977** *N.Y. Rev. Bks.* 10 Nov. 21/1 On his deathbed Frost forgave Pound his shitticisms.

shitty (ʃi·ti), *a.* [f. Shit *sb.* + -y[1].] **a.** = Shitten *a.* b.

1924 E. Hemingway *Let.* 19 July (1981) 119 In all other arts the more meazly and shitty the guy, i.e. Joyce, the greater the success in his art. **1952** S. Kauffmann *Philanderer* (1953) iv. 65 The first thing we do is change the looks of *Hearts Today.* We keep the same size but we get rid of that shitty confession look. **1970** *Guardian* 18 Nov. 11/6 You keep asking shitty questions that are irrelevant. **1977** *Spare Rib* Sept. 4/3 All the shitty jobs that most women..do every day of their lives.

b. = Shitten *a.* a.

1935 in A. W. Read *Lexical Evidence from Folk Epigr. in W.N. Amer.* 75 This Shithouse stinks like shit Because it is so shitty. **1977** C. McCullough *Thorn Birds* i. 7 If I catch you flaming little twerps touching that doll again I'll brand your shitty little arses!

shitzu, var. *shih-tzu.

shiur (ʃī·uɪ). [Heb. *šiʽūr* measure, portion.] A lesson in Jewish traditional sources.

1959 D. D. Runes *Conc. Dict. Judaism* 206/2 *Shiur*, fixed measure; generally used to designate Talmudic study hour. **1967** [see *rav]. **1973** *Jewish Chron.* 9 Feb. 21/4 Like other fortnightly meetings..it began with a shiur on the sidra of the week given by Rabbi Rosin.

shiv (ʃiv), **shive**[3], *sb.* = *chiv *sb.*[1], Chive[3]. Also *attrib.*

1915 *N.Y. World* 9 May (Suppl.) 14/3 *Shive*, a razor. **1926** J. Black *You can't Win* (1927) vii. 87 'Better get busy with your 'shive', kid.' I started cutting on the side opposite the boarding house. **1926** *Clues* Nov. 162/2 *Shiv*, a knife. **1930** *Sat. Even. Post* 5 Apr. 46/1 Those he does not shoot he sticks with his shiv—which is a knife. **1951** F. Brown *Murder can be Fun* viii. 120, I won't use no shiv. I'll take him apart with my bare hands. **1959** 'M. Ainsworth' *Murder is Catching* vi. 72 Has he any criminal connections...could he get hold of shiv-boys, for instance? **1959** H. Hobson *Mission House Murder* xiii. 88 He held a white-handled open razor... ''Strewth!' he said, 'a shiv!' **1972** *Daily Progress* (Charlottesville, Va.) 17 Feb. B. 11/5 The guards even planted a 'shive'—a tableknife—in McKinney's cell. **1976** L. Deighton *Twinkle, twinkle, Little Spy* ix. 89, I never heard of the K.G.B. using a shiv artist who hit the wrong target, and.. let them grab the knife.

shiv (ʃiv), **shive**[3], *v.* = *chiv *v.*, Chive *v.*

1926 [see *jam *sb.*[1] 1 b]. **1959** 'M. Ainsworth' *Murder is Catching* xv. 163 The boys been shiving you? **1967** 'E. Queen' *Face to Face* xxx. 136 'When was that?' 'The night they found Spotty shivved.' **1980** J. Wainwright *Venus Fly-Trap* 165 Two guys. So much hatred—eh? One shivs the other.

shiva(h (ʃi·vă). [Heb. *šiḇ'â* seven.] A period of seven days' mourning for the dead, beginning immediately after the funeral; *to sit shiva*, to observe this period. Also *attrib.*

1892 I. ZANGWILL *Childr. Ghetto* I. 177 If you had come round when he was sitting *Shivah* for Benjamin—peace be upon him!—you would have known. **1910** *Jewish Chron.* 29 Apr. 15/2 As an orthodox family we 'sat shiva'; and we took to the low seats with great heaviness of heart and in utter distress. **1938** *Ibid.* 10 June 15/2 The mourners requested that three 'shiva' chairs be sent to the house. **1959** B. KOPS *Hamlet of Stepney Green* II. i. 33 The Shiva is starting soon. Oh, those seven days of mourning. **1964** D. GRAY *Devil wore Scarlet* vi. 41 For seven days from the day of the funeral onwards a Jewish family sits Shiva. They sit on low stools in the drawing-room..and they sort of receive their friends and relations and get their sympathy. **1976** B. WILLIAMS *Making of Manchester Jewry* xi. 279 Members paid..4*d* a week, which entitled them..to *shiva* benefits, and to free burial. **1977** *New Yorker* 23 May 38/3 Elka's husband, Yontche, died, but Elka didn't observe shivah.

shivaree, *sb.* (Earlier examples.) Also in Cornwall. Also *fig.*

1805 J. F. WATSON in *Amer. Pioneer* (1843) May 229 When a *sherrie-varrie* is announced, it is done by a running cry through the streets. **1843** 'R. CARLTON' *New Purchase* II. lv. 231 The musicians..letting off at each repetition of the demand peals of shiver-ree. **1876** 'MARK TWAIN' *Old Times* 55, I started such a rattling 'shivaree' down below as never had astounded an engineer in this world before. **1926** GALSWORTHY *Silver Spoon* III. v. 251 And now came the usual 'shivaree' about such and such a case. **1942** A. L. ROWSE *Cornish Childhood* 9 The most splendid of 'shivarees' given at Tregonissey was for the wedding of Eliza Dyer to Eneas (pronounced Enas) Kellow. **1966** G. E. EVANS *Pattern under Plough* xi. 115 It was called the *Kiddly Band* in Cornwall..and it took part in the *shivaree* or wedding junketings there until the 'twenties. **1977** *Western Morning News* 30 Aug. 6/4 There was another word for a shallal: perhaps imported, or re-imported, from America. This is a shivaree, probably a corruption of charivari.

shivaree, *v.* (Earlier examples.)

1805 J. F. WATSON in *Amer. Pioneer* (1843) May 229 Edward Livingston, esq., was *sherri-varried* here; on which occasion the parties came out promptly to the balcony and thanked the populace for their attention. **1872** E. EGGLESTON *End of World* xlvi. 294 Among the manly recreations which they have proposed to themselves is that of shivereeing 'that Dutchman, Gus Wehle'.

shive, *sb.*² Restrict '*Obs.* exc. *dial.*' to sense in Dict. and add: **2.** With pronunc. (ʃəiv). *Paper-making.* A dark particle in finished paper resulting from incomplete digestion of impurities in the raw material; such particles collectively. Cf. *SHEAVE *sb.*² 3.

1922 *Manuf. Pulp & Paper* III. VIII. 1 The difference between shives and slivers should be clearly understood. **1937** E. J. LABARRE *Dict. Paper & Paper-Making Terms* 207/2 *Sheave*, also spelt *shive*..are dark specks in the finished paper, due to impurities in raw materials, rags and esparto grass, [etc.].., hence 'shivery' or 'shivey' paper. **1952** F. H. NORRIS *Paper & Paper Making* xx. 291 Shives are usually light in colour..and..shaped like a minute splinter. **1968** R. R. A. HIGHAM *Handbk. Papermaking* (ed. 2) ii. 79 Shive, knots..and similar impurities, cause breaks in the web.

3. *Comb.*: **shivelight** *nonce-wd.*, a sliver of light.

1888 G. M. HOPKINS *Poems* (1967) 105 Shivelights and shadowtackle in long lashes lace, lance, and pair.

shive, *sb.*³, *v.*³: see *SHIV *sb.*, *v.*

shiveau (ʃivō^u·). *dial.* Now *rare* or *Obs.* exc. as *SHIVOO. Also 8 **chevaux,** 9 **chiveau, shebo, sheevo.** [Origin unknown.] = *SHIVOO.

1798 C. CATHCART *Let.* 6 May in Fraser & Gibbons *Soldier & Sailor Words* (1925) 255 We have just left Gibraltar... Sir John Orde gave a grand chevaux to which he was so good as to invite me. **1828** 'JON BEE' *Living Pict. Lond.* ii. 83 A pressing invitation to what he calls a '*Chiveau*', or merry dinner. **1849** A. HARRIS *Emigrant Family* I. vii. 114 A 'shiveau' at the hut. **1862** C. C. ROBINSON *Dial. Leeds* 402 *Sheevo*, a shindy. 'A bonny sheevo thuh wor.' **1877** F. ROSS et al. *Gloss. Words Holderness* 123/2 We'd a meetin ī vesthry las' neet aboot a new cess, and them at didn't want yan kick'd up a riglar *shebo*. **1880** M. A. COURTNEY *Gloss. W. Cornwall* 50/2 *Shee-vo*, a disturbance; a row. 'There was such a grand *shee-vo*.'

shivering, *vbl. sb.*¹ Add: **1. b.** *Pottery.* Peeling and splitting of the glaze.

1921 A. B. SEARLE *Clayworkers' Hand-bk.* (ed. 3) xi. 208 Shivering is a variety of 'peeling' which may be produced by adding flint which has been too finely ground or an excess of fine silica to a body. **1947** J. C. RICH *Materials & Methods of Sculpture* ii. 51 Another cause of shivering is firing at too low a temperature. **1964** H. HODGES *Artifacts* ii. 52 Peeling..or shivering of a glaze usually results from a failure to fit the glaze to the body, the contraction of the glaze being less than that of the body.

shivering, *vbl. sb.*² Add: **2.** *Vet. Sci.* A pathological condition of horses in which certain muscles undergo rapid spasms, most commonly those in the hindquarters.

1847 *Vet. Record* III. 4 'Shivering', an affection of the stifle-joint, associated with luxation of the patella. **1907** J. W. AXE *Horse* VIII. 374 During this test it will be noticed whether the action is close,..and whether there are any indications of stringhalt or shivering. **1978** C. GEDDES *Horse* 218 The most common conditions are:... Shivering, a condition of the hind limbs, characterized by shaking movements of the hind limb and tail when the leg is flexed and lowered to the ground.

shiversome (ʃi·vəɪsəm), *a.* [f. SHIVER *sb.*³ + -SOME¹.] Causing shivers.

1930 *Observer* 28 Sept. 8 As shiversome a phase of sociology as the world has known. **1948** I. BROWN *No Idle Words* 53 Fever is a hideous paradox, being cold heat and shiversome ardour. **1970** *Daily Tel.* 17 Nov. 12/4 As brilliantly shiversome a film as I have seen for years.

shivery, *a.*² Add: **2.** Also *shivery-shaky.*

1864 *Derby Day* iv. 50 He's all shivery shakey as if he'd got the staggers or the cold shivers. **1934** J. JOYCE *Let.* 13 Aug. (1966) III. 317, I have a fit of ague for the past 24 hours... O Lord, the one day I feel so shivery-shaky!

shivey, *a.* Delete *dial.* and add a further example from *Paper-making.*

1937 [see *SHIVE *sb.*² 2].

shivoo (ʃivū·). *Austral. colloq.* Also **chivoo.** [Var. *SHIVEAU.] **a.** A celebration, a party, a spree. **b.** A disturbance, a row.

1889 J. I. HUNT *Hunt's Bk. Bonanzas* 82 Jones had been to a lodge night shivoo, and he and the boys had a gay old time. **1919** W. H. DOWNING *Digger Dialects* 16 *Chivoo*, a celebration. **1924** LAWRENCE & SKINNER *Boy in Bush* i. 15 There was a chivoo. They held me on their shoulders and I smashed the principal's windows. **1933** *Bulletin* (Sydney) 18 Oct. 11/3 Calling for a juvenile descendant at a children's birthday party, I thought of my own similar shivoo 50 years ago. **1940** F. D. DAVISON *Woman at Mill* 59 Wally had a head full of the bush balladists and aspirations toward performing at bush shivoos. **1961** P. WHITE *Riders in Chariot* ix. 314 Friday is the big shivoo, when the swells begin to swell. **1979** *Sunday Mail Mag.* (Brisbane) 14 Jan. 6/5 More than 200,000 revellers packed the forecourt of Sydney's Opera House for the big shivoo on New Year's Eve.

Shkyipetar, Shkypetar, varr. *SHQIPETAR.

shl-, var. *schl-* in many words (mostly German or Yiddish), qq.v. under this latter spelling. **shlanter,** var. *SCHLENTER *sb.* and *a.* **shlemozzle,** var. *SHEMOZZLE. **Shl(e)uh,** varr. *SHILHA. **shlinter,** var. *SCHLENTER *sb.* and *a.*

shm-, var. *schm-* in many words (mostly German or Yiddish), qq.v. under this latter spelling (cf. *SCHM-). **shmear,** var. *SCHMEER. **shmock,** var. *SCHMUCK.

shmoo (ʃmū). *U.S.* [Invented word.] A fabulous animal invented by the U.S. cartoonist Al Capp in 1948. It is small and round, and ready to fulfil immediately any of man's material wants. Also, a model or toy version of this animal. Also *Comb.*, as *shmoo-like* adj.

1948 *Newsweek* 12 July 56/3 Scheduled for appearance in August, the nature of the 'Shmoo' is a well-kept Capp secret. **1948** *Times-Herald* (Washington, D.C.) 25 Aug. 32/2 Too bad this fine, young specimen done heard th'call o' th'shmoo. **1948** *Sun* (Baltimore) 9 Dec. 16/3 The Berlin airlift..has ferried everything from coal to shmoos. **1964** R. T. PETERSON et al. *Birds* i. 13 Certainly they [*sc.* kiwis] are the most unbird-like of all birds, shmoo-like creatures shaped like large, hairy footballs. **1978** *Washington Post* 8 Sept. A13/1 Cloning would..even put an end to world hunger. Those who can discuss these things make them sound like Al Capp's 'shmoos'.

shmoos, var. *SCHMOOZE *v.*, *sb.*

‖ **sho** (ʃǭ), *sb.*¹ Pl. **sho.** [Jap.] A Japanese unit of capacity equal to ten *go*; equivalent to approximately 3·18 pints (1·80 litres).

1876 W. E. GRIFFIS *Mikado's Empire* (1877) II. Notes & App. 609 Measures of capacity. The unit is the *masū* or *shō*, a wooden box, usually with a transverse bar of iron across the top for a handle. **1902** L. HEARN *Kottō* xii. 148 No less than five shō—that is to say about one peck—of dead fireflies. **1938** D. T. SUZUKI *Zen Buddhism & its Influence on Jap. Culture* II. iii. 243 Half a *shō* (less than one quart) of rice.

‖ **shō** (ʃǭ), *sb.*² [Jap.] A small Japanese organ, made from seventeen vertical bamboo pipes, which is held in the hand and blown into.

1888 L. A. SMITH *Music of Waters* 281 The 'shō'..seems to correspond to our organ, but only in so far as it has pipes. **1936** K. SUNAGA *Jap. Music* 27 The *shō* is an instrument of which there seems to be no equivalent outside oriental music, though it is sometimes spoken of as a mouth organ. **1972** *Times* 18 Sept. 5/4 The head priest showed the instruments to Mr Heath, who took special interest in the sho pipes... He watched closely as a musician demonstraated the sho.

‖ **sho** (ʃǭ), *sb.*³ [Tibetan.] A former Tibetan unit of currency; a coin of this value.

1902 S. C. DAS *Journey to Lhasa & Central Tibet* vii. 182 Shopkeepers and pedlars pay five *sho* (1¼ rupee) annually. **1970** R. D. TARING *Daughter of Tibet* ix. 107 Ten *sho* made one *sang*.

sho, sho' (ʃǭ), repr. U.S. Blacks' pronunc. of SURE *adv.*

1893 H. A. SHANDS *Some Peculiarities of Speech in Mississippi* 56 *Sho*.., the common negro pronunciation for *sure*. *Sholy* is likewise used for *surely*. *Sho* is sometimes used for *surely*. **1926** N. N. PUCKETT in A. Dundes *Mother Wit* (1973) 7/2 A person who eats too fast 'will sho marry too young'. **1942** S. KENNEDY *Palmetto Country* 144 Sho nuff there was the preacher's buggy. **1966** *Massachusetts Rev.* VII. IV. 664 Sholey. Sho, hit'll be jes fine. Yo' done real good. **1973** E. BULLINS *Theme is Blackness* 99, I sho feel sorry for you when Cliff gets here, Bummie.

shoal, *a.* (and *adv.*). Add: **1. c.** The phr. *shoal water* used *fig.*

1884 'MARK TWAIN' *Huck. Finn* xxviii. 284 It jolted her up like everything, of course; but I was over the shoal water now, so I went right along..and told her every blame thing. **1941** J. MASEFIELD *In Mill* 105, I had.. plenty of money in the bank to tide me over the shoal-water.

shochet. (Later examples.)

1907 I. ZANGWILL *Ghetto Comedies* 386 The *Shomer* and the *Shochet* are the official twain of ritual butchery. **1961** A. W. MOSS *Valiant Crusade* vi. 81 In Shechita, the Shochet, or official who actually does the killing, has to be specially trained. **1972** *Daily Tel.* 8 June 18 Before the Shochet can use his knife the animal has to be got into the correct position.

‖ **shochu** (ʃō^u·tʃū). [Jap.] A rough Japanese spirit distilled from various ingredients, including sake dregs. Also *attrib.*

1938 BUSH & KAGAMI *Japanalia* 143/1 *Saké* contains 12 to 14 per cent. alcohol... *Shōchū*, distilled from *saké* dregs contains up to 60 per cent. alcohol. **1964** I. FLEMING *You only live Twice* x. 124 The herdsman..handed Bond a bottle of what appeared to be water. Tiger said, 'This is *shochu*. It is a very raw gin.' **1970** J. KIRKUP *Japan behind Fan* 80 Cheap Japanese spirits known as *shochu*. **1980** 'J. MELVILLE' *Chrysanthemum Chain* 88 A bottle of cheap *shochu* rotgut.

shock, *sb.*¹ Add: **3.** *shock corn, fodder.*

1865 *Trans. Illinois Agric. Soc.* V. 27 So long as the present system of..placing shock-corn on the ground.. shall prevail. **1925** R. R. SNAPP *Beef Cattle* xv. 179 Before the silo became common, corn fodder or shock corn was used extensively for wintering cattle. **1845** W. SEWALL *Diary* 10 Dec. (1930) 280/2 Shucked out a little shock fodder. **1949** H. HORNSBY *Lonesome Valley* i. 12 Chester was up in the cornfield, getting a sledload of shock fodder.

shock, *sb.*³ Add: **2.** (Further examples.) Also, a sudden large application of energy other than mechanical energy, esp. thermal energy (cf. **thermal shock*); a shock wave.

1904, 1907 [see *SHOCK WAVE a]. **1932** *Trans. Amer. Soc. Mech. Engineers* LIV. 310/2 The actual deflection can be estimated..from the location of the strong compression shock waves which follow the shock between the convergent streams. **1950** D. Q. KERN *Process Heat Transfer* xx. 733 While scale may be loosened by thermal shock, the shock does not necessarily cause it to drop off the tubes. **1955** K. F. HERZFELD in F. D. Rossini *Thermodynamics & Physics of Matter* H. ii. 686 In this method a shock travels down a shock tube. Behind it, the gas is adiabatically..compressed and is at higher temperature. The shock itself is only a few mean free paths thick. **1966** *McGraw-Hill Encycl. Sci. & Technol.* XIII. 552/1 Such shock arises when a body at one uniform temperature is suddenly accelerated to or decelerated from high supersonic or hypersonic speeds. **1974** *Acustica* XXX. 260 A reproducible acoustic shock pulse is generated in an aluminium bar by means of a transducer of the electro-magnetic induction type.

4. a. Also *ironically* in apposition with *horror*; so *shock-horror* used *attrib.*

1977 *Gay News* 7–20 Apr. 15/3 The message must have got through: certainly there were no shock-horror reactions and fun was had by all. **1980** *Times Lit. Suppl.* 31 Oct. 1240/4 The shock-horror world of the media men. **1981** *Brit. Med. Jrnl.* 18 Apr. 1312/2 The shock-horror *TV Eye* of recent weeks.

d. (*a*) *culture* (or *cultural*) *shock*: a state of distress or disorientation brought about by sudden subjection to an unfamiliar culture; (*b*) *future shock*: an analogous state brought about by too rapid a pace of social or technological change.

a. 1940 J. B. HOLT in *Amer. Sociol. Rev.* Oct. 744 All these citations suggest the 'culture shock' arising from the precipitation of a rural person or group into an urban situation. **1952** *Human Organization* Spring 16 (*heading*) The Papuan Ovokaiva vs Mt. Lamington: Cultural shock and its aftermath. **1960** [see *culture shock* s.v. *CULTURE *sb.* 5d]. **1970** A. TOFFLER *Future Shock* i. 12 Culture shock is the effect that, immersion in a strange culture has on the unprepared visitor... Culture shock is what happens when a traveler suddenly finds himself in a place where yes may mean no, where a 'fixed price' is negotiable, where to be kept waiting in an outer office is no cause for insult, where laughter may signify anger. **1978** *Lancashire Life* July 43/3 To see a defender in a protective helmet playing at cover point can cause culture shock in newcomers to the game.

b. 1965 A. TOFFLER in *Horizon* Summer 109/1 Culture shock is relatively mild in comparison with a much more serious malady that might be called 'future shock'. Future shock is the dizzying disorientation brought on by the premature arrival of the future. It may well be the most important disease of tomorrow. **1972** *Newsweek* 17 July 34 Fortunately, Japan's innate self discipline and sense of harmony have cushioned much of the 'future shock'..and so far Japan is relatively free of the..disorders so prevalent in other industrialized societies. **1975** *Whig-Standard* (Kingston, Ontario) 7 Jan. 6/3 Canada's foreign policy is in poor health these days—suffering from a severe case of future shock complicated by a crippling inferiority complex.

5. a. (Further examples.) Now used more precisely in *Med.* for a condition whose principal characteristic is low blood volume (see quot. 1968); also *ellipt.* for *shell shock* s.v. *SHELL *sb.* 39; *in shock*, in a state of shock; incapacitated by very low blood pressure and associated symptoms, or debilitated by ill-treatment or bad news; so *into shock, out of shock.*

1889 *Amer. Jrnl. Med. Sci.* XCVII. 282 For the purpose of stimulating a patient in shock it is more rational to give ether than to give alcohol. **1917** W. OWEN *Let.* 23 May (1967) 463 Sorrel was mentioned for Shock [in the Casualty List]. **1928** *Jrnl. Amer. Med. Assoc.* 9 June 1859/2 The blood pressure..suddenly fell to 52 systolic and 44 diastolic as he went into shock. **1958** J. CANNAN *And be Villain* vi. 137 Mrs Hallow was subjected to quite an ordeal this morning and is practically in shock. **1959** *Woman's Own* 27 June 44/2 She's in shock, of course, but we're giving her a transfusion. **1968** PASSMORE & ROBSON *Compan. Med. Stud.* I. xxviii. 41/1 Loss of blood volume is an important but not the only cause of shock; a similar state of shock occurs in acute heart failure and in severe infections in which the responsible haemodynamic mechanisms are different. **1975** *Publishers Weekly* 21 July 67/2 When Joe signed his first pro contract, Rose..went into shock. **1980** M. RUSSELL *Death Fuse* xvi. 149, I think she's able to talk. She's out of shock.

b. A paralytic seizure or stroke. Chiefly *Sc.* and *U.S. dial.*

1794 J. WOODFORDE *Diary* 13 Oct. (1929) IV. 143 Mr. Whitmell had a kind of Paralytic Shock this last Spring. **1896** H. JOHNSTON *Dr. Congalton's Legacy* xxiv. 315 The mistress of Windy-yett had taken 'a terrible turn—a shock or something'. **1903** K. D. WIGGIN *Rebecca of Sunnybrook Farm* xxvi. 279 We had three o' the worst shocks in our family that there ever was..and I know every symptom of 'em better 'n the doctors. **1951** E. GRAHAM *My Window looks down East* xi. 96 That was when he came the nearest to the stroke. (In Maine we call them 'shocks'.) **1955** W. F. MILNE *Eppie Elrick* xxx. 284 Haein teen a shock an' soocht awa in 'is sleep. **1981** M. CANTWELL in *N.Y. Times Mag.* 9 Aug. 6/4 One cause of my future demise might be that I 'took a shock.' In other places, a person in that condition would be said to have suffered a paralytic stroke.

c. *anaphylactic shock*: see s.v. *ANAPHYLAXIS.

6. (Earlier example of sense 'electric shock'.)

1746 W. WATSON *Sequel to Experiments in Electr.* 10 He receives a violent shock through both his arms.

6*. ellipt. for *shock-absorber.* Chiefly *U.S.*

1961 in WEBSTER. **1968** *Hot Car* Nov. 14/2 (Advt.), These are the shocks to end all shocks. **1977** *Transatlantic Rev.* LX. 22 He told her that the car would also need new shocks, brakes, a muffler, a starter and an engine job. **1979** *Guardian* 4 June 6/7 Shock-absorber people who will swop your worn-out shocks.

7. a. *shock effect, -value*; *shock-resistant* adj.; also, of things that startle or shock, as *shock headline, language, news, story*; **shock cone** *Aeronaut.*, a nose cone or other conical fairing which serves to streamline an aircraft for supersonic flight; **shock cord,** heavy elasticated cord designed to absorb or resist mechanical shock; a length of this; **shock excitation,** the excitation of natural oscillations in a system by a sudden impulse of energy from an external source; so **shock-excited** *ppl. a.*; **shock front,** the wave front of a shock wave; **shock measure,** a severe or exceptional measure taken usu. to deal with an emergency; **shock-mount** *sb.*, a mounting designed to absorb or resist mechanical shock; also as *v. trans.*, to attach by means of such a mounting; **shock-mounted** *ppl. a.*, **shock-mounting** *vbl. sb.*; **shock police,** in Spain, a republican force of specially armed police for use in assault operations; **shock-proof** *a.*, proof against damage by mechanical shock or by a surge of electrical power; also *fig.*; hence **shock-proofing** *vbl. sb.*, the process of rendering shock-proof; **shock stall** *Aeronaut.*, a stalling condition undergone by an aircraft at a speed close to that of sound, involving increased air resistance and loss of lift and control; also **shock stalling** *vbl. sb.*; **shock strut** *Aeronaut.*, a strut containing a shock absorber in the landing gear of an aircraft; **shock-tactics,** add: also *transf.* and *fig.*; also occas. **shock-tactic**; **shock test,** a test in which an object is subjected to mechanical shock; hence **shock-testing** *vbl. sb.*; **shock therapy, treatment,** treatment by means of artificially induced shock, whether anaphylactic, electrical, or drug-induced; *spec.* electro-convulsive therapy; also *fig.*; **shock tube,** an apparatus for producing shock waves by making a gas at high pressure expand suddenly into a low-pressure tube or cavity.

1947 *Shell Aviation News* No. 112. 6/3 Republic is building a fighter aircraft with a needle-nose shock cone to permit supersonic speed. **1961** *Aeroplane* CI. 548/1 The 'shock cones' are merely fairings over the boundary-layer bleed, which brings the intakes proud of the fuselage. **1930** P. WHITE *How to fly Airplane* xx. 279 (*caption*) Two boys at the rear are holding against the pull of the shock cord. **1980** *TWA Ambassador* Oct. 32/3 Secure all gear, such as the coffee-cans, in the canoe with rope or shock cord. **1959** *N. & Q.* CCIV. 36/2 The most intense shock effects come from the imposition of war's horrible destruction upon familiar places usually associated with quiet and peace. **1977** A. GIDDENS *Stud. in Social & Polit. Theory* ix. 317 Suicide attempts do appear to have a 'shock' effect on relatives and friends. **1920** E. W. STONE *Elem. Radiotelegr.* iii. 54 Exciting a vibratory circuit into oscillation is variously termed impulse excitation, shock excitation, and whip-crack excitation. **1930** A. B. WOOD *Textbk. Sound* 213 A single explosion impulse is often sufficient to set a resonator into vibration, thereby producing a musical note or a noise by shock excitation. **1967** R. F. GRAF *Mod. Dict. Electronics* 138/2 *Free oscillations*, commonly referred to as shock-excited oscillations. **1975** D. G. FINK *Electronics Engineers' Handbk.* XIX. 17 The sound levels of shock-excited tones are more difficult to specify because they vary so much during decay and can be excited over a very wide range. **1949** L. M. MILNE-THOMSON *Theoret. Hydrodynamics* (ed. 2) xx. 577 If the shock front is sufficiently oblique to the oncoming air, the conditions behind may still be supersonic. **1969** *New Scientist* 28 Aug. 434/2 The boom signature appears to coalesce at a relatively short distance from the flightpath into two shockfronts. **1977** M. WALKER *National Front* iii. 60 Shock headlines like 'Five Million Coloured Asians now in Britain?' (*RPS News*). **1959** *Listener* 13 Aug. 253/1 One is reminded more of the shock-language of the *avant-garde* Russian poets of the time. **1962** *Daily Tel.* 13 Dec. 10/2 Mr. Marples's shock measures..will be more than justified if this savage record [of death and injury on the roads] can be substantially improved. **1939** *Interavia* 5 Dec. 10 Two sets of shock mounts on either side of the blades are employed. **1942** P. C. SANDRETTO *Princ. Aeronaut. Radio Engin.* i. 10 Shock mounting in the past consisted of certain rubber shock absorbers mounted to the radio units; however, the trend is toward the use of shock-mounted shelves permanently installed in the airplane. **1947** B. W. PIKE et al. in A. Roberts *Radar Beacons* xvi. 361 The beacon should be either internally shock-mounted or carried in a padded case. **1964** R. F. FICCHI *Electr. Interference* iv. 40 Since many equipments are presently being installed on shock mountings so they will not be affected by vibration, it is important to bond adequately across shock mounts. **1973** *Times* 31 Oct. (Suppl.) p. viii, His company believe they can avoid fatigue failure..by overdesign of various components and by shock-mounting valves, pipes and other equipment. **1976** *National Observer* (U.S.) 1 May 3/4 (Advt.), Precision, shock-mounted lucite level. **1974** *Times* 3 Apr. 1/1 (*heading*) Shock news is broken to EEC ministers. **1937** *Ann. Reg. 1936* 249 The murder, on July 12, of Lieutenant Castillo of the Shock Police (known to have Socialist sympathies) by gangsters of the Right. **1957** P. KEMP *Mine were of Trouble* i. 16 Shock Police (*Guardias de Asalto*), posted in side streets on motor cycles. **1911** T. DREISER *Jennie Gerhardt* xviii. 138 He was..curiously elated beneath a sturdy, shock-proof exterior. **1925** *Wireless World* 8 Apr. 280/3 (*heading*) Shock-proof valve holder. **1930** R. MACAULAY *Staying with Relations* xiv. 203 They needed a shock-proof screen between them, to deaden the assaults of each on the other's strained nerves. **1952** H. R. CLAUSER *Pract. Radiogr. for Industry* iii. 37 Protection is obtained by immersing the [X-ray] tube in oil inside a shockproof casing. **1971** J. WAINWRIGHT *Dig Grave & let him Lie* 20 He was shockproof—the ultimate example of what bobbying can do to a man. **1978** R. GOOD *Watches in Colour* viii. 116 Shock-proof bearings for the balance pivots. **1952** H. R. CLAUSER *Pract. Radiogr. for Industry* iii. 37 Shockproofing of x-ray tubes can be done by enclosing the tube in a casing which is at ground potential. **1946** D. DE CARLE *Practical Watch Repairing* (1947) xx. 262 The shock-resistant watch cannot be looked upon as a novelty, in the sense that it is a passing phase. **1963** *New Yorker* 7 Dec. 136/1 (Advt.), Self-winding, thin, water- and shock-resistant. **1938** *Proc. R. Soc.* A. CLXIX. 188 This critical speed at which the sound wave condenses into a single pressure discontinuity is probably the shock stall or compressibility stall. **1948** *Sci. News* VII. 30 The use of swept-back wings raises the critical Mach number for the aircraft and allows the higher speeds to be reached without the danger of shock stall. **1966** D. STINTON *Anat. of Aeroplane* vi. 103 The buffeting and sharp loss of lift (Shockstall) caused by compressibility gave rise to the early misconception of a 'sound-barrier', beyond which man might not fly. **1937** *Flight* 4 Nov. 450/1 The elliptic cylinder..has a lower maximum velocity..and therefore presumably a higher shock stalling speed. **1952** W. J. DUNCAN *Princ. Control & Stability of Aircraft* xiii. 310 The separation of the shock stalling and critical Mach numbers may vary from almost zero to about 0·2. **1946** *Sun* (Baltimore) 5 Nov. 9/6 (Advt.), You'll see the shock story of the year. **1931** F. D. BRADBROOKE *Light Aeroplane Man.* vi. 92 When the advantages of the divided undercarriage began to compel attention the shock-absorbing gear had to be incorporated in the compression or shock strut. This was done by having a telescopic strut, generally with projections in each portion which were lashed with rubber cord in such a way that a shortening of the strut stretched the cord. **1949** J. W. VALE *Aviation Mechanic's Aircraft Man.* xii. 343 The fluid used in the Pneudraulic shock struts..may be used for initial filling or for partial refilling. **1919** *Manch. Guardian* 4 Feb. 5/1 It was the 'shock Tactics' of labour warfare. **1954** *Essays & Studies* VII. 84 To judge from the vehement reactions of the critics, the revolutionary shock-tactics seem in this aim to have succeeded remarkably well. **1959** *Listener* 19 Nov. 895/2 This definition of Zen as a kind of natural mysticism whose shock-tactic and other techniques are designed to stimulate the intuitive and..religious awareness. **1960** G. E. EVANS *Horse in Furrow* xx. 239 His initial shock tactics were successful: he gained control of the horse. **1961** *Encounter* Apr. 56/2 This shock-tactic had by no means the same general appeal as his witch being burnt at the stake. **1977** R. BARNARD *Blood Brotherhood* ix. 92 There was a hidden design behind..Chief Inspector Plunkett's questions, or perhaps..he was trying shock tactics. **1904** *Proc. Inst. Mech. Engineers* 1135 Considerable movement has been made of late towards the establishment of a shock test for steel. **1949** J. F. BLACKBURN *Components Handbk.* xiii. 516 In certain cases the shock tests resulted in permanent mechanical damage to the relays, often without opening the contacts. **1974** *Jrnl. Soc. Environmental Engineers* XIII. 17/1 Maximum displacement during a shock test can be obtained in several ways, one of the simplest is to measure the deformation of a piece of plasticine. **1917** *Jrnl. Iron & Steel Inst.* XCVI. 65 The regularity of the results which can be obtained with carefully manipulated shock-testing machines. *Ibid.*, A system of calibrating apparatus for the shock-testing of metals. **1963** C. T. MORROW *Shock & Vibration Engin.* I. v. 114 The advantages of an asymmetrical pulse shape in shock testing. **1917** *Jrnl. Exper. Med.* XXVI. 699 The mechanism of recovery following the so called 'protein shock therapy'. *Ibid.* 705 Bacterial infection not confined to the lymph spaces will not be influenced by shock therapy to the same extent. **1939** *Jrnl. Amer. Med. Assoc.* 16 Sept. 1170/2 Dislocations and fractures occur in insulin and metrazol shock therapy. *Ibid.* 2 Dec. 2100/2 The author recommends the use of electric shock therapy for old cases of depressive psychosis in which other therapeutic methods have failed. **1953** H. READ *True Voice of Feeling* I. viii. 149 There may be more sense in [Ezra] Pound's shock-therapy. **1973** W. BARLOW *Alexander Principle* i. 13 The psychiatrists..treated her with shock therapy and anti-depressant drugs. **1979** *Tucson Mag.* Jan. 24/1 The shock therapy that was Simon's murder induced a spirited public outcry. **1938** M. SAKEL (*title*) The pharmacological shock treatment of schizophrenia. **1939** *Jrnl. Amer. Med. Assoc.* 16 Sept. 1170/2 (*heading*) Faradic shock treatment of 'functional' psychoses. **1945** KOESTLER *Yogi & Commissar* III. iii. 202 That diplomatic shock-treatment of which they have so far only had a faint foretaste. **1947** *Sun* (Baltimore) 20 Jan. 7/1 We believe that the 'shock treatment' of prompt action is needed to halt the insane spiral of mounting costs and rising prices. **1974** *Listener* 24 Jan. 124/3 Munch suffered a complete breakdown, received shock treatment at a clinic in Copenhagen. **1949** *Sci. Amer.* Nov. 18/2 These pictures illustrate the great potentiality of the shock tube in observing and recording supersonic flow patterns. **1977** I. M. CAMPBELL *Energy & Atmosphere* v. 105 In the shock tube these conditions are produced by the rapid adiabatic compression of air or N_2–O_2 mixtures across the shock front created by the sudden release of high-pressure driver gas at one end of the tube. **1933** *Archit. Rev.* LXXIV. 68/1 *The Daily Mail*, drawn naturally to the new medium by its tradition of public-spirited interest in aviation and its awareness of the shock-value of surprise. **1959** *Encounter* Nov. 59/2 He had never dreamt that his [ballet] company would have such shock-value.

b. shock troops [tr. G. *stosstruppen*], forces of selected and specially armed men trained for deployment in assault operations, especially against strong positions or large numbers; (rarely) *sing.*, such a force. Also *fig.* and *attrib.* (in *sing.*). Hence **shock trooper.**

1917 *Times* 20 June 5/5 The second shock-troop battalion of the Third Army. **1918** E. S. FARROW *Dict. Mil. Terms* 553 *Shock Troops*, troops especially selected for assault work. They usually wear steel breastplates and other protection strong enough to turn a bullet at 50 or 60 feet. **1927** *Daily Express* 14 July 9/4 The G.P.U. troops..in..a war against Poland and Britain..would be used as shock troops. **1928** *Dict. Amer. Biogr.* I. 382/2 A master of strategy usually stays behind the lines. Not so Bishop Asbury. He asked no more of his skirmishers and shock troops than he was himself prepared to undergo. **1934** W. A. EDWARDS in F. R. Leavis *Determinations* 155 Swinburne, like some Soviet shock-trooper exhorting feeble comrades, batters and bullies us into thinking every playwright a demi-god. **1938** AUDEN & ISHERWOOD *On Frontier* I. i. 30 As for the Shock Troops..the whole organization's rotten from top to bottom. *Ibid.* II. i. 61 Such a nice boy! And quite high up in his shock-troop already. *Ibid.* ii. 84 My Peace Speech. I shall stand before my shock troopers and I shall tell them [etc.]. **1940** *Ann. Reg. 1939* 225, 54 front-line divisions..of which 14 divisions represented shock troops. **1940** *War Illustr.* 12 Apr. 353 Those who man the submarines may well be called the 'shock troops' of the sea, for of all the seafaring men their task is surely the most arduous and the most dangerous. **1952** C. DAY LEWIS tr. *Virgil's Aeneid* II. 48 At the Scaean gate, panoplied Juno Heads the shock-troops. **1955** M. BANKS *Commando Climber* i. 6 As the war developed, the general trend of commando operations had been..towards the amphibious shock-troop variety of fighting, usually on a brigade or at least on a commando scale. **1955** A. GALLAND *First & Last* xii. 91 The fighter supporting land operations of the army is exclusively a tactical arm, a kind of 'flying shock-troop', for attacking at low level enemy positions and troop movements in the front line, even with bombs, rockets and small arms. **1959** *Listener* 10 Dec. 1031/1 The main line of Chartist stock in the north is poorly represented. Where are those shock troops of Feargus O'Connor, from whose enduring loyalty his influence in the movement was derived? **1962** *Daily Tel.* 14 Sept. 24/5 While Mr. Macmillan was having longish talks with Mr. Menzies of Australia and Mr. Diefenbaker of Canada and others, his shocktroop Ministers, Mr. Sandys and Mr. Heath were standing up to all comers.

1968 *Economist* 16 Nov. 67/1 The National Union of Mineworkers' leaders voted to accept exactly the same percentage pay rise for their men, once the shocktroops of the wage struggle. **1973** R. L. Fox *Alexander* iv. 78 The Shield Bearers..served as shock troops on night raids, hill climbs and forced marches. **1975** *Guardian* 21 Jan. 14/1 The cliché about the Jesuits as the 'Pope's shock troops'. **1977** *Times* 21 Nov. 15/6 Many members of the Waffen SS..were used simply as shock troops during Hitler's War.

c. Applied to a worker in the U.S.S.R. who voluntarily exceeds the production quotas and is regarded as exemplary, and to a brigade formed by such workers and used for the achievement of arduous or urgent tasks; also to such methods of work.

1931 S. N. Harper *Making Bolsheviks* iii. 52 The so-called 'shock-brigade movement' among workmen, which is interpreted by the Communists as an illustration of a new attitude and as a new and vital force produced by the Revolution. *Ibid.* 53 The shock-brigade of a given factory or mine is a voluntary organization of workmen who have come together to fulfil and, if possible, exceed the quota of production assigned to the factory under the Five-Year Plan of expansion. **1931** *Times Lit. Suppl.* 9 July 536/4 'Cultural work' is still in effect a kind of propagandist 'shock work'. **1931** *Morning Post* 11 Aug. 11/7 Three hundred and fifty Russian 'shock workers' landed in London from the S.S. Ukraine yesterday for a two days' 'holiday'. **1934** *Spectator* 26 Oct. 615/2 The 'shock-brigaders' and star 'go-getters'. **1938** *Times* 25 July 13/6 The other projects undertaken by the groups include organization of labour to help in times of special agricultural pressure (like the Shock Brigades in Russia). **1939** R. Campbell *Flowering Rifle* v. 124 Each grim, shock-working Stakhanov. **1946** —— *Talking Bronco* 16 For us mere Shock-workers of the Camp and City Whose sweat, and life-blood, is their beer. **1949** F. Maclean *Eastern Approaches* I. xi. 157 From what I had heard of Soviet 'shock' methods a group of Stakhanovites or shock-workers should be able to put any paddle boat in order in an hour or two. **1962** E. Snow *Red China Today* (1963) lviii. 441 By intensive cultivation, luck and shock-brigade methods, we brought in a rich harvest in record time. **1981** I. Boland tr. *Ginzburg's Within Whirlwind* I. x. 84 The management did not want to use force... These girls were shock workers.

shock, *a.* Add: **b.** *shock-maned* adj.

1922 [see *shaggy-chested* s.v. *Shaggy *a* 3].

shock, *v.*[2] Add: **3. c.** To subject to or transform by mechanical shock. Cf. *Shocked *ppl. a.* 3.

1950 D. Q. Kern *Process Heat Transfer* xiv. 382 Hard scale which can be shocked from the tube. **1965** *Ann. N.Y. Acad. Sci.* CXXIII. 602 Salt shocked by a chemical explosion adjusted mainly by plastic glide along close-spaced slip planes. **1968** Ahrens & Rosenberg in French & Short *Shock Metamorphism of Natural Materials* 59/2 The Hugoniot curve is defined as the locus of pressure-volume-energy states that may be achieved within the material by shocking it from a given initial state.

4. b. (Later example.) Also *intr.* for *pass.*, to suffer shock.

1959 N. Clad *Love & Money* (1960) 15 She liked to say things to shock Clarence, partly because he shocked so easily. **1967** *Listener* 5 Oct. 448/3 Triana's play does shock.

shockability (ʃǫkăbi·lĭti). [f. Shockable *a.*: see -ity.] The capacity for being shocked. Also *attrib.*

1929 G. Gould *Democritus* 89 What we want is to preserve the precious gift of shockability while remaining too intelligent to be shocked. **1963** O. Stewart in C. Irving *Scandal '63* xix. 213 In England shockability is primarily sexual. **1969** J. Elliot *Duel* III. iii. 259 She had a low shockability threshold when it came to language. **1977** *Zigzag* Aug. 5/2 The new wave audiences have been beaten into applauding what they can get while ignoring any new trends that don't quite fit the Sunday People blueprint for shockability.

shockable, *a.* Delete *nonce-wd.* and add later examples. Also *absol.* in pl. sense (with *the*). Hence **sho·ckableness** = *Shockability.

1929 M. Arlen *Babes in Wood* 254 How..nice I think you are—to be so shockable. How different from your books! **1939** H. G. Wells *Holy Terror* III. i. 207 Shockableness is still high. Reverence is something that survives belief. **1965** *Listener* 1 July 12/1 Experimental plays, full of loose living and talk..should be put on at a rather late hour at regular intervals, so that the shockable know not to look. **1976** S. Barstow *Right True End* III. xii. 183, I think she's shockable. I'm not certain how her loyalty to me would stand the strain if she knew I was knocking off a colleague's wife.

shock-absorber. [Shock *sb.*[3]] **1.** A device, esp. on a motor vehicle, aircraft undercarriage, etc., which serves to absorb mechanical shock and to damp vibration.

1906 [in Dict. s.v. Shock *sb.*[3] 7]. **1929** *Times* 31 Oct. 21/3 The considerable number of cars which were fitted with the Luvax hydraulic shock absorbers. **1931** *Henley's ABC of Gliding & Sailflying* 193 If the landing gear is not provided with shock absorbers, it is desirable to pad the pilot's seat well. **1945** Crocker & King *Piping Handbk.* (ed. 4) xviii. 1319 Hydraulic piping can be supported in box guides so as to permit free longitudinal movement except as restrained by the shock absorbers. This arrangement is..effective in cushioning shocks which are due to water hammer. **1951** *Engineering* 26 Oct. 533/2 Long semi-elliptical reverse-camber springs of conventional design are used for the rear suspension, which is.. controlled by double-acting hydraulic shock absorbers. **1973** *Times* 15 Oct. 21/8 British Leyland have admitted that fires have occurred in 18 of the new buses and shock-absorber brackets have broken off.

2. *fig.* Something which (or someone who) reduces or mitigates the worst effects of a new and unpleasant occurrence or experience. Also *attrib.*

1924 *Foundry* 15 Feb. 105 (Advt.), Where lower production costs are necessary our products are real shock-absorbers. **1954** Koestler *Invisible Writing* iv. 52 The elastic shock-absorbers of my Party training began to operate at once. **1954** B. & R. North tr. *M. Duverger's Pol. Parties* I. ii. 83 Stable and stabilizing communities, playing some part as political shock-absorbers. **1957** *Economist* 28 Sept. 1003/1 The process..would close when the promised elections set up an all-Korean government—perhaps with a degree of regional autonomy, and with shock-absorber clauses wirtten into the constitution to cushion the losers. **1969** *Listener* 15 May 666/1 They cannot rely on help from friends or families in emergency—they are people without shock-absorbers. Often a single misfortune gives the push towards disintegration. **1977** *Time* 15 Aug. 13/1 Black labor acts as a shock absorber enabling Italy to survive economic crisis.

Hence **shock-absorbent** *a.*, **shock-absorbing** *ppl. a.* and *vbl. sb.*

1909 Shock-absorbing [in Dict. s.v. Shock *sb.*[3] 7]. **1946** D. de Carle *Pract. Watch Repairing* xx. 262 Had the balance been fitted with some shock absorbent device the damage would not have occurred. **1958** *Listener* 30 Oct. 683/1, I think you want a car that has adequate shock absorbing. **1973** *Times* 13 July 9/1 Each [crash-helmet] has a shock-absorbent liner as well as ear and cheek pads. **1973** J. G. Tweeddale *Materials Technol.* II. iii. 56 Drums..may be lined with shock-absorbing material, to minimise wear of the drum and to reduce noise.

shocked, *ppl. a.*[1] Add: **2.** (Earlier example.)

1840 Queen Victoria *Let.* 21 Jan. in B. Connell *Regina v. Palmerston* (1962) i. 20 A letter..which she has kept near three years, she is shocked to say.

3. Subjected to mechanical shock, esp. by the passage of a shock wave.

1962 E. M. Shoemaker in Z. Kopol *Physics & Astron. Moon* viii. 317 Part of the kinetic energy of the meteorite engulfed by shock is converted to internal energy in the meteorite, and part is transferred as kinetic and internal energy to the shocked rock ahead of the meteorite. **1973** *Nature* 27 July 211/2 Hypervelocity impact cratering studies have shown that about ninety-nine volumes of crushed and shocked rock are formed and ejected for each volume of liquid melt (glass) that is formed and ejected. **1976** *Ibid.* 11 Nov. 114/3 This ionisation front is preceded by a shock front, and after a time there is a shocked layer of neutral gas between these two fronts.

Hence **shockedly** (ʃǫ·kėdli, ʃǫ·ktli), *adv.*

1926 Fowler *Mod. Eng. Usage* 531/2 *Shockedly.* A bad form. **1963** D. Hughes in Sissons & French *Age of Austerity* 93 Then, rather shockedly, a knight's name figured in court.

shocker[1]**.** Add: **1.** (Further examples.) Also, something or someone shockingly bad.

1954 M. Croft *Spare Rod* I. ix. 62 A lot of people believe that to be a good writer a man must have a well-nigh perfect character... On the contrary, many of them have been perfect shockers. **1958** *Manch. Guardian* 7 June 4/7 The 'musical' is still in the ascendant. I caught one real shocker—'Jamaica'. But the others..were fun. **1960** J. Stroud *Shorn Lamb* xxiii. 248, I remember a girl we had..an absolute shocker, never settled anywhere. **1965** Mrs. L. B. Johnson *White House Diary* 17 June (1970) 291 Then Lyndon delivered the shocker of the evening. **1973** *Express* (Trinidad & Tobago) 9 Apr. 1/3 The series will be the sort of shocker that should cast out smug complacency. **1976** *Daily Times* (Lagos) 12 Oct. 1/3 This is the shocker for teachers in Bomo State. **1977** *Time* 17 Jan. 9/1 What began as a shocker killing has grown steadily more sensational. **1977** *Horse & Hound* 10 June 8/2 Lucky Sovereign ran a shocker, presumably either unable or unwilling to give his true running on this firm ground and/or the Epsom course. **1977** *Time* 8 Aug. 39/1 Then on Wednesday came a shocker from Bethlehem Steel, which reported an operating loss of $75·4 million for the first half. **1978** *Chicago* June 119/2 The jury found the guy guilty on only one count. A real shocker, and entirely due to Sullivan's work.

2. A shock-absorber. *colloq.*

1949 Partridge *Dict. Slang* (ed. 3) 1168/1 *Shocker*,..a shock-absorber: motorists': since ca. 1925. **1969** *Guardian* 23 Aug. 5/8 The models with worn shockers were thrown from side to side. **1977** *Caravan World* (Austral.) Jan. 19/2 Incorrect loading on the tow-ball..results in overloaded tyres, springs and shockers if the weight is forward.

shocker[2]**.** (Earlier U.S. example.)

1786 G. Washington *Diaries* 15 July (1925) III. 91 For every two Cradlers to allow 4 rakes, 1 shocker, and two Carriers.

shock-headed, *a.* Add: *shock-headed Peter* = *Struwwelpeter.

1848 tr. *H. Hoffmann's English Struwwelpeter* (ed. 4) 2 Any thing to me is sweeter Than to see Shock-headed Peter. **1895** R. Stephens *Cruciform Mark* ix. 47 'Shock-headed Peter', as he was familiarly dubbed..was a very interesting personality... Red-haired and red-bearded, his head was a perfect burning bush. **1905** C. Mackenzie *Diary* 23 May in *My Life & Times* (1964) III. 224 Went to see Martin Harvey as Hamlet... He looked like..shock-headed Peter. **1926** D. L. Sayers *Clouds of Witness* vii. 159 Shaking her head so angrily that she looked like shock-headed Peter.

shocking, *ppl. a.* Add: **3. d.** *shocking pink*: a vivid, garish shade of pink.

1938 *Encycl. Brit. Bk. of Year* 248/2 Only one new colour arrived; it is 'Shocking Pink', introduced by Schiaparelli in Feb. 1937, then taken up by other designers, with the result that the vanguard of fashionable women everywhere are now seen wearing this crude, cruel shade of rose. **1939** *Archit. Rev.* LXXXV. 305/3 There it is, in its gay 'shocking pink' cover, compact, comprehensive and invaluable. **1954** E. Schiaparelli *Shocking Life* ix. 97 My friends and executives..began to say that I was crazy and that nobody would want it because it was really 'nigger pink'... The colour 'shocking' established itself for ever as a classic. Even Dali dyed an enormous stuffed bear in shocking pink. **1960** M. Stewart *My Brother Michael* x. 136 They [*sc.* socks] were luminous, and of a startling shade of shocking pink. **1977** C. McCullough *Thorn Birds* xix. 520 An involuntary grimace at first sight of her shocking-pink slipper satin.

Shockley (ʃǫ·kli). The name of William B. *Shockley* (b. 1910), British-born U.S. physicist, used *attrib.* to designate concepts and devices he invented, as **Shockley diode,** a semiconductor diode consisting of four regions of alternate conductivity types (*n* and *p*), with the anode and the cathode connected to the end ones; **Shockley partial (dislocation),** a partial dislocation in which the lattice displacement, as represented by the Burgers vector, lies in the fault plane, so that the dislocation is capable of gliding.

1962 *Instrument Pract.* XVI. 1466/2 The arrangement will then have the characteristics of the Shockley or four layer diode which has only two terminals. **1965** *Wireless World* Aug. 397/2 Transistors, unijunction transistors or Shockley diodes can be used. **1975** T. D. Towers *Semiconductor Circuit Elements* xii. 146 A Shockley diode represents a switch with an off resistance of megohms and an on resistance of ohms. **1953** W. T. Read *Dislocations in Crystals* vii. 98 The Shockley partial is one of the three types of partial dislocations associated with plane faults in f.c.c. **1969** [see *partial *sb.* 2]. **1976** M. T. Sprackling *Plastic Deformation Simple Ionic Crystals* iv. 51 Shockley partial dislocations can glide in the fault plane; Frank partial dislocations cannot.

shock wave. Also **sho·ck-wave, sho·ckwave.** [f. Shock *sb.*[3]; cf. F. *onde de choc* (common in early 20th-cent. Fr. writings on fluid dynamics).] **a.** A disturbance that travels through a fluid as a narrow region in which there is a large, abrupt change in pressure and related quantities, esp. one separating regions of subsonic and supersonic fluid flow such as is created by an object moving faster than sound or by an explosion; *loosely*, any pressure wave of large amplitude.

[**1904** *Sci. Abstr.* A. VII. 646 Quasi-waves of shock propagating a dilatation in accordance with Hugoniot's law.] **1907** *Chem. Abstr.* I. 1470 The explosive wave is a shock wave accompanied by a decided combustion. **1931** *Proc. Nat. Acad. Sci.* XVII. 534 Let us regard a plane discontinuity or 'shock wave' from the point of view of the observer moving with it, so that the shock wave will appear to us stationary. **1945** *Times* 8 Nov. 2/2 When the oncoming aeroplane is travelling at, say, 600 m.p.h. or more the steadiness of the air-flow over the wing then breaks down with the result that what is known as a shock-wave occurs at the thickest part of the wing. **1950** *Sci. News* XV. Plate 5 (*caption*) The segmented appearance of the flame is due to the shock wave which is formed in the jet as it leaves the nozzle and which is reflected to and fro within the jet. **1958** *N. & Q.* CCIII. 139/1 Aside from other factors in nuclear explosions, the shock-wave, or blast, is possibly the greatest source of danger. **1973** C. Mason *Hostage* v. 65 The building was meanwhile hit by a shockwave so severe it felt like an earthquake. **1979** *Jrnl. R. Soc. Arts* CXXVII. 403/1 A small explosive charge is detonated in the ground and the resulting shock waves picked up by sensitive microphones called geophones.

b. *fig.*

1969 *Harper's Mag.* Dec. 125 The last writer who sent shock waves through Western literature. **1974** I. Murdoch *Sacred & Profane Love Machine* 145 The shock wave had not yet really come... Awful grief and pain hovered somewhere near to her. **1979** P. Harcourt *Sleep of Spies* I. iv. 56 The question caused shock waves round the room.

shod, *ppl. a.* Add: **2. a.** (Earlier mod. example.)

1840 J. Rowand *Let.* 8 July in G. P. de T. Glazebrook *Hargrave Corr.* (1938) 317 A couple of blood Indians got afighting..which ended by driving two shod arrows through one fellows body.

b. Of a motor vehicle: having tyres of a certain quality, as *well shod.* Cf. *Shoe *v.* 2.

1967 Partridge *Dict. Slang* Suppl. 1356/1 *Shod.* 'Colloquially applied to motor vehicles. A car with good tyres is described as '*well shod*' (B.P.): Australian: since ca. 1945. **1977** *Horse & Hound* 14 Jan. 44/2 (Advt.), Bedford T.K. diesel, 1964, horse/cattle box... Well shod.

shodden, *a.* (Earlier example.)

1829 J. F. Cooper *Borderers* vi. 74 His beast hath had a shodden hoof.

shoddy, *sb.* Add: **4*.** = **reclaimed rubber.* Now *rare.*

1892 *Sci. Amer.* 7 May 293/2 Mould work of the lower

grades is often made of shoddy with no addition of pure rubber. **1898** *India-Rubber & Gutta-Percha & Electr. Trades' Jrnl.* XVI. 190/2 It is not surprising..that the volume of mechanical 'shoddy' should be placed by the best estimates at not above one-sixth of the total production of reclaimed rubber in the United States. **1974** K. F. Heinisch *Dict. Rubber* 428/2 *Shoddy*, jargon formerly used for reclaim; now rarely used.

5. shoddy dropper *Austral.* and *N.Z. slang*, a pedlar of cheap or falsely described clothing; a hawker.

1941 Baker *N.Z. Slang* vi. 52 We have [this century]..acquired some underworld slang of our own..[e.g.] *shoddy dropper*, a seller of cheap serge; [etc.]. **1964** *Australasian Post* 28 May 38/3 The 'shoddy droppers' (Indian hawkers) always carried a supply of patent medicines..with them on their rounds. **1972** *Telegraph* (Brisbane) 30 Aug. 24/6 The operators were known as dudders and professional shoddy-droppers.

shoddy, *a.* Add: **2.** Also, cheap, inferior; displaying signs of use, shabby, dilapidated.

1927 *Melody Maker* Apr. 305/1 The great majority of dance bands have settled down to a very stereotyped and shoddy sort of music. **1929** V. Woolf *Room of one's Own* v. 133 She will still wear the shoddy old fetters of class on her feet. **1932** E. Waugh *Black Mischief* vii. 255 The royal box was still there, shoddy sort of affair, but it provided a platform. **1952** *Manch. Guardian Weekly* 31 July 7/2 Because Stevenson was the man to beat, and Kefauver was their man, they had to fall back on the shoddy pretence that Stevenson was the tool of the big city machines.

shoddyism. (In Dict. s.v. Shoddy *sb.*) (Earlier example.)

1865 *Three Years among Working Classes in U.S.* vi. 124 Shoddyism among a large class of the people, corruption in official stations, an absorbing passion for making money..are the prevailing characteristics of the day.

shoe, *sb.* Add: **2. b.** Also, *the shoe is on the other foot*: the facts are otherwise, the position is reversed. Cf. *the boot is on the other leg* s.v. Boot *sb.*[3] 1 b.

1933 *Mystery* May 122/1 Inspector Queen has not been able to discover our man-about-town's source of income. A gigolo? Gigolos do not pay for ladies' apartments; the shoe is rather on the other foot. **1939** B. K. Harris *Purslane* 179, I tell him if he had the waitin' on him to do the shoes would be on the other foot. **1953** J. S. Huxley *Evolution in Action* ii. 49 All the objections to a selectionist explanation of evolution that are based on the improbability of its results, simply fall to the ground. In fact the shoe is now on the other foot. Improbability is to be *expected* as the result of natural selection. **1976** *Times Lit. Suppl.* 2 Jan. 13/4 Most obviously, the shoe is on the other foot. Anyone who knows what rigour is will find it lacking in most of Hegel's transitions.

5. c. (Later examples.)

1972 L. M. Harris *Introd. Deepwater Floating Drilling Operations* ix. 90 The shoe of the foundation pile is equipped with a breakaway guide frame. **1976** *Offshore Platforms & Pipelining* 8/2 Deviation will begin about 100 ft below the conductor shoe.

q. A tyre. *slang.*

1917 E. E. Cummings *Let.* 2 Aug. (1969) 32 The rear axle looked like a mosquito's beak, and there were 2 shoes blown. **1934** R. Blaker *Night-Shift* vii. 87 If the tyres were worn to the fabric smooth as an egg, he could dismiss this outlay as 'a set of new shoes'.

r. A box for dealing the cards in baccarat or *chemin de fer*. Also, a game of baccarat.

1923 W. J. Locke *Moordius & Co.* xi. 149 Moordius dealt from the shoe. One card to the right, one to the left, one to himself. **1930** D. Byrne *Golden Goat* i. 8 They were only interested in the passing of the 'shoe' as the *chemin-de-fer* box is called. **1960** O. Manning *Great Fortune* i. 54 Hadjimoscos took his place before the shoe. As soon as he had drawn cards, he became serious and businesslike. **1964** A. Wykes *Gambling* xiii. 324 Zographos could remember every card that was played throughout a game (or 'shoe') of baccarat. **1965** D. Francis *Odds Against* iv. 52 He kept his side of the bargain by digging out the chemmy shoe. **1976** 'J. Welcome' *Grand National* iv. 54 The bank passed and the polished walnut and silver shoe slid along the table to a gaunt, henna-haired woman.

s. On a camera, a socket or other mounting for the temporary attachment of an accessory.

1953 A. Matheson *Leica Way* 47 The Leica If and Ic models carry a detachable brilliant viewfinder..in one of the two accessory shoes. **1971**, etc. [see *hot shoe* s.v. *hot *a.* 12 c]. **1979** *SLR Camera* Feb. 74/1 The modification consists of adding an extra contact to the shoe of the sensor lead.

6. a. *shoe-bag, -factory, -store* (for U.S. read orig. U.S. and add earlier and later examples).

1873 S. Coolidge *What Katy did at School* vii. 139 Hang your dresses up..and put your shoes in the shoe-bag. **1972** J. Wilson *Hide & Seek* i. 7 The children began to pour out into the playground. Alice was..dragging her shoe bag along after her. **1855** J. Holbrook *Ten Years among Mail Bags* 276 How many persons are employed in that shoe factory? **1960** M. Spark *Ballad Peckham Rye* vi. 111 She told him all of her life in the shoe factory. **1789** *Boston Directory* 175 Bond and Bryant, shoe-store. **1976** *Milton Keynes Express* 11 June 12/2 The shoe store of Leslie Wheeler at New Bradwell.

b. *shoe-repairer.*

1933 *Radio Times* 14 Apr. 127/1 The well-known Kensington Shoe Repairers. **1976** M. Hinxman *End of Good Woman* vii. 94 Shoe repairer, now that was 'poshe' if you like!

c. shoe-bench *U.S.*, a shoemaker's bench; **shoe-bill,** (*a*) (earlier example); so **shoe-bill(ed) stork**; **shoe-brush** (earlier example); also *attrib.* of an object shaped like a shoe-brush; **shoe-button,** a button used for fastening a boot or a shoe; freq. *attrib.* of a small expressionless eye; **shoe-deep** *a. U.S.*, deep enough to cover a person's shoes; **shoe-flower** (earlier example); **shoe-last,** also *fig.*; also used *attrib.* in *Archæol.* to designate or with reference to polished stone implements, flat on one side and curved on the other, found in the area of neolithic Danubian culture; **shoe-piece,** (*a*) (in Dict., sense 6 a); (*b*) a piece of wood at the back of a chair, supporting the splat; **shoe-shine, shoeshine** (orig. and chiefly *U.S.*), a polish given to shoes, esp. by a shoe-shiner; freq. *attrib.*; **shoe-shiner,** one who polishes shoes for money; **shoe-tree** (earlier example).

1841 *Knickerbocker* May 362 A few weeks' rumination on the shoe-bench, or cogitation on the tailor's board. **1891** *Harper's Mag.* June 57/1 An express wagon was..loaded with the old shoe bench. **1861** Geo. Eliot *Let.* 20 Feb. (1954) III. 381 There is a shoe-bill, a great bird of grotesque ugliness. **1957** *Bull. Brit. Mus. (Nat. Hist.): Zool.* V. 111 (*heading*) The Pelecaniform characters of the skeleton of the Shoe-bill Stork. **1964** E. A. Nida *Towards Sci. Transl.* iii. 40 A person points to the beak of a shoe-billed stork and says *That's a big bill.* **1975** *Daily Colonist* (Victoria, B.C.) 17 Dec. 6/3 Shoebill stork..is one of only eight. **1740** E. Purefoy *Let.* 8 Mar. (1931) II. x. 248, I received Mr Robotham's letter..with half a dozen of oranges, a dozen of Delft plates, & 2 shoe Brushes. **1968** J. Arnold *Shell Bk. Country Crafts* 185 For use in difficult angles an extra leggat is used, having a shoe-brush handle to make it easy to use in those awkard places. **1895** *Montgomery Ward Catal.* Spring & Summer 525/2 Button Machine... No family should be without this machine..for putting on their own shoe buttons. **1928** E. O'Neill *Strange Interlude* v. 170 Lust ogling me for a dollar with oily shoe-button Italian eyes! **1973** 'A. Gilbert' *Is she Dead Too?* (rev. ed.) ii. 29 Her eyes round and hard as shoe buttons. **1773** P. V. Fithian *Jrnl.* 28 Dec. (1900) I. 75 Last night there fell a snow, which is about half Shoe-deep. **1891** M. E. Wilkins *New England Nun* 174 There had been a light fall of snow..but it was not shoe-deep. **1814** J. Lunan *Hortus Jamaicensis* I. 176 They are also put to a use which seems little consistent with their elegance and beauty, that of blacking shoes, whence their names of *rosæ calceolariæ* and shoe-flower. **1879** G. M. Hopkins *Lett. to R. Bridges* (1955) 76 Look upon them [*sc.* suggestions] as shoelasts on which to shape your final handiwork. **1927** Peake & Fleure *Priests & Kings* vi. 126 They had..stone celts or hoes, among which is a type, not unlike that found in the Danube basin, known as the shoe-last celt. **1961** G. Clark *World Prehist.* vi. 126 Boian pioneers..used a variety of stone tools, including adze-blades of bevelled and shoe-last form. **1970** Bray & Trump *Dict. Archaeol.* 210/2 *Shoe-last adze* or *celt*, a long thin stone adze employed by the Danubian farmers of the Early Neolithic, possibly as a hoe for cultivating their fields. **1923** J. C. Rogers *Eng. Furnit.* ii. ii. 63 The splat..rose from a shaped shoe-piece planted on the rear seat rail. **1969** J. Gloag *Short Dict. Furnit.* (rev. ed.) 607 *Shoe-piece*, the shaped projection that rises from the back rail of a chair seat, into which the base of the splat is socketed. **1911** H. P. Fairchild *Greek Immigration to U.S.* vii. 127 In 1904 there were but three shoe-shine parlors in the hands of Greeks in the city. **1931** *Kansas City Times* 29 Oct., Cecil, the Negro shoe shine boy at the City barber shop, has organized a band. **1957** *New Yorker* 5 Oct. 35/1 President Romano,..resting tensely in his shirtsleeves, getting a shoeshine. **1958** X. Fielding *Corsair Country* i. 20 Where's the nobility in..these importunate shoe-shine boys? **1976** *National Observer* (U.S.) 21 Feb. 4/2 Complaints about the all-female shoeshine parlors in Salt Lake City may diminish... The commissioners said that the parlors..must not allow the shoe shiners to mingle with the customers or sit on their laps. **1910** *Chambers's Jrnl.* July 431/1 The hotel will not be bothered with boot-cleaning, that service being performed by the 'shoe-shiner' in the basement. **1976** Shoe shiner [see *shoe-shine* above]. **1827** Drake & Mansfield *Cincinnati* viii. 60 In the third story the manufacture of shoe trees is carried on.

shoe, *v.* Add: **2.** Also, to provide (a motor vehicle) with tyres of a specified type or quality. Cf. *shoe *sb.* 5 q.

1925 *Morris Owner's Man.* p. lxx (Advt.), Every car is turned out in sound order and condition, shod with good tyres. **1971** *Drive* Summer 121/1 The test car was shod with radial tyres. **1976** *Southern Even. Echo* (Southampton) 2 Nov. 15/3 Braking is by servo-assisted discs at the front and rear drums, with radial tyres as standard shoeing equipment.

shoe (ʃū), *a. U.S. slang.* [Origin obscure.] Conforming to the dress, behaviour, or attitudes of students at exclusive educational establishments; acceptable to or commended by such people.

1962 *Punch* 13 June 895/3 A girl at these institutions [*sc.* schools] must prove herself to be 'shoe'—and woe betide her if her dress and manner don't manifest..'shoeness'. **1973** *N.Y. Times Mag.* 17 June 38/3 Perhaps it is significant that one favourite mode of protest in the fifties was satire. We—a lot of us—were cool, ironic, 'shoe'. **1980** L. Birnbach et al. *Official Preppy Handbk.* 222/2 *Shoe, adj.* Top-drawer. Very acceptable.

shoeblack. Add: **b.** Also simply *shoeblack*. (Earlier and later examples.)

1837 J. Macfadyen *Flora Jamaica* I. 66 The flowers, from the mucilaginous juice they contain, are employed to give a polish to the leather of shoes; and hence the plant has received the name of the shoe-black. **1965** *Harper's Bazaar* Feb. 18/3 The scarlet blossoms of the bush they [*sc.* Jamaicans] call the Shoe-Black.

shoe-box, shoebox (ʃū·bɒks). [Shoe *sb.*] **1.** A box in which a pair of shoes is packed.

1860, 1897 [in Dict. s.v. Shoe *sb.*[1] 6 a]. **1930** J. Dos Passos *42nd Parallel* i. 101 A small house like a shoebox. **1970** J. Earl *Tuners & Amplifiers* i. 14 A modern stereo amplifier capable of yielding 20 watts..is nowadays barely larger than a shoe box.

2. *fig.* A building or part of a building resembling a shoe-box. Also *attrib.*

1968 *Listener* 1 Aug. 134/2 Leeds hasn't changed much. There are a few changes. Some of those glass shoe-boxes have been plonked down at random in the city centre. **1972** *Times* 8 June (Birmingham Suppl.) p. v/4 The mandatory shoe-box buildings. **1978** N. Freeling *Night Lords* xxxiii. 153 Bianchi..waved casually at the building; the usual pile of open shoe-boxes. **1979** M. A. Sharp *Sunflower* iii. 29 Shoebox buildings, nestled together like children's blocks.

shoe-horn, *v.* Add: **2. b.** To manœuvre or compress (someone or something) *into* (*in*, *on to*) an inadequate space (occas. *into* an inadequate period of time).

1927 D. L. Sayers *Unnatural Death* vi. 64 He shoe-horned himself into his seat [in a motor car]. **1954** *Archit. Rev.* CXVI. 212/1 For the second edition he shoehorned in material on Eiffel, Maillart and Alto, thus playing havoc with his illustration numbers. **1968** *Economist* 18 May 69/1 Big aircraft are shoe-horned on to small landing strips with only elementary navigation aids. **1969** J. Wainwright *Take-over Men* iii. 37 Lewis..was shoe-horning himself behind the steering wheel. **1972** *Real Estate Rev.* Winter 107/1 The logical-thought input might be assumed to have been forcibly pressed and shoe-horned into a preconceived formal framework. **1974** *Daily Tel.* (Colour Suppl.) 23 Aug. 7/2 In order to shoe-horn in more people airlines and aircraft manufacturers have given up any interest at all in comfort. **1978** *Science* 17 Mar. 1161/2 Nearly 140 symposia and almost 1000 speakers shoehorned into five days and nights. **1979** R. L. Simon *Peking Duck* ii. 19 The houses were..shoe-horned onto thirty feet of beachfront land.

shoepack (ʃū·pæk). *N. Amer.* Also **shoepac, shupac.** [ad. Delaware Jargon *seppock, sippack* shoes, f. Unami Delaware *čipahko* moccasins, infl. by Shoe *sb.*] Orig., and still locally, a moccasin with an extra sole; more recently, a commercially manufactured oiled leather boot, usually with a rubber sole. Cf. *pac.

1755 in S. M. Hamilton *Lett. to Washington* (1898) I. 99 It would be a good thing to have Shoe-packs or Moccosons for the Scouts. **1824** [in Dict. s.v. Shoe *sb.* 6 c]. **1853** S. Strickland *Twenty-Seven Years in Canada West* II. 286 Shoe-packs, a species of mocassin peculiar to the Lower Province, cow-hide boots, and a *bonnet rouge* for the head, complete the costume of the Canadian lumberman. **1882** J. M. LeMoine *Picturesque Quebec* 201 He came pounding along Notre Dame street, in Montreal, in his red shirt and tan-colored *shupac* boots, all dripping wet. **1903** S. E. White *Forest* x. 120 He brought to light..oil-tanned shoepacs, with and without the flexible sole. **1940** R. Marshall *Arctic Village* 101 It is only in the fall and the spring that the snow is soggy, and in those seasons shoepacks with rubber bottoms and leather uppers replace the moccasins. **1977** *New Yorker* 20 June 69/2 After the cast comes off, I can walk with a shoepac and a cane.

shoe-string, shoestring. 1. (In Dict. s.v. Shoe *sb.* 6 c.)

2. A small or inadequate amount of money; a very little capital; a small margin. Chiefly in phr. *on a shoe-string. colloq.* (orig. *U.S.*).

[**1882** *Century Mag.* Apr. 884/2 [He] could draw to a shoe-string, as the saying went, and obtain a tan-yard!] **1904** *Cosmopolitan* May 89 He..speculated 'on a shoe-string'—an exceedingly slim margin. **1926** J. Black *You can't Win* viii. 90 The new owners had no bankroll, just opened up on a shoestring. **1932** *Atlantic Monthly* Mar. 310/1 Every business man who has made a big success of himself started on a shoestring. **1957** *Listener* 28 Nov. 893/3 Reformative efforts have to be..as they say, 'run on a shoe-string'. **1977** C. McCullough *Thorn Birds* xvii. 441 Australians in England, youth-hosteling on a shoestring.

3. = *shoe-string potato*, sense 4 c below.

1931 B. Starke *Touch & Go* x. 156, I..found that the word 'shoe-strings' on the menu really meant Julienne potatoes. I ate every last shoe-string.

4. *attrib.* and *Comb.* **a.** *attrib.* Narrow (*lit.* and *fig.*).

1878 *Congress. Rec.* App. 13 June 478/2, I will promise to meet him on the northern border of 'the shoe-string district'. **1897** *Pop. Sci. Monthly* L. 309 Bad roads and shoestring paths..fringe them. **1953** *Times* 30 July 7 A shoe-string majority.

b. *attrib.* Operating on a shoe-string, costing or spending little; cheap, informal; petty.

1890 J. P. Quinn *Fools of Fortune* 494 The gamblers, aside from a lot of 'hangers on', known as 'shoestring' or 'tin horn' gamblers, do not figure in the criminal records. **1923** 'B. M. Bower' *Parowan Bonanza* xi. 137 The little shoestring propositions that go broke and leave empty houses behind them. **1936** *Sun* (Baltimore) 20 Nov. 1/5 The governors of the Federal Reserve System today proposed steps to plug up loopholes through which 'shoe-string' and other operators have been able to trade extensively without even posting margins. **1941** B. Schulberg *What makes Sammy Run?* vi. 123 A shoe-string producer..had bought the stock shots from *Hell's Angels* and *Wings* and needed an airplane story. **1958** *Vogue* Oct. 203 Winter after winter ski-crazy students flock to the snow for shoestring holidays which have been planned to the last farthing. **1959** 'M. Neville' *Sweet Night for Murder* i. 17 She talked, thought, dreamed clothes. On a shoe-string allowance, however, she could do little about them. **1977** *S. Wales Guardian* 27 Oct. 1/3 The Education Committee was being penny wise and pound foolish by giving some contracts to small private contractors running on a shoe-string budget and using non-union labour. **1978** J. Krantz *Scruples* iii. 78 The ad that launched Spider was for a new type of fingernail hardener, put out by a shoe-string company.

c. Special comb.: **shoe-string catch** *Baseball*, a running catch made close to the ground; **shoe-string fungus** = *honey fungus* s.v. *honey *sb.* (*a*) 7 b; **shoe-string potato** *U.S.*, a julienne potato (see *julienne 2) (chiefly *pl.*); **shoe-string (root) rot**, the disease caused by shoe-string fungus; **shoe-string tie**, a very narrow neck-tie.

1926 *N.Y. Times* 11 Oct. 25/2 Haley ran up on it and tried to make a shoestring catch of it. **1957** *New Yorker* 13 July 17/1 Like a shoestring catch in center field, make it and you're the hero. Muff it and you're a dope. **1926** F. D. Heald *Man. Plant Diseases* xxvi. 794 The causal fungus is generally referred to as the 'honey agaric'..or the 'shoestring fungus'. **1978** T. A. Tattar *Diseases of Shade Trees* xxiii. 315 The shoestring-fungus..and the two-lined chestnut borer..are the most common organisms of secondary action. **1906** 'H. McHugh' *Skiddoo!* ii. 30 The next course was French fried potatoes with some shoe-string potatoes on the side. **1940** *Amer. Mercury* Sept. 72 Old Fred Harvey started turning a shoestring potato into a 2500-mile of railroad eating-places. **1976** U. Curtiss *Birthday Gift* xv. 141 As fruitless as looking for shoestring potatoes in strange supermarkets. **1978** T. A. Tattar *Diseases of Shade Trees* x. 140 Shoestring root rot affects a wide range of shrubs and trees. **1931** E. E. Hubert *Outl. Forest Pathol.* ix. 417 Shoestring rot is a disease well known to the forest pathologist. **1903** F. Norris *Pit* 337 His shoestring tie straggled over his frayed shirt front. **1961** *Sunday Express* 29 Jan. 15/6 A short, dark Frenchman in a shoe-string tie.

shoey (ʃū·i). *slang.* [f. Shoe *v.* + -y[6].] A shoeing-smith in a cavalry regiment.

1919 in *War Terms* in *Athenæum* 1 Aug. 695/2. **1925** in Fraser & Gibbons *Soldier & Sailor Words* 256. **1969** S. Mays *Fall out Officers* xii. 93 Shoey..Slap some shoes on my new horse.

shoful. Add: Also **shofel. 1.** (Earlier examples.)

1828 *Sessions' Papers Old Bailey 1827–28* 602/2 The twenty counterfeit shillings were found on me; the sister came to me and asked if I had any *shofle* about me, if I had to put it away. **1846** *Swell's Night Guide* 61 The shiser thinks to bounce us by passing a shofel quid.

shog, *v.* Add: **1. a.** Also, to shake *off* a load. *rare.*

1949 D. L. Sayers tr. *Dante's Divine Comedy* I. xvii. 178 Having shogged our burden off..away he bounded.

3. b. (Later *Lit.* examples.)

1884 C. M. Yonge *Armourer's Prentices* I. x. 192 Bolt..bade him shog off, and not come sneaking after other folks' shoes. **1929** J. C. Powys *Wolf Solent* vii. 154 Lob began to swagger slowly away. 'I knows why you wants me to shog off,' he called back. *Ibid.* ix. 208 Wolf shogged off by himself. **1962** L. R. Banks *End to Running* I. v. 71 I'll just say to hell with her, to hell with the money and the house and everything else—I'll just shog off.

‖**shogi** (ʃōu·gi). Also **Sho-gi**, † **Sho-Ho-Ye, Shongi.** [Jap.] A Japanese board game resembling chess.

1858 *Japan Opened* (Relig. Tract Soc.) vii. 267 The game is called *Sho-Ho-Ye*, and is a great favourite among the Japanese. **1884** tr. *J. J. Rein's Japan* II. ii. 430 Among those of which adults of all classes..are very fond, the most conspicuous at present are Shôgi, or chess, and Go. **1890** B. H. Chamberlain *Things Japanese* 66 Japanese chess (*shōgi*) was introduced from China centuries ago. **1905** Cho-Yo *Japanese Chess* (*Shō-ngi*) 27 The governing class of people valued the chessological Art or Science of struggles, commonly known as *Shōngi* (Chess). **1969** R. C. Bell *Board & Table Games* II. ii. 38 There are about ten million Sho-gi players in Japan. **1975** *Way to Play* 50/1 There have been many forms of shogi since its introduction in about the eighth century.

shogunate. (Earlier example.)

1871 A. B. Mitford *Tales Old Japan* I. 99 After..the abolition of the Shogunate, he accompanied the last of the Shoguns in his retirement.

Shoho, var. *Saho *sb.* and *a.*

‖**shoji** (ʃōu·dʒi). [Jap.] **1.** In Japanese architecture, a sliding outer or inner door made of a latticed screen covered usu. with white paper.

1880 I. L. Bird *Unbeaten Tracks in Japan* I. 90, I closed the sliding windows, with translucent paper for window panes, called *shōji*. **1922** J. Street *Mysterious Japan* ii. 24 Children glimpsed through the open wood and paper *shoji* of their matchbox houses. **1959** R. Kirkbride *Tamiko* iv. 28 He swung himself over the sill and dropped into her room, closing the shoji behind him. **1979** H. McCloy *Smoking Mirror* Inside the house there were..sliding partitions like the panels on a Japanese shoji.

2. *attrib.* or as *adj.*

1886 J. La Farge *Let.* 1 Sept. in *Artist's Lett. Japan* (1897) 217 To look out of the *shoji* screens into the garden. **1896** L. Hearn *Kokoro* ii. 19 The light *shōji* frames serving at once for windows and walls, and repapered twice a year. **1958** R. Gannon *New Ways with Dried Flowers* x. 126 (*caption*) Shoji type screen decorated with a variety of pressed leaves. **1967** M. M. Pegler *Dict. Interior Design* 407 The shoji panels are used as screens, dividers, doors that slide behind one another on a track (Japanese style), or as window coverings. **1977** *Time* 24 Jan. 17/1 The hero tears his way through the hard paper covering of a shoji screen.

‖**shokku** (ʃǫ·kū). [Jap., f. Shock *sb.*[3]] Used *joc.* to denote a shock or surprise in political or economic affairs concerning Japan.

1971 *Time* 4 Oct. 36/1 The President had convulsed Japan..with the 'Nixon *shokku*'—his spectacular policy shifts on China and the economy. **1973** *Time* 3 Sept. 18 Indeed, the Nixon Administration's diplomatic *shokkus* in 1971 did lasting damage to Japan's relations with the U.S. **1978** *Encounter* Sept. 56/2 The Japanese were able to cope with their frightful '*oil shokku*' with far more self-restraint than marked the response of other countries to the oil embargo.

sholy (ʃōu·li). Also **sholey.** Representation of U.S. Black and Southern dial. pronunc. of Surely *adv.*

1929 H. W. Odum in *Amer. Mercury* Sept. 48/1 Camp sholy was roughish place. **1940** W. Faulkner *Hamlet* I. ii. 56 'You brought it to me?' 'Sholy,' Ratliff said. 'Take it.' **1966** M. Thelwell in A. Chapman *New Black Voices* (1972) 140 Sholey. Sho, hit'll be jes fine.

‖**shomer** (ʃōu·məɹ). Pl. **shomrim.** [ad. Heb. *šōmēr* watchman.] **1.** (See quot. 1971.)

1909 *Cent. Dict.* Suppl., Shomer. **1923** H. Trager *Pioneers in Palestine* II. iii. 147 The other passengers talk of the killing of one of the Shomrim by an Arab. **1935** *Zionist Review* Mar. 10/2 At 4-30 a.m...pounded the shomer (night watch) on my door. **1938** *Ibid.* Feb. 35/1 The renowned old Jewish watchmen..have been in the country for twenty-five years and more, having been members of the '*shomrim*' organisation. **1944** M. Samuel *Harvest in Desert* xiii. 121 From Gomel came the members of first group of *Shomrim* ('Guards') who organized in Palestine. **1971** *Encycl. Zionism & Israel* I. 462 *Hashomer* (*Shomer*) Self-defence organization of Jewish pioneers.. established in Palestine in 1909 to protect Jewish settlements there... Each..colony..was supplied with Shomrim (watchmen).

2. An inspector who verifies that food is prepared in accordance with Jewish religious laws.

1909 *Cent. Dict.* Suppl., Shomer. **1923** H. M. Lazarus *Ways of her Household* I. i. 8 There is need for a special supervisor—*shomer*—to be appointed for licensed butcher-shops. **1954** A. H. Hyamson *London Board for Shechita* vi. 33 The shomer visited the community in Paris..and was given every facility to investigate the methods of porging. **1980** *Times* 28 May 14/4, I am quite happy to accept supervision of our food supplies by a shomer appointed by the local Jewish authorities.

Shona (ʃōu·nă). = *Mashona *sb.* and *a.*

1930 C. M. Doke *Rep. Unification Shona Dialects* 61 The Language Committee..hope to unify..the dialects of the area..known as Mashonaland and the name for the language should..be one which indicates this width of range. No name but 'Shona' has been suggested which can do this. **1930** C. G. Seligman *Races of Africa* viii. 187 The Shona peoples of Southern Rhodesia and of Portuguese East Africa immediately south of the Zambesi as far as the Sabi River. **1936** *Discovery* June 179/1 The Shona..were the later or perhaps the military occupiers of the Hill which we call Mapungubwe. **1955** G. Fortune (*title*) An analytical grammar of Shona. **1976** *Times* 26 Aug. 12/6 The Shona..comprise about 75 per cent of the ..population. *Ibid.* 12/7 Mr. Joshua Nkomo..is apparently a Kalanga..one of the smallest Shona groups.. whose language is furthest from basic Shona. **1979** *Financial Times* 29 Jan. 16/4 The right wing says there is still time to negotiate a three tier federal solution which would avoid domination of the minority Ndebele and the minority Whites by the majority Shonas.

Shonee, var. *shawnee *a.* and *sb.*

shoneen. Add: Used (esp. *attrib.*) to indicate a person's inclination towards English rather than Irish standards and attitudes in cultural life, sport, etc. (Later examples.) Hence **shonee·nism.**

1918 F. Hackett *Ireland* iii. 65 West Britonism makes us what we are, shoneenism and toadyism, so it is, they're the curse of Ireland. **1920** B. MacNamara *Clanking of Chains* iv. 44 But the shoneenism of Ambrose was in more perfect keeping with the shoneen heart of Ballycullen... The songs which he sang were out of the English music halls, the books which he read were English drivel. **1922** Joyce *Ulysses* 311 Irish sport and shoneen games. **1927** [see *pro-Britisher* s.v. *pro-[1] 5 b]. **1958** B. Behan *Borstal Boy* III. 326 Now, there was a lot of shoneen writing and playing up to the herrenvolk by Rugby writers. **1960** *20th Cent.* Oct. 324 This aunt practically invented the whole concept of shoneenism... She believed that God was Anglo-Saxon, Protestant.

shonicker (ʃǫ·nikəɹ). *U.S. slang.* Also **shoniker, shonniker.** [Orig. uncertain: see quots. 1966, 1970.] An offensive name for a Jew (see also quot. 1914).

1914 Jackson & Hellyer *Vocab. Criminal Slang* 75 *Shoniker*, current among cosmopolitan thieves, especially Jews. A neophyte or inexperienced hand at the game. **1927** *Dialect Notes* V. 462 *Shonniker*, n., a Jewish pawnbroker. **1932** J. T. Farrell *Young Lonigan* vi. 269 Two hooknoses..did come along. Andy and Johnny O'Brien.. stopped the shonickers. **1966** *Publ. Amer. Dial. Soc. 1964* XLII. 45 Thus folk etymology derives *shonicker* from Yiddish *schnozzle*... My colleague..suggests a derivation from Hanukkah. **1970** L. M. Feinsilver *Taste of Yiddish* 338 *Shon, shonk, shonky, shoncker, shonniker.* These opprobrious terms for a Jew in England are supposed to have come from Yiddish *shoniker* (petty trader or peddler).

shonk (ʃǫŋk). *slang.* (Shortened form of *shonicker.) An offensive name for a Jew. Hence **sho·nky** *a.*[1] (see quot. 1951).

1938 W. Matthews *Cockney Past & Present* v. 153, I diffidently suggest the following words as the most familiar slang terms rarely used except by cockneys.. *shonk*, nose, Jew. **1940** R. Postgate *Verdict of Twelve* I. v. 75 Let's have a bit of fun with the shonks. **1951** Partridge *Dict. Slang* (ed. 4) Add. 1168/1 *Shonky*, adj., mean; money-grubbing: late C. 19–20. **1981** 'W. Haggard' *Money Men* xv. 174 'Brighton?..It's full of shonks.'..'Which means there are hotels with night clerks.'

shonkinite (ʃǫ·ŋkinəit). *Geol.* [f. *Shonkin*, Indian name for the Highwood Mountains, Montana + -ite[1].] A dark granular form of syenite consisting largely of augite and orthoclase. Hence **shonkini·tic** *a.*, having the character or consisting of shonkinite.

1895 Weed & Pirsson in *Bull. Geol. Soc. Amer.* VI. 415 For this type of rock, then, we propose the name of shonkinite,..and shonkinite we define as a granular plutonic rock consisting of essential augite and orthoclase, and thereby related to the syenite family. **1900** *Bull. Geol. Soc. Amer.* XI. 395 The relations of the 'fine grained' (shonkinitic) syenite to the leucite-porpyhry are uncertain. *a* **1928** Peach & Horne *Chapters Geol. Scott.* (1930) iv. 112 A discontinuous zone of fine-grained shonkinite and pulaskite. **1943** S. J. Shand *Eruptive Rocks* (ed. 2) xiv. 259 There are no lavas of shonkinitic composition. **1951** Turner & Verhoogen *Igneous & Metamorphic Petrology* viii. 169 The syenite undoubtedly is a differentiate derived from a parent shonkinite magma. **1978** S. R. Nockolds et al. *Petrology for Students* v. 61 Other shonkinites from the Highwood Mountains and from the Bearpaw Mountains, Montana, may have a little plagioclase.

shonky (ʃǫ·ŋki), *a.*[2] *Austral. slang.* Also **shonkie.** [Perh. f. *shonky *a.*[1]: see *shonk.] Unreliable, dishonest, 'crooked'. Hence as *sb.*, one engaged in irregular or illegal business activities.

1970 R. Beilby *No Medals for Aphrodite* 116 You shonkie sod! **1976** *Sunday Mail* (Brisbane) 2 May 8/4 Queensland has some 'shonky' charities. I cannot name them because of libel. **1979** *Financial Rev.* (Sydney) 25 July 11/6 Mr Groom is right when he refers to the building industry as being characterized by initiative and drive, but unless something is done to eliminate these 'shonkies' quickly, then such qualities will be characteristics of the past. **1981** *Australian* 2 Feb. 7/7 The woman..was forthright about the cut-price air fares... 'We call these tickets shonky,' she said.

sho' nuff: see *nuff b.

shoo, *v.* Add: **1. a.** Also, to do this by means of a movement or gesture. Also *transf.*

1919 Conrad *Arrow of Gold* I. i. 9 Shells were falling all round till a tiny French gunboat..shooed the *Numancia* away out of territorial waters. **1938** W. de la Mare *Memory* 14 She shoo'd it away with her gloves. **1959** D. Beaty *Cone of Silence* ii. 25 Then she shooed cups and plate away from her. **1959** *Listener* 15 Jan. 113/2 He shakes or nods his head to shoo the flies away. **1973** 'H. Carmichael' *Too Late for Tears* viii. 108 Hope you won't mind if I shoo you out now. I've got work to do. **1977** *Time* 22 Aug. 10/1 Israeli artillery regularly fires into south Lebanon to shoo away Palestinian guerrillas from Lebanese Christian enclaves in the border area.

b. To drive or urge (a person, animal, etc.) in a desired direction.

1903 *N.Y. Sun* 17 Nov. 12 The police shoo everybody to the south side of the loops. **1923** 'B. M. Bower' *Parowan Bonanza* xiii. 151 You're supposed to shoo a lady gently before you down the aisle. **1946** M. Dickens *Happy Prisoner* xi. 267 The first pony had already been shooed into the ring. **1973** M. Amis *Rachel Papers* 150, I do not churlishly flatten her on to the sofa nor shoo her downstairs.

4. *trans.* With *in*, to allow a racehorse to win easily. *U.S. slang.* Cf. *shoo-in.

1908 G. E. Smith *Racing Maxims & Methods of 'Pittsburgh Phil'* ix. 123 There were many times presumably that 'Tod' would win through such manipulations, being 'shooed in', as it were. **1935** D. Runyon *Money from Home* 128 They are going to shoo in Never Despair. **1976**

New Yorker 22 Mar. 85/2 To be sure, Shoemaker's confreres could have shooed him in long before this, but jockeys never, never do such things.

shoo-fly (ʃū·flɔi), *vbl. phr.* and *sb. U.S.* Also **shoofly, shoo fly.** [f. SHOO *int.*[1] + FLY *v.*[1] and *sb.*[1]]

A. *vbl. phr.* A catch phrase, popularized by a song, used as an exclamation of annoyance. *Obs.*

1867 *Chicago Republican* 24 July 8/1 [Baseball] players invariably say 'Shoo-fly', when they make a miss. **1889** FARMER *Americanisms* 484/2 *Shoo! fly! don't bother me!* An exclamation of impatience is *shoo* and *fly* are both common ejaculations in country districts when driving wandering fowls or cattle from gardens etc., to legitimate pastures... The full phrase is now familiarly colloquial. **1919** MENCKEN *Amer. Lang.* 311 *Shoo-fly* afflicted the American people for at least two years, and 'I *don't* think' and *aber nit* quite as long.

B. *sb.* † **1.** A device or structure intended to afford protection from flies. *Obs.*

1879 *Glendale* (Montana) *Atlantis* 28 Dec. 4/4 A Dutchman drove rapidly along Main Street, with a new shoo-fly attached to his wagon, making forty flips a second and striking back and forth with the vigor of a hewgag. **1896** J. RALPH *Dixie* iv. 126 In many cases they order great pavilions like giant nests built around their trees, and.. they call them 'shoo-flies', a name utterly without significance in that connection.

2. A policeman, usu. in plain clothes, whose duty is to watch and report on other policemen. *slang.*

1877 *Daily Graphic* May 1 A 'shoofly' is the term applied by a policeman to another officer who is detailed to watch him. **1903** H. HAPGOOD *Autobiogr. Thief* (1904) xii. 265, I was gathered in to make a reputation for those two shoo-flies. **1931** *Detective Fiction Weekly* 27 June 790/2 A force of 'shoo flies'—roundsmen in civilian clothes —were sent out regularly from headquarters to sweep into a precinct and look over the men. **1952** *Sun* (Baltimore) 10 May (B ed.) 2/2 Evans said he spent eighteen months on 'shoo-fly duty'—on the chief inspector's squad that worked out of headquarters keeping other policemen in line and honest. **1980** 'E. MCBAIN' *Ghosts* vii. 127 'You want a beer?..Officially I'm still on duty, but fuck it.' 'Shooflies are heavy around the holidays.'

3. A rocking horse in which the seat is placed between two rockers representing the animal. Freq. *attrib.* as *shoo-fly rocker.*

1887 *Chicago Tribune* 27 Nov. 16/7 (Advt.), Shoo fly hobby horse, 75 c. **1895** *Montgomery Ward Catal.* Spring & Summer 563/2 Shoo-fly rockers... Shoo-fly 12 × 40 inches; painted and dappled. **1947** *Chicago Tribune* 30 Dec. 15/1 The Teaneck, N.J., library has installed something called a shoo-fly, an enclosed rocker in which little Elmer..can rock his head off.

4. A temporary railway track constructed for use while the main track is obstructed or under repair. Also *transf.* (see quot. 1907).

1905 *N.Y. Even. Post* 29 July 1 The Southern Pacific Company's 'shoo-fly' around the tracks now submerged will be completed in a few days. **1907** *Dialect Notes* III. 249 *Shoo-fly, n.*, suburban railway train. **1929** *Macon* (Georgia) *Tel.* 2 July, There comes into Macon every morning on the Eatonton Shoo Fly a very old white woman named Mary Loring. **1937** *Highway Mag.* Jan. 9/1 Beginning in the spring of 1936 the railroad built two temporary 'shoo fly' tracks about 75 feet west of the existing tracks. **1961** *Washington Post* 17 Feb. B4 (*caption*) Workers on top of a construction train adjust the overhead wires for a bypass—or 'Shoo-fly' in railroad parlance—of the main railroad tracks serving the area to the south of Washington.

5. *Printing.* In some flat-bed presses, a set of narrow strips which lift the edge of the sheet off the cylinder ready for delivery. Also *shoofly finger.*

1908 *Inland Printer* XL. 551/2 Where the delivery construction uses shoo-fly fingers to give the forward edge of the sheet a lift as it passes out onto the delivery, the proper setting of these fingers or shoo-flies, as they are usually called, is of prime importance. **1927** E. ST. JOHN *Pract. Hints Presswork* ii. 10 When farthest open the shoofly fingers should be five-sixteenth of an inch away from the drawsheet. **1962** *Theory & Practice of Presswork* (U.S. Govt. Printing Office) (rev. ed.) xxviii. 170 The shooflies, stripper fingers, and tape delivery have all been eliminated on the newer chain-delivery Miehle presses.

6. In needlework, a traditional patchwork design.

1931 R. S. MCKIM *One Hundred & One Patchwork Patterns* 84/1 As shoo fly is one of the simplest of old-fashioned patchworks, both to cut and to piece, it would be a good choice for one on which a little girl could learn sewing. **1977** E. Y. WOOD *Amer. Patchwork Quilts* 15 Four-patch designs are here, such as the classic 'Shoo Fly'.

7. *attrib.* and *Comb.* **a.** (Examples in various unspecified senses.)

1870 *North Alabamian & Times* (Tuscumbia, Alabama) 21 Apr. 2/7 The gentlemen can gratify their taste by ornamenting themselves with the latest style of 'Shoo Fly' Hats. **1886** M. B. BUCKLEY *Diary Tour in Amer.* viii. 223 There were 'Shoo fly neckties' and 'Shoo fly hats'. **1891** O. WISTER *Jrnl.* 17 June (1958) 106 That's a terrible plain woman Hank's got. All driven and dried up. Looks like a picture on one of these shoo-fly boxes. **1897** *Sears, Roebuck Catal.* 35/3 Shoo-fly flasks..½ pints..pints.. quarts. **1946** C. RICHTER *Fields* 278 Huldah had gone with Amy MacMahon, a red shoofly ribbon low on both their necks.

b. shoo-fly pie, a rich tart made of molasses baked in a pastry case with a crumble topping; **shoo-fly plant**, a large annual herb, *Nicandra physalodes*, belonging to the family Solanaceæ, native to Peru, and bearing pale blue flowers followed by berries enclosed in the enlarged calyx.

1935 *Esquire* Dec. 200/1 'Shoo-fly pie'—a brown-and-white crumb-cake, faintly spiced. **1971** *Daily Colonist* (Victoria, B.C.) 9 July 3/4 The pair is helping their father sell shoo-fly Pie and other Pennsylvania items. **1979** *United States 1980/81* (Penguin Travel Guides) 48 Vermont cheese and maple syrup,.. and shoofly pie and pretzels in the Pennsylvania Dutch country are all specialties of their respective regions. [**1902** L. H. BAILEY *Cycl. Amer. Hort.* IV. 1664/1 Shoo-fly plant. A name proposed by one seedsman for Physalis.] **1949** L. H. BAILEY *Man. Cultivated Plants* (ed. 2) 871 N[*icandra*] *Physalodes*..Apple-of-Peru, Shoo-fly Plant. **1973** *Times* 20 Oct. 16/7 Left-over seeds thrown out for the birds from special mixtures..are responsible for appearances of casual weeds like..the Apple of Peru, or 'shoo-fly plant', and its pale blue flowers that are succeeded by swollen, green berry-enclosing lanterns.

shoo-in. *N. Amer.* [f. vbl. phr. *to shoo in*: see *SHOO *v.* 4.] **1.** In horseracing, a predetermined or 'fixed' race, or the winner of it. Hence *loosely*, a horse which is a certain winner.

1928 *National Turf Digest* (Baltimore) Dec. 929/2 A 'skate' is a horse having no class whatever, and rarely wins only in case of a 'fluke' or 'shoo in'. **1937** *Collier's* 11 Sept. 11/3 Sharp Practice wins by so far it looks like as if he is a shoo-in. **1950** *Sun* (Baltimore) 1 June 22/4 Some horsemen wondered whether Chris Chenery's Virginia flyer would be such a shoo-in for the Belmont Stakes..after all. **1969** R. LOCKRIDGE *Risky Way to Kill* xii. 152 Got two hunters entered in the Ridgewood show... One of them doesn't like wet going... Figuring him to be pretty much of a shoo-in for the..hunter championship.

2. *transf.* (esp. *Pol.*). A certain or easy winner; a certainty, a 'walk-over'.

1939 *News* (San Francisco) 30 Jan. 15/5 (*heading*) Bear cagers appear shoo-in for southern division title. **1948** *Tuscaloosa* (Alabama) *News* 30 July 4/2 This type of registration might endanger their balloting in the local elections, where Democratic candidates are usually chosen on a 'shoo-in' basis. **1962** K. ORVIS *Damned & Destroyed* (1966) xxv. 183 The rest was a shoo-in. The house dick nailed the room number, then waltzed down and checked the register. **1968** *Economist* 20 Jan. 29/1 Governor Rockefeller became the Republicans' leading presidential hopeful for 1964. The press thought him a shoo-in for the nomination. **1976** *Islander* (Victoria, B.C.) 10 Oct. 15/3 From then on, in spite of the fog, it [*sc.* the sailing] was a shoo-in. **1981** *Time* 13 May 68/1 If they gave a good sport Oscar, she would be a shoo-in.

shook, *ppl. a* **2.** *colloq.* **a.** *to be shook on*: to be enamoured of or enthusiastic about. *Austral.* and *N.Z.*

1888 'R. BOLDREWOOD' *Robbery under Arms* II. iii. 46 He was awful shook on Mad; but she wouldn't look at him. *Ibid.* xix. 291 I'm regular shook on the polka. **1926** J. DEVANNEY *Butcher Shop* iv. 43 She had but fallen victim to the state of mind described by girls she knew as being 'shook' on a man. **1965** S. T. OLLIVIER *Petticoat Farm* vii. 100 Tom said he wasn't too shook on makin' a public fool of himself. **1975** *Sunday Tel.* (Sydney) 29 June 49 Like Chappell, I'm not all that shook on cocktail parties myself.

b. Emotionally or physically disturbed, discomposed, upset. Usu. const. *up.* orig. and chiefly *U.S.*

1891 KIPLING in *Macmillan's Mag.* Oct. 473/2 He took my 'and an' pulled me up, an' I was pretty shook. **1897** —— *Captains Courageous* ii. 31 You was shook up and silly. **1914** *Dialect Notes* IV. 79 *Shook, p.a.*, startled, shocked, grieved. 'Jed was pow'ful shook when Minervy pegged out.' **1953** *Sun* (Baltimore) 24 Apr. (B ed.) 20/2 Ken Jackson..should qualify for the nickname Stonewall... Ken..fell two floors down a freight elevator shaft and as he said was only 'shook up'. **1959** H. SALISBURY (*title*) The shook-up generation. **1960** *Washington Post* 25 May 1 'Elva behaved all the way through it just like a good policeman,' Liverman said of his wife's role in the chase. 'But she still gets a little shook thinking about the ride.' **1976** *Daily Mirror* 11 Mar. 1/1 Rock superstar Rod Stewart was all shook up last night after a lovers' tiff with..Britt Ekland.

shool, var. *SHUL.

shoot, *sb.*[1] Add: **1. i.** *transf.* The action of shooting a film. Cf. *SHOOT *v.* 22 f.

1929 *Morning Post* 24 May 12/7 A Wembly 'Shoot' Described... A 'talkie' sequence is being 'shot' in the studio. **1978** *Broadcast* 13 Nov. 24/1 Had you crewed in features or television productions and then suddenly found yourself part of a commercial shoot?

j. *Mil.* An act of bombardment; esp., an exercise in which anti-aircraft drill is practised.

1941 *Hutchinson's Pictorial Hist. War* July–Sept. (*caption*) 162 Bofors guns, of proved efficiency against low-flying aircraft, are included in Malaya's defence programme... A practice shoot is in progress. **1961** B. FERGUSON *Watery Maze* xiv. 344 The prize shoot was executed by *Ajax* and *Argonaut* on a troublesome battery at Longues. **1977** *R.A.F. News* 8–21 June 11/2 Such blank days, and other times when 'shoots' are cancelled..can be as disappointing and frustrating to the range team as to the fliers and their units.

3. f. In slang phr. *to give* (a person) *the shoot*: to dismiss from employment, sack; also *transf.* So *to get the shoot.* Cf. *BOOT *sb.*[3] 1 c.

1846 *Swell's Night Guide* 50 'You nasty old man,' said she, 'and your doss gorger cracked a wid about you to me, and said she must give you the shoot.' **1906** [see *MOVE *sb.* 6].

g. = *SHOT *sb.*[1] 7 h. *U.S.*

1959 *Time* 5 Jan. 24/2 Another 20 or 30 Atlas shoots must be made. **1961** *N.Y. Times Mag.* 5 May 28/2 (*caption*) In a recent 'shoot' the capsule was picked up at sea fifty-six minutes after take-off.

6. c. (Earlier example.) Also *Austral.*, an opening and ramp leading from one pen to another in a sheep-shearing shed. Cf. *CHUTE *sb.* 3 b.

1873 J. H. BEADLE *Undevel. West* xxii. 432 About a quarter section of cattle-yards and 'shoots' extend around the depot. **1900, 1905** [see *PEN *sb.*[1] 1 c]. **1955** STEWART & KEESING *Austral. Bush Ballads* 239 The shearers squint along the pens, they squint along the shoots; The shearers squint along the board to catch the Boss's boots.

shoot, *v.* Add: **I. 1. i.** (Earlier example.)

1816 W. LAMBERT *Instructions & Rules of Cricket* 29 When a ball is pitched short of its usual and proper length ..it may cut or shoot on the ground.

2. a. (Further examples with *off.*)

1828 W. CARR *Dial. Craven* (ed. 2) II. 121 *To shoot off*, to go off precipitately. **1930** J. DEVANNY *Bushman Burke* xii. 72 Whatja shoot off for? Had great time after you left. **1946** [see *COAST *sb.* 4 c].

d. *colloq.* To depart, go away. Freq. *int.*

1897 *Leeds Mercury* 19 June Suppl., Nah, then, shooit, or ah'll mak yo! **1970** G. F. NEWMAN *Sir, You Bastard* viii. 230 I'll shoot then, if it's all right. Nothing else? **1974** H. L. FOSTER *Ribbin', Jivin', & Playin' Dozens* v. 203 Two of them said, 'Shoot.' They all turned and walked away.

e. *to shoot through*: to escape, abscond; to depart, leave. *Austral.* and *N.Z. slang.* Cf. *GO *v.* 89 d.

1947 *Pix* 20 Sept. 15 *Shoot through*, escape, abscond. **1951** S. MACKENZIE *Dead Men Rising* 37 I'm shooting through—my woman's sick and I've waited longer than I should have. **1965** M. SHADBOLT *Among Cinders* xviii. 168 'Well,' I said... 'I guess I'd better be shooting through. Thanks for the sausage.' **1978** *Telegraph* (Brisbane) 11 Jan. 28/1 I've been advised to shoot through and forget about the debts.

4. f. U.S. *to shoot the chute(s*: = *to chute the chute(s* s.v. *CHUTE *v.* 1. Also *shoot-the-chute* used as *sb.*

1895 *N.Y. Dramatic News* 30 Nov. 17/4 Shooting the Chutes, the latest craze that has struck the town, is.. drawing large crowds. **1920** R. FROST *Let.* 23 July (1964) 116 This man's island..will be full of divers and entertainment dives such as movies, con games, and shoot-the-chutes. **1946** E. O'NEILL *Iceman Cometh* III. 165 We're goin' to beat it down to Coney Island and shoot the chutes. **1977** *Time* 4 July 26/2 They are the not-so-spiritual descendants..of the Parisians who in 1817 rode the original shoot-the-chute.

8. a. Also of prices, sales, etc.: to rise sharply.

1968 *Listener* 27 June 826/3 The sales of vodka in Moscow shot up by 25 per cent. **1977** *Evening Gaz.* (Middlesbrough) 11 Jan. 1/6 The pound shot up two cents against the dollar.

II. 11. h. Also, to dispatch (a thing) rapidly.

1926 *S.P.E. Tract* XXIV. 126 If the article is ready, shoot it in. **1942** *Tee Emm* (Air Ministry) II. 129 You have grumbled at the amount of bumph the Group has shot at you. **1971** *Black Scholar* June 54/2, I don't have a picture at this time, but when I get one I will shoot it to you.

j. To discard, get rid of; orig. in *shoot that hat*, etc., as a mild imprecation. Also *to shoot trouble* = *TROUBLE-SHOOT *v. slang* (orig. *U.S.*).

1877 in Bartlett *Dict. Amer.* (ed. 4) 586 One lady.. with derisive scorn..observed in the language of the day, 'Oh, shoot that hat!'..The slang the gang is using now, You'll hear from every lip; It's *shoot the hat!* and get it boiled; And don't you lose your grip. **1884** J. HAY *Bread-Winners* xvi. 249 If I had all the cash he takes in to-night, I'd buy an island and shoot the machine business. **1902** FARMER & HENLEY *Slang* VI. 188/1 *Shoot that* (*hat, man*—anything)!..a mild imprecation, 'Bother!' **1928** *Sunday Express* 18 Mar. 9/2 'Tell him to shoot that song-and-dance outfit'.., and jump into some plain overalls. **1965** 'W. HAGGARD' *Hard Sell* xiv. 154 When there was trouble..then Murco Monti shot it. Political trouble especially. **1980** P. HARCOURT *Tomorrow's Treason* I. v. 72, I want you to shoot trouble for me till the conference is over.

k. *Cricket.* To bowl (a side or part of one) *out* quickly and cheaply.

1900 P. F. WARNER *Cricket in Many Climes* IV. ii. 159 Next day Ainsworth and 'Bos' shot the opposing side out for 30. **1976** J. SNOW *Cricket Rebel* 112 Half the Warwickshire side had been shot out for 46.

l. Slang phr. *to shoot a card*: to leave a visiting card. ? *Obs.*

1901 *Captain* V. 7/2 The second-year man is always careful to 'shoot' his card when the fresher is abroad. **1924** 'SAPPER' *Third Round* vi. 139 He may have heard that Mrs. Goodman is here, and has come to shoot a card.

12. a. Also *spec.* in *Angling*, to allow a quantity of (line) to run out through the hand at the forward motion of the rod in casting.

1931 *Hardy's Anglers' Guide* 13 In Figs. 1 and 2 the left hand gathers slack line, while in Fig. 3 this line is released during the forward stroke. This is termed 'shooting' line. **1977** *Chicago Tribune* 2 Oct. III. 10/2 The current will pull on the line, making casting and 'shooting' of fly line on the next cast extremely difficult.

15. Also *colloq.*, to convey or transfer (a person) with speed.

1919 F. Hurst *Humoresque* 200 Come; I'll shoot you to the club. **1921** E. B. White *Let.* 15 Sept. (1976) 24, I go to one person and he says hello and shoots me on to another. **1972** T. Stoppard *Jumpers* I. 50 I'll shoot him in here... You can try your charms on him.

17. d. Now usu. *to shoot one's cuffs.* Also *fig.*

1909 M. Beerbohm *Yet Again* 230 The large young man, shooting his cuffs, strode forward. **1929** W. Deeping *Roper's Row* iii. 25 You felt that you had shot your cuffs and scored a point when you wiped Moorhouse's stately eye. **1942** L. A. G. Strong *Unpractised Heart* 27 The millionaire pulled out a gold pencil and shot his cuff. **1974** S. Coulter *Château* I. xvii. 133 He shot his cuffs and walked resolutely towards Mademoiselle Aurélie. **1977** J. Cheever *Falconer* 129 He shot his cuff to check the time.

18. Restrict † to first three senses in Dict. and add: **e.** *intr.* To ejaculate; orig. in phr. *to shoot one's roe. slang.*

1879–80 *Pearl* (1970) 217 And the little creatures found, When they dragged him to the ground, That, while lecturing, he'd shot his noble roe, roe, roe. **1922** Joyce *Ulysses* 553 Bloom: (*His eyes wildly dilated, clasps himself*). Show! Hide! Show! Plough her! More! Shoot! **1969** [see *come *v.* 16*]. **1972** H. C. Rae *Shooting Gallery* III. 191, I wanted him to shoot and get it over.

III. 22. c. Also used in sports involving the scoring of goals. Cf. sense 27 in Dict. and Suppl.

1981 E. North *Dames* xiii. 255 'Well shot! Well shot!' Some feeble cheering on the touchline.

d. (*e*) In phr. *to shoot to kill* (cf. *kill *v.* 6 c), implying the desire to kill, rather than frighten or wound, a living target. Also *shoot-to-kill* adj. phr.

1867 *Harper's Mag.* Feb. 274/2 Wild Bill with his own hands has killed hundreds of men... 'He shoots to kill', as they say on the border. **1949** N. Marsh *Swing, Brother, Swing* iii. 48 Plays like he shoots an' he shoots to kill. **1956** 'J. Christopher' *Death of Grass* v. 79 'Must you shoot to kill?' He began to say: 'It's a matter of safety.' **1973** *Black Panther* 7 Apr. 10/3 LEAA was the liberal establishment's attempt to modernize police techniques as a substitute for 'shoot to kill' repression. **1977** *New Yorker* 15 Aug. 67/1 A Cuban businessman.. recalled favorably Mayor Richard Daley's calling for the National Guard and giving the police shoot-to-kill orders because of the Chicago riots.

(*f*) *to shoot it out*: to settle (a dispute) by shooting or by the exchange of military fire. Cf. Fight *v.* 8.

1912 W. M. Raine *Brand Blotters* xii. 327 Had he shown any sign of indecision, they would have taken a chance and shot it out. **1939** *War Illustr.* 18 Dec. 458/3 Two gangsters have temporarily joined hands to plunder the wealthier citizens, on the understanding that they will 'shoot it out' between them later. **1949** F. Maclean *Eastern Approaches* II. iv. 221 To try and shoot it out with them would bring the whole place about our ears.

f. Now usu. in extended sense: *trans.* To photograph (a scene, action, person, etc.) with a cinematographic camera; to take (cinematographic film), to film; occas. with the actor as subject. Also *intr.*

1916 'B. M. Bower' *Phantom Herd* ii. 22 He..debated whether it should be 'shot' with two cameras or three. **1919** *Conquest* Dec. 70/2 First, the camera man 'shoots' on the tank containing the fishes with one half of the lens open. **1930** E. Waugh *Vile Bodies* ix. 156 'All right,' said one of the men with megaphones... 'We'll shoot the duel now.' **1953** *Manch. Guardian Weekly* 27 Aug. 7/1 While the big-city exhibitors were pondering this expensive outlay a small studio in Hollywood shot a poor film with two interlocking lenses. **1962** Montagu & Leyda tr. *Nizhny's Lessons with Eisenstein* iii. 66 Could the set-up be so changed as to shoot past Dessalines' back? **1976** *Observer* (Colour Suppl.) 9 May 10/2 She has also shot the odd film here. **1978** J. Krantz *Scruples* iii. 77 If anyone was going to go down to the Virgin Islands and shoot three models in next year's monokinis..it was Hank.

g. *to shoot a profile*: see *profile *sb.* 4 e.

23. g. For '*U.S.* slang' read '*slang* (orig. *U.S.*)' and add: Also, to talk unrestrainedly or at length, to assert one's opinions; to boast or brag. Also *to shoot one's mouth off* and similar phrases.

1864 *Rocky Mountain News* (Denver, Colorado) 3 Aug. 4/2 A Dutch married woman..was taxed $17·80 for 'shooting off her mouth' against the virtue and morality of a neighbouring maiden. **1880** *News & Press* (Cimarron, New Mexico) 8 Apr. 1/5 Nobby, you've..never yit shot off yer mouth on the marryin' biz. **1919** O. W. Holmes *Let.* 5 Apr. (1964) iii. 184 They make me want to write a letter to ease my mind and shoot off my mouth; but of course I keep a judicial silence. **1933** D. L. Sayers *Murder must Advertise* x. 165 That don't prove nothing... Not without you know 'ow long it took Mr. Tompkin to shoot 'is mouth off. **1946** E. O. O'Neill *Iceman Cometh* II. 99 He ought to do it, and not just shook off his old bazoo about it. **1954** Wodehouse *Jeeves & Feudal Spirit* xiii. 123 So this was how the woman was accustomed to shoot off her bally head about me in my absence. **1967** *Boston Globe* 5 Apr. 51/5 The only way we can keep Red..quiet is to beat Boston... I'm tired of hearing him shoot off his mouth. **1973** W. J. Burley *Death in Salubrious Place* i. 24 With Matthew Eva shooting his mouth off about Peters it could turn ugly.

h. *trans.* and *intr.* To inject by means of a hypodermic syringe (used esp. with reference to the taking of addictive drugs). Also *refl.* Freq. const. *up. slang* (orig. *U.S.*).

1914 Jackson & Hellyer *Vocab. Criminal Slang* 75 *Shoot*, verb, current amongst hypodermic habitues. To inject morphine or other drug with a syringe. Example; 'How many times do you shoot a day?' **1926** J. Black *You can't Win* xii. 161 They grew so despondent over their plight..they decided to 'shoot up' the small portion of white stuff they had left. **1951** *Life* 25 June 120/1 But furnishes hypodermics and other paraphernalia so he may 'shoot himself' on the spot. **1953** W. Burroughs *Junkie* i. 23 He shot another syrette. *Ibid.* iii. 36, I began shooting in the main line to save stuff and because the immediate kick was better. **1969** H. Waugh *Young Prey* iv. 65 The junkies..need a place to go where they can shoot themselves and where an expert can shoot the novices. **1971** *Oz* May 5/2 They were using those needles man, they were shooting up. **1979** R. Jaffe *Class Reunion* (1980) II. iv. 204 He [*sc.* a dermatologist] would be the magician who would..peel off wrinkles, shoot silicone into laugh lines.

i. *intr.* To proceed, go ahead (with a speech, question, etc.), to 'fire away'. Usu. *imp.*, as an invitation to introduce a topic. Also *trans.* to direct (words); to say, speak; occas. *imp.* with *it*, and *to shoot back*, to riposte, retort. *colloq.* (orig. *U.S.*)

1915 *Dialect Notes* IV. 235 *Shoot, imper.*, continue; go ahead. **1917** Ade *Let.* 12 June (1973) 64 The other day a harelipped man working for me stopped me and said he wished to ask a question. I told him to shoot. **1920** S. Lewis *Main Street* 121 'Shall we try 'The Idylls of the King'? They're so full of color.' 'Go to it. Shoot.' **1934** J. M. Cain *Postman always rings Twice* ii. 9, I shot it right close to her ear, almost in a whisper. 'How come you married this Greek, anyway?' **1935** W. D. Hubbard *Thousandth Frog* 157 'Well,' said Gratton. 'Shoot it.' **1942** *Amer. Mercury* July 90 Dat what you shooting ain't worth a damn! **1951** J. G. Fennessy *Sonnet in Bottle* VII. iii. 259 'I want to ask your advice about something.'.. Rupert said, 'Well, shoot.' **1974** 'E. Lathen' *Sweet & Low* xi. 112 'Where's Amory?'... 'How do I know?' Yeoman shot back. **1978** H. Wouk *War & Remembrance* xxxvii. 388 'Can I pick your brain on one more point?' 'Shoot.'

j. Chiefly U.S. slang. *to shoot the works*: to effect something to the fullest extent; *spec.* to discharge the necessary business; to tell the truth, reveal all; *to shoot the bull*: to talk nonsense (cf. *bull *sb.*[4] 3); *to shoot a line*: see *line *sb.*[2] 13 g.

1922 E. O'Neill *Hairy Ape* vii. 74 Can't youse see I belong? Sure! I'm reg'lar. I'll stick, get me? I'll shoot de woiks for youse. **1930** *Amer. Speech* V. 197 (*heading*) Shooting the bull. **1946** Mezzrow & Wolfe *Really Blues* i. 5 We had a yen..to strut and act biggity and shoot the works. **1951** W. Stevens *Let.* 27 Dec. (1967) 735 We have people who seem to hand a list of names to a stenographer and tell her to shoot the works. **1972** *Maclean's Mag.* Mar. 41/2 'Writes all my speeches,' he'd say and slap me on the back. 'Smart boy! He can sure shoot the bull.'

k. *Bridge.* To play abnormally in a tournament in order to achieve a high score, e.g. one needed to win a tournament.

1957 M. Miles *How to win at Duplicate Bridge* vii. 318 Why do people invariably overbid when they are shooting? There are many better opportunities to shoot by underbidding. **1972** *Times* 3 June 8/6 It was the 98th deal of a 100 board match and North South were 'shooting' for top scores.

l. To strive *for*, to aim at. *U.S. colloq.*

1967 *Technology Week* 23 Jan. 15/3 The space agency is currently shooting for a nuclear engine that would operate for 1,000 hours before refueling. **1976** *Billings* (Montana) *Gaz.* 20 June 6-E/2 Mississippi College long jumper Larry Myricks is shooting for a jump of 27 feet.

26. a. Also *U.S.*, to throw a die or dice; to play at dice. *colloq.*

1909 Webster 526/1 The caster throws or 'shoots' the dice, and wins if the throw is 7 or 11. **1929** *Amer. Mercury* Sept. 49/2 We got to stop shootin' dices. **1932** W. Faulkner *Light in August* 34, I would have thought that maybe shooting dice would be the one thing he could do. **1940** —— *Hamlet* 258 Vagrancy or razor fights or shooting dice for ten or fifteen cents.

b. *U.S. colloq.* To play (a game), as in *to shoot pool, casino*, etc. Cf. *to shoot crap(s)* s.v. *crap *sb.*[4] 1, *craps.

1926 E. Hemingway *In our Time* 183 They talk and tell stories and shoot pool. **1935** A. Squire *Sing Sing Doctor* xiv. 207 Perhaps he goes for a walk, or attends a movie, or shoots a practice game of pool. **1949** A. Miller *Death of Salesman* I. 48 Come in later, we'll shoot a little casino. **1979** R. Jaffe *Class Reunion* (1980) II. ii. 187 He liked to dance, play golf, drink, shoot skeet, and laugh.

27. Now widely used in other sports, as *Basketball, Netball*, etc. **a.** (Later examples.) Also with *basket*, etc., as object.

1900 *Springfield Daily Republican* 4 Dec. 3/1 Both teams warmed up slowly and played open polo. Curtis shot the first goal in from the side. **1901** A. Farrell *Ice Hockey & Polo Guide* 54 This sudden movement surprises the man and he is liable to shoot the puck inaccurately. **1908** in H. A. Fisher *Basket Ball Guide 1908–9* 67 It was he who shot Williams' two baskets in the first overtime period. **1935** F. Hewitt *Down Ice* (rev. ed.) iv. 88 The best play is to shoot the puck at the boards and jump ahead to receive the carom. **1975** *New Yorker* 7 Apr. 112/2 He went over to shoot some baskets by himself, and while he was doing this it suddenly hit him that the game meant too much to him to give up.

b. (Later examples.)

1917 *N.Y. Times* 4 Feb. VIII. 1/5 The Aggies won the game in the final period when D. Ross shot at random from the centre of the rink. **1929** J. G. Buss *Basketball* vi. 71 *Shoot high*—and do not aim at the rim of the basket. **1951** *Netball* ('Know the Game' Series) 28/2 The player.. must..aim directly at the goal... If she shoots and then catches the ball again, she must not shoot again directly. **1978** *Washington Post* 26 Oct. A 19/5 The 'problem' is that the girls' game has only forwards and guards, and the three guards do not shoot.

c. *Golf* (orig. *U.S.*). *trans.* To record (a score) for a round or part of one; also *to shoot a birdie*, to achieve a score of one under par for a hole. Also *intr.*

1922 *Golfers Mag.* Aug. 28/1 This class of golfers, the fellows who shoot from 90 up, make golf possible in this country. **1923** [see *birdie 2]. **1933** *Amer. Golfer* July 34/1 How about birdies and eagles?..In order to shoot a birdie, you'd have to play the hole in 3.3 strokes. **1941** *Sat. Even. Post* 19 Apr. 118/3 They shot a twelve-under-par score in winning their first match. **1977** *Rolling Stone* 5 May 47/5 He played a round every day, shooting in the low 100s.

IV. 30. a. (Later *fig.* examples of *to shoot to pieces.*) Also in similar phrases. Cf. Blow *v.*[1] 24 in Dict. and Suppl.

1939 R. G. Collingwood *Autobiogr.* vi. 49 A philosophical doctrine was stuck up and shot to pieces by the 'realistic' criticism. **1946** W. H. Auden in *Harvard Alumni Bull.* 15 June 707 And nerves that never flinched at slaughter Are shot to pieces by the shorter Poems of Donne. **1955** E. Pound *Section: Rock-Drill* xcii. 81 Semele's personality shot to atoms. **1973** *Black Panther* 31 Mar. 2/1 These same pilot officers..are now being encouraged to avenge their injured pride which was shot to hell because many of the anti-war enlisted men were Black. **1979** *Homes & Gardens* June 81/1 The Season has been shot to pieces this century.

c. Now freq. to bring down (an aircraft, hence a pilot, etc.) by shooting; freq. in phr. *to shoot down in flames.* Also *fig.*, to overwhelm (a person) in argument, to destroy (an argument or theory); to assail with objections; to bring down to size.

1918 W. A. Bishop *Winged Warfare* xii. 160, I turned on the nearer of the two-seaters and..managed to shoot him down. **1928** E. Wallace *Tam* iii. 29 Captain Muller shot down his twenty-seventh aeroplane. **1943** N. Balchin *Small Back Room* 5 'Just army conservatism,' he said wearily. 'Just the army's usual trick of shooting things down.' **1943** C. H. Ward-Jackson *It's a Piece of Cake* 54 *Shot down in flames*, hopelessly beaten at anything. **1948** *Daily Tel.* 26 May 4/5 Another enemy aircraft was shot down in flames. **1958** *Times* 18 Dec. 11/4 To be shot down in flames may be an exaggerated description of getting the worse of an argument. **1959** *Listener* 3 Sept. 351/1 This is the way in which we shoot down cosmological theories. **1962** J. F. Powers *Morte d'Urban* iv. 98 He had no choice but to shoot the woman down. **1969** M. O'Brine *Mills* xi. 43 She, herself, had been a little shocked by his answer, but had secretly enjoyed seeing Eileen shot down in flames. **1977** *R.A.F. News* 11–24 May 8/6 He saw..Baron von Richtofen, shot down. **1981** J. B. Hilton *Playground of Death* vi. 81 Please shoot me down in flames if you think I'm making a bloody idiot of myself.

e. *colloq.* (orig. *U.S.*). *to shoot up*: to assail (a person, thing) by shooting; to terrorize or rampage around (a place). Also *R.A.F. slang* of an aircraft or its pilot: to dive over (a person, thing) as if or in order to attack.

1890 *Stock Grower & Farmer* 18 Jan. 5/2 This so enraged the boys that they began shooting up the town. *Ibid.* 21 June 3/1 Three cowboys shot each other up. **1909** *Chambers's Jrnl.* Feb. 104/1 Armed and masked men..took entire possession of it [*sc.* Princeton], 'shot it up' until opposition subsided. **1926** *Daily Colonist* (Victoria, B.C.) 22 July 15/7 Paul Davis..wounded after 'shooting up' rooming houses here early yesterday morning, died in hospital today. **1937** *New Statesman & Nation* 20 Feb. 288/2 Mr. Partridge is not quite so strong with regard to the slang of flying... I think..to *shoot-up*, to dive onto, and the *wind-sock* should all find a place. **1946** D. Hamson *We fell among Greeks* xvii. 180 When he had finished unloading his parachutes and parcels, he would take a long circle round and 'shoot us up', i.e. dive and roar over us at less than fifty feet, and, as he zoomed up, dip his wings left and right in salute. **1973** L. M. Boston *Memory in House* iv. 40 A squadron would roar over the house from which one plane swooped down to shoot us up. **1976** *Daily Tel.* 5 July 1, The Air France airbus which was skyjacked..a week ago, was also 'shot up'.

f. With *out*: to render (something) useless with a shot; *spec.* to puncture (a tyre), extinguish (a lamp) by shooting.

1972 *Daily Tel.* 9 Feb. 4/5 The vehicle was halted when police shot its tyres out. **1976** D. Barnes *Yesterday is Dead* (1977) II. 267 Couple of cut-'em-up family disputes and a guy that shot out fourteen street lights. **1977** J. Cartwright *Fighting Men* viii. 102 He was sorely tempted to shoot out the plane's tyres.

31. (Earlier examples.)

1761 Sterne *Tr. Shandy* IV. xiv. 85 Can'st thou carry *Trismegistus* in thy head... If she can, I'll be shot, said my father. **1803** J. Kenney *Raising Wind* II. i. 24 What a fine seal; and I'll be shot if it [*sc.* a letter] don't feel like a bank note.

32. d. *shot in the neck* (earlier example); *to shoot the breeze* (U.S.): to chat, talk idly; *to* *shoot the crow* (Sc.): to steal away without paying one's bill; to depart hurriedly, abscond, 'do a bunk' (see *S.N.D.*).

1830 *Cherokee Phoenix* (New Echota, Georgia) 21 Apr. 4/3 *Counsel.* What do you mean by *corned? Witness.* I mean, pretty well *shot in the neck.* **1887** *Fun* 8 June 246/2 A canny Scot was recently sentenced to ten days' hard for shooting the crow—*i.e.* ordering half-a-quarter of whiskey, drinking it rapidly, and neglecting to pay. **1941** *Guide to U.S. Naval Academy* 149 *Breeze, shoot the*, to refight the Civil War, etc. **1943** *Sun* (Baltimore) 4 June 30/2 He can..walk across the camp to meet some friend in another outfit, and 'shoot the breeze'. **1971** R. K. SMITH *Ransom* (1972) III. 113 There were other negative signs, too. No one had come by to shoot the breeze, to have a cup of coffee. **1973** 'J. PATRICK' *Glasgow Gang Observed* xi. 97 He had been serving a sentence of twenty-eight days detention in the last week of which he had 'shot the crow' and 'jolted', i.e. absconded. **1977** W. MCILVANNEY *Laidlaw* xliv. 206 There'll only be his mother in the house. His father shot the crow years ago.

34. Also *Oil Industry*, to detonate an explosive charge in (a well) in order to increase the flow of oil or gas.

c **1870** [in Dict.]. **1903** *Dialect Notes* II. 344 *Shoot (the well)*, to cause an explosion of several quarts of nitroglycerine at the depth of the *pay-streak*..so as to break and crack the oil rock, enabling the oil to flow faster from the pores. **1921** *Daily Colonist* (Victoria, B.C.) 11 Mar. 12/3 The report states that in Ironville No. 1 a good showing of thick oil was obtained at various depths... It was decided to shoot this well, but owing to water it was not yet known what result this would have. **1949** *Our Industry* (Anglo-Iranian Oil Co.) (ed. 2) ii. 52 Some rocks..containing oil are..compact and 'tight'... In such cases the well is often 'shot' in order to shatter the rock.

37. b. For *dial.* read 'Now *colloq.*' and add later examples.

1952 'R. GORDON' *Doctor in House* i 9 His love for his old hospital, like one's affection for the youthful homestead, increased steadily with the length of time he had been shot of it. **1976** *Daily Tel.* 22 Sept. 16/1 Advising its members to make haste to get shot of unsuitable employees.

shoot, *int. U.S. slang.* An arbitrary alteration of *SHIT *int.*

In some instances this may perh. be regarded as an imp. use of *SHOOT *v.* 11 j.

1934 WEBSTER 2319/2 *Shoot.., interj.* Pshaw! Bother!—often with *it.* **1941** E. WELTY *Curtain of Green* 42 Oh, shoot, that was about three and a half years ago. **1950** R. MOORE *Candlemas Bay* 301 'Oh shoot,' she told Jen, when Jen suggested they'd better write the next batch of boarders not to come. **1979** *Tucson Mag.* Feb. 42/1 Back in high school, I tried other so-called sports, but I always went back to rodeo. Shoot, that's the only sport there is.

shoot-'em-up (ʃū·təmʌp). *slang* (orig. *U.S.*). Also **shoot-em-up, shootemup.** [f. vbl. phr. *to shoot them up*: see *SHOOT *v.* 30 e.] A fast-moving story or film, esp. a Western, of which gun-play is a dominant feature. Also *attrib.* (or as *adj.*) and *Comb.*

1953 *Variety* 11 Feb. 6/2 A standard outdoor action plot is unfolded in 'Gunsmoke' to make it a Western feature for the shoot-'em-up market. **1958** *Washington Post* 30 July A25/7 That doesn't leave much room for anything except shoot-'em-ups. **1968** *Listener* 18 July 86/1 A racetrack-gang, shoot-em-up-bang plot and one of Mr Hawkes's disturbingly discontinuous surfaces of experience are yoked by violence together. **1973** *N.Y. Times* 10 June VII. 28/2 The new or free-form Western has several choice entries..'Oklahoma Crude', a splendid shootemup about a lady wildcatter in the oil fields. **1976** *Publishers Weekly* 15 Mar. 50/2 Her decision to put expediency ahead of love nearly costs Corey his life when the shoot-'em-up finale swings the action back to North Africa.

shooter. Add: **I. 2. b.** *Sport.* One who kicks or drives a ball at goal; also in extended use in *Basketball, Netball*, etc.

1901 A. FARRELL *Ice Hockey & Ice Polo Guide* 54 The goaler..may skate out to meet him, being careful that he is directly in line between shooter and goal. **1922** W. E. MEANWELL *Basket Ball for Men* vii. 68 Line throwing is the chief fault with most shooters. **1957** *Encycl. Brit.* III. 181/1 Previously, a star shooter could attempt all free throws for his team. **1963** C. GLYN *Don't knock Corners Off* xxi. 178, I stood and shivered as Miss Pratt picked people for the netball teams... 'You can be Shooter.' **1978** T. L. SMITH *Money War* (1979) III. 218 The only gambit he could think of was darts. He was the fifth best shooter in the very active St. Louis league.

c. One who throws a die or marble. Cf. also *crap-shooter* s.v. *CRAP *sb.*[4] 2.

1910 A. BENNETT *Clayhanger* I. i. 9 The bearded shooter, pleased by this tribute..twisted his white apron. **1926** [see *little Joe* s.v. *LITTLE *a.* 13]. **1969** R. C. BELL *Board & Table Games* II. v. 84 When any pair is thrown and the third die is 2, 3, 4, or 5, the number of the third die becomes the shooter's point.

II. 5. (Later example.)

1981 *Country Life* 18 June 1772/1 Sappy shooters, from which to take cuttings now.

8. b. (Further examples.)

1931 E. O'NEILL *Hunted* IV, in *Mourning becomes Electra* 156 Easy goes, shipmate! Stow that pistol!.. Not that I'm skeered o' you or your shooter! **1970** G. F. NEWMAN *Sir, you Bastard* v. 138 Why did you pull the shooter on the two detectives? **1972** L. HENDERSON *Cage until Tame* ix. 77 We'll need a shooter, one barrel into the ceiling straight off.

9. (Earlier example.)

1843 'WYKHAMIST' *Pract. Hints Cricket* 7 Another advantage of this mode of holding the Bat close to the ground, is the greater facility the player has in stopping 'shooters'.

10. *Public School slang.* A black morning coat. ? *Obs.*

1870 *Harrovian* 9 Apr. 134/2 Although the use of slang words and phrases has now become almost universal among the greater portion of the community, we generally find that each University or School possesses a dialect peculiar to itself... *Shooter*, a shooting coat. **1920** GALSWORTHY *In Chancery* II. vii. 181 'I suppose I'd better change into a 'shooter',' he muttered, escaping to his room. He put on the 'shooter', a high collar, a pearl pin, and his neatest grey spats.

11. *U.S. slang.* A measure or drink of spirit, esp. whisky.

1971 *Car & Driver* Jan. 75/1 He made his famous call for 'shooters'. Now in case you haven't heard, a 'shooter' is a Turner variation of the word 'shot', as in a 'shot of likker', and..refers to a shot of Canadian Club mixed into a few fingers of 'Co-cola'. **1973** W. MCCARTHY *Detail* i. 61 Let's have a shooter and a beer. **1981** W. SAFIRE in *N.Y. Times Mag.* 2 May 16/4 The word coming up fast for a *straight shot* is a *shooter.* 'A shooter is a shot of liquor swallowed in one quick gulp,' says Jeff Dee.

shooting, *vbl. sb.* Add: **1. a.** Also, an incident in which a person is shot with a firearm.

1873 'MARK TWAIN' *Gilded Age* xlvi. 425 What some of the journals lacked in suitable length..they made up in encyclopaedic information about other similar murders and shootings. **1977** *Whitaker's Almanack 1978* 590/2 During the election campaign 50 people were reported killed in shootings and bombings.

e. *Oil Industry.* Detonation of an explosive charge in a well to increase the flow of oil or gas. Cf. *SHOOT *v.* 34.

1914 F. A. TALBOT *Oil Conquest of World* v. 64 'Shooting' is undertaken only when the limestone or sandstone is of such a nature that it restricts the flow of oil. **1937** *Amer. Speech* XII. 154/1 *Shooting a well*, using nitroglycerine to make oil flow. **1946** [see *OIL WELL]. **1969** *Times* 2 May 25/1 The international oil companies are stepping up their interest in the Irish Sea in search for oil and gas... The area involved covers at least 15,000 miles and although the 'shooting' will be selective, the cost will..be..high.

5. Also, in extended use in other sports, as *Basketball, Netball, Hockey*, etc.

1897 *Encycl. Sport* I. 518/2 The goalkeeper should run forward..so as to attempt to tackle him [*sc.* the hockey player] before he can get within shooting range. **1935** *Encycl. Sports* 436/1 It [*sc.* the game of netball] proceeds when..the ball..is received by one standing within the shooting circle. **1961** *Netball* ('Know the Game' Series) (ed. 5) 20 (*heading*) Footwork for throwing and shooting. **1974** *Plain Dealer* (Cleveland, Ohio) 26 Oct. 4-D/1 This system paid off in the team's shooting this week.

6. b. The action or process of taking film with a cinematographic camera.

1920 I. P. GORE in *Stage Year Book* 56 Many companies are paying trips to the Continent for the 'shooting' of certain scenes in the actual 'locations'. **1941** B. SCHULBERG *What makes Sammy Run?* xi. 284 A director exhausted from the day's shooting. **1955** *Times* 31 May 10/3 Mr. Orson Welles, for one, has shown..the methods of 'shooting' which lay emphasis on rehearsals. **1979** *Beautiful Brit. Columbia* Spring 4 Victoria was one of the shooting locations for Harry in Your Pocket.

c. The action or process of injecting an (addictive) drug intravenously. *slang* (orig. *U.S.*).

1951 *Evening Sun* (Baltimore) 27 Mar. 4/1 A powerful combination of 'bernice snorting' and heroin 'shooting' was called 'blowing speed balls'. **1953** W. BURROUGHS *Junkie* 8 You don't wake up one morning and decide to be a drug addict. It takes at least three months' shooting twice a day to get any habit at all. **1971** *Black Scholar* Apr.–May 46 Mugging, theft, pimping and shooting dope are not themselves political actions.

8. a. *shooting-season* (earlier and later examples); (sense *6 b) *shooting schedule, script.* Also *shooting-boot* (later examples; also (*fig.*) in sense 5), *dress, jacket* (earlier example), *shoe, suit* (example).

1894 *Country Gentleman's Catal.* 154 Fagg Brothers,.. makers of shooting boots to *H.R.H. The Duke of Saxe-Coburg.* **1947** *Sporting Mirror* 7 Nov. 11/3 Grimsby were having a sad and sorry season until the unexpected revival at Manchester United when Cairns found his shooting boots. **1948** C. DAY LEWIS *Otterbury Incident* 26 Everyone knows he's a deadly shot when his shooting-boots are on. **1978** *Cornish Guardian* 27 Apr. 5/5 Tintagel found their shooting boots in the second half of their game. **1794** J. WOODFORDE *Diary* 27 Oct. (1929) IV. 149, I met Mr. Stoughton..in a Shooting Dress. **1852** J. R. PLANCHÉ *Day of Reckoning* III. i. 30 *Claude*..in a shooting dress, is seated on the steps of the terrace, examining the lock of his gun. **1796** JANE AUSTEN *Let.* 5 Sept. (1952) 11 Let me know..how many of the Gentlemen, Musicians & Waiters, he will have persuaded to come in their Shooting Jackets. **1950** 'E. CRISPIN' *Frequent Hearses* i. 36 'It would be possible for me to meet her?'..'That depends on the shooting schedules. The film's on the floor.' **1976** M. MAGUIRE *Scratchproof* i. 11 Shooting schedules were being delayed and people were beginning to say the film was jinxed. **1929** I. MONTAGU tr. *Pudovkin's On Film Technique* vi. 176 The *Shooting-script* is the scenario in its final cinematographic form. **1933** A. BRUNEL *Filmcraft* 141 Here follow two sequences of the actual shooting script of 'A Light Woman'. **1976** H. OREL in M. Drabble *Genius of T. Hardy* 103 Perhaps John Wain exaggerates by describing the entire work [*sc. The Dynasts*] as a shooting script. **1781** G. SELWYN *Let.* 19 May in *15th Rep. R. Comm. Hist. Manuscripts* App. VI. 484 in *Parl. Papers 1897* (c. 8551) LI. 1 Boothby proposes to go to you in the shooting season, that is near Christmas. **1981** C. MILLER *Childhood in Scotland* 54 The opening of the shooting seasons varied with the type of game. **1839** A. MATHEWS *Mem. Charles Mathews* III. vii. 162, I had them made after a plan of my own, for shooting-shoes. **1976** *Shooting Times & Country Mag.* 18–24 Nov. (Advt.), The golden boot—our famous shooting shoe. **1893** KIPLING *Day's Work* (1898) 43 The Rao Sahib, in tweed shooting-suit and a seven-hued turban.

b. shooting booth, a booth at a fair in which shooting for prizes is carried out (cf. *shooting gallery* (*a*)); **shooting brake,** an estate car, now *rare*; orig. a light, horse-drawn wagonette designed to accommodate passengers and goods (cf. BREAK *sb.*[2]); **shooting-gallery,** (*a*) also *fig.* in colloq. phr. *the whole shooting gallery* = *the whole shoot* s.v. SHOOT *sb.*[1] 8; (*b*) *U.S. slang*, a place where addictive drugs may be obtained and 'shot' or taken by injection; **shooting-ground,** (*a*) (earlier and later examples); **shooting-iron** (earlier example); **shooting match** (later examples); also *fig.* in colloq. phr. *the whole shooting match* = *the whole shoot* s.v. SHOOT *sb.*[1] 8; **shooting phaeton** = *shooting brake* (orig. sense) above; **shooting seat** = *shooting stick* (*c*) below, now *rare*; **shooting-stick,** (*b*) *slang* = *shooting iron* (obs.); (*c*) a walking-stick with a handle that may be opened to form an impromptu seat, first used by shooters; **shooting war,** hostilities involving armed conflict, as opposed to *cold war* s.v. *COLD *a.* 19; first used with reference to U.S. involvement in the war of 1939–45.

1900 *Times* 7 July 10/1 We may soon expect swings erected in the practice-ground, shooting booths under.. the big stand. **1970** R. LOWELL *Notebk.* 202 The shags Flying in straight lines like duck in a shooting booth. **1912** H. J. BUTLER *Motor Bodies & Chassis* iv. 48 Wagonettes, Shooting Brakes, and Luggage Cars.—This type of body fulfils the requirements of the sporting dogcart, and generally has sufficient capacity to replace two of these horsed vehicles. **1934** A. G. STREET *Endless Furrow* xvii. 301 After a few minutes occupied with introductions and drinking a glass of sherry James found himself in the shooting brake, and soon the four-in-hand swept through the gates into the town. **1948** H. MCCAUSLAND *Eng. Carriage* iv. 77 A very neat, very sporting little brake.. intended for private use in the country with a team or pair, was the Shooting Brake, which had, behind its high box, a strong suggestion of the dog-cart in its bodywork. **1958** *Times* 13 Aug. 4/5 One man was killed and 11 people were injured when a shooting brake and a motor coach were in collision at Holcombe Brook, Bury, to-night. **1951** *Life* 11 June 120/1 Sometimes he runs a 'shooting gallery', an establishment which not only sells the addict dope but furnishes hypodermics. *a* **1966** 'M. NA GOPALEEN' *Best of Myles* (1968) 323 Put the whole shooting gallery into a saucepan of cold water. **1972** J. WAMBAUGH *Blue Knight* (1973) ii. 36 He knows this boss dyke, a real mean bull dagger. Her pad's a shooting gallery for some of us. **1973** R. BUSBY *Pattern of Violence* v. 79 'Did you call in?'.. 'Yeah... The whole shooting gallery 'll be here in a few minutes.' **1835** J. J. AUDUBON *Ornith. Biogr.* III. 37 There is no lack of shooting grounds, for every creek of salt-water swarms with Marsh Hens. **1897** *Outing* Mar. 536/2 A shooting friend..and myself were staying at a farmhouse, near the shooting-grounds. **1775** S. ADAMS *Let.* 31 Jan. in *Writings* (1907) III. 172 It puts me in mind of what I remember to have heard you observe, that we may all be soon under the necessity of keeping *Shooting Irons.* **1813** *Niles' Weekly Register* IV. 35/1, I..gained their applause for my activity at our shooting matches. **1896** [see *CON b]. **1922** D. H. LAWRENCE in *N.Y. Times* 24 Dec. 9/4 What a lively shooting match will go on between all the Jacks and the Juans! **1953** K. REISZ *Technique Film Editing* II. 76 The final chase..was best presented as a 'battle of wits', instead of a wild action-packed shooting match. **1974** *BP Shield Internat.* Oct. 2/4 This had the effect of tilting up the whole shooting match. **1890** *Coach Builders' Jrnl.* 15 Nov. 181/2 Another of this firm's exhibits was a shooting phaeton... It was furnished with luncheon basket. **1898** *Carriage Builders' Jrnl.* Dec. p. ix/2 (Advt.), Four-wheel shooting phaeton; varnished walnut; pigskin cushions, brass mounts and lamps, mat, and gun-box complete. **1895** *Army & Navy Co-op Soc. Price List* 15 Sept. 954 Cane shooting seat. *Ibid.*, Wood, folding Shooting Seat, can be used as a Walking Stick. **1917** *Harrods Gen. Catal.* 1089/2 Mills' Patent Shooting Seats. Strongly recommended as being the lightest and best seat, it is also telescopic. **1845** E. J. WAKEFIELD *Adventure N.Z.* I. xi. 319 Every article of trade with the natives has its slang term,—in order that they may converse with each other respecting a purchase without initiating the natives into their calculations, thus pigs and potatoes were respectively represented by '*grunters*' and '*spuds*', guns..by '*shooting-sticks*'. **1866** 'F. KIRKLAND' *Pictorial Bk. Anecdotes* 237/2 Sambo.. fell back in confusion when the 'shooting stick' was brandished toward his own breast. **1926** E. P. OPPENHEIM *Golden Beast* I. xvii. 163 Judith had already disappeared, swinging her shooting stick in her hand. **1967** *Guardian* 23 May 2/6 The shooting sticks will prod the roots of every stately garden. **1941** *Time* 4 Aug. 15/3, 55%..are ready to risk some kind of shooting war at once. **1956** F. CASTLE *Violent Hours* vi. 51, I got into the real shooting war towards the close, at Okinawa. **1978** L. HEREN *Growing up on The Times* iii. 86 Pat had joined me before the end of the shooting war, and was almost killed in Jerusalem.

shootist. (Earlier and later U.S. examples.)
1864 *Gold Hill* (Nevada) *News* 15 Jan. 3/1 (*heading*) A Shootist. **1976** *National Observer* (U.S.) 4 Sept. 18/2 J. B. Books, the protagonist of Wayne's new movie, *The Shootist*,..not only restores the legend but expands it, giving the man and his memory grace and dignity. A shootist is a man good with a gun, and J. B. Books is a retired marshal who was good enough to kill 30 men.

shoo·t-out. orig. *U.S.* Also **shootout.** [f. vbl. phr. *to shoot it out*: see *SHOOT *v.* 22 d (*f*).]
1. A sustained exchange of shooting, a gun-fight. Also *fig.*, a dispute or competition.
1953 *N.Y. Times* 5 July VII. 13/2 The justly famous shoot-out between the Earps and the Clantons in the O–K Corral. **1968** 'R. MACDONALD' *Instant Enemy* xxx. 188 The last thing needed was the kind of shoot-out in which innocent people could get hurt. **1969** *Daily Tel.* (Colour Suppl.) 17 Jan. 15/3 In one 'shoot-out' that developed, Oakland police killed a 17-year-old Panther, Bobby Hutton, while he was unarmed. **1975** *Atlanta Jrnl.* 20 Jan. 1/2 In the ensuing shootout Sunday, the man who fired the shot was killed. **1976** *Washington Post* 19 Apr. A4/1 Church's strategy is to have the decisive shoot-out on the Senate floor in a major public debate. **1978** *Fortune* 31 Dec. 59 In the quick-draw tradition of the Old Wild West stagecoach, the two major lines have responded to adversity..by taking on one another in a fierce and profitless shootout over passenger fares. **1981** *Economist* 8 Aug. 34/1 The normal run of muggings, burglaries and rapes has been exacerbated by shootouts.. among 'cocaine cowboys'.
2. *transf.* In *Football*, a tie-breaker (see quot. 1978).
1978 *Guardian Weekly* 16 June 19/4 If the match is still tied..the teams resort to a shoot-out. Five different members of each team take a free shot at goal, starting from the 25 yard line and having five seconds to dribble the ball before shooting. If even these ten shots fail to produce a decision, they play a sudden death shoot-out until one side wins. **1979** *Globe & Mail* (Toronto) 1 May 48/9 Johann Scharmann converted the deciding shot in a shootout to win it for Detroit Express.

shoo·t-up. [f. vbl. phr. *to shoot up*: see *SHOOT *v.* 30 e.] **1.** A furious exchange of shooting, a gun-battle, a shoot-out; also, an assault by gun-fire.
1922 *Blackw. Mag.* Oct. 441/2 A favourite form of amusement of the I.R.A. used to consist in what was commonly called 'shooting up' a district: these outrages took the form of shooting at every Loyalist who appeared within range for a whole evening... Before one of these shoot-ups you might search every house in the district to be shot-up till dusk, and not find any arms..; but soon after dusk..men would..distribute arms to the gunmen. **1942** BERREY & VAN DEN BARK *Amer. Thes. Slang* § 348/4 *Gun battle*,..shoot-up. **1962** *Listener* 20 Sept. 438/3 A shoot-up in Alcatraz. **1972** P. DICKINSON *Lizard in Cup* ix. 122 The cops in New Jersey got him in a shoot-up with the Black Panthers. **1978** *New York* 3 Apr. 10/2 Were the Egyptian commandos killed by Cypriot soldiers—as the Cyprus government claims—or by the PLO? Was the shoot-up at Larnaca airport a 'misunderstanding' or a well-conceived plan?
2. The act of flying low over a target as if to or actually to attack. *R.A.F. slang.*
1942 I. GLEED *Arise to Conquer* vi. 62 We do a gentle shoot-up of our billets.

shop, *sb.* Add: **2. a.** *Shop!* (earlier example).
1888 KIPLING *Plain Tales from Hills* 242 A little wife to call 'shorp!' 'shorp!' when the door-bell rung.
e. [Back-formation f. SHOP *v.* 4.] An act of shopping for purchases. *colloq.*
1960 *Housewife* May 121/2 You should find it possible to have one big 'shop' a week with a small mid-week 'shop' for perishables. **1978** D. MURPHY *Place Apart* ix. 198 It was a Saturday morning, when many go into the city centre to do their weekly 'big shop'.
f. *shop-within-a-shop*, a shop which functions independently within the premises of a larger store, usu. dealing in the goods of one manufacturer.
1962 E. GODFREY *Retail Selling & Organ.* i. 5 Another practice..is that of opening a shop-within-a-shop, selling the manufacturer's goods and staffed by his employees. **1978** *Country Life* 5 Oct. 1054/1 Mulberry Company.. makers of..high fashion accessories are opening shops-within-shops at nine Nieman Marcus stores.
3. b. (Earlier *absol.* example.)
a **1779** 'J. H. ST. JOHN DE CRÈVECŒUR' *Sk. 18th-Cent. Amer.* (1925) 143 The truly economical farmer has always what we call a shop, that is, a house big enough to contain a loom. There..our wives can..weave.
d. *Glass-making.* A team or gang of workers (see quots.).
1889 *Harper's New Monthly Mag.* July 259/1 Generally four [glass factory workers] constitute a shop, the most skilful workman (the blower) at the head, the gatherer (a young fellow) next, and two boys, one handling moulds or tools, and the other carrying the products to the annealing oven. **1905** *28th Ann. Rep. New Jersey Bureau Statistics of Labor* III. 201 A case in point..is the change from single blower method of doing work, which prevailed previous to 1870, to what is now known as the 'shop system'; that is to say, three men now work together, two of them gathering glass and blowing the ware, while the third makes the neck smooth. **1949** P. DAVIS *Devel. Amer. Glass Industry* x. 230 The operation was performed by a three-worker shop composed of a gatherer, a blower, and a crimper. **1970** *Awake* (Austral.) 8 Jan. 23/1 The glassblowers function as a 'shop' of six or seven men.
e. *N. Amer.* A schoolroom equipped for teaching the arts of the workshop; this study as a classroom discipline. Cf. *shop class*, sense 9 c below.
1914 J. S. TAYLOR *Handbook of Vocational Education* iii. 54 The school shop now resembles the abode of the cabinet maker. *Ibid.* v. 65 The student learns much of what industrial life is like..in the successful operations of..the school shop. **1941** *School Shop* Oct. 2/2 *School Shop* has been established to serve shop teachers. **1948** G. O. WILBUR *Industrial Arts in General Educ.* ix. 127 There is some evidence which seems to indicate a close correlation between the measure of the school shop and the type of learning which takes place there. **1974** J. HELLER *Something Happened* 224 The new teachers, the old teachers,..the shop teacher, and the science teacher (he has always been leery of shop teachers and science teachers. Perhaps because they are men.) **1978** *Detroit Free Press* 2 Apr. 3D/1 A school..cannot prevent a girl from taking shop or a boy from taking home economics.
4. (Earlier examples.) *The Shop:* (later example); also (*Austral. slang*), the University of Melbourne.
1779 E. GIBBON *Let.* 15 May (1956) II. 215 So much remains to be done, that I can hardly spare a single day from the Shop. **1827** T. SURR *Richmond* II. i. 5, I hurried off with Bucks to the office, or *shop*, as he called it. **1889** *Centennial Mag.* II. III. 218 It related how 'a medical student came up to the Shop' as a freshman, and 'thought through exams. he would speedily pop'. **1918** G. WALL *Lett. of Airman* 15, I would be quite glad to get the Shop exam results. **1964** G. JOHNSTON *My Brother Jack* 260 The years at the Shop gave me nothing except a worthless B.A. and the privilege of being thrown into the University lake. **1978** G. M. FRASER *Flashman at Charge* 110 We treated each other decently, and weren't one jot more incompetent than this Sandhurst-and-Shop crowd.
b. (Earlier and later examples.) Also in gen. use (*rare*).
1885 J. K. JEROME *On Stage & Off* 126 After that it was next to impossible for him to get a shop (this expression is not slang, it is a bit of local colour). **1922** E. WALLACE *Flying Fifty-Five* xxx. 178 Fired, are you?..Well, what are you going to do? Get another shop? **1978** G. MITCHELL *Wraiths & Changelings* xii. 128 He was an out-of-work actor and was very anxious to get a shop, as he called it.
5. *to talk shop* (earlier example).
1860 C. FOX *Jrnl.* 28 Sept. (1972) 232 Holman Hunt.. does not talk 'shop', but is perfectly willing to tell you anything you really wish to know of his painting.
8. b. *to set up shop* (*fig.* example); *to live over the shop*, to live on the premises where one works; *to mind the shop*: see *MIND *v.* 11.
1930 D. L. SAYERS *Strong Poison* i. 23 'He's put her into a house somewhere round about, I fancy,' said Freddy, 'with a typewriting office to look after and live over the shop and run those comic charity stunts of his.' **1963** A. HUXLEY *Let.* 27 Mar. (1969) 952, I..heard of his plans for an LSD institute... He may be more successful in setting up shop within the US. **1976** H. WILSON *Governance of Britain* iv. 83 In 1964–70 I lived in No. 10. In 1974 I decided that I did not want to live over the shop again, and I slept each night in my home in Lord North Street.
c. Also, in a state of confusion. (Earlier and later examples.)
1874 HOTTEN *Slang Dict.* 288 In pugilistic slang, to punish a man severely is 'to knock him all over the shop'. **1916** 'TAFFRAIL' *Pincher Martin* xiv. 267 'Wagglin' about a bit,' the coxswain answered, gazing at his compass-card. .. 'She's all over the shop. Up to sou'-east one minute, an' back to south-eighty the next.' **1926** G. B. SHAW *Intell. Woman's Guide* lxxi. 345 The unconventional ones are all over the shop with all sorts of opinions. **1935** F. M. FORD *Let.* 15 Oct. (1965) 245 He is in the greatest danger of going slack all over the shop. **1978** J. I. M. STEWART *Full Term* ix. 93 At one of Anthea Gender's [parties] one was substantially although not too obtrusively in the presence of grandees drawn from all over the shop.
9. a. (*a*) *shop-bell*, *-counter*, *-door* (later examples), *-front* (earlier example: also *attrib.* and *fig.*), *sign*; (*c*) *shop-goods* (later examples); (*d*) *shop hours*; (*e*) *shop-boy* (earlier and later examples), *-clerk*, *-girl* (earlier and later examples), *-worker*.
1853 MRS. GASKELL *Cranford* xv. 299 She..was only extricated from her dilemma by the sound of the shop-bell. **1972** J. THOMSON *Not One of Us* viii. 90 The tinkle of the shop bell severed the conversation and she went through to serve. **1813** JANE AUSTEN *Pride & Prejudice* I. xv. 166 Mr. Jones's shop boy..had told her that they were not to send any more draughts to Netherfield. **1903** G. B. SHAW *Man & Superman* III. 132, I breathe an atmosphere of sweetness, like a confectioner's shopboy. **1977** *Daily Times* (Lagos) 25 Dec. 22/4 (Advt.), Drivers—Houseboys, Shopboys, Shopgirls, Housegirls. **1911** H. S. HARRISON *Queed* xiii. 151 There is your public..shop-clerks, stenographers [etc.]. **1921** *Dict. Occup. Terms* (1927) § 939 *Shopclerk*.., keeps record of amount of work done by piece workers for purpose of calculating cost and wages. **1822** D. WORDSWORTH *Jrnl.* 21 Sept. (1941) II. viii. 361 One a gentlemanly, middle aged man; the other rather younger, with a dash of the shop-counter. **1972** *Listener* 23 Nov. 690/1 'Voluntary price control'..has certainly not worked over the shop counter where it was most needed. *a* **1745** SWIFT *Works* (1766) XIII. 47 Our shop-doors will be no longer crowded with so many thieves and pick-pockets. **1832** *Chambers's Edin. Jrnl.* I. 277/1 Transported, he through the shop-door pops his head. **1977** A. HUNTER *Gently Instrumental* v. 60 The hour of the lunchtime siesta when every shop door was closed. **1835** DICKENS in *Evening Chron.* 14 July 3/3 He..got his butcher to skewer them up on conspicuous joints in his shop-front. **1934** *Times Lit. Suppl.* 25 Jan. 61/1 (*title*) Modern shopfront construction. **1961** D. HOLBROOK *Eng. for Maturity* 15, I never knew how much shop-front is behind—or perhaps in front of—teaching. **1975** *Sunday Times* 3 Aug. 24/6 The keening nature of the sounds resembles so often the seizing music one has heard in shop-front gospel churches all over America. **1820** M. EDGEWORTH *Let.* 21 May (1979) 134 The fishwomen, criers and shopgirls whose manners to customers are in general a curious mixture of the affected indifference.. and of the real anxiety for your custom. *c* **1855** GEO. ELIOT in J. W. Cross *George Eliot's Life* (1885) I. vi. 364 She looked like a shop-girl who has donned a masquerade dress impromptu. **1951** A. BARON *Rosie Hogarth* 176 She forced herself to speak calmly, in her precise shopgirl's voice. **1796** J. WOODFORDE *Diary* 2 Apr. (1929) IV. 268 Betty Cary went wth. him, to bring home some Shop Goods. **1875** [see *ABUSEFULLY *adv.*]. **1972** *Morning Star* 11 Oct. 1 Wage earners might receive more in their pay packets than they do at present but might pay more than they gained in the extra tax paid on shop goods. **1892** *Act* 55 & 56 *Vict.* c. 62 § 1 This Act may be cited as the Shop Hours Act, 1892. **1967** *Observer* 14 May 28/7 Shop hours are 10–7 p.m. **1930** *Daily Express* 6 Oct. 3/5 A great flame which lit up the whole sky..and clearly illuminated the shop signs. **1969** E. H. PINTO *Treen* 410/2 Trade labels on London goods sold between 1765 and 1770, are sometimes printed with the old shop sign. **1896** *Shop Assistant* Aug. 11/2 Manchester may again be counted as a stronghold of unionism amongst shop workers, eager and ready for the fray..which shall emancipate the shop slaves from slavery. **1966** *Listener* 25 Aug. 264/2 Shop-workers' union is to join the opposition to the Government's wage freeze.
b. *shop-done* adj. (nonce use).
1888 G. M. HOPKINS *Let.* 1 May (1956) 291, I may be able to send you one [*sc.* a photograph] of me, not shop-done but artistically better.
b*. Applied to food, goods, etc., produced commercially for sale, as (often unfavourably) opposed to home-made or made to order, as *shop-bread*, *cake*, etc.; shop-bought.
1859 GEO. ELIOT *Adam Bede* II. I. xx. 95 A cloth made of homespun linen... None of your bleached 'shop-rag' that would wear into holes in no time. **1876** C. M. YONGE *Three Brides* II. i. 304 I'm sent for one of Herbert's shirts... I believe their hearts would break outright if he took to shop ones. **1928** E. G. MILLAR *Eng. Illuminated MSS. of XIVth & XVth Cent.* iii. 38 Sarum Horae... These are seldom of more than mediocre quality, and are merely 'shop' copies. **1949** D. SMITH *I capture Castle* xii. 203, I had..two slices of cake (real shop cake) and milk. **1957** J. BRAINE *Room at Top* xxi. 180 It must have seemed that she was offering me a good home-cooked dinner and that I was rejecting it in favour of a slice of chalky shop bread spread with factory-made meat paste. **1975** *Times* 22 Nov. 11/6 As late as the 1930s the better-off continued to look down on those who..spread 'shop' jam on their bread. **1978** D. MURPHY *Place Apart* xi. 229 She brought out a slice of Christmas cake... 'It's only shop,' she apologised.
c. shop assistant, a salesman or saleswoman in a retail shop or store; **shop class** *N. Amer.*, a class in which the arts of the workshop are taught (cf. sense 3 e above); **shop committee** *U.S.* (see quot. 1923); **shopcraft** *N. Amer.*, an association of railway employees working in repair shops, etc.; **shop-dropper** *local Austral. colloq.* (see quot. 1957) (cf. *DROPPER 1 d); **shop-finish,** the professional finish of an article produced in a commercial workshop (sometimes depreciatory); also *transf.*; hence **shop-finished** *ppl. a.*; **shop-fitting,** (*a*) *pl.*, the fitments (as counters and shelves) with which a shop is equipped; (*b*) the action or process of fitting out a shop with these; hence **shop-fitter; shop-gaze** *v. intr.*, to window-shop; **shop-house,** in S.E. Asia, a shop opening on to the pavement and also used as the residence of the proprietor; **shop-soiled** *a.*, also *fig.*; **shop steward,** a person elected by his or her fellow-workers in a factory, etc., or a branch of it as their spokesman on conditions of work, etc.; **shop-talk** (later examples); **shop-walker** (earlier example); so **shop-walk** *v. intr.*, to act as a shop-walker; **shop-work,** work done in a shop or workshop; **shop-worn** *a.* orig. *U.S.* (earlier examples).
1880 *Girl's Own Paper* 25 Sept. 612/1 There are two great enemies for the shop assistant—the severe shop-walker..and the inconsiderate lady-customer. **1921** *Dict. Occup. Terms* (1927) § 775 *Shop assistant*.., serves customers with goods in retail shop or store, makes out bill or docket. **1977** D. JAMES *Spy at Evening* xii. 86 They were mostly school kids..or young shop assistants and working boys. **1948** G. O. WILBUR *Industrial Arts in General Educ.* xiv. 212 If students go home enthusiastic about the work in their shop classes, a general approval of the whole school program by the parents is apt to follow. **1962** A. LURIE *Love & Friendship* iv. 70 On the last day of school he would take home the present he had made for his mother in shop class. **1978** M. PUZO *Fools Die* xxxix. 435 In the shop class of the asylum school I made myself such a hat. **1908** *Mod. Business* Aug. 69/1 With a good shop committee the men will not be afraid to ventilate their grievances. **1923** J. D. HACKETT *Labor Terms* in *Managem. Engin.* May 344/2 *Shop Committee*, a committee appointed by members of a works committee

for the consideration of some special labor problem. **1954** C. E. Dankert *Introd. Labor* x. 187 In many labor organizations there are structural units smaller than, and subordinate to, the locals. These are the so-called shop committees, which are under the leadership of shop stewards. **1973** S. Aronowitz in G. Hunnius et al. *Workers' Control* I. 105 The impulse to dual forms of struggle—shop committees, wild cat strikes, steward movements—may become important in the labor movements of the future. **1919** W. Hines *Let.* 10 Nov. in *Official Proc. 5th Biennial Convention Railway Employees Dept. Amer. Fed. Labor* (1920) 133 The fullest cooperation of..the national officers of the Shop Crafts organizations. **1942** H. E. Jones *Wages & Labor Relations in Railroad Industry 1900–1941* 14 For shop craft employees, annual compensation stood at $1,754 in 1922. **1973** *Daily Colonist* (Victoria, B.C.) 7 Sept. 1/4 Latest union flareup occurred ..as members of Canadian National Railways shopcraft unions walked off the job. **1957** *Courier-Mail* (Brisbane) 26 Nov. 2 'Shop-droppers' are truck owners who buy large quantities of fruit and vegetables at the market and sell them to shopkeepers in and around Brisbane. **1967** *Sunday Mail* (Brisbane) 12 Feb. 18 The suppliers—known as 'shop-droppers'—have been operating for several years. **1923** *New Statesman* 6 Oct. 738/1 They [*sc.* early plays by Somerset Maugham] had the handy compactness, shop-finish and alluring shinyness of a new dressing-case. **1931** R. Fry in W. Rose *Outl. Mod. Knowl.* 914 This last perfection of finish, for which craftsmen have adopted the excellent term 'shop-finish'. **1938** R. G. Collingwood *Princ. Art* xv. 329 The slick shop-finish of a ready-made article. **1932** R. Fry *Characteristics French Art* II. 43 Elsheimer's pictures are so tight, so horribly shop-finished and over-polished. **1885** *List of Subscribers, Classified* (United Telephone Co.) (ed. 6) 188 (*heading*) Shop fitters. **1921** *Dict. Occup. Terms* (1927) § 483 *Shop fitter*, receives wooden parts or sections of counters, desks,..and other shop-fittings..fits and joins these parts or sections together. **1951** A. Baron *Rosie Hogarth* 13 Fred was an engineer and Jack a shopfitter by trade. **1978** *Detroit Free Press* 16 Apr. (Parade Suppl.) 21/1 The 33 indicted..included..a shopfitter. **1858** P. L. Simmonds *Dict. Trade Products* 342 *Shop-fittings*, the counters, desks, shelves, gas-burners, and other fixtures of a shop. **1911** *Rep. Labour & Soc. Cond. Germany* III. vi–vii. 29 The building and shopfitting trade. **1939** C. Vernon *Sweet Shop* xii. xlix. 178 We give in this chapter some general hints on shop fitting and decoration. **1959** R. Buckner *Design for Selling* ii. 14 So many bakers are altering their shop fittings to comply with the hygiene regulations. **1977** *Centuryan* (Office Cleaning Services) Christmas 2/4 The firm was concentrating too much on shopfitting for one client. **1876** L. Troubridge *Life amongst Troubridges* (1966) 143 Shopped the whole morning—*flanéed* down Regent Street, shop-gazing with true country zeal. **1946** S. Spender *European Witness* 21 Crowds who a few years ago were shop-gazing in their city. **1949** *Malayan Pictorial Observer* Aug. 9 Shop-houses line the main street. **1957** G. W. Skinner *Chinese Society in Thailand* iii. 107 By the 1880's..the junk bazaar was..a thing of the past... The former floating population of Chinese tradesmen moved to the two-story shop-houses built in rows along the new streets. **1966** 'A. Hall' *9th Directive* i. 7 Where the trishaw had dropped me..was a narrow street of shop-houses. **1978** L. Heren *Growing up on The Times* v. 182 The shophouse had four small rooms. The front room, or shop, was given over to a dispensary... Behind were two small bedrooms and a kitchen. **1926** T. E. Lawrence *Seven Pillars* (1935) v. lix. 333 Beyrout was the door of Syria, a chromatic Levantine screen through which cheap or shop-soiled foreign influences entered. **1927** M. Arlen *Young Men in Love* II. 137 Always together... That shop-soiled man and the tall girl with the curly gleaming hair. **1977** J. Wainwright *Day of Peppercorn Kill* 33 Not the love of a wife... A shop-soiled love—which..he'd reject. **1904** *Rules Amalg. Soc. Engineers* 46 Committees may also appoint shop-stewards to..keep the committee posted with all events occurring in the various shops. **1928** *Britain's Industr. Future* (Liberal Industr. Inquiry) III. xviii. 226 The shop-steward movement, which reached such magnitude during the War, was essentially an attempt to base the struggle for better conditions upon the natural unit of the factory. **1950** A. P. Herbert *Independent Member* 251 At Short's works at Rochester..the shop-stewards threatened a strike. *a* **1974** R. Crossman *Diaries* (1975) I. 478 This is the first big event of this election campaign—the revelation of a so-called kangaroo trial by shop stewards at the B.M.C. works. **1922** S. Lewis *Babbitt* x. 143 The shop-talk roused Paul Riesling... He was..a very able salesman. **1971** D. E. Westlake *I gave at Office* 76, I must have given her my complete life story..and virtually tons of shoptalk about my job. **1905** H. G. Wells *Kipps* I. vi. 135 Buggins, whose place it was to shopwalk while Carshot served, shopwalked with quite unparallelled dignity. **1825** in A. Nicoll *Hist. Eng. Drama 1660–1900* (1959) VI. 459 (*title of play*) The shop-walker. **1899** W. James *Talks to Teachers* v. 35 Laboratory work and shop work engender a habit of observation,..a knowledge of the difference between accuracy and vagueness. **1932** O. E. Saunders *Hist. Eng. Art in Middle Ages* xiii. 157 Countless lesser Books of Hours were turned out all through the fifteenth and sixteenth centuries for private patrons, but they represent mere shop-work. **1974** J. Burnett *Useful Toil* II. 141 Girls could now go into shop work, into the new light factory trades and into.. clerical work. **1838** *Amer. Comic All-I-Make for 1839* 7 The piece of goods got kinder shop worn, and the old man thought he'd never get her off his hands. **1849** Thoreau *Week Concord Riv.* 220 He is even envied by his shop-worn neighbours. **1871** P. T. Barnum *Struggles & Triumphs* 40 A large quantity of tin ware which had been in the shop for years and was considerably 'shop-worn'.

shop, *v.* Add: **1. b.** To dismiss (a person) from a position or post. *rare.*

1864 Hotten *Slang Dict.* 228 *Shop*, to discharge a shopman. **1915** H. L. Wilson *Ruggles of Red Gap* xvii. 308, I would have shopped the fellow in an instant,..had it been at any other time. He was most impertinent.

4. a. Also *transf.*

1951 M. McCarthy in *Holiday* May 47/2 He determined to attach his name to some lasting benevolent enterprise and settled on woman's education after cautious shopping and advice-seeking. **1973** *Times* 27 Feb. 16/3 The National Portrait Gallery went shopping at Phillips sale room yesterday.

b. With *around.* To visit different shops examining the prices of comparable goods offered for sale before making a purchase; to make purchases at different shops according to which offers the best price. Freq. *transf.* and *fig.*

1922 *Management Engineering* Feb. 89/1 During the war, although orders greatly exceeded production, absenteeism increased. Men took days off to 'shop around', knowing that if unsuccessful they would be welcomed back. **1936** D. Powell *Turn, Magic Wheel* II. 195 Can't you just see those little embryos shopping around for security. **1948** *Economist* 31 July 171/2 It is impossible to shop around for cheaper raw materials. **1952** A. Huxley *Let. c* 20 July (1969) 647 Since success depends on a satisfactory relation between the hypnotised person and the operator you must be prepared to 'shop around' until you find someone sympathetic as well as skilful. **1960** W. Taplin *Advertising* iv. 83 We have.. noticed the..case..of the people who buy advertised products and in effect accept the advertiser's persuasion rather than spend time 'shopping around'. **1976** J. I. M. Stewart *Memorial Service* ii. 35 It's usual to shop around a little. To send in a list of three or four colleges.

c. *trans.* To shop at (a store); to examine goods on sale in (a shop). *N. Amer.*

1955 in H. Galinsky *Amerikanisches und Britisches Englisch* (1957) 49 Shop the store that gives you more. **1961** *Ford Times* Mar. 28 (*heading*) Shopping the southern roadside. **1974** S. Marcus *Minding Store* iv. 85 One man who had shopped the entire store complained that he hadn't found what he was looking for. **1980** 'E. McBain' *Ghosts* ii. 18 Maybe all the burglars..were out shopping the department stores.

5. (Earlier example.)

1808 *Rules of Journeymen, Hat-Makers & Finishers of Stockport* in A. Aspinall *Early Eng. Trade Unions* (1949) iv. 110 And when any person comes wishing to be asked for, the person that goes and asks for him, to take his ticket, and in case that man is shopped, he must leave his ticket at the place he is shopped.

Shope (ʃōᵘp). *Biol.* The name of Richard Edwin *Shope* (1902–66), U.S. physician, used *attrib.* to designate a transmissible papilloma of rabbits described by him in 1932 (*Jrnl. Exper. Med.* LVI. 793, 803), and the DNA virus which causes it.

1934 *Jrnl. Exper. Med.* LX. 756 The Shope papilloma, as occurring in nature, manifestly falls into the group of infectious warts, condylomas, and papillomas. **1935** *Proc. Soc. Exper. Biol. & Med.* XXXIII. 193 Shope virus from some sources gives rise to progressively enlarging papillomas, and that from others to growths which tend to disappear. **1938** *Ann. Reg. 1937* 349 A high molecular weight protein apparently associated with the viral activity was isolated from the Shope rabbit papilloma. **1961** R. D. Baker *Essent. Path.* xiii. 311 Carcinogenic viruses are known to produce the Rous sarcoma in chickens and the Shope papilloma of rabbits. **1970** *New Scientist* 29 Jan. 194/1 The Shope virus..induces warts on the skins of rabbits.

shop floor. [f. Shop *sb.* + Floor *sb.*^{1}] **1.** The floor of a workshop or factory, where the operatives work; the part of a factory or workshop concerned with productive as opp. to administrative work. Freq. (with hyphen) *attrib.* Also in phr. *on the shop floor.*

1951 E. Jacques *Changing Culture of Factory* III. xii. 316 The workers' representatives..were regarded as a more reliable source of information about shop floor matters. **1956** *Nature* 18 Feb. 300/2 It is difficult to see how, in a Handbook of this kind, the real challenge and opportunity which shop-floor industry presents could be presented. **1962** *B.S.I. News* Apr. 17/2 Polymethylmethacrylate might be understood by a chemist but 'Perspex' (a trade name) would be understood at shop-floor level. **1962** *Listener* 12 July 44/2 The lack of participation on the shop floor may be one of the underlying causes of malaise. **1967** C. Margerison in Wills & Yearsley *Handbk. Management Technol.* 31 The worker on the shop floor does not tend to identify himself either with the values or the goals of the manager. **1970** *Guardian* 11 July 11/6 The unanimous decision of a dockers' delegate conference—shop floor democracy at its most democratic. **1977** M. Walker *National Front* vi. 156 The new trade union policy did not focus solely on the exploitation of racialism on the shop floor.

2. By extension, the workers on the shop floor considered *collect.*

1958 *Listener* 30 Oct. 680/2 A dispute between management and shop floor about the number of men to be employed upon a machine. **1977** *Times* 20 Apr. 4/7 They have decided to cancel... The shop floor is upset about it.

shophar. Add: The standard form is now **shofar.** (Earlier and further examples.)

1833 *Children's Mag.* V. 113 The crooked trumpet, or *shophar*, was appointed by the Law of Moses to be blown ..when the year of jubilee was proclaimed. **1891** M. Friedlander *Jewish Relig.* 403 The *shofar* is intended to awaken us. **1931** *Times Lit. Suppl.* 24 Sept. 722/2 The blowing of the Shofar turns out to have been originally the imitation of the voice of the dying God. **1973** *Synagogue Light* Sept. 41/2 Every morning at the conclusion of the service a blast of the shofar reminds us of the approaching Day of Judgment.

shoplift, *v.* [Back-formation f. Shoplifting *vbl. sb.*] To steal from a shop while pretending to be a customer. **a.** *intr.*

1820 [see Sheep-steal *v.*]. **1843** *Punch* 8 Apr. 150/1 Policeman, here's a wench Shoplifting, take the customer to jail. **1959** *Times* 9 Mar. (Britain's Food Suppl.) p. ix/3 The temptation to shop-lift is one facet of the principle on which every self-service store depends. **1971** *Guardian* 22 Feb. 9/1 When Mrs Brown gets depressed, she starts to shoplift.

b. *trans.*

1922 Joyce *Ulysses* 741 A whore always shoplifting anything she could. **1979** K. Conlon *Move in Game* I. iii. 39 She'd shoplifted a bottle of nail varnish remover.

shopman. Add: **3.** A man employed in a railway workshop.

1926 *Times* 8 Mar. 9/4 He was glad to be able to state that the case of the railway shopmen had been advanced. **1960** *Listener* 18 Aug. 250/1 They were trainmen, shopmen, telegraph operators, and so on, all highly specialized in their respective callings.

shoppe (ʃɒp, ʃɒ·pi), an archaic form of Shop *sb.* now used affectedly (as in the names of tea-shops, etc.) to suggest quaint, old-world charm. Cf. *olde *a.*

1933 J. Betjeman *Ghastly Good Taste* 138 Arts and Crafts. Gentle folk weaving and spinning; Modern Church Furnishing; Old Tea Shoppes. **1948** [see *gift shop* s.v. *gift *sb.* 9 b]. **1957** E. Pound tr. *Rimbaud* 15 What lures the aintient truss-maker from his shoppe whose luxury Sucked in the passers-by. **1979** L. Kallen *Introducing C. B. Greenfield* i. 10 This is a business office, not a tea shoppe.

shopper. Add: **1. a.** (Earlier example.)

1860 Mrs. Gaskell *Let.* 27 Aug. (1966) 632 She is very dainty-fingered, a beautiful ready workwoman, a capital shopper &c.

b. An advertising sheet or newspaper.

1958 Palmer & Gilmore in W. C. Clark *Journalism Tomorrow* iii. 32 The little advertising sheet, often called a shopper... In a few cases, the shopper can be converted into a fine-looking, profitable weekly newspaper. **1976** *National Observer* (U.S.) 16 Oct., He would junk a lot of the expensive radio and TV commercials, spend the money instead in shoppers and small town weeklies, where you can buy the whole back page for $65.

c. A shopping bag or trolley.

1968 H. C. Rae *Few Small Bones* II. v. 113 He bought enough tinned food..to last him a full week, then lugging the laden shopper, set out along the main street. **1970** *Kay & Co.* (Worcester) *Catal. 1970–71* Autumn/Winter 934 (*caption*) Giant size trolley shoppers. *Ibid.*, Tartan shopper. Novelty-shaped large capacity zip-top Shopping bag in Black Watch Tartan. **1978** H. R. F. Keating *Long Walk to Wimbledon* ix. 137 The wheels of Marigold's shopper squeaked.

2. *slang.* An informer.

1924 E. Wallace *Room 13* xxxi. 300 Jeffrey's going to shop you sooner or later, because he's a natural born shopper. **1955** P. Wildeblood *Against Law* 105 'Shoppers'...people who go to the cop-shop and squeal on their friends.

shoppie (ʃɒ·pi). *Sc.* [f. Shop *sb.* + -ie.] A little shop.

1872 Queen Victoria *Jrnl.* 13 June in D. Duff *Victoria in Highlands* (1968) 260 At half-past ten drove out in the waggonette..and drove beyond Mrs. Patterson's 'shoppie' a little way. **1887** W. Carnie *Waifs of Rhyme* 17, I ken a winsome wifikie that keeps a snug bit shoppie.

shoppie, var. *shoppy *sb.*

shopping, *vbl. sb.* Add: **1. a.** Also with *around.* Freq. *transf.*

1940 *Sun* (Baltimore) 16 Feb. 24/2 By the simple expedient of 'shopping around' before making a deal, Walter N. Kirkman..has succeeded in saving the State $13,300 a year in office rent here. **1971** *Nature* 10 Dec. 368/1 An author does much better by bargaining hard and honestly with almost any single good publishing house than by 'shopping around'.

b. *transf.* The goods that have been purchased (in quot. 1934, 'something that has been purchased').

1934 *Punch* 2 May 489/1 Thank you so much, darling, for those marvellous Shoppings... The pyjamas are divine. **1948** P. Wentworth *Traveller Returns* i. 6 There were three people in front of her—a very stout woman with a basket full of shopping.., and a stooping elderly man. **1975** *Oxford Consumer* June 4 There are those, i.e. the elderly, the infirm, people with shopping,..for whom cycling is not always possible.

c. = *shop *sb.* 2 e. *colloq.*

1934 *Punch* 2 May 489/1 Would you think me the most terrific pest if I asked you to do yet another shopping for me? **1980** M. Forster *Bride of Lowther Hall* xviii. 272, I could perhaps go to Wigton and do a mammoth shopping.

2. *attrib.* and *Comb.* Simple attrib.: *shopping bag, basket, day, expedition, hours, spree, tour, trip*; in the names of places where shopping is performed, as *shopping arcade, area, centre, complex, mall* (chiefly *N. Amer.*), *parade, plaza* (chiefly *N. Amer.*), *precinct, street*; **shopping-bag lady** *U.S.*, a vagrant woman carrying her possessions in shopping bags; **shopping cart** orig. *N. Amer.*, a large wire basket on wheels provided for the use of supermarket customers; **shopping net,** a shopping bag made of string or plastic net; **shopping service,** a department or organization offering advice or assistance with shopping; **shopping tray,** an open wire receptacle for shopping designed to fit over the chassis of a pram; **shopping trolley,** (*a*) a shopping bag set on a wheeled frame; (*b*) = *shopping cart* above. See also *SHOPPING LIST.

1933 *Radio Times* 14 Apr. 72/2 Dear Covent Garden.. we hear, alas, that you are soon to..make way for shopping-arcades. **1977** J. BINGHAM *Marriage Bureau Murder* xvi. 184 There was a shopping arcade... He often shopped there. **1959** *Manch. Guardian* 11 Aug. 6/5 More shopping areas for pedestrians only. **1974** A. MORICE *Killing with Kindness* ii. 18 You have to pass through the shopping area to get to the main road. **1886** S. COOLIDGE *What Katy did Next* ix. 247 In her shopping-bag one or two of the Carnival bonbons still remained. **1973** J. STRANGER *Walk Lonely Road* xiii. 97 Millie came in with a brimming shopping-bag. [**1972** S. R. CURTIN *Nobody ever died of Old Age* vi. 85 Letty the Bag Lady..would pack all her valuables in two large shopping bags and carry them with her.] **1976** *N.Y. Times* 30 Sept. 43/5 The chief thing about Sally, the former 'shopping bag lady', is that she has personality. **1978** *Harper's Mag.* Mar. 104 On a nearby bench, apparently keeping an intermittent vigil on the vigil, were two shopping-bag ladies. **1979** *N.Y. Times* 10 Jan. B 7 An elderly 'shopping bag lady', ..one of the legion of homeless, independent, often eccentric women who live on the city's streets. **1923** E. BOWEN *Encounters* 166 She had forgotten her shopping basket and her purse. **1977** *Times* 29 June 5/7 She arrived at the court by bus carrying a shopping basket containing her dressing gown. **1956** *Sun* (Baltimore) (B ed.) 19 Jan. 14/1 A feature of the supermarket is the now familiar shopping cart, a contraption of recent invention. **1958** M. DICKENS *Man Overboard* v. 83 A woman with a shopping cart bumped into him. **1976** G. A. BROWNE *Slide* (1977) ix. 74 The shopping cart somehow getting fuller than intended. **1898** Shopping centre [see *CENTRE *sb.* 6 a]. **1933** L. E. NEAL *Retailing & Public* v. 25 There is..great competition between multiple branch organisations..to acquire the best positions in the popular shopping centres. **1944** H. G. WELLS *'42 to '44* 136 In Welwyn Garden City to-day there is a single 'shopping centre' associated with one bazaar. **1971** P. GRESSWELL *Environment* 183 Very few shopping centres are imaginatively designed. **1977** B. GARFIELD *Recoil* v. 62 Caruso..drove him..to a shopping center in Santa Monica. **1970** *Times* 27 Feb. 19/7 Fram Gerrard, of Manchester, has won the building contract for the £1·5m. shopping complex in Leicester. **1861** C. M. YONGE *Young Step-Mother* xxix. 439 This was a grand shopping day, an endless business. **1973** D. MILLER *Chinese Jade Affair* xxiii. 220 'Only thirty Shopping Days to Christmas!' advised the big department stores. **1847** A. BRONTË *Agnes Grey* xxv. 358, I took a little more pains with my attire than if I had merely been going on some shopping expedition alone. **1885** [in Dict.]. **1979** L. MEYNELL *Hooky & Villainous Chauffeur* xi. 139 What with cooking..and the necessary shopping expeditions she didn't have much time over. **1964** A. ADBURGHAM *Shops & Shopping* i. 7 There were no stated shopping hours. **1967** *Canad. Ann. Rev. 1966* 137 Its proposals for..restriction of billboards, abolition of overhanging signs and overhead wires, closed pedestrian shopping malls, [etc.]. **1972** *N.Z. News* 26 Jan. 7 (*caption*) This scene is taken from the Cuba Street shopping mall, Wellington. **1979** *Jrnl. R. Soc. Arts* July 505/1 Shopping malls are the nearest thing to the market place which you could find in North America. **1955** T. STERLING *Evil of Day* i. 1 Within the cabin, women with shopping nets and men with folded newspapers awaited their turns. **1969** P. HIGHSMITH *Tremor of Forgery* xxi. 195 Adams had a shopping net in his hand. He was putting things away in the kitchen. **1969** *Morning Star* 1 Dec. 4/1 There will be various amenities when Stage 1 and Stage 2 are completed, [including] a shopping parade. **1957** *Ottawa Jrnl.* 6 Aug. 1/1 The break-ins were compared with the noisy June 3 'tow-truck' robbery at another grocery store in the shopping plaza. **1981** P. THEROUX *Mosquito Coast* vi. 44 We came to a shopping plaza, where we parked. **1958** Shopping precinct [see *PRECINCT *sb.* 4]. **1980** A. AUSWAKS *Trick of Diamonds* iii. 75 At the end of the High Street stood a new shipping precinct. **1925** *Eaton's News Weekly* 26 Sept. 18 When Ordering by Mail..Address Letter to *Shopping Service.* **1972** S. ELLIN *Mirror, Mirror on Wall* 79 The lady happens to work for a shopping service... If you want to do some shopping for your wife ..these people take you to the right places and pick the right stuff. **1962** M. SUMMERTON *Nightingale at Noon* (1963) iv. 55 A shopping spree to purge a memory. **1976** 'S. WOODS' *My Life is Done* 69 Ana had been on a shopping spree. **1914** A. BENNETT *Price of Love* xiv. 283 Her first apparition in the shopping streets of the town.. as Mrs. Louis Fores, married woman. **1975** P. MOYES *Black Widower* ii. 19 The great shopping street that bisects the area. **1878** Shopping tour [in Dict.]. **1970** *Kay & Co.* (Worcester) *Catal. 1970–71* Autumn/Winter 227 Leeway shopping tray provides secure storage space and is readily adaptable to most prams. **1977** *Cornish Times* 19 Aug. 7/3 (Advt.), Silver Cross pram, detachable body..with shopping tray. **1969** G. LYALL *Venus with Pistol* xviii. 116 Henri has been *killed*... Doesn't that mean more than this—shopping trip? **1976** *Economist* 17 Apr. 79/3 A motorised pram-cum-shopping-trolley would arguably be the most egalitarian form of transport. **1978** *Green Shield Stamp Catal.* Feb. 113 *Shopping trolley.* Adjustable telescopic handle. Detachable shopping bag. **1979** *Criminal Appeal Reports (Sentencing)* (1980) I. 255 On the morning of January 25, 1979 at Brent Cross Shopping Centre she went into a Waitrose Supermarket and loaded up a shopping trolley with groceries.

shopping list. [f. SHOPPING *vbl. sb.* + LIST *sb.*[6]] **1.** A list of purchases to be made or shops to be visited.

1913 *Vanity Fair* Sept. 7/2 You can easily clip half a dozen and attach them to your own shopping list. **1921** *Daily Colonist* (Victoria, B.C.) 31 Mar. 6/5 We have a beautiful selection of Oriental Rugs and Jewels. Put our name on your shopping list. **1947** W. STEVENS *Let.* 5 Sept. (1967) 567 But now that the weather is growing cooler, I begin to look at my shopping list. **1977** 'E. CRISPIN' *Glimpses of Moon* xii. 256 He went to investigate, finding a message..scribbled on a sheet torn from a Shopping List pad.

2. *transf.* and *fig.* A list of items to be considered, acted upon, etc.; *spec.* a list of weaponry sought for purchase.

1959 *Manch. Guardian* 8 July 3/3 He..did not want to put down a shopping-list of industries to be nationalised. **1963** *Times* 21 Feb. 11/3 Ground-to-air missiles were on the 'shopping list' of defence equipment taken to Moscow by the Secretary-General of the External Affairs Ministry. **1969** *Nature* 2 Aug. 436/2 The council should say which fields of medical and biological research come at the top of its shopping-list—biological organization, arterial disease, population control and drug dependence. **1970** *Cape Times* 28 Oct. 26/5 His shopping list will include a full-back..and a creative mid-field player. **1975** *N.Y. Times* 8 Sept. 1/3 The Israeli sources said negotiations had resumed on a shopping list that includes..F-15 fighter planes to match the MIG-23's deployed by Egypt and Syria. **1977** *Times* 10 June 17/1 The [French] left have indeed a fearsome shopping list for nationalization.

shoppy, *a.* **3.** (Later example used disparagingly.)

1914 W. OWEN *Let.* 10 May (1967) 249 Miss H— who, you confess, is 'shoppy'. Now that is distressing. The fact of being employed in a shop does not matter; but shoppiness does matter.

shoppy (ʃǫ·pi), *sb. slang.* Also **shoppie.** [f. SHOP *sb.* + -Y[6].] A shop assistant.

1909 P. WEBLING *Story of Virginia Perfect* i. 6 Her manner towards him..had none of the affectation of the ordinary 'young lady in business', or the vulgar intimacy of a poorer class of 'shoppie'. **1916** 'TAFFRAIL' *Pincher Martin* vii. 114 She's in Skeets the draper's... Never could stand them shoppies; they give themselves such airs. **1934** H. A. VACHELL *Disappearance of Martha Penny* i. 20 Her sparkling eyes, her fine figure, were gifts rarely bestowed upon urban 'shoppies'.

shop-window. Add: **2.** (Later examples.)

1929 C. CONNOLLY *Let.* Nov. in *Romantic Friendship* (1975) 328 [In America] a wife is a man's shop window. **1933** P. GODFREY *Back-Stage* iii. 34 A 'shop-window' is a part which carries a low salary, but which, nevertheless, is likely to enhance his acting reputation. Certain small theatres are also 'shop-windows', like the Everyman Theatre in its early days. **1954** [see *END *sb.* 7c]. **1961** *Radio Times* 6 Apr. 4/2 Once a year the BBC..stages a couple of all-star concerts as a shop-window for the kind of 'pop' programmes that it broadcasts..during the rest of the year. **1977** *Listener* 17 Mar. 347/3 London was to be a city of individuals..rather than a shop-window of state, monarchy and empire.

Hence **shop-wi·ndowful,** as much or as many as a shop-window will hold.

1898 G. B. SHAW *Mrs. Warren's Prof.* IV. 231, I shouldn't enjoy..being bored at the opera to shew off a shop windowful of diamonds.

shor (ʃǭɹ). [Turki *shōr.*] In Turkistan, an elongated saline depression in desert sand.

1888 *Encycl. Brit.* XXIII. 512/1 A feature distinctive of the Turcoman desert is seen in the very numerous *shors*, or elongated depressions, the lower portions of which are occupied mostly with sand impregnated with brackish water. **1898** *Geogr. Jrnl.* XII. 308 The *shors*.. are seen on the southern border of the Kara-kum sands. **1951** N. T. MIROV *Geogr. of Russia* xv. 155 Lower depressions, so-called sor or shor, equally extensive, are occupied with alkaline soil of the solonchak type.

shoran (ʃōᵊ·-, ʃǫ·ræn). orig. *U.S.* Also **Shoran.** [f. the initial letters of *sho*rt-*ra*nge *n*avigation.] A secondary radar system, used for precision navigation and for distance measurement, in which an aircraft or ship determines its distance from two widely-spaced ground stations which it interrogates alternately with radio pulses. Freq. *attrib.* Cf. *LORAN.

1946 *N.Y. Times* 28 Apr. 1/3 Those who have..tested shoran call it 'perhaps the greatest single invention of its type for long-range mapping to come from the family of radar in the war'. **1946** *Trans. Amer. Geophys. Union* XXVII. 459 Basically, the shoran equipment consists of three main units, the airborne transmitter-receiver-indicator and the two ground station transponders. **1949** *Sun* (Baltimore) 2 Mar. 13/2 What prompted the use of the Superforts was the belief that the development of Shoran (Short Range Navigation) equipment had reached the point where it could be put to work for the astronomer. **1966** *McGraw-Hill Encycl. Sci. & Technol.* IX. 18/2 The single-path round-trip system is the basis of distance determination in all radars. It is the system employed by Benito, Condar, Oboe, shoran, and the distance-measuring portion of Tacan equipment. **1970** *Canad. Cartographer* VII. 23/1, 12 shoran ground stations. **1977** *Sci. Amer.* Oct. 92/3 At each one a transponder was set up for a shoran radio-positioning system.

shore, *sb.*[1] Add: **1. b.** Similarly in *Geomorphol.*

1919 D. W. JOHNSON *Shore Processes & Shoreline Devel.* iv. 160 The most important of the four zones extends from low water mark to the base of the cliff,.. which usually marks the landward limit of effective wave action. This is the zone over which the water line, the line of contact between land and sea, migrates; and it will here be called the shore. **1968** R. W. FAIRBRIDGE *Encycl. Geomorphol.* 62/1 The shore is technically the coastal zone extending from the low tide limit to the maximum swash line. **1978** A. L. BLOOM *Geomorphology* xix. 437 The shore zone, or simply shore, is the zone affected by wave action.

5. a. *shore clothes, duty, -ice* (earlier and later examples), *suit; shore-based* adj.; **shore break** *Surfing* (see quot. 1962); **shore dinner** *U.S.*, a dinner consisting mainly of sea-food; **shore face** (see quots.); **shore fishery** *N. Amer.* (see quot. 1948); **shore leave,** leave of absence granted to a sailor to go on shore; **shore liberty** = prec.; **shore-loafer** *Naut. slang*, a civilian; **shore party,** (*a*) *N.Z.*, a body of whalers using a land-based station (*obs.*); (*b*) a body of persons going ashore from a ship; *spec.* a body of soldiers sent ashore; **shore patrol** *U.S.*, a naval police organization responsible for the conduct of sailors on land; hence **shore patrolman; shore platform,** a horizontal or gently sloping platform cut at about sea level in a cliff by wave action; **shore seine,** a seine used near the shore; **shore-shooting** (earlier example); **shore station,** a base on land used for shore-whaling; **shore-whaling** (earlier examples); also *spec.* = *bay whaling* s.v. *BAY *sb.*[2] 5; hence **shore whaler,** a person engaged in shore-whaling; **shore zone,** the intertidal zone, or the zone affected by wave action; = SHORE *sb.*[1] 1 b in Dict. and Suppl.

1927 *Daily Tel.* 22 Mar. 10/7 The limitation of air armaments shall be effected by limiting the number of shore-based aircraft of service type maintained in commission. **1950** A. LEE *Soviet Air Force* 34 Its naval force was shore-based except for a few reconnaissance machines on cruisers. **1980** *Jrnl. R. Soc. Arts* July 521/2 The professional mariner currently gives cautious approval to shore-based information services. **1962** T. MASTERS *Surfing made Easy* 65 *Shore break*, waves which break close to the beach. **1965** J. POLLARD *Surfrider* ii. 20 The next one you might take right to the 'shore break', the waves breaking on the very edge of the beach. **1972** Y. MALEY in G. W. Turner *Good Austral. Eng.* iv. 77 Drouyn gets it on,..hangs five, re-enters the shore break, then steps off onto the sand. **1862** E. HODDER *Mem. N.Z. Life* 24 Shore clothes were unpacked, the ship was made tidy. **1922** E. O'NEILL *Anna Christie* I. 100 He is dressed in a wrinkled, ill-fitting dark suit of shore clothes. **1895** *Outing* XXVI. 408/2 Happy-Go-Lucky Beach is proud of their achievements..in the ordering of and presiding at a good shore-dinner. **1947** E. H. PAUL *Linden on Saugus Branch* 267 It was arranged for the party to eat at the Massasoit a shore dinner cooked by Jeff. **1881** *Library Universal Knowl.* XI. 408 Paymasters..on shore-duty are employed in the naval purchasing agencies. **1901** *Chambers's Jrnl.* Aug. 551/2 Four keepers are employed in connection with the lighthouse, three being in constant attendance while the fourth is on shore-duty. **1912** J. BARRELL in *Bull. Geol. Soc. Amer.* XXIII. 385 The shore face is the relatively narrow slope developed by the breaking waves, a slope which separates the subaerial plain above from the subaqueous below. **1944** A. HOLMES *Princ. Physical Geol.* xiv. 291 In appropriate circumstances some of the sediment in transit across the wave-cut platform accumulates in the deeper water beyond, to form a shoreface terrace which grows forward like a broad embankment with its upper surface in smooth continuity with the platform. **1972** *Gloss. Geol.* (Amer. Geol. Inst.) 654/2 *Shoreface*,..the narrow, rather steeply sloping zone seaward or lakeward from the low-water shoreline, permanently covered by water, and over which beach sands and gravels actively oscillate with changing wave conditions. **1767** T. HUTCHINSON *Hist. Province Mass.-Bay* II. iv. 445 In what they call a sedentaire and we a shore fishery we shall always outdo them. **1948** R. DE KERCHOVE *Internat. Maritime Dict.* 671/1 *Shore fisheries.* Under this head are included all those fisheries prosecuted from small boats or from the shore without the aid or use of vessels. **1971** E. R. SEARY *Place Names Avalon Peninsula* iv. 65 [The Killigrews] either settled permanently or had a summer plantation at Killigrews for the shore fishery. **1752** J. ROBSON *Acct. Six Years Residence in Hudson's Bay* 58 At York-fort and Churchill-river I have observed that the ice did not break off close at the shore, but gradually; the first field leaving the shore-ice two or three miles broad, the second less, and so on till it was cleared away. **1953** *Beaver* June 22 They walked across the shore ice, perhaps as far as two miles. **1977** *New Yorker* 10 June 55/1 The river's edges are lined with ice that is stationary —'shelf ice', 'shore ice', the first to freeze at the start of winter and the last to go in spring. **1888** E. L. DORSEY *Midshipman Bob* 205 They set about making the most of their shore-leave. **1941** C. S. FORRESTER *Captain from Connecticut* xv. 216 Shore leave..meant rum and women. **1974** M. HASTINGS *Dragon Island* iv. 37 Darley was leaning on the rail. 'Shore leave?' he asked. **1906** J. LONDON *Let.* 17 Nov. (1966) 220 You can depend upon me giving good opportunities for shore-liberty. **1971** S. E. MORISON *European Discovery Amer.: Northern Voy.* ix. 287 *La Dauphine* almost always anchored in an uncomfortable roadstead, and they had shore liberty but once in the entire voyage. **1916** 'TAFFRAIL' *Carry On!* 25 If an ordinary 'shore-loafer', as a bluejacket sometimes calls a civilian, were suddenly transported to one of His Majesty's battleships he would probably spend his first few days on board in a state of hopeless bewilderment. **1841** H. W. Petre *Acct. Settlements N.Z. Co.* iv. 77 System of 'shore-parties'..is much more economical than the pursuit of the whale by ships equipped for the purpose. **1901** G. B. Shaw *Caesar & Cleopatra* III. 160 My men at the barricades are between the sea party and the shore party. **1974** M. Hastings *Dragon Island* v. 42 Tallander's concern regarding any shore parties from our ship. **1917** *Blue Jacket's Man.* (ed. 5) 644 Perhaps the establishment of the Shore Patrol has done more than any other one institution to make petty officers realize their duty as a class. **1973** H. Gruppe *Truxton Cipher* xvii. 176 The phone rang urgently in Shore Patrol headquarters at the fleet landing. **1944** *Bull. Bur. Naval Personnel Information* (U.S.) Sept. 12/1 The shore patrolman could have barged in to break up the argument. **1973** H. Gruppe *Truxton Cipher* xx. 208 Dieter leaped..straight into the arms of two waiting Shore Patrolmen. **1895** J. D. Dana *Man. Geol.* (ed. 4) 220 Besides battering and degrading cliffs, wave-action makes shore-platforms, by shearing away the rocks of coasts down to a horizontal surface near low-tide level. **1978** A. L. Bloom *Geomorphology* xix. 448 Shore platforms are developed by water-level weathering at various heights, relative to tide level, depending on structural factors..and also on wave energy, tidal range, and climate. **1884** G. B. Goode et al. *Fisheries & Fishery Industries of U.S.* I. 289 It seems..absurd that the Massachusetts people should have supposed that the use of shore-seines was exterminating the Mackerel on the coast of Massachusetts. **1973** W. Elmer *Terminol. Fishing* ii. 69 The shore seine is worked with a boat and a shore party. **1829** G. Griffin *Collegians* III. xxxi. 2 He had gone down to the Dairy farm, for the purpose of shore-shooting. **1966** *Austral. Encycl.* IX. 276/2 In 1947 a small chaser fed a shore station at Albany. **1966** *Encycl. N.Z.* III. 639/1 Hunting, therefore, occurred from vessels ranging considerable distances off shore, from others at bay anchorages, and also from a large number of open boats based on shore stations. **1885** W. D. Howells *Rise S. Lapham* xxiii. 415 A young fellow in the shabby shore-suit of a sailor. **1924** J. Masefield *Sard Harker* I. 30 Steward, will you have the goodness to set out my shore-suit presently? **1872** *Trans. & Proc. N.Z. Inst.* V. 156 The females visit the bays and inlets round the coast to calve..where they are captured by the shore whalers. **1966** *Encycl. N.Z.* III. 640/1 Hundreds of right whales killed by pelagic whalers off shore and in the bays where ships' boats were often in direct competition with those of the shore whalers. **1841** S. Revans *Lett. to H. S. Chapman* (typescript) II. 163 If no shore whaling were allowed the cow would rear the calf and get fat. **1851** H. Melville *Moby Dick* II. xxxix. 273 In the Shore Whaling.., when a Right Whale gives token of sinking, they fasten buoys to him. **1922** E. C. Starks *Hist. Calif. Shore Whaling* 6 Whaling may be classified under three heads:.. Third.—For want of a better term we may call the third form modern shore whaling. The whales are not taken from small boats, but from a seaworthy steam whaler... The whaler stays out until it has secured one or more whales, which it tows to a whaling station on shore. **1959** A. H. McLintock *Descr. Atlas N.Z.* p. xvii, Today there is a shore whaling station at the seaward entrance to Tory Channel. **1921** A. W. Grabau *Textbk. Geol.* I. xvii. 518 This [littoral] district naturally falls into two zones, (*a*) that of the shore between high and low tide (shore zone) and (*b*) that permanently submerged..(neritic zone). **1978** A. L. Bloom *Geomorphology* xix. 444 Where the postglacial rise of sea level has created a shoreline on a former hill slope, shore-zone processes cut a cliff and bench.

b. shore-bug, a bug belonging to the family Saldidæ; shore fly, a small black fly of the family Ephydridæ, found in damp or marshy places.

1895 J. H. Comstock *Man. Study Insects* 134 Some of the Shore-bugs dig burrows, and live for a part of the time beneath the ground. **1968** *Oxf. Bk. Insects* 28/2 The most common and widespread British shore bug..lives around the margins of ponds, ditches, and semi-stagnant streams and lakes. **1942** E. O. Essig *College Entomology* xxxv. 743 (Shore Flies, Ephydrid Flies.) Ephydridæ. **1954** Borror & DeLong *Introd. Study Insects* xxvii. 633 The shore flies are small to very small; most of them are dark coloured. **1979** *Nature* 29 Nov. 501/2 Eighty per cent of their diet comprises three insect species, the shore fly, *Ephydra riparia*, the waterboatman, *Trichocorixa reticulata*, and the mosquito, *Aedes dorsalis*.

Shore (ʃōᵊɹ), *sb.*[5] *Metallurgy.* The name of Albert F. *Shore* (fl. 1907), U.S. manufacturer, used *attrib.* with reference to the *Scleroscope he invented and to a scale of relative hardness associated with the use of this instrument, as *Shore hardness, Scleroscope, test,* etc.

1908 *Iron Age* LXXXII. 555 (*heading*) The Shore Scleroscope. **1908** *Jrnl. Iron & Steel Inst.* LXXVIII. 639 Maurer also gives an account of his investigations on the Shore hardness test. **1924** Jeffries & Archer *Sci. of Metals* i. 21 The Shore numbers are more representative of the yield point than of the tensile strength. **1937** R. T. Rolfe *Steels for User* vi. 110 Thus a Brinell hardness of 131 should be equivalent to a Shore figure of..22, which is the same as the Shore hardness determined. **1967** E. Chambers *Photolitho-Offset* xv. 226 The Shore hardness of the rubber stock should be between 8 to 16. **1979** J. Neely *Pract. Metall. & Materials of Industry* vi. 71/2 Elastic hardness is measured by an instrument called a Shore Scleroscope.

shore (ʃōᵊɹ), repr. *colloq.* or (in *U.S.*) *dial.* pronunc. of Sure *a.* and *adv.*

1890 *Dialect Notes* I. 71 *Shore*, sure. **1898** G. B. Shaw *Candida* I. 97 Glad to meet you, I'm shore. **1932** V. Randolph *Ozark Mountain Folks* ix. 163 Hit shore was a bad night at our place. Yas, sir, hit *shore* was! **1938** M. K. Rawlings *Yearling* vii. 62 Well, stay, then, if these folks is shore you're welcome. **1973** R. Hoban *Lion of Boaz-Jachin & Jachin-Boaz* xviii. 100 It's a proper thing for a man to do—not like running a restaurant or some shore thing like that. **1979–80** *Verbatim* Winter 14/1 My cousin Sharon, a University of Missouri homecoming queen, shore did look pretty, and her mother shore could fry chicken.

shore, *v.*[1] **1.** Delete (now *rarely*) and add later *fig.* examples with *up.*

1892 'Mark Twain' *Amer. Claimant* xxii. 219 This prop shored him up and kept him from floundering back into democracy and re-renouncing aristocracy. **1959** *Listener* 10 Dec. 1021/1 These are all signs that local authorities are likely to shore up their position for the time being. **1978** *N.Y. Times* 30 Mar. D9/4 The Carter Administration was not contemplating any emergency measures to shore up the dollar.

shore-going, *vbl. sb.* (Earlier *attrib.* examples.)

1846 *Knickerbocker* XXVIII. 64 He rigged himself in his 'shore-going togs' after supper. **1887** B. Harte *Crusade of 'Excelsior'* 63 Captain Bunker..wore a shore-going suit of black broadcloth.

shoreside. Add: *attrib.* passing into *adj.* (later examples).

1937 *Sun* (Baltimore) 4 Sept. 3/1 Harry Bridges, leader of the longshoremen, proclaimed his union's aim of a 'march inland'—to organize all shoreside transportation and commodity handling under the stevedores. **1966** *Economist* 25 June 1439/3 Norway makes sure of a flow of young men into the merchant service. Bachelors pay half the income tax of workers ashore; married men pay a little more, though still less than the shoreside worker. **1979** D. Lowden *Boudapesti 3* xxx. 160 Buildings going up...Shoreside villages, without a fishing boat in sight.

Hence as *adv.*, to the shore, to land (*rare*).

1948 Partridge *Dict. Forces' Slang* 168 Are you coming shore-side this afternoon? **1949** *Sun* (Baltimore) 6 July 10/2 A desolate peninsula in Venezuela, expected to become the Western Hemisphere's largest oil port, needed facilities for seamen going 'shoreside'.

shoreward, *adv.* Add: **3.** *shoreward of*: towards the shore in respect of; on the shoreward side of.

1941 *Sun* (Baltimore) 12 July 7/3 All interested parties are urged to be present, particularly those engaged in fishing or operating boats shoreward of or adjacent to existing authorized fishing areas. **1974** R. Adams *Shardik* xvi. 110 They came ashore..close to..the cluster of storage huts and servants' quarters lying shoreward of the Sindrad.

shorn, *ppl. a.* Add: **4.** *shorn lamb*: also applied to the dressed fur of the sheep used in garment-making.

1945 N. Mitford *Pursuit of Love* xxi. 183 Linda.. comes back covered with rich furs, while you and I..get ..three-quarter-length shorn lamb. **1968** J. Ironside *Fashion Alphabet* 153 *American broadtail.* This was the trade-name for the fur of the very young Argentine lamb... The name is now prohibited in the U.S.A. and the fur is sold under its true name of 'shorn lamb'. **1978** *Lancashire Life* Oct. 101/1 (*caption*) The 'Rambler' jacket in shorn lamb with leather piping all round and on the pockets, plus leather belt, is about £130.

short, *a.*, *sb.* and *adv.* Add: **A.** *adj.* **I. 1. b.** *to get by the short hairs*: see *hair *sb.* 8 p. Also, in same sense, *to get* or *have* (a person) *by the short and curlies. slang* (orig. *Mil.*).

1948 Partridge *Dict. Forces' Slang* 168 *Short and curlies*, the short hairs, in the phrase 'He got me by the short and curlies'—he caught me out properly. **1956** P. Scott *Male Child* III. i. 191 'Is there any point in going on, if you can't fool yourself?'..'Of course not. That's where we're got by the short and curlies. We cling on.' **1969** J. Gardner *Founder Member* iv. 72 'Stalemate?'..'Looks like it... Got us hard by the short and curlies. I wouldn't try arguing.' **1971** D. Francis *Bonecrack* xii. 153 Suppose..that I abducted Alessandro. ..I would then have Enso by the short and curlies. **1976** P. Hill *Hunters* xi. 164 There is no need for kid gloves now, we've got him by the short and curlies.

II. 5. a. *in short order*: see *order *sb.* 27 d.

8. a. Colloq. phr. *the short answer to* (something) *is* (and variants), used to introduce a straightforward, immediate, or peremptory response or solution. Also *transf.* and *fig.*

1955 *New Statesman* 24 Dec. 851/1, I suppose the short answer is money. **1962** *Times* 24 Nov. 4/6 The short answer is that they seem to indicate a far less cavalier attitude to viewers' wishes on the part of the television companies than has previously been manifest. **1966** W. Cooper *Memoirs of New Man* I. iv. 47 'The short answer to that, my dear, is No.' 'But what about the *long* answer?' **1968** *Guardian* 10 June 7/6 There's no short answer. We have tried..to persuade our dealers that giving service increases sales. **1978** A. Price *'44 Vintage* vi. 69 We don't get captured, Jack—that's the short answer. **1980** *N.Y. Times Book Rev.* 23 Mar. 11/3 The short answer is: yes, it is ill will.

b. *short story* (earlier and later examples). Hence *short-storyist.* Also *short short story*, a very short story; also *ellipt.* as *short-short.*

1877 *Independent* 17 May 9/2 His various books have been eminently readable, in the highest sense of the adjective, and some of his short stories have been almost without a flaw in their glittering beauty. *a* **1882** Trollope *Autobiogr.* (1883) I. viii. 182, I had..written from time to time certain short stories, which had been published in different periodicals. **1902** H. Belloc *Path to Rome* 140 Terror..is half the plot of their insane 'short stories'. **1923** J. M. Murry *Pencillings* 82 Mr H. G. Wells's definition of the short story as a fiction that can be read in a quarter of an hour. **1929** *Science Wonder Stories* Nov. 485/1 A few years ago, a short story was anywhere from ten thousand to twenty thousand words. Of late the short, *short* story has gained ascendency in a number of magazines. A short, *short* story is one that runs to not more than fifteen hundred words. **1936** E. Bowen *Faber Bk. Mod. Short Stories* 17 H. E. Bates has, as a shortstoryist, already a substantial body of work to his name. **1940** G. V. Martin *For our Vines have Tender Grapes* iv. 32 Unemployed unemployables..typing endlessly the Great American Saga..cannot sell a short-short to the *Chicago Daily News.* **1957** R. Hoggart *Uses of Literacy* vi. 166 The magazines go beyond the stories to the 'short short stories' or the 'one-minute stories'. **1962** E. Lacy *Freeloaders* vi. 106 An airmail letter from my agent telling me he'd sold a short-short of mine. **1972** J. Symons *Bloody Murder* xiii. 164 The 'short short story' of 2,000 words or less. **1977** V. S. Pritchett *Gentle Barbarian* vi. 90 From a short-story writer's point of view, the timing..is perfect... Turgenev is a master of his craft.

c. *short and sweet* (further examples).

1866 *Harper's Mag.* Oct. 674/2 The letter-book was consulted, and there stood, short and sweet, and right to the point: 'Dear Sir' [etc.]. **1882** H. Munby *Let.* 9 June in D. Hudson *Munby* (1972) 408, I don't like burning your letters & I don't like to *keep* them either—short & sweet is what I like from you. **1970** W. Smith *Gold Mine* xxxv. 92 Reasons first. I'll make it short and sweet, right?

13. (Further examples of *short vowel.*)

1952 [see *checked *ppl. a.*[1] 1 b]. **1962** [see *duration 1 c].

14. a. *short drink*: a small measure of liquor; a drink which is relatively strong in alcohol and hence drunk in small measures; a dram of spirits or the like.

1883 *Daily Tel.* 2 July 5/3 All these are short drinks—that is to say, drams. **1937** A. J. Cronin *Citadel* II. vii. 155 Challis..was successfully and cheerfully despatching his third short drink. **1957** M. Spark *Comforters* iv. 85 Caroline and Laurence had been on short drinks, and both were rather lit up. **1973** J. Aiken in V. Whitaker *Winter's Crimes* 5 22 A large Whisky Mac—his favourite short drink.

III. 15. a. Also *short change* (Change *sb.* 7 b); *short commons*: also *fig.* Phr. *in short supply*: inadequate to demand.

1852 Disraeli in *Hansard Commons* 9 Feb. 303, I cannot, however, help congratulating Parliamentary reformers on the content with which they have accepted the repast provided for them; the voracity of their appetites seems to me satisfied with very short commons. **1874** Short change [see Fluff *sb.*[1] 3 a]. **1908** U. B. Sinclair *Metropolis* 351 Three times in a single day in another of these great caravansaries, Montague was offered short change. **1928** Foy & Harlow *Clowning through Life* 81 Our Peanut and juice vendors were all short change artists. **1942** *Times Rev. 1941* 3 Jan. p. v/4 There has been an exemplary pooling of machine tools and of other requisites in short supply. **1943** *Sun* (Baltimore) 7 Jan. 24/2 The State's lawmakers are going to be on 'short commons' and the employes are going to be comparatively flush. **1951** D. Howarth *Shetland Bus* xi. 150 Larsen..now found himself in urgent need of bootlaces, so he tried to take the opportunity to buy some; but they were 'in short supply', and he had to make do with string. **1970** *Observer* 13 Sept. 38/5 It's shortcommons for tourists unless they're white.

b. *short ton*: see Ton[1] 4.

18. f. (Earlier and later examples.) Also followed by a sb. or an expression of quantity. *a shingle short*: see Shingle *sb.*[1] 1 b.

1873 Trollope *Phineas Redux* in *Graphic* 22 Nov. 486/2 He did take the key with him... We were a key short at the time he was away. **1923** Kipling *Irish Guards in Great War* I. 1 They were short one officer. **1944** M. Paneth *Branch Street* 97 Our last warden left us... Now we were two people short. **1976** J. Snow *Cricket Rebel* 43 We were more than 150 short when Derek joined me at the wicket. **1977** *Cork Examiner* 6 June 10/1 Cork.. were short three of their regulars.

g. *U.S. Stock Exch.* Having sold as yet unacquired stock which the seller hopes can be bought at a lower price before the time fixed for delivery. Also *short of* (such stock). Cf. Short *adv.* 11.

1849 *Merchants' Mag.* (U.S.) XXI. 118 If he does not own the stock he is 'short', or what is the same thing, a 'bear'. **1865** *Harper's Mag.* Apr. 616/2 If he has sold 500 Hudson for future delivery, expecting it to fall, he is pronounced 'short of Hudson'. **1884** A. Daly *Big Bonanza* 20 The market opened lively with a demand for speculative shares by those who have been 'short' of the leading stocks.

h. *short on*: having an insufficient quantity of, deficient in respect of.

1922 P. A. Rollins *Cowboy* iii. 54 The actual 'bad man' was 'short on conversation'. **1942** E. Waugh *Put out More Flags* ii. 113 It's just this kind of influence these children need... They're rather short on culture at the moment. **1959** *Omaha World-Herald* 20 Dec. D 18/3 Many a gypsy, short on funds and long on nerve, is a master at avoiding inspections. **1977** *Lancet* 13 Aug. 357/1 Dr Bartsch's comment, though interesting, is short on facts.

i. *U.S.* Of a race-horse, not in top form. Also in *attrib.* use.

1942 *Sun* (Baltimore) 1 May 17/1 Ben would prefer to pass the Derby altogether and point his guns at the Preakners' $50,000 the following week, rather than take a chance on setting a 'short' horse back farther in the Derby. **1960** *Washington Post* 23 May A 22 He said..that Venetian Way was 'short', meaning the horse wasn't quite ready for the 1¼ mile race. **1977** *Time* 20 June 51/2 Horsemen were quick to point out that he was slightly 'short'—not in peak form—for the Kentucky Derby.

V. 23. *short-date, -form, -grain* (see also sense 26 below), *-haul* (*HAUL *sb.* 1 c), *-leaf* (earlier and later examples), *-life, -line, -persistence, -stroke* (later examples), *-take-off, -vowel.*

1909 *Q. Rev.* Oct. 358 British railways offer facilities for cheap, short-date bookings. **1947** *Sun* (Baltimore) 15 May 2/8 The bill carries a new set of tables for the so-called short-form taxpayers—those with adjusted gross incomes of $5,000 or less. **1961** R. B. Long *Sentence & its Parts* x. 234 The Appalachians, the Rockies..are short-form phrasal proper names. **1972** *Accountant* 19 Oct. 487/2 The position [should] be clarified by an appropriate reference in the short-form report. **1947** L. P. De Gouy *Gold Cookery Bk.* xi. 766 There are many varieties of rice produced in the United States. They are ..of three general types, long grain, medium grain, and short grain. **1970** Simon & Howe *Dict. Gastronomy* 326/2 Rice generally can be divided into long, medium and short grain types. **1895** *Funk's Stand. Dict.* II. 1658/1 The interstate commerce law forbids a greater charge in the aggregate for a shorter than for a longer distance over the same line..and is commonly called the long and short haul clause. **1939** *Jrnl. R. Aeronaut. Soc.* XLIII. 900 This figure represents about 3 lbs. per rated h.p. of the engines, which is appreciably better than the figure for most modern short-haul air liners. **1960** *Times* 14 Nov. 13/6 The most popular aircraft in use for short-haul work is the Bristol Freighter. **1976** P. R. White *Planning for Public Transport* ix. 190 Increased fuel costs affect short-haul operations more radically than long-haul. **1979** *Arizona Daily Star* 5 Aug. I. 3/1 It's mainly on short-haul trains. **1796** B. Hawkins *Let.* 4 Dec. in *Coll. Georgia Hist. Soc.* (1916) IX. 24, I..came..to oak and short leaf pine. **1969** T. H. Everett *Living Trees of World* iv. 51/1 The shortleaf pine..is found from New York to Florida and Texas and has dark bluish-green foliage. **1966** M. Woodhouse *Tree Frog* xix. 144 A self-contained short-life powerplant. **1973** *Guardian* 16 Feb. 6/1 Foods classified by the Ministry as 'short-life'—that is with a storage capacity after packing of less than three months—would eventually all be stamped with a 'sell by' date. **1977** *Spare Rib* July 40/3 (Advt.), Willing to expand the project into emergency and shortlife housing and building coops. **1941** L. MacNeice *Poetry of W. B. Yeats* vi. 114 Yeats.. is outstanding among modern poets for his mastery of the short-line poem with three or four stresses to a line. **1974** *Aiken* (S. Carolina) *Standard* 24 Apr. 1-B/1 (*caption*) Train enthusiast Larry Raid, Denmark, Iowa, stands on the tracks of a shortline railroad that he has rebuilt from Keithburg, Ill., to Oakville, Iowa. **1965** *Math. in Biol. & Med.* (Med. Res. Council) iv. 192 The 1·5-mil-spot cathode ray tube..produces the short-persistence flying spot, with a sweep diameter of 10 cm. **1973** *Gloss. Electrotechnical, Power Terms* (*B.S.I.*) I. vi. 16 *Short-persistence screen*, of a cathode ray tube. A screen whose luminance decays rapidly after the stimulus has been reduced or removed. **1921** A. W. Judge *Automobile & Aircraft Engines* iv. 167 Tests..show that at low piston speeds the short stroke engine has a somewhat better thermal efficiency. **1977** D. Bastow *W. O. Bentley—Engineer* xx. 337 The short stroke engine would be at least no worse off in terms of specific weight per horse-power. **1959** *Times Lit. Suppl.* 27 Feb. 115/2 The Army pressed for ample supplies of vertical or short take-off aircraft to move troops on the battlefield. **1973** *Lebende Sprachen* XVIII. 69/1 Britain's aircraft manufacturers also have in mind a new medium size short take-off aircraft to replace the Hawker Siddeley 748. **1965** *Language* XLI. 25 We can posit for Proto-Germanic a short-vowel system consisting of four phonemes.

24. *short-barrelled, -frocked, -handled, -leaved* (earlier example), *-necked* (later examples), *-nosed* (later examples), *-vowelled.*

1978 R. Ludlum *Holcroft Covenant* xxxi. 365 He withdrew a small, short-barreled revolver and handed it to Tennyson. **1915** G. Frankau *Tid'apa* ii. 17 Perched sideways, short-frocked, on the mattress, he thought her a child in the gloom. **1933** Dylan Thomas *Let.* Nov. (1966) 52 My only sister passed through the stages of..short-frocked flappery and social snobbery into a comfortable married life. **1851** H. Melville *Moby Dick* II. xxxvi. 241 A short-handled sharp spade being sent up to him, he diligently searches for the proper place to begin breaking into the Tun. **1964** W. L. Goodman *Hist. Woodworking Tools* 29 The T- axe was gradually superseded from the middle of the 14th century onwards by the short-handled version of type 3. **1748** M. Catesby *Nat. Hist. Carolina* App. p. xxii, The short-leav'd Pine is usually a small tree. **1955** *Archaeol. News Let.* VI. 15 Professor Piggott proposed the replacement of the alphabetical classification by descriptive terms... Classes A and C should be known as 'necked beakers'... Abercromby..suggested that Class C—short necked beakers—was derived from Class A. **1970** Bray & Trump *Dict. Archaeol.* 36/2 The international bell-beakers are uncommon in Britain, where they are replaced by local variants, the long-necked (formerly A) beakers of eastern England and the short-necked (formerly C) beakers of Scotland. **1910** *Blackw. Mag.* Feb. 287/1 The Jumna, like all Indian rivers, is full of crocodiles both of the short- and long-nosed descriptions. **1948** C. L. B. Hubbard *Dogs in Britain* 3 Such breeds as the Pug and short-nosed dogs. **1935** G. O. Curme *Gram. Eng. Lang.* II. xii. 307 In early Modern English there was alongside of the long-voweled *bete* or *beat* the short-voweled *bett.*

26. short-arc *a.* (see quot. 1972); **short-arm** *a.*, (*a*) designating a punch thrown with the arm not fully extended; also *ellipt.* as *sb.*; (*b*) *slang* (orig. and chiefly *Mil.*), designating an inspection of the penis for venereal disease or other infection; also *ellipt.* as *sb.*; **short-arse, -ass** *slang*, a person of small stature; a person of little account; hence **short-arsed, -assed** *a.*, of small stature; **short back and sides,** a hair-cut in which the hair is cut short at the back and sides of the head; also *attrib.*; **short ballot** *U.S.*, a ballot in which only the more important offices are held up for election, the minor offices being filled by appointment; *spec.* (see quot. 1940); also, a form for such a ballot; also *attrib.*; **short cards** *U.S.*, one of various card games played for money (see quots.); also *attrib.* in *sing.*; **short chain** *Chem.* [*CHAIN *sb.* 5 g], a relatively small number of atoms (usu. of carbon) linked together in a line; usu. *attrib.* (with hyphen); **short clothes,** an infant's short-coats (see Short-coat *sb.* 2); also *fig.*; **short con** *U.S. slang*, a small-scale confidence racket; also (with hyphen) *attrib.*; **short corner** *Hockey*, a penalty hit taken from a spot on the goal-line up to within ten yards of the goal-posts, a penalty corner; **short-cycle(d** *adjs. Bot.*, (of a rust fungus) not having a complete life cycle; **short-day** *a.*, (of a plant) not flowering until the period of light each day falls below some limit; **short-eat** *Sri Lanka*, a snack; **short end,** (*c*) a remnant of cloth; (*d*) *U.S. slang*, the inferior part or share (*of* something), the losing end, a bad deal; (*e*) *Comm.* that part of a stock market which deals in short-term stocks; **short focus,** a focal point that is near to the lens; chiefly *attrib.*, esp. in *short-focus lens*, spec., a photographic lens whose focal length is less than the length of the diagonal of the negative or plate with which it is used; **short-frock** (earlier example); **short fuse** *U.S. slang*, a quick temper; hence **short-fused** *a.*; **short game** *Golf*, the style of golf played at the approach to and on the green; **short grain,** a condition of the fibres which gives rise to brittleness in wood (cf. Short-grained *a.*); **short-grass,** (*b*) used, usu. *attrib.*, to designate the vegetation of certain prairies; **short-hairs** (earlier example); also *attrib.* in *sing.*; **short head** *Racing*, a distance less than the length of a horse's head; a horse that has lost by a short head; also *attrib.* and *fig.*; hence **short-head** *v. trans.*, to defeat by a short head; also *transf.* and *fig.*; **short horse** *U.S.*, (*a*) = *QUARTER-HORSE; also *attrib.*; (*b*) (see sense 18 i above); **short octave** (further examples); also in keyboard instruments other than the organ; **short order** *U.S.*, an order for food to be prepared and served up quickly; a dish so served; also *attrib.*; **short-period** *a.*, extending over or lasting for a brief period of time; recurring at short intervals; **short-punt** *v. intr. Rugby Football*, to punt the ball a short distance; **short sauce:** see Sauce *sb.* 4 a; **short score** *Mus.* (see quots. 1876, 1954); **short-sea(s)** *a.*, of or pertaining to short sea crossings; **short-service** (earlier example); **short shorts** *U.S.*, very short drawers or trousers; briefs; † **short-six,** (*a*) = Six *sb.* 3 h; (*b*) *U.S.*, a type of cigar (cf. *LONG NINE); **short sleeve,** a sleeve which does not reach below the elbow; also *attrib.*; hence **short-sleeved** *a.*, having short sleeves; **short-snorter** *U.S. Mil. slang*, (see quot. 1954); also, a person who collects a short-snorter; also *attrib.*; **short spoon** *Golf*, a short wooden club (see Spoon *sb.* 4 c); **short-staffed** *a.*, not adequately provided with staff, understaffed; **short-stage** *a.*, with short distances between stopping places; also *ellipt.* as *sb.*, a coach travelling in this way (*obs.* exc. *Hist.*); **short staple** *a.* (earlier example); **Short Street,** an imaginary street where people in financial difficulty are supposed to reside; **short suit** *Cards*, a suit of which a player has few cards; also *attrib.*; hence **short-suited** *a.*, having a short suit; also *fig.*; **short sweetening** *U.S. dial.*, (*a*) cane sugar (as opposed to molasses); (*b*) maple sugar (as opposed to cane sugar); **short-title,** also, an abbreviated form of a full title of any work; also *attrib.*; **short-weight** *v. trans.*, to give short weight to (see sense 15 a in Dict.) (*U.S.*); **short whist**: see Whist *sb.*[3] a.

1955 *Sci. News Let.* 27 Aug. 136/2 Use of xenon and platinum eliminates the usual warm-up period required before today's signaling searchlights can be used. The bulb, called a short-arc mercury-xenon lamp, was developed by Westinghouse Electric Corporation. **1972** *Gloss. Electrotechnical, Power Terms* (*B.S.I.*) iv. iii. 14 *Short-arc lamp*, discharge lamp in which the distance between the electrodes is small (of the order 1 mm to 10 mm). **1906** 'H. McHugh' *Skiddoo!* 10 To the Bury Little Bunch of Newspaper knockers who have so assiduously plied hammer and harpoon since this series began, I want to say that 575,000 John Henry books were sold up to March 1st, 1906. There is your answer, O Beloved of the Short Arm Jab! **1911** J. Masefield *Everlasting Mercy* 11 Billy bats Some stinging short-arms in my slats. **1919** in *Wine, Women & War* (1926) 307 Short arm inspection between vomits. Doctor sicker than patients. **1953** *Sun* (Baltimore) 5 Jan. (B ed.) 12/5 At the Gay street station you are taken to the second floor for a brief physical check, the army 'short-arm', given in this case to see if anything has turned up since your preinduction physical. **1975** C. Allen *Plain Tales from Raj* xv. 159 Periodical medical checks, known as 'short arm inspections', ensured that any man who availed himself of the 'tree rats' or 'grass *bidis*' was properly dealt with. **1978** M. Puzo *Fools Die* xl. 450 Before you go to bed with a guy, give him a short arm... You strip down his penis, you know, like you're masturbating him, and if there's a yellow fluid coming out like a drippage, you know he's infected. **1706** Short-arse [see Spud *sb.* 4]. **1949** D. M. Davin *Roads from Home* 212 That little shortarse tried to report him. **1973** M. Amis *Rachel Papers* 54 'What's her real name?' I implored. 'Jean.' 'Oh. The short-arse? Yeah, she's all right. Boring dress.' **1951** Partridge *Dict. Slang* (ed. 4) 1168/2 *Short-arsed*, (of a person) that is short. **1973** M. Amis *Rachel Papers* 114 He was a short-arsed little bastard—about five-five. **1962** H. Hood in R. Weaver *Canad. Short Stories* (1968) 2nd Ser. 203 'Now this Pearson,' said one of the revellers, 'he's just a little short-ass. He's just a little fellow without any brains.' **1962** *Canadian Jrnl. Linguistics* Autumn 49 Short-ass(ed). **1965** M. Allingham *Mind Readers* xxii. 241 A bony young man who..wore 'short back and sides'. **1972** N. Bentley *Events of that Week* 72 The gents, in tweed caps or with their silvery short-backs-and-sides exposed to the unrelenting sun. **1974** 'G. Black' *Golden Cockatrice* v. 81 Mr Long favoured short back and sides hair-cuts for his personnel. **1982** *Observer* 16 May 4/3 Bejeaned teenagers seemed to outnumber the elderly short-back-and-sides 'sweats'. **1909** R. S. Childs in *Outlook* 17 July 638/2 On such a short ballot basis the entry of our best men into public life becomes possible. **1914** *Cycl. Amer. Government* I. 104/2 A short ballot is any voting paper which requires the selection of only a few important candidates. **1940** *Amer. Pol. Sci. Rev.* Oct. 955 The term 'presidential short ballot' is applied to the ballot form in which the names of candidates for presidential electors are omitted, and only the names of the candidates for president and vice-president appear. **1952** R. Rienow *Introd. to Government* iv. xix. 362 A suggested reform would limit the offices upon which people vote to those which..have a broad policy-making function. The plan is called the short ballot. **1968** *Economist* 27 July 33/3 As for the electors themselves, they could scarcely be more anonymous. In fact, thirty-five states have abandoned any attempt to tell the voters who they are. Instead these states only use what is called 'the short ballot'. **1845** J. J. Hooper *Some Adventures Simon Suggs* 134 Thar never were a *peaceablier* or more *gentlemanlier* game o' short cards played. **1876** *Scribner's Monthly* May 45 It is worthy of a short-card sharp and a keno flopper. **1935** A. J. Pollock *Underworld Speaks* 105/2 *Short card player*, a gambler who plays all card games well except draw poker. **1938** H. Asbury *Sucker's Progress* 286 Short card games predominated, the favorites being Brag, Poker, Seven-Up and Whist. **1942** Berrey & Van den Bark *Amer. Thes. Slang* § 743/1 *Short-card player*, a poker player, esp. a cardsharp. **1940** *Jrnl. Dairy Sci.* XXIII. 1054 The short chain fatty acids are by products of this synthesis. **1961** *Lancet* 12 Aug. 343/1 There was a high content of short-chain acids and unidentified long-chain..acids in the cholesterol esters. **1972** *Jrnl. Chromatogr.* LXXIV. 335 Measurement of short-chain fatty acids in various biological materials is becoming increasingly important in the physiology and taxonomy of microorganisms and in the dairy, food, and beverage industries. **1816** E. Weeton *Jrnl. of Governess* (1969) II. 140, I have been..making short-clothes for Mary... I think of having her weaned in a few weeks. **1843** C. Ridley *Let.* Nov. in *Cecilia* (1958) xii. 138, I believe it is much better for children to be put early into short clothes if they are well. **1921** J. Buchan *Path of King* xii. 246 He held that the country had grown up and couldn't be kept much longer in short clothes. **1932** *Detective Fiction Weekly* 6 Feb. 126/1 Little tricks known as the 'short con'. **1948** Mencken *Amer. Lang.* Suppl. II. 667 Short-con workers operate on a modest scale, and are usually content with whatever money the victim has on him at the time he is rooked. **1965** H. Gold *Man who was not with It* viii. 67 This was better than..any of the other short-con moments of which Grack had told. **1967** J. Potter *Foul Play* i. 10 His team had failed to score from the resulting short corner. **1976** *Southern Even. Echo* (Southampton) 2 Nov. 22/5 Yateley..reduced the arrears from a short corner. **1915** H. C. Travelbee in *Proc. Indiana Acad. Sci. 1914* 231 We note the teliospores of a short-cycled rust appearing on the æcial host of a long-cycled heterœcious rust. **1926** Short-cycle [see *MACROCYCLIC *a.* 1]. **1950** E. A. Bessey *Morphol. & Taxon. Fungi* xii. 396 Another anomaly in the life cycle of a short-cycle rust. *Ibid.* 397 In most of the short-cycled rusts studied..it has been shown that the mycelium is of monocaryon type until the telium or aecium is formed, when dicaryon cells appear. **1920** Garner & Allard in *Jrnl. Agric. Res.* XVIII. 559 It will be convenient to use the expressions 'long day' as meaning exposure to light for more than 12 hours and 'short day' as referring to an exposure of 12 hours or less. *Ibid.* 576 It [*sc. Aster linearifolius*] is a typical short-day' flowering perennial.

1947 *Sci. News* IV. 129 By and large, short day plants flower if they receive 8-9 hours of light a day, and long day plants flower if they receive 14-16 hours of light a day. **1980** *Sci. Amer.* May 105 (*caption*) The cocklebier is a short-day plant and will flower only if it receives at least 8·5 hours of continuous total darkness each day. **1962** *Housewife* (Ceylon) Feb. 25 (Advt.), Order your:—Short Eats..Cakes & Pastries From Grosvenor Caterers. **1971** *Times Weekender* (Ceylon) 3 Oct. 4/7 She wanted to go to a creamery and after looking at the short-eats on display, ordered a special bun. **1860** Short end [see *BALK *sb.*[1]]. **1904** ADE *True Bills* 14 Each Partner naturally believed that he was getting the Short End of the Arrangement. **1942** BERREY & VAN DEN BARK *Amer. Thes. Slang* § 371/2 Lose,..get the short end. **1960** *Lebende Sprachen* V. 35/1 Left-overs, remnants, *short ends.* **1964** *Financial Times* 10 Feb. 9/1 A fair business was done in temporary funds in the Local Authorities loans market last week. Rates tended to move erratically at the short end. **1976** *Scottish Daily Express* 24 Dec. 12/1 At the short end of the market prices were clipped by £1/8. **1977** *Time* 8 Aug. 28/2 *Annie* went back to Broadway on the short end of a 6–2 score. **1979** E. NEWMAN *Sunday Punch* xxiii. 205 You're getting the very short end of the purse. **1845** *Encycl. Metrop.* IV. 408 Another.. method is to substitute for the sun its image formed in the focus of a convex lens of short focus. **1862** *Illustr. Catal. Internat. Exhib., Industr. Dept., Brit. Div.* II. No. 3154 The same camera can be used for either short-focus portrait or long-focus landscape lenses. **1882** *Encycl. Brit.* XIV. 580/2 The sun's image formed by a lens or burning glass of short focus is our best mode of attempting to realize the conception of a luminous point. **1935** *Discovery* Jan. 25/1 The picture [*sc.* the oldest existing photograph] was taken on sensitised paper, probably with a small short-focus camera having a large-aperture lens. **1973** *Focal Dict. Photogr. Technol.* 559 Short focus lenses of normal angle are used in macro-photography at natural size or larger scales of reproduction. **1885** KIPLING in *Pioneer* 27 Jan. 5/2 Clad in short frocks in the West, Are you growing the charms that shall capture and ravish the heart from my breast? **1968** *N.Y. Times* 13 Oct. IV. 10 Tully, a fellow notorious around Sausalito for his short fuse. **1980** G. THOMPSON *Murder Mystery* xix. 149 Postel's first-rate but he's got a short fuse. You lie to him..and he'll walk off your case. **1979** *Observer* 16 Dec. 9/1 He's quite short-fused, but he knows how to control his temper. **1858** *Chambers's Jrnl.* 4 Sept. 157/2 The 'short game'—coming into play when the ball lies from a hundred to one hundred and fifty yards from the hole. **1903** H. G. HUTCHINSON et al. *Bk. Golf* IV. ii. 238 Treat the combination of mashies (sometimes irons) and putting together, calling it the short game. **1976** *Webster's Sports Dict.* 386/2 *Short game*.., the aspect of play in which control of relatively short shots (as approach shots or putts) is of primary importance. **1947** J. C. S. BROUGH *Timbers for Woodwork* iv. 30 Short grain means that the fibres lie in such a direction that the timber may snap or fracture with practically no splintering. **1956** F. W. JANE *Struct. Wood* xi. 254 Where this type of grain occurs it is clearly impossible to produce lumber which is straight grained—the wood must, inevitably, have short grain and suffer from the defects associated with such a structural peculiarity. **1916** *Jrnl. Ecol.* IV. 49 This *Bouteloua* mixed consocies, representing the most radical departure from the typical short-grass, really differs mainly in the possession of a derived element. **1929** WEAVER & CLEMENTS *Plant Ecol.* xvii. 401 The short-grass plains extend over areas in western Nebraska and include much of the western half of Kansas, eastern Colorado, [etc.]. **1961** *Listener* 7 Sept. 346/2 The short-grass plains of the Serengeti. **1867** *Ball Players' Chron.* 4 July 2/1 Being assisted by their brutish followers of the short-hair grade, they generally manage to make large hauls of plunder. **1875** *Nation* 1 Apr. 218 A very real division of the Democratic party in this city into two sets of politicians known familiarly as 'Short Hairs' and 'Swallow Tails'—the former comprising the rank and file of voters, and the latter 'the property owners and substantial men'. **1883** J. GREENWOOD *Odd People in Odd Places* 107 Fancy him having that horribly anathematized 'short head' all his own and in hand to do as he likes with—to revile it, and punch it. **1898** A. E. T. WATSON *Turf* 133 There are legends of judges having made mistakes in short head verdicts. **1922** *Weekly Dispatch* 12 Nov. 7 Danny caught him napping and shortheaded him on the post. **1932** A. J. WORRALL *Eng. Idioms* VII. 55 Teckla took the lead on the straight and won by a short-head from Bomba II. **1935** N. MITCHISON *We have been Warned* I. 55 She successfully short-headed a wool merchant for the bath. **1963** J. PRESCOT *Case for Hearing* iii. 44 The favourite was beaten on the post... I was short-headed out of a fiver. **1976** LD. HOME *Way Wind Blows* xiii. 186 Had these two pulled their weight, I have no doubt at all that our short-head defeat would have been converted into a narrow victory, and a win at that time for the Conservative Party could well have smashed the Socialists. **1977** *Irish Times* 8 June 2/1 Frozen Tiger beat the flying outsider, Poppy Fields, by a diminishing short head. **1922** *Breeders' Gaz.* 24 Aug. 212/4 There is little doubt he came from Southern Illinois, the home of many well-known 'short-horses'. **1971** *Amer. N. & Q.* Apr. 127/2 They..have had many and strong infusions of thoroughbred blood through the years, but not such that the prized short horse characteristics were lost. **1880** GROVE *Dict. Mus.* II. 588/1 In the short octave two of the natural keys were omitted, and the succession stood thus:— CC (on the EE key), FF, G, A, B, C. **1961** A. BAINES *Musical Instruments through Ages* iv. 77 The earlier instruments [of the harpsichord family] very generally had a 'short' or 'broken' octave in the bass. **1980** *Early Music* Apr. 215/1 In my own field of keyboard instruments, the important questions used to be how the jack mechanism worked and how the short octave was tuned. **1906** 'O. HENRY' *Four Million* 103 The clatter of steel, the screaming of 'short orders', the cries of the hungering and all the horrid tumult of feeding men. **1927** *Amer. Speech* II. 414/1 The nomenclature of the short-order restaurant. **1928** S. LEWIS *Man who knew Coolidge* I. 31 We plan to have a restaurant there serving short-orders twenty-four hours a day. **1956** J. POTTS *Death of Stray Cat* vii. 75 Working..as a short-order cook in his diner. **1978** J. UPDIKE *Coup* (1979) iv. 137, I..worked as waiter and short-order cook in various eating establishments. **1887** *Encycl. Brit.* XXII. 509/1 Short-period fluctuations between a maximum and minimum, within the limits of each single stroke [of a piston]. **1895** *Knowledge* 1 May 111/2 There is no longer any reason to doubt that all 'short-period variables' are really close binaries. **1900** *Ibid.* 1 Dec. 285/2 Brorsen's Comet... This interesting short-period comet. **1923** P. B. BALLARD *New Examiner* 107 For..an overwhelming majority, short-period testing, when properly carried out, is as sound and as valid as long-period testing. **1962** L. S. SASIENI *Optical Dispensing* viii. 195 A second pair of lenses for special purposes, or for short-period use. **1967** *Oceanogr. & Marine Biol.* V. 128 Such a rise is a normal aspect of the short-period low-amplitude, climatic oscillations of the Holocene epoch. **1937** C. DAY LEWIS *Starting Point* I. iii. 48 The next time he received the ball, he short-punted ahead. **1954** J. B. G. THOMAS *On Tour* 184 Morgan was half through before he short-punted. **1876** STAINER & BARRETT *Dict. Mus. Terms* 388/2 A *short* or compressed score is when all the parts are arranged or transcribed so that they shall appear in two staves... In transcribing four-part music into short score, the two upper parts are arranged in the treble stave. **1946** A. HUTCHINGS in A. L. Bacharach *Brit. Music* xvi. 207, I do not think that, even now, Rubbra finds it easy to bring off the orchestration conceived in his mind's ear while writing his 'short score'. **1954** *Grove's Dict. Music* (ed. 5) VII. 765/1 *Short score*, a term meaning either (*a*) a condensation of a vocal or instrumental full score for pianoforte or organ for use at rehearsal or (*b*) a composer's first draft of a full score in which a large orchestral lay-out is reduced to a few staves. **1980** *Early Music* July 414/3 The collection is most unusual in that it..has..a fully notated 'short-score' keyboard accompaniment. **1952** J. W. DAY *New Yeomen of England* iii. 40 The bargemen were a race apart, born and brought up to the short-seas trade. **1966** *Guardian* 28 Feb. 16/7 The coastal and short-sea container services. **1976** *Daily Tel.* 9 Sept. 1/2 All cross-Channel and short-sea vessels crewed by union members will be affected immediately the strike starts. **1882** E. W. HAMILTON *Diary* 19 Nov. (1972) I. 361 What struck him [*sc.* Mr. Gladstone] most was the magnificent appearance of the line regiments—an unanswerable proof against the charges of short service. **1946** *Sun* (Baltimore) 24 Apr. 7/2 'What are briefs,' asked Senator Millikin... Cheney dug into his satchel, came up with a pair, and waved them at Millikin. 'Oh,' said the senator. 'Short shorts.' **1964** [see *JAMAICA b]. **1976** *Billings* (Montana) *Gaz.* 2 July 2-A (Advt.), Coordinate your tops with shorts from the great selection of short shorts cuffed or uncuffed and jamaica length shorts. **1831** H. J. FINN *Amer. Comic Ann.* 219, I wus drest all in white, and lookt like a short-six goin to be dipt. **1838** W. E. BURTON *Burton's Comic Songster* 188 Give me some short six's. **1843** [see SIX *sb.* 3]. **1865** C. F. BROWNE *A. Ward: his Trav.* 57 Tom Slink, who used to smoke short-sixes and get acquainted with the little circus-boys. **1885** *Pioneer* 19 Aug. 5/1, I buy me not twelve-button gloves, 'short sixes' eke, or rings. **1890** J. JEFFERSON *Autobiogr.* 146 The very cornerstone of Juliet's balcony contained twenty pounds of the best 'short sixes'. **1639** in *Rec. Governor & Co. Massachusetts Bay* (1853) I. 274 No garment shalbee made wth short sleeves, whereby the nakedness of the arme may be discovered. **1976** *Lady's Mag.* Dec. 564/2 Short sleeves in small plaits. **1847** DICKENS *Dombey* (1848) xxxv. 354 Mrs Skewton..in a very youthful costume, with short sleeves. **1931** *Mod. Woman* Feb. 46 Length of short sleeve seam, 4½ ins. **1969** *Sears Catal.* Spring/Summer 11/1 Short sleeve tops in windowpane printed plaid. **1839** C. BRONTË *Caroline Vernon* in W. Gérin *C. Brontë* (1967) viii. 133 [A] short-sleeved frock, worked trousers and streaming sash that would better have suited the age of 9 or 10 than that of 15. **1973** D. E. WESTLAKE *Cops & Robbers* 7 With the heat the way it was, I was glad the Police Department let its people wear a short-sleeved shirt in the summer. **1944** *Sun* (Baltimore) 1 May 13/5 A 'short-snorter' made up of 18 pieces of currency. *Ibid.*, The short-snorter fellowship consists of persons who have flown over salt water. Its 'membership card' is a piece of currency signed by other short-snorters. **1954** BERREY & VAN DEN BARK *Amer. Ther. Slang* (ed. 2) § 896/1 *Short snorter*, an autograph list on a string of attached bills, usually of the currency in the countries visited. **1976** R. M. STERN *Will* ii. 15 On the study wall in a plain wood frame were the connected, signature-scrawled dollar bills..called short-snorters, or some such silly name. 'They were the in thing,' his father had told him... 'You carried them with you..and got as many signatures as you could... If there ever was a reason, I've forgotten it.' **1858** *Chambers's Jrnl.* 4 Sept. 157/1 The names of the wooden-headed clubs..short-spoon. **1901** *Encycl. Sport* II. 459/2 The long spoon, mid spoon, short spoon and baffing spoon..are now rarely seen, having been supplanted by the brassy, and the modern irons and mashies. **1970** F. C. AVIS *Golf Dict.* 196 Long spoon, the No. 3 wood; short spoon, the No. 4 wood. **1953** K. TENNANT *Joyful Condemned* xxxiv. 334, I should get my patients to bed. They're very short-staffed. **1968** 'M. CARROLL' *Dead Trouble* ii. 27 They've got a room but they're short-staffed. I said we'd take our cases up. **1977** J. SHERWOOD *Honesty will get you Nowhere* I. 16 Matron.. was short-staffed, at her wits' end to keep the place going. **1837** DICKENS *Pickwick Papers* xxxii. 339 Numerous cads and drivers of short stages. **1903** W. GILBEY *Early Carriages & Roads* 56 It seems..certain that the year 1662 saw a great increase in the number of 'short stages'—that is to say, coaches running between London and towns twenty, thirty, forty miles distant. **1963** *Times* 24 May (London Underground Suppl.) p. vi/4 Local transport in and around the Metropolis was by short-stage carriages, which ran from point to point (usually an inn). **1969** J. E. TUFFS *Essex Coaching Days* vii. 63 Spreading out from London in all directions was the net-work of short-stage coach routes. **1802** J. SIMONS *Let.* 15 Dec. in *Steele Papers* (1924) I. 341 Short Stable [*sic*], or Green seed Cotton if the best Quality, 16 cents. **1920** in *Further Lett. from Man of No Importance* (1932) 79 Soldiering is an honourable but not a profitable profession, and landed property is apt to land the owner in 'Short Street'. **1938** *Daily Tel.* 25 July 9/1 She was finally unable to help Wilde, then penniless, for his defence: and having lived in 'Short Street' myself, I quite understood. **1876** A. CAMPBELL-WALKER *Correct Card* p. xiii, *Short suit*, one of which you hold originally not more than three cards. **1893** 'L. HOFFMAN' tr. *Hertefeld's Game of Skat* 8 As..a suit consists of seven cards only, three or more constitute a long suit; and two or less a short suit. **1931** E. CULBERTSON *Contract Bridge at Glance* 43 With an Ace, a King, or honours not in sequence in one or two suits, and a *worthless* doubleton or a singleton in the third suit, lead the short suit. **1964** FREY & TRUSCOTT *Official Encycl. Bridge* 499/1 The short-suit lead is also indicated when there is a bidding inference that this is partner's suit. **1935** AUDEN & ISHERWOOD *Dog beneath Skin* II. ii. 82 Hullo, you short-suited? Here, let's see your hand. **1940** C. WOOLRICH in *Ellery Queen's Magicians of Mystery* (1976) 281 Did I say she was beautiful? Double it in spades, and you're still short-suited. **1850** *Quincy* (Illinois) *Whig* 19 Nov. 2/2 He put.. all the money she had in short sweetening, and left her without a cent. **1883** [see *long sweetening* s.v. LONG *a.*[1] 18]. **1914** B. T. WASHINGTON *Selected Speeches* 218 This good lady asked whether we wanted long or short sweetening in our coffee. **1948** E. N. DICK *Dixie Frontier* 291 'Short sweetening', or maple sugar, was also obtained in its raw state from the trees. **1896** in A. H. Chester *Dict. Names Minerals* 1 (Advt.), Short-Title Catalogue of..Publications... Arranged under subjects. **1945–51** D. WING (*title*) Short-title catalogue of books printed in England, Scotland, Ireland, Wales, and British America.., 1641–1700. **1978** *Amer. N. & Q.* XVI. 151/1 The short-title lists.. ought to be based on meticulous bibliographical descriptions. **1932** T. S. STRIBLING *Store* vii. 73 It is much mo' dangerous to accuse a white man of shawt-weightin' you when he ain't 'an when he is. **1952** *Sun* (Baltimore) 8 Apr. (B ed.) 30/5 Many Harford county coal dealers apparently are short-weighting their customers. **1977** *Time* 7 Nov. 72/3 A leading Catholic contractor short-weights the church.

b. short-eared owl, a light-coloured owl flecked with brown or black, *Asio flammeus flammeus*, distinguished by short ear-tufts and found in Europe, northern Africa, and North America.

1766 T. PENNANT *Brit. Zool.* I. 71 The Short eared Owl ..is found in the mountanous [*sic*] wooded parts of our island. **1833** [in Dict., sense 24]. **1974** *Times* 20 Mar. 18/4 Twenty short-eared owls have settled on a Humber nature reserve.

d. In Cricket: **short leg** (examples); **short slip**: see *SLIP *sb.*[3] 14; **short square (leg)**, a square leg standing close in to the wicket; **short stop** = *short slip* (see also in Baseball, below). In Baseball: **short field**, that part of the field in which the short stop plays; also, = *short fielder*; **short fielder** (earlier example); **short stop** (earlier and later examples); also *fig.*; see also in Cricket, above.

1856 *Spirit of Times* 6 Dec. 229/1 *Adams*, as short field has for many years, been deservedly distinguished. **1948** *N.Y. Times* 25 Apr. 51/6 Jack Conway was shifted to the short field. **1961** J. S. SALAK *Dict. Amer. Sports* 397 *Shortfield*,..area around shortstop position, between second and third bases. **1857** *Spirit of Times* 18 July 309/3 He is a splendid short fielder. **1843** 'WYKHAMIST' *Pract. Hints Cricket*, (*caption*) Short leg or Middle On. **1851** J. PYCROFT *Cricket Field* x. 191 Short-leg is often a very hardly used personage, expected to save runs that seem easy, but are actual impossibilities. **1877, 1894** [see LEG *sb.* 6 c]. **1963** *Times* 14 Jan. 8/3 Jarman overbalanced in pushing the first ball he received to forward short leg. **1860** *Baily's Mag.* Aug. 364 Willsher, too, made a rare catch at short square leg. **1963** *Times* 1 May 4/5 (*caption*) M. J. K. Smith (M.C.C.), at short square leg, ducks as P. J. Sharpe (Yorkshire) hooks a ball from J. A. Flavell during the match at Lord's yesterday. **1977** *Sunday Times* 30 Jan. 30/4 He made it strike like a snake and Fletcher was caught at short square. *c* **1837** W. MARTIN *Bk. Sports* vi. 104 *Order of the Players*... 4 Long stop. 5 Short stop. **1857** *Spirit of Times* 25 July 324/3 Second Nine Fahys, pitcher;..Smith, short stop. **1860** in H. T. Peters *Currier & Ives* (1942) Pl. 162, I thought our fusion would be a 'short stop' to his career. **1877** *London Soc.* XXXI. 533/1 Dorrington was almost as good at cover as Hillyer was at short-stop. **1912** *Australasian* 6 Jan. 21/2 Hobbs..was caught at short-stop by Carter. **1950** *Nature Mag.* Mar. 131/2 A sudden lunge with the net will often cut off its escape. If the net misses, a lucky shortstop may nab the lizard in passing. **1977** *Time* 8 Aug. 28/3 Andrea played shortstop and first base. **1978** *Verbatim* Feb. 2/2 If a batter hits safely between the shortstop and second, or second and first, the announcer will call that 'a seeing-eye base hit'.

e. Designating or pertaining to transactions in which a seller sells stock or goods that he does not at the time possess (cf. sense *A. 18 g and C. 11), as *short operation, position, sale, selling, side*; **short covering**, the buying in of stock or goods to cover a short sale; **short interest** (see quot. 1900); **short market** (see quot.).

1930 *Daily Express* 22 May 2/6 In late dealings the downward trend was more pronounced, but finally sporadic short covering resulted in some improvement from the day's levels. **1937** *Sun* (Baltimore) 17 Feb. 15/5 Steels, after putting on a draggy performance during the morning, whittled down part of the early losses with the aid of what brokers described as short covering. **1973** *Times* 13 July 21/8 Prices by now were really moving. Record after record was smashed. Massive short covering helped to keep prices on the boil. **1866** *Comm. & Fin. Chron.* III. 75/2 During the week a moderate short interest has been drawn out by the dullness of the market. **1900** S. A. NELSON *ABC of Wall St.* 159 *Short interest*, that interest in the market whichi s represented by the aggregate sales of men who have sold at a price with the expectation of buying in at a cheaper price. **1949** *Time* 30 May 73/1 By mid-May, the short interest had risen 130,058 in a month to 1,628,551 shares. **1900** S. A. Nelson *ABC of Wall St.* 159 *Short market*, an oversold market, with the aggregate contracts for the delivery of stocks exceeding the supply at a certain range of prices. **1870** J. K. Medbery *Men & Mysteries Wall St.* 175 With ..realizations upon short sales, Jerome felt rich enough to dissolve partnership. *Ibid.* 202 A sale profit either in a 'long' or 'short' operation. **1931** *Daily Express* 22 Sept. 2/1 Short selling in the present circumstances would demoralise the market. Consequently all short positions carried must be reported in detail each day. **1911** *Amer. Year Bk. 1910* 385/2 All of these bills were directed against the use of 'options', 'short sales', and transactions in 'futures'. **1930** *Daily Express* 23 May 2/6 Short-selling in Case Threshing Machine, which declined more than 18 points, was an unsettling factor. **1966** 'H. MacDiarmid' *Company I've Kept* iii. 71 We find..fantastic spectacles which, like short-selling, are, as the late Otto Kahn stigmatised that operation, 'inherently repellent to a right-thinking man'. **1902** A. D. McFaul *Ike Glidden* xviii. 139 He bought and sold on the short side for cash and sold on the long side on credit.

B. II. *sb.* **4. f.** (Further examples.) Also more widely = *short drink* (see *A. 14 a).

1953 *Word for Word* (Whitbread & Co.) 32/1 *Short*, a colloquial name for a gin or whisky drink, usually taken before a meal. **1973** J. Wainwright *Touch of Malice* 89, I wouldn't have thought..you were a beer man. I'd have said shorts. **1978** R. Barnard *Unruly Son* xvi. 176 There was a man and his wife... Didn't talk much, just sat and drank shorts. **1980** G. Mitchell *Whispering Knights* i. 7 They only drank shorts... Gin, and doubles at that.

g. Delete ? *nonce-use* and add earlier and later examples. Also, a contraction of a phrase.

1873 L. Troubridge *Life amongst Troubridges* (1966) vi. 53 We..have *names* for some of our relations... Uncle Tum and Aunt Kitty are Tumbo and Kitginx. *Of course* these names we never tell *anybody*..but only use them as *shorts.* **1879** Grove *Dict. Mus.* I. 332/2 *Change*..the word used as the short for change of key or *Modulation*. **1914** H. Stretton *Alone in London* iii. 28 Dolly was the short for Dorothy, and in early times he had often called his wife by that name. **1920** *Black's Domestic Dict.* 28/2 Bouquet is the short for 'Bouquet garni'.

h. In the Morse code, a dot (opp. 'long'); a short buzz, etc., sounded as a signal.

1875, etc. [see *long *a.*[1] B. 4 b]. **1978** P. Niesewand *Underground Connection* 91 Ziad pressed the bell for flat 23, two shorts, a long and a short, and waited for the entrance buzzer to sound. **1978** J. H. Bentley in *Islands* (N.Z.) Aug. 79 'I was waiting for the proper knock,' I said. Three shorts, one long.

i. A short story or article.

1912 E. A. Parry *What Judge Saw* xiv. 245 For many years I wrote dramatic criticism and reviewed books, and wrote 'shorts' and occasionally full-dress leaders for the *Manchester Guardian*. **1937** D. L. Sayers *Busman's Honeymoon* xiv. 297 That was a special effort. Three five-thousand-word shorts at forty guineas each for the *Thrill Magazine*. **1965** *Listener* 10 June 873/1 How many 'shorts' appear in comparable circumstances in this country today? Two dozen a year? The others have to make their bows between hard covers.

j. *U.S. slang.* A street-car; a car.

1914 Jackson & Hellyer *Vocab. Criminal Slang* 76 *Short*,..a street car. Derived from the limited extent of a street car ride compared with the distances negotiable by railroad transportation. **1932** *Literary Digest* 9 Apr. 36 *Short*, an automobile, used especially in the phrase 'hot short', for a stolen car. **1961** 'D. Shannon' *Ace of Spades* vi. 70 This perfectly good almost brand new Caddy I got for him, a *present*, an' he says he can't handle it..comes back with this piece of old junk, my God, pickin' up a thing like—stickin' me with a hot short to get rid of! **1975** W. McCarthy *Fourth Man* I. 26 Everybody brings him hot cars..shorts, we get up north, he fixes 'em up and then sells 'em.

k. *Mil.* A shot that falls short of its target.

1922 [see *ladder *sb.* 3 c]. **1969** I. Kemp *Brit. G.I. in Vietnam* vii. 150 We were watching the shells bursting among them when a 'short' exploded right in front of us.

l. A short film for cinema or television.

1929 *N.Y. Times* 20 Oct. ix. 8 *Shorts*, short, audible pictures. **1930** *Times* 26 Mar. 14/2 The production of several multilingual talking pictures and a series of talking comedy 'shorts'. **1935** *Life & Letters* Sept. 195 This film is actually an advertising short. **1961** *Sunday Express* 2 Apr. 19/6 A half-hour 'short'..made by a brand-new director. **1980** A. Cornelisen *Flight from Torregreca* i. 19 A young actor, who was in town making a television short.

m. *U.S.* A pair of shorts (see B. 6 d in Dict. and Suppl.).

1936 *Institute News* (Underwear Institute, N.Y.) 15 Dec. 11/2 The knitted trunk short has done very well indeed. **1956** *Amer. Speech* XXXI. 109 *A short* (a pair of drawers). **1974** *State* (Columbia, S. Carolina) 28 Mar. 2-A (Advt.), Western jean short with pockets and belt loops in navy cotton denim.

5. (Earlier example.)

1849 G. G. Foster *N.Y. in Slices* 19 Some wild-looking 'short'..rushes down and hysterically inquires of his obliging neighbour, Mr. Smith, whether he hasn't a few hundred over.

5*. *Baseball.* = *short stop* (see A. 26 d).

1856 *Spirit of Times* 4 Oct. 86/1 The Eagle Club now made a very judicious change by placing..Mr. Place as short, which effectually prevented their opponents from making any more such scores as was done in the first innings. **1897** *Outing* May 203/1 Chandler at short is being very hard pushed. **1967** C. Potok *Chosen* I. i. 34 The first one hit a single, and the second one sent a high fly to short, which Sidney Goldberg caught without having to move a step. **1976** *National Observer* (U.S.) 14 Aug. 6/5, 'I try to imagine what I'd throw to get the guy out,' says Stone. 'You know, to get him to ground out to short or something.'

6. d. Substitute for def.: Trousers reaching only to the knees or higher. In the U.S. also *spec.* underpants. (Further examples.)

1927 *Amer. Speech* II. 278/1 *Shorts*, athletic trousers. **1933** *Sun* (Baltimore) 29 Sept. 14/3 Too long has man.. allowed himself to be made miserable by a summer garb which is anything but summery. We thrill to the bold challenge issued by A. Van Dyke.., 'Shorts for men!' **1941** B. Schulberg *What makes Sammy Run?* x. 253 He was stripped down to his silk shorts. **1965** H. Gold *Man who was not with It* i. 6 He..plucked a tricksie in shorts as she wiggled by. **1973** G. Robyns *Wimbledon* xx. 137 In the thirties Wimbledon abounded in beauty... Eileen Bennett..was the girl who dared to wear shorts for the first time in public. **1974** *Caribbean Contact* Mar. 10/5 Bishop's wife came to my hotel and reported that her husband had spent the night in his 'shorts' (or underwear) ..after being stripped.

g. (*b*) (Earlier example.)

1868 *Territorial Enterprise* (Virginia, Nevada) 11 Feb. 3/2 We believe..this rise is attributable to 'cornering' of the 'shorts' below.

h. *Comm.* Short-dated securities.

1932 *Manch. Guardian* 28 Jan. 15/1 The 'shorts' are all due for repayment at par at various dates between 1933 and 1936. **1940** *Economist* 13 July 48/2 If the above sequence of interest rates reveals an artificially wide gap, it is between the yields on medium shorts and the irredeemables. **1963** H. D. Berman *Stock Exch.* (ed. 4) v. 40 U.K. Government loans with less than five years to go to the final redemption date (known as 'shorts') are always dealt in plus accrued interest. **1980** *Times* 15 Jan. 14 Gains of up to £2 were seen in long gilts and of up to ⅛ in shorts.

C. *adv.* **5. b.** *to take* (a person) *short.* (*a*) In passive freq. *spec.* to have an urgent need to urinate or defecate. *colloq.*

1890 [in Dict.]. **1928** R. Campbell *Wayzgoose* i. 30 'Tis Nature's whim that dogs, when taken short, Still to the loftiest monument resort. **1967** 'J. Ashford' *Forget what you Saw* xx. 180 Simon was in such a terrible state of nerves that he had already been taken short twice and had to rush for the lavatory. **1977** *Private Eye* 11 Nov. 10/2 Taken badly short when on his way to work, and finding that both of the public lavatories in Putney were closed, Mr. Peter Herring entered a police station and asked if he could use their convenience.

11. *to sell short*: (*a*) (earlier examples); (*b*) *fig.* to undervalue; to belittle.

1852 *Hunt's Merch. Mag.* XXVI. 738 The writer of the *Aurora* phillipic complains of the practice of 'selling short'. **1861** in *Rebellion Rec.* (1862) I. iii. 27 When one of the members of the Board offered to sell Government Stock 'short' on time, he was instantly hissed down. **1936** B. & S. Spewack *Boy meets Girl* i. 35 Larry: You can't act with a baby. They steal every scene—Law: Are you selling motherhood short? **1959** *Times* 1 Sept. 3/5 Brown, the man who knocked out the present British featherweight champion..has been sold short before. **1972** *Guardian* 21 June 1/2 Who, throughout the Labour Government, spent his time 'selling sterling short' in speeches both at home and abroad? **1974** J. Cleary *Peter's Pence* x. 281 *Domine, non sum dignus*... Martin would always sell himself short. **1980** *Times Lit. Suppl.* 24 Oct. 1194/5 It is poetry that is being sold short by such determined efforts to be funny and clever.

12. *short-pitched* adj.; **short-acting** *a. Pharm.*, relatively transient in effect.

1951 A. Grollman *Pharmacol. & Therapeutics* vi. 143 In insomnia, where there is difficulty in falling asleep, the short acting drugs are indicated. **1978** *Price's Textbk. Practice of Med.* (ed. 12) iii. 260/1 The short-acting barbiturates are apt to cause profound depression. **1867** G. H. Selkirk *Guide to Cricket Ground* ii. 36 A ball which grounds nearer the bowler than a length ball is 'short-pitched'. **1977** *World of Cricket Monthly* June 32/2 Some pointless, short-pitched bowling by Imran and Sarfraz.

short, *v.*[2] Add: (Earlier example.) Also with *out* and *fig.* Hence **sho·rting** *vbl. sb.*[2] and *ppl. a.*

1904 *Electr. Rev.* 3 Sept. 341 Should any line become 'shorted' or 'grounded'. **1912** *Motor Manual* Advt. facing p. iii, The separators allow the plates to be placed closer together and yet make 'shorting' impossible. **1957** *Practical Wireless* XXXIII. 734/1 A 150Ω resistor with a shorting switch. **1971** B. W. Aldiss *Soldier Erect* 87 Both men were immediately sympathetic, and Di made a lot of clicking noises like a shorting Morse key. **1971** P. O'Donnell *Impossible Virgin* x. 198 I'll take the Land-Rover and short out the ignition. **1974** *Sumter* (S. Carolina) *Daily Item* 24 Apr. 2A/6 The fire was started by an electric fence shorting out. **1976** *National Observer* (U.S.) 14 Aug. 9/2 A calcium-lead battery requires an inorganic sack around the lead grids to prevent materials of erosion from shorting out the battery. **1979** *N.Y. Rev. Bks.* 8 Feb. 12/2, I cannot see for the life of me why Miss Renault, that dedicated Hellenophile, should choose to live anywhere rather than the Aegean—unless she is anxious to avoid shorting out the overloaded circuits of fantasy by the insistent presence of the real world.

shortall (ʃǭ·ɹtǭl). *U.S.* [f. Short *a.* + Over)all *sb.*] Freq. *pl.* A child's one-piece suit with short sleeves and short trouser legs.

1966 *N.Y. Times* 17 Apr. 1-97/2 (Advt.), Both dress and shortalls have the fresh-from-the-laundry look of striped cotton seersucker that survives even after a hard day's play. **1969** *Sears Catal.* Spring/Summer 23 Shortall with soil release. **1976** *Billings* (Montana) *Gaz.* 5 July 3-B (Advt.), Infants & Toddler Shortalls, Orig. 4.00.

short-cha·nge, *v.* orig. *U.S.* [f. *short change*: see *short *a.* 15 a.] *trans.* To rob by giving insufficient change. Also *fig.*, to deprive (a person) of his due; to cheat, deceive. So **short-cha·nged** *ppl. a.*; **short-cha·nger**; **short-cha·nging** *vbl. sb.*

1903 Ade *People you Know* 30 Brad was out in the back Townships short-changing the Farmers. **1914** [see *gyp *sb.*[1] 3]. **1920** C. R. Cooper *Under Big Top* 205 The gambling and the graft of the side shows, the short-changers in the 'connection', the constant form of Temptation ever beckoning! **1928** L. North *Parasites* 304 The girl at the cash-register short-changed him. **1946** *Richmond* (Va.) *Times-Dispatch* 14 Feb. 4/1 Henry C. Clausen..told Pearl Harbor investigators tonight that the Navy in the South Pacific was 'short-changing' the Army right up to the latter months of the war on the information it received from decoding Japanese messages. **1958** *Photoplay* Oct. 33/2 As a child, I felt that life had short-changed me. **1959** J. Braine *Vodi* vii. 108 He'd never bought a drink for a barmaid in his life; he said that..the bitches always short-changed you anyway. **1962** A. Lurie *Love & Friendship* xiv. 278 Short-changing in the stores. **1964** D. Francis *Nerve* i. 9 He probably shot himself because that whey-faced bitch short-changed him in bed. **1976** 'D. Halliday' *Dolly & Nanny Bird* i. 14 The cultural circuit for short-changed minorities. **1978** J. A. Michener *Chesapeake* 788 My mom and pop have worked fourteen hours a day, six days a week for more than fifty years... From birth to death they've been short-changed.

short circuit, *sb.* Add: (Earlier example.) Also *attrib.* and *fig.*

1854 *Q. Rev.* XCV. 146 If the insulator should happen to get wet, the electric fluid will sometimes..run down the post to the earth, and make a short circuit home again to its battery. **1920** *Whittaker's Electr. Engineer's Pocket-bk.* (ed. 4) 253 The short-circuit test consists in measuring the voltage and power required to send current through the windings of the machine, and results in ascertaining.. the power lost in heat during the passage of the current through them. **1937** Koestler *Spanish Testament* ii. 311 True, at least once a day there is a short-circuit in my consciousness. **1970** J. Shepherd et al. *Higher Electr. Engin.* (ed. 2) xvii. 547 The circuit-breakers..must be capable of dealing with the maximum possible short-circuit current that can occur at their points of connexion. **1972** D. Bloodworth *Any Number can Play* xvi. 149 You could both only be relied upon to play it straight if you didn't know everything about each other? As soon as you get a security short-circuit and double agents giggling..someone is bound to give the game away.

short-circuit, *v.* Add: **1. a.** (Earlier example.)

1867 R. S. Culley *Handbk. Practical Telegr.* (ed. 2) viii. 166 *To short circuit a battery*, to connect the poles by a wire.

d. *intr.* Of electrical apparatus: to fail or cease working as a result of a short circuit occurring in it.

1902 *Electr. Rev.* 31 Oct. 732/1 Many a motor..condemned for short-circuiting when it is really the fault of the brakes. **1975** *New Yorker* 21 Apr. 34/2 It was a gutsy performance,..recalling Margo's near-rendezvous with Rock 'n Roll Heaven last September, when another jump-suit-cum-guitar short-circuited during an impromptu hailstorm in Louisville. **1976** *Evening Post* (Nottingham) 15 Dec. 5/3 The machine short-circuited with a bang when it was switched on.

3. *fig.* To interrupt, to cut short; to bypass by taking more direct action. Also *absol.*

1899 [in Dict., sense 1 c]. **1924** J. Buchan *Three Hostages* iii. 48 If you had happened to look at that rag you might have short-circuited your inquiry. **1938** *Ann. Reg. 1937* 159 The Council decision naturally short-circuited much of the debate which might have been expected in the Assembly. **1953** E. M. Forster *Hill of Devi* 40 Dewas and King-Emperor! In Dewas it often seemed that they might have much in common. Could one but short-circuit, all might yet be well. **1978** D. Bloodworth *Crosstalk* v. 40 It was..essential to have a secure means of short-circuiting the usual channels. **1979** D. Cupitt in M. Goulder *Incarnation & Myth* iii. 32 Here is matter for a great deal of controversy. I propose to short-circuit it by simply stipulating that [etc.].

Hence **short-ci·rcuited** *ppl. a.*; **short-ci·rcuiting** *vbl. sb.*

1896 [see *entero-enterostomy* s.v. *entero-]. **1919** H. E. Penrose *Wireless Telegr.* iv. 75 Examine the band of the magnetic detector, the magnets, and the short-circuiting contacts of the manipulating key. **1949** Koestler *Insight & Outlook* iv. 39 The concept of bisociation implies a short-circuiting of two separate mental patterns. **1951** M. McLuhan *Mech. Bride* 145/2 A kind of streamlined or short-circuited version of the usual success pattern. **1972** *Jrnl. Social Psychol.* LXXXVIII. 247 It may be postulated that the more empathic two people are with one another, the more short-circuited or 'efficient' their communication.

short crust. Sense b also **shortcrust.** [Short *a.* 20 a.] **a.** A crust of pastry made short with butter or other fat. **b.** (Also *shortcrust pastry.*) A type of short pastry.

1747 [see Short *a.* 20 a]. **1868** M. Jewry *Warne's Model Cookery* 411/1 (*heading*) To make a short crust with dripping. **1951** *Good Housek. Home Encycl.* 586/1 Lard is suitable for shortcrust and flaky pastry. **1970** Simon & Howe *Dict. Gastronomy* 290/2 Shortcrust (basically 1 lb. flour to ½ lb. fat) is crumbly when cooked.

sho·rt-cut, *v.* Also **shortcut.** [f. Short cut

sb.[1]] **1.** *trans.* **a.** To overtake by taking a short cut. **b.** To traverse by a short cut.
1915 J. London *Let.* 26 Jan. (1966) 443 If I could short-cut men to such success, I'd quit writing for a living. *a* **1951** H. G. Lamond in *Austral. Short Stories* (1951) 211 But he short-cut her on one circle. **1960** *Times* 19 Sept. 3/5 An attempt to short-cut the way to success.

2. *intr.* To take a short cut. Also const. *it.*
1925 M. Arlen *May Fair* 210 You'll go short-cutting alone... I've heard enough tales about Carmion Wood to last me a life-time. **1933** J. Steinbeck *Red Pony* in *N. Amer. Rev.* Nov. 425/1 They crossed a stubble-field to shortcut to the barn. **1960** E. Bowen *Time in Rome* v. 137 He rushed up..the Janiculum hill, short-cutting from level to level. **1970** K. Giles *Death in Church* i. 11 He knows London... He's short-cutting it towards the South Bank all right. **1977** *S. Wales Echo* 18 Jan., 'This way,' says Dai Dogs. 'We'll short cut.' The short cut is through Abertridwr's dead pit.

So **sho·rt-cutting** *ppl. a.*
1901 Kipling *Kim* xiii. 330 Though low-lying clouds might be a hindrance to a short-cutting stranger, they made no earthly difference to a thoughtful man.

shortening, *vbl. sb.* Add: **2.** Substitute for def.: A fat or oil used to make pastry, etc., short. (Earlier and later examples.)
1796 A. Simmons *Amer. Cookery* 34 *Loaf Cakes* No. 2 Rub 4 pound of sugar, 3 and a half pound of shortning, (half butter and half lard) into 9 pound of flour. **1970** Simon & Howe *Dict. Gastronomy* 347/2 *Shortening*, a culinary term used more in the United States than in Britain and it applies to fats used in making breads, cakes, pastry etc. All fats, even oils, come under this nomenclature and are used because they make mixtures 'short' or tender. **1980** *Blair & Ketchum's Country Jrnl.* Oct. 34/3, 2 tablespoons shortening.

short-fall. Add: Also **short fall, shortfall.** (Further examples.) Also, a decline; a shortcoming, a fault; a deficit, a gap; a loss. Also *attrib.*
1928 *London Mercury* May 4 We notice in Mr. Churchill's Budget Speech the repeated use of the word 'shortfall'. The word is used to indicate the difference between the amount estimated and the amount received, when the difference is on the wrong side. **1941** W. S. Churchill *2nd World War* (1950) III. 748 We cannot afford losses on that scale in view of the short fall of the American bomber programme. **1953** *Economist* 3 Jan. 35/1 The Exchequer return as a whole..showed a deficit of £951 million, in contrast with one of £602 million in the first nine months of 1951/52. These comparisons, moreover, understate the extent of the shortfall. **1960** *Times Rev. Industry* Mar. 99/3 The report estimates that the changes in American shares of these markets alone cost just over $500m. in 1958. This total is called a shortfall, for want of a better name, but is the equivalent value in 1958 of the net change in the United States share of these six markets for a list of 45 classes of manufactured goods. **1960** *Catholic Herald* 1 Apr. 3/3 He has..no illusions about her [*sc.* France's] immediate shortfall from that high level of being. **1960** *Washington Post* 16 Nov. A 16 West Germany is now running a foreign payment surplus about half the size of the country's deficit, which in view of the disparity in gross product suggests a considerable shortfall by the Federal republic in the assumption of common obligations. **1966** *Economist* 28 May 970/3 Lord Moran's apology for his [*sc.* Churchill's] shortfalls in world and domestic decisions is based too often on a too simple fallacy. **1969** *Times* 14 Feb. 25/4 The shortfall between exports and imports in January was $216m. **1971** 'D. Halliday' *Dolly & Doctor Bird* ii. 23 A scene of continuous short-fall pandemonium. **1976** *Ann. Rep. Manpower Services Comm. 1975–76* iii. 25/2 To make good the shortfall in employers' recruitment into long-term training occupations ITBs made available 'training awards' where the level of recruitment overall into long-term training was likely to fall below the particular industry's long-term needs. **1981** *Times* 4 Aug. 16/5 Half year figures from Standard Telephone & Cables revealed a profits shortfall.

short-grained, *a.* Add: **2.** Of rice: having a relatively short grain.
1953 N. Heaton *Cassell's Cooking Dict.* 422 Rice may be short-grained.., or long-grained and brightly polished. ..The former is used chiefly for puddings. **1978** J. Passmore *All Asian Cookbk.* (1979) 8 Chinese like their rice reasonably dry, short-grained.

shorthand. Add: **b.** (Further examples.)
1931 E. A. Robertson *Four Frightened People* ii. 57 Arnold Ainger spoke exactly the same language as we did... It is possible to talk from the first in mental shorthand with such an acquaintance. **1960** N. Mitford *Don't tell Alfred* xiv. 158 Americans..need the dissertation; the kind of shorthand that we talk would be useless to them. **1970** *Guardian* 10 July 10/6 'Oxfash' is undergraduate shorthand for the establishment of councillors, planners, shopkeepers, and dons.

c. *shorthand notebook, pad, reporter* (earlier example), *-writer*; **shorthand typist,** one who takes down dictation in shorthand and then types out the text.
1903 G. B. Shaw *Man & Superman* i. 2 He has no secretary with a shorthand notebook. **1977** A. Morice *Scared to Death* xxiii. 154 A single page of lined paper, perforated at the top and obviously torn from a shorthand notebook. **1960** C. Morris *Unloved* 463 Janet is making notes on a shorthand pad. **1977** M. Babson *Lord Mayor of Death* iv. 36 The recording officer began noting the words in his shorthand pad. **1881** 'Mark Twain' *Lett. to Publishers* (1967) 147 A short-hand reporter to travel with us in the spring. **1901** *Phonetic Jrnl.* 24 Aug. 541 To a large extent the occupation of the shorthand-typist has hitherto been synonymous with the lady typist. **1926** I. Pitman *Dictation Practice in Bus. Corr.* Pref. p. i, In addition to business correspondence, the shorthand-typist is frequently called upon to complete forms. **1973** J. R. L. Anderson *Death on Rocks* i. 21 She had worked as a shorthand typist. **1922** Joyce *Ulysses* 140 There was not even one shorthandwriter in the hall. **1964** T. L. Kinsey *Audio-Typing & Electric Typewriters* ii. 7 Any audio-typist can transcribe audio-dictation—the dictation is never lost, as can be the case with written notes recorded in an absent shorthand-writer's notebook.

Hence **sho·rthand** *v.*, (*a*) *trans.*, to transcribe in shorthand; also *fig.*; (*b*) *intr.*, to use shorthand.
1928 *John Blunt* 11 Aug. 1/3 (*heading*) Shorthand it! **1936** *Punch* 15 Jan. 60/1 All I wanted..was a secretary—just an ordinary girl who could shorthand and typewrite and answer a telephone and so on. **1975** *Times Lit. Suppl.* 28 Feb. 210/4 The urbanized cluster of inlets and coastal fringe the Venetians shorthanded as *La Dominante.* **1975** I. K. Martin *Regan & Manhattan File* 37 One of Broughton's silent colleagues had a notebook out, shorthanding Regan's words. **1977** *Monitor* (McAllen, Texas) 17 July 5F/6 'Shorthand' has also become quite popular in what is jocularly referred to in Hollywood as the 'creative community'. Ask a producer what his show is all about and he'll never say, 'I don't know.' He says instead, 'There's no way to shorthand that.'

short-handed, *a.*[2] Add: **2.** *spec.* in *Ice Hockey*, having fewer players on the ice than the opposing team because a penalty has been imposed; also, of a goal: scored while a team is short-handed.
1939 R. F. Vaughan *Hockey* 364 *Short handed*, a team with one or more players in the penalty box. **1951** L. Percival *Hockey Handbk.* iv. 126/2 The fundamental weapons are..aggressive use of the body, getting the puck into the opposing defensive zone and keeping it there with five men up, forcing the game (even though shorthanded), and generally keeping the pace of the play high. **1969** *Official Rule Bk. & Schedule of National Hockey League 1969–70* 30 'Short-handed' means that the team must be below the numerical strength of its opponents on the ice at the time the goal is scored... Thus coincident minor penalties to both teams do *not* cause either side to be 'short-handed'. **1970** B. Orr *Orr on Ice* 96 Our men attempt to get the puck down to the other end and keep it, for even a possible shorthanded score. **1976** *Washington Post* 19 Apr. D3/1 Serge Savard scored a short-handed goal..to lead the Montreal Canadians to a 4–1 victory over the Chicago Black Hawks.

shorthorn. Add: **2.** A small round carrot belonging to the variety so called. Also *attrib.*
1873 *Young Englishwoman* Oct. 499/1 There are several sorts of carrots: the earliest of which are generally termed short-horn. **1885** W. Robinson tr. *Vilmorin-Andrieux's Veg. Garden* 162 French Horn, or Early Short Horn, Carrot... Root almost globular, or slightly top-shaped. **1930** *Times Educ. Suppl.* 26 Apr. (Home & Classroom Suppl.) p. iv/3 Attend to the successional sowing of such crops as peas, spinach,..short-horn carrots, and lettuces. **1976** *Publishers Weekly* 19 Apr. 77/1 Such virtually unknown and unavailable items as perennial broccoli and short horn carrots.

3. *U.S. slang.* A new arrival, a greenhorn.
1888 *Outing* Nov. 129/2 Besides a few snipe killed at a swamp called by Shorthorns 'cineky', from the Spanish *sienica*, we still depended upon Uncle Sam's subsistence stores for our daily bread. **1905** A. H. Lewis *Sunset Trail* ii. 34 Don't let no shorthorn have my room. **1907** J. London *Road* 173 Gay-cats are short-horns, *chechaquos*, new chums, or tenderfeet. A gay-cat is a new-comer on The Road who is man-grown, or, at least, youth-grown. **1942** Berrey & Van den Bark *Amer. Thes. Slang* § 456/1 Inexperienced person;..*shorthorn.*

shortia (ʃǭᵊ·ɹtiă). [mod.L., f. the name of Charles W. *Short* (1794–1863), American botanist + -ia[1].] A small stemless evergreen herb of the genus so called, belonging to the family Diapensiaceæ, native to eastern North America and temperate parts of Asia, and bearing glossy leaves and white, pink, or blue flowers.

Shortia galacifolia was first described by Asa Gray from a dried specimen seen in Paris in 1839, which had been collected by André Michaux in 1798. The plant was not rediscovered in the wild until 1878.

[**1839** A. Gray *Jrnl.* 8 Apr. in *Lett. A. Gray* (1893) I. iii. 178 As this is a good North American genus and comes from near Kentucky, it shall be christened Shortia, to which we will stand as godfathers.] **1877** *Field & Forest* Sept. 40 More than once I was greeted with the query 'Found "Shortey" yet?' By which I suppose was meant the mythical Shortia of Michaux, for which any enthusiastic young or old botanist is at liberty to hunt. **1948** *Hyde Park Shopper* (Chicago) 29 Apr. 8/5 The rare flower, shortia, is found only in the mountains of North Carolina and Japan. **1962** *Times* 8 Dec. 11/3 The shortias, too, do well in a moist..position. **1974** *Country Life* 12 Dec. 1896/1 American woodlanders, such as shortias, schizocodons,..and erythroniums especially revel in it [*sc.* beech leaf-mould].

shortie, var. *shorty *sb.* and *a.*

shortite (ʃǭ·ɹtəit). *Min.* [f. the name of Maxwell N. *Short* (1889–1952), U.S. mineralogist + -ite[1].] A double carbonate of sodium and calcium, $Na_2Ca_2(CO_3)_3$, found as colourless to pale yellow wedge-shaped, orthorhombic crystals that are strongly pyroelectric.
1939 J. J. Fahey in *Amer. Mineralogist* XXIV. 514 Crystals of shortite..were found in cores of clay shale from Sweetwater County, Wyoming, at depths between 1258 and 1805 feet. *Ibid.*, Shortite is named in honor of Dr. Maxwell N. Short, Professor of optical mineralogy at the University of Arizona..and widely known for his contributions to the study of opaque minerals. **1973** *Jrnl. Geol.* LXXXI. 229 Shortite..occurs in the groundmass of micaceous kimberlite dikes from the Upper Canada Gold Mine, Ontario.

short list. [f. Short *a.* + List *sb.*[6]] A list of selected names, *esp.* of candidates for a post, from which the final selection is to be made. Hence **sho·rt-list** *v. trans.*, to put on a short list; **sho·rt-listing** *vbl. sb.*; **sho·rt-listed** *ppl. a.*
1927 W. E. Collinson *Contemp. Eng.* 124 Selection committees to University posts first familiarised me with the meaning of the short list. **1929** J. Van Druten *Young Woodley* ii. 28 He dreamed of a Headship elsewhere, always pulling wires and toadying to achieve it. He had applied for six, and lost them all; in only one case had he ever been on the Short List. **1955** M. Gilbert *Sky High* ii. 26 The police have got a short list of suspects. **1955** *Times* 12 July 2/3 Further particulars may be obtained from the Registrar, with whom applications (five copies) and the names of two referees, must be lodged not later than 23rd July, 1955. Candidates short-listed will be interviewed on 27th July, 1955. **1958** *New Statesman* 3 May 559/3 It is said that there is a Catholic majority on the party executive which did the short-listing. **1961** *Guardian* 4 Feb. 6/4 A documentary film..has been shortlisted for a 1961 British Academy award. **1962** *Listener* 4 Jan. 23/2 The mass of short-listed poems was taken to Farringford. **1974** *Country Life* 17 Jan. (Suppl.) 25 Discussions..in England will 'short list' the properties that should interest you. **1977** *Wandsworth Borough News* 7 Oct. 2/2 The local party's General Management Committee will vote for their choice next Monday evening after hearing each of the short-listed candidates give a 10-minute talk. **1979** *Financial Rev.* (Austral.) 3 July 26/1 A two-ship shortlist for the Melbourne aircraft carrier replacement.

short-lived, *a.* Add: Now usu. with pronunc. (-livd). **2. c.** Of a radioisotope or sub-atomic particle: having a relatively short half-life.
1926 R. W. Lawson tr. *Hevesy & Paneth's Man. Radioactivity* xxiii. 170 Short-lived thorium isotopes like uranium X, radiothorium, etc. **1947** *Radiology* XLIX. 286/2 The tracer and therapeutic studies with 'short-lived' artificially produced radioactive isotopes were not directed toward the study of the more general biologic effects. **1973** L. J. Tassie *Physics of Elem. Particles* ix. 91 Since the weak interaction causing the decay of the neutral kaon does not conserve *CP*, the short-lived neutral kaon and the long-lived neutral kaon are not necessarily eigenstates of *CP*.

short run, *sb.* and (with hyphen) *a.* [f. Short *a.* + Run *sb.*[1]] **A.** *sb.* **1.** (See Short *a.* 26 d.)
1830 [in Dict. s.v. Short *a.* 26 d]. **1921** P. F. Warner *My Cricketing Life* xi. 203 One of the features of his [*sc.* J. B. Hobbs's] long partnerships with Rhodes was the number of short runs they ran.

2. A relatively brief passage of time within a sequence of events (opp. Long run, long-run), usu. in phr. *in the short run.*
1879 Geo. Eliot *Let.* 18 Oct. (1956) VII. 212 Mrs. Healy's marriage is surely what you expected in the long or short run. **1928** *Britain's Industr. Future* (Liberal Industr. Inquiry) iv. xxvii. 396 But we do not believe that in anything but the very short run industry benefits from displacing adult workers by successive relays of young boys and girls. **1940** F. Pickersgill *Let.* 19 Jan. (1948) 151 Chamberlain is of course succeeding in the short run in getting rid of all the energetic and intelligent people in the Party. **1952** Isard & Whitney *Atomic Power* ix. 185 The question arises whether the economic benefits of atomic power may be greater for such a country as Russia in the short-run and middle-run as well. **1965** *New Statesman* 7 May 718/3 In the long run you will obtain substantial benefit from professional business schools like the one at Harvard... In the short run—well, I don't envy George Brown. **1971** D. C. Hague *Managerial Econ.* ii. v. 112 In economic theory, the short run is defined as that period of time during which the physical capacity of the firm is fixed.

3. *Theatr.* A short period of being represented on the stage. Also *attrib.*
1922 H. Granville-Barker *Exemplary Theatre* vi. 260 To replace the long run by the short run..or the hastily concocted 'repertory' season, is no remedy. *Ibid.* 262 Most of the 'short-run' theatres..by misplaced courtesy are dubbed 'repertory'. **1961** *Twentieth Century* Feb. 101 The short-run system of provincial repertory. **1967** *Oxf. Compan. Theatre* (ed. 3) 797/1 In Stratford-upon-Avon plays are now introduced into the bill one at a time, and given a short run before being merged in a changing bill.

4. A class or line of goods produced in limited quantity. Also *attrib.*
1957 *Times* 4 Nov. 13/1 The blot on the British copybook is the complaint from a number of stores that most manufacturers [of furniture] will not consider what are known in the trade as short runs. **1959** *Times* 14 Jan. 12/4 Printing short-run quality bookwork. **1967** V. Strauss *Printing Industry* x. 660/1 Foot-operated wire stitchers.. are used for short runs or for jobs that cannot be handled on more automatic machinery. **1970** *Publishers' Weekly* 8 June 152 Many speakers complained about printing short-run jobs: price is too high, quality is not good, and.. deliveries are too slow. **1976** *Scotsman* 25 Nov. 4/3 (Advt.), Craft Bookbinding. Contemporary style bindings

in leather and cloth: short-runs re-backing and general restoration.

B. *adj.* Occurring in or relating to the short run; = *SHORT-TERM *a.*

1947 *Partisan Rev.* XIV. 240 There is certainly a short-run tendency in critical situations toward reliance on reactionaries as counter to communists. **1958** *Listener* 9 Oct. 548/1 A combination of short-run and long-term programming on two different political and geographical levels. **1966** *Philos.* XLI. 294 Any cyclical view of history can harbour only a short-run optimism. **1979** *Internat. Jrnl. Sociol. of Law* VII. 308 Larceny, some of it responsive to short-run price changes.

short-stay, *a.* [f. SHORT *a.* + STAY *sb.*[3]]

1. (See SHORT *a.* 26 a.)

2. That makes a short stay, *spec.* in a hospital or other institution providing care or treatment; providing accommodation for a short stay; of or pertaining to those who make a short stay.

1946 *Nature* 26 Oct. 578/2 It is proposed to establish a diagnostic and research centre at the teaching hospital.. to deal with short-stay in-patients and out-patients. **1952** C. P. BLACKER *Eugenics: Galton & After* xi. 316 These mainly consist of nursery services (long- and short-stay residential nurseries; part and full-time day nurseries; nursery schools). **1960** J. STROUD *Shorn Lamb* i. 14 A short-stay case..[is] a case where..the children are only going to be In Care for a very short time. **1965** J. POLLITT *Depression & its Treatment* vi. 85 Out-patient treatment and short-stay admission is now widely practised for all psychiatrically ill patients. **1976** *Howard Jrnl.* XV. I. 45 Readers working with homeless alcoholics will appreciate the accounts of the birth and growth of two long-stay hostels and a short-stay house. **1981** D. KAVANAGH *Fiddle City* ii. 31 Short-stay car parks, long-stay car parks.

short-term, *a.* [f. SHORT *a.* + TERM *sb.*] Lasting for, pertaining to, or involving a relatively short period of time; maturing or becoming effective after a short period. Also quasi-*advb.*

1901 [in Dict. s.v. SHORT *a.* 23]. **1932** *Ann. Reg. 1931* 194 The withdrawal of French short-term credits has given the impetus to the original crisis, and other foreign creditors had followed suit. **1943** J. S. HUXLEY *Evolutionary Ethics* iv. 31 All existing societies manifest considerable ethical disunity, and..this is an expression of the conflicts and contradictions inherent in the situation—conflicts between classes and groups, between long-term and short-term good, [etc.]. **1948** 'N. SHUTE' *No Highway* 2 Short-term *ad hoc* experiments to solve a particular problem. **1956** *Planning* XXII. 41 The short-term forecasts, up to one year, are the basis for current production and buying and sales planning. **1959** *Times* 20 Jan. 9/3 It will not be enough, however, for the Government to solve the problems short-term. **1970** *Money Which?* Mar. 56/3 A gain counts as a short-term gain if, in general, you had held the asset for a year or less. **1972** *New Scientist* 24 Feb. 428 This type of memory is referred to as short-term memory because the number of events we can hold in this fashion is strictly limited, and forgetting is extremely rapid once our attention is diverted. **1980** *Daily Tel.* 28 June 16 The Minister of the Environment is seeking ways to control local high-spending by councils such as Manchester. Short-term, his powers are fairly limited.

short time. Also (attrib.) short-time. [f. SHORT *a.* + TIME *sb.*] **1.** The state or condition of working less than the regular number of hours per day or of days per week. Also *attrib.* and quasi-*advb.*

1848 W. FAGAN *O'Connell* II. 561 A supporter of 'short time' work for children in the Factories. **1861** J. S. MILL *Let.* 1 Mar. (1910) I. 245 The equality, if not superiority,.. of the short-time pupils. **1861** J. WARD *Diary* 16 Nov. in J. Burnett *Useful Toil* (1974) I. 80 The manufacturing districts..are all running short time through the scarcity of cotton. **1864** R. A. ARNOLD *Hist. Cotton Famine* iii. 84 Short time means short wages. **1906** *Daily Colonist* (Victoria, B.C.) 1 Jan. 13/2 Disorderly scenes were witnessed recently in Newcastle-on-Tyne..owing to an intimation that fifty [employees] would be put on short time. **1930** *Economist* 22 Feb. 411/1 Several watchmaking factories are working short time. **1955** *Times* 14 May 5/6 Three years ago more than 80,000 textile and clothing workers were flung out of work, and thousands more were on short time. **1961** *Ann. Reg. 1960* p. xix, Unemployment was at a low level but in the latter half of the year there was much short-time working particularly in the motor-car industry. **1978** P. BAILEY *Leisure & Class in Victorian England* iv. 80 In the early 1870s... the success of the Short Time agitation encouraged further campaigns to cut working hours.

2. *slang.* A brief visit to a prostitute; a brief sojourn in a hotel for sexual purposes. Also *attrib.*

1937 PARTRIDGE *Dict. Slang* 763/1 *Short time*, a visit to a prostitute for one copulation only. **1939** G. GREENE *Confidential Agent* I. ii. 48 It's no bother. It's the 'short times' that are the bother. In and out three times in a night. **1961** R. SETH *Anat. Spying* ii. 30 Ninety-five per cent of any ship's company, as soon as they are able to get ashore,..make straight for the nearest bar for a 'quick one', and then on to the nearest brothel for what is known in the jargon as 'a short time'. **1971** *Guardian* 8 July 3/1 Miles of girlie bars, short time hotels. **1979** J. WAINWRIGHT *Take Murder* i. 23 Three hours. Not the proverbial 'short time'... It means a bed somewhere.

short-ti·mer. [f. SHORT *a.* + TIMER 4.]

1. (See SHORT *a.* 26 a.) *Obs.* exc. *Hist.*

1863 DICKENS *Uncommercial Traveller* in *All Year Round* 20 June 400/2 The Short-Timers, in a writing competition, beat the Long-Timers of a first-class National School. **1883** [in Dict. s.v. SHORT *a.* 26 a].

2. *U.S. Mil. slang.* One nearing the end of his period of military service.

1906 T. BEYER *Amer. Battleship in Commission* 73 In most cases..'short-timers' are sent home before their enlistment expires. **1918** L. E. RUGGLES *Navy Explained* 132 Any man who has less than six months to do on his enlistment is called a 'short timer'. **1952** M. RUSS *Last Parallel* (1957) 16 Being what is known as a short-timer..I'm at peace with service life. **1977** *Chicago Tribune* 2 Oct. II. 4/6 An inspecting officer discovered a 'short-timer's calendar' centrally positioned in a foot-locker display.

3. *slang.* One serving a short prison sentence.

1915 J. LONDON *Jacket* iv. 25 He was a pallid-faced, little dope-fiend of a short-timer.

4. *slang.* One who makes a brief sojourn in a hotel for sexual purposes; one who visits a prostitute. Cf. *SHORT TIME 2.

1923 J. MANCHON *Le Slang* 267 *Short-timers*,..un couple (amoureux) qui loue en meublé pour peu de temps. **1939** G. GREENE *Confidential Agent* I. ii. 87 The shabby hotel to which 'short timers' come. **1960** *Amer. Speech* XXXV. 120 When the GI visited a *movie star*, it was usually for a *short-time*. *Short-time*..also..had an agent noun, a *short-timer*.

short-toed, *a.* [SHORT *a.* 24.] Having short toes; esp. in *short-toed lark*, any of various larks of the genera *Calandrella* and *Spizocorys*, which comprise small gregarious birds widely distributed in Europe, Africa, and Asia, esp. in deserts and steppes.

1837 [in Dict. s.v. SHORT *a.* 24]. **1863** T. C. JERDON *Birds of India* II. I. 425 The short-toed Lark appears in India in October and November, in flocks. **1869–73** [in Dict. s.v. SHORT *a.* 24]. **1933** *Discovery* July 224/1 The short-toed lark, whose protective colouring makes him almost invisible on sandy soil. **1963** *Times* 27 Feb. 11/6 Overhead range the 14 species of birds of prey, which breed here or within everyday range, including the imperial, short-toed and booted eagles. **1972** ALI & RIPLEY *Handbk. Birds India* V. 21 Short-toed Larks become excessively fat before emigration and are then netted everywhere in vast quantities. **1980** HOWARD & MOORE *Compl. Checklist Birds of World* 347/1 *Spizocorys starki* (Stark's Short-toed Lark). Angola to W. Transvaal.

sho·rtwall. *Mining.* [f. SHORT *a.* + WALL *sb.*[1]] A short coalface. Freq. *attrib.*, denoting (equipment designed for) a method of mining in which shortwalls are worked. Cf. *longwall* s.v. LONG *a.*[1] 18 a.

1912 F. D. POWER *Coalfields & Collieries Austral.* 409 *Shortwall machine*, a coal cutter for use in bords, which, when once the cutting part has made the sumping cut, is drawn across the face automatically by ropes, undercutting as it proceeds. **1931** *Trans. Inst. Mining Engineers* LXXXI. 474 The thin seams are extracted on a 'shortwall' (retreating) method. **1942** *Ibid.* CII. 42 The shortwall is antagonistic to the basic principle that the maximum area of seam should be won with the minimum of roadway consistent with roadway costs. **1958** I. C. F. STATHAM *Coal Mining Pract.* I. vii. 298 Mechanised methods are now generally adopted for the coal-cutting in these narrow opening-up places, using either a shortwall coal-cutter, a Universal coal-cutting machine or in some cases a long-wall machine. **1964** A. NELSON *Dict. Mining* 406 A shortwall face may be any length between about 5 and 30 yd and is generally employed in pillar methods of working. **1973** L. J. THOMAS *Introd. Mining* vii. 258 A group of shortwalls are mined adjacent to each other with rib-pillars left between.

shortward(s (ʃǭ·ɹtwǭɹd(z), *adv.* [f. SHORT *a.*, *sb.*, and *adv.* + -WARD, -WARDS.] Towards shorter wavelengths; on the short-wavelength side *of*.

1972 *Science* 1 Sept. 789/3 Figure 4c..shows features shortward of Lyman-α, which are attributed to the Birge-Hopfield bands of N_2. **1974** [see *LONGWARD(S *adv.*]. **1978** *Nature* 5 Oct. 414/1 IUE provides an excellent way for acquiring UV spectra in the wavelength region shortwards of the Earth's ozone cutoff (about 3,100 Å).

short wave. Also sho·rt-wave, shortwave. [f. SHORT *a.* + WAVE *sb.*] **a.** An electromagnetic wave of relatively short wavelength, *spec.* a radio wavelength of less than about 100 metres, corresponding to a frequency of more than 3000 kilohertz; radio communication or broadcasting employing such waves. Usu. *attrib.* or as *adj.*; also in adverbial use.

1839 [see *long wave* s.v. *LONG *a.*[1] 18]. **1902** *Encycl. Brit.* XXVIII. 68/2 With very fine wires the condition *na* small can be fulfilled with quite short waves. **1907** J. ERSKINE-MURRAY *Handbk. Wireless Telegr.* i. 5 Short-wave Hertzian telegraphy has never been successful at distances beyond a mile or two. **1928** D. BRUNT *Meteorology* v. 40 We have thus to picture a beam of short-wave light from the sun reaching the outer boundary of the earth's atmosphere. **1928** *Daily Mail Year Bk.* 240/2 The B.B.C.'s slowness to recognise the importance of short-wave Empire broadcasting. **1941** J. STEINBECK *Sea of Cortez* i. 7 In all the crackle and noise of the short-wave one of our men made contact with another boat. **1943** D. POWELL *Time to be Born* xiii. 308 They..drove to N.B.C. studios where he broadcast short-wave to London. **1961** *Ann. Reg. 1960* 447 The mass-produced short-wave transistor. **1972** *Sci. Amer.* Sept. 109/1 Finally it was discovered that 'shortwave' frequencies (from three to 30 megahertz) can travel halfway around the earth and more by being repeatedly reflected between the *F* layer and the earth. **1978** W. F. BUCKLEY *Stained Glass* xviii. 182 The Director rose and turned off the impressive short-wave speaker that had brought in the press conference.

b. *Med.* Used *attrib.* or as *adj.* to denote diathermy in which energy is applied to the tissues by means of oscillating electric fields having frequencies within the short-wave radio range.

1935 R. KOVÁCS *Electrotherapy & Light Therapy* (ed. 2) xviii. 306 Short-wave diathermy comprises wave lengths from 12 to 30 meters... Ultra short-wave diathermy comprises wave lengths below 12 meters. **1935** WILSON & DOWSE tr. *Holzer & Weissenberg's Found. Short Wave Therapy* 160 Short wave therapy has been used for about eight years, and..not a single case of irreparable injury has been published. **1965** E. D. R. CAMPBELL in C. W. H. Havard *Fund. Current Med. Treatment* xvi. 596 Short-wave diathermy causes heat to be more evenly distributed through the bulk of a limb by two distinct processes. **1965** N. FREELING *Criminal Conversation* I. ii. 18 Dr Hubert van der Post, neurologist, specialist in short-wave and other electrical treatments.

short-winded, *a.* **b.** (Later examples.)

1934 C. LAMBERT *Music Ho!* I. 36 His [*sc.* Debussy's] melodies may be a little short-winded. **1976** *Gramophone* May 1772/3 The first movements, if short-winded for Bach, have an easy fluency.

short-windedness. Add: Also *fig.*

1934 C. LAMBERT *Music Ho!* II. 102 His [*sc.* Stravinsky's] melodic style has always been marked by extreme shortwindedness.

shorty (ʃǭ·ɹti), *sb.* and *a.* *colloq.* or *slang.* Also **shortie.** [f. SHORT *a.* + -Y[6], -IE.] **A.** *sb.*

1. *Sc.* (spelt *shortie.*) Shortbread; a piece of shortbread.

1882 in JAMIESON, s.v. Short-Bread. **1919** C. ORR *Glorious Thing* i. 11 Home wouldn't be home to Minnie without your shorties, Jenny. **1974** *Sunday Post* (Glasgow) 27 Oct. 17/5 Shortie made with butter and browned real good is sold in St. Andrews.

2. A person of short stature; freq. with capital initial as a nickname or form of address.

1888 *Texas Siftings* 7 Jan. 10/3 One boy yelled out: 'Go it, Shorty!' **1908** S. FORD *Side-Stepping with Shorty* xix. 306 'Hello, Shorty!' says he, in that little squeak of his. **1914** 'BARTIMEUS' *Naval Occasions* xxiii. 213 Your middle watch, Shortie? *a* **1935** T. E. LAWRENCE *Mint* (1950) 152 The figure gives a large surplus of shorties. **1960** V. NABOKOV *Invitation to Beheading* vi. 70 The door of this cell was wide open, and inside, the likable shorty whom he had seen before..was standing on a chair. **1978** *Oxford Times* 20 Oct. 13/2 A reader who is 5ft 1½in tall has sent me a delightful document entitled 'Reflections of a Suicidal Shortie'.

3. A drink of spirits; a short drink. orig. *U.S.*

1931 *Amer. Speech* VII. 83 *Shorty*, and *apple-jack* are illicit drinks. **1942** BERREY & VAN DEN BARK *Amer. Thes. Slang* § 99/8 Strong liquor,..*shorty* (esp. hard, illicit liquor). *Ibid.* § 101/2 *Shorty*, a straight gin with a ginger ale chaser. **1963** *Freedomways* III. 523 Yarborough ..yelled, 'Bartender. Give the professor another shorty of gin there.' **1971** *Scope* (S. Afr.) 19 Mar. 77/2 Also popular are the tall cylindrical tumblers for long drinks, and the chunky tumbler for 'shorties'.

4. A short story, article, film, etc.

1934 M. H. WESEEN *Dict. Amer. Slang* 151 *Shorties*, short motion picture films. **1968** *Listener* 4 July 22/1 Half the time we wanted to kill its crippling name and start on a new formula, with nudes and shorties to rival the money-making *Lilliput* and *Men Only*. **1976** 'K. ROYCE' *Bustillo* x. 137, I read rather an interesting article. Just a shortie. About your man Warton.

5. A short article of clothing; pl. *spec.* shorts.

1942 BERREY & VAN DEN BARK *Amer. Thes. Slang* § 87/37 Underwear,..*shorties*, shorts. **1945** *Richmond* (Va.) *News Leader* 2 Mar. 19 (Advt.), Shorties: More popular than ever this spring! 100% wool Shetlands, in a belted all-around style. **1957** M. B. PICKEN *Fashion Dict.* 151/1 *Shortie*, glove, either slip-on or having one button; extending to wrist or a little beyond. **1958** *Vogue* Jan. 2 Jackets..just right for spring..like the jaunty shortie. **1959** 'D. BUCKINGHAM' *Wind Tunnel* xix. 157 She was already in her nightdress—a silly little nylon shorty. **1962** *Times* 19 Nov. 14/4 Among modern 'shorties' and light-weight garments in my wardrobe. **1963** [see *PEEP-HOLE].

B. *adj.* Designating products which are shorter than the norm.

1949 *Sun* (Baltimore) 19 Mar. 7/7 (Advt.), Short and sugary..cool and comfy..these delicious Rayon Jersey Shortie Pajamas in pastel shades. **1952** *N.Y. Times* 6 May 33/8 A black suede shorty glove. **1954** *Wall St. Jrnl.* 16 Apr. 1/1 Promoters of Florida tourist attractions are energetically courting a new, inexpensive and very rewarding publicity medium. It's the 'shortie' TV feature—films which Floridians make and which the networks admit they're eager to show without charge. **1956** J. POTTS *Diehard* x. 165 Her bright-green shortie coat was spotted with rain. **1960** *News Chron.* 5 July 1/7 They were sacked..after a party in which they staged their own version of Florence Nightingale in the nurses' home, dancing about in 'shortie' nighties waving lighted candles. **1971** *Scope* (S. Afr.) 19 Mar. 64/1 The girls changed into shortie cat-suits. **1972** D. HASTON *In High Places* v. 69 To go anywhere in the winter you have to be able to ski, so I had borrowed a pair of shorty skis from Grahame Tiso. **1980** *Dirt Bike* Oct. 64/3 Both bikes are using Oakley II grips and DeHandler shorty levers.

‖**shosagoto** (ʃosăgōᵘ·to). [Jap., f. *shosa* acting, conduct + *koto* matter, affair.] In Japanese Kabuki drama: a dance play; a mime performed to music.

1911 *Encycl. Brit.* XV. 170/1 Mimetic posture-dances (*Shosagoto*) were always introduced as interludes. **1957** *Oxf. Compan. Theatre* (ed. 2) 412/2 The Japanese theatre recognizes three main classes, the *jidaimono* or histories..; the *sewamono* or melodramas; and the *shosagoto* or dances. **1967** 'J. H. Roberts' *February Plan* I. iii. 92 The play today was a *shosagoto*, a Kabuki drama adapted from a Noh play. **1975** J. R. Brandon *Kabuki* 5 In the late seventeenth century, three major divisions of kabuki drama were recognized: *sewamono..jidaimono*; and dance pieces, called *shosagoto*.

Shoshone (ʃoʃōᵘ·ni), *sb.* and *a.* Also 9 Shoshonee, -ie; 9– Shoshoni. [From an unidentified American Indian language; the folk-etymology given in quot. 1918 is rejected by scholars.] **A.** *sb.* **1.** (A member of) a North American Indian people of Wyoming, Idaho, Nevada, and neighbouring states.

1805 M. Lewis *Jrnl.* 19 Aug. in *Orig. Jrnls. Lewis & Clark Exped.* (1904) II. xv. 370 The Shoshonees may be estimated at about 100 warriors. **1830** *Western Monthly Rev.* III. 562 The Shoshonee are a numerous and powerful tribe of Indians. **1834** A. Pike *Prose Sketches & Poems* 200 The Shoshones are the Snakes. **1836** W. Irving *Astoria* II. xi. 132 The Shoshonies are a branch of the once powerful and prosperous tribe of the Snakes. **1884** W. Shepherd *Prairie Exper.* 59 The Crows..came down to visit the Rapahoes, Shoshones, and other tribes. **1918** J. E. Rees *Idaho Chronol., Nomenclature, Bibliogr.* 111 The name comes from two Indian words, 'Shawnt', meaning 'abundance', and 'shaw-nip', 'grass', which was etymologically changed to the euphonious name 'Shoshoni' and in English conveys the thought of 'abundance of grass'. **1938** *Bull. U.S. Bureau Amer. Ethnol.* No. 120. 238 Shoshoni and Ute were periodically at grips. **1959** E. Tunis *Indians* 91/1 In time, the Shoshone in the far west were following social patterns that had been folkways along the Missouri. **1977** J. Gunn in Hill & Gunn *Individual in Prehistory* ix. 190 If it is assumed that Shoshoni ware is truly diagnostic of Shoshoni population movement, these data are incongruent with the proposed 1000-year-later migration of the Shoshoni into the Great Basin.

2. The language of this people, a member of the Uto-Aztecan family (formerly also applied to a grouping of languages including Shoshone).

1843 F. Marryat *Travels & Adventures of Monsieur Violet* xiv. 33/2, I addressed him in Shoshone, which beautiful dialect is common to the Comanches, Apaches, and Arrapahoes. **1933** [see *Paiute *sb.* b]. **1977** *Language* LIII. 459 The correlations with Cupan *yax* 'to be', Shoshoni *yikʷɨ* 'to sit (pl.)', and a present-tense suffix in Southern Paiute are improbable.

B. *adj.* Of or pertaining to the Shoshone or their language or a former grouping of languages to which this language was assigned.

1805 M. Lewis *Jrnl.* 17 Aug. in *Orig. Jrnls. Lewis & Clark Exped.* (1904) II. xv. 364, I was to bring on the party and baggage to the Shoshone Camp. **1837** W. Irving *Adventures Capt. Bonneville* I. xvi. 260 There was but little chance of meeting the Shoshonie bands. **1886** *Outing* Dec. 198/2 Dick had..a Shoshone woman for his wife. **1926** D. Branch in J. F. Dobie *Rainbow in Morning* (1965) 128 The precarious, abject living of the Shoshone Diggers. **1956** J. Whatmough *Lang.* xii. 221 A Shoshoni dialect spoken in southwestern Utah. **1976** *Billings* (Montana) *Gaz.* 16 June 1-A/6 What more fitting tribute to those who fought and died in this struggle, U.S. soldiers, Sioux, Cheyenne, Crow and Shoshone warriors, than to protect it for those who follow us?

Shoshonean (ʃoʃōᵘ·niăn), *a.* and *sb.* Also -ian. [f. prec. + -an.] (Designating) a branch of the Uto-Aztecan languages including Shoshone; of or pertaining to speakers of these languages.

1891 J. W. Powell in *Ann. Rep. U.S. Bureau Amer. Ethnol.* VII. 109 Very likely much of the area occupied by the Atsina was formerly Shoshonean territory. **1893** A. F. Chamberlain in *Rep. Brit. Assoc. Adv. Sci. 1892* 589 A seeming similarity in a few points of general structure to the Shoshonian and to the Siouan tongues. **1904** *Rep. U.S. Nat. Museum 1901–2* 472 All the Shoshonean types of weaving, all their forms of baskets, and most of the patterns on them are ancient. **1921** A. F. Hall *Handbk. Yosemite Nat. Park* 51 The Mono..are an offshoot from the Paiutes and other Shoshoneans of Nevada and the Great Basin country. **1929** E. Sapir in *Encycl. Brit.* V. 138/1 *Shoshonean*..occupies the greater part of the Great Basin area and contiguous territory in southern California and the southwestern Plains. **1932** [see *Pima]. **1940** M. J. Rogers in E. C. Jaeger *California Deserts* xi. 117 In historic times the Mohave Desert had fallen almost entirely into the hands of the Shoshoneans. **1950** F. Eggan *Social Organization of Western Pueblos* i. 13 By comparing the Hopi system with other Shoshonean systems, he came to the conclusion that 'linguistic conservatism has been of slight importance in the history of the present Hopi nomenclature'. **1974** *Amer. Anthropologist* LXXVI. 11 (*heading*) An archaeological perspective on Shoshonean bands.

shoshonite (ʃoʃōᵘ·nəit). *Petrogr.* [f. the name of the *Shoshone* River, Wyoming (cf. *Shoshone) + -ite¹.] A type of basaltic rock varying quite widely in composition and distinguished by containing, in addition to augite, labradorite, and usu. olivine, significant amounts of potassium feldspar.

1895 J. P. Iddings in *Jrnl. Geol.* III. 938 The classes will be described in the order just given under the names: *Absarokite, Shoshonite* and *Banakite*. *Ibid.* 943 The rocks classed as shoshonites are more numerous than the absarokites, and embrace a somewhat wider range of composition. They occupy the middle ground, as it were, in the series. **1937** Holmes & Harwood *Volcanic Area of Bufumbira* (Mem. Geol. Survey Uganda No. 3) xii. 269 The xenoliths of the shoshonites of Sabinyo include aggregates referable to kentallenite and olivine-monzonite. **1976** *Nature* 12 Feb. 472/1 The calc-alkaline lavas.. range from 'normal' basalts, basaltic-andesites and andesites to highly potassic varieties having all the compositional and modal characteristics of shoshonites.

Hence **shoshoni·tic** *a.*, resembling or consisting of shoshonite.

1937 Holmes & Harwood *Volcanic Area of Bufumbira* (Mem. Geol. Survey Uganda No. 3) ii. 16 These rocks are more feldspathic than the shoshonitic absarokites of Muhavura and Mgahinga. **1964** G. A. Joplin *Petrogr. Austral. Igneous Rocks* vii. 90 The different shoshonitic rocks show many common characteristics.

shot, *sb.*¹ Add: **I. 7. e.** (*b*) Also, a picture (or sequence of pictures) continuously shot by a single film or television camera; the action or process of taking such a picture.

1923 'B. M. Bower' *Parowan Bonanza* xxvi. 303 Bill and Tommy were both below examining the effect of their 'shots' of the evening before. **1937** *Discovery* Nov. 330/2 For each unit of programme transmission, called a shot, on account of similarity with sound-film technique, several electron cameras may be in use. **1957** W. Alwyn in Manvell & Huntley *Film Music* 9 Chapter 4 shows the various dramatic forms film music takes, and analyses in each case shot-by-shot and phase-by-phase a particular sequence [etc.]. **1963** *Movie* Jan. 8/1 The sequence in the Albert Hall auditorium..lasts about twelve minutes, 124 shots without any dialogue. **1972** *Listener* 21 Dec. 852/1 Sequence of calls before a shot. Production Assistant: 'Quiet. Going for a take. Standing by.' Director: 'Right.' **1979** D. Gurr *Troika* i. 2 The first picture is on the screen... He never told me they had that shot.

g. (*a*) A hypodermic injection of a narcotic, hallucinogen, or the like, or of a vaccine; a measure of a substance for injection. Also *fig. colloq.* (orig. *U.S.*).

1904 *San Francisco Chron. Suppl.* 30 Oct. 4/1, I varied hardly a minute each day in the time of taking my injection. My first shot was when I awoke in the morning. **1921** S. Lewis *Let.* 12 July in C. Mackenzie *My Life & Times* (1966) V. 199 Your book..was..at once a Social Document, and an opiate—or, as we say in the States, a shot of dope! **1936** L. C. Douglas *White Banners* xviii. 373 That reminds me—I've to take some typhoid shots. **1948** G. H. Johnston *Death takes Small Bites* iv. 81 If you've never had a plague shot and you've been here for five hours you might have contracted the disease. **1953** W. Burroughs *Junkie* viii. 74 About fifteen minutes later the attendant called, 'Shot line!' Everyone in the ward lined up. **1957** *London Mag.* Sept. 40 They were persons of a kind needing shots of the notion of art as others need shots of insulin. **1969** A. Lurie *Real People* 154 A doctor had come and given Charlie a shot and put him to bed. **1978** G. A. Sheehan *Running & Being* x. 136 We begin to hear about Butazolidine and cortisone shots.

(*b*) In *fig.* phr. *a shot in the arm*, a much needed stimulant or encouragement. *colloq.* (orig. *U.S.*).

1922 S. Lewis *Babbitt* viii. 108 All afternoon he snorted and chuckled and gurgled over his ability to 'give the Boys a real shot in the arm tonight'. **1939** I. Baird *Waste Heritage* xii. 157 He saw the thing because he recognized it and knew how the shot-in-the-arm worked. **1949** *Hansard Commons* 27 Sept. 82 The brake..will lead rapidly to that dollar competition..in which we..and the Belgians will use this 'shot-in-the-arm' only for the purpose of making our positions worse. **1951** M. McLuhan *Mech. Bride* (1967) 47/1 Their masters, who then decide what sort of shot in the arm the public needs. **1961** *Daily Tel.* 11 May 20/6 A 'shot in the arm' will be given to Minehead if Mr. Billy Butlin is allowed to build a holiday camp there. **1976** 'A. Garve' *Home to Roost* i. 21 Everyone felt better for seeing her. She was a shot in the arm.

(*c*) A measure of lubricant injected into the petrol tank of a motor vehicle.

1965 L. Sands *Something to Hide* v. 82 'Four gallons, Will, and four shots.'..The shots were squirted in. **1978** *Reader's Digest* Sept. 130 (Advt.), Regular shots of Redex can save you well over £30 a year at current petrol prices... Add one shot of Redex for every gallon of petrol you buy.

h. (See quots.) Cf. *moon-shot* s.v. *Moon *sb.* 16; *space shot* s.v. *Space *sb.*¹ 19.

1934 *Scoops* 19 May 456/1 Shot..a rocket flight. **1957** Williams & Epstein *Rocket Pioneers* viii. 188 The last moments before a rocket shot are always tense. **1959** F. D. Adams *Aeronaut. Dict.* 152/2 *Shot*, an act or instance of firing a rocket, esp. from the earth's surface.

i. *to call the shots*, to make the decisions; to exercise control over events. *colloq.* (orig. and chiefly *U.S.*).

1967 E. Liebow *Tally's Corner* v. 157 Sea Cat made no secret of the fact that Gloria was calling the shots in this relationship. **1972** *N.Y. Times* 3 Nov. 38/3 It is the majority party which calls the 'shots' on the rules and legislative policies affecting our city. **1978** S. Brill *Teamsters* v. 164 They stand off in a corner as if to say, 'I'm calling the shots here.' **1981** *Sunday Tel.* 5 July 8/5 They felt that an anti-Old Etonian cabal was calling the shots.

8. a. *in(to), out of shot*: also *Photogr., Cinemat.*, and *Television*, in(to) or out of view of the camera.

1958 *Spectator* 18 July 87/1 One Coco-Cola-clutching teenager..darting little glances at the camera to see if he was still in shot. **1960** N. Kneale *Mrs. Wickens in Fall* 174 The maid Cecile hurried into Shot with a tray heaped with cut bread. **1960** I. MacCormick *Small Victory* 69 Thompson looks at each of them disgustedly, then he turns away and moves out of shot. **1969** J. Elliot *Duel* iii. iii. 248 You'll have to move the mike up... Unless you want it in shot. **1976** M. Maguire *Scratchproof* iii. 40 The camera pulled back as she dashed into shot. **1980** D. Francis *Reflex* x. 120 [He] told me it was important that he should be included in my photographs..prominently in shot.

9. b. Also *cheap shot* (*N. Amer. colloq.*).

1973 W. Just *Congressman who loved Flaubert* 97 He tells me it's going to be a sympathetic show... No cheap shots. **1979** R. Jaffe *Class Reunion* (1980) ii. xi. 288 'Every time you come back from those faggots you hang around with in New York you act like a bitch.'..A cheap shot.

d. *Not...by a long shot.* Substitute for entry: *by a long shot*, by a considerable amount, by far; freq. negative in emphatic use. *colloq.* (orig. *U.S.*). (Earlier and later examples.)

1848 in Bartlett *Dict. Americanisms* 215 Mr. Divver offered a resolution summarily removing the superintendent, and was quickly told..that he was going too fast by a long shot. **1861** M. B. Chesnut *Diary* 26 Aug. in C. V. Woodward *M. Chesnut's Civil War* (1981) 163 'They dont pay the soldiers every week.' 'Not by a long shot,' cried a soldier laddie. **1884** in I. M. Tarbell *Hist. Standard Oil Co.* (1904) II. xiii. 114 They are not the Democracy of Ohio by a long shot. **1931** Wyndham Lewis *Apes of God* 17 If those were my last wishes as they are not by a long shot, would they be perfectly clear or not? **1957** W. Saroyan *Whole Voyald* 17 It wasn't only to have pretty women swarm around that I hustled my first book into print. It wasn't that alone by a long shot.

10. a. Also, *a shot in the dark*, a guess, a random attempt. Cf. Dark *sb.* 5.

1895 G. B. Shaw in *Sat. Rev.* 9 Feb. 183/1 Never did man make a worse shot in the dark. **1935** C. Isherwood *Mr. Norris changes Trains* xii. 184, I could no longer resist trying a shot in the dark. 'But you get paid from Paris?' I had scored a bull. **1950** G. Greene *Third Man* iv. 39 'There's something queer about Harry's death.' It was a shot in the dark, but already he had this firm instinctive sense that there was something wrong. **1963** *Listener* 7 Mar. 420/2 It can have been nothing more than a 'shot in dark' [*sic*], but it was a strange prediction none the less.

c. Something which has a chance to succeed (as a racehorse, etc.): usu. preceded by the odds. *colloq.*

1923 Wodehouse *Inimitable Jeeves* iv. 49, It was one of those occasions about which I shall prattle to my grandchildren—if I ever have any, which at the moment of going to press seems more or less of a hundred-to-one shot. **1931** *Daily Express* 23 Sept. 17/6 Mick..will be a neat shot for anybody when the St. Leger is run. **1936** Wodehouse *Laughing Gas* i. 9 As far as my chances of ever copping the title went, I don't suppose I was originally more than about a hundred-to-eight shot, if that. **1941** *Sun* (Baltimore) 14 Aug. 13/6 I've seen 10-to-1 shots that I knew were better horses in certain races than 2-to-1 shots. **1977** *New Yorker* 10 Oct. 174/1 Proud Birdie, a lightly weighted, 4-1 shot in the betting, was next to last going down the back-stretch.

d. *U.S. Billiards. to call one's shot*, to announce which ball one intends to shoot into which pocket; also *fig.* (Properly distinguished from sense 7 i above.)

1953 *Official Rule Bk. Pocket & Carom Billiard Games* 27 Player does not have to 'call his shot' on opening stroke. **1954** Berrey & Van den Bark *Amer. Thesaurus Slang* (ed. 2) § 179/4 Call one's shot,..*to guess or predict rightly*. **1959** N. Mailer *Advts. for Myself* 22 It will be fine if I can write so well and so strongly as to call my shot. **1962** Wodehouse *Service with Smile* vi. 83 In making this statement, he called his shots correctly. **1976** *Billings* (Montana) *Sunday Gaz.* 20 June 1-A/3 There was no question in my mind that Nixon was calling his own shots.

11. f. In Cricket, tennis, golf, etc.: (*oh,*) *shot!*, an applauding exclamation used when a player makes a good stroke, or on an accurate throw; also used when a boxer delivers an effective blow. Freq. *good shot!*

1906 Wodehouse *Love among Chickens* 311 Oh, shot, sir! Shot, indeed! **1907** 'I. Hay' *Pip* x. 309 Here are two young men worth watching. Number One is addressing his ball for an approach shot... 'Good shot!' remarks Number Two. **1922** Wodehouse *Clicking of Cuthbert* ix. 218 He drove a perfect ball, hard and low with a lot of roll. Even Eunice was impressed. 'Good shot, partner!' she said. **1933** D. L. Sayers *Murder must Advertise* xviii. 310 He always hits out. I like to see a batsman hitting out, you know. There! Good shot! Good shot! **1940** E. F. Benson *Final Edition* iii. 52 Everybody chorused 'Good shot, my lord' on the smallest excuse. **1972** J. Burmeister *Running Scared* vii. 95 The resonant bonk of a tennis racket..a distant cry of 'Oh, shot!'

22. c. *big shot* (formerly also *great* or *high shot*), an important person; a prominent member of a profession, organization, etc. Also *attrib.* Chiefly *U.S.*

1861 G. Meredith *Let.* 9 July (1970) I. 91 The great 'shots' of Stanz parade the town with their prizes in their hats. **1929** *Cincinnati* (Ohio) *Enquirer* 5 Oct. 10/3 One of them is just as likely to win the series as one of the 'big shots'. **1933** D. Runyon in *Collier's* 28 Jan. 41/1 Many of these guys are very high shots during the gold rush. **1935** C. Odets *Waiting for Lefty* in *3 Plays* (1936) iii. 135 Sure, the big shot money men want us like that. **1941** Auden *New Year Letter* II. 33 Unlike the big-shots of the day. **1957** H. Roosenburg *Walls came tumbling Down* iii. 74 Who are these new prisoners? Are they all the big-shot Nazis? **1960** *New Statesman* 9 Jan. 31/1 On arrival I was asked to dine with Thomas Lamont, along with a number of big-shots in the American newspaper world, including..Henry Luce of *Time-Life*. **1974** K. Millet *Flying* (1975) III. 300 He would still go for his man in an interview. Used the program to get the big shots.

IV. 23. g. A dram of spirits.

1928 Wodehouse *Good Morning, Bill* II. 72, I think *I'll* take a shot in a glass. **1935** J. T. Farrell *Judgment Day* II. xviii. 449 Near White City he stopped in front of a speakeasy, deciding that one good, stiff shot would jack him up. **1955** 'A. Gilbert' *Is She dead Too?* vi. 112 Edwin..produced a very little whisky in a bottle. Lamb ..gave himself a generous shot in the cup of tea. **1979** R. Jaffe *Class Reunion* (1980) II. v. 235 He poured two shots of vodka, one for her and one for himself.

V. 28*. *that's the shot!* and varr.: in expressions of approval, that's a good idea, or the 'very thing'. *Austral. colloq.*

1953 T. A. G. Hungerford *Riverslake* 142 That's the shot. Buy a bit of land and grow things. **1958** R. Stow *To Islands* ii. 46 Cattle's the shot... They worked it before. **1963** J. Cleary *Flight of Chariots* 370, I think a good strong cuppa brew would be the shot. **1976** D. Ireland *Glass Canoe* 227 'That's the shot,' said Mick. 'Stick around and guard the place.'

30. **shot drill** (later example); **shot effect** [tr. G. *schroteffekt* (W. Schottky 1918, in *Ann. der Physik* LVII. 547), f. *schrot* small shot], the fluctuation in the magnitude of the anode current in a thermionic valve due to the random character of electron emission; also *transf.*, any fluctuation having a similar stochastic character; **shot-firer,** (*a*) a man employed to fire the shot (sense 7 f) in blasting; (*b*) an electrical device for detonating the shot; hence **shot-firing; shot glass,** (*b*) *U.S.* a glass for holding a short drink; **shot gold** orig. *U.S.*, gold occurring in the form of small spheres like lead shot; **shot line** = *shot rope* below; **shot list** *Cinematogr.* and *Television*, a list of shots made by a camera; **shotmaking** *U.S.*, in golf, tennis, etc.: the playing of (esp. successful or attacking) strokes; also **shot-maker; shot noise** = *shot effect* above; **shot-peening** [see Peen, pene *v.* in Dict. and Suppl.], the use of a stream of hard metal particles directed against a metal part to harden and strengthen its surface; so **shot-peen** *v. trans.*; **shot-peened** *ppl. a.*; **shot rope,** a weighted rope hung over the side of a boat and used to guide the descent and ascent of divers.

1936 'R. Hyde' *Passport to Hell* xv. 232 Either he didn't know I was supposed to be in Le Havre doing shot drill, or he'd forgotten. [**1921** *Sci. Abstr.* A. XXIV. 759 The object is the measurement of the spontaneous current variations in high-vacuum discharge tubes, a subject which has been previously dealt with theoretically by Schottky and called by him the 'Schrot effect' (literally, the small shot effect).] **1923** *Chem. Abstr.* XVII. 924 (*heading*) The present state of the shot effect problem. **1930** *Proc. IRE* XVIII. 243 In the absence of space charge the noise has been termed by Schottky the 'schroteffekt', or 'small shot effect', from the analogy which the flight of electrons from the filament to the plate of a vacuum tube bears to the spattering of small shot fired from a shot gun. The simple term 'shot effect' will be used in this paper to denote this noise either with or without space charge. **1947** *Electronic Engin.* XIX. 82/1 Shot effect is more pronounced when the negative grid bias is greater than the usual value. **1964** N. Wiener *God & Golem* 41 There are..cases..where these irregularities are just what we wish to produce, and there are commercial devices for producing them. These are known as shot-effect generators. **1968** P. A. P. Moran *Introd. Probability Theory* ix. 423 Campbell's theorem originally arose in the study of the 'shot effect' in thermionic vacuum tubes. **1883** W. S. Gresley *Gloss. Terms Coal Mining* 219 *Shot firer*, a man specially appointed by the manager of a mine to fire off every shot in a certain number of stalls or heads during the shift. **1886** [in Dict., sense 29]. **1891** C. Pamely *Colliery Manager's Handbk.* xiv. 472 Shots are fired by the aid of litter straws, paper squibs.., safety fuze or by an electric shot-firer. **1939** G. Heyer *No Wind of Blame* xvi. 315 'What's that thing called that they use in mines when they want to blast? Electrical thing they touch off the dynamite with?' 'A shot-firer, do you mean? **1973** 'J. Patrick' *Glasgow Gang Observed* xvii. 140 He began work as a shot firer in a factory close to the approved school. **1884** *Engineering* 31 Oct. 420/2 (*heading*) Shot-firing in mines. **1959** *Times Rev. Industry* Feb. 14/1 For many years the infusion of coal *in situ* by water under pressure has been employed to reduce the dust hazard. Recently this procedure has been combined with that of shot-firing. **1955** A. Miller *Mem. Two Mondays* in *View from Bridge* 43 Enter Bert, carefully carrying a shotglass of whisky. **1970** A. Maling *Lambert's Son* (1972) xxxviii. 157, I put the lemon twists in a shot glass. **1858** *Pike's Peak Guide Book* 222 Those who have prospected over in the parks..say that they find the shot gold there. **1929** E. J. Dunn *Geol. Gold* xvii. 185 Spherical grains and small pieces of gold are found in the alluvial wash at Creswick... They are often quite spherical, generally of small size, but occasionally up to several dwts. in weight, and are known as 'shot gold'. **1971** A. P. McInnes *Dunlevy* 113 Shot gold..is always considered a coarse gold prospect, indicating coarser gold lower down. **1968** A. P. Balder *Compl. Man. Skin Diving* xiii. 248 A shot line..should be used from a boat when diving in bad visibility. **1976** Zanelli & Skuse *Sub-Aqua Illustr. Dict.* 84/2 *Shot line*, a line to which a very heavy weight (or 'shot') is fixed. It is used to guide the descent and ascent of divers. It must not be used as an anchor, because shot lines should be hung vertically. **1969** J. Elliot *Duel* III. ii. 233 She..learned how to make production breakdowns, set out commentary scripts, type shot lists. **1971** P. Purser *Holy Father's Navy* xxi. 101 The film was back from the labs, the shot list neatly typed up, the editing facilities booked. **1974** *Union* (S. Carolina) *Daily Times* 23 Apr. 9/5 The best five shot-makers in each team. **1969** *New Yorker* 14 June 45/1 My style is playmaking—consistent, percentage tennis—and his style is shotmaking. **1977** *Ibid.* 8 Aug. 48/3 These statistics..give no indication of the absolutely superb shotmaking that Bolt produced on an exceedingly narrow, fast, and exacting course. **1930** *Proc. IRE* XVIII. 255 The solid line curve *D* is the sum of the calculated shot and thermal noises. **1978** *Nature* 8 June 432/1 Individual QSO continuum magnitudes, which are also affected by the added uncertainty introduced by shot noise were generally accurate to $\pm 7\%$. **1944** H. F. Moore *Shot Peening & Fatigue of Metals* (Amer. Foundry Equipment Co.) 5/1 The metal just below the shot-peened layer is somewhat affected by the shot peening. **1944** *Proc. Soc. Exper. Stress Analysis* II. 172/2 These pieces..were shot-peened on both flat faces. **1956** F. H. Keating *Chromium-Nickel Austenitic Steels* v. 70 Well substantiated claims have been made for improvement in fatigue-resistance by shot-peening, which introduces compressive stresses in the surface layers. **1962** *Engineering* 23 Mar. 403/2, 85 per cent of the metal is machined away on electronically controlled milling machines before being curved by press or shot-peening. **1972** L. M. Harris *Introd. Deepwater Floating Drilling Operations* xii. 138 Each weld should be ground inside and out, and the transition area and weld shotpeened. **1972** H. T. Jensen in Mann & Milligan *Aircraft Fatigue* 156 We established an allowable strength of two-thirds of the strength of the machined and shot-peened strength for components that retain their as-forged surfaces. **1909** *Man. Seamanship* (Admiralty) II. vi. 116 As soon as the diver sees anything he can signal for shot rope to be lowered. **1940** 'N. Shute' *Landfall* 257 Then in slow motion he [*sc.* a diver] reached out and grasped the shot-rope, stepped off the ladder and was gone. **1960** Brookes & Broadhurst *Diving Manual* (ed. 2) 105 A shot rope should be very heavily weighted so that it will hang vertically in the water, uninfluenced by tides and currents.

shot, *ppl. a.* Add: **4. a.** Also with *down*: of an aircraft or its crew.

1943 'M. Coles' *Without Lawful Authority* ix. 115 'The 'plane..crashed in flames just this side of the Polish frontier... One of our fellows..says there were bullet-holes in the wings.' 'Shot down, eh?' **1957** H. Roosenburg *Walls came tumbling Down* 7 A local resistance group ..concentrated on picking up shot-down Allied pilots. **1968** *Listener* 26 Dec. 858/2 He was also the source of her story..of the shot-down pilot who told his captors that his sister in the States was a rich '*industrielle*'. **1980** E. Behr *Getting Even* x. 120 Organising escape routes for shot-down R.A.F. and U.S. air crews on the run.

b. Drunk. *slang* (chiefly *U.S.*, *Austral.*, and *N.Z.*). Cf. Shoot *v.* 32 d.

1864 *Harper's Mag.* May 856/2 He again sat down by the fire..by which time he was pretty well 'shot'. **1896** W. C. Gore in *Inlander* Jan. 146 *Shot*, a. Intoxicated. **1930** *Sat. Even. Post* 26 July 145/2 'I'm half shot,' he said... 'An' so are you. You're just as drunk as I am.' **1943** N. Marsh *Colour Scheme* x. 187 The chap was half-shot... He smelt of booze. **1957** *Nelson* (N.Z.) *Even. Mail* 18 May 7 He asked the man: 'Are you shot?' The man said: 'Yes.'..It was ascertained that he had fallen down while intoxicated. **1972** T. Lilley *K Section* ix. 43 He was well shot last night. Staggering.

c. In fig. phr. *shot through* (also *to hell* or *pieces*), in a state of ruin or collapse. *colloq.* (chiefly *U.S.*).

1926 E. Hemingway *Fiesta* (1927) III. xix. 277 That meant San Sebastian all shot to hell. **1932** L. Golding *Magnolia St.* I. iv. 67 The old man was all shot to pieces... He had fallen into a sort of torpor. **1937** H. G. Wells *Brynhild* xi. 243 To-day I feel shot through. I feel shot to pieces. **1977** M. Babson *Murder, Murder, Little Star* vii. 50 Look at the price I pay. My private life is shot to hell.

d. Of things: worn out, ruined, used up, spent. *slang* (chiefly *U.S.*).

1933 C. K. Stewart *Speech Amer. Airman* (Univ. Akron thesis) 89 *Shot*, an adjective meaning 'useless' 'gone', or 'worn out'. **1960** *Analog Science Fact/Fiction* Oct. 136/1 With him gone, the interstellar drive project would've been shot. **1970** I. Petite *Meander to Alaska* I. vii. 66 At that point they discovered that the transmission bearings were 'shot'. **1981** G. V. Higgins *Rat on Fire* vii. 54 Your boiler is one of those old things... I think it's about shot.

e. With *up*, severely wounded or damaged by shooting. Also *fig.* (*colloq.*) and *transf.* drugged (*U.S. slang*).

1934 V. M. Yeates *Winged Victory* I. xviii. 146 If he tried to do anything on his own he would probably get himself shot down, or at least shot up. **1938** [see *pollu-ted *ppl. a.* b]. **1945** *Richmond* (Va.) *Times-Dispatch* 22 May 2/8 The Forty-fifth Division's 'most shot up soldier to return alive' is back in the States. **1964** L. Nkosi *Rhythm of Violence* 63 Stop Shouting!..Are you all shot up or something! **1978** *Detroit Free Press* 2 Apr. (Detroit Suppl.) 8/1 Starting up the stairs, she steps around a recently shot-up addict who is just nodding off.

f. Of people: exhausted. *slang* (chiefly *U.S.*).

1939 [see *cosy *v.* 2]. **1945** G. Casey *Downhill is Easier* IV. 183 Late at night you could easily walk the twelve miles..without seeing a vehicle. I realized I was shot. **1951** E. B. White *Let.* 11 Dec. (1976) 346 Ross died last week and we have been in something of a scramble here, as well as feeling quite shot. **1967** 'V. Siller' *Biltmore Call* 120, I thought she was shot and her nerves had given out. **1972** J. Gores *Dead Skip* (1973) xii. 83 He..[was] literally too tired to move... Shot. Utterly shot.

sho·t-bag. Chiefly *U.S.* [Shot *sb.*[1]] A bag for carrying shot; a shot-pouch. Also *transf.* a purse.

1638 in *Archives of Maryland* (1887) IV. 32 It[em] one fowling piece & shott bagge. **1756** P. Hog *Let.* 14 May in S. M. Hamilton *Lett. to Washington* (1898) I. 260 Going to Load he missed his Shot Bag which had been Carried away by one of the Shots. **1800** A. Henry *Jrnl.* 4 Oct. (1897) I. iii. 111 The Indians were standing in the fort with nothing on but their breech-clouts, powder-horns, shot bags, and guns in their hands. **1872** 'Mark Twain' *Roughing It* ii. 5 We also took with us a little shot-bag of silver coin. **1946** *Aircraft Engineering* XVIII. 109/2 The time-honoured method of loading with shot bags the structure to be tested in an inverted position is still current practice across the Atlantic.

sho·t-blast. [Shot *sb.*[1]] A high-speed stream of steel particles directed at a surface to clean and roughen it.

1923 *Foundry* 1 Feb. 13 Have you noticed how the modern shot-blast and grit-blast are replacing the old dust breeding sand-blast? **1934** *Foundry Trade Jrnl.* LI. 340 The barrel..is essentially a contrivance for mechanically exposing every part of the casting or forging to be cleaned to the effect of the shot-blast. **1958** *Engineering* 21 Mar. 382/3 An airless type shot-blast plant has been installed, to deal with 35 tons of castings a day.

Hence **shot-blasting,** the use of a shot-blast; also **shot-blast** *v. trans.*, to subject to shot-blasting; **shot-blasted** *ppl. a.*; **shot-blaster,** a person using a shot-blast.

1934 F. W. Partington *G. F. Charnock's Mech. Technol.* (ed. 2) xxxi. 415 Steel castings are frequently cleaned of both sand and scale by subjecting them to shot-blasting. **1937** *Jrnl. Iron & Steel Inst.* CXXXV. 160A (*heading*) Buick shotblasts large castings automatically. **1941** W. K. Wilson *Pract. Solution Torsional Vibration Problems* (ed. 2) II. vii. 146 Shot-blasted springs are very susceptible to rusting. **1946** *Engineer* 15 Feb. 152/1 A large-capacity dust extractor, coupled to the shot-blasting chamber, exhausts all the fine dust and sand. **1959** *Times* 27 Apr. (Suppl.) p. xi/4 It has first to be shot-blasted to provide an absolutely clean surface. **1961** *Evening Standard* 26 July 18/5 (Advt.), Shot blasters & metal sprayers..reqd. **1964** S. Crawford *Basic Engin. Processes* iii. 87 Prior to bronze welding the joint faces or edges are cleaned by shot blasting. **1975** *Offshore Engineer* Sept. 143/4 A new version of their shot-blaster's helmet has been introduced by Martindale Protection. **1977** *Exchange & Mart* (South) 24 Feb. 19 M/3 One bodiless chassis, stripped, shotblasted, etc. partly reassembled.

shot-bush. (Earlier example.)

1785 [see *pigeon-weed* s.v. *pigeon *sb.* 6].

shot-gun, shotgun. For **a, b** read **1, 2** and add: **1. b.** *ellipt.* for (*a*) a shotgun building (sense 3 b below); (*b*) = *shotgun formation* (U.S. Football), sense 2 below.

1945 B. A. Botkin *Lay my Burden Down* 98 They had to go out and live in sod houses and little old boxed shotguns and turn their Negroes loose. **1966** [see *shotgun formation* below]. **1976** *Time* 19 Jan. 43 Staubach's talent is throwing from the shotgun. **1977** *New Yorker* 10 Oct. 178/2 Buckley, operating from the shotgun, threw some forty, of which some twenty were valid.

2. shotgun formation *U.S. Football* (see quot. 1966); also *fig.*; **shotgun marriage** orig. *U.S.* = *shotgun wedding* below; also *fig.*; **shotgun microphone** (or *colloq.* **mike**)**,** a highly directional microphone with a long barrel that is pointed at a distant source of sound; **shotgun wedding** orig. *U.S.*, a wedding made in haste or under duress by reason of the bride's pregnancy; also *fig.*

[**1966** Rote & Winter *Lang. of Pro Football* III. 137 *Shotgun*, offensive formation where quarterback sets four or five yards behind center with other backfield men split out as flankers or slot backs; an offensive formation designed to facilitate sending out as many pass receivers as possible while passer is in safer position to throw.] **1967** *Wall St. Jrnl.* (Eastern ed.) 30 Jan. 8/5 Mr. Hornung's argument [that his accomplishments constituted educational, artistic, scientific and civic achievements] constitutes 'a shotgun formation', the court said. **1972** J. Mosedale *Football* vi. 91 Hickey installed the shotgun formation, putting the quarterback at tailback where he could pass or run. **1929** E. W. Howe *Plain People* xxix. 267 Two people cordially disliked me for years because I thought it best to mention very briefly and respectfully their shot gun marriage. **1958** *Manch. Guardian* 22 Mar. 4/6 There were references to..the possible shotgun marriage of the 'Daily Herald' and the 'News Chronicle'. **1973** 'H. Carmichael' *Too Late for Tears* xv. 179 Shot-gun marriages went out with the advent of the Pill. **1968** J. M. Ullman *Lady on Fire* (1969) viii. 111 Even if they walked around Curley..could pick up the conversation with a shotgun microphone. The device had a range of several hundred feet. **1972** *Jrnl. Social Psychol.* LXXXVI. 30 A shotgun microphone was located to one side of the group to record the verbal interactions. **1978** T. GIFFORD *Glendower Legacy* (1979) 187 We used that miserable shotgun mike and believe me, Brennan was watching television and sneezing. **1927** S. LEWIS *Elmer Gantry* ix. 134 There were, in those parts and those days, not infrequent ceremonies known as 'shotgun weddings'. **1946** *Sun* (Baltimore) 29 Oct. 1/1 Charges that the veto system was a 'shotgun wedding' forced upon the small nations. **1974** E. HUXLEY *Gallipot Eyes* (1976) 61 She can't have been more than fourteen when she married. A shot-gun wedding, clearly.

3. a. Passing into *adj.* Made or done hastily or under pressure of necessity.

1937 *Sun* (Baltimore) 18 Aug. 8/2 Shotgun legislation... Measures pushed through in a last-hour rush. **1962** *Economist* 7 Apr. 73/1 Mr Sandys's shot-gun reorganisation of the aircraft industry. **1977** *Observer* 13 Mar. 13/2 By the end of last year, 464 men had been forced to quit, 74 after formal proceedings, the remainder in shotgun resignations.

b. Designating a house or other building with rooms set in a line on either side of a long central hallway. *U.S.*

1938 J. STUART *Beyond Dark Hills* vi. 156 Their faces wore the blank expression of the Armco plant's shotgun dwelling houses. **1944** T. D. CLARK *Pills, Petticoats & Plows* iii. 56 There was no wiser spot on earth than the porches which jutted out from the long shotgun buildings. **1950** *Penguin New Writing* XL. 67 Your Riverbottom Nigras lived in little shotgun houses. **1964** *Amer. Folk Music Occasional* I. 92 De Ole souf unroll... Dog-trots and shotgun shantys. **1974** *Times* 14 Jan. 12/3 The American South is still unmistakably southern..grits at breakfast, blacks living in shotgun shacks.

c. quasi-adv. *to ride shotgun*: see *RIDE *v.* 1 m.

shot-hole. Add: **1. a.** (Earlier example.)

1745 CAPT. DURRELL *Jrnl.* 20 May in J. S. McLennan *Louisbourg* (1918) 177 We had several Shott holes in all our sides.

b. (Examples.)

[**1889** E. A. ORMEROD *Rep. Observations Injurious Insects* 94, I found that the injury [to the tree] began by a small hole like a shot-hole in the side of the attacked stem.] **1946** *Nature* 13 July 52/2 Dry rot..is the result of the operations of fungi, and not of insects—the attacks of the latter being usually discernible by the presence of small pin or 'shot' holes in the wood. **1972** *Gloss. Terms Timber (B.S.I.)* 17 Shothole, a worm-hole usually more than 1·5 mm and not more than 3 mm in diameter.

c. A small round hole made in a leaf by a fungus or bacterium; also, a condition in which such holes occur.

1897 [implied in sense 4 below]. **1902** D. McALPINE *Fungus Dis.* iii. 33 There is a very familiar appearance in the leaves of many of our stone-fruit trees, where they are more or less punctured with round holes, as if riddled with shot; hence the name 'shot-hole' applied to the injury. **1926** F. D. HEALD *Man. Plant Dis.* ii. 33 Some varieties are prone to shot hole whenever localized areas of leaf tissue are killed. **1946** H. WORMALD *Dis. Fruits & Hops* 143 The chief agent of leaf spotting in plums is the organism which causes Bacterial Canker... Eventually the infected parts are killed and drop out, leaving 'shot holes'. **1976** A. HELLYER *Collingridge Encycl. Gardening* 259 Small round holes appear in the leaves, a symptom which is sometimes known as shot-hole and was once believed to be a separate disease [from bacterial canker caused by *Pseudomonas morsprunorum*].

4. *Comb.*, as **shot-hole borer**, a small bark beetle of the family Scolytidæ, esp. *Anisandrus dispar* (cf. *SCOLYTID); **shot-hole disease**, a plant disease characterized by shot-holes in the leaves; **shot-hole fungus**, a fungus which causes shot-holes, esp. in certain fruit trees.

[**1890** E. A. ORMEROD *Man. Injur. Insects* (ed. 2) 331, I found that the cause of the injury was the 'Shot-borer' Beetle (as it is called in America).] **1916** *Farmers' Bull.* (U.S. Dept. Agric.) No. 763. 2 The shot-hole borers or barkbeetles burrow into the bark. **1968** *Oxf. Bk. Insects* 190/2 The Shot-hole Borer.., one of the Ambrosia Beetles, is found locally in southern England. **1926** F. D. HEALD *Man. Plant Dis.* xx. 511 The disease [*sc.* cherry leaf spot] is known by various common names, such as 'leaf blight', 'leaf spot', 'yellows', 'yellow leaf', and the 'shot-hole disease'. **1946** Shot-hole disease [see *ABSCISSION 3]. **1897** W. G. SMITH tr. *von Tubeuf's Dis. Plant* II. 463 *Phyllosticta persicae*... The name 'shot-hole fungus' has sometimes been applied to this and allied forms. **1906** M. C. COOK *Fungoid Pests* 131 A shot-hole fungus has been found lately, several times affecting Peach leaves in this country.

shott. Add: (Later examples.) Also **shat.** Cf. *SABKHA.

1898 *Geogr. Jrnl.* June 604 The shats, or salt lakes, of the south of Tunis are rather a disappointment to the traveller. **1902** *Encycl. Brit.* XXXIII. 482/1 These shats ..are, strictly speaking, not lakes at all at the present day. **1957** G. E. HUTCHINSON *Treat. Limnol.* I. i. 136 In north Africa there is a series of inland drainage basins or shotts between the Greater and Lesser Atlas Mountains. **1969** J. MAVOR *Voyage to Atlantis* ii. 46 Paul Borchardt. in 1927..placed the lesser island of Atlantis..a few miles inland of the gulf of Gabès in Tunisia in the region of 'shotts'.

shotty, *a.* Add: *spec.* of gold: in the form of small, roundish lumps. (Earlier and later examples.)

1860 *Mining Surveyors' Rep.* (Mining Dept., Victoria) Aug. 236 There were also some very good patches of shotty gold and small nuggets found in the vicinity of this nugget. **1929** E. J. DUNN *Geol. Gold* xix. 222 Pounds weight of 'shotty' gold..were washed from a dish of gravel. **1959** *Observer* 17 May 8/3 Odd old prospectors still fossick in the hills in search of shotty gold.

shoulda, shouldda (ʃu·də), repr. colloq. or vulgar pronunc. of *should have* (see SHALL *v.* 18).

1933 [see *JUNK *sb.*[2] 1 e]. **1943** C. HIMES *Black on Black* (1973) 194 Man, you shoulda seen them cats. **1956** 'E. McBAIN' *Cop Hater* in *87th Precinct* (1959) 77 The kid was a Junior... Nobody shoulda given him a reefer. **1967** V. S. NAIPAUL *Mystic Masseur* iv. 55, I shoulda get married long before now. **1978** J. IRVING *World according to Garp* xviii. 393, I guess I shoulda *knocked*.

should-be, *sb.* and *a.* (Later examples.)

1878 W. JAMES in *Jrnl. Speculative Philos.* XII. 14 The interest of survival..has hitherto been treated as an ideal *should-be*. **1885** G. M. HOPKINS *Let.* 24 Apr. (1938) 107 God grant it may not be..that the should-be receiver was dead. **1951** [see *IS *sb.*].

shoulder, *sb.* Add: **2. f.** (*straight*) *from the shoulder*: also *fig.*

1904 W. H. SMITH *Promoters* v. 103 You'll..be in a shape to talk business, right from the shoulder. **1911** R. D. SAUNDERS *Col. Todhunter* ix. 118 A man that talks old-fashioned American Democracy straight from the shoulder. **1926** N. COWARD *Easy Virtue* I. 10, I must.. have a talk to her... A straight-from-the-shoulder chat might make her see things in a better light. **1947** L. P. HARTLEY *Eustace & Hilda* xi. 182 That letter had been written straight from the shoulder, or the heart. **1963** V. NABOKOV *Gift* iv. 214 He subsequently wrote it right down, straight from the shoulder, in three nights. **1977** *Gramophone* Aug. 291/3 As to the power and authority, he takes Beethoven at his word when he sees an *ff* mark and lets you have it right from the shoulder.

h. *to weep* (or *cry*) *on* (a person's) *shoulder*: to pour out one's troubles to a person; also in phr. *a shoulder to cry on*, a sympathetic and consoling listener to a person's troubles.

1935 H. L. ICKES *Diary* 10 Feb. (1953) I. 292, I called Tugwell yesterday afternoon to tell him that if he wanted any shoulder to weep on, mine was a broad one. **1942** T. BAILEY *Pink Camellia* iii. 19 She likes to talk of her troubles and weep on people's shoulders. **1966** L. DEIGHTON *Billion Dollar Brain* xvi. 163 I'm always weeping on your shoulder. **1974** 'J. LE CARRÉ' *Tinker, Tailor, Soldier, Spy* xviii. 158, I asked 'What did he want?' And Ann said 'A shoulder to cry on.' Bill..wanted to pour out his heart, she said.

i. *off-the-shoulder* (attrib. phr.): of a dress, blouse, etc., that leaves the shoulders bare.

[**1813** JANE AUSTEN *Let.* 15 Sept. (1932) 322 Stays now are not made to force the bosom up at all... I was really glad to hear that they are not to be so much off the shoulders as they were.] **1952** S. KAUFFMANN *Philanderer* (1953) xiv. 232 She was wearing an off-the-shoulder white blouse. **1960** *Guardian* 5 Jan. 6/7 A golden off-the-shoulder evening dress of only eight years ago. **1974** *Country Life* 17 Jan. 106/3 Off-the-shoulder and square necklines.

4. c. (*b*) *shoulder of mutton sail* (later examples).

1880 *Harper's Mag.* LXI. 350/2 But the Hampton boat —a modified pink-stern, with shoulder-of-mutton sails on its small masts—was the 'abler'..to stand the exigencies of all sorts of weather. **1961** F. H. BURGESS *Dict. Sailing* 187 *Shoulder-of-mutton sail*, name given to the triangular Bermudan sail.

6. j. The edge of a road; *spec.* a strip at the side of the main carriageway on which vehicles may stop in an emergency. Cf. *hard shoulder* s.v. *HARD *a.* 22 b; *soft shoulder* s.v. *SOFT *a.* 27. orig. *U.S.*

1933 *Sun* (Baltimore) 27 Dec. 8/7, I..stayed well over on the shoulder. But..only one of the numerous cars.. bothered to move nearer the middle of the road. Repeatedly, I stepped back into the bushes and mud. **1942** *Short Guide Gr. Brit.* (U.S. War Dept.) 32 *Shoulder*, (of road)—verge. **1965** 'E. McBAIN' *Doll* (1966) x. 127 The road was winding and narrow... The shoulders were muddy and soft. **1979** G. SEYMOUR *Red Fox* xii. 185 The engine coughed and died, barren of petrol... They were about to stop on the hard shoulder.

k. A poorly resolved subsidiary maximum interrupting a part of a graph otherwise having a fairly uniform or smoothly varying slope.

1956 *Jrnl. Exper. Med.* CIII. 657 The existence of the shoulder in the survival curve..is unequivocal and constitutes evidence for a multiple hit killing mechanism. **1964** *Physics in Med. & Biol.* IX. 167 If the log of the surviving fraction is plotted against dose on a linear scale, after an initial shoulder, a straight-line graph is obtained. **1977** *Nature* 17 Feb. 660/2 The asymmetry evident in the low resolution scan is revealed to be a shoulder at $\sim 10\ cm^{-1}$ to lower energy than the main band which occurs at $1{,}528\ cm^{-1}$.

l. *Surfing.* (See quots.)

1962 T. MASTERS *Surfing made Easy* 65 *Shoulder*, the unbroken section to the side of a breaking wave. **1965** J. POLLARD *Surfrider* ii. 20 Take this one near the 'shoulder', the unbroken part of the wave reached at the end of a slide. **1968** *Surfer Mag.* Jan. 65/1 Positively the shoulder-hoppers paradise.

9. a. *shoulder belt, blanket, harness, pad, sack, -socket.*

1968 *N.Y. Times* 15 Sept. I. 46 A new safety seat, with built-in shoulder belts, is being developed by the General Motors Corporation. **1976** *Billings* (Montana) *Gaz.* 24 June 7-A/5 Ontario on Jan. 1 became the first jurisdiction on the North American continent to require the wearing of available lap or shoulder belts. **1973** A. H. WHITEFORD *North Amer. Indian Arts* 69 Shoulder blankets, worn by males, have checkered or tartan patterns. **1968** *Time* 5 Apr. 38 Padded roll bars and shoulder harnesses are standard on the Shelby Cobra. **1974** HAWKEY & BINGHAM *Wild Card* xxii. 180 Wallcroft unfastened his seatbelt and shoulder harness and got out [of the car]. **1868** C. L. EASTLAKE *Hints on Household Taste* iii. 80 The 'Cromwell' chair..is..copied from examples of the seventeenth century... Both the seat and shoulder-pad are stuffed.. with horsehair. **1904** *Sci. Amer.* 21 May 406/1 Every coat has a shoulder-pad of various thicknesses made of wadding. **1951** *Sport* 16–22 Mar. 14/3 A slight 'teacup storm' occurred in Yorkshire Rugby Union circles because a Leeds team were alleged to be wearing shoulder pads. **1979** R. PERRY *Bishop's Pawn* iii. 51 He ripped seams, split shoulder pads and carved up shoes. **1923** D. H. LAWRENCE *Captain's Doll* 232 Alexander was putting the bread back into his shoulder-sack. **1953** *Scrutiny* XIX. 289 He pulls out the picture from his shoulder-sack. **1921** D. H. LAWRENCE *Birds, Beasts & Flowers* (1923) 81 Shall great wings flame from his shoulder-sockets Assyrian-wise?

b. *shoulder-fired, -launched* adjs.

1967 J. S. TOMPKINS *Weapons of World War III* viii. 105 There is also a shoulder-fired descendant of the bazooka called the LAW, or Light Antitank weapon. **1974** *Times* 5 Mar. 6/8 Guards now are equipped with the General Dynamics Redeye infra-red-guided, shoulder-launched anti-aircraft missile. **1977** *Belfast Tel.* 22 Feb. 17/4 Our new Blowpipe shoulder-launched missile which is in service with the armed forces of both the United Kingdom and Canada.

c. shoulder-bag, a bag carried by a strap or straps slung over the shoulder; **shoulder board** chiefly *U.S.*, each of the two stiffened pieces of material worn at the shoulders of military uniform and bearing the insignia of rank; **shoulder charge**, a charge in which the shoulder is directed at the target; hence as *v. trans.*; **shoulder holster**, a holster suspended from a shoulder-strap; **shoulder-length** *a.*: of hair, etc., that reaches down to the shoulders; **shoulder line**, (*a*) a line drawn on the shoulder (of an object); (*b*) the line of a woman's garment over the shoulders; **shoulder patch**, a patch attached to the shoulder of a garment and bearing an emblem or insignia; **shoulder plane** *Woodworking* (see quot. 1954); **shoulder pod** [cf. TRIPOD *sb.*], a support for a camera that rests against the shoulder; **shoulder stand**, a position in which the body and legs are held up in the air and supported on the shoulders; **shoulder tab**, each of the two pieces of material worn at the shoulders of military or other uniform and bearing insignia of rank; **shoulder throw** *Judo* (see quot. 1968); **shoulder wing**, a monoplane wing mounted high on the fuselage but not in the highest position; usu. *attrib.*

1912 D. H. LAWRENCE *Let.* 19 Aug. (1932) 49 We walked from the Isarthal down here—F. and I—with our German shoulder-bags on our backs. **1960** L. DAVIDSON *Night of Wenceslas* ii. 32 She was wearing a gaily coloured cotton frock and a shoulder bag. **1977** P. THEROUX *Consul's File* 48 She sat down and threw her shoulder-bag on a side-table. **1949** J. STEINBECK *Russian Jrnl.* 20 The uniforms were without insignia and without shoulder boards. **1980** 'J. LE CARRÉ' *Smiley's People* xxv. 295, I saw no shoulder-boards, the guards wore plain clothes. **1930** *Daily Express* 6 Oct. 16/2 They exchanged good shoulder charges, and honours were about even. **1971** *Sunday Australian* 8 Aug. 3/4 Twice outside the motel where the Springboks were staying they were shoulder-charged by police. **1973** *Weekly News* (Glasgow) 11 Aug. 7/2 He shoulder-charged the door pushing it open. **1895** *Montgomery Ward Catal.* 481/2 Shoulder Holster, with breast and shoulder strap to wear under coat on left side. **1935** M. M. ATWATER *Murder in Midsummer* xxi. 193 Mr. Henry Smith..buckled on his shoulder-holster, weighted by his old six-shooter. **1973** 'I. DRUMMOND' *Jaws of Watchdog* xiii. 166 Sandro's own gun was in its shoulder-holster. **1951** Shoulder-length [see *CUT *sb.*[2] 16 a]. **1976** C. DEXTER *Last seen Wearing* xxix. 202 Long shoulder-length hair..brushed forward over her face. **1916–17** *T. Eaton & Co. Catal.* Fall & Winter 414/2 Semi-porcelain dinner set has..gold edges and green shoulder line. **1931** *McCall's Mag.* Sept. 74 A significant self-fabric cuff and a very notable shoulder line. **1979** *Guardian* 13 June 12/4 The best of this year's T-shirts..are loose with a dropped shoulderline. **1947** A. P. GASKELL *Big Game* 82 He recalled their first issue of shoulder-patches. **1970** N. ARMSTRONG et al. *First on Moon* v. 101 An Apollo 1 shoulder patch..would be left on the moon. **1935** N. R. ROGERS *Technol. Woodwork & Metalwork* I. iv. 56 The Shoulder Plane is intended, as its name implies, for trueing tenon shoulders (end grain). **1954** W. E. KELSEY *Carpentry, Joinery & Woodcutting Machinery* i. 16 Shoulder planes..are metal rebate planes with a narrow mouth and a low-pitched cutter... They are used chiefly for planing against the end grain and are specially suitable for hardwoods. **1979** A. B. EMARY *Woodworking* xxviii. 121 The bevelled portion of the mouldings can be made with a shoulder plane or a badger plane. **1963** D. BOTTING in A. Smith *Throw out Two Hands* 263 It was possible to make hand-held movie shots (using pistol-grip or shoulder pod) with lenses of longer focus than usual. **1981** *Birds* Autumn 18/3 With miniaturisation and the wide use of telephoto lenses,..the stalking technique evolved, using shoulderpods rather than tripods. **1956** KUNZLE & THOMAS *Freestanding* iv. 44 *Inverted shoulder stand.* Start from back lying and raise the legs and hips until vertical. **1977** 'M. YORKE' *Cost of Silence* iv. 32 Sarah was practising the shoulder stand upstairs. **1966** D. FRANCIS *Flying Finish* v. 66 Gold-braided shoulder tabs on his navy uniform jacket. **1956** K. TOMIKI *Judo* iii. 73 *Seoi-Iage* (Shoulder throw). **1960** *Oxford Mail* 10 Mar. 8/3 Milsom scored a half-point for a shoulder throw then full points for a hip throw and a stranglehold. **1968** K. SMITH *Judo Dict.* 186 *Shoulder throws,* those made from a standing position and using principally the action of the hands and arms. **1941** R. A. SAVILLE-SNEATH *Aircraft Recognition* I. ii. 15 Variants of the *high-wing* type are..*Shoulder-wing,* a type in which..the wing-roots join the fuselage at the 'shoulder', i.e. lower than the normal high-wing but appreciably higher than the mid-wing position. **1962** L. DEIGHTON *Ipcress File* v. 33, I noticed a twin-engined shoulder wing Grumman S2F-3. **1969** K. MUNSON *Pioneer Aircraft 1903–14* 149/1 The Type A was a single-seat, warp-controlled, shoulder-wing monoplane with a 50 h.p. gnome rotary.

shoulder, *v.* Add: **7. a.** Also *spec.* of a race-horse, to carry (a specified weight) on the back.

1939 *Country Life* 11 Feb. 156/2 Last year, when shouldering 10st. 2lb., he fell at Becher's Brook on the second circuit. **1977** *Western Morning News* 30 Aug. 11/7 The six-year-old was returning to the course of his previous success this season, and for that win was shouldering a 7lb. penalty.

8. b. *to shoulder arms*: also *fig.* in *Cricket* (see quot. 1966).

1966 *Armchair Cricket 1966* 111 *Shoulder arms,* an expression used to describe a batsman's action when he holds the bat aloft over his shoulder as he allows the ball to go by on the off-side without attempting a stroke. **1975** *Daily Mirror* 16 Aug. 28/2 Ross Edwards immediately walked into the next ball, shouldered arms and was leg before. **1977** *Sunday Times* 30 Jan. 30/3 The next ball hit Gaekwad on the pad as he shouldered arms.

shou·lderless, *a.* [f. SHOULDER *sb.*] Without a shoulder or shoulders, esp. of garments.

1928 PEAKE & FLEURE *Steppe & Sown* vi. 78 Keller figures two shoulderless sleeves from Meilen, which Schenk placed in the third or Morgienne period. **1963** C. R. COWELL et al. *Inlays, Crowns, & Bridges* vi. 62 Shoulderless crowns present fewer difficulties in fitting than those with shoulders. **1979** *N.Y. Times Mag.* 30 Sept. 68/3 Giorgio Armani..has put together a take-off on classic men's wear that may be the most significant look to come out of Italy this season: the 'shoulderless' suit.

shouse (ʃaus). *Austral. slang.* [Syncopated form of *shit-house* (SHIT *sb.* 3).] A privy.

1941 S. J. BAKER *Dict. Austral. Slang* 66 *Shouse,* a privy. **1951** D. STIVENS *Jimmy Brocket* 214, I seen that now as plain as a country shouse. **1957** 'N. CULOTTA' *They're a Weird Mob* (1958) 43 Yeah, chuck 'em ter the shouse. **1968** T. KENEALLY *Three Cheers for Paraclete* 84 I'd like some trees on it, pines and gums, so you don't have to see your neighbour's shouse first thing each morning. **1975** L. RYAN *Shearers* 98 Dewlap, who had been standing at the back of the ring, all alone like a country s'house, now sidled up.

shout, *sb.*[2] Add: **1. d.** *U.S.* Among American Blacks, a form of dancing accompanied by much loud singing, of religious origin (cf. *ring-shout* s.v. *RING *sb.*[1] 18); a song of the type sung during such a performance. Also *attrib.*

1862 in E. W. Pearson *Lett. from Port Royal* (1906) 27 As we walked home we asked Cuffy if they considered the 'shout' as part of their religious worship. **1908** *Sears, Roebuck Catal.* 199/3 *Negro Shouts.* Songs with laughing and whistling choruses. **1937** [see *praying band* s.v. *PRAYING *ppl. a.* b]. **1938** *Mississippi* (Amer. Guide Ser.) 24 Soon a woman leaps out into the aisle. She is 'moved by the spirit', she cries, and slowly, rigidly, she begins 'the shout', or if it is a Holiness meeting, the 'Holy Dance'. It is shuffling, intricate; her heels thud on the floor. **1955** KEEPNEWS & GRAUER *Pictorial Hist. Jazz* xii. 127 Stomping variations of rags, known as 'shouts', were the show-pieces most often used in competition. **1972** *Listener* 10 Aug. 187/1 A musical innovator with tremendous vocal power, he brings gospel and shout singing to the blues.

e. *shout-up,* a noisy argument. *colloq.*

1965 G. MELLY *Owning Up* ix. 107 Whenever one of us was describing to the other some drunken shout-up with a third party. **1973** *Times* 3 Nov. 11, I didn't mention it until it seemed to become a pattern and then we had a good old shout up.

2. For *Colonial slang* read *slang* (orig. *Colonial*) and add earlier and later examples.

1854 F. FYANS *Let.* in T. F. Bride *Lett. fr. Victorian Pioneers* (1898) 127 Do you forget the shout you stood—the shout for all hands? **1886** H. BAUMANN *Londinismen* 177/1 *It's my shout,* jetzt will ich euch traktieren. **1911** C. E. W. BEAN *'Dreadnought' of Darling* xxxii. 282 'Boys,' he says, 'help yourselves. This is my shout.' **1914** *Bulletin* (Sydney) 17 Dec. 44/2 The..bloke..ses t' me: 'Your shout mate.' **1954** S. MACKENZIE *Refuge* 16 Come up and have a cup of coffee—my shout. **1977** D. BAGLEY *Enemy* xxvii. 212 Honnister addressed the landlord. 'Hi, Monte: a large scotch and a pint of Director's.' 'My shout,' I said.

shout, *v.* Add: **1. g.** (Earlier example.)

1876 *Scribner's Monthly* Nov. 142/1 'Then why prevaricate?' Said he perversely, 'Now yer shoutin'!'

† **i.** To be loud in support of a candidate. Cf. ROOT *v.*[2] 1 d. *U.S. Obs.*

1875 [implied in *SHOUTER[2] 1 b]. **1907** *N.Y. Evening Post* (semi-weekly ed.) 21 Nov. 4 Federal office-holders in various Southern States have been dutifully shouting for Roosevelt.

2. c. *fig.* To indicate plainly.

1931 E. F. BENSON *Mapp & Lucia* ii. 30 Red-brick houses with tiled roofs, that shouted Queen Anne and George I in Lucia's enraptured ears. **1976** D. FRANCIS *In Frame* iii. 48 From laquered hair via crocodile handbag to gold-trimmed shoes she shouted money.

4. Restrict *dial.* to senses in Dict. **f.** To howl *down* or reduce to silence by shouts of disapproval. Also *fig.*

1924 G. B. SHAW *St. Joan* vi. 89, I know that there is no faith in a Frenchman. [*Tumult, which he shouts down.*] **1965** M. SPARK *Mandelbaum Gate* iii. 59 Freddy's thoughts whispered on, refusing to be shouted down by any other voice that might arise in his brain to hush them up. **1967** N. FREELING *Strike out where not Applicable* 36 Francis forces things sometimes by simply shouting her down. **1978** P. MOORE *Man, Woman, & Priesthood* xi. 171 This challenge may be not only right, but vindicated; it cannot, however, be ignored and shouted down.

5. Also *N.Z.* **a.** (Earlier and further examples.)

1855 R. CARBONI *Eureka Stockade* 68 You shouted nobblers round for all hands—that's all right; it's no more than fair and square now for the boys to shout for you. **1856** H. W. HARPER *Lett. from N.Z.* (1914) 10 The first person in New Zealand to 'shout' for me, which here means to ask you into a house of call and stand treat. **1873** J. H. H. ST. JOHN *Pakeha Rambles through Maori Lands* v. 82 Our friend set to work pumping him, and 'shouted' liberally till the old fellow's tongue was unloosed. **1916** J. B. COOPER *Coo-oo-ee* iii. 36 Passing that stage of drunkenness, they started to quarrel over the question as to whose turn it was 'to shout'. **1963** N. HILLIARD *Piece of Land* 32 'Going to shout, Horace?' Clarrie pulled out some change. **1981** *National Times* (Austral.) 25–31 Jan. 23/1 The tightwad..wouldn't shout if a shark bit him.

b. (Earlier example.) Also *to shout* (a person) *to* (a treat) and with indirect obj.

1855 [see sense a above]. **1906** E. DYSON *Fact'ry 'Ands* xiv. 185 He gave up beer..in order to have it in his power to shout the young lady to 2 s. seats at the Royal. **1940** F. SARGESON *Man & his Wife* (1944) 64 If he had a win he'd shouts us plenty of beer and cigarettes. **1964** V. M. GRAYLAND *Grave-Digger's Apprentice* xx. 119 If my luck's in..I'll shout you to the pictures tonight for helping me out. **1965** S. T. OLLIVIER *Petticoat Farm* vii. 98 'Mingy old skinflints!' hissed Jane. 'They could have shouted us an ice-cream!' **1977** *Caravan World* (Austral.) Jan. 35/1 On meeting an old friend a miner would shout him, not a drink as in other places, but a bath.

shouter[2]**.** Add: **1.** † **b.** One who loudly supports a particular candidate. Cf. *SHOUT *v.* 1 i. *U.S. Obs.*

1875 *Weekly New Mexican* 13 Oct. 2/1 The Carleton and Perea 'shouters', got up a procession with banners, transparencies and noise. **1904** *Rochester* (N.Y.) *Post-Express* 26 May 4 The canvass..was very thorough, Hearst shouters being busily engaged in every city.

2. b. In the West Indies, a member of a Baptist sect influenced by African religious practices.

1950 *Caribbean Q.* II. II. 17 The Shouters and Shakers ..may practise a pseudo Christianity strongly influenced by African cult practices. **1956** M. STEARNS *Story of Jazz* (1957) iii. 30 The northern religion did not make much headway except with a small group of converts to the Baptist faith in Toco, a village in the northeastern part of the island. They are called Shouters with some accuracy, for they generated enough excitement and noise to be officially banned. **1974** *Encycl. Brit. Macropædia* III. 906/1 Charismatic leaders frequently organize distinctive local variants of Christianity, such as the Baptist sects graphically termed 'Shouters' or 'Jumpers'.

3. Also *N.Z.* (Earlier example.)

1863 *Lyttelton* (N.Z.) *Times* 31 Dec. 4/1 Perhaps some of our readers do not know the extent to which the practice of 'shouting', or of inviting to drink at the 'shouter's' expense, is carried even here.

4. One who participates in a shout (*SHOUT *sb.*[2] 1 d); a gospel-singer; a type of blues-singer. *U.S.*

1867 *Nation* 30 May 433/1 A band, composed of the best singers and of tired shouters stand at the side of the room to 'base' the others. **1931** R. W. GORDON in A. T. Smythe et al. *Carolina Low-Country* 199 The shouters form a circle and proceed around and around in a sort of slow processional. **1946** R. BLESH *Shining Trumpets* xiii. 311 In barrel-house vein are his records..with vocals by Joe Turner, then an unspoiled shouter. **1976** A. MURRAY *Stomping Blues* ix. 169 Joe Turner..has long been considered the Big Daddy of traditional blues shouters.

shouting, *vbl. sb.* Add: **1. d.** (Later examples.) Now usu. in form *bar the shouting.* No longer restricted to contests.

1869 A. L. GORDON *How We beat Favourite* in *Poems* (1912) 140 The race is all over, bar shouting. **1897** *Nat. Police Gaz.* (U.S.) 26 May 7/4 It was all over 'bar' the shouting, but the youngster refused emphatically to give way. **1909** A. BENNETT *What Public Wants* iv. 54 If I wasn't sure that it's all over except the shouting, I wouldn't touch it. **1959** *Times* 12 June 5/3 In the absence of rain or miracles it was all over bar the shouting at Romford last evening. **1976** *Western Morning News* 25 Sept. 8/2 But if the Rhodesia affair is all over bar the shouting, can the same be said about South Africa?

† **e.** Loud support for a particular candidate. *U.S. Obs.*

1904 *Minneapolis Times* 29 May 6 Thus far most of the enthusiastic shouting for Gorman can be traced to the Gorman press bureau.

2. (Earlier and further examples.)

1862 E. HODDER *Memories N.Z. Life* 123 Among this class, going to these [public houses] and 'shouting'..is considered the acmé of pleasure. **1874** A. BATHGATE *Colonial Experiences* viii. 99 One of the greatest social evils in the gold-fields is the system of 'shouting'. **1911** E. M. CLOWES *On Wallaby* iv. 106 Of course, men still go 'on the bust', cheques are planked down, and 'shouting'—the Australian equivalent for 'treating'—indulged in till all the money is finished. **1963** *Evening Post* (Wellington, N.Z.) 10 July 13/5 Costs incurred by licensing trusts in dispensing free liquor or 'shouting' ostensibly for the purpose of encouraging patronage are under fire.

3. The performing of a shout (*SHOUT *sb.*[2] 1 d); a declamatory style of singing among American Blacks.

1871 in *Rep. 42nd U.S. Congress 2 Sess. Joint Select Comm. Condition of Affairs Late Insurrectionary States: Georgia* (1872) I. 306, I have attended what they call their religious meetings; and they have what they call 'shouting'. **1927** *N.Y. Times Mag.* 24 Apr. 4/1 The type of song used in shouting is peculiar and has had much to do with molding and changing spirituals. **1946** R. BLESH *Shining Trumpets* (1949) v. 109 The rhythmic style of singing which we shall call *shouting,* a style clearly derived from, or related to, the declamatory sermons of the rural preacher.

4. *Comb.,* as **shouting distance** = *hailing distance* s.v. HAILING *vbl. sb.* b; chiefly in phr. *to be within shouting distance* (*of*) (also *fig.*); **shouting match,** a loud altercation.

1930 E. H. YOUNG *Miss Mole* iii. 29 She must be within shouting distance of the rich old gentleman who was going to leave her a fortune. **1958** L. A. G. STRONG *Light above Lake* 11 This is not to say that..O'Hara was an angel, or within shouting distance of one. **1961** *Guardian* 20 Jan. 22/7 Different ways of making..thermo-nuclear weapons cheaply are already within shouting distance. **1977** R. GADNEY *Champagne Marxist* xiii. 83 I'll station two men outside... One will be within shouting distance. **1970** M. BRAITHWAITE *Never sleep Three in Bed* vi. 68 We would begin a full-scale debate on which way we should have turned. Soon it would develop into a shouting match. **1981** V. GLENDINNING *Edith Sitwell* xv. 189 Edith was able to field, in this shouting match, one impressive new ally—John Sparrow.

shouting, *ppl. a.* Add: **2.** *U.S.* Denoting religious sects whose congregations express themselves by shouting, esp. in phr. *shouting Methodist.*

1851 T. A. BURKE *Polly Peablossom's Wedding* 87 Forgeron was from that time 'a shouting Methodist'. **1876** J. BURROUGHS *Winter Sunshine* I. 23 About the only genuine shouting Methodists that remain are to be found in the coloured churches. **1941** W. C. HANDY *Father of Blues* (1957) xi. 158 My mother was a 'shouting Methodist'. **1959** [see *religio-musical* s.v. *RELIGIO-].

shoutingly, *adv.* Add: Also *fig.*

1894 'MARK TWAIN' *Those Extraordinary Twins* ii. 335 The new lodger, rather shoutingly dressed.

shove, *v.* Add: **3. c.** *intr.* Of persons: to depart, go away. Const. with advbs., as *off,* † *out,* etc. Cf. *PUSH *v.* 1 h. *colloq.* (orig. *U.S.*).

1844 *Spirit of Times* 24 Aug. 302/2 As we shoved off from Fort P. our boys made the welkin ring, and away we dashed down the Apalachicola. **1856** 'MARK TWAIN' *Adv. T. J. Snodgrass* (1928) 31, I shoved out for the Massasawit House. **1904** 'O. HENRY' in *McClure's Mag.* Apr. 612/1 When dark came we fagged 'em a batch of bullets and shoved out the back door for the rocks. **1909** J. R. WARE *Passing Eng. Victorian Era* 223/1 *Shove off* (Navy), to quit, go, flee, depart—from shoving off a boat from land or ship. **1916** 'TAFFRAIL' *Pincher Martin* vii. 105 'Ere, 'arf a mo'!..Don't shove orf. **1922** JOYCE *Ulysses* 591 Well, I'll shove along. **1936** J. STEINBECK *In Dubious Battle* viii. 133 Them deputies knew we was goin' to shove off before daylight. **1956** P. SCOTT *Male Child* III. ii. 206, I wouldn't dream of telling you to shove off. You're there by Alan's invitation. **1979** D. ANTHONY *Long Hard Cure* xiv. 113 My, look at the hour. I'd better shove off.

d. Similarly without adv.

1866 'MARK TWAIN' *Lett. from Hawaii* (1967) 43, I then took what small change he had and 'shoved'. **1884** —— *Huckleberry Finn* xl. 409 We just unfurled our heels and shoved. **1944** *Sat. Even. Post* 9 Dec. 82/3 Well, I guess I'll shove. Good-by. **1954** C. WILLIAMS *Touch of Death* vii. 61 I'm going to shove. I can get away. **1975** N. FREELING *What are Bugles blowing For?* iv. 17, I have to ferry you down to the office... Let's shove, shall we?

4. e. To put or place. (In *colloq.* and casual use without notion of effort.) Also with *up, down.*

1902 WODEHOUSE *Pothunters* v. 93 You might shove up the list to-night. **1927** W. E. COLLINSON *Contemp. Eng.* 23 At Dulwich..we plunked things down, we shoved down notes or we shoved up lists. **1938** N. STREATFEILD *Circus is Coming* vi. 76 He threw an envelope across to Santa. 'Shove yours to Mr Stibbings in there, and lick it up.' **1974** A. FOWLES *Pastime* ii. 12 Shove your coat on the chair.

10. a. *to shove* (*the*) *queer* (examples). Now *Obs.* or *rare.*

1859 [implied in *SHOVER^1 b]. **1873** G. W. PERRIE *Buckskin Mose* ii. 36 If I had been detected in 'shoving the queer',..they wouldn't have cared one red cent. **1915** A. CONAN DOYLE *Valley of Fear* II. ii. 189 This man Pinto helped me to shove the queer... It means to pass the dollars out into circulation.

e. *to shove it*: to depart; to desist from a course of action. Usu. in *imp.*, as an expression of contemptuous dismissal. Cf. *STICK *v.*^{1} 18 d.

1941 BAKER *Dict. Austral. Slang* 71 *Stick it!*, a contemptuous ejaculation. Also, '*shove it!*' **1956** B. HOLIDAY *Lady sings Blues* (1973) viii. 84 It wasn't long after I left that he told them to shove it like I had. **1973** J. WAINWRIGHT *Devil You Don't* 18 'What say we pick one?'.. McGuire said: 'Shove it. It's not why we're here.' **1978** L. STEWART *Same Time, Next Year* (1979) xiii. 145 If he doesn't like it he can shove it, but don't worry—he won't.

11. (Earlier example.)

1836 *Montreal Transcript* 29 Dec. 2/2 About one it [*sc.* the ice] shoved for the second time, when it remained stationary till dark.

12. shove-halfpenny: delete *slang* and 'gambling', and add later examples; now usu. in form **-ha'penny.**

1915 T. BURKE *Nights in Town* 126 She shot knife, fork, and spoon across the table with a neat shove-ha'p'ny stroke. **1942** *R.A.F. Jrnl.* 3 Oct. 5 Moving from bar to shove ha'penny table. **1969** *Listener* 20 Mar. 381/3 The Camley Arms sounded such a nice pub, with piano on most nights and darts and shove-ha'penny in the public bar.

shovel, *sb.* Add: **1. g.** *shovel and broom*: rhyming slang for 'room'. Chiefly *U.S.*

1928 M. C. SHARPE *Chicago May* 288/2 *Shovel and broom*, room. **1929** [see *LINE *sb.*^{2} 13 f]. **1938** *Detective Fiction Weekly* 23 Apr. 75/1 In Australian slang...a house is a 'rat and mouse' and a room a 'shovel and broom'.

7. a. *shovel-footed* (later example).

1836 E. A. POE in *Southern Lit. Messenger* Aug. 595/2 Not a shovel-footed negro waddles across the stage

b. shovel pass *U.S. Sports*, an underarm, forward pass made with a shovelling movement of the arms; so as *v. trans.* and *intr.*

1948 *News-Age-Herald* (Birmingham, Alabama) 31 Oct. C-5/2 Frank Tripucka..then shovel-passed to Sitko. *Ibid.*, Frank Tripucka..faked a handoff to Bill Gay then shovel-passed it to Sitko. **1976** *Honolulu Star Bull.* 21 Dec. H-1/1 Alabama trotted out such gimmicks as..an underhand shovel pass for a key 19-yard gain and an unbalanced line.

shovel-board, shuffleboard. Add: **2.** (Earlier and later examples.) Also, a variant of this game played on a court not necessarily on shipboard.

The usual form is now *shuffleboard.*

1836 T. POWER *Impressions of Amer.* I. 14 Shuffleboard, chess, and backgammon, with exercise and pleasant converse, will while away the intervening hours. **1851** J. D. LEWIS *Across Atlantic* 6 That ignominious game called shovel-board, which consists in stooping down and projecting flat slabs of wood at figures chalked on the deck. **1932** E. WAUGH *Cruise* in *Work Suspended* (1949) Papa is very good at the deck games especially one called shuffle board. **1967** *Boston Sunday Herald* 26 Mar. VI. 7/7 (Advt.), 500-ft. sandy beach, 3 pools, putting green, tennis, shuffleboard, supervised Kiddie Playground. **1977** 'J. LE CARRÉ' *Hon. Schoolboy* iv. 90 Sometimes she stayed for old-tyme dancing or a game of shuffleboard.

shover^1. b. (Earlier example.)

1859 *National Police Gaz.* (U.S.) 14 May 4/3 A 'shover' named Flynn,..obtained a quantity of 'queer' and went with it to Mrs. Beemer's house and left it on her table.

shover^2 (ʃʊ·vəɹ). Also **shovver, shuv(v)er.** Jocular alteration of *CHAUFFEUR. Hence (as back-formation) **shove** *v.*^{2} *intr.*, **sho·ving** *vbl. sb.*^{2}

1905 S. A. BARNETT *Let.* 17 Aug. in H. Barnett *Canon S. A. Barnett* (1918) II. xli. 192 Dick Batston had to leave us and we are waiting here till a 'shover' comes from London... Dick drives splendidly. **1912** *World* 5 Nov. 707/2 She can drive as well as any 'shuver'. **1914** *Professional Chauffeurs' Club Jrnl.* May 15/2 When Tommy, the bad boy of the family, has received the Order of the Boot..his fond mama..says, 'Let us make him a shuvver.' **1925** *Chambers's Jrnl.* Feb. 146/1 Joseph—our 'shover'—was in the back of the car. **1932** E. M. KEATE *Mimic* vi. 77 'Paulett come and shove for me on Monday... My shover's ill.' Timothy enjoyed 'shoving'. **1953** J. TRENCH *Docken Dead* ix. 127 Sir R. went out first to tell the shuvver to bring the car round to the front. **1974** E. LEMARCHAND *Buried in Past* v. 95 It was class, for one thing. His Dad had been shovver to old Mrs P's mother and father. **1976** 'J. CHARLTON' *Remington Set* xiii. 63 Rabbiting on with the Pritchards' shover.

show, *sb.*^{1} Add: **I. 3. a.** Also *to put up a* (good, etc.) *show*: to give (such) an account of oneself.

1934 A. P. HERBERT *Holy Deadlock* 265 They've got to run the thing as they find it; and I think they put up a jolly good show. **1941** 'G. ORWELL' in *World Rev.* (1950) June 41 Impossible to guess what kind of show the Russians can put up.

c. (Earlier modern examples.) Also *N.Z.*

1864 'MARK TWAIN' in Harte & 'Twain' *Sk. Sixties* (1926) iv. 141 Give him another show. **1866** H. W. HARPER *Lett. from N.Z.* (1914) 102 There was a general response: 'We'll be there, and give you a show', a bit of diggers' slang, which I found meant—'Here's your chance, can you use it?' **1876–7** 'R. BOLDREWOOD' *Colonial Reformer* (1890) II. xvi. 42 As he's a gentleman, he's bound to give you a show.

5. c. (*a*) (Earlier and later examples.)

1756 W. FAIRFAX *Let.* 26 Apr. in S. M. Hamilton *Lett. to Washington* (1898) I. 231 Prospect of great Wealth from his Share of a Copper Mine..which has a Show of much rich Ore. **1864** *Harper's Mag.* Dec. 60/2 A young farmer.. was eloquent upon the 'show' the new well had made. **1916** *Daily Colonist* (Victoria, B.C.) 29 July 4/3 The copper deposits which have been examined have not advanced beyond the stage of prospectors' shows. **1949** *Amer. Speech* XXIV. 34 *Black gold, crude, crude oil,.. show*, and *showing* are synonyms. **1975** *North Sea Background Notes* (Brit. Petroleum Co.) 19 Ten days later a more encouraging show was found at a deeper level, but it was two months before the company was able to announce that it had indeed made the first commercial discovery of gas in the North Sea.

(*b*) *Austral.* A mine.

1931 V. PALMER *Separate Lives* 186 He's sitting on twelve thousand since he got rid of his cobalt show, and he can't spend that here. **1942** [see *NEVER *adv.* 9]. **1948** V. PALMER *Golconda* ii. 9 During the war they had rehabilitated themselves by carting wolfram on camels from a show they had discovered on the Western Australian border.

7. d. *to put on* (or *up*) *a show*: to present a good appearance that conceals the reality; to put a good or brave face on something.

1953 B. GORDON-CUMMING *Gentle Rain* 140 'It was encouraging to see her looking so nice, wasn't it?'..'I expect she was putting on a show for our sakes.' **1960** O. MANNING *Great Fortune* III. xviii. 215 He had learnt to 'put up a show'. He had hidden his fears and uncertainties.

II. 12. a. (Earlier example.)

1816 JANE AUSTEN *Emma* III. xviii. 338 You were both talking of other things; of business, shows of cattle, or new drills.

15. a. Restrict *colloq.* or *jocularly* to senses other than those of an exhibition of works of art or a dramatic performance, and add earlier and further examples.

1830 J. CONSTABLE *Let.* (1965) III. 26, I have laid by my Wood, to enable me to pay some old and just debts, to Smith, to Woodburn, & others—which I shall have ready for the 'show' I hope. **1844** J. COWELL *Thirty Years passed among Players* xvii. 42/2, I consented to become his guest for a week, and 'show my show' in the town-hall. **1896** *N.Y. Dramatic News* 4 July 12/1 [The circus] well merited its title of the 'greatest show on earth'. **1912** W. OWEN *Let.* 23 June (1967) 142 Methought I was treating you to a Show at a Picture Palace! **1935** J. REITH *Diary* 4 July (1975) 121 This was a very good show, interesting people, plenty of room, and plenty to eat. **1963** *Listener* 31 Jan. 210/1 That these painters were not a handful of isolated figures was made plain by the Whitechapel show devoted to recent Australian painting. This show..was, however eclectic it may have been, still an intelligent reflection of one man's taste. **1978** *Lancashire Life* Sept. 89/2 My favourite Blackpool show? Unhesitatingly, I nominate *No, No, Nanette.*

b. *Mil. slang.* An engagement, battle, or raid; a war. Also *big show*, a major campaign. Cf. *DO *sb.*^{1} 2 b.

1892 KIPLING *Barrack-Room Ballads* 59 What was the end of all the show, Johnnie, Johnnie? Ask my Colonel, for I don't know. **1914** R. BROOKE *Let.* Dec. (1968) 644, I entered this show (Sub-lieutenant R. Brooke R.N.D. at your service) in September and by the end of the month was in a trench. **1915** T. E. LAWRENCE *Let.* 29 Aug. (1938) 199 This Dardanelles show lags all the time... The big show must go wrong or go right first. **1918** E. A. MACKINTOSH *War, the Liberator* IV. 129 'Oh, God,' he whispered, 'don't let us get casualties before we start the show.' **1924** J. GALSWORTHY *White Monkey* II. xi. 205, I should very much dislike being blown up..but I should still more dislike missing the next show. **1939** A. B. CALLAWAY *With Packs & Rifles* ii. 20 With less than a month's training I was on my way across to the big show. **1942** *R.A.F. Jrnl.* 18 Apr. 10 At the end of the show I flew to Mosul. **1944** V. G. GARVIN tr. *Gary's Forest of Anger* xxvi. 110 The convoy was strongly guarded... Scenting 'a big show', the three Zborowski brothers spent their nights prowling round the lorries. **1977** *Daily Tel.* 15 Mar. 12/6 He was there in '98, I think, for the Malakand show. **1980** P. FITZGERALD *Human Voices* ix. 135 The pale pink smoke of London's fires..reminded him of a quiet sector of the line in the last show.

c. In radio and television, a light entertainment programme; more generally in the U.S., any kind of broadcast.

1932, etc. [see *radio show* s.v. *RADIO *sb.* 7]. **1937** *Amer. Speech* XII. 101 *Show* is used to designate nearly every type of broadcast. **1949** [see *SERVICE *sb.*^{1} 31 c]. **1956** B. HOLIDAY *Lady sings Blues* (1973) xv. 124 If you're an American citizen and unless you go to bed early these nights, you're liable to see me on the late-late show. **1964** MRS L. B. JOHNSON *White House Diary* 22 Apr. (1970) 116 In a few minutes I got a call from Lyndon's office saying, 'Turn on TV and watch the David Brinkley Show.' **1972** *Listener* 22 Jan. 124/3 If we do get breakfast television, the chat show will flourish.

16. a. (Earlier U.S. examples); also with qualifying word (esp. *good, bad*); *to run the show* (examples); also *to run one's own show*: to be independent; *to give the show away* (earlier example).

1797 H. W. FOSTER *Coquette* 138 The show is over, as we yankees say; and the girl is my own. **1851** N. KINGSLEY *Diary* 29 Jan. (1914) 171 He got 500 dollars for his share, which takeing the show as we now have it I think was a plenty. **1879** L. TROUBRIDGE *Life amongst Troubridges* (1966) 152 Tanner [the maid] was tweaked up in a cap as our 'Aunt'. She rather gave the show away by dashing forward to open the cab door! **1900** W. S. CHURCHILL in *Morning Post* 12 Apr. 5/7 'Yes,' replied the subaltern laconically, 'shoulder smashed up.' We expressed our sympathy. 'Oh, that's all right; good show wasn't it? The men are awfully pleased.' **1922** 'R. CROMPTON' *More William* ix. 156 Life was a rotten show. **1927** E. M. FORSTER *Aspects of Novel* viii. 205 James..has..a very short list of characters... For so fine a novelist it is a poor show. **1932** *Sun* (Baltimore) 23 Sept. 1/5 Farm representatives viewed the decision as another victory for the banker element which they fear intends to 'run the show'. **1946** L. P. HARTLEY *Sixth Heaven* iv. 95 You made a mistake..to absent yourself from the 'rag'—it was a really good show. **1955** *Times* 15 Aug. 6/1 They wanted to be independent... The Sudanese people wanted to 'run their own show'. **1957** J. BRAINE *Room at Top* vii. 61 The accountants and the engineers run the show no matter who's in charge. **1959** *Listener* 5 Nov. 766/1 He..came back with the bowl empty, which was taken by his mother as a jolly good show. **1969** *New Yorker* 12 Apr. 115 The astronauts..like to think they are running their own show. **1974** D. SEAMAN *Bomb that could Lip-Read* xi. 92 It's a bad show, Dickie... Why didn't you go straight in to clobber those terrorists?

b. *bad* (also *poor*) *show!*: an expression of dismay or disapprobation. Opp. *good show!* = an excellent performance or production! fine! splendid!

1916 H. YOXALL *Jrnl.* 18 Sept. in *Fashion of Life* (1966) iv. 37 They intend to do nothing to provide us with battle hdqrs. Bad show. **1936** 'M. INNES' *Death at President's Lodgings* x. 187 'Poor show,' said Horace. 'Distinctly where we step off,' said Mike. **1940** 'GUN BUSTER' *Return via Dunkirk* II. xvi. 195 The Battle of All Time is about to commence. Probably shan't get back. Jolly good show, chaps. Jolly good show. **1956** J. SYMONS *Paper Chase* iv. 12 Transport definitely not laid on to time. Bad show. **1963** N. MARSH *Dead Water* (1964) v. 123 'Bad show,' he said. 'Apologise. Not myself.'

c. *the show must go on*: things (orig. a circus or theatrical performance) must carry on as planned despite difficulty, calamity, etc.; *to get the show on the road*: to get started (*colloq.*); *to steal the show*: see *STEAL *v.*^{1} 4 h; *to stop the show*: see *STOP *v.* 23 c.

1941 E. HOLDING *Speak of Devil* xvii. 281 The hotel business is like the theatre. No matter what happens, the show must go on. **1943** *Amer. N. & Q.* Jan. 159/1 The Show Must Go On..is still primarily a circus slogan, although it can certainly be regarded as an axiom, in a lesser degree, of any form of show business, including the theatre. **1957** J. BLISH *Fallen Star* II. vii. 88 They came trooping into the thawing shack...'That's enough,' Jayne said at last. 'Let's get this show on the road.' **1957** 'GYPSY ROSE LEE' *Gypsy* xxxiv. 309 Gertrude Lawrence, with a true show-must-go-on attitude had accepted my degree *in absentia.* **1961** L. MUMFORD *City in History* viii. 231 For the Roman the whole routine of the spectacle became a compulsive one: *The show must go on!* **1973** M. RUSSELL *Double Hit* ix. 67 Now we can start to make plans... There's no harm in getting the show on the road. **1978** R. HILL *Pinch of Snuff* i. 10 How'd she look at the end of the film? I've heard that the show must go on, but this is ridiculous.

d. *all over the show* = *all over the shop* s.v. SHOP *sb.* 8 c in Dict. and Suppl.

1947 'A. P. GASKELL' *Big Game* 24 Is he very shickered? Yes; he's all over the show. **1980** M. DRABBLE *Middle Ground* 171 The district's not what it was... Arabs, all over the show. Shocking, isn't it?

III. 18. b. *U.S. horse-racing.* The third place in a race. Freq. *attrib.*

1925 W. L. COMFORT in *Sat. Even. Post* 11 July 13/3 He had broken into show money this afternoon. Yesterday he had won and placed. *Ibid.* 124/4, I wouldn't back Black Ball right now for any better than place or show. **1944** *Sun* (Baltimore) 14 Apr. 14/1 Rougemont won by three lengths... So Bluesteel took the place and Sea fight, the favorite, got the show award. **1964** A. WYKES *Gambling* vii. 197 There is no 'show' betting in England. **1975** *Cleveland* (Ohio) *Plain Dealer* 23 Mar. 13-C/2 Hail to Springtime was moved into the show spot and Top of the Morn dropped to fourth.

IV. 20. *show field, -ground, jump, -ring, saddle.*

1843 W. DYOTT *Diary* Sept. (1907) II. 374 Both attended in the show field, and afterwards at the dinner. **1846** *Amer. Agriculturist* V. 333/1 The show-ground was located in the heart of the village. **1870** H. H. DIXON *Saddle & Sirloin* iv. 89 When they met in the show-ring. **1930** J. L. M. BARRETT *Pract. Jumping* ix. 94 Blinks.. admitted to having had a whole set of show-jumps..made by the local carpenter. **1931** *Times Lit. Suppl.* 29 Oct. 840/4 The chapter on The Hound, with its warning against over-estimating the importance of success in the show-ring. **1955** *Times* 4 July 5/7 The showground, extending over 166 acres,..will be fully occupied by the trade stands..and the livestock lines, judging rings, and the pavilions. **1963** E. H. EDWARDS *Saddlery* xvii. 126 The English show saddle, confined in its use purely to the show ring, approximates more nearly to the dressage saddle than any other type, but its design is directed at displaying the horse's conformation rather than giving the rider any assistance in showing off the action of the horse. **1973** *Country Life* 8 Mar. 654/2 Large assortment of B.S.J.A. Show Jumps. All brightly painted and bolted construction. **1976** T. HEALD *Let Sleeping Dogs Die* v. 100 'Judging of the Dog-lovers' League Dog of the Year will commence..in the main ring.'.. The crowds were already gathered round the main show-ring. **1977** *Western Morning News* 1 Sept. 8/5 This year a vast number of traders throughout the area will be displaying their goods in the large marquee on the showfield.

21. a. (Further examples.)

a **1855** C. Brontë *Emma* in *Cornhill Mag.* (1860) I. 480 To judge whether the acquisition now offered was likely to answer well as a show-pupil. **1869** S. R. Hole *Bk. about Roses* ix. 138 *Paul Ricaut*..is not reliable as a show Rose, expanding rapidly..on his arrival at the exhibition. **1915** W. B. Yeats *Reveries* 173 My friend, now in his last year at school, was a show boy, and had beaten all Ireland again and again. **1941** F. Thompson *Over to Candleford* xiii. 200 She was the show pupil of the school; good at every subject. **1950** Blunden *John Keats* 33 His friends..cultivated him with vague praise, as though they were raising the most scented, gorgeous show-rose ever exhibited. **1952** A. G. L. Hellyer *Sanders' Encycl. Gardening* (ed. 22) 159 Sweet Williams, Show-type—smooth-edged petals with dark centres. **1961** C. H. D. Todd *Popular Whippet* iv. 54 The exact type of brood bitch for which I was seeking in preference to the most brilliant show-type bitch.

22. show band, a jazz band which performs with verve and theatrical extravagance; **show flat,** a flat decorated and furnished for exhibition as an advertisement, usu. for others of similar construction (cf. *show house 2 b); **show-folk** (earlier example); **show-people** = *show-folk*; **show piece,** an item of work presented for exhibition or display; freq. *transf.*; **show-stopper,** an item (esp. a song or other performance) in a show that wins so much applause as to bring the show to a temporary stop; also *fig.*; hence **show-stopping** *a.*; **show trial,** a judicial trial attended by great publicity: usu. used with specific reference to a prejudged trial of political dissidents by a Communist government; **show tune,** a popular tune from a light musical entertainment; **show-window:** for *U.S.* read orig. *U.S.* and add earlier and *fig.* examples; examples; **show-woman** (earlier example in second sense); also, a female guide in a show-place; **show wood,** the exposed wood of the frame of an upholstered chair (chiefly *attrib.*). See also *show biz, *-boat, *-business, etc.

1927 *Melody Maker* Aug. 759/2 (*heading*) South African show band in England. **1933** *Fortune* Aug. 48/1 Ellington has never compromised with the public taste for..'show bands' combining music with scenic effects, low comedy, and flag drills. **1952** B. Ulanov *Hist. Jazz in Amer.* (1958) xiv. 162 The Cotton Pickers were best known as a show band. **1970** J. Wainwright *Freeze thy Blood less Coldly* 55 He could be corner-man in any showband in the country. **1962** *Guardian* 7 Feb. 8/2 Those show flats where colour seems to have been interpreted on a liquorice all-sorts plan. **1974** *Country Life* 14 Mar. 602/1 The first five-storey block of 20 flats is expected to be completed at the end of the year... A show flat is expected to be ready in the summer. **1755** C. Charke *Life* vii. 252 The very chairmen had something to say, by way of exultation, on the misfortunes of the poor show-folk, as they impudently and ignorantly termed them. **1853** *Diogenes* 9 Apr. 159/2 Here is a description of the President's inauguration costume, to which we call the attention of Tussaud, Springthorpe, and other waxwork show-people. **1954** *Encounter* Feb. 63/2 Arthur Helliwell..treats it [*sc.* society] as a kind of *demi-monde*, dominated by show-people and speculators. **1962** 'K. Orvis' *Damned & Destroyed* xii. 82 I'm showpeople. Well, anyway, I was once. I headlined in vaudeville for fifteen years. **1838** Dickens *Sk. Young Gentlemen* 52 He likes to place implicit reliance upon the play-bills when he goes to see a show-piece. **1885** [in Dict., sense 21 a]. **1928** W. de la Mare *Come Hither* (ed. 2) 773 The sampler..the show-pieces on canvas or linen of a little girl (aged six or upwards) to prove her skill and diligence with the needle. **1941** Blunden *Thomas Hardy* iv. 84 The poet John Clare..had become a sort of show-piece in a lunatic asylum. **1978** G. Household *Last Two Weeks Georges Rivac* ii. 23 He looked suspiciously international..a show piece to impress the foreigner. **1926** *Variety* 18 Aug. 63/1 The first half [of the programme] held two show-stoppers in the Dixie Four..who stopped the show..with their 'itch' dance finish, and Dave Apollon and Co., who stopped it, closing the first half. **1945** [see *gasser 2]. **1953** N. Coward *Noël Coward Song Bk.* 76 'The Stately Homes of England' was what is colloquially known as a 'show stopper'. **1960** *Sunday Express* 18 Dec. 14/3 A show-stopper of shimmering silver lamé. **1967** T. Stoppard *Rosencrantz & Guildenstern are Dead* ii. 50 *Rosencrantz*: I can't remember how I did it. *Guildenstern*: It probably comes natural to you. *Rosencrantz*: Yes, I've got a show-stopper there. **1981** *Times Lit. Suppl.* 20 Feb. 202/3 Despite the inclusion of..other operatic items, and the Handel and Mendelssohn oratio arias which Lind loved to sing, the real show-stoppers were the 'Bird Song', [etc.]. **1962** *Times* 7 Dec. 8/7 There are few show-stopping solos of any length. **1975** *Listener* 2 Jan. 25/3 The song.. is one of the few heart-seizing, if not show-stopping, moments in Western theatre. **1937** E. Lyons *Assignment in Utopia* (1938) iii. x. 370 The Ramzin affair..in my mind..figures as the classic example of the demonstration trial—those attributes which set the show trial off from ordinary trials..seem..sharply delineated. *Ibid.* 373 Sitmin..was the one whose young son had demanded his death... This was by now a standardized piece of business in important show trials. **1949** Koestler *Promise & Fulfilment* i. vii. 87 The Administration resorted to the eccentric and rather un-British expedient of staging several show-trials. **1966** M. Woodhouse *Tree Frog* viii. 63 The Russians had U2 sorted out... They were able to go to town on it, show trial, the lot. **1978** P. P. Read *Train Robbers* viii. 145 Because it was a show trial..many of the best barristers in England were retained. **1981** *Ann. Reg. 1980* 302 Jiang Qing constantly harangued witnesses and shouted defiance at the court—to such effect that she was forcibly removed on two occasions. Thus the trial was not equivalent to the Stalinist show trials of the 1950s. **1962** J. Heller *Catch-22* vii. 59 He was a short-legged, wide-shouldered, smiling young soul who whistled bouncy show tunes continuously. **1977** *New Yorker* 10 Oct. 177/1 The Brown band..opened up its offensive with one of those breezy, quickstep middle-period Jule Styne show tunes. **1826** 'N. Nondescript' *The —* I. iii. 30 Have you not noticed a *shew window* full of pictures, and a sign with the words 'visiting cards for sale'? **1855** 'Q. K. P. Doesticks' *Doesticks, what he Says* xiv. 118 Those.. ladies who used to perform their perpetual gyrations in the show-windows. **1914** 'B. M. Bower' *Flying U Ranch* 33 Where do you keep him when he ain't in the show window? **1958** S. Spender *Engaged in Writing* 125 The glass-making was a show-window of Venice. **1965** *Navy News* Apr. Suppl. 2/5 Yeovilton is the most suitable and convenient venue for show window air displays throughout the country. **1820** M. Edgeworth *Let.* 26 Dec. (1971) 231 A holy family by Leonardo da Vinci which the woman who shewed the pictures told us was by *Vincy* Ma'am... A cabinet brought from Italy by the 3d Duke of Beaufort as said shew-woman always carefully told us. **1848** Mrs. Gaskell *Mary Barton* I. iii. 37 Her beauty would have made her desirable as a show-woman. **1977** G. M. Hopkins *Let.* 15 Aug. in *Further Lett.* (1956) 147 Mary's photographs are of Snowdon, Cadair Idris, and Valley Crucis Abbey: in the foreground of the last is the show-woman Miss Lloyd in her green shade, a quaint old character. **1919** V. Woolf *Night & Day* xxiv. 335 While Katharine went on steadily with her duties as show-woman, Rodney examined intently a row of little drawings. **1909** Wells & Hooper *Mod. Cabinet Wk.* 368 *Show wood,* applied to stuffed chairs with part of the frame showing. **1921** F. Palmer *Pract. Upholstering* xii. 39 In some show-wood frames the whole surface is polished. **1958** *House & Garden* Mar. 5 The showwood legs can be polished to any shade. **1976** *Canadian Collector* (Toronto) Sept.–Oct. 16/2 The show-wood in this piece [*sc.* a sofa] is mahogany and the frame is birch.

show, *v.* Add: **II. 2. h.** *to show the flag*: see *flag *sb.*[4] 1 c.

l. To exhibit (an animal) in a show or display.

1854 *Poultry Chron.* I. 572/2 The best [birds] should never be shown more than once a month. **1976** T. Heald *Let Sleeping Dogs Die* i. 25 The best dog I ever had..went to a Count in Florence. He paid £3000 and never showed him.

m. To display (a slide, film, etc.) on a screen by projection for public viewing. Also *absol.* for *pass.*

1911 [see *film *sb.* 3 c]. **1931** B. Brown *Talking Pictures* xii. 290 Some of the first talking pictures to be shown in this country were from Fox Movietone News. **1942** E. Waugh *Put out More Flags* iii. 219 A film was showing in the Ministry theatre: it dealt with otter-hunting. **1964** G. McDonald *Running Scared* (1977) i. ii. 22 It was Sunday and there would be a new film showing. **1976** *Oxf. Compan. Film* 118/2 Local councils.. gradually accepted the principle that a film passed by the Board could be shown without fear of prosecution under the 1909 Act.

n. *absol.* Of an artist, fashion designer, etc.: to hold an exhibition of one's work.

1912 R. Fry *Let.* (1972) I. 357 I'm delighted that [Augustus] John wants to show. **1958** *Listener* 28 Aug. 310/3 Mr. Pooley, a young painter showing at the Hammersmith Gallery..is worth watching. **1960** *Guardian* 21 July 7/7 The autumn collections of the Incorporated Society of London Fashion Designers began yesterday... John Cavanagh and Lachasse showed on this the first of the three days. **1972** E. Lucie-Smith in Cox & Dyson *20th-Cent. Mind* ii. xiv. 486 Other American artists who showed there included Robert Motherwell. **1977** *Times* 24 Feb. 8/1 Emanuel Ungaro was showing in the hotel.

4. b. (Later examples.)

1853 Lytton *My Novel* III. x. xxiv. 217 The Great Commoner had, indeed, 'something to show' for the money he had disdained and squandered. **1976** J. R. L. Anderson *Redundancy Pay* i. 11 He had been earning quite a lot of money, but had nothing real to show for it... They spent his salary as it came in.

7. Also in film.

1963 *Movie* June 29/1 The early part of the film shows their reactions to the death of Toni's wife.

9. f. *to show a leg*: see *leg *sb.* 2 a.

V. 22. d. (Later example.)

1916 'B. M. Bower' *Phantom Herd* vii. 112 As to the break I made in getting those boys out here, you'll have to show me—that's all. **1976** J. E. Taylor in L. Wing *Early Childhood Autism* (ed. 2) viii. 209 He [*sc.* the autistic child] should not be shown how to perform, since this strengthens his dependence on other people.

g. Used as an expression of defiance or self-assertion. With ellipsis of obj. clause.

1894 Mrs. H. Ward *Marcella* I. i. ii. 28 'They shall see—I will show them!' she said to herself with angry energy. **1910** A. Bennett *Clayhanger* i. ii. 16 'I'll show 'em!' he muttered. And he meant that he would show the world. **1921** H. Williamson *Beautiful Years* 170 My aunt, what a riff-raff of new bugs, Spotty. We'll show 'em, eh? **1935** C. S. Forester *African Queen* vi. 116 They hadn't believed anyone would try to get down those gorges... Well, this'd show 'em. **1952** M. Laski *Village* xvi. 215 Never did I think I'd live to hear my friends making excuses for me... I'll show them, she thought, I'll show them. **1974** M. Babson *Stalking Lamb* iv. 32 Perhaps she wouldn't come back and collect her at all—that would show her!

25. d. *to go to show*: see *go *v.* 42; freq. absol. in colloq. phr. *it just* (or *only*) *goes to show*. Also simply *it just* (or *only*) *shows*. Occas. with indirect obj.

1926 F. Scott Fitzgerald *Great Gatsby* ix. 209 It just shows you, don't it?..Jimmy was bound to get ahead. **1937** M. Sharp *Nutmeg Tree* xiv. 182 'Do you care for Galsworthy?' asked Julia... Sir William replied that he did. Which just showed. **1945** E. Waugh *Brideshead Revisited* ii. i. 222 My wife's in a terrible way. She's an experienced sailor. Only shows, doesn't it. **1952** M. Laski *Village* iv. 68 An elementary school-teacher, that's what she was... Well, it just shows. **1977** J. Bingham *Marriage Bureau Murders* xi. 140, I was a little worried about you..but..here you are safe and sound, well, well, it just shows!

VI. 28. a. Also *transf.*, of a woman: to manifest visible signs of pregnancy. *colloq.*

1936 M. Mitchell *Gone with Wind* xxxviii. 681 Comforting herself..with the belief that she did not show at all when thus covered. **1957** [see *mistake *sb.* 1 d]. **1966** B. Askwith *Step out of Time* vi. 95 How the old lady knew, miss, we have no idea. Rose certainly hadn't begun to show. **1979** R. Rendell *Make Death love Me* iii. 25 In that field Christopher was conceived... Pam would marry before she began to 'show'.

f. Of an oil well: to give an indication of the presence of oil. Cf. Show *sb.*[1] 5 c.

1904 *Dialect Notes* II. 389 *Show*, v., to promise oil. **1977** *Times* 2 Nov. 3 Almost five years ago to the day, Beryl [*sc.* an oil well] showed.

g. In catch phr. *your slip* (etc.) *is showing* (cf. Slip *sb.*[3] 10, *4 c), addressed to someone thought to be unwittingly exposing a fault. Also in similar contexts.

1943 D. Powell *Time to be Born* v. 103 Pardon me, lady, your slip is showing. **1958** *Spectator* 1 Aug. 174/2 There were still standards, and hypocrisy, the homage of vice and virtue, was the duty of all public figures. But in a gratifying number of cases the slip showed and the shocked and gratified public learned that 'Anything Goes'. **1968** [see *credibility gap* s.v. *credibility c]. **1971** C. Fick *Danziger Transcript* (1973) 33 Your defense mechanisms are showing, Mr. Danziger. **1976** A. Miller *Inside Outside* vii. 83, I see in you a new broom, though your slip is still showing in places.

29. a. Also in weakened sense, an *ellipt.* use of sense 35 c, to put in an appearance, 'turn up'.

1864 Dickens *Mut. Fr.* (1865) I. i. xiii. 127 What if I.. take a look round?..None of you need show. **1907** B. M. Croker *Company's Servant* xxxiii. 335 'Gojar never shows by day,' explained Talbot. **1951** T. Sterling *House without Door* vii. 81 Big-shots like that didn't come to the police... The guy would never show. **1969** W. Garner *Us or Them War* xxxvii. 276 Jagger said flatly, 'I'm staying until she shows.' **1974** 'J. le Carré' *Tinker, Tailor, Soldier, Spy* vii. 56 She didn't show... It was the first time she'd broken a date.

d. (Later examples.)

1982 *Times* 13 July 16/1 Glaxo showed strongly, moving up 12p on revised profit forecasts. *Ibid.* 17 July 12/1 Mixconcrete showed very firm.

e. *N. Amer. Horse-racing.* To finish third or in the first three in a race.

1903 J. Ullman *What's the Odds?* 129 The customary limit of the handbooks around Chicago was twenty, eight and four, to win, place and show. **1936** [see *place *v.* 5 f]. **1968** *Globe & Mail* (Toronto) 13 Feb. 27/1, I myself..usually bet $200 to show, or $50-$100-$200 across the board. **1977** *New Yorker* 16 May 130/1 In the OTB betting shops..he paid three dollars straight, three dollars to place, and three dollars to show.

30. f. With ppl. adj. *to show willing,* to display readiness to please or satisfy. *colloq.*

Willing is sometimes construed as a noun, in which case the verb belongs to branch IV.

1957 *Loneliness* (Women's Group on Public Welfare) iii. 29 The older woman..must 'show willing' and be adaptable. **1959** P. Bull *I know Face* i. 11 My father wanted me to be a chartered accountant... However, in order to show willing, I did settle for 'journalism'. **1964** A. Wilson *Late Call* iii. 121 Luckily the poor creature was very willing, and there was one rule Sylvia always made—never turn off anyone who shows willing. **1973** J. Wilson *Truth or Dare* x. 121, I feel I've got to go, Claire, just to show willing.

34. show out. a. (Earlier *fig.* example.)

1839 M. Walker *Diary* 9 Feb. in C. M. Drury *First White Women over Rockies* (1963) II. 143 Mrs. W. on first reaching us seemed in good humor & I hoped she had made her a better heart. But at supper table & even before she began to show out.

VII. 35*. show-and-tell. *N. Amer.* A method used in teaching young children, who are encouraged to bring objects to school and describe them to their classmates. Usu. as *attrib. phr.*

[**1948** *Q. Jrnl. Speech* XXXIV. 361/1 Those who volunteered to speak during the regular classroom share-and-tell period.] **1950** *Amer. Childhood* Sept. 18/1 Woodridge Elementary School in Austin, Texas, along with many other schools in the nation, began solving this problem three years ago through a 'Show and Tell' period, conducted almost every day in the first, second, and third grades. *Ibid.* 18/3 Pictures cause a great sensation at 'Show and Tell'. **1958** J. E. Leavitt *Nursery-Kindergarten Educ.* xi. 235 The virtues of 'show and tell' are too often dissipated in either agonies of shyness, or frantic last minute panics at home to 'find something for show and tell'. **1962** P. Bracken *I hate to housekeep Bk.* (1963) vi. 62 The children might, at their Show-and-Tell sessions at school. **1980** in S. Terkel *Amer. Dreams* 112 No courses in show-and-tell and personality adjustment.

37, 38. See also as main entries in Suppl.

38*. show-through. *Printing.* The fact of print on one side of a sheet of paper being visible from the other side. Cf. *PRINT-THROUGH 2, *strike-through* s.v. *STRIKE *v.* 88.

1947 *New Book Faces* (Lanston Monotype Machine Co., Philadelphia) 3/2 The 'show through' which is the result of printing in heavy color on thin or semi-transparent papers results in a loss of visibility and thereby affects readability. **1961** *N. & Q.* Apr. 160/2 A comparison of the facsimile with the original has shown that the facsimile is not so clear, but it has an adequate definition and the show-through, which occurs on several pages, does not seriously interfere with the reproduction. **1971** *British Printer* Jan. 80/2 The show-through is slight enough to permit printing both sides.

39. show up. a. Also, an instance of this; an exposé.

a **1854** MILL *Early Draft Autobiogr.* (1961) ii. 93 In my father's article the detailed shew-up of the Edinburgh Review had been left unfinished. **1937** W. H. S. SMITH *Let.* 30 Oct. in *Young Man's Country* (1977) ii. 97, I am beguiling myself..by reading Sinclair Lewis's *Elmer Gantry*, a show-up of American Nonconformists. **1949** 'G. ORWELL' *Let.* 16 June in *Coll. Essays* (1968) IV. 502 My recent novel is *not* intended as an attack on Socialism ..but as a show-up of the perversions to which a centralised economy is liable. **1961** *Guardian* 9 June 9/2 One of those tough, sexy, ostensibly moralistic show-ups.

b. A police identification parade. *U.S. slang.*

1929 M. A. GILL *Underworld Slang* 11/1 *Show-up*, where suspects are viewed by the police. **1932** *Sun* (Baltimore) 12 Dec. 1/3 The authorities conducted a mysterious 'show up' today for De Larm..police endeavoring to learn whether he had been seen in the vicinity..at the time of the killing. **1949** *Penguin New Writing* XXXVI. 96 They were real cops though. I had.. to stand the showup..and to put in twenty days at Juvenile. **1955** *Sun* (Baltimore) 22 Nov. 3/1 Lyman Brown..picked Graham out of a 'showup' of seven jail inmates.

showable, *a.* **3.** (Earlier example.)

1813 F. BURNEY 15 July *Let.* (1978) VII. 157 It was most fortunate that bit was shewable, for it gave propriety to the Measure.

show biz. Also **show-biz** and as one word.

a. Colloq. (orig. *U.S.*) abbrev. of *SHOW BUSINESS.

1945 *Variety* 13 June 25/4 Big-league baseball already had rearranged its team travel schedules to a minimum. However show biz has done nothing about this yet. **1948** *N.Y. Times* 18 July 2E/7 Jack Pulaski... helped coin much of *Variety*'s lingo, such as 'show biz'. **1953** [see *IMPRESSION *sb.* 6 d]. **1959** R. LONGRIGG *Wrong Number* iv. 60 Got to extemporise in show biz. **1960** M. T. WILLIAMS *Art of Jazz* p. i, A strange branch of big-time show biz. **1960** *New Left Rev.* May–June 33/2 They have their 'Pop Page'..their key to Showbiz. **1971** 'A. BURGESS' *MF* xv. 162 A lot of science gets turned into showbiz as they call it. **1976** *Liverpool Echo* 23 Nov. 6/4 Blackpool remains..the heartland of Northern showbiz.

b. *attrib.*

1945 *Variety* 30 May 28/3 (*heading*) Cantor's Showbiz tribute. **1946** J. B. PRIESTLEY *Bright Day* viii. 243 Wouldn't it be heavenly if you could mix them up —.. the retired majors..and the Show Biz boys. **1959** *News Chron.* 17 Oct. 4/2 Skirmishes with showbiz brigands. **1976** A. DAVIS *Television: First Forty Years* 42 Many of the public had misgivings, for the word 'newscaster' suggested a show-biz American approach.

Hence **show-bizzy** *a.*

1969 *Listener* 9 Jan. 62/2 The first night..was a show-bizzy occasion. **1973** S. COHEN *Diane Game* (1974) xvii. 149 After the welcoming speeches and..show-bizzy, bouquet-throwing speeches, the stage was cleared. **1981** *Times* 20 May 14/5 Even more controversial, however, is Cardin's idea to make. Maxim's more showbizzy with a series of monthly soirees starring international artists.

show-boat. *U.S.* [SHOW *sb.*[1]] A river steamer on which theatrical performances are given.

1869 *Atlantic Monthly* July 85/1 The little steamer Banjo, a show-boat belonging to Dr. Spaulding, the manager of the Floating Palace, was advertised to be at Cape Girardeau. **1909** A. C. RICE *Mr. Opp* vii. 98 A new and handsome Show Boat will tie up at the Cove. **1926** E. FERBER *Show Boat* i. 13 Eager for entertainment as the dwellers were along the little Illinois and Missouri town,..they came sparsely to the show boat. **1952** M. ALLINGHAM *Tiger in Smoke* v. 88 Lighted buses crawling by looked as big as showboats. **1977** N. ADAM *Triplehip Cracksman* xii. 124 They were a mixed bunch.. drinker..showboat gambler.

show·boater. *U.S.* [f. prec. + -ER[1].] An actor on or manager of a showboat. Also *fig.*, one who performs (in other contexts) in the theatrical style characteristic of a showboat player.

1951 P. GRAHAM *Showboats* ii. 15 Green River..was in later years to become showboaters' paradise. **1952** *Times Lit. Suppl.* 4 Apr. 239/4 The show that Mr. Chapman, the first 'showboater', presented to the Mississippi Valley. **1968** 'G. BAGBY' *Another Day* iii. 45 'What was wrong with him?' 'He was a clown. He was a showboater. He had a big mouth.' **1969** *Wall St. Jrnl.* 10 Oct. 14/1 Some of the best umpires in baseball today are almost unknown to the fans... They're not the showboaters. **1977** *Time* Jan. 56/2 Streisand is a showboater, a sort of one-woman Hippodrome whose roots are in the brassiest tradition of the American musical theatre.

Also **show·boating.**

1951 P. GRAHAM *Showboats* vii. 66 The years 1884–1889 were important..to the growing institution of showboating. **1972** D. RAMSAY *Little Murder Music* 71 Maybe there's some other reason behind the recent tendency towards showboating. The fact is, there have been a lot of gimmicks lately. **1975** W. SAFIRE *Before Fall* VI. 384 The proposal was what Nixon would call..'showboating', presented primarily for its political impact in the States.. with little chance of its acceptance by the North Vietnamese.

show business. orig. *U.S.* [SHOW *sb.*[1]] **1. a.** The entertainment industry, esp. light entertainment (formerly, always with *the*). Occas., people engaged in show business collectively. Cf. *SHOW BIZ.

1850 T. FORD *Peep behind Curtain* vii. 26 This gentleman has been engaged..in the show-business, and is, beyond all question, the best. **1870** D. J. KIRWAN *Palace & Hovel* v. 65 I've been in the show business for sixteen years... I fust began jumpin', as a hacrobat in the penny gaffs. **1886** [see PERFORMING *ppl. a.* 2]. **1903** *Century Mag.* Apr. 819/1 General Grant..declined to remain in town for the occasion, saying that he had had enough of 'show business'. **1911** G. K. CHESTERTON *Innoc. Father Brown* v. 126 He happened to be picked up by some travelling show, and..got on quite well in the show business. **1936** 'P. QUENTIN' *Puzzle for Fools* iv. 26 He was crazy to get into show business; stunts and strong-man acts. **1956** H. GRISEWOOD in A. Pryce-Jones *New Outl. Mod. Knowl.* 426 The cinema and broadcasting to a large extent are part of what is called show-business. **1962** J. MCCABE *Mr. Laurel & Mr. Hardy* i. 28 He had a great opening. All show business on the British Isles came to it. **1978** M. MUGGERIDGE in R. Trevivian *So you're Lonely* 11 The Religious Broadcasting Department of the BBC..itself a curious no-man's-land lying between show business and evangelism.

b. In catch-phr. *there's no business like show business.*

1946 I. BERLIN (*song-title*) There's no business like show business. **1956** B. HOLIDAY *Lady sings Blues* (1973) vi. 62 It's like they say, there's no damn business like show business. You have to smile to keep from throwing up. **1972** *Guardian* 24 June 11/7 There is, as they say, no business like show business.

2. *attrib.*

1958 *Punch* 26 Feb. 278/1, I was delighted to see that Frankie Vaughan had been selected as Show Business Personality of the Year. **1961** *Radio Times* 6 Apr. 53/2 No..illusions about the permanence of show-business reputations. **1976** M. BUTTERWORTH *Festival!* xi. 187 Feature stories on the show business stars.

showcase, *sb.* (*a.*) (In Dict. s.v. SHOW *sb.*[1] 22.). Add: **1.** (Earlier and later examples.)

1835 F. LIEBER *Stranger in Amer.* II. ii. 64, I..found there..all the companions of my earliest youth, the show-cases..with their old Nuremberg prints. **1879** [see SHOW *sb.*[1] 22]. **1897** R. M. STUART *In Simpkinsville* 121 Old Dr. Jenkins stood behind the showcase in his drug-store. **1935** D. L. SAYERS *Gaudy Night* vi. 124 What a blessing I hadn't put the Folio Chaucer and the other valuables in the show-cases. **1952** P. WENTWORTH *Brading Collection* xii. 69 Round the sides there were glass-topped show-cases. **1970** J. S. HARDMAN tr. *R. Boulanger's Turkey* 201 In the showcases against the wall..are various glass objects.

2. *fig.* A place or medium for presenting (esp. attractively) to general attention (freq. in Theatr. contexts). Chiefly *U.S.*

1937 'M. INNES' *Hamlet, Revenge!* II. iii. 131 Scamnum is..simply a Crispin show-case, dukedom and all. **1958** D. EWEN *Compl. Bk. Amer. Musical Theater* 79 It [sc. *Walk a little Faster*]..deserves to be remembered if only because it was the showcase for..Duke's most popular song, 'April in Paris'. **1967** N. FREELING *Strike out where not Applicable* i. 7 Its park has been turned into a landscaped garden which is a showcase for the bulb industry. **1976** M. BUTTERWORTH *Festival* xi. 173 The entertainment world fell over itself to get into this, the biggest 'showcase' on earth. **1978** S. BRILL *Teamsters* x. 364 Gibbons' local was becoming a showcase of progressive unionism.

3. *attrib.* or as *adj.* Freq. *fig.*

1903 A. H. LEWIS *Boss* 189 He's no show-case proposition!..To look at him folks might take him for a fool. **1934** *Architect. Record* Sept. 189 Show case height for standard selling. **1937** 'M. INNES' *Hamlet, Revenge!* II. iii. 131 The Duke has a show-case role. He's an Elder Statesman. **1955** *Times* 10 May 3/5 The London Philharmonic Orchestra has broken out for the summer season with some showcase programmes. **1975** B. GARFIELD *Death Sentence* (1976) vi. 36 The First Ward [of Chicago].. included the showcase hoop.

Hence as *v. trans.* (orig. *U.S.*), to place in or as in a showcase (chiefly *fig.*).

1945 H. L. MENCKEN *Amer. Lang.* Suppl. I. v. 387 A few of its [sc. *Variety*'s] characteristic inventions will suffice: *to ash-can, to angel, to showcase* [etc.]. **1949** *Jrnl.* (Baltimore) 20 July 2/1 They showcase new acts, who want to be on TV. **1959** *Spectator* 14 Aug. 192/1 It [*sc.* the Festival Ballet] has show-cased any number of notable performers. **1961** *Times* 4 Feb. 11/5 An album which introduces a new verb to the English language. It has been recorded 'to showcase' 10 different bands at a *Jazz Festival in Hi-Fi.* **1982** *Time Out* 16 July 39/5 The film..showcases both sides of Young's music.

show-down (in Dict. s.v. SHOW *v.* 37). Add: **1.** *Card-playing.* (Earlier example.) Also **show-down poker** (see quot. 1901).

1892 W. J. FLORENCE *Handbk. Poker* 42 If a player miscalls his hands, innocently, and on the show-down has enough to win the pot, it remains his. **1901** R. F. FOSTER *Poker* 16 If the limit is ten cents only, and the blind is one, the game becomes 'showdown Poker' because a player will bet the limit on anything and everything. **1973** D. WESTHEIMER *Going Public* v. 79 How about one hand of showdown poker?..Low man does the job?

2. *fig.* Delete Chiefly *U.S.* and add: also, a declaration or trial of one's strength or position; a final confrontation, a reckoning (intended to be conclusive).

1904 F. LYNDE *Grafters* ix. 131 'You don't mean to say there is any doubt about our ability to do it?' 'Oh, no; I suppose not, if it comes to a show-down.' **1916** *Daily Colonist* (Victoria, B.C.) 9 July 4/4 It is quite time that there should be what is vulgarly known as a 'show down', and this 'show down' is what I have been endeavoring to bring about. **1927** *Glasgow Herald* 19 Aug. 10 An opportunity of 'forcing a show-down' concerning British flights in China. **1936** M. ALLINGHAM *Flowers for Judge* ix. 143 Salley has been stewing up for a row with his critics for some time and is spoiling for a show-down. **1945** E. WAUGH *Brideshead Revisited* 241 If he has a show down with the old gang, they'll just disappear. **1950** T. S. ELIOT *Cocktail Party* III. 161, I believe, Henry, if I may put it vulgarly, That Lavinia has forced you to a show-down. **1962** A. LURIE *Love & Friendship* xvi. 310 When it comes to a showdown, women stick to their husbands. **1977** J. CROSBY *Company of Friends* xvii. 113 Never had she told him her code name. Some things a woman needed—for the final showdown.

3. *Comb.*, as **showdown inspection** *U.S. Mil.*, a surprise inspection of kit. Also *ellipt.*

1920 in H. S. Duell *Hist. 306th Field Artillery* 4/1 First of numerous 'show-down' inspections for the missing 'Laces, shoe, russet, pair, extra'. **1928** L. H. NASON *Top Kick* 27 When we get back to billets they'll have a show-down, an' anyone that's shy, finds it on the payroll. **1943** *Yank* 2 Apr. 19 The Army custom of show-down inspection is unnerving. **1963** J. O. KILLENS *And then We heard Thunder* ii. 14 Showdown Inspection with all of your equipment spread out before you to be checked by the pink-cheeked officers.

shower, *sb.*[1] Add: **1. d.** A dust-storm: freq. qualified by a place-name. *Austral.*

1898 E. E. MORRIS *Austral Eng.* 115/1 *Darling Shower*, a local name in the interior of Australia, and especially on the River Darling, for a dust storm, caused by cyclonic winds. **1903** 'T. COLLINS' *Such is Life* (1944) 329 (*heading*) Wilcannia shower. *Ibid.* 331 The steady intensity of the shower augmented as I went on... The increasing broadside pressure, with the sand and dust, was becoming too much for the horses. **1933** A. B. PATERSON *Animals Noah Forgot* 36 The Bogan shower, that is mostly dust. **1949** *Geogr. Mag.* Feb. 373 Duststorms are called, in various parts of the country as indicated by the change in operative names, *Darling shower, Cobar shower, Bedourie shower* and *Wilcannia shower.*

e. In prov. phr. *I didn't come down in the last shower*, indicating that one is not inexperienced, or not so raw as to be easily fooled. Chiefly *Austral.*

[**1906** 'T. COLLINS' *Rigby's Romance* (1946) 256 *He* didn't come down with the las' rain. Pity that sort of bloke ever dies.] **1944** L. GLASSOP *We were Rats* 51 I'm awake-up, I am.. I didden come down in the last shower. **1951** F. HARDY *Power without Glory* 259 'It's no use lying to me, Arty,' John West said. 'I didn't come down in the last shower.' *a* **1966** 'M. NA GOPALEEN' *Best of Myles* (1968) 277 No damn fear. I didn't come down in the last shower. **1971** B. VERNON *Big Day at Bellbird* 135, I didn't come down in the last shower, and neither did you.

f. A group or crowd (of people). Usu. *derog.*, a pitiful collection or rabble. *slang.*

1942 G. KERSH *Nine Lives Bill Nelson* ii. 13 I've seen him with some of the lousiest showers of rooks you ever saw in your life. **1958** A. HACKNEY *Private Life* xiv. 139 That unit was an absolute shower. **1962** 'H. CALVIN' *System* xiii. 176, I bet none of your shower ever even looked at Challen and his mob. **1967** M. PROCTER *Exercise Hoodwink* xiv. 100 'Have you still got the same shower in your lot?' 'Mainly. One or two new faces.' **1973** *Observer* 1 Apr. 13/3 Some of the people who go out with the hounds these days are a shower... We can't have people turning up as if they have been wearing the same pyjamas for a month. **1978** L. DAVIDSON *Chelsea Murders* I. v. 29 It's a group. What I was thinking..the Manson shower.

g. A term of mild abuse used of one person as opp. to a group. *slang.*

1949 M. LEIGH *Cross of Fire* iv. 71 You bat-eyed, buttock-brained..shower! **1959** S. GIBBONS *Pink Front Door* ii. 23 Hasn't he [*sc.* a baby] lain down *yet*? He is a little shower. **1966** O. NORTON *School of Liars* iv. 63 I'm of finer stuff, personally. I don't know why I waste my time playing with a shower like you. **1973** 'P. ALDING' *Field of Fire* xv. 123 'You're a right shower,' said Welland.

2. c. (Earlier and later examples.) (Now the more usual term.)

1873 'MARK TWAIN' & WARNER *Gilded Age* xxxiii. 308 He has fell back on hot foot-baths at night and cold showers in the morning. **1930** P. MACDONALD *Link* xi. 218, I had a shower and rammed on some clothes. **1953** R. LEHMANN *Echoing Grove* 48 Must have a shower. I've been in a muck sweat all day. **1973** J. WAINWRIGHT *Pride of Pigs* 59 The bathroom..was small, but lush..with..a bidet and a corner shower.

e. *N.Z.* (See quot. 1943.)

1943 J. A. W. BENNETT in *Amer. Speech* XVIII. 86 A *shower* is..a light decorated covering spread over cups and saucers set out on a tray or table. **1957** J. FRAME *Owls do Cry* I. vi. 24 Parcels from the handwork sale, tablerunners and tea-showers in lazy-daisy and chain and shadow stitch. **1967** F. SARGESON *Hangover* xiv. 108 All was out of sight beneath a large and snowy fabric..—the kind of gossamer thing he could remember his mother had coveted many years ago in a shop window and described as a shower

3. b. An abundance of gifts of a similar kind presented by guests at a party to celebrate esp. a wedding or birth; a party given for this purpose. Also *attrib.* Also as second element in *kitchen shower* s.v. *KITCHEN *sb.* 7, *linen shower* s.v. *LINEN *sb.* 5, *wedding shower*, etc. *U.S.*

1904 *Grand Rapids* (Michigan) *Even. Press* 22 June 4 The 'shower parties' that through mistaken hospitality the wedded couple are forced to attend. **1926** *Publishers' Weekly* 26 June 2031/1 First comes June, then the showers, the wedding and after the honeymoon the settling down to a home life. **1949** *Los Angeles Times Home Mag.* 8 May 14/3 Wedding showers..are a particularly warmhearted American custom. **1958** *Even. Standard* 10 Apr. 8/2 A shower..is really a gift-giving party centred round a luncheon, tea or supper party. **1978** J. CARROLL *Mortal Friends* IV. ii. 394 She didn't explain, but implied that she wanted to discuss her trousseau and her silver and china patterns and the sort of showers she would want.

4. b. *Physics.* A number of high-energy particles appearing together; *spec.* a group generated in the atmosphere by cosmic radiation.

1933 *Proc. R. Soc.* A. CXXXIX. 702 Particles of great energy are thrown backwards in a direction nearly opposite to that of the incident shower. **1947** *Sci. News* IV. 125 Sixty-five Geiger-Muller counters have been used to follow the direction of some of the rays and establish the width of one shower. **1966** *McGraw-Hill Encycl. Sci. & Technol.* III. 498/1 The electrons and photons of such showers are referred to as the soft component of the atmospheric (secondary) cosmic rays, reaching a maximum intensity at an atmospheric depth of 150–200 g/cm². **1977** J. NARLIKAR *Struct. Universe* iii. 99 These showers contain particles produced after the cosmic rays have interacted with the atoms of the atmosphere.

6. *shower-cap, -coat, shoe*; **shower box** *N.Z.*, = next; **shower cubicle**, a cubicle containing a shower bath; **shower curtain**, a waterproof curtain separating the shower-bath from the rest of the room; **shower head**, a rose or nozzle from which the water issues in a shower-bath; **shower-room**, a room housing one or more shower-baths; **shower stall** *U.S.* = *shower cubicle* above; **shower unit**, a shower-bath or the principal apparatus of a shower-bath.

1965 F. SARGESON *Memoirs of Peon* vii. 201 Beyond that a shower-box of such microscopic dimensions. **1977** *N.Z. Herald* 5 Jan. 2–16/8 (Advt.), Must be good value, with..shower box, basement garage plus carport. **1964** *Punch* 19 Feb. 289/1 Shower-cap and bath-towel. **1972** R. K. SMITH *Ransom* III. 125 She..stepped into the shower, remembering only at the last minute to slip on a shower cap. **1964** *Punch* 14 Oct. p. xiii, Rainwear shop ..includes velvet showercoats. **1976** *Evening Standard* 29 Dec. (Advt.), Quelrayn showercoats, fleecey lined. **1966** P. O'DONNELL *Sabre-Tooth* iii. 56 She..padded into the big shower-cubicle. **1938** L. BEMELMANS *Life Class* II. iv. 158 He was inside his shower-curtain, whistling. **1974** HAWKEY & BINGHAM *Wild Card* xviii. 145 She pulled aside the shower curtains and leaned out. **1967** *Gloss. Sanitation Terms* (*B.S.I.*) 44 *Shower head*, a water fitting, for use in a shower bath, from which water issues as a film or spray. **1978** R. NIXON *Mem.* 369 The shower in the President's private bathroom in the Residence.. consisted of half a dozen different jets and showerheads. **1939** 'E. QUEEN' *Mind Over Matter* in *Blue Book* Oct. 21/2 The crowd was so dense it overflowed into the adjoining shower-room. **1951** *Good Housek. Home Encycl.* 20/2 The ideal is of course to have a separate 'shower room'. **1965** F. SARGESON *Memoirs of Peon* iv. 90 He..was washing his hands at a basin in the far corner of the shower-room. **1975** W. CRAIG *Strasbourg Legacy* (1976) i. 8 Hoess, the commandant at Auschwitz,..refused to take credit for killing three million inmates. He had been on leave of absence while a portion of them died in the shower rooms. **1960** *Amer. Speech* XXV. 264 From the verb *edewa* [*sc.* 'come here'], sandals or shower shoes were generally called *edewa shoes*. **1978** *Sat. Even. Post* July/Aug. 105/1 (Advt.), Swim sneaks. All-rubber bathing and shower shoes. Sure-footed protection on rocks, decks, or shower floors. **1956** 'E. MCBAIN' *Cop Hater* (1958) ix. 81 The café still served as a sort of no-man's-land..served the same purpose as the shower stall does in a honeymoon suite. **1975** J. F. BURKE *Death Trick* (1976) ii. 12 He took a quick look in the bathroom, noted that the shower stall was wet. **1973** *Times* 15 Dec. 3/1 (Advt.), Shower Units, Taps, Mixers, Splashbacks.

shower, *v.* Add: **4. b.** *intr.* To have a shower-bath. Rarely *refl.* or *trans.*, to give (oneself or someone) a shower-bath.

1930 U. PARROTT *Strangers may Kiss* 196 He..asked if he could do anything helpful about dinner, and when she said, 'no', went to shower himself. **1939** R. CHANDLER *Big Sleep* xxii. 213, I shaved and showered and dressed. **1948** *Sun* (Baltimore) 1 Oct. 15/4 Jockeys..had to shower before donning silks for their next riding assignment. **1956** K. HULME *Nun's Story* viii. 128 Time to shower and put on a fresh guimpe. **1966** T. PYNCHON *Crying of Lot 49* v. 115 The executive undressed, showered and hung his suit out on the line to dry. **1977** *Listener* 7 Apr. 446/2 The condemned man..will have been showered and then been dressed in his brown burial suit. **1978** R. LUDLUM *Holcroft Covenant* xiii. 153 Holcroft showered, shaved, put the soiled clothes in a hamper outside the door, and called the car-rental agency.

showered *ppl. a.*, also, having had a shower-bath.

1953 A. UPFIELD *Murder must Wait* xxiv. 209 Shaved showered and dressed, Boney sat at his desk. **1971** D. E. WESTLAKE *I gave at Office* (1972) 139 Dressed in..new clothes..showered, fed beef stew and beer, my basic optimism..began slowly to rise.

shower-bath. Add: **b.** Also in *fig.* phr. *to pull the string of the shower-bath*, to cause (something concealed) to be released or made known suddenly. *colloq. rare.*

1928 KIPLING *Limits & Renewals* (1932) 20 If I pull the string of the shower-bath in the papers..Castorley might go off his veray parfit gentil nut. **1937** V. WOOLF *Years* 441 Why can't he flow? Why can't he pull the string of the shower bath? Why's it all locked up, refrigerated? Because he's a priest, a mystery monger.

show·erproof, *a.* (*sb.*) [f. SHOWER *sb.*¹ + PROOF *a.*, after *rainproof*, etc.] **1.** Resistant to light rain.

1895 [in Dict. s.v. SHOWER *sb.* 6]. **1907** *Army & Navy Stores Catal.* 751 A Large Variety of Showerproof Garments in all the Newest Shapes. **1923** *T. Eaton & Co. Catal.* Spring & Summer 214/4 There is no coat more popular than the English Gabardine. It is stylish, light in weight, yet firm in the weave, making it showerproof. **1960** *Farmer & Stockbreeder* 9 Feb. Suppl. 5/2 (Advt), Showerproof coat..is in a simulated leather material. **1969** A. J. HALL *Stand. Handbk. Textiles* (ed. 7) v. 333 Silicones ..are now much used for making textile fabrics showerproof. **1973** *Times* 9 Apr. 6/1 Within the trade, 'showerproof' apparently means only that the garment will not soak through at the first hint of drizzle.

2. As *sb.*, a showerproof garment, esp. a raincoat.

1972 *Guardian* 6 June 13/3 Showerproofs will stand up to short sharp showers... But they are not for the drenching downpour. **1974** M. BIRMINGHAM *You can help Me* i. 14 A slight girl in a short off-white shower-proof, a crimson scarf at her neck.

Hence as *v. trans.*, to render showerproof; **show·erproofed** *ppl. a.*, **show·erproofing** *vbl. sb.* and *ppl. a.*

1933 *Dyer* 28 Apr. 450/3 Where a shower proofing effect is desired, many of the difficulties..are less in evidence. **1951** *Good Housek. Home Encycl.* 314/2 It is sometimes advisable to showerproof outer garments. **1958** *Vogue* Apr. 104 Reversible coat in showerproofed poplin. **1962** J. T. MARSH *Self-Smoothing Fabrics* ix. 123 With urea-formaldehyde and Velan..the latter can act as a catalyst as well as the shower-proofing agent or softener. **1970** *UK Trade Names* 73/3 Marriner Handknitting Wools..Halyard showerproofed, nylonised, chunky. **1973** *Country Life* 23 Aug. 529/1 Alligator are still shower-proofing melton cloth.

show·girl. [SHOW *sb.*¹] **1. a.** An actress whose role is decorative rather than histrionic.

1836 G. SOANE (*title*) Lilian, the show girl. *Ibid.* (Duncombe ed.) I. ix. 8 The tinsel dress of the poor show girl. **1903** 'C. E. MERRIMAN' *Lett. from Son* xv. 208 Not quite all the modern Venuses have been corralled for the 'show-girl' department of musical comedy. **1923** A. TRAIN *Children's Children* xv. 192 He found it hard to believe that she was an actress, and a show-girl at that. **1936** J. BEYNON *Planet Plane* viii. 73 Give a show-girl smile, and everyone is only too glad to have you along. **1960** 'N. SHUTE' *Trustee from Toolroom* i. 5 She had gone with a party of show girls..to the Queen's Hotel after the performance. **1977** W. M. SPACKMAN *Armful of Warm Girl* 38 A leathery cousin of his own who when divorced had set up this show girl in a little flat.

b. *transf.* A mannequin.

1929 *Punch* 17 Apr. 444/3 Not the least interesting thing about these parades is that among the show-girls are many well-known titled heiresses, doing it purely for cigarette-money. **1936** J. B. PRIESTLEY *They Walk in City* i. 16 Manniekin. One o' them show girls in the big shops.

2. A girl in charge of a booth at a fair. *rare.*

1912 A. BENNETT *Matador of Five Towns* 91 The showmen and the showgirls and the showboys were titivating their booths.

show house. Add: **2. b.** A house specially finished for exhibition as an advertisement, usu. for others of similar construction (on a housing estate). Also *fig.* Cf. *show flat* s.v. *SHOW *sb.*¹ 22.

1962 *Listener* 15 Nov. 799/1 It [*sc.* the Labour Party] wished, as it were, to paddle its own canoe—to build in Britain a show-house of democratic socialism which the rest of Europe might inspect and then draw the lesson. **1963** *Times* 9 May 9/4 The first showhouse of a new private development which will ultimately provide 800 low-cost homes was opened here today. **1970** *Times* 4 Mar. 15/1 (Advt.), Don't miss the 'House and Garden' showhouse. **1974** *Country Life* 19 Dec. Suppl. 19 Family houses to be constructed... Showhouse available for visiting. **1978** J. SHERWOOD *Limericks of Lachasse* iii. 34 Frau Hoffmann's got the place looking like a show house in an exhibition.

3. A building used for staging theatrical performances; a travelling theatre.

1920 D. H. LAWRENCE *Lost Girl* vi. 105 A certain wooden show-house..an old travelling theatre. **1930** I. GOLDBERG *Tin Pan Alley* 217 The showhouses, too.. are taxed for this privilege, on the basis of their seating capacity.

showing, *vbl. sb.* Add: **1. b.** *showing-off* (later examples). Also with *up*.

1887 'F. ANSTEY' in *Graphic* 31 Dec. 727/3 He was annoyed with them for what he considered was 'showing off'. **1923** 'K. MANSFIELD' *Doves' Nest* 143 She detected that morning just the very faintest boyish showing off. **1962** N. STREATFEILD *Apple Bough* xviii. 255 Wolfgang put on his showing-off voice... 'I'm starring in this new picture.' **1973** J. PATRICK *Glasgow Gang Observed* vi. 64 Tim summed up..the boy's loss of face: 'Whit a showin' up in front o' aw the boays.'

d. *Cinemat.* and *Television.* The projection of a film on to a screen; the exhibition or broadcasting of a film. Also, an instance of this.

1947 *Ann. Reg. 1946* 376 British films..have brought $8,000,000 back to this country in 1946 from their American showings. **1967** *Listener* 6 July 15/1 The first London showings of..*New Faces* filled a cinema in Tooting with a stream of unaccustomed patrons. **1972** 'E. FERRARS' *Breath of Suspicion* iii. 45 They had arrived just as the earlier showing of the film was ending.

e. A public exhibition of the work of an artist or fashion designer; an art or fashion show.

1967 'T. WELLS' *Dead by Light of Moon* (1968) i. 8 Wouldn't you know something like this would happen at my first important showing? All the big art critics here, and somebody has to jinx the lights! **1969** 'H. PENTECOST' *Girl Watcher's Funeral* (1970) III. i. 136 It's about my showing on Friday... The fashion writers and the trade journals haven't given me much of a play. **1982** *Times* 3 Aug. 6/1 A decade or so ago, the couture salons of Paris were filled with American store buyers. At the showings this week, there weren't any store buyers.

8. a. Delete † and read *Obs.* exc. *Hist.* (Later examples.)

1859 GEO ELIOT *Adam Bede* III. l. 224 It is a vain thought to flee from the work that God appoints us... But now, I believe, I have a clear showing that my work lies elsewhere. **1978** F. BEER *Julian of Norwich's Revelations* 28 These four shewings seem without question to fall into the first of Julian's 'thre partyes'.

c. = SHOW *sb.*¹ 5 c.

1926 *Daily Colonist* (Victoria, B.C.) 28 July 7/2 The work now in progress at the property consists in the stripping downwards of the showings in these workings, which will afford..an idea of the character of the ore showings over a depth of 900 feet. **1977** J. B. HILTON *Dead-Nettle* ii. 20 'I'll drive deep. Happen there's another seam.' 'Then your first job is to collect your showing.'

showing, *ppl. a.* Add: **4.** With advbs., as *showing-up*. *rare.*

a **1941** V. WOOLF *New Dress* in *Haunted House* (1943) 49 The looking-glass..that dreadfully showing-up blue pool.

show-jumping, *vbl. sb.* [SHOW *sb.*¹] Competitive jumping on horseback over a prepared course of hurdles or show jumps (also with horse as subj.).

1929 G. BROOKE *Way of Man with Horse* xvii. 235 Show jumping is a thing apart from steeplechasing... Riding over the ordinary English show-jumping course,.. necessitates a horse that will not rush. **1936** [see *show-jumper* below]. **1958** S. WILLCOX *Three Days Running* xii. 141 Chips led after the dressage and did a clear round of show-jumping. **1963** E. H. EDWARDS *Saddlery* xvi. 121 Recently there has been much correspondence as to whether..the National Hunt jockeys, should employ a saddle incorporating the features of a show-jumping saddle and so conform to something approaching a show-jumping seat. **1973** *Country Life* 13 Sept. 697/1 The second fence, to him, was simply a show jumping fence.

Hence [as a back-formation] **show-jump** *v. intr.*, to compete in show-jumping; **show jumper**, a horse or rider that competes in show-jumping competitions.

1929 G. BROOKE *Way of Man with Horse* xvii. 236 A large percentage of show jumpers are half-bred horses. **1936** P. RODZIANKO *Mod. Horsemanship* xi. 193 A horse that has hunted is usually more successful as a show jumper than a horse that has never hunted... Hunting helps show jumping. **1943** R. S. SUMMERHAYS *Elements of Riding* (ed. 2) xix. 91 The method I have described is universally accepted as being the true way to show-jump. **1954** I. TOPTANI *Mod. Show Jumping* ii. 41 No normally trained show jumper will make for every single jump it encounters on its way. **1966** M. CATTO *Bird on Wing* iii. 58 I've show-jumped at the Tivoli. **1974** *Radio Times* 14 Mar. 4/2 Olympic silver medallist show jumper Ann Moore. **1977** N. MARSH *Last Ditch* v. 145 Dulce fancied it, though. Thought she'd make a show-jumper of it. **1980** 'E. ANTHONY' *Defector* iii. 69 She used to show-jump as a teenager.

showman. Add: **1. b.** Also *transf.* (in sports, politics, etc.), one who performs with a display of style or panache.

1964 *Guardian* 2 Mar. 7/6 There's two kinds of workers in the game, shooters and showmen. The shooter's the real wrestler... The showman's in there to make a splash, do the theatricals. **1967** C. SETON-WATSON *Italy from Liberalism to Fascism* xii. 547 In politics he [*sc.* D'Annunzio] was never more than a dilettante and a theatrical showman. **1977** *Irish Press* 29 Sept. 13/2 Meanwhile, showman Brian Barnes, was giving the small crowd their money's worth by nominating to them the type of shots he was going to play.

showmanship: restrict *nonce-wds.* to other derivative forms and add later (chiefly *transf.* and *fig.*) examples.

1874 G. H. LEWES *Let.* 19 Feb. in *Geo. Eliot Lett.* (1956) VI. 20 The story is very well told... But there is a chorus of objection against the excessive *showmanship* of the commentary. **1926** A. BENNETT *Ld. Raingo* II.

lxiv. 287 He had made a fine display of courage and wit on the doctor's declaration of his malady, but it was only a display, a proud piece of showmanship perhaps unworthy of so solemn an occasion. **1927** *Daily Express* 12 Aug. 9/3 She held a great reception yesterday, sitting in her red caravan, and chatted of the olden times and the present conditions of showmanship. **1906** *People* 13 May 4/5 But Tony, no slouch when it comes to showmanship, helped it along by wearing..a rose brocade dinner jacket. **1972** *Newsweek* 10 Jan. 8/1 Pragmatism—coupled with some of the showmanship for which he has long been known—stood as the hallmark of Bhutto's first fortnight as President.

show-me, *attrib. phr. U.S.* [Show *v.*] That demands demonstration; believing only on clear evidence, extremely sceptical. (Orig. used to describe the people of Missouri: see *Missouri 2.)

1909 *N.Y. Even. Post* (semi-weekly ed.) 19 Apr. 88 Everything indicative of the 'show-me' State of Missouri. **1909** R. A. Wason *Happy Hawkins* 283 He belonged to the show-me club. **1933** *Sun* (Baltimore) 29 July 6/1 These administrators are going to spend a great deal of their time..trying to get money from Secretary Ickes, who appears to be a show-me man. **1949** *Manch. Guardian Weekly* 20 Oct. 2 A typically materialistic 'show-me' American. **1978** J. Updike *Coup* (1979) i. 37 The premature gray and show-me squint of these Yankees is muddled in with their something eternally puerile awkward, winning, and hopeful.

show-off, *sb.* (*a.*) (in Dict. s.v. Show *v.* 38). Add: **c.** (Earlier example.)

1843 S. Bamford *Passages in Life of Radical* II. iii. 18 After some show off, by Mr Hunt, without which indeed, he scarcely knew how to get out of any matter, we left the dock.

c*. A person given to showing off. (The principal sense.)

1924 G. E. Kelly (*title*) The show-off. **1925** [see *go *v.* 58 g]. **1932** W. S. Maugham *For Services Rendered* II. 42 Lois: Well, I've always looked upon you as rather a show-off. **1943** D. Powell *Time to be Born* ii. 52 We.. don't like to show off. Our women aren't show-offs. **1954** C. Armstrong *Better to eat You* iv. 34 He knew how to deflate the show-offs and encourage the shy. **1960** T. Griffith *Waist-high Culture* I. ii. 24 Grateful for an adult audience..we must have been unbearable showoffs. **1972** 'E. Ferrars' *Breath of Suspicion* vii. 102 That honeymoon couple... What show-offs they both are, acting as if no one else had ever had a love affair before them.

d. (Earlier and later examples.) Also, ostentatious, showy.

1818 S. Ferrier *Marriage* II. xxii. 298 Colonel Lennox was evidently not a shew-off character. **1843** *Punch* Feb. 79/1 We never see this show-off style of living. **1934** T. N. Wilder *Heaven's my Destination* iii. 48 He was one of that loud show-off kind. **1954** Koestler *Trail of Dinosaur* (1955) II. 89 The perfect symbol of it all is the show-off TV aerial on the roof of suburban houses. **1977** H. Innes *Big Footprints* IV. i. 317 You stupid show-off bastard.

Hence **show-offish, show-o·ffy** *adjs.*

1942 H. Haycraft *Murder for Pleasure* ix. 189 He has too often stooped to merely show-offish quotation-spouting. **1952** S. Kauffman *Philanderer* (1953) iii. 54 My sweet, dear husband. My darling, show-offy, gentle husband. **1971** Laver & Collins *Educ. Tennis Player* xxv. 292. I hadn't jumped a net in a dozen years. I thought it was a bit show-offish for one thing. **1978** A. Maling *Lucky Devil* xxix. 155 He just came along to write the check. And he was kind of show-offy about it.

show-place. 2. (Earlier example.)

1794 J. B. S. Morritt *Let.* 19 Mar. (1914) i. 10 This [*sc.* Dresden] I hear is a very fine show-place, particularly for pictures.

showroom. Add: **3.** (Earlier examples.) Occas. in *sing.*

1820 T. Creevey *Let.* 23 Jan. in J. Gore *Creevey* (1948) xiii. 179 She is like one of her numerous gold and silver musical dickey birds, that are in all the show rooms of this house. **1820** D. Wordsworth *Jrnl.* 29 Sept. (1941) II. 322 Having paced through every show-room of the palace, we surveyed again the exterior.

shox (ʃǫks), *sb. pl.* [Re-spelling of *shocks* (chiefly in advertising and trade journalism).] Shock absorbers.

1976 *Hot Car* Mar. 20/2 (Advt.), Full range of automatic adjusting shox for American and European cars. **1977** *Custom Car* Nov. 13/1 The Fiesta 1·3S feels like a dry-sprung Mini on competition shox.

‖ **shoyu** (ʃōᵘ·yu). Also **sho-yu,** † **soeju.** [Jap.: see Soy^1.] = Soy^1 1. Freq. *attrib.* as *shoyu sauce.*

1727 J. G. Scheuchzer tr. *Kæmpfer's Hist. Japan* I. ix. 121 What they call Soeju, is also made of it, which is a sort of an *Embamma,* as they call it, which they eat at meals to get a good stomach. **1880** I. L. Bird *Unbeaten Tracks in Japan* I. 232 Eels and other dainties are served with soy (*shô-yu*), the great Japanese sauce. **1920** *Japan Advertiser* 22 Aug. 5/1 The eel is laid out flat and broiled over a charcoal fire with a special shoyu sauce. **1936** K. W. Colegrove *Militarism in Japan* iv. 45 He came from a most humble home, and he worked as a boy for a manufacturer of *shoyu* (a Japanese sauce). **1960** B. Leach *Potter in Japan* vi. 132 We ate it first with shoyu sauce. **1976** *Sci. Amer.* Sept. 172/1 Tempeh, ragi, sufu, shoyu, ang-kak, tea fungus and mizo are among those [fermentation products] eaten in Asian countries.

Shqip (ʃkyip). Also **Shqup, Shqyp.** [Alb.] = *Albanian *sb.*^{2} 2. Cf. next.

1969 'R. Stark' *Blackbird* xxv. 169 In Albania, they speak Shqyp... And in Shqyp,..Albania is Shqipenija. That means eagle country. **1974** *Encycl. Brit. Macropædia* I. 422/1 The origins of the general name Albanian.. and of the current official name Shqip or Shqipëri, which may well be derived from a term meaning 'pronounce clearly, intelligibly', are still disputed. **1976** W. H. Canaway *Willow-Pattern War* iii. 25 'From now on we speak only Shqyp'—which is what Albanians call Albanian.

Shqipetar (ʃkyi·pətāɹ). Also **Shkyipetar, Skipitar,** etc. [Alb.] = *Albanian *sb.*^{2} 1. Cf. prec.

1833 *Penny Cycl.* I. 256/2 The Albanian..calls himself Skipitar, and his native land Skiperi. **1860** *Chambers's Encycl.* I. 104/2 The *inhabitants,* estimated at 1,900,000, form a peculiar people, the Albanians or Arnauts; they call themselves Skypetars. **1876** [see *Latin *sb.* 3 c]. **1902** *Encycl. Brit.* XXV. 246/2 The Albanians, both Ghegs and Tosks, call themselves *Shkyipetar,* and their land *Shkyipenia* or *Shkyiperia,* the former being the Gheg, the latter the Tosk form of the word. **1935** *Chambers's Encycl.* I. 122/2 The name Shkypetar is derived by some from *shkip,* a rock, and thus signifies Hillmen; while others derive it from *shkyup,* an eagle, signifying Sons of the Eagle. **1971** *Guardian* 10 Aug. 4/5 Shquiptars prefer folk songs..rather than the Internationale.

‖ **shraddha, sraddha.** Add: Also † **seradeh.** (Earlier example.) Now freq. with spelling *shradh.*

1776 N. B. Halhed tr. *Code Gentoo Laws* ii. 73 Who, after his Father's Death, performs not the *Serâdeh* (religious Offices to his Father's Memory). **1969** *Hindu Weekly Mag.* (Madras) 3 Aug. p. ii/4 Nimai performed the necessary rituals and ceremonies—tarpan, shradh, ablution, offering of oblations. **1971** *Illustr. Weekly India* 4 Apr. 13/2 Females and children whose *yagyopavit* has not been done are not permitted to perform the *shradh* ceremony.

shrap (ʃræp). Colloq. abbrev. of Shrapnel.

1918 in Hamilton & Corbin *Echoes from Over There* (1919) xi. 125 They come fast at times too... I mean shrap and heavies. **1920** *Amer. Legion Weekly* 4 June 15 Top kicks whose skulls no shrap could dent. **1944** *Yank* 7 Apr. 3 The shrap is flying like rain.

shrapnel, *sb.* Add: **1.** (Later *attrib.* and *Comb.* examples.)

1918 G. Frankau *Judgement of Valhalla* 7 And floundered, torn and bleeding, Over trenches, through the wire, With the shrapnel-barrage leading To the prey of our desire. **1923** Kipling *Irish Guards in Gt. War* I. 222 A shrapnel-barrage fell also on the supports. **1939** Auden & Isherwood *Journey to War* 71 If you looked closely you could see dull red shrapnel bursts. **1940** [see sense 3 below]. **1944** *Daily Tel.* 22 Feb. 4/6 Most people know what a shrapnel shell (now temporarily obsolete) used to be.

2. *Austral.* and *N.Z. Mil. slang.* Small change, notes, or coins of low denominations.

1919 W. H. Downing *Digger Dialects* 44 *Shrapnel,*.. tattered French bank notes of small denominations. **1977** *Camera & Ciné* Nov. 24 'I don't suppose you'd have a bit of shrapnel?'..I shook fifty cents out of my purse and handed it to him.

3. Fragments from shells or bombs (see quot. 1940^1).

1940 *N. & Q.* CLXXIX. 278/1 The public has chosen to ignore the facts that shrapnel shell has become obsolete and that anti-aircraft guns fire high-explosive only. In consequence the shell fragments which are at present descending upon its devoted head are unhesitatingly referred to by the public as 'shrapnel' and the correct expression, 'shell fragments', has begun to verge on pedantry. **1940** W. S. Churchill *Secret Session Speeches* (1946) 20 Our barrage will be firing, and..great numbers of shell splinters usually described most erroneously as shrapnel, will be falling in the streets. **1946** *Chambers's Jrnl.* May 228/2 A viciously singing piece of shrapnel put his helmet straight for him. **1976** *Times* 18 Aug. 12/5 What journalists and other non-gunners call shrapnel are in fact fragments from high explosive bombs or shells. **1982** *Times* 21 June 4/5 One found a piece of shrapnel from the bomb in the pocket of his overalls.

shraum (ʃrǭm). *rare*$^{-1}$. [ad. Ir. *sream* corrupt matter, phlegm, running from the eyes.] A mucous deposit.

1922 Joyce *Ulysses* 241 He wiped away the heavy shraums that clogged his eyes.

shrdlu (ʃru·dlū). Also **shrdlu etaoin** (-eta,oin). A sequence of letters appearing on the keyboard of a type-setting machine, used as an example of an absurd or unintelligible utterance. Cf. *qwert, qwerty.

1943 D. Powell *Time to be Born* xii. 290 She read..the words... For all the sense they made to Vicky they might have been a trail of 'shrdlu etaoin's'. **1970** *New Statesman* 25 Dec. 863/2 Those witty literals, exotic printers' pies and secret messages in the *shrdlu* code.

shred, *v.* Add: **4. b.** Also *spec.* to reduce (documents) to unreadable strips or fragments by means of a shredder. Cf. *shredding *vbl. sb.* 3*.

1950 *Paper-Maker* Aug. 151 (Advt.), The 'Watford' Shredder and Duster..gives most excellent results in shredding and dusting waste papers. **1974** Bernstein & Woodward *All President's Men* xiii. 267 People became afraid that the newspapers might be discovered, so someone said, 'Shred them.' **1980** *Daily Tel.* 3 Nov. 1/4 One of his jobs was to check and shred hundreds of bundles of secret and confidential papers.

shredded, *ppl. a.* Add: *shredded wheat*: freq. eaten as a breakfast cereal (earlier and later examples).

Often written with capital initials as if a proprietary term.

1899 *T. Eaton & Co. Catal.* Spring & Summer 171/3 Shredded wheat drink, 1-lb. package. **1906** *Mrs. Beeton's Bk. Househ. Managem.* lxvii. 1721 Menus for simple breakfasts..Buttered shredded wheat. **1944** [see *puffed, puft *ppl. a.* c]. **1980** *Times* 6 Feb. 13/8 The arrival of a truck loaded with packets of Shredded Wheat.

shredder. Add: **3.** Also *spec.*, a machine for reducing documents to small unreadable fragments.

1950 [see *shred *v.* 4 b]. **1962, 1973** [see *paper shredder* s.v. *paper *sb.* 12]. **1977** *New Yorker* 27 June 23/1 Papers were discussed behind sealed doors..and tossed into shredders.

shredding, *vbl. sb.* Add: **3*.** Reducing to shreds; *spec.* the reducing of documents to small strips or fragments by a machine esp. for reasons of security.

1954 *Paper-Maker* Dec. 94 (Advt.), Watford Shredder and Duster. A speedy and efficient method of shredding, dusting and cleaning. **1966** *Punch* 15 June 864/3 The special executive type shredder involved the user in actually removing pins from documents before shredding. **1973** *Times* 18 May 11/4 Mr Odle said he did not know what documents Mr Liddy was destroying in the paper shredder but in retrospect he conceded that the shredding had been very significant.

4. *shredding machine.*

1975 R. L. Simon *Wild Turkey* xii. 77 I was in my office..when I heard someone at the shredding machine. **1980** P. Kinsley *Vatchman Switch* xvii. 115 He switched on the shredding machine.

shredding, *ppl. a.* (Earlier example.)

1883 'Mark Twain' *Life on Mississippi* li. 501 Spectral trees, dimly glimpsed through the shredding fog.

shrew, *sb.*^{1} Add: **2.** *shrew-faced* adj.

1913 D. H. Lawrence *Sons & Lovers* iv. 97 A tall, thin shrew-faced woman.

shrew, *sb.*^{2} Add: **4.** *shrew-ridden* adj.

1922 Joyce *Ulysses* 425 We have shrewridden Shakespeare and henpecked Socrates.

shrewd, *a.* Add: **15.** *shrewd-eyed* adj.; shrewd-head *Austral.* and *N.Z. slang*, a cunning person.

1856 J. G. Whittier *Panorama* 9 The shrewd-eyed salesman, garrulous and loud. **1959** *Daily Tel.* 20 May 17/1 A smiling, shrewd-eyed woman. **1916** C. J. Dennis *Songs Sentimental Bloke* 43 Now, this 'ere gorspil bloke's a fair shrewd 'ead. **1946** J. Morrison in *Coast to Coast* 163 Some shrewd-head overseas will get the blame for that pillaged case. **1960** N. Hilliard *Maori Girl* III. i. 177 Only the shrewd-heads go for that hard stuff: the shysters the takes.

shrewd (ʃrūd), *sb. rare.* [f. the adj.] **1.** A shrewd or cunning person (see also quot. 1954).

c **1858** E. Dickinson *Poems* (1955) I. 14 Could a shrewd advise me We might e'en divide—Should a shrewd betray me—Atropos decide! **1954** *Picture Post* 2 Jan. 34 The word 'Spiv', it seems, is out of date. The new word, we are reliably informed, is 'Shrewd'—and it is used as a noun, adjective and verb... The 'shrewd' is not an American by-product. He is home-bred and thoroughly English, in style and slang.

2. Shrewdness, sagacity, cunning.

1977 F. Branston *Up & Coming Man* xii. 126 All you needed was some capital and a lot of shrewd and you couldn't go wrong.

shrewdie (ʃrū·di). *colloq.* (orig. *Austral.* and *N.Z.*). Also **shrewdy.** [f. Shrewd *a.* + -ie.]

1. A shrewd or cunning person.

1916 A. Wright *Under Cloud* 35 Look here, Wilson, you're not such a shrewdie as you imagine. **1933** E. Partridge *Words, Words, Words!* III. 199 *Flankenheinrich,* to build a 'flank(ing) Henry', to show oneself a 'shrewdy'. **1949** F. Sargeson *I saw it in my Dream* 116 Johnny's a shrewdy. **1956** D. M. Davin *Sullen Bell* II. viii. 161 There'd been none of the shrewdies who dug themselves into good hospital jobs. **1967** 'E. Queen' *Face to Face* xx. 95 She couldn't have kept it under wraps indefinitely. Not with a shrewdie like Geegee Guild to account to. **1970** *Daily Tel.* 14 May 13/5 In the train of each social upheaval in America, like jackals at a carcase, come the shrewdies and hucksters in search of a quick dollar. **1979** J. Drummond *I saw him Die* ii. 16 'A shrewdie, would you say?' 'Very shrewd.'

2. A cunning trick. *rare.*

1961 B. Crump *Hang on a Minute* 27 Everything was as good as he said it was, but I knew he was pulling a shrewdie on me somewhere.

Shrewsbury. Add: **2.** In phrases. *by Shrewsbury clock*: added (in allusion to quot. 1596) to statements of duration as a proverbial phr., esp. to indicate exaggeration; *as exact* (or *regular*) *as Shrewsbury clock*: very exact or regular.

[**1596**, SHAKES. *I Hen. IV* v. iv. 151 We rose both at an instant, and fought a long houre by Shrewsburie clocke.] **1681** *Poor Robin Almanack* Mar. 12 A great many people shall feed (according as Sir John Falstaffe used to sight) three hours together by Shrewsbury Clock. **1784** H. COWLEY *More Ways than One* I. i. 1 My master is as exact as Shrewsbury clock. **1796** J. WHITE *Orig. Lett. Sir J. Falstaff* 17 Fifteen minutes, as thou say'st, by Shrewsbury clock. **1835** J. KINCAID *Random Shots from Rifleman* xiii. 332 Sir Arthur, in all his movements for twenty years, had been as regular as Shrewsbury clock. **1891** R. L. STEVENSON *Let.* in *Wks.* (1923) XXII. xi. 386, I remember, when I first saw this, laughing for an hour by Shrewsbury clock. **1901** G. B. SHAW *Admirable Bashville* III. 324 On the impenetrable sarcolobe That holds his seedling brain these fists have pounded By Shrewsb'ry clock an hour.

‖ **Shri, Sri** (ʃrī). [Skr. *Srī*, the name of Lakshmī (goddess of prosperity or beauty and the wife of Vishnu); hence, as an honorific title.] In India, a title prefixed to the names of deities and distinguished persons (and to the titles of sacred books, etc.) as a mark of respect; also, more recently, used as the Indian equivalent of Mr.

1799 *Asiatick Researches* VI. 475 *Sitá* was an incarnation of *Deví*: for *Srí-De'ví* the wife of Daisha, and daughter of *Adima* and *Iva*, entreated the Goddess, to give her one daughter exactly like herself. **1832** *Ibid.* XVII. 178 The *Kerala Utpatti*..calls him [*sc.* Sankara] the offspring of adultery, for which his mother *Sri Mahádevi* was expelled her caste. **1924** E. M. FORSTER *Passage to India* xxxiii. 289 Infinite love took upon itself the form of Shri Krishna, and saved the world. **1938** M. K. GANDHI in D. G. Tendulkar *Mahatma* (1952) IV. 348 The readers will remember that in the heyday of non-co-operation, the terms 'Mr.' and 'Esquire', were dropped by Congressmen and the nationalist press, and 'Shri' was the title largely used for all, irrespective of religion. **1969** 'E. PETERS' *Mourning Raga* iii. 44 'We are looking for the house of Shri Satyavan Kumar.'..'Yes, this is house of Mr Kumar.' **1981** S. RUSHDIE *Midnight's Children* I. 77 My cousin, Shri Ramram Seth, is a great seer.

shriek, *sb.* Add: **d.** Also, an outcry of alarm, surprise, or reproof. *colloq.*

1929 'SEAMARK' *Down River* i. 22 'Yet this man is getting through?' 'Yes—and with bags of it, too, judging from the shriek we got from the Yard.'

e. (Later examples.) Also *shriek-mark*.

1864 H. ALFORD *Queen's Eng.* 93 Our friend the compositor is sure to write '*Oh*' with a shriek (!) and to put another shriek after 'Sir'. **1933** BLUNDEN & NORMAN *We'll shift our Ground* 16 It remained only to add the shriek-marks and to discover a heroine. **1969** A. GLYN *Dragon Variation* i. 9 In her mind's eye she saw the printed score-sheet, 'N × P!!', shriek-mark, shriek-mark. **1977** *Time Lit. Suppl.* 29 Apr. 521/1 He reviewed *Principia Mathematica*... He was the only man at the college who could read its curlicues, shrieks, and hooks.

shriek, *v.* Add: **4.** *fig.* **a.** *trans.* To indicate clearly or blatantly. **b.** *intr.* To provide a clear or blatant indication *of*.

1920 'O. DOUGLAS' *Penny Plain* xii. 127 The ospreys in her hat seem to shriek money. **1938** E. AMBLER *Cause for Alarm* xiv. 225 That hat of yours..shrieks English to high Heaven. **1944** M. LASKI *Love on Supertax* v. 57 In that gathering her dress, she felt with a hot rush of shame, simply shrieked of Grosvenor Street. **1972** K. BENTON *Spy in Chancery* xi. 106 The furniture was old, well-worn and miscellaneous, fairly shrieking of 'furnished let'.

shrieking, *ppl. a.* Add: **2.** *fig.* **a.** Great, excellent, splendid. **b.** Of colours: excessively bright; lurid, glaring.

1926 N. COWARD *Queen was in Parlour* I. i. 15 My first experience was such a shrieking success. **1958** P. POLLACK *Pict. Hist. Photogr.* xii. 155/1 Satin blouses of shrieking colors. **1966** [see *CAPRI 2].

shrill, *a.* and *adv.* Add: **4.** Also of colours: bright, glaring.

1973 D. LESSING *Coll. Afr. Stories* II. 117 She wore a tight shrill green dress.

5. *shrill-sounding, -voiced* (later *transf.* and *fig.* examples) adjs.

1838 POE *Narr. Arthur Gordon Pym* xxiii. 188 A shrill-sounding and phantom voice screamed within my ears. **1920** A. HUXLEY *Leda* 15 The sky Was full of strange tumult suddenly—Beating of mighty wings and shrill-voiced fear. **1960** R. CAMPBELL tr. *Paço d'Arcos's Nostalgia* 44 The voiceless city of the shrill-voiced lights.

shrill, *v.* Add: **3.** Also with *out* (later examples).

1947 A. RANSOME *Great Northern?* i. 16 Roger's voice shrilled out, 'Sail HO!' **1975** *New Yorker* 16 June 97/3 It was a lapse on Miss Sills' part to shrill out a high E flat at the end of the first finale, but otherwise she was tender, touching, and sensitive.

shrimp, *sb.* Add: **1. c.** A shrimp or prawn used as a bait in angling.

1856 'STONEHENGE' *Man. Brit. Rural Sports* 236/2 *Shrimps* are used for angling in docks and canals, and are good baits for perch, if used alive. **1910** *Encycl. Brit.* II. 29/1 Odd attractions such as boiled shrimps, caddis-grubs, small frogs, maggots, wasp-grubs, &c. are sometimes successful. **1924** *Blackw. Mag.* Apr. 489/1, I would not trust the most experienced salmon with Michael Lydon and a Galway 'shrimp'. **1931** *Hardy's Anglers' Guide* 31 The shrimp will wake the lazy dozer, and he'll take it or your fly with a rush. *Ibid.* 180 Prawn and Shrimp Tackles. **1962** *L. L. Bean Catal.* 52 Bean's shrimp fly is an excellent imitation of the natural food for trout.

d. A colour resembling that of a cooked shrimp, a bright shade of pink.

1895 *Montgomery Ward Catal.* Spring & Summer 12/1 Colored Surah silks..in the following colors: green.. shrimp, wine. **1927** T. WOODHOUSE *Artificial Silk* 81 The particulars of the colours and patterns are as under—No. 1. A shrimp ordinary crochet pattern. **1975** *New Yorker* 26 May 81 (Advt.), This plain white steerhide belt reverses to cool summer shades including seafoam green, shrimp, bone.

3. a. *shrimp net* (earlier example), *paste, -pink* (earlier and later examples), *-red*; *shrimp-brown, -coloured* adjs.

1932 A. HUXLEY *Brave New World* iii. 38 Two shrimp-brown children emerged from a neighbouring shrubbery. **1889** 'MARK TWAIN' *Connecticut Yankee* ii. 34 An airy slim boy in shrimp-colored tights. **1859** A. J. MUNBY *Diary* 18 July in D. Hudson *Munby* (1972) 39 She stood there leaning on her shrimp net (for she had been fishing). **1918** Shrimp paste [see *Gentleman's Relish* s.v. *GENTLEMAN 7 c]. **1976** *Western Living* (Vancouver, B.C.) June 50/2 A fishing village, processing salt fish, making shrimp paste, and doing a bit of duck-farming. **1882** *Cassell's Fam. Mag.* 236/1 Shrimp-pink with white is one of the happiest and latest combinations. **1973** J. ROSSITER *Manipulators* viii. 90 A shrimp-pink shirt. **1923** D. H. LAWRENCE *Kangaroo* vii. 137 The different shells, their sea-colours of pink and brown and rainbow and..shrimp-red.

b. **shrimp-boat** a boat engaged in fishing for shrimps; **shrimp cocktail** [COCKTAIL *sb.* 4], a dish of boiled shrimps served cold in a sauce; **shrimp cracker,** a light, crisp cracker flavoured with shrimp and served as an accompaniment to Oriental food; **shrimp gumbo** *U.S.*, a shrimp soup thickened with okra pods; **shrimp plant,** an evergreen shrub, *Justicia brandegeana* (formerly *Beloperone guttata*), belonging to the family Acanthaceæ, native to Mexico, and bearing small white flowers hidden in clusters of pinkish-brown bracts.

1872 B. JERROLD *London* p. viii, Smacks, barges shrimp-boats. **1979** *Guardian* 22 Oct. 26/7 The size of mesh permitted on shrimp boats in British waters. **1937** *America's Cook Bk.* 180 Lobster or shrimp cocktail... Chill thoroughly and serve in cocktail glasses. **1977** J. WAINWRIGHT *Nest of Rats* I. vi. 38 It was a nice meal. Shrimp cocktails, followed by a good mixed grill. **1969** *Listener* 12 June 814/1 The village chief himself asked us to a dinner of dried deer and shrimp crackers, chicken and lettuce. **1975** J. VAN DE WETERING *Outsider in Amsterdam* (1976) vi. 79 He..broke a piece of shrimp-crackers and grabbed the noodles. [**1805** Shrimp gumbo: see *GUMBO 1 b.]. **1885** L. HEARN *La Cuisine Creole* 21 (*heading*) Maigre shrimp gombo for Lent. **1889** J. WHITEHEAD *Steward's Handbk.* IV. 337/2 Shrimp-gumbo..not boiled after gumbo is in. **1938** C. H. MATSCHAT *Suwanee River* 255 The supper was fresh shrimp gumbo, hot and highly spiced. **1941** L. H. & E. Z. BAILEY *Hortus Second* 101 [*Beloperone*] *guttàta*. Shrimp-plant. **1946** M. FREE *All about House Plants* xvii. 153 The Shrimp Plant..is a comparatively new introduction to the house-plant scene. **1956** X. FIELD *Housewife Bk. House Plants* III. 74 The Shrimp Plant has always been a favourite of mine. I delight in its prawn-like flowers. **1975** J. VAN DE WETERING *Tumbleweed* (1976) ii. 18 There were plants on all window-sills..the shrimp plant with a pink growth at the end of each stalk.

shrimp (ʃrimp), *v.* [f. the sb.] **a.** *intr.* To fish for shrimps. **b.** *trans.* To fish (a pool, etc.) with shrimp as a bait.

1844 M. HOLE *Diary* 26 Aug. in B. Massingham *Turn on Fountains* (1974) ii. 39 Making the most of our last day at old Blackpool... Loafed. Shrimped. **1926** R. MACAULAY *Crewe Train* II. v. 119 Torquay wasn't bad. One could shrimp and prawn and fish. **1931** *Hardy's Anglers' Guide* 31 And remember too that you may shrimp a pool in this manner and revert to fly without any fear of your pool being disturbed. **1938** *Mississippi* (U.S. Works Progress Admin.) 169 In many instances, however, boats are oystering at one season and shrimping at another.

shrimping, *vbl. sb.* Add: **2.** Fishing with shrimp as a bait.

1931 *Hardy's Anglers' Guide* 31, I have had splendid sport, owing to this way of shrimping.

shrine, *sb.* Add: **6. b.** With reference to the Order of Nobles of the Mystic Shrine. Cf. *SHRINER.

1968 *Chicago Tribune* 7 July I. 1/1 More than 2,500 Shriners gathered..to kick off the 94th annual Shrine convention. **1974** *Sunday Advocate-News* (Barbados) 3 Mar. 11/4 [The] Prime Minister..received members of the Manito Shrine Club. **1976** *Columbus* (Montana) *News* 27 May 6/3 Tom participated in the clown unit of the Shrine Ceremonial parade.

Shriner (ʃrəi·nəɹ). orig. and chiefly *U.S.* [f. SHRINE *sb.* + -ER¹.] A member of the Order of Nobles of the Mystic Shrine, established in the U.S. in 1872. Also **Shrinite.**

1884 *Proc. Imperial Council Anc. Arabic Order Nobles of Mystic Shrine* 54 His brother..was a Noble of the Shrine, and well up in all that makes an efficient and sincere Shrinite. **1886** *Ibid.* 85 The Walee..was made a Shriner in 1883. **1927** E. O'NEILL *Marco Millions* II. i. 95 This costume is a queer jumble of stunning effects that recall the parade uniforms of our modern Knights Templar, of Columbus, of Pythias, Mystic Shriners, the Klan, etc. **1966** *Economist* 24 Dec. 1332/2 It appears that the celebrated Shriners are a sub-class of masons. **1979** P. THEROUX *Old Patagonian Express* xii. 193 It was Clubgoing Hour. At the officers mess and the VFW,..the Shriners Club, the Masons..the day's work was done.

shrink, *sb.* Add: Also *spec.* in *Textiles*, the reduction in dimension of a fibre or fabric, usu. caused by treatment with water.

1947 J. T. MARSH *Introd. Textile Finishing* ix. 244 Modern anti-shrink treatments are based on..two methods. **1954** A. J. HALL *Standard Handbk. Textiles* (ed. 4) v. 280 The well-known London shrink treatment is widely used to remove residual stretch in a wool fabric. **1967** SHAW & ECKERSLEY *Cotton* xv. 131 (*heading*) Dimensional stability (shrink resistance).

2. A psychiatrist. Cf. *head-shrinker* s.v. *HEAD sb. 66. *slang* (orig. *U.S.*).

1966 T. PYNCHON *Crying of Lot 49* i. 16 It was Dr Hilarius, her shrink or psychotherapist. **1969** C. YOUNG *Todd Dossier* 78 What you've written may prove helpful. That's what the man said, the shrink. **1973** *Nation Rev.* (Melbourne) 31 Aug.–6 Sept. 1434/1 A number of value judgments were offered..by a couple of the shrinks. **1978** M. WALKER *Infiltrator* iii. 39 He could have gone to a pricey shrink who would have certified him too delicate for the Army. **1980** *Times Lit. Suppl.* 3 Oct. 117/2 It does not take a shrink to see that a man so humanly flawed and artistically inept has got to be a loser.

3. *attrib.* and *Comb.*, as (sense 1) *shrink-proofing, -resistance*; *shrink-controlled, -proof, -resist, -resistant*, adjs.

1967 KARCH & BUBER *Offset Processes* ii. 31 Controlled sheets of rubber with shrink-controlled material in the centre of the plate. **1969** *Sears, Roebuck Catal.* Spring/Summer 44/2 Shrink-controlled..cotton. **1928** Shrink-proof [see *colour-fast* s.v. *COLOUR *sb.*¹ 18]. **1965** A. J. HALL *Stand. Handbk. Textiles* (ed. 6) v. 307 In recent years three important shrinkproof treatments have come into use. **1962** J. T. MARSH *Self-Smoothing Fabrics* ii. 11 The work is based fundamentally on the shrinkproofing of wool. **1963** A. J. HALL *Textile Sci.* v. 236 (*heading*) Shrink-resist finishes for cellulose fibre fabrics. **1958** *Times* 20 Oct. 13/2 This tweed has been woven for the school..and tested for washability, shrink-resistance. **1946** A. J. HALL *Stand. Handbk. Textiles* v. 275 (*caption*) Sanforising machine for making fabric shrink resistant in washing. **1973** *Times* 9 Apr. 6/3 The main terms covered by the new standard will be..'shrink resistant', 'crease shedding'.

shrink, *v.* Add: **17.** **shrink film** = *SHRINK-WRAP *sb.*; **shrink fit** = *shrinkage fit* s.v. SHRINKAGE 4.

1967 *Times Rev. Industry* May 76/3 *Shrink film*: as a replacement for fibre-board cartons in containing canned and bottled goods during distribution. **1969** L. S. MOUNTS in W. R. R. Park *Plastics Film Technol.* v. 124 Shrink films are sealed by special point sealers, hot wire.. or impulse. **1882** *Amer. Machinist* 8 Apr. 9/1 How much should be allowed in making a shrink fit of a wrought iron crank to the shaft? **1941** L. S. MARKS *Mech. Engineer's Handbk.* (ed. 4) 923 Shrink fits are used in places where a force fit would be difficult to assemble, as for example, locomotive wheel tires. **1970** K. BALL *Fiat 600, 600D Autobook* i. 16/1 The starter ring is a shrink-fit on the flywheel.

shrinkable, *a.* Add: (Example.)

1969 W. R. R. PARK *Plastics Film Technol.* viii. 181 Heat shrinkable polyvinyl chloride tubes in a range of diameters are becoming available.

Hence **shrinkabi·lity.**

1946 A. J. HALL *Stand. Handbk. Textiles* 273 Shrinkability in washing is a feature of textile materials to which a great deal of attention has been given. **1975** I. STEWART *Concepts Mod. Math.* xiii. 189 The 'shrinkability' of a closed curve is clearly a topological property.

shrinkage. Add: **3. a.** (Earlier example.)

1873 'MARK TWAIN' *Gilded Age* xliv. 397 They invariably allowed a half for shrinkage in his statements.

b. *spec.* in *Comm.*, an allowance made for the reduction in takings due to wastage, theft, etc.

1961 *Times* 6 Jan. 6/3 An allowance of up to 1 per cent is made for pilfering, the euphemistic word for it being 'shrinkage'. **1972** *Guardian* 14 July 12/6 Around £300 is lost each year..through..shrinkage. Shrinkage is not just customer pilferage. It includes errors, incompetence and inexperience. **1981** *Times* 4 Mar. 16/1 For some time supermarkets and department stores have referred to shoplifting euphemistically as shrinkage on their balance sheets.

4. *shrinkage-resistant* adj.; **shrinkage cavity,** a cavity in metal caused by shrinkage; **shrinkage crack,** also, a crack similarly formed in other materials; **shrinkage fit** (examples).

1923 GLAZEBROOK *Dict. Appl. Physics* V. 358 (*caption*) Shrinkage cavities at surface of aluminium alloy ingot. **1973** G. J. DAVIES *Solidification & Casting* ix. 180 (*caption*) A large shrinkage cavity in the interior of an aluminium-bronze sand casting. **1930** *New Statesman* 27 Dec. 357/2 And even as regards telegraph poles and the like a preference is given to those with long shrinkage cracks. **1895** W. KENT *Mech. Engineer's Pocket-bk.* 973 (*heading*) Shrinkage fits. **1928** F. D. JONES *Handbk. Encycl. Engin.*

977 A cylindrical part which is to be held in position by a shrinkage fit is first turned a few thousandths of an inch larger than the hole in which it is to fit; the diameter of the latter is increased by heating, and after the port is inserted, the heated outer member is cooled, causing it to grip the pin or shaft with tremendous pressure. **1946** *Nature* 14 Sept. 386/1 The greatly increased demand for shrinkage-resistant garments by the Forces.

shrinker. Add: **2.** A person employed in shrinking materials in various manufacturing processes.
1921 *Dict. Occup. Terms* (1927) § 190 Tyre shrinker. *Ibid.* § 384 *Crabber; cloth shrinker, potter, shrinker,*.. tends crabbing machine, which passes cloth, at a suitable tension, through weighted rollers in a succession of troughs of water,.. where it is expanded or reduced to a specified width. **1960** *Classification of Occupations* (Gen. Register Office) 99/2 Shrinker and dyer.

shrinking, *ppl. a.* Add: **2. d.** *shrinking violet*, a shy or modest person.
1915 N. L. McClung *In Times like These* vi. 83 Voting will not be compulsory; the shrinking violets will not be torn from their shady fence-corner; the 'home bodies' will be able to still sit in rapt contemplation of their own fireside. **1949** E. Coxhead *Wind in West* iii. 83 You believe in the shrinking-violet technique, do you? **1966** R. Severn *Desperate Rendezvous* viii. 70 'Time will convince you both how indispensable I *have* been...' Wilson scowled. 'A real shrinking violet, aren't you?' he said. **1976** *Listener* 22 July 90/1 Frayn has not forgotten the underdog... The shrinking violet (as he rightly recognizes) is the most dangerous plant in the glades of privilege.

shrink-wrapping (ʃri·ŋk,ræ:piŋ), *vbl. sb.* [f. Shrink *v.* + Wrapping *vbl. sb.*] The process of packaging an article by causing a thin plastic film to contract around it so as to cling tightly to its surface.
1959 *Packaging & Display Encycl.* (ed. 5) iv. 352 Polyvinylidene films..are still mostly connected with the shrink-wrapping of meats. **1968** *Packaging* Feb. 61/2 The..machine..represents a major forward step in the shrink-wrapping field. **1971** *British Printer* Jan. 99/2 Müller can now produce machinery for..shrink-wrapping.
Hence **shri·nk-wrap** *sb.*, the plastic film used in shrink-wrapping; also (as a back-formation) as *v. trans.*; hence **shri·nk-wrapped** *ppl. a.*; **shri·nk-wrapper**, a machine used for shrink-wrapping.
1961 *Packaging Rev. Data Bk.* 283/2 Oriented film..is under development as a shrink-wrap for poultry, hams, cheese and preserve pot covers. **1968** *Packaging* Feb. 61/2 One unit..replaces the tray-erector, product-loader, and shrink-wrapper. **1969** *Ibid.* Apr. 33 (*caption*) A..principle ..of..shrinkwrapping the entire load—in one continuous sequence. **1970** *Register of Packaging* 19 Up to 30 shrink wrapped packs per minute. **1978** *Listener* 20 July 73/3 Apples that..keep well..shrink-wrapped on the supermarket shelves. **1981** *Times Lit. Suppl.* 30 Jan. 108/3 *The Writers' and Poets' Yearbook*..is cased in boards coated with a shrinkwrap, transparent laminate that looks like a badly fitting condom.

shroud, *sb.*¹ Add: **7. d.** *Engin.* A circular band attached to the circumference of the rotor of a turbine; a flange on the tip of a turbine rotor blade (flanges on adjacent blades usu. interlocking so as to form a continuous band).
1906 J. W. Sothern *Marine Steam Turbine* (ed. 2) II. 54 At the outer ends..the blades fit..into a channel-shaped brass ring, or 'shroud', as it is called. **1951** Cohen & Rogers *Gas Turbine Theory* v. 106 Although shrouds have been used on superchargers, they have not come into general use so far on impellers for gas turbines. **1967** N. E. Borden *Jet-Engine Fundamentals* 93 The shrouds form a band around the perimeter of the turbine rotor which interlocks the blades at their tips and reduces vibration. **1971** P. J. McMahon *Aircraft Propulsion* v. 162 What may show the difference between a turbine and a compressor stage would be the fitting of shrouds on turbine blades.
e. A temporary covering for part of a spacecraft, esp. one which protects and streamlines the payload of a rocket during launching.
1965 W. R. Corliss *Space Probes & Planetary Exploration* x. 235 The shroud gives probes that customary conical appearance before the ejection of the articulated sections. **1966** [see *dock *v.*³ 5]. **1975** K. W. Gatland *Missiles & Rockets* viii. 184 Above that, enclosed in a shroud, were the Airlock Module, Multiple Docking Adapter and Apollo Telescope Mount.
8. (sense 2) *shroud-plait* (poet.).
c **1864** G. M. Hopkins *Poems* (1967) 117, I desire They swathe and lace the shroud-plaits o'er my face.

shroud, *sb.*² Add: **2. b.** = *shroud line* below.
1942 F. H. Colvin *Aircraft Handbk.* (ed. 5) 679 (*caption*) Drawing the shrouds into their pockets in the seat pack. **1957** L. L. Beckford *A.B.C. of Aeronaut.* 74/1 Fastened firmly between the gores are strong cords, called Shrouds, which distribute the load evenly over the Canopy. **1973** 'A. Hall' *Tango Briefing* x. 119 Watch the ground. The whisper of wind in the shrouds... He'd had to give me five seconds..so that the 'chute wouldn't foul each other.
3. shroud line, any of the straps joining the canopy of a parachute to the harness. Usu. *pl.* Cf. *rigging lines* s.v. *rigging (*vbl.*) *sb.*² 2 c.
1929 A. F. Collins *Aviation* xii. 184 The pilot chute and big parachute, together with its shroud lines that hold it to the harness, are made so that they fold up in a very small pack. **1973** 'A. Hall' *Tango Briefing* xix. 240 The supply 'chute was draped across a spur of rock... The shroud lines were badly twisted.

shroud, *v.*² Add: **9.** Also in gen. use with reference to the provision of a shroud in var. technical senses. Cf. Shroud *sb.*¹ 7 in Dict. and Suppl.
1913 S. J. Reed *Turbines applied to Marine Propulsion* iii. 41 In both of the above systems the tips of the blades are shrouded with a steel strip, a projecting piece being left on the blade tip which passes through a hole in the shroud and which is eventually riveted over. **1948** *Chambers's Jrnl.* July 392/2 Mica is used to support the input sockets, thus preventing breakdowns owing to heat, and the sockets are also shrouded for safety and the prevention of shock. **1966** *McGraw-Hill Encycl. Sci. & Technol.* IV. 292/2 Shrouding a propeller may be used on a ship to decrease interference of propeller and hull.

shrub, *sb.*¹ Add: **4. a.** *shrub border.*
1933 A. Osborn *Shrubs & Trees* v. 38 Endeavour to visualize the shrub-border when its inmates are fully grown. **1978** R. E. Heath *Miniature Shrubs* p. vii, A shrub border once planted needs very little after care.
b. shrub rose, a rose, esp. a species or variety long in cultivation, allowed to follow its natural pattern of growth. Cf. *old rose a.
1948 G. S. Thomas in *Jrnl. R. Hort. Soc.* LXXIII. 170 (*heading*) Shrub roses for the modern garden. **1980** A. Wilson *Setting World on Fire* II. iv. 117 She runs a shrub rose nursery garden in Sussex.

shrubbery. Add: **3.** *transf.* A beard or whiskers. *joc.*
1937 Wodehouse *Lord Emsworth & Others* ii. 101 Something has eaten off Sir Preston's moustache... I met him outside, and the shrubbery had completely disappeared. **1966** J. S. Cox *Illustr. Dict. Hairdressing* 137/2 *Shrubbery*, a false beard; also the natural beard.

shrug, *sb.* Add: **5.** A short, close-fitting woman's jacket or shoulder stole with sleeves, orig. knitted or crocheted. Also *attrib.*, as *shrug jacket.* orig. *U.S.*
1957 *Knitted Outerwear Times* 12 Aug. 23/2 Women are buying the Orlon shrug for wear over sleeveless dresses and in air conditioned rooms. **1962** *Guardian* 5 Oct. 8/5 (*caption*) This ensemble..is made up of skirt and shrug in royal blue loose weave mockknit. **1973** *Country Life* 25 Jan. 250/2 Lucca lamb shrug. **1980** *Times* 12 Feb. 7/6 Camisole top and shrug jacket takes 7 50g balls of 3 Suisses Barbara.

shrug, *v.* Add: **3. b.** *fig. to shrug* (something) *off* or *aside*: to dismiss or reject (something) in an offhand manner; to be unaffected by.
1909 Webster, Shrug off. **1932** *Now & Then* Spring 15/2 He might shrug aside or be bored or even disgusted by *Strange Interlude* or *Mourning Becomes Electra.* **1949** *Catholic Times* 4 Mar. 5/1 The disgrace of Yalta can never be shrugged off. **1963** *Observer* 17 Feb. 23/5 Some house-flies and mosquitoes can now shrug off not one but several of the most lethal poisons. **1981** *Times* 18 Apr. 21/5 The stockmarket has also shrugged aside the collapse of Hedderwick Stirling Grumbar.
10. *intr.* To manœuvre one's arms and shoulders *into* a garment. Also *refl.*
1930 H. Ashton *Dr. Serocold* I. iii. 43 She shrugged herself into her stiff overcoat and began to button it all the way up to her chin. **1937** D. Aldis *Time at her Heels* ii. 33 And shrugging into her brown suit coat she followed her sons and daughter downstairs. **1974** J. Dowell *Look-off Bear* 6, I shrugged into my warm red-and-black-checked mackinaw jacket.
shrugged *ppl. a.* Also *fig.*
1874 G. M. Hopkins *Jrnl.* 23 May (1937) 195 Trees, clouds, and mountaintops 'seized' or 'shrugged' as in Turner.

shtchee, shtchi, varr. Stchi in Dict. and Suppl.

‖ **shtetl** (ʃte·t'l, ʃtē·t'l). Also **shtetel.** Pl. **shtetlach, shtetlakh, shtetls.** [Yiddish, 'little town', f. G. *stadt.*] A small Jewish town or village in Eastern Europe. Now *Hist.* Also *transf.*
1949 *Yivo Ann. Jewish Soc. Sci.* IV. 87 Swistocz..was considered one of the larger towns (*shtetl*) in the district of Grodno. **1963** M. Samuel *Little did I Know* ix. 137 The *Shtetlach!* Those forlorn little settlements in a vast and hostile wilderness, isolated alike from Jewish and non-Jewish centers of civilization. **1968** L. Rosten *Joys of Yiddish* 370 The world of the Jews in Germany..was vastly different from the world of *shtetl* Jews in eastern Europe. **1972** *New Society* 3 Aug. 228/1 People who, in former reincarnations, were clerks and schoolmarms in the *shtetls* of Minsk, Pinsk and Milwaukee. **1973** *Times* 3 Feb. 13/4 Jewish food is the diet of the *shtetel*—the small village. **1976** *Nat. Observer* (U.S.) 6 Mar. 19/1 In the *shtetlakh*, the small towns, they lived lives of grinding poverty amid the constant expectation of external attack. **1977** *Listener* 31 Mar. 422/4 The little Jewish townships of Russia, the *shtetlach.* **1978** *Times Lit. Suppl.* 10 Nov. 1314/2 Hitler swept away the *shtetls* of Eastern Europe.

‖ **shtibl** (ʃti·b'l). Also **shtiebel, shtieble, stiebel.** Pl. **shtibblach.** [Yiddish; cf. Ger. dial. *stüberl* small room.] A small synagogue or Jewish house of worship.
1929 I. Goller *Five Bks. Mr. Moses* I. i. 10 Reb Zalman, Rabbi of the *Shtiebel* off Commerical Street. *Ibid.* ii. 15 A single, large room the *Shtiebel*, combination of synagogue, house of study, library and club-room for the disciples of Reb Zalman. **1960** H. Rabinowicz *Guide to Hassidism* x. 120 The *stiebel* (literally 'room')..played a vital rôle. It served both as place of worship and as house of study... In the *stiebel* the Hassidim communed with God and with themselves. **1967** C. Porok *Chosen* vii. 116 Each Hasidic sect had its own house of worship—shtibblach, they were called. **1973** *Jewish Chron.* 14 Sept. 22/1 The new cathedral synagogue of Jerusalem..will make Herod's temple look like a shtibl. **1976** C. Bermant *Coming Home* II. iv. 173, I belong to two synagogues, a large one..and a gilded little bethel with about two dozen members called a *shtieble.*

‖ **shtik** (ʃtik). *U.S. slang.* Also **schtick, schtik, shtick.** [Yiddish, f. G. *stück* piece, play.] **1.** An act or stage routine; a joke, a 'gag'. Hence *transf.* (freq. slightly *derog.*), a patter, a 'line'; a gimmick or characteristic style. orig. *Theatr.*
1961 A. Berkman *Singers' Gloss. Show Business* 78 A piece of business; a gag or joke..*shtik.* **1962** 'E. McBain' *Empty Hours* 129 The girl didn't say a word. She didn't have to. The effect was almost comic, akin to the cock-tail-party scene... The word '*shtik*' crossed Meyer's mind. **1964** S. Bellow *Herzog* 60 'Let's cut out all the *shtick*,' said Gersbach. 'Let's say you're a crumb.' **1968** P. Tamony *Americanisms* (typescript) No. 19. 2 Consistency is not the schtick of protestors. **1973** *Times* 30 July 5/5 Emotionally controlled..and minus the usual Streisand shtick, it [*sc.* a film] is arguably the best performance of her career. **1974** P. Gzowski *Bk. about this Country* 46/1 People who are professionally funny—guys who do schticks—are less funny than he is. **1977** *Time* 19 Dec. 12/2 The former Prime Minister is not at all apologetic about his Yuletide shtik, pointing out that he has chosen to write books and sell records rather than go the David Frost route.
2. A particular area of activity or interest, a sphere or 'scene'.
1968 *Atlantic Monthly* Sept. 50/1 My first assignment was to a gentle middle-aged Jewish household, hardly my schtik. **1972** *New York* 1 May 13/2 This unfortunately overlong satire on the sexology schtick of our times. **1976** *Publishers Weekly* 15 Mar. 55/2 A husband trying to puzzle out his woman, women-God-bless-them in general, and the whole female *shtick.*

Shtokavian, Shtokavski: see *Štokavian.

‖ **shtook** (ʃtuk) *slang.* Also **schtook, schtuck, shtuck,** etc. [Origin unknown: app. not a Yiddish word.] Trouble; esp. in phr. *in* (*dead*) *shtook.*
1936 G. Ingram *Muffled Man* iv. 68, I to come to you if I'm in 'stook'. **1960** *News Chron.* 16 Feb. 6 In fact, I'm in shtook. **1970** G. F. Newman *Sir, You Bastard* 280 The filth, who was supposed to be in dead shtook, was sitting there like he owned the gaff. **1971** F. Norman *Dodger-Greaser* vii. 136 It'd be a terrible fing if none or us could 'elp each uvva aht nar an' then wen we're in dead schtook. **1975** *Observer* 27 Apr. 33/1 The scheme went awry, landing David in shtuck with the Law and jeopardising his lucrative future. **1978** J. Gardner *Dancing Dodo* xxxi. 246 You know I'm in schtuck with my bosses.

‖ **shtoom** (ʃtum), *a.* and *v. slang.* Also **schtoom, shtum(m),** etc. [Yiddish, f. G. *stumm* silent, mute.] **A.** *adj.* Silent, speechless, dumb. Esp. in phr. *to keep* (or *stay*) *shtoom.* Occas. also as *sb.*
1958 F. Norman *Bang to Rights* 15, I think it's much better to keep shtoom. **1972** J. Caine *Hamlet, my Boy* x. 141 Keep *shtumm* and you won't get plugged. **1981** J. Barnett *Firing Squad* ii. 14 Stay schtoom. If the law does come round you don't go near... It's got to be total schtoom on this.
B. *v. intr.* To be quiet, to shut *up.* Also *trans.*: cf. *shut it* s.v. *shut *v.* 4 b(*c*).
1958 F. Norman *Bang to Rights* 72 You can always shtoomup if any screws are earholeing. **1973** Boyd & Parkes *Dark Number* ii. 21 You start something, and then just when it's getting interesting you shtoom up. **1982** 'J. Gash' *Firefly Gadroon* xvii. 185 Shtum it. Sounds carry in this.

shtshi, var. Stchi in Dict. and Suppl.
shtuck, var. *shtook.

‖ **shtup** (ʃtup), *v. slang.* [Yiddish; cf. Ger. dial. *stupfen* to nudge, jog.] **1.** *trans.* To push. Hence also as *sb.*
1968 L. Rosten *Joys of Yiddish* 374 'Don't *shtup*', means 'Don't push'—both literally and figuratively... A man who *shtups* himself in 'di hoykhe fenster' (the high windows) is a man who is a social climber. **1977** M. T. Bloom *13th Man* vii. 136 What the fuck hell is now holding up the works?..Give them a *shtup.* *Ibid.* xi. 182 I'm trying to give fate a *shtup*, a push, to hurry up and resolve matters.
2. *trans.* and *intr.* To copulate (with).
1969 P. Roth *Portnoy's Complaint* 83 Why, *of course* he was *shtupping* her. **1974** D. Westlake *Help* v. 35 He'd go on home..shtup the wife..then shlep on back here. **1977** *Custom Car* Nov. 67/2 Italian men can actually murder their wives if they find 'em shtupping around.

Shuboth, var. *Shabbat.

shubunkin (ʃubʊ·ŋkin). Also **Shubunkin.** [Jap., f. *shu* vermilion + *bun* portion, division + *kin* gold.] A goldfish, *Carassius auratus*, that is multicoloured with black spots and red patches and has elongated fins and tail.

1917 W. T. Innes *Goldfish Varieties* ii. 26 One of the more recent introductions is the Shubunkin. **1928** *Daily Express* 5 July 8/4 'I'll just bring these Shubunkins to the front for you.' And he coaxed into view a magnificent creature with a blue body covered with red, black, yellow and brown spots. **1971** *Country Life* 1 Apr. 774/3 For common goldfish and shubunkins this [depth of water] can be reduced to 9 or 12 inches. **1980** *West Lancs. Evening Gaz.* 25 Aug. 17 First in the shubunkins..came second in the any variety of goldfish section.

shuck, *sb.*[2] Add: **1. e.** Phr. *to light a shuck*: to leave in a hurry, to hurry away.

1905 *Dial. Notes* III. 86 *Light a shuck*, to go in a hurry, to move on, to keep away from danger. **1938** in B. A. Botkin *Treas. S. Folklore* (1949) III. i. 459 He jumped outen the water and lit a shuck for camp. **1947** *True* Nov. 108/2 But the Espinosas lit a shuck for the mountains. **1971** J. V. Allen *Cowboy Lore* iv. 71 So he saddled up old Chaw one night and lit a shuck this way.

2. e. Nonsense, deception, sham.

1958 G. Lea *Somewhere there's Music* 163, I know about double negative too, but that's a lot of shuck. **1959** *Encounter* June 43 Despite his rejection of marriage as middle-class 'shuck' (phoney), the Beatnik's Wedding is an important event. **1972** *Islander* (Victoria, B.C.) 25 June 14/4 This is a good book and as they say in..Texas: 'I'm not putting the shuck on you' so get it and read it. **1980** A. Toffler *Third Wave* xix. 261 The recently graduated son..proclaims the nine-to-five job a degrading sham and a shuck.

3. (Earlier example.)

1847 J. M. Field *Drama in Pokerville* 68 And Mr. Bagly was there..[to shoot] any gentleman who might say 'shucks!'.

4. *shuck-mattress* (earlier example); (sense 2 e) *shuck-shark.*

1843 W. Frazier *Jrnl.* July (1930) 27 Our cargo..was a motley pile..from broken skillets, up to rickety bedsteads and *shuck*-mattresses. **1952** A. Lomax *Mister Jelly Roll* 136 I want you shuck-sharks and crooks to get out of town.

shuck, *v.*[2] Add: **2. a.** (Later examples.) (Now also occas. used outside N. Amer.)

1966 *Listener* 3 Nov. 650/2, I regard it as a great fortune to have shucked off this amount of remorse about intellectual achievement. **1968** *N.Y. Times Book Rev.* 23 June vii. 1/1 That an actively practicing attorney.. should ever be able to shuck them off long enough to produce a book..struck me as a most unlikely miracle. **1969** G. Macbeth *War Quartet* 28 The deflector bag Filled with loose cases, shucked out. **1969** *New Yorker* 12 Apr. 86/2 Then the astronaut shucks the box from the tube, which he discards as a doctor might throw away the protective part of a syringe. **1975** *Times Lit. Suppl.* 4 July 725/1 The work of a British historian that shucks off the weight of this ponderous tradition. **1976** *New Yorker* 19 Apr. 98/2 Odd thing: Joanne, now living in Connecticut, has hung on to her Southern accent; the two others, both New Yorkers, have shucked theirs. **1978** *Guardian Weekly* 1 Jan. 18/4 Spanish boys and girls have shucked the race for money... Marriage and children are not a goal. Neither is wealth.

3. a. *trans.* and *intr.* To deceive, fool or 'kid' (someone). *slang.*

1959 L. Lipton *Holy Barbarians* 25, I didn't shuck the customers enough to please the crook who was running the car lot. **1966** [see sense b below]. **1969** S. Greenlee *Spook who sat by Door* xiii. 114 He soothed them and told them to go home..and he did not shuck. You either work at a cover or forget it. **1976** C. Weston *Rouse Demon* xviii. 88 You shucking me, man, I didn't get rid of nobody! **1979** *Maclean's Mag.* 4 June 6/3 The petulant Keith Jarrett is an example: 'He's shucking.'

b. *shucking and jiving*: fooling. Cf. *Jive *v.* 1 a. *U.S. Blacks.*

[**1966** E. Bullins *Theme is Blackness* (1973) 27 Yawhl jivin'...yawhl shuckin'.] **1969** H. R. Brown *Die Nigger Die!* ii. 25, I told him he should think about it, but I knew I was schuckin' and jivin'. **1974** H. L. Foster *Ribbin', Jivin', & Playin' Dozens* v. 195 For many blacks, shuckin' and jivin' is a survival technique to avoid and stay out of trouble.

shucker (earlier example).

1872 *Golden Hours* iv. 397/1 The colored shuckers are considered the best because they will throw down a small oyster, and only open the large or medium-sized ones.

shudder, *v.* Add: **1. d.** Esp. in colloq. phr. *I shudder to think* with obj. clause.

1872 Geo. Eliot *Let.* 4 Aug. (1956) V. 297, I shudder a little to think what a long book it will be. **1952** M. Laski *Village* iii. 53 What they're going to think of us abroad, I shudder to think. **1970** A. Price *Labyrinth Makers* xii. 161 What he'll make of you I shudder to think!

4. For *nonce-use* read *rare* and add earlier and later examples.

1639 Chapman & Shirly *Tragedie of Chabot Admirall of France* i. sig. B, Loud conscience has a voyce to shadder greatnesse. **1925** E. Blunden *English Poems* 58 A drowned sheep lodged In a black holt of alders, Its poor fleece brown and vile, To shudder young beholders.

shuddersome, *a.* Add: (Later example.) Also *transf.*, inclined to shudder. Hence **shu·dder-somely** *adv.*

1903 A. M. Binstead *Pitcher in Paradise* ii. 52 One of those shuddersomely refined affairs that are supposed to be meat and drink to the giddy suburbanite. **1941** I. L. Idriess *Great Boomerang* xxii. 168 Eastern daggers of shuddersome shape, weapons of many nations. **1969** O. Blakiston *For crying out Shroud* iii. 29, I don't.. really feel so shuddersome about the smallest of bald patches.

shuddup (ʃʊdʊ·p), vulgar corruption of imp. *shut up* (see Shut *v.* 19 m). Cf. *shaddup, *shurrup.

1940 C. McCullers *Heart is Lonely Hunter* ii. xii. 217 'You dumb dumb·dumb dumb—' 'Shuddup! Shuddup!' **1978** F. Mullally *Deadly Payoff* xiii. 180 'Shuddup,' Macdonald snorted.

shuffle, *sb.* Add: **5.** (Earlier example of *double shuffle.*) Also *spec.* a modern popular dance to jazz or rock and roll music, evolved orig. from Negro folk-dance; the music to which this is danced.

1821 P. Egan *Life in London* ii. v. 287 The *kidwys* and *kiddiesses* were footing the double shuffle against each other. **1925** (*jazz music title*) Shanghai Shuffle. [**1935** K. Burchill *Step Dancing* iv. 14 Swing the leg forward from the knee, so that the ball of your foot strikes the ground as it comes through... From this position swing the lower part of the leg back to its original position, striking the ground at the same time with the ball of the foot... These two movements..done in this order, constitute what is known as the 'Shuffle'.] **1955** Keepnews & Grauer *Pictorial Hist. Jazz.* ix 97 Such slightly later recordings as *Riverboat Shuffle.* **1956** M. Stearns *Story of Jazz* xvii. 203 The arrangements now sound heavy and cluttered and the rhythm was almost of the 'shuffle' variety. **1976** J. van de Wetering *Corpse on Dike* (1977) xvi. 159 The combo..played a slow shuffle, very easy to get into.

6. b. phr. *lost in the shuffle*: overlooked or missed in the mêlée or multitude. *U.S.*

1930 D. Runyon in *Collier's* 22 Mar. 21/4, I find we are about lost in the shuffle of guys with little mustaches. **1955** *New Yorker* 11 June 74/3 Mr. Ewell's efforts to be quietly funny are lost in the shuffle. **1981** W. Safire in *N.Y. Times Mag.* 8 Feb. 12/2 The book itself would then get lost in the shuffle.

c. *transf.* A redistribution of ministerial posts within a government or cabinet. Cf. Reshuffle *sb.* in Dict. and Suppl.

1941 C. Mackenzie *Red Tapeworm* xxii. 296, I hope we shall have no more of these Cabinet shuffles for the time being! **1966** —— *Paper Lives* xiv. 184 Mr Williamson, who was hoping like Mr Upjohn to find himself in the Cabinet at the next shuffle, ceased to argue. **1976** J. I. M. Stewart *Memorial Service* xiii. 204 The government was judged likely soon to undergo one of those 'shuffles' that English political mythology declares to be periodically essential.

shuffle, *v.* Add: **1. a.** Also *fig.* with *off* to die. (In playful allusion to *Hamlet*: see sense 5 d, quot. 1602.) *colloq.*

1922 A. Huxley *Mortal Coils* 124 One has to bring them [*sc.* obituary notices] up to date every year or so for fear of being caught napping if one of these old birds chooses to shuffle off suddenly. **1977** *N.Y. Rev. Bks.* 4 Aug. 29/3 She thought—if one had to 'shuffle off'—it would be terrific to be electrocuted while playing a bass guitar in a rock group.

12. shuffle beat = next; **shuffle rhythm,** a slow strongly syncopated rhythm (see quot. 1940); **shuffle-wing,** for *Accentor* substitute *Prunella*; (later examples).

1955 Shapiro & Hentoff *Hear me talkin' to Ya* 21 They played the shuffle beat on the snare drum. **1977** *National Observer* (U.S.) 22 Jan. 22/4 A lot of it's the old southern shuffle beat. Music you could get up and dance to. **1940** *Swing* June 13/3 The typifying characteristic of the Savitt band is its 'shuffle rhythm', which is distinguished..by its..4/4 jazz time. **1967** *Boston Sunday Herald* 30 Apr. 14/4 From shuffle rhythm to rock he waxed them all. **1909** W. H. Hudson *Afoot in England* xxiv. 289, I also love the smaller vocalists—the modest shufflewing and the lesser whitethroat. **1977** *Sunday Tel.* 6 Feb. 15/7 This is a day on which to..watch truly aggressive chaffinches competing with shufflewings.

shuffly (ʃʊ·fli), *a.* [f. Shuffle *v.* + -y[1].] Characterized by shuffling; inclined to shuffle.

1926 *Blackw. Mag.* Oct. 539/2 The step slower and, if possible, more shuffly. **1952** J. Masters *Deceivers* xxi. 240 That shuffly, shy old fool. **1974** N. Freeling *Dressing of Diamond* 66 He banged on the counter, brought the shuffly man out.

shufti, shufty (ʃu·fti, ʃʊ-), *sb. slang* (orig. *Mil.*). [f. next.]

1. A look or glance. Esp. in phr. *to take* (or *have*) *a shufti.*

1943 *Gen* 16 Jan. 11/2 Take a shufti at that. That's Stephanie. **1947** D. M. Davin *Gorse blooms Pale* 201 She took another good shufty at us. **1965** J. Porter *Dover Two* x. 133 Take a shufty at this lot! **1971** Whillans & Ormerod *Don Whillans* x. 81 'Let's have a shufti at that description then,' said Joe, and we both examined the piece of paper covered with Snell's handwriting. **1980** R. Adams *Girl in Swing* xix. 245 Good idea, old boy. I'm game. Let's 'ave a crafty shufti round with that in mind, shall we?

2. *Comb.*, as **shufti-kite,** a reconnaissance aircraft; **shufti-scope,** a probe (see quots.).

1944 T. H. Wisdom *Triumph over Tunisia* 172 When the Hun shufti-kites were kept away..the U.S. Second Corps moved..to the coastal stretch in the north. **1948** Partridge *Dict. Forces' Slang* 169 *Shuftiscope*, instrument used by doctors for exploring the interior of a dysentery case. A telescope or periscope. **1962** *Times* 12 Apr. 9/4 When officers were making a routine check of the vehicle with an instrument they call a 'shufti-scope' they found the watches. Mr. Eaton explained that the 'shufti-scope' is an instrument consisting of a probe with a light through which it is possible to see into cavities.

shufty (ʃu·fti, ʃʊ-), *v. slang* (chiefly *Mil.*). Now *rare.* [f. Arab. *šufti* have you seen?, f. *šāf* to see.] *intr.* To look or watch; to glance. Freq. in *imp.*

1943 C. H. Ward-Jackson *It's Piece of Cake* 54 *Shufty*, look, watch. Thus, the orderly room sergeant to a Waaf clerk as he sights a squadron of Liberators through the headquarters' window, 'Shufty!' **1947** *Amer. Speech* XXII. 267 The word *shufti* was among the most commonly used, comprehending in its meaning both the noun and the verb 'look'..'to shufti around' [etc.].

‖ **shugo** (ʃū·go). Also **Shugo.** [Jap.] In the Japanese feudal system: a military governor.

1893 F. Brinkley tr. *Hist. Empire Japan* iv. 171 His Majesty sanctioned the appointment of High Constables (*Shugo*) in the various provinces. **1933** F. C. Jones *Japan* i. 13 As is usual under feudal conditions, the *Shugo*..made their posts hereditary. **1974** *Encycl. Brit. Macropædia* X. 64/2 It was the job of the *shugo* to recruit metropolitan guards and keep strict control over subversives and criminals.

‖ **shuka** (ʃū·kă). Also **Shukkah.** [Swahili.] A long piece of fabric, now commonly worn as a shawl-like garment in East Africa.

1856 R. F. Burton *First Footsteps E. Africa* ii. 29 As regards the word Tobe, it signifies, in Arabic, a garment generally: the Somal call it 'Maro', and the half Tobe a 'Shukkah'. **1936** F. Stark *Southern Gates Arabia* xi. 123 The visitors from outside came wrapped in their shuka, a square black shawl with two fringed sides which they wore draped over their heads and bodies, the two lower corners knotted together and the upper ones thrown over one arm. **1971** *Standard* (Dar es Salaam) 7 Apr. 6/3 (Advt.), Tasini leads the way in the latest dress print designs. Shukas, Vitenges etc.

‖ **shul** (ʃūl). Also **shool.** [Yiddish, f. G. *schule* school.] The synagogue.

[**1804** M. Wilmot *Let.* 17 July in *Russian Jrnls.* (1934) i. 114 They walked with down cast eyes and penitent countenances to the School (as the Synagogue is call'd).] **1874** Hotten *Slang Dict.* 288 *Shool*, Jews' term for their synagogue. **1876** Geo. Eliot *D. Deronda* IV. xxxiii. 136/1 This evening is the Sabbath..and I go to the *Shool.* **1892** [see *hesped]. **1932** L. Golding *Magnolia Street* i. xiii. 235 The presentation will be at night, after *shool.* **1957** L. Stern *Midas Touch* i. 19 The Kosher food, the ceremonial prayers, coming here to *shul.* **1977** *New Yorker* 9 May 41/3 Her great-uncle Zindel, a former shammes in a shul that had been torn down.

‖ **Shulchan Aruch** (ʃu·lχăn ā·ruχ). Also **Shulh(h)an Arukh.** [Heb., lit. table prepared.] The name of a work on Jewish religious practice by Joseph ben Ephraim Caro (1488–1575) now accepted as the standard guide to Orthodox observance.

1901 M. Gaster *Hist. Anc. Synagogue Spanish & Portuguese Jews* 47 It is an abstract of the *Shulhhan Arukh of Caro* containing all the laws and ceremonies of a practical utility, condensed into a very small form. **1922** *Aspects Jewish Life & Thought* 43 This popular edition of the greater work is the *Shulchan Aruch*..which was first published in the year 1565. **1957** *Encycl. Brit.* X. 18/2 The codes, especially Joseph Qaro's *Shulḥan Arukh*, became the halachic authority in Jewry. **1978** I. B. Singer *Shosha* ii. 22 He breaks every law of the Shulchan Aruch, yet at the same time he preaches Jewishness.

shulwar. Add: Also † **shalwar.** (Earlier example.)

1824 J. Morier *Adventures Hajji Baba* II. ix. 144 Can I offer him five tomâuns, and a pair of crimson *shalwars*?

shun, *v.* Add: **9. shun-pike** (earlier example); hence **shunpike** *v. intr.*, to drive along minor roads, avoiding the toll on turnpikes, or for pleasure; **shunpiker; shun-piking** *vbl. sb.*

1853 *Albany Even. Atlas* 9 Apr. 4 The Oswego Canal.. has been called a 'shun pike'. Produce sent by Lake Ontario and the Oswego Canal, avoids tolls on the canals west of Syracuse. **1964** *Collier's Encycl. Yearbk.* 70 Besides making long trips at high speed, motorists could take part in sports car rallies, chug about in antiques, 'shunpike' on quiet back roads. **1967** *Sat. Rev.* (U.S.) 22 Apr. 55 (Advt.), Smooth roads, beautiful scenery—what more could a shunpiker want? **1961** M. Beadle *These Ruins are Inhabited* iv. 41 George's reaction was to avoid all main roads—which is a good idea anyway if you're not in a hurry, the virtues of shun-piking being self-evident. **1972** *Alberta Motorist* (Edmonton) Apr. 6/3 There are, of course, many times when shunpiking is preferable for the traveller.

'shun (ʃʊn). Colloq. abbrev. of Attention 5, representing the verbal distortion and stress when used as a military command.

1888 Kipling *Plain Tales from Hills* 242 Stan'at—*hease*, *'Shun.* **1928** *Granta* 2 Nov. 76/1 Prisoner! 'Shun.

Move to the right in fours. **1955** W. FAULKNER *Fable* 108 'Bridesman,' he said but at that moment the major said "Shun!'

‖ **shunga** (ʃu·ŋgä). Also **shun-ga.** [Jap., f. *shun* spring + *ga* picture.] An example of Japanese erotic art; a painting or print of a pornographic nature.

1964 *New Society* 17 Dec. 20/2 These paintings were *shunga*, 'Spring Pictures', which is the delicate Japanese euphemism for..erotic art. **1970** *Oxf. Compan. Art* 1172 With the exception of Sharaku almost all the 600 to 700 artists in the movement produced pornographic prints, known as *shun-ga* or 'spring pictures'. **1981** G. MACBETH *Kind of Treason* ii. 23 Quite a good collection of [Japanese] prints. A Hiroshige. Some *shunga*.

shungite (ʃu·ŋgəit). *Min.* Also **schungite.** [ad. G. *schungit* (A. von Inostranzeff 1886, in *Neues Jahrb. für Mineral.* I. 92), f. *Schunga* (Russ. *Shunga*), name of a village in Russia close to the Finnish border: see -ITE[1].] (See quote. 1972.)

1892 E. S. DANA *Dana's Syst. Min.* (ed. 6) 8 Schungite from the Olonets Government, Russia, is a similar amorphous form of carbon intermediate between anthracite and graphite, occurring in phyllite. **1916** *Trans. & Proc. Geol. Soc. S. Africa* XVIII. 130 Schungite and graphitoid merge into graphite, but the difference is not crystalline merely, for the latter yields graphitic acid on oxidation, while the former do not. **1941** *Compt. Rend. (Doklady) de l'Acad. des Sci. de l'URSS* XXXIII. 358 Other authors arrived at an opposite conclusion, to the effect that the crystalline phase existing in anthracite and shungite is graphite, but..in a highly dispersed state. **1946** *Mineral. Abstr.* IX. 202 Eleven analyses of shungite from Shunga, Lake Onega, and other localities in eastern Karelia show C 46–99, ash 1–46, V_2O_5 0·016–0·77%, &c. **1968** *Ibid.* XIX. 102/1 The use of schungite to obtain combustible gases. **1972** *Gloss. Geol.* (Amer. Geol. Inst.) 656/2 *Shungite*, a hard, black, amorphous, coal-like material containing over 98% carbon, found interbedded among Precambrian schists. It is probably the metamorphic equivalent of bitumen, but it may represent merely impure graphite.

shunt, *sb.* Add: **1. b.** (Earlier example.)

1862 J. SIMMONS *Railway Traveller's Handy Bk.* 12 A thin line in the middle of trains..represents a shunt.

c. *slang.* A motor accident, a crash: esp. a nose-to-tail collision. Also **shunt-up** (on analogy with *PILE-UP 1), a multiple crash.

1959 in *Chambers's Twentieth Cent. Dict.* Add. **1967** *Economist* 11 Feb. 544/3 The characteristic American accident is a multivehicle shunt on a freeway. **1976** J. WAINWRIGHT *Bastard* vii. 91 Mist..happens on motorways, and is the cause of multi-car shunt-ups, where radiators kiss bumper bars. **1978** G. VAUGHAN *Belgrade Drop* vi. 41 'Another bloody shunt,' Yardley groaned. The Zagreb trunk was notorious for accidents.

2. c. *Med.* A natural or artificial route, esp. from a vein to an artery, whereby blood may bypass a capillary bed; the passage of blood along such a route. Also, the surgical construction of such a route.

1923 *Medicine* II. 20 Deficient oxygenation of the arterial blood..caused..by an unaerated shunt of venous blood into arterial. *Ibid.* 33 The readiness with which cyanosis develops or increases, during exercise, in a patient with an unaerated shunt. **1937** BEST & TAYLOR *Physiol. Basis Med. Pract.* xxxv. 581 (*caption*) A portion of the blood passes through unaerated channels (shunt) from the venous to the arterial system. **1961** *Lancet* 30 Sept. 728/2 2 patients..had both undergone splenectomy some time before portocaval shunt was performed. **1980** *Amer. Speech* LV. 47 Clamps used to stop blood flow through a shunt when kidney dialysis is initiated.

d. *Biochem.* An alternative metabolic pathway; *spec.* (freq. as *hexose monophosphate shunt*) the pentose phosphate cycle.

1953 *Jrnl. Bacteriol.* LXVI. 17 It has been possible to infer..the existence of a sequence of reactions, the hexosemonophosphate shunt, which may serve in nature as a major pathway for the aerobic breakdown of carbohydrate by filamentous microorganisms. **1964** [see pentose phosphate shunt s.v. *PENTOSE 2]. **1967** M. E. HALE *Biol. Lichens* viii. 118 Insoluble metabolic shunt products often serve as reserve food. **1970** [see *RIBOSE].

5. a. shunt machine, motor, a direct-current motor in which the field and armature windings are connected in parallel with respect to the supply.

1888 *Rep. Brit. Assoc. Adv. Sci. 1887* 616 In a shunt machine the current through the coils of the second magnet may be controlled by the addition of a resistance in series with it. **1953** E. MOLLOY *Small Motors & Transformers* ii. 17 [Differential compounding] is sometimes employed to secure further improvement of the speed characteristic of a shunt machine, in cases where the load is variable. **1883** *Jrnl. Soc. Telegr. Engineers & Electricians* XII. 310 A coiled magneto-machine.., in which we have a magneto-generator acting as a brake, and a shunt motor. **1977** *N.Z. Herald* 5 Jan. 3/7 And once in Auckland, tied up by traffic lights and other vehicles, he switches over completely to his shunt motor for a quiet, anxiety-free tour of the town.

shunt, *v.* Add: **4. a.** (Earlier example.)

1845 *Min. Proc. Inst. Civil Engin.* IV. 252 At intermediate stations, the waggons are now 'shunted' to their proper places, in a siding, by the engine which has propelled them along the main line.

6. b. *Med.* To pass (blood) through a shunt. Cf. *SHUNT *sb.* 2 c.

1923 *Medicine* II. 18 A condition..in patients with congenital perforate septum of the heart, where a fraction of the blood is shunted directly from the right heart to the left without passing through the lungs. **1950** BEST & TAYLOR *Physiol. Basis of Med. Pract.* (ed. 5) xxxv. 435/1 Most of the blood is shunted to the arterial side through channels which normally close at, or shortly after, birth.

shunting, *vbl. sb.* (Later examples in *Med.*)

1961 *Lancet* 23 Sept. 693/2 Arteriovenous shunting may be..applicable to more mammalian species..than has been previously considered. **1974** *Nature* 9 Aug. 489/1 Because of the incompletely divided ventricle, shunting of venous blood from the right atrium to the systemic circuit..may occur.

shupac, var. *SHOEPACK.

shurrup (ʃʊrʊ·p, ʃuru·p), vulgar corruption of imp. *shut up* (see SHUT *v.* 19 m). Also **shurr up.** Cf. *SHADDUP, *SHUDDUP.

1893 S. GRAND *Heavenly Twins* I. I. iv. 27 Barbara politely requested her to 'shurrup!' a word of the boys which she permitted herself to borrow. **1929** J. B. PRIESTLEY *Good Companions* III. iv. 553 'Shurr up!' the voice jeered, before anybody else could make a sound. **1960** C. RAY *Merry England* 173 You shurrup, shurrup: I've just about had enough of you. **1978** J. WAINWRIGHT *Ripple of Murders* 40 Shurrup, Richard, don't show your ignorance.

shush (ʃuʃ, ʃʊʃ), *v.* [Echoic, representing a repetition of SH *int.* Cf. SHSHSH.] **1.** *trans.* To call or reduce (someone) to silence by uttering the sounds denoted by *sh-sh.* Also const. advs.

1925 P. GIBBS *Unchanging Quest* xvii. 127 She would.. 'shush' away any intruders who came to interrupt her private conversation. **1930** E. FERBER *Cimarron* i. 6 The woman listened... They shushed their children when they moved or whimpered. **1949** 'J. TEY' *Brat Farrar* xxv. 225 'The Ashbys cleaning up as usual,' the voice said, and was instantly shushed. **1961** J. HELLER *Catch 22* (1962) xxii. 223 'Stop shouting, will you?' Yossarian shushed him. **1971** WODEHOUSE *Much Obliged, Jeeves* xv. 152 The ancestor..would, I think, have developed the theme had I not shushed her down with a raised hand. **1980** *Christian Sci. Monitor* (Midwestern ed.) 4 Dec. B3/2 He shushes them or storms at them or coaches them.

2. a. *intr.* To call for silence in this manner. Freq. *imp.* **b.** To become or remain silent.

1924 'O. DOUGLAS' *Pink Sugar* v. 52, I stood patiently while Nellie 'shushed' under her breath as she brushed, directing me at intervals to 'Stand still, will ye!' **1929** J. B. PRIESTLEY *Good Companions* II. i. 273 He gets no further, being fiercely requested by several of his colleagues to 'shush'. *Ibid.* III. iv. 553 Some people laughed. The remainder indignantly shushed again and then clapped. **1969** M. PUGH *Last Place Left* xix. 140 'Shush, you bloody pig,' he said, for the collie was growing impatient. **1972** J. WILSON *Hide & Seek* v. 81 'Sh, now, there's a good girl.' 'I won't shush. I want to go home.' **1977** 'J. BELL' *Such a Nice Client* vi. 63 'That's the idea. Shush!' The manageress was back.

shush (ʃuʃ, ʃʊʃ), *sb. colloq.* [f. the vb.] An utterance of the exclamation 'Sh!' Also *transf.*, quiet. Cf. HUSH *sb.*[2] 1 a.

1954 R. FULLER *Fantasy & Fugue* v. 115, I got him out among the shushes and tut-tuts before the attendants could reach him. **1959** I. & P. OPIE *Lore & Lang. Schoolch.* x. 193 Let's 'ave a bit of shush. **1971** 'A. BURGESS' *MF* vi. 71 There was a response of frightened shushes. **1982** *Observer* (Colour Suppl.) 25 Apr. 11/2 Can we have a little shush please?

shushing (ʃu·ʃiŋ, ʃʊ·ʃiŋ), *vbl. sb.* [f. *SHUSH *v.* + -ING[1].] The action of the verb. Also *attrib.*, as *shushing, noise, sound.*

1929 J. B. PRIESTLEY *Good Companions* III. iv. 552 It raised a loud and jeering laugh from that quarter, though the rest of the audience immediately made shushing noises. **1937** *Richmond* (Va.) *News-Leader* 9 Sept. 3/1 (*heading*) No 'shushing' at Nazi parley. **1972** *Listener* 15 June 806 The sound of a gourd rattle to make a 'shushing' sound. **1981** A. EDWARDS *Sonya* i. 27 There was much shushing in the front parlor if the children came in.

shush-shush, *a. rare.* [Reduplicated form of *SHUSH *v.* or *sb.*] **a.** Echoic, designating something that makes a repeated soft sound like a shush. **b.** = *HUSH-HUSH.

1954 *New World Writing* VI. 44, I measured..his shush-shush tread in my presence. **1963** *Listener* 24 Jan. 182/1 It is his [*sc.* the defence correspondent's] job to know what is going on in the shush-shush world behind the 'D' notices.

Shuswap (ʃu·swɒp), *sb.* and *a.* Also † **Shooshap, Shouswap, Shushwap.** [ad. Shuswap *səxʷepmx* Shuswap Indians.] **A.** *sb.* **a.** A North American Indian tribe inhabiting southern British Columbia. **b.** Their language. **B.** *adj.* Of or pertaining to this tribe or their language.

1838 S. PARKER *Jrnl. Exploring Tour* (1842) 313 West of these [*sc.* the Kettle Falls Indians] are the Sinpauēlish ..; and below these are the Shooshaps, having a population of five hundred and seventy-five. **1845** [see *CARRIER 2 b]. **1904** A. G. MORICE *Hist. Northern Interior Brit. Columbia* 6 In case of death the bodies were buried among the Chilcotins and the Shushwaps. *Ibid.* iv. 51 This so-called Carrier vocabulary is made up of Shushwap words. **1927** *Internat. Jrnl. Amer. Linguistics* IV. 120 Salisham—Interior dialects: Shuswap; Lillooet. **1959** E. TUNIS *Indians* 130/2 The Shushwap were a typical tribe of the interior Salish. **1965** *Canad. Jrnl. Linguistics* Spring 86 Terms found in those Salisham languages which are geographically the closest, particularly Kalispel..and Shuswap where available. **1976** *Shuswap Visitor's Guide* 10/3 According to a Shuswap Indian legend, you will find a place of perpetual summer.

shut, *sb.* Add: **6.** *Comb.*, as **shut-knife** *dial.*, a clasp-knife, a pocket-knife.

1879 J. SPILLING *Johnny's Jaunt* i. 8, I took out my shet-knife and cut her a..huncheon off the loaf. **1913** D. H. LAWRENCE *Sons & Lovers* vii. 210 But they managed to procure a loaf and a currant-loaf, which they hacked into pieces with shut-knives, and ate sitting on the wall near the bridge. **1979** in R. Blythe *View in Winter* i. 63 He'd whittle away at things... He was that cliver [*sic*] with his shutknife.

shut, *v.* Add: **I. 3.** Also in pa. pple. with verbs of movement, as *draw, push,* etc., denoting completion of an action; equivalent to To *adv.* 4. orig. *U.S.*

1884 *Century Mag.* Nov. 13 He..pushed the ground-glass door shut. **1902** O. WISTER *Virginian* xiv. 163 Our wheels clucked over the main-line switch. A train-hand threw it shut after. **1911** H. S. HARRISON *Queed* ii. 23 The last boarder rising drew shut the folding-doors into the parlor. **1933** E. O'NEILL *Ah, Wilderness!* I. 18 She slams the door shut. **1957** T. SLESSOR *First Overland* 256 We slam shut the windows, as the car slides down through the rocks.

4. b. (*a*) *to shut* (one's) *face*: see *FACE *sb.* 2 a for examples.

(*c*) *shut it* (in imperative): close one's mouth, hold one's tongue.

1886–96 in Farmer & Henley *Slang* (1903) VI. 202/1 Oh, shut it! Close your mouth until I tell you when. **1908** G. SANGER *Seventy Years Showman* x. 33 'Shut it!' said one of the showmen roughly; 'save your breath for the next scene.' **1945** G. MILLAR *Maquis* viii. 163 'Enough,' cried Boulaya. 'Shut it, Frisé... You know nothing.'

6. (Later examples.)

1949 K. S. WOODS *Rural Crafts England* II. ii. 33 The tyres have to be tightened by cutting out a piece and rejoining or shutting them with a smaller circumference to grip the wheel. **1964** H. HODGES *Artifacts* v. 86 For nearly all purposes the most effective way of joining iron was by welding or shutting.

11. a. Also (*dial.*) *shut on* and *ellipt.*

1848 MRS. GASKELL *Mary Barton* I. v. 68 As for a bad man, one's glad enough to get shut on him. **1914** D. H. LAWRENCE *Widowing of Mrs. Holroyd* III. 84 Who dost think wor goin' ter stop when we knowed 'e on'y kep on so's to get shut on us. **1976** S. BARSTOW *Right True End* I. iv. 65 'I haven't *got* her.' 'You're well shut, from all I hear.'

II. 13. shut down. a. (Earlier example of night.)

1880 'MARK TWAIN' *Tramp Abroad* xix. 182 We got to ..Heidelberg before the night shut down.

d. *Mech.* To stop or switch off (a device or machine, esp. an engine); to cause to stop working or running. Also *absol.*

1895 G. W. LUMMIS-PATERSON *Management of Dynamos* x. 148 When shutting down a machine, the load should first be gradually reduced..by easing down the engine. **1911** MARSHALL & SANKEY *Gas Engines* vi. 175 [Filling the reservoir] is done when shutting down the engine so soon as the gas is turned off. **1948** H. CONSTANT *Gas Turbines* xi. 137 The best that can be done is to shut down as many engines as possible and operate the remainder at a power output giving reasonable efficiency. **1969** I. KEMP *Brit. G.I. in Vietnam* viii. 163 We all 'shut down'—switched off our engines and made fast the rotor blades to the tails of the helicopters. **1976** *Physics Bull.* Aug. 339/2 Two samples were taken from the low-sulphur plant: one at ambient temperatures 30 days after the boiler had been shut down. **1980** *Daily Tel.* 10 Mar. 3/2 A nagging 'oil migration' problem..could eventually have forced a pilot to shut down the engine.

e. *Physics.* To stop (the chain reaction) in a nuclear reactor; to stop (a nuclear reactor) from producing useful power by making the fuel assembly subcritical.

1945 HAWLEY & LEIFSON *Atomic Energy* 157 Knoowing just when to shut down the chain-reaction..would be quite a problem. **1951** *Nucleonics* Jan. 5/2 If the temperature of the uranium exceeds 60°C, the pile is automatically shut down. **1963** B. FOZARD *Instrumentation Nuclear Reactors* xiii. 164 Unless a heavy-water reactor is shut down for such a long period that there is a significant fall in the activity of the high-energy gamma emitters, it has a built-in neutron source. **1976** *Sci. Amer.* Jan. 27/2 The level of radioactivity in a standard 1,000-megawatt reactor is very high: about 10 billion curies half an hour after the reactor is shut down.

f. *intr.* Of a device, machine, or installation, esp. a nuclear reactor: to cease to operate.

1945 H. D. SMYTH *Gen. Account Devel. Atomic Energy for Military Purposes 1940–45* viii. 81 The half-life of the U-239 is so short that its concentration becomes negligible soon after the pile shuts down. **1960** *Engineering Index 1959* 246/2 During power failures of up to 1·5 sec duration..synchronous motors usually shut down. **1976** *Sci. Amer.* July 36/1 After the reactor had shut down, the evidence of its activity was preserved virtually undisturbed through the succeeding ages of geological activity. **1978** *Nature* 19 Oct. 576/2 As the voltage dropped rapidly various sensors began to shut down, and within a few minutes the satellite ceased to respond to commands sent up from ground control stations. **1979** *Daily Tel.* 15 Aug. 32/3 The Sea Kings will operate throughout the night but the others do not have night capability and will have to shut down for the night.

15. *shut in.* **c*.** *Oil Industry.* To cease drawing oil or gas from (a well).

1931 W. H. EMMONS *Geol. Petroleum* (ed. 2) xvi. 527 In 1923, during a period of overproduction, certain groups of wells were shut in while others near by were pumped. **1962** T. C. FRICK *Petroleum Production Handbk.* II. xxx. 8 Pressure readings obtained while the well is being cleaned before the well is shut in. **1971** *West Indian World* 5 Nov. 16/2 All 17 wells had encountered satisfactory oil sand sections and were at present 'shut in' and awaiting the installation of an eight-inch pipeline.

d. For † *Obs.* read 'Now *rare*' and add later example.

1924 [implied at *SHUTTING *vbl. sb.* 3].

16. shut off. c. *intr.* To come to a halt; to cease talking or writing. *U.S.*

1896 'MARK TWAIN' in *Harper's Mag.* Sept. 526/1 'Now who—' He shut off sudden. **1902** J. LONDON *Let.* 12 July (1966) 136 Someone is going down town, so I'll shut off and give them a chance to mail this. **1938** V. WOOLF *Let.* 18 June (1980) VI. 241 He rang me up late on Wednesday... He said he had travelled post haste from Prague to see Leonard. I said, A misunderstanding. Then we shut off.

17. shut out. d. (Earlier examples.) Also *transf.* in other games and *fig. N. Amer.*

1881 *N.Y. Herald* 17 July 10/3 The Domestics were shut out in every inning up to the eighth, when by bunching their hits they scored two earned runs on a single by Mahny. **1894** *Spalding's Base Ball Guide* 40 Nichols..shut out the St. Louis team without a game to their credit out of four games played. **1952** in Wentworth & Flexner *Amer. Dict. Slang* (1960) 475/2 The last time [the Princeton football players] were shut out Penn did it on Nov. 3, 1946. **1957** *Northland News* (Uranium City, Sask.) 7 Jan. 7/2 [Ice hockey] The Flyers shut-out the blue and gold for the second time by a 2–0 count. **1976** *National Observer* (U.S.) 15 May 2/1 Reagan shut out Ford in Texas, winning all 96 delegates to the National Convention.

19. shut up. l. (Earlier example.)

1814 JANE AUSTEN *Mansfield Park* III. xvi. 305 Her son, who was always guided by the last speaker, by the person who could get hold of and shut him up.

m. (Earlier example.)

1840 *Picayune* (New Orleans) 10 Oct. 2/4 The Dutchman got a hint to 'shut up' from one of the officers.

shut, *ppl. a.* Add: **2.** *shut-away* adj. Also with adjs., as *shut-eyed*, *-minded* (so *-mindedness*), *-mouthed*.

1911 GALSWORTHY *Patrician* II. xvi. 253 Her face had a strange, brooding, shut-away look, as though he had frightened her. **1913** 'SAKI' *When William Came* (1914) xvi. 272 He looked round again at the rolling stretches of brown hills; before he had regarded them merely as the background to this little shut-away world. **1959** *Listener* 12 Mar. 473/1 The sensitive, shut-away man. **1934** J. A. LEE *Children of Poor* (1949) III. 68 Prayer was tiring in the extreme, in an atmosphere of tense, sweaty, shut-eyed sanctity. **1956** H. GOLD *Man who was not with It* (1965) xxx. 283, I watched Belle's shut-eyed face compose with fatigue. **1960** T. HUGHES *Lupercal* 37 And look in at the byre's Blaze of darkness: a sudden shut-eyed look Backward into the head. **1977** *Sunday Mail* (Brisbane) 20 Nov. 27/4, I don't want to get shut-minded as I get older. **1981** *Times Lit. Suppl.* 16 Jan. 60/4 At this stage in such a review it is a common *topos* to remark that thanks are due to the editor or author for raising weighty questions. It may seem churlish or shut-minded, but for £45 one might also expect a few answers. **1933** C. C. MARTINDALE in M. Leahy *Conversions to Catholic Church* ix. 91 A priestly work of incredible shut-mindedness, but..homage-worthiness. **1936** C. SANDBURG *People, Yes* 113 In Vermont a shut-mouthed husband finally broke forth to his wife. **1959** W. R. BIRD *These are Maritimes* viii. 217 That made him awful mad but he wouldn't say anything. He's what you'd call 'shut-mouthed'.

shut, var. *SHUTT.

shut-down. Add: **1. a.** (Earlier and later examples.)

The sense in quot. 1857 is uncertain.

1857 *Knickerbocker* XLIX. 35 'I'll be just exactly shot if you *don't!*' he added with a patent diabolical shut-down. **1884** *Boston Jrnl.* 16 Oct. 7 The Acushnet paper-mill at New Bedford has started up after a shut-down of two months. **1901** *Chambers's Jrnl.* Jan. 29/1 In the old days when we had a grievance we could talk it over with the boss; but today if there is a shut-down nobody knows anything about it except that it has been ordered from headquarters in New York. **1931** *Economist* 15 Aug. 308/2 The Ford shutdown will restrict August production. **1959** *News Chron.* 2 July 4/3 What do you propose..to prevent a shutdown of the national papers? **1967** *N.Y. Times* (Internat. Ed.) 11 Feb. 2/2 Classes resumed quietly at Madrid University today after a 10-day shutdown because of campus battles between students and the police. **1972** M. JONES *Life on Dole* vi. 51 The Dowlais shut-down had several consequences. It took away the one industrial enterprise that kept going all through the week.

b. The cessation of broadcasting for the day on any particular channel or station; the time at which this occurs.

1959 *Listener* 19 Mar. 499/1 The peak viewing-hours from 7.0 p.m. to shut-down. **1973** *Times* 15 Dec. 2/7 (*heading*) TV staggers shutdown.

2. a. The cessation of operation of a machine, device, or installation, esp. as a result of a fault.

1911 J. F. C. SNELL *Power House Design* x. 352 The..security against a shut-down arising from the duplicate sets of bus bars. **1916** *Standard. Rules Amer. Inst. Electr. Engin.* 35 This method consists in the measurement of the temperature of windings by their increase in resistance, corrected to the instant of shut-down when necessary. **1936** *Discovery* Apr. 113/2 In the event of a shut-down of the power unit, an alternative supply is available from the storage battery. **1953** [see *INPUT *v.* 3]. **1971** *New Scientist* 7 Jan. 19/1 An abrupt shutdown is a very different affair from the computer operator pushing the computer 'off' buttons. **1976** M. MACHLIN *Pipeline* liv. 542 The breakdown at Pump Station One and Three..resulted in an automatic shutdown of the entire pipeline.

b. *Physics.* The stopping of the chain reaction in a nuclear reactor when the fuel assembly is made subcritical.

1945 H. D. SMYTH *Gen. Acct. Devel. Atomic Energy for Military Purposes 1940–45* vii. 71 A shut-down for servicing could be effected. **1951** *Nucleonics* Jan. 5/1 There are two sets..of emergency shut-down rods. **1963** B. FOZARD *Instrumentation Nuclear Reactors* xiii. 162 The delay due to xenon poisoning in restarting after a shut down cannot be reduced or eliminated. **1978** N. L. FRANKIN in Foley & Van Buren *Nuclear or Not?* 120 [Boron steel control rods] drop down into the core ensuring a rapid shutdown.

shute[2]. Add: **2.** A variety of raw silk; tram silk.

1839 URE *Dict. Arts* 1102 There are three denominations of raw silk; viz., organzine, *trame* (shute or tram), and floss. **1868** [see TRAM *sb.*[1] 1].

shute[3]. Add: **5.** = *CHUTE *sb.* 3 b.

1961 R. P. HOBSON *Rancher takes Wife* iii. 47 Each had a corral system with shute and squeeze, and a log horse-pasture. **1971** J. S. GUNN *Distrib. Shearing Terms N.S.W.* 10 *Shute*, the opening through which a shorn sheep is pushed. *Ibid.*, *Shute*, the ramp outside down which a shorn sheep is pushed to the counting-out pen.

shu·t-eye. *colloq.* [f. SHUT *v.* + EYE *sb.*[1]] Sleep; sleeping.

[**1896** KIPLING *Seven Seas* 217 (*heading*) The shut-eye sentry.] **1899** *Navy & Army Illustr.* 9 Dec. 307 The remainder of the dinner hour..is spent in smoking and perhaps dozing (a little shut-eye). **1923** C. E. MONTAGUE *Fiery Particles* 174 'We'll go on to-morrow,' I said. 'A bit of shut-eye for me now.' **1936** A. HUXLEY *Eyeless in Gaza* xxiv. 346 Time for your spot of shut-eye. **1942** 'M. INNES' *Daffodil Affair* II. 68 Or game of cards... After a long party nothing like a hand or two before shut-eye. **1958** 'CASTLE' & 'HAILEY' *Flight into Danger* i. 25 Good-night... I can sure use some shut-eye. **1977** *Time* 31 Jan. 6/1 Air Force Two indeed came equipped with a place to catch up on shut-eye between stops. 'Can you sleep on a plane?' asked Ford. Said Mondale, 'I'm going to find out.'

shu·t-in, *a.* and *sb.* orig. *U.S.* [SHUT *ppl. a.* 2: cf. SHUT *v.* 15.] **A.** *adj.* **1.** Enclosed, hemmed in; *esp.* of a person: confined by severe weather or by physical or mental disability; isolated by self-absorption; abstracted.

1849 [in Dict. s.v. SHUT *ppl. a.* 2]. **1909** *Sunday School Times* (Philadelphia) 27 Feb. 110 She had brought a handful of flowers and a heart full of sunshine to the shut-in mother. **1912** [see *AUTISM]. **1932** *Brit. Jrnl. Psychol.* Apr. 301 Subject 6 has fewer friends..because she is so 'shut in' and difficult to get to know. **1943** J. B. PRIESTLEY *Daylight on Saturday* xviii. 133 You could tell by the shut-in look on their faces as they worked that they were busy thinking about these things. **1957** [see *CLAUSTROPHOBIC *a.* b]. **1975** *Budget* (Sugarcreek, Ohio) 20 Mar. 7/4 Neal C. Troyer..and Dan L. Schwartz's spent Sat. at Nappanee visiting shut-in relatives, Bis. John L. Schwartz and Mrs. Lizzie Borkholder who is blind.

2. *Oil Industry.* Of or pertaining to oil and gas wells that are shut in; applied *esp.* to production capacity that is available but not being utilized.

1931 *Economist* 28 Mar. 671/2 Production from the new East Texas fields is weakening prices, and the vast amount of shut-in production is a constant menace. **1960** *Fortnightly Rev.* (Anderson & Strudwick, Richmond, Va.) 19 Aug., The long struggle to obtain markets for Canada's large shut-in natural gas reserves was finally concluded last week. **1962** *Listener* 10 May 796/2 There remains a huge quantity of shut-in oil capacity overhanging the market and depressing prices. **1974** P. L. MOORE et al. *Drilling Practices Manual* xii. 314 The shut-in drill pipe pressure is easy to obtain if there is no back-pressure valve in the drill string.

B. *sb.* **1.** A person who is confined by severe weather or by a physical or mental disability; a withdrawn person, one who is isolated from normal social interaction.

1904 [in Dict. s.v. SHUT *ppl. a.* 2]. **1949** *Richmond* (Va.) *Times-Dispatch* 1 Feb. 9/2 (*heading*) Salad dressing diet palls on storm shut-ins. **1952** *Catholic Times* 25 July 7/4 It is the 'shut-ins' and sufferers who give the greatest of all contributions—their sufferings. **1966** *Daily Tel.* 25 May 19/5 The first Sunday in June is Shut-In's Day, a special day set aside each year to remember the sick and housebound. **1975** C. POTOK *In Beginning* ii. 118 Better a man..who is a man of the world and can also learn than a bearded shut-in with the brain of a genius and the soul of a calf. **1979** *Arizona Daily Star* 22 July J6/4 Volunteers are needed to grocery shop for elderly shut-ins.

2. *Oil Industry.* A state or period of being shut in.

1962 T. C. FRICK *Petroleum Production Handbk.* II. xxx. 7 Subsurface-pressure gauges are very useful in wells where liquids accumulate in the wellbore during shut-in. **1977** R. D. LANGENKAMP *Handbk. Oil Industry Terms & Phrases* (ed. 2) 152 There is a great difference between a shut-down and a shut-in... A well is shut in when its wellhead valves are closed, shutting off production.

Hence **shut-i·n-ness**, the quality of being confined, secluded, or withdrawn into oneself.

1913 D. H. LAWRENCE *Let.* ?10 June (1962) I. 210 The world gets a queer feeling of shut-in-ness, as if it stifled one, the horizon being too near, the sky too low. **1920** *Chambers's Jrnl.* Jan. 23/2 Leaving the bowl of the crater with its strange sense of shut-in-ness. **1952** *Jrnl. Mental Sci.* XCVIII. 310 There is evidence that shy, shut-in people are more liable to schizophrenia than outgoing folk, but this is disputed, and some psychiatrists maintain that the 'shut-inness' is just an early stage of the illness.

shut-off. Add: Also **shutoff. 1.** (Further examples.) Also, something used for stopping the operation of anything.

1951 *Nucleonics* Nov. 16/2 Two..plates are used in controlling the reactor; the other two act as emergency shut-offs. **1970** N. ARMSTRONG et al. *First on Moon* xiii. 313 Okay, I'm going to open up the main shutoffs. Ascent feed closed. **1973** R. LUDLUM *Matlock Paper* xxii. 188 He found the shut-off button and pressed it. **1978** *N.Y. Times* 30 Mar. B 8 (Advt.), A pocket-size recorder that's perfect for school, office or home. Has end-of-tape shut-off.

2. A cessation of flow, supply, or activity.

1889 *Cent. Dict.* 5606/1 *Shut-off*, stoppage of anything. **1919** *Summary of Operations Calif. Oil Fields* (Calif. State Mining Bur.) V. I. 8 *Collar shut-off*, an accidental 'shut-of' supposed to be occasioned by the accumulation of material between the walls of a well and the casing at, or just above, a collar. **1942** *Sun* (Baltimore) 28 Dec. 18/4 A threatened shutoff of tin containers. **1974** *Spartanburg* (S. Carolina) *Herald-Jrnl.* 21 Apr. A2 (Advt.), Easily adjusts from powerful stream to fine spray to complete water shut-off. **1977** *Nature* 6 Jan. 29/1 Neither *alt* nor *mod* mutants affect the shutoff of host protein or rRNA synthesis *in vivo*.

B. *adj.* [SHUT *ppl. a.* 2.] Disconnected, stopped; isolated, withdrawn.

1913 D. H. LAWRENCE *Sons & Lovers* v. 96 That peculiar shut-off look of the poor who have to depend on the favour of others. **1933** S. SPENDER *Poems* 45 The airliner with shut-off engines Glides over suburbs. **1939** C. ISHERWOOD *Goodbye to Berlin* 91, I felt a most marvellous sort of shut-off feeling from all the rest of the world. **1982** 'J. Ross' *Death's Head* iv. 30 She said nothing more, waiting in a shut-off silence.

shut-o·ut, *a.* and *sb.* [SHUT *ppl. a.* 2: cf. SHUT *v.* 17.] **A.** *adj.* **1.** That is shut out or excluded; isolated, remote.

1853 [in Dict. s.v. SHUT *ppl. a.* 2]. **1853** MRS. GASKELL *Let.* Sept. (1966) 245 He..was rather intimate with Lord Palmerston at Cambridge, a pleasant soothing reflection now, in his shut-out life. **1860** GEO. ELIOT *Let.* 5 Sept. (1954) III. 342 It is a better house than I care to have, but as it is more shut out than anything we have seen..I accept the luxury.

2. In Bridge, of a bid: pre-emptive or otherwise intended to discourage the opposition from bidding. Also *transf.* of a financial bid.

1916 [see *PRE-EMPTIVE *a.* 2]. **1921** A. E. M. FOSTER *Auction Bridge* 52 Pre-emptive bids are, in my opinion, a mistake, unless they are of the nature of necessary shut-out bids. **1932** [see *PRE-EMPTIVE *a.* 2]. **1959** REESE & DORMER *Bridge Players' Dict.* 167 An opening bid of three or four in a suit is in nearly all systems a weak shutout bid, based on a long suit with little or no outside strength. **1969** *Observer* 12 Jan. 11/1 Joe Hyman, chairman of Viyella International, ought to be worried by Courtaulds' 15s. 6d. a share shut-out bid for English Calico. **1982** *Times* 22 Jan. 13/5 The Council for the Securities Industry moved yesterday to ban 'shut out' takeover bids. It has become popular for one company to take control of another by buying or obtaining promises which give it 50 per cent control before anyone else can make counter proposals.

3. In Baseball and other games: characterized by the failure of the losers to score; that prevents the opponents from scoring. Chiefly *N. Amer.*

1949 *Minot* (North Dakota) *Daily News* 22 July 8/8 He led his Grand Forks team to a one-hit shutout victory over Duluth. **1974** *News & Press* (Darlington, S. Carolina) 25 Apr. 11/1 Riding to victory on the two hit shutout pitching of Reece Ammons and the strong bat of Darrell Lloyd, the St. John's Blue Devils blitzed the Manning Monarchs 6–0. **1978** *Monitor* (McAllen, Texas) 21 May 3B/5 The Purple team scoring a 9–0 shutout win over the White unit in a controlled scrimmage.

B. *sb.* **1.** In Baseball and other games: a match or innings in which one side does not score; prevention from scoring. Also *fig.* Chiefly *N. Amer.*

1889 *Pueblo* (Colorado) *Opinion* 21 July 4/5 The Springs were 'fated' from the start, and narrowly escaped a shut out. **1897** [in Dict. s.v. SHUT *ppl. a.* 2]. **1936** *N.Y. Herald Tribune* 2 Oct. 10/2 The national scoreboard looked pretty bad. In fact it looked so much like a shutout for the team that you voted a change of management in order to give the country a chance to win the game. **1937** *Evening Standard* 25 Feb. 31 The Swiss may fully extend Britain, and maybe even break Foster's proud run of 'shut-outs'. **1955** *Edmonton Jrnl.* 4 Jan. 10/4 A few hours later he secured that elusive shutout that had escaped him so far this season. **1972** *Newsweek* 31 July 43/3 Fischer routed Mark Taimanov..6 to 0, for the first shutout in the history of grandmaster chess. **1972** *N.Y. Times* 3 Nov. 39/1 Senator McGovern may lose every state in the Union, and..his only chance of avoiding a shut-out lies with the people..in California and the District of Columbia. **1977** *Wandsworth Borough News* 16 Sept. 10/3 Putney St. Mary's Senior 'D' and U/12 'A' teams were in good scoring form, both winning their matches after scoring 10 goals apiece. For the 'D' team it was a complete shut-out. **1978** J. IRVING *World according to Garp* xix. 426 Roberta pitched a shutout.

2. A shut-out bid: see sense 2 of the adj. above.

1936 E. CULBERTSON *Contract Bridge Complete* 17 *Shut-out*, an unnecessarily high bid, designed to make it difficult for the other side to enter the auction. **1982** *Observer* 17 Jan. 17/5 The Takeover Panel's consent to the 'shut-out'.

shutt (ʃʊt). *local.* Also shut. [See SHOAT¹.] = GRAYLING 1 a.

1939, 1952 [see *PINK *sb.*² 2 b].

shutter, *sb.* Add: **2. a.** *to put up the shutters* (earlier example).

[**1837** DICKENS *O. Twist* (1838) I. iv. 62 The undertaker had just put up the shutters of his shop, and was making some entries in his day-book.] **1877** TROLLOPE *Amer. Senator* I. iii. 27 If..you won't have any client that isn't a gentleman, you might as well put up your shutters at once.

j. A device for regulating the supply of cooling air to the radiator of an internal-combustion engine.

1918 *Aëronaut. Jrnl.* XXII. 119 A metal ring is in position on the underside of the radiators within reach of the pilot. This is apparently intended to carry a semi-circular disc to act as a radiator shutter. **1935** *Times* 2 Oct. 6/5 The temperature of the water is controlled by thermostatically-operated radiator shutters. **1957** FRAZEE & ESHELMAN *Tractors & Crawlers* v. 173 Shutters..are used on some tractors to reduce the air flow through the radiator. **1971** M. TAK *Truck Talk* 142 *Shutters*, louvers that are located between the tractor's grill and the radiator of the engine and that open and close like venetian blinds.

3. a. shutter eye (see quot. *a* 1884); **shutter weir,** a type of movable weir consisting of one or more leaves pivoted about a horizontal axis at or towards the bottom and held nearly vertical until released.

a **1884** KNIGHT *Dict. Mech.* Suppl. 807/2 *Shutter eye*, an eye for hanging a shutter to, having a projecting flange or support, which is built into the wall. **1930** *Gen. Catal. Tools & Supplies* (Buck & Hickman Ltd.) 1081 (*heading*) Pointed gate and shutter hooks and eyes. **1880** *Engineering* 30 Jan. 102/1 The needle and shutter weirs had been the most extensively adopted, and were the best types of movable weirs... The shutter weir was the most suitable for high weirs across rapid rivers, and where the navigation was conducted by flushing. **1928** F. JOHNSTONE-TAYLOR *River Engin.* iii. 69 The shutter weir, as a form of barrage, is not a new introduction, having been used..principally in Central Europe, for a number of years.

b. shutter-bug *slang* (orig. *U.S.*), an enthusiastic photographer; also *attrib.*; **shutter priority** *Photogr.*, used *attrib.* and *absol.* to designate automatic working in which the user sets the shutter speed and leaves the appropriate aperture to be set by the camera when the exposure is made; **shutter release,** the button on a camera that is pressed to cause the shutter to open; **shutter speed,** the nominal time for which a shutter is open at a given setting.

1940 *Amer. Speech* XV. 357 The amateur..is known as a clicker, a snapper,..a shutterbug. **1972** *New Nation* (Singapore) 25 Nov. 9/8 It is unspoilt by shutter-bug tourists. **1979** *Arizona Daily Star* 8 Apr. I. 3/6 (Advt.), 4 canyon tours... Our best for shutterbugs includes round trip transportation & lodgings plus photo stop at Casa Grande Ruins. **1974** L. GAUNT *Canon Reflex Way* 24 The system can be converted to shutter-priority automatic working. **1978** *SLR Camera* Aug. 31/1 (Advt.), With the new Minolta XD7 a flick of a switch allows you to change the system to suit the subject—shutter priority *or* aperture priority *or* fully manual. **1958** *Newnes Compl. Amat. Photogr.* 37 At the B setting, the shutter remains open as long as the shutter release is kept pressed. **1979** *Amat. Photographer* 30 May 97/3 Initial pressure on the shutter release lights the viewfinder LEDs which indicate the speed to be chosen by the camera. **1889** Shutter speed [in Dict.]. **1906** R. C. BAYLEY *Compl. Photographer* xiii. 158 In the Frena camera a method of regulating the shutter speed by regulating the size of the opening in a rotating disc was employed. **1977** J. HEDGECOE *Photographer's Handbk.* 162 Fast shutter speeds—say 1/250 sec or shorter—usually eliminate problems of camera shake.

shuttered, *ppl. a.* Add: Also *fig.*

1927 J. R. THEOBALD in *Oxf. Poetry* 34 A clothèd woman all alone Beneath her shuttered sky. **1930** R. CAMPBELL *Adamastor* 76 The day burns through their blood Like a white candle through a shuttered hand. **1957** M. STEWART *Thunder on Right* i. 15 Her heart began to beat lightly and fast, but her face was shuttered, and she gave no sign.

shuttering, *vbl. sb.* Add: **2. a.** = *formwork* s.v. *FORM *sb.* 22. **b.** = *FORM *sb.* 18 b.

1895 E. DE V. BUCKINGHAM *Contractors' Price-Bk.* 371 (*heading*) Concrete building casing and shuttering (per yard super). **1902** *Min. Proc. Inst. Civil Engin.* CXLIX. 298 If the shutterings or drums are well made and kept well greased, a fairly good and even face can be obtained by mixing the concrete rather wet, and well chopping down behind the shutterings or drums. **1919** *Spectator* 25 Oct. 539/2 The soil..to be used without admixture.. and to be thrown direct into the shutterings. **1939** *Archit. Rev.* LXXXVI. 35 The facing slabs..can be used, when braced, as external shuttering to a reinforced concrete wall. **1959** *Listener* 27 Aug. 316/2 Exposed concrete shows the least incidents of the shuttering, the joints of the planks, the fibres and knots of the wood. **1976** *Star* (Sheffield) 20 Nov. (Advt.), Shuttering joiners required.

shutting, *vbl. sb.* Add: **3.** (Later example.)

1924 C. MACKENZIE *Heavenly Ladder* xix. 247 They finished decorating the church just before the shutting in of a still and humid dusk.

5. *attrib.*, as **shutting joint, post,** the joint or post against which a door or gate closes; **shutting stile** (see quot. 1955).

1823 *Practical Builder* iii. 182 (*heading*) On the formation of the shutting-joints of doors. **1929** T. CORKHILL in R. Greenhalgh *Joinery & Carpentry* I. III. 171 The hinge is on the concave and the result is an extremely awkward shutting joint. **1944** N. W. KAY *Pract. Carpenter & Joiner* vi. 140 As a curved rebate is not always possible the shutting joint is set out to a straight surface tangential to the greatest radius on the framing. *a* **1877** KNIGHT *Dict. Mech.* III. 2170/1 *Shutting post*, the post or joint against which a gate or door is closed. **1909** *Chambers's Jrnl.* Nov. 764/1 On the under side of the shutting post is a small roller which runs on to a bracket on the shutting post itself, thus taking up the whole weight of the gate when it is closed. **1909** WEBSTER, Shutting stile. **1955** N. W. KAY *Mod. Building Encycl.* 613 *Shutting stile*, door or window stile opposite the hanging stile.

shuttle, *sb.*¹ Add: **8. b.** A shuttle service of aircraft; *esp.* one operated by an airline for which reservation of seats is not a requirement; an aircraft flying on such a service.

1942 [see *shuttle route*, sense 9 a below]. **1944, 1961** [see *shuttle service*, sense 9 b below]. **1964** MRS. L. B. JOHNSON *White House Diary* 9 Apr. (1970) 104, I could have caught a much later plane if I could only have ridden the shuttle. **1971** R. THOMAS *Backup Men* x. 84, I got in line for the Eastern shuttle... It's rumored that if Eastern doesn't have a seat for you on its regular shuttle to New York, it will roll out a special plane just for you. **1973** *Daily Tel.* 11 Sept. 6/4 British Caledonian is to extend its low fare 'Moonjet Service'—Britain's first no-reservation walk-on, walk-off shuttle—to Belfast. **1977** *Time* 10 Oct. 4/1 Freddie Laker's bargain-basement transatlantic shuttle, the no-frills, no-reservations Skytrain, was finally aloft, carrying passengers between London and New York at the rock-bottom round-trip fare of $236. **1978** R. LUDLUM *Holcroft Covenant* xiii. 153 The shuttles to Paris were frequent, the customs procedures lax.

c. More fully, *space shuttle.* A space rocket with wings enabling it to land like an aircraft and be used repeatedly.

Quot. 1960 is fictional.

1960 'J. WYNDHAM' in *New Worlds* Nov. 41 The acceleration in that shuttle would spread you all over the floor. **1969** *New Scientist* 5 June 513/2 NASA has announced the formation of task groups to look into..a re-usable low-cost 'Space Shuttle' to relay men and materials to and from the [space] station... The space shuttle..would be fired off vertically, shed its fuel tanks and, upon return, land horizontally at an airport. *Ibid.* 2 Oct. 7/1 Another shuttle plying on a regular basis between Cape Kennedy and this large space laboratory. **1972** *National Observer* (U.S.) 27 May 6/3 The shuttle's primary mission is to carry satellites into earth orbit and release them, at a cost below that of the expendable rockets now used to launch satellites. **1981** *Daily Tel.* 15 Apr. 1 The American space shuttle landed on a dry lake bed in California's Mojave Desert yesterday to complete the maiden flight of the first re-usable rocketship.

d. A series of journeys for the purpose of shuttle diplomacy (see sense 9 b below).

1975 *Daily Tel.* 29 Aug. 24/3 (*heading*) Raid as peace shuttle nears end. *Ibid.*, Dr Kissinger completed the last legs of his Middle East shuttle yesterday. **1977** *Time* 17 Jan. 30 It was a diplomatic shuttle, but not exactly in the Kissinger mode. *Ibid.*, Thus [Ivor] Richard's shuttle has been dubbed by some officials and journalists in southern Africa a safari of salvation.

9. a. (sense 3) *shuttle-winder*; (sense 8) *shuttle bus, flight, plane, raid, rocket, route, ship.*

1951 *Sun* (Baltimore) 18 May 3/1 The cars—some are called 'shuttle busses' because they operate from the West (executive offices) Wing to the East Wing [of the White House]—carry messengers too. **1972** *Times* 8 June 7/2 Traffic jams..that officials hoped would be averted by the bicycles and shuttle buses. **1979** *United States 1980/81* (Penguin Travel Guides) 259 During the summer, a shuttlebus runs from the lakefront to the courthouse. **1944** *News* (Tuscaloosa, Ala.) 25 June 1/3 Three crewmen also were lost as a result of the attack on the fields, apparently those used by Italian based and Britain-based bombers in the shuttle flights over Axis targets. **1961** *N.Y. Times* 10 May 90/5 The shuttle flights between the two pairs of cities carried 6,147 passengers in their first week... Passengers arriving by bus, cab or car would be able to step out at the terminal door within 150 feet of the shuttle planes. **1977** *New Yorker* 19 Sept. 40/1 She had to drive home alone, while he took a shuttle flight in the opposite direction. **1944** *Britannica Bk. Year* 770/1 *Shuttle*, combining form. Involving vehicles, especially aircraft, making repeated trips between fixed points, as ..'shuttle raid', 'shuttle plane'. **1961** [see *shuttle flight* above]. **1976** J. CROSBY *Nightfall* xii. 68 [He] left for the shuttle plane to New York. **1943** *Time* 18 Oct. 85/1 The..pilot flew on his first mission eight weeks ago, joined the first shuttle raid on Germany, flew safely to Africa, [etc.]. **1953** J. N. LEONARD *Flight into Space* 87 They say that von Braun's great shuttle rockets—to say nothing of his space station—would surely fail. **1942** *R.A.F. Jrnl.* 30 May 22 The danger zone, which is the shuttle route of the German Fock-Wulf Condors. **1959** *Amazing Stories* June 12/1 Hubbard visited the spaceport ..and watched the shuttle-ships come and go. *a* **1877** KNIGHT *Dict. Mech.* III. 2171/2 *Shuttle-winder*, a device for winding a shuttle, such as the round shuttle of the Wheeler and Wilson sewing-machine, or a tatting-shuttle.

b. † **shuttle armature** *Electr.*, an armature having a single coil wound upon an elongated iron former shaped like a shuttle (*obs.*); **shuttle bombing,** bombing carried out by planes taking off from one base and landing at another; so **shuttle bomber; shuttle car,** a vehicle for making frequent short journeys, *spec.* one for the underground haulage of coal; **shuttle diplomacy,** diplomatic activity involving a series of journeys to and fro, *esp.* by a mediator travelling between disputing parties; hence **shuttle diplomat; shuttle service** (earlier and later examples); more widely, any transport service in which vehicles or aircraft travel to and fro between fixed points at frequent intervals; **shuttle-train** (examples); † **shuttle-wound armature** *Electr.* = **shuttle armature* above (*obs.*).

1890 SLINGO & BROOKER *Electr. Engin.* viii. 241 That the design of the shuttle armature is faulty may easily be proved, for, after being rotated for a little time, the iron shuttle or core gets quite warm. **1924** S. R. ROGET *Dict. Elect. Terms* 226/2 *Shuttle armature*, a simple form of armature now rarely used, except in very small machines, with a single coil connected to a two-part commutator and lying in the two broad slots in an elongated core built up of stampings in the shape of an H with rounded sides. Also called *Siemens 'H' armature.* **1944** *Yank* 28 July 7 They are not shuttle bombers, and they did not fly from Italy to Russia intentionally. **1944** *Newsweek* 10 Jan. 27 Last summer the RAF and the Eighth both tried shuttle bombing. **1954** *Times* 10 Aug. 4/1 The city may be important for another reason—as one end of a shuttle-bombing route similar to those which worked so effectively in Europe. **1905** CALKINS & HOLDEN *Mod. Advertising* v. 89 They also have many shuttle cars, or [street]cars that make short runs. **1956** ATKINSON & WHITE in D. L. Linton *Sheffield* 276 The shuttle cars transport the ore to the main-road conveyors which discharge the ironstone at the surface into wagons. **1979** *Jrnl. R. Soc. Arts* CXXVII. 89/2 Rubber tyred shuttle cars can be used from the continuous miner to the main transport system if the floor is hard enough. **1974** *Between Lines* (Newtown, Pa.) 15 Feb. 2/3 So beware of an over-celebration of Kissinger's shuttle diplomacy, heroic as it's been. **1976** *Birmingham Post* 16 Dec. 2/5 Mr. Richard plans a round of 'shuttle diplomacy' in Southern Africa seeking support for more direct British involvement in the decolonisation of Rhodesia. **1979** H. KISSINGER *White House Years* p. xxi, The October 1973 Middle East war and the 'shuttle diplomacy' that followed. **1977** *Time* 13 June 80 Or consider Henry Kissinger. Understandably, Citizen K's style has changed perceptibly from that of the shuttle diplomat. **1892** *Q. Rev.* Oct. 486 The South-Eastern used, twenty years back, to run a 'shuttle' service every ten minutes between Charing Cross and Cannon St. **1933** *Times* 28 Feb. 9/4 Shuttle services from the outer districts connecting with the trunk and City routes can be substituted for through services from the suburbs to the City. **1944** A. JACOB *Traveller's War* xxviii. 419 It is the same kind of non-stop bombing shuttle service with which Conyngham, the A.O.C. Western Desert, achieved such great results in Africa. **1961** *Wall St. Jrnl.* 20 Mar. 2/3 Eastern Airlines said it wants to start a low-cost air 'shuttle' service between Boston, New York and Washington. **1966** 'H. MACDIARMID' *Company I've Kept* viii. 189 About..the ..date of my birthday, Biggar Post Office had to run what was virtually a shuttle-service several times a day to deliver the masses of mail. **1969** *Guardian* 18 Jan. 1/4 We can expect to see a permanent Russian space station in orbit.., probably with a shuttle service of Russian scientists from earth. **1978** *Detroit Free Press* 5 Mar. D. 16/3 It is more a commercial than a resort hotel, but it has a pool and runs a daily shuttle service to nearby public beaches for guests. **1888** A. R. DIEHL *Two Thousand Words* 190 *Shuttle-train*, one that takes short runs back and forth. **1923** *World Almanac* 503/2 A shuttle train runs between 50th Street and 59th Street on Sixth Avenue. **1942** *Sun* (Baltimore) 7 Mar. 20 When loss of tires has forced the automobile from use, shuttle trains, supplemented by busses, will be the most practical ..means for the transportation of workers in this area. **1974** *Encycl. Brit. Macropædia* XV. 494/2 In 1965 the first Freightliner container..shuttle trains began running on British Railways. **1893** G. KAPP *Dynamos, Alternators, & Transformers* ix. 209 The simplest example of an open-coil armature is the so-called shuttle-wound armature. **1902** *Encycl. Brit.* XXVII. 577/1 The second or drum method was used in the original 'shuttle-wound' armatures invented by Dr. Werner von Siemens in 1856.

shuttle, *v.* Restrict *Obs.* exc. *dial.* to senses 1 and 2 in Dict. and add: **1. b.** To transport in a vehicle or craft operating a shuttle service. Also *transf.*

1930 E. FERBER *Cimarron* xxi. 334 With his geological knowledge..and his familiarity with the region, he was shuttled back and forth from one end of the state to the other. **1945** *Times* 13 Sept. 5/7 There has been no difficulty about shuttling prisoners resident in the British and American zones. **1965** *Listener* 30 Sept. 482/2 So what happens to the old patient? Does he or she get shuttled around to one hospital after another? **1971** *Nature* 27 Aug. 632/1 That malate may serve to 'shuttle' reducing equivalents from cytoplasm to mitochondria. **1975** *Daily Tel.* 1 May 1 Scores of transport aircraft shuttle Vietnamese evacuees from Guam, Wake Island, and the Philippines to America at the rate of up to 5,000 a day. **1977** *Offshore Engineer* May 49/2 Two 15,000t tankers shuttle the oil to Spanish refineries. **1978** H. Wouk *War & Remembrance* xiv. 148 Trains devoted to shuttling the Jews rolled eastward jam-packed and went back empty.

2. (Further examples.) Also, to travel in one direction using a shuttle service. Also *transf.*

1935 M. M. Atwater *Murder in Midsummer* i. 6 A few automobiles, like overgrown beetles, shuttled back and forth along the concrete highways. **1966** *Aviation Week & Space Technol.* 5 Dec. 95/1 Analyses could be made automatically or by astronauts shuttling from earth to the satellite laboratory, staying one month or more and then returning to earth. **1971** 'A. Burgess' *MF* iv. 42 He was not to be seen: perhaps he had shuttled off to Boston or somewhere. **1973** *Internat. Relations Dict.* (U.S. Dept. State Library) 38/1 Henry Kissinger personally shuttled back and forth between Jerusalem and Cairo. **1975** *Sci. Amer.* Jan. 13/3, I moved 'temporarily' to the University of Liverpool in 1965 and have shuttled between the departments of genetics and zoology ever since. **1977** *Time* 15 Aug. 19/3 Although it was not on his original schedule, Vance decided to shuttle back to Amman, Damascus and Alexandria to convey Israeli views to Sadat and Assad. **1978** R. Ludlum *Holcroft Covenant* xiii. 157 France's domestic airline shuttled about the country with splendid irregularity. **1979** *Sci. Amer.* Jan. 29/1 (*caption*) The trains shuttle back and forth without being uncoupled, acting much like a conveyor belt.

shuttlecock, *v.* Add: **1.** (Further *fig.* example.)

1955 *Times* 10 Aug. 5/2 What Rostand lightly shuttlecocks to and fro across this barrier M. Anouilh might nowadays have said more sadly.

2. (Later example.)

1960 *Times* 23 Feb. 4/5 Miss Maxine Audley..played a part shuttle-cocking between lover, son, and husband.

shuttleless, *a.* Delete *rare* and add further examples.

1961 *Textile World* July 30 Shuttleless looms. **1967** *Economist* 29 Apr. 459/3 Popularly known as 'the green box', the BD 200, together with the shuttleless jet loom, could revolutionise the Czech industry. **1975** *Guardian* 27 Jan. 15/1 Most loom-builders were thinking in terms of shuttleless machines.

shuttling, *vbl. sb.* Add: **2.** Travelling to and fro.

1937 R. S. Morton *Woman Surgeon* i. 15 This periodical shuttling between Virginia and New Jersey entailed as much preparation and inconvenience as a modern voyage to the Antarctic.

shu·t-up, *a.* [Shut *ppl. a.* 2: cf. Shut *v.* 19.] **1.** That has been shut up: see Shut *ppl. a.* 2.

2. That can be shut up; foldable.

1799 Jane Austen *Let.* 8 Jan. (1952) 50 Martha kindly made room for me in her bed, which was the shut-up one in the new nursery. **1911** R. Nevill *Floreat Etona* x. 307 The furniture of the rooms... For the most part..consisted of a shut-up bed, a 'burry' (bureau) washstand, which also closed up, and sock cupboard.

shuv(v)er, var. *shover. **shva,** var. *sheva. **shvartze, shvartzer,** varr. *schvartze, schvartzer. **shwa,** var. *schwa.

shy, *sb.*[2] Add: **2. b.** (Earlier example.)

1824 P. Egan *Boxiana* IV. 149 'I am sure you are too generous to let a brave man want; and I never knew an appeal made here in vain.' 'Well then, go it' echoed one of the East-enders; 'I like to have a shy for my money.' Half crowns, shillings and sixpences were instantly thrown upon the stage.

3. b. *coconut shy*: see *coco, cocoa 4 d.

shy, *a.* Add: **2. d.** As last element in Combs.: frightened (of), averse or reluctant (to).

1884, etc. [see Gun-shy *a.*]. **1928,** etc. [see *work-shy* adj. s.v. *work *sb.* 34]. **1934,** etc. [see *book-shy a.* s.v. *book *sb.* 18]. **1938** *Amer. Speech* XIII. 188/1 *Needle-shy*, a phobia..which manifests itself in a revulsion against using the hypodermic needle or seeing it used. **1972** *Sat. Rev.* (U.S.) 28 Oct. 33/3 The extent to which rather sophisticated people remain telephone-shy is remarkable. **1972** *Guardian* 24 Nov. 32/1 Traffic shy commuters.

3. (Later example without const.)

1940 *Ann. Reg.* *1939* 362 So much money had already been lost..that investors were shy.

6. b. Also const. *on.*

1903 [see *long green* s.v. *long *a.*[1] A. 18]. **1975** R. Stout *Family Affair* (1976) iv. 46, I merely thought *some* women were a little shy on brains, present company not excepted.

7. b. (Earlier example.)

1821 D. Haggart *Life* 39 Although I had not been idle during these three months, I found my blunt getting shy.

9. *shy-eyed, -footed* adjs.; *shy-making* ppl. adj.; *shy-brightly* adv.

1922 Joyce *Ulysses* 205 Eglintoneyes..looked up shybrightly. **1910** J. Masefield *Ballads & Poems* 80 The shy-eyed delicate deer. **1952** R. Finlayson *Schooner came to Atia* 118 Shy-eyed kiddies ran out to look. **1917** J. Masefield *Lollingdow Downs* 86 Shy-footed beauty dear. **1930** E. Waugh *Vile Bodies* ii. 19, I shall just ring up every Cabinet Minister and *all* the newspapers and give them all the most shy-making details. **1940** M. Allingham *Black Plumes* xv. 175 Great heroism, like great cowardice, is shy-making, and they were all.. embarrassed. **1974** *Listener* 21 Nov. 677/1 Dr Ray rightly quotes enough of their shy-making exchanges.

shy, *v.*[2] **2. a.** (Earlier example.)

1793 W. B. Stevens *Jrnl.* 26 Mar. (1965) 1. 74 It was but the other day he thought that every man ought to *shy* Jack Dawson from their Houses and Lo now he is his *dear friend.*

Shylock. Add: (Further examples.) Also, a Jew, a pawnbroker; in *U.S.* (with small initial), an abusive term for a moneylender; = *loan-shark* s.v. *loan *sb.*[1] 5. (These uses are considered offensive.)

1786 R. Cumberland *Observer* (ed. 2) III. No. 64. 30 Smoke the Jew!..Out with Shylock. **1898** W. J. Locke *Idols* vi. 81 He could raise the money, cry quits with the urbane and gentle-mannered Shylock. **1930** *Sat. Even. Post* 5 Apr. 48/1 There are also guys present who are called Shylocks, because they will lend you dough when you go broke at the table, on watches or rings..at very good interest. **1935** *Sun* (Baltimore) 28 Dec. 1/3 The jury held the backbone of the 'shylock' or usury racket had been broken in the city by Dewey. **1951** Turkus & Feder *Murder, Inc.* v. 121 'Sometimes it's as good as 3,000 per cent,' one of the shylocks..explained. **1959** I. & P. Opie *Lore & Lang. Schoolch.* xvi. 346 Today, children colloquially refer to a Jew as a Yid, Shylock, or Hooknose. **1972** J. Mills *Report to Commissioner* 121 The Panthers are worse than the shylocks... They keep bleeding you. **1976** *Sunday Times* (Lagos) 1 Aug. 21/4 They are expected to alleviate the suffering of the common man who for long has been a victim of Shylock landlords. **1978** S. Brill *Teamsters* iv. 150 A member who couldn't meet his shylock payments often found that the union people he 'elected' became enforcers against him.

Hence **Shy·lock** *v. trans.*, to force (a person) to repay a debt, esp. at an exorbitant rate of interest; **shy·locker** *U.S.*, one who charges an exorbitant rate of interest; **shy·locking** *vbl. sb.* (*U.S.*)

1930 H. G. Wells *Autocracy of Mr. Parham* iv. v. 308 They bullied and quarrelled when we were only too ready for acquiescent action. They Shylocked Europe. **1933** A. G. Macdonell *England, their England* xiii. 242 One or two of them have had a bit of hard luck lately, and one can't Shylock the poor devils. **1951** Turkus & Feder *Murder, Inc.* v. 120 Loan-sharking. 'Shylocking,' it is called. **1961** *Brooklyn Law Rev.* XXVIII. 41 Such activities are the 'shakedown racket', 'shylocking' (where interest of 20% per week is charged..) and labor extortion. **1973** *Listener* 27 Jan. 878/3 Today's Dillinger.. controls vice, dope and shylocking (usury) throughout his State. **1973** J. Gores *Final Notice* xii. 73 He's an enforcer for a shylocker..with lots of sweet loans to push the vigorish up.

shypoo (ʃəi·pū, ʃəipū·). *Austral. slang.* Also **shipoo.** [Origin unknown.] Inferior liquor; a public house that sells this. Also *attrib.*

1901 *Bulletin Reciter* 30 We drank the shypoo deeply, till the lateness of the night. **1908** E. G. Murphy *Jarrahland Jingles* 108 The swell exclusive club, Have swept the shypoo shanty from its lair amid the scrub. **1917** [see *Aussie *sb.* and *a.* 1]. **1934** *Bulletin* (Sydney) 22 Aug. 20/1 That bubbling drink and spuming We used to call shypoo? **1936** H. Drake-Brockman *Sheba Lane* 237 How about managing that shipoo for me? **1962** T. Ronan *Deep of Sky* 218 A hostelry...restricted to the sale of beer and wine. Locally this was known as the 'Shypoo Shop'. I'm not sure of the derivation of 'Shypoo'. I think it is bastard Chinese for soft drink. To the sturdy second wave of pioneers of West Kimberley, beer and wine were soft drinks.

shyster. Add: **1.** For *U.S. slang* read 'orig. and chiefly *U.S. slang*' and add earlier U.S. and later non-U.S. examples.

1844 G. Wilkes *Mysteries of Tombs* 44/1 He is consulted by the magistrates on all important points of law, and the inferior shysters look upon him with a reverence approaching veneration. **1849** G. G. Foster *New York in Slices* 20 He must..wait next day for the visits of the 'shyster' lawyers—a set of turkey-buzzards whose touch is pollution and whose breath is pestilence. **1943** M. H. Harris *Vegetative Eye* 15 Not to Memory, with its shyster lackey, Association. **1952** *Manch. Guardian Weekly* 19 June 3 They call Taft's 'shyster methods' so necessary. **1961** *Listener* 14 Dec. 1046/1 A solicitor's chief clerk who persuades his shyster employer to leave the country to avoid embezzlement charges. **1981** J. Wainwright *All on Summer's Day* 31 The shyster lawyers..swear blind the client's been manhandled while in police custody.

2. *Austral.* Alteration of Shicer.

1938 X. Herbert *Capricornia* (1939) xxi. 306 You lousy sweatin' old shyster you. **1941** Baker *Dict. Austral. Slang* 66 *Shyster*, a worthless mine.

siafu (sī,ā·fu). [Swahili.] = *safari ant* s.v. *safari 3 d. Also *attrib.*

[**1920** G. D. H. Carpenter *Naturalist on Lake Victoria* xii. 276 The ant that most obtrusively calls for notice is the well known *Dorylus* or 'Safari ant',..in Kiswahili called 'Siafu'.] **1959** E. Huxley *Flame Trees of Thika* xv. 154 The rain brought out the *siafu*. Those fearful black rivers of implacable insects poured between their low mud banks over the garden. **1976** [see *safari ant* s.v. *safari 3]. **1977** Reader & Croze *Pyramids of Life* 212/1 The most effective and thorough carnivore hunter in the forest is a colony of siafu (*Dorylus*), the so-called army ant.

sial (səi·al). *Geol.* Also **Sial.** [a. G. *sial*, f. *si-licium* Silicon + *al-uminium* Aluminium.

The name was altered from *sal* (see *sal[4] 2) by G. Pfeffer in order to avoid confusion with other meanings of that word (see A. Wegener *Die Entstehung der Kontinente und Ozeane* (1920) iii. 22 and quot. 1924 below).]

The discontinuous upper layer of the earth's crust represented by the continental masses, which are composed of relatively light rocks rich in silica and alumina and may be regarded as floating on a lower crustal layer of sima; the material of which these masses are composed.

1922 [see *sal[4] 2]. **1923** *Rep. Brit. Assoc. Adv. Sci.* *1922* 364 Sial masses drift through the Sima like icebergs through the sea. **1924** J. G. A. Skerl tr. *Wegener's Orig. Continents & Oceans* iii. 36 Following a short communication from Pfeffer I should like to write 'Sial' instead of 'Sal' in order that there may be no confusion with the Latin word for Salt. **1927** Peake & Fleure *Apes & Men* ii. 18 Various crises have led to the splitting of the Sial, and..its fragments have wandered off in many directions. **1950** P. H. Kuenen *Marine Geol.* ii. 118 The isostatic equilibrium of the crust requires a considerable thickness of granitic sial in the continents and a rock of greater density in the oceanic sections. **1954** [see *sal[4] 2]. **1978** D. Bridgwater et al. in D. H. Tarling *Evol. Earth's Crust* ii. 63 In the type of Archaean craton displayed in southern Africa break up and partial destruction of earlier sial probably took place in a different tectonic regime.

Hence **sia·lic** *a.*[1], of or pertaining to the continental crust or the material of which it is made.

1924 J. G. A. Skerl tr. *Wegener's Orig. Continents & Oceans* iv. 59 Molten sialic masses (granite) from the under side of the South American block.. have emerged on its posterior edge. **1944** A. Holmes *Princ. Physical Geol.* ii. 14 There should be bulges..where gravity is relatively low; that is to say, wherever the outer part of the crust is composed of light sialic rocks. Such places are the continents. **1955** *Sci. Amer.* Sept. 62/1 Because granite is the chief sialic rock and basalt the chief simatic one, the continents are most commonly described as granitic and the ocean basins as basaltic. **1970** *Ibid.* Feb. 32/3 Stresses in the earth's crust may crack the sialic layer, producing faults and fissures that can be as much as 20 meters wide. **1975** *Nature* 3 Apr. 397/2 Localised partial melting of ancient, sialic crust may..occur in the zone of heating above large bodies of basic igneous magma introduced into high crustal levels.

sialadenitis: see s.v. *sialo-.

sialectasis (səi,ăle·ktăsis). *Path.* [f. *sialo- + Gr. ἔκτασις dilatation.] Dilatation of the ducts of the salivary glands, usu. the parotids.

1940 *Brit. Jrnl. Surg.* XXVII. 713 The term 'sialectasis' which has been used to describe the condition is not strictly correct etymologically, translating as 'a stretching out or dilatation of the saliva'. **1953** *Brit. Med. Jrnl.* 19 Dec. 1359/2 The underlying pathology in..sialectasis, sialangiectasis, or chronic recurrent parotitis, is obscure, but the essential feature is obstruction of the parotid ducts. **1974** J. D. Maynard in R. M. Kirk et al. *Surgery* ix. 201 The parotid architecture may be normal or reveal the curious appearance reminiscent of radiographs of bronchiectasis, called sialectasis. **1977** [see *sicca[2]].

sialic (səi·ălik), *a.*[2] *Biochem.* [f. Gr. σίαλ-ον saliva + -ic.] *sialic acid*: any acyl or related derivative of a neuraminic acid.

Orig. applied *spec.* to a substance of this type (then of unknown structure) isolated from the salivary glands of cattle.

1952 G. Blix et al. in *Acta Chem. Scand.* VI. 359 Besides this substance, for which we propose the provisional name sialic acid, the mucin contains small amounts of carbohydrate of the dihexose-hexosamine type. **1957** —— in *Nature* 25 May 1088/2 Sialic acid is suggested as group name for the acylated neuraminic acids. **1967** *New Scientist* 16 Feb. 414/1 Twenty years elapsed before the structure of this complex sugar was determined, and by then it was clear that it was only one of a family of sugars called sialic acids, all of which had an unusually long backbone of nine carbon atoms. **1978** *Nature* 16 Feb. 674/2 Sialic acids..of the red blood cell (RBC) membrane are considered to play an important part in the physiology of the RBC.

sialidase (səi,æ·lidēⁱz). *Biochem.* [f. prec. + -id[4] + *-ase.] = *neuraminidase.

1956 Heimer & Meyer in *Proc. Nat. Acad. Sci.* XLII. 731 The bond split must be O-glycosidic rather than N-glycosidic... The name 'sialidase' is proposed for the enzyme responsible for this action. **1963** Barka & Anderson *Histochemistry* iii. 94 Sialidase, an enzyme that selectively removes sialic acid..from mucopolysaccharides, eliminates the metachromatic staining and Alcian blue affinity of some acid mucopolysaccharides. **1978** A. White et al. *Princ. Biochem.* (ed. 6) xxix. 916 It remains unclear how sialic acid in mammals or galactose in birds and reptiles is removed in vivo from plasma glycoproteins, although sialidase and β-galactosidases are present in many tissues.

siallite (səi·ăləit). *Geol.* [ad. G. *siallit* (H. Harrassowitz 1926, in *Fortschr. Geol. Palæont.* IV. 263), f. as *sial: see -ite[1].] Weathered rock that is largely composed of hydrous aluminium silicates and is highly leached of alkalis. So **sialli·tic** *a.*

1933 H. Greene tr. *Vageler's Introd. Tropical Soils* v. 127 Where the amount of water is small and the period of action is short, as in the case of arid and semi-arid districts, siallitic and allitic bodies are formed in small amount. *Ibid.* 140 The soil becomes podsolised. The long-held opinion that this produces not merely siallites in general but a quite special kaolin and kaolinite can no longer be maintained. **1965** B. T. Bunting *Geogr. of Soil* xiv. 168 Other forms of brown earth are formed on siallitic parent materials which may overlie chalk.

sialo- (səiˌălo), before a vowel also **sial-**, comb. form of Gr. *σίαλον* saliva, used as a formative element in *Med.*, as **si:al(o)adeni·tis** [Gr. *ἀδήν* gland], inflammation of a salivary gland; **si·alolith** [-LITH], a calculus in a salivary gland; hence **si:alolithi·asis,** the presence of such a calculus; **sialorrhœa** (-rī·ă) [*-RRHŒA, -RRHEA], excessive flow of saliva.

1859 Mayne *Expos. Lex.* (1860) 1159/2 Sialadenitis. **1925** Marshall & Piney *Textbk. Surg. Path.* vi. 123 Chronic sialo-adenitis may affect either the parotid or submaxillary and may be associated with calculi. **1977** *Arch. Virol.* LIV. 352 Sialoadenitis produced by PRCV.. was morphologically compatible with SDAV-induced lesions. [**1855** Dunglison *Dict. Med. Sci.* (ed. 12) 787/2 *Sialolithi*, calculi, salivary.] **1862** Mayne *Med. Vocab.* (ed. 2) 373/2 *Sialolithus*, a salival calculus; a sialolith. **1910** Adami & Nicholls *Princ. Path.* II. xvii. 396 Concretions composed of phosphate or carbonate of lime are not uncommonly found within the [salivary] duct (sialoliths), sometimes causing or associated with cystic dilatation of the ducts and acini. **1973** *Brit. Dental Jrnl.* CXXXV. 292/2 The sialolith was club-shaped, yellow in colour and measured 14 mm in length. **1859** Mayne *Expos. Lex.* (1860) 1160/1 Sialolithiasis. **1916** L. F. Barker *Monagraphic Med.* III. viii. 264 Stone is sometimes palpable in a salivary duct (sialolithiasis). **1973** *Brit. Dental Jrnl.* CXXXV. 291/1 Sialolithiasis, the formation of a calculus in the duct or gland substance of a major or minor salivary gland, occurs most commonly in the middle-aged adult. **1846** *Lond. Med. Gaz.* XXXVII. 379/1 In the idiopathic sialorrhœa..the flow takes place as well in the night as in the day time. **1888** *Buck's Handbk. Med. Sci.* VI. 251/1 The term sialorrhea, while indicating an abnormal flow, does not necessarily imply abnormal secretion. **1933** *Ann. Rep. London County Council* IV. iii. 135 At the same time the face may be distorted into a spasmodic grimace, accompanied by flushing, lachrymation and sialorrhœa. **1978** *Jrnl. R. Soc. Med.* LXXI. 346 Abnormal conditions, such as excessive diarrhoea, sialorrhoea or sweating.

sialoglycoprotein (səi:ălogləikoprōᵘ·tīn). *Biochem.* [f. *SIAL(IC *a.*[2] + -O + *glycoprotein* (s.v. *GLYCO-).] Any glycoprotein in which sialic acid residues form a major constituent of the side chains.

1963 A. Gottschalk in Florkin & Stotz *Comprehensive Biochem.* VIII. i. 29 All sialo-glycoproteins have some features in common. Invariably their sialic acid residues occupy a terminal position and are linked through a neuraminidase susceptible α-ketosidic linkage to another sugar residue. **1965** *Biochimica & Biophysica Acta* CI. 166 A homogeneous 7·1 S sialoglycoprotein..composed of 5·9% neutral carbohydrates, 4·8% aminosugars and 4·4% sialic acid. **1976** *Nature* 20 May 236/2 Liposomes bearing sialoglycoproteins can participate in agglutination reactions mediated by appropriate lectins.

sialography (səiˌălǫ·grăfi). *Med.* [f. *SIALO- + -GRAPHY.] Radiography of the ducts of a salivary gland after they have been injected with a radio-opaque fluid.

1931 *Brit. Jrnl. Surg.* XIX. 142 Sialography will demonstrate abnormalities, dilatations, and obstructions of the larger and smaller parotid ducts. **1960** *Radiology* LXXIV. 138/1 Secretory sialography has been a useful aid in determining whether tumors in the submaxillary and parotid regions are within or adjacent to the major salivary glands. **1975** *Ibid.* CXVII. 220/1 Sialography, the demonstration of ducts and parenchyma of the major salivary glands by injection of contrast material in the gland's main secretory duct, has been practiced since its first description by Arcelin in 1913. **1977** [see *SICCA[2]].

Hence **si·alogram**, an X-ray photograph made by this technique; **sialogra·phic** *a.*

1931 *Brit. Jrnl. Surg.* XIX. 144 The sialogram shows the main duct of the gland, the larger branches, and the ductules, all well filled with lipiodol. **1938** *Surg., Gynecol. & Obstetr.* LXVII. 777 A sialographic study of 23 normal parotid glands and 76 cases of neoplastic disease of the parotid. **1974** J. D. Maynard in R. M. Kirk et al. *Surgery* ix. 201 If symptoms are sufficiently worrying to the patient and a sialogram reveals gross dilatation of the main duct, ablative..surgery is indicated. **1976** *Radiology* CXXI. 747/1 A..curved side-hole cannula for use in sialographic procedures.

sialomucin (səiˌălomiū·sin). *Biochem.* [f. *SIAL(IC *a.*[2] + -O + MUCIN in Dict. and Suppl.] Any mucin containing sialic acid residues in the molecule.

1958 L. Odin in Wolstenholme & O'Connor *Ciba Found. Symp. Chem. & Biol. Mucopolysaccharides* 235 The second main type of epithelial glycoprotein contains sialic acid as its characteristic carbohydrate constituent. .. This type of glycoprotein will for convenience be called sialomucin. **1976** *Path. Ann.* XI. 172 A recent study of the mucin..suggests that it is a sialomucin with minor sulphomucin and neutral mucin components.

sialon (səi·ălǫn). *Chem.* [f. the chemical symbols for silicon (*Si*), aluminium (*Al*), oxygen (*O*), and nitrogen (*N*).] Any of a large class of refractory materials which have crystal structures similar to those of silica and the silicates but contain aluminium and nitrogen in the polymeric framework in addition to silicon and oxygen.

1973 K. H. Jack in *Trans. & Jrnl. Brit. Ceramic Soc.* LXXII. 380/1 The structural unit of β-silicon nitride is SiN_4; of α it is on average $SiN_{3\cdot9}O_{0\cdot1}$; of oxynitride it is SiN_3O; and of the new 'sialons' it is $(Si, Al)(O, N)_4$. **1975** P. Popper *Special Ceramics* VI. p. ix, Several papers deal with materials in the Si-Al-O-N or Mg-Si-Al-O-N system. Colloquially, workers in this field have become accustomed to refer to them as 'sialons'. **1981** *Economist* 11 Apr. 98/3 The new materials mentioned at last week's conference included..very strong ceramics called sialons.

Siamese, *a.* and *sb.* Add: **A.** *adj.* **1. b.** *Siamese cat,* a lightly built shorthaired cat belonging to a breed originally found in Thailand (formerly Siam), distinguished by buff-coloured fur with points of brown, blue, or other colours, and a narrow head with large ears and slanting blue eyes; so *Siamese kitten.*

1871 *Illustr. London News* 22 July 63/2 It [*sc.* the variety class at the Crystal Palace cat show] contained.. a singular Siamese cat, coloured precisely like a black-faced pug-dog. **1889** H. Weir *Our Cats* 73 Siamese Cat. Among the beautiful varieties of the domestic cat brought into notice by cat shows, none deserve more attention than 'The Royal Cat of Siam'. **1942** Siamese kitten [see *pet-shop* s.v. *PET *sb.*[1] 3 d]. **1958** *Listener* 18 Sept. 410/1 There are many legends and stories about the origin of Siamese cats but few facts. **1972** Ing & Pond *Champion Cats of World* 109 The Siamese Cat Club was founded in 1901.

c. *Siamese fighter, fighting fish,* a brightly coloured, often red, tropical fish, *Betta splendens,* native to Malaysia and Thailand, and distinguished by enlarged fins and tail.

1929 W. T. Innes *Goldfish Varieties* (ed. 11) 256 (*caption*) *Betta splendens*, Cambodia variety, or Veiltail Siamese Albino Fighting Fish. **1968** R. Clapperton *No News on Monday* i. 9 Fifty bucks' worth of aquarium: two purple Siamese fighters hovering motionless, separated by glass. **1971** *Ceylon Observer* (Mag. ed.) 19 Sept. 2/6 (Advt.), Goldfish..Siamese Fighters. **1977** D. J. Coffey *Encycl. Aquarium Fish* 67/1 Siamese Fighting-fish are aggressive.

2. *Siamese twins*: For '1814' read '1811' and add: Also *gen.,* any pair of twins physically united by their tissues; *sing.* one of a pair of such twins. Also *attrib.* (in sing.) and *fig.* (Further examples.)

1835 Dickens in *Evening Chron.* 18 June 4 They were three long graces in drapery, with..another..the three fates with another sister—the Siamese twins multiplied by two. **1859** Geo. Eliot *Let.* 27 Feb. (1954) III. 27 People who have been inseparable and found *all* their happiness in each other for five years are in a sort of Siamese-twin condition that other people are not likely to regard with tolerance or even with belief. **1879** *Mind* IV. 331 Should the empiricists succeed in their attempt to resolve such Siamese-twin elements into habitual juxtapositions. **1883** E. W. Hamilton *Diary* 18 Dec. (1972) II. 526 Chamberlain also spoke briefly. He passed a high eulogy on Dilke—they are the Siamese twins of politicians. **1922** Joyce *Ulysses* 404 Heated argument..regarding the juridical and theological dilemma in the event of one Siamese twin predeceasing the other. **1926** J. S. Huxley *Ess. Pop. Sci.* 235 Partial constriction [of a newt embryo] produces partial doubling or 'Siamese twins'. **1937** H. H. Newman et al. *Twins* xiii. 355 Conjoined twins (Siamese twins) show marked differences in height, weight, features, and intelligence. **1957** Mankowicz & Haggar *Encycl. Eng. Pott. & Porc.* 202/1 The Kentish Siamese twins, Eliza and Mary Chalkhurst (who died in 1734 at the age of 34) were apparently made in redware. **1957** E. H. Shepard *Drawn from Memory* ix. 172 She was a queer experiment in ship design, a sort of Siamese twin of a ship; two complete hulls joined together in the middle. She had two sets of engines and two funnels. **1961** R. B. Long *Sentence & its Parts* iv. 106 Here *on Thursdays* is followed by two complete nucleuses, tied together in Siamese-twin fashion by joint possession of the introductory adjunct. **1965** E. Gowers *Fowler's Mod. Eng. Usage* (ed. 2) 554/1 *Siamese twins.* This seems a suitable term for the many words which, linked in pairs by *and* or *or*, are used to convey a single meaning. *Ibid.* 554/2 Whenever a Siamese twin suggests itself to a writer, he should be on his guard; it may be just the phrase he wants, but it is more likely to be one of those clichés that are always lying in wait to fill a vacuum in the brain. **1970** G. Greer *Female Eunuch* 245 The bitter animosity..of divorce is unknown where individuals have not become Siamese twins. **1972** Miller & Keane *Encycl. & Dict. Med. & Nursing* 876/1 New techniques in surgery..are making it possible to separate some Siamese twins whose physical links are highly complex. **1981** *Birds* Spring 63/1 My neighbour found Siamese twin starlings caught on some old wire... They had two legs each, but only three feet. The inner leg of each bird was joined together with one foot between them. **1981** *N.Y. Times Mag.* 19 July 6/4 The Kennedy prose style was a product of him and his Siamese twin, Theodore Sorensen, writing freely with his free arm.

b. Also, pertaining to or characteristic of Siamese twins.

1851 H. Melville *Moby Dick* II. xxx. 206 So, then, an elongated Siamese ligature [*sc.* monkey-rope] united us. **1955** E. Bowen *World of Love* v. 87 In step, in Siamese closeness, they paced towards it. **1969** N. J. Berrill *Person in Womb* xiii. 158 Siamese conditions meant death of mother and offspring during the agony of delivery.

c. Also *Siamese connection.*

1914 J. Kenlon *Fires & Firefighters* xxii. 322 A length of three-inch hose is attached to the pipe and strapped to the ladder with a siamese connection on the ground.

B. *sb.* **2.** (Earlier example.)

1759 *Universal Hist., Mod.* VII. 238 The Siamese resembles the Chinese in several respects: it consists mostly in monosyllables, and has neither declensions nor conjugations.

3. A Siamese cat.

1893 J. Jennings *Domestic or Fancy Cats* ii. 17 A pure-bred Siamese is a valuable cat. **1939** T. S. Eliot *Old Possum's Practical Cats* 15 It was a Siamese had mauled his missing ear. **1950** W. de la Mare *Inward Companion* 70 That crafty cat, a buff-black Siamese, Sniffing through wild wood. **1973** 'E. McBain' *Let's hear it for Deaf Man* iii. 37 Janik himself resembled a cross-eyed Siamese, blue eyes magnified behind bifocals..a tuft of black hair behind each ear.

4. A Siamese coupling or connection.

1914 J. Kenlon *Fires & Firefighting* xxii. 322 Run in two lines, connect to the siamese, raise the bed ladder to the desired position and the stream is controlled from the street by guys. **1969** *Publ. Amer. Dial. Soc.* lii. 55 *Siamese*,..a connector joint used for reducing two lines into one line. 'A Siamese will allow more pressure than a single line.'

Siamesed, *ppl. a.* (Later examples.)

1914 J. Kenlon *Fires & Firefighting* 377 For siamesed lines, an allowance was made for the loss in the siamese connection and for 20 feet of 3½-inch lead hose. **1942** Potts & Harriss *Fire Pumps & Hydraulics* viii. 59 Where series pumping has to be resorted to it is desirable to employ 'Siamesed' lines, i.e. to duplicate the deliveries from the pump or pumps in the series up to the final pump. **1970** B. Knox *Children of Mist* i. 20 The Jaguar ..had twin carburetters plus a siamesed exhaust.

sib, *a.* and *sb.*[2] Add: **1. a.** (Earlier and later examples in *spec.* sense.)

1875 R. L. Wallace *Canary Bk.* iii. 51 He said, very gravely, 'Weel, sib bred is sib bred, an I thocht that anybody kenned what that was.' However, I found that the meaning of the words was consanguinity. **1902** Bateson & Saunders *Rep. Evolution Comm. R. Soc.* I. 4 The possibility..should not be forgotten that the prepotency of the sib-bred hens may have been an original character of their particular strain. **1961** R. B. Bennett *Budgerigars, Canaries & Foreign Finches* xxi. 155 *Sib-bred*, the young from related birds bred in and in for many years. In-bred.

3. a. *spec.* in *Anthrop.* A group of people of either sex that are recognized by an individual as his kindred, and who freq. form an exogamic unit. (Further examples.)

1919 *Amer. Anthropologist* XXI. 28 The sib, like the family, is a kinship group... On the one hand, it excludes one half of the blood-kindred—the father's side of the family in matronymic, the mother's side in patronymic societies. On the other hand, it admits on equal terms all kindred of the favored side regardless of degree and even individuals considered blood-relatives merely through legal fiction. **1950** A. R. Radcliffe-Brown in Radcliffe-Brown & Forde *African Systems of Kinship & Marriage* 15 The arrangement of kin by degrees of nearness or distance was based on sib-ship... A man's sib were all his cognates within a certain degree. *Ibid.*, It is evident that no two persons can have the same sib, though for two unmarried full brothers, *A* and *B*, every person who was sib to *A* was sib to *B*, and *A* and *B* were sib-kinsmen of one another. A person cannot be said to 'belong' to a sib or be a member of a sib in the sense in which he can be said to belong to a lineage or a clan or a village community. **1967** R. Fox *Kinship & Marriage* vi. 167 The kindred..was known as the sib... Amongst the Teutonic peoples, the sib was the exogamic unit. **1968** G. D. Mitchell *Dict. Sociol.* 160 The British usage confines *sib* to an ego-centred group of cognates within a certain degree; it is thus synonymous with some meanings of kindred.

c. *Anthrop.* A kinship sub-group whose members claim unilineal descent from a single ancestor of either sex; a clan. Cf. sense 3 a in Dict. and Suppl. orig. and chiefly *U.S.*

1890 F. B. Jevons tr. *Schrader's Prehist. Antiq. of Aryan Peoples* iv. xii. 398 The Teutonic sib.., as long as it was an agrarian and military unit, is to be conceived as having been purely agnatic. **1901** *Jrnl. R. Anthrop. Inst.* IV. 68 Two brothers, and still more, a father and son, cannot fall into two different sibs. **1918** F. S. Philbrick tr. *Huebner's Hist. Gmc. Private Law* i. iii. 114 The primitive Germans lived in..sibs that based their kinship solely upon descent from a common tribal male ancestor. **1949** G. P. Murdock *Social Structure* iii. 47 If all persons born with the name Smith in our society regarded themselves as related, they would constitute a patri-sib. Some unilinear societies lack true sibs, possessing only lineages. The great majority, however, possess sibs... A sib normally includes several lineages. **1967** R. Fox *Kinship & Marriage* i. 50 There are other usages [for *clan* and *lineage*] which cause considerable confusion. .. American writers often use *sib* as the generic term with *patri-sib* and *matri-sib* as the sub varieties. This is quite wrong... The Anglo-Saxon *sib*..was not a descent group at all.

d. Chiefly *Genetics.* A brother or sister, another individual of the same parentage (see also quot. 1933).

1919 *Genetics* IV. 496 The observations..show themselves to be a strictly homogeneous population, with correlation much larger than that between sibs. **1931** E. & C. Paul tr. E. Baur et al. *Human Heredity* xi. 508 The methods..known as the brother-and-sister method or as the sib method. [*Note*] The word 'sib' or 'sibling' is coming into use in genetics in the English-speaking world, as an equivalent of the convenient German term 'Geschwister'. **1933** *Proc. R. Soc. Edin.* LIII. 106 A comparison of the resemblance between ordinary sibs and fraternal twins may be used. [Note] Here and throughout sib is used to denote brothers and sisters of different birth-rank. **1937** *Nature* 2 Oct. 573/1 Genetical research shows that height has little value as an indicator of relationships and specific distinctness, since a plant two inches high may be a sib to a plant twenty inches high. **1958** *Times* 18 Jan. 4/3 Among other problems possibly was the danger of sibs—offspring of the same parent—marrying. **1974** *Nature* 12 Apr. 594/2 The foundation stock of the highly resistant flock had parents and sibs that did not develop scrapie.

e. *attrib.*, as *sib bond, group, -mate, -mating, -pair, selection, system.*

1938 *Jrnl. R. Anthrop. Inst.* LXVIII. 301 With Trobriands and Hopi the successive sib bond exists through females. **1901** *Ibid.* XXXI. 68 The size of the sib group has always been determined by economic facts. **1920** R. H. LOWIE *Primitive Society* vi. 107 Sib-mates of the same generation usually call one another siblings, and from this..it is but a step to feeling that marriage between sib-mates would be incestuous. Hence we find as one of the most common traits of the sib the law of exogamy. **1949** G. P. MURDOCK *Social Structure* iv. 73 They are wives and clansmen of one group of disputant men, sisters and sibmates of the other. **1949** R. A. FISHER *Inbreeding* iii. 47 A mating of parent and offspring interpolated in a series of sib-matings does not advance the inbreeding process so much as a sib-mating would have done. **1971** *Brit. Med. Bull.* XXVII. 45/2 Sib-pair comparisons have also been used to separate the effects of family size..upon intelligence. **1956** *Genetics* XLI. 367 (*heading*) Isolation of preadaptive mutants in bacteria by sib selection. **1934** *Nature* 19 May 743/1 The sib system, and its attendant naming habits, is the most flourishing part of the old thought system.

sib (sib), *sb.*³ Also **Sib.** Colloq. abbrev. of *SIBILANT *sb.* 2.

1957 D. E. WALKER *Lunch with Stranger* 142 British memoirs published since the war have confirmed both the speed with which the Sibs reached the German High Command and the disruptive influence they had there. **1958** *Punch* 8 Jan. 96/1 A Sib, short for sibilant, is a story or rumour concocted to promote a set purpose, generally the sales of a particular product. **1965** B. SWEET-ESCOTT *Baker Street Irregular* iii. 98 The rumours or 'sibs', as they were called, were devised by a high-powered committee in London... Success or failure was judged by the degree to which the sibs were repeated by enemy or neutral newspapers and broadcasting transmissions. **1975** P. FUSSELL *Gt. War & Mod. Memory* ix. 328 One department [of the Special Operations Executive] did nothing but contrive 'sibs'—bizarre and hair-raising rumours to be spread over the Continent.

Sibbald (si·băld). The name of Sir Robert Sibbald (1641–1722), Scottish naturalist, used in the possessive to designate the blue whale, *Balænoptera musculus.*

1897 R. LYDEKKER *Conc. Knowledge Nat. Hist.* 173 The largest..of all whales, is the blue, or Sibbald's rorqual.., commonly known to the American whalers by the name of 'sulphur-bottom'. **1937** [see *blue whale* s.v. *BLUE *a.* 12 a]. **1972** *Oxf. Bk. Vertebrates* 190/1 Sibbald's Rorqual..has a world-wide distribution and migrates between high and low latitudes.

Sibelian (sibē̆ⁱ·liăn), *a.* and *sb.* [f. *Sibelius* (see below) + -AN.] **A.** *adj.* Of, pertaining to, or characteristic of the Finnish composer Jean Sibelius (1865–1957) or his music. **B.** *sb.* An admirer or adherent of Sibelius; an interpreter of his works.

1935 C. GRAY *Sibelius* 64 The instrumental roles are reversed, with the strings constituting a background of a typically Sibelian kind. **1937** *Sunday Times* 29 Aug. 5/2 The No. 4..is of exceptional interest to the Sibelian student now in the light thrown on it by the No. 7 and 'Tapiola'. **1943** *Scrutiny* XI. 171 Some passages of characteristically Sibelian cross-rhythmed moto perpetuo. **1966** *Punch* 23 Feb. 291/2 The Sibelian atmosphere of magic, melancholy and old solitude. **1975** *Gramophone* Oct. 598/2 Shostakovich's view of the symphony is Mahlerian rather than Sibelian. **1976** *Ibid.* June 52/2 She has put all Sibelians in her debt by including the inspired Serenades on her record. *Ibid.* Oct. 608/2 Last month Decca released a version of the *Four Legends* conducted by no less a Sibelian than Jussi Jalas, the composer's son-in-law.

Siberia (səibīə·riă). The name of a region of the U.S.S.R. in Asia used as a type of a cold, inhospitable place, or a place of exile, banishment, or imprisonment. Also *fig.*

1841 GEO. ELIOT *Let.* 17 Feb. (1954) I. 81 Probably this projected transportation may prove to be a Cape of Good Hope instead of a Siberia. **1876** C. M. YONGE *Three Brides* I. x. 159, I used to be Camilla to all the neighbourhood, and here I find myself..banished to Siberia. **1926** C. PLUMB in *Oxf. Poetry 1925* 40 The seas shall not seem vast Siberias of Time. **1952** R. CAMPBELL tr. *Baudelaire's Poems* 80 In my Siberia a bright explosion as of tropic heat. **1972** *Listener* 21 Dec. 857/3 In 1830 Andrew Jackson..[ordered] that all the Indian tribes..be removed to the west of the Mississippi..to the 'Siberia' of the Far West. **1974** 'J. LE CARRÉ' *Tinker, Tailor, Soldier, Spy* xi. 82 Guillam departed for the siberias of Brixton.

Siberian, *a.* and *sb.* Add: **A.** *adj.* **2. a.** *Siberian husky, thrush, tiger.*

1930 *Amer. Kennel Gaz.* Jan. 26/1 The Siberian huskies are recognized as the ideal dogs for driving. *Ibid.* Nov. 73/1 The breed of dog known as the Siberian Husky has been recognized by the Stud Book Committee. **1950** J. HAMBLETON *Abitibi Adventure* 74 In their equipment was included a two-dog team, made up of Siberian huskies, blue-eyed beauties trained for generations to pull their hearts out and to survive the utmost rigors of the north. **1972** *Even. Telegram* (St. John's, Newfoundland) 24 June 14/1 Various types of Northern dogs were used including Siberian Huskies. **1901** *Ibis* 417 Siberian Thrush... The nest was found on the Yenesei River by Mr. Popham in 1895. **1954** D. A. BANNERMAN *Birds Brit. Isles* III. 166 There is some reason to suppose that the Siberian thrush..has occurred in Britain. **1895** R. LYDEKKER *Hand-bk. Carnivora* I. 150 A specimen of the Siberian Tiger, apparently the first brought alive to Europe, was exhibited recently in Hagenbeck's menagerie in Amsterdam. **1956** M. L. TAYLOR *Tiger's Claw* vii. 59 'Can you read the Chinese ideogram on his head?' he inquired of me. 'It is *wang* meaning king. In the north it is believed that only Siberian tigers carry this mark.' **1978** *Times* 27 Oct. 32/8 (Advt.), Large Siberian tiger skin mounted on red satin, £600.

b. *Siberian cedar, elm, larch, pine* (later example), (*stone*) *pine* (earlier and later examples), *wallflower.*

1763 J. BELL *Trav. St. Petersburg* I. 250 Towards the Baykall lake, are high hills..covered with tall trees; among which are many..Siberian cedars. **1838** J. C. LOUDON *Arboretum & Fruticetum Britannicum* IV. 2275 The Siberian Stone Pine, or Siberian Cedar..—The cones are said to be longer, and the scales larger, than in the Swiss variety. **1967** M. T. MIROV *Genus Pinus* iii. 233 Russians call *P. sibirica* 'Siberian cedar', which causes a great deal of confusion. **1974** *Nomencl. Commerc. Timbers* (*B.S.I.*) 69 'Siberian cedar' (UK)... This name is liable to be confusing and its use should be discontinued. **1904** *Outing* Oct. 84/2 The English elm and the cork-bark and Siberian elms are also desirable. **1981** *Sci. Amer.* Aug. 40/3 Many Asian species, such as the Chinese elm ..and the Siberian elm.., are comparatively resistant to infection. **1838** J. C. LOUDON *Arboretum & Fruticetum Britannicum* IV. 2352 The Siberian larch was introduced into England by Messrs. Loddiges..about the end of the last century. **1969** T. H. EVERETT *Living Trees of World* iv. 41/1 The Siberian larch.., a close relative of the European larch, grows to 120 feet tall. **1958** *N.Z. Timber Jrnl.* Sept. 87/1 Siberian pine: *Pinus cembra* var. *sibirica* ..and *P. koraiensis*... Shipped from Vladivostok. **1838** Siberian stone pine [see *Siberian cedar* above]. **1923** A. REHDER in L. H. Bailey *Cultivated Evergreens* v. 303 Siberian Stone P[ine]. A form with shorter leaves and larger cones [than *Pinus cembra*]. **1967** N. T. MIROV *Genus Pinus* iii. 233 Its 'common' English name, 'Siberian stone pine', is rather inappropriate. **1925** G. W. DEEPING *Sorrell & Son* xxxvii. 375 A half wild patch of..purple and gold tulips, and burning orange siberian wallflowers. **1933** *Jrnl. R. Hort. Soc.* LVIII. 172 The Siberian Wallflower..probably merits that name as little as the one by which it is commonly known. **1979** C. E. L. PHILLIPS *New Small Garden* x. 137 The slightly later Siberian wallflower..is a glowing orange ball of fire.

B. *sb.* **3.** A Siberian husky.

1928 *N.Y. Times* 29 Jan. II. 1/5 Seppala left the line without a word to his furry, sharp-eared Siberians. **1944** C. CLAY *Phantom Fur Thieves* 137 The Siberian..was originally bred and raised in Siberia, is smaller in size than a huskie, more stockily built, more heavily furred.

sibilance. Delete *rare* and add: (Further examples.) Also, an undue prominence of sibilants, *esp.* in reproduced sound.

1939 A. CLARKE *Coll. Plays* (1963) 92 The words of the Chorus become a mere sibilance. **1943** A. L. ROWSE *Cornish Childhood* 87 Her voluminous skirts which made such a lovely sibillance [*sic*] whenever she moved. **1960** G. A. BRIGGS *A to Z in Audio* 183 *Sibilance*, a fault in reproduction in which consonants and, in particular, 's' sounds are given unnatural prominence. **1962** A. NISBETT *Technique Sound Studio* iv. 82 'Tilting' such a ribbon was at one time commonly used as a means of discriminating against sibilance (a voice defect which seems to be less of a nuisance than it has been in the past). **1974** —— *Use of Microphones* 24 Sometimes intelligibility is improved by using a microphone with a peak..in the 6000–8000 Hz frequency range... But this may also enhance the natural sibilance of some voices. **1979** *Amer. Poetry Rev.* Mar./Apr. 26/1 Now if we take out the first one we risk sibilance by having the *s* of 'Ignatius' run into the *s* of 'swallows'.

sibilant, *sb.* Add: **1.** (Earlier example.)

1788 W. JONES in *Asiatick Researches* I. 11 Next come different classes of *dentals*, and among the first of them should be placed the *sibilants.*

2. A rumour started and spread for propaganda or advertising purposes. Cf. WHISPER *sb.* 2.

1957 *Observer* 27 Oct. 18/7 The sib-spreader, that fortunate extrovert with a cast-iron digestion who is employed to dash about bars and cocktail parties spreading carefully composed sibilants or selling rumours. **1958** [see *SIB *sb.*³].

sibilate, *v.* Add: **2. a.** More generally, to say with a hissing sound.

1903 K. D. WIGGIN *Rebecca of Sunnybrook Farm* xix. 199 'How about cookies?' 'Do you think it's worth while?' sibilated Miss Miranda. **1910** O. BROWNING *Mem. Sixty Yrs.* xx. 318 Two portly gentlemen..turned round towards me, hissed violently and sibilated the word 'Poet' thinking, I suppose, that I was Robert.

Sibiriak (sibi·ryæk). Also **Sibiryak.** [Russ. *Sibiryák* Siberian.] A Siberian descended from European Russian settlers. Also *attrib.* or as *adj.*

1903 W. GERRARE *Greater-Russia* viii. 105 The Siberiaks, as the descendants of the early settlers in the west province are called, are of average height. **1916** M. A. CZAPLICKA *My Siberian Year* xii. 243 The Sibiriak—that is, broadly speaking, the colonial whose ancestors have been settling in Siberia, voluntarily or involuntarily, since, say, the end of the Middle Ages. *Ibid.* 245 An anthology of Sibiriak songs..would provide an illuminating document for the student of Siberian life. **1974** *Encycl. Brit. Macropædia* XVI. 726/1 There were long-established Russian peasant societies in certain parts of Siberia, in many cases the descendants of exiled religious dissidents. Such people, known as Sibiryaks or 'local Russians', have a culture and an outlook differing markedly from those of the people of European Russia.

sibling. Restrict † *Obs.* to sense in Dict. and add: Pronunc. (si·bliŋ). **2.** = *SIB *sb.*² 3 d. Also (chiefly *Anthrop.*), each of two or more children belonging to a family or kinship group having at least one parent in common. Also *fig.*

1903 K. PEARSON in *Biometrika* II. 369 These [calculations] will enable us..to predict the probable character in any individual from a knowledge of one or more parents or brethren ('siblings', = brothers or sisters). **1930** *Nature* 15 Nov. 766 A few were odd twins who had a brother or sister at school, and the remainder were either siblings of twins, or pairs of siblings unconnected with twins. **1933** L. SPIER *Yuman Tribes* vii. 209 She needed to know no more than the sex and relative ages of the siblings from whom the lines were traced to give..the terms used between any pair in the succeeding generations. **1941** *Jrnl. R. Anthrop. Inst.* LXXI. 7/2 A group of siblings is constituted by the sons and daughters of a man and his wife in monogamous societies, or of a man and his wives where there is polygyny, or of a woman and her husbands in polyandrous communities. **1950** M. FORTES in Radcliffe-Brown & Forde *Afr. Systems of Kinship* 273 Next to the bond between mother and child none is so strong as that between siblings by the same mother. **1957** V. W. TURNER *Schism & Continuity in Afr. Soc.* iii. 68 Thus uterine siblings and matrilineal parallel cousins remained together throughout life. **1957** *Observer* 24 Nov. 15/1 There are..echoes of 'Death of a Salesman'—the loyal, harassed wife, the two disenchanted siblings, and the salesman father with an unfulfilled dream. **1970** *Nature* 19 Dec. 1221/2 In the herring gull.., the chick hatching from this third egg suffers a much higher mortality than either of its siblings. **1972** *Daily Tel.* 20 Mar. 2/7 The line dividing the Kevin Street Sinn Fein organisation and its terrorist sibling, the Provisional IRA, is almost invisible. **1974** 'J. MELVILLE' *Nun's Castle* vii. 153 Siblings and kinsfolk did not have to be friends.

3. *attrib.* and *Comb.*, as *sibling group*; **sibling rivalry,** rivalry arising from the jealousy that can exist between siblings; **sibling species** *Biol.*, one of a pair or group of reproductively isolated populations whose members are morphologically very similar; cf. *twin species.*

1957 V. W. TURNER *Schism & Continuity in Afr. Soc.* p. xx, The headman's uterine sibling group. **1975** H. & C. GEERTZ *Kinship in Bali* ii. 57 One brother may farm the plot of land as sharecropper to the sibling group as a whole. **1930** *Smith Coll. Stud. in Social Wk.* I. 6 (*title*) Two studies in sibling rivalry. **1959** MARTIN & STENDLER *Child Behav. & Devel.* (rev. ed.) xvi. 553 The most common form of jealousy in young children is sibling rivalry. **1972** C. RAPHAEL *Feast of History* iv. 118 Moses..shows more than a hint of sibling rivalry in his attitude to his brother Aaron. **1979** WATSON & LINDGREN *Psychol. of Child* (ed. 4) iv. 125 Adler was also keenly aware of the conflicts and tensions among siblings..the intense competition—sibling rivalry—for status, power, and parental attention. **1940** E. MAYR in *Amer. Naturalist* LXXIV. 258 Sibling species: The opposite condition exists where pairs or larger groups of related species are so similar that they are generally considered as one species. **1942** —— *Systematics & Origin of Species* vii. 151, I call..morphologically similar and closely related, but sympatric species, sibling species. This corresponds to the 'dual species' of Pryer and of Hering (1935). **1979** *Nature* 7 June 557/2 The eastern meadowlark (*Sturnella magna*) and western meadowlark (*S. neglecta*) are sibling species of songbirds in secondary contact throughout a narrow zone of sympatry in central North America.

Hence **si·blingship** = *SIBSHIP 1.

1950 M. FORTES in Radcliffe-Brown & Forde *Afr. Syst. of Kinship & Marriage* 273 The range within which the bond of siblingship is accepted as automatically binding. **1957** V. W. TURNER *Schism & Continuity Afr. Soc.* vii. 226 These are all means..of reducing the strength of interine siblingship. **1970** [see *KINSHIP 1 b].

sibship (si·bʃip). [f. SIB *sb.*² + -SHIP.]

1. *Anthrop.* The state of belonging to a sib, or to the same sib (*SIB *a.* and *sb.*² 3 a, c).

1908 *Rep. Brit. Assoc. Adv. Sci. 1907* 654 *Sib and sibship*, the old word *sib* may be used for the relationship set up by membership of the sept. **1924** W. H. R. RIVERS *Soc. Organ.* ii. 22 All the people of a village or district.. believe themselves to be related to one another, and thus form a characteristic example of sibship. **1950** [see *SIB *a.* and *sb.*² 3 a].

2. *Biol.* and *Med.* A group comprising all the individuals born to a particular pair of parents.

1919 *Genetics* IV. 489 Fraternal resemblance is usually not far from ·54, so that 46 percent of the variance of the population occurs within the sibship. **1925** *Jrnl. Genetics* XV. 259 An acre of F_2 plants and an acre of F_3 sibships. **1939** *Nature* 18 Mar. 484/2 The fall in the birth-rate may be due to diminution in family size... Thus the average sibship in Great Britain now is said to be half of what it was fifty years ago. **1949** C. STERN *Princ. Human Genetics* 389 In sibships of 10, chance alone will give rise, on the average, to 1 sibship in 1024 of all boys. **1958** *Immunology* I. 49 Eight goldfish from the same sibship as before. **1978**

Brit. Med. Jrnl. 14 Jan. 72/1 There is a high incidence of spontaneous abortion in sibships in which a case of anencephaly or spina bifida has occurred.

sic, *adv.* Add: Also as *sb.*, an instance of 'sic'.
1910 [used s.v. Sic *v.*]. **1937** *Scrutiny* Sept. 131 As for what Miss Lynch calls 'his really serious affair with Harriet' (I feel this deserves a *sic*), it is purely theatrical. **1963** J. Mitford *Amer. Way Death* ii. 27, I do not like repeated use of *sic*... The reader who is fastidious about usage will hereafter have to supply his own *sics*. **1973** E. Taylor *Serpent under It* (1974) xiv. 224 He called the librarian..and asked him to check... Hence the 'sic'.

sic, var. Sick *v.*[2] in Dict. and Suppl.

Sican (si·kăn). Also **Sikan.** [ad. L. *Sicānus*, pl. *-ī*: see Sicanian *a.*] A member of an ancient people inhabiting Sicily at the time of the coming of the Sicels (see *Sicel *sb.* and *a.*).
1887 *Encycl. Brit.* XXII. 15/1 It is possible..that..the Sikans..belonged to the earlier non-Aryan population of western Europe. **1911** *Ibid.* XXV. 24/2 They [*sc.* the Sicels] found in the island a people called Sicans. **1968** M. Finley *Hist. Sicily* ii. 23 The Sicans who were apparently thinner on the ground than the Sicels, seem also to have been more resistant to Hellenization. **1970** *Oxf. Classical Dict.* (ed. 2) 985/1 Thucydides..attributes an Iberian origin to the Sicans.

Sicanian, *a.* Restrict *poet.* to sense in Dict. and add: Pronunc. (sikē[i]·niăn). **A.** *adj.* **b.** *Archæol.* Denoting the Neolithic period in Sicily. **c.** Of or pertaining to the Sicans. **B.** *sb.* = *Sican.
1629 T. Hobbes tr. *Thucydides' Peloponnesian War* vi. 350 After them, the first that appear to have dwelt therein, are the Sicanians. **1876** F. Tozer *Class. Geogr.* x. 117 The original inhabitants of Sicily were two tribes, the Sicanians in the west, and the Sicels in the east, both of whom belonged to the same Graeco-Italian stock as the Greeks themselves. **1909** T. E. Peet *Stone & Bronze Ages Italy & Sicily* v. 123 By Professor Orsi..the pre-Hellenic period in the island, excluding the palaeolithic, is divided into five divisions. To the first of these he gives the name Sicanian; the other four are called respectively First, Second, Third and Fourth Siculan periods. **1911** *Encycl. Brit.* XXV. 20/1 The most important of the towns to which a Sicanian origin can be with certainty assigned..are: Hyccara..; Omphakē..; and Camicus. **1957** *Ibid.* XX. 603/1 The term Sicanian is applied to that period of the Stone Age which followed the palaeolithic period exemplified in the remarkable rock engravings of the cave near Palermo.

sicca[2] (si·kă). *Path.* [ellipt. for mod.L. *keratoconjunctivitis sicca.*] The symptom of reduced or no lachrymation, with consequent dryness and inflammation of the conjunctiva, characteristic of Sjögren's syndrome; used *attrib.* as *sicca syndrome* to designate the occurrence of this symptom in the absence of rheumatoid arthritis.
1938 *Acta Ophthalmologica* XVI. 176 (*heading*) The initial stage of glandular changes in the sicca syndrome. **1949** *Ibid.* XXVII. Suppl. 33. 1 (*heading*) Keratoconjunctivitis sicca and the sicca syndrome. *Ibid.* 9 The bulk of the sicca patients in my material are rheumatics. **1967** *Amer. Jrnl. Med.* XLIII. 50/1 Sjögren's syndrome is characterized clinically by dryness of the conjunctiva and mucous membranes (sicca syndrome), and by frequent episodes of salivary and lacrimal gland enlargement. **1977** *Proc. R. Soc. Med.* LXX. 483/2 In the 'sicca' or Sjogren syndrome, Patey & Thackray (1955) have described lymphoid tissue in and around intralobar ducts which breaches the walls and allows radiopaque dye to escape during sialography, causing 'punctate sialectasis'.

Sicel (si·sĕl, si·kĕl), *sb.* and *a.* Also **Sikel.** [ad. Gr. Σικελός.] **A.** *sb.* **a.** A member of an ancient people of Sicily. **b.** The language of this people. **B.** *adj.* **a.** Of or pertaining to the Sicels or their language. **b.** *poet.* Sicilian.
1838 C. Thirlwall *Hist. Greece* II. xii. 92 The Sicels and the Phœnicians gradually retreated before the Greeks. **1881** B. Jowett tr. *Thucydides* I. 409 The Sicels were originally inhabitants of Italy,..there are Sicels still in Italy, and the country itself was so called from Italus a Sicel king. **1887** *Encycl. Brit.* XXII. 15/1 Some Sikel elements made their way into the Greek life of Sicily. **1895** L. Johnson *Poems* 37 Oh! Hellas lies far hence, Far the blue Sicel sea. **1911** *Encycl. Brit.* XXV. 24/2 That the Sicels spoke a tongue closely akin to Latin is plain from several Sicel words which crept into Sicilian Greek, and from the Siceliot system of weights and measures. **1939** L. H. Gray *Foundations of Lang.* 335 Besides the Italic dialects proper, mention must also be made of *Sicel*, of which a few glosses and an inscription of three lines have been preserved, and which seems to have belonged either to this group or to Ligurian. **1948** T. J. Dunbabin *Western Greeks* i. 40 It appears that the Sikels moved from Sicily to Italy, not vice versa. **1974** *Encycl. Brit. Micropædia* IX. 182/2 The most important Sicel gods were the Palici..; Adranus..; and the goddess Hybla. **1977** *Canad. Jrnl. Linguistics* Spring 31 Messapic and Sicel in the south take on new significance vis à vis Iberian.

Siceliot (sis-, sike·liǫt), *sb.* and *a.* Also **Sikeliot, -ote.** [ad. Gr. Σικελιώτης, f. Σικελία Sicily: see -ot[2], -ote.] **A.** *sb.* One of the ancient Greeks who colonized Sicily, distinguished from the Sicels who had settled in Sicily before their coming. **B.** *adj.* Of or pertaining to the Siceliots.
1836 C. Thirlwall *Hist. Greece* III. xxii. 263 [They were] linked together by the common name of Siceliots. **1842** *Penny Cycl.* XXIV. 407/1 The intimate knowledge which he [*sc.* Thucydides] shows respecting the history of the Italiotes and Siceliots. **1887** *Encycl. Brit.* XXII. 16/1 The ancient kingship was perhaps kept on or renewed in some of the Sikeliot and Italiot towns. **1892** *Athenæum* 7 May 597/3 In Syracuse then lay the last hopes of rescue for the Siceliot Greeks. **1931** D. Maciver *Greek Cities in Italy & Sicily* xii. 172 Gela was chosen for the Pan-Sikeliot conference of Greek Cities in 424 B.C.

‖ **Sicherheitsdienst** (zi·χ[y]ərhəitsdīnst). [G., f. *sicherheit* security + *dienst* service.] The security branch of the Schutzstaffel (SS) of the Nazi party, set up in 1931–2. Also *attrib.*
1947 [see S.D. s.v. *S 4 a.]. **1958** P. Kemp *No Colours or Crest* i. 9 His murder at the hands of Gestapo or *Sicherheitsdienst*. **1966** N. Freeling *Dresden Green* i. 44 The highly successful delivery of five of the area Sicherheitsdienst group, trousers round their ankles. **1976** T. Allbeury *Only Good German* iv. 23 The SD, the Sicherheitsdienst, were an SS outfit under Walter Schellenberg.

Sichuana, obs. var. *Sechuana.

Sicilian, *a.* and *sb.* Add: **A.** *adj.* **1. b.** Of or pertaining to the Italian dialect of Sicily.
1842 [in Dict.]. **1881** *Encycl. Brit.* XIII. 495/1 The Sicilian vocalism is conspicuously etymological. **1975** *Times Lit. Suppl.* 31 Oct. 1296/3 Dialect seems diminishing and parochial to the serious writer... We can meet good Sicilian or Venetian or Roman dialogue, but not good Italian dialogue.

2. a. (Chess) *Sicilian defence, game, opening* (earlier example).
1847 H. Staunton *Chess-Player's Handbk.* v. ii. 371 The Sicilian Game... In the opinion of Jaenisch..this is the best possible reply to the move of I.P. to K's 4th. **1852** —— *Chess Tournament* 29, I have before taken occasion to remark that in this position of the Sicilian Opening, the first player may gain time..by taking off the Kt. at once. **1875** G. H. D. Gossip *Chess-Player's Manual* iv. xxx. 799 The 'Sicilian' is now considered by most modern authorities to be a comparatively weak mode of play... We are of the opinion that the Sicilian defence is not so bad as it has been represented. **1900** *Knowledge* 1 Aug. 192/1 The success attending the Sicilian defence is especially noteworthy. **1975** *Amer. Speech 1971* XLVI. 232 One can hear heated arguments on the virtues of the Maroczy Variation of the Scheveningen System in the Sicilian Defence to the King's Pawn Opening.

B. *sb.* **4.** A language or dialect spoken in Sicily, *spec.* a dialect of modern Italian.
1818 Keats *Let.* 3 May in R. M. Milnes *Life, Lett., &c. J. Keats* (1848) I. 135 Or may I woo thee In earlier Sicilian? **1859** B. W. Dwight *Mod. Philol.* i. 187 Italian: (Dialects, Lombard; Genoese; Florentine; Neapolitan, Sicilian,..&c.). **1880** A. H. Sayce *Introd. Sci. Lang.* II. vii. 119 Sicilian, for instance, reads like a new language. **1933** L. Bloomfield *Language* iv. 64 *Ligurian* (round the present Riviera) and *Sicilian* in Sicily, may have been close to Italic. **1968** D. Mack Smith *Medieval Sicily* v. 63 Giacomo of Lentini, author of a Provençal-type lyric which is the first poem in true Sicilian that has survived. **1978** *Language* LIV. 184 Sicilian reflects the seven-vowel Southern Romance vocalism.

Siciliana. Add: (Further examples.) Also **Siciliano, siciliano**; pl. **sicilianos, siciliani.** Also, a piece in $\frac{6}{8}$ or $\frac{12}{8}$ time resembling this music. Also *attrib.*
1883 Grove *Dict. Mus.* III. 491/2 *Siciliana, Siciliano, Sicilienne*, a dance rhythm closely allied to the Pastorale. **1947** C. Gray *Contingencies & Other Essays* v. 118 The frequent recurrence in Bellini's music of 12–8 rhythms, called in seventeenth- and eighteenth-century music *Siciliani*, seems always to have been a feature of the popular music of his countrymen. **1959** D. Cooke *Lang. of Music* ii. 100 The siciliano movement in Brahms's St. Anthony Variations. **1968** *Listener* 20 June 814/1 Their variety was astonishing, from the lyrical sicilianos which the history books praise, to vigorous virtuoso pieces. **1970** W. Apel *Harvard Dict. Music* (ed. 2) 774/2 The *siciliana* occurs as a slow movement in early sonatas..as well as in vocal music..whenever gentle pastoral scenes are to be represented musically. **1974** *Early Music* July 197/1 A delightful siciliano aria for alto to the words 'Qui sedes ad dexteram Patris'. **1979** *Ibid.* Oct. 545/2 A profusion of characteristic ideas, charming *Sicilianos*, bubbling *Allegros*, idiomatic and elegant writing for the instrument.

Sicilienne. Add: **1.** (Earlier example.)
1873 *Young Englishwoman* Jan. 24/1 Sicilienne, a new kind of silk, both soft and glossy.

2. *Mus.* = Siciliana in Dict. and Suppl.
1883 [see *Siciliana]. **1927** *Daily Tel.* 12 Feb. 5/2 The Sicilienne was quiet and restful.

sick, *a.* and *sb.* Add: **A.** *adj.* **I. 1. a.** Delete 'Now chiefly literary and *U.S.*' and add further examples. Also, *to go sick*, to become ill, to report sick.
1879 [see sense 1 f below]. **1902** W. B. Yeats *Where there is Nothing* (1903) iv. i. 77 No fear, they won't refuse a sick man. **1915** D. O. Barnett *Lett.* 53 He's lots better this morning,..and he is not 'going sick' at all. **1927** E. J. Thompson *These Men thy Friends* 12 Filthy climate. No fun. But she just carries on. Hasn't gone sick once in six months. **1936** G. B. Shaw *Millionairess* ii. 164 You are my doctor: do you hear? I am a sick woman: you cannot abandon me to die. **1945** *Chambers's Jrnl.* Sept. 452/1 'And you're telling me that you've never had a few days off?.. Not even for sick-leave?' 'I was never sick, sir.' **1952** [see *Lead *sb.*[1] 6 b]. **1956** D. Jacobson *Dance in Sun* ii. ix. 91 'Hey,' he said rudely to Fletcher, 'are you sick?' **1959** V. Watkins *Cypress & Acacia* 23, I found him feeble and sick. And cold. **1962** G. Lawton *John Wesley's English* iii. 57 When Wesley is sick he is 'laid-up.' **1976** *Evening Post* (Nottingham) 15 Dec. 24/4 Willis went sick during the opening match in Poona.

d. (Further *transf.* examples.) Also *fig.*, orig. applied to Turkey and hence to other countries, regions, etc., and in extended uses.
1860 S. S. Cox *Eight Years in Congress* (1865) 129 'Mexico is our "sick man".' 'Yes; she is to America what Turkey is to Europe.' **1868** C. Schurz *Speeches, Corr. & Pol. Papers* (1913) I. 456 The South is our 'sick man'... The 'sick man' has been operated upon by Democratic doctors once more. **1888** S. Lane-Pool *Turkey* xvii. 343 The Powers have always acted on the principle that somebody must serve as a dyke between Russia and the Bosphorus, and that Turkey, being there, had better be maintained in her position. The 'Sick Man' of the morbid mind of Nicholas must be galvanized into sufficient vitality to sit up and pretend to be well. **1897** *Japan Times* 30 Mar. 3/4 Mr Valentine Chirol, who shortly after the war published in the London *Times* a series of remarkable articles exposing the rottenness of China..has recently been in the East again..and has commenced a second series of equally striking articles on the 'Sick Man of Asia'. **1918** *Times* 3 Jan. 5/1 The Sick Man of Europe has changed his doctors, and the new doctors..have prescribed participation in the European war. *Ibid.* 5/2 The Sick Man finds himself less sick than his neighbour, and Russia defenceless offers her flanks to Turkey's sharpest blades. **1929** H. M. Kallen *Frontiers of Hope* 451 Under the terms of the Peace the Jew has simply been made to replace the Turk as the Sick Man of Europe. **1959** *Listener* 30 July 168/2 It was Italy which turned the Austrian empire into a second 'sick man'. **1961** N. Smart in I. Ramsey *Prospect for Metaphysics* v. 80 Natural theology is the Sick Man of Europe. **1963** *Times* 31 Jan. 11/1 There is no imminent threat to it, but once that is passed India would be on the way to becoming in economic terms the sick man of Asia. **1967** *Listener* 26 Jan. 116/2 In December 1958 France was the sick man of Europe; it had no exchange reserves and was incapable of facing the Common Market. **1970** R. Lowell *Notebook* 205 The movie's not always the sick man of the arts. **1974** *Times* 4 May 8/4, I have been wondering who now qualifies for the title of Sick Man of Sound Broadcasting. **1979** G. St. Aubyn *Edward VII* vii. 319 China was the sick man of the Orient over whose corpse the vultures hovered.

† **f.** Said of pigeons which have lost their young and so have no recipient for the soft food that they regurgitate. *Obs.*
1765 *Treat. Domestic Pigeons* 21 If your Pigeons do not hatch, because their eggs are addle, or otherwise, you should give them a pair, or at least one young one, to feed off their soft meat, which would be apt to make them sick. **1854** L. A. Meall *Moubray's Poultry* viii. 455 We have never observed the old birds 'sick' (as most books assert they are) when the young have died. **1879** L. Wright *Pract. Pigeon Keeper* iii. 37 In order that another young one from some other pair..may be given the parents to feed off their soft meat, and save them from 'going sick' with it.

g. *slang* (orig. *U.S.*). Of a drug addict, craving for a dose of a drug, suffering from withdrawal symptoms.
1951 *N.Y. Times* 15 June 14/6, I..would walk up and..ask the bartender: 'Say, have you seen so-and-so yet?' I says: 'Man, I'm sick.' **1953** W. Burroughs *Junkie* vii. 69 The usual routine is to grab someone with junk on him, and let him stew in jail until he is good and sick. **1967** M. M. Glatt et al. *Drug Scene* vii. 91 Even now, more than two years after leaving hospital, I still feel sometimes sick in the morning when I am tense or upset, and I feel sick whenever I see syringes or 'addicts' in TV plays.

2. b. Delete ? *Obs.* and add later examples. Also *sick to the stomach.*
1863 Trollope *Small House at Allington* xxxvi, in *Cornh. Mag.* Aug. 228 How well can I remember the terror created within me by..a certain fine old gentleman...I would become sick in my stomach. **1923** [see *Here *adv.* 5 b]. **1947** A. Huxley *Let.* 9 Apr. (1969) 570, I heard a bit of the *Parsifal* Good Friday music at Easter-time.., and it made me feel even more 'sick to my stomach', as the Americans say, than in the past. **1948** 'J. Tey' *Franchise Affair* xiii. 139 You make me sick—Cat-sick. Sick to my stomach. **1955** *Jrnl. Canad. Linguistic Assoc.* Mar. 17 Another expression which has some striking variants depending on the choice of preposition is *sick at the stomach*. In the Northern speech area of the United States the usual equivalent is *sick to the stomach*; in the Midland and Southern areas, *at* is the usual preposition... In New England..and most of the Yankee settlement areas, *to* enjoys a virtual monopoly. In northwest New York State, however, *sick at the stomach* is unusually common. **1975** *Times* 30 June 17/5 If all the factories are nationalized I shall walk out of here sick to the stomach.

c. (Further examples: sense sometimes merging with 4.) Also *sick as a parrot* (a fanciful catch-phrase, chiefly used *joc.*)
1861 Hughes *Tom Brown at Oxf.* III. xi. 207 It turned me as sick as a dog. *a* **1906** 'T. Collins' *Rigby's Romance* (1946) xli. 221 Well, by-and-by I woke up, sick as a dog, with my face all scorched, and I lay down again. **1915** J. Buchan *39 Steps* vii. 161, I had a crushing headache, and felt as sick as a cat. **1947** A. Ransome *Great Northern?* xix. 238 'Sick as cats with himself,' said Nancy. **1979** *Private Eye* 16 Feb. 12/1 The Moggatollah admitted frankly that he was 'sick as a parrot' at the way events

had been unfolding. **1982** *Daily Star* 5 Feb. 5/6 Peter the budgie was sick as a parrot until a vet diagnosed his problem yesterday. Peter..has got gout!

d. In phrases *to worry* (oneself), *be worried*, *sick*.

1952 M. Laski *Village* v. 89 Edith Wilson had heard about Wendy's illness, and worried herself sick, not knowing what to do for the best. **1961** 'J. le Carré' *Call for Dead* iv. 37 You look worried sick. **1977** R. Ludlum *Chancellor Ms.* xxx. 320 She hasn't been able to sleep. She's worried sick.

II. 4. a. (*d*) Freq. in phr. *to make* (a person) *sick*.

1819, 1860 [in Dict.]. **1911** G. B. Shaw *Blanco Posnet* 30 A man like you makes me sick. **1937** 'G. Orwell' *Road to Wigan Pier* xii. 228 It makes one sick to see.. men sweating their guts out to dig a trench.., when some easily devised machine would scoop the earth out in a couple of minutes. **1944** M. Laski *Love on Supertax* i. 18 The Duchess lost her temper. 'You make me sick!' she shouted. **1978** T. Allbeury *Lantern Network* iii. 34 He talks like a schoolboy. All that 'knocking the Germans for six' stuff, it makes me sick.

5. b. In phrases *sick and tired of* (cf. *sick-tired*, sense 11 in Dict.), *sick to death of*.

1783 'J. H. St. John de Crèvecœur' *Sk. 18th-Cent. Amer.* (1925) 298, I am quite sick and tired of these pretended conscientious non-fighting mortals. **1884** E. W. Nye *Baled Hay* 124 We are sick and tired of pointing out different avenues of wealth to be laughed at and ridiculed. **1890** E. Dowson *Let. c* 11 Sept. (1967) 166, I am sick to death of this place. **1925** F. S. Fitzgerald *Great Gatsby* ix. 205 'You young men think you can force your way in any time,' she scolded. 'We're getting sick in tired of it.' **1953** R. Lehmann *Echoing Grove* 117 He was sick to death of the sound of these three crass monosyllables which he seemed always to be reiterating. **1976** *Milton Keynes Express* 9 July 2/6, I believe people are sick and tired of half-truths and evasions.

III. 6. Also, morbid, enjoying sick humour (see sense 7 f below).

1959, 1960 [see sense 7 f below]. **1961** *Times* 17 July 14/5 Mr. Sahl is disapproving of the so-called 'sick' comedians of America. **1961** Webster s.v. [1]*sick*, A sick personality. **1962** *Listener* 25 Oct. 692/3 From Korea James Mossman reported on the Panmunjom truce-line (a raree-show for tourists these days, I gather: how sick can people get?). **1964** L. Nkosi *Rhythm of Violence* 45 Don't mind them, honey! They're the sickest bunch of people you ever saw.

7. a. (Further examples.)

1817 in *Trans. Ill. State Hist. Soc. 1910* (1912) 147 Sick Milk, Sick Wheat, a plenty of Ague near the large streams. **1847** H. Howe *Hist. Collect. Ohio* 274 Those lands were too sick for wheat, making 'sick' wheat, so termed, because when made into bread, it had the effect of an emetic. **1915** *Rep. Brit. Assoc. Adv. Sci. 1914* 672 The fertility of this 'sick' soil can be restored by merely heating it for an hour or two to a temperature approaching that of boiling water. **1921** *Brit. Mus. Return* 74 in *Parl. Papers* XXVII. 651 The treatment and cleaning of sick and dirty coins. **1930** *N. & Q.* 16 Aug. 124/2 A cheese..is sick when it has been over soured or over acidulated, and in time 'weeps', gradually becoming soft inside. **1947** I. L. Idriess *Isles of Despair* xvi. 106 Some roots are 'sick', eaten through and through by boring insects. **1965** *Listener* 2 Sept. 358/1 Soils can be said to be 'potato sick', 'rose sick', 'flax sick', etc.

fig. **1931** H. Crane *Let.* 13 June (1965) 371 As for Mexico..you were right, it's a sick country. **1959** *Washington Post* 18 Nov. A 16/2 Some czars in the labor movement will scream over this resort to the courts to straighten out so-called internal affairs of sick unions, but for racket-harassed workers it is an event of the first importance. **1960** *Wall St. Jrnl.* 2 Feb. 4 He has taken other sick businesses and has done a marvelous job with them. **1973** *Black Panther* 14 July 6/2, I was basically looking at myself..people of my complexion struggling for their liberation. I saw how sick conditions were. **1976** Smythies & Corbett *Psychiatry* iii. 29 Concepts like a 'sick' society have become commonplace.

f. *colloq.* Of humour, a joke, etc.: macabre, providing amusement by reference to something that is thoroughly unpleasant.

1959 *Punch* 2 Sept. 106/1 The prototype of sick jokes is one that goes 'But apart from that, Mrs. Lincoln, how did you enjoy the play?' **1959** *Guardian* 16 Oct. 10/3 Feiffer..belongs..to the new American fashion of sick humour... Like those gifted sick comedians Mort Sahl and Lenny Bruce..he is able to go straight to the springs of derision and aggression where so much humour begins. **1959** *Washington Post* 26 Nov. D 22/1 'Sick comedy,' defines Berman carefully, 'is comic material which violates what we regard as the limits of sensitivity—poking fun at a cripple..or kidding a typhoon that killed thousands.' **1960** *Guardian* 7 Oct. 15/3 Jules Feiffer, regarded as one of the 'sick' school of cartoonists, is not as sick as all that... No one is sicker than Charles Addams. **1961** *Harper's Bazaar* Feb. 84/2 To enjoy..the sick joke.. you have to..swallow jokes about cancer, corruption, homosexuality, third degree, race prejudice and insanity. **1965** *Times Lit. Suppl.* 25 Nov. 1035/4 This has been a time of sick laughter. **1968** M. Woodhouse *Rock Baby* xvii. 164 How long exactly does it take to become a bomb-disposal expert? And don't tell me that you learn by your mistakes because I'm not in the mood for sick jokes. **1975** P. Fussell *Gt. War & Mod. Memory* vi. 228 There is extant a postwar version of such a record [of battle],..aimed at what today might be called the Sick Nostalgia Market. **1978** D. Devine *Sunk without Trace* xxv. 226 'How does it feel..to be back in the bosom of your family?' Judy said sharply: 'I'm not in the mood for sick jokes.'

10. a. *sick bay* (later examples).

1919 W. Lang *Sea Lawyer's Log* i. 6 Then our guide, a Leading Seaman,..conducted us to the doctor's quarters—or 'sick bay', as he expressed it. **1971** P. D. James *Shroud for Nightingale* iii. 60 She's in the sick bay... It's part of the private wing.

b. *sick-benefit*, *-leave* (later examples).

1909 *Chambers's Jrnl.* 26 Dec. 56/2 Members who..may have received sick-benefit. **1952** Sick benefit [see *approved *ppl. a.* 6]. **1943** J. B. Priestley *Daylight on Saturday* xxix. 231 He'll be home on sick leave.., the doctor says. **1976** *Times* 8 Mar. 12/8 Staff are entitled to paid sick leave only if there is a reasonable prospect of their return to duty.

11. *sick-making* ppl. adj. and vbl. sb.; *sick-sweet* adj.

1930 E. Waugh *Vile Bodies* i. 7 Sometimes the ship pitched and sometimes she rolled... 'Too, too sick-making,' said Miss Runcible, with one of her rare flashes of accuracy. **1938** Dylan Thomas *Let. c* 6 July (1966) 203 There will be speechmaking, drunkmaking, sickmaking and we must all dress up. **1949** N. Mitford *Love in Cold Climate* i. vi. 59 I'm in a terrible do about my [stolen] bracelet of lucky charms—no value to anybody else—really—too too sick-making. **1976** I. Illich *Limits to Medicine* 7 What has turned health care into a sick-making enterprise is the very intensity of an engineering endeavour. **1978** *Times* 5 Oct. 2/4 What is sickmaking is the IBA..trying to make the BBC out as the monster and them the viewers' guardian. **1922** Joyce *Ulysses* 444 The odour of the sicksweet weed floats towards him.

12. Special combs., as **sick-bag**, a bag provided in aircraft, ships, etc., as a receptacle for vomit; **sick call**, (*a*) (orig. and chiefly *Mil.*), a call sounded to summon those reporting sick to a place of treatment; an assembly for medical treatment; (*b*) a visit made to a sick person; (*c*) a summons to visit a sick person; **sick headache** = Migraine; also in phrases as a type of something useless or unhelpful; **sick parade** *Mil.*, an inspection of those who are ill; the people on sick parade; **sick visiting** (see quot. 1933).

1962 W. Schirra in *Into Orbit* 33 On the plane, John Glenn and Al Shepard took one of the brown paper 'sick-bags' and scribbled on it: 'Here is the answer to the air sickness problem.' **1976** 'D. Halliday' *Dolly & Nanny Bird* vi. 71 The accustomed routine with Kleenex and sick bags..and barley sugar. **1836** J. Hildreth *Dragoon Campaigns to Rocky Mountains* 114 Every morning..'sick call' blows. **1850** E. Price (*title*) Sick calls: from the diary of a missionary priest. **1883** Lady Herbert tr. *Life St. John Baptist de Rossi* iii. iv. 147 The servants never again dared to fail to warn him of any sick call. **1930** F. A. Pottle *Stretchers* 31 Sick call is blown before the dispensary door. **1931** P. J. Joyce *John Healy* ii. 37 That imperious, unmistakable sick-call knock. **1945** *Yank* 13 July 19/2 A punitive measure to discourage falling out for sick call. **1976** *Billings* (Montana) *Gaz.* 27 June 1-B/4 There is a daily sick call by a local doctor for the inmates. **1977** *New Yorker* 24 Oct. 106/2 A third way for an inmate to see a doctor is to go to sick call, which is held each weekday morning at Green Haven on the first floor of the Hospital-Segregation Building. **1978** J. Carroll *Mortal Friends* iv. ii. 389, I was a young priest at the time, see, and I get this sick-call. **1778** Fothergill in *Med. Observ.* (1784) VI. 103 Remarks on that Complaint commonly known under the Name of the Sick Head-ach. **1799** [in Dict., sense 9]. **1857** M. O. Colt *Jrnl.* 18 May (1862) xii. 218, I..was obliged..to..stay two nights and one day, suffering with a sick headache. **1915** D. O. Barnett *Lett.* 153 Shrapnel is for defenders, to stop an advance of infantry, but no more use against prepared positions than a sick headache. **1977** 'E. Crispin' *Glimpses of Moon* xii. 252 That pair in the back, between them, are about as much use as a sick headache. **1915** 'I. Hay' *First Hundred Thousand* xi. 137 M'Splae departs, grumbling, and reappears on sick parade a few days later. **1927** R. H. Mottram *Spanish Farm Trilogy* 258 Do you know what a sick parade I've got? Eighty! Yes, I have. **1966** *Times* 9 July 9/7 Command Orders say... Sick Parade has now become 'sick list'. **1933** *O.E.D. Suppl.* s.v. Sick *a.* and *sb.* 10 b, *Sick visiting*, the visiting of the sick, esp. by a minister of religion. **1960** N. Nicholson *William Cowper* 13 A most exacting life of piety, prayer-meetings, self-denial, and sick-visiting. **1977** *West Briton* 25 Aug. 11/1 He paid tribute to Mr. Clay's work, especially his sick visiting.

B. *sb.* **3. a.** For *rare* read '*rare* exc. in phr. *to give* (a person) *the sick*, to nauseate, to disgust'.

1849 *Sessions Paper* 26 Nov. 5 If I have many such markets as this, it will give me the sick. **1897** [in Dict.]. **1939** 'G. Orwell' *Coming up for Air* IV. v. 257 As for the picturesqueness,..it merely gives me the sick. **1960** *Spectator* 11 Nov. 751 Rackham and all give me the sick.

b. Colloq. phr. *on the sick*, incapacitated by illness, receiving sickness benefit.

1976 *News of World* 14 Mar. 11/2 My Dad used to be on the sick for a long time and couldn't work. **1976** *Par Golf* Aug. 39/3, I didn't realise this would get in the papers. It could cost me my job. I'm on the sick. **1976** L. Thomas *Dangerous Davies* vii. 68, I took it [*sc.* an allotment] on.. but then I was on the sick for months..and the council.. takes it off me.

4. Vomited matter.

1959 I. & P. Opie *Lore & Lang. Schoolch.* ix. 162 Spread it on the butty nice and thick, Swallow it down with a bucket of sick. **1966** *Listener* 3 Nov. 651/3 Middle-aged Chelsea ladies are crawling about in each others' sick. **1977** *Ibid.* 3 Mar. 282/4 There's blood on the windscreen, sick on the trousers.

sick, *v.*[1] Add: **2.** For † *Obs.* read 'Now *rare*' and add later example.

1909 J. Masefield *Tragedy of Nan* iii. 64 You talk rude to the quality... Talk as'd sick a savage.

4. *trans.* and *intr.* To vomit, to spew *up*. Also *fig.*

1924 C. Mackenzie *Old Men of Sea* xix. 333 The volcano started in sicking up red-hot pitch and all. **1930** Kipling *Thy Servant a Dog* 25, I have ate grass and sicked up. **1930** *Dial. Notes* VI. 83 [Child loq.] I sicked all over my yew dress. **1937** L. A. G. Strong *Swift Shadow* 209 But the snow do turn my stomach and I sicked in the hedge. **1948** 'N. Shute' *No Highway* 162 It can't do me any good if I sick it all up. **1954** 'N. Blake' *Whisper in Gloom* vii. 100, I can't go sicking it all up to the police. **1966** C. Sweeney *Scurrying Bush* xiii. 188 On the way the reptile sicked up another hen, and half-way it regurgitated a third hen on the floor of my vehicle. **1975** *Times* 16 Jan. 18/3 A planeload of passengers sicking their breakfast. **1980** *Sunday Tel.* (Colour Suppl.) 21 Dec. 11/3 She sings *Away in a Manger*..and drinks lots of drinks and then she sicks up.

sick, *v.*[2] Add: **1.** (Earlier and later examples.)

1845 J. J. Hooper *Some Adv. S. Suggs* 154 Sick him Pomp,..sick, sick, si-c-k him Bull. **1908** *Westm. Gaz.* 19 Sept. 16/1 'Sick' un then.' Now 'sicking' a hedgehog is a job which few dogs care to tackle. **1933** 'R. Crompton' *William—the Rebel* i. 14 The small white dog, evidently mistaking William's contemptuous 'Huh!' for a new form of 'Sick him!' gave a low growl and sprang forthwith upon the astonished Wotan. **1952** Wodehouse *Barmy in Wonderland* v. 53 'Sic 'em, Tulip,' he said. **1977** *Globe & Mail* (Toronto) 2 Mar. 5/2 All my dogs are attack-trained ..but they won't respond to English commands... It's so little kids can't tell him to sic someone.

2. a. (Earlier example.) Also, to set (a dog or other animal) *on* or *at*.

1845 J. J. Hooper *Some Adv. S. Suggs* 151 If I was to sick them on your old hoss yonder, they'd eat him up afore you could say Jack Robinson. **1899** B. Tarkington *Gentl. Indiana* viii. 131 Seems some of the boys..sicked the dogs on him. **1909** J. Masefield *Tragedy of Nan* ii. 28 Hope they'll catch 'im and 'ang 'im. I'd like to sick the dogs at 'em. **1932** W. Faulkner *Light in August* xiii. 286 They couldn't run him away if they was to sick them bloodhounds on him. **1977** J. Hodgins *Invention of World* iii. 75 He threatened to turn the stones into slobbering wolves and sic them on her.

b. *fig.* To set (a person) to work *on*; to set (a person) to pursue, observe, accompany, etc. (const. *on* or *on to*).

1923 E. B. White *Let.* 2 Jan. (1976) 62 The Times sicks me on feature stuff because the city editor discovered early in the game that city politics appear only in humorous light to me. **1929** R. Lardner *Round Up* xxvi. 327 All I told him was that he'd have to let me pick my own roommate after this and not sic no wild man on to me. **1939** Wodehouse *Uncle Fred in Springtime* i. 18 Why should you barge in here, gnashing your bally teeth, just because Horace sicked Claude Polt, private investigator, on to you? **1958** 'E. Dundy' *Dud Avocado* ii. iv. 221 I'll never forgive you for..sic-ing the sort of person the Contessa is on him. **1958** R. Stout *Champagne for One* (1959) xiv. 172 He had cleared away some underbrush, for instance who had sicked the cops on Laidlaw. **1972** R. Thomas *Porkchoppers* (1974) xxviii. 240 Penry works for me. If you need something done..then I'll sic him on it.

sicken, *v.* Add: **1. d.** *to sicken for*: to be in the early stages of (a disease which is not yet manifest); to be 'coming down' with.

1883 F. Montgomery *Blue Veil* ii. vii. 218, I was sickening for the mumps. **1977** *Sunday Times* 16 Jan. 30/5 Amiss, sickening for the flu which prevented him fielding, got his bat caught in his pads.

sickening, *ppl. a.* Add: **2.** Also in weakened sense.

1922 [see *fed *pa. pple.*]. **1924** M. Arlen *Green Hat* ii. 67 In ten years' time..Hilary will be the only Liberal left in Parliament, looking happier and younger and more sickening than ever. **1925** D. Mackail *Greenery Street* viii. 179 But, Ian, Daphne's thing is a subscription dance. ..*Please* don't be so sickening. **1937** W. H. Saumarez Smith *Let.* 8 Feb. in *Young Man's Country* (1977) ii. 56 Isn't it too sickening that I shall get to Singapore just after Margaret's and Ronald's departure.

Sickertian (sikɜ·ɹtiăn), *a.* [f. *Sickert* (see below) + -ian.] Reminiscent of, or in the manner of, the works of the English painter W. R. Sickert (1860–1942).

1959 *Times* 27 May 7/3 He would seem to be an unwilling draughtsman—although a few delightful drawings in a Sickertian manner are shown. **1964** L. Deighton *Funeral in Berlin* xiv. 85 The Sickertian backwaters of Camden Town. **1976** *Times* 1 May 7/1 Sylvia Gosse.. became a competent artist, practising in a Sickertian style.

sickie (si·ki). Also **sicky**. [f. Sick *a.* and *sb.* + -ie.] **1.** *Austral.* and *N.Z. colloq.* A day's sick leave, usu. taken without sufficient medical reason.

1953 T. A. G. Hungerford *Riverslake* 11 Now and then there would be one or more off on a sickie—they changed their jobs so frequently that they never let their sick leave accumulate. **1959** D. Hewett *Bobbin Up* 81 She wished she could take a sickie tomorrer, but it was payday. **1969** *Telegraph* (Brisbane) 28 Oct. 8/2 If we don't feel just right we don't go up. We have a 'sickie' and everyone understands. **1974** *N.Z. Woman's Weekly* 8 July 5/3 Because of the nature of the work it was impossible to plan time off for social functions at short notice. As a result a small percentage of cabin crew staff resorted to 'sickies'. **1981** *Courier-Mail* (Brisbane) 5 Sept.

5/2 A part-time fireman's sense of duty cost him his job after he answered an emergency call when he was taking a 'sickie' from work.

2. *N. Amer. slang.* One who is mentally ill or perverted. Also *attrib.* or as *adj.*

1973 *Ottawa Jrnl.* 1 Aug. 34/2, I hope she gets professional help because these sickies usually get worse, not better. **1974** P. DE VRIES *Glory of Hummingbird* (1975) x. 135 'Shall I..make it clear..I'm a sickie?' 'No!.. this—ailment of yours..it's an expression of some deep-seated conflict.' **1975** *Chronicle-Herald* (Halifax, N.S.) 2 Aug. 26/2 Dade County's entire homicide squad was mobilized..to search for a 'sickie' who murdered two attractive young women. **1977** *Chicago Tribune* 2 Oct. VII. 3/2 A sickie Army lieutenant who tries to run off with the reporter's daughter.

sick-in (si·kˌin). *U.S.* [f. SICK *a.* + *-IN³.] Industrial action in which a group of workers absent themselves from work on the pretext of sickness. Cf. *SICKOUT, SICK-OUT.

1974 *Spartanburg* (S. Carolina) *Herald* 25 Apr. B 8/9 The 'sick-in' forced cancellation of eight of the 11 scheduled U.N. meetings Tuesday. **1976** *N.Y. Times* 7 Sept. 35/4 New Orleans police stage sick-in. **1977** *Monitor* (McAllen, Texas) 12 June 54/1 Millard Holden,..president of the Independent Produce Haulers of America, said he had heard 'sick-in' by independent truckers would be called over the July 4 holiday.

sickish, *a.* **2.** (Earlier example.)

1727 S. J. *Vineyard* 36 Your Grapes..must not be over Ripe, for..the Wine will be Sickish and Ropey.

sickle, *sb.* Add: **4. sickle scaler** *Dentistry*, an instrument with a curved blade for removing scale from teeth.

1930 W. H. O. McGEHEE *Text-bk. Operative Dentistry* 930/2 (Index), Sickle scalers. **1956** H. M. GOLDMAN et al. *Periodontal Therapy* v. 94 The sickle scaler has a blade with two or four cutting edges. **1962** BLAKE & TROTT *Periodontology* x. 97 Fine sickle scalers are used for subgingival scaling.

sickle (si·k'l), *v.*² [f. SICKLE *sb.*: cf. SICKLED *ppl. a.* b, SICKLING¹.] **1.** *trans.* To cut with a sickle. Also *absol.*

1922 J. MASEFIELD *Dream* 13 All golden ripe and ready to be shorn By sickling sunburnt reapers singing staves. **1927** H. E. FOSDICK *Pilgrimage to Palestine* i. 4 The harvesters were sickling golden grain on the Shephelah hills. **1971** *Country Life* 2 Dec. 1501/1 The English labourer sickles his corn in August, the French labourer has it in by that time.

2. *Path.* **a.** *intr.* Of red blood cells: to become crescent- or sickle-shaped. Of blood: to exhibit sickling.

1923 *Amer. Jrnl. Dis. Children* XXVI. 133 The blood of the father..was normal on being drawn, but 'sickled' after standing for variable periods of time at room temperature. **1946** *Lancet* 10 Aug. 204/1 Severely anæmic blood always sickles far more readily than blood which is not anæmic. **1970** R. W. McGILVERY *Biochem.* iv. 75 Even the cells of heterozygotes will sickle if the oxygen tension is low enough. **1981** *Sci. Amer.* Mar. 117/1 After cyanate treatment and washing, the *AS* cells remained competent as hosts for *P. falciparum*, but now they did not sickle as readily.

b. *trans.* To cause to sickle.

1977 *Lancet* 20 Aug. 411/1 The desickling agent..reacts with red cells which had been deoxygenated and sickled with sodium metabisulphite.

sickle cell. *Path.* [f. SICKLE *sb.* + CELL *sb.*¹] **1.** One of the characteristic crescent-shaped red cells found in the blood of people with sickle cell anæmia.

[**1910** *Arch. Internal Med.* VI. 517 (*heading*) Peculiar elongated and sickle-shaped red blood corpuscles in a case of severe anemia.] **1923** *Johns Hopkins Hosp. Bull.* XXXIV. 42/2 It may..be appropriate to mention here the relationships of blood grouping to another phenomenon occurring in this family, namely, the presence of the so-called 'sickle cells' or crescentic red blood corpuscles. **1946** *Lancet* 10 Aug. 204/1 As long as the diagnosis rested on the presence of sickle cells in stained films, the condition was rarely identified. **1968** *Times* 13 Nov. 16/1 The membranes of sickle cells took longer to remove than those of normal cells, a difference that could be related to the impaired ability of sickle cells to carry oxygen.

2. *attrib.*, as *sickle cell count, family, individual, phenomenon*; **sickle cell anæmia, disease,** a frequently fatal form of anæmia, characterized by the presence of red blood cells that are rich in sickle cell hæmoglobin and sickle readily, and occurring in individuals homozygous for the sickle cell gene; **sickle cell gene,** an autosomal gene found in man, which when heterozygous produces the sickle cell trait and when homozygous sickle cell anæmia, and which is especially common in tropical Africa; **sickle cell hæmoglobin,** an abnormal hæmoglobin which tends to produce a characteristic crescent shape in red cells containing it; **sickle cell trait,** a relatively harmless condition, characterized by the presence of red blood cells containing some sickle cell hæmoglobin and conferring some resistance to malaria; (formerly applied to the characteristic sickling of the red cells which is seen *a fortiori* in sickle cell anæmia).

1922 *Jrnl. Amer. Med. Assoc.* 14 Oct. 1318/2 (*heading*) Sickle cell anemia. **1924** *Ibid.* 5 July 16/1 Several new phases have been brought out since the time, fourteen years ago, when I described what for want of a better term, I [*sc.* J. B. Herrick] called sickle cell anemia. **1969** *Times* 28 Aug. 8/2 The gene for sickle cell anaemia.. persists in certain African populations because it confers resistance against malaria. **1977** *Rolling Stone* 21 Apr. 8/1 He missed..the appearance of a frightening new phenomenon in the American black community: the replacement of sickle cell anemia with Potomac Fever as *the* crippling disease among blacks. **1970** P. OLIVER *Savannah Syncopators* 41 Those [tribes] on the coast include a large proportion with high counts of the sickle-cell gene making them resistant to malaria and able to withstand heat and high humidity; those in the savannah belt include large numbers of tribes with low sickle-cell counts and lower resistance to malaria. **1949** *Science* 25 Nov. 547/2 (*heading*) On the genetics of sickle cell disease. **1961** R. D. BAKER *Essent. Path.* xviii. 492 In sickle cell disease the spleen is often enlarged with intensely red cut surface. **1981** *Westindian World* 28 Aug. 13/2 Sickle cell disease is a blood disorder. It only affects African, Afro-Caribbean and Asian people. **1972** *Science* 13 Oct. 138/3 Physicians who treat sickle cell families emphasize the difference between sickle cell anaemia..and sickle cell trait. **1946** *Lancet* 10 Aug. 204/1 It seems clear that the sickle-cell gene originated in Africa and was carried by slaves to North and South America. **1961** *Times* 21 July 9/5 The population has a genetic resistance to malaria... They possess what is known as a sickle-cell gene, which results in their haemoglobin being abnormal. **1950** *Nature* 21 Oct. 677/1 Dr. F. Eirich, who had first directed our attention to this peculiar disease, gave us a sample of sickle-cell hæmoglobin solution. **1971** *New Scientist* 24 June 762/2 He found that in sickle cell haemoglobin one negatively charged glutamic acid in each of the two normal β chains was replaced by an electrically neutral valine. **1958** *Oxf. Univ. Gaz.* 23 Apr. 892 A study of the physique, growth, and fertility of sickle cell and normal individuals in malarious and non-malarious areas of Nigeria. **1926** *Amer. Jrnl. Dis. Children* XXXII. 334 (*heading*) The sickle cell phenomenon. **1928** *Lancet* 24 Mar. 614/1 Sickle cell or drepanocytic anæmia is found only in negroes with the sickle cell trait—that is, whose red cells become distorted into sickle-shaped cells under certain conditions. **1959** *Listener* 26 Nov. 919/2 Sickle cell trait can be found in parts of Africa, in some Mediterranean countries, and in parts of India. **1978** R. B. SCOTT *Price's Textbk. Pract. of Med.* (ed. 12) xiv. 1156/1 In sickle-cell trait where there is only 30–40 per cent haemoglobin S, symptoms are rare.

sickled, *ppl. a.* Add: **2.** *Path.* [or f. *SICKLE *v*².] Of a red blood cell: sickle-shaped.

1923 *Johns Hopkins Hosp. Bull.* XXXIV. 339/1 All the cells in the preparation kept in the dark had reversed within two days, whereas the controls remained sickled for a period of three days to one month. **1949** *Science* 25 Nov. 543/1 Under sufficiently low oxygen pressure.. all the cells of both types assume the sickled form. **1971** *New Scientist* 24 June 762/1 The sickled cells tend to clog the circulation and to break up before they reach the life span of normal red cells.

sicklemia (sik'lī·miă). *Path.* [contraction of *sickle (cell anæ)mia.] Sickle cell anæmia or the sickle cell trait. Hence **sickle·mic** *a.*

1932 *Amer. Jrnl. Med. Sci.* CLXXXIII. 386 The term sicklemia has been suggested instead of sickle-cell anemia because a grave anemia is not constantly found in these patients. It is perhaps best reserved for those cases that show sickling without anemia. **1949** *Science* 25 Nov. 543/1 Less than 1 percent of those [erythrocytes] in the venous circulation of sicklemic individuals..are normally sickled. *Ibid.* 545/2 We have assumed that one of the two components of sicklemia hemoglobin is identical with sickle cell anemia hemoglobin and the other is identical with the normal compound. **1961** R. D. BAKER *Essent. Path.* xviii. 492 The hereditary trait of sickling of red corpuscles is usually found in apparently normal individuals. However, 2 to 4 per cent of Negroes with sicklemia have sickle cell anemia because of hemolysis of the abnormal red cells. **1973** B. J. WILLIAMS *Evolution & Human Origins* iv. 61/1 In thalassemia and, to a less marked extent, sicklemia, there are changes in bone marrow.

sickler. Add: **2.** *Path.* A person with sickle cell anæmia or the sickle cell trait.

1932 *Amer. Jrnl. Med. Sci.* CLXXXIII. 388 Normal gall bladders have been observed in 'sicklers' at autopsy who have had attacks of severe pain and rigidity in the upper right quadrant of the abdomen. **1954** *Brit. Med. Jrnl.* 6 Feb. 291/2 In a group of 102 sicklers from the Balovale district of Northern Rhodesia only 10 (9·8%) had blood slides showing malaria parasites, whereas in a comparable group of 491 non-sicklers 75 (15·3%) had malaria parasites. **1978** *Observer* (Colour Suppl.) 26 Nov. 58/1 In the old days, 'sicklers' rarely reached adulthood.

sicklerite (si·klərəit). *Min.* [f. the name *Sickler* (see quot. 1912) + -ITE¹.] A phosphate of lithium, bivalent manganese, and ferric iron, $Li(Mn,Fe)(PO_4)$, found as masses of brown orthorhombic crystals.

1912 W. T. SCHALLER in *Jrnl. Washington Acad. Sci.* II. 145 Sicklerite. Named after the Sickler family, formerly of Pala [in San Diego county, California]. Found in cleavable masses..on Hiriart Hill near Pala... Results from the alteration of lithiophilite. **1975** *Fortschritte der Mineral.* LII. Special Issue 299 A large suite of secondary phosphates including sicklerite,..heterosite and others were derived from the primary minerals by hydrothermal alterations which leached alkali ions from the structures with concomitant oxidation of bivalent iron and manganese.

sickling¹. Add: **2.** *Path.* The adoption of a crescent shape by red blood cells.

1923 *Johns Hopkins Hosp. Bull.* XXXIV. 339/1 From these experiments it may be concluded that the sickling is an inherent property of the red blood cells and that the patients' sera are without effect on normal erythrocytes. **1961** R. D. BAKER *Essent. Path.* xviii. 491 In the absence of oxygen the hemoglobin S forms crystals which cause the erythrocytes to assume peculiar sickled or oat forms. The sickling can be demonstrated in Negroes with sicklemia by allowing moist preparations of blood to stand, thus using up the oxygen. **1977** *Time* 28 Nov. 56/3 The Rockefeller scientists realized that any treatment for this genetic disease..had to be directed at stopping the characteristic sickling, or distortion, of the red blood cells that occurs after they unload their cargo of oxygen.

sick-list. (Earlier and later examples.)

1748 SMOLLETT *R. Random* I. xxvii. 246 After the captain came on board, our first mate..went to wait on him with a sick list. **1883** 'MARK TWAIN' *Life on Miss.* 309 Which one numbered the biggest sick-list? **1951** *Sport* 27 Jan.–2 Feb. 4/2 With Flewin, Thompson and Spence all cluttering up the Fratton sick-list, Jack volunteered his services in the pivotal position.

sickly, *a.* Add: **8.** *sickly-scented, -sweet.*

1932 D. GASCOYNE *Roman Balcony* 85 The courtesan in the sickly-scented secrecy of her thick-curtained chamber. **1951** S. SPENDER *World within World* 267 We had to distinguish between those which smelt like pear-drops, carnations and sickly-scented hay. **1912** R. A. FREEMAN *Singing Bone* 136 The same idea having occurred to me, I applied the handle of the knife to my nose and instantly detected the sickly-sweet odour of musk. **1965** G. McINNES *Road to Gundagai* xiii. 222 The room was..sickly-sweet.

sickness. Add: **6.** *sickness insurance.*

1911 *Q. Rev.* July 209 Sickness-insurance. *a* **1974** R. CROSSMAN *Diaries* (1976) II. 745 This sickness insurance provides that if you are sick for ten days or more you are paid at the end of the tenth day and the three waiting days at the beginning are included.

sicknik (si·knik). *U.S. slang.* Also **sicknic.** [f. SICK *a.* + *-NIK.] **a.** One who is mentally ill. **b.** One who indulges in sick humour.

1959 R. BLOCH *Blood Runs Cold* (1963) 161 This is a real sicknik. A masochist, like. **1961–2** *Amer. Scholar* XXXI. 108/1 Then all at once (seemingly), in 1959, the sicknics were at hand. **1966** *New Statesman* 19 Aug. 261/1 The silliest definition of the art of Lenny Bruce is that of a 'sick' comedian (or 'sicknik', according to *Time* magazine), since it is so manifestly the sicknesses of society he was getting at. **1968** [see *-NIK].

sick-nurse, *sb.* (Earlier example.)

1816 SCOTT *Antiquary* III. xiii. 284 He has had an infernal tumble..and..I have sent your friend, Sweep-clean..to act as his sick-nurse.

sicko (si·ko). *U.S. slang.* [f. SICK *a.* + *-O².] = *SICKIE 2.

1977 J. WAMBAUGH *Black Marble* (1978) xi. 245 But, Clarence, listen! She's a sicko. Some kinda fruitcake or somethin. **1982** *Chicago Sun-Times* 25 Nov. 7/2 Is it asking too much for these sickos to stop bothering decent women?

sickout, sick-out (si·kˌaut). orig. and chiefly *U.S.* [f. SICK *a.* + OUT *adv.*, on the analogy of 'walk-out'.] = *SICK-IN. Also *attrib.*

1970 *Wall St. Jrnl.* 13 Apr. 1/3 The air controllers' 'sickout' is showing 'continuing improvement', the Government reported yesterday. On Saturday a Federal district judge ordered leaders of the Professional Air Traffic Controllers Organization to tell their members to go back to work or produce medical certificates of illness. **1974** *Trinidad Guardian* (Port-of-Spain) 16 Oct. 4/1 (Advt.), After all these strikes, sickouts, go-slows, and not a penny increase yet, now these merciless taxis up by 25% plus. **1977** *N.Y. Post* 18 June 1 The Yonkers police sickout crisis. **1978** *Telegraph* (Brisbane) 30 Oct. 12/1 Flights worldwide were delayed by a 'sick-out' of [Pan-American] flight attendants who had voted against a strike at the weekend.

sicky, var. *SICKIE.

‖ **sic transit** (sĭk træ·nzit). Also erron. **transitur.** [L.] A catch-phrase expressing the impermanence of things, in full *sic transit gloria mundi*, 'thus passes the glory of the world'.

The phrase is possibly an adaptation of a passage of Thomas à Kempis (see quot. *a* 1471). For the use of these words in papal coronations see *King's Classical & Foreign Quotations* (ed. 3, 1904) 319.

[*a* **1471** T. À KEMPIS *Imitatio Christi* (1827) I. iii. 7 O quam cito transit gloria mundi.] **1601** JONSON *Every Man in his Humour* v. i. sig. Mᵛ, See, see, how our Poets glory shines brighter and brighter, still, still it increaseth, oh now its at the highest, and now it declines as fast: you may see gallants, *sic transit gloria mundi.* **1777** H. WALPOLE *Let.* 5 Dec. (1904) X. 163 General Howe must probably return to defend New York. *Sic transit gloria mundi!* **1833** LORD LYTTON *Godolph.* III. xxiii. 250 His breathing..died away as insensibly as an infant. *Sic transit gloria mundi!* **1851** GEO. ELIOT *Let.*

4 Oct. (1954) I. 364 Sic transitur—i.e. the money from my pocket. **1915** D. H. LAWRENCE *Crown* in *Reflections on Death of Porcupine* (1925) 92 Despair comes over us when it [*sc.* the body] passes away. '*Sic transit*', we say, in agony. **1951** 'J. WYNDHAM' *Day of Triffids* v. 104 'Never—never again now will you see a sight like that,' I told myself. '*Sic transit*—.' **1965** A. NICOL *Truly Married Woman* 16 They looked at it [*sc.* a Roman ruin] silently... 'Sic transit,' he'd said as they drove away. **1971** S. JEPSON *Let. to Dead Girl* v. 50 What was once my dressing room is dismantled..(*Sic transit gloria mundi*, and so on).

sicula (si·kiulă). *Palæont.* [a. L. *sīcula*, dim. of *sīca* curved dagger.] The small conical or dagger-shaped structure secreted by and containing the initial member of a colony of graptolites.

1893 *Lunds Univ. Årsskrift* XXIX. XII. 3 The sicula is seen to project from the right side obliquely upwards towards the median groove, thus separating the rounded bases of the two moieties of the rhabdosoma. **1910** [see *rhabdosome* s.v. *RHABDO-]. **1970** R. M. BLACK *Elements Palaeont.* xiv. 211 The sicula was secreted by the first members (a zooid) of the colony and the thecae were formed by the subsequent zooids by a process of budding.

Siculan (si·kiulăn), *a.* and *sb.* [f. L. *Sicul-us*, ad. Gr. *Σικελ-ός* (see *SICEL *sb.* and *a.*) + -AN.] **A.** *adj.* **a.** *Archæol.* Denoting the Chalcolithic, Bronze, and Iron Ages in Sicily. **b.** *poet.* Sicilian. **B.** *sb. Archæol.* A member of a people of Siculan culture. Also **Siculian, Siculic.**

1896 *Jrnl. Hellenic Studies* XVI. 134 Orsi's investigations during the last seven years have included nearly every period, from the pure stone-age with its pre-Siculic indigenous population, to the time of the Christian catacombs... Orsi has been able to follow down to the fifth century B.C. traces of this strange Siculian civilization. **1901** G. SEIGI *Mediterranean Race* xiv. 283 The presence..of objects of Mycenean character in the first Siculic period. **1909** [see *SICANIAN *a.*]. **1928** *Antiquity* II. 145 The veil has been half lifted from the romantic history of the Siculans who lived near Locri Epizephyrii. **1948** T. J. DUNBABIN *Western Greeks* i. 40 The Siculan culture of prehellenic Lokroi and kindred sites in Bruttium is not older than the tenth century. **1957** *Encycl. Brit.* XX. 603/2 A few rock-hewn tombs of the first Siculan period have been discovered near Palermo. **1975** G. EWART *Be my Guest!* II. 45 Not Siculan feastings sweet will bring forth smell.

Siculo-. Add: *Siculo-American, -Arabic.*

1939 *Burlington Mag.* Oct. 171/1 Twelfth-century Siculo-Arabic combs and croziers. **1966** *Economist* 2 July 51/1 It [*sc.* the Mafia] revived with the help of the Siculo-American gangsters employed to ease the Allied landings in Sicily. **1974** K. CLARK *Another Part of Wood* iii. 115 Leigh Ashton..had a good eye for art of all kinds, but what he really loved was a small fragment of Sassanian silk, a Persian pot or a Siculo-Arabic ivory.

Sicyonian (sikiōu·niăn), *sb.* and *a.* Also 7 **Sicionian; Sikyonian.** [f. L. *Sicyōnius*, f. *Sicyōn*, a. Gr. *Σικυών*: see -IAN.] **A.** *sb.* A native or inhabitant of Sicyon, an ancient Greek city in the northern Peloponnese. **B.** *adj.* Of or pertaining to Sicyon.

1642 J. HOWELL *Forraine Travell* xvi. 206 Among the Sicionians there were admitted..[no] Physitians. **1841** *Penny Cycl.* XXI. 126/2 They [*sc.* Dipœnus and Scyllis] were employed by the Sicyonians to make for them certain statues of their gods. **1887** *Encycl. Brit.* XXII. 32/2 Clisthenes was the most powerful and famous of the Sicyonian despots. **1958** R. LIDDELL *Morea* II. i. 41 There is also a small sanctuary of the nymphs: here Sicyonian brides made offerings. **1976** R. J. HOPPER *Early Greeks* viii. 214 His victorious chariot was later preserved at Delphi under a form of *baldacchino*, the 'Sikyonian *monopteros*' decorated with archaic sculpture.

sidalcea (sidæ·lsiă). [mod.L. (A. Gray in G. Bentham *Plantas Hartwegianas* (1848) 300), f. SIDA + *Alcea*, the names of related genera.] An annual or perennial herb of the genus so called, belonging to the family Malvaceæ, native to western North America, and bearing racemes of white, pink, or purple flowers.

1882 *Gardener's Chron.* XVIII. 439 The remark applies with full force to the Sidalcea. **1922** A. J. MACSELF *Hardy Perennials* II. 190 The Sidalceas grow erect with spikes of bloom resembling small Hollyhocks. **1962** R. PAGE *Educ. Gardener* vii. 213 One of the sidalceas..has spikes of soft rose-pink flowers and rather dull green foliage. **1976** *Country Life* 11 Mar. 619/1 Gardeners are..dividing treasured perennials..sidalceas, ligularias and chelone among them.

Sidamo (sidā·mo). Also **Sidama, Sydama.** [Native name.] A group of Cushitic-speaking peoples in southwestern Ethiopia; a member of one of these peoples. Also, the language of these peoples. Also *attrib.* or as *adj.*

1834 S. GOBAT *Jrnl. Three Years' Residence in Abyssinia* ii. 166 A month's journey to the w.s.w. of Shoa he had found a little Christian empire, who have a particular language, called Sidama, and books. *Ibid.* iv. 305 Kidam Mariam had with him a slave..of Sidama... He said that the Sidamas are Christians. **1868** J. C. HOTTEN *Abyssinia & its People* II. v. 200 Kaffa is a wealthy and fertile kingdom; the inhabitants are proud and handsome... They still retain a recollection and traces of the Christian faith... The Gallas, with whom they are incessantly at war, call them, in derision, 'Sydama', originally signifying Christian. **1910** *Encycl. Brit.* XII. 894/1 Similar dialects are those of the Sid(d)âma tribes, south of Abyssinia. **1939** L. H. GRAY *Foundations of Language* 366 Mixed with Ethiopic-speakers are the Agaw dialects..; and in the south-west are the Sidama (Gudella, Kaffa, Kullo-Walamo, Bambala, etc.). **1972** *Bk. of Thousand Tongues* (ed. 2) 392/2 Sidamo is spoken by an estimated 100,000 people in highland areas north and east of Lake Abaya, southwestern Ethiopia. **1974** *Encycl. Brit. Macropædia* VI. 1013/1 Those Galla and Sidamo who retain their traditional cosmologies..are more firmly anchored in the present.

Sidcot (si·dkǫt). Also **sidcot**, (*erron.*) **Sidcott.** [f. the name of the Australian-born aviator *Sid*ney *Cot*ton (1894–1969), who designed it.] In full *Sidcot (flying) suit.* A warm one-piece suit worn by aviators or the like (see quot. 1969). Hence **Si·dcotted** *a.*, dressed in a Sidcot.

1921 *Flight* XIII. 635/2 When Mr. Courtney was testing the 'D.H.6' fuselage fitted with the experimental 'Alula' wing at Brough..the weather was rather cold, and he was wearing his 'Sidcot' suit. **1927** T. E. LAWRENCE *Let.* 30 Dec. (1938) 563, I often think of you, and always as a rather shapeless Sidcotted bundle, peering over the rim.. of a Virgin in mid air. **1928** *Motor-Cycling* 11 Jan. 240/1 An objection frequently raised against it, is that the Sidcot leaves the ankles entirely unprotected. **1940** *War Illustr.* 26 Jan. 19 Here are the two pilots of the Meteorological Flight, wearing warm Sidcot flying suits and oxygen masks, before taking to the air. **1942** R. HILLARY *Last Enemy* ii 45, I pulled on my sidcot and gloves and slipped my feet into the comforting warmth of my fur-lined boots. **1954** W. FAULKNER *Fable* 113 He took the pistol from the Sidcott's knee-pocket. **1964** G. LYALL *Most Dangerous Game* xxii. 186 Climbing into the Sidcot suit and slinging a Sten gun round my neck. **1969** BARKER & COTTON *Aviator Extraordinary* iii. 33 The suit had a warm lining of thin fur, then a layer of airproof silk, then an outside layer of light Burberry material, the whole being made in one piece just like a set of overalls... For a name I took the first three letters of my Christian and surnames—'Sidcot'.

‖ **siddha** (si·dă). Also **Siddha.** [Skr., f. *sidh-* to be fulfilled.] In Indian religions, one who has attained perfection, a saint, a semi-divine being; *spec.* in Jainism, a perfected, bodyless being, freed from the cycle of rebirths.

1846 [see *GANDHARVA]. **1883** M. M. WILLIAMS *Relig. Thought & Life in India* vii. 191 All who are uninitiated into this system [*sc.* Śāktism] are styled 'beasts' (pasu), the initiated being called Siddha, 'the perfect ones'. **1971** *Illustr. Weekly India* 11 Apr. 11/3 At the end of a period of thirty years, the venerable ascetic Mahavir became a *siddha*, freed from the cycle of birth.

‖ **siddhi** (si·di). Also **Siddhi.** [Skr., lit. 'fulfilment', f. as prec.] In Indian and Tibetan religion, a collective name for supernatural or magical powers acquired by meditation or other practices. Also in *pl.* in same sense.

[**1863** E. SCHLAGINTWEIT *Buddhism in Tibet* vi. 56 The reciting of Dhāranīs, if combined with the practise of magical rites and supported by morality and contemplation, leads to superhuman faculties (in Sanskrit Siddhi).] **1882** [see *MANDALA]. **1921** C. ELIOT *Hinduism & Buddhism* II. xxxii. 282 The religious life prescribed in the Tantras commences with the initiation and requires the supervision of the Guru. The object of it is *Siddhi* or success, the highest form of which is spiritual perfection. **1941** A. HUXLEY *Grey Eminence* ix. 218 He was deeply impressed by any manifestation of the *siddhis*, as the Indians call them, the psychic powers which may be aroused by meditation and to which the wiser mystics pay as little attention as possible. **1960** [see *MUDRA]. **1970** *Man, Myth & Magic* v. 146/3 The idea of an astral body is very old. Ancient Indian writings describe the eight *siddhis* or supernormal powers which can be acquired through a type of yoga called *Pranayama*. **1977** *Time* 8 Aug. 44/2 The teachers have now brought those wares to the American market: lessons that will lead trainees to the Siddhis, or supernatural powers.

Siddonian (sidōu·niăn), *a.* [f. *Siddon(s* (see below) + -IAN.] In the style of, or typical of, the acting of the English tragic actress Mrs. S. Siddons (1755–1831).

1795 T. WILKINSON *Wandering Patentee* III. 120, I have not observed the audience ever thought of heat in the Dog-days, when the Siddonian queen was followed. **1894** W. ARCHER *Theatrical World of 1893* 192 She is an imposing artist of the Siddonian school. **1931** C. ST. JOHN *Ellen Terry & Bernard Shaw* 64 The concealment of her ears, and her Siddonian deportment, made an indelible impression on him [*sc.* Shaw]. **1946** G. B. SHAW in *Drama* Winter 8 [She] burst in on me and demanded a Siddonian part.

siddown (sidau·n), repr. a colloq. pronunc. of the imperative *sit down!* (see SIT *v.* 21).

1936 J. CURTIS *Gilt Kid* iv. 44 'Siddown,' he retorted waving an imperious hand. **1953** K. TENNANT *Joyful Condemned* iii. 22 'Siddown,' he advised Jake Fletcher, who took the straight-backed chair. **1967** G. GREENE *May we borrow your Husband?* 110 'Siddown,' he said, 'make yourself comfortable.' **1975** D. BEATY *Electric Train* 165 What do you know about it, sonny?..Siddown! Siddown!

Siddur (si·duəɹ). Also **Sidoor, Sidur,** and with small initial. Pl. **Siddurim.** [Heb. *siddūr*, lit. 'order'.] A Jewish prayer book containing prayers and other information relevant to the daily liturgy. Cf. *MACHZOR.

1864 *Chambers's Encycl.* VI. 155/1 These early collections of prayers generally contained also compositions from the hand of the compiler, and minor additions, such as ethical tracts, almanacs, &c., and were called *Siddurim* (Orders, Rituals), embracing the whole calendar year, week-days and new moons, fasts and festivals. **1905** *Jewish Encycl.* X. 171/1 The collection, in one book, of the year's prayers for week-days, Sabbaths, holy days and fast-days is generally known as the 'Seder Tefillot', or simply the 'Siddur'. **1911** Z. HODES (*title*) Studies in Sidoor. **1925** W. O. E. OESTERLEY *Jewish Background of Christian Liturgy* i. 35 The next [extant collection of prayers] in date is the Siddur ('Order' of prayers..) of Sa'adya (A.D. 892–942). **1949** S. GAON *Devel. Jewish Prayer* 6 Collections of prayers..called..*sidur*..from the noun 'seder', which..originally..meant 'collection'. **1976** H. KEMELMAN *Wednesday Rabbi got Wet* li. 297 He had forgotten to take the prayerbook with him... She picked up the *siddur* and followed him.

side, *sb.*[1] Add: **I. 2. b.** *side by side*: also (hyphened) as *attrib. phr.*

1908 *Daily Chron.* 29 Nov. 9/5 The side-car..has the advantages of ready convertibility, low cost, and high speed..together with the far greater sociability afforded by the side-by-side accommodation. **1930** *Times Educ. Suppl.* 27 Dec. p. i/3 Side-by-side valves instead of the overhead valves. **1956** R. REDFIELD *Peasant Society & Culture* i. 20 Those early comparisons were side-by-side comparisons of societies unaffected by cities and civilization. **1970** *Gloss. Aeronaut. & Astronaut. Terms (B.S.I.)* VIII. 9 *Side-by-side assembly*, an assembly of connecting rods in which a number of similar plain connecting rods are arranged successively side-by-side with narrow big-ends usually carrying roller bearings.

c. Designating a double-barrelled shotgun with barrels set side by side (cf. *OVER-AND-UNDER *a.*). Also *absol.* and *ellipt.* as *sb.*

1950 R. SHAUGHNESSY *Skeet & Trapshooting* iii. 30 Double-barreled guns are manufactured in two styles, one known as the *over-and-under*, the other as the *side-by-side*. **1961** Side-by-side *sb.* in WEBSTER. **1964** H. L. PETERSON *Encycl. Firearms* 139/1 Henry Nock's patent breech of 1787... It was possible to shorten barrels..for a sporting gun... Shortening the barrels made the guns still lighter, and this in turn made the side-by-side double-barreled fowling piece practical. **1979** G. HAMMOND *Dead Game* ii. 32, I saw all the guns... Two..were over-and-unders, the rest side-by-sides. **1980** *Outdoor Life* (U.S.) (Northeast ed.) Oct. 53/1, I had this double-barreled side-by-side 20-gauge Savage-Fox, the ugliest thing ever made.

II. 8. c. In prov. phr. *the other side of the coin* (*penny*, etc.) = *the reverse of the medal* s.v. MEDAL *sb.* 3 b; *the other side of the shield*: see *SHIELD *sb.* 1 d.

1904 YEATS *Let.* ? 20 Jan. (1954) III. 425 *The Shadowy Waters*..is more of a ritual than a human story... *Cuchullain* or *The King's Threshold* are the other side of the halfpenny. *Ibid.* Apr. 433, I am reckless in mere speech that is not written. You are the other side of the penny, for you are admirably careful in speech. **1966** *Listener* 19 May 713/1 The social and psychological pressures are not different things but often just different sides of the same penny. **1975** M. RUSSELL *Murder by Mile* ix. 92 Angus Hamilton's..to address members and answer questions. He thought it might present an opportunity to put across the other side of the coin.

d. Each of the two grooved faces of a gramophone record. Also *slang*, a recording made on this; a record. In extended use, of tape recording. Cf. *flip side* s.v. *FLIP *sb.*[2] 7.

1936 *Rhythm* Apr. 28/1 American Brunswick, Columbia and Vocalion have a blanket contract with Irving Mills for so many sides a year. **1948** *N.Y. Age* 18 Dec. 2/6 We expect 'Skiffle Blues' to be one of our big sides in the coming weeks. **1950** *Down Beat* 14 July 11 (*heading*) Will the Louis sides on cylinder ever turn up? **1960** J. BALDWIN *Another Country* (1962) II. iii. 310 'How about some sides?'.. Lorenzo put on something..by the Modern Jazz Quartet. **1971** D. E. WESTLAKE *I gave at Office* 133 There was some tape left. Tape three, side two, the one just before this. **1979** *Guardian* 9 June 12/7, I had to wait until side two for any bloom of Schubertian joy.

9. c. *Theatr.* A page of typescript containing an actor's part and cue words (usu. *pl.*).

1933 P. GODFREY *Back-Stage* iii. 37 An experienced actor, being offered a part, is unimpressed by the number of 'sides' it contains, a 'side' being a half-quarto sheet of typescript. **1963** 'E. MCBAIN' *Ten plus One* (1964) vii. 73 'She had memorized all of her sides—' Richardson paused here to see whether or not anyone had caught his use of the professional term 'sides'..—'in the first two nights of rehearsal.' **1976** R. JAMES *House is Dark* xiii. 135 'Don't see why actors ever gave up sides... They're so much easier.'.. 'Haidee, it wasn't for the sake of the actors that they used sides. It was supposed to prevent actors from duplicating a hit script and going off with it on their own.'

10. Also *to look on* (or *to*) *the bright* (or *worst*, etc.) *side*: see *LOOK *v.* 18 d.

III. 12. a. *fig. the other side*: see *OTHER *a.* 2 d (*a*).

c. *fig. on the* (adjective) *side*, tending towards the condition or aspect described. Cf. *on the safe side* s.v. SAFE *a.* 9 c in Dict. and Suppl.

1713 [see RIGHT *a.* 10 c]. *c* **1805** G. COLMAN in M. R.

Booth *Eng. Plays of 19th Cent.* (1973) III. 69 It's prophesying on the sure side, to foretell a thing when it has happened. **1864** TROLLOPE *Can You forgive Her?* I. xi. 90 He is just a shade too good... But it's a fault on the right side. **1923** A. J. ANDERSON *Soul Sifters* xxiv. 252 'Michelmore was always on the rough side!' he remarked aloud. **1952** A. J. CRONIN *Adventures in Two Worlds* xii. 97 She was on the thin side..and her liquid, brownish eyes were too large. **1974** A. MORICE *Killing with Kindness* ii. 14 He was a bit on the tired side, but..he's accustomed to long hours.

d. *on this* (or *the other*) *side*: with reference to the Atlantic Ocean. Cf. *this* (etc.) *side of the puddle* s.v. *PUDDLE *sb.* 1 c. *colloq.* (chiefly *U.S.*).

1884 *Naturalist's World* Sept. 155/2 Canadian Postal Science College..is a society which has grown up very rapidly 'on the other side'. **1928** WODEHOUSE *Money for Nothing* vii. 129 There's dozens of people on the other side who'll buy it.

13. e. In *fig.* phr. *the other side of the hill*, those aspects of a situation which are unknown at present. Also *transf.*, the latter part of life, and in *Mil.* contexts, the enemy position or activities.

1852 DUKE OF WELLINGTON in *Croker Papers* (1884) III. xxviii. 275 We amused ourselves by guessing what sort of a country we should find at the other side of the hills we drove up... When I expressed surprise at some extraordinary good guesses he [*sc.* Croker] had made, he said, 'Why, I have spent all my life in trying *to guess what was at the other side of the hill*.' **1926** C. B. WATERLOW in H. Golding *Wonder Bk. of Motors* 12 It is not only what is on the other side of the hill that matters, but everything along the road. **1948** B. H. L. HART (*title*) The other side of the hill. **1957** C. SMITH *Case of Torches* i. 5, I had to go through a lot of badinage..about..how old I was getting and what it was like on the other side of the hill. **1960** G. MARTELLI *Agent Extraordinary* 15, I..wish..to express my gratitude..to [the]..technical director of the flying bomb sites..for allowing me a glimpse of the 'other side of the hill'. **1978** *Times* 30 Jan. 13/2 Mr Peyton..began to argue for a revalued green pound... He..correctly read what was on the other side of the hill (that is, the Government itself would soon have to revalue).

14. e. *on the side* (orig. *U.S.*). (*a*) Served separately from the main dish.

1884 *Bad Lands Cow Boy* (Little Missouri, Dakota Terr.) 7 Feb. 1/5 'Gimme that snake rare—milk gravy on the side,' was hallooed to the cook. **1916** *Literary Digest* 18 Mar. 766/3 'Beef stew and a cup of tea for me,' the new arrival said. 'Bossy in a bowl—boiled leaves on the side,' sang the waiter. **1975** D. LODGE *Changing Places* ii. 95 A club sandwich with french fries on the side.

(*b*) In addition; surreptitiously, without acknowledgement. (Freq. with connotation of dishonesty: illicitly; outside wedlock.)

1893 *Congress. Rec.* 18 Dec. 360/1 He will have no pension attorney, for a silent partner, no relative doing business 'on the side' with that bureau. **1904** *N.Y. Times* 22 June 3 To attend the big fair and receive the entertainment of St. Louis on the side. **1927** *Daily News* 11 Mar. 2/2 Y' see, Bill's in the rag-and-bone trade and he does a bit [of receiving] on the side. Just anythink he can pick up. **1937** D. L. SAYERS *Zeal of thy House* II. 44 Pocketing commissions and that sort of thing? Doing little deals on the side? **1953** R. LEHMANN *Echoing Grove* IV. 226 An independent career-woman with a successful love life on the side. **1968** R. L. HUDSON *Grace is not Blue-eyed Blond* xi. 145 What would some of you say if I told you that I, as a married man, have had three women on the side? **1977** *Gay News* 24 Mar. 14/4 They may.. gear their expectations to include sexual contacts on the side.

(*c*) *spec.* in addition to one's regular or ordinary occupation; as a subsidiary source of income (also with occas. implication of irregularity).

1898 *N.Y. Jrnl.* 26 Aug. 9/3 Samuel..started an ice cream parlor, with cigars, tobacco and delicatessen on the side. **1915** WODEHOUSE *Something Fresh* iv. 107 'I'm not asking you to be a valet and nothing else.' 'You would want me to do some cooking and plain sewing on the side, perhaps?' **1928** S. LEWIS *Man who knew Coolidge* I. 13 I'd never made a peep about how maybe it'd be a good stunt for him to go out and maybe earn a little money on the side. **1945** *Reader's Digest* July 22/1 There is a good job teaching music theory..lined up for him. And he is composing on the side. **1960** N. MARSH *False Scent* i. 29 I'm trying, on the side, to break out in a rash of serious writing. **1977** *Navy News* Dec. 1/3 We do not have information about how many people do jobs on the side, but I suspect that that practice is not confined to the Armed Forces.

15. b. Also succeeding or suffixed to the names of places or regions to form adj. or advb. phrases in the sense 'in (or on, towards) the area specified', esp. as *STATESIDE *a.* and *adv.*

1726 [see SOUTH-SIDE b]. **1924** E. M. FORSTER *Passage to India* xxxvii. 323 Jolly good poems, I'm getting published Bombay side. **1966** K. GILES *Provenance of Death* ii. 58 An Italian industrialist who does a lot of business Moscow-side.

e. *side-of-the-mouth* adj. phr., spoken aside or (as) from the side of the mouth; delivered in a rough drawling manner; pungently demotic. Also, of the style of such utterances.

1958 *Listener* 7 Aug. 203/1 Hoarse, side-of-the-mouth cracks of quite shattering pessimism. **1960** G. COULTER in M. T. Williams *Art of Jazz* 170 A racy, side-of-the-mouth idiom. **1974** *Publishers Weekly* 25 Mar. 52/3 Describes in blunt, side-of-the-mouth prose how he was given the 'contract' [to kill someone].

f. Also *to laugh on the other, wrong side* (*of one's face, mouth*): see LAUGH *v.* 1 b in Dict. and Suppl.

16. b. *side-to-side* adj. phr., characterized by movement from one side to the other.

1934 in WEBSTER. **1950** J. DEMPSEY *Championship Fighting* xxii. 157 Motions that made my head an elusive side-to-side target. **1955** W. W. DENLINGER *Compl. Boston* I. 132 This formation [*sc.* bandy legs] results in a side-to-side gait. **1962** 'K. ORVIS' *Damned & Destroyed* ix. 59 Her head began a loose, disjointed, side-to-side swaying.

IV. 18. a. Also in prov. phr. *on the side of the angels*: in favour of a spiritual interpretation (of human nature); more loosely, on the side of right despite the risk of unpopularity.

1864 DISRAELI *Church Policy* 26 Is man an ape or an angel?.. I am on the side of the angels. **1926** *Punch* 22 Dec. 700/1 Miss Marguerite Williams..is so firmly posted on the side of the angels that I can forgive her if she occasionally seems rather to force the note. **1941** A. L. ROWSE *Tudor Cornwall* ii. 52 Mr. Tawney tells us.. that 'their silence was the taciturnity of men, not the speechlessness of dumb beasts'. Though that may a little be questioned, no doubt he is on the side of the angels. **1956** G. H. VALLINS *Pattern of Eng.* vii. 171 'Different from' reminds the reader that whatever other men have done.., Fowler himself is on the side of the angels. **1979** 'C. AIRD' *Some die Eloquent* vii. 99 He had always in any case been on the side of the angels anyway. Apes were less appealing.

20. b. (Later examples.)

1898 J. A. GIBBS *Cotswold Village* xi. 230 The rest of our team included the jovial miller;..the village curate, who captained the side..; one or two farmers; [etc.]. **1947** N. CARDUS *Autobiogr.* II. ii. 194 A boy fixes figures painted on square bits of tin—just the total of the batting side, the fall of the wickets, and the score of the last man out. **1977** C. MARTIN-JENKINS *Jubilee Tests* II. iv. 87 England's only difference from their Centenary Test side was the replacement of Fletcher by Barlow.

c. (so many)*-a-side*, indicating the number of players that may compose a team on the field of play. Usu. *attrib.* of a sport or match, as *five-a-side football*, etc. Cf. *SEVEN *a.* 2 g.

1900 [see *SEVEN *a.* 2 g]. **1926** *Times* 12 Apr. 6/5 The following are the results of yesterday's matches in the Seven-a-side Tournament. **1932** *Times Lit. Suppl.* 30 June 484/2 It is now over a century since it [*sc.* shinty] was played, seventy-five or so a-side. **1951** *Sport* 27 Apr.–3 May 4/3 A five-a-side football match is being played between Glasgow's Celtic and Rangers. **1973** J. M. WHITE *Garden Game* 104 We do sanction two-a-side encounters from time to time, or even three-a-side. **1978** *Cornish Guardian* 27 Apr. 13 At a Cub Scout's six-a-side football competition..Mrs. M. Dean..presented the winners' shield.

d. *to let the side down*: see *LET *v.*[1] 29 b.

V. 23. a. *side-entrance, outlet, -path* (earlier and *fig.* examples), *turning, ward, -window* (examples of motor vehicles), *-yard.*

1907 *Daily Mail Year Bk.* 74/2 In turn the prevailing form of body has been the..side-entrance phaeton, and the landaulet and limousine. **1926** W. W. JACOBS *Sea Whispers* v. 113 To leave by the side-entrance was the best way of avoiding trouble. **1976** *Northumberland Gaz.* 26 Nov. 18/1 (Advt.), Hall, sitting room,..side entrance, porch. **1967** *Gloss. Sanitation Terms* (*B.S.I.*) 10 *Side outlet tee*, a tee which incorporates an additional branch at 90° both to the main pipe and to the leg of the tee. **1972** L. M. HARRIS *Introd. Deepwater Floating Drilling Operations* x. 98 The subsea blowout-preventer stack..should have two side outlets for the choke and kill-line connections. **1854** DICKENS *Hard Times* II. xii. 250 Indifferent to the rain,..she struck into a side-path parallel with the ride. **1924** R. S. HICHENS *After Verdict* II. vii. 181 She's always in the wholesome centre... No false steps into side-paths for her. **1946** *Law Rep.* 5 Oct. 334 She was executing a manoeuvre of turning from the near side into a side turning on her off-side. **1965** M. SPARK *Mandelbaum Gate* iii. 54 He dodged down a side-turning into the shop of an Arab dealer. **1968** M. ALLINGHAM *Cargo of Eagles* iii. 42 She shared a side ward..with two other old ladies. **1959** M. SUMMERTON *Small Wilderness* x. 131, I rolled down the side window. Instantly the car was hazed with incoming fog. **1976** *Derbyshire Times* (Peak ed.) 3 Sept. 6/2 The youth admitted kicking the side window of the car twice. **1879** W. WHITMAN *Daybooks & Notebooks* (1978) I. 139 The window where I sit ..opens on a spacious side-yard. **1979** *Kingston* (Ontario) *Whig-Standard* 29 Mar. 21/2 Narrow side yards could block fire trucks.

b. *side-curtain* (examples of use on early open motor vehicles), *parting, -whiskers* (earlier example).

1912 *Motor Manual* (ed. 14) iv. 161 The only car for such weather conditions is a covered one, either one with a Cape cart hood with side curtains well down,..or the more complete enclosure of limousine or landaulet. **1980** L. LEWIS *Private Life of Country House* iii. 35 We bought a secondhand T model Ford... It..had a hood and talc side-curtains. **1942** Side parting [see *PIPE *sb.*[1] 1 c]. **1982** D. PHILLIPS *Coconut Kiss* v. 43 Grace asked if she could do her hair with a side parting and a slide. **1867** *Amer. Naturalist* Aug. 287 Their ears are often tufted, and one species, at least, has 'side-whiskers' formed by the true fur, in addition to the labial bristles which ordinarily receive this name.

24. a. *side-beam, -eye, -glimpse.*

1935 *Discovery* Nov. 341 (*caption*) The advantages of a side-beam:..the beam can be followed as it strikes the objects bordering a country road. **1978** R. V. JONES *Most Secret War* xx. 169 If another aircraft flew down one of the side beams, the result should be a second line intersecting with the first at the exact location of the station. **1922** JOYCE *Ulysses* 48 A side-eye at my Hamlet hat. **1958** J. KEROUAC *On Road* 189 Looking at me with the same wary insolent side-eye. **1890** 'MARK TWAIN' *Let.* 11 Feb. in J. Brown *Lett.* (1912) 452 The charm of the painter is so strong that one can't keep his entire attention on the developing portrait, but must steal side-glimpses of the artist.

c. *side-remark, -talk.*

a **1910** 'MARK TWAIN' *What is Man?* in *Harper's Mag.* Oct. 673/1 He was treated to many side remarks by his fellows. **1968** *Economist* 3 Feb. 13/1 Formal statistical tables.., so that everybody can tell what each Wilsonian side-remark is meant to mean. **1917** G. S. GORDON *Let.* 14 Feb. (1943) 70 This is all side-talk compared with the great thing that has happened to you. **1931** B. BROWN *Talking Pictures* x. 250 The need for silence in the studio is increased, since side talk, coughs, etc., are liable to be picked up.

26. *side-lock.*

1907 *Yesterday's Shopping* (1969) 629/2 Plain quality side-lock hammerless guns. **1955** R. CHURCHILL *Game Shooting* IV. ii. 193 Apart from the action of fully-automatic guns, all game guns are built either with what is called the sidelock action or the box lock.

27. side action *Pharm.* = *SIDE EFFECT 2; **side band** *Telecommunication*, a band of frequencies above or below a carrier frequency, within which lie the frequencies produced by modulation of the carrier; **side boy** (earlier and later examples); **side-burn** [alteration of *BURNSIDE, after *side-hair*, etc.], for *U.S.* read orig. *U.S.* and add: usu. *pl.* (later examples); hence **side-burned** *a.*; **side chair**, an upright wooden chair without arms; **side circuit** *Teleph.* (see quot. 1916); **side cut** *Oil Industry* = *side stream* (*b*) below; **side drift** *Mining*, etc., a horizontal tunnel leading off the main passage (cf. DRIFT *sb.* 15); **side-drum**, also, in *Jazz*, etc.: a drum (usu. part of a set) placed on a stand beside the performer; **side-entry**, (*a*) a side-entrance; an area outside the side-door of a house; (*b*) *Bridge*, a card providing access to a hand in a suit other than trumps (cf. *ENTRY 1 f); **side frequency** *Telecommunication*, a particular frequency in a side band, equal, in the case of amplitude modulation, to the carrier frequency plus or minus a particular modulating frequency; **side gallery**, either of the two galleries along the side of the debating chamber of the House of Commons, divided to seat Members and others; **side-head(ing)** *Journalism* (see quot. 1889); **side-hold** *Mountaineering*, a hold in which the rock is gripped from the side; **side lamp**, a lamp placed at the side (see also quot. 1885); *spec.* of a motor vehicle = *SIDE-LIGHT 3 c; **side-lay** (later example in *Printing*); **side lever** *Mech.*, each of two beams located on the sides of some forms of steam engine, which transmit motion from the cross-head of the pistons to the connecting rods; **side-loader**, a fork-lift truck in which the fork is located at the side of the vehicle; **side lobe**, any lobe in the response or radiation pattern of a radio aerial other than the central, or main, lobe; **side-lock**, † (*a*) *pl.* that part of a wig that covers the ears and neck; (*b*) a lock of hair worn at the side of the head (also *fig.*); **side mill** *Engin.*, a circular milling cutter with teeth on its face, so that it cuts in the direction of its axis of rotation; also, a cylindrical cutter used with its axis parallel to the surface of the work-piece, so that the cutting action occurs along its length; hence **side milling** *vbl. sb.*; **side-note** (earlier example); **side-partner** *U.S. colloq.*, a close associate at work; hence, a colleague or 'side kick'; **side-piece** (*gen.* examples); **side play** *Mech.*, freedom of movement from side to side; **side reaction** *Chem.*, a subsidiary reaction taking place in a chemical system at the same time as a more important reaction; **side road**, (*a*) a minor or subsidiary road; a road leading from or to a main road; (*b*) *spec.* (*Canad.*) in Ontario, a road which passes along the side boundary of a concession; **side salad**, a salad served as a side dish; **side scraper** *Archæol.*, a broad flint implement with a scraping edge on one of the longer sides of the flake (cf. *RACLOIR); **side-screen**, † (*a*) in landscape, a secondary feature set on both sides of the principal to show perspective; (*b*) one of the side-curtains of an open motor vehicle (in quot. 1970, of the cab of a railway locomotive); **side-seat**, (*b*) a seat facing or placed at the side in any form of transport;

side-split *Canad.*, a split-level house with fewer storeys on one side than the other; **side-splitter** (examples); **side-splitting** *a.* (earlier example); hence **side-splittingly** *adv.*; **side-stream,** (*a*) a tributary stream or subsidiary current; also *fig.*; (*b*) *Oil Industry*, a fraction drawn off at an intermediate tray in a distillation column; **side-stroke** *Swimming*, a stroke employed in swimming on the side; also as advb.; **side suit,** in *Cards*, a suit other than trumps, esp. (in *Bridge*) a long suit; **side-sway,** (*a*) a rolling motion from side to side in a moving vehicle; (*b*) a sideways movement or displacement of the upper part of a building or structure as a result of wind pressure; **side tone,** *Teleph.*, the reproduction of the user's voice in a telephone receiver; a sound so heard; **side-trawler,** a trawler in which the nets are set and hauled over the sides; **side trip,** a detour or deviation (also *fig.*); a voyage or excursion aside from the main journey, esp. for sightseeing; **side valve** *Mech.*, a valve that is mounted alongside the cylinder in an internal-combustion engine and opens into a sideways extension of the combustion chamber; freq. *attrib.*; **side-wheeler,** (*b*) *U.S. Baseball*, a side-arm or left-handed pitcher; (*c*) *U.S.*, a pacing horse with a rolling gait (see quots.); **side-wing** *Theatr.* = WING *sb.* 9 c; also *transf.* in *pl.*, side-whiskers (*slang*).

1933 M. B. MUSE *Pharmacol. & Therapeutics* i. 42 Morphine sulphate..when administered as an analgesic has numerous side actions some of which are harmless. **1922** *Proc. I.R.E.* X. 363 A modulated radio telephone wave consists of two components, one, the carrier frequency itself and the other, the so-called side bands, which are the actual modulated components. **1943** *Electronic Engin.* XV. 339/2 If only one side-band is received, a local oscillator must supply the suppressed carrier frequency.. before the detector stage. **1974** *Physics Bull.* Mar. 91/2 Attention was drawn to..the use of side bands generated in the visible region by laser mixing techniques as an alternative to direct comparison of infrared and visible wavelengths. **1823** J. F. COOPER *Pilot* I. iii. 31 The shrill whistle of the boat-swains mate, as he recalled the side-boys. **1916** 'TAFFRAIL' *Pincher Martin* i. 2 Eyed critically by the grinning side-boy and the messenger. **1977** *Navy News* Sept. 25/2 Shipmate Fred Talbot was nominated 'side boy' for the evening and he piped the Mayor aboard. **1936** G. GREENE *Journey without Maps* II. iv. 197 He was ..handsome in his native robe and his sideburns. **1977** 'J. LE CARRÉ' *Hon. Schoolboy* xii. 264 Cy..had sideburns and..looked like a Mormon missionary. **1941** B. SCHULBERG *What makes Sammy Run?* iv. 75 A swarthy, sideburned Latin. **1976** *Listener* 29 July 103/1 The headmaster, the richly sideburned Mr Terry Ellis. **1905** Side chair [see *ROCKER[1] 4 b]. **1968** *Canadian Antiques Collector* July 32 (Advt.), Sheraton side chairs in mahogany with red damask upholstery. Circa 1810. **1916** *Standard. Rules Amer. Inst. Electr. Engineers* 95 A side circuit is a two-wire circuit forming one side of a phantom circuit. **1957** W. FRASER *Telecommunications* v. 122 It is possible to transmit speech on the phantom circuit without interference to either side-circuit. **1949** *Our Industry* (Anglo-Iranian Oil Co. Ltd.) (ed. 2) iii. 95 Reverting now to the question of drawing off 'side-cuts', the product on any one tray must always be contaminated by some traces of lighter components. **1970** W. G. ROBERTS *Quest for Oil* viii. 85 At the point where we wish to draw off side-cuts or intermediate fractions, special trays are put in. **1872** 'MARK TWAIN' *Roughing It* 279 He disappeared in the gloom of a 'side drift' just as a head appeared in the mouth of the shaft. **1940** *Chambers's Techn. Dict.* 768/1 *Side drift*, an adit. **1926–7** Side-drum [see *gong-drum* s.v. *GONG[2] 1 c]. **1956** Side-drum [see *BOOMY *a.*]. **1885** S. O. JEWETT *Marsh Island* 195 The old farmer and his crony moved their chairs into the square side-entry. **1901** W. CHURCHILL *Crisis* 13 He did not discuss his ambitions at dinner with the other clerks in the side entry. **1958** *Listener* 23 Oct. 669/2 North is unlikely to have the heart suit and a side entry. **1977** *Homes & Gardens* Feb. 14 The hand with the long suit has few side-entries. **1925** *Proc. I.R.E.* XIII. 295 In the case of the side frequencies produced by the modulator tube and delivered through the circuit..there will be no emfs. to balance them out and they will be impressed upon the amplifier. **1978** P. H. SMALE *Telecommunication Systems* ii. 18 The sum of carrier and modulating signal frequencies is called the upper sidefrequency. **1883** T. E. MAY *Treat. on Law, Privileges, Proc. & Usage of Parliament* (ed. 9) xi. 341 A member may speak from the side galleries, appropriated to members, but not from below the bar. **1930** B. FELL *Palace of Westminster* 41 The seating on the floor of the House accommodates 368 members and there is room in the side galleries for another 82. *a* **1974** R. CROSSMAN *Diaries* (1976) II. 402 During the all-night sitting on the Abortion Bill the side galleries would have to be closed because otherwise there would be no door-keepers. **1889** *Cent. Dict., Side-head...* In *printing*, a heading or a sub-head run in at the beginning of a paragraph, instead of being made a separate line. **1964** *New Statesman* 21 Feb. 303/3 We shall present these pieces in a way which makes their character as editorial opinion less equivocal, by prefixing a generic side-head. **1971** D. AYERST *Guardian* xxiv. 347 The *Guardian* gave Churchill only those two or three lines towards the end of the story below a modest side-head: 'The Home Secretary'. **1968** *Heidelberg News* Sept. 4/1 Send him a picture and supply a caption as a side heading. **1920** G. W. YOUNG *Mountain Craft* iv. 162 'Side'-holds, where the edge or point of rock projects and is grasped sideways. **1977** D. LAW *Starting Mountaineering & Rock Climbing* vi. 68 Most of the holds for jamming are side holds, but some can be used for a vertical pull-up. **1826** J. O'KEEFE *Recoll. Life* I. x. 376 His shaggy dress took fire from the side-lamps. **1885** E. B. IVATTS *Railway Management at Stations* 550 *Lamp* (*side*), lamps for showing red lights at the two sides of guards' vans at the end of a train, as signals to an approaching train..and white lights towards the engine driver to enable him looking back to see that no portion of his train has broken away. **1912** *Motor Manual* (ed. 14) iii. 124 It is possible..to adapt electric lighting very successfully to any car, both for interior lighting of limousines and landaulets, and for head, side and rear lamps. **1963** *Times* 30 Apr. 13/4 The many heavy lorries which..only have one pin-head size nearside sidelamp in the town. **1946** A. MONKMAN in H. Whetton *Pract. Printing & Binding* v. 64/2 Assuming the ordinary half-sheet of sixteens is on the machine, and the side-lay for printing the first side is at the foot of page 1, there would be a regular and accurate margin from page 1. **1839** Side lever [see *sway-beam* s.v. SWAY-]. **1846** [in Dict., sense 23 b]. **1882** SENNETT & ORAM *Marine Steam Engine* I. i. 3 The side-lever type of engine, though very heavy and occupying a large space for the power developed, was safe and reliable. **1939** H. W. DICKINSON *Short Hist. Steam Engine* vi. 108 This type was taken up by other makers under the name of the side-lever engine, and remained for about forty years the established type for marine-engine practice. **1960** *Times* 16 Mar. (Canberra Suppl.) p. iv/6 The forward bulkhead.. must move one frame aft to accommodate the mechanism of the side-loader. **1973** *Scotsman* 19 Feb. 3/1 (Advt.), We produce the largest and most versatile range of frontlift and sideloader trucks in the UK. **1946** *Proc. I.R.E.* XXXIV. 335/2 After either the side-lobe level or the position of the first null is specified, the position of the other nulls and of the side lobes can be found by simple calculation. **1975** D. G. FINK *Electronics Engineers' Handbk.* xxv. 25 In angle, the response function $\chi(\theta,\phi)$ is simply the antenna pattern... It has a main lobe in the direction to which it is matched, and side lobes extending over all visible space. **1688** R. HOLME *Academy of Armory* II. xviii. 463/2 The *side Locks*, are those as cover and keep warm the ears and neck, being a degree shorter than the former [*sc.* 'The *Bottom Locks*']. **1848** [in Dict., sense 23 b]. **1889** *Century Mag.* Sept. 710/1 The monuments represent him as a prince and nothing more, still wearing the side-lock of juniority. **1944** S. BELLOW *Dangling Man* 23 The street..presented itself in one of its winter aspects, creased and with thin sidelocks of snow. **1978** I. B. SINGER *Shosha* xi. 196 Old women in bonnets of beads and ribbons, men with white beards and sidelocks. **1898** H. S. WILSON *Practical Tool-Maker & Designer* i. 15 Select some good-sized straddle or side mills. **1954** H. W. PORTER et al. *Machine Shop Operations & Setups* ix. 312 This makes it possible to finish two or more parallel surfaces at the same time by using two or more side mills. **1910** D. DE VRIES *Milling Machines* xv. 449 The sharpening of the left side teeth of a side milling cutter with a cup wheel. **1954** H. W. PORTER et al. *Machine Shop Operations & Setups* ix. 312 Straddle milling requires two side-milling cutters. **1973** J. G. TWEEDDALE *Materials Technol.* II. vi. 146 Side-milling uses a cylindrical multifluted cutter (usually spirally fluted) which rotates on an axis parallel to the workpiece and is traversed across it to cut, progressively, tangentially into it. **1776** W. ROBERTSON *Let.* 8 Apr. in *Corr. Adam Smith* (1977) 193, I should wish that in the 2d Edition you would give..what the Book-sellers call Side-notes. **1890** *N.Y. Even. Post* 23 May 8/2 The arrest was made by the witness's side partner, it being his night off. **1921** R. D. PAINE *Comrades Rolling Ocean* ix. 159 We shall have to consult my side-partner, Briscoe. **1849** Side-piece [see MOB-CAP]. **1928** *Daily Express* 16 Aug. 5/2 A car (with a left-hand drive and a hood but no side-pieces). **1861** J. BOURNE *Treat. Steam-Engine* (ed. 5) viii. 352/1 The guide blocks are of brass, and in wearing down they maintain their position in the groove. This mode of construction prevents side play. **1905** E. C. C. BALY *Spectroscopy* iii. 50 It is..necessary that the jaws move smoothly in their grooves without any trace of side play. **1934** WEBSTER, Side reaction. **1936** *Jrnl. Amer. Chem. Soc.* LVIII. 2210/2 The small deviations observed..may be due to the fact that the side reactions..are more prominent in one case than in the other. **1973** *Sci. Amer.* Oct. 60/3 High-energy intermediates are frequently formed in chemical syntheses, but if they are not isolated from water or other reactive substances, they decompose in side reactions that lower the yield of the reaction. **1854** T. C. KEEFER *Ottawa* 72 The municipalities have taxed themselves too heavily for the main road..to be able to build also the side roads. **1873** *Woodstock* (Ontario) *Sentinel* 5 Dec. 3/4 To Joseph Whaley for pine timber for culvert on first side road, $1.00. **1958** R. LIDDELL *Morea* II. viii. 190 South of Argos, a side-road, off the main road to Tripolis, leads to Kefalári. **1968** *Globe & Mail* (Toronto) 13 Feb. 3/6 The partly frozen body..was found Sunday beside the Nixon Side-road. **1976** *Western Mail* (Cardiff) 22 Nov. 1/2 The other man was seen standing..near a vehicle on a little-used side road. [**1951** F. BROBECK *Good Salad Bk.* 9 A small salad served with the main course, or after it, on a decorative plate is the old-fashioned side dish salad.] **1972** D. SALE *Love Bite* II. xvii. 212 She..helped herself to a side salad of avocado in French dressing. **1980** P. ABLEMAN *Shoestring's Finest Hour* iv. 73, I queued for a hefty portion of shepherd's pie and a side salad. **1872** J. EVANS *Anc. Stone Implements* xiii. 272 When the instrument is broader than it is long, it has been termed a side scraper. **1921** R. A. S. MACALISTER *Text-Bk. European Archaeol.* I. vii. 321 The side-scraper.., a flake with secondary chipping along one edge, making it fit to scrape the interior of hides in preparing garments. **1977** *Sci. Amer.* Nov. 126/2 Among the Upper Industry tools at Hoxne were a small number of the flake implements that are traditionally called 'side scrapers' and are presumed to have played a role in the dressing of hides. **1782** W. GILPIN *Observ. on River Wye* ii. 8 Every view on a river, thus circumstanced [with steep banks], is composed of four grand parts; the area, which is the river itself; the two side-screens, which are the opposite banks, and mark the perspective; and the front-screen, which points out the winding of the river. *a* **1817** JANE AUSTEN *Northanger Abbey* (1818) I. xiv. 263 He talked of fore-grounds, distances, and second distances—side-screens and perspectives. **1932** *News Chron.* 6 Aug. 3/5 The assailant thrust a six-chambered revolver through a side-screen and fired. **1958** L. DURRELL *Mountolive* xv. 276 He drove up..in his pennoned car, rejoicing in..the whickering of wind at the side-screens. **1970** N. FLEMING *Czech Point* xiv. 191 The canvas sidescreens to the cab flapped in the wind. **1978** A. PRICE *'44 Vintage* xiii. 160 The staff car..with a closed canvas hood and side-screens. **1889** *Cent. Dict., Side-seat,*..in a vehicle of any kind, a seat with the back against the side of the vehicle, as usually in a horse-car or omnibus. **1901** *Daily News* 5 July 4 In the stern with the side-seats out there is room for 3 or 4 drift-nets. **1922** JOYCE *Ulysses* 591 The car and horse..turn. Corny Kelleher on the sideseat sways his head to and fro in sign of mirth at Bloom's plight. **1968** *Globe & Mail* (Toronto) 15 Jan. 23/1 (Advt.), Why not see this spacious side-split..in Etobicoke? **1864** *Harper's Mag.* Feb. 422/1, I send you three samples [of letters].., hoping thereby to reciprocate some of your side-splitters. **1903** A. M. BINSTEAD *Pitcher in Paradise* v. 133 As regards poetry I have already had a sidesplitter entitled 'Don't chalk your cue before a lady' accepted by Mr Arthur Roberts. **1860** S. MORDECAI *Virginia* xiv. 188 These among other side-splitting tales, which he told and acted with the skill of a Matthews. **1907** A. BENNETT *Grim Smile Five Towns* 7 Something side-splittingly funny—one of the best jokes that ever occurred. **1970** *Daily Tel.* 6 Aug. 6/2 The reader is..given an at times side-splittingly funny account of the eccentricities of Frazer and his wife. **1900** *Knowledge* 1 Dec. 273/1 The rotten condition of the surface is seen when one of the larger side-streams cuts its way down to the Durance. **1935** *Petroleum* (Inst. Petroleum Technologists) 84 The provision made for taking side-streams has greatly extended the usefulness of the fractionating tower. **1939** *John o' London's Weekly* (Suppl.) 9 June p. ii/2 The cliffs of Norfolk and Suffolk are menaced by the sidestream of a tidal current that flows westwards into the Wash. **1960** *Times* 29 Sept. 15/7 His writings are in the stimulating side-stream of scholarly diaries. **1973** D. ANDERSEN *Ways Harsh & Wild* i. 42 You'll see the waves splashing up the sides of the canyon and falling back to form a hogsback in midstream that's a yard higher than the sidestreams. **1973** R. PRIESTLEY in G. D. Hobson *Mod. Petroleum Technol.* (ed. 4) viii. 271 Products of a volatility intermediate between the overhead and bottoms products are withdrawn as sidestreams. **1867** C. STEEDMAN *Man. Swimming* 105 The five movements—three for the legs and two for the arms—required for the performance of the side stroke. *a* **1936** KIPLING *Something of Myself* (1937) ii. 34 One set of verses which exactly set the time for my side-stroke when I bathed in the big rollers. **1962** A. SEXTON *All my Pretty Ones* 55 The old-fashioned side stroke. **1976** J. MCCLURE *Rogue Eagle* xi. 185 Buchanan ..waded in and swam sidestroke downstream of the gelding. **1952** I. MACLEOD *Bridge is Easy Game* xiv. 181 The commonest case is when dummy has a long solid side suit. **1960** C. H. GOREN *New Contract Bridge in Nutshel* 13 In a side suit, the fourth card is considered a long card. **1974** *National Skat & Sheepshead Q.* Mar./Apr. 29 This decision is based upon the official rule of calling a side suit ace. **1930** Sidesway [see *ROLLING *vbl. sb.*[2] 6 b]. **1932** CROSS & MORGAN *Continuous Frames of Reinforced Concrete* iv. 108 In many problems in the analysis of rigid frames..a solution assuming no movement of the joints does not satisfy statistics because the shear in all columns of any one story is not equal to the known shear in that story. This indicates sidesway..of the frame sufficient to make $\Sigma H = O$. **1961** E. LIGHTFOOT *Moment Distribution* v. 123 After moments have been apportioned to the frame,..a single or a double cycle of joint balance and carry-over is performed (with the frame restrained against sidesway). **1980** *Daily Tel.* 11 June 14/5 [In the Princess] fast cornering produces rather a lot of side-sway. **1917** G. D. SHEPARDSON *Telephone Apparatus* xiv. 234 Some arrangements seem to give more trouble than others from 'side-tones', whereby the speaker hears his own words too strongly. *a* **1944** K. DOUGLAS *Alamein to Zem Zem* (1946) 38 The operator..breathed and hummed into the microphone, listening for sidetone. **1978** *Sci. Amer.* Mar. 59/1 Too little side tone gives the telephone an unnatural 'dead' sound and tends to cause the user to talk too loudly. **1962** J. TUNSTALL *Fishermen* ii. 46 The whole-freezer side-trawler is a..compromise solution in which conventional side-trawling is retained. *a* **1911** D. G. PHILLIPS *Susan Lenox* (1917) II. viii. 212 He's got a nasty streak in him... He put me on the Island once for a little side trip I made. **1929** L. F. CARR *Amer. Challenged* 3 He was forced to borrow money for a little side trip to New York. **1966** *Guardian* 24 Dec. 4/3 Another family..spent three weeks in Jutland, with a side trip of a couple of days in Copenhagen. **1979** N. & I. LYONS *Champagne Blues* 78, I..make arrangements for special side trips, room supplements, extended tour packages. **1928** *Daily Mail Year Bk.* p. lxiv, 3·49 H.P. side valve 'sports' model. **1946** [see *L 3]. **1973** J. LEASOR *Host of Extras* ix. 179 My heart was pounding like an old side-valve engine on a long hill when the ignition's too retarded. **1911** *Spalding's Official Base Ball Guide* 277 Redfern, side-wheeler, with Flowers, McFarlin and Reis with the other end up, made the pitching department a clever one. **1926** *Amer. Speech* I. 369/2 [Baseball] They are 'south-paws' or 'port-siders' or 'side-wheelers' when they are left-handed. **1936** *Literary Digest* 1 Aug. 35/2 Pacers have a rolling, lunging movement that has earned them the nickname of 'wigglers' or 'side-wheelers'. Left front and left rear legs come up together, followed by a counterbalancing lunge to the right. **1948** *Times Digest* (Richmond, Va.) 15 Mar. 17/4 The lanky Cincinnati Reds' sidewheeler has added a new pitch to his repertoire. **1953** *Sun* (Baltimore) 10 Aug. B15/2 Mac Hayman [will]..handle the speedy sidewheeler in her three stake engagements at the Ocean Downs Raceway. **1707** E. SETTLE *Siege of Troy* III. 23 The Scene opens and discovers a Grove..over a Tarras Walk, is seen a Beautiful Garden of six side Wings. **1811** L. SUMBEL *Mem. Life* III. 220 And a fourth, with locks *bushed* out on his temples, burlesquing the side-wings of your noble head. **1814** JANE AUSTEN *Mansfield Park* I. xiii. 257 Just a side wing or two run up..and three or four scenes to be let down. **1881** *Atlantic Monthly* Sept. 402/1 It seems as if certain actors in some preceding comedy of his were standing at the side-wings, and critically watching the progress of the after-piece.

side, *v.*[2] *slang* (now *rare*). [f. SIDE *sb.*[2]] *intr.* To be conceited or boastful; to 'put on side'. Also with *about.*

1906 R. BROOKE *Let.* 4 June (1968) 54 This school-life.. calls to me... I play my part with zest, alternately 'siding' and ragging. **1909** WODEHOUSE *Mike* v. 26 There's just a chance you might try to side about a bit soon.

si·de-arm, *a.* (and *adv.*) [SIDE *sb.*[1] 26.] **1.** Performed or delivered with a swing of the arm extended sideways, esp. in *Baseball.* Cf. ROUND-ARM *a.* and *adv.*

1908 *Baseball Mag.* June 32/1 The spit ball..when pitched with a side arm movement will go out. **1909** *Amer. Mag.* Aug. 402/2 He pitched..two fast side arm balls, high and outside. **1939** 'N. BLAKE' *Smiler with Knife* xii. 188 The unerring side-arm flick..had surprised many confident run-stealers before now. **1948** *Sun* (Baltimore) 15 Mar. 17/8 Blackwell said his best pitch was a fast sidearm ball. **1978** *Detroit Free Press* 5 Mar. c8/3 'He struck me out three times one day,' said Williams. 'He threw that sidearm slider and it would come into your face and explode.'

2. as *adv.* With a sweep of the arm extended sideways; in a side-arm manner.

1958 I. CROSS *God Boy* vii. 55 She swam sidearm alongside me. **1973** C. SAGAN *Cosmic Connection* (1975) xv. 112 As pitcher, he could throw the ball sidearm—at the horizon at between twenty and thirty miles per hour.

side-bar. Add: **5. side-bar whiskers** *U.S. local,* side-whiskers, side-burns.

1882 G. W. PECK *Peck's Sunshine* 55 He was a red-faced man, with these side-bar whiskers. **1975** *Amer. Speech 1972* XLVII. 155 Some of my earliest memories of childhood in the Up Country of South Carolina..center upon the hearing of the lively and colorful word *tea-hounds*... Invariably the expression was employed humorously..when a person referred to side-bar whiskers, rather bushy projections extending from the hairline to below the ears and worn with an unbearded chin.

6. A secondary newspaper article featuring some aspect of a main story in the same publication. *U.S. Journalism.*

1948 C. D. MACDOUGALL *Interpretive Reporting* (rev. ed.) 695 *Sidebar,* a complete article on one phase of a longer story, run separately. **1967** R. J. SERLING *President's Plane is Missing* iv. 70 Bat us out a good sidebar on anything that's ever happened to a presidential plane. **1977** *Time* 17 Jan. 5/2 The cover story was written by Morrison, with a sidebar on Felker by Michael Demarest.

sideboard. Add: **3. a.** (Example.)

1874 'UNCLE BOB' *Lett. to Children* (1875) xiv. 87 Starting with our standing collars on, we managed to get to the church... Some mischievous boy would cry out, 'Come out of those sideboards.'

b. (Examples.)

1907 *Daily Chron.* 7 Dec. 5/7 You have described the duke as having small whiskers?—Yes, they were sideboards. Where did you get that name?—I have been in America... You call them sideboards?—Yes, or sideburns. **1956** D. M. DAVIN *Sullen Bell* II. iv. 136 He was a miserable little sod, with sideboards and an American tie. **1961** H. S. TURNER *Something Extraordinary* i. 9 The boys are dressed in the Teddy style, with tight trousers and sideboards. **1975** M. BRADBURY *History Man* vi. 97 He takes his razor..clipping at the line of the sideboards.

si·decar. Also **side-car, side car.** [SIDE *sb.*[1]] **1. a.** (See SIDE *sb.*[1] 27.) Now *Hist.*

1881 [see SIDE *sb.*[1] 27]. **1963** 'A. BRIDGE' *Dangerous Islands* ix. 140 The Irish side-car, now almost extinct, is one of the least comfortable vehicles imaginable. The driver sits easily foursquare behind the horse, but the passengers perch on two long seats with a high back between them, parallel with the direction of the vehicle —and since side-cars are now never used except on very rough roads, they are jerked about, clinging to the back between the seats. **1974** *Encycl. Brit. Micropædia* V. 529/2 *Jaunting car,* also called *jaunty car* or *side-car,* two-wheeled, open vehicle, popular in Ireland from the 19th century, was unusual in having lengthwise passenger seats, either facing each other (inside the car) or back to back (outside).

b. A vehicle designed to be attached to the (near-)side of a motor-cycle to accommodate one or more passengers. Occas. attached to a bicycle.

1903 *Hardwareman* 13 June 520/1 The side car is..the most sociable attachment for a motor bicycle. **1927** KIPLING *Limits & Renewals* (1932) 177 'What did he do afterwards?' 'Bought a side-car to his bike, to hold more vegetables.' **1935** H. MOORE *Compl. Cyclist* v. 44 Until recently the cycling of a married couple was seriously restricted by the birth of a child... Now, the tandem-cum-sidecar, bearing a family of three (or more), is a fairly common sight. **1951** T. STERLING *House without Door* ii. 12 He sat on a bicycle which had a large white sidecar. **1978** J. IRVING *World according to Garp* i. 17 The pilot hurried to have Garp transferred to the sidecar of a medic's motorcycle.

2. A cocktail made of brandy and lemon juice with a dash of an orange liqueur.

1928 S. LEWIS *Man who knew Coolidge* I. 61 Mame took a Bronx, and Delmerine took a side-car. **1930** AUDEN *Poems* 12 I'll have a sidecar, thanks. **1952** S. KAUFFMANN *Philanderer* (1953) v. 77 They ordered sidecars and Suzy said.., 'Not too strong... I've got a lot of drinking to do to-night.' **1978** M. DICKENS *Open Book* vi. 49 Once or twice at cocktail parties, I saw someone I knew and had to..keep my head down as I cruised the crowd with my tray of sidecars and white ladies.

Hence as *v. intr.*, to drive a motor-cycle with a side-car attached; to travel in a side-car; also **si·de-car(r)ing** *vbl. sb.*; **si·decarist,** one who drives or travels in a motor-cycle combination. Now *rare.*

1911 *Motor Cycle* 19 Jan. 21 (Advt.), Best after tests for sidecaring,..for economy. **1914** *Motor Cycling* 12 May 8, 3½ h.p. is insufficient for sidecarring at a satisfactory speed. **1920** *Motor Cycle* 29 Apr. 487/2, I make this request because of its importance to sidecarists. **1923** *Ibid.* 25 Oct. 665/2 No doubt she would feel small and lonely when sidecarring by herself in one of these ample-looking bodies.

side chain. [SIDE *sb.*[1]] † **1.** A chain mounted at the side of a vehicle for any purpose (see quots.). *Obs.*

1849–50 J. WEALE *Dict. Terms, Side Chains,* chains and hooks fixed to the sides of the tender and engine for safety, should the central drag-bar give way. **1883** W. S. GRESLEY *Gloss. Coal-Mining* 221 *Side chain,* a chain hooked on to the sides of tubs when running upon an engine-plane or jig, to keep all the tubs together in case a coupling breaks. **1886** *Encycl. Brit.* XX. 247/2 Some [railway] companies have gone further and placed the guard or side chains upon springs.

2. a. *Chem.* A chain of atoms attached to the principal part of a molecule.

1886 ROSCOE & SCHORLEMMER *Treat. Chem.* III. III. 7 If two atoms of hydrogen [in benzene] be replaced by elements or radicals, termed 'side chains', three isomeric compounds may be formed whether the entering element or side chain be identical or different. **1927** HALDANE & HUXLEY *Animal Biol.* ii. 73 The whole [chromosome] is like a gigantic single organic chemical compound, since the molecules of such a chemical compound are all made up of smaller parts—the side-chains and radicals and single atoms. **1974** *Sci. Amer.* June 59/3 They [*sc.* the catecholamines] have in common a chemical structure that consists of a benzene ring on which there are two adjacent hydroxyl groups and an ethylamine side chain.

b. *Physiol.* A structure postulated to project from the surface of a cell and to constitute a receptor (RECEPTOR 3 a in Dict. and Suppl.) in Ehrlich's theory of immunological action; so *side-chain theory.*

1900 tr. P. Ehrlich in *Proc. R. Soc.* LXVI. 433 We may assume that the protoplasm consists of a special executive centre..in connection with which are nutritive side-chains, which possess a certain degree of independence, and which may differ from one another according to the requirements of the different cells. *Ibid.* 440, I have now laid before you the fundamental facts which up to the present constitute our knowledge in the field pertaining to immunity, and which can be most easily and successfully explained through the agency of 'side-chain theory'. **1911** *Rep. Brit. Assoc. Adv. Sci. 1910* 635 Ehrlich has given a graphic representation of this process in his side-chain theory. **1935** N. P. SHERWOOD *Immunol.* vi. 121 In Ehrlich's theory these free chemical entities or cast-off side chains constitute the antibodies found in the circulation. **1974** *Encycl. Brit. Macropædia* VI. 510/1 Only if the haptophore group of a toxic molecule combines with the side chain of the cell can a bacterial toxin act upon a cell. The affected organism then produces great quantities of the side chains, all of them 'gauged' to the disease-producing agent. These immune bodies prevent a renewed infection.

si·de-comb. orig. *U.S.* [SIDE *sb.*[1] 23 b.] A comb used to secure a woman's hair, esp. at the side of the head.

1824 *Missouri* (Columbia) *Intelligencer* 8 May 3/3 (Advt.), Tortoise shell, tuck and side combs. **1851** H. MAYHEW *London Labour* I. 346/1 A few earrings and ear-drops, and sometimes a few side-combs. **1897** [see SIDE *sb.*[1] 23 b]. *c* **1909** D. H. LAWRENCE *Collier's Friday Night* (1934) II. 28 She finishes stroking her hair up with her side-combs. **1966** *Olney Amsden & Sons Ltd. Price List* 35 *Side comb*..boxed 3 dozen singles 10/- per box.

sided, *ppl. a.* Add: **1.** (Later examples.)

1904 *N.Y. Sun* 7 Aug. 20 The yard is sided with cabins. **1952** DYLAN THOMAS *Coll. Poems* 21 The boy she dropped from darkness at her side Into the sided lap of light grew strong.

sidedness, (*b*) one-sidedness; lack of symmetry in a superficially symmetrical structure or system.

1970 A. L. LEYNINGER *Biochem.* xxvii. 617 (*heading*) Sidedness of the transport process. **1972** *Sci. Amer.* Feb. 32/2 Such proteins are evidently located exclusively on only one side of the membrane. This information lends credence to the concept of sidedness in membranes. **1976** *Word 1971* XXVII. 240 The above contention finds support from another aspect of human evolution, that is, the sidedness or dominancy in either of the two hemispheres of our brain.

side-door. Add: **1. b.** *fig.*

1930 *Times* 21 Mar. 15/5 We maintain that these 'side door' credits are endangering our chances of securing recognition of our bonds. **1965** *New Statesman* 30 Apr. 676/1 The proposed conference on Cambodia—an attempt to settle Vietnam through a side-door—may prove abortive.

2. side-door Pullman *N. Amer. slang* (chiefly *Tramps'*), a railway goods wagon with sliding doors in the sides, a box-car; a freight car.

1887 M. ROBERTS *Western Avernus* xvii. 237 When the engine..started out, I lighted a match and took a look at my..travelling carriage, or 'side-door Pullman', as the 'tramps'..facetiously call them. **1918** R. W. LARDNER *Treat 'em Rough* 10 If they didn't have all the luck in the world they would be rideing [*sic*] around the country in a side door Pullman with all their baggage on. **1927** L. F. RANLETT *Let's Go* 34 A train of 'side-door Pullmans' ..drew up at the railway station.

si·de-effect. [SIDE *sb.*[1] 24 d.] **1.** *gen.* A subsidiary consequence of an action, occurrence, or state of affairs; an unintended secondary result.

1884 [see SIDE *sb.*[1] 24 d]. **1933** E. BLUNDEN *Mind's Eye* (1934) I. 59 Here the side-effects of the quarrels south of the Canal..were felt and paid for in some casualties. **1959** B. WOOTTON *Social Sci. & Social Pathol.* xi. 336 The problem is, moreover, made more difficult still by the second of the potentially unfortunate side-effects of reformative penal treatment. **1974** 'D. CRAIG' *Whose Little Girl are You?* ii. 23 A side effect of sobriety he had found to be deadly fatigue.

2. *Med.* An effect (usu. for the worse) of a drug or other chemical other than that for which it is administered; usu. *pl.*

1939 WRIGHT & MONTAG *Textbk. Materia Med. Pharmacol. & Therapeutics* x. 112 The effects which are not desired in any particular case are referred to as 'side effects' or 'side actions' and, in some instances, these may be so powerful as to limit seriously the therapeutic usefulness of the drug. **1952** *Chambers's Jrnl.* June 384 A new alkaloid, built to the same molecular pattern, but with slight modifications, has been synthesised; it is equally anti-malarial but its side-effects are less toxic. **1961** *Lancet* 19 Aug. 390/1 The commonest complication of anticoagulant therapy is hæmorrhage. Numerous reports describe the frequency and nature of this side-effect. **1978** E. HARTMANN *Sleeping Pill* ii. 16 In the usual doses, paraldehyde does not produce severe side effects.

si·de-foot, *v. Association Football.* [SIDE *sb.*[1]] *trans.* To strike (the ball) with the (out)side of the foot.

1950 *Sport* 22–28 Sept. 10/2, I like to see the player who ..sidefoots the ball to a nearby colleague and starts a quick-passing movement. **1960** *Times* 19 Sept. 17/4 Robson side-footing the ball into the net. **1977** *Irish Press* 29 Sept. 18/5 He sent a cross to Jovanovic, who side-footed the ball into the net.

Hence as *adv.*, with the side of the foot; **si·de-footed** *ppl. a.*

1968 *Listener* 23 May 682/3 It's the way I kick, side-foot. **1974** *Observer* 1 Sept. 18/5 Latchford..steered a side-footed volley to Rimmer's left.

si·de-issue. [SIDE *sb.*[1] 24 d.] A subsidiary issue.

1873 [see SIDE *sb.*[1] 24 d]. **1928** *Sat. Rev.* 20 Oct. 515/2 The secret is well kept and the various side issues are interesting and bewildering. **1938** [see *CREATIVE *a.* 1 b]. **1958** *Times* 29 Sept. 11/2 The floor will go down fighting on the side-issue of the platform's acceptance of the *status quo* for the public schools. **1982** F. DAVIES *Death of Hit-Man* ix. 151 Zio must be here for something far more important. Not just to kill Denton. That must have been a side-issue.

si·de-kick. *slang* (orig. *U.S.*). [Back-formation from next.] **1.** A companion or close associate; *spec.* an accomplice or partner in crime; a subordinate member of a pair or group. More *loosely,* a friend, a colleague.

1906 H. GREEN *At Actors' Boarding House* 85 The Red Swede..sat over a pint of champagne with Dopey Polly.. and his side kick, the Runt. *a* **1911** D. G. PHILLIPS *Susan Lenox* (1917) II. xvii. 394 'Now, what d'ye think of that?' said Black Mustache to his 'side-kick'.. 'Guess we'd better run her in, Pete.' **1927** J. M. SAUNDERS *Wings* iv. 173 'I want two of you,' the Major said, 'who is your side-kick?' 'Armstrong,' Johnny admitted unwillingly. **1934** *Bulletin* (Sydney) 25 July 47/1 Snowy was good at soft things; as a rule, you could trust him as a sidekick to help you to a clear getaway. **1956** M. PROCTER *Pub Crawler* viii. 102 He's Frank McGeen's sidekick. They team up together in jobs of this sort. **1960** *Times* 14 Oct. 18/7 Miss Moira Redmond, as an ex-wife.., made a takingly crisp and sub-acid side-kick. **1976** *New Yorker* 23 Feb. 82/3 Christopher Lloyd was funny as a drug-ridden sidekick of the defunct singer. **1981** 'J. MCVEAN' *Seabird Nine* xiii. 154 It was the White House... And not just some little cotton-tail sidekick either, but counsel to the President.

2. *Criminals' slang.* = SIDE-POCKET 1. *U.S.*

1916 *Lit. Digest* 19 Aug. 424/2 Pockets range from 'side kicks' to 'double insiders'. **1935** *Amer. Speech* X. 20/2 *Side-kick* [formerly] one's pal. In modern argot a side pocket in the coat; it is doubtful if there is any connection. **1955** D. W. MAURER in *Publ. Amer. Dial. Soc.* XXIV. 125 The outside pockets in an overcoat are called *side kicks* (from which we get a venerable American idiom).

3. An incidental criticism; a passing or indirect attack, a 'side-swipe'.

1958 *Economist* 1 Feb. 384/2 Two intriguing passages in Mr. Thorneycroft's speech were, first, what could be taken as a sidekick at the Government's insistence on Britain having the H-bomb. **1971** *Scotsman* 20 May 10/1 Parents came in for a good many side-kicks these days, he said. 'Blame the parents' was a recurring cry.

si·de-kicker. *slang* (orig. *U.S.*). Now *rare.* [SIDE *sb.*[1]] = *SIDE-KICK 1.

1903 'O. HENRY' in *McClure's Mag.* Feb. 432 Billy was my side-kicker in New York. **1926** J. BLACK *You can't Win* xiv. 189, I cast about for a 'sidekicker'. **1929** *Papers Mich. Acad. Sci., Arts & Lett.* X. 322/1 *Side-kicker,* sleeping companion; bosom chum. **1933** *Bulletin* (Sydney) 6 Sept. 41/2 'One's known as Yargus,' George says, 'and his sidekicker as the Snake.'

side-light. Add: **1. b.** (Earlier example.)
1862 J. Brown *Let.* 4 Feb. (1912) 193, I like so much your saying that about the breeding of my mind, and all the side-lights and sub-suggestions.

3. c. One of the small warning lights on either side of the front (or rear) of a motor vehicle, which when lit show the position and width of the vehicle, esp. at night; a side-lamp.
1912 *Motor Manual* (ed. 14) iii. 120 Much better side lights have been provided than ever existed before. **1955** *Times* 16 Aug. 2/7 British motorists are singularly reluctant to use the lights of their cars—motorists abroad invariably switch on their sidelights much earlier. **1973** A. Behrend *Samarai Affair* xi. 108 One headlamp and both sidelights had been broken.

side-line, *sb.* Add: **1. a.** For '(see quot. 1862)' read 'and other sports: a line marking the edge of the playing area at the side; a touch-line. Also, the area immediately outside this.' (Further examples.) Also *fig.* with allusion to the position of a spectator observing but removed from the action of a game, esp. in phr. *on* or *from the sidelines*.
1886 J. Dwight *Lawn-Tennis* II. i. 41 He may play down the side-line or he may lob. **1899** H. A. Quinn *Pennsylvania Stories* 24 The coaches on the side lines were not so jubilant. **1962** [see *bye *sb.* 1 c]. **1977** *Cleethorpes News* 27 May 15/2 It was a close game, with plenty of support on the sidelines.
fig. **1934** Webster, *Side-line*... The standpoint of those not immediately participating. **1939** *Times* 2 Nov. 8/3 The Russian Government were well satisfied with the policy announced by the Supreme Soviet two months ago —standing on the sidelines and watching Germany, England, and France fight out the war. **1954** T. S. Eliot *Confidential Clerk* I. 18 But as you're here, Eggers, I can just relax. I'm going to enjoy the game from the sidelines. **1974** J. Mann *Sticking Place* x. 151, I can't sit on the sidelines all my life, producing academic dissertations.
b. (Earlier example.)
1890 Kipling *From Sea to Sea* (1899) II. xxix. 62 Livingstone is..the junction for the little side-line that takes you to the Yellowstone National Park.
c. *Canad.* = *side road* (*b*) s.v. *side *sb.*[1] 27.
1834 in W. A. Langton *Early Days in Upper Canada* (1926) 91 The concession lines run N.17 1/2W. and the side lines I am told are not exactly perpendicular. **1896** J. L. Gourlay *Hist. Ottawa Valley* 34 The concessions and sidelines in these townships were 66 feet wide.
3. (Further examples.)
1937 'G. Orwell' *Road to Wigan Pier* i. 8 Brooker.. was a miner by trade, but he and his wife had been keeping shops of various kinds as a side-line all their lives. **1966** *Listener* 13 Jan. 67/3 Few of them managed to make a good living out of their art alone, without running a side-line such as a brewery or an insurance office. **1977** *New Yorker* 29 Aug. 47/2 His sideline computer-service business thrived. **1979** D. Gageby in J. J. Lee *Ireland 1945–70* 130 It caused suspicion among journalists whose sideline earnings on correspondence for English or American papers seemed to be threatened.

side-line, *v.* Add: **I.** *trans.* **1.** (Earlier U.S. example.)
1837 W. Irving *Rocky Mountains* I. ii. 36 The horses were 'side lined', as it is termed: that is to say, the fore and hind foot on the same side of the animal were tied together, so as to be within eighteen inches of each other.
2. *pass.* (or as *ppl. a.*) Of a sportsman: to be forced to remain out of competition on the side-lines, esp. through injury. Also *fig.* Occas. *actively*, of an injury, etc. orig. and chiefly *U.S.*
1945 *Sun* (Baltimore) 30 June 8/2 Snead is once more sidelined with his back ailment. **1947** *News-Age-Herald* (Birmingham, Alabama) 20 July 1B/7 Charley Keller..is recovering..from an operation to relieve the back ailment that has sidelined him for several weeks. **1949** *Cavalier Daily* (Univ. of Virginia) 22 Oct. 1/5 Gene Schroeder, still side-lined with a shoulder injury. **1966** *N.Y. Times* (Internat. ed.) 22 Apr. 12/8 Buckpasser..is sidelined with a hoof injury. **1970** [see *defenceman* s.v. *defence *sb.* 9]. **1975** *Amer. Speech 1972* XLVII. 143 Although polio cruelly limited her for many years to the use of one arm, Betty Adler was never sidelined. **1977** *Daily Express* 29 Jan. 38/4 Ian Wallace and Mick Ferguson, their first-choice front men who have been side-lined for the last six weeks.
3. To mark (a passage of text) for special attention by a line or lines drawn in the margin; *spec.* (of confidential matter) to indicate that it should not be printed or published.
1968 *Guardian* 24 July 8/1 The..witnesses had been encouraged to speak freely with the assurance that they would be allowed to 'sideline' those parts of the evidence that they did not wish to see published. **1978** *Observer* 10 Dec. 1/7 The all-party committee..is expected to exercise traditional discretion in 'sidelining' or censoring Cabinet minutes.
4. *fig.* To remove from the centre of activity or attention; to place in an inferior position.
1973 H. Gruppe *Truxton Cipher* (1974) xx. 218 He even persuaded the brass to put him in charge of the special project... The Navy was glad to do it. Sideline him for a bit. **1976** *National Observer* (U.S.) 22 May 10/2 President Nixon vetoed the legislation in 1971, and since then, a lack of congressional and Administration support has sidelined the Mondale approach.
II. 5. *intr.* To engage *in* as a subsidiary occupation or sport.
1944 *College Topics* (Univ. of Virginia) 30 Mar. 3 Captain Nat Boyd is specializing in the hurdles and broad jumping and sidelining in the high jump. **1975** B. Garfield *Hopscotch* xv. 147 The kingpin in town was a back-porch country lawyer who..sidelined in real estate.

si·de-looking, *a.* [Side *sb.*[1]] **1.** Characterized by looking sideways.
1829 J. F. Cooper *Wept of Wish-ton-Wish* I. iii. 37 A demure, side-looking young woman kept her great wheel in motion. **1956** H. Gold *Man who was not with It* (1965) iv. 36 Those others turned me back..to the side-looking cast in Phyl's eyes, her black hair short-cropped with a calculated wildness.
2. Producing or being a radar or sonar beam transmitted sideways and downwards, usu. from an aircraft for the mapping of relief.
1961 B. L. Cordry et al. in G. Merrill *Airborne Radar* xiv. 777 In side-looking systems..the orientation of the antenna may not be changed easily. **1964** *Jrnl. Geophysics Res.* LXIX. 3824/1 Narrow-beam lateral echo sounders are similar to standard echo sounders except that the transducer is mounted to give a side-looking beam that is a few degrees below horizontal. **1971** P. O'Donnell *Impossible Virgin* i. 6 From film taken by side-looking radar he could penetrate..the earth's skin, to..the bedrock below. **1977** *Sci. Amer.* Oct. 93/2 The acute grazing angle of the microwave illumination of side-looking radar emphasizes the form of the land, and the large areas that can be surveyed under constant conditions favor the recognition of extensive features.

sideman. Restrict † *Obs.* to senses in Dict. and add: **5.** A supporting musician in a jazz or dance band. Cf. *front man* (ii) s.v. *front *sb.* 14. orig. *U.S.*
1936 *Amer. Mercury* XXXVIII. p. x/2 *Side man*, any musician in the band except the leader. **1943** P. E. Miller *Yearbk. Pop. Music* 7/2 He began playing in bands just a few years later, and was soon accepted as a desirable sideman. **1961** *Radio Times* 21 Dec. 53/4 *Jazz Club*. Humphrey Lyttelton..welcomes as his guests two former Lyttelton sidemen Jimmy Skidmore on tenor sax and Johnny Picard on trombone. **1977** J. Wainwright *Do Nothin' till You hear from Me* v. 67 Goodman and Dorsey..had tight section work, when needed—but they let their sidemen cut loose, and weave their own patterns.

side meat. *N. Amer.* (chiefly *Southern* and *Western U.S.*). [Side *sb.*[1]] Salt pork or bacon, usu. cut from the side of the pig.
1868 *Overland Monthly* Nov. 468/1 But they do not thrive after transplanting any better than do the corn pone of Virginia..and the 'side-meat' of Missouri. **1873** J. H. Beadle *Undevel. West* xxiv. 482 Two bright-eyed, graceful, copper-colored *señoritas* bring me a supper of coffee, side meat, eggs, and *tortillas de mais*. **1939** J. Steinbeck *Grapes of Wrath* v. 43 But—you see, a bank or a company can't do that, because those creatures don't breathe air, don't eat side-meat. **1957** M. Shulman *Rally round Flag, Boys!* (1958) xiv. 158 Accents that recalled hominy grits and sidemeat. **1975** G. V. Higgins *City on Hill* viii. 208 None of these intellectual-emotional phenomena is an adequate substitute for side meat and greens.

side-on, *adv.* and *a.* [Side *sb.*[1] + On *adv.* 7 b; cf. *head-on *adv.* and *a.*] **A.** *adv.* (*si·de-o·n*). With one side directed towards the point of reference; from the side. **B.** *adj.* (*si·de-on*) Directed from or towards one side; indirect. Of a collision: involving the meeting of one side of a vehicle with an object.
1909 L. M. Montgomery *Anne of Avonlea* xiv. 154 His farm is side-on to the Newbridge road. **1928** *Daily Mail* 16 Aug. 13/7 Side-on collisions frequently occur owing to blurred side curtains. **1960** *Times* 10 June 19/1 He may have been a little more side-on at the moment of delivery. **1976** Ld. Home *Way Wind Blows* xi. 156 One of our delegation was sitting with a side-on view of the rostrum. **1977** J. Cleary *Vortex* viii. 204 Wind was hitting the car side-on.

sidero-[1]. Add: **1. siderona·trite** [ad. Sp. *sideronatrita* (A. Raimondi *Minerales del Perú* (1878) 209)], an orthorhombic hydrated basic sulphate of ferric iron and sodium, $Na_2Fe(OH)(SO_4)_2.3H_2O$, which is a secondary mineral found in very arid regions as yellow masses or crusts, and can be prepared artificially as needle-shaped crystals; **siderophy·llite** [Gr. φύλλον leaf], a variety of biotite containing a high proportion of ferrous iron and aluminium but little ferric iron and little or no magnesium; **si·derotil** (-til, -təil) [a. G. *siderotil* (A. Schrauf 1891, in *Jahrb. d. k.-k. geol. Reichanstalt* XLI. 381), f. Gr. τίλ-ος anything plucked (f. τίλλειν to pluck)], a hydrated ferrous sulphate, $FeSO_4.5H_2O$, found as triclinic fibrous crusts and needles of a white or pale yellow or green colour (see also quot. 1964).
1890 *Amer. Jrnl. Sci.* CXL. 202 Associated with the sideronatrite..is a grayish white laminated mineral, ferronatrite, which is also often intermixed through the whole mass of the sideronatrite. **1935** J. W. Mellor *Comprehensive Treat. Inorg. & Theoret. Chem.* XIV. 345 Sideronatrite occurs in orange-yellow or straw-yellow, crystalline masses of fine, fibrous structure which separate into thin splinters. **1975** *Nature* 5 June 472/1 Alteration has produced haematite and goethite on the outer parts of the concretions, whereas the inner parts contain jarosite, gypsum, baryte, celestine and sideronatrite. **1880** H. C. Lewis in *Proc. Acad. Nat. Sci. Philadelphia* XXXII. 255 The name of *Siderophyllite*..has been given in allusion to the large percentage of iron which it contains. **1967** *Mineral. Abstr.* XVIII. 142/1 High temperature metasomatically altered granites of Jurassic and Cretaceous age [in Upper Kolyma, Russian S.F.S.R.] locally include fayalite and siderophyllite greisens in association with Sn deposits. **1897** *Mineral. Mag.* XI. 335 Siderotil... $FeSO_4 + 5H_2O$. Idria, Carniola. **1920** *Amer. Jrnl. Sci.* CCL. 229 Melanterite, either natural or artificial, is commonly coated with a white powder of siderotil and the fine powder [of the former] will dehydrate after standing for some months to the pentahydrate. **1964** *Amer. Mineralogist* XLIX. 820 From a study of natural and synthetic iron sulfates, it is concluded that the name siderotil should be applied to $(Fe,X)SO_4.5H_2O$, where X is any cation or group of cations individually less abundant than Fe. The pure compound probably does not exist in nature, but several examples of the cuprian variety are known.

2. si:deroachrestic (-ăkre·stik) *a. Path.* [ad. mod.L. *sideroachrestica* (coined in Ger. by L. Heilmeyer et al. 1957, in *Schweiz. med. Wochenschr.* LXXXVII. 1237/2), f. Gr. ἄχρηστ-ος useless (f. ἀ- A- 14 + χρῆσθαι to use)], designating a form of hypochromic anæmia in which impaired synthesis of hæmoglobin renders treatment with iron of no avail; **si·derochrome** *Biochem.* [ad. G. *siderochrom* (H. Bickel et al. 1960, in *Experientia* XVI. 131/2), f. Gr. χρῶμα colour], any of various compounds concerned with the transport of iron in bacteria; **siderope·nia** *Med.* [*-penia], an abnormally low concentration of iron in the blood; hence **siderope·nic** *a.*; **si·derophage** *Med.* [Gr. φαγεῖν to eat, devour] (see quot. 1970); **si·derophil(e, siderophi·lic** *adjs. Geol.* and *Chem.* [ad. G. *siderophil* (V. M. Goldschmidt 1923, in *Skrifter utgit av Videnskapsselsk. I: Mat.-nat. Kl.* III. 5); see -phil, -phile], applied to elements which are commonly found in metallic phases (sometimes *spec.* in association with iron) rather than combined as silicates or sulphides, and are supposed to have become concentrated in the earth's core; **siderophi·lin** *Biochem.* [-phil, -phile + -in[1]] = *transferrin; **si·derosome** *Med.* [*-some[4]], a particle of non-hæmoglobin iron in a cell.
1961 *Amer. Jrnl. Clinical Path.* XXXV. 338/1 The patients suffered from an anemia which was resistant to all forms of therapy except blood transfusion and had an erythroid hyperplasia of the bone marrow with a conspicuous accumulation of iron-staining granules in the developing erythrocytes. Similar instances have been described..under the term 'sideroachrestic anemia'. **1970** A. E. Lewis *Princ. Hematol.* xiii. 205 Sideroachrestic anemia is a very rare, hereditary anemia, refractory to treatment with iron, vitamins, or folic acid. **1961** *Chem. Abstr.* LV. 23684 Sideromycins, sideramines, and other unidentified Fe-contg. biol. active substances are taken together as a group called siderochromes. **1976** *Nature* 19 Aug. 722/2 Microbial iron-transport compounds, or siderochromes are of two general structural types, the phenolates and the hydroxamates. **1938** J. Waldenström in *Acta Med. Scand.* Suppl. XC. 395 All these factors may lead to the same result, most suitably called sideropenia. **1946** M. M. Wintrobe *Clinical Hematol.* (ed. 2) xii. 533 Anemia was not present in all of his cases but low plasma iron (sideropenia) was consistently found. **1971** J. H. Dagg et al. in Goldberg & Brain *Rec. Adv. Haematol.* ii. 107 Sideropenia causes well-defined chemical and biochemical changes, and may be associated with the clinical tissue signs found in iron deficiency states. **1939** *Acta Radiol.* XX. (*heading*) 618 The roentgenological diagnosis of sideropenic dysphagia. **1971** J. H. Dagg et al. in Goldberg & Brain *Rec. Adv. Haematol.* ii. 105 An erythrocyte protoporphyrin level above 40·0 μg per 100 ml. erythrocytes and a transferrin saturation of less than 16 per cent taken together, allow a firm diagnosis of the sideropenic state without the necessity for marrow biopsy. **1970** Passmore & Robson *Compan. Med. Stud.* II. xxi. 11/1 In lesions where there has been much haemorrhage, phagocytosis of iron pigment results in a pigmented stippling of the cytoplasm [of macrophages], and such cells are termed siderophages. **1977** *Lancet* 30 July 244/1 No siderophages were found in the cerebrospinal fluid on the 10th day. **1923** Siderophil [see *lithophil(e* adj. s.v. *litho-]. **1950** Rankama & Sahama *Geochem.* iv. 93 It may be assumed that the typically siderophile elements..are enriched in the nickel-iron core of the Earth. **1954** A. Muir *Goldschmidt's Geochem.* 680 The scarcity of all the platinum metals in the lithosphere is due to their extremely siderophil nature. **1977** *Nature* 20 Jan. 197/3 The siderophile and volatile elements on the Moon are depleted relative to the Earth and meteorites. **1971** C. B. Moore in B. Mason *Handbk. Elemental Abundances in Meteorites* xiv. 127 Although by definition silicon is a lithophilic element, evidence also shows that under highly reducing conditions in meteorites it may also be siderophilic. **1949** A. L. Schade et al. in *Arch. Biochem.* XX. 170 (*heading*) Carbon dioxide in complex formation with iron and siderophilin, the iron-binding

component of human plasma. **1971** *Nature* 28 May 250/1 Transferrin (siderophilin) is a beta-globulin found universally in vertebrate serum. **1970** *Haematologia* IV. 301 In spite of the active rhopheocytosis, ferritin aggregates (siderosomes) were found in the erythroblasts only exceptionally. **1972** W. J. WILLIAMS et al. *Hematology* viii. 80/2 Cells containing siderosomes or 'iron bodies' are usually reticulocytes. **1979** *Experientia* XXXV. 256/1 The hepatic increase of ferric deposits (ferritin, siderosomes and lipofuscin aggregates) more or less overloaded in iron in relatives of idiopathic hemochromatosis is well-known.

sideroblast (si·dĕroblɑst). *Med.* [f. SIDERO-[1] + -BLAST.] A normoblast containing one or more granules of ferritin.

1954 E. KAPLAN et al. in *Blood* IX. 204 For the purpose of this report these cells were designated as 'sideroblasts' in analogy to the term siderocyte already generally accepted for erythrocytes with iron-staining inclusions. *Ibid.* 212 The term sideroblast was proposed for normoblasts with nonstaining inclusions. **1962** BOTHWELL & FINCH *Iron Metabolism* 289 Sideroblasts are absent in iron-deficiency anemia. **1972** PASSMORE & ROBSON *Compan. Med. Stud.* III. xxi. 29/2 Ring sideroblasts were first observed in 1949 in guinea-pigs suffering from lead poisoning. They were first described in man in 1953. **1976** *Lancet* 18 Dec. 1364/1 The patient's bone-marrow exhibited a variable number of normal sideroblasts ranging from 20 to 70%.

Hence **siderobla·stic** *a.*, of, pertaining to, or characterized by the presence of sideroblasts; *esp.* in *sideroblastic anæmia*.

1956 *Blood* XI. 250 (*heading*) Chronic refractory anemia with sideroblastic bone marrow. **1972** *Nature* 10 Mar. 73/1 A similar although lesser degree of defective synthesis is seen in two other conditions due to haem deficiency, namely sideroblastic anaemia, and iron deficiency anaemia. **1977** *Blood* L. 165/2 Sideroblastic anemia..is a heterogeneous group of disorders with different basic biochemical abnormalities.

siderocyte (si·dĕrosəit). *Med.* [f. SIDERO-[1] + -CYTE.] An erythrocyte containing one or more granules of non-hæmoglobin iron.

1941 H. GRÜNEBERG in *Nature* 26 July 114/2 The 'iron cells' or 'siderocytes' do not stain diffusely, but show blue granules which vary in number from one to a dozen or more and in size from fairly large blobs down to the finest dust-like stipples. **1944** WHITBY & BRITTON *Disorders of Blood* (ed. 4) ii. 36 In some conditions, especially after splenectomy, iron granules may be found in red cells by the prussian blue reaction. The significance of these so-called siderocytes..is unknown. **1966** [see *PAPPENHEIMER]. **1977** *Blood* L. 165 The excessive non-heme iron accumulated in *f/f* fetal siderocytes is located within mitochondria.

Hence **siderocy·tic** *a.*, of, pertaining to, or characterized by the presence of siderocytes.

1957 *Blood* XII. 168 Neither red cells nor inclusion bodies were lost when siderocytic blood was transfused into a recipient without a spleen.

siderosis. For etym. read: [mod.L. (F. A. Zenker 1866, in *Deutsch. Arch. f. klin. Med.* II. 70), f. Gr. σίδηρος iron; see -OSIS.] and add: **2.** The accumulation in the tissues of siderotic material.

1890 G. M. GOULD *New Med. Dict.* 401/1 *Siderosis*, the pigmentation of the lymphatic glands, liver and kidneys, so called from the presence of iron in the pigment. **1906** J. L. SALINGER tr. Ehrlich & Lazarus in R. C. Cabot *Dis. of Metabolism of Blood, Animal Parasites, Toxicology* 314 Siderosis is *always* found [in progressive pernicious anemia], that is, an abnormally increased amount of iron in the internal organs, especially in the liver, in the spleen, in the bone marrow, and in the lymph-glands. **1966** WRIGHT & SYMMERS *Systemic Path.* I. xxi. 661/1 The Bantu people of South Africa show a very high incidence of cirrhosis of the Laënnec type in association with extensive siderosis.

3. The condition in which the lens of the eye is stained with rust derived from an embedded particle of iron. [f. mod.L. *siderosis bulbi* (G. von Bunge 1891, in *Verhandl. des X. Internat. Med. Congr., 1900* IV. x. 151).]

1895 H. R. SWANZY *Handbk. Dis. of Eye* (ed. 5) vi. 190 A discoloration occurs in cases where particles of iron have been imbedded in the eye. Siderosis..is the name given to this..condition. **1926** *Trans. Ophthalm. Soc.* XLV. 281 Particles [of iron] embedded deeply in the sclera do not give rise to siderosis. **1962** D. G. COGAN in A. Pirie *Lens Metabolism Rel. Cataract* 292 One curious property of the epithelium is its capacity to bind and accumulate iron. The entity, called siderosis lentis, may result..from an intraocular foreign body of iron.

Hence **sidero·tic** *a*, formed from or rich in insoluble iron compounds derived from the breakdown of hæmoglobin; of or pertaining to siderosis.

1932 W. BOYD *Text-Bk. Path.* xxviii. 719 All the cases of splenic anemia do not show siderotic nodules, nor are the nodules confined to this disease. **1941** *Nature* 18 Oct. 470/1 The amount of siderotic material per siderocyte is generally small. **1978** J. BATTEN in R. B. Scott *Price's Textbk. Pract. Med.* IX. 909/2 Siderotic lung disease.

'sides, *prep.* and *adv.* For 'Now *dial.*' read 'Now *dial.* and *colloq.*' and add later examples.

1918 C. MACKENZIE *Sylvia Scarlett* II. iv. 331, I didn't seem to want them no more. 'Sides, I've got seven already. **1936** M. MITCHELL *Gone with Wind* v. 79 It's too late den. Dey's already mahied[*sc.* married]. 'Sides, gempmums specs dey wives ter have sense. **1968** J. WHEELER SMITH in W. King *Black Short Story Anthol.* (1972) 37 'He didn't hurt you none, did he?' 'No, he didn't bother me, sides looking mean.' **1975** 'J. LYMINGTON' *Spider in Bath* i. 11 It's not like that. Sides, the job helps his pension.

si·de-scan, *a.* Also **side scan, sidescan.** [SIDE *sb.*[1] 24.] Applied to side-looking sonar (and radar), esp. on a ship.

1967 *Undersea Technol.* Apr. 24/2 The most important feature of side scan sonar..is its ability to produce a permanent, continuous, graphic record of what it 'sees'. **1969** *New Scientist* 20 Feb. 393/2 A range of sidescan sonars is now available. **1978** *Nature* 5 Jan. 49/2 Side-scan sonar has been used previously to profile icebergs, by lowering a sonar transducer vertically, at a known rate, from the side of a boat. **1979** *Ibid.* 29 Mar. 399/1 These surfaces were revealed by side-scan radar from aircraft in surveys made by the Brazilian government.

So **si·de-scanner; si·descanning** *a.*

1960 *Guardian* 20 July 2/6 In view of the development of side-scanning photography these flights were provocative while not violating international air-space. **1968** *Observer* 4 Feb. 3/3 A standard sonar device is used to sweep a large area and echoes of all possible wrecks are picked up and charted. The side-scanner then moves in to check each echo in detail. **1968** *Proc. 5th Symp. Remote Sensing of Environment* 534 The resolution of a side-scanning sonar instrument depends primarily on the width of the beam in the horizontal plane..and on the duration of the pulses. **1978** *Navy News* Oct. 5/1 She is equipped with echo sounders to measure the depth of water as well as side-scanning sonar which gives a view of the sea bed when locating wrecks.

side-show. Add: (Earlier U.S. and later *fig.* examples, esp. in *Mil.* contexts: cf. *SHOW *sb.*[1] 15 b.)

1866 C. H. SMITH (*title*) Bill Arp, so called. A side show of the Southern side of the War. **1869** 'MARK TWAIN' *Innoc. Abr.* liii. 573 And so I close my chapter on the Church of the Holy Sepulchre... With all its clap-trap side-shows and unseemly impostures of every kind. **1915** D. H. LAWRENCE *Rainbow* xiii. 381 But Ursula never told about Winifred Inger. That was a sort of secret side-show to her life. **1919** *Daily Express* (Dublin) 18 Mar. 3/6 (*heading*) Side shows. Sir Chas. Monro's despatch. Important minor operations. **1931** T. E. LAWRENCE *Let.* 13 Apr. (1938) 718 Your war-history has become one of my constant reference books, for the main war; and that its chapters on the side-shows are so crisply black-and-white as to make exciting stories of them. **1959** *Listener* 12 Mar. 444/1 Not even sideshows in the Yemen or police operations by the army in a riotous colony will save them. **1977** P. MOYES *To kill Coconut* xiii. 178 'What in hell is going on up in the forest.'.. 'I told you, that's a side-show.'

side-slip, *sb.* Add: **5. b.** *Aeronaut.* = *SLIP *sb.*[3] 9 j; also, a manœuvre in which this is deliberately produced.

1910 *Flight* 25 June 493/1 Is the banking..sufficient to overcome centrifugal movement (which is of course a sort of side-slip) or not? **1915** [see *OVERBANK *v.* 2 a]. **1928** *Observer* 1 July 17/3 With the greatest of ease they performed side-slips, vertical dives, and loops. **1969** K. MUNSON *Pioneer Aircraft 1903–14* 108/1 He eventually made a safe landing after the machine was put into a side-slip—a manoeuvre which, as Dallas Brett later recorded, was then 'popularly regarded as being in the nature of a preliminary funeral rite'. **1978** *Sci. Amer.* Nov. 137/1 The fixed rear fin had tended to correct this condition by causing the machine to turn in the direction of the sideslip.

c. *Skiing* and *Surfing.* The action of descending (a slope or wave).

1913 [see *SIDE-SLIP *v.* c]. **1959** P. MOYES *Dead Men don't Ski* iv. 51 Now they were tackling the sideslip—skidding sideways down icy slopes, their skis flat against the mountain-side. **1968** *Surfer Mag.* Jan. 24/3 Sliding sideways in a controlled sideslip until you reach the bottom of the wave. **1970** N. FLEMING *Czech Point* i. 10, I..went into a twenty foot long sideslip and stopped.

d. *fig.*

1916 H. BARBER *Aeroplane Speaks* p. v, The dreadful haltings, the many side-slips, the irregular speed, and, in short, the altogether disconcerting ways of a pen. **1921** GALSWORTHY *To Let* II. p. vi, He therefore confined himself to discussing with Dumetrius whether Monticellis would come again..and the future of Johns, with a side-slip into Buxton Knights.

side-slip, *v.* Add: **b.** *Aeronaut.* Of an aeroplane: to move sideways, *esp.* towards the centre of curvature while turning (cf. *SKID *v.*[1] 3 c). Also *trans.*, to cause to do this. Cf. *SLIP *v.*[1] 9 c.

1911 *Flight* 23 Sept. 830/2 He turned sharply to the left, permitting the machine to bank up too much, whereupon it side-slipped to the ground. **1928** *Rep. & Mem. Aeronaut. Res. Comm.* No. 1187. 6 The aeroplane is side-slipped with the rudder bar central. **1935** C. DAY LEWIS *Time to Dance* 36 From three thousand feet they tilted Over, side-slipped away. **1941** POPE & OTIS *Elem. Aeronaut.* ix. 84 It is possible..to sideslip the plane even during a turn of the 'S'. **1966** M. WOODHOUSE *Tree Frog* xxv. 183 The whole plane felt dead and we sideslipped fast. **1978** *Sci. Amer.* Nov. 139/1 Every so often the machine would lose control and simply sideslip into the ground.

c. *Skiing.* To descend sideways. Cf. sense 5 c of the *sb.*

1913 A. LUNN *Ski-ing* iii. 79 The expert makes great use of the side-slip for getting down difficult ground... Run with your ski in the normal position for traversing a slope... Flatten them against the slope and slip sideways. Then run a little way in the normal position and again side-slip. **1952** ISELIN & SPECTORSKY *Invitation to Skiing* vi. 101 When you can side slip and stop at will, you are ready for the next exercise. **1972** 'M. YORKE' *Silent Witness* II. 13 Knees flexed..he had side-slipped down the sheer drop from the shoulder of the mountain.

d. *transf.* and *fig.* Also occas. *trans.*

1917 'CONTACT' *Airman's Outings* v. 139 Snatches of familiar flying-talk..side-slipped away from Archie. **1921** GALSWORTHY *To Let* I. iii. 36 His heart moved in a disconcerting manner, as if it had side-slipped within his chest. **1930** *London Mercury* Feb. 319 Here he was suddenly realising that they controlled another mode of clutching. Better to side-slip that too—if he could. **1931** *Technol. Rev.* Nov. 67/1, I was cruising along 43d Street when along came Bill, Sam, and Charlie in formation, and we all side-slipped into a speakeasy and did a lot of barroom flying. **1960** T. MCLEAN *Kings of Rugby* xi. 120 He offered dummy passes, sidestepped, sideslipped. **1964** D. MACARTHUR *Reminiscences* v. 125 The problem was to sideslip my troops westward..before their path would be cut off from the north.

So **side-slipping** *vbl. sb.* and *ppl. a.*

1887 [in Dict.]. **1904** *Motor Cycle* 18 Apr. 361/3 Side-slipping is a great bugbear to motor cyclists. **1916** 'BOYD CABLE' *Action Front* 1 A wet night, a greasy road, and a side-slipping motor-bike. **1930** [see *NOSE-DIVE *v.* 1 a]. **1949** A. FAWCUS *Skiing Simplified* ii. 49 Sideslipping is the easiest way to get down a steep slope without having to turn. **1950** *Gloss. Aeronaut. Terms* (*B.S.I.*) I. 10 *Side-slipping*, motion of an aircraft relative to the air such that the air flow has a component along the lateral axis. **1975** *Oxf. Compan. Sports & Games* 957/1 The secret of giant slalom is good control of the ski edges to prevent wasteful sideslipping.

side-step, *sb.* Add: **1.** (Earlier example.) Also *spec.* in *Rugby Football*, a step to the side, as to avoid a tackle, made while running with the ball. Also *fig.*

1789 *Rules & Reg. Field Exercises Army in Ireland* I. 8 The *Side-step*, or march, is very necessary on many occasions when halted. **1927** [see *JINK *v.*[1]]. **1940** 'GUN BUSTER' *Return via Dunkirk* II. viii. 148 We've got to make a side-step, giving up part of the ridge we're now holding. **1960** V. JENKINS *Lions down Under* xi. 161 Risman did the rest with two perfect side-steps.

side-step, *v.* Add: **1. a.** *intr.* (Later examples.) Also *transf.*, to go aside from the direct route; to make a side-trip.

1927 *Ladies' Home Jrnl.* Jan. 62, I was glad I side stepped, for the journey..was worth a deviation. **1951** *Sport* 6–12 Apr. 15/2 He twists, turns, side-steps and swerves beautifully. **1973** 'D. HALLIDAY' *Dolly & Starry Bird* xv. 230 Sophia sidestepped and walked sharply past Charles.

b. *fig.* To practise evasion; to avoid an issue or prevaricate.

a **1911** D. G. PHILLIPS *Susan Lenox* (1917) II. xi. 276 What do you think of that, Terry? I offered her a twenty and she sidestepped. **1930** P. MACDONALD *Link* vii. 114 I've even asked Dinwater that flat out on two occasions. But he's always side-stepped.

c. *Skiing.* (See quots.)

1924 *Ski Terms* in *Tourist* Winter Sports No. 12/2 *Side stepping*, climbing by lifting the skis horizontally. **1976** *Webster's Sports Dict.* 390/2 *Sidestep*, to climb a slope by employing a sidestep.

2. a. *trans.* To avoid by stepping to the side; *spec.* in *Football.*

1905 'O. HENRY' in *N.Y. World* (Mag. section) 12 Mar. 5/4 I've lost two inches of my tail trying to sidestep those swinging doors. **1920** W. CAMP *Football without Coach* 93 The man who catches the ball will not be able to sidestep him or pass him. **1931** *Times* 16 Feb. 5/1 Once, Arigho.. managed to side-step Reeve. **1976** *Sunday Mail* (Glasgow) 28 Nov. 46/6 The striker took his time, sidestepped a tackle and neatly shot low past Rennie.

b. *fig.*

1900 ADE *Fables in Slang* 56 The Parents decided to give Clarence a large Measure of Liberty, that he might become Acquainted with the Snares and Temptations of the World when he was Young, and thus be Prepared to side-step the Pitfalls when he was Older. **1906** *Springfield* (Mass.) *Weekly Republ.* 27 Sept. 8 The Idaho republicans are deftly side-stepping the anti-Mormon issue. **1915** WODEHOUSE *Psmith Journalist* xxiii. 173 If I can put him away, it gets me into line with Jimmy, and he can't side-step me. **1932** E. WALLACE *When Gangs came to London* xxviii. 287 One of the best gunmen that ever sidestepped the chair. **1947** E. O. SCHLUNKE in *Coast to Coast 1946* 51 But to make sure he wasn't 'side-stepped', Krantz turned up at the railway station. **1964** *English Studies* XLV. 21 Many people side-step the recognition of a plurality of Englishes by such judgments as: 'Oh, that's not English, that's American.' **1977** *Time* 8 Aug. 25/1 If the British government continues on the line it appears to be following, we will be able to sidestep them and arrive at an internal settlement.

3. *trans.* To cause (a person or thing) to move sideways; to transfer to the side.

1969 A. GLYN *Dragon Variation* viii. 245 Jeff's Queen was *en prise*, and he side-stepped her one square where she would still be able to defend the Rook's Pawn. **1974** *Daily Tel.* 26 Mar. 16 Peter Dimmock, general manager of BBC Enterprises... Mr Dimmock, formerly general manager of BBC Outside Broadcasts, was sidestepped to his present job.

Hence **si·de-stepper**, one who steps sideways or avoids a direct course or issue; **si·de-stepping** *vbl. sb.*, stepping sideways, evasiveness, avoidance; also as *ppl. a.*

1901 G. V. HOBART *Down Line with John Henry* 100, I was the likeliest side-stepper that ever did a grass-chopping speciality. **1909** *N.Y. Even. Post* (semi-weekly ed.) 1 Mar. 1 Had not Mr. Fairbanks been a really wonderful side-stepper, their essential differences might have long ago become public property. **1912** J. SANDILANDS *Western Canad. Dict. & Phrase-Bk.*, *Sidestepping*, wandering from the argument, evading the question. **1932** *Blue Valley Farmer* (Oklahoma City) 17 Mar. 6/5 When America is grappling with things fundamental, tired and disgusted with side-stepping, buck-passing and plain lying..the country must content itself with a stone when it asked for bread. **1949** 'J. TEY' *Brat Farrar* xii. 100 The conversational ground he moved on was firm. There was need for neither side-stepping nor manoeuvre. **1960** *Times* 16 June 16/2 'Autumn' with its evocative side-stepping harmonies, was delightfully sung. **1970** *Times* 28 Sept. 12/7 The sidestepping at blinding speed of Gerald Davies on the right wing. **1980** N. FREELING *Castang's City* xvi. 105 A dodgy rapid sidestepper, a clever elusive runner.

sides to mi·ddle, *adv.* (and *adj.*) *phr.* Also -into-, side to middle. [SIDE *sb.*[1]] Of a sheet of bed-linen: with the sides and middle changing places, as a worn sheet cut down the centre and resewn thus to prolong its useful life. Also (hyphened) as *adj. phr.*

1861 MRS. BEETON *Bk. Househ. Managem.* ii. 24 Sheets should be turned 'sides to middle' before they are allowed to get very thin. **1884** E. NESBIT *Let.* in D. Langley Moore *E. Nesbit* (1933) v. 71, I have done 2 sheets 'sides into middle'. **1949** H. ASHTON *Parson Austen's Daughter* viii. 309 She..had to sleep on sheets which had been turned side to middle. **1950** B. PYM *Some Tame Gazelle* xv. 161 Although the Archdeacon had not personally made the bed, he knew that there were sides-to-middle sheets on it. **1963** 'J. M. BERRISFORD' *Gardening in Lime* ii. 24 After six to eight weeks the whole [compost] heap may be turned, sides to middle, with the top material becoming the bottom. **1972** 'S. WOODS' *They love not Poison* viii. 112 Jenny [was] diligently hemming a sheet that Mrs. Dibb wanted turned 'sides to middle'.

si·de-swipe, *sb.* [f. the vb.; cf. also SIDE-WIPE.] **1.** A glancing blow from or on the side (esp. of a motor vehicle). Chiefly *U.S.*

1917 *Dialect Notes* IV. 400 He struck it with a *side-swipe*. **1935** *Evening Sun* (Baltimore) 7 Mar. 25/3 A few days ago we said there is no such word as *sideswipe* in the dictionary... *Side-wiping* puts the shine on the car—*side-swiping* takes it off. **1964** D. SOLOMON *Accidents on Main Rural Highways* 1. 2 Nearly half of all accident involvements were either rear-end collisions or same-direction sideswipes. **1968** *Autocar* 14 Mar. 24/3 With adjustable front seats there is weakness in sideswipe. **1977** *Time* 24 Jan. 2/3 (Advt.), The ESV's have proved their life-saving value in head-on and rear-end collisions, side-swipes and roll-overs.

2. A passing jibe or verbal attack; an indirect rebuke or criticism.

1924 KIPLING *Prophet & Country* in *Debits & Credits* (1926) 193 A side-swipe at the practically non-existent birth-rate. **1959** *Sunday Times* 29 Nov. 25/6 Wolf Mankowitz has reshaped his satire on show business... A few side-swipes are allowed. **1964** *Ann. Reg. 1963* 26 He allowed himself one side-swipe at the security services, declaring that 'the £60 million spent on these services under the right hon. gentleman's premiership have been less productive..than the security services of the *News of the World*.' **1977** M. WALKER *National Front* vii. 179 Martin Webster..again warned of the enemy within in an article..which included a series of side-swipes against 'the trimmers, the popularity-seekers and moderates'.

si·de-swipe, *v.* Chiefly *U.S.* [SIDE *sb.*[1]] *trans.* To strike (something) a glancing blow on or with the side (esp. of a motor vehicle).

1904 *Philadelphia Even. Tel.* 12 Nov. 16 The west-bound St. Louis Express, while pulling on to a siding, was sideswiped by the east-bound Pittsburg Limited. **1916** *Daily Colonist* (Victoria, B.C.) 15 July 2/4 Five persons were injured..when a motor car..overturned on the boulevard, after sideswiping a stalled car. **1938** D. BAKER *Young Man with Horn* I. v. 41 No sidewalks there, and one out of ten cars doing its best to sideswipe them. **1960** I. CROSS *Backward Sex* iii. 66 The cup slid from one end of the tray to the other, sideswiping the teapot on the way. **1973** K. GILES *File on Death* ii. 29 A grey car.. came up fast... It side-swiped her and drove on.

side-track, *sb.* Add: **a.** (Earlier examples.)

1835 *Maine Farmer* 24 July 198/1 One of the principle [*sic*] dealers here has offered to lay a side track from the road to his own storehouse. **1876** G. A. CROFUTT *Trans-Continental Tourist* 41 Waterloo is a small side-track station.

b. A side-path.

1892 [see *MIDDLE-OF-THE-ROAD]. **1966** 'J. HACKSTON' *Father clears Out* 113 Trooper Caldecott riding along the soft, silent side-tracks that led to the Sunday trading.

c. *transf.* and *fig.*

1901 *Congress. Rec.* XXXIV. III. 2476/1, I do not propose to be side tracked by any Senator from the other side of the Chamber. I myself will decide when I will go on the side track. **1935** B. MALINOWSKI *Coral Gardens & their Magic* II. VI. v. 239 Man never runs on the sidetrack of magical verbiage. **1972** J. PHILIPS *Vanishing Senator* (1973) III. ii. 136 Couldn't you try rental agencies? It wouldn't be a side track for you, Inspector.

side-track, *v.* Add: **1.** *fig.* (Earlier and later examples.) Also *spec.* to divert or lead (a person) from the main course; to turn (something) aside from prominence.

1880 *News & Press* (Cimarron, New Mexico) 19 Feb. 4/3 Short skirts are now worn for dancing dresses, and the gentlemen are no longer obliged to wait for the ladies to side-track their trains before they can pass. **1887** *Scribner's Mag.* in Farmer *Americanisms* (1889) 487/1 Mebbe them thar lieyers side-tracked him with their everlastin' quashtuns, an' ef so, he warn't so pow'ful much ter blame. **1891** F. H. SMITH *Col. Carter* 139 Yancey broke away again, but Fitz side-tracked him with a gesture, and asked the colonel to repeat Klutchem's exact words. **1918** W. S. CHURCHILL *Let.* 12 Jan. in M. Gilbert *Winston S. Churchill* (1977) IV. Compan. I. 231 Munitions are everywhere being side-tracked to the claims of food, of civil imports, of Allies, and of dollars. **1929** C. CONNOLLY *Let.* in *Romantic Friendship* (1975) 325 Delicious people not so young are all somehow sidetracked. **1931** L. A. G. STRONG *Garden* xxxv. 324 He'd be all the worse to deal with, if he saw he'd been sidetracked. **1970** C. JAMES in Rubinstein & Stoneman *Education for Democracy* 157 Acknowledgement of special interests is vitally important in adolescence and should not be side-tracked into extra-curricular events. **1978** T. ALLBEURY *Lantern Network* xi. 160 Bailey disliked the fruity voice..and..the attempt to side-track him.

side-tracking *vbl. sb.* (*fig.* examples).

1947 *Mind* LVI. 291 The abnormal violence of the reaction against Idealism must, I think, be held primarily responsible for the side-tracking of its doctrine of judgment. **1981** A. PRICE *I'll soldier no More* 54 Through all the verbiage and side-tracking he held to his primary objectives.

sidewalk. 2. For 'Now *U.S.*' read 'Now chiefly *U.S.*' and add further examples outside the U.S.

1824 F. BURNEY in *Jrnls. & Lett.* (1980) VIII. 525 The streets [of Trier] were dreadfully ill paved, without any side Walk. **1826** *United Empire Loyalist* (Toronto) 1 July 39/4 Some regulation with respect to the improvement of the sidewalks, may be considered as necessary. **1891** G. MEREDITH *Let.* 27 May (1970) II. 1030 The way to propitiate them [*sc.* reviewers] is to keep along the side-walks, out of the sun. **1936** D. GASCOYNE *Man's Life is this Meat* 29 On the sidewalks houses eat the afternoon. **1951** R. CAMPBELL *Light on Dark Horse* ii. 27 The sidewalk..was still unpaved in those days. **1966** G. W. TURNER *Eng. Lang. in Austral. & N.Z.* viii 172 Cities have footpaths, though pavement is also used and Aucklanders seem to be able to use side-walk as well. **1971** *Rand Daily Mail* 27 Mar. 6/4 Wait on the sidewalk after getting off a bus. **1977** 'J. D. WHITE' *Salzburg Affair* xiii. 111 The sidewalks with their cheerful.. tourists, street musicians, girls.

3. Comb., as *sidewalk cafe, skate*; **sidewalk superintendent** *joc.* (chiefly *U.S.*), an idler who watches and gives unsolicited advice at construction works, road repairs, etc.; **sidewalk surfing** *slang* (orig. *U.S.*) = *SKATEBOARDING *vbl. sb.*; hence **sidewalk surfer.**

1940 R. CHANDLER *Farewell, my Lovely* viii. 54 The sidewalk café..was bright and cheerful inside, but the.. tables outside under the striped awning were empty. **1979** P. HARCOURT *Sleep of Spies* I. vii. 96 The week in Paris passed very quickly... We spent a lot of time..idling in sidewalk cafés. **1925** *Sears Catal.* (ed. 150) 751 Improved extension sidewalk skates. **1977** *Montgomery Ward Catal.* Spring–Summer 509/1 Junior rink-style sidewalk skates. **1940** *Sun* (Baltimore) 30 Mar. 20/7 The walk..is covered so that the sidewalk superintendents can meet in rainy weather. **1970** R. P. WARREN *Incarnations* 46 Sidewalk superintendents turn now From their duties and at you stare. **1976** A. CASSORLA *Skateboarder's Bible* 9 Weird-wheeling sidewalk surfers can be seen whipping over the blacktop from Reno to Rio de Janeiro. **1965** *National Observer* (U.S.) 5 Apr. 12/1 Remember the hula hoop? The popularity attained by that hip-swinging fad in the late 1950s is fast being dwarfed by a new teen-age craze known as sidewalk surfing or skateboarding.

sidewall. Add: **2.** *Sport* (esp. *Squash Rackets*). A wall forming one side of a court.

1902 [see *BOAST *v.*[3], *sb.*[3]]. **1935** *Encycl. Sports* 582/2 [Squash] If..the server makes his ball hit the side wall or roof or floor before it hits the front wall,..he loses his innings. **1963** *Times* 4 Feb. 4/3 This service was nothing more than an astutely placed lob, but which, when hit with reverse spin, clung to the sidewall. **1975** *Oxf. Compan. Sports & Games* 823/1 [Real tennis] The side walls are in play up to a height of about 18 ft. (5·5 m.), where the windows begin.

3. a. The side of a vehicle's tyre (TYRE *sb.*[5] 2), usu. untreaded and freq. marked or coloured distinctively. Freq. *attrib.*, as *side-wall tyre* (also *absol.* as sb.).

1922 *Encycl. Brit.* XXXII. 729/2 The outside of the [tyre's] carcass is entirely covered with rubber; the sides with a 'sidewall' layer. *c* **1949** in M. McLuhan *Mech. Bride* (1967) 83 White sidewall tires..available at extra cost. **1972** *Daily Tel.* (Colour Suppl.) 20 Oct. 10/4 Hans Galli, their chief test-pilot, was..convinced that radial-ply tyres were unsuitable for aircraft because of their flexible sidewalls. **1976** J. LEE *Ninth Man* 70 The car... White sidewalls. Radio and heater.

b. A surface at either side of a hovercraft that projects downwards underneath it and helps to contain the air-cushion. Freq. *attrib.*

1960 *Aeroplane* XCIX. 149/1 This is a type of Hovercraft with side walls which are partially immersed in water. **1960** *Economist* 6 Aug. 585/3 William Denny..is to enter a new field for British companies and develop what are called side-wall craft. **1968** *Economist* 18 May 76/3 The car ferry versions of the sidewall hovercraft now being planned..should provide direct competition with the biggest hydrofoil..now building. **1975** *Nature* 6 Feb. 391/1 The development of a 200-passenger sidewall hover-ferry.

sidewards, *adv.* **1.** (Later example.)

1912 J. STEPHENS *Crock of Gold* vi. 57 He was not looking at her but far away sidewards across the spreading hill.

sideways, *adv.* Add: **2. c.** Const. *on* (ON *adv.* 7 b): = *SIDE-ON adv.; also (hyphened) as *adj.*

1972 *Guardian* 28 Jan. 6/1 Methods of reducing injuries when a car is hit sideways-on by another car. **1973** W. BARLOW *Alexander Principle* ix. 141 We need to look once more at our spines and our stance sideways on. **1976** J. SNOW *Cricket Rebel* 37 By the time I returned to Sussex..I was very much more a 'sideways-on' bowler.

3. b. *to look sideways*: also, to regard something in a furtive or improper manner; *spec.* to glance amorously or suspiciously *at.*

1844 'J. SLICK' *High Life in N.Y.* I. xiv. 217 If he dared look sideways at his [i.e. another's] wife or sister. **1895** CONRAD *Almayer's Folly* 160 This thought caused him to pluck up heart and look at Nina sideways. **1921** B. GILBERT *Old England* 70 But he was known to be paying to three different women for a child each, And his housekeeper beginning to look sideways. **1974** N. MARSH *Black as he's Painted* vi. 162 It wouldn't..be anything out of the way if they got round to looking sideways at each other.

c. In colloq. phr. *to knock sideways*: to astound, as with pleasure or shock; to dumbfound, to amaze.

1925 B. TRAVERS *Mischief* iv. 60 She could have engaged in a viva voce competition with the editor of *The Dog World* and knocked him sideways. **1942** J. B. PRIESTLEY *Black-Out in Gretley* vii. 169 When anybody ..does something or has something that suddenly knocks me sideways, I feel I ought to mention it... It's like paying a debt. **1957** R. MASON *World of Suzie Wong* II. iv. 149 Their attitude is basically commercial... But my guess is that this stuff will knock them sideways. **1960** M. STEWART *My Brother Michael* xvi. 203, I can't seem to think straight... I feel knocked kind of sideways.

d. *Comb.*, as *sideways-looking* adj. = *SIDE-LOOKING *a.*

1962 *Daily Tel.* 29 Oct. 22/3 A new method of obtaining aerial pictures is by 'sideways looking' radar. **1966** *Geo-Marine Technol.* Oct. 18 Sideways-looking sonars produce acoustic pictures of the surface of the sea-bed. **1979** 'M. M. KAYE' *Shadow of Moon* (ed. 2) xxxiv. 408 The dark, secretive, sideways-looking eyes.

side-winder[1]. (Earlier examples.)

1840 *Daily Pennant* (St. Louis) 14 May (Th. s.v. Sockdologer), Tim gives him a sockdologer and two side-winders, and leaves him for dead on the spot. **1846** J. CODMAN *Sailor's Life & Sailor's Yarns* 31 'Take that then, for want of a shillaleh!' said the lumper, giving him a side-winder with his fist.

side-winder[2]. Add: **1.** (Earlier and later examples.) Also, one of several other small rattlesnakes.

1875 H. C. YARROW in *Rep. U.S. Geogr. Surveys West of 100th Meridian* V. 535 They were also seen in Arizona, and are called 'side-winders' by the settlers, owing to their peculiar lateral progressive motion. **1906** *Out West* Feb. 136 It is..a land of the side-winder, the Gila monster, the scorpion and the centipede. **1949** *Nat. Hist.* May 212/2 Among other interesting tracks are the slanting 'ladder-rung' trails of the sidewinder rattlesnakes. **1971** 'D. SHANNON' *Ringer* ix. 149 Royce shied back at the sight of him as if he'd been a sidewinder.

2. *transf.* and *fig.*

1906 *McClure's Mag.* XXVI. 414 You never could tell where Texas Pete was goin' to jump next. He was a sidewinder and a diamond-back and a little black rattle-snake all rolled into one. **1936** G. ROUNDS *Ol' Paul* 21 It was known as the orneriest river... It was an old 'side winder' for fair. **1940** W. FAULKNER *Hamlet* IV. i. 244 Hup, you broom-tailed hay-burning sidewinders. **1964** R. MURPHY *Pond* ix. 129 'They grew up with her and knew what a sidewinder she was.' 'What's a sidewinder?' Joey asked. 'It's a rattlesnake, but I meant it as a sort of troublemaker.'

Hence as a back-formation, **si·de-winding** *ppl. a.*, moving like a side-winder (also *fig.*); also as *vbl. sb.*; **si·de-wind** *v. intr.*

1902 H. DAY *Pine Tree Ballads* 150 That was a side-windin' answer for him. **1954** J. A. PRINGLE *Common Snakes* p. vi, Some of the adders have a peculiar side-winding movement for crawling over loose sand. **1969** A. BELLAIRS *Life of Reptiles* I. iii. 105 It is generally believed that sidewinding is the most efficient type of locomotion which a snake can use over a smooth sandy surface... *Crotalus cerastes* can sidewind at about 2 mph. **1972** *World of Wild Wheels* (Custom Car) 65/1. His side-winding Anglia symbolises everything that Hot Rod racing is all about. **1977** 'J. LE CARRÉ' *Hon. Schoolboy* xvii. 403 Occasionally a yellow bus came sidewinding down the hill toward them.

sidewise, *adv.* and *a.* Add: **6.** as *adj.* (*fig.* example).

a **1914** JOYCE *Stephen Hero* (1944) 48 You're a 'cute fellow, said Stephen in a sidewise fashion.

sidey: see SIDY *a.*[2] in Dict. and Suppl.

Sidhe (ʃī), *sb. pl. Ir. Mythol.* Also **sidhe** and (*sing.*) **Sidh.** [Ellipsis (not found in Irish) of Ir. (*aos*) *sidhe* people of the fairy mound: cf. *folk of peace* s.v. *FOLK 3 c and BANSHEE.] The hills of the fairies; fairyland, faerie. Hence (esp. in the writings of W. B. Yeats), the fairy folk, fairies, freq. regarded as the mythical gods of ancient Ireland. Cf. *SHEOGUE.

1793 J. HELY tr. *O'Flaherty's Ogygia* II. III. xxii. 55 When the princesses saw these venerable gentlemen.. they looked upon them to be the people of the Sidhe. The Irish call these Sidhe, aërial spirits or phantoms; because they are seen to come out of pleasant hills, where the common people imagine they reside: which fictitious habitations are called by us Sidhe or Siodha. **1880** S. FERGUSON *Conary* in *Poems* 95 These wicked sprites,.. men of the *Sidhs*..Who played their pipes before us, led us on Into..the night. **1899** W. B. YEATS *Wind among Reeds* 1 (*title*) The hosting of the Sidhe. **1899** —— *Let.* 21 June (1954) 321, I myself try to avoid the word 'fairy'. ..*Sidhe* or 'gentry' or 'the others' is better. **1906** S. GWYNN *Fair Hills Irel.* ii. 34 The heroes of the mysterious Tuatha de Danann who after their defeat by the Milesians withdrew from daylight into the recesses of the earth—and who are still there, fairy folk, the people of the *Sidhe.* **1919** W. B. YEATS *Only Jealousy of Emer* in *Two Plays for Dancers* 25 What one among the Sidhe has dared to lie Upon Cuchulain's bed and take his image? **1941** L. MACNEICE *Poetry of W. B. Yeats* iv. 79 Yeats's world of the Sidhe and curlews. **1977** N. ARROWSMITH *Field Guide to Little People* 20 The Sidhe live a very domestic life if undisturbed, caring for their animals, drinking whisky, borrowing milk and meal. *Ibid.* 21 The Sidhe are thin, up to six feet in height, handsome and young-looking despite their great age.

sidi. Add: *sidi-boy* (earlier example).

1867 G. E. CLARK *Seven Years of Sailor's Life* viii. 86, I wandered off alone to the 'Seide' boys village of fishermen.

siding, *vbl. sb.* Add: **II. 5. b.** For *U.S.* read orig. and chiefly *U.S.* and add: (Earlier and later examples.) Also made of materials other than timber.

1829 J. F. COOPER *Wept of Wish-ton-wish* I. xvii. 246 [Dwellings] constructed of a firm frame-work, neatly covered with sidings of boards. **1946** E. HODGINS *Mr Blandings builds his Dream House* xiii. 191 The mason subcontractor was stalled in his tracks since..no finished siding could even begin to be nailed to the sheathing. **1958** *N.Z. Timber Jrnl.* Sept. 87/1 *Sidings*, weatherboards for vertical surfaces. Varieties incude: feather-edge, novelty, rebated, ship-lap. **1968** *Globe & Mail* (Toronto) 17 Feb. 1/2 Outside the house, a black hole in the white siding showed where one bullet had driven through the living room wall. **1970** *Washington Post* 30 Sept. B. 13/7 (Advt.), A sparkling white home is yours with Reynolds aluminum siding installed by Hechinger.

c. = SIDELING *sb.* 2. *Austral.* and *N.Z.*

1891 G. CHAMIER *Philosopher Dick* I. xiii. 360 He told him to mind the siding by the shoot. **1902** H. LAWSON *Joe Wilson* in *Prose Works* (1946) 350 The dark box-scrub-covered ridges ended in steep 'sidings' coming down to the creek-bank. **1904** G. B. LANCASTER *Sons o'Men* 28 Must have gone over the siding. **1931** F. D. DAVISON *Man-Shy* (1934) xii. 165 The scrubbers were grazing along an ironbark siding. **1975** *N.Z. Jrnl. Agric.* Sept. 27/2 The animal which grazes mostly on non-treated areas—such as gullies or sidings—..will not be fully protected.

sidle, *v.* Add: **1. b.** To make one's way in a horizontal or transverse direction about an incline; *spec.* in *Mountaineering* = TRAVERSE *v.* 21. *N.Z.*

1950 *N.Z. Jrnl. Agric.* Oct. 295/1 Sowing was done following the contours and from higher to lower altitudes, as a man tends to climb when sidling. **1958** *Tararua* XII. 29 To *sidle*, to go around the side or across the face of a hill, is a characteristic New Zealand expression, strange to the Englishman or Australian. **1971** *N.Z. Listener* 19 Apr. 56/5 They got up the lower scree, sidled across the first face into a couloir, but they were getting bombed so they cramponed up to just below a gendarme.

Sidneian (si·dniăn, sidnī·ăn), *a.* Also 7 **Sydnæan, Sydnian; Sidneyan.** [f. the name of Sir Philip *Sidney* (1554–86), English statesman and man of letters, + -AN.] Of, pertaining to, or characteristic of the life and works of Sidney.

c **1610** CHAPMAN *Sonnet* [to the Earl of Montgomery] in *Homer Prince of Poets* sig. Ee3ᵛ, There runs a blood, faire Earle, through your cleare vains,.. Which still the liuing Sydnian soule maintaines. **1646** CRASHAW *Steps to Temple* 137 Sydnæan showers Of sweet discourse, whose powers Can Crowne old Winters head with flowers.

1931 E. BLUNDEN in *Mind's Eye* (1934) I. 53 It was Sidneian virtue in our colonel to invite even F. into the log cabin for a drink and a tune. **1952** D. DAVIE *Purity of Diction in Eng. Verse* App. B. 199 The 'sprezzatura' of Castiglione and the Sidneyan ideal. **1965** K. GRAHAM *Eng. Criticism of Novel* ii. 39 Hardy's..eventual abandonment of the novel for poetry can perhaps be foreseen in the high, Sidneyan aims he set for it.

Sidoor, Sidur, varr. *SIDDUR. **Sidra(h,** varr. *SEDRA. **Sidur,** var. *SIDDUR.

sidy, *a.*[2] (Later examples.)

1913 C. MACKENZIE *Sinister St.* I. II. iii. 179 The porter was frightfully sick at having to give me a telegram. He is a sidy swine. **1935** 'N. BLAKE' *Question of Proof* viii. 154 'It is possible that he could have thought he had a chance of being elected?' 'Oh, I should think so; he was sidey enough.' **1946** B. MARSHALL *George Brown's Schooldays* xxviii. 115 He couldn't very well put himself in first because people might think it rather sidey.

Siebel (sī·b'l), the name of *Siebel* Flugzeugwerke K.G., a German aircraft manufacturing company, used *attrib.* in *Siebel ferry*, a power-driven troop and freight landing-craft developed by them during the war of 1939–45. Also *absol.*

1942 *R.A.F. Jrnl.* 18 Apr. 4 (*caption*) This is the largest scale photograph yet taken of..a Siebel Ferry. Gun positions are visible at the four extremities. **1946** R. CAPELL *Simiomata* I. 36 A Siebel ferry was moving out of the harbour. *Ibid.*, The Siebel..made things unpleasant with air-bursts. These ferries, accommodating about 150 troops, carry two 88 mm. guns. **1973** D. HAMILTON-HILL *SOE Assignment* vii. 100 Siebel Ferries—the special invention of the German Kriegsmarine—double (in parallel) enlarged canoe-type gun boats.

siege, *sb.* Add: **I. 1. e.** *Siege Perilous*: the vacant seat at King Arthur's Round Table which could be occupied without peril only by the Knight destined to achieve the Grail. Also *fig.*

[*c* **1230** *La Queste del Saint Graal* (1967) 4 Et einsi alerent tant qu'il vindrent au grant siege que len apeloit le Siege Perilleux. *Ibid.* 7 Tuit li compaignon de la Table Reonde furent venu et li siege aempli, fors seulement cil que len apeloit le Siege Perilleus.] *c* **1470** MALORY *Works* (1967) I. 102 But in the Sege Perelous there shall nevir man sitte but one, and yf there be ony so hardy to do hit he shall be destroyed, and he that shall sitte therein shall have no felowe. **1870** TENNYSON *Holy Grail & Other Poems* 43 There stood a vacant chair... And Merlin call'd it 'The Siege perilous', Perilous for good and ill. **1922** J. BUCHAN *Huntingtower* xiii. 256 There in a coign of the old battlements he would prove an ugly customer to the pursuit. Only one at a time could reach that siege perilous. **1959** P. LE GENTIL in R. S. Loomis *Arthurian Lit. in Middle Ages* xix. 261 Three scenes, the fateful occupation of the Siege Perilous and the two visits to the Grail castle, constitute the main pattern.

2. c. (Later examples in *collect.* sense.)

1801 J. STRUTT *Sports & Pastimes* I. ii. 28 A *sege* of herons, and of bitterns. **1937** J. W. DAY *Sporting Adventure* 106 They [*sc.* herons] are about in pairs instead of the 'sieges' of half a dozen or more which one met only a month ago fishing on the tide line. **1977** *Islander* (Victoria, B.C.) 5 June 3/2 A siege of herons flying home against a sunset sky.

II. 6. a. Also *transf.*

1911 *Times* 5 Jan. 6/2 (*heading*) Foreign opinion on the Stepney siege. **1980** *Daily Tel.* 5 June 8/6 Police forced their way into a flat..after a man had barricaded himself in... During the two-hour siege the man's wife sustained a broken nose.

c. A period of illness, struggle, or difficulty. *U.S.*

1840 [in Dict., sense 6 a]. **1898** E. C. HALL *Aunt Jane* 9 She was as pale and peaked as if she had been through a siege of typhoid. **1929** *Randolph* (W. Va.) *Enterprise* 11 Apr. 1/1 The..Literary Society had another heavy siege Tuesday night of this week. **1952** R. CHANDLER *Let.* 31 July (1966) 27 She is weakened by a long siege of bronchitis. **1975** *Publishers Weekly* 11 Aug. 113/1 After her own siege with breast cancer, the author consulted with other victims.

7. a. (In *transf.* senses) *siege action, tactics.*

1977 *Evening Post* (Nottingham) 24 Jan. 5/8 The threat to car jobs in the Midlands grew today as delivery drivers began another week of 'siege action' at three big Leyland factories. **1977** P. HILL *Fanatics* 109 Those two have been trained in siege tactics.

b. siege economy, an economic situation in which the availability of imported goods is severely restricted by import controls and the export of capital is curtailed; **siege mentality,** a defensive or paranoid attitude of mind based on an assumption of hostility in others.

1962 S. E. FINER *Man on Horseback* vii. 92 By 1940 the parties had been dissolved, the zaibitsu harnessed to a siege economy. **1979** H. S. KENT *In on Act* xii. 131 The phrase 'siege economy' is sometimes used today to conjure up a last desperate plight in which, under the protection of high tariff walls, we would try to grow our own food, labour grimly in our mines and make the things we needed most; and so control our foreign trade as to bring in the additional supplies that we could not do without. **1969** J. L. MCKENZIE *Roman Catholic Church* III. iv. 222 This revival could not have come about without relaxation of the 'siege mentality'. **1976** *Deb. Senate Canada* 8 Mar. 11590/2 With the growing siege mentality in the suburbs of our major urban areas, the people know that crime is not under control.

Siegenian (sīge·niăn), *a. Geol.* [f. *Siegen*, name of a town and region in North Rhine-Westphalia, W. Germany, + -IAN.] Pertaining to or designating a stage of the Lower Devonian in N.W. Europe, immediately above the Gedinnian, or the epoch or age during which it was deposited. Also *absol.*

1922 *Proc. Geologists' Assoc.* XXXIII. 12 The higher horizon also includes many Siegenian species. **1928** E. NEAVERSON *Stratigraphical Palaeont.* xi. 255 In Britain.. the Siegenian stage is best represented by the Meadfoot beds of South Devon. **1931** [see *FAMENNIAN *a.*] **1967** M. R. HOUSE in W. B. Harland et al. *Fossil Record* I. 47 The goniatites appear in the mid-Siegenian as simple primitive types which soon diversify rapidly. **1979** R. ANDERTON et al. *Dynamic Stratigr. Brit. Isles* x. 130/2 Non-marine faunas of ostracoderm and placoderm fish fragments and plant remains..indicate a lower Devonian (Siegenian) age for the group.

Siegfried Line (sī·gfrīd ləin). [tr. G. *Siegfriedlinie*, f. the name of the hero *Siegfried* of Wagner's *Ring* cycle (and of the MHG epic poem the *Nibelungenlied*).] The line of fortifications occupied by the Germans in France during the war of 1914–18. Similarly, the line of defence constructed along Germany's western frontier before the war of 1939–45.

[**1923** KIPLING *Irish Guards in Great War* I. 204 The Hindenburg line, known to the Germans as 'Siegfried'.] **1936** H. A. L. FISHER *Hist. Europe* III. xxxiii. 1144 A position which had been fortified with elaborate care, and was known by the Germans as the Siegfried and by the English as the Hindenburg line. **1938** *Times* 25 Oct. 14/4 The evening newspapers [in Berlin] published to-day the first photographs of the so-called 'Siegfried Line', the massive fortifications which are being erected on the western frontiers of the Reich. **1939** *Times* 22 Sept. 6/7 What song is to be the 'Tipperary' of this war? The first candidate would seem to be 'The Washing on the Siegfried Line'. Its chorus is sufficiently simple and singable:—We're gonna hang out the washing on the Siegfried Line. Have you any dirty washing, mother dear? We're gonna hang out the washing on the Siegfried Line... If the Siegfried Line's still there. **1946** *R.A.F. Jrnl.* May 157, I rode straight through the Siegfried Line with dug-outs and then a line of anti-tank traps strung out across the countryside. **1978** E. MALPASS *Wind brings up Rain* xxiv. 221 Cholera..had broken out..in the Siegfried Line.

‖ **Sieg Heil** (zīg həil), *int.* Also **Sieg-heil, sieg heil,** etc. [Ger., lit. 'Hail victory'.] The victory salute used by the Germans during the Nazi regime, esp. at political rallies, etc. Also as *sb.* and *v. intr.* Hence **sieg-hei·ling** *ppl. a.* Cf. *HEIL *int.*

1940 'N. BLAKE' *Malice in Wonderland* ii. 31 The hysterical pitch of the Sieg Heils at a Nazi congress. **1944** V. G. GARVIN tr. *R. Gary's Forest of Anger* xxii. 89 He has only done his duty. Nothing else. Sieg-heil! **1967** R. M. STERN *Kessler Legacy* iii. 29 Your newspaper character probably..marched and *Sieg Heiled* with the rest of the boys. **1968** *Guardian* 25 Apr. 1/1, 200 dockers arrived..to shout 'Enoch! Enoch! Enoch!' in 'Sieg heil' tempo. **1968** *Listener* 26 Sept. 403/3 Thus, by 1935, her pictorial records of militarised youngsters, marching young men and sieg-heiling fathers of families were worth uncountable battalions to the Fuehrer. **1976** *Scotsman* 20 Nov. (Weekend Suppl.) 2/6 The film, with its 'Sieg Heils' and hysterical atmosphere, is still trotted out in documentaries about the 1930s. **1978** A. NEAVE *Nuremberg* xxii. 257, I half expected them to rise, salute and cry '*Sieg Heil*'!

Siemens (sī·mĕnz, ‖ zī·mĕns). The name of four German-born brothers, Ernst Werner (1816–92), Karl Wilhelm or Charles William (1823–83), Friedrich (1826–1904), and Karl (1829–1906) (von) *Siemens*, used *attrib.* and in the possessive: **1.** To denote processes or devices discovered, invented, or developed by one or more of the brothers.

The brothers were closely associated in invention and manufacturing, and it is frequently not possible to attribute a given invention or process to any one of them. Their name is often combined with that of another inventor.

a. *Steel-making.* Sometimes in Comb. with the name of Pierre Blaise Emile *Martin* (1824–1915), French engineer, as *Siemens pyrometer, regenerator*; **Siemens('s) furnace,** an open-hearth furnace; **Siemens-Martin furnace** = *Siemens furnace*; **Siemens-Martin process,** the process, invented by Martin, of melting pig iron and scrap steel together in a Siemens furnace, usu. in alkaline conditions; **Siemens process,** a process similar to the Siemens–Martin process, but usu. carried out in acidic conditions; **Siemens producer,** a form of gas producer developed by the Siemens brothers (see PRODUCER 3).

1866 *Chambers's Jrnl.* 25 Aug. 543/2 For..any..process in which an intense heat is required, the Siemens furnace is eminently suitable. **1875** *Ure's Dict. Arts* (ed. 7) III. 909 Another modification of the Siemens process consists in the use of finely-divided iron in the spongy state..instead of bars or other manufactured forms of malleable iron. *Ibid.* 910 Two processes are employed at the Landore works: the Siemens-Martin process, which consists..in dissolving scrap-metal or steel in a bath of pig-metal, to which spiegeleisen is finally added; and the ore-reducing process. *a* **1877** KNIGHT *Dict. Mech.* III. 2365/2 In the Martin-Siemens reverberatory furnace the decarbonization of the pig-iron is effected by the reactions, upon the molten bath, of wrought-iron or ore and of the furnace-flame. **1877** Siemens producer [see REGENERATOR 2 a]. **1879** *Encycl. Brit.* IX. 846/1 The most perfect method of utilizing the waste heat hitherto applied is that of the Siemens regenerator, in which the spent gases are made to travel through chambers, known as regenerators or recuperators of heat. **1881** *Ibid.* XIII. 294/2 The calorific value of a unit of weight of gas from a Siemens producer is about 650. *Ibid.* 304/1 The other Siemens pyrometer depends on the alteration of the electrical resistance of a platinum wire when heated. *Ibid.* 305/1 The ball of a Siemens pyrometer can be introduced into the tuyere through the orifice. *Ibid.* 348/2 The Pernot furnace..is substantially a Siemens-Martin furnace with a rotating bed. **1923** GLAZEBROOK *Dict. Appl. Physics* V. 515/1 The development of the mass production of steel by the Bessemer, Siemens, and subsequent processes rendered modern engineering possible on the present scale. **1973** R. D. PEHLKE *Unit Processes Extractive Metallurgy* iv. 88 The Siemens-Martin process, commonly referred to as the open hearth process, was developed at about the same time as the Thomas process. **1974** *Encycl. Brit. Macropædia* XVII. 640/1 The Siemens furnace used a grate for burning solid fuel,..and the ductwork necessary to convey the gases from one end of the furnace to the regenerator chamber and the hot air to the grate at the other end was complex and inefficient. *Ibid.*, Pierre and Emile Martin in France in 1864 built a furnace that was fired by gas and placed a set of two Siemens regenerator chambers at each end of the furnace. *Ibid.*, This furnace became known as the Siemens–Martin furnace, or, more commonly, as the open-hearth furnace.

b. In similar technical applications, as *Siemens('s) direction finder, dynamo, (electro-)-dynamometer, relay, wattmeter,* and in the names of various forms of lamp.

1867 R. S. CULLEY *Handbk. Pract. Telegr.* (ed. 2) IX. 184 Siemens' relay consists of an electromagnet of the usual horse-shoe form. **1879** *Telegr. Jrnl.* VII. 318/2 (*heading*) Siemens' electric lamp. *Ibid.* 412/2 (*heading*) Siemens' differential electric lamp. **1882** *Encycl. Brit.* XIV. 633/1 In the Siemens differential lamp,..a potential or shunt coil and a current coil oppose each other; as the arc lengthens the current becomes less, and the potential greater, each acting to cause the carbons to approach. **1884** H. R. KEMPE *Handbk. Electr. Testing* (ed. 3) xii. 284 Like galvanometers, the Siemens electro-dynamometer is not susceptible of great accuracy when readings are very low. **1886** J. MAIER *Arc & Blow Lamps* v. 40 A large Siemens' dynamo at 450 revolutions after two hours' work became so hot that the electro-magnets began to fire. **1892** W. P. MAYCOCK *Electr. Lighting & Power Distribution* I. v. 122 Siemens' wattmeter is very similar in appearance to the electro-dynamometer. **1912** *Motor Manual* (ed. 14) iii. 125 The Siemens metallic tungsten lamps are practically unaffected by shock. **1922** GLAZEBROOK *Dict. Appl. Physics* II. 4/1 If the current measured passes through both coils the scale division will approximately follow a 'square law', as in the case of the Siemens dynamometer. **1927** S. H. LONG *Navigational Wireless* v. 86 (*heading*) Instructions for operating the Siemens direction finder. **1930** T. E. HERBERT *Telegraphy* (ed. 5) viii. 258 Siemens–Halske Relay. This relay is developed from the original Siemen's [*sic*] relay. **1966** *McGraw-Hill Encyl. Sci. & Technol.* IV. 476/2 If the same current flows through all coils in series, as in the early Siemen's [*sic*] electrodynamometer.., the instrument can be calibrated as an ammeter.

2. *Electr.* † **a.** A unit of resistance, used esp. in Germany, slightly smaller than the ohm. Usu. in the possessive, as *Siemens'(s) unit. Obs.*

1867 R. S. CULLEY *Handbk. Pract. Telegr.* (ed. 2) II. 30 'Siemens' Unit' is one metre of pure mercury, of one square millimetre section, at a temperature of 32°. Thus the Ohm and the Siemens are really alike. **1899** J. E. YOUNG *Electr. Testing for Telegraph Engineers* iv. 48 A third standard, Siemens's unit, equals 0·954 B.A. ohm.

b. (Usu. written **siemens.**) [Named after Charles William *Siemens.*] A unit of conductance, equivalent to the mho.

1935 *Proc. Nat. Acad. Sci.* XXI. 579 (*table*) Siemens. **1936** *Jrnl. Inst. Electr. Engineers* LXXVIII. 238/2 The names 'hertz' and 'siemens' likewise were voted for the names of the practical units of frequency and conductance respectively. **1963** JERRARD & MCNEILL *Dict. Sci. Units* 128 The siemens is the practical unit of conductance and is equivalent to the mho... The unit, although approved by the I.E.C. in 1933 has not yet replaced the mho. **1972** [see *PASCAL 2]. **1978** *Nature* 27 July 379/1 Unit ion conductances of a few picosiemens or greater have been reported.

Siena: see *SIENNA.

Sienese, *sb.* and *a.* Add: Now usu. with pronunc. (sīĕnī·z). **A.** *sb.* **2.** An artist belonging to the Italian school of painting developed at Siena during the 14th and 15th centuries. Also *transf.*, a painting produced by such an artist.

1888 H. ATTWELL *Italian Masters* 6 The Sienese lack the robust simplicity of Giotto, and were little influenced by the austere spirit of Dante. **1921** A. HUXLEY *Crome Yellow* ii. 12 Henry Wimbush was forced to sell some of his Primitives..four or five nameless Sienese—to the Americans. **1959** *Listener* 26 Nov. 940/2 Minor Sienese are thick on the ground and so are lesser painters of the Dutch school. **1977** 'R. WEST' *Celebration* 541 Oh, your Florentines, your Sienese, your Umbrians!

B. *adj.* (Earlier example.)

1814 J. MAYNE *Jrnl.* 20 Oct. (1909) ix. 154 We walked through the principal parts of the town..and enjoyed the pure Siennese tongue.

Sienna. Substitute for entry:

Siena (si,e·nă). Also **Sienna,** † **Syenna.** [The name of a city and province in the Tuscany region of central Italy. In sense 1, *ellipt.* for TERRA SIENNA.]

1. a, b. (In Dict.)

2. *Siena marble,* a reddish mottled stone obtained from the neighbourhood of Siena.

1774 *Builder's Magazine* 129 The body of the work may be of statuary, and the columns of Syenna marble. **1802** MRS. EDGEWORTH *Let.* 6 Dec. in C. Colvin *Maria Edgeworth in France & Switzerland* (1979) 46 The Salle for public Lectures is..30 feet high supported by 4 pillars of Sienna Marble. **1848** E. RUSKIN *Let.* 20 July in M. Lutyens *Ruskins & Grays* (1972) xiv. 126 The pillars of polished Sienna marble... John said..it made him quite sick. **1894** A. HEATON *Record of Work* Pl. 8 (*caption*) Grate with brass mouldings, Sienna marble slips, and plain..tiles. **1947** J. C. RICH *Materials & Methods of Sculpture* viii. 228 Most of the Siena marbles are veined. Siena Unie, a bright yellow variety, appears to be the only one with little or no marking. **1975** *Country Life* May (*Suppl.*) 35 George III painted console table, with..fine Siena marble tops.

sierozem (sīᵊ·rozem). *Soil Sci.* Also **serozem.** [ad. Russ. *serozém,* f. *sér̈yĭ* grey + *zemlyá* earth, soil.] A type of soil, usu. calcareous and poor in organic material, that is characterized by a brownish-grey surface horizon grading into harder, carbonate-rich lower layers, and is developed typically under mixed shrub vegetation in arid climates.

1934 *Soil Sci.* XXXVIII. 485 On the steeper, and consequently drier, slopes sierozems (gray soils) are developed. **1965** B. T. BUNTING *Geogr. Soil* xii. 142 The cooler Russian and Argentine deserts have light grey serozem. **1976** H. E. DREGNE *Soil of Arid Regions* 79 A typical Serozem..from near Isfahan in Iran..had a 1 cm. thick desert pavement of fairly angular volcanic rocks overlying a loose, light brownish-gray, coarse sandy loam 4 cm. thick. **1977** J. C. F. TEDROW *Soils of Polar Landscapes* viii. 138 Traditionally, pedologists have focused their taxonomic investigations on the mature terrestric soils—Podzol, Chernozem, Sierozem, and so forth.

sierra. Add: **1. b.** (Earlier example.)

1807 R. SOUTHEY *Lett. from England* II. xxxiv. 95 A range of mountains standing in the three provinces of Worcester, Gloucester, and Hereford... This sierra is justly admired for the beauty of its form.

3. = *CERO.

1889 in *Cent. Dict.* **1905** D. S. JORDAN *Guide Study of Fishes* II. xvi. 266 Almost exactly like it [*sc.* the Spanish mackerel] in appearance is the pintado, or sierra. **1965** A. J. MCCLANE *Stand. Fishing Encycl.* 793/2 Sierra are found along the Pacific coast of America from San Diego to Peru.

Sierra Leone (si,e·ră lĭōᵘ·n), the name of a republic of West Africa, used *attrib.* in **Sierra Leone peach,** a shrub or small tree, *Nauclea latifolia* (formerly *Sarcocephalus esculentus*) of the family Rubiaceæ, native to tropical Africa, or its edible reddish fruit; = *Guinea peach* s.v. GUINEA 1.

1866 LINDLEY & MOORE *Treas. Bot.* II. 1020/1 *S[arcocephalus] esculentus* has pink flowers and an edible fruit, of the size of a peach, whence it has been called the Sierra Leone Peach. **1965** M. S. NIELSEN *Introd. Flowering Plants W. Afr.* ix. 173 Sierra Leone or Guinea Peach..is a bush or small tree in savanna with dark red, juicy fruit balls.

Hence **Sierra Leo·nean, -ian,** an inhabitant or native of Sierra Leone; also as *adj.*, of or pertaining to Sierra Leone.

1791 A. M. FALCONBRIDGE *Let.* 8 June in *Narr. Two Voyages to River Sierra Leone* (1802) iv. 83 The people appear more inclined to industry than the Sierra Leonians. **1897** M. H. KINGSLEY *Travels W. Afr.* 680 Bishop Ingram would have been able to write a more cheerful and hopeful book..if the Sierra Leonians had had a thorough grounding in technical culture. **1910** T. J. ALLDRIDGE *Transformed Colony* ix. 75 The Sierra Leonean trader feels all this pretty badly, especially as every Sierra Leonean wants to trade. **1926** *Chambers's Jrnl.* Nov. 660/1 Sierra-Leonean solicitors were hurrying to final interviews with retained advocates. **1957** M. BANTON *W. Afr. City* vi. 104 At the [1931] census the term 'Sierra Leonian' was adopted for persons previously classified as 'Liberated Africans and their descendants'. **1974** *Times* 4 May (Sierra Leone Suppl.) p. i/1 Rhythm plays a particularly important role in the way of life of all Sierra Leoneans. **1976** *Sunday Times* (Lagos) 31 Oct. 5/4 The Sierra Leonian repatriates..played a much greater role.

sies, var. *SIS int.

siesta. Delete || and add: **a.** Also *transf.*

1946 D. C. PEATTIE *Road of Naturalist* i. 19 Its crepuscular flowers are large as those of a wild rose when they open..great mothlike petals languidly expanding, as if still oppressed with the long siesta of the day. **1947** J. STEVENSON-HAMILTON *Wild Life S. Afr.* iii. 27 The rhinoceros, startled suddenly from his midday siesta, rushes blindly at the intruder.

Hence as *v. intr.*, to take a siesta.

1899 C. J. C. HYNE *Further Adventures Capt. Kettle* ii. 30 'Right,' said Kettle. 'I'll siesta too.' **1956** G. DURRELL *My Family & Other Animals* xv. 201 The rest of the family, finding they could not siesta with the argument going on, assembled to find out the trouble. **1976** L. DEIGHTON *Twinkle, twinkle Little Spy* i. 7 The staff have noisy arguments about who should siesta on the cold stone floor.

Siesta² (si,e·stă). *Chess.* The name of a town in Italy, used *attrib.* in *Siesta gambit, variation,* a continuation of the *RUY LOPEZ opening popularized in a tournament held there (see quot. 1965).

1935 SMITH & DASH tr. *Znosko-Borovsky's How to play Chess Openings* 54 This line is known as the Siesta Gambit and has been much played in recent years. **1948** G. ABRAHAMS *Teach yourself Chess* III. v. 195 P to KB4 gives the Siesta variation which is playable. **1965** *Listener* 29 Apr. 651/3, 1 P–K4 P–K4 2 N–KB3 N–QB3 3 B–N5 P–QR3 4 B–R4 P–Q3 5 P–B3 P–B4: the so-called 'Siesta' variation, which, despite its name, leads to lively play and provides an early counter to White's positional grip on the centre.

|| **sieur¹** (syǒı). Now *arch.* [Fr.: cf. MONSIEUR.] Used as a courtesy title or form of address.

1772 in D. Arundell *Sadler's Wells* (1965) iii. 28 Principal dancers. Sieur Daigueville and his pupils. **1893** S. WEYMAN *Gentleman of France* I. iii. 66 You have not told me yet, sieur, where we stay to-night. **1901** G. B. SHAW *Admirable Bashville* III. 124 Bumpkin Fitz Algernon de Courcy Cashel Byron, sieur of Park Lane and overlord of Dorset. **1981** P. VANSITTART *Death of Robin Hood* II. ii. 40 John's dwarf, Sieur Marc,..now discarded winter as he might a cloak.

|| **sieur²** (syǒı). *S. Afr.* [ad. Afrikaans *seur,* f. Du. *sinjeur* lord, master: ultimately related and assimilated to prec.] A respectful form of address or reference to a superior; master, 'sir'.

1812 A. PLUMPTRE tr. *Lichtenstein's Trav. S. Afr.* I. 118 The former [*sc.* the Hottentots] only address their master by the title of *Baas* (Master), while the slaves address him as *Sieur* (lord). **1886** G. A. FARINI *Through Kalahari Desert* 312 You ought not to have stayed here last night; the klein Sieur was very anxious. **1942** 'B. KNIGHT' *Sun climbs Slowly* xviii. 154 'Missis, *Sieur*,' she shrilled excitedly. 'The veld is on fire.' **1968** K. MCMAGH *Dinner of Herbs* 56 The maid who took the early morning coffee reported this to the sieur.

sieva (sī·vă). [Origin unknown.] A kidney bean belonging to an American variety of *Phaseolus lunatus,* or its edible seed.

1888 G. D. MERRILL *Hist. Coös County* v. 42 The Indians had..a kind of bean called now 'seiva [*sic*] bean'. **1949** *Nat. Geogr. Mag.* Aug. 159/1 The lima beans grown by the various Indian tribes..varied from the present small types used by the Hopi Indians in the Southwest to the Sieva type found in the East. **1972** Y. LOVELOCK *Veg. Bk.* I. 55 The scimitar-podded kidney bean.., also known as Hibbert, sieva or sugar bean, grows wild in tropical America and is also cultivated.

sieve, *sb.* Add: **4*.** *Math.* **a.** In full *sieve of Eratosthenes* [tr. Gr. *κόσκινον 'Ερατοσθένους,* f. the name of the Greek scientific writer of the 3rd c. B.C. who devised it]. A method of finding the prime numbers in a (usu. consecutive) list of numbers by deleting in turn all the multiples of all possible prime factors.

1803 tr. *Bossut's Gen. Hist. Math.* 18 The famous sieve of Eratosthenes..affords an easy and commodious method of finding prime numbers. **1857** *Proc. Ashmolean Soc.* III. 128 To Eratosthenes of Alexandria..is attributed the invention of the method by which the primes may successively be determined in order of magnitude. It is termed..'the sieve of Eratosthenes'. **1945** E. T. BELL *Development of Math.* (ed. 2) iv. 89 Boethius reproduced the sieve of Eratosthenes and offered some amusing trifles on figurate numbers. **1966** OGILVY & ANDERSON *Excurs. Number Theory* viii. 97 There is no known formula that turns out the prime numbers. Essentially the only way to find them is by the use of the 'sieve' devised by Eratosthenes.

b. A method of estimating or finding upper and lower limits for the number of primes, or of numbers not having factors within a stated set, that fall within a stated interval.

1897 *Nature* 6 May 10/2 (*heading*) Sieve for primes. **1952** *Proc. Internat. Congr. Mathematicians* I. 286 Ever since Viggo Brun introduced his ingenious sieve-method, it has been a very important tool in connection with problems in the theory of primes. **1972** M. N. HUXLEY (*title*) The distribution of prime numbers: large sieves and zero-density theorems.

6. a. sieve analysis, a particle-size analysis of a powdered or granular material made by passing it through sieves of increasing fineness; **sieve map,** a map upon which the distribution of a number of features is depicted by means of transparent overlays.

1928 C. C. WILEY *Princ. Highway Engin.* ii. 25 Gravel should be well graded from fine to coarse. This is determined by a sieve analysis. The sieve analysis curve for a high-grade gravel should approximate a straight line. **1971** R. HARDBOTTLE tr. *Grassmann's Physical Princ. Chem. Engin.* v. 302 Sieve analysis, in which the grains are passed in succession through sieves of various finenesses, gives directly a cumulative curve, in which..the masses or weights of the different fractions are given. [**1938** E. G. R. TAYLOR in *Geogr. Jrnl.* XCII. 25 The last map..is constructed on what I have termed the sieve method.] **1952** MONKHOUSE & WILKINSON *Maps & Diagrams* iv. 190 E. G. R. Taylor produced a map upon which all areas in Great Britain unsuitable for industrial location were indicated in solid black. These areas were determined by superimposing isopleths representing certain specific factors... This process was termed 'sieving out' and the resultant maps are sometimes referred to as 'sieve-maps'. **1965** *Listener* 27 May 774/2 When to these were added those areas of real natural beauty within the conurbation..and areas of the highest agricultural value..the result (which we called the regional sieve map) was an exceedingly complex jig-saw puzzle.

sieved (sivd), *ppl. a.* [f. SIEVE *v.* + -ED[1].] Passed through a sieve.

1949 *Nat. Geogr. Mag.* Aug. 172/2 [Kale and collards] ..in a finely chopped or 'sieved' form as food for babies. **1971** *Nature* 30 Apr. 559/2 Sanidines were extracted by elutriation of crushed and sieved pumice breccia.

Sievers (sī·vəɪz, ‖ zī·fərs), the name of Eduard *Sievers* (1850–1932), German philologist, used *attrib.* of the rule formulated by him, (*Beitr. z. Gesch. d. deutschen Sprache u. Lit.* (1878) V. 129) that in Indo-European, (post-consonantal) unaccented *i* and *u* before a vowel were consonantal after a short syllable and vocalic after a long syllable; also, this rule as modified by later scholars, or as applied by them to particular early Indo-European languages.

F. Edgerton (*Language* X (1934) 235 f. and elsewhere) played an important part in developing and modifying the rule, which is now sometimes called 'Sievers-Edgerton's Law'.

1934 *Language* X. 235 (*title*) Sievers's law and IE. weak-grade vocalism. **1939** E. PROKOSCH *Compar. Gmc. Gram.* 92 The difference in treatment according to the character of the preceding syllable..may have been Indo-European; this view was first expressed by Sievers... It is frequently referred to as 'Sievers' Law'. **1953** *Jrnl. Eng. & Gmc. Philol.* LII. 149 The essential characteristic of the P[roto-]I[ndo-]E[uropean] resonants was their threefold function as vowel, e.g. [i], consonant, [y], or vowel plus consonant [iy], as conditioned by the preceding phonemes; the description of this variation is generally known as Sievers' Law. It is most clearly apparent in our Vedic Sanskrit documents. **1959** A. CAMPBELL *Old Eng. Gram.* 164 This interchange of *i̯* and *ii̯* is called Sievers' law. **1966** M. B. EMENEAU in Birnbaum & Puhvel *Anc. Indo-Europ. Dialects* 126 While Sievers-Edgerton's law was in full working order, something other than *pūrva-* must have been the phonemic form. **1975** LASS & ANDERSON *Old Eng. Phonol.* 273 The earliest instance in Germanic..of an important role being played by the long/short syllable dichotomy, is the set of phenomena associated with the *vokalischen Auslautsgesetz* ('law of vocalic finals'), now usually called 'Sievers's Law', or the 'Sievers-Edgerton Law'.

Sievert (sī·vəɪt). The name of R. M. *Sievert*, 20th-c. Swedish radiologist, used to denote either of two units of dose of ionizing radiation. †**a.** *Sievert unit* (see quot. 1955). *Obs.* **b.** (Written *sievert.*) (See quot. 1977.)

1945 C. W. WILSON *Radium Therapy* iii. 70 For the practical determination of the Sievert unit dose by this method, the measurement is made..with a chamber having walls of a finite thickness. **1955** *Gloss. Terms Radiology* (*B.S.I.*) 19 *Sievert unit*, a unit of gamma-ray dose, being the dose of radiation delivered in one hour at a distance of 1 cm from a point source of 1 mg of radium element enclosed in platinum 0·5 mm thick. It is numerically equal to about 8·4 röntgens. **1977** *Ann. ICRP* I. III. 4/1 The special name for the unit of dose equivalent is the sievert (Sv): 1 Sv = 1 J kg^{-1} (= 100 rem). **1982** *Sci. Amer.* Feb. 34/2 The data come from fairly high doses of radiation (·5 sievert to two sieverts).

sif, var. *SEIF.

sifaka (sĭfæ·kă). Also **sifac.** [Malagasy.] A small arboreal primate belonging to the genus *Propithecus* of the family Indriidæ, native to Madagascar and distinguished by whitish silky fur with darker patches on the head and limbs, a hairless black face, and a long tail.

1845 *Encycl. Metrop.* XVI. 429/1 It [sc. *Cercopithecus Memæus* Cuv.] is a native of Cochin China and Madagascar, where it is called *Sifac.* **1901** W. RICE *Animals* 37 A smaller indri with a long tail is the sifaka, the native name of a pretty animal which..goes about by day in bands of six or eight. **1930** *Times Educ. Suppl.* 1 Mar. (Home & Classroom Suppl.) p. ix/2 The monkey-lemurs, or sifakas, are purely arboreal. **1961** *Listener* 2 Nov. 709/1 A sifaka lemur seen in David Attenborough's 'Zoo Quest to Madagascar'. **1978** *Nature* 19 Oct. 587/1 White sifaka and ringtailed lemur populations have remained stable since 1963 in the privately protected 100-hectare reserve at Berenty.

siff, var. *SYPH.

1947 C. WILLINGHAM *End as Man* ii. 18 Why don't you tell us about that time you got siff from your nigger maid? **1971** B. W. ALDISS *Soldier Erect* 157 Them mankey whores in yon knocking-shop'll give you a dose as soon as look at you. There's no' a one of them as isn't rotten with siff.

siffleur (sĭflör). Also †*erron. pl.* **siffleux.** [Fr., lit. a whistler.] **1.** *Canad.* One of several animals that make a whistling noise, esp. the hoary marmot, *Marmota caligata*, or its flesh used as food. Cf. WHISTLER 2 b.

1703 tr. *La Hontan's New Voy. N. Amer.* I. 62 Certain little Beasts, call'd Siffleurs, or Whistlers. **1808** S. FRASER *Jrnl.* 18 June (1960) 86 They gave us a *siffleur* (marmot) which is the first fresh meat we tasted since our departure. **1858** J. PALLISER *Jrnl.* 22 Aug. in *Palliser Papers* (1968) 274 The only animal which we have seen is the siffleur, whose shrill whistle we heard for the first time close to our encampment. **1898** F. RUSSELL *Expl. Far North* 249 Ground squirrels or 'siffleux' as they are known to the Company's people, are a characteristic feature of the barren portions of Arctic America. **1949** *Canad. Alpine Jrnl.* May 32 They dined on 'delicious siffleur' which tasted on the tongue like 'very delicate mutton or the fat of sucking pig'. **1968** R. M. PATTERSON *Finlay's River* 209 La Guarde shot a couple of siffleurs—marmots or whistlers—lean, miserable things at that season.

2. (with fem. *-euse*). One who entertains professionally by whistling.

1827 T. DIBDIN *Reminiscences* II. vi. 122 The following is from a celebrated *siffleur*:..'I Take the Liberty of Inclosing a few Lines, to Inform you that I am a Beautyfull Whistler If you Please to Give Me one Trial on the Stage.' **1912** *Music Hall & Theatre Review* 11 Jan. 31/1 'Who is He', a clever siffleur, charms everyone with his mimicry of birds. **1981** *Times* 26 Feb. 13/1 Melba's friend Adeline Murrelli was not a singer but that almost forgotten artist, a siffleuse, or whistler.

sift, *sb.* **3.** (Examples.)

1876 G. M. HOPKINS *Wr. Deutschland* iv, in *Poems* (1967) 52, I am soft sift In an hourglass. **1962** M. E. MURIE *Far North* II. ix. 192 The little sift of snow on the ice was marked only by tracks of ox.

sig, *sb.* Add: **2.** A solution applied to the grain side of leather before it is stained black. ? *Obs.*

1897 C. T. DAVIS *Manuf. Leather* (ed. 2) 623 In the making of 'sig' stains, blacks and pastes for leather, borax is the currier's friend. **1900** H. C. STANDAGE *Leather Worker's Manual* iv. 69 *Seasoning for Oil-Grain Leathers*—This is sometimes called 'sig'. It is a fluid which is put onto the skin, so as to dye or stain it, or otherwise prepare it for being blackened on the grain side. **1903** L. A. FLEMMING *Pract. Tanning* 51 A good 'sig' is made of forty gallons of water, twelve pounds of salts of tartar, five pounds of bichromate of potash and one quart of ammonia.

sig., abbrev. of SIGNATURE. (Examples.)

1866 G. SIMPSON *Let.* 30 May in *Geo. Eliot Lett.* (1956) IV. 263 Vol. II. is on the Machines up to Sig. K. 9 and the whole of it will be on to morrow. **1959** *N. & Q.* Dec. 461/1 In the Preface to the Lay-Reader of Richard Baxter's *Gildas Salvianus: The Reformed Pastor* (1656), sig. C. 8, the following passage occurs. **1972** P. GASKELL *New Introd. Bibliogr.* 99 (*caption*) Sheet of duodecimo.. with two signatures..(12° in 8s and 4s, 2 sigs.).

Sigatoka (siŋgătō^u·kă). Also **Sing-.** [Name of the district of Fiji where the disease was first observed.] Used *attrib.* and *absol.* to designate a disease of banana plants caused by the fungus *Cercospora musæ*, characterized by the appearance on the leaves of elongated spots, followed by rotting of the entire leaves.

1925 *Agric. Circular Dept. Agric. Fiji* V. 68 Sigatoka Disease—This is by far the most important of the banana diseases of Fiji. **1958** *New Scientist* 26 June 258/1 Sigatoka has spread to virtually all the banana growing areas since it was discovered in 1903. **1963** A. BURNS *Fiji* II. iii. 197 Leaf-spot disease, which affects bananas in various parts of the world, is often referred to as Singatoka Disease, because it was first identified in the Singatoka area of Viti Levu. **1972** C. W. WARDLAW *Banana Dis.* xi. 314 In Fiji, it became notorious in 1913 in the Sigatoka valley —hence the name 'Sigatoka Disease' or simply 'Sigatoka'.

sigh, *sb.* **3.** *sigh-like* (later examples).

1911 J. A. THOMSON *Biol. of Seasons* II. 193 When the young bird appears to be contented and very comfortable, it utters a plaintive, almost sigh-like cheep. **1964** J. C. CATFORD in D. Abercrombie et al. *Daniel Jones* 32 Auditory effect, 'sigh-like' mixture of breath and voice: one form of voiced [h].

sigh, *v.* Add: **3. c.** With cognate obj.

1789 BLAKE *Songs Innoc.* f. 6, Think not, thou canst sigh a sigh, And thy maker is not by. **1847** C. BRONTE *J. Eyre* II. ii. 37 She sighed a sigh of ineffable satisfaction, as if her cup of happiness were now full. **1888** MRS. H. WARD *R. Elsmere* III. xli. 225 Robert sighed a long sigh.

sighfully, *adv.* (Later examples.)

1905 W. J. LOCKE *Morals Marcus Ordeyne* x. 213 My aunt sighfully acquiesced, and for a while we discussed the depravity of human nature. **1925** T. DREISER *Amer. Trag.* (1926) II. III. xxv. 321 And here he wearily and sighfully drew forth his large white handkerchief once more.

sight, *sb.*[1] Add: **I. 1. d.** In colloq. phr. *a sight for sore eyes*: a person or thing one is glad to see, esp. a welcome visitor.

[**1738** SWIFT *Polite Conv.* I. 7 The Sight of you is good for sore Eyes.] **1826** HAZLITT in *New Monthly Mag.* XVI. 38 Garrick's name was..proposed..on condition he should act in tragedy and comedy... What a *sight for sore eyes* that would be! **1871** *Monthly Pkt.* Christmas 108 You're a sight for sair ee'n the now! I'm just aboot in the awfuest swither ever a body was. **1897** R. MARSH *Crime & Criminal* xxiii. 192 He was a sight for sore eyes... I like to see a man that is a man. **1931** E. O'NEILL *Mourning becomes Electra* (1932) 125 You certainly are a sight for sore eyes, Vinnie! **1973** *People's Jrnl.* (Inverness) 28 July 4/5 Elizabeth..and Sheena had done wonders,.. and the buffet was a sight for sore eyes.

e. Something which calls forth contemptuous, horrified, or amused glances; a shocking, repulsive, or ridiculous spectacle. *colloq.*

[**1694** W. PENN *Rise of Quakers* ii. 53 It was not very easie to our Primitive Friends, to make themselves Sights and Spectacles, and the Scorn and Derision of the World.] **1862** F. W. ROBINSON *Owen* II. v. iv. 288 I'm getting better now,..I was a sight last week. **1911** M. BEERBOHM *Zuleika Dobson* xx. 296 Clarence curbed the brotherly intention of telling her she looked 'a sight' in them. **1940** W. FAULKNER *Hamlet* III. i. 229 'Aint he a sight now,' Snopes cackled.

f. *sight unseen*: without previous inspection, without seeing the object to be acquired. orig. *U.S.*

1892 *Dialect Notes* I. 231 To trade knives *sight unseen* is to swap without seeing each other's knife. **1898** *Yearbk. U.S. Dept. Agric. 1897* 427 The intelligent farmer of to-day has got beyond trading 'sight unseen' or 'buying a cat in a bag' when it comes to fertilizers. **1940** F. D. DAVISON *Woman at Mill* 94, I learned that he had selected sight-unseen, that he had now come to look over his property for the first time. **1962** V. NABOKOV *Pale Fire* 82, I have had occasion to say something about the amenities of my habitation. The charming, charmingly vague lady ..who secured it for me, sight unseen, meant well, no doubt. **1968** *Listener* 7 Mar. 303, I said you were mad to advertise our modest needs—sight unseen—in the New Statesman. **1979** *Daily Tel.* 3 Feb. 34/2, I am recommending this [TV film], sight unseen, because the first offering in the series..was so good.

2. b. (Further examples.)

1931 R. CAMPBELL *Georgiad* i. 12 He could be..heterosexual with either, too—A damn sight more than you or I could do! **1958** *Times* 16 Oct. 17/1 Surrey..will have to do a sight better than they did yesterday if they are to make their presence fittingly felt in the current Rugby Union county championship. **1977** 'E. CRISPIN' *Glimpses of Moon* xii. 241 Be a sight cooler there than it is here, I reckon. **1979** C. P. SNOW *Coat of Varnish* xvi. 133 Money might be fun, but if I had to choose I'd a damn sight rather try for the top jobs.

c. Phr. *by a long, damn,* etc., *sight*, by a long way, by a good deal (usu. in negative contexts). *U.S. colloq.*

1834 C. A. DAVIS *Lett. J. Downing* 41 'General, do you want another report?' 'Not by a darn'd sight.' **1840** *Niles' Register* 9 May 149/2 He asked him if he was not going for Harrison and the whigs. 'No,' said he, 'not by a d—d sight.' **1844** *Republican Sentinel* (Richmond, Va.) 22 June 1/2 These animals begin to venture out a little of nights, since the Baltimore Convention, but are slyer by a long sight than foxes. **1884** 'MARK TWAIN' *Huck. Finn* i. 5, I asked her if she reckoned Tom Sawyer would go there, and she said not by a considerable sight. **1894** —— in *Century Mag.* Mar. 779/2 It ain't on'y jist Essex blood dat's in you, not by a long sight. **1931** E. O'NEILL *Mourning becomes Electra* (1932) 248 But I don't wish to convey that he approves of all I've set down—not by a damned sight! **1959** E. POUND *Thrones* ciii. 88 But not his fault by a damn sight. **1976** M. MACHLIN *Pipeline* xxii. 272 The excitement ain't through here by a damn sight.

II. 5. e. *Poker.* A show of hands; *spec.* one called for by a player who has insufficient chips or money to equal another's bet, but bets as much as he can. *U.S.*

1821 G. LONG *Hoyle's Games Improved* 162 The youngest hand..may *call a sight*... If he *calls a sight* the cards must be shown in rotation, the player who calls showing last, and the best hand shown wins the pool. **1850** H. G. BOHN *Bohn's New Hand-bk. Games* 381 Should one of the party over-reach the amount that is in possession of an adversary, a '*sight*' may be demanded. **1887** *Courier-Jrnl.* (Louisville, Kentucky) 23 Jan. 15/7 Then a rule sprang up that a man should be allowed a sight for his money. **1940** O. JACOBY *On Poker* 150 Even though a player's hand is beaten in sight, he should make no move to fold it except in his proper turn. **1964** E. SINCLAIR *Poker* v. 142 If a player who is beaten in sight bets against the cinch hand, he will be allowed to withdraw his bet from the pot after his attention had been drawn to the fact that he is beaten in sight.

f. A sale of packets of uncut diamonds.

1940 *Economist* 2 Mar. 385/1 A significant hint on the likely evolution of the British exchange control technique was provided last week on the occasion of the latest diamond 'sights' held in London. **1966** J. WAINWRIGHT *Crystallised Carbon Pig* xv. 74 The Diamond Corporation hold monthly 'sights'—auctions, I suppose you could call them. They sell anything between three million and five million pounds' worth of stones at each 'sight'. **1978** *Times* 9 Mar. 23/6 The rough gems are sold by the CSO at 10 'sights' (sales) a year... London holds the most important sights.

7. a. For 'Now *rare*' read 'Now *rare* except in slang phr. *to take sights*, to observe, to watch.' (Further examples.)

1934 P. ALLINGHAM *Cheapjack* xiv. 175 He pointed out a Rolls-Royce which stopped at the entrance of the fair... 'Take sights at that Rolls,' he said. 'There'll be some right mugs turn up in a minute.' **1950** R. M. HOWE *Gross's Criminal Investigation* (ed. 4) viii. 163/1 *Take sights*, looking out (especially for suitable house to break into). **1962** *New Statesman* 21 Dec. 897/3 Once we have all this information, we start 'taking sights', and this means watching the house, from the grounds, for the best part of a week.

b. (Earlier example.)

1834 *Reg. Deb. Congr. U.S.* 25 Feb. 691, I supposed for once in my life I saw gentlemen in the open field, and might be able to draw a fine sight upon them.

d. (Example.)

1848 BARTLETT *Dict. Amer.* 303 In North Carolina the distance that can be seen on a road is called a *sight.*

III. 8. b. With definite article, *spec.* = SECOND SIGHT. Chiefly *Sc.*

1924 W. HOLTBY *Crowded Street* xxix. 195 They say she's got the 'sight'—you know, second sight. **1925** W. DUKE *Scotland's Heir* x. 223 At the last the Sight came upon him, and he reared upright, crying with outflung arms that he saw bloody claymores. **1959** E. H. CLEMENTS *High Tension* v. 80 The factor stared at him. 'Why, Kilmorrin ,you have the sight!' **1977** C. MCCARRY *Secret*

Lovers x. 129, I do believe you see me in everything I do. If you haven't the sight, then what is the explanation?

c. Contrasted with *faith*.

c **1382** BIBLE (Wyclif) *2 Cor.* v. 7 For we walken bi feith, and not bi cleer siȝt. **1611** *Ibid.* (A.V.), For we walke by faith, not by sight. **1834** J. H. NEWMAN *Parochial Sermons* I. xvii. 258 And all these inducements to live by sight and not by faith are greatly increased, when men are engaged in any pursuit which properly *belongs* to the intellect. **1858** W. BROCK *Sir H. Havelock* xiii. 216 He might well have doubted of success had he walked by sight. **1871** H. ALFORD in *Hymns Anc. & Mod.* (1875) 285/1 Forward, marching eastward Where the heaven is bright, Till the veil be lifted, Till our faith be sight. **1981** M. GREEN *I believe in Satan's Downfall* vii. 201 To walk by sight would be the very antithesis of the trusting walk of faith to which God's Messiah, along with all men, was called.

10. b. See also *OUT-OF-SIGHT *adj. phr.* (*sb.*).

11. c. *line of sight* (further examples); also *transf.* with reference to the transmission of radio waves, etc.; freq. *attrib.* (with hyphens); *line-of-sight velocity* = **radial velocity*.

1920 A. S. EDDINGTON *Space, Time & Gravitation* viii. 135 In the case of the sun we know by other evidence exactly what the line-of-sight velocity should be; but we have not this knowledge for other stars. **1955** *Times* 18 July 8/2 The others [*sc.* ways of transmitting radio waves], employing in one case 'very high', and in the other 'ultra high' frequencies, are extremely reliable but until now they have been limited to line-of-sight transmission. **1956** H. S. JONES in A. Pryce-Jones *New Outl. Mod. Knowledge* 129 When the first measurements of the line-of-sight velocities of some of these objects [*sc.* spiral nebulae] were made, they were found to be surprisingly large. **1963** G. TROUP *Masers & Lasers* (ed. 2) ix. 158 Infra-red masers might be applied to line-of-sight terrestrial communications. **1972** *Sci. Amer.* Feb. 76/1 Microwave radio links are limited to line-of-sight operation.

IV. 14. b. Also, a telescopic device or other optical aid designed for this purpose; *in one's sights*, visible through the sights of one's gun; also *fig.*, esp. in phr. *to raise one's sights*, to adopt a more ambitious objective.

1942 T. RATTIGAN *Flare Path* I. 20 I've got 'im in my sights, and 'e's getting bigger all the time. **1950** *Economist* 9 Dec. 1002/2 The United States must now raise its sights, in terms of both manpower and production. **1956** A. H. COMPTON *Atomic Quest* 151 Colonel Marshall..had helped greatly in raising our sights as to the magnitude of the production task. *Ibid.* 339 It is in part the competition between societies that is forcing us to readjust our educational sights. **1959** *N.Z. Listener* 10 July 4/2, I did, for many months, seeing apprehensively that the Army would be raising its sights on compulsory marshalling of our manpower little by little. **1962** *Times* 26 Apr. 7/3 Set your sights a little higher than the kitchen and try to trim your appearance to the job. *Ibid.* 5 Dec. 4/3 Lawry setting his sights on a century. **1967** MRS. L. B. JOHNSON *White House Diary* 5 Dec. (1970) 596 First, he said, we have raised our sights. We have set our national goals to have a clean country. **1971** *Nature* 31 Dec. 499/2 Two years ago, the Government Actuary was estimating that the population would have grown from 56 million at present to..68 million by the turn of the century, but he has since been forced by more recent trends to lower his sights. **1976** J. SNOW *Cricket Rebel* 35 They were not Gloucestershire batsmen at the other end of my sights that day but the England selectors.

c. Any of a number of nails in the sides and ends of a billiard table, used in marking out the table for some forms of carom billiards.

1864 W. B. DICK *Amer. Hoyle* 419 A line is drawn down the centre of the table, from the centre nails or sights in the *head* and *lower* cushions. **1890** CHAMPLIN & BOSTWICK *Cycl. Games & Sports* 81/1 Each carom table has on it two spots, along an imaginary line drawn lengthways through the centre from the middle rails or 'sights' in the head and lower cushions: the first, opposite the second 'sight', is sometimes called the light red spot, the second, opposite the sixth 'sight', the dark red spot. **1910** *Encycl. Brit.* III. 939/1 In the case of the Triangular Baulk-line, lines are drawn at the four corners from the second 'sight' on the side-rails to the first sight on the end-rails, forming four triangles within which only a limited number of caroms may be made.

V. 16. a. *sight-seeker* (earlier example).

1814 F. BURNEY *Let.* 24 Aug. (1978) VII. 438 But for Heaven's sake send him no more sight-seekers, who expect 'The Hero' to give dinners, & shew Lyons!

b. *sight-piece* (earlier example).

1835 C. F. HOFFMAN *Winter in West* II. 171 The long western rifle has three sight-pieces on the barrel.

c. In terms relating to the practice of watching the keys of a typewriter while typing, as *sight method, system, technique, typing, typist, writer, writing*. Cf. *touch-typing*, etc. s.v. *TOUCH-.

1904 A. E. MORTON *Mod. Typewriting* (ed. 2) 12 There are two methods of manipulation, one the 'touch', and the other the 'sight' system. **1918** M. B. OWEN *Typewriting Speed* 145 The constant shifting of the eyes in sight writing. *Ibid.* 147 The sight typist writes spasmodically. *Ibid.* 153 Many sight writers use all the fingers. **1928** M. CROOKS *Touch Typewriting for Teachers* ii. 10 A typist writing by the Sight method expends about six times as much..energy..as that expended by the Touch typist. *Ibid.* 11 The properly trained Touch typist is capable of greater speed than the Sight typist. **1935** A. C. MARSHALL *Princ. Teaching Typewriting* i. 1 It is..hardly necessary now to advocate the 'touch' system as against 'sight-typing'. *Ibid.* 2 The maximum speed ever attained by a sight-typist has never exceeded 60 per cent of that of equivalent touch experts. **1969** L. J. WEST *Acquisition of Typewriting Skills* viii. 183 Will not early sight typists form a habit of sight typing?..How does one wean learners away from sight techniques?

17. sight bar, a metal bar forming part of the breech-sight of a gun; **sight bill** *U.S.*, a bill of exchange payable on presentation; **sight-board** = *sight-screen* below; **sight cheque, draft** *U.S.*, a cheque or draft payable on presentation; **sight edge** *Naut.*, (see quot. 1948); **sight feed,** a device through which the feeding of lubricant or fuel may be seen; also (with hyphen) *attrib.*; **sight gag,** a joke which achieves its effect visually; **sight-holder,** a diamond merchant entitled to buy diamonds at a sight (see sense 5 f above); **sight liability,** an obligation to pay money on presentation of a cheque or bill of exchange; **sight-line,** (*a*) (see sense 16 b in Dict.); (*b*) a straight line extending from the eye of a spectator to an object or area being watched; *spec.* a line from the eye of a spectator in a theatre to the edge of the part of the stage which that spectator can see; **sight-player,** one who is able to play music at sight; so **sight-playing; sight-read** *v. intr.* and *trans.*, to read (a piece of music) at sight; **sight record** *Ornith.*, a record of the sighting (not the capture) of a bird; **sight-screen** = *SCREEN *sb.*^{1} 1 h; **sight-setter,** on a warship, a member of a gun-crew whose duty is to keep the gun-sight at the correct elevation as shown by the range indicator (see also quot. 1973); **sight tube,** (*a*) a tube through which observations are made; (*b*) a transparent tube connected to a tank or cistern so as to display the level of the liquid inside it.

1884 *Naval Encycl.* 751/2 *Sight-bar*, a metal bar on which the range in yards, or in degrees, is marked. It is a part of the breech-sight, and, by raising or lowering it, different ranges are obtained. **1920** CARTER & ARNOLD *Field Artillery Instruction* iii. 47 The rocking bar sight consists of a rocking bar..and a sight bar. **1853** *Southern Literary Messenger* XIX. 89/2 Mr. Thompson agreed to accommodate him with a sight bill on his correspondent in Raleigh. **1887** *Courier-Jrnl.* (Louisville, Kentucky) 5 May 7/3 Eastern exchange was firm, and there were more buyers than sellers of New York sight bills at 80c per $1,000 premium. **1898** K. S. RANJITSINHJI *With Stoddart's Team* (ed. 4) iii. 49 [At Adelaide] the sight-boards behind the bowler's arm appeared to be but reminders of the existence of such things for a better purpose in England. **1955** MILLER & WHITTINGTON *Cricket Typhoon* I. i. 13 Tiny white pavilion and tinier white sight-boards. **1975** N. NICHOLSON *Wednesday Early Closing* vi. 129 Every..excuse for hindrance and delay was..tried—asking for the sight-boards to be moved,..looking round at the fielders, testing the bat. **1863** 'E. KIRKE' *My Southern Friends* xxii. 232, I enclose you sight check of Branch Bank of Cape Fear on Bank of Republic, for $10,820. **1850** G. N. JONES *Florida Plantation Rec.* (1927) 60 Your favor of the 22nd ult. enclosing sight draft on Messrs Habersham for $200. **1904** 'O. HENRY' *Cabbages & Kings* xiv. 254 It's a gold mine. It's a sight-draft on your president man for twenty thousand dollars. **1979** O. SELA *Petrograd Consignment* 34 At the bank..letters of authority were presented, mandates altered and instructions given for the preparation of sight drafts. **1911** *Encycl. Brit.* XXIV. 971/1 The projections of the plate and longitudinal sight edges are drawn in the body plan on the floor. **1948** R. DE KERCHOVE *Internat. Maritime Dict.* 676/2 *Sight edge*, the edges of the plates, in clinker-built plating, which are visible on the outside of the shell, on the top of decks and tank top, and on the opposite side from the stiffeners on bulkheads. **1888** *Lockwood's Dict. Mech. Engin.* 319 *Sight feed lubricator*, a lubricator..in which the flowing or non-flowing of the oil is always apparent at sight, being enclosed in, or having to pass through a glass vessel. **1902** A. C. HARMSWORTH et al. *Motors* ix. 172 If a Dubrulle mechanical lubricator is used, examine the ball valves sometimes, and do not trust entirely to the sight feed. **1928** *Daily Tel.* 16 Oct. 7 Non-crushable backlamps and sight-feed fuel gauges on the dashboard are in demand for the new cars. **1957** *N.Y. Herald Tribune* 7 Nov. 24/4 The line gags are like the sight gags: they're not quite sturdy enough to be up and around yet. **1977** *Time* 2 May 49/3 *I Love My Wife*..is dotted with paralyzingly funny sight gags. **1973** *Times* 19 June (Bombay Suppl.) p. xii/3 Bombay has at least 2,000 diamond businesses, of which about 1,400 are members of the Diamond Merchants' Association. Of these 43 are 'sight-holders' of the Diamond Trading Company of London, which means that they are notified of the 10 'sightings' which the DTC holds every year. The sight-holders are the only people in India to whom the DTC will sell. **1930** *Economist* 27 Sept. 556/2 It may be desirable to modify present standards as regards the ratio of gold cover to notes and sight liabilities. **1958** *Spectator* 24 Jan. 97/2 The proportion of sight-liabilities covered by reserves is no better than in 1945. **1917** E. B. KINSILA *Mod. Theatre Construction* iv. 60 One of the most important requisites in designing an auditorium is the establishment of correct sight lines. **1957** J. OSBORNE *Entertainer* 11 The sight-lines are preserved by swagging. **1958** *Archit. Rev.* CXXIII. 352/2 The second case [for the substitution of wire fence for hedgerow] is to provide sightlines at corners. **1971** P. GRESSWELL *Environment* 264 Sight lines have to be kept open at bends and corners. **1975** I. MELCHIOR *Sleeper Agent* (1976) II. 65 He positioned himself so that he had optimum sight lines down the side street. **1977** *Time Out* 28 Jan.–3 Feb. 43/2 Check seating plan before buying tickets as many seats have restricted sight lines. **1909** *Chambers's Jrnl.* May 334/2 Ask an accomplished sight-player how he is able to translate so readily the symbols he reads with the eye into their relative notes. *Ibid.* 334/1 He maintains that sight-playing does not depend upon an accurate knowledge of the relationship between notes and keys. **1944** W. APEL *Harvard Dict. Music* 680/1 The greatest enemy of sight-playing is playing by heart. **1903** A. W. PATTERSON *Schumann* 181 We want more than a facility to 'sight read' in order to fully comprehend. **1959** 'F. NEWTON' *Jazz Scene* ii. 30 Jazz cannot at present be adequately noted down on paper, and if it could, would almost certainly be far too complex for players to sight-read. **1974** *Guardian* 22 Mar. 14/4 Paul Beard, the [orchestra] leader, asked him whether he would like to stay on, making him sight-read part of Vaughan Williams's Fourth Symphony as an audition. **1934** *Brit. Birds* XXVIII. 31 All but one of these are 'sight-records', but in some cases the writer had already made the acquaintance of the species in other lands. **1959** D. A. BANNERMAN *Birds Brit. Isles* VIII. 35 A sight-record of a frigate bird observed off the south-west coast of Ireland on 25th May 1953 by W. K. Richmond, was published in the *Fair Isle Bulletin*. **1956** N. CARDUS *Close of Play* 20 The sixth ball..was fielded on the boundary's edge at the sight-screen behind MacDonald's arm. **1977** T. HEALD *Just Desserts* v. 92 At either end of the ground were white sightscreens on wheels. **1909** *Cent. Dict.* Suppl., Sight-setter. **1916** 'TAFFRAIL' *Pincher Martin* xvi. 307 Some order came through a voice-pipe to the gun; whereupon the sight-setter twiddled a small wheel and peered anxiously at a graduated dial. **1920** *Blackw. Mag.* Mar. 332/2 Dully from the concealed gun positions echoed the calls of the sight-setters. **1973** J. QUICK *Dict. Weapons & Military Terms* 400/1 *Sight setter*, the gun-crew member who sets the range and deflection data ordered by the officer controlling the fire. **1851** H. MELVILLE *Moby Dick* III. xxxviii. 221 The crushed copper sight-tubes of the quadrant. **1859** *Times* 7 Jan. 8/4 He can enter an enemy's harbour under water and make surveys, only showing above the surface a sight tube, no more than one half inch in diameter, and retire still under water. **1900** W. M. STINE *Photometrical Measurements* iii. 77 Adjust the telescopic sight tube until the different portions of the field are sharply outlined. **1905** *Motor Manual* (ed. 7) iv. 78 The oil..enters a series of sight tubes. **1951** *Proc. Physical Soc.* B. LXIV. 49 The level of the liquid in the annular gap can be deduced from observations of its level in a vertical sight-tube attached to the filling apparatus.

sight, *v.*^{1} Add: **2. c.** To take aim at (an object); to level or aim (a fire-arm, etc.) at a target.

1871 *Harper's Mag.* Dec. 48/2 No sooner, however, did he 'sight', or try to sight, the horseman in question,..than the thumping against the ribs again began. **1901** F. NORRIS *Octopus* II. vi. 521 With the words, he dropped to one knee, and sighting his rifle carefully, fired into the group of armed men. **1976** D. STOREY *Saville* I. iv. 36 Take out the bullets, and sight it at various objects outside the window.

3. a. (Earlier example.)

1787 in *Maryland Hist. Mag.* (1924) XIX. 265 The mother of the complainants wife sighted with a compass from the tree.

b. With *in*. To correct the sights of (a fire-arm, etc.) by testing and adjustment. *N. Amer.*

1958 *Washington Post* 31 Oct. D6/3 The Berwyn Rod & Gun Club invites deer hunters to sight-in their rifles during all-day open house sessions on Nov. 2 and Nov. 9. **1971** W. HILLEN *Blackwater River* x. 91, I started him off right by sighting-in his new rifle, and soon he was hitting the apple box every time. **1972** *Islander* (Victoria, B.C.) 24 Sept. 13/1 Heading into the woods with a rifle that hasn't been sighted-in makes no more sense than driving an automobile without a gasoline gauge. **1980** *Outdoor Life* (U.S.) (Northeast ed.) Oct. 94/3 A Leupold 4X compact scope (made specially for the Kimber rifle) mounted and sighted in at the factory.

sighter. Add: **3.** Also *transf.* and *fig.*

1920 G. S. GORDON *Let.* 17 Sept. (1943) 139 You were charming about my article... Richmond, in a brief post-card, called the thing a 'bull's-eye'. I call it a sighter; and some day I shall have the second shot. **1960** *Times* 11 Apr. 3/7 An early sighter by Albaladejo gave some inkling of what was in store in the matter of dropped goals.

sighting, *vbl. sb.*^{1} Add: **2.** Also, an instance of catching sight of (esp. something rare or unusual).

1955 W. GIRVAN *Flying Saucers & Common Sense* i. 13 It was not long before sightings were being reported elsewhere than in Scandinavia. **1968** *Listener* 4 July 18/2 Our objection is against the extraterrestrial origin of the phenomena, and most of us base our disbelief on the very large number of 'sightings' that have been reported. **1976** *Scotsman* 15 Dec. 9/4 The experiment to reintroduce the white-tailed eagle to the Isle of Rhum National Nature Reserve is reported to be going well, with sightings of the released birds.

3. b. *sighting-in*, the action of correcting the sights of a fire-arm, etc. Cf. *SIGHT *v.*^{1} 3 b. *N. Amer.*

1958 *Washington Post* 31 Oct. D6/3 (*heading*) 2 Days are Set for Sighting-In. **1962** *Wildlife Rev.* Dec. 9 The opening of a sighting-in range at Maiden Creek some 12 miles north of Cache Creek has been welcomed with enthusiasm by sportsmen. **1970** R. A. STEINDLER *Firearms Dict.* 229/1 *Sighting-in*, process of adjusting the sights, usually the rear one, or the elevation..& windage.. adjustments of a scope, so that the bullet will hit a predetermined point of aim on the target at a specific distance. Much of the trial & error method of sighting-in a rifle can be eliminated by the use of a collimator.

4. *sighting-hood, -tube.*

1909 *Cent. Dict.* Suppl. 1217/1 Modern turrets usually have three sighting-hoods, one in the center line for the turret training-pointer and one on each side for the two gun-pointers. **1973** J. QUICK *Dict. Weapons & Military Terms* 400/1 *Sighting hood*, an armored hood with viewing slits in the sides, as on the top of a turret, a submarine, etc. **1946** *Nature* 12 Oct. 518/2 Radiation from a 5 sq. mm. area of tyre falls on to the cell via an arrangement which comprises a water-cooled copper sighting-tube and a rotating slotted disk which serves as the radiation chopper. **1958** J. NEEDHAM in *Aspects of Translation* 86 And there are holes which take the place of the sighting-tube for looking up (at the heavenly bodies).

sight-see, *v.* Add: **1.** (Earlier and later examples.)

1824 R. HEBER *Narr. Journey Upper Provinces India* (1828) I. xii. 302, I had been sight-seeing from five till nearly ten o'clock. **1913** E. WHARTON *Custom of Country* xxx. 412 'I suppose you've been to that old church over there?'.. 'Oh, of course; when I used to sightsee. Have you never been to Paris before?' **1925** C. CONNOLLY *Let.* 28 Feb. in *Romantic Friendship* (1975) 61 Nor is there anywhere near to tempt one to sightsee. **1976** *Church Times* 30 July 7/3 It seems to me infinitely more absurd —if art and architecture mean anything to you at all, and if you can sight-see in reasonably unhurried and uncongested comfort—*not* to want to see the best in this line that civilisation has to offer. **1979** R. JAFFE *Class Reunion* II. v. 168 'And then I thought I'd just sightsee.' Dutifully she told him everything she had seen.

2. *trans.* To visit the principal sights of (a place).

1968 J. WAINWRIGHT *Web of Silence* 109, I spent the day sight-seeing Berlin. **1976** *New Yorker* 29 Mar. 95/2 (Advt.), Meet the chefs, inspect kitchens, plus sightsee the highlights from Cortina to Rome. **1977** *Daily Colonist* (Victoria, B.C.) 19 June 25/3 Macao is only 2½ miles long. Has 300,000 people. You sightsee it in an hour.

sight-seeing, *vbl. sb.* (Earlier example.)

1824 R. HEBER *Narr. Journey Upper Provinces India* 1828) I. xv. 380 Morning rides, evening sight-seeing.

attrib. (Earlier and later examples.)

1827 MRS. B. HALL *Let.* 13 Dec. in *Aristocratic Journey* (1931) 146 This has been another regular sight-seeing day. **1916** *Daily Colonist* (Victoria, B.C.) 9 July 6/3 The picnic party left the Gorge terminus during the early forenoon in the special sight-seeing car of the B.C. Electric Railway. **1925** C. MORLEY *Thunder on Left* xiii. 170 People were always driving up in crowds to visit his secrets. Like sight-seeing busses loaded with excursionists. **1976** *National Observer* (U.S.) 30 Oct. 5/1, I spotted an empty sightseeing bus moving slowly up Collins Avenue.

sight-seer. (Earlier example.)

1834 G. CRABBE JUN. in *Poet. Wks. G. Crabbe* I. viii. 207 A friend in town procured us those very eligible rooms for sight-seers, in Osborne's Hotel, Adelphi.

‖ **sigillata** (sidʒilēⁱ·tă, sigilā·tă). Also **Sigillata.** [L., = sealed: see TERRA SIGILLATA.] = *TERRA SIGILLATA 3. Also *attrib.*

1903 *Amer. Jrnl. Archaeol.* VII. 485 This study of the origin of the Gallo-Roman *sigillata* is preliminary to a complete publication. **1936** J. H. ILIFFE (*title*) Sigillata wares in the Near East. **1938** *Burlington Mag.* Jan. p. xiv/2 Southern Spain has already been known as one of the chief pottery centres of the Roman Empire... But that 'sigillata-ware' was actually made there is not so clear. **1948** *Proc. Prehistoric Soc.* XIV. 79 Sea-borne trade with the Province is shown by a sherd of Sigillata. **1966** G. SIMPSON in Oswald & Pryce *Introd. Study of Terra Sigillata* (ed. 2) p. iii, No attempt was made originally to give an exhaustive description of varieties of Sigillata which had no definite chronological value.

sigillum. For *rare*⁻¹ read *rare* and add: **2.** *R. C. Ch.* The seal of confession. Cf. SEAL *sb.*² 2 b.

1927 F. A. MARKS tr. *Kurtscheid's Hist. Seal of Confession* 1 Since the Middle Ages we have for this obligation the technical term Seal of Confession (*sigillum, signaculum confessionis*). **1937** S. O'FAOLÁIN *Purse of Coppers* 49 To add to his difficulty—for it was no help to know what, under the *sigillum*, he must pretend not to know—he had just been told in the sacristy by her employer that a pair of her best boots was missing.

3. A sign or symbol; an abbreviation; an identifying character.

1966 B. MALAMUD *Fixer* iii. 83 Please note, if you will, the sigillum on my coat lapel. **1978** *Language* LIV. 5 The true picture of dialect classification, either regionally or socially, is not known; nor is it implied by the sigilla of *DED*.

SIGINT, Sigint (si·gint), abbrev. of *signal(s) intelligence* s.v. *SIGNAL *sb.* 5 e.

1969 THOMAS & CROWLEY *New Acronyms & Initialisms 1969* 376 SIGINT, Signal Intelligence (Military). **1972** *New Scientist* 2 Mar. 467 Generally speaking the larger part of the staff of all Sigint headquarters consists of scientists and engineers. Apart from actual cryptanalysis, there is a continuing need to improve intercept equipment. **1976** *Time Out* 21 May 8/2 Each country's signals intelligence (SIGINT) agency has authority to monitor communications in one area. **1979** J. BARNETT *Backfire is Hostile!* ii. 29 She was in charge of Sigint... Signals intelligence. **1980** J. MCNEIL *Spy Game* xviii. 182 What do you know about SIGINT?.. Signals Intelligence?.. You know that's the Agency's main role over here?

sigla. Add: **a.** Also *transf.* and *fig.*

1963 V. NABOKOV *Gift* ii. 86 On the soft red sand one could make out the sigla of a summer day: the imprints of a dog's paws, the beaded tracks of a wagtail. **1973** D. OSMOND-SMITH tr. *Bettetini's Lang & Technique of Film* i. 61 If this image comes to be interpreted as the *sigla* of the preconceptual schema..it will only be of value for its semantic content.

b. Editorial designations of versions of an early literary text, esp. those used in the preparation of an edition. Also *sing.* **siglum.**

1939 R. B. MCKERROW *Prolegomena for Oxf. Shakespeare* iii. 83 Round brackets enclosing a siglum are also used as a warning that the edition thus indicated has a reading which differs. **1950** *Classica et Medievalia* XI. 7, I prefer to use the same *siglum* for the New Testament and the Patrick section [of a manuscript]. **1962** E. J. DOBSON in Davis & Wrenn *Eng. & Medieval Studies* 128, I use the following sigla: A = MS. C.C.C.C. 402 (ed. J. R. R. Tolkien, E.E.T.S. 249, 1962); C = MS. Cotton Cleopatra C VI; [etc.]. *Ibid.*, References to any text other than A are preceded by the siglum of that text. **1975** *N. & Q.* Feb. 53/2 Twenty texts of the *Epistola Cuthberti* are not recorded by Dobbie. We give them below; for each of those that Brotanek enumerates we give his siglum..; we also give some versions not listed by Brotanek, with our sigla.

‖ **siglos** (si·glǫs). Pl. **sigli, sigloi.** [Gr.] **a.** A unit of weight (see quot. 1911). Also *attrib.* **b.** A silver coin of ancient Persia.

1911 *Encycl. Brit.* XIX. 871/2 The unit of weight in the East was the shekel (*siglos*)... Starting from the siglos as unit, they [*sc.* the Greeks] invented a money-mina of 50 sigli... The siglos-units..chiefly employed in Asia Minor were the following [etc.]. *Ibid.* 903/2 Darius chose two weights, the gold shekel of 8·4 grammes and the silver drachm of 5·58 grammes... The gold coin was called the daric, the silver the siglos. *Ibid.* The regal coinage is of darics..and subdivisions in gold and of sigli and subdivisions in silver. **1962** R. A. G. CARSON *Coins* 82 Both the gold darics and the silver sigloi are bean-shaped pieces with a type on obverse only and an oblong incuse on the reverse. **1962** D. HARDEN *Phoenicians* xii. 166 The Persians themselves..minted their *darics* and *sigloi* primarily for use in their Greek dominions in Asia Minor. **1972** *Oxf. Univ. Gaz.* CII. Suppl. No. 3. 46 Perhaps the most important aspect of this hoard is the inclusion of a number of worn (and countermarked) Persian sigloi.

siglum: see *SIGLA b.

sigma. Add: **3.** *Physics* and *Chem.* **a.** [After *S 5.] Used to designate electrons, orbitals, molecular states, etc., possessing zero angular momentum about an internuclear axis; *sigma-* (or *σ-*) *bond*, a bond formed by a *σ*-orbital.

Usu. written *σ* when it refers to one electron and *Σ* when it refers to a molecule as a whole.

1929, etc. [see *PI *sb.* 3]. **1939** J. W. T. SPINKS tr. *Herzberg's Diatomic Molecules* v. 260 For multiplet *Σ* states the character positive-negative depends on whether *K*..is even or odd. **1952** L. N. FERGUSON *Electron Structures of Org. Molecules* ii. 21 In butadiene, each carbon atom forms three *σ* bonds. **1963** W. J. MOORE *Physical Chem.* (ed. 4) xiv. 600 In the electronic excitation an electron is removed from a *π* orbital and placed in a *σ* orbital. **1964** R. G. PARR *Quantum Theory of Molec. Electronic Structure* iii. 41 It is supposed that somehow the effect of the others, the sigma electrons, can be lumped into the Hamiltonian for the pi electrons. **1966** PHILLIPS & WILLIAMS *Inorg. Chem.* II. xxviii. 341 The vinyl anion, $C_2H_3^-$, binds directly to cobalt (III) of vitamin B_{12} as a simple *σ*-bonded ligand. **1972** DEPUY & CHAPMAN *Molec. Reactions & Photochem.* vi. 103 The numbers refer to the atoms at either end of the sigma bond which is thought of as moving. **1978** P. W. ATKINS *Physical Chem.* xv. 471 Thus an oxygen molecule, which.. has two *π**-electrons, could be in either a *Σ* state (the electrons orbiting in opposite directions) or in a *Δ* state (the electrons orbiting in the same sense around the bond).

b. *Particle Physics.* Used, usu. *attrib.*, to denote any of a triplet of hyperons (and their antiparticles) having an average mass of approximately 1190 MeV (2340 times that of the electron), a spin of ½, zero hypercharge, and unit isospin, and which on decaying usu. produce a nucleon and a pion (if charged) or a lambda particle and a photon (if neutral). Freq. written as *Σ*.

1954 GELL-MANN & PAIS in *Proc. Glasgow Conf. Nuclear & Pleson Physics* (1955) 347 The..apparent existence of both a positive and a negative hyperon which we shall call Σ^+ with the decay schemes $\Sigma^\pm \rightarrow N + \pi^\pm +$ ($\sim$115 MeV), $\Sigma^\pm \rightarrow P + \pi^0 +$ ($\sim$115 MeV). **1955** *Nuovo Cimento* II. 824 An event, interpreted as the disappearance of a charged *Σ*-hyperon in flight, has been observed ..in the Brookhaven cosmotron. **1961** W. S. C. WILLIAMS *Introd. Elementary Particles* xii. 298 Any subsequent *Σ* decays in flight. **1963** K. W. FORD *World of Elementary Particles* vi. 179 (*caption*) A negative pion..collides with a proton and produces two strange particles, a neutral sigma and a neutral kaon... The sigma particle lives too short a time to move a measurable distance.., decaying almost at once into a lambda and a photon. **1976** *Sci. Amer.* Jan. 46/2 The baryons with the lowest mass are those with a spin of 1/2. There are eight of them: two nucleons (*N*).., a lambda particle (*Λ*).., three sigma particles (*Σ*)..and two cascade particles (*Ξ*).

4. Biochem. *ellipt.* for *sigma factor*, sense 6 below.

1970 *New Scientist* 23 July 176/1 Soon after infection.. the phage makes its *own* sigma, which redirects the host core enzyme to start making a different set of phage proteins.

5. *Statistics.* A standard deviation: used in the singular as if the name of a unit.

1978 N. R. ULLMAN *Elem. Statistics* iii. 68 The difference is 0·5 inches, or, since $\sigma = 0{\cdot}29$..1·72 standard deviations apart or 1·72 *σ* (1·72 sigma) apart. *Ibid.* 69 You can express values in terms of sigma or in terms of 'so many sigma units from the mean'. **1979** *Nature* 29 Mar. 411/1 On each radiocarbon analysis, one sigma counting errors are given.

6. *Comb.*, as **sigma factor** *Biochem.*, a component of RNA polymerase which determines where transcription begins.

[**1969** R. R. BURGESS et al. in *Nature* 4 Jan. 44/2 GG enzyme contains, in addition, two extra bands which we shall designate *σ* and *τ*. *Ibid.* 46/1 The presence of the stimulating factor, *σ*, greatly enhances the amount of RNA synthesis. *Ibid.* 46/2 *σ* and similar factors could.. act as positive control elements regulating the amount of synthesis of different classes of RNA.] **1969** *Times* 9 May 12/6 The sigma factor helps to specify which genes are expressed. **1970** *Nature* 29 Aug. 886/1 Today sigma factor proteins..are central to all attempts to explain the positive control of gene expression. **1976** *Proc. Nat. Acad. Sci.* LXXIII. 3961 (*heading*) Purification and characterization of a putative sigma factor from *Chlamydomonas reinhardi*. *Ibid.* 4405 (*heading*) Induction of sigma factor synthesis in *Escherichia coli* by the N gene product of bacteriophage lambda.

sigmatism. (In Dict. s.v. SIGMA.) Add: **b.** Defective articulation of sibilants.

1888 A. H. BUCK *Reference Handbk. Med. Sci.* VI. 617/1 Lisping, or Sigmatism, is the most common form of stammering. It consists of giving *s* a wrong sound, usually that of *th*, by carrying the tip of the tongue too far forward, so as to touch the upper teeth. **1933** S. M. STINCHFIELD *Speech Disorders* iv. 76 The boys led in the number of cases of sigmatism, stuttering.., deafness and speech defects as a whole. **1957** *Dental Practitioner* VII. 220/2 Speech may be 'thick', which I tend to associate with the large tongue and the lateral sigmatism which suggests tongue behaviour. **1965** W. R. BRAIN *Speech Disorders* 154 Various disorders of the production of s (sigmatism) have been recognized.

sigmatropic (sigmătrǫ·pik), *a.* *Chem.* [f. SIGMA + *-TROPIC.] Involving the movement of a sigma bond to a new pair of atoms within a molecule.

1965 WOODWARD & HOFFMANN *in Jrnl. Amer. Chem. Soc.* LXXXVII. 2511/2 We define as a sigmatropic change of order [*i, j*] the migration of a *σ*-bond, flanked by one or more *π*-electron systems, to a new position whose termini are $i-1$ and $j-1$ atoms removed from the original bonded loci, in an uncatalyzed intramolecular process. **1974** GILL & WILLIS *Pericyclic Reactions* iii. 84 The transition state of a sigmatropic change is..reminiscent of the transition state of a cyclo-addition reaction.

sigmoid, *a.* and *sb.* Add: **A.** *adj.* **2.** *sigmoid colon=sigmoid flexure* in Dict.

1896 *Quain's Elem. Anat.* (ed. 10) III. IV. 113 The sigmoid colon may be defined as that part of the colon which is attached to the left iliac fossa from the iliac crest to the brim of the true pelvis. **1962** *Lancet* 5 May 951/2 Anterior resection of the rectum with primary sigmoid-rectal anastomosis for neoplasm of the rectosigmoid region and sigmoid colon.

Hence **sigmoide·ctomy** [*-ECTOMY], surgical excision of the sigmoid flexure; **sigmoidi·city,** the extent to which a curve is sigmoid (S-shaped); **sigmoidi·tis,** inflammation of the sigmoid flexure.

1906 P. L. MUMMERY *Sigmoidoscope* 55 In the cases of acute proctitis or sigmoiditis an examination with the sigmoidoscope may afford useful information. **1915** B. G. A. MOYNIHAN *Abdominal Operations* (ed. 3) II. 490/1 (Index), Sigmoidectomy. **1938** H. E. BACON *Anus, Rectum, Sigmoid Colon* xix. 695 (*heading*) Abdominal resection (sigmoidectomy)—one-stage procedure. **1968** A. WHITE et al. *Princ. Biochem.* (ed. 4) xi. 243 For hemoglobin, a similar plot yields a sigmoidal curve.. which obeys the relationship known as the Hill equation $y = Kx^n/(1 + Kx^n)$ where..the exponent n gives a measure of the sigmoidicity of the curve. **1977** *Arch. Biochem. & Biophys.* CLXXXIV. 300/1 With the enzyme from *Am*[*aranthus*] *edulis*, the response to increasing malate was qualitatively similar to that recorded for the *At*[*riplex*] *spongiosa* enzyme but sigmoidicity was more pronounced.

sigmoidoscope (sigmoi·dŏskōᵘp). *Med.* [f. prec. + -O + -SCOPE.] A speculum for examining the lower bowel and for assisting in minor operations therein. Cf. SIGMOIDSCOPE.

1900 in DORLAND *Med. Dict.* 599/2. **1906** P. L. MUMMERY *Sigmoidoscope* 7 The introduction of the electric pneumatic sigmoidoscope represents a great advance in our powers of accurate diagnosis. **1974** R. M. KIRK et al. *Surgery* vi. 123 Polyps can be removed through a sigmoidoscope using a snare.

Hence as *v. trans.*; also **sigmoidosco·pic** *a.*, performed or ascertained by means of a sigmoidoscope; **sigmoidosco·pically** *adv.*; **sigmoido·scopist,** one who uses a sigmoidoscope; **sigmoido·scopy,** examination by means of a sigmoidoscope.

1900 DORLAND *Med. Dict.* 599/2 Sigmoidoscopy. **1906** P. L. MUMMERY *Sigmoidoscope* 37 A sigmoidoscopic examination will give valuable information if there is any question of being able to remove the growth. **1961** L. MARTIN *Clinical Endocrinol.* (ed. 3) vi. 163 Intestinal symptoms and sigmoidoscopy or barium enema appearances will be diagnostic. **1962** *Lancet* 26 May 1095/1 Of the 20 patients receiving control treatment only 7 improved symptomatically and 8 sigmoidoscopically. **1966** *Ibid.* 25 June 1420/2 Heaven forbid that some future 'Chief of Service' should licence me to sigmoidoscope my cases of earache in this surgery. **1976** *Path. Ann.* XI. 28 Rectal examination may reveal blood, as may sigmoidoscopy, when the blood can often be seen coming from higher in the bowel. **1977** *Proc. R. Soc. Med.* LXX. 273/2 Sigmoidoscopic biopsy of the stricture at 14 cm showed chronically inflamed mucosa with no tumour tissue. **1977** *Lancet* 29 Oct. 893/2 The sigmoidoscopist was not able to recognise the type of enema a patient was receiving by the sigmoidoscopic appearances on the morning after an overnight retention enema.

sign, *sb.* Add: **I. 2. e.** *Math.* That aspect of a quantity which may be either positive or negative.

1820 G. Peacock *Differential & Integral Calculus* 112 The sign of d^2u may be easily determined. **1836** A. de Morgan *Differential & Integral Calculus* xiv. 369 When there is a change of sign, y is a maximum (M), or a minimum (m), according as the change is from + to − or from − to + (x increasing). **1924** G. F. Swain *Structural Engin.* xiii. 350 It is obvious that n_1 will have the same sign as f_t, and n_2 the opposite sign. **1957** G. E. Hutchinson *Treat. Limnol.* I. ix. 597 Where biochemical oxygen uptake or production occurs, no general rule as to the sign of the divergence from saturation will be possible. **1978** C. P. McKeague *Elem. Algebra* i. 23 To multiply any two real numbers simply multiply their absolute values, the sign of the answer is 1. positive if both numbers had the same sign..2. negative if the numbers had opposite signs.

6. Also, a board giving information, directions, etc.

1904, etc. [see *road sign* s.v. *road *sb.* 9 b].

II. 7. a. Also *the signs of the times*, indications of current trends. Now freq. as *sing.* phr. with leading indef. article.

1525 Bible (Tyndale) (1526) *Matt.* xvi. 3 Can ye not discerne the sygnes of the tymes? **1833** *Daily Nat. Intelligencer* 17 July 3/3 We have stood upon our '*reserved rights*' of neutrality, to watch the signs of the times. **1907** *Nature* 14 Mar. 459/1 This book is an interesting sign of the times. **1921** J. Galsworthy *To Let* II. xi. 214 '*He's* a sign of the times,' muttered Soames, 'if you like.' **1953** A. J. Toynbee *World & West* vi. 93 The people who have read the signs of the times and have taken action in the light of these indications are the obscure missionaries of half-a-dozen Oriental religions. **1977** *Gay News* 24 Mar. 19/3 Last year, perhaps as a sign of the times, Take Six notched up over 80 mentions in everything from the *Daily Mirror* to the Italian glossioso *L'Uomo*.

b. (*a*) (Examples in *Linguistics* and *Semiotics*.)

1890 W. James *Princ. Psychol.* II. xxii. 356 Language is a system of signs, different from the things signified, but able to suggest them. *c* **1902** C. S. Peirce *Coll. Papers* (1932) II. § 92 Genuine mediation is the character of a *Sign*. **1922** tr. *Wittgenstein's Tractatus* 53 The sign is the part of the symbol perceptible by the senses. **1938** C. W. Morris (*title*) Foundations of the theory of signs. **1947, 1949** [see *signifiant]. **1954** [see *signifier b]. **1964** Gould & Kolb *Dict. Soc. Sci.* 641/2 Sign denotes any stimulus which, because of association with another stimulus, elicits a response appropriate to but in the absence of the original stimulus. **1978** *Incorporated Linguist* Summer 60/3 Modern society's haste to read inadvertently into signs (in the Barthesian sense) rather than decipher the simple message. **1979** S. G. J. Hervey *Axiomatic Semantics* vii. 61 By the law of excluded middle, any given sign is either simple or complex, but not both.

(*b*) *Theol.* Phr. *outward visible sign* and varr., in sacramental ordinances, the outward and visible aspect which symbolizes the inward and spiritual aspect. Also *transf.*

1553 J. Bradford in Coverdale *Lett. Martyrs* (1564) 293 There is Idolatry in worshipping the outwarde signe of breade and wyne. **1604** *Bk. Com. Prayer, Catechism, Q.* How many partes be there in a Sacrament? *A.* Two: the Outward visible signe, and the Inward spirituall Grace. *c* **1816** J. Marriott *Hymn*, Grant to this child the inward grace, While we the outward sign impart. **1861** tr. *O Food that Weary Pilgrims Love!* in *Hymns, Anc. & Mod.* (Introits & Anthems) p. xvii, O Jesu, Whom, by power divine Now hidden 'neath the outward sign, We worship and adore. **1898** A. G. Mortimer *Cath. Faith & Practice* I. 124 The matter [of a sacrament] is the outward sign; the form that which determines the matter to its special use or purpose. **1921** J. Galsworthy *To Let* III. x. 288 In the union of the great-granddaughter..with the heir of a ninth baronet was the outward and visible sign of that merger of class in class which buttresses the political stability of a realm. **1931** V. Dixon *Sebastian Wile* II. ii. § 1 Her governess had said farewell, outward and visible sign that Martha's days of childish servitude were over. **1938** *Doctrine in Church of England* II. 127 The ordinary scholastic use is to employ the word [*sc.* sacrament] as meaning the outward and visible sign. **1951** A. Powell *Question of Upbringing* iii. 157 Monsieur Dubuisson accepted the brandy as the outward and visible sign of reconciliation. **1962** Wilson & Templeton *Anglican Teaching* ix. 180 The Catechism..defines a Sacrament as 'an outward and visible sign of an inward and spiritual grace..ordained by Christ Himself'.

d. (Earlier examples.)

1692 *Cal. Virginia St. Papers* (1875) I. 44 We Ranged about to see if we could find ye tract of any Indians, but we could not see any fresh signe. **1746** *New Hampsh. Hist. Soc. Coll.* (1834) IV. 208 By the sign of this ambush, and by the sign of their going off, in a single file, it was supposed there could not be less than 50 or 60 Indians. **1821** J. Fowler *Jrnl.* 3 Nov. (1898) 33 Heare We find the first fresh Sign of bever. *Ibid.* 7 Nov. 36 We see old sign of Indeans... We again See the Sign of White men a Head of us.

e. *Med.* An objective evidence or indication of disease (as opposed to a subjective one, or *symptom*); often used with the name of one who associated an indication with a disease characterized by it, to designate the former.

1842 W. A. Guy *Hooper's Physician's Vademecum* (new ed.) I. iii. 16 The word sign has not precisely the same meaning as the term symptom, though the two terms are sometimes used without much discrimination... Cough, expectoration, dyspnœa, hectic fever, night sweats, and emaciation, are *symptoms* of pulmonary consumption, but they are not *signs*, for each of them may occur in other diseases; but cavernous respiration and pectoriloquy are signs. *Ibid.*, The term *physical* sign is in common use among medical men: it means a sign which is an object of sense. Thus heat, redness, and swelling are physical signs of inflammation, pectoriloquy of phthisis, coagulable urine of disease of the kidney. **1851** R. P. Cotton *Phthisis & Stethoscope* i. 12 Physical signs by themselves, as a general rule, determine nothing more than physical conditions..; hence it is, that we require the use of other rules, as well as a knowledge of the patient's history and general symptoms. *Ibid.* ii. 24 Diminished resonance is one of the earliest and most characteristic signs of phthisis. **1872** W. Williams *Princ. & Pract. Vet. Surg.* xiii. 244 The diagnostic signs of elbow-joint lameness are, first, the semi-flexed position of the limb..whilst standing still; and the dropping of the head and anterior parts of the body during action. **1886** J. Finlayson *Clin. Manual for Study Med. Cases* (ed. 2) ii. 51 A pain is a 'Symptom' (subjective); a bulging chest, to which it may be due, is a 'Sign' (objective): giddiness is a 'Symptom' (subjective); the staggering resulting from it is a 'Sign' (objective). **1908** *Practitioner* Jan. 10 We do not obtain ankle clonus, or Babinsky's, or Oppenheim's sign. **1927** G. W. Deeping *Kitty* xv. 193 Mr. St. George had an undoubted paraplegia. There was definite spasticity of the lower limbs... Babinski's sign was present. **1956** A. I. Littlejohn tr. *D. Wirth's Vet. Clin. Diagnosis* 1 Symptoms in the medical sense are not available to the veterinary diagnostician, but the substitution of the term 'symptom' for 'sign' in veterinary usage is widespread. **1971** S. Magalini *Dict. Med. Syndromes* 148/1 Dercum's [syndrome]... *Symptoms.* Prevalent in women 40 to 60 years of age. Pain in part of body where localized accumulation of fat occurs. Asthenia, headache... *Signs.* Subcutaneous accumulation of fat elevated, dry, reddish, or bluish, anesthesia and diminished cutaneous sensibility. **1974** T. McGinnis *Well Dog Bk.* (1979) 95 Because your dog cannot describe their feelings in words, they technically have no symptoms, only *signs* which are any objective evidence of disease or injury you can detect.

III. 12. a. (sense 1) *sign-language* (earlier and later examples; also *fig.*); (sense 6) *sign-painter* (earlier and later examples), *-writer* (Writer 1 b), *-writing*; (sense 7) *sign-situation, -system, -using* vbl. sb. and ppl. adj.

1847 T. H. Gallandet in *Amer. Ann. Deaf & Dumb* I. 59 They originate from elements of this sign-language which nature furnishes to man wherever he is found, whether barbarous or civilized. **1960** S. Plath *Colossus* 39 These..sheets..Speak in sign language of a lost otherworld. **1981** *Amer. Speech* LVI. 130 Sign language is as adequate for the deaf as any vocal-auditory language is for a hearing person. **1725** *New-Eng. Courant* 15 Feb. 1/2, I would oblige every Sign-Painter to serve seven Years at College, before he presum'd to handle Pencil or Paint-Box. **1942** *Burlington Mag.* Jan. 9/1 Ireland takes this sketch as a proof that Hogarth contemplated setting up as a sign-painter. **1923** Ogden & Richards *Meaning of Meaning* i. 15 There may be a very long chain of sign-situations intervening between the act and its referent. **1977** *Dædalus* Fall 105 Literature..though it is..a form of communication..is cut off from the immediate pragmatic purposes which simplify other sign situations. **1924** R. H. Bell *Mystery of Words* 101 A study of the general principles of language has brought out the nature of the linguistic sign-system. **1977** R. H. Brown in Douglas & Johnson *Existential Sociol.* ii. 90 These norms and rules form a sign system that is itself subject to the feedback of experience. **1890** W. James *Princ. Psychol.* II. xxii. 357 In the human child..these ruptures of contiguous association are very soon made; far off cases of sign-using arise when we make a sign now; and soon language is launched. **1938** C. W. Morris *Found. of Theory of Signs* i. 1 Men are the dominant sign-using animals. **1957** C. E. Osgood et al. *Measurement of Meaning* i. 3 The behavior of the sign-using organism. **1871** J. Callingham *Sign Writing* i. 1 It is curious that the term 'sign-writer' is not to be found in any encyclopædia or dictionary, ancient or modern... Even Kelly's ponderous 'Post Office London Directory' does not deem the sign-writer worthy of separate enumeration in its list of trades. **1977** J. McClure *Sunday Hangman* xiii. 151 A family of losers trying to find the right words for the signwriter. **1871** J. Callingham (*title*) Sign writing. **1954** 'J. Wyndham' *Jizzle* 49 Elmer was a house-painter who doubled in the less spacious art of sign-writing. **1978** *Dumfries & Galloway Standard* 21 Oct. 21/2 (Advt.), All types of signwriting undertaken.

b. Special combs., as **sign-behaviour,** behaviour that is dependent on a sign (sense 7); **sign bit** *Computers*, a sign digit located in a sequence of binary digits; **sign-design** (see quot. 1942); **sign digit** *Computers*, a digit, located in a sequence of digits, whose value depends on the algebraic sign of the number represented; **sign-event,** a particular occurrence of the use of a sign (sense 7); **sign-process,** the process whereby a token or indication becomes operative or functions as a sign; **sign stimulus** *Biol.*, the component or characteristic of an external stimulus which is effective in initiating a particular innate behavioural response in an animal perceiving it, regardless of the presence or absence of the remainder of the stimulus; **sign-vehicle,** the token or indication that acts as a sign.

1946 C. W. Morris *Signs, Lang. & Behav.* i. 7 And goal-seeking behavior in which signs exercise control may be called sign-behavior. **1964** Gould & Kolb *Dict. Soc. Sci.* 641/2 Sign-behaviour is found in all levels of animal life. **1962** *Gloss. Terms Automatic Data Proc.* (*B.S.I.*) 19 Where the sign digit is a binary digit it is often known as a sign bit. **1975** T. Bartee *Introd. Computer Sci.* ii. 47 The sign bit is set apart from the magnitude bits by a . in each word... An alternate technique uses a box for the sign bit. **1942** R. Carnap *Introd. Semantics* § 3.5 The word 'sign' is ambiguous. It means sometimes a single object or event, sometimes a kind to which many objects belong. Whenever necessary, we shall use 'sign-*event*' in the first case, 'sign-*design*' in the second. **1944** *Mind* LIII. 36 The sign-design is what is usually meant when we use such words as 'symbol', 'word', 'sentence'. It is the form or structure common to a set of actual occurrences (sounds, marks, gestures) whereby they function symbolically. **1974** M. Taylor tr. *Metz's Film Lang.* iii. 90 Between words—pure 'sign events' as they are called in American semiotics, events that never occur twice..and language.. there is room for the study of 'sign designs', sentence patterns. **1947** A. W. Burks et al. in J. von Neumann *Coll. Wks.* (1963) V. 46 Our numbers are 40 digit aggregates, the left-most digit being the sign digit. **1950** *Proc. R. Soc.* A. CCII. 574 The first digit is regarded as a sign digit and a 'binary point' supposed to exist before the second digit. **1969** J. J. Sparkes *Transistor Switching* viii. 194 The sign digit is normally '0' for positive numbers. **1942** Sign-event [see *sign-design* above]. **1973** *Screen* Spring/Summer 164 *Spoken words*..are pure 'sign-events' incapable of being reproduced twice over and therefore impossible to study scientifically. **1946** C. W. Morris *Signs, Lang. & Behav.* i. 3 Terms which are commonly used in describing sign-processes. **1957** C. E. Osgood et al. *Measurement of Meaning* i. 5 A first step toward a behavioral interpretation of the sign-process. **1934** E. S. Russell *Behaviour of Animals* ii. 33 The principle of representative stimuli, or sign stimuli as we may call them for short, is illustrated not only in the flight reactions of animals..but even more clearly in..food-finding behaviour. **1967** A. Manning *Introd. Animal Behaviour* iii. 39 There are many examples of auditory and chemical sign-stimuli too. Turkey hens which are breeding for the first time will accept as chicks any object which makes the typical cheeping call. On the other hand..deaf turkey hens kill most of their chicks because they never receive the auditory sign-stimulus for parental behaviour. **1975, 1980** Sign stimulus [see *releaser c]. **1938** C. W. Morris *Found. of Theory of Signs* i. 4 In such cases *S* is the sign vehicle.., *D* the designatum, and *I* the interpretant of the interpreter. **1955** T. H. Pear *Eng. Soc. Differences* i. 33 Status symbols are sign-vehicles, cues which determine the status to be imputed to a person.

sign, *v.*[1] Add: **I. 4. c.** With *in*. To secure the admittance of (a person) to a hotel, club, etc., by signing a register; to record the entrance of (a person) into a building, etc.

1930 A. P. Herbert *Water Gipsies* xxv. 368 Isn't he sleeping in the hotel himself?.. Didn't want to sign you in as his wife, I shouldn't wonder. **1957** C. MacInnes *City of Spades* I. xi. 79, I shall sign you in till Johnny come, and check with him later. **1971** R. Hill *Advancement of Learning* xvi. 222 'Have you been signed in?'.. Of course, it was a club. 'Then you can't buy a drink, can you?' **1977** J. P. Anderson in Douglas & Johnson *Existential Sociol.* vi. 191 His face fell a foot when the social worker told him that Viejas Rehabilitation Center was the only place he could get in, that he would have to sign himself in for from three to six months. **1978** M. Z. Lewin *Silent Salesman* xviii. 107, I know of at least one person who was in Research [Laboratory] Three on the twenty-seventh who wasn't signed in or out.

d. With *out*. To secure the release of (a person or thing) by signing; to record the removal of (a thing) or the departure of (a person) from a building, etc.

1963 V. Nabokov *Gift* iii. 187 He signed out the complete works of Chernyshevski from the state library. **1968** *Globe & Mail* (Toronto) 13 Feb. 11/6 The nurse replied that he had been signed out by the doctor. **1972** D. E. Westlake *Cops & Robbers* (1973) x. 137 Why don't you shlep on back to the [police] station and sign us both out? **1978** [see sense 4 c above].

5. a. Also const. *for*, as authorization or acknowledgement of receipt. Also, to make a written contract *with*. *to sign on the dotted line*: see *dotted *ppl. a.* 1 c.

1938 L. Bemelmans *Life Class* II. iv. 160, I won't pay for anything that isn't properly ordered... I pay only for things I sign for. **1956** B. Holiday *Lady sings Blues* (1973) xxii. 181 The only royalties I get are on my records made after I signed with Decca. **1957** C. Smith *Case of Torches* i. 10 'Some of the boys in the laboratory ..think they compromise their independence if they sign for something.' 'All the other boxes have been signed for.' **1966** J. B. Priestley *Salt is Leaving* v. 61 If a Miss Tiller asks for me, tell her we've gone in. I've already signed for her. **1967** E. S. Gardner *Case of Queenly Contestant* xvi. 206 He said he would take care of all my expenses... I.. sign for meals in the hotel restaurant. **1974** *Times* 5 Feb. 11/7 John Alderton and Pauline Collins..have signed with London Weekend Television to appear as husband and wife in a new comedy series. **1977** P. D. James *Death of Expert Witness* II. 100 We let them borrow the key and they sign for it in a book in the office.

b. (*a*) With *off*. (Further examples.) *gen.*, to record that one is bringing something to an end, to stop doing something; *spec.* (i) *Broadcasting*, to cease broadcasting, to announce the end of a broadcast; (ii) to fall silent, to withdraw one's attention; (iii) to record leaving one's work, to stop work; (iv) *Bridge*, to indicate by a conventional bid that one is ending the bidding.

1923 *Sci. Amer.* Nov. 310/3 The local broadcasting stations have 'signed off' for the night. **1929** Wodehouse *Mr. Mulliner Speaking* vi. 206 If you're trying to propose to me, sign off. There is nothing doing. **1933** A. McCabe *Contract without Tears* 165 Had North wished to sign-off at this point he would have bid five diamonds. **1937** *Speculum* Apr. 268 Tired copyists expressed their relief at signing off from their labors. **1948** *Times* 2 Sept. 2/7 Reluctance to sign off with no additional values has led to many [Contract Bridge] players getting out of their depth. **1953** W. R. Burnett *Vanity Row* xxi. 188 Lynch was..listening to a comedy programme... 'Be with you in a minute... They're just about to sign off.' **1954** M. Procter *Hell is City* I. v. 30 What time did you sign off? ..Since then you've been in some pub... You've been working on that murder, I suppose. **1957** F. Hoyle *Black Cloud* xi. 210 If the politicians started..arguing.. the Cloud would sign off altogether. It's not going to waste its time talking to gibbering idiots. **1962** *Listener* 1 Mar. 394/3 He bid 5 N.T., which by convention asked his partner to bid Six Diamonds if he held the King of the agreed suit, hearts, and otherwise to sign off in Six Hearts. **1965** 'J. le Carré' *Looking-Glass War* xxiii.241 'The transmission's stopped.'..'Did he sign off?' **1971** H. Trevelyan *Worlds Apart* xvii. 193 By the summer of 1964 Khrushchev had decided to have nothing to do with Vietnam either and virtually signed off. **1974** R. M. Pirsig *Zen & Art of Motorcycle Maintenance* i. 23 John signs off every time the subject of cycle repair comes up. **1976** *Times* 1 May 12/7 North can hardly be blamed for seeking a slam when his partner could have 'signed off' by responding Five Diamonds to Five Clubs. **1976** *Milton Keynes Express* 30 July 13/1 In a statement Hawkins said he did not sign off because the Works job was only temporary and he was afraid he would not be able to sign on again. **1979** *Irish Times* 28 Sept. 3/1 A decision will be made later as to whether this progressive three-year-old will sign off for the season in the St Simon Stakes or the Champion Stakes.

(*b*) With *on*. (Earlier and later examples.) *spec.* (i) to record one's arrival at work, to begin work; (ii) to sign a contract to join an organization, etc.; (iii) to register at the Department of Social Security (formerly Labour or Employment Exchange) in order to obtain unemployment benefit.

1862 *Railway Traveller's Handy Bk.* 8 In most Government offices the *employés* are compelled to 'sign on', as it is called, when they arrive in the morning. **1930** E. Pound *XXX Cantos* ix. 37 Until he signed on with Siena. **1936** N. Mitchison *Fourth Pig* 29 If I didn't keep it up, there'd be a dozen knocking themselves over to get my job. And then it would be signing on again at the Labour. **1941** *Illustrated* 6 Sept. 21 She hands him the emergency slip. It says that he must sign on at 8 a.m. for the 9.30 special. **1955** *Times* 18 Aug. 5/1 Some of our men there had signed on for three or five years because they had been told they would learn a trade, but they were just batmen and doing no training at all. **1960** C. MacInnes *Mr. Love & Justice* 45 Frankie had paid his last visit to the Labour because..he wasn't going through the comedy of 'signing on' any more. **1974** P. Wright *Lang. Brit. Industry* ii. 31 Bus drivers and conductors have instead to *sign on*... They may have to make a personal appearance before the traffic inspector to show that they are not drunk or otherwise unfit. **1976** *Yorkshire Evening Press* 9 Dec. 3/4 If you gave up work voluntarily then you could be disqualified from receipt of unemployment benefit for up to six weeks, and you would have to 'sign on' and hold yourself available for employment every week. **1981** B. Hines *Looks & Smiles* 18 You take this [card] up to the Social Security office and sign on at the time it says here. *Ibid.* 44 Miserable bunch of bastards, the sergeant said... Anybody'd think they'd been forced to sign on.

c. With *up*. To enrol, to enlist; to give support *to*.

1903 A. H. Lewis *Boss* 186 You can tell by th'way they go to bat, whether th' Blackberry has signed up to them to kill our franchise. **1926** *Ladies' Home Jrnl.* Apr. 25 So she signed up for evening classes. **1942** E. Paul *Narrow St.* xxxiv. 306 It was generally accepted in our street after that that France was eager to sign up with Russia against Hitler. **1942** E. Waugh *Put out More Flags* i. 69 What I thought of doing was to sign up with you... It's a great help to start in a decent regiment. **1951** *Listener* 31 Jan. 172/2 Inducing other governments to sign up to professions of high moral and legal principles. **1975** M. Bradbury *History Man* vi. 99 I've signed up for an evening class. **1977** T. Heald *Just Desserts* i. 11 Collingdale had had to sign up as a novice friar.

d. With *out, in*. To record one's departure from, arrival at, a hotel, club, etc., by signing a register; also *fig.*

1951 G. Greene *End of Affair* ii. ii. 65 It was..as though I had signed out of the war. **1966** G. Burnett *Dead Account* xii. 97 And my name's Brook. Where do we sign in? **1968** 'G. Bagby' *Another Day—Another Death* vii. 142 It seemed impossible that..all the police who'd been poring over the book could have missed someone who signed in and hadn't signed out. **1978** M. Z. Lewin *Silent Salesman* xviii. 108 I'd like a list of all the people who signed in or out of Research Three.

6. c. Also with *up*; also *fig.*

1927 Wodehouse *Meet Mr Mulliner* i. 29 If George had been a member of the Olympic Games Selection Committee, he would have signed this woman up immediately. **1932** *Radio Times* 1 Apr. 5/2 Seversky immediately signed the violinist up for his broadcast. **1956** B. Holiday *Lady sings Blues* (1973) iii. 35 Joe Glaser, the big agent and manager..signed me up on the spot. **1963** Wodehouse *Stiff Upper Lip, Jeeves* iii. 26 While I personally..would run a mile in tight shoes to avoid marrying Stiffy, I knew him to be strongly in favour of signing her up. **1980** G. M. Fraser *Mr American* xxiii. 442 Your friend Pip is to be one of the top turns in the cabaret—I suppose they signed her up as soon as they saw the early editions.

II. 9. a. Also *spec.* to use a sign language.

1909 in Webster. **1977** *Rolling Stone* 16 June 46/1 Washoe used to sign to the others quite a bit, but of course the chimps she was signing to didn't respond. **1978** *Detroit Free Press* 5 Mar. 10/4 Strangely, many educators of deaf students don't sign (use sign language). **1980** *Nat. Geographic* June 849 Bin was picking up sign language... He didn't talk to Princess; he signed to her as he also did with other non-signing orangutans.

b. Also *spec.* to communicate or express (something) in a sign language.

1909 in Webster. **1975** J. Goulet *Oh's Profit* i. 4 Liedlich and his wife, Nancy, had signed the month, the hand-dance that was the month April. **1975** *Church Times* 15 Aug. 2/2 The lessons will be signed by deaf readers and the Lord's Prayer by one who is also blind. **1978** *Oxford Times* 16 June 2 The British Deaf Association Choir..'signed' the hymns.

III. 10. Comb., as **sign-in**, the action of signing in (see senses *4 c and *5 d); also used *attrib.* and *absol.* of a register in which people sign in; **sign-off**, the action of signing off (see sense *5 b (*a*)); *Broadcasting*, the end of transmission, an announcement of this; also *attrib.*; **sign-on**, the action of signing on (see senses *5 b (*b*) and 6 c); *Broadcasting*, the start of transmission; **sign-out**, the action of signing out (see senses *4 d and *5 d); the signature of one who has signed out; **sign-up**, the action of signing up or the state of having signed up (see senses *5 c and *6 c); also, a person who has signed up; also *attrib.*

1968 'G. Bagby' *Another Day—Another Death* vii. 142 He showed me the porter's sign-in. The man had come in quite early. **1972** 'J. Lange' *Binary* 8 A guard with a sign-in book stood in front of the elevator. Graves..took the pen and wrote his name, his authorization, and the time. **1978** S. Brill *Teamsters* iii. 115 Their names were the first entered every morning in the sign-in register at the Fund's reception desk. **1942** E. Culbertson *Official Bk. Contract Bridge* xv. 187 Finally, there is the sign-off bid... The sign-off may be made even if the responder hold one Ace. **1949** *Cavalier Daily* (Univ. Virginia) 23 Sept. 1/3 A non-affiliated station..will be on the air only during the daylight hours. Sign-on and sign-off times will vary from month to month. **1958** *Listener* 30 Oct. 709/2 The sign-off for his partner would clearly be Five Hearts. **1960** *News Chron.* 27 June 3/1 One [question]..was used by the producer as a rather abrupt sign-off. **1961** [see *sign-on* below]. **1962** H. T. Moore *Coll. Lett. D. H. Lawrence* I. p. xxi, Lawrence's sign-off line was often a foreign phrase. **1971** H. Trevelyan *Worlds Apart* xvii. 194 So now they could no longer stay silent and issued the expected 'sign-off' statement on Vietnam, evidence that they were powerless to take any diplomatic initiative. **1976** *Time* 20 Dec. 47/2 Remember his sign-off as he was being expelled from a Democratic Convention: 'This is John Chancellor, somewhere in custody.' **1948** *Seafarers' Log* 9 Jan. 5/2 One thing about the pay-offs and sign-ons we had: All the beefs were settled aboard ship to everybody's satisfaction. **1949** [see *sign-off* above]. **1961** *Time* 19 May 53/1 The toughest TV critic..dared the station and network operators and owners to sit down in front of their sets from sign-on to sign-off. **1968** 'G. Bagby' *Another Day—Another Death* vii. 142, I looked at the later sign-outs. Those covered the mob of cleaning women. **1940** *Sun* (Baltimore) 17 Sept. 9/7 Talbot, with a 'sign up' of 391,..led all the counties. **1941** *Ibid.* 14 Feb. 7/1 'There is a direct need for immediate sign-up' of nurses for army duty. **1945** *National Legionnaire* (U.S.) Sept. 1 (*heading*) Legion speeds sign-up of 12,000,000 War II victors. **1951** *Daily Progress* (Charlottesville, Va.) 5 Mar. 3/2 Sign-ups through the end of last month totaled 1,033. **1972** *Jrnl. Social Psychol.* LXXXVII. 118 A sign-up sheet was then distributed and students were asked to indicate whether..they would be willing to volunteer for the experiment. **1974** *News & Reporter* (Chester, S. Carolina) 22 Apr. 10-A/1 This will be a singles tournament and sign up will start Saturday morning at 10 a.m. **1980** *Dirt Bike* Oct. 5/1 The little gray-haired lady at the sign-up booth is your wife, or your girlfriend.

signal, *sb.* Add: **4. c.** A modulation of an electric current, electromagnetic wave, or the like by means of which information is conveyed from one place to another; the current or wave itself; also, a current or wave whose presence is regarded as conveying information about the source from which it comes. Also = *signal strength*, sense 5 e below.

1855 D. Lardner *Electric Telegraph* v. § 121 The signals transmitted appear upon the telegraphic instrument informing the agent whence the dispatch will come. **1873** *Trans. Inst. Engineers & Shipbuilders in Scotland* XVI. 119 If several thousand Leyden Jars were distributed along an aerial line of telegraph..the signals through the line would exhibit exactly the same inductive retardation as those sent through the actual submarine line. **1902** *Proc. R. Soc.* LXX. 256 For transmitting signals, an aerial wire or wires were attached to one of two spark balls fitted to an induction coil, the other ball being earthed. **1923** *Radio Times* 28 Sept. 2/2 After sunset signals may increase very considerably. **1958** *Times* 18 Jan. 7/3 The problem of how to reach Iraq and the Persian Gulf area with an adequate signal has yet to be solved. **1961** *New Scientist* 26 Jan. 199/3 The picture signal which indicates by amplitude modulation of a carrier wave how bright each point on a line should be, is interrupted at the ends of each line by synchronizing pulses. **1961** G. Millerson *Technique Telev. Production* ii. 19 The current, known as the video or picture signal, is subsequently amplified and passed to the video switching console. **1965** *New Statesman* 30 Apr. 674/2 The signals received from it [*sc.* Early Bird satellite] on the ground are extremely weak—about one-millionth of a normal TV signal in a fringe area. **1970** J. Earl *Tuners & Amplifiers* iv. 78 Signal delivered by the control section..is just right for feeding into the power amplifier section. **1978** Pasachoff & Kutner *University Astron.* xi. 302 Various objects in space emit electromagnetic signals in the radio part of the spectrum.

5. a. *signal arm* (Arm *sb.*[1] 6 c), *code, gun* (earlier and later examples), *lamp* (further examples), *light* (further examples), *strip*; also, denoting something used in receiving a signal or signals, as *signal pad* (Pad *sb.*[3] 4). Also objective, as *signal-processing*.

1901 *Railway Mag.* May 463/2 A neighbouring signal-arm falls. **1949** M. Taylor *Railway Signalling* i. 6 Near the top of the post is the signal arm which is always on the left of the post when the viewer is facing the signal. **1962** A. Lurie *Love & Friendship* xv. 293 Coarse grass grew along the track, and the signal arm was rusted at all clear. **1877** J. Habberton *Jericho Road* 94 Between the societies of neighboring counties there often existed signal-codes, and unwritten extradition and reciprocity treaties. **1952** M. K. Wilson tr. *Lorenz's King Solomon's Ring* viii. 82 The whole complicated 'signal code' of the jackdaw. **1758** in J. S. McLennan *Louisbourg* (1918) 414 Light gales and fair weather, later thick fog. Fired signal gun. **1930** R. Campbell *Adamastor* 74 The rocks, spray-clouded, are your signal guns. **1902** *Chambers's Jrnl.* July 479/2 The apparatus is simply a new glass for the signal-lamp, facing along the same way and throwing a powerful beam of light over the whole length of the arm. **1932** G. Greene *Stamboul Train* I. i. 5 A signal lamp turned from red to green. **1881** Signal-light [see *running light* s.v. *Running *vbl. sb.* 17 a]. **1936** *Discovery* Sept. 289/2 Motor-car headlights, signal lights and searchlights. **1976** *Billings* (Montana) *Gaz.* 5 July 8-A/6 The Utah Highway Patrol requested drivers to stay off the roads as signal lights were off through much of the state. **1958** P. Kemp *No Colours or Crest* iv. 54 By the operator's stool..were some signal pads. **1975** T. Allbeury *Palomino Blonde* x. 63 The Morse came and he was getting it down on his signal pad. **1964** R. F. Ficchi *Electr. Interference* vi. 99 Another way to reduce susceptibility to unwanted signals in cables is to use various signal-processing methods to improve the signal-to-noise ratio. **1917** 'Contact' *Airman's Outings* 261 The whole party circles round the aerodrome until the signal strips for 'Carry on' are laid out on the ground. **1954** W. Faulkner *Fable* 87 He reached the aerodrome and saw the ground signal-strip laid out on it;..not until he saw the other aeroplanes on the ground or landing or coming into land did he recognise it to be the peremptory emergency signal to all aircraft to come down.

b. *signal gantry*.

1927 A. Mee *Children's Treasure House* III. 1819/1 A signal gantry (one of those large bridges covered with signals which stand near important junctions or great termini). **1939** [see *Gantry 2 b]. **1976** *Physics Bull.* Dec. 556/1 A total of 15 signal gantries span the roadway for a distance of about 8 km.

c. *signal corps* (earlier example).

a **1885** G. B. McClellan *Own Story* (1887) 135 The weak point in the signal corps..was that its officers were not trained soldiers.

d. With other parts of speech, as *signal-like* adj.

1935 *Amer. Speech* X. 250/1 The result obtained..are functionally independent groups of sounds, each of the groups reflecting one of the basic, signal-like values in the given language. **1961** *Brno Studies in English* III. 51 Its survival may be satisfactorily explained by the signal-like character of *ρi* in foreign and emotionally coloured words.

e. Special combs., as **signal anxiety** *Psychol.*, anxiety which, according to the theory put forward by Freud in 1926, acts as a signal of danger to the ego; **signal-caller** *N. Amer. Football*, a player who signals to other members of his team what the next move and formation should be; **signal detection** *Psychol.*, the detection of signals, esp. with regard to the observer's vigilance and sensitivity; also *attrib.*; **signal generator** *Electronics*, an instrument that can generate modulated or unmodulated electrical waveforms of known amplitude and frequency, used in adjusting and testing electronic apparatus; **signal intelligence**: see *signals intelligence* below; **signal-noise ratio** = *signal-to-noise ratio* below; **signal plate** *Television*, in some types of camera tube, a plate electrode whose capacitance relative to the adjacent photo-electric surface is used to provide the picture signal; **signal reaction** (see quot. 1976); **signal red**, a vermilion colour; **signal(s) intelligence**, intelligence derived from the monitoring, interception, and interpretation of radio signals and similar transmissions (cf. *SIGINT, Sigint); **signal strength**, the amplitude or power of a signal, esp. of a broadcast signal as it reaches a given location or is received by a given aerial; **signal-to-noise ratio** *Radio* and *Electronics*, the ratio of the strength of a desired signal to that of unwanted noise interference, usu. expressed in decibels; also *transf.* to non-electrical systems.

[**1928** J. Rickman in *Internat. Jrnl. Psychoanal.* (Suppl. 2) 63 The situation which conditions the anticipation is the danger situation which gives, so to speak, the 'Anxiety Signal' of impending helplessness.] **1948** E. Jones *Papers on Psycho-Anal.* (ed. 5) xiv. 315 Primary anxiety, no less than the later 'signal' anxiety, belongs essentially to these defensive measures. **1968** C. Rycroft *Crit. Dict. Psychoanal.* 154 Signal anxiety..in Freud's formulation is the response of the ego to internal danger and the stimulus to the formation and use of defence-mechanisms. **1975** in S. Arieti *Amer. Handbk. Psychiatry* (ed. 2) IV. xxi. 485/1 The finely modulated, discrete and homeostatically balanced responses of the adult, such as 'signal anxiety'. **1971** L. Koppett *Guide to Spectator Sports* ii. 48 The quarterback now handles the ball on every play... He must be the signal-caller, too, because the attack is now concentrated in his hands. **1979** *Arizona Daily Star* 5 Aug. c 9/1 John Banaszak jarred the ball loose from Bills signal caller David Mays. **1954** Tanner & Swets in *Psychol. Rev.* LXI. 409/2 The mathematical model of signal detection is applicable to problems of visual detection. **1971** D. E. Broadbent *Decision & Stress* iii. 75 We cannot..take the success of signal detection theory in psychophysics as if it guaranteed its adequacy in the case of vigilance. **1979** in Hamilton & Warburton *Hum. Stress & Cognition* v. 148 Signal detection methodology is now the more widely used approach in the study of vigilance. **1929** K. Henney *Princ. Radio* xv. 376 The circuit diagram is that of the General Radio Signal Generator, a device which consists of a radio-frequency oscillator, a means of measuring and controlling its output, and a means of using any desired part of this output for purposes of measuring receivers. **1950** J. H. Reyner *Encycl. Radio & Television* 564/1 For the testing and alignment of receivers, signal generators giving modulated waves are available. **1972** *Jrnl. Social Psychol.* LXXXVII. 119 These tapes were made by recording square wave pulses produced by a Hewlet-Packard low-frequency signal generator. **1958** *Guardian* 22 May 3/1 Thompson and Miller trained for 'a specialised and secret duty in Signal Intelligence', Mr Jones continued. **1969** Signal intelligence [see *SIGINT, Sigint]. **1972** *New Scientist* 2 Mar. 466/1 The generic term for the business today is Signal Intelligence (Sigint). **1934** A. L. Albert *Electr. Communication* xv. 412 Just as in transmission over wires, it is necessary that the signal-noise ratio is high, and that fading is not excessive. **1962** *Daily Tel.* 6 July 21/7 However efficient the detectors and however good the signal-noise ratio, there will always be the possibility of doubt. **1934** V. K. Zworykin in *Jrnl. Franklin Inst.* CCXVII. 10 Consider the circuit of a single photo-electric element in the mosaic... Here *P* represents such an element, and *C* its capacity to a plate common to all the elements, which hereafter will be called the 'signal plate'. **1975** K. Wicks *Television* 19 After striking the signal plate, the electron beam returns along the tube, attracted by the positive charge on a series of five electrodes called dynodes. **1946** F. P. Chisholm in W. S. Knickerbocker *Twentieth Century English* 183 Signal-reactions..and other neuro-semantic disorders are often combined with brilliant verbal facility. **1976** N. Postman *Crazy Talk* 195 A signal reaction is what happens when words have lost their referential or symbolic aspect and instead assume the character of religious icons. **1936** *Times Educ. Suppl.* 21 Nov. p. iv/1 Gules..is not included in the range, but signal-red, similar but not quite so yellow, takes its place. **1977** *Western Morning News* 30 Aug. 2/7 Jaguar XJS; brand new;..signal red; beige trim. **1976**, etc. Signals intelligence [see *SIGINT, Sigint]. **1912** *Marconigraph* II. 269/2 Observations..showed that during totality the signal strength was increased. **1935** *Discovery* Sept. 278/1 The successive signal strengths are proportioned to the corresponding light and shade areas of the image focused by the lens upon the mosaic. **1968** M. Woodhouse *Rock Baby* xiii. 130 He..showed me..the tiny signal-strength meter on the side. **1978** *Broadcast* 20 Nov. 16/1 The report of the meeting..referred only to discussion of [Radio] Hallam's signal strength. **1935** *Proc. IRE* XXIII. 713 A single tone was used to modulate the transmitter when measuring signal-to-noise ratios. **1966** D. G. Brandon *Mod. Techniques Metallogr.* 239 The overall quantum efficiency for high-energy electrons can be of the order of 0·2 and is only limited by the necessity to achieve a reasonable signal-to-noise ratio in the emulsion. **1974** Harvey & Bohlman *Stereo F.M. Radio Handbk.* ii. 32 A reduction in carrier deviation means that a smaller signal is available at the output of the receiver demodulator and consequently the signal-to-noise ratio is lowered.

signal, *v.* Add: **2. b.** Also, to indicate, esp. unofficially or indirectly. Cf. *signalize *v.* 5.

1962 *Amer. Speech* XXXVII. 214 Since one member of the pair [of pronominal forms] is functionally redundant, the usage in different dialects may be expected to vary far more than for forms which signal significant differences. **1963** *Ibid.* XXXVIII. 52 The slots, or, more accurately, the units that can fill the slots, signal their meanings by their positions relative to each other... Some units signal their meaning without regard to position. **1978** *Times* 24 Apr. 2/1 The government seemed yesterday to be signalling its willingness to concede a reduction in the highest rates of income tax. **1979** *Tucson* (Arizona) *Citizen* 20 Sept. 1A/5 U.S. economic indicators signal the dollar should be lower than current rates. **1981** *Times* 25 Sept. 19/1 Sterling is now lower than when the Bank of England signalled higher interest rates a week last Monday.

signalization (signălaizēⁱ·ʃən). *Psychol.* [f. Signaliz(e *v.* 4 + -ation.] A term derived from the work of I. P. Pavlov (1849–1936) for the process whereby a signal comes to elicit the same response as the original stimulus.

1927 G. V. Anrep tr. *Pavlov's Conditioned Reflexes* ii. 22 The underlying principle of this activity is signalization. The sound of the metronome is the signal for food, and the animal reacts to the signal in the same way as if it were food. **1969** in K. H. Pribram *Memory Mechanisms* 137 The conditioned reflex..enables the animal to adjust itself to the essential factors of the external and internal world on the basis of the principle of signalization.

signalize, *v.* Add: **5.** Also, to indicate.

1961 *Texas Stud. Lit. & Lang.* III. 283 Pip's abject leave-taking of Miss Haversham..signalizes his homage to a supposed patroness. **1964** W. H. Dray *Philos. Hist.* 53 The willingness of the revisionists to apportion blame, however, does not signalize a return to the sectional type of partisanship. **1966** R. S. Rudner *Philos. Social Sci.* 15 A definition signalizes the redundancy or eliminability of a term. **1976** *Network* (Brit. Social. Assoc.) No. 6. 2/1 When people are trying to change their status..they seek to change their name, both to signalize the change that has taken place and to give form to the identity they are trying to shape.

6. [Signal *sb.*] *U.S.* and *Austral.* To provide (an intersection, etc.) with traffic signals.

1961 in Webster. **1977** *Sunday Mail* (Brisbane) 29 June 2/2 We had 158 signalised intersections at June 30 last year, 65 signalised pedestrian crossings..and 281 floodlit ones.

signans (si·gnænz). *Linguistics* and *Semiotics.* [L., pr. pple. of *signāre* to signify.] = *signifiant. Opp. *signatum.

1953 C. E. Bazell *Linguistic Form* 29 Multiple oppositions, rare or unknown in the signans, are normal in the signatum. **1954** *Litera* (Istanbul) I. 31 In a code, each discrete signans has a discrete signatum; for instance in the Morse code a certain combination of dots and dashes signifies a certain combination of strokes and points. **1956** Jakobson & Halle *Fundamentals of Lang.* I. ii. 15 The 'expression plane' of language, as he christened the aspect named *signans* in Stoic and Scholastic tradition,..is to be studied without any recourse to phonetic premises. **1959** *Jrnl. Individual Psychol.* XV. 62 The *signans* is perceptible, the *signatum* intelligible... Thus we perceive the sound-shape of the word *tree* and, on the other hand, we may translate this word by other verbal signs with more or less equivalent *signata* but each with a different *signans.*

signary (si·gnări). [f. L. *signum* sign + -ary[1], after *syllabary.*] An arrangement of signs; the signs which constitute the syllabic or alphabetic symbols of a language.

1902 *Encycl. Brit.* XXVII. 730/2 Probably all the signs in the hieroglyphic signary can be employed in their primary sense. **1909** A. J. Evans *Scripta Minoa* I. p. v, I have endeavoured to supply a preliminary apparatus criticus in the form of tables and explanatory catalogues of the different signaries. **1924** L. Eckenstein *Tutankh-aten* v. 42 There were other scribes of other signaries and languages who inscribed soft clay tablets with a copper stilus. **1932** *Antiquity* VI. 375 Nearly all the Phoenician signs were already in use in Egypt as far back as the 1st dynasty, part of the larger series of the Mediterranean signary.

signatum (signā·tɒm). *Linguistics* and *Semiotics.* [L., neut. sing. pa. pple. of *signāre* to signify.] = *signifié. Opp. *signans.

1953, etc. [see *signans]. **1962** R. Jakobson *Sel. Writings* I. 658 This criticism has been repeatedly mistaken for an attempt to withdraw the *signatum* from the scope of any phonemic analysis.

signature, *sb.* Add: **4. b.** (Further examples.)

1940 R. Morrish *Police & Crime-Detection* xii. 114 All these marks, however minute in themselves, form the specific 'signature' or identity of any fire-arm. **1952** M. Allingham *Tiger in Smoke* xi. 185 You knifed three people..and..you went and left your signature all over the shop. **1960** T. Hughes *Lupercal* 27 No Signature but this threshold-held hollow Remained of some vigorous souls That had Englished for Elizabeth. **1966** *Listener* 17 Nov. 746/1 An obvious pointer..is the prevalence of Shostakovich's musical 'signature'—D-S-C-H (D-E flat-C-B)—and its derivatives. **1971** *Daily Tel.* 22 Jan. 13/2 Signature of his collection: the V-necked pullover on every outfit. **1979** F. Kermode *Genesis of Secrecy* iii. 56 The episode..is a sort of reticent signature, like Alfred Hitchcock's appearances in his own films. **1979** *Studies in Eng. Lit.: Eng. Number* (Tokyo) 109 Indeed, this prosodic 'signature' is written on page after page of the *Pisan Cantos.*

d. *spec.* = *signature tune,* sense 9 below.

1932 [see *signature tune,* sense 9 below]. **1937** *Printers' Ink Monthly* May 42/2 *Signature,* the musical number or sound effect which regularly identifies a program. **1962** A. Nisbett *Technique Sound Studio* ix. 160 It is not so common for the start of a record to provide a good crisp opening signature.

e. Any pattern or characteristic in the physical properties or behaviour of a particular object, substance, etc., by which it can be identified; freq. a characteristic response which it gives to a test.

1960 *Jrnl. Histochem. & Cytochem.* VIII. 288/1 Failure to demonstrate striking differences in 'pH signature' between analogous components of normal and carcinoma cells did not particularly surprise us. **1967** *Electronics* 6 Mar. 50/3 The new radar will gather 'signatures' of orbital vehicles as well as reentering missiles. **1969** *New Scientist* 2 Oct. 21/2 The Concorde's signature from a given height will be less ponderous than that of the Boeing. **1971** *Sci. Amer.* July 77/3 The characteristic signature of a supernova remnant is the emission of radio waves whose distribution of energy with wavelength is nonthermal. **1973** D. Kyle *Raft of Swords* (1974) iii. 21 Super-sensitive acoustic receivers..which can instantly identify a vessel's 'signature'; in other words, identify the distinctive sounds made by a particular vessel. **1977** A. Hallam *Planet Earth* 41/3 Its magnetic signature allowed an age to be assigned to each piece of ocean floor. **1980** *Globe & Mail* (Toronto) 23 Aug. 2/5 The concept includes means of reducing the infra-red 'signature' given off by engine heat, thus defeating the ability of sensors to 'see' aircraft or vehicles even in darkness.

6. b. (Later examples.)

1901 D. Cockerell *Bookbinding* i. 34 The sheets of a newly printed book are arranged in piles in the printer's warehouse, each pile being made up of the same sheet or 'signature'. **1965** *Times Lit. Suppl.* 14 Oct. 928/3 This word 'signature' is..often used when the user appears to mean either 'leaf' or 'quire'. **1981** *Printing World* 28 Jan. 13/3 Signatures can be perforated down the back for 'slotted' (also known as 'notched' or 'burst') binding.

8. *Pharm.* (See quot. 1951.)

1856 E. Parrish *Introd. Pract. Pharmacy* v. ii. 418 The prescription may be divided, for the purpose of study, into the following parts..: 1. The superscription. 2. The inscription. 3. The subscription. 4. The signature. **1901** T. Sollmann *Textbk. Pharmacol.* vi. 105 The directions to the patient (signature) are always written in English, so that the patient can read them. **1951** A. Grollman *Pharmacol. & Therapeutics* 753 A prescription traditionally includes the following parts: 1. The superscription... 2. The inscription or body of the prescription... 3. The subscription... 4. The signature.., which includes the directions for the patient.

9. Special Comb.: **signature tune,** a piece of music that always precedes or follows a particular programme or a performance by a particular entertainer or band; also *transf.* and *fig.*

1932 *Daily Mail* 4 Mar. 11/4 B.B.C. Band's 'Signature'. 'Just the Time for Dancing' and 'Till Next Time' are the titles of the 'signature' tunes selected by Mr. Henry Hall for his new B.B.C. Dance Band, to be used every time the band begins or concludes a broadcast. **1934** *Punch* 8 Aug. 164/2 My dearest memory of the place [*sc.* Bilgesea] is that there was never a moment at which wailing could not be heard. It is..the 'signature-tune'..of English holiday-makers throughout the country. **1938** O. Sitwell *Those were Days* iv. iii. 462 Diminutive moonstones and giant chrysanthemums were her signature-tune, her speciality almost, you might say, what she lived for. **1950** E. Partridge *Here, There & Everywhere* 181 With Lewis Carroll the verse-form often serves the same purpose as a signature-tune. **1958** P. Gammond *Duke Ellington* ii. 72 The Duke and Bubber wrote *East St Louis toodle-oo*..and this became..the band's signature tune. **1962** A. Nisbett *Technique Sound Studio* ix. 161 Vocal music is not usually suitable for prefading, and is therefore rarely used for a closing signature tune. **1972** T. Lilley *'K' Section* xl. 192 The six o'clock news signature tune. The familiar introductory pictures. **1977** *N.Y. Rev. Bks.* 26 May 3/3 'And trod so sweetly proud' and 'In this blind bitter land' come from Yeats's well-recognized signature tune rather than from an imagination strenuously engaged with its experience.

sign-board. Add: Also *fig.*

1934 V. Woolf *Oliver Goldsmith* in *Captain's Death Bed* (1950) 15 Bodies and hearts are attached to these sign-board faces.

2. Chiefly *U.S.* A board on a guide-post to direct travellers, etc.

1829 A. Royall *Mrs. Royall's Pennsylvania* II. 38 You scarcely go a mile in Pennsylvania but you see a *Preacher* —as signboards are called. They point out the road but never travel it. **1883** *Wheelman* I. 298 They found a sign-board pointing to Swampscott and Lynn. **1972** *Straits Times* 25 Nov. 18/4 Although there are sign boards on either side of the estate indicating that it is closed to lorry traffic, these lorries continue to rumble through the estate.

signed[1], *ppl. a.* Add: **2.** (Later examples.) Also *fig.*

c **1893** H. G. Wells *Let.* in *Experiment in Autobiog.* (1934) I. vi. 392 They have let me sign an article in the *Pall Mall Gazette,*..and signed articles in dailies is a distinct advance for a poor wretch like me. **1930** G. B. Shaw *Apple Cart* I. 30 The ultimatum is here..and I shall not leave this room until I have His Majesty's signed pledge that its conditions will be observed. **1942** *World Rev.* Apr. 38/1 Key features of the newspaper contents were signed articles, and dramatic and literary *critiques* contributed by the greatest writers. **1959** *Times Lit. Suppl.* 5 June 334/2 It is a signed portrait. It is also a highly appealing, fair and convincing one. **1973** *Times* 28 Apr. 11/3 Both recordings contain versions of the 'signed' motet *Illibata Dei,* so called because the composer's name is spelled out in the text as an acrostic.

signed[3] (səind), *a. Arith.* [f. Sign *sb.* + -ed[2].] Having a (plus or minus) sign; esp. as *signed number,* a positive or negative integer.

1873 *Proc. Lond. Math. Soc.* IV. 111 A signed magnitude. **1905** *Proc. R. Soc. Edin.* XXV. 372 The sum of the signed primary minors of a determinant. **1950** *Math. Tables & Other Aids to Computation* IV. 103 A word may represent a signed-binary number lying somewhere between -2^{40} and $+2^{40}$. **1966** J. H. Cadwell *Topics in Recreational Math.* xiv. 160 We shall prove that all derivatives at these points are signed integers or zero. **1969** J. J. Sparkes *Transistor Switching* viii. 193 When writing 'signed' numbers the sign digit is identified with a bar over it.

signee (səinī·). [f. Sign *v.*[1] + -ee[1].] One who has signed a contract or register.

1953 *Sun* (Baltimore) 24 Apr. B20/2 Ken Jackson.. became the thirty-third Colt signee yesterday. **1970** G. F. NEWMAN *Sir, You Bastard* i. 13 Generally the officials were never so subtle, nor the signees so sensitive, as to be influenced by surroundings. **1977** *Times of Zambia* 12 Sept. 8/7 Montgomery, a recent signee from Celtic of the Scottish Premier League in UK.

signer. Add: **1. b.** *U.S.* (Usu. with capital initial.) *spec.* One of the signatories to the Declaration of Independence.

1865 M. B. CHESNUT *Diary* 29 Mar. in C. V. Woodward *M. Chesnut's Civil War* (1981) xxxiii. 772 What is the use of being the grandson of a signer if one is not a loyal gentleman? **1913** E. WHARTON *Custom of Country* vii. 90 The high dark dining-room with..dim portraits of 'Signers' and their females. **1928** W. A. WHITE *Masks in Pageant* 67 The grandson of a President and the great-grandson of a Signer. **1973** A. POWELL *Temporary Kings* i. 48 He is descended..from what is known as a 'Signer', one Bulton Gwinnett, who set his name to the Declaration of Independence.

signet-ring. Add: **2.** *Path.* Used, usu. *attrib.*, to describe cells and organisms that resemble signet rings in appearance.

1901 J. EWING in *Jrnl. Exper. Med.* V. 446 At a very early period of its development the æstivo-autumnal parasite in the present cases assumed a very characteristic ring shape. Many of these rings early developed a thickening of one segment, and to these bodies of various sizes the term 'signet-ring' very aptly applies. *Ibid.* 448 In six cases taking quinine typical signet-ring forms were seen in the peripheral blood 60 to 72 hours after the beginning of the paroxysm. **1928** L. E. H. WHITBY *Med. Bacteriol.* xxi. 209 The most characteristic form of the trophozoite is the so-called 'signet-ring' form, in which the chromatin granule or 'dot' is at one side. **1961** [see *KRUKENBERG]. **1966** WRIGHT & SYMMERS *Systemic Path.* I. xv. 511/1 When the mucus-secreting cells are anaplastic they appear as rounded cells, with the nucleus displaced to one side by a globule of mucus in the cytoplasm ('signet-ring cells'); 'signet-ring cell' carcinomas are highly malignant.

signifiable, *a.* (Earlier example.)

1857 *Encycl. Brit.* XIII. 610/2 It might then be determinable, and signifiable through the form of expression.

‖**signifiant** (sinʸifiaṅ). *Linguistics* and *Semiotics.* [Fr., pres. pple. of *signifier* to signify.] A sound, symbol, or image, or a sequence of sounds, etc., as opposed to the meaning expressed; the physical element of a sign. Opp. *SIGNIFIÉ.

[**1916** F. DE SAUSSURE *Cours de Linguistique Générale* I. i. 101 Nous appelons *signe* la combinaison du concept et de l'image acoustique; mais dans l'usage courant ce terme désigne généralement l'image acoustique seule... Nous proposons de conserver le mot *signe* pour désigner le total, et de remplacer *concept* et *image acoustique* respectivement par *signifié* et *signifiant*; ces derniers termes ont l'avantage de marquer l'opposition qui les sépare soit entre eux, soit du total dont ils font partie.] **1939** [see *SAUSSUREAN *a.*] **1947** *Word* III. 8 Signs are the primary objects of linguistic study. Words, word-groups, and sentences are all signs—signifiants linked with signifiés. **1949** *Archivum Linguisticum* I. 1 But the morpheme is a sign in the sense of de Saussure, an association of a *signifiant* and a *signifié* upon equal terms. **1964** *Language* XL. 307 He [*sc.* Firth] rejected all distinction between langue and parole, and signifiant and signifié. **1973** [see *MENTALISM 2]. **1973** *Screen* Spring/Summer 220 A *signifiant* (the pattern of alternating images) and a *signifié* (the indication of a simultaneity between the corresponding actions).

signific (signi·fik). *Linguistics.* [f. SIGNIFIC(ANT *sb.*] = *RADICAL *sb.* 1 c. Also *attrib.* Cf. *PHONETIC *sb.*

1923 B. KARLGREN *Analytic Dict. Chinese & Sino-Japanese* 1, I never use the term 'radical', as it wrongly conveys the idea of 'radix, racine, root' which is quite a different notion in general philology from that of signific: the meaning indicating part in the Chinese character. *Ibid.* 4 Nine tenths of all Chinese characters consist of one 'signific' and one 'phonetic'. **1948** R. A. D. FORREST *Chinese Lang.* ii. 38 The signific element in each case [*sc.* a character] denotes, or, more commonly, merely suggests, an order of ideas to which the meaning of the whole belongs. **1951** SHAU WING CHAN *Elementary Chinese* p. xvi, The last category is known as Chuañchù... It includes characters having identical significs and somewhat similar meanings but different phonetics. **1964** *Language* XL. 104 What sometimes appeared..to be a graphic element totally unrelated to the phonemic shape of the morph in question and hence by default a semantic 'key' or 'signific' was often in reality a phonetic element in the script. **1973** *Sci. Amer.* Feb. 54/2 When the 'horse' phonetic is combined with the signific for 'jade', we have *mǎ*, which means 'agate'.

‖**significacio** (signifikā·sio). Also **significatio.** [med.L. :— L. *significātio* significance.] An allegorical meaning; an innuendo.

1933 R. TUVE *Seasons & Months* iii. 85 The commonplace *significatio* of Phoebus is to be explained..as a literary inheritance rather than the last faint rumbling of wheels in a pagan festival of the Sun. **1936** C. S. LEWIS *Allegory of Love* i. 1 It is essential to this form that the iteral narrative and the *significacio* should be separable. **1968** J. A. W. BENNETT *Chaucer's Book of Fame* iii. 104 The emphatic negative is not a mere trope; it underlines the double *significacio*. **1969** R. A. LANHAM *Handlist Rhetorical Terms* 92 *Significatio*,..an innuendo.

significance. Add: **3.** *Statistics.* The level at or extent to which a result is statistically significant; freq. *attrib.*, as *significance level*; **significance test,** a method used to calculate the significance of a result; hence *significance testing* vbl. sb.

1888 J. VENN *Logic of Chance* (ed. 3) xix. 486 As before, common sense would feel little doubt that such a difference was significant, but it could give no numerical estimate of the significance. **1907** *Biometrika* V. 183 Let it be reasonable to suppose a quantity significant when it is β times its standard deviation, or $\beta/\cdot67449$ times its probable error, then we have for significance test: $m - M >$ [etc.]. Several other cases of probable error tests of significance deserve reconsideration. **1947** *Ibid.* XLVII. 139 The problem of testing the significance of difference between two proportions..receives early attention in textbooks on mathematical statistics. *Ibid.*, Such a difference in levels of significance in the solution of an everyday problem is obviously puzzling. **1960** *Amer. Sociol. Rev.* XXV. 202/2 In the test of this hypothesis a Chi-square of 34·34 was obtained, considerably lower than Chi-square at the ten per cent significance level for 34 degrees of freedom. **1970** *Nature* 25 July 384/2 Calculations of significance are based on the significance of the difference between paired observations using Student's *t* test. **1972** A. W. F. EDWARDS *Likelihood* i. 2 The rejection of the theory led to the flowering of alternative methods of inference, particularly significance-testing and estimation, to which we are heirs today. **1977** P. JOHNSON *Enemies of Society* xi. 157 In psychology, for example, it is notorious that 'results' used to confirm hypotheses are often no better than random data because significance tests would validate almost anything.

significans (signi·fikænz). *Linguistics* and *Semiotics.* [L., pres. pple. of *significāre* to signify.] = *SIGNIFIANT. Opp. *SIGNIFICATUM.

1964 E. PALMER tr. *Martinet's Elem. General Linguistics* i. 24 Every linguistic sign comprises a significatum, its meaning or value..and a significans through which the sign is made manifest. **1972** HARTMANN & STORK *Dict. Lang. & Linguistics* 209/1 *Signifier*... Alternative term: significans,..signifiant.

significant, *a.* Add: **2. b.** Substitute for leading phrase and def.: Conveying information about the value of a quantity; esp. in *significant digit, figure,* a digit which has its precise numerical meaning in the number containing it, and is not a zero used simply to fill a vacant place at the beginning or end. (Further examples.)

1938 A. E. WAUGH *Elem. Statistical Method* ii. 8 If we are told that the distance is 1000·00 miles, there are six significant figures, since it was not necessary to put in the zeros to locate the decimal point. **1957** R. A. BUCKINGHAM *Numerical Methods* i. 6 The numbers 0·000101 and 0·000999, both of which have the same absolute accuracy afforded by 6 decimals, and 3 significant figures, may yet have relative errors differing by an order of magnitude. **1962** C. BELL et al. *Fund. Arith. for Teachers* xi. 192 The value 3·1416 is said to be accurate to five significant figures. *Ibid.* xv. 231 If a measurement is expressed as a natural number, it is not always possible to determine the number of significant digits. **1965** I. ADLER *New Look at Arith.* iv. 228 Zeros which are not significant can always be replaced by words which serve the same function. *Ibid.* 231 When two approximate numbers are multiplied, the product has at most as many significant digits as there are in that one of the two numbers that has the fewer significant digits. **1968** *Brit. Med. Bull.* XXIV. 216/2 This [*sc.* a mathematical value] is not 'significant' but is printed out routinely. **1971** *Physics Bull.* Oct. 597/3 Does any analyst doing routine tests have the right to quote his result to four figures, and pretend that the fourth is also significant?

c. *Significant Form, significant form* Aesthetics, a hypothetical quality, thought to be common to all great works of art, that evokes an aesthetic response and is considered to be more significant than the subject-matter.

1914 C. BELL *Art* II. i. 8 What quality is shared by all objects that provoke our aesthetic emotions?.. In each, lines and colours combined in a particular way, certain forms and relations of forms, stir our aesthetic emotions. These relations and combinations..I call 'Significant Form'; and 'Significant Form' is the one quality common to all works of visual art. **1914** R. FRY in *Nation* 7 Mar. 938/2 Why must the potter who is to make a superbly beautiful pot not think only of its significant form, but think first and most passionately about its functions as a pot? **1929** D. H. LAWRENCE *Paintings* 20 The critics stepped forth and abstracted his good apple into Significant Form, and henceforth Cézanne was Saved. **1959** H. B. ALLSOPP *Future of Arts* xiv. 120 Some abstractionists persist in seeking what Clive Bell called 'significant form' which is significant without being significant of anything. I suspect that this idea is nonsense. **1965** *Brit. Jrnl. Aesthetics* V. 113 Significant form cannot be attributed primarily to works of art on the ground that aesthetic emotion obtained from works of art is more intense than that felt in the contemplation of natural objects and pure forms.

5. *Statistics.* Of an observed or calculated result, such as the difference between the means of two samples: having a low probability of occurrence if the null hypothesis is true; *statistically significant,* significant at some conventionally chosen level, freq. five per cent.

A result is said to be significant at a specified level of probability if it will be obtained or exceeded with not more than that probability when the null hypothesis is true.

1885 *Jrnl. R. Statistical Soc.* (Jubilee Vol.) 187 In order to determine whether the observed difference between the mean stature of 2,315 criminals and the mean stature of 8,585 British adult males belonging to the general population is significant [etc.]. **1907** *Biometrika* V. 318 Relative local differences falling beyond +2 and −2 may be regarded as probably significant since the number of asylums is small (22). **1925** R. A. FISHER *Stat. Methods Res. Workers* iii. 47 Deviations exceeding twice the standard deviation are thus formally regarded as significant. **1931** L. H. C. TIPPETT *Methods Statistics* iii. 48 It is conventional to regard all deviations greater than those with probabilities of 0·05 as real, or statistically significant. **1969** *Sci. Jrnl.* Nov. 57/1 The attitude scores differed only slightly and the differences were not statistically significant. **1970** *Nature* 25 July 376/2 Analysis of variance gave highly significant population and fertilizer effects. **1971** *Daily Tel.* (Colour Suppl.) 29 Oct. 35/4 The result, although occurring more often than other conjunctions, did not occur often enough to be statistically significant; i.e. a statistician would have said it was a chance occurrence. **1971** *Nature* 26 Nov. 231/2 If.. fifteen experiments are performed to detect a relationship which is not present, the probability that one or more experiments will give a result significant at the 0·05 level is 0·54.

significatio, var. *SIGNIFICACIO.

signification. Add: **1. c.** *Semiotics.* The process of signifying; the production of signs.

1946 C. MORRIS *Signs, Language & Behavior* iv. 111 Since a sign can denote without its interpreter knowing whether or not it denotes..it is evident that signification and knowledge are not limited to that portion of the world which acts as a direct stimulus to an interpreter's behavior. **1957** J. MARITAIN in R. N. Anshen *Language* I. v. 88 Animals make use of signs without perceiving the relation of signification. To perceive the relation of signification is to have an *idea*, i.e., a spiritual sign. **1973** *Screen* Spring/Summer 94 Each of them is in other contexts the signifying substance of one or more signification systems other than the cinema. *Ibid.* 109 In cinema signification (the process of the production of signs) is described by Metz as always more or less motivated, that is non-arbitrary.

2. (Examples in *Semiotics.*)

1964 C. MORRIS *Signification & Significance* i. 3 'Significations'..are not 'entities' in any objectionable sense, but certain describable aspects of complex behavioral processes in the natural world. **1976** T. EAGLETON *Crit. & Ideology* iii. 72 The text takes as its object, not the real, but certain significations by which the real lives itself—significations which are themselves the product of its partial abolition.

Hence **significa·tional** *a.*

1953 H. H. PRICE *Thinking & Exper.* iv. 117 Our question concerning the 'tied' (as opposed to 'free') character of significational thinking.

significatum (signifikā·tŏm). *Linguistics* and *Semiotics.* [L., neut. sing. pa. pple. of *significāre* to signify.] That which is signified or denoted; *spec.* = *SIGNIFIÉ. Opp. *SIGNIFICANS.

1865 S. HODGSON *Time & Space* ii. 44 It is of the utmost importance in reasoning to distinguish which kind of object or significatum it is which is expressed, or concealed, by a word or set of words. **1946** C. MORRIS *Signs, Lang. & Behavior* 17 Those conditions which are such that whatever fulfills them is a denotatum will be called the significatum of the sign. **1964** [see *SIGNIFICANS]. **1974** G. LEECH *Semantics* v. 73 The set of conditions (e.g. the qualities of being edible, tasty, nourishing) which make the bone a denotatum of S_1 [*sc.* a buzzer sound] constitute the *significatum* of the sign.

‖**signifié** (sinʸifie). *Linguistics* and *Semiotics.* [Fr., pa. pple. of *signifier* to signify.] A concept or meaning as opposed to its expression in a physical medium (phonetic, graphic, etc.); the semantic element of a sign. Opp. *SIGNIFIANT.

[**1916**: see *SIGNIFIANT.] **1939** [see *SAUSSUREAN *a.*]. **1947**, etc. [see *SIGNIFIANT]. **1963** J. LYONS *Structural Semantics* iii. 41 Here it may be noted that there is no need whatsoever to posit a common conceptual 'signifié', or 'meaning', to account for identity of application between different languages.

signified, *ppl. a.* Add: **B.** *absol.* as *sb.* That which is indicated; *Linguistics* and *Semiotics* = *SIGNIFIÉ (opp. *SIGNIFIER b).

1939 L. H. GRAY *Foundations of Lang.* 16 In the speaker's mind a concept arises... This concept is termed the *signified.* **1954**, etc. [see *SIGNIFIER b].

signifier. Add: **b.** *Linguistics* and *Semiotics.* = *SIGNIFIANT. Opp. *SIGNIFIED *sb.*

1954 U. WEINREICH *Languages in Contact* ii. 9 It becomes possible for the bilingual to interpret two signs whose sementemes, or signifieds, he has identified as a compound sign with a single signified and two signifiers, one in each language. **1960** W. BASKIN tr. *de Saussure's Course in Gen. Linguistics* I. i. 67 The bond between the signifier and the signified is arbitrary. **1967** LAVERS & SMITH tr. *Barthes's Elements of Semiology* III. 65 The commutation test consists of artificially introducing a change in the plane of expression (signifiers) and in observing whether this change brings about a correlative modification on the plane of content (signifieds). **1973** *Screen*

Spring/Summer 89 In a great many cases the term 'form' designates the film *signifier*..and the term 'content' its *signified*. **1976** T. Eagleton *Crit. & Ideology* iii. 72 History, one might say, is the *ultimate* signifier of literature, as it is the ultimate signified. **1977** A. Sheridan tr. *Lacan's Écrits* iii. 69 The symptom is here the signifier of a signified repressed from the consciousness of the subject. **1979** *Dædalus* Summer 72 He has only to offer the Signifier, 'Lie'—which could mean 'tell an untruth'—for Othello to snatch the Signified, 'lie with'.

c. *U.S. slang* (chiefly *Blacks'*). One who boasts or makes insulting remarks or insinuations, esp. in an attempt to exceed others in exaggeration.

1962 *Jrnl. Amer. Folklore* July–Sept. 212 The monkey is a 'signifier', and one of the methods he uses for inflaming the lion is to indicate that the elephant has been 'sounding' on the lion. **1965** H. Gold *Man who was not with It* xxii. 204 When he bragged like any carnie signifier, then I wondered where and why I was going. **1972** J. Maryland in T. Kochman *Rappin' & Stylin' Out* 209 The following verbal play is indicative of the type that might be found in any of a number of shine parlors..or street corners where the signifiers can be found congregating each day.

signify, *v.* Add: **7. b.** (Later examples.)

1903 Somerville & 'Ross' *All on Irish Shore* iii. 75 'Did many people say it?' asked Mr Gunning... 'Oh, no one whose opinion signified!' retorted Fanny Fitz. **1930** A. P. Herbert *Water Gipsies* ii. 16 Don't worry, Fred. It don't signify.

8. *intr. U.S. slang* (chiefly *Blacks'*). To boast or brag; to make insulting remarks or insinuations.

1932 *Evening Sun* (Baltimore) 9 Dec. 31/5 *Signify*, to pretend to have knowledge of a matter or subject in which one is poorly informed. **1935** Z. N. Hurston *Mules & Men* I. vii. 161 'Aw, woman, quit tryin' to signify.' 'Ah kin signify all Ah please, Mr. Nappy-chin.' **1948** *Common Ground* Summer 42/2 He was signifying and getting his revenge through songs. **1968** *Down Beat* 7 Mar. 38/3 One night Billie brought the personal element into focus by 'signifying', which in Harlemese means making a series of pointed but oblique remarks apparently addressed to no one in particular, but unmistakable in intention in such a close-knit circle. **1969** C. Mitchell *Lang. Behavior in Black Urban Community* iii. 96, I wasn't signifying at her, but..if the shoe fits, wear it. **1973** A. Dundes *Mother Wit* 141/2 A sample of some of the special techniques and forms of extended word play should convince even the most adamant sceptic that no black child who can signify or play the dozens can rightly be called lacking in verbal skills.

signifying, *vbl. sb.* Add: **b.** *U.S. slang* (chiefly *Blacks'*). The act of boasting, baiting, insulting, or making insinuations. Also *attrib.*

1959 A. Anderson *Lover Man* 21 'Y'all hush your signifying,' I said. 'That there's a *lady*, and I won't have y'all signifying 'bout her like that.' **1964** *Amer. Folk Music Occasional* I. 75 'Signifying' is a children's device, and is severely 'put down' by adults. **1970** [see *joning *vbl. sb.*]. **1974** H. L. Foster *Ribbin', Jivin', & Playin' Dozens* v. 206 Mezzrow describes a signifying scene in Big John's bar in Harlem. **1977** *Maledicta* Summer 15 Young blacks have verbal contests like this in anti-family insults, called *sounding* or *signifying*.

signifying, *ppl. a.* Add: **b.** *U.S. slang* (chiefly *Blacks'*). That boasts, insults, or makes insinuations.

1956 M. Stearns *Story of Jazz* (1957) i. 11 The language is Creole French and the New Orleans Creoles call it a 'signifying song'. In spite of its gaiety and rhumba-like rhythms, this song cuts two ways and the *sali dame* (dirty lady) to which it is addressed is about to have her reputation shredded. **1969** *Negro Digest* Sept. 14 *Signifying* poetry holds a special fascination for me. **1974** H. L. Foster *Ribbin', Jivin', & Playin' Dozens* v. 207 Deep down in the jungle where the coconuts grow/Lived the signifyingest motherfucker that the world ever know.

signing, *vbl. sb.* Add: **1. b.** With adverbs, as *signing-in, -off, -on, -out, -up*. Also *attrib.*

1925 Paterson & Webster *Man. Locomotive Running Shed Management* viii. 103 The signing-on times of cleaners are arranged with due regard to the finishing times of the engines they are required to clean. **1948** H. Innes *Blue Ice* iii. 77 He gave the signing-off whistle.. then our attention was called back to the radio. **1950** *Sport* 7–11 Apr. 14/3 He is Allenby Chilton,..to whom Liverpool gave a trial before the United engaged him, for a £10 signing-on fee, in 1938. **1965** 'T. Hinde' *Games of Chance* II. iv. 203 The purpose of the signing-in book..is to ascertain that all staff are arriving punctually. **1968** *Brit. Med. Bull.* XXIV. 222/1 The computer equivalent of the signing out inspection of the report by the laboratory staff. **1973** *Guardian* 23 May 6/8 There is no signing-on at the new job centre. **1974** Hawkey & Bingham *Wild Card* xiv. 124 A laxness among certain members of staff regarding signing-out procedures for items drawn from stock. **1976** E. Dunphy *Only a Game?* v. 159 The signing-on fee is crucial in football these days. **1981** J. Scott *Distant View of Death* xii. 162 Signing in and signing out meant nothing to Rosher... He simply worked.

3. *transf.* One who has signed a contract.

1974 *Motor Cycle* 23 Mar. 10/6 (*caption*) Hackney's new signing, Norwegian Dag Lovaas (left) chats with Kings Lynn international Malcolm Simmons. **1977** *Times* 4 Aug. 6/6 Macdonald, a £330,000 buy from Newcastle..and Hudson, a £200,000 signing from Stoke..were sent home ..because of alleged misconduct on the tour.

sign-post, *sb.* Add: **2.** Also *fig.* and *attrib.*

1961 *Atlanta Constitution* 17 Aug. 5 In the..breathless state of being in love the usual signposts that guide you to lasting and satisfying relationships are sometimes obscured. **1962** *Listener* 6 Dec. 958/2 He therefore studies talk more closely and discovers that..by selecting signpost phrases, he can convey what is being felt by what is unsaid. **1969** I. & P. Opie *Children's Games* p. viii, Full use has been made of the signposts, clearly marked for those willing to look for them, that are provided by *The Oxford English Dictionary* and *The English Dialect Dictionary*.

So **si·gnpostless** *a.*, not equipped with or marked by sign-posts.

1962 *Times* 22 Feb. 14/4 The signpost-less lanes of Surrey. **1968** *Economist* 16 Mar. 12/2 A preposterous, unanalysable, ignorant, signpostless, meandering mess.

si·gnpost, *v.* Also **sign-post.** [f. prec.] *trans.* To direct or indicate by means of or in the manner of a sign-post; to equip or provide with sign-posts. Also *fig.* Hence **si·gnposted** *ppl. a.*, **si·gnposting** *ppl. a.* and *vbl. sb.*

1895 A. A. Grace *Maoriland Stories* 105, I shall just sign-post 'em up to the station when they come. **1922** W. J. Locke *Tale of Triona* xxiii. 265 The road undulated ..with a steeply sloping drop of thirty feet to the valley. Such spots were grimly sign-posted for motorists. **1923** *Daily Mail* 19 May 5 Where the road is not so good and badly needs proper signposting. *Ibid.* 21 May 4 Dartmoor is moderately well signposted. **1930** *Aberdeen Press & Jrnl.* 8 May 5 The R.A.C. propose only to signpost the main arteries. **1938** *Sun* (Baltimore) 16 May 8/1 Even more marked improvements have been made. There are what are called 'sign-posted' reviews. **1946** E. Linklater *Private Angelo* viii. 81 They had reconnoitred, by routes that camel-ribs signposted, the farthest Libyan oases. **1953** X. Fielding *Stronghold* 57 A forbidden area metaphorically signposted 'noli me tangere'. **1955** *Times* 6 Jan. 6/1 They were also signposting a ring road for through traffic avoiding the central London area. **1961** *N. & Q.* Nov. 440/1 There are textual notes at the foot of each page, ludicrously signposted by a system of expanding alphabetical cycles. **1971** P. Gresswell *Environment* 104 Some councils are prepared to spend money on signposting. **1975** J. B. Harley *O.S. Maps* p. xiii, A principal objective is to indicate what the map user is likely to find on a particular map series and..to signpost what is omitted. **1976** *Howard Jrnl.* XV. I. 39 The different themes and possible groupings of the essays could perhaps have been signposted better to make the reader's task easier. **1978** A. & G. Ritchie *Anc. Monuments Orkney* 22 This cairn is approached by a signposted path on the N side of the Trumland to Westness road. **1981** *Times* 2 Sept. 21/1 It was as recently as June that the board [of Trusthouse Forte] reported on the six months to last April. This signposted a dreadful year for hotels.

‖ **sigri** (si·grī). [Gujarati *sagḍī*.] A fire or stove used for cooking.

1949 J. R. Lawrence *Indian Embers* 56 All day our bedding is spread over wicker cages enclosing a charcoal sigri. **1954** J. Masters *Bhowani Junction* 127 The invisible charcoal fumes from the sigri tingled in my nostrils. **1964** M. Malgonkar *Bend in Ganges* xxxiv. 334 Sundari was bending over the sigri..turning the toast. **1970** 'B. Mather' *Break in Line* xx. 245 Out here, away from the charcoal *sigri*, the cold was intense.

‖ **sijo** (sī·dʒo). [Korean.] **a.** A type of Korean vocal music. **b.** A Korean lyric poem usu. consisting of twenty-four syllables divided into three lines. Also *attrib.*

1898 I. L. Bird *Korea & her Neighbours* xii. 191 There are three classes of Korean vocal music, the first being the *Si-jo* or 'classical' style, *andante tremuloso*, and 'punctuated with drums'. **1954** W. Stevens *Let.* 9 July (1967) 840 Here are your sijos... The poems are charming, at least to me. But Korean poetry..is a delicacy, like bees' knees and apple hips. **1960** P. Hyun *Voices of Dawn* 28 The metaphysical *sijo* poets. **1971** *Korean Folklore & Classics* III. 86 The satto read sijo silently shaking himself..to forget his tediousness. **1972** *Korea Past & Present* xiv. 319 Kagok is a five-stanza form which is accompanied by an orchestra, whereas Sijo is a three-stanza form without orchestra. But they are similar in the sense that both use Sijo poems as words. **1977** *Korea* (Korean Overseas Information Service, Seoul) 57/3 The most popular Korean poetic form, the *Sijo*.

sika[1]. Substitute for def.: A small red deer, *Sika nippon*, native to Japan and eastern China and widely naturalized elsewhere. Also *attrib.* (Later examples.)

1909 E. Protheroe *Handy Nat. Hist.: Mammals* x. 365 The Sika..is a beautiful brilliant chestnut, thickly spotted with white. **1957** O. Breland *Animal Friends & Foes* i. 38 Important deer..include..the sika deer of eastern Asia. **1966** *Punch* 19 Oct. 596/2 The sika-deer of Brownsea Island left its restricted space some years ago for the Dorset mainland. **1978** *Lancashire Life* Nov. 70/1 The last Lord Ribblesdale..also introduced the Sika deer which roam the district to this day. **1981–2** *Deer Farmer* (N.Z.) Summer 3 But we have farmed other breeds, such as fallow and sika.

‖ **sika**[2] (sī·kă). [Bengali, ad. Skr. *śikyà* sling.] A rope hanger for suspending baskets, etc.

1974 *Observer* (Colour Suppl.) 15 Sept. 40 (Advt.), Sikas are traditionally used in Bangladesh village homes instead of kitchen cupboards. **1979** *Church Times* 26 Oct. 13/3 Jute *sikas* (basket hangers), bags and place-mats from Bangladesh form an attractive part of Traidcraft's range.

Sikan, var. *Sican. **Sikel,** var. *Sicel *sb.* and *a.* **Sikeliot(e,** varr. *Siceliot *sb.* and *a.*

Sikh. 1. For definition read: A member of a monotheistic religious group, originally established in India (chiefly in the Punjab) by Guru Nanak in the early part of the 16th century.

The majority of Sikhs are still located in the Punjab in northern India, but many are now living in other parts of India, and in Africa, Europe, the United States, and elsewhere. Sikhs became famous for their military prowess in the 19th century during the period of British imperialism. The Sikh religion requires its members, among other institutionalized customs, to wear a turban, and this has brought Sikhs into conflict with authorities in some countries outside India in the second half of the present century, mainly because of local regulations about the wearing of crash helmets on motor cycles.

Sikhara, var. *shikhara.

Sikhism. (Earlier example.)

1849 J. D. Cunningham *Hist. Sikhs* iii. 96/1 There are also elements of change within Sikhism itself.

Sikkimese (sikimī·z), *a.* and *sb.* [f. *Sikkim* (see below) + -ese.] **A.** *adj.* Of or pertaining to Sikkim, a country in the eastern Himalayas. **B.** *sb.* A native or inhabitant of Sikkim; *collect.* the people of Sikkim.

1861 J. C. Gawler *Dispatch* 15 Feb. in H. St. G. M. Mcrea *Regimental Hist. 45th Rattray's Sikhs* (1933) I. 149 Captain Impey's column surprised the Sikkimese camp at Temi. **1938** G. Gorer *Himalayan Village* i. 36 During the eighteenth and early nineteenth centuries the Lepchas fought with the Sikkimese against the continued invasions of the Nepali and Bhutanese. **1955** *Times* 3 June 7/3 The devout Sikkimese who asked that no human foot should profane the final high places that their faith holds sacred. **1960** 'S. Harvester' *Chinese Hammer* i. 10 Sikkimese metalwork and Kashmiri brocades. **1973** *Times* 12 Apr. 8/7 The Bhutia-Lepchas and the Sikkimese Nepalis have, however, parity in the State Council. **1978** C. Humphreys *Both Sides Circle* xx. 212 The inhabitants were a blend of Lepcha, Bhutia and other races besides the native Sikkimese.

sikr(a, varr. *shikhara.

Siksika (si·ksikă). Also † **Seksikai, Siksikai.** [Blackfoot, f. *siksi-* black + *-ka* foot.] The Blackfoot Indians, *esp.* those of the northernmost of the three tribes which comprise the Blackfoot.

1843 tr. *Wied-Neuwied's Trav. Interior N. Amer.* xix. 245 The Blackfeet form a numerous nation, which is divided into three tribes, speaking one and the same language. These tribes are—1. The Siksekai or Seksekai, the Blackfeet properly so called. *Ibid.*, The Siksekai signifies, in their language, Blackfoot. **1902** *Encycl. Brit.* XXIX. 466/1 Blackfeet (Siksika). **1910** in F. Hodge *Handbk. Amer. Indians* II. 570/1 A band of the Kainah division of the Siksika. **1923** M. Barbeau *Indian Days in Canadian Rockies* Addenda, 197 The Blackfoot..were the Bedouins of the Plains... Their three subdivisions, consisting of the Blackfoot proper (or Siksika), the Blood, and the Piegan..considered themselves as of one family. **1942** O. Lewis *Effects of White Contact upon Blackfoot Culture* ii. 7 The Blackfoot, Blood and Piegan tribes are at present time located on four reserves, of which three are in Alberta, Canada, and one in Montana... To avoid confusion we shall use the Blackfoot term 'Siksika' to refer to the Northern Blackfoot, and the term Blackfoot to refer to all three tribes. **1952** J. R. Swanton *Indian Tribes N. Amer.* 396 The Siksika are divided into the following subtribes: The Siksika or Blackfeet proper, [etc.].

Sikyonian, var. *Sicyonian *sb.* and *a.*

silage. Add: **2.** *attrib.* and *Comb.*, as *silage clamp* (Clamp *sb.*[3]), *loader, -maker, stack*; *silage-feeding, -making* vbl. sbs.; *silage-fed* ppl. adj.; **silage cutter,** a stationary machine for chopping a crop into short lengths for silage and elevating it into a silo; also, a silage harvester; **silage harvester,** a machine for cutting a standing crop as it travels, chopping it into short lengths for silage, and elevating it into another vehicle.

1961 *Farmers' Weekly* 6 Oct. 117/1 The loose housing and the self-feed silage clamps. **1978** *Cornish Guardian* 27 Apr. 15/7 (Advt.), 131 acre accredited dairy farm..milking parlour, silage clamp. **1962** *Trans. Amer. Soc. Agric. Engin.* XIX. 117 (*heading*) Code for testing silage cutters. **1967** Martin & Leonard *Princ. Field Crop Production* (ed. 2) viii. 208 Corn and sorghum row crops for silage are harvested with a field silage cutter or a forage harvester. **1972** *Country Life* 15 June 1580/1 Silage feeding to the flock..usually begins just before Christmas. *Ibid.* 1580/3 It is usually the practice in silage-fed flocks to introduce a cereal supplement just before lambing. **1931** J. B. Davidson *Agric. Machinery* xxv. 266 To reduce the labor of handling green fodder and to dispense with the use of binding twine, the operations of cutting and harvesting silage are combined in the silage harvester, and the cut silage is delivered to a wagon as it is drawn beside the harvester through the field. **1977** *Cork Examiner* 8 June 15/5 (Advt.), Used Kidd silage harvester, good working condition, £525. **1971** *Power Farming* Mar. 8/3 The operation of the American silage loader..is explained in the captions to the accompanying photographs. **1924** W. J. MALDEN *Grassland Farming* xi. 152 The silage-maker has two points to consider. **1960** *Farmer & Stock-breeder* 2 Feb. 55/2 Most of the people I have talked to have been experienced silage-makers. **1924** W. J. MALDEN *Grassland Farming* xi. 149 Heating is really an aid in silage-making, because under the moist heat the stiffest stems yield, and compression becomes easy. **1960** *Farmer & Stockbreeder* 16 Feb. 73/2 In spite of the great progress in silage-making in the last few years, the amount of permanent grass and temporary leys made into hay in Britain still far exceeded the amount conserved by all the other processes put together. **1888** Silage stack [in Dict.].

silajit (si·lădʒit). Also **shilajatu, sillajeet,** etc. [a. Hind. *shila-jit*, Skr. *śilājit, śilājatu* bitumen, f. Skr. *śilā* rock + *jit* conquering or *jatu* essence.] A name given to various solid or viscous substances found on rock in India and Nepal (see quot. 1903), esp. a usu. dark-brown odoriferous substance which is used in traditional Indian medicine and probably consists principally of dried animal urine.

1811–12 F. BUCHANAN *Acct. Bihar & Patna* (1936) II. III. iii. 467 About three miles farther in the same direction..a very peculiar substance called silajit exudes. **1833** G. PLAYFAIR tr. *Taleef Shereef* 96 *Sillajeet* is the urine of the hill wild goat, which when the animal is rutting, is discharged on the stones and evaporated by the sun's heat. **1903** *Jrnl. R. Asiatic Soc. Bengal* LXII. II. 98 One of the most peculiar medicinal substances of the East is that called Silajit or Shilajatu. It is known by the former name in Hindi and Persian, and by the latter in Bengali and Sanskrit. **1964** *New Statesman* 3 Apr. 517/2 He was extolling the miraculous properties of his ointment, guaranteed to contain the purest silajit brought from Tibet.

silane (səi·lēⁱn). *Chem.* [ad. G. *silan* (A. Stock 1916, in *Ber. d. Deut. Chem. Ges.* XLIX. 108): see SILICON and -ANE.] Any of the large class of hydrides of silicon analogous to the alkanes; *spec.* silicon tetrahydride, SiH_4, a colourless gas which has strong reducing properties and is spontaneously flammable in air.

1916 *Jrnl. Chem. Soc.* CX. II. 319 The suggestion is made that the term 'silanes' be accepted generally for the saturated compounds of silicon and hydrogen, the various members being distinguished thus: SiH_4, monosilane; Si_2H_6, disilane; [etc.]. **1935** *Nature* 9 Mar. 397/2 The oxidation of silane resembles very closely that of phosphine rather than that of methane. **1958** *Times Rev. Industry* June 26/3 The gaseous compound silane, SiH_4, is produced by reacting silicon tetrachloride with lithium aluminium hydride. **1977** *Whitaker's Almanack 1978* 1034/1 Work has now begun on cleaning and repairing these figures [on Wells Cathedral] and..it is hoped that the use of lime and silanes will prevent further decay of the stone surfaces.

silanize (səi·lănəiz), *v.* [f. *SILAN(E + -IZE.] *trans.* To treat (silica-based material, esp. support material for chromatography) with reagents which render the surface more inert by converting reactive groups to organo-silicon groups. Hence **si·lanized** *ppl. a.*, **si·lanizing** *vbl. sb.* Also **silaniza·tion,** treatment of this kind.

1962 *Analytical Chem.* XXXIV. 891/3 To eliminate possible adsorption effects, the material was silanized with Siliclad. *Ibid.*, Silanizing reduced the specific surface to about 2 sq. meters per gram. *Ibid.* 892/1 A weighed amount of silanized Chromosorb-R. **1968** *Jrnl. Chromatogr.* XXXIV. 305 By silanizing the support surface we obtained changes in the chemical character of the surface. *Ibid.* 308 The effect of surface silanization on the structure of the internal support pores is obvious. **1973** *Nature* 30 Mar. 339/1 A 5·75 inch disposable pipette plugged with silanized glass-wool. **1975** WILLIAMS & WILSON *Biologist's Guide to Princ. & Techniques Pract. Biochem.* iii. 70 This is normally achieved by silanization of the support with such compounds as hexamethyl-disilazane.

Silastic (silæ·stik). *Chem.* Also **silastic.** [f. SI(LICON + E)LASTIC *a.* and *sb.*] A proprietary name for silicone rubber. Freq. *attrib.*

1946 *Rubber Age* Feb. 580/1 Silastic is an almost entirely inorganic synthetic elastomer. **1947** *Official Gaz.* (U.S. Patent Office) 2 Dec. 26/1 Dow Corning Corporation... *Silastic.* For compositions..comparable to..rubber prior to vulcanization but containing organosilicon polymers... Claims use since July, 1945. **1953** *Electronic Engin.* XXV. 309/1 Also recently introduced is a range of tropical suppressor filter units which are hermetically sealed in a metal container with silastic terminals. **1965** *Trade Marks Jrnl.* 12 May 632/1 Silastic. **1980** *Recent Advances in Surgery* X. 66 A silastic strain gauge.

‖ **silat** (silæ·t). Also **Silat.** [Mal.] The Malay art of self-defence, practised in a series of exercises as a martial art or accompanied by drums as a ceremonial display or dance.

[**1900** W. W. SKEAT *Malay Magic* vi. 381 Those who have any skill amuse the company with exhibitions of Malay fencing (*main silat*).] **1910** R. J. WILKINSON *Papers on Malay Subjects: Life & Customs* III. 27 Even if it does drag on..as a game for Malay boys, the *main silat* will never preserve in its new form the curious wealth of technicalities associated with the national weapon of the country. **1972** M. SHEPPARD *Taman Indera* vi. 85 The first henna dance..took place in the palace garden... The only accompaniment to this dance was supplied by *Silat* drums—double-headed barrel drums. *Ibid.* x. 142 There are a great many varieties of Silat and different teachers specialize in different types. **1978** T. WILLIAMSON *Technicians of Death* xiii. 112 Silat, the Malayan martial art where the hands and arms are used for defence and the knees and feet for attack.

‖ **silbador** (silbădōə·ɹ). Pl. **silbadores, silbadors.** [Sp., = whistler.] One who uses the whistled language *silbo* (see next).

1957 *Archivum Linguisticum* IX. I. 44 The melodies whistled to silbadores proved completely unintelligible. **1965** *Sun* 24 July 5/5 A top silbador can be heard up to nine miles away... The silbadors have a voice range of two octaves.

‖ **silbo** (si·lbo). Also **Silbo.** [Sp., = a whistle, whistling.] A form of whistled Spanish used by the inhabitants of Gomera in the Canary Islands, in order to communicate across long distances. Also known as *Silbo Gomero.*

1957 *Archivum Linguisticum* IX. I. 44 There are abundant references to the silbo and at least two full-length studies. **1964** A. CLASSE in D. Abercrombie et al. *Daniel Jones* 43 The investigation of a whistled form of Spanish (Silbo Gomero)... We tested one group of consonants which are invariably confused in the Silbo. **1977** *Sci. Amer.* May 141/2 In the Spanish Civil War military signals were on occasion cast in Silbo, but there were Gomerans on both sides and so the measure-countermeasure drama soon ran its course. **1978** *Verbatim* Sept. 13/1 A phonetic analysis of the Silbo Gomero of Canarian Spanish is extended feature by feature to the articulated whistle.

silcott (si·lkǫt). ? *Obs.* Also **silcot, Sillcott.** [f. SIL(K *sb.* + COTT(ON *sb.*¹] A material made of cotton finished to resemble silk, chiefly used for underskirts. Cf. SILKETTE.

1894 J. E. DAVIS *Elem. Mod. Dressmaking* (1895) 93 Varieties of silkette or silcot (cotton finished to look and feel like silk). **1923** *Daily Mail* 17 Feb. 10 (Advt.), Petticoat of Sillcott edged with pleated and hemstitched flounce. *Ibid.* 28 Feb. 5 Silcott Petticoat with small crystal frill.

silcrete (si·lkrīt). *Geol.* [f. SIL(ICA + CON)-CRETE *sb.*] A quartzite formed of sand grains or pebbles cemented together by silica; a siliceous duricrust.

1902 G. W. LAMPLUGH in *Geol. Mag.* IX. 575, I have the hardihood to suggest that the term might be complemented by equivalents,—'silcrete', for sporadic masses in loose material of the 'greywether' type, indurated by a siliceous cement. **1950** *Antiquity* XXIV. 209 More than 90 per cent of these implements are of 'ferricrete sandstone', the others being of 'silcrete sandstone'. **1977** A. HALLAM *Planet Earth* 85 Bedrock became deeply weathered to give striking weathering crusts (duricrusts) composed of iron and aluminum oxides (in the case of ferricretes) or silica (in the case of silcretes).

sild (silt). [a. Da., Norw. *sild* herring: cf. SILE *sb.*³.] A small immature herring, *Clupea harengus*, esp. one caught in northern European seas.

1921 *Handbk. Norway & Sweden* (Admiralty) viii. 157 The true sardine..does not occur in northern waters. Norwegian 'sardines' are now known in commerce as 'sild'. **1962** E. M. CRUICKSHANK in G. Borgstrom *Fish as Food* II. iv. 195 With small fish like the sild, the entire fish is processed.

silence, *sb.* Add: **1. a.** (Later pl. and *personif.* examples.)

a **1875** G. M. HOPKINS *Poems* (1967) 31 Elected Silence, sing to me. **1967** G. STEINER *Lang. & Silence* 415 Dickens, Hopkins, Kipling are examples of modern writers whose root sensibility was oral, and who tried to adapt essentially oral means to the silences of print.

e. The renunciation of speech chosen or vowed by certain religious or monastic orders, *esp.* the Trappists. Also in extended sense. Freq. in phr. *the rule of silence.*

1387, *c* **1450** [see sense 7 in Dict.]. *a* **1631** DONNE *Poems* (1633) 69 Harmelesse fish monastique silence keepe. **1884** ADDIS & ARNOLD *Cath. Dict.* 804/1 Probably the most trying part of all the discipline is the silence, no monk being allowed to speak to his brother on any occasion. **1921** G. O'DONOVAN *Vocations* xxii. 305 Hush, Sister. The rule of silence is no joke. **1957** P. L. FERMOR *Time to keep Silence* 67 There is a special dispensation from the rule of silence for the monks who deal with the abbey livestock when they are actually addressing their dumb charges. **1978** *Oxford Diocesan Mag.* Dec. 17/1 Then there was the two days' retreat... At no time..was the sense of fellowship more apparent than during the silence.

f. Proverbial phr. *silence is golden.*

1834 CARLYLE *Sart. Res.* III. iii, in *Fraser's Mag.* June 668/1 As the Swiss Inscription says: *Sprechen ist silbern, Schweigen ist golden* (Speech is silvern, Silence is golden). **1865** W. WHITE *Eastern England* II. ix. 129 Silence is golden, says the proverb. We apprehended the full significance thereof when far away from busy thoroughfares. **1935** M. V. HUGHES *Vivians* vii. 138 'Did you tell him about that?' 'No, and I'm wondering whether I ought to?' 'I shouldn't if I were you. Silence is golden.' **1980** J. O'NEILL *Spy Game* xxv. 239 'I'll tell you the rest.. on the way back.' He sealed her lips with a finger. 'Meanwhile, silence is golden.'

2. d. Phr. *the rest is silence* and varr., in allusion to the last words of the dying Hamlet (SHAKES. *Ham.* v. ii. 368).

1910 GALSWORTHY *Justice* II. 49 Once this cheque was altered and presented, the work of four minutes—four mad minutes—the rest has been silence. **1939** A. HUXLEY *After Many a Summer* II. i. 187 If only the rest were silence!.. What joy if the rest of Wordsworth had been silence, the rest of Coleridge, the rest of Shelley! **1982** *Daily Tel.* 2 June 16/4 In most of the countries involved the eternal tug-of-war between Government and news media has long since ended. The curtain has fallen. The rest is silence.

e. A period of silence observed in memory of the dead, *esp.* the two minutes' silence kept on the anniversary of Armistice Day (11 Nov. 1918) or, since 1946, on Remembrance Sunday.

1919 *Times* 12 Nov. 15/6 The Great Silence... At 11 o'clock yesterday morning the nation, in response to the King's invitation, paid homage to the Glorious Dead by keeping a two minutes' silence for prayer and remembrance. *Ibid.* 16/1 On the Stock Exchange, after the silence, a gong was sounded. **1926** A. TOPHAM *Chron. Prussian Court* xx. 245 We discussed among other things the *Titanic* disaster [1912] which had recently happened, and I remember referring to 'the silence' of two minutes by which the Canadian railways and churches had honoured the memory of the Canadians who had perished. **1929** *B.B.C. Year-bk. 1930* 78 Broadcasting the Silence November 11th, 1928. **1972** 'E. LATHEN' *Murder without Icing* (1973) xxii. 188 The game was preceded by a two-minute silence in memory of Billy Sicagusa. **1982** D. PHILLIPS *Coconut Kiss* vi. 52 You march once round the playground and salute the flag... Then you go in for the two minutes' silence.

7. *silence-box* (earlier example), *room* (examples); *silence-loving* adj.; **silence cabinet,** (*a*) = *silence-box*; (*b*) (see quot. 1929).

1889 *Telephone* I. 471/1 The public is also admitted to a silence-box at the Nottingham Post Office. **1893** PREECE & STUBBS *Man. Teleph.* 227 At most telephone exchanges a 'silence cabinet' is provided in the public office. **1929** *B.B.C. Year-bk. 1930* 309 In Savoy Hill there are nine studios, six of which are equipped with silence cabinets (these are small rooms adjacent to the studios from which the announcer can speak before switching over to the studio itself). **1855** F. W. FABER *Growth in Holiness* ix. 147 It wrung a cry even from the silence-loving Heart of our ever-blessed Saviour. **1912** W. OWEN *Let.* 23 June (1967) 142 The firm Superintendent of their Sunday School, the silence-loving, and the melancholy-voiced, on that day capered about the lawn among them. **1958** S. HYLAND *Who goes Hang?* xviii. 77 They were in the Silence Room of the Library, a room in which conversation..is..a tabu. **1959** T. S. ELIOT *Elder Statesman* II. 47 And remember, when you want to be *very* quiet There's the Silence Room. With a television set.

silenced, *ppl. a.* Add: **b.** Of a gun: fitted with a silencer.

1965 [see *GUNSEL 2]. **1974** 'I. DRUMMOND' *Power of Bug* vii. 106 Why *did* the chap poke a silenced pistol through the window? **1980** *Daily Tel.* 15 Oct. 3 He would not shoot Henry MacKenny with a silenced fire-arm.

silencer. Add: **2.** For 'or rifle' read 'rifle, etc.' and add later examples. Hence **si·lencered** *a.*, of guns: fitted with a silencer (cf. *SILENCED *ppl. a.* b.).

1905 *Engineering* 20 Oct. 529/3 This form of silencer is not necessarily confined to marine motors. **1926** G. HUNTING *Vicarion* vi. 98 He must have had a silencer on his gun. **1950** G. BRENAN *Face of Spain* vii. 149 Nine hours in a bus without a silencer..over mountain roads full of pot-holes. **1958** *Economist* 25 Oct. 349/3 Silencers on the engines reduce their efficiency by 4 to 5 per cent, and the total weight of silencing equipment is 1,600 lb, equivalent to 8 passengers. **1967** J. WAINWRIGHT *Worms must Wait* lxxxii. 214 They heard the tiny crack of the silencered Luger. **1978** R. LUDLUM *Holcroft Covenant* iii. 44 He opened the door, pulled out his revolver and fired, the gunshot muted by a silencer.

silent, *a.* and *sb.* Add: **A.** *adj.* **1. a.** Also in phr. *strong silent man* (or *person, type*, etc.): a man who conceals and controls his feelings.

1840 CARLYLE *Chartism* iv. 30 With this strong silent people have the noisy vehement Irish now at length got common cause made. **1905** M. BEERBOHM in *Sat. Rev.* 23 Sept. 401/1 He is going to cry? No, the hero is one of those strong, silent men. **1913** C. MACKENZIE *Sinister Street* I. II. xv. 407 She said I must be careful not to grow up into a strong silent Englishman, because their day was done. **1919** A. A. MILNE *Not that it Matters* 142 It is useless to model ourselves now on the strong, silent man of the novel whose face is a shutter to hide his emotions. **1936** W. S. MAUGHAM *Cosmopolitans* 260 These for the most part are strong silent men who waste no words. **1978** L. CHARTERIS *Saint & Templar Treasure* (1979) i. 25 I've always fancied myself as the strong silent type.

d. *as silent as the grave*: of a place, hushed, containing no natural noise; of a person, secretive, discreet.

1823 J. F. COOPER *Pilot* I. vi. 78 'Does he keep silent?' 'As the grave.' **1829** W. SCOTT *Jrnl.* 1 July (1946) 89 The house..became silent as the grave. **1889** R. L. STEVENSON *Master of Ball.* iii. 62 We..lowered ourselves softly into a skiff, and left that ship behind us as silent as the grave. **1936** W. S. Maugham *Cosmopolitans* 269, I will be as silent as the grave, but honestly I don't understand. What does it all mean?

3. c. (Later example.)

1981 Macniven & Moore *Literary Lifelines* p. v, Silent corrections have been limited to restoring transposed letters.

e. Of a cinema film: unaccompanied by sound recording. Also in extended use to designate that which is related to or concerned with the silent film industry.

1914 [see *filmdom]. **1918** *N.Y. Times* 25 Nov. 11/3 (*heading*) Two opera stars in silent films. **1927** *Melody Maker* Sept. 933/3, I can see very little difference between the music appropriate to the spoken drama and that for the silent screen. **1941** B. Schulberg *What makes Sammy Run?* iv. 59 He was married to one of the big silent stars. **1967** *Listener* 30 Nov. 712/2 Rooming houses full of stars of silent pictures whom nobody remembers. **1977** R. Barnard *Death on High C's* ii. 19 In Owen's production.. you will be the silent-film heroine, and I will be the silent-film handsome seducer.

4. c. Of machinery, etc.: operating with or causing a minimum of noise.

1887 *Encycl. Brit.* XXII. 524/1 Dr. Otto's 'silent' engine, introduced in 1876, was the first successful motor of the modern type. **1904** A. B. F. Young *Compl. Motorist* (ed. 2) iv. 103 The silent working of the Lanchester car makes it also an extremely useful carriage for town use. *a* **1943** H. A. Whitcombe in J. Joyce *Trams of Past* (1979) 25 The citizens of Birmingham were proud of their steam trams and acclaimed them before all others for their..smooth and silent running.

5. b. (Later examples.)

1974 *Nature* 1 Feb. 295/2 Enhancing serum as used in series *b* was then absorbed to remove Ag-B antibodies but possibly not antibodies against (? serologically silent) products of other genes in the MHC, if such exist. **1979** *Ibid.* 5 July 12/3 The recessive scrapie allele is likely to be widespread but clinically 'silent' in these breeds.

d. *Med.* Not giving rise to or showing readily apparent signs or symptoms.

1928 W. Overend *Radiogr. of Chest* II. iv. 49 There are two forms of silent pneumonia: a hilar which does not reach the pleura; and a cortical which does not reach the hilum. **1951** [see *latent *a.* d]. **1979** *Jrnl. R. Soc. Arts* CXXVII. 171/2 We have had no great disease problem associated with them as yet but I have a feeling that the natural host is often a silent carrier.

6. b. *silent-footed* (earlier example).

1845 J. R. Lowell *To Future* in *Graham's Mag.* XXVIII. 52 And he can see the grim-eyed Doom From out the trembling gloom Its silent-footed steeds toward his palace goading.

7. Special collocations: *silent band* = *silent majority* (*b*) below; *silent cop* (*Austral.*) (see quot. 1934); *silent* (*dog*) *whistle,* a high-frequency whistle producing a note audible to a dog but scarcely audible to a human being; *silent heat* (*Vet.*), ovulation occurring without the signs of œstrus; † *silent highway,* a river or canal (*obs.*); *Silent Land,* used allusively to denote the state beyond this life; *silent majority,* (*a*) the dead; (*b*) the mass of people whose views remain unexpressed, esp. in political contexts; those who are usu. overlooked because of their moderation; *silent partner* (*U.S.*) = *sleeping partner* s.v. Sleeping *ppl. a.* 5 a; *silent policeman* (*N.Z.*) = *silent cop* above; *silent service* (see quot. 1929); *silent spring,* in allusion to the title of the work by R. Carson (see quot. 1962), which drew attention to the danger to the natural environment inherent in the use of toxic chemicals; *silent vote* (*U.S.*), the vote of those whose political leanings are not known in advance of their vote being cast; so *silent voter.*

1866 G. Meredith *Let.* 15 Jan. (1970) I. 326 Will bawlings in the street avail?.. They irritate the slumbering dominant party, without strengthening the insurgent. What is being done in the *Fortnightly,* for instance..does strengthen, while it increases the silent band. **1934** T. Wood *Cobbers* x. 122 A circle in the middle of cross-roads, for example, round which all traffic changing direction must swing; a round yellow blob, known here [*sc.* in Adelaide] as the Silent Cop, or the Poached Egg. **1959** D. Hewitt *Bobbin Up* 2 This was the corner, by the silent cop, where she and Roy had come to grief. **1961** C. Willock *Death in Covert* iv. 64 Attached..to the lapel of Gumbe-Howard's coat was a silent dog whistle, and attached..to his heels was a silent dog. **1965** D. Francis *For Kicks* xiii. 173 That's a silent whistle... For dogs... You can't hear it very well..but of course a dog can. **1980** J. W. Hill *Intermediate Physics* xvi. 150 The 'silent' dog whistle produces a note too high for the human ear but heard by a dog. **1950** N. Barron *Dairy Farmer's Vet. Bk.* vi. 65 Cows sometimes have short and possibly 'silent' heats that pass unnoticed, when the ovary produces the egg but the cow does not show any outward sign of being in season. **1970** W. H. Parker *Health & Dis. Farm Animals* vi. 58 The cow tends to be more generous with her signs of oestrus unless she is on a low plane of nutrition, when she may have a 'silent heat' like the ewe. **1848** *Punch* XV. 158/1 New towns have lately sprung up..on each side of the Thames. If the population manages to keep pace with the mania for building, the 'silent highway' will soon become as noisy as the New Cut. **1875** *Birmingham Daily Mail* 5 Mar. 2/5, I speculate on the incalculable good that a 'Home' would do in rescuing girl-babies of the silent highway from the unwomanly scenes of their wasted young lives. **1935** *Times* 28 Feb. 14/2 This Cinderella of the bridges that span London's silent highway. **1853** *Working Man's Way in World* xiv. 320 (*heading*) Parents and friends in the Silent Land. **1939** L. M. Montgomery *Anne of Ingleside* xxvii. 186 Ah well, Anne dearie, they've both passed long since into the Silent Land. **1874** *Harper's New Monthly Mag.* Sept. 468 (*heading*) The silent majority. **1910** *Motor World* 31 Mar. 851/1 (*heading*) Two join the 'silent majority'. Death calls at Detroit and Buffalo and claims well known men. **1955** C. V. Wedgwood *Great Rebellion* I. ii. iv. 256 The King in his natural optimism still believed that a silent majority in Scotland were in his favour. **1970** *Guardian* 11 May 10/2 The Midwest..is 'silent majority' country. **1976** *National Observer* (U.S.) 1 May B4/4 Two-thirds of all marriages in the United States still succeed. So often silent majorities of this kind are too readily forgotten. **1828–32** Silent partner [in Dict., sense 5 b]. **1894** S. Leavitt *Our Money Wars* 221 His Wall St. concern.. came to grief in 1890; also a concern in Buffalo in which he was a silent partner. **1974** R. L. Simon *Wild Turkey* xii. 82 They're only the directors. There's someone behind them. Another investor... It's a silent partner. **1965** F. Sargeson *Memoirs of Peon* iv. 88 A silent policeman had been prised from its street-moorings. **1929** *Papers Mich. Acad. Sci., Arts & Lett.* X. 323/2 *Silent Service,* the Navy. This is a reference to the long silent vigil of the British Fleet. **1937** T. Rattigan *French without Tears* I. 40 You naval people never talk about yourselves, do you? *Rogers.* Well, you know, silent service and all that. **1982** *Daily Tel.* 2 June 16/3 The Army learned certain lessons in Northern Ireland. The silent service did not share that experience. **1962** R. Carson (*title*) Silent spring. **1970** *N.Y. Times* 12 June 38 The Caspian Sea is probably the most dramatic battle-ground of Soviet Russia's looming silent spring and to date this battle is being lost to oil, petroleum products, industrial and city sewage, ballast and waste from ships. *Ibid.* 27 June 28 If we don't develop suitable pesticides—and use them—we really will have Silent Spring because there won't be any trees left for the birds to sing in. **1981** J. Sutherland *Bestsellers* x. 112 Guilt about man's depredation of his and other species' environment, at the 'silent spring' which he has brought. **1936** *Durant* (Okla.) *Daily Democrat* 2 Nov. 2/4 The regents and police pensions amendments have the best chances of carrying, but even they are endangered by the 'silent vote'. **1952** *Economist* 6 Sept. 556/1 It is believed that there will be a substantial 'silent' vote against Mr McCarthy by other citizens unwilling or unable to take a public stand against him. **1884** *Judge* 12 Nov. 140/2 To the Silent Voter, who was to make himself Felt for Cleveland: Tell me where you are and all will be forgiven.

B. *sb.* **3.** A silent film (see sense 3 e of the adj.).

1929 *Morning Post* 24 May 12/7 Every recognised tradition of the 'silents' seems to have gone by the board. **1977** 'J. le Carré' *Hon. Schoolboy* xvii. 404 Even the latest films up here are silents.

silentish, *a.* (Later example.)

1948 E. Blunden *Shakespeare to Hardy* (1956) xii. 168 Among those who were present..at Dickens's public readings, a 'silentish young man'.

Silesian, *a.* and *sb.* Add: **A.** *adj.* **b.** *Silesian stem,* a shouldered stem of a goblet or candlestick, supposed to have been so named in honour of George I for whom a goblet with such a stem was first made. Hence *Silesian-stemmed* adj.

[**1925** F. Buckley *Hist. Old Eng. Glass* ix. 72 The waisted bowl,..and the pediment, or Silesian-shouldered stem, were both novelties at this time.] **1929** W. A. Thorpe *Hist. Eng. & Irish Glass* I. v. 171 The shouldered stem is commonly known as 'Silesian', but it is certainly not exclusive to that part of Germany. *Ibid.* vi. 204 For about twenty years..the Silesian stem remained constant and English stem growth was at a standstill. **1961** E. M. Elville *Collector's Dict. Glass* 166 (*caption*) Silesian-stemmed glass moulded on the four shoulders with GR in relief. **1978** *Country Life* 19 Oct. 1170/2 It is a very pretty glass (I always fall for the high-shouldered, so-called Silesian stem which is apparently not Silesian at all). **1979** 'J. Gash' *Grail Tree* ii. 22 An engraved lead-glass cordial glass..among some Silesian-stemmed glasses.

Silex[2] (səi·leks). The proprietary name of a coffee-making machine in which boiling water is drawn through ground coffee in a filter by the creation of a vacuum.

1914 *Official Gaz.* (U.S. Patent Office) 31 Mar. 1370/2 Silex. Particular description of goods.—Coffee-percolators. **1934** *Trade Marks Jrnl.* 12 Sept. 1187/2 *Silex...* Coffee making appliances, kettles and kettle stands, milk heating and pasteurizing utensils, urns and urn stands, coffee sets [etc.]... The Silex Company.., State of Connecticut, United States of America; manufacturers. **1949** H. MacLennan *Precipice* iv. 267 The coffee had bubbled into the top of the Silex. **1971** J. Henderson *Copperhead* xv. 191 A girl appeared with a Silex of coffee and the usual paper cups.

silhouette, *sb.* Add: **2. a.** (Earlier example.)

1843 Thackeray *Irish Sketch-Bk.* II. xiii. 233 Ghostly looking *silhouettes.*

b. The contour or outline of a garment.

1920 *Glasgow Herald* 27 Nov. 4 The silhouette of this season is..much more attractive than that last year approved by Dame Fashion. *Ibid.* 4 Dec. 4 See that you preserve the silhouette of the gown. **1978** *Country Life* 17 Aug. 472/1 The new silhouette..is straight, narrow and short, with well defined, padded shoulders.

silica. Add: **b.** *silica dust*; **silica glass** = *quartz glass* s.v. *quartz 2 a; **silica gel,** hydrated silica in a hard granular form which is very hygroscopic and is used as a desiccant; **silica wool** = *slag wool* s.v. Slag *sb.* 5.

1918 *Act* 8 & 9 *Geo. V* c. 14 § 1 (3) Any industry.. involving exposure to silica dust. **1920** *Jrnl. Amer. Chem. Soc.* XLII. 971 The mere fact that a chemically inert substance like silica gel is found exhibiting such marked absorptive properties is sufficient in itself to indicate that the cause of adsorption does not lie in the interaction of adsorbent and adsorbed substance. **1956** *Nature* 18 Feb. 329/1 The acid mixture was separated on a silica gel column into acetic and propionic acids. **1977** J. Hedgecoe *Photographer's Handbk.* 36 If you are storing a camera in an unfavorable climate put it in a plastic bag with the packet of silica gel which is supplied with most new cameras. **1916** *Chem. Abstr.* X. 103 (*heading*) Silica glass. **1919** *Nature* 23 Oct. 153/1, I have recently observed that 'silica glass' possesses a remarkable crystalline or quasi-crystalline structure when examined in the polariscope. **1965** B. J. Moody *Compar. Inorg. Chem.* xviii. 268/2 Silica may be fused in the oxy-hydrogen blowpipe flame, softening at 1500–1600° C and fusing above 1700° C... The amorphous vitreous product is a supercooled liquid, silica glass, quartz glass, fused quartz or just silica. **1906** *Chambers's Jrnl.* Aug. 599/1 Slag-wool, or silica-wool, is in appearance and properties similar to asbestos.

silicate. a. Substitute for def.: Any salt, ester, or anion of a silicic acid; any substance (e.g. very many minerals and rocks) which is regarded as being formed from silica together with other oxides, and has an extended polymeric anionic structure built up from linked (SiO_4) tetrahedra. (Later examples.)

1891 *Jrnl. Chem. Soc.* LX. ii. 814 (*heading*) Action of phosphorus oxychloride on ethereal silicates and their chloro-derivatives. **1937** W. L. Bragg *Atomic Structure of Minerals* ix. 146 The classification of the silicates by their silicon-oxygen structures..corresponds to a large extent to the usual mineralogical classification. The structure is so rigid in the pyroxenes and amphiboles, micas, felspars and zeolites that it decides the crystal form. **1959** Berry & Mason *Mineralogy* xv. 462 Silicate classification is based on the types of linkages, which are as follows: 1. Independent tetrahedral groups... 2. Double tetrahedra structures [etc.]. **1962** P. J. & B. Durrant *Introd. Adv. Inorg. Chem.* xviii. 605 In most silicates the SiO_4 tetrahedra are not discrete, but are parts of larger systems in which certain oxygen atoms are held in common by two tetrahedra.

silication. (Later examples.)

1904 *Monogr. U.S. Geol. Survey* XLVII. viii. 667 Silication of carbonates, forming silicates and releasing carbon dioxide, is one of the chief reactions of the zone of anamorphism. **1923** *Jrnl. Geol.* XXXI. 176 Magnetic end-stage emanations..produce a bewildering series of silication..silicification, gametization and metallic-mineralization effects.

silici-. Add: **silicicla·stic** *a. Petrol.,* applied to clastic rocks and deposits that are not carbonates; **si·licicole, silici·colous** *adjs. Bot.* [L. *colĕre* to inhabit], growing best in siliceous soil.

1961 J. Braunstein in *Bull. Amer. Assoc. Petroleum Geologists* XLV. 2017/2, I dare to submit two new terms... These are, 'calciclastic'.., referring to clastic carbonate rocks, and, 'siliciclastic'.., referring to clastic non-carbonate rocks (which are almost exclusively silicon-bearing, either as forms of quartz or as silicates). **1976** *Nature* 3 June 440/1 Two major subdivisions are considered—the siliciclastic and carbonate tidal deposits. Recent siliciclastic examples include the classic tidal flats of the North Sea, [etc.]. **1965** Bell & Coombe tr. *Strasburger's Textbk. Bot.* 753 Species characteristic of particular soils have long been known,..e.g. halophytes.., or calcicole or silicicole (calcifuge) plants. **1901** *Jrnl. R. Microsc. Soc.* 53 J. A. Cl. Roux has grown a number of silicicolous (arenaceous) plants in calcareous soils, and finds that..the seedling plants develope tardily and imperfectly. **1932** Fuller & Conrad tr. *Braun-Blanquet's Plant Sociol.* vi. 187 In humid regions the leaching of carbonates sets in upon dolomite.., and acidophilous plants follow in the train of the progressive acidification of the dolomite soil. This occurrence of silicicolous plants on dolomite substrata was first noticed by Sendtner.

silicic, *a.* Add: *silicic acid,* a very weakly acidic substance obtained esp. by the action of acids on solutions of silicates and usu. existing in the form of colloidal solutions which contain H_4SiO_4 (*orthosilicic acid*) but consist mainly of polymeric oxyacids derived from this; any of these constituent acids. (Later examples.)

1898 [see *lactonitrile* s.v. *lacto- 2]. **1913** E. Hatschek *Physics & Chem. of Colloids* v. 41 If a solution of sodium silicate..is decomposed by a slight excess of hydrochloric acid, and the mixture is dialysed until the free acid and the sodium chloride have been removed, there remains in the dialyser a perfectly clear colourless sol of silicic acid. **1955** *Sci. Amer.* Sept. 65/3 The more volatile or acidic or silicic constituents of the fluid rock beneath the surface may have concentrated in the original uplifts. **1973** E. G. Rochow in J. C. Bailar et al. *Comprehensive Inorg. Chem.* I. xv. 1409 The relations between silicon dioxide and water are so close..that it often is difficult to distinguish between solutions of silica, solutions of distinct molecular silicic acids, colloidal dispersions of silica, the definite hydrates of SiO_2, hydrated silica in general, and silica gel.

silicium. Add: Now *Obs.*

silico-. Add: **b. silicoca·rnotite** [cf. *CARNOTITE, an unrelated mineral named after the same person], a silicate and phosphate of calcium, $Ca_5(PO_4)_2SiO_4$, found as orthorhombic crystals (coloured blue by impurities) in basic slag from steelmaking processes; **silico-ma·nganese**, a ferro-alloy containing relatively high proportions of manganese and silicon, *spec.* one containing 65 to 70 per cent. manganese and 12 to 25 per cent. silicon which is used in steel-making as a manganese-containing additive and as a deoxidizer; **si:licomoly·bdic acid**, any of a class of polyanionic oxyacids obtained when mixed solutions containing a molybdate and a silicate are acidified; *esp.* a yellow crystalline solid of this kind whose formation is the basis of a colorimetric determination of silicon; so **silicomo·lybdate**, an anion or a salt of such an acid; **silicopho·sphate** = *phosphosilicate* s.v. *PHOSPHO-.

1911 V. A. KROLL in *Jrnl. Iron & Steel Inst.* LXXXIV. 126 These crystals, which are of a beautiful dichroic-blue colour, will be distinguished in the present paper by the name Silico-Carnotite. **1949** *Mineral. Mag.* XXVIII. 496 Silicocarnotite is found in basic slags rich in phosphorus. **1971** *Tschermaks Mineral. und Petrogr. Mitteilungen* XVI. 19 The nature of the PO_4/SiO_4 substitution in silicocarnotite should be resolved by collecting X-ray intensity data from a crystal known to be free from impurities. **1895** E. L. RHEAD *Metallurgy* ix. 112 Siliconeisen and silico-manganese are irons containing silicon, or silicon and manganese... They are employed in steel manufacture. **1941** *Trans. Amer. Soc. Mech. Engineers* LXIII. 367/2 Both high-manganese and silicomanganese steels equal the chrome-vanadium steel tested and may have commercial advantages. **1956** W. D. HARGREAVES in D. L. Linton *Sheffield* 280 The city therefore uses quite large tonnages of pig-iron and of alloying metals..such as ..silico-manganese. **1881** *Jrnl. Chem. Soc.* XL. 880 Ammonium silico-molybdate is obtained in small yellow octahedrons, by mixing nitric acid solutions of ammonium molybdate and an alkaline silicate. **1928** J. H. YOE *Photometric Chem. Analysis* I. xxxi. 366 Silicates and phosphates form yellow silico- and phosphomolybdates with ammonium molybdate in acid solution. On treatment with sodium sulfite the silico- and phosphomolybdates give a blue reduction product. **1973** E. G. ROCHOW in J. C. Bailar et al. *Comprehensive Inorg. Chem.* I. xv. 1466 Silicon is one of 36 elements which have been reported as central atoms of heteropoly acid aggregates (borotungstates, phosphovanadates, silicomolybdates, etc.). **1871** *Jrnl. Chem. Soc.* XXIV. 157 (*heading*) A few remarks on the yellow precipitate containing silico-molybdic acid. **1956** *Nature* 3 Mar. 435/1 Analysis was carried out by measuring absorptiometrically the colour produced by the reduction of the silico-molybdic acid complex with ascorbic acid. **1927** *Jrnl. Agric. Sci.* XVII. 143 Stead..concluded that the most soluble phosphate was a silico-phosphate represented by $5CaO.P_2O_5.SiO_2$. **1963** C. R. COWELL et al. *Inlays, Crowns, & Bridges* vii. 77 A fine-grain silicophosphate cement of the appropriate shade is most suitable for cementation because it possesses some degree of translucency.

silicoflagellate (si:likoflæ·dʒĕlĕⁱt). [f. SILICO- + *FLAGELLATE *sb.*] A marine flagellate of the family Silicoflagellidæ, distinguished by a siliceous skeleton and radiating spines.

1906 M. HARTOG in Harmer & Shipley *Cambr. Nat. Hist.* I. iii. 86 The Silicoflagellate family Dictyochidae..have a skeleton of a similar nature. **1961** R. D. MANWELL *Introd. Protozool.* iii. 29 Living silicoflagellates are almost exclusively marine and pelagic in habit. **1978** *Nature* 16 Mar. 244/2 Apart from being an important structural component of diatoms and silicoflagellates..it [*sc.* silicon] is necessary for DNA polymerase activity in diatoms.

silicon. Add: **2.** Special comb.: **silicon carbide**, a hard refractory compound of silicon and carbon SiC: see *CARBORUNDUM; **silicon chip**, a chip (*CHIP *sb.*[1] 2 f) of silicon; **silicon ester**, any ester of silicic acid, *spec.* tetraethyl orthosilicate, $Si(OC_2H_5)_4$, a colourless flammable liquid which is readily hydrolysed to silica and is used in paints, weatherproof coatings for masonry, etc., and as a binding agent for moulds; **silicon iron, steel,** cast iron, or steel (respectively) containing a relatively high proportion of silicon, added to increase the magnetic permeability and/or the resistance to corrosion and heat; **Silicon Valley** orig. *U.S.* [from the use made of silicon chips], the Santa Clara valley, S.E. of San Francisco, where many leading U.S. microelectronic firms are located; **silicon wafer**, a wafer of silicon from which individual silicon chips can be separated (cf. *WAFER *sb.*).

1893 *Chem. News* LXVIII. 3A/2 (*heading*) The analysis of silicon carbide. **1982** JACKSON & DAY *Better than New* 138/2 Silicon carbide abrasives are used extensively for furniture renovation. **1965** *Sci. Amer.* Nov. 66/3 Engineers..saw the posibility of producing complete circuits within a silicon chip by forming all the circuit elements by diffusion. **1979** *Daily Tel.* 3 Oct. 14/4 Perhaps..the biggest gains will be possible from the sophisticated electronic 'engine management' control systems now being developed with the aid of the silicon chip and mini computer. **1923** A. P. LAURIE *Brit. Pat. 221, 342* 1/1 According to my earlier application silicon esters are applied to the stone and allowed gradually to hydrolise in position. **1969** *Kirk-Othmer Encycl. Chem. Technol.* (ed. 2) XVIII. 217 The silicon esters of organic acids, or silicon carboxylates, are also known and are prepared by the reaction of the acid with silicon halides. **1878** *Chem. News* 27 Dec. 299/2 This metallic mass is a silicon iron, remarkably rich in silicon, and evidently the product of a blast-furnace. **1970** *Materials & Technol.* III. x 769 These principles have been incorporated in the manufacture of conventional materials such as silicon-iron for electrical transformers. **1882** *Jrnl. Iron & Steel Inst.* 376 Peculiarities of silicon steel are: the adhesive scale which covers it; a low degree of weldability; and a very fine grain. **1975** D. G. FINK *Electronics Engineers' Handbk.* VI. 80 Silicon steels, known as electrical steels, are very widely used for low- and intermediate-frequency applications. **1974** *Fortune* June 135/2 They have turned part of Santa Clara County into 'Silicon Valley', the world capital of semiconductor technology. **1980** *N.Y. Times* 22 June IV. 8E In more recent years 'Silicon Valley' has grown up along the peninsula from San Francisco through Stanford University to San Jose. **1956** *Bell Syst. Technical Jrnl.* XXXV. 3 After diffusion the entire surface of the silicon wafer is covered with the diffused n- and p-type layers. **1977** *Sci. Amer.* Sept. 111/3 The pure, single-crystal silicon wafers that bear the circuits are much larger: currently three or four inches in diameter.

silicone (si·likōⁿn). *Chem.* [f. SILIC(O- + -ONE.] † **1.** Also **-on.** [ad. G. *silicon* (F. Wöhler 1863, in *Ann. d. Chem. u. Pharm.* CXXVII. 263).] A yellow solid obtained by the action of concentrated hydrochloric acid on calcium silicide and said to be a compound of silicon, hydrogen, and oxygen. *Obs.*

1863 F. WOHLER in *Chem. News* 10 Oct. 172 The relative proportions of the combined silicium and calcium are in general those necessary to form the compound $CaSi_2$... It is only by means of this compound that we can..explain the composition and mode of formation of the yellow body which is obtained by the action [on it] of hydrochloric acid, and which I shall now describe under the name of *Silicon*. **1909** *Jrnl. Chem. Soc.* XCVI. II. 806 The colourless substance, leucone, which is produced by exposing silicone to light and air, represents an intermediate step in the oxidation of silicone to silicon dioxide. **1946** J. R. PARTINGTON *Gen. & Inorg. Chem.* xviii. 506 By the action of concentrated hydrochloric acid on calcium silicide Wöhler (1863) obtained a yellow solid which he called silicone and formulated $Si_4H_4O_3$.

2. a. Formerly, the name given to any supposed compound of silicon analogous to the ketones, having a formula RR′SiO (R, R′ being organic radicals); in mod. use, any of a large group of synthetic organosilicon polymers (siloxanes) based on chains or networks of alternating silicon and oxygen atoms, many of these being good electrical insulators with high durability, and finding uses as liquids, greases, rubbers (notably in cosmetic surgery), or resins.

[**1906** *Jrnl. Chem. Soc.* XC. I. 128 The gelatinous diphenylsilicone (diphenyl silicoketone).] *Ibid.* 563 The silicones present in the residues..are mixtures, in variable proportions, of silicoformic anhydride and silico-oxalic acid. **1912** *Ibid.* CI. II. 2106 The term *silicone* has already been used to denote the analogues of the ketones, and may be advantageously retained for this purpose. **1948** *Q. Rev. Chem. Soc.* II. 26 The word 'silicone' was originally used by Kipping to denote the silicon analogues of ketones (RR′Si:O, cf. RR′C:O) but he soon recognised that monomeric silicones are incapable of existence; in fact, no compound containing the group Si:O is yet known. **1957** *Listener* 31 Oct. 719/2 The manufacturers use silicones partly because they give some resistance to spilled liquids and because dust does not readily adhere to the film of polish. **1979** [see *SHOOT *v.* 23 h].

b. *attrib.*, as *silicone polish, resin, rubber*, etc.

1944 *Chem. & Engin. News* 10 July 1134/3 Silicone resins, used as insulating varnishes and bonds, definitely fill the void between organic and inorganic insulating materials. *Ibid.* 25 Nov. 2016/1 Silicone rubber..has been developed by the General Electric Co., Schenectady, and was demonstrated at the Engineers' Club in New York on November 14. **1955** *Radio Times* 22 Apr. 52/1 (Advt.), New Goddard's Silicone Wax has revolutionized polishing. It's put wonder-working silicones into hard wax. **1958** *Times Rev. Industry* May 26/3 The core is clamped with steel clamps, and while still under pressure is bound with silicone varnish. **1960** *Farmer & Stockbreeder* 22 Mar. (Suppl.) 10/2 First, put the pointing in good repair, then treat the wall with a silicone waterproofing liquid. **1969** T. C. THORSTENSEN *Pract. Leather Technol.* xiv. 235 As a result of silicone treatment, shoes can be made that are for all practical purposes completely water-repellent. **1971** A. DIMENT *Think Inc.* vii. 129 Her breasts were.. very firm... Maybe a few silicone injections I thought cynically. **1973** *Materials & Technol.* VI. viii. 602 Silicone resins, being thermally stable, are used as impregnating varnishes, moulding compounds, encapsulants, and in laminates. **1974** *Sci. Amer.* Mar. 71/1 Artificial heart valves and experimental heart-bypass pumps are often fabricated from silicone rubber because the polymer has a lower tendency than most organic polymers to trigger the clotting of blood. **1976** *Gramophone* Nov. 755/3, I recommend the use..of silicone polish, applied thinly and evenly with a soft cloth, starting from the label to take up the surplus, and working outwards.

c. *Comb.*, as *silicone-impregnated, -proofed, -treated* adjs.; *silicone-treat* vb. trans.

1956 *Nature* 25 Feb. 365/2 Reversed-phase chromatography using silicone-impregnated kieselguhr columns. **1976** *Shooting Times & Country Mag.* 9–15 Dec. 7/1 (Advt.), The GARCIA gun and reel silicone impregnated cloth. Protects and cleans all metal. **1956** *Good Housek. Home Encycl.* (ed. 4) 251/2 Silicone-proofed rainwear and ski-clothes. **1958** *Times* 20 Jan. 11/5 Where traditional upholstery material is used on chairs..they should be silicone-treated. **1946** *Canad. Med. Assoc. Jrnl.* LV. 29/1 The difference between clotting times in untreated..and silicone-treated..tubes is equally marked with plasma. **1956** *Good Housek. Home Encycl.* (ed. 4) 99/2 Silicone-treated furnishing fabrics.

Hence **si·liconed** *ppl. a.*, coated, impregnated, or otherwise treated with a silicone or silicone-based material; **si·liconing** *vbl. sb.* Also (as a back-formation) **si·licone** *v. trans.*

1950 *Jrnl. Appl. Physiol.* III. 366 Venous blood was collected in a 10-ml. siliconed syringe. *Ibid.* 375 Siliconing of the syringe appears a worth-while precaution. **1959** *Listener* 1 Jan. 43/1 Siliconing really does prevent the food from sticking [to the frying pan]. **1973** 'E. MCBAIN' *Let's hear it for Deaf Man* viii. 124 A woman..with bleached blond hair and siliconed breasts. **1977** *Listener* 10 Nov. 611/2 The motel on the dunes, its beams shiny and siliconed in the clear light. **1978** *Morecambe Guardian* 14 Mar. 29/1 (Advt.), Sandblasting and siliconing. **1980** 'D. KAVANAGH' *Duffy* iv. 68 She was naked, thinnish, with..breasts which had probably been siliconed.

siliconize, *v.* (In Dict. s.v. SILICON.) **1.** *trans.* Substitute for def.: To cause to combine with silicon or its compounds; esp. to subject (a metal) to a process in which the surface is impregnated with silicon so as to form a protective coating.

1880 [implied in *siliconizing* below]. **1948** N. E. WOLDMAN *Metal Process Engin.* viii. 222 The iron or steel to be siliconized is subjected to the action of silicon carbide or ferrosilicon, or a mixture of the two and chlorine at temperatures of 1700 to 1850° F. **1977** R. B. ROSS *Handbk. Metal Treatments & Testing* 349 It is generally more economical to produce components in high-silicon cast iron rather than cast irons which are subsequently Siliconized.

2. [f. *SILICONE.] To impregnate, coat, or otherwise treat with silicones or silicone-based material. Usu. in ppl. adj. (see below).

1957 [implied in *siliconized* below]. **1963** *Obstetr. & Gynecol.* XXI. 47/1 The glassware was siliconized to prevent adsorption of the isotopes.

So **si·liconized** *ppl. a.*, **si·liconizing** *vbl. sb.*; also **si:liconiza·tion**, treatment or combination with silicon or a silicone.

1880 Siliconizing [in Dict. s.v. SILICONIZE *v.*]. **1920** WEBSTER, Siliconized. **1924** *Industr. & Engin. Chem.* Nov. 1112/1 An oxidizing atmosphere would tend to oxidize both the silicon and the iron simultaneously and prevent true siliconization. **1946** *Iron Age* 4 Apr. 75/2 These siliconized shafts replaced shafts made of stainless and nitrided steel. **1947** KIRK & OTHMER *Encycl. Chem. Technol.* I. 579 Other diffusion treatments for mild and other steels are calorizing, chromizing, and siliconizing. **1950** *Chem. Abstr.* XLIV. 4856 This method of siliconization permits a further increase of corrosion resistance of 18Cr-8Ni stainless steel, of Monel metal, and of pure Ni. **1957** *Archit. Rev.* CXXII. 354/2 T. & W. Farmiloe will demonstrate the qualities of their siliconized paints, put on the market since the last exhibition. **1977** *Hot Car* Oct. 97/3 (Advt.), Tough, resilient, siliconised enamel cuts out labour. **1978** *Nature* 28 Sept. 322/2 A double-barrelled glass micro-pipette, pretreated with a siliconising agent.

silicosis. Substitute for etym.: [ad. It. *silicosi* (A. Visconti: see C. L. Rovida in *Annali di Chim. applicata alla Med.* (1871) LIII. 103), ult. f. L. *silic-* SILEX + -OSIS.] and add: (Earlier example.)

1881 *Jrnl. Anat. & Physiol.* XV. 395 According to the nature and character of the irritant, certain forms [of pneumokoniosis] are distinguished, the chief of which are anthracosis, chalicosis or silicosis, and siderosis.

Hence **silico·tic** *a.*, affected by silicosis. Also as *sb.*

1913 *Mem. S. Afr. Inst. Med. Res.* No 3. 120 The amount of silica in the ash is greater in that from the silicotic lung than in that from the normal lung. **1938** *Jrnl. Amer. Med. Assoc.* 19 Nov. 1928/1 Clinicians, who see only the disabled silicotic patient with advanced lesions, often complicated by tuberculosis, are insisting that only such conditions represent the true picture of silicosis. **1948** [see *pneumoconiotic* s.v. *PNEUMO-]. **1980** D. POWNALL *Between Ribble & Lune* i. 20 Aaron's disease, a form of silicotic lung infection caused by the dust.

siliqua. Add: Pl. **siliquae. 4.** A Roman silver coin of the 4th and 5th centuries A.D., of the value of $\frac{1}{24}$th of a solidus.

1889 *Jrnl. Hellenic Stud.* X. 95 All the mediaeval standards were based upon the gold solidus of Constantine the Great..divided into 24 *siliquae* or *κεράτια* (from whence comes *carat*). **1927** A. R. BURNS *Money & Monetary Policy Early Times* x. 243 From about the middle of the 4th century A.D. the *siliqua*, the half of the *miliarense*, became increasingly important. **1940** [see *AUREUS]. **1962** R. A. G. CARSON *Coins* 185 Siliquae were struck mainly by Italian mints for Arcadius and Honorius and by the Gallic mints for the usurpers in control there.

silk, *sb.* and *a.* Add: **I. 1. e.** Silk sold in the form of thread or twist for sewing; freq. with defining word, as *embroidery, sewing silk,* etc.

1480–1826 Sewing silk [see SEWING *vbl. sb.*[1] 4]. **1851** *Illustr. Catal. Gt. Exhib.* III. III. 506/1 Veil, vest, and shawl embroidering silk. **1920** A. K. ARTHUR *Embroidery Bk.* ii. 10 Silks of different makes, embroidery or knitting, filosel,..and..'Tyrian', are all good for various purposes. **1951** L. TOWN *Bookbinding by Hand* xiv. 175 This is necessary to prevent fraying of the sewing silk as it passes round the headband. **1973** C. GAVIN *Snow Mountain* xxiii. 392 The drawn-thread work they were doing, on coarse linen with silks brought from their home.

f. *artificial silk* [cf. F. *soie artificielle* (de Chardonnet 1884, in *French Pat. 165,349*)] = *RAYON[1] 3. Also shortened to *art silk* (also *artsilk*).

1885 *Jrnl. Soc. Chem. Industry* 29 Jan. 34 Mr. J. B. Payne exhibited..some samples of 'artificial silk', a new filament produced by pressure through a die, from pyroxylin, the invention of Mr. J. W. Swan. **1922** *Daily Mail* 2 Dec. 1 (Advt.), Three charming designs in silcot, cotton, satin and art silk stockinette. **1924** [see *RAYON[1] 3 a]. **1928** *Lancet* 24 Mar. 631/2 Mr. Kelly asked the Home Secretary whether the Home Office had received any reports as to the conditions of health of workpeople employed in artificial silk factories. **1928** *Daily Mail* 3 Aug. 18/2 Snias and British Enkas were firmer among Artsilks. **1935** *Economist* 2 Nov. 854/1 Swedish exports to Italy consist to a large extent of chemical pulp..most of it rayon cellulose for artificial silk. **1944** A. L. BOWLEY *Stud. Nat. Income 1924–1938* 170 The excise on Artificial Silk has been charged since July 1925. **1957** H. CROOME *Forgotten Place* 15 A brilliant orange artsilk coverlet on a double bed..artsilk curtains of a different shade framing the windows.

2. b. (Earlier and later examples of *to take silk.*) Also (*rare*), *to have silk.*

1866 A. J. MUNBY *Diary* 2 Nov. (1972) 229 Dined in Hall..the talk was of who is to have silk presently and make way for us rising juniors. **1875** TROLLOPE *Prime Minister* (1876) I. iii. 36 He had..worked in a stuff gown till he was nearly sixty... He would take his silk as an honour for his declining years. **1925** W. S. MAUGHAM *Painted Veil* vii. 25 He was still a junior and many younger men than he had already taken silk. **1979** G. WAGNER *Barnardo* viii. 130 Thesiger..had become a QC... He had two juniors..who later took silk.

c. Esp. in phr. *to sport, don,* or *wear silk*: to ride (in a race). (Earlier and later examples.)

1884 H. SMART *From Post to Finish* I. xv. 243 Next week Gerald would 'don silk'..and be embarked on the career she had marked out... Had she done right?.. And yet, with his aptitude for riding..what better path.. was open to him? **1898** A. E. T. WATSON *Turf* x. 189 A gentleman, when this misfortune happens to him..can cease to wear silk, or at any rate need not ride over hurdles or fences.

d. A parachute; chiefly in phr. *to take to* or *hit the silk,* to bale out of an aircraft by parachute. *U.S. Air Force slang.*

1933 *Jrnl. R. Aeronaut. Soc.* XXXVII. 828 The American pilot..remarked that if he had engine trouble over England he would 'take to the silk', in other words abandon his machine and come down by parachute. **1943** R. WHELAN *Flying Tigers* 100 After gaining altitude Mott's plane burst into flames and he 'hit the silk'. **1956** N. MARSH *Off with his Head* (1957) viii. 177 Over Germany ..we got clobbered and I hit the silk.

3. b. Also *spec.* a jockey's cap and jacket carrying the horse-owner's colours. Cf. sense 2 c above.

1946 *Sun* (Baltimore) 31 May 15/1 Lovely Imp, carrying the Maryland silks of R. Bruce Livie's..Stable, won on a disqualification. **1955** *Radio Times* 22 Apr. 9/3 The jockeys..in gaudy silks. **1977** *New Yorker* 4 July 71/1 Last Thursday, in his first appearance in silks since the accident, he won with his first mount..by a length and a quarter.

c. (Earlier examples.)

1793 F. BURNEY *Let.* 4 Feb. (1972) II. 12 My love & thanks to my dear Sarah; though she ought to send my black silk. **1819** M. EDGEWORTH *Let.* ? 10 Mar. (1971) 181 Fanny wore her green silk and it looked beautiful.

e. A silk hat.

1906 JOYCE *Let.* 12 Aug. (1966) II. 148, I am curious to know how he looked in a tall silk. **1930** D. H. LAWRENCE *Love among Haystacks* 87, I assured her her hat was adorable, and, much to my relief, I got rid of my silk and into a dressing gown.

4. a For *U.S.* read 'orig. and chiefly *U.S.*' (Earlier and later examples.) Phr. *in silk,* at that stage when the silk is prominent.

[*c* **1662** in *New England Q.* (1937) X. 126 There groweth within the Huske upon the Corne a matter like small threads which appeare out of the top of the Eare like a tuft of haire or Silke.] **1770** G. WASHINGTON *Diary* 25 Aug. (1925) I. 395 Many Stalks were putting out entire new Shoots with young and tender Silk. **1774** P. V. FITHIAN *Jrnl.* 19 July (1900) 212 The Corn is beginning pretty generally to tassel, & I saw one hill in Silk, and in Blossom. **1847** D. DRAKE *Pioneer Life Kentucky* (1870) 52 By the month of August the corn is in silk. **1914** J. BURDETT-DAVY *Maize* v. 233 In some cases, and in the same breed, the silks appear before the tassels. **1950** *New Biol.* VIII. 46 Pollen from each plant is then poured on to the silks of the same plant. **1980** *Sci. Amer.* Jan. 101 Primitive corn and teosinte, with their tiny ears, have small pollen grains that cannot fertilize the kernels of large modern ears with their long silks.

b. A silky lustre in some rubies and sapphires, due to microscopic crystals, and considered a defect.

1886 *Jrnl. Franklin Inst.* CXXII. 380 In many genuine rubies we find a silky structure (called *silk* by jewellers). **1903** W. R. CATTELLE *Precious Stones* 47 Rubies generally contain clusters of light or dark-colored spots... White, glistening streaks in the grain of the stone, called silk, are of frequent occurrence... If silk shows plainly when the stone is faced up, it is one of the most serious defects. **1929** M. WEINSTEIN *Precious & Semi-Precious Stones* i. 6 The peculiar optical effect shown by many natural rubies and sapphires, known as 'silk', is never seen in synthetic stones. **1976** B. W. ANDERSON *Gemstones for Everyman* xii. 152 The Burma rubies..usually..show small patches of 'silk' consisting of fine needles of rutile intersecting at 60°. These have a silky appearance by reflected light.

II. 6. a. (Later examples of proverbial use.) Also used *allusively.*

1907 E. GOSSE *Father & Son* ix. 239 'Even the Lord can't make a silk purse out of a sow's ear,' said Miss Marks. **1929** D. H. LAWRENCE *Pansies* 129 Women.. want to change the man himself And turn the poor silk glove into a lusty sow's ear. **1932** R. ALDINGTON *Soft Answers* 47 Too late Julia realised that the best and most self-sacrificing of wives cannot make a silk purse out of a sow's ear, an Arnold Bennett out of an Oswald. **1959** M. BRADBURY *Eating People is Wrong* ii. 55 For the mass of men there is not too much to be said or done; you can't make a silk purse out of a sow's ear. **1978** *Jrnl. R. Soc. Arts* CXXVI. 339/2 She and her colleagues in the teaching profession are expected to turn children like that into silk purses, able to count, to spell, to read, to write, to understand, and so on.

b. *silk chiffon, gauze* (later example), *jersey, velvet* (later examples).

1965 *Which?* Mar. 95/1 *Silk chiffon,* a light, open mesh fabric, soft and smooth. For scarves, lingerie, evening dresses, millinery. **1976** *Times* 9 Mar. 9 (Advt.), Hand made silk chiffon blouse. **1965** T. R. TREGEAR *Geogr. China* ii. 81 It was not the finely woven Chinese brocades and damasks that were wanted in Rome, for when they arrived they were unravelled and re-woven into lighter, flimsier silk gauzes. **1897** *Sears, Roebuck Catal.* 231/1 Ladies' black pure silk jersey mitts. **1925** *Eaton's News Weekly* 26 Sept. 17 Very new, the Gossard Dancelette girdle of silk jersey. **1980** D. CREED *Scarab* xviii. 173 Her camel-coloured silk-jersey dress. **1880** L. TROUBRIDGE *Life amongst Troubridges* (1966) xi. 156 It was silk velvet and ten shillings a yard. **1966** P. O'DONNELL *Sabre-Tooth* vi. 91 Ilse..put on a white silk-velvet dressing gown.

d. (Later examples.)

1879 G. M. HOPKINS *Poems* (1967) 84 The vault and scope and schooling..In silk-ash kept from cooling. **1888** in *Ibid.* 198 Silk-beech, scrolled ash.

8. a. *silk grower* (earlier example).

1842 in *Proc. Vermont Hist. Soc.* (1940) VIII. 156 Called on Mr. Dexter the silk grower.

9. *silk-hatted, -hung, -lined, -socked.*

1903 W. LE QUEUX *Seven Secrets* (ed. 2) xxii. 219 The silk-hatted, frock-coated existence of the fashionable physician. **1976** L. ST. CLAIR *Fortune in Death* iii. 27 A bank messenger, very properly silk-hatted and frock-coated. **1947** AUDEN *Age of Anxiety* (1948) ii. 35 And mother wrote Swift and sure in the silk-hung saloon Her large round letters. **1901** *Westm. Gaz.* 29 Nov. 7/2 A romantic American,..after living as a hermit for fifteen years in consequence of an unhappy love affair, has been buried in a silk-lined grave. **1979** *Country Life* 1 Feb. 309/1 (Advt.), Silk-lined mohair coats. **1918** G. FRANKAU *One of Them* in *Poet. Wks.* (1923) II. xix. 123 Silk-socked; bright monocled; gallant. **1922** JOYCE *Ulysses* 517 Bella ..lifts..a plump buskined hoof and a full pastern, silk-socked.

10. a. silk embroidery, embroidery worked with silk threads; **silk road, route** (freq. with initial capitals), a trade route from China through India to the West, used in ancient times by traders in silk; **silk waste,** the fibres which remain after the reeling of silk yarn, or those obtained from damaged cocoons; † **silk wool,** a mixed yarn made of wool and either silk or staple fibre (*obs.*).

1837 *Penny Cycl.* VII. 77/1 A piece of silk embroidery. **1889** J. J. REIN *Industries of Japan* III. iv. 389 Oftentimes this silk embroidery is connected very skilfully with the painting or printing of the material. **1982** E. NORTH *Ancient Enemies* iii. 32 I've never yet told her about the private [American] college..where you can major in any subject... I met a girl who'd been there majoring in something like silk embroidery. **1931** J. W. GREGORY *Story of Road* I. iii. 43 The northern silk road in Asia crossed Persia and Kashgar to the Tarim Basin in Chinese Turkestan. **1936** P. FLEMING *News from Tartary* I. iv. 29 The Silk Road takes..you through Sinkiang to Kashgar and the Himalayan passes by one of two alternative routes. **1982** *Times* 25 Feb. 10/5 A community of some 200 Chinese-Jewish descendants of Silk Road traders in the ancient capital of Kaifeng, who no longer identify with Judaism. **1913** J. BUCHAN *Divus Johnson* in *Runagates Club* (1928) vi. 152 Russian geographers were interesting themselves in the line of the old silk route to Cathay. **1949** D. CARRUTHERS *Beyond Caspian* iv. 95 The Silk Route was not a disjointed affair, built up in sections, linking likely markets. **1981** *Daily Tel.* 30 Mar. 18/5 Tartar hats..recall the Silk Route of Marco Polo. **1842** *Encycl. Brit.* (ed. 7) XX. 350/2 To introduce such alterations in the spinning of silk waste as will supersede the cutting, carding, and scutching processes... The art of silk waste spinning..is still in its infancy. **1965** A. BREARLEY *Woollen Industry* v. 27 Silk wastes are used in woollen blends for their own distinctive merits. **1859** L. OLIPHANT *Narr. Earl of Elgin's Mission China & Japan* (1860) II. 255 The Japanese wear in winter garments thickly padded either with cotton or silk wool. **1908** *Practitioner* Nov. 760 Silcool is a form of vegetable silk-wool. **1928** F. M. ROWE tr. *Reinthaler's Artificial Silk* vii. 128 Staple fibre yarn..cannot belie its cellulose nature; it lacks..the tenacity of wool. This can be remedied..by spinning staple fibre in admixture with wool or recovered wool... Such mixed yarns (carded or combed) termed 'silk-wool',..are still used for needlework and machine knitting.

b. silk-bark, a small evergreen tree, *Maytenus acuminata,* belonging to the family Celastraceæ and native to southern Africa; **silk-tassel (bush, tree)** = *GARRYA; **silk wood,** (*b*) = CALABUR TREE; (*c*) = *Queensland maple* s.v. *QUEENSLAND.

1894 T. R. SIM *Flora of Kaffraria* 28 (*heading*) Silkbark. **1907** —— *Forests & Forest Flora Cape of Good Hope* xiv. 184 Silk-bark... A small branched unarmed tree. **1912** *Cape Times* 12 Oct. 9/8 In the gorge beneath the fall an indigenous thicket, yellow-wood, Hottentot cherry, silk-bark, has been allowed to remain. **1972** PALMER & PITMAN *Trees S. Afr.* II. 1285 The silkbark or sybas has a wide distribution, occurring from eastern tropical Africa to the Cape. **1897** M. E. PARSONS *Wild Flowers of California* 370 (*heading*) Silk-tassel tree. Quinine-bush. **1949** J. T. HOWELL *Marin Flora* 211 The graceful catkins of the staminate plants make the silk tassel bush one of the most beautiful shrubs in the chaparral. **1976** *Hortus Third* (L. H. Bailey Hortorium) 495/2 *Garrya* Dougl[as]. Silk-tassel, silk-tassel bush... The garryas are ornamentals flowering in late winter and early spring. **1888** Silk wood: used in def. of *Calabur tree.* **1891** [in Dict.]. **1909** F. M. BAILEY *Comprehensive Catal. Queensland Plants* 91 *Flindersia..Brayleyana..* Wood has been cut under the name of 'Silkwood'. **1948** A. L. HOWARD *Man. Timbers World* (ed. 3) 354 Maple silkwood is moderately elastic.

c. silk-spinner, a spider or a silk-moth.

1868 C. M. YONGE *Chaplet of Pearls* II. xlii. 246 A colony of silk-spinners, attracted by the mulberry-leaves of the old abbey garden. **1869** 'MARK TWAIN' *Innoc. Abr.* xxxiii. 365 This old dried-up reservoir is occupied by a few ghostly silk-spinners now. **1896** R. LYDEKKER *Royal Nat. Hist.* VI. iii. 95 (*heading*) The silk-spinners,—Family *Bombycidæ.*

silk, *v.* [f. the sb.] **a.** *trans.* To remove the silk from (maize). *U.S.*

1847 D. DRAKE *Pioneer Life Kentucky* (1870) 52 My first business in the morning was to pull, and husk and silk enough [corn] for breakfast. **1892** *Hist. Rev. Industr. & Commercial Growth York County* (Pa., U.S.) 59 [They] make a specialty of..'silkers' for silking corn. **1972** E. WIGGINTON *Foxfire Bk.* 177 Shuck and silk corn that is in roasting ear.

b. *intr.* Of maize: to produce the silk. *U.S.*

1878 J. H. BEADLE *Western Wilds* xv. 245 The summers are short and the nights cool. Corn will not silk. **1939** *Sun* (Baltimore) 21 July 13/4 The corn in the county is later..as the farmers have planted it so it will silk after August 10 when the danger from beetles is over. **1948** *Clarke County Democrat* (Grove Hill, Alabama) 3 June 1/3 This worm usually waits until corn bunches for tasseling or begins to silk before they attack.

silked, *a.* Add: **1.** (Earlier example.) Also, clothed in or covered with silk.

1837 *Annals Electricity, Magnetism & Chem.* I. 112 The bar is covered with several coils of silked copper wire. **1864** C. ROSSETTI *Farm Walk* in *Prince's Progress* (1866) 152 I've seen grand ladies plumed and silked. **1909** M. B. SAUNDERS *Litany Lane* iii. 33 Gorgeously furred and laced and scented and silked.

2. Of (the pages of) a book, etc.: having been strengthened by silking (sense *2).

1943 *Amer. Archivist* VI. 153 Upon subjection to accelerated aging tests..it was found that the silked papers had lost 52 per cent of their folding endurance. **1971** *Catal. Mildred C. Esty Coll. MSS Rob. Burns* (Christie's) 7, 1 p., 4to., with conjoint address leaf (considerably repaired, silked, a few words rubbed along fold).

silken, *a.* **II. 7. a.** (Later example.)

1955 E. POUND *Classic Anthol.* I. 20 Lady of silken word.

silker (si·lkəɹ). [f. SILK *sb.* + -ER[1].] One who works in or with silk; in various technical uses.

1881 *Instr. Census Clerks* (1885) 50 Piano Manufacturing... Silker. *Ibid.* 69 Cotton.. Silker. **1903** *Sci. Amer. Suppl.* 24 Jan. 22629/3 From the cutters' room the leather, which has assumed the shape of the glove, is sent to the 'silkers', who embroider the back. **1921** *Dict. Occup. Terms* (1927) 200/1 *Taper,..silker*; stitches tape by machine, down seam, in closing upper of a boot or shoe. *Ibid.* 203/1 *Silker*; (i) finishes cloth piece..by stitching folds together, by hand, with a silk thread to hold them in position; (ii) sews selvedges of cloth pieces with different coloured threads of silk or of mercerised cotton.

silkette. (Later example.)

1922 JOYCE *Ulysses* 735 The second pair of silkette stockings is laddered.

silkie (si·lki). Also **Silkie.** [f. SILK *sb.* + -IE.] A small chicken belonging to the variety so called, distinguished by long, soft plumage.

1885 [in Dict. s.v. SILKY *a.* 6 b]. **1937** W. W. BROOMHEAD *Poultry Breeding & Management* ix. 325/1 Silkies are quaint little fowls. *Ibid.* 326/1 (*caption*) A White Silkie Cock. **1978** *Country Life* 11 May 1285/1, I have a clutch of pure-bred Silkies being incubated now... I am not sure where the Silkie stands in bantam genealogy.

silkie, var. SEALCHIE, -KIE in Dict. and Suppl.

silkily, *adv.* Add: **a.** (Later examples.)
1947 A. P. GASKELL *Big Game* 91 Flash young things with lipstick, long-legged in high-heeled shoes, stood silkily, smoking tailormades. **1980** K. FOLLETT *Key to Rebecca* iii. 37 'Thank heaven you're back,' he said silkily.
b. Smoothly, quietly; used esp. of the running of an engine or machine.
1923 *Daily Mail* 7 Aug. 3 (Advt.), I was much impressed with the vehicle.. beautifully suspended and runs very silkily. **1962** I. MURDOCH *Unofficial Rose* xxix. 280 He drew it [*sc.* the dagger] silkily out of its sheath. **1978** *Lancashire Life* Apr. 141/1 The 132-2000..would slip silkily into top at anything from 25 m.p.h. upwards.

silking, *vbl. sb.* Add: **2.** The attachment of a piece of silk or other fine material to one or both sides of a sheet of paper in order to strengthen or preserve it.
1943 *Amer. Archivist* VI. 152 The two principal methods of restoration employed at the present time, silking and lamination with cellulose acetate foil, are described below. **1980** S. G. SWARTZBURG *Preserving Library Materials* vii. 74 The sheets can be strengthened by a covering of a thin sheet of japan tissue, pasted over the original page... This process is often called 'silking' because originally a fine chiffon fabric was used.
3. Development of the silk in maize.
1976 R. W. JUGENHEIMER *Corn* xiii. 206 The most desirable strains of corn over a period of years often have been those in which the individual plants varied considerably in date of silking and tasseling. **1977** *N.Z. Jrnl. Agric.* Jan. 13/4 The optimum time for spraying is a fortnight either side of silking.

silkoline (si·lkolīn). Also **silkaline, silkolene, S-.** [f. SILK *sb.*, after CRINOLINE.] A soft cotton fabric with a smooth finish resembling that of silk.
1896 *Proc. Internat. Typogr. Union* 64/1, 12 yds. silkaline, $1.80. **1907** *Yesterday's Shopping* (1969) 742/2 Dress Linings..Silkoline, black..yd. 0/10. **1911** *Everybody's Mag.* XXV. 795/2 The last wrinkle and darn of their blue silkolene cotton tights had vanished from the stage. **1918** *Sears Catal.* 1164/1 A beautiful rose design in a border Silkoline. **1921** *Daily Colonist* (Victoria, B.C.) 8 Apr. 20/3 (Advt.), Silkolene, 36 inches wide, in a full selection of colorings and designs. **1950** '*Mercury*' *Dict. of Textile Terms* 465/1 Silkaline, a very light printed, plain weave, glossy cotton fabric, made in the grey and calendered. **1970** *Kay & Co.* (Worcester) *Catal.* 1970–71 Autumn/Winter 448/2 Bonsoir 'Silkaline' Pyjamas are fashionably styled in 100% cotton.

silk screen, *sb.* [f. SILK *sb.* + SCREEN *sb.*[1]]
1. A screen (*SCREEN *sb.*[1] 6 *b) made of silk for use in screen printing. Usu. *attrib.*, esp. in *silk screen printing, process* (also *absol.*).
1930 B. ZAHN *Silk Screen Methods of Reproduction* 9 There is no other phase of the graphic arts which presents so many possibilities as the Silk Screen Process. *Ibid.* 10 A silk screen has the advantage of making a perfect imprint at low cost. **1934** F. A. BAKER *Silk Screen Practice* i. 13 The Silk Screen Process has become a necessity to all businesses that deal in colour reproduction work. **1950** *Atomics* Jan. 22/2 The silk screen press consists simply of a piece of silk stretched wet on a frame which taughtens on drying. **1952** *Print* (U.S.) July 1/1 André Girard..has been the first to apply silk screen to the art of making books. Silk screen has gone far in the scant thirty years of its existence. **1959** *Daily Mail* 14 Aug. 1/3 Robert, a silk screen printer, and Rosemary, a typist, first met about eighteen months ago. **1967** M. CHANDLER *Ceramics in Mod. World* iii. 111 The ceramist may make use of silk-screen printing. **1981** *West Lancs. Even. Gaz.* 20 Feb. 21 (Advt.), Wanted: Silk screen printer with artistic and modelling abilities.
2. A print made by the silk screen process.
1977 J. DIDION *Bk. Common Prayer* II. ii. 59 The thin FBI man gazed over Charlotte's head at the 10' by 16' silk screen of Mao Tse-tung. **1979** *Farmington* (New Mexico) *Daily Times* 27 May (Entertainment Suppl.) 22/5 'Mural-sized graphics', which will be reproduced as signed, limited-edition silk-screens.
Hence **silk-screen** *v. trans.*, to print, decorate, or reproduce by the silk screen process; **silk-screened** *ppl. a.*, **silk-screening** *vbl. sb.*; also **silk-screener**, a silk-screen printer.
1961 M. JONES *Potbank* xxv. 110 Joan..was silk-screening coffee-pots. **1967** *Listener* 21 Dec. 829/3 Andy Warhol's carrier bag beautifully silk-screened with a Campbell's soup can. **1976** WOODWARD & BERNSTEIN *Final Days* xi. 138 As the sheer mechanics of preparing the transcripts for public consumption intensified, David Hoopes..summoned the State Department silk-screener from a baseball game. **1976** *National Observer* (U.S.) 28 Aug. 9/2 She worked in the farm's silk-screening shop, helping to print Christmas cards. **1978** *Detroit Free Press* 16 Apr. (Detroit Suppl.) 34 (Advt.), Each is silk-screened several times to produce the most subtle of shading on multi-colored cotton prints.

silk stocking. Add: **2. a.** Hence in extended sense, a member of the wealthy or upper class. (Later examples.) *U.S.*
1896 [see sense 2 b in Dict.]. **1903** *Independent* 12 Nov. 2663/1 The mass of voters look upon him as a 'silk stocking'—as one who neither understands nor sympathizes with their life.
b. (Earlier example.)
1840 *Niles' Nat. Reg.* (Baltimore) 14 Mar. 22/1 They cried out in derision of locofoco slang—'Here go the silk stockings.'
3. *attrib.* and *Comb.* **a.** Simple *attrib.*, as (sense 2 a) *silk-stocking company, gentry*, etc. *U.S.*
1798 *Deb. Congress U.S.* 15 June (1851) 1948 If they wished to place them in a ridiculous point of view, or to produce for them the name of the *Silk Stocking Company*, or any other term of derision, they could not take a more effectual course to obtain it. **1812** T. JEFFERSON *Writings* (1904) XIII. 163, I trust..the Gores and Pickerings will find their levees crowded with silk stocking gentry, but no yeomanry. **1836** *Col. Crockett's Exploits & Adventures Texas* iv. 58 You may be called a drunken dog by some of the clean shirt and silk stocking gentry. **1874** 'H. CHURTON' *Toinette* xiii. 154 She had managed to pick up.. 'a tolerable English education',..[possibly] through the charity of some teacher at the 'Silk-Stocking Academy', on 'Gentleman Ridge'. **1903** *N.Y. Sun* 28 Nov. 4 He is the representative of the wealthy intellectual, the cultured, the 'silk stocking' element, for which the people in general have no abiding affection. **1980** *Verbatim* Autumn 1/2 Next after *hill* the commonest generic is *row* (several examples already given). The most frequent response of this type was *Silk Stocking Row*.
b. Special combs.: **silk-stocking district** (or **quarter**), a district inhabited mainly by supporters of the (Whig or) Republican party.
1893 *World's Fair Puck* 18 Sept. 231/2 Mr. Astorbilt (*of the silk-stocking district*)—No; I thought I was a thousand miles away from Tammany! **1903** *N.Y. Even. Post* 30 Oct. 2 Political conditions change even in the 'silk-stocking' quarter—the middle reaches of Manhattan, between 14th Street and 96th Street. **1964** *Economist* 2 May 486/2 Mr Wallace may do well, both in the silk stocking districts, and on the waterfront.

silkweed. 1. (Earlier and later examples.)
1784 *Mem. Amer. Acad.* I. 424 The seeds are contained in large pods, and are crowned with white down,.. resembling silk, which has occasioned the name of Silkweed. **1814** [see *MILKWEED 2]. **1940** J. STUART *Trees of Heaven* 48 There is the musty smell of ironweeds, milkweeds, silkweeds,..and bull grass on the lazy wind.

silky, *a.* (*sb.*) Add: **1. b.** As *sb.* (See quot. 1976.)
1822 T. BEWICK *Memoir* (1975) ii. 16, I..was only to walk along the dark passage to the back Door and to repeat something (rather ominous indeed) about 'Silkey & Hedley Kow'. **1866** W. HENDERSON *Folk Lore Northern Counties* vii. 230 Black Heddon..was greatly disturbed by a supernatural being, popularly called Silky, from the nature of her robes. **1912** in R. Tongue *Forgotten Folk-Tales English Counties* (1970) III. v. 202 Gilsland's lord had a silky who cleaned the house-place, devilled and punched lazy serving-wenches and kept all shining clean. **1967** *Tablet* 16 Dec. 1307/2 Nearly all peoples, the world over, have believed in beings they called elves, silkies, trolls, elementals or fairies. **1976** K. M. BRIGGS *Dict. Fairies* 365 The Northumbrian and Border silky..is always female... She is a spirit dressed in rustling silk, who does domestic chores about the house and is a terror to idle servants.
3. c. Of a machine, mechanism, etc. or its motion: smooth.
1935 *Times* 23 Apr. 17/6 The engine is silky and quiet throughout its range. **1977** *Gramophone* Nov. 960/2 To provide a silky movement of the tuning control, and gearing down of the knob, the Tandberg engineers have made use of a two-gang variable capacitor with its inbuilt gearing.
5. b. silky cornel = next; **silky dogwood,** a large shrub, *Cornus amomum,* native to eastern North America, whose leaves have silky hairs on their lower sides; **silky oak,** one of several Australian trees of the family Proteaceæ, esp. *Grevillea robusta* or *Cardwellia sublimis,* or the oak-like timber produced by them.
1848 A. GRAY *Man. Botany Northern U.S.* 168 (*heading*) Silky cornel. **1891** J. M. COULTER *Bot. W. Texas* I. 150 Silky cornel... Common in the Atlantic States and extending into eastern and northern Texas. **1900** B. B. SMYTH *Plants & Flowers Kansas* ii. 25 It is the Silky Dogwood; grows in clumps; and had blue berries when ripe, in broad cymose clusters. **1957** W. C. GRIMM *Bk. Shrubs* 351 The Silky Dogwood is sometimes called the Silky Cornel, Swamp Dogwood, or Kinnikinnick. **1866** Silky oak [in Dict.]. **1888** F. M. BAILEY *Queensland Woods* 104 S[*tenocarpus*] *salignus*... One of the woods called Silky Oak. **1889** Silky oak [in Dict.]. **1965** *Austral. Encycl.* II. 180/2 The northern silky oak, *Cardwellia sublimis* of Queensland, is also sometimes known as bull oak.

silky, var. SEALCHIE, -KIE in Dict. and Suppl.

sill, *sb.*[1] Add: **1. c.** The lower horizontal members of the frame of a motor vehicle.
1959 *Motor Man.* (ed. 36) i. 17 In the case of the Austin, a normal pressed-steel body was used, the channel-section sills of which were joined to the open faces of the channel section side-members to form substantial box sections. **1976** *Drive* Sept.–Oct. 75/1 The high boxed sills were a necessary structural link between the front and rear of the car. **1980** *Daily Tel.* 11 Sept. 7 (Advt.), Full underbody sealing and wax injection of sills and cross-members.
2. a. (Earlier and later *Comb.* examples.)
1885 C. M. YONGE *Nuttie's Father* I. i. 6 Lovely sill boxes full of flowers in the windows. **1955** *Archit. Rev.* CXVIII. 126/1 Panels of woven cane hanging from the sillboards cover the radiators.
3. a. Also *Comb.*
1870 *Jrnl. Ethnological Soc.* II. 417 At each end of this passage, and at right angles to it, are two square or somewhat oblong chambers. The first..was about 3 feet in width. Where it joined the central passage was a sillstone. **1981** *Glasgow Archaeol. Jrnl.* VIII. 52/2 The main uprights were set in newly dug postholes, linked by sillbeam trenches.
e. A high ridge on the sea bed that effectively separates the bodies of water on either side.
1933 *Geogr. Jrnl.* LXXXI. 571 Hamish island, situated on the shallow sill of the Red Sea. **1942** O. VON ENGELN *Geomorphol.* xix. 468 They [*sc.* fiords] are closed at the seaward end by a distinct rock sill at shallow depth, beyond which the descent to the deeper ocean waters begins. **1978** *Nature* 14 Dec. 680/2 Outflowing Mediterranean subsurface waters... They spill over the sill at Gibraltar (330 m).
4. b. In mod. use, a tabular igneous intrusion lying parallel to the surrounding strata. (Later examples.)
1914 J. P. IDDINGS *Problem of Volcanism* vii. 222 Intrusions along bedding planes of stratified rocks are commonly called sills at whatever angle they may be tilted, and intrusions in fractures that transgress stratified beds are usually classed as dikes. **1977** A. HALLAM *Planet Earth* 68 Fine examples of sills are the Carboniferous dolerite sill that forms Salisbury Crags in Edinburgh, Scotland, and the Palisades sill, up to 350m (1000ft) thick, along the west bank of the Hudson River near New York.

sillabub. Add: **1. a.** (Later examples.)
1911 M. A. FAIRCLOUGH *Ideal Cookery Book* 722 Syllabubs... Fill some custard glasses rather more than half full with the mixture. **1976** *Sat. Even. Post All-American Cookbk.* 259/2 A syllabub is a ladylike version of eggnog.
b. *syllabub glass, jug, pot* (later examples).
1677 in S. Young *Hist. Worshipful Company Glass Sellers of London* (1913) App. 68 All covers for drinking or 'Sullibub' glasses ribbed and plain shall be delivered at 3*s.* per lb. **1723** J. NOTT *Cook's & Confectioner's Dict.* sig. Ll[1], Scum off the Froth, and put it into Syllabub Glasses. **1897** A. HARTSHORNE *Old Eng. Glasses* xix. 308 In Mr. Cuming's collection is an open-mouthed glass tumbler, a family relic, 3½ inches high, said to be of the first part of the last century, and called from time immemorial 'a syllabub or whip glass'. **1970** G. SAVAGE *Dict. Antiques* 418/2 In the 1770s the old syllabub glass, which was always on a stem and a foot, became unfashionable and was replaced by a stemless glass. **1975** *Country Life* 2 Jan. 11/3 A Syllabub Jug in Ravenscroft Glass. **1723** J. NOTT *Cook's & Confectioner's Dict.* No. 188 S, Fill your Syllabub-Pot with Cyder..Sugar.. Cream. **1910** *Queen* 9 July 65/1 This syllabub or posset pot is very interesting and..the date of it has been fixed at about 1700.

silladar. Add: Also **silladari, sillahdari.** (Later examples.)
1931 E. HOWELL *Mizh* i. 9 The men were on a sillahdari basis. **1960** LD. ISMAY *Memoirs* i. 7 The 21st Cavalry, like nearly all other Indian Cavalry regiments, was organised on what was known as the *silladar* system. **1974** P. MASON *Matter of Honour* i. 26 Until 1914 many regiments of cavalry were still *sillādāri*—that is to say, the regiment was a kind of joint-stock company in which the trooper paid for his horse and equipment when he joined and sold them back when he left.

sillapak (sī·ləpăk). [ad. Eskimo *silapak.*] Also **sealapack, seelapak.** A white outer garment worn as camouflage by Eskimo hunters of Labrador.
[**1916** E. W. HAWKES *Labrador Eskimo* 39 Over the fur or duffle dicky a cotton slip (ci'l·apaq) is drawn.] **1942** *Beaver* (Winnipeg) Dec. 37/2 The cold pierced through his thin sillapak so that all night he jumped about to prevent the fatal drowsiness which precedes death from creeping upon him. **1952** *Ibid.* Dec. 10/2 Sometimes the hunter dons a white 'seelapak' to make himself even less conspicuous. **1959** *Weekend Mag.* (Montreal) 22 Aug. 9 A tightly-woven poplin of cotton and nylon takes the place of the wind-blocking fabric Eskimos first used for the outer garment known as sealapack.

sillar (sīlyā·ɹ). *Geol.* [Sp.] An ignimbrite or volcanic tuff that has not become indurated by welding.
1948 C. N. FENNER in *Bull. Geol. Soc. Amer.* LIX. 883 There has been a tendency to call all such deposits 'welded tuffs'... For those in which induration is primarily the result of recrystallization, and for those in which the fragments have little cohesion, another term is desirable. The local term 'sillar'.., commonly used in the Arequipa region [in Peru], has been applied in the present paper. *Ibid.* 887 These occurrences of both white and salmon sillar contain scattered inclusions of white pumice. **1965** F. H. HATCH et al. *Petrol. Sedimentary Rocks* (ed. 4) xv. 322 Both sillars and welded tuffs frequently exhibit columnar jointing, somewhat akin to that in lava flows proper. **1978** *Nature* 24 Aug. 750/1 In the outcrops visited, two distinct flow units, each up to 30 m thick, were consistently present, both exhibiting the properties of classic sillar.

Sillonist (si·lŏnist). *Ch. Hist.* Also ‖ **Silloniste.** [ad. F. *silloniste,* f. the name of the review *Le Sillon,* founded in 1894 by Paul Renaudin.] A member of a French Catholic movement for social reform led from *c* 1902 to 1910 by Marc Sangnier. Hence **Si·llonism**, the principles and policies of the Sillonists.

1910 *Amer. Cath. Q. Rev.* XXXV. 707 The result..can only be a democracy which will be neither Catholic nor Protestant, nor Jewish; a religion (for Sillonism, its chief state, is a religion) more universal than the Catholic Church. **1910** *Daily News* 2 Sept. 5 The Sillonists believed in certain forms of private property. **1957** *Church Hist.* XXVI. 229 Certain theologians..pretended to find errors in *Silloniste* doctrine. *Ibid.* 241 The *Sillonistes* appeared to contravene in their actions the two basic principles of the papal policy in France. **1978** J. SONDHEIMER tr. *Aubert's Church in Secularised Soc.* I. iii. 49 This was an aspect..in which Sillonism marked itself out as being the best tradition of the liberal Catholicism of the nineteenth century. *Ibid.* 50 The Sillonists had envisaged forming a spiritual polity.

silly, *a. sb.*, and *adv.* Add: **A.** *adj.* **5. c.** *silly season* (earlier example); also *transf.* and *attrib.*

1861 *Sat. Rev.* 13 July 37/2 We have, however, observed this year very strong symptoms of the Silly Season of 1861 setting in a month or two before its time. **1910** H. G. WELLS in *Eng. Rev.* Sept. 308, I got..Burkett of the *Dial* to try over a silly-season discussion of State Help for Mothers. **1930** *Forum* Dec. 375/2 The silly season was formally launched and the Big Parade began. **1952** M. TRIPP *Faith is Windsock* i. 20 Fat daily newspapers, silly-season follies, cries of 'Give Chamberlain a peerage!' after Munich. **1971** *Jrnl. Gen. Psychol.* Jan. 151 (*heading*) The psychobiological silly season—or—what happens when neurophysiological data become psychological theories. **1976** T. HEALD *Let Sleeping Dogs Die* vii. 129 The reporters were..embarrassed at having to attend such a..silly-season event.

d. (Earlier example.)

1888 R. H. LYTTELTON in Steel & Lyttelton *Cricket* vi. 287 The English captain acceded to W. G. Grace's wish and allowed him to go forward point, or, as it is familiarly called, 'silly' point.

d*. *to play silly buggers* (also *bleeders, b-s*), to fool about, to mess around. Cf. *to play buggery* s.v. *BUGGERY c. *slang.*

1961 PARTRIDGE *Dict. Slang* Suppl. 1274/1 *Silly buggers, play*, to indulge in provocative horse-play; hence, to feign stupidity: low: since ca. 1920. **1968** M. WOODHOUSE *Rock Baby* ix. 95 If they want to play silly bleeders, let them. We're technicians. **1969** M. PUGH *Last Place Left* ii. 13 You know that whatever it is, it doesn't affect humans? Don't play silly bugger, Rab. **1972** J. MCCLURE *Caterpillar Cop* iii. 43 It was too easy..and too like what happened when the gods played silly buggers. **1972** 'K. ROYCE' *Miniatures Frame* iv. 50, I have to pin something on him to stop him playing silly b's. **1976** K. WATERHOUSE *Mondays, Thursdays* 45 I'm sure none of this had anything to do with the supposed threat to our privacy. It was our God-given right to play silly buggers that was threatened, and the nation responded magnificently. **1979** *Guardian* 9 Aug. 22/8 We don't want people jeopardising our position by playing silly bs.

d.** Proverbial phr. *ask a silly question (and you get a silly answer).*

1969 'A. GILBERT' *Missing from her Home* v. 73 No, don't bother to answer that. Ask a silly question and you get a silly answer. **1970** M. PEREIRA *Pigeon's Blood* xi. 122 'John? Tell me straight: do you or don't you?' John Raze looked at his friend. 'Ask a silly question...' he said. Then after a pause: 'No.' **1974** *Guardian* 26 Mar. 24/6 Questionnaires..coming under the heading of 'Ask a silly question, and you get a silly answer' get their just deserts.

e. *silly-clever.*

1896 G. B. SHAW in *Sat. Rev.* 11 July 36/2 Greene was really amusing, Marston spirited and silly-clever. **1946** 'G. ORWELL' in *Polemic* Sept.-Oct. 8 Innumerable silly-clever Conservatives..like Sir Alan Herbert, Professor G. M. Young, Lord Elton. **1963** *Economist* 11 May 538/1 Mr Khrushchev's silly-clever forward pass in Cuba.

7. Special collocations: **silly ass,** a foolish or stupid person (cf. ASS 2); *spec.* an amiable upper-class idiot; freq. *attrib.*; **silly billy,** a foolish or feeble-minded person; used *spec.* as a nickname of William Frederick, Duke of Gloucester (1776–1834), and of William IV (1765–1837); **silly house** *slang*, a mental hospital (cf. *funny farm* s.v. *FUNNY *a.* 4); † **sillypop** *slang*, a foolish or light-headed woman (cf. POP *sb.*[2]); also *attrib.* (*obs.*); **Silly Putty** orig. *U.S.*, the proprietary name of an elastic putty-like substance with the remarkable properties of stretching, shattering, and bouncing sharply when appropriately handled, sold chiefly as a plaything; also *fig.* and with small initials; **Silly Symphony,** any of a series of animated cartoons (see quot. 1976) designed by the American cartoonist Walter Elias ('Walt') Disney (1901–66).

1901 G. B. SHAW *Captain Brassbound's Conversion* III. 290 You silly ass, you. **1905** *Punch* 22 Mar. 214/2 He inquired if Phyllis 'had done the Academy yet'? Which, as it didn't open for some days, was a silly-ass thing to say. **1945** 'G. ORWELL' in *Windmill* No. 2. 18 The silly-ass Englishman with his spats and his monocle. **1973** [see *KNUT]. **1978** R. V. JONES *Most Secret War* vii. 60 In the best manner of the silly-ass Englishman he blundered into one door after another in an apparent search for the lavatory. **1834** J. ROMILLY *Diary* 13 Apr. (1967) 55 He was in a towering passion for a minute but soon got into a good humour by laughing at the D. of Gloster. 'Did you see silly Billy squirted on last night? it was worth 5£.' **1872** B. JERROLD *London* xv. 124 The silly-Billy of the neighbourhood—on whom the neighbourhood is merciless. **1908** L. H. DAWSON *Nicknames & Pseudonyms* 269 *Silly Billy*, a nickname of William Frederick (1776–1834), Duke of Gloucester; also of William IV (1765–1837). **1934** R. NICHOLS *Fisbo* 48 Come, come, don't be a silly-billy. **1958** N. MARSH *Singing in Shrouds* 173 You'll think me a frightful silly-billy. **1969** A. CHRISTIE *Hallowe'en Party* xvi. 173 The King what had a head like a pear was on the throne—Silly Billy, wasn't it, William IVth. **1977** in Lewis & Baker *Wordpower* II. vi. 15 Mr Healey is a Silly Billy to have waited so long before doing so little of what everyone knew was necessary. **1969** K. GILES *Death cracks Bottle* x. 116 They used to allow me my *News of the World* in the silly house. **1894** M. BEERBOHM *Defence of Cosmetics* in *Yellow Bk.* Apr. 70 She is the veriest little sillypop. **1895** *Punch* 18 May 230/3 On styge or on cinder-path, sillypop things As want to play Man and *be* Woman are trying to fly without wings. **1950** *New Yorker* 26 Aug. 20 After absorbing the elementary facts about Silly Putty..we sought out Mr. Lee Weber, the manager of the bookshop... He told us that Silly Putty is the most terrific item the Doubleday shops have been privileged to handle since 'Forever Amber'. **1952** *Official Gaz.* (U.S. Patent Office) 341 Peter Hodgson, New Haven, Conn... Silly Putty... For the Plastic Known as Organo Silicone Designed and Sold for Use as a Modeling Clay and Amusement..by Children. Claims used since July 1949. **1954** 'E. Box' *Death in Fifth Position* v. 111 Silly putty is a pink substance which, if rolled in a ball, will bounce better than rubber, which will shatter if you hit it with a hammer and which will stretch to an unbelievable length. **1963** *Punch* 2 Oct. 495/1 What children today call 'silly putty', which can be pinched and stretched into any shape or length, like toffee. **1964** *Trade Marks Jrnl.* 19 Aug. 1364/2 *Silly Putty*... Playthings made of mouldable plastics. Peter Hodgson,..New Haven, State of Connecticut, United States of America; manufacturer. **1974** P. DE VRIES *Glory of Hummingbird* (1975) v. 79 It's only your hands I'm putty in... Silly putty I'm afraid. **1929** *Exhibitors Herald World* 16 Nov. 53/3 Booked into the Tivoli at Toronto for a week's run, 'The Skeleton Dance', one of the Disney Silly Symphonies which are being released by Columbia Pictures, has already made three weeks there. **1936** G. GREENE *Journey without Maps* I. iii. 67 Natives..looked like grasshoppers in a Silly Symphony. **1976** *Oxf. Compan. Film* 22/1 He [*sc.* Disney] pioneered the precise integration of the animated image with sound—particularly music—in the Silly Symphony series which began in 1928.

silly, *v.* **1. b.** (Earlier example.)

1859 *Sessions Papers Central Criminal Court* 10 May 17, I felt great pain from the blows... It half *sillied* me at the time.

silo, *sb.* Add: **1, 2.** Also, a cylindrical tower or other structure erected above ground for this purpose. Cf. *pit silo* s.v. *PIT *sb.*[1] 14.

1886 STALLMAIER & FUX tr. *Luther's Constr. & Equipment of Grain Magazines* 11 A silo is erected with outside walls, and sometimes covered with slates. **1904** WILCOX & SMITH *Farmer's Cycl. Agric.* 377/1 The first silos were simply pits dug in the ground... Since about 1875 silos of stone, brick and wood have come into use. **1948** *Coast to Coast 1947* 240 The silos stood up tall and straight, grey against the dazzling sky. A line of wheat-laden vehicles moved slowly up towards the hopper. **1950** *Amer. Speech* XXV. 165 Wherever it is possible to find ground that will be dry all seasons of the year, farmers build 'pit silos' and 'trench silos' rather than the cylindrical silos entirely aboveground. **1977** *Daily Tel.* 18 Mar. 8/3 The Norfolk agricultural engineering firm, Rowlands Engineers,..has started a three-shift system..to cope with export orders of more than £400,000 for grain, coffee and cocoa storage silos.

3. = SILAGE. *rare.*

1889 M. S. VAN DE VELDE *Cosmopolitan Recoll.* II. ii. 44 Near the spot where Mademoiselle de Montpensier, the daughter of Gaston d'Orléans, held her little court, rise the new constructions for the storage of silo. **1898** F. P. DUNNE *Mr. Dooley in Peace & War* 17 If they'd put blinders on th' mules, they wuddent be scared back be wan iv thim Spanish fleets that a jackass sees whin he's been up all night, secretly stuffing himsilf with silo.

4. *transf.* A large bin used for the storage of loose materials, as cement, etc.

1920 *Glasgow Herald* 2 Sept. 3/8 The coal silos are of sufficient capacity to maintain the supply for about 20 hours in the event of the stoppage of the conveyors. **1958** *Times Rev. Industry* May 64/3 Sulphur will be imported at wharves nearby and stored in a concrete silo with a capacity of 5,000 tons. **1961** *Engineering* 9 June 794 Cement now comes in tankers and is stored in silos. **1973** *Daily Tel.* 25 July 2/3 Another [boy]..was trapped up to his waist in a cement silo for nearly three hours.

5. a. An underground structure in which a guided missile is stored and from which it may be fired. Also *attrib.* Cf. *HARD *a.* 14 f, *SOFT *a.* 19 d.

1958 *N.Y. Times* 15 June 24/4 The system will be protected against neutralization in an enemy attack because the missiles will be installed in concrete-lined underground silos. **1960** *Aeroplane* XLIX. 18/1 For these 'silo' squadrons each missile will be emplaced vertically in a reinforced concrete-lined hole, 52 ft. in diameter and about 175 ft. deep. An elevator raises the missile to the surface a few minutes before launching. **1962** *Engineering* 5 Jan. 13 The Atlas-F [rocket] variant is to be housed within a 'silo' 174 feet deep and 52 feet in diameter... The first silos for Atlas-F are already under construction. **1968** *Economist* 31 Aug. 14/1 On present plans Minuteman III is scheduled gradually to replace Minuteman I and Minuteman II in the silos that dot the prairies and mountains of the western United States. **1975** 'A. HALL' *Mandarin Cypher* xiii. 196 The Chinese Republic had silos all over the mainland for reaction-take-off missiles. **1978** *Daily Tel.* 27 July 1/2 Loading the Revenge's 16 ballistic missiles from their hillside silos at Coulport started..yesterday.

b. *Comb.* **silo buster** *slang*, a missile which can destroy an enemy missile in its silo; so **silo-busting** *ppl. a.*

1970 *Nature* 3 Oct. 11/1 The smaller but more accurate multiple warheads..are, like the SS-9, silo-busting weapons. **1977** *Time* 3 Oct. 22/3 The U.S. has also become increasingly concerned..about existing rockets that may become 'silo busters', with the explosive force and pinpoint accuracy to destroy U.S. missiles in their underground launchers.

siloxane (silǫ·ksēⁱn). *Chem.* [ad. G. *siloxan* (A. Stock 1917, in *Ber. d. Deut. Chem. Ges.* L. 170): see SILICON, OXYGEN, and -ANE.] Any compound having a molecular structure consisting of a chain of alternate silicon and oxygen atoms, the silicon atoms being bonded to hydrogen atoms or to organic radicals. Cf. *SILICONE 2 a. Freq. *attrib.*

1917 *Jrnl. Chem. Soc.* CXII. II. 204 Perhaps the greatest confusion in the nomenclature of silicon compounds is to be found in the case of substances containing the —Si—O—Si— system. It is proposed to call the parent hydrogen compounds of this type 'siloxanes', and to specify the number of silicon and oxygen atoms in such terms as 'disiloxane', 'disildioxane', etc. **1941** *Jrnl. Amer. Chem. Soc.* LXIII. 800/2 A cross-linked structure of siloxane chains. **1948** *Electronic Engin.* XX. 82/3 The silicone oils are semi-inorganic polymers in which carbon atoms of organic radicals are linked to the silicon atoms of the so-called siloxane chain. **1960** *New Scientist* 12 May 1205/2 Silicone rubber..is built up from purified siloxanes. **1974** *Encycl. Brit. Macropædia* IV. 104/2 The most useful of man-made inorganic polymers are the siloxanes (also known as silicones).

Silsbee (si·lzbi). *Physics.* The name of Francis Briggs *Silsbee* (b. 1889), American physicist, used *attrib.* and in the possessive with reference to the phenomenon (discovered by Kamerlingh Onnes and explained by Silsbee) of the destruction of the superconducting properties of a superconductor when a current exceeding a certain critical value (the *Silsbee current*) is passed through it.

1926 *Jrnl. Franklin Inst.* CCI. 407 As is demanded for the correctness of Silsbee's hypothesis the supra-conductivity, which was disturbed by exceeding the threshold current, was restored by applying an external magnetic field. **1932** *Proc. R. Soc.* A. CXXXVI. 65 There remained the possibility..that the effect was a manifestation of the Silsbee effect, in which the current through the superconductor produces, by its own magnetic field, a depression of the critical temperature. **1968** C. G. KUPER *Introd. Theory Superconductivity* v. 89 If a current *I* in excess of the Silsbee current..is passed through a cylindrical wire.., some destruction of superconductivity must occur. **1975** M. TINKHAM *Introd. Superconductivity* iii. 99 Silsbee's rule that the critical current cannot exceed that which produces a critical magnetic field at the superconductor.

silt, *sb.* Add: **1. c.** *Soil Sci.* Applied *spec.* to particles whose sizes fall within a specified size range between those of sand and clay and to soils having a specified proportion of such particles (see quots.). Hence *silt-grade*; *silt-size* sb. (adj.).

1873 *Amer. Jrnl. Sci.* CVI. 288 It makes a material difference whether the grains of sand contained in a soil or clay are prevalently half a millimeter in diameter, or the tenth or twentieth part of that amount. Sand (or more properly silt) of the latter size is by no means impalpable. **1909** A. G. MCCALL *Physical Properties of Soils* 88 Stir up the soil remaining in the centrifugal tube and allow to stand for about one minute, or until all particles larger than silt (0·05 [mm.]) have settled. **1920** Silt grade [see *SILTSTONE]. **1958** I. W. CORNWALL *Soils for Archaeologist* xi. 125 Once the silt-grade is reached (below 0·06 mm.) a moderate wind is able to transport the grains..for long distances. **1967** *Gloss. Highway Engin. Terms* (B.S.I.) 23 *Silt.* (1) A natural sediment of grading finer than sand consisting of granular products of rock weathering: it is gritty to the touch. (2) In soil analysis it comprises the fraction between 0·06 mm and 0·002 mm. **1968** R. W. FAIRBRIDGE *Encycl. Geomorphol.* 675/1 Primary forms of lime include minute grains, incrustations on silt-size grain aggregates and snail shells. **1971** *Gloss. Soil Sci. Terms* (Soil Sci. Soc. Amer.) 15/1 *Silt*, a soil separate consisting of particles between 0·05 and 0·002 mm in equivalent diameter. **1972** [see *SAND *sb.*[2] 1 h]. **1976** L. F. CURTIS et al. *Soils in Brit. Isles* i. 3 The mineral matter [of soil] includes particles of clay (less than 2 μm diameter), silt (2–50 μm diameter) and sand (50 μm–2 mm diameter).

4. *silt-land, -trap*; **silt loam,** a soil composed at least half of silt; **siltstone** *Petrol.* (see quot. 1920).

1927 *Daily Express* 11 July 11/3 Both fenland and silt-land in these counties boast rich alluvial soil. **1963** *Times* 1 Feb. 13/6 Being essentially a study of the silt lands that border the Wash, it did not attempt to deal in detail with the equally interesting Roman occupation of the southern part of the region. **1917** MOSIER & GUSTAFSON *Soil Physics & Management* x. 138 The silt loam soils cover extensive areas in the middle west of the United States and owe their origin to loess. **1957** H. B. VANDERFORD *Managing Southern Soils* iv. 93 Surface soils which have medium to coarse textures (sandy loams, silt loams, and clay loams) are suitable for cultivation and relatively easy to keep in good tilth. **1920** A. Holmes *Nomencl. Petrol.* 211 *Siltstone*, a very fine-grained sandstone, the particles of which are predominantly of silt grade. **1946** L. D. Stamp *Britain's Struct. & Scenery* xii. 116 The lower Carboniferous deposits in the Central Lowlands of Scotland are sandstones, shales, cementstones and siltstones with only occasional bands of limestones. **1977** A. Hallam *Planet Earth* 264 The graptolites..are often common in offshore black shales and siltstones. **1946** F. D. Davison *Dusty* viii. 84 They..were going to clear out the silt-trap of one of the tanks. **1966** E. Palmer *Plains of Camdeboo* xviii. 301 Dams, water-troughs, silt traps.

silt, *v.* Add: **1. a.** Also *fig.*

1955 *Times* 10 June 7/3 [The] streets of London silt up with the swelling torrent of motor traffic.

silted *ppl. a.*: also with *up*.

1960 *Archaeologia Cambrensis* CIX. 56 The excavations ..revealed a massive stone platform built partly on the peat filling of a silted-up cistern.

siltation (siltēⁱ·ʃən). [f. Silt *v.* + -ation.] The action or result of silting. Freq. *attrib.*

1932 *Min. Proc. Inst. Civil Engin.* CCXXXII. 70 Siltation Records.—As there is a considerable quantity of silt in circulation in Bombay harbour, a detailed investigation was carried out. **1949** *Radio Times* 15 July 7/3 On the foreshore the cunning Dutch made 'siltation fields'... The incoming tides deposit mud in these fields which gradually rise until they are above sea level. Then a dyke is built. **1967** L. E. Cronin in G. H. Lauff *Estuaries* 671/1 The Potomac is a very flashy river... Droughts, floods, heavy siltation,..all present problems in its control. **1977** *Offshore Engineer* Aug. 48/4 The Port needed accurate and quick surveying to assess the siltation characteristics.

silumin (si·liŭmin). *Metallurgy.* [a. G. *silumin*: see Silicon and Aluminium.] Any of a series of casting alloys of aluminium containing about 9 to 13 per cent silicon.

1922 *Chem. Abstr.* XVI. 3861 Silumin... A new Al-Si alloy has been prepd. at the Metallbank in Frankfurt. **1930** *Engineering* 18 Apr. 508/1 This difficulty was partly overcome by resting the tent on slabs of Silumin. **1967** *Chem. Abstr.* LXVI. 21573 Effect of 0·0016–0·00072% Na on the kinetics of gas absorption under a steam-satd. atm. was investigated on silumins differing only in the initial Na content.

Silurian, *a.* and *sb.*[1] Add: **2. a.** (Further examples.) In mod. use, the name is restricted to a system of Lower Palæozoic rocks underlying the Devonian and overlying the Ordovician, so corresponding to the Upper Silurian as originally defined.

As orig. defined by Murchison the Silurian included what was subsequently called the Ordovician, and this use continued for a time after the introduction of the Ordovician in 1879.

1879 C. Lapworth in *Geol. Mag.* VI. 3 The Lyell-Hicks division of *Cambrian* and *Lower Silurian* are as rightly entitled to the rank of separate systems as the true or *Upper Silurian* itself. *Ibid.* 9 The general restriction of the title Silurian to the strata that are comprehended between the line marking the base of the Lower Llandovery, and that denoting the commencement of the brackish or fresh-water conditions of the typical Old Red Sandstone, appears..inevitable. *Ibid.* 15 The ideas of the extreme party which claims all the Lower Palæozoics for the Silurian are fated soon to become wholly extinct. **1902** A. J. Jukes-Browne *Student's Handbk. Stratigr. Geol.* vii. 64 Murchison supposed that Sedgwick's Cambrian lay entirely below his Silurian, but when the fossils were collected and described, it was found that the Upper Cambrian was equivalent to the Lower Silurian... Group after group of Sedgwick's Cambrian was gradually absorbed into it [*sc.* the Lower Silurian], till the Lower Silurian came to include the whole of the rocks (below the Upper Silurian) in which any fossils had been found. **1903** A. Geikie *Text-Bk. Geol.* (ed. 4) II. 934 Murchison's 'Lower Silurian' has by many writers been replaced by 'Ordovician', and his 'Upper Silurian' is in a similar manner being ousted by some other term... I shall continue to employ Murchison's terminology. **1912** *Q. Jrnl. Geol. Soc.* LXVIII. 332 In fixing the boundary between the Ordovician and the Silurian the peculiar characters and mode of weathering of the Lower Birkhill rocks have been found useful. **1931** Gregory & Barrett *Gen. Stratigr.* v. 77 The Silurian is now usually restricted to the strata between the Ordovician and Devonian. **1955** [see *Gotlandian, Gothlandian *a.*]. **1964** *Rep. Internat. Geol. Congr. XXI Sess., 1960* XXVIII. 254 The Commission transmits to the Congress the following proposals on the terminology of the Silurian and Ordovician... 1) Two systems are to be recognized between the Cambrian and Devonian systems. 2) The name of the lower shall be Ordovician. 3) The name of the upper shall be Silurian. **1971** *Jrnl. Geol. Soc.* CXXVII. 106 When the standard classification of the correlation charts is considered in relationship to local successions the Silurian of the British Isles is found to be something of a monument to stratigraphical chaos.

c. *transf.*, loosely designating a primitive age or period in the remote past.

1875 'Mark Twain' in *Atlantic Monthly* Aug. 193/2 In the Old Oölitic Silurian Period, just a million years ago next November. **1962** E. Snow *Red China Today* (1963) xvi. 116 When I last saw Mao..China was weak, disunited and bankrupt. Since then China's Silurian age had ended. 'China has stood up,' as Mao proclaimed.

3. Also with small initial. **a.** Of, pertaining to, or designating a paper showing two or more contrasting colours on its surface; usu. applied to stationery of a blue-grey appearance. Also, of the colour itself.

1892 J. Heywood *Wholesale Catal. Stationery & Stationers' Sundries* 22 Scotch Tinted Writings... Silurian—5 8. **1930** W. de la Mare *On the Edge* 28 The drawer beneath contained only envelopes and letter paper—*Montrésor*, in large pale-blue letters on a 'Silurian' background. **1937** E. J. Labarre *Dict. Paper* 153/1 *Granite* paper, also termed French grey, Ingres, Silurian grey, Mottled, Ingrain, is paper which clearly shows two or more contrasting colours of pulp on its surface. **1964** M. Clive *Day of Reckoning* viii. 73 Their correspondents wrote on double sheets of grey 'silurian' paper which looked hairy but was slippery.

b. As *sb.*, paper or stationery of this type.

1942 H. A. Maddox *Dict. Stationery* (ed. 2) 100 *Silurian*, a tinted writing paper formerly much in favour for note and envelopes. Characterised by a blue-grey mottled colour which gave rise to the occasional term, French Granite. **1954** *Paper Terminol.* (Spalding & Hodge) 54 *Silurian*, coloured paper, usually a writing or cover, produced by introducing into the coloured pulp, fibres dyed a deeper shade. **1960** D. Holman-Hunt *My Grandmothers & I* i. 24, I..sucked the pen and began to scratch at the grey silurian.

Silva (Si·lva). The name of José *Silva* (b. 1914), American electrician, used *attrib.* to denote the theory or methods devised by him to improve the functioning of one's mind.

1971 *Nat. Observer* (U.S.) 23 Aug. 16/1 Dr. Green faults the Silva method. **1976** *New Yorker* 15 Mar. 140/3 This book traces the frantic pilgrimage he undertook to pull himself together, running through EST, gestalt therapy,.. Esalen, hypnotism, modern dance, meditation, Silva Mind Control, Arica, [etc.]. **1978** Silva & Miele *Silva Mind Control Method* 12 The city planner had been trained in Silva Mind Control.

silva, see Sylva in Dict. and Suppl.

silver, *sb.* and *a.* Add: **I. 1. d.** *ellipt.* for *silver medal* (see sense 21a below).

1960 [see *gold[1] 1 b]. **1968** *Guardian* 22 Oct. 1/1 Major Alhusen, aged 55, won the silver in the individual event, and was only two points off taking the gold. **1979** 'D. Grant' *Moscow 5000* i. 19 Notes that would help him to win an Olympic medal. Because he would have the Silver, he told himself.

7. a. (Examples of the silver salmon.)

1934 *Nat. Geogr. Mag.* Feb. 211 There are four distinct species of salmon which run up the Columbia: the chinook, silver, sockeye, and chum. **1955** [see *Chinook b].

II. 10. d. (Earlier example.)

1879 *Bradstreet's* 22 Oct. 5/1 The silver men are as violent and rampant as ever.

III. 16. a. *silver-miner* (earlier example), *-plater* (earlier example).

1815 *Niles' Register* VIII. 141/2 There are..2 silver platers; 3 trunk makers [etc.]. **1869** 'Mark Twain' *Innoc. Abroad* vi. 57 To speak after the fashion of the silver-miners.

c. *silver-mining* (earlier example).

1872 'Mark Twain' *Roughing It* p. iv, The silver-mining fever in Nevada.

17. a. *silver-bowed, -buckled, -laced* (later example), *-mounted* (earlier example), *-plated* (earlier example), *-sandalled, -stringed, -studded, -topped, -veined.*

1894 'Mark Twain' *Those Twins* v. 393 The Judge.. laid aside his silver-bowed spectacles. **1922** Joyce *Ulysses* 506 He carries a silverstringed inlaid dulcimer... He wears dark velvet hose and silverbuckled pumps. **1939** D. Cecil *Young Melbourne* vi. 155 She also created scandal by appearing..imperfectly disguised as a page, in a plumed hat, silver-laced jacket and tight scarlet pantaloons. **1748** Smollett *R. Random* II. xliv. 79 A pair of silver mounted pistols. **1843** Dickens *Mart. Chuz.* (1844) xix. 237 To provide silver-plated handles of the very best description. **1881** O. Wilde *Poems* 67 Sweeter far if silver-sandalled foot Of some long-hidden God should ever tread The Nuneham meadows. **1916** Blunden *Harbingers* 63 So silver-sandalled down those golden ways He triumphs. **1922** Silverstringed [see *silver-buckled* above]. **1944** W. Fortescue *Mountain Madness* i. 22 A wide silver-studded black leather belt. **1928** 'Brent of Bin Bin' *Up Country* xv. 258 He was filling a bolster with articles of jewellery, silver-backed brushes, hand mirrors, candlesticks, silver-topped bottles, &c. **1976** 'D. Halliday' *Dolly & Nanny Bird* xiii. 170 There's a white leather gift box in every cabin, fitted out with..silver-topped crystal bottles. **1916** Joyce *Portrait of Artist* (1969) v. 176 He would think of the cloistral silverveined prose of Newman.

c. *silver-breasted, -flecked, -sanded, -suited, -winged* (later example).

1881 O. Wilde *Poems* 24 Lure the silver-breasted Helena Back from the lotus meadows of the dead. **1926** *Spectator* 11 Sept. 370/1 Wide silver-breasted rivers flowing to a sunlit sea. **1937** *Burlington Mag.* May 252/2 Two bowls of *Chien yao*... One is of the silver-flecked variety. **1967** *Coast to Coast 1965–6* 32 All manner of fabulous creatures of the deep surged and surfaced amid the molten silver-flecked arrowing lines of foaming waves. **1851** J. G. Whittier in *National Era* 3 Jan. 106/4 Whose small waves on a silver-sanded shore Whisper of peace. **1957** R. Campbell *Coll. Poems* II. 121 On the silver-sanded shores. **1962** *Daily Tel.* 5 Oct. 22/2 The silver-suited astronaut. **1903** Kipling *Five Nations* 2 The inrolling walls of the fog and the silver-winged breeze that disperses.

18. *silver-shining* (later examples).

1932 D. Gascoyne *Roman Balcony* 33 And through their long-nailed fingers Glide the silver-shining minnows. **1944** W. de la Mare *Coll. Rhymes & Verses* 99 There silver-shining Hesper Smiles at Mars.

19. *silver-blue, -bright* (later example), *-green, -pink, -silent.*

1959 W. Thesiger *Arabian Sands* xii. 242 We came to a succession of dune-chains, each of which..showed up in turn as a wavy silver-blue wall. **1973** J. Seabrook *Loneliness* 117 A quiet, rather subdued woman; smart, with silver-blue hair. **1959** R. Graves *Coll. Poems* 315 And next the silver-bright Hyperborean Queendom. **1914** L. Woolf *Wise Virgins* iv. 110 The silver-green water glided by him. **1923** D. H. Lawrence *Birds, Beasts & Flowers* 19 Silver-pink peach, venetian green glass of medlars and sorb-apples. **1976** 'D. Halliday' *Dolly & Nanny Bird* xiii. 165 The pearly capped teeth and silver-pink mouth. **1922** Joyce *Ulysses* 537 Through silver-silent summer air the dummy of Bloom, rolled in a mummy, rolls rotatingly.

IV. 21. a. silver band, a brass band with silver-coloured instruments; **silver beggar** (earlier example); **silver blond(e)** *a.*, of hair: of a very light, silvery colour, esp. as the result of bleaching (cf. *platinum blond(e)* s.v. *platinum 2 c); **silver collection,** a collection of 'silver' coins (or of money of no denomination lower than these) made at a meeting, etc.; **silver cord,** (*a*) used in phr. *the silver cord is loosed* and varr. (in allusion to Eccl. xii. 6) to signify the dissolution of life at death; (*b*) a symbol of excessive devotion between mother and child; **silver doctor,** an artificial fishing fly having a body of tinsel; **silver-fizz,** an effervescing drink based on gin and egg-white (cf. *fizz, fiz *sb.* 3); **silver-fork** (earlier example); also applied to later novelists displaying similar characteristics; **silver handshake,** a gratuity given on retirement or as compensation for dismissal from one's occupation (of less value than a golden handshake); † **silver hell** *slang*, a low-class gambling saloon (cf. Hell *sb.* 8) (*obs.*); **silver jubilee:** see Jubilee *sb.* 3 a; **Silver Lady,** an epithet applied to Miss Elizabeth Baxter (d. 1972), philanthropist, from her custom of giving silver coin to the down-and-outs of the Embankment in London, used *attrib.* to describe a charitable organization (and its appurtenances) which distributes food and hot drinks to vagrants; **silver medal,** a medal made of or resembling silver, awarded as the second prize in a contest, esp. in the Olympic Games; hence **silver medallist; silver point,** (*b*) the freezing point of silver under normal atmospheric pressure (about 962°C), as a thermometric fixed point; **silver-pointed** *a.*, coloured or tinged in the manner of a silver-point drawing; hence, as a back-formation, **silver-point** *v. trans.*, to cause to appear so; **silver polish,** a polish used for cleaning and brightening silver; **silver ring** *Racing* (see quot. 1921) (cf. *Tattersall 1 b); also *attrib.*; **silver screen,** a cinematographic projection screen covered with metallic paint to produce a highly reflective silver-coloured surface; usu. *transf.*, the cinema generically, considered as a medium for such film projection; **silver service** (see quot. 1970); **Silver Shirts** *U.S.*, the name applied to the Silver Legion, an American fascist, anti-Semitic paramilitary group founded in 1933 and disbanded in 1940 (cf. *blackshirt); **silver-side** (earlier example); **Silver Star,** a decoration for gallantry awarded to members of the U.S. Army and Navy (see quot. 1941); also *Silver Star medal*; **silver state** *U.S.*, a state producing silver, or advocating free coinage of silver; *spec.* (with initial capitals) Nevada or, less freq., Colorado; **silver table,** (*a*) a table made of or plated with silver; (*b*) a table used for the display of silverware, freq. with raised edges (and a glass lid); **silver-tail** (later examples); **silver tea** *N. Amer.*, a tea-party at which the guests make contributions (typically, of 'silver' coin) to charity; **silver thaw** (earlier N. Amer. example); **silver wedding** (earlier examples) (see also Wedding *vbl. sb.* 2 b).

1933 *Radio Times* 14 Apr. 126/5 The Tullis Russell Silver Band. **1949** 'J. Tey' *Brat Farrar* xxv. 228 'Thump! Thump! Thump!' said the drum of the Bures Silver Band. **1976** *Times* 3 May 12/4 The Eastbourne silver band, in bright red jackets, played *California Here I Come.* c **1842** *Exposure of Impositions practised by Vagrants* 4, I shall begin with those vagrants who, generally, obtain the most, and are considered of the first class, and by some termed 'Silver Beggars', but by travellers they are called 'Lurkers'. **1951** J. C. Fennessy *Sonnet in Bottle* I. 29 Silver-blond hair, silver-grey eyes. **1959** M. Summerton *Small Wilderness* i. 8 The silver-blonde hair that curved.. to her shoulders. **1974** D. Francis *Knock Down* iii. 37 She had silver shoes and silver-blonde hair. **1957** B. & S. G. Hulme Beaman *Ernest the Brave* 8 'I was referring to the pence expected as a result of this disgraceful exhibition!' 'Oh, Mr. Growser, sir,' Larry interrupted. 'This is supposed to be a silver collection.' **1972** H. Kemelman *Monday Rabbi took Off* xxii. 145 Imagine, Katz, no charge. Not even a silver collection. **1911** J. A. Thomson *Introd. Sci.* vi. 177 If we can use such a word, the silver cord of the bundle of life is loosed, and earth returns to earth. The microbes of decay break down the dead, and there is a return to air and water and salts. **1934** F. S. Fitzgerald *Tender is Night* I. xiii. 76 'The silver cord is cut and the golden bowl is broken and all that, but an old romantic like me can't do anything about it.' 'I'm romantic too.' They came out of the neat restored trench, and faced a memorial to the Newfoundland dead. **1942** P. Wylie *Generation of Vipers* xi. 185 Our land, subjectively mapped, would have more silver cords and apron strings crisscrossing it than railroads and telephone wires. **1959** J. Braine *Vodi* xxi. 232 Her mother, as usual, had won. And, what was hardest to forgive, had won fairly; she wasn't the Silver Cord type, she'd never been possessive. **1973** G. Mackay Brown *Magnus* vii. 156 Magnus Erlendson would live out his life, until such time as the silver cord was loosed, and the golden bowl broken, and the pitcher broken at the fountain. **1875** *Encycl. Brit.* II. 40/2 *The silver doctor*, also a very great favourite. Tag, silver tinsel; tail, a topping; but, a turn of red crewel; body of silver tinsel entirely; [etc.]. **1931** *Hardy's Anglers' Guide* 31 Your fairy shrimp, just as pretty..as any Jock Scott or Silver Doctor. **1901** O. Wister *Philos. 4* in *Stories of Colleges* 68 It must have been that extra silver-fizz you took before dinner. **1977** E. Ambler *Send no More Roses* vi. 121 He was drinking a silver-fizz, a long drink made of gin and egg-whites. [**1827** *Examiner* 18 Nov. 722/2 A writer of this accomplished stamp..also informs you that the quality eat fish with silver forks.] **1831** *Times* 15 Dec. 5/3 A single chapter of any one of them is worth more than the whole bundle of those contemptible productions of the silver-fork school, which are called 'fashionable novels'. **1974** *Times Lit. Suppl.* 4 Oct. 1092/5 The suspicion grows that this is a new-style 'silver fork' novel, with merchant bankers taking the place of noble dukes. **1958** M. Pugh *Wilderness of Monkeys* 84 Flash Willy is just about to go back to London, pick up his silver handshake, his sacking money, and get himself a corner in the 'I will photograph your child in your home' lark. **1979** C. Dexter *Service of All Dead* ii. 17 A little silver handshake, a little farewell party. **1835** T. Power *Jrnl.* 13 Jan. in *Impressions of Amer.* (1836) II. 196 With here and there a couple of the same sort of gemman to be met with about the silver hells of London. **1843** 'W. I. Moncrieff' *Scamps of London* I. i. 5 in *Sel. Dramatic Wks.* (1851) I, He's the principal partner in all the silver hells at the west end. **1961** *Ann. Charities Reg. & Digest* 208/2 *Silver Lady Fund.* Mobile café out on Embankment serving hot tea and food free to the needy. Miss Betty Baxter.., E.C.4. **1978** C. A. Berry *Gentleman of Road* xv. 171 The Silver Lady van arrived and mugs of tea and meat pies were distributed. **1908** Silver medal [see *gold[1] 1 b]. **1958** [see *baton *sb.* 2 b]. **1976** *All about the Games* (Com. Org. des Jeux Olympiques) 24 Canada's 74 athletes won one silver medal. **1911** Silver medallist [listed in Dict. at sense 8 a]. **1976** *Daily Tel.* 20 July 1/7 The cheating by Boris Onischenko, silver medallist at the Mexico City and Munich Olympics. **1928** *Bureau of Standards Jrnl. Res.* (U.S.) I. 637 The constants *a*, *b*, and *c* are to be determined by calibration at the freezing point of antimony, and at the silver and gold points. **1967** Condon & Odishaw *Handbk. Physics* (ed. 2) v. iii. 41/1 In the neighbourhood of 1000°C new determinants of the silver point and gold point have been made in recent years. **1976** I. Murdoch *Henry & Cato* I. 46 A bright half moon was.. silverpointing the slates and making pendant shadows beneath the..eaves. **1913** C. Mackenzie *Sinister St.* I. ii. xx. 483 They moved to Geneva, whose silverpointed beauty for a while deceived them. **1930** R. Campbell *Poems* 1 Two sisters... Whose fingers glint with silver-pointed nails. **1895** *Montgomery Ward Catal.* Spring & Summer 193 Thorn's Silver Polish, Liquid Form, 15c. per Bottle. **1974** 'D. Fletcher' *Lovable Man* I. 37 He memorised the exact position of the silver polish and.. began to polish the lighter. **1921** E. Wallace *Law Four Just Men* ix. 261, I found a poor little bookmaker in the silver ring—the silver ring is the enclosure where smaller bets are made in Tattersall's reservation. **1926** J. Masefield *Odtaa* xv. 257 A vile, taunting, silver-ring tick. **1939** Wodehouse *Uncle Fred in Springtime* xx. 306 She is the daughter of a retired Silver Ring bookie. **1973** 'I. Drummond' *Jaws of Watchdog* xvii. 227 Sandro was in Tatt's... He could also go down the social and financial scale into the Silver Ring and the cheapest enclosures. [**1921** 'M. Pickford' *Let.* in V. Burnett *Romantick Lady* (1927) xxxii. 398 It is not always easy to take a classic like 'Little Lord Fauntleroy' and place it on the cold, silver screen.] **1924** *Amer. Hebrew* 22 Feb. 439 (*heading*) 'Shooting' news for the silver screen; Pathe film editor who brings home to millions timely pictures of world events. **1931** B. Brown *Talking Pictures* i. 19 Somehow there had crept into this new field of endeavour the romance of the silver screen. **1959** *Times Lit. Suppl.* 6 Nov. 636/4 Not a night passes without one aspect or another of the far western frontier holding children from play and old men from the chimney corner on the silver screen or on 'the Telly'. **1979** A. Hailey *Overload* III. xii. 256 Cameron Clarke objected to Tunipah and the god of the silver screen had spoken. **1970** *Drive* Spring 43/1 Silver service means that your plate is put before you empty and the various parts of your dish are served separately from silver. **1976** *Evening Standard* 14 June 25/3 (Advt.), Commis de rang for our high class Prince's Room Restaurant—must have silver service experience. **1934** *Sun* (Baltimore) 6 Aug. 6/2 A California newspaper has published the exciting news that the Silver Shirts of America plan to put down the Communists and then take over control of the American Government. **1959** W. Faulkner *Mansion* 303 When the Silver Shirts appeared, Clarence was one of the first in Mississippi to join it. [**1845** E. Acton *Mod. Cookery* viii. 206 The natural division of the meat will show where the silver-side of the round is to be separated from the upper, or tongue side.] **1861** Mrs. Beeton *Bk. Househ. Managem.* 283 As a whole round of beef..is too large for small families..we here give the recipes for dressing a portion of the silver side of the round. **1932** *U.S. Army Regulations* 8 Aug. No. 600-45 p. 1 The authorized decorations awarded by the United States are: *a. Awarded by the War Department*... (4) Silver Star. **1932** *N.Y. Times* 18 Dec. II. 2/5 Captain Herbert G. Rosboro..received the Silver Star medal today from the War Department for gallantry in action in October, 1918. **1941** J. McDowell Morgan *Military Medals & Insignia of U.S.* 76 The Silver Star was established..on July 9, 1918. This originally was a unique badge of honor, being a small silver star, 3/16-inch in diameter, designed to be worn on the ribbon of a campaign medal to indicate..'a citation for gallantry in action'... On August 8, 1932, a distinct medal, known as the Silver Star Decoration, was established as a reward to those persons previously cited in orders for gallantry in action. **1948** E. E. Cummings *Let.* 27 Aug. (1969) 185 The hyperscientific climax of this hero (a prominent killer, holder of Silver Stars & Clusters & Purple Hearts galore)'s experience. **1969** I. Kemp *Brit. G.I. in Vietnam* vii. 153 You've been awarded the Silver Star for your action at Dak To. **1982** H. Lieberman *Late Call* lxiii. 308 I'm a veteran with a silver star and a purple heart. **1866** *Eastern Slope* (Washoe, Nevada) 15 Sept. 4/1 The Silver State struck it rich when they elected H. G. Blasdel to the Gubernatorial chair. **1871** *Harper's Mag.* Oct. 799/1 In our early days in the Silver State females were rarely to be seen in the frontier mining camps. **1885** *Weekly New Mexican Rev.* 8 Jan. 4/2 All the silver states and territories [should] organize to resist the effort which the single standard advocates are making in congress to suspend the coinage of silver. **1946** *Trail & Timberline* May 74/1 Colorado miners had been looking for gold but silver became of such importance that when the Territory became a state in 1876, it was known as the Silver State and Georgetown was called the Silver Queen. **1976** *Billings* (Montana) *Gaz.* 20 June 10-c/2 It was a bluish-gray ore—silver—and Nevada is now appropriately nicknamed 'The Silver State'. *c* **1792** C. Fiennes *Journeys* (1947) III. xii. 279 Here's a silver table and stands and glass frame. **1897** [in Dict., sense 10 c]. **1926** A. Christie *Murder of R. Ackroyd* iv. 33 What..is called a silver table, the lid of which lifts, and through the glass of which you can see the contents. **1975** *Country Life* 10 Apr. Suppl. 48 j/1 (*caption*) A really fine Chippendale period silver table of superb quality. **1908** E. G. Murphy *Jarrahland Jingles* 116 And when they're playing billiards in their flannel tennis suits, We feel like heaving something at these silvertail galoots. **1947** G. Casey *Wits are Out* ix. 125 'Mr Fleming doesn't build for basic-wage earners,' Bill said nastily. 'He hangs around waiting his chance to build for the silvertails.' **1978** *Listener* 9 Feb. 163/3 Mr Whitlam's enemies in his own Labor Party have called him a 'silvertail', meaning a social climber. **1979** *Sunday Mail Mag.* (Brisbane) 11 Feb. 16/1 The Governor-General was, in the Premier's opinion, a super silvertail. **1921** *Daily Colonist* (Victoria) 18 Mar. 9/4 A silver tea will be held at the home of Mrs. H. Lloyd-Young..on Friday afternoon. **1770** G. Cartwright *Jrnl.* 22 Dec. (1792) I. 73 There was a silver thaw in the morning, and it rained freely: very mild weather all the rest of the day. **1845** A. H. Clough in *Ambarvalia* (1849) 28 The Silver Wedding! on some pensive ear..A silvery faint memorial music swells. **1861** Queen Victoria *Let.* 13 Feb. in R. Fulford *Dearest Child* (1964) 307 You must promise to be with us for our silver wedding D. V. which will be in four years.

b. silverback, a mature male mountain gorilla, *Gorilla gorilla beringei*, distinguished by one or more patches of white or silvery hair just below the back of the neck; **silver fox**, (*a*) (earlier example); also *transf.*, the fur of this animal, esp. as a fashion item; (*b*) a fennec, *Vulpes chama*, found in southern Africa; **silver-tip** (earlier example).

1963 G. B. Schaller *Year of Gorilla* viii. 221 He was a silverback in the prime of life. **1975** J. Goulet *Human Ape* (1977) i. 5 The old silverback was having trouble breathing. **1770** G. Cartwright *Jrnl.* 30 Dec. (1792) I. 76 On Niger Sound we saw a good silver fox. **1892** *T. Eaton & Co. Catal.* Fall & Winter 11/2 Three-quarter capes, quilted lined, trimmed silver fox, $4. **1912** J. Stevenson-Hamilton *Anim. Life Afr.* xv. 231 The Silver Fox (*Vulpes chama*)..is silvery-grey, the underneath parts being tawny in hue. **1936** A. Christie *ABC Murders* xix. 143 [She] wears very lovely clothes. That crêpe marocain and the silver fox collar—*dernier cri*! **1940** [see *battle bowler* s.v. *battle *sb.* 14]. **1972** *Stand. Encycl. S.Afr.* VI. 170/2 The Cape or silver fox is found throughout the drier regions of South Africa. **1886** *Turf, Field & Farm* 26 Mar. 238/1 A silver tip is bad enough when he's wounded, and about as active a bear as there is.

c. silver-eye, substitute for def.: one of several birds of the genus *Zosterops*, distinguished by white rings round the eyes; (earlier and later examples).

1875 [see *makomako[1]]. **1911** A. E. Mack *Bush Days* 2 You will hear a whole chorus of bird notes..calling all together—thrushes, thickheads, silvereyes and peewees. **1965** [see *blight-bird* s.v. *blight *sb.*]. **1977** *Kuwait Times* 23 Nov. 6/8 Three fell to Man, including a pigeon and a parrakeet. The rats have been responsible for at least five more (a thrush, a warbler, a fantail, a silvereye and a starling).

d. silver eel, also, a young eel before the adult coloration is developed; (earlier and later examples); **silver salmon** (earlier example); **silver-sides**: also **silver-side** and as one word; (earlier and later examples); **silver trout** *N. Amer.*, one of several silvery trout, esp. *Salmo gairdneri kamloops*; also, = *kokanee.

1735 Swift & Sheridan *Let.* 28 Nov. in *Wks. J. Swift* (1768) XIII. 143 For the rest, we are forced to take up with..silver eels, and such trash. **1952** *New Biol.* XIII. 76 At the silver-eel stage..it is ready to descend the river again. **1878** J. G. Brady *Let.* May in S. Jackson *Alaska* (1880) vii. 209 A silver salmon, weighing thirty-eight to forty pounds, is sold for fifteen or twenty cents. **1820** C. S. Rafinesque in *Western Rev.* II. 240 Silverside Fallfish... Vulgar names, Silverside, Shiner, [etc.]. **1851** R. Glisan *Jrnl. Army Life* (1874) viii. 88 The purer streams from the hills abound in..silver-sides. **1911** *Rep. Fisheries 1908* (U.S.) 316/2 Some of the silversides (*Atherinidæ*) are wrongly called 'smelts'. **1962** K. F. Lagler et al. *Ichthyology* x. 284 In the brook silverside..there is a single elongate filament that serves first for temporary flotation. *Ibid.* xi. 373 Refractive errors change by several diopters during such measurements on schooling fishes, such as the silver-side (*Menidia*). **1873** C. Hallock *Fishing Tourist* I. v. 30 To the above should be added the..brook-trout, the silver-trout, and the..salmon-trout. **1907** T. W. Lambert *Fishing in Brit. Columbia* 43 Every local fisherman speaks of having caught a red side or a silver trout, and firmly believes they are distinct species. **1937, 1970** Silver trout [see *kokanee].

e. silver beech, an evergreen tree, *Nothofagus menziesii*, native to New Zealand (cf. *nothofagus); also, the timber of this tree; **silver beet** *Austral.* and *N.Z.*, the seakale beet, *Beta vulgaris*; = Chard[2]; (later examples); **silver bell (tree)** (earlier example); **silver poplar** *U.S.* (earlier example); = *white poplar* s.v. Poplar 1 b; **silversword**, a perennial herb, *Argyroxiphium sandwicense*, of the family Compositæ, native to Hawaii and bearing linear leaves with silvery hairs and clusters of purplish flowers; **silver wattle** (earlier example); **silver willow**, a variety of the white willow, *Salix alba* var. *sericea*, distinguished by silvery foliage.

1889 T. Kirk *Forest Flora N.Z.* 175 The silver-beech.. is known as 'tawhai' or 'tawai' by the Natives. **1950** *N.Z. Jrnl. Agric.* July 8/3 Durability of..less than five years.. Silver beech. **1966** *Encycl. N.Z.* I. 177/2 Silver beech.., a tree with small, thick, double-toothed leaves and a cherry-like bark on the branches and young trees, reaches heights of about 100 ft. **1915** *N.Z. Jrnl. Agric.* 20 Jan. 75 Early in February is a good time to sow silver-beet. **1951** J. Frame *Lagoon* 98 For dinner I had semolina and silver beet. **1973** *Islander* (Victoria, B.C.) 18 Feb. 2/4 Their hulls loaded down with taro, yams, chinese cabbage (rather like silver beet) and bananas. **1977** *N.Z. Herald* 5 Jan. 2-2/1 The novelty value of spaghetti bolognaise can often get over the hurdle of the silverbeet hidden in the sauce. **1785** H. Marshall *Arbustrum Americanum* 57 Silver-Bell Tree... The Corolla is of one petal, bell'd and bellied. **1847** W. Darlington *Agric. Bot.* 332 Silver Poplar... Some of the grass-plats in the public squares of New York have been quite over-run by the wide-spreading suckers of this tree. **1888** W. Hillebrand *Flora of Hawaiian Islands* 219 The 'Ahinahina' of the natives and 'Silversword' of the foreigners. **1937** *Discovery* Mar. 83 Not the least puzzling of the specialised animal and plant species of the Hawaiian Islands is the six-foot Silversword flower. **1965** P. Wylie *They Both were Naked* II. vi. 302 A silver-sword plant..grows only on a few high places on two islands [of Hawaii]. **1859** D. Bunce *Trav. Dr. Leichhardt* iii. 19 We camped among the butts of the *Acacia affinis*, or silver wattle. **1914** W. J. Bean *Trees & Shrubs Hardy in Brit. Isles* II. 475 Silver Willow.—This is the most striking of all the forms of *S[alix] alba* in the intense silvery hue of its leaves. **1976** *Country Life* 18 Mar. 682/3 A group of silver willows..are annually pollarded.

Silver age. Add: **1. c.** A period of Russian literature and art at the beginning of the twentieth century, considered in comparison with the golden era of the mid-nineteenth century.

1965 P. Benno in Hayward & Crawley *Soviet Lit. in Sixties* 179 The works of the generation of Russia's 'Silver Age' in the first three decades of the present century. **1974** T. P. Whitney tr. *Solzhenitsyn's Gulag Archipelago* I. I. ix. 336 Even though the Silver Age of art, four State Dumas, three wars, and three revolutions had come and gone, all Moscow drank Oldenborger's water. **1976** *Times Lit. Suppl.* 16 Apr. 450/3 The poet's life in pre-war St Petersburg... She grew up in the capital at a time when its artistic life was at its most febrile and brilliant, the height of the 'Silver Age', not only in poetry but in painting, ballet, music.

Silverblu (si·lvəɹblū). Also **Silver Blu(e.** [f. Silver *a.* + Blu(e *a.*] A mink belonging to a mutated form distinguished by silvery fur; also, the fur of an animal of this kind. Also *attrib.*

1941 *Amer. Fur Breeder* June 8/3 Miss Esther Wyman of Harper's Bazaar magazine was shown a couple of these Platinum pelts... She..suggested that a better fur name be given them such as Silver Blue. **1942** *Ibid.* Oct. 8/3 Of the mutations the platinum or Silver Blu mink are the most prominent. **1944** *Fur Trade Jrnl. Canada* XXI. 10/1 The first offering of 'Silverblu' mink..brought a top price. **1945, 1956** [see *mutation mink* s.v. *mutation 7]. **1966** A. Leonard *Mod. Mink Management* 202 (*caption*) The late William Whittingham developed the Silver Blu mink, the grandaddy of all mutations. **1968** J. Ironside *Fashion Alphabet* vii. 159 Silverblu (also called Platinum): The original mutation mink, introduced in 1942.

silver-foil. Add: **2.** = *SILVER PAPER 2. Cf. *FOIL *sb.*[1] 4 d.

1944 N. MAILER in E. Seaver *Cross-Section* 338 The captain took out a chocolate bar... He separated a piece of silver foil from his teeth. **1974** N. BENTLEY *Inside Information* i. 8 He slid the outside wrapping off his bar of Whole Nut... Hidden between the wrapping and the silver foil underneath was a small piece of paper.

silver-grey, *sb.* **b.** (Earlier example.)

1850 *N.Y. Tribune* 18 Oct. 5/2, I shall gladly fight on in this cause so long as I shall live, and ask no higher post than the proud one of a private in the Silver Grays.

silver-headed, *a.* **2.** (Later example.)

1981 M. MCMULLEN *Other Shoe* (1982) ii. 14 She got about slowly..with the help of a silver-headed ebony cane.

silverily (si·lvərili), *adv. rare.* [f. SILVERY *a.* + -LY[2].] = SILVERLY *adv.* 1, 2.

1929 D. H. LAWRENCE *Pansies* 44 This wet white gleam Twitches, and ebbs hitting, washing inwardly, silverily against his ribs. *a* **1930** —— *Phoenix* (1936) 40 You hear the nightingale silverily shouting.

silver-leaf. 3. Delete *local* and substitute for def.: A disease of *Prunus* and other woody plants caused by the fungus *Stereum purpureum*, which is frequently associated with a silvery sheen of the leaves and often fatal to affected branches. (Further examples.)

1902 *Jrnl. Linn. Soc. Bot.* XXXV. 390 The disease known as 'Silver-leaf' is, so far as I am aware, confined to the *Pruneæ*, and has been the subject of observation and investigation for more than a quarter of a century. **1929** *Trans. Brit. Mycol. Soc.* XIV. 163 Silver leaf, *Stereum purpureum* Pers. **1946** H. WORMALD *Diseases of Fruit & Hops* iii. 57 The Silver Leaf Order of 1923 requires growers to cut off and burn all dead wood of plum and apple trees before 15th of July each year. **1969** P. THROWER *Every Day Gardening* xiii. 292/2 (*caption*) Branches and even complete trees can be killed by Silver Leaf disease, and fungal outgrowths form on the dead wood. First, however, the leaves take on a silvery sheen. **1977** *Field* 13 Jan. 66/1 Pruning [of plum trees] should be carried out in late spring..and preferably in dry weather. This is to avoid infection by the silver leaf fungus.

silver paper. Add: **1.** (Earlier example.)

1800 M. EDGEWORTH *Birth-Day Present* in *Parent's Assistant* (ed. 3) II. 14 She was obliged to go down with her basket but half wrapped up in silver paper.

2. Also, thin metal foil, used chiefly as a damp-proof wrapping for tobacco and confectionery.

1905 *Strand Mag.* XXIX. 274/1 He has been sorting out the pieces of 'silver paper', as he calls them, in which packets of tobacco are wrapped. **1929** *B.B.C. Year-bk. 1930* 404 The balance of the subscriptions..is paid into the local Radio Circle Funds, which are further increased in various ways such as by the sale of 'silver paper'. **1976** W. TREVOR *Children of Dynmouth* iii. 65 The one he'd taken had green silver paper on it, a chocolate-covered toffee.

silver plate. Add: **3.** Used as a jocular representation of Fr. *s'il vous plaît* please. *slang.*

1919 *Yank Talk* 4/1 (*caption*) Silver plate! Loan me a coupla francs! **1920** *Dialect Notes* V. 79 *Silver plate*, s'il vous plaît. 'More of the mutton, Mr. Brown, silver plate.'

silversmith. Add: Hence **si·lversmi:thing.**

1931 E. WENHAM *Domestic Silver* ii. 8 No period in the history of British silversmithing manifests more varying foreign influences than that of the sixteenth century. **1969** T. LLOYD in R. Blythe *Akenfield* xiv. 222 There is something else I do—silversmithing. I learnt it at evening classes. **1981** *Times Lit. Suppl.* 20 Feb. 194/5 Ashbee'n emerges as a many-sided creativity, embracing architecture, silversmithing and printing.

silvery, *a.* Add: **2. a. silvery pout,** a small marine fish, *Gadiculus argenteus thori*, belonging to the cod family and found in north-western Europe and the Mediterranean.

1925 J. T. JENKINS *Fishes Brit. Isles* 155 The Silvery Pout is not often met with close inshore. **1959** A. C. HARDY *Open Sea* II. ii. 229 The little silvery pout..is an even more deep-water species.

5. b. *silvery-tongued* (example).

1885 E. W. HAMILTON *Diary* 29 Jan. (1972) II. 783 The German Ambassador whom Bismarck suspects of being too silvery-tongued over here.

silvex (si·lveks). [f. L. *silv-a* wood, woodland + Eng. *-ex*.] A hormone weedkiller that is also effective against some woody plants; 2-(2,4,5-trichlorophenoxy)propionic acid.

1954 *Proc. Southern Weed Conf.* VII. 268 Silver was active in causing cell elongation and adventitious root formation but not active in causing formative effects. **1973** ASHTON & CRAFTS *Mode of Action of Herbicides* ix. 131 These growth regulators enhance the herbicidal effect of silvex on poison ivy. **1976** *Columbus* (Montana) *News* 3 June (Joliet Suppl.) 4/5 Dandelions are more difficult to control after they flower. Spraying with 2, 4-D, silvex or dicamba (Banvel) is recommended...Silvex also gives excellent control of chickweed.

silvi- (si·lvi), comb. form of L. *silva* wood, woodland. Cf. also SYLVICULTURE, SILVI-.

silvical (si·lvikăl), *a.* [f. as SYLVICS + -ICAL.] Of or pertaining to silvics.

1909 in WEBSTER. **1919** *Jrnl. Forestry* XVII. 276 The Commission of Conservation of Canada has during several seasons conducted silvical investigations... Studies of natural regeneration, with special reference to the effects of repeated fires, have been carried out. **1931** *Ecology* XII. 568 Müller was probably the first to look upon the humus layer in the forest as a natural biological unit, and..he was able to characterize two main types of humus layer and their biological and silvical properties. **1977** *Jrnl. Arnold Arboretum Harvard Univ.* LVIII. 307 (*heading*) Silvical characteristics of sugar maple..in northern Cape Breton Island.

silvichemical (silvike·mikăl). [f. *SILVI- + CHEMICAL *a.*] Any chemical obtained from part of a tree.

1963 L. C. BRATT in *Abstr. Papers 144th Meeting Amer. Chem. Soc.* 11D The name 'silvichemicals' is used in this paper to define chemicals and special products made from tree components, primarily wood, bark, and oleoresins as well as from pulp mill by-products. **1965** *Jrnl. Forestry* LXIII. 163/1 The silvichemicals may be divided into the two broad classifications of complex polymers or mixtures and pure organic chemicals. **1974** *Finnish Chem. Lett.* VII. 262 There are clear opportunities for the creation of a profitable enterprise producing silvichemicals from technical foliage.

silvicide (si·lvisəid). [f. *SILVI- + -CIDE[1].] A substance that kills trees.

1950 in *Forestry Terminol.* (Soc. Amer. Foresters) (ed. 2) 75/1. **1960** *Jrnl. Forestry* LVIII. 403/2 Thinning white pine stands with silvicides might be expected to result in serious backflash damage. **1976** *Amer. Industr. Hygiene Assoc. Jrnl.* XXXVII. 418/1 The increasing use of organic arsenicals..as silvicides in forestry has raised questions concerning the health and safety of exposed workers.

silvics: see SYLVICS in Dict. and Suppl.

silyl (səi·ləil, -lil). *Chem.* [f. *SIL(ANE + -YL.] The univalent group or radical —SiH_3; any substituted derivative of this, esp. one in which alkyl groups replace the hydrogen atoms. Usu. *attrib.*

1916 *Jrnl. Chem. Soc.* CX. II. 319 The radicles ·SiH_3, ·Si_2H_5, and ·Si_2H_3 would be respectively designated silyl, disilyl, and disilenyl. **1939** *Ibid.* 1030 Some of the other possible reactions of the silyl radicals are more favoured than that with ethylene. **1970** *Nature* 25 July 335/2 The preparation of silylated ylides of phosphorus, arsenic and sulphur, in which the silyl group is both a stabilizing and an efficient leaving group.

Hence **silyla·tion,** a reaction or process in which a substance is converted into a form having silyl substituents; also **si·lylate** *v. trans.*, to subject to silylation; **si·lylated** *ppl. a.*; **si·lylating** *vbl. sb.*

1938 *Nature* 3 Dec. 997/1 Trimethylsilylammonium chloride is a convenient silylating agent. **1949** *Chem. Abstr. Subject Index 1937–1946* 8856/2 Silylation. **1966** *Jrnl. Amer. Chem. Soc.* LXXXVIII. 3390/1 Bis(trimethylsilyl)acetamide..is a silylating agent superior, in many respects, to the presently used methods. *Ibid.* 3390/2 Silylations of 'good' acceptors—alcohols, amines, carboxylic acids—can be carried out with monosilylamides since the rapidly established equilibria lie far on the product side. *Ibid.* 3391/1 The vapor pressure of the silylated product. **1969** *Kirk-Othmer Encyl. Chem. Technol.* (ed. 2) XVIII. 262 A method of silylating biologically active compounds. **1972** *Science* 12 May 683/3 Silylation was effected in pyridine with a mixture of hexamethyldisilazane and trimethylchlorosilane. **1978** *Experientia* XXXIV. 1380/1 The material..was silylated with 200μl of trimethylsilylimidazole at 65°C for 12–15h.

sima (səi·mă). *Geol.* Also **Sima.** [a. G. *sima* (E. Suess *Das Antlitz der Erde* (1909) III. II. xxiv. 626), f. L. *si-licium* SILICON + *magnesium* MAGNESIUM.] The continuous basal layer of the earth's crust, composed of relatively heavy, basic rocks rich in silica and magnesia, that underlies the sialic continental masses and forms the crust under the oceans; the material of which it is composed.

The lower limit of the sima is generally taken to be the Mohorovičić discontinuity.

1909 [see *NIFE]. **1925** *Glasgow Herald* 29 Sept. 9 In continental regions it [*sc.* sial] both rises higher to form the land surface, and extends downwards into or displaces somewhat the sima, just as a ship floats on and displaces the water. **1944** A. HOLMES *Princ. Physical Geol.* iv. 41 Certain rocks of the kinds grouped together as sima (*e.g.* basalt) contain calcic plagioclase, but others are free from felspar. All of the sima rocks, however, are characterized by the abundance or predominance of heavy, greenish silicate minerals. **1950** P. H. KUENEN *Marine Geol.* ii. 127 If America were plowing through the sima westwards.. one would expect a raising of the sima in front of the continent. **1970** L. KNOPOFF in Johnson & Smith *Megatectonics of Continents & Oceans* vi. 120 It seemed plausible to assert that the top of the mantle was a chemically homogeneous material. In many of the older geology texts, this material was simply called sima to describe a dense, basic rock from which the less dense, more acidic sialic crust could be derived by some process of differentiation.

Hence **sima·tic** *a.*, of or pertaining to the basal crust or the material of which it is made.

1942 R. A. DALY *Floor of Ocean* ii. 59 The oceanic sectors of the earth are characteristically simatic... Also simatic is any vitreous basalt which may form 'pockets' in the crust. **1955** [see *SIALIC *a.*[1]]. **1971** *Proc. 2nd Symposium Upper Mantle Project* (Council of Sci. & Industr. Res., New Delhi) p. xix, Resting on the simatic crust, the continental blocks move, as if riding on the conveyor belt.

simandro, simantron, varr. *SEMANTRON.

simazine (si·m-, səi·măzīn). Formerly also **-in** (-in). Also with capital initial. [f. *sim-* (ad. SYM(METRIC *a.*) + TRI)AZINE.] A colourless crystalline compound, 2-chloro-4,6-bis-(ethylamino)-1,3,5-triazine, $C_7H_{12}N_5Cl$, which is a selective weedkiller applied as an emulsion or wettable powder.

1956 *Proc. 13th Meeting N. Central Weed Control Conf.* 57/1 During 1956, an experimental herbicide..designated as Simazin, was released to experiment stations for test purposes. **1957** *Chem. Abstr.* LI. 9995 The herbicides CMU..and Simazine..are used..to prevent weed growth in grafting vineyards after the spring weeding. **1958** *Times* 10 Nov. 19/2 Another chemical on which interest is focused is Simazin..which kills a wide range of weeds. **1971** *Ideal Home* Apr. 120 Keep it weed free with an annual application of a simazine weedkiller like Weedex *before* weeds appear. **1978** *Financial Times* 2 Dec. 13/3 Rose beds kept clear of weeds by small annual applications of simazine.

simba (si·mbă). Also **Simba.** [Swahili.] A lion. Also *fig.*, a warrior; a leader.

1918 E. R. BURROUGHS *Tarzan & Jewels* iii. 30 The strange white man must certainly succumb to terrible Simba. **1935** E. HEMINGWAY *Green Hills of Africa* ii. 42 A stream of..words in Wakamba ending in the word '*Simba*'. **1966** *Transition* (Uganda) XXVI. 39/1 In battle, the simbas had to walk straight forward, and keep their eyes to the front to avoid loss of invulnerability. **1975** T. DINESEN *My Sister, Isak Dinesen* v. 56 A large simba had been lying at the river-crossing and hadn't moved as he went by, only stared menacingly at him. **1976** *Drum* (E. Afr. ed.) Sept. 3/1 Has Amin now recognised his weakness? What does he now think and say? Does he still claim to be the *simba* of Africa?

simchah (si·mχă). Also **simcha, Simchah.** [a. Heb. *śimḥā* rejoicing.] A Jewish private party or celebration.

1932 L. GOLDING *Magnolia Street* II. ii. 295 Perhaps, after all, it'll be a good match. There will be a *simchah.* **1959** H. PINTER *Birthday Party* II. 35 Mazoltov! And may we only meet at Simchahs! **1973** *Jewish Chron.* 19 Jan. 42/2 (Advt.), Arkay caterers. Specialists in home, hall and marquee catering for all simchas.

Simchat Torah (si·mχăt tōᵊ·ra). Also **Simchas, Simchath, Simhat** and hyphened. [a. Heb. *śimḥat tōrā*, f. *śimḥat*, construct case of *śimḥa* *SIMCHAH, + TORAH.] The final day of the festival of Succoth, on which the annual cycle of the reading of the Torah reaches its completion.

1891 M. FRIEDLÄNDER *Jewish Relig.* II. 480 Twice a year we have special occasion for fulfilment of this duty, viz., on *Simchath-torah* and on the *Seder*-evening. **1905** *Jewish Encycl.* XI. 365/1 The name 'Simhat Torah' came into use after the introduction of the one-year cycle for the reading of the Law. **1907** OESTERLEY & BOX *Relig. & Worship Synagogue* III. xx. 374 In some places it has.. been customary for the children to tear down the 'booths' (*sukkoth*), and burn them on *Simchath Torah.* **1927** A. FELDMAN *Sabbath Spice & Festival Fare* 30 On Simchas Torah..there is a 'procession' of the Scrolls. **1960** *Jewish Chron.* 8 Apr. 35/3 To dance on *Simchat Torah*, Is there a greater pleasure? **1973** *Synagogue Light* Sept. 56 (*caption*) Israeli Hassidim celebrating Simhat Torah at the Western Wall. **1975** C. POTOK *In Beginning* iv. 213, I thought of the way my father..had danced with the Torah on Simchat Torah. **1978** I. B. SINGER *Shosha* v. 98 Only on Simchas Torah were girls allowed inside a house of worship.

Simeonite. Add: Hence **Si·meonism,** adherence to the doctrines of Simeon.

a **1902** S. BUTLER *Way of All Flesh* (1903) xlvii. 213 These poor fellows formed a class apart..and it was among them that Simeonism chiefly flourished.

simetite (si·m-, sī·mĕtəit). *Min.* Also **Simetite.** [a. It. *simetite* (O. Helm 1887, in *Malpighia* I. 54), f. *Simeto*, name of a river in Sicily: see -ITE[1].] A variety of amber, usu. reddish, found in Sicily.

1892 E. S. DANA *Dana's Syst. Mineral.* (ed. 6) 1005 Simetite... A resin near amber from near Mt. Etna, Sicily. Remarkable for its deep red color and often showing a beautiful fluorescence. **1915** R. LANKESTER *Diversions of Naturalist* ix. 71 The Sicilian amber (called 'Simetite') was not known to the ancients. **1932** G. C. WILLIAMSON *Bk. of Amber* 209 Some of the very clearest pieces of golden Simetite possess bloom and flashes of blue. **1969** *Beaver* Summer 29/2 Reddish amber from Sicily, called simetite, is also a succinite.

Simhat Torah, var. *SIMCHAT TORAH.

simi (si·mi). [ad. Swahili *sime*.] In East Africa: a large knife; a short two-edged sword (see also quot. 1980).

1955 *Times* 7 June 6/6 Small boys in feathers, with cowbells at their ankles and brandishing tiny *simis* (swords), stamp and dance in circles. **1961** *Encounter* Jan. 24/2 He had killed two of the Masai morans..cutting the throat of the other with his simi. **1977** D. Beaty *Excellency* ix. 108 An African was..holding up a thin-bladed simi knife. **1980** *Times* 3 Apr. 8/1 Mrs Joy Adamson, the naturalist and authoress of *Born Free*, was murdered with a simi (a two-edged farming implement like a sword), and an iron bar, a police witness said.

similar, *a.* Add:

3. c. *Math.* Of two square matrices: such that one of them is equal to the other pre-multiplied by some matrix whose determinant is not zero and postmultiplied by the inverse of the same matrix.

1907 M. Bôcher *Introd. Higher Algebra* xxi. 283 Two matrices connected by a relation of the form (13) are sometimes called similar matrices. **1937** A. A. Albert *Mod. Higher Algebra* iv. 78 Every square matrix is similar to its transpose. **1979** S. H. Friedberg et al. *Linear Algebra* v. 232 Prove that similar matrices have the same trace.

similarity. Add: **3.** *attrib.*, as *similarity continuum, set*; (cf. *similar *a.* 3 c) *similarity class, group, transformation.*

1952 R. R. Stoll *Linear Algebra & Matrix Theory* vii. 176 The similarity classes of transformations are in one-one correspondence with the similarity classes of $n \times n$ matrices. **1975** S. Koh et al. tr. *Satake's Linear Algebra* iii. 141 The set of all matrices which are similar to a given matrix is called the 'similarity class' of this matrix. **1960** M. Rokeach *Open & Closed Mind* ii. 46 Recall again that we conceive of the disbelief system as a similarity continuum. **1937** A. A. Albert *Mod. Higher Algebra* iv. 76 We are studying the invariants of matrices A under a group of transformations $A \leftrightarrow PAP^{-1}$ called the similarity group. **1977** R. Holland *Self & Social Context* viii. 232 Objects normally grouped together in similarity sets may change their relationships following a revolution in science. **1961** G. Hadley *Linear Algebra* vii. 239 Either $\mathbf{PAP}^{-1}$ or $\mathbf{P}^{-1}\mathbf{AP}$ represents a similarity transformation on **A**. **1968** Fox & Mayers *Computing Methods for Scientists & Engineers* v. 113 A final important iterative method.. succeeds in reducing the matrix by similarity transformation to triangular form. **1976** G. Strang *Linear Algebra & its Applications* v. 222 Similarity transformations leave the eigenvalues unchanged.

similative (si·milătiv), *a.* and *sb. Gram.* [f. L. *similis* like + -ative.] **A.** *adj.* Denoting or expressing similarity or likeness. **B.** *sb.* A similative word, case, verbal element, or compound. Cf. Similitive *a.*

1884 in *N.E.D.* s.v. Air *sb.* B. 3. **1903** *Amer. Anthropologist* Jan.–Mar. 13 Besides these, comitatives, similatives, partitives, and suffixes expressing similar ideas, are found. **1911** H. Bradley in *Encycl. Brit.* XXV. 209/1 The many jocularly similative uses of ordinary words, such as 'tin' for money. **1930** F. R. Blake in J. T. Hatfield et al. *Curme Vol. Ling. Stud.* 37 The immaterial adnominal cases are..similative—an animal *like a pig*. **1954** Pei & Gaynor *Dict. Linguistics* 197 *Similative*, a declensional case in certain non-Indo-European languages, denoting resemblance. (Also termed *conformative*.)

simile, *v.* (Later example.)

1972 G. Jones *Kings, Beasts, & Heroes* ii. i. 75 We are told the colour of her hair and hands, her flesh and bosom, but she stays cool to view as..a wax doll. A clean doll, admittedly... And one most nobly similied.

similize, *v.* **3. b.** (Later examples.)

1925 V. Woolf *Common Reader* 106 She similised.. eternally; the sea became a meadow, the sailors shepherds, the mast a maypole. **1976** *N.Y. Times Mag.* 10 Oct. 111/3 Have a story or anecdote for every point you wish to make. Similize. Exaggerate, euphemize, elide.

simillimum (simi·limɒm). *Homœopathy.* [L., neut. of *simillimus*, superl. of *similis*, like, similar.] The remedy indicated in a particular case, as producing in a healthy person symptoms most like those of the person to be treated.

1849 R. E. Dudgeon tr. *Hahnemann's Organon Med.* 157 But even granting this could be done..the cure is effected only by opposing a *simillimum* to a *simillimum*. **1891** J. C. Burnett *Greater Dis. Liver* 42 With me it is an axiom to relieve uncomfortable or dangerous organ-states with simple organ-remedies, leaving the more remote and deeper-going to be..treated, if possible, with its pathological simillimum. **1938** [see *potentization]. **1972** D. V. Tansley *Radionics* viii. 84 This may be dispersed radionically or with the appropriate homoeopathic similimum [*sic*].

simlin. Add: Also **cimbeline, cymblin(g), cymlin. 1.** (Earlier and further examples.)

1775 N. Cresswell *Jrnl.* 5 July (1925) 95 The rest plundered about the plantation and got some young cabbages, squashes and Cimbelines. **1785** T. Jefferson *Notes Virginia* vi. 68 Cymlings. *Cucurbita verrucosa.* **1796** B. Hawkins *Let.* 2 Dec. (1916) 21 They made beans, ground peas, cymblins. **1832** J. P. Kennedy *Swallow Barn* IV. vi. 100 Little garden-patches..where cymblings ..flourished. *a* **1883** G. W. Bagby *Sel. Misc. Writings* (1885) II. 17 A true Virginian..must have..old hare, butter-beans, new potatoes, squirrel, cymlings, snaps. **1981** *Farmstead Mag.* Winter 41/1 Common pumpkins are actually a form of the same plant from which has also been developed vegetable marrows, cymlings, or cymlins (also spelled simlins), summer crookneck squashes, and yellow-flowered gourds.

Simmental (si·məntăl). Also **Simmenthal, Zimmenthal.** [a. Ger. name of the Simme valley in the canton of Berne, Switzerland.] A bull or cow of the breed of cattle so called, first developed in Switzerland, distinguished by their large size and red and white coats, and used for both milk and meat production. Also *attrib.*

1959 R. B. Kelley *Native & Adapted Cattle* iv. 62 Red Danes, Simmental, and Friesians..were seen..outside Rome. **1970** *Times* 6 Apr. 10/6 The shorthorn men are also interested in the Simmental, a big dual-purpose animal which is to be found over much of central and eastern Europe. **1973** [see *Limousin 2]. **1973** *Country Life* 12 July 80/2 Of the exotic breeds, the Simmenthal are second in popularity only to the Charolais. **1980** H. M. & D. M. Briggs *Mod. Breeds Livestock* (ed. 4) vii. 156 The first purebred Simmental bull came to the United States in 1971. *Ibid.* 157 Simmentals are large, long, and very muscular cattle.

simmer, *v.*[1] Add: **1. d.** *to simmer down*: to calm down from an angry or excited state. orig. *U.S.*

1871 'Mark Twain' *Lett. to Publishers* (1967) 58, I must and will keep shady and quiet till Bret Harte simmers down a little. **1897** W. Beatty *Secretar* xiii. 102 In a while..he simmered down. **1902** C. J. C. Hyne *Mr. Horrocks, Purser* 42 First Class passengers..don't handicap matters by interference—once they have simmered down. **1972** *Times Lit. Suppl.* 22 Dec. 1561/5 There they simmer down for a space, forget their mundane cares.

Simmerstat (si·məɹstæt). Also **simmerstat.** [f. Simmer *v.*[1] + Thermo)stat.] The proprietary name of a thermostatic control which regulates the temperature of the hot-plates or grill of an electric cooker or similar heating appliance.

1938 *Trade Marks Jrnl.* 7 Sept. 1097/1 *Simmerstat*... All goods included in Class 8. Sun-Vic Controls Limited.., London W.C. 2; manufacturers. **1951** *Good Housek. Home Encycl.* 76/1 A radiant hot-plate operated by a 'simmerstat'. **1954** *Archit. Rev.* CXVI. 270 (*caption*) Polished stainless steel and plate glass; fitted with three 60-watt lamps between the heaters and simmerstat control. **1962** *Listener* 13 Sept. 411/2 The middle-priced model is distinguished by simmerstat-controlled radiant plates. **1979** *Nature* 19 Apr. p. xiv/3 The temperature of the hotplate is controlled by a Simmerstat which regulates it between 50° and 325°C.

'simmon (si·mŏn), *sb.*[3] *U.S.* Colloq. abbrev. of Persimmon. Freq. *attrib.*, esp. as *'simmon beer.*

a **1775** J. Boucher *Gloss. Archaic & Provincial Words* (1832) p. l, Brown linen shirts, and cotton jackets wear, Or only *wring-jaw* drink, and *'simmon beer.* **1839** *Southern Lit. Messenger* V. 378/2, I ask you no odds—the longest pole, you know, takes the simmon. **1883** P. M. Hale *Woods & Timbers N. Carolina* 117 The basis of a beverage, by no means despicable, called 'Simmon Beer. **1909** 'O. Henry' *Roads of Destiny* xxi. 350 That's why you see me cake-walking with the ex-rebs to the illegitimate tune about 'simmon-seeds and cotton. **1945** B. A. Botkin *Lay my Burden Down* 66 'Simmon beer was good in the cold freezing weather too. **1949** [see *possum hunt* s.v. *possum *sb.*[1] 1 d].

Simmonds (si·məndz). *Path.* [The name of Morris *Simmonds* (1855–1925), German pathologist, who described the disease in 1914 (*Deutsch. med. Wochenschr.* 12 Feb. 322).] *Simmonds'* (also *Simmonds's*, ¶ *Simmond's*) *disease*: pituitary insufficiency caused by destruction of the gland, characterized by weakness, loss of body hair, and progressive gonadal, adrenocortical, and thyroidal failure, and occurring chiefly in women; *esp.* the chronic form (cf. **Sheehan's syndrome*).

1928 *Q. Cumulative Index Medicus* II. 993/2 Pituitary cachexia (Simmonds' disease). **1937** *Jrnl. Path. & Bacteriol.* XLV. 189 The significance of necrosis of the anterior pituitary chiefly concerns its relationship to the series of disorders of pituitary function which culminate in Simmonds's disease. **1970** Passmore & Robson *Compan. Med. Stud.* II. xxv. 6/2 The necrosis of anterior pituitary cells is followed by pituitary hypofunction (Simmond's disease).

simo (səi·mo). [Abbrev. of *si*multaneous *mo*tion-cycle.] *simo chart*: a chart in which the bodily movements of a worker are represented in relation to a time scale. Hence *simo-charting* vbl. sb.

1928 L. M. Gilbreth in *Bull. Taylor Soc.* June 127/2 The simo charts and the synthesis work demand both time and effort. **1937** R. M. Barnes *Motion & Time Study* ix. 77 The time for each therblig recorded on the analysis sheet may be shown to scale by means of a simultaneous motion-cycle chart, commonly called a 'simo chart'. **1961** *Engineering* 15 Sept. 353/1 Fig. 2 shows the simo-charts produced by a member of a recent course; they promise particularly high savings and provide a very good example of simo-charting. **1969** P. E. Randall *Introd. Work Study & Organization & Methods* iv. 27 A simo chart breaks hand movements down into eighteen categories.

simoleon (simōᵘ·līǫn). *U.S. slang.* Also **samoleon.** [Origin obscure: perh. modelled on Napoleon 1.] A dollar.

1896 G. Ade *Artie* vii. 63 He said I could have it for four hundred samoleons. **1913** C. E. Mulford *Coming of Cassidy* vii. 112 Sixty-two bucks, three score an' two simoleons; all I've got, every cent. **1952** A. Lomax *Mister Jelly Roll* 194 By the late twenties the golden simoleons began rolling in. **1977** D. Anthony *Stud Game* i. 8, I bet the limit, five thousand simoleons.

Simonite (səi·mŏnəit). [f. the name of Sir John Allsebrook *Simon* (1873–1954), Liberal politician + -ite[1].] A supporter of Sir John Simon; used *spec.* to designate a member of the Liberal National Party which seceded in 1931 from the official Liberal Party led by Sir Herbert Samuel. Freq. *attrib.* Cf. *Samuelite.

1931 [see *Samuelite]. **1932** [see *mosleyite]. **1957** J. Bowle *Viscount Samuel* xvii. 287 The Liberals had to accept a measure of Protection... But the rift with the Simonites continued. **1966** T. Wilson *Downfall of Liberal Party 1914–1935* xix. 352 The dismissed employee was to appear in Parliament in 1931 as a Simonite (anti-Lloyd George) M.P. **1977** D. Marquand *Ramsay Macdonald* xxvii. 677 On the fiscal question..he sided with the Conservatives and Simonite Liberals against Snowden and the Samuelite Liberals. **1979** G. Pottinger *Secretaries of State for Scotland 1926–76* vi. 54 It was natural for him to take the Simonites' side when the split with the Samuel faction came in 1931.

simonize (səi·mŏnəiz), *v.* Also **Simonize.** [f. *Simoniz* proprietary name of a type of car polish.] *trans.* To polish by the application of Simoniz. Also *transf.* and *fig.* So **si·monizing** *vbl. sb.*; hence **si·monized** *ppl. a.*

1934 *Amer. Speech* IX. 114/1 The work on the car may include..vulcanizing tire cuts, and simonizing. **1942** Berrey & Van den Bark *Amer. Thes. Slang* § 125/6 *Simonize*, to brilliantine the hair. *Ibid.* § 291/4 Curry favour; toady... *simonize the apple* or *orange.* **1949** A. Miller *Death of Salesman* i. 17 Remember those days? The way Biff used to simonize that car? **1953** *Economist* 25 July 258/1, I have heard it said that Harvard University humanises the scientist and simonises the humanist. **1968** R. H. R. Smithies *Shoplifter* (1969) ix. 189 The lovingly simonized fenders, hubcaps, and bumpers. **1975** *New Yorker* 19 May 116/2 He writes of someone's being 'Nixonized', which is apparently like having a car Simonized. **1977** *Chicago Tribune* 2 Oct. xii. 73/3 (Advt.), Will do Blue Coral waxing, Simonizing & interiors.

Simon Pure. Add: Also **Simon-Pure. a.** (Earlier example.)

[**1785** 'P. Pindar' *Lyric Odes* ix. 28 Flattery's a Mountebank so *spruce*—gets riches; Truth, a plain Simon Pure, a Quaker Preacher.] **1795** T. Wilkinson *Wandering Patentee* III. 34 She in her rage denounced vengeance heartily, and said that she would advertise my production as a flimsy disgraceful imposture: But she was mistaken—for mine was the true *Simon Pure.*

b. (Earlier and later examples.) Also, pure, unadulterated; honest, upright.

1869 'Mark Twain' *Innoc. Abr.* xli. 436 Soon the bell—a genuine, simon-pure bell—rang. **1913** *Jrnl. Industr. & Engin. Chem.* June 504/1 Willard Gibbs..was simon pure—in his best days he did not soil his hands even with the grime of a laboratory. **1945** R. Hargreaves *Enemy at Gate* 282 The unsullied, Simon-Pure principles of proletarian ideology. **1951** *Manch. Guardian Weekly* 28 June 2/3 The [drug] peddlers have gone underground and the specified retailers have turned Simon-pure. **1974** *Jrnl. Ecumenical Stud.* Winter 119 The simon-pure neutrality of church leaders, paralyzed by their own myth of 'even-handedness', has embarrassed in a new way the relations between individual Christians and Jews.

simool. Add: Also **semal, semul.** For *malabaricum* substitute *ceiba.* (Earlier and later examples.)

1835 *Penny Cycl.* IV. 2/2 The Semul, or cotton-tree. **1889** *Dict. Econ. Prod. India* I. 489 The semul cotton supplied them was better known as kapok. **1902** T. W. Webber *Forests Upper India* xviii. 232 The semal or cotton tree. **1932** Pearson & Brown *Comm. Timbers India* 138 The primary use of semul is for tea and rubber boxes.

simoom, *sb.* Add: Also **samoon, samum, samun, semoun. a.** (Further examples.)

α. **1832** Semoum [see *samiel]. **1947** M. A. Garbell *Tropical & Equatorial Meteorol.* xiii. 200/2 Algerian and Syrian samum.

β. **1926** W. N. Shaw *Man. Metereol.* I. ii. 28 The principal of these are..the bora of the Adriatic, the scirocco of Southern Italy, the samun of Algeria which is also called scirocco. **1931** A. A. Miller *Climatol.* xiv. 253 Similar winds to the foehn occur in all mountain districts, where cyclonic storms occur... The Chinook..is exactly similar, so are the Samun of Persia, descending from the mountains of Kurdistan,..and many others. **1968** G. R. Rumney *Climatol.* xiii. 254/1 The sirocco is known as the khamsin in Egypt, leveche in southeastern Spain, where it is usually quite dry, garbi in the Aegean, samoon in Algeria, sahat in Morocco, and ghibli in Libya.

simp (simp). Colloq. abbrev. of SIMPLE *sb.* 2 b or SIMPLETON 1: a fool, a simpleton.

1903 W. C. THOMPSON *On Road with Circus* i. 23 In circus dialect 'yap' and 'simp' indicate a credulous rustic who is easy prey for sharpers. **1924** WODEHOUSE *Bill the Conqueror* vi. 133 You poor simp, you've got about as much chance of havin' me sneak those books for you as—well, I don't know what. **1937** N. MARSH *Vintage Murder* xv. 165 You looked a big simp, Cass. **1973** *Sat. Rev. Society* (U.S.) Mar. 72/3 Wonder Woman almost (but never quite) loses her head and heart to a weak simp, a U.S. Army Intelligence pilot. **1976** *Publishers Weekly* 19 Apr. 82/3 The book's assumption is that single men are simps who don't know the difference between a pepper mill and a can opener.

simpatico (simpæ·tiko), *a.* Also (fem.) **simpatica.** [It. or Sp.: see SYMPATHIC *a.*] Pleasing, likeable; congenial, understanding; sensitive, sympathetic.

1864 H. SIDGWICK *Let.* 21 Oct. in *Memoir* (1906) ii. 119 The Frau Professorin was less 'simpatica'. **1905** E. M. FORSTER *Where Angels fear to Tread* iii. 86 The person who understands us at first sight, who never irritates us, who never bores..that is what I mean by *simpatico*. **1908** W. JAMES *Let.* 4 Oct. (1920) II. 314, I find him [*sc.* Boutroux] very *simpatico*. **1936** E. AMBLER *Dark Frontier* 80 She was infinitely—as those appreciative Italians put it—infinitely *simpatica*. **1952** A. HUXLEY *Let.* 20 May (1969) 644 There is something *simpatico* about Pascal—he is a kind of Central European Baron Munchausen. **1964** MRS. L. B. JOHNSON *White House Diary* 19 Mar. (1970) 96 Although he is very attached to the Kennedys, I thought we had established a certain simpatico relationship with him. **1976** *Observer* 22 Feb. 26/7 Sylvia reluctantly committed Ralph into the care of a blunt but *simpatico* medico who didn't talk down either to her or to us.

simple, *a.* and *sb.* Add: **A.** *adj.* **II. 6. b.** *simple life* (further examples); also *attrib.* Hence *simple-lifer*, a follower or proponent of the simple life. Also *simple-liver*; *simple-living* vbl. sb. and ppl. adj.

1736 J. THOMSON *Liberty* IV. 30 That simple Life, the quiet-whispering Grove. **1862** A. J. SYMONDS *Let.* 7 Aug. (1967) I. 355, I read through..Scotch Bothie, lured on by its intense savour of nature & love of simple life. **1909** H. G. WELLS *Ann Veronica* vii. 138 The Goopes were..following a fruitarian career..and they had reduced simple living to the finest of fine arts. *Ibid.* viii. 165 The chatter of the studios and the..discussions of the simple-life homes. **1927** W. E. COLLINSON *Contemp. Eng.* 38 During my school-days..I remember first hearing the term simple-lifers. **1933** M. ALLINGHAM *Sweet Danger* xvii. 211 If it weren't for the simple-livers on the heath..the affair would be almost plain sailing. **1956** 'J. WYNDHAM' *Seeds of Time* 231 It's mostly Janet's economies and simple-living that's built up the savings. **1978** *Listener* 14 Sept. 324/1 Members may be 'arty-crafty' and 'simple-lifers'—rather like the sort of people who nowadays promote *Vole* magazine. **1979** *Ibid.* 11 Jan. 63/3 In Cornwall..simple-living James and earth-mother Anna are variously threatened by authority, rural squalor and true terror.

10. b. (*b*) *U.S. Rhyming slang.* A diamond.

1928 M. C. SHARPE *Chicago May* 287/2 *Simple simon*, diamond. **1929** D. RUNYON in *Cosmopolitan* July 58/1, I do not see any Simple Simon on your lean and linger.

III. 14. b. (*d*) † *simple tone* = *pure tone* s.v. *PURE *a.* 1 e. *Obs.*

1875 A. J. ELLIS tr. *H. L. F. von Helmholtz's Sensations of Tone* vii. 235 Whenever the vibrations of the air or of other elastic bodies which are set in motion at the same time by two generating simple tones, are so powerful that they can no longer be considered infinitely small, mathematical theory shows that vibrations of the air must arise which have the same vibrational numbers as the combination tones. **1878** *Proc. R. Soc. Edin.* IX. 602 According to a usage which has been adopted from the German of Helmholtz by the best English scientific writers on sound, a sound is called a 'simple tone', or without qualification a 'tone', when the variation of pressure of the air..is according to a simple harmonic function of the time. **1910** H. LAMB *Dynamical Theory of Sound* 3 The sensation corresponding to a simple-harmonic vibration is called a 'simple tone',..or merely a 'tone'.

d. *Math.* (*a*) Applied to a group that has no proper normal subgroup; and hence to an algebra or ring that has no proper ideal.

1888 G. G. MORRICE tr. *Klein's Lectures on Ikosahedron* I. i. 7 If a group contains, apart from these improper cases, no self-conjugate sub-groups, it is called simple, otherwise it is called composite. **1900** *Ann. Math.* I. 151 We have here..an example of two simple abstract groups of the same order which are not identical. **1939** H. WEYL *Classical Groups* iii. 85 A simple algebra..is one capable of a faithful irreducible representation. **1965** PATTERSON & RUTHERFORD *Elem. Abstract Algebra* iii. 100 The above theorem shows that a field is simple. There exist simple rings which are not fields. **1971** E. C. DADE in Powell & Higman *Finite Simple Groups* viii. 255 An algebra A is simple if $A \neq \{o\}$ and if A and $\{o\}$ are the only two-sided ideals of A. **1980** *Sci. Amer.* May 68/1 The building blocks of group theory, analogous to the elementary particles of matter or the prime factors of integers, are called simple groups.

(*b*) Used variously (see quots.). (See also sense 15 b (*b*) in Dict.)

1889 *Proc. London Math. Soc.* XX. 70 It may happen that G_p consists of powers of one of its elements a, and has no other elements... In this case G_p is called a simple group. **1965** PATTERSON & RUTHERFORD *Elem. Abstract Algebra* iv. 135 Let $p\,t$ $P(F)$ be an irreducible polynomial. Then the field $P_p(F)$ contains a sub-field isomorphic with F... We call the field $P_p(F)$ a simple algebraic extension of the field F. **1972** R. J. WILSON *Introd. Graph Theory* ii. 9 There can never be more than one edge joining a given pair of vertices of a simple graph. **1975** *Sci. Amer.* May 102/2 A simple polyhedron is one that is topologically equivalent to a sphere and whose faces are all simple polygons: polygons topologically equivalent to a disk.

e. *simple structure* (Statistics): a model in which numerous variables, showing various degrees of correlation, have their variances assigned to a smaller number of factors in such a way that no factor affects all of the variables.

1935 L. L. THURSTONE *Vectors of Mind* p. viii, One of the principal problems of factor analysis is to find a unique set of co-ordinate axes, either orthogonal or oblique, which shall represent scientifically meaningful categories in terms of which the tests may be comprehended. This problem has been solved in terms of what I have called 'simple structure' of a trait configuration. *Ibid.* vi. 154 If a set of r hyperplanes of dimensionality (r−1) exists such that each trait vector is in one or more of the hyperplanes, then the combined configuration of the trait vectors and the reference vectors will be called a simple structure or an oblique simple structure. **1972** [see *ROTATION 1 d]. **1972** *Jrnl. Social Psychol.* LXXXVI. 188 There is no good scientific reason to expect agreement from analyses on..orthogonal pseudo-simple structure and oblique maximized simple structure.

15. b. (*e*) Applied to those vows which are taken by members of a religious order in the early stage of their profession and from which they may be dispensed; opp. to *solemn* (SOLEMN *a.* 5 a).

1759 A. BUTLER *Lives Saints* IV. 86/2 In some houses these Gray Sisters make solemn vows, but in most they content themselves with simple vows of poverty, obedience, and chastity. **1823** C. BUTLER *Continuation A. Butler's Lives Saints* 191 He entered into the society of Jesus, and made his simple vows. **1884** ADDIS & ARNOLD *Cath. Dict.* 848/1 Whereas a simple vow makes marriage unlawful and deprives the person who has made it of the right to use his property, a solemn vow makes marriage invalid and takes away all dominion over property. **1957** *Oxf. Dict. Christian Ch.* 1451/1 Since *c.* the 13th cent. canon law has also distinguished between 'simple' and 'solemn' vows. The exact scope of the distinction is disputed, but acc. to a common view the solemnity of vows is determined by their irrevocable acceptance.

(*f*) *Anthropol.*

1929 *N. & Q. Anthropol.* (ed. 5) 63 We might expect the simple patrilineal family to resemble our own, but this is not necessarily so. **1951** *Ibid.* (ed. 6) 70 The elementary or simple family is a group consisting of a father and a mother and their children, whether they are living together or not. **1977** P. LASLETT *Family Life* i. 13 The shape and membership of the familial group. In the West this has been confined for the most part to the parents and children themselves, what is called the nuclear family form or simple family household.

c. In adj. phrs., as *simple-to-follow, simple-to-operate*, etc.

1960 *Times* 18 Jan. 15/7 A simple-to-fit filter removes dust. **1960** *Farmer & Stockbreeder* 15 Mar. (Suppl.) 13 A robust motor with a completely reliable and simple-to-operate starting unit. **1971** *Woman's Own* 27 Mar. 52/1 We have combined simple-to-build shelves with..sliding transparent drawers. **1976** *BSI News* May 11/2 The BS 4264 range is set out in a simple-to-follow table giving 26 sizes.

IV. 18. *simple-natured, -sounding* adjs.

1875 'MARK TWAIN' in *Atlantic Monthly* Aug. 195/1 Good-hearted, simple-natured young Yates. **1930** E. BLUNDEN *De Bello Germanico* 16 The simple-sounding matter of pushing a truck along a French tramway is rather complex on a dark..night.

simple-minded, *a.* Add: Hence **simple-mi·ndedly** *adv.*

1934 A. HUXLEY *Beyond Mexique Bay* 255 An Indian who has given up his *Fiestas* would not be the simple-mindedly happy peasant beloved of Mr. Chase. **1981** *Christian Order* XXII. 264 Abandoned simple-mindedly and irresponsibly.

simplex, *a.* and *sb.* Add: **A.** *adj.* **2.** *Telegr.* and *Teleph.* Designating a system in which signals can be sent along a line in only one direction at a time. Also, in *Computers*, applied to a circuit along which commands can flow in only one direction, usu. from the central processor to a peripheral. Also *absol.*

1891 C. LANGDON-DAVIES *Explanation of Phonopore* vii. 28/1 The ordinary simplex telegraph is the one most in general use (except, possibly, in Great Britain). **1929** *Amer. Speech* IV. 290 One type of printer, which records the message on tape after the manner of a stock ticker, is known as the 'simplex'. **1967** DAVIDSON & KOENIG *Computers* xv. 525 These data communication lines are generally simplex, that is, they carry data in one direction only. **1975** *Sci. Amer.* Jan. 55 (Advt.), We have a range of modems, from 50 to 2400 bits per second, both for simplex and duplex traffic. **1977** J. R. L. ANDERSON *Death in City* xi. 170 The Radio Officer handed me a telephone... 'It's simplex, remember..you have to take it in turns to speak and listen.'

3. *Biol.* Of an eye: having pigment on the posterior surface of the iris only, not on the anterior surface, and so appearing blue.

1908 C. C. HURST in *Proc. R. Soc.* B. LXXX. 86 The eyes in which the posterior pigment alone is present in the iris, the anterior pigment being absent. Such eyes may be called simplex. **1946** [see *DUPLEX *a.* 1 d].

4. *Genetics.* Of a polyploid individual: having the dominant allele at any particular locus represented once.

1921 [see *NULLIPLEX *a.*]. **1931** *Genetics* XVI. 178 When R is simplex (Rrr) the expected gametic ratio is $1R{:}2Rr{:}1rr{:}2r$. *Ibid.* 183 A simplex plant (Rrr). **1932, 1963** [see *QUADRUPLEX *a.*].

B. *sb.* **1. b.** *Linguistics.* In transformational grammar, a sentence analysed as having a single kernel structure. Cf. *KERNEL *sb.*[1] 8 b (ii).

1960 R. B. LEES *Gram. Eng. Nominalizations* iii. 101 Within the *matrix*-sentence, or any other simplex, the subject governs *-self.* **1963** *Language* XXXIX. 20 Since the second occurrence of the noun *John* repeats a noun within the same simplex, it is pronominalized to the corresponding *-self* pronoun. **1965** *Ibid.* XLI. 269 These differences in the treatment of repeated and nonrepeated material are evident in both simplexes (single-kernel sentences) and complexes (multikernel sentences).

2. *Geom.* The figure, in any given number of dimensions, that is bounded by the least possible number of hyperplanes: the two-dimensional simplex is the triangle, the three-dimensional simplex is the tetrahedron, and the four-dimensional simplex is bounded by five tetrahedra.

1914 H. P. MANNING *Geom. Four Dimensions* viii. 317 In the space of five dimensions there are only three possible types of regular (convex) figures: the simplex, corresponding to the tetrahedron and pentahedroid, the orthogonal, corresponding to the cube and hypercube, and the figure reciprocal to the latter, constructed on a set of mutually perpendicular diagonals and corresponding to the octahedron and the 16-hedroid. **1929** D. M. Y. SOMMERVILLE *Introd. Geom. Four Dimensions* vii. 96 The simplest polytope in S_n is the simplex $S(n+1)$, which is bounded by $n+1$ hyperplanes. **1975** *Sci. Amer.* May 102/2 The graph is isomorphic with the skeleton of a six-dimensional simplex, the 6-space analogue of the tetrahedron.

3. *Comb.*, as **simplex method,** a method of maximizing a linear function of several variables under several constraints on other linear functions; **simplex tableau,** a table displaying the constraints in problems of the type soluble by the simplex method.

[**1951** G. B. DANTZIG in T. C. Koopmans *Activity Analysis of Production & Allocation* xxi. 339 The general nature of the 'simplex' approach (as the method discussed here is known).] **1951** R. DORFMAN in *Ibid.* xxii. 351 The simplex method makes use of the fact that any point in an *n*-dimensional space can be expressed as a sum of *n* linearly independent points. **1966** S. BEER *Decision & Control* viii. 149 There are also variants of the original set of rules for finding the answer (to which the name algorithm is applied); Dantzig's own algorithm is called the Simplex Method. **1980** A. J. JONES *Game Theory* iii. 155 The relationship with our earlier notation is simply that we have replaced A^T by A because this is the natural and universally accepted thing to do in setting up the simplex method. **1953** A. CHARNES in W. W. Cooper et al. *Introd. Linear Programming* II. vi. 66 As far as computations are concerned it is most convenient to arrange the data at each stage in a 'simplex tableau' as shown in Table I. **1966** A. BATTERSBY *Math. in Management* v. 125 A more usual form of presentation is the Simplex tableau in which all the variables have columns allocated to them.

simplex munditiis (si·mpleks mundi·ti,īs). *Lat. phr.* [L., lit. 'simple in your adornments' (Horace *Odes* I. v. 5).] Unostentatiously beautiful; elegantly simple. Also used substantively.

1766 H. BROOKE *Fool of Quality* II. xii. 274 Even the *simplex Munditiis* [sic], that ornament of a clean simplicity, recommended by Horace, can operate only by intimation of deeper purity. **1803** *Edin. Rev.* III. 8 Indeed, the *simplex munditiis* stamped every thing that he did. **1874** A. J. MUNBY *Diary* 4 May (1972) 367 Wearing a rich silk dress.., and simplex munditiis as to her beautiful hair. **1933** E. BLUNDEN *Charles Lamb* 42 The same grace, the *simplex munditiis*, haunted all through his sonnets. **1949** E. POUND *Pisan Cantos* lxxx. 84 To go far and come to an end Simplex munditiis, as the hair of Circe; perhaps without the munditiis.

simplicial (simpli·ʃəl), *a.* [f. L. *simplic-*, *simplex* single (see SIMPLEX *a.* and *sb.*) + -IAL.] Of, being, or pertaining to simplexes (sense *B. 2).

1926 [see *HOMŒOMORPH c]. **1959** E. M. PATTERSON *Topology* (ed. 2) v. 95 A geometrical simplicial complex K consists of a finite set of simplexes. **1976** *European Econ. Rev.* VIII. 305 The simplicial sub-division methods modelled by Scarf (1973) can be replaced by quicker Newton methods.

simplicist, *sb.* and *a.* Restrict † *Obs. rare* to sense in Dict. and add: **A.** *sb.* **2.** One who simplifies. *rare.*

1924 *Glasgow Herald* 24 Mar. 8 Can we ever simplify things again? Can we ever produce that statement of scientific method which will..give us an idea of how to conduct our conduct? I believe the day of the great simplicist is beginning to dawn again.

B. *adj.* That simplifies; characterized by simplicity, uncomplicated.

1934 in WEBSTER. **1949** *Sun* (Baltimore) 19 July 12/2 In the best manner of the simplicist versions of Keynes-ism, Mr. Nathan insists that the recession through which we are moving is due to the heavy capital formation of the last two years. **1951** S. SPENDER *World within World* 63 He had a simplicist view of things which did me good. **1979** *Church Times* 5 Oct. 13/3 Even the somewhat simplicist approach is justified by the need and desire to make the argument intelligible.

Hence **simplici·stic** *a.*, characterized by over-simplicity.

1950 *Archivum Linguisticum* II. 142 Streitberg's and Buck's explanations..are both of this simplicistic..type. **1970** *Nature* 7 Nov. 589/2 Attempts to relate simplicistic finite set theory and automata to faculties of mind and the mechanisms of the brain inevitably leads [*sic*] to such difficulties.

|| **simpliciter,** *adv.* Delete 'Chiefly in *Sc. Law.*' and add later examples.

1929 A. N. WHITEHEAD *Process & Reality* 69 The Aristotelian phrase suggests the crude notion that one actual entity is added to another *simpliciter*. **1936** C. S. LEWIS *Allegory of Love* v. 222 He [*sc.* Gower] says too much, not at this point or that, but too much *simpliciter*. **1963** *Times* 28 May 9/2 Substantial damages were not awarded..for physical injury *simpliciter*, but only for the pain and suffering and general loss of happiness which it occasioned. **1970** *N. & Q.* Dec. 453/1, I know of no evidence that 'shambles' *simpliciter* was ever used for 'brothel'. **1977** G. W. H. LAMPE *God as Spirit* vii. 178 It may suggest that the community which the Spirit creates is to be identified *simpliciter* with the institutional Church.

simplicity. Add: **1. c.** *spec.* in *Linguistics*, used *attrib.* with reference to the use of simplicity or economy as a criterion for evaluating a grammatical theory or description, as *simplicity criterion, metric*, etc.

1953 F. J. WHITFIELD tr. *Hjelmslev's Prolegom. Theory Lang.* 11 If..linguistic theory ends by constructing several possible methods of procedure.., that one shall be chosen that results in the simplest possible description. ..This principle, which is deduced from our so-called empirical principle, we call the *simplicity principle*. **1962** M. HALLE in *Word* XVIII. 55, I shall..exhibit the manner in which, by mechanical application of the proposed simplicity measure, certain formulations are chosen from among several alternatives. The plausibility and intrinsic appeal of the descriptions so selected will provide the primary justification not only for the proposed simplicity criterion, but also for the theory of generative grammar, of which the criterion is an integral part. **1968** *Glossa* II. 128 (*title*) Two proposals concerning the simplicity metric in phonology. **1976** J. S. GRUBER *Lexical Structures in Syntax & Semantics* II. ii. 330 The simplicity criterion will be useful in determining which of the two alternate forms of a definition is to be chosen for the lexical entry. **1977** *Canad. Jrnl. Linguistics* Spring 2 Such constraints..entail a fundamental reassessment of current formulations of the simplicity metric.

simplification. Add: **2.** *Logic.* One of the principles of inference used esp. in the calculus of propositions (see quot. 1903).

1903 B. RUSSELL *Princ. Math.* ii. 16 We can now state the six main principles of inference, to each of which ..a name is to be given... If *p* implies *p* and *q* implies *q*, then *pq* implies *p*. This is called *simplification*, and asserts merely that the joint assertion of two propositions implies the assertion of the first of the two. **1934** COHEN & NAGEL *Introd. Logic & Scientific Method* vi. 124 In order to get the calculus [of classes] started, we must state a number of fundamental principles... The following..are those which are usually assumed..Principle of simplification, [etc.]. **1954** I. M. COPI *Symbolic Logic* iii. 43 Simplification (Simp.): *p.q*.∴*p*. **1969** F. I. DRETSKE *Seeing & Knowing* ii. 57 The logical equivalence which goes under the name of simplification (P is logically equivalent to P and P).

si:mplifica·tory, *a.* [f. SIMPLIFICAT(ION + -ORY[2].] That simplifies.

1936 W. F. R. HARDIE *Study in Plato* xi. 141 Aristotle.. makes use of the misleading simplificatory language according to which the rational soul commands the irrational soul. **1972** *N. & Q.* Dec. 446/2 Simplificatory changes like the loss of unstressed syllables.

simplified, *ppl. a.* Add: *simplified spelling*: a system of writing English with greater phonetic consistency than in conventional spelling; any of various schemes for such a spelling reform. Hence *simplified speller* (nonce-word): an advocate or practitioner of simplified spelling.

1879 J. H. GLADSTONE *Spelling Reform* (ed. 2) p. v, Other advantages of a simplified spelling. **1899** 'MARK TWAIN' *What is Man?* (1917) 256, I have had a kindly feeling toward Simplified Spelling from the beginning of the movement three years ago. *Ibid.* 262, I myself am a Simplified Speller. **1907** W. JAMES *Pragmatism* vii. 260 Now the idea of this loose universe affects your typical rationalists in much the same way..as 'simplified spelling' might affect an elderly schoolmistress. **1908** W. W. SKEAT *Presidential Address delivered at first Meeting of Simplified Spelling Society* 3 The object of the Simplified Spelling Society is to consider carefully the whole subject of our modern English spelling, with a view to the initiation of..a moderate system of reforms. **1955** AUDEN in *Encounter* Feb. 11 In my Eden our only source of political news is gossip: In his New Jerusalem there will be a special daily in simplified spelling for non-verbal types. **1977** K. M. E. MURRAY *Caught in Web of Words* vi. 102 In 1905..he [*sc.* James Murray] joined the American Simplified Spelling Board. **1979** *Guardian* 7 Aug. 3/1 September 30 has been nominated by the Simplified Spelling Society as an international day of Speling [*sic*] Watching.

simplify, *v.* Add: **2. b.** *intr.* To become (more) simple; to admit of simplification.

1955 G. GREENE *Quiet American* IV. ii. 230 When we are young we are a jungle of complications. We simplify as we get older. **1964** K. G. LOCKYER *Introd. Critical Path Analysis* ii. 21 Thus the diagram will simplify to the following [etc.].

simplism. Restrict *nonce-word* to sense in Dict. and add: Also || **simplisme. 2.** [Cf. F. *simplisme.*] A tendency to over-simplify; an over-simplification.

1955 M. REIFER *Dict. New Words* 189/1 *Simplism, n.*, oversimplification of any matter and elimination of all complicating aspects; usually aimed at promoting uncritical conformity. **1969** C. LEECH *Tragedy* iii. 42 Wilbur Sanders..has declared that 'Necessity neither requires nor invites cooperation'.., but this appears to be simplism. **1974** *New Society* 13 June 623/1 A fair number of marxist academics have been alarmed at this anti-fascist *simplisme* coming home to roost. **1976** P. ALEXANDER *Death Thin-Skinned Animal* x. 104 It was impossible to argue against that sort of simplism. **1977** *Times Lit. Suppl.* 11 Feb. 150/2 Gladstone's complaint in 1874 that the opposition fomented by the *Daily News* had been 'one main cause' of the weakness of his late government was, of course, a simplism.

|| **simpliste** (sæ̃pli·st, si·mplist), *sb.* and *a.* Also **simplist** [Fr.] **A.** *sb.* One who adopts an over-simplified or one-sided view of something.

1918 W. O'BRIEN *Downfall of Parliamentarianism* i. 5 The simplest of simplists will now own..that the choice of Ireland in 1890 was not that..choice between vice and virtue..which would make human judgments in great affairs an enviably easy process. **1924** *Amer. Mercury* Apr. 465/2 But Nature and History, alas! are not *simplistes*. **1967** A. COMFORT *Anxiety Makers* vi. 197 These are *simplistes*, anxious about ritual obligations, unanxious about phenomena which genuinely threaten us with death and racial extinction. **1970** *Guardian* 12 Nov. 9/1 Robert Ardrey..is..a natural and disabling *simpliste*.

B. *adj.* That over-simplifies, one-sided; plain or uncomplicated in style.

1926 L. A. CLARE tr. *Lévy-Bruhl's How Natives Think* 15 Mental processes are infinitely more elastic, complex, and subtle, and they comprise more elements of the psychic life than a too 'simplist' intellectualism would allow. **1930** *N. & Q.* CLIX. 272/2 Rather a *simpliste*, facile doctrine perhaps. **1950** T. H. MARSHALL *Citizenship & Social Class* 84 The policy, in fact, may not be *simpliste* at all. **1960** *Encounter* Jan. 86/1 He accepts a wholly *simpliste* leftist view. **1966** N. FREELING *Dresden Green* I. 38 The *Golden Age of Landscape Gardening*, simplist, giving you the idea you could do it yourself. **1973** *Times* 25 Apr. 14/6 The familiar story of the parting of the seas is told directly in Williamson's most *simplist* vein. **1977** *Church Times* 13 May 10/2 Shouldn't some kind of theology, even though it's a bit simpliste, come in here.

simplistic, *a.* Add: **2.** (Later examples.) Now usu. with the connotation of excessive or misleading simplification.

1934 *Eng. Studies* XVI. 77 Some of the attempts at elucidating the origin of slang phrases do not seem very successful... It hardly admits of such a simplistic explanation. **1954** *Encounter* July 21/1 The Pluralists oppose the simplistic interpretations which we..inherit.. from Walter Millis' accounts of war as the product of war-mongering. **1967** *Guardian* 3 July 6/1 To see the issue as an attack on middle-class values..is so much simplistic and dangerous nonsense. **1976** T. STOPPARD *Dirty Linen* 40 She's quite right... It is simplistic to speak of malice. **1980** *Jrnl. R. Soc. Arts* Mar. 215/2 It was quite evident that these rather simplistic models were inadequate.

Hence **simpli·stically** *adv.*

1963 F. W. FREY in L. W. Pye *Communications & Political Devel.* xvii. 307 Changes which we simplistically call Westernization. **1974** *Times Lit. Suppl.* 25 Jan. 65/1 The German Democratic Republic from the first made Heine one of its classics, though sometimes reading his politics simplistically in the process. **1978** *Nature* 23 Mar. 306/1 Their basic chain mechanisms can be written simplistically as [etc.].

simply, *adv.* Add: **3. d.** *Logic.* In the simple mode of conversion applicable to propositions; opp. *per accidens* s.v. PER *prep.* 1 b. Cf. CONVERSION 4.

1599 T. BLUNDEVILLE *Art of Logike* III. 69 They say that the disiunct being like to an absolute or simple Proposition, may be converted both simplie and per accidens. **1677** T. GOOD *Brief Eng. Tract of Logick* 31 That is S. denotes the Proposition designed by the preceeding vowel, to be converted simply. **1864** [see sense 3 c in Dict.]. **1884** J. N. KEYNES *Formal Logic* II. iii. 74 This, being an E proposition, may be converted simply, giving, No one deserving of the fair is not brave. **1955** A. N. PRIOR *Formal Logic* II. i. 109 *Oba* and *Oab* do not convert either *per accidens* or simply.

6. b. Freq. in phr. *simply and solely*.

1872 C. S. CALVERLEY *Fly Leaves* 111 All least furlable things got 'furled'..simply and solely to rhyme with 'world'. **1920** *Act* 10 & 11 *Geo. V* c. 48 Sched. II. 314 Any loss or damage due simply and solely to the existence of a state of war. **1940** *Daily Tel.* 15 Feb. 6/1 What has been done is simply and solely to adjust our domestic legislation to the pressing requirements of a particular occasion.

7. Math. *simply connected:* (of a surface or other continuous set of points) connected in such a way that every closed curve lying within it forms the boundary of some surface lying within it.

1893 A. R. FORSYTH *Theory of Functions* xiv. 316 A simply connected surface is resolved by n cross-cuts into n + 1 distinct pieces, each simply connected [etc.]. **1939** M. H. A. NEWMAN *Elem. Topology Plane Sets of Points* vi. 135 The complement of a simply connected domain in the open plane may have any number of components. **1976** *Physics Bull.* Sept. 388/2 The torus is not simply connected but is otherwise a uniformly structured 2-manifold.

simpsonite (si·mpsənəit). *Min.* [f. the name of E. S. *Simpson* (1875–1939), Australian mineralogist + -ITE[1].] An oxide essentially of aluminium and tantalum, approximately $Al_4Ta_3O_{13}(F,OH)$, found as colourless hexagonal crystals externally altered to a dull cream.

1939 H. BOWLEY in *Jrnl. R. Soc. W. Australia* XXV. 89 This was sufficient to indicate that it was a mineral not previously recorded so it was decided to give it the name Simpsonite in honour of Dr. E. S. Simpson.., who..has made many outstanding contributions to our knowledge of Western Australian minerals, particularly..tantalum-bearing minerals. **1959** *Mineral. Abstr.* XIV. 274/1 Simpsonite is found in a pegmatite vein near Leshai in the northern part of Kola peninsula. **1964** *Doklady Acad. Sci. U.S.S.R.: Earth Sci. Sect.* CXLVII. 147 The crystal structure of simpsonite is close-packed and has seven octahedra as its repeat distance.

Simpson's rule (si·mpsən). *Math.* [Named after Thomas *Simpson* (1710–61), English mathematician, who proposed the rule in 1743 (*Math. Dissertations* 109).] An arithmetical rule for estimating the area under a curve where the values of an odd number of ordinates, including those at the limits, are known: the approximate area is given by the sum of the first and last ordinates, double all the other odd ordinates, and quadruple all the even ordinates, multiplied by one third of the distance between adjacent ordinates. Also applied to other analogous rules (see quot. 1909).

1875 B. WILLIAMSON *Integral Calculus* vii. 196 This and the preceding are commonly called 'Simpson's rules' for calculating areas; they were however previously noticed by Newton. **1909** *Cent. Dict.* Suppl. 1158/2 *Simpson's rules*... In *Simpson's first rule* the number of ordinates is odd... *Simpson's second rule*. In this rule the area is divided into groups of three intervals... *Simpson's* 5–8 *rule* is used for obtaining the area of a curve between the first pair of three equally-spaced ordinates. **1930** [see *RUNGE–KUTTA]. **1933** L. M. MILNE-THOMSON *Calculus of Finite Differences* vii. 197 Show that Simpson's rule is tantamount to considering the curve between two consecutive odd ordinates as parabolic. **1980** [see *RUNGE–KUTTA].

simpy (si·mpi), *a. U.S. colloq.* [Perh. f. *SIMP + -Y[1].] Foolish, dull-witted, simple-minded.

1942 BERREY & VAN DEN BARK *Amer. Thes. Slang* § 151/9 Foolish; silly;..*simpy*. **1946** MEZZROW & WOLFE *Really Blues* ix. 139 Some hammy clowning up on the bandstand to tickle the simpy customers. **1976** *Washington Post* 24 Oct. B 7/1 The usual questions—Who is your favorite author? Who in the world would you most like to dine with?—seem out of place at the presidential level. They are, in a word, too simpy.

sim-sim (si·msim). Also simsin. [Arab.: see SESAME.] = SESAME. Also *attrib.*

1917 *Chambers's Jrnl.* May 294/1 Sesamum-seed, also known as..sim-sim,..is the product of an annual plant. **1930** C. G. SELIGMAN *Races Afr.* vii. 170 He smears the rain-stone with simsin oil. **1960** *Guardian* 25 Apr. 4/4 Meat and vegetables are fried in groundnut or sim-sim oil. **1972** Y. LOVELOCK *Veg. Bk.* III. 352 Sesame, also known variously as simsim, gingelly, beniseed and til, is grown in Africa, Asia, South and Central America, for the sake of its seeds, which are used to express an oil used on salads and in cooking.

simul (si·mʊ̆l). *Chess.* [f. *SIMUL(TANEOUS *a.* 1 c.] A display in which one player plays simultaneously against a number of opponents at a number of games of chess.

1969 A. GLYN *Dragon Variation* iv. 89 He's playing twenty-four of us at once. It's a simul, simultaneous display. **1973** *Daily Tel.* 27 Jan. 11/4 Up to quite recently 'simuls' were considered very small beer by some players. **1974** SAIDY & LESSING *World of Chess* i. 26/1 (*caption*) Senior Master Edman Mednis conducts a 'simul' exhibition.

simulacral, *a.* For *rare*[−1] read *rare* and add later example.

1957 *Psychol. Rev.* LXIV. 126/1 We have long since given up simulacral theories of representation.

simuland (si·miŭlænd). [f. L. *simuland-um*, gerundive of *simulāre* SIMULATE *v.*: cf. *-AND[2].] That which is simulated by a (mathematical or computer) model.

1968 R. D. BRENNAN in J. McLeod *Simulation* i. 6/2 There should be a one-to-one correspondence between the mathematical equations and the functions of the elements of the simuland on the one hand, and between the equations and the components or algorithms of the computer on the other. **1972** G. A. MIHRAM *Simulation* v. 222 The goal is to structure entities and events that are as nearly isomorphic as possible to the elements and transformations which exist in the simuland.

simulant, *sb.* (Later examples.)

1979 MILLS & MANSFIELD *Genuine Article* vii. 110 The studio audience were challenged to tell the difference between a genuine diamond and an imitation. A tray of simulants containing a genuine diamond..was produced. **1979** *Nature* 6 Dec. 655/3 Yttrium aluminium garnet (YAG) and cubic zirconia are both used as diamond simulants.

simulate, *v.* Add: **1. d.** To imitate the conditions or behaviour of (a situation or process) by means of a model, esp. for the purpose of study or of training; *spec.* to produce a computer model of (a process).

1947 WILLIAMS & RITSON in *Jrnl. Inst. Electr. Engineers* XCIV. IIA. 123/2 If the control system contains discontinuous devices such as relays, these must be simulated by purely electronic means. **1958** GOTLIEB & HUME *High-Speed Data Processing* xiii. 258 A computer can simulate a warehouse, a factory, an oil refinery, or a river system, and if due regard is paid to detail the imitation can be very exact. **1966** *Guardian* 16 May 3/7 Games in which the situation before the 1914–18 war or the American Mexican war is simulated repeat the original situation with up to 70 per cent reliability. **1972** *Nature* 28 Apr. 462/1 Future population changes were simulated by computer.

simulated, *ppl. a.* Add: **1. b.** Imitative of particular conditions or circumstances, usu. for purposes of experiment or training.

1966 *Word Study* Dec. 3/1 Three-year training in simulated space flight. **1971** *Sci. Amer.* Oct. 44/2 For the purposes of the test four specially trained subjects..spent 25 consecutive days in one of the Institute's high-pressure chambers being exposed to simulated extreme depths. **1978** *Times* 4 Feb. 12/6, I was strapped into a rocket for a simulated flight through space..a ride..not so exhilarating as the old rollercoaster.

2. Of materials, artefacts, etc.: manufactured in imitation of other (usu. more expensive) materials or goods.

1942 *Amer. Speech* XVII. 120 In the trade it is practically impossible to find plain words for *small, artificial,* and *second grade*... *Artificial* and *imitation* appear as *simulated*. **1948** H. LAWRENCE *Death of Doll* ii. 40 'A double strand of pink pearls—' 'Simulated,' said Poke. 'Phony,' agreed Moke. **1960** *Harper's Bazaar* July 67/1 Eyelash curlers in simulated gold. **1973** *Country Life* 17 May (Suppl.) 80b, A set of 8 Regency Period Simulated Rosewood Dining Chairs.

simulation. Add: **3.** The technique of imitating the behaviour of some situation or process (whether economic, military, mechanical, etc.) by means of a suitably analogous situation or apparatus, esp. for the purpose of study or personnel training. Freq. *attrib.*

1947 *Jrnl. Inst. Electr. Engineers* XCIV. IIA. 117/1 The ensuing sections will..describe the simulations of the separate [servo] units. **1958** *Business Week* 29 Nov. 76/3 Men began to raise questions..about their models of the real world. They did this by inventing games such as chess and checkers to simulate battle, games like backgammon and Parcheesi to simulate racing. H. J. R. Murray, in his History of Board Games (Oxford, 1952), finds that such simulation games go back to the beginning of recorded history and are found in every culture. **1966** A. BATTERSBY *Math. in Managem.* vii. 159 Simulation enables a manager to study the system which he controls by imitating or 'simulating' its behaviour. **1972** *Computers & Humanities* VII. 38 The application of computer simulation techniques to the modeling of archaeological situations is one of the newest developments in computer use in archaeology. **1978** *Nature* 28 Sept. 305/1 Simulation studies on the towing of unprotected icebergs to southern continents suggest that the towing distance, ocean currents and the iceberg deterioration rate are of major importance.

simulator. Add: **2. b.** An apparatus designed to simulate the behaviour of a more complicated system; *esp.* one for training purposes that simulates the response of a vehicle, craft, or the like, having a similar set of controls and giving the illusion to the operator of responding like the real thing.

1947 WILLIAMS & RITSON in *Jrnl. Inst. Electr. Engineers* XCIV. IIA. 112 The paper presents an outline of a method which will allow automatic control systems to be studied experimentally by means of an electronic apparatus called a 'simulator', which is constructed so as to have the same characteristic equation as the control system. **1950**, etc. [see *flight simulator* s.v. *FLIGHT *sb.*[1] 15]. **1958** *Engineering* 21 Mar. 374/1 A colour print simulator will be demonstrated... The basis of the new equipment is a closed-circuit colour-television system, whose characteristics can be adjusted to match those of a desired printing system. **1967** *Guardian* 6 Mar. 12/2 The world's first locomotive simulator for driver training at the Willesden electric depot. **1970** *Daily Tel.* 16 Feb. 3/3 For the make-believe flight, Prince Philip and Young had climbed into a lunar-landing craft simulator. **1972** *Sci. Amer.* Apr. 106/3 Both mathematical and experimental demonstrations have established that the behavior of ethyl alcohol in the simulator closely approximates the behavior of propellants such as liquid hydrogen in full-scale, three-dimensional tanks that are subjected to comparable gravitational fields. **1980** P. ABLEMAN *Shoestring's Finest Hour* i. 13 Motorways have never appealed to me. It's like driving in a simulator.

c. *Computers.* Also *simulator program.* A program enabling a computer to execute programs written for a different computer.

1960 GREGORY & VAN HORN *Automatic Data-Processing Systems* viii. 272 A simulator program is essentially a group of subroutines. *Ibid.*, A simulator is useful when changing from one computer to another. **1977** *Sci. Amer.* Sept. 153/1 Thus users of large computer systems and time-sharing services have access to cross-software assemblers, compilers and simulators (programs that enable a computer of one make or model to duplicate the actions of another). **1978** J. C. CLULEY *Programming for Minicomputers* ix. 216 In order to help tracing errors, the simulator program has many of the features of a minicomputer debugging program.

simulcast (si·mǝlkɑst), *v.* orig. *U.S.* [f. SIMUL(TANEOUS *a.* + *BROADCAST *v.* 3.] *trans.* To broadcast (a programme) simultaneously on radio and television. Also, to transmit (a television programme) on two or more channels or networks at the same time. Also *absol.*

1948 *Amer. N. & Q.* May 26/2 *To simulcast*, to broadcast by radio and television simultaneously. **1948** *N.Y. Herald Tribune* 15 June 16/6 A press agent at WCAU-TV in Philadelphia has rather timorously launched the verb 'simulcast' into the uneasy seas of the English language. **1951** *Time* 16 July 58/2 Allen alone of the top announcers 'simulcasts'—broadcasts games simultaneously for both radio and TV. **1977** *Globe & Mail* (Toronto) 8 Jan. 34/3 It used to be they'd play at different times than on the U.S. stations, but not any more. Today the Canadian stations simulcast them as much as possible.

Hence as *sb.*, a programme transmitted simultaneously by radio and television; **si·mulcasting** *vbl. sb.*

1949 *Richmond* (Va.) *News Leader* 30 Aug. 12/1 NBC has announced that it will go in for simulcasting in a big way starting this Fall. **1964** M. MCLUHAN *Understanding Media* xxxi. 311 In a group of simulcasts of several media done in Toronto a few years back, TV did a strange flip. **1976** *Broadcast* 29 Nov. 6/2 A performance of Benjamin Britten's Cantata for St Nicholas..will be networked..by both the ITV companies and ILR, making it the first nationwide stereo simulcast link-up. **1977** *Ibid.* 28 Mar. 15/3 No simulcasting of PPBs (except during elections).

simulfix (si·mǝlfiks). *Gram.* [f. L. *simul* at the same time + *-fix* as in AFFIX *sb.*, PREFIX *sb.*, etc.] A formative element occurring as a modification of an element in the basic word or root (i.e. an intonation sequence or a stress pattern). So **si:mulfixa·tion**, the action of affixing a simulfix; **si·mulfixed** *a.*, of an element, employed as a simulfix.

1954 *Word* X. 212 The term 'superfix' is no more apt than 'subfix', and (the bad Latin) 'simulfix' might be even better. **1956** *Language* XXXII. 454 The process of simulfixation may be represented by a pseudo-fractional formula..+X/Y– (=simulfixed aspect marker/underlying root-initial). **1964** [see *INCOMPLETIVE *a.* (*sb.*)]. **1965** *Language* XLI. 74 Chord structures may occur—tagmemes occurring simultaneously (tone replacives, simulfixes).

simulium (simiū·li,ǝm). [mod.L. (P. A. Latreille *Hist. Nat. Crustacés & Insectes* (1802) III. 426), f. L. *simul-āre* to imitate + *-ium.*] A small dark-coloured blood-sucking fly of the genus *Simulium*, which may be the vector of certain diseases. Also *collect.* Cf. *buffalo fly* s.v. *BUFFALO *sb.* 5.

1902 L. O. HOWARD *Insect Bk.* 120 Simulium larvae frequent well aerated and frequently swiftly running streams. **1914** G. D. H. CARPENTER *Jrnl.* 26 July in *Naturalist on Lake Victoria* (1920) iv. 80, I went down to the rocky shore before breakfast, and was set upon by a swarm of viciously biting *Simulium*. **1932** RILEY & JOHANNSEN *Med. Entom.* xviii. 292 The Simulium flies abound in hilly regions of swift-flowing, well-aerated water. **1955** *Times* 8 July 9/7 The disease [*sc.* river blindness]..is caused by the bite of the simulium fly. **1977** *Observer* (Colour Suppl.) 6 Mar. 47/1 The agile simulium can fly twice as far as was previously thought possible.

simultanagnosia (si:mǝltănægnōᵘ·siă). *Psychol.* [ad. G. *simultanagnosie* (I. Wolpert 1924, in *Zentralbl. f. d. Gesamte Neurol. u. Psychiatrie* XXXV. 445), f. G. *simultan* simultaneous + Gr. ἀγνωσία ignorance (cf. *AGNOSIA).] The loss or absence of the ability to experience perceived elements, such as the details of a picture, as components of a whole.

The form *simultagnosia* appears to have arisen as a misprint (see quot. 1961); and afterwards to have been taken, on the basis of its supposed etymology, to be a term for the ability that is absent in simultanagnosia (see quot. 1970).

1936 J. M. NIELSEN *Agnosia, Apraxia, Aphasia* vii. 84 Another term for miscellaneous classification is Simultanagnosia of Wolpert. This is not an agnosia but a psychological loss on a high plane. **1959** *Brain* LXXXII. 437 There may be gross incapacity to combine the elements of the perceptual display into a coherent and integrated whole. To this type of deficit the term 'simultanagnosia' is commonly applied. **1961** W. R. BRAIN *Speech Disorders* 173 The term simultagnosia [*ed.* 2, 1965: simultanagnosia] was coined by Wolpert to describe a condition in which the patient, looking at pictures which exhibited action, failed to recognize the meaning of the whole, while the details were correctly appreciated. **1964** M. CRITCHLEY *Developmental Dyslexia* ix. 58 He observed a veritable simultagnosia, that is, an inability to grasp the meaning of a picture as a whole. **1970** HINSIE & CAMPBELL *Psychiatric Dict.* (ed. 4) 701/2 *Simultagnosia*, inability to describe the action represented in a picture. *Ibid.* 702/1 Simultanagnosia is the lack of, or any disability in, such simultaneous form perception, and is suggestive of a lesion in the anterior part of the left occipital lobe.

simultane (simǝltēⁱ·n), *v.* orig. *U.S.* [f. SIMULTANE(OUS *a.*] **a.** *trans.* and *intr.* To do (something) simultaneously with something else. **b.** *intr.* To occur or take place at the same time.

Used only by or with reference to 'Mark Twain'.

1880 'MARK TWAIN' *Lett. to Publishers* (1967) 127, I mean to have the 'Atlantic' people delay my articles hereafter, so that I can 'simultane' with you. **1881** *Ibid.* 142 If they don't want it, *then* we'll go to the Century... I want to 'simultane' it with some grave enough London magazine. **1897** —— *Following Equator* lxvii. 668 They..did do them all, but only in turn, not simultaneously. In the nature of things they could not be made to simultane. **1979** *UCT Studies in English* (Univ. Cape Town) Sept. 77 The failure of Bliss to simultane and the pirating of the book by the Canadian, Belford, put a great deal of stress on the young relationship, which nevertheless withstood it.

Simultaneism (simǝltēⁱ·nĭ,iz'm, -ēⁱ·niz'm). Also ‖ **Simultanéisme, Simultanism.** [ad. F. *Simultanéisme.*] **1.** A name given to *ORPHISM 2, because of its use of the principle of simultaneous contrast (*SIMULTANEOUS *a.* 1 b) (see also quot. 1959).

1915 [see *ORPHISM 2]. **1940** R. H. WILENSKI *Mod. French Painters* 238 Delaunay produced a series of Flat-pattern pictures with brightly coloured fragments of revolving discs—a type of Futurist-Dynamism which he called *Simultanéisme* and which Apollinaire christened '*Orphism*'. **1959** H. READ *Conc. Hist. Mod. Painting* iii. 94 [Delaunay] strove in particular to combine different aspects of figures and objects in the same painting. He himself gave the name of *Simultanéisme* to this kind of painting and was later to characterize it in these words: 'Nothing horizontal or vertical—light deforms everything, breaks everything up.' **1969** R. MAYER *Dict. Art Terms & Techniques* 273/1 The chief exponent of the style [*sc.* Orphism], Robert Delaunay (1885–1941), preferred the name Simultaneism.

2. A movement in modern French poetry, led by Henri-Martin Barzun (b. 1881), which aimed at the effect of simultaneity of both images and sounds.

1959 *Oxf. Compan. French Lit.* 676/2 *Simultanéisme*, one of the more ephemeral movements in modern poetry, an exaggerated mixture of *Cubisme* and *Unanimisme*. **1964** *Listener* 27 Aug. 315/3 Simultanism..has so far defeated its exponents..because we are not willing to appraise words other than intellectually, which means in logical succession. **1970** C. CAMPOS in J. Cruickshank *French Lit. & its Background* xi. 153 'Simultanéisme' was to be more influential as a technique for gathering impressions about reality than as a means of expressing a broader experience.

Hence **simulta·neist**, a practitioner of Simultaneism; also as *adj.*, in the manner of Simultaneism. Also ‖ **simultanéiste, simultanist** *adjs.*

1923 J. GORDON *Mod. French Painters* viii. 87 It is safer to throw most recent 'isms' out of the window... The..crop of Orphists, Futurists, Synchromists, Purists, Simultaneists, Dada-ists and so on, are as a rule irritating adjectives with no real meaning. **1930** *Times Educ. Suppl.* 3 May 197/2 A short introductory chapter on 'French Poetry after 1870' briefly describes the schools or coteries of the last few decades—the symbolists,.. simultaneists, cubists, unanimists, and so forth. **1959** *Oxf. Compan. French Lit.* 219/2 His [*sc.* Divoire's] collections of *simultanéiste* verse include: La Malediction des enfants (1910). **1975** T. STOPPARD *Travesties* I. 59 Herr Tristan Tzara was the initiator of a performance..of simultanist verse.

simultaneity. Add: **1.** (Earlier examples.) Also *spec.* in *Art*, the simultaneous representation of several views of the same object.

1652 N. CULVERWEL *Light of Nature* 118 There's no succession in God,..there's a compleat simultaneity in all his knowledge. **1798** A. F. M. WILLICH *Elem. Crit.*

Philos. 46 All the predicates of time, simultaneity, succession, &c...belong to it [*sc.* a sensible object]. **1957** *Encycl. Brit.* XVII. 64/2 Both the Cubists and the Italian Futurists used a device known as simultaneity—the practice of combining various parts of an object, or profiles of face and figure within a design concept. **1980** *Illustr. London News* Mar. 58/3 The Italian Futurists took up the notion of simultaneity in a relatively simple-minded way.

simultaneous, *a.* Add: **1. b.** *simultaneous contrast*: the effect of mutual modification of two contiguous areas of colour.

1848 M. CHEVREUL in T. Graham *Chem. Rep. & Mem.* v. 187, I will designate by the term *simultaneous contrast* the modification of colour and height of tone experienced by two differently coloured objects when seen simultaneously. **1890** [see *BORDER-LINE 1]. **1961** G. MILLERSON *Technique Television Production* iii. 45 The final values of any surface will vary with..simultaneous contrast. **1977** *Jrnl. R. Soc. Arts* CXXV. 616/2 Equally clear from the painting in the Fitzwilliam is Titian's awareness of what has since become known as the law of simultaneous contrast: the interaction of forms at the edges, so that the tone and colour of each is intensified by reaction with the other.

c. In *Chess*, denoting a number of games played against a number of opponents simultaneously by one player. Also *absol.*

1883 G. A. MACDONNELL *Chess Life-Pictures* II. 109 One of his strongest opponents in a simultaneous *sans voir* performance lost his game. **1938** P. W. SERGEANT *Championship Chess* ii. 34 Steinitz..gave a simultaneous display against twenty-two opponents at the New Vienna Chess Club. **1964** NABOKOV & SCAMMELL tr. *Nabokov's Defence* v. 77 An onlooker knowing nothing about simultaneous chess would be utterly baffled at the sight of these elderly men in black sitting gloomily behind boards that bristle thickly with curiously cut manikins, while a nimble..lad..walks lightly from table to table. **1974** SAIDY & LESSING *World of Chess* i. 24/1 The simultaneous exhibition places a premium on quick recognition of tactical threats, strong legs, and sheer physical endurance.

d. *Broadcasting.* (See quots.) Cf. S.B. s.v. *S 4 a.

1923 *Radio Times* 28 Sept. 2/3 Simultaneous broadcasting is a combination of ordinary and wireless telephony, whereby it becomes possible to broadcast at one or more stations a performance given at any other station in the country. **1971** *Gloss. Electrotechnical, Power Terms* (*B.S.I.*) III. iv. 6 *Simultaneous broadcast*, broadcast by a number of transmitters of the same programme at the same time.

e. Denoting a running oral translation of the spoken word or one skilled in this art, as *simultaneous interpreter, translation, translator*, etc.

1958 R. GLÉMET in A. H. Smith *Aspects of Translation* 120 With simultaneous interpretation..your 'intellection' of the speech need not be so thorough, but your response to words must be still quicker than before—the speaker speaks, and you are speaking too. **1965** M. SPARK *Mandelbaum Gate* vi. 187 Barbara turned the switch of her earphones to other simultaneous translations—French, Italian, then back to English. **1968** 'D. TORR' *Treason Line* 40 The simultaneous interpreters in their sound-proof boxes adjusting their earphones. **1971** *Guardian* 24 Mar. 3/5 The theatre, which only performs in Yiddish, has to have earphones with simultaneous translations for the audience. **1974** *Spartanburg* (S. Carolina) *Herald* 25 Apr. B 8/9 Simultaneous interpreters returned to their glass booths at the United Nations on Wednesday. **1977** M. T. BLOOM *13th Man* (1978) ii. 18 She's a simultaneous translator... Does a lot of work for the UN and international conferences.

sin, *sb.* Add: **1. a.** *for my sins*: (earlier and further examples).

1808 LADY LYTTELTON *Let.* 9 May (1912) 11 Now, would not you have thought he was a partisan of boxing? I did for my sins. **1906** R. BROOKE *Let.* 1 Apr. (1968) 47 About a year ago I got, for my sins, into the top form of the school. **1961** I. MURDOCH *Severed Head* v. 44 Rosemary..is for her sins a Mrs Michelis, having got married young.., to a dislikeable stockbroker called Bill Michelis, who subsequently left her. **1973** *Times* 2 Nov. 23/3 Take the BSA case in which, for my sins and much against my will, I was concerned.

2. c. Also *like* (or *worse than*) *sin*: vehemently, intensely, vigorously. Cf. *like the devil* s.v. DEVIL *sb.* 16.

1840 T. C. HALIBURTON *Clockmaker* 3rd Ser. viii. 102 Who the plague can live on sugar-candy? I am sure I couldn't. Nothin' does for me like honey; arter a while I get to hate it like sin. **1868** 'MARK TWAIN' *Let.* 8 Jan. (1917) I. 143, I have been working like sin all night to get a lecture written. **1929** W. SCOTT *Mask* i. 16 By the way, Father, dear—*who* is it that Peter Marlin hates worse than sin?

d. *to live in sin*: to cohabit outside marriage.

1838 *Ann. Rep. Bath City Mission* in G. R. Taylor *Angel-Makers* (1958) 67 Front attic, two aged people living in sin. **1855** C. KINGSLEY *Westw. Ho!* II. vii. 213 Why, not..to know whether..she's married to him or not..and I not to know whether she's living in sin or not, Mr. William. **1925** A. P. HERBERT *Laughing Ann* 92 Don't tell my mother I'm living in sin. **1974** R. B. PARKER *Godwulf Manuscript* vii. 56 A couple of freaky kids living in what my aunt used to call sin.

3. a. (Example of mod. colloquial use.) See also *Sc. Nat. Dict.*

1831 C. DARWIN *Let.* 6 Sept. in F. Darwin *Life* (1887) I. v. 207 He takes out twenty chronometers, and it will be a 'sin' not to settle the longitude.

4. a. *sin-stained.*

1843 J. G. WHITTIER *Hum. Sacrifice* in *Lays of my Home* 475 Oh! Never yet upon the scroll Of the sin-stained, but priceless soul, Hath Heaven inscribed '*Despair!*' **1896** E. DOWSON *Let.* May (1967) 363 Except that I want to see your classically sin-stained countenance, I should not even think of a week in Paris.

d. *sin-dark.*

a **1915** JOYCE *Giacomo Joyce* (1968) 10 She stands beside me, pale and chill, clothed with the shadows of the sindark nave.

6. sin-bin *slang* (chiefly *N. Amer.*) = *penalty box* (*a*) s.v. *PENALTY *sb.* 5; also *transf.*; **sin bosun** *Naval slang*, a ship's chaplain; **sin-buster** *U.S. slang*, an evangelist; a clergyman; **sin city** *slang*, a title applied jocularly or otherwise to a city considered to be a place of vice; **sin-shifter** *slang*, a clergyman.

1950 *Amer. Speech* XXV. 104/2 *Sin bin*, the penalty box where hockey players are sent for a few moments for infraction of rules, etc. **1958** *Herald Tribune* (Grand Prairie, Alberta) 11 Mar. 5/3 [The] game saw 37 minutes spent in the sin-bin. **1973** *Times* 10 Dec. 8/2 This game showed that it would be worth while trying the ice-hockey system of on-the-spot discipline with a 'sin-bin' to allow players to cool down. **1982** *Daily Tel.* 25 Feb. 19/5 It often took several months for an infant who has created chaos to be removed to a special school or a 'sin bin'. **1948** PARTRIDGE *Dict. Forces' Slang* 170 *Sin boson* [sic], *the*, the Chaplain, R.N. (Lower-deck.) **1964** *Navy News* Dec. (*H.M.S. Royal Arthur* Suppl.) 1/2 Well, at least the Sin Bosun doesn't seem too old, and did you see him get all punchy during deck-hockey yesterday? **1931** L. COCHRAN *Flood Tides* vi. 56 'The Reverend Billy Swinnerton is to conduct a revival here.'..'Not that ole sin-buster?' **1973** *Guardian* 17 Oct. 15/3 Leicester people ..saw Nottingham as a sort of sin city because people there went to the pub at night. **1975** 'A. THACKERAY' *One Way Ticket* II. 95 What's going to happen in Chicago? ..All you want to do is run amok in 'Sin City'. *a* **1912** 'T. COLLINS' *Rigby's Romance* (1946) 187 'Not a proper sin shifter,' objected Dixon. 'You can't chris'n a kid, nor yet say the (adj.) words over people.' **1919** W. H. DOWNING *Digger Dialects* 45 *Sin-shifter*, an army chaplain. **1966** 'L. LANE' *ABZ of Scouse* II. 98 *Sin-shifter*, a parson, priest, or rabbi.

‖ **sinagot** (sinagō). [Fr., f. *Séné*, a fishing village on the Gulf of Morbihan, on the west coast of France.] A two-masted Breton fishing-boat.

1927 L. RICHARDSON *Brittany & Loire* 213 Very red are the sails of the *sinagots*. **1975** *Mariner's Mirror* LXI. 93 The name for this type, which, like a Chinese junk, sets its two yards at almost right angles to their respective masts, is *sinagot*.

Sinanthropus (sinæ·nþrop*ǫ*s). [mod.L. (D. Black 1927, in *Palæontologica Sinica* D.VII. I. 21), f. SIN(O- + Gr. ἄνθρωπος man.] = *Peking man* s.v. *PEKIN 3. Hence **Sinanthro·pic** *a.*, of or pertaining to a fossil hominid of this kind; **Sina·nthropoid** *a.* [-OID], resembling Sinanthropus.

1928 *Daily Tel.* 17 Apr. 9/3 A human tooth as old as the Java ape man..has been named Sinanthropus, or 'the Peking man'. **1931** A. KEITH *New Discoveries Antiquity of Man* xvii. 260 The Sinanthropic mandibular fragment is broken short at the socket for the second incisor. **1937** *Ann. Reg. 1936* 52 Parts of three skulls of Palaeoanthropus showing Sinanthropoid features..were found in the Upper Pleistocene in Tanganyika. **1965** B. E. FREEMAN tr. *Vandel's Biospeleology* iii. 22 *Sinanthropus* used caves for shelter. **1978** *Nagel's Encycl.-Guide: China* 298 Great pride was taken in the discovery of remains of 'sinanthropus' which were older still than those found at Zhou Kou dian by Teilhard de Chardin.

‖ **Sinarquista** (sinaɹki·sta). Also (anglicized) **Sinarquist** and with small initial. [Amer.-Sp., after Sp. *anarquista* ANARCHIST; cf. SYNARCHY.] A member or adherent of the right-wing authoritarian Unión Nacional Sinarquista in Mexico, which was active between 1938 and 1960 (esp. in rural areas) and sought to restore the old order of the Catholic church and Spanish tradition, and opposed Communism, liberalism, and the policies imposed after the Revolution of 1911. Also *attrib.* or as *adj.*

1941 *N.Y. Times* 27 Dec. 8/8 An organized campaign to combat the Sinarquista Movement in Mexico will be launched next month... The Sinarquistas, often charged with favoring totalitarian nations, have begun large-scale agrarian colonization of Lower California. **1943** *Free World* May 413/1 These are reactionary leaders among the clergy who would go much farther with the Sinarquists. **1946** M. LOWRY *Let.* 2 Jan. (1967) 88 You can even see the German submarine officers taking revenge on the Consul in the form of the *sinarquistas*. **1970** G. HUIZER in I. L. Horowitz *Masses in Lat. Amer.* xiii. 474 The danger from extremely conservative and fascist forces, such as the Sinarquist movement, was alarmingly strong. **1973** P. CALVERT *Mexico* xxii. 284 The Sinarquistas were only the tip of the iceberg.

Hence ‖ **Sinarqui·smo** (anglicized **-ism**), the political doctrine of the Sinarquistas.

1943 *Free World* May 410/2 The enigma of Sinarquism is created by the character of Mexican politics. **1953** H. F. CLINE *U.S. & Mexico* xiv. 293 *Sinarquismo*—Sinarchism—is the opposite of anarchism; the word means 'with order'. Sinarquistas are believers in 'order'. **1963** D. JAMES *Mexico & Americans* xiii. 346 Sinarquismo was essentially a rural movement arising out of peasant discontent. **1971** R. MARETT *Mexico* x. 162 The fascist phenomenon of Sinarquismo, which came to a head in the late 1930's in opposition to the radical policies of Cárdenas.

since, *conj.* Add: **3. c.** In various, chiefly jocular, comparisons, as *since Christ was a corporal*, etc. *colloq.* (chiefly *U.S.* and *Mil.*).

1601 SHAKS. *Twel. N.* III. ii. 18 And they haue beene grande Iurie men, since before Noah was a Saylor. **1816** KEATS *Endymion* II. 443 Never, I aver, Since Ariadne was a vintager, So cool a purple. **1900** I. L. REEVES *Bamboo Tales* 20 Private McCoy..had been in the service since George Washington was a 'lance jack'. **1921** J. DOS PASSOS *Three Soldiers* II. ii. 75 Ain't had any pay since Christ was a corporal. I've forgotten what it looks like. **1961** PARTRIDGE *Dict. Slang* Suppl. 1274/2 *Since Pontius was a pilot*, as in 'He's been in that mob since..' R.A.F. c[atch] p[hrase], testifying to long service: since ca. 1944. **1970** *N.Y. Post* 7 Apr. 5 Dana Stone had been in Vietnam since Christ was a corporal, as the grunts in the field would say.

d. *since when?*: used *ellipt.* as an inquiry into the duration of a state of affairs mentioned in a previous statement (freq. expressing doubt or incredulity); also, with full interrogative clause. *colloq.*

1907 G. B. SHAW *John Bull's Other Island* IV. 84 *Broadbent* (*very solemnly*): No: I am a teetotaller. *Aunt Judy* (*incredulously*): Arra since when? **1966** 'G. BLACK' *You want to die, Johnny?* v. 105 'Lil's disappeared.'..'Since when?' **1977** C. WATSON *One Man's Meat* vii. 64 'Since when has Digger's father been a V.C.?' 'Since when has Digger had a father?'

‖ **sindaco** (si·ndako). [It.: see SYNDIC *sb.*] In Italy: a mayor.

[**1881** *Encycl. Brit.* XIII. 464/1 The syndic (*sindaco*) or chief magistrate of the commune is appointed by the king for three years.] **1902** H. BELLOC *Path to Rome* 342 We came to the house of the Sindaco or Mayor. **1969** M. GILBERT *Etruscan Net* I. v. 64 Broke had been looking at the Sindaco. **1975** S. JOHNSON *Urbane Guerilla* II. 81 He would seek the permission of the Sindaco and Commune of Siena for the staging of a special or *straordinario* Palio.

Sindebele: see *NDEBELE.

Sindhi (si·ndi), *sb.* and *a.* Also † **Sindee; Sindi.** [a. Hind. *Sindhi*, ult. f. Skr. *sindhu* river, *spec.* the Indus or the surrounding area.] **A.** *sb.* **1.** A native or inhabitant of Sind, now a province in the south-east of Pakistan, through which the Indus passes to the Arabian Sea.

1815 M. ELPHINSTONE *Acct. Kingdom of Caubul* IV. v. 500 The Sindees with whom I have conversed. **1836** in *Corresp. relative to Sinde 1836–1838* 20 in *Parl. Papers 1843* XXXIX. 9 The notions of the most enlightened (if I may apply the term) Sindees are..at utter variance with our customs. **1887** *Encycl. Brit.* XXII. 91/2 The Mohammedans [in Sind] may be divided into two great bodies—the Sindis proper and the naturalized Sindis. The Sindi proper is a descendant of the original Hindu. **1927** *Chambers's Jrnl.* Jan. 11/1 The little Sindi could distinguish every hoofprint and point out the goat which had made it. **1978** F. OLBRICH *Desouza pays Price* xxi. 131 Most of the Sindhis..had gathered their wealth together.. by Independence Day and descended on Bombay.

2. The name of a language consisting of several dialects spoken principally in Sind, but also in adjacent districts of north-west India.

1838 *Penny Cycl.* XII. 227/2 *Sindhí*, spoken in Sinde as far as the mouths of the Indus. **1908** [see *NEPALESE *a.* and *sb.*]. **1948** D. DIRINGER *Alphabet* II. vi. 376 Sindhi, spoken by three and a half million people in Sind. **1968** *Guardian* 14 Nov. 3/3 'Jiye Sind' (Long live Sind) has become among many Sindhis a form of salutation and there are demands for the elevation of Sindhi to the status of national language. **1981** V. POWELL *Flora Annie Steel* vii. 52 The strictly local dialect, a variety of Sindhi, made the setting up of female schools impracticable.

B. *adj.* Of or pertaining to this people or their language.

1836 W. H. WATHEN *Gram. Sindhi Lang.* 1 There are several different alphabets used in writing the Sindhi language. **1899** *Folk-Lore* X. 413 The far renowned.. Sindhi story of Sassi and Punnun. **1946** *Civil & Mil. Gaz.* 31 Aug. 8/3 Three Sindhi merchants. **1979** V. S. NAIPAUL *Bend in River* xiv. 244 There was this Sindhi girl who had studied in England.

Also **Si·nd(h)ian** *a.* and *sb.*

1849 J. D. CUNNINGHAM *Hist. Sikhs* i. 19 The occupation, by the Sindhian Daoodpotras of the Lower Sutlej, took place within the last hundred years. **1911** D. S. MARGOLIOUTH *Mohammedanism* i. 26 An outrage committed by a Sindian on a noble Moslem. **1964** in *Panjab Past & Present* (1978) XII. 412 The Sindhian Amirs were of course alarmed to learn that Ranjit Singh positively entertained the intention of attacking Shikarpur.

‖ **sindicato** (sindikā·to). [Sp., Pg.; cf. SYNDICATE *sb.*] In Spain, Portugal, Latin America, etc.: a trade union. *spec.* (usu. in *pl.*) a

Spanish trade union of a type originally established during the regime of General Franco, and subject to close government control. Cf. SYNDICAL *a.* in Dict. and Suppl.

1936 *Times* 21 Aug. 9/1 The newly created *sindicatos*, or labour unions. **1957** LD. HAILEY *Afr. Survey 1956* xx. 1451 The *sindicatos* have powers of investigating grievances or disputes, and provision is made for arbitration; they also try to find employment for members who are out of work. **1964** *Ann. Reg. 1963* 285 During the year it became evident that the Catholic Workers' Brotherhoods had become trade unions in all but name..but legally the government-controlled *sindicatos* maintained their monopoly. **1965** *New Statesman* 16 Apr. 599/1 Before his death Rodolfo Romero was the secretary-general of the peasant *sindicato* at Tapatapa. **1976** *National Observer* (U.S.) 28 Feb. 16/3 Underground leaders of the workers' commissions were widely elected to the above-ground negotiating committees of sindicatos.

sindon. Add: **2. a.** (Later examples in *spec.* use.) Also in It. form ‖ **sindone.**

1902 tr. *P. Vignon's Shroud of Christ* ii. 50 If 'the napkin' of St. John *were* the face-kerchief, where would have been the Shroud (*sindon*)? **1912** H. THURSTON in *Month* Nov. 539 One could well imagine that when the body had been laid out and covered back and front with the long impregnated sindon, strips of linen were used to secure the feet..keeping the sindon in its place. **1933** *Dublin Rev.* Jan. 36 St. Nino, a Georgian princess..was told that the Sindon was formerly in the possession of St. Peter. **1963** *Guardian* 31 May 12/3 The famous Holy Shroud, or Sindone, of Turin.

sindonology (sindǒnǫ·lodʒi). [f. SINDON + -OLOGY.] The study of the Holy Shroud of Turin, in which the body of Christ was reputedly wrapped. So **si:ndonolo·gical** *a.*

1950 *Catholic Digest* May 77/1 Dr Wuenschel..will give an address on 'The Shroud of Turin and the Burial of Christ' this May in Rome at the International Syndonological convention. **1953** E. WUENSCHEL *Holy Shroud of Turin* (rev. ed.) 4 In 1950, he was invited to read a paper at the First Sindonological Congress at Rome—a meeting of internationally recognized authorities on the Holy Shroud of Turin. **1964** J. WALSH *Shroud* xii. 117 By the start of the Second World War the Shroud had been studied more closely than in all its previous history... The investigation..assumed the stature of a separate discipline and was given a name, *sindonology*. **1978** *Church Times* 6 Oct. 6/4 This book..alarms by an account of a visit to a Sindonological Library in New York. **1979** *Radio Times* 7–13 Apr. 86/2 Don Pietro Borga is the general secretary of the International Centre for Sindonology (study of the shroud).

Hence **si:ndono·logist**, a student of the Shroud.

1953 E. WUENSCHEL *Holy Shroud of Turin* (rev. ed.) 4 He collaborated with Dr. Paul Vignon, the greatest of all sindonologists. **1980** *Observer* 28 Dec. 3/1 It has been a disappointment to sindologists (the name for shroud students) that the Roman Catholic authorities have refused to allow this [*sc.* carbon dating].

sine². Add: **4. sine bar** *Mech.*, a device used to set out or measure angles accurately, in which one end of a bar of known length is raised on gauge blocks; **sine tone** = *pure tone* s.v. *PURE *a.* 1 e; **sine wave,** a periodic oscillation of pure and simple form in which the displacement at any point is proportional to the sine of the phase angle at that point; a wave or curve resembling (a segment of) this in form.

1915 *Engineering* 8 Jan. 42/3 A sine-bar is a flat strip of steel, planed true all over, upon which are fixed two hardened and ground plugs, 1 in. in diameter, 10 in. apart. **1975** BRAM & DOWNS *Manuf. Technol.* i. 19 The sine bar is commonly used for marking off and checking the angle of a workpiece. **1962** Sine tone [see *LINE *v.*² 8 a]. **1976** *Times Lit. Suppl.* 3 Dec. 1522/5 Stockhausen's recent memoirs of his early years, which are sometimes strangely at odds with his correspondence of the period (particularly vis-à-vis the whole question of sine-tone synthesis). **1893** D. E. JONES tr. *H. Hertz's Electric Waves* 17 The vibration of the primary conductor is, at any rate to a first approximation, a uniformly damped sine-wave of determinate period. **1916** *Electrician* LXXVI. 800/1 The alternating current produced in the telephones is almost a pure sine wave. **1965** *Wireless World* Sept. 455/1 To verify the rated output of an amplifier a 1 kc/s sinewave is fed through it at a level sufficient to produce the rated output power. **1972** *Islander* (Victoria, B.C.) 21 May 15/2 Some of the flat fishes, such as flounders and rays, move by undulating their bodies in a flattened sine wave. Visualize this movement as a flag held horizontally in a stiff wind.

sine³ (səi·ni). *Eton College slang.* [a. fanciful mod.L. *sine* (*coloribus*), without (colours).] At Eton College: a House team, which excludes those awarded colours; the members of this considered *collect.*

1922 S. LESLIE *Oppidan* xxii. 276 The *sine* was made to forego the sweetness of a long lie in order to run..before breakfast. *Ibid.* 277 As match after match was lost by the *sine*, Mouler put up a notice to say that in future *sine* were expected to do a training walk as well as their morning run. **1940** M. MARPLES *Public School Slang* 112 Idioms such as these are probably not of great age... [e.g.] *sine* (Eton): used to describe a House team excluding colours, from the dog Latin *sine coloribus*, without colours: hence *2nd sine* wrongly used = 2nd XI.

Sinemurian (sinĕmiū·riăn), *a. Geol.* [ad. F. *Sinémurien* (A. d'Orbigny *Paléont. Française. Mollusques et Rayonnés Fossiles. Terrains Jurassiques* (1842–9) I. 604), f. L. *Sinemurum*, ancient name of Sémur-en-Auxois, a town in Côte d'Or department, France + *-ien* -IAN.] Of, pertaining to, or designating a stage of the Lower Jurassic in Europe which in the modern division is next below the Pliensbachian. Freq. *absol.*

1863 J. D. DANA *Man. Geol.* III. iii. 449 The Sinemurian (Lower Lias, named from the locality at Sémur). **1888** J. PRESTWICH *Geol.* II. xvi. 242 M. Gosselet includes the Lower- and Infra-Lias in one division—the Sinemurian, which he divides into two subdivisions—the Upper Sinemurian and the Lower Sinemurian or Hettangian. **1928** E. NEAVERSON *Stratigraphical Palaeont.* xv. 331 The most familiar Sinemurian brachiopod is the broad-plaited *Spiriferina walcotti.* **1969** BENNISON & WRIGHT *Geol. Hist. Brit. Isles* xiii. 289 A cyclic sequence of thin limestones and clays of Blue Lias type comprise the Hettangian followed by clays chiefly, although locally limestones may occur as high as the top of the Sinemurian.

Sineque, var. *SENECA.

‖ **sinfonia** (sinfonī·ă, sinfōᵘ·niˌă). *Mus.* Pl. **sinfonie, -ias.** [It., = SYMPHONY.] **a.** In early Italian opera: the overture. **b.** A symphony. **c.** (Used in the title of) a small symphony orchestra or chamber orchestra.

1773 C. BURNEY *Present State of Music in France & Italy* 382, I heard a *sinfonia* or overture and a chorus.. which were excellent. **1818** W. GARDNER tr. *Bombet's Lives of Haydn & Mozart* 256 The sinfonia in *The Creation*, which represents the rising of the sun, is an exemplification of this theory. **1828** E. HOLMES *Ramble among Musicians of Germany* 180 The composition given this afternoon was Mozart's Jupiter sinfonia. **1884** *Encycl. Brit.* XVII. 87/1 The sinfonia or overture which is often associated with his [*sc.* Scarlatti's] name. **1924** A. HAM *Outl. Mus. Form* xix. 82 An Overture..is an expansion of the Sinfonia or Symphony. **1946** DAVID & MENDEL *Bach Reader* I. 39 Neither the Inventions and the Sinfonias nor the two books of the *Well-Tempered Clavier*..were printed during Bach's lifetime. **1967** I. SPINK *Hist. Approach to Mus. Form* iii. 98 These operas were not in recitative throughout. They also included choruses, dances and instrumental pieces or *sinfonie*. **1976** *Leicester Mercury* 16 July, He had recently contacted about 60 top class instrumentalists.. with the intention of forming an orchestra which..would be called the Rutland Sinfonia.

Also **sinfonia concertante** (kontʃerta·nte) [CONCERTANTE], a symphonic work exhibiting characteristics of the concerto.

1903 R. HUGHES *Mus. Guide* I. 266/2 *S. concertan'te, concerta'ta, concertate...* concerto for many instrs., a concerto symphony. **1928** *Musical Times* 1 Feb. 165/1 M. Ansermet..conducted William Walton's new 'Sinfonia Concertante' for orchestra and pianoforte. **1946** MENDEL & BRODER tr. *Einstein's Mozart* xvi. 274 Mozart cultivated this form less and less as the years went on. He abandoned the *sinfonia concertante*, and separated its ingredients. **1950** R. HUGHES *Haydn* vii. 80 At the fourth concert on 9th March [1792] the endearing *Sinfonia concertante* for violin, cello, oboe and bassoon was performed for the first time. **1959** [see *ARGUABLY *adv.*]. **1979** *Early Music* July 415/2 Clarinettists will find in the E flat Symphony by the Earl of Kelly..what amounts to a *sinfonia concertante*.

‖ **sinfonietta** (sinfoniˌe·tă, sinfonye·tă). *Mus.* [It., dim. of prec.] **a.** A short, simple form of symphony. **b.** = *SINFONIA c.

1907 T. S. WOTTON *Dict. Mus. Terms* 180 *Sinfonietta*, a little Symphony, e.g. Raff's sinfonietta for 10 wind instruments. **1923** *Daily Mail* 20 Feb. 7 Mr. Eugene Goossens..introduced..his first symphony (shyly entitled a 'Sinfonietta'). **1947** A. EINSTEIN *Music in Romantic Era* xi. 131 But does not the lack of a slow movement make even a sinfonietta into a suite, a more or less disconnected succession of movements? **1970** *Music & Musicians* June 53 Playing at the Elizabeth Hall on March 25 before a miserably small audience, the Bournemouth Sinfonietta, ably directed by Nicholas Braithwaite. **1973** D. EWEN *Orchestral Music* xii. 207 His [*sc.* Hindemith's] major works..included..two compositions with humorous overtones: the Concerto for Woodwinds, Harp and Orchestra (1949) and Sinfonietta in E (1950). **1982** *Times* 29 Nov. 11/1 The London Sinfonietta settled down last night to become a string orchestra in a stabler sort of programme.

sinful, *a.* and *sb.* Add: **2. b.** Also, as a strong intensive: excessive in manner or extent; 'dreadful', 'wicked'. *colloq.*

1880 J. C. HARRIS *Uncle Remus* xxviii. 122 De way he stir up dem bees wuz sinful. **1920** WODEHOUSE *Damsel in Distress* ii. 35 The money that boy makes is sinful.

sinfully, *adv.* Add: **2.** (Earlier and later examples.) Also in weakened use: excessively.

1869 'MARK TWAIN' *Innoc. Abroad* xlv. 475 So sinfully ugly that she couldn't smile after ten o'clock Saturday night without breaking the Sabbath. **1912** [see *JUMP *sb.*¹ 7]. **1976** *New Yorker* 24 May 113/3 It's also guaranteed to be *sinfully* comfortable with its built-in headrest and body-conforming mattress.

sing, *sb.* Add: **1. a.** For 'bullet' read 'bullet or other projectile' and add later examples.

1917 E. C. MIDDLETON *Way of Air* 70 The familiar 'sing' of an approaching shell. **1930** *Carmina* Oct. 45 The sing Of a stone from the sling.

2. a. (Earlier and later examples.) Also, a hearty sing-song or round of collective singing (chiefly *U.S.*).

1850 N. KINGSLEY *Diary* 1 Sept. (1914) 140 We had a fine sing in the Evening which put me in mind of home. **1875** I. L. BIRD *Six Months in Sandwich Islands* xii. 175 There have been pleasant little gatherings for sewing.. and on Sunday evenings what is colloquially termed, 'a sing'. **1932** A. HUXLEY *Brave New World* iv. 73 In the Ealing stadium a Delta gymnastic display and community sing was in progress. **1964** 'J. H. ROBERTS' *'Q' Document* (1965) ix. 211 Skiers were gathered around in an alcoholic community sing. **1972** *Village Voice* (N.Y.) 1 June 96/4 Open sing, Verdi's Requiem. **1981** *Libr. Congr. Inf. Bull.* 16 Jan. (Staff News), Staff members and their families gather in the Great Hall for the annual carol sing.

b. *on the sing*: (of a kettle) singing. Cf. SING *v.*¹ 6 a.

1927 W. DEEPING *Kitty* xxx. 384 'All the kettles—'.. 'Two are boiling, miss; the other's on the sing.'

sing, *v.*¹ Add: **I. 1. d.** *to sing for one's supper* (also † *dinner*): for lack of money. Usu. *fig.*, to provide entertainment or a service in return for a benefit received (often, a meal).

c **1744** *Little Tommy Tucker* in *Tommy Thumb's Pretty Little Song Bk.* 10 Little Tom Tucker Sings for his Supper What shall he Eat White bread and Butter. **1803** J. KENNEY *Raising the Wind* I. i. 4 As you sometimes sing for your dinner, now you may whistle for your breakfast. **1949** N. MITFORD *Love in Cold Climate* I. iii. 30 [At] the various house parties..I had been to..I knew that I was expected..to sing for my supper by being, if possible, amusing. **1972** T. P. MCMAHON *Issue of Bishop's Blood* (1973) ix. 134 Thanks for the dinner... Is it too bad a pun to say I'm ready to sing for it?

e. *to sing along*: to sing in accompaniment to a song or piece of music. Also const. *with* the performer. Cf. *SING-ALONG *sb.* and *a.*

1959 *Time* 17 Aug. 60/3 Whether anyone actually sings along with the sing-along albums probably does not bother..Miller. **1973** *Observer* (Colour Suppl.) 29 Apr. 41/3 They all stand on the tables and sing along and stamp their feet. **1977** R. L. DUNCAN *Temple Dogs* (1978) I. ii. 46 He was singing along with the piano player, his voice shrill.

4. d. *Criminals' slang* (now chiefly *U.S.*). = *sing out* (sense 5 c in Dict.). Also *to sing like a canary*. Orig. in proverbial phr. † *he that sings once, weeps all his life after* and varr.

1612 T. SHELTON tr. *Cervantes' Don-Quixote* I. III. viii. 193 Here it is quite contrary, quoth the slave, for He that sings once, weepes all his life after. **1710** S. PALMER *Moral Essays on Proverbs* lxxii. 197 He that Sings in Disaster, shall Weep all his Life-time After. 'Tis generally suppos'd, that this Proverb was born in a Jail. *Sing*..is, when one of the Gang Tattles, Confesses, and Accuses the Rest.

1929 HOSTETTER & BEESLEY *It's a Racket!* 238 *Sing*, to confess. **1937** [implied at *SINGING *vbl. sb.* 1 d]. **1946** *Sun* (Baltimore) 10 Dec. 1/3 A former army colonel 'sang' about the operation of military government there. **1950** R. HIMMEL *I'll find You* (1958) xvii. 117 She's singing like a canary. She turned up at headquarters..and said she had some information on a killing. **1964** L. NKOSI *Rhythm of Violence* 65 Who knows, maybe he's even goin' to sing to the police! **1981** P. NIESEWAND *Word of Gentleman* xix. 126 You don't think they'd sing like canaries?..They'll sing, Claud... If they thought it would help them, they'd tell on their mothers.

II. 13. e. Of the Aboriginal inhabitants of Australia: to endow (an object) with magical properties by singing; to bring a magical influence to bear on (a person or thing) by singing.

1899 SPENCER & GILLEN *Native Tribes Central Austral.* xvi. 537 The wound was not serious..but he persisted in saying that the spear had been sung, and that..he was going to die, which accordingly he did. **1914** B. SPENCER *Native Tribes N. Territory* iii. 140 As soon as the ground was cleared..all the men retired to one side and, to the accompaniment of trumpets..and clapping of hands, it was 'sung'. This 'singing' was supposed to make the ground..in good order so that the performers could dance well. **1959** A. UPFIELD *Bony & Black Virgin* xvii. 158 The aborigines..dug up their rainstones and rubbed them with their magic stones, and 'sang' them in a secret camp. And then it rained. **1975** *Times* 8 Nov. 5/1 The Premier of Queensland was put under a death spell by Aborigines last night... An Aboriginal..said 'These people have sung him and he should start dying from now on.'

III. 14. sing-in [*IN³], a musical performance in which the audience participates in the singing.

1968 *Lebende Sprachen* XIII. 67/1 Neologismen mit *in* im Englischen und Deutschen...sing-in, sit-in, [etc.]. **1970** *New Yorker* 19 Dec. 16 Sing-in at Philharmonic Hall —Handel's 'Messiah' directed (seriatim fortunately) by nineteen directors. **1976** *Flintshire Leader* 10 Dec. 13/2 (*heading*) Penyffordd 'sing-in'.

sing, var. *SHENG.

si·ng-along, *sb.* and *a.* Also **sing-a-long** and as one word. [f. the vbl. phr. *to sing along*: see *SING *v.*¹ 1 e.] **A.** *sb.* **1.** A song or recording to which one can sing along in accompaniment (esp. a light popular song with an easy rhythm).

1959 *Time* 17 Aug. 60/3 The nation's mature citizens are merely striking back at rock'n'roll, buying the sing-alongs. **1968** *Globe & Mail* (Toronto) 3 Feb. 23/1 A Gay Nineties room with sing-alongs, familiar tunes of that era. **1971** *Ink* 31 July 16/2 Those ringing certainties which made 'Woodstock' and 'Big Yellow Taxi' into such cosy sing-alongs. **1981** J. Wainwright *Urge for Justice* I. xii. 84 He could tickle the old ivories..could hammer out a singalong with the best.

2. A sing-song to the accompaniment of a song-leader or tune.

1973 B. Broadfoot *Ten Lost Years* xxii. 256 There would be a sing-along, or the manager maybe would just pull a lucky number from a hat. **1975** *Daily Mail* 9 June 18/1 Someone in the next room's having a sing-along! **1979** *Guardian* 27 June 11/8 The insulting..notion that working-class audiences want only a beery community sing-along on their night out.

B. *adj.* Of a song, recording, etc.: to which one can sing along in accompaniment. Of or characterized by this unsophisticated but cheerful style.

1959 [see *sing *v.*[1] 1 e]. **1967** *Melody Maker* 1 Apr. 9 How can the Beatles' best..single yet be ousted by so many sing-along melodies and slush-ridden lyrics? **1974** *Financ. Times* 24 Apr. 2/3 Happy music in singalong style. **1977** P. Hill *Liars* ii. 9 A group of relatives were following the words of a sing-along record.

Singapore (siŋăpōə·r, siŋg-). The name of a city and island-republic (formerly, British Crown Colony) in South-East Asia, used *attrib.*, usu. as *Singapore* (*gin*) *sling*, to designate a cocktail with a base of gin and cherry brandy.

1930 *Savoy Cocktail Book* 1. 190 Singapore Sling. The Juice of ¼ Lemon. ¼ Dry Gin. ½ Cherry Brandy. Shake well and strain into medium size glass, and fill with soda water. Add 1 lump of ice. **1948** D. S. Embury *Fine Art of mixing Drinks* xi. 299 Singapore Gin Sling. Of all the recipes published for this drink I have never seen any two that were alike. Essentially it is simply a Gin Sling with the addition of cherry brandy. **1960** J. J. Rowlands *Spindrift from House by Sea* i. 28 Building your own house, he told us after his third Singapore gimlet, is an experience akin to a spiritual awakening. **1969** R. Thomas *Singapore Wink* xi. 118 I'm going to have a Singapore Sling in the bar of the Raffles Hotel. **1976** *Times* (Singapore Suppl.) 19 July p. iv/4 In 1915 a barman, Mr Ngian Tong Dron, tried mixing two measures of gin with one of cherry brandy and one of orange, pineapple and lime juice..the Singapore gin sling was born.

Singaporean (siŋăpōə·riăn, siŋg-), *a.* and *sb.* Also (occas.) **-ian.** [f. prec. + -an.] **A.** *adj.* Of or pertaining to Singapore.

1880 [see *moth orchid* s.v. Moth *sb.* 3]. **1927** *Malaya Tribune* 27 Dec. 7/6 Feckless Singaporean Scots. **1972** *Times* (Singapore Suppl.) 4 July p. ii/3 The Government has been alleged..to have sacrificed important aspects of Chinese culture and language in order to create its image of the Singaporian nation. **1977** *Hongkong Standard* 12 Apr. 16/5 He spoke to 360 striking Singaporean metal workers earlier in the day.

B. *sb.* A native or inhabitant of Singapore.

1927 *Malaya Tribune* 5 Jan. 9/2 (*heading*) World's motor record by Singaporeans. **1956** D. Davies *More Old Singapore* 40 A working day in the life of a Singaporean. **1965** *Times* 12 Aug. 8/1 Speaking to Malay journalists, Mr. Lee begged the Malays not to worry. He ..insisted that 'Singapore is not a Chinese country nor a Malay country nor an Indian country... It belongs to the Singaporeans.' **1975** P. Theroux *Great Railway Bazaar* xxiii. 238 Singaporeans are great assemblers of appliances.

Singatoka, var. *Sigatoka.

singed, *ppl. a.*[1] Add: **b.** (Earlier examples.) (Parallel Sc. allusive uses incorporate the related form Singed *ppl. a.*[2] (cf. quot. 1737).)

1836 *Spirit of Times* 9 Apr. 61/1 Without our Jersey friends bring on a 'singed cat', or some nag, now outside the fence, turns up a trump, the above comprise the entries for the 4 mile day. **1837** J. C. Neal *Charcoal Sketches* 48 His new friend, however, proved..to be like a singed cat, much better than he looked.

singer[1]. Add: **1. c.** An informer. Cf. *sing *v.*[1] 4 d. *Criminals' slang.*

1935 *Amer. Speech* X. 20/2 *Singer*, a stool pigeon or trusty who carries tales to the administration. (Obs.) **1961** *John o' London's* 30 Nov. 610/3 An informer, then a *squealer*, is now more often referred to..as a *singer*.

3. Special Combinations with *singer's*: **singer's node, nodule** *Path.*, a small pale swelling on a vocal cord; **singer's seat** *U.S.*, a choir-seat or bench (cf. *singing-seat* s.v. Singing *vbl. sb.* 4 b).

1953 C. Wakely *Faber Med. Dict.* 389/2 *Singers' nodes*, or *nodules*... Syn. *chorditis tuberosa.* **1961** R. D. Baker *Essent. Path.* xv. 360 Overuse of the voice can cause traumatic laryngitis and 'singer's nodes', and a biopsy will demonstrate minute hematomas in various stages of scarring. **1967** *Punch* 29 Mar. 458 Singer's Nodule, the name for a minute warty excrescence on overworked vocal apparatus. **1974** Passmore & Robson *Compan. Med. Stud.* III. xxxii. 22/2 Vocal nodules. These are called singer's nodes because they are seen in singers, particularly sopranos and tenors, but they also occur in others who use their voices excessively, with faulty voice production. **1777** Singer's seat [see *chorister 1 a]. **1861** Mrs. Stowe *Pearl of Orr's Island* (1862) ix. 84 Aunt Ruey.. had in her youth been one of the foremost leaders in the 'singers' seats'.

‖ **singerie** (sæ̃ʒəri). [Fr., apish behaviour or trick, a collection of monkeys; cf. Chinoiserie.] A piece of porcelain, painting, etc., in which monkeys are represented in anthropomorphic (often quasi-Chinese) attitude; work done in this style (esp. popular in the eighteenth cent.). Also *transf.* Cf. *monkey band, orchestra* s.v. *monkey *sb.* 17 a.

[**1820** M. Edgeworth *Let.* 4 June (1979) 142 The white wainscot..is painted with grey imitation of Indian ink pictures of monkeys in mens and womens clothes... I have some notion of having somewhere read of this cabinet of monkeys.] **1920** A. Stratton *Eng. Interior* 61 So many influences were tending to shape the arts in that century, that it is not surprising to find reflections of the French 'Chinoiserie' and 'Singerie' styles in English houses. The French painters Jean François Clermont.. and Jean Pillement..both worked in this country, and their fanciful 'Singeries', in which monkeys play the rôle of horsemen and sportsmen, have a certain charm. **1920** E. Sitwell *Wooden Pegasus* 13 (*title*) Singerie. **1957** *Economist* 9 Nov. (Suppl.) 15/2 This style..gives excessive weight to the rest of their lives, which is that of the characters in Miss Mitford's novels: one-tenth genuine emotion (a bit more for Voltaire) and nine-tenths *singerie*. **1963** N. Pevsner *Wiltshire* 520 Ceiling with *singeries* by *Andieu de Clermont*,..far too finicky for Inigo's architecture. **1977** Fleming & Honour *Penguin Dict. Decorative Arts* 742/1 The vogue for *singeries* did not begin much before the end of the c17 and reached its height of popularity in the c18 when it became associated with *chinoiserie*... *Singeries* were painted on walls, in porcelain and faience, worked in piqué and in marquetry, embroidered and printed in textiles.

Singh (siŋ). Also † **Sing(e.** [a. Hind. *siṅgh* lion, f. Skr. *siṁha* lion, 'the powerful one'.]

1. A great warrior: a cognomen or title of respect borne by several of the warrior castes of northern India, or a surname adopted by male Sikhs.

1623 N. Bangham et al. *Let.* 5 Apr. in W. Foster *Eng. Factories in India* (1908) 218 Beinge soe hotly persued by Abdala Chan and Rajae Sursinge. **1797** *Encycl. Brit.* IX. 213/2 In 1770 the rajah died, and was succeeded by his son Cheit Sing. **1841** *Penny Cycl.* XIX. 276/2 The bravery and talents of the regent Zalim Singh. **1888** Kipling *Departmental Ditties* (1890) 18 Chimbu Singh from Bikaneer..Jowar Singh the Sikh. **1955** *Times* 5 July 13/3 Maharana Sir Fateh Singh Bahadur, the head of the Sessodia Rajputs..had personal as well as dynastic claims to veneration.

2. As a simple noun.

1851 J. Thackwell *Narr. Second Sikh War* 227 The British guns were so overwhelming..and their fire so rapid and precise, that the enemy declared there was a ball for every Sing. **1914** J. J. H. Gordon *Sikhs* iv. 39 They were then hailed as 'Singhs' or lions of their race, and declared to be the Khalsa—the select... All the rest of the disciples present were similarly baptised and declared Singhs. **1930** G. B. Scott *Relig. & Short Hist. Sikhs* iii. 30 After receiving the Pahal, the novice is no longer a Sikh or scholar only, he is *Singh*, a lion, and is entitled to affix that word to his name. **1973** 'S. Harvester' *Corner of Playground* II. viii. 150 He thought about his grandfather Swaran,..first Singh of the family in Africa, a coolie who came..to build the railway from Mombasa to Victoria Nyanza.

singing, *vbl. sb.* Add: **1. b.** Now *N. Amer.* (chiefly *Southern*). A gathering joined for collective singing, esp. at a church; a hearty sing-song.

1860 O. L. Jackson *Colonel's Diary* (1922) 17, I was at a singing at Woodward Church. **1934** C. Carmer *Stars fell on Alabama* II. ii. 49 Ain't seen him since the singin' down at Samanthy. **1949** B. A. Botkin *Treas. S. Folklore* I. iv. 93 All through the South, of course, the church is an important social and cultural force, its sociability running the gamut of church-going..bush-arbor revivals, all-day singings with dinner on the grounds, church suppers, singing schools, [etc.]. **1962** E. Lucia *Klondike Kate* viii. 172 Families got together for 'singings' around the parlor piano and to play games. **1975** *Budget* (Sugarcreek, Ohio) 20 Mar. 3/5 They all had supper at the Lehman home and a singing was held later in the evening.

d. The action of turning informer or laying information against someone. Cf. sense *4 d of the vb. *Criminals' slang.*

1937 *Sat. Even. Post* 18 Dec. 85/1 One actually preferred a three-year penitentiary term to singing. **1940** *Daily Progress* (Charlottesville, Va.) 21 Mar. 3 (*heading*) 'Singing' at murder syndicate's hunting ground. **1973** *Times* 12 Apr. 7/4 The terrified 'singing' of the Sicilian 'Valachi' to delighted magistrates in Palermo has landed 36 Mafia suspects in jail.

2. b. *Teleph.* A continuous self-excited oscillation of audible frequency in a telephone circuit, normally resulting from excessive positive feedback.

1923 T. E. Herbert *Telephony* xxvi. 829 If two repeaters are in circuit, spaced so closely that the line loss between them is less than the gain given by each 'singing' or 'howling' will persist continuously. **1962** C. F. Boyce *Open-Wire Carrier Telephone Transmission* xi. 231 Singing affects not only the channel which is unstable but may also cause crosstalk into another system or overloaning of line amplifiers. **1975** R. L. Freeman *Telecommunication Transmission Handbk.* vi. 48 To control singing all four-wire paths must have some loss.

4. a. *singing commercial, -master* (later examples); **singing book** (later U.S. examples); **singing game,** a traditional children's game in which singing accompanies associated actions; **singing point** *Teleph.*, the maximum gain that a telephone repeater can have without being liable to self-oscillation in the circuit.

1793 in *Essex Inst. Hist. Coll.* (1885) XXII. 148 Voted to obtain 6 Psalm Books and 6 Singing Books for the use of the Parish. **1872** Mrs. Stowe *Oldtown Fireside Stories* 130 They tore out all the leaves of the hymn-books, and the singin'-books besides. **1948** B. Rose *Wine, Women & Words* 11, I wrote the first singing commercial. **1955** *New Yorker* 23 Apr. 74/1, I approached Mr. Chayefsky's film with no great hope that the thing would prove to be much more interesting than a singing commercial. **1881** *Folk-Lore Rec.* III. II. 169 The following 'Singing Games' are still played and sung by the children of Bocking, in Essex..I. Mary's gone a-milking..II. Thread the Tailor's needle..III. Nuts in May [etc.]. **1905** G. Ade *Let.* 7 Nov. (1973) 33 One or two of the old-fashioned singing games which went as well in the *Sho-Gun*. **1975** B. Meyrick *Behind Light* xiv. 183 Playing the singing games 'Jenny is a-weeping', 'In and out the stalky bluebells'. **1754** *N.Y. Mercury* 11 Mar. 3/2 William Tuckey, Singing-Master, Desires to inform all lovers of Psalmody, that.. all persons may be taught by him on very reasonable terms. **1891** *Harper's Mag.* Oct. 813/1 The precentor, or singing-master, as he was called, was a tall young man in a black suit with white ruffles. **1928** W. B. Yeats *Tower* 2 And to be the singing masters of my soul. **1976** J. Drummond *Funeral Urn* xvii. 89 He was planning to make a concert singer of her. He'd engaged a singing-master—ostensibly to train the Amber choir, but in fact for Bess. **1924** K. S. Johnson *Transmission Circuits for Telephonic Communications* xiv. 166 The singing point or the limiting condition beyond which satisfactory operation of the repeater cannot be maintained. **1934** *Post Office Electr. Engineers Jrnl.* XXVII. 231/2 The vertical scale gives the singing point of a repeater in decibels.

b. *singing-gallery* (earlier example), *-room*, *-seat* (earlier and later examples).

1774 in *Essex Inst. Hist. Coll.* (1884) XXI. 271 Voted Liberty to beuld a singing Seat in the front of the Gallearry Pues. **1842** F. Witts *Diary* 22 Oct. (1978) 167 The remains were to be deposited at the west end of Upton St. Leonards church, under the singing gallery, near the font. **1851** J. W. Hudson *Hist. Adult Educ.* 157 Singing-rooms are numerous, prosperous and constantly well-attended. **1902** A. Bennett *Anna of Five Towns* ii. 34 Mynors.. should have been in his place in the 'orchestra' (or, as some term it, the 'singing-seat') of the [Methodist] chapel. **1976** *S. Wales Echo* 27 Nov. 12/6 (Advt.), Sing along with Mike and Charles at the newly decorated singing-room upstairs.

singing, *ppl. a.* Add: **4. b.** *singing arc*, a direct current arc across which is connected a tuned circuit, causing the arc to oscillate and emit a sound at the frequency of the tuned circuit; *singing sand*, desert or beach sand that emits a singing, whistling, humming, or other continuous sound when disturbed.

1903 *Sci. Abstr.* VI. 30 The author suggests replacing the ordinary high-capacity condensers necessary to produce Duddell's 'singing arc' by the much less costly aluminium condenser. **1906** *Electrician* 21 Dec. 375/1 Limitations as to frequency..beset the use of the singing arc as a transformer of the direct mains current into uninterrupted high-frequency alternating current. **1950** Starling & Woodall *Physics* xxxvi. 874 The singing arc..where electrical and thermal factors are involved in the maintenance of oscillations. [**1884** *Proc. Amer. Assoc. Adv. Sci. 1883* 251 (*heading*) The singing beach of Manchester, Mass.] **1897** Singing sand [in Dict., sense 4 a]. **1941** R. A. Bagnold *Physics of Blown Sand & Desert Dunes* xvii. 251, I have found singing sand on the slip-faces of both seif and barchan dunes and of drifts formed under the shelter of cliffs. **1970** R. Johnston *Black Camels of Qashran* viii. 133 The night-long background music of the dunes was silenced. They were through the singing sands.

single, *sb.* Add: **3. h.** (Earlier example.) Also in *Baseball, spec.* = *one-base hit* s.v. *one *numeral a.* 33.

1851 J. Pycroft *Cricket Field* ii. 24 Ever and anon a single or a double are safely played away. **1867** *N.Y. Mercury* 2 Aug. 6/5 The sharp fielding of the Athletics caused the retirement of their opponents for a single. **1880** *Chicago Inter-Ocean* 29 June 8/3 Force's winning run came off a wild throw by Ward, a sacrifice and single. **1948** *Herald-Press* (St. Joseph, Mich.) 14 Aug. 7/2 Green also bashed out a triple and single during the game. **1974** *Anderson* (S. Carolina) *Independent* 23 Apr. 6A/2 The Astros broke a scoreless tie in the fourth on Bob Watson's single, a wild pitch, and Doug Rader's double.

j. A locomotive engine having a single pair of driving-wheels. Now only *Hist.*

1901 *Railway Mag.* Jan. 31/2 The engine hauling the 9.45 a.m. was No. 22, one of the rebuilt 8 ft. singles. **1931** *Times Educ. Suppl.* 27 June p. iii/3 A famous locomotive, ..one of the original 9 ft. singles built for the Bristol and Exeter Railway.

k. *pl.* Single-screened coal.

1921 *Glasgow Herald* 7 Dec. 9 Coals used in smithwork say 'pearls' and 'singles', varied from 15*s.* to 18*s.* per ton f.o.b. **1931** [see *double *sb.* 3 r].

l. *U.S. Theatr.* (See quot. 1923.) Cf. *single act* s.v. *SINGLE *a.* 17 a.

1923 *N.Y. Times* 7 Oct. IX. 2/1 *Single*, an artist working alone as an act. **1955** L. FEATHER *Encycl. Jazz* (1956) 118/2 After Keaton broke up temporarily in 1949, she worked as a single, but rejoined Keaton for several tours. **1962** J. MCCABE *Mr. Laurel & Mr. Hardy* i. 26 Following the *Sleeping Beauty* season, he went on as a single again.. for a few odd engagements. **1976** *National Observer* (U.S.) 24 Jan. 18/5 For the past 18 years George Burns has practiced his profession as a single. He has worked..in night clubs and concert halls; he has appeared..on television talk shows.

m. A one-dollar bill (*U.S.*). Also *occas.*, a one-pound note. Cf. *ONCER 2. *slang.*

1936 J. WEIDMAN in *Amer. Mercury* May 86/2, I took out my wallet... I pulled out two singles. **1961** 'J. LE CARRÉ' *Call for Dead* vii. 78 There he was..showering old singles on me like used tote tickets. **1964** L. DEIGHTON *Funeral in Berlin* xlii. 258 'Do you have a pistol or a knife or a persuader?' 'I have a persuader... Two hundred dollars in singles.' **1977** H. FAST *Immigrants* I. 35 He.. took out a wad of bills, peeling off two fives and two singles.

n. A gramophone record having only one item (typically, of popular music) on each side; an item of music on such a record.

1949 [see *pop single* s.v. *POP *a.* 1 c]. **1958** *Gramophone* Dec. 328/1 There is a single by Nino Rico and his Orchestra. **1965** G. MELLY *Owning Up* xi. 135 His version of 'Rock Island Line', originally part of a Chris Barber in Concert LP, was requested so often on the radio that it was put out as a single and rose to be top of the Hit Parade. **1981** *Listener* 1 Jan. 31/2 A track released as a single..topped the singles chart.

o. An engine with only one cylinder; a motor-cycle or car having such an engine.

1951 B. OSBORNE *Mod. Motorcycles* iii. 19 The designer of hot-stuff singles will scornfully mention Italy's Monza, ..where riders of high-revving Italian 'fours' have been.. completely licked by one of the finest single-cylinder racers ever turned out of a Birmingham factory. **1955** D. SCOTT-MONCRIEFF *Veteran & Edwardian Motor-Cars* vi. 111 The old long-stroke singles and twins were no longer allowed [in 1911]; only four- and six-cylinder cars. **1963** BIRD & HUTTON-STOTT *Veteran Motor Car Pocketbk.* 189 It was soon apparent that the small 4-cylinder engine was destined to supplant the big singles and twins which had served so long for light car work. **1976** *New Motorcycling Monthly* Oct. 24/3 It is every inch a purpose-built motorcycle, and must have been a welcome addition to a scene that still reveres our own BSA 'Gold Star' and Matchless singles.

5. *ellipt.* in general application. **a.** = *single ticket* s.v. *SINGLE *a.* 17 a.

1889 E. DOWSON *Let.* 1–2 Apr. (1967) 59 If I could see things..as he does I would take a first class single for La Trappe to-morrow. **1903** L. MERRICK *Quaint Companions* iv. 49 She congratulated herself on having taken only a 'third single' at Brighton. **1936** *Punch* 5 Feb. 141/1 'Single to Liverpool Street,' I said with easy hauteur. **1972** 'R. CRAWFORD' *Whip Hand* I. ix. 55 He..booked a single on the next flight to London.

b. A single bedroom, esp. in a hotel. Cf. SINGLE *a.* 11 d.

1963 [see *DOUBLE *sb.* 3 n]. **1967** A. HUNTER *Gently Continental* ii. 12 He goes up to Clooney's room... Number 7 is a small single at the end of the landing. **1973** E. PACE *Any War* I. 5 Yes, sir, the hotel could provide two singles with bath. **1977** B. ALDISS in *Winter's Tales* 23 12 She opened a door to a narrow room...'It's a bit noisy, but it's the only single I've got.'

c. An unmarried or unaccompanied man or woman; a person living alone. Freq. *pl.*

1964 W. & J. BREEDLOVE *Swap Clubs* ii. 57 A *single* is a man or woman who swings alone, without someone to swap. **1967** D. FRANCIS *Blood Sport* viii. 97 Family groups, mostly, and three married couples. No singles except me. **1972** P. A. WHITNEY *Snowfire* (1973) iv. 52, I had met most of the guests... Some were married, but there were a few young singles too. **1980** R. L. DUNCAN *Brimstone* iii. 59 We have a club rule against singles.

6. Special combination, in *pl.*: **singles bar** *U.S.*, a bar which caters esp. for young unmarried people in search of social companions.

1969 S. M. COY *Single Girl's Bk.* vii. 34 Singles bars.. are generally frequented by those under thirty... The good singles bars are crowded, which provides protective covering for the girl who is timid. **1971** D. E. WESTLAKE *I gave at Office* 141, I looked around to find myself in a sort of New York singles' bar without people. **1974** R. M. STROZIER in *Atlantic Monthly* Mar. 44 When I visit the East Side singles bars, some of these upper-class snooty girls look down on you. **1979** *United States 1980/81* (Penguin Travel Guides) 228 Like the Rangoon, the Saloon draws a healthy singles-bar crowd.

single, *a.* Add: **I. 6. a.** Also used for emphasis with a superlative.

1969 [see *LOOP *v.*[1] 7]. **1972** *New Yorker* 8 July 1 (Advt.), The single biggest travel buy to anywhere, ever. **1978** *Church Times* 15 Dec. 11/2 Sir Ronald has also, since last September, been chairman of the Central Board of Finance in Church House, and is thus the single most powerful figure in Church finance.

II. 8. c. Designating a person who is bringing up a child or children without the assistance of a marital partner. Chiefly in phr. *single parent* (*family*).

1969 J. SPREY in B. Schlesinger *One-Parent Family* 16 Stigmatization of the single-parent family, and especially of single parents, does occur. **1976** *Women's Report* Sept./Oct. 7/1 This, coupled with the fact that more women are voluntarily becoming single mothers by refusing to have their babies adopted has caused the government to set up a Cabinet Committee on Family Affairs. **1977** C. FREMLIN *Spider-Orchid* vii. 55 Peggy Summers was having teenage troubles at last, and wasn't managing so marvellously as a single parent after all. **1980** *Times* 24 Jan. 9/8 Gingerbread caters for all categories of single parents; the divorced, separated, widowed, unmarried, or those whose partners may be in hospital or prison.

13. b. Of whisky: pure, not mixed or blended.

1920 *Glasgow Herald* 22 July 4 No man who knows whisky when he tastes it would prefer them [*sc.* advertised blends] to a 'single' whisky. **1958** *Spectator* 27 June 838/1 It would have been before the days of proprietary whiskies; it would be interesting to know which 'single' or 'self' whisky he used and its strength. **1968** I. C. TAYLOR *Highland Whisky* (An Comunn Gaidhealach) 5 It is an excellent dry single malt. **1977** C. MCCULLOUGH *Thorn Birds* vii. 136 Twelve-year-old single-malt Scotch.

III. 17. a. *single act* (*Theatr.*), a performance (orig. in vaudeville) by one entertainer; also, an entertainer who performs unaccompanied; *single anchor* (earlier *fig.* example); *single bond* (*Chem.*), a chemical bond in which the two atoms share one pair of electrons only; *single cream*, cream with a low fat content; *single crown* (*Naut.*), a single crowning given to a knot (see CROWN *v.*[1] 14, CROWNING *vbl. sb.* 4); *single end* (*Sc.*, chiefly Glasgow), a one-roomed flat; *single entry*, (*b*) listing of a title at only one place in a catalogue, bibliography, or index, without cross-references; an entry so created; *single fare*, the charge for conveyance on an outward journey (but not back); *single-jack* (*N. Amer.*), a short hammer used in percussive hand-drilling by one person alone; *single premium*, a sum which covers the entire cost of insurance in a single payment; *single reed* (*Mus.*), a reed or blade of other material that serves as the sounding apparatus of certain wind instruments; *single shot*, used, usu. *attrib.*, with reference to a facility for producing a single event where repeated action is normal, as on an automatic weapon; *single side band* (*Telecommunication*), either of the two side bands normally associated with the carrier of a broadcast transmission; freq. *attrib.* with reference to a method of transmission in which only one side band is transmitted, the other being suppressed along with the carrier; also short for *single side band transmission*; *single ticket*, a ticket entitling a traveller to a single journey outward, as opp. to a return ticket (cf. RETURN *sb.* 1 e in Dict. and Suppl.).

1952 GRANVILLE *Dict. Theatrical Terms* 163 *Single act*, a solo performance in vaudeville, e.g. a ballad singer, a juggler, an acrobat, an impersonator, or a *raconteur*. **1960** B. KEATON *My Wonderful World of Slapstick* v. 89, I went to New York to see if I could get work there on my own. As a single act. That's what vaudeville people called it. **1822** C. ARBUTHNOT *Let.* 2 Sept. (1941) 31, I wish you to keep yrself at single anchor, for shd. the Govt. be broken up, you must hurry to me. [**1889** G. M'GOWAN tr. *Bernthsen's Text-bk Org. Chem.* i. 50 A double bond between two carbon atoms is looser, and therefore more easily broken than a single one.] **1903** WALKER & MOTT tr. *Holleman's Text-bk. Org. Chem.* I. 150 When a single bond between two carbon atoms is converted into a double one, the directions of the affinities of each of the two carbon atoms must undergo an appreciable alteration. **1966** WILLIAMS & FLEMING *Spectrosc. Methods in Org. Chem.* iii. 45 The stretching vibrations of single bonds to hydrogen give rise to the absorption at the high frequency end of the spectrum. **1955** J. G. DAVIS *Dict. Dairying* 320 The manufacture of cream was prohibited during the war but in 1951 sale was permitted for a few weeks. The standards laid down were: single cream 18 per cent. (usually homogenised), double cream 48 per cent. **1962** *Listener* 26 July 155/1, ¼ pint of real single cream. **1979** A. PARKER *Country Recipe Notebk.* viii. 108 Single cream is thin cream for pouring. It will not whip. **1808** Single crown [see *DOUBLE WALL]. **1883** *Man. Seamanship Boys' Training Ships* (Admiralty) (1886) 121 Form a double-wall, single-crowned, then lay the strands by the sides of those in the single-crown. **1897** J. WRIGHT *Scenes Sc. Life* 27 'A single en', or one apartment. **1935** MCARTHUR & LONG *No Mean City* i. 1 Cavity beds are..a feature of the Glasgow slums... The ordinary 'room-and-kitchen' apartment, and even the one-roomed 'single-end', always include a cavity bed or beds. **1981** P. TURNBULL *Deep & Crisp & Even* iv. 60 He took a single end in Maryhill and sent for his wife. **1963** *Guide to Universal Decimal Classification* (B.S.I.) i. 7 Generally speaking, each document gets only one entry in the classified file, and this method of 'single entry' is assumed for the time being. Many UDC users, however, favour a method of 'multiple entry', whereby a document on Harvesting of cereals, for instance, would get an entry under both Cereals and Harvesting. **1976** B. BUCHANAN *Gloss. Indexing Terms* 123 Single entry systems fail to correct completely the separations caused by the application of a citation order..; for this, multiple entry systems are necessary. **1777** P. THICKNESSE *Year's Journey* I. vii. 52, I could not refrain from giving her a double fee, for a single fare. **1841** C. DICKENS *Let.* 14 Sept. (1969) II. 383, I wish you'd take an opportunity..of asking all about the Fares—what a single fare is—what a double fare—what a cabin with child-stowage. **1972** C. FREMLIN *Appointment with Yesterday* i. 11 A small oblong of cardboard... 'Single fare, £1.40' is what it said. **1961** *Press* (Vancouver) 1 Sept. 11 The mechanization of mines in 1890—the replacing of hand-steel, single-jack and double-jack, by drilling machines—had created new problems. **1877** *Cassell's Family Mag.* Jan. 83/2 Net Single and Annual Premiums. **1880** *Encycl. Brit.* XIII. 171/2 We conclude..that the single premium at age 20 for a whole-term assurance of £1 according to the Hm mortality table, reckoning interest at 3 per cent., is £·32886 or 6*s.* 7*d.* **1975** R. L. CARTER *Handbk. Insurance* II. § i.2.8 The single premium bond is essentially an investment contract in which a lump sum is paid to the insurance company at the inception of the policy, and..invested in units. **1883** GROVE *Dict. Mus.* III. 90/1 It is possible to replace it [*sc.* the Double reed] in both these instruments by a single reed of clarinet shape, beating against a small wooden mouthpiece. **1920** U. DAUBENY *Orchestral Wind Instruments* vi. 55 There are no instances of the single reed in Egyptian sculpture, but cylindrical pipes of great age, fitted with single-beating reeds have been found in Greece. **1964** S. MARCUSE *Musical Instr.* 478/1 Single reeds are idioglott or heteroglott... The beating reed is the most common among Western single reeds (the clarinet reed, for example). **1942** *R.A.F. Jrnl.* 3 Oct. 29 We fired three rounds with the Tommy gun from the hip (with the single-shot mechanism). **1971** J. M. SMITH *Digital Logic* iv. 67 The one-shot or single-shot generator is a device for producing a pulse output from a trigger signal input. **1977** 'J. MCVEAN' *Bloodspoor* xx. 263 Hanson switched the Schmeisser regulator to single-shot and started to fire back. **1923** *Proc. IRE* XI. 40 It is of particular importance for long wave radio telephone transmission where the width of a single side-band is so large a fraction of the total frequency range available that the number of independent channels is at best very limited. *Ibid.* 41 The use of single side-band transmission has probably progressed farthest in connection with carrier telephony over wires. **1959** K. HENNEY *Radio Engin. Handbk.* (ed. 5) xviii. 8 In most commercial single-side-band transmitters the SSB signal is generated in an SSB generator at a frequency in the range of 100 to 500 kc. **1976** *Electronics Today Internat.* July 10/3 In areas around cities, these channels are congested and so many stations have changed over to Single Sideband, which gives higher communications efficiency and an extra 48 channels. **1859** *A.B.C. or Alphabetical Railway Guide* Aug. 121 London, Paris, and the Continent... Fares throughout (Single Tickets, available for four days), First Class, 28/0; Second Class, 20/0. **1979** 'J. LE CARRÉ' *Smiley's People* (1980) xvii. 212 He bought a second-class single ticket to Hamburg.

b. *single-boater* (see quot. 1933); *single-decker*, † (*a*) *U.S.* (see quot. 1896); (*b*) an aircraft, tramcar, etc., having only one deck; now usu. a single-decked bus; freq. *attrib.*; *single-hander*, (*a*) an action performed single-handedly or without assistance (in quot. 1877, a chase) (*rare*); (*b*) one who sails a boat single-handed; a single-handed yachtsman; *single-seater* (attrib. uses at sense *18).

1933 S. BRADFORD *Shell-backs* 70 A single boater is a trawler not fishing with a fleet but on its own. **1934** W. WOOD *Fleeters* iv. 59 The single-boaters..far outnumbered the fleeters. **1896** C. H. HASWELL *Reminisc. Octogenarian in N.Y.* xv. 332 James P. Allaire had constructed..a four-story house designed for many tenants... It is what is now termed a 'single-decker', that is, but one suite of rooms on a floor. **1910** *Sphere* 20 Aug. 176/1 The first aeroplane illustrated is the Santos Dumont aeroplane or single-decker. **1930** *Aberdeen Press & Jrnl.* 12 Feb. 6/3, I see that the L.C.C. has been selling off old single-decker tramcars at £5 apiece. **1935** S. BECKETT *Echo's Bones*, The little single-decker. **1935** *Discovery* Feb. 58/2 In these vehicles the main entrance is in front, beside the driver as in many single-decker coaches already on the road. **1954** M. PROCTER *Hell is City* I. i. 11 A red-and-white bus ..was approaching... It was a..single decker. **1962** L. DEIGHTON *Ipcress File* xxx. 196 At the bottom of the street was a single-decker bus. **1976** P. R. WHITE *Planning for Public Transport* iii. 56 The rear-engine layout was also adopted for single-deckers. **1877** *Coursing Calendar Autumn 1876* 217 War Note never seeing the hare, Adventurer fell in for a single-hander of great length, the first-named being drawn ultimately. **1893** [in Dict.]. **1954** H. INNES *Strange Land* I. 18 'There should be two men on board her.' 'Well, this bloke was single-handed.'..'He was a single-hander all right.' **1976** P. HEATON *Single-handers* i. 26 Alain Colas..is a racing singlehander, a competitor. **1916** H. BARBER *Aeroplane Speaks* Pl. xxvi, A 50 h.p. Gnome single-seater. **1972** 'M. YORKE' *Silent Witness* II. ii. 19 Twin chairs were not so bad...But this chair-lift was a single-seater and you rode alone.

18. Used attributively. Also, *single-bar*, *-cause*, *-channel*, *-class*, *-coil*, *-colour*, *-column*, *-crystal*, *-deck*, *-electron*, *-engine*, *-family*, *-issue*, *-language*, *-layer*, *-lens*, *-letter*, *-manual*, *-member* (earlier example), *-morpheme*, *-note*, *-pane*, *-particle*, *-party*, *-pass*, *-person*, *-phase*, *-ply*, *-point*, *-pole*, *-purpose*, *-reed*, *-seat*, *-seater*, *-set*, *-sex*, *-speed*, *-stage*, *-storey*, *-stress*, *-syllable*, *-tier*, *-tube*, *-turn*, *-unit*, *-use*, *-word*; *single-cell protein*, protein derived from a culture of single-celled organisms; *single-electrode* (*Chem.*), with reference to a half-cell considered in isolation; *single-lens reflex* (*camera*) (*Photogr.*), a reflex camera in which the lens that forms the image on the film is also used to provide the image in the viewfinder (by means of a mirror behind the lens that is automatically moved out of the way when the shutter release is operated) (cf. *SLR* s.v. *S 4 a); *single-plate clutch* (see quot. 1940); *single-start* (*Engin.*), designating a screw-thread or worm gear that has one continuous thread along its entire length; *single-vision* (*Ophthalm.*), (of spectacles) of which each lens is a single optical element; not bifocal, etc.; *single-wire*, designating an electrical wiring system in which current is carried by one wire, the return being provided by the chassis or frame of the apparatus or installation or the earth.

1964 *Amer. Speech* XXXIX. 104 There is a break—in speech, a single-bar juncture; in writing, a comma or dash—between the noun and its juncture. **1966** 'M. Halliday' *Wicked as Devil* iv. 36 Helen switched on a single-bar electric fire. **1977** P. Johnson *Enemies of Society* ix. 127 Marx, by contrast, has a single-cause theory: all the evils of society arise from private property; abolish that, and they will disappear. **1968** Mateles & Tannenbaum *Single-Cell Protein* i. 7 Some may wonder where the name 'Single-Cell Protein' came from and why it was adopted. It was invented at M.I.T. in May 1966, as a result of the insistent prodding of Professor Carroll Wilson. **1970** *Daily Tel.* (Colour Suppl.) 19 June 14 Single cell protein is one of the most 'exotic' of various new food sources. **1977** Single cell protein [see *single-celled*, sense 19 below]. **1962** A. Nisbett *Technique Sound Studio* ii. 33 Single-channel 'monophonic' recordings. **1977** *Proc. R. Soc. Med.* LXX. 382/1 Single-channel extracochlear stimulation will only provide low frequency information. **1967** *N.Y. Herald Tribune* (Internat. ed.) 11–12 Feb. 3/7 (Advt.), Walk on or drive on to one of these fine ultra-modern single-class ships for an overnight crossing in absolute comfort. **1977** *Listener* 17 Mar. 347/3 They built..for the propagation of middle-class values..a vast process of specialised, single-class development. **1962** Simpson & Richards *Physical Princ. Junction Transistors* iii. 38 One pass of the specimen is then equivalent to several passes in a single-coil apparatus and the removal of impurities is accelerated. **1935** B. Rackham in *Chinese Art* (Burlington Mag. Monographs) 20 The beauty of celadon, turquoise, crackled white and other single-colour glazes. **1964** *Gloss. Letterpress Rotary Printing Terms* (*B.S.I.*) 19 *Single colour unit*, a section of the press embodying one printing couple to print one side of the web in one colour. **1960** *Guardian* 9 Nov. 8/3 The 'News Chronicle'..charged for display advertising at the rate of £13 per single column inch. **1976** J. Bingham *God's Defector* iv. 43 A single-column picture of himself at the church door. **1956** *Nature* 14 Jan. 77/2 In fundamental research, much work is being done on single-crystal specimens, whereby grain-boundary effects and some other variables are eliminated. **1955** *Notes on Science in USA 1954* (Brit. Commonwealth Scientific Office, N. Amer.) 29 The large number of experiments that are now being performed on single crystal specimens. **1929** *Times* 2 Nov. 4/7 The chassis, with rather lighter driving axles and springs is sold for single-deck and coach operation. **1967** M. Chandler *Ceramics in Mod. World* ii. 84 Single-deck tunnel kilns. **1913** *Jrnl. Amer. Chem. Soc.* XXXV. 24 No satisfactory method has been found for determining the absolute magnitude of any single electrode potential. **1965** Phillips & Williams *Inorg. Chem.* I. ix. 312 It has proved very difficult, some believe impossible, to measure absolute single-electrode potentials. **1944** Stewart & Wilson *Rec. Adv. Physical & Inorg. Chem.* (ed. 7) 384 It is probable that single electron bonds..enter into the *average* final structure for diborane. **1968** M. S. Livingston *Particle Physics* iii. 39 The spectra of single-electron atoms such as He^+ and Li^{+7}. **1942** *R.A.F. Jrnl.* 27 June 1 A service between London and Paris with single-engine modified Service aircraft. **1978** R. Ludlum *Holcroft Covenant* xxxvii. 423 A small single-engine plane circled in the night sky above the flat pasture in Chambéry. **1967** R. Ardrey *Territorial Imperative* iii. 93 Unlike any other ape and like few monkeys, the gibbon lives in a single-family group, paired on a territory usually for life. **1980** *Washington Post* 4 Dec. DC1, 49 buildings containing about 600 units are being transfered from rental status or private single-family ownership to condominiums. **1977** *Time* 19 Dec. 29/3 The right-to-lifers are single-issue individuals... They vote on what he or she says about abortion. **1946** H. Jacob *On Choice of Common Lang.* 39 Four single-language frequency lists. **1978** *Language* LIV. 8 Table 2 shows the number of entries which fulfill the structural conditions for apical displacement, after we eliminate single-language entries and the disqualified ones. **1940** *Chambers's Techn. Dict.* 772/1 *Single-layer winding*, a type of armature winding in which there is only one coil-side per slot. **1946** *Nature* 21 Sept. 422/1 The reflectors consist of single-layer and multiple-layer films. **1936** *Discovery* Aug. 237/1 The camera..has 4½ times the stereoscopic parallax of the single-lens and five-lens cameras. **1940** A. L. M. Sowerby *Wall's Dict. Photogr.* (ed. 15) 547 In a single-lens reflex, pressure on the release first lifts the mirror.., and then releases the focal-plane shutter. **1955** T. A. Longmore *Med. Photogr.* (ed. 5) iii. 374 Being a single lens reflex camera there is a complete absence of parallax, so that the image seen on the focusing screen is exactly the same as that which will be recorded on the film. **1957** *Encycl. Brit.* XVII. 825/2 A single-lens camera may be provided with a beam splitter..,giving two adjacent photographs on the normal picture area. **1962** L. S. Sasieni *Optical Dispensing* xiii. 334 Apart from the single-lens magnifiers..there are a number of telescopic units. **1977** L. Gaunt *Olympus Bk.* 8 The final part of the 35 mm single-lens reflex viewing system is the eye-piece lens, focused on the viewfinder screen via the reflecting surfaces of the prism. **1878** H. MacColl in *Proc. Lond. Math. Soc.* X. 26 The monomial (or single-letter) statements. **1964** D. Ward in D. Abercrombie et al. *Daniel Jones* 393 For the convenience of readers not familiar with Cyrillic a single-letter transliteration system is given. **1880** Grove *Dict. Mus.* II. 591/2 Soon after the Restoration, Ralph Dallam built an organ for St. George's Chapel, Windsor... It was a single-manual organ only. **1978** *Early Music* Oct. 585/1 An Italian single-manual harpsichord bearing a spurious inscription dated 1740 but actually of earlier date. **1884** E. W. Hamilton *Diary* 2 Dec. (1972) II. 746 Lord Hampden..likes the system of single-member Districts, for which he has long been an advocate. **1956** J. Lotz in L. White *Frontiers of Knowl.* xiv. 221 The single-word, or better, single-morpheme sentences of the young child..cannot be analyzed into phonemes nor combined into sentences. **1949** L. Feather *Inside Be-bop* i. 6 The single-note solo style was a complete departure from the pattern of solos in chords established by..conventional jazz guitarists. **1922** Joyce *Ulysses* 698 Water closet..with opaque singlepane oblong window. **1892** A. M. Worthington *Dynamics of Rotation* ii. 20 Any rigid body may be regarded as made up of such ideal single-particle systems. **1970** G. K. Woodgate *Elem. Atomic Struct.* v. 87 For *N* non-interacting electrons with no spin–orbit interaction we find it convenient to go back to the single-particle representation. **1941** *Pacific Affairs* XIV. 76 The emergence of a fully totalitarian 'single-party State'. **1979** E. Norman *Christianity & World Order* v. 66 Tanzania—a country with a rigidly enforced socialist collectivization and a single-party constitution. **1964** S. Crawford *Basic Engin. Processes* iii. 93 The vertical plate is tack-welded in position..and then finally welded by either the single-pass or the multiple-pass techniques. **1969** *Computers & Humanities* IV. 43 Clearly, there should be much less occasion for careless errors and omissions in a multiple-pass system like Regener's than in a single-pass system like IML. **1957** *Loneliness* (Women's Group on Public Welfare) iii. 41 The number of single-person households..increased by 104 per cent between 1931 and 1951. **1900** *Jrnl. Brit. Inst. Electr. Engin.* XXIX. 246 The motor is being supplied with single-phase currents. **1946** *Nature* 31 Aug. 307/2 The electrolytic polishing of multi-phase metals is usually more difficult than that of single-phase metals owing to differing properties..of the different phases. **1979** *Dictionaries* I. 31 Editors are not restricted to single-phrase descriptions. **1926** *Motor Man.* (ed. 26) iii. 49 (*caption*) Single-plate clutch, showing internal details. **1940** *Chambers's Techn. Dict.* 772/2 *Single-plate clutch*, a friction clutch..in which the disc-shaped or annular driven member, fabric-faced, is pressed against a similar face on the driving member by springs. **1970** K. Ball *Fiat 600, 600D Autobk.* v. 45/1 The clutch, common to both the 600 and 600D series engines, is a conventional dry, single plate type with a spring cushioned hub as part of the driven plate. **1957** Simpson & Weir *Weaver's Craft* iii. 25 A tightly packed weft of thick hand-spun or single-ply rug wool. **1967** *Jane's Surface Skimmer Systems 1967–68* 13/2 A segmented skirt of single-ply neoprene-nylon fabric. **1935, 1959** Single-point [see *instantaneous *a.* 1 d]. **1979** *North Sea Progress* (Shell Internat. Petroleum Co.) 6 The field will be served by tankers at single-point mooring buoys to take the oil production. **1931** *Illustr. London News* 29 Aug. 342/3 The electrical system is 12 volts, with single-pole wiring. **1975** G. J. King *Audio Handbk.* x. 223 The slope of a single pole RC network always ultimately assumes a rate close to 6 dB/octave. **1919** *Daily Mail Year Bk.* 112/2 Many thousands of these are in service; to which the term 'single-purpose machines' is applied. **1943** J. S. Huxley *TVA* v. 27 The single-purpose costs which can be directly allocated to one or other of the functions. **1971** *Fremdsprachen* XV. 46 Each single-purpose use may be justified on its own, but the complete effect of piecemeal development can be chaos. **1931** G. Jacob *Orchestral Technique* iii. 23 *The Clarinet* (single-reed instrument). **1976** D. Munrow *Instr. Middle Ages & Renaissance* vi. 39/4 The French word *chalumeau* has been applied to the shawm as well as a detached double-reed bagpipe chanter..and the single-reed precursor of the clarinet. **1946** *Nature* 5 Oct. 469/1 The aircraft rocket enabling a single-seat fighter to deliver a salvo equal in hitting power to the broadside from a small cruiser. **1967** *Jane's Surface Skimmer Systems 1967–68* 8/1 It has built a single-seat vehicle designated Naviplane N 101. **1910** R. Loraine *Diary* 10 Apr. in W. Loraine *Robert Loraine* (1938) vi. 104 A small single-seater monoplane. **1930** *Engineering* 7 Mar. 316/1 Following upon a recent order for five Bristol Bulldog all-steel single-seater fighter aeroplanes, the Latvian Government has placed a further order..for seven additional Bulldog machines. **1973** J. Leasor *Host of Extras* i. 21 In 1911..with a single-seater body..a Rolls-Royce covered a quarter-mile stretch at Brooklands at 101 miles an hour. **1961** *Guardian* 11 Dec. 7/7 Higher salaries..have made a single-set drama..cost more nearly $100,000. **1971** J. Elsom *Theatre outside London* x. 181 Low-cast, single-set comedies, with the occasional mystery play or classic revival. **1939** A. H. Whipple *Educ. up to Fifteen Years* 36 Experiments should be conducted in single-sex schools to ascertain..whether or not the education of girls should differ in important respects from that of boys. **1980** *Times* 19 Feb. 2 Applications to Oriel, the only remaining men's single-sex college, are down again. **1958** M. L. Hall *Newnes Compl. Amat. Photogr.* ii. 32 Single-speed rotary or single-leaf shutters, placed either in front of or behind the lens. **1975** *Language for Life* (Dept. Educ. & Sci.) vi. 95 Unfortunately, if most of their reading is of the single-speed kind, children will be habituated to becoming single-speed readers. **1922** Glazebrook *Dict. Appl. Physics* II. 891/2 Single-stage amplifiers. **1945** H. D. Smyth *Gen. Acct. Devel. Atomic Energy Mil. Purposes* iv. 40 Single-stage separators had effected the enrichment of the U-235 on a laboratory scale to about the degree predicted theoretically. **1956** *Spaceflight* I. 24/1 The first stage resembles the Viking rocket which attained a record altitude (for single-stage rockets) of 158·4 miles in 1954. **1964** S. Crawford *Basic Engin. Processes* xiv. 301 On a single-start thread the lead and the pitch are identical. **1975** Bram & Downs *Manuf. Technol.* iv. 120 The depth of a single-start thread stands in a definite relationship to its pitch. **1947** A. Waring *Approach to Better Housing* ii. 33 While not advocating the provision of single-storey dwellings for large families..nevertheless these can be planned for small families and aged people..quite as successfully as the two-storey dwelling. **1970** D. Goldrich et al. in I. L. Horowitz *Masses in Lat. Amer.* v. 183 They are housed predominantly in single-story dwellings on individual plots. **1964** C. Barber *Linguistic Change in Present-Day Eng.* iv. 86 The word *greatcoat* is a modern example of a transitional state between a double-stress and a single-stress form. **1959** Wimsatt & Beardsley in *Publ. Mod. Lang. Assoc. Amer.* LXXIV. 595 The single-syllable foot occurs in lines that sound like this: 'Weave, weave, the sunlight in your hair'. **1959** *Daily Tel.* 6 Mar. 21/3 The Ministry has suggested that single-tier highway authorities with less than 200,000 people in their areas should be set up in Greater London. **1977** *Whitaker's Almanack 1978* 624 For the purpose of local government Northern Ireland has a system of 26 single-tier district councils. **1904** A. B. F. Young *Compl. Motorist* xi. 247 There are some single-tube pneumatic tyres in which the whole of the fabric is constructed in one piece. **1935** *Discovery* Feb. 44/1 (*caption*) Guide-cradle for launching single-tube rockets. **1963** *Gloss. Mining Terms* (*B.S.I.*) iii. 13 *Single-tube core barrel*, the simplest core barrel, having only a single cylindrical tube. **1940** *Chambers's Techn. Dict.* 772/2 *Single-turn coil*, an armature coil consisting of a single turn of copper bar. **1962** Corson & Lorrain *Introd. Electromagn. Fields* vi. 236 We consider single-turn coils for simplicity. **1936** *Discovery* Aug. 237/1 The world's largest single unit multi-lens aerial mapping camera. **1973** *Tucson* (Ariz.) *Daily Citizen* 22 Aug. 27/2 We have passed the time when we can afford the luxury of building single-unit homes. **1959** *Gloss. Terms Packaging* (*B.S.I.*) 43 *Single-use tube*, a tube with sufficient contents for one use only. **1969** *Computers & Humanities* III. 138 The heavy-duty Selectric typewriter also requires frequent adjustments for uniform impressions, plus a single-use ribbon for publication output. **1962** L. S. Sasieni *Optical Dispensing* vii. 174 Logically a single-vision lens prescribed for reading would be the most comfortable. **1971** *Optometry Today* 24 This team is capable of examining, prescribing, fabricating and dispensing single-vision lenses, mounted in frames, on the spot. **1902** *Encycl. Brit.* XXXIII. 228/2 In 1892..he established communication between Lavernock Point and an island called Flat Holme..by placing at these positions insulated single-wire circuits, earthed at both ends. **1913** V. B. Lewes *Oil Fuel* iv. 108 The single-wire system must not be adopted for any part of the electric lighting installation in vessels carrying petroleum. **1907** W. James *Pragmatism* vii. 239 All the great single-word answers to the world's riddle, such as God, the One, Reason, Law, [etc.]. **1964** R. H. Robins *Gen. Linguistics* 284 Compound verbal expressions..fulfil some of the semantic functions of the single-word tense forms of other languages.

19. *single-barrelled* (earlier and *fig.* examples), *-bedded, -celled, -coloured, -decked, -ended, -engined, -purposed, -reeded, -roomed, -sexed, -sided, -spaced, -storeyed* (*-storied*), *-syllabled, -worded*; *single-stranded* (*Biochem.*), (of a nucleic acid) consisting of only one sequence of nucleotides; hence *single-strandedness*.

1821 E. Baker *Remarks on Rifle Guns* (ed. 8) 114 The average weight of a single-barrelled gun should be from 6lbs to 6lbs 4oz. **1880** 'Mark Twain' *Speeches* (1923) 83 He possessed a single-barrelled fame before; he will possess a double-barrelled fame now. **1788** J. Woodforde *Diary* 20 May (1927) III. 27, I had a very good single bedded Room to night. **1892** I. Zangwill *Childr. Ghetto* III. 188 Here single-bedded cabins could be had as low as fourpence a night. **1972** 'G. North' *Sergeant Cluff rings True* xix. 146 The single-bedded ward had its memories... A constable..watched the bed in which the Sergeant had once lain wounded. **1899** W. James *Talks to Teachers* xiv. 163 In biology, we used to have interminable discussion as to whether certain single-celled organisms were animals or vegetables, until Haeckel introduced the new appercep-tive name of Protista, which ended the disputes. **1977** G. Scott *Hot Pursuit* xii. 105 Single cell protein is produced by single-celled animals: bacteria, yeasts, fungi, that sort of thing. **1703** tr. H. van Oosten *Dutch Gardener* II. iv. 60, I think the single colour'd to be the best..because the tulip that is already changed and striped, doth easily mix her colours together; and this is the reason why the single colours that come from them, have not so strong a colour as those from the single coloured ones. **1940** W. Stevens in *Accent* Autumn 12 The single-colored, colorless, primitive. **1869** Single-decked [see *double-deck]. **1972** 'G. North' *Sergeant Cluff rings True* xiv. 112 The single-decked bus..laboured up the hill. **1952** *Proc. IRE* XL. 11/1 Since the output is single ended, the feedback can be made directly from the midpoint of the output stage to a preceding single-ended stage. **1975** *Official Transcript Techn. Papers Ann. Nat. Cable Television Assoc. Convention* (New Orleans) 24 Investigations were conducted on an operating cable television system to explore methods of increasing the channel capacity of broadband single-ended amplifiers. **1964** *Oceanogr. & Marine Biol.* II. 47 Transportation was by means of single-engined aircraft. **1978** R. V. Jones *Most Secret War* xxxiv. 301 It happened that a unit of single-engined fighters had been formed in the preceding weeks by Major Hajo Herrmann. **1905** J. London *Let.* 4 Apr. (1966) 169 You and I are both fighters, and single-purposed fighters too. **1933** 'R. Crompton' *William—the Rebel* viii. 164 They were all large, single-purposed, unsmiling men. **1920** U. Daubeny *Orchestral Wind Instruments* vi. 55 Somewhat similar rude single-reeded pipes are still used by Italian shepherds and Roman pifferari. **1911** G. B. Shaw *Getting Married* 129 Very few couples can live in a single-roomed tenement without exchanging blows quite frequently. **1903** —— *Man & Superman* iii. 112 She [*sc.* Nature] created him in order to produce something better than the single-sexed process can produce. **1934** L. B. Pekin *Progressive Schools* iv. 62, I cannot imagine any teacher who has given co-education a fair trial..ever returning to a single-sexed school. **1937** *Discovery* Sept. 284/1 Single-sided, long-playing, unbreakable durium-type records so popular a few years ago. **1977** *Gramophone* Aug. 262/3 Frank Andrews (London, NW10) points out that Zonophones were single-sided until June 1911. **1956** *Nature* 18 Feb. 334/2 A number of strains [of lucerne] planted as single-spaced plants in the field. **1959** J. Thurber *Years with Ross* xi. 191 Ross sat down at his typewriter..and wrote..a remarkable five-page single-spaced letter. **1975** T. ALLBEURY *Special Collection* xv. 99 A foolscap sheet in single-spaced typing. **1835** J. E. ALEXANDER *Sk. in Portugal* v. 113 By the side of the road to Santarem was the quarter of Colonel Shaw, a long single-storied peasant's house in a vineyard. **1967** *Antiquaries Jrnl.* XLVII. 275 The hall probably rose clear above this east room, which may have been roofed as a single-storeyed lean-to. **1954** *Proc. R. Soc.* A. CCXXIII. 94 Most of these earlier formulations..have involved single stranded structures and must be rejected. **1964** G. H. HAGGIS et al. *Introd. Molecular Biol.* iv. 79 The RNA component of the virus is a long single-stranded nucleic acid chain. **1978** *BioSystems* X. 102/1 Double stranded DNA would be unsuitable because, unlike single-stranded RNA it cannot fold up on its own to form specific and complex 3D structures. **1974** *Nature* 5 Apr. 507/1 They..exhibit greater buoyant densities due to the presence of RNA sequences and/or some degree of single strandedness. **1890** W. JAMES *Princ. Psychol.* I. xiv. 558 The 'cue' was given by single-syllabled words called out by an assistant. **1948** E. SITWELL *Notebk. on Shakespeare* vi. 72 In such lines [from *King Lear*]..the single-syllabled words take on the hugeness of those new-made stones that Deucalion and Pyrrha, the Deluge being over, found and cast behind their backs. *a* **1832** J. BENTHAM *Logic* vii, in *Wks.* (1843) VIII. 252/1 Finding a more appropriate single-worded denomination for the species. **1893** W. MINTO *Logic* I. ii. 68 Whether this is single-worded or many-worded is..a grammatical question.

20. a. *single-tuned* adj. (*Electronics*), having a single tuned circuit between two active devices.

1947 F. E. TERMAN *Radio Engin.* (ed. 3) vii. 346 The band width in the case of an amplifier system employing double-tuned circuits is defined in the same manner as for a system employing single-tuned circuits. **1975** D. G. FINK *Electronics Engineers' Handbk.* XIII. 43 The two common types [of tuned interstage] are the single- and double-tuned interstage.

b. Also with vbl. sbs., as *single-boating*, *-manning*, *-spacing*.

1934 W. WOOD *Fleeters* iv. 59 Men who are only used to Iceland and single-boatin' aren't any good at this fleetin' job. **1965** *Times* 22 Oct. 8/7 The proposal that single manning of locomotives should be introduced within a year or two. **1973** *Guardian* 31 Dec. 13/8 London Transport..has launched..single-manning... But the single-manned buses..take up to five times as long at stops. **1956** F. C. AVIS *Bookman's Conc. Dict.* 273/1 *Single spacing*, the style of typewriting in which the lines of characters follow immediately after each other without any interlinear spacing, equivalent to 'Solid' typesetting. **1958** E. NEWBY *Short Walk in Hindu Kush* ii. 21 A great spate of letters..neatly typed in single spacing. **1978** *Church Times* 21 July 5/4 A letter of more than two pages in single-spacing.

c. With vb. *single-space*.

1961 *Guardian* 6 Feb. 9/5 Press releases would be single-spaced to save paper. **1963** D. HEYES *12th of Never* (1964) i. 8 He..continued typing..and..single-spaced the final line to squeeze it in.

single, *v.*[1] Add: **8. c.** With *up*: to cast off all turns of rope except one. Also *intr. Naut.*

1900 J. C. CANTWELL *Diary* 17 May in *Rep. Operations U.S. Revenue Steamer Nunivak* (1904) iv. 57 The lines by which the *Nunivak* was held to the shore were singled up. **1925** R. CLEMENTS *Gipsy of Horn* vi. 103 Our moorings had been singled up. **1959** C. S. FORESTER *Hunting Bismarck* 8 Already sailors at the lines were singling up and then casting off. **1966** T. PYNCHON *Crying of Lot 49* ii. 31 The little submarine..was at the quai, singling up all lines.

9. d. *Baseball.* Of a batter: to hit a single (sense *3 h); to make a one-base hit. Also *trans.*, by singling to enable (another player) to reach home base.

1916 *Chicago Tribune* 7 Oct. 13/1 In the ninth, the first man up singled. **1949** *Clarke County Democrat* (Grove Hill, Alabama) 22 Sept. 2/5 The first St. Michael batter singled. **1966** *N.Y. Times* (Internat. ed.) 22 Apr. 12/1 Felipe Alou singled in the first inning off Ray Culp. **1970** *Globe & Mail* (Toronto) 28 Sept. 19/3 Adolfo Phillips singled home Ron Brand in the 11th inning. **1978** *N.Y. Times* 30 Mar. D 19/4 In the third, Ken Henderson doubled, John Stearns singled and it was 4–0.

single-bli·nd, *a.* [f. SINGLE *a.*, after *DOUBLE(-)BLIND *a.*] Applied to a test or experiment conducted by one person on another in which information about the test that may lead to bias in the results is concealed from one of the parties.

1963 *Amer. Jrnl. Psychiatry* CXX. 67/1 The single-blind study showed relief of symptoms with mephenoxalone in 3 of 9 patients. **1976** *Sci. Amer.* Jan. 8/3 The test was not even single-blind. **1978** *Nature* 20 Apr. 729/1 The studies were performed open or single-blind, in most cases with randomised placebo controls. **1981** *Brit. Med. Jrnl.* 11 July 122/2 If the identity of the treatment is concealed only from the assessor then the trial is single-masked or single-blind... The term 'single-blind' has also been applied to trials in which only the patient is in the dark, although this is not nearly so important as the assessor being in the dark.

single grave. *Archæol.* [f. SINGLE *a.* 17, 18: tr. Du. *enkelgraf* single grave.] A barrow-grave containing the remains of only one person. Freq. *attrib.*, *spec.* (esp. with initial capitals) designating a culture characterized by individual burial which first flourished in northern Germany and Scandinavia during the later Neolithic Age, or representatives of this.

[**1898** S. MÜLLER in *Aarb. f. nord Oldk.* 157 (*heading*) De jydske Enkeltgraver fra Stenalderen.] **1936** J. G. D. CLARK *Mesolithic Settlement of Northern Europe* ii. 73 The triangular-sectioned flake arrowhead..is abundant in passage-graves and occurs in single-graves. **1937** E. V. GORDON tr. *Shetelig & Falk's Scand. Arch.* v. 66 It can be shown that the single-grave people, with their characteristic battle-axes and their own pottery, came from..central Europe. **1954** S. PIGGOTT *Neolithic Cultures* xii. 378 In Denmark the Single-grave invasion takes place after the LG IV marine transgression. **1955** *Univ. Lond. Inst. Archaeol. Ann. Rep.* XI. 39 The discovery at Ohlenburg,..of a devolved Single-Grave beaker. **1957** V. G. CHILDE *Dawn Europ. Civilization* (ed. 6) ix. 160 Archaeologically these graziers are known only by little cemeteries of barrows, and so they are termed the Single Grave folk. **1963** S. PIGGOTT in Foster & Alcock *Culture & Environment* iv. 60 Glasbergen and Van der Waals have shown the Single Grave element to be represented by their Footed Beakers, with an absolute date of *c.* 2200 B.C. **1970** BRAY & TRUMP *Dict. Archaeol.* 212/2 This [burial] rite..links the Single-Grave cultures with the great Corded Ware-Battleaxe complex.

single-handed, *a.* Add: **2. a.** Also passing into *adv.* (Later examples.)

1900 J. SLOCUM *Sailing Alone around World* xxi. 272 On the 4th of June, 1898, the *Spray* cleared from the United States consulate, and her license to sail single-handed, even round the world, was returned to her for the last time. **1939** G. B. SHAW *Geneva* I. 4, I have to do it singlehanded too: I havnt even an office boy to help me. **1970** G. M. FRASER *General danced at Dawn* 144 Lance-Corporal Michael O'Leary, who took on crowds of Germans singlehanded.

singlehandedly *adv.* (later examples).

1964 *Duckett's Reg.* Mar. 41/2 America's most famous Franciscan, who almost singlehandedly Christianised America's Pacific Coast. **1979** *N.Y. Rev. Bks.* 25 Oct. 10/1 Barbara Underwood..boasts that she singlehandedly made *one quarter of a million dollars* for the cult.

single-line, *a.* Add: **1.** Also, of or pertaining to things ranged in a single line; spec. *single-line traffic* (see quot. 1954).

1924 *Beaver* (Winnipeg) Aug. 410 In the extreme north, single-line hitching [of dogs to sleds], and fan hitching is in general use. **1937** *Burlington Mag.* Feb. 93/2 The National Gallery led the way..towards the open, single- or double-line hanging which is now the rule. **1954** *Gloss. Highway Engin. Terms* (*B.S.I.*) 54 *Single-line traffic*, traffic constrained to movement in one direction in a single traffic lane. **1967** G. F. FIENNES *I tried to run Railway* i. 3, I had learned by heart the Block Regulations for double and single lines, the Guard's Rules and the Rules of Single Line Working. **1967** E. LEMARCHAND *Death of Old Girl* xx. 226 There was a bad smash and a big pile-up... It was an hour before they got even single-line traffic going again. **1970** O. JOHN *Diamond Dress* iii. 39 Part of the autostrada is down to single line traffic... Road repairs.

single-o, *sb.*, *a.*, and *adv. U.S. slang* (chiefly *Criminals'*). [f. SINGLE *a.* 1; cf. O *int.* 3.]

A. *sb.* **a.** In gaming: ? the number one. **b.** A crime perpetrated without an assistant. Also, a solitary or single person, a loner; *spec.* a criminal who works alone.

1916 H. L. WILSON *Somewhere in Red Gap* vi. 262 She exposed some very distressing facts about his [*sc.* her husband's] nature the time she put five apiece on the three numbers and the single-o come up. **1930** R. CHADWICK in *Liberty* 5 July 20/2, I have my first experience in single-o jobs... The first single-o is a street heist. **1931** G. IRWIN *Amer. Tramp & Underworld Slang* 170 *Single O*, one working a lone 'game' or 'racket'. One travelling alone for preference. **1942** BERREY & VAN DEN BARK *Amer. Thes. Slang* §461/3 *Single O*, who who works without a confederate.

B. *adj.* Solitary, lone; unaccompanied; *spec.* of (one who engages in) criminal activity without an accomplice.

1930 [see the sb. above]. **1950** *Harper's Mag.* Feb. 71/2 There are 'single-o' heist-men, such as the one known in the papers as Slick Willie, who has robbed large and well-protected banks single-handed, but the vast majority of the brotherhood work in mobs. **1955** D. W. MAURER in *Publ. Amer. Dial. Soc.* XXIV. 83 He [*sc.* a lone pickpocket] is usually referred to as a *single o tool*, a *single handed tool*, or a *single o cannon*.

C. *adv.* Alone; independently; without an accomplice.

1948 *Even. Bull.* (Philadelphia) 7 Apr. 39/7 Instead of working single-o as was his custom. Ernie used an accomplice to drive the getaway car. **1955** D. W. MAURER in *Publ. Amer. Dial. Soc.* XXIV. 100 He's a guy that will muzzle around single o. **1962** 'K. ORVIS' *Damned & Destroyed* xii. 83 Little Faysy wants to go dream-streeting single-o.

singlet. Add: **3. a.** *Physics* and *Chem.* A single line in a spectrum, not part of a multiplet; an atomic or molecular energy level or state possessing (in the case of fine structure) zero electronic spin and orbital angular momenta giving only one value of the quantum number *J*, or (in the case of hyperfine structure) zero electronic and nuclear angular momenta, giving only one value of the quantum number *F*; a molecular state in which all electron spins are paired. Freq. *attrib.*

1920 *Astrophysical Jrnl.* LII. 2 An investigation of the Doppler effect led Stark to the conclusion that the parhelium (singlet) series are due to electronic disturbances in helium atoms which have lost two electrons. **1922** *Phil. Trans. R. Soc.* A. CCXXIII. 137 In the arc spectra of the alkaline-earth elements, in addition to triplet series, there are series of singlets and also certain 'intercombination' lines. **1928** *Proc. R. Soc.* A. CXVII. 147 The general equations of type (18) apply to orthohelium (considered as a singlet system) as well as parhelium. **1934, 1937** [see *INTERCOMBINATION]. **1972** DEPUY & CHAPMAN *Molec. Reactions & Photochem.* iii. 33 Molecular states with all electrons paired are called singlet states. **1977** *Nature* 3 Nov. 15/3 A number of papers dealt with experimental techniques, especially interesting were those on the use of dye lasers for excitation of singlet oxygen.

b. *Particle Physics.* A multiplet (sense *b) of one sub-atomic particle.

1937 *Physical Rev.* LI. 119/2 For an element of the mass [*formula follows*] certain states in which the neutrons are in the doublet, the protons in the triplet state, exactly coincides [*sic*] in approximation (1) with a state in which the neutrons are in the quartet, the protons in the singlet state. **1961, 1962** [see *OCTET, OCTETTE 3 c]. **1977** *Nature* 21 July 202/1 Before the advent of charm in 1976 all known mesons were found to come in multiplets of 9 (nonets) and all known baryons in groups of 1, 8 or 10 (singlets, octets or decuplets).

single tax. *Econ.* [f. SINGLE *a.*: tr. Fr. *impôt unique.*] **a.** A tax on that part of land value known as unearned profit (*produit net*), proposed by François Quesnay (1694–1774) and favoured by the Physiocrats. (See esp. quot. 1931.)

1853 J. R. MCCULLOCH *Sketch Life & Writings F. Quesnay* in *Treat. & Ess. Econ. Policy* 436 It is needless to make any remarks on the exploded notion of Quesnay with respect to agriculture being the only source of wealth, or on his project for consolidating all taxes into a single tax (*l'impôt unique*), to be laid direct on land! **1880** *Nation* 12 Aug. 118/2 All this is accomplished by adopting the *impôt unique* of the physiocrats—the single tax on land—provided the tax be high enough to leave the cultivator nothing but wages [etc.]. **1931** *Amer. Econ. Rev.* XXI. 607 The peculiar characteristic of the Physiocrats' single tax is to be found in the idea of *produit net*. It was not essentially a single tax on land at all. It was a single tax on surplus agricultural products. **1966** A. GILPIN *Dict. Econ. Terms* 185 The Physiocrats..favoured a single tax—an 'impôt unique'—on land, arguing that the cultivation of land was the only work really productive of wealth.

b. A tax on land value as the sole source of public revenue, proposed by Henry George (1839–97). Freq. *attrib.*

1879 H. GEORGE *Progress & Poverty* VIII. iv. 383 The effect of substituting for the manifold taxes now imposed a single tax on the value of land would hardly lessen the number of conscious taxpayers, for the division of land now held on speculation would much increase the number of tax payers. **1891** *Century Mag.* Sept. 795/1 Here we have the core and essence of the single-tax philosophy—confiscation. **1917** *Amer. City* Apr. 384/1 May I..call serious attention to land value taxation—the single tax—which I believe should be regarded as..a satisfactory and just system of revenue. **1926** *Daily Colonist* (Victoria, B.C.) 14 July 2/5 The single tax method of taxation was praised enthusiastically. **1933** H. G. WELLS *Shape of Things to Come* II. 244 Utah had become a practically autonomous Single-Tax State. **1944** G. B. SHAW *Everybody's Political What's What?* xxxvii. 322 If he proves that he knows as much about economic rent as Thomas De Quincey and Henry George did..he must not be asked whether his conclusions are the Conservative ones of De Quincey, the Single Tax of George, or the revolutionary ones of Marx. **1950** *World-Herald Mag.* (Omaha) 26 Mar. 9/2 The once prominent single tax movement, no longer a red hot political issue, is one which has continued on unobtrusively. **1979** *Vole* 8 Nov. 25/1 His [*sc.* George's] Single Tax would confiscate, not the land, but the rents presently paid to owners.

c. *Single Tax Party*, the English name for a Danish political party inspired by the economic principles of Henry George (see sense b above).

1950 *Manch. Guardian* 15 Sept. 6/2 The most remarkable feature, however, was the rise of the Danish single-tax party (disciples of Henry George who call themselves the Union of Justice). **1961** *Denmark* 91/2 Of new parties the Communist Party and the Single-Tax Party proved to be durable. **1970** W. G. JONES *Denmark* vi. 134 A new party called Danmarks Retsforbund—normally known in English as the Single Tax Party..has had parliamentary representation and is still in existence.

Hence **single-taxer** (also with initial capitals), a believer in the advantages of a single tax; a member of the Single Tax Party.

1889 *20th Cent.* (N.Y.) 6 Apr. 102/1 He says that is a fair question which no Single-taxer ever answers, but that if it is evaded the whole single-tax theory vanishes. **1934** B. RUSSELL *Freedom & Organization 1814–1914* xi. 124 Both Socialists and Single-Taxers derived their proposals from him [*sc.* Ricardo]. **1941** [see *JEHOVAH 2]. **1968** *Times Lit. Suppl.* 25 Apr. 436/5 A front-parlour discussion group that included communists, spiritualists, psychic researchers and single taxers.

singleton[2]. Add: **2. b.** *Bibliogr.* (See quot. 1952.)

1952 J. CARTER *ABC for Book-Collectors* 166 *Singleton*, a jargon word (of recent origin in this sense), meaning a single leaf, where a conjugate pair would be expected... A singleton will either be the surviving leaf where the other has been severed for insertion elsewhere, or the severed half in its inset position, or an extra leaf. **1957** [see *BIFOLIUM]. **1975** *Anglo-Saxon Eng.* IV. 116 Leaves 5 and 8 in quire 43 are singletons.

4. a. A child resulting from a single rather than a multiple birth.

1931 A. GESELL in C. Murchison *Handbk. Child Psychol.* vi. 158 Twins have always captured much attention from singletons! **1942** E. B. HURLOCK *Child Devel.* vii. 186 In the size of vocabulary, mean length of sentence, and articulation, twins were retarded as contrasted with singletons of the same age. **1980** *Daily Tel.* 5 Nov. 3/2 Identical twins tend to marry less often than singletons.

b. One who is alone or unaccompanied, as an only child or unmarried person. Also *spec.* an undercover agent who operates alone.

1937 E. M. CHANNON *Son of his Parents* iii. 63 I'm a singleton. But we had an Anglo-Indian kid here for a couple of years, and he and I did our lessons together. **1969** *Daily Tel.* 9 Apr. 14/7 Two wealthy singletons with £5,000 a year apiece would each pay £2,400 10s od and their combined net income would be £5,199; married they would pay £6,083 10s od in tax. **1977** C. MCCARRY *Secret Lovers* iii. 32 He was alone, a singleton in the jargon, living under deep cover, with an ordinary passport and no protection from his government.

c. The only one of its kind or class; a set having only one member. Also *attrib.*

1966 [see *INJECTIVE *a.*]. **1975** *Language* LI. 648 A singleton like *perdition* (or *conflagration*)..has no relatives like **perdite* **perditive*. **1977** *Canad. Jrnl. Linguistics* 1976 XXI. 144 The speaker uses the definite description as a characterization of a (singleton) set, whose members he wants to say something about.

single track, *sb.* and *a.* [SINGLE *a.*] **A.** *sb.* **1.** A single pair of railway lines (occas. of tramlines). Also (with hyphen) *attrib.*

1832 *Amer. Rail Road Jrnl.* I. 245/1 The entire length of single track [is] yet to be laid. **1837** H. MARTINEAU *Society in Amer.* II. II. ii. 192 On the 26th of November, 1833, the first car traversed the whole length of the single track. **1869** *Bradshaw's Railway Man.* XXI. 422 There are..190 miles of double track, and 130 miles of sidings.., making the entire length of track equal to 1,137 miles of single track. **1898** *McClure's Mag.* Mar. 390/1 Running a first-class train on a single-track branch. **1942** 'N. SHUTE' *Pied Piper* i. 18 The little engine puffed along its single track, pulling its two old coaches through a country dripping with thawing snow. **1955** A. ROSS *Australia 55* ix. 108 A river runs through it, also a single-track railway line. **1976** P. R. WHITE *Planning for Public Transport* viii. 164 A number of single-track control systems exist, in which the overriding principle is that only one train has authority to occupy a section at any one time.

2. A recorded strip on magnetic tape that does not have another strip alongside it, usu. occupying almost the full width of the tape. Also *attrib.* and as *adv.*

1959 W. S. SHARPS *Dict. Cinemat.* 129/1 *Single-track recorder*, a magnetic tape recorder using a single track, usually the full width of the tape. **1962** A. NISBETT *Technique Sound Studio* vi. 116 It is best to do all original recording single track, and to use other tracks only when copying. **1975** G. N. PATCHETT *F. M. Reception* III. xvi. 162 The whole tape is normally used for professional recording. It is known as single track.

B. *adj.* Concentrated on or capable of only one line of thought or action, obsessional, esp. in phr. *single-track mind* (chiefly *U.S.*) (cf. *one-track* adj. s.v. *ONE *numeral a.* 33); affording no choice or opportunity of divergence.

1919 *Ladies' Home Jrnl.* Feb. 35/1 The average girl no longer has a single-track mind. **1924** A. J. SMALL *Frozen Gold* iv. 108 Sitka Charley's was a single-track mind; dour and grim and devilishly dogged, but still, single-track. **1933** *Times Educ. Suppl.* 21 Oct. 349/3 In every school, no matter whether it be 'single-track' or 'multi-bias', there will always be a certain number who fail to come up to the standard set by the school. *c* **1942** L. MUMFORD *City Devel.* (1946) 152 To make up for a single-track concentration, there must be range of vision and comprehensiveness of understanding. **1964** *Listener* 26 Mar. 508/1 Under the Criminal Justice Act 1948, the double-track system of preventive detention was replaced by a single-track system. **1978** S. SHELDON *Bloodline* xxxi. 302 Max Hornung had a single-track mind.

single-valued, *a.* *Math.* [SINGLE *a.*]. Having a unique value for each value of its argument(s); that maps to one and only one point, number, etc. Hence **single-valuedness,** the property of being single-valued.

1879 [in Dict., s.v. SINGLE *a.* 19]. **1882** [see REVERSE *sb.* I a]. **1946** *Nature* 27 July 128/2 In Indian longitudes.. the base of the stratosphere is always sharp and clear-cut and single-valued in summer, but is just one of several inversions in winter. **1968** C. G. KUPER *Introd. Theory Superconductivity* iii. 52 To guarantee single-valuedness, we must impose the flux quantization condition. **1970** G. K. WOODGATE *Elem. Atomic Struct.* ii. 17 Thus Φ, like Θ, is a single-valued function of its argument. This single-valuedness is not a necessary postulate of wave mechanics, but a result derived from the condition that we are working in a central field in (r, θ, ϕ) space.

singling, *vbl. sb.* **1.** (Later examples with *out.*)

1911 M. BEERBOHM *Let.* 3 Nov. (1964) 210 Your singling-out of that phrase..is a proof that Rothenstein and Ruskin are right about reverence for nature. **1964** F. BOWERS *Bibliogr. & Textual Crit.* VI. iv. 200 Sir Walter Greg's singling-out of this as the clinching evidence.

singly, *adv.* Add: **4.** *singly-charged.*

1924 *Phil. Mag.* XLVII. 282 The number of particles due to doubly-charged, singly-charged, and neutral helium atoms..varied in number over..a wide range. **1965** PHILLIPS & WILLIAMS *Inorg. Chem.* I. v. 176, $h\nu$ may be taken as the ionization potential of an ion (i.e. for a singly-charged positive ion, the second ionization potential of the element, and for a singly-charged negative ion, the electron affinity of the element).

sing-sing[3]. [Reduplicative pidgin formation f. SING *v.*[1]] In Papua New Guinea: an occasion of feasting and musical celebration.

1899 C. M. E. DAVID *Funafuti* v. 58 Opataia..came to say that there was to be a sing-sing that night in the schoolroom, in honour of the expedition. **1924** E. RAFF *Let.* 10 Jan. in F. E. Williams *Orokaiva Magic* (1928) I. 100 At one of the 'sing sings' (dances) a follower who fell down 'dead' was promptly revived. **1943** S. W. REED *Making of Mod. New Guinea* vii. 211 In the native villages the initiation ceremonies, tribal dances, and *singsing* will continue to express a mode of life utterly foreign to the European. **1968** *Telegraph* (Brisbane) 3 Sept. 18/6 Cattle given to New Guinean farmers for breeding are being killed and eaten at 'sing sings' (festivals).

sing-song, *sb.* Add: **4. a.** Now more usu. a gathering for, or session of, community singing.

1869 J. GREENWOOD *Seven Curses of London* ii. 19 The London factory-bred girl..has her 'young man', and accompanies him of evenings to 'sing-songs' and raffles. **1899** KIPLING *Stalky & Co.* II. 252 'Had some rippin' sing-songs in camp, too,' said Tertius. **1914** D. O. BARNETT *Let.* 18 Dec. (1915) 28 We've got some sing-songs and smokers on for Christmas. **1933** *Sun* (Baltimore) 21 Oct. 14/6 Harvard students will..learn old German drinking songs at the German Sing-Song conducted by James W. Hawkes. **1968** 'J. LE CARRÉ' *Small Town in Germany* ix. 147 Wednesday was welfare. Ping pong night. Sing song night. **1974** J. AIKEN *Midnight is Place* i. 30 Ey, David! Coom to t'sing-song at t'Mason's Arms tonight?

6. Special Comb.: **sing-song girl,** a Chinese girl who entertains men by singing and dancing (*euphem.* one of easy virtue); **sing-song theory,** the theory (propounded by Jespersen) that language evolved from primitive singing.

1934 'A. BRIDGE' *Ginger Griffin* 326 So there will be more war in China because of a foreigner's idle love-letter to a sing-song girl. **1939** AUDEN & ISHERWOOD *Journey to War* 157 Even the singsong girls have changed their style. **1965** J. VON STERNBERG *Fun in Chinese Laundry* iv. 82 On the first floor were gambling tables, singsong girls. **1978** *China Now* Mar./Apr. 19/2 The shocking thing was that in the cities—where officials danced or played with sing song girls—there were grain and food. **1939** L. H. GRAY *Foundations of Lang.* 40 Language has been traced by some to primitive rhythmic chants and to singing (the sing-song theory). **1973** *Current Anthropol.* XIV. 27/3 He makes no reference to Jespersen's classic 'sing-song' theory of language origin (1922). Though this label was applied to Jespersen's hypothesis..by his critics, there seems little doubt that he believed language to have been chanted before it was spoken.

sing-songy *a.* (earlier example).

1892 E. LYTTON *Let.* 20 July in E. Lutyens *Blessed Girl* (1953) viii. 155 Vic is made to read poetry aloud to us. He has a very sing-songy voice.

sing-song, *v.* Add: **1. b.** Also, with direct speech as obj.

1931 [see *CALLER *sb.* 1 e]. **1963** R. WOLFF *I, Keturah* II. iv. 171 'You can't catch me. You can't catch me,' he singsonged. **1976** P. A. LAKE *Leffert's Disease* 173 'I'm sorry, he's not here,' she sing-songed with her nasal twang.

‖**singspiel** (zi·ŋʃpīl). *Mus.* Also **Singspiel.** [Ger., f. *singen* to sing + *spiel* play.] A semi-dramatic performance in which song and dialogue alternate, popular in Germany in the latter part of the eighteenth century.

1876 F. L. RITTER *Hist. Mus.* 266 The 'Singspiel' or 'operette' as constructed by Hiller, makes use of the spoken dialogue, as does the French comic opera. **1880** *Grove's Dict. Mus.* II. 519/1 That best and truest form of German Opera, the 'Singspiel'. **1911** E. J. DENT *Mozart's Opera 'The Magic Flute'* 4 [Schikaneder] gave a season of German 'Singspiel' (comic opera) at Vienna in the winter of 1784–5. **1930** *Observer* 23 Mar. 25 Many [operettas] of the German 'singspiel' type could be done. **1942** E. BLOM *Music in Eng.* ii. 24 English ballad opera crept into Germany by the back door and served as the direct model for the German *Singspiel.* **1962** *Guardian* 7 Feb. 9/1 Cherubini..evolved a style of *opéra comique*.. not unlike the *singspiel* of Mozart ('Seraglio'). **1977** *Times Lit. Suppl.* 10 June 710/5 A more general discussion of *opera seria, Singspiel*, etc.

singular, *a.* Add: **I. 3. c.** *singular matrix* (see quots. 1964, 1972); *singular solution*, a solution of a differential equation that cannot be obtained directly from the complete primitive; *esp.* a solution whose graph is the envelope of the graphs of the complete primitive.

1836 A. DE MORGAN *Differential & Integral Calculus* xi. 191 If there be a singular solution it is $y = a$... We have only found the singular solution from the primitive itself. **1873** A. CAYLEY in *Messenger of Math.* II. 12, I consider the singular solution to be that given by the equation which belongs to the envelope-locus (viz. I do not recognise any singular solution which is not of the envelope species). **1957** L. FOX *Two-Point Boundary Probl.* i. 2 The most general solution of an ordinary differential equation of order n contains n arbitrary constants. This general solution is called the Complete Primitive, and a Particular Integral is obtained by giving specific values to these arbitrary constants. Non-linear equations may also have singular solutions, not obtainable from the complete primitive. **1964** N. N. HANCOCK *Matrix Anal. Electr. Machinery* ii. 18 A 'singular' matrix is one for which the determinant formed by the same array is of zero value. **1972** A. G. HOWSON *Handbk. Terms Algebra & Anal.* viii. 43 If there is no matrix B..such that $AB = BA = I$, then A is said to be singular.

‖**singulare tantum** (siŋgiŭlā·re tæ·ntŏm). *Gram.* Also **singularis tantum.** Pl. **singularia tantum.** [L. neut. phr., 'singular only'.] A word which has only a singular form: usu. applied to mass (or uncountable) nouns. Cf. *PLURALE TANTUM.

1940 A. H. GARDINER *Theory of Proper Names* 27 A *singulare tantum* has developed a plural by cutting the designated entity, like a worm, into two parts. **1962** H. M. HOENIGSWALD in Householder & Saporta *Probl. Lexicogr.* 109 The ordinary coverage of singularia tantum, is mostly limited to mass nouns. **1979** *Trans. Philol. Soc.* 160 This is why the plural of *dahyu-* in the sense of 'nations' would have been *translatable* into Elamite only by *taššup*, a word which at xwāning was doomed to come out as the singularis tantum *kāra-*.

singularism (si·ŋgiŭlăriz'm). [See -ISM.] A philosophy which explains the phenomena of the universe from a single principle: opp. to PLURALISM. Cf. MONISM.

1897 PILLSBURY & TITCHENER tr. *Külpe's Introd. Philos.* iii. 107 It is customary to distinguish the various views that can be held upon this question by the terms *monism, dualism* and *pluralism.* But as the difference expressed by the first two is..predominantly qualitative, it seems better to make a..quantitative antithesis, and to speak only of *singularism* and *pluralism.* The former explains or deduces all the phenomena of the universe from one single principle. **1911** J. WARD *Realm of Ends* 24 If the difficulties of Pluralism point the way to Singularism they will at least serve to make the character of the One clearer than any 'cheap and easy monism'.. can ever do. **1931** A. WOLF in W. Rose *Outl. Mod. Knowl.* xiii. 576 The philosophy of James is perhaps best understood as a reaction against the excessive intellectualism, and the monism or singularism of absolute idealism.

singularity. Add: **9. d.** *Math.* A point at which a function takes an infinite value.

1893 A. R. FORSYTH *Theory of Functions* xxi. 606 All the essential singularities of a discontinuous group lie on the axis of a when the group is real. **1939** [see *SCHWARZSCHILD 2]. **1959** *Listener* 27 Aug. 320/1 At the start of the expansion certain quantities in our differential equations become infinite. This frequently happens with differential equations, and when it does the equation is said to contain a mathematical singularity. **1977** *Sci. Amer.* July 126/3 Gauss did much more with complex numbers. In 1811 he discovered what is now called Cauchy's theorem: The integral of a complex analytical function around a closed curve that encloses no singularities is zero.

e. *Astr.* A region in space-time at which matter is infinitely dense.

1965 *Physical Rev. Lett.* XIV. 58/1 An exterior observer will always see matter outside $r = 2m$, the collapse through $r = 2m$ to the singularity at $r = 0$ being invisible to him. **1972** *Nature* 21 Apr. 378/2 In the physical world..we may take the phrase 'space-time singularity' to mean a region in which space and time have become so locally distorted that the present laws of physics are no longer applicable. **1979** *Jrnl. R. Soc. Arts* CXXVII. 579/1 A central 'singularity' where tidal forces (the difference between the gravitational acceleration of his head and his feet) would become infinite, and he would be crushed out of existence.

singulary (si·ŋgiŭlări), *a.* *Logic.* [f. L. *singulāris* SINGULAR *a.*: see -ARY[2].] Involving just one element.

1940 W. V. O. QUINE *Math. Logic* i. 13 Conjunction and alternation are binary, in that they combine statements two at a time. But denial..is singulary. [*Note*] The series of adjectives 'binary', 'ternary', 'quaternary', 'quinary',..leaves mathematicians in a quandary when $n = 1$. It is customary to stammer out some such makeshift as 'unary' or 'uninary' or 'unitary'. But the proper word is apparent if we reflect that the series of Latin distributives 'bini', 'terni', 'quaterni', 'quini',..begins with 'singuli'. **1954** *Word* X. 227 There are singulary operations, but no singulary relations... An example of a singulary operation in mathematics is 'reciprocal of'. **1965** N. CHOMSKY *Aspects of Theory of Syntax* iii. 132 Many of the optional singulary transformations of Chomsky..must be reformulated as obligatory transformations.

singulative (si·ŋgiŭlătiv). *Gram.* [ad. F. *singulatif*: cf. SINGULAR *a.* and -ATIVE.] (See quot. 1966); also, a singular form.

[**1952** MEILLET & COHEN *Langues du Monde* (ed. 2) 1279 *Singulatif*, morphème ayant pour fonction de donner à un mot une valeur de singulier, généralement par opposition à un collectif.] **1966** M. PEI *Gloss. Linguistic Ter-*

minol. 250 *Singulative*, a morpheme having for its function to give a word the force of a singular, usually by way of opposition to a collective (*rice, rice-grain*). **1970** J. McN. Dodgson *Pl.-Names Cheshire* I. 151 The *-inn, -enn* suffix is not diminutive but a singulative... The singulative effect would indicate some particularised aspect of a location—e.g. a particular piece of moorland in a general area of moors. **1977** *Word 1972* XXVIII. 194 *Clocs*: plural *clocsiau*...; doubly characterized plural, with a new 'singulative' *clocsen*.

sinh (ʃəin, sin(t)ʃ, səinˌēi·tʃ). *Math.* Abbrev. of *hyperbolic sine* s.v. Hyperbolic *a.* 2 b.

1873 *Messenger of Math.* II. 190 Sinh *x* and cosh *x* are of course the hyperbolic sine and cosine of *x*, viz. $\frac{1}{2}(e^x - e^{-x})$ and $\frac{1}{2}(e^x + e^{-x})$. **1891** [see *cosh]. **1972** A. G. Howson *Handbk. Terms Algebra & Anal.* xxxiii. 164 Sinh and cosh both have domain R; the image of sinh is R.

Sinhala (sinhā·la), *sb.* and *a.* [a. Skr. (see Sinhalese).] **A.** *sb.* = Sinhalese *sb.* and *a.* 2.

1954 Pei & Gaynor *Dict. Linguistics* 198 *Sinhala*, modern vernacular Sinhalese, mixed with foreign words. **1961** *Times* 27 June 13 The Official Language Act of 1958 came into effect at the beginning of this year, and without reference to Tamil prescribes Sinhala as the sole official language of Ceylon. **1977** *Economist* 3 Sept. 62/1 Mrs Bandaranaike fought an election on a platform of 'Sinhala only' as Sri Lanka's state language.

B. *adj.* = Sinhalese *sb.* and *a.* 3.

1926 M. C. Rasanayagam *Anc. Jaffna* vi. 231 The Pallava king..says in one of his inscriptions that he vanquished 'the Sinhala king who was proud of the strength of his arms'. **1962** *Housewife* (Ceylon) Feb. 9 Local hand-made clay tiles based on traditional Sinhala designs. **1963** *Guardian* 2 May 10/3 An Act of 1956 prescribed the Sinhala language as the one official language of Ceylon.

Sinhalese, *sb.* and *a.* Add: The Sinhalese are properly members of an Aryan people deriving from N. India and now forming the majority of the population of Sri Lanka.

1. (Earlier example.) Also *sing.*, a Sinhalese native of Sri Lanka.

1801 *Asiatick Researches* VII. 32 The *Singhalais* assert, from record, the total destruction and regeneration of the universe, many other times. **1913** L. Woolf *Village in Jungle* iii. 45 He was tall for a Sinhalese, broad-shouldered, and big-boned. **1948** [see *Ceylonese *a.* and *sb.*].

2. (Earlier example.)

1801 *Asiatick Researches* VII. 401 The end of the soul is called, in Singalese, *Nivani*.

sinhalite (si·nhăləit). *Min.* [f. as Sinhal(ese *sb.* and *a.* + -ite[1].] A borate of aluminium and magnesium, $MgAlBO_4$ (usu. also containing iron), which forms pale yellow to deep brown orthorhombic crystals resembling olivine and frequently of gem quality.

1952 Claringbull & Hey in *Mineral. Mag.* XXIX. 843 For this new mineral the name *sinhalite* is proposed, from Sinhala the Sanskrit name for Ceylon. **1952** *Times* 4 Dec. 3/3 Sinhalite..was previously thought to be an olivine rich in iron. **1965** *Amer. Mineralogist* L. 1979 The sinhalite from Ceylon had a density of 3·494, corresponding to a composition $(Al,Mg)_{1\cdot95}Fe_{0\cdot05}BO_4$. Judging from the absorption data, most of the iron in sinhalite is divalent. **1971** *Jrnl. Gemmology* XII. 154 One of the few sinhalites we have officially tested..was an attractive golden brown specimen.

Sinico- (si·niko), combining form of med.L. *Sinicus* Sinic *a.*, as in *Sinico-Annamitic*; **Sinico-Japanese** *sb.* and *a.* = *Sino-Japanese* s.v. *Sino-[1] 2, 3. Now *rare*.

1838 P. S. du Ponceau *Diss. Nature & Char. Chinese Syst. Writing* p. xxix, Those Sinico-anamitic words, if they are really in use, do not belong to the original language. **1866** F. V. Dickins tr. *Teika's Hyak Nin Is'shiu* p. vii, Such ill-sounding Sinico-Japanese syllables as rets', bats' mats', teats', shuts', and the like. **1884** tr. *J. J. Rein's Japan* 396 The Japanese Language... Yamato- and Sinico-Japanese. **1902** *Encycl. Brit.* XXIX. 729/1 Like all fine specimens of the Sinico-Japanese school, the prices are too high to attract wide custom.

sinification. (Later examples.)

1966 D. Wilson *Quarter of Mankind* xxi. 206 There is no separate Hongkong nationality. Sinification of public life proceeds very slowly. **1977** *Daily Tel.* 12 Feb. 16 The aim is 'sinification' of Tibet.

sinify, *v.* (Later examples.)

1942 A. J. Grajdanzev *Formosa Today* iii. 35 Only 95,400 of them are classified as 'savages'..the remaining 60,500 being 'civilized', that is, they are 'sinified'. **1966** *Economist* 1 Oct. 58/1 But he [*sc.* Mao] did not sinify the basic philosophical principles of Marxism. **1977** *Times* 12 Oct. (China Suppl.) p. vii/7 The central Government has often been accused of 'sinifying' the minority nationality areas of China.

sinister, *a.* Add: **4. b.** *sinister interest* (earlier examples in the works of the Utilitarian philosophers).

1817 J. Bentham *Plan Parl. Reform* iii. p. xi, Here we have one partial, one separate, one sinister interest..with which the universal..interest has to anatagonise. **1824** J. S. Mill in *Westm. Rev.* II. 347 When romance assumes the garb of history,..it infallibly allies itself with the sinister interests of the few. **1827** J. Bentham *Rationale Evid.* V. ix. i. 6 Interest when acting in such a direction and with such effect as to give birth to falsehood may be termed sinister interest. **1861** J. S. Mill *Repr. Govt.* vi. 118 The evils arising from the prevalence of modes of action in the representative body dictated by sinister interests (to employ the useful phrase introduced by Bentham), that is, interests conflicting more or less with the general good of the community.

sinisterly, *adv.* **1.** Delete *rare* and add later examples.

1930 D. H. Lawrence *A Propos of Lady Chatterley's Lover* 6 The effect is peculiarly depressing, sinisterly high-brow. **1946** G. Millar *Horned Pigeon* xxi. 346 The ducks looked happy and healthy, perhaps sinisterly so. **1969** [see *rentier]. **1974** E. Jones *Barlow comes to Judgement* 48 There is nothing sinisterly secret about the WHY Club.

sinistral, *a.* Add: **8.** Also as *sb.*, a left-handed person.

1927 [see *dextral *a.* 1 c]. **1964** M. Critchley *Developmental Dyslexia* xiv. 84 The patient declared herself to be right-handed, but she wore her wrist-watch on the right arm like many sinistrals do.

9. *Geol.* Being or pertaining to a strike-slip fault in which the motion of the block on the farther side of the fault from an observer is towards the left. Opp. *dextral*.

1942 E. M. Anderson *Dynamics of Faulting* v. 55 E. E. L. Dixon has distinguished the types of displacement as right-hand and left-hand heaves... The two classes of fault-planes may well be termed 'dextral' and 'sinistral'. *Ibid.* 71 The Bala fault-zone..is undoubtedly sinistral. **1964** A. Holmes *Princ. Physical Geol.* (ed. 2) ix. 219 In strike-slip faults the relative displacement of the block on the far side of the fault, as viewed from the ground, may have been either to the right (giving a right-lateral or dextral fault) or to the left (giving a left-lateral or sinistral fault). **1978** *Nature* 5 Jan. 50/2 The Bathurst and McDonald faults.., which form the boundaries of the Slave wedge are major sinistral and dextral strike-slip fault systems that extend for hundreds of kilometres.

sink, *sb.*[1] Add: **I. 2. f.** In semi-proverbial phr. *a mind like a sink*, an imagination that tends to put an indecent or lewd construction on events. *slang*.

1932 A. Christie *Thirteen Problems* x. 170 And if one tries to warn them..they tell one that one has a Victorian mind—and that, they say, is like a *sink*. **1949** Wodehouse *Uncle Dynamite* viii. 129 He concluded by saying that it was a pity that some people, whose identity he did not specify, had minds like sinks. **1970** S. Taylor *Murder grows Roots* ii. 16 [She] said he'd probably gone off with some woman. Her mind's like a sink!

g. Used *attrib.* of a (school, estate, etc., in a) socially deprived area.

1972 *Daily Mail* 4 Oct. 25/3 The downward spiral of decline in the 'sink' areas could be broken if the school led the way. **1972** *Guardian* 17 Oct. 17/4 It is a pity.. that there is not a 'sink' schools conference, like the Headmasters' Conference of the public schools, to act as a general champion of the rights of urban schools. **1976** *New Society* 18 Nov. 365/2 Somewhere, in every town that has council houses at all, there's a 'sink' estate—the roughest and shabbiest on the books, disproportionately tenanted by families with problems, and despised both by those who live there and the town at large. **1981** *Observer* 8 Feb. 29/4 None of its problems has reduced Callow to a 'sink' school: it has great achievements, including children in its first sixth form about to depart bright-eyed and bushy-tailed to university.

II. 8. Delete *Kinematics* and add: The opposite of *source* in any scientific sense; a place where or a process by which energy (esp. heat) is removed from a system, or some specific component of a system is removed from circulation and either stored or destroyed; a device whose function is to act as a sink. (Earlier and later examples.)

1855 J. C. Maxwell in *Trans. Cambr. Philos. Soc.* (1864) X. 32 If the origin of the tube or its termination be within the space under consideration, then we must conceive the fluid to be supplied by a source within that space, capable of creating and emitting unity of fluid in unity of time, and to be afterwards swallowed up by a sink capable of receiving and destroying the same amount continually. **1885** *Electrician* 3 July 134/1 There will..be transfer of energy through the medium from sources to sinks of energy. **1902** *Encycl. Brit.* XXVIII. 18/2 In the case of current flow in plane sheets, we have to consider certain points called sources at which the current flows into the sheet, and certain points called sinks at which it leaves. **1951** *Jrnl. Brit. Interplanetary Soc.* X. 256 The generation of electrical power by means of a heat engine requires that the heat produced at a temperature T_1 be conveyed to a 'sink' at a temperature T_2. **1966** *Economist* 8 Oct. 180/1 They [*sc.* power stations] could be used as a 'sink' for the gas while the distribution system is geared up to take it elsewhere. **1977** I. M. Campbell *Energy & Atmosphere* viii. 263 The main sink for hydroperoxy radicals in the troposphere appears, at present, to be identified as reaction with nitrogen oxides.

III. 11. c. *gen.* An instance or act of sinking. *rare*.

1818 Keats *Let.* 13 Mar. (1958) I. 240 When a poor devil is drowning, it is said he comes thrice to the surface, ere he makes his final sink.

d. *Aeronautics.* Loss of altitude, esp. in gliding flight; the rate of this.

1943 [see *rate *sb.*[1] 7 b]. **1955** A. Welch et al. *Soaring Pilot* iii. 33 Minimum sink will occur at some lower lift coefficient (i.e. a higher speed). **1962** R. C. S. Allen *Theory of Flight for Glider Pilots* iv. 28 When the power is a minimum, the sink is a minimum. **1973** *Sci. Amer.* Dec. 103/3 The effect of the vulture's lower wing loading is that it can turn in much smaller circles at a similar rate of sink.

12. c. (Earlier example.)

1840 A. Bunn *Stage both before & behind Curtain* III. viii. 280 The scenery..described, in the glowing language of the stage, under the head of flats, wings, side-pieces, borders, sinks, flies, &c.., has been painted..by a Stanfield and Grieve.

IV. 14. sink garden, a miniature garden, comprising a group of small plants (often alpine varieties) grown in an old stone sink or similar container; **sink rate** *Aeronaut.* = *sinking speed* s.v. *sinking *vbl. sb.* 4; **sink tidy**, a perforated receptacle for kitchen waste, placed on a sink unit; **sink unit**, a kitchen unit comprising a sink and draining-board, usu. with cupboards below.

[**1923** *Gardeners' Chron.* 2 June 306/2 Quite a novel feature of the rock gardens [at Chelsea] were the miniature gardens..in stone sinks.] **1935** C. Elliott *Rock Garden Plants* 10, I at first intended to devote chapters to the building of rock gardens, the making of screes, to sink gardens, [etc.]. **1954** R. Pearson *Town Gardening* xii. 109 (*heading*) Trough and sink gardens. **1966** *National Observer* (U.S.) 21 Feb. 9/3 Attention so far has focused on the 727's 'sink rate', or rate of descent as it comes down from its 25,000-foot cruising altitude on an approach to landing. **1978** A. Welch *Bk. Airsports* vi. 92/2 Most Para-Commander 'chutes..have a sink rate of about 13 feet per second. **1951** *Catal. of Exhibits, South Bank Exhib., Festival of Britain* 52/1 Deep sink tidy. **1958** *New Scientist* 9 Jan. 13/1 Polyethylene..well known in recent years for its use in the manufacture of..sink-tidies, buckets and washing-up bowls. **1981** R. Barnard *Mother's Boys* v. 52 She took out the sink-tidy, with the rubbish from breakfast, and slapped the contents into the dust-bin. **1939** Martin & Speight *Flat Bk.* 66 Wringer unit which can be fixed permanently to an 'Easiwork' sink unit in an ideal position between the sink and copper. **1971** R. Rendell *One across, Two Down* v. 45, I would have it painted throughout for you and a sink unit put in.

sink, *v.* Add: **I. 1. a.** Also in fig. phr. *to sink without trace*; usu. *pass.* [tr. Ger.: see *spurlos versenkt.]

1925 Fraser & Gibbons *Soldier & Sailor Words* 267 *Spurlos versenkt*, gone entirely. Disappeared. Specifically—sunk without trace, with all on board. **1936** 'D. Yates' *And Berry came Too* viii. 313 'That has gone, sir.' ..'Sunk without trace,' said Berry. 'What a very beautiful thought.' **1946** W. S. Churchill *Compl. Speeches* (1974) VII. 7337 He has departed '*spurlos versenkt*' as the German expression says—sunk without leaving a trace behind. **1965** A. Fairfax-Lucy in Battiscombe & Laski *Chaplet for Charlotte Yonge* 92 *Kenneth* has sunk without a trace, but *The Little Duke* lives. **1974** 'J. le Carré' *Tinker, Tailor* xii. 104 'And the third? Viktorov?' 'Sunk without trace... Trained and disappeared.'

b. Also in phr. *to sink through the floor*, used to express deep embarrassment.

1908 L. M. Montgomery *Anne of Green Gables* xii. 118 She thought she would sink through the floor when she saw you come in all rigged out like that. **1956** 'C. Blackstock' *Dewey Death* iv. 79 The pause was long enough to make Barbara wish she could sink through the floor. **1969** E. Gébler *Shall I eat You Now?* 36 The fear he might suddenly say *anything*—well something really that would make you sink through the floor.

6. c. Of an oil painting: to develop dull spots on the surface where the pigments have sunk into the ground. Also const. *in*. Cf. *sinking *vbl. sb.* 1 e.

1939 H. Hubbard *Materia Pictoria* 231 During the process of painting, and after completion, Oil Paintings are liable to sink-in and become dull in parts. **1968** M. Noakes *Prof. Approach to Oil Painting* ii. 12 Linseed oil can be used for 'oiling out' when a picture shows signs of sinking... Varnish seals and protects the surface of a painting, as well as reviving any areas that have sunk.

III. 17. d. *Golf.* To hole a ball from (a putt); to hole (a ball) by putting.

1916 Travers & Rice *Winning Shot* i. 23 After coming up in three and then sinking a ten or a fifteen putt for a four, the situation had suddenly changed. **1933** F. Ouimet *Game of Golf* xiv. 203, I murmured a few mild prayers before putting again, and this time I succeeded in sinking the ball. **1955** Keeler & Rice *Bobby Jones Story* xxi. 119 Mrs. Vanderbeck did sink that putt of 25-feet,..and..Alexa did sink hers for a win. **1971** 'D. Halliday' *Dolly & Doctor Bird* xv. 215 Arrived on the green, he pursued the ball round the pin..and finally sank it at nine.

e. To consume (an alcoholic drink); to drink down (esp. rapidly); = *down *v.*[2] 1 c. *colloq.*

1932 G. Holt *Drums beat at Night* ii. 30 Let's go out and sink a few beers. We can talk at the pub. **1947** L. MacNeice *Dark Tower* 157 I'll sink a pint in The Dog Returns. **1953** A. Neave *They have their Exits* xii. 144 Each man spoke of what he would do first on arrival in England. 'I shall sink three pints of mild and bitter,' said one. **1962** L. Deighton *Ipcress File* ii. 19, I..sank a quick grappa. **1977** M. Kenyon *Rapist* xiv. 182 Get a couple of cups, Sergeant, we'll sink a fast one.

f. *Basketball.* To score a goal or basket from (a shot). Also *absol.*

1935 *N.Y. Times* 24 Feb. iii. 4/1 O'Donnell sank a long field goal and Kozloff threw a foul to give Penn a 4–1 lead. **1950** N. Holman *Holman on Basketball* 50 With Norm Mager sinking five and Floyd Layne making four set shots..the City College five won. **1962** *Sports Illustr.*

Bk. Basketball iv. 83 Cousy..leaped into the air and sank a left-hander that won the game. **1972** *Sports Illustr.* 3 Jan. 51/1 The Rainbows' John Pennebacker sank from free throws.

20. d. Hunting. *to sink the wind*: to move downwind of another; *spec.* of a fox: to pass below the line of scent. Cf. WIND *sb.*[1] 4.

1778 G. CARTWRIGHT *Jrnl.* 26 Sept. (1792) II. 374, I saw a large stag upon the south hill..and I let him pass; crossing his route and sinking the wind, I made all possible speed to the foot of Gravel Hills, where I headed him. **1847** R. S. SURTEES *Hawbuck Grange* v. 96 We..found a hare by Clipstone Clump, who went as straight as an arrow to Gatley Coppice, from whence, sinking the wind all the way, she ran to Silverspring. **1896** T. SMITH *Life of Fox* 299 When men go down wind to hear the cry, it is called sinking the wind of the hounds. **1948** F. PITT *Hounds, Horses & Hunting* 271 *Sink the Wind*, to go downwind.

sink, var. *SYNC.

‖ **sinkeh** (si·ŋke). [Malay *singke(h*, a. Hokkien *sinkheh* (also used), f. *sin* new + *kheh* visitor.] In Malaysia, a newcomer (esp. a labourer) recently arrived from China.

1879 J. D. VAUGHAN *Manners & Customs of Chinese of Straits Settlements* 6 The Chinaman on first landing in the Straits is called a Sinkeh. **1927** R. J. H. SIDNEY *In Brit. Malaya Today* 145 The Secret Societies were really Friendly Societies which each *sinkeh* (new-comer) joined. **1948** V. PURCELL *Chinese in Malaya* iii. 58 The staple article of local commerce was the *sinkheh* (Hokkien), *sankah* (Cantonese), the new recruit from China. **1972** C. M. TURNBULL *Straits Settlements 1826–67* i. 44 The employer obtained full right to their labour for a period usually of one year, during which the *sinkhehs* were fed, clothed, housed and given a small allowance.

sinker, *sb.*[1] Add: **II. 5. d.** *slang* (orig. *U.S.*). A doughy cake, esp. a doughnut; a dumpling. Now *rare*.

1870 J. H. BEADLE *Utah* 223 Our favorite dinner, when we could get the meat, was of fried ham and 'sinkers'. **1903** F. B. SMITH *How Paris amuses Itself* 48 The New York Dairy Lunch, with..its elevating Bible texts, and depressing 'sinkers',..would never make a success with Parisians. **1906** *N.Y. Even. Post* 10 Dec. 14 Without 'sinkers', corn cakes, cream puffs, 'cookies', and other standard foodstuffs at reasonable prices to appease the appetite between lectures, it is simply impossible to go on studying. **1926** E. FERBER *Show Boat* xiii. 268 The coffee was hot, strong, revivifying; the sinkers crisp and fresh. **1946** J. IRVING *Royal Navalese* 157 *Sinkers*, dumplings. **1975** *Amer. Speech 1971* XLVI. 172 Round fried cake with hole in the centre..*sinker*.

III. A person or thing that sinks. Chiefly *N. Amer.* **6*. a.** One who sinks. *rare*.

1851 H. MELVILLE *Moby Dick* II. lxxviii. 78 No sign of either the sinker or the diver.

b. A sunken or partly submerged log.

1884 *Redwood & Lumbering in Calif. Forests* (Edgar Cherry & Co.) 95 The well matured heartwood of the base of these trees is so solid as to sink in water—hence designated as 'sinkers'. **1905** *Terms Forestry & Logging* 34 *Deadhead*, a sunken or partly sunken log... Syn[onym]: sinker. **1915** P. B. KYNE *Cappy Ricks* 28 A sinker is a heavy, close-grained clear redwood butt-log, which, if cut in the spring,..is so heavy it will not float in the mill-pond. **1969** *Marine Digest* 4 Jan. 6/2 Ferry manager.. blamed the accident on a sinker.

c. *Baseball.* A ball which drops markedly after being pitched or hit.

1932 *Baseball Mag.* Oct. 496/1 Outfield skill depends a lot on the player's quickness in detecting whether it's a 'sailer' or a 'sinker'. **1943** [see *OUTCURVE 1]. **1952** *Sun* (Baltimore) 19 Apr. 13/1 A baffling repertoire of sliders and lazy sinkers. **1967** *Boston Traveler* 1 June 31/3 I've developed a good sinker and my fastball and curve are moving. **1975** *Cleveland* (Ohio) *Plain Dealer* 29 Mar. 2-c/5 He's missing bad with his sinker.

sinker (si·ŋkəɪ), *sb.*[2] *Bot.* Also 9 **senker.** [a. G. *senker* process, shoot, now assimilated to SINKER *sb.*[1]] A process of the root system of a mistletoe that grows radially into the tissues of the stem of the host.

1863 J. HARLEY in *Trans. Linn. Soc.* XXIV. 176 The young plant [*sc.* mistletoe] first sends into the bark of the nourishing plant a single root, sucker, or *senker*. **1894** SOMERVILLE & WARD tr. *Hartig's Dis' Trees* I. 27 Once a year, very seldom twice, often only each alternate year, a 'sinker' originates on the inner side of the cortex-root near the apex. **1938** J. S. BOYCE *Forest Path.* xv. 347 From the cortical haustoria are developed the sinkers which grow radially through the inner bark to the cambium, later becoming embedded in the wood by the formation of new annual rings. **1970** W. H. SMITH *Tree Path.* xxi. 220 Generally, sinkers are located within the rays of host xylem tissue, where they appear to grow coincidentally with the host.

sinkful (si·ŋkful). Also **sink-full.** [f. SINK *sb.*[1] + -FUL.] As much or as many as will fill a kitchen sink.

1961 'A. A. FAIR' *Shills can't cash Chips* viii. 148, I hate to come home to a sinkful of dirty dishes. **1976** W. J. BURLEY *Wycliffe & Schoolgirls* iii. 64 The kitchen..had.. a sink-full of dirty dishes. **1982** J. B. HILTON *Sunset Law* i. 7 Mock exasperation about the third sinkful of crockery that day.

sink-hole. Add: **1.** (Further examples.)

1949 *Reader's Digest* June 45/1 The French industrialist behaves as if he believed his country were headed toward the sink-hole. **1976** N. THORNBURG *Cutter & Bone* v. 124 'In this world!' Cutter's grin did not believe... 'This jailhouse. This sinkhole of piss and misery.' **1978** H. WOUK *War & Remembrance* xlviii. 488 Hollywood's such a sinkhole.

2. (Earlier example.)

1780 W. FLEMING *Diary* 20 Mar. in N. D. Mereness *Travels in Amer. Colonies* (1916) 639 Springs..appear again either in Sink holes immediately vanishing or bursting out.

sinking, *vbl. sb.* Add: **1. b.** Also with *in*.

1937 W. B. YEATS *Vision* 178 A sinking-in of the body upon its supersensual life.

e. *Painting.* A dull matt spot on the surface of an oil painting caused by the absorption of the pigments by the ground; the process by which the pigments sink into or become absorbed by the ground. Also *sinking-in*.

1915 P. YOUNG tr. *Vibert's Science Painting* ix. 118 Where, in the execution of a picture on account of repeated re-touching, embus or sinkings appear, it is possible..to make them disappear with a light scumbling of re-touching varnish. **1939** H. HUBBARD *Materia Pictoria* 231 The chief causes of sinking-in are: (A) The porousness of the Painting-ground or Priming [etc.]. **1951** R. MAYER *Artist's Handbk. Materials & Techniques* xii. 433 *Embu*, (French), in an oil painting, a dull spot in an otherwise glossy surface, caused by a sinking-in of the oil color. **1971** B. DORF *Beginner's Guide to Painting in Oils* xiii. 158 *Sinking*, dull patches in oil paint, caused by too absorbent ground, wrong medium, or too much dilutant.

f. Also *attrib.*, as *sinking feeling*.

1890 H. G. HUTCHINSON *Golf* (Badm. Libr.) ix. 246 The nerves and muscles must be fed for the work before them; otherwise there will ensue a dreadful sinking feeling before the end of the round. **1920** *Poster*, Bovril.. Prevents that sinking feeling. **1920** C. A. W. MONCKTON *Some Experiences of New Guinea Resident Magistrate* xxv. 302 'Do you feel devilish hungry half an hour before meals?'..'Yes,..sometimes so hungry that I have a sinking feeling.' **1937** *Discovery* Oct. 295/1 The slight sinking feeling experienced by pedestrian members.., when faced by the considerable uphill trudge. **1961** W. BUCHAN *Helen All Alone* 196, I just have a sinking feeling. **1979** L. MEYER *Fake Front* xiii. 108, I got that nasty sinking feeling again. We..couldn't get the story into the paper.

4. Special comb.: **sinking speed**, the vertical downward component of the velocity of a gliding body.

1930 V. W. PAGÉ *Henley's ABC of Gliding & Sailflying* (1931) ii. 40 The falling or sinking speed depends on the weight of the glider loaded and the skill of the pilot in manipulating the controls. **1953** *New Biol.* XIV. 72 One requirement of a bird which is to soar in upcurrents is that it should have a low 'sinking speed'; that is to say, it must lose height slowly when gliding in still air. **1973** *Sci. Amer.* Dec. 102/2 If the air through which the bird is flying happens to be rising at a speed greater than the sinking speed, the bird is carried up with it and acquires potential energy it can use later to glide through air that is not rising.

sinneress. (Later example.)

1929 S. LESLIE *Anglo-Catholic* xii. 165 Veronica's card was the tell-tale finger pointing to her as a sinneress.

sinnerite (si·nərəit). *Min.* [See quot. 1964 and -ITE[1].] A sulpharsenite of copper, $Cu_6As_4S_9$, found as brittle, grey, triclinic crystals.

1964 MARUMO & NOWACKI in *Schweiz. Min. u. Petrogr. Mitt.* XLIV. 440 In the course of the systematical study of the sulfosalt minerals from Lengenbach, Binnatal, a new mineral, a copper arsensulfide was found, which has some similarity to binnite and lautite... The mineral was named sinnerite in honour of the late Rudolf von Sinner, president of the Commission of the Naturhistorisches Museum Bern. **1975** *Amer. Mineralogist* LX. 998/2 Both natural and synthetic crystals of sinnerite are complexly twinned.

Sinn Fein (ʃin fēɪ·n). [f. Ir. *sinn féin* we ourselves.] The name of an Irish movement founded in 1905 by Arthur Griffith (1872–1922), Irish journalist and politician, orig. aiming at the independence of Ireland and a revival of Irish culture and language and now dedicated to the political unification of Northern Ireland and the Republic of Ireland. Freq. *attrib.*

1905 *United Irishman* 18 Mar. 4/4 The Sinn Fein policy which we have propounded for Ireland, will henceforth be the policy of the National Council. **1906** A. GRIFFITH *Sinn Fein Policy* 4 The policy for which the National Council stands is summarised in its title—'*Sinn Fein*'. *Ibid.* 32 Increase of employment, industrial effort and advancement should be everywhere the principal means towards the national aims of Sinn Fein Policy. **1907** *Westm. Gaz.* 31 Aug. 7/1 Sinn Fein is not as yet a movement of much political moment. **1920** *Public Opinion* 16 July 58/3 The intellectual leaders of Sinn Fein can by no means bind the extremists. **1930** W. K. HANCOCK *Australia* x. 213 Labour politicians preached Australia for the Australians and a sort of Sinn Fein exclusiveness. **1936** E. CURTIS *Hist. Ireland* xx. 386 Sinn Fein came out as a political force by winning an election in Roscommon in February 1917. **1944** M. J. MACMANUS *Eamon de Valera* iv. 69 De Valera..had been co-opted on the National Council of Sinn Fein after his release. **1955** *Times* 16 May 3/5 The fact that Sinn Fein has put forward candidates for West Belfast, Mid-Ulster, [etc.]..may mean that a Unionist gain will be recorded. **1962** A. LURIE *Love & Friendship* ii. 29 He looked over-excited, as if he were about to..lead a small raid for the Sinn Fein. **1971** *Eire Nua: Soc. & Econ. Programme of Sinn Fein* 3 The Constitution of Sinn Fein advocates not merely the complete overthrow of English rule in Ireland but also the setting up of a Democratic Socialist Republic. **1972** R. KEE *Green Flag* ix. 452 From May 1905 Griffith's new policy generally began to be called the 'Sinn Fein' rather than the 'Hungarian' policy. The suggestion for the new name had been made to him by a young woman named Mary Butler, late in 1904, though the words had long been fairly commonly used as a motto for Irish self-reliance and had in fact been the early motto of the Gaelic League. **1978** P. BOARDMAN *Worlds of Patrick Geddes* vii. 248 The never-ending nemesis of Sinn Fein Rebellion.

Hence **Sinn Fei·ner**, a member or adherent of Sinn Fein; **Sinn Fei·nism**, the methods, aims, or policies of Sinn Fein.

1907 *Daily Chron.* 13 Aug. 6/2 Sir Thomas Esmonde's action in adopting Sinn Feinism as against Parliamentary agitation. **1907** *Westm. Gaz.* 31 Aug. 7/1 Sinn Feiners further suggest that the Irish representatives, having withdrawn from Westminster, should assemble in Dublin. **1917** A. HUXLEY *Let.* May (1969) 124 The best part of political life after the war will be an unofficial Sinn Feinism. **1928** *Daily Express* 17 Nov. 3/5 The Sinn Feiners desired to strengthen this protest by obtaining the withdrawal from Parliament of the whole O'Brien party. **1945** R. CHANDLER *Let.* 1 Jan. (1981) 41, I have a great many Irish relatives..some of them Sinn Feiners. **1979** W. NELSON *Minstrel Code* ix. 75 The spot where Sinn Feiners gunned down a British Field-Marshal, Sir Henry Wilson, in 1922, on the doorstep of his home.

sinningia (sini·ŋgi,ă). [mod.L. (C. G. Nees von Esenbeck 1825, in *Ann. Sci. Nat.* VI. 296), f. the name of Wilhelm *Sinning* (1794–1874), German botanist + -IA[1].] A hairy herbaceous plant of the genus so called, belonging to the family Gesneriaceæ, native to Brazil, and bearing bell-shaped flowers.

Sinningia speciosa is the parent of many varieties commonly known as gloxinias.

1826 *Bot. Reg.* XII. 997 (*heading*) Green Brazilian Sinningia. **1902** L. H. BAILEY *Cycl. Amer. Hort.* IV. 1670/2 The Sinningias are little known horticulturally. **1936** E. SITWELL *Victoria of England* xix. 226 Flowers from the Queen's hothouses at Osborne—the lyonia with its waxlike bells.., the velvety sinningia with dark leaves. **1979** *Homes & Gardens* Feb. 25/1 Gloxinias, or sinningias as they are now called, are old favourites as house and cottage plants.

Sino-[1]. Add: Also with pronunc. (səi·no). **1. Sinological** *a.* (examples); **Sinologist** (earlier example); **Sinologue** (earlier example); **Si·nophile** [-PHILE], a lover of China or things Chinese; also as *adj.* and **Sinophi·lia,** love of China or that which is Chinese; contrasted with **Sinopho·bia,** dread or hatred of these; also **Sinopho·bic** and **Si·nophobe** *adjs.*; **Sino-xenic** *a.* [f. XEN- (see XENO-) + -IC], of a language: unrelated to a Chinese language but containing some Chinese linguistic elements.

1877 *Trübner's Amer. & Oriental Lit. Record* XI. 2/1 It is significant of the preponderance assigned in sinological studies to the English language, that Mr. von Möllendorff has thought it desirable to publish his work in English. **1970** *Guardian* 26 Nov. 15/6 This very readable and also scholarly collection..has all kinds of Sinological goodies too. **1816** P. DU PONCEAU *Let.* 31 July in *Trans. Hist. & Lit. Comm. Amer. Philos. Soc. 1816* I. 400 As I am no Sinologist, I will not undertake to say that the description which I have attempted to give of this language.. is very accurate. **1853** *North-China Herald* 21 May 167/2 Prince of Sinologues. **1900** E. R. SCIDMORE *China* i. 7 One agrees and disagrees, too, with the sinologues, who are usually sinophiles, that the Chinese are the one great race and flower of all Asia. **1977** R. LUDLUM *Chancellor MS.* xxxiii. 350 He's a Sinophile..He has one of the most extensive Chinese art collections in the world. **1974** *Daily Colonist* (Victoria, B.C.) 17 July 17/7 Ireland attributed the herbal pill fad to the public's 'sinophilia' or ardent interest in Chinese culture including medicine. **1920** W. J. LOCKE *House of Baltazar* iii. 31 Water-End became divided into two camps—Sinophile and Sinophobe. **1966** *New Statesman* 22 Apr. 601/2 Siam..exhibits considerable Sinophobia. **1977** *New Yorker* 24 Oct. 177/1 The Korean war and the Sinophobic diplomacy of John Foster Dulles. **1972** *Computers & Humanities* VI. 259 The term 'dialect' in this article refers loosely to all the sources of information in DOC: Middle Chinese,..18 modern Chinese dialects, and 3 Sino-Xenic sources.

2. Combined with adjectives of nationality to mean 'Chinese and..' or 'between China or the Chinese and (the country or people designated)', as *Sino-Albanian, -American, -Australian, -British, -Indian, -Japanese, -Malay, -Mongolian, -Russian, -Soviet, -Tibetan.*

1976 W. H. CANAWAY *Willow-Pattern War* v. 55 The Sino-Albanian axis. **1931** H. B. MORSE *Far Eastern International Relations* 750 (*caption*) Significance of the Sino-American treaty of 1928. **1978** D. BLOODWORTH *Crosstalk* iii. 28 Sino-American exchanges..had yielded a private understanding. **1904** *Amer. Naturalist* Sept. 676 The restriction of the Sino-Australian continent to a certain part of the Cretaceous times consequently would meet the postulates of geography and zoögeography. **1977** *South China Morning Post* (Hong Kong) 15 Apr. 2/1 An insight into how Sino-British relations, already good, are likely to develop. **1959** *Listener* 25 June 1093/2 The Sino-Indian agreement of April 1954. **1903** *Burlington Mag.* Oct. 13/1 We must place to the front the fact that Sino-Japanese design is almost exclusively an art of contours. **1978** *Jrnl. R. Soc. Arts* CXXVI. 652/1 The terms of the Sino-Japanese Trade Agreement are, I would judge, likely to prove more beneficial to both parties than the EEC/China Agreement. **1975** 'G. Black' *Big Wind for Summer* ii. 22 The girl..was..Sino-Malay. **1976** *Times Lit. Suppl.* 20 Feb. 206/2 In Central Asia..the Sino-Soviet frontier is straddled by a homogeneous Muslim population, while the Sino-Mongolian frontier is similarly straddled by a Mongolian population. **1926** *Glasgow Herald* 23 Jan. 9 The rift in the Sino-Russian lute. **1929** A. J. Toynbee *Survey Internat. Affairs 1928* 434 The zone ..had reverted to Chinese administration in virtue of the Sino-Soviet Russian agreement of the 31st May 1924. **1959** *Listener* 2 Apr. 598/3 The Sino-Soviet zone of nations. **1971** H. Trevelyan *Worlds Apart* x. 125 Sino-Soviet companies were formed to exploit minerals and oil, to develop Sinkiang in which the Soviet Union had a close interest, and to manage civil aviation. **1973** *Times* 14 Nov. 18/3 The Nagas are a group of 20 tribes of Sino-Tibetan origin.

3. Used similarly with sbs. to form sbs. (freq. *attrib.*) with the meaning 'a language (family) or subsection of this, characterized by a relationship between Chinese and the language (family) specified', as *Sino-Japanese, -Korean, -Siamese*; **Sino-Tibetan,** a family of languages comprising the Chinese, Tibeto-Burman, and (according to some scholars) the Tai languages.

1923 B. Karlgren *Analytic Dict. Chinese & Sino-Japanese* 7 After the Sino-Japanese readings I often add in parenthesis the Kana spelling. **1954** M. Pei *Dict. Linguistics* 198 *Sino-Japanese*, a term applied to Chinese loan-words in the Japanese language, the spoken form of which is different from the form or forms occurring in any of the spoken Chinese vernaculars. **1975** *Amer. Speech 1973* XLVIII. 122 If Japanese is indeed the source of the term, a more plausible model would be *nemaki*, the colloquial equivalent of *shin-i*, which is the learned or Sino-Japanese term. **1953** Sino-Korean [see *hangul[2]]. **1975** *Language* LI. 257 Each representing a lexical item with information regarding..its pronunciation in the 21 major dialects of China and in the Sino-xenic languages, i.e. Sino-Japanese and Sino-Korean. **1948** D. Diringer *Alphabet* 402 The Sino-Siamese sub-family of languages. **1954** M. Pei *Dict. Linguistics* 198 Many linguists classify Chinese and Tai into one Tai-Chinese or Sino-Siamese sub-family. **1933** L. Bloomfield *Language* iv. 69 The great *Indo-Chinese* (or *Sino-Tibetan*) family consists of three branches. **1948** R. A. D. Forrest *Chinese Lang.* i. 21 Chinese is reckoned as an independent member of the Sino-Tibetan, Indo-Chinese, or Sinitic family of languages. **1977** C. F. & F. M. Voegelin *Classification & Index of World's Langs.* 307 It is the older, more liberal, classifications of Sino-Tibetan that have now come under critical scrutiny.

sino-[2] (səi·no), comb. form of Sinus.

sino-atrial (səino,ēi·triăl), *a. Anat.* Also **sinoatrial.** [f. *sino-[2] + Atrial *a.*] Of, pertaining to, or designating a small body of tissue (the *sino-atrial node*) in the wall of the right atrium of the heart that acts as a pacemaker by producing a contractile signal at regular intervals; (so called because it arises in the embryo at the junction of the sinus venosus and the atrium). Cf. *sinuatrial *a.*

1913 *Gray's Anat.* (ed. 18) 552 The sino-atrial node is situated on the anterior border of the opening of the superior vena cava. **1962** *Listener* 10 May 810/1 A small mass of specialized muscle cells within the heart, the sino-atrial node, discharges a brief electric 'spark' regularly seventy-two times a minute or thereabouts. **1969** [see *dysrhythmia* s.v. *dys-].

sino-auricular (səino,ōri·kiŭlăɹ), *a. Anat.* [f. *sino-[2] + Auricular *a.*] = prec.

1907 Keith & Flack in *Jrnl. Anat. & Physiol.* XLI. 181 We use the term 'sino-auricular' in preference to 'sino-canalar' because, although a true sino-canalar junction exists on the dorsal side in the most primitive hearts,.. yet in all but these the part of the canal between the sinus and the auricle disappears, and the dorsal junction becomes really a sino-auricular junction. **1942** Bramwell & King *Princ. & Pract. Cardiol.* v. 87 Closely related to sinus arrhythmia is the disorder known as sino-auricular heart-block. **1976** *Archives Internationales de Physiologie et de Biochimie* LXXXIV. 81 (*heading*) Chronotropic responses to experimental ischemia of the canine sino auricular node.

sinogram (səi·nogræm). *Med.* [f. *sino-[2] + -gram.] An X-ray photograph of a sinus into which a contrast medium has been introduced.

1961 *Lancet* 5 Aug. 296/1 A sinogram showed narrowing of the sagittal sinus anterior to the fontanelle. **1974** J. D. Maynard in R. M. Kirk et al. *Surgery* x. 220/1 Such sinograms..can be repeated regularly until the cavity has decreased until it is the size of the tube it contains.

So **sino·graphy,** the radiographic examination of sinuses.

1957 in Dorland *Med. Dict.* (ed. 23) 1254/2. **1974** A. Henry in R. M. Kirk et al. *Surgery* xv. 295/2 When a sinus is present it is worth while performing sinography.. in an effort to delineate a communication with an intraosseous abscess cavity possibly containing a sequestrum.

sinoite (səi·no,əit). *Min.* [f. the chemical symbols for silicon (*Si*), nitrogen (*N*) and oxygen (*O*) + -ite[1].] Silicon oxynitride, Si_2N_2O, found as colourless orthorhombic crystals in some chondritic meteorites.

1964 C. A. Andersen et al. in *Science* 9 Oct. 257/3 We propose the name *sinoite*, which is derived directly from the chemical formula, for this new mineral. **1966** *Geochimica & Cosmochimica Acta* XXX. 367 Sinoite has only been found in the enstatite chondrites. **1972** *Nature* 22 Dec. 461/2 The relatively high nitrogen content in some enstatite chondrites is partly due to the presence of the mineral sinoite, Si_2N_2O, which so far has been found only in two meteorites.

sinopia (sinōᵘ·piă). [It.; cf. Sinoper, Sinople.] **1.** = Sinoper 2 a.

1844 Mrs. Merrifield tr. *Cennini's Treatise on Painting* xxxviii. 22 There is a natural red pigment, which is called sinopia or porphyry. **1910** A. P. Laurie *Materials of Painter's Craft* x. 208 *Sinopia*..is one of the many names under which red ochres are mentioned. **1978** *Times Lit. Suppl.* 20 Oct. 1208/3 Trecento fresco painters normally drew direct on the wall in sinopia without preliminary drawings.

2. *transf.* The preliminary rough sketch for a fresco, covered by the final work. Pl. *sinopie.*

1958 *Times* 10 Dec. 3/4 During the process of detaching a fresco from the wall it is often possible to separate it also from the *sinopia*—that is, the preliminary rough sketch. **1969** *Daily Tel.* (Colour Suppl.) 28 Mar. 28/3 Their long hidden *sinopie*, as the preparatory full-size wall-drawings are called, are generally our only witness to the evolution of their ideas. **1975** E. H. Gombrich *Let.* 14 Nov. in *Ideas & Idols* (1979) 182 Are the sinopie really better than the frescoes? **1981** M. Delahaye *Sale of Lot 236* xxiii. 197 The sinopia..had also to be right technically... He was safe in the materials. Charcoal, ochre, and sinopite were all natural substances.

sinsemilla (sinsəmi·lă). [a. Amer. Sp., lit. 'without seed'.] A plant belonging to a strain of *Cannabis sativa* having a particularly high narcotic content; also, the narcotic produced from a plant of this kind. Also *attrib.*

1975 *High Times* Dec. 68/2 Last year a guy bit the dust in Arizona in a PBY—a big-ass World War II Navy amphibian—full of prime Mexican sinsemilla. **1978** *Time* 12 June 22 Studies show that *sinsemillas* weed contains five times more tetrahydrocannabinol (pot's narcotic ingredient) than the common Mexican variety. **1980** *Daily Tel.* 19 Sept. 11/2 This year sinsemilla buds are fetching from $2,200 (£917) to $3,000 (£1,250) a pound. **1982** *Newsweek* 25 Oct. 60 Sinsemilla retails for up to $250 an ounce these days, and every plant produces up to two pounds of marketable buds.

sinter, *sb.* Add: **3.** Material which has been subjected to sintering; *spec.* iron ore prepared for smelting by sintering the powdered material, usu. together with coke and other materials; (see also quot. 1958).

1909 *Chem. Abstr.* III. 167 Process of treating metal-bearing ore in a uniformly formed mass of fine particles containing combustible elements to form relatively large agglomerated bodies of sinter by internal combustion. **1926** *Jrnl. Iron & Steel Inst.* CXIV. 61 Both the briquettes and the sinter are crushed to a somewhat coarser size than the lump ore before charging in the furnace. **1956** *Planning* 9 Apr. 64 Sinter has other advantages—it may rid the furnace of unwanted sulphur and volatile constituents and..increase furnace output while reducing coke consumption. **1958** A. D. Merriman *Dict. Metall.* 323/2 *Sinter*, a term used in reference to the solid waste from smelting or refining operations. It is also used to denote a product of a sintering operation. **1973** *Times* 12 Feb. (Suppl.) p. ii/4 The mixture of foreign and Frodingham ores will produce a sinter containing about 54 per cent iron.

4. Special Comb.: **sinter plant,** a furnace for sintering iron ore.

1938 R. H. Sweetser *Blast Furnace Practice* i. 57 Three types of sinter plant were erected in this country.. all based on the principle of down-draft suction, ignition on the top of a mixture of flue dust, and fine iron pyrites cinder. **1980** *Times* 29 Feb. 2 The coke ovens at Redcar ..are part of the steel complex, along with a sinter plant.

sinter (si·ntəɹ), *v.* [f. the sb.] **a.** *intr.* Of particles or particulate material: to coalesce into a solid mass under the influence of heat without liquefaction. Also with *together.* **b.** *trans.* To cause to coalesce in this way.

1871 [implied at Sintering *vbl. sb.*]. **1903** *Amer. Chem. Jrnl.* XXIX. 487. On heating, it [*sc.* methylmercaptothymine] sintered at about 225°. **1907** *Trans. Inst. Mining & Metall.* XVI. 321 The formation of ferrous silicate aids..in sintering the material. **1938** R. H. Sweetser *Blast Furnace Practice* i. 58 This plant sinters red ore, fines and flue dust. **1948** *Electronic Engin.* XX. 68 To the surface thus formed a nickel powder is sintered to provide a base for brazing materials. **1953** *Sci. News* XXIX. 43 Many small metal components are now made by sintering metal powders, which have previously been pressed into the desired shape. **1973** *Sci. Amer.* Oct. 129/2 At high temperatures the effect is even stronger: metal powders sinter together under pressure. **1976** *Ceramurgia Internat.* II. 90/2 Attempts were made to sinter material which was dried at 125°C and not calcined.

sintered (si·ntəɹd), *ppl. a.* Substitute for def.: That has been subjected to or formed by sintering; *sintered carbide*, a very hard material manufactured by sintering a pulverized mixture of cobalt or nickel and carbides of metals such as tungsten and tantalum, and used in the cutting parts of tools; *sintered glass*, a porous form of glass made by sintering glass powder and used esp. in chemical filtration apparatus.

1877 [in Dict.]. **1907** *Trans. Inst. Mining & Metall.* XVI. 313 The product obtained consists of a porous sintered mass of ferrous silicate. **1937** *Machinery* L. 773 (*heading*) The production of sintered carbides. **1940** *Jrnl. Sci. Instruments* XVII. 139 (*heading*) Sintered glass filters. **1951** O. W. Boston *Metal Processing* (ed. 2) v. 103 Sintered-carbide tools were introduced commercially in this country in 1928. **1959** *Economist* 21 Feb. 719/2 The process of manufacturing small pellets of sintered reactor fuel..follows the normal practice of the ceramics industry. **1962** J. T. Marsh *Self-Smoothing Fabrics* xxii. 365 The liquid is then decanted through a weighed sintered-glass crucible. **1964** S. Crawford *Basic Engin. Processes* iv. 104 Sintered carbide is fully hard when cooled to room temperature. **1982** D. Clark *Doone Walk* vii. 147 Front and back wheels have disc brakes with sintered pads to cure the problem of grip on wet roads.

sintering (si·ntəriŋ), *vbl. sb.* Substitute for def.: The process or action of the vb.; *spec.* as applied to iron ore (see *sinter *sb.* 3). Freq. *attrib.*

1871 [in Dict.]. **1907** *Trans. Inst. Mining & Metall.* XVI. 314 These..difficulties are overcome by the use of the sintering process, as the loss is small owing to the ore being wet. **1914** *Iron Trade Rev.* LV. 292 (*heading*) Sintering plant at Pottstown. **1930** *Engineering* 16 May 650/2 Sintering occurs when charges of partially reduced ores are maintained for considerable periods at temperatures above 750 deg. C. **1958** [see *sinter *sb.* 3]. **1958** N. Levine *Canada made Me* ii. 78 Above us a steel cable carried large buckets of iron ore from the Mine to the Sintering Plant. **1977** *Western Mail* (Cardiff) 5 Mar. 6/1 South Wales exports about one million tons a year, much of it anthracite duff used in briquetting and sintering in steel production.

sintoc. Add: Also **sintok.**

1900 W. W. Skeat *Malay Magic* v. 278 In Penang a root called *sintok* is usually preferred to limes. **1972** A. Amin tr. *Ahmad's No Harvest but Thorn* iv. 32 The *sintok*-wood *tajak*-handle.

sinuatrial (səiniu,ēi·triăl), *a. Anat.* Also **sinu-atrial.** [f. L. *sinu-*, stem of Sinus + Atrial *a.*] = *sino-atrial *a.*

1935 *Gray's Anat.* (ed. 26) 67 The sinu-atrial and atrio-ventricular nodes, the atrioventricular bundle and its right fasciculus, are supplied by the right coronary artery. **1962** *Ibid.* (ed. 33) 747 The sinuatrial node is a narrow, horse-shoe shaped structure situated in the upper part of the sulcus terminalis of the right atrium. **1968** Passmore & Robson *Compan. Med. Stud.* I. xxviii. 9/2 The part of the heart with the highest spontaneous rate..provides the source of excitation of the whole heart, and this pacemaker is normally the sinuatrial (SA) node.

sinuous, *a.* Add: **3.** Also of people.

1906 B. Vaughan *Sins of Society* 129 The lithesome, sinuous girl trips with it across the stage to her mother.

Hence **si·nuousness** (*b*) in this sense.

1924 R. Macaulay *Orphan Island* xiii. § 4 Like a sturdy little boy without feminine elegances, or any of Flora's wild-animal sinuousness. **1980** *Early Music* July 308/1 Any actor reciting them..would certainly emphasize the contrast between the biting *sk* sound at the beginning of these two words and the powerful sinuousness of 'l'onde'.

sinus. Add: **6.** *sinus infection*; **sinus gland** *Zool.* [tr. G. *sinusdrüse* (B. Hanström 1937, in *K. Svenska Vetenskapsakad. Handl.* XVI. iii. 3)], a structure in the eye stalk or head of crustaceans orig. thought to be a gland but now recognized as a neurohæmal organ in which are stored various hormones concerned with growth, reproduction, and metabolism; **sinus rhythm,** the normal rhythm of the heart, proceeding from the sino-atrial node; **sinus venosus** [mod.L., f. *venōsus* venous], a part of some vertebrate hearts into which the veins lead and which empties into the atrium.

1938 *Arkiv för Zoologi* XXX B. viii. 1 When investigating the nervous system and the organs of sense of the crustaceans, Hanström found (1931–1935) two organs which he called the blood gland (the sinus gland) and the X-organ. **1972** M. S. Gardiner *Biol. Invertebrates* xvii. 714/1 Molting in decapod crustaceans is also influenced by hormones discharged from the sinus glands. **1936** *Discovery* Dec. 380/1, I was suffering from widespread sinus infection. **1911** T. Lewis *Mechanism of Heart Beat* xii. 132 The compensatory pause fails; that is to say, disturbance of sinus rhythm may be demonstrated. **1980** *Brit. Med. Jrnl.* 29 Mar. 922/2 Ventricular fibrillation was converted to sinus rhythm with a 'thump' on the chest. **1836–9** R. B. Todd *Cycl. Anat. & Physiol.* II. 579/2 This division of the auricle into proper auricle and sinus venosus is more distinct in the left than in the right auricle. **1926** J. S. Huxley *Ess. Pop. Sci.* 199 The ventricle of the frog's heart has its own independent rate of beat when isolated. But in the intact animal this independent rate is all the time being speeded up by the faster-beating sinus venosus. **1970** *Encycl. Biol. Sci.* (ed.

2) 400/2 In the fish, amphibians, and reptiles the contraction starts in the thin muscle wall of the sinus venosus... In birds and mammals the sinus venosus is absent.

sinusitis (səinǝ̆sai·tis). [f. SINUS + -ITIS, prob. ad. F. *sinusite.*] Inflammation of a sinus, esp. a nasal sinus.

1896 *Jrnl. Laryngol.* X. 37 (*heading*) Treatment of sinusitis. **1935** IMPERATORI & BURMAN *Dis. Nose & Throat* xi. 146 Morning frontal headache increasing in intensity towards afternoon usually indicates maxillary sinusitis. **1951** M. LOWRY *Let.* 25 Aug. (1961) 252 Water.. nearly makes him die of dysentery, and milk..gives him sinusitis. **1977** W. MARSHALL *Thin Air* vii. 87 The smell.. came up the rickety stairs..like a poisonous cloud of pollen at the height of the sinusitis season.

sinusoid. Add: **2.** A blood vessel similar in size to a capillary but irregular in shape and without the continuous endothelial lining of capillaries. (Later examples.)

1920 *Nature* 27 May 411/1 A system of wide sinusoids (renal venous meshwork), which has no connection with the intertubular plexus. **1974** D. & M. WEBSTER *Compar. Vertebr. Morphol.* xiii. 315 In the mammalian adrenal cortex the steroidogenic tissues can be divided into zones on the basis of the arrangement of cells and their relationships to the numerous blood sinusoids.

sinusoidal, *a.* Add: Having the form of a sinusoid; varying periodically (with time, distance, etc.) as a sine varies with an angle; (see also quot. 1910). (Further examples.)

1910 N. HAWKINS *Electr. Dict.* 400/2 *Sinusoidal alternator,* an alternating current dynamo which generates simple harmonic or sinusoidal currents. **1948** *Nature* 28 Feb. 295/1 Along with the detailed solutions of the differential equations for step velocity input..is given a brief development of the solutions for sinusoidal input. **1957** G. E. HUTCHINSON *Treat. Limnol.* I. v. 357 The height of the wave at first decreases slightly, then increases as the wave approaches breaking. During the final phase of the rise in height, the sinusoidal or trochoidal form is lost. **1975** *Nature* 23 Oct. 674/1 Patterns of alternating light and dark bars with a sinusoidal luminance profile across the bars—sinusoidal gratings—are commonly used to study spatial interactions in the visual system.

sinusoidally (later examples).

1929 J. A. RATCLIFFE *Physical Princ. Wireless* i. 3 The simplest form of alternating current is one in which the current varies sinusoidally with the time. **1947** *Jrnl. Inst. Electr. Engineers* CXIV. III. 279/1 When the hemispherical end of a reproducing stylus is moved in contact with a sinusoidal surface of comparable curvature, the stylus tip does not itself move sinusoidally. **1974** *Sci. Amer.* Nov. 34/3 Voltages and current vary sinusoidally at a frequency of 60 hertz (cycles per second) in the U.S. and Canada and 50 hertz in most other countries of the world.

‖ **siot** (ʃǫt). [Welsh, evidently a loanword from an unrecorded regional sense of SHOT *sb.*[1]] In North Wales, a cereal mash of buttermilk and crushed oat-bread.

1936 *Farmhouse Fare* 148 *Siot.* ½ cupful oat bread. 1 pint buttermilk. Crush the bread..and put into a basin. Pour in the buttermilk, and let the bread soak for 1 hour, when it will be ready to serve. **1949** 'M. INNES' *Journeying Boy* xiv. 172 For breakfast it was impossible that they should have anything but siot or skirlie-mirlie. **1974** *Country Life* 12 Dec. 1845/2 Siot..was a pint of buttermilk poured on to a half cup of crushed oat bread... The 'mash' was served with bread and butter.

Siouan (sū·ăn), *a.* and *sb.* [f. *SIOU(X *a.* and *sb.* + -AN.] **A.** *adj.* = *SIOUX *a.* b. **B.** *sb.* **a.** = *SIOUX *sb.* 2 a. Also *Comb.* **b.** = *SIOUX *sb.* 1 b.

1885 J. O. DORSEY in *Smithsonian Inst. Rep. 1883* 919 The term 'Siouan' has been applied to that family of Indians which has been known heretofore as the 'Dakotan Family'. It is unfortunate that we are obliged to use this adjective, which is derived from 'Sioux', as the latter is not a genuine Indian word... In honor of Albert Gallatin, who was the first to classify the Indians of this family as the 'Sioux', the Bureau of Ethnology of the Smithsonian Institution has adopted the new term, 'Siouan', as the name of this family. **1889** *Amer. Naturalist* Jan. 75 The Siouan group had its habitat on the prairies between the Mississippi and Missouri. **1900, 1907** [see *CROW *sb.*[4] and *a.*]. **1929** E. SAPIR in *Encycl. Brit.* V. 139/2 Hokan-Siouan... Eastern group (1) Siouan-Yuchi..(2) Natchez-Muskogian. **1937** R. H. LOWIE *Hist. Ethnol. Theory* (1938) vi. 63 [Morgan] recognized the criteria of..the 'Omaha' system and indicated its occurrence among the Algonkian as well as the Siouan family. **1949** B. A. BOTKIN *Treas. S. Folklore* III. ii. 497 Enough Biloxi were left..to enable investigators to identify them..as members of the Siouan linguistic family. **1977** H. LANDAR in T. A. Sebeok *Native Langs. Americas* II. III. 352 Gallatin (1836) assigned the Shyenne language to his Sioux group on the basis of several names of 'Shyennes' who signed a treaty in July, 1825. The signers were possessed of Siouan, not Algonquian, names. **1978** C. CALLENDER in B. G. Trigger *Handbk. N. Amer. Indians* XV. 610/1 The societies that at the time of European contact were established in the upper Great Lakes area..were mostly Algonquian but included the Siouan-speaking Winnebago.

Sioux (sū), *a.* and *sb.* Also 8 **Sous,** 9 **Suouex.** [a. N. Amer. Fr., earlier *Nadouessioux,* etc., ad. Ojibwa (Ottawa dial.) *nātowēssiwak*: Fr. pl. termination *-x* replaced the equivalent Ojibwa feature *-ak.*] **A.** *adj.* **a.** Of or pertaining to the Sioux people or their language (see the sb. below). **b.** Formerly, of or pertaining to the Siouan languages or language grouping; = *SIOUAN *a.*

1761 D. CLAUS *Let.* 19 Mar. in J. Sullivan *Papers Sir W. Johnson* (1921) III. 363, I picked up a pair of shoes made by the Sioux Ind[in]. to the Westward. **1805** Z. N. PIKE *Jrnl.* 8 Sept. in *Sources of Mississippi* (1810) I. 14 His design was to winter with some of the Sioux bands. **1824** W. H. KEATING *Narr. Exped. St. Peter's River* I. viii. 376 Account of the Dacotas or Sioux Indians. **1836** A. GALLATIN in *Trans. & Coll. Amer. Antiquarian Soc.* II. 120 The nations which speak the Sioux language may be considered..as consisting of four subdivisions, viz. the Winnebagoes; the Sioux proper and Assiniboins; [etc.]. **1893** L. WAGNER *Significance of Names* 36 The Sioux State [is] the territory of the Sioux tribe of Indians. **1919** S. LEWIS *Free Air* ix. 101 She fancied that on it the Sioux scout still sat sentinel. **1949** *Amer. Photogr.* Jan. 40/1 Following a speech in Siouan language, in which God was asked for rain, the real Sun Dance now started. **1973** *Black Panther* 1 Sept. 17/1 Chief Fools Crow..damned the Executors in Sioux language.

B. *sb.* **1. a.** = *DAKOTA *sb.* 1. **b.** Formerly also, more generally, a (member of a) linguistic grouping of North American Indian peoples that includes the Sioux, Crow, Omaha, and others.

1762 D. CLAUS Let. 2 June in J. Sullivan *Papers Sir W. Johnson* (1921) III. 754 Missisages, Ottawawas, Renards & Sioux, were the Nations assembled at Cataracqui. **1768** [see *hot war* s.v. *HOT *a.* 12]. **1785** T. JEFFERSON *Notes on Virginia* xi. 185 Sioux. On the heads of the Mississippi and westward of that river. **1827** J. F. COOPER *Prairie* III. vii. 227 The keen weapon..meeting the naked breast of the impetuous Sioux, the blade was buried to the buck-horn haft. **1836** A. GALLATIN in *Trans. & Coll. Amer. Antiquarian Soc.* II. 120 The Indians..east of the mountains are the Sioux; the Pawnees; the Fall, Rapid, or Paunch Indians; [etc.]. **1908** *Rep. Brit. Assoc.* 851 They [*sc.* the mound-builders] seem to have been followed by the Sioux (Dakotas), Iroquois, who are probably of Aztec origin. **1937** R. H. LOWIE *Hist. Ethnol. Theory* (1938) xiv. 262 The signs of Queenslanders and Sioux lend little support to psychic unity. **1957** P. WORSLEY *Trumpet shall Sound* 222 To the Sioux..the coming of the Dance helped to set off a train of events which culminated in the bloody massacre at Wounded Knee. **1964** MRS. L. B. JOHNSON *White House Diary* 11 Jan. (1970) 40 George Catlin..painted the Sioux... His paintings line the second-floor hall of the White House. **1975** D. PITTS *This City is Ours* xiv. 48 His name was Mick Dull Knife; he was a full-blooded Sioux and a graduate of Princeton.

2. a. Formerly, the language family to which the Sioux and related peoples belong; = *SIOUAN *sb.* **b.** The language of the Sioux or Dakota Indians.

1783 J. O. JUSTAMOND tr. *Raynal's Philos. & Polit. Hist. Settlements & Trade of Europeans in E. & W. Indies* VI. xv. 439 Three original languages were spoken in Canada, the Algonquin, the Sioux, and the Huron. **1915** J. BUCHAN *Salute to Adventurers* ix. 141 He said something in Sioux to one of the warriors. **1971** *Guardian* 18 Sept. 10/4 She spoke only Cheyenne and Sioux.

Sip (sip), *sb.*[2] Also **sip.** Black English abbrev. of *Mississippi* (cf. *MISSISSIPPIAN *sb.* and *a.*); *the Sip*: the State of Mississippi.

1969 P. CROSS in *Folklore Forum* II. VI. 141 There's this nigga who went to the 'Sip', you know, uh—Mississippi, that is. **1971** *Black Scholar* Jan. 41/1 He loaded up the trunk with all his fine clothes and lit' out for the 'sip'.

Sipapu (sī·papū). Also **Shipap(u.** [ad. Hopi *sípâ·pɨ̀.*] In the beliefs of Pueblo Indians, an opening in the earth, variously located by different tribes, through which their mythical ancestors emerged into the present world; a symbolic representation of this opening, as a hole in the floor of a kiva.

1891 A. F. BANDELIER in *Jrnl. Amer. Ethnol. & Archaeol.* (1892) III. 111 Cibobe is the same as Shipapu, the lagune where the deceased go to rest. **1896** J. W. FEWKES in *16th Ann. Rep. Bur. Amer. Ethnol.* (1897) 279 The Snake chief at Cipaulovi has no *tiponi,* and consequently no altar. The only objects at the end of the altar ..was a row of twenty snake whips leaning against the ledge of the rear wall, behind the *sipapû.* **1931** R. BENEDICT in *U.S. Bur. Amer. Ethnol. Bull.* XCVIII. 3 When the people who came up out of Shipap found these people who had been saved they called them Tsauwan yahana. **1939** E. C. PARSONS *Pueblo Indian Religion* I. iii. 216 On the road to the *sipapu* in the west, the place of emergence where the Hopi dead return..an actual spot in the wall of the Grand Canyon.., the breath body is met by..an Agave spirit sentinel. **1955** PRIESTLEY & HAWKES *Journey down Rainbow* vii. 115 Although the Sun Father was worshipped as the great cosmic power, Pueblo religion was mainly directed downwards towards the realm of the Earth Mother, the realm that was reached by way of the *Sipapu,* the home of the spirits whence the newborn came and the dead returned. **1977** M. JENKINSON *Land of Clear Light* I. 69 Man came up through the opening, the Sipapu, and flourished upon the surface of the earth... The image of the Sipapu has been likened by non-Indians to the birth process.

Siphnian (si·fniăn), *sb.* and *a.* [f. Gr. Σίφνιος, L. *Siphnius* + -AN.] **A.** *sb.* A native or inhabitant of the Greek Cycladic island of Siphnos. **B.** *adj.* Of, pertaining to, or characteristic of Siphnos.

1709 I. LITTLEBURY tr. *Herodotus' Hist.* I. III. 282 The Siphnians drawing all their forces together, fought a battle, and were defeated by the Samians, who took many prisoners in the pursuit. **1845** *Encycl. Metropol.* XVII. 494/2 The soft stone, whence the ancient Siphnians used to cut pots and cauldrons. **1886** J. H. FRERE *Aristophanes* 18 It appears by what Herodotus says of the oracle addressed to the Siphnians, that the 'red cheeks' must have gone out of fashion in his time. **1895** *Jrnl. Hellenic Studies* XV. 208 The school to which the sculpture of the Siphnian treasury must be assigned has already caused some discussion. **1932** R. FRY *Let.* 1 May (1972) II. 669 The early Ionian sculptures—above all the Siphnian treasure. **1956** PARKE & WORMELL *Delphic Oracle* I. II. vi. 150 Siphnos had a..rich source of income in gold and silver mines. From the proceeds of these mines the Siphnians became after the mid-sixth century the richest of the islanders. **1977** *Antiquaries Jrnl.* LVII. 348 Chemical tests have shed no further light on the origin of the wares conventionally known as 'Melian' and 'Siphnian'.

siphon, *v.* Add: **1. b.** *fig.* To draw off or from, as if by means of a siphon; to divert. Const. advbs. (chiefly *off*: *spec.* illicitly, of money) and preps.

1940 E. WILSON *To Finland Station* II. i. 75 All the fervor of which they were still capable was siphoned off into the revolutionary army. **1952** *N.Y. Times* 8 Sept. (late City ed.) 45/7 The police said order was gradually restored as the screaming crowd was slowly siphoned out of the stadium. **1955** H. ROTH *Sleeper* ix. 69 We are positive he wasn't siphoning out information. **1957** *Economist* 7 Dec. 842/1 If he were to siphon off the more than 20 per cent of the poll which Liberals won at Gloucester and Ipswich..the Tories' majority..would be reduced. **1965** H. I. ANSOFF *Corporate Strategy* (1968) iv. 61 This personal objective [of maximum current earnings] can have a shattering effect on a firm when control is taken over by a person or a group with the explicit aim of siphoning out of the firm most of its liquid..assets. **1976** F. WARNER *Killing Time* I. ii. 12 Society depends on the integration of those functions that prostitution siphons off. **1979** 'A. HAILEY' *Overload* III. xiii. 261 So how about the remainder [of the income of an organization]? The best guess was that Birdsong, who controlled p & lfp totally, was siphoning it off.

siphonaceous (səifǒnē[i]·ʃəs), *a. Bot.* [f. SIPHON *sb.* + -ACEOUS.] Characterized by or being an algal thallus that is tubular and largely without septa; = SIPHONEOUS *a.* in Dict. and Suppl.

1916 G. S. WEST *Algæ* I. 223 There are a number of undoubted fossil siphonaceous Algæ, the calcified thallus of various forms having lent itself to preservation. **1933** G. M. SMITH *Fresh-Water Algae U.S.* 299 Continued growth of such a coenocyte..would lead to a simple siphonaceous form such as *Protosiphon.* **1969** F. E. ROUND *Introd. Lower Plants* ii. 30 One of the simplest completely siphonaceous genera is *Bryopsis.*

siphonapteran (səifǒnæ·ptərăn), *a.* (*sb.*) [f. mod.L. order name *Siphonaptera* (P. A. Latreille *Familles Naturelles du Règne Animal* (1825) 334), (f. combining form of Gr. σίφων SIPHON- + ἄπτερος wingless) + -AN: cf. APTERAN *a.* and *sb.*] Of or pertaining to a flea of the order Siphonaptera. Also as *sb.*

1842 [in Dict., s.v. SIPHON-]. **1941** I. FOX in *Proc. Entomol. Soc. Washington* XLIII. 6 (*title*) The siphonapteran thorax. **1962** GORDON & LAVOIPIERRE *Entomol. for Students of Med.* xxxv. 218 The egg is similar to that of other fleas and the larvae which emerge after 3 to 4 days incubation are typical siphonapteran larvae.

siphonein (səi·fǒnīn). *Biochem.* [f. SIPHON(O- + *-ein,* perh. after LUTEIN.] An ester of siphonoxanthin present in certain green algæ.

1949 H. H. STRAIN in Franck & Loomis *Photosynthesis in Plants* vi. 162 Siphonein. In most algae containing siphonaxanthin one finds about equivalent amounts of a spectroscopically similar carotenoid which is converted into siphonaxanthin by saponification with alcoholic potassium hydroxide. **1964** [see *siphonoxanthin* s.v. *SIPHONO-]. **1969** *Tetrahedron Lett.* No. 59. 5141 Siphonein is an ester of siphonaxanthin characterized by the esterification of the primary hydroxyl group with a fatty acid.

siphoneous, *a.* Add: = *SIPHONACEOUS *a.* (Later examples.)

1967 I. MORRIS *Introd. Algae* ii. 21 Multicellular thalli may be regarded as being of five main types: 1. Colonial.. 2. Aggregatious..3. Filamentous..4. Siphoneous..5. Parenchymatous. **1971** KUMAR & SINGH *Textbk. Algae* ii. 24 A siphoneous thallus is multinucleate lacking septation except during the formation of reproductive organs.

siphoner (səi·fǒnəɹ). [f. SIPHON *v.* + -ER[1].] One who draws off (liquid, etc.) by siphoning; *spec.* a petrol-thief.

1961 E. S. TURNER *Phoney War* vii. 44 The scarcity of petrol bred a new type of sneak-thief, the siphoner, who went round with a length of rubber tubing and a can, helping himself to the contents of car tanks. **1979** *Tucson Mag.* Sept. 35/1 Mass cruising [in cars] is dying rapidly. About the only people who can do it anymore are the filthy rich and the skillful siphoners.

siphonet. Add: Now *rare* or † *Obs.*, *siphunculus* (q.v., sense *2) or more commonly *cornicle* being used instead.

siphono-. Add: **si·phonostele** *Bot.*, a stele consisting of a core of pith surrounded by concentric layers of xylem and phloem; so **si:phonoste·lic** *a.*; also (*rare*) **si·phonostely,** the state of being or having such a stele; **si:phonoxa·nthin** (also **siphona-)**, a xanthophyll pigment, $C_{40}H_{56}O_4$, present in certain green algæ.

1899 E. C. JEFFREY in *Mem. Boston Soc. Nat. Hist.* V. 160 The two primitive types of stele described above may ..be appropriately designated, protostelic and siphonostelic respectively. *Ibid.*, The primary vascular axes of living Lycopodiales rarely present the phenomena of siphonostely. **1902** Siphonostele [see *MESARCH 1]. **1969** F. E. ROUND *Introd. Lower Plants* x. 123 A simple stele is formed. This consists either of a stellate mass of xylem surrounded by a few rows of simple phloem cells or, in the aerial parts of *Psilotum* and *Tmesipteris*, becoming siphonostelic. *Ibid.*, The central tissue in the siphonosteles is often sclerified. **1949** H. H. STRAIN in Franck & Loomis *Photosynthesis in Plants* vi. 162 Siphonaxanthin. Green algae of the order Siphonales yield significant quantities of this ketonic pigment that closely resembles fucoxanthin with respect to spectral absorption properties. **1964** *Oceanogr. & Marine Biol.* II. 217 Within the Chlorophyta, the Siphonales differ from the other members in possessing siphonein and siphonoxanthin. **1973** V. J. & D. J. CHAPMAN *Algae* (ed. 2) vi. 137 The discoid chloroplasts..lack siphonaxanthin so characteristic of the siphonaceous Chlorophyceae.

siphuncle. Add: **2.** *spec.* = *SIPHUNCULUS 2.

1899 *Cambr. Nat. Hist.* VI. 589 Another highly peculiar structure [in aphids] is the siphons, frequently called nectaries, honey-tubes, or siphuncles. **1962** G. A. TULLOCH *J. R. de la Torre-Bueno's Gloss. Entomol.* (rev. ed.) 268 *Siphuncle*, the cornicle of the aphids.

siphuncular, *a.* Add: Also, of or pertaining to a siphunculus. (Later example.)

1975 *Jrnl. Zool.* CLXXV. 278 Prodding the abdomen and pinching the legs of a sycamore aphid induces it to produce siphuncular exudate.

siphunculus. Add: **2.** *Ent.* A tubular appendage on the abdomen of aphids, which lets out a waxy substance when the animal is attacked that acts as an alarm pheromone; (formerly believed to be the tube from which honeydew comes). Usu. called a *cornicle*.

1939 V. B. WIGGLESWORTH *Princ. Insect Physiol.* x. 233 At the apex of the abdominal tubes or siphunculi of Aphids are ostioles..which allow wax-laden blood cells to escape. **1975** *Jrnl. Zool.* CLXXV. 280 When prodded or attacked by parasites or predators aphids often exude these cells bathed in fluid from their siphunculi.

Siporex (si·pǫreks). A proprietary name for a type of cement or concrete (see quots.).

1938 *Trade Marks Jrnl.* 27 July 913/1 *Siporex* 583, 757. Slates, bricks, blocks, beams, piles, pillars, posts, tiles, pipes, drains and shaped pieces, all made of cement or concrete for use in building or construction. *Internationella Siporex Aktiebolaget*..Sweden..24th February 1938. **1943** *Archit. Rev.* XCIV. 68/1 The Mässhallen in Gothenburg—a large covered sports hall in steel, concrete and siporex—is also by Eriksson. **1965** *Economist* 5 June 1176/2 Siporex is an autoclaved lightweight aerated concrete product which was first developed in Sweden some thirty years ago, and is now used all over the world.

sippers (si·pəɹz). *Naut. slang.* [f. SIP *sb.*: see *-ER[6].] A sip (of rum), esp. taken from another's tot, as a reward for some service or in celebration; *spec.* (see quot. 1944).

1944 J. P. W. MALLALIEU *Very Ordinary Seaman* 99 For his service in measuring the rum the Leading Hand of the mess was entitled to 'sippers' from every man, a 'sipper' being a taste of each tot. **1945** *Penguin New Writing* XXIII. 49 Old three-badge A.B.'s offer him 'sippers' from their tots of rum and protect him from over-zealous killicks. **1956** H. TUNSTALL-BEHRENS *Pamir* 25 A bottle appeared with enough in it to give us all 'sippers'. **1977** R. BAKER *Dry Ginger* viii. 100 Two brothers, one old enough to be allowed his tot of rum, and the other too young..known respectively as 'Gulpers' and 'Sippers' Young.

sipunculan (səipɒ·ŋkiŭlăn), *sb.* and *a.* [f. mod.L. name of phylum *Sipuncula*: see *SIPUNCULID.] **a.** *sb.* A burrowing unsegmented worm of the phylum Sipuncula, found in sandy littoral regions. **b.** *adj.* Of or pertaining to a worm of this kind or the group as a whole.

1975 *Nature* 30 Oct. 818/2 There is convincing evidence that myohaemerythrin, a monomeric protein found in the retractor muscles of the sipunculan worm *Themiste pyroides*, and the protomers of haemerythrin have quite similar tertiary structures. **1977** P. E. GIBBS *Brit. Sipunculans* 7 Whilst sipunculans show clear embryological affinities with the Annelida, it is now generally agreed that..they are best regarded as a distinct and separate phylum.

sipunculid. For 'as prec.' in etym. substitute: mod.L. (Linnæus *Systema Naturæ* (ed. 12, 1766) I. II. 1078). (Later examples.) Also as *adj.*

1928 RUSSELL & YONGE *Seas* i. 20 The Sipunculids.. have a protrusible proboscis and a tough leathery body. **1941, 1967** [see *ECHIUROID *a.* and *sb.*]. **1974** *Sci. Amer.* Apr. 88/2 Probably a fourth type consisted of unsegmented burrowers that fed on surface detritus and gave rise to the modern sipunculid worms.

sir, *sb.* Add: **I. 1. b. Sir Berkeley** *coarse slang* [after *Berkeley* Hunt: see *BERK], the female genital organs; hence *transf.*, sexual intercourse, 'sex'; **Sir Garnet**: see *GARNET[5].

1937 J. CURTIS *There ain't no Justice* xvii. 175 She gives me plenty of the old Sir Berkeley, but she knows how to look after herself, I guess.

II. 6. *sir knight* (later examples).

1939 *Sun* (Baltimore) 30 Sept. 7/8 We stand here today to watch you, sir knights, just in friendly tournament. **1977** *Belfast Tel.* 19 Jan. 2/4 The Officers and Sir Knights of the United Sons of Ulster R.B.P. 1041, regret the death of the Sister of their esteemed Sir Knight Robert Scott, P.M.

7. a. Also, used by schoolchildren in addressing a master.

1838 DICKENS *Nickleby* (1839) viii. 69 'Third boy, what's a horse?' 'A beast, Sir,' replied the boy. **1899** KIPLING *Stalky & Co.* 108 Please, sir, what am I to do about prep.? *a* **1930** D. H. LAWRENCE *Phoenix II* (1968) 25 Please Sir, do tortoises bite? **1955** E. BLISHEN *Roaring Boys* i. 31 'The cane,' said Sims vaguely. 'Sir can't,' said Pottell... 'Is it because you're too young, sir?' **1974** 'J. LE CARRÉ' *Tinker, Tailor* xiv. 118 'Sir, please sir, I think he's to do with the church, sir,' said Cole Slaw. 'I saw him, talking to Wells Fargo, sir, after the service.'

8. b. (Earlier and later examples.)

1768 STERNE *Sent. Journey* I. 38 Figure to yourself, my dear Sir, that in giving you a chaise which would fall to pieces before you had got half way to Paris..how much I should suffer. **1776** *Critical Rev.* XLII. 89 It is usual, we are told, with the Scots..to address the person with whom they converse by the appellation My dear Sir. **1893** G. B. SHAW *Widowers' Houses* II. iii. 43 *Sartorius*: Will you excuse me for ten minutes? *Cokane*: My dear sir!—*Trench*: Certainly. **1983** A. VENTERS *Blood on Rocks* xiii. 122 'You must have something to eat, my dear sir,' he cried.

c. *yes, sir*: an emphatic assertion; *no, sir*: see *NOSSIR. Chiefly *U.S. colloq.*

1799 *Aurora* (Philadelphia) 8 Aug. (Th.), Yes Sir! and [France] has been successful beyond any former experience. **1889** 'C. E. CRADDOCK' *Despot of Broomsedge Cove* 40 Yes, sir... None like 'em now. **1929** W. FAULKNER *Sartoris* II. v. 124 'Yes sir,' he repeated, 'he's sure some joker.' **1942** J. B. PRIESTLEY in *R.A.F. Jrnl.* 3 Oct. 2, I could take it and I could dish it out. Yes, Sir!

10. a. Also more recently, a knight or baronet.

1922 W. J. LOCKE *Tale of Triona* i. 9 A proud old Anglo-Indian family, all Generals and Colonels and Sirs and Ladies. **1952** 'W. COOPER' *Struggles of Albert Woods* IV. i. 202 Albert thought..there must be a connection between Jameson's appointments and his becoming a Sir. **1974** P. GORE-BOOTH *With Great Truth & Respect* 374, I argued hard and explicitly on behalf of my diplomatic colleagues because becoming a 'Sir' is one of the tools of the trade.

b. *spec.* a schoolmaster. *colloq.* or *humorous.*

1955 [see sense 7 a above]. **1961** *Guardian* 1 Dec. 7/2 [The] users will be grateful to Sir for providing..a smashing set of answers. **1968, 1973** [see *MISS *sb.*[2] 3 f]. **1980** *Daily Tel.* 31 Mar. 10/3 Sir never repeated any part of a question.

sirab, var. *SERAB.

siratro (siræ·tro). [f. initial letters (as indicated) of Commonwealth *S*cientific and *I*ndustrial *R*esearch Organization + *atro*(*purpureus* the specific epithet of the parent plants.] A tropical legume of the variety so called, developed at the C.S.I.R.O. Pasture Research Station, Samford, near Brisbane, by E. M. Hutton in the early 1960s from Mexican strains of *Macroptilium* (*Phaseolus*) *atropurpureum.*

1962 E. M. HUTTON in *Austral. Jrnl. Exper. Agric.* II. 117/1 Two Mexican strains of *P*[*haseolus*] *atropurpureus*.. were crossed, and this resulted in the development of a new bred strain which has been named Siratro. **1975** *Nature* 31 July 409/1 An isolate from nodules of *Trema cannabina*..is a strain able to nodulate siratro. **1978** *Jrnl. R. Soc. Arts* CXXVI. 628/2 The Legume Siratro is probably the most outstanding example of pasture plant breeding... It is now the most widely grown pasture legume in southern and central Queensland.

sirdar. Add: **1.** *β.* (Later examples.)

1899 P. S. ALLEN *Let.* 15 Feb. (1939) 19 A Sardar of this neighbourhood whom we met in Khewra station sent us.. a present. **1969** S. M. SADEEK *Windswept & Other Stories* 36 An arsenal of life pulsed and throbbed between the harsh rasping orders of the sardars echoing through the native compound.

siree, var. SIRREE in Dict. and Suppl.

sireen (səirī·n). Also **syreen.** Repr. colloq. (now chiefly *U.S.*) pronunc. of SIREN *sb.* (esp sense 7 b in Dict. and Suppl.).

1915 KIPLING *Fringes of Fleet* 11 Five damned trawlers with their syreens blowing. **1940** *Economist* 28 Sept. 398/2 The air raids have produced some more new war words... A quite inexplicable new word is the 'sireen', which has widely ousted the siren. Its slight resemblance to Eileen and Doreen suggests that it may have arisen from a desire to give the noise a feminine personality. **1943** G. GREENE *Ministry of Fear* I. i. 16 This time of night... It's the sireens. **1957** W. FAULKNER *Town* xxiv. 363 Mr. Connors went to his [car] that had the red light and the sireen on it. **1977** J. CLEARY *Vortex* i. 20 The siren began to wail again:..'I wish he'd blow up that goddam si-reen.'

sireland (səiᵊ·ɹlæ̆nd). *nonce-wd.* [f. SIRE *sb.*, punningly after *Ireland.*] The land of one's birth; one's native country or fatherland.

1922 JOYCE *Ulysses* 182 Cranly's eleven true Wicklowmen to free their sireland. **1939** —— *Finnegans Wake* (1964) 428 Sireland calls you.

siren, *sb.* Add: **I. 7. b.** Also, more generally, a device which produces a piercing note (freq. of varying tone), used as an air-raid warning, or to signify the approach of a police car, etc.; the noise itself. Formerly, a motor-horn.

1907 [see *CUT-OUT *sb.* 1 b]. **1917** *Flying* 25 July 2/2 Tests with various sirens were made in Central London in order to ascertain whether they would be audible. **1940** S. O'CASEY *Let.* 20 Aug. (1975) I. 866 We have a kind of a cellar that we are to go to when the siren sounds. **1943** *Times* (Weekly ed.) 18 Aug. 12/3 The Luftwaffe helps the Church Army. How?—every night there isn't a siren, a Church Army friend puts sixpence in her box and when there is she puts 2s. 6d. in as soon as the 'All Clear' goes. **1963** MRS. L. B. JOHNSON *White House Diary* 22 Nov. (1970) 5 We got in [the car]. Lyndon told the agents to stop the sirens. **1969** G. MACBETH *War Quartet* 43 Then the sirens went, Sucking life underground. **1971** *Daily Tel.* (Colour Suppl.) 22 Oct. 19/3 Pursued by cops, lights flashing, siren wailing, up Brighton Road.

II. 8. b. *siren-bird.*

1923 E. SITWELL *Bucolic Comedies* 90 Where siren-birds sip Bohea.

10. *siren alarm*; **siren suit**, a one-piece costume resembling overalls or a boiler-suit, orig. designed for wear by women in air-raid shelters; later, worn by either sex, and as a fashion garment.

1950 G. B. SHAW *Farfetched Fables* II. 107 He is interrupted by a siren alarm, followed by an artillery salvo. **1976** LD. HOME *Way Wind Blows* iv. 72 Some time in the early hours of the next morning there was a siren alarm, and we all trooped down to the basement of No. 10. **1939** *English* Autumn 346 Ladies' dress-shops ambiguously advertise 'siren suits' for the Air Raid Shelter. **1942** C. KING *Jrnl.* 17 July in *With Malice toward None* (1970) 183 The Prime Minister..was in his blue siren-suit. **1959** R. COLLIER *City that wouldn't Die* vii. 102 In a minute he [*sc.* Winston Churchill] came—black silk dressing-gown embroidered with gold pheasants over the baby-blue siren suit he called 'my rompers'. **1977** *Belfast Tel.* 19 Jan. 18/7 (Advt.), Good reductions in children's coats and fur siren suits.

siren, *v.* Restrict *rare* to sense 1 and add: **1.** (Later examples.)

1935 L. MACNEICE *Poems* 14 Two [women] there are, as I drive in the city... The one sirening me to draw up by the kerb. **1960** T. STACEY *Brothers* xxx. 353 They heard brilliant rippling music like some huge wooden xylophone. With this intricate sound still sirening them they found themselves on a hill top.

2. Also (of a police car, etc.), to proceed with siren blaring; to make *one's way* thus. Also **si·rening** *ppl. a.*

1940 'M. INNES' *Secret Vanguard* x. 106 A sirening ambulance or fire-engine. **1951** R. BRADBURY *Silver Locusts* 50 They slammed the police-wagon door and drove him off into the early morning, his face pressed to the rear window, and just before they sirened over a hill, he saw the red fire..on an ordinary Monday morning on the ordinary planet Earth. **1960** *Guardian* 21 Oct. 13/4 He was sirening up the Henry Hudson parkway. **1965** D. S. DAVIS *Pale Betrayer* xxviii. 206 Fitzgerald sirened his way through the crowd, not leaving the car. **1978** J. I. M. STEWART *Full Term* viii. 86 An ambulance went wildly sirening into St. Giles'.

Sirenian, var. *SIRYENIAN *sb.* and *a.*

sirex (səi·reks). *Ent.* Also **Sirex.** [mod.L. (Linnæus *Fauna Suecica* (ed. 2, 1761) 396), f. Gr. σειρήν siren, a solitary bee or wasp.] A wood-wasp or horntail of the genus *Sirex*, whose larvæ burrow into the trunks of trees. Also *attrib.*

1895 *Cambr. Nat. Hist.* V. 509 The *Sirex* will..attack a perfectly healthy tree immediately after it has been felled. **1908** A. T. GILLANDERS *Forest Entomol.* v. 190 The female *Sirex*..is armed with a long ovipositor. **1928** *Bull. Entomol. Res.* XIX. 219 (*heading*) The *Sirex* woodwasps and their importance in forestry. **1958** *N.Z. Timber Jrnl.* Sept. 87/1 The sirex woodwasp..attacks live and freshly felled trees. **1969** *Sun* (Melbourne) 26 June 16/2 The dreaded sirex wasp has been found in pine plantations.

sirih. Add: Also **sireh.** Substitute for def.: A trailing tropical shrub, *Piper betle*, of the family Piperaceæ, native to Indonesia, where the pungent leaves are chewed with areca nuts; also, the leaves of the shrub; = BETEL 1. (Earlier examples.)

1779 T. Forrest *Voyage to New Guinea* vi. 75 The Malays call the betel leaf, Ciry. **1783** W. Marsden *Hist. Sumatra* 74 The *Seeree*, a creeping plant, whole leaf, of a strong aromatic flavor, they eat with the betel nut. **1795** tr. *C. P. Thunberg's Trav.* (ed. 2) II. 268 The betel leaves, called Siri (*Piper betel*), are therefore brought in fresh every day for sale. **1839** T. J. Newbold *Straits of Malacca* I. ii. 87 The parents..offer a small present of plantains, sirih, tobacco, etc.

b. *sirih-box* (earlier example), *juice, leaf* (earlier example), *vine*.

1839 *Chinese Repository* VII. 130 His betel and siri box. **1939** A. Keith *Land below Wind* xiii. 211, I looked back at the kampong women..; their lips, red with *sireh* juice, like cerise flowers. **1846** H. Keppel *Exped. to Borneo of H.M.S. Dido* II. i. 13 His majesty chewed his sirih-leaf and betel-nut. **1893** F. A. Swettenham *About Perak* 38 Here the Malay lives under his sireh-vine and durian tree.

sirki. (Earlier example.)

1801 *Asiatick Researches* VII. 463 *Hoogla* or *Sirkee* mats.

sirocco. Add: **1. a.** (Earlier *transf.* examples.)

1848 J. S. Robinson *Sk. Gt. West* 17 The dreaded Sirocco..burns us even through our clothes. **1870** *Weekly Standard* (Buenos Aires) 21 Dec. (Suppl.) col. 6 The Sirocco on Wednesday was so terrible that in the effort to keep cool, the mind reverted to icebergs and Polar travels but all in vain.

b. (Earlier example.)

1700 J. Jackson *Let.* 2 Feb. in *Private Corr. S. Pepys* (1926) I. 278 But the weather being changed and the Sciroccos now blowing into the place of the Tramontains, this design is become impracticable.

siro·cco, *v. rare.* Also **scirocco.** [f. the sb.] *intr.* and *trans.* To blow (about) like the sirocco.

1921 D. H. Lawrence *Let.* 16 Nov. (1962) II. 677 It has blown, the wind, and snowed on Calabria, and sciroccoed till we are all of us in fragments. **1937** J. Squire *Honeysuckle & Bee* vi. 170 The monotonous maudlin refrain of a song about the Isle of Capri... As it faded away, I remembered where, when it had already sciroccoed the world for six months, I had last heard it.

‖ **sirop** (siro, si·rǫp). [Fr.: see Syrup *sb.*] (A drink made from) a sweetened fruit-juice concentrate.

1871 *Monthly Packet* Oct. 369 The sirops and Savoy cakes had been disposed of. **1889** E. Simcox in K. A. McKenzie *E. Simcox & G. Eliot* (1961) ii. 55 Ending up.. with *sirop* at some café in the small hours. **1933** 'G. Orwell' *Down & Out* xvii. 126 Two children..sharing a glass of *sirop*. **1966** H. Yoxall *Fashion of Life* xxiii. 206 We consumed *sirops* called *citronade, grenadine, framboise*. **1978** *Times* 22 July 8/7 The continental 'sirops', in mint, grenadine and blackcurrant flavours, are available in good delicatessens..for under £1.50.

sirree. See also *no siree, *yes siree.

Siryenian (siryī·niăn), *sb.* and *a.* Also **Sirenian, Syrianian, -jenian, Syryenian, Ziranian, Zyrenian.** [f. mod.L. *Syriænus* (ad. Russ. *zyryánin, -áne* *Zyrian *sb.* and *a.*) + -ian.] = *Zyrian *sb.* and *a.*

1851 *Illustr. Catal. Gt. Exhib.* iii. 552/1 Sirenian St. Matthew. **1878** *Encycl. Brit.* VIII. 700/1 Finnic or Ugrian represented by..Siryenian. **1879** *Ibid.* IX. 291/2 The Permian Finns comprise the Siryenians,.. the Permian proper,..and the Votyak. **1908** [see *Permian *a.* (*sb.*) 2]. **1910** *Encycl. Brit.* X. 389/1 The Syryenian headquarters are at the town of Ishma on the Pechora. **1911** *Ibid.* XXVI. 317/2 Syryenians (also Sirianian, Syrjenian, Zyrenian, Ziranian, Zyrian and Zirian), a tribe belonging to the Permian division of the eastern Finns. **1930** Liddell & Scott *Gr.-Eng. Lex.*, *Κάνναβις*..borrowed perh. fr. Ugro-Finnish, cf...Syrianian *piš* 'hemp'.

sis (sis), *sb.* Also **siss.** Colloq. abbrev. of Sister *sb.* (in Dict. and Suppl.).

1656 Dr. Denton *Let.* 20 Nov. in M. M. Verney *Memoirs* (1894) III. ix. 315 We had need call a councell for marryinge and givinge in marriage, you for your sis, she for hers, and I for mine. **1808** Lady Lyttelton *Let.* 18 Dec. (1912) ii. 53 But oh, Bob, pity your poor Mam and Sis, when they will have to set out on a bleak morning, over such rough, splashy, squashy, jolting and jumbling roads as ours. **1835** *Knickerbocker* VI. 293 All the friends called her sister,..which, as the half was easier to be bandied about than the whole,..soon dwindled into 'sis'. **1859** [see Siss *sb.*[1]]. **1872** C. M. Yonge *P's & Q's* iii. 19 'I knew you were a jolly old sis,' said Horace with a hug. **1891** M. E. Ryan *Pagan of Alleghanies* 133 Folks call boys 'bud' sometimes, jist like they call girls 'sis'. **1924** Lawrence & Skinner *Boy in Bush* vi. 86 Skippin' up an' down like sis. **1935** Z. N. Hurston *Mules & Men* (1970) i. x. 220 Sis Cat, we both got a li'l money. **1948** M. Allingham *More Work for Undertaker* ii. 26 'Who was she? Your only love?' 'Gawd, no! My sis.' **1970** M. Walker *Prophets for New Day* in S. Henderson *Understanding New Black Poetry* (1973) ii. 161, I run down to Sis Avery's. **1974** D. Gray *Dead Give Away* i. 14 You'll be wearing clothes at the Private View, won't you, Sis?

‖ **sis** (sis, sis), *int. S. Afr.* Also †**cess.** [ad. Afrikaans *sies* (also used), perh. ad. Hottentot *si* or *tsi*.] An ejaculation expressing disgust or disappointment.

1862 A. W. Drayson *Tales at Outspan* 67, I have lost more cattle from the attacks of hyænas than I have from lions, or leopards, and as to sheep, *cess*, I've had nearly a whole flock worried by them. **1909** *Cape* 30 Apr. 6 Sis for her. She gave me nothing to eat but semalina and kofee. **1926** E. Lewis *Mantis* i. iv. 79 'Sis, man!' Hugo had scolded him, 'you go to see one of these private fellows.' **1949** *Forum* 26 Mar. 15 The elegant word 'sies!' is in evidence when persons to whom objection is taken are present or even mentioned. **1972** *Star* (Johannesburg) 15 Nov. 18 The majority of young Afrikaans people.. cannot speak English and..have no intention of doing so. Ag sis! Praat English.

-sis, *suffix*, repr. Gr. -σις in nouns of action, as in Analysis, Arsis, *merisis, Peristalsis, etc. Also in some nouns denoting a specified diseased state, as *filariasis, Phthisis, *psittacosis, Sepsis.

sisal. Add: Now usu. with pronunc. (səi·s'l).

3. Special combs., as **sisalcraft, -kraft,** a waterproof material with a core of sisal fibres.

1940 *Chambers's Techn. Dict.* 774/1 Sisalcraft. **1945** *Jrnl. R. Army Med. Corps* LXXXIV. 98 The sisalcraft and blankets already sewn up. **1948** *Spectator* 9 Apr. 430/1 The wooden huts in which the occupants of Antarctic bases live are specially designed with layers of tinfoil and sisalkraft between the inner and outer walls. **1961** [see *sark *v.* 2]. **1962** *Economist* 8 Sept. 956/1 The conventional materials..such as bituminised sisalcraft and burlap.

sis-boom-bah (sis,būm,bā·), *int.* and *sb. U.S.* Also **-ah.** [Echoic, repr. the sound of a skyrocket: a hissing flight (*sis*), an explosion (*boom*), and an exclamation of delight from the spectators (*bah, ah*): see *skyrocket 2.] A shout expressive of support or encouragement to a college team. Hence as *sb.*, enthusiastic or partisan support of spectator sports, esp. football.

[**1867**: see *sky-rocket *sb.* 2]. **1924** *Dialect Notes* V. 276 *Sis-boom:* —— ah, —— bah (college yells). **1961** M. Beadle *These Ruins are Inhabited* (1963) iv. 48 Fresh from the land of sis-boom-bah.., the Americans had a hard time at first learning to applaud good play by *either* team. **1970** *Time* 17 Aug. 64 For the next 2½ years it was girls, flasks and sis-boom-bah. But the public image concealed an all-night reader.

siserskite, var. *sysertskite.

sisham, var. Shisham.

1890 Kipling *Soldiers Three* 31 We three were comfortably settled under the big *sisham* [ed. 1889 *shisham*].

sisi, var. *seesee. **sisith,** var. *zizith.

siss, *sb.*[1] Substitute for entry:
siss, var. *sis *sb.*

sisserskite, obs. var. *sysertskite.

sissonne. Delete *rare*, substitute for def. '(See quot. 1957.)', and add later examples.

1892, 1913 [see *ciseaux]. **1930** Craske & Beaumont *Theory & Pract. Allegro in Class. Ballet* 47 *Sissonne dessus*... Other *sissonnes* are *sissonne dessous, s. en avant, s. en arrière*, etc. **1947** N. Nicolaeva-Legat *Ballet Education* iv. 109 *Sissone* is another step which has many variations. *Sissone simple* on the *cou-de-pied* is taken from V pos., the right leg in front; a spring into the air, pushing from the ground equally with both feet and with straight knees; land on the left leg. **1957** G. B. L. Wilson *Dict. Ballet* 247 *Sissonne*, or *pas de sissonne*, probably from *pas de ciseaux*, a scissor-like movement... With a slight plié, the dancer springs into the air to the fifth position, alighting on one foot with a demi-plié, with the other leg extended to the back, front, or side; the back foot is then closed to the supporting foot (a sissonne fermée)... If the dancer lands on one foot with the other on the coup-de-pied..it is a sissonne simple (or ordinaire). **1968** J. Winearls *Mod. Dance* (ed. 2) iii. 87 This sissonne is a combination of the three elements, light—quick—and peripheral.

sissy (si·si). *colloq.* [f. *sis *sb.* + -y[6]; cf. *cissy *sb.* and *a.*] **1.** A sister.

1846 *Dollar Newspaper* (Philadelphia) 22 Apr. 1/7 'Sissy Jane' smoothed back my hair, and smiled at me. **1854** Dickens *Hard Times* i. vi. 41 When Sissy got into the school here..her father was as pleased as Punch. **1859** [see Siss *sb.*[1]]. **1865** K. H. Digby *Short Poems* 39 The little one grasping, with such a tight hold, The frock of sweet sissy, herself not too bold. **1901** M. Franklin *My Brilliant Career* xiii. 107 Don't be frightened, sissy, I never kiss girls. **1939** Joyce *Finnegans Wake* 94 It made ma make merry and sissy so shy.

2. An effeminate person; a coward.

1887 *Lantern* (New Orleans) 27 Aug. 3/2 Look and walk too much like sissies to do much fightin'. **1899** T. Hall *Tales* 131 'Well, you are a sissy,' said Blinks contemptuously. **1926** *British Weekly* 9 Sept. 473/3 A religious 'sissy' was anathema to me. **1932** S. Gibbons *Cold Comfort Farm* xvii. 237, I want red blood. I don't want no sissies, see? **1938** L. MacNeice *Zoo* iv. 74 The Sealyham, say the older breeders, is becoming a sissy. **1969** C. Himes *Blind Man with Pistol* ii. 25 The sissies..were colored and mostly young. They all had straightened hair..; long false eyelashes. **1977** *Time* 21 Feb. 40/2 Smokers proved to be sissies when deprived of cigarettes.

3. *attrib.* or as *adj.* **a.** Effeminate; cowardly.

1891 *Harper's Mag.* Aug. 485/2 He approached and sat near me, deep in conversation with a young gentleman with sissy whiskers. **1893** *Sunday Mercury* (N.Y.) 14 May 15/5 (*heading*) Sissy men in Society.—Powdered, Painted and Laced. They swarm at Afternoon Teas. **1899** T. Hall *Tales* 121 Scotty was, in the newspaper vernacular, 'a sissy boy', or, in other words, a bit effeminate. **1926** *British Weekly* 2 Sept. 452/3 There was nothing 'sissy' about him. He was a born fighter. **1932** S. Gibbons *Cold Comfort Farm* xvii. 241 Thassa sissy sort of a name, but it'll do. **1941** 'R. West' *Black Lamb & Grey Falcon* II. 152 The monuments..had apparently been produced by a pastry-cook under the influence of Persian art. Such sugary little scrolls and swaps, such sissy little flowers in pots, such coy little etchings of swords on the soldiers' tombs. **1959** *Spectator* 25 Sept. 408/2 All the kudos goes to the campaign-scarred, ink-stained veteran: none to the new bug in his sissy clean blazer. **1970** P. Dickinson tr. *Aristophanes' Wasps* in *Plays* I. 192 That sissy son of Chaireas prances In with his mincing walk. **1977** C. McCullough *Thorn Birds* xi. 260 No cutter ever wore gloves. They slowed a man down... Besides, gloves were sissy.

b. sissy bar, a metal loop rising from behind the seat of a bicycle or motor-cycle.

1969 *Daily Colonist* (Victoria, B.C.) 19 June 40/1 (Advt.), The 'Super Cycle' breed with hi-rise handlebars on a cantilever frame...the 36" Sissy bar, [etc.]. **1974** R. B. Parker *God save Child* vi. 49 Another motorcycle... A big one,..small front wheel, sissy bar behind.

Hence **sissifica·tion,** effeminacy; **si·ssified** *a.*, effeminate; **si·ssiness,** effeminacy; **si·ssyish** *a.*, somewhat effeminate.

1889 W. D. Howells *Hazard of New Fortunes* II. 64 The New York fellows carried canes..; and they were both sissyish and fast. **1905** J. C. Lincoln *Partners of Tide* iv. 78 To be seen with girls was not so 'sissified' in his mind as it used to be. **1926** *Harper's Mag.* Feb. 350/2 In spite of his funny sissiness there was not a dog in town that did not love him. **1938** I. Goldberg *Wonder of Words* xv. 305 Mr Sokolsky establishes a correlation between high blood-pressure and masculinity, and between low blood-pressure and femininity or sissification. **1959** E. Pound *Thrones* xcix. 57 In statement, answer; in conversation Not with sissified fussiness (chiao') Always want your own way. **1973** *Guardian* 1 June 10/5 The much-publicised Warhol Factory mystique..thinly veils a highly reactionary, bigoted and sissified neo-Nazi boutique. **1975** *N.Y. Times* 12 Sept. 38/6 Mr. Mahan said that the other cowboys on the rodeo circuit had generally accepted his fashion business, and that none of them considered it 'sissyish or effeminate'.

sister, *sb.* Add: **I. 2.** (Further examples.) *spec.* (*a*) a (fellow) prostitute; (*b*) a (fellow) feminist; (*c*) among Blacks, a Black woman. *sisters under the skin*: see *skin *sb.* 5 j.

1847 A. Harris *Settlers & Convicts* vi. 94 When 'her sister' (so they usually speak in the *sisterhood of sorrow*) came here, she came too. **1870** *Free Lance* 16 Apr. 123/1 The working sisters of this great city are waking up to a sense of what they ought to do in making future provision for themselves. **1889** *Girl's Own Paper* 28 Sept. 824/3 A better day..has dawned..on our sisters, the working girls of this country. **1899** 'J. Flynt' *Tramping* i. iv. 94 If he can only have some outcast woman, or 'sister', as he calls her..he is a comparatively happy fellow. **1912** H. Ellis *Task of Social Hygiene* iii. 104 'La femme libre'.. must be a woman of reflection and intellect who, having meditated on the fate of her 'sisters'..shall give forth the confession of her sex..in such a manner as to furnish the indispensable elements for formulating the rights and duties of woman. **1912** in C. McKay *Songs of Jamaica* 16 Me watch de vine dem grow, S'er t'row dung a de root. **1926** L. Hughes *Weary Blues* 37, I got a railroad ticket, Pack my trunk and ride. Sing 'em sister! Got a railroad ticket, Pack my trunk and ride. **1935** Z. N. Hurston *Mules & Men* (1970) i. vii. 164 De cow went bustin' on down de back-road wid de ole man till they met a sister he knowed. **1940** J. Crad *Traders in Women* v. 130 Then she left her 'selling position' and it was immediately occupied by one of her 'sisters'. **1944** *Publ. Amer. Dial. Soc.* ii. 36 *Sister, n.*, a woman. W. N[orth] C[arolina]. **1968** *Ramparts* May 12 Our sisters in Vietnam have taught us many lessons. **1973** *Black World* June 90/2 Sister Williams breaks her book down into three major parts. **1976** R. B. Parker *Promised Land* xix. 110 When the sisters call you... Talk to them of obligation and sororal affiliation. **1977** C. McFadden *Serial* (1978) iii. 13/1 The sisters weren't invariably as supportive as she'd hoped they'd be. **1979** *Guardian* 5 May 12/2 Becoming Britain's first woman Prime Minister is one [achievement], whatever the sisters may say, that can only change perceptions of what women can aspire to.

3. d. (Earlier and later examples.) Also, prefixed as a title to the name of a nurse. *Sister Dora* [f. the name of the celebrated nurse Dorothy ('Dora') Pattison, 1832–78], a type of nurse's cap (see quot. 1971).

1860 [see *nursing *vbl. sb.* 1 b]. **1924** 'R. Hall' *Unlit Lamp* xlvi. 314, I made swabs at the Town Hall at Seabourne... I had a Sister Dora arrangement on my head; we all had, it made us look important. Some of the women wore aprons with large red crosses on their bibs. **1949** N. Mitford *Love in Cold Climate* ii. viii. 276 Doesn't it seem funny to have talcum powder and..boring old Sister waiting..for somebody who doesn't exist? **1971** J. Manton *Sister Dora* xvi. 266 [Dora Pattison] made herself up a new cap, still tied with a butterfly bow and streamers under the chin but folded smoothly back over her dark hair. It was to be known to generations of nurses as 'a Sister Dora'. **1976** C. Storr *Unnatural Fathers* iii. 34 Kind Sister Tucker..faithful in her professional code of discretion, bustled upstairs..to attend to her interesting patients. **1978** *Church Times* 29 Dec. 11/3 The little white cap worn by nurses everywhere became known within the profession as 'a Sister Dora'. **1979** 'C. Aird' *Some die Eloquent* i. 11 When Sister Casualty..had trouble-makers in her patch she would ring down to the police station.

Ibid. iii. 37 Sister Stork's on the other phone to the delivery ward.

5. (Further examples.) Also *colloq.* as a mode of address to an unrelated woman, esp. one whose name is not known.

1906 H. GREEN *At Actors' Boarding House* 56 He got up and walked over to her bench. 'You up agin it too, sister?' he said, gently. **1926** E. O'NEILL *Great God Brown* I. iii. 40 Blessed are the pitiful, Sister! **1929** W. FAULKNER *Sartoris* II. iii. 97 A voice in the other room boomed in rich rolling waves 'Mawnin', sister,' it said. **1934** 'E. M. DELAFIELD' *Provincial Lady in Amer.* 60 Shouted at by a policeman who tells her: Put your lights on, sister! **1943** *Amer. Speech* XVIII. 88 [New Zealand English] Sister is also used for a girl as a term of address. It is not..a recent adoption from American films, but a relic of the whaling slang of a century ago. **1944** M. LASKI *Love on Supertax* xi. 103 Just waiting for your boy friend, duckie..? You want the best, we got 'em, eh, sister? **1953** H. MILLER *Plexus* (1963) iii. 127 'He doesn't need advice,' she replied. 'He knows what he's doing.' 'O.K. sister, have it your way then!' With this he turned abruptly to me again. **1976** 'R. BOYLE' *Cry Rape* i. 6 Come on, sister... Why won't you stay and talk to me? I'm a nice guy.

II. 9. For † read '*Obs.* exc. *arch.* in *sister-son.*' (Later examples.)

1955 J. R. R. TOLKIEN *Return of King* vi. 255 Fréalaf, Helm's sister-son. *a* **1973** —— *Silmarillion* (1977) xvi. 136 The King..looked with liking upon Maeglin his sister-son.

10. a. *sister woman.*

a **1786** BURNS *Address to Unco Guid* in *Poems* (1968) I. 53 Then gently scan your brother Man, Still gentler sister Woman. **1856** DICKENS *Little Dorrit* (1857) xxvii. 243 A woman, who..has a perverted delight in making a sister-woman as wretched as she is. **1939** N. MARSH *Overture to Death* vii. 76, I have judged my sister-woman in my heart and condemned her.

b. *sister state* (earlier example).

1777 *Rec. Early Hist. Boston* (1887) XVIII. 285 We are sure, that very large, & much wanted Supplies, the Property of this State & expected here, are now ordered into some of the Sister States.

c. *sister island* (further example), *isle, science, ship* (further examples), *soul.*

1936 *Discovery* June 187/1 The *waganga*, who specialise in *pepo*-exorcism, go through a special training. The art is at its highest in Pemba, the sister-island of Zanzibar. **1838** T. LANGTON in H. H. Langton *Gentlewoman in Upper Canada* (1950) 58 William Jones is from the sister isle. **1939** JOYCE *Finnegans Wake* 51 A native of the sisterisle..by his brogue. **1901** W. JAMES *Mem. & Stud.* (1911) vii. 169 Whether his name [*sc.* F. Myers'] will have in psychology as honorable a place as their names [*sc.* Cuvier and Agassiz's] have gained in the sister-science, will depend on whether future inquirers shall adopt or reject his theories. **1966** N. NICOLSON in *Diaries & Lett. H. Nicolson* (1966) 56 The airship, R.101, was contracted by the Government in 1925 as a sister-ship to R.100. **1974** E. R. H. IVAMY *Marine Insurance* (ed. 2) xv. 216 This clause is known as the 'sister ship' clause and was introduced to state the legal position where two ships belonging to the same owner come into collision. **1897** J. WARING tr. *Balzac's Lily of Valley* 74 Feeling now that we were twins of the same nurture, she could not conceive of semi-confidences between sister souls that had drunk of the same spring. **1933** *Times Lit. Suppl.* 16 Nov. 792/2 The influence of the visiting Cousin Nellie, who finds a sister-soul in the comfortable person of an Aug [*sc.* August visitor] of her own age.

d. sister chromatid *Biol.*, each of a pair of chromatids derived from a common parent chromosome.

1942 *Jrnl. Genetics* XLIII. 195 A single chromatid may be broken and fail to rejoin, the chromatid fragment almost always remaining paired to its sister chromatid. **1975** *Nature* 13 Nov. 122/1 Techniques have been developed which distinguish between sister chromatids without using radioisotopes and autoradiography.

11. sister act (see quot. 1952); **sister tutor,** a nursing sister who teaches trainee nurses.

1908 G. V. HOBART *Go to It* 56 Their names were Millie and Tillie, and they..did a sister act. **1908** *Variety* 18 Apr. 4/4 There may be a number of new 'sister' acts in vaudeville next season. **1952** W. GRANVILLE *Dict. Theatrical Terms* 163 *Sister act*, a variety act performed by two or more sisters; e.g. the famous Dolly Sisters, the singing Green Sisters of the stage and radio. **1968** R. RENDELL *Secret House of Death* vi. 62 An even temperature, that's one thing my sister tutor always impressed on me. **1971** P. D. JAMES *Shroud for Nightingale* iv. 119 I'm not a qualified Sister Tutor. I was only deputizing.

sisterhood. Add: **1.** (Later examples in feminist use.)

1968 *Notes from First Year* June 18 Sisterhood is powerful! **1974** *Time* 6 May 80 Sisterhood across class lines is a myth. **1980** J. R. RICHARDS *Sceptical Feminist* i. 28 Basic to much recent feminist practice has been the idea of *sisterhood*, which..involves a determination among members of the women's movement to work together as equals.

2. b. (Later examples, of feminists.)

1972 *Newsweek* 9 Oct. 104 That book's stinging attack on the women's lib movement achieved for its author a place in the sisterhood's demonology right next to Hugh Hefner. **1981** *Times* 9 Sept. 9/3 At the age of 24 Sarah Daniels must count as a second generation feminist, and if this first play is a portent of what the sisterhood is now brewing up then male chauvinism can breathe again.

Sistine (si·stīn), *a.* and *sb.* [ad. It. *sistino* of Sixtus.] **A.** *adj.* Pertaining to Pope Sixtus IV (1471–84); *spec.* as epithet of the chapel built by him; hence, of or belonging to the Sistine Chapel, as *Sistine Madonna*, a picture by Raphael originally hung there. **B.** *sb.* The Sistine Chapel.

[**1769** J. REYNOLDS *Discourse delivered at Opening of Royal Academy* 5 On the sight of the Capella Sistina, he [*sc.* Raphael] immediately..assumed that grand style of painting.] **1771** C. BURNEY *Pres. State Music in France & Italy* p. vi, The Pope's chapel is sometimes called the Sistine chapel, from Sextus Quintus, who built it. **1863** J. A. SYMONDS *Let.* 19 Dec. (1967) I. 435 The Sistine Chapel too gains everything by being seen in the original. **1869** 'MARK TWAIN' *Innoc. Abroad* xxvii. 288 He has shown us the great picture in the Sistine Chapel..by Michael Angelo. **1885** *Encycl. Brit.* XIX. 64/1 San Sisto.. lost its chief attraction when Raphael's Sistine Madonna (now in Dresden) was sold by the monks. **1887** 'J. OLDCASTLE' *Leo XIII* vi. 36 The conclave assembled to-day in the Sistine. **1889** GROVE *Dict. Mus.* IV. 122/1 The traditions of the Sistine Choir. **1920** W. B. YEATS *Michael Robartes & Dancer* 2 While Michael Angelo's Sistine roof His 'Morning' and his 'Night' disclose How sinew that has been pulled tight,..Can rule by supernatural right. **1950** *New Yorker* 25 Feb. 82/3 In the vesper Mass, the Sistine's famous boy sopranos let loose their voices. **1968** A. DIMENT *Bang Bang Birds* x. 182 All I could hear was a choir singing in the Sistine Chapel. **1975** 'R. PLAYER' *Let's talk of Graves* iii. 81 The Czar Nicholas the First.. was kneeling in the Sistine. *Ibid.* 82 The clouds of Sistine incense around the yellow tapers. **1977** R. L. WOLFF *Gains & Losses* ii. 131 Guy [Morville]..looks like one of the angels in the Sistine Madonna.

sisyrinchium (siziri·nkiŏm). [mod.L. (L. Plukenet *Almagestum Botanicum* (1696) 348), f. Gr. σισυρίγχιον a plant name used by Theophrastus.] An annual or perennial herb of the genus so called, belonging to the family Iridaceæ, native to North or South America, and bearing linear leaves and clusters of small blue, yellow, red, or white flowers; = *blue-eyed grass* s.v. BLUE-EYED *a.* in Dict. and Suppl. and *satin-flower* (*e*) s.v. *SATIN *sb.* (and *a.*) 8 b.

1772 R. WESTON *Universal Botanist* III. 664 (*heading*) Narrow-leaved Virginian Sisyrinchium. **1919** R. FARRER *Eng. Rock-Garden* II. 367 An unknown Sisyrinchium may often prove to be a *Marica* lurking in ambush for the unwary. **1955** L. D. HILLS *Alpine Gardening* v. 137 The Sisyrinchiums are good imitation rushes by the stream side. **1971** B. MILES *Bluebells & Bittersweet* 120/2 Sisyrinchiums will never be accused of flamboyancy [*sic*], but they are darlings.

sit, *sb.*[1] Add: **1. c.** (Earlier example.)

1820 M. EDGEWORTH *Let.* 10 Aug. (1979) 208 Their bodies look as if..they had taken an eternal *sit* from the stiff square stays of former day.

2. a. (Further example.)

1971 N. FREELING *Over High Side* I. 8 He wanted a nice cup of tea and a sit.

sit, *sb.*[2] For *Printers' slang* read 'orig. *Printers' slang*' and add earlier and later examples. Now esp. in *sit(s) vac,* situation(s) vacant (see *SITUATION 6 b).

1853 'MARK TWAIN' in *Hannibal* (Missouri) *Jrnl.* 8 Sept. 2/1, I shall look out for a sit; for they say there is plenty of work to be had for *sober* compositors. **1878** W. WHITMAN *Daybks. & Notebks.* (1978) I. 110 Applied to Bart Bonsall, for a sit. for Harry. **1901** [see *BOVRILIZE *v.*]. **1914** JOYCE *Dubliners* 91 But Hogan has a good sit, hasn't he? **1969** *Guardian* 29 July 4/8 Asians.., with the sort of skills that the 'Sits vac' columns of British newspapers are clamouring for—nurses, motor mechanics, turners, secretaries. **1970** *Ibid.* 14 Nov. 9/2 (*heading*) 'I felt I could do the job.'..Peter Terson on the Sit. Vac. he didn't fill. **1973** *Ibid.* 12 Feb. 11/4 June Moelzer wants.. a job... She sifts through the 'sit vac' columns, becoming less and less choosy as the months go by. **1975** *Listener* 8 May 609/3 Raking through the sits. vac., John Timpson ..reported an advertisement in a Devon local paper for a person 'to move Earth—about two days' work'. **1980** D. FRANCIS *Reflex* xiii. 161 No rides, no income. You start looking at 'sits vac'.

sit, *sb.*[3] Also sitt. Abbrev. of SITTING-ROOM.

1937 A. CHRISTIE *Dumb Witness* vi. 58 We've a nice bungalow at Hemel End, two bed., one sitt. **1961** [see *BED *sb.* 1 e].

sit, *v.* Add: **I. 1. f.** To sit down in a public place as a form of protest; to take part in a sit-in.

1961 *Daily Tel.* 21 Oct. 7/1 A tailor..was yesterday preparing to 'sit' for nine years, if necessary, in the path of a £1,500,000 redevelopment scheme. **1963** G. BUTLER *Coffin for Baby* iii. 49 My boy said to me this morning: Shall I sit or shan't I? You must do as your conscience tells you, I said. **1966** WODEHOUSE *Plum Pie* v. 121 Every now and then we march from Aldermaston, protesting like a ton of bricks... And then we sit a good deal. **1970** P. LAURIE *Scotland Yard* x. 259 The demonstrators.. could 'sit' as long as they liked.

g. To baby-sit.

1966 J. GLOAG *Sentence of Life* xxiii. 192 He wondered if Willy would be able to get Mrs Hillman in to sit. Friday was a bad night. **1968** J. UPDIKE *Couples* iii. 247 It was easier for the Saltzes to leave Bernard, who stays up forever reading anyway, to sit for his brother. **1975** M. BRADBURY *History Man* vii. 121 I'll have to get a sitter... I shouldn't have any trouble finding someone to sit. One of the students.

2. c. With *through.*

1889 J. L. TOOLE *Reminisc.* I. viii. 263 Quite different in its acceptance of fun or pathos from the audience that sits through the same piece the next night. **1932** D. L. SAYERS *Have his Carcase* xix. 255 She sat on right through the programme, but when it came to God Save the King, she chucked it. **1981** L. DEIGHTON *XPD* xxix. 236 Sir Sydney..gallantly sat through another half-hour of finer points of script editing.

3. b. *to sit pretty*: see *PRETTY *adv.* 2 a; *to sit tight*: see TIGHT *adv.* 2 b in Dict. and Suppl.

c. *to sit at the feet of* (a person), to be the disciple or pupil of (a teacher); *to sit on one's hands,* (*a*) *U.S. colloq.*, to withhold or be sparing of applause; (*b*) to be inactive.

1535 BIBLE (Coverdale) *Luke* x., Mary..sat hir downe at Iesus fete, and herkened vnto his worde. **1611** *Ibid.* (A.V.) *Luke* x. 39 Mary..also sate at Iesus feet, and heard his word. **1633** [in Dict.]. **1907** KIPLING *Sons of Martha*, They sit at the Feet, and they hear The Word—they see how truly the Promise runs. **1926** G. M. TREVELYAN *Hist. England* v. iii. 557 They [*sc.* the Whigs] had sat at the feet of Edmund Burke. **1952** G. SARTON *Hist. Sci.* I. xxi. 547 He came to Athens to sit at Plato's feet. **1971** *Nature* 5 Mar. 2/2 It is clear that there are far more universities per square mile in Britain than are necessary to enable students to sit at the feet of some teacher or other. **1926** E. FERBER *Show Boat* vi. 106 Well, they were sitting on their hands to-night, all right. Seemed they never would warm up. **1948** *Newsweek* 16 July 19/1 Listlessly, the convention sat on its hands at all mentions of Mr. Truman in the opening speeches. **1959** *Listener* 1 Jan. 4/1 This helped to reduce the number of constituency associations, who had to be persuaded by MacDonald or Gladstone to sit on their hands or, worse still, toil for their ally. **1961** *IUD Digest* Fall 74/1 Organized labour can ill afford to sit on its hands. **1972** *Guardian* 19 May 12/3 Opposition MPs who only yesterday sat on their hands to let Herr Brandt's Ostpolitik treaties through the Bundestag were back on their feet again this morning. **1976** *New Yorker* 8 Mar. 57/1 'Don't clap too hard—it's a very old building,' he cautions the audience, which is sitting on its hands. **1979** M. A. SHARP *Sunflower* xvi. 148, I should have learned *something* by now. I haven't exactly been sitting on my hands.

6. c. Also, to present oneself *for* an examination, etc.

1929 R. GRAVES *Goodbye to All That* xxvii. 362 My tutor..warned me that I must on no account disparage the eighteenth century when I sat for my final examination. **1955** *Times* 30 June 6/5 Pupils sitting for the examination for entry to secondary schools. **1963** R. PEDLEY *Comprehensive School* i. 14 In some of the 3900 'modern' schools in England and Wales it is possible for the cleverer pupils to sit for GCE at ordinary level. **1968** G. MAXWELL *Raven seek thy Brother* viii. 102, I appealed to my guardian to be allowed to retire..from the scene on the grounds of ill-health... The refusal was absolute..; I was to sit for my degree, no matter what the outcome. **1980** *Radio Times* 1–7 Mar. 16/4 It is possible to take an A-level without having sat for the O-level.

II. 13. a. (Later examples.)

1976 M. MACHLIN *Pipeline* liii. 526 Occasionally a guard was left when equipment sat in the field, but now it was lunch hour. **1977** *Oxford Jrnl.* 10 June 1/5 There were a dozen eggs still sitting on the front porch and the dustbin sat at the back of the house where the binmen had left it. **1978** *Sci. Amer.* May 65/2 The idea of an exploding clump of matter sitting somewhere in space offers no natural way to account for the existence of the cosmic background radiation.

c. (Later examples.)

1878 D. KEMP *Man. Yacht & Boat Sailing* 368/2 Sails are said to 'sit' well when they do not girt, pucker, belly, or shake. **1958** *Listener* 28 Aug. 309/3 Slots must be cut in the bottom half of them [*sc.* the horizontal pieces] where they meet the posts, so that they will sit nicely. **1971** *Good Motoring* Sept. 18/1 Where the 33 tended to hang out its back end on fast corners the 44 sat steadily on the road.

16. d. *fig.* Without compl.

1964 G. C. KUNZLE *Parallel Bars* ix. 410 Make certain that you can do an individual movement with perfect technique before you include it in the exercise. Then try it out in minor competitions until it 'sits'. **1971** B. GRAHAM *Spy Trap* ii. 19 It was too pat, too smug, like a well-turned-out radio script. It didn't sit.

17. c. Also *poet.*

1878 J. J. AUBERTIN tr. *Camoens' Lusiads* II. VIII. lxiv. 129 With a proud confidence, which sat him well.

IV. *With adverbs.* **20*. sit around,** orig. *N. Amer.* To be idle; to lounge.

1915 N. L. MCCLUNG *In Times like These* iv. 42 Personally I sympathize with the young man and believe it would be a happier home if she were as interested in the paper as he and were reading the other half of it instead of sitting around feeling hurt. **1935** *Time* 29 July 42/2 *Accent on Youth* suffers less than most pieces on translation to the screen, for, although its people sit around and talk a lot, they at least talk with wit. **1939** I. BAIRD *Waste Heritage* xix. 267 A lot of them sat around in shirtsleeves. **1959** J. THURBER *Years with Ross* iv. 61 Ross had asked me..to sit around and talk with him and H. L. Mencken. **1971** C. WHITMAN *Death Suspended* v. 95 All they did was to sit around looking decorative. **1979** *Times* 13 Nov. 2/8, I could not sit around twiddling my thumbs and doing nothing.

20. sit back.** To be inactive or passive.

1943 D. POWELL *Time to be Born* xi. 276 One can't sit back and see one's brother..made a monkey of that way! **1953** E. SIMON *Past Masters* III. 156 Harriet is the ideal executive... I can just sit back and let her get on with it. **1970** J. SANGSTER *Touchfeather, Too* ii. 38 Here then was my contact... I sat back and waited for him to make his play. **1982** *Times* 22 Feb. 1/3 We cannot sit back and let them walk all over us.

21. sit down. e. *spec.* To sit down on strike in one's place of work; to sit down in a public place as a form of protest.

1936 *Sun* (Baltimore) 2 Nov. 14/1 Various of the men reporting for picket duty yesterday came from ships where cooks had been the first to 'sit down' in sympathy with the West Coast strikers and hadn't had any food for forty-eight hours. **1942** Berrey & Van den Bark *Amer. Thes. Slang* § 528/7 *Sit down*, to go on a 'sit-down strike'. **1962** P. Mortimer *Pumpkin Eater* xxi. 179 'She paints Ban the Bomb on everything.'..'I suppose she sits down all over the place?' **1963** D. V. Baker *Door is always Open* ix. 190 Parents sitting down on a dangerous highway, children sitting down to protect a play-street, workers sitting down to achieve some change in conditions. **1965** J. Porter *Dover Three* iii. 34 If she's been sitting down again, she'll have to go... Having members of the staff arrested and flung into jail is bad for the school's reputation.

22. sit in. d. To attend or be present at an event. (*a*) orig. and chiefly *U.S.* To take part in a game or other event. Also const. *on, to, with.* Cf. sense 22 a in Dict.

1868 S. Hale *Let.* 5 Jan. (1919) ii. 44 Before we got to lunch two Englishmen *sot in*. **1916** C. Sandburg *Chicago Poems* 63 He didn't sit in with the big thieves. *a* **1922** T. S. Eliot *Waste Land Drafts* (1971) 5 Sopped up some gin, sat in to the cork game. **1929** Wodehouse *Gentleman of Leisure* x. 79 You'll be able to let me sit in on de game, won't you? **1962** D. Francis *Dead Cert* ii. 19, I took ten of Henry's chips and sat in with them. Joan dealt. **1973** 'H. Howard' *Highway to Murder* viii. 102 You weren't invited to sit in on this deal, but you elected to take a hand.

(*b*) To attend an event or occasion as a spectator or observer. Also const. *at, on, with.*

1919 C. S. Parker *Amer. Idyll* x. 103, I sat in on a meeting of the Building Trades Board. **1931** *Oil & Gas Jrnl.* 5 Mar. 197/4 Any oil man or state or federal official may 'sit in' on the proceedings of the state wide committee. **1945** A. Huxley *Time must have Stop* viii. 91 Paul De Vries had already sat in at a number of the old lady's séances. **1949** 'J. Tey' *Brat Farrar* viii. 66 Kevin Macdermott had 'sat in' at one of these office conferences. **1959** *Times Lit. Suppl.* 10 July 411/1 Mrs. Bennett sat in, in 1928, on the experiment which produced Dr. I. A. Richards's *Practical Criticism.* **1962** 'S. Ransome' *Without Trace* iii. 31 'He has something to talk over with me.'..'Would he mind if I sat in?' **1965** *Listener* 13 May 703/2, I sat in with a class and saw the *Antigone* and *The Caucasian Chalk Circle* cut up into weekly twenty-minute doses. **1967** *Daily Tel.* 15 May 9/4 To sit in at a play of this sort is to realise quite soon that you are being asked a riddle. **1970** *Morning Star* 11 May 4/4 The headmaster will therefore sit in on some lessons and try to pinpoint the weaknesses so that the teacher is helped. **1977** *Spare Rib* July 17/1 If you sat in on some of the interviews I've been through you'd know.

e. To co-operate, to collaborate. Also const. *with, on.* (Only in P. G. Wodehouse.)

1925 Wodehouse *Sam the Sudden* xiii. 96 Do you mean to say..that if Soapy was sitting in with the Archbishop of Canterbury on a plan for skinning a sucker, the archbish wouldn't split Even Stephen? **1937** —— *Lord Emsworth & Others* ii. 96 Can I count on your co-operation?..Sit in, and I shall be able to marry the girl I adore. Refuse to do your bit, and I drift through the remainder of my life a soured, blighted bachelor. *a* **1975** —— *Sunset at Blandings* (1977) xi. 77 Jeff refused to sit in on your chuckleheaded idea of eloping for a very good reason.

f. orig. *U.S.* To join in playing or singing with a (*spec.* jazz) band or orchestra of which one is not a regular member. Also const. *with.*

1936 *Delineator* Nov. 102/ Those on the drawn-up chairs are *sitting in*; they have dropped in with their instruments to jam. **1937** *New Republic* 24 Nov. 69/2 Jess saw Bix Beiderbecke and sat in with him later. **1943** H. L. Mencken *Heathen Days* vii. 91 Once, when a baron sat in for a few sessions, we called him Count. **1949** L. Feather *Inside Be-bop* i. 8 On these occasions Kansas Fields or Jack Parker might sit in on drums. **1956** E. Delaney in S. Traill *Play that Music* v. 57 Another thing which influences the playing of today is the fact that no longer can one 'sit-in'. Before the war any player could walk into a club and 'sit-in' with the band. **1965** G. Melly *Owning Up* vii. 75 Buying a barrel of cider for the musicians who came along to sit in. **1971** *Melody Maker* 4 Sept. 20 Mungo Jerry, with Joe Rush, of the Country Jug band sitting in on washboard, sounded like a five man Jesse Fuller. **1982** *New Yorker* 30 Aug. 63/2 His unique playing ..alienated club owners and other musicians, and he found little work. He even had trouble sitting in.

g. orig. *U.S.* (Often written with a hyphen.) To occupy a building as a demonstration of protest.

1941 *Sun* (Baltimore) 15 Apr. 3/3 More than 700 of the city's brighter-than-average students spurned their Easter Monday holiday today and marched to their city college preparatory school to 'sit in and work' as a protest against Mayor LaGuardia's proposal to close the school. **1961** *Look* 25 Apr. 46/2 Negroes who picket, sit-in, crowd our jails, advance on white schools and otherwise approach prevailing privilege. **1967** *Economist* 8 Apr. 142/2 Young people who..defend the virtues of marijuana and LSD and march, demonstrate, sit-in or lie-in to prove their faith in assorted causes. **1974** K. Millett *Flying* (1975) v. 517 Rosset had my friends arrested when they sat in at his publishing house. **1976** C. Hollis *Oxford in Twenties* 128 A few [undergraduates]..sit-in, demonstrate, occupy buildings, demand higher grants and more adequate lodgings.

24. sit out. b. (Earlier example.)

1805 E. Cavanagh *Let.* 20 Aug. in Londonderry & Hyde *Russian Jrnls.* (1934) ii. 179, I sat out & made a Gown while we were going along.

25. sit up. b. (Examples with *for.*) Also, *S. Afr.* and *dial.*, to stay up for part of the night (*with* a person) as a sign of or during courtship, to keep company *with.* Cf. *opsit *v.*

1786 J. Woodforde *Diary* 18 Feb. (1926) II. 228 The Captain..did not return till 12 at Night, just as I was going to bed after sitting up for him till that time. **1869** Geo. Eliot *Let.* 15 Nov. (1956) V. 67, I admire your courage and endurance in sitting up for the meteors. **1878** H. A. Roche *On Trek in Transvaal* 136 The question of questions is, whether she will 'sit up and keep company with him!' If she has consented to do this she has virtually consented to 'sit up' with him as long as they both shall live. **1892** O. Schreiner *Thoughts on S. Afr.* iv. 181 Having made up his mind which daughter he desires to pay his attention to, it is now necessary he should request the parents' permission to sit up with her. **1893** *West Cumberland Times* (Holiday No.) 6/2 (E.D.D.), The custom being for the lad to sit up with the lass. **1896** *Dial. Notes* I. 424 *Sit up with*, to receive courtship from. **1951** L. Craig *Singing Hills* 99 Then he asked if he could sit up with me that night. He was merely asking for a date so I said yes. **1961** F. G. Cassidy *Jamaica Talk* x. 221 Courting..is still described by the terms to *sit up* or to *walk out.* **1961** D. Rooke *Lover for Estelle* 36 He had solemnly shown a candle which he carried in his pocket as a hint to Estelle that they should sit up together that night. **1974** *Daily Dispatch* (S. Afr.) 29 Mar. 12 Clinton, you've been sitting up with Nellie..an car riding and nothings come of it.

c. Also *spec.*, to remain in a sitting posture during an overnight train journey, in contrast to taking a sleeper. *to sit up and take nourishment*, to be convalescent.

1909 Wodehouse *Mike* lv. 311 'How's Adair?'..'Sitting up and taking nourishment once more.' **1918** E. V. Lucas *'Twixt Eagle & Dove* 152 The well-worn phrase 'to sit up and take nourishment'. **1947** L. P. Hartley *Eustace & Hilda* i. ix. 162 'But could you cancel your wagon-lit ticket?' 'I don't need to. I'm going to sit up.' **1953** K. Tennant *Joyful Condemned* xxviii. 277 Now there are no sleepers, you'd have to sit up in the train. **1967** O. Wynd *Walk Softly* vii. 107 'You've got a sleeper reservation?' 'No, I was going to sit up.' **1982** N. Painting *Reluctant Archer* v. 82 'Book a sleeper,' said Reggie airily. There were no sleepers. I sat up all night.

f. (Earlier example.) Also *to sit up and take notice*, to become suddenly interested, to pay attention.

1886 H. Baumann *Londinismen* 179/2 *To make a person sit up*, jemand in Erstaunen setzen. [**1898** Kipling *Stalky & Co.* (1899) 84 If they make such a row now, what will they do when she really begins to look up an' take notice?] **1909** *N.Y. Even. Post* 6 Mar. 1/3 The crowd that fell upon Washington was of such a size that the District authorities sat up and took serious notice. **1929** *Burton Evening Gaz.* 1 Jan. 5/1 By the time that the Oxford English Dictionary compilers reach the 'E' section of additions to that great work..they will have to sit up and take some notice of a new and curious borrowing from the French. **1954** A. Huxley *Let.* 18 Jan. (1969) 694 If you want them to sit up and take notice, prepare your way with a barrage of heavy guns from respectable institutions. **1968** H. C. Rae *Few Small Bones* ii. viii. 141 Look at him..stuffed full of pet theories, praying I'll sit up and take notice of him. **1977** M. Allen *Spence in Petal Park* xvii. 77 When I see him I sit up and take notice.

g. *to sit up and beg* (cf. *beg *v.* 2 i): used *fig.*; also (with hyphens) as *adj. phr.*

1917 R. Barnes *Let.* 20 July in M. Gilbert *W. S. Churchill* (1977) IV. Compan. i. 105 Pile up the guns & shells & we will make the Hun sit up & beg, but we haven't got enough yet. **1919** W. H. Berry *New Traffic* (*Aircraft*) viii. 46 Our gallant youth is quite prepared..to make his seventy miles per hour motor-bike sit-up-and-beg as he would put it. **1958** *Listener* 16 Oct. 603/2 In the 'sit-up-and-beg' attitude in which some modern fighter aircraft come in to land. **1961** Partridge *Dict. Slang* Suppl. 1275/1 'He can make it sit up and beg' indicates that a man has become extremely proficient in working some material, e.g. a metal. **1963** Bird & Hutton-Stott *Veteran Motor Car* 215 They were usually endowed with handsome 'sporty' bucket seat bodies in marked contrast to the usual sit-up-and-beg auntification of the time. **1968** *New Scientist* 3 Oct. 8/2 The pilot is thus in a sit-up-and-beg attitude. **1973** G. Talbot *Ten Seconds from Now* xvi. 200 He rode, incongruously, in a vintage, sit-up-and-beg, hearse-like black limousine. **1978** *Lancashire Life* Apr. 65/1 Old Luke's sit-up-and-beg bike was propped against one of the sandstone gateposts. **1978** *Times* 4 July 19/4 Ramirez tucked away a net cord by his opponent that sat up and simply begged. **1980** *Radio Times* 4–10 Oct. 13/1 A midwife in London's dockland, travelling around on a sit-up-and-beg bike.

h. *to sit up like Jacky* (Austral.), to sit up straight, to comport oneself in a prim and proper manner.

1941 Baker *Dict. Austral. Slang* 38 *Jacky, sit up like*, to behave, sit up straight. **1969** P. A. Smith *Folklore Austral. Railwaymen* 180 As we were rattling along north to Darwin I happened to look back out of the guard's van and there they [*sc.* the hoboes] were—sitting up like Jacky in the commissioner's car behind us. **1975** H. Porter *Extra* 139 He's telling Edinburgh, and those writers sitting up like jacky in tiers behind him, about the construction of his next book.

26. *With prepositions, in special senses.* **sit on** or **upon. d.** (Examples with *on.*)

1892 I. Zangwill *Childr. Ghetto* I. xi. 238 'Odious prig!' thought Hannah. 'He actually doesn't see I'm sitting on him.' **1894** Somerville & 'Ross' *Real Charlotte* I. vi. 76 If you're going to sit on me every time I open my mouth, I'd better shut up. **1936** N. Streatfeild *Ballet Shoes* xiv. 225 In the tube going home, Pauline and Petrova pestered Posy for criticism of the production; but the moment she made any, they sat on her, asking her what she thought she knew about it. **1969** *New Yorker* 14 June 46/2 Someone should have sat on him when he was young. **1975** *Guardian* 22 Jan. 1/2 The TUC general secretary..proceeded to sit heavily on the CBI's suggestion.

e. To hold back, to keep to oneself without acting upon.

1906 Kipling *Actions & Reactions* (1909) 203 A three-million pound insurrection caused by a deputy Under-Secretary sitting upon a mass of green-labelled correspondence instead of reading it. **1967** F. Clifford *All Men are Lonely Now* i. iv. 64 Where have all the yellows gone?..Seriously, who's sitting on them? **1983** M. Hinxman *Corpse Now Arriving* vii. 45 She'd 'sat' on the article..until..a deadline had galvanized her into putting words on paper.

f. To suppress, to silence.

1915 A. Huxley *Let.* Nov. (1969) 85 What an odd business it was about the suppression of Lawrence's book, *The Rainbow*. It is always the serious books that get sat on. **1925** 'R. Hall' *Saturday Life* iv. 51 But she sat on her conscience. **1972** D. McLachlan *No Case for Crown* iii. 39, I want this story sat on till midnight. **1976** M. Machlin *Pipeline* ii. 32 There had to be a scout on that plane—this one's going to be hard to sit on. **1977** *Undercurrents* June–July 18/1 These huge public charivari were sat upon heavily by the police.

g. To wait for (something or someone) to change or develop; to observe or trail.

1958 *Spectator* 11 July 62/2 Two children..were brought to my hospital..suffering from appendicitis, which had been treated conservatively (or in hospital slang 'sat on') for several days. **1966** I. Jefferies *House-Surgeon* vi. 118, I couldn't make up my mind either, so we decided to sit on her and see what happened.

h. *to sit on the splice* (Cricket): see *splice *sb.* 1 c.

27. sit over. Also, to linger over (a meal, etc.) while sitting. (Further examples.)

1952 M. Laski *Village* x. 156 The dinner was cleared away and they sat over their coffee. **1971** 'E. Ferrars' *Stranger & Afraid* vi. 112 They..had lunch, sitting over it until about two o'clock.

28. sit under. Also, to listen to (a teacher), to be the pupil of.

1899 J. London *Let.* 20 Sept. (1966) 56 Stopped over at Stanford, where I..sat under the various profs. **1952** 'J. Tey' *Singing Sands* iii. 39 He 'sat under' a bank clerk in Glasgow, a chap from Uist, and swotted up some Gaelic.

29. sit with. c. To be received in a specified manner by; to be consonant with.

1961 in Webster s.v. [1]*sit*, Setting an example that may not sit well with the more obedient Communist leaders. **1972** *Listener* 1 June 705/2 In the meanwhile sanctions would be continued, and this did not sit well with right-wing opinion inside the Conservative Party.

V. 31. a. Also *transf.*

1814 Jane Austen *Mansfield Park* II. ii. 33 Poor old coachman would attend us..though he was hardly able to sit the box on account of the rheumatism. **1977** *New Yorker* 11 July 19/1 She sits a bicycle with the feckless insouciance of an eleven-year-old gliding down a country lane.

c. Add to def.: using one's body-weight to adjust its balance. (Earlier example.)

1865 *Etoniana* xi. 170 The time-honoured custom of 'sitting a boat'.

36. d. To act as a baby-sitter for (a child). Also *transf.*

1950 *Here & Now* (N.Z.) Nov. 28/2 He is a nice domestic chap: speaks on international affairs; helps old ladies across the street; can sit a baby. **1971** E. Fenwick *Impeccable People* xx. 110 He can help sit Granny, too. **1976** *Billings* (Montana) *Gaz.* 16 June 9-c/6 (Advt.), 'Grandma' needed to sit 3 pre-school boys, in my home ½ days beginning late August.

e. To take (an examination).

1957 A. Wilson *Bit off Map* 40 With the degree behind me, I shall sit the Administrative in June. **1966** *Rep. Comm. Inquiry Univ. Oxf.* II. 152 Collections are college examinations, usually sat at the beginning of a term. **1980** *Radio Times* 1–7 Mar. 16/4 A child can..enter for and sit an examination without being put forward by the school.

37. sit out. a. (Earlier example of a dance.) Also *transf.*

c **1869** Taylor & Dubourg in M. R. Booth *Eng. Plays of 19th Cent.* (1973) III. 251, I didn't sit out one dance. **1957** *Economist* 19 Oct. 208/2 Only two countries —Holland and Australia—gave a majority in favour of getting involved [in a war with Russia]. In the rest, all but two of which are allies of America, most people said they would rather sit this one out. **1978** G. A. Sheehan *Running & Being* xv. 211, I hadn't realized this..until the 1976 Boston Marathon... Any thinking adult would have sat this one out.

c. (Earlier examples.)

1751 Fielding *Amelia* II. v. v. 127 She resolved to come to an eclaircissement, and having sat out some company that came in, when they were alone together, [etc.]. **1808** Jane Austen *Let.* 9 Dec. (1952) 237 We found Mrs. Lance at home & alone, & sat out three other Ladies who soon came in.

sit-. Add: **sit-me-down (-upon)** *colloq.*, the buttocks, the posterior.

1926 D. L. Sayers *Clouds of Witness* ii. 55 He's left the impression of his sit-me-down-upon on the cushion. **1935** 'G. Orwell' *Clergyman's Daughter* iii. 187 Shift yourself..and make room for my little sit-me-down. **1942** Partridge *Usage & Abusage* 351/2 Euphemism..is often employed, sometimes in such childish form as *sit-me-down.*

sitar. Add: Also with pronunc. (sitā·ɹ). Also **setar.** Delete *Anglo-Ind.* and substitute for def.: A long-necked, guitar-like, Indian musical instrument, having from three to seven strings which the player plucks. Also *attrib.* and *Comb.* (Further examples.)

1954 *Grove's Dict. Mus.* (ed. 5) IV. 459/1 The *Setar* is the most popular instrument in northern India. **1957** *New Oxf. Hist. Music* I. iv. 224 Another favourite plucked instrument is the *setar*, of Persian origin. **1959** D. Cooke *Lang. Music* ii. 55 A recent improvisation on a *raga*, by one of India's leading sitar-players. **1966** *Melody Maker* 7 May 10 Since George Harrison introduced the sitar on 'Norwegian Wood' on the Beatles' 'Rubber Soul' album there has been an intense interest in this Indian instrument. **1975** D. Lodge *Changing Places* ii. 85 Someone dimmed the lights and turned up the sitar music. **1978** P. Griffiths *Conc. Hist. Mod. Music* ix. 139 The use of sitars in rock bands.

sitarist (sitā·rist). [f. Sitar + -ist.] One who plays the sitar.

1966 *Guardian* 16 Aug. 6/5 Jayasri..gave her first public recital at the age of 15 accompanying her father, who is himself a well-known sitarist. **1977** *Times* 23 July 9/3 It provides opportunities for the sitarist to engage in musical small-talk with Menuhin's violin and Jean-Pierre Rampal's flute. **1982** *Listener* 18 Nov. 21/2 They were Indian sitarists, and they went at their sitars with a will.

sitatunga, var. *situtunga.

sitcom (si·tkǫm). orig. *U.S.* Also **sit-com, sit.-com.** Abbreviation of *situation comedy* s.v. *situation 11.

1964 *Life* 18 Sept. 24/2 Even Bing Crosby has succumbed to series TV and will appear in a sitcom as an electrical engineer who happens to break into song once a week. **1970** *Globe & Mail* (Toronto) 25 Sept. 14/4 A domestic sitcom about a pair of newlyweds. **1972** P. Black *Biggest Aspidistra in World* iii. v. 195 The only sitcom shows to see the possibility of success..were *Dear Dotty* and *Friends and Neighbours*. **1973** *Times* 2 June 8/4 *My Good Woman*, the new peak time sit-com spot on Monday evenings. **1978** *Encounter* Feb. 32/2 The nearest thing is the comedian Les Dawson, when he relies on words and not on sit.-com. conventions. **1980** *Times Lit. Suppl.* 2 May 492/5 His [*sc.* N. Simon's] stage comedy is hardly distinguishable from television sitcom.

sit-down, *a.* and *sb.* Add: **A.** *adj.* **3.** Of a strike, demonstration, etc.: in which persons sit down in a work-place, public building, etc.; also *fig.* Of a person: participating in such a strike or demonstration.

1936 *N.Y. Times* 30 Jan. 7/6, 1000 workers of the Firestone Tire and Rubber Company remained idle in a 'sit down' protest. **1936** *Sun* (Baltimore) 2 Nov. 14/2 Claiming 2,300 men already were affected by a 'sit down' strike on eighteen ships, the insurgent seamen's defense committee tonight set out to extend its work embargo on all United States vessels in this port. **1937** *Times* 25 Jan. 19/4 The General Motors Corporation has decided to remain in possession of such of its plants as are occupied by sit-down strikers. *Ibid.* 22 Nov. 12/5 'Business' says it is hampered by Government interference and unwise taxation; the Government seem convinced that political enmity has provoked capital investors to a sit-down strike. **1940** H. Brighouse *Man who ignored War* 23 You're on a sit-down strike, sitting there and saying to Hitler, 'Go away, little man, I'm busy creating beauty.' **1948** *Sun* (Baltimore) 8 Apr. 1/6 A small bloc of Republicans is conducting a deliberate 'sit-down strike' on the ECA and other legislation in an attempt to block as much of the Administration's program as it can. **1958** *San Francisco Examiner* 24 Aug. i. 25/2 (*heading*) New sit-down battle in Jim Crow cafes. *Ibid.* 25/6 The 'sit-down' endeavor at Brown's [luncheonette] was the latest in a series which began Tuesday night. **1959** *Listener* 15 Jan. 118/1 London Transport appeals for an end to sit-down strikes on the underground railways. **1960** *Washington Post* 24 Feb. 33/7 White college students joined Negroes today in 'sitdown' lunch counter protests in Winston-Salem. **1960** *Sunday Express* 18 Dec. 12/8 Bertrand Russell proposes to stage a 'sit-down' demonstration outside the Ministry of Defence. **1961** *Daily Tel.* 18 Oct. 1/1 Four members of the anti-nuclear Committee of 100 staged a sit-down protest for over four hours last night in a sitting-room at the Russian Embassy in London. **1962** *Listener* 15 Mar. 458/2 The reasonable sit-down demonstrator. **1972** G. Durrell *Catch me Colobus* x. 221 Remember that animals and plants have no M.P. they can write to; they can't perform sit-down strikes..they have nobody to speak for them except us.

B. *sb.* **1. a.** (Earlier and later examples.) Also, an opportunity to sit down and relax.

1861 Mrs. Stowe *Pearl of Orr's Island* I. xii. 104, I am come here for a good sit-down by your kitchen-fire. **1932** D. L. Sayers *Have his Carcase* iv. 56 'A nice sit-down in the lounge,' said Wimsey, sitting down. **1937** 'J. Bell' *Murder in Hospital* i. 6 By the nurse's desk a constant stream came in with..heads done up in dirty, blood-stained rags..some with nerves on edge from witnessing so many..gruesome sights, some all the better for a good sit down. **1967** N. Freeling *Strike out where not Applicable* 69 The sit-down had done his leg..some good. **1982** J. Sherwood *Shot in Arm* iii. 32 If Verney wanted to go back..it would mean a sit-down and a cup of tea.

b. *N. Amer. Tramps' slang.* A free sit-down meal.

1919 *Dialect Notes* V. 42 *Sit-down*, a meal sitting down. 'A sit-down, with hot Java.' **1926** J. Black *You can't Win* vi. 67 She'll give you a sit-down for yourself, chances are, but bring back a 'lump' for us. **1927** F. Niven *Queer Fellows* iv. 45 There must be houses where we could get a hand-out for sure... We might even get a sit-down. **1936** *New Republic* 15 July 289/1 Upon the occasions referred to, 'sit downs', or invitations to eat at the family table, are more apt to be given.

c. A sit-down strike or demonstration.

1936 *N.Y. Times* 2 Feb. 26/1 The Akron rubber industry's second 'sit-down' of the week was in progress today. **1938** *Times* 23 May 13/4 About 1200 single unemployed men entered three Vancouver buildings..on Friday..and began a 'sit down' in order to obtain immediate work and wages. **1958** *Economist* 1 Nov. 421/1 The Japanese government has long been irked by the failure of the police to deal effectively with demonstrators who stage sit-downs at American air bases and also inside government offices. **1960** *N.Y. Times* 3 Apr. iv. 7/1 (*caption*) Negro students at Southern University in Louisiana apply at registrar's office to withdraw from the university to protest expulsion of classmates for lunch-counter sitdowns. **1961** *Guardian* 3 Feb. 5/6, 1,200 volunteers..have so far agreed to take part in a sitdown outside the Ministry of Defence... The sitdown is in protest against the Polaris agreement. **1967** *Times* 28 Feb. (Canada Suppl.) 34 Young Canadians have joined sit-downs against nuclear arms. **1972** R. Thomas *Porkchoppers* (1974) xxvi. 228, I spent forty-one days in that place... It was a sit-down and the old man sent me in to sit with them. **1978** *Peace News* 25 Aug. 3/1 The next day, 2,100 workers turned up for a 'sit-down', and another 300 were dismissed. **1982** M. Wallace *Brit. Govt. N. Ireland* ii. 29 Measures to deal with street sit-downs and the occupation of public buildings.

Hence **si·t-downer,** a participant in a sit-down strike or demonstration.

1936 *Time* 30 Nov. 15/1 Most of the 4,300 workers obeyed, but 1,100 sit-downers sat pat. **1949** *Sun* (Baltimore) 6 July 9/4 The local Communist association aided the sitdowners. **1960** *N.Y. Times* 15 May 12E/1 (*heading*) Sit-downers score a quiet victory. **1961** *Guardian* 27 Sept. 20/6 Lord Russell..has won the sit-downers' enthusiasm. **1963** D. V. Baker *Door is always Open* ix. 187 We had finally reached Hyde Park, where the Committee had arranged for the sit-downers to meet before marching to Whitehall.

site, *sb.*[2] Add: **2. b.** In scientific use, a position or location in or on something, esp. one where some activity happens or is done.

1950 *Sci. News* XV. 70 Even a perfect crystal will contain a certain number of vacant lattice positions. The proportion of such sites depends only on the temperature. **1954** A. White et al. *Princ. Biochem.* xii. 259 This inhibition may be a result..of combination of the inhibitor with the same site on the enzyme at which the substrate would combine. **1956** M. Demerec in *Publ. Carnegie Inst. Washington* No. 612. 2 The specific properties of an allele are determined by changes at a specific part of the gene locus. Thus it is now evident that a gene locus is composed of a number of units, separable by crossing over, which we call 'sites'. **1966** T. S. & C. R. Leeson *Histology* viii. 140/1 In the fetus..blood cells are formed in different sites at different ages. **1968** Passmore & Robson *Compan. Med. Stud.* I. vii. 2/2 The high specificity of most enzymes..suggests that on the surface of the enzyme molecule there is one or perhaps a few sites specifically adapted for binding the correct substrate and bringing about the reaction. **1971** Levitan & Montagu *Textbk. Human Genetics* xv. 576 On this view the several factors belonging to the same polypeptide..would be determined by different mutable sites on one of the genes. **1982** K. H. Muench in T. M. Devlin *Textbk. Biochem.* xix. 943 (*caption*) Human proinsulin. After cleavage at the two sites indicated..the arginine residues..and the lysine residue..are removed to give insulin and C-peptide.

3. a. (Further examples.) Also, in wider use, a piece of ground or an area which has been appropriated for some purpose; the scene of a specified activity. Freq. in comb. with the first element indicating the (intended) use of the area as *building, caravan, landing, launching, picnic* (etc.) *site*: see these words in Dict. and Suppl.

1888 [see *nesting-site* s.v. Nesting *vbl. sb.* b]. **1930** [see *nest-site* s.v. *nest *sb.* 8]. **1953** N. Tinbergen *Herring Gull's World* xvii. 152 The bird usually developed a clear preference in favour of one of the two nests,..a site-preference. **1963** *Camping* ('Know the Game' Ser.) 43/2 (*heading*) Choosing a camp site. *Ibid.* 46/2 Have consideration for other campers. Do not stroll into someone else's site just as they are in the middle of morning ablutions. **1965** A. J. P. Taylor *Eng. Hist. 1914–1945* xvi. 578 The use of the pilotless aeroplanes and of the rockets was delayed..by bombing their launching sites in France. **1973** E. F. Schumacher *Small is Beautiful* ii. iv. 129 There will be a continuous traffic of radioactive substances..from the stations to waste-processing plants; and from there to disposal sites. **1980** J. McNeil *Spy Game* xix. 189 It was shoe-horned between the radar assembly sheds, a piece of open ground which had miraculously escaped the rash of building covering the rest of the site.

c. *Archæol.* A place containing the remains of former human habitation; an excavation.

1911 T. E. Lawrence *Let.* Apr. (1954) 149 The dig has proved a failure to the present (tho' there is still hope of one part of the site). **1963** E. S. Wood *Collins Field Guide Archaeol.* ii. ii. 200 Bronze Age sacred sites, such as the circles at Knowlton (Dorset), which has a church inside it,..indicate continuity of sacred sites. **1977** *Times* 13 Aug. 14/4 More than four fifths of the villa's walls have been destroyed by ploughing and erosion, and Mr Sumpter feels that the site would not have survived another year's ploughing. **1980** *Rescue News* Dec. 7/5 A cliff site near Northskaill. The site is a great kitchen-midden at least 3·5m thick.

5. *U.S. Naut. slang.* A job, a situation.

1930 *Amer. Speech* V. 393 *Site*, a place as fisherman aboard a fishing vessel. **1957** *Maine Coast Fisherman* July 21/1 Skipper Farrell won't offer a site to a cook who will only cook. **1967** *National Fisherman* June 19-c/2 Palmer was to have a steady job ('site') aboard until he quit or was discharged for cause. **1977** *New Yorker* 15 Aug. 46/3 Joe, who generally keeps his own counsel, tells me that he is hoping to get a site—a job—on the Sniktaw.

6. *attrib.* and *Comb.*, as (sense 3) *site clerk, foreman, manager*; **site assembly,** assembly of building components on the site; **site value,** the amount for which a site may be sold (see also quot. 1893).

1958 *Listener* 6 Nov. 726/2 The mechanization of building and rapid site-assembly of light-weight factory-produced components is a priority item in the current five-year plan. **1961** *Evening Standard* 20 July 18/3 (Advt.), Site Clerk required by..contractors. **1969** T. Parker *Twisting Lane* 57 I'd got a fairly decent job as a site-clerk with a small firm of builders. **1964** K. G. Lockyer *Introd. Critical Path Anal.* iii. 27 Departmental managers, site foremen. **1981** J. B. Hilton *Playground of Death* viii. 97 Three site foremen in succession suffered accidents. **1961** *Technology* May 121/3 There was a need..for a new sort of foreman for the larger projects, a site manager. **1976** R. Lewis *Distant Banner* iii. 85 The bosses had obviously been on the site manager's back. **1893** Site value [in Dict., sense 3 a]. **1904** G. B. Shaw *Common Sense of Municipal Trading* x. 92 The popular remedy is to tax site values directly. **1941** H. Nicolson *Diary* 17 Mar. (1967) 152 It gives a magnificent vista of St Paul's... To get that permanently cleared is worth 40 million pounds in site-value. **1973** E. Page *Fortnight by Sea* vi. 67 Hunston's had been losing trade..had been glad to sell out in the end for the very considerable site value.

site, *v.*[2] 1, **siting,** *vbl. sb.* (Later examples in general use.) See also *sited *ppl. a.*

1918 *Cornhill Mag.* June 621 The short-sighted policy adopted in the siting and construction of schools. **1920** *Discovery* Apr. 116/1 It is advisable to avoid siting a wireless station close to higher ground. **1931** *Times Lit. Suppl.* 16 Apr. 310/2 A practical handbook on the siting, construction and upkeep of garden pools. **1946** *Nature* 2 Nov. 600/2 Areas of exceptional natural beauty or great historic interest should be avoided if their character would be impaired by the siting of a town. **1955** *Times* 29 June 7/1 New proposals for siting Rodin's sculptured group of the Burghers of Calais. **1980** *New Age* (U.S.) Oct. 37/2 This arrangement..has resulted today in more than sixty so-called 'energy wars' going on in this country between utilities or siting authorities and the politically weaker rural people.

sited, *ppl. a.* Restrict † *Obs.* to sense 2 in Dict. and add: **1.** (Later examples.)

1975 *No Through Road* (Automobile Assoc.), This unusually sited lake, halfway up a steep hillside, was created when a glacial overflow channel became blocked. **1979** *Weekend Bargain Breaks* (Trusthouse Forte) 17/1 The hotel..is well sited in this peaceful town.

sitha, sithee (si·ðă, si·ði), repr. dial. pronunciations of *see thou* (see See *v.* 5 f), used esp. as an interjection to draw attention or as a conversation filler.

For further material see *Eng. Dial. Dict.*

1885 [see *plonker 1 a]. **1887** Kipling *Plain Tales from Hills* (1888) 62 Now, *sitha*, tak' a *tat* an' a *lookri*, an' ride tha domdest. **1920** D. H. Lawrence *Touch & Go* iii. ii. 86 See's motor?—comin' up—sithee? **1932** Kipling *Limits & Renewals* 309 She's proud of hersen!—Sitha! She's tryin' to admire of her own belly! **1969** *Listener* 15 May 700/3 My first awareness of Castleford was as a young sports writer looking round for the press box when an official said: 'Sitha, lad, it's up there, on't top deck.' **1974** J. Aiken *Midnight is Place* iv. 135 They're needing a place to lodge too, sithee.

sit-in, *a.* and *sb.* orig. *U.S.* [The phrase *sit in* (see Sit *v.* 22 in Dict. and Suppl. and -in[3]) used attrib. and as sb.] **A.** *adj.* Of a strike, demonstration, etc.: in which persons occupy a work place, public building, etc., esp. in protest against alleged activities there. Of a person: participating in such a strike or dmonstration. Also, of or pertaining to such a strike or demonstration.

1937 *Sun* (Baltimore) 3 Apr. 7/2 (*caption*) The Synthetic Yarn Federation Local 2214..is staging a 'sit-in' strike at Covington. **1938** *Topeka* (Kansas) *Capital* 26 Nov. 12/5 [Daladier] used..police to eject sit-in strikers from factories. **1941** *Sun* (Baltimore) 15 Apr. 3/3 (*heading*) New York students stage 'sit-in' protest. Spurn holiday to make demonstration against proposed school closing. **1948** *Ibid.* 25 Nov. 1/4 Passengers aboard the strike-bound luxury liner Queen Elizabeth today were ordered to get off by Friday, but approximately 900 said no and voted for a 'sit-in' strike. **1959** *Times* 10 Jan. 6/7 A warning to passengers not to repeat the recent 'sit-in' strikes on the London Underground was given yesterday. **1960** *Time* 14 Mar. 21/1 Negro 'sit-in' demonstrations at segregated lunch counters. **1960** *Guardian* 25 July 7/3 The two men had agreed..to express 'support for the objectives of the sit-in demonstrators' in the South. **1973** *Black World* Mar. 37 Pressure for opening the main-stream of American life to Blacks mounted in the 1950's—the sit-in kids, the Supreme Court School Desegregation Decision, [etc.]. **1973** *Times* 17 Nov. 8/2 During May [1936] the French

Treasury almost ran out of funds... There was..a great wave of 'sit-in' strikes. **1980** *Washington Post* 1 Feb. A2/1 Their refusal to budge officially launched the sit-in phase of the civil rights movement.

B. *sb.* **1.** A sit-in strike or demonstration.

1937 *N.Y. Times* 29 May 1/7 Fifty members of the Workers Alliance who tried to stage a sit-in at City Hall yesterday were removed..by a dozen policemen. **1941** *Sun* (Baltimore) 15 Apr. 3/3 He approved the 'sit in' as an 'orderly and dignified protest'. **1960** *Newsweek* 22 Feb. 27 What some Negroes were calling the 'sit-down' and some the 'sit-in'. **1960** *Commentary* June 525/2 The spread of similar picket lines to other cities..seems to have been as spontaneous as the sit-ins themselves. **1965** MRS. L. B. JOHNSON *White House Diary* 11 Mar. (1970) 250 Some of the Civil Rights marchers had walked into the White House..and refused to budge. A sit-in in the White House! **1973** *Law Reports: Appeal Cases* Nov. 858 A sit-in per se is not threatening, abusive or insulting behaviour. **1976** *Times* 10 May 20/5 Sit-ins and work-ins are used by employees..increasingly..as a tactic in collective bargaining. **1978** *Cornish Guardian* 27 Apr. 1/1 Mothers who last year threatened to stage a sit-in on St. Austell's Truro Road are again worried that a child is going to be knocked down and killed there.

2. A participant in a sit-in strike or demonstration. *U.S.*

1963 R. I. McDAVID *Mencken's Amer. Lang.* 557 Most lay newspapers would simply describe such persons [*sc.* sitters-in] as sit-ins. **1970** *Daily Progress* (Charlottesville, Va.) 19 Mar. 1/8 A group of people willing to commit civil disobedience will sit down on the pavement in front of the building, obstructing the entrance. If these sit-ins are arrested, another group will take their place.

Hence **si·t-inner** = *SIT-IN *sb.* 2.

1946 *Sun* (Baltimore) 26 Oct. 3/1 Sixty American War Department civilian employés..held to their rooms in the luxury Hotel Excelsior tonight as the midnight deadline approached for them to obey army orders to move out. Officially an army spokesman said no action was contemplated against the defiant 'sit-inners' until after midnight. **1960** *New Left Rev.* Sept.–Oct. 39/2 The police hosed and clubbed the sit-inners.

sit-in-'ems, sitinems (si·tinĕmz), *sb. pl. slang* (now *rare* or *Obs.*). [Repr. a colloq. pronunciation of *sit in them* + pl. *-s.*] Trousers.

1886 in H. BAUMANN *Londinismen* 179/2. **1922** JOYCE *Ulysses* 418 Don't stain my brandnew sitinems.

siting, *vbl. sb.* Add: Also in general use: see quots. s.v. *SITE *v.*[2]

Sitka (si·tka). [a. Tlingit *sheet'ká* (town of) Sitka, lit. 'outer side of Baranof Island'.] **1.** (A member of) a local group of Tlingit Indians formerly living principally in this North American Indian town. Also formerly, the variety of the Tlingit language spoken there. Also *attrib.* or as *adj.*

1829 J. S. GREEN in *Missionary Herald* (1830) XXVI. 343 The Sitka Indians have built their village under the guns of the fort, so the Russians can easily defend themselves from their depredations. *Ibid.* 344 The Sitka I think is peculiarly soft and musical. **1836** [see *CHILKAT]. **1873** *Alaska Herald* 9 July 4/2 The Hydahs, Chilcats, Tarkous, Ouchanons, and Sitkas participated. **1879** W. G. MORRIS *Public Service of Alaska* 14 In the fall of 1877, a potlatch was given at Sitka by Jack, chief of the Sitkas, and it is estimated correctly he gave away on that occasion 500 blankets. **1910** F. W. HODGE *Handbk. Amer. Indians* II. 582/2 *Sitka*,..a Tlingit tribe..on the w. coast of Baranof id., Alaska.

2. The name of the town, used *attrib.* or *absol.* to designate trees native to the region, as **Sitka cedar, cypress,** the Alaska cedar, *Chamæcyparis nootkatensis,* of the family Cupressaceæ; **Sitka pine, spruce,** a large conifer, *Picea sitchensis,* of the family Pinaceæ, or its light softwood timber.

1884 C. S. SARGENT *Rep. Forests N. Amer.* 580 The most valuable tree of this region [*sc.* Alaska] is the Sitka cedar. *Ibid.* 178 *Chamæcyparis Nutkaensis*... Yellow Cypress. Sitka Cypress. **1884** *N.Y. Times* 5 Oct. 5/2 The white spruce, or Sitka pine..grows to a height of 150 and 175 feet. **1895** FUNSTON & COVILLE in *Contrib. U.S. Nat. Herbarium* III. 328 The great bulk of this forest is composed of Sitka spruce. **1920** *Nature* 29 July 692/1 The Sitka or silver spruce..might be called the aluminium of timbers. **1928** *Daily Mail* 9 Aug. 13/4 The Duchy estates on Dartmoor, where it is hoped to plant 5,000 acres with sitka, Norway spruce, and Douglas fir. **1948** *Antioch Rev.* Winter 48 This would be the first step toward cutting off the magnificent Douglas fir and Sitka pine from 300,000 acres. **1965** G. MAXWELL *House of Elrig* vi. 98 The needles of unthinned sitka. **1975** W. CONDRY *Pathway to Wild* ix. 151 If that other western American, the Sitka spruce, now planted so multitudinously in Britain, were also going to be given the chance of making forests of giant trees..then conservationists might be less unhappy with it. **1977** *Chicago Tribune* 2 Oct. I. 39/2 (Advt.), This fine piano was made specially for us. Its quality features include..solid Sitka spruce soundboard.

‖ **sitkamer** (si·tkamər). *S. Afr.* Also **sitkamer, zitkamer, zit-kamer.** [Afrikaans, f. Du. *sit* sitting + *kamer* room.] A sitting-room, a lounge.

1902 'INTELLIGENCE OFFICER' *On Heels of De Wet* 88 Those cushions you have on your front seat came out of the Nieuwjaarsfontein *sitkomer* [sic]. **1904** *Argus* (Cape Town) *Christmas Ann.* 12 He saw his mother standing at the door of the *zitkamer.* **1912** F. BANCROFT *Veldt Dwellers* 31 It was smoke-room, bar-room, and general zit-kamer combined. **1929** J. G. VAN ALPHEN *Jan Venter, S.A.P.* 249 The *sitkamer* was packed with visitors. **1935** P. SMITH *Platkops Children* 84 The sit-kamer is so beautiful you know, that Ou-ma Carel never lets the sun shine in it excep' for a little on Sundays. **1955** W. ROBERTSON *Blue Wagon* i. 3 Van Zyl and John..entered the *sit-kamer*, as the general living-room of the place was called. **1964** J. NEINTJES *Manor House* 7 We entered a lounge on the right, the *sitkamer*—a large room with a high ceiling on beams. **1971** J. A. BROWN *Return* 79 The door of the cuckoo-clock in the *sitkamer* banged in and out.

sitosterol (saitǫ·stĕrǫl). *Biochem.* [ad. G. *sitosterin* (R. Burián 1897, in *Sitzungsber. der K. Akad. der Wissensch. (Math.-Nat. Classe)* CVI. IIb. 549), f. Gr. σῖτο-ς grain, bread + G. *-sterin* after *phytosterin* (see PHYTO-); cf. *PHYTOSTEROL, *-STEROL.] Any of a number of closely similar crystalline sterols, most of them isomers of formula $C_{29}H_{50}O$, first isolated from corn oil and widely distributed in plants; *spec.* the most common such substance, *β-sitosterol,* also called *CINCHOL.

Before 1926 considered to be a single substance.

1898 *Jrnl. Chem. Soc.* LXXIV. I. 72 A substance..is obtained which resembles the cholesterol of bile in external appearance and in composition..; it is named sitosterol. **1926** *Jrnl. Amer. Chem. Soc.* XLVIII. 2986 The substance corresponding in composition to sitosterol..is not homogeneous. It is a mixture containing at least three isomeric sterols... It is proposed to name these isomers α-, β- and γ-sitosterol. **1943** *Ann. Reg. 1942* 358 Work on algal chemistry showed that sitosterol, the characteristic sterol of the phanerogams, is common to the green algæ. **1962** H. BURN *Drugs, Med. & Man* v. 57 The substance sitosterol can be given which prevents the cholesterol which is in the diet from being absorbed through the wall of the intestine. **1974** M. C. GERALD *Pharmacol.* xxii. 401 Sitosterols enhance the elimination of cholesterol in the feces.

sitrep (si·tˌrep). *Mil.* Also **Sit. Rep., Sitrep, Sit-rep.** Abbrev. of *situation report* s.v. *SITUATION II.

1943 J. H. FULLARTON *Troop Target* xxiii. 173 The daily Sit. Rep. had now identified seven Italian and at least three German divisions in the line. **1947** D. M. DAVIN *For Rest of our Lives* 307 He thumbed through his log with its patrol reports, phone messages, sitreps, all the raw material from which he must first form in his mind a clear picture of what the enemy was up to. **1955** E. WAUGH *Officers & Gentlemen* 264 The B.G.S. said: 'We got a sitrep from the Halberdiers three hours ago.' **1961** I. FLEMING *Thunderball* xxiii. 240 I'm going to..get a signal off to Navy Department, give them a Sitrep. **1968** P. KINSLEY *Pimpernel 60* ii. 37 Look over a couple of Sit-reps which I received yesterday. **1975** D. W. S. HUNT *On Spot* i. 11 In fact what he [*sc.* Wellington] wrote was a succinct report on the fighting of the past four days. It was in the first place the equivalent of the modern 'Sitrep', which a general, or his staff in his name, telegraphs every night.

sitringee. Add: Also **satrangi, -ji, shatranji;** 7 **citterengee,** 8 **sittringe,** 9 **satrin-, sattran-, satrun-, sut(t)rin-, -gee, -jee.** (Further examples.)

1688 J. PEACHEY in W. Hedges *Diary* (1888) II. cclxv, 2 Citterengees, charged before. **1785** *Calcutta Gaz.* 3 Mar. 7/2 To be sold by public auction..The valuable effects of Warren Hastings, Esq... Carpets and Sittringes. **1851** *Illustr. Catal. Gt. Exhib.* IV. 917/2 Cotton carpets (*Satrunjees*) of different sizes—from Bengal. **1858** P. L. SIMMONDS *Dict. Trade Products, Sattrangee, Satringee,* a kind of fibrous striped mat or carpet made in India. **1859** M. THOMSON *Story of Cawnpore* xii. 189 They provided us with straw to lie upon, and gave us a sutringee each (a piece of carpet) to cover our bodies. **1876** *Encycl. Brit.* V. 129/2 Cotton carpets or *Suttringees* are a cheap substitute for woollen fabrics in almost universal use throughout India. **1881** *Ibid.* XII. 762/1 Carpets and rugs may be classified into those made of cotton and those made of wool. The former, called *satranjis* and *daris,* are made chiefly in Bengal and northern India. **1904** G. WATT *Indian Art at Delhi 1903* 273 If to this list be added..the rug the *dari* or *satranji*, the series of chief artistic textile articles of Native dress and household use may be regarded as complete. *Ibid.* 446 A larger market might be found in India for *shatranjis* than has as yet been attained. **1969** E. BHARNANI *Decorative Designs & Craftsmanship of India* iii. 33 In North India..cotton rugs (*Daris* and *Satrangis*) have been produced in several areas since a long time.

sits vac: see *SIT *sb.*[2]

sitter[1]**.** Add: **1. g.** One who has a sitting with a medium.

1909 in WEBSTER. **1928** *Daily Mail* 25 July 6/2 If media were unable to get into a trance the sitting was cancelled and the money returned to the sitter. **1961** W. H. SALTER *Zoar* vi. 73 The sitter brings with him marked plates which he gives the medium. **1977** 'L. EGAN' *Blind Search* ii. 32 One of their perennial sitters, Claire Ewing..a researcher herself, not an emotion-harried sentimentalist seeking reassurance.

h. *U.S. slang.* (See quots. 1938, 1948[2].)

1938 S. HART *New Yorkers* 183 Bowery barkeeps employed homeless men and women as 'sitters' to shiver near the fire on wintry nights and thus evoke the sympathy of cash customers who would treat them to drinks to the great profit of the house. **1948** *Sun* (Baltimore) 7 Aug. 5/4 Violations, particularly of sitters' rules, would mean suspension or barring women from the licensed premises. **1948** H. L. MENCKEN *Amer. Lang.* Suppl. II. 682 Women who frequent taverns or night-clubs, getting a percentage on the drinks they induce male patrons to buy, are..*sitters.*

i. A baby-sitter.

1943 *Life* 8 Nov. 100/2 (*caption*) Matt Thomson stays home with baby... Once they would have hired capable 'sitter'. Now only inexperienced girls are available. **1951** H. MACINNES *Neither Five nor Three* I. i. 11 She and Jon couldn't come to the party because the baby was sick or they couldn't get a sitter. **1960** *Sunday Express* 26 June 5/3 He has a first-class nurse and a 'sitter' while I am away. **1975** [see *SIT *v.* 1 g].

j. A participant in a sit-in or sit-down.

1961 *Britannica Bk. of Year* 537/2 *Sit in,*..and *sitter,* terms used in connection with the attempts by Negroes to eat in cafés and restaurants from which they were normally excluded. **1961** *Guardian* 22 Sept. 12/4 There are still people who think that marchers and sitters can be dismissed because some are oddly dressed.

5. *sitter-in*: (*a*) a baby-sitter; (*b*) one who takes part in a sit-in; (*c*) one who sits in with a band (*SIT *v.* 22 f); *sitter-out*: (*b*) one who sits out at cards.

1947 J. L. BURN *Recent Advances in Public Health* ix. 132 To enable husband and wife to go out together, a 'sitters in' service to look after the baby has been established in some areas. **1951** M. KENNEDY *Lucy Carmichael* VII. iv. 330 'We shan't even be able to go to the club.' 'We'll get a sitter-in for them.' **1960** *Guardian* 30 Dec. 10/5 The husband..[acted] as the sitter-in when his wife was on evening shift. **1962** *Maroon* (Univ. of Chicago) 20 July 1 (*heading*) Convict Cairo sitters-in; fine each $300. **1963** *Economist* 8 June 1013/1 Negro 'sitters-in'..gather daily to decide who shall court arrest. **1968** *Blues Unlimited* Dec. 12 Jake recorded with his current group..plus assorted sitters-in. **1976** *Southern Even. Echo* (Southampton) 6 Nov. 7/2 Members of the Jess Roden Band are some of our favourite 'sitters-in'. **1976** J. I. M. STEWART *Memorial Service* vi. 92 There would be eruptions. 'Demos' would be held, buildings sat in by sitters-in.

1853 MRS. GASKELL *Cranford* i. 14 Miss Jessie could not play cards: but she talked to the sitters-out.

6. Anything easy or (apparently) certain of performance; an easy catch, stroke, or shot; a sitting target; a certain winner; a certainty.

1898 *Tit-Bits* 25 June 252/3 A 'sitter' is a catch which falls absolutely into the hands. **1903** G. L. JESSOP in H. G. Hutchinson *Cricket* v. 117 The missing of a 'sitter' by some lazy fieldsman whose thoughts were anywhere but on the game. **1908** A. S. M. HUTCHINSON *Once aboard Lugger* I. iv. 50 'You know I got ploughed?'..'Bad luck, I suppose? I thought it was a sitter for you this time.' **1917** H. A. VACHELL *Fishpingle* ix. 183 'Down ours,' enjoined Lionel to his [golfing] partner. 'You'll do it, Joyce. It's a sitter.' **1918** *Chambers's Jrnl.* Apr. 239/1 'A sitter, by the Great Hook Block!' cried Carstairs. 'A transport full of Boches!' **1923** WODEHOUSE *Inimitable Jeeves* v. 54 An absolute sitter came unstitched in the second race at Haydock Park. **1927** *Observer* 3 July 18/1 A series of very bad shots, including a double fault by Borotra, the missing of absolute 'sitters' by both players and the driving of many easy balls into the net well over the baseline. **1946** *Sunday Dispatch* 8 Sept. 6/2 Midway through the second half Bradley missed a sitter when Roper centred across an open goal. **1951** N. M. GUNN *Well at World's End* xix. 156 A pheasant showed, an old cock. The bird stood. We stood. 'Granville, my boy,' he said to me, 'I always want you to remember this: Confucius never shot at a sitter.' **1973** A. HUNTER *Gently French* ii. 16 They use two [routes]... The trouble is they just alternate them... So they were sitters for a villain like Quarles. **1977** *Times of Swaziland* 11 Feb. 14/2 When Wire Kunene was given a sitter on a plate by the evergreen Sugar Ray Zulu, Kunene let slip the chance. **1980** *Amer. Speech 1976* LI. 294 *Sitter,* ball that is soft and easy to return.

sitter[2] (si·tər). *Oxford University slang.* [*-ER.[6]: cf. *BED-SITTER.] A sitting-room.

1904 [see *-ER[6]]. **1925** *Glasgow Herald* 24 Oct. 6 If lectures are to be broadcast, the temptation to listen to them in the quiet and comfort of one's own sitter will be irresistible.

sitting, *vbl. sb.* Add: **1. d.** For *rare*⁻¹ read *rare* and add further example.

1816 JANE AUSTEN *Emma* II. iv. 69 His air as he walked by the house—the very sitting of his hat.

5. e. One in a series of (esp. two) servings of a meal, *spec.* in the restaurant-car of a train.

1959 P. MOYES *Dead Men don't Ski* i. 13 The lights of the train came on..and..the bell sounded..for First Dinner. Jimmy..was..due to dine at the first sitting. **1962** N. STREATFEILD *Apple Bough* vii. 101 An attendant from the restaurant-car looked in. 'Luncheon tickets?' he asked. The man said: 'Second sitting, please.' **1965** E. BROWN *Big Man* ix. 74 I'll clean up the cabin while you are at lunch. You are second sitting. **1977** C. ALLEN *Raj* i. 25/2 Gongs were sounded to mark the arrival of each course... Older travellers preferred the second sitting.

6. a. With *in, up* (further examples).

1817 JANE AUSTEN *Let.* 22 May (1932) 493 Words..fail ..to describe what a Nurse she has been to me... There was never any sitting-up necessary. **1900** M. BEERBOHM in *Sat. Rev.* 6 Jan. 12/2 Was not a pantomime..the most brilliant occasion for 'sitting-up'? **1946** R. BLESH *Shining Trumpets* x. 237 The band instrumentation was kept normal, and men alternated with one another in the process known as *sitting in.* **1977** 'C. AIRD' *Parting Breath*

iv. 54 The students..squatted on the floor... 'Sitting-in means sitting down, I reckon,' remarked one student.

b. (Earlier and further examples.)

1874 W. LENNOX *My Recollections* II. 29 A sitting-down supper was announced. **1895** E. F. BENSON *Dodo* II. xi. 232 The music..was quite loud enough to be heard distinctly in a small, rather unfrequented sitting-out room. **1900** *Traveller* 4 Aug. 106/2 On the *Caledonia* there was a minimum of space... There were no sitting-out places. **1939** *Sun* (Baltimore) 5 Apr. 26/2 An abundance of unoccupied land for playgrounds, sitting-out areas, walks and service streets. **1964** V. J. CHAPMAN *Coastal Veg.* ix. 212 Maritime cliffs are often the haunt of sea birds, either as nesting areas or as 'sitting out' places. **1976** *National Observer* (U.S.) 19 June 17 (Advt.), It gives full pillow support to head and back for firm sitting-up comfort.

sitting, *ppl. a.* Add: **4. d.** Of a huntsman's target: stationary, and so easily hit. Freq. *fig.* (orig. *Mil.*) in *sitting bird, duck*, etc.

1867 TROLLOPE *Claverings* I. x. 126 The man who fires at a sitting bird is known to be no sportsman. **1944** *R.A.F. Jrnl.* Aug. 270 Carriers are sitting birds for enemy surface craft. **1944** *Reader's Digest* May 53 (*heading*) Why tankers are no longer sitting ducks. **1948** *Harper's Mag.* Apr. 290/2 Ever since Sinclair Lewis gave the first lessons in marksmanship, men of the Senator's type have been sitting ducks for the opposition. **1949** *Sat. Even. Post* 16 July 23/3 (*caption*) Rescuing downed aviators sometimes got a sitting-duck submarine fired on by our own quick-triggered forces. **1954** J. BLISH in *If; Worlds Sci. Fict.* No. 4. 38/2 You're a sitting duck for a real infection if you abuse your time during convalescence. **1958** 'A. GILBERT' *Death against Clock* vi. 89 'It could be he was financin' another establishment and didn't want Mrs M. to know. And Wife No. 2 might be makin' trouble.' 'Simpler to put *her* light out in that case,'... 'Ah, but then he'd be a sitting duck for the police. Someone always comes forward in cases like these to say he..saw the dear departed with a gent.' **1961** B. FERGUSSON *Watery Maze* vii. 183 We had learned that for tanks to land before tank obstacles had been breached was lethal; they would inevitably be halted, and would become sitting ducks. **1977** 'J. D. WHITE' *Salzburg Affair* xiii. 109 Narrow streets, he'd be a sitting target. **1978** J. WAINWRIGHT *Thief of Time* 195, I have no 'gentlemanly' distaste at shooting sitting targets; wood pigeons, rabbits, hares..let them be motionless..and I have meat for supper.

b. *fig.* That can hardly be bungled.

1932 *Evening Standard* 28 Jan. 11/2 They had a hand which contained a 'sitting' game in Spades—one of two had five to the four top honours. **1960** I. PEEBLES *Bowler's Turn* 190 Against these two Dexter with a bit of luck (dropped at square leg at 30 and off a sitting return by Worrell at 32) played confidently.

sitting-room. Add: **1.** (Earlier examples.)

1771 H. PELHAM *Let.* 25 Aug. in *Mass. Hist. Soc. Coll.* (1914) LXXI. 147 The Arches at the sides of the Chimnie in the Sitting Room, I like. **1797** J. WOODFORDE *Diary* 31 Jan. (1931) V. 8 Our sitting Room smoked very much all the Morning.

2. (Earlier example.)

1881 'MARK TWAIN' *Prince & Pauper* xxxii. 365 Trying to find sitting-room in the galleries.

situate, *v.* For 'Now *rare*' read 'Now *rare* in lit. sense' and add: **1.** (Further examples.) Now usu. *fig.*, to establish or indicate the place of, to put in a context, to bring into defined relations.

1953 *Sunday Times* 20 Sept. 5/7 From Baudelaire to Balchin, Swinburne to Sansom, Virginia Woolf to Angus Wilson, he situates us all, and hands out a ticket to the celestial garden-party of modern literature which assigns us to our table. **1961** *Encounter* May 49/2 The key to 'situating' her..is to grasp..that she was not an 'Edwardian natural' at all. **1964** E. PALMER tr. *Martinet's Elem. General Linguistics* ii. 44 Their linguistic behaviour, whereby *maison* appears in exactly the same contexts in which I would situate it myself. **1973** *Mod. Eucharistic Agreement* 74 We have sought..to situate the role of the presiding minister in relation to the sacerdotal ministry of the Church. **1977** *Proc. Roy. Soc. Med.* LXX. 425/2 Since I know less about medicine than about Molière, I have woven into my paper a brief review of his career with a view to situating the seven comedies in which medicine is parodied or satirized. **1982** *Times Lit. Suppl.* 13 Aug. 872/1 The title of John Allett's book indicates that this is where he wishes to situate Hobson.

situation. Add: **II. 6. b.** (Earlier example.) *situations vacant*: jobs to be filled, *spec.* as advertised in a column or page of a newspaper; a newspaper column or page advertising jobs; also *attrib.* Also *situations wanted.*

1803 G. COLMAN *John Bull* III. ii. 36 Service? Nonsense ..I'll put you into a situation in town. *a* **1911** D. G. PHILLIPS *Susan Lenox* (1917) II. iv. 73 Want ads.. closely printed columns of advertisements of help wanted and situations wanted. **1931** M. ALLINGHAM *Look to Lady* xx. 207 I'll be readin' the Situations Vacant before I know where I am. 'E aint even left me a reference. **1944** M. LASKI *Love on Supertax* ii. 14 'Is it Situations Wanted day?'..If so, give me the outside sheet.'..The Duke pulled his newspaper to pieces. **1949** E. COXHEAD *Wind in West* i. 19 She began to look through the situations-vacant columns in the farming papers. **1967** R. RENDELL *New Lease of Death* ix. 88 Elizabeth Crilling sat..reading the Situations Vacant in last week's local paper. **1971** D. LEES *Rainbow Company* ii. 29 An obvious commercial traveller reading the situations vacant column of the *Telegraph*.

9. a. Also in mod. usage, preceded by an attributive word or phrase, and designating: (*a*) the state or general circumstances of something at a particular time, as *coal situation*, etc. (and which is acknowledged to change from time to time); (*b*) a particular state of affairs or occasion existing independently, as *standing credit situation, crisis situation*, etc.

Objections have been raised to both usages, but the latter is often especially decried as an ugly and sometimes tautological formation.

1934 *Times* 22 Aug. 11/3 A popular dodge at present is to add the word 'situation' or 'position' to a noun; by this means apparently it has been discovered that the most pregnant meanings can be expressed with the least effort. The 'coal situation' remains unchanged; the 'herring position' is grave. **1935** *Jrnl. Pediatrics* VI. 115 The group that is treated at the Children's Hospital,..may be received after an attempt has been made in an outlying home or hospital to make the best of a premature baby situation. **1941** J. S. HUXLEY *Uniqueness of Man* ix. 193 A crab can react to various situations—a food-situation, a hunger-situation, a fear-situation, a sex-situation. **1952** *Amer. Speech* XXVII. 13 Corn-shortage situation, draft-evasion situation. **1966** [see *LEAST *a.* 1 e]. **1972** *Where* Jan. 18/1 A school hall or playground, festooned with bunting, with colourful stalls and the sound of the tombola rolling, assumes less of an institutional atmosphere and more of a face-to-face primary group situation. **1973** *Art Internat.* Mar. 26/1 What comes to such galleries is filtered through all kinds of art situations. **1975** *N.Y. Times* 17 Sept. 47/3 We can run innovative or traditional programs here, whereas in an old-fashioned building the architecture limited us to traditional teaching situations. **1976** *Local Council Rev.* Summer 3 (Advt.), These chairs are ideally suitable for multiple seating situations for use in Town Halls, Village Halls, Community Centres, etc. **1977** H. FAST *Immigrants* I. 74 This is not a loan but a standing credit situation. **1978** *Oxford Times* 13 Jan. 4/3 Unless catchment areas are re-drawn Lord Williams's school will go through a crisis situation for at least five years.

11. Special combs.: **situation comedy,** a comedy (serial) in which the humour derives largely from the particular conjunction of characters and circumstances; **situation ethics, morality,** the belief that individual circumstances or particular situations may call for flexibility in the application of moral laws; **situation report** *Mil.* (see quot. 1918); also *transf.*; **situation(s) room,** a room set aside by a military or governmental agency for giving reports on the current state of any action, operation, etc.

1953 *TV Guide* (N.Y. Metro ed.) 23 Oct. 19/1 Ever since *I love Lucy* zoomed to the top rung on the rating ladder, it seems the networks have been filling every available half-hour with another situation comedy. **1967** *Listener* 10 Aug. 161/1 The two best situation-comedy shows this country has ever produced are..*Steptoe and Son* and.. *Till Death Us Do Part.* **1972** *Time* 17 Apr. 39/1 NBC plans *The Little People*, about a Hawaiian pediatrician and his pediatrician daughter, and ABC has *Temperature's Rising*, about the chief surgeon in a big city hospital. Both shows will combine the medical genre with the situation-comedy formula. [**1950** K. RAHNER in *Stimmen der Zeit* CXLV. 330 (*heading*) Situationsethik und Sündenmystik.] **1955** *Cross Currents* Winter 79/2 Father Rahner wished to demonstrate..that..situation-ethics was the most modern and fashionable form of laxity; that it was..an attempt of half-Christians to dodge the effort demanded by the notion of morality and the rigor of the law, by appealing to 'the situation'. **1966** J. FLETCHER *Situation Ethics* i. 26 Situation ethics goes part of the way with natural law, by accepting reason as the instrument of moral judgment while rejecting the notion that the good is 'given' in the nature of things, objectively. **1979** B. G. SKINNER *Robert Exon* vi. 56 The so-called Situation Ethics, where the Christian in a spirit of prayer and love decides for himself what is the right course of action to take. **1962** *Dict. Moral Theol.* 801/1 Situation morality, carried to extremes, must not be understood as an escape from the heavy burden of moral integrity. **1918** E. S. FARROW *Dict. Mil. Terms* 561 *Situation reports*, reports designed to keep superior officers and neighboring units informed of the progress of events and any important changes in the situation or movement of their own or enemy troops. **1960** *Mag. Fantasy & SF* (N.Y.) Nov. 58/1, I assume that I will be attacked, and decide to file a situation report. **1970** C. WHITMAN *Death out of Focus* vii. 104 No doubt her precious father had telephoned her and given her the latest situation report. **1977** W. H. SAUMAREZ SMITH *Young Man's Country* ii. 33 One regular chore was the 'fortnightly confidential report' to the District Magistrate, which was a general 'situation report' about anything interesting happening in the subdivision. **1967** *Sunday Times* 21 May 7 The intelligence 'situation room' will keep the 15 permanent ambassadors of the NATO countries and their key military commands more fully up-to-date on Russia's political and military build-up than they have ever been before. **1970** M. KELLY *Spinifex* ii. 28 Hopkins was sitting on the edge of a table in the Situations Room. **1976** *National Observer* (U.S.) 28 Aug. 2/5 In the Situation Room of the White House, Secretary of State Kissinger convened the Washington Special Action Group, a subcommittee of the National Security Council, to plot possible U.S. responses to the deaths.

situational (sitiu,ē·ʃənăl), *a.* [f. SITUATION + -AL.] Of or pertaining to a situation or situations; dependent on, determined by, or in relation to position, situation, or circumstances. *situational analysis, logic* (see quot. 1977[2]); *situational ethics, morality* = *situation ethics, morality* s.v. *SITUATION 11.

1903 *Academy* 27 June 632/1 As situational drama (if we may coin the term) always is rhetorical. **1927** *Observer* 24 Apr. 14/5 The main defect of this book seems to lie in the way in which literary or dramatic or situational clues are allowed to dictate musical judgments. **1935** *Jrnl. Philos.* XXXII. 650 Psychology has an incontestable claim if it will but stake it out and work it properly. By working at a meaningful level—not of physical stimulus and meaningless sensation—its products will be observable meaningful properties of situational things. **1945** K. R. POPPER *Open Soc.* II. xiv. 90 The method of applying a situational logic to the social sciences is not based on any psychological assumption concerning the rationality ..of 'human nature'. **1949** M. MEAD *Male & Female* xiv. 286 It [*sc.* the dating pattern] defines the relationship between a male and a female as situational. **1952** *Essays in Criticism* II. 95 The situational analogies are clear enough by the end of the first episode. **1959** J. L. M. TRIM in R. Quirk et al. *Teaching of English* iii. 87 Nouns, principal verbs, adjectives and adverbs are indefinite in number and therefore subject to primarily situational constraints. **1968** *Meta* XIII. 16 Situational meaning reflects the influence of context on utterances. Asking someone about his troubles is likely to produce different responses in a bank and in a hospital regardless of the speaker's intention. **1969** *Observer* 21 Dec. (Colour Suppl.) 38/3 As for sin—situational ethics could take care of that. **1972** K. R. POPPER *Objective Knowl.* iv. 179 By a situational analysis I mean a certain kind of tentative or conjectural explanation of some human action which appeals to the situation in which the agent finds himself. **1975** *Language for Life* (Dept. Educ. & Sci.) x. 157 It is this 'situational context', as a linguist would term it, that calls for improvisation. **1977** J. D. DOUGLAS in Douglas & Johnson *Existential Sociol.* i. 14 Man is fundamentally grounded, situational—existential. **1977** in Bullock & Stallybrass *Fontana Dict. Mod. Thought* 575/1 *Situational analysis*; *situational logic*.., an approach to the explanation of social action in which a detailed reconstruction of the circumstances of action (incuding both objective conditions and the participant's aims, knowledge, beliefs, values, and subjective 'definitions' of the situation) is taken as a basis for hypothesizing rational courses of action for the individual involved, through which their observed behaviour may be rendered intelligible. **1978** J. M. GUSTAFSON *Protestant & Roman Catholic Ethics* ii. 48 Rahner's criticisms warned against the radical extension of situational morality. **1980** *English World-Wide* I. 1. 3 Relating linguistic to situational factors.

Hence **situa·tionalism** = *SITUATIONISM 2; **situa·tionalist** *a.*, of or pertaining to situation ethics; **situa·tionally** *adv.*, with respect to situation; in a situational manner.

1935 *Word Study* Feb. 1/2 *Situationally* is a regular adverbial formation from the adjective situational. **1939** P. CHRISTOPHERSEN *Articles* 38 The article is of course situationally determined here. **1964** R. H. ROBINS *Gen. Linguistics* 191 A sentence is by definition grammatically complete (the alleged 'incomplete' or 'elliptical' situationally tied sentences are complete in those situations). **1970** W. K. FRANKENA in Pahel & Schiller *Readings in Contemp. Ethical Theory* 542 Views variously referred to as antinomian,..existentialist, situationalist, or contextualist. **1971** N. H. G. ROBINSON *Groundwk. Christian Ethics* ix. 242 Nor indeed may we expect any other outcome, unless..the logical successor to Bonhoeffer is to be found either in secularization or in situationalism. **1977** J. D. DOUGLAS in Douglas & Johnson *Existential Sociol.* i. 60 There are other reasons why we see experience as necessarily problematic, as necessarily free and situationally contingent. **1977** J. M. JOHNSON in *Ibid.* v. 161 This extreme situationalism is perhaps best illustrated by Zimmerman and Pollner's (1970) discussion of the *occasioned corpus*. **1979** *Guardian* 9 June 10/3 Since the Bible was written in a very different age from ours, its commands must be interpreted situationally.

situationer (sitiu,ē·ʃənəɹ). [f. SITUATION + -ER[1].] In *Journalism*, an article or report constituting a general essay on a situation.

1959 *Observer* 15 Nov. 20/5 I.T.V.'s *This Week*..was struggling to condense an African situationer—ranging from Oxford undergraduates boycotting South African sherry to forecasts of the future of Federation and the White Highlands—and a profile of Mao Tse-tung into a few minutes each. **1972** D. BLOODWORTH *Any Number can Play* xi. 93 Ivansong had written and cabled a one-thousand-word situationer on Mekong. **1977** *Radio Times* 2–8 July 13/2 Newspapers..had far more word-space than radio..so newspapers found it easier to accommodate 'situationers'.

situationism (sitiu,ē·ʃəniz'm). [f. SITUATION + -ISM.] **1.** The revolutionary ideas relating to culture associated with the Situationist International (see quot. 1971 s.v. *SITUATIONIST *sb.* 1).

1964 *Times Lit. Suppl.* 3 Sept. 781/4 Our International ..coming after the development both of our philosophy and of our art, at once refuses to proclaim any sort of doctrine and rejects the term 'situationism' as used only by enemies of the situationist programme. **1973** *Listener* 2 Aug. 152/1 The Angry Brigade['s]..communiqués suggest..a combination of situationism and Syndicalism. **1978** *Radio Times* 28 Jan.–3 Feb. 15/3 One philosophical strain, peculiar to developed countries, was 'Situationism'. At its simplest, its followers believe the working class has been bamboozled out of its legitimate rights by a capitalist conspiracy that 'appropriated' trade unionism and socialism, then 'laundered' and returned them as harmless institutions.

2. Adherence to situation ethics.

1966 J. FLETCHER *Situation Ethics* i. 29 There are various names for this approach: situationism, contextualism, occasionalism, circumstantialism, even actualism. **1977** A. KOLNAI *Ethics, Value, & Reality* vii. 145 The wide variety of reductionist and constructivist types of Ethics ranging, say, from utilitarianism to prescriptivism or from metaphysical perfectionism to situationism.

situationist (sitiu,ēⁱ·ʃənist), *a.* and *sb.* [f. SITUATION + -IST; in sense A. 1 ad. Fr. *situationniste.*] **A.** *adj.* **1.** Of or pertaining to certain revolutionary views about the situation of man in modern culture (see quot. 1971, sense B. 1 below); *Situationist International,* a movement started in Paris in the 1950s to promote these views.

1958 *Archit. Rev.* CXXIV. 1/2 Snap judgments on the publications of the Situationist International had best be restrained until the documents have been frisked for hidden persuaders. **1963** *Listener* 31 Jan. 202/2 What she has to say about the uses of diversity seems to derive as uniquely from this particular urban scene as does the Situationist vision from the psychogeography of Paris. **1975** *Observer* (Colour Suppl.) 13 July 26/1 The sergeant discovered that the word 'spectacles' was a concept, an emblem, almost, of a group subscribing to the views of the so-called Situationist International. **1980** *Times Lit. Suppl.* 4 Apr. 387 The walls and statues of the Sorbonne were plastered with posters of Marx, Lenin, Che and Mao, with situationist slogans and Red Flags.

2. Dependent on or determined by circumstances; situationalist.

1970 G. GREER *Female Eunuch* 328 Women's revolution is necessarily situationist. **1972** *Times Lit. Suppl.* 19 May 580/4 His own view involves contextual considerations without being situationist. The relevant context is that of a particular social system.

B. *sb.* **1.** An adherent of the Situationist International or of situationism.

1963 *Listener* 31 Jan. 201/1 The Situationists are best-known as one of the most subversive anti-art groups of the post-war epoch. **1964** *Times Lit. Suppl.* 3 Sept. 781/5 True situationists are much more strongly opposed to all the prevailing mechanisms of culture and information. **1971** R. GOMBIN in Apter & Joll *Anarchism Today* 19 For the situationists, the bureaucratic system of industrial society has considerably increased the sum total of the exploitation and repression of man... The tremendous development of science and technology has led to the individual being completely taken over by the system; the individual is no more than a commodity..manipulated by the specialists in cultural repression: artists, psychiatrists,..sociologists and 'experts' of all kinds. To fight against a 'spectacular' society, in which everything is treated as a commodity and in which creative energy spends itself in the fabrication of pseudo-needs, one must attack on all fronts simultaneously. **1977** *It* May 5/1 Debord was (is?) a Situationist—a member of perhaps the most radical group to emerge in France in the years approaching the 1968 eruption: they were radical in the sense that they explored most deeply the critique of modern industrial society, which formed the ideological basis for the French upheaval.

2. An upholder of situation ethics.

1966 J. FLETCHER *Situation Ethics* i. 26 The situationist follows a moral law or violates it according to love's need.

situla (si·tiulă). *Archæol.* Pl. **situlae, -las.** [L., = bucket.] Any of various bucket-shaped vessels. Also *attrib.*

1897 *Knowledge* 1 Oct. 229/1 Situla (Bucket), of Apulian fabric, with scene representing Dionysos espousing Ariadne. **1905** *Brit. Mus. Guide Early Iron Age* 14 The succeeding (iron-sword) period..is richly represented by articles decorated in the *situla* style. Such is the name given to a method of ornamenting vessels of the bucket-type..by means of horizontal bands. **1928** D. RANDALL-MACIVER *Italy before Romans* 61 An early example of the situla or bronze bucket for which Bologna no less than Este was to become famous in future years. **1942** *Oxoniensia* VII. 45 (*caption*) Everted rim; general form approaching carinated situlas of Long Wittenham type. **1970** *Ashmolean Mus.: Rep. Visitors 1969* 14 Luristan bronze situla decorated with a feast scene. **1972** *Times* 18 May (Egypt Suppl.) p. iv/6 (*caption*) A *situla*, or temple ritual vessel.

Hence **si·tulate, situ·liform** *adjs.*, having the form of a situla.

1937 *Oxoniensia* II. 26 The Iron Age A2 wares also call for some remark. The situliform jar passes through the usual stages of degradation, and finger-tip ornament goes out of use. **1945** *Proc. Prehistoric Soc.* XI. 32 Shouldered and situlate vessels, either plain or with simple finger-tip ornament. **1946** *Ibid.* XII. 125 A tall situliform urn which may owe some features to Iron Age A forms. **1967** *Antiquaries Jrnl.* XLVII. 181 The rim of a coarse, situlate jar with short upright rim and weak shoulder of Early Iron Age affinities.

sit-up, *sb.* and *a.* Add: **A.** *sb.* **2. a.** An act of sitting up.

1843 R. CARLTON *New Purchase* I. ix. 64 This sit-up we instantly performed—as well, at least, as we could.

b. A physical exercise in which the upper half of the body is raised to a sitting from a supine posture. Also *attrib.*

1955 V. FALLON *Figure Correction & Beauty for You* xx. 112 Sit-up—2 sets of twenty repetitions. **1960** J. HEWITT *Yoga* III. 56 The well-known 'sit-up' exercise... Paschimatanasana differs from an ordinary sit-up in that the movement is continued until the face comes close to the knees. **1971** A. A. MICHELE *You don't have to Ache* 93 Do five to ten sit-ups in a curling fashion bringing your body straight forward. Then do five sit-ups twisting your body to the left, and five twisting your body to the right. **1977** J. F. FIXX *Compl. Bk. Running* xv. 179 To strengthen your stomach muscles,..do twenty or so sit-ups with your knees bent.

B. *adj.* Also, at or against which one sits up.

1960 *Times* 16 Mar. (Canberra Suppl.) p. v/4 A tavern, with a sit-up bar. **1980** L. BIRNBACH et al. *Official Preppy Handbk.* 93 To Buy (or otherwise obtain as soon as possible:..Sit-up pillow.

sit-upon. Add: **2.** The buttocks, the posterior.

1920 C. A. W. MONCKTON *Some Experiences of New Guinea Resident Magistrate* xxv. 302 You have a big boil on your sit-upon. **1955** E. WAUGH *Officers & Gentlemen* II. i. 169 Mrs Stitch immediately sat in the place he vacated. 'Hot-sit-upon,' she remarked. **1976** 'J. WELCOME' *Grand National* viii. 130 I've got something to eat off and to put me sit-upon on in the evenings.

situs. Restrict *rare* to gen. sense in Dict. and add: **2.** *Law.* **a.** Chiefly *U.S.* The place to which for purposes of legal jurisdiction or taxation a property is deemed to belong.

1834 J. STORY *Commentaries on Conflict of Laws* xiv. 462 Moveables are, for many purposes, to be deemed to have no *situs*, except that of the domicil of the owner. **1884** R. DESTY *Amer. Law of Taxation* I. v. 97 The legislature has the power to fix the *situs* of property for purposes of taxation. **1926** *Pacific Reporter* CCXLVIII. 341/1 Actual situs of personal property is necessary for taxation. ..In order to tax the cars in controversy as personal property, they must have actual situs at common law in this state. **1956** *All England Law Reports* 19 Jan. 134 If, however, the situs of the debt be German, he submits that the moratorium law is confiscatory. **1970** *Southwestern Reporter* CCCCXLV. Ser. II. 57/1 Bulldozers, which were regularly moved from one temporary location to another, did not have actual situs of their own, and were not subject to ad valorem taxation. **1977** JOHNS & GREENFIELD *Dymond's Capital Transfer Tax* xxiii. 491 Seven of the agreements provide *situs* codes (for determining the locality of assets).

b. *U.S.* A work-site, esp. (*common situs*) one occupied by two or more employers. Freq. *attrib.*

1950 *Fed. Suppl.* XCI. 698/2 The Act..was intended to keep the situs of a labor dispute confined to actual functions of the parties involved... It is 'stranger picketing', i.e., picketing in aid of a secondary boycott. **1952** *Cornell Law Q.* Winter 247 In such 'common-situs cases' additional criteria necessarily must be invoked. **1959** *Missouri Law Rev.* Jan. 89 Common-premises or common-situs picketing occurs where a labor organization pickets premises where the employees of two or more employers are working and the labor organization has a dispute with only one of the employers. **1977** *Time* 4 July 47/1 With smoothly coordinated pressure, business lobbyists have managed..to defeat organized labor's bid to pass a common situs picketing bill that would have allowed a single union to shut down a construction site.

situs inversus (səi·tŏs, sī·tŏs invɔ̄·ɹsŏs). *Med.* [L., in full *situs inversus viscerum* inverted disposition of the internal organs.] The condition in which the organs of the body are transposed through the sagittal plane (so that the heart lies on the right side, etc.).

1896 J. T. WHITTAKER in T. L. Stedman *Twentieth Century Pract. Med.* IV. 59 Malformations of individual organs are very rare in typical situs inversus. **1966** WRIGHT & SYMMERS *Systemic Path.* I. xv. 484/2 Situs inversus due to malrotation of the foetal gut..is very rare. **1976** *Sci. Amer.* Sept. 68/2 Patients exhibiting situs inversus frequently suffer from chronic sinusitis and bronchitis.

situtunga (situtŭ·ŋgă). Also **sitatunga.** [Swahili.] A medium-sized brown or greyish antelope, *Tragelaphus spekei,* found in east and central Africa, and distinguished by elongated, splayed hooves that enable the animal to walk on marshy ground, and spiral horns in the male. Also *attrib.*

1881 F. C. SELOUS *Hunter's Wanderings Afr.* x. 158 These men told me that in some thick beds of reeds near their town were some situtunga antelope. **1899** [see *HARNESSED *ppl. a.* 4]. **1920** G. D. H. CARPENTER *Naturalist on Lake Victoria* iv. 80 The thunderous snortings of hippos, the muffled bark of the Situtunga, break in. **1947** L. HASTINGS *Dragons are Extra* viii. 191 The highly specialised sitatunga, lord of the swamps. **1949** *Cape Argus* 11 Aug. 7/6 Lions in the swamp appeared to live on Situtunga bush buck. **1955** P. A. BUXTON *Nat. Hist. Tsetse Flies* vi. 144 On some uninhabited islands in Lake Victoria, Uganda, the sitatunga antelope (*Limnotragus s. spekii*) multiplies and with it *G. palpalis.* **1973** *Stand. Encycl. S. Afr.* IX. 650/1 The sitatunga has coarse, shaggy hair.

sit vac: see *SIT *sb.*[2]

Sitwellian (sitwe·liăn), *a.* and *sb.* [f. the name *Sitwell* (see below) + -IAN.] **A.** *adj.* Of, pertaining to, or characteristic of the writers Edith Sitwell (1887–1964), and her brothers Osbert (1892–1969) and Sacheverell (b. 1897). **B.** *sb.* An admirer of the Sitwells.

1923 A. BENNETT in *Adelphi* Aug. 237 This book..is a characteristically Sitwellian beauty. **1927** *Observer* 5 June 4 The Sitwells are known to everyone who has even a casual acquaintance with modern literature, though many who talk of them seem to have read about their doings rather than studied them in their own works. This is a necessary consequence of the Sitwellian methods of publicity. **1937** *Times Lit. Suppl.* 1 May 322/1 Mr. Courtenay's extremely modern simile with its oozy vowels —Sitwellian, surely. **1952** *Scrutiny* Oct. 6 Rajan's examination of Milton's verse keeps turning into Sitwellian clap-trap. **1960** V. SACKVILLE-WEST *Let.* 23 Mar. in H. Nicolson *Diaries* (1968) 382 Edith has built up her personality in many fortuitous ways—her strange appearance,..and all the Sitwellian legend. **1978** J. PEARSON *Façades* xi. 196 The society was conducted with true Sitwellian panache. *Ibid.* 212 Thomas Balston at Duckworth's—himself an enthusiastic Sitwellian—had taken over from Grant Richards as the trio's publisher.

So **Si·twellism,** the style or behaviour of the Sitwells.

1927 R. L. MÉGROZ *Three Sitwells* vi. 105 The phenomenon of Sitwellism. **1932** F. R. LEAVIS *New Bearings in Eng. Poetry* ii. 73 The opposition to the Georgians was already..(just after the war) Sitwellism. **1981** V. GLENDINNING *E. Sitwell* v. 80 The Sitwells defence was attack... Sitwellism at its silliest and most inflated.

‖ **Sitzfleisch** (zi·tsfləiʃ). Also **sitzfleisch.** [Ger., f. *sitz-en* to sit + *fleisch* flesh.] The ability to endure or persist in some activity.

a **1930** D. H. LAWRENCE *Lovely Lady* (1932) 165 They simply hadn't enough *Sitzfleisch* to squat under a bho-tree. **1971** *Atlantic Monthly* May 106 It takes not only special training but a liberal endowment of *Sitzfleisch* to hear one of his [*sc.* Messiaen's] pieces out from one end to the other. **1975** *Harpers & Queen* May 127/3 Lenny hadn't got the patience, the concentration, the sitzfleisch. **1977** *Time* 26 Dec. 31/1 Some of the games now filtering into the general consciousness are distance runs indeed, taking anything from several hours to several months to play, and requiring formidable *Sitzfleisch* (German for sitting flesh).

‖ **Sitz im Leben** (zi·ts im lēbən). *Theol.* Also hyphened. [Ger., lit. 'place in life'.] In Biblical criticism, the circumstances in which a tradition developed, considered as determining the form of that tradition.

1934 M. DIBELIUS *From Tradition to Gospel* i. 7 The categories enable us to draw a conclusion as to what is called the 'Sitz im Leben', i.e. the historical and social stratum in which precisely these literary forms were developed. **1955** D. E. NINEHAM *Stud. Gospels* 230 They [*sc.* the Form-critics] have shown the importance of the factor they call *Sitz-im-Leben* in the preservation of the material included in our gospels. **1956** *Scottish Jrnl. Theol.* IX. 403 Events in Jesus' life are seen by Mark from the *Sitz im Leben* which they have in the early Church. **1976** *Expository Times* LXXXVII. v. 139/2 We may therefore accept without hesitation the doctrine of *Sitz im Leben,* provided that we clearly understand what it is and what are its limitations.

sitzkrieg (si·tskrīg). Also **Sitzkrieg.** [Formed on the analogy of *BLITZKRIEG, as if f. G. *sitz-en* to sit + *krieg* war.] A war, or part of a war, marked by a (relative) absence of active hostilities; *spec.* that phase of the war of 1939–45 lasting from September 1939 to May 1940; a 'phoney war'. Also *fig.*

1940 *N.Y. Times* 21 Feb. 4/7 The R.A.F. referred to the war as a 'Sitzkrieg', which it translated as 'sit-down war'. **1940** *Newsweek* 11 Mar. 28/2 The European 'sitzkrieg' has definitely taught the usually turbulent Balkan states that their safety and independence can best be attained through at least a modicum of unity. **1943** *Sun* (Baltimore) 12 Nov. 1/6 (*heading*) Temporary 'sitzkrieg' on Garigliano sector. **1954** W. K. HANCOCK *Country & Calling* vii. 187 The *sitzkrieg* had at least given me a golden chance to visit West Africa and had thereby enabled me to finish my book. **1967** B. B. GILBERT *Britain Since 1918* iv. 118 As the German conquest of Poland had been termed a '*blitzkrieg*', a lightning war, the new phase of the war that lasted from the end of September [1939] until the beginning of April was frequently designated a '*sitzkrieg*'. **1970** *Courier-Mail* (Brisbane) 22 Dec. 3/1 (*heading*) Old men prepare for sit-in battle... Thirty-six old men..yesterday settled down to a 'sitzkrieg' in the Battle of Rosebank—the Glebe, Sydney, aged men's home. **1980** *Christian Sci. Monitor* (Midwestern ed.) 4 Dec. 6/1 Most observers think the two armies will become involved in a 'sitzkrieg', meaning a long military waiting game.

sitzmark (si·tsmāɹk). *Skiing.* [App. f. G. *sitz-en* to sit + MARK *sb.*[1]] The impression in the snow made by a skier falling backwards on his posterior; an act of so falling. Hence **si·tzmark** *v. intr.*, to fall in this manner.

1935 *Punch* 13 Feb. 176/2 One seems to see as in an inspired flash..the insidious vileness of a sitzmark. [*Note*] Deliberately sitting down in the snow when no other method of stopping seems possible. Very degrading. **1935** *Sierra Club Bull.* Feb. 7 One should be ashamed to make a long descent by 'sitzmarking' at every turn. **1947** F. S. SMYTHE *Again Switzerland* ii. 22 While to fall backwards and *sitzmark* is the hallmark of the craven. **1964** *Harper's Bazaar* Nov. 140/2 The wintersporter who prefers..a bar stool to sitting repeatedly in a *sitzmark.* **1973** P. A. WHITNEY *Snowfire* xvi. 306, I sat down and let my skis go out from under me, sliding a little way on the seat of my pants, leaving sitzmarks behind me. **1977** *Globe & Mail* (Toronto) 16 Nov. 37/6 My rump has had much practice from last winter's skiing—sitzmarks were almost second nature to it.

Siva (ʃī·va, sī·vă). Also **Shiva.** [a. Skr. *śiva,* lit. 'the auspicious one'.] **1.** The third deity of the Hindu triad, to whom are attributed the powers of reproduction and dissolution. Also *transf.*, a representation of this deity.

1788 *Asiatick Res.* I. 248 Siva is believed to have *three* eyes. **1862** J. B. SPEID *Our Last Years in India* iv. 73 The horrid Churruckpuja..festival..in honour of Kali, the consort of Siva, the God of Destruction. **1903** J. C. OMAN *Mystics, Ascetics, & Saints of India* vii. 110 Siva, regarded by his special followers as the Supreme Being, commands their adoration in many different and even seemingly contradictory characters. **1931** *Times Lit. Suppl.* 28 May 429/2 Soon he had brought a haunting fear to the minds of several people, turning upon the possession of an old bronze dancing Siva. **1963** *Times* 23 May 14/6 They [*sc.* deformed cattle] are taken as avatars of.. the riding bull of the Lord Shiva. **1977** *Jrnl. R. Soc. Arts* CXXV. 583/2 The famous dancing Śiva from Ujjain in the Gwālior Museum.

2. *attrib.* and *Comb.*, as *Siva-complex, -worship.*

1876 *Encycl. Brit.* V. 243/1 The Mahávinayaka Peak.. has been consecrated for ages to Siva-worship by ascetics and pilgrims. **1937** H. NICOLSON *Helen's Tower* ix. 191 Was it (as the Viennese might further contend) some Siva-complex, some dread of the destruction-principle? **1967** SPATE & LEARMONTH *India & Pakistan* (ed. 3) vi. 174 Artistically, the best things are a handful of..seals. These..carry an undeciphered script, and their symbolism suggests that some elements in Hinduism, notably Siva-worship, may stem from Harappan culture.

Sivaism. Add: Also **Shivaism.** Cf. *S(h)aivism* s.v. *SAIVA.

1931 *Times Lit. Suppl.* 19 Mar. 228/2 Vishnuism and Shivaism. **1962** A. HUXLEY *Island* xi. 178 The local brand of Mahayana Buddhism, with a bit of Shivaism, probably, on the side.

Sivaist (ʃī·văˌist, sī·văˌist), *a.* [f. as prec. + -IST.] Of or pertaining to the worship of Siva.

1937 M. COVARRUBIAS *Island of Bali* I. vii. 173 It was within this period, from the seventh to the ninth centuries,..that the finest monuments of Java were built, the Buddhist *Borobudur* and the Sivaist *Lora Djongrang* in Prambanan.

Sivaite. Add: Also **Shivaite, shivaite.** Cf. *S(h)aivite* s.v. *SAIVA.

1958 A. HUXLEY *Let.* 22 June (1969) 850 The process of turning old Shivaite-cum-Mahayana-Buddhist society into something combining the best features of East and West was inaugurated in the eighteen-forties by a Scottish surgeon. **1962** —— *Island* vi. 82 We're still Buddhists or Shivaites. **1970** *Guardian* 10 Aug. 9/4 A 1,000-year-old shivaite temple..on the border between Cambodia and Thailand.

Sivan (sī·vān). Also 4–5 **Ciban, Siban, Siwan.** [a. Heb. *sīwān.*] The ninth month of the Jewish year, though named third in the traditional month-list, corresponding to the latter part of May and the earlier part of June.

c **1382** BIBLE (Wycliffe) *Esther* viii. 9 The thridde moneth, that is clepid Ciban [*later text* Siban], that is June. **1535** *Ibid.* (Coverdale), In the thirde moneth, that is the moneth Siuan. **1737** W. WHISTON tr. *Josephus' Jewish War* III. vii. § 29 This fight happened upon the twentieth day of the month Desius (Sivan). **1816** J. ALLEN *Mod. Judaism* xxi. 386 The feast of Pentecost is on the *sixth* day of the month of *Sivan*, the *fiftieth* of the *Omer*. **1891** M. FRIEDLÄNDER *Jewish Relig.* ii. 393 The Feast of Weeks, the 6th and 7th of *Sivan*, commemorates ..an historical event. **1952** *Jewish Q. Rev.* XLIII. II. 181 On Siwan 7..Moses ascended the mountain. **1977** *Jewish Chron.* 20 May 17/1 Friday, May 20 (Sivan 3), Sabbath begins in London at 8.38.

Siwalik (siwā·lik). Also †**Sewalik; Sivalik.** [Hind.]

a. The name of the southern outlying foothills of the Himalayas, extending from Sikkim through Nepal and India to Pakistan, used *attrib.* with reference to the thick sequence of fluviatile and lacustrine sediments, rich in fossil vertebrates, of which they are composed and the time in the Pliocene (or late Miocene) to early Pleistocene when they were deposited.

1836 CAUTLEY & FALCONER in *Asiatic Researches* XIX. xiii. 200 There existed along with the Mastodon, Sivatherium, Fossil Camel, &c. of the Sivalik deposits, a large distinct species of Bear, equalling if not exceeding the largest known of the genus. **1864** *Q. Jrnl. Geol. Soc.* XX. 383 He refers the rocks observed [in the north-western Himalayas] to the following formations:—1. The fluvio-lacustrine series. 2. The Siwalik series... 6. The Palæozoic series. **1902** *Encycl. Brit.* XXV. 466/1 Dr. Dubois..excavated from a bed, considered by him to be of Sivalik formation (Pliocene), a thighbone which competent anatomists decide to be human. **1908** H. B. C. SOLLAS tr. *Suess's Face of Earth* III. IV. vi. 218 Sediments possibly of Siwalik age. **1955** BROWN & DEY *India's Mineral Wealth* (ed. 3) xix. 697 The outer margin of the Himalayas is formed by a continuous fringe of foot-hills built of the rocks of the Siwalik Series. **1975** A. M. DAVIES et al. *Tertiary Faunas* (ed. 2) II. vi. 359 From the Indian subcontinent the Middle Siwalik succession is of Late Miocene equivalent.

b. *absol.* The Siwalik series or period.

1877 *Rec. Geol. Survey India* X. 121 Upper Siwalik. This division includes the great conglomerates and associated beds which terminate the tertiary series of the country. **1938** *Q. Jrnl. Geol. Soc.* XCIV. 407 The alluvial deposits of the Bannu and Derajat plains probably conceal..a geological record more or less continuous from the latest Siwalik. **1974** *Encycl. Brit. Micropædia* IX. 246/2 Remains of the first clearly hominid forms..are known from the Siwalik. **1978** MITCHELL & READING in H. G. Reading *Sedimentary Environments & Facies* xiv. 464/2 Stratabound deposits of uranium with minor vanadium occur in the late Miocene to early Pliocene Middle Siwaliks.

Siwash (səi·wɒʃ), *sb. N. Amer.* Also **Si-wash, siwash.** [Chinook Jargon, a N. Amer. Fr. dial. form of Fr. *sauvage* (SAVAGE *a.*) in same sense.] **1. a.** An Indian, *spec.* of the North Pacific Coast. Freq. *attrib.* (Now considered perjorative.)

1847 J. PALMER *Jrnl. Trav. Rocky Mts.* 150 Si-wash Indians. *a* **1861** T. WINTHROP *Canoe & Saddle* (1883) ii. 18 The three unsavory..mat-haired, truculent siwashes. **1869** [see *HAIDA *a.* and *sb.*]. **1870** [see*ALEUTIAN *a.* and *sb.*]. **1897** *Outing* XXX. 541/1 As we neared the Narrows other Siwashes in other queer-looking canoes paddled out. **1904** E. ROBINS *Magnetic North* 293 You soon learn it is the Siwash custom. **1949** *Boston Globe* 15 May (Fiction Mag.) 3/2 The Siwash showed him a poke of coarse gold. **1967** C. L. EVANS *Newe! Post* 6 He was looking portly in a heavy Siwash sweater, and unselfconsciously wearing the knitted hat to match.

b. *transf.* A name of opprobrium; occas. joc.

1882 *Edmonton Bull.* 3 June 4/3 Does this great chieftain think new settlers are a community of Siwashes or cringing dependants. **1924** C. E. MULFORD *Rustlers' Valley* xiii. 158 So-long, you Siwash! **1964** P. BERTON *Golden Trail* 23, I wouldn't go across the river on that old Siwash's word.

2. Chinook Jargon, the lingua franca of the North Pacific Coast Indians.

1902 *Skagway Daily Alaskan* 23 Aug. 3/1 The governor was forced back upon his ability to talk siwash, hoping thereby to control the Indian vote. **1908** R. E. BEACH *Barrier* 56 Address me in Siwash or in English unless we are alone. **1936** W. B. MOWERY *Paradise Trail* 14 That's what Saghelia means in Siwash—the purty land..paradise.

3. *Comb.*, as **siwash camp,** an open camp with no tent; **Siwash duck,** a scoter of the genus *Melonitta.*

1922 *19th Cent.* Feb. 267 At night they would build a 'siwash' camp, digging a big hole in the snow, lining it with green spruce boughs and building up a three-foot wall of green spruce trees for a windbreak on back and sides. **1962** M. F. MURIE *Two in Far North* II. x. 197 We had only about twelve miles to travel from our siwash camp to Tramway Bar. **1911** *Daily Colonist* (Victoria, B.C.) 30 Apr. 10/1, I finally caught Mr. Indian just as he was coming ashore with his ducks, he had about 60 or 70 in the canoe, but they were mostly scoter or what is more commonly called Siwash ducks. **1927** *Blackw. Mag.* Aug. 207/2 He could see when any siwash ducks were on a shallow part of the lagoon. **1966** *Daily Colonist* (Victoria, B.C.) 20 Mar. 11/4 It is a rare occurrence for a Siwash duck, as the species [*sc.* surf scoter] is commonly called, to be found on such a shoreline.

siwash, *v. N. Amer.* [f. prec.] **1.** *intr.* To camp without a tent, like an Indian.

1938 T. C. STANWELL-FLETCHER *Driftwood Valley* (1946) v. 94 Since we can't carry the additional weight of a tent, we'll have to siwash under trees. **1977** *New Yorker* 20 June 64/3 In discrete valleys were a few cabins, and they stayed in them or siwashed (camped on the trail).

2. *trans.* To bar (a person) from purchasing alcoholic drink. *colloq.*

1948 C. W. HOLLIDAY *Valley of Youth* 144 It [*sc.* Painkiller] was in great demand by the old inebriates during the periods when they had been 'Siwashed'—which meant that it was illegal to serve them with a drink over the bar or sell them liquor. **1957** A. R. BARRATT *Coronets & Buckskins* 9 Wen a wite man gets so's no one will sell him drinks—well folks say e's been siwashed.

So (sense 1) **si·washing** *vbl. sb.*

1904 *Churchman* 21 May 626, I have a lame shoulder, the result of continuous 'siwashing' and sleeping in the snow. **1938** T. C. STANWELL-FLETCHER *Driftwood Valley* (1946) vi. 110 The day after our siwashing trip, we lounged about the cabin, luxuriating in a paradise of warmth and rest. **1962** M. E. MURIE *Two in Far North* II. ix. 194 South Fork Henry no doubt thought we were young fools to be looking forward to a night of siwashing.

six, *a.* and *sb.* Add: **A.** *adj.* **1. d.** *Six Acts* (earlier example); *Six Counties,* the Ulster counties of Antrim, Down, Armagh, Londonderry, Tyrone, and Fermanagh, which have since 1920 comprised the province of Northern Ireland; (cf. *twenty-six counties* s.v. *TWENTY-SIX *a.*); *Six Dynasties,* a collective term for the Chinese dynasties of Ch'en, Eastern Chin, Liang, Liu-Sung, Southern Ch'i and Wu, belonging to the period AD 220–589; freq. used *attrib.* to denote this period of history in China; *Six Nations* (earlier examples).

1834 *Times* 22 Apr. 5/6 Every man that dared to open his mouth against the Castlereagh and Sidmouth despotism must have set the Six Acts at defiance. **1921** *Notes from Ireland* 40/1 The Unionists of the 'Six Counties'. **1922** C. J. C. STREET *Ireland in 1921* ix. 226 The House of Commons contained only Unionist members, who were obviously deeply concerned at the position of affairs while anxious to say nothing which might compromise the position of the Six Counties. **1935** *Frontier Sentinel* (Newry) 22 June 4/4 The Six-County Premier. **1949** [see *ENGLISHIZE *v.*]. **1960** J. STROUD *Shorn Lamb* iv. 49 Suppose..she turns out to be some one-eyed horror in the Six Counties looney-bin. **1974** *Irish Democrat* Nov. 5/2 The significance of the six county election results has been widely debated. **1934** K. S. LATOURETTE *Chinese* I. iv. 155 The fall of the Eastern Chin..is usually said to mark the beginning of the era known to the Chinese as the..Southern and Northern Dynasties, which lasted until 589. Another classification—inclusive of a longer period—employed by Chinese historians is the Six Dynasties, by which are meant the six kingdoms and dynasties between the downfall of the Han and the reunification of China in 589. **1966** F. SCHURMANN *Ideology & Organization in Communist China* vii. 407 The most ambitious attempt of this sort occurred during the Six Dynasties Period (third to sixth century A.D.). This was a period of serious political and social breakdown. **1973** T. R. TREGEAR *Chinese* i. 26 Monks from India..so impressed the barbarians of the Six Dynasties..that they adopted Buddhism. **1980** E. BEHR *Getting Even* v. 59 A huge 'Six Dynasties' celadon jar and a horseman of the Northern Wei period. **1710** in J. W. Lydekker *Faithful Mohawks* (1938) ii. 28 And as a sure Token of the sincerity of the six Nations, We do..present Our Great Queen with these Belts of Wampum. **1785** T. JEFFERSON *Notes Virginia* 390 The Mingo or Six-nation Indians. *Ibid.*, The Mingos are a war colony from the six nations.

e. Colloq. phr. *six feet under* and varr.: dead and buried; in or into the grave.

1942 BERREY & VAN DEN BARK *Amer. Thes. Slang* § 117/19 *Dead and buried*..six feet under. **1968** J. SANGSTER *Touchfeather* xv. 184 Bill didn't realise it, but he was as dead now as he would be when they lowered him six feet under. **1976** A. PRICE *War Game* v. 107 He never cared for nobody born... He never did, and he never will. Not till he's six foot under. **1979** J. GERSON *Omega Factor* 78 In Islay..we make sure the dead are stiff and cold and six feet under.

2. g. Naut. slang phr. *six upon four*: (on) short rations (i.e. four men's food shared between six men). ? *Obs.*

1829 D. JERROLD *Black-ey'd Susan* II. ii. 31 May you live a life of ban-yan days, and be put six upon four for't. **1843** J. F. COOPER *Ned Myers* 78 As to food, we were kept 'six upon four' the whole time I was prisoner. *Ibid.* 86 Put at 'six upon four' again.

h. *Cricket.* With omission of *runs.* (i) Six runs scored by striking the ball clear over the boundary. Cf. sense 6 of the sb., below.

1857 T. HUGHES *Tom Brown's School Days* II. viii. 392 When you or Raggles hit a ball hard away for six, I am delighted. **1951** G. BRODRIBB *All Round Wicket* vi. 39 A lusty hit for six gives many people intense pleasure... There were..many outstanding feats of six-hitting. **1979** *Daily Tel.* 29 May 17/3 The ball was hit for six.. into the vicarage grounds.

(ii) Also *transf.* and *fig.* in various colloq. phrases: *to knock* (someone) *for six,* to wrench from a state of composure; to defeat (soundly); to astonish; also in extended uses, and with inanimate obj. Similarly, *to go for six* (see also quot. 1943); *to hit for six*: see *HIT *v.* 8 f.

1902 J. MILNE *Epistles of Atkins* vi. 107 'It knocked me for six', is the statement we have about a bullet in the knee. **1934** A. BERKELEY *Panic Party* iv. 69 It's a crashing bore..to think of those dim cads knocking us for six like this, but..it's no use getting strenuous about it. **1941** L. A. G. STRONG *John McCormack* viii. 129 John ..hurled his Santuzza from him with such vigour that she went for six, landing in the wings on the far side of the stage. **1943** C. H. W. JACKSON *It's a Piece of Cake* 32 *Gone for six*, killed, missing. **1949** R. GOW *Ann Veronica* I, in *Plays of Year 1949* I. 240 You're just like an angel yourself sitting there. You knock me for six, if I may borrow a sporting metaphor. **1955** *Times* 6 Aug. 7/4 It is a song that knocks for six the illusion..that little creatures probably know by instinct how to do their stuffs. **1973** 'B. GRAEME' *Two & Two make Five* vi. 58 A glass of his home-made cider..knocks you for six.

i. Chiefly as Fr. phr. *Les Six* (le sis) a Parisian group of six composers, Louis Durey (1888–1979), Arthur Honegger (1892–1955), Darius Milhaud (1892–1974), Germaine Tailleferre (b. 1892), Georges Auric (b. 1899), and Francis Poulenc (1899–1963), formed after the war of 1914–18, whose music represents a reaction against romanticism and impressionism.

[**1920** H. COLLET in *Comœdia* 16 Jan. 2/6 Les artistes conscients reconnaissent en Satie un maître. Voyons maintenant ce que valent les 'Six' qu'il précéda sur la voie nouvelle.] **1927** *Grove's Dict. Mus.* (ed. 3) II. 662/1 Although a member of the group of French musicians known as the 'Six', he [*sc.* Honegger] is of Swiss parentage. **1934** C. LAMBERT *Music Ho!* III. 194 Chabrier.. may be considered..the father of the post-war movement associated with the names of Les Six. **1952** B. ULANOV *Hist. Jazz in Amer.* (1958) x. 113 The lessons the composer had learned from..the music of Ravel and *les six* were poorly applied. **1978** P. GRIFFITHS *Conc. Hist. Mod. Music* vi. 72 Les Six did not exist as a group for more than a few years.

j. *the Six,* the group of countries (Belgium, France, the German Federal Republic, Holland, Italy, and Luxembourg) which were the original members of the European Economic Community from 1958 until the admission of others in 1973.

1957 [see *EUROPEAN *a.* 1 c]. **1958** *Economist* 18 Oct. 207/1 The Six are the European Community, forerunner of the continental political union..that is to be when General de Gaulle is gone. **1981** *Times* 30 June

7/1 In 1977 Britain..threatened to bring down the whole European edifice built up painstakingly by the original Six.

B. *sb.* **2. b.** (*b*) *spec.* a group of six Brownie Guides or Cub Scouts.

1916 R. BADEN-POWELL *Wolf Cub's Handbk.* II. 59 Each Six is called after a Wolf by its colour. **1920** —— *Brownies or Blue Birds* ii. 11 The Brownies are divided into parties of six; each 'Six' is under the leader who is called a 'Sixer'. **1972** TRINKY & PETERS *Cub Scout Games* 26 Cubs enjoy Six relays and will compete fiercely for their Six.

3. i. Substitute for def.: Large flower-pots, six of which are formed from a cast of clay. (Earlier example.)

1824 J. C. LOUDON *Encycl. Gardening* II. 327 The Flower Pot, is a cylindrical tapering vessel of burnt clay, with a perforated bottom, and of which there are ten sorts, distinguished by their sizes thus: the..third [size has] 6 [to the cast, and are called] sixes [, being] 9 [inches diameter] 8 [inches deep].

k. *U.S. slang.* A prison sentence of six months.

1844 J. H. INGRAHAM *La Bonita Cigarera* vi. 27/1 I've served two sixes in her, and that's enough for me to give to the service o' my country! **1928** J. O'CONNOR *Broadway Racketeers* xvii. 182 Even if its only a sixer in the pen, too many sixes are bad for the health.

l. A six-cylinder motor car or engine.

1920 *Motor Man.* (ed. 23) 19 The chief constructional difference between the six and the four is in the crankshaft. **1977** *Chicago Tribune* 2 Oct. XIII. 18/2 The use of fours, sixes, and small V-8's is more prevalent in 1978.

4. a. Also *old six* (see quot. 1890).

1890 BARRÈRE & LELAND *Dict. Slang* II. 98 *Old six* (common), old ale at sixpence a quart. *Spoken*—Look what I've got to do tonight! There's fourteen 'pubs' on my beat... That means that I've got fourteen pints of old six to get down me. **1898** J. D. BRAYSHAW *Slum Silhouettes* 155 Tell 'er ter send for an hexty pint of old six. *Ibid.* 156 The foaming jug of 'old six' was placed on the table.

6. *Cricket.* A score of six runs made by striking the ball clear over the boundary; a shot which achieves this.

1920 D. J. KNIGHT in P. F. Warner *Cricket* i. 34 If accurately timed—remember that flick of the wrists at the psychological moment—there goes the easiest six in cricket to your credit! **1933** H. LARWOOD *Body-Line?* 8 Mr. Wyatt again bats well... He ends a fiery rubber with a crashing six! **1949** J. SYMONS *Bland Beginning* 217 The ball sailed high into the air... The umpire signalled a six. **1957** G. LYTTELTON *Let.* 27 June in *Lyttelton–Hart-Davis Lett.* (1979) II. 120 His [*sc.* F. Trueman's] three sixes off consecutive balls were worth seeing. **1976** J. SNOW *Cricket Rebel* 16 Shortly after my six-hitting effort the school was sold and the ground used for building.

7. *the deep six*: used in various slang phrs. to denote death or the grave (perh. from the custom of burial at sea, at a depth of six fathoms); also *fig.* Hence as *v. trans.*, to submerge in water; also *fig.*, to reject, abandon, conceal. orig. and chiefly *U.S.*

1929 M. A. GILL *Underworld Slang* 4/2 *Deep six*, grave. **1947** S. PALMER *Miss Withers Regrets* (1948) xii. 135 My old lady went over the hill with my bank account before I was out of boot camp. I'd have given her the deep-six if I coulda got a furlough. **1966** T. PYNCHON *Crying of Lot 49* iii. 50 Attack, retaliation, both projectiles deep-sixed forever and the Pacific rolls on. **1973** *Times* 26 July 8/3 Mr Dean has testified that Mr Ehrlichman told him to 'deep six' the documents... He said he threw the documents into the Potomac river. **1975** *Publishers Weekly* 28 July 116/1 They discovered that Americans..have been hung up on the wisdom of Franklin's 'Poor Richard's Almanack'..: 'work hard, be thrifty, don't borrow.'.. They tell their readers to 'deep six' Poor Richard and put his advice into reverse. **1976** *Listener* 28 Oct. 524/3 The more serious charge from Dean that he [*sc.* President Ford] tried to 'deep six' the Watergate investigation. **1977** *Islander* (Victoria, B.C.) 21 Aug. 2/3, I heard later that Bruce had taken them [*sc.* three guns] out into the saltchuck and deep-sixed them. **1978** *Sunday Mail Color Mag.* (Brisbane) 7 May 13 'Fraid the rest of the treasure *and* your gear have gone for the deep six!..It's over three hundred feet to the bottom of that trench!

C. 1. a. *six-ball* (over), *six-bit* (code, row), *six-cylinder* (engine, motor vehicle) (also *absol.*); *six-piece* (band), *six-water* (grog) (earlier example).

1910 *Blackw. Mag.* Jan. 97/2 He covered something between 250 and 300 yards in the course of each six-ball over. **1979** *Times* 29 Nov. 19/1 England..made 211 for eight in their 50 six-ball overs. **1964** T. W. MCRAE *Impact of Computers on Accounting* i. 9 A computer using a 'six-bit' binary code. **1964** C. DENT *Quantity Surveying by Computer* vi. 72 These word trains, forming blocks of data, are directed to the tape via the tape control unit, which breaks them into six-bit rows. **1905** G. B. SHAW in *Grand Mag.* Feb. 116 An old crock of a 1904 six-cylinder car. **1938** *New Statesman* 22 Jan. 142/2 At one period the Morris interests were building a couple of dozen six-cylinders, all different. **1977** 'D. RUTHERFORD' *Return Load* iv. 83 Under the shiny cellulose lid..lurked a six-cylinder engine. **1948** A. BARON *From City from Plough* 39 On the dais at the end of the ballroom a six-piece band thumped and brayed. **1959** *Encounter* Oct. 49/1 In the dining-room a six-piece dance-band plays. **1829** D. JERROLD *Black-Ey'd Susan* II. i. 27 May I be put on six-water grog for a lubber.

2. *six-holed, -membered, -pointed* (earlier example), *-toothed* (earlier example), *-wheeled* (later example); *six-belted, -striped*.

1908 R. SOUTH *Moths Brit. Isles* II. 358 Six-belted Clearwing... The body of the male has seven yellow belts, and that of the female one less. **1958** W. J. STOKOE *Caterpillars Brit. Moths* II. 244 The Six-belted Clearwing ..*Dipsosphecia scopigera*. The haunts of this moth are on chalk downs. **1955** E. POUND *Classic Anthol.* II. 135 With six-holed flutes That were bamboo shoots. **1956** I. L. FINAR *Org. Chem.* II. viii. 252 Bicyclic monoterpenes contain a six-membered ring and a three-, four-, or five-membered ring. **1978** A. J. BIRCH in *Further Perspectives Organic Chem.* (Ciba Symposium) 6 A similar cyclization to a six-membered ring from the C_{20}-precursor geranylgeranyl pyrophosphate would not yield this group. **1764** T. H. CROKER et al. *Compl. Dict. Arts & Sciences* I. s.v. *Diamond*, These [diamonds] the jewellers call six-pointed stones. **1907** R. SOUTH *Moths Brit. Isles* I. 227 The Six-striped Rustic..is also generally distributed over our islands. **1742** W. ELLIS *Mod. Husbandman* Sept. xxvi. 124 The Sheep..are generally six-toothed Wethers. *a* **1976** A. CHRISTIE *Autobiogr.* (1977) VIII. i. 372 It was at this time of day when the big six-wheeled cars most often went off the track.

3. *six-bitter* [*BIT *sb.*² 8 b], *-roomer* (earlier example), *-seater*.

1928 *Coast Guard* Aug. 6/1 (*caption*) A fleet of 'six-bitters', or 75-footers, at maneuvers. **1964** M. F. WILLOUGHBY *Rum War at Sea* vii. 88 Many six-bitters were used offshore to picket larger rum vessels. **1853** DICKENS *Bleak Ho.* lxiv. 612 'It's a six roomer, exclusive of kitchens,' said Mr. Guppy, 'and in the opinion of my friends, a commodious tenement.' **1932** T. S. ELIOT *Sweeney Agonistes* 24 There's no motor cars No two-seaters, no six-seaters. **1977** *Herald* (Melbourne) 18 Jan. 2/2 A six-seater antique dining table, and two antique chairs were among the $4000 haul.

5. six-ale (earlier example); **six by six** *U.S. Mil. slang* (see quot. 1966); also written *6 × 6*, *6 by 6* and *ellipt.* as **six-by; six chamber**: also in full **six chamber revolver; Six Day(s) War**, an Arab–Israeli war that lasted from 5 to 10 June 1967; **six-eight tempo, time** *Mus.*, time or rhythm having a bar length of six quavers' duration divided into two equal beats; also *ellipt.* and as $\frac{6}{8}$; **six-figure** *a.*, (*a*) evaluated to or containing six significant figures or six decimal places; (*b*) containing or represented by six digits; *spec.* worth hundreds of thousands (of pounds, dollars, etc.); also in phr. *in six figures*; **six-four** (later example); **six-four measure, meter, time** *Mus.*, time or rhythm having a bar length of six crotchets' duration divided into two equal beats; also *ellipt.* and as $\frac{6}{4}$; **six-gun** *N. Amer.* = SIX-SHOOTER; cf. *six-chamber* (*revolver*) in Dict. and Suppl.; **six o'clock**: see sense 2 c of the adj.; also denoting any position resembling that of the hands of a clock at six o'clock; **six-pack** orig. and chiefly *U.S.*, a package containing six cans or bottles of a drink; **six-two time** *Mus.*, time or rhythm having a bar length of six minims' duration divided into two equal beats; also written $\frac{6}{2}$.

1871 *N.Y. Almanac* 40/1 And a glass of 'six ale', punctually every morning at eleven o'clock, was absolutely necessary to his existence. **1942** *Infantry Jrnl.* Sept. 41/1 A group of upturned faces stands out to an aerial observer like a 6 × 6 in a flock of jeeps. **1943** *Yank* 3 Sept. 7/2 I'm herding a 6 by 6. **1966** *Sunday Times* (Colour Suppl.) 4 Dec. 73/4 GI Jargon. *Six by six*, six wheel truck with six-wheel drive. **1973** D. FAIRBAIRN *Shoot* xiv. 109, I want you to load everything onto a six-by, and I want you to have the six-by all gassed up and ready to go. **1922** JOYCE *Ulysses* 642 The sixchamber revolver anecdotes verging on the tropical. **1967** *Times* 14 June 1/3 The purpose of this move is clearly to have the Assembly condemn Israel and demand that she withdraw her armed forces to the armistice demarcation lines as they existed before the six-day war that started on June 5. **1967** *Listener* 17 Aug. 196/3 In the euphoria that followed the Six Days War, the Israelis appear to be convinced that they can work miracles. **1977** P. JOHNSON *Enemies of Society* xviii. 241 The impetus which created the political terrorism of the 1970s was undoubtedly provided by the Arab defeat in the 1967 Six Day war. **1873** *Illustr. London News* 2 Aug. 114/2 'Sleep, baby darling,' a lullaby..is in the six-eight tempo conventionally associated with slumber-songs. **1884** GROVE *Dict. Mus.* IV. 119/1 Six-eight time..with two Beats in the Bar, each represented by a dotted Crotchet—or its equivalent, three Quavers. **1936** F. G. HAWKES *Stud. in Time & Tempo* xii. 74 $\frac{2}{4}$, $\frac{6}{8}$, and $\frac{6}{4}$ are much alike so far as the movements of the baton are concerned. **1965** *New Yorker* 8 May 173/1 McFarland's rhythms are full of stop-times, double time-passages, six-eight time, and shuffle rhythms. **1978** G. READ *Mod. Rhythmic Notation* v. 158 In essence, the $\frac{6}{8}$ violin part constitutes triplets in duple time. **1840** R. FARLEY (*title*) Tables of six-figure logarithms. **1873** 'MARK TWAIN' & WARNER *Gilded Age* xiii. 123 He always talked in six figures. It was as natural for the dear boy to be rich as it is for most of us to be poor. **1963** P. DRACKETT *Motor Rallying* iii. 40 To illustrate, let's take a six-figure reference, the type normally employed. It may be, say 386 443. **1970** J. McN. DODGSON *Pl.-Names Cheshire* I. p. xliv, A four- or six-figure National Grid reference to the location of the principal hamlet. **1971** *Daily Tel.* 7 July 14, 64 pictures in 75 minutes, three in the six-figure class, and Monet's great painting..not far behind. **1981** R. ADAMS *Girl in Swing* (rev. ed.) xxi. 291 If you were to decide to put it into auction it would be almost bound to go for a very large sum—in the six-figure range. **1884** GROVE *Dict. Mus.* IV. 119/1 Six-four Time..with two Beats in the bar, each represented by a dotted Minim—or its equivalent, three Crotchets. **1936** Six-four [see *six-eight* above]. **1938** *Oxf. Compan. Mus.* 409/1 If the fifth [is in the bass] it is a Second Inversion (also spoken of as 'six-four' chord). **1968** *Listener* 6 June 748/3 An unmetrical vocal line in six-four against an accompaniment in four-four. **1978** G. READ *Mod. Rhythmic Notation* v. 159 Combining two $\frac{3}{4}$ measures into one $\frac{6}{4}$ measure does not simplify the issue, nor would altering the $\frac{6}{4}$ meter to $\frac{6}{8}$. **1912** W. M. RAINE *Brand Blotters* 336 My carbine was gone. It was too far for a six-gun. **1968** E. MCCOURT *Saskatchewan* v. 61 The Canadian cowboys rode unarmed, the Americans carried six-guns. **1979** G. SWARTHOUT *Skeletons* 30 I'll..order a shot of red-eye and lay my six-gun on the bar. **1684** *Phil. Trans. R. Soc.* XVII. 672 The Courses [i.e. veins of ore] usually lying from East to West, or at Six a Clock as their Term is. **1915** 'I. HAY' *First Hundred Thousand* vii. 82 He..touched 'six o' clock' on the distant bull..and took the second pull for the last time. **1927** W. E. COLLINSON *Contemp. Eng.* 92 Expressions I learnt..when doing target-practice..viz. the six o'clock aim (from position on target focussed). **1961** *Wall St. Jrnl.* 19 Oct. 1/5 One leading brand which retailed for $2·09 a six-pack last January now is sold for $1·79. **1972** M. J. BOSSE *Incident at Naha* iii. 138, I took her a pound of bacon and a six-pack of diet cola. **1981** *TV Picture Life* Mar. 46/2 'I went out and borrowed a pickup truck and wore my hat out in the rain for a couple of days, got a six-pack of beer and didn't shower,' John remembers. **1884** GROVE *Dict. Mus.* IV. 119/1 Six-two time, $\frac{6}{2}$; with two beats in each Bar; each represented by a dotted Semibreve—or its equivalent, three Minims. **1978** G. READ *Mod. Rhythmic Notation* ii. 19 In more traditional symbology, $\frac{3}{1}$ or $\frac{3}{1}$.

sixer. Add: **2. a.** Also, six months' imprisonment.

1849 *Session Papers* 1 Feb. 324 The prisoner said he should not mind if he got off with a *sixer*—that means six months' imprisonment. **1887** J. W. HORSLEY *Jottings from Jail* i. 23 Neddie, from City Road, smugged for attempt up the Grove, expects a sixer..and is reconciling himself to an absence from his oriental home for half a year. **1903** [see *CARPET *sb.* 7]. **1926** J. BLACK *You can't Win* xii. 161 We'll both get a 'sixer' in the morning if we go in front of the judge. **1955** D. W. MAURER in *Publ. Amer. Dial. Soc.* XXIV. 151 Maybe he will get off with a *bit*..or a *sixer*, which is six months in jail.

d. Six strokes of the cane administered as punishment in school. Cf. *six of the best* s.v. *BEST *a.* 10 d.

1927 *Chambers's Jrnl.* 10 Sept. 645/2 About a dozen boys..ranged up in front of the Doctor, who, stepping off his pedestal, administered a 'sixer' to each of the culprits with a long and stout cane. **1977** C. MCCULLOUGH *Thorn Birds* ii. 29 They all got sixers, but Meggie was terribly upset because she thought she ought to have been the only one punished.

3. A Brownie Guide or Cub Scout in charge of a six.

1916 R. BADEN-POWELL *Wolf Cub's Handbk.* III. 216 The average Cub when promoted to Sixer does not carry so much authority. **1920** [see *SIX *sb.* 2 b (*b*)]. **1965** G. MCINNES *Road to Gundagai* x. 161, I was promoted to be Sixer of the Whites. **1978** *Lochaber News* 31 Mar. 7/5 On Thursday, March 23 the sixers and seconds went to Raigmore Hospital to present a cheque to Dr John Burton for the kidney unit at the hospital.

sixpence. Add: **1.** (Earlier *Comb.* example.)

1780 J. WOODFORDE *Diary* 20 June (1924) I. 286 Gave on going—O.I.O. For which you have 6d worth of anything at the Bar.

2. b. (Further examples.)

1818 H. B. FEARON *Sk. Amer.* 13 A beggar came in, and was relieved with a Spanish silver piece called a sixpence. **1891** S. M. WELCH *Home Hist.* 169 It was common, particularly in New England, to call a sixpence or a half dime, a *fip*.

sixpenny, *a.* and *sb.* Add: **2.** (Later examples.) Also of things.

1878 H. H. JACKSON *Travel at Home* 11 She didn't never want to see any o' them sixpenny towns agin. **1911** G. B. SHAW *Doctor's Dilemma* p. xxvi, The sixpenny doctor, with his low prices and quick turnover of patients, visibly makes much more than you. **1927** KIPLING *Limits & Renewals* (1932) 164 When I was a sixpenny doctor at Lambeth.

3. c. (Earlier example.)

1840 *Knickerbocker* XV. 138 The larger newspaper establishments, satirically termed by their Lilliputian rivals, 'the respectable sixpennies'.

d. As *sb.* A cinema seat that costs sixpence.

1958 *Listener* 4 Dec. 927/2 A small boy sitting in the sixpennies at the Bijou Cinema.

4. *sixpenny piece* (earlier example).

1897 M. H. KINGSLEY *Travels in W. Afr.* xxvi. 589 A piece of ground the size of a sixpenny piece.

sixpennyworth. Add: Also **sixpennorth.**

1933 [see *BACCO, BACCY].

six-shooter. Add: (Earlier example.)

1844 *Nauvoo* (Illinois) *Neighbor* 24 July 3/1 Joseph.. opening the door..discharged one barrel of a six shooter (Pistol) in the entry.

six-shooting *ppl. a.* (earlier example). Also **si·x-shoo:ter** *v.*; **si·x shoo:tering** *vbl. sb.*

1858 T. VIELE *Following Drum* 224 A belt full of pistols,..and a six-shooting rifle. **1904** P. FOUNTAIN *Great North-West* xx. 242, I never was so near six-shootering myself as I was that night. **1909** 'O. HENRY' *Roads of Destiny* xxii. 371 We heard a yelling and a six-shootering.

sixteen, *a.* and *sb.* Add: **B.** *sb.* **5.** A medium-sized flower-pot, sixteen of which are formed from a cast of clay.

1802 W. Forsyth *Treat. Culture & Managem. Fruit-Trees* viii. 114 The 1st size of 8 in the Cast is called Eights. 2[nd size of] 12 [in the Cast is called] Twelves. . . Sixteens . . . Twenty-fours. **1852** G. W. Johnson *Cottage Gardener's Dict.* 392/2 Nine-inch pot. . 16s. [= sixteens]. **1895** *Culture of Veg. & Flowers* (Sutton & Sons) (ed. 6) 323 Small 60. . 2⅜ [inches]. Mid. 60. . 3. Large 60. . 3½. . . 16. . 8½. . . 6. . 12½. **1955** W. E. Shewell-Cooper *Pot Plants* ii. 19 The tendency is to use smaller pots and, whereas years ago we grew all our late Chrysanthemums in 12's, we try to do them today in 16's or even 24's. **1962** [see *sixty *sb.* 4 c].

C. 1. sixteen millimetre, (more usually) **16mm,** a cine film which is sixteen millimetres wide; in full **sixteen millimetre film;** also *attrib.*

1926–7 *Army & Navy Stores Catal.* 971/1 The Bell Howell 'Filmo' automatic camera. . Accommodates newly standardized 16 m/m films. **1951** R. Spottiswoode *Film & its Techniques* i. 9 The producer must also make up his mind whether to shoot in color or black and white, in standard theater 35 mm. film, or nontheatrical 16 mm. film. **1969** G. Greene *Travels with my Aunt* i. viii. 82 The films, of course, had all been shot on sixteen millimetre, and. . they were enlarged practically to cinerama size. **1977** *New Yorker* 29 Aug. 66/2 Traveling, then, at almost six hundred miles an hour, we watch this innovative sixteen-millimetre movie, projected with infinite difficulty at thirty-six feet a minute.

sixteener. 2. (Later example.)

1966 *Daily Tel.* 5 Nov. 7/6 The world's biggest organization of young motor-cyclists. . launched a petition against the sixteener ban.

sixteensome (sikstī·nsəm). [f. Sixteen *a.* + -some[2].] A group of sixteen persons. Usu. *attrib.* in *sixteensome reel,* a Scottish dance performed in sets of sixteen persons. Also *absol.*

1926 [see *eightsome *a.*]. **1938** *St. Andrews Citizen* 13 Aug. 9 He is much in request to teach. . eightsomes, sixteensomes, and thirty-twosomes. **1954** H. A. Thurston *Scotland's Dances* 51 The same process can be applied to the eightsome reel: the result is the *double eightsome* or *sixteensome reel.* **1964** J. & T. Flett *Trad. Dancing* i. 18 Mr Reid taught. . the Eightsome Reel, and the Sixteensome Reel. **1979** *Harper's & Queen* July 157/3 They led the sixteensome of Atholl Highlanders down the stairs two by two.

sixth, *a.* and *sb.* Add: **A.** *adj.* **2.** With omission of *form* (later examples), *former.*

c **1898** W. Lewis *Let.* (1963) 6 First a fellow got a 'sixth licking' (stripes from every sixth in the house). **1906** R. Brooke *Let.* 3 Feb. (1968) 39 [He] has been discovered. . showing up proses done for him by a wee & terrified Sixth. **1914** 'I. Hay' *Lighter Side School Life* i. 5 The Head. . probably takes the Sixth for an hour or two a day. **1963** *Sunday Times* 8 Sept. 29/3 Cool Shakespeare thrives in the sixth and phrases like 'Pox on't'. . are in present usage. **1977** R. Rendell *Judgement in Stone* vi. 50 You're no longer the naughtiest girl in the sixth.

C. 2. *sixth day,* the name given to Friday by members of the Society of Friends; *sixth form:* see Form *sb.* 6 b (later examples); hence *sixth-former:* see *-former; *sixth-form college,* a college for pupils over the age of sixteen, chiefly providing A-level courses.

1655 G. Fox *Jrnl.* (1694) 152 On the Sixth day of that Week I had a meeting near Colchester. **1858** M. Tuckett *Diary* 26 Sept. in H. Fox *Mariana's Diary* (*c* 1975) 8 Sixth day morning was bright and fine. **1976** *Minutes Ohio Yearly Meeting of Friends* 30 (*heading*) Sixth day afternoon session, eighth month 27th. **1938** C. Morgan *Flashing Stream* 31 He who wrote the Sonnets, or Hamlet's bidding to Ophelia. . had no moderation, no smell of the sixth form, no sense of humour. **1965** H. L. Elvin *Educ. & Contemp. Soc.* ii. vii. 134 There is little doubt that the sixth form college would be welcomed by most of the young people who would go to it. **1967** *Listener* 18 May 645/1 The eighteen-year-old emerging from our sixth forms has a level of knowledge as good as a second year student in a North American university. **1976** *Times* 18 Aug. 3/2 Tameside council has decided not to introduce two proposed sixth form colleges.

sixth sense (siksþ sens). [f. Sixth *a.* + Sense *sb.*] A supposed intuitive faculty by which a person or animal perceives facts and regulates action without the direct use of any of the five senses. Hence **sixth-sense** *v. trans.,* to discover by means of a sixth sense; **sixth-sensed** *a.,* possessing a sixth sense.

[**1687** W. Domvile tr. *B. de Fontenelle's Plurality of Worlds* iii. 50 It has been thought that we want a sixth natural Sense, by which we might know many things more than we do.] **1761** L. Sterne *Tristram Shandy* IV. i. 75 There seems in some passages to want a sixth sense to do it rightly. **1807** R. Southey *Lett. from England* II. xl. 176 It was surprising to see them [*sc.* the blind] move about the room,. . as if they had possessed that sixth sense, which experimental naturalists. . are said to have discovered in bats, when they have put out their eyes. **1841** Dickens *Barnaby Rudge* xxxiii. 122 People. . doing exactly the same things for a great many years, acquire a sixth sense, or some unknown power of influencing each other. **1903** *Science Siftings* 31 Oct. 46/1 The 'sixth sense' by which blind persons perceive certain objects. **1958** R. Godden *Greengage Summer* xvi. 199 Did she have some sixth-sense warning? **1967** *Punch* 25 Oct. 609/2 This, I sixth-sensed, could well be it. **1976** J. Crosby *Nightfall* xxx. 176 About Elf I am second-sighted, sixth-sensed, magicked. **1979** R. Jaffe *Class Reunion* (1980) ii. iii. 199 There was something about living together and being very close that gave people a sort of sixth sense.

sixty, *a.* and *sb.* Add: **A.** *adj.* **2. b.** *sixty-six* (earlier example); *sixty-nine, 69* = *soixante-neuf.

1857 T. Frere *Hoyle's Games* 4 The German game of 'Sechs und Sechszig', or Sixty-six, has never before, that we are aware of, been dressed in an English garb. **1888** [see *soixante-neuf]. **1973** D. Lang *Freaks* 90 We spent many hours lying on her bed, more or less in the classical 69 position, but motionless. **1978** *Guardian Weekly* 23 Apr. 21/5 When I first met him, I thought 69 was a bottle of Scotch.

B. *sb.* **1. b.** (Later examples.)

1910 *Dialect Notes* III. 445 That child cuts up like sixty. **1975** J. D. Fitzgerald *Great Brain does it Again* ii. 20 We ran like sixty to the front porch.

3. (Example of years in a person's life.) Now *spec.* the period 1960–9.

1964 M. McLuhan *Understanding Media* ii. xxxi. 320 TV in the Fifties and Sixties spread to the entire population. **1978** *Listener* 3 Aug. 145/1, I was, alas, one of those who spent the Sixties sneering at the notion of parish-pump broadcasting. **1981** 'D. Shannon' *Murder most Strange* ii. 34 They were both in the sixties, middle-sized, sandy coloring. **1983** D. Gethin *Wyatt* xiv. 99 An ageing sixties swinger with the elegant mannerisms of a professional hotelier.

4. c. A small flower-pot, sixty of which are formed from a cast of clay.

1802 W. Forsyth *Treat. Culture & Managem. Fruit-Trees* viii. 114 There are some [pots] smaller than sixtys, for seedlings and heaths. **1895** [see *sixteen *sb.* 5]. **1962** A. J. Huxley *Garden Terms Simplified* 69 Above are shown, to scale top row from left to right, an 8½in. pot (16),. . and a 3½ in. pot (large 60).

C. a. *sixty-miler* (Austral.), a small cargo vessel which transports coal along the coast from Newcastle to Sydney; *sixty-pounder* (later example).

1933 I. Hamilton *Nights Ashore* 29 The *Five Stars* was a few tons larger than the average ancient sixty miler. *Ibid.* 210 During the slack 'sixty-miler' season. **1940** Blunden *Poems 1930–40* 202 And as the stream's last murmer stilled, Our sixty-pounders started talking. **1948** *Sydney Morning Herald* 28 Jan. 1/7 Sydney's gas supply now depends on the '60-milers'.

c. Also called *sixty-fours.*

1805 in E. Howe *London Compositor* (1947) ii. 92 Forty-eights to be paid two shillings per sheet extra, and sixty-fours two shillings and sixpence per sheet extra.

d. *sixty-four dollar question, $64 question,* orig. the question posed at the climax of a U.S. radio quiz for a prize of sixty-four dollars, used *transf.* to denote a difficult or crucial question; also *sixty-four dollar answer, sixty-four thousand dollar question,* and varr.

1942 J. R. Tunis *All American* vii. 240 Here's the sixty-four dollar question. Will the team go to Miami? **1942** *Time* 18 May 22/3 The Jap. . could still sweat over the $64 question. **1955** M. Gilbert *Sky High* xii. 176 'What have these receivers got to do with us?. . 'That's the sixty-four dollar question.' **1957** R. Hoggart *Uses of Literacy* vi. 150 All the time he had the sixty-four dollar answer but did not know it. **1957** *Observer* 21 July 1/3 Mr. Macmillan said. . there was only one answer to the 64,000-dollar question—to increase production. **1958** *Listener* 4 Dec. 930/1, I come now to what you probably feel is the sixty-four-dollar question. How is all this to be paid for? **1963** *N.Y. Times* 2 Dec. 37/1 Mr. Baker. . left the air, to return in 1942 as master of ceremonies on 'Take it or Leave it'. . . He posed 'the $64 question', a term that became part of everyday language. **1967** *N.Y. Rev. Bks.* 7 Dec. 27/1 On June 1, 1955, 'The $64,000 Question' was born and commercial television was never the same again. **1979** *Jrnl. R. Soc. Arts* CXXVII. 143/2 Like his predecessor on this rostrum he left it to Mr. Tyrrell Burgess, our lecturer tonight, to tackle the sixty-four dollar question—What now? **1981** B. Healey *Last Ferry from Lido* vi. 101 It still leaves the sixty-four thousand dollar question. Where do we go from here?

size, *sb.*[1] **II. 10. d.** For *rare* read: *rare* exc. in phr. *to cut* (*chop,* etc.) *down to size:* see *cut *v.* 53 h. *colloq.*

1953 *Time* 20 July 40/3 He kept Stalin down to size. **1962** *Listener* 17 May 883/1 The complexity and psychological depth abandoned in hacking the novel down to size. **1972** *N.Y. Times* 3 Nov. 39/6 Once the warlord armies supporting him were chopped down to size. ., he was content to fade away.

f. In colloq. phr. *that's* (*about*) *the size of it,* etc.: that is what it amounts to, that is the situation.

1860 [in Dict., sense 12 a]. **1880** 'Mark Twain' *Tramp Abroad* vii. 71 'Bloodshed!' 'That's about the size of it,' I said. **1914** G. Atherton *Perch of Devil* i. 89 That's the size of it, only I couldn't ever say it like that. **1922** Joyce *Ulysses* 305 Talking about the Gaelic league and the antitreating league and drink, the curse of Ireland. Antitreating is about the size of it. **1966** D. Francis *Flying Finish* ii. 21 'He just went to Italy and didn't come back?' 'That's about the size of it,' Simon agreed. **1973** 'M. Innes' *Appleby's Answer* xv. 134 It's money that's really in his head. . . That's about the size of it, wouldn't you say?

11. c. *to try* (something) (*on*) *for size:* to consider (an idea, theory, etc.) to see whether it fits the facts. Also *loosely,* to try out or sample. *colloq.* (orig. *U.S.*).

1956 'E. McBain' *Cop Hater* (1958) viii. 70 'Try this for size,' Bush said. 'I'm listening,' Carella said. **1967** 'E. Queen' *Face to Face* xxix. 127 'All right,' said the Inspector. 'Let's try this on for size: You knew what Spotty had to sell, didn't you?' **1969** 'J. Fraser' *Cock-pit of Roses* x. 81 'I know some bugger's been pinching 'em, if that's what you're getting at.' Try that on for size, you devil, his look seemed to say. **1979** A. Boyle *Climate of Treason* (1980) viii. 258 Trying his boss's desk for size, Philby noticed the untidy array of memoranda and pending files in the in-tray. **1980** J. McClure *Blood of Englishman* xxiv. 221 She was shaking the sardines into a saucer. 'There, kitty! Try those for size.'

13. size distribution, the way in which size varies among members of a population of particles; **size effect,** an effect due to size; **size-group,** those constituents of a population whose sizes fall within a specific range; **size-range,** a range of sizes; a size group.

1925 *Trans. Faraday Soc.* XXI. 381 (*heading*) A simple method of obtaining the size distribution of particles in soils and precipitates. **1966** D. G. Brandon *Mod. Techniques Metallogr.* v. 250 In the past, size-distribution analysis has usually involved time-consuming measurements on individual grains or particles. **1943** *Ann. Appl. Biol.* XXX. 216/2 The loss in weight increases progressively from *I* to *IV* indicating the existence of a size effect. **1968** C. G. Kuper *Introd. Theory Superconductivity* v. 92 The discrepancy between the experiments and the London theory has been interpreted as a size effect, arising from the scattering of normal electrons by the n-s boundary. **1944** J. S. Huxley *On Living in Revolution* 110 The total population can be separated into four size-groups, corresponding to the produce of the four successive years that each grub lives in the soil before it turns into a beetle. **1971** I. G. Gass et al. *Understanding Earth* ix. 132/2 They contain both filamentous and globular structures, and the latter occur in more than one size-group. **1924** *Industr. & Engin. Chem.* XVI. 930/2 The figures given. . for the size range were calculated in this way. **1955** *New Biol.* XIX. 95 Some particles in the mitochondrial size-range appear to be proplastids. **1962** *Science Survey* III. 296 Shoals of large salmon were observed to remain inactive at the tail of the pool while a smaller size-range of salmon and trout ascended successfully.

size, *v.*[1] Add: **4. a.** (Later U.S. examples.)

1862 *Trans. Ill. Agric. Soc.* (1865) V. 233 There is no provision made for 'sizing the gavels' [in reaping]. **1897** F. C. Moore *How to build Home* 90 The first-story beams are to be sized and leveled upon the sill and upon the foundation wall. **1981** *Sci. Amer.* Apr. 30/1 Second, says Dr. Derry, the book was sized to fit into a briefcase.

fig. **1899** [see *panhandler 1].

6. For *rare*[−1] read † *Obs.* and add later examples.

1853 J. G. Baldwin *Flush Times Alabama* 113 The jury shortly after returned into court with a verdict which 'sized their pile'. **1873** J. H. Beadle *Undevel. West* xii. 198 They are satisfied to 'size your pile' and take quarter of it. **1889** 'Mark Twain' *Conn. Yankee* 300, I was resolved he should have at least one [bath]. . if it sized up my whole influence and bankrupted the pile.

7. a. (Later examples.) Hence **si·ze-up** *sb.,* an estimate. *U.S.*

1924 E. O'Neill *All God's Chillun got Wings* 103 John scrutinizes their faces keenly, sizing up the situation. **1945** E. S. Gardner *Case of Golddigger's Purse* v. 35, I always like to plan my campaign after I've sized up my man. **1949** *Security* (Charlottesville, Va.) May 1/2 Reminded him how wrong a bright man can be in his size-up of other folks. **1952** *Sun* (Baltimore) 22 Oct. 19/7 Casey's size-up of Woodling as a pinch-hitter was verified in the eighth inning. **1978** *N.Y. Times* 30 Mar. B3/1 A teen-ager in sneakers, sizing up the drinkers in the darkened bar as easy marks, whispered to a friend, 'I wonder if they've got any change.'

b. (Later example.)

1912 A. Conan Doyle *Lost World* vi. 87, I want a man I can bank on. So I sized you down, and I'm bound to say that you came well out of it.

8. b. (Earlier and later examples.)

a **1631** Donne *Poems* (1633) 63 So As they waxe lesser, fall, as they sise, grow. *c* **1866** G. M. Hopkins *Poems* (1967) 36 That a quince I pore upon? O no it is the sizing moon. **1926** *Daily Colonist* (Victoria, B.C.) 13 July 4/5 Pears and apples are sizing well and developing nicely. **1940** *Sun* (Baltimore) 5 Sept. 7/5 Sweet potato tubers are developing and sizing in Western Maryland.

c. With *up:* to develop or take shape; to amount (*to* something); to reach the necessary standard. Cf. *to measure up to* s.v. *measure *v.* 4 c. *U.S.*

1884 E. W. Nye *Baled Hay* 126 Time, at last, makes all things size up in proper shape. **1905** *N.Y. Even. Post* 21 Nov. 1 If the President does not think that Mr. Halpin sizes up as chairman of the County Committee, [etc.]. **1910** J. Hart *Vigilante Girl* ii. 28 Burke isn't a bad sort—he sizes up about as well as most of them. **1917** H. James *Ivory Tower* ii. i. 89 The question of what Gray's 'interest'. . might size up to.

sizeless, *a.* (Later examples.)

1896 L. T. Hobhouse *Theory Knowl.* 47 Can we now stigmatise the sizeless, figureless, positionless extension in the same way? **1935** W. de la Mare *Early One Morning* xv. 195 A universe that was nothing but a sizeless point.

sizing, *vbl. sb.*[1] Add: **4.** *sizing up,* the process of assessing or evaluating.

1967 *Coast to Coast 1965–6* 136 No doubt he guessed I'd been doing a bit of sizing up and decided he had better help me get my ideas into order.

sizzle, *sb.* Add: **1.** Also *fig.*

1964 *Economist* 1 Feb. 400/1 The Jesuit sanctuary at Loyola..was a sizzle of sex-appeal. **1976** *National Observer* (U.S.) 17 July 6/1 You've reached middle age, and your marriage has lost its sizzle.

2. *Comb.*, as **sizzle cymbal**, a cymbal, used chiefly in jazz and dance bands, with several small rivets set loosely through it to make a sizzling sound when the cymbal is struck.

1944 W. Apel *Harvard Dict. Mus.* 198/1 Various modifications are used in jazz bands, e.g., the Choke cymbal, the Sizzle cymbal. **1964** R. Burns *Selection, Care, & Use of Cymbals* 7 Sizzle cymbals are immensely popular with drummers playing with jazz groups. **1967** *New Yorker* 21 Jan. 52/2 Marsala told me just to play with wood-blocks and a sizzle cymbal.

sizzle, *v.* Add: **2.** (Later *fig.* examples.)

1928 'Brent of Bin Bin' *Up Country* xv. 266 As Little River was in the same direction he sizzled away to old Healey at the point of the spur. **1966** *Daily Tel.* 15 Nov. 13/3 Some colours vibrate when they are used together and I often use them to make a dull corner sizzle. **1979** *Fisherman's Weekly* 21 June 27/1 When a run comes, line can sizzle off the reel, so be sure to use an open bale-arm plus indicator.

sizzler (si·zləɹ). *colloq.* [f. Sizzle *v.* + -er[1].] **1.** *U.S.* A sizzling heat, day, etc.; a 'scorcher'.

1901 *Emporia* (Kansas) *Gaz.* 1 July 9 The drought which is a sizzler and frier and boiler is a good thing for Kansas. **1904** G. H. Lorimer *Old Gorgon Graham* ii. 37 Satan may be down in Arizona cooking up a sizzler for the corn belt.

2. a. Something salacious or *risqué*. Cf. *scorcher 3 d.

1957 'N. Blake' *End of Chapter* xi. 169 A lot of morons who only wanted to curl up with a nice sizzler by Elinor Glyn. **1977** *News of World* 17 Apr. 9/9 A blue movie being shown to a judge in court was a real sizzler. In fact, it was so hot that it began to melt.

b. A very fast shot or hit. Cf. *scorcher 3 c.

1960 E. W. Swanton *West Indies* iii. 51 The one chance he gave..was a sizzler to the gully. **1976** *Sunday Times* (Lagos) 26 Sept. 1/3 Buffaloes goalkeeper Chilongwe positioned himself to record an amazing save off a sizzler.

sizzling, *ppl. a.* Add: Also *fig.*

1923 [see *picture *sb.* 2 j]. **1947** *Sporting Mirror* 7 Nov. 8/1 His intended tap back to goalkeeper Hesford, from a long way out, became a sizzling shot which won the game for Charlton. **1977** *Time* 30 May 51/2 The sizzling increases [in personal income] of February and March.

sizzlingly (si·zliŋli), *adv.* [f. prec. + -ly[2].] So as to sizzle. Used to give emphasis to expressions of warmth, intensity, etc.

1956 *Essays in Crit.* VI. 204 You, too, were once not allegoric But blazed with passions sizzlingly phosphoric. **1963** *Listener* 21 Feb. 327/2 Unless one has some sizzlingly hot contributions to make, one somehow feels that a mere dialogue is perhaps not enough.

sizzly (si·zli), *a.* [f. Sizzle *v.* + -y[1].] Sizzling, effervescent, exciting.

1936 J. Dos Passos *Big Money* 17 The sizzly smell of champagne and welshrabbit. **1948** D. Ballantyne *Cunninghams* xii. 70 Carole Plowman..was the most beautiful girl in the hall... 'A few good-looking girls here,' he said. 'About three,' Phil said. 'That Plowman tart's sizzly.'

sjambok, *sb.* Add: Also 8 **chanboc(k),** 9 **samboc, sambok, schambok, shambo.** (Earlier and further examples of var. forms.)

α. **1790** E. Helme tr. *Le Vaillant's Trav. Interior Parts Afr.* I. xxi. 412 The next day my men employed themselves in cutting the skin off the Hippopotamus, to make what, in this country, the[y] call *Chanboc*, which are whips, used to drive the oxen. **1804** J. Barrow *Trav. Interior S. Afr.* II. ii. 96 One of those infernal whips, made from the hide of a rhinoceros or sea-cow, known by the name of *sambocs*. **1808** J. Read in G. E. Cory *Rise of S. Afr.* (1921) I. vii. 203 Terribly flogged with a sambok or whip made of the skin of a rhinoceros. **1850** T. Shone *Diary* III. 19 Mar. in *Voorloper* (1976) 717 Lost my Samboc, the Horse Broke his bridle. **1852** M. B. Hudson *S. African Frontier Life* I. 40 No coaxing nor threats, after sambok persuasion, Could cure him of sulks on the present occasion.

β. **1791** tr. *Le Vaillant's Trav. Interior Parts Afr.* I. 195 My people were busied in cutting to pieces the hide of the hippopotamus, to make what the country folks call *chanboc*. **1801** J. Barrow *Trav. S. Afr.* iii. 145 These sort of whips which they call *shambos* are most horrid instruments. **1812** A. Plumptre tr. *Lichtenstein's Trav. S. Afr.* I. i. vii. 98 The skin is the only thing valuable to the colonists, to cut into strips for making the driving whips known here by the Malay name of Schamboks. **1822** W. J. Burchell *Trav. Interior S. Afr.* I. 86 Sometimes encouraged by good words, at other times terrified into exertion by ten blows of the *shambok.* **1911** L. Cohen *Reminisc. Kimberley* xviii. 320 'All right,' he replied... 'Bring me a shambok.'

sjambok, *v.* Add: Also **sjambook.** (Earlier examples.)

1881 *Blackw. Mag.* Dec. 756/1 To associate or have anything to do with blacks, except to make them work, or *sjambook* them if they don't work hard is an unpardonable offence in a Boer's eyes. **1894** E. Glanville *Fair Colonist* xv. 116, I would cheerfully sjambok a stock-lifter until he dropped.

Hence **sja·mbokker**, one who uses a sjambok.

1953 *Cape Times* 30 Mar. 1/1 The sjambokker came outside and hit..Mr. Eddy..on the legs.

sjamboking, *vbl. sb.* Add: Also spelt *sjambokking*. Also *fig.*

1908 D. Blackburn *I came & Saw* 208 Your sjambokking of Sixpence gave me the idea for the Humanitarian Company. **1953** *Cape Times* 30 Mar. 1/1 A police investigation into the alleged sjambokking of two United Party canvassers. **1980** *Listener* 17 Apr. 487/3 Lilford, landowner and power behind Smith and the Rhodesian Front, gave me a verbal sjambokking over the telephone.

Sjögren (ʃə·grĕn). *Path.* [The name of H. S. C. *Sjögren*, Swedish ophthalmologist, who described the condition in 1933 (*Acta Ophthalm.* Suppl. No. 2. 1–151); used after G. *Sjögrens-syndrom* (Weber & Schlüter 1937, in *Deutsch. Arch. für klin. Med.* CLXXX. 333).] *Sjögren's disease* or *syndrome*: a condition characterized by chronic inflammatory swelling of the salivary and lachrymal glands and by auto-immune antibodies in the blood.

1938 *Proc. R. Soc. Med.* XXXII. 255 (*heading*) Sjögren's syndrome associated with pigmentation and sclerodermia of the legs. **1954** [see *keratoconjunctivitis* s.v. *kerato-]. **1961** *Lancet* 26 Aug. 456/2 The diagnosis of Sjögren's disease was made from the case-history and clinical condition, supported by positive Schirmer and rose-bengal tests. **1974** Passmore & Robson *Compan. Med. Stud.* III. xxv. 18/2 Sjögren's syndrome rivals systemic lupus erythematosus in the multiplicity of auto-antibodies present in the serum.

sjögrenite (ʃə·grĕnəit). *Min.* [f. the name of S. A. Hjalmar *Sjögren* (1856–1922), Swedish mineralogist + -ite[1].] A hydrated basic carbonate of iron and magnesium found as yellowish or brownish thin transparent plates formed by hydrothermal action.

1941 C. Frondel in *Amer. Mineralogist* XXVI. 303 The hexagonal mineral commonly admixed with pyroaurite is described on a following page under the name sjögrenite. **1968** *Acta Crystallographica* B. XXIV. 972/1 The carbonate-hydroxides $Mg_6M_2^{III}(OH)_{16}CO_3.4H_2O$ (M^{III} = Fe, Al, or Cr) are known to occur in two dimorphic forms: the hexagonal sjögrenite group has $a \sim 3{\cdot}1$ and $c \sim 15{\cdot}5$ Å; the rhombohedral pyroaurite group has the same *a* value but *c* is about 23·2 Å. **1973** *Mineral. Mag.* XXXIX. 378 Two sub-groups could be distinguished, which would today be described as polytypes differing only in layer stacking; these are represented by pyroaurite and sjögrenite respectively.

ska (skā). [Origin unknown, perh. echoic.] A kind of popular music of Jamaican origin, characterized by a fast tempo and emphasis of the off-beat. Also, a dance to such music. Cf. *reggae, *rocksteady.

1964 [see *game *sb.* 3 b]. **1969,** etc. [see *rocksteady]. **1971** *Guardian* 25 Feb. 10/4 West Indian ska or blue beat music, latterly taken up by skinheads. **1980** *Rolling Stone* (Austral.) 26 June 16/5 'We don't see it as a ska revival,' Davies says, 'because we don't play pure ska.'..The group is also quick to point out the differences between the various 'ska' bands.

skaapsteker (skā·pstē·kəɹ). Also **scarpsticker, scha(a)psteeker, -steker, -sticker.** [Afrikaans, f. Du. *skaap* sheep + *steker* stinger.] A venomous but usually harmless snake of the genus *Psammophylax*, esp. the spotted skaapsteker, *P. rhombeatus*, or the striped skaapsteker, *P. tritæniatus*, which are both greyish-brown with darker markings.

1818 C. I. Latrobe *Jrnl. Visit S. Afr.* xxii. 353 Our good-natured Hottentots, perceiving that I had begun to collect serpents, brought me several kinds, among which were the..schaapsteker, (sheep-stinger); and copra di capella. **1834** T. Pringle *Afr. Sketches* 280 There are several species of snakes..such as the nacht-slang (night adder), the schaap-steeker (sheep-stinger), [etc.]. **1856** F. Fleming *S. Afr.* 406 The 'Scarpsticker' of the Dutch, or Night-Adder; a small dingy-brown Adder, spotted with black, about eighteen inches long. **1887** *Encycl. Brit.* XXII. 197/1 The second African snake of this family is the 'schapsticker' (Sheep Stinger). **1915** *Chambers's Jrnl.* June 437/2 The schaap-sticker..is a short, silvery snake about the thickness of a man's finger. **1931** *Discovery* Mar. 73/2 We have droves of skaapstekers, night-adders, and house snakes. **1952** *Cape Argus* 7 June (Mag. Sect.) 2/4, I..'bagged' a good collection of the local snakes; mostly of a harmless variety, such as mole snakes, water snakes, herald snakes, schaapstekers. **1973** *Stand. Encycl. S. Afr.* IX. 651/2 The name skaapsteker is quite misleading and unfortunate, as there is certainly no truth in the widespread belief that these snakes are in the habit of biting and killing sheep.

skad, var. *scad[7]. **skaffie,** var. *scaf. **skag,** var. *scag. **skål,** var. Skoal *sb.* in Dict. and Suppl.

‖ **skandalon** (skæ·ndălǫn). *Theol.* Also **scandalon.** [Gr. σκάνδαλον stumbling-block; cf. I *Cor.* i. 23 Χριστὸν ἐσταυρωμένον, Ἰουδαίοις μεν σκάνδαλον Christ crucified, to the Jews a stumbling-block.] A stumbling-block, cause of offence, scandal (sense 1 b).

1945 *Theology* XLVIII. 104 Any particular 'Thou' may become a *skandalon* at any time. **1948** *Scott. Jrnl. Theol.* I. 113 It is not a truth which can be arrived at by scientific investigation, and on that account it is a *scandalon* to the scientist, and to this scientifically minded generation. **1957** *Ibid.* X. 86 The scandalon of Christian faith is accepted, and the essay aims at being the account which biblical thinking must give of itself, taking itself seriously and simply. **1972** *Times Lit. Suppl.* 28 Jan. 105/4 Belief in God is *the* skandalon barring men and women in their thousands from a secular faith in Jesus Christ.

skans, var. Schanse in Dict. and Suppl.

skarn (skāɹn). *Geol.* Also **scarn.** [a. Sw. *skarn* lit. 'dung, filth', in same sense, f. ON. *skarn* (cf. north. dial. *scarn* dung (E.D.D.)).] Orig. applied to the silicate gangue of certain Archæan iron-ore or other mineral deposits, esp. where these occur in limestone or dolomite; now extended to any lime-bearing siliceous rock produced by metamorphism (esp. of limestone or dolomite) and the introduction of new elements. Freq. *attrib.*

1901 H. Louis in *Trans. Inst. Mining & Metallurgy* X. 49, I have of late years adopted a very convenient Scandinavian word, *skarn*, for the zone of altered rock, usually calcareous, that contains such minerals as epidote, schorl, idocrase, at times augite, hornblende, mica, etc., and I speak of these altered rocks as epidote skarn, etc. **1911** *Econ. Geol.* VI. 708 Very characteristic of this zone, especially in connection with ore deposits, are the 'scarn' rocks—iron-rich silicate rocks produced by the addition of iron and silica to limestones. **1932** A. Harker *Metamorphism* ix. 129 The skarn type of metasomatism is found at numerous British localities, but usually as a narrow belt and with little of the impregnation with sulphides. **1954** *Econ. Geol.* XLIX. 633 The skarn is a hard dense green rock characterized by the presence of quartz, green ferro-magnesian silicates..and garnet. **1966** [see *sakhaite]. **1978** [see *serendibite].

skate, *sb.*[1] **3. skate-barrow** (earlier example).

1851 Thoreau *Jrnl.* 27 July in *Writings* (1906) VIII. 354 Skates' eggs, called in England skate-barrows from their form, on the sand.

skate, *sb.*[2] Add: **1. a.** (Examples = Roller-skate.) In slang (orig. *Mil.*) phr. *to get* (or *put*) *one's skates on*, to hurry up (see also quot. 1925).

(*a*) **1876** J. A. Harwood *Rinks & Rollers* iii. 39 The skates used had four wheels of iron placed in one line from the foot to the heel. **1925** *Sears Roebuck & Co. Catal.* 751 Children's Extension Skates With Steel Self Contained Ball Bearing Rolls. **1959** *Ice & Roller Skating* 20 Wooden wheels are essential for rink skating and the skate should be screwed onto the boot by an expert. **1975** *Man. Artistic Roller Skating* 24 The change-of-edge..should be as short as possible, not materially longer than the length of the skate.

(*b*) **1895** W. C. Gore in *Inlander* Dec. 113 *Get your skates on*, hurry up. **1919** *War Slang* in *Athenæum* 8 Aug. 727/2 To evade duty or get clear, you 'put your skates on'. **1925** Fraser & Gibbons *Soldier & Sailor Words* 260 *Skates, to put on*, to hurry up. Also to evade duty. To desert. **1938** F. D. Sharpe *Sharpe of Flying Squad* xxvi. 263 'Jack, guy for your b— life. The Squad are here.'..Said Jack: 'I very soon put my skates on.' **1969** G. Lyall *Venus with Pistol* ix. 54 It was Carlos telling me to get my skates on and down to the Doelen plenty chop-chop. **1976** W. J. Burley *Wycliffe & Schoolgirls* i. 33 I'd better be getting my skates on, I'm catching the night train and I haven't done a thing about getting ready.

c. *U.S.* A sledge runner.

1781 S. Peters *Gen. Hist. Connecticut* 320 In the winter, the sleigh is used; a vehicle..carrying six persons in its box, which hangs on four posts standing on two steel sliders, or large scates. **1907** *St. Nicholas* July 781/1 You make a framework of timbers..and stick a skate or runner at each corner.

d. *transf.* A device with a set of rollers or wheels on which something moves; a device which can be placed under a heavy object to facilitate its movement.

1905 *Engineering Rev.* XIII. 103/1 The Dolter system.. consists of a skate suspended from the under part of the car; this makes contact with a small iron block embedded in the road. **1940** *Chambers's Techn. Dict.* 774/2 *Skate, sidetracking.* (1) A device to move an aeroplane sideways on the ground, for manoeuvring in confined spaces, as when packing into sheds. (2) A shoe for slipping beneath the wheels for handling an aeroplane on soft snow. **1961** *Daily Tel.* 4 Oct. 15/2 An engineering firm has offered to supply skates for the Arch. *Ibid.*, The skates, or tracked skids, are made of steel plates. **1972** *Police Rev.* 10 Nov. 1477/1 It appears that the 'skates' shown in ..last week's *Police Review* (page 1405) would combat the above criticisms. **1976** *Southern Even. Echo* (Southampton) 18 Nov. 17/7 Terry Maine..invented a 'skate' to go under the damaged wheel—which enables the aircraft to be moved quickly into a hanger for repairs.

e. N. Amer. A set of tackle for halibut-fishing, etc., used chiefly on the Pacific Coast of N. Amer.

1882 J. W. Collins in *Fishermen's Own Book* 96 We set twenty skates of trawl—the whole string. **1897** Kipling *Captains Courageous* iii. 75 'How many skates you reckon we'll need?' ''Baout three. Hurry!' 'There's three-hundred fathom to each tub,' Dan explained. **1960** M. Sharcott *Place of Many Winds* vii. 127 Either the night before or in the morning before the skates of gear are set they must be baited. *Ibid.* 129 Trolling fishermen often curse the skates of halibut gear. **1972** F. Ford *Atush Inlet* ix. 85 The marker, then the anchor, then two-three hundred yards of halibut line with a baited hook every ten feet, then another anchor and a marker. That's a skate.

3. b. *skate-iron* (earlier example); **skate key,** a key for tightening roller-skates; **skatepark,** a park or rink for skateboarding.

1838 J. H. Ingraham *Burton* I. x. 143 It was placed on runners sixteen inches high, shaped like skate-irons. **1962** 'E. McBain' *Like Love* xiv. 193 A little girl..was sitting on the steps tightening her skates with a skate key. **1977** *Montgomery Ward Catal.* Spring–Summer 509/1 Clamp-on sidewalk skates... Skate key included. **1976** *N.Y. Times Mag.* 12 Sept. 85/2 A $60,000 15 thousand-square-feet-of-concrete skatepark. **1977** *Sunday Times* 27 Nov. (Colour Suppl.) 27/4 Use purpose-built skate-parks as they have a variety of bowls and slaloms which allow you freedom to develop tricks away from other skaters and spectators.

skate (skē^{i}t), *sb.*^{3} *slang* (chiefly *U.S.*). [Origin uncertain.] **1.** A poor, worn-out, decrepit horse.

1894 Kipling in *Cent. Mag.* Dec. 295/2 This yaller-backed skate comes to our pastur'. **1923** E. Hemingway *Three Stories* 29 They'd kill that bunch of skates for their hides and hoofs up at Paris. **1935** H. Davis *Honey in Horn* vi. 61 Joel Hardcastle's horses were underfed, badly shod, and skates. **1978** E. Tidyman *Table Stakes* I. iv. 68 The man was a gambler... A pony player. Used to bet thousands on the worst-looking skates you've ever seen.

2. a. A mean or contemptible person. Esp. in *cheap skate* (also *attrib.* or as *adj.*).

1896 Cheap skate [see *horse *sb.* 17]. **1898** F. P. Dunne *Mr. Dooley in Peace & War* 198 If th' skate fr'm Oklahoma is allowed f'r to belch anny in this here assimblage, th' diligates fr'm th' imperyal Territ'ry iv New Mexico'll lave th' hall. **1904** J. C. Lincoln *Cap'n Eri* xxi. 383 Offered me a hundred dollars a week, the skate! **1935** D. L. Sayers *Gaudy Night* xix. 399 'It would suit them very well,' thought Harriet, 'the cheap skates!' **1947** *Partisan Rev.* XIV. 259 Samuel lost his temper and told the boss what he thought of him, what a cheap skate he was. **1958** *New Statesman* 4 Oct. 444/2 A cheapskate doctor he employed to save a few dollars gave his wife, Mary, morphine to ease her pains after delivering her youngest son, Edmund, and she has become an addict. **1960** H. Pinter *Caretaker* I. 9 *Aston*: I saw him have a go at you. *Davies*:..The filthy skate, an old-man like me. **1973** J. Porter *It's Murder with Dover* xii. 119 They were hardened women of the world and knew a cheap skate when they saw one.

b. *labour skate* (U.S.), a trade-union official.

1930 *Amer. Mercury* Dec. 456/2 *Labor-skate*, an official of a labor union. **1978** *Washington Post* 27 Jan. D7/3 Most of the crowd consisted of labor skates, members of Jewish groups, and friends of Jackson and Moynihan.

skate, *v.* Add: **1. a.** *fig.* Esp. in phr. (*a*) *to skate over* (or *on*) *thin ice*; (*b*) *to skate over* or *round* (a fact, subject, etc.), to pass by or over hurriedly, to avoid mentioning.

(*a*) **1897** A. Beardsley *Let.* 15 Sept. (1970) 368, I hardly like to think now of all the thin ice I must have skated over since March 31st—a miraculous patinage! **1897** [in Dict.]. **1926** P. Guedalla *Palmerston* V. iii. 356 Even *Punch* regaled its readers with a princely figure of slightly sinister aspect skating perilously on the thin ice of foreign affairs. **1945** E. Waugh *Brideshead Revisited* I. v. 98 He..could talk at length of..how this or that Jesuit or Dominican had skated on thin ice or sailed near the wind in his Lenten discourses. **1978** H. Carpenter *Inklings* IV. i. 216 He skated on thin ice in the opening chapter of *The Problem of Pain*, where he offered his readers a 'proof' of the existence of God which..tackled this immense issue 'on the scale of a pamphlet in a church porch'.

(*b*) **1928** *Manch. Guardian Weekly* 30 Mar. 243/1 The Premier did not do more than skate round the problem. **1948** 'N. Shute' *No Highway* v. 123 We both skated over the implications of that. **1957** *Economist* 7 Dec. 860/1 The reason for the outbreak of the second Balkan war in 1913..is gracefully skated over. **1965** *New Statesman* 16 Apr. 622/3 Mr Brown's latest paper on prices and incomes skates carefully around this point. **1971** *Where* Sept. 266/1 It also skates over the fact that it is an offence to be in possession of the drugs listed if they have not been legally prescribed. **1979** C. Moule in M. Goulder *Incarnation & Myth* v. 135 It has been claimed that Mark's christology is authoritative and as much part of the New Testament as Paul's... But this is to skate over the question, What was Mark's intention?

c. *colloq.* To depart speedily.

1915 in C. Johnson *Battleground Adventures* liv. 418 Holt met the ol' man comin' from the barn as hard as he could run. Oh! he was comin' from thar skatin'. *c* **1926** 'Mixer' *Transport Workers' Song Bk.* 31 Well, I'm skating. Coming, 'Slasher'? **1937** G. Frankau *More of Us* v. 63 When one's happy—well, time simply flies. Me for the hay. Let's get our bill, and skate.

d. *U.S. slang.* (See quots.)

1945 L. Shelly *Jive Talk Dict.* 17/1 *Skate*, to get away with something. **1977** *Amer. Speech* 1975 L. 66 *Skate vi*, shirk duties. 'The new pledges are really skating this week.' **1979** *Observer* 18 Mar. (Colour Suppl.) 56 I'm not a woman's libber but I don't want to skate (shirk).

2. c. To slide or glide over. Also *fig.*

1900 [see *fenner]. **1970** G. F. Newman *Sir, you Bastard* i. 22 Sneed skated the passing out examination with the highest marks on record. **1971** B. Patten *Irrelevant Song* 27 Quick as the autumn marigold Skates the borders of whitening grass.

skateboard (skē^{i}·tbō^{ə}ɹd), *sb.* orig. *U.S.* Also **skate board** [f. Skate *sb.*^{2}, after *surfboard.*] A narrow platform mounted on roller-skate wheels, on which the rider coasts along, usu. in a standing position (orig. developed from surf-riding, chiefly as a pastime). Also *attrib.*

1964 *Life* 5 June 89 Skateboards appeared last fall in southern California. **1964** *Surfer* Sept. 72 No one, except possibly the skateboard manufacturers, took them seriously until recently. *Ibid.* 76 When they can't go out in the water and surf, they can do it on land with a skateboard. **1965** *Globe & Mail* (Toronto) 21 Apr. 5/6 Hundreds of vacationing teen-agers..wheeled to City Hall yesterday on their skate boards to demand an off-the-street area to carry on their latest fad. **1974** *Daily Colonist* (Victoria, B.C.) 21 Aug. 18/6 He was..a legless cripple whose only means of locomotion was a skate board. **1976** A. Cassorla *Skateboarder's Bible* i. 9 Already in the works are extensive skateboard parks. **1976** C. Weston *Rouse Demon* (1977) xxi. 96 A boy on a skateboard whirled by on the sidewalk. **1978** K. Amis *Jake's Thing* xx. 204 The local authorities wanted..a skateboard park built on the site. **1978** *Cornish Guardian* 27 Apr. 23/1 (Advt.), Used Car Parts (fronting the quay, adjoining skateboard rink). **1980** P. Harcourt *Tomorrow's Treason* I. i. 28 An even smaller boy..seemingly unable to get off his skateboard..was careering straight into the path of my car.

Hence **ska·teboard** *v. intr.*, to ride on a skateboard; **ska·teboarder**; **ska·teboarding** *vbl. sb.*

1964 *Life* 5 June 89 Skateboarding requires only a tapered piece of wood flexibly mounted on roller-skate wheels and a stretch of pavement. *Ibid.*, A good skateboarder can do all a surfer's tricks and more. **1964** *Surfer* Sept. 74 Some of the skateboarders have set up slalom courses, timing each other from stand-still starts. **1968** W. Warwick *Surfriding in N.Z.* 19/1 To skateboard properly the rider should have a reasonable sense of balance. **1976** *National Observer* (U.S.) 3 July 12/2 They're..'taking it to the limit': skateboarding up the sides of empty swimming pools and pipelines. **1977** *Times* 15 Oct. 24/2 The odd skateboarder en route for the adventure playground. **1978** *Morecambe Guardian* 14 Mar. 4/5 Coun. Mrs Taylor said that if any children still felt strongly about having no skateboarding park they should contact her so that a united effort could be made. **1979** V. S. Naipaul *Bend in River* xv. 249 A wide, sloping avenue..with boys skateboarding.

skater. Add: Occas. = *skateboarder.

1977 *Times* 19 Nov. 26/6 Many a skate park, rightly, refuses admittance unless skaters wear protective helmets and pads. **1977** [see *skatepark* s.v. *skate *sb.*^{2} 3 b].

skating, *vbl. sb.* Add: **a.** (Examples = Roller-skating.)

1876 J. A. Harwood *Rinks & Rollers* iv. 63 There are few more lively..sights than..the young engaged in skating and flirting, while the elder ones sip tea between the trees. **1948** C. Beastall *Int. Roller Skating Annual* 15 The RSROA, who banned metal wheels, introduced skating and proficiency tests..in their rinks. **1975** *Man. Artistic Roller Skating* 38 The candidate is required to compose..an original dance..suitable for skating in public skating sessions.

b. *skating pond, -rink* (further examples; also *fig.*), *skirt.*

1903 Skating pond [see *live wire* s.v. *live *a.* 8]. **1981** *Northeast Woods & Waters* Jan. 24/3 Osborndale in Derby even offers a large skating pond, lighted for night skating. **1875** *Building News* 19 Nov. 579/1 Skating Rinks. The [roller-]skating rink is an institution that has rapidly grown in..popularity. **1926** Maines & Grant *Wise-Crack Dict.* 14/2 *Skating rink for flies*, baldheaded man. **1958** *Roller Dance Skating Man.* 32 (Advt.), Skating Rinks at: Skating Rink & Cafeteria, Granby Halls, Leicester. **1976** *Flintshire Leader* 10 Dec. 2/8 Freezing conditions this week turned a road in Carmel near Holywell into a skating rink. **1968** J. Ironside *Fashion Alphabet* 62 *Skating skirt.* Traditionally this is cut circular and very short, worn with tights. **1971** *Petticoat* 24 July 3/4 They'll be taking hemlines just about as high as they can go, even to skating-skirt length.

‖ **skaz** (skaz). [Russ.] First-person narrative in which the author assumes a persona. Also *attrib.*

1926 D. S. Mirsky *Contemp. Russ. Lit.* vii. 311 Michael Zoshchenko..is a more narrative writer: he is also an ornamentalist, but his ornamentalism is a purely colloquial skaz, which proceeds from Leskov. **1957** W. E. Harkins *Dict. Russ. Lit.* 360 *Skaz*, a Russian word designating a narrative told by a fictitious narrator, rather than by the author directly. **1967** *Russ. Review* XXVI. 177 In succeeding works Solzhenitsyn resorts to *skaz* only occasionally. **1974** Moore & Parry *Twentieth-Cent. Russ. Lit.* i. 10 Remizov was a sharp stylist who often wrote in the vein of folklore; he carried on Nikolai Leskov's tradition of *skaz*, an attempt to reproduce the exact idiom of each speaker in a story. **1980** *Times Lit. Suppl.* 7 Nov. 1264/4 The narrator [is] a typically Russian busybody in the 'skaz' tradition.

sked (sked), colloq. abbrev. (orig. *U.S.*) of (*a*) Schedule *sb.*; (*b*) Schedule *v.*; (*c*) Scheduled *ppl. a.*; also *ellipt.*, a scheduled flight.

1929 *Amer. Speech* IV. 289 A 'sked' (schedule) is a message to the central office briefly sketching the contents of a story offered for transmission. **1942** Berrey & Van den Bark *Amer. Thes. Slang* § 597/5 *Bill* [verb]; *schedule*, sked. **1949** *Daily Progress* (Charlottesville, Va.) 26 Aug. 12/3 (*heading*) W[illiam] & M[ary] skeds tour for court team. **1953** Scott & Fisher *Thousand Geese* ix. 103 If we were to get back for our radio sked..we thought we should start home. **1972** *Sat. Rev.* (U.S.) 4 Mar. 33/2 The ultimate answer..is for the skeds to become competitive with the charters. **1977** *New Day* Summer 6/1 All mission stations [in Papua New Guinea] are connected by radio, and different times (skeds) are assigned for their use. The Post Office has radio skeds for Government traffic. **1981** *Beautiful Brit. Columbia* Fall 22 Near the Dean, at Eliguk or Gatcho lakes you can be flown out to Nimpo Lake at Highway 20; thence by car, 'sked-flight' (a Cariboo phrase for a scheduled flight). **1981** L. Leamer *Assignment* i. 8, I don't mind when it's skedded right..but..I don't ever want to work with Henderson again.

skedaddle, *v.* Add: Also **skiddaddle. 1.** (Earlier example.)

1861 *N.Y. Tribune* 10 Aug. 5/5 No sooner did the traitors discover their approach than they 'skiddaddled', (a phrase the Union boys up here apply to the good use the seceshers make of their legs in time of danger).

Skee-Ball (skī·bǭl). Also **skeeball.** [f. Ski *sb.* or *v.* + Ball *sb.*^{1}] An indoor game in which balls set rolling down an alley are projected over a hump or otherwise into targets. Also *attrib.*

Skee-Ball is a proprietary term in the U.S.

1923 *Daily Mail* 11 June 3 The game of Skeeball is an American invention which has been in increasing operation in the United States for some six years. It is the latest development of the game of bowls, sharply distinguished from all similar games by a hump in the centre of the alley which causes the ball to leap high in the air and enter a target. **1930** A. P. Herbert *Water Gipsies* xviii. 258 Ernest played skeeball because it was the nearest thing to skittles, and he won a china dog. **1974** J. Wainwright *Evidence I shall Give* xxiv. 121 A Skee-Ball set-up with six lanes.

skeeler (skī·ləɹ). [Perh. f. Ski *sb.* + Rol)ler *sb.*^{1}] (See quots.) Hence **skee·ling** *vbl. sb.*, skating on skeelers.

1968 *Daily Tel.* 28 Dec. 23/4 (*caption*) 'Skeelers', a cross between ice and roller skates. *Ibid.* 23/6 The skates, called 'Skeelers'.., are just part of the fun for the children at the *Daily Mail* New Year Show. **1969** *Ibid.* 31 Jan. 17/5 Skeeling, launched last autumn, gives some of the exhilarating feeling of skating—but without ice. Skeelers are like ice skates but three wheels replace the blade; they will slide on any hard surface. **1972** *Kingston* (Ontario) *Whig-Standard* 13 June 15/6 Skeeling, according to the publicity releases, is iceless skating; a summer hockey equivalent. Skeelers are a cross between roller skates and ice skates and were originally developed by the Russians to help condition speed skaters during the off-season.

skeesicks, var. *skeezicks.

skeet (skīt), *sb.*^{2} orig. *U.S.* [Proposed for the name of the sport (see quot. 1926) as an 'old' form of Shoot *v.*] A form of clay-pigeon shooting in which targets are projected at a variety of shooting angles in a semicircular range. Also, in some *attrib.* uses (see below), a clay pigeon; so *to shoot skeet.*

1926 *National Sportsman* (U.S.) May 18 (*heading*) Skeet, the new sport. *Ibid.*, Since the prize of $100 was offered for the most suitable name for the new shooting sport.., nearly 10,000 suggestions have been received... After careful consideration, the name that seemed to apply itself the best was '*skeet*', a very old form of our present word 'shoot'... Mrs. Gertrude Hurlbutt, Dayton, Montana, sent in the suggestion. **1931** *Daily Progress* (Charlottesville, Va.) 26 Oct. 3/2 Skeets [*sic*] is unlike regular trap-shooting in that the birds come from oppositely located houses and that, in one position two birds come at once. **1931** L. B. Smith (*title*) Better trapshooting. With a section on skeet. **1939** *Country Life* 11 Feb. p. xxi/3 (Advt.), Clay bird shooting.—Practice and Coaching; every flight imitated; skeet; automatic traps. **1955** R. Churchill *Game Shooting* III. i. 173 In 1927, I myself introduced the game of skeet to England. **1976** *Webster's Sports Dict.* 395/1 A round of skeet consists of 25 shots. **1979** R. Jaffe *Class Reunion* II. ii. 139 He liked to dance, play golf, drink, shoot skeet, and laugh.

b. *attrib.* and *Comb.*, as *skeet championship, contest, ground, gun, match, range, shoot, shooter, shooting.*

1942 *Tee Emm* (Air Ministry) II. 75 He has won the Skeet championship several times. **1975** *Oxf. Compan. Sports & Games* 927/1 The first U.S. national skeet championships were held in 1935. **1952** *Times* 14 July 5/5 Colonel C. T. Edwinson..won the skeet (clay pigeon) contest in the world shooting championships here yesterday. **1926** *National Sportsman* (U.S.) Sept. 22 (*heading*) News from the skeet grounds. **1975** *Oxf. Compan. Sports & Games* 925/2 On a skeet ground layout there are two spring-release traps. **1976** *Shooting Times & Country Mag.* 9–15 Dec. 5/1 (Advt.), David Price..can testify to the suitability of his Miroku 800SW Skeet gun for game shooting. **1970** *Cape Times* 28 Oct. 24/4 Evgeny Petrov, of Russia, set an unofficial world record here, breaking 200 straight targets in the International skeet match of the world shooting championships here. **1942** *Tee Emm* (Air Ministry) II. 75 We had an article on Training with Clay Targets and the Skeet Range in our April, 1942, issue. **1970** G. Jackson *Let.* 21 May in *Soledad Brother* (1971) 255 Quietly..I would have my fronts open as many skeet, trap, rifle, and pistol ranges as I could rent space for in and around the black community. **1926** *National Sportsman* (U.S.) June 18 A group of about twenty good sportsmen in the town of Maynard, Mass. held their first skeet shoot. **1959** *Times* 1 Aug. 9/5 In addition to tests which simulate the different types of game-shooting, 'skeet' and 'down the line' shoots are held. **1926** *National Sportsman* (U.S.) June 18 If the skeet shooter were in hot competition..he would probably choose small shot. **1967** *Boston Sunday Herald* 26 Mar. VI. 6/5 A rifle range for the skeet shooter. **1926** *National Sportsman* (U.S.) May 19/2 (Advt.), The Western Practice Trap is ideal for 'Skeet' shooting, or for any kind of shotgun practice. **1971** *Courier-Mail* (Brisbane) 11 June 7/3 Winner..was

Graham Bailey,..who took the final of the Winchester Australia skeet shooting championship at the Belmont range.

Hence **skee·ting** *vbl. sb.*², participating in the sport of skeet, skeet shooting.

1926 *National Sportsman* (U.S.) May 18/2 It is as easy to say *skeet, skeeting, skeeter* as it is to say shoot, shooting, shooter. *Ibid.* Sept. 22/3 The game of *skeeting* is just like a ball game. *Ibid.*, Hunt's Club and *skeeting* field is a public place. **1968** *Daily Mail* 23 Oct 16/7 Skeeting is a precise form of shooting which is in the Olympic Games for the first time.

skeet (skīt), *v.*² *dial.* [Alteration of (esp. *U.S.*) Scoot *v.* or (esp. *Sc.*) Skite *v.*² or Skate *v.* in Dict. and Suppl.] **1.** *intr.* To move swiftly; to hurry; to run. Usu. with advbs.

1838 J. C. Neal *Charcoal Sk.* 97 You must skeete, even if you have to cut high-dutchers with your irons loose. *a* **1855** J. F. Kelly *Humors of Falconbridge* (1856) 251, I skeeted down them steps into the Common to let off my corked up risibilities. **1861** in L. C. Baker *Hist. U.S. Secret Service* (1867) v. 101 Burn the letter..and then get in your hole and skeet for Dixie. **1877** G. Stewart *Fireside Tales* 89 Skeet howe hame, guid folk! **1922** Joyce *Ulysses* 748 That icy wind skeeting across from those mountains. **1924** C. Greer-Petrie *Angeline of Hill Country* 18 Here comes a mighty impudent lookin' darky a-skeetin' towards us. **1929** L. Robinson in *Lett. Sean O'Casey* (1975) I. 358 Johnny Perrin..got married yesterday and skeeted off to Wales for a few days.

2. *trans.* To squirt, to eject (fluid). Also *absol.*

1880 Courtney & Couch *Gloss. Words in Use in Cornwall* 51/2 *Skeet, v.*, to eject saliva through the teeth. **1886** J. J. H. Burgess *Shetland Sk. & Poems* 114 Every platch 'at he med skeetit it up and doon ower every ane 'at cam' near. **1908** *Dial. Notes* III. 370 *Skeet, v. tr.*, to scoot (water), spew out of the mouth, especially between the teeth. **1912** J. Nicolson *Hame-Spun* 45, I was skeetit frae head ta foot, sae 'at I'm not onlookin'. **1935** Z. N. Hurston *Mules & Men* I. iii. 64 Julius spat out into the yard, trying to give the impression that he was skeeting tobacco juice like a man. **1946** C. McCullers *Member of Wedding* I. 48 She loved to..lightly meddle with their things—with Mrs Marlowe's atomizer which skeeted perfume, the grey-pink powder puff, [etc.].

skeeter, *sb.*¹ (Earlier example.)

1839 *Spirit of Times* 21 Dec. 495/2, I was fas asleep, and dreaming dat a big skeeter was a biten me.

skeeter (skī·təɹ), *sb.*² [f. *Skeet *sb.*² + -er¹.] One who participates in the sport of skeet, a skeet shooter.

1926 *National Sportsman* (U.S.) May 18/1 From this station Skeeter faces each trap in turn and shoots at the target coming directly over his head. **1968** *Daily Mail* 23 Oct. 16/8 The skeeter loses a point if he fails to destroy the pigeon as it passes invisibly over his head.

skeeter (skī·təɹ), *v.* Var. Skitter *v.*² I.

1964 J. Hillaby *Journey to Jade Sea* 101 Three geese promptly took off, skeetering up into a gust of wind. **1971** C. McCullers in *Redbook* Oct. 196/1 She had one of those grotesque little imaginings... She saw herself and Marshall... Skeetering angrily up and down the cold blank glass like minute monkeys. **1972** *Observer* (Colour Suppl.) 23 Apr. 35/4 Fiennes and Stanley Cribbett skeeter through the savage waters of the Bridge River rapids.

skeeze (skīz), *v. rare.* [Origin uncertain.] *intr.* ? To peer, to glance obliquely.

1922 Joyce *Ulysses* 298 Old Garryowen started growling again at Bloom that was skeezing round the door.—Come in, come on, he won't eat you, says the citizen. *Ibid.* 731 Hes mad on the subject of drawers..always skeezing at those brazenfaced things on the bicycles with their skirts blowing up to their navels.

skeezicks (skī·ziks). *U.S. slang.* Also **skeesicks, -zacks, -zecks.** [? Fanciful.] A good-for-nothing, a rascal, a rogue. (Now usu. playfully of children.)

1850 *Frontier Guardian* (Kanesville, Iowa) 2 Oct. 3/5 Though Kister that skeezecks with Hall at his back, Should come again thieving [etc.]. **1869** B. Harte in *Overland Monthly* June 572/1 Thar aint nobody but him within ten mile of the shanty, and that 'ar d—d old skeesicks knows it. **1875** J. G. Holland *Sevenoaks* iii. 40 If there's anything awful bad..in [the word] Skeezacks—I should say that Tom Buffum was an old Skeezacks. **1908** *Everybody's* Dec. 796/2 This is a poor skeezicks that's got nothing to eat but an onion. **1939** P. A. Rollins *Gone Haywire* v. 117 Eb Hawkins, that ol' skeesicks you met on th' railway train an' liked, is th' feller that's acted as th' owners' agent in sellin' rights to your uncle.

skeg, *sb.*¹ Add: **2. b.** *Surfboarding.* The fin of a surfboard.

1962 T. Masters *Surfing Made Easy* 65 *Skeg*, the rudder or fin of a surfboard. **1964** *Sunday Mail Mag.* (Brisbane) 17 May 1 These were the now famous Malibu boards. 10 feet long, and made of balsa, with a fin or skeg for greater control. **1968** *Surfer Mag.* Jan. 73/2 He showed them skeg-first take offs.

skein, *sb.*¹ Add: **1. b.** (Further examples.)

1932 W. B. Yeats *Words for Music* 26 For love is but a skein unwound Between the dark and dawn. **1935** T. S. Eliot *Murder in Cathedral* I. 37 You hold the skein: wind, Thomas, wind The thread of eternal life and death. **1939** Dylan Thomas *Map of Love* 16, I with a living skein, Tongue and ear in the thread, angle the temple-bound Curl-locked and animal cavepools of spells and bone.

†**2. c.** *Cytology.* The chromosomal strands in a cell undergoing mitosis; used *attrib.* to denote the stage of mitosis now known as *prophase; = *spireme. *Obs.*

1889 *Q. Jrnl. Microsc. Sci.* XXX. 164 The first stage of karyokinesis, the so-called 'dense skein' ('dichter Knäuel'). *Ibid.* 173 Rable says definitely that he has always found the longitudinal splitting of the chromatic threads to be completed at the end of the skein phase. **1904** *Science* 4 Mar. 393/1 No sign of chromatin thread (linin or skein) is apparent.

3. *skein-winder.*

1920 L. Hooper *Weaving for Beginner* x. 76 A skein winder..is only required if the weft is supplied to the weaver in skeins. **1964** O. G. Tod *Joy of Hand Weaving* (ed. 2) xviii. 87 If winding from a skein, place the skein around an adjustable *skein-winder.*

skein, *v.* Add: Also *fig.* Hence **skeined** *ppl. a.*

c **1885** G. M. Hopkins *Poems* (1967) 98 Let life, waned, ah let life wind Off her once skeined stained veined variety upon, all on two spools. **1955** E. Bowen *World of Love* xi. 219 Water skeined the landscape. **1971** 'D. Halliday' *Dolly & Doctor Bird* v. 62 The Florida coast. Flat land skeined with sheets of flat water. **1977** P. Scupham *Hinterland* 8 When Vulcan beat new armour out for Rome..Skeined cupids hooded their toy bacchanals.

Hence **skei·ner,** one who or that which makes yarn into skeins.

1921 *Dict. Occup. Terms* (1927) 169/1 *Skeiner* (twine); minds skein or rand machine, which winds finished twine into skeins. *Ibid.* 367/2 *Bundler* (flax and hemp); *skeiner*; puts together necessary number of hanks of yarn to form a bundle. **1931** M. L. Davies *Life as we have known It* 74 As a 'skeiner' her work was to separate and twist up the skeins from the 'bond' (on a silk mill). **1969** E. H. Pinto *Treen* 318/2 The niddy-noddy was a combined measure and skeiner.

skeletal, *a.* Add: The pronunciation (skelī·tăl) is occasionally heard. **b.** *skeletal muscle*, add to def.: or transmitting force to connective tissue sheets, and in most cases under voluntary control; striated muscle other than cardiac muscle. (Further examples.)

1936 L. B. Arey *Developmental Anat.* (ed. 3) xiii. 361 With the exception of those muscles of the head and neck which differentiate out of the branchial arches, the skeletal muscles originate from that portion of the mesodermal segment designated a myotome, or muscle plate. **1978** D. R. Lamb *Physiol. of Exercise* ii. 15 The skeletal muscles consume most of the oxygen and require most of the body's blood during heavy exercise. **1982** *Sci. Amer.* June 48/2 It was found that in skeletal and cardiac muscle (which is called striated muscle because of its striped appearance in a micrograph) calcium binds to a protein called troponin *c.*

c. *skeletal soil* = *lithosol* s.v. *litho-.

[**1928** *Proc. 1st Internat. Congr. Soil Sci.* IV. 31 [Soils] developing in a normal way..whose profile is imperfect wholly because of lack of time to complete their development have never been given any designation covering them as a whole. They have been designated as *skeleton soils* but this term is not applicable to the group as a whole.] **1932** G. W. Robinson *Soils* xvi. 320 Immature skeletal soils are found in the south [of Germany]. **1939** [see *lithosol* s.v. *litho-]. **1977** J. C. F. Tedrow *Soils of Polar Landscapes* xxii. 568 Ohsumi reviewed the characteristics of the alpine soils in Japan and established four varieties: (1) Alpine grassland soils, (2) Alpine podzols, (3) Alpine wet meadow soils, and (4) Skeletal soils.

d. Having or consisting of only a framework or outline; bare, meagre.

1961 W. Brown *Bedeviled* 106 Once Dr. Hazel had pieced together this skeletal tale, he notified Captain Brill. **1967** T. Keneally *Bring Larks* ii. 17 She stood business-like against the skeletal tracery of her master's sick vines. **1967** A. N. Sherwin-White *Racial Prejudice in Imperial Rome* Pref. p. vii, They have been printed much as delivered, with the addition only of source references, a skeletal bibliography, and translations of most quotations. **1971** *Physics Bull.* Aug. 462/1 Some body can be given to these skeletal facts by an order-of-magnitude calculation.

Hence **ske·letally** *adv.*, as regards the skeleton.

1956 *Nature* 18 Feb. 342/2 The history of the Amphibia Salientia can readily be traced back to the Jurassic when it appears that, skeletally at least, they were already typical, modern Anura. **1974** *Ibid.* 13 Sept. 137/2 In Detroit..serum antirachitic activity..was significantly less in symptomatic osteoporotic subjects than in the skeletally normal.

skeleton, *sb.* Add: **1. d.** *Hist.* A member of a 'skeleton army' (see sense 7 d below).

1882 *Eastern Post* 4 Nov. 3/3 There was nothing to fear from the latest born army; there would be 'skeletons' enough in it. **1950** R. Sandall *Hist. Salvation Army* xxxiii. 196 The police..dispersed the 'skeletons'. **1981** C. Scott *Heavenly Witch* viii. 120 The Judge of Assize..condemned the Skeletons as the aggressive party.

3. b. *Chem.* The basic atomic framework of a molecule, disregarding substituents (and sometimes also side chains or bond type).

1907 J. B. Cohen *Org. Chem. Adv. Students* I. xiii. 472 It will be at once perceived how very large a number of possible menthadienes can be derived from these two skeleton structures. **1910** *Jrnl. Physiol.* XLI. 29 The carbon-skeleton of β-phenylethylamine is..identical with that of adrenine. **1926** [see **isoprene unit*]. **1956** I. L. Finar *Org. Chem.* II. viii. 310 The nature of the sesquiterpene skeleton is also characterised by the number of double bonds present in the molecule. **1975** *Jrnl. Chem. Soc. Dalton Trans.* 31/1 Internal vibrations of nitrate, the imidazole ligands.., and the ML_6 skeleton.

6. d. A skeleton forme.

1938 F. T. Bowers in *Library* XIX. 315 When the term skeleton is used it will indicate the imposed cross-bars, furniture, and running-titles of a forme. **1950** *Studies in Bibliography* III. 246 The first five sheets of the play were printed with three skeletons used in a pattern somewhat different from that in *Lear.* **1978** *Studies in Eng. Lit.: Eng. Number* (Tokyo) 22 Skeleton II was used for the outer forme of sheets B, C, D.

7. c. (Further examples.) Also, in wider use, applied to any staff, company, etc., of the minimum size for carrying on the work to be done; so *skeleton service*, a service reduced to a bare minimum.

1914 in W. S. Churchill *World Crisis* (1923) xix. 445 There is only a skeleton force of patrol vessels available on the East Coast. **1925** *Strand Mag.* Sept. 255/2 A skeleton staff were working nervously under the direction of a chartered accountant. **1926** *Times* 6 May 3/1 On the railways skeleton services were run on main and suburban lines, and more trains are promised to-day. **1928** *Daily Mail* 7 Aug. 2/5 The establishment of skeleton air defence formations on the northern coast. **1937** W. H. Saumarez Smith *Let.* 23 Jan. in *Young Man's Country* (1977) ii. 53 All my officers have gone out to the mofussil..and all the clerks except 6, a mere skeleton staff to keep the work going. **1938** *Sun* (Baltimore) 20 Jan. 6/3 A skeleton crew of 125 men will take the ship to Scotland. **1957** P. Kemp *Mine were of Trouble* ii. 29 Skeleton crews whose task was to train Spaniards in the use of their weapons. **1973** 'I. Drummond' *Jaws of Watchdog* xviii. 255 A skeleton staff was still on duty, juniors, message-takers. **1976** *S. Wales Echo* 25 Nov. 4/2 Buses will not run in Cardiff for three consecutive days over Christmas despite a last-ditch effort to have a skeleton service on one day.

d. *skeleton frame, framework*; also applied to a vehicle or other conveyance of basic or light construction, as *skeleton bob* [*Bob *sb.*¹ 2 e], *brake, break* [Break *sb.*²], *car, gig, sleigh, wagon*; **skeleton army** *Hist.*, a group of people attempting to disrupt the activities of the Salvation Army or Church Army; **skeleton brass,** a memorial brass representing a skeleton; **skeleton construction** (see quot.); **skeleton drill** *Mil.*, infantry drill for the instruction of officers, in which a small number of men represents a battalion; also *fig.*; **skeleton forme** (see quot. 1972); **skeleton weed,** a perennial herb, *Chondrilla juncea*, of the family Compositæ, native to the Mediterranean region and naturalized in Australia, where it is a troublesome weed of cereal crops.

1881 *War Cry* Christmas No. 6/2 The chief officers of 'The Skeleton Army', raised to oppose us at Exeter, were converted. **1888** C. M. Yonge *Beechcroft at Rockstone* I. iii. 64 The Salvation Army was marching that way, and ..yells and cat-calls behind showed that the Skeleton Army was on its way to meet them. **1920** H. Begbie *Life W. Booth* I. xxix. 482 'Skeleton Armies'..set themselves up to break up the processions of the Salvation Army. **1950** R. Sandall *Hist. Salvation Army* xxxiii. 196 These skeleton armies carried flags usually bearing a skull and crossbones device. **1980** F. K. Prochaska *Women & Philanthropy in 19th-Cent. England* vi. 193 A 'Skeleton Army' of rowdies often shadowed volunteers of the Church Army and..pelted them. **1954** R. Martin *Your Ski Holiday* xiii. 91 Racing on the 'skeleton bob' is a very different affair... The 'skeleton bob' is a steel chassis with two steel runners, about 3 feet long and about 13 inches apart. On this chassis is a sliding seat. **1963** I. Fleming *On H.M. Secret Service* xii. 133 A little 'garage' that housed the bob-sleighs and one-man skeleton-bobs. **1898** *Carriage Builders' Jrnl.* Nov. p. viii/2 (Advt.), Wanted, Pair-horse Skeleton Brake. **1935** *Automobile & Carriage Builders' Jrnl.* Apr. 68/2 The skeleton brake has a high driving seat with the fore and hind carriages connected by a perch only. **1890** H. W. Macklin *Monumental Brasses* i. 17 Shroud and skeleton brasses came into general use. **1956** A. C. Bouquet *Church Brasses* vii. 147 There is a skeleton brass at Weybridge, Surrey, with three effigies. **1972** R. le Strange *Compl. Descriptive Guide Brit. Monumental Brasses* 9 Between the two, the shroud and skeleton brasses, lay the cadavers. **1974** S. Walrond *Encycl. Driving* 237 Skeleton Break... This vehicle..was used for breaking and training when a youngster would be put in alongside an older schoolmaster. **1936** '*ABC*' *Brit. Columbia Lumber Trade Directory* 73 Elco Logging Co. Ltd... Three High Leads;.. 45 Skeleton Cars. **1942** R. L. Haig-Brown *Timber* 253 *Skeleton car*, a railroad car made up of two sets of four wheels joined by a heavy timber across which the steel bunks are set to carry the logs. **1891** *Archit. Record* Oct.–Dec. 228 Within the past three or four years a new method of constructing very high buildings in New York has come into vogue. It is known as the skeleton construction and consists in the use of iron or steel columns, with thin curtain walls between, in place of solid thick brick walls. **1876** Voyle & Stevenson *Military Dict.* 387/2 *Skeleton drill*, which is a method of instructing officers and non-commissioned officers in drill, when a sufficient number of men cannot be collected to form a battalion in single rank. **1897** Hardy *Well-Beloved* III. v. 278 Pierston..could consider, and practise thoroughly a species of skeleton-drill in receiving visitors when the pair should announce themselves as married. **1888** Skeleton forme [in Dict.]. **1964** F. Bowers *Bibliogr. & Textual Crit.* I. i. 10 An examination of the running-titles..discloses that the text of the play in sheet B was imposed in two different skeleton-formes. **1972** P. Gaskell *New Introd. Bibliogr.* 109 All these re-usable parts, the typographical parts which left their mark upon the paper, and the chase, quoins, and furniture which did not, are known collectively today as the 'skeleton forme'. **1951** KOESTLER *Age of Longing* iv. 84 Towers of wood and towers of metal, towers which had merely a skeleton-frame and towers that were panelled in from all sides. **1897** *Building Construction* (new ed.) I. 17 The combination of columns and girders which form the 'skeleton' framework. **1867** 'T. LACKLAND' *Homespun* II. 181 At all hours of the day..a fly, a sulky, or a skeleton gig could be seen somewhere about the yard. **1974** S. WALROND *Encycl. Driving* 238 *Skeleton gig*, a light gig with a curved open stick-back seat which is suspended by iron stays on two side and one cross-spring. The shafts run outside the bootless body. **1902** *Hub* Aug. 172/1 The skeleton sleigh as seen last winter had a black body, cream gear and black irons. **1955** E. A. COLLARD *Canadian Yesterdays* 232 Next comes a stunner—a skeleton sleigh, red as fire, drawn by a trotter black as coal. **1868** H. WOODRUFF *Trotting Horse Amer.* x. 112 If the race is to be run in harness, it will be advisable to change the sulky for a skeleton wagon occasionally. **1974** S. WALROND *Encycl. Driving* 238 *Skeleton waggon*, an American four-wheeled single-seat vehicle which was built for racing. **1935** ROSS & TAYLOR in *Agric. Gaz. N.S.W.* XLVI. 16/1 Skeleton weed is well liked by sheep, especially when it is in the young stages. **1965** *Austral. Encycl.* IX. 225/2 Skeleton weed..is a close relative of the dandelion and chicory, having a spindly habit of growth.

8. *skeleton-gaunt* adj.

1929 W. B. YEATS *Winding Stair* 3 When withered old and skeleton-gaunt.

skeletonized, *ppl. a.* Add: Also, possessing or having developed a skeleton. (Further examples.)

1976 *Nature* 29 Jan. 271/1 Some 500 million years ago.. all but two of the living phyla that are well skeletonised had already appeared. **1978** *Sci. Amer.* Sept. 108/1 These durable skeletonized invertebrates seem to have one thing in common: they all originally lived on the sea floor rather than burrowing in it.

skellum, *sb.* and *a.* Add: The usual spelling is now **skelm.** Also **schelm** (for examples attributed to German speakers see SCHELM).

A. *sb.* **1.** (Further examples.)

1827 *Scenes & Occurrences in Albany & Caffer-Land* ii. 38 The Caffer flew into a violent passion, and said that he was no *schelm*:— that a *schelm* was a man that ought to be strangled. **1858** A. W. DRAYSON *Sporting Scenes* xviii. 314 A thorough Cape 'schelm' would..beat the best English swindler living. **1910** D. FAIRBRIDGE *That which hath Been* xxiii. 281 That poor nervous woman called out in Dutch: 'I will open the door, you schelms'. **1916** J. BUCHAN *Greenmantle* iii. 35, I got into German territory all right, and then a *skellum* of an officer came along, and commandeered all my mules. **1939** S. CLOETE *Watch for Dawn* i. 7 A thieving skelm of a Hottentot. **1950** *Cape Argus* 26 July 2/5 There are very few fools in Johannesburg, but a lot of skelms. **1956** E. U. T. HUDDLESTON *Naught for your Comfort* ii. 29 As for Absalom—he is a 'skellum', a 'tsotsi'—the kind of Kaffir who ought to be sjambokked every day: it would teach him sense. **1961** L. VAN DER POST *Heart of Hunter* I. v. 95 'Moren!' he said hoarsely, 'you're more of a skelm than any spirit.' **1976** J. MCCLURE *Rogue Eagle* v. 90 Vorster pardoned that *skelm* who was always breaking out of jail and shooting policemen.

2. (Earlier and later examples.)

1827 G. THOMPSON *Travels in S. Afr.* 467 Both the lion and the saddle had disappeared, and nothing could be found but the horse's clean picked bones. Lucas said he could excuse the schelm for killing the horse. **1909** P. FITZPATRICK *Jock of Bushveld* 260 The natives told us it was quite useless to follow it up as it was a real 'schelm'. **1939** S. CLOETE *Watch for Dawn* v. 67 'I am not dead,' Kaspar said, having quieted his horse, 'and I do not think anything is broken,..but your horse is a skelm.'

B. *attrib.* or as *adj.* Rascally, villainous; sly; untrustworthy; of an animal: vicious, bad-tempered. Chiefly and now only *S. Afr.*

1673 [in Dict., sense 1]. **1801** G. M. THEAL *Records Cape Colony* (1899) IV. 442 Owing to the present hostile disposition of the Skellam Hottentots.., I sent the Euphrosyne with the Dispatch. **1827** *Scenes & Occurrences in Albany & Caffer-Land* vii. 151 Diederik..determined on shooting it, declaring, that no *schelm* beast should kill his horse. **1828** T. PRINGLE *Ephemerides* 114 'Tis his lair—'tis his voice! from your saddles alight, For the bold skelm-beast is preparing to fight. **1829** C. ROSE *4 Yrs. in S. Africa* 115, I joined a party of Schelm (robber) Hottentots and Kaffers, and we had horses, and arms, and we would attack the boors' houses. **1852** M. B. HUDSON *S. Afr. Frontier Life* I. 16 We had in our drove a most skellum young mare. *c* **1902** I. VAUGHAN *Diary* (1958) 3 Joseph it is my feet that are skelm. They go by themselves, before I know. **1911** L. COHEN *Reminisc. Kimberley* xxiii. 397 'Hi, skilum Pontac!' (crack) 'Ah! you verdompt England!' (crack, whack, bang) and poor England would plunge into the yoke mad with pain and terror. **1972** *Sunday Tribune* (Natal) 25 June 23 You've got to be 'skelm' (sly) when you're working on a project like this.

skelp, *sb.*^{2} **2.** *skelp-forger* (earlier example).

1804 *Aris's Gaz.* (Birmingham) 23 Apr. 3/3 (Advt.), Wanted a good skelp-forger, who has a perfect knowledge of drawing skelps for all kinds of binding, military, and African gun barrels.

skelp, *v.*^{2} Add: Hence **ske·lping** *vbl. sb.*^{2} (in quot. *attrib.*).

1803 *Aris's Gaz.* (Birmingham) 26 Dec. 2/4 (Advt), Lot 1. A forge and mill..recently used as a plating or skelping forge.

Skeltonic, *a.* and *sb.* Add: **a.** *adj.* (Later examples.)

1938 L. MACNEICE *Mod. Poetry* 190 Witness his [*sc.* Auden's] Skeltonic polemic. **1954** C. S. LEWIS *Eng. Lit. in Sixteenth Cent.* I. i. 72 *Pars Prima* is in rough trimeters of Skeltonic type. *Ibid.* ii. 137 There would be no problem if all Skelton's Skeltonic poems had been on this level.

b. *sb.* (Later examples.) Also *sing.*

1923 A. HUXLEY in *Athenæum* 12 Nov. 655/2 Skelton, whose..variations on the decasyllable are mostly..rough skeltonics. **1936** *N. & Q.* 21 Nov. 362/1 The Skeltonic consists of short verses of two, three or four accents.. varying in syllabic content..and rhyming in groups of anything from two to five or more lines at a time. **1954** C. S. LEWIS *Eng. Lit. in Sixteenth Cent.* I. ii. 136 The problem about the source of Skeltonics sinks into insignificance beside the critical problem. **1976** *Times Lit. Suppl.* 12 Mar. 295/3 [Hood's] 'A Public Dinner' catches exactly in its breathless Skeltonics the noise and hurry of the occasion.

Skene (skīn). *Anat.* The name of Alexander Johnston Chalmers *Skene* (1838–1900), Scottish-born U.S. gynæcologist, used in the possessive to designate two small, blind ducts which open into the female urethra and the glands which they drain, homologous to the ducts of the male prostate gland; (described by Skene in 1880).

1890 BILLINGS *Med. Dict.* II. 543/2 *Skene's tubules*, small blind canals, 3 to 6 mm. in length, lying along the urethra of the female and opening near the meatus. **1910** *Practitioner* Mar. 393 Two of these spots..probably represent the opening of Skene's ducts. **1932** C. J. MILLER *Clin. Gynecol.* ii. 35 The cure of a chronic urethritis cannot be expected while there remains an active infection in Skene's glands. **1963** *Lancet* 5 Jan. 23/2 The urethra is often tender on palpation, and thick yellow mucus can be expressed from Skene's glands.

skeow-ways (skiau·wēⁱz), *adv. Ir. dial.* [f. SKEW *a.* and *adv.* + -WAYS.] = ASKEW *adv.*

1869 P. KENNEDY *Evenings in Duffrey* xii. 108 Down I flew *Skeow ways* across the river. **1922** JOYCE *Ulysses* 99 Horse looking round at it with his plume skeowways. **1947** P. C. O'NEILL *North-County Dublin Gloss.* xvii. 279 He went skeow-ways down the field.

‖ **skepsel** (ske·psəl). *S. Afr. colloq.* Also **schepsel.** [Afrikaans *skepsel*, Du. *schepsel*, f. *scheppen* to create.] A creature; freq. used as a derogatory designation for a Black or Coloured person. Also *attrib.* or as *adj.*

1844 J. BACKHOUSE *Narr. Visit to Mauritius & S. Afr.* xxxiv. 620 The coloured, who are generally styled Heathens, Schepsels, *Creatures*. **1899** B. MITFORD *Weird of Deadly Hollow* 125 Your baas? Confound you, it's my buck. Leave it alone, you schepsel. **1920** R. Y. STORMBERG *Mrs. Pieter de Bruyn* 96 Swartz was called a Hottentot, a Shangaan, a skepsel and a few other elegant compliments, and being a full-blooded and very proud Basuto his eyes rolled at the insult. **1943** J. BURGER *Black Man's Burden* 67 The Boer farmer treats his workers in a kindly and tolerant fashion; he does not refer to them as 'bloody niggers', but as *skepsels*. **1951** P. ABRAHAM *Wild Conquest* I. i. 48 All they are going to do is to stop working for us. So that *skepsel* Johannes says. **1953** M. MURRAY *Fire Raisers* xiv. 131 How can we bring up our children decently when there are skepsels like that about? **1968** K. MCMAGH *Dinner of Herbs* 32 You know how the volk love meat and don't mind where it comes from. Poor skepsels! **1975** W. M. MACMILLAN *My S. Afr. Years* 143 There was I remember one terrible case of a horrible old rascal who sold his step-daughter to a Hottentot. I remember that the *schepsel* was soundly punished.

skerm, var. SCHERM in Dict. and Suppl.

skerrick (ske·rik). Now chiefly *Austral. colloq.* (orig. *dial.*). Also **skerrik,** *Sc.* **skourick;** 9 **scurrick, skirrack, skirrick, skurrick.** [Origin uncertain: cf. SCUDDICK.] † **1.** (See quot.) *Obs.*

1823 [see SCUDDICK].

2. A small amount; a small fragment; the slightest bit. Usu. in neg. contexts.

1825 JAMIESON *Etym. Dict. Sc. Lang.* Suppl. 407/2, I care nae a *skourick*. **1841** R. W. HAMILTON *Nugae Literariae* 359 *Skerrick*, the smallest thing or fraction. 'Not a skerrick remaining.' 'Not worth a skerrick.' **1859** W. DICKINSON *Gloss. Words & Phr. Cumberland* 104 Nay, *aal* nut give a *skurrick* mair. **1863** *Bairnsla Foak's Annual* 14 A son ov hiz woddant gie a skirrick a nowt ta noabdy. **1873** *Halifax Orig. Illuminated Clock Almanack* 11 He cooarted a lass 'at didn't care a skirrack fur him. **1890** J. D. ROBERTSON *Gloss. Dial. & Arch. Words used in County of Gloucester* 135 You shan't use a *scurrick* of anything that belongs to me. **1916** *Bulletin* (Sydney, N.S.W.) 16 Mar. 47/1 Nothing found at all of them? Not. a skerrick. **1936** F. CLUNE *Roaming round Darling* xxv. 269 These wadless blokes of the Never-Never have to pay road, car, petrol, State, Federal and Unemployment Relief taxes, and never get a skerrick in exchange. **1947** H. DRAKE-BROCKMAN *Fatal Days* 116 Eddie had rushed off without leaving a skerrick of kindling; he often did. **1962** A. UPFIELD *Will of Tribe* i. 13 'And no tracks..you said.' 'Not a skerrik of a track.' **1969** D. CLARK *Nobody's Perfect* v. 139 'Any luck?' 'Not a skerrick,' said Green. **1972** *South China Morning Post* 18 Aug. 5/2 The felon was made to pick up every skerrick of refuse. **1977** C. MCCULLOUGH *Thorn Birds* vii. 143 If I had paid you a skerrick of attention it would have been all over Gilly in record time.

sketch, *sb.* Add: **4. a.** (Earlier examples.)

1789 W. DUNLAP *Darby's Return* (title-page), A comic sketch. As performed..for the benefit of Mr. Wignell. **1829** H. FOOTE *Compan. to Theatres* 74 Satirical sketches, or slight comic pieces on the follies of the day, have likewise been produced here with good effect.

5*. A ridiculous sight, a very amusing person; so *hot sketch*, a comical or colourful person. *slang.*

1917 S. LEWIS *Job* xx. 299 You women cer'nly are a sketch! **1921** H. C. WITWER *Leather Pushers* x. 269 This Roberts is a hot sketch for a fighter, anyways! **1925** E. HEMINGWAY *In Our Time* (1926) 84 You're a hot sketch. Who the hell asked you to butt in here? **1926** MAINES & GRANT *Wise-Crack Dict.* 9/2 *He's a sketch*, he's comical. **1930** J. DOS PASSOS *42nd Parallel* v. 399 'He's a hot sketch,' said one of the girls to the other. **1930** J. B. PRIESTLEY *Angel Pavement* xi. 604 You do look a sight, Dad... I never saw such a sketch.

6. *sketch-pad* [PAD *sb.*^{3}].

1961 M. SPARK *Prime of Miss Jean Brodie* iii. 64, I went to get a new sketch pad. **1981** *Listener* 5 Nov. 546/2 The drawings..offering imaginative ideas to any child with a sketch-pad.

sketching, *vbl. sb.* Add: **2.** *sketching-basket*, *-block* (earlier example), *-club* (earlier example), *-tour*, *-umbrella.*

1843 D. G. ROSSETTI *Let.* 7 July (1965) I. 16 There have been two meetings of the Sketching Club since your departure. **1852** C. M. YONGE *Two Guardians* i. 9 They set off..Marian carrying her little sketching-basket. **1865** G. M. HOPKINS *Jrnls. & Papers* (1959) 86 Shewing a sketching-block, he asked if there would be any objection to his sketching there. **1890** C. M. YONGE *More Bywords* viii. 269 There's..our sketching tour in August. **1902** A. BENNETT *Anna of Five Towns* x. 247 Beatrice, with easel and sketching-umbrella. **1939–40** *Army & Navy Stores Catal.* 375/1 *Sketching umbrellas.* Cream cover, lined green, wind valve, jointed stick, and spike, closes up to 34½ in.—42/-.

sketchy, *a.* Add: **3.** Also *fig.*

1943 E. B. WHITE *Let.* 13 Mar. (1976) 238, I am hoping that my health (which has been rather sketchy lately) will improve. **1977** *Horse & Hound* 14 Jan. 7/3 He survived some decidedly sketchy jumps in the early stages.

skeuomorph (skiū·omǭɹf). [f. Gr. σκεῦος vessel, implement + μορφή form.] **1.** An ornament or ornamental design on an artefact resulting from the nature of the material used or the method of working it.

1889 H. COLLEY MARCH in *Trans. Lancs. & Cheshire Antiq. Soc.* VII. 166 The forms of ornament demonstrably due to structure require a name. If those taken from animals are called zoomorphs, and those from plants phyllomorphs, it will be convenient to call those derived from structure, skeuomorphs. **1979** *Nature* 6 Dec. 632/2 So-called 'skeuomorphs' in architecture that involve conversion of originally necessary features into purely decorative patterns.

2. An object or feature copying the design of a similar artefact in another material.

1938 *Proc. Prehistoric Soc.* IV. 82 This necklace type is best known in jet from northern Britain, where it has.. provided the type of which the gold lunula is a skeuomorph. **1943** *Antiquity* XVII. 7 Stone skeuomorphs of wooden fences. **1977** [see SKEUOMORPHIC *a.* below]. **1981** *Chartered Mechanical Engineer* Sept. 20/3 'Skeuomorphs' seem to be very common in motor car design, particularly where changes are made from ferrous metals to nonferrous metals or plastics.

Hence **skeuomo·rphic** *a.*, of, pertaining to, decorated with, or having the character of a skeuomorph or skeuomorphs.

1889 H. COLLEY MARCH in *Trans. Lancs. & Cheshire Antiq. Soc.* VII. 168 The transfer of thong-work from the flint axe, where it was functional, to the bronze celt, where it was skeuomorphic. **1895** A. C. HADDON *Evol. Art* 6 The reader is referred to the section on skeuomorphic pottery. **1905** [see *ANTHROPOMORPHIC *a.* 2]. **1928** R. A. S. MACALISTER *Archaeol. Ireland* vi. 277 Celtic interlacement..is *skeuomorphic*; that is, it is derived from the patterns produced by a technical process—in this case, by weaving. **1930** J. L. MYRES *Who were Greeks?* viii. 464 When a potter, working in red clay..fashions clay vessels so that..they resemble metal work or leather work or basketry..his style is 'skeuomorphic'. **1951** B. Z. SELIGMAN *N. & Q. Anthropol.* (ed. 6) III. 311 Note whether the design is..skeuomorphic. **1959** J. D. EVANS *Malta* iii. 127 The skeuomorphic carving of some of the inner halls of the rock-cut monument of Hal Saflieni. **1977** T. SHAW *Unearthing Igbo-Ukwu* 15 When something is originally made in one material and is then translated into another, but by its form and decoration reveals the original model which it imitates, this is called a 'skeuomorph', and the object in the new material is said to be 'skeuomorphic'. Thus the bronze pot described is skeuomorphic of an ordinary pottery vessel.

skew, *sb.*^{3} **1.** For *Obs.*$^{-1}$ read *Obs. rare* and add further example.

1884 G. FORBES in W. Thomson *Molecular Dynamics* 289 So the coefficients sighed and gave a last tangential skew And *a* shook hands with *b* & *c* and S and T and U, And with a tear they parted.

4. *Statistics.* Skewness.

1974 *Listener* 7 Nov. 595/2 The skew in the graph is at both ends. **1978** *Nature* 2 Mar. 39/1 The distribution is not symmetrical but displays positive skew, a feature held in common with observations at lower frequencies.

skew, *a.* Add: **1. c.** *Statistics.* Of a statistical distribution: not symmetrical about its mean. Cf. *SKEWED *a.*[2] 2.

A distribution is said to be *skew* (or *skewed*) *positively* or *to the right* if its third moment about its mean is positive, so that its larger tail lies to the right; and conversely.

1894 *Phil. Trans. R. Soc.* CLXXXV. 107, I have succeeded in resolving this mortality-curve into components which are not..all of the normal type, but become, as we approach infinite mortality, of the skew form. **1905** *Drapers' Co. Res. Mem.* (Biometric Ser.) II. 22 The theory of skew variation will give regression curves..containing product terms in *x* and *y*. **1929** *Jrnl. du Conseil* IV. 219 The area of the curve has been reduced to about half its original dimensions, but it has not been rendered very skew. **1936** *Bot. Rev.* II. 229 The distributions of the less common grasses are markedly skew. **1968** *Brit. Med. Bull.* XXIV. 210/2 The first is fairly symmetrical but discloses one outlying value; the second is notably skew to the right.

2. a. *skew gearing,* gearing consisting of two cog-wheels having non-parallel, non-intersecting axes; so *skew gear*; *skew nail, nailing* (cf. *skew-nail* vb., sense 3 in Dict.).

1908 J. Richardson *Mod. Steam Engine* ix. 159 Fig. 150 shows the usual bevel gear, and Fig. 151 the skew gear now used in preference. **1929** *Times* 2 Nov. 4/7 The oil pump, driven by skew gear from the camshaft, is in the sump. **1975** Ryder & Bennett *Mechanics of Machines* iv. 112 Skew or spiral gears (which are helical gears of differing helix angles forming a mating pair) are used to transmit motion between non-intersecting shafts. *a* **1877** Knight *Dict. Mech.* III. 2194/2 *Skew-gearing,* cog-wheels with teeth placed obliquely, so as to slide into each other and avoid clashing. **1902** A. C. Harmsworth et al. *Motors & Motor-Driving* x. 191 Another plan..substitutes for the bevel gearing what is known as skew or screw gearing. **1954** W. E. Kelsey *Carpentry, Joinery & Woodcutting Machinery* xiv. 394 In practice, skew nails are driven in various places..to prevent any movement. **1958** *Times* 27 Mar. 5/2 In one case there was a double skew nail. **1929** T. Corkhill in R. Greenhalgh *Joinery & Carpentry* VI. 1561 *Skew nailing,* nails driven with an inclination to the surface to give greater security. **1958** *Times* 27 Mar. 5/2 Double skew nailing was an old traditional practice. **1973** P. Hutchinson *Home Carpenter* ii. 13 (*caption*) Skew nailing locks timber framing firmly in place.

b. *skew field,* a ring whose non-zero elements form a group with respect to multiplication; a set which satisfies the axioms for a field except that multiplication is not commutative.

1965 Patterson & Rutherford *Elem. Abstract Algebra* iii. 75 In certain cases we encounter systems which satisfy all the required properties for a field with one exception, the commutative law of multiplication. Such systems are known as..skew fields. **1969** F. M. Hall *Introd. Abstr. Algebra* II. iv. 114 The only skew field of any importance is the set of quaternions.

3. a. *skew-eyed* adj. (later example; also as *adv.*).

1922 Joyce *Ulysses* 30 And skeweyed Walter sirring his father. **1976** I. Levin *Boys from Brazil* ii. 57 He.. smiled skew-eyed at him.

b. skew-symmetric *a. Math.*, (of a matrix or other square array of elements) having all the elements of the principal diagonal equal to zero, and each of the remaining elements equal to the negative of the element in the corresponding position on the other side of the diagonal; more generally, applied to an array of any dimension in which every element having a repeated subscript is zero and every other element is equal to the negative of elements having an odd permutation of the same subscripts; also **skew-symmetrical** *a.*; hence **skew-symmetry.**

[**1849** A. Cayley in *Jrnl. für die reine und angewandte Math.* XXXVIII. 93 On a $\lambda_{r.s} = -\lambda_{s.r}$ $(r \neq 0)$; $\lambda_{r.r} = 0$. Ces déterminants peuvent être nommés 'gauches et symmétriques'.] **1911** T. Muir *Hist. Determinants* II. ix. 255 Any skew determinant is expressible in terms of skew symmetric determinants and those of the original determinant which are not included in the latter. *Ibid.* 269 The identity..is the twin theorem to one given in his previous paper regarding a bordered skew symmetrical determinant of even order. **1955** W. Pauli *Niels Bohr* 45 The vectors and skew-symmetric tensors transform just like the analogous electromagnetic quantities. **1967** [see *bilinear *a.* 2]. **1980** A. J. Jones *Game Theory* i. 44 Thus a matrix game is symmetric if its matrix is skew-symmetric. **1927** *Proc. R. Soc.* A. CXVI. 249 In any example the quickest way of showing the skew-symmetry is to write T symbolically as a determinant. **1980** A. J. Jones *Game Theory* i. 46 Skew-symmetry of the matrix is preserved by this operation.

skew, *v.*[2] Add: **6.** Also, to distort, bias.

1975 *Amer. Speech 1972* XLVII. 284 If he sings the song, he pronounces the name and possibly skews the results. **1979** *Sci. Amer.* Feb. 105/2 Whatever was skewing the eye-color ratio had its effect only in the course of sperm formation, not in egg formation. **1981** *Amer. Speech* LVI. 45 If we count those informants using both *big daddy* and *big mamma* only once, to avoid falsely skewing the data, fully 39 percent of the 38 different informants..are black.

8. *Statistics.* To make skew (*skew *a.* 1 c).

1929 *Jrnl. du Conseil* IV. 219 The frequency curve has been reduced to a very small proportion of the original, the mode has been shifted 1⅞ cms., and the group has been distinctly 'skewed'. **1931** *Brit. Jrnl. Psychol.* XXII. 85 The raising of the level of difficulty of test *A* will tend to skew the score-scatter positively.

skewed, *a.*[2] Add: **1. b.** *fig.*

1960 *Economist* 25 June 1330/1 This triple structure [of a book] is a magnificent achievement,..but its magnificence is..skewed at its foundation... The skewness derives from Professor Hayek's perfectly legitimate definition of freedom. **1977** *New Yorker* 17 Oct. 78/2 She quickly came to share her husband's feelings about the skewed state of the world.

2. a. *Statistics.* = *skew *a.* 1 c.

1940 *Brit. Jrnl. Psychol.* XXX. 259 A difficult test tends to produce a positively skewed score-scatter. **1953** E. Mayr et al. *Methods & Princ. Systematic Zool.* vii. 134 A skewed curve is a curve in which the mode..is above or below the mean. **1977** *Lancet* 5 Feb. 311/1 In our hands, the crude breath-test results are highly skewed, but logarithmic transformation does produce a distribution which is indistinguishable from normal. **1977** R. E. Megill *Introd. Risk Analysis* iii. 22 The distribution shown in Fig. 3.1 is skewed to the right; i.e. it has more values to the right of its highest frequency (mode) than to the left.

b. Of a sample or data: biased, not representative.

1975 *Amer. Speech 1973* XLVIII. 6 Since the data used for restructuring would have been external and skewed, one would expect attempts at restructuring to be only partially successful. **1977** *Times* 12 May 23/2 Quotas.. are at present heavily skewed in favour of those countries which were economically powerful when the [International Monetary] Fund was set up.

3. Distorted; shifted in emphasis or character.

1935 G. K. Zipf *Psycho-Biol. of Lang.* iii. 105 A range of frequency where the skewed phoneme *t* in *ts* would be most stable. **1965** E. Haugen *Norwegian Eng. Dict.* 40/1 The typical East Norwegian (Oslo) [vowel] system is markedly skewed (in the same direction as Swedish)... The whole system has undergone a counterclockwise movement. **1980** *Nature* 17 Jan. 234/1 Critics..argued that the military control of research meant such research would inevitably be skewed towards the production of weapons of mass destruction. **1981** *Time* 7 Dec. 79/2 The wildness of the cat, its..skewed version of reality.

skewer, *sb.* Add: **1. d.** (Further examples.)

1848 *Sinks of London Laid Open* 124/2 *Skewer,* sword. **1934** A. Russell *Tramp-Royal in Wild Australia* xxxviii. 254 There'd be 'skewers' flying in all directions. Rotten wounds they'd make—barbed, you know.

Skewes (skiū·ėz, skiūz). *Math.* The name of S. *Skewes* (b. 1899), South African born mathematician, used *attrib.* and in the possessive to designate an extremely large number, relevant in the theory of the distribution of prime numbers, having the value exp(exp (exp 79)).

The first pronunc. is that used by the Skewes family. In 1933 (*Jrnl. London Math. Soc.* VIII. 277) Skewes claimed that, for some value of *a* less than this number, the number of primes less than *a* exceeds $\int_0^a \frac{dx}{\ln x}$.

1949 Kasner & Newman *Math. & Imagination* ii. 32 A veritable giant is Skewes' number, even bigger than a gogolplex. **1955** *Math. Rev.* XVI. 676/1 In a previous paper..the author has obtained a larger value of X_1 (the so-called Skewes number) on the assumption of the Riemann hypothesis.

skewgy-mewgy, var. *soogee-moogee.

skewing, *vbl. sb.*[1] (in Dict. s.v. Skew *v.*[2]). Add: **2.** Bias, distortion.

1969 *Language* XLV. 487 In reality the transfer at the kernel level can generally be made with far less danger of skewing than if one follows the highly involved processes. **1975** *Nature* 13 Mar. 139/2 The degree of skewing would depend on factors such as the length of time between the act of volunteering and actual participation in the experiment.

skewness. (Further examples.)

1905 K. Pearson in *Biometrika* IV. 173 The chief physical differences between actual frequency distributions and the Gaussian theoretical distribution are:... (ii) The ratio of this separation between mean and mode to the variability of the character—a quantity I have termed the skewness. **1935** G. K. Zipf *Psycho-Biol. of Lang.* iii. 99 The varying degrees of difficulty in the articulation of a phoneme resulting from the different combinations in which it occurs, together with the various relative frequencies of occurrences of the phoneme in its different combinations, may introduce a modification in the normal distribution of speech-sounds about the phonemic norm which, it seems, may well be termed *skewness.* **1936** *Hereditas* XXI. 330 The difference is probably not significant (the standard error could not be calculated owing to a marked skewness in both series). **1965** *Language* XLI. 189 A 'sound system'..of a complexity and skewness out of line with anything attested by languages known to us. **1968** *Economist* 30 Nov. 63/1 The latest crisis..has been about the skewness of certain European currencies and not about the dollar or gold at all. **1970** *Watsonia* VIII. 124 A similar distribution of this character was found in most of the plants included in Table 1; in only four of them was the skewness more markedly positive.

skew-whiff (skiū,wi·f, -hwi·f), *a.* and *adv. dial.* and *colloq.* Also **skew-wiff, -wift,** etc.; 8 **scew-.** [f. Skew *a.* and *adv.* + Whiff *sb.*[1] or *v.*[1]] Askew, awry (*lit.* and *fig.*).

1754 *Scots Mag.* July 337/2 Behind, with a coach-horse short dock, cut your hair; Stick a flower before, scew-whiff, with an air. **1839** W. Holloway *General Dict. Provincialisms* 154/1 *Skew-whift, adj.* (Askew, from Skef, Belg. oblique; and perhaps Whiffed, blown.) Awry. **1854** A. E. Baker *Gloss. Northamptonshire Words & Phrases* II. 239 *Skew-whiff,* awry, aslant. 'It's all *skew-whiff.*' Probably blown on one side by a whiff or puff. **1879** G. F. Jackson *Shropshire Word-Bk.* 386 *Skew-whiff,.. adv.* awry; irregular; zigzag. **1895** J. T. Clegg *Stories, Sketches, & Rhymes in Rochdale Dialect* 228 Her judgment's getten thrut skew-wift. **1899** *Shetland News* 20 May 7/2, I hed ta geng skewquieff. **1935** A. P. Herbert *What a Word!* iv. 101 Go on cackling..until the orator has to stop and ask you why you cackle. Then tell him. He won't get *Frankenstein* skew-whiff again. **1946** D. L. Sayers *Unpopular Opinions* 59 When Neptune shouldered Britain out of the sea, he did not make a neat engineering job of it. Characteristically, Britain came up skew-wiff, with one edge thick and hard and the other soft and thin, like a slice of wedding-cake. **1959** I. & P. Opie *Lore & Lang. Schoolch.* iii. 47 If a boy's cap is on skew-whiff: 'Are you wearing that cap or just walking underneath it?' **1959** *N.Z. Listener* 12 June 20/3 A breaker turned the bow skew-wiff. **1974** J. Cleary *Peter's Pence* iii. 82 Our plans seem to have gone a bit skew-wiff, don't they? That's the trouble with the Irish. **1977** *Lancashire Life* Feb. 53/4 Thi tie's put on skew-wiff.

skewy (skiū·i), *a. colloq.* [f. Skew *a.* and *adv.* + -y[1].] Somewhat askew, awry, or twisted. So **skew·iness,** the quality of being skewy.

1862 'G. Hamilton' *Country Living* 62 Though freedom from foreign growth discovered an intention of straightness, the most casual observer could not but see that skewiness had usurped its place. **1898** A. T. Slosson *Dumb Foxglove* 71 Narrer an' p'inted like a pear, or skewy an' knobby like a quince. **1940** *Amer. Speech* XV. 131/2 They have the same meaning as awry or 'skewy'. **1960** E. H. Gombrich *Art & Illusion* viii. 248 The right-hand one is really a distorted, skewy object which only assumes the appearance of a chair.

‖ **skhod** (sχǫd). [Russ.] In the U.S.S.R. (and pre-Revolutionary Russia), an assembly of villagers. Also *selskii skhod.*

1877 D. M. Wallace *Russia* viii. 120 All important communal affairs are regulated by the *Selski Skhod,* or Village Assembly. **1914** H. W. Williams *Russia of Russians* xi. 348 The affairs of the community are managed by a *skhod,* or mote of which all the adult males are members. **1948** J. Towster *Political Power in U.S.S.R.* x. 201 In small rural settlements the place of a village soviet was to be taken by a *skhod*—a general meeting of electors. **1959** E. H. Carr *Socialism in One Country* II. 307 The *skhod,* which dated from Tsarist times, was the village meeting... It was not, strictly speaking, a public body. It had no constitutional status, no officially recognized duties..but it sometimes performed primitive functions of local government. **1972** T. Shanin *Awkward Class* ix. 164 A 'rural gathering' (*sel'skii skhod*) was to be established in parallel with the 'land gathering'. The 'rural gathering' would consist of all the inhabitants with Soviet electoral rights within the area of a Rural Soviet.

ski, *sb.* Delete ‖ and add: Now only with pronunc. (skī) and usu. with pl. **skis. 1. a.** (Earlier and later examples.) Also *fig.*

Quot. 1755 is an isolated early use.

1755 *Monthly Rev.* XII. 451 He says they have *skies,* or long and thin pieces of board, so smooth, that the peasants wade through the snow with them. **1923** D. H. Lawrence *Birds, Beasts & Flowers* 177 So she..goes off in slow sad leaps On the long flat skis of her legs. **1933** *Illustr. London News* 9 Dec. 942/1 A German soldier named Schuhmacher, said to have belonged to an infantry battalion training on ski in the Bavarian Alps, was shot dead by Austrian frontier guards. **1960** A. S. Neill in *Id* III. 4 The snow was deep and we all had to go out on skis.

b. Each of two or three runners forming part of the landing gear of an aeroplane designed to land on snow or ice. Cf. *ski-plane,* sense 2 b below.

1912 *Flight* 17 Feb. 137 (*caption*) Note the special skis attached for landing purposes. **1931** F. D. Bradbrooke *Light Aeroplane Man.* vi. 96 For work on ice and snow skis are fitted to the undercarriage instead of wheels. **1948** 'N. Shute' *No Highway* ii. 41 They flew up in a Norseman fitted with skis and landed in deep snow. **1959** Green & Pollinger *World's Fighting Planes* (ed. 3) 21 The Otter may be fitted with wheels, floats or skis.

c. *transf.* = *water ski. Usu. *pl.*

1930 *Literary Digest* 11 Oct. 48/3 Many games have been introduced this summer for those who walk on water with skis. **1964** G. McDonald *Running Scared* xii. 160 Tom suggested water skiing... Tom's skis surfaced easily and beautifully. **1974** *Encycl. Brit. Micropædia* X. 574/3 Typical all-purpose skis are of wood 6½ inches wide and 5 feet 9 inches..long, with a stabilizing fin on the bottom near the heel.

d. A launching site for flying bombs. Freq. *attrib.*

1953 P. C. Berg *Dict. New Words* (ed. 2) 146/1 *Ski,* the launching apparatus for the flying bomb, from its fancied resemblance to a gigantic ski. (1944.) **1957** P. J. de la Ferte *Rocket* vi. 89 The Allied Air Forces launched a massive assault on the ramps, ski constructions and preparation huts. **1958** C. B. Smith *Evidence in Camera* ix. 224 A launching site..which also matched up with the foundations for ramps at the ski sites... The ski buildings provided storage space for twenty flying bombs on each site. **1978** R. A. Young *Flying Bomb* ii. 27 (*caption*) The left-hand 'ski' has not yet been roofed. *Ibid.* 30 When components arrived at the sites they could be most easily stored in one of the 'ski' buildings.

2. a. *ski-runner* (earlier example); *ski-racing, -running* (later examples); (= *ski-ing* vbl. sb.), as *ski boot, -cap, centre, chalet, clothes, club, goggles, -hut, instructor, -jacket -lodge, pants, parka, -race, resort, -room, school, shop, slope, suit, track, trail, troops, trousers, -wear.*

1907 E. C. RICHARDSON *Ski-Running* 48 In the Black Forest ski boots are often made of dog or calf skin. **1972** *Guardian* 31 Oct. 11/3 Ski boots are now injection-moulded plastic shells lined with foam padding. **1937** *Sierra Club Bull.* Feb. 46 There follows, however, our usual clothing list..ski-boots and ski-caps. **1975** E. HILLARY *Nothing Venture, Nothing Win* ii. 39, I had an icicle about five inches long hanging from the strap of my ski-cap. **1942** Ski center [see *ski trail* below]. **1948** [see *ORIENTEERING]. **1960** *Sunday Express* 27 Nov. 15/5 On the same railway line..there are nine other ski centres. **1971** *Country Life* 23 Dec. 1814/4 (Advt.), Ski Chalets. Top resorts in France, Switzerland and Austria. **1975** *Times* 2 Jan. 4/7 President Ford continued to study a report he received at his ski chalet. **1965** 'J. LE CARRÉ' *Looking-Glass War* i. 3 A group of children... Some wore ski clothes. **1913** F. H. HARRIS *Dartmouth out o' Doors* 104 In our own country ski clubs are flourishing. **1963** *Ski-ing* ('Know the Game' Series) 12 There are a number of ski clubs which are affiliated to the Ski Club of Great Britain. **1971** C. BONINGTON *Annapurna South Face* 244 Ski-goggles..proved ideal in bad weather conditions. **1958** E. DUNDY *Dud Avocado* I. vi. 93 Dressed for the Select as for a ski-hut..in a checkered wool-shirt, G.I. pants and ski-boots. **1973** *Times* 8 Jan. 5/1 The party.. had arrived back at a skihut at Abisko. **1959** P. MOYES *Dead Men don't Ski* iv. 45 It is..traditional for ski instructors to be handsome. **1978** S. SHELDON *Bloodline* ii. 28 On her thirty-fifth birthday Anna had gone to Kitzbühel, in Austria, and there she had met Walther Gassner, a ski instructor thirteen years younger than she. **1968** M. WOODHOUSE *Rock Baby* xxiv. 234 He was wearing a blue ski-jacket and denim trousers. **1966** —— *Tree Frog* xii. 86 A hunting-lodge modernised to make a ski-lodge. **1978** *Chicago* June 36/1 Once a ski lodge, then a theatre, this rural listening room now provides one of the most relaxed settings for good pop, jazz, and folk. **1937** *Sierra Club Bull.* Feb. 46 There follows..our usual clothing list... Ski-pants. **1977** C. FORBES *Avalanche Express* xxv. 267 Six men clad in ski-masks and ski-pants. **1974** *Amer. Speech 1970* XLV. 180 A variety of wearing apparel, such as children's clothes, men's slacks, ski parkas and sweaters. **1936** C. M. DOLE *Amer. Ski Ann.* 53 There should be a competent course patrol for all ski races made up from the personnel of the club ski patrols. **1973** D. FRANCIS *Slay-Ride* ii. 23 He used to win across-country ski races. **1898** *Encycl. Sport* II. 379/1 About a hundred competitors come from various parts of the country to strive for these blue ribbons of the ski-racing world. **1975** *Times* 19 Dec. 9/5 In ski racing..one's position in the starting order is based on one's previous results. **1965** 'J. LE CARRÉ' *Looking-Glass War* iii. 33 The town..feeds the main ski resorts. **1972** D. HASTON *In High Places* vi. 72 We..tried to be as inconspicuous as four laden climbers can be in a ski resort. **1963** I. FLEMING *On H.M. Secret Service* xii. 129 There was a ski-room and workshop to the left of the exit. **1887** *Appleton's Ann. Cycl. 1886* XI. 805/1 The distance covered by an expert skee-runner is from fifty to sixty miles a day. **1911** A. BENNETT *Card* xi. 273 No sport was true sport save the sport of ski-running. **1969** H. MACINNES *Salzburg Connection* ii. 37 We have no ski lift here..no special slopes. But there is good ski-running. That is the best sport anyway... Let me show you on this map... You can ski for thirty kilometres. **1934** *Leisure* Jan. 23 This run..will probably be used by the official Ski School of the U.S. Eastern Amateur Ski Association. **1954** R. MARTIN *Your Ski Holiday* vi. 44 Some people nowadays go to one of the 'dry ski schools' which are being set up in several of the large towns of England. **1980** J. CARTWRIGHT *Horse of Darius* iii. 42 She..made her way along to the office of the ski school. **1969** H. MACINNES *Salzburg Connection* viii. 114 Just beyond Bad Aussee..where Johann Kronsteiner has his ski-shop. **1934** *Discovery* Oct. 297/2 (*caption*) The new 'tower-hotels' at Colle di Sestrières in the Italian Alps, with a background of ski-slopes. **1976** A. WHITE *Long Silence* xi. 104 A fall of snow at the wrong time can start an avalanche on the ski slopes. **1956** R. BRADDON *Nancy Wake* vi. 55 She accordingly bought herself a new ski suit. **1978** J. A. MICHENER *Chesapeake* 809 They walked together, bundled in ski suits, to all corners of their estate. **1948** H. INNES *Blue Ice* vii. 194 Three ski tracks ran off at an angle, crossing the tracks we were following. **1975** D. BAGLEY *Snow Tiger* xxxii. 281 Here is an enlargement of the breakaway point of the avalanche. There is a ski track going into it. **1942** *Economic Geogr.* July 318/2 Lack of overnight accommodations, or their location at inconvenient distances from the ski trails and slopes, has, and will, retard the popularity of many otherwise excellent ski centers. **1973** P. A. WHITNEY *Snowfire* vi. 108 The immediate problem of getting myself down a ski trail without breaking my neck. **1934** S. SPENDER *Vienna* iii. 32 Like diving monoplanes..curled down on them the ski-troops. **1974** *Encycl. Brit. Macropædia* XVI. 835/1 Ski troops were..used in Sweden as early as 1452. **1946** P. BOTTOME *Lifeline* vii. 71 Ida, dressed in long ski trousers and a black pullover. **1969** N. FREELING *Tsing-Boum* xxii. 158 Tight black ski trousers and excessively brilliant orange sweater. **1961** *Sports & Camping Goods Dealer* Nov. 9/1 Big demand for Ski-wear... Sales of skiwear continue to rise. **1980** L. BIRNBACH et al. *Official Preppy Handbk.* 152/2 The latest and most expensive skiwear and equipment.

b. Special Combs. **ski-boat,** (*a*) *S. Afr.*, a raftlike boat with two outboard motors used esp. for offshore fishing; (*b*) a small powerboat used for towing water-skiers; **ski-bob** [*BOB *sb.*[1] 2 d, e], a vehicle resembling a bicycle with skis instead of wheels, which slides quickly over snow; hence as *v. intr.*, to ride a ski-bob; **ski-bobber,** one who ski-bobs; **ski-bobbing** *vbl. sb.*, the action of riding a ski-bob, esp. as a sport; **ski bum** *N. Amer. slang*, a skiing enthusiast who works casually at a resort in order to ski; hence **ski bumming; ski carrier** = *ski rack* below; **ski flying** (see quot. 1974); **skijamas** *N. Amer.*, a pair of pyjamas in the style of a ski suit; **ski-jump,** (*a*) the artificial structure built on a natural slope, from which a ski-jumper takes off; also *transf.* and *fig.*; (*b*) a leap made by a ski-jumper; **ski-jumper,** one who takes part in ski-jumping; **ski-jumping,** a winter sport in which skiers 'jump' from the end of a snow-covered chute built high on a slope, marks being usu. awarded for style and distance covered by the leap; also, this action; **ski-lift:** see *LIFT *sb.*[2] 10 b; **ski-mask,** a protective covering for the face, of the type worn by skiers (and adopted by others to conceal identity); hence **ski-masked** *a.*; **ski pack,** an arrangement whereby a tour company offers holiday facilities and the hire of skiing equipment at one inclusive price; **ski patrol** *N. Amer.*, a group of expert skiers who patrol ski slopes to check on conditions and assist skiers in difficulties; hence **ski patrolman,** a member of a ski patrol; **ski-plane,** an aeroplane having its undercarriage fitted with skis (sense 1 c above) for landing on snow or ice; **ski pole** *U.S.* = *ski stick* below; **ski rack,** a frame (usu. fixed to the roof of a car) on which skis are placed for transportation; **ski ramp,** a ramp constructed for skiing practice; also *transf.*; **ski run,** (*a*) a spell of travelling on skis; (*b*) a skiing piste; **ski stick,** one of two long sticks held by a skier to assist in propulsion or braking and in balancing; **ski tour,** a tour made by cross-country skiing; hence **ski-tourer, ski-touring; ski tow,** (*a*) a mechanical device for conveying skiers up a slope, in the form of an endless moving rope or of bars or seats suspended from an overhead cable; (*b*) a tow-rope for water-skiers; hence **ski-tow** *v. trans.*, to pull with a ski tow; **ski-walking,** cross-country skiing (cf. *NORDIC *a.* b); so **ski-walk** *v. trans.*, to travel over by ski-walking; **ski-wax,** wax applied to the undersides of skis to improve performance; **ski-wheel,** on the undercarriage of an aircraft: a combination of ski and wheel (see quots.); hence **ski-wheeled** *a.*, having a ski-wheel landing gear.

1964 A. TREW *Smoke Island* ii. 43 José brought the ski-boat round and Andy recovered some of the lost line as he scrambled into the fighting-chair. **1971** 'D. HALLIDAY' *Dolly & Doctor Bird* viii. 103 The holidaymakers..hissing past..in the ski boat. **1974** *Argus* (Cape Town) 2 Aug. 11/4 Many of the ski-boats operating in that area had 60, 80 or 100 snoek. **1966** *Skier* Sept. 7/1, 1962: I became German and Bavarian Women's ski-bob Champion. **1968** *Guardian* 21 Sept. 10/3 The ski-bob is a small bicycle on skis with short skis for the feet with braking claws on them. **1969** *Winter Sports Ann.* 20/1 One can learn to ski-bob very quickly. **1976** *Daily Tel.* (Colour Suppl.) 6 Aug. 6/2 A ski-bob can exceed speeds of 80mph on a steep, straight run. *Ibid.* 6/3 Captain John Beckett..who once taught a lady journalist to ski-bob in one-and-a-half hours. **1967** Ski bobber [see *mini-ski* s.v. *MINI-]. **1976** *Daily Tel.* (Colour Suppl.) 6 Aug. 6/1 Ski-bobbers are now eligible for grants from the National Council for Physical Recreation. **1966** *Skier* Sept. 6/2 Ski-bobbing has come a long way since those first laughing days. **1971** *Daily Tel.* 30 Jan. 7/5 Ski-bobbing (not yet so popular in France as elsewhere, but rapidly catching on). **1976** *Ibid.* (Colour Suppl.) 6 Aug. 6/1 In 1971, the Army included ski-bobbing in their own skiing championships. **1960** *Washington Post* 4 Mar. c5/3 John Kerr..is firmly settled in the picturesque ex-mining town of Aspen, Colo., and happily pursuing one of the world's newest professions—ski bumming... By ski bum standards, John Kerr has struck it rich. **1978** *N.Y. Times* 16 Jan. c8/1 (*headline*) Ski-bum shortage shakes the resorts. **1978** S. SHELDON *Bloodline* ii. 34 'What can a ski bum contribute to Roffe and Sons?' he asked. **1965** 'D. SHANNON' *Death-Bringers* xiv. 187 It was the right Anglia. It had ski carriers on its roof. **1970** *Globe & Mail* (Toronto) 25 Sept. 32/7 (Advt.), 100 Accessories..from ski carriers to repair bases, we have them all at spectacular savings. **1952** *Sun* (Baltimore) 3 Mar. (B ed.) 15/7 Toivo Lauren..won the international 'ski-flying' contest today with a jump of approximately 429 feet 9 inches. **1974** R. SCHARFF *Ski Magazine's Encycl. Skiing* 420/2 *Ski flying*, a form of jumping on hills where distances of 100 meters or more can be reached. **1958** L. WHISHAW *As Far as you'll take Me* vii. 104, I..then, dressed in my skijamas, ate my dinner in peace. **1964** *N.Y. Times* 29 Nov. 132 Reis 'ski-jamas' are set for winter slumber. **1907** E. C. RICHARDSON *Ski-Running* 89 The outlook from the top of a ski-jump of any magnitude is indeed alarming. **1922** E. E. CUMMINGS *Enormous Room* i.18 A face all ski-jumps and toboggan slides. **1948** H. INNES *Blue Ice* x. 250 He was going to do a ski jump..on to the top of the moving train. **1953** X. FIELDING *Stronghold* 42 At last I reached a scree, as long and steep as a ski-jump. **1960** C. H. GIBBS-SMITH *Aeroplane* 3/5 A later illustration shows a long 'ski-jump' ramp. **1971** L. KOPPETT *N.Y. Times Guide Spectator Sports* xvi. 222 One of the most spectacular sights in any sport is the ski jump. **1978** *Navy News* Aug. 40/4 The invention of the Ski Jump take-off ramp to be fitted in Royal Navy ships carrying Harrier aircraft has won an award of £25,000. **1894** *Engineering News* 1 Mar. 169/3 Ski-jumpers..have for some time been holding tournaments in Minnesota. **1981** 'E. LATHEN' *Going for Gold* i. 15 People..were taking up stations from which they could watch the last of the ski jumpers. **1904** *Sandow's Mag.* Mar. 200 (*caption*) A ski-jumping competition. **1927** A. HUXLEY *Let.* 14 Feb. (1969) 283 We had an international ski jumping competition here last week. **1960** *Guardian* 8 Dec. 10/6 In 1950 and 1951 there was ski jumping..on Hampstead Heath. **1973** *Country Life* 29 Nov. 1807 Ski-jumping and cross-country (*langlauf*) racing. **1973** 'D. SHANNON' *No Holiday for Crime* xiv. 208 It had been a professional job: ski-masks, a look-out at the door. **1980** J. BALL *Then came Violence* xiii. 103 Since ski masks had been used..there were no descriptions. **1976** *Time* 20 Dec. 7/2 Graziella Quartuccio, 43, was snatched away in her nightgown..by a machine-gun-toting gang of ski-masked Mafiosi. **1969** *Guardian* 11 Oct. 10/6 See which holidays give the best value in terms of ski packs. **1936** C. M. DOLE *Amer. Ski Ann.* 52 A definite organization is necessary. The Ski Patrol has been suggested..and..has been instituted in one locality. **1963** *Amer. Speech* XXXVIII. 204 The warning signs erected in ski areas by the ski patrol. **1978** *Globe & Mail* (Toronto) 8 Feb. 31/1 The Canadian Ski Patrol system is again this season doing on-the-slopes testing of bindings for skiers. **1957** *Today's Health* Jan. 54/3 Two ski patrolmen.. lashed their skis together to make an emergency toboggan. **1930** O. H. KNEEN *Everyman's Bk. Flying* xiii. 231 The Fairchild Airplane Company and others use the term *ski-plane* for Canadian machines, convertible to seaplanes in the summer. **1936** J. GRIERSON *High Failure* xiii. 281 For Canadian conditions the most useful machines are seaplanes in summer and ski-planes in winter. **1964** G. LYALL *Most Dangerous Game* xxi. 172, I came in from Spitzbergen, in an old Noorduyn Norseman ski-plane. **1975** E. HILLARY *Nothing Venture, Nothing Win* vi. 82 Access to the mountains is often long and difficult—or used to be before the development of ski-planes and helicopters. **1920** *Literary Digest* 14 Feb. 115, I need not describe these poles to you, as any dealer will know what you mean by ski-poles. **1978** W. F. BUCKLEY *Stained Glass* xv. 155 The accordion player, without ski poles, and making music all the way, began the three-mile ski down the mountain. **1968** *Globe & Mail* (Toronto) 5 Feb. 26/8 (Advt.), 67 Austin Cooper, tachometer, ski rack. **1980** L. BIRNBACH et al. *Official Preppy Handbk.* 204/2 In the winter, the car is heading north, topped with a ski rack. **1973** *Houston Post* (Spotlight Suppl.) 14 Oct. 9/5 The fair is free, including hourly ski demonstrations by Ed Williams on a ski ramp. **1976** *Southern Even. Echo* (Southampton) 11 Nov. 17/2 Ships with 'ski-ramps' at the bow for the launching jump-jet aircraft were forecast by the chief designer of the Harrier at Southampton University last night. **1924** O. POULSEN *Skiing* 72 It is on one of these long ski-runs alone that a man can think out his problems best. **1951** M. KENNEDY *Lucy Carmichael* V. iii. 222 The next few seconds had been as good as a first class ski run. **1953** DYLAN THOMAS *Let.* 27 Feb. (1966) 395 We could go anywhere on that, except Laughlin's heart and ski-run. **1977** N. FREELING *Gadget* ii. 92 The climb..was steep as a downhill ski-run. **1907** E. C. RICHARDSON *Ski-Running* 46 (*caption*) Disc for bottom of ski stick. **1924** E. HEMINGWAY in *Transatlantic Rev.* Dec. 635 Nick knocked his clamps loose with one of his ski sticks. **1970** N. FLEMING *Czech Point* (1971) i. 7, I hooked my skisticks on to the T-bar. **1949** E. COXHEAD *Wind in West* vii. 180 Ilse knew..nothing of nature except what she could see from a ski-tour. **1972** *Guardian* 11 Mar. 13/1 The standard yardstick for these ski-tourers and ski-mountaineers has been..a mountain obstacle race between..Chamonix, and Zermatt. **1960** *Ibid.* 24 Oct. 11/4 In Scotland..after April only high-level ski-touring is possible. **1972** DEAN & SMITH *Wisconsin* 161/1 Call it ski touring, Nordic skiing,.. or simply X-C, but it all boils down to the same thing—the art of walking on skis. **1942** *Economic Geogr.* July 307/2 The invention of the ski tow at about this time.. gave great impetus to the growing interest in skiing. **1967** *Spectator* 15 Sept. 301/1 One laird explained his resistance ..to..building a ski tow in the snowy heights he owned—by saying simply, 'Look what happened to Switzerland.' **1971** J. YARDLEY *Kiss a Day* vii. 121 He..trailed the ski-tow over the side for her to catch. Five minutes later they were cutting a white wake across the lagoon. **1976** P. CAVE *High Flying Birds* iii. 28 Ski-towing a hang-glider is reckoned on being a pretty dangerous sport at the best of times. **1970** R. LOWELL *Notebk.* 148 We ski-walked the eggshell at the Mittersill. **1974** *Observer* 3 Nov. 34/2 The age-old Nordic ski-ing that is both easier to learn and cheaper to enjoy. Essentially it is walking, or running, on skis over undulating countryside... Ski-walking, Nordic ski-ing, *Skiwandern, ski de vandonnée, Ski du fond, Langlauf*—the variety of names given to the sport perhaps causes confusion. **1910** W. R. RICKMERS *Ski-ing* 35 Ski-wax can be obtained hard or in tubes. **1979** R. FIENNES *Hell on Ice* v. 68, I needed feeling in my fingers to..feel for my map, change the ski-wax and many other things. **1938** C. WINCHESTER *Wonders of World Aviation* 979/2 It sometimes happens that flights to the northern parts of Canada necessitate a take-off fit only for wheels and a destination with ground fit only for skis. This indicates that there is a need for a ski-wheel combination. **1958** *Edmonton* (Alberta) *Jrnl.* 24 June III. 17/8 A pilot on ski-wheels who runs into trouble will pick a lake or river, set down parallel to the shore, and ski neatly up onto the beach before his aircraft loses its forward momentum and sinks. **1976** *Jrnl. R. Soc. Arts* CXXIV. 634/2 Two ski-wheeled de Havilland Twin Otter aircraft are operational in the Antarctic between November and March.

ski, *v.* Add: **1. b.** To water-ski.

1947 *Life* 17 Feb. 7/3 Lumber dealers..have seen pictures of her skiing among the cypresses and want to know how they can purchase the trees. **1956** PETERSON & FISHER *Wild Amer.* ix. 101 A girl came by at breakneck speed on one water ski,..then three daredevil young men

..skied up and jumped over an inclined platform. **1970** 'D. Halliday' *Dolly & Cookie Bird* viii. 130 'Does Louie ski?' He swooped away, the spray flying.

2. *trans.* To travel over (a slope, etc.) on skis; to ski at (a place).

1973 P. A. Whitney *Snowfire* xii. 236 It's easier to ski a steep slope than a gentle one. **1980** *Sunday Times* 21 Sept. 8 Ski the top resorts in Europe..and now the U.S.A.

skiable (skī·ăb'l), *a.* [f. Ski *v.* + -able.] Of a slope, snow, etc.: capable of being skied on; fit for skiing.

1961 in Webster. **1963** *Amer. Speech* XXXVIII. 205 Inferior..heavy snow that is hardly 'skiable' for the average skier. **1969** *Observer* 14 Sept. 35/1 In every skiable side-valley, new resorts have sprouted. **1979** *United States 1980/81* (Penguin Travel Guides) 486 This..blown-out volcano is skiable from late October.

skiagraph, *sb.* Add: (Later examples.)

1925 [see *roetgenological* adj. s.v. *roentgen-, roentgeno-]. **1940** E. F. Benson *Final Edition* x. 208 When.. one of them suggested that an X-ray skiagraph should be taken, it showed osteo-arthritis in an advanced stage.

skiagrapher, (*b*) = Sciagrapher.

1957 V. Nabokov *Pnin* iv. 98 Lads..would spend years grinding colors in the workshop of some great Italian skiagrapher.

skiascopy (skəiæ·skŏ̆pi). *Med.* [ad. F. *skiascopie* (Chibret 1886, in *Arch. d'Ophthalmol.* VI. 147), f. Gr. σκιά shadow: see *-scopy.] Retinoscopy, esp. by means of a skiascope.

1886 *Amer. Jrnl. Med. Sci.* XCII. 248 Chibret proposes to employ the term 'skiascopy', in place of the terms keratoscopy, retinoscopy, pupilloscopy, and phantoscopy ..to designate this..method of determining the ocular refraction based upon the examination of the shadows which are formed in the eye when light is thrown into it. **1933** *Arch. Ophthalmol.* X. 689 Cycloskiascopy is more difficult than the classic method of cylinder skiascopy. **1958** *Ophthalmic Lit.* XII. 557 The term 'skiascopy' was proposed by Chibret instead of retinoscopy, as the retina is not normally in focus. **1976** *Ophthalmic Res.* VIII. 115 Data of skiascopy are not very exact because of the difficult procedure of measurement.

Hence **ski·ascope,** an instrument that directs light into a patient's eye along the line of sight of the examiner, so that the latter can judge the refraction of the eye from the movement of the illuminated area and the shadows as the light source is moved; **skiasco·pic** *a.*, of or pertaining to skiascopy; **skiasco·pically** *adv.*

1892 *Arch. Ophthalmol.* XXI. 422 A skiascope is now used at the Utrecht Clinique with glasses on each side which by combinations make a series of plus and minus D from 1 to 10. **1897** *Ibid.* XXVI. 598 A new hand at the sciascopic test. **1903** E. Clarke *Errors Accommodation & Refraction of Eye* vi. 77 Marple's skiascopes, made by Meyrowitz of New York, are very useful, and obviate the necessity for keeping a separate test case in the dark room. **1930** *Amer. Jrnl. Ophthalmol.* XIII. 102/1 Jackson measured skiascopically the symmetrical aberration in one hundred eyes. **1958** *Ophthalmic Lit.* XII. 557 Four important skiascopic fields are to be considered. **1971** *Biol. Abstr.* LII. 5247/1 (*heading*) Focal ophthalmoscopy with the help of a modified electric skiascope.

Skiatron (skəi·ătrǫn). *Electronics.* Also **skiatron.** [f. Gr. σκιά shadow + *-tron.] A proprietary name for a type of cathode-ray tube in which the electron beam produces a dark trace. Also *attrib.*, esp. as *Skiatron tube.*

1940 A. H. Rosenthal in *Electronics & Television & Short-Wave World* XIII. 52 (*heading*) The Skiatron—a new scophony development towards large-screen television projection. **1946** *Trade Marks Jrnl.* 26 June 330/2 *Skiatron*... Scientific apparatus and instruments, electrical apparatus and instruments included in Class 9. Scophony Limited... 17th Sept. 1945. **1947** L. J. Haworth in L. N. Ridenour *Radar Systems Engin.* xiii. 483 The alkali halides..have the property of darkening for a time at a point where they have been struck by an electron beam of sufficient energy. This phenomenon has been made use of in one form of cathode-ray tube, known as the 'skiatron'..used for projection purposes. **1948** *Electronic Engin.* XX. 21/2 (*caption*) Large screen plan position indicator with 'Skiatron' tube, as used by the Admiralty. **1953** *Official Gaz.* (U.S. Patent Office) 3 Nov. 21/2 *Skiatron*..for cathode ray tubes... Claims use since Aug. 1, 1942. **1966** H. H. Poole *Fund. Display Systems* ii. 32 The dark trace tube, also referred to as the Skiatron tube, is currently manufactured by National Union. It is available in screen sizes of 5, 7, 10, and 12 inches. **1973** C. J. Richards *Electronic Display & Data Systems* iii. 76 During the Second World War..the skiatron projection tube was used... Today a family of 'deformographic' tubes exists which can project a picture several metres across.

skid, *sb.* Add: **1. c.** *Oil Industry.* A skid beam (see sense 5 below).

1975 *Offshore Engin.* Oct. 66/1 The order for the skids went to Hopson, Co Durham. **1976** *Offshore Platforms & Pipelining* 20/2 Major items of drilling equipment represent skid sizes of available components.

2. c. (Earlier example.)

1782 'J. H. St. John de Crèvecoeur' *Lett. from Amer. Farmer* iii. 110 The logs were placed with skids, and the usual contrivances: thus the rude house was raised.

f. A runner attached to the underside of an aircraft. Cf. **tail skid*, **wing skid.*

1909 *Aëronaut. Jrnl.* XIII. 119/2 The tail of the machine rests on a small skid fixed to the frame. *Ibid.* 120/1 The wing tips are provided with light wheels and skids. **1909** A. Berget *Conquest of Air* ii. iii. 194 The planes rest upon two skids which form a kind of sleigh. **1947** A. C. Douglas *Gliding & Advanced Soaring* x. 259 Very close to the usual position of the release, will be the nose fitting of the skid. **1981** 'A. Hall' *Pekin Target* i. 11 We put the chopper down..on one skid and a rotor tip.

g. *pl.* In *fig.* phrases describing impending downfall or defeat; the way to failure or ruin: *to put the skids under* (a person or thing), to arrange the downfall of; to remove or oust (esp. from office), to get rid of; to cause to fail; *to hit the skids,* to enter a rapid decline or deterioration; *on the skids,* on the way to defeat or ruin; in a steadily worsening state. *colloq.* (orig. *U.S.*).

1918 H. C. Witwer in *Collier's* 9 Mar. 16/3 Me and Jeanne is gonna have a flat over in Brooklyn as soon as we put the skids under the Kaiser. **1920** —— in *Ibid.* 5 June 36/3 Kane Halliday, as the butlers was wonted to announce him previous to the time he hit the skids, was merely engaged to this gold mine. **1921** A. G. Empey *Madonna of Hills* lxi. 363 As yet it would be too dangerous to flaunt Davis openly, even if he was on the 'skids'. **1929** D. Hammett *Red Harvest* xii. 119 'What did Noonan put the skids under you for?' 'Skids? What skids? I quit.' **1938** A. J. Liebling *Back where I came From* 48 The men on the Bowery..had taken to hanging around saloons, drinking on empty stomachs. Eventually they had hit the skids and been forced to abscond from the genteel communities where their wives still lingered. **1943** M. McCarthy *Company she Keeps* v. 128 Capitalism was on the skids, and everybody ought to know about it. **1954** A. Melville in *Plays of Year 1954* (1955) XI. 26 You're too pigheaded to realise that the skids are well and truly under you. **1962** 'K. Orvis' *Damned & Destroyed* ix. 61 I'm on the skids. For good, it looks like. **1975** J. Symons *Three Pipe Problem* xvi. 165 A plan by one gang to put the skids under another. **1976** *Daily Mirror* 12 Mar. 23/4 They were only 378p when the £ hit the skids a week ago. **1977** *Irish Press* 29 Sept. 12/6 The Irish shoe industry, after being on the skids for six years, may be finding its feet again.

4. a. (Examples.)

1907 A. Bennett *Grim Smile of Five Towns* 192 At the bottom they had a severe skid. **1933** Kipling in *Strand Mag.* Feb. 131 The Cars put up an average bag of twenty dead per diem... And so began, in skid and stink, the real blood-sport of Britain. **1972** 'H. Calvin' *Take Two Popes* xi. 111 The cars touched gently at 100 kph, went into a skid together and slid on to the roadside verge.

b. *Aeronaut.* A movement of an aircraft that includes a sideways component, esp. away from the centre of curvature of a turn. Cf. *slip *sb.*[3] 9 j.

1916 H. Barber *Aeroplane Speaks* 83 The velocity of the 'skid', or sideways movement. **1942** *Tee Emm* (Air Ministry) II. 65 Do a quick barrel half roll with plenty of skid. **1952** A. Y. Bramble *Air-plane Flight* xiii. 199 Some pilots use the term 'slip' loosely to mean a skid. It is important to note the difference. A side-slip may occur whilst flying straight or *inwards* during a turn, but 'skidding' of the machine can occur only during yawing motion, and strictly, is always in the direction outwards, away from the turn.

5. skid beam: also *transf.*, a horizontal beam supporting a deck on an oil or natural gas platform; **skid-lid** *slang*, a motor-cyclist's crash-helmet; **skid mark,** the mark made on the road by the tyre of a skidding vehicle (usu. *pl.*); **skid-mounted** *a.*, mounted on runners; **skid-pan,** (*b*) a slippery road surface prepared to enable drivers to practise skid-correction; also *transf.*; **skid-proof** *a.*, of a road, etc.: on which one cannot skid or slip (esp. in wet conditions); designed to prevent skidding; hence as *v. trans.*, to render skid-proof; **skid road,** (*b*) N. Amer., orig. a downtown area frequented by loggers; now *gen.* = *skid row.

1976 *Offshore Platforms & Pipelining* 23 The distance between skid beams is the first dimension to consider when designing a platform rig. **1958** *Oxf. Mail* 8 Feb. 8/7 Skid-lids' importance stressed. **1968** R. V. Beste *Repeat Instructions* vii. 71 He wore the leather jacket and round skid-lid..usual to ton-up tearaways. **1977** C. Watson *One Man's Meat* xiii. 120 This bird in motor-cycle get-up ..with that great skid-lid hiding half her face. **1937** M. Allingham *Dancers in Mourning* iv. 59 The skid marks were easily discernible on the flint road. **1978** M. Gilbert *Empty House* v. 47 There were no skid marks, which would..indicate that he made no attempt to brake. **1960** *Farmer & Stockbreeder* 16 Feb. Suppl. 24/2 Being skid-mounted, it can readily be moved to a new site. **1975** *Petroleum Rev.* XXIX. 135/1 AOT will provide complete prefabricated skid mounted systems into which are built flowmeters, [etc.]. **1958** *Times* 17 June 9/6 On the skid pan (which is equivalent to a road covered with wet ice). **1959** *News Chron.* 12 Oct. 1/4 Rain turned many roads into skid-pans and caused hundreds of accidents. **1972** C. Mudie *Motor Boats & Boating* 108 The control of a car is exact and direct whereas a boat is on the skid pan of the sea. **1976** *Norwich Mercury* 17 Dec. 10/3 This thrilling game played at a terrific pace..on a greasy treacherous skidpan at Skinners Lane on Saturday. **1980** *Sunday Times* (Colour Suppl.) 21 Sept. 58/2 The first days of the course are instruction in evasive driving, done on a nearby skidpan. **1937** *Daily Express* 20 Feb. 10/2 Some roads are practically skid-proof, others not. **1958** *Washington Post* 25 Oct. B10/1 To skidproof concrete porch steps, it has long been the custom to sprinkle sand on freshly painted surfaces. **1906** *Log of 'Columbia'* i. 8/1 'We'll likely see him in town.'.. 'He'll be in the Skid road somewhere.' **1925** *Amer. Speech* I. 135 When the logger of to-day speaks of the 'skid-road' he means the place where loggers gather when they are in town. **1940** *Amer. Mercury* Dec. 412 Most of the skid-road bars provide either a floor show..or a hill-billy band. **1962** E. Lucia *Klondike Kate* iii. 98 Arriving in Dawson like some little tramp from Seattle's Skid Road. **1971** *Daily Colonist* (Victoria, B.C.) 15 May 5/5 Young heroin users are replacing the Skid Road addicts in British Columbia. **1980** *Washington Post* 1 Mar. A13/4 In Seattle, where the 'Skid Row' term originated 'from flophouses built along the 'Skid Road' of lumber being 'skidded' to the water front', reminders of that age remain.

Hence **ski·dded** *a.*, provided with a skid or skids.

1935 *Charlottesville* (Va.) *Daily Progress* 22 Feb. 1/1 He streaked off into the stratosphere at dawn today on a 2,447 mile flight to New York City where he planned to land on the wood skidded belly of the ship. **1961** *Flight* LXXX. 471/2 The lift platform was variously adjusted to handle simple cargo, general 'skidded' cargo and fully loaded vehicles.

skid, *v.*[1] Add: **3. b.** Also, of the vehicle itself.

1907 G. B. Shaw in *Neolith* Nov. 3 'The bus skidded.' 'So would any bus skid in this mud, going at that rate.' **1926** E. F. Spanner *Naviators* i. 13 A car that looks as though it is going straight can be dodged, but one that skids about like a demented dog chasing its tail is not to be faced with assurance. **1927** Kipling *Limits & Renewals* (1932) 159 It was raining hard, and the car skidded badly. **1966** G. Greene *Comedians* III. iii. 280 The car because of my momentary inattention skidded sideways.

c. *Aeronaut.* Of an aircraft: to move sideways, esp. away from the centre of curvature while turning. Cf. *slip *v.*[1] 9 c.

1911 *Daily Colonist* (Victoria, B.C.) (Mag. Section) 9 Apr. 9/5 If the rag points up, the operator knows his machine is going down..but if it points to the side, the operator knows he is 'skidding'. **1916** H. Barber *Aeroplane Speaks* 22 When an aeroplane is turned to the left or the right the centrifugal force of its momentum causes it to skid sideways and outwards away from the centre of the turn. **1942** *R.A.F. Jrnl.* 3 Oct. 35 He lost speed suddenly and skidded to the starboard. **1965** C. N. Van Deventer *Introd. Gen. Aeronaut.* x. 233/2 If the ball moves in the direction of the turn, it indicates that the airplane is slipping toward the inside of the turn... If the ball moves in the opposite direction, the airplane is skidding toward the outside of the turn.

d. *fig.* To follow an incorrect or unprofitable course; to make a mistake, to err or fail. Also of prices, etc.: to fall or decline rapidly. *colloq.* (chiefly *U.S.*).

1920 *Literary Digest* 22 May 120 Time was when the unsuccessful man merely failed, but these days, in a world scurrying about in motor-cars and breathing gasoline, he is said to 'skid'. **1937** G. Frankau *More of Us* vi. 67 Next morning woke a damsel heavy-lidded To wonder had she not, or had she, skidded. **1962** K. Orvis *Damned & Destroyed* iv. 29 He had skidded until he had become merely a brilliant young pianist. **1970** *Computers & Humanities* V. 11 Alabama Populists..tended mainly to be unsuccessful yeoman farmers who were skidding toward tenancy. **1976** *National Observer* (U.S.) 21 Aug. 8/6 A good investment..if some unforeseen misfortune causes currencies to skid.

4. *trans.* To cause (a vehicle, its wheels, etc.) to skid; to turn (a corner, etc.) by means of a skidding movement.

1924 'J. Sutherland' *Circle of Stars* xxiii. 238 Carter skidded the Ford to a standstill. **1928** *Sunday Express* 19 Aug. 1/1 Viscount Curzon..was cheered as he skilfully skidded the corners. **1931** G. Le Q. Martel *In Wake of Tank* 84 A turn through to a right angle absorbed so much power in skidding the track round that it was usually necessary to change down to first gear on the machine.

skidder, (*a*) (earlier example); (*b*) a tractor or other machine for skidding logs.

1870 *Overland Monthly* V. 56/1 Another, called the 'skidder', skids the road. **1905** [see *bummer 4]. **1945** B. MacDonald *Egg & I* (1946) 184 These toots were the signals given by the 'whistle punk' to direct the operations of the skidder bringing in the logs. **1965** *Weekend Mag.* 2 Oct. 3/3 Then it lays the denuded trunk on the ground and another machine, called 'a skidder', takes it to a landing area where it is cut into pulpwood lengths. **1976** *New Yorker* 3 May 52/2 The skidder, which vaguely resembles a pair of tractors coupled together..replaced the horse not long ago as the means of 'twitching' a tree ..from the cutter to the truck.

skid, *v.*[2] Add: **1.** Also, = Scud *v.*[1] 2.

1940 L. MacNeice *Last Ditch* 32 Toy sail skidding on Whitestone Pond at the peak of London.

2. *trans.* = Scud *v.*[1] 5 a.

1891 in *Eng. Dial. Dict.* **1897** G. B. Shaw *Let.* 1 Mar. in *Ellen Terry & Shaw* (1931) 159 Get ten sovereigns and skid them out from the beach into the sea.

skiddaddle, var. Skedaddle *v.* in Dict. and Suppl.

Skiddavian (skidē̆ⁱ·viăn), *a. Geol.* [f. *Skiddav-*, stem of latinized form of next + -ian.] = *Skiddaw *b*. Also *absol.*

1905 J. E. Marr in *Q. Jrnl. Geol. Soc.* LXI. p. lxxxi, The time-divisions which I would..propose to adopt for the rocks of this [Ordovician] system are as follows:— Ashgillian. Caradocian. Llandeilian. Skiddavian. *Ibid.* p. lxxxii, The beds tabulated above may..be taken as defining the upper and lower limits of the Skiddavian Series. *Ibid.* p. lxxxiii, *Didymograptus bifidus*..belongs to the top of the Skiddavian. **1929** W. W. Watts in Evans & Stubblefield *Handbk. Geol. Brit. Isles* 63 The Skiddavian fauna includes many species of *Didymograptus*. *Ibid.*, The Manx Slates of the Isle of Man are probably in part of Skiddavian age. **1955** G. G. Woodford tr. *Gignoux's Stratigr. Geol.* iii. 83 (*caption*) Upper Skiddavian: shales and sandstones of the upper Arenig. Lower Skiddavian: basal sandstone of the Arenig.

Skiddaw (ski·dǭ). *Geol.* The name of a mountain in the English Lake District, used *attrib.*: (*a*) in **Skiddaw slate(s)** (or **Slate(s)**), a thick group of slates, flags, and mudstones that outcrops in the northern part of the Lake District and out of which Skiddaw and neighbouring mountains have been eroded; (*b*) to designate the lowest division of the Ordovician in Britain, esp. in the Lake District.

1832 *Proc. Geol. Soc.* I. 401 Skiddaw slate.—The author briefly describes the range and extent of this group. **1855** J. Phillips *Man. Geol.* vi. 108 These..occupy a long range of mountains parallel to the Skiddaw slates. **1897** *Index Vols. I.–L. Q. Jrnl. Geol. Soc.* 357/1 Skiddaw age of Easdale Slates. **1900** *Proc. & Trans. R. Soc. Canada* VI. iv. 200 There is a remarkable similarity between the Ordovician of..Quebec and New Brunswick and the Ordovician of western Europe as developed in Great Britain: The Skiddaw and Arenig, the Hartfell and Llandeilo formations, being easily recognized in Canada. **1933** H. H. Symonds *Walking in Lake District* x. 255 Thus came the 'Skiddaw slate', that earliest rock of Cumberland, found *par excellence* in Skiddaw himself. **1969** Bennison & Wright *Geol. Hist. Brit. Isles* v. 102 The Skiddaw Slates have been slightly metamorphosed.. by later intrusions... However, the early Ordovician seems to have been devoid of igneous activity—unlike Wales—and only late in Skiddaw times did it commence. **1977** R. Prosser *Geol. explained in Lake District* i. 13 The oldest rocks [of the Lake District massif], the Skiddaw Slates.., have their main exposures north of a line from Ennerdale Water, past Derwentwater to Troutbeck and include the hill masses of the Skiddaw range.

skiddy (ski·di), *a.* [f. Skid *v.*[1] + -y[1].] Of surfaces, etc.: on which one is liable to skid; treacherously slippery. Also, characterized by skidding.

1902 *Car* 4 June 72/2 The state of a road which constitutes a 'skiddy' and a 'non-skiddy' surface. **1928** *Daily Express* 10 Dec. 19 Motorists drove with caution on skiddy roads. **1935** *Punch* 27 Mar. 358/3 Drive frightfully cautiously and go slowly round the corners.., because you *know* how skiddy it is these days. **1947** A. C. Douglas *Gliding & Soaring* 56 Another range of difficulties..caused by..dislike of being out of normal position in the air, resulting in flat skiddy turns, and so on. **1977** D. Murphy *Where Indus is Young* xi. 233 Skiddy mud making it impossible to keep upright.

skidoo (skidū·), *v.* *N. Amer. slang.* Also **skiddoo.** [Orig. uncertain, perh. f. Skedaddle *v.*] **1.** *intr.* To go away, leave, or depart hurriedly. Freq. *imp.*

1905 'H. McHugh' *You can search Me* i. 13 Skidoo, skidoo, and quit me, Mr. Josheimer! **1911** G. B. Shaw *Shewing-up of B. Posnet* 404 Outside, Nestor. Out you go... Skiddoo, Nestor. **1949** *New Yorker* 2 Apr. 26/3, I skiddoo and take a trip. **1963** B. Malamud *Idiots First* 135 'If you skidoo now..you'll get spit.' 'Who's skidooing?'

2. In catch-phrases. **a.** Used as an exclamation of disrespect (*for* a person). Esp. in nonsense association with *twenty-three.* (*temporary.*)

1906 J. F. Kelly *Man with Grip* (ed. 2) 99 As for Belmont and Ryan and the rest of that bunch, Skidoo for that crowd when we pass. *Ibid.* 118 'I can see a reason for 'skidoo',' said one, 'and for '23' also. Skidoo from skids and '23' from 23rd Street that has ferries and depots for 80 per cent. of the railroads leaving New York.' **1911** *Maclean's Mag.* Oct. 348/1 Surrounded by this conglomerate procession as I went on my way, the urchins would yell 'Skidoo,' '23 for you!'

b. *spec.* as *twenty-three skidoo*: formerly, a exclamation of uncertain meaning; later used *imp.*, go away, 'scram'.

1926 C. T. Ryan in *Amer. Speech* II. 92/1, I really do not recall which appeared first in my vocabulary, the use of 'some' for emphasis or that effective but horrible '23-Skiddoo'—perhaps they were simultaneous. **1929** *Amer. Speech* IV. 430 Among the terms which the daily press credits Mr. Dorgan with inventing are:..twenty-three skiddoo (go away). **1957** W. Faulkner *Town* iii. 56 Almost any time now Father would walk in rubbing his hands and saying 'oh you kid' or 'twenty-three skidoo'. **1978** D. Bagley *Flyaway* xi. 80 This elderly, profane woman..used an antique American slang... I expected her to come out with 'twenty-three, skidoo'.

Ski-doo, Skidoo (skidū·, skī·dū). orig. *N. Amer.* Also **skidoo.** The proprietary name of a motorized toboggan; hence *gen.* (with small initial), any motorized toboggan.

1961 *Time* (Canada ed.) 29 Dec. 10/1 To hear the Eskimos tell it, the Ski-doo is the greatest thing to hit the north since stripped blubber. **1963** *Globe & Mail* (Toronto) 2 Mar. 30/2 Fishermen..were getting to the choice spots the easy way, using skidoos. **1964** *Star Weekly* (Toronto) 19 Dec. 13/1 The first of these open-air snowmobiles was the Skidoo, originated by the late Armand Bombardier of Valcourt, Que., seven years ago. **1966** *Beaver* Winter 29/2 A trapper with a fast skidoo is able to cover his lines in a third of the time that it took him to do it by dog-team. **1969** *Trade Marks Jrnl.* (Canada) 23 July 961/2 Ski-doo... Filing date: Oct. 31 1968. Bombardier Limited, Valcourt, Quebec. **1969** *Guardian* 30 Aug. 4/5 It was this valley which one had originally proposed to travel along with the skidoos. **1973** C. Bonington *Next Horizon* xvii. 238 Do you want to go by Skidoo, or dog-team? **1977** *Courier-Mail* (Brisbane) 8 Mar. 5/5 One man..gave me a thrilling but hair-raising lift on his skidoo.

Hence as *v. intr.*, to travel by Skidoo; **skidoo·ing** *vbl. sb.*, **skidoo·er.**

1966 *North* (Ottawa) Nov.–Dec. 38 She now substitutes skidooing under the Midnight Sun for surfing on subtropical seas. **1968** J. G. Vermandel *So Long at Fair* xvii. 129 It was near one of those small hills that a skidooer came upon the body. **1975** W. S. Avis in *Occasional Papers Dept. English R. Military Coll. Canada* (1978) No. 2. 25 To skidoo. **1979** R. Fiennes *Hell on Ice* viii. 120 Charlie and I skidooed back to our abandoned tents. **1980** *Beautiful British Columbia* Winter 9 (*caption*) Skidooing near Fort St. John.

skid row (skid rōᵘ). Chiefly *N. Amer.* Also with capital initials. [Altered f. *skid road* (*b*) s.v. *Skid *sb.* 5.] **a.** Any run-down area of a town where the unemployed, vagrants, alcoholics, etc., tend to congregate. Also *fig.*

1931 G. Irwin *Amer. Tramp & Underworld Slang* 170 *Skid row*, the district where workers congregate when in town or away from their job. **1935** A. J. Pollock *Underworld Speaks* 107/1 *Skid row*, district in a city where tramps (bums) congregate. **1942** *Crisis* Oct. 314/1 Here, a short walk up from 'Skid Row',..is haven for men of all races. **1944** *N. & Q.* Nov. 120/2 A skidrow..is a district (mostly in western cities) where unskilled workers.. gather to look for jobs—a district of employment agencies, cheap flop-houses, etc. **1953** W. Burroughs *Junkie* viii. 80 When the time came for my sendoff shot, I was assigned to Ward B—'Skid Row', it was called. **1959** *New Statesman* 26 Dec. 899/2 Described in a report by a church mission as the nearest thing to 'Skid Row' that we have, it is a festering slum hidden in a narrow valley between the backs of lush shops in Firth Street, and Caxton Hill. **1963** *Economist* 13 July 125/1 The grisly inhabitants of the numerous urban 'skid rows'. **1977** D. M. Smith *Human Geogr.* xi. 338 The concentration of social deviants in the local 'Skid Row' produces freak figures.

b. *attrib.*

1948 *Sun* (Baltimore) 18 Sept. 3/2 Salisbury was a skid-row alcoholic when he was committed to Eloise. **1962** *Times* 1 Feb. 5/3 The 'skid-row' pictures painted in Seattle. **1973** E. B. Ritson in Howe & Loraine *Environmental Med.* xvi. 216 The grim environment of the skid-row districts of cities tends to attract social misfits. **1980** N. Marsh *Photo-Finish* i. 18 He disguises himself..like a Skid Row drop-out.

skier. (In Dict. s.v. Ski *sb.*) Add: (*a*) (later examples); (*b*) a water-skier. See also *Ski-ing *vbl. sb.*

1924 K. Furse *Ski-Running* 56 By his tracks shall a Ski-er be judged! **1941** *Life* 4 Aug. 54/1 In water-skiing the skiers hang on to a 75-ft. rope behind a speeding motorboat and skim along the water as fast as 45 m.p.h. **1959** P. Moyes *Dead Men don't Ski* iv. 48 Not a bad skier... Could have used him in the Team in the old days. **1973** V. Canning *Finger of Saturn* v. 97 The boat was moving into the small quay now. Its speed slackened and the skier dropped low into the water.

skiff, *sb.*[2] For *Sc.* read Chiefly *Sc.* and add: **1.** Also, a light flurry or cover *of* snow (N. Amer. examples).

1928 *Dialect Notes* VI. 88 *Skiff or skift* as applied to snow..means a thin coating. **1959** E. Collier *Three against Wilderness* xix. 193, I saw the track in a skiff of snow, half a mile from the cabin. **1966** M. & O. Murie *Wapiti Wilderness* iv. 44 We were glad enough to have a skiff of snow, it made study and counting of tracks so much easier. **1975** *Budget* (Sugarcreek, Ohio) 20 Mar. 10/5 The weather..has been colder with skiffs of snow here and there.

skiffle (ski·f'l). orig. *U.S.* [Origin unknown.] **1.** Formerly (*U.S.*), a style of jazz music popular at rent parties, deriving from blues, ragtime, and folk music, and played on standard and improvised instruments. Later, a form of popular music developed from this in the 1950s (esp. in the United Kingdom), in which the vocal part is supported by a rhythmic accompaniment of guitars or banjos and other more or less conventional instruments; a song written in this style. Cf. *Washboard.

1926 (*jazz-music title*) Chicago skiffle. **1930** *Paramount Dealers' List* Apr. 2/1, 12886—Home Town Skiffle—Part I. Descriptive Novelty—All Star. **1946** in Carey & McCarthy *Jazz Directory* (1949) 167 Dan Burley and his Skiffle Boys..Skiffle Blues. **1948** *N.Y. Age* 9 Oct. 2/7 Fletcher insisted on looking over the Skiffler's shoulder trying to dig the riffle that make the skiffle. **1957** *Times* 3 May 13/4 Earnest young women will not consent to hear even skiffle, unless they are sure of the reverberation factor of the sitting room. **1959** *Times* 27 June 7/3 Skiffle is a form of Do it Yourself that depends entirely on song and has the supreme merit of persuading its devotees to make music for themselves. **1966** P. J. Kavanagh *Perfect Stranger* xiv. 199 It was the age of skiffle but the ethos had reached Djakarta before the technique. **1973** 'J. Marks' *Mick Jagger* (1974) 55 Chris Barber and Ken Colyer were the leaders of the skiffle movement. I was with the very first Barber–Colyer Skiffle Band, and when they split up, I left because I didn't actually enjoy skiffle. **1976** *Jrnl. R. Soc. Arts* CXXIV. 603/2 One of the most cheering things that came out of skiffle was the fact that it got children singing, because they sang in groups.

2. *U.S. Blacks.* = *rent party* s.v. *Rent *sb.*[1] 4 c. (Perhaps the original sense.)

1946 [see *Percolator c]. **1956** S. Longstreet *Real Jazz Old & New* 126 You could always get together and charge a few coins and have a skiffle... The money paid the rent. **1974** [see *Percolator c].

3. a. *attrib.*, as *skiffle band, group, music.*

1957 *Sing Out!* Spring 30 In the first decade of the 20th Century, these New Orleans boys called themselves a 'Skiffle' band. **1981** *Washington Post* 8 Jan. DC7 The Sunshine Skiffle Band..has become a favorite at area folk festivals. **1953** *Melody Maker* 10 Oct. 15/1 London Jazz Club..Ken Colyer's Sensational Jazzmen and Skiffle Group. **1957** C. Brooke-Rose *Languages of Love* 215 A skiffle group—consisting of two guitarists, a thimble-fingered drummer with a wooden washboard, and a man sweeping a carpet-brush rhythmically over three metal strings drawn taut across a saucepan. **1976** *Dumfries & Galloway Standard* 25 Dec. 7/8 The 'Vipers' comprise five well-known artistes in their own right who get together to form a skiffle group. **1948** *Record Changer* June 5/2 The Jazz Room..will feature only the best of jazz and opening night featured..Freddy Moore, Kansas Fields, Dan Burley and his skiffle music. **1958** J. Asman in P. Gammond *Decca Bk. Jazz* xiv. 173 The phenomenon of skiffle music, peculiar only to Britain as yet, is well under way. **1978** *New York* 3 Apr. 73/2 Lonnie Donnegan was already a veteran performer in England when, in 1961, his recording of 'Does Your Chewing Gum Lose Its Flavor on the Bedpost Overnight?' introduced skiffle music to America.

b. General *attrib.* uses.

1946 [see sense 1 above]. **1948** *Record Changer* Aug. 5 Dan Burley, the skiffle man, is now a disc jockey. **1953** *Melody Maker* 19 Sept. 15/2 Club Calendar... London Jazz Club... Ken Colyer's Sensational Jazzmen, every Monday, with skiffle party. **1957** *Universe* 30 Aug. 8/3 There were lots of children's playclothes..'skiffle outfits' of jersey and jeans. **1965** G. Melly *Owning Up* xi. 135 He [*sc.* Ken Colyer] called these interludes 'Skiffle Sessions', to differentiate them from the more serious activity of playing blues, rags, [etc.].

Hence as *v. intr.*, to play skiffle music; **ski·ffler,** one who plays skiffle; a devotee of skiffle; **ski·ffling** *vbl. sb.*[2]

1948 *N.Y. Age* 9 Oct. 3/2 The skiffler's Club is one in which members control the titles of records selected for such programs. **1956** *Observer* 21 Oct. 13/3 The clientele whom the skifflers serve are almost wholly under-thirty, non-drinkers.., mainly middle-class. **1957** *Auckland* (N.Z.) *Weekly News* 2 Oct. 5 'Skiffling' is the latest craze to come to New Zealand. **1957** [see *Rock and roll *v.*]. **1959** H. Hobson *Mission House Murder* iii. 21 Anybody with floppy hair, a pair of tight jeans and a cheap guitar can be a skiffler in three easy lessons. **1974** *Times* 9 Jan. 12/7 That was the time when..those who did not rock skiffled away merrily.

skiffling (ski·fliŋ), *vbl. sb.*[1] [Cf. Scabbling, Scaffling, Scappling *vbl. sbs.*] (See quot. *a* 1877.)

a **1877** Knight *Dict. Mech.* III. 2195/1 *Skiffling*, knobbing. Knocking off the rough corners of ashlar in the preliminary dressing. **1901** J. Black *Masonry* 23 For ragstone ashlar work, the stone, when quarried, has its rough projections knocked off with a heavy double-pointed hammer... This operation is locally [*sc.* in Kent] called 'skiffling', and is the same as that known in the neighbourhood of London and other parts of the country by the term of 'knobbling'.

skift, *sb.*[3] (Earlier and later N. Amer. examples.)

1808 B. Hunt *Diary* 25 Dec. in *Chester Co.* (Pa.) *Hist. Soc. Bull.* (1898) 17 May be call'd green Christmass: a small skift of snow. **1927** *Amer. Speech* II. 364 *Skift of snow*, a small amount of snow. **1947** *Canad. Cattlemen* (Winnipeg) Dec. 148 Farmers regard 'a skift o' rain' as an adjunct to the fermentation of the natural juices in the semi-green corn blown into the [silo]. **1970** I. Petite *Meander to Alaska* iv. 34 We had seen practically every rock, headland, light, skift of sea birds rising, tree, and deserted beach cabin.

skift (skift), *sb.*[4] Var. Skiff *sb.*[1] *U.S. dial.*

1656 *Suffolk Co.* (Mass.) *Deeds* (1880) I. 2 [We are] desired by Jno. Blackman to App[rize] a smale skifte taken vp adrift. **1807** J. R. Bedford in *Tenn. Hist. Mag.* (1919) V. 118 They would board us in their skift without the inconvenience to us of going to shore. **1816** U. Brown *Jrnl.* 12 Sept. in *Maryland Hist. Mag.* (1916) XI. 222 Wm. Wells..prevails with me to go with him down the River 1½ Miles to what he called a skift. **1885** *Century Mag.* Aug. 505/2 Visitors call it a skiff, natives a skift. **1935** G. Santayana *Last Puritan* iii. x. 395 You were perfectly happy here, sculling in your skift.

ski-ing, *vbl. sb.* (in Dict. s.v. Ski *sb.*). Add: Also **skiing. 1.** (Later examples.)

1911 A. Bennett *Card* xi. 273 Ski-ing became the rage... The Captain said 'skee', but he did not object to 'shee'... People with no shame..said brazenly 'sky'. **1927** E. Hemingway in V. W. Brooks *Amer. Caravan* 46 In the Silvretta the ski-ing had been all right, but it was spring ski-ing. **1975** *New Yorker* 21 Apr. 40/3 It has been raining a lot, ruining the skiing.

2. Water-skiing.

1971 'D. Halliday' *Dolly & Doctor Bird* xii. 161, I have never yet met..a man who with greater clarity could teach me to water-ski... I made a reasonable success, for a beginner, at skiing.

3. *attrib.*

1921 A. LUNN *Alpine Ski-ing* 16 (*caption*) Ski-ing slopes at Scheidegg. **1932** AUDEN in *Rev. Eng. Stud.* (1978) Aug. 283 A waxen sandboy in skiing kit. **1946** G. MILLAR *Horned Pigeon* xx. 306 The first passengers to arrive.. wore ski-ing clothes. **1951** 'J. WYNDHAM' *Day of Triffids* vi. 107 She had chosen a dark-blue skiing suit. **1961** 'J. LE CARRÉ' *Call for Dead* xviii. 191 She met Dieter on a skiing holiday in Germany. **1978** S. SHELDON *Bloodline* ii. 30 He skipped skiing lessons in order to go into the village with Anna.

ski-joring (skīdʒōᵊ·riŋ). Also **skijoring.** [Semi-naturalized alteration of Norw. *ski-kjøring*, f. *ski* SKI *sb.* + *kjøring* driving (f. *kjøre* to drive).] A winter sport in which a skier is pulled over the snow by a horse or horses (or by a motorized vehicle).

1920 *Punch* 17 Mar. 204/1 Skating, sliding, curling and yodelling in the intervals of ski-ing, skijoring, skilacking and skihandlung. **1927** *Sunday Times* 13 Feb. 17/2 In the skijoring races on the Lake,..the well-known Swiss hockey player fell. **1946** G. STIMPSON *Bk. about Thousand Things* 473 The winter sport in which a person on skis is drawn over the snow or ice by a horse is called *skijoring*. **1963** *Guardian* 13 Feb. 13/3 Every type of winter sport.. skating, skijöring, bob-sledding. **1980** G. M. FRASER *Mr. American* xvi. 296 Ski-joring..is when you have horses to pull you along on skis.

Also **ski-jo·rer,** a skier who engages in ski-joring.

1936 'F. BEEDING' *Nine Waxed Faces* 193 Then..I led t back to where Granby was bending over the skijörer.

skil (skil). [a. Haida *sqil.*] = *SABLEFISH. Also **ski·lfish.**

1886 *Encycl. Brit.* XX. 170/1 Halibut, herring, salmon, cod, and coal-fish or 'skil' (this last also rich in oil and a valuable food-fish) are likewise abundant [off the coast of British Columbia]. **1897** C. R. TUTTLE *Golden North* 124 One of the most delicious of deep water fish is the skil, or black cod, as it is sometimes called. **1910** F. W. HODGE *Handbk. Amer. Indians* II. 591/1 Skil. A local name of the black candle-fish. **1923** D. K. TRESSLER *Marine Prod. Commerce* 736/2 Skilfish (*Anoploma fimbria*). A common food fish from Unalaska to Monterey. **1964** G. C. CARL *Some Common Marine Fishes Brit. Columbia* 48 The giant skilfish..may attain a weight of 200 pounds.

skilful, *a.* and *adv.* For 6 **skillful** read 6, 9— (chiefly *U.S.*) **skillful** and add examples of this form.

1891 J. W. STEVENS *Leather Manuf.* vii. 75 There are several machines for this work each of which will perform satisfactory work when managed by skillful hands. **1952** G. SARTON *Hist. Sci.* I. ix. 225 The power of Athens was based..also..upon the skillful use of all the resources that such places as Delos and Delphi offered. **1969** R. BUCKMINSTER FULLER *Operating Man. Spaceship Earth* i. 19 The myriad of physical, muscle, and craft-skill specializations which their intellect and their skillful swordplay commanded. **1972** P. H. KOCHER *Master of Middle-Earth* ii. 25 Their skillful blending as achieved by Tolkien requires some sophistication of understanding.

skill, *sb.*[1] Add: **6. a.** Also, an ability to perform a function, acquired or learnt with practice (usu. *pl.*).

1932 H. G. WELLS *Work, Wealth & Happiness of Mankind* xvi. 808 Unforgettable memories, obstinate prepossessions, life-worn traditions, obsolete skills and responses. **1938** *English* II. 20 It is the function of the educator..to enable the pupils to appropriate and use all that preceding generations have learnt, the useful skills, the practical knowledge, the social organizations, the moral principles. **1945** *Times* 29 Sept. 4/6 There is a sizeable body in Congress which believes..that this country should secure the greatest possible political advantage from its present monopoly of the actual manufacturing skills. **1958** *Listener* 12 June 976/2 There are ages of maturation at which it is appropriate to teach children skills like reading. **1964** P. STREVENS *Papers in Lang.* (1965) ii. 25 The national needs for foreign language skills in the nineteen-sixties are of a different order. **1975** *Language for Life* (Dept. Educ. & Sci.) xiii. 198 The advocates of this form of organisation say that these conditions lead to an assured attention to the 'basic skills'. **1980** *Times* 29 Feb. 19 For the advertising agencies a restricted market means that their skills will be needed more than ever.

9. a. skill centre orig. *U.S.*, a local training institution providing instruction in practical and technical skills, *spec.* in U.K. (**Skillcentre, skillcentre**), one sponsored by the government (cf. *job centre* s.v. *JOB *sb.*[2] 7).

1963 *Amer. Vocational Jrnl.* Dec. 33/2 The industrial situation assures the future of the area schools, but two problems involved are: (a) a common agreement on the type of regional education programs (i.e. state vocational schools,..vocational departments in comprehensive high schools, state skill centers), [etc.]. **1975** *Manpower Services Commission Ann. Rep. 1974–75* 8/3 The government training centres under their new name of 'skillcentres' were to be expanded. **1976** *Ibid. 1975–76* 16/3 These services include sponsored training at Skillcentres designed to enable firms to send employees to be trained to meet the firms' own precisely defined needs. **1977** *Daily Tel.* 12 Sept. 11 Technicians from the Government Skillcentres, who are of much higher standard. **1978** *Church Times* 27 Jan. 2/2 Skill centres and other training provisions for school-leavers and the young unemployed.

b. In *pl.*

1967 COULTHARD & SMITH in Wills & Yearsley *Handbk. Management Technol.* 196 Techniques of management by objectives, performance planning, and skills analysis are being more widely applied as they become increasingly effective in contributing to success. *Ibid.* 212 *Skills analysis*, the setting down of the underlying knowledge and dexterity which an operative will require in order to perform a given industrial operation. **1971** R. N. EVANS *Foundations of Vocational Education* III. xiv. 231 Unlike earlier manpower and anti-poverty training programs, Skills Centers could accept trainees whenever a training slot was open. **1976** *National Observer* (U.S.) 17 Apr. 14/5 The English teaching profession..has progressed..well beyond thinking of writing instruction solely or principally in terms of basic skills instruction. **1977** P. STREVENS *New Orientations Teaching of English* vi. 78 Shortcomings in demonstration and practice facilities affect the skills component.

skillet[1]. Add: **1.** Now chiefly *N. Amer.*, a frying-pan, a (heavy) cooking-pan.

1917 C. MATHEWSON *Second Base Sloan* vi. 73 [Nearby lay] an iron skillet with the handle broken off. **1932** W. FAULKNER *Light in August* xvii. 382 He stands, tall, misshapen, lonely in his lonely and illkept kitchen, holding in his hand an iron skillet in which yesterday's old grease is bleakly caked. **1959** A. SEXTON in *Audience* Autumn 31, I have found the warm caves in the woods, filled them with skillets, carvings, shelves, closets. **1968** *Globe & Mail Mag.* (Toronto) 13 Jan. 16/3 Cook, stirring constantly, over medium heat, until slightly thickened. Add frankfurters. Cover skillet, simmer 8 to 10 minutes. **1979** *Arizona Daily Star* 5 Aug. (Parade Suppl.) 12/4 Heat oil in paella pan or wide skillet.

skillet[2]. Add: **1.** (Later examples.) Also in more general applications.

1959 *Gloss. Terms Packaging* (*B.S.I.*) 19 *Skillet*, a piece of scored timber rotarily cut into veneers which forms part of the finished punnet. **1968** *Guardian* 18 Nov. 6/4 Mr Moreland keeps a selection of 'skillets' (flattened out matchboxes) in his wallet to pass round at social gatherings.

skillful, chiefly U.S. var. *SKILFUL *a.* and *adv.*

skilling, *sb.*[1] Add: Also 9 **skillen. 1. b.** (Earlier examples.)

1799 R. JOHNSON *Let.* 26 Aug. in *Evangelical Mag.* (1800) July 299 Blood was discovered in different parts, particularly in a small skilling, where, as afterwards appeared, my friend was dragged. **1826** J. ATKINSON *Acct. State of Agric. & Grazing in N.S.W.* 100 The barn may be built with lean-to's or skillings all round.

attrib. **1852** *Colonial Church Chron.* VI. 294 As is usually the case with bush houses, two skillen-rooms were to be added behind.

skillinger (ski·liŋgəɹ). *East Anglian local.* [f. corruption of *Terschelling*, the name of one of the West Frisian Islands in north-western Netherlands + -ER[1].] An East Anglian oyster smack operating off the north-western coast of Holland (see quots.).

1933 *Yachting Monthly* Aug. 265 Used for oyster dredging off the Terschelling light on the Dutch coast they [*sc.* large Brightlingsea smacks] were known locally as 'Skillingers'. **1959** P. NORTON *End of Voyage* xv. 107 Many of these larger smacks were ketch rigged... They were called 'Skillingers'. **1970** E. MARCH *Inshore Craft Gt. Brit.* I. vi. 192 Another ground lay off the Terschilling Light on the Dutch coast, which gave its name to the vessels working there—'Skillingers'.

skillion. For *Austr.* read *Austral.* and *N.Z.*, and add: Also 9 **skilion. 1.** (Earlier examples.)

1843 C. ROWCROFT *Tales of Colonies* I. vii. 120 At the back of the long room of twenty feet, a skillion, to serve as a kitchen, &c.

attrib. **1866** MRS. N. CHEVALIER *Reminisc. Journey* 23 The house consisted of a front room..a skillion kitchen with big fire, and one end of this skillion had a kind of shed.

2. (See quot. 1933.) Now *Hist.*

1846 C. P. HODGSON *Reminisc. Austral.* 39 Skillions formed by a sloping verandah to receive the sheep in from the fold as required. **1863** S. BUTLER *First Year Canterbury Settlement* x. 158 The wool-shed..[has] a large central space, and an aisle-like partition on each side.. for holding the sheep at night... In a wool-shed, the aisles would be called skilions. **1871** M. A. BROOME *Christmas Cake in Four Quarters* IV. iii. 279 There was the skillions standing empty, and the shearers lounging about idling when Christmas Day came. **1933** L. ACLAND in *Press* (Christchurch, N.Z.) 2 Dec. 15/7 *Skillion.* In old Australian and New Zealand books (up to about 1880) it is common and means the sheep-holding part of a woolshed.

3. Special Comb. **skillion roof,** a roof sloping from the side of a building; hence **skillion-roofed** *a.*

1911 J. NANGLE *Australian Building Practice* 171 *Lean-to Roof.* This kind (sometimes called a Skillion Roof) ..is generally used only in rear buildings, or verandahs where no ceilings are required. **1977** *N.Z. Jrnl. Science* XIX. 312 A skillion roof and other thin roof forms. **1967** J. MORRISON in *Coast to Coast 1965–66* 136 It was little more than a skillion-roofed shack.

skilly, *sb.* Add: **2.** *transf.* An insipid beverage; tea or coffee. Also *attrib.* and *Comb.* Chiefly *Naut. slang.*

1927 [see *MADAM *sb.* 3 c (*e*)]. **1933** J. MASEFIELD *Bird of Dawning* 214 The skilly-can, which may have contained a hot drink of some sort, was rolling with the whack-pots. **1935** —— *Victorious Troy* 37 There was a big old battered tin coffee pot containing skilly, or a brown, hot liquid, which the crew called 'tea' at night, and 'coffee' in the morning. **1936** B. M. ADAMS *Ships & Women* iii. 59 They said it was tea. Skilly, they called it. **1953** J. MASEFIELD *Conway* (ed. 2) III. 250 A cup of skilly completed the repast.

skim, *sb.* Add: **1. c.** (Earlier examples.)

1807 J. R. BEDFORD *Jrnl.* 22 Jan. in *Tennessee Hist. Mag.* (1919) V. 50 Nothing worth noting..but the intense severity of the cold..occasioning a very thin skim of ice on the river. **1869** 'MARK TWAIN' *Innoc. Abr.* xx. 206 It never has even a skim of ice upon its surface.

d. The fraction of latex which is poor in globules of rubber and is separated from the cream by centrifugation in the manufacture of rubber.

1928 *Brit. Pat. 319,410* 2/1 The concentrate contained approximately 0·07 and the skim about 0·14 per cent of ammonia. **1937** H. BARRON *Mod. Rubber Chem.* v. 57 Latex is separated into two portions, one containing about 60 per cent of rubber and very little serum constituents, while the 'skim' contains about 6 per cent rubber and nearly all the serum constituents. **1952** *Ann. Rep. Progress of Rubber Technol.* xvi. 21 A producer of latex concentrate has described a procedure for recovering the residual rubber from centrifuge skim or cream underlayer. **1972** *Materials & Technol.* V. xiv. 471 The whey or skim obtained after the concentration of latex still contains small amounts of rubber, which can be recovered as skim rubber.

5. *skim ice*; **skim-board,** a type of surf-board used for riding shallow water; **skim money** *slang*, a portion of the takings at a casino illicitly diverted in order to evade taxes.

1965 P. L. DIXON *Compl. Bk. Surfing* 143 Riding a skim board is simple to define, difficult to accomplish. **1972** *National Geographic* Nov. 688 Riding a skimboard, a youth glides over a comber-laved beach. **1938** W. FAULKNER *Unvanquished* 211 It lay with its body on the land and its head fixed in the skim ice like it was set into a mirror. **1974** J. KEATS *Of Time & Island* v. 74 You can see them [*sc.* fish] lying under skim ice in the shallows in the spring. **1973** W. MCCARTHY *Detail* iii. 144 They used her as a courier for skim money.

skim, *v.* Add: **2. b.** (Later *fig.* example.)

1926 W. R. INGE *Lay Thoughts of Dean* II. x. 157 Civilisation tends to sterilise the ablest part of a nation. In each generation it skims off the cream and leaves the milk thinner.

d. To conceal or divert (some of one's earnings or takings, freq. from gambling) to avoid paying tax on them; also *absol.* Also with *off.* *U.S. slang.*

1966 *Nat. Observer* (U.S.) 5 Sept. 7/3 Certain Las Vegas gamblers have been 'skimming' millions of dollars in casino winnings—taking a cut of the receipts before the tax collector had a chance to get his share. **1973** *Sun* (Baltimore) 24 July A7/8 Noting the frequent discrepancies in amounts of cash transferred between people and the huge sums involved, he asked: 'Do you have any information, Mr Strachan, of anyone skimming?' **1978** M. PUZO *Fools Die* xviii. 194 Gronevelt felt that hotel owners who skimmed money in the casino counting room were jerks, that the FBI would catch up with them sooner or later.

skimble-skamble, *sb.* Add: Also, writing of this nature.

1818 BYRON *Let.* 1 June in *Works* (1900) IV. xvii. 238 Did you read his skimble-skamble about Wordsworth being at the head of his own profession, in the eyes of those who followed it?

skimi, var. *SHIKIMI.

skimish (ski·miʃ). *slang.* [ad. Shelta *škimis* to drink, *škimišk* drunk.] Alcoholic drink; liquor. Also **ski·mished** *a.*, drunk.

1908 W. H. DAVIES *Autobiogr. Super-Tramp* xxiv. 211, I seldom lie down at night but what I am half skimished (half drunk), for I assure you I never go short of my skimish. **1936** J. CURTIS *Gilt Kid* iv. 40 He had been drinking all that skimish without having had a bite to eat.

skimmer, *sb.* Add: **1. c.** Esp. the black clam, *Cyprina islandica* (examples.)

1881 E. INGERSOLL *Oyster Industry* 248 *Skimmer*, the *Cyprina islandica*, or big beach clam. (South shore of Long Island.) **1949** R. J. SIM *Pages from Past* 65 The big surf clam, or skimmer (Mactra solidissima Chemn.), lies bedded down in great colonies off shore.

d. A device or craft designed to collect oil spilled on water.

1971 *Petroleum Rev.* May 203/2 (*caption*) The skimmer straddles the boom and the suction box is about to be immersed to suck up the oil floating on the surface of the water. **1976** M. MACHLIN *Pipeline* li. 516 Heavy duty floating skimmers will be deployed to recover as much oil as is feasible. **1977** *Times* 25 Apr. 1/4 A fleet of skimmers is steaming from Stavanger to suck up the oil and transfer it to waiting tankers.

3. b. One who conceals or diverts some of his earnings or takings in order to avoid paying tax on them. *U.S. slang.* Cf. *SKIM *v.* 2 d.

1970 *Wall St. Jrnl.* 23 Mar. 13/1 Some skimmers..give themselves away by keeping track of their true earnings. A New York dentist, for instance, devised a dot-dash code for his office records. **1978** S. Brill *Teamsters* vi. 241 The cash was being split, some to be counted for taxes and the rest to go to the skimmers.

6. c. A metal hook for trundling a child's iron hoop. Now chiefly *Hist.*

1891 R. Pearse Chope *Dial. Hartland, Devonshire* 70 *Skimmer*, a hooked iron rod used by children for trundling iron hoops without striking them. **1953** L. Daiken *Children's Toys* iii. 38 In Victorian times the old-fashioned metal hoop was controlled by a 'skimmer', the vernacular name for the hook-and-handle apparatus held in the hand. **1961** *Listener* 12 Oct. 549/2 For boys they [*sc.* hoops] were of iron, driven along and steered by an iron hook we called a skimmer. **1979** *This England* Winter 66/3 The tool used to both drive and check the hoop had a hook at the end of a short length of steel with a wooden handle, and was called the 'skimmer'.

7. b. (Later examples.) Also, a hydroplane, hydrofoil, hovercraft, or other vessel that has little or no displacement at speed.

1909 J. I. Thornycroft in *Engineering* 12 Mar. 365/1 Vessels which greatly reduce their displacement when travelling at high speeds are generally called 'hydroplanes', but this name is not altogether satisfactory, as the surfaces on which they glide are not always planes. To call such vessels 'gliders' or 'skimmers' has been suggested as more appropriate... The latter word will be used to describe boats which at high speeds are heavier than the water they displace. **1920** *Yachting Monthly* XXIX. 20 Owing to the fact that she was an unballasted skimmer she had an unfortunate habit of capsizing at moorings. **1945** J. J. Fahey *Pacific War Diary* 308 The General, Admiral, Captain and a few other officers left the ship in a skimmer for a picnic. **1967** (*title*) Jane's surface skimmer systems 1967–68. **1971** *Morning Star* 30 Mar. 9/1 Soviet sea-going skimmers type Kometa-M are furnished with log, radio, radar and other navigation safety instruments. **1975** *Sunday Mail Mag.* (Brisbane) 22 June 5/1 They are not hovercraft or hydrofoils but 'skimmers'—ships which can take off from the water and thunder along a few score cm above it, supported on huge airliner-type wings.

c. A hat; a broad-brimmed boater, esp. of straw. Formerly, *skimmer hat. slang* (chiefly *U.S.*).

1830 J. F. Watson *Annals of Philadelphia* 176 Other articles of female wear..[include] a 'skimmer hat',..of a very small flat crown and big brim, not unlike the present Leghorn flats. **1929** *Amer. Speech* IV. 430 Among the terms which the daily press credits Mr. Dorgan with inventing are:..skimmer (hat). **1939** M. B. Picken *Lang. Fashion* 73/3 *Skimmer*, flat-crowned sailor, usually of straw, having wide, straight brim. Worn and so-called by students at Eton College. **1946** *Sun* (Baltimore) 14 Jan. 12/1 New Yorkers who patronize such places pay several times over the original cost of their skimmers, in tips alone, during the course of a year. **1974** P. de Vries *Glory of Hummingbird* ii. 13 The thoroughly incompatible straw hat... The brightly banded boater, or 'skimmer' or 'katy'.

d. A sheath-like dress that fits closely to the lines of the body. Chiefly *U.S.*

1964 *N.Y. Times* 9 Dec. 5 Irish linen skimmer with a flirty scalloped hemline! **1968** *Tel.* (Brisbane) 2 Feb. 14/7 Cotton crepe skimmers..finished with set-in sleeves and a self bow trim. **1974** *News & Press* (Darlington, S. Carolina) 25 Apr. 3 (Advt.), Our large collection includes wraps, skimmers, pleated coat dresses, fit 'n flares [etc.].

8. b. *Cricket*, etc. A ball that travels with a low trajectory.

c **1868** in H. Chadwick *Scrapbks.* XI. 5/1 An over-throw of Hatfield allowed Wilkins to seize second; he then stole to third, and ran in on Fisler's 'skimmer' to left field. **1897** K. S. Ranjitsinhji *Jubilee Bk. Cricket* iii. 119 Strawyard promptly drives it just as expected—a real 'skimmer' 6 feet over extra-cover's head. **1908** *N.Y. Even. Jrnl.* 11 June 17/1 Twice Honus dug up slashing skimmers that Mike shot past Leach. **1911** P. F. Warner *Bk. of Cricket* v. 114 Haigh was bowling, and..Palairet batting, when a 'skimmer' came towards the pavilion straight for me. **1930** A. P. F. Chapman in Lonsdale & Parker *Game of Cricket* vii. 114 The catches sent him are a varied assortment—'skiers and skimmers'—but he rarely gets an easy one. **1980** *Amer. Speech 1976* LI. 294 Tennis slang... *skimmer*, ball gliding lightly and rapidly over the net.

9. skimmer-cake (earlier example); † **skimmer hat**: see sense 7 c above; **skimmer shell** *U.S.*, the shell of a clam or scallop (cf. sense 1 c in Dict. and Suppl.).

1795 J. Woodforde *Diary* 9 Feb. (1929) IV. 172 Dinner to day, boiled Beef & a Skimmer-Cake. **1880** *Golden Hours* XII. 520/1 Two pretty shells of the kind that children call 'skimmer shells'.

skimmi, var. *shikimi.

skimmia. In etym. for (Thunberg, 1784) substitute (C. P. Thunberg *Nova Genera Plantarum* (1783) iii. 57) and for def. read: An evergreen shrub of the genus so called, belonging to the family Rutaceæ, native to Japan, China, or the Himalayas, and bearing panicles of small white flowers followed by red berries. Cf. *shikimi. (Earlier and later examples.)

1853 *Curtis's Bot. Mag.* LXXIX. 4719 (*heading*) Japan Skimmia. **1908** G. Jekyll *Colour in Flower Garden* xi. 104 Here are green Aucubas and Skimmias. **1925** A. J. Macself *Flowering Trees & Shrubs* xi. 179 Cuttings of Skimmias root very well in sandy peat under bell-glasses. **1960** *Times* 24 Sept. 9/3 There are..the skimmias, but here we have to be..more careful, because some of them are monosexual. **1980** *Plantsman* I. 237 Skimmias prefer deep heavy fertile acid moist soils.

skimming, *vbl. sb.* Add: **2. b.** The practice of concealing or diverting some of one's earnings or takings to avoid paying tax on them. *U.S. slang.* Cf. *skim *v.* 2 d.

1966 *Economist* 10 Sept. 1023/3 The report ascribed the allegations of skimming and underworld connections to excessive zeal displayed by the department. **1966** *Wall St. Jrnl.* (Eastern ed.) 23 Nov. 32 The term 'skimming' refers to the alleged practice of some casino operators of failing to report the full amount of their gambling revenues to state and Federal tax authorities, and often distributing this unreported income to alleged secret interests in their casinos. **1970** *Ibid.* 23 Mar. 13/1 A few years ago in Philadelphia, the owner of a large pizza parlour was suspected of skimming. **1976** *National Observer* (U.S.) 23 Oct. 2/4 To correct the common practice of 'skimming' (underreporting the income from bingo games), the commission suggests that all states require operators to report the percentage of the take that actually goes to the intended charity. **1982** *Daily Tel.* 24 Aug. 11/2 Charged in connection with a 'skimming' operation—siphoning off money to avoid tax—at a Las Vegas casino.

4. skimming net, a fishing-net with a handle, a dip-net (earlier example).

1806 Lewis & Clark *Orig. Jrnls. Lewis & Clark Exped.* (1905) IV. xxv. 292 Those people have a number of buffalow robes. They have great number of skimming nets.

skimming, *ppl. a.* Add: **4.** *Cricket.* Of a bowler: that bowls the ball with a low trajectory (now *rare*). Also, of a shot which carries low and fast. Cf. *skimmer 8 b.

1851 W. Clark in W. Bolland *Cricket Notes* 132 Suppose you have what I call a skimming Bowler. **1888** A. G. Steel in Steel & Lyttelton *Cricket* iii. 165 The low skimming fast bowler is generally an easy man to play. **1930** *Morning Post* 9 Aug. 14/1 Woolley..made a low skimming drive over the ring at long-on for 6 off S. Staples.

skimobile (skī·mŏbīl). *N. Amer.* [f. Ski *sb.* + *-mobile.] **1.** A car or chain of cars used to carry skiers up a mountain; a ski-lift.

1946 *Richmond* (Va.) *News Leader* 9 Jan. 4/2 A skimobile ascends Mount Cranmore, near North Conway, N.H., taking skiers to the top of a 2,052 foot rundown. **1979** *United States 1980/81* (Penguin Travel Guides) 483 Its oddball skimobile is one of the oldest lifts in New England.

2. A small vehicle for travelling over snow, with caterpillar tracks at the back and steerable skis in front. Cf. *snowmobile. (Now the usual sense.)

1955 *Kingston* (Ont.) *Whig-Standard* 6 Apr. 25/3 With the advent of snowmobiles and skimobiles, most dog teams are now used for dog races. **1969** 'R. Stark' *Blackbird* (1970) xx. 127 There were a couple of skimobiles down there, little open scooters with skis in front and treads in back. **1974** R. B. Parker *God save Child* ii. 8 Shopping centers, a fish market, a skimobile shop.

skimp, *a.* (Later examples.)

1926 [see *love-curl* s.v. *love *sb.*[1] 16]. **1970** G. F. Newman *Sir, You Bastard* viii. 244 Sneed turned his attention to considering the skimp possibles; there were no probables for the job.

skimp (skimp), *sb.* Chiefly *dial.* and *colloq.* [f. the adj.] A small or insignificant piece *of* something; a small or scanty article, esp. a fashionably skimpy garment.

1862 C. C. Robinson *Dial. Leeds* 118 He thowt 'at t' moin was necessary tul his existence, and..he hed one māade o' white pāaper, an' oiled here an' thear, so as to resemble skimps o' cloud, as seen to the physical eye. **1925** *Bulletin* (Glasgow) 11 Apr. 10/2 She surreptitiously dabbed a little skimp of a handkerchief in her eyes. **1966** *Seventeen* June 92 A skimp..of stinging green French cotton. **1979** B. Malamud *Dubin's Lives* vi. 211 She wore a yellow skimp, her bosom snug in the fabric, her legs.. good to see in short dresses.

ski·mping, *vbl. sb.* [f. Skimp *v.* + -ing[1].] The action of the verb.

1898 A. Beardsley *Let.* Jan. (1970) 425, I must try and boil the book down but it's so rich and full of chances that skimping would be a sin. **1977** *Hot Car* Oct. 125/3 (Advt.), No skimping to cut cost.

skimpy, *a.* (Earlier example.)

1842 C. Ridley *Let.* 9 Oct. in *Cecilia* (1958) viii. 101 She had on her wedding dress which was very skimpy.

skin, *sb.* Add: **I. 1. c.** (Earlier and further examples in sense: a purse.) Also, a wallet, or a pocket-book.

a **1790** H. Potter *New Dict. Cant & Flash* (1795) 53 *Skin*, a purse. **1902** S. Clapin *New Dict. Americanisms* 365 *Skin*... A purse; a pocket-book. **1935** A. J. Pollock *Underworld Speaks* 107/1 *Skin*, a pocketbook or wallet. **1936** J. Curtis *Gilt Kid* xii. 137 Proper jobs I mean. Not nicking skins from blokes what are lit up. **1955** D. W. Maurer in *Publ. Amer. Dialect Soc.* xxiv. 114 Synonymous terms [of billfold] are *hide*, *skin*, or *poke*.

d. The integument of a bird or mammal, which is preserved but not mounted.

1840 W. Swainson *Taxidermy* i. iii. 84 The preservation of birds in skins, or, more properly, in an unmounted state, is, above all others, the best for scientific purposes. **1888** *Encycl. Brit.* XXIII. 90/1 Powders consisting of tannin, pepper, camphor, and burnt alum are sometimes used for 'making skins', but they dry them too rapidly for the purposes of 'mounting'... When 'skins' only are to be made for the cabinet, it is sufficient to fill the head and neck with chopped tow, [etc.]. **1964** G. Corbet in H. N. Southern *Handbk. Brit. Mammals* i. 117 There are two current methods of preparing study skins, resulting in 'round' and 'flat' skins respectively. The round skin, in which the skin is filled to simulate the shape of the body, is the traditional method..but flat skins are now usually preferred.

e. *spec.* A piece of sealskin or the like attached to the running surface of a ski to prevent slipping backwards during climbing. Also called *climbing skin.* Usu. *pl.*

1924 E. C. Richardson *'Shilling' Ski-Runner* (ed. 3) 11 Sealskins..are useful where long, unbroken ascents are to be made. By far the best kind are those which are stuck temporarily to the bottom of the ski... They are called, after their inventor, 'Sohm' skins. **1924** K. Furse *Ski-Running* 39 Skins are used for climbing uphill on tour. They consist of long strips of sealskin, which are attached to the running surface of the Skis. **1948** H. Innes *Blue Ice* vii. 192 The Norwegians use different waxes, not skins, for climbing through snow. **1966** M. Woodhouse *Tree Frog* xvi. 123 The back room, damp and musty with stored rugs and climbing skins. **1980** J. Cartwright *Horse of Darius* xii. 175 He fastened his skis, attached some skins and made the climb.

2. b. *U.S. slang.* A dollar.

1930 [see *by *prep.* 33 e]. **1950** [see *lip *sb.* 3 d]. **1976** R. B. Parker *Promised Land* xx. 121, I got a buyer with about a hundred thousand dollars..a hundred thousand skins.

3*. Chiefly *Jazz.* (*a*) A drum-head; (*b*) *slang*, a drum. Usu. *pl.*

1927 *Melody Maker* Aug. 756/1 Moisture from the breathing of the dancers will also condense on your side drum and the skins absorb this immediately. **1938** *Manch. Guardian Weekly* 2 Sept. 188/3 The swing musicians called 'cats' play..'skins' (drums) and 'woodpiles' (xylophones). **1945** L. Shelly *Jive Talk Dict.* 21 *Beatin' the skins*, striking the drums. **1980** *Musicians Only* 26 Apr. 12/5 They come in with skins with holes in.

II. 4. d. The bare (human) skin.

1922 Joyce *Ulysses* 748, I in my skin hopping around. **1956** H. Gold *Man who was not with It* (1965) xvi. 142, I asked her to bring her swimming clothes..because we were not to swim in our skins today. **1976** *Western Mail* (Cardiff) 27 Nov., The great day dawned, Wales v Africa, Wales in skins and Jack Sharkey's and S. Africa in white (skins meant no jerseys).

e. *U.S. Blacks' slang.* The skin of the palm of the hand, as making contact in shaking or slapping hands in friendship or solidarity. Freq. in phr. *to give* (*some*) *skin*, imp. *gimme some skin* (also as *sb.*).

1942 Z. N. Hurston in A. Dundes *Mother Wit* (1973) 223/2 'Gimme some skin!' 'Lay de skin on me, pal!' Sweet Back grabbed Jelly's outstretched hand and shook hard. **1944** D. Burley *Handbk. Jive* 85 The act of 'Gimme-some-skin' involves some theatricals, an intricate sense of timing, plenty of gestures. **1967** *Harper's Mag.* Nov. 62/2 Once—when I came in on the break behind him at precisely the right point—Pops gave me some skin. He reached out his dark old hand..and I turned my hand, palm up... Pops lightly brushed my open palm in a half-slap, the jive set's seal of approval. **1972** B. G. Cooke in T. Kochman *Rappin' & Stylin' Out* 33 The gestural expressions of 'giving skin' and 'getting skin' are very common in the black community. **1974** H. L. Foster *Ribbin', Jivin', & Playin' Dozens* iv. 119 The viewer of TV sporting events will often observe black athletes, and whites too now, giving skin after a home run, a touchdown, or at the start of a basketball game.

5. b. *skin and bone*(*s*) (further examples); hence *skin-and-bony* adj. Also *skin and grief.*

1886 H. Baumann *Londinismen* 180/2 *Skin-and-bones..*, *skin-and-grief*..haut und knochen, dürre Person. **1906** [see *gramophone]. **1912** D. H. Lawrence *Let.* 24 Dec. (1962) I. 172 They want me to have form: that means, they want me to have *their* pernicious ossiferous skin-and-grief form, and I won't. **1935** C. Day Lewis *Time to Dance* 61 You silly great fulminating bogeyman! You're nothing but a laugh and a daft skin-and-bony man. **1955** G. Greene *Loser takes All* i. vii. 43 The horse was all skin and bone and I had forgotten that the road was uphill. **1981** B. Granger *Schism* i. 9 The old man ..was just skin and bones. Maybe they could fatten him up.

e. (Later examples.)

c **1885** A. W. Pinero in M. R. Booth *Eng. Plays of 19th Cent.* (1973) IV. 338, I'm wet to the skin and frightfully hungry! **1938** R. D. Finlayson *Brown Man's Burden* 60 It was useless to try and find shelter, and the two runaways were soaked to the skin in a minute. **1974** S. Milligan *Rommel* 128 The rain had temporarily stopped... We were all soaked to the skin and bloody miserable.

i. (Further examples: cf. quot. 1896, sense 4 b, and sense *5 k (*b*).)

1886 G. B. Shaw *How to become Musical Critic* (1960) 115 The one [*sc.* actor] gets into the skin of one character: the other only puts on the clothes of twelve. **1916** J. R. Towse *Sixty Years of Theater* xxiii. 361 In the church scene, Miss Rehan won her audience by a fine display of honest womanly indignation, but she never really 'got into the skin' of Beatrice. **1959** M. Summerton *Small Wilderness* i. 11 He got under the skin of the rôle and lived it... He was given a small part in the spring production. **1963** *Listener* 28 Mar. 564/2 Those who enjoy the fun of getting inside someone else's skin.

j. *under the skin*, in reality, as opposed to superficial appearances. Esp. in phr. *sisters under the skin* (after quot. 1896).

1896 KIPLING *Seven Seas* 193 For the Colonel's lady an' Judy O'Grady Are sisters under their skins! **1946** A. CHRISTIE *Hollow* iii. 31 They were the same, sisters under the skin, Mrs. Pearstock from Tottenham and Mrs. Forrester of Park Lane. **1959** [see *IMPULSE *sb.* 5 c]. **1960** P. GALLICO *Mrs Harris goes to New York* ii. 24 Mrs Schreiber poured it all forth to her sympathetic sister-under-the-skin, Mrs Harris. **1960** *Economist* 8 Oct. 149/1 The old ladies who booed him..are sisters under the skin to the dockers who met him with a placard curtly advising him to 'drop dead, you bum'. **1975** D. FRANCIS *High Stakes* xi. 160 Merchant bankers are pirates under the skin. **1977** *Times* 19 Apr. 14/2 *Sub specie aeternitatis*, you might say, the Richmond dustmen and Jimmy Edwards are brothers under the skin.

k. *to get under* (a person's) *skin*, (*a*) to affect the deep feelings of; to irritate, to annoy; (*b*) to come to an understanding of, to empathize with.

1896 ADE *Artie* vi. 54 Say, Miller, if I was to beat his whole face off I could n't ketch even. He got way under the skin on me. **1927** H. T. LOWE-PORTER tr. *T. Mann's Magic Mountain* I. v. 300 What's the matter? Has anything got under your skin? **1927** H. CRANE *Let.* 12 Sept. (1965) 307, I think I really succeed in getting under the skin of this glorious and dying animal [*sc.* the Indian]. **1933** F. BALDWIN *Innocent Bystander* (1935) vii. 132 That pleased her, she had got under his skin, he had at least admitted something. **1938** E. BOWEN *Death of Heart* I. viii. 143 'That is why she annoys me so.' 'You once said she'd been very kind.' 'Indeed she has—that's her way of getting under my skin.' **1942** A. CHRISTIE *Five Little Pigs* I. iv. 32, I think you are interested in—character, shall we say?.. To get under the skin, as it were, of your criminal. **1948** L. A. G. STRONG *Trevannion* xvi. 297 'Aren't you perhaps afraid the inadequacy may be on your side?'.. 'Damn you, Walter. You do get under a man's skin.' **1972** D. DELMAN *Sudden Death* iii. 58 Do I bug you, Mr Mathews? Do I get under your skin? **1977** C. MCCULLOUGH *Thorn Birds* xvii. 455, I can keep you, because I'll never let you get under my skin.

l. *no skin off one's nose* and varr. (*colloq.*), a matter of indifference to one.

1920 S. LEWIS *Main Street* xxv. 312 Go to it. No skin off my ear, Nat. Think I want to be fifth wheel in the coach? **1926** —— *Mantrap* viii. 95 If you think..that it's any skin off my nose to lose the pleasures of your company..you got another think coming. **1930** *Amer. Mercury* Dec. 420/1 It ain't no skin off of Hymie's bugle. **1934** J. O'HARA *Appointment in Samarra* vi. 158 Okay. No skin off my ass. **1938** D. BAKER *Young Man with Horn* I. iv. 30 It was no skin off Jeff what color his old lady painted the piano. **1955** A. MILLER *View from Bridge* 102 Don't thank me... It's no skin off me. **1960** D. LYTTON *Goddam White Man* v. 113 But it was no skin off my nose that she was dead. **1963** *Australasian Post* 14 Mar. 51/2 If you want to yap on like a drongo in the DTs it's no skin off *my* bugle. Go ahead: be a gig! See if I care! **1966** J. PORTER *Sour Cream* v. 60 Our arrival was no skin off her nose and she didn't pay all that much attention to us. **1971** B. MALAMUD *Tenants* 35 Make it like eight [o'clock] or around that if it's no skin off you. If I miss a day don't fret on it. **1972** R. MILNER in W. King *Black Short Story Anthol.* 378 Then Clyde said it was no skin off his ass. **1978** L. MEYNELL *Papersnake* xiv. 188 It was no skin off my nose... My heart wasn't hurt, even if my pride was.

m. (*here's to the*) *skin off your nose* and varr.: used as a toast.

1925 FRASER & GIBBONS *Soldier & Sailor Words* 260 *Here's to the skin off your nose:* Your good health! **1936** WODEHOUSE *Young Men in Spats* ii. 42 'Well, skin off your nose,' said Pongo. 'Fluff in your latchkey,' said Barmy. **1949** [see *MUD *sb.*[1] 3]. **1959** D. EDEN *Sleeping Bride* ix. 85 Philip handed her a drink and she added, 'Here's the skin off your nose.'

n. *skin and blister*, sister. *Rhyming slang.*

1925 FRASER & GIBBONS *Soldier & Sailor Words* 260 *Skin and blister*, sister. (Rhyming slang.) **1935** G. INGRAM *Cockney Cavalcade* x. 170, I saw your skin and blister last night. **1972** G. F. NEWMAN *You Nice Bastard* 348 *Skin and blister*, sister.

7. f. The outermost layer of a pearl.

1885 *Encycl. Brit.* XVIII. 446/2 A pearl of the first water should possess, in jewellers' language, a perfect 'skin' and a fine 'orient'. **1935** L. KORNITZER *Pearls & Men* xix. 165 Keep on inspecting your pearl... When the blemish has been removed and a clean bright skin shows up, the worst is over. Smooth the skin with the finest emery paper you can obtain. **1976** B. W. ANDERSON *Gemstones for Everyman* xxiii. 300 The finest cultured pearls have come from waters off the north Australian coast... The oyster used here is the large *pinctada maxima*. The resultant cultured pearls are also large and have very thick skins.

g. The outer or surface layers of a conductor, in which alternating current tends to be concentrated at high frequencies.

1891 [see *skin effect*, sense 13 below]. **1891** [see *skin resistance*, sense 13 below]. **1893** J. J. THOMSON *Recent Res. Electr. & Magn.* iv. 260 When the vibrations are very rapid the currents are practically confined to a thin skin on the outside of the conductor. **1943** C. L. BOLTZ *Basic Radio* vii. 121 As the frequency is increased, the current is concentrated more and more in the outer layer—the 'skin'—of a conductor. **1958** J. SHEPHERD et al. *Higher Electr. Engin.* vii. 182 The effect increases with frequency, until at high frequencies the current is almost entirely in the 'outer skin' of the conductor.

h. *slang.* A tyre.

1954 *Rocky Mountain News* (Denver) 2 Sept. in *Amer. Speech* (1956) XXXI. 305 *Skin*, a tire. **1977** *Hot Car* Oct. 62/1 The answer is to run at the *same pressure* as the standard tyres, as by dropping the pressure any more than two pounds, you could cause sidewall failure, even in the big American skins.

i. A duplicating stencil; *spec.* the part that actually goes on the duplicator.

1965 G. M. BEER *Machines for Office Workers* iv. 73 When the [correcting] fluid is applied [to the stencil] it will..seep through the incisions and make the carbon.. adhere to the wax sheet; subsequently, at the duplicator, the carbon and backing sheets are removed, and in doing this it is..possible that the re-formed skin will also be detached so that both the incorrect letter, and the correction over it, appear on the duplicated sheet. **1972** T. LILLEY *'K' Section* xl. 203 She had typed the 'skin'; he would check it and then run off about four hundred copies. **1973** *Daily Tel.* 25 Apr. 13/8 It was then discovered that one foolscap duplicating skin could produce only 10,000 copies. Four skins had to be typed and 'run off'

8. c. *transf.* The outer covering of any craft or vehicle (or a constituent layer of this); esp. of an aircraft or spacecraft.

1921 *Flight* XIII. 247/2 The skin below the chines is formed of two thicknesses of mahogany planking... One ply of varnished cotton fabric is laid between the mahogany skins. **1937** *Jrnl. R. Aeronaut. Soc.* XLI. 846 It is proposed to form the skin of the wing from two separated sheets of plywood. **1948** 'N. SHUTE' *No Highway* iii. 64 Here in the aircraft everything was firm and steady and secure; the even tremor of the engines, the faintly heard rush of air over the outer skin, these bred confidence. **1962** G. COOPER in *Into Orbit* 29 The crews are equipped with.. a fire axe for cutting through the capsule's skin. **1973** *Times* 3 May 4/1 They found that the whole of the skin of the caravan was full of blocks of cannabis. **1973** TERRY & BAKER *Racing Car Design & Development* vi. 135 Increasing safety-consciousness caused the FIA to stipulate that, for 1972, the outer skins of all Formula 1 monocoques had to have a maximum thickness of 16 swg. **1977** D. BEATY *Excellency* i. 8 The company to which it [*sc.* an aircraft] belonged had been painted out... What remained against the silver duralumin skin was AN—.

9. b. *U.S. slang.* = SKINFLINT.

1900 ADE *More Fables* 30 Some of the Folks.. used to say that Henry was a Skin, and was too Stingy to give his Family enough to eat.

c. Without contemptuous implications: a person (of a specified kind). Chiefly *Anglo-Ir.*

1914 JOYCE *Dubliners* 152 Ah, poor Joe is a decent skin. **1939** 'F. O'BRIEN' *At Swim-Two-Birds* 166 A decent skin if ever there was one, said Slug with warmth, a man that didn't stint the porter. **1958** B. BEHAN *Borstal Boy* III. 258 These were lies..that Cragg was muttering about the Colonel, who wasn't a bad old skin at all,..since he got to know us. *Ibid* 266 He seemed a decent old skin. **1966** F. SHAW et al. *Lern Yerself Scouse* 22 *Ee's a good skin*, he is an agreeable fellow.

d. *slang.* A horse or mule.

1923 E. HEMINGWAY *Three Stories & Ten Poems* 32 They take the first batch of skins out to gallop. **1925** FRASER & GIBBONS *Soldier & Sailor Words* 260 *A skin*, a horse: mule. **1941** BAKER *Dict. Austral. Slang* 67 *Skin*, a horse, 'generally the property of a professional wayfarer'.

e. *slang.* = *SKINHEAD 2 (*b*).

1970 *Daily Progress* (Charlottesville, Va.) 15 Apr. 7/1 You gotta decide what family you are going to join, the hairies or the skins. **1978** R. WESTALL *Devil on Road* iv. 26 Those Midland sods must be crazy... I shouted the rudest things you can shout at skins. **1981** *Times* 22 July 11/3 'There's good and bad skinheads,' is as far as he will go... The picture is complicated: there are black skins, and there are non-violent skins... Certainly, many of the skins are thugs.

9*. *U.S.* A card game in which each player has one card which he bets will not be the first to be matched by a card dealt from the pack.

1925 *Messenger* Dec. 386/1 Playing 'skin' for matches. **1935** Z. N. HURSTON *Mules & Men* I. iii. 72 Ah played skin wid de Devil for mah life. **1973** J. SCARNE *Scarne's Encycl. Games* xvi. 310/1 The game of Skin is dead even; that is, dealer and player have exactly equal chances of winning. **1978** MOORE & LEVINE *Big Paddle* (1979) i. 15 Larsen loves skin. He'll go all over looking for a skin game.

9.** *the Skins*, the nickname of the 5th Royal Inniskilling Dragoon Guards or, formerly, the Royal Inniskilling Fusiliers [properly a corruption of *Inniskilling*, assimilated to the sb.].

1938 R. HAYWARD *In Praise of Ulster* 235 The Indian Mutiny, South Africa and the Great War brought fresh glories to the valiant 'Skins'. **1949** ST. J. ERVINE *Craigavon* II. xlvi. 233 The history of 'the Skins', the nickname of the Inniskilling Fusiliers, is rich with the jewels of courage. **1954** L. MACNEICE *Autumn Sequel* 67 The Skins have gone to Kenya with their trousers smartly creased. **1981** J. JOHNSTON *Christmas Tree* 25 Did you have a brother in the Skins?

III. 10. a. *skin care, colour, -flake, -tissue.*

1954 V. DENGEL *All about You* vi. 141 There are four points to proper, daily skin care. **1969** V. J-R. KEHOE *Technique Film & Television Make-Up* (ed. 2) iii. 40 (*heading*) Skin care products. **1972** *Sat. Rev.* (U.S.) 27 May 18/2 The idea of discrimination based on skin color is beyond their comprehension. **1930** E. POUND *XXX Cantos* xv. 66 Skin-flakes, repetitions, erosions. **1944** *Horizon* Mar. 172 The grey matter of the brain-rind was originally skin-tissue. **1949** M. MEAD *Male & Female* i. 19 The sensitivity of our skin-tissues.

b. *skin-bag, -boat* (earlier and later examples), *-cover.*

1860 Skin-bag [see *ATTA]. **1910** W. DE LA MARE *Three Mulla-Mulgars* xxviii. 237 Having cut one of their skin-bags to pieces. **1804** W. CLARK in *Orig. Jrnls. Lewis & Clark Expedition* (1904) I. 87 The Indians pass this river in Skin Boats which is flat and will not turn over. **1968** G. JONES *Hist. Vikings* I. i. 17 These hunters, fishermen, and food-gatherers from the south..developed the skin-boat. **1954** J. R. R. TOLKIEN *Fellowship of Ring* ix. 408 They drew the skin-covers over their boats.

11. a. *skin-fitting.*

1915 D. H. LAWRENCE *Rainbow* iv. 91 She wore an elegant, skin-fitting coat. **1947** *Science News* IV. 11 The men who went into enemy ports during the war wore skinfitting dresses.

b. *skin-grafting* (earlier examples).

1870 *Lancet* 27 Aug. 306/2 (*heading*) Skin-grafting. *Ibid.* 22 Oct. 566/2 Mr. Francis Mason has performed the operation of skin grafting on granulating surfaces in nine instances.

12. a. *skin-covered.*

1897 YEATS *Secret Rose* 1 A large house with skin-covered wattles for the assembly. **1977** *Proc. R. Soc. Med.* LXX. 234/1 Any open lesion is more dangerous than a skin-covered one.

b. *skin-thin* adj.

1946 W. DE LA MARE *Traveller* 12 Their skin-thin gills. **1966** P. SCOTT *Jewel in Crown* IV. 171 The tough little shell of skin-thin masculinity that used to harden the outward appearance of the British military wives.

13. skin-beater *slang* (now *Obs.* or *rare*), in a jazz- or dance-band: a drummer; **skin beetle** *U.S.*, a greyish-brown beetle of the genus *Trox* or a brown, hairy beetle of the family Dermestidæ, feeding on carrion or other organic material; **skin-changer,** one supposedly able to metamorphose himself or herself; **skin cream,** an oleaginous cosmetic preparation for care of the skin; **skin depth** *Electr.* [cf. sense *7 g], the distance from the surface of a conductor at which an electromagnetic wave of a given frequency is attenuated by a factor of $1/e$ ($e = 2{\cdot}718\ldots$); also *fig.*; **skin-drying** *vbl. sb.* (*Founding*), drying of the surface of a greensand mould before casting; so **skin-dried** *a.*; **skin effect** *Electr.*, the tendency of an alternating current of high frequency to flow through the outer layers only of a conductor, resulting in an increase in effective resistance; **skin flap** *Surg.*, a portion of living skin attached to the body by one edge so that it remains alive while it is used to close a wound after amputation, or in plastic surgery; **skin-flick** *slang*, a film of a pornographic type; **skin-food** (examples); **skin friction,** add: *esp.* the friction between the surface of an aircraft or the like and the air; (further examples); **skin game,** (*a*) (earlier example); also *transf.* and *fig.*; (*b*) the pornography trade; (*c*) = sense 9* above; a game of this; **skin graft,** a piece of living skin which has been surgically transferred to a new site or to a different individual; also, the process of making such a transfer; **skin house** *slang*, (*a*) a gambling establishment; (*b*) an establishment providing pornographic entertainment; **skin magazine** *colloq.*, a magazine containing nude photographs, a pornographic magazine; **skinman** (further examples); **skin packaging,** a method of packaging in which the article, placed on a backing plate which is to form part of the package, has a plastic film cover thermoformed on to it; **skin pass** *Metallurgy*, a final cold-rolling, effecting a small reduction in thickness, given to heat-treated strip steel in order to improve surface and mechinical properties; **skin-pop** *v. intr.* (*slang*, orig. *U.S.*), to inject a drug subcutaneously (cf. *MAIN-LINE *v.*); so as *sb.*, the action of skin-popping; also *fig.*; hence **skin-popper; skin-popping** *vbl. sb.*; **skin potential,** the electrical potential between different points on the skin, esp. as exhibited in the galvanic skin response; **skin resistance,** † (*a*) = *skin friction* above; † (*b*) the resistance of the skin (sense *7 g) of an electrical conductor; (*c*) the electrical resistance of the skin of an organism; **skin-search** *sb.* and *v.* (*slang*) = *strip-search* sb. and vb. s.v. *STRIP *v.*[1] 24 a; **skin test** *sb.*, a test to see whether an immune reaction is elicited when a substance is applied to or injected into the skin; so **skin-test** *v. trans.*, **skin testing** *vbl. sb.*; **skin tonic,** a cosmetic astringent for the skin; **skin trade** (orig. *U.S.*), commerce in animals' skins; also *fig.*; also = *skin game* (*b*) above.

1936 *Amer. Mercury* XXXVIII. p. x/2 *Skin beater*, the drummer man. **1953** *N.Y. Times Book Rev.* 13 Sept. 33/3 Red, the reefer-smitten skin beater. **1842** T. W. HARRIS *Treat. Insects New Eng. Injurious to Vegetation* 11 Skin-beetles.., bone-beetles..act the useful part of scavengers. **1895** J. H. & A. B. COMSTOCK *Man. Study Insects* 559 The skin-beetles..are small or of medium size. **1942** [see *larder beetle* s.v. *LARDER[1] 3]. **1972** SWAN & PAPP *Common Insects N. Amer.* xx. 436 Skin beetles feed on carrion, skin, feathers, and dung. **1927** E. V. GORDON *Introd. Old Norse* 224 Berserks were probably named 'bear-shirts' from a superstition that they were 'skin-changers'. **1937** J. R. R. TOLKIEN *Hobbit* vi. 121 He is a skin-changer. He changes his skin: sometimes he is a huge black bear, sometimes he is a great strong black-haired man with huge arms and a great beard. **1907** *Yesterday's Shopping* (1969) 537/1 Violet oatmeal skin cream. **1979** P. FERRIS *Talk to me about England* III. 133, I appear to be missing a pot of special vitamin skin-cream. **1941** J. A. STRATTON *Electromagn. Theory* ix. 536 One may assume for conductors of arbitrary cross section that the field and current distributions near the surface differ negligibly from those near the surface of an infinite plane provided the radius of curvature is very much greater than the skin depth. **1962** CORSON & LORRAIN *Introd. Electromagn. Fields* x. 338 The skin depth decreases if either the conductivity σ, the permeability K_m, or the frequency f increases. **1966** *Listener* 5 May 653/3 Myshkin's apparent niceness and gentleness, his ridiculousness, are the surface, the skin depth of his assumed role. **1954** Skin-dried [see *skin-drying* vbl. sb. below]. **1970** E. PARKES et al. in K. Strauss *Appl. Sci. in Casting Metals* ix. 321 (*heading*) Skin dried and dry sand moulding. **1888** *Lockwood's Dict. Mech. Engin.* 324 Skin drying effects the removal of a portion of the moisture and diminishes the risk of a blown or a scabbed casting. **1954** J. E. GARSIDE in A. J. Murphy *Non-Ferrous Foundry Metall.* v. 171 Pouring should be completed as soon as possible after skin-drying owing to the fact that the moisture from the backing sand slowly penetrates towards the skin-dried mould face. **1891** *Electrician* 29 May 91/1 Sir William Thomson recalled attention to the tendency of alternating currents to avoid the central portions of metallic conductors, thereby giving rise to an increase of resistance which has been occasionally alluded to under the name of the 'skin effect'. **1965** *Wireless World* Aug. 401/1 The h.f. resistance is increased partly by skin effect, and more significantly by eddy currents induced in the lossy magnet system. **1873** *Brit. Med. Jrnl.* 15 Mar. 286/2 He took a large skin-flap from the front below the knee, a smaller flap behind, and left just enough of the bones to fit an apparatus. **1974** R. M. KIRK et al. *Surgery* v. 73/2 Skin flaps are used to close large defects in situations where sound healing is essential, when good quality of skin is desirable and when the local blood supply would not sustain free grafts. **1968–70** *Current Slang* (Univ. S. Dakota) III–IV. 110 *Skin flick, n.* A pornographic movie. **1969** *Daily Colonist* (Victoria, B.C.) 7 June 13/3 We ran family movies for nine years and almost went broke. For the last three years, we've been showing skinflicks and doing much better financially. **1975** P. WEBB *Erotic Arts* viii. 280 In the '60s..film-makers became aware of the commercial possibilities of the voyeur film, or 'skin-flick'. **1898**, etc. Skin-food [see *FOOD *sb.* 2 b]. **1977** B. PYM *Quartet in Autumn* ix. 81 Turning her attention to the wash basin she noted..a jar of skinfood and a tube of Steradent tablets. **1907** F. W. LANCHESTER *Aerodynamics* vi. 220 In actual planes it is impossible to do away with thickness, so that in addition to skin friction there must be the possibility of a longitudinal pressure component due to the shape of the plane. **1919** R. H. GODDARD *Method of Reaching Extreme Altitudes* 9 The resistance, R, may be taken as independent of the length of the rocket by neglecting 'skin friction'. **1948** *Sci. News* VII. 24 In the same way a body moving through air loses energy by skin friction (analogous to conduction). **1978** *Jrnl. R. Soc. Arts* CXXVI. 683/1 During acceleration to supersonic speeds the external surface of the structure becomes hotter due to skin friction from the air flow. **1868** M. H. SMITH *Sunshine & Shadow in New York* 405 The square game..is played only by gentlemen, and in first-class houses;..the skin game..is played in all the dens and chambers, and in the thousand low hells of New York. **1904** W. H. SMITH *Promoters* 98 We built the bridges finally,..for we weren't really working a skin game. **1920** GALSWORTHY *Skin Game* I. 19 She wants to sell, an' she'll get her price, whatever it is. *Hillcrist.* (*With deep anger*) If that isn't a skin game..I don't know what is. **1958** *Economist* 1 Feb. 398/2 The..ironies of German political life: the strange mixture of elements.. that mingle in the Bonn skin game. **1970** *Times Educ. Suppl.* 18 Dec. 1/1 The censor and the skin game. **1973** J. SCARNE *Scarne's Encycl. Games* xvi. 308 (*heading*) The skin game. **1973** E. MCGIRR *Bardel's Murder* i. 10 As a very small [antiques] dealer, I was no opposition... His business is rather a skin game. **1976** *Globe & Mail* (Toronto) 7 Jan. 10/3 The long-respected publication had been sold and new publishers had changed big game to the skin game. **1978** Skin game [see sense 9* above]. **1871** *Lancet* 22 Apr. 535/1 On taking off the plaster the skin-grafts were found adhering. **1930** A. H. DAVIS *Burns* xxi. 195 Most surgeons..find that heteroplastic skin grafts are universally unsuccessful. **1935** P. H. MITCHINER *Mod. Treatment of Burns & Scalds* v. 54 Riverdin's or Thiersch's skin grafts give excellent results. **1977** D. BAGLEY *Enemy* xxxi. 251 Gillian..had just had the operation for the first of the skin grafts. **1871** *Galaxy* XII. 61 A 'skin' house, as the dens where cheating games are played are called. **1902** FARMER & HENLEY *Slang* VI. 227/1 *Skin-house*, a gambling den. **1970** *Harper's Mag.* July 34 The skin houses were mostly playing short subjects—a girl taking a bath in a sylvan stream, a volleyball game in a nudist camp. **1972** *Dict. Contemp. & Colloq. Usage* (Eng. Lang. Inst. Amer.) 27/1 *Skin house*, a theater featuring nude women or films of nude women. **1972** J. WAMBAUGH *Blue Knight* (1973) i. 29 Some gunsel I'd heard was hanging out in the skin houses and taxi-dance joints. **1968** *Rat* 13–16 May 11/1 Two prophylactics and a skin magazine was found in President Kirk's drawer. **1980** *Cosmopolitan* May 319/1 Men often use pictures as stimulation when they masturbate (hence the popularity of so-called skin magazines), but women do so much less often. **1829** P. EGAN *Boxiana* 2nd Ser. II. 220 At a proper age, JEM turned out to earn an honest penny, and was apprenticed to a *skyver*, or skinman, in Newcastle-upon-Tyne. **1970** M. TARMEY *Skinman* vi. 128 He sat hunched and helpless in the chair.., a skinman without any skins. **1962** A. L. GRIFF *Plastics Extrusion Technol.* vi. 122 In skin-packaging, the coated board can now be the base, while coated flexible film can be the skin. **1971** *Engineering* Apr. 63/2 Two commercial systems of skin packaging are in general use. The Soag-Stanley process uses an uncoated board, the other a coated and perforated board. **1939** J. DEARDEN *Iron & Steel Today* x. 149 A single pass through a skin pass mill then brings it to its final thickness. **1977** R. B. ROSS *Handbk. Metal Treatments & Testing* 351 On the production side, the Skin pass will be used to produce the final surface finish and simultaneously achieve slightly improved mechanical properties. **1953** KRAMER & KARR *Teen-Age Gangs* i. 35 You get a big fat mouth every time you give that leg of yours a skin-pop. *Ibid.* 243 *Skin-pop*, to inject drugs, usually heroin, under skin into body. **1959, 1964** [see *MAIN-LINE *v.*]. **1971** 'D. HALLIDAY' *Dolly & Doctor Bird* xvi. 242 You can't deny we gave your social habits a skin-pop. **1970** *Daily Tel.* 30 Jan. 19/1 She had also 'skin-popped' (injected drugs just below the surface of the skin) and taken a vast assortment of pills. **1953** KRAMER & KARR *Teen-age Gangs* i. 35 A very expert skin-popper, Hoppy is. **1970** H. WAUGH *Finish me Off* 48 No marks. She must be a skin-popper. **1952** *Sunday Times* 3 Feb. 5/4 'Skin popping'..consists of scratching open a place in the skin and injecting heroin or morphine there. **1970** *Observer* 3 May 3/1 When the addicts run out of veins to inject, because of scars and ulcers, they try skin-popping—injecting just under the skin or into a muscle. **1936** *Amer. Jrnl. Physiol.* CXVII. 189 (*heading*) Skin potential and impedance responses with recurring shock stimulation. **1967** VENABLES & MARTIN *Man. Psychophysiol. Methods* ii. 58 The permeability of the cell membrane is a physiological phenomenon, and measurements of skin resistance and skin potential must be made within physiological limits. **1875** *English Mechanic* 3 Sept. 634/3 We have sufficient data from which the skin-resistance [of a ship's hull] can be determined. **1891** *Jrnl. Inst. Electr. Engineers* XX. 479 When we deal with conductors of about a centimetre in diameter there is no apparent effect of this skin resistance. **1895** H. LAMB *Hydrodynamics* xi. 575 The frictional or 'skin-resistance' experienced by a solid of 'easy' shape moving through a liquid. **1904** *Jrnl. Franklin Inst.* CLVII. 248 The skin resistance of copper bonds increases with time. **1927** *Brain* L. 231 We have learned that the skin resistance is invariably decreased both by pain and by elevation of body temperature. **1942** S. R. HATHAWAY *Physiol. Psychol.* xi. 236 The level of skin resistance has a low inverse correlation with neuroticism. **1971** *Jrnl. Gen. Psychol.* LXXXV. 88 Each record was analyzed by recording the averaged skin resistances for the last two minutes of the resting period and for each minute of the stimulus film period. **1935** A. J. POLLOCK *Underworld Speaks* 107/2 *Skin search*, an arrested person who is stripped naked and his body thoroughly searched for narcotics. **1970** G. JACKSON *Let.* 4 Apr. in *Soledad Brother* (1971) 212 Our cells were being invaded by the goon squad: you wake up, take your licks, get skin-searched. **1973** *Time* 26 Mar. 64 So far, none of the three new guards in California's state prison system for men have been assigned to conduct 'skin searches' of nude prisoners for contraband. **1979** F. FORSYTH *Devil's Alternative* xvii. 386 If you are thinking of giving me a weapon, don't bother. On my return I am to be skin-searched. **1925** W. W. DUKE *Allergy* xv. 207 She gave positive skin tests to a number of extracts including wheat. **1943** W. C. BOYD *Fund. Immunol.* xi. 424 Patients should not be skin tested without previous adequate history and physical examination. **1961** *New Scientist* 16 Mar. 696/1 All the components cause a positive reaction in the skin tests commonly used for allergic responses. **1971** R. SCOTT *Wedding Man* ii. 65 Every Asian child was skin-tested [for tuberculosis] as soon as possible after arrival. **1925** W. W. DUKE *Allergy* xv. 206 One's first impression of skin testing is likely to be one of disappointment. **1963** L. V. CRAWFORD in F. Speer *Allergic Child* xxvii. 420 Although the mechanics of skin testing are simple, considerable experience is required for proper interpretation. **1906** *Daily Colonist* (Victoria, B.C.) 27 Jan. 5/1 (Advt.), Special Sales. Toilet Goods..Skin Tonics. Perfumes. **1971** M. LEE *Dying for Fun* xxxiv. 167 The fragrance of Lapsang Souchong, mingled with the tang of skin tonic. **1710** W. BYRD *Secret Diary* (1941) 186 About 5 o'clock Robin Hix and Robin Mumford came to discourse about the skin trade. **1885** *List of Subscribers, Classified* (United Telephone Co.) (ed. 6) 101 (*heading*) Fur and skin trade. *a* **1953** DYLAN THOMAS (*title*) Adventures in the skin trade. **1977** *Time* 19 Sept. 41/1 The city [*sc.* Boston] set aside this seedy downtown area three years ago for X-rated movies, porn shops and other facets of the skin trade—in hopes of being able to contain them.

skin, *v.* Add: **II. 4. d.** *to skin the cat* (U.S.), to perform a gymnastic exercise involving passing the feet and legs between the arms while hanging by the hands from a horizontal bar and so drawing the body up and over the bar; also *transf.* and *fig.*

1845 S. JUDD *Margaret* II. i. 199 Their several diversions, snapping-the-whip, skinning-the-cat, racing round the Meeting-house, or what not. **1888** 'C. E. CRADDOCK' *Story of Keedon Bluffs* v. 88 He did not wait a second but 'skinned the cat' among the rafters. **1905** *N.Y. Even. Post* 14 Oct., We have learned how to hide behind the back log of 'environment' or to 'skin the cat' in morality on the score of 'heredity'. **1907** C. E. MULFORD *Bar-20* viii. 80, I used to shinny up this here wall an' skin th' cat getting through that hole up there. **1931** *Sun* (Baltimore) 29 May 12/7 You saw them skin the cat On the high trapeze. **1946** B. TREADWELL *Big Bk. Swing* 125/2 Skin he cat; ride, brother, ride.

e. To keep (one's eyes) open. *U.S. colloq.*

1865 *N.Y. Herald* in Farmer & Henley *Slang* (1891) II. 361, Keep a padlock on yer mouth and skin yer weather eye. **1875** J. G. HOLLAND *Sevenoaks* x. 133 Skin yer eyes, now, Mr. Balfour, we're comin' to a lick.

f. *fig.* To beat or overcome completely. *U.S. slang.*

1862 *Charleston* (S. Carolina) *Mercury* 9 Aug. 1/5 They were 'skinning' the soldiers of other regiments the 'tallest kind'. **1911** H. QUICK *Yellowstone Nights* iv. 110 'Purty good little places,' said he, 'but the home place skins 'em all.' **1981** *Verbatim* VII. III. 7/2 Puns ('Eagles *skin* Washington')..offer limitless possibilities to the enterprising sports journalist.

7. b. (Earlier examples.)

1819 *Massachusetts Spy* 24 Mar. 3/1 They will not be able to skin the people as deep as they did during their former reign. **1839** C. F. BRIGGS *Harry Franco* II. vi. 76, I wish I may be blown into a gin shop if I warnt skinned clean O! The young woman had..picked my pockets of every cent.

9. a. (Earlier examples.) *Obs.*

1835 J. TODD *Student's Manual* (ed. 3) 115 Should you allow yourself to think of going into the recitation-room, and there trust to 'skinning', as it is called in some colleges. **1837** *Yale Lit. Mag.* Feb. 138 A student is said to skin a problem, when he places the most implicit faith in the correctness of his neighbor's solution of it, or at least sufficient to warrant bestowing upon it the rites of adoption.

b. For *trans.* read *intr.* and add: Also with *through*, to slip through, to pass by a narrow margin. *U.S.*

1902 G. H. LORIMER *Lett. Self-Made Merchant* xi. 141 If you would make a downright failure or a clean-cut success once in a while, instead of always just skinning through this way. **1920** W. CAMP *Football without Coach* 57 The best a runner can hope for is a chance to skin through that opening before it ceases to exist.

c. (Earlier example.)

1873 J. MILLER *Life amongst Modocs* iv. 44 Four aces! and what else? Skin 'em out, skin 'em out!

III. 11. *trans.* and *intr.* To inject (a drug) subcutaneously. Cf. *skin-pop* v. s.v. *SKIN *sb.* 13. *slang.*

1953 W. BURROUGHS *Junkie* vi. 57 He had to shoot in the skin about half the time. But he only gave up and 'skinned' a shot after an agonizing half-hour of probing and poking and cleaning out the needle, which would clog up with blood. **1970, 1972** [see *MAIN *v.* 2].

skinch (skintʃ), *v.* and *int. north* and *Midland dial.* [Origin unknown.] **A.** *v. intr.* To encroach, to cheat. **B.** *int.* A formula used by children in a game to demand a truce.

1891 S. O. ADDY *Gloss. Words Sheffield* Suppl. 52 *Skinch, v.* to encroach, to shorten distance. When a boy playing at marbles moves his taw nearer to the ring than he ought to do he is said to *skinch, i.e.*, to encroach unfairly. **1893–4** O. HESLOP *Northumberland Words* II. 649 *Skinch!* the cry for parley in a boys' game. **1914** D. H. LAWRENCE *Prussian Officer* 262 Willy could hear the endless calling and shouting of men's voices. 'Tha'rt skinchin!' **1959** I. & P. OPIE *Lore & Lang. Schoolch.* viii. 150 'Croggie' is..general in West Hartlepool although the usual term in County Durham is 'skinch'.

skin-diver. [f. SKIN *sb.* + DIVER.] One who dives or swims underwater without a full diving suit or a fixed line to the surface. Hence **skin-diving** *vbl. sb.* and *ppl. a.*; [as back-formation] **skin-dive** *v. intr.*, to dive or swim underwater as a skin-diver; also as *sb.*, an act or instance of skin-diving.

1932 *Blackw. Mag.* Jan. 20/1 They relied solely upon their skin divers—the divers' technical term for a naked man. **1938** D. LONG *Sailing all Seas in Idle Hour* ix. 121 The finest 'skin' divers in the world come from lonely atolls such as Penrhyn, where only 'skin' diving is allowed. **1950** SCHENK & KENDALL *Shallow Water Diving* iv. 74 This equipment is used in the sport commonly known as 'Goggling' or 'Skindiving'. **1951** *Skin Diver* Dec. 2 The name of *The Skin Diver* was picked because it includes everyone interested and participating in underwater fishing and hunting. *Ibid.*, We want to publish any and all items of interest to our skin diving readers. **1952** *Time* 17 Nov. 50/3 Bucher, poised on the rail of the small ship bobbing in the rough water, was aiming to become the first man ever to 'skin-dive' (*i.e.*, without the aid of artificial breathing apparatus) deeper than 115 ft. **1953** J. Y. COUSTEAU *Silent World* i. 9 Vanity coloured our early skin dives. We plumed ourselves at the thought that we latecomers could attain the working depths of pearl and sponge divers who had made their first plunges as infants. *Ibid.*, Dumas's skin-diving technique consisted of floating face under water and breathing through a schnorkel tube. **1959** L. SMITH *One Hour* v. 69 For hours, we'd engage in this philosophical skin-diving. **1964** M. MCLUHAN *Understanding Media* xxiii. 233 The smarter advertisers have made free with fur and fuzz, and blur and buzz. They have, in a word, taken a skin-dive. For that is what the TV viewer is. He is a skin-diver, and he no longer likes garish daylight on hard, shiny surfaces. **1966** T. PYNCHON *Crying of Lot 49* iii. 57 There stood Di Presso, in a skin-diving suit and wraparound shades. **1970** *Daily Colonist* (Victoria, B.C.) 14 Oct. 7/6 At Taveuni, the prince took time off to swim and skindive. **1973** J. LEASOR *Host of Extras* vii. 127 He adjusted his mask and went over backwards in the way of the trained skin-diver. **1975** *N.Y. Times* 6 Nov. 20/2 Skindiving Israeli scientists are exploring the sunken fortifications of the city of Acre. **1977** B. PYM *Quartet in Autumn* iv. 37 'It's the swimming that would attract me.' 'You mean skin-diving and that sort of thing?'

skinflinty, *a.* (Earlier example.)

1886 F. R. STOCKTON *Casting away of Mrs. Lecks & Mrs. Aleshine* II. 122 If he undertook to be skinflinty he'd better try it on somebody else besides us.

skin fold. *Med.* Also **skin-fold, skinfold.** [f. SKIN *sb.* + FOLD *sb.*[3]] A fold of skin and underlying fat formed by pinching, as a measure of nutritional status; freq. *attrib.*, as *skinfold thickness*; **skinfold cal(l)iper(s)**, a pair of callipers for measuring the thickness of such a fold.

1921 *Amer. Jrnl. Physical Anthrop.* IV. 224 For the estimate of the quantity of the skin and of the subcutaneous fat, the writer uses the thickness of the skin fold on the upper arm, above the biceps; on the forearm ..and on the abdomen. **1950** *Nutrition Abstr. & Rev.* XX. 250 Pinching a skinfold to obtain a rough estimate of the thickness of the subcutaneous adipose tissue and, by inference, of the fatness or leanness of a subject, is an old clinical procedure. **1954** *Jrnl. Lab. & Clin. Med.* XLIII. 969 The skinfold thickness is read to the nearest half millimeter on the slide scale. *Ibid.* 970 A skinfold caliper..which is easily manipulated with one hand. **1961** L. MARTIN *Clin. Endocrinol.* (ed. 3) ii. 54 Measurements by skin-fold calipers have shown that from birth until three months..there is a rapid increase in fat deposition. **1973** *Times* 17 May 20/1 Using skinfold calipers, designed by and for doctors working on obesity, the thickness of the fat layer at four sites on the body is measured. **1977** *Lancet* 1 Jan. 17/2 Skinfold thickness measurements provide a non-invasive and reproducible means of measuring subcutaneous fat in newborn babies.

skinful. 3. a. (Earlier example.)

1788 *Columbian Mag.* Oct. 557/2 Determined, as they said, once more to get *a skin-full of liquor.*

ski·nhead. *colloq.* [f. SKIN *sb.* + HEAD *sb.*] **1.** (A person with) a bald head.

1953 BERREY & VAN DEN BARK *Amer. Thes. Slang* (1954) §430/5 Bald-headed man,..cue ball, skinhead, turret top. **1957** M. SHULMAN *Rally round Flag, Boys!* vi. 66 Oscar was a bow-legged, barrel-chested man with a skin head. **1976** 'O. JACKS' *Assassination Day* v. 85 'Ow long you gonna be, skinhead?.. Your wig's slipping.

2. A person with a shaven head or closely cropped hair; *spec.* (*a*) a recruit to the U.S. Marine Corps; (*b*) in the U.K., a youth (often one of a gang), also typically characterized by wearing workman-like clothing and heavy boots, and by a tendency to aggressive behaviour.

1953 BERREY & VAN DEN BARK *Amer. Thes. Slang* (1954) §825/2 Cue ball, skinhead, a fellow with a crew haircut. **1956** *Amer. Speech* XXXI. 190 He will administer a royal chewing out (tongue lashing) to the hapless skinheads (recruits; so-called because of their completely shaven heads). **1969** *Daily Mirror* 3 Sept. 12/1 A group of teenagers..wear tight and rather short jeans, collarless T-shirts, exposed braces, big steel-capped boots and hair erased almost to their scalps. The lack of hair is what gives them their generic names..crop-heads, skin-heads or peanuts. The boots are good for kicking. **1971** *Daily Tel.* 13 Apr. 1 Gangs of Hell's Angels and skinheads marred Easter Monday seaside outings. **1973** C. MULLARD *Black Britain* IV. xi. 131 According to an eye-witness a gang of white skinheads savagely attacked a black youth who today is nearly blind as a result. **1975** I. SHAW *Nightwork* vii. 84 The skinheads are preparing the ground... One morning we'll wake up and the tanks will be rolling down Pennsylvania Avenue and the machine guns will be on every roof. **1978** *Lancashire Life* Apr. 27/1 The index can be visualised: Beats, Jesus Freaks, Groupies, Skinheads, Punks..the procession seems endless, and to many is evoked by one word—Hippies. **1980** *Herald* (Melbourne) 9 Apr. 5/3 Thousands of skinheads shouting Nazi slogans invaded the resort in special trains.

skinless, *a.* Add: *spec.* of sausages and similar meats.

1954 *Food Manufacture* 1 Nov. p. xi (Advt.), Visking food and sausage casings are..available through Viskase Limited... Visking Nojax for skinless sausages. **1959** E. H. CLEMENTS *High Tension* vi. 119 'He'd bring.. *cevabcici*—'... 'Sausages, you mean.' 'Oh yes... Special skinless ones..from a shop in Soho.' **1968** R. CLAPPERTON *No News on Monday* v. 52, I helped myself to a couple of skinless sausages from the refrigerator. **1972** D. BLOODWORTH *Any Number can Play* xvii. 170 He..had..eaten a tin of skinless frankfurters with a purée of mashed yam.

skinned, *ppl. a.* Add: **II. 4. b.** (Earlier example.)

1833 *Political Examiner* (Shelbyville, Kentucky) 22 June 4/1, I wish I may be shot if I dont think you had better keep your eyes skinned so that you can look powerful sharp, lest we get rowed up the river this heat.

c. Beaten, bested, overcome completely; esp. in *to have* (*got*) (a person or object) *skinned. colloq.* (orig. *U.S.*).

1904 'O. HENRY' *Cabbages & Kings* iii. 56, I guess you've got us skinned on the animal and vegetation question. **1908** 'YESLAH' *Tenderfoot S. Calif.* ii. 22 When it rains in California, it's got all the rest of the country skinned to death. **1913** R. BROOKE *Let. c* 23 July in *Coll. Poems* (1918) Mem. p. lxxxiv, 'Sir, I may tell you that in my opinion you have Mr. Noyes skinned.' That means I'm better than him. **1927** E. WALLACE *Feathered Serpent* iv. 47, I came down here to make a few inquiries... I've got these reporter guys skinned to death!

d. = *SKINT *a.* Also with *out. colloq.*

1935 A. J. POLLOCK *Underworld Speaks* 107/1 *Skinned out*, broke; without funds. **1957** C. MACINNES *City of Spades* I. xii. 93 Why's he left me skinned in hopeless destitution? **1958** *Observer* 14 Dec. 7/8 I'm skinned, I know I can always count on someone helpin' me.

skinner[1]. Add: **2. b.** An implement used for skinning animals.

1872 *Amer. Naturalist* VI. 223 The specimen could have been used as a knife, or 'skinner', although now its edge is too irregular and dull for skinning.

4. b. (Later examples.)

Esp. common in Australia to mean (*a*) a horse that wins a race at very long odds; (*b*) any betting coup.

1903 A. M. BINSTEAD *Pitcher in Paradise* xii. 292 A skinner!—great-balls-of-fire! a skinner! **1907** A. WRIGHT *Keane of Kalgoorlie* 66 Although he had gone up in the weights considerably, his owner decreed that he should win the Rosehill handicap, and give the 'shop' another 'skinner'. **1930** *Technique of Betting* 7 Frequently a race is won by a horse against which the bookmaker has not laid any bet, and the book then shows a profit of 100%—the bookmaker has what he calls a 'skinner'. **1934** T. WOOD *Cobbers* viii. 96 Charles..would lay two to one port-wine jelly, five to apple-pie... Tonight we had college pudding and jam tart. Charles..said it was a skinner for the books. **1974** *Sydney Morning Herald* 8 Oct. 17 Skinner for bookmakers. **1977** A. C. H. SMITH *Jericho Gun* v. 60 At twelve to one, which is the forecast SP here, it's a skinner.

7. A driver of a team of horses or mules; occas. also, a lorry driver. *N. Amer.*

1870 [see *mule skinner* s.v. *MULE[1] 5 c]. **1910** E. FERGUSON *Janey Canuck in West* 91 The teamsters are called 'skinners'. I met them all on the log road. **1924** *Scribner's Mag.* Dec. 645/1 The skinner with the longest words travels the fastest. **1929** *Amer. Speech* V. 147 Since the driver of the old time orecar was called a *mule-skinner* or *mule-whacker*, the driver of the modern motor-propelled car is a *motor-skinner*, sometimes just a *trammer*. **1939** J. STEINBECK *Grapes of Wrath* ii. 14 A guy that never been a truck skinner don't know nothin' what it's like. **1954** E. F. HAGELL *When Grass was Free* 3 A single line attached to the next leader's bit and passed back along the teams to the teamster or 'skinner'.

8. *a skinner* semi-adj.: 'skint', broke; empty. *N.Z. colloq.*

1943 *New Writing* XVIII. 68 So I paid for the pair of us, which left me practically a skinner. **1967** *Landfall* XXI. 241 Sure you're a skinner? Not a drop in the place, I mean? **1981** *Macquarie Dict.* (s.v. *skinner*), The beer's a skinner.

Skinner[2] (ski·nəɹ). The name of the American psychologist, B. F. *Skinner* (b. 1904), used *attrib.* to indicate the theories or methods concerned with conditioning human or animal behaviour associated with him; esp. as *Skinner box*, a box in which an animal is isolated, equipped essentially with a bar or other device that it learns to use either to obtain a reward or to escape punishment.

1938 *Jrnl. Exper. Psychol.* XXIII. 507 A modified form of the Skinner apparatus. **1940** *Ibid.* XXVI. 614 (*heading*) The variability of extinction scores in 'Skinner-box' experiments. **1951** E. R. HILGARD in S. S. Stevens *Handbk. Exper. Psychol.* 530/1 It is possible to train animals in the Skinner box to do what the experimenter wishes. **1962** *Listener* 13 Sept. 390/1 The technique for measuring the pressure applied to a lever by a rat in a Skinner-box. **1973** *Nature* 27 July 241/3 The method of 'operant conditioning' in a Skinner box can be used to investigate physiological changes that accompany habit formation. **1980** BROWN & WALLACE *Physiol. Psychol.* xv. 457 Most of the principles of learning were derived from studies on a single animal (the white rat) in a single learning situation (instrumental conditioning in the Skinner box).

Skinnerian (skinīə·riăn), *a.* and *sb.* [f. prec. + -IAN.] **A.** *adj.* Of or pertaining to B. F. Skinner's behaviourist theories or methods. **B.** *sb.* A follower or adherent of B. F. Skinner.

1958 *Psychol. Bull.* LV. 148/2 The studies to be reviewed in this paper follow this Skinnerian paradigm. **1964** H. J. EYSENCK *Exper. Behav. Therapy* II. 187 One possible reason why Skinnerians have restricted themselves in this fashion. **1965** *Language* XLI. 98 The extreme Skinnerian view that the correct inductive generalization can be accomplished with no need for anything more than positive instances. **1977** H. J. EYSENCK *You & Neurosis* v. 168 Skinnerian behaviourism has become a 'school', in the same way as Freudianism did many years earlier. Skinnerians concentrate exclusively on a very small area of psychology. **1979** *Nature* 29 Nov. 440/1 The sales techniques used in Iran, and no doubt they are now being used in other Third World countries, were a balanced compound of Skinnerian Psychology and gangsterism.

So **Ski·nnerism**, Skinnerian behaviourism.

1969 *Times Educ. Suppl.* 16 May 1640/2, I fear the growth of Skinnerism and its rats and pigeons. **1979** *Nature* 24 May 355/1 They bring us a metatheoretical commitment to a hard-line Skinnerism, according to which even the editorial policy of the *Journal of the Experimental Analysis of Behavior* is dangerously revisionist.

skinning, *vbl. sb.* Add: **2. c.** (Earlier example.)

1856 *Trans. Michigan State Agric. Soc.* VII. 171 The old plan of constant cropping without manure, or 'skinning', will ruin the land.

d. A physical or verbal beating; a hammering. *U.S. slang.*

1929 *Chicagoan* 17 Aug. 22/2 In this period he [*sc.* Carl Sandburg] wrote the poetic denunciation of the Rev. Billy Sunday that..remains as the most thorough skinning that the evangelist ever received. **1972** J. W. THOMPSON in W. King *Black Short Story Anthol.* 260 Daddy..has taught me several different ways to skin a cat, and that redhead doesn't know it yet, but he's got a skinning coming.

2*. (See quot.) *slang.* Cf. *SKIN *v.* 11.

1973 *Daily Mail* 3 Apr. 19/4 *Skinning*, injecting drugs under the skin.

3. *skinning knife* (earlier example).

1859 G. A. JACKSON *Diary* 8 Jan. in F. Hall *Hist. Colorado* (1890) II. 521 Dug and panned to-day until my belt knife was worn out; so will have to quit or use my skinning knife.

skinny, *a.* Add: **A.** *adj.* **5.** Of clothing: tight-fitting.

1970 'D. HALLIDAY' *Dolly & Cookie Bird* vii. 96 Janey's friends..in skinny sweaters and bell-bottomed corduroy trousers. **1972** *Vogue* Feb. 63 Long skinny jacket over beautifully cut pants. **1982** *Times* 2 Apr. 10/3 Teddy bear fur over skinny suede skirts.

6. Special collocations, as **Skinny Liz**, a thin girl or woman (see also quot. 1940); **skinny-malink, -links, -linky** (chiefly *Sc.*), a thin or emaciated person or animal; also *attrib.* or as *adj.*; **skinny-rib** *a.*, of a sweater, etc., fitting tightly across the ribs [the apparent connection with *rib stitch* is accidental]; also *ellipt.* as *sb.*

1940 M. MARPLES *Public School Slang* 190 St. Bees.. used *wimp* (a corruption of *women*) and the Arabic *bint* of women in general, while *skinny liz* was applied, almost as a nickname, to any elderly woman. **1959** I. & P. OPIE *Lore & Lang. Schoolch.* ix. 169 Thin people..skin and bones, skinny,..skinny guts, Skinny Liz, skinny-malink. **1961** N. FITZGERALD *Black Welcome* iv. 95 She takes no interest in..eatin'. That's why she's such a Skinny Liz. **1892** *Brechin Advertiser* 6 Sept. 3 Twa skinamalinks o' the genus horse. **1904** 'H. FOULIS' *Erchie* iii. 15 Wee skinamalink craturs dottin' up the passages in U.F. kirks carryin' the books. **1916** *Dialect Notes* IV. 280 *Skinny-malink*, a very thin person. 'O, she's a regular skinny-malink.' Usage jocular. **1935** S. BECKETT *Echo's Bones*, The chagrin of the old skinnymalinks. **1956** *Sunday Times* 22 Jan. 2/5 There used to be a children's song in Aberdeen relating the adventures of a thin man called 'Skinamalinky Lang Legs', which is still sung as a skipping song, etc.: Skinamalinky lang legs Umbrella feet. **1979** L. DERWENT *Border Bairn* vi. 71 A skinnymalink of a laddie with holes in his stockings. **1973** *Tucson* (Arizona) *Daily Citizen* 22 Aug. 48/2 (Advt.), Men's fashionable, skinny-rib..acrylic pullover. **1976** *Milton Keynes Express* 25 June 11/1 (Advt.), Skirts, blouses, and skinny ribs.

B. *sb.* **1. a.** *Austral.* A girl or woman. ? *Obs.* **b.** A thin person.

1941 BAKER *Dict. Austral. Slang* 67 *Skinny*, a girl or young woman. **1959** [see *Skinny Liz*, sense A. 6 above]. **1977** *Time* 6 June 48/2 The skinnies of the world have, in effect, righteously established fitness standards that reward their own strengths and forgive their weaknesses.

2. Information; rumour (see also quot. 1959). *slang* (chiefly *U.S.*).

1959 *Amer. Speech* XXXIV. 156 *What's the skinny* means 'What's up?' **1974** E. BRAWLEY *Rap* (1975) II. xxiii. 363 Come to lay some skinny on you that I picked up off the vine. **1979** D. ANTHONY *Long Hard Cure* xxi. 162 Who killed her, Butler? Let's have the skinny. **1980** L. CODY *Dupe* xxiii. 165 Give them the skinny but keep the kudos.

ski·nny, *v.* [f. the adj.] *intr.* To lose flesh; to become skinny or skinnier. Usu. with *down.*

1939 J. STEINBECK *Grapes of Wrath* xxii. 423 She thinned out and she skinnied out, an'—she dropped that baby, dead. **1976** *Billings* (Montana) *Gaz.* 30 June 6-B/3 She joined TOPS after a neighbor started skinnying down to the system. **1981** *TV Picture Life* Mar. 61/1 (Advt.), All the difficult 'skinnying-down' has been done for you while you slept.

ski·nny-dip, *v. slang* (orig. *U.S.*). [f. SKINNY *a.* 3 + DIP *v.* 8.] *intr.* To swim naked. So as *sb.*, a naked swim; **ski·nny-dipper**, a person who swims naked; **ski·nny-dipping** *vbl. sb.*

1966 *Punch* 12 Oct. 557/2 Nearly a year has passed since three members of the San Francisco Sexual Freedom League went skinny-dipping in the San Francisco bay. **1967** WENTWORTH & FLEXNER *Dict. Amer. Slang* Suppl. 704/2 *Skinny-dip*, to swim in the nude. **1970** J. HOWARD *Please Touch* 14 Except for a couple of furtive midnight skinny-dips I had never taken off my clothes in public. **1971** *Daily Colonist* (Victoria, B.C.) 26 May 19/4 It was never resolved if the chickens got over the light problem or the skinny dippers were apprehended by the constable. **1971** *Daily Progress* (Charlottesville, Va.) 17 July 1/7 Two young men decided to skinny-dip near Rexburg, Idaho and left their clothes in their sail boat, but the boat sailed out of reach. **1975** *Sunday Mail* (Brisbane) 9 Mar. 30/6 *Perth.*—Skinny-dippers breathed a collective sigh of relief last week when Police Minister Ray O'Connor said ..they could carry on stripping. **1977** *Times* 11 Apr. 5/7 His guests took skinny-dips in baths of champagne. **1980** L. BIRNBACH et al. *Official Preppy Handbk.* 190/1 Once every summer, teenagers are caught skinny-dipping after dark. **1981** *Times* 20 Apr. 4/8 One weekend no less than 36 people were arrested for 'skinny-dipping'.

skint (skint), *a. colloq.* [Var. *SKINNED *ppl. a.* (see sense 4 d).] Penniless, broke.

1925 FRASER & GIBBONS *Soldier & Sailor Words* 260 *Skint, to be*, hard up. **1935** G. INGRAM *Cockney Cavalcade* vii. 97 Edina [*sic*] offered him a shilling. 'That's all right... I ain't "skint" yet.' **1955** G. FREEMAN *Liberty Man* III. iv. 158 If he had enough to pay, it would just about leave him skint. **1962** *New Statesman* 18 May 708/3 All I want is a bike and ten pounds a week in me pocket—there's one thing I can't stand and that's being skint. **1977** S. MILLIGAN in *Observer* (Colour Suppl.) 6 Nov. 32/2 McGonagall..journeyed on foot (he was skint) from Dundee to Balmoral. **1981** *Times* 27 Aug. 17/3 Are the British really as skint as we tend to make out?

skin-tight, *a.* Add: Also *fig.*

1916 JOYCE *Portrait of Artist* v. 280 They..gave orders to jarvies in highpitched provincial voices which pierced through their skintight accents. **1977** *Sounds* 9 July 31/1 'Cathedral', 'Dark Star', 'Cold Rain' and 'In My Dreams' are all skintight songs, questioning, but personal and without pretension.

skip, *sb.*[1] Add: **2. d.** *Poker.* = *skip straight* s.v. *SKIP *v.*[1] 8.

1880 J. BLACKBRIDGE *Compl. Poker-Player* vii. 48 'Skips' consisting of alternate cards in sequence for instance, 3, 5, 7, 9, Jack. **1905** R. F. FOSTER *Practical Poker* 75 A skip is almost twice as difficult to get as any other straight, the exact odds against it being 423 to 1.

e. *Radio.* The phenomenon of the poor or non-existent reception of signals from a particular station which occurs between points where signals propagated directly from the station become undetectable and points where signals begin again to be received owing to reflection in the upper atmosphere. Also applied to the silent region itself, and to radio signals received from beyond it.

1925 [see *skip region*, sense 5 below]. **1927** O. F. BROWN *Elem. Radio-Communication* xvi. 203 The existence of the skip is explained by there being insufficient electrons to bring the wave down again until the angle of incidence becomes that corresponding to the 500 range. **1931** *Observer* 8 Nov. 18/5 Because of 'skip' it will hardly ever be audible in this country. **1965** B. SWEET-ESCOTT *Baker St. Irregular* iv. 114 The 'skip' was explained..as being the heavenward arc made by the path of the waves emitted by the short-wave transmitters. **1976** PERKOWSKI & STRAL *Joy of CB* vii. 68 The FCC purposely limited CB operations to distances under 150 miles to preclude the use of skip. **1976** *S9* (N.Y.) Feb. 88/2 When CB skip starts rolling in, he says that's the time to start tuning 25 to 50 MHz.

f. In automatic data processing, the action of a machine (e.g. a punch) in passing over material not requiring the functioning of the machine; a computer instruction or routine specifying such action.

1946 [see *skip bar*, sense 5 below]. **1962** *Gloss. Terms Automatic Data Processing* (*B.S.I.*) 91 Machines in current use can perform the function called skip wherein a field in which no punching is required is rapidly passed under the punch knives, which are not active at the time. **1966** H. P. HARTKEMEIER *Data Processing* iv. 199/1 All functions of the machine are stopped while a skip is taking place. **1969** P. B. JOURDAIN *Condensed Computer Encycl.* 468 An unconditional skip is a computer instruction demanding that the next *n* instructions be ignored. **1976** KERNIGAN & PLAUGER *Software Tools* iii. 80 Skip produces n blank lines.

4. *N. Amer. colloq.* One who absconds, *spec.* to avoid paying debts; one who defaults in payment.

1915 J. R. FOOTE *Mod. Collection Methods* 32 In some lines of business, much, and in some, most of the collection department work is the tracing of skips. A skip is a handy term used to describe a debtor who finds it easy to forget to leave any tracks when he moves his earthly possessions. **1939** *Amer. Speech* XIV. 240 *Skip*, guest who leaves without paying his bill. **1949** *Collier's* 8 Jan. 27/1 Kleinman's book of procedures lists exactly 110 ways to trace a skip. **1978** *Detroit Free Press* 14 Apr. 2c/2 Jean Phelan traces all kinds of hard-to-locate 'skips'—the defaulters who have 'skipped' out.

5. *attrib.* and *Comb.*, as (sense *2 e) *skip distance, region, zone*; (sense *2 f) *skip bar*; (sense *4) *skip-trace, -tracer, -tracing* vbl. sb.

1946 *Ann. Harvard Computation Laboratory* I. 274 Cards may be punched containing a function in the first columns of the cards and a serial number in the last columns of the cards. After the function is punched, a duplicating card and skip bar control the punch. **1926** *Physical Rev.* XXVII. 189 Larmor's theory of refraction due to the electrons of the Kennelly-Heaviside layer does not explain the 'skip distances' for short radio waves. **1977** T. ALLBEURY *Man with President's Mind* vii. 75 The radiated strength was fifty kilowatts..a power of about seventy-five kilometres due east. It would be the skip distance that carried it to Washington, or a relay from London. **1925** *Proc. IRE* XIII. 680 An uncertain region not far from the transmitter has been introduced between 100 and 350 miles during the summer night range and a skip, or entirely-missed, region, occurs in the winter night ranges between 100–350 miles. **1970** K. CONWAY *Naked Nemesis* ii. 18 The last one hadn't paid me... There wasn't enough involved for me to start a skip-trace on him. **1980** J. GARDNER *Garden of Weapons* II. i. 119 The Yanks think we need it [*sc.* a safe house] for a skip-trace outfit. They think we've lost somebody. **1953** BERREY & VAN DEN BARK *Amer. Thes. Slang* (1954) § 460/18 *Skip tracer*, a tracer of defaulting debtors. **1960** P. S. BEAGLE *Fine & Private Place* i. 12 You ran away from it [*sc.* life] nineteen years ago, and it follows you like a skip-tracer. **1978** *Globe & Mail* (Toronto) 14 Sept. 3/2 Mr. Lillie testified that he is a skip-tracer who tracks down persons who default on their debts then change addresses. **1960** J. BLISH *Galactic Cluster* 124 If he has rebuilt..the Universe to accommodate a private skip-tracing firm..I..see no reason why we can't counter-check him. **1977** B. GARFIELD *Recoil* xi. 134 This is.. better than repossessing cars and skip-tracing. **1926** *Physical Rev.* XXVII. 192 The skip zone was not very sharply defined. **1946** *Richmond* (Va.) *Times-Dispatch* 27 Jan. I. 16/6 The skip zone is one of the knottiest problems of present-day radio communications.

skip, *sb.*[2] Add: Also *gen.*, a large container for the reception and conveyance of materials or rubbish.

1940 *Chambers's Techn. Dict.* 775/2 *Skip*,..a bucket used for the transport of spoil or materials and hung for this purpose from a crane or cableway. **1950** *Landfall* (N.Z.) IV. 125 We start loading seasoned timber into one of the skips. **1972** *Daily Tel.* 17 Jan. 3/3 Householders who leave builders' skips—large containers which can be hired to take away rubble—at the kerbside for collection by a special vehicle face fines of up to £100 under a law coming into force today. **1978** *Cornish Guardian* 27 Apr. 8/8 There will be a skip placed at the Town Hall, St. Columb and at the entrance to Halloon Avenue, St. Columb Road, on Friday, 28th. April, and at the Town Hall and Public Conveniences, Indian Queens on Friday, 12th. May, 1978 for Bulk Household refuse collections.

attrib. (Further examples.)

1951 J. CLEMO in D. V. Baker *One & All* 260 He had worked as a loader in a clay-pit near Pengarth, and one winter's day he had been crushed by a skip-waggon. **1972** CONYUS in A. Chapman *New Black Voices* 219 Shoveling straw Into the mouth of the skip loader. **1976** *Star* (Sheffield) 29 Nov. 12/5 (Advt.), Sale, TK skip lorry. 12 months' test.

skip, *sb.*[3] For *Sc.* read 'orig. *Sc.*' and add further examples. Also *gen.*, a captain, a commanding officer, a manager, a boss.

1921 *Amer. Legion Weekly* 28 Jan. 7 The skip wanted to investigate. **1930** T. FREDENBURGH *Soldiers March!* xxv. 201 Better get into a wagon somewhere..in case the Skip starts prowling. **1948** M. ALLINGHAM *More Work for Undertaker* xiii. 163 I've been chinning with the old Skip and he says Bang on, jolly good show. **1955** *Times* 15 Aug. 8/5 In rink games the 'skip', or captain, of each side stands near the jack to direct his men by voice or signal where their next shot should arrive. **1968** *Globe & Mail* (Toronto) 3 Feb. 35/5 In addition to winning several minor bonspiels, the Thornhill skip is in the last 16 for the Ontario Curling Association Championship. **1970** *Wall St. Jrnl.* 8 July 18/6 If you're ever called up to play baseball in the big leagues, be sure to call the manager 'Skip'. Managers like to be called Skip. **1973** D. KYLE *Raft of Swords* (1974) viii. 81 On the flight deck..the young navigator said, 'I don't really understand what we're looking *for*, skip.' 'Just Russian warships.' **1977** *N.Z. Herald* 8 Jan. 1-10/3 Who are Arthur Connew's great heroes in all those many years and thousands of ends of bowling? J.S. Martin in the singles and Jimmy Mingins and Mort Squire as skips. **1977** *S. Wales Guardian* 27 Oct. 4/5 Skip Mr. Cliff Davies invested new members to the scout troop.

skip (skip), *sb.*[7] orig. *Sc.* [Origin obscure.] The peak of a cap.

1888 A. G. MURDOCH *Scotch Readings* (Ser. 2) 29 Ye're surely no ettlin' to put on that ugly twa-faced kep..wi' the skip baith back an' fore? **1969** M. PUGH *Last Place Left* ii. 11 He adjusted his American fatigue cap so that the skip almost covered his eyes. **1974** H. MACINNES *Climb to Lost World* xi. 207 'Hiya, Jo. Did you make it?' asked Don, peering up from beneath his cap skip.

skip, *v.*[1] Add: **I. 2. b.** For 'Now *U.S. colloq.*' read 'Now *colloq.*' and add: Also with *out* and as *to skip it*.

1865 M. GRIGSBY *Diary* 3 Jan. in *Smoked Yank* (1888) xxi. 179 Thirteen [paroled men]..skipped out to-day. **1902** 'MARK TWAIN' in *Harper's Mag.* Jan. 265/2 Skip out for the coast some night. **1959** I. & P. OPIE *Lore & Lang. Schoolch.* x. 193 Juvenile language is well stocked..with expressions inviting a person's departure, for instance:.. skip it, sling your hook, [etc.]. *a* **1966** 'M. NA GOPALEEN' *Best of Myles* (1977) 308 The son turned out to be a very bad bit of work, sold all the furniture to buy drink and then skipped it to America. **1969** G. LYALL *Venus with Pistol* xxxv. 231 He tells Dona Margarita we seem to have skipped out together. **1977** J. THOMSON *Case Closed* ii. 21 Bibby hadn't turned up. He wondered if he had skipped out.

II. 5. e. Phr. *skip it, let's skip it*: an exhortation or command to drop a subject or forget something. orig. *U.S.*

1934 M. H. WESEEN *Dict. Amer. Slang* 395 *Skip it*, drop the matter. **1939** R. CHANDLER *Big Sleep* xiii. 97, I started to say: 'What the hell—!' 'Oh, skip it,' Eddie Mars sighed. **1943** M. MCCARTHY *Company she Keeps* vi. 195 'Oh, Dr James,' she sighed. 'Let's skip it this time.' **1945** E. WAUGH *Brideshead Revisited* 17 Oh, very conscientious, I'm sure. Skip it and get a move on. **1955** E. CADELL *Lark shall Sing* x. 116 'I hate to seem to butt in on your—' 'Skip it. Go ahead and help me.' **1971** R. DENTRY *Encounter at Kharmel* ii. 31 At home..we cope and never give it a second thought. Out here we—oh, skip it! **1977** *New Yorker* 3 Oct. 40/3 Forgive me... Let's skip it, then, she says.

f. To forgo, to abstain from; to omit to take part in or to do.

1961 in WEBSTER s.v. [1]*skip*, The president skipped his regular Thursday press conference. **1970** K. H. COOPER *New Aerobics* ix. 137 Women suffering from cramps find exercise extremely uncomfortable. Common sense alone tells them to skip exercise during those days. **1979** R. JAFFE *Class Reunion* II. ix. 209 They picked at their dinner, unable to eat the roast pigeon..or the salad, and skipping dessert.

6. b. (Earlier and later examples.)

c **1810** W. HICKEY *Memoirs* (1960) ii. 28, I had intended to skip school, and take the usual march with the Guards to Kensington. **1951** J. D. SALINGER *Catcher in Rye* xxv. 270 If I let you skip school this afternoon and go for a little walk, will you cut out the crazy stuff? **1976** *National Observer* (U.S.) 17 Jan. 1/2 School phobia is a fairly common reason why some kids skip school.

c. For '(the country)' read '(a place)' and add further examples.

1885 *Santa Fé Weekly New Mexican* 10 Sept. 4/7 George Handley, a laundryman at Albuquerque, has skipped the town. **1906** U. SINCLAIR *Jungle* xxv. 307 The offending gambler had got wind of what was coming to him, and had skipped the town. **1977** *Detroit Free Press* 11 Dec. 11-B/1 Cliff won't go along with Molly's scheme to take Olive's $10,000 and skip town.

d. *to skip* (*one's*) *bail* = *to jump* (*one's*) *bail* (see JUMP *v.* 10 a in Dict. and Suppl.).

1900 *Congr. Rec.* 5 Feb. 1521/2, I should like the gentleman to know that one lot of those ballot-box stuffers are in jail and every one of the others has skipped his bail. **1930** P. W. SLOSSON *Great Crusade* (1931) 88 The I.W.W. leader who had 'skipped bail' and fled abroad. **1973** *Black Panther* 16 June 3/3 Eldridge Cleaver..skipped bail to avoid prosecution.

III. 8. skip-bombing (see quot. 1973); also *attrib.*; **skip-read** *v. trans.* and *intr.*, to read (a book) while skipping the passages of less importance; so **skip-reader**; **skip straight** *Poker*, a straight (STRAIGHT *sb.* 5) consisting of cards of alternate values.

1943 *Time* 18 Jan. 68/3 A U.S. Flying Fortress thundered into the Jap Harbor at Rabaul..to make the first test in the South Pacific of a new technique—'skip-bombing'. **1944** W. W. ELTON et al. *Guide Naval Aviation* ix. 172 A skip-bombing airplane must be fast and maneuverable... Tanks and ships are often attacked with skip bombing. **1964** D. MACARTHUR *Reminisc.* VI. 171 Special preparations were made to carry out a new technique of skip-bombing in the event of unfavorable weather and low cloud formations. **1973** J. QUICK *Dict. Weapons & Mil. Terms* 401/2 *Skip bombing*, a method of aerial bombing in which the bomb is released from such a low altitude that it slides or glances along the surface of the water or ground and strikes the target at or above water level or ground level. **1977** M. T. BLOOM *13th Man* (1978) p. ii, Skip-read all you want through the book, but go through the last page word by word. **1977** *Modern Railways* Dec. 490/1 Once taken up it is not a book which can be skip-read, for every page is packed solid with information. **1973** *Howard Jrnl.* XIII. 342 A very clear and easy to read book which should present no difficulties to the skip-reader. **1887** J. W. KELLER *Game of Draw Poker* 17 Efforts have been made to introduce into the game of Draw Poker what is known as the 'skip' straight—a sequence of alternate cards. **1944** A. H. MOREHEAD *Mod. Hoyle* 31 *Skip straight*, a sequence of cards once separated in rank. Examples: A—Q—10—8—6, or J—9—7—5—3.

skipjack, *sb.* Add: **4.** Also *attrib.*, esp. in **skipjack tuna**, a tropical pelagic food fish, *Katsuwonus pelamis*, of the family Scombridæ, distinguished by its large size and striped body. (Later examples.)

1920 BLUNDEN *Waggoner* 2 Where flock and shine the skip-jack dace. **1936** P. S. BARNHART *Marine Fishes S. Calif.* 36 Skipjack..a pelagic fish of a wide range. **1937** L. A. WALFORD *Marine Game Fishes Pacific Coast* 17 The skipjack is the smallest of the tunas, rarely exceeding 25 inches in length. **1949** THOMAS & LOVETT in Vesey-Fitzgerald & Lamonte *Game Fish of World* II. 132 There are the oceanic bonito, known locally as the skipjack, and the California bonito. **1961** E. S. HERALD *Living Fishes of World* 229 (*caption*) Skipjack Tuna..world-wide in tropical waters. **1973** *Sunday Times* 10 June (Colour Suppl.) 44/3 The most valuable fish in Papua New Guinea waters are skipjack tuna.

6. *U.S.* A kind of sailing-boat (see quot. 1976). Also *attrib.*

1887 *Forest & Stream* IX. 75 The 'skip-jack' is a connecting link between the skiff and the round-bottom boat. **1941** H. I. CHAPELLE *Boatbuilding* i. 36 The well-known Chesapeake Bay Skipjacks may be taken to represent the next type, having a good deal of beam and more dead rise than the modified sharpies. **1968** *Washington Star* 27 May B-1/2 They were watching last October's Chesapeake Appreciation Day skipjack races, off Annapolis. **1976** *Oxf. Compan. Ships & Sea* 807/2 *Skipjack*, a work-boat of the east coast of the U.S.A., sloop-rigged with a jib-headed mainsail and a foresail set on a bowsprit. They were hard-chined boats with a large wooden centreboard. **1978** J. A. MICHENER *Chesapeake* 725 In winter months he labored aboard a white man's skipjack dredging oysters... In spring he helped the skipjack captain haul timber to Baltimore.

skipper, *sb.*[2] Add: **4.** *Services' slang.* A commanding officer in the army; the captain of an aircraft or squadron.

1906 *Soldier Slang* in C. McGovern *Sarjint Larry an' Frinds*, *Skipper*, the commanding officer. **1926** *Sat. Even. Post* 6 Mar. 154/3 The skipper told us to look after yuh. **1929** *Papers Mich. Acad. Sci., Arts & Lett.* X. 323 *Skipper*, the squadron commander in the Royal Naval Air Service. **1958** P. KEMP *No Colours or Crest* v. 86 The Skipper wondered if you'd like to go forward to the flight deck for a look around. **1977** *R.A.F. News* 11–24 May 9/1 The headmaster..will join his wartime Whitley skipper, Gp Capt Leonard Cheshire.

5. *slang* (orig. *U.S.*). A police captain or sergeant; a police chief.

1929 HOSTETTER & BEESLEY *It's a Racket!* 238 *Skipper*, a police captain in command of a police station, bureau, or district. **1930** *Amer. Mercury* Dec. 457/2, I goes to the skipper and fronts for the mutt. **1962** *John o' London's* 25 Jan. 82/2 A police sergeant is called *skipper*. **1976** D. BARNES *Yesterday is Dead* (1977) II. 262 Good piece of police work... I'll fill the skipper in. I'm sure he'll be pleased.

skipper, *sb.*[3] Restrict † *Obs.* to sense in Dict. and add: **1. b.** Any sleeping-place for a vagrant.

1925 *Flynn's* 3 Jan. 661/2 *Skipper*,..a lodging house; a tramp. **1935** 'G. ORWELL' *Clergyman's Daughter* ii. 101 We ain't got a brown between us, and we..got to tap for our tommy and skipper at nights. **1939** J. WORBY *Spiv's Progress* i. 9 I'm going north. Do you know any good skippers up the road? **1978** *Country Life* 20 July 189/2 He had painfully to learn the rudiments of vagrant survival: to make sure of his 'skipper' or kip before dark.

2. A vagrant; one who sleeps rough.

1925 [see sense 1 b above]. **1965** *Guardian* 9 Dec. 9/1 It was the night of the big Government census of the 'skippers'—the people who sleep rough. **1977** *Listener* 28 July 103/3 On the rubble-strewn redevelopment sites of central Glasgow, you find the groups of 'skippers', the men who live rough... These are the ones who admit that alcohol has won.

3. An act of sleeping rough; esp. in *to do a skipper*.

1935 H. NEVILLE *Sneak Thief on Road* 347 *Skipper*, a liedown in a spinney or anywhere where no rent is paid. **1937** J. CURTIS *You're in Racket Too* i. 9 It would be no fun doing a skipper on a November night. **1962** *Observer* 11 Mar. 35/1 There are not enough beds. Many will be turned away and have to do a 'skipper' in station, park or ruin.

skipper, *v.*[1] (Further examples.)

1950 *Sport* 7–11 Apr. 14/1 Dick skippered the City side who, in 1938, wrote a chapter of Cup history. **1951** N. M. GUNN *Well at World's End* xxvi. 239 The idea..was to get the old man to skipper her for a couple of seasons. **1977** *R.A.F. News* 27 Apr.–10 May 5/1 Brian, then a flight lieutenant, had skippered the Sunderland on three flights.

skipping, *vbl. sb.*[1] **1.** (Earlier example of the pastime using a skipping-rope.)

1800 *Infant's Library* IX. 7 Skipping. This is a very healthful play in winter; it will make you nice and warm in frosty weather.

attrib. (Further examples.)

1959 I. & P. OPIE *Lore & Lang. Schoolch.* ii. 38 Norman Douglas gives it as a skipping rhyme in 'London Street Games'. **1977** N. FREELING *Gadget* II. 70 How many skipping rhymes do I know? Sixty? A hundred?

2. (Earlier example in sense 5a of SKIP *v.*[1])

1824 SCOTT *Redgauntlet* II. i. 15 Such as are addicted to the laudable practice of *skipping*.

skipping-rope. (Earlier example.)

1802 F. BURNEY *Jrnl.* (1975) V. 388 He interests himself warmly about them, since he has seen the Cuttings, especially of the skipping ropes.

skirlie (skɜ̄·ɹli). *Sc.* Also **skirley.** [Shortened dim. form of *skirl-in-the-pan* s.v. SKIRL *sb.* 2 b: see -Y[6], -IE.] A dish of oatmeal and onions, etc., fried together.

1914 *Trans. Banffshire Field Club* 26/27 June 26 Crackens, bayheads, and skirlie are formed of fish livers and oatmeal cooked together. **1929** F. M. MCNEILL *Scots Kitchen* 205 *Skirlie*... Chop two ounces of suet finely. Have a pan very hot and put in the suet. When..melted, add one or two finely chopped onions and brown them well. Now add enough oatmeal to absorb the fat. **1947** *Sc. Women's Rural Inst. Cookery Bk.* x. 184 *Skirley*..3 handfuls of oatmeal.., ½ lb. suet, 2 onions.., pepper, salt. **1969** *Observer* 12 Jan. 33/4 *Skirley* (oatmeal, onions, suet, seasoned and fried in a cake).

skirmish, *v.* Add: **1. c.** *colloq.* (orig. *U.S.*). To make excursions in order to see what one can find; to scout *round* in search of something.

1864 'MARK TWAIN' in Harte & 'Twain' *Sk. Sixties* (1926) 129 His first cousin..is a skirmisher and is with the parson—he goes through the camp-meetings and skirmishes for raw converts. **1869** —— *Innocents Abroad* ix. 86 When the commissary department fails they 'skirmish', as Jack terms it in his sinful, slangy way. **1893** M. HOLLEY *Samantha at World's Fair* xix. 608 The males, from creation down, have been left free to skirmish round and git a livin' for themselves. **1894** 'R. ANDOM' *We Three & Troddles* xxiii. 220 He left the room to skirmish after a clean handkerchief. *Ibid.* xxiv. 231 We had them downstairs and into the cab before they could skirmish after more substantial fare. **1907** S. E. WHITE *Arizona Nights* 17 We skirmished around and found a condemned army pack saddle with aparejos.

skirrack, obs. var. *SKERRICK.

skirret[1]. **1.** (Earlier *attrib.* example.)

1728 E. SMITH *Compleat Housewife* (ed. 2) 113 (*heading*) To make a skirret-pye.

skirret[2]. (Earlier example.)

1825 *Republican* 29 July 123 The skirret is an implement which acts on a centre pin, from whence a centre line is drawn, chalked and struck, to mark out the ground for the foundation of the intended structure.

skirrick, obs. var. *SKERRICK.

skirt, *sb.* Add: **I. 1. a.** *divided skirt* (earlier example).

1885 'V. LEE' *Let.* in P. Gunn *V. Lee* (1964) x. 127 A very bright blue paper dress suggestive of divided skirts and ulster to match.

b. (Further examples.) *a bit of skirt*: a woman; esp. an attractive one.

1914 S. LEWIS *Our Mr. Wrenn* iv. 55 Pete was..singing hoarsely, 'Dey was a skoit and 'er name was Goity.' **1916** C. J. DENNIS *Doreen & Sentimental Bloke* 89 *Skirt, or bit of skirt*, a female. **1928** D. H. LAWRENCE *Woman who rode Away* 283 And what about your American skirt?—I told him, there was nothing to say about her. **1934** J. BROPHY *Waterfront* ii. 42 A nice juicy bit of skirt, eh? **1958** 'N. CULOTTA' *They're a Weird Mob* 190 'Reckon we better stick ter beer?' 'Until them other two skirts turn up.' **1974** K. MILLETT *Flying* (1975) v. 469 The two patriarchs, never tired of chasing twenty-year-old skirts in their old age. **1977** J. I. M. STEWART *Madonna of Astrolabe* xx. 280 They mustn't quarrel over a bit of skirt.

c. An underskirt or petticoat.

1862 *Catal. Internat. Exhib., Industr. Dept., Brit. Div.* II. No. 3674 Counterpanes, toilette-covers, skirts. *Ibid.* No. 4935 Spiral Crinoline Steel and Bronze for Ladies' Skirts. **1908** M. E. MORGAN *How to dress Doll* v. 51 The flannel skirt is cut from a straight piece of fine white flannel.

3. *to hide behind the skirts of*, to take refuge behind, to use for protection.

1938 G. GRAHAM *Swiss Sonata* 356 Is *she* hiding behind your skirts too? **1975** *Current Hist.* Dec. 230/2 In terms of foreign dominance, Thailand asserted her independence from China only as she was able to hide behind the skirts of the Western giants, Great Britain, France and, most important, the United States.

II. 4. c. Also in other *techn.* senses (see quots.).

1951 *Gloss. Aeronaut. Terms* (*B.S.I.*) III. 15 *Skirt*, the lower portion of the canopy [of a parachute]. **1962** J. GLENN et al. in *Into Orbit* 245 Parachutes used on Mercury capsules are reefed by means of ropes tied around the skirt of the parachute. **1964** J. L. NAYLER *Dict. Astronautics* 252 *Skirt*, the lower outer part of a rocket vehicle. It acts as a fairing to the rocket motor or booster. **1969** *Times* 22 July (Moon Rep. Suppl.) p. iii/7 There's one picture I'm taking now of the right rear of the spacecraft looking at the skirts of the descent stage. **1970** *Gloss. Aeronaut. & Astronaut. Terms* (*B.S.I.*) VI. 2 *Skirt*, an aerodynamic fairing to influence the airflow in the vicinity of the propelling nozzles.

e. A surface that conceals or protects the wheels or underneath of a vehicle or aircraft; *spec.* (*a*) a detachable panel concealing part of the wheel of a car and fitted flush with the bodywork; (*b*) a surface designed to deflect the air so as to produce a downward force on the car aerodynamically.

1912 C. B. HAYWARD *Practical Aeronautics* 286 There are six landing wheels forward, three on each side of the center and enclosed in what is termed a 'skirt'. **1953** FRAZEE & SPICER *Automotive Collision Work* i. 55 Sometimes fender skirts are used on the rear fenders of cars. These skirts cover the wheel opening and are attached to the fender by clamps. **1965** M. C. OAKS *Fell's Guide to Mobile Home Living* vi. 97 Many mobile home owners enclose the space beneath their mobile homes with skirts or siding. These skirts..provide enclosed storage space, protect your tires from the sun, and..provide extra insulation. **1974** *Country Life* 21 Mar. 659/1 The Triumph Dolomite Sprint..is recognized by its..discreet spoiler beneath the front skirt. **1981** *Times* 5 Feb. 13/1 The South African Grand Prix will take place at Kyalmi... The cars will be equipped with skirts, almost certainly for the last time. **1981** *Sci. Amer.* Aug. 25/3 Most new main battle tanks have lightly armored 'skirts' to cover vulnerable treads and wheels.

f. *Mech.* The lower part of the curved surface of a piston in a piston engine, below the grooves for piston rings. Also *piston skirt*.

1913 W. E. DOMMETT *Motor Car Mech.* 12 For the sake of lightness and more particularly for use on racing cars, holes are drilled around the lower part or skirt of the piston and two rings only may be used. **1929** NEWTON & STEEDS *Motor Vehicle* vi. 57 In order that finer clearances may be used without risk of seizure, many different designs of semi-flexible skirt have been introduced. **1970** K. BALL *Fiat 600, 600 D Autobook* i. 14/2 In each case, the number is on the opposite side to the slot in the piston skirt.

g. A flexible surface that projects downwards underneath a hovercraft to contain or divide the air-cushion.

1962 *Daily Tel.* 12 Apr. 15/7 The cushion of pressurised air can take any proportion of the weight off the wheels. It is in an adjustable synthetic rubber 'skirt' below the waist-line of the vehicle. **1968** *Economist* 7 Sept. 81/1 The skirt of the hovercraft is one of its most sensitive parts. If the design is not right, the ride is uncomfortable and skirt edges flap up and down on the surface of the sea causing excessive wear. **1977** *Hovering Craft & Hydrofoil* XVII. 18/2 SEDAM, the French manufacturer, claims that their skirt is better than ours, but these claims will be put to the acid test when the N 500 and the SR.N4 Mk 3 run alongside each other on the Channel next year.

6. c. Chiefly *pl.* = SKIRTING *vbl. sb.* 5.

1851 F. A. WELD *Hints to Intending Sheep-Farmers N.Z.* 8 The Merino has the more valuable wool, being finer, and particularly superior in the 'skirts', which are remarkably deficient in the crossed sheep. **1886** [see sense 6 b in Dict.]. **1965** J. S. GUNN *Terminol. Shearing Industry* II. 23 *Skirt, skirting*. This word is generally used in the plural and refers to the wool round the edge of the fleece which is pulled off by the 'skirter'..or woolroller... In original English practice the skirts were handled by the 'wool sorter'..and not processed quite so carefully as in Australia.

III. 8. c. The lower sloping portions of a peak or rise on a graph, esp. of one representing electrical resonance.

1940 *Chambers's Techn. Dict.* 775/2 *Skirt*, the lower side portions of a resonance curve. **1962** SIMPSON & RICHARDS *Physical Princ. Junction Transistors* xiv. 341 This would be partly overcome if the top of the amplitude response curve were made flatter and the 'skirts' made steeper. **1965** *Wireless World* Sept. 33 (Advt.), Bandwidth skirts are better than 80-dB down. **1970** J. EARL *Tuners & Amplifiers* ii. 43 In such sets..the element is arranged in the form of a bandpass coupling or filter, giving sharp response skirts while handling signals in the required bandwidth.

11. *skirt-guard, -length*; *skirt-like* adj.; **skirt-board,** (*b*) a board to iron skirts on; **skirt-chaser** *slang*, one who pursues women with amorous attentions; hence **skirt-chase** *v. intr.*; **skirt-chasing** *vbl. sb.*; **skirt-dance** *sb.* (examples); **skirt-dancer** (examples); **skirt duty** *slang*, (*a*) acting in a way designed to attract men; (*b*) keeping company with women, regarded as a military duty; **skirt-knicker(s)** (see quot. 1913); **skirt-land,** land having skirt soil (see below); **skirt patrol** *slang* (orig. *U.S.*) (see quot. 1941); **skirt soil,** a loam composed of a mixture of peat and clay or sand or silt (cf. SKIRTY *a.*).

1861 MRS. BEETON *Bk. Househ. Managem.* 1013 The skirts of muslin dresses should be ironed on a skirt-board covered with flannel. **1932** D. C. MINTER *Mod. Needlecraft* 107/2 Almost indispensable to successful dress-making are..sleeve and skirt board for pressing, [etc.]. **1943** J. B. PRIESTLEY *Daylight on Saturday* xi. 70 Don't be a dam' fool, Percy. I'm not skirt-chasing. **1942** BERREY & VAN DEN BARK *Amer. Thes. Slang* § 438/2 Lascivious man... *Skirt* or *woman chaser*. **1962** L. PETERS *Snatch of Music* iii. 45 He had always despised..the indiscriminate skirt-chaser. **1974** L. LAMB *Man in Mist* xvi. 106, I don't suppose that Settle is a skirt chaser. He probably wanted to frighten the girl away. **1950** 'S. RANSOME' *Deadly Miss Ashley* xiv. 167, I always told you you'd regret your skirt-chasing... A man should stick with his wife and family. **1981** D. BOGGIS *Time to Betray* vii. 40 Chevalier went skirt-chasing at a disco. **1895** G. B. SHAW *Let.* 1 Nov. in *E. Terry & B. Shaw* (1931) 17 Mrs Pat Campbell entrances all London as Juliet, with a skirt dance. **1961** WODEHOUSE *Ice in Bedroom* vi. 47, I feel like dancing a skirt dance. **1974** D. SMITH *Look back with Love* xii. 113 There was usually one skirt-dance, during which the boys lolled..looking tolerant and slightly cynical. **1895** G. B. SHAW in *Sat. Rev.* 6 Apr. 445/1 Our skirt dancers are all petticoats. **1922** Skirt-dancer [see *high-kicker* s.v. *HIGH *a.* 21]. **1922** JOYCE *Ulysses* 758 He was throwing his sheeps eyes at those two doing skirt duty up and down. **1925** in *Amer. Speech 1972* (1975) XLVII. 102 That evening, Jim detailed himself to some more 'skirt duty'. **1932** C. MORGAN *Fountain* II. ii. 100 A woman's bicycle with the broken strings of its skirt-guard dangling in a melancholy fringe over its spokes. **1982** J. HONE *Valley of Fox* vii. 105 A big, black old-fashioned woman's bicycle, with cord skirt-guards forming a fan over the back wheel. **1908** in C. W. Cunnington *Eng. Women's Clothing in Present Cent.* (1952) ii. 84 The skirt-knickers which the up-to-date maiden delights in. **1913** *Queen* 13 Dec. 1091/2 The tango and peg-top fashion between them are responsible for an entirely new form of skirt-knicker... The characteristic of the new garment..is that it is formed entirely of one length of material falling from the waist in front to the knees and up again to the waist at the back, slits or openings occurring at the sides through which the legs are passed. **1946** J. W. DAY *Harvest Adventure* x. 145 Those cows are fed for more than nine months of the year on by-products of the farm—such as beet-tops, beet-pulp, kale—and on skirt-land, and marsh grazings. **1981** P. SALWAY *Roman Britain* 268 The skirtlands of the southern Fens were the worst hit by these troubles. **1920** *T. Eaton & Co. Catal.* Spring & Summer 1/1 Skirt Lengths 35 ins. 37 ins. 38 ins. **1980** L. LEWIS *Private Life Country House* xii. 166 Skirt lengths remained what you had been wearing for some time. **1862** W. C. BRYANT *Tale of Cloudland* in *Poet. Wks.* (1883) II. 315, I plainly saw a chariot cushioned deep With sides that seemed of down, and skirt-like wings On which they nestled. **1980** *Motor* 16 Feb. 31/1 Deep, 'skirt-like' door sills. **1941** *Amer. Speech* XVI. 168/2 *Skirt patrol*, search for feminine companionship. **1967** Skirt patrol [see OAO s.v. *O 5 d]. **1960** *Times* 5 July (Suppl. on Agric.) p. vi/3 Lying between the areas of silt and peat there are indeterminate areas of what are now called 'skirt' soils. The soil physicist has classified them as organic silty clay loams. **1968** *Economist* 27 Apr. 52/2 Only two-thirds of the original acreage of peat in the fens—over 300,000 acres—are now covered with more than a 'skirt soil'.

skirted, *ppl. a.* Add: **1. c.** Of a hovercraft, having a skirt. Cf. *SKIRT *sb.* 4 g.

1967 *Jane's Surface Skimmer Systems 1967–68* 1/2 The relative sophistication of the 80 knot skirted hovercraft.

skirting, *vbl. sb.* Add: **4.** *skirting radiator*, a radiator running along a wall at the level of the skirting.

1970 *Home & Garden* Mar. 94/4 Skirting radiators have a great deal to recommend them. **1978** *Cornish Guardian* 27 Apr. 16/6 (Advt.), Superbly renovated cottage with full central heating, unobtrusive skirting radiators [etc.].

skirty (skɜ·ɹti), *sb. colloq.* [f. SKIRT *sb.* + -Y[6].] A skirt or underskirt.

1922 JOYCE *Ulysses* 47 A woman and a man. I see her skirties. Pinned up, I bet. **1977** *Sounds* 9 July 18/2 I'd like to dirty up Their little skirties up.

skish (skiʃ). *U.S.* [perh. f. *SK(EET *sb.*[2] or SK(ILL *sb.*[1] + F)ISH *sb.*[1]] A game in which participants use fishing tackle to cast a plug or fly at a target on dry land. Also *attrib.*

1940 *Outdoor America* Jan. 11/3 Skish—the new name chosen for the casting game originally known as Fish-O was selected on January 6 by the judges of the Fish-O change-of-name contest. **1942** *Sun* (Baltimore) 8 July 13/3 He said the best score he ever made in 'skish'—dry-land 'fishing' in which participants cast at thirty-inch rings at distances from forty to eighty feet—was in the eighties out of a possible 100 points. **1965** *Richmond* (Va.) *Times-Dispatch* 5 Feb. 25/2 Skish..is a game devised for indoor anglers who want to improve their casting techniques by casting at targets rather than for fish. **1976** *Webster's Sports Dict.* 399/1 There are 3 different skish events: skish bait, skish spinning, and skish fly casting.

skit (skit), *sb.*⁴ *colloq.* [Origin obscure.] A large number, a crowd; *pl.* 'lots'.
1913 C. Mackenzie *Sinister St.* I. II. ix. 287, I met an odd sort of chap..who told me a skit of things—you—know—about a bad life. **1925** A. S. M. Hutchinson *One Increasing Purpose* III. ix. 268 'What was that little red rosette he had on his left arm? I see skits of people with it.' 'Been vaccinated, of course.' **1927** *Blackw. Mag.* Nov. 594/1 The Kachins were in the jungle, a skit of them, trying to stop us at the ford.

skit (skit), *a.*² *Anglo-Ir.* [App. colloq. adjectival use of Ir. *sciót* cut, bit, laugh.] Amusing; *to be right skit*, to be a great laugh (cf. *LAUGH *sb.* 4 b).
1914 Joyce *Dubliners* 26 Mahoney said it would be right skit to run away to sea on one of those big ships.

skite, *sb.* Add: Also *Austral.* and *N.Z. colloq.*
3. a. (Earlier example.)
1790 W. Maclay *Jrnl.* 28 June (1890) x. 310 Hamilton has a very boyish, giddy manner, and Scotch-Irish people could well call him a 'skite'.
4. *Austral.* and *N.Z. colloq.* **a.** Boasting, boastfulness; ostentation, show; conceit.
1860 C. Thatcher *Victoria Songster* v. 160 You don't often see a chap given to 'skite, Can do very much when it comes to a fight. **1910** E. W. Hornung *Boss of Taroomba* 180 'Then none o' your skite, mate,' said Bill, knocking out a clay pipe against his heel. **1918** G. Wall *Lett. Airman* 85 This notepaper is a part of it, quite unnecessary skite. I thought you might like a sample of it, though. **1933** N. Lindsay *Saturdee* 115 Ponk's the bloke to take the skite outer him. **1958** I. Cross *God Boy* vi. 44 You started us off with your skite about not caring about fifty bangs and now you say shut up. **1965** S. T. Ollivier *Petticoat Farm* ii. 31 'Alister Bridgeman says it's mostly skite,' Sarah said breezily. **1972** P. Newton *Sheep Thief* xviii. 149, I thought I had a good district run but you've taken the skite out of me.
b. A braggart, a boaster; a conceited person.
1906 'T. Collins' in *Barrier Truth* (Broken Hill, N.S.W.) 1 June, In spite of Rigby's very complimentary insinuation that I'm a skite and a liar, the wagon was gone. **1928** *Bulletin* (Sydney) 29 Feb. 21/1 To the mug, the skite and the liar, to the nark and the hypocrite A fellow can always jerry. **1941** S. J. Baker *N.Z. Slang* vii. 61 Our borrowings [from Australia] of what might be described as 'social' slang..[include] *skite*. **1952** D. Niland in *Coast to Coast 1951–1952* 198 And what a skite! You should have seen him. **1958** I. Cross *God Boy* i. 8 I'm not a skite but if I was fighting a man it would be the same. **1965** G. McInnes *Road to Gundagai* ii. 30 He had no time for 'skites', that is, boastful know-it-alls. **1969** *Australian* 23 Sept. 2 Australians should not see themselves as boastful, arrogant skites, the Governor-General, Sir Paul Hasluck, said yesterday.
5. Orig. and chiefly *Sc.* A jollification, a spree, a binge. Freq. in phr. *on the skite*.
1869 *St. Andrews Gaz.* 27 Nov. 3/6 A correspondent.. sends the following..catalogue of synonyms of whisky and whisky drinking in the West of Scotland:—..on the skyte. **1895** W. Stewart *Lilts* 65 When ye went on the 'skite' an' sent railway things glee'd. **1909** J. J. Bell *Oh! Christina* xiv. 112 You an' me's gaun to ha'e an' awfu' skite, eh, auntie? **1946** J. Irving *Royal Navalese* 158 *Skite (skyte), on the*, indulging in an orgy; on 'the tiles'. **1954** *Times* 16 Nov. 4/1 The Bejant skite (the party of the first-year students). **1972** N. Smythe in E. Berman *Ten of Best* (1979) 113, I was a bit too fond of the old jar, Went on the skite once too often.

skite, *v.*² Restrict '*Sc.* and *dial.*' to senses in Dict. and add:
For further material see also *Sc. Nat. Dict.*
3. *Austral.* and *N.Z. colloq.* To brag, to boast.
1857 C. R. Thatcher *Colonial Songster* 18 If ever you get into a fight, Of course you'll not forget to skite. **1896** E. Turner *Little Larrikin* xxiv. 295 It used to make me a bit sick sometimes to hear him skite, knowing how much chance I had. **1902** *N.Z. Illustr. Mag.* V. 486 They had him skiting about his moonlight stroll with someone. **1940** F. Sargeson *Man & his Wife* (1944) 79, I suppose he went back to his ship and skited about the time he'd had. **1956** G. Casey in *Coast to Coast 1955–56* 82 Spent most of the forty-eight hours skiting to his wife and young Les that he had got old Spend's goat thoroughly. **1968** A. Holden *Death after School* xxv. 181 They did save my life... I don't mind *how* much they skite. **1978** P. Grace *Mutuwhenua* xiv. 102 Everyone laughing, hugging Nanny who was skiting about her hat.
Hence (sense *3) **ski·ter; ski·ting** *vbl. sb.*
1898 *Bulletin* (Sydney) 17 Dec. (Red Page) An incessant talker is a *skiter* or a *fluter*. **1916** *Anzac Bk.* 99 If there's one thing I hate, it is skiting... So you won't think I boast when I tell you. **1936** F. Clune *Roaming round Darling* ix. 77 A fellow, fed up with city skiters, came out west to the edge of beyond, and began this village, where he could do his own skiting. **1957** R. Lawler *Summer of Seventeenth Doll* III. 113 Lyin' comes as natural to him as skiting.

skither (ski·ðəɹ), var. Skitter *v.*²
1904 *Eng. Dial. Dict.* V. 483/1 Leeak at mah scoperil, hoo it skithers across teeable. **1922** H. Quick *Vandemark's Folly* viii. 143, I remembered..how she had skithered back to the carriage. **1929** S. Leacock *Iron Man* v. 205 When we drive the ball..skithers off sideways. **1977** *Meanjin* (Austral.) XXXVI. I. 68, I skither down barefeet first.

skitter, *sb.*¹ Add: Also *colloq.* **1.** (Further examples.) Now freq. in *pl.*
1939 J. Steinbeck *Grapes of Wrath* xxii. 431 They et green grapes. They all five got the howlin' skitters. Run out ever' ten minutes. **1940** M. Marples *Public School Slang* 159 *Skitters, squitters*, diarrhœa. **1948** Partridge *Dict. Forces' Slang* 180 *Squitters, skitters*, a symptom of dysentery and other stomach troubles.

skitter, *sb.*² Delete *U.S.* and for def. read: A light scampering or skipping movement or the sound caused by this. (Further examples.)
1959 E. Allen *Man who chose Death* xiii. 130 A quick skitter of footsteps like mice in the rafters. **1961** S. Bunce *No Sainted City* xxiii. 170 A confusion of sounds. A skitter of light footfalls.

skitter, *v.*² Add: **1. a.** (Further examples.) Freq. with advbs.
1903 Kipling in *Windsor Mag.* Sept. 363/2 She skittered about in the bracken, being a 'citable child. **1935** M. Eberhart *Cases of S. Dare* 64 The monkey darted out from under the sofa and was suddenly skittering across the room again. **1946** C. McCullers *Member of Wedding* III. 178 Frances watched the Portuguese who..played a mock piano on the counter to the music-box tune. He swayed as he played and his fingers skittered up and down the counter. **1949** B. Marshall *To Every Man a Penny* xlix. 151 The limousines, the taxicabs, the lorries and the buses roared round the church, skittering away to Neuilly, Auteuil and Montmartre. **1968** B. Hines *Kestrel for Knave* 57 The boys began to swallow their Adam's apples, their eyes skittering about in still heads. **1976** *Church Times* 26 Nov. (Bk. Suppl.) p. iv/2 He skittered through a fantastic mass of scientific evidence for the scarcely believable and downright unbelievable. **1977** *Listener* 17 Feb. 215/3 Not only is the tenor-saxophonist playing his usual devious game but..Basie is joining in... Both men skittering around the melody line in high good humour. **1977** *New Yorker* 24 Oct. 33/1, I found, skittering in nervous computer printout across the bottom of my bill, the words 'Thank you very much for your prompt payment'.
b. For *U.S.* read 'orig. *dial.*' and add: Also with other advbs. and advb. phrases. (Earlier and later examples.)
1847 J. O. Halliwell *Dict. Archaic & Provincial Words* II. 750 A countryman who was leading me up a steep hill, when we came to a place which was inaccessible, said 'We had better *skitter* under here, and it won't be so steep.' (Kent). **1931** W. Faulkner *Sanctuary* xxv. 298 A second man flew out and skittered along the floor on his back. **1951** J. C. Fennessy *Sonnet in Bottle* II. i. 40 The little whitish-silver flying fish skittering over the ship's bow wave. **1956** C. Evans *Kanchenjunga* xii. 121 Fragments of snow kept skittering down the slope and bombarding the tent. **1969** *New Yorker* 12 Apr. 127/1 The astronauts will start back to the LM—first tossing the universal handling tool..across the black *mare*, where it may skitter to rest inside a small crater. **1970** *Globe & Mail* (Toronto) 28 Sept. 21/7 His long blast was deflected by defenseman Jim McKenny's glove and skittered past a surprised Bruce Gamble in goal who was moving the opposite way to cover. **1978** M. Puzo *Fools Die* ii. 15 He was tired of the glittering red dice skittering across green felt.
2. b. In various senses, with reference to the impartation of a rapid or sliding motion (see quots.).
1902 Kipling *Just So Stories* 61 Let's say things to the bunnies, and watch 'em skitter their tails! **1907** *Harper's Mag.* Feb. 460 The younger boy skittered rocks at a chicken-hawk. **1919** J. Masefield *Reynard* 112 The great hooves skittered The Blood Brook's shallows to sheets that glittered. **1968** A. Diment *Bang Bang Birds* ii. 22 She produced a 6 × 4 glossy..and skittered it across the desk to me. **1972** M. J. Bosse *Incident at Naha* i. 54 Edgar Gear blinked and skittered his hand through his hair.

skittery, *a.* Add: **2.** Skittish, restless.
1941 *Sun* (Baltimore) 29 Aug. 17/2 The little fellers—the skittery moths, and the 11½-foot penguin dinghies, complete the list. **1974** D. Sears *Lark in Clear Air* x. 123 You can see that kind of eye in a skittery horse. **1976** *Gramophone* Oct. 607/1 The only two points at which I was aware of any lack of finish were in the finale of Op. 13 (sometimes a bit skittery) and the 'Dance' of Op. 14.
3. *Textiles.* Producing or taking on an undesired speckly appearance in dyeing.
1955 *Jrnl. Soc. Dyers & Colourists* LXXI. 707/1 A dye which is selective, i.e. skittery, in dyeing behaviour, however, will show marked differences in the rate of exhaustion. **1970** E. R. Trotman *Dyeing & Chem. Technol. Textile Fibres* (ed. 4) xvii. 442 It [*sc.* water solubility] increases the tendency to give 'skittery' shades, caused by the emphasis of variations in affinity from one fibre to another.
Hence **ski·tteriness.**
1952 *Jrnl. Soc. Dyers & Colourists* LXVIII. 306/1 *Skitteriness*, an undesired speckled effect in a yarn or fabric arising from differences in colour or depth of dyeing between adjacent fibres or portions of the same fibre. **1955** *Ibid.* LXXI. 707/1 Skitteriness is a specific property of the dye... Skitteriness comes about through selective dyeing of different wool fibres. **1964** *Dyeing of Polyester Fibres* (I.C.I.) (ed. 3) viii. 237 Although the..dyes recommended..are those with superior levelling properties, it is still essential to ensure initial level application of the wool dye if excessive 'skitteriness' is to be avoided.

skittle, *sb.* Add: **1. b.** (Further examples.)
1857 T. Hughes *Tom Brown's School Days* I. ii. 46 Life isn't all beer and skittles. **1931** A. Christie *Sittaford Mystery* xxvi. 211 'It's an experience, isn't it?' 'Teach him life can't be all beer and skittles,' said Robert Gardner maliciously. **1963** D. Ogilvy *Confessions Advert. Man* (1964) i. 12 Managing an advertising agency isn't all beer and skittles.
c. (Earlier examples.)
1864 *Orchestra* 12 Nov. 104/1 *Se faire applaudir* is not 'to make onesself applauded', and 'joyous comedian' is simply skittles. **1886** Kipling *Departmental Ditties* (ed. 2) 43 'Where is your heat?' says he, 'Coming,' says I to Pagett. 'Skittles!' says Pagett, M.P.
d. *colloq.* Chess played without serious application.
1856 C. Tomlinson *Chess Player's Ann.* 61 Nor will our royal Game less royal sound, If shallow men play skittles on the ground, Where first-rate Chess sedately sits in state, And spends long hours accomplishing a mate. **1894** *Daily News* 30 May 3/6 There is, as every experienced chessist knows, all the difference in the world between what is known as off-hand play or 'skittles' and chess. **1940** Prins & Wood tr. *Euwe's Meet Masters* i. 14 Every game of chess, serious or 'skittles',
3. a. *skittle-ground* (earlier and later examples).
1737 *London Mag.* Sept. 477/2 Such days would still be much better employed in that Way, than in sotting at an Ale-House, or loitering in a Skettle or Nine-Pin Ground. **1971** *Country Life* 9 Dec. 1673/3 In 1773, the spring was covered over, and the site reverted to a simple public house with a skittle-ground attached.

skittle, *v.* Add: **2. b.** To knock down (skittles, etc.); *Cricket*, to bowl out (batsmen) in rapid succession. Also *fig.*, to kill, defeat easily.
1880 *Wisden's Cricketers' Almanack* 18 Mr. Chatterton 'skittled' the wickets down so rapidly. **1919** W. H. Downing *Digger Dial.* 45 *Skittled*, killed. **1928** *Daily Express* 31 Mar. 3/4 Mine host and Mr. Herbert swung their arms, flung the cheeses, and skittled the pins. **1977** *World of Cricket Monthly* June 92/3 The Warwickshire bowling attack..skittled the students for a mere 59 in just 2½ hours.
c. *Cricket.* Similarly with *out*. Also, to dismiss (a team) cheaply.
1906 A. E. Knight *Compl. Cricketer* v. 172 Jim Jones thinks Sir Arthur Squire a rotten captain, who never gives him a chance to 'skittle the rabbits out'. **1949** J. Symons *Bland Beginning* 216 Now that Anthony had found a length, he began to skittle out the batsmen. **1979** *Daily Tel.* 9 Aug. 1/3 Somerset's West Indian fast bowler, Joel Garner, took five wickets for 11 runs, helping to skittle out Kent for 60.

skittler. Add: **1.** (Later example.)
1958 G. Usher *Death in Bag* vii. 64 He'd go and see how the skittlers was doin'.
2. One who plays chess without serious application.
1868 *Westminster Chess Club Papers* I. 87 We consider it quite possible to diffuse the game [of chess] without affording encouragement to the mere 'skittler'. **1911** *Daily News* 24 Apr. 4 The spread of chess literature, which has made every 'skittler' a book player.

skive (skəiv), *sb.*³ *slang.* [f. *SKIVE *v.*³] An act of shirking; an opportunity for avoiding a difficult or unpleasant task, an easy option.
1958 F. Norman *Bang to Rights* III. 90 Not many of us wanted to learn english and only went on the class for a skive. **1960** [see *CHUFFED *a.* a]. **1968** *Guardian* 1 Oct. 6/1 'Isn't just a skive,' he told them. 'At any time, any time, you may be parachuted behind the Russian lines.' **1976** *Times Higher Educ. Suppl.* 26 Mar. 7/1 I'd always thought that science degrees with a non-scientific element would be attractive but perhaps students associate them with the general studies they do in the sixth form and think of them either as a skive or a nuisance. **1980** J. Ditton *Copley's Hunch* I. ii. 68 He thought the sentry was on the skive. Thought he'd come down..for a cup of coffee.

skive (skəiv), *v.*³ *slang* (orig. *Mil.*). Also **scive, skyve.** [perh. ad. Fr. *esquiver*, to dodge, slink away, but cf. Skive *v.*²] *intr.* To evade a duty, to shirk; to avoid work by absenting oneself, to play truant. Also with *off*.
1919 *Athenæum* 1 Aug. 695/1 'To skive,' to dodge a fatigue. **1925** Fraser & Gibbons *Soldier & Sailor Words & Phrases* 260 *To skive*, to dodge a duty or fatigue. **1960** *Twentieth Cent.* Nov. 390 Who hasn't bought black-market, possibly stolen goods, who hasn't skived off work? **1960** J. Birley *Time of Cuckoo* 139 'But a second is what you aimed for, isn't it? I mean one has to be pretty brilliant for the other, anyway, and if not, why work all that hard?' 'Oh, yes, yes, I dare say... I've been skyving all my life, certainly, if that's what you mean.' **1961** *New Statesman* 21 July 82/2 If one of the other cleaners offered advice, it was usually on how to scive off better. **1962** *Listener* 27 Dec. 1104/3 Anyone who thinks of the Fire Service as a soft option that literary types skived into during the war ought to have watched 'Fire Rescue'. **1965** [see *free period* s.v. *FREE *a.* D. 2]. **1971** *Times Educ. Suppl.* 25 June 69 People work—and skyve—openly at any time. **1973** J. Mann *Only Security* vi. 58 The girls who dig are always glad of an excuse to skive off and have a rest. **1976** *Sunday Post* (Glasgow) 26 Dec., A Dundee bus conductor was chatting to three young boys as he took their fares last

Monday. He asked if they were on holiday. They replied they were 'just skiving'. **1982** *Sunday Times* 31 Jan. 3/6 These people work, skive and fiddle in packs.

Hence **ski·ving** *vbl. sb.*[2]

1958 *Daily Mail* 18 July 3/3 You do two hours' work a day and spend the rest of the time dodging. In the Army we called it swinging the lead, but on the railway it's called skiving. **1974** *New Society* 19 Sept. 727/1 It is among managerial and professional workers that sponging, skiving and malingering is epidemic. **1977** *Ibid.* 25 Aug. 381/3 Some of the overseers connive at, even join in, this skyving. **1978** P. Marsh et al. *Rules of Disorder* ii. 33 Skiving was not infrequent—the pupils slipping out once the register had been called.

skiver, *sb.*[2] **2.** (Earlier examples.)

1829 P. Egan *Boxiana* 2nd Ser. II. 220 At a proper age, Jem turned out to earn an honest penny, and was apprenticed to a *skyver*, or skinman, in Newcastle-upon-Tyne. **1850** *Rep. Comm. Patents 1849* (U.S.) I. 313, I claim..the application of a gauge or gauges to a skiver.

skiver (skəi·vəɹ), *sb.*[3] *slang.* Also **sciver, skyver.** [f. *skive *v.*[3] + -er[1].] One who avoids work; a shirker; a truant.

1941 G. Kersh *They die with their Boots Clean* 219 Well, mud in your eye, old skivers! **1942** —— *Nine Lives Bill Nelson* xi. 71 You end up like them old skivers that mooch about the Naffy Library. **1959** I. & P. Opie *Lore & Lang. Schoolch.* xvii. 372 A few children in Kirkcaldy give 'sciver' as a name for a truant. **1961** *New Statesman* 26 May 830/1 As it was day-time, everyone in the coffee bar was a sciver, on the dole or on the fiddle or just plain hopeful. **1971** [see *fruit gum* s.v. *fruit *sb.* 9]. **1977** *Daily Tel.* 24 Nov. 8/6 A Labour-controlled council is to crack down on 'skivers' following a report which alleges large scale absenteeism and sick leave among its manual workers. **1982** *Times* 20 Apr. 4/8, I frequently came across cases at depots where there were skivers galore.

skiving, *vbl. sb.*[2]: see *skive *v.*[3]

skivvy (ski·vi), *sb.*[1] *colloq.* (usu. *derogatory*). Also **scivey, skivey.** [Of obscure origin.] A female domestic servant, esp. a maid-of-all-work. Also *transf.*

1902 H. Baumann *Londinismen* (ed. 2) 211/2 *Skivey*,.. slav(e)y. **1913** C. Mackenzie *Sinister St.* I. ii. iv. 195 The ball had landed twice..on the same balcony to the great annoyance of the 'skivvy', who was..invited to bung it down. **1915** W. Owen *Let.* 23 Nov. (1967) 367, I never thought myself capable of such strenuosities as to do skivvy's drudgery. **1938** L. Durrell *Black Book* 240 Gwen, that dirty little skivvy, smelling of..grease from the sink! **1947** E. Wilson *Europe without Baedeker* viii. 206 You were waited on by slovenly skivvies so pallidly unappetizing that they made the meager food seem more tasteless. **1961** 'F. O'Brien' *Hard Life* vii. 52 The young people of today think the daddy is a tramp and the mammy a poor skivvy. **1974** *Times* 1 May 4/5 This represents a change in the nurses' attitude. No longer will you be the skivvies of the health service. **1977** *Punch* 31 Aug.–6 Sept. 331/1 Blossom, the strikingly handsome new scivvy, is mixing her a posset.

Hence **ski·vvy** *v. intr.*, to work as a skivvy; **ski·vvying** *vbl. sb.*

1931 R. Campbell *Georgiad* ii. 44 Every Nellie, Gertie Or Daisy that..ever left her own unlettered stews To skivvy in the kitchen of the Muse. **1968** *Punch* 21 Feb. 287/1 There are now better jobs than skivvying to look for, and wages sometimes comparable with what the job-seeking housewife herself might be earning. **1973** J. Thomson *Death Cap* ii. 33 It wasn't no skivvying job... Mrs King treated me like a friend. **1974** W. Foley *Child in Forest* ii. 156 She come up to skivvy in the same place as you, then?

skivvy (ski·vi), *sb.*[2] Also **scivvy, skivie, skivvie.** [Of unknown origin.] **1.** *N. Amer. slang* (orig. *Naut.*). **a.** An undershirt, a vest. Also *skivvy shirt.* **b.** *pl.* Underclothes.

1932 J. L. D'Esque *Count in Fo'c'sle* 216 He cut away the unconscious engineer's shirt and skivie with his jack-knife. **1942** Berrey & Van den Bark *Amer. Thes. Slang* §900/6 *Skivvie shirt*, an undervest. **1944** C. Mackenzie *Sailors of Fortune* 95 The Red Cross woman brought me khaki trousers, scivvy shirt and a left shoe. **1945** *Seafarers' Log* 9 Nov. 6/3 Chips appeared, also gassed up, in his skivvies. **1946** T. Heggen *Mister Roberts* 7 It now contained a soiled scivvy shirt. **1953** S. Bellow *Adventures Augie March* 28 We had to brush our teeth with salt..and sleeping in skivvies was outlawed; we had to wear pajamas. **1967** 'J. Cross' *To Hell for Half-a-Crown* ii. 36 The..biceps straining at the white skivvy shirt. **1972** R. White *Be not Afraid* xvii. 206 We jumped out of our sleeping bags.., only realizing after we had recovered the gear that we were barefoot and in skivvies in subzero weather. **1978** W. Hjortsberg *Falling Angel* xxxviii. 184 Ethan Krusemark, wearing boxer shorts and a skivvy, lay on his back..doing leg presses.

2. A high-necked lightweight pullover or jumper.

1967 *Telegraph* (Brisbane) 27 Feb. 14/4 (*caption*) This waistcoat should be a winner on the winter scene teamed with white long-sleeved skivvy. **1972** *New York* 8 May 20/1 (Advt.), Sleeveless skivvy (shown under the cardigans) in peach or pale blue. **1972** D. Sale *Love Bite* xix. 239 She was wearing a navy-blue jump suit over a black skivvy, so that she wouldn't be seen in the dark.

sklodowskite (sklǫdǭ·vskəit). *Min.* [a. F. *sklodowskite* (A. Schoep 1924, in *Compt. Rend.* CLXXIX. 415), f. *Sklodowska*, maiden name of Marie Curie (1867–1934), Polish-born chemist and co-discoverer of radium: see -ite[1].] A hydrated uranyl magnesium silicate, $Mg(UO_2)_2Si_2O_7.6H_2O$, which occurs as a secondary mineral, forming lemon-yellow monoclinic crystals.

1924 *Chem. Abstr.* XVIII. 3577 (*heading*) Sklodowskite, a new radioactive mineral. **1957** *Amer. Mineralogist* XLII. 617 Sklodowskite, which is considered iso-structural with uranophane, and beta-uranophane may have structures based on uranophane. **1972** *Canad. Mineralogist* XI. 562 A mixture of uranophane and sklodowskite forms a coating on a specimen of quartz with magnetite.

skoal, *sb.* Add: Now usu. with pronunc. (skǫl) and in form **skol.** Also **skal, sköl.** (Further examples of use as a toast.)

1924 *Vogue* late Jan. 64/2 If only I could make out why nobody dared touch his glass before someone else had said 'Skål', and why you yourself were at it the whole time. **1935** J. D. Carr *Death-Watch* xix. 187 'Skoal,' wheezed Dr. Fell absently. He pushed his glass away. **1948** F. Brown *Murder can be Fun* (1951) ii. 24 'Skoal!' he said. They drank. **1961** *Guardian* 8 Feb. 12/5 'Skol' which we imagine to be a jolly kind of 'Cheerio' on lifting a glass, is an essential part of Swedish etiquette. **1961** M. Beadle *These Ruins are Inhabited* (1963) ix. 116 We.. learned the etiquette of *sköl*. The Swedes are enthusiastic drinkers. **1973** D. Francis *Slay-Ride* i. 17 '*Skol*' they said. '*Skol*' I repeated. They watched interestedly while I drank.

skoal, *v.* Delete † *Obs.*, for *Sc.* read 'orig. *Sc.*', and add: Also **skol. a.** (Later examples.) **b.** *trans.* To drink the health of.

1909 E. Pound *Personae* 17, I skoal to the eyes as grey-blown mere..Wineing the ghosts of yester-year. **1928** H. Crane *Let.* 27 Mar. (1965) 320 Many bottles of dubious gin and whiskey—with much 'skoling'. **1935** G. Greene *England made Me* i. 1 She swallowed it at a draught.. skoal, skoal, but there was no one to skoal. **1963** *Times* 23 Jan. 12/7 There was ample time to *skol* one another. **1980** P. Harcourt *Tomorrow's Treason* i. iv. 67 We had skolled in champagne the bonfires being lit around the fjord.

Skoda (skōᵘ·dă). The name of the Czech engineer and industrialist Emil von *Skoda* (1839–1900), used *attrib.* and *ellipt.* to designate guns manufactured in the factories established by him.

1902 *Encycl. Brit.* XXIX. 166/1 In the Hotchkiss and also in the Skoda systems the mechanism is of the vertical breech block type. **1933** J. Buchan *Prince of Captivity* i. 78 Skoda mountain howitzers which had once been destined for the Hedjaz. **1973** J. Quick *Dict. Weapons & Mil. Terms* 402/1 The first Skoda machine gun appeared in 1888 and was a delayed-blowback weapon.

‖ **skoff** (skǫf). *S. Afr.* Also **schoft, skof, skoft.** Pl. **skoffs, skofte.** [Afrikaans *skof*, f. Du. *schoft* (see Scoff *sb.*[2]).] A stage of a journey, a period of travel between outspans.

1785 G. Forster tr. *Sparrman's Voyage to Cape of Good Hope* I. 132 Four such hours with a horse, or with eight oxen, are reckoned to make one *skoft*. **1801** J. Barrow *Acct. Trav. S. Afr.* I. ii. 55 Each day's journey is called a *skoff*; and the length of these is generally regulated by local circumstances, being from five to fifteen hours. **1835** H. I. Venable in D. J. Kotzé *Lett. Amer. Missionaries* (1950) 70 The Dutch call a day's journey a *schoft*. For oxen in good condition a schoft is from twenty to twenty-four miles. **1892** R. Churchill *Men, Mines & Animals in S. Afr.* ix. 134 We have done twenty-five miles from Silika in three 'skoffs', which is excellent trekking. **1932** L. Fouche in C. Fuller *Louis Trigardt's Trek* p. xv, It became imperative to ascertain the value of Trigardt's unit, the length of a 'skof'. **1969** A. Fugard *Boesman & Lena* i. 2 That last skof was hard. Against the wind... Heavier and heavier. Every step. **1972** L. G. Green *When Journey's Over* (1973) v. 50 The normal day on the road was made up of two or three stages known as *skofte*.

skoff, var. Scoff *sb.*[2] and *v.*[2] in Dict. and Suppl.

skokiaan (skǫ·kiān). *S. Afr.* Also **skokian.** [Poss. of Nguni origin.] An intoxicating home-brewed liquor fermented with yeast. Also *attrib.*

1926 S. G. Millin *S. Africans* vii. ii. 223 Sometimes a group of Kaffirs are found drinking a rapidly fermenting preparation called *skokiaan* in the outbuilding of a European's home. **1936** Williams & May *I am Black* iv. xvii. 175 The white men call me a skokiaan queen. **1946** P. Abrahams *Mine Boy* xi. 135 He knew she was one of the foremost Skokiaan Queens—for that is what they call the women who deal in illicit liquor. **1953** D. Lessing *Five* 286 Skokian is a wicked and dangerous drink, and it is illegal. It is made quickly, in one day, and may contain many different substances. On this night it has mealie-meal, sugar, tobacco, methylated spirits, boot polish and yeast. Some skokian queens use magic, such as the limb of a dead person. **1970** G. Lord *Marshmallow Pie* iv. 33 He didn't hate the blacks... All they wanted was a quiet life and some *skokiaan* on Saturday nights. **1976** *Globe & Mail* (Toronto) 13 Nov. 16/5 The rougher shebeens lack refinements and sell often-questionable products, ranging from commercial and homemade beers to a variety of moonshine liquors, including the legendary skokiaan.

skol, var. Skoal *sb.*, *v.*, in Dict. and Suppl.

sköl, var. Skoal *sb.* in Dict. and Suppl.

skolly (skǫ·li). *S. Afr.* Also **scolly, -ie.** [a. Afrikaans, prob. ad. Du. *schoelje* scoundrel, rascal.] A Black or Coloured African hooligan, gangster, hoodlum; a vagrant. Also *attrib.*, as *skolly boy.* Hence **sko·llydom,** the condition or activity of a skolly; **sko·llyism,** the way of life of a skolly.

1934 *Cape Argus* 8 Jan. 10/6 The accused..were actually several degrees lower than the average 'scolly-boy' who commits most of the crimes of violence and theft in the Peninsula. **1934** *Cape Times* 12 Jan. 9/7 The 'scollie' boys could be rounded up and sent to labour colonies. **1949** *Ibid.* 10 Sept. 8/8 The cure for skollydom is not mollycoddling. **1954** R. St. John *Through Malan's Africa* v. 32 Experts say that dagga is one of the least harmful of the narcotics, and yet in District 6 it leads to the shebeens and skollyism. **1961** *Cape Times* 28 Jan. 11/1 Don't you realize that your son is becoming a White skolly?.. He is going to land in gaol unless you do something about him. **1972** *East Cape Post* 14 Mar., Tsotsis and skollies who lurk in street corners, waiting to assault and rob innocent people. **1980** J. McClure *Blood of Englishman* ix. 82 Look at the clientele... All the top-notch... You won't find skolly boys in here.

skoob (skūb). [Reversal of *books*: not in general use (see quots.).] A pile of books assembled in order to be destroyed as a gesture against the proliferation and undue veneration of the printed word (see quot. 1967); the ceremonial burning of a book or books.

1963 *Guardian* 14 Feb. 6/5 The Skoob Image—the mangled books. **1966** *Archit. Rev.* Dec. 441/2 A skoob tower by John Latham—a construction of art books destined to be detonated. **1967** *Listener* 18 May 654/3 Latham's earlier works were assemblages of torn and paint-covered books... His 'skoob' (books spelt backwards) are a cathartic topsy-turvying of the natural reaction of horror at the destruction of the printed word. **1968** *Guardian* 14 Sept. 3/3 Mr. Stone said it was the first time that a 'skoob', the burning of a book, had taken place in Kensington Church Walk.

skookum (skū·kǫ̈m), *sb.* and *a.* *N. Amer.* Also † **scocum, scokum,** etc. [a. Chinook Jargon.] **A.** *sb.* An evil spirit; a disease. *Obs.* exc. *Hist.*

1838 S. Parker *Jrnl. of Exploring Tour beyond Rocky Mts.* 336 Evil spirit, skookoom. Hell, skookoom. **1844** Lee & Frost *Ten Yrs. in Oregon* xvi. 180 He [*sc.* the medicine man] transfers the 'sko-koms', or 'tam-an-a-was', or disease, wholly or in part from the patient to himself. **1846** Johnson & Winter *Route Across Rocky Mts.* iii. 54 Several loud shouts are uttered in as frightful a manner as they are able. They then open their fingers gradually, to allow the terrified Scocum, (evil spirit,) to make his escape. **1900** *Oregon Hist. Soc. Q.* I. 185 The benefits of his fishery had gone, not to the people, but to the wicked skookum.

B. *adj.* **a.** Strong, stout, brave; fine, splendid.

1847 J. Palmer *Jrnl. Trav. Rocky Mts.* 151/1 *Skookum*, strong, stout. **1891** H. W. Seton-Karr *Bear Hunting in White Mts.* viii. 83 He believed that a bear would hold out its paw towards a man at a distance and feel whether he was *skookum*—brave. **1901** *Daily Colonist* (Victoria, B.C.) 29 Oct. 6/3, I would have gone up myself but could not stand the five days' tramp with 40 or 50 pounds on my back. It takes a 'skookum' man to stand a trip like that. **1913** [see *rough lock, rough-lock]. **1941** J. Smiley *Hash House Lingo* 50 *Skookum*, good; all right. **1949** *Sierra Club. Bull.* (San Francisco) June 105 Billy and Pete were skookum, and I was pretty good myself in those days. **1962** E. Lucia *Klondike Kate* 12 As Klondike Kate, she was a mighty skookum gal. **1975** *Islander* (Victoria, B.C.) 6 July 4/2 Ted, by this time a skookum young fellow of 20, then turned his eyes further west.

b. Special collocations. **skookum chuck** [*chuck *sb.*[6]], a fast-moving body of water, a torrent, rapids; an ocean; **skookum house,** a gaol.

1888 Lees & Clutterbuck *B.C. 1887: Ramble in British Columbia* xvii. 184 We arranged to meet at the Skookumchuck Creek ('the stream of the rapid torrent'). **1899** *Bull. U.S. Fish Comm. 1898* XVIII. 73 The passage is a 'skookum chuck', through which the water runs in whirls and rapids almost constantly and with great velocity. **1911** E. P. Johnson *Legends of Vancouver* 47 You have listened to the call of the Skookum Chuck, as the Chinook speakers call the rollicking, tumbling streams that sing their way through the canyons. **1940** K. S. Pinkerton *Three's Crew* x. 102 A tidal rapids is a 'skookum chuck'. **1959** *Times* (Queen in Canada Suppl.) 18 June p. xii/1 This is the salt chuck, the skookum chuck..in fact the Pacific. **1873** R. C. L. Brown *Klatsassan* 165 It was only after much *waw-waw* (parley) and sundry threats of the skookum-house (gaol).. that one of them was got to undertake to carry him. **1901** *Daily Colonist* (Victoria, B.C.) 5 Oct. 3/2 There were no less than fourteen inmates of the 'skookum house' on Cormorant Street last night. **1965** *Islander* (Victoria, B.C.) 9 May 6/2 In 1872, Frederick Brent was appointed Justice of the Peace and a skookum-house (jail) was built on his land.

skoptophilia, var. *scopophilia.

Skoptsi (skǫ·ptsi), *sb. pl.* Also occas. **Skoptzi, Skopzy,** etc. [Russ., pl. of *skopéts*, eunuch, member of Skoptsi.] An ascetic Russian Christian sect, known since the eighteenth century and now forbidden, given to self-mutilation (see quots.). Also *rarely* as *sing.* Hence **Sko·ptsism,** the faith and practice of the Skoptsi.

1856 [see *KHLIST]. **1874** J. H. BLUNT *Dict. Sects* 564/1 *Skoptzi*, a name signifying 'eunuchs', given to a Russian sect of the Bezpopoftschin Dissenters, and derived from their practice of self-mutilation, which they supposed to be warranted by Scripture (Matt. xix. 12). **1887** A. F. HEARD *Russ. Ch. & Russ. Dissent* xi. 270 Notwithstanding their precautions, the Skoptsi are betrayed by their pale, sallow complexion, their scanty beard, shrill voice, effeminate, peculiar gait, and hesitating, wavering look. **1888** 'STEPNIAK' *Russ. Peasantry* II. iii. 439 The *Skopzy* or *Castrati*, founded by Selivanov at the close of the eighteenth century. **1911** *Encycl. Brit.* XXV. 194/1 Skoptsism was, however, not exterminated, and grave scandals constantly arose. **1957** *Ibid.* XXIII. 873/1 The Skoptsi..settled in Yakut in the 1860s and introduced agriculture... The clean, well-built Skoptsi villages were a striking contrast to the dirty Yakutsh settlements. **1960** O. MANNING *Great Fortune* I. 25 A *Skopit*. One of the sights of the city. The *Skopits* belong to a Russian sect. **1970** B. WALKER *Sex & Supernatural* ix. 84 The best known of the modern castrant cults called the Skoptsi, or 'eunuchs', a mystical Russian sect which first came into prominence in the middle of the 18th century but which was said to have been in existence for at least three centuries before that.

‖ **skothending** (skǫ·tˌhendiŋ). *Pros.* [ON.] Chiefly in Scaldic verse: rhyme formed with the same consonant or consonant cluster preceded by differing vowels; half-rhyme.

1838 G. P. MARSH *Compendious Gram. Old-Northern or Icel. Lang.* IV. 144 The same consonants with different vowels (skothending, *half-rhyme*, or *assonance*). **1860, 1873–4** [see *half-rhyme* s.v. *HALF- II. n]. **1945** L. M. HOLLANDER *Skalds* 10 The *skothending* in the odd, and the *aðalhending* in the even, half-line always involve the second but last syllable. **1977** J. MILROY *Lang. G. M. Hopkins* v. 144 We are not accustomed to notice *skothending* (end-consonant rhyme) when it occurs in English. Hopkins uses it very liberally.

skotophil(e, var. *SCOTOPHIL *a.* **skourick,** Sc. var. *SKERRICK.

Skraeling (skrǣ·liŋ). *Scandinavian Hist.* Also † **Schrelling, Skrelling, Skrælling,** etc.; **Skræling.** [ad. ON. *Skræling(j)ar* pl., the Norse name for the inhabitants of Greenland at the time of the Norse settlement.] A member of a savage people encountered by the early Norse settlers on Greenland, of uncertain origin but often considered to be of Eskimo descent. Also applied similarly to the inhabitants of Vinland (sometimes identified with the NE. coast of N. America). Usu. *pl.*

1767 tr. *Crantz's Hist. Greenland* I. III. i. 132 The Greenlanders call themselves..*Innuit*... The Icelanders, who many hundred years ago discovered..this country and the neighbouring coasts of America, called them in form *Skrællings*, because they are little of stature. **1797** *Encycl. Brit.* VIII. 129/2 This nation, called *Schrellings*, at length prevailed against the Iceland settlers who inhabited the western district [of Greenland]. **1875** *Ibid.* I. 706/2 They had some intercourse..with a people who came in leathern boats, and were called *Skrælings*, from their dwarfish size... The Skrælings were of course Esquimaux... The hostilities of the Skrælings was no doubt the principal cause of the abandonment of the colony [of Vinland]. **1891** KIPLING in *Contemp. Rev.* July 21 He.. said:—'When they heard *our* bulls bellow the Skrælings ran away!' **1921** G. M. GATHORNE-HARDY *Norse Discoverers of Amer.* II. iv. 172 In so far..as the descriptions of the Skrælings of Wineland are realistic, and differ materially from anything which can have been derived from Eskimo sources, these descriptions form probably the most convincing proof of the historical accuracy of these stories. **1979** N. DAVIES *Voyagers to New World* 227 When spring came the skraelings once more appeared.

Skraup (skraup). *Chem.* The name of Zdenko Hans *Skraup* (1850–1910), Czech chemist, used *attrib.* and in the possessive to denote a reaction which he discovered (*Sitzungsber. der K. Akad. der Wissensch.* (*Math.-Nat. Classe*) (1880) LXXXI. II. 593), in which a quinoline is synthesized by heating a primary aromatic amine with glycerol, sulphuric acid, and an oxidizing agent.

1886 *Jrnl. Chem. Soc.* L. 79 Chloromethylquinoline..is prepared by Skraup's method from parachlorometatoluidine. **1935** L. F. MAREK in P. H. Groggins *Unit Processes in Org. Synthesis* vii. 350 Quinoline is prepared from aniline and glycerol by the Skraup reaction. **1954** I. L. FINAR *Org. Chem.* (ed. 2) I. xxxi. 691 Alizarin Blue..may be prepared by first reducing Alizarin Orange to the corresponding amino-compound and then heating this with glycerol, sulphuric acid and nitrobenzene (Skraup's synthesis). **1975** R. F. BROWN *Org. Chem.* xxviii. 908 The Skraup synthesis involves a dehydration, a Michael addition, an electrophilic substitution (the ring-closing reaction), and an oxidation, all occurring in one flask during a relatively short period of refluxing.

skreef, obs. var. *SCREEF *sb.*

‖ **skrik** (skrik). *S. Afr. colloq.* Also **schreik, schrick, schrijk, schrik, scrick.** [Afrikaans, f. Du. *schrik* fright.] A sudden fright, start; a shock or *frisson*. Freq. in phr. *to get, have* or *give* (someone) *a skrik.*

1887 A. A. ANDERSON *Twenty-Five Years in Waggon* i. 21 They heard the rattling of wheels in a manner which made them think that the oxen must have had a 'scrick' (scare) from a lion. **1896** H. A. BRYDEN *Tales of S. Afr.* 68 It gave me a very nasty *schrijk* at the time. **1897** E. GLANVILLE *Tales from Veld* xxiii. 173 Lor' bless yer, the *schreik* he gave me. **1899** D. BLACKBURN *Prinsloo of Prinsloosdorp* 30 Piet had a bad schrick, but he thought out a plan. **1913** J. J. DOKE *Secret City* xxx. 255 How you do frighten me. You gave me quite a schrik. **1942** S. CLOETE *Hill of Doves* xxxi. 440 'It's Reuter,' someone said. 'What are you doing to give us a skrik like this? It is a joke. It is Reuter.' **1969** A. FUGARD *Boesman & Lena* I. 7 Remember that night the water came up so high?.. You got such a skrik you ran the wrong way. **1975** *Darling* 12 Feb. 119 'Who, me?' I tune him, meantime, feeling the skriks running up and down my spine.

skrike, *v.* Now the more usual form of SCRIKE *v.* Add: **2.** To weep, cry.

1905 *Eng. Dial. Dict.* V. s.v., Hoo skrite't so when hur mother deed I thow't hoo'd ne'er ha done. *Ibid.*, I can tell by yur een as yo'n bin skrikin'. **1977** P. CARTER *Under Goliath* xxvi. 142, I stood there..skriking my eyes out like a mammy's boy... I really cried my eyes out in the loft. **1978** *Lancashire Life* Apr. 42/3 Second un poor little soul Did nuthin' else but skrike.

skriking *vbl. sb.* (later example); **skriker** (later example).

1937 J. R. R. TOLKIEN *Hobbit* iv. 76 The yells and yammering, croaking, jibbering and jabbering; howls, growls and curses; shrieking and skriking, that followed were beyond description. **1959** I. & P. OPIE *Lore & Lang. Schoolch.* x. 186 In the area of Blackburn, Bolton, Manchester, Stockport, and Halifax the term 'skriking' [*sc.* for 'crying'] is common, the noun being 'skriker'.

skulduggery. (In Dict. s.v. SCULDUDDERY 3.) For *U.S.* read orig. *U.S.* and add: 9 **scull-duggery; skullduggery.** Substitute for def.: underhand dealing, roguish intrigue or machination, trickery. (Earlier and later examples.)

1867 A. D. RICHARDSON *Beyond Mississippi* xi. 134 From Minnesota had been imported the mysterious term 'scull-duggery', used to signify political or other trickery. **1911** H. QUICK *Yellowstone Nights* ix. 239 It began to look to me like Hen was up to some skulduggery. **1929** M. A. GILL *Underworld Slang* 11/1 *Skull duggery*, dirty work. **1936** H. HAGEDORN *Brookings* iii. 49 America at ..its worst in financiering, political machination and the skullduggery of the stock market. **1949** J. STEINBECK *Russian Jrnl.* ix. 215 The political skulduggery of the Kremlin. **1957** A. GRIMBLE *Return to Islands* vii. 130 Disgraceful stories of all the skulduggeries he had got away with by suborning government officials. **1962** D. FRANCIS *Dead Cert* ix. 108 The skulduggery that goes on in respectable little old Brighton. **1980** *Times* 3 Jan. 10/2 Watergate was such a sensational piece of skulduggery.

Hence [as back-formation] **sku·ldug** *v. trans.*, to extract by trickery. *nonce-wd.*

1936 W. FAULKNER *Absalom, Absalom!* vi. 178 This Faustus who..skuldugged a hundred miles of land out of a poor ignorant Indian.

skulk, *sb.* **1.** (Earlier modern U.S. example.)

1838 *Knickerbocker* XI. 448 Spotswood had told the middie that Tudor was a great 'skulk', and would probably be reluctant to turn out.

skull, *sb.*[1] Add: **1. b.** Also in slang phr. *out of one's skull*, out of one's mind, crazy. Also succeeding pa. pple., as *bored out of one's skull*, beside oneself with boredom, bored stiff.

1967 *Listener* 7 Dec. 740/2, 12 good men and true, glumly spruce, resigned to a long haul and bored, bored out of their skulls. **1968** T. WOLFE *Electric Kool-Aid Acid Test* xv. 205 They [*sc.* the Beatles] have brought this whole mass of human beings to the point where they are.. out of their skulls. **1973** W. SHEED *People will always be Kind* II. v. 301 You'd have had to be out of your skull not to in those days. **1978** G. VIDAL *Kalki* iii. 83, I thought that Kalki was out of his skull.

d. Also *skull and crossbones*, a representation of a bare skull with two thigh-bones crossed beneath it as an emblem of death, esp. as depicted on a pirate's flag (later examples). Cf. *The Jolly Roger* s.v. ROGER[2] 4. Also *attrib.* and *fig.* Hence *skull-and-crossboned* adj.

1911 D. H. LAWRENCE *Let.* c11 May (1979) I. 268 I've got a grinning skull-and-crossbones headache. **1924** WODEHOUSE *Bill the Conqueror* xvii. 254 This was open rebellion. This was hoisting the skull and cross-bones. **1928** J. M. BARRIE *Peter Pan* in *Plays* v. 73 We see what is happening on the deck of the *Jolly Roger*, which is flying the skull and crossbones. **1930** *Times Lit. Suppl.* 5 June 481/4 The pirates on the Spanish Main in the old skull-and-crossbones days were pleasant and picturesque fellows. **1931** A. RANSOME *Swallowdale* iii. 50 A small varnished dinghy..was sailing in between the headlands. At the masthead was a black flag with the skull and crossbones on it in white. **1955** J. KENWARD *Suburban Child* xxxii. 94 Further down the street where I lived there lived a pirate five years old, the very thing in appearance as in temperament, with a cutlass (silver painted) and a black triangular hat (skull-and-crossboned) both home-made by his understanding parents. **1982** *Times* 5 July 4/3 The nuclear submarine..[was] flying the Jolly Roger to denote their success in sinking the Argentine cruiser... The Skull-and-Crossbones denotes a 'kill'.

e. *slang.* (So much) *a skull*, per person. Cf. HEAD *sb.* 7 b.

1922 JOYCE *Ulysses* 299 They chop up the rope after and sell the bits for a few bob a skull. **1950** *Chambers's Jrnl.* Apr. 213/2 'What difference would the five of clubs make? Sure he had a cast-iron hand.' The Sergeant drew slow caressing fingers along his jaw. That'll be two bob a skull, boys,' he reminded them pleasantly.

5. a. *skull-eye, -neck.*

1928 BLUNDEN *Retreat* 32 The stone skull-eyes look down most drearily. **1922** JOYCE *Ulysses* 509 His eye agonising in his flat skullneck.

6. b. *skull-hunter* (earlier example).

1866 'MARK TWAIN' *Lett. from Hawaii* (1967) 62 In spite of the depredations of 'skull hunters', we rode a considerable distance over ground..thickly strewn with human bones.

7. skull-buster *U.S. slang*, something that taxes the mind; a complicated problem; **skull session** *U.S. slang*, a discussion, conference.

1926 *University Mag.* (Univ. Va.) Oct. 17 *Skull-buster*, a particularly hard course. **1946** MEZZROW & WOLFE *Really Blues* i. 18 Most of my skullbusters got solved at The School. **1959** J. BLISH *Clash of Cymbals* iv. 97 Web and Estelle..had become accepted silent partners at such skull-sessions. **1973** 'D. JORDAN' *Nile Green* xi. 49 Joe was ready for the skull session.

skull (skɒl), *v.* [f. SKULL *sb.*[1]] **1.** *trans.* (with *up*) and *intr.* *Metallurgy.* Of molten metal: to freeze and form a skull (in). Cf. SKULL *sb.*[1] 4.

1941 *Engineers' Digest* II. 409/2 Very low sulphur iron, or slow-running iron, would skull up the ladles if much scrap were used. **1953** D. J. O. BRANDT *Manuf. Iron & Steel* xxiii. 174 Neither may the ladle be emptied too slowly, for if it is the steel will get too cold and will 'scull' [*ed.* 2: skull], i.e., freeze.

2. *trans.* To strike (someone) on the head. *slang* (chiefly *U.S.*).

1945 BAKER *Austral. Lang.* viii. 157 *Skull*, to strike (someone). **1952** B. MALAMUD *Natural* 32 My father? Well, maybe I did want to skull him sometimes. **1956** F. CASTLE *Violent Hours* vii. 58 'You didn't get skulled backing away from him,' Webb said dryly. **1975** A. BERGMAN *Hollywood & Le Vine* (1976) viii. 97 My waking came in drugged stages... I had been skulled.

skull-cap. Add: **1. b.** *fig.*

1960 S. BECKER tr. *A. Schwarz-Bart's Last of Just* (1961) VI. 305 Everything under the skullcap of the heavens that called itself a democracy. **1978** *Amer. Poetry Rev.* July/Aug. 35/2, I remember the moon is a skullcap not placed properly on the head.

skullduggery, var. *SKULDUGGERY.

skun, occas. pa. t. or pa. pple. of SKIN *v. dial.* and *colloq.* (chiefly *U.S.*). (See also Wentworth *Amer. Dial. Dict.*)

1917 R. FROST *Let.* 3 Dec. (1972) 20 They might have skun him alive if he had been a mere pupil in their classes. **1927** *Bulletin* (Glasgow) 26 Sept. 12/3 When it comes to breakfast foods America has got Great Britain skun a mile. **1936** J. G. BRANDON *Pawnshop Murder* xxvi. 260 The toff Wibley is working for might be connected with the old dame Widgett skun for her 'ice'? **1942** W. FAULKNER *Go down, Moses* 23 You run a hard race and you run a good one, but you skun the hen-house one time too many.

skunge, var. *SCUNGE *sb.*

skunk, *sb.* Add: **2. b.** Something unpleasant or rotten; rubbish, nonsense.

1929 D. H. LAWRENCE *Pansies* 148 Once and for all, have done with it, all the silly bunk of upper-class superiority; that superior stuff is just holy skunk. **1976** *Daily Times* (Lagos) 8 Oct. 7/6 However, for throwing away the skunk of a national anthem that was unashamedly saddled to this federation for 16 long years, a thousand cheers to the father of this nation, late Murtala Muhammed.

c. *U.S. Mil. slang.* An unidentified surface craft. Cf. *BOGY[1], BOGEY[1] 6.

1945 J. BRYAN *Diary* 24 Mar. in *Aircraft Carrier* (1954) 112 'Skunk' is code for a surface contact, a companion term to 'bogey' in the air. **1952** *N.Y. Times Mag.* 19 Oct. 14/4 The cruiser is..useful at times for coastal bombardment or to seek out and destroy enemy 'skunks' (surface craft). **1957** *Ibid.* 19 May 22/3 A Skunk is an unidentified surface ship, as opposed to a Bogie, which is an unidentified aircraft.

3. skunk bear = WOLVERENE, -INE, 1; **skunk spruce,** one of several aromatic North American spruces, esp. the eastern *Picea glauca* or the western *Picea engelmannii.*

1876 G. B. GRINNELL in W. Ludlow *U.S. Army Corps of Engineers Rep. Reconn. to Yellowstone Nat. Park* i. 65 *Gulo luscus*... In this region, they were spoken of as the 'Skunk-bear'. **1911** J. E. ROGERS *Wild Animals* 112 The wolverine, largest of all the weasels, looks more like a bear and a skunk combined. 'Skunk-bear' is one of his many nicknames. **1961** *Tamarack Rev.* Spring 9 He slouched.. but never preventing the fear from settling in him, never preventing it from turning his eye wary and cruel as any skunkbear's. **1894** *Amer. Folk-Lore* VII. 99 *Picea alba*,.. skunk-spruce. **1921** P. B. KYNE *Go-getter* iii. 32 Have you ever had any experience selling skunk spruce?.. It's coarse and stringy and wet and heavy and smells just like a skunk. **1948** *Sun* (Baltimore) 21 Dec. 14/2 They are not, it seems, 'real Christmas trees: only skunk spruce'.

skunky *a.*: also, evil-smelling.

1946 D. C. PEATTIE *Road of Naturalist* i. 21 Nicolletia with off-shade yellow-pinks and mustardy green-yellows and a skunky odour that simply would not wash off the fingers. **1960** *Tamarack Rev.* Winter 127 He called.. 'Skunky small one?' Tommy Moore turned his soapy face upward. He was used to being summoned this way. **1973** *Globe & Mail* (Toronto) 3 July 28/1 The thousands of blue-jeaned teenagers..drink beer in the sun, drinking it fast so it doesn't go skunky. **1981** P. THEROUX *Mosquito Coast* xxi. 277 In very hot weather..the jungle odour is skunky and as strong as garbage.

skunk, *v.* Substitute for entry:

skunk (skʌŋk), *v. slang* (orig. and chiefly *N. Amer.*). [f. the sb.] **1. a.** *intr.* To fail. *rare.*

1831 *Constellation* 1 Jan. 54/1 It is a common expression in New-England, to say of a person, who does not get a king in the game of chequers, he *skunked*.

b. *trans.* To defeat or get the better of; to inflict defeat upon.

In some quots. in passive = 'defeated without making any score'.

1843 *Quincy* (Illinois) *Herald* 24 Nov. 2/1 The Legislature will be Democratic by an overwhelming majority; it is more than probable that the Whigs have been skunked. **1845** *Spirit of Times* 9 Aug. 273/2 In the second hand of the third game, I made high, low, game, and 'skunked' him, outright. **1848** BARTLETT *Dict. Amer.* 409 In games of chance, if one of the players fails to make a point, he is said to be *skunked*. A presidential candidate who fails to secure one electoral vote is also skunked. **1876** W. WRIGHT *Big Bonanza* lxxi. 541 'Skunked, by the holy spoons', cried he. **1898** N. BROOKS *Boys of Fairport* ii. 37 Their only hope now was to 'skunk' the White Bears, who were coming to bat. **1904** F. CRISSEY *Tattlings* xvii. 365 A certain trio of choice scamps from the city hall gang would make a strong committee that could skunk the enemy. **1921** *Daily Colonist* (Victoria, B.C.) 18 Oct. 10/1 Very few hunters who went after the pheasants..did not get some at any rate, and the man who was 'skunked' probably would be very hard to find. **1939** *Sun* (Baltimore) 4 Dec. 18/1 The outcome of that battle..was Navy 10, Army 0... 'Which means,' one of them explained to his girl friend, 'We got 10 and they got skunked.' **1944** DUNCAN & NICKOLS *Mentor Graham* xvi. 170 Lincoln, with a short, logical speech in which no words were wasted, 'skunked' his adversary. **1948** *Field & Stream* June 86/2, I have fished on opening day in the snow.., only to get skunked. **1971** D. CONOVER *One Man's Island* 33 When the Colonel comes home from fishing, by his vociferous oaths we know that he was skunked. **1972** D. DELMAN *Sudden Death* (1973) vi. 64 She'll skunk Nell Duncan today, and win.

2. a. *trans.* To fail to pay (a bill or a creditor).

1851 B. H. HALL *College Words* 284 *Skunk*, at Princeton College, to fail to pay a debt; used actively; e.g. to skunk a tailor, i.e. not to pay him. **1859** [in Dict.]. **1961** WEBSTER s.v., Made a practice of skunking hotels.

b. To cheat; in *pass.*, to be cheated *out of*.

1890 C. W. HASKINS *Argonauts of Calif.* xvii. 250, I got skunked once out of a good claim. **1971** E. FENWICK *Impeccable People* iii. 21 I'm beginning to think we skunked you over the price.

skunk-cabbage. Add: Also **skunk's cabbage.** Also used, esp. on the Pacific Coast, to designate *Lysichiton camtschatcense*, another member of the family Araceæ, or a false hellebore of the genus *Veratrum*, of the family Liliaceæ. (Earlier and later examples.)

1751 J. ELIOT *Ess. Field-Husbandry* iii. 66 Take the Roots of Swamp Hellebore, sometimes called Skunk Cabbage, Tickle Weed. **1849** N. KINGSLEY *Jrnl.* 3 May (1914) 15 The fruit grows on the extreme top with a blow or flower resembling our Skunks Cabbage. **1868** H. W. BEECHER *Norwood* 91 The great, succulent leaves of the skunk's cabbage were fully expanded. **1906** *Atlantic Monthly* Oct. 495 The first flower to bloom in this latitude when the winter frost loosens its grip upon the sod is the gross, uncouth, and noisome skunk cabbage. **1950** *Chicago Tribune* 28 Mar. 14/3 Some watch for skunk cabbages poking mottled brown snouts thru the swamp muck. **1968** PETERSON & MCKENNY *Field Guide to Wildflowers* 368 Skunk Cabbage... The sheathing, shell-like spathe, mottled and varying from green to purple-brown, envelops the heavy rounded spadix. **1976** *Hortus Third* (L. H. Bailey Hortorium) 1148/1 *Veratrum*..*californicum* E. Durand. Corn lily, skunk cabbage.

‖ **Skupština** (sku·pʃtinā). Also 9 **Scubsch'tina, Skoupschina,** etc.; **Skupshtina.** [Serbo-Croatian *skupština*, f. *skupa* together, *skupiti* to assemble.] The national assembly of Yugoslavia; formerly, of Serbia or Montenegro.

1847 A. KERR tr. *von Ranke's Hist. Servia* x. 190 Soon after New Year's Day, all the Woiwodes, with their suites, assembled at a Diet called Skupschtina. **1862** W. DENTON *Servia & Servians* xii. 241 Immediately after the Servians had succeeded in liberating themselves from the Turkish rule they set about forming political institutions for themselves. Among the earliest is the assembly called the Skoupschina. **1866** *Chambers's Encycl.* VIII. 629/2 Each circle..sends a deputy to the *Scubsch'tina*. **1883** *Encycl. Brit.* XVI. 781/2 In 1851, Danilo..prevailed on the 'skuptchina' to declare Montenegro a secular state with the hereditary government of a prince. **1902** *Ibid.* XXX. 821/1 A *Skupshtina*, or popular assembly, is summoned on rare occasions of national importance. **1911** R. W. SETON-WATSON *Southern Slav Question* ix. 194 The Skupština had sufficient self-restraint and sanity to decide against war. **1923** [see *Serbo-Bulgarian* adj. s.v. *SERBO-]. **1940** C. SFORZA *Fifty Years of War & Diplomacy in Balkans* iv. 22 In the elections..Pashich won a complete victory. In the Skupshtina, an imposing majority was ready to follow him. **1968** F. W. HONDIUS *Yugoslav Community of Nations* ii. 74 This Constitution.. created a precedent by recognizing the concept of popular sovereignty, reflected in a powerful one-chamber Skupština. **1976** F. SINGLETON *Twentieth-Cent. Yugoslavia* I. iv. 48 The regency introduced constitutional reforms which provided for a Skupština of 120 members.

skurrick, obs. var. *SKERRICK. **skut,** var. *SCUT *sb.*[4]

skutterudite (sku·tərŭdəit). *Min.* [ad. G. *skutterudit* (W. von Haidinger *Handb. der bestimm. Mineral.*, etc. (1845) IV. 560), f. *Skutterud*, name of a village in SE. Norway (now called *Skotterud*): see -ITE[1].] An arsenide of cobalt, ideally $CoAs_3$, that commonly contains other elements, esp. nickel, iron, bismuth, and sulphur, and is found as grey cubic crystals with a metallic lustre.

1850 J. D. DANA *Syst. Mineral.* (ed. 3) 474 Skutterudite... Lustre bright metallic. Color between tin-white and pale lead-grey, sometimes iridescent. **1892** [see *nickel-skutterudite* s.v. *NICKEL *sb.* 3 b]. **1902** H. A. MIERS *Mineralogy* 332 It is remarkable that there is another arsenide of cobalt of quite different composition, $CoAs_3$, known as skutterudite, which is also cubic and pyritohedral. **1947** *Bull. Geol. Soc. Amer.* LVIII. 317 In spite of repeated attempts, varying the conditions of temperature and using different fluxes, no higher cobalt arsenide other than skutterudite $CoAs_3$ was obtained. **1968** I. KOSTOV *Mineral.* 135 Skutterudite, smaltite, and chloanthite are typical intermediate- or high-temperature hydrothermal minerals.

sky, *sb.*[1] Add: **3. d.** (*a*) Also, *out of a clear* (or *blue*) *sky* and varr. = *out of the blue* s.v. *BLUE *sb.* 5 a; (*b*) *to the skies* (later examples); (*d*) *the sky's the limit*, there is no apparent limit.

(*a*) **1875** TENNYSON *Q. Mary* v. iii. 264 So from a clear sky falls the thunderbolt! **1897** [in Dict.]. **1903** WODEHOUSE *Tales of St. Austin's* 2 To spring an examination on you in the middle of the term out of a blue sky, as it were, was underhand and unsportsmanlike. **1924** E. O'NEILL *Welded* I, in *All God's Chillun got Wings* I. 98 It was revelation, then—a miracle out of the sky! **1958** G. GREENE *Our Man in Havana* III. ii. 115 She's had two unhappy *coups de foudre* herself. They came quite suddenly, out of a clear sky.

(*b*) **1915** W. S. MAUGHAM *Of Human Bondage* xlii. 198 Red-nosed comedians were lauded to the skies for their sense of character. **1955** D. GARNETT *Golden Echo* II. i. 16 If he had praised it to the skies or damned it, or even told the truth, not much harm would have been done. **1973** P. J. SEYBOLD *Revolutionary Educ. in China* xiv. 156 At one time they shouted 'Long live the teachers'.., praising them to the skies.

(*d*) **1920** *Current History* (U.S.) Oct. 142/2 (*caption*) The sky is now her limit. **1933** *Daily Mirror* 26 Oct. 12/4 To say 'the sky was his limit' definitely adds something to the usual 'he succeeded' or 'he rose in the world'. **1934** WEBSTER s.v. *sky*, the sky is the limit. **1936** C. SANDBURG *People, Yes* 160 'Did you say the sky is the limit?' 'Yes, we won't go any higher than the sky.' **1942** E. PAUL *Narrow St.* xxiv. 211 Every municipality, excepting small villages, had its official Mont-de-Piété, and the sky was the limit. **1952** W. R. BURNETT *Vanity Row* vii. 68 If there's ever anything we can do for you... You know. Sky's the limit, as people say. **1961** L. MUMFORD *City in History* ii. 52 The cult of power exulted in its own boundless display... The sky was the limit. **1977** H. FAST *Immigrants* II. 97 As far as the Pacific passage is concerned, rates are going up and the sky's the limit.

4. c. In joc. phr. *the* (or *that*) *great* —— *in the sky*: with personal subj., God considered as the omniscient exponent of an earthly art or profession; of a place or structure, the type of a paradise especially suited to the deceased.

1977 MCKNIGHT & TOBLER *Bob Marley* v. 62 Chuck Willis, the 'Sheik of the Stroll' became one of the first members of the great rock group in the sky. **1979** *Times* 24 Nov. 15/7 It is up to that Great Film Critic in the sky to deal with *Life of Brian* in His own way. **1980** D. BLOODWORTH *Trapdoor* xvii. 107 There's a Director of Central Intelligence up there in that great Langley in the sky. **1982** *Times* 26 Jan. 10/3 Daphne, the pelican, has gone to that great aviary in the sky after 25 years residence..in St James's Park.

5. a. (Examples illustrating use as a fashion shade.)

1851 *Illustr. Catal. Gt. Exhib.* III. 506/2 Pink, white, sky, and maize gros de Naples for ladies' bonnets. **1894** [see *HELIO[2]]. **1923** *Weekly Dispatch* 11 Feb. 14 (Advt.), Will not Fade... Silky finish. Ivory, Biscuit, Sky, Coral [etc.]. **1949** *Radio Times* 15 July 44/3 Lovely pastel shades—Peach, Apple, Sky. **1976** *National Observer* (U.S.) 22 May 17/4 (Advt.), The plain shades... Rust, Beige, Tan, Sky, White, Black.

7*. *Rhyming slang. ellipt.* for *SKY-ROCKET *sb.* 3: pocket.

1890 in Barrère & Leland *Dict. Slang* II. 248/2 The Oof Bird's scarce and the landlady's fly, And there isn't a mash with a mag in his sky. **1898** A. M. BINSTEAD *Pink 'Un & Pelican* xi. 237 After thirty-six 'ands 'ad bin all over him, tore his trowseys an' left 'im as naked as Barth-Sheber—why, even *then* we never found his sky! **1928** E. WALLACE *Gunner* xviii. 140 'Put that in your sky... In your pocket,' she said impatiently. **1979** P. HILL *Washermen* lx. 132 Said 'ee found it [*sc.* a gun] on the rattler. Put it in 'is sky when 'ee got off at Leicester Square.

8. Now chiefly *Lit.* and *poet.* **a.** Simple *attrib.* (Later examples.)

1904 W. B. YEATS *Pot of Broth* in *Hour-Glass* 78 Give me some vessel till I give this sky-woman a taste of it. **1916** BLUNDEN *Harbingers* 64 He stells the meadows in similitude Of stars in black sky-spaces. **1920** D. H. LAWRENCE *Lost Girl* xiv. 320 White clouds, in the sort of hollow sky-dome. **1930** W. H. AUDEN *Poems* 9 Though heart fears all heart cries for, rebuffs with mortal beat Skyfall, the legs sucked under, adder's bite. **1946** L. B. LYON *Rough Walk Home* 11 Lift arm or lift an eyebrow, He'll weave his sky-brow Spell round the offender. **1959** D. DAVIE *Forests of Lithuania* vi. 59 Fires cluster and dart Cross over, light over light Overarches the sky-round. **1979** D. WILLIAMS *Genesis & Exodus* vii. 127 He enjoyed the wide sky-sweep of the fens.

b. *sky-gazer.*

1930 V. WOOLF *On being Ill* 19 Pedestrians would be impeded and disconcerted by a public sky-gazer.

c. With pa. pples. (Earlier and further examples.)

1589 R. GREENE *Menaphon* Sig. F1[v], A Skie borne forme. **1807** J. BARLOW *Columbiad* III. 110 Far beneath, the sky-borne waters ride, Veil the dark deep and sheet the mountain's side. **1923** D. H. LAWRENCE *Birds, Beasts & Flowers* 17 And sipped down, perhaps, with a sip of Marsala So that the rambling, sky-dropped grape can add its music to yours. **1934** L. B. LYON *White Hare* 14 Wind-scoured and sky-burned The fell was. **1946** DYLAN THOMAS *Deaths & Entrances* 27 May his hunger go howling on bare white bones Past the statues of the stables and the sky roofed sties. **1977** *Hongkong Standard* 12 Apr. 3/3 Aides say Mr Peres originated and pushed the idea of last July's skyborne rescue from Uganda of 100 hostages.

d. With pres. pples. (Further examples.)

1788 P. FRENEAU *Hermit of Saba* in *Misc. Works* 31 When thou, sky-pointing Saba, Shall tremble on thy base most fearfully! **1819** Sky-aspiring [see *BALMILY *adv.*]. **1844** J. R. LOWELL *Poems* 274 They tell us that our land was made for song, With its huge rivers and sky-piercing peaks. **1922** JOYCE *Ulysses* 563 Stephen with hat ashplant frogsplits in middle highkicks with skykicking mouth shut hand clasp part under thigh. **1933** C. DAY LEWIS *Magnetic Mountain* 9 Void are the valleys.. And dumb the sky-dividing hills. **1957** L. MACNEICE *Visitations* 42 Felt suddenly harassed, a sky-splitting headache with nothing to cause it. **1977** *New Scientist* 24 Feb. 478/1 A spiky, sky-piercing crenellation of buildings running down the Royal Mile from the hunched bulk of the castle to the rounded towers of the Palace of Holyroodhouse.

9. sky bear *N. Amer. slang*, (an officer in) a police helicopter (cf. *SMOKEY BEAR 2); **sky border** *Theatr.*, a border of painted cloth, used both to represent sky and to conceal the top of the stage from the audience; **skycap** *N. Amer.* [after *REDCAP 5], a porter at an airport; **sky-clad** *a. slang*, nude, unclothed (esp. in *Witchcraft*); **sky cloth** *Theatr.*, a backcloth painted or coloured to represent the sky (cf. *sky border* above); **sky-clothed** *a.* = *sky-clad* adj. above; **sky-diving,** the sport of parachuting from an aeroplane with a long period of (freq. acrobatic) free fall before the parachute is opened; also as adj., **sky-diver** and (as back-formation) **sky-dive** *v. intr.*; **sky-drop** *Theatr.* = *sky cloth* above; **sky fighter,** an aeroplane or airman that engages in aerial combat; hence **sky-fight; sky filter,** a filter (usu. yellow and denser at the top than at the bottom) for improving the rendering of a bright sky in black and white photography; **sky-fire** (later *poet.* example); **sky-flower,** a shrub or small tree, *Duranta repens*, of the family Verbenaceæ, native to Central and South America and bearing clusters of pale blue flowers followed by yellow berries (cf. *PIGEON-BERRY 1); **sky-god** *Religion* and *Mythol.*, a god of or in the sky; also **sky-goddess; skyman** *Journalists' slang*, a paratrooper; **sky-marker** *Mil.*, a parachute flare used by raiding aircraft to mark a target (cf. *PARACHUTE *sb.* 5); also Comb., as *sky-marker bomb*; also *sky-marking*; **sky marshal** *U.S.* a plain-clothes armed guard on an aeroplane employed to counter hi-jacking; **sky-path,** a route taken through the sky, a skyway; **sky pilot** *slang* (earlier and later examples); also, a chaplain in any of the armed forces, prison service, etc., and *gen.*, a priest or parson, a clergyman; † **sky race,** in British India, an amateur steeplechase; **sky-ride** *U.S.*, a device for conveying passengers at a considerable height above ground, spec. one at the World Fair at Chicago in 1933–4; **sky screen,** an array of photocells used to record or detect the travel of an aircraft, projectile, etc.; **sky shade** *Photogr.* (see quots.); **sky-ship,** a very large craft for air or space travel; **sky-shouting,** the sending of advertisements or messages from an aircraft to the ground by means of a loudspeaker; also as adj. and **sky-shouter; sky-surfing** *U.S.* =

hang-gliding s.v. *HANG-; hence **sky-surfer; skywatch** orig. *U.S.*, the process or activity of watching the sky for aircraft or other phenomena; hence **skywatcher; sky wave,** a radio wave reflected back towards the earth's surface by the ionosphere (cf. *ground wave* s.v. *GROUND *sb.* 18 a).

1975 L. DILLS *CB Slanguage Dict.* 54 *Sky bear*, police helicopter. **1977** *Daily Colonist* (Victoria, B.C.) 3 July 1/2 (*heading*) Sky bear keeps eye on Island's drivers. **1846** G. A. A'BECKETT *Quizziology Brit. Drama* 16 Pointing with a property sword to the sky borders. **1896** W. ARCHER *Theatr. World of 1895* iv. 28 Above it hang mathematically horizontal 'sky-borders', apparently representing a flat layer of fog in the upper air. **1918** G. B. SHAW in *Nation* 22 June 310/1 The scenery made Old Drury feel young again. Wings, sky-borders, set pieces: nothing was missing. **1950** *Official Gaz.* (U.S. Patent Office) 26 Dec. 1066/2 Sky Cap. For General Porter Service. **1966** *National Observer* (U.S.) 7 Nov. 6/5 They would reduce the number of Negro 'sky caps' employed at the airport. **1972** T. KENRICK *Tough One to Lose* ii. 33 He took a job as a skycap at the International Airport. **1977** J. WAMBAUGH *Black Marble* (1978) xv. 342 He spotted a skycap carrying some bags towards the front. **1909** WEBSTER, Sky-clad. **1970** R. BUCKLAND in K. Singer *Tales from Unknown* 296 Witches always work naked or, as they call it, *skyclad*. **1933** Sky-cloth [see *BATTEN *sb.*[1] 1 b]. **1981** *Times Lit. Suppl.* 4 Sept. 998/3 Instead of a naturalistically painted backcloth he used a plain sheet of colour (what we should call a sky cloth). **1924** EARL OF RONALDSHAY *India* xxiv. 305 The Digambara, or sky-clothed ascetic, must live stark naked. **1965** *N.Y. Times* 24 Apr. 21 Mary Cushing..snorkles, surfs, skis and sky-dives. **1961** *Times* 3 July 6/4 The screech of the skydiver was heard above Hereford this weekend as.. people saw a demonstration of the latest 'official' British Army sport. **1970** *Daily Tel.* 5 Oct. 1/1 Two women skydivers and a man were injured when they parachuted at 2,500ft from a De Havilland aircraft..last night. **1979** P. NIESEWAND *Member of Club* xii. 84 A flypast might be nice... How about some sky-divers? Everyone likes them. **1959** *News Chron.* 8 July 4/7 The sport..of 'sky-diving' in which certain adventurous types turn somersaults in the air before opening their parachutes. **1962** *Daily Tel.* 7 Aug. 11/7 A sky-diving team will leave London Airport today..to compete in the sixth world sport parachuting championships. **1979** R. JAFFE *Class Reunion* (1980) II. ix. 275 Apparently she's taken up skydiving... She's going to kill herself. **1901** C. MORRIS *Life on Stage* xii. 84 In this tableau the circular opening in the flat, backed by a sky-drop and with blue clouds hanging about the opening, represented heaven. **1969** G. MACBETH *War Quartet* 36 He was dead to this Antarctic sky-fight. **1937** *Sun* (Baltimore) 2 Mar. 1/3 The first of the army's super sky-fighters, a four-engined Boeing bomber, dropped to a perfect landing on snow-covered Langley Field at 2.09 P.M. today. **1943** R. WHELAN *Flying Tigers* ix. 97 George Paxton..moved to break up this shocking attack on a helpless airman, which violated the code of sky fighters. **1930** G. E. BROWN *Clerc's Photogr.* xi. 83 Sky filters are made in the shape of a long rectangle, which is carried in a mount, allowing it to be raised or lowered. **1970** M. J. SETHNA *Photogr.* v. 102 Where the sky is light and bright, but the landscape is less bright or is dark, the balance of tones can well be secured through the use of what is known as 'the graduated sky filter'. **1906** Sky-fire [see *night-web* s.v. *NIGHT *sb.* 13 a]. **1938** D. WYMAN *Hedges, Screens & Windbreaks* II. 77 Tall Broad-leaved Evergreens... *Duranta plumieri*, Skyflower. **1971** Sky-flower [see *PIGEON-BERRY 1]. **1907** H. M. CHADWICK *Orig. Eng. Nation* x. 245 On the strength of this passage [in *Gylfaginning*] it has been supposed that Frey was originally a sky-god or sun-god. **1938** E. BEVAN *Symbolism & Belief* ii. 30 The belief in the Sky-God may have, of course, two forms according as the sky itself is personified, is identified with the Person up there, or as the Person is conceived more anthropomorphically. **1948** B. G. M. SUNDKLER *Bantu Prophets in S. Afr.* i. 24 The lightning-magician, the priest of the sky-god, arrives much sooner..at proficiency in his particular speciality. **1979** *N.Y. Rev. Bks.* 25 Oct. 19/3 Now the Heavenly Father, or Aryan sky-god, is found to be..simply irrelevant. **1959** *New Larousse Encycl. Mythol.* 23/2 *Hathor*... A sky-goddess, she was originally described as the daughter of Ra and the wife of Horus. **1982** N. FRYE *Great Code* iii. 70 Zeus..third in a line of sky-gods. The earth-mother..tends to take on the characteristics of a sky-goddess. **1952** *John o' London's Weekly* 18 Jan. 54/1 The failure of Fleet Street to make paratroopers into skymen. **1958** *Daily Mail* 18 July 1/2 Skymen saved Hussein's life... But for the arrival of our paratroops yesterday,..Hussein..would almost certainly have been assassinated. **1964** *Sunday Tel.* 14 June 3/4 (*heading*) Skymen hit the target. **1943** *Times* 31 Dec. 4/6 The Pathfinder force used parachute flares known as 'sky-markers' which drift downwards very slowly, to mark the target area. **1944** *Times* 17 Feb. 4/4 Flak was so violent when the first sky-marker bombs were dropped that it was evident that the main night fighter force was late. **1946** *R.A.F. Jrnl.* May 169 The red, yellow and green T.I.s and the skymarker flares, remained the principal weapons of P.F.F. throughout the war... The 'wanganni' skymarkers went down over Germany and load after load of destruction followed. **1944** R. DIMBLEBY in *War Report* (B.B.C.) (1946) 281 Our job was to replenish the flares already dropped by the Pathfinders ahead... This was 'sky-marking'. **1968** *Sunday Mail* (Brisbane) 23 June 32/6 He is a member of a new elite breed of law enforcement officers in America—the sky marshals. His job is to prevent airliner hi-jacking... All the sky marshals are volunteers from the ranks of the F.A.A.'s regular inspectors. **1971** *Daily Colonist* (Victoria, B.C.) 13 Mar. 25/6 A number of women trained in marksmanship and hand-to-hand combat will join the men assigned to the skymarshal force recently created to protect U.S. airliners from hijackers. **1931** F. SIMPICH in *Nat. Geogr. Mag.* Jan. 1 (*heading*) Skypaths through Latin America. **1958** *Times* 27 Oct. 10/1 Nearly 400 Glacier dry bearings assist each Comet 4 on its smooth skypath. **1883** G. W. PECK *Peck's Bad Boy* 177 Look-a-here you sky-pilot, this thing has gone far enough. **1910** *Busy Man's Mag.* Mar. 71/1, I was hailed as a 'sky pilot' by the trio and invited to be sociable over a whisky bottle. **1922** JOYCE *Ulysses* 305 One or two sky pilots having an eye around that there was no goings on with the females. **1935** AUDEN & ISHERWOOD *Dog beneath Skin* II. v. 114 Ort ter 'ave bin a sky pilot, you ort! **1973** B. BROADFOOT *Ten Lost Years* xii. 140 At the missions you would get a sermon, say 15 minutes of religion from a sky pilot. **1982** *New Scientist* 18 Mar. 740/3 The first issue includes an attack on the accuracy of radiocarbon dating by an English skypilot called Charles Foley. **1858** G. F. ATKINSON *Curry & Rice* (ed. 2) xviii, The Sky Races, which to the uninitiated may be explained as a meeting for horses that have enjoyed no specific training beyond what could be accomplished during the interval of the 'get-up' and the 'come-off'. **1885** LADY DUFFERIN *Jrnl.* 11 June in *Our Viceregal Life in India* (1889) I. iv. 157 The Simla sky races began today. **1933** *Sun* (Baltimore) 22 July 10/3 Two Concordia women, who attended the World's Fair at Chicago recently ventured on the 'sky ride', the device which carries passengers across the grounds at a height of 200 feet. **1966** E. MCCULLOGH *World's Fair Midways* viii. 93 One of the features of the fair [*sc.* Century of Progress Exposition] was the Sky Ride, a monorail structure whose two giant towers stretched up sixty-four stories... They were connected at the twenty-fourth story by cables, from which so-called rocket cars were suspended. **1945** L. E. SIMON *German Sci. Establishments* (PB Rep. No. 19849) II. ii. 48 One thing that was particularly notable was a large number of photoelectric 'sky screens'. **1969** *New Scientist* 2 Oct. 25/3 The accuracy of the sky screens is said to be two metres in azimuth, and 1·5 metres in elevation. **1889** E. J. WALL *Dict. Photogr.* 177 *Sky shade*, a piece of wood or card used to shade the lens during exposure, to prevent reflections from the sky or sun. **1909** G. L. JOHNSON *Photographic Optics & Colour Photogr.* ii. 152 Skyshades are of great value in colour photography..as without some such screen the skies are invariably spoilt through overexposure. **1930** G. E. BROWN *Clerc's Photogr.* xi. 83 The most usual form of commercial sky shade..consists of a uniformly graduated filter of gelatine or glass. **1973** D. A. SPENCER *Focal Dict. Photogr. Technol.* 568 *Sky shade*, any form of shield attached to the lens mount for preventing direct rays of the sun reaching the camera lens. In USA, the term is sometimes used as another name for lens hood. **1923** L. PAUER *Day of Judgment* 16 If possible ..we are going to board that sky-ship. **1960** *Analog Science Fact/Fiction* Dec. 10/1 When we first heard of the Sky Ship, we were on an island whose name..was Yarzik. **1975** *Times* 18 Apr. 6/3 The Sky Ship, with a diameter of 30ft and in the shape of a flying saucer..is a scaled-down prototype of a planned vehicle..which will be 700 ft in diameter..able to carry a payload of up to 400 tons. **1932** *Children's Newspaper* 23 Jan. 6/1 The inventor..can now quote terms for Sky Shouting or Sky Advertising. Concerning the sky-shouters a really alarming invention has been successfully tried. **1932** *Flight* 8 July 638/1 They recommend that sky-shouting (by means of a loud speaker) should be prohibited by law for all private purposes. **1955** *Times* 9 June 8/2 The withdrawal of the surrender offer was being conveyed to the terrorists by all possible means, including radio and sky-shouting aircraft. **1962** *Engineering* 26 Oct. 564 The practicability of long range speech transmission was seen during British army operations in Malaya when a 'sky-shouting' installation in an aircraft was used for propaganda purposes. **1973** *Times* 15 May 8/4 Last year 2,285 hours were logged by aircraft flying 'sky-shouting' patrols in which recorded propaganda messages were relayed to Africans living in the bush. **1972** *Popular Mechanics* June 102/2 How long a sky surfer can stay in the air depends on wind strength and skill. **1972** *Popular Sci.* June 94/2 Today's hang-glider pilots like to call their sport 'sky-surfing'. **1974** *Sci. Amer.* Dec. 138/1 The rapidly evolving sport, which is known as sky surfing or hang gliding, makes about equal demands on the enthusiast's skills as a pilot and as an aerodynamicist. **1952** *Sun* (Baltimore) 17 July B7/5 (*heading*) 18,000 in Britain serve on skywatch. **1958** A. BUDRYS in Aldiss & Harrison *Decade 1950s* (1976) 68, I made it. Got to this Navy skywatch station. **1972** *Oxford Times* 21 Jan. 3/7 A full house is expected for next week's UFO convention in Banbury... 'Many of those attending are the people who made sightings over North Oxon last year which ended with us having a skywatch, which was unfortunately rained off.' **1973** *Daily Tel.* 30 July 1/5 Skylab, at present, is not visible to British skywatchers since its orbital track does not take it over Britain. **1928** STERLING & KRUSE *Radio Manual* xiv. 524 The day signal which reappears at 850 miles may be considered the sky wave. **1944** *Proc. IRE* XXXII. 668/1 Design of directional antennas for broadcast stations to prevent skywave interference to another station. **1971** K. KENT in C. Bonington *Annapurna South Face* 277 The near-link radios had to be h/f sets capable of voice/cw and able to utilize a sky-wave and surface-wave mode of operation.

sky, *v.*[1] Add: **1. a.** Also used of other objects, as a hat, etc.; spec. *to sky the wipe* Austral. Boxing slang = *to throw up the sponge* s.v. SPONGE *sb.*[1] 1 c.

1898 A. M. BINSTEAD *Pink 'Un & Pelican* x. 215 He skied his tile in the most approved fashion..literally beaming with good-nature as he shook his jockey by the hand. **1916** C. J. DENNIS *Songs of Sentimental Bloke* xi. 87 Fer 'arf a mo' I 'as a fight; Then conscience skies the wipe... Sez I 'Orright'. **1933** *Bulletin* (Sydney) 14 June 27/2 It is generally understood that a boxer must consider himself beaten when his seconds 'sky the wipe'.

b. (Earlier example.) Also in *Golf*, etc.

1868 *J. Lillywhite's Cricketers' Compan.* 102 He..sometimes gets deceived by a short one, and 'skies' it. **1909** [see *FLUFF *v.*[1] 5 e]. **1922** E. F. BENSON *Miss Mapp* iii. 73 Major Flint drove, skying the ball to a prodigious height. **1976** *Morecambe Guardian* 7 Dec. 8/1 Worksop came back into the attack when Wall started a good move but Joe Johnson skied the ball high over.

c. At an auction: to raise the price of (an item) by high bidding; to raise (the bidding) by a considerable amount.

1892 STEVENSON & OSBOURNE *Wrecker* ix. 146 All of a sudden he appeared as a third competitor, skied the *Flying Scud* with four fat bids of a thousand dollars each, and then as suddenly fled the field. **1928** D. L. SAYERS *Ld. Peter views Body* x. 236 Wimsey, entering into the spirit of the thing, skied the bidding with enthusiasm. The dealers,..fancying that there must be some special excellence about the book.., joined in.

sky-blue, *sb.* Add: **1. b.** Comb., as *sky-blue-pink*, a fantasy colour. Also as adj. *joc.*

1942 G. KERSH *Nine Lives Bill Nelson* xi. 66 Bill could swear that black was white, or green was sky-blue-pink. **1967** L. J. BRAUN *Cat who ate Danish Modern* xv. 131 What colours do you mix to get sky-blue-pink? **1982** S. T. HAYMON *Ritual Murder* xvii. 116 Caught him out red-handed... Not to say green and yellow an' sky-blue-pink.

3. b. Barley broth (*Naut.*); any vegetable soup.

1887 S. SAMUELS *Forecastle to Cabin* iv. 53 Sky-blue (boiled barley), hard tack, and tea sweetened with treacle was Jack's fare for the morning meal. **1908** J. M. SULLIVAN *Criminal Slang* 23 *Sky-blue*, vegetable soup. **1910** H. Y. MOFFAT *Ship's Boy to Skipper* xiii. 204 Once a week we had for dinner what we called 'Sky Blue'. It was made by putting a small quantity of barley into a large quantity of water.

Skybus (skəi·bʌs). *U.S.* Also **skybus, sky bus.** [SKY *sb.*[1]] **1.** The proprietary name of a regular air service for which passengers need not book in advance. Cf. *SKYTRAIN 2.

1945 *Aviation* Feb. 132 Douglas Skybus. Designed for feeder line operations, seating 24 passengers. **1966** *Official Gaz.* (U.S. Patent Office) 8 Feb. TM 65/1 New York Airways, Inc... *Skybus* for air service for passengers, mail, and freight. First use Oct. 15, 1952. **1972** *Times* 28 Sept. 1/1 Trans International Airlines today proposed to the Civil Aeronautics Board a daily New York to London 'sky bus' service at a fare of $75. **1977** *Time* 10 Oct. 5/1 Trans International Airlines..borrowed a leaf from Laker's book and last month proposed a 'Skybus' service from the U.S. to Tokyo and Hong Kong.

2. (See quots.)

1966 *Daily Tel.* 21 Apr. 16/4 (*caption*) In Pittsburgh.. tests are being carried out with a Skybus... The bus itself is a lightweight aluminium car with light rubber wheels, which run on two small concrete rails. It picks up current from a centre beam. **1967** *Guardian* 2 Feb. 3/3 Westinghouse Electric Corporation, of Pittsburgh..have developed a driverless 'skybus' for the US Government... The skybus is a cross between a bus and a train and can run in tunnels, on the ground, or elevated.

Skye. Add: **a.** *Skye terrier* (earlier and later examples).

1847 H. D. RICHARDSON *Dogs* vii. 71 The Skye Terrier, so called from its being found in greatest perfection in the Western Isles of Scotland, and the Isle of Skye in particular. **1971** F. HAMILTON *World Encycl. Dogs* 478 The show Skye Terrier's profuse, well groomed coat.., its veil of thick hair shielding fore-face, and the silky feathering of ears and tail, are not attained and maintained without considerable trouble.

skyer. (Earlier examples.)

1853 *Bell's Life in London* 24 July 6/2 Mr Walker gave a few 'skyers' in scoring 20, for which number he brought out his bat. **1867** *Australasian* 26 Jan. 107/4 Fowler hit a skyer to leg, no one in the road.

sky-ful. Add: Now usu. **skyful.** (Later examples.)

1910 KIPLING *Rewards & Fairies* 152 Presently I heard guns... I stopped fiddling to listen, and I heard a whole skyful o' French up in the fog. **1966** D. VARADAY *Gara-Yaka's Domain* xiii. 146 They slept under the trees, with a skyful of stars for their blankets.

sky-high, *adv.* and *a.* Add: **A.** *adv.* Also, freq. in *fig.* phr. *to blow sky-high*, to refute utterly; = EXPLODE *v.* 3.

1845 A. JACKSON *Let.* 6 June in M. James *A. Jackson* (1937) xxiii. 498 Put your veto upon them both, or you and your Secretary will be blown sky high. **1948** *Daily Tel.* 29 May 2/6 [He] blew sky-high the complacent superstition of a war-time 'renaissance'. **1951** N. MITFORD *Blessing* I. viii. 83 At this dinner Grace's preconceived ideas about the French..were blown sky high. **1955** *Times* 26 May 3/3 Matters which had been put forward in the course of that case had either fallen by the wayside or had been blown 'sky-high'.

B. *adj.* Also *fig.*, very high.

1959 *Times* 7 Sept. 11/6 The current miracle of labour-saving flats, sky-high wages, and welfare state. **1975** A. BERGMAN *Hollywood & Le Vine* (1976) v. 67 We don't pay writers whatever sky-high figures their agents talk them into demanding.

sky-hook. Also **sky hook, skyhook.** [SKY *sb.*[1]] **1. a.** orig. *Aeronaut.* An imaginary contrivance for attachment to the sky; an imaginary means of suspension in the sky.

1915 *Aeroplane* 10 Mar. 222 The battery signaller sent a message: 'Battery out of action for an hour, remain aloft awaiting orders.' Back came the reply with remarkable promptitude: 'Submitted; that this machine is not fitted with sky-hooks.' **1933** *Ibid.* 11 Jan. 47/1 They [*sc.* slots] have in fact been used as..sky-hooks on the wing tips. **1948** *Register* Sept. 262 Mr. Shaw's plea..is, at bottom, a plea for a skyhook. For that common agreement which it assumes hung from a skyhook and was broken when we severed it from its support. **1960** R. W. MARKS *Dymaxion World of B. Fuller* 28/1 With each thrust of his wings, the duck generates a momentary vacuum sky-hook above each wing. **1970** D. WATERFIELD *Continental Waterboy* i. 6, I..was prepared to..fetch him a left-handed wrench, a skyhook, anything.

b. Applied to various devices or craft capable of lifting something into the air, as: a hook on an aircraft; an aerial cableway; a a balloon, helicopter, etc., designed for lifting. orig. *U.S.*

1935 MEIER & LINDBERGH in *Sci. Monthly* (N.Y.) Jan. 5 An instrument new to transatlantic airplanes..which, being untried, was noncommittally called the 'sky hook'. **1945** *Collier's Mag.* 27 Jan. 38/4 He tried building a model of one of these seed pods, blowing it up to the size of a man and loading its hollow container with cargo. It spiraled down vertically and could safely bring 100 pounds to earth from any height... The device, now nicknamed the 'skyhook', is fluttering down on many Allied battlefields. **1949** *Sun* (Baltimore) 13 Aug. 12/3 That long renowned but hitherto incredible gadget, the sky-hook, is now a reality... It is known as 'The Aerial Track Airport: a cable runway for landing and launching airplanes'. **1951** *N.Y. Times* 13 Feb. 1/7 The balloons, called skyhooks by the Navy researchers, were released at many points in the country. **1966** *Science* 11 Feb. 682 (*heading*) Satellite elongation into a true 'sky-hook'. **1970** [see *dogman* s.v. *DOG *sb.* 18 a]. **1982** *Monitor* (McAllen, Texas) 25 Mar. 1-A/1 The shuttle's robot arm lifted a space environment monitor out of the payload bay today in an important 'first' that proved the remotely controlled skyhook will be able to launch satellites.

2. *Mountaineering.* A hook fixed into a rock-face, from which ropes, etc., may depend.

1957 *Appalachia* 15 Dec. 452 On the one occasion when I carried a 'skyhook' among my pitons I was no less than delighted to find it really could be used to circumvent the placing of a bolt. **1968** P. CREW *Encycl. Dict. Mountaineering* 108/2 *Sky-hook*..consists of a flattened hook of high quality steel... Sky-hooks have a small eye, to which a sling and étrier can be attached... They are particularly useful on loose flakes..which would probably break off if a piton was used. **1976** [see *RURP].

skyhoot, *v.* ? Fanciful perversion of SCOOT *v.* Freq. as pres. pple.

1888 *Boy's Own Paper* Summer 38/1 Something's sky-hooted in my shoulder... That brute threw me on my head. **1900** H. F. DAY *Up in Maine* 56 That air pessle ..come sky-hootin' like a ten-inch bomb. **1911** [see *LICKETY *adv.*]. **1928** E. WALLACE *Double* i. 7 Why I'm sky-hooting down to Brighton for two days, heaven knows!

skyjack (skəi·dʒæk), *v.* Also **sky-jack.** [f. SKY *sb.*[1] + *HI)JACK *v.*] *trans.* To hijack (an aeroplane). Also const. *to* (a destination).

1961 *N.Y. Mirror* 10 Aug. 1 (*heading*) Pan Am Jet skyjacked to Havana. **1968** *Tel.* (Brisbane) 13 Mar. 24/7 Over the years scores of light planes, in addition to larger passenger airliners, have been skyjacked and flown to Cuba. **1970** *Time* 12 Oct. 38/3 Aboard the plane was Leila Khaled, 24, the Palestinian guerrilla who attempted to skyjack an El Al airliner over Britain last month. **1971** *Daily Tel.* 1 Feb. 20/3 Sentence of death on a Lithuanian ..for trying to skyjack a Soviet airliner to Sweden, has been commuted. **1977** *Whitaker's Almanack 1978* 604/2 A Russian engineer who skyjacked a Soviet airliner surrendered to Swedish police when the plane landed at Stockholm.

Hence **sky·jacked** *ppl. a.*, **sky·jacking** *vbl. sb.*

1961 *N.Y. Mirror* 5 Aug. 3 (*heading*) Rush stiff skyjacking law. **1969** *Daily Tel.* 1 Nov. 1/1 All air traffic was warned..to avoid the sky-jacked airliner as special preparations were made at Shannon Airport to receive the Trans-World airliner. **1977** D. E. WESTLAKE *Nobody's Perfect* (1978) 227 Listen to this. We fake a skyjacking, but what we *really* do—.

skyjack (skəi·dʒæk), *sb.* [f. the vb.] An instance of skyjacking.

1968 *Tel.* (Brisbane) 13 Mar. 24/7 In the third skyjack in 16 days, a U.S. National Airlines DC8 with 59 people aboard landed at Havana, Cuba, today. **1969** *Cavalier Daily* (Univ. Va.) 5 Feb., United Airlines Tuesday reported an unsuccessful skyjack attempt. **1975** A. OSMOND *Saladin!* I. v. 39 The wars and the riots, the skyjacks and terrorists' bombs. **1978** R. JANSSON *News Caper* iv. 46 This is a skyjack. We have a hostage at either end of the plane.

skyjacker (skəi·dʒækəɹ). Also **sky-jacker.** [f. SKY *sb.*[1] + *HI)JACKER.] One who hijacks an aeroplane.

1961 *N.Y. Mirror* 4 Aug. 1 (*caption*) JFK directed capture of skyjackers. **1970** *Pacifist* Sept. 5/2 The death of hostages will not necessarily lead to the release of..the woman sky-jacker, Leila Khaled. **1976** P. HENISSART *Winter Quarry* ix. 91 You're probably a skyjacker or a bigamist on the run. **1982** *Daily Tel.* 24 July 4/6 The skyjackers..were said to have threatened crew members.

Skylab (skəi·læb). [f. SKY *sb.*[1] + *LAB *sb.*[2]] The name of a space laboratory launched into earth orbit by the U.S. in 1973. Freq. *attrib.* Occas. (with small initial) in *gen.* use.

The laboratory itself was more precisely designated *Skylab 1*; *Skylabs 2, 3,* and *4* were the spacecraft which successively ferried crews to it. The laboratory was manned until 1974, and disintegrated in the atmosphere in 1979.

1970 *Nature* 13 June 1001/2 There are now only four journeys to the Moon before autumn 1972 when the engineers at the Cape and in Houston turn their attention to the Skylab programme—the renamed Apollo applications programme. *Ibid.* 22 Aug. 774/1 Cancelling two of the [Apollo] flights so as to conserve the Saturn V launcher vehicles for ambitions nearer home, such as Skylab and the space station project. **1972** *Daily Progress* (Charlottesville, Va.) 19 Jan. B9/8 The first three-man crew is scheduled to spend 28 days aboard the Skylab mission starting next May. **1973** *Guardian* 11 Apr. 4/3 Preparations are precisely on schedule at Cape Kennedy for the launching on May 14 of Skylab-1, the first US experimental space station. **1975** *McGraw-Hill Yearbk. Sci. & Technol.* 43 With the recovery of the *Skylab 4* command module and crew on Feb. 8, 1974, the active operational phase of the Skylab Program was brought to a successful conclusion. **1979** *Guardian* 12 July 1/8 Skylab fell to earth last night... Its debris scattered into the sea and on to a sparsely inhabited Australian desert. **1982** M. DUKE *Flashpoint* xiii. 98 Scientifically equipped satellites and sky labs.

skylark, *sb.* Add: **3.** With initial capital in catch-phr. *any more for the Skylark?* (from a boatman's cry at seaside resorts), used to offer an open invitation, usu. for a ride or lift.

1931 M. ALLINGHAM *Look to Lady* x. 107 What a good job there's no more for the Skylark... I love riding in other people's motor-cars. **1977** E. DEWHURST *Curtain Fall* v. 46 You hoping for a lift, Miss Rhoda?.. Come along, then, ducky. Any more for the *Skylark*?

sky-larker. Add: †**2.** *Cricket.* = SKYER. *Obs.*

1839 *Bell's Life* 30 June 4/1 Wells..soon retired, giving a 'skylarker', which Button caught.

skylight, *sb.* Add: **4.** Special Comb.: **skylight filter**, a pale filter for use when taking colour photographs to counter excessive blueness from skylight.

1955 G. R. SHARP tr. *Lorelle's Colour Bk. Photogr.* 77 A pale yellow haze or skylight filter may be desirable for shots of people or groups in the shade under a blue sky. **1965** *Focal Encycl. Photogr.* I. 615/2 General correction filters for colour include haze and skylight filters, which mainly absorb ultraviolet and a certain amount of blue light. **1978** *SLR Camera* Sept. 45/1 In addition to performing this very useful warming task, the Skylight filter also gets rid of a lot of UV and gives a mild degree of haze penetration.

skylighted *ppl. a.* (earlier example).

1849 DICKENS *Dav. Copp.* (1850) xxiii. 246 The sky-lighted offices of Spenlow and Jorkins.

sky-line. Add: **1. a.** (Earlier examples.) Also, the representation of this in painting or another art.

1824 SCOTT *St. Ronan's* I. iv. 84 Some boy's daubing, I suppose... Eh! What..is this?.. Who can this be?.. Do but see the sky-line—why, this is..an exquisite little bit. **1849** LYTTON *Caxtons* III. XIV. ii. 10 Seeing only the roof of that palace boldly breaking the sky-line, how serene your contemplations!

b. The outline or silhouette of a building or number of buildings or other objects seen against the sky.

1896 G. B. SHAW in *Sat. Rev.* 10 Oct. 386/2 A tall and beautiful figure, rising like a delicate spire above a skyline of city chimney-pots. **1928** *Daily Mail Year Bk.* 48/1 A traveller returning to the metropolis after some years' absence has difficulty in recognising some of our famous streets; the sky-line is different, salients have disappeared. **1932** *News Chron.* 5 July 9/5 The city's skyline of roofs was silhouetted against a blaze of gold. **1962** *Economist* 27 Oct. 347/1 The decision to free London from the sixty-year-old 100-foot ceiling which cramped ground space and deadened the skyline. **1971** P. GRESSWELL *Environment* 230 Consideration of skylines should be one of the prerequisites of planning.

2. *Forestry.* An overhead cable for the transport of logs.

1925 A. PHILIP *Crimson West* 144 Preparing the spar-tree for 'high-lead' or 'sky-line' rigging, is the most spectacular and thrilling performance in the logging industry. **1942** R. L. HAIG-BROWN *Timber* 254 In the case of a yarder the sky line is the same as the main-line, going from the spar tree through a block attached to a tree stump at the back of the setting. **1958** W. F. MCCULLOCH *Woods Words* 168 Perhaps the first skyline in the Northwest was rigged by Bob Barr at the Bridal Veil Lumber Company in Oregon in 1899. **1963** *Press* (Vancouver) Apr. 9 There's where the donkeys puff and strain As they pull the logs on the road And the skyline moans, as if in pain As it bears its heavy load.

Hence **sky·lined** *ppl. a.*, visible or silhouetted on the skyline.

1946 G. MILLAR *Horned Pigeon* ii. 33 We heard trucks behind us. When we dropped flat we saw them sky-lined. **1969** 'J. FRASER' *Cock-pit of Roses* xvi. 126 Out past the hedge you'll be sky-lined, flashing like neon. **1978** L. HEREN *Growing up on The Times* v. 170 The bear was briefly skylined on another false crest, and I fired..and finally killed it.

skylit (skəi·lit), *ppl. a.* [Pa. pple. of SKY-LIGHT *v.*] = SKYLIGHTED *ppl. a.*

1923 A. E. HOUSMAN *Shropshire Lad* xli. 62 And like a skylit water stood The bluebells in the azured wood. **1978** *Jrnl. R. Soc. Arts* CXXVI. 237/2 It occupies eight of the Royal Academy skylit galleries. **1979** *United States 1980/81* (Penguin Travel Guides) 191 Rooms full of medieval and Renaissance art,..ranged around a skylit, plant-filled courtyard.

Skylon, skylon (skəi·lǫn). *Archit.* [f. SKY *sb.*[1], prob. after PYLON.] The name of a spindle-shaped filigree spire, illuminated at night, forming a prominent feature of the South Bank exhibition at the Festival of Britain in 1951. Also used *transf.* of other similar structures.

1950 *Times* 11 Nov. 4/4 Mrs. A. G. S. Fidler, the wife of the chief architect to the Crawley Development Corporation, was informed yesterday that her suggestion of the name of 'Skylon' for the vertical feature of the Festival of Britain exhibition had been accepted. **1951** *John o' London's Weekly* 11 May 280/2 Skylon..denoting something streamlined and precariously poised. **1959** I. & P. OPIE *Lore & Lang. Schoolch.* ix. 169 The term Skylon..was found two years later [*sc.* after the Festival of Britain] to be a name for the lanky not only in London but as far away as Ruthin. **1961** *Daily Tel.* 9 Nov. 28/5 The centrepiece of decoration is, perhaps, a gold skylon on the road from the airport [in Accra]. **1966** *Guardian* 5 Nov. 7/5 There is an elegant skylon with a revolving restaurant on top. **1977** *Times* 9 Feb. 16/3 Dominating the exhibition will be a Skylon-type structure recalling the Festival of Britain.

skyphos (skəi·fǫs). *Gr. Antiq.* [Gr. σκύφος SCYPHUS.] A large drinking-cup or bowl, having two handles not extending above the rim, and no foot.

1858 S. BIRCH *Anc. Pottery* II. 103 The Heracleotan *scyphos* had its handle ornamented with the Heraclean knot. **1921** *Brit. Museum Return* 61 in *Parl. Papers 1921* XXVII. 555 Attic black-figure skyphos. **1942** J. D. BEAZLEY *Attic Red-Figure Vase-Painters* xii. 301 The vases..are by Makron, whose name appears on his masterpiece, the Boston skyphos. **1960** *Oxf. Univ. Gaz.* 4 Mar. 805/2 From Cyprus:..a painted skyphos imitating a class of pottery made at al Mina under East Greek influence (8th century B.C.). **1979** *Nature* 29 Feb. 643/2 Samples were taken from the base, sides and handles of an Attic skyphos which had been fired between 440 and 425 BC.

sky-rocket, *sb.* Add: **2.** *transf.* An enthusiastic cheer, raised esp. by college students; = *SIS-BOOM-BAH. *U.S. slang.*

1867 *Ball Players' Chron.* (N.Y.) 25 July 2/2 After cheers had been interchanged, and the Nationals had let off a 'sky rocket'—namely a sort of finish to three cheers, with a 'hiss—boom—ah!'—an adjournment was had to the clubhouse. **1894** [in Dict.] **1947** G. S. PERRY *Cities of Amer.* 222 He is such a stimulating lecturer that many of his classes are preceded by a 'skyrocket': a Wisconsin yell reserved for its heroes.

3. *Rhyming slang* for 'pocket'. Cf. *SKY *sb.*[1] 7*.

1879 *Macmillan's Mag.* Oct. 502/1 A slavey piped the spoons sticking out of my skyrocket (pocket), so I got smugged. **1898** [see *OUTER colloq. var. OUT OF *prep. phr.*]. **1936** J. CURTIS *Gilt Kid* ix. 98 There's no sense in hanging around in the West End with a cane and Christ knows what else in my sky-rocket. **1962** F. NORMAN *Guntz* i. 8 He put the letter in an envelope and..handed it to me. I took it and stuffed it in my sky rocket. **1973** 'B. MATHER' *Snowline* xv. 180 Ten trouble-free runs.. and you're back in England with five thousand quid in your skyrocket.

sky·rocket, *v.* [f. the sb.] **1.** *trans.* In *Cricket*, = SKY *v.*[1] 1 b. *rare*$^{-1}$.

1851 W. CLARKE *Pract. Hints Cricket* in W. Bolland *Cricket Notes* 134 It's enough to make you bite your thumbs to see your best balls pulled and sky-rocketed about.

2. a. *intr.* To rise abruptly and rapidly; to increase dramatically (in number, amount, etc.). Cf. *ROCKET *v.* 2 c. Chiefly *U.S.*

1895 in *Funk's Stand. Dict.* **1923** *Nation* (N.Y.) 22 Aug. 181 The supply runs short and prices go skyrocketing. **1935** *Motion Picture* Nov. 40/2 Frances Dee..skyrockets to new importance with an amazingly fine performance. **1936** M. MITCHELL *Gone with Wind* xii. 217 Even the cheapest cotton goods had skyrocketed in price. **1943** J. STEINBECK in *N.Y. Herald Tribune* 29 Sept. 21/8 The incidence of GI dysentery skyrocketed. **1951** E. PAUL *Springtime in Paris* iv. 80 After World War I,.. the mark skyrocketed from 100 to the dollar to 3,000,000 or more. **1968** MRS. L. B. JOHNSON *White House Diary* 14 Mar. (1970) 638 The headlines ran:—'Mad Rush in Europe'..'Gold Buying Skyrockets'. **1974** 'E. LATHEN' *Sweet & Low* xviii. 173 It had taken only twenty-four hours in the hinterland for his opinion of Milan to skyrocket.

b. To jump or fly up suddenly, in the manner of a sky-rocket. *rare.*

1907 G. B. SHAW *John Bull's Other Island* II. 30 Here! where are you jumpin to? Wheres your manners to go skyrocketin like that out o the box in the middle o your confession? **1946** J. W. DAY *Harvest Adventure* iv. 48 Partridges sky-rocketed and screwballed overhead and fled to safety.

2. a. *trans.* To destroy utterly; = EXPLODE *v.* 3. **b.** To cause to rise abruptly and rapidly: to propel rapidly forward or upward; to increase sharply.

1928 *Daily Express* 24 Nov. 3/5 A careful 'once-over' of some of London's most prominent public men has.. sky-rocketed the popular American idea that all Englishmen are snappy dressers! **1950** BLESH & JANIS *They all played Ragtime* v. 102 His 1896 success at Keith's and Tony Pastor's in New York skyrocketed him into the public eye. **1976** *National Observer* (U.S.) 31 Jan. 6/1 If I had a disease that skyrocketed my chances of dying early.., would I take the drugs that would control my disease.

So **sky·rocketing** *vbl. sb.* and *ppl. a.* Cf. *ROCKETING *ppl. a.*

1849 POE *Marginalia* in *Compl. Wks.* (1902) XVI. 166 The German 'Schwärmerei'—not exactly 'hum-bug', but 'sky-rocketing'—..that peculiar style of criticism which has lately come into fashion, through the influence of certain..people who live..about Boston. **1933** *Sun* (Baltimore) 18 Aug. 16/5 Skyrocketing of all grain values immediately ensued. **1962** [see *EXPLOSION 4 b]. **1979** *Vole* 8 Nov. 26/1 Land-prices..are a key element in the sky-rocketing costs of both housing and food.

sky-scraper. Add: **2. a.** [A horse named Skyscraper, sired by Highflyer, won the Epsom Derby in 1789:

1788 *Racing Calendar* 269 Mr. Dutton named the D. of Bedford's c. Skyscraper, by Highflyer. **1810** T. H. MORLAND *Geneal. English Race Horse* 147 Skyscraper mare produced Brainworm by Buzzard. *Ibid.* 160 [Death] Skyscraper, 1807.]

† **d.** A tall hat or bonnet. *Obs.*

1800 W. SCOTT *Let.* 5 Apr. (1937) XII. 159 The trumpets call me to swagger in a cockd skyscraper and sword. **1847** J. A. EAMES *Budget of Lett.* 397 She gave me a black silk bonnet..which stuck right up in the air after the fashion of the old 'sky scrapers'.

e. In *Baseball, Cricket*, etc., a ball propelled high in the air; a towering hit, a skyer.

1866 *N.Y. Herald* 27 June 5/5 Goodspeed made three handsome fly catches; Mehl, Sweet and Dupignac each paying their share of attention to the 'skyscrapers'. **1907** *St. Nicholas* (N.Y.) Sept. 996 A 'skyscraper' throw to first. **1943** *Amer. Speech* XVIII. 104 Fly balls include the *skyscraper*, the *cloud-buster*, [etc.]. **1963** *Times* 28 Feb. 3/6 Alabaster's skyscraper to Titmus at midwicket demonstrated only the extraordinary sureness of Titmus in the field.

4. (Earlier and later examples.)

[**1883** J. MOSER in *Amer. Architect & Building News* 30 June 305 The capitol building should always have a dome. I should raise thereon a gigantic 'sky-scraper', contrary to all precedent in practice.] **1888** *Inter-Ocean* 30 Dec. 10/5 The 'sky-scrapers' of Chicago outrival anything of their kind in the world. **1903** O. KILDARE *My Mamie Rose* xix. 288 We reach our stoop in the yawning dark cañon of the skyscrapers. **1928** W. A. STARRETT *Skyscrapers & Men who build Them* i. 1 The skyscraper is the most distinctively American thing in the world. **1942** *Short Guide Gt. Brit.* (U.S. War Dept.) 7 London has no skyscrapers. **1951** *Manch. Guardian Weekly* 19 Apr. 5 Theatres will have skyscrapers superimposed on them. **1976** *Sunday Mail* (Glasgow) 28 Nov. 20/2 Babs Marchant ..lives 18 storeys up in an Ibrox, Glasgow, skyscraper.

Hence **sky-scrapered** *a.*, characterized by the presence of or full of sky-scrapers; surrounded by sky-scrapers; built very tall.

1947 *Ann. Reg. 1946* 212 The new home [for the U.N.] would be sky-scrapered, congested and expensive. **1963** *Harper's Bazaar* Jan. 21/2 Cagliari..is now a busy sky-scrapered seaport. **1963** C. L. COOPER *Black!* x. 151 The skyscrapered trillion-bricked dwellings. **1965** *Guardian* 4 Oct. 9/4 Salisbury is brittle, skyscrapered, centralised, and carefully zoned into European and African residential areas.

sky-scraping, *a.* (Further examples.)

1884 *Chicago Daily Tribune* 9 Mar. 19/1 The sky-scraping buildings that have been and will be erected down-town will never endanger human life, because they will only be occupied by people wide awake. **1904** *N.Y. Even. Post* 12 Mar. 10 (*heading*) Sky-scraping prices at last Brandus picture sale. **1905** KIPLING *Actions & Reactions* (1909) 123 What under the stars are you doing here, you sky-scraping chimney-sweep? **1961** P. FLEMING *Bayonets to Lhasa* xviii. 230 The force camped..less than a mile from the sky-scraping Potala. **1973** *Washington Post* 13 Jan. C1/1 Man's most wondrous, skyscraping community, the 110-story Brobdingnagian shafts stand ..at the western edge of Manhattan island.

sky-sign. Add: **1.** (Later example.)

1940 C. DAY LEWIS tr. *Virgil's Georgics* I. 23 Well for us that we watch the rise and fall of the sky-signs And the four different seasons that divide the year equally.

2. a. (Later examples.) Also *spec.* an electrically illuminated sign or message similarly placed.

1903 *Building News* 10 Apr. 510/2 Mr Caudwell..contended..that a sky sign was any sign which could be seen against the sky by a person standing beneath. **1916** A. BENNETT *Lion's Share* ix. 64 They crossed a thoroughfare that twinkled and glittered from end to end with moving sky-signs. **1926** *Socialist Rev.* June 13 In Piccadilly a large crowd—mostly strikers—watched a *Daily Dispatch* news bulletin thrown up on a huge sky-sign. **1938** F. BRETT YOUNG *Dr. Bradley Remembers* iii. 121 He was to see the dim, discreet streets of the city centre..garish with neon lights and sky-signs. **1954** *Times* 17 Dec. 9/4 London County Council gives notice of a Bill..'To repeal the provisions of the London Building Acts, 1930 to 1939, prohibiting the erection of sky signs.' **1966** *Punch* 16 Mar. 368/2 There's to be one of those electric sky-sign newscasters in Piccadilly Circus at last. But remember how easy it is to get hold of the wrong end of those revolving messages.

b. An advertisement or other message in sky-writing.

1922 *Flight* XIV. 330/2 This week has witnessed the first practical application of the invention of Major J. C. Savage, by means of which chemical smoke trailing from an aeroplane can be used for writing words or tracing figures in the sky... His first 'sky sign' took the form of the word 'Castrol'. **1931** C. DAY LEWIS *From Feathers to Iron* 53 Now shall the airman vertically banking Out of the blue write a new sky-sign.

skytrain (skəi·trē^{i}n). Also with hyphen and as two words. [SKY *sb.*^{1}] **1.** *U.S.* A convoy consisting of a number of gliders towed in line by an aeroplane, and used for the transport of freight, etc. and in *Mil.* applications. (*temporary.*)

1934 *Sun* (Baltimore) 4 Aug. 4/2 Glider lands from airmail 'train' in pioneer flight... Lustig sky trains. **1935** *Evening Sun* (Baltimore) 14 May 1/7 The sky-train..—two gliders towed by an airplane—took off at Miami on its one-stop flight under perfect weather conditions. **1944** C. MILBURN *Diary* 18 June (1979) 221 Wounded men..are evacuated from Normandy by 'sky trains', which carry a flight nurse and two medical officers. **1946** A. LEE *German Air Force* xii. 165 The fighter units in Western Germany..carried out only one or two thrusts against the long sky train of tempting Dakotas and their gliders.

2. Skytrain. Also **skytrain.** The name of a privately-owned passenger air service seeking to provide regular, low-cost, transatlantic travel facilities. (No longer in operation.)

A proprietary name in the U.S.

1971 *Daily Tel.* 20 Oct. 2/6 Laker Airways applied yesterday..for permission to operate a 'sky train' service to New York for a winter single fare of £32.50 per passenger. **1972** *Ibid.* 27 Sept. 1 Mr Freddy Laker..said last night: 'Skytrain is a walk on, walk off, no frills, no reservation service similar to a train service.' **1977** *Arab Times* 14 Dec. 6/2 Freddie Laker, creator of the cut-rate London-New York Skytrain air service, said Monday his airline has applied to operate a similar Skytrain service between London and Los Angeles. **1978** *Official Gaz.* (U.S. Patent Office) 23 May 345/2 Laker Airways Limited ..*Skytrain*..For air passenger services—namely, the transportation of passengers by air.

skyve, -er, -ing, varr. *SKIVE *v.*^{3}, *SKIVER *sb.*^{3}, *SKIVING *vbl. sb.*^{2}

skyward, *a.* (Earlier and later examples.)

1831 W. HOWITT *Bk. of Seasons* 325 The sky-ward and inaccessible pinnacles. **1935** C. DAY LEWIS *Time to Dance* 22 Speak up, speak up, you skyward man, Speak up and tell us true.

skyway (skəi·wē^i). Chiefly *U.S.* [SKY *sb.*^{1}]

1. The sky as a medium of transport or a route used by aircraft; = *AIRWAY 2.

1919 *Pearson's Mag.* Dec. 547/1 The letters will tell.. the nationality of the ship passing along the world's skyways. **1928** L. THOMAS (*title*) European skyways. The story of a tour of Europe by aeroplane. **1934** *Sun* (Baltimore) 15 May 1/3 Theirs is the great-circle route over the North Atlantic—the skyway emblazoned by Byrd, Acosta, [etc.]. **1952** *N.Y. Times* 7 Aug. 39/8 The team of precision flyers will fly the skyway route on the way to their home base at Corpus Christi, Tex. **1967** M. CRAVEN *I heard Owl call my Name* xi. 68 High in the skyways wild geese called exultantly on their first early passages back from the south.

2. An overhead motorway. Also *transf.* (see quot. 1960).

1940 *Sun* (Baltimore) 6 Sept. 13/4 It has been suggested that a skyway be built along Pratt street from Monroe to the Fallsway, the western end to connect with the route to Washington. **1958** *Wall St. Jrnl.* 10 Nov. 18/3 A reduction in toll rates charged on the Sunshine Skyway ..is expected to be approved by the State Road Department Board. **1960** *Daily Tel.* 10 Feb. 20/6 The system, known as Skyway, runs on a concrete way 15 ft above ground. It has a speed of 50 m.p.h. and it is estimated operates for as little as a penny a mile. **1972** J. GORES *Dead Skip* (1973) i. 7 Heslip unlocked the chain-link storage lot under the concrete abutments of the skyway adjacent to the DICA office.

3. Chiefly in Minneapolis: (see quot. 1975^1); an aerial walkway between buildings. *U.S.*

[**1968** *Archit. Forum* Jan.–Feb. 83/2 The first pedestrian bridge of an elaborate second-story network has been completed in downtown St. Paul. Part of the 12-block urban renewal project, the 'Skyway' will eventually comprise an elevated system of bridges and concourses.] **1969** *Ibid.* Jan.–Feb. 75/3 The overpass idea, now called a 'Skyway', is being carried out several blocks to the east. **1970** *Business Week* 26 Dec. 48/2 Shelter from summer heat and winter weather is one advantage of skyways—especially in Minneapolis, where it is below or near freezing for five months of the year. **1975** *Country Life* 2 Jan. 36/3 There has been a great incentive to construct the Skyway system... Skyways are broad, carpeted, heated, air-conditioned, glass-covered corridors, linking the main city buildings at first-floor level. **1975** *New Yorker* 24 Mar. 106/2 Walking there is a pleasure—down the carless mall, or through a glazed 'skyway' system if snow starts to fall. **1979** *United States 1980/81* (Penguin Travel Guides) 266 The most extraordinary feature of downtown Minneapolis is its internal skyway, an interconnected belt of pedestrian malls and escalators.

sky-writing, *vbl. sb.* [SKY *sb.*^{1}] The tracing of legible signs in the sky, esp. for advertising purposes, by means of smoke trails made by aircraft or (occas.) by letters and devices projected by searchlight. Also, the writing so produced.

1923 *Western Gaz.* 16 May 8/4 Sky-writing..did not commend itself to the general body of advertisers. **1926** H. BARR in *Mod. Advertising* I. 9/1 Invented in 1910 by John Clifford Savage, it was not until twelve years later that sky-writing became an accomplished fact. *Ibid.* 9/2 The corporation..is stated to have spent £320,000 on sky-writing publicity alone. **1932** *Flight* 8 July 638/1 Night sky-writing, by projection of light on to clouds at night, was considered at no little length. **1935** H. G. WELLS *Things to Come* ix. 91 Sky writing by the new planes. **1959** *Belfast Tel.* 9 Oct. 7/1 It is believed to be the first time skywriting has been used in a general election. **1966** *Punch* 13 July 54/1 Long ago You fancied many wonders that we know, The 'Telephonoscope', for one, 'Sky Writing', and the Long Range Gun. **1978** F. ROSS *Sleeping Dogs* 157 He couldn't have made his intentions universally clearer if he'd spelled them out in sky-writing.

So as *ppl. a.* and hence [as back-formation] **sky-write** *v.* (*a*) *intr.*, to practise sky-writing; (*b*) *trans.*, to trace in the sky by means of smoke trails; **sky-writer; sky-written** *ppl. a.*

1922 *Daily Mail* 8 Aug. 5/3 The Daily Mail sky-writing aeroplane was over Margate and Folkestone yesterday. **1926** *Mod. Advertising* I. 9/2, 1,450 sky-written demonstrations were carried out by eight pilots. **1927** *Pictorial Weekly* 17 Sept. 198 A window sign which reproduces in miniature the work of the sky-writer. **1932** *Times Educ. Suppl.* 22 Oct. p. iv/3 A battery of sky-writing projectors will be installed on the roofs of buildings. **1934** WEBSTER, Skywrite. **1941** B. SCHULBERG *What makes Sammy Run?* xii. 219 Feeling his words fade off into the air like a sky-writer's. **1959** J. CARY *Captive & Free* xlvii. 203 She was always calling him on the telephone with new ideas—aeroplanes sky-writing the message..; pavement-writing; ..and loudspeaker vans. **1960** *Guardian* 29 Dec. 3/2 Sky-written slogans. **1973** J. DRUMMOND *Bang! Bang!* i. 2 The plane swooped... The smoke spurted... People wondered if it was possible for a sky-writer to dot his 'i's. *Ibid.* 3 They've been sky-writing to advertise their shows.

slab, *sb.*^{1} Add: **1. a.** (Earlier and later *transf.* and further *techn.* examples.)

1881 *Encycl. Brit.* XII. 839/1 The rubber is glossy, of a bright pink colour and mottled appearance, and occurs in the form either of small balls pressed together or of irregular masses called 'slabs or 'loaf' rubber. **1903** *Imperial Inst. Techn. Rep.* 153 The 'slabs' of blackish rubber alone being worth 1*s.* 11*d.* per pound. **1964** *Amer. Speech* XXXIX. 274 *Slab*, a solid piece of rubber used as an ingredient to be melted and mixed with solvents to form rubber cements or to be milled and stripped off.

transf. **1882** *Harper's Mag.* July 32/2 From one of our exchanges..we chip off the following slab of scientific knowledge. **1951** PARTRIDGE *Dict. Slang* (ed. 4) Add. 1172/2 *Slab*..a long paragraph. **1958** *Listener* 14 Aug. 249/3 The conventional slabs of Brahms, Beethoven, and Tchaikovsky. *a* **1974** R. CROSSMAN *Diaries* (1976) II. 623 When I started, I used to dictate slabs without any real preparation.

b. *spec.* in *Metallurgy*, such a piece of metal produced from an ingot for subsequent rolling into sheet or plate.

1863 [in Dict.]. **1910** [see *BILLET *sb.*^{2} 9]. **1931** *Economist* 21 Mar. 608/1 The biggest decline occurring in billets, blooms and slabs. **1968** D. R. CLIFFE *Technical Metallurgy* iv. 70 Ingots are broken down into blooms or slabs, as a hot working process, in a cogging mill. **1972** *Times* 18 Sept. 21/6 Production of slab zinc was 35,000 tons.

c. = *slab-cake*, sense 6 below.

1908 J. KIRKLAND *Mod. Baker* III. 462 Rice Slab at 6d. per lb... Lemon Madeira at 3d. per lb... Fruit Slab at 3d. per lb. **1948** *Good Housek. Cookery Bk.* 580 Cut the Genoese slab into 2-inch squares. **1974** W. FOLEY *Child in Forest* I. iii. 39 Plain slab was a delicate luxury and this was no plain slab!

d. *Archit.* A rectangular block of pre-cast, reinforced concrete used in building, esp. in multi-storey constructions.

1927 *Archit. Rec.* Dec. 452/2 A number of experimental houses have been built with 'textile-block slab construction'... The system consists of concrete block slabs about two or three inches thick of unit sizes which can be handled, laid on end with interlocking grooves, reinforced horizontally and vertically by means of steel rods. **1930** *Amer. Architect* Apr. 32/2 A type of floor and ceiling construction light in weight, quickly erected..is being used... The system consists of two types of slabs, one for floors and another for ceilings, used in conjunction with the ordinary supporting members of steel construction. **1938** *Archit. Rev.* LXXXIII. 223 (*caption*) One of the two 'porte-cochères', in reinforced concrete column and slab construction. **1951** *Ibid.* CX. 92 The café terrace, which disappears beneath its lightly supported slab roof to become a two-level café-bar. **1973** D. FRANCIS *Slay-Ride* x. 122 A modern square-built glass and slab affair a mile out of the city centre.

e. *Archit.* A high-rise block of impersonal aspect.

[**1933** L. MUMFORD in *New Yorker* 23 Dec. 29/2 What does one find? First, a gigantic slab of a building.] **1952** *Archit. Rev.* CXI. 119/1 As is well known, the term 'slab' was coined in the 1930's in connection with publicity on the RCA Building at Rockefeller Center. **1958** *Listener* 20 Nov. 827/1 A point block of government offices is now going up at Wellington..and other high-rise slabs for offices and flats. **1969** BURCHARD & BUSH-BROWN *Archit. of Amer.* IV. 353 The early skyscrapers were massive blocks... The new characteristic form became the slab, a term applied to the buildings erected at the Rockefeller Center beginning about 1930. The slab form had appeared briefly in the early history of the skyscraper, notably in the Monadnock Building... It remained for the architects of Rockefeller Center..to modernize the slab, to make it thinner in relation to its height, to simplify it and to treat it with characteristic but underemphasized setbacks.

2. b. (Earlier and later examples.) Also *N.Z.*

1829 H. WIDOWSON *Present State Van Diemen's Land* 86 Logs, or as they are more commonly called, slabs, for erecting barns or small buildings are erected in the same manner. **1905** W.B. *Where White Man Treads* 259 It is a low whare of split slabs, adzed over, and sunk into the earth as closely as the inequalities of adze-jointing will permit. **1950** *N.Z. Jrnl. Agric.* Apr. 375/2 Floors [in very early milking sheds] were of wooden slabs, bricks, stones, or even clay. **1957** P. White *Voss* vi. 154 She was standing in front of a house, or hut, of bleached slabs, that melted into the live trunks of the surrounding trees.

3. d. A flat piece of stone, etc., immediately in front of a fire-place; a stone hearth.

1876 *Encycl. Brit.* IV. 466/2 The slab is that part of the floor of a room which is immediately before the fire-place, and along the extent of its front. In basement rooms, this slab is supported by a brick wall brought up from the ground; but in upper rooms the slab is supported by a flat half brick arch called a brick trimmer. **1883** R. L. Stevenson *Treasure Is.* xix. 153 Little had been left beside the framework of the house; but in one corner there was a stone slab laid down by way of hearth, and an old rusty iron basket to contain the fire. **1963** B. Goodson *Pract. Guide to House Repairs* iv. 50 The tiled hearth slab is bedded in about ½ in. of mortar on the existing hearth. **1977** J. S. Curl *Eng. Archit.* 154/1 *Slab*..the hearth of a fireplace.

e. The stone on which a corpse is laid in a mortuary. Also *transf.* and *fig.*

1903 A. H. Lewis *Boss* viii. 101 I've seen a bloke take a slab in th' morgue for less. It was Benny the Bite; he gets a knife between his slats. **1924** G. C. Henderson *Keys to Crookdom* 417 Slab... Undertaker's table. **1930** H. C. Bailey *Mr. Fortune Explains* 111 On a slab in the mortuary the woman's body lay and the divisional surgeon turned from it to nod at Reggie. **1932** E. Wallace *When Gangs came to London* ii. 26 My best friend is a forty-five..and the day he puts you on the slab I'm going to put diamonds all round his muzzle. **1977** 'C. Aird' *Parting Breath* x. 127 Pathologists had hobby-horses, too, and obesity was..Dr Dabbe's. He was always having a go at Sergeant Gelven..about his weight. 'See you soon,' was his favourite form of greeting to the portly detective, 'on my slab.'

4. a. (sense 2 b) *slab-and-bark house, hut; slab-and-shingle hut; slab house* (earlier and later examples), *hut* (later examples), *whare* [Whare].

1862 R. Henning *Let.* 18 Oct. (1966) 111 It is not much to move a slab house; all the woodwork takes down and puts up again. **1901** M. Franklin *My Brilliant Career* i. 5 Our comfortable, wide-veranda'ed..slab house..was ever full to overflowing. **1905** W.B. *Where White Man Treads* 293 He..who lives in a slab whare, and on a fare which his dainty collie sniffs at and rejects. **1908** E. J. Banfield *Confessions of Beachcomber* I. i. 12 According to the formula neatly printed in official journals, the building of a slab hut is absurdly easy. **1933** *Bulletin* (Sydney) 25 Jan. 20 A good three-roomed slab-and-shingle hut that had been vacated by a white family. **1945** *Salt* 12 Feb. 4/1 His earliest years were spent in a slab-and-bark hut. **1949** F. Sargeson *I saw it in my Dream* 100 A slab *whare* in a narrow valley. **1959** J. Wright *Generations of Men* 53 A slab-and-bark house in lonely fever-ridden country. **1969** F. Sargeson *Joy of Worm* i. 7 It then became pleasant to look forward to hot food, the shelter of the farmer's slab hut, and talk with the man himself.

b. (sense 2 a) *slabwood.*

1877 [in Dict.]. **1921** *Daily Colonist* (Victoria, B.C.) 2 Oct. 10/1 (Advt.), Cordwood, Slabwood, Blockwood, Dry Kindling. **1962** M. E. Murie *Two in Far North* I. ii. 20 Off at one side, a lean-to bedroom built of slab wood. **1976** *Newmarket Jrnl.* 16 Dec., (Advt.), Hardwood and softwood, slabwood and off-cuts for sale.

5. a. *slab-bridged* (earlier *fig.* example), *-walled.* Cf. Slab-sided *a.* in Dict. and Suppl.

1859 *Atlantic Monthly* Nov. 642/1 Anyone who has driven over a mountain-stream by one of those bridges made of *slabs* will feel the force of a term we once heard applied to a parson so shaky in character that no dependence could be placed on him,—'A slab-bridged kind o' feller!' **1930** L. G. D. Acland *Early Canterbury Runs* 1st Ser. viii. 213 The slab-walled, earthen-floored hut.

c. *slab-like* adj.

1899 W. James *Talks to Teachers* 214 The even forehead, the slab-like cheek, the codfish eye, may be less interesting for the moment. **1970** R. J. Small *Study of Landforms* iv. 122 On the high valley slopes above Glen Rosa great slab-like outcrops of granite, tilted at between 30° and 60°, are developed where glacial erosion and frost weathering have exposed dilatation joints.

6. Special combinations: **slab avalanche,** an avalanche in which a sheet of snow breaks cleanly away along a fracture line; **slab bacon,** unsliced bacon; **slab-cake,** (a) cake baked in a large rectangular tin (cf. sense 1 c above).

[**1920** A. Lunn in G. W. Young *Mountain Craft* ix. 431 The wind-slab is the most treacherous of all avalanches. **1936** G. Seligman *Snow Structure & Ski Fields* vii. 160 If this 'slab' of snow has formed on a steep slope it will shatter into countless blocks of hardened snow, and these, sliding downhill, will precipitate the most insidious of all avalanches—the wind-slab avalanche.] **1953** *Avalanche Handbk.* (U.S. Dept. Agric. Forest Service) iv. 34 (*caption*) Major slab-avalanche. Depth of fracture: 10 feet. **1978** C. Fraser *Avalanches & Snow Safety* v. 79 Criterion 1 is the form of break which started the avalanche and this leads to the broad division of all avalanches into two types: 'loose-snow avalanches'..and 'slab avalanches'. **1932** *Even. Sun* (Baltimore) 7 Nov. 12/7 (Advt.), Boneless Slab Bacon lb 13½c. **1975** L. & S. Lobel *All about Meat* vii. 115 Take the trouble to hunt for unsliced slab bacon. **1902** J. T. Law *Grocer's Man.* (ed. 2) 854/1 Slab Cakes, or Cut Cakes (sold by the pound).—The introduction of these ready-made cakes, as an extension of the birthday, wedding, and Christmas cake system, appears to be displacing or supplanting much of the old-fashioned retail business in currants, raisins,..spices, etc. **1935** *Economist* 22 June 1439/1 Scribbans and Company, the well known makers of slab cake, find their activities in fields where steady progress..is the natural order of things. **1974** W. Foley *Child in Forest* I. v. 57 A slice of bright slab cake.

slab, *v.*³ Add: **5.** *trans.* Of a path, climber, etc.: to traverse (the side of a slope) horizontally or at a gentle angle. *U.S.*

1889 Farmer *Americanisms* 492/2 *To slab,* to make roads round the sides of mountains. **1892** *Outing* Jan. 268/1 So we started blindly up the bank and into the forest, continuing for an hour and a half to 'slab' the mountain, as the backwoodsmen say. **1907** *Guide Paths & Camps White Mountains* (Appalachian Mountain Club) 62 The path now slabs the east side. **1916** *Ibid.* (ed. 2) 265 The path..rises by easy zigzags slabbing the S.W. flank of Eagle Cliff. **1963** *Appalachian Trailway News* Sept. 43/2 We zigzagged and slabbed mountains, finally coming..down a beautiful grassy glade where stood Big Stamp Shelter. **1968** *Ibid.* Sept. 43/2 Route slabs north-western slope of ridge.

slabber, *sb.*² Add: **c.** A workman who cuts or forms materials into slabs.

An early form of the word may occur in the proper name *Ric. Sclaber* (1327), *Ric. le Sclabber* (1333): see *N. & Q.* (1963) July 256/1.

1921 *Dict. Occup. Terms* (1927) § 118 *Slabber,* cements together tiles and other shaped articles for hearths, kerbs, etc. *Ibid.* § 159 *Slabber,*..cuts blocks of gelatine..into slabs. **1977** *New Society* 25 Aug. 387/1 His heavy manual work as a fireplace 'tile slabber'.

slabby (slæ·bi), *sb. N.Z. colloq.* [f. Slab *sb.*¹ 2 a.] A timber worker dealing with slabs of timber.

1907 'G. B. Lancaster' *Tracks We Tread* vi. 87 The..clumsiest slabby that lumped in the mill. **1916** G. Thornton *Wowser* v. 72 Barnabas the slabby (the man who wheels away the unused portions of timber).

slab-sided, *a.* For *U.S.* read orig. *U.S.* and add earlier and later examples. Also in *Archit.*: see *slab *sb.*¹ 1 d.

1817 J. K. Paulding *Lett. from South* II. 122 He was what is usually called a tall slab-sided Virginian. **1927** A. Conan Doyle *Case-Bk. Sherlock Holmes* iii. 89 The prize-fighter, a heavily built young man with a stupid, obstinate, slab-sided face. **1933** *Flight* 23 Mar. 268 The fuselage is not quite 'slab-sided'. **1964** L. Deighton *Funeral in Berlin* v. 32 The large slab-sided department store. **1981** E. Corlett *Revolution in Merchant Shipping* 35/1 High slab-sided deckhouses.

slack, *sb.*¹ Add: **2.** (Later examples.) Also, a depression among sand-dunes.

1929 [see *low *sb.* 3 a]. **1934** *Geogr. Jrnl.* LXXXIII. 498 The question that always comes to my mind in looking at dune formations is what is the primary cause of the rhythmical or ripple effect, the succession of ridges and slacks. **1963** *Times* 27 Feb. 11/6 In the lee of the high dunes lie wet slacks and attractive freshwater pools out of which grow strands of reed and reed-mace. **1964** V. J. Chapman *Coastal Vegetation* vi. 153 The damp soil of the slacks is colonized by a carpet of the Creeping Willow.

slack, *sb.*³ Add: **3. c.** In critical path analysis, the length of time by which a particular event can be delayed without delaying the completion of the overall objective.

1962 *NASA PERT & Compan. Cost System Handbk.* (U.S. Nat. Aeronaut. & Space Admin.) B-3 The accomplishment of event #3 could be delayed by three weeks without jeopardizing meeting the expected date for the end objective. This difference or cushion is called slack. **1964** K. G. Lockyer *Introd. Critical Path Anal.* v. 46 A different expression of the ability of activities to move is given by considering the head and tail events. These have 'earliest' and 'latest' times, and slack is the difference between these times. **1970** O. Dopping *Computers & Data Processing* xxii. 346 After the critical path has been found, it may be possible to transfer resources from activities with a big slack to certain critical activities.

4. a. Also *fig.*, esp. in phr. *to take up the slack,* to use up a surplus or make up a deficiency, thereby maintaining or returning to a stable condition.

1915 J. London *Jacket* viii. 63 Jones was forcing his foot into my back in order to cinch me tighter, while I was trying with my muscle to steal slack. **1930** *Economist* 21 June 1391/2 There is general agreement that the termination of the Stevenson Scheme left the industry with much more 'slack' to take up than was realised two years ago. **1933** *Sun* (Baltimore) 12 Sept. 1/6 The American Federation of Labor..was framing demands for further..wage-boosting to take up employment slack. **1957** *Economist* 16 Nov. 610/2 Sir Alexander Fleck's investigations may show just how much slack has crept into an organization that should be, if anything, over-cautious. **1967** *Times* 28 Feb. (Canada Suppl.) 33 There is the feeling that slack will develop as the year progresses. **1972** A. MacVicar *Golden Venus Affair* vi. 61 It was a comfort having somebody like Mary Jo to take up the slack of decision-making. **1980** B. Paul *First Gravedigger* v. 60 We'd no longer be handling his speciality... Our new rare books department in London would take up the slack.

c. Phr. *to give* (or *cut*) (a person) *some slack,* to show (a person) understanding or restraint, to give (one) a chance. *U.S. slang* (chiefly *Blacks'*).

1968 M. F. Jackmon in Jones & Neal *Black Fire* (1969) 555 Say, baby, light'n up on me—gimme some slack. **1969** H. Rap Brown *Die Nigger Die* ii. 29 Now, if the brother couldn't come back behind that, I usually cut him some slack. **1971** *Current Slang* (Univ. S. Dakota) VI. 3 *Cut me some slack!*, to give one a chance (imperative). **1973** *Black World* May 39/1 Tradesmen give them no slack in the unfamiliar bargaining processes.

5. *pl.* Now *spec.* loosely-cut trousers for informal wear, esp. those worn by women.

1932 D. L. Sayers *Have his Carcase* ii. 31 He wore a pair of old flannel slacks, and a khaki shirt. **1937** *Night & Day* 29 July 22/2 Deeply to be deplored are such things as sandals..slacks and sun-top dresses. **1942** A. Christie *Body in Library* xii. 139 She was wearing grey slacks and an emerald jumper. **1947** W. S. Maugham *Creatures of Circumstance* 303 He changed from his business clothes into slacks and an old coat. **1956** A. H. Compton *Atomic Quest* i. 32 Dressed casually in slacks and a sweater, he invited me cordially into his study. **1966** J. Betjeman *High & Low* 56 The debs may turn disdainful backs On Pearl's uncouth mechanic slacks. **1968** *Listener* 10 Dec. 790/3 In Jordan, girls at Amman University have been instructed not to wear..slacks either, and, moreover, to keep off heavy make-up. **1979** R. Jaffe *Class Reunion* (1980) I. i. 27 Nor could you wear slacks or any other sort of pants to class, even in the snow.

6. (Earlier example.)

1825 J. Neal *Bro. Jonathan* I. 156 'None o' your slack,' says I..'none o' your pokin' fun at me.'

7. *Pros.* A syllable or part of a foot which does not receive stress.

c **1883** G. M. Hopkins *Poems* (1967) 45 Every foot has one principal stress or accent, and this or the syllable it falls on may be called the Stress of the foot and the other part, the one or two unaccented syllables, the Slack. **1970** J. Malof *Man. Eng. Meters* i. 2 In the freer varieties of accentual verse, meter is determined simply by counting the number of stresses in the line.., ignoring the relatively unemphatic or unstressed syllables, which we call slacks. **1973** *Word 1970* XXVI. 56 None or as many as six slacks may appear between such isochronous accents, though one, two, or three slacks are more normal.

8. A street-walker or prostitute. *slang.*

1959 *Encounter* May 24 *Slack,* which is the call-girls' word for a street-girl. **1963** *Observer* 29 Sept. 31/4 A young master was asked by a boy..'Can a slack (prostitute) work hard enough to earn a living?' **1965** W. Young *Eros Denied* xiv. 141 The slack is afraid of disease, and afraid of the sex maniac who thinks it'd be fun to strangle her.

9. *Comb.* **slack suit,** a pair of slacks with a matching jacket, as a fashionable garment for women; **slack variable** *Math.*, a variable which expresses the difference between the two sides of an inequality.

1940 R. Chandler *Farewell, my Lovely* xxvii. 203 Miss Anne Riordan stood there, in a pale green slack suit. **1973** H. Nielsen *Severed Key* viii. 91 She had..changed into a lime-green knitted slack-suit. **1953** Cooper & Henderson *Introd. Linear Programming* I. ii. 6 These values λ_i (i = 10,11,... 16) so introduced may be referred to as slack variables... The requirement that the slack variables be non-negative merely extends the range of the subscript. **1974** Adby & Dempster *Introd. Optimization Methods* v. 156 At least some evidence exists which suggests that the use of slack variables is an effective method for handling inequality constraints, both linear and non-linear.

slack, *a.* and *adv.* Add: **A.** *adj.* **III. 7. e.** *Phonetics.* Of a vowel: = *lax *a.* 5 c.

1909 H. C. Wyld *Elem. Lessons Eng. Gram.* ii. 28 Vowels formed with the tongue tense we call Tense Vowels, those with the tongue soft we call Slack Vowels. **1934** C. Davies *Eng. Pronunc. from 15th to 18th Cent.* 8 It was probably a slack, round mid-back, vowel. **1970** B. M. H. Strang *Hist. Eng.* 285 The letter *æ* represents a long, low, slack front vowel /æ:/ in *dælan.*

10. *slack key* (Mus.) [tr. Hawaiian *kī hōʻalu,* f. *kī* key + *hōʻalu* slack], used *absol.* and *attrib.*, esp. as *slack-key guitar,* with reference to a style of guitar-playing originating in Hawaii, in which the strings are slightly relaxed to produce strong bass resonances; *slack party* (Naut slang) (see quots.); *slack wire* (earlier and later examples).

1975 G. S. Kanahele in *Haʻilono Mele* Jan. 2/2 Our first concert [in 1972] was memorable. It featured the slack key guitar, the first time that an entire concert was devoted to this unique style of playing. **1976** *Guitar Player* Apr. 14/2 The original style is kept alive solely by those guitarists who insist on playing only slack key. **1977** *Zigzag* Mar. 20/1 Could you explain about slack-key guitar? **1933** J. Masefield *Conway* iv. 145 For official punishments there was an institution known as 'slack party', which meant employment upon every available job..from morning till night. **1945** 'Tackline' *Holiday Sailor* 133 Jimmy's pet form of punishment was his 'slack party'. Hands tardy in going on watch or performing some allotted task with lack of zeal were enrolled in the slack party. And the slack party did not lead an especially restful existence. **1753** *N.-Y. Mercury* 20 Aug. 3/3 The Surprizing Performances of the celebrated Anthony Joseph Dugee..On a Slack Wire scarcely perceptible and without a Balance. **1866** M. Mackintosh *Stage Reminisc.* xi. 138 Andrew was at once a good tight-rope dancer and slack-wire vaulter. **1977** E. Ambler *Send no more Roses* viii. 183 A slack-wire baggy-pants act out of a third-rate circus.

IV. 11. a. *slack-jawed, -mouthed.*

1901 Kipling *Kim* iii. 76 Our colonel used to send for slack-jawed down-country men who talked too much. **1936** W. Faulkner *Absalom, Absalom!* 44 Wild-eyed and considerably slack-mouthed. **1942** —— *Go down, Moses* 32 He stood for perhaps ten seconds, slackjawed with amazed and incredulous comprehension. **1976** J. Carroll *Mortal Friends* II. iii. 170 The people were Catholics nearly to a person, and they stared slack-jawed at the line of nuns. **1976** P. Cave *High Flying Birds* iii. 42, I continued to gaze at Sonya with slack-mouthed adoration.

B. *adv.* **b.** *slack-tethered.*
1922 JOYCE *Ulysses* 98 On the towpath by the lock a slacktethered horse.

slackening, *vbl. sb.* Add: Also with *off.*
1903 CONRAD *Romance* v. i. 402, I wanted rest, woman's love, slackening off. **1951** J. M. FRASER *Psychol.* xiv. 157 It is rather more usual for a slackening-off process to take place.

slacker. Add: **2.** (Later examples.) Also, *spec.* used in *Mil.* contexts in the war of 1914–18.
1914 'BARTIMEUS' *Naval Occasions* v. 37 What about a song, you slacker! **1817** 'TAFFRAIL' *Sub* ii. 62 An habitual slacker at Osborne, however, was soon sized up, and if repeated warnings did not cause him to mend his ways, he generally got the Order of the Boot at the end of his third term. **1921** H. WILLIAMSON *Beautiful Years* 217 He was a little slacker, the kind that used cribs later on in school life. **1933** H. C. BAILEY *Mr. Fortune Wonders* 109 Eston strode past him with a laugh, 'Had enough already?' and Cicely pattered after crying, 'Slacker!' **1964** A. WHITEHOUSE *Epics & Legends of First World War* vi. 134 The..League..rendered important service in..handling the 'slacker' and conscientious-objector groups. **1969** R. MAUGHAM *Link* II. 16 'You're a slacker and you're a shirker,' he said. 'You're a little runt in many ways. But you're the best of the lot of them.'

Slack-ma-girdle (slæ·kmăgɜ̄·ɹd'l). Also **Slack-my-girdle.** [f. phr. *slack my girdle*: cf. SLACK *v.* 6.] A variety of cider apple (see quots.).
1885 HOGG & BULL *Herefordshire Pomona, List of other Cider Apples,* Slack-My-Girdle, or Slack-my-girl.—A striped Somersetshire apple of large size. It is also much grown in Devonshire. **1967** [see *HANG-DOWN *sb.* and *a.*]. **1981** *Countryman* LXXXVI. III. 42 Others..use only true cider apples, from trees with names as evocative as..Slack-ma-Girdle.

slackness. Add: **5.** *Naut.* (See quot. 1877.)
1877 W. H. WHITE *Man. Naval Archit.* 484 The contrary condition, where the resultant resistance acts abaft the resultant wind pressure, and makes the head of the ship fall off from the wind, is termed 'slackness', and can only be counteracted by keeping the helm a-lee. **1922** E. L. ATTWOOD *Theoret. Naval Archit.* (ed. 8) xi. 380 If the centre of effort is forward of the C.L.R. the bow of the ship tends to fall off from the wind (which is termed 'slackness').

slack-water. Add: **3.** (Earlier example.)
1837 J. M. PECK *Gazetteer Illinois* (ed. 2) III. 264 Fox river is susceptible of improvement by slack water at small expense.
4. *slack-water basin.*
1836 J. HALL *Statistics of West* 38 At low stages the [Ohio] river becomes resolved into a succession of ripples, with extensive slack water basins between them.

sladang, var. *SELADANG.

Slade (slēⁱd). The name of Felix Slade (1790–1868) used: **a.** *attrib.* to designate the School of Fine Art (founded 1871) at University College London and its members, and scholarships and professorships in fine art endowed by him at Oxford, Cambridge, and London.
1869 *Proc. A.G.M.* (U.C.L.) 13 At their Session on May 2nd the Council received notice of the bequest of £45,000 made by the late Mr Felix Slade, for the purpose of founding 'three or more Professorships for promoting the study of Fine Arts, to be termed the Slade Professorships of Fine Arts..one..in..Oxford, another..in..Cambridge, and one more in the University College of London'. **1872** *U.C.L. Calendar, 1871–1872* 44 Slade Scholarships. Under the will of the late Mr Felix Slade, six Scholarships of £50 per annum each..have been founded in the College. **1885** KIPLING *Let.* 18 Dec. in C. Carrington *Rudyard Kipling* (1955) iv. 71 Do you ever come to know anything about the Slade Art School and the students there—the female ones. **1925** E. BUDGE *Mummy* (ed. 2) p. vii, In the year 1892, on the recommendation of J. H. Middleton, Slade Professor of Fine Art in the University of Cambridge, the Syndics..commissioned me to make a Catalogue. **1958** *Observer* 15 June 15/2 Joan Mitchell's rather beautiful painting..which has a sensitive, tight-lipped, almost Slade School quality. **1964** K. CLARK *Ruskin Today* I. 11 In 1869 he [*sc.* John Ruskin] was appointed Slade Professor at Oxford. **1978** *Ann. Rep. 1977–78* (U.C.L.) 19 The College acknowledges ..the co-operation of the Fine Art Society Gallery.., which put on an exhibition of work by Slade artists.
b. *absol.* with *the*: the School of Fine Art itself.
1890 C. M. YONGE *More Bywords* 249 There are the art classes at the Slade, and the lectures I am down for. **1904** R. FRY *Let.* 22 June (1972) I. 222 You will..be as much disappointed, almost, as I am about the Slade. It is a very serious blow to my hopes... They have long ago realized that Waldstein was a failure as Slade Professor. **1928** R. CAMPBELL *Wayzgoose* I. 10 And surely from the stir that this one made He might have been a student at the Slade. **1961** G. SPENCER *Stanley Spencer* v. 102 His entry into the Slade proved to be a most far-reaching and valuable decision. **1980** I. MURDOCH *Nuns & Soldiers* 201 Tim described the Slade and his early experiments in painting.

slag, *sb.*¹ Add: **2. a.** (Examples referring to the use of slag in the construction of roads.)
1951 *Sources of Road Aggregate in Gt. Brit.* (Dept. Scientific & Industrial Research) (ed. 2) 4 Slags from smelting operations form a valuable source of roadstone in England and Wales... With one exception the slags are derived from iron smelters or steel works. **1955** I. D. MARGARY *Roman Roads in Britain* I. i. 15 In districts where iron was being worked the hard slag provided an almost ideal metalling [for Roman roads]. **1958** *Optima* Mar. 14/1 At Maresfield Hempstead, near Benenden, and at Slinfold, Roman roads are partly constructed of slag, and large quantities of slag have since been used.
b. (Further examples.)
1888 [see *BASIC *a.* 2 d]. **1937** *Nature* 20 Feb. 318/2 The Industrial Research Council of the British Iron and Steel Federation will show..the applications of foamed slag as an aggregate for lightweight concrete. *c* **1957** *Story of Slag* (Brit. Slag Federation) 16 (*caption*) Airfield, showing main runway coated with three-quarter inch graded bituminous slag. *Ibid.* 17 Dry slag makes excellent rail track ballast. *Ibid.* 18 Dry slag is used by many local authorities as filter-bed media. *Ibid.* 21 Foamed slag building blocks used in construction of houses at Gateshead and Middlesbrough. **1971** *Arable Farmer* Feb. 69/2 Dressings of basic slag, potassic basic slag or PK compound fertiliser at the beginning and near the end of the ley break should prove sufficient to carry three successive corn crops.
4*. *slang.* **a.** A worthless or insignificant person (freq. used as a term of contempt): *spec.* (*a*) a coward; (*b*) a rough or brutal person; (*c*) any objectionable or contemptible person; (*d*) a vagrant or a petty criminal; also, such persons collectively; (*e*) (the most usual sense) a prostitute or promiscuous woman; a slattern.
(*a*) **1788** GROSE *Dict. Vulgar Tongue* (ed. 2), *Slag,* a slack-mettled fellow, one not ready to resent an affront. **1958** F. NORMAN *Bang to Rights* II. 62 You'v got the guts of a slag.
(*b*) **1934** P. ALLINGHAM *Cheapjack* xix. 237 The Newcastle 'slag' is the sort of man who makes up the personnel of the race-gangs, and..he will pick a fight with anyone. **1961** *New Statesman* 14 Apr. 576/2 As the underworld put it, 'he steamed in like a slag and roughed them up as he topped them.'
(*c*) **1943** W. BUCHANAN-TAYLOR *Shake It Again* xxi. 199 It seemed slaggy to me. (A *slag* is a person who is not much *bottle*—not much good;..for whom you have no respect or time.) **1958** M. PUGH *Wilderness of Monkeys* 89 Sit down..you slag. **1962** PARKER & ALLERTON *Courage of his Convictions* iv. 159 When I got out there was some slag on the door, all gold braid and nose in the air, wouldn't let me in! **1981** *Daily Tel.* 8 July 3/1 As sentence was announced, the dead boy's father..shouted: 'I hope you rot in it, you slag.'
(*d*) **1955** P. WILDEBLOOD *Against Law* III. 120 Several different kinds of burglars..the rank amateurs or 'slags' who had stolen paltry sums. **1962** R. COOK *Crust on its Uppers* iii. 43 Marchmare lent it to this hatful of slag. **1962** D. WARNER *Death of Bogey* I. ii. 14 In my day, the strong-arm boys were slags. Nobody in the big-time would look at 'em. **1963** T. & P. MORRIS *Pentonville* xi. 227 Pentonville also contains at any given time a number of vagrants, drunks and similar social derelicts... Prison argot classifies them all as *slags.* **1968** J. LOCK *Lady Policeman* xii. 108 Only prostitutes, their friends, layabouts, tom watchers, petty criminals and the like are left—'the slag' we call them. **1970** P. LAURIE *Scotland Yard* vi. 141, I could get them up the nick and take their prints with ink, but that's really for slag.
(*e*) **1958** *N.Z. Listener* 10 Oct. 6/3 A 'slag' is a white girl who lives with or is friendly with coloured people of either sex. **1959** ANON. *Streetwalker* iv. 87 It's my pride he hurts, with his little slags. **1966** *New Statesman* 23 Dec. 934/2 You have to wear glasses these days if you don't want to be called a slag. **1970** 'D. CRAIG' *Young Men may Die* x. 72 Does anyone care what happens to a slag? **1973** J. SEABROOK *Loneliness* 185, I went out with a girl called Angie, who was really a bit of a slag.
b. Worthless matter, rubbish; nonsense.
1948 V. PALMER *Golconda* v. 35 'Listen,' he said... 'There's some men in every camp will get a kick out of throwing dirt. Who's been filling you up with slag about me? That old crank up on the mountain, was it?' **1970** *New Yorker* 12 Sept. 32/3 It is very depressing to think about the wonderful..letters people used to get..and then look at the slag on one's desk.
5. a. *slag-dump, -heap* (also *fig.*), *inclusion, -mound, -tip, wool* (earlier and later examples).
1923 KIPLING *Irish Guards in Gt. War* I. 109 It was a jagged, scarred and mutilated sweep of mining-villages, factories, quarries, slag-dumps, pit-heads, chalk-pits and railway embankments. **1974** *Times* 11 Jan. 16/6 Various stages of iron-working are represented by ore-roasting areas, three slag dumps, 36 smelting furnaces [etc.]. **1917** A. G. EMPEY *Over Top* 308 *Slag heap,* a pile of rubbish, tin cans, etc. **1931** C. DAY LEWIS *From Feathers to Iron* xxix. 54 Wherever radiance from ashes arises—Willow-herb glowing on abandoned slagheaps. **1963** *Times* 24 Jan. 6/2 It was not enough to put one or two council houses near the slag heaps. **1974** F. WARNER *Meeting Ends* II. ii. 39 What a bore the slagheap of matrimony! **1913** Slag inclusion [see *INCLUSION 2]. **1934** *Jrnl. R. Aeronaut. Soc.* XXXVIII. 249 Thirteen micro-photographs show forms of slag inclusion and distortion of films in butt welding. **1945** GREAVES & WRIGHTON *Practical Microsc. Metallogr.* vi. 96 Of commercial wrought irons, Swedish Bar Iron is most free from slag inclusions. **1955** J. R. R. TOLKIEN *Return of King* 374 Frodo reaches the slag-mounds. **1960** C. DAY LEWIS *Buried Day* vii. 130 The prevailing wind brought the acrid smell of slag-tips from the Mansfield collieries. **1878** J. DEBY *Rep. Iron & Steel Industries Foreign Countries* II. i. 13 The manufacture of blast furnace slag wool has recently been established commercially for the first time in America. **1979** *Nature* 19 July 183/2 The fibres are produced from glass, rock, slag and metallic oxides and include fibreglass and rock and slag wools which are widely used for home insulation as a substitute for asbestos.

b. **slag notch,** a hole in a furnace, above the level of the molten metal, which can be unstopped to let out slag.
1895 E. L. RHEAD *Metallurgy* 96 In the top of the dam is a groove, the 'slag-notch', through which the slags flow continuously, after reaching that level, and through which the blast blows to keep it clear. **1929** W. LISTER *Practical Steelmaking* xxxviii. 392 A 'Dewhurst' ladle can stand under the middle door in order to catch the slag running over the slag notch.

† **slag** (slæg), *sb.*² *Obs. Criminals' slang.* [Prob. f. SLANG *sb.*⁴, under influence of SLAG *sb.*¹ in Dict. and Suppl.] = SLANG *sb.*⁴ I.
1857 'DUCANGE ANGLICUS' *Vulgar Tongue* 19 *Slag, n.* Chain, a gold or silver one. **1926** *Clues* Nov. 159/1 Then we'll take the hot hoops and slags up to the block dealers. **1929** *Detective Fiction Weekly* 2 Mar. 694/2 One 'nips the slag' when one cuts the watch chain, a practice practically defunct now.

slag, *v.* Add: **3.** *trans.* To abuse or denigrate (a person); to criticize, insult. Also with *off. slang.*
1971 J. MANDELKAU *Buttons* v. 75 He was doing a good job of bad mouthing and slagging me to a number of the Angels. **1972** *Guardian* 17 Aug. 1/1 Mr Jack Jones, general secretary of the Transport and General Workers' Union, was 'slagged off'—in dockland jargon—several times during the day. A gang of furious dockers invaded his press conference. **1974** G. F. NEWMAN *Price* v. 156 She always put out warnings, invariably slagging Terry. **1976** E. DUNPHY *Only a Game?* v. 150 When the game starts, if things start going wrong, everyone blames them. Everyone slags them off. **1978** *Broadcast* 29 May 2/2 There's been a growing tendency for some sales organisations to slag the [television] company which used to be.. the brand leader in British sales. **1981** *Daily Tel.* 25 Feb. 17/6 He followed me down the street, slagging me off.
slagging *vbl. sb.* (examples in sense *3 of the vb.).
1971 *News-Advocate* (Barbados) 20 Mar. 9/6 You get so much slagging of bands nowadays. **1977** *Zigzag* Aug. 20/3 The gig met with quite a bit of slagging in the rock press.

slaggy, *a.* Add: **2.** *slang.* **a.** Of a person or thing: objectionable, unpleasant, offensive.
1943 [see *SLAG *sb.*¹ 4* a (*c*)]. **1962** R. COOK *Crust on its Uppers* x. 82 That slaggy basement of yours. **1972** R. QUILTY *Tenth Session* I. 20 Some sort of hippie, maybe? No roadie, he could swear to that, having tangled with some real slaggy ones.
b. Of a woman: promiscuous, 'cheap'; slatternly.
1973 H. MILLER *Open City* xiv. 160 The writer and his slaggy girl friend. **1980** R. CONNOLLY *Sunday Kind of Woman* ii. 22 He thought about some of the slaggy models he had known.

slagless (slæ·glės), *a.* [f. SLAG *sb.*¹ + -LESS.] Of iron, steel, etc.: free from slag. Hence **sla·glessness.**
1902 *Encycl. Brit.* XXIX. 571/1 (*in table*) Slagless or 'Ingot-metal' Series. *Ibid.* 571/2 But the former lack the essential quality—slaglessness—which makes the latter steel.

‖ **slainte** (slā·ntʃə), *int.* Also **slainté.** [a. Gael. *slàinte,* lit. 'health'.] A Gaelic toast: good health!
1824 SCOTT *Redgauntlet* II. vii. 159 He then took up the tankard, and saying aloud in Gaelic, '*Slaint an Rey*', just tasted the liquor. **1880** A. P. GRAVES *Irish Songs & Ballads* 71 Here's a health to you, Father O'Flynn, Slainté, and slainté, and slainté agin. **1922** JOYCE *Ulysses* 44 Well: *slainte!* **1949** E. COXHEAD *Wind in West* iv. 114 '*Slainte mhor,* Rory!' cried Kurt, who knew what was necessary in every language. **1952** 'J. TEY' *Singing Sands* vii. 105 '*Slainte!*' he said, and took a swig of it. **1966** S. FORBES *Terror touches Me* iv. 43 'Here, Brendan. Slainté.' Brendan's hand trembled as he took the full glass. **1980** M. MCMULLEN *My Cousin Death* (1981) vi. 78 Upshaw gave him his drink..'*Slainte.*'

slalom (slā·lǫm). [a. Norw. *slalåm,* f. *sla* sloping + *låm* track.] **1.** A downhill race in which skiers, descending singly, describe a zigzag course between artificial obstacles, usu. flags. Freq. *attrib.*
1921 *British Ski Year Bk.* 274 Slalom race on Inner-Arosa practice slopes. **1927** A. LUNN *Hist. Skiing* xviii. 227 However, the Slalom was worth a trial, and in 1922 the Alpine Ski Challenge Cup became a Slalom race. **1950** *Times* 13 Feb. 7/5 The Kandahar Ski Club, which originated the modern downhill racing movement (the slalom is a British invention worked out at Mürren), still insists that its candidates shall pass a test in soft snow. **1966** L. DEIGHTON *Billion-Dollar Brain* I. vii. 58 Three sets of skis..one set of which were slalom skis. **1972** C. SHORT *Naked Skier* i. 2 She did a slalom turn... I stood for a while looking at the ski tracks she had left. **1980** *Daily Tel.* 26 Jan. 32 The shadow of Switzerland's Marie-Therese Nadig, who beat her in both the downhill and giant slaloms in the 1972 Winter Games.
2. *Water-skiing.* A run along a zigzag course defined by buoys. Also *attrib.*
1949 *Sun* (Baltimore) 25 July 14/1 Mary Lois Thornhill ..yesterday added the slalom to the trick riding and jumping titles she won on Martin Lagoon. **1963** *Newsweek* 23 Sept. 66/3 Billy Spencer, the youngest of the 99 competitors in the world water-skiing championship at Vichy, France, finished his first slalom run. **1978** G.

WRIGHT *Illustr. Handbk. Sporting Terms* 154/1 In Slalom—a timed run through two lines of buoys—half a point is awarded for every buoy successfully rounded and also for returning to within the boat's wake before the next buoy.

3. A race in which canoeists weave between obstacles, esp. along a course of rapid water. Freq. *attrib.*

1956 N. MCNAUGHT *Canoeing Man.* vii. 86 Most local slaloms take place on weir-type courses. *Ibid.* 88 Slalom organizers must ensure that a rescue boat is always manned and ready. **1964, 1969** [see *KAYAKING *vbl. sb.*] **1969** *Publ. Amer. Dial. Soc.* LI. 7 *Slalom kayak*, ..a highly maneuverable kayak constructed with more curve rocker in the keel than a downriver or combination kayak. **1973** R. FIENNES *Headless Valley* vii. 111 Then in 1969 two Russians, expert slalom canoeists, set out to navigate the Liard. **1977** *Herald* (Melbourne) 17 Jan. 2/5 Kaine had a junior kayak for a year, but found it did not perform as well as the slalom boat his father built.

4. An exercise or contest in which a motor vehicle is driven along a zigzag course defined by markers. Also *attrib.*

1965 *Listener* 15 Apr. 578/1 There is a keen following of motor racing among the Swiss: entries are not lacking in their speed hill climbs, rallies, and slaloms (or 'wiggle-woggles' between pylons). **1972** *National Observer* (N.Y.) 27 May 19/2 Next came a *slalom* exercise through a long row of traffic cones. You must swerve the car to the right of the first cone, to the left of the second, back right around the third... It teaches braking and shows how much more your car can take and 'do' than you thought. **1974** *Rules of Game* 297/1 Slalom, or autotest, competitions are a test of maneuverability. Cars attempt the course singly. Each car starts with 0 points and receives 1 point for each second taken and 10 points for each marker touched. The winner is the driver with the fewest points at the finish.

5. A similar race or activity in *Skateboarding*. (See also quot. 1976[2].) Also, a track suitable for this.

1976 A. CASSORLA *Skateboarder's Bible* 11 Slaloms could not be held on a steep grade or be set up with widely spread cones because of the poor turning capacity of the boards. **1976** *National Observer* (U.S.) 3 July 12/3 Slalom, as in skiing, going downhill and weaving around markers. **1978** *Skatcat's Quiz Bk.* (R. Soc. Prevention of Accidents) 2/1 You need a 6" wide deck to start with. Flexi for slalom. Stiffer for free-style. **1978** *Cornish Guardian* 27 Apr. 13/4 The playgrounds were flat and the youngsters wanted the excitement of bowls and slaloms which the Polkyth park would have.

Hence as *v. intr.*, to perform or compete in a slalom, to make frequent rapid (slalom) turns; **sla·lomer, sla·lomist**, one who slaloms; **sla·loming** *vbl. sb.*

1956 N. MCNAUGHT *Canoeing Man.* vii. 90 An individual slalomist who overturns is disqualified on that particular run. *Ibid.*, Strength and skill are needed for successful slaloming. **1973** *Times* 28 Sept. 36/5 Forty miles of pistes where you can schuss, trek, slalom, langlauf. **1976** *Daily Tel.* (Colour Suppl.) 30 July 9/1 What they are all doing is skateboarding—zooming and slaloming and 'hanging ten' and catamaraning on four-wheeled boards. **1977** *Skateboard Special* Sept. 5/1 The best slalomists still use wide wheels to prevent the board wobbling at high speed. **1978** *Guardian Weekly* 12 Feb. 24/3 Whether he is the world's greatest ever slalomer no-one can say.

slam, *sb.*[1] Add: **1. b.** A violent blow administered to a ball. *slang* (chiefly *U.S.*).

1931 *Lit. Digest* 18 Apr. 40, I remember when a hit was a..clout,..slam..but never..just a hit. **1978** *Chicago* June 274/1 Engrossed as each team was in setting up the ball for a slam, the players' concentration was marred by the explosion of tear-gas canisters some distance away.

2. a. (Earlier example.)

a **1817** JANE AUSTEN *Persuasion* (1818) IV. viii. 147 The various noises of the room, the almost ceaseless slam of the door.

3. An insult or 'put-down'. *U.S. slang.*

1884 I. M. RITTENHOUSE *Jrnl.* in *Maud* (1939) 296 Oh! did I tell you that Mr. Hough to atone for his 'slams', said, 'I did want to make one gallant speech, but I hardly dared, about how remarkably well you looked Tuesday night.' **1944** B. A. BOTKIN *Treas. Amer. Folklore* III. 410 Certain formulae are identified with disparaging or insulting wisecracks, or 'slams'. **1980** R. L. DUNCAN *Brimstone* i. 22, I don't take that description as a slam. I was a great piece of ass.

4. = *SLAMMER 3. Usu. with *the*. Chiefly *U.S. slang.*

1960 R. G. REISNER *Jazz Titans* 164 *Slam*, jail. **1965** A. LURIE *Nowhere City* (1966) xi. 118 That was really thinking fast. I guess you saved me a night in slam. **1972** J. WAINWRIGHT *Requiem for Loser* vi. 132 Reginald Drover. Escapee from one of Her Majesty's slams. **1972** S. GREENLEE in W. King *Black Short Story Anthol.* 95 Uncle Benny told him that getting a bad teacher for a year was like being in the slam, and you just did your time and didn't let it bug you. **1978** J. GORES *Gone, no Forwarding* vii. 40 You're going to the slam for fifteen.

5. Special *Comb.* **slamdunk** *U.S. Basketball* [cf. *DUNK *v.*], a forceful shot in which a player jumps and slams the ball down into the basket.

1976 *N.Y. Times* 25 May 35 The only one-eyed candidate who would know how to put in a slamdunk on a New York playground has new financial life. **1981** *Washington Post* 25 Feb. E7/3 Robinson had 32 points and Jones put on a slam-dunk show to finish with 17.

slam, *sb.*[2] Add: **2. b.** *grand slam* (earlier examples, from the game of Boston). Also *small slam* = *little slam*, in Bridge.

1814 C. JONES *Hoyle's Games Improved* 188 These declarations will supersede that of Boston simply... The highest, called Grand Slam, is undertaking to get 13 tricks. **1921** F. IRWIN *Compl. Auction Player* i. 25 To take all, or all but one, of the tricks is to make a slam. The former is called a grand slam, and is worth 100 above the line. The latter is called a small slam, and is worth 50. **1937** N. DE V. HART *Slams à la Culbertson* I. vi. 53 If he has his maximum count.., he will bid Small Slam even without a five-card suit. **1959** *Listener* 15 Jan. 146/2 West might then content himself with the small slam. **1977** *Times* 3 Sept. 7/2 South made an overtrick in the small slam.

c. *grand slam* (transf.): (*a*) a complete success; *spec.* victory in all of a series of matches or competitions; (*b*) an attack in force; forceful or decisive behaviour; (*c*) in Baseball, *grand slam* (*homer, home run*): (see quot. 1974).

(*a*) **1920** D. H. LAWRENCE *Let.* 5 Feb. (1962) I. 619, I feel that this is the time to make our grand-slam. **1966** D. F. GALOUYE *Lost Perception* viii. 86 We're going to try for a grand slam—knock them all out at once with nuclear stuff the next time we pin down their locations. **1967** *Boston Sunday Herald* 26 Mar. II. 7/1 He was the world's No. 1 amateur in 1962 and only the second player in history to accomplish the 'Grand Slam'. **1976** *Scottish Daily Express* 24 Dec. 14/1 We are the Home International champions after a Grand Slam of victories against England, Wales and Northern Ireland.

(*b*) **1933** F. RICHARDS *Old Soldiers never Die* ix. 123 Dawn broke..and we were anxiously waiting for the time when the Grand Slam commenced. **1959** *Times Lit. Suppl.* 29 May 322/5 Churchillian impetuosity and grand-slam rashness. **1963** *Times* 7 Mar. 8/3 The most persuasive argument for retaining *Checkmate* in the Royal Ballet's repertory..is the opportunity for grand slam acting it offers to its protagonist, the malevolent Black Queen.

(*c*) **1953** *Sport* June 58/1 Bill Carr knocked his pitch over the fence for a grand-slam homer. **1961** *Sports Illustr.* 2 Oct. 10/2 Baltimore's Jim Gentile hit a grand slam homer off Don Larsen in Chicago one rainy night last week. **1967** *Boston Sunday Herald* 30 Apr. I. 8/2 (Advt.), It's as exciting as a ninth inning grand-slam! **1974** *Rules of Game* 168/3 A grand slam home run is a home run hit when the bases are loaded, i.e. when three men are on base. It scores four runs, the maximum possible from one hit. **1978** *Detroit Free Press* 16 Apr. E 3/1 The Pirates finally put it together and broke a five-game skid with a little help from a pair of homers from Bill Robinson, one a grand slam.

3. *attrib.* in *Bridge*, as *slam bid*(*ding*), *contract, hand.*

1929 M. C. WORK *Compl. Contract Bridge* p. xi, The partner..must jump if his hand warrant it—either one step..or a vault toward a slam bid. **1947** E. KLEIN *Enjoy your Bridge* II. xiii. 114 Be content to win a perfectly safe contract and leave your slam bids for a later stage. **1927** *Work-Whitehead Auction Bridge Bull.* Feb. 141 Contract in its original form, minus the recently introduced 'vulnerable' feature and slam bidding, made its first appearance abroad some fifteen years ago. **1974** *Times* 16 Feb. 13/2 Slam bidding is treated in most text books as if it..cannot be covered by ordinary approach bidding. **1938** Slam contract [see *CONTROL *sb.* 3 e]. **1959** *Listener* 8 Jan. 84/2 There is every reason to hope for a slam contract in some suit. **1977** *Times* 16 Apr. 11/8 He..bid Three Diamonds which..in conjunction with the cue-bids, produced a slam contract in the wrong suit. **1937** J. CRANE *Crane Syst. Contract Bidding* 78 (*heading*) Examples of a bidding game and slam hands from matches. **1979** REESE & FLINT *Trick 13* 17, I didn't know anything was wrong till that slam hand near the finish.

slam, *v.*[1] Add: **2.** Also with *on*, as in *to slam on the brakes*, to apply the brakes of a motor vehicle, etc. suddenly. Also *fig.*

1958 L. URIS *Exodus* IV. iii. 501 Zev slammed on the brakes and pulled over to the side of the road. **1975** *Business Week* 1 Sept. 23 The rule is designed to prevent a truck from jackknifing or jumping a lane when drivers slam on the brakes at 20 mph to 60 mph. **1975** *Economist* 4 Oct. 11 Can the driver [*sc. contextually* General Franco] be persuaded to look forward instead of back, or can someone else intervene to slam on the brakes? **1976** *Business Week* 11 Oct. 96 A radar unit in the nose..that warns the driver of road hazards ahead—and slams on the brakes if he fails to do so. **1982** *Chr. Sci. Monitor* 13 Apr. 7 Inflation has dropped dramatically as the quasi-independent Federal Reserve Board slams on the brakes of high interest rates.

c. (Earlier example.)

1870 'MARK TWAIN' *Lett. to Publishers* (1967) 49, I can slam you into the lecture field for life and secure you ten thousand dollars a year as long as you live.

4. (Later examples.)

1914 G. B. SHAW *Misalliance* 42 Theyre coming slam into the greenhouse. **1930** E. POUND *XXX Cantos* xviii. 82 An' he run damn slam on the breakwater.

5. a. To be severely critical, to utter insults. *U.S. slang. rare.*

1884 I. M. RITTENHOUSE *Jrnl.* in *Maud* (1939) 291 When I and Mr Hough arrived late Dr Benson and Mr Parsons slammed right and left at the tardiness.

b. *trans.* To criticize severely. *colloq.* (orig *U.S.*).

[**1914** 'HIGH JINKS, JR.' *Choice Slang* 18 *Slamming contest*, a condition where two or more individuals are engaged in criticism. 'A Knockfest.'] **1916** H. L. WILSON *Somewhere in Red Gap* ii. 57 Couldn't even agree on the same kind of cocktail. Both slamming the waiter. **1932** G. ATHERTON *Adventures of Novelist* VI. xiii. 380 She took care I should constantly be slammed. **1958** 'N. SHUTE' *Rainbow & Rose* 252 They come with bright and tinkling vivacity until I slam them down. **1962** J. SYMONS *Killing of Francie Lake* ii. 19 You go on the air and slam negro landlords and they'll be saying you're anti-negro. **1978** J. IRVING *World according to Garp* v. 89 A long, cocky letter, quoting Marcus Aurelius and slamming Franz Grillparzer.

6. Const. *prep.* To move violently, to crash.

1973 *Times* 2 Nov. 13/6 Rosa..savagely slamming around the kitchen. **1976** M. MACHLIN *Pipeline* lvi. 566 The lifeboat was now slamming through the choppy two and three foot high waves at over twenty knots. **1979** R. JAFFE *Class Reunion* (1980) II. iv. 209 She didn't even see the small stone wall until she had slammed into it.

slamming *vbl. sb.* (examples *spec.* of boats: see quot. 1948).

1935 *Engineering* 18 Jan. 55/1 'Pounding' or 'slamming' damage is looked upon as no more than a normal circumstance..of cargo vessels trading across the North Atlantic. **1948** R. DE KERCHOVE *Internat. Maritime Dict.* 685/1 Slamming almost always takes place forward... Slamming damage is usually ascribed to dynamic pressures arising from impact of the ship's hull upon the surface of the water, and from the actual impulsive displacement of water caused by the downward movement of the ship when pitching. **1972** C. MUDIE *Motor Boats & Boating* 17 If such a craft were to be taken to sea she would rapidly be found to be..apt to break her back from slamming when pitching.

slam-bang, *adv., a.,* and *v.* Add to etym.: cf. SLAP-BANG *adv., a.,* and *sb.* **A.** *adv.* **1.** (Earlier example.)

1840 R. M. BIRD *Robin Day* 25 Five or six hundred field pieces blazing away slambang.

B. *adj.* **1.** (Earlier and later examples.)

1823 'J. BEE' *Dict. Slang* 158 *Slam-bang shops*, places where gourmands of the fourth rate regale;..probably, from..the 'slam-banging' of the doors, plates, and tools. **1957** *Economist* 28 Sept. 999/1 With all the diplomatic finesse of a runaway bulldozer, the governments of the major powers are conducting a slambang exchange of public accusations. **1981** H. R. F. KEATING *Go West, Inspector Ghote* ii. 25 Fred Hoskin's slam-bang voice broke in on his thoughts.

2. In weakened use: exciting, impressive, first-rate. Also, vigorous, energetic. *colloq.*

1939 *Sun* (Baltimore) 4 Dec. 13/4 The balance of the card will be made up of some real slam-bang preliminaries. **1942** *Ibid.* 17 June 1/8 American heavy bombers have entered the Mediterranean sea war in slambang fashion. **1952** B. MALAMUD *Natural* 20 A slambang young pitcher who'd soon be laying them low in the big leagues. **1965** *Times Lit. Suppl.* 25 Nov. 1061/2 We have this plot for a slam-bang topical novel about the Johnson administration. **1972** D. DELMAN *Sudden Death* (1973) v. 126 You were good today. I watched you. Slam-bang. **1975** *Publishers Weekly* 2 June 49/1 A very cerebral English mystery, with..a finale that is full of slambang action. **1979** *Radio Times* 5–11 May 23/2 It was described by Judith Crist as a 'slam-bang top-quality grown-up adventure which thumbs its nose at authority and morality'.

slam-banging *vbl. sb.* (earlier example).

1823 [see sense 1 of the adj., above]. **1843** *Knickerbocker* XXII. 41 The creaking on its rusty hinges and slam-banging of the sign of the Devil-Tavern.

slammable (slæ·măb'l), *a. rare.* [f. SLAM *v.*[1] + -ABLE.] Of a door, etc.: capable of being slammed (shut).

1976 T. STOPPARD *Dirty Linen* 9 Separate table with good slammable drawers for *Maddie*.

slammakin, slammerkin, *a.* Add: (Examples of the spelling *slummocking*.)

1960 R. COLLIER *House called Memory* iv. 53 A big slummocking girl with cropped hair and braying laugh. **1978** S. RADLEY *Death & Maiden* iv. 37 They're a slummocking family..always have been.

slammer. Add: **3.** Prison, gaol. Usu. with *the*: occas. *the slammers*. Cf. *SLAM *sb.*[1] 4. *slang* (orig. *U.S.*).

1952 G. MANDEL *Flee Angry Strangers* 358 I'm hip what you was doin wit Ange while I was in the slammer. **1961** RIGNEY & SMITH *Real Bohemia* p. xvii, *Slammer*, jail. **1970** E. BULLINS *Theme is Blackness* (1973) 177 I'm into a heavy petty criminal thing, man. The Man is always ready to vamp on you and take you off 'round here or put you in the slammers. **1975** B. GARFIELD *Death Sentence* (1976) v. 31 Less than one per cent of Chicago's crimes are solved, in the sense that some joker gets tried and convicted and sent to the slammer. **1977** D. BAGLEY *Enemy* xv. 131 This one's not for the slammer. He'll go to Broadmoor for sure.

slan (slæn). [Invented word, from the novel by A. E. van Vogt: see quot. 1940.] In works of Science Fiction: a being of superior intelligence, physique, etc.; a superman. Hence used *gen.* among fans of this type of literature.

1940 A. E. VAN VOGT *Slan* in *Astounding Sci. Ficton* Oct. 27/1 They..accuse Samuel Lann, the human being and biological scientist who first created slans, and after whom slans are named—Samuel Lann: S. Lann: Slan—of fostering in his children the belief that they must rule the world. **1955** KOESTLER *Trail of Dinosaur* 143 Fen gather in clubhouses called slanshacks, 'slan' meaning a biologically mutated superman. **1969** H. WARNER *All Our Yesterdays* ii. 42 'Fans are slans!' became the rallying cry of the Cosmic Circle. **1975** E. WEINSTEIN *Fillostrated Fan Dict.* 119 *Slan shack*, a place where more than two fans live. **1980** *Verbatim* Autumn 10/1 'He's a slan' is the fannish equivalent of 'He's a helluva guy'.

slanchways, var. *SLAUNCHWAYS, -WISE *adv.* and *a.*

slang, *sb.*[3] Add: **1. b.** (Earlier example.)
1801 *Encycl. Brit.* Suppl. I. 723/1 A studied harangue, filled with that sentimental slang of philanthropy, which costs so little, promises so much, and has now corrupted all the languages of Europe.
c. (Later examples.)
1914 J. M. BARRIE *Admirable Crichton* IV. 227 In the regrettable slang of the servants' hall, my lady, the master is usually referred to as the Gov. **1925** T. DREISER *Amer. Tragedy* (1926) I. II. i. 156 Don't say 'swell'. And don't say 'huh'. Can't you learn to cut out the slang? **1937** PARTRIDGE *Dict. Slang* p. ix, *A Dictionary of Slang and Unconventional English*, i.e. of linguistically unconventional English, should be of interest to word-lovers. **1976** *Times Lit. Suppl.* 30 Apr. 520/4 In Australia, slang simply has a quite different status from slang in England. It is a *part* of 'Standard English' there, not outside 'Standard English'. Slang words are used informally, casually and naturally by all Australians regardless of class or education.
attrib. and *Comb.* **1856** G. MEREDITH *Let.* 15 Dec. (1970) I. 28 Have you..a book of Hampshire Dialect?.. Also a slang Dictionary, or book of the same with Gloss. **1926** *Variety* 29 Dec. 5/3, I was hep that the slang slingers were not crowding each other. **1977** K. F. KISTER *Dictionary Buying Guide* II. 240 The more substantial slang dictionaries provide detailed word histories and thus complement the etymological dictionaries.
d. (Earlier example.)
1805 T. CAMPBELL *Let.* 9 Feb. in W. Partington *Private Letter-bks. W. Scott* (1930) 100 In five weeks, however, her slang broke out, and within the seventh she discovered the whole catalogue of Vices of which a very ugly woman can be guilty.

slanging, *vbl. sb.* (In Dict. s.v. SLANG *v.*) Add: *slanging match*: an exchange of abuse; a vituperative argument.
1896 T. E. TAYLOR *Running Blockade* vi. 74 A slanging match went on between us, like that sometimes to be heard between two penny steamboat captains on the Thames. **1936** *Sun* (Baltimore) 14 Oct. 12/3 They [*sc.* the speeches] were made by the man who commands the highest authority and the greatest power in all the Reich, and they provoked an international slanging match. **1938** 'G. ORWELL' *Homage to Catalonia* xii. 243 The slanging-match in the newspapers. **1978** J. PORTER *Dead Easy for Dover* xiv. 140 Mrs Vincent very sensibly decided not to get involved in a slanging match with Dover. Their views on unmarried mothers were poles apart.

slangish, *a.* (Earlier example.)
1813 J. B. S. MORRITT *Let.* 3 Apr. in W. Partington *Private Letter-bks. W. Scott* (1930) 110 Poems of their own which are dull and slangish.

slangster. (In Dict. s.v. SLANGISM.) (Later examples.)
1926 *Variety* 29 Dec. 5/4 Most slangsters use the exaggerated simile when breaking into print. **1933** *Times Lit. Suppl.* 16 Nov. 781/4 Rhoda Broughton..would probably have thought Galsworthy far too much of a 'slangster'. **1945** *Gen* 5 May 24/1 His [*sc.* Walter Winchell's] slangster column..in the New York Daily Mirror. **1965** *English Studies* XLVI. 465 A *slangster* [is] a user of slang.

slanguage. (In Dict. s.v. SLANGISM.) (Earlier and later examples.)
1879 *Harvard Lampoon* 21 Nov. 88/1 (*title*) Slanguage on Angele. **1911** *Daily Colonist* (Victoria, B.C.) 7 Apr. 4/2 The 'slanguage' of a sporting reporter is a fearful and wonderful thing. **1926** *Irish Statesman* 18 Dec. 355/1 (*heading*) The American slanguage. **1926** *Variety* 29 Dec. 7/4 Every phase of our complex civilization, and every class have contributed something to what is fast becoming a national slanguage. **1927** *Vanity Fair* XXIX. 67/2 Jack Conway..is conceded to be the ace 'slanguage' hurler in the world. **1935** [see *CAT *sb.*[1] 2 c]. **1958** *Inside the ACD* (Amer. College Dict.) Nov. 2/1 Max Shulman shows in *Rally Round the Flag, Boys*, a new novel, that he can capture and record living speech including the 'slanguage' of the current cool crop of hipsters. **1963** [see *CUBE, *sb.*[1] 1 c]. **1974** *Trailer Life* Nov. 92 Our slanguage is so offbeat that during World War II American military men were able to foil the enemy by resorting to American vernacular.

slangwhang, *v.* (Earlier example.)
1880 *Punch* 11 Sept. 117/1 Over the Census Bill Honourable Members got senselessly incensed.., Orthodoxy and the other Doxies slang-whanging each other just as if they were really in earnest.

† slangwhang (slæ·ŋhwæŋ), *sb. U.S. Obs.* Also **slang-wang.** [f. as prec. + WHANG *sb.*[2]] Violent or abusive language.
1834 H. M. BRACKENRIDGE *Recollections* xvi. 183 The young lawyer..who has acquired nothing of the ordinary slangwhang. **1859** *Harper's Mag.* July 164/1 Don't allow their vulgar slang-wang to have the slightest effect upon you.

slangwhanging, *vbl. sb.* (Earlier example.)
1809 *Essex Register* (Salem, Mass.) 20 May 2/2 (*heading*) Federal Slang-whanging..or, a new comical, heroic, quizzical, serio-farcical melo drama.

slangwhanging, *ppl. a.* Add: Also **slang-wanging.** (Later example.)
1959 *Listener* 19 Feb. 325/2 A slang-wanging, stump speaker.

slangy, *a.* Add: **2. b.** (Earlier example.)
1842 R. H. DANA *Jrnl.* 14 Nov. (1968) I. 103 His letters have been careless, pretentious, & with a kind of off-hand, slang-ey, defying tone.

slant, *sb.*[1] Add: **1. e.** *Typogr.* = *OBLIQUE *sb.* 5, SOLIDUS[1] 2 in Dict. and Suppl. Used esp. of either of a pair of lines enclosing the representation of a linguistic (esp. phonemic) element.
1962 *Gen. Systems* VII. 299/2 Its mate is suffixed with a slant (virgule), thus: 4006 How to Silence. 4006/ How to Sound. **1964** E. PALMER tr. *Martinet's Elem. Gen. Linguistics* i. 24 This [*sc.* a significans] we represent between slants (/ž e mal a la tet/, /ž e mal/, /mal/). **1972** HARTMANN & STORK *Dict. Lang. & Linguistics* 172/1 Phonemic transcription is usually written between slants, e.g. /haus/.
3. a. Also *on a slant.*
1951 E. PAUL *Springtime in Paris* xv. 286 Busse.. leaped quickly, hit the lower level of the street pavement on a slant, and almost turned his ankle. **1957** D. LESSING *Going Home* ii. 35 The night was magnificent; the Southern Cross on a slant overhead.
b. *Microbiol.* A sloping surface of culture medium, usu. prepared by letting it solidify in a sloping test-tube, and used for the culture of micro-organisms. Cf. *SLOPE *sb.*[1] 3 a.
1899 T. BOWHILL *Man. Bacteriol. Technique* ii. 60 Take three freshly prepared tubes of oblique surface agar-agar —usually called 'agar-slants'—with plenty of water of condensation in the bottom. **1924** *Jrnl. Bacteriol.* IX. 398 Loops were transferred, at intervals up to four hours, to agar slants, and these were incubated overnight. **1949** *Amer. Jrnl. Path.* XXV. 7 Growth on plated media, while not unlike that on slants, was somewhat slower. **1972** *Sci. Amer.* Sept. 187/1 Dried yeast is typically sealed in an airtight envelope filled with nitrogen. Cultures can be perpetuated by inoculating slants of fresh nutrient agar under sterile conditions every 90 days.
6. (Later example.)
1868 H. WOODRUFF *Trotting Horse Amer.* iii. 58, I have known many that will be always watching slants to get an extra quart of oats for their colts.
8. A way of regarding something, a point of view or 'angle'; an interpretation; a bias. orig. *U.S.*
1905 *N.Y. Even. Post* 28 Jan. 5 The titles of articles on this subject bear an extremely pessimistic slant. **1927** C. CONNOLLY *Let.* 26 Jan. in *Romantic Friendship* (1975) 230 The slant at which I write betrays an unbearable optimism. **1935** M. M. ATWATER *Murder in Midsummer* xv. 138 Mentally he was going over his 'story'..to change the slant of some of the phrases. **1948** *Sunday Pictorial* 18 July 12/3 A new and intriguing slant on the Borgias by Nigel Balchin. **1965** *Amer. N. & Q.* Mar. 99/2 The book has a pro-Galvão slant showing the man as a romantic hero. **1973** J. WOOD *North Beat* ii. 19 New slant—timing the lunch-hour, eh? When did we have that one before?
9. *U.S. colloq.* A glance, look.
1911 E. FERBER *Dawn O'Hara* viii. 109 You're supposed t'take a slant at th'things an' make up your mind w'at you want. **1934** [see *PETTING *vbl. sb.* 3].
10. *U.S. slang.* A slant-eyed person, *spec.* used as a term of contempt for one of Oriental stock. Cf. *slant-eye(s)* s.v. *SLANT *a.* 3.
1942 BERREY & VAN DEN BARK *Amer. Thes. Slang* §385/19 Oriental..*slant.* **1969** *Time* 5 Dec. 26/1 To the G.I. the Vietnamese..is a 'gook', 'dink', 'slope' or 'slant'. **1976** M. MACHLIN *Pipeline* vii. 79 And the fuckin' Eskimo slants are tryin' to get the rest of it. **1978** J. GORES *Gone, no Forwarding* (1979) 191 He took me back to the slant broad... A slant or a Buddha-head.

slant, *a.* Add: **3. slant-drill** *v. intr. Oil Industry*, to drill a bore hole at an angle to the vertical; also *trans.*; so **slant-drilling** *vbl. sb.*; **slant-eye(s)** *slang* (orig. *U.S.*), a slant-eyed person, *spec.* an Asian (cf. *SLANT *sb.*[1] 10); **slant-line** = *SLANT *sb.*[1] 1 e; **slant-rhyme** = *half-rhyme* s.v. *HALF- II. n.
1969 *New Scientist* 24 Apr. 169/1 They suggest the search for oil..should be restricted to slant-drilling from the shore. **1975** *Offshore* Sept. 244/2 Much of the area covered by the sale can be slant-drilled from the shoreline or the barrier islands. **1976** L. ST. CLAIR *Fortune in Death* i. 8 We've wasted enough time fishing drill pipe out of this hole. Let's plug back and slant-drill. **1977** *Time* 28 Feb. 17/2 Two weeks ago the Israelis began sinking another hole on the shore at El Tur, slant-drilling into the waters whose ownership it disputes. **1929** *Amer. Speech* IV. 344 *Slant eye*, an oriental. **1962** E. SNOW *Red China Today* (1963) xii. 85 One might assume that contempt for American imperialism would by now have produced Chinese equivalents of insulting American epithets such as slopeys, slant-eyes and chinks. **1966** *Publ. Amer. Dial. Soc. 1964* XLII. 31 A few terms [for Orientals] reflect stereotype racial characteristics, i.e., *yellow-belly, yellow-man, slant eyes.* **1972** *Times* 20 May 3/4, I have engaged in campaigns against blacks, yellows and slant-eyes. Why should we have one rule for the whites and one for coloureds? **1974** *Times Lit. Suppl.* 26 July 795/4 And those Jap Ph.D.'s, their questionnaires! (Replying 'Sod off, Slant-Eyes' led to friction.) **1977** 'J. LE CARRÉ' *Hon. Schoolboy* i. 36 Renting a cottage in the New Territories, he..proposed to expire under a slanteye heaven. **1954** F. G. CASSIDY *Robertson's Devel. Mod. Eng.* (ed. 2) iv. 61 Phonemic symbols are placed between virgules (or 'slant-lines', or 'diagonals'). **1966** *Publ. Amer. Dial. Soc.* XLVI. 16 In line with Haugen's procedure..*slant lines*..used in this article perform double duty for phonemic and diaphonic representations. **1944** *Mod. Lang. Q.* V. 324 Traditional prosodists have discussed rhyme as a degree of likeness in word sounds and have catalogued its approximations, alliteration, assonance, slant rhyme, eye rhyme, [etc.]. **1976** *Times Lit. Suppl.* 16 Jan. 50/2 Wilfrid Owen and Yeats opted for slant-rhyme because it suited their poetic purposes; Fry seems to chime because sometimes he cannot rhyme.

slant, *v.* Add: **5. b.** *fig.* To give a slant (*SLANT *sb.*[1] 8) or bias to (something). orig. *U.S.*
1939 *Writer's Digest* Sept. 26/2 These types of articles are exceptionally valuable in slanting the writing for certain magazines and trade journals. **1951** H. MACINNES *Neither Five nor Three* II. xi. 166 Did that fool Weidler see that Blackworth was 'slanting' his use of material? **1960** *New Left Rev.* May–June 66/1 There is no suggestion ..that Mr. Bullock is deliberately slanting the picture he paints. **1980** M. BABSON *Dangerous to Know* vi. 41 'I suppose it *could* be slanted that way.' It was obvious that May had been considering a different slant.

slanted, *ppl. a.* Add: **2.** Biased, tendentious.
1959 *Listener* 2 Apr. 580/2 A consistently slanted picture of Soviet policy. **1967** 'R. SIMONS' *Taxed to Death* v. 80 Why are you asking me all these slanted questions about Nathin? **1978** *Detroit Free Press* 16 Apr. E8/1 'The material coming our way is so slanted on gun control and hunting's role in wildlife management, I can't, in good conscience, pass it on to our youngsters,' he had said.

slanter, var. *SCHLENTER *sb.* and *a.*

slantindicular, *a.* (*sb.*) and *adv.* Add: Also **-diclar, -dickelar, slantendikular. A.** *adj.* **a.** (Earlier examples.)
β. **1832** *Mem. of Nullifier* iv. 37 This is sorter a slantindickelar road, stranger. **1835** P. H. NICKLIN *Lett. Descr. Virginia Springs* 30 [He] makes his bivouac among the trees..under a slantindicular shed.
B. *adv.* (Earlier and later examples.)
1831 *Daily Louisville Public Advertiser* 17 Oct. 2/3 He looked up at me slantindicler [*sic*], and I looked down on him slantindiclar. **1873** C. H. SMITH *Bill Arp's Peace Papers* xxx. 202 If we could have slid into it quietly and slantendikular, if slavery could have sorter tapered out and freedom sorter tapered in, everybody could have got used to it.

slanting, *vbl. sb.* (Later examples.)
1959 *Times* 15 May 6/7 It is still an even chance that any University production of [Shakespeare's plays] one samples will not be heavily flavoured with gimmickry or slanting. **1980** M. MCMULLEN *My Cousin Death* (1981) 7 Not a gentle..rain..but an ill-natured heavy slanting from the northeast.

slantingways (slɑ·ntɪŋwēⁱz), *adv. rare.* [f. SLANTING *ppl. a.* + -WAYS.] Slantwise. Cf. SLANTWAYS *adv.*
1899 H. G. WELLS *When Sleeper Wakes* vi. 59 He walked slantingways across the room. **1916** —— *Mr. Britling* II. iv. 332 We were busy..pushing our trench out from an angle slantingways forward.

slap, *sb.*[1] Add: **1. a.** *slap on the back* (or *shoulder*): as a hearty gesture of friendship or congratulation. Also *fig.* Cf. *BACK-SLAPPING *ppl. a.* and *vbl. sb.*
1820 W. IRVING *Sketch Bk.* VI. 94 His hospitable attentions were brief, but expressive, being confined to a shake of the hand, a slap on the shoulder..and a pressing invitation to 'reach to, and help themselves'. **1863** G. MEREDITH *Let.* 19 Feb. (1970) I. 193 Did you say in it you are sorry for your virulent offensive letter that I received? ..If so, a slap on the back and we're friends again. **1883** STEVENSON *Treasure Isl.* viii. 62 He seemed in the most cheerful spirits..with a merry word or a slap on the shoulder for the most favoured of his guests. **1929** L. MACNEICE *Blind Fireworks* 5 There are lines which may, by the incautious, be (wrongly) read in a merry slap-on-the-back fashion.
e. *slap and tickle*: (a bout of) light amorous play.
1928 E. ROBERTSON *Cullum* ix. 178 She gave me a playful push... She was one of the dreadful type that Cullum called 'slap-and-tickle' girls. **1936** N. COWARD *To-Night at 8.30* 77 She won't [come back]—she's out having a bit of slap and tickle with our Albert. **1958** 'N. SHUTE' *Rainbow & Rose* vi. 243 When I want a bit of slap and tickle I'll arrange it for myself, thank you. **1977** C. MCCULLOUGH *Thorn Birds* x. 236 He'd woo her the way she obviously wanted, flowers and attention and not too much slap-and-tickle.
f. *Mech.* = *piston slap* s.v. *PISTON *sb.* 4.
1930 *Engineering* 7 Mar. 304/1 Large engines..used,.. until recently,..cast-iron pistons. This is because of required durability..and because of expansion troubles—slap, leakage, &c.
2. a. Esp. in phrs. *a slap in* (or † *on*) *the face, in the eye, on the wrist.*
1861 [in Dict.]. **1895** LLOYD GEORGE *Let.* 3 June (1973) 85 So there's another slap in the eye for the Bryn party. **1898** G. B. SHAW *Philanderer* I. 96 I'll have to apologize for her... Her going away is a downright slap in the face for these people. **1914** *Dialect Notes* IV. 112 *Slap on the wrist*, mild rebuke or criticism. **1920** D. H. LAWRENCE *Touch & Go* 5 How much will you give me for my syllogism? Not a slap in the eye, I hope. **1932** L. GOLDING *Magnolia Street* II. iii. 308 The Great War was..a slap in the face, quite simply. **1966** *Economist* 26 Feb. 801/1 The Administration has been trying to choke off North Vietnam's supplies for some time... The latest move—a 'slap on the wrist', according to the dockers—has been

to blacklist ships which visit Haiphong. **1970** P. CARLON *Death by Demonstration* vi. 73 All she said was, 'I don't want to talk about it.' That was as good as a slap in the eye. **1977** *Rolling Stone* 7 Apr. 17/3 We think we can get Anita off with a fine and a slap on the wrist, but the thing with Keith is much more serious. **1979** *Guardian* 17 Jan. 1/4 Industry will regard action to tighten price control.. as a slap in the face.

b. (Earlier example.)

1840 A. BUNN *Stage before & behind Curtain* III. 38 Enabled me to have a slap at the pretenders.

slap, *v.*[1] Add: **1. a.** Also *to slap* (someone) *on the back*: to clap (someone) on the back as a gesture of goodwill or congratulation; to treat in a hearty or jovial manner.

1908 E. M. FORSTER *Room with View* x. 173, I said, 'Hooray, old boy!' and slapped him on the back. **1914** A. C. BENSON *Jrnl.* in D. Newsome *On Edge of Paradise* (1980) x. 320 M.F. was always the sort of man who slapped everyone on the back. **1931** R. CAMPBELL *Georgiad* iii. 54 Nicolson who in his weekly crack Will slap the meanest scribbler on the back. **1941** 'R. WEST' *Black Lamb & Grey Falcon* I. 496 The stocky little men were.. lifting their glasses to him and slapping him on the back.

d. *U.S. slang.* To play (a double-bass) without a bow in jazz style, *spec.* to pull the strings so as to let them snap back on to the fingerboard.

1933 [see *DOG-HOUSE 2 b]. **1935** *Swing Music* June 83/1 The lyric, which was a masterpiece of fatuity.., had to do with the vogue of 'picking and slapping' the double bass. **1958** *Times Lit. Suppl.* 11 Apr. (Children's Literature Suppl.) p. iii/3 He takes up the violin, viola and cello, but happily stays just the right size for the double-bass, which he 'slaps' with such proficiency that he ends up in a famous jazz orchestra.

2. Delete † *Obs.* and add later example.

1884 'MARK TWAIN' *Huck. Finn* xvii. 158 She could rattle off poetry like nothing... She would slap down a line, and if she couldn't find anything to rhyme with it she would just scratch it out and slap down another one.

3. b. (Later *fig.* examples.)

1922 *Collier's* 1 July 26/1 Judge Tuckerman.. slapped on the fines and costs with a lavish hand. **1924** E. M. FORSTER *Passage to India* vii. 61 The College itself had been slapped down by the Public Works Department, but its grounds included an ancient garden. **1968** J. WAINWRIGHT *Web of Silence* 12 A 'D Notice' gets slapped on the inquiry... The newspapers are gagged from the word 'go'. **1976** *Milton Keynes Express* 23 July 38/5 The Berks and Bucks FA have slapped a severe six-week ban on Hurrell following his sending off in a charity match.

7. (Later *poet.* example.)

1966 S. HEANEY *Death of Naturalist* 57 And one Was scaresome for there, out of ferns and tall Foxgloves, a rat slapped across my reflection.

8. Also *trans.*, to throw. (In quot. *fig.*)

1957 [see *prisoner's dilemma* s.v. *PRISONER[2] 1 b].

9. *trans.* To punish (someone) *with* a penalty, sentence, etc. *N. Amer.*

1968 *Globe & Mail* (Toronto) 13 Jan. 37/2 Late in the contest coach John Petrushchak and centre Bruno Marcocchio were slapped with technical fouls for disagreeing with the referees. **1972** *Newsweek* 10 Jan. 17/3 For his indiscretion, he is slapped with a stiff $17,000 fine. **1973** *Tucson* (Arizona) *Daily Citizen* 22 Aug. 4/1 Two young stepbrothers involved in a drug-crime.. were slapped with five years partial probation.

10. In *fig.* phrs. *to slap* (a person or thing) *down*: to snub, suppress, or rebuke; *to slap* (a person's) *wrist*: to scold or reprimand; *to slap* (a person's) *face*: to administer a sharp reproof or rebuff.

1938 'E. QUEEN' *Four of Hearts* xi. 153 She's been.. leading me on just so she could turn around and slap me down. **1949** L. A. G. STRONG *Maud Cherrill* 40 Any hint of affectation or pretentiousness she would have slapped down hard. **1960** 'E. MCBAIN' *See them Die* xvi. 209 You're God, and there isn't anyone who's going to slap your wrist, no matter how you do it. **1973** *Times* 13 Aug. 4/2 Sales of this have gone up in recent years and we cannot think that the Government is going to slap the face of a very large number of users to save a little money. *Ibid.* 17 Oct. 20/3 The police sergeant who conducted the prosecutions was often slapped down by the clerk of the court for leading his witnesses. **1977** E. AMBLER *Send no More Roses* iii. 53 Thinking that he was about to deliver the admonition, I let him go ahead. He didn't even slap her wrist. **1978** *Lancashire Life* July 63/2 His seniors might well have felt he was a publicity-seeker who needed slapping-down.

11. *Comb.* **slap-bass**, a double-bass played in jazz style (see quot. 1956); **slap-you-on-the-back** *attrib. phr.*, hearty, jovial.

1949 *Sun* (Baltimore) 22 Jan. 6/3 The slap-bass virtuoso who accidentally kicks a hole in his instrument in the middle of a jam session. **1956** S. TRAILL *Play that Music* iv. 46 This was the era of the slap bass: so called because the strings were pulled away from the fingerboard of the bass and.. let smartly back to the fingerboard—thereby making a loud clicking sound. **1932** B. WORSLEY-GOUGH *Public Affairs* x. 182 'Lord,' said Venetia, 'I had forgotten the Bishop. What is he like?' 'Jovial. Jolly. Slap-you-on-the-back-for-tuppence.' **1957** *Times Lit. Suppl.* 22 Nov. 708/4 Mr Matthews has a jolly, slap-you-on-the-back approach. **1962** *Listener* 28 June 1114/2 Newbolt himself was no hearty, bluff, slap-you-on-the-back sort of man.

slap, *a.* (Earlier example.)

1840 H. COCKTON *Valentine Vox* xiv. 108 But it's a werry nice place; werry private and genteel. None o' your public 'uns!—everything slap and respectable!

sla·p-back. *U.S.* Also **slapback.** [f. SLAP *v.*[1] + BACK *adv.*] A counter-attack, retaliation.

1931 *Sun* (Baltimore) 31 Mar. 10/7 The working of Canada's tariff slap-back against our beloved Smoot-Hawley law. **1941** *New Yorker* 27 Dec. 37/1 A resounding Allied slapback at the enemy in the Pacific.

slap-bang, *adv.* Add: Also of position: directly or precisely (*in* the centre); completely, absolutely. Cf. *BANG *adv.* a.

1963 A. SMITH *Throw out Two Hands* xiv. 143 That gas was contentedly holding over three-quarters of a ton 1,500 feet above a lake and slap bang in the middle of the sky.

slap-dab, *adv. N. Amer. dial.* and *colloq.* [f. SLAP *adv.* + DAB *adv.*] = SLAP-BANG *adv.* in Dict. and Suppl. (see also quot. 1896). Cf. *SMACK-DAB *adv.*

1886 *Turf, Field & Farm* XLII. 174/3 He was goin' that fas' he run slap-dab agin me afo' he seed me. **1896** *Dialect Notes* I. 399 *Slap-dab*.., violently or awkwardly. 'He rushed in slap-dab and broke things.' **1949** *Publ. Amer. Dial. Soc.* xi. 11 It jumped slap-dab in the middle. **1973** *Victorian* (Victoria, B.C.) 1 Aug. 1/1 It occurred slap dab in the middle of what is now Centennial Square.

slap-dash, *adv.*, *a.* and *sb.* Add: Hence **slapda·shness.**

1929 *Daily Tel.* 15 Jan. 7 If he has the defects of his virtues—a certain slap-dashness visible enough in one or two of these stories—he has also the virtues of his defects. **1965** *Punch* 27 Jan. 146/2 By halfway I was finding the slapdashness of the overall pattern rather self-indulgent and the separate delights were suffering from this.

slapdashery. Delete '(in *nonce use*)' and add later examples. Also (*rare*) **slapdasherie.**

1908 KIPLING *Lett. of Travel* (1920) 144 Here and there the people are infected with the unworthy superstition of 'hustle', which means half-doing your appointed job and applauding your own slapdasherie for as long a time as would enable you to finish off two clean pieces of work. *a* **1913** F. ROLFE *Desire & Pursuit of Whole* (1934) vii. 60 That really huge romance.. which his friend.. wrote with such reprehensible slapdashery. **1966** *New Statesman* 14 Oct. 547/2 Sensibility and earthiness, obsession with detail and romantic slapdashery. **1982** *Times* 28 July 11/3 What it loses in slapdashery it gains in exuberance.

sla·p-happy, *a. colloq.* (orig. *U.S.*). Also **slaphappy.** [f. SLAP *sb.*[1] + *-HAPPY.]

1. Dazed, punch-drunk; dizzy (with happiness).

1936 J. TULLY *Bruiser* x. 89 A slap-happy bum. **1938** *Newsweek* 23 May 22/1 A sample [of talk] designed to knock philologists slap-happy. **1940** *Detective Tales* Apr. 8/1 He was a little slap-happy from a decade of slugfesting. **1947** [see *PUNCH-DRUNK *a.*]. **1973** *Maclean's Mag.* (Toronto) Feb. 32/2 It was so exhilaratingly ludicrous.. that I felt quite slaphappy.

2. Carefree, casual; careless, thoughtless, irresponsible.

1937 *N.Y. Herald Tribune* 28 Aug. 14/1 After the dust had settled he and Ernest Hemingway, the slaphappy litterateur, toured Spain together. **1940** *Nation* 6 Apr. 448/1 Unless production [of television programmes] is slap-happy, the costs promise to compare with those of Broadway shows. **1951** R. HOGGART *Auden* iii. 78 This is Auden's characteristic 'Love' again, allied to his leftism—a lyrical but vague coda to a slap-happy knocking-down of many old guys. **1958** E. H. CLEMENTS *Uncommon Cold* i. 26 The irresponsible slap-happy manners of extreme modern youth. **1977** *Meanjin* XXXVI. I. 131 The real point is that Sydney—slap-happy and extroverted—is the favoured haunt of the cultural bureaucrats.

Hence **slap-ha·ppily** *adv.*, **slap-ha·ppiness.**

1958 S. HYLAND *Who goes Hang?* xiv. 63 The impression of boisterous slap-happiness. **1968** M. BRAGG *Without City Wall* II. xxvii. 249 Spray the world with froth of slap-happiness. **1969** *Guardian* 20 Oct. 22/2 He is unlikely to display himself so slap-happily before those surging crowds.

slapjack. 1. For *U.S.* read *N. Amer.* and add earlier and further examples.

1805 'AN AMERICAN LADY' *New Amer. Cookery* 60 *Indian Slapjack.* One quart milk, 1 pint of Indian meal, 4 eggs, 4 spoons of flour. **1867** J. K. LORD *At Home in Wilderness* viii. 132 Then I can bake bread in my frying-pan, make and fry pancakes, or 'slap-jacks', as trappers call them. **1895** W. ELKINGTON *Five Years in Canada* xiii. 111 Another favourite dish.. is also made of flour and water, mixed into a batter and fried in fat; it is eaten with syrup or sugar, and is called 'slap-jack'.

slapper[1]. Add: **2. b.** In jazz, one who plays the double-bass (see *SLAP *v.*[1] 1 d).

1934 S. R. NELSON *All about Jazz* vi. 126 So a race of pickers and slappers.. sprang into being. **1936** *Swing Music* Mar. 9/2 Steve Brown, that tremendous string-bass slapper.

slapping, *vbl. sb.*[1] Add: **c.** In jazz, the action of playing a double-bass (see *SLAP *v.*[1] 1 d).

1931 *Melody Maker* Dec. 1029/3 Slapping, too, becomes next to impossible with a high bridge. **1959** 'F. NEWTON' *Jazz Scene* 289 *Slapping* for pizzicato playing.

slappy (slæ·pi), *a. U.S. slang.* [f. *SLAP(-HAPPY *a.* + -Y[1].] = *SLAP-HAPPY *a.* Also as *sb.*

1937 [see *PUNCHY *a.*[4]]. **1942** BERREY & VAN DEN BARK *Amer. Thes. Slang* § 151/9 *Foolish; silly;*.. slappy. *Ibid.* § 702/32 '*Punch-drunk*'; *dazed*.. slappy.

slap shot. *Ice Hockey.* Also **slapshot.** [f. SLAP *v.*[1] + SHOT *sb.*[1]] A shot made with a sharp slapping movement of the stick, which usu. lifts the puck off the ice. Hence **sla·p-shoot** *v. trans.*, to hit (a puck) in this manner.

1942 E. JEREMIAH *Ice Hockey* iii. 12 A slap shot.. is very effective because its suddenness has a valuable surprise element. **1956** *Roy. Canad. Air Force Coach's Manual Hockey* 40 The slap shot can be made by stopping the puck first, then teeing off on it. **1968** *Globe & Mail* (Toronto) 3 Feb. 35/1 Athlete-columnists are more common than writers who can also skate and slapshoot a hockey puck. **1972** 'E. LATHEN' *Murder without Icing* (1973) ii. 18 Billy Siragusa, the Huskies' new center, was practicing slap shots. **1974** *Los Angeles Times* 13 Oct. III. 2/3 Rene Robert got Buffalo's only goal at 14:06 of the opening period with a 30-foot slapshot.

sla·pstick. orig. *U.S.* Also **slap-stick.** [f. SLAP *v.*[1] + STICK *sb.*[1]] **1.** Two flat pieces of wood joined together at one end, used to produce a loud slapping noise; *spec.* such a device used in pantomime and low comedy to make a great noise with the pretence of dealing a heavy blow (see also quot. 1950).

1896 *N.Y. Dramatic News* 4 July 9/3 What a relief, truly, from the slap-sticks, rough-and-tumble comedy couples abounding in the variety ranks. **1907** *Weekly Budget* 19 Oct. 1/2 The special officer in the gallery, armed with a 'slap-stick', the customary weapon in American theatre galleries, made himself very officious amongst the small boys. **1925** M. W. DISHER *Clowns & Pantomimes* 13 What has caused the playgoers' sudden callousness? The slapstick. Towards the end of the seventeenth century Arlequin had introduced into England the double-lath of castigation, which made the maximum amount of noise with the minimum of injury. **1937** M. COVARRUBIAS *Island of Bali* iv. 77 Life-size scarecrows are erected, but soon the birds become familiar with them... Then watchmen circulate among the fields beating bamboo drums and cracking loud bamboo slap-sticks. **1950** *Sun* (Baltimore) 10 Apr. 3/1 The 50-year-old clown.. said that when he bent over another funnyman accidentally hit him with the wrong side of a slap-stick. He explained that a slap-stick contains a blank ·38-caliber cartridge on one side to make a bang.

2. a. *attrib.* passing into *adj.* Of or pertaining to a slapstick; of or reminiscent of knock-about comedy.

1906 *N.Y. Even. Post* 25 Oct. 10 It required all the untiring efforts of an industrious 'slap-stick' coterie.. to keep the enthusiasm up to a respectable degree. **1914** *Photoplay* Sept. 91 (*heading*) Making slap-stick comedy. **1923** *Weekly Dispatch* 4 Mar. 9 He likes good comedies.. but thinks the slapstick ones ridiculous. **1928** *Daily Sketch* 7 Aug. 4/3 The jokes.. are rapier-like in their keenness, not the usual rolling-pin or slapstick form of humour. **1936** W. HOLTBY *South Riding* IV. v. 258 She took a one-and-threepenny ticket, sat in comfort, and watched a Mickey Mouse film, a slapstick comedy, and the tragedy of Greta Garbo acting Mata Hari. **1944** [see *POCHO]. **1962** A. NISBETT *Technique Sound Studio* x. 173 Decidedly unobvious effects, such as the cork-and-resin 'creak' or the hinged slapstick 'whip'. **1977** R. L. WOLFF *Gains & Losses* II. iv. 296 The prevailing tone of the book is highly satirical, with strong overtones of slapstick farce.

b. *absol.* Knockabout comedy or humour, farce, horseplay.

1926 *Amer. Speech* I. 437/2 *Slap-stick*, low comedy in its simplest form. Named from the double paddles formerly used by circus clowns to beat each other. **1930** *Publishers' Weekly* 25 Jan. 420/2 The slapstick of 1929 was often exciting. The Joan Lowell episode was regarded as exposing the gullibility of the critics... The popularity of 'The Specialist' made the whole book business look cockeyed. **1955** *Times* 6 June 9/1 A comic parson (Mr. Noel Howlett) is added for good measure, mainly to play on the piano while other people crawl under it. Even on the level of slapstick the farce seemed to keep in motion with some difficulty and raised but moderate laughter. **1967** M. KENYON *Whole Hog* xxv. 253 A contest which had promised.. to be short and cruel, had become slapstick. **1976** *Oxf. Compan. Film* 640/1 As it developed in the decade 1910–20.. slapstick depended on frenzied, often disorganized, motion that increased in tempo as visual gags proliferated.

sla·p-tongue, *v.* Also **slaptongue, slap tongue.** [f. SLAP *v.*[1] + TONGUE *sb.*] *intr.* To produce a staccato effect in playing the saxophone by striking the tongue against the reed. So **sla·p-tonguing** *vbl. sb.*; hence **sla·p-tongue** *a.*, playing or played with this technique.

1926 WHITEMAN & MCBRIDE *Jazz* ix. 203 Slap tonguing is accomplished by sucking on the reed, thus creating a vacuum, then hitting the vacuum with the tongue, causing a pop. **1927** *Melody Maker* May 503/1 How to slap-tongue is not the easiest thing to explain in words. **1954** *Grove's Dict. Mus.* (ed. 5) VII. 433/2 Tongued staccato playing.. was at one period developed by dance musicians into a curious explosive effect termed 'slap-tonguing'. **1963** *Down Beat* 3 Jan. 20 His first solo with Henderson, a clownlike, slap-tongue effort. **1969** *Listener* 12 June 838/1 Experimentation was limited to exploiting its [*sc.* the saxophone's] agility..or producing comic effects by slap tonguing. **1971** *Daily Tel.* 18 Sept. 7/8 Henderson's Columbia sessions..despite occasional farm-yard noises and slaptongue reeds offer good Redman and Charlie Green.

slap-up, *a.* Add: **a.** (Earlier and later examples.) Now used esp. of meals.

1823 'J. Bee' *Slang* 161 *Slap-up,* used for 'bang-up'. 'Tis *northern.* **1931** W. S. Maugham in *Nash's Pall Mall Mag.* Dec. 24/1 A bottle of pop tonight, my pet, and a slap-up dinner. **1977** *Lancashire Life* Nov. 74/2 There was a slap-up tea at the institute.

slart (slāɹt). *dial.* [Origin unknown: for related senses see *Eng. Dial. Dict.*] *pl.* Left-overs, scraps.

1913, 1917 [see *ort]. **1977** Scollins & Titford *Ey up, mi Duck!* III. 50 *Slarts,* left-overs, scraps of food.

slash, *sb.*^{1} Add: **1. b.** In *Cricket,* any unorthodox attacking stroke played with a great swing of the bat.

1906 A. E. Knight *Complete Cricket* ii. 78 A slash at the ball, the bat slicing the ball instead of meeting it with the full face. **1948** *Sporting Mirror* 21 May 7/1 The first shot he made after arriving at the wickets was a glorious 'slash' to the boundary. **1977** *Daily Express* 29 Jan. 35/1 Yajuvendra, never looking the part in his first Test innings, took a full-blooded slash outside off stump at a short one from Willis.

c. *fig.* A reduction; a (swingeing) cut. Cf. *slash *v.*^{1} *1 d.

1950 *N.Y. Times* 20 Apr. 2/1 (*heading*) House group bars overall 50% slash in wartime excises. **1951** [see *consumer 2 c]. **1973** *Tucson* (Arizona) *Daily Citizen* 22 Aug. 1 This would be the second wave of base slashes in about a year. **1983** *Guardian Weekly* 6 Mar. 14/1 A 50 per cent slash in the army's budget.

3. b. (Earlier *absol.* and later *attrib.* examples.)

1839 H. Brandon *Poverty, Mendicity & Crime* 165/1 *Slash,* outside coat pocket. **1969** *Sears Catal.* Spring/Summer 47 No-iron reversible jacket... Plaid side has two slash pockets. **1973** W. Hallahan *Ross Forgery* iii. 3 The watchman pushed his hands into the slash pockets of his jacket.

4. a. An open tract or clearing in a forest, esp. one strewn with debris resulting from felling or logging, high wind, or fire. Cf. *slashing *vbl. sb.* 4 b. *N. Amer.*

1825 A. Anderson *Diary* 30 Aug. in G. Sellar *Narr.* (1916) vii. 102 We have been here scarce three months and there is a great slash. **1849** J. E. Alexander *L'Acadie* I. 272 After various difficulties..getting with our horses into 'slashes' or parts of the forest cut down.. we at last reached the small wooden hostel. **1923** H. E. Williams *Spinning Wheels & Homespun* 154 Raspberries are found oftenest in what are called 'slashes' in the woods, where the older timber has been cut down, and the new has not yet grown up to replace it. **1963** *Sun* (Vancouver) 23 Nov. 21/1 The rolling hills along the.. rivers are parklike with their copses of fir, tamarack, poplar and willow..left standing in old log slashes or burns.

b. Felled trees and other debris left in a forest after logging or the clearing of a tract, or resulting from high wind or fire. Cf. *slashing *vbl. sb.* 4 c. orig. and chiefly *N. Amer.*

In mod. use, *slash* denotes the branches and other trimmings cut from trees preparatory to removing the logs from a forest.

1841 *Bytown* (Ottawa) *Gaz.* 17 Feb. 1/3 To end of month clearing up old 'slash', which term has previously been defined. **1917** F. D. Adams in J. O. Miller *New Era in Canada* 85 In Quebec and British Columbia, settlers who desire to burn their slash must now obtain permits from the Government forest ranger, who supervises the burning. **1928** *Indian Forest Rec.* XIII. vii. 3 Comprehensively defined, *chir* slash includes all débris resulting from operations involving the felling and utilization of *chir* trees, and also from the destruction of trees of this species by such agencies as wind, snow, fire, lightning, floods, landslips, insects and fungi. **1952** P. W. Richards *Tropical Rain Forest* xvii. 379 Soil impoverishment will in turn depend on..the quantity of debris and 'slash' left on the ground after clearing. **1965** *Wildlife Rev.* Mar. 19/2 Cougars travel over long ranges and are found in various ecological types of terrain such as slash, mature forest and second growth. **1980** *Search* XI. 71/1 Planting of tubed stock on corridors cleared of slash may be another means of establishing eucalypt seedlings.

c. *attrib.* and *Comb.,* as *slash area, fire.*

1971 *Islander* (Victoria, B.C.) 30 May 12/3 After about a third of a mile you break out into a slash area where logging operations have been carried out. **1949** *Pacific Discovery* Jan.–Feb. 4/1 The river knew well the flashing draft of lightning fires in the grass but not the consuming roar of a slash fire. **1980** *Search* XI. 69/1 Slash fires result in mobilisation of large amounts of nutrients both during the fire..and subsequently as a result of stimulated biological mineralisation in the soil.

5. A thin sloping line, thus /; = *oblique *sb.* 5, Solidus^1 2 in Dict. and Suppl. *U.S.* Also *slash-mark.*

1961 in Webster. **1964** *Amer. Speech* XXXIX. 103 The number to the right of the slash is the total number of occurrences of that type of clause. **1976** T. Allbeury *Only Good German* x. 76 Reference SC49 slash two. **1979** C. E. Schorske *Fin-de-Siècle Vienna* vii. 331 Breaking the phrase with slash marks at unsuspected nodes. **1980** *Maledicta* III. ii. 206 Although it is true that . , : ; () - [] – ! ? / and * have names—in the case of /, several names: solidus, virgule, slash-mark, diagonal—there is a gap in the naming of #.

slash, *sb.*^{2} Restrict † *Obs. rare* to sense in Dict. and add: **2.** *slang.* An act of urination.

1950 P. Tempest *Lag's Lexicon* 192 *Slash, to go for a,* to visit the urinal. **1953** *Chambers's Jrnl.* June 325/1 'I'm leaving my turret for a moment. I want a slash.' 'Okay, kid, you know where to find it?' 'I should do. I've had to empty them often enough!' **1977** N. J. Crisp *Odd Job Man* i. 5 He decided to risk a quick slash, which..he needed.

slash, *sb.*^{3} **a.** Substitute for def.: Swampy ground; a swamp. (Earlier and later examples.)

1652 in N. M. Nugent *Cavaliers & Pioneers* (1934) I. 239/2 Neer a wett slash, running N.N.W. to an Easternmost branch of Richard Cr. **1717** *Prince George County* (Virginia) *Deed Bk.* 202 in *Amer. Speech* (1940) XV. 393/1 A white Oake Standing in a round Slash. **1897** *Geogr. Jrnl.* IX. 538 There are many successive ridges of shingle running in varying directions, and often with narrow strips of marsh enclosed between successive ridges. Such bands of marsh have been given the very appropriate name of 'slashes' in New Jersey. **1903** *Dialect Notes* II. 330 [S. E. Missouri] *Slash,* wet bottom land. A slash differs from a slough in having no perceptible channel. **1966** *Publ. Amer. Dial. Soc.* xlvi. 29 *Slash,* a swamp.—'It was in that slash down on the river.'

b. slash-pine, for '(see quots.)' read: a pine growing in a slash or low-lying coastal region, esp. *Pinus caribæa,* the principal native pine of south-eastern North America; also, the wood of this tree. (Later examples.)

1934 *Sun* (Baltimore) 7 Dec. 3/2 Dr. Herty recently made newsprint from slash and other southern pine. **1949** *Clarke County Democrat* (Grove Hill, Alabama) 28 July 1/3 Both have plots on which they have set out slash pine seedlings. **1974** *Calhoun Times* (St. Matthews, S. Carolina) 18 Apr. 2/1 Loblolly and slash pines are most susceptible [to rust galls].

slash, *sb.*^{4} (Later example.)

1916 [see *slatch 1].

slash, *v.*^{1} Add: **1. c.** To clear (land) of vegetation, to cut (trees or undergrowth) *down,* esp. preparatory to burning off the resulting slash. Chiefly *N. Amer.*

1821 T. McCulloch *Stepsure Letters* (1960) 20 He had slashed down a large piece of wood; and now he determined to raise a crop. **1849** C. Hursthouse *Acct. Settlement New Plymouth* vii. 93 The cane-like fern stalks.. should be cut at once,..and the 'Tutu' slashed down with a bill-hook. **1889** W. H. Withrow *Our Own Country* 362 The native forest had been 'slashed' in that particular locality. **1931** *Beaver* Sept. 276 Five acres of virgin land were slashed. **1962** A. Fry *Ranch on Cariboo* 66 Sometimes we built fence or slashed brush to extend the yard.

d. *fig.* To reduce (something) severely in size or quantity. Freq. used with reference to prices, payments, etc.

1906 *Washington Post* 29 Apr. 6 A disposition was manifested in the Senate Committee to slash the salaries of members of the commission. **1910** *Springfield* (Mass.) *Weekly Republican* 8 Dec. 8 It is not a pleasant thing to slash a presidential message to this extent. **1931** *Evening Standard* 4 Aug. 10/1 The big department stores have not merely reduced their prices; they have 'slashed' them. **1958** *Listener* 13 Nov. 777/2 After that I stuck to one garage and slashed expenditure by 50 per cent. at a single stroke. **1976** *Daily Mirror* 16 July 1/1 Labour held their seat in yesterday's vital Thurrock by-election. But their majority was slashed.

2. b. (Later U.S. example.) Also in cricket, to play a vigorous attacking stroke. Occas. *trans.* (in quot. with bowler as object).

1955 [see *gully *sb.*^{1} 2 d]. **1974** *Plain Dealer* (Cleveland, Ohio) 26 Oct. 7-d/7 Tailback Mike Newman slashed across from two yards out to cut Westlake's margin to 7-6 with 8:42 left. **1977** C. Martin-Jenkins *MCC in India* iii. 51 Viswanath slashed, snicked and was caught by Knott. **1977** *World of Cricket Monthly* June 87/1 The self-appointed England exile slashed Sarfraz for two boundaries in the first over.

9. *Comb.* **slash-hook** = Slasher 2 b.

1891 R. Wallace *Rural Econ. Austral. & N.Z.* xv. 231 Vines, creepers, supplejacks, and small saplings..require to be carefully cut by slash-hooks. **1930** Blunden *Poems* 188 Some harsh slash-hook Slit my skull and poured out all the fountains of my senses. **1942** [see *fagging *vbl. sb.*^{2}].

slash (slæʃ), *v.*^{2} *slang.* [f. *slash *sb.*^{2} 2.] *intr.* To urinate.

1973 M. Amis *Rachel Papers* 189 If you can slash in my bed (I thought) don't tell me you can't suck my cock.

slash-and-burn, *attrib. phr.* Also **slash and burn, slash-burn, slash, burn.** [f. phr. *to slash and burn*: see Slash *v.*, Burn *v.*^{1}] Designating a method of shifting cultivation in which vegetation is cut down in an area of virgin or rejuvenated forest, allowed to dry, and then burned off before seeds are planted. Also occas. in non-*attrib.* use.

1942 Chapple & Coon *Princ. Anthropol.* viii. 189 Linton has a theory that the development of confederacies by the Maya and the Indians of the southeastern States was a consequence of this aspect of the slash-and-burn system. **1951** [see *swidden 2]. **1969** G. Clark *World Prehistory* (ed. 2) vi. 126 The rapidity of their spread.. was due in part to their use of slash and burn agriculture,..and in part to the lack of opposition. **1973** J. J. McKelvey *Man against Tsetse* iii. 190 The Kibori River eradication program..obviated the need to continue with a slash-burn program. **1976** *Conservation News* Sept./Oct. 5/1 The slash, burn, short-term cultivation and migration habit of tribal populations has been forced for centuries by the intractable fact that when an area of forest is cleared crops can be grown in it for only two or three seasons before the soil nutrients are exhausted. **1977** G. Clark *World Prehistory* (ed. 3) iii. 126 The regime of slash and burn, involving the shift of cultivation every few years and the clearance of new patches of forest, inevitably implied the temporary abandonment of settlements. **1978** *Guardian Weekly* 2 Apr. 13/1 Eking out a living by fishing, picking fruit and berries and by slash-and-burn farming.

Hence **slash and burn** *v. trans.*; **slashed and burnt** *ppl. a.* Also **slash-bur·ning** *vbl. sb.,* the process or practice of slash-and-burn agriculture.

1919 *Jrnl. Forestry* XVII. 277 It is proposed..to conduct slash-burning operations under control in selected localities [in Canada] and observe the establishment of natural regeneration through a period of years. **1949** *Malayan Forester* XII. 83 The plot was established in order to ascertain the extent of soil erosion..and to study natural plant succession of the slashed and burnt..areas. **1954** *Brit. Columbia Lumberman* Mar. 78 Slash burning in a good seed year should precede seedfall, if possible. **1955** J. D. Freeman *Iban Agric.* vi. 128 Deleterious results.. ensue when healthy, young vegetation..is slashed and burnt before proper regeneration..has taken place. *Ibid.* 129 Three sample plots were established to study 'natural plant succession', on (*a*) the slashed and burnt area [etc.]. **1980** *Search* XI. 71/2 Since slash-burning has been widely used [in Australia] only for the last 20–25 years, there has been no opportunity in Australian native forests to observe its effect on the productivity of successive forest rotations. **1981** P. Theroux *Mosquito Coast* xii. 137 Slash and burn the whole area and we've got four or five acres of good growing land.

slashed, *ppl. a.* Add: **4.** Of timber: felled, esp. in an unplanned or destructive manner. *N. Amer.*

1843 *Yale Lit. Mag.* VIII. 332 His eye wandered far away over acres of slashed timber.

5. *Cricket.* Played with or resulting from a slash (*slash *sb.*^{1} 1 b).

1974 *Observer* 9 June 24/8 A slashed catch to first slip accounted for Johnson. **1976** *S. Wales Echo* 27 Nov. 18/6 Reaching his half century in 138 minutes, he gave one difficult chance off a slashed stroke when he was 55, but Glenn Turner could not hold the ball at slip.

slasher. Add: **2. b.** (Earlier U.S. and later Austral. and N.Z. examples.)

1858 J. A. Warder *Hedges & Evergreens* 98 The slasher with a wooden handle set at an angle with the edge of the blade. **1916** J. B. Cooper *Coo-oo-ee* xi. 147 Cathead ferns and bracken..soon sprang up if he neglected to use the 'slasher', a large broad half-moon knife fixed to a stout ash handle. **1947** J. Bertram *Shadow of War* 70 Native convicts kept the lawns trimmed with formidable slashers.

d. A form of circular saw used to cut logs into predetermined lengths, usu. having several blades mounted on the same shaft.

1892 P. Benjamin *Mod. Mechanism* 777 A power-feed slab slasher, which differs greatly from the ordinary type of slabbing machines..has but one saw. **1915** *Saw in Hist.* iii. 38 Then there are Slashers—Circular Saws used in a gang, and averaging four or more to each set. **1947** N. C. Brown *Lumber* ii. 108 The slasher consists of a set of circular cut-off saws, generally arranged 49″ apart on a single shaft, to cut slabs, edgings, and other sawmill refuse into suitable lengths for lath stock, broomhandle stock, fuelwood, or other purposes. **1963** R. R. A. Higham *Handbk. Papermaking* v. 111 It will be assumed that they [*sc.* the logs] have already arrived at the slasher

slashing, *vbl. sb.* Add: **2. b.** (Earlier example.)

1842 *Illustr. London News* 14 May 9/1 The slashing being fully studded..with diamonds, rubies, emeralds.

4. For *U.S.* read *N. Amer.* Delete def., transfer quot. to sense *4 b, and add: **a.** The action of felling trees, esp. as a preliminary to clearing a tract of forest by burning.

1822 *Port Folio* XIII. 68 The act of hewing down the timber is called *slashing.* **1833** A. Fergusson *Pract. Notes* 42 A mode of chopping is in use hereabouts, termed slashing. It consists in merely prostrating the trees, without any further operation for a season, and then at leisure consuming the whole by fire. **1899** W. A. MacKay *Pioneer Life in Zorra* 167 There were three ways by which the first settlers cleared the land. The first was called 'slashing'. **1963** E. C. Guillet *Pioneer Farmer & Backwoodsman* I. 309 Another easy and cheap method was 'slashing'... felling the trees and allowing them to stay where they fell for a season or two.

b. = *slash *sb.*^{1} 4 a.

1840 *Jamestown* (N.Y.) *Jrnl.* 1 July 2/5 On Monday, the body of Mr. Brown was found in a slashing. **1894** [in Dict., sense 4 a]. **1912** 'R. Connor' *Corporal Cameron of N.W. Mounted Police* 269 At the 'slashing' the wagon ruts faded out and the road narrowed to a single cow path.

c. = *slash *sb.*^{1} 4 b. Freq. *pl.*

1864 T. Weed in T. L. Nichols *40 Yrs. Amer. Life* II. 215 Cattle..were turned out to 'browse' in the 'slashings'. **1928** P. A. Taverner *Ornithol. Invest. near Belvedere, Alberta* 104 *Mountain Bluebird,* not uncommon in the burnt spruce and slashings, but scarce elsewhere.

1964 *Islander* (Victoria, B.C.) 20 Sept. 5/2 Another small fire was burning in slashing on the west side of Reef Point. **1980** *Northeast Woods & Waters* Dec. 7/3 It headed into a small swamp made up of very thick and very low alders, criss-crossed with blowdowns and slashings.

5. The sizing of yarn by means of a slasher (sense 4) (see also quot. 1960).

1895 R. Marsden *Cotton Weaving* 514 Blackburn prices for Tape-sizeing or Slashing. **1921** *Dict. Occup. Terms* (1927) § 369 *Dresser*,..one who prepares delicate and fine yarns by passing them through sizing or slashing frame. **1960** *Textile Terms & Definitions* (Textile Inst.) (ed. 4) 136 *Slashing*,..(1) A synonym for slasher sizing. (2) This term has also been adopted to indicate the process which is used to reduce the extensibility of rayon yarns... The process consists in stretching the yarn in the wet state and then drying it while maintaining the stretched length.

slashing, *ppl. a.* Add: **2.** Also of weapons with cutting edges.

1950 H. L. Lorimer *Homer & Monuments* i. 34 To give better protection against the slashing sword. **1964** C. Willock *Enormous Zoo* ix. 162 Their wrists adorned with semi-circular slashing knives and their fingers with the slashing blades they mount on rings.

3. a. Now used esp. of horses. (Later examples.)

1951 *Sport* 16–22 Mar. 20/2 A big slashing powerful chestnut with powerful limbs to support his considerable weight, he is equally good in front and behind the saddle. **1976** *Horse & Hound* 10 Dec. 8/1 Fred Winter was able to give Bula the run he needed..in Wednesday's Sundew 'Chase, named after the fine, big, slashing chestnut whom he rode to victory in..1957.

c. *spec.* in *Cricket*, playing or played in a vigorous or unrestrained manner. Cf. *slash *v.*^{1} 2 b.

1832 P. Egan *Bk. Sports* 346/1 A free slashing hitter, who holds it a crime To get any less than six runs a time. **1849** *Boy's Own Bk.* 69 Such implements as these [*sc.* the old bats] were but ill adapted even for what is termed 'slashing hitting'. **1885** [see *free *a.* 8 f].

4. (Later examples.) Now chiefly *Austral.*

1861 *Harper's Mag.* Mar. 470/1 Capin Clapp..relaxed his rigid features..as he thought of the 'slashin' cargo we had aboard. **1969** *Telegraph* (Brisbane) 16 May 15/4 Elke Sommer in some slashing fashions takes up crime in this study of computerised skullduggery. **1973** *Ibid.* 16 Aug. 26/3 Who'll win a slashing $700 wardrobe just for looking her smart, bright self?

slat, *sb.*^{1} Add: **4. c.** *pl.* The ribs. *slang* (orig. and chiefly *U.S.*).

1898 H. E. Hamblen *General Manager's Story* 33 There's nothing much the matter with him; few of his slats stove in, that's all. **1911** J. Masefield *Everlasting Mercy* 11 Billy bats Some stinging short-arms in my slats. **1916** C. J. Dennis *Ginger Mick* 28 Why don't ole England belt 'em in the slats? **1928** *New Yorker* 3 Nov. 44/2 When Mr. Kaplan pokes M. de Vos in the slats he (or it) [*sc.* the crowd] halloos rapturously for Mr. Kaplan. **1944** W. Stevens *Let.* 12 Sept. (1967) 473, I want to give the office a kick in the slats. **1976** *Observer* (Colour Suppl.) 29 Feb. 33/1 The crunch probably came with the V & G report where, to my mind unfairly, certain civil servants got a real kick in the slat.

d. *Aeronaut.* The part of an aeroplane wing that is forward of a slot near the leading edge, or that can be moved forward to create such a slot and so provide additional lift. Cf. *slot *sb.*^{2} 2 d.

1931 *Man. Rigging for Aircraft* (H.M.S.O.) (ed. 3) i. 12 Slots are a device for varying the air flow over the surface of an aerofoil, by the use of an auxiliary aerofoil, or slat, set parallel to and in front of the leading edge of the main aerofoil. **1935** C. G. Burge *Compl. Bk. Aviation* 451/2 The slat behind which the slot itself lies is mounted so that it swings forward automatically when an angle of incidence some few degrees below stalling point is reached. **1960** C. H. Gibbs-Smith *Aeroplane* i. xiii. 104 The slotted wing, matured in 1919,..was a device consisting of a curved slat (at first manually operated and then automatic) which was made to project from the leading edge of the wing and thus force air through the resulting slot and over the upper surface of the wing: the effect was to..postpone stalling.

6. b. slat-back *a.* orig. and chiefly *U.S.*, of a chair: having a back constructed of several horizontal ribs (cf. *ladder-back* (*chair*) s.v. *ladder *sb.* 6); also *absol.* as *sb.*; **slat conveyor** (see quot. 1957); **slat fence** *U.S.*, a fence made of slats.

1891 I. W. Lyon *Colonial Furnit. New England* 165 They were called in their day 'bannister back', 'split back', 'slit back', and sometimes 'slat back' chairs. **1904** W. B. Ware *Seats of Colonists* 12 *Slat-back Chair*: Now often known as *Shaker Chair*, is the simplest expression of the *Turned Chair*. **1952** J. Gloag *Short Dict. Furnit.* 434 *Slat back*, a name sometimes used for a primitive form of ladder back chair, with four or five slats between the seat and the top rail: a type made in the countryside. **1976** *Billings* (Montana) *Gaz.* 30 June 4-c/1 (Advt.), Slat-back rocker is constructed of selected hardwoods with an antique pine finish. **1916** G. F. Zimmer *Mech. Handling & Storing* (ed. 2) vii. 101 Slat conveyors are used largely to carry substance in bags, also general merchandise packed in boxes and crates. **1957** J. A. W. Huggill in H. W. Cremer *Chem. Engin. Practice* III. 413 The slat conveyor, for packages, sacks and similar unit loads, has its carrying surface made of wooden or metal slats.., each attached to the chain links. **1790** W. Bentley *Diary* 22 June (1905) I. 180 The Principal Garden is in three parts divided by an open slat fence painted white. **1938** M. K. Rawlings *Yearling* xxxiii. 424 He came to the slat fence. He felt his way along it.

slatch. 1. (Later example.)

1916 T. C. Cantrill et al. *Geol. S. Wales Coalfield* xii. xii. 116 It is probable that the circular or elliptical pockets of coal known as 'slatches' or 'slashes' are the remains or short closed synclinal masses of coal abnormally swollen out by the squeezing-down of the two sides of the syncline.

slate, *sb.*^{1} Add: **1. c.** (Earlier example.)

1854 J. E. Millais *Let.* 25 May in M. Lutyens *Millais & Ruskins* (1967) 216 Ruskin..is certainly *mad* or has a slate loose.

2. b. Also in phrs. *to wipe* (*off*) *the slate, to wipe the slate clean*: to obliterate or cancel a record, usu. of a debt, misdemeanour, etc.; hence *loosely*, to make a fresh start.

1899 [see *active *a.* 4]. **1921** G. B. Shaw *Back to Methuselah* p. lxix, We are helpless before a slate scrawled with figures of National Debts... the sensible thing to do is to wipe the slate and let the wrangling States distribute what they can spare. **1937** A. Huxley *Ends & Means* iv. 27 Where violence is pushed to its limits and the victims are totally exterminated, the slate is wiped clean and the perpetrators of violence are free to begin afresh on their own account. **1960** *Times* 2 Mar. 14/1 Tactically, Wolves must bank on all-out attack to wipe the slate clean. **1973** *Times* 28 Apr. 11/4 What I try to do each year is to wipe the slate clean. 'Now what can I do this year?'

c. For *U.S.* read 'orig. and chiefly *N. Amer.*' and substitute for def.: a list of candidates proposed for election or appointment to an official (esp. political) post; also *transf.*, the group of candidates so nominated; a group of candidates (occas. also of electors) with a set of shared political views. (Earlier and later examples.)

1842 *N.Y. Tribune* 24 Jan. 3/1 The Regency are obliged to put them on the *slate* to be rid of them, and then rub names out at leisure. **1913** R. M. LaFollette *Autobiogr.* 12 Well, the fraternities made their slate and put it through. **1931** W. G. McAdoo *Crowded Years* xii. 182 The Governor had Brandeis on the slate as Secretary of Commerce. **1952** *Manch. Guardian Weekly* 1 May 2/2 There were..nine contests between slates of delegates pledged to Taft and slates pledged to Eisenhower. **1963** *Economist* 2 Nov. 18/1 Electors were originally independent agents, not bound to any party. However, 'slates' of electors soon appeared, usually, though not always, pledged..to one or other of the parties. **1968** *Globe & Mail* (Toronto) 13 Feb. 3/2 The Eglinton Federal Liberal Association last night..selected a complete slate of delegates pledged to vote for Finance Minister Mitchell Sharp at the national Liberal leadership convention. **1970** *New Yorker* 15 Aug. 78/3 Only three slates, or thirty candidates, can be elected. **1972** R. Thomas *Porkchoppers* (1974) xxvi. 230 Cubbin voted without hesitation for himself and his slate. **1976** *National Observer* (U.S.) 12 June 2/2 Uncommitted slates led the voting in the Democratic Presidential primary. **1977** *N.Y. Rev. Bks.* 23 June 19/3 Eliav..who abandoned Labor in 1975, led a socialist and dovish slate ('Sheli') in this election. **1979** *Observer* 27 May 9/2 It was possible to see lists—Labour backbenchers are great ones for lists—giving the 'slates' of the Tribune and Manifesto Groups for the Shadow Cabinet elections.

d. A written record of a debt made when purchase of goods is allowed on credit. Also *fig.*, esp. in phr. *on the slate*, on account. (See also quot. 1909.)

1909 J. R. Ware *Passing Eng.* 188/1 *On the slate* (*Lower Peoples*'), written up against you—from the credit-slate kept in chandlers' shops. **1922** Joyce *Ulysses* 369 Lose your customers that way. Pubs do. Fellows run up a bill on the slate and then slinking around the back streets into somewhere else. **1954** *Sun* (Baltimore) 30 Oct. 1/5 [London] Many food stores are putting the bills 'on the slate' until the men go back to work. **1966** 'J. Hackston' *Father clears Out* 114 The Site Committee..made history by going on the slate and ticking up a few rounds of drinks. **1973** J. Marks *Mick Jagger* (1974) 39 He let them run a slate because they seemed like good sorts. **1980** *Observer* 7 Dec. 3/3 He knew of pharmacists who had been asked to put the bill 'on the slate' by families needing four or five prescriptions.

5. (Earlier example.)

1813 Jane Austen *Let.* 16 Sept. (1952) 327 There was but 2 y^d and a q^r of the dark slate in the Shop, but the Man promised to match it.

6. b. *slate-floored, -hung, -pointed, -roofed.*

1978 J. L. Hensley *Killing in Gold* (1979) xi. 151 The slate-floored entrance hall. **1948** J. Betjeman *Sel. Poems* 116 The slate-hung, goodly-builded house. **1930** J. Dos Passos *42nd Parallel* iv. 292 The shining gray slate-pointed roofs of Quebec. **1960** *Times* 26 Mar. 9/5 Indeed, everything here recalls France—the squares and cobbled streets, the whitewashed walls and dormered slate-pointed houses. **1981** V. Glendinning *Edith Sitwell* xi. 151 A whitewashed slate-roofed village.

d. *slate-grey* (later examples).

1937 *Discovery* Dec. 384/2 Its black or slate-grey body. **1976** *National Observer* (U.S.) 6 Nov. 21 (Advt.), Generously cut in quality wool gabardine—Mid-Fawn, Slate Grey or Lovat.

7. slate-writer, a person who practises slate-writing; **slate-writing,** in spiritualism: writing performed on a slate, attributed to the agency of a medium, but without physical contact of the medium and the writing instrument.

1902 F. Podmore *Mod. Spiritualism* II. iv. ii. 221 Professional slate-writers. **1949** G. B. Shaw *Buoyant Billions* 7 They have a cohort of Slate Writers and Writing Mediums. **1885** *Century Mag.* July 382/2 She can do the trance business, and knocks, and slate-writing, and all that sort of thing. **1898** *Sci. Amer.* 8 Oct. 229/2 There has probably been nothing that has made more converts to spiritualism than the much talked of 'Slate Writing Test'. **1930** H. Carrington *Story of Psychic Science* vi. 147 The majority of messages..have been upon *slates*—hence the former popularity of 'slate-writing' mediums. **1977** B. Inglis *Natural & Supernatural* xxviii. 277 Slade was one of the practitioners of the new technique: slate-writing.

slate, *v.*^{1} Add: **1.** (Later *absol.* example.)

1941 *Cross & Plough* Ladyday 9/2 To shelter him, man had to fell timber,..to burn bricks and tiles, to thatch and to slate.

2. a. (Later examples.) Also const. *to.* Also, to plan, propose, or schedule (an event). Chiefly *U.S.*

1904 F. Lynde *Grafters* xxvii. 343 Griggs was on for the night run eastward with the express; and 'Dutch' Tischer had found himself slated to take the fast mail west. **1936** Wodehouse *Laughing Gas* ix. 94 You ought to be thanking me on your knees for warning you. Yes, sir, unless you pull up mighty quick, you're slated to get yours. **1944** *College Topics* (Univ. of Virginia) 30 Mar. 3 No one has been slated for the 220, but Wenger may run in that event. **1960** *Times* 14 Sept. 12/6, I was intrigued to see this heading in a Charleston paper 'Church Tour slated'... It turned out to be nothing more than the announcement of an annual plantation tour..to raise funds for the local Protestant Episcopal Church. **1966** [see *locomotive *sb.* 4]. **1971** *Wall St. Jrnl.* 22 July w1/2 The Treasury is offering new 7%, 10-year bonds... Other cash-raising moves are also slated. **1973** *Oxf. Mag.* 4 May 10/1 When Americans mean to do something they *slate* it, rather than timetable or table it. When they do *table* it, they don't mean to do it. **1979** *Farmington* (New Mexico) *Daily Times* 27 May 3A/3 Gov. Bruce King and.. Navajo Tribal Chairman Peter MacDonald are slated to attend the ceremony.

b. *spec.* to propose or nominate a candidate for political office; to form a slate (*slate *sb.*^{1} 2 c) of candidates. *U.S.*

1804 J. Pearson *Let.* 26 Nov. in J. Steele *Papers* (1924) I. 441 The Federalists have not, nor do they intend slating a candidate. **1912** T. Dreiser *Financier* xxvii. 297 Stener, although he had served two terms, was slated for re-election. **1961** T. H. White *Making of President 1960* iv. 100 On one huge ballot the Charlestonian was offered *fifty-three* individual choices of candidates if he wished to ponder his selections. Such a mystifying ballot requires simplification..supplied by 'slating'. The local bosses, the union chiefs, the statewide candidates, the education-board candidates, even the veterans organizations, all make cross-alliances to settle on, then print, a 'slate' of approved candidates among the multitude of names.

3. To scrape (a skin or hide) with a slater to remove loosened hairs.

1885 C. T. Davis *Manuf. Leather* xxxii. 527 Upon removal from the bate the skins are 'slated', which is the removal of the fine hair remaining upon the skins after the unhairing operation.

slate-colour. (Earlier and later examples.)

1799 in M. Edgeworth *Parent's Assistant* (1800) VI. 119 Mr. Davis, slate-colour and straw. **1919** E. O'Neill *Rope* in *Moon of Caribbees* 180 The sea is a dark slate color.

slater^1**.** Add: **2.** (Later Austral. and N.Z. examples.)

1951 J. Frame *Lagoon* 45 She collected things, slaters and earwigs and spiders. **1965** *Austral. Encycl.* IX. 349/2 The best-known isopods are the terrestrial forms commonly called wood-lice, slaters, carpenters, or sow-bugs. **1979** *Sunday Mail Color Mag.* (Brisbane) 23 Sept. 21/3 (Advt.), Snails slugs slaters millipedes. Now Baysol kills them all.

3. A blade of slate or the like used for slating skins and hides.

1885 C. T. Davis *Manuf. Leather* xxxii. 527 The 'slater' is a tool closely resembling a 'slicker'; but the edge of the 'slater' is ground sharp.

Slater^3 (slē¹·tə.ɪ). *Physics.* [The name of John C. *Slater* (1900–76), U.S. physicist.] *Slater determinant*: a determinant which expresses the total wave function of an atom and is totally anti-symmetric with respect to an interchange of electrons, the elements being single-electron wave functions.

Described by Slater in *Physical Rev.* (1929) XXXIV. 1293.

1952 *Jrnl. Chem. Physics* XX. 769/1 The wave function of the $^3E_u^-$ state is $|\phi_0\phi_0\phi_1\phi_1\phi_{-1}\phi_{-2}|$ or $|\phi_0\phi_0\phi_{-1}\phi_{-1}\phi_1\phi_2|$, where $|...|$ means a Slater determinant, and the spin is assumed to be suitable for each state. **1964** L. Wilets *Theories Nucl. Fission* iv. 56 A Slater determinant of plane waves replaces the highly correlated true wave function. **1976** *Nature* 28 Oct. 804/2 Such determinants have ever since been known as Slater determinants and have found applications in many fields.

slath (slaþ). = Slat *sb.*^{1} 5 a.

1875 [see Slat *sb.*^{1} 5 a]. **1906** M. Corelli *Treasure of Heaven* 288 He..was now patiently mastering the technical business of forming a 'slath'. **1949** K. S. Woods *Rural Crafts of England* iii. x. 162 A base is woven first, called in the Midlands a 'slath'. **1968** J. Arnold *Shell Bk. Country Crafts* 257 A round or oval one [*sc.* base] is started with the 'slath', an interlaced cross-work of rods of at least four each way, around which the weaving begins.

slather, *v.* For 'Chiefly *dial.*' read 'Chiefly *dial.* and *U.S.*' and add: **2. a.** *trans.* To spill or slop; to scatter. Also, to use in large quantities; to squander; to paste, spread, or smear liberally. Usu. with advbs.

1866 'MARK TWAIN' *Sk. Sixties* (1926) 210 You have slathered too many frivolous sentimental tales into your paper. **1875** —— *Let.* 26 Jan. (1917) I. 247 The partialities of Providence do seem to be slathered around (as one may say). **1876** C. C. ROBINSON *Gloss. Words Dial. Mid-Yorks.* 126/1 *Slather*.., to spill. **1877** F. Ross et al. *Gloss. Words used in Holderness* 128/2 Leeak at him! he's *slatherin* pig-meeat all across hoose fleear. **1895** J. T. CLEGG *Stories, Sk., & Rhymes* 43 Some carless chilt had bin a buyin peawdher blue an' slatthert it. **1904** G. ADE *True Bills* 131 A very Rich Man who wishes to be Respected must fill his Clothes with Currency and go out and slather it around. **1928** PEASE & FAIRFAX-BLAKEBOROUGH *Dict. Dial. N. Riding Yorks.* 118/2 'Eh bud things is slather'd aboot i' that hoos!' 'T'hay an' strae war blawn clean oot o' t'stagarth an' slather'd aboot t'field ayont.' **1937** M. HILLIS *Orchids on your Budget* v. 82 You can get a good make-shift facial by slathering cream on your face after a shampoo. **1954** *Columbia* (S. Carolina) *Record* (Sat. Comic Suppl.) 27 Nov. 6, I got some American toast here, an' I'll gladly slather some jam on to sweeten it up. **1967** E. B. NICKERSON *Kayaks to Arctic* iii. 24 Slather it [*sc.* mosquito repellent] on where common sense indicates, and have confidence. **1978** J. IRVING *World according to Garp* xvii. 363 Perfume, which he remembered Roberta slathering over him.

b. To besmear; to spread or splash liberally on. Usu. with *with*.

1941 W. A. PERCY *Lanterns on Levee* xvi. 184 Another rest-camp, half completed, leaking the ample French rain, slathered with mud, awaited us. **1961** WEBSTER s.v. *slather, Slathering the cars with paint. **1977** *Time* 25 Apr. 17/1 His top chef offers such specialties as veal tongue slathered with *foie gras*. **1979** R. GILLESPIE *Crossword Mystery* iii. 53 She burned painfully. Rocky slathered her externally with Solarcaine.

3. *slang.* To thrash, defeat thoroughly, castigate.

1910 O. JOHNSON *Varmint* viii. 112 He turned on the Coffee-colored Angel and slathered him, drove him hither and thither with terrific blows. *c* **1926** 'MIXER' *Transport Workers' Song Bk.* 36 And all their Simon Puritans Are infused with great delight When an officer is slathered As chair-warmer, parasite. **1968** *Globe & Mail* (Toronto) 13 Feb. 27/1 Canadians can get slathered in Olympic hockey.

slather (slæ·ðəɹ), *sb.* [f. prec.] **1.** *U.S. colloq.* Usu. *pl.* A large amount, lots, lashings.

1857 M. D. SANFORD *Jrnl.* 30 Mar. in D. F. Danker *Mollie* (1959) 6, I believe there are 500 passengers, lots and 'slathers' of young men. **1876** 'MARK TWAIN' *Tom Sawyer* vii. 68 They get slathers of money—most a dollar a day. **1906** *N.Y. Globe* 20 Aug. 6 There is the same slather of indefinite charges. **1966** 'E. LINDALL' *Time too Soon* (1967) vii. 69 What he's giving her I don't want anyway. A whole slather of animal passion. **1970** —— *Gathering of Eagles* vi. 63 They..ate the damper with slathers of sweet, brown treacle.

2. *north.* and *Sc. dial.* Thin mud; a sloppy mass.

1876 C. C. ROBINSON *Gloss. Words Dial. Mid-Yorks.* 126/1 *Slather*, puddle, in a thin state. **1928** PEASE & FAIRFAX-BLAKEBOROUGH *Dict. Dial. N. Riding Yorks.* 118/2 *Slather*.., mud and mess. **1939** A. BORTHWICK *Always Little Further* vi. 126 Two big slabs o' breed wi' a slather o' jam in atween. **1980** J. GARDAM *Sidmouth Lett.* 134 Wear yer wellies or you'll get in a slather int yard.

3. *open slather* (*Austral.* and *N.Z. colloq.*), freedom to operate without interference, a free-for-all.

1919 J. V. MARSHALL *World of Living Dead* 71 They say she's an open slather up there. Not a demon [*sc.* a policeman] in the burg. **1949** J. MORRISON *Creeping City* xxviii. 227 You're asking to be allowed an open slather at an essential public service without being challenged. **1959** G. SLATTER *Gun in Hand* xiii. 180 It's worth a go. Come round, she said, it'll be open slather. **1974** *Sunday Sun* (Brisbane) 1 Sept. 5/1 The beef was marked and butcher shop customers had the opportunity to check the grading... Now it's open slather. **1979** *Financial Rev.* (Austral.) 9 May 5 A problem..was how to prevent an 'open slather' in the sale of tickets.

slating, *vbl. sb.*[1] Add: **4.** The process of removing hairs from skins or hides with a slater. Freq. *attrib.*

1885 C. T. DAVIS *Manuf. Leather* xvi. 313 In many.. tanneries fleshing machines have been tried..in..other tanneries experiments were made to convert them into slating..machines. **1903** L. A. FLEMMING *Pract. Tanning* 12 In some cases it is necessary to work the skins through the slating machine, or upon the beams.

slating, *vbl. sb.*[2] **1.** (Earlier example.)

1860 P. H. RATHBONE in *Trades' Societies & Strikes* 368 The society defended all men prosecuted for trade assaults or 'slatings', as the term was.

‖ **slatko** (slæ·tko). [Serbo-Croatian, lit. sugared fruit.] (See quots.)

1941 'R. WEST' *Black Lamb & Grey Falcon* II. 111 The gallery, here walled in though it is open in most monasteries, where the visitors are given slatko, the ceremonial offering of sugar or jam and glasses of cold water. **1961** *Times* 9 Sept. 11/3 In the hostelry guests.. are offered *slatko*, the ceremonial offering of sugar or jam.

slatted (slæ·tėd), *a.* [f. SLAT *sb.*[1] or *v.*[1] + -ED[2], -ED[1].] Made or furnished with slats.

1886 [see SLAT *v.*[1] 2]. **1948** W. FAULKNER *Intruder in Dust* ix. 180 The truck (it was another pickup; they..had commandeered it, with a slatted cattle frame on the bed). **1960** *Farmer & Stockbreeder* 2 Feb. 82/1 Calves..were housed in individual slatted-floor boxes until seven or eight weeks old. **1968** C. BROOKE-ROSE *Between* 30 The light pours through the slatted shutters making a slatted pattern on the left pale green wall. **1972** *Daily Tel.* 11 July 3/2 A vertically slatted radiator grille..and an XJ12 motif at the back distinguish the new car from the XJ6. **1980** *Amat. Gardening* 4 Oct. 31/3 An advantage of slatted benching against solid trays is that the slats can be opened out to permit better air circulation between the plants.

slaty, *a.* Add: **2.** *slaty cleavage*: see CLEAVAGE 1 c.

4. (Later example.)

1981 *Woman's Jrnl.* Mar. 135/3 Duck is..on the fatty side, so we need a dry, even slaty, wine to accompany it.

5. *slaty-blue* (earlier and later examples).

1854 [see *JACINTH 1 e]. **1975** H. R. F. KEATING *Remarkable Case of Burglary* i. 1 The slaty-blue eyes in his thin pale face.

slaughter, *sb.* Add: **3. a.** (Later *transf.* example.)

1971 *Rand Daily Mail* 27 Mar. 5/3 The slaughter on our roads and damage to property are apparently accepted with equanimity.

4. (Later examples.)

1911 M. BEERBOHM *Zuleika Dobson* viii. 137, I..am going to die for the love I bear this woman. And let no man think I go unwilling. I am no lamb led to the slaughter. **1926** W. R. INGE *Lay Thoughts of Dean* II. ii. 98 The Russians..were driven like sheep to the slaughter, in some cases unarmed, and always insufficiently protected by artillery. **1955** J. MASTERS *Coromandel!* iii. 203 They are on their way now... They will be goats for the slaughter. **1982** *Daily Tel.* 10 Feb. 16/5 The rank-and-file membership of the union are meekly following their so-called leaders like lambs to the slaughter.

9. a. (Further examples.)

1899 C. J. CUTCLIFFE HYNE *Further Adventures of Captain Kettle* v. 123 The foreign crew of the lifeboat, limp with scare, would have been mere slaughter-pigs on board, even if they could have been lured there. **1958** *Johannesburg Sunday Times* 14 Dec. 7/1 The highest price for slaughter stock at the Ladysmith Farmers' Association stock sale last week was £52 10s. **1968** *Globe & Mail* (Toronto) 13 Feb. B10/3 Slaughter cattle of mixed quality. **1977** *West Briton* 25 Aug. 6/1 (Advt.), We have received Ministry approval under this Order for the sale of slaughter sheep and store and breeding sheep on the same day. **1978** *Morecambe Guardian* 14 Mar. 22/1 (Advt.), Usual Sale of Livestock including..Fat Cattle and Slaughter Cows.

b. *slaughter-pen, -yard* (further examples).

1796 *Deb. Congress U.S.* 28 Dec. (1849) 1720 Georgia was a slaughter-pen during the war. **1856** W. G. SIMMS *Charlemont* ii. 27 These lads..raise hogs for the slaughter-pen. **1878** *Rep. Indian Affairs* (U.S.) 151 For the first time in the history of this agency Indians have been induced..to perform the labor of the slaughter-pen. **1928** BLUNDEN *Undertones of War* iv. 37 The casualties caused by the mine were sixty or more. Cuinchy..was a slaughter-yard. **1968** T. KINSELLA *Nightwalker* 28 Pigs in a slaughteryard that turn and savage each other.

slaughter, *v.* Add: **2. b.** To destroy by excessive felling.

1896 *Vermont Agric. Rep.* XV. 85 Our lumber forests are being slaughtered. **1903** S. E. WHITE *Blazed Trail Stories* 27 Fitzpatrick would not have the pine 'slaughtered'.

c. To defeat or demolish completely. *colloq.*

1903 *N.Y. Even. Post* 5 Oct. 3 McLaughlin's lieutenants are openly declaring that they will 'slaughter' the McClellan-Grout-Fornes ticket. **1929** C. E. MERRIAM *Chicago* 280 He was hopelessly beaten..in the primaries of 1907; and again slaughtered..in the primaries of 1915.

slaughterable (slǭ·tərăb'l), *a.* [f. SLAUGHTER *v.* + -ABLE.] That may be slaughtered; fit for slaughter.

1911 *Daily News* 25 Sept. 4 There will simply be a dearth of slaughterable cattle. **1966** *Punch* 17 Aug. 261/3 Even the angriest demon drivers are reduced to the status of slaughterable black sheep.

slaughter-house. Add: **2. a.** (Later *fig.* example.)

1918 [see *cutting-room* s.v. *CUTTING *vbl. sb.* 10].

c. *slang.* A cheap brothel.

1928 E. SUTTON tr. *Londres' Road to Buenos Ayres* vii. 55 She had got into a slaughter-house at two dollars instead of five. **1962** W. FAULKNER *Reivers* viii. 164 Both of you get to hell back to that slaughterhouse.

slaughtery (slǭ·təri). Delete † *Obs.* and add: **1.** (Later example.)

1904 HARDY *Dynasts* I. VI. iii. 196 If it indeed must be That this day Austria smoke with slaughtery, Quicken the issue as Thou knowest how.

2. (Later examples.)

1917 G. J. NICHOLLS *Bacon & Hams* 26 The exporting slaughteries or factories. *Ibid.*, There is appointed to each slaughtery at least one veterinary officer who acts as inspector.

slaum (slǭm), *v. dial.* Also **slorm.** [perh. related to SLIME *sb.*, *v.*[1]; for other uses see *Eng. Dial. Dict.*] *intr.* To slobber, to blubber; also, to flatter obsequiously. Hence **slau·ming** *ppl. a.*, (*a*) muddy, sticky; (*b*) slobbering, obsequiously flattering. Also *vbl. sb.*

1787 W. TAYLOR *Scots Poems* 99 He has a dreadfu' drouth, Whilk *slawmin* canna put awa'. **1904** in *Eng. Dial. Dict.* V. 506/2 The wet maks the road a bit slaumin'. *Ibid.*, Yer needn't come slawmin 'ere, for a don't believe yer. (Notts.) **1911** A. WARRACK *Scots Dict.* 527/1 *Slaum, v.*, to slobber; to blubber; to smear. **1920** D. H. LAWRENCE *Lost Girl* xi. 278 I'd rather have him than your smarmy slormin sort.

slaunchways, -wise (slǭ·ntʃwēɪz, -waiz), *adv.* and *a. U.S. colloq.* Also **slanch-, slawnch-.** [Alteration of SLANTWAYS *adv.*, SLANTWISE *adv.* and *a.*] Slanting(ly), oblique(ly); out of true. Also *fig.*

1913 H. KEPHART *Our Southern Highlanders* xiii. 294 Slaunchways denotes slanting. **1923** *Dialect Notes* V. 236 *Slawnch-wise*, adj., slantwise, slanting, out of true. **1933** *Amer. Speech* VIII. III. 82 A Texas colleague of mine.. said he wanted a full-width bed so that he could lie *slaunchwise* part of the time. **1941** *Sat. Even. Post* 5 Apr. 23/2 The race tide would slap him slanchways pronto. **1944** *Publ. Amer. Dial. Soc.* II. 61 'The road runs *slaunchways* across the field.' 'Don't hold your cup *slaunchways*; you'll spill your coffee.' **1981** *N.Y. Times Mag.* 19 Apr. 10 If you think Professor Cassidy's ideas are slaunchwise or skewhiffy, harass him directly.

Slav, *sb.* Add: **2.** = SLAVONIC *sb.* (Cf. Fr. *slave.*) Also *Comb.*

1924 G. G. WALSH *Emperor Charles IV* iii. 34 The right of the monks, in his presence, to recite the Offices in Slav. **1935** HUXLEY & HADDON *We Europeans* vii. 203 The Slav-speaking population of central Europe. **1972** D. DAKIN *Unification of Greece* 265 The Greek Church and the Greek communities had maintained schools where even the Slav-speaking Orthodox could acquire a knowledge of Greek.

‖ **slava** (slā·vă). [Serbo-Croatian, lit. honour, renown.] A festival of a family saint in Yugoslavia, a name-day.

1900 'ODYSSEUS' *Turkey in Europe* viii. 372 The Slava, or festival of the family saint. **1920** *Glasgow Herald* 6 July 9 They told us of that country beyond, with its mountains and rivers, its peasant homes, its Slavas and songs of heroes—an Arcadia in truth. **1970** J. BROWN *Un-melting Pot* v. 76 The household gods have had a central place in Yugoslav life since pre-Christian times and families today still have their household saints and keep their slava—their annual family days. **1976** *New Yorker* 22 Mar. 68/3 He remembers the priest blessing the house on his father's *slava*, or name day.

slave, *sb.*[1] (and *a.*) Add: **I. 1. d.** *Slave of the Lamp*, in the story of Aladdin in the *Arabian Nights*: a genie summoned by rubbing a magic lamp and bound to perform the wishes of the lamp's possessor; hence, allusively, one who performs swift miracles, or one who is under an inescapable obligation.

c **1840** LADY WILTON *Art of Needlework* xv. 238 The accommodations provided for the king..on this occasion [*sc.* The Field of Cloth of Gold] were more than magnificent; a vast and splendid edifice that seemed..to rise almost with the celerity of that prepared by the slaves of the lamp. **1841** DICKENS *Let.* 1 July (1969) II. 319, I am bound to be..constant to my plans. I am a poor Slave of the Lamp. **1853** C. BRONTË *Villette* II. xxi. 90, I almost looked to see if a huge, dark, cloudy hand—that of the Slave of the Lamp—were not..guarding its wondrous treasure. **1897** KIPLING *Stalky & Co* (1899) 38 (*title*) Slaves of the Lamp. **1953** E. COXHEAD *Midlanders* v. 120 Their working life was a deadening one. They were as near as possible machines themselves, slaves of the implacable lamp. **1959** *Encounter* Aug. 67/2 The physical scientist..is the magician. He is the contemporary equivalent of that old friend of our children, the Slave of the Lamp. Which means that he is very much an underling: he makes his magic at the command of his masters.

4*. Applied to a thing. **a.** *Naut.* = *slave jib*, sense 9 below.

1934 *Yachting Monthly* LVII. 119/2 These craft [*sc.* Bristol Channel pilot cutters], when in the pilot service, carried a heavy mainsail roped up the leech, a heavy staysail with two sets of reef points, and a working jib, generally known as 'the slave'. **1970** E. MARCH *Inshore Craft* II. vii. 263 A 'slave' slightly larger [than the storm jib] and so called because it was almost permanently set.

b. A slave device (see sense 5 c below).

1940 F. HOPE-JONES *Electr. Timekeeping* (1942) xvi. 156 Using a remontoire impulse as a synchronizing signal to control a Graham dead-beat escapement clock employed as a slave. **1965** *Jrnl. Scientific Instruments* XLII. 444/2 The whole seconds of the slave and chronometer can be matched regardless of the position of synchronization. **1969** J. J. SPARKES *Transistor Switching* v. 129 Which flip-flop is called the master and which the slave is quite arbitrary. **1975** D. PITTS *Target Manhattan* (1976) xxix. 126 'The first move is to get hold of that master computer.'..'That would stop the explosion?' 'It will if they haven't given final instructions to the slave.'

II. 5. a. *slave-boy, -girl* (later examples), *-labourer, woman.*

1848 MILL *Pol. Econ.* I. II. v. 294 No slave-labourers are worse fed, clothed, or lodged, than the free peasantry of Ireland. **1897** M. KINGSLEY *Trav. W. Afr.* iii. 70, I have myself seen..slave women who had suffered for theft. **1920** J. MASEFIELD *Enslaved* 13 They took my lady with them as a slave-girl to be sold. **1957** H. ROOSENBURG *Walls came tumbling Down* iv. 79 The Nazis had used Russian and Polish POWs as slave labourers.

1962 H. R. Loyn *Anglo-Saxon England* i. 34 From this district [of Yorkshire] came the slave-boys seen and questioned by Pope Gregory in the Roman slave-market. **1977** P. Johnson *Enemies of Society* ii. 15 We find the great fourth-century senator, Symmachus.., asking a Danubian official to buy him twenty slave-boys, 'because on the frontier it is easy to find slaves and the price is usually tolerable'. **1980** F. Warner *Light Shadows* ii. 10, I gave the Emperor that slave-girl, Acte.

c. *techn.* Used to denote a subsidiary device, *esp.* one which is controlled by, or which follows accurately the movements of, another device.

1904 D. Gill in *Rep. H.M. Astronomer at Cape of Good Hope for 1903* 7 The Clock consists of two separate instruments:—(a) A pendulum... (b) The 'slave-clock' with a wheel train and dead-beat escapement, the pendulum of which has a period of vibration slightly shorter than one second. **1930** *Engineering* 11 Apr. 466/2 A micrometer.. bearing against a 'slave' micrometer introduced to allow of the main one being set to a zero reading anywhere over a considerable range. **1938** *Jrnl. R. Aeronaut. Soc.* XLII. 907 This is a double acting liquid pressure remote control system having a number of slave cylinder units fed from a common source of pressure... The slave cylinders are arranged to effect a number of operations in a predetermined sequence when pressure is fed through one pipe line. **1945** *Electronics* Nov. 94/1 (*caption*) Master and slave stations transmit synchronized pulses, and the difference in their times of arrival determines the position of the ship or aircraft. **1963** *Wall St. Jrnl.* 13 Feb. 20/1 The 'slave' locomotive..is being tested... The 'slave' would ride in the middle of a train perhaps 200 cars long; automatic sensing devices would keep it pulling the back end of such a train in rhythm with the manned master locomotive up front. **1972** *Amat. Photographer* 12 Jan. 41/1 (*caption*) A slave flash... This gun can be clipped anywhere and will trigger its own bulb, being actuated by the flash from another bulb gun. **1976** *Pract. Householder* Nov. (Heating Suppl.) 2/1 A houseful of remote slave units (electronic, of course) and a central control system is no longer eccentric gadgetry. **1977** *Grimsby Even. Tel.* 27 May 3/9 (Advt.), 100 watt slave amplifier, £40. **1980** Keene & Haynes *Spyship* xiii. 152 With this information, beamed off a slave satellite.., set and drift can be measured.

6. a. *slave labour* (earlier examples), *-master, song, work.*

1820 *Deb. Congr. U.S.* 9 Feb. (1855) 1213 Free labor and slave labor cannot be employed together. **1842** Dickens *Amer. Notes* II. i. 16 The system of employing a great amount of slave labour in forcing crops. **1822** *Sunday Times* 20 Oct. 1/4 The Continental Monarchs were but so many slave-masters. **1869** Mill *Subj. Women* iii. 142 Servitude, except when it actually brutalizes, though corrupting to both, is less so to the slaves than to the slave-masters. **1924** W. Deeping *Three Rooms* ii. 16 His manner towards women was Oriental, playfully and tolerantly casual, but behind it was the thick hand of the slave-master. **1971** *Black Scholar* June 11/1 We were so abhorrent to our slavemasters that legal barriers were instituted to prevent the natural process of assimilation. **1881** *Harper's Mag.* May 818/2 The plaintive slave songs..have won popularity wherever the English language is spoken. **1939** *Jrnl. Negro Educ.* VIII. 641/2 The slave song was an awesome prophecy, rooted in the knowledge of what was going on and of human nature, and not in mystical lore. **1973** *Advocate-News* (Barbados) 19 Feb. 4/4 He sang an old slave song his grandmother had taught him. **1916** D. H. Lawrence *Twilight in Italy* 303 Life is now a matter of selling oneself to slave-work. **1926** J. Pedersen *Israel, its Life & Culture* I. II. 381 They..set him to the ignominious slave-work of grinding in the prison house.

b. *slave block, camp, house, pen* (further examples), *pit, quarter.*

1907 Kipling *Actions & Reactions* (1909) 188 The Hajji had often gloatingly appraised his skill..at five thousand rupees upon any slave block. **1966** *Keystone Folklore Q.* XI. 74 She was only eight when she was sold on the slave block. **1953** K. Tennant *Joyful Condemned* xxii. 208 Men all over the world making weary marches to prison camps and slave camps. **1973** R. Dougall *In & out of Box* xi. 127 The great bulk of the work was carried out manually by wretched, scarecrow figures dressed in rags... They were gangs from the notorious Stalin slave camps in the Arctic. **1939** J. Masefield *Live & Kicking Ned* 145 Inside the slave-house. **1943** H. T. Kane *Bayous of Louisiana* III. 256 A barn and a few slave houses are all that can be found today of the former grandeur of the Durands, among the trees. **1901** W. Churchill *Crisis* I. iv. 35 A score of miserable human beings waiting to be sold at auction. Mr. Lynch's slave pen had been disgorged that morning. **1951** E. M. Graham *My Window looks down East* x. 86 In the cellar they have a slavepen. **1931** *Times Lit. Suppl.* 4 June 440/3 Characteristic..are the winding entrance gangways, a feature..in the..'slave pits'. **1959** J. D. Clark *Prehist. Southern Africa* xi. 302 These pits have been popularly referred to as 'Slave pits' suggesting that they were the places where slaves were confined on their journey from the interior to the coast. This explanation is, however, more fanciful than factual. **1982** *Evening Post* (Bristol) 19 Jan. 12 (Advt.), 2 further rooms and basement, with slave pit. **1837** H. Martineau *Society in America* II. i. 49 The slave-quarter is large. **1911** G. B. Shaw *Getting Married* Pref. 160 The people whose conception of marriage is a farm-yard or slave-quarter conception are always more or less in a panic lest the slightest relaxation of the marriage laws should utterly demoralize society. **1956** G. P. Kurath in A. F. C. Wallace *Men & Cultures* (1960) 152 The hot rhythms of jazz..have emerged from slave quarters..to respectable society. **1981** P. Mallory *Killing Matter* vii. 82, I bought some groceries..and, once inside my undistinguished slave-quarter, made myself a drink.

c. *slave-class.*

1935 Huxley & Haddon *We Europeans* ix. 279 A slave-class..of markedly different ethnic type from their masters. **1977** W. M. Spackman *Armful of Warm Girl* 108 No birthright Philadelphia Quaker ever bothered his head over their slave-class preoccupation with the safety of their unappetizing souls.

7. a. (Later examples.)

1939 J. Masefield *Live & Kicking Ned* 71 A white slave who knew medicine might be worth double that to a slave-owner. **1946** *Nature* 2 Nov. 607/2 Slave-raiders were exhausting a wasting asset, the chief export of tropical Africa. **1957** V. W. Turner *Schism & Continuity in Afr. Soc.* vi. 193 The mechanisms which formerly maintained the norms governing the relations of slave-owners and slaves could no longer operate. **1973** *Black World* Oct. 68/2 Unable to live in the slave-holder's kingdom, Walker fled to Boston. **1982** *English World-Wide* III. I. 19 A majority of the planters attempted to surmount the moral conflict inherent in being a slave-holder.

b. *slave-holding* (earlier and later examples), *-making* (later examples), *-owning* (earlier and later examples).

1798 *Deb. Congr. U.S.* 29 June (1851) 2058 At present the slaveholding parts of the State are burdened with the heaviest part of the State taxes. **1959** D. K. Wilgus *Anglo-Amer. Folksong Scholarship* 353 White songs in the slave-holding areas. **1928** Slave-making [see *dulosis]. **1944** J. S. Huxley *On Living in Revolution* 61 The raids of the slave-making ants are..a curious combination of predation and parasitism. **1977** Richards & Davies *Imms' Gen. Textbk. Ent.* (ed. 10) II. III. 1243 Slave-making ants are confined to the northern hemisphere and are members of four genera only. **1828** J. F. Cooper *Notions of Americans* II. xiii. 296 The confederation is nearly equally divided into slave-owning, and what are called free states. **1934** E. O'Neill *Days without End* I. 34 They..had supplanted Him [*sc.* Almighty God] with the slave-owning State—the most grotesque god that ever came out of Asia! **1971** *Black Scholar* June 3/1 The human capital of the slave-owning class.

c. *slave-dealing* (earlier example), *-holding* (earlier example), *-raiding.*

1835 J. E. Alexander *Sk. in Portugal* ix. 212 Many of the governors have held office solely for the purpose of enriching themselves by slave-dealing. **1841** J. Sturge *Let.* 30 June in *Visit to U.S. in 1841* (1842) 33 If slave-holding were to be justified at all, the slave-trade must be also. **1933** A. N. Whitehead *Adv. of Ideas* iii. 34 Mediaeval wars were dissociated from slave-raiding expeditions. **1957** V. W. Turner *Schism & Continuity in Afr. Soc.* p. xx, The slave-trading and -raiding of the nineteenth century.

9. slave ant = sense 4 in Dict.; **slave bangle, bracelet** orig. *U.S.*: formerly, a slave's identity bracelet worn on the wrist or ankle; now, a bandle of metal, glass, bone, etc., worn for ornament, freq. above the elbow; **slave jib** *Naut.* (see quot.); **slave king** *Indian Hist.*, one of a dynasty founded by a former slave, Qutb uddin Aibak, which ruled the Delhi Sultanate from 1206 to 1290; usu. *pl.*; **slave-maker,** an ant belonging to a species that uses ants of a different species as slaves; **slave market,** a market at which slaves are bought and sold; also *fig.*, esp. (*N. Amer. slang*) an employment exchange; **slave morality** [tr. G. *sklaven-moral* (Nietzsche, *Jenseits von Gut und Böse* (1886) 231)], a morality characteristic of the weak, and rooted in resentment of the powerful, that exalts the lowly virtues of meekness, obedience, etc.; **slave worker,** in the war of 1939–45: a person put to enforced labour by the German Nazi regime, esp. a foreigner deported to Germany for this purpose.

1862 *Chambers's Jrnl.* 15 Feb. 97/2 Reaumur discovered how the ants of South America sally forth to kidnap hundreds of the black 'slave ants'. **1895** J. H. & A. Comstock *Man. Study Insects* 641 The Slave-ant, *Formica subsericea*..is usually a dark-brown or ash-colored ant with reddish legs. **1923** U. L. Silberrad *Lett. Jean Armiter* ii. 33 A green-glass slave bangle. **1931** N. Cunard *Black Man & White Ladyship* 4 The thick old Congo ivories she thinks, are slave bangles. **1975** D. Gray *Ride on Tiger* ii. 20 She wore..a silver slave bangle on her right arm. **1934** Webster, Slave bracelet. **1940** R. Chandler *Farewell, My Lovely* xxi. 164 An emerald.. that..managed to look as phony as a dime-store slave bracelet. **1976** Botham & Donnelly *Valentino* xxii. 169 Her special gift for her husband—a platinum slave bracelet. **1948** R. de Kerchove *Internat. Maritime Dict.* 685/2 *Slave jib*, a term used by yachtsmen to denote a working jib, almost permanently set. **1841** M. Elphinstone *Hist. India* II. VI. i. 1 (*heading*) Slave kings. **1882** W. W. Hunter *Indian Empire* ix. 223 Kutab-ud-dín had started life as a Túrkí slave, and several of his successors rose by valour or intrigue from the same low condition to the throne. His dynasty is accordingly known as that of the Slave Kings. **1958** O. Caroe *Pathans* i. 17 The slave-kings who followed them in Delhi were, every one, a Turk. **1971** *Illustr. Weekly India* 11 Apr. 55/1 Following Mohammed Ghori's establishment in Delhi, we had several dynasties of Muslim rulers like the so-called Slave Kings. **1859** Slave-maker [in Dict., sense 7 a]. **1915** H. St. J. K. Donisthorpe *Brit. Ants* 282 *Formica sanguinea*, the blood-red Robber Ant, our only slave-maker, is one of the most interesting species, showing great intelligence in adapting its habits to varying circumstances. **1978** *Nature* 16 Mar. 209/1 Wilson surveys a range of behaviour including that of 'slavemaker' ants who have become dependent on workers of other species. **1835** W. E. Channing *Slavery* iv. 87 Slave-markets.. turn to mockery the language of freedom in the halls of Congress. **1838, 1871** [in Dict., sense 6 b]. **1911** G. B. Shaw *Getting Married* Pref. 179 We are in the slave-market, where the conception of our relations to the persons sold is..simply commercial. **1931** 'D. Stiff' *Milk & Honey Route* 214 *Slave market*, that part of the main stem where jobs are sold. **1960** *Voice of Idle Worker* (Vancouver) 8 Feb. 2/2 The chances are that he will be a regular customer at the slave market for a few months. **1907** H. Zimmern tr. *Nietzsche's Beyond Good & Evil* ix. 227 In a tour through the many finer and coarser moralities which have hitherto prevailed or still prevail on the earth, I found certain traits recurring regularly together and connected with one another, until finally two primary types revealed themselves to me, and a radical distinction was brought to light. There is *master-morality* and *slave-morality*. **1907** G. B. Shaw *Major Barbara* Pref. 153 Nietzsche..regarded the slave-morality as having been..imposed on the world by slaves making a virtue of necessity and a religion of their servitude. Mr Stuart-Glennie regards the slave-morality as an invention of the superior white race to subjugate the minds of the inferior races whom they wished to exploit. **1960** J. O. Urmson *Conc. Encycl. Western Philos.* 282/2 It deals at length with slave morality which contrasts good and *evil*. **1946** *Ann. Reg. 1945* 185 The all-overshadowing event after the collapse of Nazi Germany was the liberation of the concentration camps and the huge army of foreign slave-workers in Germany. **1956** I. Serraillier *Silver Sword* vii. 47 Everyone over twelve had to register, and he would almost certainly have been carried off to Germany as a slave worker. **1971** P. D. James *Shroud for Nightingale* viii. 264 [They] were Jewish slave workers in Germany..they were given lethal injections.

Slave (slē[i]v), *sb.*[2] Also **Slavey;** 9 **Slavé, Slavi.** [tr. Cree *awahkān* captive, slave; the disyllabic Eng. forms reflect a local jargon var. with Fr. suffix *-ais.*] (A member of) a grouping of Athapascan-speaking North American Indians living in the boreal forest region of northwestern Canada; the language of this people. Also *attrib.* or as *adj.*

1789 A. MacKenzie *Let.* 22 May in L. R. Masson *Les Bourgeois de la Compagnie du Nord-Ouest* (1889) 30 (*Récits* section), Mr. Leroux arrived on the 22nd March from the other side of Slave Lake where he had seen a great number of Red Knives and Slave Indians. **1801** —— *Voyages from Montreal* (1903) I. viii. 340 When this country was formerly invaded by the Knisteneaux, they found the Beaver Indians inhabiting the land about Portage la Roche; and the adjoining tribe were those whome they called slaves. They drove both these tribes before them; when the latter proceeded down the river from the Lake of the Hills, in consequence of which that part of it obtained the name of the Slave River. **1851** J. Richardson *Arctic Searching Exped.* I. viii. 242 The comfort, and not unfrequently the lives, of parties of the timid Slave or Hare Indians are sacrificed. **1862** R. G. Latham *Elements Comparative Philol.* lv. 391 The *Beaver* Indian is transitional to the Slave and the Chepewyan proper. **1875** H. H. Bancroft *Native Races Pacific States* III. 587 A greater divergence from the stock language is observable in the dialect of the Tutchone Kutchin, which, with those of..the Slavé of Francis Lake..might almost be called a dialectic division of the Tinneh language. **1890** W. C. Bompas (*title*) Hymns in the Tenni or Slavi language. **1907** F. W. Hodge *Handbk. Amer. Indians N. of Mexico* I. 440 Petitot restricted the term [*sc.* Etchareottine] to the Etcheridiegottine, whom he distinguished from the Slaves proper. **1932** D. Jenness *Indians of Canada* xxiii. 390 In summer the Slave lived in conical lodges covered with brush or spruce bark. **1938** E. M. North *Bk. Thousand Tongues* 870/1 *Slave...* Spoken by Indians living along the Mackenzie River, northwestern Canada. **1946** J. J. Honigmann *Ethnogr. & Acculturation of Fort Nelson Slave* 16 He is married to a Slave woman and in his cultural affiliations and background is more Slave than Cree. **1959** E. Tunis *Indians* x. 132 There was a group, the Etchaottine (Slaves), who were kind to old people. **1974** *Sunday Tel.* 18 Aug. 5/5 In the Territorial Capital of Yellowknife barmen have noticed a substantial reduction in the number of Dogribs seeking drink—and a corresponding increase in the number of Indians claiming to be members of the Chepewyan and Slavey tribes. **1979** M. E. Krauss in Campbell & Mithun *Languages of Native Amer.* 862 These are all to a significant degree mutually intelligible, with Dogrib being the most divergent (not counting Slavey). **1981** *Handbk. N. Amer. Indians* VI. 79 No convenient name for this language exists, although Slave or Slavey was in 1980 commonly used as a self-designation by most speakers of Mountain, Bearlake, and Hare, as well as of Slavey proper.

slave, *v.*[1] Add: **1. d.** *techn.* To subject (a device) to control or regulation by another device. Const. *to* the device.

1952 [see *manipulator 2 f]. **1958** C. C. Adams *Space Flight* v. 132 The camera is synchronized with the National Bureau of Standards radio transmitter WWV, whose chief function is to broadcast time signals of incredible accuracy... It does this by means of a crystal clock..which is 'slaved' to WWV. **1978** *Broadcast* 21 Aug. 5/3 (Advt.), Picture stabilization provided by an oscillating mirror slaved to the film perforations.

2. a. (Later example.)

1925 E. O'Neill *Compl. Wks.* II. 154 Didn't he slave Maw t' death?

slaved, *ppl. a.* Add: **3.** With prep., as *slaved-for. rare.*

1952 Dylan Thomas *Coll. Poems* 132 My paid-for slaved-for own.

sla·ve-drive, *v.* [Back-formation from next.] *intr.* To exploit slave labour; to demand hard or servile labour. Also *trans.*, to demand an excessive amount of work from (a person). So **sla·ve-driven** *ppl. a.*, **sla·ve-driving** *ppl. a.* and *vbl. sb.*

1830 *Reg. Deb. Congr. U.S.* 10 May 939/1 Here they may live and flourish, until some slave-driving politician and planter of South Carolina..again chains them to a miserable dependence on South Carolina cotton and British looms. **1836** *Blackw. Mag.* Oct. 562/1 Ye slave driving hosts of factory and poor law commissioners. **1859** J. B. JONES *Wild Southern Scenes* vi. 46 The reason alleged was his alliance with the 'slave-driving' Blounts of the South. **1878** G. MEREDITH *Lett.* (1970) II. 565, I hope to propose myself to you for a night in January. At present I have the Devil behind me slave-driving. **1889** Slave-driving [in Dict. s.v. SLAVE *sb.* (and *a.*) 7 c]. **1889** G. B. SHAW in *Star* 1 June 4/1 Bully him; slave-drive him. **1933** Slave-driven [see *medium close-up* s.v. *MEDIUM B. 3 d]. *a* **1935** T. E. LAWRENCE *Mint* (1955) II. xiv. 136 Corporal Hemmings again supervised the gymnasium-work today. He slave-drove us as usual. **1952** E. O'NEILL *Moon for Misbegotten* I. 13 He's gone like Thomas and John before him to escape your slave-driving. **1957** W. CAMP *Prospects of Love* II. v. 61 You're not to let her slave-drive you. **1982** P. FITZGERALD *At Freddie's* iv. 32 There was no need for her to go back... Indeed it was probably a mistake, and might give Freddie the notion that slave-driving encourages slavery.

sla·ve-driver. orig. *U.S.* [SLAVE *sb.* + DRIVER.] An overseer of slaves; *transf.* an exacting taskmaster.

1807 *Salmagundi* 13 Feb. 42 Beautiful, Oh most puissant slave-driver, as are my wives, they are exceeded by the women of this country. **1828** *Athenæum* 29 Feb. 162/2 The scourge shall no longer sound among the Antilles, nor the image of God be trampled by the slave-driver into the likeness of the beasts that perish. **1830**, etc. [in Dict. s.v. SLAVE *sb.* (and *a.*) 7 a]. **1854** THOREAU *Walden* 10 It is..worst of all when you are the slave-driver of yourself. **1857** T. B. GUNN *Physiol. N.Y. Boarding-Houses* xv. 127 He'd been an overseer—or, as they termed it, *slave-driver*—down South. **1901** MERWIN & WEBSTER *Calumet 'K'* x. 189 Do you think it would be worth something to the men who hire you for a dirty slave-driver to be protected from a strike? **1922** E. O'NEILL *Hairy Ape* iii. 32 Bloody slave-driver! **1948** H. L. MENCKEN *Amer. Lang.* Suppl. II. 674 The [prison] guards are *shields, screws,..slave-drivers* or *herders.* **1975** *Investors Chron.* 28 Feb. 589/1 He is not a slave driver but somehow generates an extremely hard-working atmosphere.

slavey[1]. **1.** Delete † *Obs.* and add later examples.

1901 M. FRANKLIN *My Brilliant Career* xvii. 141 Harold Beecham kept a snivelling little Queensland black boy as a sort of black-your-boots, odd-jobs slavey or factotum. **1967** *Atlantic Monthly* Apr. 103/2 All his years a loyal slavey he had worked his heart out for peanuts.

Slavey, var. *SLAVE *sb.*[2] **Slavi,** obs. var. *SLAVE *sb.*[2]

Slavic, *sb.* Add: **a.** (Earlier examples.)

1812 A. MURRAY *Let.* 8 Aug. in T. Constable *A. Constable* (1873) I. 333, I wish, however, to have about 100 or 150 printed pages additional on the Latin, Slavic, Persic, and Celtic. **1850** [see *Church Slavic* s.v. *CHURCH *sb.* 18].

b. *Comb.*, as *Slavic-speaking* adj.

1942 *Amer. Council of Learned Societies Bull.* No. 34. 58 (*heading*) The Slavic-speaking groups of the United States and Canada. **1980** *Word 1979* XXX. 19 Albanians in Yugoslavia are classified as a nationality (*narodnost*) within a population consisting predominantly of Slavic-speaking peoples.

Slavicist (slā·v-, slæ·visist). [f. SLAVIC *sb.* + -IST.] = SLAVIST[2].

1930 K. MALONE in *Stud. in Honor of H. Collitz* 328 *Slavist*..actually has two meanings:..(2) an authority on Slavic, and for the second meaning *Slavicist* would be a more appropriate term. **1964** *Slavic Rev.* XXIII. 707 There does not seem to be an organized correlation between trained Slavicists and potentially available posts. **1976** *Language* LII. 108 Most Slavicists agree on two cardinal classes of denominal qualitative adjectives.

slavikite (slæ·vīkəit). *Min.* [ad. Czech. *slavíkit* (Jirkovský & Ulrich 1926, in *Věstník Státního Geol. Ústavu Česk. Repub.* II. 345), f. the name of František *Slavík* (1876–1957), Czech mineralogist: see -ITE[1].] A trigonal greenish-yellow hydrated basic sulphate of ferric iron found as an oxidation product of pyrite and usu. containing additional magnesium and sodium.

1927 *Mineral. Abstr.* III. 365 This mineral, named slavíkite (after the abstractor), forms minute, almost microscopic, crystals with the rhombohedron (10$\bar{1}$1) and the base (0001) equally developed, or tabular parallel to (0001). **1957** *Ibid.* XIII. 369 Slavikite..associated with gypsum, pickeringite, and jarosite, occurs in Belgium at Stavelot on Revinian phyllites and at Val-Dieu on Famennian sandstone. **1968** I. KOSTOV *Mineral.* 500 Slavikite is trigonal, found in minute uniaxial negative crystals tabular on {0001}.

slaving, *vbl. sb.* Add: **2.** The automatic control or regulation of one device by another.

1960 *How TV Works* ii. 17/2 This technique—known by the jargon of 'slaving'—ensures that the programmes sent out from the transmitters are no less excellent in quality when they originate from very distant studios. **1974** *Some Technical Terms & Slang* (Granada Television), *Slaving*, interlocking electronic signals between disparate sources.

Slavistic. Add: In *pl.*, Slav linguistic studies.

1956 *Archivum Linguisticum* VIII. II. 176 Slavic synchronic comparative grammar, a branch of Slavistics which does not yet exist. **1965** [see *JAT' *sb.*[3]].

Slavo-. a. *Slavo-Lithuanian* (earlier example).

1874 H. BENDALL tr. *Schleicher's Compar. Gram.* I. 7 Teutonic and Sclavo-Lithuanian.

slavocracy. (Earlier example.)

1840 *Illinois State Reg.* (Springfield) 22 Jan. 2/2 The reign of the slaveocracy is hastening to a close.

slavocrat. (Earlier example.)

1842 S. M. GATES *Let.* 24 Jan. in J. G. Birney *Lett.* (1938) II. 666 Some Slaveocrats in Georgia have lately attempted to cast odium upon Mr. Adams.

Slavonian, *a.* Add: **2.** *Slavonian oak*, the silvery timber of a European oak, esp. *Quercus robur* or *Q. petræa*, grown in the Slavonian region of Yugoslavia.

1938 E. H. P. BOULTON *Dict. Wood* 127 Oak, Slavonian... Similar to English Oak but softer. **1956** *Handbk. of Hardwoods* (Forest Prod. Res. Lab.) 167 Slavonian oak, from Yugoslavia, is typically of slow, even growth, has a uniform colour and straight grain, and is mild and easy to work. **1966** A. W. LEWIS *Gloss. Woodworking Terms* 106 Slavonian oak (throughout Europe).

slaw. For *U.S.* read *N. Amer.* and add: (Earlier and later examples.) Also, any dish the main ingredient of which is sliced cabbage.

1794, etc. [see *COLD-SLAW]. **1861** T. WINTHROP *Cecil Dreeme* 157 Pad of butter. Plate of slaw, ready vinegared. **1905** *N.Y. Even. Post* 23 Sept. 2 Mince pie, hokey-pokey ice cream, over-ripe watermelon, frankfurters with hot slaw—all the less expensive and less desirable articles of diet go to stunt the gamin's growth. **1916** *Chambers's Jrnl.* Feb. 143/1 In Canada it [*sc.* celery cabbage] is used for cold slaw. **1944** *Sun* (Baltimore) 1 Nov. 10/7 It was customary in his family in his boyhood to serve a 'hot slaw' with turkey, the slaw consisting of cabbage cooked with vinegar and sugar. **1977** *National Observer* (U.S.) 22 Jan. 9/1 If she craves tossed salad when the price of lettuce is high, she resolutely buys cabbage and makes slaw instead.

slawnchwise, var. *SLAUNCHWAYS, -WISE *adv.* and *a.*

slay, sley, *sb.*[1] Add: **2. slay sword,** each of the supports upon which the slay of a loom oscillates during the process of weaving.

1895 R. MARSDEN *Cotton Weaving* v. 166 The shaft is cranked, and by means of arms from these cranks is attached to the 'slay' or lathe..which oscillates upon the 'slay-swords'. **1963** A. J. HALL *Textile Sci.* iii. 142 This reed is fastened to the sley sword *S*, which is pivoted..so that as required it can swing to and from position *X* after the insertion of each weft thread.

slay, *v.*[1] Add: **II. 5.** *fig.* (Further examples.) *esp.* To overwhelm with delight, to convulse (someone) with laughter. Cf. *KILL *v.* 6 a.

1863 G. MEREDITH *Let.* May (1970) I. 203, I have lately been slain by a pretty face. **1927** L. MAYER *Just between Us Girls* i. 2 Well, anyways, my dear, it simply slayed me. **1937** *Amer. Speech* XII. 181 (*heading*) Satchelmouth slays 'em. **1943** H. A. SMITH *Life in Putty Knife Factory* xiii. 225 The boys who slay me..are the ones who have set pieces to recite when they answer the phone. **1953** R. CHANDLER *Long Good-Bye* xi. 68 A hoodlum with sentiment... That slays me. **1958** *Spectator* 21 Nov. 728/1 Frost,..reading naturally and roughly but with a high degree of contrivance, slaying them into calls for encores and favourite poems. **1965** D. FRANCIS *Odds Against* xi. 150 'Oh God, Dolly, you slay me,' said Chico, laughing warmly. **1975** D. O'SULLIVAN in D. Marcus *Best Irish Short Stories* (1977) II. 98 They're fun... They'll slay you! **1977** *Guardian Weekly* 23 Oct. 4/3 The earliest comment on these lines that I can find comes from Denis Thatcher in October, 1970. 'Who could meet Margaret..without being completely slain by her personality and intellectual brilliance?'

slean (slīn), var. SLANE.

1951 *Engineering* 6 Apr. 389/2 'Sleans' are used to cut the peat. **1976** J. HAYES *Missing* (1977) v. 203 The man's had his slean out for me since we cut the turf together... Had me unfrocked, he did. **1977** J. HODGINS *Invention of World* iii. 74 When some turf-cutter drives his slean into the peat in that desolate valley [etc.].

sleaze (slīz), *sb. slang.* [Back-formation from SLEAZY, SLEEZY *a.*] **1.** Squalor; sordidness, sleaziness; dilapidation; (something of) inferior quality or low moral standards. Also *attrib.*

1967 *Listener* 14 Sept. 326/2 For all its brazen sleaze, Soho is a pretty fair working model of what a city neighbourhood should be. **1975** *Publishers Weekly* 29 Dec. 68/2 Obviously written to cash in on 'Mandingo', this isn't even readable sleaze: the plot's sloppy, Gilchrist hasn't the knack for writing commercial sex, and the hero is too despicable to be seductive. **1976** *National Observer* (U.S.) 17 July 16 (*heading*) At home with the sleaze king. **1981** *New Yorker* 9 Mar. 104/1 These stores are vast, computerized sleaze centers, where you can buy almost anything—pills, toys, candy, liquor, stockings, pillows, and gadgetry.

2. A person of low moral standards.

1976 *Telegraph* (Brisbane) 3 Aug. 10/3 When I made the mistake of calling them 'sleazy' to their faces, their reaction was outrage. 'Don't call me a sleaze,' said Miss Currie. **1977** *Time* 28 Feb. 48/1 Oh God, red nail polish—I look like a sleaze.

sleaze, sleeze (slīz), *v.* [f. as prec.] **1.** *dial.* (See quots.) ? *Obs.*

1777 in *Eng. Dial. Dict.* **1825** J. JENNINGS *Observations on Some of Dialects in W. of England* 69 *To sleeze*,..to separate; to come apart: applied to cloth, when the warp and woof readily separate from each other. **1904** *Eng. Dial. Dict.* V. 513/1 *Sleeze*,..*v.* Of loosely or badly woven cloth: to separate, part asunder; to wear away; also with *away*.

2. *slang.* To move in a sleazy fashion.

1964 *Punch* 30 Dec. 986/2 Other plays, sleazing across the West End boards. **1978** W. F. BUCKLEY *Stained Glass* xxii. 211 The depressing, unseasonal föhn that sleazes over Europe with dumpy barometric pressures that enervate and depress. **1978** *Whig-Standard* (Kingston, Ontario) 31 Mar. A-6 When not thumping.., they [*sc.* a rock group] just kind of sleaze along, a little like Lou Reed at his best.

slea·zily, *adv.* [f. SLEAZY, SLEEZY *a.* + -LY[2].] In a sleazy manner.

1959 *Listener* 5 Nov. 793/2 A bloated society staggering sleazily towards decay. **1974** M. FIDO *Kipling* 119/2 Huneefa and her sleazily exotic magic. **1976** *Listener* 14 Oct. 486/4 Despising and envying the order and bourgeois contentment of the new ménage, sleazily growling in her basement flat.

sleaziness. Delete *rare* and add later examples.

1959 *Guardian* 3 Dec. 7/2 The pop-eyed sleaziness of a Master Elliot's night-boy. **1978** *Fortune* 18 Dec. 107 The classifieds represent a sleaziness of practice that I hope will be corrected by the more ethical newspapers and publishers.

sleazo (slī·zo), *a.* and *sb. U.S. slang.* [f. SLEAZY, SLEEZY *a.* + *-O[2].] (Something) sleazy, (something) pornographic.

1972 E. SANDERS *Family* iii. 68 Manson used to hang out on the Sunset Strip using the name Chuck Summers. There were a bunch of sleazo bars and cafés on or near the Sunset Strip. *Ibid.* 69 What was it that caused Manson's death-trip? The factors that seem to have fed the violent freak-out shall be termed here sleazo inputs. **1975** *Guardian Weekly* 2 Aug. 20 Her sleazo routines seem half-rehearsed. Her dirty jokes sound almost like last-gasp fill-ins for the cleaner lines she was supposed to deliver but forgot. **1978** *Courier-Mail* (Brisbane) 4 Jan. 16/2 Norman Mailer said he liked sex movies, especially 'love pornies' and 'the sleazos'.

sleazy, sleezy, *a.* Add: **2. c.** Dilapidated, filthy, slatternly, squalid; sordid, depraved, disreputable, worthless.

1941 J. FAULKNER *Men Working* i. 31 Gwendolin..had been hanging on to her dress and peering around her wide sleazy hips. **1941** W. A. PERCY *Lanterns on Levee* x. 111, I was always happening on a Hermaphrodite, in some discreet alcove, and I would examine the sleazy mock-modest little monster. **1946** 'P. QUENTIN' *Puzzle for Fiends* 248 Her glamour dissolved... Suddenly Selena seemed sleazy. **1951** S. KAYE-SMITH *Mrs Gailey* IV. xvi. 211 In her now was a real distaste for the sleazy comforts of Mrs Turner's kitchen. **1956** L. MCINTOSH *Oxford Folly* viii. 128 Beyond it was the cemetery and some sleazy suburb whose name Adrian did not know. **1958** *Punch* 27 Aug. 286/2 A kind of sleazy, leering sex for its own sake. **1959** F. USHER *Death in Error* x. 145 I've seen all the sleasy joints of Paris. **1966** *Listener* 30 June 947/2 He scratches a middle-aged living in Paris as a gigolo in a sleazy night club. **1971** B. W. ALDISS *Soldier Erect* 46 Some sleezy and probably malevolent god. **1976** *National Observer* (U.S.) 1 May 19/1 The methods used to slur the innocent grew sleazier. **1977** *Listener* 3 Mar. 282/1 The entrance of Salomé is greeted by the world's sleeziest tune, 'La Paloma'. **1979** R. JAFFE *Class Reunion* I. iv. 42 Scollay Square, an area that was sleazy, neon lit, and disreputable.

sled, *sb.*[1] Add: **1. c.** Any of various devices made to be towed along the sea bed.

1939 *Sun* (Baltimore) 25 Jan. 3/4 As the sled passes over a buried cable both coils develop electric current which is wired to the mother ship above. **1967** *Petroleum* XXX. 158/2 The jets and suction dredge are mounted on a sled lowered from a frame at the stern of the vessel and straddle the pipe, along which they move as the barge proceeds. **1978** *Nature* 9 Mar. 156/2 This hypothesis is consistent with..the detection of a large ^{3}He excess in a 'thermal plume' (thermal anomaly $\sim$0.1°C, sampled using a deep-tow sled) over the Galapagos Spreading Centre.

2. b. Also *rocket sled.* A rocket-propelled vehicle running on rails for subjecting things to controlled high accelerations and decelerations.

1948 *Richmond* (Va.) *Times-Dispatch* 13 Jan. 9 The rocket-powered sleds moved over a standard-gauge railroad track.., covering the 2,000 feet in less than two seconds. **1956** L. MALLAN *Men, Rockets & Space* vi. 84 When he decelerated from 421 m.p.h. on the new sled, he reached a peak of only 22 G's. **1967** *Technology Week* 20 Feb. 18/1 Feasibility of a new segmented solid rocket sled motor designed for multiple re-use in sled testing has been shown in recent tests. **1974** *Encycl. Brit. Macropædia* XV. 942/1 Braking is accomplished by a parachute or, more often, by extending a scoop beneath the sled into a trough of water beneath the track rails.

5. *sled-dog* (N. Amer.).

1692 H. KELSEY *Indian Belief* in *Kelsey Papers* (1929) 21 Now as for a woman they do not so much mind her for they reckon she is like a Slead dog or Bitch when she is living & when she dies they think she dyes to Eternity. **1777** G. CARTWRIGHT *Jrnl.* 18 Dec. in *Trans. Labrador* (1792) II. 277 Finding my sled-dog lame, I defered my journey. **1914, 1966** [see *MUSH *v.*[3]]. **1980** *Beautiful British Columbia* Winter 9 (*caption*) Sled dogs at Atlin's Long Distance Dog Sled Race.

sledding, *vbl. sb.* For *U.S.* read *N. Amer.* and add: **b.** With qualifying adj. (Further examples.)

1908 R. E. BEACH *Barrier* 127 Now them kind of places is all right for married men but they're tough sleddin' for single ones. **1939** L. M. MONTGOMERY *Anne of Ingleside* xxvii. 185 Ye *can* keep a house without a woman, but it's hard sledding. **1954** T. P. KELLEY *Black Donnellys* 57 Damnation—had he somehow, unknowingly, revealed himself? If so, he could sure expect some rough sledding ahead. **1968** M. WOODHOUSE *Rock Baby* iii. 20 It was hard sledding, but after a while I got him to say something definite. **1979** *Arizona Daily Sun* 19 Apr. 4/2 This part of the administration's plan likewise faces tough sledding on Capitol Hill.

sledge, *sb.*[2] Add: **1. b.** = *SLED *sb.*[1] 2 b.

1957 *New Scientist* 20 June 16/3 The isolation of such a fault may lead to simpler performance studies on restricted imitative devices... They may be built into the man-carrying centrifuge or rocket sledge to observe changes due to acceleration.

4. *sledge-driver* (earlier example), *-head*; **sledge-meter,** a wheel and counting device towed behind a sledge to measure the distance travelled.

1819 *Theatrical Inquisitor* Apr. 314 Of the literary talent of the stage manager, we have never thought highly, and his 'Land Storm; or the Sledge Driver and his Dogs' seems only a little alteration from a piece, called 'Lowina of Tobolski'..by the same author. **1924** A. J. SMALL *Frozen Gold* i. 15 A..human thunderbolt which hurled at him... A sledge-head knocked up from nowhere and connected with his chin. **1966** S. HEANEY *Death of Naturalist* 41 The cap juts like a gantry's crossbeam, Cowling plated forehead and sledgehead jaw. **1902** R. F. SCOTT *Jrnl.* 18 Nov. in *Voyage of 'Discovery'* (1905) II. xiii. 24 A dull day.., but we plodded on... Starting at 11 A.M., we pushed on for two and a half miles by our sledge-meter. **1929** J. G. HAYES *R. E. Peary* x. 166 Peary never used a sledgemeter on the Arctic pack, saying it would have been smashed by the rough surface. **1958** *Times* 2 Jan. 6/5 During last night's painful run the tractors were biting down 2 ft... The 12-hour haul wound a laborious 22 miles through the sledgemeter.

sledge-hammer, *sb.* (Earlier *attrib.* and *fig.* examples.)

1799 T. HOLCROFT *Jrnl.* 13 Jan. in *Memoirs* (1816) III. 123 Yet having read mine, you come with a sledge hammer of criticism, describe it as absolutely contemptible. **1843** DICKENS *Let.* 24 Sept. (1974) III. 572, I sent Miss Coutts a sledge-hammer account of the Ragged schools.

sledge-hammer *v.* (later examples).

1963 A. SMITH *Throw out Two Hands* xvi. 167 Sledge-hammering a steel spike into the ground. **1976** *CRC Jrnl.* July 19/1 It is perfectly possible to understand what is going on on stage without having the point sledge-hammered home.

sle·dging, *vbl. sb.*[2] *Austral. Cricket slang.* [f. SLEDGE *sb.*[1] + -ING[1].] (See quot. 1982.)

1977 *World of Cricket Monthly* June 5/1 Lillee had his views on intimidating batsmen on Melbourne television. And on *sledging*—the term comes from *subtle as a sledge-hammer.* **1979** *Age* (Melbourne) 2 July 9/6 A year or so earlier the Australian team coined 'sledging' for needling or gamesmanship. **1982** *London Portrait Mag.* May 68/3 *Sledging,* trying to disrupt batsmen's concentration by abusing, teasing them. **1983** *Guardian* 8 Feb. 23/1 Geoff Howarth says he intends to complain about the amount of swearing, sledging and unchecked short-pitched bowling New Zealand have faced.

sleek, *v.* Add: **2. d.** To draw (a comb) through hair with a smoothing effect.

1959 *Listener* 21 May 904/1 The boys sleeking combs through their hair. **1967** G. B. MAIR *Girl from Peking* vii. 73 The Admiral..was sleeking a comb through his thinning hair.

sleep, *sb.* Add: **1. d.** (Later examples.) Also *spec.*, the solid substance found in the corners of the eyes and along the edges of the eyelids after sleep.

1905 in *Eng. Dial. Dict.* **1922** 'R. WEST' *Judge* I. iv. 195 Richard was sitting in front of the fire, rubbing the sleep out of his eyes. **1951** L. MACNEICE tr. *Goethe's Faust* 241 Children, you have scarcely scrubbed your eyes of sleep—and bored already? **1955** J. D. SALINGER in *New Yorker* 29 Jan. 27/1 He began to massage the side of his face.., removing..a bit of sleep from one eye. **1973** P. WHITE *Eye of Storm* vii. 300 The girl stood..washing the sleep out of her eyes.

e. *to lose sleep over*, etc.: see *LOSE *v.*[1] 3 b.

2. Also, in hyperbolic phrase *could do something in one's sleep* and varr.

1953 E. COXHEAD *Midlanders* viii. 187 There's no difficulty. We could make them in our sleep. **1970** J. BRAINE *Stay with me till Morning* i. 9 His job didn't claim much of his energy. He could, as they say, do it in his sleep.

3. a. Also, in phr. *to have* or *get one's sleep out*, to sleep until one wakes naturally.

1685 C. GARDINER *Let.* in M. M. Verney *Mem.* (1899) IV. ix. 341 Your grandsons shall have their sleep out beefore they goe. **1911** F. H. BURNETT *Secret Garden* xvii. 183 'You must go back and get your sleep out,' she said. **1930** A. BENNETT *Imperial Palace* lvii. 434 She had told him to call her. He had refused; she must have her sleep out.

b. (Earlier *N. Amer.* and later examples.)

1670 N. CARTERET in *S. Carolina Hist. Soc. Coll.* (1897) V. 166 The Caseeka..was within one sleep of us. **1896** C. WHITNEY *On Snow-Shoes to Barren Grounds* 182 The one 'sleep' did not bring us up to the caribou, but it took us north to the lodge of another Indian. **1919** CODY & COOPER *Memories of Buffalo Bill* 312 It was many sleeps away. **1953** D. CUSHMAN *Stay away, Joe* 53 From three-four sleeps came riders to the tepee of our father.

c. *fig.* A prison term, usu. comparatively short. *slang* (orig. *U.S.*).

1911 D. LOWRIE *My Life in Prison* vi. 63 A year sentence is known as a 'sleep'. **1931** 'D. STIFF' *Milk & Honey Route* vi. 65 Any time you want to retreat to some such place for a short or long rest or 'sleep', just go to the social worker displaying the proper symptoms. **1938** J. PHELAN *Lifer* xix. 202, I wasn't interested myself [in escaping]. Three years was nothing—just a sleep, as you chaps put it. **1971** D. BAGLEY *Freedom Trap* iii. 59 In prison jargon, a 'sleep' is a sentence from six months to two years; a 'cut' is from two to four years, and a 'stretch' is anything over four years.

4. a. *to put to sleep*, to kill, esp. painlessly; also *fig.*

1942 R. GODDEN *Breakfast with Nikolides* v. 118, I want you simply to give him an injection and put him to sleep. I will muzzle him. **1966** K. A. SADDLER *Gilt Edge* ii. 37, I had to have the Allard [*sc.* a car] put to sleep... She started coughing up oil... I couldn't bear to see her in agony. **1967** A. LEWIN *Unaltered Cat* II. vi. 134 Her cousin's Siamese cat..had..a litter of four adorable seal-point kittens. Ethel's husband was for putting them to sleep, but Ethel wouldn't hear of it. **1970** *Women's Household* July 10/1 She had started to suffer, so the humane thing to do was to put her to sleep. **1975** tr. *Melchior's Sleeper Agent* (1976) III. vii. 154 The Führer's Alsatian dog, Blondi..had been ordered put to sleep. Dr. Haase had given her poison.

5. b. (Earlier example.)

1859 PRINCESS ROYAL *Let.* 12 Dec. in R. Fulford *Dearest Child* (1964) 212 Wegner..pinches his arm to see whether he feels it... He feels just a little but not much, like a part that is gone to sleep.

6. a. *sleep deprivation.*

1966 I. JEFFERIES *House-Surgeon* xii. 230 Those who are still not weakened sufficiently are eroded remorselessly by sleep-deprivation. **1980** E. BEHR *Getting Even* i. 18 We tried another tactic... Truth drugs... Even some subtle sleep deprivation. Inconclusive.

b. *sleep-producing.*

1844 E. A. Poe in *Godey's Lady's Bk.* Apr. 177/2 This *rapport* extended beyond the limits of the simple sleep-producing power... At the first attempt..the mesmerist entirely failed. **1907** W. JAMES in *Amer. Mag.* Nov. 64/2 The best sleep-producing agent which his practice had revealed to him was *prayer*.

c. *sleep-bound, -dazed, -twisted*; also with ppl. adjs., as *sleep-drunk.*

1841 J. G. WHITTIER in *Knickerbocker* May 369 Bend o'er us now, as over them, And set our sleep-bound spirits free. **1889** *Cent. Dict.*, Sleep-drunk. **1938** E. BOWEN *Death of Heart* III. v. 417 He..saw in a sleep-bound way how specious wisdom was. **1951** KOESTLER *Age of Longing* I. iii. 41 Sleep-drunk and frightened, Hydie begins to cry. **1954** —— *Invisible Writing* IV. xxxvii. 394 Sleep-dazed, he is unable to decide which of the two hostile dictators is reaching out for him this time. **1960** T. HUGHES *Lupercal* 21 Our lantern's little orange flare Made a round mask of our each sleep-dazed face. **1960** S. PLATH *Colossus* 39 Sleep-twisted sheets.

7. sleep apnœa, apnœa occurring in sleep; **sleep-coat,** a knee-length front-fastening night-shirt or dressing-gown; **sleep-learn** *a.*, pertaining to sleep-learning; **sleep-learning, -teaching** *vbl. sbs.*, learning, teaching, during sleep, esp. by exposure to radio, tape-recordings, etc. (cf. *HYPNOPÆDIA); **sleep movement** *Bot.*, a movement of a part of a plant, esp. a leaf, that occurs each nightfall and, in reverse, each daybreak; **sleep-shorts,** shorts as an item of nightwear; **sleep sofa** *U.S.*, a sofa which may be used as a bed; **sleep-talk** *v. intr.*, to speak (as) during sleep; **sleep-talker** (later examples); **sleep-talking** (later examples); **sleep-teaching** *vbl. sb.*: see *sleep-learning* vbl. sb. above; **sleep-waker** (earlier example); **sleep-wear,** night wear.

1976 *National Observer* (U.S.) 18 Dec. 16/4 Sleep apnea has three forms: central apnea [etc.]. **1980** *Brit. Med. Jrnl.* 29 Mar. 895/2 Sleep apnoea was defined as cessation of airflow at the nose and mouth lasting for at least 10 seconds. **1948** *Sun* (Baltimore) 11 Feb. 3/5 (Advt.), Rayon knit sleep-coats... What young, gay, pretty and practical sleepers! **1966** *Punch* 23 Feb. 290/2 The nearest Hardy Amies equivalent is a..short-sleeved garment called a 'sleep-coat', designed for warm climates and centrally heated homes... It is a loose neglіgé, fastening with a sash. **1976** *National Observer* (U.S.) 6 Nov. 21 (Advt.), Sleepcoats for cool knights. **1968** *Punch* 4 Dec. 804/2 Two new 'sleep-learn' devices. **1972** D. LEES *Zodiac* 151 By using an adaptation of the sleep-learn technique we can turn you into anything we want. **1953** M. L. COYNE in *Jrnl. Exper. Psychol.* (1956) LI. 97/1 (*heading*) Some problems and parameters of sleep learning. **1966** *Listener* 8 Dec. 852/3 Equally dangerous might be so-called 'sleep-learning' courses which try to teach you something special, like a new language, while you sleep. **1972** J. GORES *Dead Skip* (1973) iii. 18 Through his mind, like a sleep-learning tape, reeled Bart's words. **1880** Sleep-movement [in Dict., sense 6 a]. **1906**, etc. [see *NYCTINASTIC *a.*]. **1965** BELL & COOMBE tr. *Strasburger's Textbk. Bot.* 391 *Mimosa* also shows sleep movements, and at nightfall appears almost as if stimulated by mechanical shock. **1964** *Women's Wear Daily* 30 Nov. 50 A pair of sleepshorts in all sleepwear colors to be sold separately, worn with anything the consumer wishes. **1976** *National Observer* (U.S.) 29 May 2/6 (Advt.), Classic travel shave coat & matching sleep shorts. **1973** *Washington Post* 13 Jan. A13/3 (Advt.), Elegant traditional sleeper. Refined traditional sleep sofa from Waynline. **1960** S. PLATH *Colossus* 48 The sleep-talking virgin. **1980** *Times Lit. Suppl.* 23 May 578/5 She has a tendency to over-point,..and I can feel death around too, very little hope or heart—'although I admit I desire', she intones, sleep-talking. **1972** R. ADAMS *Watership Down* x. 44 His voice sank and became that of a sleep-talker. **1981** *Maledicta* V. 287 Each sleeptalker was asked..a series of some 25 questions and sub-questions about his/her verbalizations. **1899** Sleep-talking [see *somniloquy* s.v. SOMNILOQUACIOUS *a.*]. **1939** JOYCE *Finnegans Wake* 459 She's a fright, poor old dutch, in her sleeptalking. **1981** *Maledicta* V. 286 There has always existed the phenomenon of somniloquy, commonly known as sleeptalking. **1932** Sleep-teaching [see *HYPNOPÆDIA]. **1957** A. HUXLEY *Let.* 12 Dec. (1969) 837 A dictator..could, by the use of drugs, sleep-teaching, hypnosis, subliminal projection..establish a high degree of control over his subjects. **1970** *Times* 19 Sept. 13 In Russia more than 180 educational institutes..are now fully equipped for sleepteaching. **1844** E. A. POE in *Columbian Mag.* Aug. 70/2 As the sleep-waker pronounced these latter words..I observed upon his countenance a singular expression. **1935** A. P. HERBERT *What a Word!* iv. 115, I have been implored by many to attack..'sleep-wear', and 'swim-wear'. **1964** [see *sleep-shorts* above]. **1979** N. HYND *False Flags* xxiv. 213 You travel light... Just..some sleepwear.

sleep, *v.* Add: **I. 1. a.** *to sleep rough*: see ROUGH *adv.* 1 b; *to sleep tight*: see *TIGHT *adv.* 1.

b. (Further examples.) Also, with *around*: to engage in sexual intercourse casually with a variety of partners; to be sexually promiscuous (*colloq.*).

1898 *Sessions Paper of Central Criminal Court* Feb. 266 He has been sleeping with my wife. How would you like it? **1928** A. HUXLEY *Point Counter Point* xxvii. 445 'Sleeping around'—that was how he had heard a young American girl describe the amorous side of the ideal life, as lived in Hollywood. **1936** R. LEHMANN *Weather in Streets* II. 185 A child's out of the question now, they don't sleep together any more. **1940** W. FAULKNER *Hamlet* II. 92 All we want anyway is to keep her out of trouble until she gets old enough to sleep with a man without getting me and him both arrested. **1952** M. LASKI *Village* xvi. 218, I don't think for a minute she's been sleeping around..but you know what gossip is. **1967** J. POTTER *Foul Play* xiii. 161 He's only interested in George and Freda and whether Johnnie and Freda slept together. **1975** P. LORAINE *Wrong Man in Mirror* 78 Rose Maddox was not a loose girl; she did not sleep around with just anybody.

c. (Further examples.)

a **1907** F. THOMPSON *St Ignatius Loyola* (1909) x. 192 He discussed all measures with his brethren; and ever enjoined them to sleep on the matter, and pray the next morning before decision. **1926** V. MCNABB *Church & Land* 83 My friend rose from his seat. 'I see—we must do things ourselves. I must sleep on this.' **1959** S. SALTON-VANE *Black Whippet* ii. 32 Sleep on it. Think it over, and come and see me early tomorrow morning. **1962** P. GREGORY *Like Tigress at Bay* ix. 99 Let me think about it, though. I'd like to sleep on it. **1983** 'W. HAGGARD' *Heirloom* viii. 90 He simply looked at a problem hard and then slept on it.

g. For *Sc.* read 'orig. *Sc.*' at sense 'to over-sleep' and add earlier and later examples. Also, to lie in (*LIE *v.*[1] 23 d), to sleep late.

1827 C. I. JOHNSTONE *Eliz. de Bruce* I. iii. 56 Ye whiles sleep in on a morning. **1883** W. AITKEN *Lays of Line* 58 A'e mornin' last March, when Rab Black sleepit in. **1931** *Amer. Speech* VII. 20 *Sleep in*, to sleep late. 'I'm going to sleep in tomorrow.' **1931** D. L. SAYERS *Five Red Herrings* i. 16 Shall I tell Mrs. McLeod to let you sleep in, as they say? And call you with a couple of aspirins on toast? **1935** *Beaver* Dec. 66/2 On Sundays the chief guide usually allows his voyageurs to sleep in, which means that instead of getting up at four o'clock they get up about six-thirty. **1967** E. TAYLOR *Second Thursday* ii. 31 Susan dear, you *must* have slept in this morning. **1975** J. GRADY *Shadow of Condor* v. 90 Because he slept in and had an appointment, Malcolm excused himself from the exercises.

h. Also as *ppl. adj.*

1939 W. FORTESCUE *There's Rosemary, There's Rue* xi. 79 We crawled up to our bedroom..and got under our bed-quilts, *not* between those slept-in sheets. **1966** N. FREELING *King of Rainy Country* 140 He..changed his slept-in suit. **1976** J. CROSBY *Snake* (1977) xi. 53 She pulled the crinkly blue-and-white striped blouse as taut as she could..trying to make it look a little less slept-in.

i. With *on*: to continue sleeping, to sleep late.

1739–40 RICHARDSON *Pamela* (1741) I. 267 I'll wake her,—said I.—No, don't,—said she,—let her sleep on; we shall lie better without her. **1939** 'J. BELL' *Death at Half-Term* v. 92, I let our lot sleep on, but the other four came over from the San, and woke them up. **1958** P.

Scott *Mark of Warrior* I. ii. 44 In four hours Hussein would wake him... Esther would sleep on. **1969** J. Fraser *Clap Hands if you believe in Fairies* iv. 48 Don't worry too much if he's not sleepy. I'll let him sleep on in the morning.

j. With *over*. † (*a*) to sleep late (*obs.*); (*b*) to spend the night at a place other than one's own residence (chiefly *U.S.*).

1827 *Harvard Reg.* Sept. 202 They have indulged in the luxury of 'sleeping over'. **1871** L. H. Bagg *Four Years at Yale* 570 On Sunday mornings, too, there is an unusual amount of 'sleeping over',—breakfast being often cut as well as chapel by the votaries of Morpheus. **1975** *Sunday Advocate-News* (Barbados) 15 June 7/2 The sleep-overs will be the night of the last Thursday of each session. On that night campers sleep-over if they choose to do so. **1977** D. Anthony *Stud Game* iii. 23, I begged him to sleep over... But he had an early appointment the next day. **1978** M. Puzo *Fools Die* xxviii. 331 Those were nights I'd hop a plane to Vegas for the evening, sleep over and come back in the early morning.

k. With *out*: to spend the night in the open air; also, to sleep away from the premises on which one is employed.

1852 [implied at *sleeping *vbl. sb.* 1 c]. **1890** Kipling *Departmental Ditties, Barrack-Room Ballads* 56 'E's sleepin' out an' far to-night,' the Colour-Sergeant said. **1908** R. Brooke *Let.* 18 Aug. (1968) 139, I should love to sleep out with nothing but a few extra socks on. **1912** [used in Dict., sense 1 g]. **1936** 'J. Tey' *Shilling for Candles* xiv. 159 He might have been sleeping out, the first three nights. But you know what last night was like. Torrents... He must have found shelter. **1974** *Whig-Standard* (Kingston, Ontario) 11 Jan. 7/1 There are more dossers sleeping out in London today than there were at the turn of the century.

l. Of a bed or mattress: to afford sleep of a specified quality.

1942 W. Faulkner *Go down, Moses* 83 This here pallet sleeps all right to me. **1977** *Austral. House & Garden* Jan. 115/1 A foam mattress is generally lighter, is non-allergenic and resists mildew... Foam sleeps cooler in warm temperatures, it is claimed, and warmer in cool temperatures.

m. With *up*: to catch up on one's sleep, to stop for a sleep.

1951 *Manch. Guardian Weekly* 1 Feb. 3/3 The General.. would say nothing more than that he was off for a rest. He headed..for the..hotel to sleep-up until Wednesday. **1968** *Listener* 11 July 50/2 It was..so full and exhausting ..that, at the end of term..we used to sleep up for several days before venturing out onto the streets. **1968** in P. G. Hollowell *Lorry Driver* vii. 183 You want to give your mate a bit of a shaking up. What you do is to spot him 'sleeping up' and go quietly by him and turn your wagon round... Then hold your hands on the horn.

n. With *through*: esp. of a baby, to sleep uninterruptedly through a period of time, usually the night.

1967 'L. Egan' *Nameless Ones* i. 3 She's the most beautiful baby ever... Sleeping right through. God, when I think—. **1971** O. Norton *Corpse-Bird Cries* ii. 33, I..slept through until nearly ten o'clock on Sunday morning. **1976** 'J. Charlton' *Remington Set* xx. 104 'Baby going to be all right in the guest room?' 'She'll sleep right through,' Fran said.

4. a. *spec.*, to act as a sleeping partner (see Sleeping *ppl. a.* 5) or as a sleeper (sense *2 d).

1949 D. Leon *Ruskin* I. i. 8 Telford supplied adequate capital and otherwise 'slept' most gracefully. **1975** J. Hone *Sixth Directorate* II. 48 Once they were sure the man was with the KGB.. they had watched him... And no one had come near him... They assumed the man was sleeping.

II. 6. a. (Further examples of *to sleep the sleep of the just*.)

1927 R. Lehmann *Dusty Answer* III. i. 139 Jennifer's peaceful flushed countenance and regular breathing greeted her astonished senses. She was sleeping the sleep of the slightly intoxicated just. **1944** W. S. Maugham *Razor's Edge* vii. 276 Gray's conversation was composed of clichés... He never went to bed, but hit the hay, where he slept the sleep of the just. **1977** *Lancashire Life* Dec. 57/3 Tired and ready to go home, we went back to the river where Edith's father was still sleeping the sleep of the just.

11. (Further examples.)

1861 [see *mother's blessing* s.v. *mother *sb.*[1] 15 a]. **1923** *Daily Mail* 24 Feb. 7 A gasworks foreman..said that at present the gas included 13 per cent of carbon monoxide... 'One per cent is sufficient to kill. It sleeps you to death.'

12. (Earlier and further examples.)

1848 Bartlett *Dict. Amer.* 306 She could eat fifty people in her house, but could not sleep half the number. **1883** *Gringo & Greaser* (Manzano, New Mexico) 1 Sept. 2/1 If we can find some other philanthropist who will kindly hash, beer and sleep us, we'll be there. **1919** Mencken *Amer. Lang.* i. 24 A sleeping-car sleeps thirty passengers. **1941** W. A. Percy *Lanterns on Levee* i. 12 Welcome, messieurs, I can eat you but I cannot sleep you. **1949** *Spectator* 11 Nov. 631/2 During August some hotels were sleeping four or five guests to a room. **1965** E. O'Brien *August is Wicked Month* xi. 113 Oh we got beds, we can sleep..eighty. **1977** *Western Mail* (Cardiff) 5 Mar. 10/7 (Advt.), Farmhouse holiday flat. Sleeps six.

C. *Comb.*: **sleep-away** *a.* (*U.S.*), at which one sleeps away from home. See also *sleep-in, -out, -over *sbs.* and *adjs.*

1976 *Woman's Day* (U.S.) Nov. 244/2 Diana is told she must go to a sleep-away camp because the doctor says she needs more exercise. **1978** *Chicago* June 157/2 All the sleep-away camps have separate living quarters for boys and girls, but the tennis itself is mixed.

sleeper. Add: **I. 2. c.** A sleeping partner.

1901 *Edin. Rev.* Apr. 385 If..a director can be treated as a purely sleeping partner, it can do that company no harm that..the sleeper, on becoming a Minister, should cease to be a director. **1983** 'W. Haggard' *Heirloom* xi. 122, I might fix that. At a price... No consortium takes in a sleeper for nothing.

d. A spy, saboteur, or the like, who remains inactive for a long period before engaging in spying or sabotage or otherwise acting to achieve his ends; *loosely*, any undercover agent.

1955 H. Roth *Sleeper* ix. 66 Hollister..was a sleeper—a member of the Communist Party whose whole life was dedicated to the one big moment. **1963** J. Joesten *They call it Intelligence* I. iv. 45 A 'sleeper' is an agent planted in a strategic place for a specific purpose only. **1966** M. Woodhouse *Tree Frog* xxv. 187 Bought, or brainwashed? Or had he been a sleeper for years, waiting for just this job? **1975** *Daily Mail* 16 Aug. 2/1 They had been responsible for a year-long campaign of bombings in the city... When police cleaned up the cell, the IRA activated a reserve unit of 'sleepers'. **1976** *Times* 7 June 12/5 There almost certainly exists within our political establishment, what is known as a 'sleeper'—a high level political figure who is in fact a Soviet agent, infiltrated into the system many years ago. **1981** *Observer* 29 Mar. 15 Key members of the..Committee concluded that only the existence of a 'mole' or 'sleeper' (the preferred 'trade' word) could explain the many leaks and failures of the 1950s and 1960s.

4. b. *Gambling.* (See quots. 1864, 1897.)

1856 *San Francisco Bulletin* 4 Dec. 2/2 Some were waiting for 'sleepers', others were telling some other betters a certain card was going to win, dead 'sure'. **1864** W. B. Dick *Amer. Hoyle* 208 A bet [in faro] is said to be a sleeper, when the owner has forgotten it, when it becomes public property, any one having a right to take it. **1897** [in Dict., sense 4 a]. **1939** P. A. Rollins *Gone Haywire* 16 A Dakota miner had been detected attempting to steal 'sleepers' from the faro table. **1944** [see *heave ho b].

5. a. (Earlier and *attrib.* examples.) Also, a train made up of or including sleeping-cars.

1875 *Chicago Tribune* 11 Sept. 3/2 Every item of wood, iron, or upholstery which enters into the make-up..of a Pullman sleeper is Selected with Skilled Care. **1880** W. Whitman *Daybks. & Notebks.* (1978) I. 188 On a first-class sleeper. **1881** 'Mark Twain' *Speeches* (1910) 258, I..must change cars there and take the sleeper train. **1950** O. S. Nock *Brit. Locomotives from Footplate* vi. 118 The run with No. 46235 on the Inverness 'sleeper'..shows how great sometimes is the gulf between maximum locomotive capacity under ideal conditions and practical application on the road. **1952** 'J. Tey' *Singing Sands* iv. 62 A friend who came across him on the train. Saw his name on the sleeper list, or noticed him in passing. **1967** O. Wynd *Walk Softly, Men Praying* vii. 106 'You've got a sleeper reservation?' 'No, I was going to sit up.' 'All right... How about the eleven o'clock express.' **1969** M. Pugh *Last Place Left* xxi. 164 He made out sleeper tickets for us..and we shared a two-berth compartment. **1970** R. Adam *Stalk to Kill* xi. 158 A restless night in the sleeper train from London. **1979** P. Theroux *Old Patagonian Express* iv. 53, I was glad to be on this sleeper to the coast.

b. Used *attrib.* and *absol.* to designate a vehicle with sleeping facilities.

1939 *Nat. Geogr. Mag.* Feb. 133/2 Their covered wagons are now shiny streamliners (40 hours from Chicago), or mammoth sleeper buses (which they still call 'stages'). **1951** *Amer. Speech* XXVI. 308/2 *Sleeper*, any truck or tractor that is equipped with a sleeping berth. **1969** *Sydney Morning Herald* 24 May 9/7 Mr Ferrier plans to buy a sleeper-van and, with his wife, spend the next 18 months travelling around Australia. **1971** M. Tak *Truck Talk* 146 *Sleeper cab*, a tractor in which an adjoining bunk area is located behind the driver's seat. **1976** *Eastern Daily Press* (Norwich) 19 Nov. 14/2 (Advt.), *Scania* 32-ton tractor, sleeper cab.

5*. Something whose quality or value proves to be greater than was generally expected; a 'dark horse'. orig. *U.S.*

1892 *Outing* (U.S.) Mar. 454/2 Williams won the high and low hurdles in record time,..and Harmar a second in the mile, being beaten by Wells, a 'sleeper' from Amherst. **1903** J. P. Paret *Lawn Tennis* III. vi. 350 Sleeper, a slang expression meaning a player who is much better than was thought. **1926** *Clues* Nov. 162/2 *Sleeper*, something of value that has been overlooked. **1945** *Richmond* (Va.) *Times-Dispatch* 31 July 7/4 In film parlance, this is a *sleeper*—a picture made with the thought that it would be just another light Summer item, but which has turned out to be a surprisingly popular box-office success. **1962** W. & M. Morris *Dict. Word & Phrase Origins* I. 267 A sleeper is a stamp more rare—and thus more valuable—than the catalogue listings indicate. **1968** J. D. Watson *Double Helix* xx. 141 Bill's appearance was the sleeper of the three-day gathering... As soon as he had finished his unassuming report..everyone in the audience knew that a bombshell had exploded. **1978** *Detroit Free Press* 5 Mar. B. 12/2 In any given week of new book arrivals, there occasionally is a sleeper, a book which comes in virtually unannounced with 'best seller' written all over it. **1981** J. D. MacDonald *Free Fall in Crimson* v. 49 He made a couple of motion pictures... on a very small budget, and they were what is called sleepers. They made a lot of money, considering what they cost.

5.** Miscellaneous uses. **a.** An unbranded calf which has had a notch cut in its ear. *U.S.*

1893 O. Wister *Jrnl.* 31 Dec. (1958) 198 *Sleeper*, a cow with earmark and no brand. **1933** J. V. Allen *Cowboy Lore* I. 12 *A sleeper* is a calf ear-marked by a cattle thief who intends to come back later and steal the animal. **1949** *Boston Sunday Globe* 1 May (Fiction Mag.) 2/1 He..gave a tally of the sleepers and mavericks he had branded.

b. An earring, esp. one in the form of a simple hoop, worn not primarily as ornament but to keep the hole in a pierced ear-lobe open.

1896 G. F. Northall *Warwickshire Word-bk.* 215 *Sleepers, sb. pl.*, fine, small rings of gold, first put into the ears after boring, and afterwards worn whenever the larger ear-rings, or 'droppers', are inconvenient. Their use is to prevent the closing of the perforations of the lobes. **1959** *News Chron.* 6 Oct. 6/2 That ghastly business of turning sleepers in a fresh and often painful wound. **1971** R. Scott *Wedding Man is Nicer than Cats, Miss* i. 38 Even quite small girls had had their ears pierced... No one wore sleepers, but the ear-rings could be taken out and the holes plugged with tiny pieces of wood. **1978** J. Updike *Coup* (1979) vii. 293 Substituting for her great hoop earrings little sleepers of agate.

c. A sleeping-suit for a baby or a small child. Also *pl.* orig. *N. Amer.*

1921 *Daily Colonist* (Victoria, B.C.) 12 Oct. 7/1 (Advt.), Children's sleepers at $1.95 a suit. Made of strong quality flanelette in neat colored stripe. **1944** C. Himes *Black on Black* (1973) 247 Norma sat on the side of the bed and helped Lucy into her sleepers. **1970** *Toronto Daily Star* 24 Sept. 23/1 (Advt.), Minute imperfections should not affect wear, appearance or comfort of these cosy sleepers. **1975** *Daily Tel.* 14 Feb. 15/3 (*caption*) Lucy is in her Mothercare sleeper with vinyl feet.

d. A particle of sleep (*sleep *sb.* 1 d).

1942 Berrey & Van den Bark *Amer. Thes. Slang* § 251/1 *Sleepers*, particles in the eyes after a sound sleep. **1944** H. Croome *You've gone Astray* i. 9 He had sleepers in his eyes, ugh!

e. A sleeping-pill. *slang.*

1961 Rigney & Smith *Real Bohemia* p. xvii, *Sleepers*, barbiturates (sedatives), usually seconal, nembutal, amytal, etc. **1967** M. M. Glatt et al. *Drug Scene* vii. 91 A lot of addicts are taking liquid Methedrine with 'sleepers' now—it is getting worse. **1979** C. Dale *Helping with Inquiries* I. 11 Take a sleeper, I would, put yourself right out.

II. 10. *sleeper-beam.*

1937 *Discovery* Dec. 377/2 The house had been divided into rooms by lath and plaster walls, the sleeper-beams for which were let into shallow trenches in the chalk or gravel floors. **1970** Bray & Trump *Dict. Archæol.* 213/2 In early timber-framed buildings, Roman, Saxon and medieval, the framing was often erected not on a wall foundation but directly on a horizontal beam resting on or slightly recessed into the ground. From its recumbent position this is known as a sleeper beam.

III. 11. Special combs., as **sleeper agent** = sense 2 d above; **sleeper pass** *N. Amer. Football*, a pass unexpectedly involving a player hitherto ignored; **sleeper seat**, a reclining seat on which one can sleep during a journey; **sleeper wall** *Building*, a low wall built under a ground floor to support joists where there is no basement; so **sleeper walling.**

1973 *TV Times* (Austral.) 3 Feb. 11/1 A sleeper agent is someone who, over the years, has worked himself up into a position of trust. **1977** H. Kaplan *Damascus Cover* (1978) v. 54 Operative Sixty-six is a member of the Syrian Parliament. He was a sleeper agent for twelve years. **1954** *Sun* (Baltimore) 4 Dec. (B ed.) 11/3 The Rams pulled the old corner lot 'sleeper' pass on the first running play of the new season for a touchdown. **1966** *Globe Mag.* (Toronto) 20 Aug. 7/3 Part of Canadian football folklore is the sleeper pass Keith Spaith threw..in 1948. **1960** *Times* 11 Feb. 9/5 Whether sleeper-seats and bunks should be provided. **1980** *Sunday Times* 21 Sept. 11 (Advt.), TWA's First Class Sleeper-Seats make it easy to lie back and relax peacefully. **1836, 1893** Sleeper wall [in Dict., sense 10]. **1972** S. Smith *Brickwork* viii. 37 The sleeper walls supporting the floor are built 'honey-comb', that is, with holes left through them to permit through ventilation. **1971** *Power Farming* Mar. 9/1 The latest aid to producing a 12ft-high stack at Kexby—a 50ft square of sleeper walling—is illustrated.

slee·per, *v. rare.* [f. the sb.] **1.** *trans.* To mark (a calf) with a notch in its ear.

1910 C. E. Mulford *Hopalong Cassidy* xii. 79 Either the H2 was sleepering Bar-20 calves for their irons later on, or rustlers were at work.

2. *intr.* To travel in a railway sleeping-car.

1978 A. Fraser *Wild Island* xvii. 155 Beauregard was off..on the overnight sleeper to London. 'Flying visit... Back in the morning. Sleepering both ways.'

Hence **slee·pering** *vbl. sb.*

1910 C. E. Mulford *Hopalong Cassidy* xii. 80 'I saw a H2 sleeper, up just above th' Bend.'.. 'Lazy trick, that sleepering.'

Sleeperette (slīpəre·t). Also **sleeperette.** [f. Sleeper + -ette.] The proprietary name of a kind of reclining seat; = *sleeper seat* s.v. *sleeper 11.

1950 *Official Gaz.* (U.S. Patent Office) 11 July 443/2 Pan American Airways Inc., New York... Sleeperette. For transportation of passengers by aircraft. **1959** *Radio Times* 2 Jan. 28/2 (Advt.), Travel by sleeperettes on the 'Austropa Express'. **1966** *Punch* 31 Aug. 341/1 We could put Emma, who is three.., beside a VIP in his long-lie sleeperette. **1968** *Guardian* 27 Apr. 10/2 (Advt.), Fred Olsen car ferry from Harwich; single sleeperette fare £8 5s. **1982** *Daily Tel.* 24 Dec. 11/5 British Airways' new first class 'sleeperette' service.

slee·p-in, *sb.* and *a.* **A.** *sb.* **1.** [*-in[3].] A form of protest in which the participants sleep overnight in premises which they have occupied.

1965, 1971 [see *-in[3]].

2. [f. vbl. phr. *to sleep in*: see sense 1 g of

the vb. in Dict. and Suppl.] An act of sleeping later than usual, a lie-in.

1977 P. G. Winslow *Witch Hill Murder* II. 67 Those bells do make the damnedest racket. Nobody..can have a sleep-in on Sunday.

B. *attrib.* or as *adj.* [Sleep *v.* 1 g.] Of a person: that sleeps on the premises, resident. Of a place: at which one stays overnight, residential.

1961 in *Webster* s.v., Five sleep-in servants. **1970** L. Sanders *Anderson Tapes* xxi. 56 Apartment Four A... A sleep-in maid. **1974** H. L. Foster *Ribbin', Jivin', & Playin' Dozens* vii. 329 The first was a three-week sleep-in camp experience for 62 children and their teachers in June, 1947, at Life Camps. The second was a three-day sleep-over school camping experience..at Hudson Guild Farm, Nokong, New Jersey. **1981** J. D. MacDonald *Free Fall in Crimson* x. 106 He managed to hustle me into bed... I told him I had to quit. I wasn't going to be a sleep-in secretary.

sleeping, *vbl. sb.* Add: **1. c.** With advbs. as *around* (see *sleep *v.* 1 b), *out* (see *sleep *v.* 1 k).

1852 *Rep. Committee on Criminal & Destitute Juveniles* App. III. 427 in *Parl. Papers* VII. 389 It is his fourth committal; his offence being, 'sleeping out'. **1945** S. Lewis *C. Timberlane* xxiv. 155 Going to be none of this 'modern civilized, urbane' sleeping around and getting complicated in *our* house. **1957** J. Braine *Room at Top* xxv. 204 I'm glad you've decided to settle down. You're too old for sleeping around. **1973** E. J. Bahr *Nice Neighbourhood* xiii. 137 Her mother..did some sleeping around to help make ends meet. **1974** 'M. Innes' *Appleby's Other Story* ix. 73 One very large bush has been curiously hollowed out... The badgers use it as a sleeping-out place. **1976** V. Canning *Doomsday Carrier* iv. 68 A sleeping-out pass until six tomorrow. **1976** *Howard Jrnl.* XV. I. 43 It seems wrong to assume..that non-indictable assaults, malicious damage, begging and sleeping out [etc.],..are all associated with social dereliction, homelessness, or disturbed behaviour.

2. a. *sleeping-berth, -car* (further examples), *-place* (further examples), *-platform, -porch, -quarters, -room* (further examples).

1834 *Chambers's Edin. Jrnl.* III. 316/2 The Calais boats being small, and mounting few sleeping berths. **1939** Auden & Isherwood *Journey to War* v. 123 The bugs must have been nesting in the upholstery of the shabby old Belgian sleeping-berths. **1979** O. Sela *Petrograd Consignment* 259 The..relative comfort of a first-class sleeping berth..all the way to Stockholm. **1872** Sleeping-car [see *Pullman a]. **1903** Mrs. H. Ward *Lady Rose's Daughter* xviii. 313, I will go and get a sleeping car for you to Calais. **1954** T. S. Eliot *Confidential Clerk* I. 32, I shall go and rest now. In a sleeping-car it is quite impossible To get one's quiet hour. **1978** J. Simmons *Railway in England & Wales 1830–1914* I. viii. 195 The first sleeping cars in Britain appeared in 1873, on trains running between London and Glasgow. **1910** W. de la Mare *Three Mulla-Mulgars* 52 Let us hobble on, Mulla-mulgars, until we find a quieter sleeping-place. **1957** P. Worsley *Trumpet shall Sound* viii. 150 Existing huts were to be..replaced by communal houses..one as sleeping-place for the men and one for the women. **1935** *Discovery* Dec. 361/2 Mr E. W. Savory did not actually see any of these apes in the district, but the presence of their sleeping-platforms is proof of their residence there. **1940** R. Finnie *Lure of North* 199 His original excavation, from which most of the snow blocks needed for the house had been taken, now constituted the floor, and the rest of that space—more than half—was the sleeping platform, a foot or so higher. **1915** J. Webster *Dear Enemy* 44, I want two hundred feet of sleeping-porch running along the outside of our dormitories. **1971** *Sunday Express* (Johannesburg) (Homefinder) 28 Mar. 2/2 (Advt.), Flats 6 × 2 plus sleeping porch. **1919** E. O'Neill *Moon of Caribbees* 117 A door leading to the captain's sleeping quarters. **1944** J. S. Huxley *On Living in Revolution* 111 Many people have to share crowded sleeping-quarters. **1982** V. Mehta *Vedi* iii. 52 Mrs. Ras Mohun marched me up to her sleeping quarters. **1833** *Chambers's Edin. Jrnl.* I. 386/1, I..was shown to my sleeping-room by the waiter. **1903** W. B. Yeats in *Fortn. Rev.* Apr. 752 Maeve walked through that great hall, and with a sigh Lifted the curtain of her sleeping-room. **1978** *Chicago* June 135/2 He..leads me into a small sleeping room, which has a cot, a small desk, and a chair.

b. *sleeping-bag* (earlier and later examples), *-chair, -mask, -mat* (later examples); **sleeping dictionary** *slang*, a foreign woman with whom a man has a sexual relationship and from whom he learns her language.

1850 S. Osborn *Jrnl.* 11 Oct. in *Stray Leaves from Arctic Jrnl.* (1852) 147 Friday morning, at seven o'clock, we rolled up our beds, or rather sleeping-bags. **1933** *Discovery* Sept. 284/1 We retired to sleep in our sleeping-bags in the tiny room allotted us. **1978** *Times* 22 Nov. 5/4 She had put him..in his carrycot wrapped in a sleeping bag, romper suit and cardigan. **1675** in J. Gloag *Short Dict. Furnit.* (1969) 619 For a sleeping chaire to fall in the back of Iron Worke. *a* **1877** Knight *Dict. Mech.* I. 481/2 Car-seats..made reclining, for night travel..are termed 'sleeping-chairs'. **1924** Macquoid & Edwards *Dict. English Furnit.* I. 215 In the Queen's Closet at Ham House are two winged 'sleeping chairs'..with ratchets to let down the backs. **1928** J. B. Wharton *Squad* 21 We picked up two beauties... Oo-la-la—I've learned French —out uv a sleepin' dictionary—dat's what dey're called. **1965** *Listener* 25 Mar. 461/3 He paints the old China of bound feet,..the endless dinners, the mistress (sleeping dictionary) as fragile as a butterfly. **1979** M. Lindsay in C. Allen *Tales from Dark Continent* i. 14 In East Africa.. 'East African officers as a whole maintained a..stricter code in the matter of sleeping with African women'—sometimes referred to as 'sleeping dictionaries', from their obvious advantages as language instructors—than did their fellow-officers in West Africa. **1908** S. Ford *Side-Stepping with Shorty McCabe* ix. 139 They'd kept his face in a steam box by the hour..made him wear a sleepin' mask, and done everything but peel him alive. **1944** S. Bellow *Dangling Man* 79 A black cotton sleeping mask hung around her neck. **1965** A. Nicol *Truly Married Woman* 3 He then severely flogged his eldest son..for wetting his sleeping-mat last night. **1979** J. Melville *Wages of Zen* ii. 21 Hanae always folded the sleeping mats up and put them away during the day.

c. *sleeping-draught* (further examples), *pill, powder* (further examples), *tablet.*

1664 Lady Hobart *Let.* 23 Mar. in M. M. Verney *Mem.* (1899) IV. ii. 53 Thay had no way but to give hur a sleping pell, & she slep all night. **1790** J. Woodforde *Diary* 17 Sept. (1927) III. 214 Her Child is dead..owing it is supposed to her [having] given him a Sleeping Pill. *c* **1900** H. A. Jones in M. R. Booth *Eng. Plays of 19th Cent.* (1969) II. 414 You'll find a sleeping powder in the second drawer... We must manage to give Lionel a little sleep tonight. **1934** G. B. Shaw *Too True to be Good* I. 42 It must be that new sleeping draught the doctor gave me. **1936** *Time* 19 Oct. 66/2 It was then that she attempted to find independence in an overdose of sleeping powder. **1938** W. S. Maugham *Writer's Notebk.* (1949) 300 He feels the moment can never be excelled and so takes an overdose of sleeping-pills. **1941** C. Milburn *Diary* 4 Oct. (1979) vii. 110 A sleeping tablet last night gave me a good rest. **1973** M. Amis *Rachel Papers* 30 Dozy afternoons slugging on opiate cough mixtures, sleeping-draughts dropped at noon, stolen handfuls of Valium, a sheet of aspirins before breakfast. **1976** H. Wilson *Governance of Britain* iv. 105, I have never had a sleeping pill in No. 10. I have never needed one. **1977** K. O'Hara *Ghost of T. Penry* xv. 148 She'd taken a quadruple dose of sleeping tablets last night.

d. *sleeping sickness*: see as main entry.

e. *sleeping partner, time* (later examples; also *fig.*).

1707 E. Settle *Siege of Troy* III. 18 'Tis high sleeping Time, and so let's all home to Bed. **1833** E. B. Browning tr. *Aeschylus' Prometheus Bound* 96 The close and subtle clasping of a chain..Whose links are furnished from the common mine..From work-times, diet-times, and sleeping-times. **1903** Farmer & Henley *Slang* VI. 247/1 *Sleeping-partner*... 2. (common).—A bed-fellow. **1926** Maines & Grant *Wise-Crack Dict.* 14/1 *Sleeping time*, one year in Jail. **1959** T. S. Eliot *Elder Statesman* 5 The rhythm that governs the repose of our sleepingtime. **1967** P. D. James *Unnatural Causes* I. vi. 42 Your sleeping partner would provide you with an alibi. **1979** G. Mitchell *Mudflats of Dead* xiv. 144 Camilla wasn't the only predator... People are always changing their sleeping partners.

sleeping, *ppl. a.* Add: **1. a.** *Sleeping Beauty* (occas. *Princess*), the heroine of a fairy tale (Charles Perrault's *La belle au bois dormant*) who slept for a hundred years, until woken by the kiss of her prince; also (sometimes with small initial) applied allusively and joc. to any sleeping or unconscious person; also *attrib.* and *transf.*

1729 R. Samber *Perrault's Tales* iv. 32 (*heading*) The sleeping beauty in the wood. **1830** Tennyson (*title*) The sleeping beauty. **1893** S. J. Weyman *Gentleman of France* III. xxviii. 91 The Castle before us..might have been that of the Sleeping Princess, so fairylike it looked. **1907** E. Glyn *Three Weeks* iv. 64 The Austrians..are naturally awake, whereas you English are naturally asleep, and you yourself are the Sleeping Beauty, Paul. **1909** Mrs. H. Ward *Daphne* ii. 40 It had been a Sleeping Beauty story so far. Treasure for the winning—a thorn hedge—and slain lovers! **1936** C. Day Lewis *Friendly Tree* vii. 97 Who could wake the Sleeping Beauty with a kiss of friendship? **1955** E. Bowen *World of Love* vii. 126 Sleeping-beauty briars..swung at her. **1965** J. Porter *Dover Two* ii. 26 A rather smudgy photograph of Curdley's Sleeping Beauty lying motionless in her hospital bed. **1967** V. Nabokov *Speak, Memory* vi. 136 The terra-incognita blanks map makers of old used to call 'sleeping beauties'. **1977** D. Bagley *Enemy* xxiii. 179 You can go in and wake the sleeping beauties. **1979** A. Price *Tomorrow's Ghost* ii. 28 You can be our Sleeping Princess in the Library, and I shall come and wake you with a kiss.

d. *sleeping lizard* (earlier example).

1859 D. Bunce *Trav. with Dr Leichhardt* ix. 94 We disturbed many of the short, knobby-tailed sleeping lizard (*Agama*).

f. *sleeping policeman*: see *policeman 1 e.

sleeping sickness. (In Dict. s.v. Sleeping *vbl. sb.* 2 d.) Substitute for def.: **1.** In general and *fig.* senses.

1551 R. Robinson tr. *More's Utopia* II. M.v.[r], Is there annye man so possessed wyth stonyshe insensibilitie, or with the sleping sicknes, that he wyll not graunt health to be acceptable to hym and delectable. **1647** [in Dict. s.v. Sleeping *vbl. sb.* 2 d]. **1904** *Jrnl. R. Microsc. Soc.* Apr. 179 Sleeping Sickness of Silk-worms..is in no wise due to the micro-organisms of the mulberry leaves.

2. *Path.* Any of several similar diseases caused by protozoans of the genus *Trypanosoma* and transmitted by flies of the genus *Glossina*, prevalent in tropical Africa, and characterized by the proliferation of the trypanosomes in the blood and changes in the central nervous system leading to apathy, coma, and death. Also *attrib.*

1875, 1897 [in Dict. s.v. Sleeping *vbl. sb.* 2 d]. **1905** [see *Gambia]. **1908** W. S. Churchill *My African Journey* v. 96 On April 28th, 1903, Colonel Bruce, whose services had been obtained for the investigation of 'sleeping sickness'.., announced that he considered the disease to be due to a kind of trypanosome, conveyed from one person to another by the bite of a species of tsetse-fly called *Glossina palpalis*. **1926** *Encycl. Brit.* III. 558/1 Sleeping sickness is now treated by compounds of arsenic..; by compounds of antimony..; and by a drug of undisclosed composition called Bayer 205, or Germanin. **1958** L. van der Post *Lost World Kalahari* (1961) vi. 109 A small African outpost on the edge of the sleeping sickness country of Northern Bechuanaland. **1970** Passmore & Robson *Compan. Med. Stud.* II. xix. 7/2 Sleeping sickness in West Africa differs clinically and epidemiologically from the condition in East Africa. In the West, the disease generally runs a chronic course, in the East it is acute.

3. = *sleepy sickness 2. Now *rare.*

1918 *Proc. R. Soc. Med.* XII. (Med. Section) p. xvii, The term 'sleeping sickness'..would not be an inappropriate name for this epidemic [*sc.* encephalitis]. **1920** *Lancet* 13 Mar. 620/2 Some popular term for encephalitis lethargica less cumbrous than 'lethargic encephalitis' and free from the objection to 'sleeping sickness'. **1921** *Times* 3 Feb. 7/2 The Registrar-General's returns for the week.. show that there were 21 cases of sleeping sickness (*encephalitis lethargica*) notified..in London alone. **1961** L. E. Bollo *Introd. Med. & Med. Terminol.* xiv. 148 The von Economo type of encephalitis (encephalitis lethargica, or sleeping sickness) is said to be of unknown etiology... African sleeping sickness, caused by protozoa of the genus *Trypanosoma*, is discussed later.

slee·p-out, *sb.* and *a.* [f. vbl. phr. *to sleep out*: see *sleep *v.* 1 k.] **A.** *sb.* A veranda, porch, or outbuilding providing sleeping accommodation; a sleeping area not in the main building. *Austral.* and *N.Z.*

1941 *Coast to Coast* 84 'A nice scone and a nice cup of tea and a lay-down in the sleep-out,' Mrs Smith was saying in her warm, motherly voice. 'You'll be fine then.' **1962** A. Seymour *One Day of Year* 7 A multiple set, main areas being the kitchen; the 'lounge'; and Hughie's study, which is a glassed-in sleepout at the side of the house. **1977** *N.Z. Herald* 5 Jan. 2–15/8 (Advt.), Well-established country tearooms with 3-brm attached acom... There is almost an acre of grounds plus a sleepout to go with this bargain. **1979** *Sunday Mail Mag.* (Brisbane) 29 Apr. 26/3 The sleep-out..is now back to veranda play space.

B. *attrib.* or as *adj.* Of a person: that sleeps away from the premises, non-resident.

1958 V. P. Johns *Servant's Problem* i. 11 It concerned the household in which she was the sleep-out, full-time maid. **1961** in *Webster* s.v., The sleep-out cooks and maids were coming to work.

slee·p-over, *sb.* (and *a.*) Chiefly *U.S.* [f. vbl. phr. *to sleep over*: see *sleep *v.* 1 j.] **A.** *sb.* **a.** (See quot. 1935.) **b.** An occasion of spending the night at a place other than one's residence. **B.** *attrib.* or as *adj.* Involving spending the night away from one's residence. Of a person: that stays the night.

1935 *Amer. Speech* X. 236/1 A contributor testifies that in part of Pennsylvania, in college use, a sleep-over is a permission to stay away from church and remain in bed on Sunday morning. **1974** [see *sleep-in *a.*]. **1975** [see *sleep *v.* 1 j]. **1979** *Sunset* (Desert ed.) Apr. 156/2 (*caption*) At night wall hanging unhooks to become a feather-soft mat for sleep-over guests.

slee·p-walk, *v.* [Back-formation f. Sleep-walking *vbl. sb.* and *ppl. a.*] *intr.* To walk while asleep; to be in a state resembling that of a sleep-walker. Also *fig.*

1923 in *Englische Studien* (1935) LXX. 119 The heroine sleep-walks. **1954** *Gramophone* XXXI. 445 She sleep-walks noisily, but with dramatic vigour. **1976** E. O'Brien in *New Yorker* 16 Aug. 30/1 Every night Mrs. Reinhardt sleepwalked. **1981** I. McEwan *Comfort of Strangers* i. 18 She sleepwalked from moment to moment, and whole months slipped by without memory, without bearing the faintest imprint of her conscious will. **1982** *Daily Tel.* 21 Dec. 4/6 Mr Reagan..accused Congress of 'sleep-walking' into the future.

sleepy, *a.* Add: **1. d.** Substitute for def.: One of several Australian lizards of the family Scincidæ, esp. the shingleback, *Trachylosaurus rugosus*, found in the southern part of the country. (Earlier example.)

1883 [see *blue tongue, blue-tongue 2].

2. b. (Further examples.) See also *sleepy sickness.

1831 W. Youatt *Horse* 103 Some say that there is a yellowness of the eye..in the early stage of sleepy or stomach-staggers. **1913** Dorland *Med. Dict.* (ed. 7) 887/1 *Sleepy staggers, stomach staggers*, a disease of horses, of unknown causation but usually associated with the eating of moldy hay and grain. **1922** *Times Lit. Suppl.* 3 Aug. 511/2 The tomato suffers from the so-called 'Sleepy Disease' manifested in a wilting of the plant.

4. sleepy-bye(s), *Sc.* **-baw** *sb.*, a nursery name for sleep; also as *v. intr.*, to go to sleep; **Sleepy Hollow, sleepy hollow,** (*a*) a name given to a place with a soporific atmosphere or characterized by torpidity (in quot. 1820, to which some quots. allude, the name of a valley near Tarrytown (Irving's home) in Westchester county, N.Y. State); (*b*) a type of comfortable deep-upholstered armchair; also called *sleepy-hollow chair*; **sleepy-time** *U.S.*, bedtime.

1907 N. MUNRO *Daft Days* x. 85 Just you lie down there pet, and sleepy-baw. **1925** M. BEERBOHM *Observations* 37 Before you go to sleepy-bye I'll read it to you. **1968** A. DIMENT *Bang Bang Birds* x. 177 'Sleepy byes time, Lex,' and I just felt the prick in my arm before I was blotted out again. **1820** W. IRVING *Sk. Bk.* VI. 51 *(heading)* The legend of Sleepy Hollow. *Ibid.* 53 This sequestered glen has long been known by the name of Sleepy Hollow, and its rustic lads are called the Sleepy Hollow boys. **1834** M. EDGEWORTH *Helen* I. xv. 321 Beauclerc, who had not yet tried the chair, sank into its luxurious depth, and leaning back, asked if it might not be appropriately called the 'Sleepy-hollow'. **1836** *Madrid in 1835: Sk. by Resident Officer* I. v. 94 No friendly arm-chair; none of that somniferous form, not unaptly termed 'sleepy hollow'. **1868** L. M. ALCOTT *Little Women* v. 79 There were..Sleepy-Hollow chairs, and queer tables. **1897** [in Dict., sense 2 c]. **1922** JOYCE *Ulysses* 371 Rip van Winkle we played... Then I did Rip van Winkle coming back. She leaned on the sideboard watching. Moorish eyes. Twenty years asleep in Sleepy Hollow. **1924** GALSWORTHY *White Monkey* I. vii. 53 'First time I remember anything of the sort on that Board.' 'Sleepy hollow,' said Soames. **1955** 'A. GILBERT' *Is she Dead Too?* v. 91 There's plenty of work to be had, you don't have to stop in Sleepy Hollow. **1957** M. SWAN *Brit. Guiana* 98 It is a charming little sleepy hollow of a town with long strait streets. **1966** M. M. PEGLER *Dict. Interior Design* (1967) 412 *Sleepy hollow chair*, a mid-19th-century American chair which is upholstered and has a curved back and low, comfortable arms. The seat is usually scooped out. **1976** N. FREELING *Lake Isle* viii. 43 This bastard in Soulay is merely wanting to make a fuss. Sleepy hollow. If he were any good he wouldn't be there. **1981** *London Rev. Bks.* 2–15 July 6/4 The restless forces were never as strong in Britain as the laws of inertia and the politics of Sleepy Hollow. **1862** K. STONE *Jrnl.* 19 Aug. in *Brokenburn* (1955) 137 He was satisfied I would not sleep a wink, but at sleepy time.. we all went to bed and slept soundly. **1918** S. C. BRYANT *Stories to tell Little Ones* p. ix, I have been in the habit of singing them rhymes..a while before sleepy-time. **1950** O. NASH *Family Reunion* 81 At sleepy-time he beats a path Straight to the bedroom or the bath.

sleepy sickness. [SLEEPY *a.*] †**1.** = *SLEEPING SICKNESS 2. *Obs.*

1803, 1903 [in Dict. s.v. SLEEPY *a.* 2b].

2. Encephalitis lethargica, an often fatal disease widespread between 1916 and 1928, characterized in many of those who survived it by extreme somnolence due to physiological brain damage.

1922 ASHBY & WRIGHT *Dis. Children* (ed. 6) 389 Encephalitis lethargica. Sleepy sickness. Epidemic stupor. This disease is more common in adults. **1923** *Daily Mail* 26 Feb. 9 Sleepy sickness (encephalitis lethargica) is attacking prominent people in Winnipeg. **1930** A. CHRISTIE *Murder at Vicarage* xiv. 112 There's nothing radically wrong with him... He's had Encephalitis Lethargica, sleepy sickness, as it's commonly called. **1962** 'J. BELL' *Crime in our Time* IV. 99 Encephalitis lethargica, or sleepy sickness (not to be confused with trypanosomiasis, sleeping sickness, carried by the tsetse fly). **1973** *Daily Tel.* 27 Jan. 11/1 Survivors of the great sleepy-sickness epidemic, which claimed five million victims between 1916 and 1927, lived on in a kind of somnolence for 40 years till this drug awoke them.

3. *Vet.* A disease of pregnant ewes, provoked by imbalance between the degree of nourishment and the stage of pregnancy, and characterized by somnolence and neuromuscular disturbances; pregnancy toxæmia. Also *Comb.*

1937 *Vet. Jrnl.* XCIII. 213 In the early stages of sleepy sickness they lie in a perfectly normal recumbent position, but before long..on their side with legs stretched out. **1950** D. GASCOYNE *Vagrant* 8 Baa, Baa, O sleepy-sickness-rotted sheep, in your nice fold Are none but marketable fleeces. **1964** *N.Z. Jrnl. Agric.* Mar. 546/2 More than 80 per cent of deaths in the ewe flock occur over lambing, when losses due to blood poisoning, bearing trouble, sleepy sickness..and lambing difficulties occur.

sleet, *sb.*[1] Add: **2.** *sleet-gust; sleet-bound* adj.

1782 J. TRUMBULL *M'Fingal* III. 65 He glitter'd to the Western ray Like Sleet-bound trees in wintry skies. **1929** C. DAY LEWIS *Transitional Poem* II. 34 When bullying April bruised mine eyes With sleet-bound appetites and crude Experiments of green. **1928** BLUNDEN *Retreat* 48 Where the lashed sleet-gust foams, buffeting and blinding.

sleet, *v.* **1. b.** (Later example.)

1955 C. M. KORNBLUTH *Mindworm* 39 Her manicured hand gripped his arm in excitement and terror. Unfelt radiation sleeted through their loins.

sleety, *a.* **2.** (Earlier example.)

1816 JANE AUSTEN *Emma* II. xvii. 329 The evening of a cold sleety April day.

sleeve, *sb.* Add: **1. a.** (Further examples denoting a separate article of dress.)

1805 JANE AUSTEN *Let.* 21 Apr. (1952) 154, I wore my crape sleeves to the Concert, I had them put in on the occasion. **1897** *Montgomery Ward Catal.* 297/1 Ladies' Gossamer Rubber Sleeves, 16 inches long. **1967** G. BELLAIRS *Single Ticket to Death* v. 61 He was without jacket and wore black calico detachable sleeves reaching to the elbows of his white shirt.

2. f. *another pair of sleeves* (later examples); *to put the sleeve on* (someone): (*a*) to beg or borrow money from (someone); (*b*) to arrest (someone): to cause (someone) to be arrested; *a sleeve across the windpipe,* an assault or severe blow (usu. *fig.*).

1904 H. JAMES *Golden Bowl* I. III. xxiv. 395 'Decide to live—ah yes!—for her child.' 'Oh, bother her child!.. To live..for her father—which is another pair of sleeves!' **1930** D. RUNYON in *Sat. Even. Post* 5 Apr. 72/2 These coppers..know who he is very well indeed and will take great pleasure in putting the old sleeve on him if they only have a few charges against him, which they do not. **1931** *Amer. Speech* VI. 440 *Put the sleeve on,* to borrow; to make a touch from a fellow convict. **1934** H. N. ROSE *Thes. Slang* iii. 29/1 Wait'll I put the sleeve on Joe fer some chewin'. **1937** *Nature* 23 Jan. 130/1 Prof. Furnas's exasperating,..naive volume is altogether another pair of sleeves. **1952** WODEHOUSE *Barmy in Wonderland* i. 13 My wardrobe perished in the holocaust, of course. When you're being given the sleeve across the windpipe by Acts of God, you don't waste time fumbling around for socks and trousers. **1960** WENTWORTH & FLEXNER *Dict. Amer. Slang* 486/1 *Put the sleeve on (someone),* 1. To arrest someone; to identify someone to the police for arrest. 2. To stop a friend on the street in order to ask for a loan of money; to ask for a contribution or for money owed. **1972** WODEHOUSE *Pearls, Girls, & Monty Bodkin* ii. 17 Just as if it looked as though all they had to do was collect the bridesmaids, order the cake and sign up the Bishop and assistant clergy, along came the sleeve across the windpipe. Her father refused to give his consent to their union.

7. b. *spec.* part of a celt or prehistoric axe.

1929 V. G. CHILDE *Danube in Prehistory* 78 Possibly they were shafted with the aid of horn sleeves. *Ibid.* 107 Axes and adzes hafted in deer-horn sleeves. **1970** BRAY & TRUMP *Dict. Archaeol.* 20/1 *Antler sleeve,* a section of deer antler carved into a mortice at one end to hold a stone axe head.

c. *Electr.* A metal cylinder fitted round the full length of the core of an electromagnetic relay to modify the speeds of opening and closing. Cf. *SLUG *sb.*[2] 3 c.

1921 W. AITKEN *Autom. Telephone Systems* I. 45 The copper sleeve and heavy ring on the core of F gives it a greater range of adjustment. **1969** S. F. SMITH *Teleph. & Telegr. A* ii. 45 The skin effect, due mainly to the iron core, tends to confine alternating magnetic fluxes at speech frequencies to the nickel-iron sleeves to give the required impedance.

d. *Aeronaut.* = *DROGUE 3 (*b*) and (*c*).

1933 C. K. STEWART *Speech Amer. Airman* (thesis, Univ. Akron) 90 *Sleeve,* a towed target for anti-aircraft guns to practice shooting at. **1933** S. SPENDER *Poems* 45 The air-liner..Glides over suburbs and the sleeves set trailing tall To point the wind. **1937** *Times* 12 June 16/4 The target was the usual sleeve, towed behind a Fairey Gordon. **1942** *Tee Emm* (Air Ministry) II. 67 There's the old Henley and there's the sleeve coming up—. They're off!—..A grand salvo after a week's weary waiting.

e. A close-fitting protective cover or case, esp. one for a gramophone record; a slip-case. Cf. *record sleeve* s.v. *RECORD *sb.* 14.

1953 *N.Y. Times* 22 Mar. II. 40/6 Another group of buyers is swayed more by the art on the 'sleeve' or jacket than by the quality, or even by the title, of the music. **1954** *Melody Maker* 11 Dec. 15/2 His first LP to be released in this country..reached me without sleeve. **1976** W. GOLDMAN *Magic* III. ii. 119 She lifted the tone arm off, and..put the record back in the sleeve. **1981** *Verbatim* Spring 20/2 This is a man's pocket wallet with some plastic credit card sleeves.

8. a. (sense *7 d) *sleeve target*; (sense *7 e) *sleeve artist, design, information, -picture.*

1977 *Times* 18 Apr. (Gram. Suppl.) p. iv/6 Individual sleeve artists such as Roger Dean or Patrick Woodroffe. *Ibid.* iv/7 Jazz musicians..insisted on good sleeve design. **1966** *Melody Maker* 23 July 16/5 Bob Houston's review of the John Coltrane album 'Ascension' blindly copies the sleeve information that Freddie Hubbard plays the first trumpet solo. **1959** *Times* 10 Jan. 9/5 A disc with an imaginative if punning sleeve-picture showing wind blowing through barley. **1932** *Aeroplane* 11 May 839 *(caption),* A Fairey IIIF seaplane towing a sleeve target for gunnery practice **1955** 'N. SHUTE' *Requiem for Wren* iii. 68 Firing the Oerlikon at a sleeve target towed by an aeroplane. **1979** A. FOX *Threat Warning Red* iii. 27 Sleeve target this afternoon, an AA shoot.

8. b. sleeve bearing, a form of bearing in which an axle or shaft turns in a lubricated sleeve; **sleeve-board** (later examples); **sleeve-cap** *U.S.*, the topmost part of a sleeve; **sleeve dog,** for '(see quot.)' read: a very small Pekinese dog, usually under six pounds in weight; (later examples); **sleeve gun** *U.S.*, a miniature gun which can be concealed in the clothing; **sleeve-note,** an informative or critical note about a gramophone record, printed on the sleeve; **sleeve Pekinese** = *sleeve dog* above; **sleeve-valve,** a kind of valve, employed in certain types of internal-combustion engine, consisting of a hollow cylindrical sleeve fitting closely inside the engine cylinder and moving with the piston in such a way that inlet and exhaust ports are opened and closed at appropriate times; freq. *attrib.*; hence **sleeve-valved** *a.*

1907 W. S. BOULTON *Pract. Coal-Mining* III. 9 The 'sleeve' bearing..is intended to obviate this waste [of oil], and to secure continuously good lubrication. **1967** *Times Rev. Industry* Aug. 22/2 Exhaust silencers, anti-vibration mounts, the substitution of sleeve bearings for ball or roller bearings, [etc.]..are only a few of the attempts made to reduce the noise at source. **1975** *Sci. Amer.* July 50/1 Since many motors, engines and other machines incorporate journal bearings (sometimes designated plain bearings, sleeve bearings, fluid-film bearings or bushings), the annual production of journal bearings is in the billions. **1916** *Daily Colonist* (Victoria, B.C.) 2 July 7/6 (Advt.), Sleeve Boards, regular 75c. Our price 32c. **1969** D. CLARK *Death after Evensong* ii. 31 Trousers, with no fore-and-aft creases.., ironed on a sleeve board. **1964** *McCall's Sewing* xi. 158/1 All set-in sleeves are cut with a sleeve cap that is larger than the armhole section into which it must fit. **1978** *Detroit Free Press* 2 Apr. 50/1 All too often a knitted sweater is ruined by puckers where the sleeve cap joins the shoulder section. **1931** A. C. DIXEY *Lion Dog of Peking* iv. 12 They were petted and pampered, the smallest—the highly-prized 'sleeve' dogs—being carried in the voluminous sleeves of the long robes worn at Court by both sexes. **1970** P. TAMONY *Americanisms* (typescript) No. 27. 7 The toy or small breeds such as the Pekinese and Shih Tzu had been the sleeve dogs of women at the Imperial Court of China. **1944** R. F. ADAMS *Western Words* 146/1 *Sleeve gun,* a derringer such as a gambler carried up his sleeve. **1971** K. WHEELER *Epitaph for Mister Wynn* xxxii. 396 He..took out a snub-barreled Sharps derringer, a sleeve gun. **1974** E. MCGIRR *Murderous Journey* 153 Have a look at Pout ... Sleeve gun and I'd guess an envelope in his breast pocket. **1956** *Gramophone* Oct. 184/2 Each soloist is given his fair share of the spotlight (the sleeve notes helpfully identify which plays when). **1980** *Early Music* Jan. 85/2 A pity, though, that the programme book's translation of the libretti kept so close to the impenetrable one in the sleeve-notes to the Electrola/Reflexe recording. **1949** I. HARMAN *Pekingese* iv. 37 A Miniature or Sleeve Pekingese is, officially, any Pekingese which is not more than six pounds in weight. **1978** 'J. MELVILLE' *Axwater* i. 12 A tiny, bright-eyed, button-faced creature appeared.. and behind it another even smaller. Two sleeve Pekingese. **1910** *Engineering* 18 Nov. 688/3 Both Messrs. Panhard and Levassor..and Messrs. Milnes Daimler, Limited.. showed examples of the Knight sleeve-valve engine. **1911** *Ibid.* 3 Nov. 590/2 The usual tappet-valves are replaced by a single sleeve-valve. **1958** GIBSON & TUTEUR *Control System Components* xi. 424 A Vickers two-land sleeve valve. **1982** P. DICKINSON *Last House-Party* iv. 49 'This car makes a remarkable amount of smoke.' 'That's the trouble with these sleeve-valve engines.' **1932** *World Today* Feb. 261/2 The news that Daimlers had taken over the Lanchester Company suggested that it might be a sleeve-valved job.

sleeved, *ppl. a.* Add: **b.** Fitted or covered with a sleeve or sleeves (in sense 7 of the sb.).

1905 *Engineering Rev.* XIII. 272/1 The Hyatt bearing has..been successfully applied to sleeved axles, both in small cars and heavy 'buses and lorries. **1970** 'S. HARVESTER' *Moscow Road* i. 13 A stereophonic phonograph and two racks of sleeved discs. **1976** *Gramophone* June 51/3 The pressing is beautifully smooth, and the disc is attractively sleeved; the cover is a water colour of the composer by his son.

sleeveen (slī·vīn, slīvī·n). *Ir.* and *Newfoundland.* Also **sleiveen, slieveen.** [ad. Ir. *slighbhín, slíbhín* sly person, trickster.] An untrustworthy or cunning person.

1834 S. LOVER *Legends & Stories of Ireland* (Ser. 2) 295 How the man was chated by a *sleeveen* vagabone. **1888** W. B. YEATS *Fairy & Folk Tales Irish Peasantry* 220 In trust took he John's lands,—*Sleiveens* were all his race. **1892** J. BARLOW *Irish Idylls* viii. 215 He isn't the *slieveen* to be playin' fast and loose wid your dacint little slip of a girl. **1955** L. E. F. ENGLISH *Historic Newfoundland* 36 *Slieveen,* a deceitful person. *a* **1966** 'M. NA GOPALEEN' *Best of Myles* (1968) 104 A thief, a fly-be-night, a sleeveen and a baucagh-shool. **1973** G. PINSENT *Rowdyman* 42 Mr. Lowe told Will all about his friendship with our father and about how decent a fellow he was, but that Will had 'the looks of a sleeveen about him'. *Ibid.* 53 Well, I took my eyes off him for a half a second and that sleeveen jabbed me in the gut with two hard fingers. **1975** D. O'SULLIVAN in D. Marcus *Best Irish Short Stories* (1977) II. 95 'O, the crabbed, conniving little sleeveen.' 'She's up in London now, dancing in the Harp.'

sleeveless, *a.* **2. b.** Delete 'Now *rare*' and add later examples.

1931 L. STORM *Dragon* xvii. 293 I'd never have the courage like you..to venture forth on what might be a sleeveless errand. **1948** *Chambers's Jrnl.* 320/2 And, as soon as they were settled in, he had McGilchrist ride openly away, putting it about he was satisfied all the talk of whisky-'stilling was a pack of lies by ill-doing ones willing to give the King's officer a sleeveless errand. **1959** I. & P. OPIE *Lore & Lang. Schoolch.* iv. 58 In some [*sc.* schoolchildren's tricks] he [*sc.* the dupe] is sent on sleeveless errands.

sleever. Add: (Later example.) Also *Austral.* and *N.Z.* Also, a measure of drink (usu. of beer) contained in a sleever. Cf. *long-sleever* s.v. LONG *a.*[1] 18.

1936 'R. HYDE' *Passport to Hell* v. 89 Places where the police weren't so quick off the mark if the landlord passed a few sleevers over the counter after six o'clock. **1941** BAKER *Dict. Austral. Slang* 67 *Sleever,* a drink, esp. a large drink. **1970** 'H. CARMICHAEL' *Remote Control* i. 8 'I haven't got a glass with a handle so you'll have to make do with a sleever.'..She brought his beer. **1975** B. MEYRICK *Behind Light* viii. 99 Herby used to nip up to the New Inn, buy a 'sleever' of beer and bring it back.

sleeving, *vbl. sb.* Add: **3.** A tubular covering for a cylindrical object, esp. of insulating material for an electric cable, etc.; material used for this purpose.

1923 *Wireless World* 12 May 168/2, ½ lb. No. 20 tinned copper wire and a quantity of insulating sleeving of various colours. **1933** *Electrician* 10 Feb. 185/2 Woven sleevings, stockingettes or circular tapes of cotton or silk are varnished and used extensively for insulating wire connections of windings, radio sets,..etc. **1978** *SLR Camera* Nov. 31/3 Should it prove to be undersize, the best policy will be to use suitable piece of thin-walled aluminium tube (available from model shops) as sleeving.

sleigh, *sb.* Add: **4. sleigh bed** *N. Amer.*, a type of bed resembling a sleigh, having head- and footboards curving outwards; a French bed.

1902 F. C. Morse *Furnit. of Olden Time* iii. 77 Plainer bedsteads in this [French bed] style were made, veneered with mahogany, and they are sometimes called sleigh beds, on account of their shape. **1950** W. Bird *Nova Scotia* iii. 87 Those who spend the night in the ancient bedrooms, perhaps sleeping on the great 'sleigh bed' that remains in one. **1976** *National Observer* (U.S.) 14 Feb. 4/4 (Advt.), Antique Marketry Furniture, Ca. 1790, Dresser w/mirror, highboy, desk, two sleigh beds.

sleigh-bell. (Earlier example.)

c **1780** in *Amer. Poems* (1793) I. 208 Mind and have the sleigh-bells sent.

slei·gh-ride, *sb.* Also **sleighride, sleigh ride. 1.** A ride in a sleigh. Also *fig.*

1770 J. Hiltzheimer *Diary* (1893) 2 Apr. 20 Took a sleigh ride, the 'five mile round', with wife, sister, and son Tommy. **1828** H. J. Finn et al. *Whimwhams* 22 Such worthy gentlemen happen to remember..a winter's breakfast at a country inn, after a sleigh-ride of ten miles for an appetite. **1849** [in Dict. s.v. Sleigh *sb.* 4]. **1902** W. D. Hulbert *Forest Neighbors* (1903) 181 Not even a sleigh-ride on a winter's night can set the live blood dancing as it will dance and tingle up there above the clouds. **1956** E. B. White *Let.* 14 Jan. (1976) 412, I am cheered up when I see our political giants discovering that the lil ole writing game isn't quite the sleighride they like to think it is.

2. *U.S. slang.* The action of taking a narcotic drug, usu. cocaine; the euphoria resulting from taking a narcotic drug. Usu. in phr. *to take* (*go on*) *a sleigh ride* and varr. Cf. *snow *sb.*[1] 4 d.

1925 *Flynn's* 4 Apr. 818/2 *Sleigh-ride*, a jab of morphine from a hypodermic syringe, or the resulting state of intoxication. **1928** M. C. Sharpe *Chicago May* xxxi. 286 *Taking a sleigh ride*, getting morphine. **1938** D. Castle *Do your Own Time* xxix. 251 'He took to going on sleigh rides.' 'No! Where the hell did he get the snow?' **1942** *Detective Fiction* Apr. 56/2 Julio is very fond of his hop. Anything from the weed to a sniff of snow. Suppose he gets on a big sleigh ride and talks out of turn. **1963** 'D. Shannon' *Death of Busybody* iv. 52 It was just some dope out on a sleigh-ride.

3. *U.S. slang.* An implausible or false story; a hoax, a deliberate deception. Freq. in phr. *to take* (someone) *for a sleigh ride*, to mislead (someone). Cf. *ride *sb.*[1] 1 f (*a*).

1931 G. Irwin *Amer. Tramp & Underworld Slang* 172 An absolutely impossible or unlikely idea or action, or.. the cheating or fleecing of a victim... 'We gave him a sleigh ride'—we cheated him by a false story or by sharp practice. **1942** Berrey & Van den Bark *Amer. Thes. Slang* § 202/2 Incredible story, *sleigh ride*. **1950** *Sun* (Baltimore) 13 Mar. 1/1 House Republicans, charging that the taxpayers are being taken for a 'bureaucratic sleighride'. **1960** Wentworth & Flexner *Dict. Amer. Slang* 486/2 *Sleighride*, an instance of being cheated, believing a lie, or being taken advantage of. Almost always in the expression 'taken for a sleighride'.

Hence as *v. intr.*, (*a*) to ride in a sleigh; (*b*) to take a narcotic drug. Also **slei·gh-rider; slei·gh-riding** *vbl. sb.*

1807–8 Sleigh-riding [in Dict. s.v. Sleigh *sb.* 4]. **1833** *Knickerbocker* I. 207 Arrived at the Plains, the sleigh riders stopped at a tavern. **1845** Sleigh-ride [in Dict. s.v. Sleigh *sb.* 4]. **1883** *Wheelman* (Boston, Mass.) I. 434, I was making my first trial of it [*sc.* a bicycle] in the snow, among the sleigh-riders. **1915** G. Bronson-Howard *God's Man* vi. iii. 376 Whadda you been doing?—sleigh-riding? Stick to the long bamboo, Charley—that snow's awful bad for the imagination. *Ibid.* vii. i. 409 Petty's kind had been profitable 'sleigh-riders' when he provided 'snow' on Seventh Avenue. **1929** *Detective Fiction Weekly* 13 Apr. 599/1 He's a sleigh rider. You know, sniffs coke. Made a fortune writing papers for booze hustlers and has spent every dime of it on snow. **1934** C. de Lenoir *Hundredth Man* i. 13 Sniffing heroin or cocaine is 'sleigh-riding'. **1949** *Summit Valley Times* (Argo, Illinois) 1 Dec. 4/3 Santa, who now reigns the Christmas card realm, in 1919 managed to sleighride onto only a handful of cards for children. **1977** H. Waugh *Secret Room of Morgate House* (1978) xxxiv. 164 Between times they sleighrode, and even walked. **1982** J. Adair *Founding Fathers* xii. 267 The New Englanders adopted..skating and sleigh-riding from their Dutch neighbours.

sleiveen, var. *sleeveen.

‖ **slendang** (sle·ndæŋ). Also **selendang.** [a. Javanese *slénḍang*, Indonesian *seléndang*.] In Indonesia, a long scarf or stole worn by women.

1885 H. O. Forbes *Naturalist's Wanderings Eastern Archipelago* iii. ii. 147 Above this the body is girt with a silk *slendang*, half concealing the breasts. **1911** B. Miall tr. *Cabaton's Java* v. 125 An indispensable article of the feminine toilet is the *slendang*: a scarf in *batik*, often ornamented with fringes. **1937** M. Covarrubias *Island of Bali* iii. 48 It is necessary to be properly dressed to pay or to receive a visit. The breasts of men and women should be covered by a special breast-cloth, a *saput* for men and a *selendang* for women. **1941** *Lincoln* (Nebraska) *Sunday Jrnl. & Star* 12 Oct. D-6/1 Maria Montez, in 'White Savage', will wear a scant bit of cloth called a *slendang*, something like a sarong, only more so, or less so! **1963** J. Kirkup *Tropic Temper* 168 The men approach the women and claim their selendangs or long gauzy stoles which are used most effectively in the dance movements. **1964** Langewis & Wagner *Decorative Art in Indonesian Textiles* 27 In a certain *batik* cloth, the *slendang*, a centrally placed undecorated area always appears in the form of an elongated rhomboid.

slender, *v.* Delete † *Obs. rare*—[1] and add: **a.** *trans.* (Later example.)

1965 H. Porter *Cats of Venice* 81 These shape-gripping *cheong sams* had slendered them to elegance.

b. *intr.* To become narrower, to narrow. Also with *down*.

1871 G. M. Hopkins *Poems* (1967) 13 And slendering to his burning rim Into the flat blue mist the sun Drops out and all our day is done. **1955** E. Bowen *World of Love* iii. 55 Her strong forearms, which slendered down..to the wrists.

slender-bodied, *a.* (Later example.)

1963 *Times* 4 Feb. 13/2 Dresses..with a slender-bodied look.

slenderize (sle·ndərəiz), *v.* Also **slenderise.** [f. Slender *a.* + -ize.] **a.** *intr.* To make oneself slender, to slim. **b.** *trans.* To make (something) slender, to make (the figure) appear slender. Also *absol.*

1923 *Weekly Dispatch* 4 Feb. 15/5 A slight figure will be more essential than ever. 'You must slenderise,' said one, coining a useful word. **1923** *Daily Mail* 21 Mar. 6/1 (Advt.), Corsets for slenderising full figures. **1946** *Sun* (Baltimore) 10 May 12/1 He brought it down to within a few inches of the ground, slenderized the column on which it hangs in merry-go-round fashion. **1964** *McCall's Sewing* i. 11/1 Lines for the 'Viking' type are a problem. You'll want those which slenderise without adding height. **1976** *National Observer* (U.S.) 13 Mar. 11/5 (Advt.), Starting age 6 yrs. Slenderize. Charm... Clover Lodge [establishment for overweight girls].

Hence **sle·nderizer; sle·nderizing** *ppl. a.* and *vbl. sb.*

1927 *Daily Express* 9 Sept. 5/5 There is the high straight line that is suited to the office frock, and the graceful slenderising V-cut accentuated by removable front of deep ivory crêpe-de-chine. **1928** *Sunday Express* 29 Apr. 15/4 Chefs are searching their brains for the slenderising sweet that will tempt both men and women diners. **1932** *Woman & Beauty* Apr. 87/1 (Advt.), Slenderizing. Free book tells how you can become slim. **1935** *Amer. Speech* X. 192/2 Black velvet, we find, is the best *slenderizer*. **1958** *People* 4 May 7/1 (Advt.), A most flattering and slenderising style. **1969** *Daily Tel.* 18 Apr. 17 The skirt does a slenderising job where most women want to look slim. **1970** *Globe & Mail* (Toronto) 25 Sept. 10/2 (Advt.), The jacket is a little longer. It continues the slenderizing effect of the waist. **1978** *Detroit Free Press* 5 Mar. B12/1, I made a slenderizing lunch of cottage cheese and grapefruit sections.

slenderness. Add: **3.** *attrib.* **slenderness ratio** *Engin.*, the ratio of the effective length of a column or pillar to its least radius of gyration (formerly, to its least diameter).

1905 M. Merriman *Mechanics of Materials* (ed. 10) ix. 191 The ratio l/r is called the 'slenderness ratio' of the column. **1931** *Engineering* 9 Jan. 61/3 Experiments on eccentrically-loaded steel columns... The slenderness ratios ranged from 50 to 150. **1976** R. F. Warner et al. *Reinforced Concrete* xiii. 308 The effective strength of the column section..is divided by a reduction factor R... R is given as $R = 1{\cdot}2 - 0{\cdot}01(l/r)$ in which l/r is the maximum slenderness ratio for the column, for bending in any plane.

slenter, var. *schlenter, *sb.* and *a.* **sleughi,** var. *saluki.

sleuth, *sb.*[2] **2. b.** For *U.S.* read 'orig. *U.S.*' and add earlier and further examples. Also *transf.*

1872 *N.Y. Fireside Compan.* 13 May 4/3 The name of the story is *Sleuth, the Detective* and a more remarkable and thrilling story has seldom ever been written. **1904** 'O. Henry' *Cabbages & Kings* iv. 73 Goodwin followed at increased speed, but without any of the artful tactics that are so dear to the heart of the sleuth. **1949** *Manch. Guardian Weekly* 22 Dec. 2/3 A school of newspaper sleuths who attributed every declaration of American foreign policy to the hidden hand of George Kennan. **1958** 'J. Byrom' *Or be he Dead* v. 69, I gather you have Miss Canning as your assistant sleuth. **1979** *Oxf. Jrnl.* 16 Nov. 1 (*caption*) Amateur sleuths Gordon Murray and Jane Lawton... Their investigations launched a top-level probe into an Oxford business.

sleuth, *v.*[2] Add: **a.** Also, to investigate (something or someone). Also with *out* (in quot. 1939: to detect or expose).

1939 [see *record *sb.* 5 g]. **1949** *Sun* (Baltimore) 16 Nov. 14/3 Men who qualify for the tremendous job of sleuthing a single big industry like steel or coal—and determining the facts to make wage, hour and pension recommendations. **1956** A. Christie *Dead Man's Folly* xviii. 240 'Who hired you to sleuth me?'.. 'You are in error,' replied Poirot. 'I have not been sleuthing you.' **1968** P. Dickinson *Skin Deep* v. 108 It had been something private he'd sleuthed out, something secret. **1979** *Amer. Speech 1978* LIII. 285 Ten years ago, sleuthing a clue from Lenneberg, I wrote..'The use of tools may be much older than language.'

b. *intr.* To act as a detective; to conduct an investigation. Also with *around*.

1912 L. J. Vance *Destroying Angel* xx. 276 So I went sleuthing; traced you through the canal to Peconic. **1930** 'Sapper' *Finger of Fate* 99 My poor friend..labours under the delusion that he is a detective. He goes about with magnifying glasses, and sleuths. **1975** *High Times* Dec. 31/2 If you sleuth around—beginning at the roach-infested gringo palace, the Hotel Astorial—you can get directions to the mushroom fields overlooking San José. **1980** E. Dewhurst *Drink This* ii. 28 He had been sleuthing, unconsciously..all the time he had thought he was relaxing.

Hence **sleu·thing** *vbl. sb.*

1900 Ade *More Fables* 193 He called himself a Reformer, and he did all his Sleuthing in the line of Duty. **1924** *Weekly Westm. Gaz.* 13 Sept. 580/2 One always knew all about his theories and his sleuthing. **1946** *Reader's Digest* Sept. 76/1 Izzy knew nothing of sleuthing procedure; he simply knocked on the door. **1958** T. F. T. Plucknett *Early Eng. Legal Lit.* v. 83 Teasing as these references are, they seem too obscure and divergent to permit any plausible conclusion as the authorship of *Brevia Placitata*, in spite of the very clever sleuthing of Mr Turner. **1979** *Dædalus* Summer 111 It is possible, through conscientious sleuthing, to decode the secondary associations of symbols.

sleuth-hound. 2. (Examples in sense 'detective'.)

[**1849** A. B. Reach *Clement Lorimer* xiii. 130 There is an awful mystery which the sleuth hounds of the law may trace—a mystery of suspicion, perhaps a mystery of crime.] **1902** Wodehouse *Pothunters* iv. 66 Jim's respect for the abilities of our national sleuth-hounds was greater than Tony's, and a good deal greater than that of most people. **1929** *Bookman* Nov. 264/1 'What is it, Fra Diavolo?' he asked... 'A peeler, fellow, a sleuth-hound.' **1948** *Amer. Speech* XXIII. 306/2 The hunt for it would be engrossing to a literary sleuth-hound.

slew, *sb.*[1] Add: **1. b.** More generally, an expanse or mass of water. *rare.*

1915 D. H. Lawrence *Rainbow* ix. 227 Tilly, an old woman now, came in saying that the labourers who had been suppering up said the yard and everywhere was just a slew of water. **1941** *Penguin New Writing* II. 20 Great slews of water flushed along the deck.

slew, *sb.*[2] Add: **2.** = *slewing *vbl. sb.* 2. Usu. *attrib.*

1958 J. G. Truxal *Control Engineers' Handbk.* iii. 6 (*table*) Slew rate. **1981** *Popular Hi-Fi* Mar. 78/2 Measurements of slew rate do appear to be relevant to the performance of an amplifier.

slew (slū), *sb.*[3] *colloq.* (orig. *U.S.*). Also **slue.** [ad. Ir. *slua*(*gh*), crowd, multitude.] A very large number *of*, a great amount *of*. Also in pl.

1839 D. P. Thompson *Green Mountain Boys* II. x. 145 He has cut out a road, and drawn up a whole slew of cannon clean to the top of Mount Defiance. **1858** *Harper's Mag.* May 767/2 By gracious! three thousand dollars is a 'tarnal slue of money. **1897** R. E. Robinson *Uncle Lisha's Outing* i. 2 I've seen slews on 'em [*sc.* ducks] on the ma'shes. **1937** *Sun* (Baltimore) 13 Nov. 8/1 This fable furnishes an excuse for a whole slue of low-comedy gags and wheezes. **1958** *Listener* 19 June 1015/2, I got up and checked with another inspector. There seemed to be slews of them lounging around. **1970** *Guardian* 9 Apr. 3/2 The offer has brought in 'piles of letters'... In addition.. he has received a 'slew of calls' from other bankers asking about the offer. **1978** J. Carroll *Mortal Friends* iv. vi. 458 Should I ask a slew of questions just to draw his gaze my way? **1982** *Radio Times* 11–17 Sept. 86/2 Roger Dennhardt had served three years of a 13-year sentence for armed robbery when..he offered to give evidence for the Crown against a slew of former associates.

slew (slū), *sb.*[4] *Basketry.* [Orig. uncertain: perh. a new sense of Slew *sb.*[2]] A filling made of two or more strands worked together. Hence **slew** *v.*[2]; **sle·wing** *vbl. sb.*

1902 P. N. Hasluck *Basket Work* 50 Next fill in by working two rods together; this process is known by basket-makers as slewing. *Ibid.* 53 Start slewing with one rod, add another a few stakes farther on. **1907** [see *fitch *sb.*[3]]. **1912** T. Okey *Art of Basket-Making* vi. 27 The slath being now finished he slews up the bottom to its required size. *Ibid.* vii. 59 Any small modification..may be made, during the slewing up of the bottom. **1953** A. G. Knock *Willow Basket-Work* 47 The upsetting, which is begun with tops, consists of four rounds of three-rod waling, and the siding is a three-rod slew. **1960** E. Legg *Country Baskets* 79 It was made of coarse brown willows in the familiar slew beloved of the worker anxious to turn out as many baskets as he could. **1964** H. Hodges *Artifacts* x. 146 Both slewing and randing require an odd number of stakes.

slew, *v.* Add: **1. d.** Also *Austral.* and *N.Z.*, to outwit, to trick. Also in phr. *to get slewed*, to lose one's bearings in the bush, to be 'bushed'.

1813 V. Pyke *Wild Will Enderby* (ed. 2) i. xi. 62 The general impression seemed to be that Jack Ketch had been 'slued' (*anglice*, robbed of his dues) by the trio. **1929** K. S. Prichard *Coonardoo* xvii. 167 We separated, followin' tracks, and I managed to get slewed. **1944** *Living off Land* iv. 65 Many a bushman has become bushed before now, while even a good bushman may get slewed for a few hours in strange and difficult country.

2. Also with *over*. More recently, of motor vehicles, to skid uncontrollably (*across* a surface); to slide and turn out of the proper course, to 'career'.

1914 KIPLING *Diversities of Creatures* (1917) 389 'We overtake on the right as a rule in England.' 'Thanks!' Mr Lingnam slued over. **1943** *Sun* (Baltimore) 8 Sept. 3/2 The..luxury train..slewed crazily over four tracks when its locomotive boiler blew up. **1965** M. BRADBURY *Stepping Westward* viii. 380 On one sharp bend the car slewed across the road and angled round again just short of the edge of a deep ravine. **1982** B. CHATWIN *On Black Hill* xx. 97 The car slewed off down the yard.

3. Of a control mechanism or electronic device: to undergo slewing (*SLEWING *vbl. sb.* 2).

1958 GIBSON & TUTEUR *Control System Components* v. 237 A servo using this circuit tends to have relatively poor synchronizing characteristics when slewing, i.e., when large and rapid changes of the input are made. **1962** L. A. STOCKDALE *Servomechanisms* vii. 112 The slewing time may form part of the servo specification, i.e. the servo to slew through 90° in the minimum time.

slewed, *ppl. a.* (Earlier and later examples.)

1801 A. ELLICOTT in C. V. Mathews *Andrew Ellicott* (1908) 201 He was two thirds slewed (as the Rahway people call being in liquor). **1886** [see *BOILED *ppl. a.* c]. **1935** H. H. FINLAYSON *Red Centre* xiii. 129 When questioned closely he admitted rather sheepishly that he was 'slewed'. **1975** D. LODGE *Changing Places* iii. 106, I was somewhat slewed by this time and kept calling him Sparrow.

slew-foot. *U.S. slang.* Also **slough-, slue-foot,** etc. [f. SLEW *v.*] A person who walks with his feet turned out; a clumsy person. Also *transf.* Hence **slew-foot** *v.*; **slew-footed** *ppl. a.*

1896 BOGERT & O'BRIEN *Slew Foot Sal* (song) 3 I'll tell you of a lady, her name is Slew Foot Sal,..She's heavy and she weighs five-thirty-three. **1922** F. SCOTT FITZGERALD *Beautiful & Damned* I. iii. 122 A man in a striped blue suit, walking slue-footed in white-spatted feet. **1945** L. SAXON et al. *Gumbo Ya-Ya* xxiii. 496 She is hoping that her galloping, slue-foot, light-brown, lazy husband ..will soon find a job. **1950** R. STARNES *Another Mug for Bier* xx. 130 Haggis [*sc.* an Airedale] shrugged and slough-footed away. **1961** J. B. PRIESTLEY *Saturn over Water* iv. 53 Leaving your work to go slewfooting in South America.

slewing, *vbl. sb.* Add: **I. 2.** The response of a control mechanism or electronic device to a sudden large increase in input, esp. one that causes the device to respond at its maximum rate (the *slewing rate* or *speed*). Usu. *attrib.*

1958 O. J. M. SMITH *Feedback Control Systems* vii. 201 The infrequent large-magnitude changes of the average input to a servo produce slewing of the output at maximum velocity. **1962** R. N. CLARK *Introd. Automatic Control Systems* vii. 270 The large signal (or slewing speed) response characteristics of a system. **1975** G. J. KING *Audio Handbk.* ii. 47 The maximum frequency at which full power can be obtained is a function of the amplifier's slewing rate, which is different from rise time.

slice, *sb.*[1] Add: **2. b.** *Geol.* A relatively thin, broad mass of rock situated between two approximately parallel thrust faults, esp. when these make a small angle with the horizontal. Also *thrust slice.*

1914 PEACH & HORNE *Guide Geol. Model Assynt Mts.* 18 The slices of strata thus repeated have been driven westwards by major thrusts along planes which truncate the overlying reversed faults. **1942** M. P. BILLINGS *Structural Geol.* xvii. 327 Surrounding the basin is a zone..of outwardly-driven thrust slices. In still another zone.. rootless slices and isolated blocks of various slices are common. **1957** *Q. Jrnl. Geol. Soc.* CXIII. 59 They occur.. as infolds, and slices brought up along the Strathconon tear-fault. **1969** BENNISON & WRIGHT *Geol. Hist. Brit. Isles* iii. 46 In it [*sc.* the Laxfordian orogeny] are found fragments of earlier orogenic belts brought up as thrust slices.

c. *Electronics.* A small, thin slab of semiconducting material on which circuit elements have been formed.

1964 *Proc. IEEE* LII. 1713 (*heading*) Evolution of the concept of a computer on a slice. **1975** *Sci. Amer.* May 36/2 National Semiconductor..introduced a four-bit PMOS slice that could be used as a modular unit in the design of machines ranging from four to 32 bits.

3. b. *slice of life* [tr. F. *tranche de la vie*, a term orig. applied to French Naturalist literature: see quot. 1890], a realistic and detailed portrayal in drama, narrative, painting, etc., of incidents typical of everyday life. Freq. (usu. with hyphens) *attrib.*

[**1890** J. JULLIEN in *Art et Critique* 9 Aug. 500/2 Ce n'est donc qu'une tranche de la vie que nous pouvons mettre à la scène.] **1895** G. B. SHAW in *Sat. Rev.* 19 Oct. 503/1 The substitution of a homogeneous slice of life for the old theatrical sandwich of sentiment and comic relief. **1914** H. JAMES in *Times Lit. Suppl.* 19 Mar. 134/4 The Orgreaves..come..as near squaring aesthetically with the famous formula of the 'slice of life' as any example that could be adduced. **1938** R. G. COLLINGWOOD *Princ. Art* p. v, We have..a new drama, taking the place of the old 'slice of life' entertainment, in which the author's chief business was to represent everyday doings of ordinary people as the audience believed them to behave. **1954** M. EWER *Heart Untouched* ix. 154 This is a costume picture, not a slice-of-life drama. **1962** *Listener* 14 June 1028/2 The pure landscape, the still life, the 'slice of life', the painting for painting's sake, is a late development. **1976** *National Observer* (U.S.) 4 Dec. 20/3 Mrs McFarland is one of the just-folks who appeared in one of those slice-of-life commercials. **1981** *Daily Tel.* 19 Feb. 13/1 Yet another indigestible slice of life about 'a warm, winning, and wise and wonderful Jewish family'.

slice, *sb.*[2] Add: **2.** Similarly in *Tennis.* Cf. *SLICE *v.*[1] 5.

1969 *New Yorker* 14 June 47/3 He hits a slice so hard and with such sharp placement, close to the sideline, that the ball jumps cleanly past Graebner's racquet for a service ace. **1971** LAVER & COLLINS *Educ. Tennis Player* xi. 144 My slice (a left-hander's) will move to a right-hander's backhand, and that's convenient.

slice, *v.*[1] Add: **1. c.** In colloq. phr. *no matter how* (or *whichever way*, etc.) *you slice it*: however you look at it. orig. and chiefly *U.S.*

1936 C. SANDBURG *People, Yes* 160 No matter how thick or how thin you slice it it's still baloney. **1941** WODEHOUSE *Berlin Broadcasts* in *Performing Flea* (1961) I. 261 Slice it where you like, it is still a German prison camp. **1968** J. SANGSTER *Touchfeather* xvii. 198 Whichever way you sliced it, I had absolutely nothing on Roger Gerastan except what I had guessed. **1979** 'A. HAILEY' *Overload* III. xii. 257 Whichever way you slice it,.. Cameron Clarke has done our cause a lot of harm.

5. Also in other sports, to make a sharp stroke across a ball rather than straight on it, causing it to be propelled forward at an angle (on purpose or unintentionally); in *Lawn Tennis*, etc., to impart spin or swing in this manner. Cf. *CHOP *v.*[1] 7 d, e.

1905 H. A. VACHELL *Hill* xii. 255 Scaife has been transformed into a tremendous human machine, inexorably cutting and slicing, pulling and drawing. **1954** J. B. G. THOMAS *On Tour* 68 Birt, normally the safest of place kickers, made his mark, only for the ball to be sliced towards the corner flag. **1969** *New Yorker* 14 June 61/2 He'll slice. He'll lob. **1976** J. SNOW *Cricket Rebel* 63 Alan Smith..started to hit out boldly, slicing the ball repeatedly over and through the covers.

sliceable (sləi·săb'l), *a.* [f. SLICE *v.*[1] + -ABLE.] That can be sliced or divided.

1976 *Evening Post* (Nottingham) 16 Dec. 11/2 Other useful buys here for Christmas catering are..1 litre packs Walls sliceable vanilla ice cream. **1978** *Aslib Proc.* XXX. 33 On-line data bases..are tools which are infinitely sliceable into subsets.

sliced, *ppl. a.* Add: **1. b.** Of food: sold already cut into slices, esp. *sliced bread.* Also in colloq. phr. *the best* (or *greatest*, etc.) *thing since sliced bread*: an expression of enthusiastic appreciation, esp. of a new invention or discovery.

1958 J. MORTIMER *What shall we tell Caroline?* ii. 109 The trouble with living here, the butter gets as hard as the rock of Gibraltar. It blasts great holes in your sliced bread. **1963** L. DEIGHTON *Horse under Water* xxxi. 124 They prodded..their product... Sliced, sterilized and Cellophane-wrapped; a loaf. **1969** R. JAFFE *Fame Game* (1970) v. 106 You're the greatest thing since sliced bread. **1970** *Guardian* 28 Feb. 10/1 The biggest thing since sliced bread is now in the shops. It is called part-baked bread. **1972** WODEHOUSE *Pearls, Girls, & Monty Bodkin* xii. 183 Bodkin regards you as the best thing that's happened since sliced bread. **1973** J. THOMSON *Death Cap* ii. 34 Mrs King asked me to..buy half a pound of sliced ham and I cut the sandwiches. **1976** *National Observer* (U.S.) 21 Aug. 6/3 They're the best thing since sliced bread and they're selling like wildfire here,' says Dan Wagner, proprietor of the Georgetown Cycle Shop. **1981** *Austral. Forest Industries Jrnl.* Suppl. (Plywood & Veneer) Oct. 35 (*heading*) Sheathing—the greatest thing since sliced bread!

3. Also in tennis (see *SLICE *v.*[1] 5).

1971 LAVER & COLLINS *Educ. Tennis Player* xi. 144 Most of the time I used a sliced serve, and that seems to be the common delivery.

slicer. 1. (Further examples.)

1907 *Yesterday's Shopping* (1969) 215/2 The Sterling Slicer. Slices any kind of vegetable or fruit evenly. **1956** F. S. ATKINSON in D. L. Linton *Sheffield* xiv. 269 Intensive efforts are being made to replace the hand-loading of coal on to conveyors by mechanical power-loaders and, in seams over 3 ft. 3 in. considerable success is being achieved with Meco Moore Loaders..and Huwood Slicers. **1971** [see *PLOUGH, *PLOW *sb.*[1] 5 i].

slick, *sb.*[1] **3. a.** For *U.S.* read 'orig. *U.S.*', and add: Also, a floating mass of oil. Also *transf.*

[**1889**, etc.: see *oil slick* s.v. *OIL *sb.*[1] 6 e.] **1938** *Daily Progress* (Charlottesville, Va.) 30 July 1/8 The slick.. caused by oil from the 'Hawaii Clipper'. **1950** *Jrnl. Marine Res.* IX. 69 Artificial slicks form in harbor waters contaminated with refuse and oil. **1973** *Daily Tel.* (Colour Suppl.) 9 Mar. 12/2 You can see the mouse-run quite clearly because of the slick of oil which all rodents leave behind on walls and floors if they regularly move along a particular route. **1982** H. INNES *Black Tide* II. i. 28 The slick now stretched in a great smooth, brown, greasy layer right across the bay.

5. *U.S.* A wild, unbranded horse, cow, or other range animal; a maverick.

1890 *Stock Grower & Farmer* 12 July 6/3 Seven of them were branded, the remainder were 'slicks', or horses which had run wild from birth. **1934** in J. A. & A. Lomax *Amer. Ballads* xvi. 411 No maverick or slick will be tallied In that great book of life in His home. **1965** G. SHEPHERD *West of Yesterday* xiv. 127 By picking up slicks or unbranded cattle on the way—gathered a nice little herd.

6. *U.S.* An expensive or 'glossy' magazine (opp. *pulp magazine* s.v. *PULP *sb.* 5 c).

1934 *Writer* Mar. 73/2 Perhaps he [*sc.* the author] gets an offer for two hundred dollars from one of the 'slicks'. **1952** S. KAUFFMANN *Philanderer* (1953) iv. 65 We're going to change one of our present magazines—from a confession to a woman's slick. **1958** *Manch. Guardian* 26 Sept. 4/3 Jack Finney's stories, which have been popular in the better American slicks, point the trend all the more for not all being science fiction. **1977** *Transatlantic Rev.* LX. 57 One will keep on about 'the slicks' he wants to write for.

7. a. A smooth tyre used on various kinds of racing vehicle.

1959 *Wall St. Jrnl.* (Eastern ed.) 11 Aug. 1/4 Both Goodyear Tire & Rubber Co. and General Tire & Rubber Co. have jumped into the business..developing and building 'slicks'—smooth racing tires—for the little vehicles. **1965** *Daily Mail* 2 Oct. 5/7 The slicks (smooth, £20-a-piece racing tyres) burst into smoke and then into flame. **1978** 'D. RUTHERFORD' *Collision Course* 56 Everybody had fitted 'slicks', the smooth treadless tyres used on dry roads.

b. (See quots.)

1969 I. KEMP *Brit. G.I. in Vietnam* iii. 45 The 'slicks'—small Huey helicopters—would fly the troops to the battle zone, while the larger Chinooks brought in their heavy equipment. **1974** N. MEYER *Target Practice* (1975) v. 61 We were lifted by choppers called 'Hueys' (or 'slicks', because they land on runners instead of wheels).

8. *U.S. slang.* A clever or smart person; a cheat or swindler. Cf. *SLICKER 3; *SLICKSTER.

1959 N. MAILER *Advts. for Myself* (1961) I. 28 To try a major novel about the last war in Europe without a sense of the past is to fail in the worst way—as an over-ambitious and opportunistic slick. **1970** R. D. ABRAHAMS *Positively Black* iv. 88 These stories commonly turn on some way in which the 'slick' manages to trick the white storekeeper 'Mr. Charlie' into giving him respect and service. **1971** E. BULLINS in W. King *Black Short Story Anthol.* (1972) 76 Dandy's mother had a civil-service job in the city, and the city slick Dandy was from Philly. **1973** [see *RUN *v.* 52 h].

9. Special Comb.: **slick-licker** *Canad. colloq.*, an apparatus for removing oil floating as a slick.

1970 *Globe & Mail* (Toronto) 7 May 4 (*caption*) Slick-lickers—barges in Nova Scotia's Chedabucto Bay designed to suck in oil off the water's surface from the wrecked tanker Arrow and transfer it to 45-gallon drums. **1972** *Daily Colonist* (Victoria, B.C.) 12 Feb. 9/5 The federal transport department has placed a $150,000 order for 22 slicklicker machines... The machine..picks up oil from water surfaces by using an endless belt that has been treated chemically. **1975** *Lamp* (Exxon Corporation) Winter 24/1 Imperial Oil Limited, Exxon Corporation's Canadian affiliate, is employing a 'slicklicker' to counter the menace of oil spills on water.

slick, *a.* Add: **1.** Also, of a surface: slippery (chiefly *U.S.*). (Later examples.)

1901 A. H. RICE *Mrs Wiggs of Cabbage Patch* xi. 143 When the floor was dry and the candle sprinkled over it, Australia and Europena were detailed to slide upon it until it became slick. **1936** M. MITCHELL *Gone with Wind* xxxv. 590 The horse..plodded off, picking its way carefully down the slick road. **1979** C. FREEMAN *Portraits* (1980) vi. 31 The streets were covered with a white blanket of snow and ice so slick it was almost impossible for him to walk. **1981** *Railway Mag.* Mar. 115/3 No. 765 [*sc.* a steam locomotive] was true to her breed, losing her footing temporarily on the slick rails as she fought for adhesion.

2. b. Of range animals: unbranded, wild. *U.S.*

1955 R. HOBSON *Nothing too Good* xvii. 181 The pounding of slick horses hitting across the range. **1973** R. SYMONS *Where Wagon Led* I. iii. 39 Then brand everything that's 'slick'—provided you know they're off your own mares.

3. (Of persons or things personified.) (Further example.) See also sense 4 below.

1936 AUDEN & ISHERWOOD *Ascent of F6* (1937) I. i. 17 Evening. A slick and unctuous Time Has sold us yet another shop-soiled day.

4. (Of persons.) (Earlier and further examples.) Also (merging with sense 3), glibly clever, having easy assurance.

1807 *Lancaster* (Pa.) *Jrnl.* 16 Oct. 3/1 You are getting too slick. What a charming thing it is to see men under good discipline. **1921** E. O'NEILL *Diff'rent* I, in *Emperor Jones* 213 Jim Benson's one o' them slick jokers, same's Jack; can't keep their mouths shet or mind their own business. **1953** R. LEHMANN *Echoing Grove* 155 Give her a pen and she cannot be trusted not to express herself in clichés, like a schoolgirl with a smear of the popular slick journalist. **1951** [see *REGISTER *v.* 3 c]. **1966** 'J. HACKSTON' *Father clears Out* 98 The rest of our local colour was made up of a community of slick, quick-off-the-mark jumpers.

5. (Of things, actions, etc.) (Earlier and further examples.) Also, neat, in good order; smart, efficient, that operates smoothly; superficially attractive, glibly clever.

1833 *Jamestown* (N.Y.) *Jrnl.* 25 Sept. 2/1 Of all the inventions I've hearn on of Mr. Van Buren's, this is about the slickest. **1837** *Baltimore Commercial Transcript* 4

Sept. 2/3 Prudence guessed strawberries and cream were slick. Jonathan thought they wa'nt so slick as Pru's lips. **1860** J. G. HOLLAND *Miss Gilbert's Career* viii. 131, I love to see a young man that keeps things slick around him. **1891** *Fur, Fin & Feather* Mar. 169 They reckons to make mighty slick work in cleaning everything up on the way back. **1901** W. CHURCHILL *Crisis* I. xii. 104 'You'd die laughing, Lige, to hear how he did it.' 'Some *slickness*, I'll gamble,' grunted Captain Lige. 'Well, I reckon 'twas slick.' **1904** W. H. SMITH *Promoters* i. 19 I've seen the thing done a hundred times, with a slick word every time. **1920** E. O'NEILL *Beyond Horizon* I. ii. 35 'He'll make this one of the slickest, best-payin' farms in the state.'.. 'Seems to me it's a pretty slick place right now.' **1921** GALSWORTHY *To Let* 286 He could not go on staying here, walled in and sheltered, with everything so slick and comfortable. **1927** *New Republic* 12 Oct. 218/2 His dialogue is of that slick and well oiled kind that you may meet in good vaudeville or in the Saturday Evening Post. **1931** E. F. BENSON *Mapp & Lucia* i. 18 Let us practise that scene where I knight you. We must get it very slick. **1933** E. O'NEILL *Ah, Wilderness!* III. i. 95 How was that for a slick way of getting rid of him? **1940** M. V. HUGHES *London Family between Wars* xii. 157 America.., with its slick, fervid haste and its terrifying efficiency. **1958** *Woman* 22 Feb. 23/3 That's what 'Six-Five Special' does to you!.. We must admit that it's about the slickest light show on TV today. **1972** E. H. GOMBRICH *Story of Art* (ed. 12) xxvi. 439 He had more and more become convinced that art was in danger of becoming slick and superficial. **1978** *Electronics & Power* Nov./Dec. 824/1 When that [*sc.* the robbing of banks] became difficult we went for the cash in transit, until the professionals got their drill so slick that the game was not worth the candle. **1978** *Lancashire Life* Oct. 155/2 The Accord four-door I drove had a slick, finger-light, five-speed manual gearbox with a well chosen set of ratios. **1979** *Church Times* 6 July 16/5, I will scrap Series Three And invent something slicker. How grand to be free—A real alive Vicar!

6. a. slick ear *U.S.* = *SLICK *sb.*[1] 5; also *fig.*

1914 *World's Work* XXVII. 447/1 Any 'slick-ear' (steer not marked on the ears or branded) found on the range about which inquiry was made was promptly assigned to his ownership, and 'slick-ears' eventually became known as 'mavericks'. **1958** 'W. HENRY' *Seven Men at Mimbres Springs* vii. 74 I'd clean forgot the slick-ear son of a bitch! **1966** H. MARRIOTT *Cariboo Cowboy* iv. 48 Sometimes the cow would die for some reason or another and the calf would be left without a mother, in which case it grew up an orphan calf or a 'slick-ear'.

b. slick-paper *U.S.*, a kind of glossy paper used esp. for printing popular magazines (cf. *SLICK *sb.*[1] 6); usu. *attrib.*; hence **slick magazine, story.**

1930 D. WILHELM *Writing for Profit* iv. 102 There are between 100 and 125 pulp-paper magazines alone beside all the illustrated and 'slick paper' magazines! **1936** *Amer. Mercury* XXXVII. 286/2 Occasionally I have put aside two weeks..in which to attempt a slick magazine story. **1949** H. E. NEAL *Writing & Selling Fact & Fiction* ii. 17 The average slick story is divisible into six parts. **1976** *National Observer* (U.S.) 23 Oct. 22/5 They will come again next year with..their suitcases stuffed with slick-paper brochures full of self-praise. **1980** *TWA Ambassador* Oct. 82/3 Two distinct genres of regional business publications are trying to serve this market: the tabloid and the slick magazine.

slick, *adv.* **2.** (Earlier example.)

1818 H. B. FEARON *Sk. Amer.* 123 Did she die slick right away?

slick, *v.* Add: **1. b.** (Further examples with *up.*)

Sometimes with derogatory overtones.

1831 [see *BETTER *a.* 4 b (*b*)]. **1863** *Harper's Mag.* 55/1 He got into Peter's way by attempting..to 'slick up' the barn. **1953** R. LEHMANN *Echoing Grove* 187 Stop slicking it up into cheap melodrama. **1973** E.-J. BAHR *Nice Neighbourhood* iii. 25 I'm going to get her all slicked up in her new outfit from Aunt Joan and show her off.

d. *intr.* To smarten or tidy *up. U.S.*

1841 *Knickerbocker* XVII. 41 In a little while he recovered his self-possession, or, to make use of one of his own expressions 'he slicked up'. **1887** M. E. WILKINS *Humble Romance* 395 I'm going to slick up here a little for you while I stay... He watched her..as she flew about putting things to rights. **1948** *Family Circle* June 96/2 It's always serious when they slick up for a girl!

slicked, *ppl. a.* Add: **a.** (Later examples in sense 3 of the vb.) Also with *back, down.*

1921 E. O'NEILL *Diff'rent* I, in *Emperor Jones* 215 His hair [is] wet and slicked in a part. **1937** A. CHRISTIE *Murder in Mews* 163 It was the good-looking young man with the slicked-back hair who had spoken. **1949** E. DE MAUNY *Huntsman in his Career* II. 128 There was dandruff on the collar from his slicked-back, fair hair. **1964** *Economist* 20 June 1365/2 Mr McNamara's slicked-down patent leather hair. **1975** B. GARFIELD *Death Sentence* (1976) xi. 57 Latins, with slicked hair. **1976** N. THORNBURG *Cutter & Bone* iv. 86 He had a distinctly Arabic look about him, slicked-down black hair. **1977** *Listener* 17 Nov. 653/2 People with slicked-back hair..jitter-bugging round the radio.

b. With *up*: dressed up, smart, elegant; also *fig.*, made more sophisticated. orig. *U.S.*

1836 [in Dict. s.v. SLICK *v.* 1 b]. **1867** *Atlantic Monthly* Jan. 109/2 Is this my farm?... It looks more slicked up than ever it used to. **1928** J. GALSWORTHY *Swan Song* I. xi. 81 Montpellier Square..was all slicked up since he was last there... Builders and decorators must have done well lately. **1957** R. HOGGART *Uses of Literacy* xi. 276 The new-style popular publications..are pallid but slicked-up extensions even of nineteenth-century sensationalism. **1979** *Tucson Mag.* Apr. 34/1 In the same wave came..the new City Hall and the slicked-up El Presidio Park.

slicker. 2. a. For *U.S.* read 'orig. and chiefly *U.S.*' and add: *spec.* a loose-fitting oilskin outer garment, usu. of a bright yellow or orange colour.

1910 C. E. MULFORD *Hopalong Cassidy* xx. 126 After throwing his saddle on his horse he went back to the house to get his 'slicker', a yellow water-proof coat. **1953** M. PEAKE *Mr Pye* xxii. 176 Tintagieu..now wore a black oilskin slicker. **1971** *N.Z. Listener* 19 Apr. 56/5 One was a nuggety bloke in a sou'-wester, oilskin slicker, and bowyangs. **1978** R. LUDLUM *Holcroft Covenant* iii. 43 Police and maintenance crews were everywhere, distinguished from one another by the contrasting black and orange of their slickers.

3. = *city slicker* s.v. *CITY 9. orig. and chiefly *U.S.*

1900 'J. FLYNT' *Notes Itinerant Policeman* iii. 62 Pick-pockets!.. You just bring the slickers in. **1932** J. T. FARRELL *Young Lonigan* vi. 230 Swan, the slicker, who wore a tout's gray checked suit with narrow-cuffed trousers [etc.]. **1936** *Sat. Morning Advertiser* (Durant, Okla.) 14 Mar. 1/3 (*heading*) 'Slicker' insurance agents better be a bit wary now. **1946** WODEHOUSE *Money in Bank* xii. 106 I'm going to put it across that slicker..if it's the last thing I do. **1978** *Morecambe Guardian* 14 Mar. 15/4 He becomes a sort of Midnight Cowboy, lost and confused by the slickers around him.

4. *U.S.* = SILVER-FISH 2.

1902 L. O. HOWARD *Insect Bk.* 380 (Order *Thysanura.*) The insects of this order are usually of very small size... They comprise the little insects known as springtails, bristletails, fishmoths or slickers. **1962** METCALF & FLINT *Destructive & Useful Insects* (ed. 4) xix. 905 The silverfish or slicker..is uniform, silvery or greenish gray.

Hence as *vb. trans.*, to cheat; to defeat by being 'slick'.

1935 H. DAVIS *Honey in Horn* xxii. 376 His entertainment had mostly been swindling and slickering them. **1971** LAVER & COLLINS *Educ. Tennis Player* xiii. 157 It happens all the time, an older, less powerful team who understand the principles of doubles slickering a couple of youths who might be considerably superior in singles. **1974** *Tel.* (Brisbane) 4 Sept. 30/4, I thrive on guys who try to slicker me. **1979** *Globe & Mail* (Toronto) 16 May 41/8 What was it Charlie had said about being slickered?

slickered (sli·kəɹd), *a. U.S.* [f. SLICKER *sb.*[2] + -ED[2].] Wearing a slicker.

1972 C. L. COOPER *Black* 151, I could see..slickered cops smoking on duty. **1975** *New Yorker* 10 Mar. 29/1 About twelve horses on the track, a few running hard, their slickered riders standing tall in the stirrups.

slicking, *vbl. sb.* Add: **1*.** With *up*: the action of making (oneself, a place, etc.) neat and tidy. *U.S. colloq.*

1855 *Trans. Mich. Agric. Soc.* VI. 495 The farm needs a good deal of slicking up to make the general appearance equal to what nature has done for the land. **1907** *Springfield* (Mass.) *Weekly Republ.* 9 May 1 Denver has been having her period of spring slicking up.

slickly, *adv.* Add: **1.** (Later example.)

1973 *Daily Tel.* 11 Jan. 17/1 Walter Albini likes to see his male models with their hair oiled slickly down like George Raft's.

2. (Later examples.)

1927 *Daily Tel.* 16 Aug. 12/5 The play..needs to be more slickly produced and better acted in order to be made convincing. **1978** K. ROYCE *Satan Touch* vi. 99 Slickly he turned his hand down to indicate the chair.

slickness. Add: **1.** (Later U.S. example.)

1976 *Billings* (Montana) *Gaz.* 28 June 3-A/1 It's a three-quarter ton pickup with skid-trailer, painted the bright orange of the Montana Highway Department. It tests the slickness of the road surface.

3. (Later examples.) Now freq. *derog.*

1927 *Music & Letters* July 321 Pure artistry may decline to a mere slickness and facility. **1967** E. SHORT *Embroidery & Fabric Collage* iv. 112 Anything cheap, shoddy, shallow or clever to a degree of slickness, is out of place.

slickster (sli·kstəɹ). *U.S. slang.* [f. SLICK *sb.*[1] + -STER.] A swindler.

1965 C. BROWN *Manchild in Promised Land* xiv. 332 All the Muslims now felt as though 125th Street was theirs. It used to belong to the hustlers and the slicksters. **1973** [see *RUN *v.* 52 h].

slide, *sb.* Add: **I. 1. c.** (Examples of the sense 'portamento'.)

1908 *Grove's Dict. Mus.* (ed. 2) IV. 482/1 To violinists the 'slide' is one of the principal vehicles of expression, at the same time a means of passing from one note to another at a distance. **1913** F. THISTLETON *Mod. Violin Technique* xv. 74 The slide is one of the principal mediums of expression on the violin. **1938** L. TERTIS *Beauty of Tone in String Playing* 14 The celerity with which this is done is the secret of discreet natural portamento... There must be no drawling, languishing, or lingering in the action of the slide.

d. *fig.* A rapid decline; a downturn. Also in phr. *on the slide.*

1884 [in Dict., sense 1 b]. **1931** *Economist* 14 Mar. 569/2 Unsatisfactory traffics, and the passing of the B.A. Great Western dividend, accentuated the 'slide' of prices. **1969** N. COHN *Pop from Beginning* ix. 86 He began to flag. By early 1964, he was definitely on the slide. **1981** *Times* 5 May 18/1 A 20 per cent slide in profits at the half-way stage.

e. *Baseball.* A plunging or sliding approach made to a base along the ground.

1886 H. CHADWICK *Art of Batting* 68 A slide in time saves an out. **1934** *Baseball Mag.* Apr. 497/2 Chapman has a natural talent as a base stealer... He knows how.. to make a perfect slide. **1944** E. ALLEN *Major League Baseball* xv. 204 There are four types of slides: the hook slide, the bent leg slide, the feet first slide and the head first slide. **1972** J. MOSEDALE *Football* iii. 32 He stretched it into a triple with a daring slide [contextually in Baseball].

f. *Surfing.* A ride across the face of a wave (see quot. 1963); a wave suitable for this.

1935 D. KAHANOMOKU in T. Blake *Hawaiian Surfboard* i. 32 (*caption*) A fine illustration of the slide. The wave is coming on while the rider is sliding left across the face of the swell. **1946** J. A. BALL *Scrapbk. of Surfriding* 57 (*caption*) Tom Blake streaking along on a long belly slide. **1963** J. POLLARD *Austral. Surfrider* ii. 20/1 A 'slide' can be either 'left' or 'right', angling down the wave to one side or the other. **1968** *Surfer Mag.* Jan. 47/3 Ten-foot waves that peel off in good right and left slides.

g. *Curling.* A delivery in which a curler slides some distance forward in launching his stone.

1950 K. WATSON *Curling* i. 42 By delivering the stone at the end of a long slide, a player could be more accurate in delivery. **1962, 1969** [see *long slide* s.v. *LONG *a.*[1] A. 18].

h. *Jazz.* = *GLISSANDO.

1959 'F. NEWTON' *Jazz Scene* 289 Technical terms either duplicate existing, but unfamiliar, ones—e.g. *slide, smear*, for glissando..or they describe things for which no proper academic equivalent exists. **1973** *Black World* Nov. 48/1 Performance practices require a 'slur' and/or 'slide' when moving from tone to tone.

3. c. *Geol.* A fault formed at and associated with a fold.

1910 E. B. BAILEY in *Q. Jrnl. Geol. Soc.* LXVI. 593 'Fold-fault' itself is too cumbrous for constant repetition, and accordingly 'slide' has been introduced to take its place. **1934** —— in *Ibid.* XC. 467 'Fold-fault' is an old word for a fault formed in close causal connexion with folding... I employed the word 'slip' in this sense, but on Lapworth's suggestion exchanged it for 'slide'. Now that reversed and unreversed limbs are often distinguishable through the help of current-bedding, the word 'slide' is less necessary, since it can often conveniently be replaced by 'thrust' or 'lag'. The following are helpful though incomplete definitions:— A thrust is a slide replacing an inverted limb, actual or ideal. A lag is a slide replacing a normal limb. **1969** BENNISON & WRIGHT *Geol. Hist. Brit. Isles* iii. 55 An important structural break, the Iltay Boundary Slide, separates two contrasted sedimentary successions both in Scotland and northern Ireland.

II. 5. j. *N.Z.* A serving-hatch.

1949 J. R. COLE *It was so Late* 92, I was standing by the slide in the lounge one night. **1955** *Numbers* I. IV. 14 Charlie ordered for them both and Kate dragged back to the slide.

k. *transf.* A musical instrument equipped with a slide.

1976 A. BAINES *Brass Instruments* iv. 94 (*heading*) Renaissance slides. **1977** J. WAINWRIGHT *Do Nothin' till you hear from Me* viii. 129 Walter Green—trombonist... As a slide-player he is average.

6. Now *spec.* a clasp for fastening in the hair. (Later examples.)

1932 L. GOLDING *Magnolia Street* III. ix. 593 That slide which has just slid out of her hair on to the parquet floor. **1952** M. LASKI *Village* ii. 33 Her soft brown hair caught back with a slide. **1981** J. B. HILTON *Playground of Death* ii. 10 There wasn't a grip, clip or slide on the market that would keep my mam's hair up.

7. b. (Earlier example.) Now also, a photographic transparency for use in a slide projector.

1819 M. EDGEWORTH *Let.* 17 Apr. (1971) 199 You know him and his magic lantern of good things. Some new figures on the slides. **1940** P. E. BOUCHER *Fundamentals of Photogr.* (1941) xiii. 200 Valuable slides..which are to be subjected to considerable use should be mounted in glass. **1978** M. J. LANGFORD *Step by Step Guide to Photogr.* 176 Before presentation, your slides must be inserted in holders ready for projection.

III. 10. c. (Earlier example.)

1855 W. HOWITT *Land, Labour & Gold* I. 206 We take the fine gravel out of the slide of the cradle.

d. A structure with a smooth sloping surface used as a toy or piece of playground equipment down which children slide, or as an entertainment at a fairground. Cf. *CHUTE *sb.* 3 c.

1890 *Century Mag. Advertising Suppl.* Dec. 70 Wood's parlor toboggan slide. The most satisfactory toy yet invented for children. **1924** *Ladies' Home Jrnl.* Nov. 126/1 This kiddies' slide is more fun than the old cellar door! **1954** R. DAHL *Someone like You* 210 All week the swings and the see-saws and the high slide with steps going up to it stood deserted. **1975** I. STARSMORE *English Fairs* iv. 92 (*caption*) The Portable Slide. Height 29 ft... The three 100 ft. lanes guide 'passengers' down the slide. **1979** 'J. LE CARRÉ' *Smiley's People* (1980) xxi. 257 There was a children's slide in the garden.

11. b. *U.S. slang.* (See quot. 1932.)

1932 *Even. Sun* (Baltimore) 9 Dec. 31/5 *Slide*, a trouser's [*sic*] pocket. **1967** 'I. SLIM' *Pimp: Story of my Life* (1969) iii. 68 How would you like a half a 'G' in your 'slide'?

12. (Earlier example.)

1842 J. E. DEKAY *Zool. N.Y.* I. 40 The steel trap is placed..at the bottom of one of their slides.

slide, *v.* Add: **B. I. 1. d.** *Baseball.* To perform a slide (sense 1 e).

1891 *Harper's Weekly* 23 May 391/4 His base running, in spite of his care about sliding, is of the old-time quality that has already won two championships for Yale. **1904** J. J. McGRAW *Science of Baseball* 67 He shouldn't slide unless his pants are properly padded. **1932** *Baseball Mag.* Oct. 501/2 George Watkins, quick to grasp Dazzy's slight slip, turned on a full burst of speed and slid across home plate with the only run of the game. **1977** *Rolling Stone* 30 June 76/2 Do you always think about baseball players when you're making love?.. I couldn't figure out why you kept yelling, 'Slide!'

e. *Surfing.* To ride across the face of a wave.

1931 *Country Life in Amer.* Jan. 57 If the wave proves exceptionally steep, keep to the stern of the board and then, after you 'catch' the wave, head the board at an angle to it. This will enable you to 'slide' with the wave. **1959** J. BLOOMFIELD *Know-How in Surf* iii. 27 The gradually breaking crest enables the body to slide down its front at an angle of approximately 45 degrees.

f. *Curling.* To move forwards while delivering the stone.

1936 F. B. TALBOT *Mr Besom starts Curling* xiii. 34 Many good players slide out of the hack *as* they deliver the stone. **1950** K. WATSON *Curling* i. 1 Whether you slide or do not slide, that follow-through is essentially the smooth delivery of the stone.

4. b. (Later examples.)

1904 [see *BUSY *sb.*[2]]. **1932** E. WALLACE *When Gangs came to London* xxvii. 269 There's only one word that any sensible man can read in this situation, and that word is —slide!

slide-. Add: **a.** *slide cornet, trombone, trumpet* (earlier example), *whistle*; **slide fastener** chiefly *U.S.*, a zip-fastener; **slide-wire** *Electr.*, a resistance wire along which a contact slides in a Wheatstone bridge or similar device.

1926 WHITEMAN & MCBRIDE *Jazz* ix. 206 The jazz band has introduced some little known instruments such as..the slide cornet and the czimbalon. **1946** MEZZROW & WOLFE *Really Blues* (1957) i. 12 He showed up in the band room with a slide cornet. **1934** *Newsweek* 21 July 29/2 The Prince of Wales uses a slide fastener on his trousers. **1944** *Sun* (Baltimore) 16 Sept. 7/4 The B. F. Goodrich Company announced today development of a 'zipped lip' construction that makes a metal slide fastener watertight and airtight. **1971** N. MARSH *Tied up in Tinsel* vi. 135 'Let's have a look at the robe.'.. A slide fastener ran right down the back. **1891** C. R. DAY *Descr. Catal. Musical Instruments, R. Military Exhib.* x. 180 Slide trombone... In this instrument, as should always be the case, the taper of the bell is carried right through the tuning slides. **1934** *Hound & Horn* July–Sept. 595 The harpsichord seems a very complicated instrument to compare alongside the single-noted valve trumpet, or a slide trombone. **1977** 'E. CRISPIN' *Glimpses of Moon* xiii. 269 How we could brighten our Church Fêtes up, short of breaking all the Ten Commandments simultaneously to a fanfare of slide-trombones. **1885** G. B. SHAW in *Mag. of Music* II. 112/1 These slide trumpets are not the instruments Bach wrote for. **1939** *Sears, Roebuck Catal.* Fall–Winter 914/3 Slide whistle. Professional model... Has full chromatic scale of two octaves. **1976** *Gramophone* Feb. 1355/2 The flight grows slower to reveal gentle tones of slide-whistles, zither and harp. **1885** J. DREDGE *Electric Illumination* II. 1. 53 The Slide-Wire, or Metre Bridge..is a modification of the bridge due to Kirchoff, and is especially useful for the measurement of low resistances. **1922** GLAZEBROOK *Dict. Appl. Physics* II. 714/2 The first bridge to employ a slide wire was devised by Fleeming Jenkin in 1862 and was used to intercompare the standard coils made for the British Association Committee on Electrical Standards. **1964** *Oceanogr. & Marine Biol.* II. 359 The depth element is a Bourdon tube coupled to a slide-wire potentiometer. **1969** A. BRODGESELL in B. G. Lipták *Instrument Engineers' Handbk.* I. ix. 942 Potentiometric displacement sensors consist of a slide wire and wiper. The slide wire is powered by a constant voltage representing full scale travel.

c. *slide carrier, changer, projector, show, viewer*; *slide-in* adj.; **slide area** *U.S.*, an area in which landslips or avalanches are likely to happen; **slide-back** *Electronics*, the alteration of the grid bias of a thermionic valve which is necessary to restore the anode current to zero after the application of a signal voltage to the grid; apparatus to measure this alteration, freq. as an indirect measure of the signal voltage; also **slide-back voltmeter**; **slide guitar,** a style of guitar-playing characterized by a glissando effect produced by moving an object along the strings; usu. *attrib.*; **slide-rock,** talus rock; **slide-tape** *attrib. phr.*, involving photographic slides shown in a predetermined sequence to the accompaniment of a synchronized commentary recorded on magnetic tape.

1959 *Sunday Times* 7 June 16/6 The 'slide area' itself is that part of the Californian coast which is physically slipping, dropping and sliding towards the sea. **1970** *Wall St. Jrnl.* (Eastern ed.) 19 May 1/4 The Kildares live in what is euphemistically called here a 'slide area'. **1925** *Year-bk. Wireless Telegr.* 847 When a control room is some distance from the transmitter it is usual to install a valve voltmeter with a slideback which either measures the voltage across the output of the main amplifier or indicates when a certain voltage is exceeded. **1931** *B.B.C. Year-bk. 1932* 356 The 'slide-back'..consisted of a valve or similar device so biassed that no indication occurred until there was present and superimposed upon the bias a voltage greater than, and opposing in phase, the biassing voltage. **1938** H. A. BROWN *Radio-Frequency Electr. Measurements* (ed. 2) vi. 279 Peak, or slide-back, voltmeters are coming more and more into use. **1948** A. L. ALBERT *Radio Fundamentals* ix. 354 There is an error involved with this slide-back voltmeter, but with large signals..the error is small. **1965** *Wireless World* July 19 (Advt.), Slide-back measurement of time and amplitude by means of directly-calibrated shift controls. **1953** A. PEARLMAN *Rollei Manual* xxiii. 357 Sticky exudations may foul the slide carrier of the projector. **1971** *Sci. Amer.* Sept. 224/2 An adequate beam can be formed by making a pinhole aperture in the slide carrier of a 35-millimeter projector. **1959** *IRE Trans. Mil. Electronics* III. 97/1 Like a projection slide changer, we can observe one slide while discarding the slide already observed and replacing it with a new one. **1962** *Which?* Mar. 69/1 We did not test fully automatic projectors, but 6 had semi-automatic slide changers built in. **1968** P. OLIVER *Screening Blues* i. 35 Another..version was recorded in 1937 by Black Ace (B. K. Turner) who accompanied himself with brilliant slide guitar playing. **1976** *Morecambe Guardian* 7 Dec. 23/2 And inevitably those ubiquitous sessioners, Klaus Voorman (bass)..and Jesse Ed Davies (slide guitar), have played a major part. **1977** MCKNIGHT & TOBLER *Bob Marley* ix. 111 The Wailers version is decorated by an ethereal slide guitar solo. **1973** G. DAVEY *Fun with Hi-Fi* v. 35 The BSR MacDonald playing deck which I use has slide-in facilities for fitting the cartridge of one's choice. **1977** *Gramophone* Apr. 1629/2 The headshell has a slide-in cartridge carrier. **1956** E. S. BOMBACK *Retina Manual* xxi. 222 *(caption)* The Leitz Prado 150-watt slide projector. **1979** P. NIESEWAND *Member of Club* ii. 17 Two slide projectors were being positioned... 'Remember, when the lights go out, we'll be showing some slides.' **1901** *Yearbk. U.S. Dept. Agric. 1900* 195 In the mountains we often find the hillside slopes covered with broken rock of various sizes. This we call slide rock. **1974** FLINT & SKINNER *Physical Geol.* vii. 121/2 Weathering converts the sliderock into fine-grained regolith which, with its pores of extremely small diameter, can hold much more moisture than sliderock and thus acquire both vegetation and soil. **1956** E. S. BOMBACK *Retina Manual* xxi. 222 The color slide show has quite a lot in common with the motion picture film. **1978** *Peace News* 25 Aug. 18/3 On their last visit to Britain four years ago they did a slide show and a question and answer session. **1971** *Publishers' Weekly* 22 Mar. 20/2 The final part of the program..consisted of a slide-tape commentary. **1977** J. HEDGECOE *Photographer's Handbk.* 305 Sound for slide-tape presentations can be prepared from studio recordings using a microphone direct. **1960** *Which?* Oct. 228/2 A slide viewer should give a good *optical performance.*

slideable, *a.* Restrict *rare*[−1] to sense in Dict. and add: Also **slidable. b.** That may be slid.

1888 *Engineer* LXV. 538/4 A screw mounted in a bearing slidable in a right line. **1925** A. W. JUDGE *Carburettors & Carburation* iv. 63 M is a slidable clip. **1969** *Jane's Freight Containers 1968–69* 408/2 The bogie will be slidable along the full length of the chassis.

Hence **sli·dably** *adv.*

1907 F. W. LANCHESTER *Aerodynamics* 348 A square plane of thin brass, mounted 'slidably' on anti-friction rollers. **1954** *Patents for Inventions. Abridgments of Specifications* Group XXXIV. 23/1 The spiders 8 of which are also slidably mounted on the shafts.

slider. Add: **1. c.** (Earlier example.)

1877 *Scribner's Monthly* Nov. 11/1 'Sliders', the common river turtles of almost all the rivers of the region, grow to a much larger size.

d. *Baseball.* A fast pitch that breaks or slides away from its original path.

1936 *Sun* (Baltimore) 14 Aug. 12/6 It looks like what some of the modern pitchers call 'a slider'. **1980** *Washington Post* 1 Aug. D3/3 The human body isn't meant to throw the slider.

2. (Further example.)

1805 R. SUTCLIFF *Jrnl.* 6 Jan. in *Trav. N. Amer.* (1811) iv. 67 They make use of a boat that has two sliders, one on each side the keel.

4. e. *Bell-ringing.* (See quot. 1901.)

1871 [see STAY *sb.*[2] 2 h]. **1901** H. E. BULWER *Gloss. Techn. Terms Bells & Ringing* 4 *Slider*, usually a bar of wood pivoted at one end on one of the lower members of the 'frame', and extending across the bottom of the 'bell-pit' so that its free end may move to and fro on a bed provided for it on the opposite side of the 'pit'. **1931** E. MORRIS *Hist. & Art Change Ringing* i. 15 For many years ..bells were rung without stay or slider as we now know them. *Ibid.*, Stedman..mentions what would be the forerunner of the stay and slider adjustment. **1974** J. CAMP *Bell Ringing* ii. 30 *(caption)* The stay has pushed the slider to the limit of its movement and the bell cannot turn any further.

f. A sliding electrical contact, forming part of a variable resistance or the like, or serving as a control on electrical equipment.

1872 *Jrnl. Soc. Electr. Engineers* I. 202 The slider *n* is moved on the compensating wire so as to destroy the deflection of the galvonometer. **1923** *Popular Wireless* 13 Oct. Suppl. 1 Suppose we have a coil consisting of 500 turns of No. 22 wire,..fitted with a slider, and we wish to know approximately where to put the slider to receive the Dutch concerts. **1965** *Wireless World* Sept. 432/1 The base..is taken to the slider of a potentiometer connected across the output terminals of the power supply. **1975** *Hi-Fi Answers* Feb. 76/3 Set the input level sliders to about three-quarters of full travel and route the signal back through the amplifier by means of the tape monitor button. **1978** *Gramophone* Aug. 392/3 The latest in Bang and Olufsen's range of Beomaster tuner-amplifiers is.. distinguished by its..absence of switches and knobs—all functions being handled by sliders, press-keys, and wheels.

7. b. Ice-cream served in a sandwich form between two wafers. *colloq.*

1915 J. J. BELL *Wee Macgregor Enlists* ii, Come on oot wi' me an' I'll stan' ye a dizzen sliders. **1935** L. MACNEICE *Poems* 63 Ice cream in sliders Bought in dusty streets. **1967** R. MACKAY *House & Day* 75 'I'll have a slider too.'.. The woman took a wafer..and covered it with the thin yellow ice-cream... She put a second wafer on the top.

8. *slider bridge, clutch, control, potentiometer, switch.*

1919 S. F. WALKER *Electr. Mining Machinery* xxiii. 186 Use of the slider bridge in connection with the loop test for finding a fault to earth in a cable. **1972** *World of Wild Wheels* (Custom Car) 57/2 One of the latest innovations being tried in the States..is the slider clutch. **1978** *Detroit Free Press* 16 Apr. F14/1 (Advt.), Enderle fuel injection, 2 spd Lenco, new slider clutch, Airheart disc brks. **1973** *Wireless World* Oct. 72 (Advt.), Top quality slider controls. **1972** *Ibid.* Jan. 88/2 (Advt.), New slider potentiometers. As used on only the most exclusive of Audio Amplifiers and Mixers. **1970** *Ibid.* July 87/2 (Advt.), Slider switches. Double pole, double throw.

slide-rule. Also **slide rule.** Add: *spec.* A device whereby multiplication and division, and sometimes other mathematical operations, may be performed with speed but limited accuracy, consisting essentially of two rules marked with logarithmic scales and capable of being slid along one another, and usually also a transparent cursor marked with a line crossing the scales, so that a required result may be obtained by inspection after proper movement of these. Also *fig.* (Further examples.)

This, not *sliding rule*, is now the usual name.

1890 *Engineering News* 20 Dec. 543 In France the slide rule is seen on the desk of almost every manufacturer, miller or engineer. **1930** *Engineering* 31 Jan. 131/3 A special form of slide rule..for the purpose of simplifying calculations relating to structures of reinforced concrete. **1958** *Times Lit. Suppl.* 10 Jan. 19/1 They bring out their slide-rule at the sight of a signature, and then, by nice calculation, decide whether there has been any sense in the prose equations which precede it. **1958** *Listener* 11 Sept. 375/1 Towards the end of the war many of the operations of war, especially those concerned with aircraft, were kept under close scientific scrutiny and control. This was the era of the so-called slide-rule strategy. **1974** *Encycl. Brit. Macropædia* XI. 653/2 The first known slide rule in which the slide worked between parts of a fixed stock was made by Robert Bissaker of Great Britain in 1654. *Ibid.*, Amédée Mannheim, an officer of the French artillery, invented in 1859 what may be considered the first of the modern slide rules... This rule.. brought into general use a cursor. **1976** NICHOLS & ARMSTRONG *Workers Divided* 68 Workers were incensed by the efforts of a new manager to run their plant flat out all the time: 'You have to have a real feel for the plant not just be all slide-rule like him.'

sliding, *vbl. sb.* Add: **2. b.** *sliding motion* (earlier example).

1690 LOCKE *Essay Hum. Und.* II. xxiii. 144 All parts of Bodies must be easily separable by such a lateral sliding motion.

sliding, *ppl. a.* Add: **3. b.** (Later examples.)

1948 *Assoc. Football* ('Know the Game' Series) 31/2 A sliding tackle done fairly is not dangerous.., especially when clear contact is made with the ball, and should therefore not be penalised. **1974** *Liverpool Echo* (Football ed.) 12 Oct. 1/2 Foggon went racing through again, but Boersma took the ball off him with a splendid sliding tackle.

6. a. *sliding contact*, a connection in an electric circuit that can be slid along a length of resistance wire; see also s.v. SLIDING *vbl. sb.* 2 b; *sliding valve* = SLIDE-VALVE.

1872 *Jrnl. Soc. Telegr. Engineers* I. 208 The wire with sliding contact was apt to wear if much used. **1926** R. W. HUTCHINSON *Wireless* 77 Sliding contacts can be moved to and fro along two brass sliding rails. **1971** B. SCHARF *Engin. & its Language* xxi. 307 In order to vary the value of one of the known resistances a rheostat may be used, or two of the known resistances may be replaced by a single wire of known resistance with a sliding contact. **1909** *Westm. Gaz.* 11 Nov. 5/1 The new Daimler engine may be said to have brought us to the end of the first stage of the sliding-valve principle.

b. *sliding panel* (earlier example), *roof, shutter* (earlier example), *window.*

a **1817** JANE AUSTEN *Northanger Abbey* (1818) II. v. 76 Have you a stout heart?—Nerves fit for sliding pannels and tapestry? **1929** *Motor World* 29 Mar. 199/1 One or other of the various types of sun-saloons (folding or sliding roof) may be offered at an extra charge. **1959** *Observer* 1 Mar. 21/6 Although many will welcome the sliding roof, the handle is rather prominent. **1766** T. H. CROKER et al. *Compl. Dict. Arts & Sciences* II., s.v. *Madder* col. 4, The sliding-shutters are pulled down. **1724** in *Maryland Hist. Mag.* (1911) VI. 1 Two sliding windows ..with good frame shutters. **1880** *Dict. Leading Techn. & Trade Terms Archit. Design & Building Construction* 207/1 Another form of opening and closing window is one used in domestic structures of a humble character, and termed a 'sliding', sometimes a 'rolling window'. **1976** H. MACINNES *Agent in Place* xxv. 260 A stretch of sliding windows opening onto a balcony.

9. b. (Earlier example.)

1842 C. GUEST *Jrnl.* 14 Feb. (1950) vii. 129 His opinion that in times of scarcity the fixed duty he proposes would have to give way, which is exactly the argument the Tories use when advocating the sliding scale.

10. a. *sliding hernia* (Med.) (see quot. 1958).

1910 SPENCER & GASK *Pract. Surg.* xvii. 995 Retroperitoneal hernia... The cæcum or sigmoid flexure may slide up and down behind the peritoneum, 'Sliding hernia', 'Hernie par glissement'. **1936** Cole & Elman *Textbk. Gen. Surg.* xxv. 753 Sliding hernias descend so readily that a truss is rarely satisfactory in maintaining reduction. **1958** D. L. B. Farley in L. Oliver *Basic Surg.* xiii. 198 Hernia 'en glissade' ('sliding' hernia) refers to herniation of a viscus such as the cæcum or bladder which has an extraperitoneal surface. **1974** R. M. Kirk et al. *Surgery* vi. 78 Sliding hernia. If the lower oesophagus and cardia straighten out and slide into the chest, the competence of the cardiac sphincter may be impaired so that gastric contents reflux into the oesophagus.

b. *sliding filament* (Physiol.), used *attrib.* to designate the model of the action of striated muscle in which contraction results from filaments of actin and of myosin sliding past one another.

1957 *Jrnl. Biophys. & Biochem. Cytol.* III. 640 The results which have been described above give full support to the 'sliding filament model' of striated muscle. **1973** *Times* 14 Aug. 14/7 This..provided the main basis for the 'sliding filament' theory of muscle contraction, now universally accepted.

11. *sliding parity* (Econ.) = *crawling peg* s.v. *crawling *ppl. a.* b.

1966 *Economist* 25 June 1440/2 A tiny minority advocates completely free exchange markets... Possibly a majority favours continued official intervention to set limits to market fluctuations... But an increasing minority favours a compromise system, variously called the crawling peg..or..the sliding parity. **1970** *Times* 9 Feb. 20/1 It sets out to demolish the arguments of those who are..downright hostile to the introduction of the so called sliding parity or crawling peg.

slieveen, var. *sleeveen.

slight, *v.* **2.** For † *Obs.* read *Obs.* exc. *Hist.*, and add later examples.

1974 *Country Life* 28 Mar. 747/3 In March 1645–46, Parliament gave orders that Corfe [Castle] should be slighted. **1976** E. N. Luttwak *Grand Strategy of Roman Empire* ii. 57 It was standard practice to slight the defenses once the site was left. **1977** *Brit. Med. Jrnl.* 24 Dec. 1619/1 Mrs Barbara Castle shattered the political confidence of consultants as effectively as Henry II slighted his opponents' strongholds.

slighten, *v.* For † *Obs.* read *rare* and add: **2.** To make smaller or more slight.

1954 P. Toynbee *Friends Apart* vii. 90 Dysentery.. had thinned his face and slightened his broad body.

Hence **sli·ghtening** *ppl. a.*

1916 A. Quiller-Couch *Art of Reading* (1920) i. 14 God forbid that anyone should hint a slightening word of what our sons and brothers are doing just now.

slighting, *vbl. sb.* **2.** For † *Obs.* read *Obs.* exc. *Hist.*, and add later examples.

1936 *Times Lit. Suppl.* 6 June 479/4 In spite of Cromwellian 'slighting' and the quarrying of local builders and road-makers, so much..still remains. **1977** H. R. Loyn *Vikings in Britain* v. 95 Evidence of possible slighting of fortifications at Cricklade and Cadbury, may well indicate the confidence of the new régime at least in Wessex under Cnut and Earl Godwin.

† **slightually** (slǝi·tiuăli), *adv. Obs. U.S. joc.* [f. Slight(ly *adv.* + Act)ually *adv.*] Actually slightly.

1859 E. H. N. Patterson *Jrnl.* 29 Mar. in L. Hafen *Overland Routes to Gold Fields* (1942) 79 The weather has been beautiful, although last night was 'slightually' frosty. **1873** 'Mark Twain' *Gilded Age* xxix. 266 The Hooverville *Patriot and Clarion* had this 'item':— Slightually Overboard.

slim, *sb.* Restrict † *Obs.* to sense in Dict. and add: **2.** A course of slimming, a diet; usu. in phr. *sponsored slim.*

1977 *Gay News* 7–20 Apr. 8/1 Barrie announced his intention to go on a sponsored 'slim'. People were asked to sign pledge forms to give a certain amount of money for every pound Barrie would lose between Cambridge and Oxford. **1977** *Navy News* Aug. 30/6 Bill Skilliter went on a sponsored slim and lost 3st.

slim, *a.* Add: **1. f.** Of clothes: cut on slender lines; designed to give an appearance of slimness.

1884 [see *scoop-shovel bonnet* s.v. *scoop *sb.*[1] 7]. **1970/71** *Kay's Catal.* Autumn–Winter 145/1 Crimplene Skirt elegantly slim with a raised stripe effect. **1979** *Daily Tel.* 4 June 17/3 (Advt.), One of the most handsome and utterly wearable of this spring's suits is the linen-y slim one in a soft lilac-grey.

4. a. *slim-faced, -footed, -legged, -muzzled, -pointed, -sandalled, -shanked, -tailed, -textured, -waisted* (later example).

1838 Poe *Narr. A. G. Pym* xix. 160 Slim-legged hogs. **1862** G. M. Hopkins *Poems* (1967) 10 And spread Slim-pointed seagull plumes. **1866** —— *Jrnls. & Papers* (1959) 142 After six a very slim-textured and pale causeway of mare's tail cloud running N.E. and S.W. **1872** Hardy *Under Greenwood Tree* I. i. ii. 22 The slim-faced martel had knocked 'em down to me because I nodded to en in my friendly way. **1880** 'Mark Twain' *Tramp Abr.* x. 95 A long, slim-legged boy, he was, encased in quite a short shirt. *Ibid.* 96 Into the midst of this peaceful scene burst that slim-shanked boy in the brief shirt. **1912** W. de la Mare *Child's Day* 14 But there, Ann dear, You'd rather be A slim-tailed mermaid In the sea. **1914** D. H. Lawrence *Prussian Officer & Other Stories* 20 His slim-legged, beautiful horse. **1922** Joyce *Ulysses* 530 Milly Bloom, fairhaired, greenvested, slimsandalled.., breaks from the arms of her lover. **1923** D. H. Lawrence *Birds, Beasts & Flowers* 61 Cyclamens putting their ears back. Long, pensive, slim-muzzled greyhound buds. **1927** —— *Mornings in Mexico* 83 Donkeys, mules, on they come..great bundles bouncing against the sides of the slim-footed animals. **1978** W. F. Buckley *Stained Glass* 225 Himmelfarb..grinned at his long-legged, slim-faced, lightly freckled assistant. **1981** A. Sewart *Close your Eyes & Sleep* vi. 57 He was slim-waisted and muscular looking.

b. slim hole *Oil Industry,* a drill hole of smaller diameter than normal; usu. *attrib.* (with hyphen); **slim volume,** a book of verse by a little-known poet (freq. mildly *derog.*); hence **slim vol** *colloq. abbrev.*

1953 *World Oil* June 112/3 Analysis of areas favorable and unfavorable to slim hole drilling may have been influenced by the performance of available bits in the various types of formations encountered. **1959** *Wall St. Jrnl.* (Eastern ed.) 20 July 15/3 'Slim-hole' drilling..employs conventional equipment—but less of it. The idea is to substitute small pipe and other tinier tools to do a job historically done by larger, more costly units. **1972** L. M. Harris *Introd. Deepwater Floating Drilling Operations* iii. 16 Some companies use slim-hole designs and special-clearance couplings on casings. **1975** A. P. Szilas *Production & Transport of Oil & Gas* iv. 345 (*caption*) Bottom-hole arrangements for the sucker-rod pumping of slim holes. **1920** E. Wallace *Daffodil Mystery* iii. 23 Thornton Lyne was a store-keeper, a Bachelor of Arts,.. and the author of a slim volume. **1953** R. Lehmann *Echoing Grove* 242 The accent, I gather, is on culture—lots of slim vols in the house now. **1979** *Church Times* 1 June 5/3 Friends will..welcome a slim volume of his poems that has come out.

slim, *v.* Restrict 'Chiefly *dial.*' to senses in Dict. and add: **3. b.** *fig.* To reduce in size or extent. Freq. const. *down.*

1963 *Richmond* (Va.) *Times-Dispatch* 16 Dec. 19/1 He set out to slim the budget. **1971** *Daily Tel.* 16 Aug. 11/6, I have slimmed down my holding of Westland Aircraft.. by selling 1,250 at 46½p. **1976** A. White *Long Silence* xix. 169 We'd been able to slim our plan down considerably, to make do with the minimum of men. **1980** *Daily Tel.* 18 Jan. 1/8 Sir Charles Villiers, British Steel's chairman, ended weeks of speculation over the future of two plants..when he said both works would be slimmed.

4. *intr.* To try to reduce one's weight by dieting; to become slim. Also with *down.* Also *fig.*

1930 *Punch* 2 Apr. 366/2 The hostess ate hardly any. She is slimming. **1937** L. C. Douglas *Forgive us our Trespasses* xiii. 254 As the minutes slimmed down to four, three, two, Dinny found his heart beating rapidly. **1963** 'E. McBain' *Ten Plus One* xii. 158, I was too fat... But the funny part was, once I slimmed down, I didn't want to be an actor any more. **1975** G. Howell *In Vogue* 1/2 'Dressing on a war income' was a regular feature [in British *Vogue*],..recommending that women should slim in order to use less fabric.

Hence **sli·mmed-down** *ppl. a.*; also **sli·m-down** (usu. *attrib.*).

1978 *Detroit Free Press* 5 Mar. b14/5 Other corporations are impressed by their strong cash positions, their slimmed-down lease structures and their good earnings. **1978** *N.Y. Times Mag.* 23 July 23/2 Frye-boot chic was swept aside as big-top looks became slimdown looks. **1980** *Daily Tel.* 4 Nov. 1/2 There may be a repeat of the late-1979 confrontation over the British Leyland slimdown and efficiency programme. **1981** *Times* 7 Aug. 20/3 Mercantile House continued to advance in its slimmed-down form.

slime, *sb.* Add: **4. b.** Also *anode slime.* The deposit of insoluble material formed at the anode in the electrolytic refining of copper and some other metals; = *anode mud* s.v. *anode c.

1902 J. McCrae tr. *Arrhenius' Text-bk. Electrochem.* xvi. 276 The other impurities, such as gold, silver,..and lead, remain undissolved, or form insoluble compounds ..and falling from the anode, collect in the so-called anode slime. **1935** W. A. Koehler *Princ. & Applic. Electrochem.* II. xxiii. 170 A large part of the silver produced is obtained from the slimes which are a by-product from the electrorefining of baser metals, especially from the refining of copper, lead, nickel, and zinc. **1954** M. C. Sneed et al. *Comprehensive Inorg. Chem.* II. ii. 128 Copper refinery slime is a dirty-black mixture of very finely divided copper and metallic and nonmetallic anode impurities. **1969** H. T. Evans tr. *Hägg's Gen. & Inorg. Chem.* xxxvi. 749 Silver and gold by-products of the production of copper are collected in the anode slime during copper electrolysis.

6. c. *slimes dam* (S. Afr.); *slime-silvered* adj.

1927 Joyce *On Beach at Fontana* in *Pomes Penyeach,* A senile sea numbers each single Slimesilvered stone. **1956** *Archit. Rev.* CXX. 48/3 There are three main varieties of dump, the sand dumps.., the rock dumps.., and the slimes dams, 50 to 100 feet high, covering wide areas, flat-topped. **1971** *Sunday Times* (Johannesburg) (Mag. Section) 28 Mar. 11/5 That square outline you see at the corner of what looks like a Witwatersrand slimes dam is, in fact, the remains of a Roman army camp.

slime, *v.*[1] **3.** (Earlier examples.)

1723 J. Nott *Cook's & Confectioner's Dict.* sig. R5ᵛ, *To fry Lampreys,* Bleed them, preserve their Blood, slime them, and cut them in pieces. **1747** H. Glasse *Art of Cookery* ix. 86 Slime your Tenches.

slimed, *ppl. a.* (Later examples.)

1940 W. Faulkner *Hamlet* ii. 201 He..stooped and began to drag away the slimed and rotten branches. **1952** *Chambers's Jrnl.* Feb. 110/1 A dark, dank, and sepulchral sphere of silent stone, where passage succeeded passage in an unending monotony of slimed and moss-grown solitude. **1972** F. Warner *Lying Figures* iv. 43 Two bodies..still slimed from the womb.

sli·m-in. Also **slim in.** [f. Slim *v.* + *-in[3].] A course of (usu. sponsored) slimming undertaken by several people in competition with or in support of one another.

1973 *Inverness Courier* 31 July 5/4 A sponsored 'slim-in'..recently raised £15. **1977** *Cornish Times* 19 Aug. 10/1 The sponsored 'slim in' was won by Mrs V. Humphries.

sliming, *vbl. sb.* Add: **2.** *Mining.* The reduction of ore to slime (Slime *sb.* 4).

1920, etc. [see *all-sliming vbl. sb.* and *ppl. a.* s.v. *all 13]. **1965** G. J. Williams *Econ. Geol. N.Z.* v. 56/1 The fine grinding which was necessary to liberate the gold caused losses in scheelite through sliming.

slim jim (slim dʒim). Also **slim Jim, Slim Jim.** [Rhyming combination of Slim *a.* and the proper name *Jim.*] A very slim or thin person.

1889 'Mark Twain' *Conn. Yankee* xxxix. 500 Go it, slim Jim!

2. *transf.* (See quot. 1925.)

1916 Joyce *Portrait of Artist* ii. 104 He had..eaten slim jim out of his cricket cap. **1925** —— *Let.* 31 Oct. (1966) III. 129 This is a kind of sweet meat made of a soft marshmellow jelly which is coated first with pink sugar and then powdered, so far as I remember with cocoanut chips. It is called 'Slim Jim' because it is sold in strips about a foot or a foot and a half in length and an inch in breadth.

3. *attrib.* Designating something long and thin or narrow, as *slim-jim pants, tie,* etc. Also *ellipt.* in pl.

1916 R. Frost *Mountain Interval* 60 That ought to make you An ideal one-girl farm, And give you a chance to put some strength On your slim-jim arm. **1956** *Amer. Speech* XXXI. 307 *Frontier pants..slim jims,* long pants, tapered so closely that they must be zipped at the ankles, or must have slits. **1957** [see *jean 2 b]. **1960** *Guardian* 9 Mar. 6/1 Warm flannelette lined corduroy 'slim jims'. **1962** *Times* 13 Apr. 6/4 Worthing Museum..is asking for a Teddy boy costume, 'with narrow trousers, fancy waistcoat, three-quarter jacket, Slim Jim tie and thick-soled crepe sneakers'. **1962** *Spectator* 27 Apr. 536 The spade ties everyone wore before the slim jims came in. **1973** O. Sela *Portuguese Fragment* (1974) xi. 61 He wore a long sleeved white shirt and slim-jim tie.

slimline, slim-line (sli·mlǝin), *a.* [f. Slim *a.* + *line *sb.*[2] 14 b.] **a.** Slim, narrow, gracefully thin in style or appearance. Occas. *absol.* as *sb.*

1949 Pender & Del Mar *Electr. Engineers Handbk.* (ed. 4) xv. 33 (*headings*) Technical data on fluorescent lamps... Standard line lamps... Slimline lamps. **1961** *Economist* 28 Oct. 328/3 Stereophonic equipment, slimline television, the second wireless set. **1964** *N.Y. Post* 21 Oct. 18/2 (Advt.), Elegant long gowns..slinky slimlines and ultra-feminine bouffants. **1971** *New Scientist* 11 Feb. 323/1 Whenever I switched on the box I seemed to find pontificating doctors: podgy ones telling me to smoke cigars, slimline ones telling me to eat less. **1976** C. Egleton *State Visit* viii. 82 'What if you wanted to speak to someone outside the airport?' Mostyn pointed to a red slim-line. 'Then I would use that one [*sc.* telephone],' he said. **1978** *Times* 10 Aug. 11/1, I put on my white crepe slimline dress.

b. *fig.* Exiguous, economical, stripped of unnecessary elaboration.

1973 *Listener* 26 July 125/2 This slim-line plot is made the occasion for many a worthy animadversion on man's rape of the surface of the earth. **1975** B. J. Enright in Barr & Line *Ess. on Information & Libraries* v. 66 A hesitant and doubtful response greeted Maurice Line's forecast of 'lean muscular libraries' to replace 'fat bloated ones of the past'—the 'new slimline library' seemed a somewhat dubious proposition. **1980** *Daily Tel.* 18 Jan. 1/8 The board has decided to concentrate further consultations and discussions with the unions and the workforce on a 'slimline' operation.

slimly, *adv.* Add: **2. b.** So as to give an effect or appearance of slimness.

1970–1 *Kay's Catal.* Autumn–Winter 60/1 A casual classic that's never out of fashion; slimly styled in knitted Courtelle. **1979** *Homes & Gardens* June 103/1 The front [of the skirt] double wraps, so that it fits sleekly and slimly.

slimmer (sli·mǝɹ). [f. *slim *v.* 4 + -er[1].] One who practises slimming.

1974 *Country Life* 12 Dec. 1845/1 The horrors of a slimmer can be as awful as those of an alcoholic, at least until his stomach shrinks. **1978** J. Pudney *Thank Goodness for Cake* 124 It was not designed as a slimmer's diet but I lost weight. **1980** *West Lancs. Evening Gazette* 11 Aug. 10 (Advt.), Slimmers, have you heard that the.. new slimming method..is now available?

slimming (sli·miŋ), *ppl. a.* [f. Slim *v.* + -ing[2].] Producing an appearance of slimness; conducive to slimness.

1925 *Daily Express* 18 Nov. 6/3 The Lord Chamberlain took out the words 'slimming over the hips', which is a phrase used every day by fashionable costumiers. **1927** *Daily Chron.* 29 Mar. 15/4 Orange juice with a dash of gin in it..is said to be slimming! **1952** *Observer* 14 Sept. 8/6 Youthlines '1980'. The so-slimming girdle in marvellous American Leno. **1980** *Daily Tel.* 13 Oct. 19/3 Slimming Nehru jackets, buttoned close to the throat.

slimming (sli·miŋ), *vbl. sb.* [f. SLIM *v.* + -ING[1].] **a.** The practice of using special means, such as dieting and exercises, to produce slimness of body. Also *fig.*

1931 GALSWORTHY *Maid-in-Waiting* xi. 101 Perhaps the young of today will nevah grow fat. They do slimming—ah-ha! **1958** *Spectator* 7 Feb. 165/1 If such a drastic slimming is to be enforced on agriculture, there is little doubt that [etc.]. **1974** *Times* 17 Apr. 10/5 A medical view of slimming. **1982** *Daily Tel.* 3 Aug. 13/2 The slimming of prime rates brought investors back in force late in the session.

b. *attrib.* (passing into *adj.*)

1932 *Times* 1 Feb. 9/3 She was a bit exercised about getting too stout and might have been going in for 'slimming' exercises as sometimes ladies did. **1951** M. McLUHAN *Mech. Bride* (1967) 154/1 The plump wife who went off for a prolonged slimming course. **1979** A. MORICE *Murder in Outline* x. 85 She was taking slimming pills... She was..worried about her weight.

slimnastics (slimnæ·stiks), *sb. pl.* (const. as *sing.*). *U.S.* [Blend of *SLIM(MING *vbl. sb.* and GYM)NASTICS.] (See quots. 1970.)

1967 *New Yorker* 22 Apr. 138/2 The calendar on the Community Center bulletin board lists citizenship classes, pinochle and bridge games,..'slimnastics', ceramic classes, and dances of the Teen Club. **1970** M. PEI *Words in Sheep's Clothing* ii. 12 'Slimnastics' (gymnastics that slim you down). **1970** NOTTIDGE & LAMPLUGH *Slimnastics* i. 9 'Slimnastics' is a combination of slimming and gymnastics in a group. **1979** *Honolulu Advertiser* 8 Jan. A-4/3 Women's Slimnastics Classes. **1983** *N.Y. Times* 12 Jan. B 2/5 In a gymnasium, 40 women were exercising in a 'slimnastics' class.

sling, *sb.*[1] **1. a.** (Earlier example in sense 'boy's catapult'.)

1828 W. CLARKE *Boy's Own Bk.* (ed. 2) 25 The sling... Whirl it round several times, let go the shorter thong, and the stone will be shot to a great distance.

sling, *sb.*[2] Add: **1. b.** In mountaineering, rock-climbing, etc., a short length of rope used to provide additional support for the body in abseiling or belaying.

1920 G. W. YOUNG *Mountain Craft* iv. 194 Not only is the single sling more likely to snap under the rub of the hard ring. **1946** J. E. Q. BARFORD *Climbing in Britain* ii. 24 *Slings*. Most parties doing exposed or difficult rock climbs nowadays carry one or more slings. **1965** A. BLACKSHAW *Mountaineering* II. vii. 204 Most British climbers carry nylon slings... The use of slings has been very highly developed by British mountaineers; mainly, no doubt, because natural running belays have come to be used much more here than elsewhere. **1976** G. MOFFAT *Over Sea to Death* v. 53 She placed her slings, clipped in her rope and, watching it fall, caught her second's eye.

3. d. *to have* (one's) *ass in a sling*, etc.: (see quot. 1960); to be in trouble. Cf. *ASS, arse. *U.S. slang.*

1960 WENTWORTH & FLEXNER *Dict. Amer. Slang* 10/1 *To have one's ass in a sling*, to be or to appear to be sad, rejected, tired, or defeated. **1976** 'B. SHELBY' *Great Pebble Affair* (1977) 157, I figure there's no money in it for me, but I sure as hell want Rosale's ass in the sling. **1982** S. F. X. DEAN *Such Pretty Toys* (1983) vi. 94 Gonna get my ass in some sling if I miss that plane.

7. sling-back, used *attrib.* and *absol.* to designate (*a*) a woman's shoe which has an open back and is held on by a strap across the heel; so **sling-backed** *a.*; (*b*) a type of chair characterized by a fabric seat suspended from a rigid frame; **sling-bag,** a bag with a long strap which may be hung from the shoulder; **sling chair** *U.S.*, a sling-back chair (see *sling-back* (*b*) above); **sling-jacket** (see quot. 1900); **sling-load, sling load,** a load which is lifted in a sling; also (with hyphen) as *v. trans.*; **sling pump** *N. Amer.*, a sling-back shoe (see *sling-back* (*a*) above).

1949 *10 Eventful Years* (Encycl. Brit.) II. 312/2 They were soft suede slippers, little leather sling-backs, ankle-high boots, and ballet slippers of all colours and materials. **1950** 'S. RANSOME' *Deadly Miss Ashley* ii. 25 Neat black sling-back wedgies on small feet. **1973** 'D. JORDAN' *Nile Green* xxvii. 119, I was sitting on a sling-back chair looking out on the Nile. **1974** *Country Life* 21 Mar. 688/1 A canvas sling-back with a rope wedge sole for £5. **1976** B. BOVA *Multiple Man* iii. 34, I walked across to the Scandinavian sling back that I usually sat in... I eased myself into the slingback chair. **1978** *Vogue* 1 Mar. 131 (*caption*) Sling-back high heels..£37. **1948** 'J. BELL' *Wonderful Mrs Marriott* vii. 86 A pair of toeless sling-backed wedge-heeled shoes. **1965** M. SPARK *Mandelbaum Gate* vii. 218 Sturdily clutching with one thumb the shoulder strap of her sling-bag. **1976** *Woman's Weekly* 6 Nov. 11/1 The letter still lay in the bottom of her sling bag. **1957** *Holiday* Nov. 141/1 The sling, or Hardoy, chair, a leather suspension from a rigid metal cradle, adapted from a wooden folding chair used by Italian officers in North Africa. **1978** L. BLOCK *Burglar in Closet* ix. 75 Jillian..sat in a sling chair. **1900** HARDY in *Sphere* 21 Apr. 419/2 In those days the Hussar regiments still wore over the left shoulder that attractive attachment, or frilled half-coat, hanging loosely behind like the wounded wing of a bird, which was called the pelisse, though it was known among the troopers themselves as a 'sling-jacket'. **1908** —— *Dynasts* III. II. I Will the gay sling-jacket glow again beside the muslin gown? **1933** M. LOWRY *Ultramarine* v. 213 The cargo, chests of tea, was hoisted in slingloads of ten from the piles. **1968** *Globe & Mail* (Toronto) 3 Feb. B1/2 The union was asking for a 22-man basic work gang; extensive sling-load limitations, [etc.]. **1969** *Jane's Freight Containers 1968–69* 8/1 The line of action of the sling load is assumed to be parallel to and not more than 38 mm..from the outer face of the corner fitting. **1969** I. KEMP *Brit. G.I. in Vietnam* x. 176 A Chinook to sling-load our chopper back to Phuoc Vinh. **1941** *Women's Wear Daily* 31 Oct. I. 13/1 The shoe which so many retailers claimed they could not sell, the sling pump, is due to make another trip, very definitely an evidence that women want them and like them. **1968** *Globe & Mail* (Toronto) 17 Feb. 12 (Advt.), Cool sandal sling pump with adjustable T-strap, low heel.

sling, *sb.*[3] Add: **3.** *Austral.* A gratuity; a bribe. Also *sling back*. Cf. *SLING *v.*[1] 9.

1948 K. S. PRICHARD *Golden Miles* viii. 92 'There's some hungry bastards,' the men said, 'making big money on their ore, never give the poor bugger boggin' for 'em a sling back.' The sling back might be ten bob on pay-day, or no more than a few pots of beer, but was always appreciated. *Ibid.* ix. 102 Sling backs to the shift boss got some men their jobs. **1953** K. TENNANT *Joyful Condemned* xxiv. 232 Say I take twenty per cent of the cop for myself..all the rest goes in slings. **1969** *People* (Austral.) 15 Jan. 21/2 It is not uncommon for a [poker] machine to go into a club with what is known in the trade as 'a sling'..to someone or other of the 'power men'... These 'slings' can range up to $300 a machine sold. **1973** *Nation Rev.* (Melbourne) 31 Aug. 1450/1 The hospital.. must have been quite notorious in police circles. As far as I knew, we were exceptional in refusing to pay the customary sling.

sling, *sb.*[5] **1.** (Earlier U.S. example.)

1792 P. FRENEAU in *National Gazette* (Philadelphia) 28 June 280/1 Rum ne'er shall meet my lips..In shape of toddy, punch, grog, sling or dram.

sling, *v.*[1] Add: **2. a.** (Later *fig.* examples.)

1959 E. H. CLEMENTS *High Tension* vii. 128 He'd been slung out of the test because he'd hurt his foot. **1977** W. MARSHALL *Thin Air* vi. 69 He was so bloody stupid we slung him out.

3. b. Also in phr. *to sling hash*, to wait at tables. *U.S.* Cf. *hash-slinger* s.v. *HASH *sb.*[1] 6.

1876 [see *Calamity Jane* s.v. *CALAMITY 3]. **1906** 'O. HENRY' *Four Million* 106 I'm going back there and ask her to marry me. I guess she won't want to sling hash any more when she sees the pile of dust I've got. **1949** *Life* 24 Oct. 20/2 She..slung hash for a couple of weeks.

d. See also *HOOK *sb.*[1] 16 b.

e. (Earlier example.) Also, to speak or utter (language, etc.) well or fluently. Also, *to sling the bull*, to talk glib nonsense (*U.S.*). Cf. sense a in Dict.

1874 E. EGGLESTON *Circuit Rider* vii. 72 He was beginning to sling his rude metaphors to the right and left. **1892** KIPLING *Barrack-Room Ballads* 67 An' 'ow they would admire for to hear us sling the *bat* [= speak the language]. **1904** G. B. SHAW *Lett. to Granville Barker* (1956) 27 One of them, the stage Irishman,..might be done by, say, Neville Doone, if he can sling the dialect. **1934** T. E. LAWRENCE *Let.* 8 June (1938) 806 In such an eyewash job as this of mine, the power to sling the gab would be very helpful. **1940** A. H. MARCKWARD *Scribner Handbk. Eng.* vii. 212 Undoubtedly the chief reason for the conversational effectiveness of many individuals is their inherent ability to sling it. **1982** *Verbatim* Autumn 14/2 Watch out for..the low-down curs and dirty dogs, who sling the bull and then send you on a wild goose chase.

g. (Later example.) Also *to sling in* or *up*.

1911 G. B. SHAW *Blanco Posnet* 384 Stow it, Boozy. Sling it. Cut it. Cheese it. Shut up. **1910** G. B. LANCASTER *Jim of Ranges* ii. 48 I've slung her [*sc.* Queensland] up. Guv her the go, the ole jade. **1953** K. TENNANT *Joyful Condemned* xxxii. 309 We both slung in our jobs.. and went off after him.

8. *to sling off* (*at*), to jeer (at). *Austral.* and *N.Z. colloq.*

1911 S. RUDD *Dashwoods* 24, I heard yer both slingin' off. **1916** *Anzac Bk.* 31, I could not understand them slinging off at 'im and 'im thinking they were treatin' 'im like as 'e was one of themselves. **1921** K. S. PRICHARD *Black Opal* xiii. 112 The rest of the men continued nevertheless to 'sling off', as they said, at Bully and Roy O'Mara as they saw fit. **1941** *Coast to Coast* 232 'Why was he so wild?' 'Aw, it was just some chaps'd been slinging off at him,' I said. **1960** N. HILLIARD *Maori Girl* III. vii. 221 The *pakehas* think you're slinging off about them or saying something rude. **1963** J. CANTWELL *No Stranger to Flame* v. 86 'Stop it,' Barry said, flushing. 'Stop slinging off.' **1975** M. R. LIVERANI *Winter Sparrows* II. xv. 232 She glowered at the driver suspiciously. Was he slinging off at her?

9. To pay a bribe or gratuity. Occas. with *it*. Cf. *SLING *sb.*[3] 3. *Austral.*

1939 K. TENNANT *Foveaux* II. 172 'I'm slinging it to Hamp,' Bardy said sullenly. **1949** L. GLOSSOP *Lucky Palmer* 5 Clarrie, he ain't gone off in six months. Must sling to the cops. Wonder how much he pays 'em. **1953** T. A. G. HUNGERFORD *Riverslake* vi. 130 'Sling, Stefan!' When the Pole looked at him uncomprehendingly Murdoch whipped a ten-pound note out of the bundle and handed it to the ring-keeper. 'He don't know,' he explained. 'It's the first time he's played.' **1971** F. HARDY *Outcasts of Foolgarah* 56 On first name terms with every shire President so long as they didn't forget to sling when backhanders came in.

sling, *v.*[2] Add: **4. a.** Also in phr. *to sling one's hammock*, to have a period of time off-duty to get used to a new ship. *Naut.*

1913 T. T. JEANS *John Graham Sub-Lieutenant R.N.* iii. 58 There was no 'school' till morning, the Padré had a day off 'to sling his hammock'. **1917** 'TAFFRAIL' *Sub* iii. 92 'You'll have to-morrow to sling your hammock and to get used to the ship, youngster,' he went on. **1946** G. HACKWORTH JONES *Sixteen Bells* I. iv. 67 Reggie was hardly given a day to 'sling his hammock' before he was instructed to take over the afternoon watch.

sling-. Add: **sling-net** (later example); **sling-trot** (earlier example).

1866 MRS. GASKELL *Wives & Daughters* I. x. 112 He had been out dredging in ponds and ditches, and has his wet sling-net, with its imprisoned treasures..over his shoulder. **1853** J. PALLISER *Solitary Rambles & Adventures Hunter in Prairies* vi. 144, I saw my stag begin to fall in the rear of the band, and his pace slacken to a sling trot.

slinger, *sb.*[1] Add: **2.** (Later examples.)

1920 D. J. KNIGHT in P. F. Warner *Cricket* i. 45 The man [*sc.* fast bowler] who bowls with his arm more or less horizontal—a slinger. **1926** *Variety* 29 Dec. 5/3 The erudite word slingers. *Ibid.*, The slang *slingers*. **1944** E. BLUNDEN *Cricket Country* iv. 52 T. was soon displaced for a less expensive slinger. **1979** *Vole* June 45/2 The slingers of the mid-nineteenth century terrified lesser batsmen.

3. Chiefly *Services' slang.* Bread soaked in tea. Usu. *pl.* Also applied *loosely* to other food.

1882 F. W. P. JAGO *Anc. Lang. & Dial. Cornwall* 267 Slingers. Kettle broth made of boiling water, bread, salt, and pepper, with sometimes a little butter. **1890** BARRÈRE & LELAND *Dict. Slang* II. 256/2 *Slingers*,..bits of bread floating in tea. **1895** KIPLING in *Pall Mall Gaz.* 30 May 2/2 You won't have no mind for slingers, not to-morrow —..bein' sick! **1925** FRASER & GIBBONS *Soldier & Sailor Words* 261 *Slingers*, tea or coffee with bread soaked in it. Dumplings. **1962** W. GRANVILLE *Dict. Sailors' Slang* 108 *Slingers*, ship's biscuits or bread soaked in cocoa. A snack eaten before *slinging* one's hammock. Supper is very early in the Navy and *slingers* help to fortify the men until breakfast the next day. **1965** 'J. LE CARRÉ' *Looking Glass War* ii. 31 We had the canteen in the old days. Slinger and wadge.

slinger, *sb.*[2] (Later examples.)

1969 *Daily Tel.* 2 Apr. 1/1 The slip was dropped from an overall pocket by a slinger—a man who guides car bodies and other parts into position on the assembly track—and it showed that he was earning as much as the assembly workers themselves. **1974** P. WRIGHT *Lang. Brit. Industry* viii. 69 In heavy electrical engineering, where the crane-driver can see the slinger directing his load, they communicate by shouts. **1982** *Sunday Times* 27 June 3/1 I've been in the ropery 12 years and my husband's been in the yard, as a slinger, for 17 years.

sli·ngful. [f. SLING *sb.*[2] 1 + -FUL.] As much as a sling will hold.

1913 *Cassell's Mag. Fiction & Popular Lit.* June 183/1 A stevedore was killed by a falling slingful of railway sleepers. **1941** E. P. O'DONNELL *Great Big Doorstep* xxii. 313 She heard the donkey engines clanking aboard an approaching ship, and slingfuls of fruit splashing into the water.

slinging, *vbl. sb.*[2] (Later example.)

1901 *Business Terms, Phrases & Abbrev.* (ed. 2) 109 The buyer must attend to their being put on board, and pay the dues or the charges for slinging, should any be incurred.

sli·ngshot. orig. *U.S.* Also **sling-shot.** (In Dict. s.v. SLING-.) Add: **1. a.** (Earlier and later examples.)

1849 N. KINGSLEY *Diary* 23 Oct. (1914) 77 Many are getting up sling-shots,..but I hope we shall never have occasion to use them, but we must all do something to pass away the time. **1895** [in Dict. s.v. SLING-]. **1901** *Daily Colonist* (Victoria, B.C.) 15 Oct. 5/2 The police have started a crusade against the use of slingshots and air and pea guns by boys. **1966** *Economist* 2 July 28/2 In peasant style, they placed women and children to the fore, and used slingshots with shepherds' accuracy to defend themselves against the detachment of police cavalry. **1977** C. McCULLOUGH *Thorn Birds* i. 3 She played happily with the whistles and slingshots..her brothers discarded.

b. In various *fig.* and *transf.* uses implying propulsion from or as from a catapult (see quots.) Also as quasi-*adv.*

1951 *Sun* (Baltimore) 10 July 15/3 [In a game of softball] I've never seen a pitcher get away with an illegal pitch in the national or league play... Most of them throw just like I do—straight windmill—and out on the Coast, they throw slingshot. **1964** W. GOLDING *Spire* ix. 159 The weather..began to squeeze bursts of rain out of the air like slingshot, so that although the men were wet, they were warm with the stinging. **1975** *New Yorker* 30 June 81/1 That's the slingshot there—where the rubber is stretched between bumpers [in a pinball machine]. **1976** J. JAMES *Bridge of Sand* iii. 62 There came immediately on us a great storm of hail. The sling-shots of the Gods rattled on our helmets, bounced off our shields, almost cut our faces. **1976** *6,000 Words* 184 *Slingshot*. n, 1: a maneuver in auto racing in which a drafting car accelerates past the car in front by taking advantage of reserve power 2: a dragster in which the driver sits behind the rear wheels. **1979** 'A. Hailey' *Overload* III. vii. 222 Harry London's feet hit the floor like slingshots.

c. *Astronaut.* A space flight which uses the gravitational pull of a celestial body in order to accelerate sharply and, usu., to change course. Freq. *attrib.* (see sense 3 below.)

1970 N. Armstrong et al. *First on Moon* viii. 174 The three men on Apollo II had to decide whether to allow themselves to be 'captured' by lunar gravity—or take the slingshot and come home. **1971** *Encyclopedia Science Suppl.* 350 The next flight now scheduled is for 1973, a 'slingshot' that will pass close to Venus on its way to Mercury.

2. A weapon consisting of a heavy weight wrapped in a cloth or equivalent and used as a cosh; a blackjack. ? *Obs.*

1891 H. Herman *His Angel* ix. 149 He made a ghastly horrible sling-shot by filling a heavy tumbler with the iron tops screwed off from the fire-irons, and tying the lot in a handkerchief. **1904** *N.Y. Evening Post* 24 June 2/6 The guards..are authorized to carry slingshots... [They] are heavily loaded with lead, and are securely attached to the wrist.

3. *attrib.*, as (sense 1 a) *slingshot crotch*; (sense 1 b) *slingshot dragster*; (sense 1 c) *slingshot action, attitude, flight, manœuvre, trajectory*.

1979 *Guardian* 3 Sept. 11/3 Accelerated and turned by the slingshot action of Saturn's gravitational field, the spacecraft is heading out past Titan on a new trajectory. **1970** N. Armstrong et al. *First on Moon* iv. 83 We've completed our maneuvers to observe the slingshot attitude. **1923** W. S. Cather *Lost Lady* ii. 16 They had behaved like wild creatures all morning;..cutting slingshot crotches. **1962** *Engineering* 5 Jan. 5/1 Sydney Allard's immaculately prepared 'slingshot' dragster, with its 480 hp. Roots-blown Chrysler V8 engine. **1971** *Guardian* 16 Dec. 13/5 Designed..to use the gravitational fields of the planets for 'sling-shot' flights which—using Jupiter as the primary springboard—visit Saturn and Pluto, then Uranus and Neptune. **1970** N. Armstrong et al. *First on Moon* iv. 82 A 'slingshot' maneuver, a trajectory which would take it behind the trailing edge of the moon. **1976** *Sci. News* 18 June 391 The 'slingshot' trajectory between the worlds has carried Pioneer 11 about 16° above the plane of the ecliptic.

Hence **sli·ngshot** *v. intr.*; **sli·ng-shooting** *ppl. a.*

1969 *Daily Progress* (Charlottesville, Va.) 5 July 6/4 'I could stay with him in a draft (the two cars running one behind the other).'.. Yarborough said he purposely gave Baker two chances to slingshot past to learn if he was fast enough. **1975** B. Garfield *Death Sentence* xxi. 106 The lights were all gone: stone-throwing and sling-shooting kids routinely used them for target practice. **1980** *Dirt Bike* Oct. 68/1 Ward's body inched forward with increasing speed until he slingshotted at blurring velocity to and beyond the Yamaha.

slink, *sb.* **2. d.** (Earlier example.)

1858 Thoreau *Jrnl.* 29 Aug. in *Writings* (1906) XVII. 134 F. says they call the cardinal-flower 'slink-weed', and say that the eating it will cause cows to miscarry.

slink, *v.* Add: **2. d.** To withdraw from. *rare.*

1853 J. G. Baldwin *Flush Times Alabama* 26 Many a witness..'slunk his pitch mightily' when old Kasm put him through on the cross-examination.

e. To turn (the eyes) *round* in a stealthy or slinking manner. *rare.*

1923 Galsworthy *Captures* 162 Leaning down to our scoundrel and slinking her eyes round at the Countess, she murmured something malicious.

sli·nker, *sb.*² [f. Slink *v.* + -er¹.] One who slinks about; a shirker. So as *v. intr.*, to shirk.

1880 G. Smith *Gipsy Life* ii. 48 When the task-master perceived the 'gang' had begun to 'slinker' he would shout out. **1919** G. W. Deeping *Second Youth* xxviii. 238 It makes a man so mean, so sly, such a slinker round corners. **1923** —— *Secret Sanctuary* x. 97 He had seen the most inveterate slinker change into a creature of crude and bounding energy when a piece of leather was to be kicked about a field. **1954** J. R. R. Tolkien *Two Towers* II. iii. 247 Sam's guess was that the Sméagol and Gollum halves (or what in his own mind he called Slinker and Stinker) had made a truce and a temporary alliance.

slinky (sli·ŋki), *a.* [f. Slink *v.* + -y¹.] Of a woman, esp. from the manner of her dress: sinuous, slender, gliding; of a garment: close-fitting, as if moulded to the figure. In extended use (with varying degrees of approval): stealthy, dextrous, furtive.

1921 *Ladies' Home Jrnl.* Jan. 8/1 Even now I seem to see in memory a slinky, slant-eyed person with long, slender finger nails, who wears green. **1923** *Glasgow Herald* 21 July 6/5 Jessica was swathed in a slinky gown of flat crepe in a deep blue shade. **1932** D. L. Sayers *Have his Carcase* xviii. 235 She now selected a slinky garment, composed of what male writers call 'some soft, clinging material'. **1944** R. Chandler *Lady in Lake* 116 One of those slinky glittering females. **1951** N. C. Hunter *Waters of Moon* III. i. 69 Some really classy young man with heaps of money. A Guards officer, for instance, or something rather slinky on the Stock Exchange. **1962** *Times* 28 Dec. 9/5 Miss Ross sings a variety of songs—slinky, torchy, witty. **1973** *Country Life* 8 Mar. 633/2 Slinky dresses that have the finest of straps or are completely strapless. **1980** J. Wainwright *Eye of Beholder* 18 His missus. The slinky, brittle bint.

Hence **sli·nkily** *adv.*

1935 *Amer. Speech* X. 192/2 A long flowing gown trails slinkily on the floor.

Slinky (sli·ŋki), *sb.* Also **slinky.** [f. Slink *v.* + -y⁶.] The proprietary name of a toy consisting of a flexible helical spring which can be made to 'somersault' down steps as an inverted U. Also *Slinky toy*. Also *fig.*

1948 *Trade Marks Jrnl.* 11 Feb. 114/2 Slinky. 654,972. Games (other than ordinary playing cards) toys and sporting articles (except clothing). James Industries Inc.., 4932, Portico St., Germantown, Philadelphia..—24th Dec. 1946. **1968** *Habitat Xmas Catal.*, Slinky toy—fun for childish adults and grown up children! **1975** *Publishers Weekly* 7 Apr. 83/1 The tangled slinky-toy lives of these three turned-on folk heroes. **1979** *Early Learning 1979–80* (Early Learning Centre) 32/2 Plastic Slinky... Walks down stairs!

slinter, var. *schlenter *sb.* and *a.*

slip, *sb.*¹ Add: **4. b.** *slip house* (later examples), *kiln* (earlier example); *slip decoration, glaze*; **slip casting,** the manufacture of ceramic articles by allowing slip to solidify in a porous mould.

1901 W. P. Rix tr. *E. Bourry's Treat. Ceramic Industries* iv. 231 (*heading*) Moulding by slip casting. **1959** *Jrnl. Iron & Steel Inst.* CXCI. 208/1 A description is given of the technique of slip casting, and its application to the casting of high-temperature materials including ceramics and metallo-ceramics. **1974** F. H. Norton *Elem. Ceramics* viii. 95 The slip-casting method is much used in ceramic production as it is possible by this means to reproduce very complicated shapes in plaster molds. **1960** R. G. Haggar *Conc. Encycl. Cont. Pottery & Porc.* 458/1 Slip decoration consists of applying to the unfired clay surface of the ware, before it has been dried and fired, contrasted coloured slips, either by trailing from a quill, [etc.]. **1973** R. Fournier *Illustr. Dict. Pract. Pottery* 211/2 (*caption*) Slip decoration. An English slip-trailed dish—possibly Tickenhall. **1960** *Times* 6 Aug. 9/7 Without the slip-glaze upper decoration finish. **1902** A. Bennett *Anna of Five Towns* viii. 167 The clay travelled naturally in a circle from the slip-house by the canal to the packing-house by the canal. **1961** M. Jones *Potbank* viii. 30 The maker breaks a lump of clay off the hunk brought from the sliphouse. **1769** J. Wedgwood *Let.* 9 Apr. (1965) 73 The Slip Kiln is nearly finished.

c. *slip-decorated, -decorator, -glazing, -painting, -trailer, -trailing.*

1883 L. M. Solon *Art Eng. Potter* 27 (*heading*) Slip-decorated ware. **1900** F. Litchfield *Pottery & Porcelain* ii. 25 At Wrotham..were produced..quaint, slip-decorated posset-pots, tygs, and dishes. **1979** *Essex Jrnl.* XIV. 20 There were also a number of small sherds of slip-decorated lead-glazed jugs and plates produced at Harlow. **1921** *Dict. Occup. Terms* (1927) § 105 *Slip decorator*, applies a pattern to pottery in the green state by blowing on coloured clay slips. **1960** *Times* 6 Aug. 9/6 The dual colouring..was obtained by slip-glazing before firing. **1902** *Encycl. Brit.* XXXI. 874/2 Turning to the decorative side of pottery work, we have in *slip-painting* a method as old as primitive pottery itself. **1964** H. Hodges *Artifacts* i. 33 One particularly elaborate form of slip painting, *feather combing*, involves the use of a brush with multiple points. **1940** B. Leach *Potter's Bk.* ii. 33 There are at least half a dozen potteries in Japan where the slip-trailer is employed. **1960** H. Powell *Beginner's Bk. Pottery* II. 64 *Slip trailer*.., a small rubber bag with a narrow neck into which is fitted a thin glass tube. **1940** B. Leach *Potter's Bk.* vi. 147 One glaze can be trailed over another with the same instrument that is used in slip trailing. **1964** H. Hodges *Artifacts* i. 33 The clay may be applied in a fairly fluid form using for the purpose a container with a nozzle, much as a cake is iced by bakers. This method is called *slip-trailing*. *a* **1977** *Harrison Mayer Ltd. Catal.* 27/1 A range of coloured slips prepared for slip trailing.

slip, *sb.*² Add: **I. 3. a.** (Further examples.) Also *N.Z.*

1950 *N.Z. Jrnl. Agric.* Dec. 559/1 The usual practice is to buy the pigs as slips. **1977** *Cornish Times* 19 Aug. 1/1 (Advt.), Strong quality Slips and Pigs for slaughter accepted.

II. 4. Restrict † *Obs. rare* to sense in Dict. and add: **b.** A light under-waistcoat with the edge showing to form a border to a waistcoat worn with morning dress.

1933 C. St. J. Sprigg *Fatality in Fleet St.* viii. 98 Oakley looked like..a monkey which had surprisingly been trained to wear a morning-coat and grey slip. **1941** H. G. Wells *You can't be too Careful* III. x. 158 And you looking *lovely* in a silk hat and light grey trousers. You'll have, you know, white slips to your waistcoat.

6. b. (Later examples.)

1903 G. Jack *Wood Carving* iii. 43 For sharpening the insides of tools, 'slips' are made with rounded edges of different sizes. One slip of 'Washita' stone and one of 'Arcansas'. **1960** C. H. Hayward *Cabinet Making for Beginners* (ed. 2) iv. 104 Drawer Making... Grooved slips are glued to the sides to hold the bottom.

10. a. Also *betting slip*: see *betting *vbl. sb.*¹ 2.

III. 13. b. *slip proof.*

1892 A. Oldfield *Pract. Man. Typogr.* iii. 37 Proofs are required in various stages, and have a distinct name in each stage, as follows:—'slip', or galley proofs [etc.]. **1908** W. S. Churchill *Let.* 8 Sept. in R. S. Churchill *Winston S. Churchill* (1969) II. Compan. II. 839 Messrs Hodder & Stoughton should let me have all the *Strand* articles up to date in slip proof as soon as possible. **1973** S. Jennett *Making of Books* (ed. 5) I. vi. 99 Paging is a manual operation carried out by compositors... Each man has his share of slip proofs.

slip, *sb.*³ Add: **II. 4. c.** (Further examples.) Now, an underskirt or petticoat dependent from the waist or the shoulders and having no sleeves. Colloq. phr. *your slip is showing*: see *show *v.* 28 g.

1825 H. Wilson *Mem.* II. 103 What do you call a slip? do you mean a petticoat, or an intrigue? **1903** M. M. *How to dress & what to Wear* 185 Slips. This term is applicable either to a skirt or a bodice. A skirt slip is made of silk, satin, or even batiste, and is employed for wearing under a thin upper dress... Slips may, or may not, be provided with sleeves. **1920** M. S. Woolman *Clothing* ix. 135 Slips or underfrocks with detachable sleeves have also been designed... Many of the slips are made without sewed-in lining. **1944** H. Croome *You've gone Astray* xv. 158 He glowered at Linda, sitting on the edge of the bed in her slip with one stocking off. **1957** J. Braine *Room at Top* xi. 109 She came over in her slip... She was already a different person in the blue silk garment. **1979** R. Jaffe *Class Reunion* (1980) I. vi. 85 In her slip and pants and garter belt and stockings she would lie down.

d. (Later example.)

1977 *New Yorker* 27 June 72/3 What I want is my pillow... The slip is homemade.

f. *pl.* In full *bathing slips*: bathing-drawers. (No longer in use.)

1904 *Times* 11 Aug. 10/3 He wore a pair of bathing slips and a broad-brimmed white linen cap. **1927** W. E. Collinson *Contemp. Eng.* 62 Bathing togs consisted of a bathing suit and slips, a reduced type of bathing-drawers.

5. (Earlier example.)

1771 C. Burney *Present State of Mus. France & Italy* 244 Printed sonnets, in praise of singers and dancers, were thrown from the slips.

III. 9. a. (Further *techn.* examples.)

1888 *Lockwood's Dict. Mech. Engin.* 329 *Slip*, the sliding of riveted joints one over the other to such an extent as to be visible. **1950** *Sci. News* XV. 143 The copper-rich oxide layer..acted as a lubricant between billet and container... This particular type of oxide layer seems to favour slip or slide of the metal under it.

c. Substitute for def.: The difference between the pitch of a propeller (on a ship or aircraft) and the distance it moves through the ambient medium in one revolution. (Examples in *Aeronaut.*)

1910 R. W. A. Brewer *Art of Aviation* viii. 110 A certain amount of slip is necessary in order to obtain thrust. **1919** [see *pitch *sb.*² 25 e]. **1946** H. Rouse *Elem. Mech. Fluids* ix. 293 At peak efficiency the effective pitch of the propeller is somewhat below the geometric pitch, which results in a so-called 'slip' of the blades. **1965** C. N. Van Deventer *Introd. Gen. Aeronautics* viii. 194/1 (*caption*) A comparison of geometric pitch with working pitch and slip.

e. The sudden descent of material within a blast furnace. Cf. *slipping *vbl. sb.*¹ 1 c.

1881 *Encycl. Brit.* XIII. 305/2 A 'slip' (or sudden jerky motion downwards of a mass of material that had previously more or less 'scaffolded'). **1911** *Jrnl. Iron & Steel Inst.* LXXXIII. 587 The causes of accidents peculiar to blast-furnaces, especially explosions, slips, and break-outs. **1948** G. R. Bashforth *Manuf. Iron & Steel* I. x. 166 The sudden slip of cold solid material into a hotter zone.. may result in serious explosions. **1969** K. R. Haley in J. H. Strassburger *Blast Furnace* II. xii. 592 A slip.. causes wear on the lining.

f. Movement relative to a solid surface of the fluid immediately adjacent to it.

1887 *Encycl. Brit.* XXII. 771/1 While greater surface than is offered by [a swimmer's] hands and feet was always given, with the evident intention of reducing 'slip', much resistance took place at the neutral or negative part of the stroke. **1891** *Phil. Trans. R. Soc.* A. CLXXXI. 560 From equation (i.) it follows that the effect of slip varies inversely as the radius of the tube. **1937** Dodge & Thompson *Fluid Mech.* xii. 308 The principal reason..is the fact that the hypothesis of zero slip at the boundary of the solid has been abandoned. **1967** R. S. Brodkey *Phenomena of Fluid Motions* vii. 91 If slip at the boundary were allowed, the flow rate would become $Q =$ [etc.]. **1979** *Nature* 22 Mar. 350/2 Circumferential slip is essential if a helical object is to develop thrust in a true liquid, that is, if it is to propel itself using viscous forces.

g. *Electr. Engin.* The proportion by which the speed of an electric motor falls short of the speed of rotation of the magnetic flux inside it.

1893 *Jrnl. Inst. Electr. Engineers* XXII. 328 The machine has a frequency of 50 and a slip of 6 per cent. **1936** Say & Pink *Performance & Design of Alternating Current Machines* xii. 211 On no load the slip is generally less than..1 per cent. **1976** A. R. Daniels *Introd. Electr. Machines* vii. 122 The rotor is driven at a small slip with respect to the armature rotating m.m.f.

h. *Cryst.* The movement of one layer of ions over another in a stressed crystal.

1899 *Proc. R. Soc.* LXV. 86 The real character of the lines is apparent when the crystalline constitution of each grain is considered. They are not cracks, but *slips* along planes of cleavage or gliding planes. **1932** *Jrnl. Iron & Steel Inst.* CXXVI. 600 These results are in accord with the theory of deformation by slip. **1966** C. R. Tottle *Sci. Engin. Materials* iii. 64 In slip, a restricted number of planes are involved, and a restricted number of directions, so that whole areas of the crystal are affected. **1976** M. C. Nutt *Metallurgy & Plastics for Engineers* v. 70 Since metals deform by slip only on certain planes of atoms, it follows that anything that interferes with the slip process hardens the metal.

i. The turning of one plate of a clutch relative to the other when they are in contact.

1902 A. C. HARMSWORTH *Motors & Motor-Driving* vi. 95 On the road also, if a clutch does not act, due to slip, a small dose of water puts matters right at once if the mechanical portions are in order. **1925** *Morris Owner's Man.* 22 The more pressure there is on the foot-board the less pressure is available in the clutch, and consequently there is a danger of slip starting. **1976** C. WEBB *Be your own Car Mechanic* vii. 96 When a clutch is worn it begins to slip. The slip generates heat and can cause the clutch spring or springs to lose their strength.

j. *Aeronaut.* A movement of an aircraft that includes a sideways component, esp. downwards towards the centre of curvature of a turn. Cf. *SKID *sb.* 4 b.

1916 GRAHAME-WHITE & HARPER *Learning to Fly* v. 50 The machine being near the ground, it came into contact with the surface of the aerodrome before the 'slip' had time to develop any high rate of speed. **1929** HALL & NILES *One Man's War* 114 Our slip was a slow one. It would be impossible to come out of a fast slip because that was done by putting on the rudder nearest to the direction of the slip. **1930** R. DUNCAN *Stunt Flying* ix. 79 A slip sideways into a landing is invaluable if it is necessary to land in a small area. **1952** [see *SKID *sb.* 4 b]. **1965** C. N. VAN DEVENTER *Introd. Gen. Aeronaut.* x. 233/2 Information on slip and turn is nearly always wanted at the same time. **1983** D. STINTON *Design of Aeroplane* xiii. 465 A spiral dive..is marked by increasing airspeed and, usually, no slip or skid.

10. d. (Later examples of *a slip of the tongue*.)

1906 H. C. WYLD *Hist. Study of Mother Tongue* iv. 72 He at once perceives the difference [in his pronunciation], and 'corrects' the result as a 'mistake' or a 'slip of the tongue'. **1928** E. O'NEILL *Strange Interlude* VIII. 314 'You said "Navy".'.. 'Slip of the tongue! I meant Gordon.' **1939** G. B. SHAW *In Good King Charles's Golden Days* I. 13 'What did you call the gentleman, Mr Fox?'.. 'A slip of the tongue, Mistress Basham.' **1958** J. WAIN *Contenders* vii. 151 The Canon was still beating down Robert's attempt to explain away that slip of the tongue. **1975** *Economist* 21 June 31/2 Transcripts of the call, accurate to the last slip of the tongue, have been sent to the magazine Stern.

14. b. (Earlier example.)

1816 W. LAMBERT *Cricketer's Guide* (ed. 6) iii. 41 In *backing up*, he [*sc.* point] should take care to give the man at the slip sufficient room.

c. With qualifying words indicating the various positions in the slips, and the fieldsmen stationed there, as † *extra slip*, a man who stands outside second slip; third slip; *first slip*, the slip fielder who stands immediately to the right of the wicket-keeper (for a right-handed batsman); his position; similarly, *second* (*third*, etc.) *slip*, ranged in a line out from the wicket-keeper; *leg slip*: see *LEG *sb.* 17b; † *long slip*, a fieldsman placed as first slip, but deeper (or wider) in the field; † *middle slip*, short third man; † *short slip* = *first slip* above. Also COVER-SLIP 1 (*Obs.*).

1816 W. LAMBERT *Cricketer's Guide* (ed. 6) iii. 41 The Fieldsman that can best be spared is placed between the first Slip and Point. *Ibid.* 43 The Long Slip to cover the Short Slip. This man must stand..about the same distance from the Wicket as the Long Stop. *Ibid.* 44 This man should stand the same distance, playing between the Point and second slip. **1851** J. PYCROFT *Cricket Field* v. 75 A third man on, and a forward point,..with slow bowling, or an extra slip with fast, made a very strong field. *Ibid.* x. 193 A third man up, or a middle slip, is at times very killing. *Ibid.* xi. 222 A third slip can hardly be spared. **1892** W. G. GRACE in G. A. Hutchison *Outdoor Games* i. 26 Third man, who is, perhaps, rather a middle-slip, being long-slip placed in close enough to save the run. **1900** P. F. WARNER *Cricket in Many Climes* iii. 45, I was missed at extra slip..when I had only made a few runs. **1921** —— *My Cricketing Life* xii. 227 Jack was..a short slip of the same class as Tunnicliffe [, etc.]. **1955** *Times* 4 July 3/3 He swung the ball both ways, supported by a hostile, close-set field, Holliday taking two sharp low catches at first slip. **1976** *Times* 23 July 9/4 After adding 43 with Murray, Rowe was out to a tumbling catch at first slip; when Snow took over from Ward, Murray was well caught at second slip; when Willis came on, Holder gave third slip a catch.

IV. 15. a. (sense 4 c) *slip-dress* (U.S.); (sense 14) *slip-catch, -catcher, -catching, -fielder, -fielding, fieldsman.*

1903 S. L. JESSOP in H. G. Hutchinson *Cricket* v. 119 This range [of hits for practising catches] will include different kinds of chances, from 'slip' catches to catches in the long field. **1977** *World of Cricket Monthly* June 29/3 Raja took his third wicket through a slip-catch. **1920** LYTTELTON & WILSON in P. F. Warner *Cricket* vii. 268 As a slip catcher he was worthy to rank with R.E. and G.N. Foster. **1963** *Times* 17 Apr. 3/2 Downside are looking for proficient slip-catchers to give the required support to R. F. Thompson, a fast bowler, for whom they have high regard. **1950** W. HAMMOND *Cricketers' School* vi. 64 His slip-catching is first-rate. **1964** *Glamour* May 149 Andrea wears a bare blue linen slip-dress. **1912** P. F. WARNER *Eng. v. Australia* i. 2 The Committee..invited George Gunn, Woolley, and Mead, slip-fielders all of them. **1963** *Times* 13 June 3/5 The slip fielder is Titmus. **1906** A. E. KNIGHT *Complete Cricketer* iv. 153 The possibilities of slip fielding are so very great. **1976** *Times Lit. Suppl.* 16 July 896/5 There are a number of mistakes of fact (the editors' slip-fielding is not infallible). **1906** A. E. KNIGHT *Complete Cricketer* iv. 153 In degree it is true of all fieldsmen, yet it is more true of slip fieldsmen, that a position in the field is largely what the individual fieldsman cares to make it. **1920** G. L. JESSOP in P. F. Warner *Cricket* iv. 167 The importance of a slip fieldsman is only second to that of a wicket-keeper.

b. Special Combinations. **slip angle,** (*a*) a parameter of a screw propeller (see quots. 1878, 1902); (*b*) *Motoring,* (see quot. 1959[2]); **slip band,** a slip line, or a cluster of such lines; **slip face,** the steepest face of a sand dune, down which sand slips; **slip flow,** in fluid dynamics, a mode of flow of a gas over a surface, the gas in contact with the surface having a definite velocity relative to it; **slip line,** a fine line visible on a polished crystalline surface where it is cut by a slip plane; (*b*) a line in a solid whose tangent at any point is one of the shear directions at that point; **slip plane,** a plane along which slip occurs in a crystal; **slip ratio,** the ratio of the slip of a propeller to its pitch.

1878 W. FROUDE in *Trans. Inst. Naval Architects* XIX. 50 The difference between the direction of the plane itself ..and the direction of its motion through the water..may be called the slip angle. **1902** *Encycl. Brit.* XXXII. 587/1 The slip angle (obliquity of surface to the line of its motion) ought always to have the same value (proportional to the square root of the coefficient of friction). **1936, 1959** [see *OVERSTEER *v.*]. **1959** *Manch. Guardian* 27 July 2/3 The slip angle is the difference between the direction in which the wheels are pointing and the actual direction in which the car travels. **1899** EWING & ROSENHAIN in *Proc. R. Soc.* LXV. 87 Rotation of the stage to which the strained specimen is fixed makes the bands on one or another of the grains flash out successively, with kaleidoscopic effect. In what follows we shall speak of these lines as slip bands. **1976** C. BRADSHAW *Metallurgy for Schools* vi. 60 (*caption*) Photomicrograph showing slip bands formed on the surface of brass strip that has been stretched. **1941** R. A. BAGNOLD *Physics of Blown Sand & Desert Dunes* xiv. 224 The seif dune differs more markedly from the barchan in that its slip-face, instead of running mainly transverse to the prevailing wind, runs parallel with it. **1976** *Nature* 22 July 284/2 The beetles either burrowed into dune slipfaces when returned or remained active. **1946** HSUE-SHEN TSIEN in *Jrnl. Aeronaut. Sci.* XIII. 654/2 It was found that gas no longer sticks to the surface but slips over the surface with a definite velocity... This type of flow can be called the slip flow. **1978** *Jrnl. Fluid Mech.* LXXXV. 731 (*heading*) Slip flow past a tangential flat plate at low Reynolds numbers. **1900** *Phil. Trans. R. Soc.* A. CXCIII. 369 In gold or copper, it is very usual to find, on examining a strained specimen that one portion of a grain is covered with simple slip lines. **1931** NÁDAI & WAHL *Plasticity* xvii. 110 (*caption*) Helical slip lines on polished marble cylinder after compression. **1950** *Sci. News* XV. Plate 16 (*caption*) Slip-lines in pure zinc after exposure to 50 thermal cycles between 30°C and 150°C (× 500). **1973** JOHNSON & MELLOR *Engin. Plasticity* xii. 383 In order to determine the load necessary for a particular plastic forming operation, we must first of all obtain the slip-line field pattern. **1976** M. C. NUTT *Metallurgy & Plastics for Engineers* v. 66 In Fig. 5–2 the intersection of individual slip planes with the polished surface is observed, thus forming slip lines. **1925** *Jrnl. Iron & Steel Inst.* CXII. 87 The authors consider that the lowest value for tensile strength in an iron crystal will be obtained when two slip planes of the crystal make angles of 45° to the axis of stress. **1975** *Nature* 10 Apr. 489/1 Granular xenoliths..in which olivine and pyroxene show various strain effects, including undulose extinction.., slip-planes, and subgrain development. **1878** *Trans. Inst. Naval Architects* XIX. 50 The area which will drive the ship with a given slip ratio, is directly as the ship's resistance and is inversely as the square of her speed. **1902** *Encycl. Brit.* XXXVIII. 587/2 In combining the results from the four propellers great assistance was derived from the discovery that the curves expressing the variation of efficiency with slip-ratio had a close similarity. **1920** A. FAGE *Airscrews* vi. 70 In the writer's opinion the notion of slip is superfluous; and the introduction of a slip-ratio as a performance parameter quite unnecessary.

slip, *v.*[1] Add: **I. 2. a.** (Earlier example with *off.*)

c **1810** W. HICKEY *Mem.* (1960) xix. 309, I..might slip off *sans cérémonie* and proceed to join the Oxfordshire party.

5. b. (Examples of accidental disclosure in conversation.)

1942 T. BAILEY *Pink Camellia* xxiv. 180, I didn't mean it, darling. It just slipped out. **1979** *Homes & Gardens* June 77/2, I always know if he's worried but he never tells me the details straight out. It sometimes slips out in conversation when the crisis is over and I think, Oh, that's what it was about.

II. 8. d. For *U.S.* read orig. *U.S.* and add earlier and later examples. Freq. const. *on.*

1855 *Jrnl. Discourses* II. 67/2 Some men think the way they are going to be saviors is to get as many wives as they can, and save them; now, they may slip up on that. **1866** *Weekly New Mexican* 14 July 2/1 The knowledge that he has 'slipped up' and been exposed is more than sufficient punishment for the offense. **1923** C. J. DUTTON *Shadow on Glass* xviii. 247 All of us slipped up. **1940** J. REITH *Diary* 31 Jan. (1975) v. 240, I wish I had been City member instead of Southampton. I slipped up on that. **1959** J. VERNEY *Friday's Tunnel* viii. 80, I couldn't help feeling that Daddy had slipped up pretty badly this time. **1981** A. MORICE *Men in her Death* x. 108 Somewhere along the line I had slipped up.

e. Of a person: to fall away from a standard (in behaviour or achievement); to deteriorate; to lose one's command of things. Chiefly as *pres. pple. colloq.*

[**1907** G. B. SHAW *Major Barbara* III. 286 You are fencing, Euripides. You are weakening: your grip is slipping. **1914** 'HIGH JINKS, JR.' *Choice Slang* 18 *Slipping,* failing, 'losing out', 'going under'.] **1930** *Publishers' Weekly* 22 Feb. 933/2, I must be slipping for I turned in a measly 78 on No. 4 in the Lenz-Rendel book. **1949** 'J. TEY' *Brat Farrar* xxvii. 242 I'm behaving very badly to-night, aren't I? I seem to be slipping. **1962** 'E. FERRARS' *Busy Body* ix. 104 He'd been slipping lately, drinking too much and boasting. **1976** H. MACINNES *Agent in Place* xiii. 137 The journalist was the first to know he was slipping; next his editors; and then the public. End of a career.

9. c. *intr.* and *trans. Aeronaut.* = *SIDE-SLIP *v.* b.

1911 *Aero* July (Suppl.) 2/2 The extra weight caused the machine to slide down sideways when steeply banked round the end corner. The Blériot slipped downward. **1930** R. DUNCAN *Stunt Flying* iii. 15 Side-slipping.. enables the machine to be put down in a far shorter space than would be possible through a normal glide, forward speed being reduced to a minimum by slipping the airplane sideways down to within a few feet of the ground. **1941** POPE & OTIS *Elem. Aeronaut.* iii. 19 If the banking is insufficient for such a turn, the plane will skid, and if the banking is too great, the plane will slip toward the inside of the curve. **1952** A. Y. BRAMBLE *Air-plane Flight* xiii. 199 Slipping may be used deliberately with useful effect, providing the air-plane is of the type that may be 'slipped'. **1965** [see *SKID *v.*[1] 3 c].

10. a. (Later examples of *to slip through one's fingers.*)

1915 W. S. MAUGHAM *Of Human Bondage* xlvii. 236 He was mad to have let such an adventure slip through his fingers. **1970** J. A. T. ROBINSON *Christian Freedom in Permissive Society* p. ix, Try to net it [*sc.* the concept of freedom] in the categories of discursive knowledge,..it slips through your fingers, and you end up..by concluding that it does not exist.

c. *to slip through the net*: to evade detection or apprehension; to escape someone's vigilance; to be overlooked.

1902 G. B. SHAW *Mrs. Warren's Profession* p. xviii, Nothing can really shake the confidence of the public in the Lord Chamberlain's department except a remorseless and unbowdlerized narration of the licentious fictions which slip through its net. **1970** *Times* 21 Feb. 7/5 All those in the 'know' in the underworld..maintain that it was a man who was never on trial but who slipped through the net. **1977** M. DRABBLE *Ice Age* I. 67 The real poor..were better off than they would have been in the thirties, for Britain is, after all, a welfare state, and not many slip through its net.

III. 15. a. *spec.* (*Motoring*) in phr. *to slip* (*in*) *the clutch,* to let in, release the clutch (*CLUTCH *sb.*[1] 6 a), slightly or momentarily.

1904 A. B. F. YOUNG *Compl. Motorist* 214 When the brake lever is in the 'on' position, it is impossible to start the car by slipping in the clutch until it has been released. **1912** *Motor Man.* 73 The metal clutch..can be 'slipped' to any extent without affecting the surface of the discs. **1965** PRIESTLEY & WISDOM *Good Driving* ix. 63 It is permissible [in reversing] to slip (feather) the clutch a little so as to maintain an even rate of travel. **1972** HILLIER & PITTUCK *Fundamentals of Motor Vehicle Technol.* 20 Most modern engines have a speed range from about 400 revolutions per minute..unless the clutch is partly disconnected or slipped.

18. c. (Later examples.)

1922 E. O'NEILL *Hairy Ape* vii. 78 Man in de Moon, yuh look so wise, gimme de answer, huh? Slip me de inside dope. **1935** [see *DUCAT 2 b]. **1936** WODEHOUSE *Laughing Gas* xix. 210 You tell me..and I'll slip you that money you wanted. **1952** 'N. SHUTE' *Far Country* ix. 257 Jim must have known the man was a boozer, and he might have thought some of his mates would try to slip him something. **1968** P. H. NEWBY *Something to answer For* iii. 88 If it's money you want, give me a little time, I can slip you a few hundred. **1978** S. BRILL *Teamsters* iv. 133 At one lunch, he testified, he slipped Provenzano $1,500.

d. In *slang* phr. *to slip* (something) *over* (*on*) (someone), to take advantage of someone by trickery, to hoodwink; *to slip a fast one over on* (someone) = to pull or put over a fast one (see *FAST *a.* 11).

1912 C. MATHEWSON *Pitching in Pinch* iii. 63, I attempted to slip a fast one over on Cooley and got the ball a little too high. **1927** *Daily Tel.* 29 Mar. 10/7 If one only had the nerve and audacity one could 'slip it over' the German every time. **1936** WODEHOUSE *Laughing Gas* v. 63 Can you imagine my lawyer letting them slip that over! **1960** 'B. MCCORQUODALE' *Price is Love* iii. 53 It was something he really wanted to know and was trying to slip it over on her unexpectedly.

19. b. *to slip a disc*: to sustain a 'slipped disc' (*SLIPPED *ppl. a.*[1] 2).

1958 'J. BYROM' *Or be he Dead* v. 68 An unfortunate tramp who had slipped a disk. **1974** G. MITCHELL *Javelin for Jonah* ii. 33 He told Margot to rake the long-jump pit ..and she slipped a disc.

VI. 26. e. (Earlier and later examples.)

1840 J. GAUGAIN *Lady's Assistant* 13 Slip a stitch having wool in front, then pass the wool to the back under the left pin. **1926** E. K. MIDDLETON *New Knitting* 15 To decrease two at a time. Slip one. Knit two together. Draw the slipped stitch over. **1951** E. CLOSE *Knitting* ii. 29 Slip one stitch from the left hand to the right hand needle as if you were about to knit it. **1973** M. STRADAL *Knitting, Crochet & Looping* i. 26 Slip one stitch purlwise, thread over needle and knit together the slipped stitch and the thread-over-needle of previous row.

VII. 30. *Shipbuilding.* To place (a boat) on

a slip (Slip *sb.*³ 1 b) for inspection, repair, etc.

1950 H. M. Denham in *Jrnl. R. Cruising Club 1949* 122, I got Korby slipped (only £4) and put on a coat of antifouling. **1964** *Roving Commissions 1903* 207 We crossed to Hermione in the hopes of finding a caique yard which would slip us for a reasonable fee to check up on the bump we received at Finike. **1975** R. Butler *Where all Girls are Sweeter* iii. 23 The boat looked new. Short of slipping her she was in prime condition.

slip-. Add: **1. a. slip-case,** a close-fitting box with one side open into which a book or books are placed for protection, while allowing the spine to remain visible; also, a similar case for gramophone records or photographic equipment; hence **slipcased** *a.*, contained in a box of this kind; **slip-cover** *U.S.* = *loose cover* s.v. *loose *a.* 9; hence as *v. trans.*, to cover with a slip-cover; **slip crew** *Aviation*, an aircrew stationed at an intermediate point or carried to take over the operation of an aeroplane on a long-distance flight; **slip edition,** a special (usu. local) edition of a newspaper, carrying news items not included in the main issue; **slip gauge** *Engin.*, a Johannson block (see *Johannson); **slip-gear,** a gear designed to slip if loaded above a predetermined limit; **slip-horn,** a slide-trombone; **slip-jig** (earlier and later examples); **slip joint,** (*b*) a joint in a pipe, one section of which can move telescopically within another, to allow longitudinal expansion and contraction and so prevent damage by temperature changes or jolts; **slip-noose** (earlier example); **slip ring** *Electr. Engin.*, a ring of conducting material which is attached to and rotates with a shaft, so that electric current may be transferred to a stationary circuit through a fixed brush pressing against it; also *attrib.*; **slip road,** a short (usu. one-way) road giving access to or exit from a main highway, esp. a motorway; an approach road; **slip rope** (later examples); **slip scraper** *U.S.*, a horse-drawn earth-moving device; **slip sheet** *Printing*, a sheet of paper interleaving newly printed sheets to prevent set-off or smudging; hence **slip-sheet** *v. trans.*, **slip-sheeting** *vbl. sb.*; **slip-stitch** *sb.* (earlier and later examples); also in sewing, dressmaking, etc. (see also quot. 1964); **slip winder** (see quot. 1921); also *slip winding*.

1930 A. E. Newton *This Bk.-Collecting Game* ii. 20 Many collectors, in binding their books or in having slip cases made for them, . . have their novels . . in one colour, their poetry in another. **1942** W. Stevens *Let.* 17 Sept. (1967) 420, I should like the general effect of the binding to be light... There should, of course, be a slip case. **1966** P. J. Kavanagh *Perfect Stranger* xiii. 187 Why not put all three [volumes] into a slip-case . . and sell them as a set? **1977** *Gramophone* May 1738/2 Decca have also made again available this month an integral recording of the five Beethoven Piano Concertos, previously issued in a slip-case but now in a box. **1979** *Amat. Photographer* Feb. 54/3 Both versions are supplied in a gift outfit with flash unit, slip case and wrist chain at a price of about £85. **1969** *Times* 15 Nov. p. iv/6 (Advt.), *Magellan's Voyage*.. 2 volumes slipcased. **1978** *Amer. N. & Q.* Nov. 44/2 A handsome slip-cased volume . . seems to be under-priced. **1886** *Home Decoration* 3 Apr. 79/1 The slip covers for the furniture are of . . toile. **1911** [see *klaxon *sb.*]. **1920** *T. Eaton & Co. Catal.* Spring & Summer 395/2 Slip Covers for Ford Cars... Set consists of cover for each seat and back of seats, doors, kicking pad for front seat and complete cover for hood. **1952** S. Kauffmann *Philanderer* (1953) iii. 36 Cora had, of course, made all the curtains, slip covers and bedspreads herself. **1965** T. Capote *In Cold Blood* ii. 78 The couch . . that Nancy had slip-covered. **1978** T. Gifford *Glendower Legacy* 75 The slipcovers were wearing out at the arm. **1947** *Shell Aviation News* No. 112. 8/3 One of the most important problems is that of aircrew fatigue, and research on this question includes investigation into . . provision of 'slip' crews at strategic points, facilities for crew rest in aircraft. **1973** C. Egleton *Seven Days to Killing* xix. 196 The RAF are not carrying a slip crew on this trip. They would need to rest before the return flight. **1961** 'B. Wells' *Day Earth caught Fire* iii. 39 This is terrific stuff. We'll have a slip edition. **1975** T. Allbeury *Palomino Blonde* iv. 12 Issues of the *Northumberland Gazette* with slip editions for Morpeth and Berwick. **1919** *Engineering* 11 July 33/3 The minimeter for comparing slip gauges to an accuracy of one-millionth of an inch is another of the new precision instruments. **1971** B. Scharf *Engin. & its Language* vii. 47 In order to combine two slip gauges, they are slid together with slight pressure. **1897** E. K. Scott *Local Distribution of Electric Power in Workshops* 53 The current at starting a heavy lift can be materially reduced by having a slip gear or belt, so as to enable the motor to get up speed. **1930** *Engineering* 4 Apr. 431/2 An electric motor fitted with a centrifugal clutch and slip-gear. **1923** G. McKnight *Eng. Words & their Background* iv. 45 *Sliphorn*, trombone. **1938** D. Baker *Young Man with Horn* iii. i. 120 He doesn't play a valve trombone either, just a regular slip-horn. **1957** *Melody Maker* 4 May 6/2 Wilbur himself was somewhat subdued, using both slip-horn and valve, but what he did was pleasant trombone. **1829** G. Griffin *Collegian* I. ii. 19 Eily was dancing with a strange young gentleman . . and . . he would not let her go until she had finished the slip jig. *a* **1966** 'M. na Gopaleen' *Best of Myles* (1968) 284 The lads who believe that in slip-jigs we have a national prophylaxis make life less stark. **1930** Walker & Crocker *Piping Handbk.* vii. 504 Slip joints are used very extensively in water and saturated-steam lines. **1972** L. M. Harris *Introd. Deepwater Floating Drilling Operations* ii. 6 Slip joints compensate for vertical motion in the lower section of the drill string. **1837** Slip noose [see *lasso *sb.* 1]. **1896** S. P. Thompson *Dynamo-Electric Machinery* (ed. 4) iii. 35 There must . . be sliding contacts to maintain the coils of the revolving field-magnet part in continuous metallic connexion with the auxiliary exciting circuit. In either case the appropriate device consists of a pair of slip rings, against each of which a brush presses. **1958** *Times Rev. Industry* Feb. 46/1 Automatic starting of slip-ring electric motors has always presented many problems. **1974** *Physics Bull.* May 204/2 Special emphasis is placed on the study of aluminium as a contact material in place of copper for sliprings and commutators. **1953** *Times* 11 Feb. 3/3 A 'slip-road' a mile and a half long . . would draw away from the narrow streets of High Barnet the great number of heavy lorries now passing through this congested centre. **1968** W. Garner *Deep, Deep Freeze* iii. 36 He took the slip road on to the *Autobahn*. **1979** A. Price *Tomorrow's Ghost* ii. 17 He waited to leave the slip-road for the motorway proper. **1909** *Man. Seamanship* (Admiralty) II. iii. ix. 177 If there is much strain on the slip rope, it should be eased before letting it go. **1964** Slip rope [see *honda]. **1934** *Sun* (Baltimore) 9 Nov. 15/3 Ringle, while clearing loose dirt with the aid of a horse and slip scraper, lost his footing and fell. **1942** W. Faulkner *Go down, Moses* 113 Throwing dirt . . faster than a slip scraper could have done it. **1917** F. S. Henry *Printing for School & Shop* xiv. 237 Never use enameled paper for slipsheets, or the sheets will stick together. **1924** —— *Essent. Printing* x. 149 While an expert feeder can sometimes do his own slipsheeting, it is customary to have an assistant place the slipsheets as the printed sheets are stacked on the feedboard. **1949** Melcher & Larrick *Printing & Promotion Handbk.* 279/2 This slip sheeting assures a clean job of mimeographing where it is necessary to print on non-absorbent paper. **1957** Jackson & Cleverdon *Printing* iii. 139/2 Clean unprinted newspaper . . makes good slip sheets. **1967** V. Strauss *Printing Industry* vii. 516/2 In two-sided printing . . it may be necessary to 'slip-sheet' the job. (Slip-sheeting means that a sheet of waste paper is inserted after each printed sheet. When the ink is dry the slip sheets are removed.) **1872** *Young Englishwoman* Oct. 558/1 Work 2 slip-stitches on the first 2 chain. **1932** D. C. Minter *Mod. Needlecraft* 92/2 *Single Crochet* (*or Slip-stitch*) . . is used for making a very narrow row. **1951** *Good Housek. Home Encycl.* 58/1 Tack, and slip-stitch by hand. **1964** *McCall's Sewing* ii. 32/1 *Slip-stitch*, tiny hand-stitches taken through and under a fold of fabric where the stitching must be invisible. **1921** *Dict. Occup. Terms* (1927) § 371 *Slip winder*; winds silk threads, for use in lace making, from hanks or cops on to spools or bobbins. **1976** *Evening Post* (Nottingham) 16 Dec. 17/5 (Advt.), Wanted male or female experienced slip winder (cone to spool). **1940** *Chambers's Techn. Dict.* 778/2 *Slip winding* (Textiles), the process of transferring yarn from a hank to flanged bobbins in lace manufacture.

b. *slip-lid*.

1938 *Shelf Appeal* July 26/2 The slip-lid tin was evolved rather over fifty years ago. **1979** *Gloss. Packaging Terms* (*B.S.I.*) ii. 8 *Slip lid*, a lid that fits over the mouth of the container body.

c. *slip coach* (later examples); also in connection with other vehicles and craft, as **slip-tank,** a fuel tank that may be jettisoned from an aircraft when empty.

1932 G. Greene *Stamboul Train* i. i. 8 The party . . belonged to the slip-coach for Athens. **1978** *Lancs. Life* Apr. 52/2 The L & Y . . brought in slip coaches, notably at Rochdale where two trains from Bradford to Manchester unhitched the back two coaches without stopping. **1920** *Flight* XII. 957/1 Seventeen tanks may be readily slipped overboard to act as ballast. These slip-tanks have no bottom connections, and petrol is drawn from them by means of a semi-rotary pump.

2. slip-on (later examples); also (chiefly *U.S.*) a glove and now usu. a shoe; *attrib.*: now also as *adj.*; **slip-over** *a.*, of a garment: made without an opening at the front, and to be slipped on over the head; hence as *sb.* (usu. one word), a sweater or pullover, usu. with a V-neck and no sleeves; **slip-up,** the act of slipping up (see Slip *v.*¹ 8 d), a failure, mistake, blunder.

1920 *T. Eaton & Co. Catal.* Spring & Summer 395/3 Running Board Mat. Fastened with patent slip-on fasteners. **1923** *Ibid.* 214/3 One of the smartest of the new models [of coat] . . a double-breasted 'slip-on', with yoke. **1938** [see *scuff *sb.*¹ 4]. **1949** *Sun* (Baltimore) 8 Sept. 5/1 (Advt.), Wear Right gloves... Shorties and slipons all hand-sewn. **1956** *People* 13 May 3/7 (Advt.), Slip-on Casual. Brown Willow uppers, leather sole. **1959** *Wall St. Jrnl.* 13 Dec. (Eastern ed.) 17/4 'Slim slip-ons', or dressy shoes without laces, will be promoted for men. **1965** *N.Y. Times* 9 Dec. 5 (Advt.), Hand-in-Glove with fashion: . . Elbow-deep slipons. **1972** J. Ball *Five Pieces of Jade* xiv. 178 Tibbs . . noted the slip-on shoes which . . could be shed within a second or two. **1978** L. Charteris *Saint in Trouble* (1979) i. iii. 33 His eyes . . started with the suede slip-ons, journeyed up . . the light grey suit. **1982** Barr & York *Official Sloane Ranger Handbk.* 33/2 These are smart tough slip-ons, in black or dark blue patent or leather, with a chunky heel and gilt snaffle or chain across the top. **1919–20** *T. Eaton & Co. Catal.* Fall & Winter 153/3 Slip-over Nightgown. **1923** *Daily Mail* 6 Mar. 1 (Advt.), Elastic bust bodice of special value, slip-over shape. **1936** *Times* 10 Jan. 7/4 Bargains for men include poplin shirts at 9s. 6d. and all wool slip-overs at 10s. **1941** *Picture Post* 3 May 32/1 Pullovers, Slipovers, and Beach Shirts for men and boys. **1945** *Richmond* (Va.) *Times-Dispatch* 9 Jan. 16 (Advt.), All-wool slipover sweater. **1962** *Punch* 26 Sept. p. xvii, Burberrys have . . reversible alpaca slip-overs. **1981** *Times* 6 Jan. 12/7 According to numerous shop window displays observed during the current sales, the garment I have always called a pullover is now known as a slipover. **1909** *N.Y. Even. Post* (semi-weekly ed.) 30 Sept. 1 Should there be any slip-up in the present plans. **1948** 'G. Orwell' *Let.* 21 Dec. in *Coll. Essays* (1968) IV. 459, I suppose there *may* be some slip-up, but if not my address . . will be The Cotswold Sanatorium. **1978** H. Jobson *To die a Little* ii. 26, I . . had a slight feeling of apprehension... Had there been some legal slip-up?

slip form. *Engin.* Also **slip-form, slipform.** [f. Slip *v.*¹] A mould open at both ends in which a structure of uniform cross-section is cast by filling it with concrete and continually moving and refilling it as the concrete sets. Freq. *attrib.* with reference to this technique of construction, esp. as *slipform* (*concrete*) *paver*, a machine which continually forms the concrete surface of a road or the like by this technique.

1958 *Construction Methods & Equipment* Aug. 72/2 Slip-form placing of concrete reduced material and manpower requirements to a fraction of what they might have been with timber forms and scaffolding. *Ibid.* 73/2 The contractor supported slip forms with a number of steel yokes. **1963** *Contractors & Engineers* Jan. 40/4 Slip-form pavers are shorter this year... The early slip-form machines, with 40 to 60 feet of sliding form, amazed many people. **1964** [see *form *sb.* 18 b]. **1974** *Sci. Amer.* Dec. 145/1 The road itself, that great ribbon of concrete, is being placed by the slip-form paver, which spreads, smooths, levels, cuts the edges squarely and even finishes the surface. **1975** *Offshore* Sept. 147/1 The steel slipform is guided on rails cast into the interior surface of the cylinder wall.

Hence **sli·pform** *v. trans.*, to cast by this technique; **sli·pformed** *ppl. a.* **sli·pforming** *vbl. sb.*

1968 J. J. Waddell *Concrete Construction Handbk.* xxxiv. 1 The ultimate approach in incorporating a slip-form into building construction is to slipform all vertical concrete. *Ibid.*, Slipforming is a faster method of construction than conventional forming. *Ibid.* 2 Slipformed-concrete. **1975** *Offshore* Sept. 147/1 Tests are complete on the slip-forming of inclined legs for a deepwater concrete platform. **1981** *Times* 12 Mar. 3/6 The contractors are slip forming 2,000 metres of double track. This track-laying method was first used in 1967.

slip-knot. (Earlier *transf.* example.)

1842 T. Moore *Jrnl.* Sept. 14 in *Mem. Thomas Moore* (1856) VII. 330 Had already formed a sort of slip-knot with Easthope to dine at his country house, but he had luckily put me off till to-morrow.

slippage. Add: **2.** *Mech.* The difference between the expected and the actual output of a system.

1905 W. Rogers *Pumps & Hydraulics* II. 384 Pump slip or slippage represents the difference between the calculated and the actual discharge of a pump. **1936** *Kent's Mech. Engineers' Handbk.* (ed. 11) II. i. 41 Actual Volumetric Efficiency/Indicated Volumetric Efficiency = Slippage Efficiency [of an air compressor]. This is the ratio of the volume of measured air delivered to the apparent volume shown by the indicator diagram.

3. *transf.* and *fig.* Falling away from a standard; the measure of this. *spec.* with reference to (*a*) failure to meet a deadline or fulfil a promise, delay; (*b*) loss of public esteem, of a candidate for office in popularity ratings; (*c*) *Econ.*, decline in value.

1920 in Webster. **1960** *Washington Post* 1 Jan. A16 It is almost as if a deliberate decision had been taken to accept second-place status. This continued slippage also affects starkly the challenges that lie ahead. **1960** *Guardian* 13 May 10/5 The failure (or 'slippage' as delays are now called) of their 400-mile anti-aircraft missile. **1968** *Ibid.* 22 Aug. 9/7 The latest Gallup poll . . shows that Nixon would get 45 per cent of the votes compared with Humphrey's 29 per cent. That is an astonishing slippage for the Vice-President. **1970** *Nature* 13 June 1011/2 ESRO's biggest project . . is the half-ton TD1 astronomy satellite which was to have been launched in spring 1972, although some slippage now seems likely. **1972** *Guardian* 1 Nov. 12/2 British living standards could be eroded by a continued slippage of sterling. **1976** *Times* 20 Apr. 13/3 There is widespread concern among parents that standards of achievement and behaviour in schools have been allowed, if not to collapse, at least to slip... This apparent slippage has taken place at the time when the number of comprehensive schools has increased rapidly. **1980** M. Lee *Govt. by Pen* 211 His health had been giving way, and there were signs of mental slippage. **1982** *Sunday Times* 10 Oct. 54/3 Given the traditional slippage that occurs in the timetable on such projects, the company will not know at the outset just when it will have to draw down the cash for each stage payment.

slipped, *ppl. a.*¹ Add: **1.** (Examples in *Knitting*.)

1840 J. Gaugain *Lady's Assistant* 11 Take in back stitch of three, by slipping off backwards without working the first, . . lift over the first slipped one over the taken-in loop. **1872** *Young Englishwoman* Nov. 607/1 In decreasing . . a stitch may be slipped, the following stitch knitted and the slipped stitch drawn over it. **1926,** etc. [see *slip *v.*¹ 26 e]. **1958** J. Norbury *Knitting Adventure* i. 15 Purl slipped stitch from cable needle.

2. *slipped disc*, an intervertebral disc that is ruptured or injured, causing pain in the back or (if nerve roots are compressed) in other parts of the body. *colloq.*

1953 E. SIMON *Past Masters* III. 142 The slipped disk everybody nowadays is suffering from. **1959** *Listener* 10 Sept. 397/3 Achondroplasic breeds [of dogs] are also more apt to develop so-called 'slipped discs'. **1972** J. MINIFIE *Homesteader* x. 79 God help the farmer who 'pulled his back', as they used to say before 'slipped disc' became the fashionable term. **1974** PASSMORE & ROBSON *Compan. Med. Stud.* III. xxv. 56/2 If a load exceeds the ultimate tolerance of a disc..the nucleus may be forced through the annulus or cause it to bulge locally, a condition known as ruptured or prolapsed or slipped disc.

slipped (slipt), *ppl. a.*^{3} [f. SLIP *v.*^{3}] Painted or ornamented with slip.

1914 *Oxf. Univ. Gaz.* 11 Mar. 574 A boar's head in slipped painted ware of Late Hittite date. **1976** *Nature* 15 Apr. 581/2 This pottery includes sophisticated slipped wares.

slipper, *sb.* Add: **I. 1. e.** As an instrument of punishment with which a child (etc.) is disciplined by beating. In phr. *to take a slipper to* (someone).

[**1682**, etc.: implied at SLIPPER *v.*^{2} 1]. **1876** [see *REAR *sb.*^{3} 2 b]. **1924** GALSWORTHY *White Monkey* III. viii. 266 Teach him a sense of other people, as young as possible, with a slipper if necessary. **1932** A. J. WORRALL *Eng. Idioms* ii. 18 He is very impudent in his manner, and I should dearly like to take my slipper to him. **1978** R. MILLS *Comprehensive Educ.* 21 'I haven't done my homework, my History.' 'Ha, ha, it's the slipper for you then.' **1982** *Daily Tel.* 1 Mar. 10/7 The cane and slipper never did the likes of us any harm.

f. A temporary shoe for a horse.

1903 SOMERVILLE & 'ROSS' *All on Irish Shore* iii. 82 He [*sc.* the smith] examined each hoof in succession..and then, turning to Mr Fennessy, remarked:— 'Ye'd laugh if ye were here the day I put a slipper on this one.' **1953** G. BROOKE *Introd. Riding & Stablecraft* vi. 52 You should pull up at a shoeing-smith's, and..he will tack on what they call a slipper; that is, a shoe that fits well enough, and will see you through the day.

4. d. *Mech.* Also *slipper block*. A guide block attached to a reciprocating rod, esp. a piston rod or its cross-head, so as to slide with the motion of the rod against a fixed plate and prevent any tendency of the rod to bend.

1881 N. P. BURGH *Mod. Marine Engin.* (rev. ed.) 72/1 The guide channels..are the ordinary kind, arranged to receive slipper blocks. **1883** A. E. SEATON *Man. Marine Engin.* viii. 144 To preserve the piston-rod in its true course, a guide is provided, and the piston-rod end fitted with blocks or slippers to work in it. **1952** FOX & MCBIRNIE *Marine Steam Engines & Turbines* ix. 155 A single slipper crosshead is generally made as shown. **1971** *Naval Marine Engin. Practice* (Min. of Defence) (ed. 2) I. vi. 137 A slipper is fitted to the crosshead, and this slipper slides in a vertical guide to maintain straight reciprocating motion against the thrust of the connecting rod. The slipper may be circular..or in the form of a flat plate.

e. *Mech.* A part that is capable of sliding in the direction of its length.

1903 *Electr. World & Engin.* 21 Nov. 845/2 The buckets of the Riedler turbine resemble those of the well-known Pelton type. The steam jet is divided by a central 'slipper' in two parts. **1930** *Engineering* 25 Apr. 539/3 About half-way along this arm is attached a slipper, D, which is kept in contact with the straight-edge, E, by a weight, F. **1966** *McGraw-Hill Encycl. Sci. & Technol.* XI. 611/2 Sleds are carried on shoes or slippers that grip the railhead in order to prevent derailing.

5. (Example.)

1818 L. D. CLARK *Diary* 11 July in *Firelands Pioneer* (1920) XXI. 2314 Made a slipper for Mrs. Caufield's baby.

II. 7. b. *Cricket.* One who fields in the slips. *colloq.* Somewhat *rare*.

1903 D. L. G. JEPHSON in H. G. Hutchinson *Cricket* iv. 102 There were good slips, bad slips, fast-asleep slips, and since his time every variety of 'slipper' has passed across the stage. **1973** *Daily Tel.* 23 July 32/1 If Hayes be sufficiently rated as a slipper, Roope could be spared.

III. 10. slipper-bath: now usu. one of a number of single baths of the modern domestic style installed for hire at public baths; **slipper chair** *U.S.*, a low-seated, freq. upholstered chair with a high back; **slipper satin,** a strong, closely woven fabric with a semi-glossy appearance, used for making slippers, dresses, furnishings, etc.; **slipperslapper** *nonce-wd.*, a loose, sloppily-fitting slipper (cf. *SLIP-SLOP *sb.* 4); **slipper socks, sox** *pl.*, a pair of slippers with socks combined.

1960 L. WRIGHT *Clean & Decent* xii. 172 Confusion may arise from the fact that single baths of the ordinary modern kind, on hire at Public Baths, are there still called 'Slipper Baths'. Such, no doubt, they originally were; the term has survived the change. **1981** *Times* 25 Feb. 8/5 The council closed down a slipper bath which had been used by pensioners living in bed-sitters. **1938** *House Beautiful* Jan. 41 Slipper chair... Typical of the French Regency. Broad proportions, beech frame delicately carved. Circa 1715. **1957** M. MILLAR *Soft Talkers* x. 94 Her mother sat in a slipper chair. **1979** M. MCMULLEN *But Nellie was so Nice* (1981) I. v. 42 He..made himself pleasant to Ursula in her slipper chair. **1937** M. SHARP *Nutmeg Tree* xxiii. 297 They saw the Disgusted Lady.. marvellous in ice-blue slipper satin. **1970** D. CLARK *Deadly Pattern* v. 104 A gilt-legged Chesterfield upholstered in cream slipper satin. **1922** JOYCE *Ulysses* 86 Slop about in slipperslappers for fear he'd wake. **1950** *Sears, Roebuck Catal.* Fall/Winter 1324/6 Slipper socks. **1951** *Ibid.* Fall/Winter 371 (*heading*) Footease slipper socks for every member of the family. **1970** *Guardian* 15 Dec. 9/3 Just tee-shirts with dungarees or jeans—plus slippersox. **1973** *Sunday Advocate-News* (Barbados) 9 Dec. 25/1 Slipper socks and bow ties can be great ways to gift him.

slippered, *ppl. a.* Add: **1. b.** *fig. Lit.* and *poet.*

1851 H. MELVILLE *Moby Dick* II. xvii. 136 The slippered waves whispered together. **1912** R. BROOKE *Coll. Poems* (1970) 68 A vague unpunctual star, A slippered Hesper.

slippering, *vbl. sb.* [f. SLIPPER *v.*^{2} + -ING^{1}.] Beating with a slipper.

1851 H. MELVILLE *Moby Dick* I. iv. 41 Beseeching her as a particular favour to give me a good slippering for my misbehaviour. **1919** H. WALPOLE *Jeremy* ii. 33 A slippering from his father or idiotic punishments from the Jampot. **1934** M. V. HUGHES *London Child of Seventies* iv. 35 A threatened 'slippering' of the boys by my father if they are too noisy. **1953** J. CARY *Except the Lord* ix. 32 Beating was a punishment that could be graded from a random cuff.., through a hard smack, to a formal slippering. **1972** *Times* 9 Oct. 13/5 Children..respected striking or slippering as common..in their schools.

slipper-slopper, *a. dial.* and *colloq. rare.* [Redupl. f. SLIPPER *sb.*] Wearing loose slippers; down-at-heel, sloppy.

1825 J. JENNINGS *Observations Dial. W. Eng.* 70 *Slipper-slopper*,..having shoes or slippers down at the heel; loose. **1888** F. T. ELWORTHY *West Somerset Wd.-bk.* 680 Father, be sure you baint gwain out all slipper-slopper like that. **1904** in *Eng. Dial. Dict.* V. 525/1 Slippers trodden down at the heels are said to be slipper-slopper. **1951** J. FRAME *Lagoon* 29 Their shoes were slipper-slopper.

Hence as *v. intr.*, to walk about in loose slippers; also **slipper-slopping** *vbl. sb.*

1929 R. HUGHES *High Wind in Jamaica* viii. 192 Jonsen slipper-sloppered up and down his side of the deck. **1933** L. A. G. STRONG *Sea Wall* I. i. 13 He was roused from his meditations by a..slipper-slopping on the stairs.

slippery, *a.* Add: **1. c.** *slippery slope* fig., a course leading to disaster or destruction.

1951 J. FLEMING *Man who looked Back* x. 132 You go off down the slippery slope; it'll do you good. **1964** *Daily Tel.* 6 Jan. 12/2 While Western feet thus approach what some fear may be a 'slippery slope' towards recognition of the East, Ulbricht's ground seems as firm as ever it was. **1979** N. LASH *Theology on Dover Beach* iv. 74 It could be argued..that to give priority to love, to trust, to action, to commitment, is to start down the slippery slope along which rationality, objectivity and—eventually—truth are abandoned.

2. d. *slippery elm* (earlier examples). Cf. *red elm* s.v. RED *a.* 17 d in Dict. and Suppl.

1748 D. DRAKE *Let.* 1 Jan. in *Pioneer Life Kentucky* (1870) iv. 73 Of the whole forest the red or slippery elm was the best. **1780** W. FLEMING *Jrnl.* 20 Mar. in N. D. Mereness *Trav. Amer. Colonies* (1916) 640 Bear fat is preserved sweet and pure by putting in a bunch of the Slippery Elem [*sic*] bark into it when rendering. **1810** [see *moose elm* s.v. *MOOSE^{1} b].

4. c. Prov. phr. *as slippery as an eel*. Cf. EEL 1 c.

[*c* **1412** HOCCLEVE *Reg. Princes* (1897) 1985 Mi wit is also slipir as an eel. **1562** [see SLIPPER *a.* 1b].] **1601** HOLLAND tr. *Pliny's Nat. Hist.* I. IX. xx. 247 All that be long and slipperie as Yeels and Congres. **1622** S. ROWLANDS *Good Newes & Bad Newes* sig. B1^{v}, Fie vpon giddie Fortune, and her wheele, Vnconstant, and as slipperie as an Eele. **1739–40** RICHARDSON *Pamela* (1740) I. 245 You'll find her as slippery as an eel, I'll assure you. **1855** MRS. GASKELL *North & South* I. xvii. 209 He's as slippery as an eel, he is. He's like a cat,—as sleek, and cunning. **1914** T. DREISER *Titan* xxvi. 220, I am morally certain he uses money to get what he is after as freely as a fireman uses water. He's as slippery as an eel. **1980** J. GARDNER *Garden of Weapons* II. i. 128 He's big, but slippery as an eel.

7*. *look slippery* = *look slippy* s.v. SLIPPY *a.*^{1} 2. *dial.* or *colloq. rare.*

1922 JOYCE *Ulysses* 418 Two Ardilauns. Same here. Look slippery.

9. *slippery-footed*; **slippery hitch** *Naut.*, a knot made fast by catching part of the rope beneath the bight, released at a pull on the free end; also *fig.*; **slippery pole** = *greasy pole* s.v. GREASY *a.* 9 (in quots. *fig.*); **Slippery Sam,** a card-game (cf. *blind-hookey* s.v. BLIND *a.* 16).

1903 Slippery-footed [see *HOT-FOOT *v.*]. **1832** Slippery hitch [see HITCH *sb.* 6 b]. **1903** 'T. COLLINS' *Such is Life* vii. 273 Alf, it appeared, had left the station six or eight weeks before, bound for no-one knew where. Jack's opinion was that in so doing he had made a slippery-hitch. **1944** C. W. ASHLEY *Bk. Knots* i. 19 The *Slippery Hitch* is often found in the sheets and halyards of small boats. **1972** *Village Voice* (N.Y.) 1 June 20/1 The Voice had this wonderfully sobering policy of rejecting your stories right when you thought you had a firm grasp on the slippery pole. **1977** H. GREENE *FSO-1* xviii. 167 All of these years of clambering up the slippery pole only to find there was no top to it. **1923** L. H. DAWSON *Hoyle's Games Modernized* I. 162 Slippery Sam is a variation of and by many considered an improvement on Blind Hookey. **1954** A. S. C. ROSS in *Neuphilologische Mitteilungen* LV. 22 Solo whist..is non-U, though much 'lower' games (e.g. pontoon, nap and even slippery sam) are not necessarily so. **1978** C. STORR *Winter's End* iv. 58 The others were exclaiming and shouting at Racing Demon... They'd changed to Slippery Sam.

slippiness. Add: **b.** Speed, promptitude, alacrity. *colloq.*

1974 WODEHOUSE *Aunts aren't Gentlemen* xii. 98, I think I outlined the position..rather well, making it abundantly clear that..the cat..must be restored to its proprietor with all possible slippiness.

slipping, *vbl. sb.*^{1} Add: **1. c.** = *SLIP *sb.*^{3} 9 e.

1912 *Q. Rev.* Jan. 182 The danger attendant on the 'slipping' of a charge in a blast furnace—the descent of hunks of limestone and ore that are hurled into the air when such a 'slip' occurs. **1948** G. R. BASHFORTH *Manuf. Iron & Steel* I. x. 166 Slipping is the aftermath of scaffolding or hanging. *Ibid.*, Slipping or irregular descent of the stock may..occur due to badly designed bosh walls. **1969** K. R. HALEY in J. H. Strassburger *Blast Furnace* II. xii. 592 (*heading*) Hanging and slipping.

2. (*Lit.* and *fig.* examples in sense *15 a of the vb.)

1925 *Morris Owner's Man.* 22 Persistent slipping of the clutch must not be resorted to. **1959** *Listener* 17 Dec. 1085/3 Such statements as that on page 169..may be regarded as a momentary slipping of the clutch.

slippy, *a.*^{1} **2.** (Later examples.)

1915 [see *buck-rabbit* s.v. *BUCK *sb.*^{1} 3]. **1924** D. MOORE *Fen's First Term* i. 4 There is a hurry... Go and change and look slippy. **1972** WODEHOUSE *Pearls, Girls, & Monty Bodkin* xi. 178 Both of you get out of the car... And make it slippy, because I haven't got all day.

slip-slap, *v.* Restrict *rare*$^{-1}$ to sense in Dict. and add: **2.** = SLIP-SLOP *v.* 3. *rare.*

1926 T. E. LAWRENCE *Seven Pillars* v. lvii. 302 At Cairo my sandalled feet slip-slapped up the quiet Savoy corridors. **1965** 'LAUCHMONEN' *Old Thom's Harvest* v. 58 She slip-slapped in her cut-back slippers to the door.

slip-slop, *sb.* **4.** Restrict *U.S.* to sense in Dict. and add: **b.** A kind of beach sandal; = *FLIP-FLOP *sb.* f. Chiefly *S. Afr.*

1971 *Studies in English* (Univ. Cape Town) Feb. 29 Beach-thongs, sandles [*sic*] made of rubber..have a great many names here—sloppies, slip-slops, plakkies, etc. **1974** 'G. BLACK' *Golden Cockatrice* iv. 66, I couldn't believe they had my shoe size too, almost relieved to find only a pair of slip-slops. **1976** J. MCCLURE *Rogue Eagle* ii. 31 Knotted blouse, blue jeans and slip-slop sandals.

slip-sloppism. (Earlier example.)

1803 *Lett. Miss Riversdale* III. 228 Slip-sopism [*sic*] is not confined to females, now-a-days, I perceive.

slip stone, slipstone (sli·p,stōᵘn). [f. SLIP *sb.*^{5} + STONE *sb.*] A shaped oilstone used for sharpening gouges.

1927 H. HUBBARD *Colour Block Print Making* 209 *Slip stone*, a thin sharpening stone so shaped as to remove the burr or ragged edge from the inside of a gouge. **1947** J. C. RICH *Materials & Methods of Sculpture* x. 300 With gouges, the sharpening method is generally reversed. Specially shaped slip stones..are employed and the stone is rubbed on the gouge. **1958** J. R. BIGGS *Woodcuts* 36 Remember to have one slip-stone with its smallest curve small enough to sharpen the smallest gouge. **1976** *Billings* (Montana) *Gaz.* 27 June 4-G/5 With a slipstone, the tool is held firm while the sharpener is moved along the edges. With a whetstone, the tool is moved across it to get sharp edges.

slip-stream (sli·pstrīm). Also **slip stream, slipstream.** [f. SLIP *sb.*^{3} + STREAM *sb.*] **1. a.** The current of air or water driven backward by a propeller or downward by a rotor.

1913 A. E. BERRIMAN *Aviation* viii. 79 Each blade deflects air backwards as it moves; the combined effect of both blades operating always in the same region when the machine is standing still produces a concentrated flow of air, which becomes a very pronounced draught. Technically, this draught is called the slip stream. **1919, 1920** [see *air scoop* s.v. *AIR *sb.*^{1} B. II]. **1935** *Sun* (Baltimore) 19 Jan. 9/2 The slip stream from the propeller cast bits of mud and ice into the air during the take-off. **1963** J. ROWLAND *North to Adventure* ix. 132 Her rudder was one of those absurd little metal plates which are utterly ineffective unless the slipstream from the propeller is impinging directly upon them. **1973** C. BONNINGTON *Next Horizon* xiii. 190 The snow leapt up at me, and I was there, in one piece, with the slip-stream of the helicopter hammering at me.

b. Any localized current associated with an object, esp. a moving one.

1947 in J. A. Carruth *Loch Ness & its Monster* (1950) 31 'We unmistakably sighted,' said Mr. Cottier, 'on the placid surface of the loch a fairly long slip-stream which quickly developed in length.' **1963** *Times* 8 June 5/2 He [*sc.* a cyclist] sat at the back, carried along in the slipstream of his adversaries, and so was the least tired rider when it came to the final sprint. **1973** 'A. HALL' *Tango Briefing* v. 62 The slipstream didn't cool anything: it just circulated the heat. There were gnats already sticking to the windscreen. **1974** M. BABSON *Stalking Lamb* xxv. 183 The candles flared and died..leaving little slipstreams of smoke.

2. *fig.* An assisting force considered to draw

something along with or in the wake of the principal.

1957 *Universe* 16 Aug. 4/2 The kaleidoscope of life which has moved with such tremendous upheavals..for the people caught up in its slipstream since 1933. **1961** *Times* 30 June 4/1 Sangster it was..who proved himself the leader, drawing in his slipstream Wilson. **1970** D. MATHEW *Courtiers of Henry VIII* III. vi. 203 They stood in contrast to all the slipstream of the modern State. **1980** *Times* 29 Feb. 1/2 Some of those who were trying to get into the slipstream behind the Labour Party.

Hence as *v. trans.*, to follow closely behind (another vehicle) so that the resistance of the air to one's progress is less; also, to pass after travelling in another's slipstream; also **sli·p-streaming** *vbl. sb.*

1957 S. MOSS *In Track of Speed* ii. 18, I tried for the first time the art of slip-streaming... What you do is to tuck in behind a faster car, so that you are more or less sucked along in the 'partial vacuum'. **1960** *News Chron.* 18 July 5/4, I planned to slip-stream him on the last lap. **1969** *Man* (Austral.) Mar. 43/1 If you are in near-equal machinery, it becomes a case..of slip-streaming an inch behind him and diving out for a pass at the vital moment. **1979** L. PRYOR *Viper* viii. 156, I caught them on the pit straight as they slipstreamed each other on the left side of the road.

slipware, slip-ware (sli·pwēᵊɹ). [f. SLIP *sb.*[1] + WARE *sb.*[3]]. Pottery coated with slip. Also *fig.* and *attrib.* passing into *adj.*

1883 L. M. SOLON *Art Eng. Potter* 41 We shall conclude by mentioning another sort of Slip-ware also made now-a-days, the sham 'old Slip', of which we have to confess the possession of several pieces, bought..for genuine specimens. **1929** H. READ *Staffordshire Pottery Figures* 2 The Staffordshire potters, who had already acquired considerable skill in the manipulation of clays in the making of the type of pottery known as slipware. **1935** *Burlington Mag.* Oct. 180/1 A Wrotham slipware dish. **1957** *Listener* 17 Oct. 608/1 My second preference among English pots..would be slip ware, which seems to be the earliest which can definitely be assigned to Staffordshire. **1968** J. ARNOLD *Shell Bk. Country Crafts* 232 Slip-ware is a porous earthenware on which a creamy clay has been applied on the still damp body, before firing, either by immersion or brush trailing. **1976** 'D. HALLIDAY' *Dolly & Nanny Bird* vii. 92 Two girls in curled hats..and pink slip-ware faces.

slip-way. Add: **1.** (Examples of a ramp used by a seaplane.) Also *fig.*

1912 *Flight* 7 Dec. 1133 (*caption*) The machine being launched from the slipway that leads down to the water from the hangar. **1922** *Encycl. Brit.* XXX. 48/1 The management of these [seaplane] stations is very similar to that of an aerodrome, with the exception of slipways up and down which aircraft are moved on leaving and entering the water. **1936** *Sun* (Baltimore) 6 July 9/1 The giant four-motored plane, prototype of the airliner with which Britain is to face the Atlantic voyage, made its first appearance on the slipway at Rochester this week. **1938** G. GREENE *Brighton Rock* I. iii. 46 The coffin slid smoothly down into the fiery sea... The clergyman smiled gently from behind the slipway. **1982** P. CONNON *In Shadow of Eagle's Wing* 28 On the evening of Wednesday, August 3, the hydromonoplane was launched down the slipway into Bowness Bay.

slit, *sb.* Add: **1. d.** The vulva. *coarse slang.*

Its currency is restricted in the manner of other coarse terms: see small-type note s.v. *FUCK *v.*

1648 R. HERRICK *Hesperides* 47 Scobble for Whoredome whips his wife; and cryes, He'll slit her nose; but blubb'-ring, she replyes, Good Sir, make no more cuts i' th'out-ward skin, One slit's enough to let Adultry in. **1714** *Cabinet of Love* 18 His tarse, as soon as to my slit applied Up to the hilt into my cunt did slide. **1970** G. GREER *Female Eunuch* 265 The vagina..belittled by terms like.. *slit.* **1977** *Rolling Stone* 24 Mar. 41/4 What am I going to call it? Snatch, Twat? Pussy? Puss puss, nice kitty, nice little animal that's so goddam patronizing it's almost as bad as saying 'slit'.

e. A narrow, usu. straight aperture in an optical instrument through which a beam of light can be received.

[**1832** *Nat. Philos.* (Libr. Useful Knowl.) II. II. iii. 25/1 Instead of a row of holes, he formed one narrow slit in the shutter... By this means a spectrum of any required breadth may be formed.] **1863** E. ATKINSON tr. *Ganot's Elem. Treat. Physics* VII. iv. 410 A telescope, the eyepiece of which can be regulated by a micrometric screw... The slit is in the focus of the object-glass of the telescope. **1888** *Proc. R. Soc.* XLIII. 130 Huggins's photograph of the spectrum of Comet Wells, taken with a wide slit. **1905** E. C. C. BALY *Spectroscopy* iii. 48 As generally used at the present time the slit is formed between two metal jaws, one of which is fixed while the other is moved by a fine-pitched screw. **1926** *Jrnl. Optical Soc. Amer.* X. 186 If the spectrophotometer has a second collimator, the continuous spectrum may be formed from an incandescent light placed in front of its slit. **1969** D. W. TENQUIST et al. *University Optics* I. xi. 293 (*caption*) Fraunhofer diffraction at a double slit.

5. slit drum, a primitive percussion instrument made out of a hollowed log with a longitudinal slit; **slit fricative** *Phonetics,* a fricative or spirant sound made by expelling the breath through a narrow aperture; **slit-gong** = *slit drum* above; **slit lamp** *Ophthalm.*, a lamp which emits a narrow but intense beam of light, used for examining the interior of the eye; freq. *attrib.*; **slit pocket,** a side pocket in a garment, with a vertical opening; **slit sampler,** a device for studying the bacterial content of the air, having a slit through which it is drawn; **slit sound, spirant** *Phonetics* = *slit fricative* above; **slit-trench,** a narrow trench made to accommodate and protect a soldier or weapon in battle.

1933 *Africa* VI. 155 The deep-toned slit-drum..is assigned by ethnologists..to the matriarchal 'two-class' culture circle. **1957** *New Oxf. Hist. Music* I. ii. 185 The wooden fish, still in use among Taoists and Buddhists, is a slit-drum. **1974** *Encycl. Brit. Macropædia* XIV. 61/2 In Vietnam the slit-drum is both a temple and a watchmen's instrument. On Java slit-drums can be traced to the Hindu–Javanese period (1st–9th century AD). **1955** H. A. GLEASON *Introd. Descr. Linguistics* ii. 22 Because of the slit-like shape of the opening, these sounds are called slit fricatives. **1973** J. C. WELLS *Jamaican Pronunc. in London* 127 This feature is an extension of the..distinction between 'groove' and 'slit' fricatives. **1938** *Jrnl. R. Anthrop. Inst.* LXVIII. 241 Samara returned to the village and after beating the slit-gong gave vent to his grievance. **1970** *Times* 23 Feb. 10/4 (*caption*) A 'slit gong' which has been accepted by the Queen as a gift... The gong is used in the New Hebrides to convey messages, summon people and sound the alarm. **1922** *Arch. Ophthalm.* LI. 271 Many new phases of examination of the living eye are made possible by the use of the slit lamp. **1961** [see *GONIOSCOPE]. **1978** *Jrnl. R. Soc. Med.* LXXI. 100 Slit-lamp examination revealed a moderate number of cells in the anterior and posterior vitreous. **1933** J. E. LIBERTY *Practical Tailoring* ix. 169 Slit pockets are somewhat similar to trouser pockets and are made with jettings, or welts, but the pocket is not sewn twice. The mouth of the pocket is almost upright and at least 7 in. long for a normal size coat. **1978** M. SICHEL *Costume Reference 8: 1918–1939* 36 Many skirts worn with blouses had pockets at the sides or slit pockets and belts of the same material. **1941** R. B. BOURDILLON et al. in *Jrnl. Hygiene* XLI. 220 The range of concentrations which can be measured accurately with the slit sampler is from about 1 to 10,000 per cu. ft. **1963** WALTER & ISRAEL *Gen. Path.* xix. 295 The slit-sampler consists of a narrow slit through which air is sucked on to a rotating culture plate beneath it. **1912** Slit sound [see *RILL *sb.*[1] 4]. **1958** Slit spirant [see *RILL *sb.*[1] 4]. **1970** *Publ. Amer. Dial. Soc. 1968* L. 21 The phoneme /θ/ of *thirty, Martha, hearth* is a voiceless dental slit spirant [θ]. **1942** Slit trench [see *FOX-HOLE]. **1944** *Times* 12 May 3/2 At Manus Island the prisoners were made to dig slit trenches for the Japanese. **1971** B. W. ALDISS *Soldier Erect* 162 My slit-trench is the first on the right, next to the cookhouse. Cheerio, Ali, you old robber!

slit, *ppl. a.* Add: **3. c.** *slit iron* (earlier Amer. example); **slit skirt,** a tight skirt slit upward from the hem for ease of movement or sexual allurement.

1789 *Deb. Congress U.S.* 17 Apr. (1834) I. 167 To lay an impost of seven and a half per cent..upon..slit or rolled iron. **1913** *Punch* 30 July 101/2 Four young women who last week promenaded Fifth Avenue, New York, in slit skirts..were surrounded by an enraged mob. **1954** C. G. BRADLEY *Western World Costume* xxi. 342 The hobble skirt of 1914 was worn even on long walking excursions. The slit skirt of the same year brought protests from bishops and ministers. **1976** 'M. DELVING' *China Expert* i. 7 The slit skirt of the *ch'i pao* she always wore.

slither, *sb.* Add: **4. a.** Also *transf.* and *fig.*

1915 E. WALLACE *Man who bought London* ii. 23 So many people were following closely in that hurried slither to the platform. **1970** *Guardian* 12 Nov. 12/2 If the whole slither into inflation is not to accelerate..some private employers will have to stand firm.

b. Something smooth and slippery; a smoothly sliding mass; = SLIVER *sb.*[1] I.

1919 E. POUND *Quia Pauper Amavi* 40 If she goes in a gleam of Cos, in a slither of dyed stuff, There is a volume in the matter. **1955** N. NICHOLSON *Lakers* xi. 188 Only after rain, when..the rocks are hung with slithers of water like lace curtains against the black slate. **1966** G. GREENE *Comedians* I. v. 153 Little fenced saucers of earth where a few palm-trees grew and slithers of water gleamed between. **1981** *Daily Tel.* 27 May 15/1 Calvin Klein's newest dress is a slither of silk shaped simply like an overgrown T-shirt.

slithering, *ppl. a.* (Earlier mod. example.)

1840 M. EDGEWORTH *Let.* 30 Dec. (1971) 573 Not one name when introduced had I been able to make out from Mrs. Hollands slithering pronunciation.

slithery, *a.* For Chiefly *dial.* read orig. *dial.* and add: **a.** (Later examples).

1922 E. R. EDDISON *Worm* xxvi. 332 With rocks and pits hidden in the heather, and slithery slabs of granite. **1946** M. PEAKE *Titus Groan* 298 His lordship..was gazing at his daughter with a slithery smile upon his mouth that had once been so finely drawn. **1952** L. A. G. STRONG *Darling Tom* i. 12 Against the wall stood four slithery horse-hair chairs. **1975** E. HUXLEY *Gallipot Eyes* (1976) 168 Oaksey Wood is a morass with yellowish water lying deep in slithery tractor ruts.

b. *Comb.*, as *slithery-eyed, -slobbery* adjs.

1921 D. H. LAWRENCE *Sea & Sardinia* iii. 123 Give me the old, salty way of love. How I am nauseated with sentiment and nobility, the macaroni slithery-slobbery mess of modern adorations. **1977** *New Yorker* 8 Aug. 11/1 He picks out the very lad:..a twin..identical to the slithery-eyed boy destined to grow up into Marty Feldman.

slithy (slɔi·ði), *a.* Also † **slythy.** [Presumably a blend of SLIMY *a.* and LITHE *a.*] A word invented by 'Lewis Carroll': 'smooth and active' ('Carroll', 1855, 140) and popularized esp. in phr. *slithy toves* from *Through the Looking-Glass* (1871). Also in subsequent allusive uses.

1855 'L. CARROLL' *Rectory Umbrella & Mischmasch* (1932) 139 Twas bryllyg and the slythy [1871: slithy] toves Did gyre and gymble in the wabe. **1920** 'K. MANSFIELD' *Let.* 27 Sept. (1928) II. 48, I watched him [*sc.* a lizard] come forth to-day—*very* slithy—and eat an ant. **1928** A. S. EDDINGTON *Nature of Physical World* xiii. 291 Eight slithy toves gyre and gimble in the oxygen wabe; seven in nitrogen. **1937** G. FRANKAU *More of Us* 2 While the free-versifier gyres and gimbles The slithy tove—with his own 'private symbols'. **1960** H. MARCHAND *Categories* x. 368 Lewis Carroll's *slithy..*, *chortle..*have become common property. Shakespeare's *glaze* (f. *glare* and *gaze*) has not. **1981** *Time Out* 20–26 Mar. 54/1 Pity the slithy toves of academe.

sli·tted, *a. rare.* [f. SLIT *sb.* + -ED[2].] Having a slit or slits; shaped like a slit.

1936 B. BROOKER *Think of Earth* I. i. 20 Stale fumes of beer..were belched at the Canon as he passed the slitted swing doors of the bar. **1947** W. STEVENS *Transport to Summer* 139 A face of stone in an unending red, Red-emerald, red-slitted-blue, a face of slate. **1974** R. ADAMS *Shardik* xxiv. 184 The window-openings, rounded and slitted like key-holes, which lit the spiral stairways.

slitty (sli·ti), *a.* [f. SLIT *sb.* + -Y[1].] Of the eyes: long and narrow. Also in *Comb.*, as *slitty-eyed*, slit-eyed.

1908 R. BROUGHTON *Mamma* x. 104 Her slitty eyes, opened so wide as almost to look large. *Ibid.* xxiii. 218 Her slitty eyes dancing with mirth and benevolence. **1926** G. FRANKAU *My Unsentimental Journey* 276 Where the slitty-eyed Chinese are. **1947** M. MORRIS *Township* 9 She was a sturdy young woman.., with..bright, slitty black eyes. **1976** *Listener* 18 Mar. 324/1 The English couple who turned down the Thai baby that was procured for them 'because its eyes are too slitty'.

sliver, *sb.*[1] Add: **1. a.** (Later *fig.* examples.)

1967 T. KINSELLA *Nightwalker* I. 5 Bone-splinters, silvery slivers of screams. **1978** J. CARROLL *Mortal Friends* III. vi. 327 People on buses and on the streets of Boston traded slivers of information as if they were coins.

c. (Earlier example.)

1869 *Maine Acts & Resolves* 24 Any pumice, scraps or other offal arising from the making of oil or slivers for bait.

sliving, *ppl. a.* (Later examples.)

c **1909** D. H. LAWRENCE *Collier's Friday Night* (1934) iii. 75 I'm not a fool, if you think so. I can pay you yet, you sliving bitch! **1913** —— *Sons & Lovers* iv. 66 What should go runnin' up my arm but a mouse... They'll get in your pocket an' eat your snap, if you'll let 'em..the slivin', nibblin' little nuisances.

slivovitz (sli·vŏvits). Also **sliwowitz**; ‖ **slivovic(e), slivovitza, sljivovica.** [ad. G. *slibowitz*, f. Bulg. *slivovitza*, Serbo-Croat *šljivovica* plum brandy, f. OSl. *sliva* plum; cf. SLOE.] A central and eastern European plum brandy.

α. **1885** *Encycl. Brit.* XVIII. 692/2 Other important articles of commerce are wine, wool, cattle, timber, hides, honey, wax and 'slivovitza', an inferior spirit made from plums. **1938** C. MORGAN *Flashing Stream* I. i. 72 They have a drink called Šljivovica. It's a kind of plum-brandy. **1950** [see *plum brandy* s.v. *PLUM *sb.* 6]. **1973** S. JACKMAN *Guns covered with Flowers* vi. 98 They drank two small glasses of sljivovica.

β. **1897** B. STOKER *Dracula* i. 11 There is a flask of slivovitz..underneath the seat, if you should require it. **1900** 'ODYSSEUS' *Turkey in Europe* viii. 374 The plum-trees [of Northern Servia] that produce the national drink of slivovitz, or plum-brandy. **1940** M. HEALY *Stay me with Flagons* 273 Kirsch and Kirschwasser..never have appealed to me; and Slivovitz I have never drunk, I think. **1951** F. BROWN *Murder can be Fun* viii. 104 What are you drinking? Me, I like slivovitz. **1960** A. E. BENDER *Dict. Nutrition* 114/2 *Sliwowitz*, plum brandy originating in Yugoslavia. **1960** R. ST. JOHN *Foreign Correspondent* ix. 192 There was a young German in his compartment who had drunk too deeply of Bulgarian slivovitz. **1976** *New Yorker* 22 Mar. 47/1 He sits by the kitchen window of his little flat,..drinking the slivovitz he smuggles into Sweden each September in carefully emptied beer bottles.

γ. **1958** P. KEMP *No Colours or Crest* viii. 172 A flask of excellent Prizren slivovic. **1961** E. WAUGH *Unconditional Surrender* III. ii. 226 Once, after a jack-pot, he was offered a glass of Slivovic. **1971** *Southerly* XXXI. 17 Here's to scotch, to bourbon, to slivovic, to uyzo.

Sloane Ranger (slōᵘn rēⁱ·ndʒəɹ), *sb.* and *adj. phr.* [Blend of *Sloane* Square, London, and *Lone Ranger*, a well-known hero of western stories and films.] (Of, pertaining to, or characteristic of) a fashionable but upper class and conventional young woman in London. Also occas. extended to any member of the class to which such young women belong, and *ellipt.* as *Sloane.* Hence **Sloa·neness.**

1975 P. YORK in *Harpers & Queen* Oct. 190/3 The Sloane Rangers..are the nicest British Girl. *Ibid.* 191/2 The Sloane Rangers always *add tone.* They never put on prole accents, like self-conscious Oxford boys in the sixties. *Ibid.* 191/3 Once a Sloane marries and moves to Kennington and starts learning sociology through the Open University, she is off the rails. *Ibid.*, Sloaneness, some people would say, is a track to be liberated from

Ibid. 192/3 Sloane Ranger pet hates..incense, Norman Mailer. **1978** *Evening Standard* 21 Aug. 13/2 A way of life neither Mayfair, nor West End nor Sloane Ranger, but which is summed up in the words Cafe Society. **1978** D. MacKenzie *Deep, Dark & Dangerous* i. 55 Emma.. was a hell of a lot different to the succession of Sloane Rangers who had been her predecessors, harpies bent on getting far more than they gave. **1980** S. Allan *Dead Giveaway* xv. 154 She wore a cashmere sweater..a Sloane ranger type. **1981** J. Mann *Funeral Sites* xviii. 111 The all-English Phoebe with her Sloane Ranger voice and manners. **1982** Barr & York *Official Sloane Ranger Handbk.* 10/1 Sloane Rangers hesitate to use the term 'breeding' now (of people, not animals) but that's what background means. **1983** *Times* 16 Apr. 3/7 (*headline*) Bogus Sloane Ranger lived like a lord. *Ibid.* 3/8 He even emulated the voice of those known as Sloane Rangers and men about town.

slob, *sb.*[1] Add: **1. d.** *Canad.* = *slob-ice*, sense 4 below.

1878 *North Star* (St. John's, Newfoundland) 30 Mar. 3/1 The bay here was caught over last week, and a string of 'slob' made its appearance across the mouth, but the heavy sea of Thursday broke it all up. **1907** J. G. Millais *Newfoundland* ii. 44 They themselves had hooked seventeen white coats out o' the slob (shore ice). **1920** W. T. Grenfell *Labrador Doctor* ix. 174 This ice is of very different qualities. Now it is 'slob' mixed with snow born on the Newfoundland coast. **1951** *Beaver* Sept. 20 Wind half a gale, temperature away down and slob in harbour and around schooner turning to ice.

3. (Further examples.) Also, a lout, a fat person; one who is gullible or excessively soft-hearted, a fool; a person of little account. *slang.*

1904 'No. 1500' *Life in Sing Sing* 252/2 *Slob*, a person easy to impose upon; an untidy person. **1904** G. V. Hobart *Jim Hickey* i. 16 You're a warm young guy When you start to buy—You're a slob when you lose the price! **1927** H. V. Morton *In Search of England* x. 185 He was no beauty to look at, but then women seem to like the ugly slobs, don't they? **1938** R. Flannagan *County Court* 36 That praying old slob, Jones, has three boys and every one of 'em has run away. **1950** Wodehouse *Nothing Serious* 29 'The poor old slob,' she murmured. **1953** *If; Worlds of Sci. Fiction* Sept. 40/1 Speaking..as an ordinary slob that doesn't follow rarefied reasoning very well. **1958** S. Ellin *Eighth Circle* ii. xv. 123 A big, fat, gutless slob. **1959** I. & P. Opie *Lore & Lang. Schoolch.* ix. 168 The unfortunate fat boy..is known as:..slob, [etc.]. **1960** 'E. McBain' *Heckler* v. 60 There are people..who always look like slobs... The tendency toward sloppiness first exhibits itself when the subject is still a child. **1966** A. Cavanaugh *Children are Gone* ii. vi. 49 'I'm a slob,' Shirley said. 'I'm not an intellectual.' **1970** R. Price *Gt. Roob Revolution* 7 The hucksters who control the..mass media think they are manipulating what they refer to as 'the slobs'. **1972** T. P. McMahon *Issue of Bishop's Blood* (1973) ii. 17 He's a real slob for his employees. He buys them houses, goes to their bar mitzvahs. **1978** J. Irving *World according to Garp* ix. 184, I think you're an irresponsible slob.

4. slob ice orig. *Canad.*, densely-packed, sludgy ice, esp. sea ice; **slob trout,** a brown trout, *Salmo trutta*, which stays in a river estuary instead of going further out to sea.

1835 E. Wix *Six Months Newfoundland Missionary's Jrnl.* (1836) 16, I crossed through the 'slob ice', which was very thick in Conception Bay, to Port de Grave. **1920** W. T. Grenfell *Labrador Doctor* vi. 132 The slob ice had already made ballicaters and the biting cold of winter so far north had set in with all its vigour. **1955** *Sci. Amer.* Apr. 52/3 On the way to Little America, its first Antarctic port of call, the Atka saw very little of the drifting ice pack that surrounds the continent. It passed through a few 'bergy bits' and pieces of 'slob ice' —melting remnants of the pack. **1965** F. Russell *Secret Islands* vii. 88 The island was isolated because it was surrounded by impassable slob ice. **1907** W. L. Calderwood *Life of Salmon* i. 6 In the West of Ireland we have.. the so-called slob trout. **1930** G. H. Nall *Life Sea Trout* vi. 75 These brown Trout, feeding in brackish and salt water, are numerous, and special names have been given to them, such as 'Slob Trout', and 'Estuarine Trout'. **1960** C. Willock *Angler's Encycl.* 190/1 Slob-trout: sometimes called bull trout, are brown trout that migrate only as far as the estuary.

slob (slǫb), *v.* [f. Slob *sb.*[1]] *trans.* To slop (*out*); to express by slobbering. So **slo·bbed** *ppl. a.*

1887 Parish & Shaw *Dict. Kentish Dial.* 152 *Slobbed*, slopped, spilt. *a* **1918** W. Owen *Poems* (1963) 69 Drooping tongues from jaws that slob their relish. **1946** B. Marshall *George Brown's Schooldays* 56 The master began to slob out the tapioca.

slobber, *v.* Add: **1. d.** fig. *to slobber over*, to be over-attentive or over-affectionate towards (someone); to be exaggeratedly enthusiastic about (something).

1825 [in Dict., sense 1 b]. **1892** 'Mark Twain' *Amer. Claim.* xiii. 139 They treat you as a tramp until they find out you're a congressman, and then they slobber all over you. **1914** W. Owen *Let.* 28 Aug. (1967) 282 He received me like a lover. To use an expression of the Rev. H. Wigan's, he quite slobbered over me. **1927** D. L. Sayers *Unnatural Death* iii. xxii. 257 Miss Climpson had little difficulty in reconstructing one of those hateful and passionate 'scenes' of slighted jealousy... 'I do everything for you—you don't care a bit for me..!' And 'Don't be.. ridiculous... Oh, stop it, Vera! I hate being slobbered over.' **1978** P. Theroux *Picture Palace* viii. 50 Even if they had slobbered over every blessed picture in the place they would not have understood.

slobberhannes (slǫ·bəɹhænės). [Origin unknown. Perh. ad. Du.: cf. Du. dial. *slabberjan* the name of a game, and Du. *Hannes* Jack.] A card-game for four persons played with only high-ranking cards, in which the object is to lose tricks. Also, a point scored at this game.

1877 W. B. Dick *Mod. Pocket Hoyle* (ed. 8) 211 *Slobberhannes*... The object of the game is to *avoid* making points, as the player who first gets ten points loses the game. *Ibid.* 212 If a player scores *all* of the three foregoing points, he receives one point extra, which is called 'Slobberhannes'. **1952** J. B. Pick *Phoenix Dict. Games* 276 *Slobberhannes* (4 players). Played with a pack from which all cards below seven have been withdrawn. **1964** A. Wykes *Gambling* vii. 165 *Greek hearts*..and *slobberhannes* are slightly simpler variations on the trick-losing theme.

slobby, *a.* Add: **2. a.** Sloppy, sentimental. **b.** Of or pertaining to a slob (Slob *sb.*[1] 3 in Dict. and Suppl.).

1913 R. Brooke *Let.* 3 July (1968) 479, I had a bad fit of home-sickness this morning... I threw up quite a lot of slobby old memories. **1967** *Spectator* 4 Aug. 131/1 To be honest, backbone isn't, as it were, at the forefront of my character. I am pretty slobby within. **1970** W. Burroughs Jr. *Speed* (1971) v. 108 Vicki told me that I looked like a slobby bum. **1976** W. Goldman *Magic* iii. ix. 181 She'd end up stranded some place maybe with..some slobby dummy. **1976** *New Yorker* 9 Feb. 84/3 Peter Boyle's role is small, but..he does slobby wonders with his scenes as the gently thick Wizard.

slobgollion (slǫbgǫ·lyən). *Whaling slang.* [Origin unknown: cf. Slumgullion.] A substance found in sperm-oil (see quot.).

1851 H. Melville *Moby Dick* III. viii. 65 It is called slobgollion; an appellation original with the whalemen... It is an ineffably oozy, stringy affair, most frequently found in the tubs of sperm, after a profound squeezing, and subsequent decanting.

sloe. Add: **3.** *sloe eye.*

1957 V. J. Kehoe *Technique Film & T.V. Make-Up* ix. 107 (*caption*) Effect of sloe eye after applying latex to outer ends of lashes and eyelid and pressing them together. **1977** N. Marsh *Last Ditch* ii. 37 His sloe eyes looked out of a pale face.

slog, *sb.* **2.** (Earlier examples.)

1846 *Swell's Night Guide* 76 And she felt inclined to mug her rival, only she thought it would be no bottle, cos her rival could go in a buster at a slog. **1865** *Lillywhite's Cricketers' Compan.* 139 Too fond of losing his wicket for a 'slog'.

slog, *v.* Add: **1. a.** (Earlier example.)

1824 *Session Papers Central Criminal Court* 21 Sept. 535/1 One of them said, 'Go back and slog him.'

3. a. (Earlier example.)

1846 *Swell's Night Guide* 37 Most of them can slog, that is to say,..fight.

b. *Cricket.* To hit, or attempt to hit, the ball hard and with abandon.

1869 *Baily's Mag.* July 21 Not only did he 'slog', in the true sense of the word, which we take to be hitting blindly and high in the air, but [etc.]. **1904** F. C. Holland *Cricket* 36 You should go to the nets, not to slog, but to play. **1935** J. C. Masterman *Fate cannot harm Me* viii. 167 At the fifth ball the Admiral slogged with even crookeder bat and even more mighty effort; he missed it, and all three stumps were spreadeagled. **1980** *Cricketer International* Feb. 11/1 The incredible thing is that he never had to slog once to make his runs.

slogan. Add: **1. b.** (Further examples.)

1922 *Times* 20 June 7/4 'Post early.' New P.O. slogan on letters. **1928** *Publishers' Weekly* 9 June 2386 As an advertising man, Mr. Calkins believes the slogan 'a cent a copy to sell the art of reading', a great and revolutionary one. **1951** H. Arendt *Burden of Our Time* i. ii. 38 Antisemitic slogans were highly effective in mobilizing large strata of the population. **1958** P. H. Gibbs *Curtains of Yesterday* xix. 157 On the other side [of an ancient gateway] with big letters deeply carved was the new slogan of Lenin's Russia. 'Religion is the Opium of the People.' **1968** V. S. Pritchett *Cab at Door* ix. 163 All sects have their jargon and Father, eager as an advertising man is for slogans, had picked them all up and lived by them. **1971** H. Macmillan *Riding the Storm* xv. 478 The somewhat disingenuous slogan of 'ban the bomb'. **1972** F. Fitzgerald *Fire in Lake* viii. 277 Thousands of soldiers and civil servants marched with the dock workers shouting anti-government and occasionally anti-American slogans. **1980** R. Scruton *Meaning of Conservatism* iii. 59 One particular slogan will later occupy our attention—'equality of opportunity'.

2. Also *Comb.*, as *slogan-shouter*, *-shouting* vbl. sb. and ppl. adj.; *slogan-like* adj.

1936 Wirth & Shils tr. *Mannheim's Ideology & Utopia* i. 36 Two slogan-like concepts 'ideology and utopia'. **1975** *Language for Life* (Dept. Educ. & Sci.) xiii. 199 Public debate..has often been conducted through a series of slogan-like headings: progressive, formal, integration, basics, and several more. **1940** G. Cunningham *Jrnl.* 14 Dec. in N. Mitchell *Sir G. Cunningham* (1968) iv. 83 Heard from Peshawar that slogan shouters had been told to go home. **1968** N. Mitchell *Ibid.*, On the 12th, the slogan shouters sent notices to the Deputy Commissioner where and when they would shout their slogans on 14th December. **1940** G. Cunningham *Jrnl.* 24 Dec. in *Ibid.* 84 Slogan shouting by Satyagrahis has stopped as Gandhi has declared a holiday for Christmas. **1972** J. Biggs-Davison *Africa—Hope Deferred* x. 98 These are but a few of the problems facing independent Africa that can no longer be concealed by an excess of slogan-shouting. **1976** M. Zia-ud-din *Memoirs* 63 Wherever it stopped there were large crowds of slogan-shouting Muslims. **1978** *Jrnl. R. Soc. Arts* CXXVI. 696/2 *Medical Inspection* destroys the 'nobility' of war more readily than 1,000 slogan-shouting demonstrators.

Hence **slo·ganed** *a.*, marked with a slogan.

1966 'G. Douglas' *Odd Woman Out* ix. 60 This tall girl ..in jeans and a sloganed sweater. **1978** *Church Times* 1 Sept. 15/2 With..leather waistcoats or sloganed T-shirts. **1979** *Sci. Amer.* Apr. 30/1 A graffiti remover which was developed by the organic chemistry section in response to a government campaign to clean-up the much-sloganed areas of Belfast and Londonderry.

sloganeer (slōᵘgănīᵊ·ɹ). orig. *U.S.* [f. Slogan + -eer.] One who devises or who uses slogans.

1922 R. Connell in *Sat. Even. Post* (U.S.) 29 Apr. 100/2 (*heading*) Once a sloganeer. **1935** *Sat. Rev. Lit.* 11 May 30/3 The day may come when a West Coast sloganeer will proudly proclaim, 'If it isn't at San Marino, it isn't a book.' **1963** D. Ogilvy *Confessions Advertising Man* vii. 127 Posters are for sloganeers. **1971** *N.Z. Listener* 31 May 5 'Sloganeers'—young, sometimes older people, who do not analyse a problem but pick up a current catchcry. **1978** *Times* 7 Aug. 12/4 Questions are a favourite device of envelope sloganeers. 'Is he to be our next President?' asked one.

Hence as *v. intr.*, to express oneself in slogans (now usu. in a political context); **sloganee·ring** *vbl. sb.* and *ppl. a.*

1941 H. S. Johnson *Hell-Bent for War* ii. 37 In this modern sloganeering day,..the constant repetition of a lie has become the..weapon of the totalitarian propagandist. *Ibid.* iv. 85 We are..getting all ready to do it all over again with hardly a variation in timing sequence or superficial sloganeering. **1944** *Sun* (Baltimore) 18 Mar. 6/6 To speak of the German dead in terms of carpets is not to exaggerate or 'sloganeer'. **1949** *Ibid.* 13 Oct. 18/3 Eastern Germany's tireless Communists, still a bit breathless from the ten-day marathon of sloganeering over the new 'East German Republic', [etc.]. **1967** *Philos. Rev.* LXXVI. 105 An area where superficiality and sloganeering too often hold sway. **1970** K. Millett *Sexual Politics* iii. v. 265 What she does 'become' is only a nonentity, utterly incorporated into Birkin, his single follower, proselytizing and sloganeering. **1978** *New Statesman* 27 Oct. 556/3 The islanders have learnt to deploy the bullying sloganeering and empty hard sell of 'Westminster' politics. **1981** *Encounter* Apr. 48/2 To distinguish truth from sloganeering licence and exaggeration.

sloganize (slōᵘ·gănəiz), *v.* [f. Slogan + -ize.]

1. *trans.* **a.** To make (something) the subject of a slogan; to express in a slogan.

1929 *Bull. Amer. Library Assoc.* Apr. 70 Infected with the economy virus sloganized by recent high national executives. **1941** Auden *New Year Let.* ii. 39 Round a provincial régime that sloganized the Rights of Man. **1949** *Archit. Rev.* CV. 96/2 To sloganize the present trend in Sweden: 'Personal, organic creation in a harmonious democracy'—which should be vague enough to please everybody. **1981** *R. United Services Inst. Jrnl.* June 7/1 If you try to sloganise it I think it is quite dangerous.

b. To influence by means of slogans.

1954 *ADA World* Feb. 1M/1 Of all the economic prescriptions that have been written in Washington in the past 25 years, none is stranger or more dangerous than the current attempt to sloganize the country out of an economic decline.

2. *intr.* To compose slogans, to utter slogans.

1960 *Encounter* June 38/1 Mao's ability to sloganise and reduce complex matters to simple formulas has been one of his key assets. **1975** *Daily Tel.* 24 June 11/2 The conspirators met in a pub and sloganised about tyrants.

Hence **slo·ganized** *ppl. a.*, expressed in the form of a slogan or slogans; **slo·ganizer,** one who uses slogans; **slo·ganizing** *vbl. sb.* and *ppl. a.*

1940 *New Statesman* 2 Mar. 274/1 Snappy presentation and slick sloganising. **1965** *Ibid.* 29 Oct. 660/3 This could become mere sententiousness, the jingling or sloganising final flourish in a poem like 'Waiting'. **1970** *Times* 31 Mar. (Austral. Suppl.) p. ii/7 Throughout the 1950s and early 1960s Mr. (later Sir) Robert Menzies encapsulated this *weltanschauung* in the sloganized search for 'great and powerful friends'. **1974** *Daily Tel.* 27 June 18 The cliché-ridden sloganisers of the extreme Left. **1975** R. Lewis *M. Thatcher* v. 42 The manifesto gave an easy sloganised summary of the 'action' to which the Party was committing itself. **1981** *Times Lit. Suppl.* 15 May 548/1 The success of 'All You Need is Love'..encouraged the Beatles to try their hand at sloganizing.

slogger, *sb.* Add: **2. a.** (Earlier example.) Also, a heavy blow.

1829 P. Egan *Boxiana* 2nd Ser. II. 19 He got away from a *slogger*, but immediately commenced an exchange of blows. **1846** *Swell's Night Guide* 75 No one dares to dispute the ability of the boshman; 'cos he's..a numming slogger.

b. (Earlier example.)

1850 *County Herald* 31 Aug. 7/3 Who went in a slogger, scoring two's and three's, till the scorers called game.

c. A person or machine that works hard or with effort, often with a suggestion of ponderousness or lack of sparkle.

1928 G. B. Shaw *Intelligent Woman's Guide* xlix. 208 The employers, to find out how much work can be got out of a man, pick out an exceptionally quick and indefatigable man called a slogger. **1968** J. Sangster *Touchfeather* xiii. 138 Bill was a bloody genius... Harvey's a slogger. It takes him a year to arrive where Bill could in twenty-four hours. **1977** *Drive* Mar.–Apr. 56/2 The Manta's 1.9 engine is a solid, reliable slogger in the General Motors tradition.

sloggering, *ppl. a.* Add: **b.** (See quot. 1977.) *rare*$^{-1}$.

1876 G. M. Hopkins *Wr. Deutschland* in *Poems* (1967) 57 The inboard seas run swirling and hawling; The rash smart sloggering brine Blinds her. **1977** J. Milroy *Lang. G. M. Hopkins* 245 *Sloggering*..: Certainly imit., belonging to phonaesthetic series (*slither*, etc.), a derivative (*slog*, etc.), and a blend... Complex associations suggest the meaning: 'dashing (against the ship) repeatedly and drawing back with a sucking gurgling noise'.

slogging, *vbl. sb.* Add: (Earlier and later examples.) Also *attrib.*

1857 *Bell's Life* 31 May 6/4 Nor ought we to omit notice of Reynolds's 15 by a kind of paralytic slogging, which *sometimes* tells. **1934** [see *run *sb.*[1] 2 a]. **1958** F. C. Avis *Boxing Ref. Dict.* 103 *Slogging match*, a contest in which both men hit each other heavily and very often.

sloke[2]. (Earlier example.)

1788 *Asiatick Researches* I. 127 Thus speak the following *Slokes* from the *Dhormo Onoosaason*.

sloop, *sb.*[1] **3.** *sloop-man* (earlier examples).

1676 T. Glover *Acct. of Virginia* in *Phil. Trans. R. Soc.* XI. 625 The sloop man dropped his grap-line. **1737** *Calendar Virginia State Papers* (1875) I. 229 Paid a Sloop man for 2 gals of rum.

sloosh (slūʃ), *sb. dial.* and *colloq.* [Echoic: cf. Slosh *sb.*, Slush *sb.*[2] But perhaps partly a variant of Sluice *sb.*] A pouring of water; a wash; a noise of, or as of, heavily splashing or rushing water.

1919 *Athenæum* 11 July 582/2 Among the brand-new slang one may discern some that had an onomatopœic or at any rate an imitative origin; for instance 'sloosh', a wash. **1920** *Blackw. Mag.* Apr. 500/2 There was the sloosh of bilge-water. **1926** W. de la Mare *Connoisseur* 187 Mr. Thripp..not only tidied up his own and Tilda's bedroom..but even gave a sloosh to the bath. **1973** C. Bonington *Next Horizon* v. 88 He got about half-way up, and suddenly there was a sloosh, and he came shooting down the steep snow. **1981** P. Theroux *Mosquito Coast* xiv. 173 The only sounds were the flap and splash..and the sloosh of water in the culverts.

sloosh (slūʃ), *v. dial.* and *colloq.* [Echoic: cf. Slosh *v.*[1], Slush *v.* But perhaps partly a variant of Sluice *v.*] **1.** *trans.* **a.** To wash with a copious supply of water; to pour water or other liquid copiously over.

1912 W. de la Mare *Child's Day* 10 Elizabeth Ann.. stands slooshing herself With that 'normous sponge. **1933** G. Murray tr. *Acharnians* in *Aristophanes* i. 27 Niagara'd me and slooshed me, till—almost—In so much sewage I gave up the ghost.

b. To pour with a rush, to dash (water).

1952 L. A. G. Strong *Darling Tom* 129 The butcher's boy in his blue Sunday suit had got the gardener's wheeled tank from the park, and was slooshing water down the area.

2. *intr.* To make a heavy splashing or rushing noise; to flow or pour with a rush.

1914 [see *clicky *a.*]. **1920** *Blackw. Mag.* Apr. 502/2 The slooshing bilge-water. **1971** C. Bonington *Annapurna South Face* xii. 153 Tom knocked it [*sc.* the primus stove] over, sending the liquid slooshing over the tent floor. *Ibid.* xiii. 167 Instant porridge...a hot, palatable food that simply slooshed down the throat. **1981** P. Theroux *Mosquito Coast* xxvi. 345 She gazed at the torrent of water slooshing downstream.

So **sloo·shy** *v. trans.* = *sloosh *v.* 1 a.

1907 W. De Morgan *Alice-for-Short* xlix. 531 But Cook was turning cataracts of water into her sink, to slooshy it well out after a real good wash-up.

sloothering (slū·ðəriŋ), *vbl. sb. Anglo-Ir.* Also **sluthering.** [Perh. ad. Ir. *lúdar* fawning, flattery with prosthetic *s-* (A. J. Bliss).] Cajoling, wheedling. Hence as *ppl. a.*

1892 J. Barlow *Irish Idylls* viii. 215 There do be girls will get round a man wid their slootherin'. **1896** G. B. Shaw in *Sat. Rev.* 1 Feb. 123/1 Boucicault had a charming brogue: not even the speech of the eminent journalist.. is more musical in sound or irresistible in insinuation—'sloothering' would be the right word, were it current here—than his. **1901** J. Barlow *From Land of Shamrock* 79 Coaxing and sluthering, reinforced by a couple of.. florins. **1919** G. B. Shaw *O'Flaherty V.C.* 188 You foulmouthed, dirty minded, lying, sloothering old sow. **1922** Joyce *Ulysses* 756 He used to amuse me the things he said with the half sloothering smile on him.

slop, *sb.*[1] Add: **7. b.** *slop-clothing* (earlier example).

1802 D. Collins *Acct. Eng. Colony in New S. Wales* II. xiii. 131 For want of slop clothing and bedding, indeed, they were much distressed.

c. slop-chit *Naut.*, a note offered at a ship's stores in exchange for clothing; also *transf.*, an expense sheet.

1946 'Tackline' *You met such Nice Girls in Wrens* i. 11 Sailors come in at different times with what we call Slop-Chits, but which are really nothing but shopping lists. So the slop-chits are the things they want, such as shoes and socks and caps and things. **1969** S. Hyland *Top Bloody Secret* II. 123 Superb autobahn all the way, and a reasonably fast car on his slopchit, made Karlsruhe almost one of the nearer suburbs.

slop, *sb.*[2] Add: **2. b.** *Naut.* A choppy sea, chop.

1956 *Sun* (Baltimore) 21 Nov. 23/6 Mostly southerlies, they pick up to twenty knots and kick up a good slop. **1974** F. Mowat *Boat who wouldn't Float* xi. 120 A slop was banging against her bows, giving her life and motion. **1977** *Austral. Sailing* Jan. 65/1 The Tornados and Hobie 16s revelled in the slop.

3. b. *colloq.* (orig. *U.S.*). Sentimentality, affected sensibility.

1866 'Mark Twain' *Lett. from Hawaii* (1967) 33 You can go on writing that slop about balmy breezes and fragrant flowers, and all that sort of truck. **1917** E. Pound *Let.* Mar. (1971) 108, I would suggest that a series of this sort [*sc.* essays on French poets] by me, Eliot, and De Bosschère would at least keep out a certain amount of *slop* from the prose section. **1924** Galsworthy *White Monkey* I. xiii. 106 Sentiment being 'slop', and championship mere condescension. **1927** *Sunday Express* 24 July 4 'Seventh Heaven', the swamp of sentiment into which the critics were invited to plunge a few days ago. Personally I should describe it as the sublimity of slop. **1942** Berrey & Van den Bark *Amer. Thes. Slang* § 265/1 *Sentimentality*,..slop.

c. *U.S.* and *Austral. slang.* Beer. Usu. *pl.*

1904 'No. 1500' *Life in Sing Sing* 252/2 *Slop*, beer. **1919** *Dial. Notes* V. 42 *Slops*, beer. **1949** L. Glassop *Lucky Palmer* i. 5 Keep your shirt on. There's no harm in having a jug of slops, now is there? **1953** T. A. G. Hungerford *Riverslake* x. 197 His wife and both of his kids got burned to death when his house went up... They reckon that's what sent him onto the slops in the first place. **1963** *Australasian Post* 14 Mar. 51/2 Bung me and me mate over a droppa slops, will yer love?

4. b. *U.S. dial.* and *colloq.* Kitchen refuse or swill fed to cattle or pigs. Usu. *pl.*

1805 R. Parkinson *Tour in America* I. 39 It was natural for me to inquire, what they kept their cows and horses on during the winter. They told me—their horses on blades, and their cows on slops. **1912** T. Dreiser *Financier* xii. 127 A slop-man,..who could come with a great wagon filled with barrels and haul away the slops from your back door, was absolutely essential. **1961** *Publ. Amer. Dial. Soc.* XXXVI. 7 *Slop*, food for pigs.

c. *fig.* Nonsense, rubbish; insolence.

1952 B. Malamud *Natural* 214 Roy tore it up and told the usher to take no more slop from him. **1978** J. Irving *World according to Garp* vi. 120 'Sometimes I feel it is my responsibility to say no,' the editor was quoted as saying, 'even if I know people *do* want to read this slop.'

5*. A dance (see quot. 1962).

1962 *Punch* 16 May 761/1 In the Slop the partners face each other and perform rhythmic movements with feet stationary, the arms swinging pendulum-like in front of the body. **1966** T. Pynchon *Crying of Lot 49* v. 131 Each couple on the floor danced whatever was in the fellow's head: tango, two-step, bossa nova, slop. **1969** N. Cohn *Pop from Beginning* ix. 84 There was the Hully Gully,..the Slop and..the Frug.

6. *slop-barrel* (earlier example), *-bowl* (earlier examples), *-can*, *-pail* (earlier examples), *-tank*, *-tub*; **slop-stone** *dial.*, a stone slab used as a surface for washing.

1831 J. M. Peck *Guide for Emigrants* 172 With..a dairy and slop barrel..pork may be raised from the sow. **1810** *Columbian Centinel* 25 Aug. 4/2 For sale at Davis & Brown's Silver Ware and Jewellry Store..Sugar Basons, ..Slop-Bowls. **1861** Trollope *Orley Farm* (1862) I. xi. 85 A small pile of buttered toast on the slop-bowl, kept warm by hot water below. **1926** *Scribner's Mag.* Aug. 204/1 A strange black dog..supporting himself by raiding the slop-cans of Nigger Town. **1854** B. P. Shillaber *Life & Sayings Mrs. Partington* 212 My boy knows very well how to manage it when the slop-pail is within reach. **1860** F. Nightingale *Notes on Nursing* 14 A slop-pail should never be brought into a sick room. **1882** Nodal & Milner *Gloss. Lancs. Dial.* 245 *Slopstone*, a place for washing. **1911** A. Bennett *Card* viii. 197 A gas range and a marble slopstone with two taps. **1978** *Lancashire Life* Oct. 83/2 Ah want thad slop-stooan scrubbin'. **1968** *New Scientist* 25 Jan. 196/2 One of the ship's tanks is selected to serve as a slop tank... The tanks to be cleaned are washed in turn and washings are pumped continuously into the top of the slop tank. **1979** F. Forsyth *Devil's Alternative* ix. 223 She had sixty giant tanks, or holds... One of these was the slop tank, to be used for..gathering the slops from her fifty crude-carrying cargo tanks. **1867** 'Mark Twain' *Celebrated Jumping Frog* 169 You will proceed toward the window and sit down in that slop-tub.

slop, *v.*[2] Add: **1. c.** *Prison slang.* To empty the contents of (esp. a chamber-pot). Usu. *absol.*

1955 [implied at *slopping *vbl. sb.* b]. **1957** *Listener* 28 Nov. 893/3 He watched the prisoners 'slopping out', working, and attending classes. **1963** T. & P. Morris *Pentonville* v. 104 The next two hours are given over to getting washed, shaved, breakfasted and 'slopped out'. **1967** *Guardian* 2 June 6/1 Along the landing from his cell is a single recess for 'slopping out' chamber pots and wash-basins. **1973** *Times* 20 Dec. 2/3 At Brixton..they queue at communal lavatories to slop out their pots. **1978** 'A. Garve' *Counterstroke* I. xvi. 67 Prisoners rise at 6.30 a.m. Slop out. Clean their cells.

4. b. With *up*: to become intoxicated. *U.S. slang.*

1899 [implied at *slopping-up* s.v. *slopping *vbl. sb.* b]. **1916** 'W. Scott' *Seventeen Years in Underworld* xi. 64 The illgotten gains are spent 'slopping up' (getting drunk). **1919** *Bookman* (N.Y.) Apr. 208/2 Discuss the effect of the Prohibition Amendment on a white liner. What would be his chances after its passage of procuring sufficient powders to enable him to get slopped up (a) in the State of Maine, (b) in New York City? **1926** J. Black *You can't Win* ix. 108 No use takin' a bunch of thirsty bums along and stealin' money for them to slop up in some saloon the next day.

5. b. *colloq.* With *about*, *around*, etc.: to wander aimlessly, to move in a slovenly manner; to mess *about*.

1907 W. De Morgan *Alice-for-Short* xlv. 471 Old pictures do slop about the world in a vague way, till some aesthomenous person detects quality in them. **1922** M. Arlen '*Piracy*' III. xi. 236 When I said that you were too fine and I was too old to slop about Europe in a hole-and-corner way, I meant that this disorderly kind of life is unworthy of you. **1958** X. Fielding *Corsair Country* i. 22 So many of them slop about in cast-off men's shoes several sizes too big. **1973** *Times* 28 Nov. 13/6 Jimmy always says I mustn't slop about while I'm learning a piece, and I think that's good advice. **1982** *TV Times Mag.* 9–15 Oct. 47/1 At home..there's nothing she likes better than to 'slop around in anything that's comfy to wear'.

7. *U.S. dial.* and *colloq.* To feed (pigs or cattle) with slops.

1848 D. Drake *Pioneer Life in Kentucky* (1870) 92 To slop the cows..was another [labour]. **1920** C. Russell *Story of Nonpartisan League* 63 An angry representative told them to 'go home and slop the hogs'. **1947** *Time* 27 Jan. 21/2 Did you ever slop a hawg? **1966** R. G. Toepfer *Witness* iii. 19 First off, he'd better feed the chickens and slop the pigs. **1976** *New Yorker* 17 May 34/1 Your hosts.. will be up at dawn to slop their pig.

8. The vbl. stem in comb., as **slop-over** *U.S.*, an act or instance of slopping over; also *fig.*

1908 Z. Gale *Friendship Village* 275, I see 'em all sprinkled along comin' from the funeral—neighbours an' friends an' just folks—an' most of 'em livin' in Friendship peaceful an'—barrin' slopovers—doin' the level best they could. **1952** *Richmond* (Va.) *Times-Dispatch* 5 Jan. 17/4 The ordinary foams used in fire-fighting do the rest of the job. The job is easy because there is no slop-over, frothing or expansion of the hot oil layer. **1977** *Time* 9 May 26/2 My motive in everything I was saying or certainly thinking at the time was not to try to cover up a criminal action but—to be sure that as far as any slip-over—or should I say slop-over, I think, would be a better word—any slop-over in a way that would damage innocent people.

slope, *sb.*[1] Add: **1. a.** (Examples in *pl.* in *spec.* sense 'ski-slopes'.)

1924, etc. [see *nursery slope* s.v. *nursery 8 c]. **1972** P. A. Whitney *Snowfire* (1973) vi. 100 Snow bunny..was a term applied to beginners, usually female, who haunted the slopes. **1976** J. Farris *Fury* (1977) xviii. 306 He bought..clothing for the slopes and for après-ski.

c. (Earlier example.)

1863 *Harper's Mag.* Sept. 459/2 There is an entrance to the mine by means of an inclined plane, called a slope.

2. c. The tangent of the angle between a line and the horizontal; the ratio of the projection on the *y*-axis of an infinitesimal segment of a graph to its projection on the *x*-axis; the value of the first differential of some quantity, esp. with respect to distance.

1889 J. A. Fleming *Alternate Current Transformer* I. iii. 92 We shall call the trigonometrical tangent of the angle PTN, the slope of the tangent at the point P. *Ibid.* 93 The firm line curve is a curve of sines... The dotted line is a curve of sines, whose ordinate QN at any point represents the slope of the tangent at P on the original curve. **1898** *Proc. R. Soc.* LX. 478 If the slope of RR is positive we may say that large values of *x* are on the whole associated with large values of *y*, if it is negative large values of *x* are associated with small values of *y*. **1905** *Physical Rev.* XX. 174 The difference of temperature slope at different parts of the two bars was measured by means of thermoelectric couples. **1933** G. van Praagh *Introd. Calculus* i. 9 If *y* is a function of *x*, the differential coefficient or derivative of *y* with respect to *x* measures the rate of change of *y* with *x* for some particular value of x, x_1, and is the slope of the graph of f(x) at the point x_1. **1959** *Listener* 26 Feb. 371/2 The ball will slow up because of the gravitational 'slope'. **1971** *Physics Bull.* Feb. 86/1 A ln σ against $1/T$ plot should, at the temperature of conversion, exhibit a change of slope.

3. a. (Further examples, in sense of *slant *sb.*[1] 3 b.)

1928 L. F. H. Whitby *Med. Bacteriol.* iii. 46 Secondary cultures, or subcultures, are made by picking colonies from the plate and planting them on to slopes. **1951** —— & Hynes *Ibid.* (ed. 5) iii. 24 Slopes are made by allowing the medium to set in test-tubes or bottles tilted about 10° from the horizontal. **1974** R. K. Pawsey *Techniques with Bacteria* iv. 51 The loop is introduced to the base of the slope and a wavy line made on the slope with the loop gradually rising to the top.

5. *Electronics.* The mutual conductance of a valve (so called because it is numerically equal to the slope of one of the characteristic curves of the valve).

[**1918** *Wireless World* Nov. 458 (*heading*) A thermionic valve slopemeter. *Ibid.*, The effectiveness of a valve as a relay and amplifier depends primarily on the slope of the grid voltage-plate current characteristic.] **1932** *B.B.C. Year-bk.* 395 It is now the common practice of valve manufacturers to give a figure for the mutual conductance (or slope) of each of their products. **1948** C. A. Quarrington *Mod. Practical Radio & Television* (ed. 2) I. x. 78 The measurement of slope may be carried out under any conditions of grid voltage. **1953** A. H. W. Beck *Thermionic Valves* ix. 246 The mutual conductance or slope = $(\partial I_a/\partial V_g)$, V_a const.

6. *U.S. slang.* An oriental; more recently,

spec. a Vietnamese. (Abusive.) Cf. *slopehead* s.v. *SLOPE- a, *SLOPY *sb.*, and *SLANT *sb.*[1] 10.
1948 G. H. JOHNSTON *Death takes small Bites* v. 121 He seemed a hell of a lot more concerned with his bunch of flea-bitten slopes and his pots of medicine. **1966** *Publ. Amer. Dial. Soc. 1964* XLII. 45 *Slope* and *slopehead* were the most popular terms applied to all 'indigenous personnel' [in Korea in 1950–1]. **1966** *New Statesman* 25 Mar. 436/3 He confirms the soldiers' contempt for the Vietnamese ('slopes' and 'gooks'). **1969** [see *DINK *sb.*[3]]. **1978** R. THOMAS *Chinaman's Chance* iii. 35 All the Chinaman's gotta do is get into Saigon... Once he's in nobody's gonna notice him, because all those slopes look alike.

7. Used *attrib.* to designate a quantity defined as a rate of change or derivative instead of as a ratio; chiefly in *slope resistance*.
1931 L. B. TURNER *Wireless* vii. 203 In the metallic parts of the circuits..the slope resistance $\partial e/\partial i$ and Ohm's resistance e/i are equal. *Ibid.* viii. 235 It is necessary to allow..for the very small slope or differential permeability dB/dH of the core. **1971** *Gloss. Electrotechnical Power Terms* (*B.S.I.*) II. ii. 18 *Slope resistance*, value of forward resistance calculated from the slope of the straight line used when determining the threshold voltage from the forward current/voltage drop characteristics of a diode or thyristor in the on-state.

slope, *v.*[2] Add: **1. a.** (Earlier example.)
1830 *Palladium of Brit. N. Amer.* (Toronto) 29 Aug. 224/1 Bad climate indeed, wonder people dont all *slope*.
b. (Further examples.) Also, to move (*off*, *in*, etc.) in a leisurely manner; to amble (*in*, etc.); to depart surreptitiously, sneak off.
1876 TROLLOPE *Prime Minister* II. xvi. 265 You should have seen the policeman sloping over and putting himself in the way. **1922** JOYCE *Ulysses* 298 Come in, come on, he won't eat you... So Bloom slopes in with his cod's eye on the dog. **1980** *Private Eye* 26 Sept. 13/1 Anyway, he sloped in for a chinwag with the Boss.

slope-. Add: **a. slope circuit** *Electronics* = *slope filter* below; **slope current,** (*a*) an air current produced when wind is deflected upwards by a hill; (*b*) an ocean current that arises when the surface of the sea slopes as a result of wind action; **slope detection** *Electronics*, the detection of a frequency-modulated signal by means of a slope filter followed by a detector for amplitude-modulated signals; so **slope detector; slope filter** *Electronics*, a filter whose response increases or decreases more or less uniformly over the frequency range in which it is used; **slopehead** *U.S. slang* = *SLOPE *sb.*[1] 6 (abusive; cf. also *SLOPY *sb.*); **slope wash, slopewash** *Geomorphol.*, the downhill movement of soil or rock under the action of gravity assisted by running water not confined to a channel.
1966 M. SCHWARTZ et al. *Communication Systems & Techniques* v. 230 One side of a resonance curve is used as a 'slope circuit' in a frequency detector. **1978** S. HAYKIN *Communication Systems* iv. 342 Basically, a frequency discriminator consists of a slope circuit followed by an envelope detector. **1931** V. W. PAGÉ *Henley's ABC Gliding & Sailflying* vii. 150 This ascending air current, which is defined as a slope current, forms the source of energy for sailing flight. **1939** REVELLE & SHEPARD in P. D. Trask *Recent Marine Sediments* 277 In the Southern California region..the chief role in the transportation of débris must be played by tidal currents and non-permanent eddying 'slope currents' resulting from wind action. **1968** G. NEUMANN *Ocean Currents* iv. 195 The resulting slope of the sea surface produces horizontal pressure gradients in meridional direction which, in turn, cause slope currents to develop. **1949** B. GROB *Basic Television* xxi. 433 While slope detection is seldom used in television receivers for reception of the associated sound signal, the principle is important because it illustrates how an FM signal can be received with an AM system. **1978** D. CAMERON *Audio Technol. Systems* iv. 129 Economy-type FM tuners occasionally use some form of slope detection. **1958** A. W. KEEN *Frequency Modulation* iii. 83 This circuit, with the resonant frequency adjusted above the highest value of the f.m. signal-frequency, or below the lowest, was the first to be used..as an f.m. detector and is known as a 'slope' detector. **1977** F. G. STREMLER *Introd. Communication Systems* vi. 293 Although the slope detector is economical, it has a very limited range and its use is restricted to input signals with small frequency variations. **1937** *Proc. IRE* XXV. 474 The intermediate-frequency output of a superheterodyne receiver is fed through a limiter to a slope filter or conversion circuit which converts the frequency modulation into amplitude modulation. **1942** A. HUND *Frequency Modulation* i. 84 For the upper cutoff frequency..of the slope filter a voltage $2E$ is obtained at the output of this filter. **1966** Slopehead [see *SLOPE *sb.*[1] 6]. **1968** *Listener* 23 May 656/2 At Can Tho, two years ago, I heard American Air Force men sing a ballad about the Vietnamese, whom they then called 'slopeheads' or 'slopes'. **1938** C. F. S. SHARPE *Landslides & Related Phenomena* i. 8 The series can be represented as follows: Stream-flow (much water, small load, low angle), Slopewash, Sheetflood, Mudflow, Earth-flow, Debris-avalanche, Landslide (little water, large load, moderate to high angle). **1966** J. WYCKOFF *Rock, Time, & Landscape* iv. 71 As the ravine is cut deeper, its walls are worn back by weathering, mass wasting, and slope wash. **1978** *Nature* 23 Feb. 740/1 Slopewash seems important in sediment transport and fallen sandstone blocks and trees accumulate sediment on their upslope sides.

slopey: see *SLOPY *a.*

sloppage. For *rare*[−1] read *rare* and add: Also, the action of slopping.
1962 J. ONSLOW *Bowler-Hatted Cowboy* viii. 79, I filled the barrel among the boulders of the creek, and put a few sticks to float in it. These served as baffles and minimized the loss from sloppage.

sloppery. (Earlier example.)
1832 *Chambers's Edin. Jrnl.* I. 130/1 Their pails, and buckets, and brushes, and all their slopery, are just as rife..as they were a month earlier.

sloppily, *adv.* (Further examples.)
1909 *Chambers's Jrnl.* Sept. 572/2 The swish of the water licking sloppily against the yacht's side had a very lonesome sound. *a* **1911** D. G. PHILLIPS *Susan Lenox* (1917) II. xv. 354 She regarded his play as mediocre claptrap..fit only for the unthinking, sloppily sentimental crowd. **1942** E. PAUL *Narrow St.* xi. 83 In first class, one was slighted by the poverty-stricken employees, and served sloppily in the dining car, if any. **1952** S. KAUFFMANN *Philanderer* (1953) iii. 39 I've done it six summers now and its all a lot of crudney. Rush around and push shows together sloppily. **1979** *Country Life* 18 Jan. 134/3 The subject..is perilously near the sloppily mawkish.

sloppiness. (Further examples.)
1928 [see *animal-lover* s.v. *ANIMAL *sb.* and *a.* C. 1]. **1939** A. THIRKELL *Before Lunch* vii. 187 It had also crossed her mind that Daphne liked young Mr Bond, but..Daphne was all against what she called sloppiness. **1960** [see *SLOB *sb.*[1] 3]. **1980** *Maledicta* Summer 157 Because of the sloppiness of most original references..I have spent many years tracking down complete bibliographical data.

slopping, *vbl. sb.* Add: **b.** With advbs., as *-out* (see *SLOP *v.*[2] 1 c), *-over*; *slopping-up* (N. Amer. slang), a drinking-bout.
1899 'J. FLYNT' *Tramping* II. iv. 271 The bums intended to have a great 'sloppin'-up' (drinking-bout). **1922** H. KEMP *Tramping on Life* 133 'Slopping up' is what the tramps call a drinking jamboree. **1945** H. READ *Coat of Many Colours* lxii. 304 But there is no slopping-over of irrelevant emotion. **1948** *Richmond* (Va.) *Times-Dispatch* 9 Jan. 16/1 This [*sc.* a fulsome speech] is what is known among the hamlets of his native State as 'slopping over', and is considered as serious a breach of etiquette as..beating one's grandmother in public. **1955** *Times* 25 May 6/6 A hospital officer at the prison, said that on May 7 he was unlocking doors for 'slopping out' to be done. **1968** L. DEIGHTON *Only when I Larf* xviii. 232 You can tell a new warder; they just can't stand the smell of the slopping-out each morning. **1976** O. JACKS *Assassination Day* v. 80 A long term in prison..reviled him, from slopping out to terrible food.

sloppy, *a.* Add: **3. b.** *colloq.* Of the sea: choppy.
1970 *Studies in English* (Univ. of Cape Town) I. 26 Mushy, or sloppy surf, indicates a troubled, choppy water surface which would be difficult to ride. **1977** *Austral. Sailing* Jan. 69/1 However the sloppy Botany Bay conditions plus a series of freakish thunder storms made the series wide open.
4. b. *colloq.* Weakly sentimental.
1883 'MARK TWAIN' *Life on Miss.* xlviii. 482 The sloppy twaddle in the way of answers, furnished by Manchester. **1919** J. C. SNAITH *Love Lane* xxxi. 163 The Corporal stopped suddenly, took Melia in his arms and kissed her. It was a sloppy thing to do, unworthy of old married people. **1936** R. LEHMANN *Weather in Streets* ii. 53 Kate said with a funny look, as if she were saying something a tiny bit embarrassing, on the sloppy side. **1959** [see *DRIP *sb.* 3 c].
c. *Comb.*, as *sloppy-minded*, *-mindedness*.
1903 G. B. SHAW *Let.* 15 Sept. (1946) 18 Sloppyminded lunatics. **1965** B. SWEET-ESCOTT *Baker Street Irregular* ii. 43 He had a sharp tongue for the sloppy-minded and the half-baked. **1976** *Listener* 22 July 89/2 This final hymn to sloppy-mindedness.
6. Special collocations: **Sloppy Joe, sloppy joe** *colloq.*, (*a*) used *attrib.* and *absol.* to designate a loose-fitting sweater; (*b*) *U.S.*, a kind of hamburger in which the minced-beef filling is made into a kind of meat sauce; (*c*) a slovenly person.
1942 BERREY & VAN DEN BARK *Amer. Thes. Slang* § 87/32 *Sloppy Joe*, a loose cardigan sweater. **1943** *Knitted Outerwear Times* 15 May 1/1 You can't look like Lana Turner in a Sloppy Joe. Well—maybe Lana could. **1944** *Life* 15 May 67/1 (*caption*) Traditional garb of all school girls is 'Sloppy Joe' sweater, single string of pearls, pleated skirt, socks and shoes. **1958** E. HYAMS *Taking it Easy* II. 147 The young men were dressed in fashionable jeans and sloppy joes. **1961** R. E. CHURCH *Burger Cook Bk.* I. 42 *Sloppy Joes*...ground beef..onions..celery.. sweet pickle relish..brown sugar..Worcestershire sauce ..chili sauce..vinegar..green pepper..hamburger buns. **1961** WEBSTER, *Sloppy joe*.., a man who is negligent of his clothes or personal appearance. **1966** 'L. LANE' *ABZ of Scouse* 99 *Sloppy Joe*, a careless, shiftless person. **1974** *Washington Post* 1 Aug. D-1/2 Bill Myer..sits in the cafeteria..eating sloppy joes. **1980** *Ibid.* 17 Jan. B-5/1 Teen-agers wore a baggier variety [of sweater], often pairing 'sloppy joe' sweater..with pleated skirts.

slop-worker. Add: (Earlier example.) So **slop-working** *vbl. sb.*
1850 C. KINGSLEY *Cheap Clothes & Nasty* 22 It served as a blanket to the fever-stricken slopworker. *Ibid.* 26 Fresh victims are being driven by penury into the slop-working trade.

slopy, *a.* Add: Also **slopey. B.** *sb. U.S. slang.* An oriental, a Chinese. (Abusive.) Cf. *SLOPE *sb.*[1] 6, *slopehead* s.v. *SLOPE- a.
1948 G. H. JOHNSTON *Death takes small Bites* v. 107 'And you'll find it mighty hard, son, to convince Petroleum Developments that the fields aren't as important as a bunch of flea-bitten slopeys!' 'Well, go on.' 'Okay—as long as you understand that oil's a pretty important commodity—and Chinese ain't.' **1962** E. SNOW *Red China Today* (1963) xii. 85 One might assume that contempt for American imperialism would by now have produced Chinese equivalents of insulting American epithets such as slopeys, slant-eyes and chinks.

slorm, var. *SLAUM *v.*

slosh, *sb.* Add: **2. a.** Also, watery, sodden, or unappetizing food.
1923 BLUNDEN *Christ's Hospital* 201 *Slosh*, boiled rice. **1959** I. & P. OPIE *Lore & Lang. Schoolch.* ix. 163 Any kind of milk pudding is 'slosh' or 'baby pudding'. **1980** *Telegraph* (Brisbane) 16 Jan. 2/3 Honesty in advertising. A sign outside a Noosa Heads fast food shop 'American Slosh'.
b. (Earlier and later examples.)
1894 G. B. SHAW *Let.* 2 June (1965) I. 440 The assumption that society likes the sort of loyal, constitutional, jingo, pietistic slosh it has to pretend to like. **1915** E. M. FORSTER *Let.* 2 Aug. in P. N. Furbank *E. M. Forster* (1977) II. i. 19 He [*sc.* Rupert Brooke] was essentially hard: his hatred of slosh went rather too deep.
4. A blow, an act of striking.
1936 WODEHOUSE *Laughing Gas* x. 107, I recalled that I had noticed her hand quiver once or twice, as if itching for the slosh. **1977** *Daily Mirror* 12 Apr. 20/5 (*caption*) I'll give you such a slosh when I get up from here.
5. A game played on a billiard table with six coloured balls and one white, with which each player tries to pocket the coloured balls in a certain order.
1938 [see *HYPOMANIC *sb.*]. **1951** G. FRANKAU *Oliver Trenton* xxiii. 180 His brother-in-law was teaching her to play slosh. **1961** E. WAUGH *Unconditional Surrender* I. iv. 60 Guy spent the remaining hours of his fortieth birthday at Bellamy's playing 'slosh'. **1976** *Daily Tel.* 29 Apr. 18 The equipment was suitable not only for billiards but also for 'slosh'.

slosh, *v.*[1] Add: **3. b.** Of liquid: to splash; to flow in streams.
a **1953** E. O'NEILL *Touch of Poet* (1957) I. 35 When he attempts to raise the glass to his lips the water sloshes over his hand. **1969** L. MICHAELS *Going Places* 59, I might, as I toppled, blood sloshing through my lips, beg forgiveness. **1977** 'J. LE CARRÉ' *Honourable Schoolboy* i. 29 The rain poured off them..sloshing in red rivulets round their ankles.
4. *trans.* **a.** To pour or dash (liquid); to splash, throw, pour, or swallow carelessly. Also *fig.* Usu. with advbs. *colloq.*
1875 *Chicago Tribune* 3 Sept. 2/5 The Ring-paid scribblers and papers will slosh on the usual amount of whitewash. **1885** *Century Mag.* Nov. 63/2 If mining records was ever kep' as they'd ought to be, and not sloshed round so public like. **1899** G. B. SHAW *Let.* 26 Apr. (1972) II. 85, I dipped into the book.., and sloshed down a heap of words.. But it is a scandalously poor job of a review. **1926** E. FERBER *Show Boat* x. 221 Often he sloshed down whole gallons of river water before she came. **1936** M. MITCHELL *Gone with Wind* liv. 934 He picked up the decanter and sloshed a glassful, untidily. **1945** *Everybody's Digest* Aug. 86 He sloshed on his sombrero and went outta there, heatin' his axles. *a* **1953** E. O'NEILL *Touch of Poet* (1957) III. 100 He sloshes whiskey from the decanter into both their glasses. **1960** J. STROUD *Shorn Lamb* xxii. 239 It had..attic bedrooms and Harry used to go up there and slosh paint about. **1964** L. DEIGHTON *Funeral in Berlin* xv. 91 He laughed a deep, manly laugh and sloshed down some beer. **1978** 'J. LYMINGTON' *Waking of Stone* vi. 149 She sloshed out porridge into plates.
b. To pour or dash liquid upon, to douse. *colloq.*
1912 G. W. DEEPING *Sincerity* ii. 18, I can't stand these counter-bouncing little beasts like Threadgold. He's only fit to slosh people with treacle and water. **1917** H. GARLAND *Son of Border* xxviii. 371, I generally managed to slosh myself with cold water from the well. **1979** *Amer. Poetry Rev.* Mar./Apr. 26/2 Rain began to pelt the cars and slosh the yard and spatter down the flowers.
5. *colloq.* To hit, to strike; to crush, to defeat. Also *fig.* Cf. SLASH *v.* 2 b.
1890 KIPLING *Barrack-Room Ballads* (1892) 11 We sloshed you with Martinis, an' it wasn't 'ardly fair; But for all the odds agin' you, Fuzzy-Wuz, you broke the square. **1904** E. NESBIT *Phoenix & Carpet* v. 94, I say, slosh 'em..and get clear off with the swag. **1914** C. MACKENZIE *Sinister Street* II. IV. ii. 881, I wouldn't half slosh his jaw in, if I was a man. **1918** R. P. FLEMING *Let.* in D. Hart-Davis *Peter Fleming* (1974) ii. 33, I saw one [adder] coiled up asleep in some bushes, and picked it up by the tail..and we took it into the open and sloshed it. **1921** A. S. M. HUTCHINSON *If Winter Comes* II. vii. 138 These Balkan chaps set to, to slosh Turkey. **1933** *Punch* 18 Oct. 421/1 'I wish to contradict the rumour that I wish to slosh Sir Stafford Cripps,' says Mr. Ernest Bevin. **1967** N. FREELING *Strike out where not Applicable* 75 Somebody sloshed him, if I may be allowed the word. *a* **1974** R. CROSSMAN *Diaries* (1975) I. 399 Characteristically enough, at the end the committee chairman who had been wildest in his wrath moved the vote of thanks and said, 'Well, we have to have a good go sometimes at sloshing our Labour Minister.' **1977** 'J. GASH' *Judas Pair* x. 118 I've sloshed her..sometimes when she'd got me mad.

sloshed (slǫʃt), *ppl. a. slang.* [f. SLOSH *v.*[1] + -ED[1].] Drunk, tipsy. Also *absol.*

1946 *Word Study* May 3/1 Synonyms for *drunk* now current in England..*tiddley, oiled* or *well oiled, sloshed.* **1952** 'R. GORDON' *Doctor in House* xi. 120 Tony, you're sloshed already. **1966** L. SOUTHWORTH *Felon in Disguise* viii. 118 The D.S.O. was due to an overdose of Italian vino. I was too sloshed to care. **1978** R. LUDLUM *Holcroft Covenant* iii. 41 They drank a *great* deal... They appeared quite sloshed. **1979** *Logophile* III. II. 17/1 It started as a pub game, played for the amusement of the slightly sloshed.

sloshing, *vbl. sb.* (In Dict. s.v. SLOSH *v.*[1] 3.) Add: **2.** = HIDING *vbl. sb.*[2]

1931 T. R. G. LYELL *Slang, Phrase & Idiom* 693 He ran up against a gang of roughs in the street last night, and they gave him an awful sloshing!

sloshy, *a.* **1.** (Earlier example.)

1797 B. HAWKINS *Let.* 22 Feb. in *Coll. Georgia Hist. Soc.* (1916) IX. 88 Flat piney sloshy land.

sloshy, *a.* Add: (Further examples.) Also, sloppy, sentimental.

1913 A. LUNN *Harrovians* ii. 35 Because..if they had form games some sloshy old chaw [*Note*, i.e. Old Harrovian, a term of affection] would write to the papers. **1920** *Glasgow Herald* 30 Apr. 9 They are living not merely upon vegetables, but sloshy vegetables. **1924** E. F. BENSON *David of King's* vii. 136 'Positively his last appearance,' said David. 'Rather theatrical, but not sloshy.' **1933** *Daily Mirror* 26 Oct. 12/4 'Sloshy talk' is simply the perpetration of such phrases as 'too, too marvellous' and 'utterly divine'. **1949** [see *BOOB *sb.* 4]. **1957** D. PIPER *English Face* x. 244 Broader, indeed sloshy, effects were needed by an emulator of Reynolds, Daniel Gardner. **1978** C. STORR *Winter's End* ii. 37 You thought it was like in those rotten stories... I've read enough sloshy stuff in my time.

slot, *sb.*[2] Add: **2. b.** Also (*slang*), a slot-machine.

1950 R. BISSELL *Stretch on River* xiii. 135 The slots are going night and day. **1978** M. PUZO *Fools Die* xviii. 197 The slots usually brought in a profit of about a hundred thousand dollars a week.

c. The middle of the semi-circular or horse-shoe-shaped desk at which a newspaper's sub-editors work, occupied by the chief sub-editor. *U.S. slang.*

1917 H. GRANT *Two Sides of Atlantic* iii. 44 The man who 'sits in the slot' (the chief-sub.), will know for a certainty that the decision of 'Bill' to invade Windy City will automatically entail the departure of all who 'hunt' with Bill. **1923** [see *RIM *sb.*[1] 3 c]. **1970** R. K. KENT *Lang. Journalism* 123 *Slot*, the middle of the horseshoe-shaped copy desk where the news editor or copy editor (sometimes called *slotman*) sits. To be *in the slot* is to be in charge of the copy desk.

d. *Aeronaut.* A linear gap in an aerofoil, running parallel to its leading edge, which allows the passage of air from the lower to the upper surface and so increases the lift. Cf. *SLAT *sb.*[1] 4 d.

1920 *Flight* XII. 1124/1 It has already been mentioned that the slot separating the false from the main leading edge is contracted towards the upper surface. **1936** *Discovery* Mar. 73/2 The Weick and Hammond have..a control which is a combination of slot and aileron. This is intended to obviate the need of a rudder. **1960** C. H. GIBBS-SMITH *Aeroplane* II. 221 Ingenious as the machine undoubtedly was,..there is no visible trace of any slots, or of any wires or other gear attached to, or passing anywhere near, the wings that could be associated with slots.

e. The vulva. *coarse slang.* Cf. *SLIT *sb.* 1 d.

1942 BERREY & VAN DEN BARK *Amer. Thes. Slang* § 121/38 *Female pudendum*...shape, slot, snatch, tail. **1977** MILLER & SWIFT *Words & Women* vii. 117 No such positive connotations attach to prick, but even this word does not convey the absolute scorn of slit, slot, snatch, and gash.

f. A marked-out parking space. Chiefly *U.S.*

1944 R. CHANDLER *Lady in Lake* xiii. 74, I..parked in one of the diagonal slots at the side of the Prescott Hotel. **1968** A. DIMENT *Great Spy Race* iii. 35, I shunted my car into a small slot near the fire station. **1978** R. LUDLUM *Holcroft Covenant* xvii. 195 Holcroft backed the car out of its slot, then drove through the entrance posts onto the country road.

g. A prison cell; also, = *CELL *sb.*[1] 4 b. *Austral. slang.*

1947 *Pix* 20 Sept. 15 *Peter* or *slot*, cell. **1969** *Sydney Sunday Tel.* 21 Dec. 14/4 'I'd hate to try and tot up the number of hooks and badges (rank and good conduct insignia) that little lot's whipped away since the ship came out.'.. 'And what about the slot (cells) they've dished out. It must run into years!' **1976** *Cleo* Aug. 33 Some of the old heads are in the slot, he says. The slot is jail.

5. b. *Austral.* and *N.Z.* A crevasse.

1959 *Tararua* XIII. 46 *Slot*, for a crevasse, sometimes used by climbers, is not necessary and is merely slang. **1968** K. WEATHERLY *Roo Shooter* 58 This was the roughest bit of country yet—short, miserable, scrubby trees and stringy bushes; broken country, high slots and hollows full of water.

5*. *fig.* **a.** A position in a list, hierarchy, system, or scheme; a position to be filled; a category; a place or division in a timetable, esp. in broadcasting.

1942 BERREY & VAN DEN BARK *Amer. Thes. Slang* § 672/10 Rank or rating in league, division, percentage ladder, slot. **1947** AUDEN *Nones* (1952) 64 Among those staring blemishes that mark War's havocking slot. **1956** *Sat. Rev.* (U.S.) 2 June 50/2 No management slot is harder to fill today than the research director's post. **1956** W. H. WHYTE *Organization Man* II. viii. 104 Sales work..is about the only slot they would qualify for if they took English or history. **1964** *Economist* 25 Jan. 327/2 There is a 'slot' in the market for a medium-range supersonic airliner. *Ibid.* 20 June 1369/3 The 'slots' once gained, were never given up [by regional TV stations]. **1966** *Listener* 6 Oct. 518/1 It seems perverse that when the Monday evening 'slot' has been extended to as much as two hours for lesser fry, it should be made to stand at ninety minutes for *The Merchant of Venice* (Home Service, September 26). **1967** *Ibid.* 6 Apr. 467/3 'Theology, during the great controversies of the mid-nineteenth century, was anti-scientific.'.. (Try fitting Newman or even Kingsley into that slot!) **1969** *Times* 21 Nov. 23/5 How serious is the situation at Heathrow?.. There are no spare 'slots' into which landing and taking-off airliners can be fitted. **1970** *Daily Tel.* 3 Sept. 13/2 The first Radio London slot each day will be from 6.45 a.m. to 9 a.m., a blend of news, music, personalities and information called 'Rush Hour'. **1972** *Business Week* 18 Mar. 81/1 Although he held a top slot at SNIA, he was lured away for the even bigger job at Alitalia. **1973** C. BONNINGTON *Next Horizon* xxii. 298 An Italian millionaire..had permission for an autumn reconnaissance in 1972 to be followed by a spring attempt in 1973. Owing to sickness he gave up his autumn slot. **1974** *Guardian* 26 Mar. 14/1 Welland's script was accepted by the BBC for its 'Play For Today' slot. **1976** *National Observer* (U.S.) 24 Apr. 19A/3 Stanford has 10,009 applications for 1,450 freshman slots next fall. **1976** A. DAVIS *Television: First Forty Years* viii. 86 Suitable slots are normally of 90 to 120 minutes, with time for commercials to be taken out of this, but films are rarely obliging enough to run to exactly the length required. **1977** *Film & Television Technician* Mar. 6/4 The British programme-makers are actually pushing the Americans out of the number one slot in key Western Europe and Scandinavian countries. **1977** *Times* 25 Aug. 1/8 The importance of taking a flight 'slot' when it comes up. **1978** M. PUZO *Fools Die* xii. 131 After six months of free-lance work he offered me a magazine editor slot. **1980** *Jrnl. R. Soc. Arts* July 529/2 Many place Kokoschka in the slot 'Expressionist'.

b. *spec.* in *Linguistics* (see quot. 1960). Also *attrib.* and *Comb.*

1957 K. L. PIKE in *General Linguistics* Spring 36 The characteristics of a grammeme which in many instances are perhaps most readily recognized in current descriptions of a grammemic system are the functional slot with its class filler. **1959** [see *DIAPHONEME]. **1959** W. H. MITTINS in Quirk & Smith *Teaching of English* iv. 116 Some teachers..seek to achieve a kind of concentration and continuity by methodically working through batteries of vocabulary exercises in slot-filling..and the like. **1960** ELSON & PICKETT *Beginning Morphology-Syntax* ii. 16 A *slot* is a grammatical position or function (e.g. subject) which is *filled* by a list of mutually substitutable items (e.g. nouns). The tagmeme is the unit of grammatical arrangement involved in or resulting from this slot-class correlation. *Ibid.* 37 Make a chart with the slot names.., listing fillers below each slot name. *Ibid.* iii. 40 As a filler class they can only be united by some such term as 'subject slot fillers'. **1962** W. A. STEWART in F. A. Rice *Study of Role of Second Languages in Asia, Africa, & Latin Amer.* 21 Under various conditions, the same language may occupy more than one functional slot. **1964** E. BACH *Introd. Transformational Gram.* iii. 44 But the basic points of the slot-symbol and class-symbol description and the lack of context-sensitive rules remain untouched. **1964** *Language* XL. 314 American slot-and-filler grammatical description. **1965** *Word Study* Feb. 3/1 Word groups filling noun slots and verb slots comprise the chief building blocks of utterances. **1970** B. M. H. STRANG *Hist. English* 25 When, through cross-cultural experience, speakers of one language are conscious of an 'empty slot' in their language which is filled in another language.., they may..fill the gap by borrowing the filler. **1972** *Archivum Linguisticum* III. 22 The lexical co-occurrence restrictions which hold between the fillers of predicate and subject slots are different from the restrictions which hold between the fillers of predicate and instrument slots. **1972** *Computers & Humanities* VII. 14 Some recent publications include..'Computerized Japanese Haiku', which describes how the poems are created by slot-filling. **1972** M. L. SAMUELS *Linguistic Evolution* 65 A new slot-filler may arise from borrowing or creation, or the 'pull' of the empty slot may hasten a new process of extension in another existing word. **1981** *Word 1980* XXXI. 230 He makes use of the slot-and-filler infrastructure, characteristic of tagmemics.

7. b. Special combs., as **slot aerial, antenna,** an aerial in the form of one or more slots in a metal surface; **slot-back,** *N. Amer. Football,* (the position of) a back who stands behind a gap in the forward line; **slot car,** a miniature racing car, powered by electricity, which travels in a slot in a track; **slot-machine:** see sense 6 b in Dict.; also *fig.* and *attrib.*; **slot man** *U.S. slang,* a newspaper's chief sub-editor, a news editor; **slot racer** = **slot car*; so **slot-race** *v. intr.*, **slot-racing** *vbl. sb.*; **slot radiator** = **slot aerial*; **slot seam,** a clothing seam reinforced underneath; also, = *channel seam* s.v. *CHANNEL *sb.*[1] 12; **slot television,** a coin-operated television; **slot winding** *Electr. Engin.*, an armature winding in which the conductors are laid in slots or grooves in the core; so **slot-wound** *a.*

1946 *Jrnl. Inst. Electr. Engineers* XCIII. IIIA. 626/1 It would appear that slot aerials are capable of making a contribution to the problem of designing a radiating element that produces circular polarization in all directions of radiation. **1956** *B.B.C. Handbk. 1957* 56 To keep staff up to date, training supplements on such items as slot aerials, television lighting, frequency modulation, and other developments are issued. **1946** *Jrnl. Inst. Electr. Engineers* XCIII. IIIA. 749/2 In spite of the length of the slot antenna, this load can be treated as lumped at the position of the centre of the slot. **1975** D. G. FINK *Electronics Engineers' Handbk.* XVIII. 43 Very low profile slot antennas utilizing shallow cavities fed by coaxial cables have been designed for aircraft use. **1959** *Washington Post* 21 Nov. A14/4 He helped develop Elroy (Crazy-legs) Hirsch into a slotback with the Los Angeles Rams. **1970** *Globe & Mail* (Toronto) 28 Sept. 18/2 Slotback Dick Smith took a 12-yard pass from Sonny Wade in the second quarter for one Montreal touchdown. **1974** *Anderson* (S. Carolina) *Independent* 24 Apr. 5B/1 At slot back.. Rut Livingston..has the makings of a great player. **1966** *Maclean's Mag.* 22 Jan. 9A The track on which slot cars race is a tabletop affair. **1971** *Publishers' Weekly* 27 Sept. 129/3 (Advt.), *The New Zealand Boys' Book of Crafts, Pets, Sports and Hobbies* by Anthony Harvey and Peter Snell provides information on..model-making, rugby, sailing, slot cars, and wood-carving. **1891** *Brooklyn Daily Eagle* Index July–Dec. 155/2 Slot machine. **1892** [in Dict., sense 6 b]. *a* **1910** 'O. HENRY' *Rolling Stones* (1912) 196 Mac McGowan was to..drop his silver talent into the slit of the slot-machine of fame and fortune that gives up reputation and dough. **1929** *Sun* (Baltimore) 15 Nov. 1/6 'Spike' O'Donnell,..beer baron and bootlegger,..is acting as his own lawyer in the 'slot machine' trial. **1933** C. DAY LEWIS *Magnetic Mountain* 12 Eating chocolate creams from the slot-machines. **1957** *Observer* 1 Sept. 13/4 At Las Vegas the plane empties of passengers who, with cold passion, play the slot-machines in the concourse until ten minutes later, when it is time to go. **1978** J. WAINWRIGHT *Jury People* lxiv. 216 A slot-machine arcade. One of these pin-table places. **1928** *Amer. Speech* IV. 134 Presiding over the copy readers is the 'head of the desk' or 'slot man'. His chief duty is to judge the amount of space to be given any 'story' or news article and to designate the size of the 'headline' or 'head'. **1972** Slot man [see *REVISE *sb.* 3]. **1966** *Daily Progress* (Charlottesville, Va.) 4 Feb. 13 (*caption*) J. P. Evans..and Ed Johnson get ready to put their slot racers through a gruelling five-lap race. **1965** *Wall St. Jrnl.* 27 Aug. 22 A rapidly growing number of Americans..have caught the slot-racing bug. **1967** J. SYMONS *Man who killed Himself* I. vi. 69, I haven't joined a slot racing club... I like slot racing on my own. **1946** *Jrnl. Inst. Electr. Engineers* XCIII. IIIA. 748/2 When slot radiators which were very loosely coupled to the guide had to be measured, standing-wave measurements of single slots became unreliable. **1967** *IEEE Trans. Antennas & Propagation* XV. 826/1 If the boundaries of the dielectric cover are kept within the local reactive fields of the slot, the primary effect upon the radiation is a change in the impedance of the slot radiator. **1918** E. & M. WALLBANK *Dress Cutting & Making* x. 69 *Slot Seam*, in which both edges are overlapped on to a wrap piece or 'slot'. **1968** J. IRONSIDE *Fashion Alphabet* 99 *Channel Seam* (*slot seam*): to make a channel or slot seam, the seam turnings should be basted together. An additional strip of fabric should be laid under the basted seam and should then be machined approximately half-inch or so away from the basted seam line. **1958** *Kinematograph Weekly* (Studio Rev.) 29 May p. iv/3 If slot television gets a real hold on the public, commercial cinema..is doomed. **1977** *Grimsby Even. Tel.* 26 May 3/8 (Advt.), Slot television, bargains galore. **1900** *Jrnl. Brit. Inst. Electr. Engineers* XXIX. 802 A hole-winding produces a somewhat smoother pole than a slot-winding. **1968** FINK & CARROLL *Standard Handbk. Electr. Engineers* (ed. 10) VI. 10 Fractional slot windings, where the number of slots per phase per pole is not an integer, have unequal coil groups. **1931** L. B. TURNER *Wireless* xiv. 471 The calculation of E.M.F. in a slot-wound dynamo.

slot, *v.*[2] Add: **4.** To thread (material, etc.) *with* (ribbon).

1922 JOYCE *Ulysses* 344 She had four dinky sets,.. each set slotted with different coloured ribbons. **1975** G. HOWELL *In Vogue* 243 The flowerpot hat..in coffee cream satin slotted with a brown ribbon.

5. *intr.* **a.** To admit of being threaded through a hole or slot.

1928 *Daily Express* 9 Jan. 13 The unique collar slots through the buckle.

b. *fig.* To fit *in* or *into*; to take up a position *in* a space or slot (*SLOT *sb.*[2] 5*).

1940 H. G. WELLS *Babes in Darkling Wood* I. i. 40 We are not the people we were yesterday. We slot into the new order. **1965** *New Statesman* 7 May 715/1 Personally I never knew yet quite what I was nor where I slotted in; I suppose I was ready for total identification somewhere, but never where I happened to be. **1966** 'A. HALL' *9th Directive* xx. 187, I..watched the police-car slot in between us and the car ahead; then it pulled out and one lost it. **1971** *Daily Tel.* 9 June 2/4 Initially the trains will operate at a maximum 125 mph to 'slot in' with new-type conventional diesels. **1976** *Times* 15 Apr. 27/1 The French company augments its range in Britain with the GTL, which slots in between the 956cc TL and the high-performance TS. **1976** *Ilkeston Advertiser* 10 Dec. 19/1 They produced a great team display with new boy Henshaw slotting in well. **1980** S. BRETT *Dead Side of Mike* xiii. 149 There are quite a few details which haven't slotted into position yet, but..the outline's right.

6. *trans.* **a.** To fit (something) *in* or *into* a position, space, or slot (*SLOT *sb.*[2] 5*).

1966 A. BATTERSBY *Math. in Management* viii. 211 Certain complex calculations..are available in a form which can be readily 'slotted in' to bigger programs. **1968** *Listener* 4 Jan. 27/1 The television slotting system.. separates programmes into categories... But slotting also creates a climate in which surprise is unwelcome... Slotted into one of the arts programme times the Beatles' film would hardly have raised a whisper. **1970** O. NORTON

Dead on Prediction i. 14, I..managed to slot the Mini into the corner of the temporary car park. **1971** *Country Life* 8 Apr. 801/1 The richly Italianate façade of the Finsbury Bank for Savings..was slotted into the terrace in 1840. **1972** M. WILLIAMS *Inside Number 10* xiii. 339 The National Agent went to great pains to slot this function into the election tour. **1973** *Scotsman* 13 Feb. 8/4 Steady progress up the scale leads to a salary of £3638. It is inconceivable that the Bishop of Bath and Wells..would be slotted in at the minimum. **1977** C. DEXTER *Silent World N. Quinn* viii. 71 He slotted the book back into its shelf. **1977** *Irish Times* 8 June 8/4 Why, for instance, wasn't Sile de Valera slotted into this constituency once Vivion de Valera stood down?

b. *spec.* in *Football.* To kick (the ball, a pass) accurately through a narrow space, esp. *in* or *into* the goal; to score (a goal) in this way. Also *absol.*

1970 F. C. AVIS *Soccer Dict.* (ed. 3) 86 *Slot in*, to pass, or to score a goal, by the very skilful placing of the ball through a narrow gap between players. **1974** *Observer* 1 Sept. 18/4 Boersma hardly needed to leave the ground to slot his..header into the net. **1975** *Liverpool Echo* (Football ed.) 1 Feb. 1/4 United took the lead through Jones who slotted home. **1975** *Evening News* (Edinburgh) (Sports Final ed.) 15 Mar. 10/2 McDowell slotted the ball into the net. **1977** *Wandsworth Borough News* 7 Oct. 10/1 He beat Newton, centre-half Robinson and goalkeeper Stevenson before slotting the ball in. **1978** *Cornish Guardian* 27 Apr. 5/3 The home team were showing good touches and Hargreaves slotted in a third goal after Barker had sent a good shot screaming goalwards

slote, var. *SLUIT.

slotted, *ppl. a.* Add: **1.** (Further examples in *Aeronaut.*: cf. *SLOT *sb.*[2] 2 d.) Also, *slotted armature* (Electr. Engin.), an armature having slots or grooves to contain the conductors; a slot-wound armature; *slotted line*, a length of coaxial cable or wave guide having a slot running lengthwise in its outer conductor to receive a probe for investigating standing waves.

1902 *Encycl. Brit.* XXVII. 582/2 These wires lie side by side in the smooth-core armature with one layer, or one on the top of the other if there are two layers, as is usually the case in slotted armatures. **1921** *Jrnl. R. Aeronaut. Soc.* XXV. 274 (*heading*) Flap experiments with slotted wings. *Ibid.* 275 (*caption*) Slotted aerofoil with flap. **1926** *Ibid.* XXX. 357 With a combination of slotted aileron and forward aerofoil, complete lateral control at the stall has been obtained. **1935** C. G. BURGE *Compl. Bk. Aviation* 240/1 The Handley-Page Slotted Wing is one of the best-known devices for preventing this stalling, at least within the normal range of angles which an aeroplane is likely to reach. **1947** E. A. YUNKER et al. in H. J. Reich *Very High-Frequency Techniques* II. xxiv. 592 A notched coaxial cable is a cheap and easily made substitute for a slotted line and is satisfactory for measurements not requiring great accuracy. **1966** *McGraw-Hill Encycl. Sci. & Technol.* VII. 44/2 A commercial slotted line for measuring impedances at the lower microwave frequencies is shown. **1973** J. D. EDWARDS *Electr. Machines* ii. 53 The basic machine equations are the same for a slotted armature as for a smooth cylindrical armature, provided that the total pole flux..is unchanged. **1977** *R.A.F. Yearbk.* 31/2 On rolling or overshooting, the lifting power of the wing with full slotted flaps is an experience to behold.

2. Threaded through a hole or slot.

1932 *Woman & Beauty* Apr. 27 A slotted scarf gives a great many opportunities for freshening up an everyday frock.

slotting, *vbl. sb.* Add: **4. a.** The action of threading through a hole or slot. Also, ornamentation with threading.

1923 *Daily Mail* 18 June 1 Filet lace and hem stitching, finished ribbon slotting at low waist line.

b. The action or condition of fitting in a slot (*SLOT *sb.*[2] 5*). Also *attrib.*

1959 *Washington Post* 26 Dec. A19/1 Ratings have climbed despite the show's unhappy time slotting between 'Laramie' and 'Bronco', without a big show preceding it on the network. **1968** [see *SLOT *v.*[2] 6].

slouch, *sb.* Add: **1. b.** For *U.S. slang* read 'orig. *U.S. slang*' and add earlier and later examples.

1796 A. BARTON *Disappointment* III. i. 73 He's no slouch of a fellow. **1840** C. F. HOFFMAN *Greyslaer* II. II. x. 23 You are no slouch of a woodsman to carry a yearling of such a heft as that. **1924** GALSWORTHY *White Monkey* III. x. 281 'No slouch of a miracle!' he thought, 'modern town life!' **1956** *People* 13 May 4/5 But Tony, no slouch when it comes to showmanship, helped it along by wearing..a rose brocade dinner jacket. **1961** *Coast to Coast 1959–60* 42 Speaking of Bradman, Mr Stulpnagel, they say you were no mean slouch with the bat yourself. **1967** G. F. FIENNES *I tried to run a Railway* ii. 7 He, Happy, himself no slouch at basic English, was revolted by George's language. **1978** R. HOLLES *Spawn* v. 42 He was making his pile... He's certainly no slouch in the business world.

slouch, *a.* **3.** (Earlier example.)

1812 E. WEETON *Let.* 15 June (1969) II. 34, I had on a small slouch straw hat, a grey stuff jacket, and petticoat.

slouch-eared, *a.* (Later example.)

1855 *Trans. Mich. Agric. Soc.* VI. 511 The original English breed [of hogs]—those long-legged,..slouch-eared, big-headed..animals.

slough, *sb.*[1] **4.** For *U.S.* read *N. Amer.* and add: (Earlier and *Canad.* examples.) Also, a side channel of a river, or a natural channel that is only sporadically filled with water.

1714 *Rep. Record Commissioners* (Boston Registry Dept.) (1877) III. 217 Between his old house & the Slough or Small Bridge. **1858** W. P. BLAKE *Rep. Geol. Reconnaissance in California* i. 10 There lay outstretched the broad and green Tulares—great swamps or lowlands overgrown with rushes and threaded by the sinuous channels and sloughs of the river. **1859** *Brit. Colonist* (Victoria, B.C.) 17 Dec. 3/2 At Old Langley, the slough is entirely frozen up. **1888** D. M. GORDON *Mountain & Prairie* 143 At the same time there are many sloughs, or 'slews' so-called, where part of the river flows by some devious and half-hidden course. **1913** THOMAS & WATT *Improvement of Rivers* (ed. 2) I. i. 30 In valleys with narrow bottom lands the result is a slough or drain close to the hills which returns the water to the main channel further down, one slough succeeding another along the valley. **1924** M. H. MASON *Arctic Forests* 225 There was an Indian toboggan trail on the long slough, past Jenny Island up to the eight-mile point. **1932** C. R. LONGWELL et al. *Textbk. Geol.* I. iii. 60 Most [short cuts]..are abandoned as the flood subsides and are left as sloughs, which are slowly undercut as the meander shifts downstream. **1939** W. HÄNTZSCHEL in P. D. Trask *Recent Marine Sediments* III. 202 The sloughs (Priele) on the tidal flats are comparable to rivers and brooks. *Ibid.*, Where the range in tides in Jade Bay is as high as 3·6 meters, the sloughs are deeply incised. **1962** W. STEGNER *Wolf Willow* I. i. 8 In deep sloughs tules have rooted, and every such pond is dignified with mating mallards. **1970** LEOPOLD & WOLMAN in G. H. Dury *Rivers & River Terraces* vii. 199 Opposite the gravel island is a slough aligned with a grassed depression. Both features undoubtedly carry water during flood flow. **1974** P. GZOWSKI *Bk. about this Country* 20, I remember seeing a bunch of geese sitting in a little slough. **1976** *Prof. Paper U.S. Geol. Survey* No. 929. 150/2 The ecological model is designed to relate the wildlife in the Shark River Slough to the availability of food and water.

5. slough bass, for def. read: a black bass of the genus *Micropterus* (earlier example); **slough grass,** for def. read: one of several coarse grasses of swampy ground, esp. a species of the genus *Muhlenbergia* (earlier and later examples); **slough hay** *Canad.*, (hay made from) slough grass.

1877 C. HALLOCK *Sportsman's Gaz.* 276 Locally they are termed perch..slough bass, etc. **1860** *Trans. Ill. Agric. Soc.* IV. 488 Then [I] make a band of whatever material I have at hand, (slough grass is preferable). **1907** L. H. BAILEY *Cycl. Amer. Agric.* II. 454/1 In wet and swampy places, slough-grass (*Spartina*) furnishes a supply of coarse hay. **1980** *Country Life* 13 Nov. 1819/3 The hay is made of wild slough grass. **1934** G. BETTANY *Valley of Lost Gold* 264 In the tall slough hay beside them orange lilies raised their heads waist high. **1948** T. ONRAET *Sixty Below* 135, I have often seen them kneeling on their forelegs to feed in comfort on short willows and slough hay. **1955** *Sentinel-Courier* (Pilot Mound, Manitoba) 31 Mar. 4/1 (Advt.), For sale—Baled slough hay, wire tied. **1968** S. E. ROBERTS *Of Us & Oxen* ii. 14 This 'slough hay' is said to be less nutritious than the 'upland hay' cut from buffalo grass.

slough, *v.*[1] Add: **a.** Also without *up.* (Earlier example.)

1861 in *Daily Colonist* (Victoria, B.C.) (1911) 16 Apr. 1/6 Several of the wagons while conveying passengers and freight from the steamer on Sunday night became sloughed and the passengers were compelled to 'foot it' to town.

b. *slang.* To imprison, to lock (*up*). Usu. in passive.

1848 *Ladies' Repository* Oct. 317/1 *Slough*, to lock. **1894** 'J. FLYNT' in *Century Mag.* Feb. 518/2 I've boozed around this town..for seven years, and I've not been sloughed up yet. **1926** J. BLACK *You can't Win* vii. 87 They'll..haul us over to Martinez..an' slough us in the county jail. **1935** A. J. POLLOCK *Underworld Speaks* 108/2 *Sloughed*, arrested.

slough, *v.*[2] Add: **5.** *intr.* Of soil, rock, etc.: to fall *away* or slide *down* into an adjoining hole or depression.

1897 W. STARLING *Floods of Mississippi* i. 14/1 Water leaking through the old bank infiltrates the new earth and it sloughs away bodily. **1942** W. FAULKNER *Go down, Moses* 30 As though the whole mound had stooped roaring down at him—the entire overhang sloughed. **1955** HENNES & EKSE *Fund. Transportation Engin.* ii. 30 The processes of weathering tend to loosen surface material and cause it to slough and drift down any slope greater than the angle of repose of the dry loose material. **1957** A. C. CLARKE *Deep Range* v. 54 Sometimes, in deep ocean waters far from the eternal rain of silt which sloughs down from the edges of the continents, it was possible to see as much as two hundred feet. **1974** P. L. MOORE et al. *Drilling Practices Manual* iii. 46 Shale sloughs into the hole.

sloughed *ppl. a.* (further example).

1897 W. STARLING *Floods of Mississippi* i. 14/1 A good thick dressing of brush is laid on the sloughed mass.

sloughi, var. *SALUKI.

sloughing, *vbl. sb.* Add: **3.** The collapse of soil or rock into a hole or down a bank.

1897 W. STARLING *Floods of Mississippi* i. 14/1 There is no incident..more alarming..than the sloughing or slipping of the inside slope of a levee. **1948** TERZAGHI & PECK *Soil Mech. in Engin. Pract.* viii. 336 To prevent sloughing of the toes of the slopes, the small quantity of water that flows through the gaps between the wells is removed. **1957** *Nature* 13 July 100 (*heading*) Vernal sloughing of sludge deposits in a sewage effluent channel. **1972** L. M. HARRIS *Introd. Deepwater Floating Drilling Operations* vi. 90 On completion of drilling, the hole is normally filled with gel-water mud to prevent sloughing and fill.

sloughing, *ppl. a.* Add: **2.** Of soil or rock: collapsing, sliding.

1974 P. L. MOORE et al. *Drilling Practices Manual* iii. 46 It has been common practice to reduce water-loss when sloughing shale becomes a problem.

slougi, var. *SALUKI.

Slovak, *sb.* and *a.* Add: Now usu. with pronunc. (slō^{u}·væk). **A. 1.** For 'dwelling.. Hungary' read 'dwelling in Slovakia, formerly part of Hungary, now the Slovak Socialist Republic and part of Czechoslovakia'.

Slovakian *a.* and *sb.*: now usu. with pronunc. (slovæ·kiăn); **Slovakish** *a.* and *sb.* (earlier examples).

1850 'TALVI' *Hist. View Lang. Lit. Slavic Nations* III. i. 217 A voluminous Slovakish dictionary. *Ibid.* 219 Books written in Slovakish.

sloven, *sb.* Add: **5.** *Canad.* (See quots. 1895, 1941.) Also called *sloven-wagon.*

1895 *Dialect Notes* I. 381 *Sloven*, a low truck wagon. **1907** *Canad. Mag.* XXIX. 442/1 It is called a 'sloven-waggon' (doubtless for some good reason). **1941** H. MACLENNAN *Barometer Rising* 11 Grinding on the cobble-stones behind a pair of plunging Clydesdales came one of Halifax's most typical vehicles, a low-slung dray with a high driver's box, known as a sloven. **1964** *Atlantic Advocate* Aug. 79 As evening approached the horses were hitched to a long, low wagon, known in our country as a 'sloven', and the apples were hauled to the house.

6. *Forestry.* (See quot. 1957.)

1946 F. SARGESON *That Summer* 175 The stumps still had the sloven sticking up. **1953** H. L. EDLIN *Forester's Handbk.* xiii. 201 Only when the crown of the tree strikes the ground will the last link be broken; the 'hinge' will then break, the tree pulling an irregular splinter of wood out of the stump below it. This splinter, or sloven, is then sawn off. **1957** *Brit. Commonwealth Forest Terminol.* II. 178 *Sloven*, the torn splintered portion of timber left on a stump or the end of a butt, where the key finally broke when the tree fell.

sloven, *v.* Add: Hence **slo·vened** *ppl. a.*, done in a slovenly manner.

1937 'G. ORWELL' *Road to Wigan Pier* I. i. 17 It was not only the dirt.., but the feeling..of having got down into some subterranean place where people go creeping round and round..in an endless muddle of slovened jobs and mean grievances.

Slovene, *sb.* Add: **2.** The language of the Slovenes.

1911 *Encycl. Brit.* XXV. 245/2 Except for a few 15th-century prayers and formulæ we do not find any more specimens of Slovene until the Reformation. **1960** O. MANNING *Great Fortune* III. 174 David smiled down modestly. 'My Slovene is a little rusty,' he said. **1972** W. B. LOCKWOOD *Panorama Indo-Europ. Lang.* ix. 161 Slovene is the official language of the Constituent Republic of Slovenia. **1980** *English World-Wide* I. 256 Of the remaining essays not involving English, most are on minority languages, such as..the individual cases of Slovene in Southern Austria.

Slovenian, *a.* and *sb.* Add: **a.** *adj.* (Further examples.)

1902 *Encycl. Brit.* XXVI. 16 Of late years attempts have been made to turn the Slovenian national movement into this direction, and to attract the Slovenians also towards the Orthodox non-Austrian Slavs. **1922** M. S. STANOYEVICH *Early Jugoslav Lit.* viii. 69 The works of Croatian and Slovenian authors..hardly contributed anything towards progress in linguistics science and literature. **1960** O. MANNING *Great Fortune* I. 5 When they woke the next morning they were on the Slovenian plain.

b. *sb.* (Further examples.) Also, a Slovene.

1885 [see *CROATIAN *sb.* and *a.*]. **1902** [see sense a above]. **1955** [see *MACEDONIAN *sb.*[1] c]. **1978** *Language* LIV. 451 The beginner thus has to look in the glossary if he wishes to ascertain whether the forms cited in these examples are younger or older Old Slavonic, Old Slovenian, or 15th-century Russian spellings.

Slovincian (slovi·nsiăn). Also **Slovintian, Slovinzian.** [f. F. *Slovince*, ad. G. *Slowinze*, f. Kashubian *Słovinsći* + -IAN.] An extinct dialect of Kashubian.

1883 *Trans. Philol. Soc. 1880–1* 373 With regard to Baltic Slavonic, represented by its only surviving dialects, Slovintian and Cassubian, I shall treat it as an independent language. **1934, 1935** [see *KASHUBE]. **1939** L. H. GRAY *Foundations of Lang.* 355 Polish (closely connected with Kashubian and Slovincian). **1965** G. Y. SHEVELOV *Prehist. Slavic* i. 1 Slovincian was still extant in the early twentieth century in the district of Słupsk, now in north-western Poland. **1972** W. B. LOCKWOOD *Panorama Indo-Europ. Lang.* 158 Due west of the present Kashubian area lies the district of Slupsk (Stolp), where autochthonous Slavonic survived until the end of the last century, when it was entirely supplanted by German; here the dialects were locally termed Slovinzian. **1974** [see *POMERANIAN *a.*].

slow, *sb.* Add: **2. b.** A slow train.

1956 *Railway Mag.* Mar. 163/2 There is a daily slow, stopping at all stations between Damascus and Deraa. **1976** P. LOVESEY *Swing, swing Together* xiii. 55 We can take a train... We can catch a slow to Oxford.

c. A slow tune in popular music.

1956 B. BURNS in S. Traill *Play that Music* ii. 34 His style is hot and aggressive—pushing the beat in fast numbers and rhapsodic in slows. **1977** J. WAINWRIGHT *Do Nothin' till you hear from Me* xi. 184 In that set of standard slows, this ten-piece [band] of mine was like Ellington's piano.

3. a. (Earlier example.)

1854 F. LILLYWHITE *Guide to Cricketers* 84 [He] is a good bat, and can bowl 'slows' well.

4. b. *the slows* (colloq.), an imaginary disease or ailment accounting for slowness.

1843 *Ainsworth's Mag.* IV. 124 If somewhat troubled with 'the slows', not a hound but was as true as the sun. **1843** J. C. SHAIRP *Let.* 25 Sept. in W. A. Knight *Principal Shairp* (1888) vi. 71 This..makes good my summer's work. 'The Slows' are my bane, but I must be courageous and face what remains... If I could but secure a *second*, I should be happy. **1927** *Daily Express* 13 Dec. 16/2 Rimell's mare, How Nice, had a fit of the slows, for she was always in the next division from start to finish. **1970** D. FRANCIS *Rat Race* viii. 102 They might as well send him [*sc.* a racehorse] to the knackers. Got the slows right and proper, that one has.

slow, *a.* Add: **I. 4.** (Later examples.) *slow learner*: spec. in *Educ.* (see quot. 1981).

1938 *High Points* Apr. 33/1 The problem of the slow learner continues to grow involved as increased numbers flow into high school. **1945** 'O. MALET' *My Bird Sings* II. ii. 121 Your sister does not benefit so swiftly by her education... She is a slow learner. **1946** P. BOTTOME *Lifeline* xvi. 144 She wanted everything... I'm exactly the opposite in love. I'm a slow starter. I want little. **1963** *Times* 25 May 9/4 Here is comfort for the slow-starter who begins at the bottom. **1975** *Times* 26 Apr. 7/4, I was 24 and I'd run away from home... I was kind of a slow starter. **1977** *Wandsworth Borough News* 7 Oct. 28/2 (Advt.), Tutorials: 'A' and 'O' level, most subjects; public examinations; slow learners welcome. **1981** D. ROWNTREE *Dict. Education* 286 *Slow learner.* A term often used rather loosely of any child whose attainments have always fallen noticeably behind those of other children of the same age, without any implication as to what might be thought to be the cause..or whether the child might be enabled to speed up or catch up. Sometimes, however, the term is used to indicate children who are not only expected to remain slow learners but also to be unable ever to learn as much as others. Some people would even restrict the term to pupils who are educationally subnormal.

6. (Further examples, of solemn or tragic music.) *slow handclap*: see *HANDCLAP c.

1826 F. REYNOLDS *Life & Times* II. 144 The curtain to the new piece having risen, the heroine entered to slow music. **1895** *World* 4 Dec. 27/1, I could see the conductor of the orchestra waiting eagerly for the word 'mother'—the cue for the slow music—and I was, oh! so thankful when it came. **1926** G. B. SHAW *Translations & Tomfooleries* 78 You were not found..with the limelight streaming on your white face, and the band playing slow music.

7. b. Of an oven: of such a temperature that it cooks slowly.

1747 H. GLASSE *Art of Cookery* ix. 113 Bake it in a slow oven, with crust as above. **1846** A. SOYER *Gastronomic Regenerator* 571 Place them in a slow oven to bake. **1917** F. KLICKMANN *Between Larch-Woods & Weir* xiii. 242 She had told Dick to put the patties into a slow oven for ten or twelve minutes before eating. **1973** *Times* 1 Dec. 11 Place the casserole in a slow oven.

c. *slow burn* fig.: (*a*) (see *BURN *sb.*³ 1 d); (*b*) *Theatr.*, delayed response or slow reaction to a joke; also *attrib.*

1975 *Daily Tel.* 10 Feb. 12 For some of her jokes in public Margaret Thatcher relies..on what professional comedians call the 'slow burn'. **1975** D. LODGE *Changing Places* i. 22 The realization..strikes him, like a slow-burn gag in a movie-comedy.

8. d. *slow poke, slowpoke* (colloq., chiefly *U.S.*) = SLOW-COACH; also *attrib.* or as *adj.*, slow, idle. Cf. POKE *sb.*³ 3.

1848 BARTLETT *Dict. Americanisms* 255 'What a slow *poke* you are!' A woman's word. **1877** F. ROSS et al. *Gloss Words used in Holderness* 128/2 *Slaw-pooak*.., a dunce; a driveller. **1920** G. ADE *Hand-Made Fables* 226 He placed the Experiences of an ordinary slow-poke year into one Week. **1935** J. T. FARRELL *Judgment Day* xvi. 367 Slackers, slow-pokes, easy-going, unambitious fellows, I neither want, nor can tolerate. **1959** *Guardian* 31 Aug. 2/3 'Slowpokes'—unnecessarily slow drivers—cause other road users to take additional risks. **1971** W. H. MCNEILL in A. Bullock *Twentieth Century* 54/1 What could a slowpoke airplane do against intercontinental missiles? **1981** S. RUSHDIE *Midnight's Children* I. 112 Come on, slowpoke, you don't want to be late.

II. 9. a. *slow pass*: spec. in *Bridge* (see quot. 1934); *slow-scan* (Television), scanning at a much slower rate than in ordinary television, so that the resulting signal has a much smaller bandwidth and can be transmitted more cheaply; usu. *attrib.*

1934 *Amer. Speech* IX. 11/1 A *slow pass* is a pass preceded by a long period of thought, and since it conveys the impression that some strength is held without paying the regular price of a bid, is regarded as unethical. **1955** *Sun* (Baltimore) (B ed.) 7 Dec. 3/4 The so-called slow-scan system paints a picture every two seconds and requires only 8,000 cycles. *Ibid.* 3/5 Slow scan cannot handle objects in motion. **1960** *Guardian* 20 Apr. 4/1 The National Broadcasting Company will show short excerpts to American audiences at breakfast-time by using the 'slowscan' process and transmitting film by cable to Montreal. **1970** N. ARMSTRONG et al. *First on Moon* v. 110 TV was tried on Gordon Cooper's Mercury flight, using a slow-scan black and white camera. **1973** *Times* 2 June 10/6 It was agreed when North South protested the score that East's pass over Three Spades was a 'slow pass'. **1975** D. G. FINK *Electronics Engineers' Handbk.* XI. 62 Slow-scan tubes are useful for remotely located cameras requiring a data link to the monitor wherein the bandwidth reduction significantly lowers the data-link cost.

b. *slow bell* (Naut., N. Amer.), a bell signalling that a ship should proceed slowly; chiefly in prepositional phrases, at a reduced speed; also *fig.*; *slow puncture*, a puncture from which the air escapes gradually.

1901 *Daily Colonist* (Victoria, B.C.) 5 Nov. 3/2 Early in the evening she [*sc.* S.S. City of Seattle] had run among a number of small icebergs and she was coming down the channel under a slow bell. **1944** *Amer. Speech* XIX. 108 Another of the best [phrases], used especially in declining a drink or an extra job of work, is 'Not me, thanks; *I'm taking it on the slow bell.*' **1946** *Seafarers' Log* 19 Apr. 3/4 There will be no slow bell on the organizing drive. **1958** *Wall St. Jrnl.* 17 Dec. 26/2 We were at slow-bell for much of '58 because of the recession. **1958** E. NEWBY *Short Walk in Hindu Kush* xviii. 217 Our airbeds had slow punctures and the ground was hard. **1968** C. P. BRACKEN *Roman Ring* xv. 147 He had left the Fiat at a garage outside Rome to have a slow puncture repaired. **1974** A. MORICE *Death of Heavenly Twin* xii. 124 I've got a flat tyre. It's probably a slow puncture

10. c. (Further examples.) Also of other photographic items: necessitating longer exposures (e.g., in the case of a lens, because its aperture is small).

1902 *Encycl. Brit.* XXXI. 695/1 Owing to the small working aperture it [*sc.* a lens] seems slow, but it is not so for the definition and flatness of field obtained. **1915** D. GRANT *Manual of Photogr.* 74 'Slow' papers give plucky results from flat negatives. **1957** E. S. BOMBACK *Photogr. in Colour* x. 107 The use of slow contact printing paper.. may result in negative or partially negative images in the print. **1973** *Sci. Amer.* Dec. 39/3 Telescopes such as the 100-inch reflector on Mount Wilson, which has a focal ratio of *f*/5, are quite 'slow', that is, they require long exposure times.

d. Med. *slow* (*virus*) *disease* or *infection*, any of various progressive diseases caused by a virus or virus-like organism that multiplies slowly in the host organism and having incubation periods of months or years; hence (by a false analysis) *slow virus*.

1954 B. SIGURDSSON in *Brit. Vet. Jrnl.* CX. 350 If the word chronic is taken to mean not only protracted, but also something which lingers on, has an irregular and unpredictable course and may end in any one of several different ways, then the expression should not be used about the diseases I have discussed here; these infections should perhaps rather be called *slow* infections. *Ibid.* 352 It seems as if an important group of slow virus infections is gradually coming to light. **1967** *New England Jrnl. Med.* CCLXXVI. 392/1 (*heading*) Slow-virus infections of the nervous system. **1971** *Jrnl. Virol.* VII. 301 Progressive pneumonia virus, the causative agent of slow, pulmonary disease of Montana sheep, was shown to be antigenically related to two other slow viruses of sheep, visna and maedi. **1976** R. H. KIMBERLIN *Slow Virus Diseases of Animals & Man* i. 5 One major distinguishing feature of slow diseases..was this: once clinical signs of disease have appeared the disease then follows a regular progressive course which always ends in serious illness and usually death. **1977** *Sci. Amer.* May 140/2 A dozen fatal diseases of the human central nervous system stand suspect of slow-virus origin.

III. 13. a. *slow-pitch* (*softball*) (U.S.), a type of softball in which each pitch must travel in an arc of a specified minimum height; *slow wheel* spec., a type of potter's wheel turned at a slow speed.

1946 W. B. HONEY *Art of Potter* II. ii. 12 A device was introduced for rotating the pot while it was being built, on a horizontal pivoted table or disc..; this 'slow wheel' presumably led to the invention of the fully developed potter's wheel. **1964** H. HODGES *Artifacts* i. 28 Many archaeologists are in the habit of distinguishing between a *slow wheel*, that is to say a device in which the movement of the wheel-head is either intermittent or relatively slow, and a fast wheel. **1971** *Canadian Antiques Collector* Apr. 16/1 Most frequently Ipswich ware is formed on a 'slow wheel' which is in principle a freely-revolving turntable. Both pot and wheel were revolved by hand. **1971** *N.Y. Times* 6 June 95/5 With the opening of the annual Long Beach Slow Pitch Softball League..policemen and addicts met for the first time in friendly competition. **1976** *Billings* (Montana) *Gaz.* 2 July 1–c/1 Softball fans will have a chance to glimpse some of the top men's slowpitch teams in the northwest during the Town & Country-Corner Pocket Men's Slowpitch Softball Tournament.

c. Nuclear Physics. *slow neutron*, a neutron with little kinetic energy, esp. as a result of being slowed down by a moderator; freq. = **thermal neutron*; also *attrib.*; so *slow reactor*, a reactor in which fission is produced primarily by moderated neutrons; a thermal reactor.

1934 *Chem. Abstr.* XXVIII. 2263 The slow neutrons are probably emitted from Be when an excitation of a Be nucleus by α-particles occurs without capture. **1938** R. W. LAWSON tr. *Hevesy & Paneth's Manual of Radio-activity* (ed. 2) x. 112 These slow neutrons are produced by allowing fast neutrons, such as those emitted by a radon-beryllium source, to pass through water, paraffin wax, or other substances containing hydrogen. **1945** H. D. SMYTH *Gen. Acct. Devel. Atomic Energy Mil. Purposes* ii. 23 For a slow-neutron chain reaction using a moderator and unseparated uranium it was almost certain that tons of metal and of moderator would be required. **1949** *Atomics* Sept. 45/2 The so-called 'slow neutron reactor'. These reactors take advantage of the fact that neutrons produce fission in uranium more easily as they go slower. **1958** *Chambers's Techn. Dict.* Add. 1014/1 Slow reactor. **1964** M. GOWING *Britain & Atomic Energy 1939–1945* iv. 115 Bombs were discussed in terms of slow neutron chain reactions. **1973** *Daily Tel.* 12 Oct. 8/5 Fast reactors, cooled by sodium instead of carbon dioxide, as in slow reactors now used, can provide more heat more rapidly.

14. a. *spec.* (i) *slow motion*, (*a*) motion of slower speed than normal; also *attrib.*; (*b*) *Cinemat.*, the technique of shooting a film at a faster speed than normal so that when it is projected the action will appear to be slowed down; also *transf.*, and *attrib.*

1801 J. STRUTT *Sports & Pastimes* III. ii. 130 At a show in the country, about forty years ago, which was contrived in such a manner, that the whole group descended and ascended with a slow motion to the sound of music. **1834** *Mechanics' Mag.* 4 Oct. 16/2 The gear was changed from the quick to the slow motion. **1860** [in Dict.]. **1878** [in Dict., sense 16 d]. **1903** *Work* 4 July 341/2 Next make the ball and vertical slow-motion screw. **1924** *Spectator* 3 May 720/1 Its deliberation becomes a separate quality, akin to the slow motion of the cinema. **1929** E. WILSON *I thought of Daisy* ii. 102 A slow-motion diving picture of champion woman swimmers. **1938** W. S. CHURCHILL *Let.* 9 June in M. Gilbert *W. S. Churchill* (1976) V. xlvi. 946 In all my experience of public offices..I have never seen anything like the slow-motion picture which the work of this Committee has presented. **1943** J. B. PRIESTLEY *Daylight on Saturday* xi. 70 The sound of their slow-motion patter..just gets your goat. **1956** J. BALDWIN *Giovanni's Room* I. ii. 57 Like those figures in slow motion one sometimes sees on the screen. **1962** F. I. ORDWAY et al. *Basic Astronautics* vii. 316 This test is accomplished by firing the model engine in a wind tunnel and observing the flow of the exhaust gases with the aid of slow motion cameras. **1973** *Listener* 23 Aug. 244/1 Time on Friday moved very slowly. Everything seemed to be as if in a slow motion film.

(ii) Of a ballroom dance: with steps at walking-pace.

1928 '*H.M.V.*' *Catal.* 76/2 Slow F[ox]-T[rot]. **1949** A. CHUJOY *Dance Encycl.* 76/2 *Baston*, a form of slow waltz..in which the couples turn in circles in several directions. **1949** A. WILSON *Wrong Set* 56 She was almost lying in Bruce's arms as he carried her through the slow foxtrot. **1962** J. BRAINE *Life at Top* ii. 54 They were taking their partners for a waltz now, a slow waltz, an old waltz from the days of Carroll Gibbons and the Orpheans. **1966** 'M. HALLIDAY' *Wicked as Devil* ix. 79 The floor was crowded for a slow foxtrot. **1976** *Listener* 29 July 105/2 Going to the dancing class to practise the slow waltz and the tango.

c. (Earlier example.)

1868 *J. Lillywhite's Cricketers' Compan.* 61 The wickets were in excellent order, though somewhat 'slow' for Gravesend.

d. Also of a lane of a dual carriageway or motorway: intended for vehicles which are not overtaking; also *fig.*

1967 'M. CARREL' *Dark Edge of Violence* ix. 80 The police car..dropped back and sulked along in the slow-lane. **1969** R. PETRIE *Despatch of Dove* III. 146 He'd put himself in a silly position, in the slow lane without the chance of a turn-off. **1972** B. EVERITT *Cold Front* v. 38 'Are we conversing or making love?'..'Let's go into the slow lane for a minute. What are you doing between leaving Medicom and joining the Grand Old Man?' **1977** R. RENDELL *Judgement in Stone* xix. 151 Joan's driving had become erratic, and her jerky zigzagging from slow lane to fast was a frightening experience.

V. 16. a. Parasynthetic, as *slow-minded*, *-motioned*. Also *slow-mindedness*.

1930 D. H. LAWRENCE *A Propos of Lady Chatterley's Lover* 9 The evocative power of the so-called obscene words..perhaps are [*sic*] still too strong for slow-minded, half-evoked lower natures to-day. **1935** KIPLING *Two Forewords* 16 The seller..berated, for their slow-mindedness, men who, but for being too much urged to buy, would have bought. **1856** 'MARK TWAIN' *Let.* 10 June (1917) I. 33 They are either excessively slow motioned or very lazy. **1951** N. G. ANNAN *Leslie Stephen* x. 285 Progress for him was an incalculable and slow-motioned operation.

b. With verbs, as *slow-clap*, *-foot* (later example), *-handclap* (see *HANDCLAP c), *-march* (later examples), *-steam*, *-waltz*.

1960 Slow-clap [see *OUT-SCORE *v.*]. **1979** *Guardian* 26 Oct. 2/1 Mrs Thatcher was also slow-clapped and heckled..during her speech. **1885** W. B. YEATS in *Dublin Univ. Rev.* May 82/2, I see the night, Deep-eyed, slow-footing down the empty glade. **1927** T. E. LAWRENCE *Let.* 19 May (1938) 516 These long dreary slow-marching books are invaluable friends in Drigh Road. **1977** *Times* 30 July 2/3 The RAF colour squadron slow-marched the old colour ..off the parade ground. **1975** *Petroleum Economist* Sept. 356/3, 22 per cent of the active fleet..was estimated to be slow-steaming in July. *Ibid.* 341/2 Due to slow-steaming, fuel consumption..fell. **1977** *Living with Tanker Surplus* (Shell Internat. Petroleum Co.) 5 The financial rewards for slow-steaming small vessels are greater than for large vessels, because a small ship consumes relatively more bunkers per tonne of cargo. **1976** 'P. B. YUILL' *Hazell & Menacing Jester* viii. 81 He recovered a bit as I was slow-waltzing him to the stairs.

c. With adjs., as *slow-syruppy*.

1922 Joyce *Ulysses* 261 Neatly she poured slowsyruppy sole.

d. With sbs., as *slow-beat, -burn* (see sense *7 c), *-gait, -growth, -neutron* (see sense *13 c), *-pitch* (see sense *13 a), *-poke* (see sense *8 d), *-scan* (see sense *9 a), *-speed, -tempo*; *slow-release* adj., (*a*) *Electr.*, applied to a relay in which the delay between a de-energizing signal and the opening of the contacts is intentionally increased; (*b*) characterized by the slow release of an active substance (as by a pharmaceutical preparation); *slow-wave* adj., *spec.* applied to the commonest form of non-REM sleep, in which brain waves having a frequency of ½ to 3 hertz, lower than that of alpha or beta waves, are detectable.

1965 *Economist* 4 Sept. 857/2 Egypt's slow-beat socialism is not so agreeable to Moscow as was Algeria's hot rhythm under Mr Ben Bella. **1977** J. Wainwright *Do Nothin' till you hear from Me* viii. 125 He can blow a beautiful slow-beat chorus. **1940** C. Day Lewis tr. *Virgil's Georgics* II. 41 Waggonloads drawn home by the slow-gait oxen. **1965** H. I. Ansoff *Corporate Strategy* vi. 109 The electronics industry ranges from high growth in technologically sophisticated areas, such as optical electronics, to slow-growth consumer oriented product-markets, such as radio and television. **1970** *Globe & Mail* (Toronto) 26 Sept. B2/2 Ontario Development Corp. has granted loans totalling more than $1-million to 10 companies planning to set up plants in slow-growth areas of the province. **1928** *Jrnl. Inst. Electr. Engineers* LXVI. 342/2 The No. 2 armature is especially suitable for slow-release relays. **1961** *Lancet* 29 July 230/1 Possibly the diminished efficacy of penicillin in the treatment of uncomplicated gonorrhœa may be due to the wide use of slow-release preparations giving a prolonged, though low, blood concentration. **1969** S. F. Smith *Teleph. & Telegr. A* ii. 43 One particularly useful way of obtaining a slow release feature without making the relay slow to operate is to connect a permanent shunt across the operating coil of the relay. **1974** *Nature* 25 Jan. 199/2 The efficiency of slow-release nitrogen was investigated as an initial and maintenance fertiliser treatment. **1958** *Newnes Compl. Amat. Photogr.* 33 An older box camera with a slow-speed shutter can be speeded up very simply. **1971** *Engineering* Apr. 20/1 In the case of slow-speed engines, machining can often be confined to pin and journal diameters and web faces. **1980** *Redbook* Oct. G12/2 Slow-speed film lets you get good pictures even on a sun-drenched sandy beach or glistening ski slope. **1962** D. Francis *Dead Cert* vi. 55 We swayed lazily round the floor to some dreamy slow-tempo music. **1978** T. Williamson *Technicians of Death* viii. 60 The invisible disc jockey began to play a slow-tempo number. **1963** G. Troup *Masers & Lasers* (ed. 2) iv. 71 There are three kinds of structures suitable for slow-wave propagation in the paramagnetic maser. **1967** *Physiol. Rev.* XLVII. 118 Slow wave sleep. **1968** *Brit. Med. Bull.* XXIV. 257/1 There is a reduction in the amplitude of the evoked response during rapid eye-movement sleep as compared with slow-wave sleep. **1974** W. P. Koella in van Praag & Meinardi *Brain & Sleep* 9 Stages 1 to 4 are referred to as NREM-sleep; the term 'slow-wave-sleep' should be reserved for stages 3 and 4 which are characterized by the 'slow' delta-waves.

slow, *adv.* Add: **1. b.** *slow back*: a direction to a golfer when the club is swung back from the ball in making a stroke.

1886 H. G. Hutchinson *Hints on Golf* 17 Golfers have gone so far as to instruct their caddies to say to them, 'Slow back,' so as to keep them in mind of this precept each time they addressed themselves to drive the ball. **1909** P. A. Vaile *Mod. Golf* viii. 136 Gather speed as you go up, but do not get up much speed on the upward swing, for if you do you have to waste energy fighting it at the top of the swing. This is the reason for 'slow back'. **1922** Wodehouse *Clicking of Cuthbert* iii. 73 Slow back—keep the head.

2. a. (Further examples.) spec. *slow-reacting substance* (Physiol.), any of various substances that are produced in the body in response to various stimuli and cause slower and longer lasting contraction of smooth muscle than does histamine; *spec.* one released in anaphylaxis; abbrev. SRS (see *S 4 a); *slow-releasing* = *slow-release* adj. (*a*) s.v. *slow *a.* 16 d.

1876 'Mark Twain' *Tom Sawyer* xxxi. 237 The slow-dragging ages. **1894** Kipling *Jungle Bk.* 95 Asleep in the arms of the slow-swinging seas. **1904** —— *Traffics & Discoveries* 368 Warn them of seas that slip our yoke Of slow conspiring stars. **1904** H. G. Wells *Food of Gods* II. i. 142 They were children—slow-growing children of a new race. **1910** J. Poole *Pract. Telephone Handbk.* (ed. 4) xi. 169 A slow-acting relay. **1912** W. de la Mare *Listeners* 24 Whose feathers..Gleam with slow-gathering drops of dew. **1915** D. H. Lawrence *Rainbow* i. 1 They were fresh, blond, slow-speaking people. **1916** A. Huxley *Burning Wheel* 22 The chime Of bells slow-dying. **1920** E. Sitwell *Wooden Pegasus* 101 A slow-leaking tap. **1921** D. H. Lawrence *Tortoises* 10 You..set forward, slow-dragging, on your four-pinned toes. **1921** R. Graves *Pier glass* 44 Slow-rising smoke and nothing wrong! **1923** T. E. Herbert *Telephony* xiii. 334 The special feature of the slow releasing relay..is the extension of the core on which is placed a solid copper collar. **1924** R. Campbell *Flaming Terrapin* iii. 43 The death-cry and the agony supreme Of the slow-drowning world. **1925** Slow-running [see **idling passage*]. **1925** F. Scott Fitzgerald *Great Gatsby* iii. 59 But I am slow-thinking. **1927** T. Wilder *Bridge of San Luis Rey* II. 38 That city of large girdled Women..slow-moving and slow-smiling, a city of crystal air. **1930** E. Pound *XXX Cantos* v. 20 A Knight with slow-lifting eyelids. **1930** Blunden *Poems* 315 At last slow-mending From the hacked wounds of our proud error's field. **1931** A. Huxley *Cicadas* 33 Death in the Scorpion hunts him up the sky..round the vault of time, round the slow-curving year. **1932** W. Faulkner *Light in August* i. 23 The slowspitting and squatting men. **1932** Auden *Orators* II. 75 O charged-to-the-full-in-secret slow-beating heart. **1939** Kellaway & Trethewie in *Austral. Jrnl. Exper. Biol.* XVII. 227 The perfusate was also tested for the presence of the substance described by Feldberg and Kellaway (1938) which, after a latent interval, causes contraction of the gut followed by slow relaxation and by characteristic after-changes in the excitability of the muscle. This substance we have called S.R.S. (slow reacting substance). **1947** Crowther & Whiddington *Science at War* 160 The slow-sinking depth charges may be evaded by the submarine. **1948** R. Graves *Coll. Poems, 1914–1947* 240 Under your Milky Way And slow-revolving Bear. **1954** J. R. R. Tolkien *Fellowship of Ring* 212 A long slow-climbing slope. **1954** A. G. L. Hellyer *Encycl. Garden Work* 18/2 Basic slag is a relatively slow-acting fertilizer. *a* **1957** R. Campbell tr. *Rimbaud's Drunken Boat* in *Coll. Poems* (1960) III. 18 Where with slow-pulsing and delirious fires,..ferments the crimson bitterness of love. **1958** J. W. Freebody *Telegraphy* iv. 85/1 For slow operating or slow releasing relays three lengths of slug are employed. **1958** *Pharmacol. Rev.* X. 419 Two entirely different groups of slow reacting substances have been established; one..consists of polypeptides, the other one of lipid-soluble acids. **1964** L. MacNeice *Astrol.* ii. 66 With slow-running planets the *transits* are the things to look for. **1970** Passmore & Robson *Compan. Med. Stud.* II. xxiv. 3/2 Histamine, the slow reacting substance (SRS-A) and bradykinin may be the most important agents involved in the pathogenesis of human bronchial asthma. **1975** *New Phytologist* LXXIV. 367 In alpine regions of Africa, there are trends from erect pachycaul plants towards stout slow-growing plant forms.

b. (Further examples.)

1896 Kipling *Seven Seas* 53 To the grist of the slow-ground ages. *Ibid.* 65 Each man drew his watchful breath slow taken 'tween the teeth. **1910** W. de la Mare *Three Mulla-Mulgars* xi. 153 Between his slow-drawled, shakety notes of deep and shrill Nod listened for the least stir in the forest. **1914** Kipling *For All We have & Are* 3 Comfort, content, delight, The ages' slow-bought gain. **1916** A. Huxley *Burning Wheel* 39 While on the windy down-land..The slow-driven sun beheld us. **1944** Blunden *Shells by Stream* 43 Your eyes..Enfold the slow-bloomed scenes. **1949** —— *After Bombing* 34 All other lightning Might be as honey or kind balms slow-melted.

slow, *v.* Add: **3.** Also with *down*.

1971 *Engineering* Apr. 34/1 Most neutron radiography has been carried out using slowed-down thermal neutrons. **1976** 'J. Ross' *I know what it's like to Die* xxiv. 151 A creeping slowed-down vision with a dreamlike clarity.

slow-down. Also **slowdown.** [f. Slow *v.* + Down *adv.*] The action or process of slowing down; an instance of slowing down; *spec.* (*a*) *U.S.*, a form of industrial protest in which employees work at a deliberately slow pace; (*b*) an economic recession, a decline in productivity or demand. Also *attrib.*

1897 [in Dict. s.v. Slow *sb.* 5]. **1937** *Daily Progress* (Charlottesville, Va.) 16 Apr. 1/5 An official of the U.A.W.A. said the objective of workers in a slow-down was to 'try to see how little they can do without actually stopping work entirely'. **1939** *Sun* (Baltimore) 10 Jan. 16/3 The slow-down strike was called off late today. **1942** J. Steinbeck *Moon is Down* v. 70 'I think I fixed the mine for a while.' 'What's your trouble?'..'Oh, the usual thing with me—the slow-down and a wrecked dump car.' **1944** *Sun* (Baltimore) 28 Oct. 12/1 Low-quoted stocks..came out in blocks running to 33,000 shares and propped volume, although slowdowns were plentiful. **1950** *Ibid.* 7 Feb. 7/4 Helmstedt, Germany, checkpoint for the Russians' off-again, on-again 'slowdown' of Berlin-bound highway traffic. **1953** *Encounter* Nov. 70/1 In dozens of factories there were slow-downs..or sit-down strikes. **1957** *Economist* 28 Dec. 1132/1 At least 5,000 employees in lead-zinc mines and smelters..have lost their jobs this year... The slow-down extends even to the largest and most diversified producers. **1969** *Nature* 19 Apr. 218/2 The search will now be on for further eccentric behaviour in..the Crab Nebula pulsar which has the shortest period and the fastest slowdown rate of all. **1969** *Guardian* 2 Oct. 12/1 Has the Government any plans to protect Britain from a slowdown? **1973** *Nature* 3 Aug. 260/1 The observed evolutionary slowdown in higher primates may simply be the consequence of progressive prolongation of their generation time. **1977** *New Yorker* 24 Oct. 79/2 The mess-hall workers staged a work slowdown. **1977** J. W. Kendrick *Understanding Productivity* iv. 35 The factors explaining the 1966–69 slowdown also help to explain why productivity advance recovered..during the final complete subperiod. **1978** *Sci. Amer.* July 28/2 Energy is required, for example, to accelerate the vehicle from traffic stops and slowdowns, to climb hills and to overcome the rolling resistance of the tires. **1980** A. Coppel *Hastings Conspiracy* xxviii. 184 The switchboard operators are starting a slow-down over wages. **1981** *Washington Star* 14 Jan. F4/2 The University of the District of Columbia barely overcame the visitors' slow-down tactics and escaped with a bizarre 28–27 victory last night at D.C. Armory.

slow drag. Also **slow-drag.** [f. Slow *a.* + Drag *sb.*] A slow blues rhythm; a piece of music in this rhythm; a dance characterized by dragging of the feet, performed to this rhythm. Also *attrib.* Hence **slow-drag** *v. intr.*, to dance the slow drag.

1911 S. Joplin *Treemonisha* (music score) XXVII. 215 Directions for the Slow Drag. 1. The Slow Drag must begin on the first beat of each measure. 2. When moving forward, drag the left foot; when moving backward, drag the right foot, [etc.]. **1924** *Etude* Aug. 527/1 An exceedingly popular jazz is the slow drag. **1926** A. Niles in W. C. Handy *Blues* ii. 9 The songs were woven of the same stuff as the other overlapping items..the over-and-overs, slow-drags, pats, and stomps. **1935** Z. N. Hurston *Mules & Men* I. ix. 185 The piano was throbbing like a stringed drum and the couples slow-dragging about the floor were urging the player on to new lows. **1941** W. C Handy *Father of Blues* (1957) vi. 76 It was not easy for me to concede that a simple slow-drag and repeat could be rhythm itself. **1949** B. A. Botkin *Treas. S. Folklore* v. i. 745 This is one of the best-known of the slow-drag work songs sung by Negro prisoners in South Texas. **1968** P. Oliver *Screening Blues* iii. 94 The shuffle of the 'slow drag' would have been effective at the medium tempo of the tune. **1970** —— *Savannah Syncopators* 57 On occasions..'slow-dragging' couples may be seen to be shuffling in a manner reminiscent, perhaps, of the 'shout'. **1976** A. Murray *Stomping Blues* vi. 83 There is Bessie Smith's slow-drag version..recorded in 1925. **1980** *Amer. Speech* LV. 210 They slow-dragged to low-down blues.

slower, *sb.* For *rare*⁻¹ read *rare* and add later examples. Also with *down*.

1947 Crowther & Whiddington *Science at War* 144 The most suitable substance for use as a slower-down was heavy water. **1961** P. Frankau *Pen to Paper* 64, I know also that one fatal slower of the pace can be found in the adjectives.

slowing, *vbl. sb.* (Examples with *up*.)

1900 [see *control *sb.* 3 c]. **1960** E. Delavenay *Introd. to Machine Translation* 82 This means a slowing-up in the matching of input words with words stored in the dictionary. **1965** J. Pollitt *Depression & its Treatment* vi. 82 In the elderly, particularly those in the senium, the effects of retardation are added to the existing slowing-up process associated with aging.

slowly, *adv.* **3. a.** (Further examples.)

1921 D. H. Lawrence *Tortoises* 33 That mud-hovel of his slowly-rambling spouse. **1926** J. S. Huxley *Essays in Pop. Science* 195 They [*sc.* frogs in Arctic zones] would be so slowly-working that their growth would be prolonged over an uneconomic number of seasons. **1931** R. Campbell *Georgiad* ii. 47 A blush began to dawn As rosy as a slowly-cooking prawn. **1937** *Discovery* July 196/1 Long strings of slowly-moving camels. **1951** S. Spender tr. *Rilke's Life of Virgin Mary* 15 And if the gleam from distant flambeaux plays On slowly-nearing ceremonial dresses. **1965** Phillips & Williams *Inorg. Chem.* I. viii. 292 Now in many of these inter-combinations *dA*/*dx* is a slowly-varying function, sometimes over relatively small ranges but often over very wide ranges of composition. **1967** *Oceanography & Marine Biol.* V. 468 On soft substrata two biocoenoses may be recognized, namely, one on beaches..with quickly-drying wracks and a second where slowly-drying wracks are present.

sloyd, *sb.* Add: Also **slöijd.** (Earlier example.)

1884 [see Fad *sb.*² 1].

slub, *sb.*² Add: **2.** A yarn containing thickened parts, or slubs, at intervals; a fabric woven from such a yarn. Also *attrib.*, having an irregular effect given by a warp of uneven thickness.

1928 *Daily Express* 14 Aug. 4 Slub reps, artificial silk velour, chenille combined with artificial silk..are shown. **1940** *Chambers's Techn. Dict.* 779/1 *Slub yarns*, fancy yarns with thickened parts at frequent intervals. **1946** *Daily Progress* (Charlottesville, Va.) 30 Apr. 12/7 Solid color blue slub-weave and white striped blue chambray. **1957** *Textile Terms & Defs.* (Textile Inst.) (ed. 3) 42 Spun slubs may be produced by an intermittent acceleration of one pair of rollers during spinning. **1958** *Observer* 24 Aug. 7/7 Structured skirt fabrics come from Manchester as well as from Switzerland, but there they go by the general, somewhat unfeminine designation of 'slubs'. **1974** *News & Reporter* (Chester, S. Carolina) 24 Apr. 6-A (Advt.), Textured rayon with interesting slub highlights. **1979** *Radio Times* 5–11 May 14/1 In his choice of clothes—slub silk tie, silk pocket handkerchief, hound's-tooth jacket with turn-back cuffs—as in his choice of claret he declares himself a man of some style.

Hence **slubbed** *a.*, of fabrics: containing slubs.

1961 *Harper's Bazaar* June 55 Three piece in white slubbed rayon. **1980** M. Drabble *Middle Ground* 171 Her vast off-white, gold-tasselled, slubbed-silk settee.

slubber, *v.* Add: **4.** Also with *through*.

1941 Auden *New Year Let.* I. 24 Time and again have slubbered through With slip and slapdash what I do.

sludge, *sb.* Add: **1. a.** (Further examples: cf. *sludge *v.* 6.)

1946 L. D. Stamp *Britain's Struct. & Scenery* iii. 20 In tundra lands the sub-soil remains permanently frozen whilst the surface thaws in summer and, where there are steep slopes, masses of sludge slide downhill. **1959** G. H. Dury *Face of Earth* xv. 181 The loess records cold, very dry climate. The underlying sludge was formed in a preceding episode of moister conditions when the topsoil thawed annually.

c. The colour of sludge. Also *attrib.*

1962 *Sunday Express* 4 Feb. 19/2 Pyjama stripes—navy, 'sludge' or 'smog' on white. **1977** *Vogue* Feb. 90/1 From a commanding frilly and deep sludge dress, Merle Park changes into her working clothes.

2. *spec.* Such material formed as waste in

various industrial and mechanical processes. (Further examples.)

1920 Cross & Bevan *Paper-Making* 144 It constitutes a 'sludge', practically devoid of useful felting properties. **1933** *Charlottesville* (Va.) *Daily Progress* 22 May 6/5 The death of five men in a drainage vat at the Hess and Drucker Tannery was being investigated... The fifth was a would-be rescuer, who plunged into the tank of sludge. **1965** *New Statesman* 19 Nov. 809/4 (Advt.), Industrial Chemist required by Company dealing in sludges & effluents of all kinds. **1974** J. Dyson *Prime Minister's Boat is Missing* xxx. 180 The sludge of crude oil in the bottom of tanks.

d. A loose sediment that forms in boilers and other vessels in which water is habitually heated.

1839 [in Dict., sense 2 a]. **1912** R. B. Dole in Rogers & Aubert *Industr. Chem.* iii. 47 If magnesium and sulphates are comparatively low or if suspended matter is comparatively high the scale is soft and bulky and may be in the form of sludge that can be blown or washed from the boiler. **1937** E. Pull *Boiler-House Practice* xv. 147 Every opportunity should be taken to remove accumulations of grease, scale, sludge and soot. **1955** Kirk & Othmer *Encycl. Chem. Technol.* XIV. 940 This led to the system..of maintaining at all times in the boiler water a small but sufficient excess of phosphate ion so that all calcium ion entering with the feed water would be precipitated as a loose sludge of calcium phosphate rather than as a hard scale.

e. The mixture of water or mud fluid with cuttings that is produced in rock drilling.

1871 [see Sludger]. **1911** Dana & Saunders *Rock Drilling* ii. 21 The shales will often form a sludge containing such proportions of large and small particles as to cake on the bit. **1933** R. S. Lewis *Elements Mining* xiv. 422 Where much sludge is made it is very important to have the water return with sufficient velocity to lift the heaviest particles in the sludge. **1963** *Gloss. Mining Terms (B.S.I.)* iii. 13 *Sludge*, rock cuttings produced by the drill bit.

f. A dark viscous liquid or semi-solid mass deposited when a petroleum distillate is mixed with strong sulphuric acid during refining. Also called *sludge acid* (see sense 4 below), *acid sludge*.

1885 *Encycl. Brit.* XVIII. 719/1 The acid 'sludge', consisting of the oil of vitriol combined with the impurities of the oil and forming a black tarry liquid, settles to the bottom..and is drawn off. **1938** Oliver & Spangler in A. E. Dunstan et al. *Sci. Petroleum* IV. 2765/1 At refineries on the sea coast acid sludge was frequently discharged into the ocean. **1954** Kirk & Othmer *Encycl. Chem. Technol.* XIII. 493 Most refineries hydrolyze the light nonlube sludges, effecting an incomplete separation of acid tars from the weak impure acid. **1965** O. T. Fasullo *Sulfuric Acid* v. 127 The tendency of sludges to evolve sulfur dioxide.., in addition to the enormous quantity in which sludges are necessarily produced by the petroleum industry, makes these materials worthy subjects for the application of pollution control measures.

g. = *slime *sb.* 4 b.

1900 *Jrnl. Brit. Inst. Electr. Engin.* XXIX. 274 In copper refining with high current densities less anode sludge is formed. **1948** T. C. Elliott *Electric Accumulator Man.* iii. 26 The piling up of sludge..and the creation of possible short circuits through the growths clinging to the tubes..must be avoided. **1977** Brodd & Kordesch tr. *Bode's Lead-Acid Batteries* iii. 222 A Pb content of more than 5% is supposed to cause difficulties during the formation of positive plates (swelling or warping or extensive sludge formation).

h. A thick, semi-solid deposit that tends to form in oil when it is heated, exposed to the air, or mixed with another kind of oil.

1920 *Whittaker's Electr. Engineer's Pocket-bk.* (ed. 4) 245 When the transformer is examined, it is found that the windings and core are covered with a reddish-brown flocculent deposit or sludge. **1927** *Jrnl. Soc. Chem. Industry* 8 Apr. 135T/2 The sludge deposits which are sometimes found in hollow crankpins..are due evidently to decomposition products of the oil being thrown out by centrifugal action. **1941** D. F. Miner *Insulation Electr. Apparatus* iv. 81 The purification of oil used in circuit breakers and transformers consists principally in the removal of water, carbon, and sludge. **1973** G. Zwick *Everyman's Guide Car Maintenance* (1974) vi. 153 If the motorist has consistently been using a high grade heavy duty oil, the chances are that the interior of the engine is clean, with a bare minimum of sludge and other residues.

i. *Med.* (A quantity of) sludged blood. Cf. *sludging *vbl. sb.* 4.

1947 *Science* 7 Nov. 436/2 Many human patients have various degrees of unexplainable edema... These can now be examined for sludges. **1972** H. I. Bicher *Blood Cell Aggregation* ii. 27 All of this provides strong additional support for considering sludge as..a possible antecedent to thrombosis.

4. *sludge brown, green, grey* sbs. and adjs.; *sludge-coloured* adj.; **sludge acid** = sense 2 f above.

1885 Sludge acid [in Dict.]. **1938** Oliver & Spangler in A. E. Dunstan et al. *Sci. Petroleum* IV. 2766/2 Formerly it was possible to use some of this weak separated sludge acid for the manufacture of superphosphate fertilizer, but the objections..to the presence of evil-smelling hydrocarbon derivatives in superphosphate has practically stopped this. **1965** O. T. Fasullo *Sulfuric Acid* v. 127 Heavy sludges are generally mixed with lighter sludge acids to produce a blend with a middle-range viscosity. **1977** D. Clark *Gimmel Flask* v. 82, I thought this sort of sludge brown varnish paint went out with Queen Victoria. **1962** A. Lejeune *Duel in Shadows* vii. 91 An Englishman in a sludge-coloured raincoat. **1979** S. Gainham in G. Hardinge *Winter's Crimes* XI. 69 The woman in sludge-coloured tweed. **1971** *Vogue* 1 Oct. 127 Sludge green knit tights. **1972** *Guardian* 8 Feb. 11/2 Cheesecloth smock shirt..natural, yellow, sludge green, red or blue. **1976** *Times* 3 Feb. 9/7 Single breasted coat..sludge green with maroon overcheck **1977** *Listener* 22–29 Dec. 855/4 He's a moray eel, a sludge-grey reptilian lurker.

sludge, *v.* **I. 1.** Delete (2 b) and add later examples.

1950 *Brit. Birds* XLIII. 383 The bird was on a pool used for sludging boiler ash, which has been constructed within the last two years. **1978** *Sci. Amer.* Jan. 85 (Advt.), In industry, chromic acid and oil-water emulsions usually live only once. They do their job; then they get discharged, sludged, trucked away, and buried.

4. *intr.* To form or deposit sludge.

1941 D. F. Miner *Insulation Electr. Apparatus* iv. 80 Transformer oil that has begun to sludge will continue to do so after it has been purified by means of the centrifuge or filter press. **1977** Brodd & Kordesch tr. *Bode's Lead-Acid Batteries* iii. 271 Those plates that have been formed at 40°C with 1·06 kg/liter (acid concentration) and 74 A/m² (current density) are the last to sludge.

II. 5. *intr.* To trudge, to tramp; to labour. Cf. Slutch *v.* 3.

1908 M. & J. Findlater *Crossriggs* xxiii. 170 She had got to sludge back to the station in the rain, and then go home and give a cheerful account of her day. **1913** D. H. Lawrence *Love Poems & Others* 44 A widow o forty-five As has sludged like a horse all her life. **1954** *New Statesman* 3 Apr. 432/3 'Well, goodnight,' he said, sludging away.

III. 6. *intr.* To move slowly by solifluction.

1938 *Geol. Mag.* LXXV. 254 Only the upper 800 feet is precipitous, the lower 600 feet..consisting of vegetated scree down which recent waste is sludging. **1940** C. F. C. Hawkes *Prehistoric Foundations of Europe* ii. 7 Seasonal thawing will cause surface deposits to sludge over more deeply frozen subsoil: this phenomenon is called solifluxion. **1959** G. H. Dury *Face of Earth* xv. 177 Sludging downslope, rock-waste tends to mask the break between high and low ground. **1964** *New Scientist* 8 Oct. 105/2 Half frozen material sludges rapidly downhill in the spring thaw.

Hence **sludged** *ppl. a.*

1941 D. F. Miner *Insulation Electr. Apparatus* iv. 80 No method is yet available that will..bring sludged oil back to its original condition. **1947** *Science* 7 Nov. 435/2 The resistance of sludged blood to its own passage through the bottlenecks of the circulatory system forcibly reduces the rates of blood flow through all the open vessels of the body. **1972** H. I. Bicher *Blood Cell Aggregation* ii. 35 Ischemic changes in the myocardium as a result of sludged blood.

sludging (slʌ·dʒiŋ), *vbl. sb.* [f. Sludge *sb.* or *v.* + -ing¹.] **1.** The action of filling up crevices in dried clay by means of free-flowing mud; also, the mud so used.

1852 J. Wiggins *Embanking* 19 As these spits contract in drying, the crevices outside are therefore filled with mud, which is called 'sludging'. *a* **1877** Knight *Dict. Mech.* III. 2217/1 *Sludging*, stopping the crevices incident to the contraction of clay piled in embankments, by mud sufficiently fluid to run freely. **1940** *Chambers's Techn. Dict.* 342/1 The crevices left when the clay has dried out are filled with sludging.

2. The formation or deposition of sludge, esp. in oil.

1922 Glazebrook *Dict. Appl. Physics* II. 928/1 Various schemes and devices are used to prevent sludging, such as..by using a float on the oil surface. **1931** Hoffert & Claxton *Motor Benzole* vi. 143 The difference in the solubilities of the resinous substances in different types of wash oils, also accounts for the sludging that usually occurs when such oils are mixed. **1969** *Practical Motorist* Jan. 557/1 Most modern engine oils incorporate additives which are designed to reduce sludging. **1973** *Times* 1 June 11/5 No black sludge will be able to form in your central heating system. How horrid. I never knew sludging was going on behind those pipes.

3. = *solifluction.

1946 *Amer. Jrnl. Sci.* CCXLIV. 626 The down-slope movement of the fine-grained components is presumed to be largely a flow as mud and is called by English writers 'sludging'. **1959** G. H. Dury *Face of Earth* xv. 177 Widespread sludging is mainly responsible for the featureless aspect of many Arctic landscapes. **1964** *New Scientist* 8 Oct. 105/3 He also showed..that the much-discussed movement by freeze-thaw sludging (solifluction) is quantitatively of very little significance [in a Lappland valley]. **1975** J. G. Evans *Environment Early Man Brit. Isles* i. 7 The Upper Gravel..was most likely formed by downhill sludging under conditions of impeded drainage.

4. *Med.* The aggregation of blood cells into jelly-like masses in such a way as to impede circulation.

1950 *Amer. Jrnl. Med. Sci.* CCXIX. 538/2 We have.. found a close correlation between the blood sedimentation rate and the degree of sludging in the capillaries. **1976** *Path. Ann.* XI. 3 This hemorrhage is sustained for up to 24 hours until the deeper intact capillaries adopt a ballooned appearance due to stasis and sludging of red cells.

sludgy, *a.* Add: **3.** Of the colour of sludge.

1975 *Country Life* 18 Dec. 1770/2 'Workwear', made in sludgy colours and materials. **1978** *Daily Tel.* 6 Dec. 17/4 All colours are sludgy at the fashionable end of the market at present... Pinks, yellows and purples are just unsaleable.

sluff (slʌf), *v.* *U.S.* var. Slough *v.*² 3.

For other uses see *Engl. Dial. Dict.* s.v. *Slough* sb.¹ and vb.¹.

1934 *Amer. Ballads & Folk Songs* i. 24 And sluffed their coin for 'dago red'. **1959** T. Reese *Bridge Player's Dict.* 206 *Sluff*, to discard; to throw a card, other than a trump, of a suit different from the one led. **1964** *N.Y. Times Mag.* 6 Dec. 20 Its water-repellent finish sluffs off snow. **1966** J. dos Passos *Best Times* (1968) ii. 56, I had sluffed off Harvard indifference, but Harvard snobbery still hung on. **1972** *New York* 8 May 43/3 His [*sc.* a dog's] shedding mechanism, which now goes about building up and sluffing off the coat. **1972** *Village Voice* (N.Y.) 1 June 50/4 When I consulted a urologist he complained that he was sick of other doctors sluffing the problem off on him all the time. **1976** *National Skat & Sheepshead Q.* Mar. 5 The picker sluffed off the club king. **1978** *Detroit Free Press* 2 Apr. 19C/3 East is now squeezed in the red suits—he must either give up a trick to the jack of hearts or sluff two diamonds, which sets up declarer's third diamond. **1980** *Amer. Speech* LV. 210 Black jazzmen returned to the linguistic roots of their art which had been sidetracked and sluffed off in the *bebop/bop* movement of the 1940s.

slug, *sb.*¹ Add: **1. b.** A contemptible person; a fat person.

In some instances the influence of sense 4a is probable.

1931 A. Huxley *Let.* 25 Sept. (1969) 355, I am making notes for a short study..and tho' this cannot be specifically a retort to Murry it will in effect try to undo some of the mischief that that slug has undoubtedly done. **1940** G. & S. Lorimer *First Love Farewell* iv. 133 'He didn't love me and I felt pretty bad about it!' 'The complete and utter slug!' **1959** I. & P. Opie *Lore & Lang. Schoolch.* ix. 168 The unfortunate fat boy..is known as..slug. **1966** 'J. Hackston' *Father clears Out* 104 No more big slugs turning up, the rush lost its enthusiasm.

6. slug pellet, a pellet of bait containing a poison to kill slugs.

1960 *Do it Yourself Gardening Ann.* 100/3 The most effective way of controlling slugs and snails is to use a metaldehyde-bait mixture... The easiest way to do this is to use a proprietary brand of slug pellets. **1976** L. Thomas *Dangerous Davies* xvi. 188 A large tin of garden slug pellets.

slug, *sb.*² Add: **1. b.** For 'Now *U.S.*' read 'Now chiefly *U.S.*' and add further examples.

1916 H. L. Wilson *Somewhere in Red Gap* vi. 245 Even the new Episcopalian minister..took a slug of rye and said it was undeniably delightful. **1940** R. Chandler *Farewell, my Lovely* v. 34, I poured her a slug that would have made me float over a wall. **1958** C. Williams *Man in Motion* (1959) i. 6 Pouring another cup of coffee, I dropped a slug of bourbon in it. **1973** C. Bonington *Next Horizon* xv. 216 The scene was Hogarthian—with a soldier lying flat in the gutter,..a mother giving her eighteen-month babe a slug of the fire-water, to stop it crying. **1978** L. Heren *Growing up on The Times* v. 182 Their simple niceness was almost as good as a slug of scotch and a cigarette which I..could not enjoy in their company.

c. A compact mass of liquid regarded as retaining its identity as it travels.

1947 I. Thomas *Injection Molding of Plastics* vi. 353 If the reservoir were omitted the cold slug of material would enter the cavity and possibly cause smudge or flow marks in the molded article. **1967** *Guardian* 13 Feb. 14/6 In each pipe will be methane gas plus liquid oil called the 'slug'... Once ashore the gas and slug have to be separated and cleaned. **1971** *Nature* 21 May 181/1 A rapid intravenous injection leads to a 'slug' of relatively undispersed drug traversing the arteries on the first circuit. **1975** *Petroleum Rev.* XXIX. 315/3 A collection of liquid, known as a 'slug', can amount to several hundred thousand gallons and will travel along the pipeline at a speed of up to 10 miles per hour. **1979** *Nature* 8 Feb. 441/1 The velocity of the ejected slug of [volcanic] debris.

3. a. (Earlier examples.)

1849 *Picayune* (New Orleans) 6 June 1/6 The gold from that stream is generally in large pieces, more generally termed slugs or coarse, but very fine gold, if you please. **1855** *Golden Era* (San Francisco) 21 Jan. 2/7 We took out one slug weighing 60 ounces of pure gold, in the shape of an ox's tongue.

c. *Electr.* A metal cylinder fitted round the end of the core of an electromagnetic relay to modify the speeds of opening and closing. Cf. *sleeve *sb.* 7 c.

1928 *Jrnl. Inst. Electr. Engineers* LXVI. 346/1 A thick copper cylinder—or 'slug'—placed over part of the core, or a thin cylinder—or 'sleeve'—placed over the whole of the core, will provide a closed path of very low resistance in which currents of considerable magnitude may flow. **1943** A. L. Albert *Fund. Telephony* ix. 199 The amount of time delay can be regulated by the size and location of the copper slug. **1969** M. L. Gayford *Mod. Relay Techniques* iii. 60 A slug at the armature end slows down both operation and release. A slug at the rear or heel end has little effect on the operate time but produces suitable delay on release.

d. *Nucl. Engin.* A rod or bar of nuclear fuel.

1945 H. D. Smyth *Gen. Acct. Devel. Atomic Energy Mil. Purposes* vii. 69 The uranium would react chemically with the water,..probably to the point of disintegrating the uranium slugs. **1952** [see *plutonium 2 b]. *a* **1958** K. Edwards in 'E. Crispin' *Best SF 3* (1958) 34 The uranium slugs were short and the aluminium cans that held them in the centre of the pile..were long. **1967** J. T. Long *Engin. Nuclear Fuel Reprocessing* xi. 838 The slugs were cooled by natural convection of water in a finned tank. **1973** *Trans. Amer. Nuclear Soc.* XVII. 508/2 A charge of fuel particles, a preformed matrix slug, and a top punch are inserted.

e. *Electr.* An adjustable magnetic core used to vary the inductance of a coil containing it. Chiefly in *slug tuning* (so *slug-tuned* adj.).

1957 *Practical Wireless* XXXIII. 566/1 Now adjust trimmers or slugs of discriminator transformer to obtain a symmetrical pattern. **1959** R. L. SHRADER *Electronic Communication* xiv. 390 A few receiver RF amplifiers.. use slug tuning, having a mechanical means of pulling the slug into the desired position in the coil by a dial on the front of the equipment. **1960** *Practical Wireless* XXXVI. 416/2 Coil L2 is also heavily damped and variable tuning is hardly worthwhile; it is accordingly slug-tuned to the centre of the three transmissions to be received. **1979** A. A. LIFF *Color & Black & White Television Theory & Servicing* iv. 108 The individually tuned circuits in the oscillator section are all slug tuned.

4. c. (Earlier examples.)
1851 *Oregon Statesman* 23 Sept. 2/6 He accordingly 'pungled down' two of Moffat's $50 slugs, and of course, cut the black, there being no red spots in the pack. **1872** S. POWERS *Afoot & Alone* 303 A shining 'slug', fresh from the San Francisco mint, [was] laid scrupulously in the place.

e. *U.S. slang.* A dollar; a counterfeit coin; a token.
1887 *Lantern* (New Orleans) 4 June 5/2 She'd sooner put up her ten slugs and go back to the pipe. **1913** *Dial. Notes* IV. 28 *Slug*,..round piece of metal for slot machines. **1934** J. T. FARRELL *Young Manhood of Studs Lonigan* xvii. 259 He bought a slug from the cashier in the Chain drugstore at Prairie and walked back to the telephone booths.

f. *Journalism.* = *slug-line*, sense 6 below.
1925 G. M. HYDE *Newspaper Editing* (ed. 2) ii. 89 Use expressions that will not offend readers..if the slugs slip into print... 'Kill widow'..may be misunderstood. **1927** *Amer. Speech* II. 240/2 'Slug'..is a brief title..placed above a story for the guidance of the copy-reader and the printer. **1949** T. F. BARNHART *Weekly Newspaper Writing & Editing* xxii. 224/2 In many newspaper plants some other term is substituted for guidelines, such as catch-lines, slugs and slug-lines. **1979** 'A. HAILEY' *Overload* IV. vii. 324 The newspaper put a copyright slug over her story.

5*. *Engin.* A unit of mass equal to 32·1740 lb., being the mass of a body which accelerates at one foot per second per second when acted on by one pound force.
1902 A. M. WORTHINGTON *Dynamics of Rotation* (ed. 4) p. viii, I have ventured to give the name of a 'slug' to the British Engineer's Unit of Mass, *i.e.*, to the mass in which an acceleration of one foot-per-sec.-per-sec. is produced by a force of one pound. **1923** A. R. LOW in W. L. Marsh *Rep. Internat. Air Congr.* 62 The 'slug' of 32·2 pounds avoirdupois mass, which has actually been imposed on British aeronautics by the Advisory Committee. **1936** F. W. LANCHESTER *Theory of Dimensions & its Application for Engineers* v. 37 Even amongst the advocates of Perry's system.., the slug has never taken shape except on paper; it has, and has had no real material existence. **1944** N. A. V. PIERCY *Compl. Course Elem. Aerodynamics* iv. 86 At 15° C. and 760 mm. pressure, ρ [*sc.* the density of air]..=0·00238 slug per cubic foot. **1973** *Nature* 20 July 184/3 The statement that the unit of mass in the British system is the slug is several years out of date.

6. *slug-gun*; **slug-line** *Journalism*, an identifying title, usu. occupying one slug, accompanying a news story in draft and galleys; **slug-setting** *Printing*, the method of setting an entire line of type on a single slug; so **slug-set** *a.*
1940 *Illustr. London News* CXCVI. 53 (*caption*) Their training includes the use of tear-gas, while they are armed with 'slug-guns', ·303 rifles and staves. **1973** M. AMIS *Rachel Papers* 218 The youth, handsomely reading Tennyson on summer evenings, or trying to kill birds with feeble, rusted slug-guns. **1930** K. E. OLSON *Typogr. & Mechanics of Newspaper* xi. 360 Sometimes the printer forgets to remove the slugline when he places a story in its column, and this would appear above the story unless caught in the final check. **1976** J. MCCLURE *Rogue Eagle* ii. 27 He tapped out the name of his freelance agency and the slug-line. **1963** Slug-setting [see *FILMSET *v.*]. **1970** *Times Lit. Suppl.* 9 Apr. 387/2 It is an instance of their attention to quality that even novels are 'Monotype' set, whereas most publishers use slug-setting. **1975** J. BUTCHER *Copy-Editing* ii. 7 Slugsetting is unsuitable for complex tables, though Monotype may be used for tables in a slugset book.

slug, *sb.*³ Add: **2.** *attrib.* and *Comb.*, as **slug-fest** [*FEST] *U.S. slang*, a hard-hitting contest, *spec.* in boxing and baseball; **slug-nutty** *a.* (*U.S. slang*), punch-drunk; hence **slug-nuttiness.**
1916 *Nebraska State Jrnl.* 27 July 3/1 (*heading*) Denver wins in slugfest. **1933** G. TUNNEY *Man must Fight* 14 If Dempsey would gamble with me in a slug-fest I would beat him to the punch every time. **1943** *Amer. Speech* XVIII. 105 A good inning at bat..is a..*slug-fest.* **1969** *Daily Colonist* (Victoria, B.C.) 21 Mar. 1/4 A meeting between Canadian MPs and a high French government official turned into a verbal slugfest as the Canadians raked the Gaullist government for its policies towards Quebec and Ottawa. **1976** M. MACHLIN *Pipeline* x. 116 For a while it looked as though there was going to be a real slugfest. **1979** *Arizona Daily Star* 1 Apr. B5/4 'Back to Basics' is today's biggest educational debate topic. But so far, it has generated a mostly muddled, emotional slugfest. *Ibid.* 8 Apr. C1/2 Powers gave up four runs on seven hits, a contrast from the 33-hit slugfest of Friday night. **1943** *Gen* 16 Jan. 30/1 Though no medical man, I know enough about slug-nuttiness to tell you..how it comes about. **1933** 'P. CAIN' *Fast One* vi. 196 He shook his head sadly without looking up. 'Slug-nutty.' **1936** J. STEINBECK *In Dubious Battle* ii. 16 Don't mind Joy. He's slug-nutty. He's been smacked over the head too much. **1950** E. HEMINGWAY *Across River & into Trees* iv. 26 He's been beat up so much he's slug-nutty.

slug, *v.*² Add: **3.** *Journalism. trans.* To mark with a slug-line; with compl.: to give as a slug-line or other heading.
1925 G. M. HYDE *Newspaper Editing* (ed. 2) ii. 27 What the copywriter does..may be summarized... 'Slugs' story for record and make-up. **1928** *Amer. Speech* IV. 135 The hardened deskman merely grins, squeezes the gist of a column story into ten words and 'slugs' the article to designate the 'head' that is to accompany it. **1940** N. MACNEIL *Without Fear or Favor* v. 74 The foreign editor..may slug his stories by correspondent. **1953** B. WESTLEY *News Editing* xii. 197 When they moved a story about the possible use of bacteriological warfare.., the United Press slugged it: 'Germs'. **1974** J. BANNING *How I fooled World* xix. 77 The [news] story, slugged 'Television', ran something like this. **1976** *Daily Tel.* 13 Oct. 6/7 Members of the National Union of Journalists.. called..for all relevant copy to be marked, or 'slugged', 'Not for Preston'. *Ibid.*, There was a previous precedent for slugging copy in an outside dispute.

slug, *v.*³ Add: **1. b.** *fig.* To treat roughly; to drug; to exploit; to overcharge; to force *out* of; to churn *out.*
1925 A. S. M. HUTCHINSON *One Increasing Purpose* I. xviii. 112, I know..that really you were court-martialled and hoofed out... But what the facts were, *why* you were slugged, *how* they found out your hideous goings-on, I never could discover. **1938** J. STEINBECK *Long Valley* 116, I guess the doctor slugged me pretty hard... I feel all right now, only a little dopey. **1941** S. J. BAKER *Dict. Austral. Slang* 68 *Get slugged*, to be charged excessively. **1946** K. S. PRICHARD *Roaring Nineties* 326 Alf knew the mine-owners were slugging the prospectors and alluvial diggers. **1962** 'K. ORVIS' *Damned & Destroyed* vi. 46 She had..slugged herself insensible with a terrific overdose of heroin. **1974** P. DE VRIES *Glory of Hummingbird* ii. 14 The thankless task of slugging contributions out of the congregation. **1976** *Australasian Express* 11 June 26/2 Canberra: Big cars will be slugged for extra insurance if a report to the Government is adopted. **1977** *New Yorker* 19 Sept. 96/2 I've been slugging out so many notes of American music I'm turning into a piece of apple pie.

c. *to slug it out*: to fight it out; to stick it out.
1943 *Time* 10 May 98/3 Twice it screens exciting action: once when the sub slugs it out with a disguised German raider. **1952** M. LOWRY *Let.* 11 Jan. (1967) 286 Somehow we slugged it out, without having to abandon the house. **1970** *Listener* 23 July 127/3 It decided not to slug it out directly with *News at Ten.* **1973** *Black World* Mar. 58, I saw the two shadows boxing on the side of the brick building... It was Bernie and Bennie Speakes, twins about 10, slugging it out in the alley. **1978** *Detroit Free Press* 16 Apr. 14C/1 They'll slug it out, week by week, blow by blow, for all the world to see.

2. *intr.* To slog. Also with *along*, *away.*
1943 *Fortune* Feb. 122/1 Guns slugging at close range. **1943** *Newsweek* 9 Aug. 27/1 This found them..still slugging along at a point between the coastal villages of Tetere and Zovi. **1944** *Reader's Digest* Nov. 62/1 But always he was slugging away at novel writing on the side. **1959** *Times* 9 Mar. 3/1 In the second [half], largely an affair of forwards slugging away with barely diminished vigour, the Navy's packing became untidy.

sluggard, *sb.* **a.** *Comb.* (Later examples.)
1892 J. LUMSDEN *Sheep-head & Trotters* 301 Harvest, however, came at length, lagging on a-pace, sweet and sluggard-wise. **1910** W. DE MORGAN *Affair of Dishonour* vii. 87 That he should, simply from an idle indulgence of laziness, lie sluggard-wise till near mid-day.

sluggardry. For † *Obs.*⁻¹ read *rare* and add later examples.
1925 V. WOOLF *Common Reader* 79 The extremes of passion are not for the novelist;..he must tame his swiftness to sluggardry. **1935** W. DE LA MARE *Early One Morning* 145 Unusual discomfort of mind or body may slow down the wheels of existence to a sluggardry almost beyond endurance.

slugged (slʌgd), *a.*² [f. SLUG *sb.*² + -ED².] Having a slug or slugs.
1906 *Daily Colonist* (Victoria, B.C.) 5 Jan. 9/1 (Advt.), Boys' Calf Boots, double soles, slugged bottoms, sizes 1 to 5. **1922** *Daily Mail* 10 Nov. 4 Boys' unlined slugged soles Derbys. **1928** *Jrnl. Inst. Electr. Engineers* LXVI. 341/1 The release of slugged relays is complicated by saturation. **1958** J. W. FREEBODY *Telegraphy* iv. 84/1 The actual release lag of a slugged relay depends also on the spring tension.

slugger². For *U.S.* read 'orig. and chiefly *U.S.*' and add: **1.** (Earlier and further examples.) Also in *Baseball*, a hard-hitting batter.
1877 [see *COON *sb.* 4 b]. **1883** *Chicago Tribune* 3 July 6/5 Poor Burns fell an easy victim to the Cleveland sluggers. **1894** G. MEREDITH *Let.* 19 Feb. (1970) III. 1155 Harrison is a controversial slugger. I did not expect he would descend to the use of street missiles. Your answer hit the right tone. **1946** *Sun* (Baltimore) 27 May 15 (*caption*) Charlie Keller, the Yankee's slugger, is shown being caught in a rundown. **1952** *Manch. Guardian Weekly* 16 Oct. 2/1 Their team includes Mr. Gromyko and the notorious slugger Vyshinsky. **1967** *Boston Sunday Herald* 26 Mar. II. 3/1 Tony has the build of a slugger... Maybe some club will make an offer for him, giving a dependable pitcher in return. **1970** *Daily Tel.* (Colour Suppl.) 9 Oct. 27/3 No amateur karate exponent stands a halfway chance against an old-fashioned slugger and kicker who has real experience of street brawls. **1972** J. MOSEDALE *Football* vii. 100 One of the National League's most powerful sluggers as a Cincinnati Red. **1977** *Times of Zambia* 7 Sept. 10/7 The new holder of baseball's all-time Home Run record, Japanese slugger Sadaharu Oh.

3. Usu. *pl.* Ear-to-chin whiskers. Also called *slugger whiskers. U.S. slang.*
1898 F. P. DUNNE *Mr. Dooley in Peace & War* 211 Ganderbilk he was there, too, standin' out on th' steps in th' cold, combin' his whiskers... He wears a pair iv sluggers..with his fingers. **1900** G. ADE *More Fables* 118 The mild old Gentleman with the straw-colored Sluggers ..came near. **1960** WENTWORTH & FLEXNER *Dict. Amer. Slang* 489/2 *Slugger*.., an ear-to-ear chin beard, as worn by a stage Irishman. **1960** B. KEATON *My Wonderful World of Slapstick* i. 12 A fright wig, slugger whiskers, fancy vest.

slugger³. Add: **2.** One who attaches the top piece of the heel of a shoe to the seat.
1911 *Rep. Labour & Soc. Cond. Germany* (Tariff Reform League) III. VI–VII. 30 The average wages paid in the district were:.. Sole layer 20s. to 32s. Slugger 30s. to 35s. **1921** *Dict. Occup. Terms* (1927) § 414 *Slugger*,..operates, by means of a lever, slugging machine, which attaches top piece of heel to seat.

slugging, *vbl. sb.*² Add: (Further examples.) Also *attrib.* and *fig.*
1942 BERREY & VAN DEN BARK *Amer. Thes. Slang* § 675/3 *Game with many hits*...slugging match. **1956** A. H. COMPTON *Atomic Quest* 315 The war would become a heavy slugging match. **1959** *Economist* 30 May 819/1 The abortive Shawwaf revolt in Mosul set off a slugging match between Cairo and Baghdad. **1974** *Sumter* (S. Carolina) *Daily Item* 23 Apr. 7A/5 His slugging percentage? A whopping .860. **1978** J. CARROLL *Mortal Friends* III. vi. 339 A month's worth of slugging along a coastline through a series of towns.

sluggish, *a.* Add: **3. b.** [Rendering of Russ. *stértaya* (*shizofreniya*), worn, hackneyed (schizophrenia).] Applied to an alleged type of schizophrenia ascribed to political or religious dissidents confined in state psychiatric hospitals in the U.S.S.R.
1977 *Science News* 10 Sept. 165 'Even if one should accept the diagnosis of sluggish schizophrenia in these and similar cases,' Chodoff said, 'one must wonder why a disease without delusions, hallucinations or agitated behavior should require injections of chloropromazine (an antischizophrenic drug) for its treatment.' **1978** *Nature* 4 May 6/2 Yet, when committed, Shikhanovich was diagnosed as a 'psychopath with the possibility of the onset of sluggish schizophrenia' (the latter 'disease', of course, being unknown to non-Soviet diagnosis). **1980** *Prisoners of Conscience in USSR* (Amnesty Internat.) (ed. 2) 184 Schizophrenia, often in its 'sluggish' form, has been the diagnosis most commonly made of dissenters.

sluice, *sb.* Add: **5.** (Earlier example.)
1851 *San Francisco Picayune* 14 Oct. 2/4 In the neighbourhood of Rough and Ready, a sluice of fourteen miles in length has been constructed.

6. a. sluice-fork, a fork used to break up lumps of gravel in a gold-miner's sluice-box; **sluice-head** orig. *U.S.*, a supply or head of water sufficient for flushing out a sluice; also *fig.*
1856 *San Francisco Call* 16 Dec. 4/2 As he went—took it *puss*'nal—it commenced raining 'sluice-forks'. **1874** A. BATHGATE *Colonial Experiences* viii. 92 The large stones.. lifted out by hand..while the smaller ones are sometimes taken out with a long handled long pronged sluice-fork. **1909** H. THOMPSON in A. E. Currie *Centennial Treasury of Otago Verse* (1949) 59 Slinging stones out with his sluice-fork—what a pleasant little game. **1855** *Golden Era* (San Francisco) 4 Mar. 1/6 At Eureka there are only twelve sluiceheads of water running. **1863** V. PYKE in *App. Jrnls. House Reps. N.Z.* D. VI. 15 Head races..represent about 200 sluice heads. **1901** E. DYSON in *Austral. Short Stories* (1951) 58 Mrs. Mooney..wept sluice-heads... She had been replenishing the fountain of tears with whisky. **1906** *Daily Colonist* (Victoria, B.C.) 6 Jan. 12/3 Although little opened, the springs now have a flow of two sluice-heads. **1935** G. L. MEREDITH *Adventuring in Maoriland in Seventies* xiii. 145 The one we went to is just a boiling spring, running about five 'sluice-heads' of boiling water.

sluice-box. (Earlier examples.)
1857 *Hutching's Mag.* July 7/1 A continuous line of these troughs or 'sluice boxes', the smaller and lower end of each, inserted for three or four inches into the larger end of the next one below, form the 'sluice'. **1864** *Richmond-Atkinson Papers* (1960) II. ii. 110 You will not be quite out of the rattle of the shovel, long tom, and sluice box, for we are very golden just now.

sluice-way. (Earlier example.)
1779 W. MCKENDRY *Jrnl.* 8 Aug. in *Proc. Mass. Hist. Soc.* (1886) II. 461 The sluce way was broke up and the water filld. the river immediately.

sluit. Add: Also **slote.** (Earlier examples.)
1818 C. I. LATROBE *Jrnl. Visit to S. Afr.* x. 187 It has.. water in abundance, brought by a *slote*, or canal, from a considerable distance. **1852** C. BARTER *Dorp & Veld* iv. 33 Going one dark night to a friend's house, and keeping in the middle of the road to avoid the 'sloots', I stumbled over..a large black ox. **1862** L. DUFF GORDON *Let.* 29 Dec. in F. Galton *Vacation Tourists* (1864) 157 There is no water but what runs down the streets in the sloot, a paved channel, which brings the water from the mountain and supplies the houses and gardens.

slum, *sb.*¹ Add: **I. 2. a.** Also *rarely*, a house materially unfit for human habitation.
1955 *Times* 25 Aug. 5/5 Nowadays people who live in so-called slum houses (a 'slum', as officially defined

means a house materially unfit for habitation), set a good standard of cleanliness. **1972** *Observer* 31 Dec. 8/2 He had inherited nearly two million slums.

4. a. *slum area, -dweller, property, street*, etc. (further examples); *slum-bred* adj.

1891 *Contemp. Rev.* Oct. 548 Tens of millions will be exposed to the physical and mental blight of the 'submerged' slum-dweller. **1898** E. Howard *To-morrow* xiv. 147 What will become of this slum property?.. These wretched slums will be pulled down. **1924** *Glasgow Herald* 8 Mar. 7 The slum problem is fundamentally not one of stone and lime or cubic space, but of mental and social outlook. **1928** Galsworthy *Swan Song* i. vii. 57 Slum-dwellers were such good sorts! **1932** L. Golding *Magnolia St.* iii. vi. 537 A tribe of inconceivable people who lived in a slum street in a dark English town. **1935** C. S. Forester *Afr. Queen* iv. 86 His slum-bred father and mother. **1939** C. Day Lewis *Child of Misfortune* ii. ii. 151 The Church.. held slum-property, helped to exploit innocent native tribes and ruined their morals and physique. **1940** 'G. Orwell' *Inside Whale* 20 Low wages and the growth and shift of population had brought into existence a huge, dangerous slum-proletariat. **1959** I. & P. Opie *Lore & Lang. Schoolch.* xviii. 389 A row of crowded slum houses with front doors cheek by jowl. **1959** J. Cary *Captive & Free* ix. 41 The mid-town terraces which can and have so easily become slum tenements. **1960** 'F. Newton' *Jazz Scene* vi. 100 The penalties of the isolated, community-less life of the slum-bred entertainer. **1968** *Globe & Mail* (Toronto) 13 Feb. 27/1 Maple Leafs can muddle into the slum area of fifth place and there are few hoots of derision. *a* **1974** R. Crossman *Diaries* (1975) I. 182 The town itself has some 30,000 or 40,000 inhabitants..who don't want Birmingham slum dwellers dumped on them as overspill. **1979** G. St. Aubyn *Edward VII* viii. 379 She insisted on being shown his slum property in the East End of London. **1980** J. Melville *Chrysanthemum Chain* 135 Walker made his way out and into the shabby slum street.

b. Special Combinations: **slum clearance**, the evacuation and demolition of slums, usu. accompanied by the rehousing of the inhabitants; freq. *attrib.*; also **slum clearer, clearing** *ppl. a.*; **slumland** (later examples); **slum landlord**, one who lets slum property to tenants, esp. one who allows his property to fall into disrepair; hence **slum landlordism**, the practice of letting slum property; **slumlord** *U.S.* = *slum landlord* above; hence **slumlordship.**

[**1900** A. Smith *Housing Question* iii. 60 The clearance of slums should not be taken to make room for housing schemes.] **1907** E. R. Dewsnup *Housing Problem in Eng.* xi. 227 Local Authorities..have hesitated to shoulder the financial burden that would result from any general application of the powers of slum clearance placed at their disposal by statute law. **1930** T. E. Lawrence *Let.* 19 Jan. (1938) 678 The area it occupied turned into a public garden, in pursuance of the slum-clearance scheme. **1936** T. S. Eliot *Essays Ancient & Modern* 132 We recognize that possibility in every work of slum-clearance and housing reform. **1953** E. Smith *Guide to English Traditions & Public Life* 133 The necessity of slum-clearance had to be faced. **1961** L. Mumford *City in History* viii. 220 Such systematic slum clearance projects as Nero's great fire naturally increased the housing shortage. **1979** *Punch* 28 Nov. 1032/3 Ms Greer..does not establish much that is positive; but she has performed a monumental work of intellectual slum-clearance. **1934** 'R. Crompton' *William—the Gangster* viii. 177 They were all lofty and spacious enough to satisfy the most determined and particular of slum clearers. **1977** *Listener* 28 Apr. 531/1 If the developer had to pay over a slice to the slum-clearing authorities, this would allow them to rehouse the slum-dwellers. **1929** S. Leslie *Anglo-Catholic* i. 10 He felt at home in the East End and refreshed..when he lay back at night and sniffed the indefinable steam of slumland. **1978** D. Murphy *Place Apart* vi. 110, I..cycled back to slumland to spend the rest of the day with Catholic families. **1893** G. B. Shaw *Widowers' Houses* iii. vii. 84 The worst slum landlord in London. **1931** W. Holtby *Poor Caroline* iii. 97 There was so much to be done..slum landlords to be confronted. **1972** C. Drummond *Death at Bar* vii. 179 A slum landlord who augmented his meagre rents in strange and unlawful ways. **1892** *Black & White* 17 Dec. 698/1 As a discussion, with open doors, of the pros and cons of slum-landlordism ..Mr Shaw's *Widowers' Houses* is..a very considerable piece of work. **1967** *Sunday Times* 30 Apr. 11/1 Slum landlordism..has not been seriously curtailed. **1953** *Chicago Daily News* 12 Sept. 3/7 Reporters..found that slumlords frequently twist Illinois' trust laws into blinds for escaping detection. **1957** *N.Y. Times Mag.* 12 May 36/3 The landlord had bitterly protested..that he was not a 'slumlord' and avowed that he was ready to put the building in condition *if* he could get a guarantee that it would stay that way. **1978** S. Wilson *Dealer's Move* vii. 121 A big place in Surrey—it belonged to one of the king slum-lords. **1966** *Atlantic Monthly* Nov. 128 Within the chivalric order of slumlordship he is a very minor vassal.

II. 5. a. (Earlier example.)

1812 P. Egan *Boxiana* i. 122 The flowing harangue of some dusty cove..lavish with his slum on the beauties possessed by some distinguished pugilist.

8. *N. Amer.* **a.** Cheap or imitation jewellery. Also as *adj. Criminals' slang.*

1914 Jackson & Hellyer *Vocab. Criminal Slang* 77 *Slum*, jewelry of any description, but lately reduced in scope of meaning to include only the less valuable kinds of jewelry... 'He's got a bale of slum for sloughings.' **1924** G. C. Henderson *Keys to Crookdom* 418 *Slum*, plated jewelry. **1931** *Amer. Speech* VII. 102 Nail the stones but blow the slum. **1946** S. S. Jacobs in *Mag. Digest* Aug. 89/2 A guy buys a slum ring for ten cents. **1955** *Publ. Amer. Dialect Soc.* xxiv. 122 Any kind of jewelry, usually exclusive of watches, was—and still is—referred to as *slum*. **1962** 'K. Orvis' *Damned & Destroyed* vii. 53 Jewellery... Top stuff. No slum.

b. Cheap prizes at a fair, carnival, etc.

1929 *Sat. Even. Post* 19 Oct. 26/2 Business Opportunities hammer at every door in the advertising columns of this trade paper. Slum, 1008 pieces for tie pins, collar pins, brooches, cigarette holders, rings, $695 the lot. **1956** H. Gold *Man who was not with It* (1965) i. 5 The slum prizes dripped from their hands, taffy, teddy-bears, streamers of paper.

Hence **slu·mism** [-ism], the existence of slums; the deprivations and other ills associated with or characteristic of life in the slums.

1967 *Britannica Bk. of Year 1966* 804/2 *Slumism*, the existence of highly congested urban residential areas characterized by deteriorated unsanitary buildings, poverty, and social disorganization. **1967** *Harper's Mag.* Feb. 83 We must show the same unhesitating commitment to fighting slumism, poverty, ignorance, prejudice, and unemployment that we show to fighting Communism. **1971** L. Chester *Martin Luther King* xi. 262 We are victims of slumism!

slum, *sb.*[3] *slang.* [App. abbrev. of Slumgullion.] **1.** = Slumgullion 2 c.

1847 J. Mitchell *Reminisc. College* 117 Though the son of Vulcan found the pork and cabbage harmless, I am sure that slum would have been a match for him. **1865** 'Mark Twain' *Notebook* 28 Jan. (1935) i. 6 Chili-beans and dish-water three times today as usual and some kind of 'slum' which the Frenchman called 'hash'. **1898** E. H. Blatchford *Let.* 17 July (1920) 37 Beef stew, commonly known as slum. **1918** *Stars & Stripes* 5 Apr. 4 Everyone knows that there are at least three different kinds of slum—the watered kind, the more solid variety and the occasional special sort that wears a pie-crust. The Marines describe these three types in sea-lingo: 'slum with the tide in', 'slum with the tide out', and 'slum with an overcoat'. **1972** J. M. Minifie *Homesteader* xx. 182 There would be white table-cloths and sparkling glass and silver, instead of a mess-tin of slum on a dirty table in barracks.

2. Special Combinations. **slum burner**, an army cook; **slum gun**, a field-kitchen.

1930 *Our Army* Aug. 33 The..cook..is a 'slum-burner'. **1943** M. Hargrove *See here, Private Hargrove* xlii. 118 Oscar of the Waldorf, in the Army, would still be..a *slum-burner*. **1917** R. Batchelder *Watching & Waiting on Border* vii. 90 The regiment owned a field-kitchen, or 'slum-gun', a bulky vehicle in which food might be prepared on the march. **1947** D. Runyon *Poems for Men* 213 Our slum-gun busted down.

slum, *v.* Add: **2. b.** *intr.* (See quot. 1965.) Also *trans.*, to shear (a sheep, etc.) in this manner. *Austral. Sheep-shearing.*

1965 J. S. Gunn *Terminol. Shearing Industry* ii. 24 A shearer slums if he works as fast as he can, and perhaps carelessly, while the pen is full, and thus takes a large proportion of the easy sheep. **1966** J. Carter *People of Inland* (1967) xvii. 165 Then at shearing time, these same 'guns' can slum pen after pen of fine, clean sheep, because the opportunity to set a new record has presented itself.

4. a. Also with *it*.

1899 W. James *Let.* 8 Feb. (1920) II. 88 Kipling knows perfectly well that our camps in the tropics are not college settlements or our armies bands of philanthropists, slumming it.

b. To accept, temporarily and voluntarily, a standard (of living, travel, etc.) lower than that to which one is accustomed; to mix with one's inferiors. Freq. as *pres. pple.* and with *it*. Also *fig.*

1928 E. Wallace *Gunner* xxiii. 192 'What are you doing down here?' 'Slumming,' said Gunner Hayes coolly. 'I like now and again to establish contact with the underworld.' **1944** N. Coward *Middle East Diary* 95 We quite enjoyed slumming it in the ordinary pullman. **1946** R. G. Collingwood *Idea of Hist.* iv. 145 It is necessary to go slumming among the most unsavoury relics of third-rate historical work. **1951** E. Coxhead *One Green Bottle* ii. 57 He isn't quite a professor yet. She's just slumming till he becomes one. **1959** *Ann. Reg. 1958* 192 Mr Rockefeller, as he slummed it in New York in the battle with his fellow millionaire the Democratic Mr Harriman. **1978** P. Porter *Cost of Seriousness* 35 On its dorsal, a monster is drumming Messages for the new world—each wraith Is a spirit of old Europe slumming. **1981** *Birds* Autumn 68/1 It [*sc.* a brambling] was quite unabashed by the proximity of the feeding area to the back door and was happily 'slumming it' with the resident sparrows, chaffinches and greenfinches.

slumber, *sb.* Add: **4. slumber cap**, a light, close-fitting cap of lace, ribbon, etc., worn in bed to keep the hair tidy; **slumbercoach** *U.S.*, a railway car which provides economical private sleeping accommodation; **slumber net**, a slumber cap made of net; **slumber party** *U.S.*, a party for youngsters (esp. girls) who stay on to sleep overnight; **slumber room** *U.S.*, a room in which a corpse is laid out by an undertaker until the funeral takes place; **slumberwear**, night-clothes.

1928 *Sunday Dispatch* 8 July 16 Shingle caps or slumber caps for the seaside..in Nottingham lace, bound with pink, blue or any coloured satin ribbon. **1971** 'A. Gilbert' *Tenant for Tomb* iii. 47 She rolled up the plaits under..a slumber cap, an affair of bright blue silk and lace and a ribbon bow. **1958** *Washington Post* 26 June c19/3 B&O charges regular coach fare plus a $6 service charge for a single room..for its slumbercoaches, which are operated on only one train, the Baltimore–Washington–Chicago Columbian. **1979** *United States 1980/81* (Penguin Travel Guides) 19 Long-distance trains offer sleeping accommodations..slumbercoaches, private rooms,..roomettes. **1930** J. Rhys *After leaving Mr Mackenzie* ii. xiii. 217 Out of the second door emerged a lady in a pink dressing-gown, with her hair hidden by a slumber-net. **1950** A. Wilson *Such Darling Dodos* 79 The artifice of the black waved hair..beneath the neat mesh of the slumber net. **1966** *Olney Amsden & Sons Ltd. Price List* 23 Hair and slumber nets. [**1942** Berrey & Van den Bark *Amer. Thes. Slang* § 251/1 *Sleep*,..slumber party.] **1949** *Senior Prom* Nov. 22/2 For a girls' party you might have a brunch, lunch, dinner,..or slumber party. **1954** *Life* 26 Apr. 186/2 Because it was to be a slumber party, the 19 girls..came carrying pillows, blankets and floppy animals—but no one really expecting to get much sleep. **1974** A. Lurie *War between Tates* ix. 181 'I'm invited to Elsie's slumber party.' 'Oh? And what is a slumber party?' 'Don't you even know that? You have a party, and then you sleep overnight.' **1936** Slumber-room [see *funeral-home* s.v. *Funeral *sb.* 6]. **1963** J. Mitford *Amer. Way of Death* iv. 61 The slumber rooms are elusively reminiscent of some other feature of American life... 'So then you've got a slumber room tied up for three days or more,' he said... 'How much would it cost you to stay in a good motel for three days?'.. Motels for the dead! That's it, of course. **1979** *Sun-Times* (Chicago) 28 Sept. 4 Would it be considered improper to take a photograph of a deceased friend or relative in the slumber room during viewing hours? **1909** *Punch* 24 Mar. 206/3 The famous house so long consecrated to the habiliments of Morpheus, or 'slumberwear', as of late we have been taught to call them. **1961** L. P. Hartley *Two for River* iv. 74 If he called her now she would probably be in bed, and come down in her nightgown or her pyjamas, or whatever slumberwear she favoured, and that would never do.

slumdom. Add: Also, the condition or character of slums or slum-dwellers.

1927 G. B. Shaw in *Yorks. Even. News* 30 Nov. 9/2 Civilisation means 'Respect my life and property and I will respect yours.' Slumdom means 'Disregard my life and property and I will disregard yours.' **1962** *Economist* 18 Aug. 593/1 Another 60,000 old houses slip into slumdom. **1973** *Daily Tel.* 7 Nov. 13/1 A pre-war, cottage-type housing estate that is slipping into slumdom as fast as the downward slope will take it.

slumgullion. Add: **1.** (U.S. example.)

1872 'Mark Twain' *Roughing It* iv. 44 He poured for us a beverage which he called '*Slumgullion*'.

2. b. (Earlier and later examples.)

1887 B. Harte *Millionaire & Devil's Ford* 146 We preach at them for playing in the slumgullion, and getting themselves splashed. **1906** C. de L. Canfield *Diary of Forty-Niner* 27 The mud we were sending down the stream buried them under slumgullion. **1948** O. Weston *Mother Lode Album* 82 The miners..insisted on calling it 'Slumgullion', because when it rained the knee-deep adobe mud was no small problem.

c. (Earlier and later examples.) Occas. used outside U.S.

1902 J. London *Daughter of Snows* 45 'What do you happen to call it?' 'Slumgullion,' she responded curtly, and thereafter the meal went on in silence. **1932** J. Dos Passos *1919* 17 Bedbugs in the bunks in the stinking focastle, slumgullion for grub. **1959** A. Sillitoe *Loneliness* 7 The first thing a long-distance cross-country runner would do..would be to run as far away from the place as he could get on a bellyful of Borstal slumgullion. **1976** T. Walker *Spatsizi* x. 115 For want of a better word we called it slumgullion.

slumgum (slɒ·mgɒm). *U.S.* Also **slum gum.** [f. Slum *sb.*[2] + Gum *sb.*[2]] The residual wax, propolis, and other impurities that remain when the honey and most of the wax are extracted from honeycombs by warming them.

1890 *Gleanings Bee Culture* XVIII. 704/2 The cappings are laid on this perforated tin, and, when they melt, the wax and honey run through into the chamber below, leaving what Californians call the 'slumgum' on the tin above. **1917** *Rep. Iowa State Apiarist* 36 A third of the weight of this slumgum is wax and should be saved. **1946** R. A. Grout *Hive & Honeybee* xxii. 544 Slumgum is the material remaining after some rendering treatment has been performed on comb material. It may be more or less rich in beeswax and is usually dark brown or almost black in color. **1980** *Bee Craft* LXII. 154/2 The water.. had to heat to the extractor temperature and this allowed the dross or slum gum to coagulate on the under surface of the straining cloth.

slumless (slɒ·mlės), *a.* [f. Slum *sb.*[1] + -less.] Containing no slums.

1924 *Glasgow Herald* 8 Mar. 7 The difference between almost slumless Düsseldorf and slummy Glasgow is not altogether in municipal policy or school education. **1946** P. Bottome *Lifeline* xxx. 235 Berlin...bustling, self-determined, ordered, slumless. **1966** *Guardian* 16 May 15/3 Any big-city mayor..can successfully achieve a relatively slumless city.

slumminess. (Later examples.)

1926 A. Huxley *Two or Three Graces* 176 It was a slummy street... It was not hard to know where respectable slumminess ended and gay Bohemianism began. **1961** *Guardian* 29 Mar. 9/3 Being overcrowded does not necessarily imply slumminess.

slumming, *vbl. sb.* Add: **2. c.** *fig.* with defining adj. Cf. sense *4 b of the vb.

1933 Dylan Thomas *Let.* (1966) 70 Few understand the works of Cummings, And few James Joyce's mental slummings. **1958** [see *DEMOTIC *a.* 2]. **1977** M. DRABBLE *Ice Age* I. 35 She accused Anthony of hypocrisy, of intellectual slumming, of *folie de grandeur*, of brain fever.

slu·mmock, *sb. dial.* and *colloq.* [Var. of dial. *slammock*: see *Eng. Dial. Dict.* and SLUMMOCK *v.*] A dirty, untidy, or slovenly person; a slut. Freq. as a disrespectful term of address. Cf. SLAMMAKIN *sb.* 2.

19th.-cent. dial. examples in *Eng. Dial. Dict.* s.v. *Slammock* sb.

1932 'L. G. GIBBON' *Sunset Song* 186 Chris found herself dancing with Mistress Mutch, the great, easy-going slummock. **1953** L. HILL tr. *Anouilh's Waltz of Toreadors* in J. C. Trewin *Plays of Year* VIII. 444 A slummock, a girl who hasn't even washed! **1966** M. KELLY *Dead Corse* i. 10 'You are the greatest slummock,' she said. 'How can you bear to lie on an unmade bed?' **1974** P. FLOWER *Odd Job* ix. 59 He wiped Norah's table-top... Norah was a slummock.

slummocker (slɒ·mǒkəɹ). *dial.* Also **slummicker.** [Of obscure ulterior etym.: see SLAMMAKIN *sb.* and *a.*; SLUMMOCK *v.* This form is not recorded in dialect dicts.] = SLAMMAKIN *sb.* 2; an awkward or careless person.

1905 G. B. SHAW *Let.* 13 Aug. in A. T. Schwab *James Gibbons Huneker* (1963) xiii. 167 You will never be anything but a clever slummocker in America. **1905** —— *Let.* 16 Sept. in J. G. Huneker *Steeplejack* (1920) II. 258 The reason I call you a slummocker and heap insults on you, is that you are very useful to me in America, and quite friendly; consequently, you must be educated or you will compromise me. **1940** C. STEAD *Man who loved Children* (1941) ix. 376, I have to let that great big slummicker wash the dishes and smash every glass and plate in the house.

slummocking: see SLAMMAKIN *a.* in Dict. and Suppl.

slummocky, *a.* Add: *dial.* and *colloq.* Also (rarely) **slammocky, slommachy, slummucky.** (Further examples.) Hence **slu·mmockiness.**

? **1861** MRS. GASKELL *Let.* 28 Feb. (1966) 643 A tall, gentlemanly, slammocky-as-to-figure man. **1914** KIPLING in *Nash's Mag.* June 278/1 The rough-ironed table-linen, ..the slummocky set-out of victuals at meals. **1926** W. DE LA MARE *Connoisseur* 65 A help from the village—precious little good *she* was. Slummocky—and *stupid*! **1947** M. PENN *Manchester Fourteen Miles* iii. 34 Grandma Winstanley was..a slattern... Lizzie couldn't abide her slummockiness. **1953** J. CARY *Except the Lord* xxxviii. 169 Girls after a few months service would return on holiday not only in smart clothes but with quite new scorn for what they called our slummucky ways. **1962** J. CANNAN *All is Discovered* ii. 29 'An attractive woman?' 'No, sir. A slummacky sort. More like a gyppo.' **1973** P. WHITE *Eye of Storm* viii. 376 Her hands had been coarsened by menial grind, her body made slommacky by childbearing. **1974** H. R. F. KEATING *Underside* xix. 187 The doom-laden slummockiness of his bohemian days.

slummy (slɒ·mi), *sb. colloq.* Also **slummie.** [f. SLUM *sb.*¹ + -Y⁶.] A slum-dweller.

1934 P. O'MARA (*title*) Autobiography of a Liverpool Irish slummy. **1964** A. PRIOR *Z Cars Again* xvi. 158 The remains of many meals stood on..a newspaper... It was a typical slummie's house. **1973** 'J. PATRICK' *Glasgow Gang Observed* xii. 111 Big Fry..tauntingly called out: 'We're the slummies!'

slump, *sb.*² Add: **2. a.** Also *spec.* in *Econ.*, a sharp or sudden decline in trade or business, usu. accompanied by widespread unemployment. Freq. with reference to a particular instance, esp. the Great Depression of 1929 and subsequent years.

1922 H. A. SILVERMAN *Substance of Economics* xv. 231 Industries grew to depend increasingly on one another... It became inevitable..that a 'boom' or a 'slump' in one branch should synchronize with similar conditions elsewhere. **1930** *Engineering* 10 Jan. 42/2 To discover opportunities for employment on such jobs during industrial slumps. **1936** J. M. KEYNES *Gen. Theory Employment, Interest & Money* IV. xvi. 218 In the succeeding 'slump' the stock of capital may fall for a time below the level which will yield a marginal efficiency of zero. **1936** N. STREATFEILD *Ballet Shoes* vi. 89 'Well, I can't go back to Kuala Lumpur.' 'Why?' 'A thing called a slump.' **1952** *Granta* 15 Nov. 12/1 We wanted to fight Fascism, War and the Slump. **1953** M. SCOTT *Breakfast at Six* iii. 24 Bought all this land—got it cheap in slump time. **1957** I. CROSS *God Boy* (1958) iii. 27 Then there was the slump ..and then I never did get a chance with that hotel in Wellington. **1976** *Economist* 16 Oct. 13/2 A record rise in mortgage charges during a building slump.

b. *Geomorphol.* A landslide in which soil, sediment, or the like slides a short distance with some degree of cohesion and usu. a slight backward rotation owing to the concavity of the surface of separation from the parent mass; movement of this kind; also, a mass of material that has so fallen.

1905 CHAMBERLIN & SALISBURY *Geology* I. iv. 218 (*heading*) Creep, slumps, and landslides. **1949** F. J. PETTIJOHN *Sedimentary Rocks* iv. 145 A structure of similar appearance..is reported from some limestones and dolomites. The cause of the folding may be due to subaqueous slump. **1954** W. D. THORNBURY *Princ. Geomorphol.* v. 104 Mantle rock..is moved downslope by creep, slump, other types of mass-wasting, and by sheet-wash. **1963** D. W. & E. E. HUMPHRIES tr. *Termier's Erosion & Sedimentation* vii. 166 Water-laid phenomena (slumps, low-angle cross bedding) are observed, and suggest that eolian sands have been blown into a shallow sea. **1964** V. J. CHAPMAN *Coastal Veget.* i. 2 A large scale change induced by a major cliff-fall or slump. **1970** W. H. MATTHEWS *Geol. made Simple* (rev. ed.) viii. 117 Slump is a common occurrence along the banks of streams. **1978** A. L. BLOOM *Geomorphology* viii. 178 An elaborate engineering technology has been developed to predict the surface of rupture beneath a slump in order to drill into it and drain the water from the vicinity.

c. *Engin.* The height through which the top of a mass of fresh concrete sinks when the mould containing it is removed, as in the slump test (see sense 4 below).

1920 D. A. ABRAMS *Design of Concrete Mixes* (Bull. No. 1, Structural Materials Res. Lab., Lewis Inst., Chicago) 13 Normal consistency..requires the use of such a quantity of mixing water as will cause a slump of ½ to 1 in. in a freshly molded 6 × 12-in. cylinder of about 1:4 mix. **1934** S. C. HOLLISTER in L. C. Urquhart *Civil Engin. Handbk.* VII. 562 Concrete for buildings ranges from 4 to 6 in. slump. **1977** D. E. BRANSON *Deformation of Concrete Structures* i. 48 Creep correction factors... May be marginal but normally can be neglected for slumps up to 4 in.

3. *gen.* A slumping movement or fall.

1850 S. JUDD *Richard Edney* i. 12 Move carefully! It is a slip, or a slump, all the way through. **1867** 'T. LACKLAND' *Homespun* I. 90 A..black snake..slid down with a slump ..into the water. **1900** S. HALE *Let.* 29 Apr. (1919) 361, I let my huge bulk down with a slump.

4. *attrib.*, as (sense *2 b) *slump bed, bedding, block, series, sheet, structure*; **slump test** *Engin.*, a test of the consistency of fresh concrete in which the slump is measured following the removal of a mould of specified size and shape (usu. the frustum of a cone).

1974 *Sedimentology* XXI. 2 Exposures of banks and slump beds extend along the whole of the coast. **1949** F. J. PETTIJOHN *Sedimentary Rocks* iv. 145 The disturbance is restricted to layers a mere inch or two thick. Such deformation is usually due to subaqueous slump or gliding and has been termed 'slump' or 'glide bedding'. **1964** *Gloss. Mining Terms* (*B.S.I.*) v. 13 *Slump bedding*, disturbed strata interbedded between undisturbed strata, caused by flow of newly deposited sediment. **1969** D. J. EASTERBROOK *Princ. Geomorphol.* xi. 228 During movement of a slump block, secondary slumps may develop and produce a stair-step-like series of parallel slump blocks. **1978** A. L. BLOOM *Geomorphology* viii. 178 Vegetation or even houses may be carried intact on the surface of a large slump block. **1937** O. T. JONES in *Q. Jrnl. Geol. Soc.* XCIII. 272 In view of the fact that a thick mass.. may have been formed by successive sliding or slumping of sediments, it is proposed to speak of it as a slump series, and where it is reasonably certain that a mass is the result of a single episode, that mass is referred to as a slump sheet. A slump series is or may be..made up of several slump sheets separated by a greater or lesser thickness of normal mudstones. **1976** *Jrnl. Geol. Soc.* CXXXII. 125 Sequence 4, in the upper part of the slump sheet, is most complexly deformed, showing closed and contorted folds. **1963** *Geol. Mag.* C. 205 The slump structures which characterize the Torridonian red sandstones of North-West Scotland. **1975** J. L. WILSON *Carbonate Facies Geol. Hist.* viii. 238 The limestone..has graded beds, lamination, microbreccias and slump structure. **1920** F. L. ROMAN in *Engin. & Contracting* 3 Mar. 241/1 Cone No. 1..was far better than a cylinder for determining the consistency of concrete by means of a 'slump' test. **1975** *Concrete Inspection Procedures* (Portland Cement Assoc.) iv. 41 A slump test is made at the start of the operation each day and whenever the appearance of concrete indicates a change in consistency.

slump, *v.*² Add: **2. b.** Also, to fall or collapse clumsily or heavily. *spec.* in *Geomorphol.* of soil, sediment, etc.: to fall in a slump (sense *2 b).

1905 CHAMBERLIN & SALISBURY *Geology* I. iv. 220 Where a stream's banks are high..considerable masses sometimes slump from the bank. **1920** *Engin. & Contracting* 3 Mar. 241/1 Large voids or stone pockets tend to cause the concrete specimen to slump on one side rather than vertically. **1937** *Q. Jrnl. Geol. Soc.* XCIII. 276 Sediments accumulating on a sub-aqueous slope would slide or slump if the weight increased beyond a certain amount. **1978** FRIEDMAN & SANDERS *Princ. Sedimentol.* xii. 400/1 Strata that slumped and were deformed may be..overlain by turbidites.

c. (Earlier example with † *off.*)

1888 in Farmer *Americanisms* (1889) 495/2 'How's North-western this morning, Uncle Zeke?' asked Dick... 'Slumped off six points, hang it!' scowling viciously over his paper.

d. *transf.* and *fig.*

1925 *Sunday Times* 20 Sept. 12/6 Where one's sympathy slumps and all one's optimism fails is in face of two depressing facts. **1970** *Daily Tel.* 16 May 12 Better pay and conditions are essential if police morale is not to go on slumping. **1977** *Cork Examiner* 6 June 7/1 The overnight leader..slumped to an 80 in his second round for 150.

Hence **slumped** *ppl. a.*

1937 *Q. Jrnl. Geol. Soc.* XCIII. 277 Local after-slides.. added low ridges on the surface of the major slumped mass. **1965** G. J. WILLIAMS *Econ. Geol. N.Z.* iii. 31/2 There is a good deal of glacial debris and slumped ground under the thick forest. **1976** J. E. SANDERS et al. *Physical Geol.* vii. 244 A slumped mass usually does not travel very far nor spectacularly fast.

slumpflation (slɒmpflēⁱ·ʃən). *Econ.* [Portmanteau blend of SLUMP *sb.*² + *IN)FLATION 6: cf. *STAGFLATION.] A state of economic depression in which decreasing output and employment in industry are accompanied by increasing inflation.

1974 W. REES-MOGG *Reigning Error* iv. 75 So-called stagflation and slumpflation are the inevitable reflection of the progressive divergence between a rising nominal and a falling real supply of money. **1976** *Economic Jrnl.* LXXXVI. 171 Chronic slumpflation has given rise to much agonising reappraisal of doctrines that were hardening into orthodoxies. **1980** *Economist* 23 Feb. 13/1 The government can get less slumpflation in British industry only by making life easier for the employers' wage negotiators. **1981** J. SUTHERLAND *Bestsellers* xix. 201 Portugal wallows in the slumpflation that will eventually lead to fascism.

slumping (slɒ·mpiŋ), *vbl. sb.*² *Geomorphol.* [f. SLUMP *v.*² + -ING¹.] The fall of soil, sediment, or the like in a slump (*SLUMP *sb.*² 3 b).

1907 R. D. SALISBURY *Physiography* vi. 106 Slumping is very common on slopes composed of unconsolidated material, such as clay or accumulations of loose rock. **1944** A. HOLMES *Princ. Physical Geol.* x. 148 Similar conditions favour landslides on a bigger scale, wherever slumping (Fig. 63) or sliding (Fig. 64) can occur on the sides of undercut slopes, precipices, and cliffs. **1979** *Geogr. Mag.* July 668/3 Many sub-circular pans on the Essex marshes may be formed by the blocking-off by slumping and vegetation overgrowth of the large number of creek heads which appear rounded in outline.

slumscape (slɒ·mskēⁱp). [f. SLUM *sb.*¹, after LANDSCAPE, etc.: cf. SCAPE *sb.*³] Slum scenery, or a picture of this.

1947 WYNDHAM LEWIS *Let.* Apr. (1963) 405 Down another [road] moved a great slumscape painter. **1967** *N.Y. Times* 4 May 41/5 They walked slowly through the scarred and dreary slumscape.

slup, *v.* Delete † *Obs.*⁻¹ and add later examples. [Modern examples may represent an echoic form. Cf. SLURP *v.* in Dict. and Suppl.] Hence **slup** *sb.*, the noise of slupping; **slu·pping** *ppl. a.* and *vbl. sb.*

1947 *Time* 7 Apr. 74/2 A julep-slupping burlesque of a Southern politico. **1949** *Daily Progress* (Charlottesville, Va.) 2 Mar. 10 (*caption*) Put a muffler on that soup sluppin'. **1949** H. HORNSBY *Lonesome Valley* 11 The mule slupped the clear water. **1952** J. STEINBECK *East of Eden* 23 There was no talk at supper. The quiet was disturbed only by the slup of soup and gnash of chewing. **1971** G. EWART *Gavin Ewart Show* I. 28, I am a bottle of wine... slup me rough and homely and I'll taste fine.

slur, *sb.*² **3.** (Examples of *slur-cock.*)

1927 T. WOODHOUSE *Artificial Silk* ix. 98 The jack sinkers..are operated directly or indirectly by means of the cam of a 'slur-cock'. **1962** *Engineering* 15 June 771/1 Straight bar knitting machines..depend largely for their successful operation upon the motion given by a linear cam known as the 'slurcock'.

slurb (slɜ̄ɹb). orig. *U.S.* [App. f. *sl-* (as in *sloppy, sleazy*, etc.: see quot. 1962) + URB(AN *a.*, though later re-analysed as if from SL(UM *sb.*¹ + SUB)URB.] An area of unplanned suburban development.

1962 WOOD & HELLER *California going, Going...* 10 The character and quality of such urban sprawl is readily recognizable... These are the qualities of most of our new urban areas—of our *slurbs*—our sloppy, sleazy, slovenly, slipshod semi-cities. **1966** *Guardian* 22 Apr. 12/3 About 35 miles west of London there is a new town that no one knows about. It is in Berkshire, between Reading and Sandhurst, and it includes Wokingham and Crowthorne. It is what Californians, who have plenty of them, call a 'slurb'—an amorphous and intermittent spread of houses. **1967** *Economist* 8 July 120/2 The pattern which has turned Los Angeles into an 'un-community', into 'twenty suburbs in search of a city', into the archetypal 'slurb'. **1979** B. WARD *Progress for Small Planet* xxi. 235 The basic concept of 'urban villages' (the Chelseas, the Trasteveres, the Greenwich villages)..often allow a vitality and an attractiveness which the world's concrete suburban deserts, slurbs, and sprawls so demonstrably lack.

slurp, *v.* **1. a.** *trans.* Delete *rare* and add: Also, to eat in this manner. (See also quot. 1976). Also with *down, up.*

1917 *Dialect Notes* IV. 329 *Slurp, v.t.* and *i.*..to eat liquid food with audible inhalation of air. **1947** *Richmond* (Va.) *Times-Dispatch* 30 Dec. 15/1 The stars just whirl in.., slurp a cup of coffee and zoom out again. **1952** C. ARMSTRONG *Black-Eyed Stranger* ii. 10 'You know—' Baby slurped food, 'If you want to live you got to eat.' **1962** R. LOWELL *Imitations* 39 They are slurping their dinners quite happily. **1974** P. CAVE *Mama* (new ed.) xiii. 107 The Angels obediently slurped down the remainder of their teas and rose to their feet noisily. **1976** *Daily Tel.* 21 Jan. 15/5 After about seven years of 'slurping' (the correct professional word) tea in the tasting room he [*sc.* a tea-taster]..has prospects of becoming a buyer or blender.

b. *transf.* and *fig.*

1968 *Punch* 11 Dec. 858/1 The idiocies of British holiday habits, which tend to waver between 'slurping up the kilometres' and getting away from it all amid insanitary *souks*. **1973** M. AMIS *Rachel Papers* 15 Mrs Bladderby had an even wreckier mother, who..had, moreover, during a recent outing, got her left leg slurped into a dreadful piece of agricultural machinery.

2. a. *intr.* To make a sucking noise in drinking or eating.

1917 [see sense 1a above]. **1961** B. CRUMP *Hang on a Minute, Mate* 108, I had my head inside the can slurping happily away. **1975** A. A. THOMPSON *Message from Absolom* iv. 24 The Americans ate hungrily. At the other table, the Elberts slurped audibly.

b. *transf.* and *fig.*

1958 J. KEROUAC *On Road* vii. 155 He..stuck his finger in Marylou's dress, slurped up her knee. **1963** [see *MATIÈRE]. **1971** B. W. ALDISS *Soldier Erect* 24 On bed immediately... Fanny swimming with juice, slurps when touched. Marvellous tits, delicious underarms. **1976** P. CAVE *High Flying Birds* iv. 51 With a couple of pints of champagne slurping around her insides, she found it increasingly difficult to wrap her tongue round the hard Anglo-Saxon consonants.

Hence **slu·rping** *ppl. a.* and *vbl. sb.*

1960 W. SHEED *Middle Class Educ.* (1961) 31 The slurping roar of the undergraduates. **1976** *Daily Tel.* 21 Jan. 15/5 Mr Ronald Calvert, chief taster for Ridgways,.. wonders if women are daunted by a job entailing the 'slurping' of 200 to 400 mouthfuls of tea on an average working day. **1980** *Sunday Express* 27 July 16 No one would want them to endanger their striped pants by sitting next to spotty Coca-Cola slurping children.

slurp (slɜ̆ːp), *sb.* and *int.* [f. the vb.] **A.** *sb.* A slurping sip or lick; the noise of slurping.

1949 H. HORNSBY *Lonesome Valley* xxi. 270 The second cow..slammed her nose against her side and swiped at flies with her tongue. Almost before the slobbery slurp was over with the cow trotted after the other. **1959** A. BAILEY *Making Progress* 142 The slurps and gulps of the Danes moodily drinking their beer. **1960** I. CROSS *Backward Sex* 140 He..took a huge slurp of tea. **1977** D. CLARK *Gimmel Flask* iv. 79 Green took a slurp of his coffee, grimaced at the taste.

B. *int.* An interjection imitating the sound of a slurp.

1966 L. COHEN *Beautiful Losers* I. 16 It is recorded that she prayed incessantly. Glog, glog, dear God..slurp, flark, glamph, hiccup, jerk. **1967** W. H. CANAWAY *Mules of Borgo San Marco* iv. 51 She dipped her spoon in the soup, sipped, and said, 'Perfect!' '*Slurp*,' said Major Widdicombe. **1970** *Private Eye* 22 May 16 Leetle Germaine eez at votre service!!! (slurp!).

slurry, *sb.* Add: **1. a.** Also in extended use, any fluid mixture of a pulverized solid with a liquid (usu. water), freq. used as a convenient form in which to handle solids in bulk. (Later examples.)

1935 *Discovery* Apr. 119/1 The strata are pounded into a 'slurry' by the constant rising and falling of the heavy drilling tools. **1948** *Chambers's Jrnl.* July 388/1 The idea here is to break up the turf bank face by means of high-pressure jets, like firemen's hoses, into slurry. **1955** *Sci. News Let.* 20 Aug. 115/2 The U.S.-designed power plant.. uses..thorium oxide slurry in heavy water in another part of the device, called a homogenous reactor. **1961** *Aeroplane* CI. 342/3 Whatever form of contaminant is selected, it is first mixed with kerosene to form a 'slurry', so representing the normal state in which it would pass through a filter in service. **1975** *Nature* 30 Oct. 818/1 In a second experiment, another batch of about 3 ml of the packed cell slurry was resuspended in the culture medium.

b. *spec.* A mixture of water and fine particles of coal, produced esp. as a by-product of the washing of coal; such material in dried form, used as fuel.

1913 *Trans. Inst. Mining Engineers* XLV. 429 Where the moisture percentage is not over 5, the small dust measuring less than 1 cubic millimetre (which is the cause of all the slurry trouble) can be just as efficiently treated by dry-percussive screening as by any other method. **1930** *Ibid.* LXXVIII. 27 It cannot be claimed that slurry is a suitable fuel for pulverizing. **1955** *Times* 4 July 15/5 They [*sc.* the N.C.B.] have been using a new type of mechanical stoker, which is fully automatic, to burn slurry—fine particles of coal and soluble shale which is rejected from washeries. **1976** 'R. LEWIS' *Witness my Death* v. 180 That tip up there, it's full of water. The slurry is drifting down.

c. *spec.* A mixture of manure or farmyard waste and water; manure in fluid form.

1965 *Punch* 22 Dec. 932/2 In a modern fattening house ..the manure from several hundred swine falls through slatted floors into tanks beneath the building where a daily dose of water soon turns it into a forbidding quantity of evil-smelling slurry. **1971** *Farmers Weekly* 19 Mar. 48/4 It takes one man about six minutes a day to clear away the slurry and a bit longer to put out the hay. **1970** R. JEFFRIES *Dead Man's Bluff* i. 5 He went through from the dairy into the herringbone parlour and stared..at the two days' accumulation of slurry.

3. *attrib.*, as *slurry disposal, pipeline, pit, pump, refiner, tank, tanker*; **slurry seal** (see quot. 1967).

1970 R. JEFFRIES *Dead Man's Bluff* i. 5 He stared angrily at..the slurry disposal unit. **1969** *Daily Colonist* (Victoria, B.C.) 13 Dec. 9/3 Kaiser..was contemplating a slurry pipeline to the coast as an alternative to rail. **1976** *Cumberland News* 3 Dec. 13/4 There was a slurry pit also under a byre, made of slate. **1940** KRISTAL & ANNETT *Pumps* 338/2 (Index), Slurry pumps. **1976** *Cumberland News* 3 Dec. 34/3 (Advt.), Alfa Laval slurry pumps. **1916** *Trans. Inst. Mining Engineers* LI. 272 With the combination of this slurry-refiner and the elevated settling-tank.., it has been found possible to work a washery, year in and year out, without any outlet whatever. **1967** *Gloss. Highway Engin. Terms* (*B.S.I.*) 30 *Slurry seal*, a mixture of binder, fine aggregate and mineral filler with water added to produce a material of slurry consistency. **1974** *Globe & Mail* (Toronto) 7 Feb. 5/6 Slurry seal is a tar-like chemical substance that is spread on city streets to preserve them. It is cheaper than asphalt. **1936** *Economist* 25 Apr. 213/2 Property account has been increased to £12,557 by the addition of the slurry tanks and quartz deposit. **1971** *Farmers Weekly* (*Extra*) 19 Mar. 5/1 (Advt.), We know we have the best slurry tanker.

slurry (slɜ̆·ri), *a.* [f. SLUR *v.*[1] + -Y[1].] Blurred, indistinct: now usu. of speech. Also **slu·rrily** *adv.*

1937 *Daily Express* 12 Feb. 5/3 This is the way to detect a forgery—look for notes that are rather blurred or 'slurry'. **1969** 'H. CALVIN' *Chosen Instrument* ii. 22 'We own nothing, we need nothing,' the fat boy said slurrily. **1977** J. MCCLURE *Sunday Hangman* xv. 174 'Why leave the bodies everywhere?' Willie demanded, driven..to speak his mind, if a little slurrily.

slush, *sb.*[1] Add: **2. c.** Food, esp. of a watery consistency. *slang.*

1941 J. SMILEY *Hash House Lingo* 51 *Slush*, hash. **1955** J. THOMAS *No Banners* ix. 79 It was years since he had tasted anything but jail slush. **1962** W. GRANVILLE *Dict. Sailors' Slang* 108/2 *Slush*, any 'sloppy' food: e.g., soup or stew.

4. a. (Earlier and later examples.) Also *gen.*, nonsense, drivel; sentimental rubbish. Also as *int.*

1869 'MARK TWAIN' *Innoc. Abr.* x. 91 He'll..grind out about four reams of the awfullest slush. **1906** *Dialect Notes* III. 156 O, slush! What nonsense. **1919** C. E. VAN LOAN *Score by Innings* 332 A woman reporter..took one look at Conley..and tore off a whole page of slush. **1937** PARTRIDGE *Dict. Slang* 786/1 As = sickly sentiment, *slush* is familiar S.E. **1944** [see *blush-making* adj. s.v. *BLUSH *sb.* C.]. **1949** [see *KITSCH]. **1953** F. SCOTT FITZGERALD *Tender is Night* I. ix. 51, I mean, would I have been the sort of girl you might have—oh, slush, you know what I mean. **1961** *Observer* 26 Nov. 27/4 The ending is purest slush, and there are some cheap dramatics in the camera work. **1970** R. K. KENT *Lang. Journalism* 124 *Slush*,.. cheaply sentimental copy; trash; drivel.

b. Counterfeit paper money. *slang.*

1924 E. WALLACE *Room 13* i. 11 Young Legge's..the biggest printer of slush in the world! And it's not ord'nary slush. Experts..can't tell 'em from real Bank of England stuff. **1933** D. HUME *Crime Unlimited* vii. 64 We've been handling slush lately—ten bobs and quids. Where they were printed doesn't matter to you.

6. *slush-lamp* (earlier example), *-light*; (sense 4) *slush melodrama, novel*; **slush casting**, a method of making hollow castings in which molten metal is poured into a mould and then poured out again after a layer of metal has solidified on the inner surface of the mould; a casting produced by this method; also **slush-cast** *v.*; **slush-money** orig. *U.S.*, money paid out from a *SLUSH FUND b; **slush moulding,** a process identical to the slush casting of metal but carried out with plastic or latex; so **slush mould,** a mould for use in slush moulding; **slush-moulded** *ppl. a.*; **slush oil** *U.S.*, crude oil found in association with certain shales or sandstones (? *obs.*); **slush pit** (see quots.); **slush pump,** (*a*) a pump used to circulate mud through a rotary drilling column; (*b*) *U.S. slang*, a trombone.

1934 WEBSTER, Slush-cast, *v. t. & i.* **1965** E. TUNIS *Colonial Craftsmen* iv. 75/2 Feet and knobs were cast solid, but spouts and handles were slush cast, a system used also for such things as sand shakers and nursing bottles whose inner surfaces wouldn't be visible. **1930** M. STERN *Die-Casting Pract.* i. 16 The thickness of a slush casting depends upon the length of time that the metal is left in the mold. **1934** CHARNOCK & PARTINGTON *Mech. Technol.* (ed. 2) xxxv. 485 Slush casting is a method of producing light hollow castings without the use of cores. **1936** H. L. CAMPBELL *Metal Castings* iii. 53 Slush castings are produced by pouring the low-melting alloys of lead, antimony, and zinc into metal molds and, after a short interval, slushing out the metal which remains in a liquid state. **1963** JONES & SCHUBERT *Engin. Encycl.* (ed. 3) 1161 The process known as slush-casting is employed extensively in the production of ornamental objects made of spelter or zinc. **1871** C. L. MONEY *Knocking about N.Z.* vi. 77 An old volume of 'Household Words' to spell over at my little fire in the evenings by the light of my slush-lamp. **1887** S. SAMUELS *Forecastle to Cabin* vi. 76 This thump, we found out afterwards, was caused by a handspike; the jar from it put the slush light out. **1972** *People* (Austral.) 13 Feb. 12/2 They..lit their earth-floored bunkhouses at night with slushlights made from treacle-tins filled with fat. **1916** 'B. M. BOWER' *Phantom Herd* vii. 112 You want those stories worked up in a lot of darned, sickly slush melodramas. **1842** J. F. COOPER *Wing-and-Wing* II. 20 They were only put there yesterday..a little slush-money did it all. **1976** *National Observer* (U.S.) 24 Jan. 3/3 There have been a series of well-founded reports..that the multinational corporations have been shoveling slush money into Christian Democrat coffers. **1957** V. J. KEHOE *Technique Film & Television Make-up* xii. 148 It [*sc.* dental stone] has low absorption qualities so is not suitable for slush molds. **1965** E. TUNIS *Colonial Craftsmen* iv. 75/2 The slush mold's two halves shaped only the outside of the article. The caster poured hot metal into it, sluiced it around carefully, and then poured it out again. **1954** N. J. RAKAS *Plastics Engin. Handbk.* x. 314 The physical qualities of slush-molded plastisol are such that it is possible to do exceptionally accurate work. **1943** SIMONDS & ELLIS *Handbk. Plastics* 971 *Slush molding*, a process for molding hollow castings with accelerated thermoplastic phenolic resins. **1957** V. J. KEHOE *Technique Film & Television Make-up* xii. 154 Slush molding requires the use of a fillered latex as the unfillered variety will not build-up on itself in a plaster mold. **1963** H. R. CLAUSER *Encycl. Engin. Materials & Processes* 491/2 Vinyl foam products such as armrests..are manufactured by first forming a tough vinyl skin by spraying, slush molding or rotational molding. The interior then is formed by casting..a vinyl plastisol foam within the pregelled skin. **1977** *Listener* 3 Mar. 284/4 Communications—meaning journalism, detective fiction, slush novels, and film-making. **1880** J. F. CARLL *Geol. Oil Regions of Warren* [etc.] *Counties* 254 The measures above the Warren and Bradford 'Third sands' have produced considerable 'shale or slush oil', which may perhaps be attributed to a fissured condition of these rocks. **1884** *U.S. Tenth Census* X. 13 The first well sunk to the Bradford sands was drilled..2 miles northeast of Bradford. 'Slush oil' was found at a depth of 751 feet, and in November, 1871, producing sand was struck at 1,110 feet. **1931** *Sun* (Baltimore) 29 Apr. 1/4 Four lay in the slush pit, an earthen depression intended to catch drilling refuse. **1975** L. CROOK *Oil Terms* 105 *Slush pit*, pit used for storing drilling mud. **1913** *Oil & Gas Man's Mag.* VIII. 822/2 Two slush pumps are usually installed with each drilling outfit—one pump to operate and the other one to act as a relay. **1921**, etc. [see *mud-laden fluid* s.v. *MUD *sb.*[1] 5]. **1937** *Amer. Speech* XII. 48/2 *Slushpump*, a trombone. **1938** [see *gob-stick* s.v. *GOB *sb.*[2] b]. **1943** *N.Y. Times* 9 May II. 5/4 That man with the Slush Pump was a fine sender. **1949** *Our Industry* (Anglo-Iranian Oil Co. Ltd.) (ed. 2) ii. 37 The circuit of this mud-laden fluid..commences at the slush pumps. **1962** J. WAIN *Strike Father Dead* 141, I could see at once why he preferred the valve trombone to the ordinary slush-pump. **1974** *BP Shield Internat.* Oct. 19/3 There's always a lot of work we can do in the sheltered places—like maintaining the slush-pump. **1977** J. WAINWRIGHT *Do Nothin' till you hear from Me* x. 176 Get Walt to help on the slushpump try-outs. Walt stays first trombone.

slush, *v.* **II. 5.** (Earlier example.)

1853 MOSSMAN & BANISTER *Australia visited & Re-visited* iv. 45 The dirty work, mud, and slushing in water.. are so contrary to the habits of the many, that few can stand the training.

slusher. Add: **2.** *Mining.* A mechanical device for loading or packing broken material in which a bucket is drawn to and fro through a pile of the material by ropes wound round a drum at each end of its length of travel.

1923 *Mine & Quarry* July 1267/1 The contractor..has what is practically the double drum slusher in the ordinary drag line excavator and also in his back-filling machine. **1946** *Trans. Inst. Mining Engineers* CVI. 115 Four scours, totalling 1,200 yds., have been driven with the slusher. **1976** *Times Lit. Suppl.* 8 Oct. 1281/2 Diamonds... To mine them you need, among other things,..a double drum slusher.

slush fund. orig. and chiefly *U.S.* [SLUSH *sb.*[1] 2.] **a.** In the Navy: money collected from the sale of slush, etc., and used to buy luxuries for the crew. Also, a similar fund in the Army.

1839 W. MCNALLY *Evils & Abuses in Naval & Merchant Service* xvii. 162 The sailors in the navy are allowed salt beef... From this provision, when cooked..nearly all the fat boils off; this is carefully skimmed..and put into empty beef or pork barrels, and sold, and the money so received is called the *slush fund*. **1884** *Naval Encycl.* 759/2 *Slush-fund*, money obtained from the sale of slush. It is to be used for premiums for target firing, etc., and not for ship's purposes. **1963** T. PYNCHON *V.* i. 14 Pappy ended up borrowing 500 for 700 from Mac the cook's slush fund.

b. *transf.* A fund used to supplement the salaries of government employees; a fund used to bribe, or influence the action of, a person or group of persons, *spec.* for political ends; a fund used to support a favoured political candidate.

1874 *Congr. Record* 17 Apr. 3166/1 We have had this 'slush-fund' since 1866... It was divided among these officers to increase their salaries. **1894** *Ibid.* 16 Jan. 904/1 [Cleveland] was not elected in 1888..because of pious John Wanamaker and his $400,000 of campaign slush funds. **1924** *Glasgow Herald* 16 Feb. 10 A huge fund alleged to have been deposited in a Washington bank to the credit of a widely-known citizen very intimate with men prominent in public life... The name given to the mysterious fund is the 'slush fund'... 'Slush', in the American acceptance of the word, means illicit commission, bribery, corruption, and graft. **1931** *Economist* 10 Oct. 658/1 How candidate-deputies will react against this suppression of what has usually, in the past, been regarded as an electoral 'slush' fund remains to be seen. **1962** *Guardian* 15 Mar. 9/6 Eisenhower's running mate was accused of being the beneficiary of a 'slush fund' subscribed by wealthy backers. **1977** *Whitaker's Almanack 1978* 567/2 The Prime Minister on May 23 commissioned Mr. Dell, the Trade Secretary, to review Government policy and commercial practices in the light of the 'slush fund' allegations. **1980** *Washington Post* 1 Feb. A1/1 The company had a secret $600,000 slush fund for entertaining Pentagon officials.

slushing, *vbl. sb.* (In Dict. s.v. SLUSH *v.*) Add: *spec.* in *Mining*, the action or process of moving or scraping broken ore into a dump or on to a wagon or chute.

1923 *Mine & Quarry* July 1267/1 The scraping or slushing of ore into chutes or raises or into mine cars is only one of the many uses for the portable double drum hoists. **1946** *Trans. Inst. Mining Engineers* CVI. 116 Both for hand-filling and slushing one haulage-hand was engaged in getting the tubs away from the contractor.

1966 S. D. Woodruff *Methods of Working Coal & Metal Mines* III. b. ii. 287 As soon as a cut was completed the tramming, or slushing, floor was filled with waste before another cut was started.

slushing, *ppl. a.* (In Dict. s.v. Slush *v.*) Add: *spec.* pertaining to or designating a viscous oil or grease used to protect bright metal surfaces, when paint or other fixed coatings cannot be used.
1920 *Technologic Papers Bureau of Standards* (U.S.) No. 176. 4 Slushing oils or slushing compounds are of a varied nature, sometimes being straight mineral greases ..sometimes mixtures of mineral and animal greases.. finely divided mineral matter, and volatile solvents. **1939** Burns & Schuh *Protective Coatings for Metals* xvi. 381 The successful use of slushing compounds depends to a considerable extent upon proper cleaning of the metal surface beforehand. **1975** *Chem. Abstr.* LXXXIII. 13232 A slushing oil was prepd. from a mixt. of a metal mahogany or naphthalene sulphonate, a C_{15-60} fatty acid, a cosolvent, and mineral oil.

slushy, *sb.* Also **slushey, slushie.** Add: **a.** (Earlier example as a nickname.) Also in more gen. application: a cook; any unskilled kitchen or domestic help.
1876 F. W. H. Symondson *Two Years abaft Mast* xiii. 261 An unexpected roll of the ship sent both pig and cook sliding... There was 'Slushy' sometimes over, sometimes under the pig. **1919** W. H. Downing *Digger Dial.* 46 *Slushey*, a mess orderly. **1936** [see *poisoner b]. **1953** 'Caddie' *Sydney Barmaid* 25 Nellie, a wisp of a girl who was slushie at Mrs Murphy's boarding-house. Slushie was the name given to anyone who worked at a camp boarding-house. **1967** C. Drummond *Death at Furlong Post* xii. 153 'You could get a job as a slushy in any restaurant,' he pronounced, 'good short-order cookery.' **1970** K. Giles *Death in Church* iv. 85 A grey-headed woman was crying in a corner—'The part-time slushy,' said Porterman.
b. (Later examples.)
1904 *Bulletin* (Sydney) 15 Sept. 39/1 Terms as usual, 4s. per man per week, the cook to find his own slushy. **1936** A. Russell *Gone Nomad* iii. 14, I had to take my turn at butchering the ration sheep and as 'slushy' to 'Doughboy' Terry, the cook. **1959** H. P. Tritton *Time means Tucker* 25/2 Having over 100 men to cook for, he selected two off-siders, sometimes called 'slushies', and started his duties immediately.

slut, *sb.* Add: **3.** (Earlier example.)
1821 J. Fowler *Jrnl.* 13 Nov. (1898) 42 A large Slut Which belongs to the Party atacted the Bare.
5. slut's wool (earlier example).
1862 *Edin. Rev.* Apr. 410 Upstairs there is 'slut's wool' under the beds.

slut, *v.* Add: **2.** (Later examples.) Also, to behave like a slovenly woman or a woman of loose morals. Also with *about*.
1913 A. Lunn *Harrovians* ii. 37 They groise their horrid eyes off and get out of fagging in a term or two, while we poor devils have to slut about 'on boy' for three years. **1948** G. Greene *Heart of Matter* ii. iii. i. 200 Perhaps I'd have slutted with Bagster or killed myself. **1955** D. Barton *Glorious Life* 199 In winter she had less of the Cinderella look that slutting about in summer cottons imposed on her.

sluthering, var. *sloothering *vbl. sb.*

sluttishly, *adv.* (Later example.)
1976 J. Cooper *Harriet* xiii. 106 They had a nice, relaxed evening..sluttishly eating curry off their knees.

sly, *a., adv.,* and *sb.* Add: **A.** *adj.* **5. b.** (Earlier and later Austral. examples.)
1829 H. Widowson *Present State of Van Diemen's Land* iv. 24 To these [inns] also, I believe, I may add a like number of 'sly grog shops', as they are called. **1840** T. P. MacQueen *Australia* 23 Increased powers ought to be given the magistrates and police to prevent the nuisances usually termed sly grog shops. **1936** F. Clune *Roaming round Darling* xxiv. 265 What a promotion—a sly-grogger to king of the Toko blacks! **1941** Baker *Dict. Austral. Slang* 68 *Sly-groggery*, a sly-grog shop. **1959** M. Scott *White Elephant* xiii. 137 It's a sly-grogging hole and..I didn't go there. **1969** W. Dick *Naked Prodigal* 64 We were on our way to the sly grog joint to buy a dozen bottles.
7. slypuss [Puss 3 b], a cunning or deceitful girl, a minx; so **slypussness.**
1908 W. De Morgan *Somehow Good* ix. 79 Laetitia, whose speech..appeared to impute insight, or penetration, or sly-pussness..to her young friend. **1942** [see *nitwitted *a.*].
8. *sly-eyed, -looking.*
1967 G. Kelly in *Coast to Coast 1965–6* 97 He hated blonde women—sly-eyed, breasts..undulating above her ..tunic. **1795** P. Freneau *Poems* (1902) II. 341 A youngster was order'd to hold himself ready, A sly looking lad that was 'prentice to Snip. **1945** 'G. Orwell' *Animal Farm* vi. 47 He was a sly-looking little man.
B. *adv.* *Comb.* (Later *poet.* example.)
1931 H. Belloc *Sonnets & Verse* 80 Wine, bright avenger of sly-dealing wrong.
C. *absol.* or as *sb.* **2.** (*b*) (Earlier example.)
1818 Keats *Let.* 18 Dec. (1958) II. 13 It might have been a good joke to pour on the sly bottle after bottle into a washing tub and roar for more.

slype. Substitute for def.: A covered way or passage, esp. one lying between the transept of a cathedral or monastic church and the chapter-house, and commonly leading out from the cloister. (Earlier example.)
1860 M. E. C. Walcott *Cathedrals in U.K.* (ed. 2) 261 The slype is the passage on the south-west side of the nave.

slype (slaip), *v.* *Basket-making.* Also **slipe.** [Prob. var. Slipe *v.*[2]] *trans.* To cut away one side of (a rod or cane) with a long slanting cut, so that it comes to a point. Hence **slype** *sb.*; **slyped** *ppl. a.*; **sly·ping** *vbl. sb.*
1910 *Encycl. Brit.* III. 482/2 If the bottom is made on a hoop the butts of the stakes are 'sliped', *i.e.* cut away with a long cut of the shop-knife, and turned tightly round the hoop; they are then said to be 'scallomed' on. **1912** T. Okey *Introd. Art of Basket-making* vii. 68 Having prepared the stuff, slype six bottom-sticks. *Ibid.* 154 *Slype*, a long cut. **1953** A. G. Knock *Willow Basket-Work* 27 The blackberry basket,..requires a bow of stout rod fitted across the basket..by inserting its slyped ends down into the siding. **1959** D. Wright *Baskets & Basketry* vi. 136 *Slype*, a slanting or flat cut. **1960** E. Legg *Country Baskets* 52 The liners are duly slyped before insertion... Slyping is done whenever you need to shape a rod or cane to fit it snugly and securely against another.

smack, *sb.*[2] Add: **3. a.** *a smack in the face* (examples); also *a smack in the eye.*
1895 A. W. Pinero *Second Mrs. Tanqueray* iii. 105 One gets so many smacks in the face through interfering in matrimonial squabbles. **1930** A. P. Herbert *Water Gipsies* viii. 84 'I'm leaving here.' 'Leaving us, Mr. Bryan?' Jane thought 'Oh, Lord, another smack in the face!' **1941** Baker *Dict. Austral. Slang* 68 *Smack in the eye, a*, a disappointment, a refusal, a rebuff. **1949** E. Coxhead *Wind in West* vii. 191 Well, but it was a nice smack in the face! To keep him, with all his experience.. so completely in the dark. **1958** I. Cross *God Boy* xii. 98, I could tell that what he said was supposed to be a smack in the eye for me.
5. *Comb.*, as **smackwarm** *nonce-wd.* (see quot.).
1922 Joyce *Ulysses* 262 She let free..her nipped elastic garter smackwarm against her smackable woman's warmhosed thigh.

smack (smæk), *sb.*[4] *slang* (orig. *U.S.*). [Prob. alteration of *schmeck.] A drug, *spec.* heroin.
1942 Berrey & Van den Bark *Amer. Thes. Slang* § 509/8 *Smack*,..a small packet of drugs. **1960** R. G. Reisner *Jazz Titans* 164 *Smack*, heroin. **1964** *N.Y. Times Mag.* 23 Aug. 64/2 Cocaine..referred to as..*smack*. **1968** *Sunday Truth* (Brisbane) 6 Oct. 36/3 When I first came here you were a big swinger if you turned on with pot. Now they're going straight on to smack (another slang word for heroin). **1969** *Oz* May 36/1 In the paper today it said that Jimmy Hendrix got busted for smack. **1976** R. Condon *Whisper of Axe* ii. vii. 208 She began by having the smack pushers recruit from 53 street gangs. **1980** P. Kinsley *Vatchman Switch* xii. 91 You're dealing and.. I'm going to prove it. You're into opium and smack.

smack, *v.*[2] Add: **5. a.** (Earlier and *fig.* examples.) Also *spec.* to chastise (a child) in this manner.
1835 Dickens *Seven Dials* in *Bell's Life* 27 Sept. 1/1 Mrs. A. smacks Mrs. B.'s child for 'making faces'. **1892** G. B. Shaw *Let.* 12 Aug. (1965) I. 359 Smacking Bebel & Singer in the eye for their *dénigrement* of our programme. **1918** E. Pound *Let.* 1 Jan. (1971) 127, I liked your comment p. 89, Nov. no. Naturally pleased to see the folk song idea smacked again. **1976** *Evening Post* (Nottingham) 14 Dec. 18/9 It appeared to have been put there by her two-year-old son, who had been smacked for moving things about the house.
c. *to smack it about* (see quot. 1962). *Naut. slang.*
1914 'Bartimeus' *Naval Occasions* i. 5 Better man your boat from the boom and shove straight off. Smack it about! **1915** —— *Tall Ship* iv. 71 It's three o'clock now, so I advise you to smack it about and clean if you're going ashore. **1962** W. Granville *Dict. Sailors' Slang* 108/2 *Smack it about!*, naval exhortation to the hands to 'get a move on';..from the smacking of paint brushes about the ship's hull by the side party.
8. In *Comb.*, as **smack-bottom,** a childish expression for a smack on the bottom given in chastisement.
1970 P. Laurie *Scotland Yard* iii. 89 'Put them down, Pop, or you'll get a smack-bottom.'.. The old man has gone back to babyhood. **1978** K. Amis *Jake's Thing* xvii. 182 What he needs is a damn good smack-bottom and being told not to be so boring.

smackable (smæ·kăb'l), *a.* *rare.* [f. Smack *v.*[2] + -able.] That may be smacked.
1922 [see *smackwarm* s.v. *smack *sb.*[2] 5].

smack-dab, *adv.* *U.S. dial.* and *colloq.* Also **smack dab.** [f. Smack *v.*[2] 7 + Dab *adv.*] Exactly, precisely; with a smack. Cf. *slap-dab *adv.*
1892 *Dialect Notes* I. 232 He hit him smack dab in the mouth. **1893** H. A. Shands *Some Peculiarities of Speech in Mississippi* 75 *Smack-dab*, a term used by all classes, but more especially by the uneducated, to mean *exactly, precisely*; as, 'I hit him *smack-dab* in the face'. **1934** D. Runyon in *Collier's* 3 Mar. 8/2 The old King tumbles smack-dab into the street. **1949** H. Hornsby *Lonesome Valley* 16 He gave a little hop and landed smack-dab in the water. **1953** *Sun* (Baltimore) 30 Apr. (ed. b) 19/6 An April rain fell today where no man..would have dared tread last night—smack dab between the bristling New York Yankees and St. Louis Browns. **1967** *Boston Globe* 18 May 27/2 The university trustees apparently want to put it [*sc.* a university] smack-dab into Copley sq. **1970** N. Armstrong et al. *First on Moon* xiii. 321 Here was the LM..right smack dab where it should have been. **1979** *United States 1980/81* (Penguin Travel Guides) 395 Whether you want to be..smack-dab downtown,..or conveniently near Lambert Field Airport, quality hotels are available.

smacker, *sb.*[2] Add: **3.** *slang* (orig. *U.S.*). A coin or note of money; *spec.* a dollar; a pound.
1920 *Chicago Herald & Examiner* 2 Jan. 14/2 Along comes Earl Gray and knocks off the U.S. treasury for 13,000,000 smackers. **1924** Wodehouse *Bill the Conqueror* xvi. 261, I asked him to lend me a hundred smackers. **1928** [see *graft *sb.*[5] a]. **1935** C. W. T. Craig *Paraguayan Interlude* xxvi. 302 'I will give you a thousand beautiful smackers for your church.'.. Mac took out a thousand peso bill and handed it to me. **1937** C. W. Parmenter *Kings of Beacon Hill* i. x. 70 Easy to touch, too, whether for a cigarette or a hundred smackers. **1946** F. Sargeson *That Summer* 86, I gave him a couple of smackers. **1953** R. Lehmann *Echoing Grove* 205 Could I touch you for a smacker? I'm stony broke. **1968** *Landfall* XXII. 42, I wouldn't mind a few smackers. Enough for a case of whisky. **1979** 'L. Black' *Penny Murder* i. 5 'Gone at twelve thousand pounds.'.. Twelve thousand smackers for a tray of old coins. Whew!

smackeroo (smæ:kĕrū·). *slang* (orig. and chiefly *U.S.*). [f. Smacker *sb.*[2]: see *-eroo.] Used in senses of Smacker *sb.*[2] in Dict. and Suppl.: a coin or note of money; a kiss; a blow. Also as *int.*
Amer. Speech (1942) XVII. 14/1 gives citations of *smackeroo* 'dollar' used on U.S. radio programmes in 1940 and 1941.
1942 Berrey & Van den Bark *Amer. Thes. Slang* § 29/2 *Something excellent*...smackeroo. *Ibid.* § 559/16 *Silver dollar*..smacker,..smackeroo. *Ibid.* § 702/1 *Blow.* ..smackeroo. **1951** P. Branch *Lion in Cellar* ix. 102 She grimps up the ladder... And what happens?..*Smackeroo!* **1961** S. Price *Just for Record* viii. 71, I got out the crisp crackling smackeroos and counted out two hundred of them. **1964** C. Chaplin *Autobiogr.* xvii. 300 You're getting the Legion of Honour, kid... That's the wrong colour—that's what they give to school-teachers; you don't get the smackeroos on the cheek for that one. **1977** 'E. V. Cunningham' *One-Penny Orange* (1978) vii. 90 The price is eight thousand pounds, and the pound was five dollars then, so that makes it forty thousand smackeroos.

smahan (smæ·hăn, sma·han). *Anglo-Ir.* [ad. Ir. *smeathán.*] A drop (to drink); a taste or nip.
1914 Joyce *Dubliners* 117 Pony up, boys. We'll have just one little smahan more. **1961** 'F. O'Brien' *Hard Life* iii. 21 That reminds me—I think I deserve a smahan. Where's my crock?

small, *a.* and *sb.*[2] Add: **A.** *adj.* **II. 3. a.** Phr. *small is beautiful*: expressing a belief that small-scale institutions, systems, etc., are more desirable than large-scale ones. Also as *adj. phr.*
1973 E. F. Schumacher (*title*) Small is beautiful. **1975** *Country Life* 25 Dec. 1784/1 Adapting Schumacher's phrase, we decide that not only small but piecemeal is beautiful. **1976** *Seed* V. v. 6/3 Included are articles on self-sufficiency, 'small-is-beautiful' politics and agriculture and nutrition. **1977** D. James *Spy at Evening* xxiv. 193 Small Is Beautiful—but big pays more. **1978** *Times* 23 Mar. 16/3 Mr. St John-Stevas..has proclaimed that 'small is beautiful'. There will be 'no more of those monster schools'. **1979** *Jrnl. R. Soc. Arts* July 468/1 It is worth mentioning another and different pressure upon the nature and shape of the hospital: and that is the vague but pervasive notion that 'small is beautiful'.
b. (*it's a*) *small world* and varr.: a comment on an unexpected meeting with an acquaintance or other similar coincidence.
1895 A. W. Pinero *Second Mrs. Tanqueray* iii. 147 Mr. Ardale and I have met in London... They say the world's very small, don't they. **1959** M. Gilbert *Blood & Judgement* i. 17 He was in the pub tonight... It's a small world, isn't it? **1967** R. Rendell *Wolf to Slaughter* iii. 21 'Small world,' he said... 'That bloke was in here yesterday.' **1973** 'H. Carmichael' *Too Late for Tears* v. 69, I might've guessed even if I hadn't seen..you at the inquest in Aylesbury. Small world, isn't it? **1979** S. Barlay *Crash Course* i. 13 'How did you know?'..'It's a small world.'
c. *small boy* (earlier examples); also *small girl.* Also, of a sibling: younger.
1786 G. Washington *Diary* 5 July (1925) III. 86 That Cowpers Jack and Day, with some small boys and girls,.. were assisting the farmer. **1821** J. F. Cooper *Spy* I. i. 14 A small boy was directed to guide him to his room. **1876** C. M. Yonge *Three Brides* II. xv. 292 He still looked on the tall, young man as the small brother to be patronized, and protected. **1891** L. T. Meade *Sweet Girl Graduate* xxii. 182 Three small girls were making themselves busy with holly and ivy. **1923** E. E. Cummings *Let.* 28 July (1969) 99 What happens to my 'small' 'sister'..is not among the interests of my own completely erratic..existence. **1936** N. Streatfeild *Ballet Shoes* iv. 58 About twenty small girls..were learning tap-dancing. **1949** 'J. Tey' *Brat Farrar* xii. 100 If he had ever had a small sister he would have liked her to be just like Jane. **1973**

M. Mackintosh *King & Two Queens* i. 14 'Go away, small girl,' Frances commanded. **1977** A. Wilson *Strange Ride R. Kipling* i. 23 The strength of Rudyard's love for his small sister.

4. a. *small print*: freq. applied to the detailed information or conditions qualifying the principal text of a document, and printed in a smaller type. Also *attrib.* and *fig.* Cf. *fine print* (*fine *a.* 7 i).

1698 [in Dict.]. **1785** T. Jefferson *Notes on State of Virginia* xxii. 323 A large octavo volume of small print. **1856** [see Print *sb.* 8]. **1944** Blunden *Cricket Country* xvi. 161 What all these curious titles [of games said by Rabelais to have been played by Gargantua] meant in practice may be left to the small print of the commentaries. **1970** 'W. Haggard' *Hardliners* xi. 126 His contract had been terminated under some small-print clause he hadn't much studied. **1971** *Daily Tel.* 2 Nov. 14 Some interest attaches therefore to the 'small print' of the Queen's speech and how far it avoids firm undertakings on some of the more controversial measures. **1972** A. Price *Col. Butler's Wolf* xii. 136 There was nothing in the small print about having to like the men one served with. **1974** *Times* 17 Aug. 12/5 The collapse will.. strengthen Government moves to reform the 'small print' [holiday] booking conditions. **1979** *Sunday Times* (Colour Suppl.) 18 Nov. 35/2 The Prince of Wales reckoned he got the better of the PM in one or two exchanges on the small print of recent Cabinet memoranda.

5. c. (Later examples used of playing-cards.)

1863 *Hoyle's Games* ii. 23 Having only a few small trumps, make them when you can. **1910** W. Dalton *'Saturday' Bridge* iii. 63 Suppose that he holds ace, king, and three small diamonds, and ace, knave, and two small hearts. **1973** *Country Life* 10 May 1331/2 The declarer.. led a small Spade to dummy.

9. c. Introducing a repetition of the initial letter of a word to show that it has general rather than specific reference or that it is a less serious variety of the thing denoted. Cf. *capital *a.* 5 b, *big *a.* 3 h.

1952 *Observer* 18 May 7/6 Back to liberalism-with-a-small-l they trail. **1960** *Times* 22 Oct. 8/1 A newspaper that is serious, lively, and radical with a small r. **1968** *Globe & Mail Mag.* (Toronto) 13 Jan. 2/4 A general mood of small-c conservatism in the country. **1971** 'A. Garve' *Late Bill Smith* v. 139 They were both ardently liberal with a small 'l'. **1974** W. Garner *Big enough Wreath* xii. 165 You're not out of trouble but I'm just beginning to spell it with a small t. **1979** L. Meyer *False Front* ii. 14 They came from different sides of the track, but that wouldn't have been enough to stop a small 'd' democrat like Winston.

IV. 16. b. (Further examples.) Spec., *the small man*, the typical small businessman.

1835 C. F. Hoffman *Winter in West* I. 79 They were chiefly plain people, small farmers and graziers. **1850** C. Kingsley *Alton Locke* II. xi. 154 In helping to pass the Reform Bill, [they had] only helped to give power to the two very classes who crushed them—the great labour kings, and the small shopkeepers. **1926** Chesterton *Outl. Sanity* iv. iii. 170 If the small man found his small mechanical plant helped to the preservation of his small property, its claim would be very considerable. **1931** V. Woolf *Waves* 255 How comforting it is to watch the lights coming out in the bedrooms of small shopkeepers on the other side of the river. **1935** M. Egan *Dominant Sex* i. 27 In these days of trusts and combines the small man hardly stands an earthly. **1947** McCallum & Readman *Brit. Gen. Election 1945* iii. 63 The Conservatives..professed that they were not in favour of the growth of monopoly, and that they were anxious to curb it for the sake of the 'small man'. **1948** Koestler in *Partisan Rev.* XV. 38 The petite bourgeoisie—the storekeeper, artisan, small businessman, white-collar worker. **1960** A. Clarke *Horse-Eaters* 9 Thousands Bred yearly will fatten Small farmers. **1973** *Sat. Rev. Soc.* (U.S.) Mar. 58/1, I was a small farmer..and there's no way you can do it today. You need technology and you need efficiency..and you can't afford..it if you're down there on a small farm. **1974** *Times* 12 Nov. 14/2 The Smaller Businesses Association..set up to champion the interests of the small business man. **1976** R. Barnard *Little Local Murder* ix. 106 'Aven't you 'eard 'ow difficult things are for the small shopkeeper?

20. c. Also with *look*. Cf. sense 16 in Dict.

1784 E. Sheridan *Jrnl.* 6 Oct. (1960) 31 Linley came to see my Father, he received him very kindly but poor L. look'd very small. **1863** T. Taylor *Ticket-of-Leave Man* iv. i. 74 You've no right to be..coming after a chap, to make him look small this way.

V. 21. a. *small ad, advertisement*, a small advertisement in a newspaper, usu. in a separate section devoted to such and printed with lack of display; *small-bourgeois* adj. = *petit bourgeois; so *small bourgeoisie*; *small caps* = *small capitals* in Dict.; *small chop* [*chop *sb.*[6]] (W. Afr. colloq.), small items of food; *small end*, in a piston engine, the end of a connecting rod nearer to the piston; also *attrib.*; *smallest room* (colloq.), the lavatory of a particular building (cf. *small room* below); *small-for-dates*, (of a new-born baby) smaller than would be expected in view of the time since its conception; *small fortune*: see Fortune *sb.* 6 in Dict. and Suppl.; *small fruit* (N. Amer.) (see quot. 1892); *smallgoods* (Austral.), sausages, bacon, etc.; *small-hand* (earlier examples); *small-holder*, one who owns or works a small-holding; *small-holding*, (*b*) the practice or occupation of working a small-holding; *small paper* (later example); *small-pipe(s)*, a Northumbrian bellows-filled bagpipe; *small room* (colloq.), a lavatory (cf. *smallest room* above); *small screen*, television; also *attrib.*; *small seed* (see quot. 1950); *small slam*: see *slam *sb.*[2] 2 b; *small stores* (Naut.), (*a*) items for personal use or consumption on a sea-voyage; (*b*) *U.S.* articles of regulation issue clothing; a shop selling these; also *attrib.* (in *sing.* or *pl.*).

1922 Small ad [see *ad]. **1961** 'F. O'Brien' *Hard Life* vi. 45, I put a small ad. in one of the papers. **1969** *Sunday Times* 2 Mar. 8/3 To recruit models, they ran a string of small-ads asking: 'Are you really ugly?' **1978** J. Wainwright *Ripple of Murders* 11 A small ad. in the Personal Column..will read, 'J.D. Message received.' **1919** *Times* 6 Nov. 2 Small Advertisement order form. **1937** M. Allingham *Dancers in Mourning* xxiii. 285 Uncle William put down *The Times*. He had been looking at the small advertisements. **1930** A. Bennett *Imperial Palace* lv. 414 Customers of the small bourgeois class. **1974** N. Freeling *Dressing of Diamond* 134 A very small-bourgeois existence, with a canary. **1970** F. C. Weffort in I. L. Horowitz *Masses in Lat. Amer.* xi. 398 They did not feel so much like members of a decadent small bourgeoisie, but rather like operators with a stable position moving toward the better. **1856** Geo. Eliot in *Westm. Rev.* Oct. 454 She informs us, with all the lucidity of italics and small caps, that '*function*, not *form*,..weakly engrossed her'. **1967** *Style Man.* (U.S. Govt. Printing Off.) (rev. ed.) iii. 31 In matter set in caps and small caps..capitalize all principal words. **1963** M. Laurence in R. Weaver *Canad. Short Stories* (1968) 2nd Ser. 140, I use the shallow ones to put groundnuts in..for small-chop with drinks. **1971** J. Spencer *Eng. Lang. W. Afr.* 11 Pidgin words, known and used by almost everyone,.. who has lived in the coastal areas of West Africa..*chop* n and v, 'food' and 'eat', and its recent extensions in phrases such as *small chop*, 'cocktail eats', *chop box*,..etc. **1850** T. Tredgold *Steam Engine* (ed. 3) I. ix. 7 Into these guide-blocks are fixed the cross-heads, forming the bearings for the small ends of the connecting rods. **1908** *Autocar Handbk.* (ed. 2) ii. 38 The gudgeon pin end of the connecting rod is called the small end, and the other end the big end. **1922** *Encycl. Brit.* XXX. 36/2 The ordinary small-end bronze bush system with gudgeon pins fixed in the piston was used. **1948** A. W. Judge *Mod. Motor Engineer* (ed. 4) I. ix. 208 After a considerable period of running..the small-end bush may wear oval, due to the more or less vertical thrust of the connecting rod. **1971** B. Scharf *Engin. & its Language* xii. 122 Connecting rods... They comprise a big end..and a small end through which the gudgeon pin..passes. **1930** Smallest room [see *geography 1 d]. **1933** P. Godfrey *Back-Stage* xvi. 202 The smallest room in the house invariably has prohibitory notices of a stern and intimate character. **1960** *Guardian* 29 Apr. 12/6 Soon she had become unable..to take herself into her 'smallest room' in the midget backyard. **1973** 'H. Carmichael' *Candles for Dead* xii. 150 At a guess, I'd say he's probably in the smallest room. **1965** *Clinics in Developmental Med.* XIX. 1 Not all 'small for dates' babies should necessarily be regarded as suffering from pathological growth retardation. **1978** *Nature* 30 Mar. 404/1 During the past twenty years it has become accepted that some babies are born small not because they are premature but because their growth has been retarded in the uterus. These so-called small-for-dates babies..are at greater than normal risk at birth. **1822** J. C. Loudon *Encycl. Gardening* iii. 537 This operation [*sc.* gathering] in the case of small fruits, as the gooseberry, strawberry, &c. is generally performed by the under gardeners. **1892** A. A. Crozier *Dict. Bot. Terms* 164/2 Small fruits, a horticultural term for certain low-growing perennial, fruit-bearing plants and their product, including the strawberry, raspberry, blackberry, gooseberry, currant, huckleberry, and cranberry. **1926** *Daily Colonist* (Victoria, B.C.) 11 July 12/3 Small fruit continue to show prominence, but some varieties are becoming scarce. **1950** *Sci. Monthly* Apr. 212 The story of the evolution of the groups from which our small fruits have been derived is shrouded in the mists of the geological past. **1969** *Northern Territory News* (Focus '69) 22 (Advt.), It sells the best cuts of meat—beef, lamb, veal and pork—as well as smallgoods. **1973** *Bulletin* (Sydney) 25 Aug. 20/3 What are the smallgoods manufacturers putting in their sausages now that mutton, the backbone of their industry, has ceased to be cheap and plentiful? **1821** Small hand [see *nary *a.*]. **1847** Dickens *Dombey* (1848) xiv. 134 He would be expected to inform Doctor and Mrs. Blimber, in superfine small-hand, that Mr. P. Dombey would be happy to have the honour of waiting on them. **1837** Small-holder [in Dict., sense 16 b]. **1915** H. R. Haggard in *Times* 15 Mar. 3/2 The wives and daughters of smallholders will help their menfolk because they are labouring for themselves. **1977** *Times* 18 Aug. 14/6 A smallholder living in a hut on the duneland plantation. **1927** S. L. Bensusan *Latter-Day Rural Engl.* viii. 73 Smallholding thrives in Lincolnshire. **1936** W. M. Sale *S. Richardson* 31 It was not until the autumn of 1742 that he began to see the need for publishing his second small paper edition. **1855** in Wright *Eng. Dial. Dict.* (1904) V. 548/1 The torch was lit on point of spear—And small pipes they did sound. **1927** *Observer* 30 Oct. 8 A humble performer on the Northumbrian small-pipes. **1967** A. L. Lloyd *Folk Song in Eng.* vi. 333 The silvery-toned Northumbrian small-pipes struggling to be heard above the full shrill singing. **1975** S. Marcuse *Mus. Instruments* 482/1 The mid-18th c., when the characteristic feature of the small-pipe was developed: its chanter was stopped. **1858** Queen Victoria *Let.* 7 Feb. in R. Fulford *Dearest Child* (1964) 35 Has the railway carriage got a small room to it? **1979** D. Sanders *Queen sends for Mrs. Chadwick* 134 Where..was the nearest small room to the Queen's drawing-room, where the President would be received? **1956** *B.B.C. Handbk. 1957* 79 This unit.. provides the means for young writers to become acquainted with the requirements of the small screen. **1963** 'E. Crispin' *Best SF Five* 9 The success of the *Quatermass* series has given science fiction a limited yet tolerably regular share in the hotchpotch purveyed by the small screen. **1966** *Guardian* 29 Mar. 10/3 Both sides have studiously kept their small-screen liabilities out of the studios. **1971** *Oxford Times* 26 Nov. 31/4 The stars and the characters they portray are as in the small-screen version. **1980** *Times Lit. Suppl.* 31 Oct. 1229/4 Jonathan Miller had little success in finding the play's natural rhythms and adapting them to the small screen. **1840** W. Deans *Let.* 30 Oct. in J. Deans *Pioneers Canterbury* (1939) 29, I..have got in about two acres of potatoes and ..numerous small seeds. **1950** *N.Z. Jrnl. Agric.* Apr. 359/1 Small seeds [grown in a Canterbury district] include perennial and Italian rye-grass, cocksfoot, crested dogs-tail, and clover. **1814** G. Coggeshall *Jrnl.* 24 Mar. in *Voyages* (1851) 55 We took on board six casks of fresh water, some fresh provisions, and sundry small stores. **1877** *Nautical Mag.* XLVI. 195 Small stores as coffee, tea, or sugar was called by the 'geordies'. **1927** *U.S. Navy Bluejackets' Man.* 379 The storekeeper who issues this clothing will make out a small-store slip in duplicate. **1938** *Ibid.* 20 Besides the small stores where you can get all your clothing at very cheap prices, your station will have the following shops. **1950** *Ibid.* 124 The storekeeper who issues this clothing makes out a small-stores slip, in duplicate. **1966** Noel & Bush *Naval Terms Dict.* 93 *Clothing and small stores*, standard articles of uniform for officers and enlisted men with such related articles as buttons, brushes, etc.

22. a. *small-angle, -band, -bore* (also *fig.*), *-boy, -budget, -city, -claims, -end* (see sense *21 a), *-farm, -fry* (earlier example), *-gauge, -girl, -group, -letter* (later examples), *-plane, -power, -print* (see sense *4 a), *-sample, -screen* (see sense *21 a), *-shop, -signal, -step, -store(s)* (see sense *21 a), *-type*; **small-cell** *Path.*, used *attrib.* to designate various tumours of uncertain origin composed of small cells, esp. an oat-cell carcinoma of the bronchus; **small-scale** *a.*, operating or executed on a small scale; drawn to a small scale; of small size or extent; **small-yield** *a.* = *low-yield* adj. s.v. *low *a.* 23.

1960 *Proc. R. Soc.* A. CCLIV. 242 (*heading*) The small-angle scattering of photons. **1979** *Jrnl. R. Soc. Arts* Jan. 106/2 *Small-angle x-ray scattering*, which is another versatile structural tool for phase transformations, defects and voids, supported catalysts, polymers and various biological materials. **1941** *Jazz Information* Nov. 25/2 They are the best jazz recordings of the New Orleans small-band type. **1977** *New Yorker* 12 Sept. 122/2 Hampton was enough of a sensation to be asked by Victor in 1937 to lead a series of small-band recordings. **1898** W. S. Churchill in *Morning Post* 7 Oct. 5/7 The Dervish gunboat *Bordaine*..returned from its quest with nearly a hundred men wounded by the small-bore bullets of a civilised force which was in occupation. **1900** *Congress. Rec.* 14 Feb. 1804/2 No small-bore, two-by-four, radical politicians can hurt that great court. **1932** *Sun* (Baltimore) 15 Nov. 10/2 The thing to do is to sweep this ghastly mess out of doors, once and for all. It will not be easy to do—if small-bore statesmanship is to continue to rule us. **1976** *R.A.F. News* 11–24 May 19 (*caption*) Brawdy's small bore rifle team pictured with..the Nobel Challenge Cup. **1861** *Harper's Mag.* June 133/1 We sometimes sell skates: and buying a lot at auction last fall, we thought to monopolize all the small-boy trade by posting a flaming placard announcing that we sold skates at twenty cents a pair. **1937** M. Allingham *Dancers in Mourning* xiii. 178 He was..handsome in the downy, small boy fashion of his kind. **1973** J. Stranger *Walk Lonely Road* xiii. 92 He grinned at her, and she grinned her small-boy grin back at him. **1961** *Times* 31 July 14/7 Hardly anyone in Hollywood makes small-budget pictures any more. **1979** 'P. O'Connor' *Into Strong City* xxxiv. 122 Someone in London..would rush out a small-budget film into which they would cram every Scottish actor and actress. **1929** Clute & Smith in *Arch. Surg.* XVIII. 11 In the fourth and last group..we have another debatable form of tumor. For the purposes of classification, we have designated it as the small cell carcinoma. This is the type of tumor which is sometimes called lymphosarcoma, as it is made up of small round cells, poorly differentiated..with a prominent nucleus and an almost negligible amount of cytoplasm. **1966** Wright & Symmers *Systemic Path.* I. v. 265/1 In the earlier days of histopathology, although lymphocytic and lymphoblastic types of lymphosarcoma were recognized, various tumours were frequently confused with them, including..small-cell anaplastic carcinomas (for example, of the thyroid and bronchus). **1976** *Path. Ann.* XI. 319 In the differential diagnosis of acute leukemia the following should be considered: small cell epithelial tumors (eg, oat cell carcinoma, carcinoid, islet cell tumor), neuroblastoma, [etc.]. **1977** V. Coleman *Paper Doctors* xiii. 139 Surgery for small-cell cancer of the bronchus. **1964** S. M. Miller in I. L. Horowitz *New Sociology* 292 The small-town and small-city poor suffer from the demise of local industry. **1977** *Sat. Rev.* (U.S.) 5 Mar. 12/2 This array of small-city labor disputes. **1961** Webster, Small-claims court. **1972** M. Kaye *Lively Game of Death* vii. 38, I simply threatened him with Small Claims Court... The maximum claim there is five hundred dollars. **1978** *Listener* 3 Aug. 159/3 The London Small Claims Court..is being run on an experimental basis and only handles claims up to £350. **1960** *Farmer & Stockbreeder* 16 Feb. 60/3 This pinpoints the need for a cheaper small-farm tank of from 80 to 125 gallons capacity. **1970** S. L. Barraclough in I. L. Horowitz *Masses in Lat. Amer.* iv. 112 If any group has been systematically discriminated against, it is the small-farm producers and landless workers. **1874** 'Mark Twain' in *Atlantic Monthly* Nov. 592/2 Dey wa'n't no small-fry officers, mine you; dey was de biggest dey is. **1957** R. Frankenberg *Village on Border* 10 The small-gauge railway. *a* **1976** A. Christie *Autobiogr.* (1977) vi. i. 296 An expedition in a small-gauge train. **1980** 'A. Skinner' *Mind's Eye* v. 73 'Thank you,' she said with careful, small-girl politeness. **1951** in Rohrer & Sherif *Soc. Psychol. at Crossroads* 333 The very few small-group studies made in recent years. **1955** KEEPNEWS & GRAUER *Pictorial Hist. Jazz* xi. 117 Alternating big-band work with prolific small-group recording activity. **1964** I. L. HOROWITZ *New Sociology* 25 Even at the level..of small-group research, time must be recorded. **1972** G. LITTLE in G. W. Turner *Good Austral. Eng.* vii. 135 The pupils sit in groups face to face, and pursue a variety of small-group activities. **1974** *Melody Maker* 13 Apr. 50/7 A lovely example of small-group jazz by players who have worked together. **1979** in W. G. Lawrence *Exploring Indiv. & Organiz. Boundaries* vi. 91 The students were told that they would participate in a small group experience. **1945** E. JOHNSTON *Writing & Illuminat. & Lettering* xv. 263 More time and material than a Small-letter MS. entails. **1950** *Language* XXVI. 13 Small-letter vowels. **1964** G. LYALL *Most Dangerous Game* vi. 42 He was the only other pilot doing small-plane charter work in Lapland that year. **1956** *Nature* 18 Feb. 322/2 Specifications for two light-weight small-power sprayers. *Ibid.* 28 Jan. 160/1 Techniques of small-sample loading employing micro-pipettes. **1968** *Brit. Med. Bull.* XXIV. 220/2 The calculations in the program have been written for the particular needs of the medical research worker; thus 'small sample' statistical theory is well represented. **1852** Small-scale [in Dict.]. **1887** [see SCALE *sb.*³ 11 a]. **1935** *Discovery* Mar. 78/1 The small-scale structure of the ice will be examined. **1951** R. FIRTH *Elem. Social Organization* ii. 43 These are small-scale units..the members of which are in close personal contact in daily life. **1954** M. RICKERT *Painting in Britain: Middle Ages* v. 131 Softer, finer vellum, more suitable for the small-scale miniatures. **1960** *Farmer & Stockbreeder* 16 Feb. 75/3 The disadvantages of small-scale farming heavily outweighed the advantages. **1964** W. L. GOODMAN *Hist. Woodworking Tools* 56 The difficulties of showing detail in small-scale carvings. **1979** *N. & Q.* Feb. 16/2 Orrery was very much the literary dilettante and small-scale Mæcenas. **1937** *Discovery* Feb. 45/1 Flicker, 'rain' and a rather dim appearance make the demonstration noticeably inferior in quality to that obtained with the small screen receivers now on the market. **1868** G. MEREDITH *Let.* Oct. (1970) I. 376 Eleven a.m. plates of small-shop ham, thick cut, grisly with brine: four smashed eggs on it. **1967** KARCH & BUBER *Offset Processes* ii. 9 The graphic arts is a small-shop industry. Only about 1,000 plants employ more than 100 employees, and the average is 17. **1949** *Bell Syst. Techn. Jrnl.* XXVIII. 401 An explicit calculation of the transient phenomena outside the range of small-signal theory. **1962** SIMPSON & RICHARDS *Physical Princ. Junction Transistors* xv. 372 The equivalent circuits.. may be used in the determination of the transient response of video amplifiers by estimating their time of response to a small-step input of current or voltage. **1962** R. WILLIAMS *Communications* iii. 58 Regular columns of close print, with small-type headlines. **1976** *Amer. Speech 1974* XLIX. 267 Good lexicography keeps open a variety of approaches to defining, which include..exploiting small-type notes for added comment. **1959** *N.Y. Times* 19 Mar. 16/1 The three Project Argus detonations involved relatively small yield nuclear devices. **1963** *Listener* 7 Feb. 251/2 The introduction of compact, mobile 'small yield' weapons into service with American forces in Europe.

b. *small-boyish* (earlier example).

1882 W. JAMES *Let.* 9 Nov. (1920) I. 214 Baginsky's torrent of words was even more overwhelming than Munk's. I never felt quite so helpless and small-boyish before.

23. *small-faced* (later examples), *-headed, -printed, -propertied, -spored, -typed, -windowed.*

1932 D. H. LAWRENCE *Etruscan Places* 143 A small-faced, weedy sort of youth. **1967** KARCH & BUBER *Offset Processes* iv. 78 Sizes range from a small-faced six point to a 13-point full point sized capital letter font. **1851** H. MELVILLE *Moby Dick* I. xli. 303 The White Steed of the Prairies; a magnificent milk-white charger, large-eyed, small-headed, bluff-chested. **1931** W. FAULKNER *Sanctuary* xvii. 159 The thick small-headed shape of him would be clinging to the bars, gorilla-like. **1956** P. A. LARKIN *Less Deceived* 40 Nor the shelves stuffed with small-printed books for the Sabbath. **1951** C. W. MILLS *White Collar* I. iii. 34 The ideology suitable for a nation of small capitalists persists, as if that small-propertied world were still a going concern. **1899** *Allbutt's Syst. Med.* VIII. 854 The large-spored fungus first attacks the root of the hair and grows upwards. **1964** M. HYNES *Med. Bacteriol.* (ed. 8) xxvii. 418 (*caption*) Ringworm of hair—Small-spored ectothrix. **1891** T. HARDY *Let.* 4 Mar. (1978) I. 230 My own occupation at present is that of correcting a bundle of miserably small-typed proofs. **1902** M. BEERBOHM in *Sat. Rev.* 15 Nov. 612/2 The authentic 'star'..is a no greater person than small-typed, smuggled-in 'J. M. Barrie'. **1930** W. DE LA MARE *Poems for Children* 35 The small-windowed moonlit house. **1976** *Times* 21 Aug. 12/3 One-storeyed, small-windowed cottages.

B. *absol.* or as *sb.*² **1. b.** *sing.* A child, a little one.

1907 W. DE MORGAN *Alice-for-Short* xxx. 300 How much can you remember of all that time, Alice? You were only a small, you know. *Ibid.*, I wasn't such a small as all that. **1947** *Forum* (Johannesburg) 5 Apr. 37/1 In a dozen other ways the prefects are the right-hand men of their Housemasters and me, and many a small owes a very great debt indeed to them. **1968** *Guardian* 1 Apr. 7/3 Leave two smalls to the tender mercies of a baby sitter? **1981** P. DICKINSON *Seventh Raven* vi. 75 After each performance there's always a dozen smalls wandering miserably around.

9. a. Also, underclothes.

1943 N. COWARD *Middle East Diary* (1944) 80 Their mothers stood nearby washing out a few 'smalls' in the shallows. **1951** *People* 3 June 4/6 Most of those who do send out to the laundry still wash smalls and personal linen themselves. **1973** *Guardian* 12 Mar. 10/2 Not many Americans..can have a clear idea of what to use the bidet for, apart from soaking the smalls.

d. (Further examples.)

1919 H. ETHERIDGE *Dict. Typewriting* 125 May be in either capitals and smalls or all capitals. **1947** M. MORRIS in 'B. James' *Austral. Short Stories* (1963) 344 Make it another small... All round. **1976** *Wymondham & Attleborough Express* 10 Dec. 21/2 Mediums [*sc.* eggs] from 46p to 43p per dozen with only smalls below this rate.

e. Small advertisements.

1942 *New Statesman* 11 July 25/3 The members of staff usually responsible for selecting 'smalls' and rejecting those that are undesirable. **1959** *Times* 2 Dec. 9/4 The Press figure does not take into account the booming Classified advertising revenue, or 'Smalls'.

small, *adv.* Add: **5.** *small-drawn* adj.

a **1918** W. OWEN *Poems* (1920) 13 And terror's first constriction over, Their hearts remain small drawn.

6. *Naut.* Close to the wind.

1848 J. F. COOPER *Oak-Openings* II. xiv. 203 All the difficulty was reduced to steering so 'small', as seamen term it, as to prevent one or the other of the lugs from jibing. **1911** J. BARTEN *Compl. Naut. Pocket Dict.* 192 Steer small.

small, *v.* **1.** Delete † *Obs.* and add later example. (Still *rare.*)

1962 'K. ORVIS' *Damned & Destroyed* xiv. 95 Welch smalled his hands against his desk.

small-leaved, *a.* Also small-leafed. [SMALL *a.*] Having small leaves.

1699 M. LISTER *Journey to Paris* 209 The Tree most in use here, was the small-leaved Horne-Beam. **1731** P. MILLER *Gardeners Dict.* s.v. Tilia, The small-leav'd Lime-tree. **1827** [see SMALL *a.* 23 b]. **1884** [see SMALL *a.* 23 a]. **1889** [see SMALL *a.* 23 b]. **1962** R. PAGE *Educ. Gardener* v. 159 The small-leaved elm *Ulmus pumila*..seems resistant to elm-disease. **1967** *Coast to Coast 1965–6* 209 The dunes gave way to the..hardy small-leafed bushes. **1979** P. THEROUX *Old Patagonian Express* xxi. 322 These sparse, small-leaved thorn bushes create the illusion of green.

small-pox, *sb.* Add: **2. c.** *Comb.*, as *smallpox-pitted* adj.; also *fig.*

1897 'MARK TWAIN' *Following Equator* xlix. 465 Saharas of sand, smallpox-pitted with footprints. **1926** D. H. LAWRENCE *Plumed Serpent* v. 92 The pug-faced Mexican in charge, and his small-pox-pitted assistant.

small-poxed, *a.* Add: Also *fig.*

1901 'MARK TWAIN' *Let.* 28 July (1917) II. 711 Water, small-poxed with rain-splashes. **1952** *Landfall* Mar. 28 The smallpoxed plaster walls of the railway station that the English had shelled from the sea.

small-talk, *sb.* Add: Also *attrib.*

1905 A. BENNETT *Tales of Five Towns* I. 22 'Will Harry be late at the works to-night again?' she asked in her colder, small-talk manner, which committed her to nothing. **1977** *Gay News* 7–20 Apr. 16/3 He will begin in a very small talk kind of way about anything and before long he builds up a kind of empathy between him and the other person.

small time, small-time, *sb.* and *a.* (*phr.*) orig. and chiefly *U.S.* Also (as adj.) small-time. [SMALL *a.*] **A.** *sb. Theatr.* (See quot. 1926.) Also *transf.*

1910 *Variety* 30 Apr. 9/4 Acts on the 'small time' of any merit or quality will not play in the houses calling for 'five shows daily'. **1917** WODEHOUSE *Man with Two Left Feet* 38 He's booked me in the small time at thirty-five dollars a week. **1926** *Amer. Speech* I. 436/2 *Small time*, the lower salaried circuits or where acts must work three or more times a day. **1960** B. KEATON *My Wonderful World of Slapstick* v. 88 Rather than play the small time, other big-time acts preferred not to work. **1977** B. LANGLEY *Death Stalk* ix. 103 Small-time hoodlums looked very much alike. Perhaps it was that streak..of uniformity which kept them in the small-time.

B. *adj.* Of or pertaining to second-rate vaudeville; *gen.* operating on a small scale, second-rate, unimportant, insignificant.

1910 *Variety* 30 Apr. 9/4 The Hartford Opera House has been taken under a five-year lease by S. Z. Poli who will operate it as a 'small time' vaudeville house. **1921** A. G. EMPEY *Madonna of Hills* iii. 24 She had been given a 'tryout' before a booking agency, and had made good to the extent of working in 'small time' vaudeville. **1934** *Punch* 7 Mar. 280/2 He lumbered, mined and starved in Canada; he became an itinerant 'small-time' wrestler and pugilist all over the United States. **1938** WODEHOUSE *Code of Woosters* xiii. 278 Sidney Carton..was small-time stuff compared with you, Bertie. **1940** R. CHANDLER *Farewell, my Lovely* xxxii. 244 You think I'm a small time private dick trying to push ten times his own weight. **1949** 'J. TEY' *Brat Farrar* xv. 139 Timber..was a deliberate and intelligent rogue... There was nothing small-time about Timber. **1961** *John o' London's* 5 Jan. 22/2 A gang of big-time smugglers want to eliminate the small-time hero. **1968** P. OLIVER *Screening Blues* iv. 130 The words [of a blues song] were gauche but revealing of the anxieties of the small-time player. **1976** P. R. WHITE *Planning for Public Transport* x. 204 Many economists expert in the finer points of judging small-time savings, or the effect of taxation in determining net resource costs, have only the haziest idea of costs. **1977** I. SHAW *Beggarman, Thief* III. viii. 307 Do you intend to be a small-time tennis pro.. all your life?

Hence **small-timer,** (*a*) a small-time theatre (*rare*); (*b*) a small-time operator, an insignificant person.

1910 *Variety* 30 Apr. 9/4 S. Z. Poli..will operate it as a small time' vaudeville house, under the booking direction of J. J. Clancy, and in conjunction with the other Poli 'small timers'. **1935** A. J. POLLOCK *Underworld Speaks* 109/1 *Small timer*, a person who doesn't amount to much; a piker. **1950** *Sport* 24–30 Mar. 21/4 The small-timer is now not only demanding protection from the Guild but a rightful place in boxing affairs. **1959** R. SIMONS *Houseboat Killings* viii. 90 She was a small timer when I met 'er... Then she got so 'igh and mighty she wouldn't speak to me. **1976** 'TREVANIAN' *Main* (1977) x. 189 A couple of small-timers..who make their money by 'laundering' men for the American organized-crime market.

small-town, *a.* Also small town. [SMALL *a.*] Of, pertaining to, or characteristic of a small town; unsophisticated, provincial.

1824 *Blackw. Mag.* June 659/2 Nothing can be better than Miss Austin's [*sic*] sketches of that sober, orderly, small-town, parsonage, sort of society in which she herself had spent her life. **1859** *Bentley's Q. Rev.* July 437 If 'George Eliot' proves to be..a very young man, son of a small town tradesman [etc.]. **1881** *Harper's Mag.* Jan. 223/2 Cosmopolitans, they do not sink into the ruts of small-town life. **1930** R. MACAULAY *Staying with Relations* xvii. 254 It looked even a little more decayed and small-town than the Miramar. **1937** J. M. MURRY *Necessity of Pacifism* iii. 47 Their natural mode of feeling is still small-town and parochial. **1949** KOESTLER *Promise & Fulfilment* I. ii. 14 The Jews had..only a homogeneous lower-middle-class of Eastern European small-town origin. **1959** *Times* 30 Sept. 13/4 A lawyer who is by no means so simple and small-town as he makes himself out to be. **1964** R. MILIBAND in I. L. Horowitz *New Sociology* 80 A rural, small-town, one-man-one-gun America. **1969** A. LURIE *Real People* 105 Not a slick professional show like Saratoga; but very amateurish, small-town. **1975** *Verbatim* May 12/1 Can a small-town girl from Kansas and Indiana make good as a reporter in the wilds of Greater Boston? **1980** *Times Lit. Suppl.* 19 Sept. 1047/4 Pinning her characters..in small-town Oregon.., she uncovers the hidden principles and ambitions of little men and women as they battle against the smothering ordinariness of suburban life.

So **small-towner**, an inhabitant of a small town, one who comes from a small town; **small-townish, -towny** *adjs.*, characteristic or suggestive of a small town.

1920 S. LEWIS *Main Street* xxix. 353 It's dreadfully tabby and small-towny. **1931** H. CONCANNON *St. Patrick* xiv. 189 The smooth paths of a smug small-townish officialdom. **1945** *Sun* (Baltimore) 17 Apr. 1/2 A friendly, small-townish man of the Middle West, called suddenly to the presidency..by the death of Franklin D. Roosevelt, [etc.]. **1969** *Listener* 5 July 3/2 The small-towners gratefully seized upon this idealised portrait, using it as psychological support and insulation from the cold reality of their dependence on the mass society. **1974** Small-townish [see *OREGONIAN *a.*].

smally, *adv.* For † *Obs.* read 'Now *rare*' and add: **4.** (Later example.)

1946 B. MARSHALL *George Brown's Schooldays* xxx. 128 Abinger moved smally in between them.

5. Of a sound: with low volume.

1958 T. H. WHITE *Once & Future King* II. ii. 224 All these noises came up to the two on the tower smally, as though they were listening through the wrong end of a megaphone. **1964** F. O'ROURKE *Mule for Marquesa* 55 Hoover said, 'Good luck,' and his words died smally in the thud of seats hitting saddles.

smalm, *v.*: see *SMARM *v.* **smalmy,** var. *SMARMY *a.*

smalt, *sb.* (and *a.*). Add: **4. a.** *smalt-maker.*

1921 *Dict. Occup. Terms* (1927) § 143 *Smalt maker*, places powdered mixture of cobalt oxide, silica (pure sand) and potassium carbonate into a wheeled fireclay crucible [etc.]. **1923** *Chambers's Jrnl.* 15 Dec. 36/1 The supreme obstacle confronting the smalt-makers.

Hence **sma·lter,** one who prepares smalt.

1923 *Chambers's Jrnl.* 15 Dec. 36/1 The Venetian glass-makers..were content to purchase their requirements from the 'smalters' of Germany.

smarm, *v.* Now the usual form of SMALM *v.* For *dial.* read '*colloq.* orig. *dial.*' and add:

1. b. To make smooth with an oily or greasy substance; to smooth or slick *down*. Also *fig.*

1937 KIPLING *Something of Myself* viii. 211 The Provincial Press has been syndicated, standardized, and smarmed down out of individuality. **1953** *Chambers's Jrnl.* June 356/1, I remembered in time the need to attach a canvas, oil-filled bag to the sea-anchor, so that the thin trickle of oil would smalm the crippling seas. **1953** *Landfall* June 126 He twitted me about my orange brogues, my smarmed-down hair, my nervous attempts at wit. **1977** M. KENYON *Rapist* i. 5 The rapist looked in the looking-glass at the smarmed hair.

c. To treat in a wheedling, flattering way.

1902 *Little Folks* Mar. 221/2 You can go and smarm him over if you want to.

2. a. *intr.* To behave in a fulsomely flattering or toadying manner, to suck *up to* a person. Also const. *about, over.*

1911 O. ONIONS *Widdershins* ix. 265 It had been the usual thing..twenty years ago—smarming about Art and the Arts. **1920** 'O. DOUGLAS' *Penny Plain* xx. 218 The people you try to help will smarm to your face and blackguard you behind your back. **1924** H. DE SELINCOURT *Cricket Match* v. 184 Loving her to tease him..and not sort of smalm over him like some chaps' maters did. **1928** A. P. HERBERT *Trials of Topsy* xxiii. 138, I will *not* spend week-ends *smarming* about in your *ulcerated* town. **1942** G. R. GILBERT *Free to Laugh and Dance* vi. 29 The.. children of his two previous marriages were indignant but they couldn't do anything about it, they all hanging round and smarming up to the old man, and his marrying again in spite of them. **1950** J. CANNAN *Murder Included* vi. 108 Murder was the last thing that a toady like that doctor would look for in the family he smarmed over. **1960** F. RAPHAEL *Limits of Love* III. vi. 343 Dulles and Eden were smarming up to Nasser.

b. *to smarm one's way*, to make one's way by flattery or toadying.

1940 G. D. H. & M. COLE *Counterpoint Murder* i. 15, I am going to report you to Mr. Marston. So it's no use you thinking you can smarm your way out of it. **1975** *Times Lit. Suppl.* 20 June 692/4 He is as convincing an uncaught villain as any in crime fiction; cautious and false, smarming his way into the upper reaches of such a society as only such a man would seek to crawl into.

Hence **smarmed** *ppl. a.*; **sma·rming** *vbl. sb.* and *ppl. a.*

1950 J. CANNAN *Murder Included* ii. 22 Bunny strove to use tact and courtesy: Elizabeth accused her of 'smarming'. **1953** Smarmed [see *SMARM *v.* 1 b]. **1957** L. DURRELL *Justine* II. 143 He is a complete *parvenu* of course and rose on..judicious smarming of powerful people. **1970** E. BERCKMAN *She asked for It* ix. 108 It's wonderful how greedy people are for these smarming little compliments. **1974** D. GRAY *Dead Give Away* iii. 31 He hated her smarming ways. **1977** Smarmed [see *SMARM *v.* 1 b].

smarm (smāɹm), *sb. colloq.* Also **smalm.** [f. the vb.] An unctuous bearing; fulsome flattery; flattering or toadying behaviour.

1937 H. C. BAILEY *Clunk's Claimant* xiii. 84 That smarm of holiness..was pretty near the ruddy limit. **1962** M. URQUHART *Frail on North Circular* xiii. 72 'That's a nice new hair-do, Lil.'.. 'Don't come your smarm with me.' **1966** C. FENN *Pyramid of Night* iii. 60 The manager escorted her right to the door. There was no doubt that this kind of smarm was cute. **1969** B. COBB *Scandal at Scotland Yard* xvi. 154 He was ready to turn on the smarm with the 'Kiss and be friends again' talk. **1978** *Guardian Weekly* 19 Feb. 22/1 'George' did this, 'George' did that, all the way through. 'George' is the victim of bonhomie and smarm.

smarmy (smā·ɹmi), *a.* (and *sb.*). *colloq.* Also **smalmy.** [f. *SMARM *v.* or *sb.* + -Y[1].] **A.** *adj.* **a.** Smooth and sleek. **b.** Ingratiating, obsequious; smug, unctuous.

1909 C. HAMILTON *Plain Brown* i. 4 A tall, slight, smarmy-headed man. **1924** 'L. BROCK' *Deductions Col. Gore* iv. 51 Don't you be taken in by that smarmy swine. **1928** K. CLARK *Gothic Revival* ix. 236 If he [*sc.* Gilbert Scott] saved a few cathedrals from ruins, we must, I suppose, look more kindly on their smalmy surfaces. **1929** ST. J. ERVINE *First Mrs. Fraser* II. 49 *Janet.* But, Ninian dear, you shouldn't have said anything. *Ninian.* He was looking so smarmy and self-satisfied that I had to. **1930** *London Mercury* Aug. 380 Our forefathers rejected 'smarmy' overtures with 'Fair words butter no parsnips'. **1955** H. SPRING *These Lovers fled Away* 133 Uriah Heep's sort of smarmy humbleness. **1962** S. RAVEN *Close of Play* I. vi. 77 He's a smarmy, ingratiating swine. **1976** J. B. HILTON *Gamekeeper's Gallows* viii. 66 She used to..tell her how grateful she was. Not smarmy, like; genuine. **1979** R. JAFFE *Class Reunion* I. ix. 98 He always treated her as if she were a little bit better than he was; an attitude that was smarmy in other men.

B. *absol.* as *sb.* A smarmy person. *rare.*

1957 T. GUNN *Sense of Movement* 22 You understand ..the speculative man or passionate You know the smarmies, but side-step the grease.

Hence **sma·rmily** *adv.*; **sma·rminess.**

1934 H. NICOLSON *Let.* 17 Nov. (1966) 189 There is something about the smarminess of Americans which makes me see red. **1958** 'A. BRIDGE' *Portuguese Escape* 184 The art of making himself agreeable in his current surroundings, whatever they were; but..he rather overdid it..'smarminess' described his conversation with painful accuracy. **1968** J. PORTER *Dover goes to Pott* i. 15 Dover, sycophant and snob that he was, smarmily agreed. **1974** 'D. KYLE' *Raft of Swords* II. xii. 129 With deliberate smarminess, Gawthorpe thanked him. **1982** *Sunday Express* 30 May 6/8 It is smarmily hypocritical.

smart, *sb.*[2] Add: **3.** Usu. *pl.* Intelligence, cleverness, acumen; wits. *U.S. slang.*

1970 *It* 27 Feb.–13 Mar. 14/4 Now Abbie's a very brilliant cat. He's very far out, very freaked out, but he's still got some smarts. **1970** *New Yorker* 28 Nov. 126/3, I knew I had the smarts—the business smarts—even then. **1972** H. KEMELMAN *Monday Rabbi took Off* xlv. 263 The whole story is a little weak... I mean, this kid of yours has the normal amount of smarts. **1977** *N.Y. Times* 9 Oct. 26 Mrs. Maynard said that Mr. Miller ..'doesn't have enough smart to run a union as big as the United Mine Workers'. **1979** *Sunday Star* (Toronto) 6 May B7/4 You know—streetwise, lots of smart, lots of quick, playing pinochle with vice cops. **1981** *Guardian Weekly* 26 July 15/4 They complain that the level of intelligence is low and that the soldiers have neither the smarts nor the education to work the complicated weapons of modern warfare.

smart, *a.* Add: **I. 6. b.** (Further example.)

1870 G. M. HOPKINS *Jrnls. & Papers* (1959) 201 The day had been very bright and clear, distances smart.

7. a. (Earlier example.)

1778 S. FOOTE *Devil upon Two Sticks* II. 44 in *Wks.* IV, [Scot loq.] Ah! for the mater of that, it is a praty smart little income.

b. *right smart* (earlier and later examples).

1842 J. S. BUCKINGHAM *Slave States of America* II. 327, I asked here, whether the people made much maple-sugar in this neighbourhood; when the gentleman..answered, 'Yes, they do, I reckon, right smart.' **1932** W. FAULKNER *Light in August* i. 25 There is a right smart of folks in Jefferson I don't know. **1938** M. K. RAWLINGS *Yearling* vi. 54 'Howdy, Mr. Forrester. Proud to see you. How's your health?' 'Howdy, sir. I'm right smart tol'able, seein' as how I be near about done for.' **1949** L. NORDYKE *Cattle Empire* 81 Heard a right smart about you, Pincham.

II. 8. For † *Obs. rare* read '*Obs. rare* exc. *predic.* in *to be* or *get smart* (U.S.)'.

1933 E. O'NEILL *Ah, Wilderness* II. 60 *Tommy*... Uncle Sid's soused again. *Mrs. Miller*... You be quiet! Did I ever! You're getting too smart! **1955** W. C. GAULT *Ring around Rosa* v. 59 Don't get smart, Callahan. **1956** B. HOLIDAY *Lady sings Blues* (1973) i. 4 This time Cousin Ida beat me for being smart with her.

9. c. Healthy, well. *U.S.*

1788 J. MAY *Jrnl.* 31 Aug. (1873) 116 Didn't feel smart enough to go to meeting. **1832** J. J. STRANG *Diary* 23 Aug. in M. M. Quaife *Kingdom of St. James* (1930) 205 This commenced the sickest day I ever suffered since my remembrance but now (evening) I am again smart for a sick person. **1956** B. HOLIDAY *Lady sings Blues* (1973) i. 1 By the time she worked her way out of hock in the hospital and took me home to her folks, I was so big and smart I could sit up in a carriage.

10. c. Of a device: capable of some independent and seemingly intelligent action. Cf. *smart bomb* in sense 15 below.

1972 *Proc. IEEE* LX. 1282/1 The term 'smart terminal' is used here to identify an interactive terminal in which part of the processing is accomplished by a small computer or processor contained within the terminal itself. **1977** *Sci. Amer.* Sept. 188/1 When smart traffic signals become ubiquitous and are linked to a control center, the traffic cop at the intersection will become obsolete. **1980** *Economist* 15 Mar. 84/3 Tomorrow's vehicles are likely to have a series of 'smart' transducers attached to the engine, gear-box, brakes, etc, all sending coded messages via a common wire to the dashboard. **1982** *Times* 1 June 15/5 Smart sensors ensure a direct hit on a target.

13. *the smart set* (examples); also *transf.*

1885 E. W. HAMILTON *Diary* 20 May (1972) II. 867 Dined at Brook House... This is a house at which one meets the 'grand set' as distinct from the 'smart set'—two totally different sections of the best London Society. **1900** *Smart Set* Apr. 137 The Smart Set of London has for the last ten or fifteen years..been the chief influence of our English playwrights, plays and players. **1937** K. BLIXEN *Out of Africa* I. i. 12 Our Quasi Smart Set of the Colony. **1949** P. HASTINGS *Cases in Court* v. 265 Mrs Barney's family were well-known in Mayfair and both Mrs Barney and the dead man were notorious members of the so-called young 'smart set'. **1974** P. DICKINSON *Poison Oracle* ii. 66 Dinah [*sc.* an ape]..had indeed left the slums to join the evolutionary smart set, Man. **1981** V. GLENDINNING *E. Sitwell* ix. 131 Edith's interest in the intrigues of the smart set was minimal.

14. *smart-looking* (earlier example), *-suited.*

1770 'P. PENNYLESS' *Sentimental Lucubrations* ii. 31 A smart-looking waiter came up to me. **1922** JOYCE *Ulysses* 249 James's wax smartsuited freshcheeked models.

15. Special collocations: **smart bomb,** a powered missile which is guided to its target by an optical system; **smart money** *U.S.*, money bet or invested by persons with expert knowledge; *transf.* knowledgeable persons; **smart mouth** *U.S. slang*, one who is good at repartee, one who gives cheek; so **smart-mouth** *v. trans.* to be cheeky to, to be witty at the expense of; **smart-mouthed** *a.*

1972 *Guardian* 29 June 4/2 Three out of four [missions] have been using 'smart' bombs. **1975** *N.Y. Times* 8 Sept. 2/4 Since 1973 the Israeli Air Force has been furnished with a variety of 'smart bombs' guided by laser beams of television. **1982** *Sunday Tel.* 9 May 17/5 The American 'smart' bomb, which homes on a laser beam shone on to the target by a spotter aircraft. **1926** *Amer. Mercury* Dec. 464/2 In referring to money wagered by persons with good tips or information, the term used is *smart* money. **1930** W. R. BURNETT *Iron Man* I. 5 'Well,' said Regan, 'all the smart money's on the black boy.' **1947** *Sun* (Baltimore) 6 Aug. 10/5 Bookmakers and layoff men are gamblers and many times they add personal wages to 'smart money'. **1977** H. FAST *Immigrants* II. 87 Germany has declared war on Russia, and the smart money says that this is only the beginning. **1981** *Times* 7 Nov. 6/8 Mr Weinberger..is close to the President..much closer than Mr Haig has ever been. In a battle for Mr Reagan's ear, all the smart money would be on Mr Weinberger. **1968** *Sun Mag.* (Baltimore) 13 Oct. 19/1, I was a smart mouth, a troublemaker in school. **1976** R. B. PARKER *Promised Land* (1977) xii. 65 Don't smart-mouth me, man. You wising off at me? **1978** J. L. HENSLEY *Killing in Gold* (1979) viii. 97 He..beat up three kids..when one of them smart-mouthed him. **1976** *Publishers Weekly* 19 Apr. 82/3 Smart-mouthed film critic for *Gotham* magazine. **1978** J. IRVING *World according to Garp* xii. 229 Some smart-mouthed motorist..will..ask.., 'What are you in training for?'

smart alec (smāɹt æ·lėk). *colloq.* (orig. *U.S.*). Also **aleck, alick,** hyphenated, and with capital initial(s). [f. SMART *a.* + *Alec*, dim. of personal name *Alexander.*] A would-be clever person; a 'know-all'; occas., a man who is ostentatiously smart in dress or manner. Also *attrib.* or as *adj.*

1865 *Carson* (Nevada) *Appeal* 17 Oct. 2/3 Halloa, old smart Aleck—how is the complimentary vote for Ashley? **1873** J. H. BEADLE *Undevel. West* vii. 140, I had the pleasure of seeing at least a score of 'smart Alecks' relieved of their surplus cash. **1887** F. FRANCIS *Saddle & Mocassin* 312 You may talk about..your Smart Alicks, and your Joe-dandies and daisies. **1902** [see *RUN *v.* 64 h]. **1904** W. N. HARBEN *Georgians* ix. 92 Thar was a smart Alec of a feller from Little Dogtrot over in the mountains. **1934** C. STEAD *Seven Poor Men of Sydney* vi. 184 Rawson, from the Trades Hall, ready, assured, blatant, a political opportunist, whom Joseph called a 'real smart-alec'. **1934** H. G. WELLS *Exper. Autobiogr.* I. v. 276 Nowhere was there protection from those Smart Alecs, the primary poison of the whole process, who piled up the rents. **1941** B. SCHULBERG *What makes Sammy Run?* xii. 221 He's a smart-aleck. I can see already he thinks he knows more than I do. **1942** C. BARRETT *On Wallaby* x. 202 One smart Alick came to..offer his services in return for a large tin of pineapple slices. **1956** C. V. WEDGWOOD *Lit. & Historian* 9 The imitators of Lytton Strachey managed by their smart-aleck antics to obscure for a long decade what was really valuable in the new approach to biography. **1964** L. NKOSI *Rhythm of Violence* II. ii. 33 I'm bored with their smart-aleck talk! **1976** T. STOPPARD *Dirty Linen* 40 Smart alec-paragraphs about innocent tripe-and-onions with tittian voluptuaries? **1979** L. MEYNELL *Hooky & Villainous Chauffeur* vii. 99 Smart alec, aren't you? Smart and smug like all you intellectual lot.

Hence **smart-alec(k)ism,** smart-aleckry; an instance of this; **smart-aleckry,** behaviour characteristic of a smart alec, ostentatious or smug cleverness; **smart-alecky** *a.*, characteristic of a smart alec, ostentatiously or smugly clever.

1905 *Dialect Notes* III. II. 157 *Smart Elecky*, impertinent, impudent. 'He's too *Smart Elecky* for me.' **1926** G. J. NATHAN *House of Satan* 6 Ripples of smart-aleckry. **1929** J. B. PRIESTLEY *Good Companions* III. v. 579, I wouldn't have minded so much if he hadn't been so Smart Alecky about it. **1934** *Sun* (Baltimore) 28 Aug. 8/7 The futility of those modern writers who mistake smart aleckism for sophistication and vulgarity for art. **1938** *Scrutiny* VI. IV. 400 His [*sc.* Fauré's] supreme disregard of public opinion is difficult to parallel in an age in which composers seek consolation for their lack of popular appreciation in the formation of cliques and the cultivation of a pert smart-alecism. **1958** *Spectator* 5 Sept. 306/2 *Brouhaha* remains a hodgepodge of smartaleckry aimed.. at the intellectual teddy-boy set. **1962** *Listener* 21 June 1091/3 A sophisticated bit of smart-alecksim like the 'nine-minute opera' *Introductions and Goodbyes.* **1965** *New Statesman* 30 Apr. 690/1 The last thing the Hansons go in for is the shrug of the shoulders or the smart-alecism—unless it's at the expense of psychoanalysing critics who..suggest that Tchaikovsky was..rather odd. **1976** *National Observer* (U.S.) 10 July 8/3 She now writes regularly for New York magazine, though her cautious, measured manner of speaking doesn't seem to fit that magazine's usually brash, smart-alecky tone. **1981** *Times Lit. Suppl.* 6 Mar. 247/5 The various lists in the book have an air of Christmas competition-setting smart-aleckry.

smart-arse, -ass (smā·ɹtāɹs, -æs), *a.* and *sb. slang.* Also as one word without hyphen and as two words. [f. SMART *a.* + ARSE *sb.*, *ASS.] = *SMART ALEC.

Only the form with *-ass* is current in the U.S.

1962 J. D. MACDONALD *Girl, Gold Watch & Everything* ix. 118 Some smart-ass crowd set up all the confusion so as they could clean out them stores. **1965** W. DICK *Bunch of Ratbags* 245 Anyhow, where else could we go, do you know, smartarse? **1970** B. OAKLEY *Salute to Great McCarthy* 28 That smart arse from the city. **1972** D. DELMAN *Week to Kill* 115 But you've got a smart-ass answer for that, haven't you? **1972** P. MARKS *Collector's Choice* ii. 102 You're too pretty to be such a smart-ass. Just watch your step. **1973** *Guardian* 24 Feb. 8/5 A picture of a rose..needn't be just beautiful, or decorative, or a matter of smart-arse graphics. **1975** *Time Out* 9 May 13/2 When I'm hyping a film, as I'm doing now, I try not to get too smartass and articulate. **1977** *Private Eye* 1 Apr. 23/4 (Advt.), Get it together to put down pseuds, poseurs and general smartasses. **1981** J. BARNETT *Firing Squad* x. 92 He had indulged in reckless speculation... He was just as much a smart-arse as the Farnham D.I.

So **sma·rt-ass** *v. trans.*, to say in a smart-alecky manner; *intr.* and *trans.*, to behave in a smart-alecky manner (towards). **sma·rt-arsed, -assed** *adjs.*, smart-alecky.

1960 P. BLONDAL *Candle to light Sun* 191 A lot of smart-assed novelists would have you believe they're dirt-coat. **1962** A. SEYMOUR *One Day of Year* 49 Going round with smart-arsed little sheilas from the North Shore. It's all wrong, son. **1971** R. THOMAS *Backup Men* iv. 31 Is that supposed to be a smartassed answer? **1970** E. TIDYMAN *Shaft* (1971) vii. 95 'You can complain to the union,' he had smart-assed Persons, 'but twelve-fifty an hour is only my rate for living. I get a lot more for dying.' **1976** R. B. PARKER *Promised Land* xix. 115 Don't smart-ass with me, Johnny, or you'll be looking very close at the floor. **1977** J. WAINWRIGHT *Day of Peppercorn Kill* 68 No smart-arsed lawyer's going to shift my evidence. **1978** F. ROSS *Sleeping Dogs* 152 'I guess it's something to do with the generation gap, sir.' 'Don't smart-ass me!' **1979** *Globe & Mail* (Toronto) 15 Sept. 42/1 It is tempting to be smart-assed when reviewing a Richard Rohmer novel.

smartie, var. SMARTY in Dict. and Suppl.

smartish, *a.* Add: **B.** *adv.* Somewhat smartly.

1877 *Coursing Calendar Autumn 1876* 5 Vicar-of-Bray.. won a smartish-run trial with his extra pace. **1896** G. F. NORTHALL *Warwickshire Word-book* 218 *Smartish, adj.* and *adv.*, fairly well. 'How are you?' 'Smartish, thank you.' 'I'm getting on smartish now.' **1973** W. H. CANAWAY *Harry doing Good* II. iii. 155 You nipped off..a bit smartish, didn't you? **1979** N. FREELING *Widow* xiii. 79 Whip out smartish to the Italian grocer.

smartness. 6. (Earlier examples.)
1800 M. Edgeworth *Little Merchants* in *Parent's Assistant* (ed. 3) III. 111 His son's *smartness* was no longer useful in making bargains. **1819** M. Wilmot *Let.* 8 Dec. (1935) 34 We have got ourselves settled in..with fewer plagues than almost any family of strangers could boast. This we owe..to Willys smartness in his quiet way.

smarty, *sb.* For *U.S.* read 'orig. *U.S.*' and add: Also **smartie.** (Earlier and later examples.) Also, a smartly-dressed person; a member of a smart set.
1861 *Calif. Mag.* Aug. 39/2 'Juvenile smartys' are interesting, even to a vagabond. **1876** 'Mark Twain' *Tom Sawyer* i. 22 Smarty! You think you're *some*, now. *Ibid.* xviii. 156 That Saint Louis smarty that thinks he dresses so fine. **1929** D. H. Lawrence *Pansies* 89 But it is hard to be tolerant with the smarties. **1932** Auden *Orators* ii. 44 Poops and smarties, Who pilfer always but are never whipped. **1933** R. Strachey *Many Happy Returns* ii. 123 A gala night at the 'Shadwell Palace', dancing those Limehouse blues with her smartie. **1956** L. McIntosh *Oxford Folly* viii. 118 It's amazing how easy it is for anyone like me, with no background, to pose as an Oxford smartie. **1957** M. Millar *Soft Talkers* xxi. 204 'Do you happen to know how much it was?' 'No, and neither do you, smartie.' **1962** A. Bourne *Doctor's Creed* ii. 46 The worst payers were what we used to call the 'West End Smarties', flimsy young women who would appear from nowhere with no doctor's letter or tangible recommendations.

B. *adj.* **a.** Smart-alecky; ostentatiously smart.
1883 'Mark Twain' *Life on Mississippi* xxxiii. 370 The barkeeper..was gay and smarty and talky. **1940** *Horizon* Feb. 68 Another line of attack is to concede that the first number is interesting, but to add that it is middlebrow and 'smarty'. **1948** M. Allingham *More Work for Undertaker* vi. 83 He was full of smarty ideas and had no manners. **1960** D. Potter *Glittering Coffin* vi. 96 A smarty gossip column. **1967** G. Kelly in *Coast to Coast 1965–6* 104 The local smarty boys, the privileged class.

b. Special Combs. (also written *smarti-*), as **smarty-boots,** (orig. *U.S.*) **-pants** *colloq.*, an overly clever person, a know-all, a smart alec; also *attrib.* or as *adj.*
1962 *Times* 7 June 16/3 The phoney-ness of a smartiboots Ivy League undergraduate. **1962** *John o' London's* 22 Nov. 467/1 A cold, well-bred English smarty-boots. **1965** J. Porter *Dover Two* xiii. 166 He was grateful that smartie-boots MacGregor had overlooked the obvious, too. **1970** *Sunday Times* (Colour Suppl.) 6 Dec. 31/3 His self-confidence and satisfaction in his own life got under people's skin...phrases like 'Smartie Boots' were attached to him. **1979** *Guardian* 12 Nov. 13/7, I am not trying to be wilfully iconoclastic or smarty-boots when I say that.. Picasso simply is not the greatest painter of the 20th century. **1941** B. Schulberg *What makes Sammy Run?* iv. 57 One of those Vassar smarty-pants. **1953** M. Dickens *No More Meadows* vi. 266 [Amer. loq.] He jumped right in with his slick talk... That smarty pants. **1967** N. Marsh *Death at Dolphin* viii. 199 Hawkins, Mr. Smartypants, has a little chat. **1969** *Punch* 26 Mar. 465/3 *Cage Me a Leacock* (BBC-2) owed everything—though not, I hope, the smarty-pants title—to Braden's enormous enthusiasm for his subject. **1976** *Listener* 24 June 815/2 Technologically outclassed and outsold by pinstriped smartipants from foreign business schools. **1981** *Times Lit. Suppl.* 13 Feb. 158/3 The smarty-pants youthfulness is very period.

smash, *sb.*^{1} Add: **1. a.** (Earlier example.)
1725 E. Wigan *Let.* 25 Sept. in N. D. Mereness *Trav. Amer. Colonies* (1916) 156 They design to keep out lookouts every way and be ready to give them a Smash in their Towns.

b. Also in Badminton, Table Tennis, etc.
1950 *Badminton* ('Know the Game' Ser.) 30/1 The smash is perhaps the most vulnerable stroke in the game. **1981** G. MacBeth *Kind of Treason* xvi. 156 'Fourteen-fifteen,' said Yoshida, serving again. He'd lost the point ..by a wasted smash.

3. a. (Earlier and later examples in sense of 'collision'.)
1841 [see *railroad line* s.v. *Railroad *sb.* 3 a]. **1909** *Westm. Gaz.* 27 Apr. 4/2 If the brakes fail to hold it is impossible to avoid a bad smash. **1957** M. Spark *Comforters* viii. 196 If I hadn't had the smash I'd have got you last autumn.

5. a. (Earlier and later examples.)
1850 [see *brandy-smash* s.v. *Brandy *sb.* 2]. **1871** [see *corpse reviver* s.v. *Corpse *sb.* 6]. **1909** [see *brandy-smash* s.v. *Brandy *sb.* 2]. **1958** A. L. Simon *Dict. Wines, Spirits & Liqueurs* 147/2 *Smashes*, mixed iced drinks always with a spirit foundation and some mint flavouring. **1973** Wodehouse *Bachelors Anonymous* xiii. 170 What more likely than that he should have fetched up in Hollywood, made a packet, perished of a surfeit of brandy smashes, and left that packet to that nephew.

b. An alcoholic drink, esp. wine. *N. Amer. slang.*
1959 *Maclean's Mag.* 15 Aug. 28/2 So I had a couple of smashes and marched in. **1966** *Globe & Mail* (Toronto) 15 Mar. 35/8 Every time you wanted a smash the check girl would hand the coat to you over the counter, so you could get your mickey without actually taking the coat out. **1975** *Amer. Speech 1972* XLVII. 153 Let's get in the wind and belt some smash.

6. A great success; a film, person, play, song, etc., which enjoys popular success; a hit (*Hit *sb.* 4). Also *attrib.*, esp. in **smash hit.**
1923 *Variety* 11 Oct. 16 (*heading*) 'Rosie O'Reilly' and 'The Fool', Loop's Two Smash Hits. **1930** *Times Lit. Suppl.* 16 Oct. 841/1 An entirely strange girl; whom anyone would have admitted to be a 'smash'. **1931** *Daily Express* 21 Sept. 9/3 The magnates who had contracted to buy the picture indulged in fits of doubt concerning its prospects as a box-office 'smash'. **1935** *Amer. Speech* X. 193/2 Terminology from other fields aids the fashion editor... The sports writer is also responsible for the *smash hit* dinner dress. **1935** Wodehouse *Blandings Castle* xii. 305 Our whole programme is built around it. We are relying on it to be our big smash. **1948** W. S. Maugham *Colonel's Lady* in *Quartet* 201 The English publisher said to him: 'We've not had a success like this with a book of verse for twenty years.'.. The American publisher said to him: 'It's swell. It'll be a smash hit in America.' **1949** R. Chandler *Let.* 23 Apr. (1981) 174 You can't make me into a smash best seller. **1956** B. Holiday *Lady sings Blues* (1973) xix. 158 *Holiday on Broadway* was a sellout, and the first performance made us think we had a smash. **1961** *Amer. Speech* XXXVI. 110 It was a smash commercial success. **1969** R. Lowell *Notebk. 1967–68* 71 Eliot dead, you [*sc.* Ezra Pound] saying, 'And who is left to understand my jokes? My old Brother in the acts..and besides, he was a smash of a poet.' **1973** *Black World* Apr. 18/2 All smash Broadway musical hits. **1975** D. Francis *High Stakes* 232 The oddly mixed party proved a smash-hit success. **1978** *Times* 1 Nov. 13/1 [His] aim..has been to expand a truthful little ethnic comedy into a popular smash.

smash, *sb.*^{2} Add: **1. b.** Loose change.
1821 D. Haggart *Life* 13 M'Guire got L.7 of smash; I got a L.10 banknote. **1953** W. Burroughs *Junkie* (1972) ii. 22 Soon I was buying his drinks and meals, and he was hitting me for 'smash' (change) at regular intervals. **1953** K. Tennant *Joyful Condemned* iii. 21 Giving her his smash on pay-night so's she can blow it. **1965** *Australasian Post* 4 Mar. 47 Russell goes on to point out that all loose change is sometimes known as 'smash'.

smash, *v.*^{1} Add: **I. 3. b.** Also in Badminton, Squash Rackets, etc.
1965 *Badminton* ('Know the Game' Ser.) (ed. 2) 31/1 The man should take the shuttle as early as possible, playing drives when the shuttle is too low to smash. **1968** *Squash Rackets* ('Know the Game' Ser.) 43/1 You cannot smash a good high lob as you can at lawn tennis. *Ibid.* 44/2 A lob that was too high above the player's head has been smashed on to the tin.

III. 8. a. (Earlier example.) Also with *run.*
1818 [see Go *v.* B. 10]. **1849** T. T. Johnson *Sights Gold Region* xxii. 211 The afternoon of our 'first day out' was signalized by running smash into a big sycamore tree.

b. *to play smash*: to come to grief; to wreak havoc *with. dial.* and *U.S. colloq.*
1841 *Spirit of Times* 2 Jan. 523/2 Bill Spence got drunk and played smash with all the arrangements. **1842** D. Vedder *Poems* 84 Slates an' tiles, frae aff the houses, On the causey crown played smash. **1887** *Courier-Journal* (Louisville, Kentucky) 17 Jan. 1/7 (*caption*) Plays Smash With a Passenger Train on the Fitchburg Railroad. **1903** W. N. Harben *Abner Daniel* ii. 11 Yore pa's as bull-headed as a young steer, an' he's already played smash anyway. **1912** *Dialect Notes* III. viii. 585 *Play smash,*..a euphemism for *play hell* or *play the devil.* **1915** *Ibid.* IV. iii. 187 *Play smash,*..to make a great blunder; do a thing wholly wrong.

smash, *v.*^{2} **1.** (Earlier and later examples.)
1801 *Sporting Mag.* XIX. 88/1 He had never seen any [forged notes] that were better done; he had *smashed* several. **1898** A. M. Binstead *Pink 'Un & Pelican* x. 229 The small tradesman, afraid to smash his notes at a bureau, had them still intact when the police called upon him. **1905** —— *Mop Fair* ii. 28 The imaginary 'bailiff' who spoke about the handcuffs is well known in the neighbourhood..while the counterfeit 'tipstaff' who smashed the cheque is a dog-fighting publican.

smash-and-grab. Also **smash and grab, smash'n-grab.** [f. Smash *v.*^{1}, Grab *v.*] Used *attrib.* to designate a type of robbery in which the thief smashes a shop-window and grabs the goods there displayed. Also *transf.* and *fig.*, and *absol.* Hence **smash-and-grabber; smash and grabbing** *vbl. sb.*
1927 J. C. Goodwin *Crook Pie* ii. 52 'Smash and Grab' raids seem to be the order of the day. **1928** *Daily Tel.* 9 Oct. 12/2 Three men in a motor-car were concerned in a smash-and-grab raid... One of them threw a stone through the window. They then seized all the cameras available and returned to the car, which was driven away before a chase could be started. **1932** [see *Screwer 2]. **1933** Blunden *Charles Lamb* vii. 206 A literature of the smash-and-grab type..seems to have some chance of superseding the thorough, persuasive, modulated and interwoven style. **1937** A. L. Rowse *Sir Richard Grenville* v. 106 A smash-and-grab run upon the Isthmus of Panama. **1938** [see *Pick-up *sb.* a (vi)]. **1939** T. S. Eliot *Old Possum's Practical Cats* 23 They were..remarkably smart at a smash-and-grab. **1944** G. B. Shaw *Everybody's Political What's What?* xxvi. 232 Monstrous world wars and smash-and-grab revolutions. **1951** M. McLuhan *Mech. Bride* (1967) 145/2 A commercial society dedicated to the smash and grab and one-man fury of enterprise. **1960** *Observer* 24 Jan. 5/1 A sausage team always had to work three-handed... One to do the smash and grabbing. **1965** H. I. Ansoff *Corporate Strategy* (1968) iii. 39 In reaction to the public outrages at the 'smash'n-grab imperialism' of the nineteenth century, business has acquired a sense of social responsibility. **1970** *Oxf. Times* 23 Oct. 1/6 A smash and grab raid was carried out on the shop of Horns..shortly before midnight. **1973** W. M. Duncan *Big Timer* iv. 29 They tell me there was a smash-and-grab at Shader's, miss. **1978** *Daily Mail* 25 Jan. 12/2 Robbery with violence..used to be a 'snatch' or a 'smash-and-grab'.

smashed, *ppl. a.* Add: **1.** Also *fig.* Also *smashed-down, -up.*
1909 J. R. Ware *Passing Eng.* 227/1 *Smashed* (Navy), reduced in rank. **1915** J. Webster *Dear Enemy* 325 Our poor smashed-up doctor. **1918** W. S. Churchill in M. Gilbert *Winston S. Churchill* (1977) IV. Compan. i. 365 Ought we to build our lives & policy & the future arrangement of the world on the unreal basis of a smashed-up Russia & an invincible Germany. **1935** A. J. Pollock *Underworld Speaks* 109/1 *Smashed*, to have lost all material possessions. **1938** E. Blunden in *Times Lit. Suppl.* 8 Oct. 633/2 Nor the dead in smashed-down den. **1982** J. Hansen *Gravedigger* iii. 24 No abandoned or smashed-up Rollses.

2. Intoxicated, drunk; under the influence of drugs; 'stoned'. *slang* (orig. *U.S.*).
1962 J. D. MacDonald *Key to Suite* (1968) viii. 139 Are you figuring on getting smashed? **1968** *New Scientist* 26 Sept. 679/2 The males rapidly acquired a taste for the stuff [*sc.* alcohol], bent their elbows with great application, and soon became smashed. **1968** A. Young in A. Chapman *New Black Voices* (1972) 147 Turns out he was half-smashed and half-drunk because he'd smoked some dope when he got up that morning, then on the way to school he'd met up with Wine, so the two of them did up a fifth of Nature Boy, a brand of sweet wine. **1973** D. Laing *Freaks* 20 He would get smashed on two and a half pints of Worthington E from the wood, and fall about misquoting the poetry of the beat generation. **1977** *New Society* 27 Jan. 185/3 If you're smashed out of your skull all the time on peyote, then even the bizarre patronage of Marlon Brando must seem tolerable.

smasher^1. Add: **1. b.** A very pretty or attractive woman; an attractive man.
1948 Partridge *Dict. Forces' Slang* 173 To a Scotsman an attractive girl was 'a wee smasher'. **1949** J. R. Cole *It was so Late* 61 'Yes. No kidding,' Don said. 'But she was easier to look at than anything around here. She was a smasher—straight she was!' **1957** A. Wilson *Bit off Map & Other Stories* 74 When the jeunes filles met Rodney, Jackie..put her head on one side and said, 'I say, isn't he a smasher!' **1963** *Security Gazette* V. 1. 13/2 The applicant for a shorthand typist's job—she was a smasher. **1977** C. McCullough *Thorn Birds* xviii. 458 In a long black wig, tan body paint and my few scraps of metal I look a smasher.

2. b. (Earlier example.)
1829 P. Egan *Boxiana* 2nd Ser. II. 706 Tom, by the effect of this *smasher*, lost his equilibrium.

4. (Later examples.)
1921 [see *double-faulter* s.v. *Double *a.* C. 3]. **1928** B. Nuthall *Learning Lawn Tennis* vii. 114, I am not an expert smasher myself.

5. (Earlier example.) Also *ellipt.*
1891 E. Glanville *Fossicker* xviii. 156 The Dutchmen stared at him from under the brims of their felt 'smashers'. **1892** J. R. Couper *Mixed Humanity* i. 4 A wide-awake, called in South Africa a 'smasher'. **1894** C. H. W. Donaldson *With Wilson in Matabeleland* ix. 189 Brown cord jackets and 'smasher' hats, bandoliers and rifles.

smasher^2. Add: **3.** A receiver of stolen property. *rare.*
1929 C. Humphreys *Gt. Pearl Robbery* i. 60 The goods might be disposed of to a 'smasher'. that is, a receiver of stolen property.

smasheroo (smæːʃərūˑ). *slang* (orig. and chiefly *U.S.*). [f. Smash *sb.*^{1} + *-eroo.] A great success.
1948 *Life* 26 Jan. 47/2 The press snickeringly reported Virginia's coming-out party, a smasheroo, right down to the 500 bottles of ginger beer, the spots left on the furniture. **1960** S. Kauffmann *If it be Love* iii. iv. 211 A smasheroo. All seven reviews were great. **1962** *John o' London's* 11 Jan. 43/3 In the historical hokum-pokum bracket there's been one real smasheroo, *El Cid.* **1967** *Punch* 29 Nov. 822/2 A smasheroo musical will bring its creators vastly more. The most spectacular example of this in recent years is *Hello, Dolly!* **1975** *New Yorker* 17 Mar. 92/1 Is one going to make the burning a big Broadway smasheroo of a scene?

smashing, *ppl. a.*^{1} Add: **2.** *colloq.* Very good; greatly pleasing; excellent; sensational.
a **1911** D. G. Phillips *Susan Lenox* (1917) II. vi. 164 When you get dressed up a bit..you'll do a smashing business. **1914** W. Owen *Let.* 27 Dec. (1967) 310, I come in hungry to find a 'smashin' dinner. **1922** [see *Crack *sb.* 1 d]. **1944** M. Paneth *Branch Street* 8 When the children came..to play in the house they thought it 'smashing'. **1948** *Mind* LVII. 418 The fact is, the verification principle is a metaphysical proposition—a 'smashing' one if I may be permitted the expression. **1959** *Times Lit. Suppl.* 2 Oct. 564/2 It is not her fault that the publishers, in big letters on the jacket, promise 'as smashing a last sentence as we can recall!' That promise is not fulfilled. The final twist is surprisingly unsurprising. **1977** *Chem. in Brit.* XIII. 118/2 This is a smashing book for anyone interested in surface chemistry and physics to have available on his bookshelf.

smashingly *adv.* (later examples).
1923 *Daily Mail* 8 Sept. 6/6 Her volleying is splendid, And smashingly she serves. **1956** 'C. Blackstock' *Dewey Death* iv. 75 He was so smashingly handsome. **1970** *Daily Tel.* 21 July 13/4 The Férand evening midis of white organdie, smashingly printed with swirls of grey and cocoa.

smash-up. Add: Also (*U.S.*) **smashup. a.** (Later examples.)
1940 W. Empson *Gathering Storm* 67 Politicians, etc., living now, who made a smash-up of international affairs. **1974** [see *military police* s.v. *Military *a.* 3 b]. **1978** H. Wouk *War & Remembrance* xxxix. 399 Historians tend to miss the awful simultaneity of the fourfold smashup.

b. *spec.* A collision, esp. of road or rail vehicles; a crash. Chiefly *U.S.*

1856 M. J. Holmes '*Lena Rivers* 36 The old lady, sure of a *smash-up* this time, had attempted to rise. **1875** H. W. Shaw *Josh Billings' Farmer's Allminax* 13 Got the orfull smash up on the rale rode. **1923** M. B. Watts *Luther Nichols* 354 There had been..a smash up; a delivery-wagon..had run head-on into that there stone. **1931** *Kansas City Times* 3 Oct. E/6 What could run more typically true to form than a smashup when that bee got up a motorist's pants leg a short time ago? **1978** J. Irving *World according to Garp* xii. 236 They all drive so fast... If it weren't for you, I sometimes think they'd be having their smashups right in my living room.

S-matrix: see *S II. 11.

smatter, *v.* **1.** Restrict † *Obs.* to sense in Dict. and add: **b.** *U.S.* To splash, splatter. Also *intr.* Hence **sma·ttered** *ppl. a.*

1893 *N. & Q.* 15 July 45 In the daily reports of the interesting Lizzie Borden murder trial, recently held in Massachusetts, I notice the peculiar use of the words *smatter, smattering,* and *smattered* in reference to splashes of blood. **1958** S. A. Grau *Hard Blue Sky* III. 125 The first heavy drops fell and smattered in the dust. **1974** D. Richards *Coming of Winter* v. 144 The man had on a long grey coat, smattered with mud.

smattering, *vbl. sb.* Add: **1. c.** A small amount or number.

1973 *Nation Rev.* (Melbourne) 31 Aug. 1442/6 The news that *does* appear—other than a smattering of inconsequential rubbish—is..thinly disguised opinion. *Ibid.* 1464/2 There were 10,000 men (and a smattering of women) of letters in the UK. **1975** D. Nobbs *Death of Reginald Perrin* 154 There was a surprised pause, then a smattering of applause, which grew slowly into a tolerable ovation.

'smatter of fact. Also **smatterer fact, smatter fact,** etc. Repr. colloq. pronunc. of phr. *as a matter of fact.* Cf. Fact 6 a.

1922 S. Lewis *Babbitt* iv. 44 Besides, smatter fact, I'll tell you confidentially. *Ibid.* vi. 85 Smatter of fact, there's a whole lot of valuable time lost even at the U., studying poetry and French and subjects that never brought in anybody a cent. **1957** V. S. Naipaul *Mystic Masseur* iii. 39 But, smatterer fact, I don't like the idea. **1968** A. Clarke *Darkened Room* v. 59 Oh, I don't mind... 'Smatter o' fact..I like it. **1972** 'J. & E. Bonett' *No Time to Kill* vi. 67 'Smatter of fact, my real name's Gladys, but..I took to Carmen... 'Sides, now I've picked up the lingo, a lot of 'em tell me what good English I speak. **1978** D. Bloodworth *Crosstalk* vi. 45 S'matter of a fact, that one's a cinch.

smaze (smēⁱz). [Blend of Smoke *sb.* and Haze *sb.*] A mixture of smoke and haze.

1953 *Daily Progress* (Charlottesville, Va.) 21 Nov. 1/6 (*caption*) Manhattan skyscrapers look like misty dream-castles as a combination of smoke and haze drifts around them. Called 'smog' by most people, the smoke-haze combination might more aptly be termed 'smaze'. **1953** *N.Y. Times* 22 Nov. 1/1 From smaze and smog, the city got down to an old-fashioned ocean fog yesterday. **1958** *Manch. Guardian* 22 Nov. 4/4 Over seven million domestic chimneys emit at low level smoky particles and tarry substances which cause the urban 'haze' (or 'smaze') in industrial areas. **1960** *Daily Tel.* 16 Nov. 1/8 A Weather Bureau official described the condition as a kind of smog-like haze. 'Call it smaze,' he said. **1968** *Courier-Mail* (Brisbane) 3 July 3/7 That smoky, cloudy, dirty stuff that's been hanging around blurring the buildings of Brisbane these last few mornings is not *smog,* it's *smaze.*

smear, *sb.* Add: **3. b.** (Further examples.) *esp.* a sample of human or other cells obtained without surgery; *vaginal smear,* a smear of cells obtained from the vagina, studied to detect cervical cancer of the womb.

1917 Stockard & Papanicolaou in *Amer. Jrnl. Anat.* XXII. 227 In order to examine the vagina [of a guinea-pig] thoroughly we have introduced a small nasal speculum which facilitates clear view of the interior and a smear is made of any fluid that may be present. *Ibid.,* A study of the vaginal smears from guinea-pigs. **1920** *Proc. Nat. Conf. Social Work 1919* 58 Dr. Knight's plan of requiring a smear [for the detection of venereal disease] from every female child coming under their care would seem a wise precaution. **1925** *Jrnl. Amer. Med. Assoc.* 8 May 1422/2 The guinea-pig is a particularly suitable animal for such an investigation, on account of the regularity of its estrual cycle. The use of vaginal smear examinations makes it possible to detect the return of estrus in a very exact way. **1928** G. N. Papanicolaou in *3rd Race Betterment Conf.* 530 In a case of benign tumor everything you find in a vaginal smear is more or less normal... In contrast to this, in..cases..of malignant tumors, there are some definite characteristic changes. **1943** —— *Diagnosis Uterine Cancer* vi. 34 Vaginal smears made after the operation continued to show the carcinoma cells in considerable numbers. **1958** Cervical smear [see *Papanicolaou]. **1966** *Listener* 4 Aug. 151/1 Cervical smear centres for the early diagnosis of womb cancer..have..been outstandingly successful. **1969,** etc. [see *Pap *sb.*[4]]. **1975** *Nature* 9 Oct. 480/1 The presence of sperm cells in vaginal smears taken [from rats] the following morning was taken as positive indication of pregnancy.

c. A slanderous or defamatory remark; an attempt to defame by slander. *colloq.* (orig. *U.S.*).

1943 *Sun* (Baltimore) 22 Oct. 8/3 'This is an outright smear,' Stromberg asserted. **1953** E. Simon *Past Masters* iv. v. 256 Our only hope is to get some sort of official enquiry..to scotch all the smears. **1958** *Spectator* 15 Aug. 225/2, I would have expected from Mr. Lehmann not that implied smear but approving pats on both our heads. **1959** *Listener* 25 June 1115/1, I became aware of a gentle campaign of smear. **1977** E. Ambler *Send no More Roses* x. 246 There *is* the smear, and I'm the subject of it.

5*. In *Jazz,* a short glissando; a slurring or sliding effect produced by a brass instrument, esp. a trombone.

1926 [see *portamento]. **1944** *New Yorker* 1 July 29/2 Someone may advocate extending a note or cutting it off. The sax section may want to put an additional smear on it. **1959** M. T. Williams *Art of Jazz* (1960) iv. 36 Those devices that gave..the illusion of smear and roughness to his tone.

6. (sense *3 c) *smear document, interview, job, journalism, merchant, -monger, process, sheet, story;* **smear campaign,** a plan to discredit someone or something, or to destroy a reputation, by means of smears; **smear-glaze** (examples); hence *smear-glazed* adj.; **smear tactics,** the tactics used in a smear campaign; **smear test,** a test for cancer of the womb made by microscopic examination of a smear (see sense 3 b in Dict. and Suppl.); **smear-word,** a word which in spite of its literal meaning is used to imply something derogatory.

1938 *Sun* (Baltimore) 7 May 1/5 He called the Lobby Committee 'a snooping committee' which was engaged in 'a smear campaign', a campaign of 'terror and intimidation' against newspapers and magazines which dare to criticize activities of the New Deal. **1978** N. Freeling *Night Lords* vii. 31 We'll get accused of a smear campaign against Rolls-Royce cars. **1940** *Sun* (Baltimore) 18 Oct. 22/6 This was the pamphlet attacked by Republicans as a 'smear document'. **1977** M. Walker *National Front* vii. 183 Tyndall denied responsibility for the smear document. **1893** E. A. Barber *Pottery & Porcelain of United States* vi. 82 Glaze, which in the kiln would vaporize and form a slight deposit on the ware, technically known as '*smear*' glaze. **1971** L. A. Boger *Dict. World Pottery & Porcelain* 320/1 Smear glaze was a development following salt glaze and is frequently mistaken for it. **1963** *Times* 26 Jan. 11/7 The delicately smear-glazed porcelain more usually associated with small Victorian statuary and so suggestive of marble that it was known as parian ware. **1960** *New Statesman* 23 Jan. 96/1 But the elaborate smear interviews and paragraphs in Sydney were nobody's mistake, but just the boys obeying orders. **1970** E. Ambler *Intercom Conspiracy* iii. 73 It was a smear job hashed up to discredit one or another of his clients' competitors. **1967** *Punch* 8 Feb. 190/2 This touched the muddiest depths of smear journalism, full of cheap sneers and nasty innuendo. **1963** *Times* 15 May 9/2 The finding on this point was a bitter disappointment to the smear merchants. **1967** *Punch* 8 Feb. 190/2, I read with great satisfaction the editiorial..on the smearmongers of the Press and other vehicles of opinion. **1958** *Times* 26 Feb. 9/5 Mr Gaitskell's intention was, I imagine, to minimize the value of the report and rob it of its influence.., another application of the now well-known 'smear' process. **1951** *Observer* 16 Dec. 7/4 He is instructed to dismiss five people..accused by a smear-sheet of Communist sympathies. **1947** *New Statesman* 22 Nov. 404/3 The Garry Allighan affair has done great harm in confirming in the minds of thoughtless people the smear stories about politicians that are put about by people who are not thoughtless. **1955** 'E. C. R. Lorac' *Ask Policeman* v. 56 They didn't want the Sunday papers to write up Rosetta Towers as a smear story. **1945** *West Va. Rev.* Nov. 40/1 In recent years there has developed in his country a group of press agents who have adopted 'smear' tactics. **1974** *Times* 14 Feb. 22/3 In the old days they used to be called smear tactics but this year..mini-Watergates. **1950** *Consumer Rep.* XV. 367/1 The smear test for uterine cancer is done by scraping tissue..from the rear of the vagina. **1977** *Spare Rib* May 19/1 Yearly smear tests are important as they give early warning of a disease which takes 15 years to develop. **1938** I. Goldberg *Wonder of Words* xv. 298 The term *Bolshevik* ..becomes so encrusted with non-political significance that it loses any sharpness of outline..and grows into what has been called 'a smear-word'—a word that takes on whatever emotional color the speaker may..desire. **1961** *Twentieth Cent.* Jan. 87 'Philology', that smear-word among students everywhere.

smear, *v.* Add: **4. c.** Also (without const.), to attempt to discredit (a reputation, etc.). *colloq.* (orig. *U.S.*).

1936 W. Irwin *Propaganda & News* xxii. 292 When the Republicans began calling this line of attack the 'smear Hoover' campaign, Michelson..faced the microphone with a masterpiece of ingenious invective. **1945** G. Endore *Methinks the Lady* xi. 268 You had plenty of time..to hold up the jury while you smeared the science of psychoanalysis. **1948** *Manch. Guardian Weekly* 23 Sept. 9 He is afraid of being smeared. **1951** *Here & Now* (N.Z.) May 23/2 Mary Jane Keeny has been a target for the red-baiters who from time to time try to smear the UN as a Communist-dominated organisation. **1966** *Listener* 30 June 934/2 What the successors are trying to do seems to me not so much to prove particular corruption as to smear the previous regime. **1978** G. McDonald *Fletch's Fortune* (1979) xix. 130 Is the campaign against me going to continue? Are the March newspapers going to continue to smear me?

e. In Southern Africa, to coat over (the floor of a hut, etc.) with a mixture of cow-dung and water.

1839 W. C. Harris *Wild Sports S. Afr.* xvii. 143 The space was smeared with a mixture of mud and cow-dung, resembling that used in all parts of India for similar purposes. **1878, 1880** [see *dagga[2]]. **1893** Blennerhassett & Sleeman *Adv. Mashonaland* ii. 32 We were unsuited physically for such work as 'daghering' huts or 'smearing floors'.

6. a. (Further examples.)

1854 W. Collins *Hide & Seek* III. viii. 231 They seemed to get smeared out of my head—like we used to smear old sums off our slates at school. **1920** 'K. Mansfield' *Bliss & Other Stories* 73 And then there is the waiter... When he is not smearing over the table or flicking at a dead fly or two, he stands with one hand on the back of a chair. **1964** W. Golding *Spire* ii. 37 One delver relaxed, and smeared a hand over his sweaty face. *Ibid.* viii. 155 He peered in [a metal sheet] closer and closer until his breath dimmed his own image and he had to smear it off with his sleeve.

b. To thrash or kill; to wipe out or destroy by bombing. *slang.*

1935 A. J. Pollock *Underworld Speaks* 109/1 *Smear,* to kill. **1941** Baker *Dict. Austral. Slang* 68 *To smear someone,* to thrash a person in a bout of fisticuffs. **1944** *Amer. Speech* XIX. 187 He [*sc.* S. J. Baker] gives examples of Australian argot, of which several follow:..*smear,* to murder, [etc.]. **1957** P. Frank *Seven Days to Never* ix. 245 We can smear every base, every industrial complex, once and for all. **1958** P. Bryant *Two Hours to Doom* 43 The report on the..Russian I.C.B.M. site had removed his..doubt..whether his bombers could smear it before the missiles were fired off.

smear-case. Also **smearcase.** (Earlier and later examples.)

1829 A. Royall *Pennsylvania* I. 471 A dish, common amongst the Germans,..is curds and cream. It is very palatable, and called by the Germans *smearcase.* **1934** *Sun* (Baltimore) 21 July 4/7 Under the seat in the old wagon two jars of smearcase. **1978** *Amer. Speech* LIII. 201 The 'miscellaneous' category includes..*clabber cheese* (but more commonly *cottage cheese, Dutch cheese, smearcase*).

smeared, *ppl. a.* Add: **3. b.** *smeared out:* spread out, distributed; averaged over a volume of space or a period of time.

1931 *Nature* 8 Aug. 211/1 It can be represented..by supposing each electron to move in the field of the nucleus and the other electrons, representing it by the 'smeared out' continuous distribution which the solution of the wave equation gives, and then taking the electron atmosphere to be the sum of these distributions. **1977** *New Scientist* 21 Apr. 120/2 By measuring their extinction properties at a single wavelength we could show that the smeared-out density of dust grains is a few per cent of the density of all matter in interstellar space. **1979** *Nature* 18 Jan. 188/1 This behaviour..will be completely smeared out at experimental temperatures. **1979** *Sci. Amer.* Nov. 128/1 A wave function..often describes the electron as if it were smeared out over a large region of space.

smearer. (Later examples.)

1955 E. Pound *Classic Anthol.* II. 117 Take therefore, I say, these smearers And fellow travellers, chuck 'em To wolves and tigers. **1960** *Guardian* 7 Oct. 9/2 A common trick is for a smearer to..tell..drinkers that a candidate is a teetotaller.

smearing, *vbl. sb.* Add: **1.** (Further examples.)

1893 [see *dagga[2]]. **1940** G. Seldes *Witch Hunt* p. xiii, But surely there ought to be some restraint to the American spirit of fair play in combating underhanded smearing campaigns. **1948** E. Rosenthal *African Switzerland* iii. 34 Smearing..is a Basuto custom. You may have noticed that all the native huts are covered on the outside with a layer of mud, and this again is worked into all kinds of pretty and complicated patterns. That is smearing.

2. In *Jazz,* the production of a smear or glissando.

1934 S. R. Nelson *All about Jazz* ii. 61 The subtle slurring and smearing of to-day would have astonished some of the early players. **1952** B. Ulanov *Hist. Jazz in Amer.* (1958) vi. 66 Filhe..contrasted his low-register looping and smearing with Bab Frank.

smearing (smīᵊ·riŋ), *ppl. a.* [f. Smear *v.* + -ing[2].] **a.** In *Jazz,* pertaining to a smear or slurring effect. **b.** Slanderous.

1958 P. Gammond *Decca Bk. of Jazz* iv. 57 The smearing, broad glissandi of Christian's trombone. *a* **1974** R. Crossman *Diaries* (1976) II. 627 We also have to overcome something else—the stream of anti-government propaganda, smearing, snarky, derisive, which comes out of Fleet Street.

smeck, var. *schmeck.

smectic, *a.* Restrict *rare* to sense in Dict. and add: **2.** *Physical Chem.* Applied to (the state of) a mesophase (a liquid crystal) in which the molecules all have the same orientation and are arranged in well-defined planes. Also as *sb.,* a smectic substance. Cf. *nematic *a.* [ad. F. *smectique* (G. Friedel 1922, in *Ann. de Physique* XVIII. 276).]

1923 [see *nematic *a.*]. **1936** *Mineral. Abstr.* VI. 237 In addition to the fuller's earths and smectic clays the series includes montmorillonite, confolensite, [etc.]. **1940** Glasstone *Text-bk. Physical Chem.* vii. 505 In the smectic state normal liquid flow does not occur: the movement is of a gliding nature, in one plane. **1971** *New Scientist* 14 Jan. 63/2 Once the smectic mesophase had formed, the continuous or 'closed' bimolecular sheets would isolate the aqueous compartments from their neighbours. **1974** *Nature* 25 Jan. 178/3 As yet uncategorised smectics probably exist, for example, the smectic phase of 4′-n-octyl-4-cyanobiphenyl described by Gray.

smectite. Add: **a.** (Later examples.) Now *Obs.*

1932 *Amer. Mineralogist* XVII. 198 It seems hardly worth while to retain the two names smectite and montmorillonite for what appears to be the same mineral... It seems in the best interests of science to continue the name montmorillonite, and to drop that of smectite. **1942** *Ibid.* XXVII. 810 The differential thermal curve for the smectite sample..is like that of montmorillonite... This is in agreement with Kerr's..conclusion [*prec. quot.*] that smectite is not a valid species because of its similarity to montmorillonite.

b. = *MONTMORILLONOID. So *smectite group* = *montmorillonite group* s.v. *MONTMORILLONITE b.

1955 G. BROWN in *Clay Minerals Bull.* II. 296 *Smectites* is the name proposed for the minerals at present variously known as montmorillonoids, montmorins, minerals of the montmorillonite group and frequently even montmorillonites. Smectites are defined as minerals composed of 2:1 or triphormic layers, which, when the readily exchangeable cations are replaced by Na^+ and the material is saturated with glycerol, give a basal spacing of 18Å approximately. **1957** R. GREENE-KELLY in R. C. Mackenzie *Differential Thermal Investigation of Clays* v. 140 By far the most abundant dioctahedral smectite is montmorillonite. **1966** [see *MONTMORILLONITE a]. **1975** *Amer. Mineralogist* LX. 66/1 The significant chemical and physical properties of smectites often depend on the nature of the interlayer exchange ions. **1979** *Sci. Amer.* Apr. 78/1 (*caption*) Smectite group of clay minerals, formerly called the montmorillonite group, has extremely fine-grained, irregular and thin-layered crystals.

Smee[2] (smī). The name of Alfred *Smee* (1818–1877), English surgeon and experimenter, used *attrib.* and in the possessive to designate an obsolete type of primary cell or battery he invented (*Phil. Mag.* (1840) XVI. 315), consisting of zinc and platinum (or platinized silver) electrodes in dilute sulphuric acid.

1852 F. S. WILLIAMS *Iron Roads* 314 Great inconvenience arose from the spilling of the acid solution used in Smee's batteries. **1873** F. JENKIN *Electr. & Magnetism* xv. 215 The Smee battery is better than the copper zinc battery. **1950** G. W. VINAL *Primary Batteries* i. 16 Smee's cell of 1840 avoided..the difficulty experienced with polarization in other single-fluid batteries. *Ibid.*, The electromotive force of the Smee cell was low, about 0·5 volt, which was its principal disadvantage.

smell, *sb.* Add: **3. a.** Also, the special, indefinable, or subtle character of something.

1948 'N. SHUTE' *No Highway* ii. 38 Fifteen years in the aircraft industry... One gets to know the smell of things like this. **1974** J. THOMSON *Long Revenge* iii. 40 The smell of the case had come back to him..and he had the feeling that there was a great deal more to it.

b. (Later examples.)

1973 *Times* 19 Dec. 14/7 Things are looking up: there is a smell of success in the air. **1981** *Listener* 2 July 3/1 There's a smell of success: people really think they can shift governments.

5. smell fox, the wood anemone, *Anemone nemorosa*.

1892 C. M. YONGE *Old Woman's Outlook in Hampshire Village* 49 The beloved *Anemone nemorosa*—the windflower—or, as the village children unpoetically call it, 'smell foxes'. **1898** —— *John Keble's Parishes* xv. 172 Smellfox, anemone. **1931** M. GRIEVE *Mod. Herbal* I. 34 Anemone (Wood)..Synonyms. Crowfoot, Windflower, Smell Fox.

smell, *v.* Add: **I. 2. b.** *to smell a rat*: see RAT *sb.*[1] 2 a.

II. 6. (*c*) (Later U.S. examples.)

1912 F. J. HASKIN *Amer. Govt.* 276 He took out the cork, smelled of it, and then replaced it. **1919** E. O'NEILL *Moon of Caribbees* 30 His foot hits a bottle. He stoops down and picks it up and smells of it.

III. 8. c. (Later examples.) Also in phr. *not to smell right*, to have an air of being not quite in order.

1939 'N. BLAKE' *Smiler with Knife* x. 154 It doesn't sound like Fascism. It doesn't smell like Fascism. **1950** 'J. TEY' *To love & be Wise* xvii. 219 It's..the whole set-up... It doesn't smell right. **1969** *Sunday Times* (Colour Suppl.) 21 Dec. 11/1 Jock could not have been nicer... As a matter of fact he has been so nice that it smells bad. **1974** J. THOMSON *Long Revenge* iii. 33 Finch was inclined towards accepting the case... And yet..he hesitated... It still did not smell right to him.

d. To give rise to suspicion; to have an air of dishonesty or fraud.

1939 *Sun* (Baltimore) 12 Dec. 3/3 What 'smelled' about the..case appeared to have been saved by committee counsel for later inquiry. **1950** *Austral. Police Jrnl.* Apr. 118 *It smells*, it is something to be wary about; highly suspicious. **1970** G. F. NEWMAN *Sir, You Bastard* ii. 78 Things..wouldn't always get past the sharp-eyed QC. If a case smelt, he would smell it. **1973** 'H. HOWARD' *Highway to Murder* viii. 103 There's a wrong slant to this affair. I can't put my finger on it—but it smells.

9. c. (Later examples of *to smell of the lamp*.)

1887 [see LAMP *sb.*[1] 1 b]. **1927** GALSWORTHY *Castles in Spain* 154 At times he wrote stories unworthy of him. At times his work smelled of the lamp. **1953** G. S. FRASER *Modern Writer & his World* III. iv. 254 This desire of his..to be 'complex' and to bring in a wide range of cultural references at all costs does make his work sometimes smell a little of the lamp.

11. Also with *out*.

1978 *Lancashire Life* Oct. 83/3 Ah must 'a' smelt the class-room a'et When a' them odours mingled. **1979** 'J. Ross' *Rattling of Old Bones* ii. 17 How..can you have a dead body smelling out the house and not know it?

smellage. Substitute for etym.: [Alteration of SMALLAGE.] and add to def.: *Levisticum officinale*, of the family Umbelliferæ. (Earlier and later examples.)

1836 A. H. LINCOLN *Familiar Lect. Bot.* (ed. 5) 110 [*Ligusticum*] *levisticum* (smellage,) leaves many..Medicinal. **1889** R. T. COOKE *Steadfast* iii. 43 A nosegay of lavender, damask roses, smellage, old man, clove pinks [etc.].

smeller. Add: **5.** *fig.* Anything remarkable for exceptional violence, severity, strength, etc. **a.** = SNORTER[1] 2 b. **b.** *slang.* A heavy fall; usu. in phr. *to come a smeller*. Cf. *STINKER 6 c.

1898 KIPLING *Fleet in Being* v. 55 Good old gales—regular smellers. **1923** J. MANCHON *Le Slang* 278 *Smeller*, (2) to come a smeller, ramasser une pelle. **1934** WODEHOUSE *Right Ho, Jeeves* ix. 92 A man's brain whizzes along for years exceeding the speed limit, and then something suddenly goes wrong with the steering gear and it skids and comes a smeller in the ditch.

smellie (sme·li). [f. SMELL *v.* + -IE, after *TALKIE.] A (hypothetical) cinema or television film in which smell is synchronized with the picture. Usu. pl. Cf. *FEELY.

1929 A. P. HERBERT in *Punch* 8 May 508/3 These early smellies made a great sensation, particularly *Fish*, a strong story written 'around the life of a San Francisco fishwife of homicidal tendencies'. **1949** *Sun* (Baltimore) 12 Apr. 6/6 (*cartoon caption*) Soviet Smellies present 'Uncle Joe's Pipe'. **1958** *Spectator* 20 June 801/3 We had an Esther Williams picture and I wanted to advertise it as a smellie, with an ozonair machine in the foyer... The circuit wouldn't wear it, though. **1977** *Time* 11 Apr. 33/2 Another treat in the works: smellies—a futuristic device attached to the [T.V.] set will emit aromas into the living room.

smelling, *vbl. sb.* Add: **3. c.** (Earlier and later examples.)

1722 DEFOE *Memoirs of Plague* 239 In a Word, the whole Church was like a smelling Bottle. **1936** W. FAULKNER *Absalom, Absalom!* vi. 195 Clytie..stood impassive beside the wagon that last day, following the second ceremonial to the grave with the silk cushion and the parasol and the smelling-bottle.

smellsip (sme·lsip), *v. nonce-wd.* [f. SMELL *v.* + SIP *v.*] *trans.* To smell and sip almost simultaneously.

1922 JOYCE *Ulysses* 170 He smellsipped the cordial juice and..set his wineglass delicately down.

smelly, *a.* Add: **a.** Also *fig.* **b.** Suspicious. *rare*.

1923 J. MANCHON *Le Slang* 278 *Smelly*,..louche, véreux. **1944** [see *RIDE *v.* 9 c]. **1970** G. F. NEWMAN *Sir, You Bastard* viii. 227 Seems a bit smelly, Terry. I should blow him out.

SMERSH, Smersh (smɔ̄ɪʃ). [Russ. abbrev. of *smert' shpionam*, lit. 'death to spies'.] The popular name of the Russian counter-espionage organization, originating during the war of 1939–45, which is responsible for maintaining security within the Soviet armed and intelligence services.

1953 I. FLEMING *Casino Royale* xxvii. 217 He would take on SMERSH and hunt it down. Without SMERSH, without this cold weapon of death and revenge, the M.W.D. would be just another bunch of civil servant spies. **1955** H. HODGKINSON *Doubletalk* 1 Still to be met with are..SMERSH (*smert shpionam*: death to spies), the war-time name for the Soviet Army Counter-espionage organisation. **1961** D. MOORE *Highway of Fear* iv. 27 Faster!.. The Smersh zombies..are right behind you. **1967** E. GRIERSON *Crime of One's Own* ix. 73 All this nonsense of Calvert being some type from SMERSH—and Mason's the Man from Uncle, I suppose? **1977** *Times Lit. Suppl.* 29 Apr. 534/3 Missing..from..the *Great Soviet Encyclopedia*..are two Abakumovs, Andrei Ivanovich..and Viktor Semenovich, head of Smersh during the Second World War and Minister for State Security after it.

smetana (sme·tănă). Also with Fr. spelling **smitane** (smitan). [a. Russ. *smetána* sour cream, f. *smetat'* to sweep together, collect.] Sour cream. Freq. *attrib.* as *smetana* (or *smitane*) *sauce*, a sauce made with sour cream and seasonings, usu. served with meat.

1909 M. RONALD *Century Cook Bk.* (rev. ed.) 606 Smetana sauce... Pour a cup of thick sour cream into the pan, let it just brown, and then pour over steaks. **1938** *Zionist Rev.* 11 Aug. 13/1 For supper there is bread and *smetana*. **1939** A. L. SIMON *Conc. Encycl. Gastron.* I. 48/1 *Smitane*, Sauce. Sour cream and onions. **1963** I. FLEMING *On H.M. Secret Service* (1964) xxiii. 242 Rehrücken mit Sahne. That's saddle of roebuck with a smitane sauce. **1968** A. TACK *Spy who wasn't Exchanged* xii. 91 He ordered a sour milk and cream mixture called *Smetana*. **1978** *Chicago* June 242/2 Our favorites are the eggy cheese blintzes..Lithuanian schnitzel with smetana (sour cream) sauce, veal cordon bleu, etc. **1979** N. FREELING *Widow* xiv. 83 Any sort of sauce you like except tomato. Smitane maybe.

S meter: see *S II. 10.

smi·ckering, *ppl. a. rare*⁻¹. That smirks or smickers.

1930 W. DE LA MARE *Poems for Children* 17 All turned their heads with a smickering smile.

smidge (smidʒ). [Origin unknown, perh. f. SMITCH *sb.*[2]: cf. next.] A tiny amount. Orig. and chiefly *U.S.*

1905 *Dialect Notes* III. 65 *Smidge, smitch*, n., smallest piece, tiniest particle. **1934** *Sun* (Baltimore) 21 Sept. 1/6 Every last smidge of his record will be investigated. **1965** AUDEN *About House* (1966) 17 Surrender my smidge Of nitrogen to the World Fund. **1967** 'E. QUEEN' *Face to Face* xli. 184 Do you suppose I might have a smidge of that, Inspector? It looks so good, and I haven't had any breakfast. **1973** *Observer* 28 Oct. 48/4 Inviting us to buy their mail-order course for a smidge under £13. **1976** *Washington Post* 15 June A7/2 A Democratic Party that can't even afford..a smidge of debate.

smidgen (smi·dʒĕn). orig. and chiefly *U.S.* Also **smidgeon, smidgin, smitchin,** etc. [Origin unknown, perh. f. SMITCH *sb.*[2] + *-en, -in*, repr. dial. pronunc. of -ING[1]: cf. prec.] A tiny amount, a trace; a very small person or thing.

1845 C. M. KIRKLAND *Western Clearings* 71 They wouldn't have left a smitchin o' honey. **1878** J. H. BEADLE *Western Wilds* 611 Not a smidgeon left—just bodaciously chawed up and spit out. **1886** *Trans. Amer. Philol. Assoc.* XVII. 43 *Smidgen*, 'a small bit, a grain', as 'a *smidgen* of meal', is common in East Tennessee. **1913** [see *CLIP *sb.*[2] 4]. **1930** *Va. Quarterly Rev.* 6 Apr. 249 He can testify perhaps..that he has had a bait, a snack, or a mere smidgen of them. **1952** J. STEINBECK *East of Eden* xxiii. 289 You little, silly, half-pint, smidgin of a wife. **1954** R. MILLAR *Waiting for Gillian* in *Plays of the Year* X. 346 There's a smidgin of Gordon's in the whisky decanter. **1960** WODEHOUSE *Jeeves in Offing* iv. 45 'No will of her own?' 'Not a smidgeon.' **1968** *Globe & Mail* (Toronto) 17 Feb. 37 (Advt.), Whether you're nine months or ninety years old, plump or twiggy, tall as a tree or small as a smidgeon. **1971** *N.Z. Listener* 18 Oct. 11/5 It's an unknown quantity often combined with just a smidgen of skill. **1973** *People's Jrnl.* (Inverness & Northern Counties ed.) 15 Dec. 4/5 My family would eat mince pies to a band playing so long as there's at least a smidgeon of rum butter to wipe over the top crust. **1982** R. CONQUEST in *Times Lit. Suppl.* 17 Dec. 1385/4 Any writer allowing the merest smidgin of Soviet reality into his work was headed straight for Magadan.

smilacina (smɔilăsɔi·nă). [mod.L. (R. L. Desfontaines 1807, in *Ann. Mus. Hist. Nat.* IX. 51), f. *smilac-*, SMILAX + -INA[2].] A perennial herb of the genus so called, belonging to the family Liliaceæ, native to North America or temperate parts of Asia, and bearing terminal clusters of small white flowers; also called false Solomon's seal.

1808 *Curtis's Bot. Mag.* XXIX. 1155 (*heading*) Oval-Leaved Smilacina. **1890** *Harper's Mag.* Apr. 709/1 The little smilacina lifts its spike of tiny, fragrant blossoms. **1970** B. MILES *Bluebells & Bittersweet* viii. 141/3 Though perhaps not as well known [as Solomon's seal], smilacina wants the same situation.

smile, *sb.*[1] Add: **1. a.** (Later example of phr. *all smiles*.)

1916 G. B. SHAW *Pygmalion* III. 154 Higgins:..Dont be nervous about it. Pitch it in strong. Clara (all smiles): I will. Good-bye.

2. (Earlier example.)

1839 *Spirit of Times* 24 Aug. 294/3 We all agreed to take another smile.

3. b. *attrib.*, as *smile-line, -wrinkle*.

1921 W. DE LA MARE *Memoirs of Midget* xxiv. 158, I looked at his long, fair eyelashes and the smile-line on his cheek. **1977** *New Yorker* 19 Sept. 58/3 Firkusny is a tall, lithe, trim man with gray hair, blue eyes, and smile lines in his face which soften an almost austere handsomeness. *a* **1930** D. H. LAWRENCE *Phoenix II* (1968) III. 254 The smile-wrinkles on the fresh, pleased face, they give odd quivers.

smile, *v.* Add: **I. 1. c.** (Earlier U.S. examples.) Also in phr. *to come up smiling*: see *COME *v.* 69 b.

1883 C. H. HOYT *Bunch of Keys* III, in *Five Plays* (1944) 48 'Single room?' 'Well, I should smile.' **1889** 'MARK TWAIN' *Conn. Yank.* ix. 113 They actually wanted *me* to put in! Well, I should smile.

d. Of eyes: to express pleasure, amusement, etc.

1759 C. WESLEY in J. & C. Wesley *Funeral Hymns* 2nd Ser. 37 Those laughing eyes shall smile no more. *a* **1889** G. M. HOPKINS *Poems* (1967) 37 And May has come, hair-bound in flowers, With eyes that smile thro' the tears of the hours. **1938** DYLAN THOMAS in *Seven* Winter 17 She wept in her pain and made mouths, Talked and tore though her eyes smiled. **1940** W. FAULKNER *Hamlet* IV. i. 289 His face changed—something fleeting, quizzical, but not smiling, his eyes did not smile.

2. a. Also with *advbs.*, as *back, down, over, up*.

1845 [see *RANK *sb.*[1] 3 b]. **1860** A. J. EVANS *Beulah* xx. 177 He smiled down into her tearful face. **1866** MRS. C. J. NEWBY *Common Sense* II. 88 The cheerful rallying tone awoke something of the old pride in him, and he smiled up. **1889** R. L. Stevenson *Master of Ballantrae* iv. 111 How was he to smile back on the deceiver? **1905** E. M. Albanesi *Brown Eyes of Mary* iii. 38 She smiled up at him from under the white sunshade. **1908** *Smart Set* June 89/1 The girl pushed aside the screen and smiled over at her. **1949** A. Miller *Death of Salesman* 132 He's a man way out there in the blue, riding on a smile and a shoeshine. And when they start not smiling back—that's an earthquake. **1952** E. O'Neill *Moon for Misbegotten* I. 40 She smiles down at Jim, her face softening.

II. 6. b. Also with *down, out*.

1860 G. Meredith *Evan Harrington* xi. 111 'Another!' the hostess instantly smiled down the inhospitable outcry. **1936** R. Campbell *Mithraic Emblems* 52 It is the blossom in our blood With folded petals smiling out the sere, Brown, shuffled slippers of the limping year.

8. b. Also with direct speech as obj., to say with a smile.

1860 [in Dict.]. **1886** 'M. Gray' *Silence of Dean Maitland* III. ii. 35 'This is alarming,' smiled the dean. **1902** H. James *Wings of Dove* xv. 231 'He won't..make up his mind about me.' 'Well,' Milly smiled, 'give him time.' **1936** W. Holtby *South Riding* III. iii. 175 'Well, Dolly, I hope you're looking after these young men,' smiled Carne shyly. **1976** H. MacInnes *Agent in Place* xix. 208 'Not for me,' Georges smiled.

Smilesian (smai·lziăn), *a.* Also **Smilesean.** [f. the name of Samuel *Smiles* + -ian.] Of, pertaining to, or characteristic of Samuel Smiles (1812–1904), author of *Self-Help* (1859) and other works for those who wish to 'improve' themselves by personal effort and initiative, or his thought and writings. Also occas. **Samuel-Smi·lesian.**

1889 G. B. Shaw *Fabian Essays in Socialism* 23 With all its [*sc.* private property's] energy, its Smilesian 'self-help', its merchant-princely enterprise,..what has it heaped up, over and above the pittance of its slaves? **1928** A. Huxley *Point Counter Point* xvii. 298 Most Smilesian souls must smell rather nasty, I should think. **1929** —— *Do what you Will* 151 There are..occasions—and this is what..the Samuel-Smilesian morality refuses to admit—when a man ought to permit himself to be subdued to things. **1968** *Punch* 29 May 792/2 It was up to the individual in a Samuel Smilesian way to restore his own fortunes through personal effort. **1969** G. M. Brown *Orkney Tapestry* ii. 53 Religion was Smilesian—heaven looked with favour on those who strove to improve themselves—unto him that hath shall be given. **1981** J. S. Bratton *Impact of Victorian Children's Fiction* ii. 45 In the year after the Great Exhibition, a thrusting optimistic appeal to Smilesean self-confidence..was certainly the shape of things to come.

smilesmirk (smei·lsmɔ̄ɹk), *v. nonce-wd.* [f. Smile *v.* + Smirk *v.*] *intr.* To smile in a smirking manner.

1922 Joyce *Ulysses* 262 She smilesmirked supercilious.

smilet. (Further example.)

1845 J. J. Hooper *Taking Census* in *Some Adventures Capt. Simon Suggs* 175 The wrinkles on Mr. Kuncker's face formed themselves into fifty little smilets.

smiley, var. Smily *a.* in Dict. and Suppl.

smiling, *ppl. a.* Add: **5.** *smiling-lipped*.

1936 C. S. Lewis *Oxford Mag.* 14 May 575/2 The smiling-lipped Assyrian, cruel-bearded king.

smily, *a.* Add: Now usu. with spelling **smiley. 1. a.** (Later examples.)

1969 D. Francis *Enquiry* vii. 97 It's your eyes... Dark and sort of smiley and sad. **1976** H. Kemelman *Wednesday Rabbi got Wet* iii. 21 A short man..with a round head and smiley face.

b. Smiling; cheerful.

1970 *Sunday Times* 8 Feb. 15/2 If the instruction wasn't nice and smiley, it'd upset me. **1972** *Times* 1 Dec. 20/2 *China*—new from France with the smiley face in black on yellow. **1976** R. B. Parker *Promised Land* (1977) vii. 35, I..said goodby with smily pleasant overtones in my voice.

2. Caused by or causing a smile.

1974 *Times* 22 Jan. 11/5 For smiley lines which are too deep, just paint out the start of them with a highlight. **1977** *Rolling Stone* 13 Jan. 52/2 To the extent that he includes these fast, cheerful numbers and smiley oddities such as Cole Porter's 'True Love' and the impenetrable fable 'Crackerbox Palace', Harrison seems hoping to achieve fresh popularity.

S-mine. Also S mine. [Abbrev. and anglicization of G. *schützenmine*, lit. 'infantryman mine'.] Used, esp. in the war of 1939–45, to designate a variety of enemy anti-personnel mine.

1944 J. H. Fullarton *Troop Target* 206 The enemy had sown elaborate mine fields—heavy Teller mines and deadly anti-personnel S mines. **1945** [see *anti-personnel* s.v. *Anti-[1] 4 (iii)]. **1972** *Daily Tel.* (Colour Suppl.) 1 Sept. 16/2 In the last war the Germans devised a series of anti-personnel devices, including the S-mine & the 'butterfly-bomb'. **1977** C. McCullough *Thorn Birds* xv. 351 Sometimes a man would step on an unexploded S-mine.

smi·rkily, *adv.* [f. Smirky *a.* + -ly[2].] = Smirkingly *adv.*

a **1974** R. Crossman *Diaries* (1975) I. 135 There they were today looking at Jennie rather smugly and smirkily. **1978** *Guardian Weekly* 5 Feb. 18/3 Cryptic allusions..to padlocks and fetters, which most recent biographers have smirkily interpreted as meaning that he was a masochist.

Smirnoff (smɔ̄·ɹnof). The proprietary name of a brand of vodka.

1948 *Official Gaz.* (U.S. Patent Office) 26 Apr. 1008/1 *Smirnoff*..for vodka and kummel. Claims use since 1914. **1959** *Trade Marks Jrnl.* 15 Apr. 411/2 Smirnoff... Vodka. W. & A. Gilbey Limited. **1961** *Twining Bros.* (Oxford) *Wine List* Autumn 15 *Vodka etc.* Smirnoff 65.5° 39/4. **1965** 'M. Fallon' *Keys of Hell* v. 50 One of the bottles contained Smirnoff, his favourite vodka. **1977** *New Yorker* 3 Oct. 46/2, I got out the Smirnoff,..and finished it off.

smish. (Earlier example.)

1807 H. Tufts in E. Pearson *Autobiogr. of Criminal* (1930) II. iv. 292 *Smish*, a shirt.

smitane: see *Smetana.

smitch, *sb.*[2] Add: Also used adverbially. *rare.*

1963 M. McCarthy *Group* viii. 177 Neat but not gaudy, in a plain skirt and shirtwaist,..an old cameo brooch..—general effect a smitch Victorian.

smitchy (smi·tʃi), *a. colloq., rare.* [f. Smitch *sb.*[2] + -y.[1]] Tiny.

1888 Kipling *Plain Tales from Hills* 245 The Copper that takes you up is an old friend that tuk you up before, when you was a little, smitchy boy.

smite, *sb.*[1] Add: **1. b.** *Cricket.* A hard hit made by a batsman.

1888 R. H. Lyttelton in Steel & Lyttelton *Cricket* ii. 39 There is one hit in particular that in these days is very seldom seen—that is, the smite to long-leg with a horizontal bat. **1898** G. Giffen *With Bat & Ball* ii. 19 Since Trott hit one over [the boundary] at square leg, Jack Lyons and Tom Garrett have effected a similar smite.

2. b. A small or least amount; a particle. *U.S.* and *dial.*

1843 'R. Carlton' *New Purchase* I. xix. 175 Not a smite of noise, only my breathing and a sort of pittin-pattin sound of my heart. *a* **1852** F. M. Whitcher *Widow Bedott P.* (1856) v. 50 But it dident do a smite o' good. **1913** [see *Ream *sb.*[2] d].

smite, *v.* Add: **B. II. 3. a.** Also in phr. *to smite* (someone) *hip and thigh*: see Hip *sb.*[1] 2 d.

e. *Cricket.* To hit with great force; to defeat by hard hitting.

1891 W. G. Grace *Cricket* iv. 127 Mr. I. D. Walker.. smote them to the tune of 90. **1904** F. C. Holland *Cricket* 28 After you have smitten him [*sc.* the bowler of yorkers] full-pitch two or three times, he will soon stop bothering you in this way. **1982** P. Tinniswood *More Tales from Long Room* vii. 87 My next sermon will take as its text: 'And, lo, Harry Halliday was a plump man, yet many a six did he smite for Yorkshire.'

smiter. Add: **1. e.** *Cricket.* A hard-hitting batsman.

1897 W. J. Ford in K. S. Ranjitsinhji *Jubilee Bk. Cricket* vii. 267 A little mercy should be shown to the muscular if unscientific 'smiter'. **1897** D. Moffat *Crickety Cricket* 25 Stoddart the smiter has carried his bat For a grandly made three-figure score. **1944** E. Blunden *Cricket Country* iv. 53 Poor Charles could not solve the problem of getting this smiter caught in the deep field.

smith, *sb.* Add: **3.** *smith-shop* (earlier examples); also *smith('s) shop*. chiefly *U.S.*

1651 *Early Rec. Dedham, Mass.* (1892) III. 179 Whensoever the said shopp shall be no longer vsed for a smithes shopp.., then it shall be remoued out of the high way. **1710** *Rec. Early Hist. Boston* (1884) XI. 105 Ordered that complaint be made..against Enoch Greenliefe for making a Smith Shop in his buildings. **1743** W. Ellis *Mod. Husbandman* Oct. xxii. 236 The Ploughman here has seldom Occasion to go to a Smith's Shop. **1755** *New Hampsh. Probate Rec.* (1916) III. 705 The Corner where Geo. Warrens Smith Shop Stands. *a* **1816** B. Hawkins *Sk. Creek Country* (1848) 30 At the public establishment there is a smith's shop. **1882** *Econ. Geol. Illinois* III. 150 The coal..is..used in an adjoining smith-shop.

Smith & Wesson (we·sǝn). [The names of Horace *Smith* (1808–93) and Daniel B. *Wesson* (1825–1906), founders of a firm of gunsmiths in Springfield, Mass.] The proprietary name of a make of firearm, esp. a type of cartridge revolver.

1860 *Charleston* (S. Carolina) *Mercury* 6 Nov. 3/3 (Advt.), Smith & Wesson's seven shooters. **1865** [see *Remington]. **1881** G. W. Romspert *Western Echo* 115 The second ball from my Smith & Wesson stretched him struggling upon the earth with a bullet through his lungs. **1893** *Official Gaz.* (U.S. Patent Office) 16 May 1058/1 Revolving firearms. Smith & Wesson, Springfield, Mass... Essential feature, the word and character *Smith & Wesson*. Used since 1857. **1928** *Trade Marks Jrnl.* 14 Nov. 1822/1 Smith and Wesson. 482,778. Revolvers and Pistols. Smith and Wesson Inc. **1957** J. E. Parsons *Smith & Wesson Revolvers* i. 13 The Smith & Wesson revolver had arrived as a de luxe presentation item. **1964** E. S. Gardner *Case of Phantom Fortune* (1970) xix. 192, I show you a Smith and Wesson revolver. **1981** *Daily Tel.* 18 June 18/5 They prefer to throw truncheons rather than draw a 0.38 Smith & Wesson.

smither, *sb.* (Later example.)

1976 *Star* (Sheffield) 3 Dec. 19/4 (Advt.), Retired Smither required for part-time light Machine Knife Smithing work.

smithereen (smiðǝrī·n), *v.* [f. Smithereens *sb. pl.*] *trans.* To smash or blow up into tiny fragments. Hence **smitheree·ning** *ppl. a.*

1927 H. Crane in *Transition* Dec. 136 Lo, Lord, Thou ridest! Lord, Lord, Thy swifting heart Naught stayeth, naught now bideth But's smithereened apart! **1959** *Listener* 5 Mar. 429/2 A bomb in a suit-case timed shortly to do its smithereening work. **1964** *Economist* 16 May 699/2 Dum-dum bullets or smithereening explosives. **1973** *N.Y. News* 21 Aug. 53/1 He'd like to smithereen the crystal ball.

smithereens, *sb. pl.* Add: **a.** (Earlier and later examples.)

1829 G. Griffin *Collegians* II. xxii. 157 A body would tink it hardly safe to stand here under 'em, in dread dey'd come tumblin' down, may be, an' make *smiddereens* of him, bless de mark! **1922** Joyce *Ulysses* 372 Crew and cargo in smithereens. **1927** D. H. Lawrence *Mornings in Mexico* 16 The sun went bang, with smithereens of birds bursting in all directions. **1933** *Sun* (Baltimore) 22 Dec. 22/6 A substantial charge of dynamite—enough, in fact, to blast the bridge to smithereens. **1961** J. I. Packer *Evangelism & Sovereignty of God* ii. 31 Books like Deuteronomy and Isaiah and John's Gospel and Romans smash it [*sc.* a man-centred outlook] to smithereens. **1976** *Time* 27 Dec. 36/3 The result is another kind of supernova, a fantastic explosion that blows the star to smithereens, dispersing into space most of the remaining elements that it had manufactured during its lifetime.

Smithfield[2] (smi·þfīld). *U.S.* The name of a town in Virginia, used *attrib.* to designate a type of ham cured by a special process which originated there.

Properly applied only to hams cured within the corporate limits of Smithfield.

1908 *Sat. Even. Post* 31 Oct. 25/2 Next to singing a hymn, nothing gives him so much pleasure as a Smithfield ham. **1947** R. Berolzheimer *U.S. Regional Cookbk.* 188 *Smithfield ham*... The hogs fatten rapidly by foraging in the peanut fields after the crop is harvested, special care is taken in curing and smoking. **1973** M. R. Crowell *Greener Pastures* 113 Smithfield ham is truly worth it all. **1977** *Times* 15 Oct. 13/5 Seek out a Virginian friend..and sip mint juleps..until the Smithfield ham and spoonbread are ready.

smithiantha (smiþi,æ·nþă). [mod.L. (P. Magnus in C. E. O. Kuntze *Revisio Generum Plantarum* (1891) II. 977), f. the name of Matilda *Smith* (1854–1926), botanical artist + Gr. ἄνθος flower (with fem. ending to conform with the gender of names it superseded).] A small, perennial, rhizomatous herb of the genus so called, belonging to the family Gesneriaceæ, native to Mexico, and bearing hairy, cordate, variegated leaves and clusters of red, yellow, or orange bell-shaped flowers; = Gesnera in Dict. and Suppl.

1961 *Times* 27 Sept. 6/6 Colourful smithianthas, better known under their familiar name of gesneria. **1979** A. Huxley *Success with House Plants* 364/3 Smithianthas grow best in medium light.

smithite (smi·þait). *Min.* [f. the name of G. F. Herbert *Smith* (1872–1953), English mineralogist + -ite[1].] A sulpharsenite of silver, $AgAsS_2$, found as red tabular monoclinic crystals.

1905 *Nature* 13 Apr. 574/2 Further crystallographic and chemical details were given of the three new red minerals from the Binnenthal originally described by R. H. Solly, and named by him Smithite (after G. F. Herbert Smith), Hutchinsonite (after A. Hutchinson), and Trechmannite after C. O. Trechmann). **1905** R. H. Solly in *Mineral. Mag.* XIV. 74 Smithite is associated with hutchinsonite, sartorite, and rathite in the white dolomite of the Lengenbach. **1938** *Econ. Geol.* XXXIII. 155 Proustite occurs.. in magnificent eutectic relationships with smithite. **1968** I. Kostov *Mineral.* 173 Pyrostilpnite, aramayoite, and smithite have perfect pinacoidal cleavage... Smithite is very soft, the other minerals have a hardness between 2 and 3.

Smith-Trager (smiþ,trē·gǝɹ). *Linguistics.* = *Trager-Smith.

1959 *Canadian Jrnl. Linguistics* V. I. 8 The Smith-Trager schema for plotting the English phonemes and the diaphonemic relations between idiolects and dialects is a case in point. **1964** W. S. Allen in D. Abercrombie et al. *Daniel Jones* 9 This should not be taken to imply an acceptance of the 4-term (Smith-Trager) stress system.

smithy, *v.* Add: **1. a.** Also *fig.*

1910 J. Masefield *Ballads & Poems* 66 Until this case, this clogging mould, Be smithied all to kingly gold. **1929** A. Clarke *Pilgrimage* 19 Smithied in gloom the low day Had glowed upon the axle.

2. (Earlier example.)

1733 L. Theobald in *Works of Shakespeare* VII. 96 To *smithy*, is, to perform the Work and Office of a Smith.

smithying, *vbl. sb.* (Later *fig.* example.)
1934 E. Blunden *Challenge to Death* 336 History's smithying should not disappear Without reverberation.

smock, *sb.* Add: **2. b.** A loose garment worn by artists over their other clothes to keep them clean; a woman's or child's loose dress or blouse resembling a smock-frock in shape.
1907 *Yesterday's Shopping* (1969) 790/1 Girls' cashmere smock. In cream, sky, cardinal. **1938** N. Marsh *Artists in Crime* (1941) xiii. 192 He found..an evening dress in close proximity to a painting-smock. *Ibid.* 193 He was amused to find that even the Seacliff painting-bags and smock smelt of Worth. **1969** R. T. Wilcox *Dict. Costume* 326/2 The smock is now much worn as a coverall by professional people at work, especially artists. **1971** [see *maternity 3 b].

c. In full *camouflage smock*, a loose outer tunic of coarse material dyed brown and green and worn by troops as camouflage.
1964 L. Deighton *Funeral in Berlin* xxxii. 171 They wore camouflage smocks and steel helmets... They were front-line troops, not Waffen S.S. **1974** C. Ryan *Bridge too Far* iv. vii. 295 The only thing I could do for most of them was to take off their smocks and cover their faces. **1978** M. Walker *Infiltrator* xxi. 224 He tossed me an assault rifle and..a camouflage smock.

3. a. *smock dress, jacket, linen* (earlier example), *shirt* (later example), *sleeve* (later example); **smock-ravelled** *dial.*, perplexed.
1980 J. Hone *Flowers of Forest* i. 28 The woman in the pale smock dress. **1976** *Bridgwater Mercury* 21 Dec. 3/2 (Advt.), Half price smock jackets. **1880** L. Higgin *Handbk. Embroidery* ii. 12 *Smock Linen* is a strong even green cloth..an excellent ground for working screens. **1904** in *Eng. Dial. Dict.*, Smock-ravelled. **1913** D. H. Lawrence *Let.* 15 Sept. (1962), I feel a bit smock-ravelled—don't know where the east is, nor the north and west. **1972** *Guardian* 8 Feb. 11/6 A smock shirt is less voluminous than a smock, but has..smock details: the neck is round or square, there is usually a yoke, and often pleated or pin-tucked fronts. **1870** A. J. Munby *Diary* 25 June in D. Hudson *Munby* (1972) 288 A stout fair girl..who looked well in her cotton hoodbonnet and red neckerchief, and smocksleeves.

smock, *v.* **4.** (Later examples.)
1963 N. Streatfeild *Vicarage Family* iii. 27 Louise.. was still small enough for smocks and her mother smocked beautifully. **1980** *Daily Tel.* 24 Apr. 14/5 His mother brought him up alone on a war pension plus what she could make by smocking children's clothes.

smocked, *ppl. a.* Add: **2.** (Later examples.)
1918 E. A. Archer *Needlecraft* x. 112, I am sure you will not be contented till Sally Ann has a smocked dress. **1934** A. M. Miall *Compl. Needlecraft* 92 Smocked garments readily stretch as a child grows.

smock-faced, *a.* (Later example.)
1923 E. Sitwell *Bucolic Comedies* 16 Forlorn the smock-faced sheep sit.

smock-frock, *sb.* Add: **2.** (Earlier example.)
1858 Thackeray *Virginians* I. xv. 112 The smock-frocks did not seem to heed, and clamped out of church quite unconcerned.

smocking, *vbl. sb.* Add: (Later examples.)
1916 *T. Eaton & Co. Catal.* Spring & Summer 23/1 Shoulder yoke with neat smocking trims both sides of the front. **1934** A. M. Miall *Compl. Needlecraft* 92 Smocking is a special favourite for children's clothes. **1961** A. Liley *Craft of Embroidery* iv. 174 Smocking generally takes up three times as much fabric as the final width required. **1964** *McCall's Sewing* xiii. 242/1 The same smocking stitches can be used in both types of smocking. **1976** P. Clabburn *Needleworker's Dict.* 245/2 *(caption)* Smocking: detail of a child's dress, English, 1930.

smock-racing, *vbl. sb.* (Earlier example.)
1790 J. Woodforde *Diary* 24 May (1927) III. 192 Smock-racing at the Heart this Aft. being Whit-Monday.

smog (smǫg). [Blend of Smoke *sb.* and Fog *sb.*²] **1. a.** Fog intensified by smoke. Cf. *photochemical smog* s.v. *photochemical *a.*
1905 *Daily Graphic* 26 July 10/2 In the engineering section of the Congress Dr. H. A. des Vœux, hon. treasurer of the Coal Smoke Abatement Society, read a paper on 'Fog and Smoke'. He said it required no science to see that there was something produced in great cities which was not found in the country, and that was smoky fog, or what was known as 'smog'. **1905** *Globe* 27 July 3/5 The other day at a meeting of the Public Health Congress Dr. Des Vœux did a public service in coining a new word for the London fog, which was referred to as 'smog', a compound of 'smoke' and 'fog'. **1938** *Daily Progress* (Charlottesville, Va.) 12 May 7 In the opinion of many medical authorities, 'smog' is the principal reason why Pittsburgh has the highest pneumonia death rate in the United States. **1950** *Economist* 25 Feb. 432/2 Smog is a problem, far from completely understood as yet, of air contamination not by smoke, but by the fumes and gases —sulphur compounds, chlorine and so on—given off by modern industrial processes such as oil refining, chemical manufacturing and metallurgy. **1955** *Sci. Amer.* May 63/3 At first it was thought that smoke, dust, sulfur dioxide and hydrofluoric acid were responsible for the smog [in Los Angeles], but soon it became clear that these known pollutants, in the concentrations measured on smoggy days, could not cause the physiological effects observed... It was then that A. J. Haagen-Smit..suggested that peroxides and ozonides of hydrocarbons were responsible for smog. **1961** L. Mumford *City in History* xv. 479 Nor have they eliminated the unburned hydrocarbons which help produce the smog that blankets such a motor-ridden conurbation as Los Angeles. **1975** D. Lodge *Changing Places* ii. 71 It was difficult to tell whether the sediment thickening the atmosphere was rain or sleet or smog.

b. *fig.* A state or condition of obscurity or confusion; something designed to confuse or obscure.
1954 *Ann. Reg. 1953* i. 54 Lord Reading..described it [*sc.* the Russian Note] in the House of Lords as 18 pages of 'somewhat dismal and turgid "smog" '. **1976** *Billings* (Montana) *Gaz.* 30 June 1-a/1 When the political smog clears, Billings city government somehow continues to function. **1978** D. Bloodworth *Crosstalk* xxiv. 191 He hoped..Zoe's gift might pierce the gathering smog? Because things were getting tough, and the Russians were..accusing the Maoists of trying to flood Moscow with narcotics.

2. *attrib.* and *Comb.*, as *smog-bank, -burner, mask, producer; smog-bound, -free, -producing* adjs.
1975 *Country Life* 16 Jan. 130/2 Take a commuter jet from Los Angeles to San Francisco... You rise above the smog-bank. **1970** *New Scientist* 1 Jan. 8/3 Smogbound, noise-deafened, misanthropic Londoners..might be taking their high blood pressure with them. **1961** *Engineering* 27 Jan. 175/3 The smog-burner is a mechanical rather than a chemical or catalytic device. **1959** *News Chron.* 19 June 4/3 The six-bedroom houses hardly get dirty in California's smog-free climate. **1981** *Times* 6 Aug. 7/7 Smog-free sunsets over the Indian Ocean. **1954** *Ann. Reg. 1953* iv. 391 The year 1953 might well be remembered as the one in which 'smog' masks first appeared. **1979** *Listener* 5 July 6/1 Visiting journalists [to Tokyo].. were amazed to find they didn't have to wear smog-masks. **1951** *Sun* (Baltimore) (B ed.) 31 Dec. 14/2 More than a dozen Baltimore firms have been definitely albeit informally tagged as smog producers. **1970** *New Scientist* 13 Aug. 324/1 Efforts to curb auto-pollution concern the directly poisonous or smog-producing colourless emissions of carbon monoxide, unburnt hydrocarbons and nitrogen oxides.

Hence as *v. trans.* N. Amer. colloq., (*a*) with *out, up*: to cover or envelop in smog; (*b*) with *in*: to confine or imprison because of smog; (freq. *pass.*); **smogged** *ppl. a.*
1966 P. Tamony *Americanisms* (typescript) No. 14. 2 The era of the motor-car smogged up greenery. **1970** *Globe & Mail* (Toronto) 28 Sept. 4/1 Mr. Lewis was 'smogged in' at Sudbury..and was unable to arrive in time for the Ottawa meeting. **1974** *Science News* 24–31 Aug. 136 Conventional geodesy depends on clear lines of sight, and in the Los Angeles basin these are often smogged out. **1982** *Chr. Sci. Monitor* (Mid-Western ed.) 8 Dec. 12 Yet you can't do it because they have to meet the same pollution standards they do in heavily smogged areas.

smogger (smǫ·gəɹ). [Origin unknown.] (See quots.).
1958 F. Jennings *Men of Lanes* 217 Veteran tramps have their road-sign language, by which they communicate with each other... Vagabonds call it 'smogger', and it is said to have been introduced into England by gipsies in the time of Henry VIII. **1975** *Indexer* IX. 131/2 Supposing, for example, you see a chalk mark (a 'smogger') made by a tramp on your gate-post, consisting of two large and slightly overlapping circles, you could identify this as meaning 'tell a pathetic story', but if the sign consisted of three small circles in a line, it would mean 'money usually given here'.

smoggy (smǫ·gi), *a.* [f. *smog + -y¹.] Characterized by the presence of smog. Hence **smo·ggily** *adv.*
1905 *Daily News* 26 July 9 Observations had proved that, even in the most 'smoggy' periods, there was far less of the evil element in the early hours of the morning. **1948** *Smog Problem in Los Angeles County* 17/1 Smoggy days are usually days of high temperature. **1965** P. Wylie *They Both were Naked* ii. vi. 291 When the fourth day was smoggily born in the black-smudged, yellow opacity that was air I ordered coffee. **1978** P. Niesewand *Underground Connection* 25 A smoggy wind blew across the crowded platform as a train thundered in.

smogless (smǫ·glės), *a.* [f. *smog + -less.] Free from smog; characterized by the absence of smog.
1948 G. Marx *Let.* 27 July (1967) 192 On a smogless day our gleaming skulls can be seen as far east as Cedar Rapids. **1960** *Spectator* 30 Sept. 501/1 In an attempt to bring the smogless society a little closer, the Minister asked..the official black areas to submit their plans for smoke control. **1971** *Nature* 19 Feb. 549/1, I measured the atmospheric extinction in three wavelengths on 31 clear, smogless nights at the Mount Wilson Observatory.

smokable, *a.* and *sb.* Add: **A.** *adj.* **2.** Able to be ridiculed. Cf. Smoke *v.* 9. *rare.*
1818 Keats *Let.* 31 Dec. (1958) II. 19 The Dress Maker, the blue Stocking and the most charming sentimentalist.. are equally smokeable.

B. *sb.* Also in *sing.*
1897 'Mark Twain' *Autobiogr.* (1924) I. 98 There are people who strictly deprive themselves of each and every eatable, drinkable and smokable which has in any way acquired a shady reputation.

smoke, *sb.* Add: **I. 1. d.** Also, any large city or town. Chiefly *Austral.*
1848 H. W. Haygarth *Recoll. Bush Life in Australia* 6 As he gradually leaves behind him the 'big smoke' (as the aborigines picturesquely call the town), the accommodations become more and more scanty. **1893** J. A. Barry *Steve Brown's Bunyip* 21 You want to get away amongst the spielers and forties of the big smoke? **1903** Farmer & Henley *Slang* VI. 270 *The Smoke* = any large city: spec. London: also *The Great Smoke*. **1971** *Sunday Australian* 8 Aug. 5/3 The unhappy pilgrimage from bush to big smoke.

f. A shade of grey.
1882 *Cassell's Family Mag.* Apr. 314/2 Charming colouring.., smoke, bright blues and drabs. **1923** *Daily Mail* 13 Feb. 13 (Advt.), Wool hose..in..lt. grey, shoe grey, smoke, mole. **1971** [see *kasha¹ 2]. **1978** *Hot Car* June 98/1 (Advt.), All Portholes are supplied *domed* either in clear, blue, green, smoke, bronze or black perspex.

2. a. (Further examples.) Also, a particular kind of smoke.
1919 *Jrnl. Amer. Chem. Soc.* XLI. 312 The rate of disappearance of a finely divided smoke of a given concentration was greater than for a coarser smoke. **1950** *Thorpe's Dict. Appl. Chem.* (ed. 4) X. 787/1 Determining the particle size of a smoke. **1972** *Combustion Sci. & Technol.* VI. 55/1 Carbon smokes are generated by combustion.

c. † (*a*) *N. Amer.* = Smudge *sb.*² 2. *Obs.* (*b*) (See quot. 1961.)
1689 H. Kelsey *Jrnl.* 29 June (1929) 26 Abundance of Musketers & at night could not gett wood Enough for to make a smoke to Clear yᵐ. **1765** R. Rogers *Conc. Account N. Amer.* 140 It is difficult to sleep without a smoak in your bed-chamber, to expell [mosquitoes]. **1860** H. Y. Hind *Assiniboine* in *Canad. Red River Exped.* I. xiii. 286 At each camping place we were obliged to make 'smokes' to drive away these tormentors [*sc.* mosquitoes]. **1961** *Amateur Gardening* 4 Nov. Suppl. 47/2 Many of the modern insecticides and fungicides are sold in the form of small containers which when ignited give off clouds of vapour carrying fine chemical into all parts of the greenhouse. These devices are known simply as 'smokes'.

4. e. *spec.* in *Espionage*, false information to distract opponents.
[**1859** G. W. Matsell *Vocabulum* 82 *Smoke*, humbug; any thing said to conceal the true sentiment of the talker; to cover the intent.] **1966** 'A. Hall' *9th Directive* xxi. 200 'No go. I got myself cornered. One dead.'.. 'Do you need any smoke out?' **1977** 'J. le Carré' *Honourable Schoolboy* iv. 91 For smoke.. Molly chose a dozen other R's.

i. *to watch someone's smoke* (slang, orig. *U.S.*), to watch someone go, to observe someone's actions; chiefly imp. in phr. *watch my smoke.*
1905 G. W. Peck *Peck's Bad Boy with Circus* ix. 114 The elephant..winked at the other elephants, as much as to say: 'Watch my smoke.' **1921** R. D. Paine *Comrades Rolling Ocean* i. 10 Suspend judgement and watch my smoke. That's all I ask. **1927** Wodehouse *Meet Mr Mulliner* iii. 82 'You are a curate, eh?' 'At present. But,' said Augustine, tapping his companion on the chest, 'just watch my smoke.' **1928** C. Sandburg *Good Morning, America* 18 Let's go. Watch our smoke. Excuse our dust. **1947** Wodehouse *Full Moon* ii. 27 Look at Henry the Eighth... And Solomon. Once they started marrying, there was no holding them—you just sat back and watched their smoke.

j. *in(to) smoke* (slang, chiefly *Austral.*), in(to) hiding.
1924 C. J. Dennis *Rose of Spadgers* 72 'Jist now,' says Brannigan, 'Spike Wegg's in smoke. Oh, jist concerns a cove 'e tried to croak.' **1938** P. J. Smith *Con Man* ix. 179 Denman advised Naysmith to remain 'in smoke'—an expression meaning to hide himself—and play golf until Denman had stood his trial alone for the offence in Glasgow. **1943** K. Tennant *Ride on Stranger* xvii. 203 The New Zealand delegate returned anonymously, slipped ashore and 'went into smoke' like some famous criminal. **1967** K. S. Prichard *Subtle Flame* 252 Meanwhile Tony's got to be kept in smoke?

k. *to go up in smoke*, to be consumed by fire; to be destroyed completely; also *fig.*, to lose one's temper.
1933 [see *go *v.* 94 h]. **1939** 'N. Blake' *Smiler with Knife* 94 Oh, glory no! He'd go up in smoke. **1946** [see *Interimsethik]. **1955** [see *highbrow, high-brow *sb.*].

5. a. (*b*) Opium; (*c*) marijuana.
1884 Kipling *Plain Tales from Hills* (1888) 238 The coffin is gone—gone to China again—with the old man and a couple of *tolahs* of Smoke inside, in case he should want 'em on the way. **1946** C. McCullers *Member of Wedding* iii. 192 Made crazy one night by a marihuana cigarette, by something called smoke or snow. **1956** S. Longstreet *Real Jazz Old & New* xiii. 104 He mixed.. with studs shying a toy of opium. But there isn't much record that he went for tea-sticks or the smoke himself. **1963** H. Parkhurst *Undertow* (1964) v. 84 To her 'smoke' and the 'kicks' were the things that seemed to count. **1977** *Rolling Stone* 16 June 76/2 He wondered aloud if there were 'smoke' in the house, prompting people in the front rows to toss lit joints upon the stage.

b. Also, a marijuana cigarette.
1967 [see *joint *sb.* 14 c]. **1980** 'D. Kavanagh' *Duffy* iii. 52 He'd known who handled smokes, who handled snort and who handled smack.

6. (Earlier and further examples.) *to have* (or *take*) *a smoke*, to smoke a pipe, cigarette, or cigar.
1835 A. B. Longstreet *Georgia Scenes* 213 *Mrs. B.* [to *Mrs. S.*]. Well, let's light our pipes, and take a short smoke, and go to bed. **1860** W. H. Russell *My Diary in India* II. iii. 53 Here..were to be seen a few soldiers,.. lounging about, taking an early morning smoke. **1887** *Lantern* (New Orleans) May, in *Amer. Speech* (1948) XXIII. 247/2 A book-keeper for a large firm here begged an acquaintance for twenty-five cents to go and have a smoke with. **1922** Joyce *Ulysses* 112 Ideal spot to have

a quiet smoke and read the *Church Times*. **1926** J. Black *You can't Win* xi. 141, I..found my way into the hop joints. Curiosity was my only excuse for my first 'smoke'. **1978** O. White *Silent Reach* xix. 206 Can't say I blame you. Have another smoke?

7. b. Cheap whisky; a concoction based on raw alcohol, etc., used as a substitute for whisky. *N. Amer.*

1904 'O. Henry' *Cabbages & Kings* iii. 52 Brandy, anisada, Scotch 'smoke' and various wines. **1928** *Daily Tel.* 9 Oct. 11/3 Twelve additional deaths today are attributed to week-end 'jags', which have been traced to 'speak-easies' in the New York east-end, where the liquor is known as 'smoke'. **1940** *Sun* (Baltimore) 14 Nov. 8/2 Judge Eugene O'Dunne yesterday ruled that the sale of denatured alcohol diluted with water and known as 'smoke'—comes within the effect of the liquor laws. **1950** [see *rubby-dub* s.v. *Rubby]. **1959** *Washington Post* 18 Aug. A3/4 It was the smoke that made Heaton a loner and junk peddler in the demolition jungles of the Southwest area. **1980** *Amer. Speech* 1977 LII. 117 Blends of anti-freeze and water, sometimes including methyl alcohol, solvent or paint remover, cleaning fluid, canned heat, or other alcohol mixtures: *smoke*.

8. Also, a short-haired cat with similar blue-grey or black colouring. (Later examples.)

1933 E. Buckworth-Herne-Soame *Cats* xviii. 99 A smoke is one of the most handsome cats living. **1958** *Listener* 28 Aug. 298/2 With two exceptions, the Chinchilla and smoke, short-hairs have the same variety of colour as do long-hairs. **1972** Ing & Pond *Champion Cats of World* 79/1 The first Smokes were bred by chance. *Ibid.* 99/2 Black and Blue Smoke. Except that the fur is short rather than long, the standard is the same as..the long-haired varieties. **1976** *Southern Even. Echo* (Southampton) 11 Nov. (Advts. Suppl.) 14/3 Pedigree long-haired male kittens, black and blue smokes.

b. An abusive and offensive term for a Black. *U.S. slang.*

1913 J. T. Foote *Blister Jones* viii. 242 'Who you callin' a smoke?' says Snowball, startin' fur Micky. **1932** J. T. Farrell *Young Lonigan* i. 21 He had bashed the living moses out of that smoke who pulled a razor on him over in Carter playground. **1940** R. Chandler *Farewell, my Lovely* iii. 24 There was five smokes carved Harlem sunsets on each other. **1970** L. Sanders *Anderson Tapes* xxxiii. 109 Five men. One's a smoke.

II. 9. a. *smoke-barrage, -column, -devil, -dust, -fog, -pall, -plume, -puff, -ring* (further examples), *-trail, -wreath* (later examples).

1923 Kipling *Irish Guards in Great War* I. 317 A Guards Battalion..came up..under cover of what looked like a smoke-barrage. **1932** Blunden *Fall in Ghosts* 10 The youth scurried away to the problem of preventing that smoke-column from the cookers. **1919** J. Masefield *Battle of Somme* 5 The No Man's Land, into which our men advanced, was a strip of earth without life, made smoky, dusty, and dim by explosions which came out of the air upon it, and left black, curling, slowly fading, dust and smoke-devils behind them. **1970** R. Lowell *Notebook* 247 Smoke-dust the Chinese draftsman made eternal. **1933** *Gloss. Aeronaut. Terms* (*B.S.I.*) xiv. 88 *Smoke fog*, fog due to particles of smoke in the atmosphere. A thick haze. **1918** G. Frankau *Poetical Wks.* xx. 153 Southward, gray skies with smoke-pall overcast. **1940** W. Faulkner *Hamlet* iii. 159 He actually heard the cow's voice..from beyond the smokepall on the other hill. **1920** *Glasgow Herald* 3 July 6 We may even be deprived of some of these interesting smoke-plumes that float proudly and unafraid over public works. **1978** *Sci. Amer.* May 162/1 There are two basic types of smoke plume: the momentum jet..and the buoyant plume. **1897** W. S. Churchill in *Daily Tel.* 9 Nov. 7/6 The mountain battery..came into action and began shelling the summits, from which the smoke-puffs were most frequent and continuous. **1909** F. Barclay *Rosary* xxiv. 257 'And this pleases you?' inquired the doctor, blowing smoke rings into the air. **1959** I. & P. Opie *Lore & Lang. Schoolch.* xi. 220 A 14-year-old girl, Newbridge, Monmouthshire, writes: 'If you see a smoke ring coming from an engine you can wish once, and if you see two smoke rings you can wish twice.' **1971** *Wall St. Jrnl.* 22 July w.1/5 The industry tries all sorts of promotions from a cigar smoke ring blowing contest at Palisades Amusement Park..to cigar and cognac tasting sessions. **1933** *O.E.D.* (Suppl.) s.v. Sky *sb.*[1] 9, Smoke-trails made by aircraft. **1979** 'P. O'Connor' *Into Strong City* xxxviii. 142 A puffer making its way up the Clyde. A smoke trail. The sea calm. **1913** D. H. Lawrence *Love Poems & Others* 36 To-day a thicket of sunshine with blue smoke-wreaths. **1939** R. Campbell *Flowering Rifle* vi. 138 Through rolling smoke-wreaths, there, like ant-hills rise The kopjes in the nitre-breathing skies.

b. *smoke-hood, -vent.*

1969 'M. Renault' *Fire from Heaven* (1972) v. 199 King Archelaos had hung a smoke-hood over the hearth. **1912** J. L. M. Myres *Dawn of Hist.* viii. 185 In Crete the climate is mild enough..for portable braziers to suffice, and this release from anxiety for smoke-vents encouraged the architects to daring experiments. **1936** Smoke-vent [see *smoke-blackening*, sense 9 c below].

c. *smoke-blackening, -burn, -mark.*

1936 *Discovery* Feb. 55/2 The semi-conical apartment at the east end was evidently a fire-chamber, as traces of smoke-blackening were found on stones that had fallen from the roof and had once surrounded a smoke-vent. **1971** S. Hill *Strange Meeting* ii. 141 He had very pale, almost white eyelashes, and a curious mark, like a smoke burn, across his forehead. **1876** 'Mark Twain' *Tom Sawyer* xxxi. 23 Holding their candles aloft and reading the tangled web-work of names..with which the rocky walls [of the cave] had been frescoed (in candle smoke)... They made a smoke-mark for future guidance.

d. *smoke-grey* (later examples).

1903 [see sense 9 e in Dict.]. **1924** [see *Harris]. **1976** *Billings* (Montana) *Gaz.* 30 June 9-D/3 (Advt.), For sale 1976 Corvette... Red w/ smoke gray interior.

10. a. *smoke-belching, -chaser, -control, -detecting, -detection, -detector, -discharger, -generator.*

1963 Bird & Hutton-Stott *Veteran Motor Car* 81 They were extremely refined,..smoke-belching, costly,..and slow. **1974** Smoke-belching [see *Samlor]. **1935** L. Luard *Conquering Seas* xii. 153 Shot thirty-five miles east of Cape. Towed for three hours. Double bag. Fish hard and golden. Worked edge of Strunda four days. Good living. Shifted to avoid smoke-chasers.—Trial shoot in 45 fathoms. Nowt. **1942** *Sun* (Baltimore) 14 May 4/2 Lookouts, smoke-chasers, firemen and organized stand-by crews to prevent, detect and fight forest fires. **1956** *Ann. Reg. 1955* 4 Densely populated areas designated for smoke-control. **1967** *Economist* 30 Dec. 1277/1 The real trouble is still the old one: too few smoke control orders in the Black Areas. **1962** *Flight International* LXXXI. 190/2 The Pyrene Co Ltd have contributed smoke-detecting..equipment to the D.H.121 Trident. **1936** *Discovery* May 146/2 Other uses [of light-sensitive cells] were for..smoke detection in factory chimneys. **1957** *Practical Wireless* XXXIII. 683/2 Such devices as..a smoke detector and fire indicator. **1978** *N.Y. Times* 30 Mar. B16/5 (Advt.), 117 West 58th St... Completely re-modeled Prewar Bldg—featuring—..smoke detectors—ceramic tile kitch & bath. *a* **1944** K. Douglas *Alamein to Zem Zem* (1946) 16 There were also two smoke dischargers to be operated by me. Stacked round the sides of the turret were the six-pounder shells. **1979** P. Alexander *Show me Hero* xx. 210 Kemp threw a canister of tear-gas... Quinn threw a smoke-discharger. **1933** *Gloss. Aeronaut. Terms* (*B.S.I.*) xiii. 3 *Smoke generator*, a pyrotechnic device, placed on the ground, emitting smoke for indicating wind direction. **1961** W. Vaughan-Thomas *Anzio* ix. 211 The smoke generators, manned by cheerful coloured troops, tried to blot out observation and protect the shipping from sneak raiders.

b. *smoke-bemuffled, -blackened, -defiled, -dyed* (earlier example), *-filled, -laden, -logged, -palled, -reddened, -scorched, -sodden* (later example), *-stained, -warmed.*

1912 W. de la Mare *Listeners* 81 Vainly 'gainst that thin wall The trumpets call, Or with loud hum The smoke-bemuffled drum. **1890** A. Conan Doyle *Firm of Girdlestone* xiv. 111 Puffing at his weed and staring up at the smoke-blackened ceiling. **1976** M. Machlin *Pipeline* lvi. 567 The small smoke-blackened figure walked slowly toward the forepeak of the Globtik Alamo. **1919** Kipling *Years Between* 42 Witness thy portrait, smoke-defiled. **1817** *Jrnl. Salem Mechanic* 19 Oct. in *Essex Inst. Hist. Coll.* (1866) VIII. 234, I have not seen a handsome woman since I left Salem; they are here [*sc.* Pittsburgh] all smoke-dyed. **1920** *Evening Star* (Washington) 14 June 1/2 Harry Daugherty..predicted that about 2.11 a.m., 'in a smoke-filled room', on a certain night during the republican national convention, the next nominee would be chosen. **1965** G. McInnes *Road to Gundagai* v. 77 These damp and smokefilled holes. **1979** *Now!* 21–27 Sept. 74/3 Presidential candidates are not selected by political pros in smoke-filled rooms these days. **1903** *Work* 21 Mar. 105/1 Incrustations due to the smoke-laden atmosphere. **1975** *Economist* 6 Sept. 20/1 If you've ever tried to make clearheaded decisions in a stuffy, smoke-laden conference room, you'll appreciate what we mean. **1963** *Times* 25 May 8/4 A fire officer said: 'When we arrived ammunition was exploding everywhere. Our job was made even more difficult because the building was completely smoke-logged.' **1976** *Southern Even. Echo* (Southampton) 13 Nov. 16/2 Firemen had to wear breathing equipment to get into the smoke-logged electrical input room on the first floor. **1922** Joyce *Ulysses* 583 Two shafts of light fall on the smokepalled altarstone. **1893** Kipling *Seven Seas* (1896) 97 To the smoke-reddened eyes of Loben. **1888** —— *Departmental Ditties* (1890) 81 Anger and pain and terror Stamped on the smoke-scorched skin. **1959** C. Devlin *Sermons & Devotional Writings of G. M. Hopkins* 5 In this smoke-sodden little town he [*sc.* Hopkins] came up against people who needed him desperately. **1849** *Chambers's Edin. Jrnl.* 24 Nov. 327/2 Smoke-stained walls. **1965** J. A. Michener *Source* (1966) 71 Along the smoke-stained walls hung spears and clubs, animal skins drying for later use and baskets containing grain. **1951** L. MacNeice tr. *Goethe's Faust* ii. 193 Yon smoke-warmed garment.

c. *smoke-dim, -foul.*

1937 'G. Orwell' *Road to Wigan Pier* iv. 71 You walk through the smoke-dim slums of Manchester. **1888** G. M. Hopkins *Let.* 1 May (1938) 145, I..dislike any town..for its bad and smokefoul air.

11. smoke alarm, a device that automatically gives a warning of the presence of smoke; **smoke-boat** *Naut. slang,* a steamship; **smoke-bomb,** a bomb which produces a smoke-screen; **smoke bush** = *smoke plant*; **smoke candle** (see quot. 1962); **smoke canister,** a canister whose contents can be ignited to produce smoke; **smoke concert** *N.Z.*, a concert at which smoking is allowed; **smokefall** [after Nightfall] *rare*⁻¹, 'the moment when the wind drops and smoke that had ascended descends' (Dame Helen Gardner); **smoke goggles,** goggles that protect the eyes against smoke; **smoke grenade,** a grenade that emits a cloud of smoke on impact; **smoke-head,** (*a*) the head of a column of smoke; (*b*) *Naut.*, a funnel; **smoke helmet,** (*a*) also, a similar helmet used by others; (*b*) a form of respirator used for counteracting poison gas, etc., in the war of 1914–18; **smoke-hound** *U.S. slang,* an alcoholic who drinks smoke (see sense 7 b above); **smoke joint** [*Joint *sb.* 14] *U.S. slang,* a bar selling inferior liquor; **smoke-meter,** an instrument for measuring the density or the composition of smoke; **smoke Persian,** a long-haired smoke-coloured cat (cf. sense 8 in Dict. and Suppl.); **smoke plant:** for *Rhus cotinus* substitute *Cotinus coggygria* and add further examples; **smoke point,** (*a*) the lowest temperature at which an oil or fat gives off smoke; (*b*) the height of the tallest flame with which a particular sample of kerosene will burn; **smoke-pole** *slang,* a firearm; **smoke pot,** a tin containing substances that produce smoke or a similar opaque vapour; **smoke rocket,** a rocket that emits smoke; **smoke shell** *Mil.*, a projectile that generates a dense cloud of smoke after it is fired; **smoke-shop,** restrict † to sense in Dict. and add: now *U.S.*; (*b*) a tobacconist's shop; a place where people gather to smoke and talk; (*c*) a bar, esp. one selling inferior or cheap liquor; **smoke-signal,** a column of smoke used as a signal (cf. sense 2 a in Dict.); also *transf.* and *fig.*; **smoke-stick** *slang,* = *smoke-pole* above; **smoke tunnel,** a wind tunnel into which smoke can be introduced to make the airflow visible; **smoke-wagon** *U.S. slang,* a firearm; **smoke-writing** = *Sky-writing *vbl. sb.*

1936 *Discovery* Nov. 359/2 A smoke alarm apparatus for the small industrial chimney is also provided. **1977** *Chicago Tribune* 2 Oct. xii. 17/9 (Advt.), Full basement, low assoc. fee, central humidifier and smoke alarm. **1867** G. E. Clark *Seven Years of Sailor's Life* xii. 116 Capen and de missis go munyana in de big smoke boat. **1901** *Rudder* Jan. 9/2 The magnificent steam yacht Mayflower passed us close aboard. We had a fine contempt for any and all 'smoke boats', but the sweetness of her lines..compelled admiration. **1929** F. Bowen *Sea Slang* 127 *Smoke boat,* the old sailing ship man's term of contempt for a steamer. **1917** A. G. Empey *Over Top* 308 *Smoke bomb,* a shell which, in exploding, emits a dense white smoke, hiding the operations of troops. **1931** V. Bruce *Bluebird's Flight* iii. 29 Throwing over a smoke bomb, I descended on a nice hard piece of ground. **1973** 'I. Drummond' *Jaws of Watchdog* xv. 205 A little smoke-bomb. I put it through a window... Then I went in through another window. **1902** L. H. Bailey *Cycl. Amer. Hort.* IV. 1529/1 *Rhus*..*Cotinus,* Linn. Smoke Bush. Venice Sumach..fl[ower]s purple, in ample loose panicles. **1940** [see *partridge vine* s.v. *Partridge 5]. **1977** *Weekly Times* (Melbourne) 19 Jan. 29/4 The other sample is from the smoke bush. **1932** C. Gilson *Wild Metal* iii. i. 248 We had been provided with smoke-candles; and when we had cleared the Boche out of his trenches, the wind changed and the smoke masked our own fire. **1950** *Times* 13 May 4/5 The pilot started to descend in order to round the turning point at not more than 300 ft. for recognition purposes. The point was near a golf course..where white strips had been laid out and smoke candles were fired as the Meteor approached. **1962** *Ordnance Technical Terminol.* (U.S. Army Ordnance School, AD 660 112) 282/1 *Smoke candle,* munition which produces smoke by vaporizing a smoke producing oil. **1973** 'I. Drummond' *Jaws of Watchdog* x. 135 The smoke-canisters were not of a recognized pattern..used by any NATO army. **1974** H. MacInnes *Climb to Lost World* ix. 148 We had smoke canisters all ready, in case we heard a plane. **1888** J. D. Wickham *Casual Ramblings* 42 They had a smoke concert with a Salvation Army accompaniment till a clock was 'ayont the twal'. **1935** A. Mulgan *Pilgrim's Way in N.Z.* xiv. 90 'A man should go on to the football field,' declared a representative forward at a 'smoke' concert, 'prepared to meet his God.' **1936** T. S. Eliot *Coll. Poems 1909–1935* 188 But only in time can..The moment in the draughty church at smokefall Be remembered. **1962** *Flight International* LXXXII. 487/2 Stowage provision is made for smoke goggles at each duty station. **1976** B. Jackson *Flameout* iv. 59 Fumes and smoke..surged forward into the flight deck. The crew put on smoke goggles. *a* **1944** K. Douglas *Alamein to Zem Zem* (1946) 16 Stacked round the sides of the turret were..hand-grenades, smoke grenades and machine-gun ammunition. **1980** *Globe & Laurel* July/Aug. 229/2 Twice during the night we were attacked by a small enemy force who ran through our position throwing Chinese crackers and smoke grenades. **1915** Kipling *France at War* 11 He pointed to the large deliberate smoke-heads. **1942** H. Bloomfield *Sailing to Sun* xvi. 164 There was smoke coming from the smoke-head of the *Owl.* **1906** *Royal Mag.* Feb. 338/1 A safety smoke helmet. **1915** D. O. Barnett *Let.* 10 June 171 We've got a wonderful new respirator issued, a 'smoke helmet' made of cloth..which is soaked in a solution. **1972** *Police Rev.* 17 Nov. 1491/2 Constables equipped and wearing diving or smoke helmets. **1932** *Sun* (Baltimore) 23 Nov. 20/4 If a downpour has just started, the jungles are literally emptied into the stations... They come in by the dozen.., ancient smoke hounds and middle-aged rovers. **1931** 'D. Stiff' *Milk & Honey Route* xii. 128 Mark my word, out of the muck hole that was a 'smoke joint' will rise a lily that will outdo the old-time saloon in all those old virtues. **1941** *Jrnl. Soc. Automotive Engineers* XLVIII. 188/2 The smokemeter itself is our only means of measuring smoke density precisely. **1961** *Guardian* 24 Mar. 6/3 In..a letter..regarding..the control of diesel exhaust smoke..Mr. Marples has indicated that further detailed investigation into the possibilities of using a smokemeter would be worth while. **1904** 'Saki' *Reginald* 3 You want one of her smoke Persian kittens. **1973** *Country Life* 25 Jan. 226/3 My smoke persian was an individualist like Mr. Fearon's cat. **1888** *Garden* 18 Aug. 159/1 The Venetian Sumach, Wig Tree, or Smoke Plant..is one of the most remarkable of late-flowering shrubs. **1948** N. Catchpole *Flowering Shrubs & Small Trees* 177 Smoke Plant or Burning Bush... The common names relate to the fine, feathery inflorescence. **1933** *Petroleum Handbk.* x. 181 The smoke point only gives an indication of the burning quality of a kerosine immediately the lamp is lit. **1951** McMichael & Bailey in M. B. Jacobs *Chem. & Technol. of Food & Food Products* II. xxv. 1150 If a fat is to be used for frying..its smoke point, or smoking temperature, is of some importance. **1958** *Jrnl. Home Econ.* L. 778/1 An emulsifier lowers the smoke point of the fat to which it is added. **1975** E. M. Goodger *Hydrocarbon Fuels* vii. 134 Two kerosine types of burner fuel are classified as C1 and C2, with minimum smoke-points of 35 and 25 mm, respectively. **1929** M. A. Gill *Underworld Slang* 11/1 *Smoke pole*, gun. **1970** *N.Z. Listener* 21 Sept. 14/5 A long time since he'd fired the old smoke-pole, anyway. **1980** *Hunting Ann.* 1981 55/1 This requires the hunter to decide in advance whether he wants to hunt with an antique or modern... There is no going out later using a scoped rifle after getting zilched with a smokepole. **1950** *N.Z. Jrnl. Agric.* June 534/3 By taking one or two smoke pots into a poultry house and seeing where the smoke goes and what happens to it, improvements in ventilation are often suggested. **1965** 'Lauchmonen' *Old Thom's Harvest* x. 135 They all sit down near..their mosquito smoke-pots. **1978** J. Gardner *Dancing Dodo* xiii. 92 She would.. begin her let down west of Brussels, and start up the smoke pots housed in the starboard nacelles. **1891** A. Conan Doyle in *Strand Mag.* July 70/1 'It is nothing very formidable,' he said, taking a long cigar-shaped roll from his pocket. 'It is an ordinary plumber's smoke rocket, fitted with a cap at either end to make it self-lighting.' **1954** [see *ripple-fired* adj. s.v. *ripple *sb.*[3] 7]. **1964** J. S. Scott *Dict. Building* 265 *Smoke Rocket*.., a rocket which gives off a dense, lasting smoke which is directed into a drain under test. **1919** P. R. Worrall *Smoke Tactics* 27 Smoke shells may be used as a visible sign to Infantry and Tanks to mark the barrage. **1937** *Times* 16 Apr. 8/6 The howitzers used smoke shells mixed with their high explosive to give a screen effect. **1966** *McGraw-Hill Encycl. Sci. & Technol.* I. 539/1 The 81-mm and 4·2-in. mortars, capable of lobbing high-explosive or smoke shells onto enemy positions, round out the category of infantry weapons. **1937** C. Himes *Nigger* in *Black on Black* (1973) 125 Harold Price..was just leaving the house for his afternoon tonk session down at the smoke shop at 100th Street and Cedar. **1959** R. M. Dorson *Amer. Folklore* vii. 267 The enterprising folklorist need not journey into the back hills to scoop up tradition. He can set up his recording machine in the smokeshop or the union grill. **1972** J. Wambaugh *Blue Knight* (1973) i. 19, I walked down to the smoke shop. I picked up half a dozen fifty-cent cigars. **1977** *New Yorker* 27 June 31/1 Send out to the smoke shop for three cartons of straw-tipped Melachrinos. **1873** S. W. Cozzens *Marvellous Country* iv. 65 After leaving the Organos Mountains we had noticed Indian smoke-signals. **1923** *Beaver* Dec. 108 Another smoke signal was seen curling upward away to the north. **1944** *Living off Land* iv. 84 A very useful mode of attracting attention is by means of smoke signals. **1962** *Amer. Speech* XXXVII. 135 *Smoke signals, n.* Sometimes trains were taken on a logging railroad without authority. The men had to keep a sharp lookout for smoke from other trains in order to get onto a side track or to back up quickly: 'We had to watch for smoke signals.' **1978** *Times* 20 Jan. 4/8 Mr Enoch Powell['s].. delphic remarks certainly got Mrs Thatcher asking herself what smoke signals he intended. **1927** *Flynn's* 22 Jan. 376/2, I ups and prods him and says, 'Hand it over, er this smokestick'll do the talking.' **1940** in S. J. Baker *Austral. Lang.* (1945) viii. 153 A rifle is a smoke-stick, a machine-gun is a death-adder. **1931** *Flight* 18 Dec. 1243/2 The type of smoke tunnel used by Mr. Farren for his demonstrations had cost approximately £65. **1964** P. Bradshaw *Exper. Fluid Mech.* vi. 151 Smoke tunnels are usually of open-circuit design to prevent the accumulation of smoke in the airstream. **1975** L. J. Clancy *Aerodynamics* xiii. 365 The principal requirement of a smoke tunnel is for uniform flow with low turbulence. **1891** J. Maitland *Amer. Slang Dict.* 251 *Smoke-wagon* (Am.), a revolver. The word is used by the negroes of the Chicago levee. **1926** J. Black *You can't Win* x. 132 I'll have her buy me a pair of 'smoke wagons'. **1950** *Western Folklore* IX. 138 Familiar epithets for the revolver were equalizer, shootin' iron,..smoke wagon. **1932** *Flight* 8 July 638 The committee recommend that smoke-writing should not be prohibited or controlled.

smoke, *v.* Add: **I. 2. d.** Also const. *off*.
1961 P. White *Riders in Chariot* 415 Dubbo had gone all right. Had taken his tin box, it seemed, and smoked off.

4. (Further U.S. examples.)
1818 A. Royall *Let.* 19 Feb. (1830) 104 It's as fair cheatin says I, as ever seed in my life; and you can make him smoke for it. **1878** J. H. Beadle *Western Wilds* xxviii. 442 The residents will make him 'smoke' with high taxes on his land.

II. 6. b. Also *fig.*, to force *out* into the open (a conspirator); to bring *out* publicly. orig. *U.S.*
1914 *Dialect Notes* IV. 164 *Smoke one out, v. phr.*, to find and bring from concealment. 'I'll try and smoke him out again.' **1948** *Times* 28 Feb. 5/7 Speculators were 'smoked out' by a Congressional inquiry. **1959** *Listener* 25 June 1105/2 We were using a food guide, compiled by some daring spy who was determined to smoke out tasty food if it cost him his citizenship. **1977** G. V. Higgins *Dreamland* viii. 83, I had done it to smoke them out, and had succeeded.

III. 11. (Further examples with reference to marijuana, opium, or other illegal drugs.)
1895 Conrad *Almayer's Folly* xii. 267 'And they both smoke,' added Ali. 'Phew! Opium, you mean?' Ali nodded. **1957** *Sun* (Baltimore) 12 Jan. 11/2 Asked how he took dope, Harrod replied that he 'smoked, snorted and skin-popped'. **1972** *Guardian* 29 Jan. 9/2 Mr Williams had three previous convictions for possession of cannabis... 'I've said I smoke sometimes.' **1977** 'J. le Carré' *Honourable Schoolboy* xvi. 381 For a large *divan* secrecy was vital... The safest place to smoke would undoubtedly be upstairs.

12. a. (Further examples with marijuana as object.) Also *fig.*
1946 E. O'Neill *Iceman Cometh* I. 54 Bejees, Jimmy's started them off smoking the same hop. **1951** *Life* 25 June 21/1, I heard and saw guys who skin pop,..smoke pot, banging and shoot up the main vein in your arm and leg. **1976** *New Yorker* 8 Mar. 98/2 We smoked, sure. At one time, everybody in the platoon had smoked pot except the lieutenant.

13. Also, to 'rag' by smoking. *U.S.*
1850 in B. H. Hall *College Words* (1851) 285, I would not have you sacrifice all these advantages for the sake of smoking future Freshmen. **1880** *Harper's Mag.* Nov. 950/1 They hazed and smoked Freshmen.

15. *trans.* To furnish with tobacco. *rare.*
1897 'Mark Twain' *Following Equator* xi. 129 He will.. feed you and slake you and smoke you with the best that money can buy.

IV. 16. To shoot (a person) with a firearm. *U.S. slang.*
1926 J. Black *You can't Win* xi. 144 Git inside an' stay there or I'll smoke both of youse off. **1942** *Detective Fiction* May 53/1 You chiseling rat. You didn't figure Tommy and those heels could hold *me*, did you? I smoked them just like I'm gonna smoke you, Bugs.

smoked, *ppl. a.* Add: **1. b.** *smoked sheet*, a form of raw rubber that is preserved for transportation by drying the coagulated latex in a smoky atmosphere.
1909 *Westm. Gaz.* 26 Oct. 9/2 Buyers..appeared willing to give higher prices for smoked sheet than for crêpe. **1950** *Thorpe's Dict. Appl. Chem.* (ed. 4) 552/1 For the preparation of smoked sheet the strained, diluted latex is poured into rectangular tanks carrying vertical slots at 1½-in. intervals. **1972** P. W. Allen *Natural Rubber & Synthetics* iii. 69 The new grading method would free producers from the need to make rubber in those forms such as ribbed smoked sheet which had evolved around the need to fit the traditional grading procedures.

4. (Further examples: cf. quots. 1755, 1819, sense 2 in Dict.)
1892 H. James *Let.* 29 July (1981) III. 391 You all melt away in this hard Swiss light. But I have just bought a tinted (I believe they call it a 'smoked') pince nez, and I am attempting to focus you again. **1947** [see *bathy-thermograph* s.v. *bathy-]. **1978** *Lancashire Life* Apr. 141/1 The sun visors..are made of a dark red smoked plastic and slide away completely out of sight. **1979** G. Watson *Black Jack* xii. 82 A limousine with smoked-glass windows.

smoke-dried, *ppl. a.* Add: Also *fig.*
a **1941** V. Woolf *Death of Moth* (1942) 108 The dead weight of smoke-dried culture.

smoke-ho, -oh. Add: Chiefly *Austral., N.Z.,* and *Naut.* Also **smoke-o.** [see *-o[2].] **1.** (Earlier and further examples.) More generally, a tea-break, a rest period. Also, a cup of tea or a snack taken at work.
1874 L. J. Kennaway *Crusts* 124 Sawyers, and stockmen, carpenters, packers, shinglers and loafers, Smoke as they work to assist them, and then knock off for a '*smoke oh!*' **1881** *Adelaide Observer* 31 Dec. 46, I must go to 'smoke O'. **1930** V. Palmer *Passage* 247 At smoko, when they took a spell in the middle of loading the boat..the talk was of Lew. **1938** F. Worsley *First Voyage* iii. 56 'Five minutes' smoke-oh,' was the mate's reply. **1942** S. Campion *Bonaza* i. 21 C'm'on, now, cobbers, we'll go make ourselves smoke-o, eh? Nuthin' like a cuppa. **1953** A. Upfield *Murder must Wait* iii. 26 A billy of tea and a slice of brownie..a smoko tea suitable for a half-caste. **1954** T. Ronan *Vision Splendid* 179 If you blokes aren't coming down for your smoko I'll throw it away. **1961** G. Foulser *Seaman's Voice* ix. 136 It was then 'kaffetid' or smoko as U.K. seamen call it. **1961** P. White *Riders in Chariot* xiii. 456 It was just on smoke-o. The machines were easing... It was now time to relax. **1963** H. C. de Mierre *Long Voyage* i. 7 The stevedores broke off for their mid-morning 'smoke-ho'. **1970** D. M. Davin *Not Here, Not Now* vi. i. 274 An hour off to eat and then on again from one till three. Another smoko then, and on again till five. **1972** P. Newton *Sheep Thief* iii. 27 By 'smoko' time..the three drovers had arrived in from the back. **1978** O. White *Silent Reach* viii. 85 Margan..let the big truck roll to a standstill. 'Smoke-oh,' he announced.

2. = *smoke concert* s.v. *smoke *sb.* 11.
1918 G. A. Taylor *Those were Days* 30 The State Governor was present, and it was a rare incident for that distinguished party to grace an Art Society 'Smoko'. **1957** D. Niland *Call me when Cross turns Over* vii. 170 He chopped wood for hotels and boarding-houses, and sometimes was roped in as an entertainer at smokos and concerts. **1976** *Australian* 24 Apr. 18 The Leader of the Opposition, Mr Whitlam, worked in his Sydney office and attended a 'smoko' at Wentworthville RSL club last night.

smoke-house. Add: **3.** Chiefly *N. Amer.* (Earlier examples.)
1746 in *Lower Norfolk Co. Virginia Antiquary* (1896) I. iv. 110, I..bequeath to my wife Mary the free use & occupation of my dwelling house..with the Kitching, Store house Smoke house, Hen house [etc.]. **1841** A. Langton *Let.* 29 May (1904) 282 We intend putting up a smoke-house soon, which is the best way of keeping hung meat.

smoke-in (smōᵘ·kˌin). [*-in[3].] A gathering for the purpose of smoking or otherwise inhaling cannabis.
1968 *Courier-Mail* (Brisbane) 14 Sept. 7/9 Hashish burnt in a teaspoon held over a gas stove had been inhaled through a metal tube during a 'smoke-in' at a Clayfield flat. **1972** *Guardian* 1 July 1/5 The yippies and the Street People staged a 'smoke-in'.

smo·ke-jump, *v. N. Amer.* [f. Smoke *sb.* + Jump *v.*] To jump by parachute from an aircraft, in order to extinguish a forest fire. Chiefly as *vbl. sb.*
1942 *Fire Control Notes* VI. 95 Parachute smoke jumping..has proved according to all reports, that such a method of attack on small fires is practical. **1949** *Amer. Forests* Oct. 18/3 Smoke jumping is a hazardous occupation. **1958** *Amer. Speech* XXXIII. 180 *Smokejumping* and the verb *to smokejump* appear frequently in newspapers. **1976** *Billings* (Montana) *Gaz.* 11 July 1-D/4 As the blaze spread Friday, the state forestry agency supplied forces, and Missoula sent in two smoke-jumping crews by bus totaling about 40 men.

So **smo·ke-jumper** a forest-fire fighter who arrives by parachute.
1940 *Sci. Amer.* Feb. 97/3 These experiments have proved entirely successful and the 'smoke jumpers' will be of inestimable value in preserving our forests. **1956** Peterson & Fisher *Wild America* xxxi. 337 Fires are spotted and fought while they are still small. 'Smoke jumpers' parachute from planes to fires in the roadless back country. **1979** *Arizona Daily Star* 5 Aug. A 10/3 The lone survivor..was pulled from the wreckage by smoke jumpers called in to fight a small forest fire touched off by the crash.

smokeless, *a.* Add: **1.** (Further examples.)
1904 *Sci. Amer.* 4 June 446/3 *Smokeless fuel*,..Mr. Weeple employs a simple method of treating such carbonaceous substances as bituminous coal, coal-dust, oil residue, and the like as will produce a fuel that will burn free from 'black smoke' during combustion. **1935** *Economist* 29 June 1479/1 The main product of low-temperature carbonisation is a smokeless solid fuel. **1977** M. Russell *Mr T* xviii. 145 A fireplace..in which smokeless fuel glowed.

2. *smokeless zone*, a district in which the creation of smoke is forbidden by law.
1953 *Interim Rep. Comm. Air Pollution* 27 in *Parl. Papers* (Cmd. 9011) VIII. 655 The 'smokeless zone' provision of some local Acts..apply to domestic as well as industrial smoke. **1969** A. E. Lindop *Sight Unseen* iv. 34 In spite of the fact that we were a smokeless zone I had a comfortable coal fire. **1976** *Daily Record* (Glasgow) 4 Dec. 12/3 It came at a public meeting after Stirling District Council had tried to get a smokeless zone order on the village quashed.

smoker. Add: **2. b.** For *Obs.*$^{-1}$ read *Obs. rare* and add further example.
1849 H. A. Wise *Los Gringos* xlv. 340, I..took passage in one of them smokers, bigger than a three-decker.

e. A motor vehicle or engine that emits excessive exhaust fumes (see also quot. 1951). *colloq.*
1951 *Amer. Speech* XXVI. 309/1 *Smoker, n.*, a Diesel-motored truck. **1962** *Daily Tel.* 18 Aug. 13/4 Roadside checks..have resulted in about one diesel lorry in eight being termed a 'smoker' because it is making too much exhaust. **1976** *Globe & Mail* (Toronto) 30 Jan. 1/6 The Ontario Environment Ministry has laid its first pollution charge against the driver of a 'smoker'—a car emitting dense smoke.

3. b. *smoker's cough*, a cough caused by excessive smoking.
[**1907** B. M. Croker *Company's Servant* i. 7 D'ye hear the cough of him? That's the real Ganja smoker's cough.] **1927** F. Harris *My Life & Loves* III. xii. 178 He smoked incessantly though the cigarettes plagued him with smoker's cough. **1942** *R.A.F. Jrnl.* 13 June 17 There was one case of a heavy smoker being sent back to his unit... He had a smoker's cough which betrayed him on night exercises. **1962** *Guardian* 14 Apr. 5/1 His smoker's cough, his overdraft anxiety, his impending divorce. **1967** E. Taylor *Second Thursday* i. 9 The old truck burst into life drowning out..the hacking smokers' cough of its owner.

4. b. (Earlier and later examples.)
1887 *Referee* 9 Jan. 6/3 (Advt.), East Hill Smoking Concert Club.—The first 'smoker' of the above club will be given at the East Hill Hotel, Wandsworth, on Thursday, at 8 o'clock. **1894** W. T. Vincent *Recoll. Fred Leslie* I. xviii. 25 Come down to our concert, A Smoker 'tis called. **1939** Joyce *Finnegans Wake* 433 Tootling risky *apropos* songs at commercial travellers' smokers. **1961** E. Williams *George* xx. 319 He was..in the Ouds and last term leading lady in the 'smoker', Oxford for smoking-concert. **1976** W. Goldman *Magic* II. 79 Merlin..brought him along to an Elks' smoker.

c. *U.S.* A social gathering of men, sometimes with organized entertainment.
1899 *N.Y. Jrnl.* 7 Sept. 1/3 Smoker at the Waldorf-Astoria for the sailors of the Olympic. **1911** H. S. Harrison *Queed* 196 After the bouts or the 'exhibition' of a Saturday, there was always a smoker. **1956** E. N. Rogers *Queenie's Brood* 42 A smoker was scheduled frequently at which boxing bouts were featured, or a pie race, a wrestling match, [etc.]. **1969** A. R. Bosworth *My Love Affair with Navy* xii. 168 Both the tin cans and the subs have long been famed for the smokers they held ashore.

smoke-room. Add: Also *attrib.*
1906 *Nature* 17 May 53/2 The book is full of smoke-room gossip and snatches of sailors' songs. **1937** [see *lounge bar* s.v. *lounge *sb.* 4]. **1945** Auden *Coll. Poetry* 134 That caged rebuked question Occasionally let out at clambakes or College reunions, and which the smoke-room story Alone, ironically enough, stands up for.

smokery. Add: **3. b.** = Smoke-house 3. *rare.*
1794 T. Cooper *America* 132 His *smokery* for bacon, hams, &c. is a room about twelve feet square. **1961** N. Froud et al. tr. *Montagné's Larousse Gastronomique*

494/1 In modern smokeries, the racks are fitted into the chimney, thus avoiding a great deal of handling.

smoke-screen (smōᵘ·kˌskrīn). Also **smoke screen, smokescreen.** [f. SMOKE *sb.* + SCREEN *sb.*[1]] **1.** A screen of smoke, *spec.* one produced to conceal military or naval forces or operations, or a stretch of land or sea.

1915 F. A. TALBOT *Aeroplanes* 172 The 'smoke screen', ..an accepted and extensively practised ruse in naval strategy, and..now adopted by its mosquito colleagues of the air. **1937** [see *BLANK *v.* 5 a]. *a* **1944** K. DOUGLAS *Alamein to Zem Zem* (1946) xviii. 107 A straight path would take me behind the..smoke-screen rising and slanting from the carrier. **1977** O. JACKS *Autumn Heroes* xiv. 200 The smoke screen was breaking up patchily to reveal..charred bodies.

2. *fig.* Something designed to conceal or mislead; a deliberate distraction or diversion. Also *attrib.*

1926 R. MACAULAY *Crewe Train* II. iv. 107 The winds, doubtless, were a smoke-screen put up to conceal an advance into some more pithy topic. **1928** *Manch. Guardian Weekly* 7 Sept. 184/3 The 'diplomatic correspondents'..are putting up a smoke-screen of excuse for the Anglo-French naval accord. **1935** A. KENNEDY *Current Eng.* xiii. 567. 'Orismological sesquipedalianism' ..has been much employed of late as a form of smoke-screen writing intended to assist advertisers. **1943** H. READ *Politics of Unpolitical* II. 13 The incursions of democracy..are always accompanied by a smoke-screen of righteousness which hides their real nature and dimensions. **1954** *Encounter* Mar. 73/2 Behind the 'scientific' smoke-screen of statistical tables, graphs, codes, and rebarbative language there is a continuous propaganda for more, and more varied, sexual 'outlets' as physiologically good in themselves. **1973** 'H. CARMICHAEL' *Too Late for Tears* viii. 109 Telling you about his other women was just a smokescreen.

Hence **smo·ke-screen** *v. trans.* (*a*) to deceive by a smoke-screen; (*b*) to conceal or divert attention from by a smoke-screen; **sm·oke-screened** *ppl. a.*, hidden by smoke; **smo·ke-screening** *vbl. sb.*, concealment by smoke-screen, the use of smoke-screens.

1922 O. PARKES *Ships of R. Navy* 147 The sphere of usefulness could be extended to include..smoke screening. **1948** *Nature* 7 Feb. 194/2 Advisory duties at H.Q. Bomber Command..were followed..by duties in connexion with the meteorological aspects of smoke screening. **1950** J. D. MACDONALD *Brass Cupcake* ix. 82 Don't let her smoke-screen you, Chief. **1958** *This Week Mag.* 18 May 35/1 Earlier that day, John Foster Dulles had foxily smokescreened the operation by issuing a statement about summit talks with Russia. **1963** M. ALLINGHAM *China Governess* iii. 47 Some silly little bit..had got him into a scandal which had to be smoke-screened. **1971** N. FREELING *Over High Side* II. 106 He lit it [*sc.* a cigar]... Smoke-screened, he looked back. **1979** I. S. BLACK *Journey to Safe Place* xix. 252 You made a balls of it... Nothing is going to smoke-screen that.

smoke-stack. Add: **1. a.** For *U.S.* read 'Chiefly *U.S.*' and add earlier and later examples.

1859 *Harper's Mag.* Apr. 606/1 The hoarse breath of the smoke stacks..came from the rosin-fed furnaces. **1903** [see *salt-caked* adj. s.v. *SALT *sb.*[1] 12 b]. **1942** E. PAUL *Narrow St.* ix. 70 All tugs had smoke-stacks that could be tilted flat when the craft passed under a bridge. **1976** *National Observer* (U.S.) 7 Aug. 7/6 Her smokestacks are lowered..so she can get under some bridges.

2. (Earlier example.)

1859 *Cairo City* (Illinois) *Gaz.* 8 July 3/1 A number of mischievous boys,..lighting a bunch of fire crackers,.. threw them into the smoke stack.

smo·ke-up. *U.S. slang.* [f. SMOKE *v.* + UP *adv.*[1]] An official notice that a student's work is not up to the required standard.

1927 *Amer. Speech* II. 278/1 [Stanford Univ.] *Smoke up*, official warning of dangerously low standing in history. **1960** *Indiana Daily Student* 23 Nov., Sikes says 56 p.c. of Frosh probably had one Smoke-up.

smokey, var. SMOKY *a.* and *sb.* in Dict. and Suppl.

Smokey Bear (smōᵘ·ki bēᵊɹ). *U.S. slang.* Also **Smoky Bear**; in sense 2 **Smokey the Bear** and *ellipt.* as **Smok(e)y.** [f. *smokey* var. SMOKY *a.* and *sb.* + BEAR *sb.*[1]: the name of an animal character used in U.S. fire-prevention advertising.] **1.** Used *attrib.* and *absol.* to designate a type of wide-brimmed hat.

1969 I. KEMP *Brit. G.I. in Vietnam* ii. 23 Sergeants Sullivant, McKane and Rothweiller..wore the round, soft-brimmed hats known by Americans as 'Smokey Bear'—similar to those of the Royal Canadian Mounted Police. **1974** R. M. PIRSIG *Zen & Art of Motorcycle Maintenance* xii. 142 At the park entrance we stop and pay a man in a Smokey Bear hat.

2. A state policeman; *collect.* state police.

1974 *Rolling Stone* 26 Sept. 86 Truckers..keep Don advised for the location of 'Smokies'..so he'll know when to gear the tour bus down from its maximum speed of 82 mph. **1975** *Courier-Mail* (Brisbane) 26 Oct. 36/12 They [*sc.* CB radios] are used by lorry drivers to warn: 'Smokey down the line.' **1975** *High Times* Dec. 67/2 The cab is better outfitted..with..CB radio (for trackin' those Smokeys in the unwrapped package). **1976** PERKOWSKI & STRAL *Joy of CB* ii. 16 Truckers warned each other of the location of 'Smokey Bears' (the name state troopers were given because their hats resembled that worn by the fabled firefighter). **1976** LIEBERMAN & RHODES *Compl. CB Handbk.* vi. 137 *Smokey the bear*, State Police. **1978** *Weekend* 20–26 Dec. 22 Long distance lorry drivers in America try to avoid smokey bears and tend to drink road tar. Or, in English, avoid state police and drink coffee. **1979** O. MCNAB *Horror Story* (1980) xviii. 72 That Smoky looking at us? *Ibid.* xix. 79 We've got a Smoky Bear on the side.

smokie, obs. var. SMOKY *a.*, *Sc.* var. SMOKY *sb.* in Dict and Suppl.

smoking, *vbl. sb.* Add: **2. b.** *ellipt.* A (railway) smoking-carriage or compartment.

1889–90 KIPLING *Let.* in C. Carrington *Rudyard Kipling* (1955) vi. 140 Went home with him as far as Charing Cross in a 3rd smoking.

c. *ellipt.* A smoking-jacket; also (chiefly as a gallicism), a dinner jacket (see *DINNER *sb.* 2).

1922 M. ARLEN *Piracy* II. ix. 127 He put on a dress-suit... It suited Argentines very well, *le smoking*. But Englishmen were made of sterner stuff. **1934** S. BECKETT *More Pricks than Kicks* 77 Cinched beyond reproach in the double-breasted smoking. **1960** R. ST. JOHN *Foreign Correspondent* viii. 142, I will make you a 'smoking' of fine English material for twenty thousand lei. **1977** T. HEALD *Just Desserts* vii. 171 Guests wore tuxedos if they were American males and black dinner jackets if..European (..except for the odd Italian in tobacco brown 'smoking').

6. b. *smoking box* [BOX *sb.* [2] III], *-cap* (earlier example), *car, carriage* (earlier example), *compartment, -lamp, lounge, -suit*; **smoking machine,** a device which draws air through a lighted cigarette, etc., so that the smoke may be used for scientific study; **smoking weed** (*a*) = BEARBERRY a; cf. KINNIKINIC 2; (*b*) = *CANNABIS 1; cf. *MARIJUANA, MARIHUANA 2.

1841 DICKENS *Old Curiosity Shop* lxxiii. 220 A little cottage at Hampstead..had in its garden a smoking-box. **1841** J. ROMILLY *Diary* 9 Mar. (1967) 211 Dined with Bayne: he..wore an embroidered smoking cap. **1846** *Amer. Railroad Jrnl.* 380/3 Smoking Cars—..we mean cars expressly provided for the lovers of the 'weed'. **1931** W. FAULKNER *Sanctuary* xix. 202 Horace..went forward into the smoking car. It was full too. **1958** 'E. MCBAIN' *Killer's Payoff* (1960) vi. 59 She boarded the train and went directly to a smoking car. **1888** *Amer. Humorist* (London) 5 May 7/1 Came over from New York..in the smoking compartment of a parlor car. **1862** J. SIMMONS *Railway Traveller's Handy Book* 83 Some lines have certain smoking carriages provided. **1889** *Cent. Dict.*, *Smoking-lamp*.., a lamp hung up on board of a man-of-war during hours when smoking is permitted, for the men to light their pipes by. **1940** D. POTTER *Sailing Sulu Sea* 28 Smoking was prohibited except when the smoking-lamp—a name now almost forgotten—was authorized to be lighted. **1966** J. V. NOEL *Naval Terms Dict.* 304 *Smoking lamp*: If 'lighted', it means that smoking is permitted; if 'out', means smoking prohibited. **1951** E. PAUL *Springtime in Paris* iii. 45 He could relax like a tomcat, in an easy chair in the smoking lounge. **1968** *Globe & Mail* (Toronto) 17 Feb. 6/2 Why should the teachers have a smoking lounge and not the students? **1953** *Life* 21 Dec. 20/1 (*caption*) Smoking machine puffs on 60 cigarets in front of Dr. Evarts Graham, who, with his collaborator on the mouse cancer research, Dr. Ernest Wynder, perfected the robot. **1963** *Times* 22 Apr. 19/3 A 'smoking machine' is used to demonstrate the amount of chemicals inhaled, including those which cause cancer. **1971** *Nature* 26 Nov. 227/1 Lung explants..were..exposed in a Filtrona CSM12 smoking machine to puffs of fresh cigarette smoke. **1898** M. BEERBOHM *Let.* 12 Jan. (1964) 127, I have a smoking-suit of purple silk, with dark red facings. **1958** *Listener* 21 Aug. 261/2 Did you know..that women wore smoking suits in the 'twenties? **1857** J. HECTOR *Jrnl.* 31 Oct. in *Capt. Palliser's Exploration in Brit. N. Amer.* 65 in *Parl. Papers 1863* XXXIX. 441 A gravelly soil supporting a poor growth of grass, but in some parts covered with a dense matting of the smoking weed.., the bright red berries of which afford food for large coveys of the prairie hens. **1957** C. MACINNES *City of Spades* I. v. 27 I'd seen what plant it was in flower-pots inside there... 'It's smoking weed,' I said.

c. *smoking-concert* (later examples).

1934 T. S. ELIOT *Rock* i. 40 Dance 'alls, picture palaces, swimmin' baths, smokin' concerts, restaurants. **1945** *Daily Mirror* 15 Aug. 7/2 Anyone who could perform well enough for a private party or a smoking concert was roped in. **1971** *Sunday Nation* (Nairobi) 11 Apr. 42/5 The smoking concert will be held on Sunday evening and not on the Saturday as I stated.

d. In other senses, as *smoking-party* [PARTY *sb.* 8]; **smoking point, temperature** = *smoke point* s.v. *SMOKE *sb.* 11.

1898 'MARK TWAIN' in *Century Mag.* Nov. 100/1 This smoking-party had been gathered together partly for business. **1923** KIPLING *Irish Guards in Great War* I. 206 Leave was possible; smoking-parties made themselves in the big huts. **1915** *Jrnl. Home Econ.* VII. 538 For each case the addition of acid resulted in the lowering of the smoking point. **1931** *Industr. & Engin. Chem.* (Analyt. Ed.) 15 Oct. 348/2 Take the temperature at which the first wisp of smoke is seen rising from the top of the flask as the smoking point. **1915** *Jrnl. Home Econ.* VII. 535 The smoking temperature of a fat may be defined as the temperature at which the fat gives off visible fumes. **1945** *ABC of Cookery* (Ministry of Food) xii. 46 A good frying fat is one that can be heated to a high temperature.. before it smokes and burns, that is, it has a high smoking temperature. **1951** Smoking temperature [see *smoke point* s.v. *SMOKE *sb.* 11].

smoking, *ppl. a.* Add: **1.** fig. *smoking gun, pistol* (U.S.), a piece of incontrovertible incriminating evidence.

1974 *New Yorker* 21 Oct. 135/1 Some are still searching for what has come to be termed 'the murder weapon'—or 'the smoking gun'—the definitive piece of evidence that the President committed a crime. **1975** *Collier's Year Bk.* 10/2 After the new transcripts were disclosed..members of Congress abandoned Nixon in droves. 'I guess we have found the smoking pistol, haven't we?' asked Representative Barber Conable. **1976** WOODWARD & BERNSTEIN *Final Days* 269 Buzhardt felt that here was a potential smoking gun. *Ibid.* 271 He had heard the President approve the plan, he had heard him suggest the exact wording. Buzhardt had found the 'smoking pistol'. He had heard the President load it, aim and fire. **1977** *Time* 19 Sept. 24/2 In fact, there may well be no 'smoking gun'—no incontrovertible, black-and-white evidence of wrongdoing by Lance. **1979** *N.Y. Times* 12 Jan. D14 We haven't got a smoking pistol. Unfortunately, everyone is zeroing in on this as a cause, but the case isn't that strong.

smoky, *a.* and *sb.* Add: **smokie** (also *Sc.* as *sb.*), **smokey** (common in *U.S.*). **A.** *adj.* **3. c.** Foggy, misty. Now *rare* exc. in proper names. *U.S.*

1769 in *Essex Inst. Hist. Coll.* (1877) XIV. 262 This week much smoky. **1824** J. DODDRIDGE *Notes on Virginia* xxxi. 266 The smokey time commenced, and lasted for a considerable number of days. **1825** J. NEAL *Bro. Jonathan* I. 105 See'd him jess now, comin' over the smoky mountain there. **1971** *N.Y. Times Encycl. Almanac 1971* 243/1 In East Tennessee are the Great Smoky and Cumberland Mountains of the Appalachian range.

5. (Further examples.)

1951 E. DAVID *French Country Cooking* 26 The smoky wines of Pouilly-sur-Loire. **1978** *Sunday Times* (Colour Suppl.) 19 Feb. 17/3 *Smoky*, a delicate aroma that is found in several white wines, often originating from the volcanic soil, and also on the bouquet of Madeira as a result of the latter's special *estufado* heat treatment.

b. *fig.* Of the sound of a musical instrument or voice.

1958 G. BOATFIELD in P. Gammond *Decca Bk. Jazz* xxiv. 312 Noone's deceptively easy clarinet and Kelly's smoky trumpet are noteworthy. **1966** *Cavalier Daily* (Univ. of Virginia) 11 Nov. 1 The smooth, smoky sound of the Platters combined with their expressive hand jive will entertain students from 9 to 1 Friday night.

7. (Further examples.)

1869 [see *KENTISH *a.* 3 b]. **1934** WEBSTER, *Smoky-blue*. **1934** *Discovery* June 166/2 Plain burnished red ware and smoky grey pottery. **1974** *Men's Wear* 29 Aug. 17/2 Smokey-navy motifs on beige. **1976** H. TRACY *Death in Reserve* xi. 87 A smoky-blue spring evening. **1980** *New Age* (U.S.) Oct. 58 (Advt.), Danish Souperbag..In wilderness rust brown, battleship grey, parrot green, smokey black.

12. *smoky-tasting, -voiced, -winged.*

1925 H. CRANE *Let.* 28 Feb. (1965) 199 Delicious smoky tasting sardines. **1973** J. J. MCKELVEY *Man against Tsetse* ii. 67 He did, however, add entomology to his accomplishments by studying the life cycle of the dark-eyed, smoky-winged tsetse that was causing nagana in Zululand. **1976** *New Yorker* 29 Mar. 6/3 A promising, smoky-voiced jazz and rhythm-and-blues singer.

B. *sb.* **2.** (Further examples.)

1948 R. DE KERCHOVE *International Maritime Dict.* 690/2 *Scotch haddie* (*U.S.*)... In Great Britain called smokie. **1965** *Arbroath Guide* 3 Apr. 4 The older generation argue that the old time 'smokie' is a haddock freshly caught by line and smoked in the Arbroath way. **1974** *Sunday Tel.* 23 June 15/5 Let us make the distinction between the genuine Arbroath smokie, which gets its colour from the actual smoke when the fish is cured, and the common kipper. **1976** *Daily Record* (Glasgow) 29 Nov., Arbroath's famous 'smokie' industry will be hit by the ban on catching haddock in the North Sea.

4. See *SMOKEY BEAR.

smole (smōᵘl), joc. var. of SMILE *sb.*[1] or *v.* or *smiled* (pa. t. of SMILE *v.*). Now *rare* or *Obs.*

1858 J. C. THOMSON *Almae Matres* i. 5 Tick, Esquire, rose at our entrance, smole blandly, and mumbled something to the effect that he was glad..to make our acquaintance. **1894** 'MARK TWAIN' in *St. Nicholas* Mar. 400/2 Then he smole a smile that spread around and covered the whole Sahara. **1909** J. R. WARE *Passing Eng.* 227/1 *Smole*.., a grotesque variation of smile. **1937** PARTRIDGE *Dict. Slang* 789/1 (He) smoled a smile (or smole).

smolyaninovite (smǫlyănī·nǒvəit). *Min.* Also **smolia-.** [ad. Russ. *smolyaninovit* (L. K. Yakhontova 1956, in *Dokladȳ Akad. Nauk SSSR* CIX. 849), f. the name of N. A. *Smolyaninov*: see -ITE[1].] A hydrated arsenate of iron, cobalt, nickel, and other metals found as a yellow oxidation product of cobalt and nickel ores.

1957 *Chem. Abstr.* LI. 4885 (*heading*) Smolyaninovite, a new mineral. **1977** *Mineral. Mag.* XLI. 388 A specimen purchased by the [British] Museum in 1927..from Schneeberg, Saxony, has been found to carry small amounts of smolyaninovite, constituting a third occurrence of the mineral. **1981** K. FRYE *Encyl. Mineral.* 715/2 *Smolianinovite*, orth.

smon (smǫn). *Path.* Also **SMON.** [Acronym f. the initial letters of *s*ubacute *m*yelo-*o*ptico-

*n*europathy.] A disease of the nervous system characterized by recurrent motor, sensory, and visual symptoms, freq. including numbness of the legs.

1971 *Lancet* 3 Apr. 697/1 The Japanese S.M.O.N. syndrome occurs in patients who have not taken clioquinol or other hydroxyquinolines. **1977** *Arab Times* 31 Oct. 2/3 In June last year, the two firms admitted that the drug quinoform, also called chinoform, had 'a causal relationship' with a disease of the nervous system called smon (subacute myelo-optico-neuropathy), which affects limb movement and can cause blindness. **1979** *Guardian Weekly* 1 Apr. 15/4 Smon (subacute myelo-optico-neuropathy) outbreaks in several communities [in Japan] occurred as early as the 1950s. **1982** *Lancet* 25 Sept. 716/2 They stated that rise and fall in SMON was synchronous with consumption of clioquinol... This is a continuing controversy.

smooch, *sb.*[1] (Earlier example.)

1825 J. NEAL *Bro. Jonathan* II. 46 Cowhide shoes—newly greased..which left a 'smooch' upon whatever they came near.

smooch (smūtʃ), *sb.*[2] orig. and chiefly *U.S.* [f. *SMOOCH *v.*[3] or var. SMOUCH *sb.*[1]] A kiss; a fondling embrace or caress, a cuddle. Also, slow, close dancing; (music suitable for) a dance of this nature. Freq. *attrib.*

1942 BERREY & VAN DEN BARK *Amer. Thes. Slang* § 847/4 *Smooch*, a kiss. *Ibid.* § 830/5 *Smoochbuggy*,..an automobile used for 'necking'. **1945** *Tacoma* (Washington) *News Tribune* 27 Oct. 3/3 I'd rather have hootch And a bit of a smooch—The air corps will always do me. **1957** *Time* 2 Sept. 28/3 Ethel Merman and Fernando Lamas..found that their nightly onstage smooch grated too harshly on their star-crossed sensibilities. **1971** *New Scientist* 24 June 730/1 Two Antipodean couples joined their lips in a long-term kiss aimed at beating the standing smooch record. **1973** J. WAINWRIGHT *Pride of Pigs* 43 The smooch classics—*Mood Indigo, Lazy River, Georgia On My Mind*—slow and draggy. **1977** *Record Mirror* 16 Apr. 27/5 Perfect even-tempoed bland MOR until it slows up for a smooch.

smooch (smūtʃ), *v.*[2] *dial.* and *colloq.* [App. an altered form of MOOCH, MOUCH *v.*] **1.** *intr.* To sneak, creep; to wander or prowl *round* (somewhere).

1904 in *Eng. Dial. Dict.* **1950** R. MOORE *Candlemas Bay* 223 Then he realized his mother would probably send him back for the dish, so he smooched glumly in to retrieve it. **1960** I. JEFFERIES *Dignity & Purity* v. 76 'What are your plans?' 'I'm going to smooch round here, if that's all right.'

2. *trans.* To steal.

1941 J. M. CAIN *Mildred Pierce* xi. 229 Then she..went over to the cash box, and smooched four $10 bills.

smooch (smūtʃ), *v.*[3] orig. *U.S.* [Var. SMOUCH *v.*[1]] *intr.* To kiss; to neck or pet; *spec.* while dancing to a lazy, romantic melody.

1932 *Amer. Speech* VII. 336 *Smooch*,..to kiss. **1937** *Sat. Even. Post* 20 Feb. 89/2 Once upon a time you 'spooned',..but now you may 'smooch' or 'perch'. **1952** R. V. WILLIAMS *Hard Way* ii. 19 Maybe she smooched with them. Maybe she didn't. **1959** *Encounter* May 22/1 She would find her mother smooching away with some man. **1964** L. NKOSI *Rhythm of Violence* 41 Mary and Gama are sharing a studio couch on which they are smooching quietly. **1972** 'M. YORKE' *Silent Witness* ii. 39 'I prefer to smooch to subtle melodies,' said Patrick, clasping her closely.

Hence **smoo·ching** *vbl. sb.* and *ppl. a.*

1941 J. SMILEY *Hash House Lingo* 51 *Smooching*, employee making love to one of the opposite sex while on duty. **1951** S. J. PERELMAN in *New Yorker* 20 Oct. 29/2 No parenthetical smooching is going to upset her applecart. **1962** *John o' London's* 16 Aug. 163/3 When Miss Baxter pokes her head through the window of a smooching couple's car..it's merely funny. **1977** *Time* 8 Aug. 29/2 Stapleton, 46, danced a bit and inspired some affectionate smooching from the guest of honor. **1978** H. JOBSON *To die a Little* iii. 52 We danced on..in a cluster of smooching bodies.

smoocher (smū·tʃəɹ). orig. *U.S.* [f. *SMOOCH *v.*[3] + -ER[1].] **a.** One who smooches. **b.** A song or piece of music suitable for accompanying slow, close dancing.

1946 *Sun* (Baltimore) 18 May 2/6 Seeking out 'necking spots' to catch 'smoochers'. **1976** *Record Mirror* 3 Apr. 19/5 Ella's dreamy reading of the 'How strange the change from major to minor' tune is of course an ace smoocher at any time.

smoochy (smū·tʃi), *a.* [f. *SMOOCH *v.*[3] or *sb.*[2]: + -Y[1].] Amorous, sexy; *spec.* of music: suitable for accompanying slow, close dancing.

1966 A. E. LINDOP *I start Counting* xvi. 190 Cooings and mewings and smoochy murmurings. **1971** *Woman's Own* 27 Mar. 26/2 He led me to the dance floor... The next smoochy number was played. **1976** G. SIMS *End of Web* xvii. 120 Dated, smoochy music was being played. **1980** I. WATSON *Gardens of Delights* xvii. 111 Partnering the wench in a body-rubbing, smoochy glide.

Hence **smoo·chily** *adv.*, **smoo·chiness.**

1976 'D. HALLIDAY' *Dolly & Nanny Bird* xi. 138 Three or four couples were dancing smoochily at the end of the room. **1977** E. W. HILDICK *Loop* xi. 69 I'm still not sure whether today's callous outspokenness isn't preferable to ..sly smoochiness.

smoodge, smooge (smūdʒ), *v. Austral.* and *N.Z. colloq.* [Prob. var. SMUDGE *v.*[5]: see *Smudge* v.[1] in *Eng. Dial. Dict.*] *intr.* To act in an ingratiating or fawning manner; to display affection, to behave amorously.

1906 E. DYSON *Fact'ry 'Ands* v. 54 He would smooge to me when the boss wasn't about, 'n' he said we could run a grand little show on our lonesome. **1916** C. J. DENNIS *Songs Sentimental Bloke* 39 An' there they smooge a treat, wiv pretty words Like two love-birds. **1936** M. FRANKLIN *All that Swagger* xlii. 395 They smoodge around Roger, but they order me about like a rouseabout. **1957** P. WHITE *Voss* v. 110 That is just what ladies do not take to, some big stray tom smoodgin' round their skirts. Ladies like to fall in love. **1969** *Landfall* XXIII. 27 We'd better go in now or he'll think we're smooging with each other out here. **1973** P. WHITE *Eye of Storm* x. 480 She came smoodging up at her father, and he.. kissed her.

So **smoo·dger**, a flatterer, a sycophant; **smoo·dging** *ppl. a.* and *vbl. sb.*

1898 *Bulletin* (Sydney) 30 July 32/3 Another undesirable specimen is the 'crawler'. Always carrying yarns to the boss about the other men... He is first cousin to the 'smooger', who is only superficially a white man. **1899** *Ibid.* 7 Jan. 15/1 Lawson..*feels* for the wretch who is out battling, and is kept out by servile, 'smoodging' station lifers. **1916** T. SKEYHILL *Soldier Songs from Anzac* 59 E's a sneakin', smoogin' blighter, An' 'e'll never make a fighter. **1940** F. D. DAVISON *Woman at Mill* 218 He was a mean customer,..a petty bureaucrat, and a smooger, to boot. **1953** D. M. DAVIN in *Landfall* VII. 20 He would be putting his arms around her. 'Smooging won't get you out of it,' she said. **1958** R. STOW *To Islands* i. 19 'Sister,' she sighed lovingly, hiding her face against Helen's neck. 'You old smoodger,' Helen said. **1963** B. PEARSON *Coal Flat* xvii. 304 You do your smooging somewhere else.

smooth, *a.* Add: **1. d.** In tennis, squash, etc., of one of the two sides of the racket (see quot. 1901): used as a call when the racket is spun to decide the right to serve first or to choose ends. Opp. *ROUGH *a.* 1 d.

1890 J. MARSHALL in *Tennis, Rackets, Fives* 26 *Smooth*, the front of the racket, which shows no knots. *Spin*, the decision by a racket, thrown spinning up into the air by one player, while the other calls 'rough' or 'smooth'. **1901** *Encycl. Sport* II. 621/2 *Smooth side of racket*, the side from which the twisted gut does not project. **1911** [see *ROUGH *a.* 1 d]. **1961** *Times* 4 July 11/4 The vicar's niece, whose professed ignorance of the game [*sc.* lawn tennis] was emphasized by a call of 'heads' when she should have called 'smooth'. **1973** M. RUSSELL *Double Hit* xxv. 186 Nevil spun his racket. 'Smooth,' said Colleano. 'Rough. I'll serve.'

1*. Specialized uses in the sciences. **a.** *Anat.* Applied to those muscles of vertebrates that are neither skeletal (sense *b) nor cardiac, such as those forming the gut wall, being capable of sustained but not rapid contraction and generally not under voluntary control; also to the non-striated muscle of invertebrates.

1860 BUSK & HUXLEY tr. *Kölliker's Man. Human Microsc. Anat.* I. xxxiv. 112 In the *areola* of the nipple, the smooth muscles, which are especially well developed in the female, are disposed circularly in a delicate layer. **1866** [see STRIATED *ppl. a.* 1 a]. **1927** HALDANE & HUXLEY *Animal Biol.* ii. 117 The nervous system controls striped muscle, heart muscle, smooth muscle, and glands. **1959** W. ANDREW *Textbk. Compar. Histol.* viii. 335 Alternating with these elastic tissue laminae are the masses of smooth muscle fibers with some collagenous fibers. **1962** *Lancet* 8 Dec. 1192/2 There was swelling of the vessel walls with separation of the smooth-muscle fibres. **1971** N. GARAMVÖLGYI in K. Laki *Contractile Proteins & Muscle* 83 There is a wide variety in the different smooth muscles of invertebrate and vertebrate species. **1982** *Sci. Amer.* June 48/2 It is not known how calcium causes contraction in smooth muscle (most involuntary muscle).

b. *Bacteriol.* Applied to a bacterial phenotype characterized by smooth-looking colonies of regular outline, and by cells having polysaccharide capsules.

[**1920**: see *S 4 a.] **1921** [see *ROUGH *a.* 1 e]. **1947** *Ann. Rev. Microbiol.* I. 20 The sharply distinct antigenic pattern observed in the smooth colony of encapsulated organisms is not preserved in the rough colony of unencapsulated variants. **1973** KLAINER & GEIS *Agents of Bacterial Dis.* i. 23 Smooth (S) colonies are convex, round, and slimy and are usually regarded as the 'normal' form.

c. Of a graph, function, or distribution: having no breaks, discontinuities, or irregularities.

1929 *Jrnl. du Conseil* IV. 211 The result was a smooth unimodal curve but very skew. **1933** *Econometrica* I. 242 If the values of a variable extend over a wide range, there will be little likelihood that the distribution will be smooth and unimodal. **1946** M. G. KENDALL *Adv. Theory Statistics* II. xxix. 386 The conception of a trend as a 'smooth' or 'regular' movement is equivalent to the supposition that the trend can be represented, at least locally, by a smooth mathematical function. **1959** *Listener* 2 July 14/1 The light-curve is not entirely smooth, as the increase to maximum is steeper than the subsequent drop. **1962** A. NISBETT *Technique Sound Studio* iv. 82 Microphones with a smooth response in the upper middle frequency range have come into general use. **1966** *Rep. Comm. Inquiry Univ. Oxf.* II. 400 Scales A and B bring the total college and university stipend to the same level as far as possible with a smooth college scale.

6. c. Superior, excellent, 'classy'; clever, 'neat'. *colloq.* (orig. *U.S.*).

1893 W. K. POST *Harvard Stories* 210 'Well, you'll have a rattling good time down there.' 'A smooth time, you mean,' corrected Rattleton. **1900** ADE *Fables in Slang* 43 The Benevolent Lady..derived much Joy from the Knowledge that..People were..remarking..'Say, ain't she the Smooth Article?' **1924** WODEHOUSE *Bill the Conqueror* iii. 82 How did you come to think of this stunt?.. It was the smoothest trick I ever heard of. **1942** E. B. WHITE *Let.* 31 Jan. (1976) 222 MacLeish looks a little like Doctor Devol, and he is some smooth poet. **1946** WODEHOUSE *Joy in Morning* xxvi. 237 Smooth work, Uncle Percy... There can't be many fellows about with brains like yours. **1970** C. MAJOR *Dict. Afro-Amer. Slang* 106 *Smooth*, very adept; clever.

d. Of manners, dress, etc.: stylish, suave, chic. *colloq.*

Sometimes indistinguishable from senses 6 b and *c.

1922 WODEHOUSE *Jill the Reckless* xix. 285 'What charming manners Major Selby has. So polished... So smooth!' 'Smooth,' said Mr. Pilkington dourly, 'is right!' **1924** P. MARKS *Plastic Age* xi. 99 A 'smooth' boy who prided himself on his conquests. *Ibid.* xvi. 168 These were the 'smooth boys', interested primarily in clothes and 'parties'. **1942** BERREY & VAN DEN BARK *Amer. Thes. Slang* § 233/10 *Stylish*; '*chic*'...smooth. **1944** *Chicago Tribune* 10 Dec. (Grafic Mag.) 4 Watch those people whom you consider smooth; see how they dress. **1977** [see *SHARP *a.* 6* b].

12. a. *smooth breathing*: see BREATHING *vbl. sb.* 9; *smooth mouth*, the worn teeth without cusps found in horses more than seven or eight years old; so *smooth-mouthed* adj.

1746 Smooth breathing [see BREATHING *vbl. sb.* 9]. **1888** KING & COOKSON *Sound & Inflex. Gr. & Lat.* 172 The prefix *sm̥-* (together) appears as ἁ- with a smooth breathing in ἀ-δελφός. **1940** *Chambers's Techn. Dict.* 560/2 Mouth, smooth (Vet.). Smooth and polished grinding surface of the molar teeth of horses. **1955** R. HOBSON *Nothing too Good* vi. 51 Between eight and ten years of age..they [*sc.* horses] acquire what we call a smooth mouth. **1974** H. S. THOMAS *Horses* x. 183 At age nine the cusps are gone from the corner incisors. The horse is said to be smooth-mouthed.

b. smooth-head, a deep-sea fish belonging to the family Alepocephalidæ, resembling a herring with a larger body and dark-coloured skin.

1931 J. R. NORMAN *Hist. Fishes* viii. 150 A species of Smooth-head (*Leptoderma*) captured in the Bay of Bengal has been described as having the skin covered all over with a thick, opalescent, and uniformly luminous epidermis. **1969** A. WHEELER *Fishes Brit. Isles & N.-W. Europe* 123 Smooth-heads..are deep-water relatives of the herring family. **1975** *Times* 5 Dec. 12/3 Smooth-head is abundant, but..its flesh has the consistency of custard.

14. a. *smooth-cheeked* (later example), *-fleshed, -grained* (later example), *-lined, -lipped, -paced* (later example), *-perfumed, -plumed, -surfaced.*

1927 V. WOOLF in *Nation & Athenæum* Aug. 661/2 One of those smooth-cheeked, steady-eyed men. **1923** D. H. LAWRENCE *Birds, Beasts & Flowers* 41 Fig-trees, weird fig-trees Made of thick, smooth silver..Thick, smooth-fleshed silver. **1963** *Times* 16 May 16/1 Viennese singers are frequently smooth-grained in comparison with their Italian colleagues. **1930** W. B. YEATS *Wild Apples* 23 And land and strand and all are fair As that smooth-lined up-tilted boat From which the Foam-Born Queen stept out. **1605** MARSTON *Dutch Courtezan* sig. Hv, But yet when my discourse hath staide your quaking, You will be smoother lipt. **1862** G. M. HOPKINS *Vision of Mermaids* (1929), Or on the swell Tugg'd the boss'd, smooth-lipp'd, giant, Strombus-shell. *a* **1941** V. WOOLF *Captain's Death Bed* (1950) 151 A large, smooth-paced cart horse. **1923** E. SITWELL *Bucolic Comedies* 29 Smooth-perfumèd stephanotis. **1918** W. DE LA MARE *Motley* 72 The smooth-plumed bird. **1883** 'MARK TWAIN' *Life on Miss.* xxv. 274 The Devil's Tea Table..a great smooth-surfaced mass of rock. **1967** M. CLARK in *Coast to Coast* 1965–6 34 Fluffy, bouncy balls and not those smooth-surfaced..ones.

smooth, *adv.* Add: **2. a.** *smooth-oiled, -rounded, -trodden, -worn.*

1955 E. POUND *Classic Anthol.* I. 49 Double teams matched, smooth-oiled reins. **1916** D. H. LAWRENCE *Amores* 102 A new night pouring down shall swill Us away in an utter sleep, until We are one, smooth-rounded. **1958** R. GRAVES *Steps* 249 There are some words carry a curse with them: Smooth-trodden, abstract, slippery vocables. **1920** A. HUXLEY *Leda* 14 Smooth-worn silver, polished through the years. **1922** JOYCE *Ulysses* 525 Lifting your billowy flounces on the smooth-worn throne.

b. *smooth-rolling, -running, -weeping.*

1823 HAZLITT *Liber Amoris* III. 156 Thousands of years of smooth-rolling eternity and balmy, sainted repose. **1917** 'CONTACT' *Airman's Outings* v. 117 The smooth-running ambulances bring broken soldiers. **1941** J. MASEFIELD *Gautama the Enlightened* 14 The black-bright, smooth-running..typewriting machine. **1977** J. P. ANDERSON in Douglas & Johnson *Existential Sociol.* vi. 186 To make the screening interview a smooth-running interaction, the patient has to be able to talk about the topics the screening worker thinks are important. **1944** E. SITWELL *Green Song* 10 The amber blood of the smooth-weeping tree.

smooth, *v.* Add: **I. 1. e.** To transform or modify (a graph, distribution, or function) so as to make it smooth; to lessen irregularities or fluctuations in (something that can be represented by a graph). Cf. sense 11 c below.

1889 F. GALTON *Natural Inheritance* vii. 100 These relations] came out distinctly after I had 'smoothed' the entries. **1898** *Knowledge* 1 Oct. 235/1 Then the thirteen year series of these numbers is smoothed with averages of four. **1934** *Brit. Jrnl. Psychol.* Oct. 249 The theoretical periodogram was..made to conform... It was therefore smoothed per ten units, thus making it resemble a curve of old log. units. **1962** D. F. SHAW *Introd. Electronics* x. 203 The performance of the diode rectifier is improved by the use of a filter circuit to smooth the output. **1979** *Sci. Amer.* May 52/3 This generalization is strictly statistical, because our analysis has smoothed the gas distribution... It does not rule out the existence of isolated patches of vigorous star formation.

II. 11. b. Also, = sense 1 a in Dict.

1900 *20th Ann. Rep. U.S. Geol. Surv.* II. 196 A belt of country marked by landslide topography which was gradually smoothed out, owing to the decay and erosion of the fallen blocks of basalt.

c. = sense 1 e above; also, to lessen (irregularities or fluctuations) in something which can be described by a graph, esp. a time series.

1933 *Econometrics* I. 238 An elaborately weighted moving function..prevents the resulting curve from smoothing out fluctuations. **1945** L. A. MAVERICK *Time Series Analysis* p. vii, In smoothing out the monthly cycle..Wardwell's moving cyclical average of changing length is used. **1957** *Encycl. Brit.* XXIII. 432/1 By the provision of storage facilities at the source and of the main aqueduct service reservoirs, these various fluctuations [in demand] can be smoothed out. **1962** A. NISBETT *Technique Sound Studio* i. 30 At the 'back' [of the microphone] the response is fairly flat—the effect of the pad being to smooth out the peak. **1971** *Sci. Amer.* Oct. 69/1 Tests of nuclear weapons have shown that atmospheric mixing is rapid and that irregularities in composition are smoothed out after a few years. **1978** *Daily Tel.* 6 Jan. 17 The Americans will be very reluctant to do more than smooth out fluctuations in the exchange rate.

smooth-bore. Add: **1.** (Earlier examples.)

1812 *Niles' Weekly Reg.* II. 398/1 It was the best smooth bore he ever shot with in his life. **1834** W. A. CARRUTHERS *Kentuckians in N.Y.* I. 21 Your smooth bores waste a deal of powder and lead.

2. a. (Earlier example.)

1799 in *Deb. Congress U.S.* (1851) 7th Congress 2 Sess., App. 1402 One had a rifle, and the other a smooth-bore piece.

smoothed, *ppl. a.* Add: **2. b.** Of graphs, statistical fluctuations, etc. Cf. *SMOOTH *v.* 1 e, 11 c.

1888 *Proc. R. Soc.* XLV. 140 These smoothed values were obtained by plotting the observed values, after transmuting them as..described into their respective Q units. **1903** *Science* 17 July 91/2 Smoothed rainfall curve for the British Isles. **1933** *Econometrica* I. 240 The points of inflection should be marked in the smoothed curve, to serve as guides to the desired smoothing line. **1962** D. F. SHAW *Introd. Electronics* x. 204 The advantage of this circuit is that the smoothed d.c. output voltage has a high value and the residual ripple voltage may be reduced to a fraction of 1%. **1964** K. G. LOCKYER *Introd. Critical Path Anal.* viii. 78 Clearly it is desirable to try to shift some of the earlier over-load into the later under-load. If this could be completely done, then the load would be said to be 'smoothed'.

smoothen, *v.* Add: **3. b.** Also const. *back, out.*

1913 R. KANE *Good Friday to Easter Sunday* iii. 126 She may smoothen back His hair, thick and heavy with crimson moisture. **1945** N. COLLINS *London belongs to Me* II. xx. 189 The sound which it made as he smoothened it out flat.

smoothie (smū·ði), *sb.* and *a. colloq.* (orig. *U.S.*). Also **smoothy.** [f. SMOOTH *a.* + -Y[6], -IE.] **A.** *sb.* A person who is 'smooth' (sense 6 in Dict. and Suppl.); one who is suave or stylish in conduct or appearance: usu. a man. Occas. with unfavourable sense: a slick but shallow or insinuating fellow, a fop.

1929 *Princeton Alumni Weekly* 24 May 981/3 *Smoothie* ..indicates *savoir faire*, a certain *je ne sais quoi*... Clothes do much to make the *smoothie*. **1932** B. G. DE SYLVA et al. (*song-title*) You're an old smoothie. **1939** R. CHANDLER *Big Sleep* xxv. 213 It might be a smoothie in the detective business trying to get a noseful of somebody else's case. **1943** HUNT & PRINGLE *Service Slang* 60 *Smoothie*, a chap who fancies himself as a ladies' man. **1954** P. FRANKAU *Wreath for Enemy* I. i. 5 Laurent is a smoothy, and I do not see how anybody could be in love with him. **1957** *Listener* 14 Nov. 801/2 A television smoothie. (This last is now gossip-writer's English for a slick commentator or smiling interviewer.) **1958** C. RICE *April Robin Murders* v. 54 This poetic-looking smoothie makes a thing out of marrying women with money. **1960** *Spectator* 8 July 66 The usual smoothie with a pseudo-American accent. **1973** *Guardian* 4 May 31/2 '*They* think there's nothing but muck and pit heaps up here,' say North-easterners, referring to the southern 'smoothies'. **1979** H. JENKINS *Culture Gap* I. iv. 24, I have nothing but contempt for the international art market. It is a racket none the better for being operated by cultivated smoothies.

B. *adj.* = SMOOTH *a.* 6 in Dict. and Suppl.

1959 I. JEFFERIES *Thirteen Days* iv. 54 Stern..was a real smoothie boy..like what I intended to be when I grew up. **1972** *Times* 7 Sept. 19/1 Max's prime characteristic..is being very tactful without being at all smoothy. **1974** N. FREELING *Dressing of Diamond* 101 Bernard.. is good at the smoothie commercial stuff.

smoothing, *vbl. sb.* Add: **1. a.** (Further examples.) Also with *out.*

1929 *Jrnl. du Conseil* IV. 228 The purpose of the smoothing was to eliminate minor fluctuations of the character of lunar (monthly) cycles which are known to exist in the sardine. **1933** *Econometrica* I. 238 (*heading*) Time series: their analysis by successive smoothings. **1939** *Proc. R. Soc.* A. CLXXI. 81 The smoothing out of the stress distribution becomes less and less effective, and the maximum stress at the stress peaks rises. **1955** L. D. LANDAU in W. Pauli *Niels Bohr* 68 The great difficulties which arise in a physical 'smoothing-out' of particles, as opposed to a purely formal 'smoothing-out'..are well known. **1970** *Nature* 22 Aug. 824/1 The output signal [was] digitally recorded after smoothing with a 1 s time constant electronic filter.

b. (Later examples.)

1935 *Harvard Univ. Summ. Ph.D. Theses* 288 Under smoothing are included all monophthongizations and monophthong-retaining effects which are due to WG (originally) velar consonants. **1977** *Archivum Linguisticum* VIII. 79 It seems most probable that S[econd] F[ronting] was a rather late change, taking place after *i*-umlaut had occurred although almost certainly before back mutation and smoothing.

2. Also designating devices for reducing ripple in electrical signals, as *smoothing capacitor, choke, circuit, filter.*

1959 *Engineering* 20 Feb. 230/2 A small smoothing capacitor in the reading amplifier prevents the output from falling to zero during the transport of the wiper from one contact to the next. **1941** *P.O. Electr. Engineers Jrnl.* XXXIV. 118/1 With the development of floating battery power supply systems in telephone exchanges and repeater stations, there is a considerable demand for smoothing chokes. **1940** *Chambers's Techn. Dict.* 780/1 Smoothing circuit. **1975** G. J. KING *Audio Handbk.* iv. 96 Separate smoothing and filtering circuits are used for the supplies of the preceding stages and for the preamplifier stages of the control section. **1941** *P.O. Electr. Engineers Jrnl.* XXXIV. 118/1 The cost of the complete smoothing filter may be comparable with that of the associated motor-generator set.

smooth-leaved, *a.* Add: *smooth-leaved elm*, a large tree, *Ulmus carpinifolia*, native to Europe, North Africa, and western Asia, and distinguished by smooth leaves with shiny upper surfaces.

1731 P. MILLER *Gardeners Dict.* s.v. Ulmus; folio glabro..The Smooth-leav'd or Witch-Elm. **1811** J. E. SMITH *Eng. Bot.* XXXII. 2248 (*heading*) Smooth-leaved, or Wych Elm. **1913** ELWES & HENRY *Trees Gt. Brit. & Ireland* VII. 1887 Smooth-leaved Elm... A tree, with a straight bole, and wide-spreading branches. **1971** *Country Life* 23 Dec. 1772/2 We can be pretty certain that these trees..are forms of the smooth-leaved elm.

smoo·th-talk, *v. colloq.* (orig. *U.S.*). [f. SMOOTH *a.*] *trans.* To address or persuade with bland, specious language. Also, to win (one's way) by smooth-talking.

1950 A. LOMAX *Mister Jelly Roll* (1952) 205 If a cop stopped him he could smooth-talk his way right out of it just like they were relatives. **1956** *Sun* (Baltimore) 2 Mar. 19/6 A Michigan man was accused today of smooth-talking bankers..into sending him cash by posing over the telephone as a depositor. **1958** J. WAIN *Contenders* 171 She was transferring herself..as a result of being smooth-talked into it. **1960** *Washington Post* 2 Nov. 3/2 He and his wife had been 'smooth-talked' and later threatened. **1967** 'E. LATHEN' *Murder against Grain* ii. 18, I let him smooth-talk me into doing the Sloan's errands. **1979** F. OLBRICH *Sweet & Deadly* viii. 98 The practised politician smooth-talking his way round an awkward question.

‖ **smørbrød** (smö·rbröd). Also **smorbrodt.** [Norw.: cf. *SMØRREBRØD.] A Norwegian open sandwich: also *collect.*

1933 M. LOWRY *Ultramarine* ii. 96 Nevermore sit in a lunar park in Aalesund, holding each other's hands, or eating smorbrodt. **1980** R. BARNARD *Death in Cold Climate* i. 9 He..collected on a plate a ham smørbrød and a cheese roll.

smorgasbord (smōə·ɹgăsbōəɹd). Also ‖ **smörgåsbord,** *erron.* **smörgosbrod,** etc. [a. Sw., f. *smörgås* (slice of) bread and butter (f. *smör* butter, cogn. w. SMEAR *sb.* + *gås* goose, lump of butter) + *bord* BOARD *sb.*, table: cf. *SMØRREBRØD.] **1.** The Swedish hors d'œuvres, typically comprising a cold table of open sandwiches served with an assortment of delicacies; also provided as a separate meal or buffet.

1893 *Figaro* (Chicago) 26 Jan. 345/1 In every household..before sitting down to dinner an appetizer, or *smörgos-brod*, is partaken of. **1895** *Baedeker's Norway, Sweden & Denmark* p. xxiii, The Smörgåsbord or Brännvinsbord, where various relishes, bread-and-butter, and liqueurs are served by way of stimulant to the appetite, is peculiar to Sweden. **1926** *Ladies' Home Jrnl.* Nov. 150/2 The 'Smorgesbord', or bountifully supplied relish table, is a Scandinavian institution, though it is said the custom originated in ancient Russia. **1936** *Discovery* Apr. 109/2 Meals, which begin with the smörgåsbord, as in Sweden, are..excellent and cheap. **1948** 'J. TEY' *Franchise Affair* i. 17 'Sandwiches without tops' the girl called them. 'Smorgasbord'. **1959** *Good Food Guide 1959–60* 314 The first level offers a Swedish—Swedish, not Danish, because hot hors d'œuvres are included—smorgasbord at 8/6. **1968** [see *CHUCK WAGGON]. **1975** D. RAMSAY *Descent into Dark* ii. 66 The smorgasbord restaurant Joyce had been fond of. **1978** *New York* 3 Apr. 19 (Advt.), Wine & Dine! Gourmet menu. Smorgasbord..2 bars. Duty-free prices.

2. *fig.* A medley, miscellany; a rich variety or selection.

1948 MENJOU & MUSSELMAN *It took Nine Tailors* xxii. 176 Instead the studio offered me the lead in a piece of *smörgåsbord* called *The Sorrows of Satan*, a novel by Marie Corelli. **1961** *Encounter* Apr. 56/2 The messy smörgasbord of his hysterical whimsical ideas. **1969** T. E. B. HOWARTH *Culture, Anarchy & Public Schools* iii. 55 The smorgasbord system is a form of shorthand to describe the multiplicity of optional 'subjects' pupils in American high schools elect to study. **1978** M. PUZO *Fools Die* xii. 129 Everyday Magazines..was a group of publications that drowned the American public with information, pseudoinformation, sex and pseudosex... A real smorgasbord.

'smorning (smōə·ɹnɪŋ), colloq. or dial. abbrev. of 'this morning'.

1932 S. GIBBONS *Cold Comfort Farm* xx. 267 She took on something awful about Miss Judith going off 'smorning. **1967** 'G. DOUGLAS' *Death went Hunting* xviii. 155 Well, 'smorning Mr Bolton comes over to me. **1973** J. MANN *Only Security* xiv. 184, I found her, I did. 'Smorning, when I come rabbiting.

‖ **smørrebrød** (smö·rəbrōð). Also **smörrebröd.** [Da., f. *smør* butter + *brød* BREAD *sb.*[1]; cf. *SMØRBRØD.] A Danish open sandwich; also *collect.*

1902 M. THOMAS *Denmark, Past & Present* II. xviii. 133 Your true Dane takes a piece of bread, plasters it with butter, then searches..for the slice of meat or fish he prefers and puts it on the bread and butter... This is called 'smörrebröd' and is the national dish. **1932** G. BRÖCHNER *Wayfarer in Denmark* vi. 76 All Danish cafés ..have..a 'Smörrebröds seddel': a long narrow card with a list of the different kinds of Smörrebröd served. **1959** *Good Food Guide 1959–60* 242 It has opened a Scandinavian smörrebröd cold table in its basement. **1975** tr. *Melchior's Sleeper Agent* (1976) III. 247, I will make you some *Smørrebrød*, Rudi, the kind you like.

smother, *sb.* Add: **1. a.** (Later *fig.* example in literary use.)

1975 N. NICHOLSON *Wednesday Early Closing* ix. 176 A dull smother of hopelessness hung over the town like the smutch from a smoking rubbish dump.

2. e. *N.Z.* An incident in which sheep are lost by suffocation caused by others falling on top of them, as during a round-up.

1930 L. G. D. ACLAND *Early Canterbury Runs* 1st Ser. vi. 128 They once had a bad smother there. *Ibid.* Mt. Peel was unlucky with smothers. **1933** —— in *Press* (Christchurch, N.Z.) 2 Dec. 15/7, I believe there was a still worse smother [of sheep] on a station called Roxburgh in Otago. **1949** S. S. CRAWFORD *Sheep & Sheepmen of Canterbury* v. 42 Mt. Peel [station] was unlucky with smothers [of sheep].

3*. *Rugby Football.* A high tackle in which the player 'smothers' (sense *3 d) his opponent. In full *smother-tackle.*

1927 WAKEFIELD & MARSHALL *Rugger* iv. 248 Hoping ..that by the swiftness of your advance you may get him in a smother-tackle, taking both man and ball. **1929** *Illustr. Sporting & Dramatic News* 19 Oct. 183 (*caption*) Getting the ball away from a smother. **1960** E. S. & W. J. HIGHAM *High Speed Rugby* v. 48 *The Smother Tackle.* This tackle is a high tackle and is used when you want to prevent a player from passing or touching down.

smother, *v.* Add: **I. 1. a.** (Later *fig.* example.)

1944 [see *BLANKET. *sb* 2 c].

b. Also *spec.* of sheep, to suffocate others by falling on top of them, as during a round-up; to cause (sheep) to die in this manner. *N.Z.*

1871 M. A. BARKER *Christmas Cake in Four Quarters* IV. iii. 290, I had to bring 'em [*sc.* the mob of sheep] down uncommon easy, for it was a nasty place, and I didn't want half of 'em to be smothered in the creek. **1930** L. G. D. ACLAND *Early Canterbury Runs* 1st Ser. vi. 128 They once smothered 5000 in the gully. *a* **1948** —— *Ibid.* (1951) 397 Run sheep..are very easy to s[mother] on broken hill ground... They s[mothere]d 1,200 once..at Mount Peel.

3. c. (Earlier example.) Also in *Association Football* (see quot. 1954).

1845 N. WANOSTROCHT *Felix on Bat* I. iv. 18 Should it be pitched an inch too far, be sure to get well out at it, and smother it. **1954** F. C. AVIS *Soccer Dict.* 112 *Smother,* to put oneself in the way of an opponent's shot, especially by the goalkeeper advancing from his goal towards the opponent. **1976** *Northumberland Gaz.* 26 Nov., His shot was smothered as the final whistle went.

d. *Rugby Football.* To tackle with a bear-like hug embracing the body and arms, preventing one's opponent from releasing the ball or touching it down.

1920 W. CAMP *Football without a Coach* vii. 132 Unless experience shows that there is a certain definite play to watch or a certain player to smother. **1928** *Sunday Times* 5 Feb. 24/7 He kicked well ahead on the slippery turf, and after Hunt had smothered the full-back, scored.

II. 11. *Boxing.* (See quot. 1954.)

1916 [see *INFIGHT *v.* 2]. **1954** F. C. AVIS *Boxing Dict.* 103 *Smother*, to prevent, by clever positioning of the arms, the development of an opponent's attack.

smother crop. [f. SMOTHER *v.*] A crop which is grown to suppress weeds.

1920 W. E. BRENCHLEY *Weeds on Farm Land* iii. 51

When a smother crop is grown it is of course necessary that the crop seed should be free from weed seed. **1937** A. F. Hill *Econ. Bot.* xv. 336 Barley is also used for hay and pasturage and as a smother crop to kill out weeds. **1973** P. A. Colinvaux *Introd. Ecol.* xxi. 303 Barley is known as a 'smother crop' because it keeps down weeds in the field. This it does with root secretions, weed killers of its own.

smothered, *ppl. a.* Add: **2. b.** (Earlier example.) See also Mate *sb.*[1] b.

1804 *Introd. Hist. & Study of Chess* v. 82 *Smothered mate* is when the king is so surrounded by his own friends that he cannot move out of check for them; and this mate is generally given by the knight.

3. (Later examples.)

1877 E. S. Dallas *Kettner's Book of Table* 369 Smothered Rabbit. This is the name given in England to boiled rabbit. It is smothered with a white onion sauce. **1923** *Mrs. Beeton's Bk. Househ. Managem.* 582 (*heading*) Chicken, Smothered (Poulet étuvé). **1948** *Good Housek. Cookery Bk.* II. 237 *Smothered tongues*... Cook preferably in a double saucepan or in a basin in a steamer. **1975** tr. *Melchior's Sleeper Agent* (1976) III. 290 A juicy steak heaped with smothered onions.

smothering, *vbl. sb.* (Examples in sense *1 b of the vb.)

1950 *N.Z. Jrnl. Agric.* July 5/2 It is undesirable to have yards on a very steep slope, as the danger of smothering, particularly with lambs in a large yard, is greatly increased. **1956** G. Bowen *Wool Away!* (ed. 2) iv. 47 The 'sheepo' must keep an eye on them for smothering, the first sign of which is sheep jumping up in the pen.

smoulder, *v.* Add: **2. d.** To show suppressed anger, hatred, resentment, etc.

1934 in Webster. **1957** L. Durrell *Justine* I. 69 She seemed to smoulder like a tar-barrel on the point of explosion. **1983** 'J. Gash' *Sleepers of Erin* iv. 42 Kurak smouldered his way to the Rolls, vibing pure hate in my direction.

smudge, *sb.*[1] Add: **4.** *smudge pan*; **smudge cell** *Med.*, a degenerate leucocyte in a blood film.

[**1935** Whitby & Britton *Disorders of Blood* iv. 89 Degenerate lymphocytes usually appear as smudges and are known as 'smear cells'.] **1937** Kracke & Garver *Dis. Blood & Atlas Hematol.* vi. 84 It has been stated that smudge forms are degenerating lymphocytes and that basket cells..are degenerating granulocytes... It seems more probable that the smudge cell is an early stage and the basket cell a later stage of the same process. **1971** W. M. Dougherty *Introd. Hematol.* iii. 70/1 Most often the bare nuclei that we call smudge cells or basket cells are in fact the bare nuclei of the lymphocytes. **1798** J. Constable *Let.* 2 Dec. (1964) II. 16, I should be glad of the smudge pan as soon as convenient.

smudge, *sb.*[2] **1.** For Now *U.S.* read Now *N. Amer.* and add: esp. a smoke made to repel mosquitoes, etc. (Further examples.)

1887 E. Custer *Tenting on Plains* ii. 77 Eliza.. brought old kettles with raw cotton into our room, from which proceeded such smudges and such odors as would soon have wilted a Northern mosquito. **1939** F. P. Grove *Two Generations* v. 32 If there had been a moon, a person coming over the hills would have seen that smudge as a perfectly level sheet closing the bowl like a lid. **1971** [see *repellent *a.* 2 d].

2. a. (Earlier and later examples.)

1806 A. Henry in E. Coues *New Light on Early Hist. Greater Northwest* (1897) I. 287 The women closed the openings of the cabins, and made a smudge inside. **1936** B. Brooker *Think of Earth* III. vii. 278 'We'll make a smudge,' said Bundy, and..began gathering twigs and handfuls of scorched grass. **1952** *Chambers's Jrnl.* Aug. 503/2 Laddash greeted her, squatting in the smoke of a smudge against the mosquitoes. **1959** [see *punky *a.* a].

b. *attrib.* *smudge bonfire, fire* (earlier and later examples), *-smoke*; designating containers for the smouldering fire, as *smudge box, can, kettle, pot*, etc.

1846 *Knickerbocker* XXVIII. 241 You make a large 'smudge' fire outside that the smoke may drive these [insects] away. **1860** *Harper's Mag.* Oct. 584/1 Through the smudge-smoke issuing from the half-breeds' quarters we could catch glimpses of dark eyes. **1882** G. C. Eggleston *Wreck of Red Bird* 55 'What is a "smudge box", Ned?' 'Simply a shallow box of earth set upon a post, to build a smudge upon.' **1902** S. E. White *Blazed Trail* xx. 148 Thorpe's old tin pail was pressed into service as a smudge-kettle. **1903** *Outing* XLIII. 166/1 Other settlers keep the smudge-pot going and live in smoke. **1909** H. Bindloss *Lorimer of Northwest* 3 The dun smoke of a smudge-fire shows that Harry is in prairie fashion protecting our stock. **1923** F. Waldo *Down Mackenzie* 116 One sees the horses after a trip..released for rest, huddling to windward of smudge bonfires, or in default of these standing in a forlorn group together to get in one another's shade. **1944** *Living off Land* ii. 31 Professional beekeepers use a small smoke bellows, but the best substitute is to light a smudge fire and let the smoke drift past the entrance to the hive. **1954** A. M. Bezanson *Sodbusters invade Peace* 134 A smudge can was my constant companion in or in front of the house. **1965** H. Johnson *Bay of Pigs* III. i. 106 While one of the men put up the signs, another lighted the smudge pots. **1978** J. A. Michener *Chesapeake* 18 If he kept a smudge-fire going..he could survive. *Ibid.* 36 The mosquitoes were terrible..and people stayed close to smudge pots when the sun went down.

smudge, *v.*[1] Add: Hence **smu·dging** *vbl. sb.*[3] (in quot. *fig.*).

1873 J. Brown *Let.* 27 Dec. (1912) 288, I always feel insulted by these smudgings and besmearings.

smudge, *v.*[2] **1. b.** For *U.S.* read *N. Amer.* and add examples. Also, to cause (a fire) to smoke; to drive (mosquitoes, etc.) *away* by smoke. Now *rare*.

1860 *Harper's Mag.* Aug. 296/2 The blankets were spread in the tents, the tents smudged or mosquito nets hung. **1866** *Ibid.* Jan. 265/2 The others sat by the fire and 'smudged' it. **1880** D. Currie *Lett. of Rusticus* 56/1 Before going to bed we smudged the tent, which made the mosquitoes so drunk that they did not molest us again before morning. **1921** *Daily Colonist* (Victoria, B.C.) 30 Oct. 21/1, I piled on some brush and tried to smudge 'em away.

c. Among North American Indians, to smoke (pottery) in order to give it a black shiny finish. See also *smudging *vbl. sb.*[2]

1936 K. M. Chapman *Pottery of Santo Domingo Pueblo* 7 The ware turns light red in firing, though this is often purposely smudged to a more or less dense black after firing is complete.

Hence **smu·dging** *vbl. sb.*[2] (*spec.* in sense *1 c of the vb.).

1846 E. W. Farnham *Life in Prairie Land* II. x. 314 This process is more briefly designated by its technical name of '*smudging*'. **1955** Bushnell & Digby *Anc. Amer. Pottery* iv. 32 In these examples the colour is due rather to smudging with carbon in the fire than to chemical reaction. **1973** A. H. Whiteford *North Amer. Indian Arts* 15 Smudging is achieved by smothering the fire with fine damp manure.

smudge, *v.*[4] Add: So **smu·dging** *vbl. sb.*[1]

1789 W. Maclay *Jrnl.* 11 May (1890) 30 He will.. dimple his visage with the most silly kind of half smile which I can not well express in English. The Scotch-Irish have a word that hits it exactly—*smudging*.

smudgeless (smʌ·dʒlès), *a.* [f. Smudge *v.*[1] or *sb.*[1] + -less.] **a.** That will not smudge or smear. **b.** Without a smudge, clean.

1913 *Chambers's Jrnl.* Mar. 270/1 So-called indelible and smudgeless inks have been placed upon the market. **1924** W. Deeping *Three Rooms* xxxvi. 320 She had dealt with the silver, and it lay bright and smudgeless on a sheet of green baize. **1976** *Sci. Amer.* Jan. 15/2 (Advt.), Its built-in silent recorder prepares a permanent cardiotocogram on smudgeless thermal paper.

smug, *v.*[1] Add: **3.** [Perh. a different word: cf. Smuggle *v.*[2]] *intr.* To caress, fondle. *dial. rare.*

1813 E. Picken *Poems* I. 176 We'll cuddle baith amang the fug An' while we hug, an' kiss, an' smug, I'll haud thee firm by ilka lug. **1922** Joyce *Ulysses* 308 Blind to the world up in a shebeen in Bride street after closing time..and hugging and smugging.

smug, *v.*[2] **4.** (Earlier example.)

1887 J. W. Horsley *Jottings from Jail* i. 6 We used to go and smug snowy (steal linen) that was hung out to dry.

smuggery (smʌ·gəri). *nonce-wd.* [f. Smug *a.* + -ery.] The quality or condition of being smug, or an instance of this; smugness.

1928 A. Huxley *Point Counter Point* xi. 170 Enlargements,..by contrast with our bourgeois and Pecksniffian smuggeries. **1961** G. Frankau in P. Frankau *Pen to Paper* 221, I must pray to be redeemed from the sin of Smuggery.

smugging, *vbl. sb.*[1] (In Dict. s.v. Smug *v.*[1]) (Later *poet.* example.)

1932 Auden *Orators* III. 104 Only hard On smugging, smartness, and self-regard.

smush (smʌʃ), *sb.*[1] [Alteration of Mush *sb.*[1]: cf. Smash *sb.*[1]] **1.** = Mush *sb.*[1] 3 a; a messy pulp. *dial.*

1825 Jamieson *Sc. Dict.* (Suppl.) II. 429/1 *Gane to smush*, reduced to a friable or crumbled state, like potatoes too much boiled, &c. **1929** D. H. Lawrence *Pansies* 130 Then suddenly the mastodon rose with the wonderful lady And trampled all the listeners to a smush.

2. The mouth; = *mush *sb.*[1] 3 d. *U.S. slang. rare.*

1930 [see *haul *v.* 3 c]. **1935** D. Runyon in *Hearst's* Jan. 160/2 He grabs Miss Amelia Bodkin in his arms and kisses her kerplump on the smush.

smut, *sb.* Add: **7.** (sense 1) *smut machine* (earlier example), *mill*; (sense 5) *smut book, shop*, etc.; *smut-hunting* ppl. adj.; **smut-hound** [cf. *hound *sb.*[1] 4 e] *colloq.*, one who seeks to censor or suppress smut (sense 5), esp. in literature.

1818 *Niles' Reg.* XV. 80/1 *A smut mill*, for cleaning wheat of smut, is in operation at Plattsburg. **1850** *Mary Wedlake's Priced List Farming Implements* 25 A *Smut Machine*, to clean damaged grain. **1927** H. L. Mencken *Let.* 2 Dec. (1961) 305 Of my inventions I am vainest of Bible Belt, booboisie, smut-hound and Boobus americanus. **1928** D. H. Lawrence *Let.* 9 Mar. (1962) II. 1042 Mason wrote me rather scared about the censor and smut-hunting authorities. **1930** Auden *Poems* 69 Lawrence was brought down by smut-hounds, Blake went dotty as he sang. **1930** *Publishers' Weekly* 31 May 2737/2 The confiscation of dirty picture postals and smut books. **1961** *John o' London's* 28 Sept. 357/3 The bulk of *The High Price of Pornography* is devoted to a survey of the rancid avalanche of smut magazines..which are pulped out in the States. **1965** E. L. Myles *Emperor of Peace* I. xiii. 135 He bought..a two-inch stone burr mill complete with smut mill, cleaner and water wheel. **1967** *Spectator* 1 Dec. 683/1 Eminent men of letters would not be dismissed as fools or smuthounds. **1977** *Zigzag* Apr. 28/3 He said we were turning lunchtime into a 42nd street smut shop.

smuttily, *adv.* (Later examples.)

1737 *London Mag.* May 261/2, I suppose you do not mean an old Woman, seeing that to talk smuttily to such, would be no great Insult. **1974** P. Cave *Mama* (new ed.) xiii. 109 'Got some..business, down at the docks, have you?' asked one of the drivers and leered smuttily.

smuttiness. 2. (Later example.)

1973 *Times* 16 Nov. 5/5 Viewers are also asked.. whether..smuttiness in comedy programmes..is found offensive.

Smyrna. Add: **a.** *Smyrna carpet, fig, rug.*

1881 C. C. Harrison *Woman's Handiwork* III. 165 Curtains of French make, stamped with patterns taken from Turkish or Smyrna rugs. **1897** *Sears, Roebuck Catal.* 12/2 Imported Smyrna Figs, very choice. **1904** W. D. Ellwanger *Oriental Rug* 153 Smyrna carpets, 97, 98. **1956** S. Bedford *Legacy* III. vi. 198 Smyrna figs, grapes in cotton-wool, Turkish delight. **1966** N. Freeling *Dresden Green* I. 16 Two smyrna rugs on the polished wooden floor, that he had made on winter evenings. **1977** 'R. Player' *Month of Mangled Models* vii. 125 They were treading silently on the best Aubusson in Paris although ..the little Smyrna carpet in the boudoir was worth three times as much.

b. Also, a Smyrna carpet.

1904 W. D. Ellwanger *Oriental Rug* 97 Most other carpets are of Turkish weaving..and come under the general title of Smyrnas.

Smyrniote, *a.* (Earlier example, with spelling *Smyrniot.*)

1867 C. M. Yonge *Pupils of St. John* xii. 191 The strong spirit of contending for the purity of the faith had descended from St. John upon the great Smyrniot bishop.

smythite (smaɪ·ðəit). *Min.* [f. the name of Charles H. *Smyth* (1866–1937), U.S. geologist + -ite[1].] A sulphide of iron and probably nickel found as opaque bronze-coloured crystals that are strongly magnetic and have a metallic lustre.

1956 Erd & Evans in *Jrnl. Amer. Chem. Soc.* LXXVIII. 2017/1 We have found minute, plate-like crystal inclusions in calcite crystals..to be a new iron sulfide... The mineral is named smythite (pronounced smīth'ite) in honor of Professor C. H. Smyth, Jr. **1972** *Amer. Mineralogist* LVII. 1571 Smythite was originally described by Erd *et al.*.. as having a rhombohedral structure..and Fe_3S_4 composition. These data are in error and smythite is hereby redefined... Nickel is present in all smythites present to date..and it is suggested that smythite is *not* a phase in the Fe–S system but possibly in the Fe–Ni–S system. **1976** *Minerals Sci. & Engin.* VIII. 119/2 There is still considerable doubt about the composition range and thermal stability of natural and synthetic smythite, and even whether it should be included as a phase in the iron-sulphur system.

snack, *sb.*[2] Add: **4. c.** Also, designating a place at which snacks are sold, as *snack booth, counter, shop*; in appositive use, as *snack lunch, meal*; *snack-sized* adj. Cf. *snack bar.

1976 D. Heffron *Crusty Crossed* xxii. 147, I sat alone on the sand, watching my sisters parade over to the snack booth with their boyfriends. **1977** W. J. Weatherby *Home in Dark* viii. 44 A large woman who served behind the snack counter. **1964** N. Marsh *Dead Water* iii. 85, I..had a snack lunch in the new bar. **1977** W. Hildick *Loop* ix. 47 After a snack lunch, I walked round to the School House. **1962** *Punch* 28 Nov. 773/1 We are becoming 'increasingly a nation of tea and soft-drink consumers and snack-meal eaters'. **1976** 'K. Royce' *Bustillo* xii. 157 Bustillo was eating a snack meal. **1977** *Chicago Tribune* 2 Oct. XII. 18/2 (Advt.), Partial bldg. standing due to fire, selling as is, formerly snack shop, restaurant. **1974** E. Ambler *Doctor Frigo* III. 153 A snack-sized gobbet of raw flesh.

5. *Austral. slang.* Something easy to accomplish, a 'snip'.

1941 S. J. Baker *Austral. Slang* 68 *Snack*, a certainty. **1952** T. A. G. Hungerford *Ridge & River* 138 There was nothing to it... It was a snack. **1961** M. Calthorpe *Dyehouse* 150 In Hughie's day he'd made this a snack. **1970** R. Beilby *No Medals for Aphrodite* 274 'How could I do that, Harry?' 'Easy. It'll be a snack.'

snack, *v.* Add: **1. a.** Also *fig.*, to utter or exchange sharp, snapping words or remarks. (Not in general use.) Cf. Snap *v.* 2 a.

1956 C. P. Snow *Homecomings* I. 357 They quarrelled and snacked. *Ibid.* 358 The prickles and self-assertiveness which made them snack. **1959** P. H. Johnson *Humbler Creation* xii. 85 The usual strung-up celebrations at home, with..Libby and her mother gently snacking at each other in tones of excessive goodwill. **1960** C. P. Snow *Affair* viii. 91 Irene and I glanced at each other with discomfort, a discomfort different from just looking on at her husband and my wife snacking.

Hence **sna·cking** *vbl. sb.*

1959 P. H. Johnson *Humbler Creation* v. 30 The meeting petered away as it usually did, into desultory snackings and exchanges of fellowship. **1969** W. Cahn *Out of Cracker Barrel* xxiii. 318 Premium Saltines and Ritz crackers were used as snacks long before snacking came into vogue. **1978** *Radio Times* 18–24 Feb. 67 There are three meals a day, 'more or less regular, with no snacking in between'. **1980** P. S. Powers *Obesity* ix. 219 Snacking while watching television is notorious for increasing the total daily calories ingested.

snack bar. [f. Snack *sb.*^{2} + Bar *sb.*^{1} 28.]

1. A bar or counter at which snacks are served to customers; (part of) a restaurant containing such a bar.

1930 *Punch* 16 Apr. 433 A vegetarian snack-bar. **1937** *Archit. Rev.* Nov. p. lxii (*caption*) A restaurant and snack bar in Regent Street, London. **1943** *Sun* (Baltimore) 14 Oct. 5/1 A 'snack bar', offering sandwiches and soft drinks, is maintained at the Gold street center. **1958** S. Hyland *Who goes Hang?* xliii, 210 Arthur's highly polished snack-bar. **1965** D. Henderson *Heart of Newfoundland* 54 Marty's run a chain of snack bars in different parts of the city. **1978** S. Brill *Teamsters* vii. 284 Barkett pulled the truck into a gas station snack bar for a coffee break.

2. *attrib.* Also *fig.*

1940 'G. Orwell' *Inside Whale* 138 It is a flowing, swelling prose..with rhythms in it, something quite different from the flat cautious statements and snackbar dialects that are now in fashion. **1957** *Observer* 1 Sept. 11/7 Amongst the things most desired are seats bookable by telephone, good coffee and snack-bar service. **1982** J. Scott *Uprush of Mayhem* vi. 59 The lunch-time rush for snackbar sandwiches.

sna·ckery. Also **snackerie.** [f. Snack *sb.*^{2} + -ery.] A snack bar or other public eating-place serving snacks.

1936 *Amer. Speech* XI. 374/1 *Steve's Snackerie* is the sign over a small café in Lincoln, Nebraska. **1967** *Punch* 30 Aug. 295/2 If we want better pubs, pubs catering for the family, we must..convert them all into decent snackeries, and let them stay open for at least twelve hours a day. **1969** 'R. Crawford' *Cockleburr* i. vi. 55, I..ate a nondescript pizza in a nondescript snackery. **1981** *Nordic Skiing* Jan. 48/3 The ski shop sports rentals, needed accessories, waxing area and snackery.

snacke·tte. *W. Indies.* [f. Snack *sb.*^{2} + -ette, after *launderette.] A snack bar.

1973 *Advocate-News* (Barbados) 20 Jan. 3/1 The snackette also offers a take-away service, and customers can make their orders by telephone, and then collect them. **1973** *Trinidad & Tobago Overseas Express* 28 May 11/3 Her husband was returning from a snackette in Marabella. **1974** *Sunday Advocate-News* (Barbados) 3 Mar. 16 (Advt.), Experienced person required to manage and control Snackette and Restaurant.

snaffle, *sb.*^{1} Add: **2. snaffle-mouth,** the mouth of a horse which can be managed with a snaffle alone.

1910 *Chambers's Jrnl.* 1 Oct. 703/1 A jungle-fowl which ..causes my horse to dance a gavotte.., a feat for which his snaffle mouth and indolent disposition eminently unfit him. **1932** J. E. Hance *School for Horse & Rider* x. 85 From time to time one hears of such and such a horse possessing a 'snaffle mouth'. To be entitled to such a designation the animal would have to be capable of flexing and bending to this form of bit at all paces, and such animals are extremely rare. **1977** *Horse & Hound* 14 Jan. 36/3 (Advt.), Chestnut gelding... Snaffle mouth, quiet in every way.

snaffle, *v.*^{4} Add: **2.** To appropriate, seize, catch, snatch. Also with *up*.

1895 Kipling in *Century Mag.* Dec. 273/2 A year's leave was among the things he had 'snaffled out of the campaign', to use his own words. **1915** D. O. Barnett *Let.* 7 Aug. 218, I see they've snaffled Warsaw. **1916** 'Peter' *Trench Yarns* 10 A certain airman had engine trouble up aloft and had to come down behind the German lines. Of course they snaffled him. **1928** *Sunday Express* 15 Apr. 11/6, I soon snaffled a double role in a big spectacle. **1959** *Times* 28 May 4/7 Slade threw down Cook's wicket when Meyer tried to snaffle the strike. **1964** M. McLuhan *Understanding Media* xxxi. 331 Jack discovered how to extend the TV mosaic image..seemingly snaffling up just anybody from anywhere. *a* **1974** R. Crossman *Diaries* (1975) I. 149 There was a good deal of bleating, but I got my way and was able to snaffle the Statement for myself in the process.

snafu (snæ·fu), *phr.*, *a.*, and *sb.* Also **SNAFU.** *slang* (chiefly *U.S.*, orig. *U.S. Mil.*). [Acronym f. the initial letters of *s*ituation *n*ormal: *a*ll *f*ouled (or *f*ucked) *u*p.] **A.** Used acronymically (often with an explanation) as an expression conveying the common soldier's laconic acceptance of the disorder of war and the ineptitude of his superiors.

1941 *Amer. N. & Q.* Sept. 94/2 *Snafu*, situation normal. **1943** *Amer. Mercury* Nov. 555/2 *Snafu*—politely translated as 'situation normal; all fouled up', to indicate that things are not going too well. **1946** *Amer. Jrnl. Sociol.* Mar. 419 Interestingly, the expression 'snafu', derived from this, 'Situation normal, all f—ed up', is coming into general civilian use. **1966** *Sunday Times* (Colour Suppl.) 4 Dec. 73/4 GI Jargon... *Snafu*, Situation normal, all fouled up. **1975** *Listener* 13 Mar. 349/1 There was a barrack-room mnemonic which fits the ill-starred Dieppe raid: SNAFU, or Situation Normal, All Fouled Up.

B. *adj.* Confused, chaotic.

1942 *Time* 15 June 11/1 Last week U.S. citizens knew that gasoline rationing and rubber requisitioning were snafu. **1950** 'D. Divine' *King of Fassarai* (1951) xxviii. 245 Situation Snafu... Send for the Seabees.

C. *sb.* Now usu. with *a* and *pl.* A confusion or mix-up; a hitch, mishap; muddle, confused state.

1943 *Yank* 10 Sept. 9 They worked hard and steadily, with a minimum of snafu. **1945** *Richmond* (Va.) *Times-Dispatch* 11 Dec. 10/7 Corporations struggling with the problems of reconversion, strikes, shortages and snafu in general. **1956** C. W. Mills *Power Elite* viii. 182 The key to the bureaucratic snafu that has often characterized the navy is that as the ships and the guns and the logistics became more technically complicated, the men who ran them acquired rank less by technical specialty than by seniority. **1958** 'Castle' & 'Hailey' *Flight into Danger* i. 17 It would have to be a big show in Vancouver to justify this snafu. **1963** Mrs. L. B. Johnson *White House Diary* 28 Dec. (1970) 23 Pretty soon the German plane rolled in, overshooting the red carpet by a few feet, so there was a slight snafu and they had to hop around to get onto it. **1965** *Times Lit. Suppl.* 25 Nov. 1039/1 He must have seen enough 'snafus' to make him sceptical of 'the Brass'. **1976** *Guardian* 20 Oct. 4/8 As that monumental snafu at Domadedovo attests, Aeroflot's shortcomings are also big ones. **1978** W. F. Buckley *Stained Glass* xxi. 206 Singer then rehearsed Blackford in emergency instructions to be followed in the hideous event of a snafu. **1980** B. Mason *Solo* 117 And Holy Moses, *what* a snafu! Why foul up poor, harmless, gormless Glad?

Hence as vb. *U.S. slang*, (*a*) *trans.* to mess up, to play havoc with; (*b*) *intr.* to go wrong; also **sna·fued** *ppl. a.*

1943 *Yank* 19 Nov. 9 Then the Army snafued the romance by transferring Kinser to this post. **1944** *Life* 16 Oct. 20/2 It is a symbol of SNAFU.., and a star is rated for each snafued campaign after Guadalcanal. **1953** *Sun* (Baltimore) 1 Sept. (B ed.) 17/2 Eddie had twice this season snafued a batting order and caused men to be called out for swinging out of turn. **1955** 'J. Christopher' *Year of Comet* i. 15 Of course I didn't bring you up here simply to tell you P & M snafued your psychoplan sixteen years ago. **1975** J. Grady *Shadow of Condor* i. 31 Every now and then something snafus and there is one hell of a mess. **1981** G. Markstein *Ultimate Issue* 38 My arrangements seemed snafued. I guess the lines got crossed.

snag, *sb.*^{1} Add: **1. c.** (Later examples.) Also, a disadvantage, a hitch; a defect.

1903 *N.Y. Times* 20 Oct. 1 A conference lasting three hours took place which was plain sailing until the last moment, when a snag was struck. **1923** Wodehouse *Inimitable Jeeves* vi. 66 At this point the scenario struck another snag. **1936** W. H. Saumarez Smith *Let.* 26 Dec. in *Young Man's Country* (1977) ii. 48 The only snag..was that Grindlay's had failed to send my tickets to the U.S. Club. **1940** *Economist* 27 Jan. 142/2 Mr Gandhi referred to the 'undoubted snags' in Lord Linlithgow's statement, but a pre-requisite to tackling the 'snags' is a better spirit and some measure of confidence. **1945** C. H. Ward-Jackson *Piece of Cake* 56 *Snag*, aircraft defect. **1950** J. Cannan *Murder Included* iii. 39 The house would be all right; the snag would be the skivvies. **1962** *Daily Tel.* 19 Nov. 22/5 (*heading*) Bonn Air Force finds snags in U.S. plane. **1977** B. Pym *Quartet in Autumn* v. 44 There had been a good deal of discussion..as to whether he should go by coach or by train and the advantages and snags of each method were endlessly weighed up.

d. *N. Amer.* A standing dead tree.

1904 *Dialect Notes* II. 421 There was a big snag with a woodpecker's nest in it south of our house. **1936** *Sun* (Baltimore) 1 Aug. 11/1 Flames..have turned more than 30,000 acres of once-green forest into charred and smoldering snags. **1946** B. MacDonald *Egg & I* 94 Incredibly tall, spindly snags leaned threateningly towards me. **1960** M. Sharcott *Place of Many Winds* i. 14 The sun touched the hills behind us, lighting the dead white snags that so liberally sprinkled the live spruce. **1975** *Islander* (Victoria, B.C.) 8 June 16/1 Osprey will choose a nest site atop a dead snag from which he can command a view of the habitat around him.

4. snag-boat (earlier example).

1832 *Reg. Deb. Congress U.S.* (1833) 3 May 2722 The snag boat had been employed in improving the navigation of the Mississippi.

snag (snæg), *sb.*^{4} *Austral. colloq.* [Origin unknown: cf. *Snag* vb.^{2} and sb.^{3} 6 in E.D.D.; *Snag* sb.^{1} 2 in S.N.D.] A sausage.

1941 Baker *Dict. Austral. Slang* 68 *Snags*, sausages. **1949** R. Park *Poor Man's Orange* 33 'Let's have sausages.' .. Good old snags. They were always there to be fallen back on. **1972** *Sunday Mail Mag.* (Brisbane) 26 Mar. 13/1 The dog had an uncanny capacity for nicking in to the butcher's shop, snatching a snag and getting out again. **1980** *Bulletin* (Sydney) 6 May 112/3, I make my own snags, my own pies and pasties. The Yanks love them after you've twisted their arms to try them.

snag, *v.*^{2} Add: **1. b.** (Earlier and later examples.) Also, to impede, to inconvenience. Also with *up*.

1833 *Polit. Examiner* (Shelbyville, Kentucky) 22 June 4/1, I will agree to be shot with a paper wadding if there ar' room enough in the whole clearing for a man of ordinary parts to stand on five minutes at a time, without getting snagged by some tape and cotton yarn dealer in the street. **1929** Hall & Niles *One Man's War* 131, I decided to try clipping the German's tail with my propeller or snag him in some way. **1962** *Guardian* 19 Dec. 8/3 No place to work and insufficient funds..had snagged her. **1968** C. Burke *Elephant across Border* v. 193 He was going to do whatever he could to snag things up.

4. *N. Amer.* **a.** To catch, get hold of, grab, steal, pick up. *colloq.*

1895 *Dialect Notes* I. 399 *Snag*, to steal. **1927** *Amer. Speech* II. 278/1 *Snag a pick up*, get a free ride. *Ibid.*, *Snag the current*, get the drift. **1930** D. Runyon in *Collier's* 1 Feb. 44/2 There is plenty of trouble over Lillian snagging her Peke. **1941** B. Appel in C. Grayson *New Stories for Men* 32 Red would snag a dollar or two out of me with a promise that I should take it out of his wages. **1946** Mezzrow & Wolfe *Really Blues* xii. 226 You didn't come of age on the welfare, snagging butts out of the gutter. **1962** J. Glenn in *Into Orbit* 221 Two sailors reached over with a shepherd's hook to snag the capsule. **1966** L. J. Braun *Cat who could read Backwards* (1967) xiv. 160 I'll get to the club early and snag a quiet table. **1978** J. Carroll *Mortal Friends* v. i. 503 Colman and Janet did not snag each other with their eyes at the mention of the Ritz.

b. *Sport.* To catch or field (a ball); to receive (a pass).

1942 Berrey & Van den Bark *Amer. Thes. Slang* § 679/5 *Field a ball*..snag the oval. **1968** *Washington Post* 4 July C1/3 (*caption*) Mantle was safe as Ron Hansen's throw, after snagging a line drive by Andy Kosco, was a trifle tardy. **1977** *Time* 30 May 40/2 In their place came players tailored to Big Bill's skills: quick, sure-handed guards to snag his crisp outlet passes and start the fast break rolling.

c. *Angling.* To catch (fish), *spec.* with a bare hook; to catch illicitly or improperly.

1946 *Richmond* (Va.) *Times-Dispatch* 17 Mar. B-11/2 When the herring are in in numbers, you snag a herring about every third or fourth attempt. **1960** *Washington Post* 11 Mar. D5 Unbelievable as it may sound, the herring are so thick at the height of the run that simply jerking a bare hook through the water will snag fish. **1974** *Evening Herald* (Rock Hill, S. Carolina) 18 Apr. 7/1 The largest striper of the first week of the 10 week-long derby went to Sumter's John Benenhaly who also used cut bait to snag a 26 pound, 8 ounce fish. **1979** *Globe & Mail* (Toronto) 7 Feb. 5/6 His six-man patrol is fed up with those who snag fish illegally.

5. *intr.* **a.** To strike a snag, to get caught *on* a projection or obstacle.

1866 *Harper's Mag.* Nov. 810/1 A Mississippi steamer, that snagged and went down on 'Yazoo Bend'. **1929** W. Faulkner *Sound & Fury* 3 You snagged on that nail again. Cant you never crawl through here without snagging on that nail. **1970** G. F. Newman *Sir, You Bastard* 262 He could neither see the thorn he had snagged on, nor the path by which to pull clear. **1976** M. Machlin *Pipeline* lv. 559 The rock itself..was some seventy-five yards from the ship, which apparently had snagged on an underwater rock projection some hundred feet down.

b. Of a fabric: to be rendered imperfect by a pulled thread.

1970 *Which?* Oct. 300/2 A few brands suffered slightly from pilling..and several of the Crimplene ones snagged.

6. The verb-stem in combinations, as (sense *4 c) *snag-fishing*, *-hook*, *-line*.

1936 *Sun* (Baltimore) 8 July 8/6 They..charged all three with using snag lines and snag hooks with intent to do bodily harm to the aforesaid sturgeon. **1952** B. Harwin *Home is Upriver* viii. 86 He could get an old gasboat somewhere, cheap, some fishhooks and lines enough for snag-fishing. *Ibid.* x. 99 Kip and Lenny fished: snaglines and bushlines. **1960** *Washington Post* 11 Mar. D5 A snag hook is a huge treble hook which can be fished from either a rod or hand. Usually two or three are tied to a strong line (chalk line is a favorite), a singer is attached and the whole shebang is cast into the drink and retrieved in a series of short jerks.

snagged, *ppl. a.* Add: **2.** (Earlier and later examples.) Also *fig.*

1851 E. C. E. Stuart-Wortley *Travels in U.S.* 112 In the papers will you often see whole columns, headed, 'Snagged', containing a melancholy list of boats. **1867** A. D. Richardson *Beyond Mississippi* i. 21 A snagged steamer. **1930** D. Runyon in *Collier's* 22 Mar. 53/1 Basil is snagged if ever I see a guy snagged, and personally I do not blame him, because Miss Harriet Mackyle may not look like a million, but she has a couple. **1977** *Time* 3 Jan. 34/1 The talks have been snagged for months on how to deal with two new weapons.

snagger. Add: **2.** *Austral.* A slow, inexpert, or poor sheep-shearer.

1887 *Tibb's Popular Songbk.* 11, I found a lot of snaggers Not a shearer in the mob. *a* **1914** *Click go Shears* in R. Ward *Austral. Ballads* (1964) 120 The ringer looks round and is beaten by a blow, And curses the snagger with the bare-bellied yeo. **1945** Baker *Austral. Lang.* 63 *Snagger*, a shearer who is learning the trade and handling less than fifty sheep a day. **1969** B. Hardy *West of Darling* 106 Since they were slow, inexpert, and rough in their performances, the poorest shearers in the shed were nicknamed 'snaggers'. **1975** *Sunday Mail* (Brisbane) 14 Sept. 6/6 The younger men who have taken the old 'snaggers'' places, stand up on 'the board'..and shear along with the best of them.

3. *N. Amer.* [*snag *v.*^{2} 4 c.] One who snags fish; one who catches fish illicitly.

1946 *Richmond* (Va.) *Times-Dispatch* 17 Mar. B-11/2 Alewives which have been snagged by the many 'snaggers' on the dam. **1976** *Globe & Mail* (Toronto) 20 Oct. 36/3 Among this group were many snaggers, fish hogs using any means to trap the big fish. One man, armed only with a landing net, scooped away at fish in one pool.

snagging, *vbl. sb.*^{2} (In Dict. s.v. Snag *v.*^{2}) (Earlier and later examples.)

1775 in J. J. Henry *Campaign against Quebec* (1812) 53 The paths and carrying places we had sufficiently developed..by strong blazing and snagging of bushes. **1851** A. O. Hall *Manhattaner in N. Orleans* 179 There may sometimes occur a snagging, or a fire, with perhaps a collision. **1874** *Rep. Vermont Board Agric.* II. 550 The stumps are rotting, and it is nearly ready for the..work of snagging and bogging. **1960** *Washington Post* 11 Mar. D5/1 They're [*sc.* herrings] caught mostly by dipnets and the gentle method known as snagging. **1980** *Outdoor Life* (U.S.) (Northeast ed.) Oct. 56/2 Because Pacific Coast salmon die after spawning, snagging was introduced as a sporting way to harvest huge numbers of fish in a short time.

snaggle (snæ·g'l), *sb.* Chiefly *dial.* and *colloq.* [app. f. SNAG *sb.*¹: cf. SNAGGLE-TOOTH in Dict. and Suppl.] **1.** A snaggle-tooth; one who has snaggle-teeth. *rare.*

1823 M. WILMOT *Let.* 1 Oct. (1935) 197 Blanche [has] become *alas* a snaggle! Those dear little pearls of teeth are going. **1880** COURTNEY & COUCH *Gloss. Words Cornwall* 52/2 What snaggles the cheeld has.

2. A tangle; a knotted or projecting mass.

1904 *Eng. Dial. Dict.* V. 567/1 *Snaggle*,..a knotted, entangled condition. **1968** C. HELMERICKS *Down Wild River North* II. xxii. 336 The girls pitched our tent in the sparse, pristine plant population between rock snaggles. **1978** T. HUGHES in *Times Lit. Suppl.* 14 Apr. 409/1 All eyes watch The weathered, rooty, bushy pile of faces, A snaggle of faces.

3. *attrib.*, as *snaggle-tusk*.

1922 JOYCE *Ulysses* 424 The famished snaggletusks of an elderly bawd protrude from a doorway.

snaggled, *a.* Add: **1.** Also *transf.*

1938 J. STEINBECK *Long Valley* 58 The sharp snaggled edge of the ridge stood out above them. **1942** W. FAULKNER *Go down, Moses* 69 A few snaggled trees of what had been an orchard.

snaggle-tooth. Add: (Earlier example.) Also, one with snaggle-teeth.

1820 M. WILMOT *Let.* 12 Jan. (1935) 51 Catherine has actually lost one of her teeth!.. The poor Cat will be a rare frightful snaggle tooth. **1821** —— *Let.* 17 Mar. 99 Instead of being hideous in the snaggle tooth age..she is..improved. **1906** *Dialect Notes* III. 157 You'll be a snaggle-tooth before you're twenty, if you don't quit eating so much candy. **1909** J. R. WARE *Passing Eng.* 227/2 *Snaggle-tooth*, woman of lower order..who, lifting her upper lip when scolding, shows an irregular row of teeth.

snaggle-toothed, *a.* Delete *rare* and add later examples. Also *fig.*

1945 B. MACDONALD *Egg & I* (1946) 85 On grey winter days its snaggle-toothed horizon could be seen plainly. **1954** *Caribbean Quarterly* III. IV. 231 Albert is a bright-eyed, snaggle-toothed little man. **1971** B. W. ALDISS *Soldier Erect* 32 That snaggle-toothed chap in the comic button-up white suit,..—put him in a proper pinstripe and he'd pass for an Eastbourne estate agent! **1977** *Time* 14 Feb. 21/3 Entertainment is provided by..a Hollywood drop-cloth view of snaggle-toothed Mount Kenya.

snaggly (snæ·gli), *a.* Chiefly *dial.* and *colloq.* [f. as *SNAGGLE *sb.*: see -Y¹.] Irregular; tangled; ragged.

1794 W. CLARK *Jrnl.* 4 Aug. in *Mississippi Valley Hist. Rev.* (1914) I. 422 The army was conducted..through intolerable thick woods & the earth covered with Snagley underwoods. **1882** F. W. P. JAGO *Anc. Lang. & Dial. Cornwall* 269 'Snaggly teeth', i.e., very irregular or ill-shaped teeth. **1968** P. S. BEAGLE *Last Unicorn* xiv. 206 Squat, snaggly trees that had never yet bloomed were putting forth flowers in the wary way an army sends out scouts. **1978** R. JANSSON *News Caper* vi. 55 The bullet.. bounced off something metal before it hit her, because the wound is all snaggly.

snaggy, *a.*¹ **3.** (Earlier examples.)

1806 W. CLARK in Lewis & Clark *Orig. Jrnls. Lewis & Clark Expedition* (1905) V. 380 The Sand bars..confined the [river] to a narrow Snagey Chanel. **1843** 'R. CARLTON' *New Purchase* ix. 58 To learn the nature of 'mash land'—'rooty and snaggy land' [etc.].

snail, *sb.*¹ Add: **2. c.** (Later examples.)

1915 *Dialect Notes* IV. 198 We'll have to wait for Edith. She's such a snail. **1959** I. & P. OPIE *Lore & Lang. Schoolch.* xvii. 366 He [*sc.* a latecomer] is a..Snail.

6. a. *snail-trace, -track; snail-green, -nacreous, -nosed* adjs.

1931 V. WOOLF *Waves* 25 Louis regards the wall opposite with snail-green eyes. **1923** D. H. LAWRENCE *Birds, Beasts & Flowers* 60 Cyclamen leaves..Spurned with mud Snail-nacreous Low down. **1960** S. PLATH *Colossus* 10 In their jars the snail-nosed babies moon and glow. **1966** J. MERRILL *Nights & Days* 42 The brief snail-trace Of her withdrawal dries upon our faces. **1930** D. H. LAWRENCE *Nettles* 20 All those nasty police-eyes like snail-tracks smearing the gentle souls that figure in the paint.

7. snail darter [cf. DARTER 5], a small freshwater fish, *Percina tanasi*, belonging to the family Percidæ, and found in certain rivers of the U.S.; **snail trail** *Needlework* (see quots.); **snail-wheel** (earlier example).

1975 *U.S. Federal Reg.* 17 June 25597/2 The Fish and Wildlife Service has evidence on hand that the snail darter *Percina* (*Imostoma*) sp. is an endangered species. **1977** *Time* 11 Apr. 17/2 The Mississippi sand-hill crane and the three-inch snail darter of the Little Tennessee River have already halted state and federal bulldozers. **1981** *Science* 15 May 761/3 Populations of snail darters have been found in three new places... If they turn out to be established populations the fish may no longer be an endangered species... The snail darter may be reclassified as a 'threatened'..species. **1899** W. G. P. TOWNSEND *Embroidery* vi. 94 *Snail-trail*,..the same principle as *single coral*, only worked more on the slope. **1948** C. CHRISTOPHER *Compl. Bk. Embroidery Stitches* iii. 64 Snail Trail, or Knot Stitch, makes a series of simple knots connected with each other on the surface of the fabric. **1973** E. WILSON *Embroidery Bk.* (1975) vi. 322 Snail trail worked very close becomes Broad Rope stitch. When worked with the needle at right angles to the thread, instead of slanting, it becomes Coral. **1831** M. EDGEWORTH *Let.* 6 May (1971) 535 Inkstands that shut impervious to ink—insured by the snail wheel tightener.

snail, *v.* Add: **2. c.** To make (one's way) very slowly.

1936 M. FRANKLIN *All that Swagger* v. 56 Two bullock drays were snailing their way from the Port.

snailish, *a.* Add: Hence **snai·lishness.**

1905 M. BEERBOHM in *Sat. Rev.* 24 June 835/1 Usually, this pace in elocution does not madden me. But..I am moved to cry out against this idiotic tradition of snailishness.

snail-slow, *a.* Add: Hence as *adv.*

1901 [in Dict., sense 1]. **1951** W. DE LA MARE *Winged Chariot* 44 Snail-slow moves *everything* for which we wait. **1974** V. CANNING *Painted Tent* x. 203 The time of waiting..had passed snail-slow for Smiler.

snaily, *a.* (and *sb.*). Add: **1.** (Later examples.) Also *fig.*

1928 D. H. LAWRENCE *Let.* 17 Mar. (1932) 710 We *must* put salt on the hypocritical and snaily tails, the good public. **1979** *Sci. Amer.* Mar. 27/2 Periwinkles, snaily bivalves and the plants and animals (such as barnacles and algae) that live on other organisms each get a detailed chapter.

snake, *sb.* Add: **I. 1. c.** (Earlier and further examples.)

1839 *Spirit of Times* 17 Aug. 283/3 Snakes! such a row! **1888** 'R. BOLDREWOOD' *Robbery under Arms* II. xi. 190 So the muchacha went back on yer—snakes alive! I kinder expected it. **1922** E. RAYMOND *Tell England* ix. 122, I thought we'd be last for the Swimming Cup. But snakes alive! we'll get in the semi-final. **1927** G. D. H. & M. COLE *Murder at Crome House* xxii. 271 But, snakes, Flint—this is Exeter! **1930** G. B. SHAW *Apple Cart* I. 15 Holy snakes! look at Bill.

2. b. (Later examples.)

1907 E. GOSSE *Father & Son* xi. 281 He did not scruple to remind the Deity of various objections to a life of pleasure and of the snakes that lie hidden in the grass of evening parties. **1978** J. IRVING *World according to Garp* xiv. 271 We were playing in Dallas, when that snake in the grass..came up on my blind side.

d. *to wake snakes*: (*b*) to rouse oneself, to look lively; (*c*) see WAKE *v.* 8 c.

1835 A. B. LONGSTREET *Georgia Scenes* 6 Oh, wake snakes, and walk your chalks! *c* **1859** in Bartlett *Dict. Amer.* (1860) 498 Well, here I be; wake snakes, the day's a-breaking.

e. *snakes in Iceland*: used allusively (see quot. 1758) of something posited only to be dismissed as non-existent.

[**1758** tr. *N. Horrebow's Natural Hist. Iceland* lxxii. 91 No snakes of any kind are to be met with throughout the whole island.] **1791** BOSWELL *Life of Johnson* II. 220 Johnson had said that he could repeat a complete chapter of 'The Natural History of Iceland', from the Danish of *Horrebow*, the whole of which was exactly thus:—'Chap. lxxii. *Concerning Snakes*. There are no snakes to be met with throughout the whole island'. **1906** *Spectator* 5 May 716/1 'The Value of a Public School Education' reminds one of the chapter on the snakes in Iceland... 'So far as the school at large is concerned every Greek and Latin book should be destroyed.' **1978** C. SYKES in R. Buckle *U & Non-U Revisited* 60 And what about hats? Of them it may be said as was said of snakes in *The Natural History of Iceland*.

f. *lower than a snake's belly*: despicable, very low indeed. *Austral. slang.*

1932 L. MANN *Flesh in Armour* 191 'It was a dirty trick. He knew about me and her.' 'Dirty! Lower than a snake's belly.' **1951** D. CUSACK *Say no to Death* 20 He'd only have to take one look at Jan to be convinced in his honest old heart that his son was lower than a snake's belly. **1965** J. BEEDE *They hosed them Out* 175, I thought, 'if I have to crawl to this illegitimate I'll get lower than a snake's belly.'

3. b. *U.S.* and *Austral. slang.* (See quots.) Cf. *snake charmer*, sense 11 a below.

1929 *Bookman* (U.S.) July 526/1 A Snake has many jobs. If he's a Hump-brakey he handles the cars rolled onto a series of tracks placed on a slight incline. The engine shoves them 'over the hump' and it is his job to handle the brakes. **1934** *Amer. Speech* IX. 73/2 *Snake*, switchman. His work requires him to crawl around and over cars, and he has a reputation for never hurrying. **1945** BAKER *Austral. Lang.* xiv. 249 There are terms like ..*snake-charmers*, *snakes* or *lizards*, railway platelayers.

c. *Austral. Mil. slang.* (See quot. 1945.)

1945 BAKER *Austral. Lang.* viii. 160 *Snakes*, a sergeant. **1948** [see *SNAKE-PIT 2]. **1951** E. LAMBERT *Twenty Thousand Thieves* 314 Baxter reckoned the officers and snakes are pinching our beer.

4. e. In various technical uses.

1947 *Britannica Bk. of Year* 841/1 *Snake*, nickname of a device used during an advance to destroy wires and detonate mines. **1957** *Daily Progress* (Charlottesville, Va.) 8 Jan. 5/3 A plumber's 'snake' has succeeded where a mixed pack of rats and mongooses failed. *Ibid.*, The snakes are thin flexible cables used to clean or carry wires inside pipes. **1961** W. VAUGHAN-THOMAS *Anzio* ix. 207 The Snake was a 300-foot tube of steel packed with TNT up to about fifty feet from the tank, which first towed the tube into battle and then swung around and pushed it out over a minefield. The crew..exploded the TNT by fire from their machine-guns. **1964** 'E. MCBAIN' *Ax* v. 88 The plumber's snake had caught on one of the cross supports... Hawes reached up and shoved at the snake, coiling it back into the drawer.

f. *Econ.* A narrow range of fluctuation in rates of exchange, agreed to by certain member countries of the EEC (see quot. 1973). Hence *snake in the tunnel*: this range in relation to a wider range of fluctuation agreed in the foreign exchange markets.

1972 *Economist* 11 Mar. 87/1 Europe's currencies will try to be held inside the celebrated 'snake' wriggling within the overall 4.5 per cent dollar 'tunnel'. **1972** *Accountant* 12 Oct. 451/2 It would take over the day-to-day running of the so-called 'snake in the tunnel' system of exchange rate margins which Britain opted out of when the £ was floated on June 23rd. **1973** *Business Week* 10 Mar. 37/3 In March 1972, the six charter members of the EEC and the three nations then awaiting membership agreed to keep their currencies trading within a narrower band against one another than they do in trading against the dollar. When set down on graph paper, the snake is the narrow EEC band and the tunnel the wider dollar band. *Ibid.*, A year-old technique that is dubbed, whimsically enough, the 'snake in the tunnel'. **1975** *Sunday Tel.* 11 May 24/4 There may be an agreement on the amount the pound should be devalued..followed by a return to the European currency arrangement (the 'snake in the tunnel'). **1976** *Times* 14 Aug. 15/1 Finance ministers from the 'snake countries' (Belgium, Denmark, Germany, Luxembourg, The Netherlands, Norway and Sweden). **1979** *Dædalus* Winter 63 But the idea offers an opportunity..of avoiding the pitfalls of previous efforts that had aimed prematurely at stabilizing exchange rates in a European 'snake'. **1980** T. BARLING *Goodbye Piccadilly* viii. 155 An illuminated wallchart showed the present float of the European Money Snake.

7*. With capital initial. Applied to American Indians of various Shoshone groups, esp. those of Oregon. Freq. *attrib.*, esp. as *Snake Indian.*

1791 in *Mass. Hist. Soc. Coll.* (1794) III. 24 The tribes of Indians..were called..the Blackfeet tribe, the Snake Indians [, etc.]. **1805** P. GASS *Jrnl.* 22 Oct. (1807) xiv. 154 This..is the same river whose head waters we saw at the Snake nation. **1831** *Niles' Weekly Reg.* IV. 265/2 They happily fell in with a small party of Snake Indians. **1821** J. FOWLER *Jrnl.* 24 Nov. (1898) 55 Last night on Counting them over find now four Hundred of the following nations—Ietans—Arrapohoes—Kiawa Padduce—Cheans—Snakes. **1843** T. TALBOT *Jrnl.* 7 Sept. (1931) 45 The trappers prefer Snake Indians and Snake horses before any race of men or horses in the world. **1890** N. P. LANGFORD *Vigilante Days* xiii. 161 [With] a band of Snakes.., we can run off two thousand of the best of those animals. **1920** S. M. DRUMM in J. C. Luttig *Jrnl. Expedition Upper Missouri* 166 Snake Indians. This tribe was so generally known by this term as to almost obscure the family name of Shoshoni. **1938** M. THOMPSON *High Trails Glacier Nat. Park* 53 The Snake warriors got ready for an attack as soon as the moon should come up. **1940** *Places to see in Wyoming* p. xxiv/2 Shoshones were also referred to as Snakes or the Snake People. **1977** [see *PAIUTE *sb.* a].

II. 8. a. *snake farm, meat, -poisoning* (later example), *-venom.*

1934 *Discovery* July 207/2 The Pasteur Institute in India, the Snake Institute at Port Elizabeth, South Africa, and the Butantan 'Snake-farm' near São Paulo, Brazil, are the headquarters of snake research and cure. **1979** *United States 1980/81* (Penguin Travel Guides) 34 Traveling by car you can be flexible—making any number of stops at souvenir shops or snake farms. **1976** H. KEMELMAN *Wednesday Rabbi got Wet* xxxix. 226 As alien and outlandish as snails or snakemeat or fried termites. **1965** R. & D. MORRIS *Men & Snakes* v. 106 Normally death by snake-poisoning is a prolonged and unpleasant business. **1951** WHITBY & HYNES *Med. Bacteriol.* (ed. 5) xx. 317 It is possible that other toxins of these soil bacteria are (like the snake-venoms) primarily digestive ferments rather than aggressive mechanisms.

b. *snake ceremony, cult, cultist, -priest, -stick.*

1959 E. TUNIS *Indians* ix. 128/1 Nearly all of the rituals had the same purpose: to cajole rain from the gods. The famous Snake Ceremony had that object. **1958** C. ACHEBE *Things fall Apart* III. xxi. 159 His father was the priest of the snake cult. **1965** R. & D. MORRIS *Men & Snakes* iii. 67 It has been argued that the Egyptian contingent of the Jews in the Exodus may have been snake cultists and Moses himself a kind of snake shaman. **1900** *Outing* June 305/2 Then, like a flash, the Snake priests dart upon them grabbing in their hands all they can pick up. **1958** C. ACHEBE *Things fall Apart* III. xxii. 165 One of them was Enoch, the son of the snake-priest who was believed to have killed and eaten the sacred python. **1902** *Chambers's Jrnl.* Feb. 81/1 Readers of that delightful novel, *The World went very well Then*, will remember Mr Brinjes of the fiery eye and the snake-stick, who made every negro do his bidding. **1974** H. MACINNES *Climb to Lost World* vi. 97 We were all hypersensitive about the possibility of being stung or bitten, and kept our snake sticks handy.

c. *snake-god* (later examples), *goddess, monster.*

1863 W. K. KELLY *Curiosities Indo-Europ. Trad. & Folk-Lore* i. 9 The bird, beast, and snake-gods. **1965** R. & D. MORRIS *Men & Snakes* ii. 28 The snake god Danh-gbi of Whydah, Dahomey. **1925** A. EVANS *Ring of Nestor* 15 Besides the well-known Snake Goddess of the Temple Repository at Knossos, a series of other figures have now come to light showing this attribute. **1979** *Jrnl. R. Soc. Arts* July 511/2 But in this region they also make paper caskets on bamboo frames which are used in festivals, especially for that of the snake-goddess, Bishahari. **1965** R. & D. MORRIS *Men & Snakes* ii. 49 A similar snake monster, Typhon, who in Greek mythology merges with Typhoeus, was said to be the cause of earthquakes as well as many springs.

d. *snake bracelet, -buckle, -hook, -mark, -mask, -spiral.*

1968 *New Larousse Encycl. Mythol.* (ed. 2) 484/1 (*caption*) Snake bracelet from Dahomey. **1979** F. Morton *Nervous Splendour* (1980) ix. 89 He had long wanted to give Martha a gold snake bracelet, a status symbol. *a* **1882** H. Kendall in *Penguin Bk. Austral. Ballads* (1964) 92 A hero..With a jumper and snake-buckle belt on. **1971** P. D. James *Shroud for Nightingale* iv. 123 A schoolboy's belt..clasped with a snake buckle. **1978** M. Dickens *An Open Book* i. 6 Dining room lunch meant putting on a dress instead of the boy's shirt and flannel shorts and snake-buckle belt we wore at Chilworthy. **1944** Blunden *Cricket Country* xi. 122 Wearing a revolver holster on a snake-hook belt. **1929** D. H. Lawrence *Pansies* 39 In the odd pattern, like snake-marks on the sand It leaves its trail. **1968** K. Weatherly *Roo Shooter* 16 Two large [kangaroo] does..came in,.. their tails dragging long snake marks in the dust. **1965** R. & D. Morris *Men & Snakes* ii. 41 A snake mask set with turquoises, the emblems of the god [*sc.* Quetzalcoatl]. **1922** Joyce *Ulysses* 715 The snakespiral springs of the mattress being old.

9. *snake-bearing* adj.; *snake-charming* vbl. sb.; *snake-handling* vbl. sb. and adj.

1927 D. H. Lawrence *Mornings in Mexico* 162 The shoulders of the young, snake-bearing men. **1897** 'Mark Twain' *Foll. Equat.* xliii. 388 The girls went through a performance which represented snake-charming. **1978** *Amer. Poetry Rev.* Nov./Dec. 25 Adam and eve because they had a snakecharming act. **1940** *Sci. News Let.* 17 Aug. 103/2 Snake-handling religious cultists of Georgia are 'all of a piece' with followers of other cults who go to unusual lengths to show their faith or their access to supernatural powers. The same thing, with or without snake-handling, has been seen in various cultures and various times. **1973** R. L. Fox *Alexander the Great* iii. 45 Snake-handling is a known practice in the wilder sorts of Greek religion.

10. *snake-green, -haired* (later example), *-hipped, -locked, -tailed, -tressed* (later example).

1948 C. S. Lewis in *Punch* 23 June 543/2 Sea-chances brought To her forest-silent And crimson-fruited And snake-green island Her guests unsought. **1921** W. de la Mare *Veil* 59 Snake-haired, snow-shouldered, pure as flame and dew,..Rises the Goddess. **1976** 'G. Black' *Moon for Killers* i. 7 He looked like a Hollywood top actor of the fifties..still almost snake-hipped, with long, thrust-out legs. **1954** G. Barker *Vision of Beasts & Gods* 39 The snake-locked image of dream Hanging ahead. **1946** R. Graves *Poems 1938–45* 32 By noting that the snake-tailed chthonian winds Were answerable to fate alone, not Zeus. **1894** O. Wilde *Sphinx* 28 What snake-tressed fury fresh from Hell.

11. a. snake-bit(ten) *a.*, (*a*) bitten by a snake; (*b*) *U.S.* irremediably doomed to misfortune; **snake boot** *N. Amer.*, a boot with a high ankle worn for protection against snake-bites, or a fashion boot resembling this; **snake charmer** *Austral. slang* (see quots.); **snake eyes,** (*a*) *U.S. slang*, tapioca; (*b*) *N. Amer. slang*, a throw of two ones with a pair of dice; also *fig.*, bad luck; **snake-headed** *a. slang* (see quot. 1941); **snake hips,** (*a*) very narrow hips; (*b*) the name of a popular dance (see quot. 1970); so **snake-hip** *attrib.*; **snake juice:** for *Austr. slang* read '*slang* (chiefly *Austral.*)' and add: also *loosely*, any alcoholic drink; **snake oil,** a quack remedy or panacea; also *fig.*; freq. *attrib.*, esp. as *snake-oil salesman*; **snake poison:** for *U.S.* read *U.S.* and *Austral. slang* and add later example; **snake rail fence** *N. Amer.* = Snake-fence; **snake room** *Canad.* (see quot. 1912); **snake story** (earlier U.S. examples).

1807 Snake-bitten [in Dict., sense 10]. **1938** M. K. Rawlings *Yearling* xiv. 149 He sobbed, 'Pa—He's snake-bit.' **1942** W. Faulkner *Go down, Moses* 111 Ah'm snakebit and de pizen cant hawm me. **1957** *Daily Progress* (Charlottesville, Va.) 18 Nov. 14/1 It was another long afternoon Saturday at Scott Stadium for Coach Ben Martin, his assistants and his 'snake-bitten' football players as they fell before South Carolina, 13-0. *Ibid.*, Commenting on the game last Saturday afternoon Martin said: 'We're just snake-bit that's all there is to it.' Snake-bit is a term used by coaches when referring to a team which never seems to have a break in its favor. **1965** Mrs. L. B. Johnson *White House Diary* 10 June (1970) 283 From the first moment of the day we were 'snake-bit' —everything went wrong. **1976** *Columbus* (Montana) *News* (Joliet Suppl.) 17 June 2/3 We managed to get back to the house, not snake-bitten and not smelling *too* much like a skunk. **1965** Snakeboot [see *kinky *sb.*]. **1972** R. Reid *Canadian Style* (1973) iv. 144 'Say, what is, or are, galoshes?' 'Like rubber snake boots, but they buckle or zip up the front.' **1937** A. W. Upfield *Mr Jelly's Business* 16 'And what are the Snake Charmers?' 'They are the permanent-way men.' **1969** P. A. Smith *Folklore Austral. Railwaymen* 279 Fettlers are invariably referred to as 'snake charmers'. **1918** L. E. Ruggles *Navy Explained* 20 Tapioca is 'snake eyes'. **1929** M. A. Gill *Underworld Slang* 11/2 *Snake eyes*, aces up on the dice. **1935** *Jrnl. Abnormal Psychol.* XXX. 364 *Snake eyes*, tapioca. **1964** A. Wykes *Gambling* vi. 134 Modern craps players use..slang for various combinations of two dice: 'snake eyes' for Two, [etc.]. **1972** *Islander* (Victoria, B.C.) 30 July 12/3 But this time Baychimo's annual throw of the dice came up 'snake-eyes', and the ice closed about trapping her forever. **1978** R. Moore *Big Paddle* iv. 88 Cliff..let the dice go... He didn't have to look to know they'd come up snake eyes. **1978** G. Vidal *Kalki* vi. 138 It's like throwing dice. Let's just hope it won't be snake eyes for Jim Kelly. **1920** B. Cronin *Timber Wolves* viii. 137 Anyhow, they's no need to get snake-headed about it. **1941** S. J. Baker *Dict. Austral. Slang* 68 *Snake-headed*, angry, vindictive. **1932** *Daily Progress* (Charlottesville, Va.) 20 Apr. 4/3 There is a distinct class clash between the Harlem intelligentsia and snake-hip dancers and chanters of hot-cha-cha and skiddle-de-scow in the black and tan auberges. **1977** *Melody Maker* 26 Mar. 43/2 The biggest sensation of all..was the 'snake-hip' dancer, Bessie Dudley, waggling her bottom, clad in black satin knickers. **1933** *Fortune* Aug. 48/1 Dancers like the gelatinous 'Snake Hips' Tucker. **1956** G. P. Kurath in A. F. C. Wallace *Men & Cultures* (1960) 153 Restraints were shaken off..in an epidemic of angular, foot-twisting gyrations—the Charleston, Snake Hips, Susie-Q, and Truckin'. **1970** C. Major *Dict. Afro-Amer. Slang* 106 *Snake hips*, a Baltimore- and New York-oriented jazz dance. **1977** N. Slater *Crossfire* iii. 62 The fellows..all seem to have snake-hips, painfully tight trousers and platform shoes. **1904** E. S. Emerson *Shanty Entertainment* 70 Then he started them on snake-juice, known as Boot and Blacking Rum. **1965** M. McIntyre *Place of Quiet Waters* xii. 224, I wonder if that snake juice is fit to drink. **1973** R. Robinson *Drift of Things* 290 Broke into Eric's hut, threw the 'pickled' specimens out of the jars, and drank the methylated spirits. That must have been the real 'Snake-Juice'. **1927** S. V. Benét *John Brown's Body* 294 Crooked creatures of a thousand dubious trades, ..sellers of snake-oil balm and lucky rings. **1946** E. O'Neill *Iceman Cometh* i. 90 I'll bet he's standing on a street corner in hell right now, making suckers of the damned, telling them there's nothing like snake oil for a bad burn. **1961** *Washington Post* 10 May A4/2 Advertisers who try to 'lubricate the wheels of our economy with snake oil'. **1976** *Listener* 25 Mar. 382/1 Jimmy Savile has always had more *chutzpah* than a wagonload of snake-oil salesmen. **1977** *Rolling Stone* 21 Apr. 66/2 It was, after all, the Jew who was the perennial doubter, the archetypal outsider, longing for redemption while dismissing the claims of would-be redeemers as so much snake oil. **1978** *Times* 21 Jan. 12/7 The pseudo-graphic industry.. are snake-oil salesmen deceiving the public. **1947** K. Tennant *Lost Haven* iv. 66 If Bee-Bonnet ever again wants me to sample his snake poison, I'll pour it on him and set it alight. **1889** B. Harte *Cressy* ii. 38 Mr. McKinstry's 'snake rail' fence was already discernible in the lighter opening of the woods. **1958** H. Symons *Fences* 48 One of the early Canadian fences most popular in the east was the snake rail fence. **1912** J. Sandilands *Western Canad. Dict.* 42/1 *Snake-room*, a side room of a basement where saloon-keepers accommodate doped or drunken people until they recover their senses, presumably a place where they 'see snakes'. **1921** *Daily Colonist* (Victoria, B.C.) 29 Oct. 15/2 'Tommy' was one of a bunch who were swapping stories recently in the snake room. **1975** F. Kennedy *Alberta was my Beat* vi. 73 All adjourned to the 'snake room' in the basement. **1826** *Virginia Herald* (Fredericksburg) 6 Sept. 3/2 The New-York Spectator will probably class this with the Snake stories of the day. **1867** *Harper's Mag.* Aug. 281/3 We told snake and fish stories.

b. snake doctor *U.S.* = Dragon-fly or Hellgrammite; **snake feeder** *U.S.* = prec.

a **1883** G. W. Bagby *Old Virginia Gentleman* (1910) 92 [The water is] full of all manner of nasty and confounded 'mud-kittens', 'snap'n turtles', and snake doctors. **1948** *Field & Stream* July 42/2 Various stages of the dobson are known as..flip-flaps, snake doctors. **1978** *Amer. Speech* LIII. 201 The flora and fauna terms include.. *snake feeder* (listed as the common name for the dragon-fly, *snake doctor* being listed as 'slightly known'). **1861** *Trans. Illinois Agric. Soc.* IV. 341 A particular species of dragon-fly, or snake-feeder, as it is absurdly called in this country. **1904** G. Stratton-Porter *Freckles* xiv. 289 He shifted restlessly, and the movement sent the snake-feeders skimming. **1949** H. Kurath *Word Geogr. Eastern U.S.* 14/1 The line of demarkation over against the Midland snake feeder is remarkably clear and sharp.

c. snake-locked anemone = Opelet; **snake plant,** (*b*) = *mother-in-law's tongue* s.v. *mother-in-law.

1853 P. H. Gosse *Naturalist's Rambles Devon. Coast* iv. 96 The Snake-locked Anemone..is by no means common. **1928** Russell & Yonge *Seas* 37 Especially common in the pools is the 'Snake-locked anemone'. **1979** J. D. & J. J. George *Marine Life* 32/1 *Anemonia sulcata* ..(snakelocks anemone). A species with many sinuous tentacles. **1946** M. Free *All about House Plants* xviii. 271 The common Snake-plant..is one of the most inelegant of all plants, with its stiff, 30-inch, upright leaves. **1973** *Daily Colonist* (Victoria, B.C.) 21 Nov. 24/1 He had poured his heart out to a hardy sansevieria, otherwise known as snake plant or mother-in-law's tongues.

snake, *v.*[1] Add: **II. 5. a.** (Earlier example.)

1829 T. Flint *George Mason* ii. 21 It was so contrived that..logs..could be drawn, or, as it is technically phrased, *snaked* into church.

b. (Earlier example.)

1856 M. Thomson *Plu-ri-bus-tah* xii. 135 First he pulled the pillow-case off. Then he snaked the stars and stripes off.

snake, *v.*[2] For '*dial.* (chiefly *north.* and *Sc.*)' read '*dial.* and *U.S.*' and add: **2.** (Further examples.) Also, to cheat (someone) at cards.

a **1861** T. Winthrop *John Brent* (1862) xvi. 183 They snaked me to the figure of a slug at their cheatin' game. **1886** Kipling *Departmental Ditties* (ed. 2) 36 You will find excuse to snake Three days' 'casual' on the bust. **1921** T. Dreiser *Let.* 2 Jan. (1959) I. 333 Start the ball and if I snake the forty thousand..you get five thousand. **1959** [see *shaft *sb.*[2] 9* c]. **1977** *Amer. Speech* 1975 L. 66 *Snake*,..steal (one's date) 'Carol tried to snake my date last night'.

snake-bark (snē[i]·kbāɹk). [f. Snake *sb.* + Bark *sb.*[1] 1.] In full, *snake-bark(ed) maple.* A maple, esp. *Acer pennsylvanicum* from eastern North America or *Acer davidii* from eastern Asia, belonging to a group distinguished by bark streaked with white.

1838 J. C. Loudon *Arboretum & Fruticetum Britannicum* I. 407 The striped-barked Maple..Snake-barked Maple, Moose Wood. **1914** W. J. Bean *Trees & Shrubs Hardy in Brit. Isles* I. 153 *A. pennsylvanicum*..Snake-bark Maple... This maple is remarkable chiefly for the exceedingly handsome striping of its younger branches and stem. **1974** A. Mitchell *Field Guide Trees Brit. Isles* 341 The Snake-barked Maples are a difficult and confused group. *Ibid.* 342 Similar species. *A. distylum*..although not truly a Snake-bark. **1977** *Harpers & Queen* Nov. 274/4 Suburban gardens..are now enriched with azaleas, ..snakebark maple, winter-sweet and all sorts of curiosities. **1980** *Amat. Gardening* 25 Oct. 29/1 With the exception of *Acer pennsylvanicum*..the Snakebarks are native to China or Japan.

sna·ke dance. Also **snake-dance.** [Snake *sb.*] **1.** Among the Hopi Indians, a religious dance involving the handling of live rattle-snakes. Also, among other American Indian groups, various dances so called from the motion of the dancers or the function of the dance.

1772 D. Taitt *Jrnl.* 6 Mar. in N. D. Mereness *Trav. Amer. Colonies* (1916) 517 The women danced the Snake dance, the leader haveing her legs Covered with Turpin shells which is filled with small stones on purpose to make a noise. **1883** [in Dict. s.v. Snake *sb.* 8 b]. **1891** *Rep. Bureau Amer. Ethnol.* VIII. 136 Among the Hopi, particularly at Walpi, the snake-dance is renowned. **1927** D. H. Lawrence *Mornings in Mexico* 136 The snake dance (I am told) is held once a year. *Ibid.* 138 Three thousand people came to see the little snake dance this year. **1940** R. Chandler *Farewell, my Lovely* xx. 158 I'm no school-marm at the snake dances. **1965** R. & D. Morris *Men & Snakes* ii. 38 The snakes used in the famous Hopi Snake Dance are not worshipped, but sent as messengers to the raingods of the underworld. **1970** K. Platt *Pushbutton Butterfly* ix. 100 A Shoshone snake dance.

2. a. A dance performed as a stage entertainment in imitation of the movement of a snake or involving the handling of a snake.

1895 *N.Y. Dramatic News* 23 Nov. 4 Ida Siddons in her snake dance, two Italian pantomimists [etc.]. **1971** R. Russell tr. *Ahmad's Shore & Wave* vii. 66 'What cabaret girl?' 'The one who does the snake dance.'

b. A dance performed by a group of people linked together in a long line and moving about in a zig-zag fashion, as at parties, celebrations, etc. orig. and chiefly *U.S.*

1911 G. Burgess *Find Woman* x. 244 So he..went, reminding them of the [football] score and the snake-dance every time he opened a bottle. **1946** E. B. Thompson *Amer. Daughter* 234 A few minutes later [I] was a link in a howling, writhing snake dance that weaved itself in and out of the business section. **1960** *Daily Tel.* 15 July 19/2, 23,000 in Tokyo anti-treaty snake-dance. **1965** G. B. Schaller *Year of Gorilla* viii. 206 One grabbed the rump hairs of the first one with both hands, the third animal did the same to the second one, and then all three careened wildly down a slope in snake-dance fashion. **1976** *National Observer* (U.S.) 10 July 11/1 During the rebellious days of the 1960s, college students spurned many traditional campus pleasures, from spring proms and snake dances to the social reassurance offered by membership in fraternities and sororities.

Also (with hyphen) as *v. intr.*; so **snake-dancing** *ppl. a.*; hence **snake-dancer.**

1922 *Chicago Daily Maroon* 3 Oct. 2/1 The public.. picture..howling, snakedancing crowds whenever colleges and universities are mentioned. **1931** F. L. Allen *Only Yesterday* 17 Eight hundred Barnard College girls snake-danced on Morningside Heights in New York. **1960** *Daily Tel.* 15 July 19/2 They snake-danced through the city with their paper lanterns and red banners and dispersed quietly without incident, police said. **1977** C. McCullough *Thorn Birds* v. 93 Princess Houri the Snake Dancer (See Her Fan the Flames of a Cobra's Rage!).

snake-fence. For *U.S.* read *N. Amer.* and add earlier and further examples.

1805 R. Parkinson *Tour Amer.* I. i. 48 Snake-fences; which are rails laid with the ends of one upon the other, from eight to sixteen in number in one length. **1844** F. Marryat *Settlers in Canada* 53 A herd of cattle were grazing on a portion of the cleared land; the other was divided off by a snake-fence..and was under cultivation. **1904** C. G. D. Roberts *Watchers of Trails* 239 The snake fence of split rails which bounded the pasture. **1973** L. Russell *Everyday Life Colonial Canada* ii. 33 In constructing a snake fence the rails of adjacent bays were overlapped at a wide angle... Such a fence was a zig-zag of bays.

snake-head. Add: **2.** (Earlier example.) Now *Hist.*

1845 *Yankee* (Boston) 9 Aug. 3/4 Mr. John F. Wall ..was near being killed..by what is technically called a *snakehead*.

4. Substitute for def.: A tropical marine or fresh-water carnivorous fish of the family Channidæ, esp. one of the genus *Ophiocephalus*, found in Africa or Asia, usually mottled grey, brown, or black in colour. (Examples.)

1905 D. S. JORDAN *Guide Study of Fishes* II. xxi. 370 Snake-head mullets..seem to us nearer the labyrinthine fishes. **1961** E. S. HERALD *Living Fishes of World* 244/2 Snakeheads will live for many hours and sometimes days out of water.

sna·ke-pit. Also snakepit. [SNAKE *sb.*]

1. Among primitive peoples, a large pit containing poisonous snakes into which victims are thrown for execution or as a test of endurance.

1883 VIGFUSSON & YORK-POWELL *Corpus Poeticum Boreale* II. IX. 346 Anslaug..gives him a charmed coat, which preserves him even in the snake-pit into which he is cast by Ælla, king of the Northumbrians. **1909** *Saga-Book of Viking Club* VI. I. 73 Ragnarr was captured by King Ella, and cast into a snake pit. **1940–41** *Scandinavian Stud.* XVI. 32 We may say that the theme of the Snake Tower or Snake Pit is foreign to Europe but is a typical Oriental importation. **1961** H. TREECE *Jason* III. xxvii. 224 Medea halted at the edge of the snake-pit... Then she lowered herself to the marble rim of the pit and gently eased down among the little snakes. **1977** A. P. SMYTH *Scandinavian Kings in Brit. Isles 850–880* iii. 36 The account of Ragnarr's invasion of Northumbria and his death in the snake-pit at the hands of King Ælla is found in its most elaborate form in *Ragnars saga*.

2. *transf.* and *fig.*

1941 *Argus* (Melbourne) *Week-End Mag.* 15 Nov. 1/4 *Snake pit*, sergeants' mess. **1948** S. L. ELLIOTT in E. Hanger *Khaki, Bush & Bigotry* (1968) 91 Andy Edwards has been promoted and moved up to the snake pit with you and the other snakes. **1956** A. L. ROWSE *Early Churchills* v. 82 He was a man..simple and rigid, in that snake-pit of a Court with its twisting..creatures,.. deceitful and insincere. **1966** B. GLEMSER *Dear Hungarian Friend* ii. 36 He is at the United Nations... That is the only way to survive in the political snakepit. **1969** *N.Y. Review Bks.* 21 Aug. 8/1 The venal and compromising snakepit of American politics. **1976** *Publishers Weekly* 20 Sept. 74/3 All depicted as guilty as hell, conniving, scheming, fighting and feuding. It's a snakepit of a scene. **1977** *Listener* 25 Aug. 245/1 A snake-pit of imperfect chromatic scales.

3. *spec.* A mental hospital (after the title of the novel by M. J. Ward: see quot. 1947).

1947 M. J. WARD (*title*) The snake pit. **1960** *Sunday Express* 15 May 17/4 The snake-pit women's ward. **1968** A. LASKI *Keeper* ii. 22 They had visited him in the snake-pit. **1976** *Courier-Mail* (Brisbane) 30 Apr. 5/1 It's like going back to the days when psychiatric hospitals everywhere were called snakepits.

snake-root. Add: **2. b.** = *RAUWOLFIA.

1955 *Sci. Amer.* Oct. 81/1 Reserpine is an alkaloid extract from the snakeroot plant. **1976** W. A. R. THOMSON *Herbs that Heal* ix. 147 The root, popularly known as 'snake-root' because of its long, tapering, crooked nature, contains most of the medicinal properties of the plant.

Snakes and Ladders. Also with hyphens and small initials. [See below.]

1. The name of a board-game for children in which the hazards and advantages are provided by snakes and ladders depicted on the board.

A counter that chances to arrive on a square at the head of a snake must be withdrawn to the snake's tail, while one that arrives at the foot of a ladder can be advanced to its top.

1907 *Yesterday's Shopping* (1969) 1031/1 *Snakes and Ladders*. An interesting and most exciting game of chance. **1933** N. STREATFEILD *Tops & Bottoms* xii. 146 Felicity thought that bringing up Beaty was rather like playing Snakes and Ladders, through no fault of your own stepping on the head of a snake and sliding to the bottom again; in this case, with no ladder in view up which to shoot to regain lost ground. **1946** E. LINKLATER *Private Angelo* viii. 89 Promotion in war-time was like..a game of snakes-and-ladders. **1964** A. WYKES *Gambling* vi. 128 Backgammon..is the precursor of practically every modern board-and-pieces game in which the moves are decided by dice—even parlor games like *snakes-and-ladders*. **1980** *Daily Tel.* 25 Jan. 15/3 New and more sophisticated versions of snakes and ladders and noughts and crosses will also be provided [on trains].

2. *fig.* A series of unpredictable successes and set-backs. Hence *snake-and-ladder* adj.

1930 M. ALLINGHAM *Mystery Mile* xxiii. 213 The [fire] engines were still drawn up outside Number Thirty Four. 'Still playing Snakes and Ladders, I see,' said Campion. **1961** *Listener* 31 Aug. 319/2 The artists whose life-work does not find a place in the historical snakes and ladders of *avant-garde* development. **1978** G. GREENE *Human Factor* v. iii. 267 After so many years of concealment he was beginning to enjoy this snake-and-ladder game. **1978** G. SIMS *Rex Mundi* xix. 117 Snakes and ladders progress, old man—that's all we can hope for. A lucky throw that puts us on the ladder. **1982** *Church Times* 23 July 6/1 Nothing could illustrate more graphically the snake-and-ladder aspect of a political career than the last year of Tony Crosland's life.

snakesman. For *Obs.* read 'Now *Hist.*' and add later examples.

1973 G. BUTLER *Coffin for Pandora* vii. 153 Perhaps I did train up one or two snakesmen..and perhaps we did work together. **1975** M. CRICHTON *Great Train Robbery* v. 31 A snakesman was a child adept at wriggling through small spaces.

snaking, *vbl. sb.* Add: **4.** A rapid oscillation of an aircraft about a vertical axis; a similar motion of a caravan or trailer.

1945 *Jrnl. R. Aeronaut. Soc.* XLIX. 463/2 There is a possibility of the aeroplane developing an undamped short period oscillation in which rapid movement of the rudder from side to side plays an essential part—the tail wagging the dog. Such an oscillation is known as 'snaking'. **1949** *Aircraft Engin.* Oct. 311/1 Snaking can be cured by sticking on strips to the trailing edge of the rudder. **1966** *Caravanning* ('Know the Game' Ser.) 11 Stabilisers have been devised to overcome any side movement or 'snaking' of the caravan in relation to the direction of the car. **1972** *Nature* 18 Aug. 377/2 Detailed studies of gust effects, and of 'snaking'.

snakishly (snēⁱ·kiʃli), *adv.* [f. SNAKISH *a.* + -LY².] In the manner of a snake; treacherously, venomously.

1935 E. R. EDDISON *Mistress* xi. 204 The Vicar, regarding him snakishly, drew back his thin lips in a smile. **1963** D. HUGHES in Sissons & French *Age of Austerity* iv. 87 Heath..was accepted..as a quite normal manifestation of that time..which made his vicious sallies into madness..all the more snakishly repellent.

snaky, *a.* Add: **3. a.** (Later N. Amer. examples.)

1933 J. V. ALLEN *Cowboy Lore* IV. 101 If you reckon your mounts are some snakey and raw Just try ridin' herd on a stove that won't draw. **1966** M. & O. MURIE *Wapiti Wilderness* iv. 71 Oh, I believe he's a pretty good horse. He may be a little bit snaky. **1980** [see *shavetail* s.v. *SHAVE *v.* 13].

b. *Austral.* and *N.Z. slang.* Angry, annoyed.

1919 W. H. DOWNING *Digger Dialects* 46 *Snaky*,.. (1) angry (e.g., to turn snaky); (2) irritable. **1941** K. TENNANT *Battlers* 86 Now lay off, sport... Don't go snaky on the kid. **1943** *Amer. Speech* XVIII. 90 [In New Zealand] *To go crook* is to show anger or annoyance... The verbs *to go snaky, to go maggoty*..have the same implications. **1945** N. MARSH *Died in Wool* vii. 155 There was a hold up... Everyone was snakey. Young Doug says the sheep are dry and I say they're not. **1974** D. WILLIAMSON *Three Plays* 34 What are you snaky about this time? **1981** *Courier-Mail* (Brisbane) 28 Nov. 23/1 They remain very snaky indeed about allegedly non-impartial treatment from players and umpires in Perth.

snallygaster (snæ·ligɑstəɹ). *U.S. dial.* [ad. G. *schnelle geister*, lit. 'quick spirits'.] A mythical monster supposedly found in Maryland. Cf. *SNOLLYGOSTER.

1940 *Maryland* (Writers' Program) 348 Residents of a Negro settlement near the distillery are firm in their belief that the neighborhood has a 'snallygaster'—a fabulous reptilian bird of vast size that preys on poultry and Negro children after nightfall. **1949** *Sun* (Baltimore) 28 July 14/1 (*heading*) Could it have been a snallygaster? **1954** *Sunday Sun* (Baltimore) *Mag.* 31 Oct. (*recto front cover*), Is this, at last, the snallygaster that has been said to terrorize Western Maryland but that most people have considered legendary?

snam (snæm), *v. slang.* ? *Obs.* [Origin unknown.] *intr.* To snatch; to steal.

App. recorded only in Dicts.

1824 J. MACTAGGART *Scottish Gallovidian Encycl.* 429 *Snam*, to snap at any thing greedily. **1874** HOTTEN *Slang Dict.* 298 *Snam*, to snatch, or rob from the person. Mostly used to describe that kind of theft which consists in picking up anything lying about, and making off with it rapidly.

Hence as *sb.*; also **sna·mmer**, one who snams; a thief.

1839 H. BRANDON in W. A. Miles *Poverty, Mendicity & Crime* 164/2 *Pudding Snammer*, one who steals from a cook shop **1887** Snam [see *DUB *sb.*⁸]. **1950** PARTRIDGE *Dict. Underworld* 649/1 *On the snam*, engaged in stealing.

snap, *sb.* Add: **I. 2. b.** (Earlier examples.)

1882 *Adventures Billy Shakespoke* v. 89, I dropped in to see my old partner..and he proposed that we should try another 'snap' in Lynn. **1885** *Santa Fé Weekly New Mexican* 24 Sept. 4/6 It is the custom, during the summer months, for 'snap' companies to travel through the country and gather shekels.

c. = *soft snap* s.v. SOFT *a.* 27. chiefly *N. Amer.*

1877 H. RUEDE *Sod-House Days* 120 It is no snap, for the straw rolls out fast enough to keep them very busy. **1901** *Daily Colonist* (Victoria, B.C.) 27 Oct. 3/4 Formerly porters received as low as $15 a month and this wage in a buffet car was at one time considered a snap, as tips were wont to bring a man's income up to all the way from $100 to $200 a month. **1924** P. MARKS *Plastic Age* xxiv. 287 He had three classes in literature, one in music—partly because it was a 'snap' and partly because he really wanted to know more about music—and his composition course. **1936** V. SHEEAN *Personal Hist.* i. 3 The football players, the social lights, the pretty co-eds, and all the other students who regarded study as an inconvenient detail in college life, rushed to inscribe themselves for 'snap' courses. **1962** A. LURIE *Love & Friendship* viii. 180 The new semester has started, and I have a whole new selection of little 'creative writers' on my hands...the course is rumored to be a Snap (one thinks of those paper crackers at children's parties). **1967** *Technology Week* XX. 95/2 (Advt.), Blazing a path to the moon is no snap. Neither is charting a career.

4. (Later examples.) Also in *Comb.*

1913 D. H. LAWRENCE *Sons & Lovers* i. 25 She..put him out a clean scarf and snap-bag. *Ibid.* iv. 65, I went to put my coat on at snap-time. **1935** A. J. CRONIN *Stars look Down* I. ix. 67 'Come on, ye old beggor, and have yer snap,' Tom called out with his mouth full of bread and cheese. **1960** C. DAY LEWIS *Buried Day* vii. 131 The black-faced miners cycling home from work with their snap-tins bumping at their sides. **1980** *Guardian* 11 Nov. 8/3 At 10 o'clock the regular farm hands disappeared to the dutch barn for their 'snap'.

5. d. Add to def.: The call of 'snap' is made when two matching cards are exposed. (Earlier examples.) Also *attrib.*, as *snap-card.*

1881 *Cassell's Bk. Indoor Amusements* 144 The game of Snap may either be played with the ordinary Whist cards or with special cards prepared for the purpose. **1890** CHAMPLIN & BOSTWICK *Young Folks' Cyclopaedia Games & Sports* 659/1 *Snap*, a game played by any number of persons with 36 cards. **1916** *N. & Q.* 9 Sept. 210/1 Who designed the illustrations that appear on snap cards, and when did they first appear? **1966** J. DERRICK *Teaching English to Immigrants* v. 188 Much pre-reading apparatus can be used for this purpose, such as word-matching cards, snapcards, word lotto, and other sets of apparatus where identifying and matching single words is involved.

e. A temporary faro game.

1845 J. J. HOOPER *Some Adventures Capt. S. Suggs* x. 133 I'll never bet on two pair agin! They're peart at the snap game, theyselves; but they're badly lewed this hitch! **1864** W. B. DICK *Amer. Hoyle* 208 *Snap*, [in Faro] a temporary bank, not a regular or established game. **1938** H. ASBURY *Sucker's Progress* 280 A few of the river gamesters ran Faro snaps when ashore in St. Louis, but most of them concentrated on Poker.

f. A U.S. party game in which one of the players chases another round a ring formed by the rest.

1865 B. L. RIDLEY *Battles & Sk. Army of Tennessee* (1906) 481 Games [in Georgia] soon began—'Thimble', 'Snap', and kissing songs. **1930** *Virginia Jrnl. Educ.* Oct. 73 Social intercourse [in the mountains of Virginia] was very limited. Monthly religious meetings at widely scattered churches, occasional parties at which 'Boston', 'Snap' and 'Shaker's Dance' were played all night long. **1944** G. WILSON *Passing Institutions* 93 Our liveliest game was Snap, a game that used to seem very exciting but now somewhat resembles Drop the Handkerchief.

g. *U.S.* and *Canad. Football.* = *SNAP-BACK 1 b.

1922 P. D. HAUGHTON *Football & how to watch It* 30 Watch the offensive ends begin their mad rush downfield at the snap of the ball. **1947** *Richmond* (Va.) *Times-Dispatch* 9 Nov. B7/7 From a single-wing formation to the right, Deuber, the tailback, took the snap and set sail wide around Virginia's left end. **1958** *Edmonton Jrnl.* 7 Aug. 7/2 London kicker Legg fumbled a snap on the third down. **1974** *Plain Dealer* (Cleveland, Ohio) 27 Oct. 2-C/3 Penn State..converted a fumbled snap into the game's first score only three minutes into the first period.

9. b. (Later examples.)

1899 *St. George's Hosp. Gaz.* VII. 91 An extremely pretty set of Kodak 'snaps' are contributed by Mr. Peck. **1950** *Nat. Geogr. Mag.* Apr. 514/1 We..eventually secured a few satisfactory snaps of the ordinary garden variety of jump. **1977** *Time* 26 Sept. 31/2 They even had a prospectus put together for publishers and included some sample snaps.

11. a. (Earlier example.)

1865 *Harper's Mag.* Jan. 145/2 [They were] good enough people in their way, but had no snap about them. She liked people with snap.

b. (Earlier example.)

1870 'MARK TWAIN' *Lett. to Publishers* (1967) 49, I should write the book as if *I* went through all these adventures myself—this in order to give it snap and freshness.

II. 12. e. *U.S.* A trick, deception, trap; also in phr. *to give the snap away.*

1844 *Lexington* (Kentucky) *Observer* 18 Sept. 3/1 Mr Van Buren..with his characteristic politeness *declined to be caught in any such snap.* **1885** *Weekly New Mexican Rev.* 2 July 4/3 He was roped into this snap by Chicago sharpers. **1900** *Congress. Rec.* 15 Feb. 1850/2 Ex-Senator Vilas gave the snap away when he said [etc.]. **1919** E. HOUGH *Sagebrusher* 501 If that girl's not blind she'll get out and give this snap away.

13. e. (Later examples.)

1976 *Eastern Daily Press* (Norwich) 16 Dec. 13/4 The friction strips which make the bang are known as 'snaps' in the industry. **1980** *Daily Tel.* 25 Nov. 15/5 Those who felt inspired to make their own crackers..may have encountered some difficulty in finding the vital bangers, called snaps in the trade.

III. 14. c. *pl.* Hand-cuffs. *slang.*

1895 J. CAMINADA *Twenty-Five Years Detective Life* 49, I put the 'snaps' on 'Pudding', and conveyed him.. to Livesey Street police station. **1910** [see *NIPPER *sb.*¹ 4 c]. **1958** M. PROCTER *Man in Ambush* x. 119 We got the snaps on him and locked him up. **1967** —— *Exercise Hoodwink* xxv. 178 Sergeant, we'd better have the snaps on these three.

d. *U.S.* A press-stud or snap-fastener. *Usu. pl.*

1964 *McCall's Sewing* xii. 221/1 Snaps are used to hold fabrics together where there is little strain on the garment. They give a neat flat closure. **1968** J. UPDIKE *Couples* (1970) ii. 160 Frank's delicate hand uncoupled her bra snaps. **1977** *New Yorker* 27 June 72/3 The [pillow]slip is homemade, with snaps at one end.

15. a. *snap, crackle,* (*and*) *pop*, an advertiser's catchphrase representing the lively sound produced by a brand of breakfast cereal when milk is added; used allusively and in *transf.* senses for breakfast cereal or for vigour or energetic behaviour.

1954 *Daily Mail* 15 Dec. 2/1 (Advt.), With their fascinating 'Snap! Crackle! Pop!' as the milk's poured on, *Rice Krispies* really do seem to be talking. **1959** *Times Lit. Suppl.* 27 Mar. 179/4 In the 1950s the whole of

America, Canada, Australia, England and parts of Europe are eating cereals for breakfast—snap, crackle, pop. **1960** *Guardian* 17 Mar. 9/2 Marples..always acting with that zestful snap, crackle, pop that entertains as much as it nourishes. **1962** 'R. GORDON' *Doctor in Swim* xi. 66 Now the poor fellow was as jumpy as a plate of snap-crackle-pop when you pour the milk on. **1962** F. WILLIAMS *Amer. Invasion* ii. 20 With every snap, crackle and pop on the breakfast table the American accent carries farther. **1963** *Trade Marks Jrnl.* 1 June 730/2 Snap Crackle Pop. 851,181. Cereal preparations made of rice for food for human consumption. Kellogg Company of Great Britain Limited..Manchester, 3rd July 1963. **1965** *Times Lit. Suppl.* 22 Apr. 315/5 When due allowance has been made for the chapter's snap crackle pop style. **1977** *N.Y. Rev. Bks.* 28 Apr. 11/4 But the few paragraphs of real information are hard to find in the snap, crackle, and pop of gossip and insult. **1979** P. LEVI *Head in Soup* vii. 128 Snap, crackle, pop. The telephone went dead.

b. (Earlier U.S. examples.)

1833 S. SMITH *Life & Writings J. Downing* 43 As long as I have President Jackson to look to for paymaster, I don't care a snap about sending in any bills. *a* **1852** F. M. WHITCHER *Widow Bedott Papers* (1856) xxii. 232 If you don't care a snap for him, what makes you go with him to lecters, and concerts, and sleigh rides?

18. (Earlier examples.)

c **1770** J. RANDOLPH *Treat. Gardening* in Gardiner & Hepburn *Amer. Gardener* (1818) 275 French beans and snaps are the same. **1842** C. M. KIRKLAND *Forest Life* II. xli. 165 'Snaps' are green beans.

snap, *v.* Add: **II. 5. a.** (Earlier example in Cricket.)

1872 *Wisden* 23 John Smith stayed with Mr Grace until 63 runs were made, when Pooley snapped him.

f. *U.S.* and *Canad. Football.* To put (the ball) in play by passing it quickly backwards to begin a scrimmage; to make a snap (sense *5 g). Also with *back*.

1887 *Outing* Oct. 70/1 In a scrimmage he places it on the ground, and at a signal from his quarter, snaps the ball back by a downward and backward pressure with his foot. **1920** W. CAMP *Football without Coach* iii. 48 Now let us say the quarter calls the signal..the play would get under way and the center would snap him the ball. **1968** *Globe & Mail* (Toronto) 3 Feb. 37/6 During such periods, when a pass is incomplete or a ball goes into touch, time will not resume until the ball has been snapped on the next play. **1973** *Philadelphia Inquirer* (Today Suppl.) 7 Oct. 42/1 Moss lights up and hunches over his desk, like a linebacker waiting for signals. The ball is snapped; he's off.

g. To match (an exposed card in a game of snap); to call out 'snap!' to (an opponent).

1935 *Encycl. Sports* 568/2 In case a player calls snap when there is nothing to snap on the table, the cards in front of him go to a pool. *Ibid.*, Grimace snap is extremely simple. Instead of snapping each other, the two players are under contract to make each other laugh, to which they may do anything except speak.

7. b. (Later examples.)

1950 T. S. ELIOT *Cocktail Party* I. ii. 60 Have you looked in your bag?.. Well, don't snap my head off. **1976** J. I. M. STEWART *Memorial Service* i. 12 He adores the place... That's why he snaps your head off if you venture to say a good word for it.

III. 12. a. Also, to switch *off* or *on*, or to shut *to*, with a snapping sound; to cause (fabric, elastic, etc.) to make such a sound.

1911 H. S. HARRISON *Queed* 68 Queed cleverly bethought him to snap on an electric light. **1922** JOYCE *Ulysses* 21 Haines helped himself [to a cigarette] and snapped the case to. **1925** F. SCOTT FITZGERALD *Great Gatsby* viii. 191 About five o'clock it was blue enough outside to snap off the light. **1926** J. MASEFIELD *Odtaa* xvi. 277 He snapped-to the breech of his rifle. **1949** B. A. BOTKIN *Treas. S. Folklore* II. iii. 252 Both Bilbo and Gene Talmadge were famous for their red suspenders, which Talmadge loved to snap. **1962** J. UPDIKE *Centaur* (1963) vi. 178 He laughed and behind me I could hear all the Caucasus laughing and snapping their towels and flipping their silvery genitals. **1979** R. JAFFE *Class Reunion* (1980) II. vii. 248 Ken was dressed, snapping on his wrist-watch. *Ibid.* 254 Ken snapped off the TV with his remote control.

13. b. Also, to fit *in*, to come *off*, with a snap.

1967 *Boston Sunday Herald Mag.* 26 Mar. 26/2 (Advt.), Quality absorbent reusable cotton pad snaps in—removes easily for laundering. **1976** *Columbus* (Montana) *News* 1 July 3/3 (Advt.), Safety grilles snap off to clean. 3-speed 20″ Fan.

IV. 15. b. (Later examples.)

1927 WODEHOUSE *Meet Mr Mulliner* ix. 310 Something seemed to snap in James. The scales seemed to fall from James's eyes. **1933** E. O'NEILL *Days without End* (1934) I. 49 He knew..she was going to die... He..saw that no miracle would happen... Something snapped in him then. **1970** A. FRY *How a People Die* xxiv. 212 Something snapped. I lost my temper and I chewed that poor guy out from hell to breakfast.

d. *colloq.* To change one's behaviour or position quickly, esp. *to snap back*: to recover; *to snap (in)to*: to throw oneself smartly into (an action); *to snap out of*: to desist from (an attitude, etc.), to change a mood, pattern of behaviour, etc., by sudden effort. Freq. as imp. *snap out of it.*

1918 in F. A. Pottle *Stretchers* (1929) ix. 239 Oh, snap into it! We want to get this done. **1918** [see *HIT *v.* 22* e]. **1928** *Sat. Even. Post* 7 Jan. 9/3 Oh, for heaven's sake, Lucia, snap out of it and act like a human being. **1941** N. MARSH *Death & Dancing Footman* (1942) vi. 114 Do snap out of being all Freudian. **1943** K. TENNANT *Ride on Stranger* xviii. 205 Time we were getting a move on... Snap into it, Joe. **1944** *Sun* (Baltimore) 13 Jan. 5/1 If the Government acts quickly.., the aircraft industry will snap back quickly. **1962** J. GLENN in *Into Orbit* 18 We had to demonstrate how well we could undergo all kinds of stress and discomfort and then snap back again. **1967** [see *OWNSOME]. **1967** *Boston Sunday Herald* 14 May (This Week Mag.) 15/3 The Senator..spent half an hour persuading a very reluctant repairman to come. 'Why,' asked a guest, 'didn't you just tell him to snap to it?' **1981** M. SPARK *Loitering with Intent* x. 158 We mustn't get morbid. Let's snap out of it.

16. b. Also *spec.* in sport, to break a tie or a pattern of performance. *U.S.*

1951 *Amer. Speech* XXVI. 230 Michigan snaps Gopher streak. **1967** *Boston Herald* 8 May 16/6 His run-scoring single in the fifth inning climaxed a two-run rally that snapped a 3-3 tie. **1973** *Internat. Herald Tribune* 15 June 15/6 California held on to score a 7-5 home victory over Boston, snapping a four-game losing streak. **1976** *Washington Post* 19 Apr. D3/1 Danny Lawson's goal at 14:53 of the third period snapped a 4-4 tie.

d. To get (a person) *out of* a certain frame of mind. Cf. sense 15 d above.

1957 A. GRIMBLE *Return to Islands* iv. 78 Once they had struck their noble attitude officially..nothing but the crack of doom would ever snap them out of it. **1964** M. MCLUHAN *Understanding Media* I. v. 55 The parallel between two media holds us on the frontiers between forms that snap us out of the Narcissus-narcosis. **1968** *Globe & Mail* (Toronto) 13 Jan. 28/5 Brisk way to snap yourself out of the post holiday lethargy is to get out your little or not so little lists and decide to do some entertaining.

snap (snæp), *int.* The call in the card-game snap (SNAP *sb.* 5 d in Dict. and Suppl.); hence as an exclamation used when two similar objects turn up or two similar events take place.

1890 CHAMPLIN & BOSTWICK *Young Folks' Cycl. Games & Sports* 659/2 When a player turns a card having the same design as one on the top of another player's exposed pile, both must say 'Snap'. **1958** N. F. SIMPSON *Hole* 7 *Cerebro.* He seems to be biding his time at the moment. *Soma.* Snap! **1962** J. BRAINE *Life at Top* v. 88 He passed me his cigarette-case. The cigarettes..bore his initials. I reached for my cigarette-lighter then took out instead one of the books of matches I'd taken away from the Savoy. He looked at the matches and grinned. 'Snap,' he said. **1971** M. RUSSELL *Deadline* viii. 95 'I've read your stuff.' 'Snap.' **1980** J. WAINWRIGHT *Venus Fly-Trap* 39 Daphne, too, was wearing dark glasses... Harry ..murmured, 'Snap.'

snap-. Add: **A. a. snap action**: also used *attrib.* to designate switches and relays that make and break contact rapidly, independently of the speed of the actuating mechanism; **snap-bean** (earlier example); **snap-brim,** used *attrib.* to designate a type of hat for men with a brim which may be arranged in different ways; also *absol.*; hence **snap-brimmed** *a.*; **snap gauge** *Mech.*, a form of caliper gauge that can be used to check that a component is neither too large nor too small within stated tolerances.

1951 *Chambers's Jrnl.* Oct. 639/2 A snap-action switch ..cuts out the power supply at short and timed intervals. **1962** *Newnes Conc. Encycl. Electr. Engin.* 726/1 Many rotary switches are manufactured for d.c. operation with snap-action mechanisms. **1977** R. W. SMEATON *Switchgear & Control Handbk.* III. 4 Snap-action contacts reduce the arcing time. **1770** M. AMBLER *Jrnl.* Sept. in *Virginia Mag. Hist. & Biogr.* (1937) XLV. 156 A Breast of Veal for Dinner Snap Beans & gooseberry tart. **1928** *Daily Express* 5 July 9/4 The snap-brim (or turn-down) soft felt hat. **1941** [see *BRETON *sb.* and *a.*]. **1969** V. C. CLINTON-BADDELEY *Only Matter of Time* 45 Davie..put on his soft green hat... Why a 'snap brim', by the way? He always wondered. **1972** B. F. CONNERS *Don't embarrass Bureau* (1973) I. 3 The man was wearing a nondescript raincoat and a gray snap-brim hat. **1949** B. A. BOTKIN *Treas. S. Folklore* II. iii. 252 Loud checked suit, flaming necktie, diamond stickpin, and rakish snap-brimmed felt hat. **1976** *Maclean's Mag.* (Toronto) 15 Nov. 28/1 Al Capone wasn't talking through his snap-brimmed hat. **1918** D. T. HAMILTON *Gages, Gaging & Inspection* iii. 67 Snap gages used in general manufacturing are made in three types; namely, solid, adjustable, and built-up gages. **1964** S. CRAWFORD *Basic Engin. Processes* iv. 298 When using snap gauges for checking external diameters the component should be gauged in a number of positions along and around its surface.

b. *snap button, closing, closure, fastener, fastening, -joint, -lid, -lock, shackle*; **snap-link** (later examples); *spec.* = *KARABINER; **snap-ring,** (*a*) (later examples); (*b*) = *KARABINER; **snap switch,** a snap-action switch.

1897 *Sears, Roebuck Catal.* (1968) 228/3 Gloves... Set in thumbs, and patent snap buttons. **1976** *National Observer* (U.S.) 23 Oct. 20/2 His pearl snap-button shirt is open, his belt loosened a notch, his head propped up with a bulky, weathered arm. **1964** *McCall's Sewing* 171/2 (*heading*), Sleeve with snap closing. **1969** *Sears Catal.* Spring/Summer 16 Band waist, snap closure. **1976** *National Observer* (U.S.) 10 Apr. 16/3 (Advt.), The waist band and two patch pockets are fitted with permanent and attractive metal snap closures. No buttons to fall off. **1895** *Montgomery Ward Catal.* Spring & Summer 289/3 Men's Genuine Oil Tanned Calfskin Gloves,..one button, patent snap fastener. **1976** M. MAGUIRE *Scratchproof* xi. 165 My eyes instinctively traced the zipper, buttons and snap fasteners on her suit. **1898** *T. Eaton & Co. Catal.* Spring & Summer 124/3 Men's Klondike sleeping bags,.. envelope top, snap fastenings, riveted corners. **1981** *Sunday Express Mag.* 11 Oct. 17/2 (Advt.), And each of the two key fobs has its own snap fastening. **1956** *Archit. Rev.* CXIX. 213/2 In this case the positive fixing and covering are achieved by a simple snap-joint incorporated in the edge corrugations. **1968** *Gloss. Terms Mechanized & Hand Sheet Metal Work* (*B.S.I.*) 21 *Snap joint*, the junction between two pieces of sheet or strip, the edges of which are formed so that they can be clipped together to form a rigid joint. **1932** *N. & Q.* 13 Feb. 123/2 Portable Ink-Bottles: these were in quite common use until recent times... I frequently had in a waistcoat pocket, the small square, or oblong leathered covered box, with a snap-lid. **1946** D. R. BROWER *Man. Ski Mountaineering* (ed. 2) iii. 28 The army aluminium carabiner (snaplink) has equal strength, weighs much less. **1981** L. DEIGHTON *XPD* xxxvii. 294 Never mind all these modern contraptions—pitons, snap links and stirrups. **1913** *Strand Mag.* Nov. 103 (Advt.), Smart, neat, snap-lock links. Of all Hosiers, Outfitters, etc... *Snap-lock Link Co.* **1971** B. MALAMUD *Tenants* 12 His apartment, stoutly protected by two patent locks plus a strong snap-lock enclosing heavy circular bolts. **1941** T. A. H. PEACOCKE *Mountaineering* ii. 25 Each climber carries a loop of line... A 'karabiner' (snap-ring) is hung on the loop. **1941** *Engineers' Digest* II. 321/1 Snap rings provide an economical and effective means of facilitating machine assemblies in applications where the loading is not excessive. **1957** *Listener* 28 Nov. 882/2 The less fortunate..of us have to..join the modern school of artificial rock climbers..with their pitons, snap rings, miniature ladders, [etc.]. **1970** K. BALL *Fiat 600, 600D Autobook* i. 12/2 With a special tool..depress the valve springs, remove the split cotters and snap rings. **1974** *Islander* (Victoria, B.C.) 21 July 11/1 Another day ..a snap shackle on the mizzen staysail broke. **1926** *Gloss. Terms Electr. Engin.* (Brit. Engin. Stand. Assoc.) 159 Snap switch. **1977** R. W. SMEATON *Switchgear & Control Handbk.* III. 6 (*heading*) Resistance of control-circuit duty contacts and snap switches.

d. (Further examples.) Also, **snap freezing,** freezing done by reducing the temperature suddenly to well below freezing point; hence **snap-freeze** *v. trans.*

1841 *Congress. Globe* X. App. 42/3 This extra session of Congress, called in time of peace to take snap judgments on the American people. **1867** *J. Lillywhite's Cricketers' Companion* 13 Get some one to give you difficult catches... You will soon be good at snap-catching. **1888** A. G. STEEL in Steel & Lyttelton *Cricket* iii. 179 The object of short-slip is to pick up snicks which just miss the wicket-keeper, and although he may hold a larger proportion of these quick snap catches when a long way from the wicket, he will get an infinitely greater number when closer in. **1896** *Congress. Rec.* 27 Feb. 2214/2 When the snap tally was taken, he..went to the clerk. **1898** A. P. ATTERBURY tr. *Sombart's Socialism & Social Movement in 19th Cent.* vi. 137 A snap resolution of a working-men's congress. **1932** 'N. SHUTE' *Lonely Road* xi. 229 This isn't any snap decision on my part. I've been thinking of it for some time. **1933** *Mod. Lang. Notes* XLVIII. 393 In most cases they reflect, not conclusions drawn from research, but snap judgments based on chance observation and personal likes and dislikes. **1940** *Sun* (Baltimore) 23 Sept. 12/2 (*caption*) Charley Gehringer takes a snap throw from Shortstop Dick Bartell. **1954** X. FIELDING *Hide & Seek* v. 67 Unless we were unlucky enough to be held up by a snap Gestapo..check. **1955** *New Biol.* XVIII. 93 Slow cooling is supposed to cause more damage than rapid cooling since it results in the formation of larger ice crystals, and the use of 'snap' or ultra-rapid freezing has been advocated on the grounds that ice crystal formation may be avoided altogether, the system cooling in an amorphous state. **1959** 'A. GILBERT' *Death takes Wife* v. 54, I had to keep this snap appointment. **1959** *Punch* 27 May 704/3 You have to be constantly on the *qui vive* if you are not going to risk being behindhand with the timing of the first drop [of hail], or even missing a snap shower altogether. **1960** Snap-test [see *BREATHALYSER]. **1960** V. JENKINS *Lions down Under* xi. 161 There was no doubt about his speed and capacity for 'snap-thinking'. **1965** *Listener* 21 Oct. 637/2 The snap opinions in this programme which I have always respected are those of Patrick Campbell. **1973** *Times* 8 Jan. 3/3 The investigation..will involve snap checks at garages. **1974** HAWKEY & BINGHAM *Wild Card* ix. 95 If he builds a cryogenic tank into the spacecraft, it'll rupture on explosion, spray the tissue with liquid oxygen, snap-freeze it, and provide perfect histological specimens for the investigators. **1974** B. A. NEWTON *Trypanosomiasis & Leishmaniasis* 277 Annear (1956) described a technique for 'snap freezing' *Crithidia oncopelti* on a 'peptone plug'. **1974** 'M. INNES' *Appleby's other Story* viii. 62 One must make no snap judgement. **1974** *Socialist Worker* 26 Oct. 15/1, 2800 teachers in 90 schools staging snap strikes in support of a £15-a-week interim increase. **1976** *Alyn & Deeside Observer* 10 Dec. 16/3 The information arrives at a time which can allow only for a 'snap decision'. **1977** *Times of Zambia* 7 Sept. 2/2 A snap survey of clinics found that medical assistants in the health institutions had not been able to administer prescribed drugs for some time now.

e. *snap bill, division* (earlier example), *election.*

1883 E. W. HAMILTON *Diary* 19 July (1972) II. 461 The Agricultural Holdings Bill..is on the whole being well received, though the Government were on Tuesday defeated by a snap division on a landlords' amendment. **1940** *Sun* (Baltimore) 28 Mar. 12/3 The outcome of the voting in Canada is no surprise. It was a 'snap' election engineered with the greatest skill by Prime Minister W. L. Mackenzie King and the results have fully justified his astute political strategy. **1973** *Times* 8 Dec. 3/8 The strong majority..who do not think the Government should hold a snap general election on this issue are mainly Conservative voters. **1975** J. P. MORGAN *House of Lords & Labour Govt.* viii. 217 The reformers themselves therefore argued that the announcement should be made immediately, and the Lords' reform, including any mention of a snap Bill, indefinitely deferred.

B. Forming combinations, esp. with prepositions, used *attrib.* to designate things or appliances operating with a snap (cf. sense A. b in Dict. and Suppl.); as *snap-in, -off, -on,* etc.

1905–6 *T. Eaton & Co. Catal.* Fall & Winter 158/4 Snap-on Hose Supporters, snaps on to edge of corset. **1939–40** *Army & Navy Stores Catal.* 590 Sports seats... Pigskin covered handle, 'snap-on' ground disc. **1963** *Punch* 17 Apr. 560/3 This is a hygienic, snap-top canister-ette. **1967** *Electronics* 6 Mar. 81/1 (Advt.), Printed Circuit Pins (A) may be attached at rates up to 4,000 an hour; snap-in design holds leads in position for easy solder dipping. **1972** *N.Y. Times* 3 Nov. 3/4 (Advt.), 4 snap-close shirts. **1977** *National Observer* (U.S.) 15 Jan. 21/4 Old wine is also served up in snaptop cans in an entertainment called *The Club*, now at the downtown Circle in the Square. **1978** *Detroit Free Press* 16 Apr. (Parade Suppl.) 14/2 (Advt.), Our very special features, such as a new one-piece, snap-in drapery rod. Works like a traverse. No tabs to tear! **1979** *Nature* 29 Mar. p. xxix/2 A unique one-handed operation, using inexpensive snap-on snap-off plastic, disposable tips.

sna·p-back. Also **snapback.** [f. SNAP-.]

1. *U.S.* and *Canad. Football.* **a.** A centre player; the centre-rusher. *? Obs.*

1887 *Outing* Oct. 69/2 He it is who, receiving the ball from the 'center-rusher', or 'snap-back', as he is more commonly called, passes it to some other player for a kick or run. **1893** W. C. CAMP *College Sports* 99 This name [*sc.* center rusher] has since given place almost entirely to 'snap-back'. **1901** *Encycl. Sport* II. 426/1 The influence of the snap-back will at once be realised from the consideration that the moment he puts the ball into play through his legs behind him, he also makes six men besides himself immediately off-side.

b. A backward pass from the centre which puts the ball in play to begin a scrimmage.

1910 [see *SCRIMMAGE, SCRUMMAGE *sb.* 4 c (*a*)]. **1947** *Sun* (Baltimore) 8 Nov. 10/3 The first [attempt] fizzled when Wally Wilson fumbled the snapback, while Jones booted wide of the goal posts following the final six pointer.

2. a. A recovery of an earlier position or circumstances. **b.** A reaction or retaliation.

1949 *Sun* (Baltimore) 15 Oct. 13/1 A mild recovery movement in mid-morning cut losses... In the final hour [of trading] there was a snap-back from the lows that gave the whole market a lift. **1961** *Economist* 28 Oct. 370/3 There is little prospect of a swift snapback until the economy shows more signs of strength. **1972** P. TAMONY *Americanisms* (typescript) No. 32. 2 The snapback of the childish and immature took the form of re-mailings of obscene scrawls. **1979** *Financial Rev.* 11 June 7/1 Behind the upward move of the dollar a pressure cooker effect is building—the kind of pressure that could cause a snap-back and make last year's weakness in the currency look like strength.

3. In Boxing, a swift backward movement of the body to evade an opponent's blow.

1950 J. DEMPSEY *Championship Fighting* xxii. 169 The last and worst type of evasion is the pull-away. Some fighters call it the 'snap-back'. **1952** *Amateur Boxing* ('Know the Game' ser.) 23/1 *Snap back*, a sway backwards —a quick 'snap' back from the hips, sufficient to be out of range of the blow.

snapdragon. 5. (Earlier example in Glass-making.)

1869 *Our Young Folks* V. 85 This was taken up by a second boy on a 'snap-dragon',—a rod something like a ponty, but with a socket at the end for holding articles of glass,—and carried to a glory-hole.

snapped, *ppl. a.* Add: **2.** Designating matching exposed cards which have prompted the call 'snap!' in the game of snap. Cf. *SNAP *v.* 5 g.

1935 *Encycl. Sports, Games & Pastimes* 568/2 The one who calls first obtains all the cards which lie beneath the two snapped ones.

snapper, *sb.*[1] Add: **2. d.** (Later example.)

1980 *Times* 22 Dec. 12/8 People write to me of 'snappers' which are available at posh, probably preppy, parties in Boston, and which go pop like crackers.

e. (Later examples.) Also *attrib.*, as *snapper ending.*

1895 'MARK TWAIN' in *Youth's Companion* 3 Oct. 464/1 The..humorous story finishes with a nub, point, snapper, or whatever you like to call it. **1949** *Newsweek* 19 Dec. 13/3 Then came the snapper: 'No matter by what method we achieve security, we'll not achieve it in a bankrupt economy.' **1962** E. LACY *Freeloaders* ix. 186 This is the end of the story. I hardly think I've been steering you towards a twist, or snapper ending. **1973** *Publishesr Weekly* 10 Dec. 31/1 The second story is written as a correspondence between a clerk and an alien, and has an O. Henry snapper at the end. **1976** *New Yorker* 24 May 143/1 The first, a male ensemble with some very good martial-arts-style acrobatics, has a snapper ending that doesn't snap.

f. (Earlier and later examples.)

1817 J. SANSOM *Sk. Lower Canada* 15 One had proposed to put *a snapper* on the driver's whip. **1841** *Knickerbocker* XVII. 277 All the whips were provided with red snappers. **1903** *N.Y. Even. Post* 29 Sept. 8/2 Senator Carmack..is simply adding a snapper to the lash of his vigorous denunciation of the whole Philippine policy. **1949** B. A. BOTKIN *Treas. S. Folklore* I. v. 117 Showing off his prowess..he first split a horsefly into pieces, and then tore a bumblebee into shreds with the snapper on the end of his whip.

g. *pl.* Teeth; a set of false teeth. *slang.*

1924 WODEHOUSE *Leave it to Psmith* i. 36 You see, this fellow understands my snappers. **1958** *Listener* 31 July 154/2 Do your snappers fit snugly?

h. A sea-bed sampler that operates by enclosing material between two or more jaws that come together on contact with the bottom. Also *snapper grab, sampler.*

1925 *Proc. & Trans. R. Soc. Canada* (*Math., etc. Sciences*) 3rd Ser. XIX. IV. 51 The 'snapper' is a simple and inexpensive instrument which has long been used in connection with submarine cable laying. **1942** H. U. SVERDRUP et al. *Oceans* x. 344 Bottom samplers used for oceanographic work fall into three general categories: dredges (drag buckets), snappers, and coring tubes. *Ibid.* 345 Snapper samplers of the clamshell type have been widely used for obtaining samples of the superficial layers of the sediments. **1968** R. V. TAIT *Elements Marine Ecol.* iii. 49 For larger samples, various small spring-loaded, snapper grabs have been devised which take a shallow bite out of the sea-floor.

3. b. *U.S. Football.* Also *snapper-back* = *SNAP-BACK 1 a.

1887 in P. H. Davis *Football* (1911) 475 Rule 12 altered so as to prohibit interference with the snapper-back until the ball is in motion. **1920** W. CAMP *Football without Coach* 30 That involves a great deal harder work from the center rush or snapper back in getting the ball back to him. **1961** J. S. SALAK *Dict. Amer. Sports* 409 The snapper is the player who snaps the ball. **1974** *Rules of Game* 148/1 The snapper may not slide his hands along the ball before grasping it, nor move his feet or lift a hand until after a snap.

3*. a. A taker of snapshots; a casual photographer.

1910 *Chambers's Jrnl.* 13 Aug. 589/1 There is no relief in a protest, for the rampant 'snapper' knows that the law is on his side. **1921** *Ibid.* 30 July 546/1 He who was but a snapper, a presser of a button, and next became a photographic enthusiast. **1977** *Ripped & Torn* VI. 7/2 And thanks a lot to all you budding photographers for the offers of photos, just send 'em in you snappers.

b. *slang.* A ticket inspector.

1938 F. D. SHARPE *Sharpe of Flying Squad* 333 *A snapper*, ticket inspector. **1957** 'N. CULOTTA' *They're a Weird Mob* (1958) x. 142 'E doesn't want yer ticket. The snapper's got yer ticket.

6. a. (Further examples.) Cf. SCHNAPPER in Dict. and Suppl.

1842 W. R. WADE *Journey in Northern Island N.Z.* vii. 180 Some snappers which the lads had caught furnished us with a hearty supper. **1896** [see *NANNYGAI]. **1959** A. MCLINTOCK *Descr. Atlas N.Z.* 48 Snapper..is the most important species in the commercial catch. **1977** *Best of Austral. Angler* 9/1 The floating gar system used for tailor is also one of the very best ways to catch snapper from the rocks.

b. *red snapper*: see RED *a.* 17 c in Dict. and Suppl.

c. (Earlier example.)

1796 [see *mud-turtle* s.v. *MUD *sb.*[1] 5 b].

snappily, *adv.* Add: **2.** Smartly, nattily; crisply, deftly.

1936 J. T. FARRELL *$1,000 a Week* (1942) 141 He looked unobtrusively at two snappily dressed young fellows on his left. **1947** *People* 22 June 5/1 Another snappily-togged Ascot-bound party of bright young things noisily piling into a glittering £5,000 limousine. **1977** 'A. STUART' *Snap Judgement* 16 A strong, blue-eyed, snappily dressed young man. **1981** E. AGRY *Assault Force* v. 53 Mac reversed the Audi snappily into the nearest driveway.

snapping, *vbl. sb.* Add: **3. snapping-point,** the point at which something will snap, or someone's strength or endurance will fail.

1933 G. ARTHUR *Septuagenarian's Scrap Bk.* 272 And like all good artists, like Sarah herself, she is a '*traqueuse*' whose head feels hot and hands are cold on a first night, and who, with fever in the veins and nerves strained to snapping-point, will yet perhaps give the most inspired performance of the whole run. **1946** K. TENNANT *Lost Haven* (1947) i. 20 To have not only mud but sticky honeycomb all over her shiny, clean linoleum was the snapping-point. **1982** *India Today* 15 Feb. 125/2 Relations between the Government and the judiciary are stretched to snapping point.

snapping, *ppl. a.* Add: **2. b.** That makes a sharp cracking or snapping noise.

1891 *Outlook* Dec. 238/1 In the tender light of the rising sun he creeps downstairs, avoiding that squeaking board and that snapping step. **1942** W. FAULKNER *Go down, Moses* 170 They emerged from the narrow, roofless tunnel of snapping and hissing cane, still galloping, onto the open ridge below. **1968** B. HINES *Kestrel for Knave* 132 Every time he tried to escape [from the shower] the three boys bounced him back, stinging him with their snapping towels as he retreated.

3. b. (Earlier examples.) Also *snapping tortoise.*

1784 J. F. D. SMYTH *Tour U.S.A.* I. 338 One kind of them bites very fiercely when incensed..; these are called Snapping Turtles. **1808** T. ASHE *Trav. Amer.* II. 234 The Indians call this by a name which implies the snapping tortoise. **1828** [see *SALT RIVER 2 a]. **1840** *Knickerbocker* XVI. 54 The..snapping-tortoises, frogs, squirrels, and such small deer, are their flocks and herds.

c. *snapping shrimp*, a shrimp of the family Alpheidæ, which uses its large chelæ to make a snapping noise; also called the pistol shrimp.

1941 STEINBECK & RICKETTS *Sea of Cortez* 194 Sponges and tunicates under which small crabs and snapping shrimps hid themselves. **1964** *Oceanogr. & Marine Biol.* II. 431 The clicking of snapping shrimp..is a form of ambient sound when one is concentrating on the sounds of fish.

4. Violent, severe, extreme; usu. as quasi-*adv.*

1845 *Knickerbocker* XXV. 87 I've got a snapping headache. **1876** *Wide Awake* (Boston, Mass.) July 19/1 The night was snapping cold. **1905** K. D. WIGGIN *Rose o' the River* 93 The snapping cold weather and the depth to which the water was frozen were aiding it.

snappingly, *adv.* Add: Also, briskly, smartly. Cf. *SNAPPILY *adv.* 2.

1976 *Gramophone* Dec. 1016/1 The second subject [is] held in a more or less strict tempo but flecked with fine, subliminally caught colours, the mordents now fluttering like spread acciaccaturas, now expressive, now snappingly exact. **1978** *Ibid.* Apr. 1756/2 Bernstein, as one would expect, is ideally alive and snappingly rhythmic at the opening of the last movement's allegro section.

snappy, *a.* Add: **6. a.** (Earlier and later examples.)

1871 'MARK TWAIN' in *Galaxy* Apr. 615/2, I compressed it into a snappy foot-note at the bottom. **1955** *Times* 27 Aug. 8/4 Her clean texture, snappy rhythm, and general strength of tone and purpose all betokened a true grasp of the composer's style. **1977** *N.Z. Herald* 8 Jan. 2-12/4 (Advt.), Painting roofs, for free quotes phone the expert. Snappy service.

b. *snappy dresser*, someone who dresses in a stylish or natty manner.

1925 *New Yorker* 9 May 27/1, I always used to be a snappy dresser. **1958** [see *DUDE *v.*]. **1977** P. THEROUX *Consul's File* 174 A woman waiting for her lover..whom she would describe as a snappy dresser, a riot, a real card.

d. *U.S.* Designating weather characteristic of a cold snap (SNAP *sb.* 7 a, b).

1928 J. C. LINCOLN *Silas Bradford's Boy* 149 It was a clear, snappy early winter day. **1951** *Publ. Amer. Dial. Soc.* xv. 60 *Snappy*,..said of crispy cold weather.

7. b. Phr. *to make it snappy*: to make haste, to get a move on.

1926 G. FRANKAU *My Unsentimental Journey* ii. 31 After that we 'made it snappy' (Anglicé—got a move on). **1945** A. HUXLEY *Let.* 10 Apr. (1969) 520, I wish there had been space in my review to quote you at length on these subjects, But, alas, I had to 'make it snappy'. **1976** J. I. M. STEWART *Young Patullo* ix. 195 Make it snappy. Taxi's waiting.

snap-shooter. Add: **2.** Also **snapshooter.**

1904 *Car* X. 240 (*caption*) Mr. W. K. Vanderbilt, Jr.,.. is reluctant to pose before a camera, but occasionally falls a victim to wily 'snapshooters'. **1973** C. BONINGTON *Next Horizon* iv. 72, I had always taken a camera with me on my climbs, but had been little more than a holiday snapshooter.

snap-shooting, *vbl. sb.* (Example in *Photogr.*)

1979 G. MACDONALD *Camera* iv. 57 Snapshooting was.. a..haphazard affair... Most snaps were still portraits of family and friends.

snap-shot, *sb.* Add: **1. b.** (Earlier example.)

1845 F. TOLFREY *Sportsman in Canada* II. v. 131 It is capital practice is this snipe-shooting for a youngster; at least it makes a man a good snap-shot.

2. a. (Later examples.) Also *fig.*

1903 'O. HENRY' in *Everybody's Mag.* Aug. 194/1 You see a man doing nothing but loafing around making snapshots. **1928** *Observer* 17 June 10/2, I asked President Masaryk..if he could give me a snapshot of the difference between what he found when he came to Prague in 1918, and what he has the satisfaction of seeing now. **1930** [see *HUSTLE *v.* 5]. **1950** G. B. SHAW *Farfetched Fables* iii. 109 What are you doing here?..Only hiking round the island. May I take a snapshot? **1962** M. MCLUHAN *Gutenberg Galaxy* 241 He [*sc.* Montaigne] bred up a great race of self-portrayers by means of the mental snapshot. **1975** P. FUSSELL *Gt. War & Mod. Memory* i. 10 British and German soldiers..meeting in No Man's Land to exchange cigarets and to take snapshots. **1978** P. O'DONNELL *Dragon's Claw* iii. 47 Snapshots of sight and sound, of touch, taste, and smell.

b. *Computers.* A record of the contents of some or all of the storage locations in a computer at a particular stage in the execution of a program (see quot. 1963). Freq. *attrib.*

1963 GREGORY & VAN HORN *Automatic Data-Processing Systems* (ed. 2) xii. 473 Some simplified forms of post-mortem routines give only a storage snapshot, which is a complete copy of all storage locations at the time the processor stopped. A snapshot routine may also list the instruction that caused the program to stop, the current contents of arithmetic units and indexes, and perhaps, several of the most-recently executed jumps thus indicating the path of program control. A differential snapshot lists the contents of storage locations that have changed from their initial value or from their value in a prior snapshot. **1966** *IFIP-ICC Vocab. Information Processing* 85 When a trace program gives output only on selected instructions, or for selected conditions, it is called a snapshot program. **1973** C. W. GEAR *Introd. Computer Sci.* vi. 244 An alternative is to take a series of snapshots at points in the program section.

2*. In various sports, a quick shot (of the ball, etc.) at goal.

1961 *Times* 29 May 4/3 [In Polo.] After Hanut had

scored with a lovely snapshot to make it 3–2. **1963** *Globe & Mail* (Toronto) 21 Jan. 16/3 [In Hockey.] Hull responded by taking a quick pass from Balfour and scoring on a quick snap-shot. **1976** *Oadby & Wigston* (Leics.) *Advertiser* 26 Nov. 15/4 [In Football.] Saints hit back and a snapshot by Jim White hit the crossbar.

3. (Further examples.)

1894 [see *ENLARGER 1 b]. **1901** MERWIN & WEBSTER *Calumet 'K'* xv. 288 Young men with snap-shot cameras waylaid Bannon. **1967** J. PHILIP et al. *Best of Granta* I. 17 The winning photo in *The Granta* Holiday Snapshot Competition shows a couple kissing on a beach. **1977** R. E. HARRINGTON *Quintain* iii. 24 He searched the terrain, storing quick snapshot impressions. **1977** *N.Y. Rev. Bks.* 23 June 25/3 The crudely chronological order of snapshot-sequences pasted in family albums.

snap-shot, *v.* Add: **b.** Also *fig.*

1907 *Outlook* 17 Aug. 206/2 All the peculiar attitude of our race toward dancing was suddenly snapshotted in that absurdity. **1932** *Essays & Stud.* XVII. 84 Thackeray found them [*sc.* the railways] vulgar, but amusing for the opportunities they gave of snapshotting people. **1980** *Daily Tel.* 21 Nov. 15/1 The play snapshots pretty sharply Jimmy's furtive park meetings with his waif.

c. To shoot (something) quickly without taking deliberate aim.

1928 *Daily Express* 6 Dec. 19/3 Mr Blyth...was a fairly deliberate shot, and liked to take his high birds neatly and quietly, but could nevertheless snapshot a woodcock in thick covert with an effortless ease.

Hence **sna·pshotting** *ppl. a.*

1978 *Nature* 7 Dec. 647/2 Mr Sankhala also remarks that the snap-shotting tourist is so preoccupied with shutter speeds, lens apertures and focussing that he fails to see anything around him.

snare, *sb.* Add: **2. a.** Now often made of wire.

b. *ellipt.* for *snare-drum*, sense 3 b.

1938 D. BAKER *Young Man with Horn* I. iv. 28 He could, of course, play his snare and..sooner or later he'd have money enough to buy a piano. **1950** A. LOMAX *Mister Jelly Roll* 64, I had a drummer that hit his snares so loud that one night I gave him a couple of fly swatters for a gag. **1960** 'E. MCBAIN' *Give Boys Great Big Hand* xii. 137 The big one is the bass drum, and that round black case is what they call the snare. **1973** J. WAINWRIGHT *Pride of Pigs* 31 The drummer giving his snare a series of flicks with the wire brushes.

3. a. *snare wire.*

1804 LEWIS & CLARK *Orig. Jrnls. Lewis & Clark Exped.* (1905) VI. 274 Baling Invoice of Sundries for Indian Presents..3 Rolls Ear Wire, 3 do Snare Wire. **1953** P. PROVENCHER *I live in Woods* iv. 36, I am in no danger because I have my axe, matches, fishing lines and snare-wire. **1964** C. WILLOCK *Enormous Zoo* iv. 56 Snare wire began to make its appearance most frequently... Catching animals with wire snares attached to large logs is understandably popular.

b. *snare-drum* (earlier example), *drummer, drumming, -head* (later examples).

1873 T. B. ALDRICH *Marjorie Daw* 130 Morning and evening we heard the spiteful roll of their snare-drums. **1926** E. FERBER *Show Boat* v. 96 A snare drummer who was always called a 'sticks', and the bass drum, known as the bull. **1941** W. C. HANDY *Father of Blues* (1957) i. 5 The youngster would..beat on the strings in the manner of a snare drummer. **1961** A. BAINES *Mus. Instruments* xiv. 335 'Snares'..consist of a number of gut or wire strings stretched across the lower skin or 'snare head'. **1966** *Crescendo* Apr. 30/3 Complete with snare drumming that would make the Dagenham Girl Pipers turn green with envy. **1976** *New Yorker* 8 Mar. 108/3 He would hit the snare directly, or hit the snarehead and the rim.

snare, *v.* Add: **1. c.** *U.S.* To catch, to win by a small margin.

1942 BERREY & VAN DEN BARK *Amer. Thes. Slang* § 650/6 *Win*...snare a win. *Ibid.* § 679/5 *Field a ball; catch*...snare a hit. **1948** *Sun* (Baltimore) 26 Nov. 17/1 Double Brandy..came from next to last to snare the second money about a half length in front of Brookmeade Stable's Gnu.

snareless, *a.* Add: **b.** Without a snare.

1978 *Early Music* Jan. 29/1 Drums are often snareless, though the pictorial evidence is that the cylindrical drum almost always had a snare.

snaring, *vbl. sb.* (In Dict. s.v. SNARE *v.*) Add: Also *attrib.*

1923 *Beaver* Mar. 236/1 Having some snaring twine she killed sufficient rabbits to keep herself and child alive. **1971** A. FRY *Long Journey* iv. 18 The snaring wing, a long brush fence with a few 'escapes'.., each set with a snare. *Ibid.* ix. 52 Three or four men could work together, driving animals..toward a snaring fence.

snarky (snā·ɹki), *a. colloq.* [f. SNARK *v.* + -Y[1].] Irritable, short-tempered, 'narky'.

1906 E. NESBIT *Railway Children* ii. 49 Don't be snarky, Peter. It isn't our fault. **1913** J. VAIZEY *College Girl* xxiv. 326 'Why should you think I am "snarky"?' 'Because—you *are*! You're not a bit sociable and friendly.' **1953** E. COXHEAD *Midlanders* x. 247 I've known you were the soul of kindness, under that snarky way. *a* **1974** R. CROSSMAN *Diaries* (1976) II. 627 We also have to overcome something else—the stream of anti-government propaganda, smearing, snarky, derisive, which comes out of Fleet Street.

Hence **sna·rkily** *adv.*; **sna·rkiness**; **sna·rkish** *a.*

1912 R. FRY *Let.* 16 Mar. (1972) I. 355 So sorry I seem so snarkish just now. **1960** *Economist* 28 May 859/2 In some of his comments on bureaucracy there is a relapse into snarkiness. **1967** *Listener* 20 July 91/3 Viewers' letters are not just read out. They are commented upon by Kenneth Robinson (usually rather snarkily).

snarl, *sb.*[1] Add: **2. a.** (Later examples of sense 'a knot in the hair'.)

1966 J. S. COX *Illustr. Dict. Hairdressing & Wigmaking* 139/2 *Snarl*, a tangle in the hair. **1976** 'TREVANIAN' *Main* (1977) xiii. 243 A young slattern who tugs a snarl out of her hair with her fingers.

b. (Further examples.) *traffic snarl* (U.S. colloq.), a traffic jam.

1933 E. B. WHITE *Let.* Mar. (1976) 113 At noon I happened to be driving north on Fourth Avenue, and got held up in a traffic snarl. **1950** J. D. MACDONALD *Brass Cupcake* ii. 18, I dove slowly back into the traffic snarl. **1968** S. CHALLIS *Death on Quiet Beach* iii. 30 The traffic was a slow snarl that cost him forty minutes. **1975** *New Yorker* 19 May 99/1 The traffic snarls were impenetrable. **1979** *Arizona Daily Star* 5 Aug. D 3/3 Production snarls kept cars out of the showroom. **1980** R. L. DUNCAN *Brimstone* iv. 65 The congressional reorganization studies ..were resulting in a snarl of immense proportions.

3. (Earlier and later examples.)

1775 in O. E. Winslow *Amer. Broadside Verse* (1930) 141/2, I see another snarl of men. **1825** J. NEAL *Bro. Jonathan* I. 76 There being 'a pootty consid'r'ble snarl o' gals, I guess' the supper was bravely furnished. **1836** W. DUNLAP *Mem. Water Drinker* (1837) II. iii. 24 They swarm like a snarl of bees before hiving. **1904** *N.Y. Tribune* 10 Apr. (Suppl.) 7/3 A veritable snarl of street urchins took possession of several benches in Lincoln Park.

snarl, *v.*[1] Add: **2. c.** *to snarl up*: to throw into confusion, to mess up; to entangle, to impede the smooth running of (something). *colloq.*

1937 C. DAY LEWIS *Starting Point* I. iii. 49 He short-punted ahead, snarling up the defence. **1957** J. F. HORNER *Summary of Scientology* vi. 67 Self-processing tends only to snarl-up the person attempting it. **1960** *Economist* 22 Oct. 317/2 A..wish to snarl up the relations between the western governments. **1962** *Listener* 5 July 36/2 Private cars are increasing at such a rate.. that the roads will be snarled up. **1976** *Daily Tel.* 22 June 1/3 The Conservatives snarled up Government business by ceasing the pairing of MPs and other co-operation. **1981** *Sunday Express* 25 Oct. (*heading*) 150,000 marchers snarl up London.

3. Also *fig.* and with *up.*

1951 *Manch. Guardian Weekly* 19 Apr. 5/3 The traffic clears quickly at times, when it might otherwise snarl—which is the American way of saying it might 'cause an inextricable jam'. **1963** *Listener* 14 Feb. 300/2 The action ..snarls up into an obtrusive expressionism. **1970** G. F. NEWMAN *Sir, You Bastard* viii. 201 Traffic snarled eastwards along Brompton Road at a snail's pace.

snarled, *ppl. a.* **2.** (Further *fig.* examples.) Of road traffic: congested (orig. *U.S.*). Also with *up.*

1967 N. MARSH *Death at Dolphin* viii. 230 We've caught a snarled-up little job this time. **1973** R. HILL *Ruling Passion* I. vii. 73 Another diversionary tactic. What a snarled-up lot of people they were! **1976** R. MOORE *Dubai* i. 8 Fitz pushed his way through the..streets, walking through the snarled traffic. **1980** *Times* 8 July 6/2 One of the worst spots for snarled-up traffic.

sna·rl-up. *colloq.* [f. vbl. phr. *to snarl up*: see *SNARL *v.*[1] 2 c, 3.] A muddle, state of confusion; a mistake; a traffic jam; a blockage. Also *attrib.*

1960 M. PHILLIPS in *Analog Sci. Fact/Fiction* Nov. 24/1 Both courses..resulted in more snarl-ups. Reports that should have been sent in weeks before arrived too late; reports meant for the eyes of only one man were turned out in triplicate. **1962** J. BRAINE *Life at Top* xi. 152 There was going to be a huge snarl-up very soon. **1963** *Daily Tel.* 3 June 1/1 On what the AA described as 'snarl-up Sunday' there were queues of up to 19 miles on several major arteries. **1966** *Musical Opinion* Aug. 691/1 The main cause of the brouhaha about electronic instruments is a snarl-up in terminology. **1969** *Daily Tel.* 10 Jan. 1/2 Sixty-three people were injured and more than 100 vehicles smashed up as freezing fog gripped the M1 and M10 yesterday... The AA described it as 'the worst snarl-up since the M1 opened'. **1974** *Financial Times* 15 Mar. 23/7 Small organisation snarl-ups, such as failing to get out the Speakers' Handbook in time. **1977** 'E. CRISPIN' *Glimpses of Moon* xi. 220 A helicopter..dipped to examine the snarl-up in the lane below.

snatch, *sb.* Add: **3. d.** (*a*) An unexpected and quick robbery; an act of forcibly robbing someone; (*b*) *slang* (orig. and chiefly *U.S.*), a kidnapping; also *attrib.*

(*a*) **1866** [in Dict., sense 3 a]. **1885** M. DAVITT *Leaves from Prison Diary* I. I. xvi. 152, I did a snatch near St. Paul's. **1939** *Forum* Dec. 275/2 A piece of paper covering the slit was rolled aside in the course of a snatch. **1976** *Southern Even. Echo* (Southampton) 17 Nov. 17/2 Basingstoke police warned women to hang on to their handbags after a sixth attempted snatch in recent weeks. **1980** *West Lancs. Even. Gaz.* 6 June 1 An engineering labourer who was stabbed..during a wage snatch on Merseyside.

(*b*) **1931** D. RUNYON in *Collier's* 26 Sept. 7/2 Harry the Horse and Spanish John and Little Isadore pay no attention whatever to local sentiment and go on the snatch. **1932** E. D. SULLIVAN *Snatch Racket* p. x, Bootleg millions ..have provided the sound support for two hundred standard rackets..in the United States and among them is kidnapping—the 'snatch racket'. **1934** 'D. HUME' *Too Dangerous to Live* xix. 200 Where did this snatch take place, Inspector? **1945** —— *Come back for Body* ii. 21 Their only child..has vanished. It looks like a straightforward snatch. **1950** J. D. MACDONALD *Brass Cupcake* ii. 21, I handle it just like a snatch payment. The ransom for Junior. **1980** C. MOOREHEAD *Fortune's Hostages* ii. 26 By 1932 America was in the middle of.. the 'snatch racket'. Dozens of children had been seized... Kidnapping was happening everywhere.

e. *Weight-lifting.* A lift in which the weight is raised in a single motion from the floor to a position overhead with the arms straight.

1928, etc. [see *PRESS *sb.*[1] 6 c]. **1950** *Sun* (Baltimore) 1 May 15/4 Sheppard lifted 240 in the snatch. **1968** *Globe & Mail* (Toronto) 17 Feb. 11/3 Modern lifters do not perform one-arm lifts. Once, two of them were on the Olympic agenda: the one-arm press and the one-arm snatch. **1976** *All about Games* (Com. Org. des Jeux Olympiques) 81 There are two lifts in modern weight-lifting—the snatch and the clean and jerk.

f. Jerkiness in the working of the transmission of a motor vehicle.

1932 *Motoring Encyl.* 137/1 A little thin oil..will soften the [clutch] surfaces sufficiently to avoid snatch. **1955** *Times* 2 Aug. 10/5 Upward and downward changes were made without any trace of snatch. **1962** *Which? Car Suppl.* Oct. 139/1 The car was in excellent condition, apart from..a little 'snatch' in the transmission.

14. *dial.* and *slang.* The female pudenda. Also *attrib.* Cf. sense 6 b in Dict.

1904 in *Eng. Dial. Dict.* **1955** W. GADDIS *Recognitions* III. iv. 851 She said, See? and pulled up her dress to show me her...to show there weren't any marks on her...anywhere else on her body.—You mean on her snatch. **1961** J. HELLER *Catch-22* xxvii. 303 She..twisted away, fleeing far enough..for Yossarian to lunge forward and grab her by the snatch again. **1969** P. ROTH *Portnoy's Complaint* 193 Know what I did when I was fifteen? Sent a lock of my snatch-hair off in an envelope to Marlon Brando. **1971** B. W. ALDISS *Soldier Erect* 128, I was vexed and disappointed that the contact with the *bibi* had been so commercial, so perfunctory—why, I had not even seen or touched her snatch. **1978** J. UPDIKE *Coup* (1979) v. 191 Sooner a black man mate with a lazy shit-smeared sow..than entrust his ebony penis to the snatch of a white devil mare.

snatch, *v.* Add: **2. d.** *spec.* (*a*) To steal, esp. by snatching; (*b*) *slang* (orig. and chiefly *U.S.*), to kidnap.

1765 [in Dict., sense 2 a]. **1887** G. W. WALLING *Recollections N.Y. Chief of Police* xviii. 254 His most brilliant exploit was his 'snatching' of $100,000 from the Royal Insurance Company's office in Broadway in broad daylight. **1919** WODEHOUSE *Coming of Bill* (1920) I. i. 12 As if she had caught him in the act of endeavouring to snatch her purse. **1932** *Detective Fiction Weekly* 17 Dec. 23/2 It's dollars to doughnuts the kid was snatched up in the park. **1934** *Sun* (Baltimore) 10 Mar. 1/7 Banghart had introduced him to the Touhy mob just before the market speculator was 'snatched'. **1936** *Detective Fiction Weekly* 6 June 12/1 'It's one more sweet-running crate. Just about the sweetest I ever snatched. **1973** 'I. DRUMMOND' *Jaws of Watchdog* xii. 156 Why didn't we snatch him in the street and take him away someplace?

e. To partake hurriedly of (food, sleep, etc.).

1803 M. WILMOT *Let.* 6 Aug. in *Russian Jrnls.* (1934) I. 34 We rose with one accord, dress'd, snatch'd a cup of Coffee and got into Mdm R—'s Carriage. **1942** BERREY & VAN DEN BARK *Amer. Thes. Slang* § 94/13 *Eat a small or hurried meal*,..snatch a bite. *Ibid.* § 251/6 *Take a nap*,.. snatch a wink. **1952** M. STEEN *Phoenix Rising* i. 27 I'm snatching a sandwich at the club. **1977** M. KENYON *Rapist* x. 121 He might snatch two hours' sleep..if he swallowed a couple of sleepers.

f. *to snatch it* or *one's time*: to resign, to leave a job and take the wages due. *Austral. slang.*

1941 *Argus* (Melbourne) *Week-End Mag.* 15 Nov. 1/4 *Snatch your time*, resign from the Army, or threaten to leave. **1944** A. MARSHALL *These are my People* 158 'I suppose you struck some bad bosses in your time?' 'If they're bad, I snatch it.' **1962** T. RONAN *Deep of Sky* 55 What's more, when we pass Silverton I'm snatching my time. **1973** F. HUELIN *Keep Moving* 83 What are yous goin' to do? Snatch it or stay?

10. *intr.* Of a mechanism or its control in a motor vehicle, aircraft, etc.: to operate in a jerky or rough manner.

1932 *Motoring Encyl.* 137/1 When..fabric disks have settled down and worn smooth, they are sometimes prone to snatch and engage fiercely. **1942** B. J. ELLAN *Spitfire* xii. 65 His ailerons were obviously snatching too, as first one wing and then the other would dip violently. **1955** *Times* 12 July 12/6 The car tested was inclined to 'snatch' in the transmission if the speed was allowed to drop too low in top gear.

snatch-. Add: **c.** (Earlier example.)

1884 E. W. HAMILTON *Diary* 15 Mar. (1972) II. 577 A motion..which..the Opposition supported in the hope of taking the Government by surprise and putting them in a minority by a snatch division.

d. *snatch-thief* (earlier example); **snatch-back,** the action of taking back; also *attrib.*; (see also quot. 1905); **snatch crop,** a crop grown for quick returns without regard to the future productivity of the soil; also *attrib.* and *fig.*; **snatch squad** *Mil.*, a group of soldiers detailed to seize troublemakers in a crowd; also *transf.*

1905 *Dialect Notes* III. 94 *Snatchback*, change for the worse in circumstances... 'That's a snatchback for him.' **1949** *New Statesman* 24 Dec. 750/3 The distress caused by the snatch-back is no less tragic than would be suffered by natural parents who were forcibly deprived of their children. **1962** A. SAMPSON *Anat. of Britain* xxiii. 377 Hire-purchase..companies..could be ruthless in enforcing 'snatch-backs' if payments had lapsed. **1965** E. GUNDREY *Foot in Door* xvii. 123 'Snatchback' machines, that is ones which had to be returned to dealers by people who failed to keep up their H.P. payments. **1979** H. S. KENT *In on Act* ix. 101 The main objects of the Bill were, first, to make sure that the hire-purchaser knew what he was paying..secondly, to restrict the seller's rights to 'snatch back' the goods on default... The most dear to Ellen's heart was the ban on the snatch-back. **1937** H. G. WELLS *Brynhild* v. 58 Fellows like Blatch can reap a harvest..at ten per cent... There are too many authors. Blatch is able to live by snatch crops. **1959** *Listener* 30 July 179/2 The heart of the soil..had been weakened by the greed of the snatch-crop farmers. **1970** *Financial Times* 23 Mar. 1/1 About 150 youths moved out of Bogside.., smashing windows..and stoning the Army 'snatch squad'. **1976** *Western Mail* (Cardiff) 22 Nov. 1/2 A snatch squad of animal lovers seized 11 beagle pups in a night-time commando-style raid on a top-security breeding centre in West Wales. **1982** *Times* 1 Sept. 3/1 Snatch squads tried ineffectively to combat roaming gangs of pickpockets. **1887** *Courier-Jrnl.* (Louisville, Kentucky) 1 May 13/2 Where the bonnet-buyer is there is the pickpocket and snatch-thief also.

snatcher. Add: **1. d.** *slang* (orig. *U.S.*). A kidnapper.

1932 *Tulsa* (Okla.) *Daily World* 7 Mar. 10/5 'Snatchers' or kidnapers have not been as busy in Tulsa as they have in other cities. **1940** 'D. HUME' *Invitation to Grave* xviii. 235 Mick was reflecting upon the fact that his father's 'snatchers' had entered through this door.

snatching, *vbl. sb.* **1.** (Further examples.)

1931 D. RUNYON in *Collier's* 26 Sept. 7 (*heading*) The snatching of Bookie Bob. **1955** *Times* 26 July 6/6 As soon as the speed drops to 20 m.p.h., a change to third gear is essential to avoid 'snatching'. **1972** J. PHILIPS *Vanishing Senator* (1973) III. ii. 127 They're all in a state over the snatching of Mrs. Lloyd.

snavel (snæ·v'l), *v.*^{2} *slang and dial.* (now chiefly *Austral.*). Also **snavvle.** [Perh. var. SNABBLE *v.* or SNAFFLE *v.*^{4}] *trans.* To steal; to appropriate, to grab.

For further material see *Eng. Dial. Dict.* s.v. *Snavel* vb.^{2} and sb.^{2}

a **1790** H. T. POTTER *New Dict. Cant & Flash* (ed. 2, 1795) 54 *Snavel*, to steal when running. **1823** 'J. BEE' *Slang* 162 *Snavel*, to steal, by snatching, probably, or concealing any small property by piece-meal. **1903** 'T. COLLINS' *Such is Life* 18 Well, we had a bunch o' keys at the camp. I had snavelled 'em at the railway station. **1919** W. DOWNING *Digger Dialects* 46 *Snavvle*, take by stealth; steal; capture. **1933** *Bulletin* (Sydney) 4 Oct. 10/1 Could we but snavel *that* We'd incontestably be home and dried In this keen race. **1948** V. PALMER *Golconda* xiii. 100 They're booming the notion o' a new township and snavelling all the land within a mile o' it.

So † **sna·veller,** a thief. *Obs. rare.*

1781 G. PARKER *View of Society* II. 168 The Snaveller.. coaxes the child up some by-alley,..and grabbles the whole.

snax (snæks), commercial var. *snacks*, pl. of SNACK *sb.*^{2}

1947 I. BROWN *Say the Word* 17 Why does such shop-window spelling, Sox and Snax, irritate me so? **1965** I. FLEMING *Man with Golden Gun* v. 70 A hand-painted sign said '*Snax*'. **1980** 'M. YORKE' *Scent of Fear* vii. 62 She bought sandwiches at Takeaway Snax.

snazzy (snæ·zi), *a. slang* (orig. *U.S.*). [Origin unknown.] Excellent; attractive; classy, stylish, flashy.

1932 *Amer. Speech* VII. 336 *Snazzy*, agreeable; attractive. **1935** N. ERSINE *Underworld & Prison Slang* 68 That's a snazzy dressup you've got. **1938** W. CHAMBERS *Once too Often* i. 17 It was indeed a very snazzy setup and I wondered how many months he was in arrears with his rent. **1944** R. CHANDLER *Let.* 16 Dec. (1966) 43, I had a very snazzy beginning which they cut out, because it didn't really have anything to do with detective stories. **1946** 'P. QUENTIN' *Puzzle for Friends* iii. 27 Think what a snazzy life you've got. All the money in the world. No worries. No work. **1956** 'J. WYNDHAM' *Seeds of Time* 214 You come here with your ritzy ways and your snazzy talk. **1960** *News Chron.* 30 Sept. 4/5 Rod..takes off his snazzy smoking jacket to rescue his..girl friend. **1968** J. LOCK *Lady Policeman* ix. 82 They've made the plain uniforms look as snazzy as possible with whiter-than-white hat-bands, belts and gaiters. **1971** B. W. ALDISS *Soldier Erect* 115, I see you're all togged up... It's really snazzy you look. **1974** *Early Music* Jan. 24/2, I am convinced that the snazzy rhythms and syncopations that one often hears are wrong. **1978** C. LEOPOLD *Casablack* 1 A snazzy, loose-fitting pinstripe that was emphatically fashion in..1942.

sneak, *sb.* Add: **2. a.** Also more generally *on the sneak*, on the sly, by stealth, under concealment.

c **1863** T. TAYLOR *Ticket-of-Leave Man* I. 9 Pottering about on the sneak, flimping or smashing a little when I get the chance. **1930** *Amer. Mercury* XXI. 458/1 You got to work strictly on the sneak. All the spots are hot. **1935** *Sun* (Baltimore) 13 July 9/6 A few of them [*sc.* betting spots] were 'sneaking' with just as many customers as ever... These spots 'on the sneak' usually are located in the upper floors of Loop skyscrapers. **1955** *Publ. Amer. Dial. Soc.* XXIV. 86 If the *road mob* decides to work *on the sneak*, that is, without advance arrangements in any locality, [etc.]. **1982** *Chicago Sun-Times* 6 Aug. 71/1 He does so with all the glee of a schoolkid reading Playboy magazine on the sneak.

3. (Earlier example.)

1851 J. PYCROFT *Cricket Field* vii. 105 Cowley..put on one Tailor Humphreys to bowl twisting underhand sneaks.

4. (Earlier example.)

1862 *Female Life in Prison* I. xvii. 211 The night-officer is generally accustomed to wear a species of India-rubber shoes or goloshes on her feet. These are termed 'sneaks' by the women [of Brixton Prison].

5. *U.S. colloq.* = *sneak preview* s.v. *SNEAK- a.

1941 B. SCHULBERG *What makes Sammy Run?* iv. 60 We'll know better after the sneak... And..when we see whether Mr. and Mrs. Public buy tickets. **1967** *Boston Globe* 5 Apr. 57/1 (*heading*) Sneaks slated at music hall. **1978** E. TIDYMAN *Table Stakes* II. vi. 265 The studio agreed to give the production three previews... The first 'sneak'..took place at a small theater in Redlands.

sneak, *v.* Add: Pa. t. and pple. also (orig. and chiefly *U.S.*) **snuck.**

1887 *Lantern* (New Orleans) 17 Dec. 3/3 He grubbed ten dollars from de bums an den snuck home. **1932** J. T. FARRELL *Young Lonigan* ii. 55 They had all snuck in and were having a good time, making trouble. **1940** R. CHANDLER *Farewell, my Lovely* vi. 36, I snuck in there and grabbed it. **1958** J. KEROUAC *On Road* II. viii. 159 Four sullen fieldworkers, snuck from their chores to brawl in drinking fields. **1969** *Oz* May 3/1 It was sticking out of a dustbin—the mag I mean..so I snuck off to the park and had a good old read. **1976** S. BRETT *So Much Blood* xvi. 191 At the interval Charles and Frances snuck out to the pub. **1979** *Vassar Q.* Summer 17/3, I have come around the back way and snuck up, as we say in Nebraska, on my subject.

I. 1. d. (Earlier example.)

1896 G. ADE *Artie* 7 I'd a' sneaked early in the game.

II. 4. (Examples with a person as obj.)

1968 J. M. ULLMAN *Lady on Fire* (1969) xii. 160 You've got a new lead. Maybe something the sister told you after you snuck her out of that hotel. **1971** D. E. WESTLAKE *I gave at Office* (1972) 12 There was some suspicion that a couple of guests had snuck friends in. **1979** R. JAFFE *Class Reunion* I. vii. 69 He wanted to sneak her into his room.

6. b. (Further examples.) Also, to take or partake of surreptitiously.

1900 *Dialect Notes* II. 61 *Sneak*, to appropriate. **1921** E. O'NEILL *Emperor Jones* i. 160 When I sleeps, dey sneaks a sleep, too, and I pretends I never suspicions it. *a* **1953** —— *More Stately Mansions* (1964) II. iii. 136 Each sneaks a suspicious, probing glance at the other. **1955** J. H. O'HARA *Ten North Frederick* (1956) 34, I can sneak us another drink. **1956** M. DUGGAN *Immanuel's Land* 107 The conductor stood on the bucking platform, sneaking a cigarette. **1968** *Globe & Mail* (Toronto) 17 Feb. 6/2 If they did have these smoking areas..the students wouldn't have to sneak a smoke in the washroom. **1978** J. IRVING *World according to Garp* ii. 30 He was happy to run errands for the patients, deliver messages, sneak food.

sneak-. Also: **a. sneak-boat** (earlier example); **sneak-current** (examples); **sneak-guest,** one who makes public the events of private social gatherings at which he is a guest; **sneak-hunting,** hunting from an unobserved approach; **sneak preview** orig. *U.S.*, a showing of a (usually unnamed) cinematic film prior to regular release, to test audience reaction; also *transf.* and *fig.*; hence **sneak-preview** *v. trans.*, (*a*) to show (a film) in a sneak preview; (*b*) to have a sneak preview of (something); **sneak-thief** (earlier and later examples); also, a pickpocket, a snatch-thief; also *attrib.*; hence *sneak-thief* vb. trans. (*nonce-wd.*); *sneak-thiefery, -thievery.*

1853 *Laws General Assembly of Maryland* 220 Any person or persons [who] shall use any sink boats, sneak boats or floats,..shall be subject to a fine. **1899** K. B. MILLER *Amer. Telephone Practice* xxiii. 275 It frequently happens..that a very small current..will not be sufficient to blow the fuse... These currents are very appropriately termed 'sneak currents'. **1934** A. L. ALBERT *Electr. Commun.* xii. 325 Currents slightly in excess of the normal operating values..are often called 'sneak' currents. **1930** *Times Lit. Suppl.* 9 Jan. 18/1 Creevey..was in fact (if a very modern term may be forgiven because it is so apt) a 'sneak-guest'. **1958** *Listener* 18 Dec. 1045/1 He [*sc.* Boswell] was regarded in society as something of a 'sneak guest'. **1878** E. B. TUTTLE *Border Tales* 45 By sneak-hunting, one man can kill a whole band of elk. **1980** *Outdoor Life* (U.S.) (Northeast ed.) Oct. 84/3 Sneak hunting is a difficult and time-consuming sport. **1938** *Daily Progress* (Charlottesville, Va.) 28 Nov. 1/6 A double-barreled, two-blizzard 'sneak' pre-view of the 1938 edition of winter. **1939** *Chambers's Jrnl.* Nov. 858/1 In America, pre-views, frequently called 'sneak pre-views', have always been allowed. **1949** *Sun* (Baltimore) 28 Jan. 13/4 (Advt.), Sneak preview—tonight at 11.40 p.m. Even though the producers say we mustn't tell—we can hint it's..one of the funniest comedies you've ever seen! **1950** *Ibid.* 14 Sept. 16/1 The film was sneak-previewed in Hollywood. **1952** *Art Digest* 15 Sept. 5/1 Sneak Preview. On the theory that our readers like to know in advance about important art events, we summarize..the 1952–53 season. **1960** *Sunday Express* 18 Dec. 9/3 Paris-bound passengers were given a sneak preview of Britain's 'pennyfarthing' airliner, the Vickers Vanguard. **1972** *Guardian* 24 May 13/7 The old-established Oregon primary ..served as a sneak preview of the multimillion dollar Californian entertainment. **1975** *New Yorker* 22 Dec. 31/2 Our pal..delights in opportunities to see things in advance, so he was easily persuaded last week to accept our invitation to sneak-preview the new open-air observation platform twelve feet above the roof. **1980** *Times Lit. Suppl.* 12 Sept. 990/2 This selection brings together poems from all five of her [*sc.* P. Beer's] published collections, plus a satisfying sneak preview of what one hopes will be her sixth. **1859** G. W. MATSELL *Vocabulum* 82 *Sneak-thief*, a fellow who sneaks into areas, basement-doors or windows, or through front doors by means of latch-keys, and entering the various apartments, steals any thing he can carry off. **1866** *Harper's Mag.* Nov. 690/1 A female 'sneak thief' and a 'longshoreman now appear. *a* **1930** D. H. LAWRENCE *Last Poems* (1932) 100 That is why business seems to me despicable, and most love-affairs, just sneak-thief pocket-picking of dressed-up people. *Ibid.* 242 The jixery perhaps never picked a man's pocket But my god, they sneak-thiefed his very genitals away from him. **1959** M. CUMBERLAND *Murmurs in Rue Morgue* xix. 117 He is the sneak-thief type and the petty blackmailer. **1976** *Liverpool Echo* 6 Dec. 7/9 Wrexham Police to-day warned shoppers to be on the lookout for sneak thieves after a woman shopping in a chemist shop in the town had £200 stolen from her bag. **1923** Sneak-thiefery [see *GANGSTERDOM]. **1963** V. GIELGUD *Goggle-Box Affair* xvii. 177 Nothing else was taken, so it wasn't just sneak-thievery. **1973** E. BERCKMAN *Victorian Album* 82 So there I was, practising deceit on Christabel and sneak-thievery on Mrs Rumbold.

b. In misc. other uses, passing into adj.: that acts or is effected by stealth, deceit, or surprise; unexpected.

1938 *Sun* (Baltimore) 19 July 8/3 His 'sneak hop' from New York to Ireland terminated successfully. **1943** [see *FRINGE *sb.* 2 b]. **1943** *Sun* (Baltimore) 27 Dec. 5/2 A sneak air attack might be attempted by the enemy on Christmas Day. **1944** *Ann. Reg. 1943* I. 21 The soundness of the air defence..had compelled them to confine themselves largely to 'sneak' raids on coastal towns. **1952** *Sun* (Baltimore) 17 June 4/1 The snail-spread sneak disease, bilharzia. **1955** *Publ. Amer. Dial. Soc.* XXIV. 59 The act of theft from the person by stealth is..referred to as a *sneak job*. **1970** [see *LEAD *sb.*^{2} 5 c]. **1971** 'L. BLACK' *Death has Green Fingers* ii. 18 Horace was a wonderful sneak photographer. **1976** *Evening Post* (Nottingham) 14 Dec. 11/6 A sneak raider stole £740 takings from the Triangle toy shop.

sneaker. 3. For *U.S. colloq.* read '*colloq.* (orig. and chiefly *U.S.*)' and add further examples.

1900 G. ADE *More Fables* 193 His Job on this Earth was to put on a pair of Pneumatic Sneakers every Morning and go out and investigate Other People's Affairs. **1914** S. LEWIS *Our Mr. Wrenn* iv. 56 Firm but fearful in his rubber sneakers. **1930** 'S. S. VAN DINE' *Scarab Murder Case* iv. 61 He got relief by wearing white canvas sneakers with rubber soles. **1936** WODEHOUSE *Laughing Gas* xii. 126 You could scarcely expect to turn up in sneakers and a sweater, my good fellow. **1948** J. STEINBECK *Russ. Jrnl.* (1949) 13 She wore canvas sneakers. **1959** *Manch. Guardian* 24 June 7/2 The international uniform of jeans and sandals or sneakers. **1967** A. HENRI in *Penguin Mod. Poets* X. 55 The daughters of Albion..lacing up blue sneakers over brown ankles. **1974** A. LURIE *War between Tates* v. 95 It was Jeffrey who started it; he could not find his left sneaker. **1981** *Sunday Express Mag.* 26 July 16/3 (*caption*) Shades of throwaway chic for pop singer, Graham Bonnet. Old sneakers and a borrowed suit?

4. (Earlier example.)

1851 J. PYCROFT *Cricket Field* iv. 63 With the primitive fashion of ground bowling, called sneakers, forward play could have no place.

Hence **snea·kered** *a.*, clad in sneakers.

1961 'E. FENWICK' *Friend of Mary Rose* (1962) iv. 39 He heard..a soft jump—as of sneakered feet. **1976** 'E. McBAIN' *Guns* (1977) i. 34 He floats on sneakered feet to the back door of the car. **1979** *Listener* 3 May 613/2 Their crew-cut, pony-tailed, sneakered sons and daughters.

sneakishly, *adv.* For *rare*$^{-1}$ read *rare* and add: Also, in a sneaking or stealthy manner.

1867 'T. LACKLAND' *Homespun* I. 55 He begins with throwing a glance at her sneakishly. **1912** *Daily News* 11 May 6 When men come together to profess a creed they come courageously... When they come together in a clique they come sneakishly.

sneaky, *a.* Add: **3.** *Sneaky Pete, sneaky pete*: a name given to any of various illicit or cheap intoxicating beverages. Also *attrib. slang* (orig. and chiefly *U.S.*).

1949 *Collier's* 3 Sept. 40/1 A group which was..discussing the effects of 'sneaky-pete', a generic term for fortified wines. **1951** [see *POT *sb.*^{5} 1]. **1955** *Amer. Speech* XXX. 88 *Sneaky pete*, marijuana mixed in wine. **1965** J. S. GUNN *Terminol. Shearing Industry* I. 32 *Sneaky pete*, one of the many vivid names..which shearers and others give to cheap wine. **1971** J. H. JONES in J. H. Clarke *Harlem* 310 He walked around an unconscious Sneaky Pete drinker. **1978** J. GORES *Gone, no Forwarding* (1979) vi. 40 The stranger bought a pint of sneaky pete and he and Sammy went to sit in his short and drink it.

B. as *sb.* A small concealed microphone or other device for surveillance or espionage.

1974 M. COPELAND *Real Spy World* 317 A 'sneaky' differs from the other technical devices in that it is planted inside an intelligence target. **1977** F. WEBB *Go for Out* v. 78 His car had been fitted with a sneaky ..searching for a microscopic radio transmitter was pointless. **1978** D. BLOODWORTH *Crosstalk* xxi. 168, I never actually found the mikes or the cameras, but..I just thought I'd get away from all the sneakies.

Hence **snea·kily** *adv.*

1966 D. VARADAY *Gara-Yaka's Domain* vii. 75 As fast as he drove off one crowd of fluttering birds, another swooped in, nipping sneakily with slashing beaks. **1974** P. CAVE *Mama* (new ed.) ix. 77 Peter the publican was hovering sneakily around with his ears wide open.

sned, *v.* Restrict 'In later use *Sc.* and *north. dial.*' to sense 2 in Dict. and add: **1. b.** (Later examples.)

1953 H. L. Edlin *Forester's Handbk.* xiii. 205 As soon as the tree is down it should be lopped or snedded, by cutting the branches away from the trunk. **1971** *Timber Trades Jrnl.* 3 Apr. 58/2 Although the chainsaw has long been used for limbing hardwoods the technique of snedding softwoods with a power saw is relatively new.

sneery, *a.* (Later examples.)

1919 D. Ashford *Young Visiters* viii. 53 Ethel patted her hair and looked very sneery. **1949** D. Smith *I capture Castle* III. xv. 289 'Does he believe in it?' 'No, he's always very sneery.' **1967** *Punch* 22 Nov. 776/1 It has taken twenty years to get rid of the amateurs, and the professionals..are having a hard time breaking down the sneery reputation gained. **1977** *N.Y. Rev. Bks.* 9 June 10/4 The sneery attitude toward surgeons that many physicians..were at one time wont to affect.

sneeze, *sb.* Add: **3.** *attrib.*, as **sneeze gas,** a substance used to incapacitate people by causing them to sneeze when it is inhaled or absorbed through the skin.

1918 E. S. Farrow *Dict. Mil. Terms* 567 *Sneeze-gas*, a gas which produces paroxysms of sneezing, so that it is difficult to keep on a mask if any of the gas is inhaled. **1966** *McGraw-Hill Encycl. Sci. & Technol.* III. 45/1 Sternutators, sometimes called sneeze gases or vomiting gases, cause physical discomfort.., and general malaise to such an extent that a casualty results.

sneeze, *v.* **3.** (Later examples.)

1930 R. Campbell *Adamastor* 76 Their horses..Vast phantom shapes with eyeballs rolling white That sneeze a fiery steam about their knees. **1961** G. Durrell *Whispering Land* viii. 194 Anyway, when I had sneezed some of the dust out of my nose, I clapped dutifully outside the gate.

sneezing, *vbl. sb.* Add: **3. a.** *sneezing-powder* (later examples); **sneezing gas** = *sneeze gas* s.v. *Sneeze *sb.* 3.

1918 H. H. Tudor *Let.* 13 Nov. in M. Gilbert *Winston S. Churchill* (1977) IV. Companion I. 415 The shell you speak of may be sneezing gas, which is not deadly. **1939** H. F. Thuillier *Gas in Next War* xvi. 145 The General Disarmament Conference of the League of Nations sitting in 1932 sought to divide the known chemical war agents into..two categories [lethal and non-lethal], and to obtain agreement for the use of the non-lethal kind, *i.e.* the lachrimatory (tear gases) and the sternutatory (sneezing gases) in war. **1979** *Guardian* 25 Aug. 12/6 Soup ..always tastes the same when you have accidentally emptied the pot of fine grey sneezing powder into it. **1982** *London Mag.* June 31 Once he bought sneezing-powder from the joke-shop in New Oxford Street.

‖ **snekkja** (sne·kyă). Pl. **snekkjur,** (*erron.*) **snekkar.** [Icel.: see Snack *sb.*[1]] An ancient Icelandic or Scandinavian longship.

1847 N. H. Nicolas *Hist. R. Navy* I. i. 10 The Scandinavians are said to have possessed small boats with.. twelve seamen, and a longer kind of vessel called 'snekkar' or serpents, chiefly used for war, with twenty rowers. **1889** P. B. du Chaillu *Viking Age* II. ix. 137 The *snekkja* was a somewhat smaller long-ship, of which frequent mention is made; but sometimes it must have been as large as a dragon-ship. **1911** *Encycl. Brit.* XXIV. 865/1 The famous *snekkjur* or serpents, said to be represented on the Bayeux tapestry. **1970** Foote & Wilson *Viking Achievement* vii. 236 The longship was the real warship, with at least twenty benches. One common sort was called *snekkja*.

snell, *sb.* (Earlier example.)

1846 *Spirit of Times* 9 May 126/2 [The bass] was taken with a jointed rod, with a single gut snell, after half an hour's play.

snell, *a.* and *adv.* Add: Hence **sne·llness,** sharpness, keenness.

1915 J. Buchan *Salute to Adventurers* i. 15 That bold girl singing a martial ballad to the storm and taking pleasure in the snellness of the air.

snell, *v.* Add: Hence **snelled** *ppl. a.*

1893 [in Dict.]. **1960** *Washington Post* 29 Apr. D9 The somewhat cumbersome assembly of one or more spinner blades ahead of a snelled or long-shanked hook. **1976** *Billings* (Montana) *Gaz.* 28 June 2-D (Advt), Packages of 6 snelled hooks.

Snellen (sne·lən). *Ophthalm.* The name of Hermann *Snellen* (1834–1908), Dutch ophthalmologist, used *attrib.* and in the possessive to designate: (*a*) a scale of similar square-serifed type-faces of different sizes, all subtending the same angle at different rated distances, proposed by him in 1862 (in his *Échelle Typographique*) and used to print test cards which are presented at known distances to ophthalmic patients who are asked to read out as many lines as they can; also, the letters, test cards, etc., associated with this scale; (*b*) a fraction which expresses a patient's visual acuity as the actual reading distance over the rated distance of the smallest Snellen letters read.

1864 T. Longmore *Man. Instructions Defective Vision in Soldiers* ii. 10 The emmetropic eye can read Snellen's types at any of the indicated distances. **1866** H. W. Williams *Rec. Adv. Ophthalm. Sci.* 29 Two other series have been added as reading tests... Both of these are almost perfectly accurate in their gradations of sizes,— and correspond, the first with the same numbers of Snellen's scale, the second with those of Jaeger's test. **1912** L. Laurance *Visual Optics & Sight Testing* iv. 73 The visual acuity, as expressed by a Snellen fraction, varies..with the health of the person. **1934** C. S. Price *Improvement of Sight by Natural Methods* ii. 21 The large cards or charts bearing a series of sizes in the types are conveniently known as 'Snellen Charts'. **1960** N. Bier *Correction Subnormal Vision* i. 4 A person with visual acuity of 6/60 Snellen or better should not ordinarily be regarded as blind. **1971** *Jrnl. Gen. Psychol.* LXXXIV. 85 He measured visual acuity, using Snellen letters at 10 meters.

Snell's law (snelz). *Optics.* [Named after Willebrord van Roijen *Snell* (1591–1626), Dutch astronomer and mathematician, who formulated the law in 1621.] The law which states that for a ray of light passing from one uniform medium to another the sines of the angles of incidence and refraction are always in the same ratio.

1873 J. Tyndall *On Light* i. 24 Snell's law of refraction is one of the corner-stones of optical science, and its applications to-day are millionfold. **1935** Dawson & Porritt *Rubber* 404/1 Stretched rubber shows double refraction, i.e. a ray of light entering the rubber from air or a vacuum is split up into two rays, one of which.. obeys Snell's law of refraction, whilst the other..does not unless it travels in a certain critical direction. **1974** *Nature* 18 Jan. 156/2 Snell's law and a value of 1·67 for the refractive index of the lens were used to determine the angles of refraction at the surfaces of the lens.

‖ **snelskrif** (sne·lskrĭf). *S. Afr.* [Afrikaans, f. *snel* rapid + *skrif* writing.] A system of shorthand for the Afrikaans language. Also *attrib.*

1949 *Cape Argus* 16 Apr. 11/2 (Advt.), Take a rapid course..in book-keeping, Afrikaans, snelskrif, shorthand, [etc.]. **1952** *Cape Times* 2 Aug. 9/7 Typists who qualify for shorthand and *snelskrif* tests. **1972** *Grocott's Mail* (Grahamstown) 1 Sept. 2 Bilingualism, shorthand, snelskrif, typing..are all essential.

snib, *v.*[2] For *Sc.* read orig. *Sc.* and add: **1.** (Further examples.)

1889 A. Conan Doyle *Sign of Four* vi. 92 Your ally would..shut the window, snib it on the inside. **1934** R. Knox *Still Dead* xxii. 269 Trying to shut the door quietly, she left it not quite snibbed properly, so that it came a bit ajar. **1953** A. Upfield *Murder must Wait* i. 4 The Yale-type lock was snibbed. **1962** W. H. Murray *Maelstrom* v. 73 He snibbed all the ground-floor windows. **1967** I. Hamilton *Man with Brown Paper Face* ix. 132, I went softly to the main entrance and snibbed it from the inside and put the bolt across. **1971** *Islander* (Victoria, B.C.) 21 Nov. 2/3 The windows were not only unbroken but snibbed shut.

snick, *sb.*[2] **2.** (Earlier example.)

1857 *Bell's Life* 19 July 7/5 The last jump from 135 to 158..included many 'snicks', not hits.

Snick (snik), *sb.*[5] *U.S.* Also **SNICK.** [Alt. of *SNCC* (see S 4 a and below).] The Student Non-violent Co-ordinating Committee, an organization of Black Americans campaigning for civil rights and Black power. Also *attrib.*

1962 *Time* 12 Jan. 15/1 To fight segregation in their own way, young Negroes have organized themselves into a federation called the Student Nonviolent Coordinating Committee ('Snick' for short). **1967** *National Observer* (U.S.) 27 Nov. 1/4 Snick had its origins in the sit-in movements of 1960. *Ibid.*, Snick leaders consider elections a white man's device to deceive Negroes with false promises. **1967** *Telegraph* (Austral.) 5 Aug. 2/1 The white man has been violent towards the Negro for 400 years... If we are violent to him he deserves every bit. SNICK is respected because if we say burn, baby, burn, we'll be the first to strike a match. **1978** L. Heren *Growing up on The Times* ix. 292 In 1964..white students..met members of the student non-violent coordinating committee. Snick, as it was usually called, was still very much a genuine student movement with religious roots.

snick, *v.*[2] **2. b.** (Earlier example.)

1871 'Thomsonby' *Cricketers in Council* 3 The new trundler then put down a tice..which the Surrey colt snicked cleverly through the slips.

snick, *v.*[3] Add: **1. b.** To turn *on, off, out, up,* to push *open*, with a clicking noise.

1927 *Daily Express* 30 Aug. 3/4 As she snicks open the trellised door. **1927** *Observer* 4 Dec. 12 A Foreman with a lantern..walks down a dark platform snicking on lights. **1959** I. Jefferies *Thirteen Days* vi. 75 This corner was all wrong for..firing a pistol round..but I snicked the heat out and exposed an eye. **1973** R. Hayes *Hungarian Game* xxxiv. 207 Hagopian crested the hill and snicked off the ignition. **1977** *Detroit Free Press* 11 Dec. 15-c/1 The electric vacuum system that snicks lamps up with the tap of a toggle on modern cars.

2. b. To move *back*, to come *open*, with a click.

1963 C. D. Simak *They walked like Men* xiv. 76 The lock snicked back and the door came open. **1972** J. Potts *Trouble-Maker* (1973) xviii. 146 The back door snicked open.

snicker, *sb.*[1] (Earlier example.)

1836 *Knickerbocker* VI. 562, I was partially 'ware of a general *snicker* through the room.

snicker-snack (sniːkəɪsnæ·k, sni·kəɪsnæːk), *adv.* and *sb.* Also **snickasnack.** [Imit.: cf. *snick-snack *adv.* and *sb.*] (With) a snipping or clicking sound.

1871 'L. Carroll' *Through Looking Glass* i. 22 The vorpal blade went snicker-snack! **1913** C. Mackenzie *Sinister Street* I. II. xv. 403 Mrs Carthew snipped away, talking in sentences that matched the quick snickasnack of her weapon. **1979** P. Way *Sunrise* viii. 79 The little man next door was chopping his hedge. The shears were going snicker-snack. *Ibid.* 85 He glanced back at them fiddling with the dominoes... The pattern fell snicker-snack over.

snicket (sni·kėt). *north. dial.* [Origin obscure.] A narrow passage between houses, an alley-way.

For further senses of the word see *Eng. Dial. Dict.*

1898 B. Kirkby *Lakeland Words* 136 *Snicket*, a narrow passage between buildings. **1947** I. Brown *Say the Word* 65 We have vennels, gunnels, and snickets in our northern towns. **1957** R. Hoggart *Uses of Literacy* I. ii. 52 Street after regular street of shoddily uniform houses intersected by a dark pattern of ginnels and snickets (alleyways) and courts. **1968** B. Hines *Kestrel for Knave* 31 He cut down a snicket between two houses, out into the fields. **1981** J. Stubbs *Ironmaster* xx. 276 We are cramming poor people into ginnels and snickets and foetid courts.

snickety (sni·kėti), *a. rare.* [Origin obscure: cf. *persnickety *a.* (*adv.*).] Fussy, pernickety.

a **1960** E. M. Forster *Maurice* (1971) IV. xxxix. 186 Maurice hated cricket. It demanded a snickety neatness he could not supply.

snick-snack (sni·ksnæk, sniksnæ·k), *adv.* and *sb.* Also **snic-snac.** [Imit.: redupl. from Snick *sb.*[3]] = *snicker-snack *adv.* and *sb.*

1925 C. Day Lewis *Beechen Vigil* 11 Meanders around the rose-beds, gnarled, clay-brown, Old Tom the pruner, snic-snac up and down. **1970** *New Yorker* 28 Nov. 151/1 Big, straight scissors, from Finland..have a nice feel in the hand and a reassuring snick-snack.

sniddy, var. *snidey *a.*

snide, *a.* and *sb.* For *Cant* read '*colloq.* (orig. *Cant*)' and add: **A.** *adj.* **1.** (Earlier and further examples.) Also more widely, inferior, worthless.

1859 G. W. Matsell *Vocabulum* 83 *Snide stuff*, bad money. **1861** J. Clay *Prison Chaplain* viii. 537 The observant and experienced E.R. says 'The utterers of "*Snide pewter*" (base silver) are almost all Irish.' **1887** F. Francis *Saddle & Mocassin* i. 3 These here men don't want none of your..snide outfits, but jest good *bronchos* and a waggon, and strong harness. **1887** *Lantern* (New Orleans) 9 Apr. 2/3 Who runs dat snide hash house. **1899** 'J. Flynt' *Tramping with Tramps* II. 277 Utica..is sort of a snide place, this time of the year. **1906** E. Dyson *Fact'ry 'Ands* xiv. 180 'Tain't ther liquor wot's snide, it's ther dead hookity hides what it gets chuted into. **1926** [see *jungle *sb.* 2 c]. **1973** 'J. Patrick' *Glasgow Gang Observed* 235 Snide 'boggin': used in phrase 'snide gear', i.e. clothes that are out of fashion, contemptible, inferior.

2. Of a person: cunning, sharp.

1883 E. J. Milliken *Childe Chappie's Pilgrimage* ii. 15 They self-deemed astute and 'snide', Of *nous* bereft, low chaff the bar-queen golden dyed. **1889** *Cent. Dict.* 5730/3 *Snide*,..sharp; characterized by low cunning and sharp practice. **1950** P. Tempest *Lag's Lexicon* 193 'He's a "snide" so-and-so' = he's a slippery customer.

3. Insinuating, sneering, slyly derogatory.

1933 *N. & Q.* 14 Oct. 261/2 Our snide way of saying it was cheap, false, and counterfeit. **1939** *Sun* (Baltimore) 15 Apr. 8/1 Snide trick. Any reprehensible bills..enacted in secrecy at a session of the Legislature are bound to come to the surface after the State's lawmakers have left Annapolis. **1943** *Ibid.* 22 Apr. 30/6 It was a horrifying thing..to hear the President..making a snide attack against a group of Americans instead of defending America. **1954** M. Davenport *My Brother's Keeper* 182 She lived in a tenement..and she would fill the whole neighbourhood with snide gossip. **1961** J. Heller *Catch-22* (1962) x. 103 Ex-P.F.C. Wintergreen was a snide little punk who enjoyed working at cross-purposes. **1978** G. Greene *Human Factor* VI. ii. 318 Next day when Ivan made his snide references to 'gratitude' he broke furiously out: 'You call this gratitude.' **1981** *Maledicta* V. 123 He ..curses a great deal and writes snide letters to careless authors.

B. *sb.* **1. b.** A base, contemptible person; a swindler, cheat, liar.

1874 Hotten *Slang Dict.* 299 'He's a snide,' though this seems but a contraction of *snide 'un*. **1883** J. Hay *Bread-Winners* xix. 297 'I am right glad I got here to save you from that—' he paused, searching for a word which would be descriptive and yet not improper in the presence of a lady,..'that snide.' **1919** *Dial. Notes* V. 67 That fellow is a snide, do not trust him. **1935** Auden & Isherwood *Dog beneath Skin* II. iii. 99 Young Waters is playing too. He's no snyde at the game. **1972** L. Henderson *Cage until Tame* xii. 103 Tolly's not a snide, he's better than most, and he's been bloody unlucky.

c. Hypocrisy, pretence; malicious gossip.

1902 G. H. Lorimer *Lett. Self-made Merchant* vii. 90 Courtesy without condescension,..simplicity without snide. **1966** *New Statesman* 8 Apr. 499/2 She analysed.. the nasty state of affairs on the gossip beat. The result was spectacular—some of the popular papers changed the titles of their columns, keyhole snide was banned, [etc.].

Hence **sni·dely** *adv.*; **sni·deness**; **sni·dery** = *snide *sb.* 1 c; also, an instance of this.

1942 Berrey & Van den Bark *Amer. Thes. Slang.* § 317/1 *Treachery*...snideness. **1953** *Britannica Bk. of Year* 639/2 *Snidery*,..hypocrisy, pretence. **1956** D. Karp *All Honorable Men* 39, I drew aside the people from *Time* and asked them if they were going to treat the Institute snidely or soberly. **1961** 'B. Wells' *Day Earth caught Fire* viii. 119 'If you're right this means no private water at all.' 'Correct,' said Pete snidely. 'Just turn on the taps and hear the rude noise of progress.' **1965** P. Wylie *They both were Naked* I. ii. 92, I was 'in'...by great good luck and the use of some small snideness. **1967** *Punch* 8 Nov. 697/2 Those sardonic snideries which come too readily to one's lips. **1969** *Daily Tel.* 24 Apr. 21/5 The snidery of the humour may escape those playgoers who cannot look at it with fairly Irish eyes. **1975** *Country Life* 30 Oct. 1160/1, I have often snidely remarked, that the flowers on each spike are not half of them opened before the first are already brown. **1978** A. Noakes *William Frith* iv. 68 Frith's success with *Derby Day*.. sparked off some ill-tempered snideries.

snidey (snəi·di), *a. slang.* Also **sniddy, snidy.** [f. Snide *a.* + -y[1].] **a.** Bad, contemptible. **b.** Insinuating, cutting.

1890 in Barrère & Leland *Dict. Slang* II. 267/2 Since Bill George was nabbed for liftin' them sax things is been very sniddy, so you'll be glad to learn as I have got on a new hook. **1903** Farmer & Henley *Slang* VI. 281/1 *Snide*... As *adj.* (also *sniddy* or *snidey*) = bad, wretched, contemptible. **1928** F. Hurst *President is Born* xxii. 232 'Fraid! Snidey! Poof! 'Fraid. Poof! Poof! Poof! **1972** *Guardian* 20 Jan. 13/2 Miss Duncan will not allow snidy little one-liners to upset her. **1977** *Sounds* 9 July 33/3 The journalists thought he was being 'Hip' when he was snidey about the Dolls on TV.

Hence **sni·diness.**

1976 E. Dunphy *Only a Game?* iii. 98 Because there is glory and money and your career at stake. And that entails backbiting, snidiness, scapegoating and a whole host of other things.

snie, var. *snye.

sniff, *sb.* Add: **1. d.** *fig.* A hint, intimation.

1936 C. Day Lewis *Friendly Tree* II. ix. 124, I have been..wondering if I shall ever get a job... I have just got a sniff of one—experimental work.

5. *U.S.* A domino game in which the first double played has special significance; the first double played.

1917 J. Hergesheimer *Three Black Pennys* III. xxiv. 289 After dinner, when they were playing sniff. **1930** J. H. Appel *Business Biogr. J. Wanamaker* xxii. 336 His own favourite game was 'sniff', played with dominoes. **1961** D. C. Armanino *Pop. Domino Games* 37 A *singles* may be played off the end of singles, the sides of doubles, and the ends of Sniff. Sniff is the only double on which plays can be made on the ends. **1974** F. Berndt *Domino Bk.* 33 Sniff is yet another variation of Muggins. *Ibid.*, The first double played is called the Sniff.

sniff, *v.* Add: **1. b.** *spec.* To inhale cocaine, the fumes of glue, etc., through the nose. *slang.*

1925 *Flynn's* 4 Apr. 819/2 *Sniff*,..to use powdered cocaine as snuff. **1931** E. Wallace *On Spot* ii. 24 Red, you're..a hop-head... We got no room in this outfit for guys who sniff. **1967** C. Drummond *Death at Furlong Post* v. 62 So they send us a dipso who sniffs! **1970** *New Scientist* 13 Aug. 352/1 These young people generally 'sniffed' from a plastic bag into which they first squirted aeroplane glue, cleaning fluid or whatever. **1975** *Weekend Mag.* (Montreal) 8 Feb. 21 The Whitebear sisters began sniffing almost two years ago, Janice says. 'A friend of ours used to sniff. At first, we didn't know what he was doing, so we asked and then we tried it too.' **1977** J. van de Wetering *Death of Hawker* vii. 73 He's sniffing too... Cocaine powder.

2. a. (Later *fig.* examples.)

1973 A. Mann *Tiara* ix. 76, I want to..sniff around the Vatican again. **1977** R. Player *Month of Mangled Models* vii. 133 Sniffing around Chelsea and Kelmscott.

5. b. Also with *out.*

1946 *Sun* (Baltimore) 12 Aug. 1/2 A pilotless aircraft that is sent into the air to 'sniff out' its own enemy target. **1979** J. Barnett *Backfire is Hostile!* xi. 111 You should concentrate more on sniffing out the sex fiends than speculating on spies.

c. Phr. *to sniff the wind*: see *wind *sb.*[1]

sniffable (sni·făb'l), *a.* [f. Sniff *v.* + -able.] That can be sniffed.

1975 *Weekend Mag.* (Montreal) 8 Feb. 23/1 Stocks of the old sniffable product were being bootlegged by merchants all over Regina. **1977** J. Wambaugh *Black Marble* (1978) iv. 36 Lopez boasted that he could..have enough sniffable paint left to get three of his pals loaded.

sniffer (In Dict. s.v. Sniff *v.*). Add: **1. b.** *spec.* One who sniffs a drug or toxic substance. Cf. *glue-sniffer* s.v. *glue *sb.* 6. orig. *U.S. slang.*

1920 E. S. Bishop *Narcotic Drug Problem* iii. 23 The heroin 'sniffer' of idle and curious adolescence. **1928** *Amer. Mercury* Aug. 485/2 The Baron was..a 'sniffer' himself. **1942** J. Henry *Henry's Famous Cases* iv. 40 Cocaine addicts are known as 'sniffers'. **1968** *Guardian* 22 Mar. 11/1 Doreen was also a 'sniffer'. This is the name given to people who inhale a mixture of ether and methylated spirits and become 'blocked'. **1981** *Daily Tel.* 24 Apr. 3/1 A glue sniffer is under the influence of a drug for the purposes of the 1972 Road Traffic Act, magistrates decided yesterday when a self-confessed 'sniffer' denied being unfit to drive through drink or drugs while in charge of a motorcycle.

2. *slang.* The nose.

1858 [see *pile-driver 2]. **1962** R. Cook *Crust on its Uppers* ii. 34 They'll..look down their sniffers at you.

3. a. Any device for detecting gas, radiation, etc. *colloq.*

1945 *Richmond* (Virginia) *Times-Dispatch* 10 Oct. 2/5 The hydrogen content in copper wire annealing furnaces.. is now continuously indicated by a new sensitive apparatus called a sniffer nose. **1946** *Sun* (Baltimore) 21 June 10/3 Louis E. De La Fleur..demonstrated a small hand-borne radio fixer, known as a 'sniffer'. He said that it was so accurate that he had been able..to locate an outlaw transmitter in a New York apartment house where hundreds of legal radios and electrical devices were putting out potential inteference. **1950** *Listener* 5 Jan. 12/1 These tiny Geiger counters first came to public attention last spring in New York... Uranium can turn up anywhere so there is no reason why, if you had a 'sniffer', as they are called, you should not start prospecting here in Great Britain. **1968** *Guardian* 5 Sept. 2/7 Perch a radar sensor on the tail..: insert a diesel fume 'sniffer'. **1972** 'J. Lange' *Binary* 170 The sniffer..had been developed for use in Vietnam and had been adapted for customs operations... If the sniffer said plastic explosive was behind the door, he had to believe it. **1979** F. Pohl *Jem* iii. 26 The car was..an indispensable necessity in what he did for the agency; twice a day, other employees of the agency went over it with electronic sniffers and radio probes to make sure it had been neither bombed nor bugged.

b. Usu. *sniffer dog.* A dog trained to detect specific odours, esp. those of drugs or explosives. *colloq.*

1964 *N.Y. Times Mag.* 23 Aug. 62/3 *Sniffer*, police dog. **1975** A. Beevor *Violent Brink* iii. 66 We are using.. sniffer dogs at ports and airports so as to increase our chances of catching the explosive coming in. **1977** *Air Mail* Spring 7/1 In the first two months 'sniffer' dogs and handlers trained by the RAF Police Dog Training Flight had helped British Customs and Excise officers detect £125,000 worth of smuggled drugs. **1979** *Daily Tel.* 17 Apr. 1/6 Forty-five 'sniffer' dogs were flown into Yugoslavia from Switzerland and set to work to smell out casualties from debris in towns around Kotor Bay. **1982** *Times* 3 Sept. 10/5 Sniffer-dogs for drugs.

sniffing, *vbl. sb.* (Examples in sense 1 b of the vb.) Cf. *glue-sniffing* s.v. *glue *sb.* 6.

1968 *Guardian* 22 Mar. 11/2, I asked her what attraction there was in 'sniffing'. **1975** *Weekend Mag.* (Montreal) 8 Feb. 23/1 In any case, legislation doesn't eliminate the sniffing problem which is nation-wide. **1977** *Lancet* 8 Jan. 84/1 Investigation of the 42 patients..showed that 'sniffing' was a group activity involving mainly adolescents aged 12–19 years, all of whom had a previous history of solvent abuse.

sniffly (sni·fli), *a.* [f. Sniffle *v.* + -y[1].] Sniffling; characterized by sniffling. Also *fig.*

1927 W. E. Collinson *Contemp. Eng.* 59 They vary in intensity from the sniffling or sniffly cold to the churchyard cough! **1929** G. Ade *Let.* 8 Feb. (1973) 139 The warm weather will be welcome. Most of us have sniffly colds. Otherwise we are all right. **1960** *Guardian* 9 Apr. 6/6 We sat there in the bare little room, wet and sniffly with sentiment. **1966** R. H. Rimmer *Harrad Experiment* (1967) 79 Get out your handkerchiefs, wipe your sniffly nose. **1974** [see *luxe 1].

sniffy, *a.* Add: (Further examples.)

1915 W. S. Maugham *Of Human Bondage* lxxiv. 382 You were rather sniffy about meeting him. **1925** S. Baring-Gould *Further Reminisc.* iv. 45 Their wives were especially sniffy towards Mrs Jervis. **1965** *Listener* 3 June 834/3 He was catty about Balzac, sniffy about Stendhal, stuffy about Flaubert, and cagey about Baudelaire. **1979** *Jrnl. R. Soc. Arts* July 511/1 Sniffy comments of a patronizing nature about Victorian buildings so regrettably sprinkled throughout earlier books in *The Buildings of England* are carefully avoided.

Hence **sni·ffily** *adv.*, **sni·ffiness** (examples); **sni·ffish** *a.* (*rare*), somewhat sniffy.

1900 Kipling *Just So Stories* (1902) 108 'What will happen if I do? said the Jaguar, most sniffily and most cautious. **1927** *Blackw. Mag.* Dec. 834/1, I didn't think sniffiness was usual under the circumstances. **1928** 'M. Neville' *Kiss Proof* xviii. 163 'Oh, if that's the way you feel about it,' Toddles said sniffily. **1933** 'G. Orwell' *Let.* June (1968) I. 121 There is also a certain sniffish 'I told you so' implication. **1968** M. Collis *Somerville & Ross* iii. 45 In her *Irish Memories* (published in 1917) Edith, recalling that time, writes of the sniffyness of her brothers and uncles. **1973** *Guardian* 30 June 11/3 'He wasn't up to much as a sub-editor,' said one of the older hacks, sniffily. **1981** *Economist* 24 Jan. 22/2 Although for the past two years the United States has been Algeria's largest trading partner, the relationship between the two countries has been marked by a suspicious sniffiness.

snifter, *sb.* Add: **4.** A (small) quantity of intoxicating liquor, a drink, a 'nip'. *colloq.* (orig. *U.S.*).

See note, sense 5 below.

1844 *Spirit of Times* 20 Apr. 86/2 He swallowed a cool 'snifter' at the nearest cabaret. **1910** G. B. McCutcheon *Rose in Ring* v. 90 You need a snifter of brandy...Joey handed her a drink from his flask. **1924** Wodehouse *Ukridge* iii. 56 And now, old horse, you may lead me across the street to the Coal Hole for a short snifter. **1934** *Bulletin* (Sydney) 26 Dec. 41/1 The postboy brought George a telegram, and..on opening it George smiled and shouted snifters all round. **1942** E. Paul *Narrow St.* xxvii. 246, I..was on the point of suggesting that he step across to the Café St. Michel for a snifter. **1963** B. Pearson *Coal Flat* i. 14 Do you want a drink—or would you rather have a bit of a snifter with the boys? **1978** R. V. Jones *Most Secret War* vii. 59 What happened was that he had taken it from his own station to another for a lunch which was preceded, and doubtless followed, by a surfeit of what he termed 'lightning snifters'.

5. A glass with a wide body narrowing towards the top, used for brandy, etc. orig. and chiefly *U.S.*

The sense 'the contents of a snifter' is usu. indistinguishable from sense 4 above and may be represented in some examples there.

1937 G. Frankau *More of Us* xvi. 170 And sought that other room to drain a snifter With Herr Staatsschauspielhausmeister Kohn-Goering. **1943** D. Baker *Trio* 155 She was sitting beside me holding a brandy snifter. **1970** J. Hansen *Fadeout* i. 4 A bottle of brandy warmed on the hearth... She poured splashes from it into two small snifters. **1978** G. Vidal *Kalki* x. iii. 241, I drank brandy from a huge Baccarat snifter.

6. a. *U.S. slang.* A cocaine addict. Cf. *sniffer 1 b.

1925 *Flynn's* 4 Apr. 819/2 *Snifter*, a cocaine fiend. **1929** *Detective Fiction Weekly* 27 Apr. 31/2 A certain cocaine addict, known as Snifter Selton. **1955** *Amer. Speech* XXX. 85 *Snifter*, an addict who inhales cocaine.

b. *slang* (orig. *U.S.*). A small quantity of cocaine inhaled through the nose.

1930 *Detective Fiction Weekly* 5 July 357/1 Well, boys, take me down [to the police station]. Just one snifter of snow and I'm with you. **1934** 'D. Hume' *Too Dangerous to Live* viii. 85 He's been doping for a few months—cocaine. When he was picked up he hadn't had a snifter for nearly twenty-four hours. **1974** J. Wainwright *Evidence I shall Give* xxi. 99 A snifter when the pain's bad... It ain't for kicks. You're no junkie.

7. *U.S. slang.* A portable radio direction-finder. Cf. *sniffer 3 a.

1944 *Sci. News Let.* 12 Aug. 103 'The snifter'..is a portable, one-man direction finder that 'smells out' by radio the very room in which an illegal radio transmitter is hidden. **1949** *Life* 5 Dec. 166/2 At the start hunters with radio direction finders, called 'snifters', collect at Brookfield Zoo.

snifty, *a.* Add: **2.** *slang* (orig. and chiefly *U.S.*). Haughty, disdainful.

1889 K. Munroe *Golden Days* xvii. 188 If you notice me getting anyways snifty..you just bump me down hard. **1902** G. H. Lorimer *Lett. Self-made Merchant* xviii. 268 Clytie said..that spirits were mighty snifty and high-toned. **1909** H. G. Wells *Tono-Bungay* I. i. 40 'Snifty beast!'..That governess made things impossible. **1942** Berrey & Van den Bark *Amer. Thes. Slang* § 301/6 *Arrogant*,..snifty.

snig (snig), *v.*[2] *north. dial.*, *Austral.*, *N.Z.*, and *Canad. local.* [Origin obscure.] *trans.* To drag (a heavy load, esp. timber) by means of ropes and chains. Hence **sni·gging** *vbl. sb.* (also *attrib.*).

For further material see *Eng. Dial. Dict.*

1790 F. Grose *Provinc. Gloss.* (ed. 2), *Snig*, to drag wood without a cart. **1866** J. T. Staton *Rays fro th' Loominary* 127 He wur one ut wur brought up to sniggin timber. **1933** L. Acland in *Press* (Christchurch, N.Z.) 2 Dec. 15/7 *Snig*, to drag along the ground by horse or bullocks, especially to drag logs or other timber. The stout chain which goes round the log has a ring at one end, and a hook to which the horses' chains are attached. It is called a *snigging chain.* **1946** B. James in Murdoch & Drake-Brockman *Austral. Short Stories* (1951) 251 Peter cut timber on the hills, and snigged it down with the plough horses. **1961** B. Crump *Hang on a Minute Mate* 44 They dug their axes into a handy stump and trudged off down the snigging-track. **1968** E. R. Buckler *Ox Bells & Fireflies* xv. 221 A group of men have gathered to help another lay a new sill under his barn. 'Hadn't I better hitch up the team and snig her closer the foundation there?' **1969** *Parade* (Austral.) Dec. 17/2 He would get his horse and snig Trompson's body off the claim. **1975** *Sunday Mail* (Brisbane) 1 June 6/2 Bullock teams would snig the logs to the winder.

snig (snig), *v.*[3] *dial.* and *slang.* [Origin obscure.] *intr.* and *trans.* To steal.

1862 C. C. Robinson *Dial. Leeds* 415 *Snig*, to steal after a mean fashion, as a man who undertakes any business, or interests himself any way in the property of a person, and is 'snigging' away at it all the time. **1864** J. Ramsbottam *Phases of Distress* 37 They'll pitch an' toss an' swear, An' snig an' snatch owt wheer they con. **1892** Kipling *Barrack-Room Ballads* 31 If you've ever snigged the washin' from the line.

snip, *sb.* Add: **II. 8.** (Later examples.) Cf. *tinsnips.

1940 I. L. Idriess *Lightning Ridge* xiii. 88 As the miner's hand gently closed on the snips the jaws came together and bit a chip from the edge of the nobby. **1966** D. F. Galouye *Lost Perception* xviii. 188 He fished his snips out of the kit. 'Now we have only to cut the cables.' **1979** *Sunset* Apr. 170/2 The home owner made a pattern first, then used tin snips to cut long pieces of copper trimmings into strips.

10. a. (Earlier and later examples.)

a **1890** *Sporting Life* in Barrère & Leland *Dict. Slang* (1890) II. 268 D. is in glorious form with his wires, and is certain to keep it up next week at the above meetings, for which he knows of several snips. **1913** C. Mackenzie

Sinister St. I. II. xi. 323 You'll get your Third Fifteen cap for a snip. **1923** E. P. OPPENHEIM *Inevitable Millionaires* xxviii. 285 'You think it will be a good speculation, then?' Stephen observed, a little sadly. 'A dead snip,' Sir Philip assured them. **1945** 'N. SHUTE' *Most Secret* viii. 187 It is a snip; we will get both of them. **1954** WODEHOUSE *Jeeves & Feudal Spirit* ii. 19 Wooster..is the deadest of snips. He throws a beautiful dart.

b. A bargain, a good buy. *slang.*

1926 H. V. MORTON *Spell of London* 94 She sees a tea-gown with the authentic plainness..about it that tells her it began life in higher circles. 'Now, that's a snip, miss. Just your style!' **1933** *Camera* Aug. 7 (Advt.), Exchange your present camera for one of these guaranteed 'snips'. **1935** L. A. G. STRONG *Tuesday Afternoon* 20 The smart man comes along, looks in the window, spots the real snip. **1956** 'N. SHUTE' *Beyond Black Stump* ix. 254 Got them for only a couple of quid each, a snip. **1963** *Punch* 30 Jan. 162/1 A snip at forty bucks. **1977** *Times* 29 Oct. 10/6 At a time when Beaujolais prices are soaring it is a snip at £1·90.

c. A piece of good fortune. In phr. *a snip of a* (thing) to designate something simpler, more excellent, or more pleasing than one could have expected, a 'gift'.

1932 W. S. MAUGHAM *For Services Rendered* II. 47 It's been a snip for me having this house to come to. Except for all of you I should have had a pretty thin time. **1952** M. TRIPP *Faith is Windsock* xiv. 210 A snip of an op. Cloud over the target thwarted any searchlights, fog kept the fighters down and there was no flak. **1953** DYLAN THOMAS *Under Milk Wood* (1954) 47 Llaregyb this snip of a morning is wildfruit and warm, the streets, fields, sands and waters springing in the young sun.

snipe, *sb.* Add: **4. c.** *U.S.* The discarded stub of a cigar or cigarette.

1891 H. CAMPBELL *Darkness & Daylight* iv. 124 The 'Snipe-Shooter' was guilty of smoking cigar-stubs picked out of the gutter a habit known among the boys as 'snipe-shooting'. **1899** 'J. FLYNT' *Tramping* II. iv. 274 This 'snipe' chewing and smoking is the most popular use of tobacco in trampdom. **1914** 'HIGH JINKS, JR.' *Choice Slang* 18 *Snipe*, a cigar or a cigarette stub. **1939** J. STEINBECK *Grapes of Wrath* x. 129 Winfield was..an inveterate collector and smoker of snipes.

d. One of a group of workers, esp. on board ship (see quots.). *U.S.*

1918 L. E. RUGGLES *Navy Explained* 139 *Snipe*—Firemen in the 'black gang' always refer to each other as 'snipes'. In a gang of snipes below there is generally one dude who is known as the 'king snipe'. He is considered the leading snipe of the watch. **1932** *Santa Fé Mag.* XXVI. II. 34/1 A foreman of a section gang is a *Jerry* or a *king*; a section laborer is a *snipe*. **1951** H. WOUK *Caine Mutiny* xxvi. 289 A big sloppy chowhound named Wagner, a snipe, had made himself a wax impression of the cook's key. **1953** M. DIBNER *Deep Six* xv. 169 A snipe chief wearing a blue shirt and an oil-soiled khaki cap stood legs apart, drinking coffee.

e. *Logging.* A sloping surface or bevel cut on the fore end of a log to facilitate dragging.

1958 W. F. MCCULLOCH *Woods Words* 172 *Snipe*, a bevel hewed on the ride side of the end of a log, making it easier to pull over the skids. **1975** *Islander* (Victoria, B.C.) 2 Mar. 13/1 He took out the long, beautiful 155-foot timbers, 18 inches at the butt and tapered with a four-foot snipe to a four-inch square point.

5*. Also **Snipe.** A type of sloop-rigged sailing boat approximately 15½ ft. long and used for racing; also, the name of this class of boat.

1931 *Rudder* (U.S.) July 46 Snipe... Designed especially for the *Rudder* by William F. Crosby. *Ibid.* 47/1 Snipe is a design for a small racing sloop. **1941** *Sun* (Baltimore) 20 Aug. 13/6 For the small-boat sailors races have been arranged in the following classes: Snipe, moth, penguin, winabout, Hampton, 20-foot roundbottom, 20-foot (and under) chine built knockabout. **1942** *E. African Ann.* *1941–2* 57/1 There is always some fine sailing to be had.. some craft beating out into the bay or later in the evening some homeward bound 'Snipe' coming in before the wind. **1969** H. HORWOOD *Newfoundland* xix. 149 Holyrood has a small harbour at the mouth of a brook, and a junior sailing club with instructors and racing snipes.

5.** A long-range shot or attack from a sharp-shooter; the sound of a sniper's bullet. Also *fig.*

1969 G. MACBETH *War Quartet* 72 The return snipe struck His mouth below the helmet. **1973** E. BULLINS *Theme is Blackness* 6 For paeans of Blackness were videoed throughout Black America, between the stoccado snipe of the assassin's slug. **1977** *Rolling Stone* 13 Jan. 10/1 Rod Stewart..has transcended two years of snipes for his romance with actress Britt Ekland. **1977** *Sunday Times* 3 July 17/5 The difficulty of organising a 'snipe' (assassination by a single gunman) in the tight security of Belfast.

6. b. *snipe-nosed* (later examples referring to pliers).

1968 M. WOODHOUSE *Rock Baby* xvi. 157, I took the Allen Keys and a small pair of snipe-nosed pliers. **1969** *Gloss. Terms Dentistry* (*B.S.I.*) 48 *Snipe-nosed pliers*, pliers with square nosed flat beaks... Used for bending wire.

snipe, *v.* Add: **2. b.** *fig.* To assault with harsh sly criticism; to rebuke or censure sharply; to make a carping attack *at* (someone).

1892 [implied at *SNIPING *vbl. sb.* 1 b]. **1959** I. & P. OPIE *Lore & Lang. Schoolch.* xvi. 343 Although adult factions may have made peace with each other, their children on the way to school may continue sniping at each other for generations. **1979** 'A. HAILEY' *Overload* I. xiv. 79 The press representatives had eaten and imbibed with gusto, then in published reports, some had sniped at GSP & L for extravagant entertaining at a time of rising utility bills.

3. *trans. Logging.* To cut a snipe or bevel on (a log) to ease dragging.

1870 *Overland Monthly* 5 July 56/1 The fourth man is the 'hook-tender', whose duties are to wait on the team and 'snipe the logs'. **1902** *N.Z. Illustr. Mag.* V. 375 If the weather is favourable, the log is 'sniped' or rounded at one end, an iron grip driven into it, and to this the team is fastened. **1958** W. F. MCCULLOCH *Woods Words* 173 *Snipe*,..to hew a snipe on the end of a log. *Snipe for the ride*, to put the snipe on the side of the log which would ride on the bottom, saving the work of sniping a bevel around the entire end of the log.

4. *trans.* and *intr.* To pilfer, steal; to pick up or obtain (from the roadside, etc.); *spec.* to prospect for gold, as in old diggings. Cf. SNIPER 3. *slang* (chiefly *N. Amer.*).

1909 R. SERVICE *Ballads of Cheechako* 122, I panned and I panned in the shiny sand, and I sniped on the river bar; But I know, I know, that it's down below that the golden treasures are. **1923** J. MANCHON *Le Slang* 280 *Snipe*, escamoter [*sc.* to steal, filch]. **1932** J. T. FARRELL *Young Lonigan* iv. 169 He walked down to Fifty-seventh St, furtively looked round to see if anyone saw him, and when the coast was clear, he sniped a butt from the street. **1974** F. W. LUDDITT *Campfire Sketches of Cariboo* vi. 27 They..made small amounts of money sniping for gold. **1977** *New Yorker* 20 June 81/1 He 'sniped' a lot of his gold—just took it from likely spots without settling down to the formalities of a claim.

sniper. Add: **4.** *Logging.* One who cuts a snipe on a log.

1905 *Terms Forestry & Logging* (U.S. Dept. Agric. Bureau Forestry) 48 *Sniper*, one who noses logs before they are skidded. **1906** *Log of 'Columbia'* June 8/1 'He ought to be chased out of the woods,' said Jim, the sniper. **1914** *Chambers's Jrnl.* 3 Oct. 696/1 Summoning the sniper for an occasional undersnipe. **1956** R. W. ANDREWS *Glory Days of Logging* 14 These were..snipers who shaped the butt ends, so they [*sc.* logs] wouldn't hang up on the skids.

5. *Austral.* (See quot. 1945.)

1945 BAKER *Austral. Lang.* xiv. 248 A waterfront term of fairly recent origin is *sniper*, a non-union labourer. **1955** J. MORRISON *Black Cargo* 14 It will need only one shout of 'Sniper!' and Lamond will be lucky to get out without being knocked down. **1957** T. NELSON *Hungry Mile* 72 The W.W.F. had preference of work, wharf by wharf. The outsiders (snipers) would stand back at the gate until the W.W.F. men were all used.

sniperscope (snəi·pəɹskōᵘp). [f. SNIPER + -SCOPE.] † **1.** A device incorporating a periscope, whereby a rifle may be fired by a soldier who remains concealed. *Obs.*

1918 R. H. KNYVETT *Over There* 135 Many of the inventions are forgotten, but some are in use in France today, notably the 'periscope rifle' or 'sniperscope'.

2. A small device which converts infra-red radiation to a visible image and may be fixed to a gun so that it can be aimed in the dark.

1941 *Sun* (Baltimore) 1 Jan. 6/3 The selected few American infantrymen who tried out the 'sniperscope' at Okinawa have already had a glimpse of future warfare. **1954** W. TUCKER *Wild Talent* (1955) xi. 418 'He must have used a rifle. And had good eyesight.' 'He probably had a sniperscope on it.' **1971** F. FORSYTH *Day of Jackal* I. i. 14 A rifle with sniperscope was found at Poinard's flat.

sni·piness. [f. SNIPY *a.* + -NESS.] Undue length and pointedness of the muzzle of an animal, suggestive of a snipe's bill.

1938 J. W. DAY *Dog in Sport* xv. 204 The jaws should be long and powerful, and quite free from snipiness or exaggeration in length. **1963** B. S. VESEY-FITZGERALD *Cat Owner's Encycl.* 121 The nose is longish, but the cheeks being very prominent do away with any snipiness, which is a bad fault.

sniping, *vbl. sb.* Add: **1. b.** *fig.* The making of sly critical assaults; sharp fault-finding or carping. Freq. with *at.*

1892 MRS. H. WARD *David Grieve* I. vi. 128 Hannah's appetite for snipin' returned. **1935** E. POUND *Let.* 7 Feb. (1971) 267 Eng. print so smeared with personal sniping and clique politics that any definition of limitations..is likely to be taken as 'anti-'. **1945** *Sun* (Baltimore) 25 June 1/3 There has been a lot of unfortunate sniping at the project. **1955** *Essays in Criticism* V. 64 Mr. Liddell's 'criticisms' of his essay..are mere sniping and peripheral eroding which say next to nothing about their subject. **1969** H. PERKIN *Key Profession* vi. 229 Hence that perpetual sniping..at the universities for their supposed idleness and inefficiency. **1977** *Time* 4 July 2/3 Your sniping at the U.N. and its jobs-for-the-boys was not premature. **1980** M. FONTEYN *Magic of Dance* 214 Taglioni, tired of petty sniping and endless comparisons favouring her rival, journeyed to St. Petersburg.

3. Prospecting for gold, esp. in old diggings. *N. Amer. slang.*

1897 M. H. E. HAYNE *Pioneers of Klondyke* 93 There is little 'snipping' [*sic*]—i.e. working old bars—on Forty Mile Creek, but it does not pay much. **1963** *Placer Mining B.C.* 7/1 Chinese miners were particularly adept at sniping... Sniping and bar-combing are..carried out by individuals who would rather do this than work for wages.

4. *Austral.* Working as a non-union labourer.

1951 *Meanjin* (Melbourne) X. 334 You never scabbed, or anything like that? You never did any sniping?

snippy, *a.* Add: **2.** (Later examples.) Also, putting on airs, supercilious.

1894 P. L. FORD *Hon. Peter Stirling* xxx. 171 Before I could possibly have said or done anything to offend her, she treated me in the snippiest way. **1934** E. CARR *Jrnl.* 12 Feb. in *Hundreds & Thousands* (1966) 95, I don't want to be mean and snippy but I don't think they know. **1952** H. GARNER *Yellow Sweater* 93 There followed an explanation of why her son hadn't been attending school as regular as he should, and how snippy the teacher was getting to be. **1961** *Insurance Salesman* Jan. 47/1 One of our clerks was a snippy, opinionated girl who kept everything unsettled and rubbed everyone the wrong way. **1970** J. POTTS *Affair of Heart* viii. 65, I must say, she was very snippy. Downright rude. **1974** *Times* 28 Feb. 10/6 This irritates Mr Heath... Privately, he is quite snippy about it. **1977** D. RAMSAY *You can't call it Murder* I. 52 Daughter Sarah described as uppity and snippy.

snit². *slang* (orig. and chiefly *U.S.*). [Of uncertain origin (see quot. 1939²).] A state of agitation; a fit of rage or bad temper; a tantrum, sulk. Freq. in phr. *in a snit.*

1939 C. BOOTHE *Kiss Boys Good-bye* II. i. 105 'I declare, Mrs. Rand, I cried myself into a snit.' 'A snit?' 'I do deplore it, but when I'm in a snit I'm prone to bull the object of my wrath plumb in the tummy.' **1939** *Sat. Rev. Lit.* 23 Dec. 12/1 The membership could hardly be said to be in a snit,..as nobody in Georgia seems ever to have heard of either the word or the state of being until Miss Clare Boothe isolated and defined it. **1962** J. POTTS *Evil Wish* x. 136 If you hadn't been in such a snit when I came upstairs I'd have told you so. **1971** *Daily Progress* (Charlottesville, Va.) 21 Jan. 4A/3 If New York solves its problems through gambling, every state in the union is going to follow suit except Nevada, which will probably secede from the nation in a snit. **1975** J. GOULET *Oh's Profit* xxxvii. 208 The President of the United States had bawled him out and left Cambridge College in a fierce snit. **1980** *N.Y. Times* 8 Jan. D 16, I was recently..put in charge of six other copywriters, two of them men. The men are in a quiet snit.

snitch, *sb.* Add: **3.** (Later examples, chiefly U.S.)

1906 *Atlantic Monthly* Nov. 589 He employs that phenomenon of despicability..in Western parlance called a snitch.. to work up the lawsuit. **1930** *Forum* Dec. 375/1 A police informer in New York, for instance, is a stool or snitch. **1959** I. & P. OPIE *Lore & Lang. Schoolch.* x. 189 The tell tale is..a sly, a snitch or snitcher (common, especially in the Midlands). **1965** J. WAINWRIGHT *Death in Sleeping City* 142 The 'snitches' and the 'grassers' and the 'stoolpigeons' whispered out of the corner of their mouths, and money changed hands. **1979** S. RIFKIN *McQuaid in August* ix. 97 Lopez was an informant..a paragon among snitches.

4. Phr. *to have* (or *get*) *a snitch on* (someone): to have a grudge against or 'down' on; to dislike. *N.Z. slang.*

1943 J. A. W. BENNETT in *Amer. Speech* XVIII. 90 A person [in New Zealand] complaining of another's ill-will might also say, 'He's got a proper snitch on me'—obviously a variant of 'to snitch upon' (to inform against). **1948** *Landfall* II. 109 These jokers didn't understand the snitch Myers had on you, seemed to think it was right that Myers should always be tormenting you. **1953** O. E. MIDDLETON *Short Stories* 28 He wasn't a man to get a snitch on his neighbours because of a bit of bad luck and it wasn't long before he was his own self again. **1959** G. SLATTER *Gun in my Hand* viii. 91 Got a snitch on me and put me in crook with the boss.

5. *Comb.*, as **snitch-rag** *slang*, a handkerchief.

1940 H. G. WELLS *Babes in Darkling Wood* I. i. 25 Can I borrow your snitch-rag, Gemini?

snitch, *v.* Add: **1.** (Later examples.) Now usu. with *on*. Also, to reveal or give information *to* (someone). *slang.*

1910 'O. HENRY' *Whirligigs* xiii. 157 Say, don't snitch to the tenants about this, will yer? **1926** J. BLACK *You can't Win* xix. 279 If I get a job some copper will snitch on me to my boss. **1933** *Daily Progress* (Charlottesville, Va.) 26 Jan. 1/8 He did it, he said, because she 'snitched' on him when he played truant from school. **1941** B. SCHULBERG *What makes Sammy Run?* v. 83, I felt a little guilty about snitching on my neighbor. **1957** A. MILLER *View from Bridge* I. 33 The family had an uncle that they were hidin' in the house, and he snitched to the Immigration. **1966** P. MOLONEY *Plea for Mersey* 14 The Captain.. had snitched to the police that his cargo was being pilfered.

3. To take surreptitiously, purloin; to steal or 'pinch'. *slang.*

1904 *N.Y. Times* 6 June 9 They reached Coney Island by snitching rides. **1933** D. L. SAYERS *Murder must Advertise* iii. 46 He first of all snitched people's ideas without telling them, and then didn't give them the credit for it. **1948** L. A. G. STRONG *Trevannion* xvii. 323 You love a girl faithfully for years, and some glib sod comes along at the heel of the hunt and snitches her from you. **1958** [see *BOOKSY *a.*]. **1976** M. MACHLIN *Pipeline* xxx. 348 How about that guy who snitched a whole D-9 tractor, brand-new?

Hence **sni·tching** *vbl. sb.*

1923 W. S. MAUGHAM *Our Betters* III. 172 You really might have left Tony alone. This habit you have of snitching has got you into trouble before. **1933** *Sun* (Baltimore) 24 Aug. 6/7 Not long ago we had the fine stirring story by Neil Swanson 'The Judas Tree', and now comes a snitching of that title by Leslie Ford, who calls his new detective thriller 'The Clue of the Judas Tree'. **1961** B. MALAMUD *New Life* (1962) 298 He had been thinking of discussing with him Bullock's concern with athletes but it was too much like snitching. **1972** J. WAMBAUGH *Blue Knight* (1973) ii. 39 'Okay,' I said, giving him a chance to rationalize his snitching, which all informants have to do when they start out.

sni·tter, *v.*[2] *Sc.* and *north. dial.* [Cf. SNICKER *v.*, SNIGGER *v.*[1], SNIRT *v.*, and TITTER *v.*[1]] To laugh in a suppressed, nervous manner (*at* something). Also as *sb.*

1825 JAMIESON Suppl., *To snuister*, or *snuitter*,..to laugh in a suppressed or clandestine way through the nostrils. *Snuister, snuitter*,..a laugh of this kind. **1892** M. C. F. MORRIS *Yorkshire Folk-Talk* 374 What's ta stannin' theer snitterin' an' laffin' at? **1896** 'G. UMBER' *Ayrshire Idylls* 71 Hoo her words should provoke sae muckle snitterin' an' lauchin'. **1975** *New Society* 31 July 235/2 A prevailing snitter (cross between snigger and titter) greeted the preview of..a new play... There was plenty to snitter at. **1975** W. MCILVANNEY *Docherty* III. v. 270 'Ye micht never be heard o'.' 'Sen' in David Livingstone,' Conn said. Tom snittered. **1977** —— *Laidlaw* xxxviii. 177 Harkness began to laugh. Laidlaw stared at him, then..snittered at himself.

snivelization (sniv'ləizēɪ·ʃən). *nonce-wd.* [Melville's factitious blend of SNIVEL *sb.* and CIVILIZATION.] Civilization considered derisively as a cause of anxiety or plaintiveness. Also **sni·velize** *v. trans.*, to reduce (someone) to a state of whimpering civilization; **sni·velized** *ppl. a.*

1849 H. MELVILLE *Redburn* I. xxi. 200 Ye wouldn't have been to sea here, leadin' this dog's life, if you hadn't been snivelized... Snivelization has been the ruin on ye. *Ibid.*, Snivelized chaps only learns the way to take on 'bout life, and snivel. **1892** 'MARK TWAIN' *Satires & Burlesques* (1967) 169 He was working this character into an elaborate satire on civilization to be called 'Affeland (Snivelization)'. *c* **1938** L. MUMFORD *Report on Honolulu* in *City Development* (1946) x. 106 The restrictions and burdens imposed by what one of Herman Melville's characters derisively called 'snivelization'.

snivellingly (sni·v'liŋli), *adv.* [f. SNIVELLING *ppl. a.* + -LY[2].] In a snivelling or whimpering manner; abjectly.

1959 *Times* 31 July 9/1 Mary [Queen of Scots] is presented as a creature of radiant perfection surrounded by snivellingly devoted waiting women and surly guards. **1970** N. FLEMING *Czech Point* (1971) i. 9 Beside him I would have appeared a snivellingly puny specimen.

snob, *sb.*[1] Add: **1. b.** The last sheep to be sheared; hence, the roughest or most difficult sheep to shear; = *COBBLER 1 b. *Austral.* and *N.Z. slang.*

1945 C. E. W. BEAN *On Wool Track* (new ed.) 135 The sheep most difficult to shear, which naturally is left last in the pen, is also called the 'snob'. **1955** G. BOWEN *Wool Away!* 157 *Snob*, the last sheep in the pen. **1971** J. S. GUNN *Distrib. Shearing Terms N.S.W.* 9 As it is the practice to leave rough sheep until last it is only to be expected that *snob* and *cobbler* for both 'rough' and 'last' will occur... *Snob* and *cobbler* meant 'last' before specialising to 'rough'. **1975** L. RYAN *Shearers* i. 49 'Get on to this wrinkled bludger!' he said. It was the last sheep in the pen... 'Real snob, ain't it?'

3. d. One who despises those who are considered inferior in rank, attainment, or taste. Freq. in extended sense with defining word that limits its reference to a particular sphere.

Overlaps with sense 3 c in Dict.

1911 G. B. SHAW *Getting Married* 228 All her childish affectations of conscientious scruple and religious impulse have been applauded and deferred to until she has become an ethical snob of the first water. **1925** F. SCOTT FITZGERALD *Great Gatsby* vii. 146 Listen, Tom. If you're such a snob, why did you invite him to lunch? **1931** A. HUXLEY *Music at Night* 121, I have met several adolescent consumption-snobs...these ingenuous young tubercle-snobs. **1935** C. ISHERWOOD *Mr Norris changes Trains* iv. 58, I rather enjoyed playing with the idea that he was, in fact, a dangerous criminal... Nearly every member of my generation is a crime-snob. **1939** [see *INTELLECTUAL *a.* 1 b]. **1959** G. FREEMAN *Jack would be Gentleman* iii. 54 God knows, Moyra, I'm not a snob but that sort of person just wouldn't understand. **1960** J. O'HARA *Sermons & Soda-Water* I. 26 He doesn't want to know her any better and neither would my mother. That isn't snobbishness... You're the snob of us two. **1977** T. HEALD *Just Desserts* i. 16 He does..that frightful column in the Chronicle... The wine snob's guide to an early cirrhosis.

e. *inverted snob*: see *INVERTED *ppl. a.* 9.

5. a. *snob jargon, school, word*, etc.; *snob-free* adj.; **snob appeal,** attractiveness to snobs; **snob value,** value as a commodity prized by snobs or as an indication of superiority.

1933 LEAVIS & THOMPSON *Culture & Environment* 15 (*heading*) The snob appeal. **1943** *Scrutiny* XI. 289 There is, of course, the same snob-appeal, and just as Mr. Richards is always introducing a Shakespearean phrase.., so Jeeves is always quoting Pope. **1958** M. DICKENS *Man Overboard* xii. 192 There's a snob appeal about having a retired officer as bursar. **1978** J. PEARSON *Façades* vii. 127 Osbert and Edith [Sitwell]..had inherited.. style; their snob appeal was undeniable. **1961** D. L. MUNBY *God & Rich Society* iv. 68 Americans and Scandinavians have a lot to teach us about real social equality and snob-free education. **1952** E. PARTRIDGE *From Sanskrit to Brazil* 59 The most dangerous snob jargon of all is that used by ordinarily well-educated..men and women. **1953** R. CHANDLER *Let.* 16 Sept. (1981) 351 If your boy won't behave himself..you can send him to one of the New England snob schools like Groton. **1978** M. BIRMINGHAM *Sleep in Ditch* 113 She'd been married, very young, almost the moment she'd left her snob school. **1936** *Proc. Inst. Automobile Engineers* XXX. 762 Generally, if the big luxury car leads with any new refinement sooner or later the lower and lowest-priced cars follow, the new feature acquires from its aristocratic origin what has been aptly termed 'snob-value'. **1955** T. H. PEAR *Eng. Social Differences* 131 The terms of normal psychology have never achieved snob-value. **1969** M. FISH in A. S. C. Ross *What are U?* 78 It was an example of faulty handcraft giving a snob value to a product that could have been made more efficiently by machine. **1935** A. P. HERBERT *What a Word!* iv. 92 'Beginning' is musical and 'commencement' is not. Also, it is a Snob-word.

b. Used *predicatively* as *adj.*, fashionable, snobbish, pretentious.

1958 *Spectator* 14 Feb. 209/3 A little slower than Buchan, a little less naively snob than Dornford Yates. **1970** *Daily Tel.* 9 Apr. 17/2 Champagne we consider too snob, and we're all off hard liquor. We drink wine now as an aperitif.

snob, *sb.*[2] Add: In full, *snob-cricket*. ? Now *obs.*

1888 A. LANG in Steel & Lyttelton *Cricket* i. 1 There is a sport known at some schools as 'stump-cricket', 'snob-cricket', or ..'Dex'. **1893** J. W. BAINES in A. G. Bradley et al. *Hist. Marlborough Coll.* xxii. 220 The great thing was 'Snob' cricket, which speedily became a most popular and fashionable pursuit. **1901** *Blackw. Mag.* Oct. 490/2 The game known as 'snob-cricket', little cricket, 'stump-and-ball', and so forth, might be introduced.

snobbery. Add: **2. c.** With defining word: pretension to superior knowledge, taste, etc., in a particular sphere.

1903 [see *INTELLECTUAL *a.* 1 b]. **1937** LD. SAMUEL *Belief & Action* iii. 30 It is a kind of cosmic snobbery to expect us to feel 'humble' in the presence of astronomical dimensions merely because they are big. **1977** *Times* 15 Nov. (Italian Wine Suppl.) p. i/3 It is perhaps another instance of declining wine snobbery when people want to offer a wine that is good but cheap.

snobbism. Add: Also **snobism** [cf. next]. **1.** (Earlier and later examples.) Also, an instance or manifestation of this.

1845 *Punch* June 254/1 We never saw any living creature in such a high state of snobbism. **1895** [see *EGOMANIA]. **1923** J. M. MURRY *Pencillings* 36 Dickens is safe, so safe indeed that within the next twelve months he may become a snobism in his turn... Although I have floundered into most of the artistic snobisms of my time.. I have never deserted Mr. Micawber. **1932** P. BALFOUR *Society Racket* i. 48 'Belle's Letters', in which the great social figures..liked to be mentioned and to have their dresses described, is nauseous in its unabashed and luscious snobism. **1940** H. G. WELLS *All aboard for Ararat* iii. 84 Some mysterious process of snobism. **1966** *Punch* 20 July 124/2 It deflates a lot of irritating snobbisms and pomposities. **1972** *Science* 12 May 620/1 A union representative must cope with the inevitable snobbism of the better educated engineer or chemist.

‖ **snobisme** (snobīz'm). Also *erron.* **snobbisme.** [Fr.] = SNOBBISM in Dict. and Suppl.

1913 E. MARSH in S. Hynes *Edwardian Turn of Mind* (1968) ix. 343, I went with Denis to the Ballet... It's *delicious*, I went thoroughly meaning to dislike it, so it isn't *snobisme* on my part. **1920** A. HUXLEY *Let.* 4 Mar. (1969) 182 What you must go and see in Paris is the Cirque Medrano... It's become rather a snobisme to go. **1931** *Punch* 23 Sept. 334 For a womanly yet talented woman of good family, with enough English *snobisme* to relish Society and enough Irish irresponsibility to take its awful procedure lightly. **1958** *Spectator* 18 July 86/2 The one-eyed monster..? Oh dear, must that particular *snobbisme* be perpetuated? **1968** J. M. WHITE *Night-climber* vii. 46 Always marvellous, that English nation, compounded equally of the Bible and *Snobisme*. **1977** T. HEALD *Just Desserts* vii. 145 It was undrinkable... No ludicrous snobisme about it being an English wine, could possibly persuade any normal palate of anything else.

snobocracy. Add: (Earlier example.) Also **snobocra·tic** *a.*

1853 J. M. RICHMOND *Let.* 17 July in *Richmond-Atkinson Papers* (1960) I. 129 His impartiality..is not satisfactory to the 'snobocracy', as Jas calls the genteel of this place. **1960** *Times Lit. Suppl.* 16 Sept. 589/1 These days of tax-evader farmers and snobocratic huntsmen.

snobographer. (Later example.)

1966 *Punch* 29 June 965/3 Auchincloss has surpassed himself in this magnificent comedy of manners... He is *the* post-Freud snobographer.

SNOBOL (snōᵘ·bɒl). *Computers.* [Acronym f. the letters of '*s*tring-*o*riented sym*bol*ic *l*anguage', after *Cobol*, etc.: cf. *STRING *sb.* 15.] A high-level programming language used chiefly in literary research and symbolic computation.

1964 D. J. FARBER et al. in *Jrnl. Assoc. Computing Machinery* XI. 21 Interest in language translation, program compilation and combinatorial problems has increased... The string-orientated symbolic language SNOBOL has been developed with these problems in mind. **1969** *Computers & Humanities* IV. 74, I..began first to implement a year-long research project on rhythm in the Spanish language, using SNOBOL for text-manipulation and FORTRAN for statistical operations. **1971** *Ibid.* V. 156 SNOBOL IV..is a string manipulation and pattern-matching language and in this area makes both ALGOL and FORTRAN look clumsy... SNOBOL programs are typically shorter in character and line count than a FORTRAN or ALGOL counterpart. **1971** R. A. WISBEY *Computer in Lit. & Ling. Research* 165 The computer used in this study is the IBM 360/91. The language is SNOBOL 4, Version 3, a string manipulation language developed by Bell Telephone Laboratories, Inc.

Sno-cat (snōᵘ·kæt). orig. *U.S.* Also **sno-cat, Snocat, snocat.** [f. *sno*, an arbitrary respelling of SNOW *sb.*[1] + *CAT(ERPILLAR 1 b.] A proprietary name in the U.S. for a type of snow-cat (see *SNOWCAT).

1946 *Official Gaz.* (U.S. Patent Office) 10 Sept. 212/1 *Sno-cat*. No claim is made to the exclusive use of the word 'Sno' apart from the mark. For automotive vehicles for traveling over snow. Claims use since Sept. 1, 1941. **1957** *Times* 4 Dec. 11/7 The Snocat..came to the rescue and easily hauled both the Weasels and sledges on to better surfaces. **1958** *Listener* 13 Nov. 793/1 The popular impression that Antarctica is always and only white is matched by the suspicion that a modern expedition in those regions is all sno-cats and telecommunications. **1968** MRS. L. B. JOHNSON *White House Diary* 26 June (1970) 691 We got into a strange vehicle called a 'Sno-Cat', a long cab on caterpillar treads. **1970** *Observer* 20 Dec. 25/1 A wealthy industrialist seriously proposed running a Snocat service along the entire Haute Route. **1977** *New Scientist* 20 Jan. 123 The unloading operation was carried out with heavy cargo sledges towed in relays by snocats on the sea ice and caterpillar tractors on the ice shelf.

snockered (snɒ·kəɹd), *ppl. a. slang.* Also **snookered.** [Perh. arbitrary alteration of *SNOOKERED *ppl. a.*] Drunk, intoxicated. Cf. *SCHNOCKERED *ppl. a.*

1961 S. PRICE *Just for Record* x. 105 You rolled along half-snockered after Sunday lunch. **1969** 'R. STARK' *Dame* xx. 121 'I may be a little high,' she said, 'but I'm not snockered.' **1977** *Amer. Speech 1975* L. 66 *Snockered adj*, drunk. 'She was snockered; she didn't mean it.' **1980** *Globe & Mail* (Toronto) 4 Oct. 6/6 I'll get a bottle of Jack Daniel's for cocktails. Get them snookered on bourbon and they won't know the difference.

snodger (snɒ·dʒəɹ), *a.*, (*adv.*, and *sb.*). *Austral.* and *N.Z. slang.* ? *Obs.* [Of uncertain origin: cf. SNOD *a.* and SNOG *a.*] Excellent, very good, first-rate. Also as *adv.* and *sb.*

1919 W. H. DOWNING *Digger Dial.* 46 *Snodger* (adj.), excellent. **1924** C. J. DENNIS *Rose of Spadgers* 40 It was a snodger day!.. The apple trees was white with bloom. All things seemed good to me. **1941** BAKER *N.Z. Slang* vi. 51 Expressions..in constant use by our youngsters.. stunner, snorter, snodger, ripsnorter. **1946** *Sunday Sun* (Austral.) 11 Aug. (Suppl.) 15 There they find the conships fitted up snodger with bulkheads studded with nails. **1950** *Austral. Police Jrnl.* Apr. 119 If something is a snodger it is 'mighty' in Queensland, it is 'colossal' in N.S.W., and just 'very nice' everywhere else.

snoek. Add: The S. Afr. pronunc. is (snuk). Substitute for def.: A snake mackerel, *Thyrsites atun*, of the family Gempylidæ, a large marine food fish found in large shoals in colder parts of Southern Hemisphere oceans. Cf. *BARRACUDA. (Earlier and further examples.)

1797 A. BARNARD *Jrnl.* in *Lives of Lindsays* (1849) 388 The fish called *snook*..when salted and dried, was one of the best fish at the Cape. *a* **1823** J. EWART *Jrnl. Stay Cape Good Hope* (1970) ii. 13 Snoek, a long oily fish which being caught in great quantities and consequently cheap, forms the principal food of the slaves. **1833** *Graham's Town* (Cape Province) *Jrnl.* 14 Feb. 3 Phosphorescent glimmerings of a decayed Snoek. **1880** A. C. L. G. GÜNTHER *Introd. Study of Fishes* 436 In New Zealand it is called 'barracuda' or 'snoek'. **1913** D. FAIRBRIDGE *That which hath Been* 73 An old Malay fisherman, carrying his baskets of snoek. **1931** *Times Lit. Suppl.* 16 Apr. 301/2 The snoek..is not a pike..but a distant cousin of the mackerel. **1946** L. G. GREEN *So Few are Free* iv. 57 Snoek are caught by each boat's crew at the rate of a thousand to three thousand a day. **1963** S. COOPER in Sissons & French *Age of Austerity* 51 In October 1947.. the hungry British first heard the word 'snoek'. Ten million tins of it from South Africa were to replace Portuguese sardines. **1974** *Stand. Encycl. S. Afr.* X. 28/1 The snoek is also an important food fish in Australia.

snoek (snuk), *v. S. Afr.* [f. the sb.] *intr.* To fish for snoek. Hence **snoe·ker**; **snoe·king** *vbl. sb.*

1913 W. W. THOMPSON *Sea Fisheries Cape Colony* ii. 50 It is a pretty sight to watch a fleet of fishing boats snoeking under sail. **1937** L. G. GREEN *Great Afr. Mysteries* xii. 137 The total catch by all the snoeking vessels often amounts to a million fish. **1950** *Cape Argus* 28 Oct. (Mag. Section) 3 Fishermen declare that China snoek are caught after the ordinary snoeking season is over. **1952** L. G. GREEN *Lords of Last Frontier* xxi. 299 Snoeking, a trade that has prospered here for forty years, keeps a grand fleet of small craft in commission. **1959** *Cape Times* 5 May 2/7 (*heading*) Snoeker found ringed bird. *Ibid.*, While snoeking at St. Helena Bay, John Mentor..found a dead black sea-duiker.

snogging (snɒ·giŋ), *vbl. sb. slang.* [Origin unknown: cf. SNUG *v.*] Engagement in light, amorous play, esp. kissing and cuddling.

1945 C. H. WARD-JACKSON *It's a Piece of Cake* (ed. 2)

56 *Snogging*, courting, running around with the opposite sex. Comes from India. Thus, 'On my leave I'm going up to the hills for a bit of snogging.' Also used as a verb. **1951** *Sunday Pictorial* 28 Oct. 10/6 Few hounds can get in more than half an hour of 'snogging'—their elegant term for not-too-serious courtship. **1960** N. Epton *Love & English* vi. 341 It is all right..to cuddle. (The current term among teen-agers is 'snogging'.) **1966** P. Willmott *Adolescent Boys* iii. 40, I went upstairs with Jill and we did a bit of snogging on the bed. **1975** *Weekend* 4 Feb. 19/1 If a cinema manager tolerates snogging among his audience he is liable to lose his licence.

Also **snog** *v. intr.*, to engage in snogging; **snog** *sb.*, an instance of this; **sno·gger, sno·gging** *ppl. a.*

1945 [see *snogging *vbl. sb.*]. **1958** 'J. Brogan' *Cummings Report* xv. 156 He is a..girl-snogging.. bounder. **1959** W. Camp *Ruling Passion* xii. 82 Let's pretend we're teenagers and stop for a nice snog. **1962** A. Sampson *Anat. Britain* xxxvi. 574 The cinema has lost its hold—except among unmarried teenagers, two-thirds of whom go at least once a week, perhaps to snog in the doubles. **1965** J. Gaskell *Fabulous Heroine* 94 A most experienced snogger. **1973** M. Amis *Rachel Papers* 21 They were enjoying a kiss—well, more of a snog really. **1981** R. Barnard *Mother's Boys* ii. 20 They had..taken the side way through the little cutting known popularly as 'Snoggers Alley'.

Snohomish (snōᵘhōᵘ·miʃ), *a.* and *sb.* Also **Snow-**. [19th-cent. Puget Salish *snuhumš*.] **A.** *adj.* Of or pertaining to the Snohomish or their language. **B.** *sb.* (A member of) a Salish Indian people of western Washington; also, their language.

1856 N. D. Hill *Let.* 30 Sept. in *U.S. Congr. House Exec. Doc.* (1857) xxxvii. 77, I received a letter from you appointing me the local agent for the Snohomish, the Snoqualmi, and the Skiquamish tribes of Indians. **1874** *Field & Stream* 20 Aug. 18/3 This assertion was verified afterwards by a Snohomish Indian. **1910** F. W. Hodge *Handbk. Amer. Indians* II. 606/2 Snohomish. A Salish tribe formerly on the s. end of Whidbey id., Puget sd., and on the mainland opposite at the mouth of Snohomish r., Wash. Pop. 350 in 1850. The remnant is now on Tulalip res., Wash., mixed with other broken tribes. **1940** M. W. Smith *Puyallup–Nisqually* 17 In the Puyallup-Nisqually dialect the word means butte or rump but informants thought it might mean something else in the dialects of either the Twana or Snohomish. **1966** *Internat. Jrnl. Amer. Linguistics* XXXII. 350/2 Snowhomish..was spoken in the region around Port Gardner Bay..and along the Snowhomish River. **1977** C. F. & F. M. Voegelin *Classification & Index World's Lang.* 301 Puget Sound Salish = Puget = Toughnowawmish. D[ialect]s Northern Puget Sound (Skagit, Snohomish), Southern Puget Sound (Duwamish, Muckleshoot, Nisqualli, Puyallup, Snoqualmie, Suquamish). 10–20. Washington.

snollygoster (snǫ·ligǫstəɹ). *U.S. dial.* and *slang.* [Perh. connected with *snallygaster, which is, however, of more recent appearance.] A shrewd, unprincipled person, esp. a politician. Also in other more or less fanciful uses (see quots.).

1846 *Commonwealth* (Frankfort, Kentucky) 7 Apr. 2/6 Now here I am a rale propelling, double revolving locomotive Snolly Goster, ready to attack anything. **1863** D. Emmett *Black Brigade* 5 We am de snolly-gosters, An' lubs Jim Ribber oysters. **1895** *Columbus* (Ohio) *Dispatch* 28 Oct. 4/3 A Georgia editor kindly explains that 'a snollygoster is a fellow who wants office, regardless of party, platform or principles, and who, whenever he wins, gets there by the sheer force of monumental talknophical assumnacy'. **1912** *Dialect Notes* III. 590 *Snolly-goster*, a shyster. **1915** *Nebraska State Jrnl.* 7 Sept. 6/3 We once knew a miserly old *snollygoster* who used to look in a mirror to see the reflection of a saint. **1952** *N.Y. Herald Tribune* 3 Sept. 17/2 President Truman..said some people like to pray in public so that others will view them as honorable and religious men... 'I wish some of these snollygosters would read the New Testament and perform accordingly.' **1953** *Cavalier Daily* (Univ. of Virginia) 12 Nov. 1/2 Former President Truman may have been making a talknophical assumnacy when he said a snollygoster is what Southerners call a man born out of wedlock. **1972** A. Roudybush *Sybaritic Death* xx. 168 The deaths of a middle-aged tart and an elderly snollygoster are of little moment.

snomobile, var. *snowmobile.

snood, *sb.* Add: **1. a.** More recently, a fashionable bag-like or closed woman's hair-net, usu. worn at the back of the head. (Later examples.)

1938 *Sun* (Baltimore) 22 Oct. 5/6 (*caption*) New hats in vivid colors... Shakos, pill boxes, turbans, brims, pie plates and snoods. **1939** in C. W. Cunnington *English Women's Clothing* (1952) vii. 262 A spate of hoods and snoods. **1944** M. Laski *Love on Supertax* x. 92 She carefully placed on the top of her head a little forward-tilting black hat whose draped jersey snood just failed to conceal the mass of yellow wrinkles. **1947** E. Jenkins *Young Enthusiasts* 47 They..wore ribbon snoods secured under their buns. **1968** J. Ironside *Fashion Alphabet* 148 A knitted or open-work 'bag' over the back of the hair. Sometimes a snood is attached to a hat.

snoodle (snū·d'l), *v. dial.* (chiefly *north.*) or *nursery.* Now *rare.* [See *Eng. Dial. Dict.*: prob. rel. to Snudge *v.*², Snuggle *v.*, etc.] *intr.* To snuggle, nestle. Also *trans.*

1887 in T. Darlington *Folk-Speech S. Cheshire* 355. **1898** R. Dottie *Rambles & Recoll.* ' "R" Dick' 115 Eaur snug, white hostelry snoodlin' i' th' valley. **1904** J. Vaizey *More about Pixie* (1910) i. 9 She snoodled her head along the pillow so as to lean it against the nurse's shoulder. **1908** E. J. Banfield *Confessions of Beachcomber* i. i. 32 Snoodling beside lumps of coral or beneath weather-beaten drift-wood, they [*sc.* young birds] afford startling proof of the effect of sympathetic coloration.

snook: now the commoner form of Snooks derisive gesture (q.v. in Dict. and Suppl.); var. Snoek in Dict. and Suppl.

snooker, *sb.*² Add:

It is commonly held that the word represents an allusive use of Snooker *sb.*¹, a newly joined cadet, first applied to the game by Col. Sir Neville Chamberlain (1856–1944), a subaltern in the Devonshire Regiment stationed at Jubbulpore in central India in 1875, with reference to the rawness of the play of a fellow officer. The story is often repeated, e.g. in *The Times* (1980) 29 Dec. 9.

snooker *v.*: also *fig.* (chiefly *pass.*), to place in an impossible position; to balk, 'stymie'; **snoo·kered** *ppl. a.*, **snoo·kering** *vbl. sb.*

1915 *Morning Post* 8 Apr. 5/1 If we had fired the Germans might have sent up a light and then we should have been snookered all right. **1927** C. Mackenzie *Vestal Fire* i. i. 5 One of the recognized amusements of a Sirene dinner-party was to try to snooker Joseph R. Neave over Dante. **1935** *Times* 5 Oct. 5/6 The snookering all through was clever. **1970** K. Giles *Death in Church* iii. 65 In France they might have had a chance..but here they were snookered.

snooks. Add: The form **snook** is now usual. Chiefly in phr. *to cock a snook (at)*. (Earlier and later examples.)

1791 E. Wynne *Diary* 7 Dec. (1935) I. 90 They *cock snooks* at one on every occasion. **1929** H. S. Walpole *Hans Frost* i. vii. 78 He was like a dirty street boy cocking a snook at Sappho. **1938** E. Ambler *Cause for Alarm* viii. 128 The Rome–Berlin axis..cocked the biggest snook yet at the League of Nations idea. **1959** M. Cumberland *Murmurs in Rue Morgue* v. 38 With his right hand he made the somewhat coarse gesture known as 'cocking a snook'. The thumb and extended fingers, spread in front of the face, made a baffling disguise. **1961** B. Fergusson *Watery Maze* ii. 48 It would be idle to pretend that it was of much importance; it was really only cocking a vulgar snook. **1965** *Listener* 9 Sept. 374/2, I walked past the Thatched House..where I and other young journalists used to cock snooks at our superiors. **1980** *Times* 29 Feb. 10 East German craft last spring embarked upon a new ploy..to net a Danish torpedo,..cocking a snook at Nato's Baltic muscle.

Hence **snoo·k-cocking** *vbl. sb.*, **snook-cockingly** *adv.*; **snook-cocker.**

1950 D. Gascoyne *Vagrant* 57 And not think them impudent snook-cocking. **1958** *Economist* 6 Dec. 880/2 The seven Liberal councillors of Finchley..in snook-cocking protest against the local shortcomings of London Transport's bus service have launched a free private service of their own. **1962** *Spectator* 13 Apr. 478 A snook-cockingly 'blasphemous' film. **1965** E. Gowers *Fowler's Mod. Eng. Usage* (ed. 2) 535/2 Mere snook-cockers of whom it has been said..that their only concern is to 'find someone who is doing something..and fling a few insults at him'. **1978** Cadogan & Craig *Women & Children First* viii. 167 Spike Milligan's snook-cocking record of his wartime experiences.

Snooks² (snūks). A proper name or familiar appellation applied to a hypothetical person in a particular case (see quots.); also, any individual person. Cf. *Joe Bloggs* s.v. *Joe *sb.*² 5 c.

1860 Hotten *Dict. Slang* (ed. 2) 221 *Snooks*, an imaginary personage often brought forward as the answer to an idle question, or as the perpetrator of a senseless joke. **1919** G. B. Shaw *Inca of Perusalem* in *Heartbreak House* 214 Well, what about Snooks? **1922** Ld. Riddell *Some Things that Matter* ix. 108 '50 per cent of the inhabitants of Bunkumville who use this valuable adjunct to health and personal beauty wear Snooks's Expanders, which are undoubtedly the best.' That may be true, but I omit to mention that only two persons in Bunkumville wear chest expanders, one of whom is Snooks himself. **1959** *Times* 8 Dec. 13/4 The recommended formula goes something like this: 'This is Flaxway 5768. Mr. Snooks is out. If you wish to leave a message, go ahead.'.. Snooks, returning eventually to base, presses a button, and the machine reels off all the messages.

snookums (snū·kǝ̆mz). [Nonsense formation: cf. *diddums and prec.] A trivial term of endearment, usu. applied to children or lapdogs.

1919 *Ladies' Home Jrnl.* May 153/1 Even 'Snookums' knows and appreciates the soothing qualities of Johnson's Toilet and Baby Powder. **1928** *Chambers's Jrnl.* 21 Jan. 128/2 She is now a 'city-lady', with a couple of dear little 'snookums'.

snoop, *v.* Restrict *U.S.* to sense 1 and add: **2. a.** (Earlier and later examples.) Also with other advbs. orig. *U.S.*

In quot. 1832 unusually without following *adv.* or *prep.*

1832 R. C. Sands *Writings* (1834) II. 291 The world has realms wherein to *snoop*, And I am not a noddy. **1840** C. F. Hoffman *Greyslaer* II. iii. i. 105 Our scouts would make us believe that both he and Bradshawe are snooping about the country among the Tories. **1855** *Knickerbocker* XLVI. 317 The level which the..engineers 'snooped' round and found out, hasn't '*a parallel*' in all the adjacent region. **1902** H. L. Wilson *Spenders* iii. 26 Work..is something you want to get done; play is something you jest like to be doin'. Snoopin' up these gulches is both of 'em to me. **1931** D. L. Sayers *Five Red Herrings* xviii. 185 It is hardly possible for a local policeman in a country place to snoop about, wheedling information out of the inhabitants. **1943** J. B. Priestley *Daylight on Saturday* xxviii. 220 What are you doing here? Snooping around and then sending in a report in triplicate—eh? **1951** J. Fleming *Man who looked Back* xv. 195 You..have all the fun snooping round and I've got to wait.

b. To pry into matters one need not be concerned with. Often const. *on* (a person). *colloq.*

1921 *Daily Colonist* (Victoria, B.C.) 3 Apr. 9/3 There is the landlady who 'snoops' too much to suit her boarders. **1946** [see *ferret *sb.*¹ 1 b]. **1950** *Chicago Daily News* 14 Apr. 18/3 Another thing is that snoopers often get snooped on, in retribution. **1965** M. Spark *Mandelbaum Gate* vii. 254 Has he had any opportunity to snoop? **1975** R. Stout *Family Affair* vi. 55, I wouldn't ask you to snoop on a friend.

3. *trans.* To steal, to misappropriate. Also *absol. rare.*

1924 Galsworthy *White Monkey* i. viii. 57 If we let you snoop copies, all the packers will snoop copies. *Ibid.* iii. viii. 270 Yes, and look at that little snooper himself; he snooped to keep her alive after pneumonia.

Hence **snoo·ping** *vbl. sb.* and *ppl. a.*

1936 J. Steinbeck *In Dubious Battle* vii. 109 The health authorities are going to do plenty of snooping. If they can catch us off base, they'll bounce us. **1946** K. Tennant *Lost Haven* (1947) xvii. 288 He was just a snooping tourist. **1952** *Manch. Guardian Weekly* 14 Feb. 13 Whose job it is to engage in political snooping. **1965** D. Francis *Odds Against* iv. 49 All very normal... It was my snooping which seemed unreal. **1974** 'M. Innes' *Appleby's Other Story* xi. 87 'If you want my help—' 'A snooping copper's *help?*' **1977** *Rolling Stone* 13 Jan. 30/2 She collected the results of her snooping in a manila folder.

snoop (snūp), *sb. colloq.* (orig. *U.S.*). [f. the vb.] **1.** = Snooper 1 in Dict. and Suppl.; *spec.* one who makes official or other investigation, a detective.

1891 *Amer. Folk-lore* IV. 160 *Snoop*.—This word I have frequently heard in New England, used both as a verb and as a noun. It implies sneaking, spying, prying around. **1929** *Amer. Speech* V. 152 *Snoop*, one who noses something out. 'That woman is a snoop.' **1942** *New Statesman* 19 Sept. 186/3 *Snoops* are the Service Police, corresponding to the Army's Military Police. **1944** Dylan Thomas *Let.* 21 Sept. (1966) 267 There stinks a snoop in black. I'm thinking it Is Mr. Jones the Cake. **1948** *Time* 3 May 19/3 Every cop,..stool pigeon and neighborhood snoop in Detroit was working overtime. **1970** A. Sillitoe *Start in Life* vi. 318 His snoops already know I left Beirut. **1978** R. Thomas *Chinaman's Chance* xxxvii. 360 The Congressman seems to have been an awfully fine snoop. But then, he used to be a cop.

2. An act of snooping, prying, or investigation; a surreptitious inspection. Freq. with *(a)round*.

1908 G. H. Lorimer *Jack Spurlock—Prodigal* xi. 274 She couldn't keep her servants, for she was torn with dark doubts of their honesty... Life for her was one long snoop about the house. **1939** 'N. Blake' *Smiler with Knife* xii. 172 Why not have a snoop round in Chilton's study? **1969** M. Pugh *Last Place Left* xxii. 167 'You're going to take this to Brunner's house?' 'Not straight. Once I've had a good snoop round it.' **1972** G. Lyall *Blame Dead* xv. 107, I did a little unpacking and then went for a general snoop.

snooper. (In Dict. s.v. Snoop *v.*) Add: **1.** (Earlier and later examples.) *spec.* one who makes an intrusive official investigation. orig. *U.S.*

1889 in *Cent. Dict.* **1928** *Chicago Tribune* 11 July 10/4 Prohibition Commissioner Doran has warned dry snoopers to stop gunplay against innocent citizens. **1939** 'N. Blake' *Smiler with Knife* i. 19 What a snooper you are! **1948** *Jrnl. R. Aeronaut. Soc.* LII. 719 The difficulty with this is that the potential user is unlikely to come into the picture in the detail design stage, and the designing firm would probably not, in any case, welcome yet another 'snooper'. **1959** E. H. Clements *High Tension* vi. 103 We should consider ourselves lucky to have a professional snooper as a neighbour. **1965** M. Spark *Mandelbaum Gate* iii. 80 We know Ramdez. He's a snooper for his government. **1978** D. Grylls *Guardians & Angels* iii. 89 The parents..are tip-toeingly attentive... Of course, the adults are not depicted as snoopers.

2. A sneak-thief, a misappropriator. *rare.*

1924 [see *snoop *v.* 3]. **1927** 'J. Barbican' *Confessions Rum-Runner* ii. xxiii. 257 You rotten little cross-eyed snooper.

snooperscope (snū·pəɹskōᵘp). [f. Snooper + -scope; cf. *sniperscope.] A device which converts infra-red radiation to a visible image; esp. a pair of such devices fitted together and worn on the head to provide binocular vision in the dark.

1946 *Times-Dispatch* (Richmond, Va.) 16 Apr. 2/1 The snooperscope can be used over a special helmet. It weighs from six to seven pounds, and looks like something out of this world. *Ibid.*, The snooperscope had another use. With one on his noggin, a jeep or truck driver could go barrelling down the road to the front without lights. **1955** *Sci. News Let.* 7 May 295/3 A modified snooperscope is being used to 'see' through silicon crystals, spotting imperfections produced in manufacturing transistors, rectifiers and other semi-conducting devices. **1962** *Appl. Physics Lett.* I. 91/2 We looked at the diode output through a 'snooperscope' and above the threshold observed a very intense and narrow beam [of infrared radiation] radiating from the junction region. **1972** J. MILLS *Report to Commissioner* 227 Hanson says why not darken the floor and watch the elevator with snooperscopes.

snoo·pery. orig. *U.S.* [f. SNOOP *v.* + -ERY.] The activity of snooping or prying; surreptitious investigation, *spec.* into another's private affairs.

1935 *Sun* (Baltimore) 13 Feb. 2/6 C. Jasper Bell (Dem., Mo.) turned the Capitol Hill fight against 'innovations into snoopery' upon another law, the NIRA. Thus, the number of enactments now known to contain provisions making public the private financial affairs of citizens was brought to five. **1964** *Spectator* 13 Mar. 337/1 In time private enterprise snoopery could become a growth industry and major job-supplier for our unemployed. **1972** G. LYALL *Blame Dead* xiv. 104 'He sounds shifty as hell.'.. That..might help justify David's snoopery. **1981** A. PATON *Towards Mountain* xxii. 187 The rules were simple—no sharing of blankets, the doors to stand open, no boy to sleep in any other dormitory except the one to which he had been assigned. These rules could be evaded, but their evasion was preferable to a reign of snoopery and an encouragement of informers.

snoo·py, *a.* [f. SNOOP *v.* + -Y[1].] Inquisitive, excessively curious or prying.

1895 in *Funk's Stand. Dict.* **1921** S. FORD *Inez & Trilby May* xii. 212 With the cops so snoopy, we can't afford a scene. **1930** P. MACDONALD *Link* xi. 216 I'm not snoopy, but I opened my door and listened. **1952** *Chambers's Jrnl.* Feb. 81/2 This was a depot where the Canadian rum-runners met the American bootleggers to exchange Canadian and Scotch whisky for American dollars, and I knew enough about these operations to realise that life did not amount to much when snoopy guys butted in. **1978** J. WAINWRIGHT *Jury People* xii. 41 Don't think I was being snoopy—but..I saw you arrive, this morning.

Hence **snoo·piness.**

1969 L. HELLMAN *Unfinished Woman* iv. 39 The vicarious, excited snoopiness I knew was mixed with the kindness.

snoose (snūs, snūz). *Western N. Amer.* Also **schnoose, snooze.** [ad. Da., Norw., and Sw. *snus* snuff, shortening of Da., Sw. *snustobak*, Norw. *snustobakk* snuff tobacco; cf. SNUSH *sb.*] Chewing snuff, esp. taken by loggers. Also *fig.*

1912 H. FOOTNER *New Rivers of North* 21 Loud were the lamentations of his foreigners when his 'snooze' gave out, 'snooze' being the local familiarity for snuff. **1925** *Amer. Speech* I. 138/1 He 'fogs-up' on his pipe, or takes a 'rear of snoose'. 'Snoose' is a certain brand of Swedish snuff; it is moist and hot with pepper, and the man who is not used to it will find his gums burning and his head swimming when he tries his first 'rear'; but nearly every logger in this neck of the woods [*sc.* Northwest] has abandoned the old-time American plug for this terrific Nordic concoction. **1942** *Ibid.* XXVII. 221/2 *Give her snoose*, an order to increase power. **1955** R. HOBSON *Nothing too Good* xiii. 136 Larkie was a snoose chewer. **1965** *Sun* (Vancouver) 22 Apr. 51/7 (*caption*) Just before ya face the old lady ya shove a wad of schnoose in yer mouth.. she'll never smell yer breath. **1977** J. HODGINS *Invention of World* i. 5 He spat snoose out the broken window onto the pavement.

snoot (snūt), *sb.* [dial. var. SNOUT *sb.*[1]] **1.** = SNOUT *sb.*[1] 2. *dial.* and *slang.*

1861 J. BARR *Poems* 33 Like harrow teeth they're stickin' out, To catch the dirt below their snoot. **1866** *Galaxy* 1 Oct. 277, I had supposed that such phrases as 'I'll mash your head!' 'I'll bash you on the snoot!' 'I'll mawl yer jaws,' and similar expressive threats, were invented in the New World. **1884** E. W. NYE *Baled Hay* 209 Read our..'Ode to the Busted Snoot of a Shattered Venus de Milo'. **1905** [see SNOUT *sb.*[1] 2]. **1924** WODEHOUSE *Bill the Conqueror* v. 101 He seethed with generous indignation and even went so far as to state his intention ..of busting the fellow one on the snoot. **1938** D. RUNYON *Furthermore* v. 86 A bust in the snoot. **1956** D. M. DAVIN *Sullen Bell* II. iv. 136 At first I was all for poking the bloke in the snoot. **1971** J. AIKEN *Nightly Deadshade* iii. 33 Snell is sticking his long snoot into the middle of things.

2. The nose of an aircraft, esp. of adjustable construction (cf. *droop-snoot* s.v. *DROOP *sb.* 3). Also, the nose of a car, etc.

1945, etc. [see *droop-snoot* s.v. *DROOP *sb.* 3]. **1962** *New Scientist* 18 Jan. 135/1 As the flaps are depressed, so the snoot is tilted downwards until at full flaps it is depressed at an angle of 35°. **1977** *Drive* Mar.–Apr. 52/3 Drivers are in a poor position to judge the droop-snoot of the car. **1980** A. COPPEL *Hastings Conspiracy* iv. 32 Through the open door of the flight-deck Brede could see that the snoot had been lowered for better visibility.

3. A tubular or conical attachment used to produce a narrow beam from a spotlight.

1952 *Cinema* 7 Jan. 108/1 (Advt.), Viking Films Ltd... Lighting equipment... Spots... Cans, bashers, overhead banks, snoots, barndoors, diffusers, niggers, etc. **1972** QUICK & LA BAU *Handbk. Film Production* xi. 73 Snoots consist of metal tubes that are mounted on the front of spotlights to control the spread of their beams. **1977** J. HEDGECOE *Photographer's Handbk.* 34 Spotlight accessories include folding barn-doors..and conical snoots.. both of which restrict the beam.

snoot, *v. U.S.* [f. prec.] **1.** *intr.* = NOSE *v.* 8 b; = SNOUT *v.* 2. (In quot. *fig.*) *U.S. dial. rare.*

1890 *Dialect Notes* I. 75 *Snoot* (snût), of the human face or nose, apparently the same word as *snout*. A vulgar word in New England. 'I'll bu'st your snoot'; 'hit him on the snoot'. As a verb in 'to snoot round', *i.e.* to nose around, it is reported from *Poughkeepsie*, N.Y.

2. *trans.* To snub; to treat scornfully or with disdain. *U.S.*

1928 E. HATCH *Couple of Quick Ones* IV. 198, I followed him..up the street to where the Wright limousine was snooting the world in general at the kerb. **1939** J. P. MARQUAND *Wickford Point* xi. 124 Don't try to snoot Sue Jaeckel. **1959** V. PACKARD *Status Seekers* iii. 44 Many intellectuals..develop their own ways of snooting. **1977** *Time* 17 Jan. 28/3 Cinderella (Gemma Craven) gets snooted by her Stepsisters and gazes sorrowfully into the flames of the scullery fire.

snooter (snū·təɹ), *v.* [f. as prec. + -ER[5].] *trans.* To harass, to bedevil; to snub. (Only in P. G. Wodehouse.)

1923 WODEHOUSE *Inimit. Jeeves* iii. 30 My Aunt Agatha ..wouldn't be on hand to snooter me for at least another six weeks. **1929** —— *Mr. Mulliner Speaking* viii. 286 'As far', replied Mr. Finch, frigidly, 'as a bloke can be said to be all right..who has been..chivvied and snootered and shot in the fleshy part of the leg—.' **1932** —— *Let.* 13 Aug. in *Performing Flea* (1953) 66 Downtrodden young peer, much snootered by aunts, etc., has become engaged to two girls at once.

snootful (snū·tful). [f. *SNOOT *sb.* + -FUL.] As much (alcohol, etc.) as one can take; a quantity of alcohol, esp. one sufficient to induce drunkenness. Cf. SKINFUL 3 a.

1918 R. LARDNER *Real Dope* 43 When somebodys else husband pulls something its O.K. but if their own husband does it he must of had a snoot full. **1935** WODEHOUSE *Luck of Bodkins* xvii. 205 His whole mind was manifestly intent on reaching the smoking-room and getting a snootful. **1953** W. R. BURNETT *Vanity Row* xvi. 117 He was drunk... 'A snootful, eh?' **1969** K. VONNEGUT *Slaughterhouse-Five* ii. 40 Billy didn't usually drink much..but he certainly had a snootful now. **1977** H. GREENE *FSO-1* xi. 103 Kim..had gotten a snootful of the tear gas.

snootily (snū·tili), *adv.* [f. *SNOOTY *a.* + -LY[2].] In a snooty manner, superciliously.

1940 'G. ORWELL' *Let.* 16 Apr. in *Coll. Essays* (1968) II. 22, I get quite a lot of letters..from people snootily pointing out some mistake I've made. **1954** KOESTLER *Invisible Writing* III. xix. 220 And now, when I am down, you snootily refuse to help me with my business. **1961** *Guardian* 29 Mar. 14/3 An old lady..remarked..rather snootily..'It's where you were born that counts.' **1980** I. HUNTER *Malcolm Muggeridge* ii. 36 Vidler was unimpressed by all this and replied somewhat snootily, rejecting all his arguments.

snoo·tiness. [f. as prec. + -NESS.] The character or quality of being snooty; conceitedness, superciliousness.

1932 J. T. FARRELL *Young Lonigan* iii. 124 She said it served Helen right that she had gotten a crush on a guy like Weary, because Weary would take some of the snootiness out of her. **1942** *R.A.F. Jrnl.* 2 May 22 They in turn mistook our English reserve for 'snootiness'. **1956** S. HOPE *Diggers' Paradise* 155 One or two tourists I met were annoyed about what they described as this 'snootiness'. **1977** *Sunday Times* 15 May 40/1 All these books steer with tact between the contrasting risks of sycophancy and snootiness.

snooty (snū·ti), *a.* [f. *SNOOT *sb.* + -Y[1].] Supercilious, haughty, conceited; affecting superiority, snobbish; 'highbrow', 'stuck-up'. Occas., irritable, short-tempered.

1919 A. HUXLEY *Let.* 12 Aug. (1969) 180 A very snooty cousin and a sporty one. **1922** S. LEWIS *Babbitt* xx. 252, I didn't like..the snooty way you talked. **1931** E. LINKLATER *Juan in Amer.* II. xvi. 172 She says you were kinda snooty with her. Tried to high-hat her. **1938** E. BOWEN *Death of Heart* II. vii. 303 Reproaches and rather snooty laughs were exchanged. **1940** in Harrison & Madge *War begins at Home* xiv. 379 They're quite snooty, because you don't buy anything else. **1947** 'A. P. GASKELL' in D. M. Davin *N.Z. Short Stories* (1953) 282, I was lucky to have a girl like Betty who was keen on football. Some of the girls used to go very snooty when the blokes couldn't take them to the Friday-night hops. **1955** E. CADELL *Lark shall Sing* v. 67 One of those snooty little cafés..run by bony gentlewomen. **1959** I. & P. OPIE *Lore & Lang. Schoolch.* x. 178 A short-tempered person is spoken of as being..snappy, snooty (meaning easily irritated), and sharp-edged. **1960** O. MANNING *Great Fortune* II. 142 The English wives were a bit snooty with me. **1980** R. BARNARD *Death in Cold Climate* vi. 60 You know how the English can say 'Really?'—all cold and snooty.

snooze, *sb.* Add: **3.** *Comb.* **snooze alarm,** an alarm on a bedside clock which may be preset or reset to repeat after a short interval, allowing the sleeper a further nap; **snooze button,** a button on a clock which sets the snooze alarm.

1973 *Electrical Wholesaler* Sept. 76/1 (Advt.), Snooze alarm clock housed in finely tooled aluminium case. **1976** *Washington Post* 19 Apr. A15/6 (Advt.), Multiband clock radio. Digital Numbers. Wake to Music. Extra Snooze Alarm. **1974** *Sci. Amer.* Oct. 63/2 For years, alarm clocks were dull..even those with snooze buttons and fancy dials.

snoozer. Add: **1. b.** As a vague appellation: a fellow, a chap. *colloq.* (orig. *U.S.*).

1884 [see *BANK *v.*[2] 4 b]. **1891** 'E. PERKINS' *Thirty Years of Wit* 296 I'm the snoozer from the upper trail; I'm the reveler in murder and in gore. **1903** 'O. HENRY' in *Ainslee's* Sept. 116/2 She knows what a wild kind of a snoozer I've been. **1916** *Anzac Book* 99 The chaps of the 16th Battalion Are not easy snoozers to beat. **1923** R. D. PAINE *Comrades of Rolling Ocean* iv. 65 Do you mean to say that the wonderful old snoozer had the grit to cruise out to your country at his age? **1939** JOYCE *Finnegans Wake* 174 They had cornered him about until there was not a snoozer among them but was utterly undeceived. **1946** *Sunday Sun* (Austral.) 20 Oct. (Suppl.) 15 They'd have lamped a snoozer rigged up as an army skipper clopclopping along on a nag just behind them. **1966** H. MARRIOTT *Cariboo Cowboy* v. 52 Zim was a tough old snoozer. I know that he cut his knee open with an axe and sewed it up with some worsted yarn and his wife's darning needle.

† **2.** A thief who steals from the hotel or house in which he is staying. Cf. SNOOZE *sb.* 2. *slang. Obs.*

1862 H. MAYHEW *London Labour* Extra vol. 242/1 Some two years ago a robbery was committed by a 'snoozer' or one of those thieves who take up their quarters at hotels for the purpose of robbery. **1882** *Sydney Slang Dict.* 8/1 *Snoozers*, men and women who sleep at hotels and boarding-houses and decamp with other people's effects in the morning. **1889** FARMER *Americanisms* 501/2 *Snooser*, an hotel thief who lives in the place, and thus seeks for opportunities to carry out his depredations.

Snopes (snōᵘ·ps). Also **snopes;** *erron. pl.* **Snopes.** The family name of a series of vicious characters in the fiction of William Faulkner (first described in *Sartoris*, 1929), used as a type of an unscrupulous or heartless person.

1962 *Guardian* 3 Oct. 1/6 There are plenty of snopes waiting to take over and act as though Mr Meredith has never been. **1970** *Times* 10 Apr. 10 In the heated circumstances of the present Mr. Nixon would be joining the yahoos and the snopes. **1977** *Time* 17 Oct. 48/2 His brother, the Snopes in the woodpile, satirizes the theme by assuming the very worst of the American people and braying at them.

snore, *v.* Add: **1. b.** Also *U.S.*

1935 W. FAULKNER *As I lay Dying* 40 Beyond the porch Cash's saw snores steadily into the board.

snore-. Add: **b.** With advb. **snore-off** *colloq.* (chiefly *Austral.* and *N.Z.*), a sleep or nap, esp. after drinking.

1950 *Landfall* June 127, I notice Little Spike's legs sticking out from an empty tallow cask where he is having a snore-off. **1967** K. GILES *Death & Mr Prettyman* vi. 120 He always vowed to cut out these afternoon snore-offs. **1968** D. O'GRADY *Bottle of Sandwiches* 49 He surfaced from his plonk-induced snore-off.

snorer. Add: **1. b.** *slang.* The nose.

1891 FARMER *Slang* II. 168/1 *Conk*,..the nose... English synonyms..snorer; [etc.]. **1925** O. JESPERSEN *Mankind, Nation & Individual* viii. 156 Lastly we have Slang-words for..the Nose. Danish, *snude*... Engl., a number of expressions:..snorter, snorer. **1959** I. & P. OPIE *Lore & Lang. Schoolch.* ix. 155 Children go in for short sharp words, as in their more usual names for parts of the body:..'snorer', 'snozzle', and 'boko' for nose.

snoring, *vbl. sb.* Add: **a.** Also *transf.*

1935 A. J. CRONIN *Stars look Down* I. ix. 69 There was a silence, broken only by the snoring of air through the wind-bore cast of the pump. *Ibid.* 70 The snoring of the pump had stopped. **1951** R. HARGREAVES *This Happy Breed* ix. 102 The obscene snorings of the saxophone.

snork, *sb.* Add: **3.** *Austral.* and *N.Z. slang.* A baby.

1941 BAKER *Dict. Austral. Slang* 68 *Snork*, a baby. **1941** —— *N.Z. Slang* vi. 57 Other twentieth century New Zealand expressions of varied use include..*snork*, a baby. **1944** L. GLASSOP *We were Rats* 273 Got a scar on his hand, but probably he's had it since he was a little snork. **1956** D. M. DAVIN *Sullen Bell* II. v. 136 What I wasn't expecting was to find her living with the same bloke again and well on the way to having another snork. **1963** B. PEARSON *Coal Flat* x. 194 It's better to knock it on the head at birth, isn't it? Like a snork you don't want. **1970** D. M. DAVIN *Not Here, Not Now* II. vii. 108 Have to give up being on the bum once there's a snork or two to be looked after.

snorkel, schnorkel (snǭ·ɹkĕl, ʃnǭ·ɹkĕl). Also ‖ **Schnorchel** (ʃnǭ·ɹχəl), **Schnorkel.** [ad. G. *schnorchel.*] **1. a.** Usu. in forms **schnorkel, Schnorkel.** An airshaft, invented in the Netherlands and developed in Germany, which was fitted to diesel-engined submarines so that air could reach the engines, allowing them to function, and exhaust gases to be expelled, while the vessel was submerged; also a submarine fitted with such an airshaft. Also *Schnorkel Spirall.*

1944 *News Chron.* 11 Dec. 4/2 They are the new submarines fitted with what the Germans call the Schnorkel Spirall, the purpose of which is to extend under-water endurance. **1945** *Engineer* 19 Jan. 52/3 We hear that the

Germans are fitting their U-boats with what is called the Schnorkel. **1945** *News-Leader* (Richmond, Va.) 12 Mar. 13/3 The 'schnorkel', or stovepipe breather, and the folding kite are chief among the new German gadgets. **1946** [see *breathing-tube* s.v. *BREATHING *vbl. sb.* 10]. **1946** *Collier's* 11 May 69/2 The other the Germans called the '*Schnorchel*'. That was a pipe or tube of about periscope height, that extended from the ventilating system of the engines to the surface. **1950** *Sat. Even. Post* 11 Nov. 79 Chief credit for this went to the snorkel, a device which enables subs to breathe under water. Invented by the Dutch, stolen by the Nazis and perfected by the U.S. Navy, the snorkel has revolutionized naval warfare. **1959** *Sunday Times* 8 Feb. 13/4 In the spring of 1944 operational U-boats of the older types began to be equipped with the 'Schnorkel'. **1969** *New Scientist* 28 Aug. 418/1 The invention of the schnorkel reduced the area exposed during recharging to a single pipe extending a few feet above the surface. **1974** L. DEIGHTON *Spy Story* xviii. 192 We came up to periscope depth and let a blow of fresh air through the schnorkel.

b. Usu. in form **snorkel.** A short breathing-tube used by underwater swimmers.

1953 J. Y. COUSTEAU *Silent World* 6 They claimed we drove away fish, damaged nets, looted their seines, and caused mistrals with our schnorkels. **1958** *Oxf. Mail* 17 Apr. 6/7 The American film television series, *Sea Hunt*, claims to be boosting the sport of skin-diving. If that is true there is soon going to be a big demand for snorkels and spear-guns in the Midlands. **1962** *Underwater Swimming* ('Know the Game' ser.) 9/1 By lying on the surface with the face in the water and breathing through the snorkel, the diver can watch the underwater scene continuously. **1968** *T.V. World* 10 Feb. 18/1 It is only when she sees a swimmer's snorkel in her stepfather's room that Mandy realises how the crime could have been committed. **1977** G. DURRELL *Golden Bats & Pink Pigeons* v. 110 We had only masks and no snorkels, and my mask let in water.

2. Usu. in form **Snorkel.** A proprietary name for a piece of apparatus used in fighting fires in tall buildings, consisting of a platform which may be elevated and extended.

1959 *Official Gaz.* (U.S. Patent Office) 27 Oct. TM 140/1 Pitman Manufacturing Company, Grandview, Mo. Filed July 6, 1959. *Snorkel.* For Aerial Platform Apparatus, Particularly Such Apparatus Adapted for Use in Fire Fighting. First use June 11, 1959. **1960** *Amer City* Jan. 83/2 After re-design and further testing of pilot models, the Pitman Aerial Platform, now known as the Snorkel, was offered in July 1958. **1963** R. I. MCDAVID *Mencken's Amer. Lang.* 258 *Snorkel*... The Chicago Fire Department uses it to designate a piece with an elevated pumping platform, for fighting fires in tall buildings. **1969** *Trade Marks Jrnl.* 26 Nov. 1955/1 *Snorkel* 940,580. Mobile hydraulically operated rotatable and elevatable platforms for use in fire fighting. Simon Engineering Dudley Limited,..Dudley, Worcestershire; Manufacturers. **1973** *Lebende Sprachen* XVIII. 69/2 At Newcastle upon Tyne the Chief Fire Officer has installed a closed circuit television camera on an aerial platform known as a *snorkel*. **1977** *Monitor* (McAllen, Texas) 28 June 1A/9 The fire was declared out at 8 a.m. The Edinburg snorkel was used to wet down all parts under the collapsed roof.

3. *attrib.*

1944 [see sense 1 a above]. **1945** *Illustr. London News* 3 Mar. 229/2 The most recent move in this never-ceasing battle was the introduction..of the 'Schnorkel' apparatus. **1949** *Sun* (Baltimore) 2 Apr. 7/2 (*caption*) First photo of damaged sub... The periscope and snorkel equipment are bent. **1953** J. Y. COUSTEAU *Silent World* 1 My wife, Simone, would swim out on the surface with a schnorkel breathing-tube and watch me through her submerged mask. **1954** E. CLARK *Lady with Spear* xix. 187 He.. wasn't a strong swimmer, but he wanted to try a face mask and snorkel tube. **1958** *Times Lit. Suppl.* 9 May 257/4 'There is no tactical requirement for such a fitting,' was the crushing reply to his early suggestion for the designing of a *schnorkel* apparatus. **1962** F. I. ORDWAY et al. *Basic Astronautics* xiii. 510 These devices had snorkel attachments to prevent the entry of water into the systems. **1967** *New Scientist* 9 Mar. 457/1 Modern conventional submarines can proceed at speed for many days with nothing except their 'schnorkel' air-breathing tubes breaking the surface. **1967** O. WYND *Walk Softly, Men Praying* xii. 187 The men..might have got out in snorkel-suits and been picked up by a deep-sea fishing fleet. **1973** *People's Jrnl.* (Inverness) 28 July 10/3 (*caption*) Firemen use the 85ft. snorkel escape ladder to rescue a 'casualty' from the training tower. **1980** P. MOYES *Angel Death* iv. 47 They climbed ashore, with their snorkel masks and fins slung in a string shopping- bag.

Hence as *v. intr.* (also *erron.* **snorkle**), to use a snorkel; to swim underwater using a snorkel; **sno·rkeller, sno·rkelling** *vbl. sb.*

1959 *New Scientist* 26 Mar. 695/2 Pressure variations due to this 'snorkeling' might disturb sensitive instrumentation systems. Mark I could snorkel. **1959** *Elizabethan* June 21/2 But archaeology is really work for trained specialists. You will most likely want to know where to 'snorkel' and fish. **1960** F. M. ROBERTS *Basic Scuba* ii. 27 Snorkeling through weeds..might pull the mouthpiece from the diver's lips because the crook gets caught. **1963** *Harper's Bazaar* Jan. 30/2 Many skin divers are content to remain snorkelers, but some want to go deeper and deeper. **1968** J. UPDIKE *Couples* ii. 171 Ken liked to snorkel. **1974** *Country Life* 24 Jan. (Suppl.) 32 Vast golden bays... Each..an adventure for intrepid snorklers. **1975** D. MARLOWE *Nightshade* x. 116 Water sports, shuffleboard, scuba and snorkling. **1977** G. DURRELL *Golden Bats & Pink Pigeons* iv. 81 We went snorkling on the reef. **1980** P. MOYES *Angel Death* viii. 104 Henry and Emma swam and snorkelled and sunbathed.

snort, *sb.*[1] Add: **3. a.** *slang* (orig. *U.S.*). An alcoholic drink; a measure of spirits; a 'snifter'.

1889 FARMER *Americanisms* 501/2 A *snort* of whiskey is a dram; a nip; a small quantity. **1912** J. SANDILANDS *Western Canad. Dict. & Phrase-Book* 42/2 The sporting Canadian asks his friends, 'Will you have a snort?' **1925** WODEHOUSE *Carry on, Jeeves* iv. 80 We were taking a quiet snort in a corner. **1945** J. STEINBECK *Cannery Row* xxix. 189 She..took out a bottle and a glass and poured herself a snort. **1962** 'R. GORDON' *Doctor in Swim* xii. 75 'How about an—ah—quick snort?' I stared at him. 'But you never drink except at Christmas.' **1966** M. LAURENCE *Jest of God* xii. 199 Ladies often feel it wouldn't be very nice to drink rye at such a time [as bereavement], but a snort of sherry is usually acceptable. **1981** M. E. ATKINS *Palimpsest* viii. 83 We'll have another snort... C'mon, drink up, I'll fill your glass.

b. *slang* (orig. *U.S.*). A dose or measure of cocaine or heroin which is taken by inhalation.

1951 [see *joy-pop* s.v. *JOY *sb.* 10]. **1959** [see *MAIN LINE 1 c]. **1962** [see *HORSE *sb.* 14*]. **1972** H. C. RAE *Shooting Gallery* II. 73 How did McDowell pick up a big enough snort to do for himself? **1978** G. VIDAL *Kalki* iv. 88 'Want a snort?' Bruce produced a cocaine snifter.

snort (snǭɹt), *sb.*[2] *Naut. slang* (now only *Hist.*). [Anglicized corruption of G. *schnorchel*, after SNORT *sb.*[1]] = *SNORKEL, SCHNORKEL 1 a. Freq. *attrib.*

1944 *News Chron.* 11 Dec. 4/2 The first 'snort' U-boats are probably already at sea... 'Snort' is the Navy's nickname for them. **1944** *N.Y. Herald Tribune* 12 Dec. 1/7 (*heading*) 'Snorts' said to enable vessels to stay under 20 days. **1950** *Times* 26 Apr. 6/6 Under the programme 10 existing submarines are to be equipped with the 'Snort' breathing apparatus. **1954** H. M. BURTON tr. *Diolé's Under-Water Exploration* v. 69 The chief improvements to the standard type submarine which were introduced during the last war were the work of the Germans. They were responsible, in particular, for the *Schnorchel*, or 'snort'. **1976** *Oxf. Compan. Ships & Sea* 759/1 In the British Navy the schnorkel tube was given the name snort.

Hence as *v.*[2] *intr.*: of a submarine, to travel underwater by means of a snort; **sno·rter**[3], a submarine fitted with a snort; **sno·rting** *vbl. sb.*[2]

1953 *John o' London's Weekly* 3 July 602/2 Since the *Andrew* crossed the Atlantic in total submergence, the word snort has acquired a different significance. Said her captain after she had achieved her object: 'All we were told was: "You are going to snort back"—so we snorted.' **1957** *Jane's Fighting Ships 1957–8* 51 On 15 June 1953 *Andrew* completed a 2500 sea miles voyage under water from Bermuda to the English Channel in 15 days, a record for 'snorting' in the Royal Navy. **1962** W. GRANVILLE *Dict. Sailor's Slang* 109/1 *Snorter*, submarine fitted with the snorkel device which enables her to keep at sea for a considerable period. **1974** 'M. HEBDEN' *Pride of Dolphins* III. ii. 230 'Open Three Main vents. Periscope depth. Stand by to snort.'.. They were snorting slowly back up the Solent. **1979** *Daily Tel.* 3 May 3/3 Since Olympus could reach safety from snorting depth in about a minute, the order to dive was given 45 seconds too late.

snort, *v.* Add: **7.** *slang* (orig. *U.S.*). To inhale (a narcotic drug in powder form, esp. cocaine or heroin). Also *absol.*

1935 A. J. POLLOCK *Underworld Speaks* 110/1 *Snort*, to sniff cocaine or heroin. **1958** H. BRADDY in *Southern Folklore Q.* Sept. 134 Since ma was a viper And daddy would snort, There wasn't much more I had to be taught. **1967** M. M. GLATT et al. *Drug Scene* iii. 32, I started snorting cocaine through the nose. **1972** M. J. BOSSE *Incident at Naha* i. 38 She snorted Methedrine. I saw her do it many times. **1974** M. C. GERALD *Pharmacol.* xv. 291 Cocaine is usually administered intravenously, although some prefer to 'sniff' or 'snort' it. **1980** M. BOOTH *Bad Track* ii. 46 'Are you snorting?'.. He nodded... He inhaled the cocaine. **1982** *Daily Tel.* 4 Oct. 3/3 Mrs Pulitzer's lawyers claim that she started snorting cocaine after being sucked into the vortex of the 'Palm Beach lifestyle'.

snorter[1]. Add: **2. c.** (Examples in *Cricket.*)

1888 R. H. MITCHELL in Steel & Lyttelton *Cricket* xiii. 380 How different this..from being compelled to play a real 'snorter' before the breath is fairly recovered after the effort of running several fourers in succession! **1898** G. GIFFEN *With Bat & Ball* xi. 189, I know of no bowler whom one has to watch so closely [as T. R. McKibben], for you never know when you are going to get a 'snorter' of a break, from one side or the other. **1929** *Morning Post* 11 Mar. 16/4 When in the next Test, at Lord's, McDonald bowled him [*sc.* Hendren] for 0 with a 'snorter'. **1954** J. H. FINGLETON *Ashes crown Year* xxiv. 257 May..now hit another 'snorter' through the covers.

d. (Earlier example.)

1829 P. EGAN *Boxiana* 2nd Ser. II. 119 The latter got a severe snorter, which not only uncorked the claret, but left a stupifying quality behind it.

e. The nose itself.

1829 P. EGAN *Boxiana* 2nd Ser. II. 353 The snorter of Raines looked red! For why? Jones's mauley had given it a rum tap! **1846** *Swell's Night Guide* 132/2 *Snorter*, the nose. **1925** [see *SNORER 1 b].

snorter[2]. Add: **2.** = *SNOTTER *sb.*[2] 2.

1950 BOWN & DOVE *Port Operation & Admin.* iv. 138 The snotter, or snorter, is a length of cordage or S.W.R. with an eye spliced in each end. **1965** R. B. ORAM *Cargo Handling* v. 93 Rope snorters are used at Sydney and Brisbane to discharge the pallets and these are left on the cargo at loading.

snorter[3]: see *SNORT *sb.*[2] **snorting,** *vbl. sb.*[2]: see *SNORT *sb.*[2]

snorting, *ppl. a.* Add: **4.** Exceptionally remarkable for excellence, size, strength, etc. (In quot. as *advb.*) *colloq. rare.*

1924 GALSWORTHY *White Monkey* II. ix. 195 I've played bridge with him,..—snorting good player.

snot, *sb.* Add: **3.** (Later examples.)

1939 JOYCE *Finnegans Wake* 494, I would misdemean to rebuke to the libels of snots from the fleshambles, the canalles. **1952** B. HARWIN *Home is Upriver* xvii. 172 You want that damn' little snot now, hah? A damn' little snot ain't even dry behind the ears. **1974** N. FREELING *Dressing of Diamond* 159 She wasn't going to cry in front of that rotten-toothed snot. **1981** J. MELVILLE *Sort of Samurai* iii. 25 We've let the boy go home on bail... Miserable little snot, but no real harm in him.

5. *snot-green, -smeared* adjs.; **snotnose** *slang*, a term of contempt applied to a childish, despicable, or conceited person; = SNOTTY-NOSE; **snot-nosed** *a. slang*, foul with nasal mucus; conceited; inexperienced and contemptible; = SNOTTY-NOSED *a.*; **snot-rag** *slang*, a pocket-handkerchief; also *transf.* as a term of opprobrium.

1922 Snotgreen [see *SCROTUM b]. **1975** T. STOPPARD *Travesties* I. 23 The swiftly-gliding snot-green (mucus mutandis) Limmat River. **1941** T. WOLFE *Hills Beyond* ix. 338 How do *you* know whether it's round or flat—a little two-by-fo' snotnose like you that ain't *been* nowhere. **1949** A. MILLER *Death of Salesman* II. 97 That snotnose. Imagine that? **1963** 'E. MCBAIN' *Ten plus One* xi. 143 He was not enjoying this little snotnose..and the college girl talk. **1977** H. FAST *Immigrants* I. 72 So don't be young snotnose with me. I like serious boys. **1941** B. SCHULBERG *What makes Sammy Run?* i. 13 A snot-nosed little office boy. **1960** H. LEE *To kill Mockingbird* iii. 34 Ain't no snot-nosed slut of a schoolteacher ever born c'n make me do nothin'! You ain't makin' me go nowhere, missus. **1972** M. WOODHOUSE *Mama Doll* viii. 100 A persuasive manner you picked up at some snot-nosed advertising agency. **1886** F. T. ELWORTHY *W. Somerset Word-Bk.* 690 *Snot-rag*.., a pocket-handkerchief. **1916** 'TAFFRAIL' *Pincher Martin* vi. 95 Any schoolboy will tell you what a 'snot rag' is. **1929** T. WOLFE *Look homeward, Angel* xiv. 170, I don't give a good goddam..if you're the President's snotrag. **1959** N. MAILER *Advts. for Myself* (1961) 84 One of them said he was going to take my shirt and use it for a snotrag, and they all laughed. **1973** J. WAINWRIGHT *High-Class Kill* 241 You are a self-opinionated idiot. You, and every snivelling little snot-rag like you. **1939** AUDEN & ISHERWOOD *Journey to War* i. 48 The averted, snot-smeared, animal faces of the very humble.

snotter, *sb.*[2] Add: **2.** A length of rope with an eye spliced in each end.

1950 [see *SNORTER[2] 2]. **1956** C. L. SAUERBIER *Marine Cargo Operations* vii. 416 The sling is constructed in the same manner as the fiber rope snotter. **1961** COURSE & ORAM *Gloss. Cargo-Handling Terms* 72 The snotter is stretched out to its full length and the package placed on it centrally. The ends of the snotter are brought over it and one eye rove through the other and placed on the lifting hook.

sno·ttily, *adv.* (Examples.)

1927 *Blackw. Mag.* Dec. 816/2 'Of course I did,' he replied, rather snottily I thought. **1937** J. T. FARRELL *Fellow Countrymen* 180 A man in a hurry bumped into him, and hastening on, snottily suggested that he quit taking up the whole sidewalk. **1973** M. AMIS *Rachel Papers* 59, I had a face looking over my shoulder, no matter how snottily equivocal its expression.

snottiness. (Later examples.)

1973 *Guardian* 18 June 4/6 The snottiness of the elitist eastern [US] establishment. **1976** *New Society* 19 Aug. 407/3 The snottiness of the French..Surly waiter..snapping concierge.

snotty, *sb.* (Later examples.)

1916 'TAFFRAIL' *Pincher Martin* vi. 95 No boat ever left the ship under steam or sail without a 'snotty' in charge. **1943** HUNT & PRINGLE *Service Slang* 61 *Snotty*, midshipman. (So called after the buttons on his sleeve, which are said to be there for a purpose not unconnected with the nickname.) **1974** P. DICKINSON *Poison Oracle* ii. 47 A British Naval Party under the command of a snappily saluting little snotty.

snotty, *a.* Add: **1. b.** (Later examples.)

1958 J. C. HEROLD *Mistress to Age* (1959) III. xiii. 263 Albertine had slapped the Crown Prince and called him a snotty brat. **1967** P. WELLES *Babyhip* ii. 36 My brother tried to date her, but she rejected him. She told him she didn't admire Catholics. I think that's pretty snotty. We did go to the same Sunday School. **1974** S. ELLIN *Stronghold* 60 'Did it strike you,' Coco asks at his snotty meanest, 'that if we came properly prepared, we could have stopped him from taking off?'

c. (Later examples.) Now *esp.* supercilious, aloof, 'snooty'.

1905 JOYCE *Let.* 7 Feb. (1966) II. 80 Are the 'girls' 'snotty' about Nora? **1916** W. OWEN *Let.* 9 Dec. (1967) 417 A snotty, acid, scot, impatient, irritated wretch. **1926** E. HEMINGWAY *Sun also Rises* xviii. 218, I won't eat down-stairs with that German head waiter. He was damned snotty. **1936** J. REITH *Diary* 13 May (1975) ii. 170 This is an insult... I was very snotty and reserved with the prig. **1968** *Globe & Mail Mag.* (Toronto) 13 Jan. 12/3 Francois is not always snotty, thank heaven. **1978** T. GIFFORD *Glendower Legacy* (1979) 39 He..thought for a moment of taking up the possibility of an exchange program with the snotty bastards in Cultural Affairs.

snotty-nose. For ? *Obs.* read 'Now *rare*' and add later example.

1932 L. GOLDING *Magnolia St.* III. i. 495 A little snotty-nose like that..and he's the [boxing] champion from all the world!

snotty-nosed, *a.* Delete Now *dial.* and add later examples.

1948 *Sun* (Baltimore) 20 Aug. 15/8 It was Walker who once told the Babe on a memorable occasion never to let down 'those snotty-nosed kids' who always loved him. 1971 P. AUDEMARS *Stolen like Magic Away* v. 66 All that love and..passion—thrown away every day on a bunch of snotty-nosed kids who take it..for granted. 1978 N. J. CRISP *London Deal* vii. 109 There's a snotty nosed young DC from the Yard sitting in his car outside.

snous (snaus). Also **snouse.** [ad. Da. or Sw. *snus* snuff.] Powdered tobacco.

1962 J. ONSLOW *Bowler-Hatted Cowboy* xxi. 204 His lower lip bulged with a wad of 'snouse', or Copenhagen snuff. 1979 *Guardian* 31 Mar. 13/5 The narcotic to which most [Swedish] young people are addicted is..'snous', a concoction of powdered tobacco stuffed under the upper lip.

snout, *sb.*[1] Add: **2. c.** Phr. *to have a snout on* (someone), to bear ill-will towards someone. *Austral.*

1941 BAKER *Dict. Austral. Slang* 69 *Snout on, have a*, to bear a grudge against a person. 1949 L. GLASSOP *Lucky Palmer* 212 He's got a snout on the Kid for something. 1966 T. RONAN *Once there was Bagman* 39 The reason you blokes have such a snout on him..is that he's forgotten more Law than you've ever learned.

5*. *slang.* A police informer.

1910 C. E. B. RUSSELL *Young Gaol-Birds* xii. 176 He was in reality a 'snout' or 'nark',..and from time to time had 'given away' many of his comrades. 1938 F. D. SHARPE *Sharpe of Flying Squad* xvii. 189 A 'sneak' or 'snout' is looked upon more or less as a leper in the Underworld. 1954 [see *GRASS *sb.*[1] 11*]. 1964 *Sunday Mail Mag.* (Brisbane) 5 Apr. 5/5 Then a 'snout' (or informant) called Big Ears made a long trip just to tell me: 'You're in trouble, Monty.' 1977 'E. CRISPIN' *Glimpses of Moon* xii. 235 His previous arrests had all been..the work probably of some anonymous snout. 1982 *Observer* 15 Aug. 22/6 You may have been 'grassed'..by a 'snout'.

7. snout-face: used as a personal insult.

1923 D. H. LAWRENCE *Birds, Beasts & Flowers* 184 But you, you snout-face, you reject nothing. 1979 *Amer. Poetry Rev.* Mar./Apr. 6/2 And the people In the streets, speechless, saw them passing: The scrawny guy, the barefoot one, the fellow with The bicycle, The black, Snout-face, that gal in yellow, [etc.].

snout, *sb.*[2] Add: **1. a.** (Earlier example.)

1885 A. GRIFFITHS *Fast & Loose* III. xii. 202 He knows Joe; worked for him, with regard to snout (tobacco); and he's straight—as a rod.

b. A cigarette.

1950 P. TEMPEST *Lag's Lexicon* 193 *Snout.* Word used collectively to cover all tobacco, hand-rolled and factory-made cigarettes, cigarette ends, and pipe dottles. 1954 *Evening News* 7 Jan. 2/2 Savage was seen and said: 'You will not find any export snouts here.' 1959 H. HOBSON *Mission House Murder* xxix. 187, I would smoke it slowly and..save the butt—*snouts*, the old lags called them. 1961 R. LONGRIGG *Daughters of Mulberry* 94 'Snout?' said her Ronnie, offering the Rothman's Kingsize. 1966 P. MOLONEY *Plea for Mersey* 54 Goin down the city fer a booze an a snout. 1976 J. O'CONNOR *Eleventh Commandment* vii. 91 If you were wise you chose non-smokers as your friends because they wouldn't shop you to an unscrupulous warder for a couple of snouts.

2. *attrib.*, as *snout ash, baron* [*BARON 2 c], *case, gaff* [*GAFF *sb.*[4] 3], *paper.*

1962 R. COOK *Crust on its Uppers* i. 21 Ever had someone put snout ash in your rosie? 1950 P. TEMPEST *Lag's Lexicon* 194 Snout-baron. 1964 *Economist* 25 Jan. 317/1 The 'snout barons'—prisoners who make a profit from the shortage of tobacco within prisons. 1962 R. COOK *Crust on its Uppers* iv. 48 'I'm going to give our Brian a fag,' an' he..brings out this heavy old snout case. 1936 Snout gaff [see *GAFF *sb.*[4] 3]. 1958 *Encounter* Apr. 18/1 He hardly ever spoke to me unless he wanted something, like a smoke or a snout paper.

snout, *v.* Add: **3.** *trans.* To bear ill-will towards; to treat with disfavour, to rebuff. Freq. as pa. pple. and ppl. adj. *Austral. slang.*

1916 C. J. DENNIS *Moods of Ginger Mick* 11 An' snouted them that snouted 'im, an' never give a dam. 1916 —— *Songs of Sentimental Bloke* 13 The world 'as got me snouted jist a treat. 1944 A. MARSHALL *These are my People* 155, I was sore as a snouted sheila for weeks. 1970 R. BEILBY *No Medals for Aphrodite* 149 That officer happened to have me snouted because I got you across the river, against his orders.

4. *intr.* To act as a police informer. *slang.*

1923 E. WALLACE *Missing Million* xx. 161 The gang found he was snouting. 1930 —— *White Face* xiii. 206 Dr. Marford knows, but he's not the feller that goes snouting on his patients. 1962 D. WARNER *Death of Bogey* II. iii. 71 No one wanted to be seen talking to him in case they were afterwards accused of snouting. Nevertheless, a great many did snout. 1973 'B. MATHER' *Snowline* x. 116 I've got to live in London when I go back. How long do you think I'd last if word got round that I'd been snouting?

Hence **snou·ting** *vbl. sb.* (also *attrib.*).

1937 PARTRIDGE *Dict. Slang* 795/2 *Snouting*, vbl. n., giving information to the police. 1962 [see sense 4 above]. 1973 J. WAINWRIGHT *Pride of Pigs* 55 Arranging a 'snouting service' with those villains; the lesser hooks being pulled in for the piffling crimes, while the big boys work the blinders without..being pushed too hard. 1978 F. BRANSTON *Sergeant Ritchie's Conscience* iv. 56 He started on his snouting expedition.

Snovian (snōu·viăn), *a.* [f. the name of the English writer Charles Percy *Snow* (1905–80), on the model of *SHAVIAN *a.* and *sb.*, etc.] Of or pertaining to the writings or ideas of C. P. Snow. Hence **Sno·vianism,** the beliefs or theories of C. P. Snow.

1966 *Listener* 19 May 733/1 This twinkling dancing life and soul of these almost edible pages is also one of the Snovian Olympians. *Ibid.*, Nothing could be more depressing than this total acceptance of the doctrines of Snovianism, even down to the use of the term *mana* and the reluctance to take seriously anyone below the rank of knight bachelor. 1969 *Observer* 17 Aug. 21/2 The attack on scientific rationalism..first appears in a paper on the Snovian conception of the Two Cultures. 1977 P. JOHNSON *Enemies of Society* xii. 163 The United Kingdom, compared with other..countries..had (in 1964) 'the greatest concentration on science and technology in higher education and the biggest proportion of qualified scientists and technologists..in relation to population and labour-force'—the exact opposite of the conventional Snovian thesis.

snow, *sb.*[1] Add: **I. 2. b.** (Earlier example.)

1778 J. CARVER *Trav. N.-Amer.* 250 Those [Indians] in the interior parts..count their years by winters; or, as they express themselves, by snows.

3*. Ellipt. for *snow tyre*, sense 7 b below. *N. Amer.*

1968 *Globe & Mail* (Toronto) 13 Jan. 26/2 (Advt.), 67 Fiat,..special exhaust, snows. 1977 *Detroit Free Press* 11 Dec. 22-D/8 (Advt.), '73 F-350 V8 4spd, dual tanks, PsPb, Ranger, snows.

II. 4. b. (Further examples.) *spec.* Solid carbon dioxide.

1913 J. HALL-EDWARDS *Carbon Dioxide Snow* 28 Having prepared our cone, or stick of snow..the first step is to place the patient in a comfortable and easy position. 1931 DOUGHERTY & KEARNEY *Fire* 243 The 'snow' does not freeze the fire as is sometimes erroneously believed, but blankets or smothers it. 1951 WHITBY & HYNES *Med. Bacteriol.* (ed. 5) ii. 20 Many bacteria and viruses..may be preserved by rapid freezing to -70°C, with CO_2-snow. 1974 L. E. LONG *Geology* i. 19 A frozen 'snow' of methane and ammonia glued the dust particles into globs that eventually grew to about the size of basketballs. 1979 *Nature* 30 Aug. 738/1 Much of the distributed SO_2 snow would be expected to fall within a few tens of kilometres of the scarps [on Jupiter's satellite Io].

d. *slang* (orig. *U.S.*). Cocaine; occas. heroin or morphine.

1914 JACKSON & HELLYER *Vocab. Criminal Slang* 78 *Snow*,..derived from the extremely flocculent nature of cocaine when pulverized. 1915 *Policeman's Monthly* Dec. 17/3 One day, his pal found him depressed and told him to take a little sniff of 'snow', as heroin is known to the vernacular of the criminal. 1925 A. P. HERBERT *Laughing Ann* 92 Don't let her know about whisky and 'snow'. 1933 N. DOUGLAS *Looking Back* II. 364 He..walked up and down the room..taking, every now and then, a pinch of cocaine... 'I didn't know you took snow.' 1956 [see *JAB *v.* e]. 1966 'A. HALL' *9th Directive* iii. 25 Pangsapa was a narcotics contrabandist and would therefore know people ..prepared to kill for a fix of snow. 1967 N. LUCAS *C.I.D.* x. 135 Luckier still not to have graduated from pep pills to..'Snow'..—morphine. 1979 P. DRISCOLL *Pangolin* xx. 151 'Tell me how much this roll will get me.' 'I guess around a hundred twenty grams. That's..the purest snow you'll ever see.'

e. *slang.* (Silver) money.

1925 FRASER & GIBBONS *Soldier & Sailor Words & Phrases* 263 *Snow*, money. Silver. 1936 J. CURTIS *Gilt Kid* 173 Count up that snow while I go through the other drawers. 1970 F. MCKENNA *Gloss. Railwaymen's Talk* 38 *Snow*, small silver i.e. sixpences.

f. Spots that appear as a flickering mass filling a television or radar screen, caused by interference or a low signal-to-noise ratio.

1946 *Proc. IRE* XXXIV. 428/2 These [current] fluctuations give rise to a masking effect, often referred to as 'snow', in the transmitted picture. 1950 HELLER & SHULMAN *Television Servicing* vi. 121 Low signal input may be recognized by the characteristic presence of 'snow' in the received picture. 1977 J. CHEEVER *Falconer* 209, I took my TV... I had a little snow and asked the repairman to come in. 1978 *Sci. Amer.* Apr. 18/1 The most commonly encountered white noise is the thermal noise produced by the random motions of electrons through an electrical resistance. It causes most of the static in a radio or amplifier and the 'snow' on radar and television screens when there is no input.

III. 7. a. *snow-bank* (earlier example), *block, bridge, cave, -cloud* (earlier example), *cover, -crust, -flurry, -glare, -hut* (earlier and later examples), *-light* (earlier example), *-patch, -squall* (earlier example).

1779 E. PARKMAN *Diary* (1899) 194 Snow-Banks very high one nigh my saddle-house 6 feet high. 1893 'MARK TWAIN' in *Cosmopolitan* Nov. 54/1 My father..built this great mansion of frozen snow-blocks. 1973 W. S. AVIS in *Occasional Papers Dept. English R. Military Coll. Canada* (1978) No. 2. 152 A knife..used primarily in cutting snow blocks for igloo-building. 1982 S. B. FLEXNER *Listening to America* 22 Alaskan Eskimos often built their igloos out of animal skins, driftwood, etc., using snow-block ones only for temporary or emergency shelters. 1890 *Moose Jaw* (Saskatchewan) *Times* 20 June 1/4 Every observant passenger on the Canadian Pacific Railroad had noticed the snow bridge on the Illecillewaet, but there are records of ice bridges also. 1921 A. LUNN *Alpine Skiing* vii. 83 On the Grenz glacier a snow-bridge fourteen feet thick, and in the recent Oberaarfoch accident a snow-bridge six feet thick, collapsed beneath men on skis. 1939 [see *SCHRUND]. 1979 C. KILIAN *Icequake* xiii. 228 The snow bridges seem good and thick, but the quake probably weakened them. 1972 D. HASTON *In High Places* ix. 103 On descending they found Mick at the col installed in a snow-cave that he had dug out. 1981 *Nordic Skiing* Jan. 21/2 You can imagine me huddled in my own hastily dug snow cave waiting out the blizzard. 1879 I. BIRD *Lady's Life in Rocky Mountains* x. 168 Looming vaguely through a heavy snow-cloud. 1919 *Sci. Monthly* IX. 397 A winter snow-cover prevents deep freezing of the ground. 1956 A. GARNETT in D. L. Linton *Sheffield* 48, 1947..was phenomenal for the prolonged and severe cold weather experienced and for the long duration of a snow cover. 1824 S. BLACK *Jrnl.* 24 May (1955) 14 They left the Fort in March on the snow crust. 1957 G. E. HUTCHINSON *Treat. Limnol.* I. iii. 214 Teis (1946) examined various snow crusts and firn samples. 1979 R. FIENNES *Hell on Ice* iv. 63 The wind-firm snowcrust. 1879 I. BIRD *Lady's Life in Rocky Mountains* ix. 124 The wild flowers are gorgeous..though..the recent snow-flurries have finished them. 1936 *Geogr. Jrnl.* LXXXVII. 133 On September 1 came the first snow-flurries of the season. 1860 M. REID *Odd People* 394 More likely it is the snow-glare to which the Laplander, as well as the Esquimaux, is much exposed, that brings about the copious *watering* of the eyes. 1962 L. S. SASIENI *Optical Dispensing* xiii. 326 In snow glare protection is required against the ultra-violet. 1970 R. D. TARING *Daughter of Tibet* xix. 246 Between the smoke and the snow-glare of the day our eyes were red and watering and very sore. 1823 *Lit. Gaz.* 25 Oct. 673/3 A tribe of about fifty Esquimaux who were erecting their snow-huts. 1930 V. SACKVILLE-WEST *Edwardians* i. 28 He had been marooned..somewhere near the South Pole in a snow-hut. 1830 M. O'BRIEN *Jrnl.* (1968) I. ix. 87 It was dark—as dark as it can be with snowlight. 1909 Snow-patch [see *FLORA 3 b]. 1979 B. JOHN *World of Ice* 26 (*caption*) The peaks and mountain-sides at this time of year are almost free of snow and ice, and only a few perennial snowpatches remain. 1775 E. WILD *Jrnl.* 6 Dec. in *Mass. Hist. Soc. Proc.* (1886) II. 287 The weather is attended with Snow Squalls.

b. *snow-anchor, -board, -boot* (later examples), *buggy, chain, -coat, -fence* (earlier example), *-fencing, gallery, gauge* (further examples), *-glasses, -pants, -scoop, scooter, -shed* (earlier and later examples), *-stake, -suit, tractor, tyre, vehicle.*

1971 C. BONINGTON *Annapurna South Face* 248 The 'dead men' were an outstanding success and..gave by far the most reliable..snow anchor we were able to use on the expedition. 1972 D. HASTON *In High Places* xi. 120 Using devious combinations of snow-stakes, 'dead men' (or snow-anchors).., they took two days to come out of those overhangs. 1881 W. P. BUCHAN *Plumbing* (ed. 3) xi. 70 A style which serves both as a snow-board and as a preventive of broken chimney cans, loose slates, &c., falling over the roof. 1971 *Country Life* 14 Oct. 964/1 Notices warning of snow-board avalanches had been posted..that very morning. 1856 S. OSBORN *M'Clure's Discovery North-West Passage* xii. 160 The heavy falls the men experienced in their thick winter clothing and cloth snow-boots. 1962 A. LURIE *Love & Friendship* I. viii. 142 She came..to ask if she could borrow my snowboots to walk in the snow with. 1970 *Toronto Daily Star* 24 Sept. 16/3 (Advt.), Tamarack snow boots. The new style. 1949 *Sun* (Baltimore) 8 Feb. 15/3 Second Army headquarters..is sending 48 'snow buggy' operators..to the aid of snow-bound Nebraskans... Their main job will be to drive weasels, the Army's special vehicle for snow-covered terrain. 1965 *Kingston* (Ontario) *Whig-Standard* 27 Dec. 17 (*caption*) Roaring through the snow at speeds..approaching 35 miles-an-hour on the..new snow buggy. 1975 *Islander* (Victoria, B.C.) 9 Feb. 12/1 If you don't have snow chains, don't even try to get up the steep logging road. 1981 P. TURNBULL *Deep & Crisp & Even* i. 8 An ambulance with snow chains drove along the street. 1963 *N.Y. Times* 15 Dec. 18/7 (Advt.), This jaunty..pile-lined 'snowcoat' gets you ready for Winter's worst! 1965 *Harper's Bazaar* Nov. 95 Fir green quilted snowcoat. 1873 G. M. GRANT *Ocean to Ocean* ix. 261 The high mountains..act as natural snow fences. 1953 *Canad. Geogr. Jrnl.* XLVI. 68/2 Others made cribs out of snow fencing and piled the grain in the open fields. 1972 L. HANCOCK *Sleeping Bag* viii. 181 We dug an extensive salt-water pool and walk-in aviary..then snow-fencing enclosures for the raptorial birds. 1874 Snow gallery [see *round timber* s.v. *ROUND *a.* 15 a]. 1975 D. BAGLEY *Snow Tiger* xix. 157 They build snow galleries over roads..in Switzerland. The snow goes straight over the top. 1939 *Meteorol. Gloss.* (Met. Office) (ed. 3) 172 In the Hellmann-Fuess snow-gauge the snow is caught in a receiver supported on a balance, the displacement of which is continuously recorded. 1952 E. F. DAVIES *Illyrian Venture* ii. 32 The snow gauges on the mountain passes, dead tree trunks with marks nailed to them to show the depth of the winter drifts. 1927 E. HEMINGWAY *Men without Women* 162 Around the major's eyes were two white circles where his snow-glasses had protected his face from the sun on the snow. 1975 E. HILLARY *Nothing Venture, Nothing Win* xi. 175 Wilkins..seemed comparatively unhurt, although his snowglasses had cut his forehead. 1948 T. ONRAET *Sixty Below* 100 The ordinary snow pants and parka are made with the least possible openings. 1962 *N.Y. Post* 9 Oct. 22 (Advt.), Infants' pile snowsuits... Matching, contrasting snowpants. 1978 *Detroit Free Press* 5 Mar. D-1/1 It was still cold and your mother made you put on your coat, hat and mittens, but you could never-mind the 'snow pants' by now. 1961 J. W. ANDERSON *Fur Trader's Story* x. 80, I struck the tent, loaded the toboggan with tent, stove,..snow scoop..and so forth, and set off. 1963 *Engineering* 18 Jan. 79 The manufacturers are now considering adding the snow-scoop to their range of standard attachments. 1964 *Star Weekly* (Toronto) 19 Dec. 13/1 The odd little snow scooters you see cavorting about ..represent the newest phenomenon to revolutionize Canadian sport, family living—and business. 1969 *Daily*

Colonist (Victoria, B.C.) 5 Sept. 27/3 Reindeer-tending Lapps of northern Norway use snow scooters to round up strays and transport supplies. **1981** *Times* 14 Dec. 22/8 Four policemen..have been..to North Cape, in Norway, for charity. They reached there on snow scooters. **1868** *Oregon State Jrnl.* 22 Aug. 2/3 The Pacific Railroad advertises for a thousand men to build snow sheds on the summit. **1965** E. McCourt *Road across Canada* 177 In Glacier [B.C.] more than half a mile of snowsheds, solidly built of steel and concrete.., guard the most vulnerable spots. **1971** *Daily Tel.* 9 Jan. 9/2 The railway line runs through numerous long snow-sheds in these high lands [in Norway]. These are built over the line to keep it free of snow in winter. **1971** C. Bonington *Annapurna South Face* viii. 95, I pushed in a snow-stake, but it went in too easily and would almost certainly be pulled out if I fell on it. **1972** Snow-stake [see *snow-anchor* above]. **1942** D. Powell *Time to be Born* i. 37 The red snow suit her mother had promised. **1962** A. Lurie *Love & Friendship* I. iii. 53 Emmy put Freddy into his snow-suit. **1980** *Daily Tel.* 9 Jan. 1/8 There was no sign of the guerrillas in the rugged terrain, but Russians and their armour, including tanks, were everywhere. Some were in white snow suits. **1936** *Canad. Geogr. Jrnl.* XII. 34/2 Somebody began to work on the idea of snowmobiles and snow tractors. **1971** *Country Life* 14 Oct. 964/1 Hardly had the two children been freed when they [*sc.* a rescue team] were on the spot, having covered the ground in a snow-tractor. **1954** *Sun* (Baltimore) 23 Jan. 8/1 Now it's chains vs. snow tires, the treachery of the steep hill by the lake and stern telephone calls to warn the little woman off the roads. **1968** 'E. McBain' *Fuzz* xii. 197 The snow.. presented no major traffic problems as yet, especially if.. one had snow tyres on one's automobile. **1978** *Times* 23 Jan. 12/7 Avis..had only one car they could rent me and it had no snow tyres or chains. **1968** *Globe & Mail* (Toronto) 3 Feb. 46/3 (*heading*) Snow vehicles.

c. *snow-pinion.*

1879 G. M. Hopkins *Poems* (1967) 80 If a wuthering of his palmy snow-pinions scatter a colossal smile Off him.

d. *snow cake* (earlier example), *eggs* (earlier example).

1861 Mrs. Beeton *Bk. Househ. Managem.* 747 *Snow eggs*,..4 eggs, ¾ pint of milk,..sugar..vanilla, lemon-rind. *Ibid.* 864 *Snow cake*...½ lb. of *tous-les-mois*, ¼ lb. of ..sugar, ¼ lb. of..butter, 1 egg,..1 lemon.

8. a. *snow-backed, -blanched, -blanketed, -born, -bowered, -cooled, -dazed, -dimmed, -drowned* (later example), *-fed* (later examples), *-hooded, -packed, -shouldered, -suited.*

1897 Kipling *Five Nations* (1903) 18 While thick around the homestead Our snow-backed leaders graze. **1945** W. de la Mare *Burning-Glass* 23 The snow-blanched sunshine. **1971** R. Dentry *Encounter at Kharmel* ix. 151 The snow-blanketed hills. **1879** I. Bird *Lady's Life in Rocky Mountains* vii. 97 From this side rise, snow-born, the bright St. Vrain, and the Big and Little Thompson. **1930** R. Campbell *Adamastor* 62 Fair siren of the snow-born lake. **1919** W. de la Mare *Flora* 42 Still from the snow-bowered, link-lit street The muffled hooves of horses beat. **1920** R. Graves *Country Sentiment* 63 Or toys or meat or snow-cooled drink. *a* **1918** W. Owen *Poems* (1963) 48 We cringe in holes, back on forgotten dreams, and stare, snow-dazed, deep into grassier ditches. **1957** Blunden *Poems of Many Years* 295 In snow-dimmed moonlight. **1978** G. Greene *Human Factor* vi. ii. 322 Outside the silence of the snow-drowned street was so extreme that Castle hesitated to break it. **1936** R. Campbell *Mithraic Emblems* 31 The lily-scented blood, the snow-fed wine of scarlet stain. **1963** *Times* 6 Feb. (New Zealand Suppl.) p. vii/3 The Rangitata itself —snow-fed and treacherous. **1880** 'Mark Twain' *Tramp Abroad* xxv. 245 The stately border of snow-hooded mountain peaks. **1945** W. de la Mare *Burning-Glass* 44 A moth, snow-hooded, delicate past belief. **1973** J. M. White *Garden Game* 188 Teague drove his Mercedes..on to the snow-packed verge. **1921** W. de la Mare *Veil* 59 Snake-haired, snow-shouldered, pure as flame and dew. **1936** R. Campbell *Mithraic Emblems* 17 Each great snow-shouldered beast. **1961** 'E. Lathen' *Banking on Death* (1962) ix. 71 Snowsuited toddlers frolicking merrily in the snow. **1971** A. Bailey *In Village* (1972) xix. 189 Snow-suited small children.

b. *snow-blower, -clearer, -loader, -scraper* (earlier example), *-shifter, -thrower.*

1955 *Hamilton* (Ontario) *Spectator* 25 Jan. 24/3 Street sweepers, snow blowers, and other city equipment stored outdoors at the Elgin Street yard. **1964** S. Forbes *Long Hate* (1966) x. 92 'We'll have to shovel, I guess.'.. 'Can't you use the snow blower?' **1978** *Daily Tel.* 1 Feb. 1/7 Extra snow-clearing equipment was being sent to the area and the RAF was bringing in a large snowblower from Switzerland. **1963** *Times* 18 Feb. 4/1 The efforts of dedicated Kingsholm snow-clearers were rewarded, and the surface was unbelievably good in the circumstances. *Ibid.* 28 Jan. 9/6 Clearing is done by a continuous moving belt operation with a plough in front followed by a specially built snow loader which digs into drifts with rotating blades and funnels it into a line of waiting lorries. **1974** *Globe & Mail* (Toronto) 12 Feb. 5/3 The combined snow loader and melter was designed by Metro roads department and consultants after testing a small 75-ton snow melter during the past three winters. **1851** in H. Greeley *Recoll. Busy Life* (1868) 559 We met with a bad accident ..45 miles from Baltimore, our snow-scraper catching against some part of the track. **1962** Snow-shifter [see *Mack *sb.*⁶]. **1966** *Wall St. Jrnl.* 28 Dec. 1/4 The power-driven snowblower (or snowthrower, if you prefer), a gadget with reel-type blades that chew through the snow and push it into a chute, from whence it's blown aside. **1978** *Detroit Free Press* 16 Apr. (Gardening Guide) 6 (Advt.), Attachments include 60-inch rotary mower, 48-inch snow thrower, [etc.].

c. *snow-clear, -cool, -deep* (later example), *-proof, -soft* (later examples).

1925 E. Sitwell et al. *Poor Young People* 15 Or peck Anne's snow-clear cheek. **1919** R. Graves *Treasure Box* 11 Where Sweetheart, my brown mare,..May loll her leathern tongue In snow-cool water. **1964** J. Michie tr. *Horace's Odes* I. xii. 41 The snow-cool shoulder Of Haemus. **1920** T. S. Eliot *Ara Vos Prec* 25 Buried beneath some snow-deep Alps. **1972** 'M. Yorke' *Silent Witness* ii. 26 A small figure lightly encased in snow-proof garments. **1978** J. Cowley in *Islands* (N.Z.) Aug. 25 Padded nylon windbreakers and snow-proof pants. **1924** E. Sitwell *Sleeping Beauty* xvi. 54 Far from snow-soft sleep. **1959** E. Pound *Thrones* civ. 92 The small breasts snow-soft over tripod.

9. a. snow-belt *U.S.* [*Belt *sb.* 5 a], a region subject to heavy snowfalls; also *attrib.*; **snow-break** (later examples); **snow bunny** *N. Amer. slang*, an inexperienced (usu. female) skier; a pretty girl who frequents ski slopes; **snow-cone** *U.S.* (see quot. 1969); also *attrib.*; **snow course**, a line along which the depth of snow is periodically sampled at fixed points; **snow cruiser** *N. Amer.*, a motor vehicle designed to travel over snow; *spec.* (with capital initials) a Canadian proprietary term for a type of motorized toboggan; also *attrib.*; hence **snow-cruising** *vbl. sb.*; also *attrib.*; **snow devil**, a column of snow whirled round by the wind (cf. Devil *sb.* 11); **snow-dropper** (examples); **snow-dropping** (further examples); also as gerund; **snow-eater** *Meteorol.* [tr. G. *schneefresser*], a warm wind, esp. a föhn, that causes rapid melting of snow; **snow grain** *Meteorol.*, a small, opaque, precipitated ice particle, usu. flattened and less than 1 mm. in diameter, that does not bounce on a hard surface; cf. *snow pellet* below; **snow gun** *U.S.* = **snow-maker*; **snow-hole**, (*b*) a hole in snow used as a temporary shelter; **snow job** *slang* (orig. *U.S.*), a concerted attempt at flattery, deception, or persuasion; also *attrib.*; hence **snow-job** *v. trans.*, to do a snow job on (someone); **snow-jobbing** *vbl. sb.*, the performing of a snow job; **snow machine** *N. Amer.*, a motor vehicle designed to travel over snow; also *attrib.*; **snow-maker** (orig. *U.S.*), a device used for the artificial production of a snow-like precipitate for ski-slopes and the like; also, one who makes snow by the use of such a device; so **snow-making** *vbl. sb.* and *ppl. a.*; **snow-melt**, the melting of fallen snow; also, the water that results; **snowpack** *U.S.*, lying snow that is compressed and hardened by its own weight; **snow pellet** *Meteorol.*, an opaque precipitated ice particle, usu. a few millimetres in diameter, that will bounce on a hard surface; a soft hailstone; cf. *snow grain* above; **snow plane** *N. Amer.*, a type of snowmobile that is mounted on skis and propelled by an engine-driven propeller; **Snow Queen**, the chief character in a fairy-tale of this name by Hans Christian Andersen, used allusively to designate a cold-hearted woman; also *attrib.*; **snow-raking** *N.Z.* (see quots.); **snow roller**, a cylinder of snow formed by the action of the wind rolling it along; **snow scene**, a landscape covered with snow; **snow-skiing** *vbl. sb.* = Ski-ing *vbl. sb.* (*ski-ing *vbl. sb.* 1), opp. to water-skiing; so **snow-ski** *v. intr.*; **snow-skier**; **snow-snake(s)** *N. Amer.*, 'an Indian game played with a straight wooden rod having a weighted head resembling that of a snake, this rod being slid over a smooth field of snow or down specially constructed runways; the rod used in this game' (Dict. Canad.); hence **snow-snaking**; **snow-sports**, sports that take place on snow, *spec.* skiing; also *attrib.*

1874 *Los Angeles County Ten Thousand Questions Answered* 11/1 There are two great continental railroad routes within the snowbelt. **1933** *Amer. City* Sept. 53/1 Old-fashioned winters have not been as prevalent in the snow belt in the last few years as they were ten or twenty years ago. **1967** *Wall St. Jrnl.* 1 Feb. 1/4 Some makers predict snowmobile sales soon will surpass boat sales in snowbelt states. **1981** *Nordic Skiing* Jan. 39/1 Thanks to a 120–140 inch snowbelt location, Temple Mountain offers skiing from early December to mid-April. **1895** W. R. Fisher tr. *Hess's Forest Protection* 482 The term *snow-break* is used to denote the breakage of stems or branches. **1905** *Terms Forestry* (U.S. Dept. Agric. Bureau Forestry) 21 *Snowbreak*. 1. The breaking of trees by snow. 2. An area on which trees have been broken by snow. 3. Shelterbelt. **1928** R. S. Troup *Silvicultural Systems* v. 70 Its uneven-aged condition up to the pole stage is considered to be a protection against both snowbreak and sliding snow on steep hill-sides. **1933** *Forestry* VII. 146 In spite of the relatively high elevation there was no indication of snowbreak. **1953** P. C. Berg *Dict. New Words in Eng.* 147/2 *Snow bunny*,..n. Skiing. A beginner, esp. a girl. **1964** *Star Weekly* (Toronto) 19 Dec. 39/1 December used to be a dull month, but that was before our pretty Canadian snow bunnies..started brightening up the Canadian snow scene. **1968** *Globe & Mail* (Toronto) 13 Jan. 49/6 'Watching you for only two runs, I can see you're not just a 'snow bunny', Coral!' 'No, I was on the women's ski-team at college.' **1972** P. A. Whitney *Snowfire* (1973) vi. 100 Snow bunny..was a term applied to beginners, usually female, who haunted the slopes. **1969** *Daily Tel.* 6 June 18 A snowcone is a paper cup of flavoured shaved ice, highly popular among children. **1976** *Billings* (Montana) *Gaz.* 4 July 2-B/4 The Jolly Wagons had competition in those days from a snow-cone vendor driving an identical Cushman which contained only ice and flavored syrups. **1933** *Geogr. Rev.* XXIII. 540 It was only necessary to maintain a series of measurements carefully taken in the same spot each year. These measurements, laid out at definite intervals.., were named 'snow courses'. **1965** R. G. Kazmann *Mod. Hydrol.* ii. 36 This type of measurement, made at frequent intervals over very elaborately organized snow courses.. is the accepted practical method of measuring solid-state precipitation. **1939** *Sun* (Baltimore) 14 Nov. 11/3 A twenty-seven-ton snow cruiser..designed to serve as an igloo on wheels to help the forces inspect vast areas of unexplored ice and snow. **1956** *Canad. Trade Mark 102,409* 13 Jan., Wares: Small engine driven snow remover. Trade Mark: Snow-Cruiser. **1966** *Canad. Geogr. Jrnl.* Sept. 79/3 Outboard Marine makes..Snow Cruiser.. a small motorized toboggan on rubber tires and skis, a variation of the original snowmobile invented by Armand Bombardier of Quebec ten years ago. **1969** *Sears Catal.* Spring/Summer 14 A tent of this type would be ideal for sportsmen, hunters and Snowcruiser enthusiasts. **1966** *British Columbia Digest* Dec. 10 (Advt.), '67 is the big year for snow cruising..and you have 3 fabulous OMC Snow Cruisers to choose from! **1968** *Globe & Mail* (Toronto) 15 Jan. 24/3 (Advt.), Wonderful snow-cruising parklands. **1932** F. S. Smythe *Kamet Conquered* xii. 169 From the serene skyline of Meade's Col little 'snow devils' were rising against the deepening green of the evening sky. **1962** W. H. Murray *Maelstrom* xiv. 183 Whirling snow-devils came charging across the plateau, driving spiculae in their faces. **1847** G. W. M. Reynolds *Mysteries of London* III. xxix. 85/1 A stranger looked like a snow-dropper. **1963** T. & P. Morris *Pentonville* viii. 190 The larcenist who steals feminine underwear from clothes-lines (the 'snowdropper') is often a pathetic object of derision and contempt. **1977** *Western Mail* (Cardiff) 5 Mar. 8/1 A 'snowdropper' is a man who steals women's underwear. **1882** *Sydney Slang Dict.* 9/2 Dick's a broker and has gone out *snow-dropping*. **1930** [see *cattle-duffing* s.v. *Cattle 9]. **1967** *Telegraph* (Brisbane) 1 Mar. 26/4 Patfield had set out last November to steal sheets, but in the most systematic manner of 'snow dropping' (clothes-line thefts) he had stolen everything he could find. **1972** *Observer* 31 Dec. 3/4 He couldn't resist the temptation to go 'snow dropping' (stealing clothes from lines). **1886** *Science* 12 Mar. 242/2 Warm west winds answering to the 'Chinook' winds occur as far south as southern Colorado, though I have seldom heard the name 'Chinook' applied to them in this region. They are here [*sc.* in Colorado Springs] often called Pacific winds, also 'snow-eaters' and 'zephyrs'. **1933** F. H. Cheley *Camping Out* 197 It was the Chinook wind... The Indians call it the 'snow eater'. **1967** R. W. Fairbridge *Encycl. Atmospheric Sci. & Astrogeol.* 1151/2 The rapid melting of the snow caused by the chinook ('Snow-eater') is welcomed because it frees the higher pastures. **1944** H. R. Byers *Gen. Meteorol.* vi. 125 Granular snow, snow grains... White, opaque, snow-like grains, similar to soft hail but more or less flattened or oblong. **1967** R. W. Fairbridge *Encycl. Atmospheric Sci. & Astrogeol.* 772/1 Snow grains..neither bounce nor break when hitting the ground. **1971** *Industr. & Engin. Chem.* (*Process Design & Devel.*) Jan. 75/1 To cover a bare ski slope, 10 to 15 commercial snow guns (nozzles in which water and air are combined, usually at 100 psig) are used. **1974** *Compressed Air* Apr. 9/1 The snow-guns are 'very efficient, inexpensive and can be moved easily'. **1953** P. Provencher *I live in Woods* vii. 64 To make a snow hole, dig to a depth of five feet at the foot of a steep incline or cliff. **1965** B. E. Freeman tr. *Vandel's Biospeleology* xiii. 195 Nivicoles, the inhabitants of snow-holes. **1978** *Daily Colonist* (Victoria, B.C.) 7 May 7/8 The six men and three women spent..three nights in snow-holes—man-made snow caves—before reaching..the summit. **1943** *Amer. Mercury* Nov. 555 There he tries a *snow job* on her (hands her a line) and if she falls for it she's been *snowed under*. **1953** K. Tennant *Joyful Condemned* xx. 192 He..made a bee-line for the red-head. 'Now for the snow job,' Geechi murmured. **1962** 'K. Orvis' *Damned & Destroyed* xxi. 155 Are you going to snow-job me about finding substitutes? **1966** S. Morrow *Moonlighters* (1967) v. 53 Possibly her scepticism accounted for her success with the teenagers...kids were most apt to trust the adults who were immune to a snow job. **1969** C. Burke *God is Beautiful, Man* (1970) 52 It's better to say yes or no and mean it—than to give a lot of snow job promises anyway. **1979** D. Robinson *Eldorado Network* xliii. 291, I just saw you do another snow job. You were in North Wales..which is why it sounds so convincing. Nice try, Luis. **1966** *National Observer* (U.S.) 19 Dec. 12/2 Democratic county chairmen hereabouts have, of necessity, worked out a terrific combination of railroading, arm twisting, and snow jobbing, not necessarily involving consent or persuasion. **1973** *Whig-Standard* (Kingston, Ontario) 14 Jan. 15/7 Roads are not for snowmobiles—the snow machines and other vehicles using the highways simply do not mix. **1976** *News Miner* (Fairbanks, Alaska) 6 Nov. B17/2 Snow machine driving, in which participants may cross miles of wintry terrain on a weekend outing. **1977** *New Yorker* 4 July 42/1 Their snow machine—Ski-Doo Alpine—rests on the floor below the furs. It goes ten miles an hour on the trail, and the two of them ride it. **1955** *N.Y. Times* 30 Jan. II. 31/4 The snow makers provided a long-needed answer on how to cope with the snowless situation..in the Southern Catskills. **1963** *Engineering* 13 Sept. 321/3 Snow-makers mix air and water under pressure and blow the resulting mixture in dense 50 ft arcs. **1965** *Economist* 25 Dec. 1416/1 While the rainmakers have been failing, for a decade or more the snowmakers have been succeeding beyond their wildest dreams and as a result..more American skiers than ever are assured of at least enough snow to try out the new skis which they have been given for Christmas. **1980** J. Krantz *Princess Daisy* xxvi. 461

The snow-making machines had started... The snow-makers continued to cover the path. **1954** *U.S. Pat. 2,676,471* 7 At an ambient temperature of 31°F and less, snow has been made at any pressure from 25 to 200 lbs. per square inch by varying the water pressure to give a snow making mixture. **1956** *Compressed Air Mag.* LXI. 101/3 Snow-making at Fahnestock consists..of bringing compressed air and water together at a nozzle that acts in the same manner as a paint spray gun. **1960** *N.Y. Herald-Tribune* 13 Nov. VII. 8/1 Across the country.. dozens of snow-making machines are poised, ready to transform bare hillsides into Alpine paradises. **1976** 'A. Cross' *Question of Max* i. 8 There is a damn snow-making machine on some blasted ski slope. **1927** *Q. Jrnl. Geol. Soc.* LXXXIII. 167 We arrived just as the spring snow-melt was finishing. **1941** *Yearbk. Agric. 1941* (U.S.) 560 In cleared areas snow depths are intermediate..and snow melt is rapid. **1971** W. Hillen *Blackwater River* ii. 16 Snowmelt starting to run from exposed mountain slopes. **1979** *Field* 17 Oct. 1048/3 So far as rainfall is concerned,..the total amount of this element..in meterological records includes snowmelt. **1952** *Trans. Amer. Geophysical Union* XXXIII. 874 The water equivalent of the seasonal snow pack was observed after individual falls. **1955** *Sci. News Let.* 1 Oct. 214/3 Winter snowpack is the source of 40% of California's streamflow. **1973** R. Hayes *Hungarian Game* xxxvi. 215 Beneath the thin, brittle crust there was an inch of powder before the snowpack. **1935** *Jrnl. Faculty Sci. Hokkaido Imp. Univ.* 2nd Ser. I. 215 The snow pellet or the graupel..is one of the modified forms of snow crystal. **1967** R. W. Fairbridge *Encycl. Atmospheric Sci. & Astrogeol.* 442/2 Small hail, under 5 mm, is officially classified as ice pellets or snow pellets. **1953** R. Moon *This is Saskatchewan* ii. 9 Bob Fudge's manufacturing is not confined to snow planes. **1967** E. B. Nickerson *Kayaks to Arctic* xix. 186 He had a snow plane—an enclosed cabin on ski runners shoved along by an aeroplane propeller in the fashion of an Everglades swamp buggy. **1972** T. McHugh *Time of Buffalo* xii. 145 We rented two snowplanes for a trip into the snow-bound heartland of Yellowstone Park. **1935** Marsh & Jellett *Nursing-Home Murder* vi. 75 A very cold fishy sort of lady... A Snow Queen, in fact. **1974** L. Deighton *Spy Story* xi. 111 She gave me the inscrutable Snow-queen smile. **1977** *N.Y. Rev. Bks.* 27 Oct. 14/. Charlotte was a Snow Queen who flirted coldly and shamelessly with her son. **1919** *N.Z. Jrnl. Agric.* 20 Feb. 90 After a heavy snowfall..send out as many men as can be got together..to get the sheep on to the sunny faces, where a certain amount of thaw may have taken place... This is what is generally known as 'snow-raking'. **1958** J. Pascoe *N.Z. Sheep-Station* in *People of World* 1st Ser. 19 Then the men must stamp out a trail through the snow—a job called 'snow-raking'—and lead the sheep down to the valley flats. **1866** G. J. Symons *British Rainfall, 1865* p. vii, Snow Rollers... The snow ripples up.., and the ripples breaking into sections, the wind rolls each..until, just like a..snow-ball, they rapidly increase in size. **1876** *Meteorol. Mag.* XI. 52 This is the first instance recorded of the formation of 'Snow Rollers' in England. **1959** *Weatherwise* XII. 63/2 The area cleared of snow during the formation of snow rollers is usually V-shaped, accounting for their peculiar shape, which is cylindrical with concave ends. **1836** H. C. Robinson *Diary* 15 Jan. (1967) 152, I found a snow scene quite pleasant in this mountainous country. **1921** R. Fry *Let.* 14 Dec. (1972) II. 518 A stupendous Courbet snow scene. **1978** 'L. Black' *Foursome* i. 6 It was incongruous against the background of..correspondence files..stacks of catalogues, the snow-scene on the calendar. **1975** *New Yorker* 1 Sept. 28/1 You don't play tennis, you don't snow-ski, you don't water-ski, you don't ride a bicycle... Albert, we have nothing in common. **1941** *Life* 4 Aug. 55/2 *(caption)* Bending her knees like a snow skier, Hallie rides over the wake. *Ibid.* 54 Combining aquaplaning and snow skiing, water-skiing was imported from the Riviera several years ago. **1977** *Chicago Tribune* 2 Oct. XII. 33/3 (Advt.), We're looking for a bright, enthusiastic gal, who knows the retail clothing business, especially snow skiing attire. **1844** *Chambers's Edin. Jrnl.* I. 327 They [*sc.* Cherokee Indians]..in winter amuse themselves with their snow-snakes, which are long smooth sticks of hard wood..which they send to an extraordinary distance over the smooth surface of the snow. **1888** *Trans. R. Soc. Canada* VI. II. 44 If this is the game spoken of by other writers as 'Snow-snakes', there is nothing in the [Abenaki] name to so indicate. **1959** E. Tunis *Indians* 56/2 Snow snake was played by all the northern tribes on a level track made by dragging a log or a boy through the snow. **1973** M. Crowell *Greener Pastures* 81 The wall photograph..of Indians playing the venerable game of snow-snake. **1978** *Whig-Standard* (Kingston, Ontario) 11 Feb. A8/1 The snow snake is a smooth, thin stick about 2m long. It is thrown along a crust of smooth, hard snow. The player whose snake slides the farthest is the winner. **1979** *Ibid.* 1 Feb. 9/1 It is called snow-snaking and the Mohawk Indians have played it for centuries. It is not recognized at the Canada Winter Games but maybe it will some day. [**1905** *Country Life* Dec. 181 *(heading)* Practical side of snow and ice sports.] **1966** *Guardian* 15 Oct. 5/2 (Advt.), Snowsports. 2 weeks including full-board £29.15.0! **1974** *Country Life* 3/10 Jan. 52/1 (Advt.), *Off-season winter rates*..for skiers and snow-sports enthusiasts.

b. snow bear, a buff or brown bear, *Ursus arctos isabellinus*, found in the Himalayan region; **snow-camel**, the Bactrian camel, *Camelus bactrianus*; **snow flea**, esp. one of the genus *Achorutes*; (earlier and later examples); **snow-wolf**, a wolf that lives in snowy regions; the (imitation) fur of this animal; **snow-worm**: esp. = *ICE-WORM a; (later examples).

1869 A. A. Kinloch *Large Game Shooting Thibet & N. West* I. xv. 46 The Snow Bear varies a good deal in size. **1884** R. A. Sterndale *Nat. Hist. Mammalia India & Ceylon* 111 The bear of which we have the oldest record is almost the same as our Indian or Snow Bear. **1910** *Blackw. Mag.* Oct. 433/2 One of them..got three really good heads, and two snow-bears, in one day. **1901** Kipling *Kim* viii. 204 Nor is even a Balkh stallion..of any account in the great Northern deserts beside the snow-camels I have seen. **1850** Thoreau *Jrnl.* 16 Dec. in *Writings* (1906) VIII. 125 The snow everywhere was covered with snow-fleas like pepper. **1868** *Amer. Naturalist* II. 53 The little insects called snow-fleas..are found in winter at the foot of trees. **1943** B. Damon *Sense of Humus* 106 Snow fleas..have a disagreeable habit of putting an end to their brief existence by drowning themselves in sap buckets. **1910** W. de la Mare *Three Mulla-Mulgars* 192 So brave are these snow-wolves. **1976** *Sunday Mail* (Glasgow) 28 Nov. 46/1 (Advt.), De luxe heavy pile Silver Mink, Ocelot, Tiger, Snow Wolf, they are beautiful. **1899** H. G. Bryant in *Proc. Acad. Nat. Sci. Philadelphia* 134 The snow-worms were first observed a few hundred yards from our first camp. **1916** *Trans. Amer. Microsc. Soc.* XXXV. 102 Nothing definite is known concerning the food of these snow-worms.

d. snow bush, esp. the small silvery shrub, *Calocephalus brownii*, of the family Compositæ, native to Australia; (examples); hence *snow-bushed* adj.; **snow-grass**, substitute for def.: one of several coarse grasses of upland regions, esp., in New Zealand, a tussock grass of the genus *Danthonia*; cf. *DANTHONIA; also *attrib.*; (further examples); **snow gum**, a shrub or small tree, *Eucalyptus niphophila*, with white bark and glaucous leaves, native to high regions of New South Wales; **snow lily**, a perennial herb, *Erythronium grandiflorum*, belonging to the family Liliaceæ, native to alpine regions of western North America, and bearing white or yellow flowers; **snow pea** = *MANGE-TOUT; **snow plant**, (*b*) *Sarcodes sanguinea*; (earlier and later examples).

1909 A. E. Mack *Bush Calendar* 12 Where the trees were fewer, 'snow bushes' grew white. **1965** *Austral. Encycl.* III. 158/1 Snow-bush, a dense and intricately branched shrub..forms large and rounded, white-woolly growths. **1946** Dylan Thomas *Deaths & Entrances* 28 And the dancers move On the departed snowbushed green. **1906** T. F. Cheeseman *Man. N.Z. Flora* 887 Snow-grass. **1918** F. W. Hilgendore *Pasture Plants & Pastures N.Z.* ii. 42 Snow Grass (*Danthonia raoulii*).—This is another Tussock, growing 4 to 6 feet high. It has broad leaves shining below, and feathery oat-like heads... Its presence in quantity frequently marks the limit above which it is not safe to carry sheep in winter..as indeed its popular name of Snow Grass would indicate. **1930** L. G. D. Acland *Early Canterbury Runs* 1st Ser. vi. 131 When he was first thatching the cob house..he put the top of each bundle of snow-grass outside the bottom of the one above so that all the rain ran inwards. **1968** *N.Z. Listener* 10 May 10/4 The beast, a young stag, had its antlers hopelessly entangled in the tough-rooted snowgrass. **1972** P. Newton *Sheep Thief* ii. 18 The roof consisting of bare birch rafters with a thick layer of snow grass thatch. **1928** 'Brent of Bin Bin' *Up Country* xiv. 237 The snow-gums stood like brides in veils of perfumed lace. **1964** D. Stewart in R. Ward *Penguin Bk. Austral. Ballads* 278 Hard to say where he came from—..out of a hollow snowgum Or out of a granite boulder. **1981** *Garden* CVI. 275/1 There are..very large trees of the Tasmanian snow gum at Inverewe in Ross-shire. **1907** S. Brown *Alpine Flora of Canadian Rocky Mountains* 44 *(heading)* *Erythronium grandiflorum* Pursh. *Snow Lily.* **1936** D. McCowan *Animals Canad. Rockies* xxix. 250 Great quantities of the bulbs of Snow Lilies. **1972** *Islander* (Victoria, B.C.) 2 Apr. 13/3 The snow lily..pops its bright yellow head out as soon as the snow has left the hill-sides. **1949** *Nature Mag.* XLII. 35/2 The snow pea..is commonly listed by all large seed-firms as an edible-podded pea. **1956** 'E. McBain' *Cop Hater* (1958) xx. 172 Chinese vegetables; luscious snow peas, and water chestnuts. **1978** *Times* 17 July 14/3 We had a prolific crop of sugar peas, which the Americans call snow peas. **1870** *Old & New* Mar. 349/2 The strange snow-plant.. must be passed as a railroad traveller passes all things. **1940** *Oregon: End of Trail* 20 Deeper in the forest grow the waxy Indian pipe, the blood-red snow plant, and the rare moccasin flower. **1959** Munz & Keck *California Flora* 436 Snow Plant. Red fleshy usually pubescent saprophyte.

snow, *v.* Add: **4. b.** *fig.* To deceive or win over with plausible words; to kid, to dupe. Also with *under*. *slang* (orig. and chiefly *U.S.*).

1943 [see *snow job* s.v. *SNOW *sb.*[1] 9 a]. **1945** D. Dempsey in M. Mayorga *Best One-Act Plays of '44* 18 Give me the lid, Greenberg..who you tryin' to snow, Lou-i-siana? **1956** 'E. S. Aarons' *Assignment Treason* (1967) v. 43 Were you snowing me about Hackett doing the clobber job on you? **1963** N. Freeling *Because of Cats* xi. 175, I won't get mad. Just don't snow me with any sob-sister business. **1966** H. Waugh *Pure Poison* (1967) xiv. 87 Roger'd be alone in a corner with some girl and..looked like he was really snowing them. **1980** *Australian* 9 Dec. 6/5 Mr J. C. Moore (the new minister in charge of the Customs Bureau) has taken the most immediate and active interest in the workings of the bureau. Unfortunately, it is most likely that he also will be snowed by the bureaucrats as has been the case with previous ministers.

6. d. With *in*. To block, imprison with snow. Chiefly *N. Amer.*

1857 G. F. McDougall *Eventful Voy. 'Resolute'* xiii. 331 The fore and after parts of the upper deck were now snowed in, to the depth of nine inches on the starboard side. **1887** C. B. George *40 Yrs. on Rail* ix. 188 My train was snowed in during one of the terrible storms. **1970** *Daily Colonist* (Victoria, B.C.) 1 Jan. 1/3 Picture above taken a year ago as worst blizzard in years blanketed area shows cars snowed-in on King's Road.

7. *U.S. slang.* To drug, to dope. Also with advbs. Usu. in pa. pple.

1927 *Amer. Speech* Dec. 167/2 Snowed in, dopey, as if full of cocaine. **1934** R. Chandler in *Black Mask* July 70/2 She looked snowed, weaved around funny. **1942** Berrey & Van den Bark *Amer. Thes. Slang* § 509/30 *Snowed, snowed in, up* or *under*,..under the influence of cocaine. **1956** H. Gold *Man who was not with It* xxiii. 222 But I figured on how to get snowed.

snowball, *sb.* Add: **1. b.** Phr. *a snowball's chance in hell*: see *HELL *sb.* 10 b. Also ellipt. as *a snowball's chance*.

1934 *Esquire* Sept. 27 He wouldn't have a snowball's chance with you. **1977** *Amer. Machinist* 1 June 27 There is not a snowball's chance in Haiti of making the deadline on an across-the-board basis. **1979** 'A. Hailey' *Overload* I. 1. 4 'Told 'em there wasn't a snowball's chance,' a woman assistant dispatcher called over.

e. *transf.* A scheme or project that relies for its growth on a snowball effect (see quots.).

1892 *Whitehall Rev.* 17 Sept. 7/1 The system of 'Snowballs' is multiplication at a very rapid rate, each giver being obliged to bind himself to find a certain number of others who will not only give, but bind themselves each to find an equal number of contributors on the same terms. **1923** H. C. Bailey *Mr Fortune's Practice* v. 141 It's just like a snowball... When you want subscriptions and have a snowball where every one has to get some one else to subscribe. **1927** E. F. Benson *Lucia in London* iii. 70 Will she just pick up acquaintances, and pick up more from them, like one of those charity snowballs?

f. In bingo, etc.: a cash prize which accumulates through successive games until it is won.

1949 S. P. Llewellyn *Troopships* 5 Last house... May I remind you, gentlemen, that the snowball is now worth over fourteen pounds? **1960** *Guardian* 2 Dec. 23/5 The British Legion..club..was more or less built on Bingo... The crowds, drawn by a 'snowball' on a lucky number which had reached £16, had been growing..too large. **1971** A. Ross *Huddersfield Job* 129 The snowball—a sort of continuing competition in which the cash prizes, if not won, are carried forward to swell next week's total. **1976** *Evening Post* (Nottingham) 15 Dec. 13/2 Tote Baseball Nos. 20 & 13 & 6 Three winners. Snowball not won.

2. b. One of various cocktails (see quots.).

1930 *Savoy Cocktail Bk.* 150 Snowball Cocktail. ⅙ Crème de Violette. ⅙ White Crème de Menthe. ⅙ Anisette. ⅙ Sweet Cream. ½ Dry Gin. **1963** D. A. Embury *Fine Art of Mixing Drinks* (ed. 2) 289 Snow Ball. A Silver Fizz with whisky in place of the gin and ginger ale in place of the charged water. **1966** J. Doxat *Booth's Handbk. Cocktails & Mixed Drinks* xiv. 145 Snowball. Ice cube in tall glass. Generous measure of Advocaat; top with Fizzy Lemonade; decorate with slice of Lemon. **1972** A. Draper *Death Penalty* ii. 16 Ben ordered the drinks—a snowball for Jeannie and whisky mac for himself. **1979** R. Barnard *Posthumous Papers* xvii. 158 She ordered a snowball... 'I'm not used to coming into a pub on my own.'

c. *U.S.* and *W. Indies.* An ice-cream; a confection made of shaved or chipped ice covered in syrup, etc.

1941 J. Smiley *Hash House Lingo* 51 *Snowball*, dip of vanilla ice cream. **1946** K. Dunham *Journey to Accompong* 93 My Maroon neighbors..were lolling around..drinking the penny 'snowball' made from chipped ice with a sweet purple syrup poured over it. **1953** H. P. Morrison in *Caribbean Anthol. Short Stories* 137 Customers of every age milled round to buy 'snow-ball'—cool crushed ice in cheap glass tumblers with red, yellow or even green syrup oozing slowly through the crystalline mass. **1962** [see *MAUBY].

4. a. Also used for other species of *Viburnum*. (Later example.)

1948 W. Arnold-Forster *Shrubs for Milder Counties* iv. 184 *V. Opulus sterile*, the familiar 'Snowball', is..quite good as a hedge.

5. a. *snowball cocktail, fight, vendor.*

1930 Snowball cocktail [see sense 2 b above]. **1890** Champlin & Bostwick *Young Folks' Cycl. Games & Sports* 660/1 *Snowball fights*, contests between two parties armed with snowballs. **1948** *Sun* (Baltimore) 27 Aug. 24/3 Snowball vendors did a rush business.

b. snowball bush, tree, also = sense 4 a in Dict. and Suppl.; (later examples).

1931 W. N. Clute *Common Names Plants* 48 Guelder rose, a common name of the snow-ball bush.., is said to be properly elder rose. **1979** *Seymour* (Indiana) *Daily Tribune* 19 May 1/3 The 'snowball bush' in his side yard is in full bloom. **1902** E. T. Cook *Trees & Shrubs for Eng. Gardens* 443 Snowball tree..is too well known to need description. **1973** A. Bonar *Shrubs & Decorative Trees* III. 86 The snowball tree..is more attractive florally.

c. *snowball effect, prize.*

1941 I. L. Idriess *Great Boomerang* xxxii. 251 It will not be the amount to be spent that will be considered, but the snowball effect of the resulting benefits. **1963** *Daily Tel.* 23 Jan. 20/8 A 'snowball' prize played for evening after evening at a bingo club is legal, provided the management gives the prize money. **1979** P. Niesewand *Member of Club* xviii. 142 Hundreds of families emigrate [from South Africa] every month... Each one has a snowball effect. Other families start thinking: should we leave also?

snowball, *v.* Add: **1. b.** *fig.* To increase or grow like a snowball rolled across snow; to accumulate or gather momentum at an ever-increasing rate.

1929 E. N. Nicholson *Study of Birds* 39 Some flocks are freshly formed each day, and recruits can be watched joining the original members at intervals until it snowballs up to its full size. **1934** *Sun* (Baltimore) 9 Nov. 26/7 The [housing] program in Maryland is 'snowballing'. **1967**

R. LEHMANN *Swan in Evening* III. 104 The success of those classes delighted and amused her. How polyglot they became and how they snowballed. **1969** *New Yorker* 19 Apr. 94/2 When a man knows what to look for, his value snowballs. **1973** *Lebende Sprachen* XVIII. 69/2 Management must appreciate the extra profit that snowballs from making use of advanced techniques. **1976** *Ilkeston Advertiser* 10 Dec. 15/4 Anyone is welcome to join in at any time during the day. A coach will ferry people around the circuit and singers usually 'snowball' throughout the day.

2. (Earlier example.)

1850 L. SAWYER *Way Sk.* (1926) iii. 46 Our men amused themselves with snowballing each other.

3. (Earlier example.)

1852 F. A. BUCK *Let.* 18 Dec. in *Yankee Trader* (1930) 112 At first we snow-balled, the whole town engaging in the sport like school boys.

Hence **snowballing** *vbl. sb.* (earlier and later examples); **snow·balling** *ppl. a.*

1861 F. A. BUCK *Let.* 20 Jan. in *Yankee Trader* (1930) 186 Christmas we had a nice lot of egg nog and cake and snow balling. **1941** *Sun* (Baltimore) 3 Nov. 14/1 The constantly snow-balling defense effort may cut into the everyday things we use in normal civilian existence. **1966** *Word Study* Dec. 4/1 Dubious meaning..starts a snowballing that soon places the intended meaning beyond retrieval. **1971** *Daily Tel.* 29 Dec. 10 The snowballing success of Alan Ayckbourn's plays abroad..is a constant surprise to him. **1973** *Times* 14 Aug. 3/3 The 'snowballing' technique by which researchers were introduced to one drug taker; who introduced a second and so on. **1977** *N.Y. Times* 16 Jan. IV. 19/3 Mr. Kissinger's pet theory of 'linkage', a kind of snowballing of détente, had to be given up.

snowberry. 2. (Earlier example.)

1813 T. JEFFERSON *Let.* 8 Dec. in *Orig. Jrnls. Lewis & Clark Exped.* (1905) VII. 393 We call it the snow-berry bush, no botanical name being yet given to it.

snow-bird. Add: **3.** *U.S. slang.* One who sniffs cocaine (cf. *SNOW *sb.*[1] 4 d); *gen.* a drug addict.

1914 JACKSON & HELLYER *Vocab. Criminal Slang* 78 A 'snowbird' is the customary designation of the cocaine habitue. **1923** [see *LOADED *ppl. a.* 3 b]. **1952** *Sunday Times* 3 Feb. 5/4 Present-day New York is not..a city overrun by 'snowbirds' jabbing needles into their arms. **1963** 'M. CORRIGAN' *Why do Women—?* xxiii. 175 Don't tell me you never heard that name for a dope addict—a snowbird.

4. *U.S. slang.* **a.** (See quots.)

1905 *N.Y. Even. Post* 20 Nov. 6, 28 per cent. deserted after three months, and were presumably 'snow-birds', that is, men who enlist to get food and clothing during the winter months. **1918** *Sat. Even. Post* 23 Nov. 11/1 They belonged to a shiftless class, the members of which often enlist in the army late in the fall because they want a job for the winter—the boys call them snowbirds. **1930** W. H. WALDRON *Old Sergeant's Conferences* vii. 123 A 'Snow bird' is a deserter who surrenders in the fall to get a place to stay through the winter.

b. (See quot. 1924.)

1923 *Nation* 31 Oct. 487 In winter, when building is at a standstill in the North, northern workmen, 'snow birds' or 'white doves' in Negro parlance, flock south. **1924** 'DIGIT' *Confessions 20th Century Hobo* 12 *Snowbird*, in the Southern States a Northerner who migrates south to avoid the winter. **1962** *Economist* 22 Dec. 1206/1 The Negro, who regularly loses his job to the 'snowbirds' from New York in the winter holiday season. **1979** *United States 1980/81* (Penguin Travel Guides) 243 This figure swells..during the winter months when 'snowbirds' arrive. ('Snowbird' is a tricky term as used in Miami, it refers primarily to tourists escaping the Northeastern freeze.)

5. *colloq.* A person who likes snow; a snow-sports enthusiast.

1928 D. H. LAWRENCE *Let.* in F. Lawrence *Not I* (1934) 269, I am no snow-bird, I hate the stark and shroudy whitemen, white and fuck. **1973** *Globe & Mail* (Toronto) 8 Dec. 43/8 No joy yet for snowbirds. Snow enthusiasts will have to wait at least one more week before they can start up their snow-mobile engines or put on their skis.

snow-blind, *a.* Add: Also *fig.*

1946 DYLAN THOMAS *Deaths & Entrances* 26 It is a winter's tale That the snow blind twilight ferries over the lakes.

snowcat (snōᵘ·kæt). orig. *N. Amer.* [Re-spelling of *SNO-CAT.] A tracked vehicle designed for travelling over snow (heavier and more rugged than a snowmobile). Cf. *SNO-CAT.

1955 *Sun* (Baltimore) 10 Dec. 2/3 Two tractor-treaded snowcats will set out for a point in Byrd Land about 600 miles away. **1960** *Maclean's Mag.* 2 Jan. 15/2 The snow is brushed and groomed between one day's skiing and the next by tread-driven machines called snow cats. **1971** *Country Life* 25 Feb. 436/2 The final requiem to Isaac's services came with the Snowcat, a sort of caterpillar contrivance that could do most things bar swim. **1973** *Observer* (Colour Suppl.) 21 Jan. 35/2 You can..make the magical and distinctly tricky trip by snowcat across Iceland's vast Vatnajokull Glacier.

Snowcem (snōᵘ·sem). Also **snowcem.** [f. SNOW *sb.*[1] + CEM(ENT *sb.*] The proprietary name of a cement-based (typically white) paint, used for covering external walls. Hence **Snow·cemmed** *a.*, painted with Snowcem.

1939 *Trade Marks Jrnl.* 20 Sept. 1301 Snowcem. 608,464. Paints having a base of cement. The Cement Marketing Co. Ltd...—1st Aug. 1939. **1947** *E. African Ann. 1946–7* 120 (Advt.), Building Materials..Snowcrete, Colorcrete and Snowcem. **1966** D. FRANCIS *Flying Finish* i. 13 Its drab walls..badly needed a coat of 'Snowcem'. **1969** R. BLYTHE *Akenfield* 19 The old farmsteads, snowcemmed and trim, ride high on the hills. **1972** J. BLACKBURN *Devil Daddy* i. 15 Batterday shamed his neighbours with Snowcemmed walls. **1979** B. HINES *Price of Coal* 25 I've heard they've ordered ten thousand gallons of Snowcem to whitewash the shaft with.

snowdrop. Add: **4.** *slang.* An American military policeman; hence, any military policeman.

1944 *N.Y. Times* 9 Apr. IV. 1/7 'Snowdrops'—the London nickname for white-helmeted American military police—were patroling the sidewalks. **1946** H. NICOLSON *Diary* 30 Apr. (1968) 59 Schacht sits in the witness box ..flanked by two young Americans in white helmets. Every hour, two other snowdrops..take over from their comrades the white batons of office. **1967** 'A. CORDELL' *Bright Cantonese* ix. 100 Where are you goin'?..Running to the first Snowdrop you can find? **1978** D. KYLE *Black Camelot* xvii. 270 Special detachments of military police 'snowdrops' went from house to house.

snowdrop tree. 2. For *Halesia tetraptera* substitute 'of the genus *Halesia*, bearing clusters of drooping white flowers'. (Earlier example.)

1813 H. MUHLENBERG *Catal. Plant. Amer.* 46 Silverbell tree, or Four-winged Snow-drop tree.

snowed, *ppl. a.* Add: **3.** Also *snowed-in* (see *SNOW *v.* 6 d).

1904 *N.Y. Even. Post* 5 Feb. 3 The Wabash is devoting all its energies to clearing the line of delayed and snowed-in trains. **1982** N. FREELING *Wolfnight* 128 A winter sun on a snowed-in landscape.

snowfall. Add: **1.** Also *fig.*

1964 M. A. JOHNSON in *Oceanogr. & Marine Biol.* II. 31 In recent years there has been a fundamental change in our picture of the deep-sea floor; previously conditions were thought to be essentially 'static', with negligible currents and the only variation with time being the steady 'snowfall' of sediment to the sea bed. **1969** MRS. L. B. JOHNSON *White House Diary* 10 Jan. (1970) 762 Dinner became a very snowfall of menu cards being passed around the tables for autographs.

snowflake. Add: **6.** = *hair-line crack* s.v. *HAIR-LINE 7. *U.S.*

1919 *Bull. Amer. Inst. Mining Engineers* Feb. 183 The appearance of 'snow-flakes' is unmistakable... The white silvery area, which always has the appearance of being of a very coarsely crystalline structure, in the specimen stands out in bold contrast to the darker background, and readily justifies the use of the term 'snow-flakes'. **1925** [see *hair crack* s.v. *HAIR *sb.* 10]. **1942** [see *fish-eye* s.v. *FISH *sb.*[1] 7].

7. *attrib.*, as **snowflake curve** *Math.*, a mathematically conceived curve (see quot. 1975) whose sixfold symmetry is reminiscent of that of a snowflake, of interest because its infinite length bounds a finite area.

1956 W. G. WALTER *Further Outlook* III. iv. 100 Jim Bursley had explained the snowflake curve to me and we had discussed the projection of such a curve into three dimensions. **1975** *Sci. Amer.* Nov. 144/2 Take the analyst's 'snowflake' curve.., which is made in an elementary way from an equilateral triangle of unit side by replacing the middle third of each side with a 'cape', itself the two jutting equal sides of a triangle a third as large as the original, and so on, repeating indefinitely. **1978** *Ibid.* Apr. 21/2 Among the fractals that exhibit strong regularity the best-known are the Peano curves that completely fill the finite region and the beautiful snowflake curve discovered by the Swedish mathematician Helge von Koch in 1904.

snow-man. Add: **1. b.** *Archæol.* Used *attrib.* and *absol.* to designate a technique of clay-modelling (see quot. 1955) or the figurines so produced.

1908 [in Dict., sense 1]. **1955** L. WOOLLEY *Alalakh* viii. 244 The vast majority [of figurines]..were hand-modelled more or less in the round in what is called the 'snow-man' technique, i.e. the clay is pinched into shape with the fingers and details are added by sticking on small pellets of clay, as well as by incision with a blunt stick or..by dotted lines made with a roulette. **1962** D. HARDEN *Phoenicians* ii. 42 The site..has produced remains of the seventh century, including some surprisingly primitive snow-man figurines of clay. **1974** J. CHESTERMAN *Classical Terracotta Figures* ii. 29 A group from Cyprus.., known as 'snowmen', was being produced in relative abundance... I think they are jolly little fellows with their peaked caps, pointed beards and stumpy arms.

c. Used *attrib.* and *absol.* to designate a type of pottery figure (see quot. 1957).

1931 D. MACALISTER in *William Duesbury's London Account Bk. 1751–53* p. xxv, I have illustrated several figures in white porcelain... Certain figures of the 'snowman' type belong to this class. **1933** *Trans. Eng. Ceramic Circle* I. 46 The 'snow man' bag-piper... Another 'snow man' in white porcelain... He looks like a *poilu*, but may be meant for a Chinaman. **1957** MANKOWICZ & HAGGAR *Encycl. Eng. Pottery & Porcelain* 205/1 *'Snowman' figures*, porcelain figures heavily glazed with a thick, opaque, glassy glaze, obscuring the modelling,..now known..to be the production of William Littler of Longton Hall, or of Jenkinson at the same works. **1974** *Encycl. Brit. Micropædia* IX. 303/2 *Snowman porcelain*... Called snowmen because of their thick white enveloping glaze, they include figures of human beings and animals.

3. *Abominable Snowman*: see *ABOMINABLE *a.* 1 c. Also simply *snowman.*

1931 J. CANNAN *Ithuriel's Hour* iv. 131 His gods, to say nothing of hairless Snow Men, and the shades of his ancestors. **1937** *Times* 31 Dec. 8/3 Mr. Smythe says that the snowman superstition is known only to the Tibetan or semi-Tibetan peoples. **1959** *Times* 8 Jan. 13/5 In the case of the famous Himalayan 'snowman' the evidence.. seems to point to the existence of perhaps two unknown species..of anthropoid ape.

4. *U.S. slang.* One who snows (*SNOW *v.* 4 b) someone.

1967 P. MCGIRR *Murder is Absurd* iii. 44 You're a great snow man, Warren. But I'm not in dreamland yet. **1977** *Amer. Speech 1975* L. 66 *Snowman*, male who easily wins the affections of females.

snowmobile (snōᵘ·mŏbīl). orig. *N. Amer.* Also **snow-mobile, snow mobile, snomobile, Snomobile.** [f. SNOW *sb.* + *AUTO)MOBILE *a.* and *sb.*] Any motor vehicle designed for travelling over snow; *spec.* a small, light passenger vehicle supported on runners at the front and a traction chain at the rear. Also *attrib.*

1931 *Times Lit. Suppl.* 5 Feb. 89/1 The American expedition to the South Pole under..Admiral Byrd was.. carried out in the grand manner... It had a 'snowmobile'; but this did not travel very far before meeting disaster on the rough surface. **1934** *Canad. Patent Office Rec.* 30 Oct. 2464/1 A snowmobile comprising an automobile having a pair of runners in place of the automobile front wheels, beams extending longitudinally of the automobile and rearwardly of the rear axle, a third axle mounted adjacent the rear ends of said beams, wheels forming the sole supporting means for the rear of the snowmobile journalled on said third axle, driving gears mounted on the automobile rear axle in place of the ordinary near wheels, and traction chains connecting said wheels and driving gears. **1947** *Times* 8 Mar. 5/6 They [*sc.* the Eskimos] have seen..drums of petrol parachuted to the snowmobiles of the Canadian Army exercise 'Musk-Ox'. **1961** *Times* 24 Apr. 16/6, I can..watch the teenagers race their stripped down jalopies... There are snow-mobiles and snocats. **1966** *Popular Science* Jan. 117 Snow really flies as this snowmobile owner takes his Larson Eagle on a long, thrilling jump. **1968** *Globe & Mail* (Toronto) 3 Feb. 46/4 (Advt.), Snow mobiles, demonstrator sale. **1969** *Daily Tel.* 11 Mar. 24/8 Organisers of a fox-hunt, mounted on snowmobiles, on a frozen lake in Minnesota have been threatened with police action. **1970** *Toronto Daily Star* 24 Sept. 10/4 (Advt.), Snowmobile suits on sale. **1970** *Nature* 29 Aug. 880/1 It is powered by..air-cooled engines originally developed for the 'sno-mobiles' now so popular during the Canadian winter. **1972** C. MUDIE *Motor Boats & Boating* 82 The question of how to use your Snomobile in high summer has been met by one manufacturer who markets a float attachment and a modified propeller drive so that the basic unit quickly becomes a lakeside holiday flier. **1977** *New Yorker* 2 May 60/2 Dog teams have largely been replaced by snowmobiles. **1980** *Harpers & Queen* Jan. 79/4 Snowmobiles alone use over 117 million gallons of fuel each year in the United States.

Hence **snow·mobiler**, one who drives or rides upon a snowmobile; **snow·mobiling** *vbl. sb.*, the action or sport of using a snowmobile; **snow·mobilist** = *SNOWMOBILER.

1964 *Star Weekly* (Toronto) 19 Dec. 14/1 We'd like to see a broader approach to snowmobiling as a family-style sport. **1967** *Daily Tel.* 14 Mar. 21/1 This weekend, some 11,000 'snowmobilists' were skimming across the snow-covered Adirondacks at speeds up to 30 mph, twice those on downhill slopes. **1968** *Globe & Mail* (Toronto) 13 Jan. 41/5 Snowmobilers would be well advised to obtain from the Ontario Safety League a copy of the Ten Commandments of Snowmobile Safety. **1977** *Time* 7 Feb. 60/2 The arduous route..led the snowmobilers along busy, narrow roads, through woods and across ditches. **1981** *Northeast Woods & Waters* Jan. 4/1 Years of driving and snowmobiling have prepared me and I always carry spare parts and tools and we fixed it in a jiffy.

snow-on-the-mountain. (In Dict. s.v. SNOW *sb.*[1] 5 d.) Substitute for def.:

1. *U.S.* An annual spurge, *Euphorbia marginata*, of the family Euphorbiaceæ, native to the central southern United States, and bearing white bracts.

1873 *Kansas Mag.* June 502/2 Their miller's-plant, or snow-on-the-mountain, is nothing but our spurge. **1878–80** [in Dict. s.v. SNOW *sb.* [1]5 d]. **1918** W. CATHER *My Antonia* IV. iv. 364 Every sunflower stalk and clump of snow-on-the-mountain drew itself up high and pointed. **1966** Mrs. L. B. JOHNSON *White House Diary* 27 Aug. (1970) 416 And there is snow-on-the-mountains—everywhere—especially in the meadows.

2. One of several low-growing, white-flowered, cruciferous plants, esp. white alyssum, *Arabis alpina*, or *Alyssum maritimum.*

1882 H. FRIEND *Gloss. Devon. Plant Names* 51 Snow-on-the-Mountain. *Alyssum maritimum*, L. **1886** [in Dict. s.v. SNOW *sb.*[1] 5 d]. **1890** J. D. ROBERTSON *Gloss. Dial. & Archaic Words Gloucestershire* 145 Snow-on-the-mountain. *Arabis alpina*, L. **1933** *Downside Rev.* LI. 523 The 'snow-on-the-mountains' was in full bloom, groups of crocuses were holding out their golden fingers just behind it, and the yellow and white looked like strips of spring sunshine.

snow-plough, *sb.* Add: **2.** *Skiing.* = *double stem* s.v. *DOUBLE *a.* A. 6. Also *attrib.*

1905 RICKMERS & RICHARDSON in D. M. M. C. Somerville et al. *Ski-Running* (ed. 2) 69 Stemming is akin to snow-ploughing, and by some German writers the stemming position is termed the half-snow-plough position. **1922** V. CAULFEILD *Ski-ing Turns* vii. 134 Although it is unsafe for any one but an expert to take the snow-plough position when travelling at all fast, this Snow-plough Christiania can be done at a good deal higher speed than the Pure Snow-plough turn. **1936** [see *double stem* s.v. *DOUBLE *a.* A 6]. **1948** P. LUNN *Ski-ing Primer* xi. 56 The snow-plough..is not only a useful manœuvre in itself, but is also the basis of the stem turn. **1953** A. WOODBURN tr. *Jacques's Downhill Skiing* I. iii. 79 The snow plough position..is one of the few that the beginner finds quite natural. **1966** A. N. GOODING *Basic Ski-ing* vi. 37 You first learn how to stop by using the Snowplough Brake. **1978** *Observer* 29 Jan. 35/1 Our instructor starts us on snowplough turns (with the tips of the skis pointing inwards). **1981** *Northeast Woods & Waters* Jan. 27/2 The snowplow, the 'dinking on the ski tips inward to make turns or to stop' is definitely a beginner maneuver.

So **snow-·plough** *v. intr.*, to execute a snow-plough in skiing; **snow-·ploughing** *vbl. sb.*

1904 D. M. M. C. SOMERVILLE et al. *Ski-Running* 39 The Norwegians call it 'snow-ploughing', but 'stemming' is shorter, and, we think, more expressive. **1928** E. JESSUP *Skis & Ski-ing* ix. 124 Very often it suffices to brake with the skis fairly flat on snow. In such cases, bend your knees inward only slightly... When you 'snowplough' in the foregoing fashion, both of your skis are serving as brakes. **1959** P. MOYES *Dead Men don't Ski* iv. 50 They had learnt, now, to snow-plough—putting the tips of their skis together to slow down or stop. **1961** *Times* 14 Feb. 14/7 The usual portly Frenchman..who charges along, skis wide apart and braking hard by stemming or 'snowploughing'. **1979** N. SLATER *Falcon* ix. 161 He snow-ploughed down towards her..snapped off his ski-bindings.

snowshoe. Add: **3. snowshoe hare**, the North American varying hare, *Lepus americanus*; **snowshoe rabbit** = *snowshoe hare* above (further examples).

1921 *Frontier* May 11 In a zig-zag pattern in the snow were the tracks of the snow-shoe hares. **1977** *New Yorker* 9 May 96/2 We kicked at some wolf scat, old as winter. It was woolly and white and filled with the hair of a snowshoe hare. **1903** J. LONDON *Call of Wild* 90 Leap by leap, like some pale frost wraith, the snowshoe rabbit flashed on ahead. **1971** W. HILLEN *Blackwater River* iii. 21 Snowshoe rabbits, so called because their large hairy feet serve as snowshoes.

snow-shoed *a.*: also *fig.*; **snow-shoeing** *vbl. sb.* (earlier example); **snow-shoer** (earlier example).

1946 DYLAN THOMAS *Deaths & Entrances* 30 The singing breaks in the snow shoed villages of wishes. **1867** *Territorial Enterprise* (Virginia City, Nevada) 12 Mar. 3/2 A race for a gold buckle, free to all lady snow-shoers, was also announced. **1884** H. CHADWICK *Sports & Pastimes Amer. Boys* 205 One of the favorite winter sports of the Canadians is snowshoeing, which is enjoyed to a great extent by the clubs of Montreal, who engage in races and long tramps over the hills on snowshoes.

snow-storm. Add: **1.** (Earlier *lit.* and *fig.* examples.)

1771 A. G. WINSLOW *Diary* 6 Dec. (1895) 8, I was prevented dining at unkle Joshua's by a snow storm. **1869** 'MARK TWAIN' *Innocents Abroad* xiii. 125 A snow-storm of waving handkerchiefs.

2. A paperweight or toy in the form of a transparent dome or globe containing a representation of a scene and loose snow-like particles, which, when shaken, creates the appearance of a snow-storm. Also *attrib.*

1926 'O. DOUGLAS' *Proper Place* xvii. 149 A round glass globe containing a miniature cottage, which, when shaken, became surrounded with whirling snow-flakes. 'It's a snow-storm,' she declared triumphantly. **1931** E. SACKVILLE-WEST *Simpson* II. 144 Salathiel held up a glass globe, inside which was a minute Scotch-baronial castle..He shook the globe and a whirlwind of white flakes swirled up... The Snowstorm jerked downwards in his hand. **1939** C. MORLEY *Kitty Foyle* (1940) xxxii. 332 It's good to have a person call your attention to something you're so used to you almost forgot thinking about it. I mean the glass snowstorm ball. Molly's back in Chicago and I take the glass ball and give it a whirl. **1947** 'D. YATES' *Berry Scene* x. 273 My eye was caught by a snowstorm—one of those little glass balls, with a baby cottage inside. And when you shake it, snow-flakes begin to fall. **1967** M. DRABBLE *Jerusalem the Golden* v. 101 Toys..a tower of bricks, a weather house, a huge pendant snowstorm globe containing a small palace and a small forest. **1975** S. LAUDER *Killing Time on Corvo* ix. 85, I recalled, as a child, staring entranced into Modrinka's snowstorm paper-weight.

3. *fig.* An appearance of dense snow on a television or radar screen. Cf. *SNOW *sb.*[1] 4 f.

1948 *Nature* 31 Jan. 167/1 The visual effect was that of a violent snowstorm of the type well known to televiewers due to motor-car ignition interference, but at a very much more intense level. **1974** L. DEIGHTON *Spy Story* xviii. 195 The radar screen was a snowstorm that dashed..in a mad rhythm. **1980** J. B. HILTON *Anathema Stone* I. 16 The television set..produced a snow-storm on every channel.

snowy, *a.* Add: **3. b.** Of the picture on a television screen: affected with snow (*SNOW *sb.*[1] 4 f).

1959 LEVY & FRANKEL *Television Servicing* xiv. 442 The picture may become weak and snowy. **1976** H. KEMELMAN *Wednesday Rabbi got Wet* xxiii. 73 She turned the set on... There was a lot of static, and the picture wavered and became snowy.

snozzle (snǫz'l), var. *SCHNOZZLE. Also *transf.*

1930 D. RUNYON in *Collier's* 20 Dec. 13/2 He no sooner pokes his snozzle into the joint than a guy by the name of Louie the Lug..jumps up. **1931** *Ibid.* 26 Sept. 9/2, I put the old convincer on him by letting him peer down the snozzle of my John Roscoe. **1959** I. & P. OPIE *Lore & Lang. Schoolch.* ix. 155 Children go in for short sharp words, as..'snozzle'..for nose. **1968** D. O'GRADY *Bottle of Sandwiches* (1969) iv. 60 The poor Old Girl [*sc.* a truck] was mud from anus to snozzle.

snub, *sb.*[1] Add: **I. 1. b.** *pl.* As *int.*, expressing total indifference or contempt. *slang.*

1934 *Neuphilologische Mitteilungen* XXXV. 130 Prep-school slang..*snubs* interj. accompanied by making a long nose. **1945** E. WAUGH *Brideshead Revisited* I. vi. 135 Now I shall tell her I have had it straight from a real artist, and snubs to her.

II. 4. For † *Obs.* read *rare* and add later example.

1925 W. DE LA MARE *Broomsticks* 220 Not so much as an ole scrubbin'-brush or a snub of soap.

5. Also *fig.*

1973 R. D. SYMONS *Where Wagon Led* p. xiii, A man who cannot put a snub on his temper had better leave horses alone.

snub, *sb.*[3] and *a.* Add: **A.** *sb.* **2.** *Geom.* A snub polyhedron or polytope.

1948 H. S. M. COXETER *Regular Polytopes* viii. 151 (*heading*) The snub {3, 4, 3}. **1952** CUNDY & ROLLETT *Math. Models* iii. 94 It can be proved..that..there are only thirteen Archimedean solids, two of which occur in two forms. Those two are the two 'snubs'. **1971** M. J. WENNINGER *Polyhedron Models* III. 179 Great inverted snub icosidodecahedron. This polyhedron is another snub that is simpler in construction than most of the others in this set.

B. *adj.* **3.** *Geom.* Used to designate certain symmetrical polyhedra and polytopes; in general, they have no mirror symmetry and occur in enantiomorphic pairs. [tr. L. *sīmus* squashed (Kepler *Harmonices Mundi* (1619) V. II. xxviii. 62).]

A snub cube has as its faces 6 squares and 32 equilateral triangles; a snub dodecahedron has 12 pentagons and 80 equilateral triangles: they are more nearly spherical than the cube and dodecahedron to which Kepler related them, hence the name.

1934 *Proc. London Math. Soc.* XXXVIII. 338 We might symbolize such a snub polytope by ringing all the dots in the graph. [*Note*] The word 'snub' is a free translation of Kepler's *simus*. **1952** CUNDY & ROLLETT *Math. Models* iii. 101 (*caption*) Snub cube. *Ibid.* 108 (*caption*) Snub dodecahedron. **1971** M. J. WENNINGER *Polyhedron Models* I. 32 The snub dodecahedron. This polyhedron has the same relation to the regular dodecahedron that the snub cube has to the regular hexahedron.

snubbed, *ppl. a.* Add: **2. b.** Shortened, stumpy.

1835 J. H. INGRAHAM *South-West* I. iii. 27 With swallow-tailed sterns, snubbed bows, and black hulls. **1903** *Trans. Inst. Naval Archit.* XLV. 26 Conditions in which you may have the 'snubbed' finish of the curve of areas.

snubber. Add: **3. a.** A simple form of shock-absorber used esp. in motor vehicles. Freq. *attrib.*

1921 *Daily Colonist* (Victoria, B.C.) 22 Oct. 10/7 (Advt.), Gabriel snubbers increase the riding comfort of any car. **1928** *Sunday Dispatch* 19 Aug. 8 New snubber plates are fitted on the front springs. **1956** TOBOLDT & PURVIS *Automotive Encycl.* 30d/1 The first so called 'shock absorbers' were simple rebound absorbers or snubbers. **1961** *Aeroplane* C. 429/1 The second-stage rotor blades have been fitted with 'snubbers' at approximately their mean height. **1970** *Telegraph* (Brisbane) 18 Dec. 8/1 The trouble with our washing machine..was that it needed a new snubber spring. **1973** R. L. ESHLEMAN in Snowdon & Ungar *Isolation of Mech. Vibration, Impact, & Noise* 228 The friction snubber utilizes coulomb friction between a liner material and the snubber wall. **1980** *Truck & Bus Transportation* (Austral.) Jan. 32/3 The snubber consists of an endless circle of chain encased in a solid block of rubber.

b. *Electronics.* A circuit intended to suppress voltage spikes.

1968 *IEEE Trans. Industry & General Applications* IV. 666/2 With properly damped snubber circuits the commutation transient waveshapes are such that the initial *dv/dt* is highest. **1977** *Design Engin.* July 27/1 All thyristor installations normally require a snubber, or dv/dt suppression network consisting of a capacitor and resistor in series across the device.

c. A device used to damp pulsations in, or check the flow of, a fluid.

1972 L. J. LORTIE in Blake & Mitchell *Vibration & Acoustic Measurement Handbk.* xxvii. 542 Using the simple snubber (expansion chamber)..which is made of standard piping components, an original pulse amplitude of 100 pressure units may usually be reduced to the order of ten or five units. **1977** *Sci. Amer.* June 46/2 The rate of descent of the piston is predetermined by the setting of the flow snubber in the dividing plate, which admits the water into the lower half of the cylinder.

snubbing, *vbl. sb.* Add: **3.** The action of reducing or suppressing oscillation; damping.

1951 C. E. CREDE *Vibration & Shock Isolation* iii. 112 (*heading*) Effect of snubbing. **1961** HARRIS & —— *Shock & Vibration Handbk.* III. xlv. 24 Because car loading can change from trip to trip, practical considerations dictate a compromise both in the selection of load springs and in the design of a snubbing means.

snub-nosed, *a.* Add: **2.** *fig.* Stumpy; short and broad at the front; abbreviated.

1925 F. SCOTT FITZGERALD *Great Gatsby* i. 9 A snub-nosed motor-boat..bumped the tide offshore. **1961** E. S. GARDNER in *Webster* s.v., A snub-nosed revolver. **1963** *Times* 5 Feb. 7/5 These snub-nosed,..two-stroke machines. **1966** P. O'DONNELL *Sabre-Tooth* x. 137 A Smith & Wesson Centennial, a snub-nosed hammerless revolver. **1978** S. SHELDON *Bloodline* l. 405 Others carried snub-nosed tear gas rifles.

snuck, chiefly U.S. pa. t. and pple. of SNEAK *v.* in Dict. and Suppl.

snuff, *sb.*[1] Add: **I. 1.** *Comb.* (Earlier and later examples.)

1709 in J. S. Moore *Goods & Chattels of our Forefathers* (1976) 196 Two brasse Snuffers and Snuff panns, one latten hoop for Cakes, a greater Chayr. **1963** *Times* 11 May 11/1 Candle-snuffers fitted with snuff pans were being used in Britain by the mid-fifteenth-century.

II. 7. Used *attrib.* to designate pornographic photographs or films involving the actual killing of a woman. Cf. *SNUFF *v.*[1] 1 d.

1975 *Whig-Standard* (Kingston, Ontario) 2 Oct. 3/6 New York City police detective Joseph Horman said.. that the 8-millimetre, eight-reel films called 'snuff' or 'slasher' movies had been in tightly controlled distribution for a month. **1975** *Globe & Mail* (Toronto) 20 Nov. 7/4 There are reports of 'snuff films' in the United States, pornographic movies that contain all the usual perversions but culminate with women being mutilated and killed—for real. **1976** *New Musical Express* 31 Jan. 11/3 The 'snuff movie', a kind of ultimate pornography that has at its climax the supposedly unfaked murder of a young woman. **1977** *Daily Colonist* (Victoria, B.C.) 23 July 3/2 Charged with attempted murder in the making of 'snuff' photographic stills. **1978** S. SHELDON *Bloodline* xlii. 360 For the last several years we have been hearing increasing rumors of snuff films, pornographic films in which at the end of the sexual act the victim is murdered on camera. **1981** *Observer* 12 July 39/4 The merchants and devotees of 'snuff porn' require that the masochistic models who pose for it actually die while receiving some hideous sexual punishment. At the actual moment of death the models are photographed in full colour, with very good lighting.

snuff, *sb.*[3] Add: **1. a.** Add to def.: In the Southern United States, usually taken orally. (Further examples.)

1849 [see *DIP *v.* 5]. **1891** M. E. RYAN *Pagan of Alleghanies* 105 [Does] your deity of the lower world.. chew snuff? **1907** *Dialect Notes* III. 230 *Dip* (*snuff*), *v.t.*, to smear snuff on the gums with a brush made by chewing the end of a small stick. **1913** [see *DIP *v.* 5]. **1951** W. FAULKNER *Knight's Gambit* 87 We watched him take..a tin of snuff and tilt a measure of it into the lid and then into his lower lip, tapping the final grain from the lid with..deliberation.

c. The colour of snuff. Also *attrib.* or as *adj.*

1951 [see *MUSTARD *sb.* 1 f]. **1974** *Times* 26 Nov. 19/6 Colour combinations..snuff/ice, blue/white.

3. a. *up to snuff*, also, up to the required or usual standard, up to scratch.

1906 J. LONDON *Let.* 31 May (1966) 204 As usual, your criticisms are right up to snuff. **1931** *Punch* 4 Nov. 495/2 Now Romney painted well enough, And Reynolds too, they say, And Gainsborough's things are up to snuff, And Lawrence had his day. **1943** E. B. WHITE *Let.* 20 Mar. (1976) 239 The Central Park piece..is up to snuff or better. **1944** R. LEHMANN *Ballad & Source* 204 Madame Jardine says you're to go and see her for a few minutes. Only a *few* to-day. She's not quite up to snuff. **1974** S. ELLIN *Stronghold* 33 He did not..go as far as some Quakers by convincement and suggest that birthright Quakers are not quite up to snuff. **1982** *N. & Q.* Feb. 83/1 The publisher's rejection of such received proceedings reflects, I suppose, their commitment to a databank, annual slices of which will suffice to bring future editions of their guides up to snuff.

4. *snuff-bottle* (earlier example), *-stain.*

1850 *Spirit of Times* 16 Mar. 41/3 Did you see..that old snuff-bottle? **1914** JOYCE *Dubliners* 13 The red handkerchief,..blackened..with the snuff-stains of a week.

5. snuff-dipper (earlier example); **snuff-dipping** (earlier example); **snuff-gourd**, a bottle gourd, the dried shell of the fruit of *Lagenaria siceraria*, a white-flowered annual vine; = *snuff-box gourd* s.v. SNUFF-BOX 3.

1845 T. J. GREEN *Texian Exped.* x. 137 We believe the most filthy of all practices is that of your..'snuff-dippers'. **1860** E. M. COWELL *Jrnl.* 22 Apr. in M. W. Disher *Cowells in Amer.* (1934) 65 The ladies have a habit.., 'snuff dipping' which is openly practised in the South, and privately indulged in, in the North. **1901** KIPLING *Kim* iv. 99 The lama dipped deep into his snuff-gourd. **1921** *United Free Church Missionary Rec.* June 190/2 Her dress consists simply of a ragged apron of goatskin, and a snuff-gourd hung round her neck.

snuff, *v.*[1] Add: **1. d.** *slang.* = sense 2 d below.

1973 C. ALVERSON *Fighting Back* xxv. 129 Wait'll you see what you've got when Speranza finds out that you put Gino in a position to get snuffed. **1976** F. WARNER *Killing Time* I. i. 7 They had to sneak over and come back with a prisoner, and most got snuffed themselves. **1978** T. GIFFORD *Glendower Legacy* (1979) 158 We should have snuffed this little shit when we had the chance.

2. c. Also, to terminate (life).

1929 HALL & NILES *One Man's War* iii. 25 We..knew ..that many lives would be snuffed out ere long. **1981** *Telegraph* (Brisbane) 23 Jan. 4/5 A prosecution witness today admitted she was content that the life of the man known as 'Mr Asia' should be snuffed out.

d. *slang.* To kill, to murder.

1932 E. WALLACE *When Gangs came to London* xxviii. 285 Eddie would have snuffed out Cora. **1973** *Philadelphia Inquirer* 7 Oct. (Today Suppl.) 12/1 'You're saying you're going to snuff that guy out before you know?'.. 'The people who are murdered didn't get an equal chance.' **1980** E. BEHR *Getting Even* xv. 174 If I cause too much embarrassment, they'll just snuff me out.

3. Also without *out*.

1916 C. J. DENNIS *Songs of Sentimental Bloke* v. 43 They think she's snuffed, an' plant 'er in 'er tomb.

snuff-box. 2. (Earlier example.)

1829 P. EGAN *Boxiana* 2nd Ser. II. 251 He came up with a frown..and, without the slightest ceremony, opened with a fillip on the Gipsy's snuff-box.

snuffer[1]. Add: **3.** *snuffer(s)-box, -handle, -stand, -tray* (later examples).

1843 *Ainsworth's Mag.* III. 180 Spectacle cases and snuffer-stands. **1898** G. B. SHAW *Man of Destiny* 203 With a couple of candles alight, and a broad snuffers tray in the other. **1952** B. & T. HUGHES *Three Centuries of Eng. Domestic Silver* v. 82 The upright snuffer stand, with a vertical socket to receive the snuffer box, was a late Charles II innovation. *Ibid.* 84 An immense amount of ingenuity now began to be lavished upon the ornamentation of snuffer handles. **1960** H. HAYWARD *Handbk. Antique Coll.* 260/1 *Snuffer-tray*, oblong or oval tray with or without small feet and scroll and ring handle at side for holding snuffers. **1971** *Country Life* 10 June 1434/1 A snuffers tray inscribed four years after it was made 'In Memory of Mrs. Jane Parsons, Oct. 11th, 1750'.

snuffer[2]. **3.** (Earlier example.)

1882 J. SNODGRASS tr. *Heine's Relig. & Philos. in Germany* II. 89 You know that he [*sc.* Frederick the Great] composed French verses,..was a prodigious snuffer, and believed in nothing but cannon.

4. (Earlier example.)

1829 T. C. HALIBURTON *Hist. & Statist. Acct. Nova-Scotia* II. ix. 404 Fish—Whale Species... Snuffer.

snuffing, *vbl. sb.*[1] Add: **3.** With *out*: dying.

1922 P. A. ROLLINS *Cowboy* iii. 55 His demise was sometimes referred to as his 'snuffing out'..or 'passing in his checks'.

snuffiness. (Earlier example.)

1862 J. A. SYMONDS *Let.* c 28 Feb. (1967) I. 336 Nothing cd have exceeded the snuffiness of my journey yesterday. I..did my cold no good.

snuff-mull. (Earlier example.)

1808 *Monthly Pantheon* I. 598/2 He was..famous for making Highland dirks and snuff mulls.

snuffy, *a.*[1] Add: **2.** Of cattle or horses: excitable, spirited, wild.

1955 R. HOBSON *Nothing too Good* xviii. 186 Any ball-up or milling around business up in front of the mile-and-a-half line of snuffy range beef could easily cause the critters to split into the spruce. **1964** *Penguin Bk. Austral. Ballads* 131 I'll yard them snuffy cattle in a way that's safe to swear. **1973** R. SYMONS *Where Wagon Led* vi. xix. 290 When he worked, he worked. Otherwise he played, mostly at breaking-in the snuffy ones.

snuffy, *a.*[2] Add: **2. b.** (Earlier and *fig.* examples.)

1765 STERNE *Tr. Shandy* VIII. 51 A plan..upon the lower corner of which..there is still remaining the marks of a snuffy finger and thumb. *a* **1846** B. R. HAYDON *Autobiogr.* (1927) III. xiii. 229 Brighton gay, gambling, dissipated..Dieppe dark, old, snuffy and picturesque. **1925** E. SITWELL *Troy Park* 67 Trees periwigged and snuffy.

3. (Earlier example.)

1823 'J. BEE' *Slang* 162 *Snuffy*—drunk, with a nasal delivery. *Snuffy*—drunk in the feminine application, and applied but seldom to puling fellows.

snug, *sb.*[2] Add: **1.** (Earlier example.)

1757 S. FOOTE *Author* I. i. 8 You love the snug, the Chimney-Corner of Life; and retire to this obscure Nook.

2. a. (Earlier and later examples.) Also *snug bar*.

1838 *Actors by Daylight* I. 84 Act-drop..the signal for the stage-manager to run in from the snug, and bully everybody. **1903** SOMERVILLE & 'ROSS' *All on Irish Shore* 226 'Don't be afraid,' said our hostess reassuringly, 'he'll never see ye—sure I have him safe back in the snug!' **1956** J. M. MOGEY *Family & Neighbourhood* 105 Solitary women drinkers prefer the snug in a larger public-house. **1967** *Punch* 17 May 736/3 Old women's gossip in the snug-bar..at 'The Garibaldi'. **1977** *Ibid.* 31 Aug.–6 Sept. 331/2 Angus Beakley's cart-horse went berserk and crashed into the snug of *The Flat Pig And Hat*.

b. Delete *Sc.* and add earlier example.

1860 DICKENS *Uncommercial Traveller* (1861) v. 63 Across the room, a series of open pews for Jack..at the other end, a larger pew..entitled *snug*, and reserved for mates.

snug, *a.*[1] **2. b.** (Further examples.)

1886 F. T. ELWORTHY *W. Somerset Word-bk.* 691 'So snug's a bug in a rug' is the common superlative expression. **1934** J. BUCHAN *Free Fishers* xiii. 211 Jem hung up his hat and ever since has been as snug as a flea in a blanket. **1936** D. POWELL *Turn, Magic Wheel* I. 93 The fetish of permanency, the snug-as-a-bug-in-a-rug fetish. **1974** P. DICKINSON *Poison Oracle* ii. 42 You just wait here, snug as a bug in a rug, learning it all second hand.

snug, *v.* Add: **1.** *transf.* and *fig.* (Later example.)

1978 T. L. SMITH *Money War* (1979) I. 74 Folding bipod which snugs under the barrel when not in use; large winter trigger.

c. *U.S.* With *up*.

1868 M. M. POMEROY *Nonsense* xxvi. 248 She 'snugged up' toward us as gently as a juvenile dove. **1873** J. H. BEADLE *Undeveloped West* v. 106 He used to complain that I 'snugged up' altogether too much.

6. b. Also *transf.*

1918 KIPLING *Land & Sea Tales* (1923) 116 They snugged her down. I don't know how one snugs down an aeroplane.

snuggery. Add: **1. a.** (Earlier example.)

1812 M. EDGEWORTH *Tales of Fashionable Life* V. 268 Let me establish you comfortably in this, which I call my sanctuary—my *snuggery*.

b. (Earlier example.)

1829 P. EGAN *Boxiana* 2nd Ser. II. 206 Shelton, on Friday evening after the fight, made his *bow* to the *Daffy Club*, at the Castle Tavern, Holborn: and, in the *snuggery*, Tom received the £100 stakes, as the reward of his victory.

2. b. (Further example.)

1953 DYLAN THOMAS *Under Milk Wood* (1954) 2 It is night neddying among the snuggeries of babies.

3. For *rare*[−1] read *rare* and add later example.

1958 [see *DO-GOOD].

snuggle, *sb.* Add: Also, a group of persons or things which are snuggled together.

a **1910** 'MARK TWAIN' *Autobiogr.* (1924) I. 103 In the early cold mornings a snuggle of children..occupying the hearthstone. **1935** E. BOWEN *House in Paris* II. i. 87 A snuggle of gothic villas. **1966** J. S. COX *Illustr. Dict. Hairdressing & Wigmaking* p. ix, Words which, when used in conjunction with the word *curls*, are indicative of either the quantity,..or arrangement of a *group of curls*: ..Ruffle, Snuggle, Soufflé.

snu·ggle-pup. *U.S. slang.* ? *Obs.* Also **-pupper, -puppy.** [f. SNUGGLE *v.* + *PUP *sb.*[1] 2 b.] An attractive young girl.

1922 [see *jazz queen* s.v. *JAZZ *sb.* 5]. **1925** LINDSEY & EVANS *Revolt Mod. Youth* v. 58 We go to parties with these young crumpet munchers and snuggle pups. **1933** *Forum & Century* (N.Y.) Dec. 367/2, I glimmed him with a snuggle-puppy.

snuggler (snʌ·gləɹ). [f. SNUGGLE *v.* + -ER[1].] One who snuggles.

1887 E. B. CUSTER *Tenting on Plains* xii. 379 It finally dawned upon us that the little horse was a constitutional snuggler. **1939** JOYCE *Finnegans Wake* 548, I chained her chastemate to grippe fiuming snugglers.

snuggly (snʌ·gli), *a. colloq.* [f. SNUGGLE *v.* + -Y[1].] Characterized by or inviting snuggling; snug, close-fitting. Also redupl. as *snuggly-wuggly*.

1928 A. HUXLEY *Point Counter Point* xvi. 287 Such a dear snuggly-wuggly, lovey-dovey little chap. **1966** R. H. RIMMER *Harrad Experiment* 36 It's [*sc.* sexual intercourse is] going to be nice and snuggly, and lots of fun. **1976** *National Observer* (U.S.) 28 Aug. 15/4 (Advt.), Our own grown-up version of the classic favorite for children. The snuggly fashion that will make any 'Lig kid' a beautiful baby all over again. Deliciously tantalizing on *her*, and..ruggedly good-looking on *him*.

snum (snʌm), *v. U.S. colloq.* Alteration of *swear*, esp. in *I snum* as exclamation. Also as *sb.* in *by snum!* (*obs.*). Cf. VUM *v.*, *sb.*

1825 J. NEAL *Brother Jonathan* II. 315 By snum; but you're a precious fellow! **1839** *Yale Lit. Mag.* IV. 357 I snum, 'tain't the thing for me. **1904** J. C. LINCOLN *Cap'n Eri* i. 4, I ain't quite a fool yit, Eri Hedge. I guess I know—well, I snum! I forgot that upper vest pocket! **1916** H. L. WILSON *Somewhere in Red Gap* viii. 333 Now, I snum! Here she's two-thirty! **1951** *Publ. Amer. Dial. Soc.* xv. 67 *I snum!*, exclamation of amazement.

snurge (snɜːdʒ), *sb. slang.* [Cf. SNEAK *sb.*] **a.** In schools, an informer, a tell-tale. **b.** One who curries favour, a toady; generally, an obnoxious person.

1933 M. HODGE *Wind & Rain* (1934) I. i. 19 He's probably only a kid. He may be a perfect little snurge...for all you know. **1955** M. GILBERT *Sky High* ii. 29 He's such a little snurge... He's so bogus. **1955** *People* (Austral.) 13 July 47/4 She was going to cut off my allowance. But do you know, it was that out-and-out snurge that pleaded for me? **1956** C. P. SNOW *Homecomings* xliv. 308 He had got on a good deal better as a snurge than he would have done as a malcontent.

snye (snai). *Canad.* and *local U.S.* Also **snie, sny.** [ad. Canad. Fr. *chenail*, Fr. *chenal* CHANNEL *sb.*[1]] A side-channel, esp. one creating an island.

1819 W. KEYES *Diary* 17 Apr. in *Wisconsin Mag. Hist.* (1920) III. 457 Evening, anchor a little above the upper snie (or channel) that leads to the Mississippi. **1826** *Kingston* (Ontario) *Chron.* 3 Nov. 2/5 We are also busy forming a channel through the rapids, for the sake of the raftsmen—this is done by building two strong dams, and deepening what is called a *dry snie*. **1829** J. MACTAGGART *Three Years in Canada* I. 136 At this place, there are numbers of islands formed by snies winding round the Falls. **1886** in *Alberta Hist. Rev.* (1971) Summer 16/2 And from there to the snye which is a short cut into Fort Resolution. **1893** 'MARK TWAIN' in *St. Nicholas* Nov. 24/2 Ef we..slips acrost de river to-night arter de moon's gone down, en kills dat sick fam'ly dat's over on the Sny. **1908** C. MAIR *Through Mackenzie Basin* 40 Much of [the tracking]..is in the water, wading up 'snies', or tortuous shallow channels..floundering in gumbo slides. **1921** *Beaver* Aug.–Sept. 15/1 The Imperial Oil Company narrowly escaped the loss of their machines, which were lying on the snye at the back of the Fort awaiting favorable weather. **1948** *Canad. Geogr. Jrnl.* Mar. 150/2 The word *snye, sny* or *snie* has been used for many years to describe a channel behind an island, with slack current or partly dried, or some such similar feature. **1967** E. B. NICKERSON *Kayaks to Arctic* ii. 17 There is a snye for float planes. **1969** E. W. MORSE *Fur Trade Canoe Routes* II. v. 57 The brigades shot the Allumette Rapids in their main (north) channel, the 'Timber Snye', where a safe canoe course passes.

so, *adv.* and *conj.* Add: **B. I. 5. g.** Ellipt. for *is that so?* expressing (*a*) recognition or realization of a fact or (*b*) questioning or dismissal of a statement (cf. *so what*, sense 10 c below).

1803 G. COLMAN *John Bull* I. 7 *Peregrine.* Is your house far from the sea-shore? *Mrs. Brulgruddery.* About three miles, Sir. *Peregrine.* So! I have been wandering about since day-break. **1886** *Liverpool Even. Express* 9 Jan. 3/4 'Oh, Mr. Blobbs, you can form no idea of the terrible dream I had last night.'.. 'So?' remarked Mr. Blobbs, continuing the perusal of the morning paper. **1903** FARMER & HENLEY *Slang* VI. 289/1 'The King returns to town to-day' 'So?' **1973** H. NIELSEN *Severed Key* i. 6 'Small craft warnings are out.' 'So?' Simon queried. **1977** W. TUTE *Cairo Sleeper* vii. 122 'You will see whoever Major Masri decides you should see,' the officer said curtly... 'So!' she said to herself. **1978** A. MORICE *Murder by Proxy* i. 13 'He's an estate agent.'.. 'So?' 'So nothing.'

h. Used to add emphasis to a statement contradicting a negative assertion made by the previous speaker. *dial.* or *colloq.* (chiefly *U.S.*).

1913 *Dialect Notes* IV. 55 *So, adj.*, used sometimes as 'too' and 'just the same' are used to intensify an assertion in reply to an expression of scepticism. 'You don't know anything about it!' 'I do *so*!' **1931** *Amer. Speech* VII. 20 *So*, emphatic in absolute use. 'I was—so!' **1937** L. B. MURPHY *Social Behavior & Child Personality* ii. 62 Eunice, 'I don't.' Anne, 'You do so.' **1951** N. M. GUNN *Well at World's End* xiv. 101 'You don't like butter!' she cried. 'I do so like butter!' 'You don't! You don't!'.. 'I do so!' he yelled. **1953** K. TENNANT *Joyful Condemned* xii. 103 'How old are you?' 'Eighteen.' 'Eighteen, my fat aunt.'.. 'I am so eighteen.' **1979** G. SWARTHOUT *Skeletons* 28 'I've published nineteen!' 'You haven't.' 'I have so.'

7. a. so-fashion *adv.*, in this or that manner. *U.S. dial.*

1890 *Dialect Notes* I. 23 *So fashion*, meaning *so*, *in that way*. Is this known all over New England? **1903** G. S. WASSON *Cap'n Simeon's Store* v. 86 It don't look right for nobody..to take and hang on to them tormented ole witch-bridles so-fashion! **1913** R. FROST in *Poetry & Drama* Dec. 415 I'll knock so-fashion and peep round the door When I come back, so you'll know who it is.

† b. *slang.* Homosexual. *Obs.*

1937 in PARTRIDGE *Dict. Slang.* **1963** C. MACKENZIE *Life & Times* II. 254 'I've come to the conclusion,' he told me, 'that I'm not really "so" at all. I much prefer girls.' At this date [*sc.* 1899] the cant word among homosexuals for their proclivities was 'so'. That seems to have vanished completely from current cant. **1968** J. R. ACKERLEY *My Father & Myself* xvi. 192 A young 'so' man, picked up by Arthur in a Hyde Park urinal. **1973** *Daily Tel.* (Colour Suppl.) 23 Feb. 51/4 Wilde used to call him 'the architect of the moon'. Rothenstein, Beerbohm,..and Epstein were his more predictable friends, as he was not..at all 'gay', as it is now called, or, as it was then called, 'so'.

II. 10. b. (*b*) [Reflecting Yiddish idioms.] Without implication of a preceding statement, or with concessive force: = well then, in that case, very well; also (introducing interrogative clauses) with adversative force: = but then, anyway.

1950 B. MALAMUD in *Partisan Rev.* XVII. 666 Miriam returned after 11.30... 'So where did you go?' Feld asked pleasantly. **1952** M. PEI *Story of English* 182 The adverb *so* at the beginning of a sentence ('So I'll pay for it!'), probably of Yiddish origin, occurs frequently in conversation. **1960** 'E. MCBAIN' *Give Boys Great Big Hand* i. 4 'I warn you..I ain't got no wine.' 'So who wants wine?' **1977** F. BRANSTON *Up & Coming Man* v. 49 'How much profit..?' 'Impossible to do more than make a wild guess.' 'So make a wild guess.'

c. *so what?*: a retort made to an assertion, implying that the problem expressed has no immediate interest or obvious solution. Also as *attrib. phr.* orig. *U.S.*

1934 M. H. WESEEN *Dict. Amer. Slang* 399 So what?—What of it? What does it matter?.. What does that have to do with the matter? Your remark has no bearing or significance. **1935** F. BALDWIN *Innocent Bystander* v. 83

He has a wife,' said the girl gloomily. 'So what?' asked Angela carelessly. **1938** C. Landery (*title*) So what? a young man's odyssey. **1949** *Hansard Commons* 21 Nov. 104 That is unfortunate and disappointing but, to use an American expression, 'So what?' **1953** in *Shorter Oxf. Eng. Dict.* (1955). Add., The tragedy of the 'So what?' generation. **1960** M. A. Sindall *Matey* xiii. 177 She suddenly yawned and flung the magazine on to the seat. 'So what!' she murmured. **1968** C. Watson *Charity ends at Home* x. 126 No, the fact is that Henny and I got along as well as most. Not around each other's necks all the time, but so what? **1970** T. Hilton *Pre-Raphaelites* viii. 201 Burne-Jones pushed art so far away from this world that our reactions to some of his paintings are of a merely so-what kind.

III. 13. *not so* preceding an adj., in the sense 'not very, none too—': see *not *adv.* and *sb.* 15 d.

14. g. With an adj. of size or quantity, with the implication of an accompanying gesture: = as — as this. Esp. in phr. *when I (he,* etc.) *was so high*, when I (etc.) was a small child. Hence *so-high* adj. Cf. That *dem. adv.* b, quot. 1870.

1876 Geo. Eliot *Dan. Der.* IV. vii. liii. 89 'You would have me love what I have from the time I was so high'—here she held her left hand a yard from the floor. **1899** Kipling *Stalky & Co.* 226 'Do 'ee lov' me, Mary?' 'Iss—fai! Talled 'ee zo since yeou was zo high!' **1916** A. Huxley *Let.* c 12 July (1969) 105 Vassall..seems..to have known me when I was 'so high'. **1963** 'B. Graeme' *Almost without Murder* xiv. 157 As a so-high kid I had 'liked' ice cream.

V. 23. For '† rarely' read 'also', and add later, chiefly *colloq.*, examples of *so* alone.

In the revived use, orig. *U.S.*

1851 H. Melville *Moby Dick* III. 564 Take your leg off from the crown of the anchor here, though, so I can pass the rope. **1902** E. L. Banks *Autobiogr. Newspaper Girl* xii. 143 One of the books in front of mine was six shillings. I bought it so mine would show. **1913** [see sense 7 a above]. **1949** W. Rogers *Autobiogr.* 44 The reason they leave some of our boys over there..is so they can get mail that was sent to them during the war. **1951** C. P. Snow *Masters* i. 3 Shovelling coal up the back of the chimney, throwing it on so it would burn for hours. **1968** *Los Angeles Times* 3 Mar. E6/3 The main reason Gender is back in the classroom is so he can converse in the many languages he knows. **1977** A. Thwaite *Portion for Foxes* 28, I shall make it simple so you understand.

VII. 35. f. (Earlier examples.)

1721 J. Kelly *Scottish Proverbs* 300 *So far, so good*. So much is done to good purpose. **1754** Richardson *Sir Charles Grandison* V. x. 56 'So far, so good,' said aunt Eleanor.

soak, *v.* Add. **I. 1. d.** Of metal: to become heated uniformly throughout its mass.

1843 [in Dict., sense 1 b]. **1939** J. Dearden *Iron & Steel To-day* x. 134 Here the ingots are allowed to 'soak' until they are the same heat all through, and then they are rolled.

2. e. *transf.* Of heat: to penetrate *through* the mass of an ingot until it is at a uniform temperature.

1902 *Encycl. Brit.* XXIX. 587/1 Bringing such an ingot..to the rolling temperature is not really an operation of heating,..but one of equalizing the temperature, by allowing the internal excess of heat to 'soak' through the mass. **1970** F. Simons *Dict. Ferrous Metals* 191 *Soaked steel*, steel heated in a furnace and held at the chosen temperature sufficiently long for the heat to have 'soaked' right through to the centre of the mass, which is only then uniformly heated.

II. 6. b. To maintain (metal or ceramics) at a constant temperature for a period to ensure that they are uniformly heated.

1925 *Jrnl. Iron & Steel Inst.* CXII. 491 The ingots should be stripped, soaked, and forged before reaching the temperature of the critical range. **1956** A. K. Osborne *Encycl. Iron & Steel Industry* 392/1 The pit was for soaking the ingots or permitting the heat contained in the still molten steel in its interior to penetrate to the outer portions until the temperature of the entire ingot was reasonably uniform. **1966** *McGraw-Hill Encycl. Sci. & Technol.* VII. 346/1 In this type of kiln the cycle of setting ware in the kiln, heating up, 'soaking' or holding at peak temperature for some time, cooling and removing or 'drawing' the ware is repeated for each batch.

7. e. (Earlier and further examples.) Also, to criticize harshly, to 'knock'; *to soak it to* (one) = *to sock it to* (one) (see Sock *v.*² 1 c in Dict. and Suppl.).

1892 *Columbus* (Ohio) *Even. Dispatch* 29 July 1/4 To-day's Washington Post 'soaks' it to the Southern Democrats in the House who were so rallied in 1885 in their support of the bill making an appropriation to the New Orleans Exposition, but are now opposed to a similar appropriation for the World's Fair. **1896** S. Crane *George's Mother* xiii. 152 At the gang's corner, they asked: 'Who soaked yeh, Fidsey?' **1908** G. H. Lorimer *Jack Spurlock* ii. 44 Yes, he done it! Soak it to him good! *Ibid.* vi. 107 My troubles came at me from all sides, and soaked it to me till my conscience fairly ached. **1915** H. L. Wilson *Ruggles of Red Gap* (1917) xii. 210 If he gets fancy with you, soak him again. You done it once. **1920** Wodehouse *Coming of Bill* ii. xiv. 239 Soak it to him, kid. **1925** H. L. Foster *Trop. Tramp Tourists* iii. 21, I found that we had on board..the man whose newspaper soaked my last book. **1936** [see *button *sb.* 5 g].

f. To impose upon (a person, etc.) by an extortionate charge or price; to charge or tax heavily; to borrow or extort money from; to cost a high price. Freq. const. *for* or with indirect object expressing a sum of money. *slang* (orig. *U.S.*).

1895 *N.Y. Dramatic News* 23 Nov. 2/2 This little scheme sometimes..enables the photographer to 'soak' them. **1904** *Newspaperdom* 21 Apr. 8 When a local merchant asks you to give his business a friendly notice, soak him 10 or 15 cents a line. **1915** Wodehouse *Something Fresh* ii. 37 Especially after poor old Percy had just got soaked for such a pile of money. **1932** D. L. Sayers *Have his Carcase* xiii. 164 Poor, but not mercenary or dishonest, since he refused to soak Mrs W. **1936** N. Coward *To-night at 8.30* ii. 60 She soaked her old man plenty, I'm sure—before he took to soaking himself! **1949** [see *brass *v.*¹ 2]. **1958** *Times* 17 Mar. 12/6, I hope the Court-Leet soaked the Air Ministry, and I expect it did, for these Berkshire men knew their own value. **1966** 'L. Lane' *ABZ of Scouse* 101 Can I soak yer fer a coupler bob? **1971** *Farmers Weekly* 19 Mar. 42/3 If you think this is a soak-the-housewives review, nobody knows more about soaking the housewives than you. **1977** *Time* 21 Nov. 59/2 Then add the investment in sophisticated equipment: a single stainless-steel 1,000-gal. vat can soak the vintner for some $6,000.

Hence **soak-the-rich,** *attrib. phr.* applied to a policy of progressive taxation (*progressive *a.* 3 f); also in similar phrases, as *soak-the-poor*, etc. orig. *U.S.*

1935 J. Warburg *Hell Bent for Election* 72 He [*sc.* F. D. Roosevelt] thought he was being 'clever' when he tried to steal Huey Long's thunder by suddenly coming out with his 'soak the rich' tax message. **1935** H. L. Ickes in *Lit. Digest* 14 Dec. 6/3 Soak the Rich (Antonym, Soak the Poor)—Newspaperese for a system of taxation founded upon the absurd and revolutionary theory that a man should be assessed taxes in proportion to his ability to pay. **1949** A. Christie *Crooked House* i. 8 No Soak-the-rich taxes would have any effect on him. He'd just soak the soakers. **1959** *Economist* 7 Feb. 498/1 The Democratic cry that this is a 'soak-the-poor' Budget. **1970** *Wall St. Jrnl.* 29 Apr. 1/5 Soak-the-sinner tax policy remains a stand-by... Taxes on alcoholic beverages and on cigarets have been the most frequent targets for increases. **1972** *Listener* 28 Dec. 898/3 Advocates of populist soak-the-rich policies.

III. 9. d. *pass.* with *in*: to be imbued with, to be profoundly acquainted with (a subject of study).

1937 *Ann. Reg. 1936* 56 It was generally agreed that the best speeches were made more or less extempore by speakers who were 'soaked' in their subject. *a* **1960** E. M. Forster *Maurice* (1971) i. i. 4 Mr Ducie would smile, for he was soaked in evolution.

IV. 11. *Comb.*, as *soak-dike, -ditch, -drain*; † **soakpit** = *soakaway (*obs.*); **soakway** [Way *adv.*] = *soakaway.

1970 S. J. Hallam in C. W. Phillips *Fenland in Roman Times* 23 Settlers clung tenaciously to these rich soils, and we can read from the air the story of their constant efforts to cope with deteriorating drainage: silting, the digging of soak-dykes, renewed silting, re-digging. *Ibid.* 33 The modern soak ditches take the drainage from the field ditches and discharge it into the main channel at regulated points; the Roman soak ditches must have had a similar function. **1963** *Times* 1 Feb. 13/7 The southern fringes of the planned settlement went first; water courses were provided with parallel soak-drains, which in their turn proved inadequate. **1970** P. Salway in C. W. Phillips *Fenland in Roman Times* 18 On the silts, continued occupation must have depended on keeping the system of soak-drains in operation. These drains imply sluices to let the water drain out of field and settlement ditches into the main watercourses at low tide and to prevent or control river water entering the ditches at high tide. **1898** E. C. S. Moore *Sanitary Engin.* i. 5 If made in porous soils so that the liquid soaks away they are called soak-pits; they are dangerous to neighbouring wells. **1956** C. D. Pigott in D. L. Linton *Sheffield* 83 Now only *Sphagnum recurvum* is at all frequent and this is no doubt due to its occupation of the wettest soakways which are avoided by sheep. **1978** *Jrnl. R. Soc. Arts* CXXVI. 438/2 These latter [*sc.* rain water channels]..empty into soakways at the base of the building.

soakage. Add: **3.** Also *attrib.*, in *Austral.* and *N.Z.* use.

1921 H. Guthrie-Smith *Tutira* xx. 196 These surface swellings are the result of a blocked soakage system. **1936** I. L. Idriess *Cattle King* iv. 30 Often you can dig in a dry creek-bed and obtain soakage water if you dig in the right place. **1937** E. Hill *Great Austral. Loneliness* vi. 53 At the crude soakage wells provided, he [*sc.* a white man] camps in the evenings.

soakaway (sōᵘ·kăwēⁱ). Also **soak-away.** [f. Soak *v.* + Away *adv.*] A pit, usu. filled with hard-core, into which water or other liquids may flow and from which they may percolate slowly into the surrounding subsoil.

1916 H. G. Wells *Mr. Britling* ii. iv. 331 Every now and then someone stumbles into a soakaway for rain-water. **1928** *Daily Express* 31 May 5/3 Be sure to find out if your kitchen sink drains to a 'soak-away'. If it does, you must not let much water go down it, but throw out washing-up water and suchlike on the garden. **1951** *Archit. Rev.* CIX. 291 The drainage system..consists of a series of septic tanks for soil drains and soakaways for stormwater. **1976** *Sunday Times* (Lagos) 26 Sept. 4/3 He says he can as well repair blocked soak-aways or any job a qualified plumber can do.

soaked, *ppl. a.* Add: **3.** Intoxicated. Freq. as second element of a *Comb.*

Some of these quotations may be regarded as further examples of Soak *v.* 7 b.

1737 *Pennsylvania Gaz.* 6–13 Jan. 2/2 He carries too much Sail, Stew'd, Stubb'd, Soak'd, Soft. **1899, 1908** [see *gin-soaked* adj. s.v. *gin *sb.*² 2 b]. **1939** Joyce *Finnegans Wake* i. 85 The prisoner, soaked in methylated, appeared in dry dock. *a* **1953** E. O'Neill *Touch of Poet* (1957) iv. 158 Like a rum-soaked trooper, brawling before a brothel on a Saturday night.

soaker. Add: **4. b.** (Earlier example.)

1789 J. Byng *Jrnl.* 29 May in *Torrington Diaries* (1938) IV. 95 An approaching Storm made me pull up near the Grey Hound Inn; and well I did, for it came down a Soaker.

c. A soaking pit.

1928 *Jrnl. Iron & Steel Inst.* CXVII. 201 The heated soakers are fired by blast-furnace gas. **1959** *Ibid.* CXCIII. 368/2 The soaking pit used was an electric soaker with a single trough coke resistor. **1976** *Steel USSR* VI. 194/2 The holding period from the end of casting to charging into the soakers was maintained constant as far as possible.

soaking, *vbl. sb.* Add: **2.** Also, a similar process in which ingots of other metals or ceramic objects are brought to a uniform temperature in a furnace or kiln. (Further examples.)

1926 *Jrnl. Iron & Steel Inst.* CXIII. 648 A cooling curve taken of the 0·48 carbon steel after heating up to 1000°C., and cooled immediately without soaking, gave the ferrite point at the normal temperature. **1964** H. Hodges *Artifacts* i. 39 The early stages of firing [of pottery] are thus slow..; the temperature is allowed to rise slowly by stages, each rise being followed by a period at which a steady temperature is maintained for a time, a process known as soaking. **1966** *McGraw-Hill Encycl. Sci. & Technol.* VI. 379/1 If the alloy is heated to a temperature not far below its freezing temperature and held at that temperature for a long time, interdiffusion of the alloy constituents will tend to eliminate segregation. Such homogenization treatment is frequently called soaking.

3. *soaking pit* (further examples).

1913 *Jrnl. Iron & Steel Inst.* LXXXVII. i. 67 With a view to having a regular sequence of hot ingots delivered to Gjers soaking-pits, whilst the centre of the ingot was still liquid,..a central casting-pit was substituted, designed on the Bessemer principle. **1962** *Gloss. Terms Glass Ind.* (*B.S.I.*) 12 *Soaking pit*, a conditioning furnace used to bring glass in open pots to a uniform temperature for castings. **1976** *Steel USSR* VI. 196/2 The duration of holding in the soaking pits for 13–18 t ingots from the end of casting to the start of stripping must not exceed 1 h 10 min.

Soamin (sōᵘ·ămin). *Pharm.* Also **soamin.** [f. So(dium + *amin(o-.] A proprietary term for, sodium *p*-aminophenylarsonate (= *atoxyl), formerly used to treat skin diseases.

1908 *Trade Marks Jrnl.* 13 May 763/2 *Soamin*... Chemical substances prepared for use in Medicine and Pharmacy. Henry Solomon Wellcome, trading as Burroughs, Wellcome and Co.,..London EC.; Manufacturing Chemist. **1909** *Official Gaz.* (U.S. Patent Office) 19 Jan. 759/2 Henry Solomon Wellcome, London, England. Filed Nov. 2, 1908. *Soamin*... Sodium Para-amino-phenylarsonates. **1918** J. H. Parsons *Dis. Eye* (ed. 3) xvii. 354 Arsenic is specially liable to cause optic atrophy, usually total, when administered in the form of trivalent benzol-ring compounds such as atoxyl or soamin. **1920** J. M. H. McLeod *Dis. Skin* vi. 111 Arylarsonate Group, which consists of atoxyl or soamin, arsacetin, and orsudan, was at one time much in favour but has fallen into disuse recently.

so-and-so, *sb.*, *a.*, and *adv.* Add: Also **soandso. A.** *sb.* **2.** Used *euphem.* as a term of abuse for a person (occas. a thing). Also, with weakened force, as a term of affection.

1897 W. S. Maugham *Liza of Lambeth* iii. 42 'You little so-and-so!' said Liza, somewhat inelegantly, making a dash at him. **1931** D. L. Sayers *Five Red Herrings* xii. 132 Some rigmarole about always finding the so-and-so hanging round his place and he wanted to have it out with him. **1943** *Lafayette Alumnus* (Lafayette College, Easton, Pa.) Nov. 5/1 Hiya, Joe, you old so-and-so, haven't seen you since that time, etc., etc. **1945** *Penguin New Writing* XXVI. 55, I told 'em all that but they wouldn't listen, the ignorant soandsos. **1956** B. Goolden *At Foot of Hills* vi. 124 'He felt he oughtn't to leave his work.' 'Poor old so-and-so.' **1958** 'A. Bridge' *Portuguese Escape* i. 13 The Countess is a hard-baked, publicity-minded old So-and-so, with about as much consideration for other people as a sack of dried beans! **1968** K. Weatherly *Roo Shooter* 107 It's not much good you staying out if some other so-and-so is going to work it, is there? **1973** *Times* 28 Nov. 13/5 The set [of an opera] is an absolute so-and-so to walk about on. **1977** B. Pym *Quartet in Autumn* i. 9 'Hoping to get off early, lazy little so-and-so,' said Norman.

B. *adj.* **2.** *euphem.* as a term of abuse.

1929 E. Wallace *Kennedy the Con Man* iv. in *Red Aces* 173 'That's what we pay rates and taxes for, and no so-and-so policemen in sight!' He did not say 'so-and-so', but Mr. Reeder thought his profanity was excusable. **1942** B. Himes *Lunching at Ritzmore* in *Black on Black* (1973) 177 You would..resume your discussions..on defense..or the F.B.I., or the 'so and so' owners of Lockheed, or that (unprintable) Aimee Semple McPherson. **1959** *Listener* 30 July 186/2 Some [clients] are good, some are indifferent, some are a so-and-so nuisance.

C. *adv.* **4.** As a mere intensive.

1959 'A. Fraser' *High Tension* v. 60 'Why can't Hugh help then? Or won't he?' 'Not so-and-so likely.'

Soanean (sōᵘ·nian), *a.* [f. the name of Sir John *Soane* (see below) + -an.] Of, pertaining to, or characteristic of Sir John Soane (1753–1837), British architect, or the buildings designed by him. Also **Soane·sque** [-ESQUE], **Soa·nic** [-IC], *adjs.*

1842 *Penny Cycl.* XXII. 168/2 He thought proper to limit the time of the 'Soanean Museum' being opened to the public to two days in each week for three months in the year. **1945** E. WAUGH *Brideshead Revisited* I. iv. 72 It was an aesthetic education to live within those walls, to wander from room to room, from the Soanesque library to the Chinese drawing-room. **1948** *Archit. Rev.* CIV. 64/1 An extravagant blend of Soanic abstraction and Italian *grotesquerie*. **1974** SHERWOOD & PEVSNER *Oxfordshire* 815 A doorway with Soanean incised decoration.

soap, *sb.* Add: **I. 1. a.** Now usu. distinguished from DETERGENT *sb.* in Dict. and Suppl.: soap is prepared from natural oils and fats and is precipitated by the ions (notably calcium) present in hard water. (Further examples.)

1940 J. H. WIGNER *Soap Manufacture* i. 20 In the textile trades soap is largely used for removing the natural impurities from the fibre and detergent properties are the main consideration. **1966** *McGraw-Hill Encycl. Sci. & Technol.* XII. 393/1 In ordinary usage the term soap specifies an alkali metal or substituted ammonium salt of a straight-chain carboxylic acid 10–18 carbon atoms in length, and the name detergent is given to synthetic materials of similar structure. **1972** *Materials & Technol.* V. x. 295 In synthetic anionic detergents, the main weaknesses associated with the traditional carboxylate soaps, namely, precipitation in hard water and decomposition in acidic solutions, are avoided by the use of other hydrophilic groups in place of the carboxylate group.

d. (Earlier and later examples.)

1854 D. G. ROSSETTI *Let.* 11 May (1965) I. 193, I heard from MacCrae who offers £50 for the water-colour, with all manner of soap and sawder into the bargain. **1957** W. FAULKNER *Town* (1958) x. 149 'The pattern,' Uncle Gavin said. 'First the soap, then the threat, then the bribe.'

f. *no soap*: an announcement of refusal of a request or offer, failure in an attempt, etc.; 'nothing doing'. *slang* (orig. and chiefly *U.S.*).

1926 MAINES & GRANT *Wise-Crack Dict.* 11/2 *No soap*, can't talk business. **1929** E. WILSON *I thought of Daisy* iii. 153 If he tries to cut in on you, don't letum—I'll just tellum, no soap! **1932** J. T. FARRELL *Young Lonigan* vi. 216 Studs said he'd take a dozen or two when Nate brought them around. Nate tried to collect in advance; but Studs was no soap for that. **1939** W. FAULKNER *Wild Palms* 42, I told him. Not that I was to meet you at a hotel. I just said, suppose I did. And he still said no soap. **1948** A. N. KEITH *Three came Home* iii. 72 We would.. call across.. 'No-soap!' or 'Not to-night!' **1957** J. KEROUAC *On Road* (1958) I. xiii. 86 Terry and I tried to find work at the drive-ins. It was no soap anywhere. **1977** 'E. CRISPIN' *Glimpses of Moon* vi. 93 'The police tried to trace the handkerchief, I take it?' 'They did, but no soap.'

g. *not to know* (someone) *from a bar of soap*: not to have the slightest acquaintance with. *Austral. colloq.*

1938 *Smith's Weekly* 26 Nov. 23 (*caption*), I don't know you from a bar of soap. **1943** K. TENNANT *Ride on Stranger* xxv. 319 'Why doesn't she marry the child's father?'..'It's my belief she doesn't know him from a bar of soap.' **1970** J. CLEARY *Helga's Web* vii. 130 I've never met any of his—interests. Certainly not this girl. I dunno her from a bar of soap.

h. = *SOAP OPERA 1 a.

1943 *N.Y. Times Mag.* 28 Mar. 19 Within these specifications, there is a deal of shrewd craftsmanship in the preparation of the 'soaps'. **1958** *New Statesman* 12 Apr. 455/3 Pay-TV will lure whatever is good in television now and leave those who cannot afford to pay for programmes stuck with an unvaried diet of soap and corn. **1969** A. ARENT *Laying on of Hands* vi. 46, I was one of five writers doing a daytime soap. One script a week. **1974** *Anderson* (S. Carolina) *Independent* 20 Apr. 5A/2 Agnes..had landed a job dialoging soaps for well-known television writer Irna Phillips. **1978** *Amer. Poetry Rev.* July/Aug. 19/3 If you turn on day-time T.V. you will see most of his actors playing rather similar roles in the soaps.

II. 4. a. *soap-film*, *-lather* (earlier example), *-pad*, *-pipe*, *-tablet*.

1924 R. M. OGDEN tr. *Koffka's Growth of Mind* iii. 105 A soap-film is produced upon a wire-frame..and upon it a little noose of thread is cast in whatever form it may take. **1976** *Sci. Amer.* July 93/3 The area-minimizing principle alone is sufficient to account for the overall geometry of soap films and soap bubbles. **1771** SMOLLETT *Humph. Cl.* I. 238 His face frothed up to the eyes with soap lather. **1958** *Listener* 16 Oct. 627/1 Scour round the inside with a steel wool soap-pad. **1956** S. BECKETT *Malone Dies* (1958) 21, I remember the soap-pipe with which, as a child, I used to blow bubbles. **1920** D. H. LAWRENCE *Lost Girl* iv. 52 Happiness is a sort of soap-tablet—he won't be happy till he gets it.

c. *soap basket*.

1926–7 *Army & Navy Stores Catal.* 122 Wire sponge and soap basket. For hanging on bath, etc.—1/-. **1975** *New Yorker* 17 Nov. 145/1 We found an assortment of brass soap baskets to hook over the side of the tub.

d. (in sense *1 h), *soap fan*, *land*, *star*, *watcher*.

1976 *National Observer* (U.S.) 10 July 16/2 Real soap fans have a dozen or so fan magazines, newspapers, and newsletters. **1948** Soapland: see *SOAP OPERA 1 a. **1977** *Guardian Weekly* 17 Apr. 18/1 People who resent the behaviour of a character she plays don't walk up and slap her, as has happened to more than one American soap star. **1978** *Times* 29 Aug. 1/8 The dedicated soap watcher..can switch channels for a solid five hours.. until, at 4.30 p.m...soap-land is closed for another day.

5. a. *soap-saver*.

1919 *T. Eaton & Co. Catal.* Spring & Summer 366/4 Wire soap saver 7c. **1973** *Listener* 25 Jan. 117/2 The soap-saver..was made like a diffuser-spoon, but bigger, with a basket of open wire-mesh.

c. *soap-smooth* adj.

1949 E. POUND *Pisan Cantos* lxxvi. 45 By the soap-smooth stone posts.

d. Instrumental, as *soap-filled* adj.

1970 *Which?* May 149/2 The cheapest soap-filled pads cost nearly 2d each.

6. a. soap flakes *pl.*, soap in the form of thin flakes for washing clothes, etc.; **soap leaf**, a leaf of soap (see *LEAF *sb.*[1] 10 b); **soap-lock** (earlier examples); **soap powder** (earlier example); also *loosely*, detergent in the form of a powder; **soap-stock, soapstock**, a crude, partially saponified mixture of fatty acids formed as a by-product in the refining of natural fats.

1926–7 *Army & Navy Stores Catal.* 38/2 Soap Flakes—lb., -/8. **1933** 'G. ORWELL' *Down & Out in Paris & London* xii. 91 There are no soap-flakes, only the treacly soft soap. **1967** N. FREELING *Strike out where not Applicable* 137 It was a little like a copywriter presenting an advertising campaign to a soapflakes manufacturer. **1909** *Cent. Dict.* Suppl., Soap-leaf. **1925** [see *LEAF *sb.* 10 b]. **1978** *Times* 4 Nov. 24/5 Good presents for adults: a book of soap leaves. **1840** *Picayune* (New Orleans) 30 Aug. 2/2 Howard..is described as..wearing moustaches and soap-locks. **1842** 'UNCLE SAM' *Peculiarities* I. 119 You are an incendiary, a robber by profession, a soap-lock and a loafer. **1865** H. MAYHEW *Shops & Companies of London* 199/1, I can always make quick work of *my* washing by using 'Harper Twelvetrees' Glycerine Soap-Powder', and it makes the clothes beautifully clean and white. **1964** M. DRABBLE *Garrick Year* xii. 193 Putting in my second instalment of soap-powder. **1970** G. GREER *Female Eunuch* 325 Some of the mark-up on soap powders.. could be avoided. **1895** J. LEWKOWITSCH tr. *Benedikt's Chem. Analysis of Oils, Fats, Waxes* xii. 632 (*heading*) Examination of the fatty matter ('soap stock'). **1924** MYDDLETON & BARRY *Fats* iii. 35 The recovery of oil from the soap-stock depends for its commercial success upon the ruling prices of the edible oil. **1972** *Materials & Technol.* V. x. 279 [In soap-making] use is also made of by-product fatty materials such as soapstocks and curd oils.

soap and water. [SOAP *sb.*] The commonest method of washing, used in phrases referring to standards of personal cleanliness. Also *attrib.*

1837 H. MARTINEAU *Society in Amer.* II. III. ii. 151 The demand of society for fresh air and soap and water has considerably increased. **1861** GEO. ELIOT *Silas Marner* xiv. 243 A great ceremony with soap and water, from which baby came out in new beauty. **1907** G. B. SHAW *Major Barbara* in *John Bull's Other Island* 168 Transfigured men and women carry their gospel through a transfigured world..practising what the world will let them practise, including soap and water, color and music. **1922** E. O'NEILL *Hairy Ape* iv. 37 Their faces and bodies shine from a soap and water scrubbing. **1961** L. MUMFORD *City in History* xv. 469 The spread of the soap-and-water habit might well account for the lowering of infant mortality rates. **1973** A. MACVICAR *Painted Doll Affair* iii. 39 She was an enthusiast for soap and water, as her schoolgirl complexion showed.

Hence **soap-and-water** *v. trans.*

1848, 1883 [in Dict. s.v. SOAP *v.* 1 *Comb.*].

soapberry. Add: **2. c.** *N. Amer.* A deciduous shrub, *Shepherdia canadensis*, of the family Elæagnaceæ, native to North America, and bearing small yellow flowers followed by edible red berries; also, the berries of this shrub; = *buffalo-berry* s.v. BUFFALO 5.

1904 A. G. MORICE *Hist. N. Interior Brit. Columbia* 61 The soap-berries were ripening. **1923** *Beaver* Dec. 104 In Central British Columbia it [*sc.* Indian ice cream] was made by working to a lather the dried soap berry. **1957** J. R. & I. M. CHRISTIE *Story Okanagan Falls* 42 Soap-berry..bears its gay red-currant-like berries now only for the birds to enjoy. **1963** *Beaver* Autumn 40/1 The interior fresh-water Indians..readily gave soapberries, kinninnick leaves and bark for smoking.

soa·p-box. [f. SOAP *sb.* + BOX *sb.*[2]] **a.** A box for holding soap; orig. and still occas., a small receptacle for a ball or bar of soap; later *esp.* a wooden case in which soap is or may be packed, traditionally used as a makeshift stand for a speaker; hence used *fig.* and allusively.

1660 [in Dict. s.v. SOAP *sb.* 4 c]. **1834** *Chambers's Edin. Jrnl.* III. 143/3 A soap-box! A thing with a lid which is found on almost every wash-stand in Great Britain. **1862** [in Dict. s.v. SOAP *sb.* 4 c]. **1907** J. LONDON *Road* 211, I get up on a soap-box to trot out the particular economic bees that buzz in my bonnet. **1912** *Town Topics* 16 Nov. 3/4 The days when a couple of..clerks on inverted soap boxes..were his staff. **1926–7** *Army & Navy Stores Catal.* 104/3 Soap box. Useful for travellers—each 1/6. **1928** *Observer* 1 Apr. 21/4 To use the language of Australian politics, 'Soapbox must be met by soapbox.' **1933** E. O'NEILL *Days without End* I. 32 If you knew what a burden he made my life for years with his preaching. Letter upon letter—each with a soap box inclosed, so to speak. **1943** K. TENNANT *Ride on Stranger* xxiii. 295 She made no answer to this outburst which, she felt, was only old Shanno blowing off steam... 'Back to your soap box,' she said briefly. **1945** N. MITFORD *Pursuit of Love* xiii. 97 She became an out-and-out Communist..preaching her new-found doctrine..from a soap-box in Hyde Park. **1948** M. LASKI *Tory Heaven* xi. 153 At his feet, a wax-faced baby moaned incessantly in a soap-box. **1960** H. HAYWARD *Antique Coll.* 260/1 *Soap-box*, spherical box of silver, pewter or brass for soap-ball, standing on moulded base with screw-on or hinged pierced or plain cover. **1968** *Daily Tel.* (Colour Suppl.) 13 Dec. 19/2, I look upon my wealth, and now the House of Lords, as useful soap boxes. **1977** *Time* 14 Nov. 59/3 The primary U.S. condition for rejoining is that the I.L.O. get off its political soapbox.

b. *attrib.* (chiefly with reference to public speaking from a soap-box); **soap-box cart**, a child's cart made from a soap-box; so **soap-box derby** [*DERBY 1 d].

1918 *National Geographic* July 8/1 (*caption*) The soap-box orator and his auditors. **1924** *Telephone Topics* XVIII. 262 (*heading*) Public address system supersedes soap box oratory. **1927** T. C. PEASE *United States* 546 The choice of party candidates by manipulation of party conventions and soap-box primaries. **1933** DYLAN THOMAS *Let.* Sept. (1966) 21 You must excuse my slight soap-box attitude. **1942** E. WAUGH *Put out More Flags* i. 72 Soap-box orators screaming their envy of the rich. **1950** *Manch. Guardian Weekly* 4 May 3/2 The 'Soap Box Derby' is an American festival rather more important to some..youngsters than the Fourth of July. **1960** *Times* 1 Mar. 13/1 The theatrical appeal of her soap-box oratory. **1977** J. VAN DE WETERING *Death of Hawker* xiii. 119, I like inventing. I was always making soap box carts when I was a child.

Hence (U.S.) **soap-box** *v. intr.*, to speak from or as from a soap-box; **soap-boxer**, one who speaks from a soap-box; **soap-boxing** *vbl. sb.*

1913 *Industrial Worker* (Spokane, Washington) 10 Apr. 4/1 They do want all the publicity that can be given them by the press, by the locals, soap-boxers, and by individual conversation. **1919** U. SINCLAIR *Jimmie Higgins* iv. 42 If he could have an assistant..the soap-boxing could go on every night. **1926** E. O'NEILL *Great God Brown* I. iii. 41 When you got to love to live it's hard to love living. I better join the A.F. of L. and soap-box for the eight-hour night! **1972** *Village Voice* (N.Y.) 1 June 78/3 He's been a soap boxer for the IWW (actually he sang and his brother spoke).

soap-bubble. (Earlier example.)

1800 M. EDGEWORTH *Parent's Assistant* (ed. 3) V. 100 Two other little children..came to him to beg, that he would blow some soap bubbles for them.

soaper. Add: **1. d.** A manufacturer of soap.

1965 *Economist* 16 Oct. 303/2 Denied any real difference to exploit, the soapers have not even got an expanding market to sell in. **1979** *Jrnl. R. Soc. Arts* Dec. 60/1 The glassmakers and soapers responded to the growing shortage of domestic potash in several ways. **1982** *Shell Technol.* No. 3. 6/2 Manufacturing the surfactant molecules known as detergent active matter falls, normally, into the domain of the chemicals industry. Combining this active matter with the other constituents of a modern synthetic detergent and marketing the finished product is the concern of 'soapers'.

3. = *SOAP OPERA 1 a. *N. Amer.*

1946 *Time* 26 Aug. 56/3 The result: *Pepper Young's Family*, one of radio's most popular soapers. **1972** *Daily Colonist* (Victoria, B.C.) 4 Feb. 2/1 The CBC soaper Whiteoaks of Jalna rates only slightly higher than a documentary on the mating habits of the tsetse fly. **1981** *TV Picture Life* Mar. 6/1 Daytime soapers were dealing with sex and violence far more explicitly than their night-time brothers for quite a while.

soapie (sǭᵘ·pi). *colloq.* [f. SOAP *sb.* + -IE.] = *SOAP OPERA 1 a.

1964 F. POHL in *Galaxy* Oct. 190/2 You had a nervous breakdown..space cafard, as they call it on the soapies. **1978** *N.Y. Times* 30 Mar. C21/6 Movie: 'Daughters Courageous'... A soapie, granted. And dated. But pleasantly cheerful.

soapily, *adv.* Add: (Later examples.) Also in sense 4 of SOAPY *adj.*

1976 A. E. LINDOP in H. Watson *Winter's Crimes 8* 200 Soapily he would say, 'Darling, don't worry.' **1979** *Sci. Amer.* Jan. 26/1 The breakdown of the insulator may have many causes from the death of the maintaining cells to the appearance of a detergentlike metabolite capable of soapily cleaning off the invaluable lipid layers.

soapless, *a.* Add: **a.** (Later *lit.* example.)

1906 [see *CANDLELESS *a.*].

b. Of shampoo, detergent, etc.: not containing soap.

1936 *Chemist & Druggist* CXXIV. 56/2 The alternative to sulphonated lorol [*sic*] for soapless shampoos is saponin. **1959** *Which?* Nov. 152/2 All the liquid and cream shampoos, since they are all based on very similar soapless detergents, would clean the hair effectively in hard or soft water. **1966** J. S. COX *Illustr. Dict. Hairdressing & Wigmaking* 140/1 Sulphonated vegetable oils are also used in another type of soapless detergent.

soapolallie (sǭᵘ·polæli). *N. Amer.* Also **soapol(l)ali(e), soopolallie, sopelalee**, etc. [f. SOAP *sb.* + Chinook Jargon *olallie* berry.] **1.** A thick drink made from crushed soap-berries. Cf. *SOAPBERRY 2 c.

1895 *Canad. Mag.* Aug. 344/1 We were fortunate enough to see some Indians eating 'soapolali'. **1944** C. BARBEAU *Mountain Cloud* 199 Here are the stems of blackberries and the wild fruit of the hills that gives sopelalee. **1966** *Islander* (Victoria, B.C.) 27 Feb. 6/2 There was [at the potlatch] also a great deal of oolachan-grease and soapollalie.

2. = *SOAPBERRY 2c. Also *attrib.*
1937 T. STANWELL-FLETCHER *Jrnl.* 23 Sept. in *Driftwood Valley* (1946) 33 On drier, more open ridges..are.. dense thickets of small Shepherdia, or soopolallie, bushes. **1953** A. F. FLUKE *Kwakiutl* 21 The berries of the 'soopolally' bush..were dried and stored whole. **1957** J. R. & I. M. CHRISTIE *Story of Okanagan Falls* 42 One little shrub, the Indians' 'soopolallie'..bears its gay red currant-like berries now only for the birds to enjoy. **1976** T. WALKER *Spatsizi* xii. 139 The soap olallie leaves were a darker green, and the fruit larger.

soap opera. *colloq.* (orig. *U.S.*). [f. SOAP *sb.* + OPERA.
So called because some of the early sponsors of the programmes were soap manufacturers. For the use of *opera*, cf. *horse opera* s.v. *HORSE sb. 27 a.]
1. a. A radio or television serial dealing esp. with domestic situations and freq. characterized by melodrama and sentimentality; this type of serial considered as a genre.
[**1938** *Christian Cent.* 24 Aug. 1011/1 These fifteen-minute tragedies..I call the 'soap tragedies'..because it is by the grace of soap I am allowed to shed tears for these characters who suffer so much from life.] **1939** *Newsweek* 13 Nov. 44/2 Transcontinental Network bubbled up out of the 'soap operas'. **1948** *Time* 11 Oct. 40/3 *The Beast in Me* also includes such matter as Humorist Thurber's grimly unhumorous 'Soapland' (studies in contemporary soap opera). **1953** M. DICKENS *No More Meadows* iv. 180 More and more soap operas had hit the air to sell detergents and deodorants and headache pills. **1978** J. IRVING *World according to Garp* xvi. 321 Hoping that the visceral reality of Garp's language.. somehow rescued the book from sheer soap opera. **1980** *Times Lit. Suppl.* 24 Oct. 1210/5 Some advertising campaigns [on ITV] have become mini soap-operas.
b. *transf.* and *fig.*
1944 R. CHANDLER *Lady in Lake* v. 36, I haven't heard a word from Muriel in the whole month... I don't have any idea at all where's she's at. With some other guy maybe. I hope he treats her better than I did... Thanks for listening to the soap opera. **1958** *Spectator* 19 Sept. 369/2 Eugene O'Neill's wordy autobiographical play is an endlessly tragic soap-opera, a sort of Mrs. Dale's Diarrhœa. **1962** [see *HUFF *sb.* 1]. **1971** 'A. BURGESS' *MF* ii. 25 The act of robbery..near 39th Street... This was daily soap-opera of the streets.
2. *attrib.*
1942 W. STEGNER *Mormon Country* 347 They deal with impressionable virgins caught in the net of polygamy and agonizing worse than any soap-opera heroine through endless difficulties. **1951** M. MCLUHAN *Mech. Bride* (1967) 157/1 Soap-opera serials are short on action, long on situations. **1958** *Punch* 9 July 59/2 The revival of 'The Royalty' (BBC) is the latest development in the soap-opera world, on a Channel that has no soap to sell. **1978** S. BRILL *Teamsters* ix. 349 Most of the soap-opera intrigue of innuendo and in-fighting was not terribly subtle.
Hence **soap-opera·tic, -operatical** *adjs.*, of or characteristic of a soap opera.
1963 *New Yorker* 1 June 66 'The L-Shaped Room'... A sentimental piece of work, but so justly and successfully sentimental that it nearly always avoids seeming soap-operatic. **1975** *Country Life* 20 Mar. 742/3 A few weeks ago the BBC concluded a soap-operatical version of the loves of Georges Sand. **1979** *Boston Globe* 18 May 39 From her soap-operatic point of view, Watergate was not a national tragedy but rather was the personal pathos of a woman with nothing to give a husband in need.

soapy, *a.* Add: **5. a.** (Earlier example.)
1854 E. TWISLETON *Let.* 22 June (1928) xi. 202 The Bishop of Oxford I never do like..his manner, when Lords are in presence, richly merits his popular sobriquet of 'Soapy Sam'.
5*. Of style, tone, etc.: smooth, bland, sickly, sentimental.
1889 G. B. SHAW in *Star* 12 Aug. 3/4 Miss Nettie Carpenter played Svendsen's Romance for Violin, and played it very well, though her tone is just a little soapy—if I may be permitted to use such an expression. **1926** C. CONNOLLY *Let.* 1 June in *Romantic Friendship* (1975) 139 Benson's style is pretty soapy. **1973** *Publishers Weekly* 17 Sept. 59/3 Romance, which gets a bit soapy at times.

soar, *v.* Add: **I. 1. f.** *Aeronaut.* Of an aircraft or its pilot: to fly without the aid of an engine, esp. for an extended period without significant loss of altitude.
1893 O. CHANUTE in *Amer. Engineer & Railroad Jrnl.* Feb. 85/2 M. de Sanderval..is to be commended for having made an earnest if unsuccessful effort to learn how to soar in a wind like a bird. **1903** W. WRIGHT in *Jrnl. Western Soc. Engineers* VIII. 402 On trial we found that the machine would soar on the side of a hill having a slope of about 7 degrees. *Ibid.* 407 It would be easy to soar in front of any hill of suitable slope, whenever the wind blew with sufficient force to furnish support. **1931** V. W. PAGÉ *ABC of Gliding* vii. 159 An expert in Germany recently soared for a distance of 42 miles. **1940** L. B. BARRINGER *Flight without Power* xii. 218 After being checked out in two-seaters, they are allowed to soar in single-seaters. **1976** D. PIGGOTT *Gliding* (ed. 4) viii. 49 In general, it is not wise to attempt to soar by circling if you are below 500 feet.
3. c. Of an amount, price, etc.: to rise or increase rapidly. Hence, of a commodity: to increase rapidly in price.
1929 T. WOLFE *Look Homeward, Angel* xv. 196 She realized that in a very short time land values would soar beyond her present means. **1965** *New Statesman* 30 Apr. 672/3 The improvement..cannot be more than a stopgap whilst numbers continue to soar. **1978** I. B. SINGER *Shosha* i. 12 The price of meat soared. **1979** *Tucson* (Arizona) *Citizen* 20 Sept. 1A/4 Gold soared to another record of $380 at London's five major bullion firms.
7. To cause to soar.
1661 J. HEATH in J. W. Draper *Cent. Broadside Elegies* (1928) No. 43 A Cherubs wing hath soar'd him to this Hight. **1930** R. CAMPBELL *Adamastor* 88 Partaking the strain of the heavenward pride That soars me away from the earth I deride. **1978** A. WELCH *Book of Airports* ii. 28/1 Soaring the glider all the way back to where you started from is both exciting and satisfying. **1982** *Sci. Amer.* July 60/1 With the engine off the craft can be soared like a hang glider.

soarable (sōᵊ·răb'l), *a.* [f. SOAR *v.* + -ABLE.] Suitable for soaring flight. Hence **soarabi·lity,** a soarable condition.
1922 *Nature* 17 June 799/1 When the air at the level of the fin-ray was 'soarable', as shown by the behavior of dragon-flies. **1922** *Flight* XIV. 620/2 How machines will fare..remains to be seen. The southern slopes are not nearly so steep, and the extent to which they give soarability is at present a matter for speculation. **1961** *Aeroplane & Astronautics* CI. 163/2 The second day.. suffered from clamp in the middle but produced soarable periods at either end. *Ibid.*, Nobody went away in the morning soarability, because the post-frontal sky, when it came in late afternoon, should theoretically have been worth waiting for.

soaraway (sōᵊ·răwēⁱ), *a.* [f. SOAR *v.* + AWAY *adv.*] Soaring, making rapid or impressive progress.
1977 *Zigzag* Aug. 6/1 All the great American pop styles rolled into one but fueled with the energy of the super soaraway seventies. **1978** *Oxford Jrnl.* 6 Jan. 1/1 The team which has made the Journal a soaraway success. **1982** *Observer* 26 Sept. 9/4 He'll soon be writing for Britain's best and liveliest soaraway Sunday newspaper.

soarer. Add: **1.** (Further examples.)
1900 W. WRIGHT in M. W. McFarland *Papers W. & O. Wright* (1953) I. 34 Hawks are better soarers than buzzards. **1910** *Times* 18 May 14/5 The albatross is pre-eminently the gliding soarer of the bird kingdom. **1978** *Sci. Amer.* July 102/1 Those master soarers, the great albatrosses.
2. An aircraft designed for soaring.
1909 *Flight* 20 Feb. 110/1 For a machine heavier-than-air, the true distinctive expression should decidedly be, 'flying machine', comprising 'flyers', 'gliders', 'soarers', &c. **1931** V. W. PAGÉ *ABC of Gliding* viii. 164 The primary training or school machines..are gliders rather than soarers. **1941** S. P. JOHNSTON *Horizons Unlimited* 30 Sailplanes or soarers are simply light and efficient gliders that may be made to take advantage of up currents of air to attain altitudes far above their launching points.

soaring, *vbl. sb.* Add: **1. b.** *Aeronaut.* Gliding; now *esp.* gliding for extended periods without significant loss of altitude. Freq. *attrib.*
[**1864** *Leisure Hour* 21 May 328/1 The sciences of aerostation and meteorology must progress together as wedded sciences... The effect of a mutual reaction upon each other we are unable to conjecture, further than to anticipate..more than probable extension of the properties and simple soaring power of the balloon.] **1893** *Amer. Engineer & Railroad Jrnl.* LXVII. 396/1 It seems now reasonably possible for designers of soaring machines..to experiment with their apparatus without further search for some hidden secret. **1894** O. CHANUTE *Progr. Flying Machines* p. iv, Aeroplanes for soaring flight. **1896** [see *GLIDING *vbl. sb.* 2]. **1903** W. WRIGHT in *Jrnl. Western Soc. Engineers* VIII. 401 In principle Soaring is exactly equivalent to gliding, the practical difference being that in one case the wind moves with an upward trend against a motionless surface, while in the other the surface moves with a downward trend against motionless air. **1931** V. W. PAGÉ *ABC of Gliding* p. vii, Soaring machines or sailplanes are usually monoplanes with a higher aspect ratio than found in the training planes. **1931** P. & M. WHITE *Gliding & Soaring* xviii. 145 Soaring differs from gliding in that the ship, instead of losing altitude, either pursues a level course or gains height. **1952** F. GREEN *ABC of Gliding* 90 Ridge soaring depends basically on the wind. **1958** D. PIGGOTT *Gliding* xviii. 118 Many glider pilots become anxious to start cross-country flying as soon as they have made one or two soaring flights. **1974** *Sci. Amer.* Aug. 14/2 His memberships.. reflect several of his outside interests, which he lists as 'camping, canoeing, gliding and soaring and gardening'. **1979** *Yale Alumni Mag.* Apr. (Suppl.) CN 20/1 He is fully recovered..and still believes that soaring is a great sport.

soave (soā·ve), *adv. Mus.* [It.] As a direction to the performer: softly, gently, with delicacy and tenderness. Also **soaveme·nte.**
1740 J. GRASSINEAU *Mus. Dict.* 228 *Soave*, or *Soavement*, sweetly or agreeably. **1876** STAINER & BARRETT *Dict. Mus. Terms* 399/2 *Soave, Soavemente* (*It.*), agreeably, delicately, gently, softly, sweetly. **1959** *Collins Mus. Encycl.* 609/2 *Soave*,..in a smooth and gentle manner.

Soave (soā·ve). The name of a town in northern Italy, used *attrib.* and *absol.* to designate a dry white wine made there.
1935 SCHOONMAKER & MARVEL *Compl. Wine Bk.* v. 130 The most widely sold and the best white wine of Veneto is the dry Soave. **1960** *Spectator* 15 July 114 *Soave* in Italian means 'suave' in English, but the wine gets its name..after the battlemented little town of Soave... It is a white wine, very dry indeed as Italian wines go, with a refreshing acidity. **1969** R. AIRTH *Snatch!* ix. 90 We had a bottle of Soave Bolla, chilled, with the lobster. **1975** *Observer* (Colour Suppl.) 3 Aug. 12/2 Soave, a light dry white from Italy, is getting into more and more shops. It comes from around Verona.

Soay (sōᵘ·ə). Also **Soa.** The name of an island in the Western Isles, used *absol.* or *attrib.* to designate a small, brownish, short-tailed sheep, *Ovis aries*, belonging to a variety once restricted to the island.
1906 J. G. MILLAIS *Mammals Gt. Brit.* III. 210 The history of the Soay sheep is unknown. **1912** R. LYDEKKER *Sheep & its Cousins* iv. 59 These small and half-wild Soa sheep belong to a group of breeds, or sub-breeds, which are widely distributed over Northern Europe. **1922** *Nature* 6 May 595/1 It will be gathered that the primitive sheep of Europe was of the Soay type. **1949** E. COXHEAD *Wind in West* vi. 161 A chap..on a wee island north of Skye who's experimenting with the Soay sheep. **1970** *Observer* 26 Apr. (Colour Suppl.) 35/2 The unusually leggy sheep..is a Soay. **1974** R. N. CAMPBELL in P. A. Jewell *Island Survivors* ii. 28 The Soay sheep..is the most primitive domestic form in Europe. *Ibid.* 31 The flocks..of Soays on Soay were left behind. **1979** *Vole* Feb. 45/2 The sheep that are used are Soays, small, brown, attractive animals. A few years ago this very ancient breed faced extinction. Today its future is assured.

sob, *sb.*[1] Add: **3. b.** *colloq.* (orig. *U.S.*) with reference to sentimental appeals to the emotions, as *sob act, -raiser, -reporter, -singer, -song, specialist, squad, -talk, tune*; **sob brother,** *U.S. colloq.*, a sentimental man; **sob sister,** a female journalist who writes sentimental reports or articles; a writer of sob stories; hence in various *transf.* uses, *esp.*: an actress who plays pathetic roles; a sentimental, impractical person, a do-gooder; a journalist who gives advice on readers' problems; **sob story,** a report or article designed to make a sentimental appeal to the emotions; *transf.* a narrative of one's misfortunes, a 'hard luck story'; **sob-stuff,** speech or writing which makes a sentimental appeal to the emotions; also *attrib.*
a **1953** E. O'NEILL *Long Day's Journey into Night* (1956) IV. 157 He's been putting on the old sob act for you, eh? **1914** J. LONDON *Let.* 23 Sept. (1966) 430 All I can say is that he is a weak-brother, a sob-brother. **1917** S. GRAHAM *Priest of Ideal* xxix. 278 Our great sob-raiser who persistently pleads in the *Primer* for all causes which obviously evoke pity and rage. **1929** *McGraw-Hill Book Notes* 11 Feb., The story in that announcement..looked too much like the efforts of a newspaper sob-reporter. **1955** *Star* (Johannesburg) 10 Oct. 8/2 Should a squad of police be seconded..to guard the American 'sob singer' Johnnie Ray? **1912** *Sat. Even. Post* (N.Y.) 7 Dec. 9/3 Of the Daily Blatt's seven sob sisters six had husbands; and of the six it was more or less pure coincidence that five were supported by their wives. **1922** *Opportunities in Motion Picture Ind.* (Photoplay Research Soc.) 5 Some sob-sisters have gratified their ambition to play comedy, and have played it well. **1927** *Sat. Even. Post* (N.Y.) 24 Dec. 62/3 The sob sisters and the sob brothers..who didn't raise their boys to be soldiers. **1936** WODEHOUSE *Laughing Gas* xviii. 196 It's one of the things the sob-sisters are sure to write up. **1939** *Sun* (Baltimore) 21 Feb. 9/8 Forecasting opposition to his plan by 'sob-sisters' Goodwin said 'it wouldn't do any harm to give these sob-sisters a couple of wallops too'. **1963** J. MITFORD *Amer. Way Death* x. 153 Mrs. St. Johns is best known as one of the original sob sisters, a Hearst reporter in her youth. **1967** *Boston Herald* 8 May 19/5 Now that Svetlana has become America's newest millionaire glamor girl sob-sister, American interest in peeking or looking through the iron curtain is at a new all-time high. **1972** *Listener* 20 July 72/3 Sob sisters, those ladies who advise the unhappy about their problems. **1927** *New Republic* 12 Oct. 211/1 He has possibly scored some moderate hits: in 'Manhattan Mary', 'Broadway', 'The Five Step'..,a curiously constructed sob-song called 'Memories', and the title-piece. **1964** J. P. CLARK *Three Plays* 114 So you turn your broad back Upon me and will continue with your sob-songs? **1931** *Kansas City* (Missouri) *Star* 3 Nov. 22/5 It is gratifying..that the sob specialists can find practically nothing..to be sorry about. **1912** G. M. HYDE *Newspaper Reporting* 236 The search for human interest material is a modification of the 'sob squad' work of the sensational papers, on more delicate lines. **1913** *Writer's Mag.* Nov. 174/2, I wrote the 'sob' story of 'the City that Turned Down Santa'. **1923** C. E. MONTAGUE *Fiery Particles* 177 Thomas Curtayne, the greatest of Irishmen, was to be buried in homely state... Here was a sob-story, manifestly. **1949** *Los Angeles Times* 15 June II. 4/4 How anyone could heed such a sob story is beyond me. **1979** N. HYND *False Flags* xxi. 188 'Sometimes a man tries to do too much.'.. 'I'm familiar with the old sob story.' **1982** A. MATHER *Impetuous Masquerade* xi. 170 And give him some sob-story? **1918** H. C. WITWER in *Collier's* 11 May 15/2 Well, Joe, we gotta lot of new songs over here now, besides 'Where Do We Go From Here?' which same is our favourite and a lot more of the old stand-bys, which runs more to the sob stuff. **1922** C. SIDGWICK *Victorian* xxvi. 193 When the girls talked sobstuff at school I always told them I meant to marry a millionaire. **1929** D. H. LAWRENCE *Pansies* 128 A sickly people will slay us If we touch the sob-stuff crown of such martyrs. **1937** A. CHRISTIE *Murder in Mews* ix. 223 Of course I'm sorry. I don't indulge in sob-stuff. But I shall miss him. **1978** N. MARSH *Grave Mistake* iii. 90 He puts on a bit of an act like a guide doing his sob-stuff over Mary Queen of Scots in Edinburgh Castle. **1946** KOESTLER *Thieves in Night* 219 'That's so much sob-talk,' said Matthews. **1926** E. O'NEILL *Great God Brown* II. i. 46 I love those rotten old sob tunes.

sob (sǫb), *sb.*² *slang.* [prob. altered form of Sov.] A pound.

1970 G. F. Newman *Sir, You Bastard* iii. 113 Two hundred sobs was a small piece of fifty grand. **1973** 'K. Royce' *Spider Underground* v. 79 Norman could have back his fifty sobs; when I failed I didn't want compensation.

sob, *v.*¹ Add: **3. b.** (Earlier example with direct speech.)

1861 C. M. Yonge *Young Step-mother* iv. 42 'Things didn't use to be stupid when Ned was there!' sobbed Gilbert.

‖ **soba** (sōᵘ·bă). [Jap.] A type of noodle that is made from buckwheat and is a popular Japanese food. Also *attrib.*

1896 *Far East* 20 Dec. 33/1 A strange custom of eating *Soba* (a kind of vermicelli made of buckwheat) on the last day of December prevails among a large class of people. **1928** K. Yamato *Shoji* vi. 90 We were presented with bowls of vermicelli, or *soba.* **1936** K. Tezuka *Jap. Food* 25 Sometimes *udon*.. or *soba* (buckwheat noodles) are used in place of boiled rice. **1965** W. Swaan *Jap. Lantern* i. 6 Bowls of steaming *soba*, a type of Chinese noodle dearly beloved by the Japanese. **1971** *Ashmolean Mus. Rep. of Visitors 1970* 54 Soba cup, blue and white decoration of bamboos, probably Arita ware.

Hence **sobaya** (soba·ya), in Japan, a shop or restaurant which serves *soba.*

1958 *Japan* (Unesco) (1964) 727/1 The term *sobaya* is used in eastern Japan for vendors and shops that sell *udon* and *soba.* **1960** B. Leach *Potter in Japan* vi. 132 We made our way to a Sobaya (buckwheat macaroni restaurant) and ate 'Zaru Soba'.

sober, *a.* Add: **II. 4. b.** *sober sadness* (later *arch.* example).

1819 J. Keats *Let.* 21 Sept. (1931) II. 426 Isabella is what I should call..'A weak-sided Poem' with an amusing sober-sadness about it.

IV. 14. *sober-coloured, -living, -looking, -spoken* adjs.

1851 Borrow *Lavengro* I. xxv. 317 They were dressed in sober-coloured habiliments. **1892** 'Mark Twain' *Amer. Claimant* xvi. 168 He drops into the stoodio as sober-colored as anything you ever see. **1960** *Times* 4 Mar. 13/7 There is a hard-working, sober-living, self-respecting section among them. *a* **1817** Jane Austen *Northanger Abbey* (1818) I. xi. 183 The morrow brought a very sober looking morning. **1934** W. S. Churchill *Marlborough* II. xiv. 304 These were very unusual expressions for the sober-spoken and matter-of-fact Marlborough.

sober, *v.* Add: **II. 5.** Also with *up.* Hence as *attrib. phr.*

1884 [see Sobering *vbl. sb.*]. **1901** *Daily Colonist* (Victoria, B.C.) 2 Nov. 5/2 The police yesterday gathered in an Indian woman who was rolling along in the street in a drunken condition with a baby in her arms. She was released as soon as she had sobered up. **1938** E. Waugh *Scoop* iii. ii. 284 'Aunt Agnes and I very much fear that he has taken too much.'..'Oh, he'll sober up,' said Uncle Theodore, from deep experience. **1963** Auden *Dyer's Hand* 261 When he [*sc.* Cassio] sobers up, his regret is.. that he has lost his reputation. **1967** *Listener* 23 Nov. 669/3 The National Federation of Licensed Victuallers announced that they're to back the search for a sober-up pill—an alcohol antidote.

sobering *ppl. a.* (earlier examples); also with *down.*

1816 Jane Austen *Emma* II. ii. 24 The sobering suggestions of her own good understanding. *a* **1817** —— *Persuasion* (1818) III. vii. 141 These were words which could not but dwell with her... They were of sobering tendency. **1975** B. Meyrick *Behind Light* xiv. 183 The sobering-down item of community hymn singing.

Soberano (sobera·no). [Sp., lit. 'sovereign'.] A Spanish brandy; also, a drink of this.

1963 'D. Cory' *Hammerhead* iv. 59 He called the barman over and ordered a Soberano. *Ibid.* vii. 109 Downing three fingers of cognac, more exactly Soberano. **1969** R. V. Beste *Next Time I'll pay my own Fare* vii. 88 Gage opted for..a 'Soberano' which he found to be the least syrupy of the Spanish brandies. **1974** R. Jeffries *Mistakenly in Mallorca* xxii. 199 He..went through to the larder for a bottle of Soberano and three glasses... Back on the patio, he poured out three brandies.

sobersides. Add: (Earlier *transf.* example.)

1779 J. Wedgwood *Let.* 25 Feb. (1965) 229, I am sorry you have been again out of luck with a horse; but do not despair. I have got a *sober sides* on trial for a week past.

sober-sided *a.* (later examples).

1880 G. W. Cable *Grandissimes* i. 4 Honoré in mask? he is too sober-sided to do such a thing. **1892** [see *choral *a.*¹ 2 c]. **1950** *Psychiatry* Feb. 8/2 A sober-sided, meticulous investigator. **1970** N. Armstrong et al. *First on Moon* ii. 41 The Apollo news center at Cape Kennedy issued a sobersided 'status report'.

sobful (sǫ·bfŭl), *a. rare.* [f. Sob *sb.* or *v.*¹ + -ful.] Full of sobs, given to sobbing; provocative of sobs.

1921 W. J. Turner *Music & Life* 8 The composer of the most sobful ballad that ever made a drunkard weep. **1924** *Blackw. Mag.* Nov. 692/2 He was not really in a very sobful mood.

‖ **sobornost** (sǫbǭ·rnǫst). *Theol.* [a. Russ. *sobórnost'* conciliarism, catholicity.] A unity of persons in a loving fellowship in which each member retains freedom and integrity without excessive individualism.

1935 O. F. Clarke tr. *Berdyaev's Freedom & Spirit* iii. 91 The revelation of the Trinity is, however, not that of a heavenly monarchy..but that of heavenly love, the divine *sobornost.* **1962** *Listener* 30 Aug. 317/1 How are we to achieve what Berdyaeff would call a valid *sobornost* —a really felt community? **1976** N. V. Riasanovsky *Parting of Ways* iv. 177 Khomiakov's concept of *sobornost*, an association in love, freedom, and truth of believers. **1977** *Church Times* 21 Jan. 13/3 *Sobornost* furthermore provides a further incentive to Roman Catholic officialdom not to regard Church unity too exclusively from a juridical point of view.

Sobranie (sǫ̆brā·ni). [Proprietary name: cf. next.] A kind of tobacco or a cigarette made from it. Also *Balkan Sobranie*, and *attrib.*

1899 *Tobacco* 1 Mar. p. lxvi/2 Register of specialities... cigarettes... Balkan Sobranie—Robt. Lewis, 20, St. James St., Lon., S.W. **1923** *Trade Marks Jrnl.* 19 Sept. 1969 *Sobraine* [sic]... Cigarettes. Isaiah Redstone.. cigarette manufacturer. *Ibid.* 19 Dec. 2707 The Balkan Sobranie... Cigarettes. **1927** D. L. Sayers *Unnatural Death* iii. 31 Lord Peter wriggled into the window seat, lit a Sobranie and clasped his hands about his knees. **1955** N. Fitzgerald *House is Falling* xi. 188 When three Sobranies had been lighted, Lake continued. **1966** L. Southworth *Felon in Disguise* vii. 116, I will leave it at the tobacconists... All you have to do is to..ask for the pound tin of Balkan Sobranie you ordered. **1966** 'A. York' *Eliminator* iii. 49 She put the pistol away in her bedside drawer and lit a Balkan Sobranie. **1977** *Punch* 31 Aug.–6 Sept. 355/1 Insouciant Senior Lecturers smoked Sobranie.

Sobranye (səbrā·n(i)ye). Also **Sobraniye, -je, Subranie.** [ad. Bulg. *sŭbránie* assembly; cf. Russ. *sobránie* and quot. 1902.] The parliament or national assembly of Bulgaria.

1894 E. Dicey *Peasant State* xv. 142 There are..three Estates in Bulgaria: the Crown, the Ministers, and the Sobranje. **1902** *Encycl. Brit.* XXVI. 448/2 The national representation is embodied in the Sobranye, or ordinary assembly (Bulgarian, *Sŭbranie*, the Russian form *Sobranye* being usually employed by foreign writers), and the Grand Sobranye, which is convoked in extraordinary circumstances. **1923** G. Buchanan *My Mission to Russia* I. ii. 22 In spite, however, of his declaring the elections invalid, the Grand Sobranje met and occupied itself with the difficult task of finding a prince willing to accept the thorny crown which Prince Alexander had laid down. **1957** *Times* 21 Dec. 5/4 Some 4,500,000 to five million Bulgarians will go through the motions of 'electing' a new Sobranye. **1974** J. Rothschild *East Central Europe between Two World Wars* vii. 334 The Peasantists won 85 seats in the Sŭbranie, the unicameral national legislature.

soc. (sǫk), abbrev. of Society 8 and 10.

1890 Barrère & Leland *Dict. Slang* II. 274 *Soc* (printers), this is an abbreviation of the word 'Society'. To be a member of the *Soc.* (compositors'), hence not a 'rat'. **1903** Farmer & Henley *Slang* VI. 291/2 *Non-Soc-man*, a *rat*.., a blackleg, a non-Union-man. **1980** 'J. Marcus' *Marsh Blood* v. 73 The overwhelming number of the Art Soc.'s members were amateurs.

so-called, *ppl. a.* Add: Also as one word. **2.** (*a*) Also *loosely* or *catachr.* as a term of abuse. (*b*) Now freq. used without implication of incorrectness.

(*a*) **1888** O. Wilde in *Woman's World* I. 134/2 'This so-called nineteenth century'—as an impassioned young orator once termed it, after a contemptuous diatribe against the evils of modern civilisation. **1960** C. S. Lewis *Studies in Words* ix. 226 Rose Macaulay noticed a tendency to prefix 'so called' to almost any adjective when it was used of those the speaker hated; the final absurdity being reached when people referred to the Germans as 'these so-called Germans'. **1980** W. Safire in *N.Y. Times Mag.* 13 Jan. 6/1 Examples of sneer words are 'self-proclaimed', 'would-be', 'purported' and that Soviet favorite, 'so-called'.

(*b*) *a* **1961** in Webster, s.v., His heavy working schedule did not keep the student out of so-called campus politics. **1962** R. Carson *Silent Spring* viii. 86 The so-called Dutch elm disease entered the United States from Europe about 1930. **1966** G. Greene *Comedians* i. ii. 46 New buildings ..built for an international exhibition in so-called modern style. **1968** *Physics Bull.* Nov. 373/1 The socalled Schrödinger representation. **1977** C. Sagan *Dragons of Eden* ii. 41 Many spinal-cord neurons seem to have about 10,000 synapses, and the so-called Purkinje cells of the cerebellum may have still more. **1979** P. Nihalani et al. *Indian & Brit. English* i. 164 A number of so-called transformational grammarians are to attend the teachers' conference at Krishnapur next week.

soccer. Now the usual form of Socker in Dict. and Suppl.

sociability. Add: **2.** *Ecol.* The extent to which the plants of a species are found in proximity to one another. [The sense is due to Braun-Blanquet and Pavillard, who used F. *sociabilité* (*Vocabulaire de Sociologie végétale* (1922) 3).]

1922 *Jrnl. Ecol.* X. 246 Where the French terms are practically identical with the English equivalents..they are simply translated... La Sociabilité (Soziabilität, Geselligkeit): disposition of individuals in the interior of an association. Five grades of sociability are expressed as follows. **1932** Fuller & Conard tr. *Braun-Blanquet's Plant Sociol.* iii. 36 Gregariousness or 'sociability' expresses a space relationship of individual plants, answering the question, how are the individuals or shoots of a species grouped? **1961** Hanson & Churchill *Plant Community* iii. 97 Species that spread only by seed may also show a high degree of sociability, especially in the early stages of succession, as in abandoned fields where certain annual weeds may become very dense. **1973** P. A. Colinvaux *Introd. Ecol.* v. 65 *Zea mays*..had a cover abundance rating of only '3' since, although the commonest plant, it by no means covered nearly all the ground as it must to rate a '5', and a sociability of '1', earned because it was evenly spaced and thus the extreme loner.

sociable, *a.* and *sb.* Add: **A.** *adj.* **5.** *Math.* Designating a cycle of three or more integers such that each is the sum of the factors of the previous one; cf. Perfect *a.* B. 8. [The sense is due to P. Poulet, who used F. *sociable* (*L'Intermédiaire des Mathématiciens* (1918) XXV. 101).]

1970 *Math. Computation* XXIV. 428 Until now only two groups of sociable numbers were known, respectively of order 5 and 28... I have made an exhaustive search for sociable groups of order $t \leq 10$ of which the lesser number is smaller than 6.10^7. This search has yielded 9 new groups,..all of order 4. **1972** C. S. Ogilvy *Tomorrow's Math* (ed. 2) v. 113 The numbers 12496→14288→15472→14536→14264→12496 form what has been called a sociable chain of 5 links... The sum of factors of 12496 is 14288, the sum of factors of 14288 is 15472, and so on around the chain.

B. *sb.* **1.** Restrict † *Obs.* to sense in Dict. and add: **b.** A sociable person. *rare.*

1927 A. Huxley *Proper Studies* 190 The ratio of solitaries to sociables will remain much as it is.

2. a. (Earlier example.)

1780 *Pennsylvania Jrnl. & Weekly Advertiser* 15 Mar. 4/1 Wanted to exchange, a neat sulkey, almost new, for a sociable or one horse chair, equally good.

c. (Examples.)

1851 C. Cist *Sketches & Statistics of Cincinnati in 1851* 202 Dressing bureaus, sociables, and *vis-à-vis* are sure to catch the visitor's eye, and to open the visitor's purse. **1872** *Atlantic Monthly* May 544 She was lying on a little sociable or sofa, as he entered. **1930** V. Sackville-West *Edwardians* iii. 133 In the centre of the room stood a sociable..on which two persons might sit, facing one another, but properly divided by the arm and wriggle of the S. **1959** *Times* 8 Aug. 9/4, I would venture to claim for something like the double sofa of the illustration the honour of representing the ideals of this whole decade... The seats revolve so that the two occupants—there is ample space for broad backs and expansive crinolines—have room for manoeuvre. It was called a 'sociable'. **1961** L. G. G. Ramsey *Connoisseur New Guide Antique Eng. Furnit.* 120 The variant known as the 'sociable', 'conversation sofa', or 'tête-à-tête', with the two ends facing each other on the lines of the French 'causeuse'..was popular for a short time during the 1840's, but seems to have already gone out of favour by the mid-1850's.

social, *a.* and *sb.* Add: **4. a.** (Further examples.) *social evening* (later examples); similarly *social tea.*

1785 Boswell *Jrnl. Tour Hebr.* 142 His benevolent, gay, social intercourse. **1857** Dickens *Little Dorrit* ii. xiv. 441 He took pains, on all social occasions, to draw Mr Sparkler out. **1877** *Independent* 8 Feb. 4/3 The social event of the season! **1887** [see Visit *sb* 1 a]. **1896** W. James *Mem. & Stud.* (1911) i. 3 On this social occasion it has seemed that what Agassiz stood for in the way of character and influence is the more fitting to commemorate. **1899** J. London *Let.* 17 Apr. (1966) 28 So you grow a-weary of the social whirl. **1911** G. Stratton-Porter *Harvester* xvi. 342 Wait until afternoon, and pretend you are making a social call. **1915** F. M. Hueffer *Good Soldier* iii. iv. 178 He would dine and pass the evening..at social functions of one kind or another. **1926** Social tea [see *bridge roll* s.v. *bridge *sb.*² c]. **1943** G. Greene *Ministry of Fear* iii. ii. 193 Haven't we met—? ..On one of the doctor's social evenings. **1946** L. P. Hartley *Sixth Heaven* iii. 67 We saw him chattering away... He loves the social round. **1958** A. Huxley *Let.* 20 Oct. (1969) 855, I have been revolving in the social whirl—seeing everybody. **1959** B. Bernardi *Mugwe, Failing Prophet* i. 6 Social intercourse between the main section of the Tharaka and the Thagichu has never been broken off. **1976** *Eastern Even. News* (Norwich) 9 Dec. 12/7 Patients of St. Andrews Hospital, Thorpe, enjoyed a social evening in the Octagon Centre at the hospital. **1977** P. Scott *Staying On* (1978) xiii. 204 In all the years they'd known one another they had never exchanged social visits. **1980** *Jewish Chron.* 4 Jan. 9/3 Brighton and Hove Emunah held a social tea at the Talmud Torah hall of Hove Hebrew Congregation.

c. Of, relating to, or connected with fashionable or leisured society (cf. Society 3 c). See also *social column, social register*, sense 12 below.

1873 Trollope *Eustace Diamonds* iii. lxxviii. 331 The police..had..succeeded in sending two scoundrels out of the social world, probably for life. **1894** *Harper's New Monthly Mag.* Oct. 697/2 But who looked so far from their faces, so certain to reveal the types of all styles of the beauty of our theatrical and social queens? **1896** M. Corelli *Thelma* II. ii. ii. 137 In the social world, Fashion, the capricious deity, must be followed. **1903** A. Bennett *Truth about Author* vi. 80 The editor was enchanted with my social paragraphs. **1911** M. Corelli *Life Everlasting* xi. 237 It was supposed then..that as I found myself the possessor of an income of between five and six thousand a year, I would naturally..enter upon what is called a social career. **1925** *Ladies' Home Jrnl.* Apr. 163/3 After you married Jack Hollsworth you went into a sort of social eclipse and almost kept out of things entirely. **1930** G. B. Shaw *Apple Cart* i. 39 The King's displeasure is still a sentence of social death within range of St James's Palace. **1938** L. Bemelmans *Life Class* II. v. 164 Their committee selected their dates..at the beginning of the season, but late enough to give them some knowledge of the social calendar. **1977** G. Scott *Hot Pursuit* v. 51 Little country towns where the social calendar revolved gently around race meetings and the seasons.

5. c. (Earlier and further examples.)

1792 N. Webster in E. E. Ford *Notes on Life of N. Webster* (1912) I. 363 A number of Gentlemen meet at my house for the purpose of forming a social Club. **1817** Coleridge *Biographia Literaria* II. xxii. 136 In the social circles of private life we often find a striking use of the latter put a stop to the general flow of conversation. **1843** Mill *Logic* II. iv. v. 264 The accident that one of the words was used and not the other on a particular occasion or in a particular social circle. **1872** B. Jerrold *London* xix. 155 The [Covent Garden] piazzas..where a few noteworthy social clubs still linger. **1935** *Burlington Mag.* Apr. 161/2 All social circles allied to the Court. **1966** J. Cleary *High Commissioner* ix. 185 He..belonged to none of the social clubs. He played golf..at a public course. **1977** *Evening Post* (Nottingham) 24 Jan. 7/6 But the couple who lived there escaped with their lives—because just two hours earlier a neighbour had persuaded them to go with him to a local social club.

d. Of a room, a building, etc.: used for friendly intercourse or association. See also *social centre*, sense 12 below.

1889 Kipling *From Sea to Sea* (1899) I. xxii. 426 The ladies' saloon..according to American custom, was labelled 'Social Hall'. **1975** C. Potok *In Beginning* (1976) iv. 234 After the service we all went to the social hall downstairs and there was wine and whiskey and cake.

6. a. (Further examples.)

1842 *Boston Quarterly Rev.* 184 Man is a social Being. **1966** G. N. Leech *Eng. in Advertising* i. 3 Yet the study of language can be regarded as central to man's study of himself, whether as an individual or as a social being.

c. *social whale* (earlier example); = *pilot whale* s.v. Pilot *sb.* 6.

1865 H. D. Thoreau *Cape Cod* vii. 130 In the summer and fall sometimes, hundreds of blackfish (the Social Whale..)..are driven ashore.

7. a, b. (Earlier and further examples.)

1695 Locke *Some Thoughts concerning Educ.* (ed. 3) 191 Careful guard ought to be kept over them [*sc.* children]; and every least slip in this great social vertue taken notice of and rectified. *a* **1704** —— *Conduct of Understanding* (1754) 164 We should love our neighbour as ourselves, is such a fundamental truth for the regulating human society, that, I think, by that alone, one might without difficulty, determine all the cases and doubts in social morality. **1801** M. Edgeworth *Belinda* (1833) I. xvi. 135 His social prejudices were such as..to supply the place of the power and habit of reasoning. **1814** M. Birkbeck *Journey through France* 22 The labouring class here is certainly much higher, on the social scale, than with us. **1830** J. S. Mill *Let.* 9 Feb. in *Wks.* (1963) XII. 48 Those parts of our social institutions and policy which at present oppose improvement. **1833** —— in *Monthly Repos.* VII. 801 The St. Simonians are, just now, the only association of public writers existing in the world who systematically stir up from the foundation all the great social questions. **1843** Social phenomenon [see Historical *a.* (*sb.*) 2 c]. *a* **1854** Mill *Draft Autobiogr.* (1961) 173 The social problem of the future we considered to be, how to unite the greatest individual liberty of action with an equal ownership of all in the raw material of the globe & an equal participation of all in the benefits of combined labour. **1856** Geo. Eliot in *Westm. Rev.* X. 70 The study of at least one social group—namely, the factory operatives. **1857** *Edin. Rev.* CVI. 223 Goethe's early experiences at first led him to view the whole social fabric with contempt. **1858** Trollope *Dr. Thorne* I. i. 2 Its social graces, and the general air of clanship which pervades it [*sc.* Barsetshire]. **1859** Thackeray *Virginians* II. xxxiii. 266 To marry without a competence is..a crime against our social codes. **1861** J. S. Mill in *Fraser's Mag.* Dec. 672/1 This is the highest abstract standard of social and distributive justice. **1863** *Home & Foreign Rev.* Oct. 546 The multiplicity of her characters,..the richness of her social backgrounds. **1864** Social hierarchy [see Hierarchy 4]. **1869** Mill *Subj. Women* iv. 163 Self-respect, self-help, and self-control..are the essential conditions both of individual prosperity and of social virtue. **1871** A. C. Fraser *Life of Berkeley* ii. 88 He was shocked by the tone of social morality, which so appallingly greeted him on his return. **1876** H. Spencer *Princ. Sociol.* I. iii. ii. 629 After welfare of the social group and welfare of progeny, comes welfare of parents. **1887** J. Bascom *Sociol.* i. 9 But, with fitting modifications, they shape also the social contact of diverse ranks. **1887** J. Payn *Holiday Tasks* 123 If people would only say what they really think concerning this and that..social life would be much more interesting. **1892** Social welfare [see Welfare *sb.* 1]. **1897** *Amer. Jrnl. Sociol.* Nov. 343 As we say in sociological language, there was a very low degree of social consciousness. **1901** W. James *Mem. & Stud.* (1911) vii. 150 There are social prejudices which scientific men themselves obey. **1901** *Amer. Jrnl. Sociol.* Nov. 399 He makes a better home and moves upward in the social scale, perhaps, faster than the immigrant from any other country. **1902** Social justice [see *environmental *a.*]. **1911** M. Corelli *Life Everlasting* ix. 210 He doesn't fit into any accepted social code at all. **1927** B. Russell *Outl. Philos.* ii. 27 Knowledge..as a social phenomenon..is something displayed in bodily movements. **1935** H. Edib *Clown & his Daughter* xxv. 137 The shadow of a social barrier was added to the damnable shadow of separation! **1935** T. S. Eliot *Murder in Cathedral* ii. 80 There are times when violence is the only way in which social justice can be secured. **1938** L. MacNeice *I crossed Minch* ix. 130 A mind must be conditioned by education and social context. **1940** *Economist* 5 Oct. 428/1 More than two decades of extremely divergent developments in contrasting social climates had to be undone. **1947** *Mind* LVI. 327 If we speak of 'social problems', that is something different. **1949** M. Fortes *Social Structure* 55 The British House of Commons is a familiar instance of growth in social institutions and organization. **1955** T. Williams in S. J. Kunitz *20th Cent. Authors* Suppl. I. 1088/1 In St. Louis we suddenly discovered there were two kinds of people, the rich and the poor, and that we belonged more to the latter... It was the beginning of the social-consciousness which I think has marked most of my writing. **1957** *Practical Wireless* XXXIII. 727/2 (Advt.), You get a welcome break from the usual routine, with sports, games and a great social life. **1964** M. Argyle *Psychol. & Social Probl.* xvi. 199 In limited spheres advice is also given by social scientists,..on the social welfare of the old, young, and poor. **1966** G. N. Leech *Eng. in Advertising* v. 49 Slang and familiar forms of language..help..to fix the identity and social background of the speaker. **1967** Social mix [see *mix *sb.*[2] 1 a]. **1970** *Guardian* 3 June 8/6 The Arts Council and its affiliated agencies..are seen as a vital part of the social fabric for which society must be responsible. **1970** F. C. Weffort in I. L. Horowitz *Masses in Lat. Amer.* xi. 391 It legalized the 'social question'; that is, it formally recognised that the masses have a right to express their aspirations. **1974** in *Wertheim's Evolution & Revolution* 91 In looking for the structural features of social life we look first for the existence of social groups of all kinds. **1978** *Bookseller* 17 June 3186/3 A school with only 170 children, a high percentage of whom have severe social problems. **1981** G. Priestland *Priestland's Progress* ii. 34 The compilers of the gospels had other things on their minds than ..Jewish social problems. **1982** *Times* 14 June 9/5 The bribery, abuse of privilege, and indifference to social welfare on his own [*sc.* the Labour Party] side.

c. (Earlier and later examples.)

1835 H. Reeve tr. *de Tocqueville's Democracy in Amer.* II. ix. 256 The Anglo-Americans settled in the New World in a state of social equality. **1840** *Ibid.* IV. iii. xii. 106 They have allowed the social inferiority of woman to subsist. **1840** J. S. Mill in *Westm. Rev.* Mar. 262 The demoralizing effect of great inequalities in wealth and social rank. *a* **1876** H. Martineau *Autobiogr.* (1877) (ed. 3) I. 297 Norwich..has now no claims to social superiority. **1885** W. Harris *Hist. Radical Party* xvii. 429 Whigs and Conservatives alike desired..conditions and limitations which should preserve power to the same social class which had now the control of so many of the constituencies. **1888** E. Bellamy *Looking Backward* xi. 164 Who are willing to be domestic servants..where all are social equals? Our ladies found it hard enough to find such even when there was little pretense of social equality. **1917** N. Douglas *South Wind* xxxix. 453 Her home broken up; her child a bastard; herself and Meadows—social outcasts. **1925** *New Yorker* 11 July 6/1 The fact that Davis is a social outcast because of his want of faith..wouldn't cut any ice. **1928** Mrs. Belloc Lowndes *Diary* 20 Feb. (1971) 113 One of Curzon's most unfortunate peculiarities was his rudeness to those whom he considered his social inferiors. **1934** M. V. Hughes *London Child of Seventies* xiii. 159 One must never suppose that any other people whatsoever are one's social superiors. **1944** L. P. Hartley *Shrimp & Anemone* xiv. 200 The social superiority of the South over all parts of England. **1948** 'G. Orwell' in *Observer* 28 Nov. 4/4 The social misfit..should learn to be contented in his own station. **1958** J. K. Galbraith *Affluent Society* vi. 55 In the central tradition of economic theory, the existence of social classes—of capitalists, middle class, and proletarians—was only surreptitiously conceded. **1964** T. B. Bottomore *Elites & Society* i. 23 S. F. Nadel..emphasizes 'social superiority' as the distinguishing feature of an elite. **1967** A. L. Lloyd *Folk Song in Eng.* ii. 86 The medieval peasant..his illiteracy, his social inferiority. **1970** N. A. Victoria in I. L. Horowitz *Masses in Lat. Amer.* xv. 549 Among the remaining social classes, the split was reflected in general skepticism. **1973** *Listener* 28 June 863/2 The Industrial Revolution..became in time a social revolution and established that social equality on which we all depend.

e. *Social Sciences.* Pertaining or due to the interrelations resulting from an individual's association with others or connected with the functions and structures necessary to membership of a group or society. Also *transf.* in *Zool.*

There is no rigid demarcation between this sense and the primary meaning of 7 a and b; the examples given illustrate some of the uses commonly found among writers on the social sciences.

1840 J. S. Mill in *Edin. Rev.* Oct. 5 By Democracy M. de Tocqueville understands equality of conditions; the absence of all aristocracy, whether constituted by political privileges, or by superiority in individual importance and social power. **1843** Social organism [see Dynamics 1 b]. **1852** J. S. Mill in *Westm. Rev.* II. 380 Attention is due to those opinions and feelings,..not as matter of history, but as social forces in present being. **1861** —— *Repr. Govt.* iii. 68 Where this school of public spirit does not exist, scarcely any sense is entertained that private persons, in no eminent social situation, owe any duties to society, except to obey the laws and submit to the government. **1876** H. Spencer *Princ. Sociol.* I. ii. iii. 487 That social integration that results from the clustering of clusters, is joined with augmentation of the number contained by each cluster. **1877** G. H. Lewes *Problems* III. 5 A new factor, namely, the social factor. **1878** W. James *Let.* 25 Nov. in R. B. Perry *Tht. & Char. of W. James* (1935) II. 35 Their only weakness would lie in the fact of their social environment not recognizing this as the ultimate interest. **1890** —— *Princ. Psychol.* I. x. 293 A man's Social Self is the recognition which he gets from his mates. **1904** —— *Mem. & Stud.* (1911) vi. 138 It would never occur to a reader of his [*sc.* Spencer's] pages that a social force proper might be anything that acted as a stimulus of social change. **1905** A. W. Small *Gen. Sociol.* xxvii. 381 It is the factor which is essential in the end, to economize and co-ordinate all the details of social adjustment. **1920** Thomas & Znaniecki *Polish Peasant* IV. p. xii, Many individuals..consider the social isolation and relatively low cultural level of the peasant communities an undesirable phenomenon. **1934** C. W. Morris in G. H. Mead *Mind, Self & Soc.* p. xvi, Though not used by Mead, the term 'social behaviorism' may serve to characterize the relation of Mead's position to that of John B. Watson. **1936** M. Sherif *Psychol. of Social Norms* 3 We shall consider customs, traditions, standards, rules, values, fashions, and all other criteria of conduct which are standardized as a consequence of the contact of individuals, as specific cases of 'social norms'. **1936** *Amer. Jrnl. Orthopsychiatry* VI. 416 (*title*) Trends in social therapy. **1941** Miller & Dollard (*title*) Social learning and imitation. **1941** *Mind* L. 396 Boodin's reflections on society and the social behaviour of men have, obviously, been deeply influenced by these two special sorts of experiences. **1944** *Mind* LIII. 351 It is said to be evident 'on evolutionary grounds' that the individual is 'higher than the state or the social organism'. **1945** E. Mayo *Social Problems of Industrial Civilization* i. 13 Social skill shows itself as a capacity to receive communications from others, and to respond to the attitudes and ideas of others in such fashion as to promote congenial participation in a common task. **1949** M. Mead *Male & Female* i. 10 None of these powers—to kill individuals, to destroy the social integration of groups..are new. **1951** Gerth & Bramstedt tr. *Mannheim's Freedom, Power & Democratic Planning* i. 6 By social techniques I refer to all methods of influencing human behavior so that it fits into the prevailing patterns of social interaction and organization. **1959** W. F. Leopold in J. A. Fishman *Readings Sociol. of Lang.* (1968) 349 The colloquial standard [speech] of an individual has several layers suitable for a variety of social situations. **1964** M. Argyle *Psychol. & Social Probl.* viii. 108 Social factors are of considerable importance in job satisfaction, according to a number of early studies. **1975** E. O. Wilson *Sociobiol.* ii. vii. 160/1 Although the development of 'social behavior' has not been analyzed in these animals, the visible responses are..elementary and stereotyped. **1978** D. Grylls *Guardians & Angels* i. 31 Traherne..blames the social environment instead of original sin.

9. a. (Earlier and further examples.)

1833 J. S. Mill in *Monthly Repos.* VII. 269 An error which many..of our social reformers, habitually fall into. **1859** G. A. Sala *Twice Round Clock* 36, I am glad to observe, for the edification of social economists. **1885** W. Harris *Hist. Radical Party* vii. 120 Some immediate remedy such as the Spencean and other social theorists had to offer. **1919** Branford & Geddes *Coming Polity* (ed. 2) iii. i. 223 Compound these three insurgent types of social critic..and you have the disorders of Revolution. **1926** B. Webb *My Apprenticeship* v. 217 In comparison with the preceding generation of social researchers, I suggest that his [*sc.* Charles Booth's] method of analysis constitutes..the first sign-post directing the student on one of the main ways to discovery. **1931** *Times Lit. Suppl.* 22 Oct. 809/2 Like the work of so many of the 'social' novelists of his period, it is to a large extent a sort of narrative journalism of contemporary events. **1941** J. S. Huxley *Uniqueness of Man* xi. 251 Our social planners would undoubtedly benefit from a study of the evolution of individuality in animals. **1949** M. Fortes *Social Structure* p. ix, Their theme was the comparative study of human society by the methods of the natural sciences, and the difference between such studies and those of social philosophers. **1970** R. A. H. Robinson *Origins of Franco's Spain* v. 224 In the terminology of European Catholic thought, the Spanish Monarchists of the 1930s were social-romantics, the *Cedistas* social-reformists. **1970** *Guardian* 7 Aug. 10/5 [Notting Hill's] over-exposure is the result of the number of social agencies and sheer do-gooders that have moved into the area.

b. (Earlier and further examples.)

1828 J. S. Mill in *Westm. Rev.* IX. 257 In political and social philosophy his [*sc.* Sir Walter Scott's] principles are all summed up in the orthodox one, that whatever is English is best. **1835** H. Reeve tr. *de Tocqueville's Democracy in America* I. ii. 23 The..main ideas which constitute the basis of the social theory of the United States. **1836** J. S. Mill in *Westm. Rev.* XXVI. 11 *Laws* of society, or laws of human nature in the social state..form the subject of a branch of science which may be aptly designated from the title of *social economy*; somewhat less happily by that of *speculative politics*, or the *science* of politics, as contra-distinguished from the art. **1837** —— in *Ibid.* XXVIII. 100 These men raised the cry of social reform. **1887** B. Webb *My Apprenticeship* (1926) 418 Seeking justification in social research. **1899** *Amer. Jrnl. Sociol.* May 765 But they have all come by experience to discover that the social ethics of Christianity can indeed supply a moral basis of a general kind for social work and social politics. **1901** *Amer. Jrnl. Sociol.* Jan. 472 We have a social technology—a system of conscious and purposeful organization of persons in which every actual, natural social organization finds its true place, and all factors..cooperate to realize an increasing aggregate and better proportions of the 'health, wealth, beauty, knowledge, sociability, and rightness' desires. **1914** G. B. Shaw *Dark Lady of Sonnets* 129 Our plays of poverty and squalor..will then be..read only by historical students of social pathology. **1914** *New Republic* 14 Nov. 28/2 The author believes that one way to write best sellers is to write filth. This is not as it should be. These two propositions, taken together, are social criticism. **1920** W. R. Sorley *Hist. Eng. Philos.* xii. 265 Maurice's..work, both in social reform and in religion, derived stimulus and direction from philosophical ideas. **1931** *Proc. Nat. Conf. Social Work 1930* 448 Social planning suggests activity on the part of groups in making planning effective in action. **1937** L. C. Knights in *Scrutiny* VI. 137 It is just possible to claim that Restoration comedy contains 'social criticism' in its handling of 'the vulgar'. **1949** *Mind* LVIII. 383 'Social theory' is the general study of the whole field of social phenomena. **1957** P. Coveney *Poor Monkey* iv. 54 The social novel of Disraeli, Mrs. Gaskell, and Kingsley..represents something essential to the literary consciousness of the age. **1964** M. Argyle *Psychol. & Social Probl.* xvi. 202 Another objection to social planning is that it is felt to increase the power of the state and restrict individual freedom. **1976** *Listener* 3 June 705/3 A different style of thought in social philosophy..post-Marxist critique. **1979** A.

Easson *Elizabeth Gaskell* ii. 61 *Mary Barton* and *North and South* are often spoken of in the context of social fiction. **1980** *Times* 9 Jan. 10/3 The British tradition of politically committed social research.

c. Of activities, etc., carried out (esp. by government agencies) to improve the condition of society or for the benefit of society as a whole.

1964 *Times Rev. Industry & Technol.* Jan. 65/3 The large backlog in 'social' investments—schools, hospitals, public and private housing. **1965** B. Pearce tr. *Preobrazhensky's New Economics* 222 Where the tractor is acquired by society as a whole it will facilitate the transition to the social cultivation of the land throughout the countryside. **1973** *Listener* 1 Mar. 287/2 Love of the poor needs social legislation to stiffen it up. **1977** *Spare Rib* Jan. 25/1 Legislation is ineffectual while cuts in social spending continue.

10. *social chauvinism*, a communist term for the attitude or action of a socialist party which supports the non-socialist government of its country in the prosecution of a war; so *social chauvinist* sb. and adj.; *social democracy*, (the advocacy of) a socialist system achieved by democratic means (formerly also a general term for socialism and communism); *social democrat* (further examples); also applied *spec.* to a member of the communist party in Russia and elsewhere; now applied chiefly to one who advocates the achievement of socialism by democratic means; *esp.* in the U.K., a member of the Social Democratic Party; hence *social democratic* adj., now *esp.* in the U.K. designating a party founded in March 1981 by a group of former Labour MPs; also in extended use; *social fascist*, term used by communists for a member of any other left-wing party (implying the identity of non-communist socialism with fascism); hence *social fascism*; *social-imperialism*, a term used at one time in China (and occas. elsewhere) for policies held to conceal imperialist aims beneath a socialist veneer; hence *social imperialist*; *social revolutionary* adj., advocating or supporting social revolution (applied *spec.* to a former political party in Russia); also as *sb.*

1976 H. T. Willetts tr. *A. Solzhenitsyn's Lenin in Zurich* 256 'The development of the international socialist movement', he [*sc.* Lenin] wrote, 'is moving slowly..but definitely in the direction of "a break" with opportunism and social chauvinism.' **1957** R. N. Carew Hunt *Guide to Communist Jargon* xliv. 147 The social chauvinists are the socialist leaders who were supporting their bourgeois governments in prosecuting the war as one of national defence. **1974** J. White tr. *Poulantzas's Fascism & Dictatorship* iv. ii. 185 It was during this same period, mainly after 1930, that the *social-chauvinist* side of KPD policy grew decisively. **1888** G. B. Shaw in *Fabian Essays in Socialism* (1889) 183 What then does a gradual transition to Social Democracy mean specifically? It means the gradual extension of the franchise; and the transfer of rent and interest to the State. **1928** [see *centrist b]. **1947** *Vogue* May 104/3 Sweden represents the best way of existence a flourishing social-democracy has yet found. **1974** J. White tr. *Poulantzas's Fascism & Dictatorship* iv. i. 151 Social democracy, except sometimes in revolutionary periods, has in principle a permanent mass basis in a capitalist formation. **1981** *Times* 10 Mar. 1/6 Mr Jenkins said that 'well before Easter' the Council for Social Democracy would have been turned into the Social Democrat Party. **1881** Social democrat [see *proletariate, -at 2 a]. **1918** [see *minimalist 1]. **1947** *Partisan Rev.* XIV. 312 Barea was one of those gray murky middle-class Social Democrats who made of his adherence a means of avoiding rather than of engaging in political thought. **1965** *New Statesman* 14 May 753/2 A preference for the Social Democrat stronghold [*sc.* Berlin] over the Christian Democrat capital [*sc.* Bonn]. **1974** tr. *Sniečkus's Soviet Lithuania* 13 During the revolution, increasing numbers of Lithuanian Social-Democrats urged that their party unite with the Russian Social-Democratic Labour Party. **1981** *Times* 26 Mar. 14/8 We have gained the sympathy of a quarter of Britain's voters, and between a third and two-fifths if Social Democrats fight together with Liberals. **1870** *Times* 10 Oct. 3/2 General von Falkenstein has issued the following order:— 'The prohibition to hold social Democratic meetings is rescinded.' **1887** [see International *a.* b]. **1893** [in Dict., sense 11]. **1966** I. Deutscher in *Marxism in Our Time* (1972) 36 Trotsky..represents the Marxist school of thought in its purity, as it existed before its debasement by the social-democratic and Stalinist orthodoxies. **1975** *Times Lit. Suppl.* 23 May 563/4 Recommendations which ranged from orthodox socialist models to moderately social-democratic solutions. **1981** *Guardian* 26 Mar. 4/8 The Social Democratic Party will be launched today. **1981** *Times* 12 Dec. 7/1 It is essential..to divine in good time which of the two mutually exclusive positions on the subject [of snow] will be taken by each person one meets. As far as snow is concerned, there is no middle ground, no Social Democratic stance. **1941** 'G. Orwell' in V. Gollancz *Betrayal of Left* 210 All orthodox Communists were committed to the belief that 'Social-fascism' (i.e. Socialism) was the real enemy of the workers. **1974** J. White tr. *Poulantzas's Fascism & Dictatorship* iv. i. 149 It was no accident that the theory of social fascism was unfailingly accompanied by the identification of fascism with the other forms of bourgeois State. *a* **1937** J. Bell in *Essays, Poems & Lett.* (1938) ii. 294 'The adversary.' He takes the form of an enthusiastic member of the Young Communist League and he bellows incessantly. That I am a social-democratic, social-fascist, weak-kneed traitor. That I am a bourgeois intellectual. **1961** [see *Fascist *sb.* and *a.*]. **1975** *Guardian* 19 Mar. 2/3 Their [*sc.* the Portuguese Maoists'] stated philosophy is that the Armed Forces movement, the Communist Party, and other left-wing groups are 'Social Fascists'. **1965** tr. *Lenin's Tasks of Third International* in *Coll. Works* XXIX. 502 'Fabian imperialism' and 'social-imperialism' are one and the same thing: socialism in words, imperialism in deeds. **1971** Social imperialism [see *revisionist *a.*]. **1978** Hua Kuo-feng in *Peking Rev.* 10 Mar. 35/2 The people's struggle against them, and in particular against Soviet social-imperialism, is on a higher upsurge than ever. **1974** *China Reconstructs* July 4/1 The Soviet revisionist social-imperialists bill Confucius as 'the most holy sage and foremost teacher of China.' **1907** Social revolutionary [see *integralist *sb.*]. **1918** [see *minimalist 1]. **1931** E. Wilson *Axel's Castle* viii. 270 He [*sc.* Rimbaud] had flamed up, at the fall of the Second Empire, with social-revolutionary idealism. **1978** *Listener* 17 Aug. 206/2 Lenin proposed that the land should be given to the peasants. The indignant social revolutionaries shouted out, 'But that's our programme..and you have opposed it.'

11. *social-conscious*, *-cultural*, *-economic*, *-emotional*, *-ethical*, *-minded*, *-philosophical*, *-political* (earlier example), *-relational*, *-situational*.

1856 Geo. Eliot in *Westm. Rev.* X. 68 The views at which he has arrived.., he sums up in the term—*social-political-conservatism*. **1919** M. Beer *Hist. Brit. Socialism* I. i. v. 71 A serious contribution to social-economic speculation. **1932** *Addresses & Proc. Nat. Educ. Assoc. of U.S.* LXX. 231 It has been thought that social-economic planning in the United States would break down our democratic form of government. **1939** A. Huxley *After Many a Summer* ii. v. 229 For these..'normality' in sexual behaviour would be quite different from what it was for the more social-minded. **1940** K. Mannheim *Ideology & Utopia* 35 The discovery of the social-situational roots of thought at first, therefore, took the form of unmasking. **1942** C. Himes *Black on Black* (1973) 183 His social-conscious protestations of hurt had leapt the bounds of amateur sincerity. **1951** Parsons & Shils *Toward General Theory of Action* i. i. 18 Fundamentals of behavior psychology..primary viscerogenic and possibly social-relational needs, cognition and learning. **1956** J. Klein *Study of Groups* viii. 118 Social-emotional behaviour. **1960** C. S. Lewis *Studies in Words* i. 22 Thus from the very first the social-ethical meaning, merely by existing, is bound to separate itself from the status-meaning. **1970** A. G. Frank in I. L. Horowitz *Masses in Lat. Amer.* vi. 220 There are undoubtedly differences in..various social-cultural indices between the self-built and the other two types of low-income urban settlements. **1977** A. Giddens *Stud. in Social & Polit. Theory* viii. 291 Durkheim..was very critical of some features of Comte's social-philosophical writings.

12. Special collocations. **social action,** deliberate action that results in the restructuring of institutions or a change in the conditions of life in a society; **social anthropology,** the study of (esp. primitive) peoples comparatively through their kinship systems, associations, institutions, culture, etc., and the forces that affect their social systems; hence **social anthropological** *a.*, **social anthropologist**; **social benefit,** (*a*) a benefit to society resulting from technological innovation and the like; (*b*) a benefit (*benefit *sb.* 4 d) payable under a system of social security; **social butterfly,** a person who flits from one social entertainment to another or is chiefly occupied with social activities, a socialite; **social case-work, case-worker** = *case-work, *case-worker; **social causation,** the causation of human actions by social factors, or their analysis in these terms; **social centre,** any place in which people gather for communal activities, recreations, etc., *esp.* a building designed for this purpose; **social change,** change in the customs, institutions, or culture of a society brought about by some new, esp. technological or ideological, element; **social character** (see quots.); **social climber,** one who seeks to advance himself socially, esp. by gaining acceptance in fashionable society; hence (as back-formations) **social climb** *sb.* and *v. intr.*, **social climbing** *vbl. sb.* and *ppl. a.*; **social column,** a column in a newspaper or magazine that reports the activities of members of fashionable or leisured society; hence **social columnist**; **social compact** = *social contract*, below; **social conscience,** a conscience that is sensitive to or preoccupied with the problems and injustices of society; **social contract,** (*a*) (see sense 7 b in Dict.) (*b*) *transf.*, a mutual agreement between specific groups or elements within a society; **social control,** control of the individual by the social group to which he belongs; control by government, on behalf of society as a whole, of particular sectors of society; **social cost,** the cost to society in terms of effort, ill-health, inconvenience, etc., of some enterprise or innovation; **social cycle** (see quot. 1963); **social Darwinism** *Sociol.*, the Darwinian theory of evolution extended and applied to various aspects of the concept of social progress; hence **social Darwinist** *sb.* and *a.*; **social deprivation,** deprivation of social interaction or of the ordinary benefits of social life; **social dialectology,** the study of the dialects spoken by particular social groups; hence **social dialectologist; social differentiation,** the process whereby a group or community becomes separate or distinct; the process whereby the different roles and functions of individuals become institutionalized; **social disease,** any social evil such as poverty, starvation, etc.; *spec. U.S.*, venereal disease (orig. a euphemism); **social disorganization** (see quot. 1920); **social distance** *Social Psychol.*, (*a*) the degree of remoteness that a member of one social group would like to exist or feels to exist between himself and the members of another, expressed (for example) in terms of the relationships to which he would admit them; (*b*) the physical distance between individuals that they find acceptable in social contexts; **social document,** a literary work embodying an authentic and informative description of the social conditions of its time; also *transf.*; **social drinking** *vbl. sb.*, the drinking of alcoholic liquor as a stimulus to, or an accompaniment of, social intercourse; hence as *ppl. a.* and (as back-formations) **social drink** *sb.*, **social drinker; social dynamics,** (the branch of sociology treating of) the forces at work in social change; **social engineering** orig. *U.S.*, the application of sociological principles to specific social problems; hence **social engineer,** a specialist in this field; **social evolution:** see *evolution 9; **social fact,** something originating in the institutions or culture of a society which affects the behaviour or attitudes of the individual member of that society; **social geography** (see quot. 1929); hence **social geographer; social gospel,** an understanding of the gospel as having especially a social application; used esp. with reference to many U.S. churchmen of the late nineteenth and early twentieth centuries who advocated social reform through the Christian gospel; also *gen.*, a message of salvation for society; **social history,** (*a*) the history of social behaviour or of society (the usual sense); (*b*) the background and circumstances of a social worker's client; hence (in sense (*a*)) **social historian, social-historical** *a.*; **social inquiry report** (see quot. 1967); **social insurance,** the insurance of the citizen against loss of income through sickness, unemployment, etc., with the participation of the government and the employer; also in extended use and *attrib.*; **social lie,** an untrue statement designed to facilitate social relations; hence **social liar; social medicine** (see quot. 1925); **social mobility** = *mobility[1] 1 c; **social mobilization** *Sociol.*, (see quot. 1961); **social morphology,** (the study of) the various forms of social structure and the changes that take place within them or govern them; **social order,** (*a*) orderliness within society, absence of disorder and unrest; (*b*) the way in which society is organized at a given time, the constituted social system; **social organization:** see *organization 2 c; **social position:** see *position *sb.* 9 b; **social process,** a pattern that can be discerned in the way a society coheres and adapts to change over a period of years; **social psychiatry,** the branch of mental health concerned with the social causes and social consequences of mental illness and with the various social methods which may be used to treat such illness; hence **social psychiatric** *a.*, **social psychiatrist; social psychology,** the study of human behaviour as it is affected by social factors; hence **social-psychological** *a.*, **social psychologist;** cf. *collective psychology* s.v. *collective *a.* 2 d; **social realism,** realism in art and literature that has a specifically social or political content or message; sometimes applied *spec.* to a movement in U.S. art in the 1930s; also *attrib.*;

hence **social realist** *sb.* and *a.*, **social realistic** *a.*; **social reality,** a conception of what exists that is affected by the customs and beliefs of the group; **social register** orig. *U.S.*, a register or directory of those who are socially prominent; *transf.*, a union black list; also *attrib.* or as *adj.*; **social releaser** = *RELEASER c; **social revolution,** a revolution in the structure and nature of society; *spec.* that anticipated or fostered by socialists and communists (cf. *social revolutionary a.* and *sb.*, sense 10 above); **social role** = *RÔLE 2; **social secretary,** a secretary whose function it is to make arrangements for the social activities of a person or society; **social space** *Sociol.*, the 'space', in terms of the difference in social position or individual freedom of action, that is felt to exist between one person and another; **social statics** *Sociol.*, the study of the organization and structure of a stable society or social group; **social status:** see *STATUS 3; **social stratification,** the division of society into strata based on social position or class; **social strata, stratum:** see *STRATUM 6; **social structure,** the established set of customs, relationships, institutions, etc., of which a social system is composed; hence **social structural** *a.*; **social studies,** an inclusive term for various aspects or branches of the study of human society; **social survey,** a comprehensive and detailed examination of some aspect of the social life, history, problems, etc., of a particular locality; **social system,** a set of interdependent relationships, customs, institutions, etc., that constitute a society; **social table** (see quot. 1952); **social unit,** an individual considered as one of the separate parts of which a society or group is composed; a community or group considered as having a separate identity within a larger whole; **social wage** (see quot. 1975); also *transf.*; **social will,** a term for the desires regarding the affairs of a society or group expressed by its members in general.

1853 H. MARTINEAU tr. *Comte's Positive Philos.* II. viii. 246 Its distinctive social action..was well represented by the noble Fabricius. **1873** H. SPENCER *Study of Sociol.* i. 2 Minds in which the conceptions of social actions are thus rudimentary, are also minds ready to harbour wild hopes of benefits to be achieved by administrative agencies. **1937** T. PARSONS (*title*) The structure of social action. **1951** R. FIRTH *Elements of Social Organization* i. 33 No social action, no element of culture, can be adequately studied or defined in isolation. **1953** in S. Tax et al. *Appraisal of Anthropology Today* xiii. 220/2 The outline ..does not vary much from subjects..considered to be in the cultural/social-anthropological field. **1927** OGBURN & GOLDENWEISER *Social Sciences* ii. 11 Then there are the social anthropologists who make economic activity the basis of social anthropology. **1896** *Academy* 18 Jan. 49/1 Dr. Steinmetz..found processes of moral, political, and religious development so intricately entwined, that his researches had to spread far over the field of social anthropology. **1908** J. G. FRAZER *Psyche's Task* (1913) 159 (*heading*) The scope of social anthropology, an Inaugural Lecture. **1975** M. BRADBURY *History Man* ix. 147, I worked in social anthropology with him..he's certainly not a racist. **1872** GEO. ELIOT *Middlemarch* III. lvi. 241 Your neatly-carved argument for a social benefit which they [*sc.* rustics] do *not* feel. **1963** *Listener* 23 May 855/1 Dr Beesley..and I have attempted a so-called social-benefit study or, as it is sometimes called, a cost-benefit analysis, of the London Victoria line. **1963** J. R. SARGENT in M. Shanks *Lessons of Public Enterprise* xv. 250 A balancing of social benefits against social costs. **1972** *Guardian* 30 Dec. 4/1 From Monday every citizen of the nine nations..is entitled to the same pay and.. social benefits..as fellow Europeans. **1910** A. E. HOUSMAN *Let.* 4 Mar. (1971) 108 People are asking me out a great deal too often..I am not a social butterfly. **1938** D. DU MAURIER *Rebecca* ix. 117 A social butterfly, very modern and plastered with paint. **1975** D. RAMSAY *Descent into Dark* i. 15 To be a social butterfly and make my wife happy. **1917** M. E. RICHMOND *Social Diagnosis* 5 The methods and aims of social case work were or should be the same in every type of service. *Ibid.*, The ground which all social case workers could occupy in common. **1896** F. H. GIDDINGS *Princ. Sociol.* i. 20 Thus the cycle of social causation begins and ends in the physical process. **1937** R. M. MACIVER *Society* xxvi. 476 In social causation there is a logical order of relationship between the factors that we do not find in physical causation. **1964** GOULD & KOLB *Dict. Social Sciences* 647/1 There has been much discussion about the relationship between ideas of social causation and the problem of the freedom of the individual will. **1901** *Amer. Jrnl. Sociol.* Sept. 206 Is there not room for the school..in providing accessible and agreeable social centers? **1922** L. MUMFORD in H. Stearns *Civilization in U.S.* 6 The social centre and the community centre, which in a singularly hard and consciously beatific way have sought to organize fellowship and mutual aid.., are products of the last decade. **1937** *Discovery* Feb. 47/1 Social amelioration through a special milk scheme, a special housing scheme, and the encouragement of camps and social centres. **1978** J. ANDERSON *Angel of Death* v. 42 The main saloon..was the social centre of the yacht. **1836** J. S. MILL in *London & Westm. Rev.* Jan. 28 The main thing which social changes can do for the..higher classes..is gradually to put an end to every kind of unearned distinction. **1856** A. C. FRASER *Ess. Philos.* i. 11 The most memorable religious and social change which the world has witnessed since the introduction of Christianity. **1952** GERTH & MARTINDALE in *Weber's Ancient Judaism* p. xviii, A second sociological issue of concern to Weber is the examination of social changes due to territorial organization and urbanization. **1942** E. FROMM *Fear of Freedom* 239 The social character comprises only a selection of traits, the essential nucleus of the character structure of most members of a group which has developed as the result of the basic experiences and mode of life common to that group. **1961** R. H. WILLIAMS *Long Revol.* I. iii. 79 The 'social character' is a selective response to experience, a learned system of feeling and acting, in a majority of the community into which the child is born. **1975** G. HOWELL *In Vogue* 151/2 Sweaters appear... Their social climb touches its peak..over a grandly outsize evening skirt. **1962** *Sunday Express* 21 Jan. 1/3 Allegations that I was social-climbing among royalty. **1926** S. LEWIS *Mantrap* viii. 95 You sniveling little social climber! **1941** A. CHRISTIE *Evil under Sun* ix. 178 There are many of your English idioms that describe him. The rough diamond! The self-made man! The social climber! **1973** *Black World* Mar. 21 Whatever the shortcomings of our early literary efforts, they ought not be considered in the main as the reprehensible fumblings of middle-class social-climbers. **1924** W. HOLTBY *Crowded Street* xxxviii. 294 The careful tact of years of social climbing. **1927** P. SOROKIN *Social Mobility* vii. 133 There are two types of vertical mobility:..*social climbing* and *social sinking*. **1938** AUDEN & ISHERWOOD *On Frontier* III. ii. 107 A social-climbing wife and a playboy son. **1960** *Twentieth Century* Dec. 588 A political thriller about a middle-aged reporter who learns of a major scandal involving a Minister of the Crown... Good pictures of the social-climbing Minister,..and various Fleet Street characters. **1978** *Trans. Yorks. Dial. Soc.* LXXVIII. 12 He takes the opportunity to castigate the creeping hypocrisy and social climbing which had always called forth his most bitter satire. **1936** 'R. WEST' *Thinking Reed* vii. 223 A crowded paragraph in the social column of the Paris New York *Herald*. **1952** M. ALLINGHAM *Tiger in Smoke* i. 9 Every social column in the country had announced that she was about to marry him. **1976** 'R. MACDONALD' *Blue Hammer* ix. 43, I don't intend to write a social column for the rest of my life. **1976** M. GREEN *Children of Sun* vi. 209 Hannen Swaffer was the first social columnist who knew from inside the world he wrote about. **1793,** etc. Social compact [see COMPACT *sb.*[1] 1 b]. **1974** *Times* 26 Feb. 12/3 Mr Wilson has sought to defend this rubbish by arguing that a great new 'social compact' with the unions will be achieved, by the terms of which they will agree to forgo wage-increases in return for all the splendidly socialist things Mr Wilson's Government will be doing. **1883** B. POTTER *Let.* July in *Lett. Sidney & Beatrice Webb* (1978) I. 16 So ends the London Season! and I shall return with clear social conscience to my dowdy dress. **1888** G. B. SHAW in *Fabian Essays in Socialism* (1889) 185 The value of Trade Unionism in awakening the social conscience of the skilled workers. **1925** A. HUXLEY *Those Barren Leaves* I. iii. 35 When our dividends came rolling in..we did, it is true, feel almost a twinge of social conscience. **1978** *Architectural Design* 5 June 311/3 Public libraries and art galleries were built by..millionaires with a social conscience. **1967** B. R. WILLIAMS *New Social Contract* 4 In a modern industrial nation..the individual and the community enter in effect into a Social Contract, by which the group as a whole agrees to dedicate a certain part of its total assets..to the provision of benefits for its members. **1972** *Times* 3 Oct. 1/1 'We say that what Britain needs is a new social contract,' Mr Callaghan said. **1974** *Socialist Worker* 23 Nov. 3/4 The last week has seen two massive holes punched through the Social Contract. First by the Rolls-Royce workers in getting their £8 a week rise, then [etc.]. **1977** *Guardian Weekly* 11 Sept. 5/5 The greatest strength of our unarmed police force lies..in its social contract with the public. **1859** MILL *Liberty* i. 14 The practical question, where to place the limit—how to make the fitting adjustment between individual independence and social control—is a subject on which nearly everything remains to be done. **1896** E. A. ROSS in *Amer. Jrnl. Sociol.* Mar. 519 By Social Control, on the other hand, I mean that ascendancy over the aims and acts of the individual which is exercised on behalf of the group. **1898** F. H. GIDDINGS *Elem. Sociol.* xix. 217 Social control, manifesting itself in the authoritative organization of society as the state, and acting through the organs of government, is sovereignty. **1913** L. T. HOBHOUSE *Devel. & Purpose* p. xvii, A new demand for the extension of collective responsibility and the social control of industrial life. **1951** N. ANNAN *Leslie Stephen* vii. 218 The field of what is now called social control. How do law, custom, religion and moral codes govern men's actions? **1972** *Guardian* 29 Mar. 14/3 By closing its doors relatively early, the public transport system is an effective measure of social control over non-car owners. **1901** *Amer. Jrnl. Sociol.* July 137 For marginal social cost always equals marginal social utility. **1927** G. D. H. COLE *Econ. System* vii. 62 Social cost simply cannot be measured in terms of money, but only in the last resort in terms of human effort and destruction of natural resources. **1977** *N.Y. Rev. Bks.* 31 Mar. 21/2 Rehabilitation [of housing]..has proved to be cheaper in social costs. **1961** *B.S.I. News* Nov. 11/2 The new regulations..also lay down requirements about the lights to be carried on four-wheeled 'social cycles', now common in holiday areas. **1963** *Daily Tel.* 8 July 11/8 A young woman holidaymaker riding a 'social-cycle' was killed... The cycles are often seen at seaside resorts. They are like tricycles with two people sitting beside each other on a bench. **1887** *Mind* XII. 627 There can be no 'social Darwinism'. Social progress is not essentially the result of a struggle, but of intelligence. **1972** P. B. MEDAWAR *Hope of Progress* 71 Social Darwinism in the form expounded by Haeckel provided a theoretical justification for the great biological crimes of Fascism. **1907** *Amer. Jrnl. Sociol.* XII. 709 The great writers on race-struggles never use the term 'social Darwinism' but a number of sociologists have called them 'social Darwinists'. **1945** R. HOFSTADTER *Social Darwinism in Amer. Thought* ii. 25 In applying evolution to society, Spencer, and after him the Social Darwinists, were simply doing poetic justice to its origins. **1981** J. SUTHERLAND *Bestsellers* iv. 57 There is no room for.. cosiness in Hailey's social-Darwinist universe. **1958** *Jrnl. Abnormal & Social Psychol.* LVI. 49 (*title*) The effect of brief social deprivation on behaviors for a social reinforcer. **1979** W. J. FISHMAN *Streets of E. London* 52/2 The social deprivation inherent in East End life. **1977** *Publ. Amer. Dial. Soc.* 1974 LXI/LXII. 4 Social dialectologists in recent years have made numerous attempts to describe the speech of black Americans. **1981** *Amer. Speech* LVI. 104 Social dialectologists..have also neglected important work of the area linguists. **1970** *Jrnl. Eng. Linguistics* IV. 46 (*title*) Social dialectology in America: a critical survey. *Ibid.*, Although..Mencken.. and others had discussed American social dialects, the systematic study of the sociology of American English really began in the late 1920's. **1976** *General Linguistics* XVI. 32 *Rustic* is an example of social dialectology at its thoroughly honest best. **1872** H. SPENCER in *Contemp. Rev.* XX. 317 The primary social differentiation which we have noted between the regulative part and the operative part, is presently followed by a distinction..between the internal arrangements of the two parts. **1903** L. F. WARD *Pure Sociol.* II. x. 202, I propose to use..the sufficiently vague..term *race*..for all the different kinds of social groups that were formed during the process of social differentiation. **1926** C. C. NORTH *Social Differentiation* i. 5 It is essential to any proper understanding of social differentiation that some effort be made to distinguish between the biological and the social in the sources or causes of social distinctions. **1971** F. R. ALLEN *Socio-Cultural Dynamics* iii. 72 Social differentiation as a major view of change. **1891** T. H. HUXLEY (*title*) Social diseases and worse remedies. **1907** *Amer. Jrnl. Sociol.* July 20 (*title*) Prophylaxis of social diseases. **1945** G. ENDORE *Methinks the Lady* vii. 138 What rights? Overtime pay, maybe? Union hours? Sure. Social security, maybe? Or social diseases? **1970** *Guardian* 28 Apr. 10/1 Hard drugs addiction..is a contagious social disease. **1978** R. LUDLUM *Holcroft Covenant* xxvii. 314 She was probably an ODESSA agent and you've come down with a social disease, as planned. **1920** THOMAS & ZNANIECKI *Polish Peasant* IV. i. 2 The question of social disorganization. We can define the latter briefly as a decrease of the influence of existing social rules of behavior upon individual members of the group. **1958** M. ARGYLE *Relig. Behaviour* xi. 136 The evidence showing how the level of mental disorder increases with social disorganization. **1924** R. E. PARK in *Jrnl. Appl. Sociol.* VIII. 344 Prejudice is..a sort of spontaneous conservation which tends to preserve the social order and the social distances upon which that order rests. **1948** M. SHERIF *Outl. Social Psychol.* xiv. 341 The *average*..member of a group exhibits the degree of prejudice toward the member of another group prescribed by the social distance scale of his group. **1955** G. SIRCOM tr. *Hediger's Psychol. & Behaviour Captive Animals* vi. 83 According to its species, each individual keeps at a greater or lesser distance from its group; that is, the group shows specific social distance. **1960** *Jrnl. Abnormal & Social Psychol.* LXI. 110/1 Bogardus'..ordinal scale of social distance in which a subject indicated zero social distance by stating that he was willing to marry a member of a particular ethnic group, and maximum social distance by stating that he would exclude such a person from the country. **1966** E. T. HALL *Hidden Dimension* x. 115 Desks in the offices of important people are large enough to hold visitors at the far phase of social distance. **1978** P. BAILEY *Leisure & Class in Victorian Eng.* iv. 105 The middle classes were acutely concerned to reinforce, not reduce, social distance. **1921** Social document [see *SHOT *sb.*[1] 7 g (a)]. **1937** S. JAMESON in *Fact* May 87/1 Several times on the road to Wigan pier George Orwell stops to give us his frank opinion of socialists as he has met them... In the first part of the book he has provided a social document as vivid, bitter, and telling as one could have asked. **1959** I. & P. OPIE *Lore & Lang. Schoolch.* p. v, This pioneer work and social document of first importance is ..something of a curiosity. **1974** *Country Life* 30 May 1339/3 This painting of the *Lawn at Goodwood* 1886..has been purchased by the Goodwood Trust for 7,000 gn. I find it a decided non-event in the world of art, but a social document of real importance. **1976** *New Yorker* 12 Jan. 47/2 He's been boozing. And I don't mean he's just had a 'social' drink or two. **1969** in Halpert & Story *Christmas Mumming in Newfoundland* 84 Deep Harbour fishermen have traditionally celebrated Christmas by group visiting, whether as mummers or as 'social drinkers'. **1977** E. LEONARD *Unknown Man* xiv. 120 I wasn't an alcoholic. I was a heavy social drinker. **1901** B. S. ROWNTREE *Poverty* 316 This [public] house is evidently one where 'social' drinking is carried on. **1958** KELLER & SEELEY *Alcohol Lang.* 22 *Social drinking.* 1. Moderate drinking on social occasions. 2. Drinking to comply with the expectation of companions. 3. Drinking in a way and within the limits accepted by a cultural group. **1969** in Halpert & Story *Christmas Mumming in Newfoundland* 82 At night throngs of 'social-drinking' men threading their way along the narrow footpaths sing between visits. **1843** Social dynamics [see DYNAMICS 1 b]. **1938** B. RUSSELL *Power* i. 11 The laws of social dynamics are laws which can only be stated in terms of power, not in terms of this or that form of power. **1974** *Howard Jrnl.* XIV. 97 Overcrowding and..the introduction of strangers into the resident group, or other alterations in the social dynamics. **1900** W. H. TOLMAN *Industrial Betterment* II. 81 'Of course you are too busy..and..need someone on your staff whose sole business will be the planning and direction of movements to improve industrial conditions; in other words you need a social engineer.' Social engineering is a new profession. **1980** *Gazette* (Montreal) 22 Mar. 109/2 Woodward and Armstrong..revile the efforts of President and Congress to appoint Supreme Court judges who will not act as left-of-center social engineers. **1899** *Social Engineering* Sept. 18 The following subjects were adopted for A Course of Lectures on Modern Social Problems... Social Engineering a New Profession. **1919** M. BEER *Hist. Brit. Socialism* II. xiv. 287 The Fabian Society appears to form an institute for social engineering. **1945**

K. R. Popper *Open Society* I. ix. 138 The Platonic approach..can be called *Utopian engineering*, as opposed to that kind of social engineering..which may be described by the name of *piecemeal engineering*. **1980** *Jrnl. R. Soc. Arts* May 351/2 A sort of extension of Architecture ..as a vast subject in its own right with a powerful social-engineering content. **1843** J. S. Mill *Logic* II. iv. v. 273 There is hardly a single name, expressive of any moral or social fact calculated to call forth strong affections.., which does not carry with it..a connotation of those strong affections. **1887** Moore & Aveling tr. *Marx's Capital* I. i. 44 The mutual exchangeability of all kinds of useful private labour is an established social fact. **1938** Solovay & Mueller tr. *Durkheim's Rules Sociol. Method* p. liii, We gave a definition of social facts as ways of acting or thinking with the peculiar characteristic of exercising a coercive influence on individual consciousnesses. **1977** P. Laslett *Family Life* 2 History stands as much in need of a theory of itself as of any other form of generalization about social facts. **1929** P. Geddes in *Sociol. Rev.* XXI. 7 It is a commonplace to every social geographer, that of all forms of rural development over Europe, it is the forest which most definitely thrives and prospers under collective ownership. **1980** *Verbatim* Autumn 1/1 Social geographers are aware of this, of course; it is interesting to find concurrent evidence from a linguistic survey. **1907** G. W. Hoke in *Geogr. Jrnl.* XXIX. 67 In addition to the physiographical group of factors which are by common consent held to be fundamental, the sociological factors are no less fundamental to social geography. **1929** Huntington & Carlson *Environmental Basis of Social Geogr.* i. 5 Social geography examines it [*sc.* the relationship between man and his environment] from the point of view of man and his activities, that is, the social aspect. **1886** C. O. Brown *Talks on Labor Troubles* i. 9 These views..are being read as a new social gospel by hundreds of thousands of people. **1890** *Dawn* II. Suppl. 1 In man's relation to man, Jesus Christ preached a *social* gospel; accordingly, in those relations, his disciples must be socialists. **1917** W. Rauschenbusch *Theol. for Social Gospel* i. 1 We have a social gospel. We need a systematic theology large enough to match it. *Ibid.* 2 The social gospel has become orthodox. *Ibid.* xix. 279 The social gospel is the voice of prophecy in modern life. **1958** M. Argyle *Relig. Behaviour* v. 45 A small college at which it seems that a modernistic and social gospel was widely held among the staff. **1969** A. Richardson *Dict. Christian Theol.* 313/2 The christology of the social gospel focuses on the way the divine life of Christ can get control of human society. *Ibid.*, There were other conspicuous leaders of the social gospel. **1912** A. Conan Doyle in *Strand Mag.* Dec. 603/1 There are few social historians of those days who have not told of the long and fierce struggle between..Sir Charles Tregellis and Lord Barrymore. **1973** *Listener* 25 Oct. 571/1 Social historians must do the best they can with such evidence as they have. **1897** *Library Jrnl.* Mar. 139 'Colonial Days in old New York'..is really of the social historical order rather than a book of travel. **1937** *Burlington Mag.* June 310/1 The historical section..is sketchy..and its lack of concentration results in an apparent insufficiency of social-historical facts to explain stylistic changes. **1977** A. Wilson *Strange Ride of R. Kipling* vii. 342, I prefer..a social-historical description of long generations of Evangelical belief ending in post-Darwinian doubt. **1856** G. Roberts *Social Hist. of People of Southern Counties of England in Past Centuries* p. v, Researches..disclosed many particulars of the former condition of our countrymen... These have been made available for the express correction of a very general ignorance of our Social History that prevails. **1907** L. H. Morgan *Ancient Society* ii. i. 50 It represents a striking phase of the ancient social history of our race. **1950** McDougall & Cormack in C. Morris *Social Casework in Great Britain* ii. 40 The social history..is the essential basis of constructive help. It does not follow from this that..every client's story must be fully investigated. **1970** D. C. Gibbons *Delinquent Behaviour* iii. 48 The social history document prepared by the probation officer..looms large in the disposition of the case. **1976** W. Gérin *Elizabeth Gaskell* xiv. 152 From the point of view of social history, *North and South* is but a poor successor to the realities of *Mary Barton*. **1967** *Act Eliz. II* c.80 § 57 A court of any prescribed class shall before passing on any person a sentence to which the rules apply consider a social inquiry report, that is to say a report about him and his circumstances, made by a probation officer or any other person authorised to do so by the rules. **1977** *Grimsby Even. Tel.* 27 May 13/1 The case had been adjourned for social inquiry and psychiatric reports. **1909** C. R. Henderson *Ann. Amer. Acad. Pol. & Social Sci.* Mar. 265 It is time..to adopt some such description as 'social insurance' to cover the methods of guaranteeing income to wage earners and their families in case of sickness, accident, invalidism, feebleness of old age, death of the breadwinner and unemployment. *Ibid.* 270 No voluntary system of social insurance can be economically administered, save upon a foundation of compulsory insurance. **1922** S. A. Queen *Social Work in Light of Hist.* xii. 209 The ideal purpose of social insurance is to prevent, and finally to eradicate poverty and the consequent need of relief by meeting the problem at its origin. **1970** *Internat. & Compar. Law Quarterly* 4th Ser. XIX. ii. 301 The District Court of Kiel held that payments from a social insurance authority had to be set off against the child's right to maintenance against his father's heirs. **1977** *Times* 10 Sept. 2/6 Research in this field is..a piece of social insurance. **1976** R. Harris *Three Candles for Dark* iv. 27 I'm not a liar, or not a real one. A social liar, maybe, like everyone else. **1941** Auden *New Year Letter* iii. 64 And yet although the social lie Looks double to the dreamer's eye. **1969** M. Drabble *Waterfall* 94 She might have invented the information as a social lie (a felicitous duplicity). **1971** W. Tute *Tarnham Connection* vii. 135 [He] said he was expected back home, which Mado knew to be a social lie. **1919** *Lancet* 24 May 921/1 (*heading*) Social medicine in Vienna. **1925** F. L. Dunham *Approach to Social Medicine* i. 14 A need arises in welfare work for a field of preventive science to which social science, psychology, psychiatry and various other departments shall contribute... It may be called *Social Medicine*. **1977** *Lancet* 24 & 31 Dec. 1336/1 What has been the contribution of social medicine to social policy in general and to health-services policy in particular. **1925** P. Sorokin in *Social Forces* May 635/2 We used to think that in the United States 'social mobility' was greatest. **1954** D. V. Glass (*title*) Social mobility in Britain. **1978** *Listener* 26 Jan. 107/2 The patterns of social mobility over the past generation. **1953** K. W. Deutsch *Nationalism & Social Communication* vi. 114 If there is economic growth, social communication will probably spread and social mobilization will progress. **1961** —— in *Amer. Pol. Sci. Rev.* Sept. 493/1 Social mobilization is a name given to an overall process of change, which happens to substantial parts of the population in countries which are moving from traditional to modern ways of life. **1905** E. A. Ross *Foundations Sociol.* viii. 182 The term..social morphology..will describe, not only human relations and groupings, but also their mutations in the course of time. **1960** *Amer. Sociol. Rev.* XXV. 193/2 Durkheim proposed the examination and comparison of languages..in order to find 'the manner in which social representations adhere to and repel one another', and how any such 'social morphology' is to be explained. **1797** *Encycl. Brit.* XVII. 570/2 Though social order is no longer unknown nor unobserved, yet the form of government is still extremely simple. **1817** [in Dict., sense 7 b]. **1853** H. Martineau tr. *Comte's Positive Philos.* II. vi. i. 6 A polity that could not hold its ground before the natural progress of intelligence and of society can never again serve as a basis of social order. **1909** H. G. Wells *Ann Veronica* vi. 129, I know that our social order is dreadful enough..and sacrifices all that is best and most beautiful in life. **1920** B. Russell *Pract. & Theory Bolshevism* i. ii. 28 He [*sc.* the Communist] is.. aiming at the creation of a new social order. **1955** M. Gluckman *Custom & Conflict in Africa* i. 17 What emerges, I think, is that if there are sufficient conflicts of loyalties at work, settlement will be achieved..and social order maintained. **1977** P. Laslett *Family Life* i. 46 The traditional social order on our continent. **1835** H. Reeve tr. *de Tocqueville's Democracy in Amer.* II. x. 429 If republican principles are to perish in America, they can only yield after a laborious social process. **1887** [see *process *sb.* 5 b]. **1947** Henderson & Parsons tr. *Weber's Theory of Social & Econ. Organization* i. 96 Charisma..is thus the bearer of many dynamic tendencies of social processes. **1974** tr. *Wertheim's Evolution & Revolution* 164 The aim of this study is to deal with revolutions as social processes. **1966** G. Tannenbaum in S. Arieti *Amer. Handbk. Psychiatry* xxxv. 577/1 The social psychiatric model is based on public health principles rather than on the traditional clinical prototype. **1964** *Observer* 23 Aug. 1/1 The social psychiatrists..believe that the answers to mental health can only be found by.. studying the patient in relation to the groups he moves in. **1924** *Amer. Jrnl. Psychiatry* LXXXI. 149 The Round Table Conferences..were well attended..36 formed the group which discussed problems of social psychiatry. **1958** D. McK. Rioch in *Symposium on Preventive & Social Psychiatry 1957* p. iv, The last two sessions..are devoted to organizational, therapeutic and other clinical developments of social psychiatry in recent years. **1976** B. H. Kaplan et al. (*title*) Further explorations in social psychiatry. **1909** W. M. Urban *Valuation* i. 2 A collection of social-psychological monographs. **1978** *Language* LIV. 160 It is more surprising..that he does not refer to the rich social-psychological literature on language attitudes. **1899** *Amer. Jrnl. Sociol.* Mar. 661 To the social psychologist, however, it is evident that economic crises are phenomena that lie wholly within the psychical process of group-life. **1972** M. Argyle *Social Psychol. of Work* i. 3 There are a number of very important social problems in industry today which fall into the sphere of the social psychologist. **1891** E. A. Ross *Let.* 13 Dec. in *Amer. Sociol. Rev.* (1938) III. 364 Do we not need an *Origin of Species* in the dawn of Esthetic and Social Psychology? **1927** *Mod. Philology* Nov. 213 Or, we may study the group, observing every act of a given type... This is social psychology. **1964** Gould & Kolb *Dict. Soc. Sciences* 663/1 Only psychology and sociology include social psychology as part of their explicit subject-matter. **1977** R. Holland *Self & Social Context* v. 167 On the other side of psychology stands sociology, sharing with psychology the field of social psychology, since there are sociologically trained and psychologically trained social psychologists. **1937** L. Cheskin in *Education* Nov. 186/2 Current art..expresses mainly group action, mass movement, class struggle, not individual characters. The artists of today seek to express mainly social realism, not organic realism or naturalism. **1940** C. Connolly in *Horizon* Feb. 70 The flight of Auden and Isherwood..is also a symptom of the failure of social realism as an aesthetic doctrine. **1959** *Times Lit. Suppl.* 6 Nov. p. xxix/4 The collapse of social realism from its heyday during the 1930s... Generally to-day..American art is aloof and bent on wrestling with private problems. Even Ben Shahn, the outstanding social realist of twenty years ago, has come to prefer the expression of emotion through symbolism of his own devising from which political satire is absent. **1972** *Sat. Rev.* (U.S.) 27 May 14/3 The dismal social-realism caricatures that passed for art in the Thirties. **1940** Social realist [see *communist-inspired* s.v. *communist 3 b]. **1956** *New Yorker* 14 Jan. 71/1 Perhaps the only really native Italian schools..are the one called Spazialismo..and a social-realist one. **1959** [see *social realism* above]. **1976** *Listener* 19 Aug. 218/3 Twenty years ago, the most modern artists in England were called the 'kitchen-sink school'... John Berger wrote social realist reviews of their exhibitions. **1960** *Guardian* 18 Oct. 5/5 The group has..a distinct social realistic bias. **1859** D. Masson *Brit. Novelists* iv. 308 It may be that the representation of social reality is..the proper business of the Novel. **1887** Moore & Aveling tr. *Marx's Capital* I. i. 15 The value of commodities has a purely social reality. **1949** W. L. Warner in M. Fortes *Social Structure* 4 Agreement among the informants assures the status analyst that the social class sytem derived from their statements is..an ever present..social reality. **1978** *Language* LIV. 449 It may be noted that O's social realities of the West German job market refer more to the over-employment of the 1960's than to the under-employment of the 1970's. **1889** (*title*) Social Register, New York. **1945** *Seafarers' Log* 6 July 6/4 The crew recommended that the 'advantages' of the social register be extended to William Chance and J. D. Bell, both trip carders. **1949** *Sat. Even. Post* 15 Oct. 142/3 The student body..has a heavy sprinkling of millionaires' sons and Social Register families. **1981** *Newsweek* 20 July 24 Martha von Bulow was pure Social Register, born into wealth, educated in the best private schools, and married for a time to an Austrian prince. **1953** N. Tinbergen *Herring Gull's World* ii. 13 Colour can act as a 'social releaser' by releasing a response in another individual just as a call often does. **1962** *Listener* 9 Aug. 207/2 In such tribes we see something very like social releasers. **1831** J. S. Mill *Ess.* (1962) 20 There must be a moral and social revolution,..which shall leave to no man one fraction of unearned distinction or unearned importance. **1890** W. Booth *In Darkest England* i. ix. 80 The Socialist tells me that the great Social Revolution is looming large on the horizon. **1910** H. G. Wells *New Machiavelli* (1911) i. iv. 121 The social revolution and the triumph of the Proletariat after the class war. **1941** *Time* 19 May 98/1 World War II is a social revolution, but not the kind of social revolution almost everybody thinks it is. **1974** tr. *Wertheim's Evolution & Revolution* 173 However, true social revolutions in earlier times showed a religious component as well. **1928** *Psychol. Abstr.* 889 Social role of language. **1949** [see *rôle 2]. **1977** Social role [see *role set* s.v. *rôle 4]. **1905** E. Wharton *House of Mirth* ii. viii. 417 Carry promised to find somebody who wants a kind of social secretary—you know she makes a speciality of the helpless rich. **1949** 'J. Tey' *Brat Farrar* xxii. 195 She moved him on from one group to another as expertly as a social secretary. **1978** 'J. Horbury' *Diplomatic Affair* i. iv. 43 'Never neglect *placement* if you wish to rise.'..'By the time you rise to the point where it matters, some charming social secretary will worry about it for you.' **1925** P. Sorokin *Sociol. of Revol.* xii. 250 Some of their members in two or three years cover an enormous distance in 'social space': from ordinary lawyers,.. workers, peasants,..etc., they become persons..occupying high posts. **1927** —— *Social Mobility* i. 3 Persons near each other in geometrical space—*e.g.*, a king and his servant..—are often separated by the greatest distance in social space. **1961** J. N. Findlay *Values & Intentions* ix. 398 The first encounter with social space is normally that of a being without formed views, abilities or values, with a range of beings surpassingly mature,..decided, powerful and in general benign. **1977** T. M. Kando *Social Interaction* xi. 260/1 The study of space becomes truly interesting when it is conceived of as social space. **1843** Social statics [see Dynamics 1 b]. **1851** H. Spencer (*title*) Social statics. **1958** A. R. Radcliffe-Brown *Meth. in Social Anthropol.* i. v. 128 For social anthropology the task is to formulate and validate statements about the conditions of existence of social systems (laws of social statics) and the regularities that are observable in social change (laws of social dynamics). **1927** P. Sorokin *Social Mobility* ii. 11 Social stratification means the differentiation of a given population into hierarchically superposed classes. **1979** G. Ritzer et al. *Sociol.* ix. 238 Their contention that because social stratification is universal, it must be a functional necessity. **1972** P. Laslett *Household & Family* 58 In the relations of children to servants we may..find..important and revealing social structural differences. **1835** H. Reeve tr. *de Tocqueville's Democracy in Amer.* I. v. 69 The Constitution of the United States..consists of two distinct social structures, connected, and..encased one within the other. **1872** H. Spencer in *Contemp. Rev.* XX. 311 Social influences which..facilitate further aggregation with consequent further complexity of social structure. **1949** M. Fortes *Social Structure* p. xiii, The study of kinship systems and..the concept of social structure. **1968** Jacobson & Schoepf tr. *Levi-Strauss's Structural Anthropol.* I. xv. 277 Studies in social structure have to do with the formal aspects of social phenomena. *a* **1854** Mill *Early Draft Autobiogr.* (1961) 108 The social studies of myself and several of my companions assumed a shape which contributed very much to my mental development. **1926** B. Webb *My Apprenticeship* v. 217 A subtle combination of quantitative and qualitative analysis is a necessary factor in social studies. **1938** S. Chase *Tyranny of Words* vii. 78 The social studies are..backward compared to the physical sciences. **1977** *Lancashire Life* Nov. 136/3 In some schools R.E. is lumped together with history and geography and called Humanities or Social Studies. **1927** *Amer. Jrnl. Sociol.* XXXIII. 424 (*title*) The social survey of Tyneside: an English regional social survey. **1948** [see *participant *sb.* 1]. **1956** *B.B.C. Handbk.* 1957 106 Two major enquiries by this section, both making use of social-survey methods. **1979** J. MacKenzie *Victorian Courtship* iii. 40 Mary Booth.. welcomed the help Beatrice [Potter] proposed to give her husband in his ambitious social survey. **1782** 'J. H. St. John de Crèvecœur' *Lett. from Amer. Farmer* iii. 50 New laws, a new mode of living, a new social system. **1853** H. Martineau tr. *Comte's Positive Philos.* II. vi. i. 11 The passage from one social system to another can never be continuous and direct. **1917** Kipling *Diversity of Creatures* 335, I cannot think it right that any human being should exercise mastery over others in the merciless fashion our tom-fool social system permits. **1951** E. E. Evans-Pritchard *Social Anthropol.* i. 11 The social anthropologist studies societies as wholes. He studies their oecologies, their economics.., their technologies, their arts, *etc.* as parts of general social systems. **1971** P. Worsthorne *Socialist Myth* vii. 143 Socialism has a conception of the role of government which can only be realized in a social system that exalts authority. **1797** in J. Gloag *Short Dict. Furniture* (1969) 626 A Gentleman's social table. **1952** *Ibid.* 436 *Social table*, a small, kidney-shaped table with four legs, and a revolving, cylindrical receptacle for wine bottles, supported on a pillar-and-claw stand, which fitted into the concave curve of the table. . It allowed two or three people to sit with their wine near a fire. **1962** 'M. Innes' *Connoisseur's Case* xvi. 190 A gentleman's social table by Hepplewhite. **1873** H. Spencer *Study of Sociol.* xv. 372 No one doubts that the spendthrift or the gambler..is inferior as a social unit. *a* **1899** [see *super-organism* s.v. Super- 6 b]. **1907** W. James *Pragmatism* vi. 232 Must my thoughts dwell night and day on my personal sins and blemishes..or sink may I and ignore them in order to be a decent social unit? **1939** AUDEN in *I Believe* (1940) 26 Recent technical advances, such as cheap electrical power, are making smaller social units more of a practical possibility than they seemed fifty years ago. **1978** *Country Life* 17 Aug. 467/1 The family as a social unit. **1969** *Daily Tel.* (Colour Suppl.) 14 Mar. 5/1 Wage rises might have been slightly checked but 'the social wage' has gone up steadily. ..'The social wage', in plain English, means Government hand-outs, the exact opposite of a wage. **1971** *Guardian* 7 July 12/4 The real social wage of many low-paid workers has been adversely affected. **1975** M. THATCHER in *Let Children Grow Tall* (1977) 18 People..complain that government takes too much of their incomes for what is now called the 'Social Wage'—the estimated annual value of the services provided out of public funds for each individual. **1977** *Daily News* (Perth, Austral.) 19 Jan. 8/1 If, on becoming a mother, every woman became entitled to a social wage of $100 a week, tax free, then this might achieve a great deal in terms of righting the lot of some women. **1892** L. F. WARD *Let.* 17 Mar. in *Amer. Sociol. Rev.* (1938) June 371 (*heading*) The social will. **1911** J. WARD *Realm of Ends* vi. 118 Is there in any exact sense a social spirit, a social will, a social end, a social conscience? **1942** R. G. COLLINGWOOD *New Leviathan* xxi. 152 There is always a discrepancy between the social will and its products

B. *sb.* **2.** (Earlier example.)

1870 *Mainland Guardian* (New Westminster, Brit. Columbia) 8 Jan. 3/4 A very pleasant Social was given by the ladies and friends in our new mission church on Christmas day.

3. *ellipt* for *SOCIAL SECURITY 1 a or b. *colloq.*

1981 *Times* 20 May 3/8 I'm getting two wages, one from prison, and one from the social. **1983** J. WAINWRIGHT *Their Evil Ways* 17 They were both 'on the social'. *Ibid.* 26 She applied for extra 'social'. She was.. sure she was *entitled* to some extra.

Social Credit. [f. SOCIAL *a.* + CREDIT *sb.*] **1.** A political theory advocated by C. H. Douglas (see *DOUGLAS[3]), according to which the supposed chronic deficiency in the purchasing power of consumers was to be remedied through a reduction of prices by means of subsidies to producers or through the giving of additional money to consumers; occas. also, a subsidy under this system. Also short for *Social Credit Party* or *League*.

1920 A. R. ORAGE in C. H. Douglas *Credit-Power & Democracy* 166 The effect is inherent in the separation of Real Credit from Financial Credit—Social Credit, that is to say, from Financial Credit privately controlled. **1922** C. H. DOUGLAS *Labour Party & Social Credit* 17 It is an important Report, not..as advancing any valid..criticism of the principles or details of Social Credit. **1935** *Calgary Typo News* 15 Mar. 1/1 We wonder..what is the policy of The Albertan? Liberal, Social Credit or Independent? **1936** S. E. THOMAS *This Social Credit Business* 16 If the A+B Theorem is sound, what is the necessity for 'National Dividends' *as well as* Social Credits to retailers? **1944** G. B. SHAW *Everybody's Political What's What?* xi. 84 The apostles of Social Credit once actually persuaded a Canadian legislature to budget on its imaginary riches. **1966** R. S. MILNE *Political Parties in New Zealand* iii. 78 *Potentially*, therefore, the Democrats, Democratic Labour, and Social Credit were 'national' parties. **1974** E. MCGIRR *Murderous Journey* 127 Ricardo's political grin..calculated to warm the cockles of any voter way back to Douglas Social Credit.

2. *attrib.* and *Comb.*, as *Social Credit analysis*, *group*, *leader*, etc.; **Social Credit League** (*a*) *Canad.*, an organization outside party politics corresponding to the Social Credit Party; (*b*) *N.Z.* (also *Social Credit Political League*), a political party advocating Social Credit; **Social Credit Party** *Canad.*, a political party whose policies are based on the theory of Social Credit.

1922 C. H. DOUGLAS *Labour Party & Social Credit* 26 This article successfully avoided any mention or indication of the Social Credit Proposals. *Ibid.* 29 The Social Credit Movement..is in sharp opposition to the official Labour Party and High Finance jointly. **1931** V. A. DEMANT *This Unemployment* vi. 121 The *Social Credit* analysis of C. H. Douglas, costing expert for the Government during the War. **1934** T. S. ELIOT *Rock* i. 12 Ain't you ever 'eard me speak o' the principles of Social Credit Reform? **1935** *Economist* 29 June 1474/1 A Social Credit scheme for Alberta under which he promised to guarantee every adult inhabitant of the Province $25 per week. **1958** *Maclean's Mag.* 10 May 97/4 When the two factions separated Wicks and Savage took the name and formed the Social Credit League. **1958** *Time* (Canadian ed.) 15 Sept. 16/3 The leader of the badly mauled Social Credit party. **1961** *Canada Month* Nov. 11/3 The B.C. Social Credit League offered alternative solutions to his problem. **1965** *Oxf. N.Z. Encyl.* 277/2 Two splinter parties, the Social Credit League and the Communist Party, have contested seats in elections, but neither has ever secured a seat in the House of Representatives. **1966** *Encycl. N.Z.* II. 812/1 In May 1953, the New Zealand Social Credit Political League was formed. **1966** 'H. MACDIARMID' *Company I've Kept* iv. 106 Douglas's Social Credit system (or a partial form of it) was tried out by Alberta, Canada, in the inter-war years. **1967** *Canad. Ann. Rev. 1966* 5 Both the NDP and the small Social Credit group indicated that they were willing to co-operate with the government. **1968** *Globe & Mail* (Toronto) 17 Feb. 8/1 The national Social Credit Party could drive forward to counteract its 'inaccurate image'. **1968** *Landfall* XXII. 365 The men armed with Social Credit conversation for the interval. **1969** *N.Z. News* 5 Nov. 8/5 The Social Credit Leader, Mr. Cracknell, may have all too often been dismissed as something of a political lightweight.

Hence **Social Crediter, Social Creditor,** an advocate of Social Credit; also occas. **Social Creditist** (cf. *CREDITISTE).

1938 *Social Crediter* 17 Sept. 2/1 What I (a Social Crediter) should say to that, is that I don't know whether Sir Oswald agrees with me or not. **1953** M. LOWRY *Sel. Lett.* (1967) 337 The Social Crediters fell, after having made some demonstrations of power. **1963** *Daily Tel.* 31 Oct. 14/2 The Social Creditists, appealing mainly to Quebec nationalism, could muster only 27 votes against 210. **1965** *Economist* 13 Nov. 713/1 In the new [Canadian] house there will still be nine Creditistes attached to Mr Caouette, and five Social Crediters of the Thompson variety. **1976** H. WILSON *Governance of Britain* viii. 161 In past times, not recently, they were told, the number of committed Henry Georgeites, or Douglas Social Creditors, might have put forward similar claims.

socialism. Add: **1.** (Earlier example.) *Christian socialism* (example).

1837 *Leeds Times* 12 Aug. 5/1 *Socialism.*—Messrs. Fleming and Rigby.—On Monday evening..these two gentlemen attended [*sic*] an audience..on the topics of the real nature of man. **1850** *Daily News* 13 Mar. 5/2 The infection of..'Christian Socialism' is spreading to Whitehall.

socialist. Add: **1. a.** (Earlier example.)

1827 *Co-operative Magazine* Nov. 509 The chief question..between the modern,..Political Economists, and the Communionists or Socialists, is whether it is more beneficial that this capital should be individual or in common.

b. *Comb.*, as *socialist-controlled*, *-dominated*, *-ridden*.

1929 *Times* 16 Aug. 11/3 Mr. Moore, the Leader of the Opposition, appealed to the people of this Socialist-ridden State on a promise to substitute for Socialism 'private effort and enterprise'. **1976** N. O'SULLIVAN *Conservatism* v. 124 Whenever important bills were opposed by the House of Lords, he suggested, there might be an appeal, in the form of a mass referendum, over the heads of a socialist-dominated House of Commons to the people. **1976** *Southern Even. Echo* (Southampton) 1 Nov. 3/3 There are many Socialist-controlled local authorities on which the dominant group doesn't give the opposition any places on any committees.

2. c. In *Combs.* used *attrib.* or as *adj.*, as *socialist-chauvinist*, *-feminist*, *-rebel*, *-revolutionary*, *-workman*.

1919 A. SIRNIS tr. *Lenin's Collapse of Second International* x. 65 This group, the only one which had performed systematic work amongst the masses..turned Socialist-Chauvinist. **1921** D. H. LAWRENCE *Sea & Sardinia* ii. 76 He immediately put on the socialist-workman indignation. **1952** E. HOBSBAWM in *Granta* 15 Nov. 10/2 The Radical age of the 1820s and 1830s, and the mixed socialist-rebel age which overlapped the first world war. **1976** H. T. WILLETTS tr. *Solzhenitsyn's Lenin in Zurich* 253 The Socialist-Revolutionary Party was born at the end of 1901 out of the merging of the Populist groups. **1976** *Women's Report* Sept./Oct. 17/1 They would like feedback from the last issue, articles from individuals and groups giving a socialist-feminist analysis of activities.

socialist realism. [tr. Russ. *sotsialisticheskiĭ realizm.*] The official theory of art and literature of the Soviet Communist party, according to which the artist's or writer's work should reflect and commend the life and ideals of socialist society. Also *attrib.*

1934 M. EASTMAN *Artists in Uniform* (rev. ed.) I. ii. 16 The present creative method in proletarian art and literature..is 'Socialist Realism'. *Ibid.* 17 Socialist Realism means seeing all reality as a development toward socialism. **1940** GRAVES & HODGE *Long Week-End* xxiii. 402 The hope that fact-finding would bring to fruition the theory of socialist realism. **1967** G. STEINER *Lang. & Silence* 390 Her recent novels betray the contortions of a genuine artist trying to come to terms with the grey half-truths of 'socialist realism'. **1978** *Jrnl. R. Soc. Arts* Dec. 64/2 In 1934 the term 'socialist realism' came into current use, and architecture suffered from various interpretations of it.

Hence **socialist-realist** *sb.* and *a.*

1935 G. STRUVE *Soviet Russ. Literature* xiv. 247 It is difficult to say why Sholokhov's *Upturned Soil* should be regarded as a work of a Socialist Realist and not of a realist *tout court*. **1945** H. READ *Coat of Many Colours* vi. 27 The 'socialist-realists' in Russia, who believe that the function of art is primarily to further the cause of socialism. **1958** *Listener* 6 Nov. 727/2 The whole fabric of the so-called 'socialist-realist' architectural philosophy [in the U.S.S.R.], which was actually pseudo-classical, has collapsed. **1964** *Ann. Reg. 1963* 229 He [*sc.* Mr Gomulka] ..announced that socialist-realist art would receive special support. **1977** V. S. PRITCHETT *Gentle Barbarian* xiii. 218 The crude, black and white, schematic works of the Socialist Realists of our time.

socialite (sōᵘ·ʃǎləit). *colloq.* (orig. *U.S.*). [f. SOCIAL *a.* and *sb.* + -ITE[1].] A person who is prominent in fashionable society; one who is fond of social activities and entertainments. Also *attrib.*

1928 *Time* 31 Dec. 30/3 Splendorous as hostess & socialite was Princess Clara in both Germany and England. **1937** D. B. WYNDHAM LEWIS in L. Russell *Press Gang!* 249 *Eric Daintee*, wealthy lissom Mayfair filmamateur, socialite, dressdesigner, surrealist. **1938** E. LYONS *Assignment in Utopia* II. xiv. 226 The main body of amateur sociologists,..earnest probers, socialite thrill-hunters, and miscellaneous neurotics did not take possession [of Moscow] until the following years. **1949** R. MANVELL *Film* II. vi. 139, I do not think a working girl should take her standards from a socialite. **1956** J. C. MASTERMAN *Case of Four Friends* vii. 125 A rather irresponsible *bon viveur* or socialite (as the young call them). **1960** *Harper's Bazaar* July 19/1 Private citizens in the socialite belt even distribute matches bearing their own monograms. **1978** J. KRANTZ *Scruples* iii. 79 At *Vogue* there are something like twenty-one editors of varying degrees of importance, including those stationed in Paris, Rome, and Madrid who are socialites first, editors second. **1980** *Times Lit. Suppl.* 12 Sept. 1000/4 Although a professional naturalist.., he [*sc.* Victor Jacquemont] was by nature something of a dilettante and very much a socialite.

sociality. Add: **2.** (*a*) (Further examples.)

1932 S. ZUCKERMAN *Soc. Life Monkeys & Apes* xvii. 291 The monkey's sociality. **1966** R. M. LOCKLEY *Grey Seal, Common Seal* ix. 125 The puzzling feature of the sociality of the Farne grey seals is that they continue to crowd together to nurse their pups on certain of the islets only. **1978** *Sci. Amer.* Sept. 139/1 The order also includes many nonsocial species, and the surprising fact is that sociality has originated on a number of separate occasions among the bees, the ants and the wasps.

socialization. Add: **1.** (Earlier and later examples.)

1884 W. MORRIS in *Justice* 31 May 2/1 The socialisation of labour which ought to have been a blessing to the community has been turned into a curse by the appropriation of the products of its labour by individuals..; the result of which to the workers has been a dire slavery, of which long hours of labour,..and complete repulsiveness in the work itself have been the greatest evils. **1957** *Ann. Reg. 1956* 311 The Chinese People's Republic remained largely preoccupied with the drive for greater industrialization and for the 'socialization' of agriculture. **1965** B. PEARCE tr. *Preobrazhensky's New Economics* 6 The socialization of industry means by its very essence a transference of responsibility in economic leadership to science, to an extent quite unknown in capitalist economics. **1977** D. M. SMITH *Human Geogr.* xii. 359 The effective socialization of production under capitalism.. stands in supreme contradiction with private appropriation.

2. *Social Sciences.* The process of forming associations or of adapting oneself to them; esp. the process whereby an individual acquires the modifications of behaviour and the values necessary for the stability of the social group of which he is or becomes a member. Also *attrib.*, esp. in *socialization process*.

1841 *London Phalanx* 6 Nov. 505/1 Fourier in his analysis of universal movement in society..forms a scale of seven degrees or periods of general progress between.. *Edenism*, or the primitive state of humanity..and.. *Socialization*, or complete simple association. **1895** G. SIMMEL in *Ann. Amer. Acad. Pol. Sci.* VI. III. 417 The investigation of the forces, forms and development of socialization, of co-operation, of association of individuals, should be the single object of sociology as a special science. **1924** F. H. ALLPORT *Soc. Psychol.* xiv. 378 It is..possible that the evils mentioned are not *necessary* accompaniments of contemporary civilization or of the socialization of mankind. **1924** E. S. BOGARDUS *Fundamentals Soc. Psychol.* xx. 235 The best way to understand the socialization process is to consider the experiences of persons who have..a broad social vision and understanding. **1951** *Mind* LX. 288 This process of 'socialisation'— to use the standard term—produces..the 'personality' of the individual. **1953** WHITING & CHILD *Child Training & Personality* xi. 247 A relatively unimportant role in the total socialization process. **1964** M. ARGYLE *Psychol. & Social Probl.* v. 72 The socialization factor [in reducing the crime rate] is already being manipulated to some extent by placing children from very bad homes in foster homes. **1965** G. P. MURDOCK *Ess.* 44 The processes by which it [*sc.* culture]..is transmitted from one generation to the next (education and socialization). **1980** in N. Warren *Stud. in Cross-Cultural Psychol.* II. v. 215 We know relatively little about an area I shall label 'intellectual socialization'.

socialize, *v.* Add: **1.** esp. in *Social Sciences*. Also, to transmit to an individual the cultural values and standards of behaviour of the social group of which he is regarded as a member.

1932 M. GABAIN tr. *Piaget's Moral Judgment of Child* iv. 350 This assumption gains force if..social constraint does not really suffice to 'socialize' the child but accentuates its egocentrism. **1957** O. R. MCGREGOR *Divorce in Eng.* iii. 79 With horrifying overcrowding..the family could not be a stable, ongoing concern. Children were brutally socialised. **1971** *Mod. Law Rev.* XXXIV. VI. 643 New lawyers are..informally 'socialised', taught the norms and behaviour patterns which are the basis of a stable legal profession. **1976** *National Observer* (U.S.) 31 July 1/2 She is convinced..that women traditionally have failed to excel physically because they were socialized to think they could not.

2. (Later examples.) Also in extended uses: to administer or organize with social aims in view (rather than predominantly for profit); to finance with public funds; to bring under public control. Also *absol.*

1920 M. BEER *Hist. Brit. Socialism* II. III. ix. 181 Maurice's main idea was to socialise the Christian and to Christianise the socialist. **1920** *Westm. Gaz.* 2 Dec. 6/1 The Fehrenbach Cabinet is being increasingly pressed to Socialise, and first of all to Socialise coal. **1926** J. M. KEYNES *End of Laissez-Faire* iv. 42 One of the most interesting and unnoticed developments of recent decades has been the tendency of big enterprise to socialise itself.

1938 *Sun* (Baltimore) 15 June 2/3 Discussions as to what the medical association and the Government might do about 'socializing' or financing with public funds the medical treatment of economically submerged individuals. **1948** *News Chron.* 20 Sept. 3/3 In fact, we have to socialise men's minds—without destroying their individuality and enterprise—as well as socialising the physical assets. **1975** J. De Bres tr. *Mandel's Late Capitalism* vii. 233 Within the company labour is directly socialized in the sense that the overall plan of the company..directly determines the output of the various factories, workshops and conveyor belts. **1976** *Ilkeston Advertiser* 10 Dec. 20/3 It could do this by compulsory purchase, saying that it was merely 'socialising' the land by buying it at current use value and preventing a capitalist developer from doing the same, and then re-selling the land at a profit.

3. *intr.* To be sociable, participate in social activities. Freq. const. *with.* orig. *U.S.*

1895 in *Funk's Stand. Dict.* **1900** *Dialect Notes* II. 62 *Socialize*,..to talk with one of the opposite sex. **1934** *Amer. Speech* IX. 76 Did you socialize much in Atlantic City?..I am not going to socialize much this winter. **1939** Joyce *Finnegans Wake* (1964) iii. 498 After plenty of his fresh stout and his good balls of malt,..socializing and communicanting in the deification of his members. **1959** V. Packard *Status Seekers* xii. 167 Trying to socialize across class barriers can be a strain. **1966** J. Pearl *Crucifixion of Pete McCabe* ii. 21 McCabe could socialize with any of his three neighbours. **1970** *Daily Tel.* 25 Feb. 15/3, I prefer to socialise outside the team but wouldn't go out with any man who was shattered by my job. **1978** *Detroit Free Press* 5 Mar. 6/2 They're hard to spot because they don't like to sit around in trees and socialize with other birds.

socialized, *ppl. a.* Add: (Later examples.) *socialized medicine*: a system of medical care that is financed and administered by the state.

1892 G. B. Shaw *Fabian Soc.* (Fabian Tract No. 41) 20 Thousands of thoroughly Socialized Radicals..who would have resisted Socialism fiercely if it had been forced on them. **1935** *Sun* (Baltimore) 16 Feb. 9/1 Traditionally hostile to socialized medical care, the organized medical profession will decide tomorrow whether to temper its stand to the trend of the day toward State control. **1936** J. M. Keynes *Gen. Theory Employment, Interest & Money* v. xix. 267 Except in a socialised community where wage-policy is settled by decree, there is no means of securing uniform wage reductions for every class of labour. **1939** *Time* 30 Jan. 52/2 Although socialized medicine would certainly limit a patient's free choice of a physician, few people today are free to choose their doctors. **1949** Koestler *Insight & Outlook* xiv. 195 The listing together of such different phenomena as, for example, optical projective illusions, hypnosis, and socialized behaviour as manifestations of 'self-transcendence' is arbitrary. **1949** *Sun* (Baltimore) 15 June 12/3 For instance, at this moment the socialized railways of Britain face labor unrest of great intensity, the basic quarrel being over wages. **1964** R. Braddon *Year Angry Rabbit* ix. 82 'Goddam,' muttered the American sourly, 'why can't you Australians have Socialized Medicine like the Limies?' **1973** *Sci. Amer.* Jan. 33/1 One [*sc.* primate] in particular—the chimpanzee—not only cooperates in the work of the chase but also engages in a remarkably socialized distribution of the prey after the kill. **1976** *Howard Jrnl.* XV. i. 51 The juvenile courts dispensed unchallenged what the Americans call socialized justice. (Socialized simply means individualized civil justice which focuses upon social conditions. It has no party political connotations.) **1977** *Lancet* 17 Sept. 596/1 Why socialised medicine should so often be equated with socialist medicine I fail to understand

socializee (sōu·ʃăləizī·). [f. Socialize *v.* + -ee[1].] One who is being socialized (in sense 1 of the vb.)

1952 T. Parsons *Social System* vi. 209 Thus not only the socializing agents *but the socializee* must be conceived as acting in roles. **1975** *Jrnl. Politics* XXXVII. 83 Yet socialization within the family is not simply a two-generation phenomenon, for the parents themselves were once the socializees instead of the socializers.

socializer (sōu·ʃăləizəɹ). [f. Socialize *v.* + -er[1].] **1.** One who socializes an industry, an economy, or the like. Cf. *socialize *v.* 2.

1947 [see *decartel(l)ization].

2. One who or that which makes a person social or sociable; that which induces a sociable atmosphere.

1974 H. L. Foster *Ribbin', Jivin', & Playin' Dozens* iv. 162 The right language at the proper time can serve as a socializer, a relaxing agent, and a positive catalyst to enhance communication. **1975** [see prec.]. **1976** *Word 1971* XXVII. 476 They are *socializers* which function as the verbal oil to ease friction in communication... A's phrase 'How are you?' is a socializer; A does not usually expect to learn B's physiological or psychological problems. **1981** *Underground Grammarian* Oct. 4/1 Our educationists are socializers with political intentions.

3. One who likes to participate in social activities.

1977 J. Anderson *Appearance of Evil* iv. 21 She was the quietest member of the family, was less of a socializer than Victor. **1978** G. A. Sheehan *Running & Being* ii. 29 His 'good life' is quite different from that of an aggressive football player and the relaxed socializer.

socializing, *vbl. sb.* (In Dict. s.v. Socialize *v.*) (Later examples.)

1944 J. S. Huxley *On Living in Revolution* 21 This humanizing and socializing of sectional groups is one way in which the new social order will differ from the old. **1959** V. Packard *Status Seekers* xii. 168 Status is attached to the act of socializing. **1965** B. Pearce tr. *Preobrazhensky's New Economics* 76 The whole system of regulation of the economy cannot but be affected by the socializing of industry and transport. **1970** *Globe & Mail* (Toronto) 28 Sept. 13/2 Having no brothers or sisters to toughen her, socializing is probably bewildering. **1976** Botham & Donnelly *Valentino* vi. 45 Lunchtime socialising.. brought him into contact with members of a motion picture company.

socializing, *ppl. a.* Add: Also, that revels in participating in social activities.

1965 F. L. Utley in Bessinger & Creed *Medieval & Linguistic Stud.* 308 A multiple martyr, to a fretful socializing wife, to the chthonic Mother, to the Judas Wilkes, to and for the Nation. **1980** *London Mag.* July 81/2 Mostly he [*sc.* Somerset Maugham] dealt in types, such as the rich bitch, the honest whore, the socializing snob.

socially, *adv.* Add: **4.** (Later examples.) Freq. regarded as forming a *Comb.* with a following *adj.* or *ppl. adj.*

1890 W. H. Dawson *Unearned Increment* iv. 47 The socially-created value of land. **1909** *Daily Chron.* 3 Nov. 1/1 The Budget taxes one form of 'socially-created wealth'. **1937** L. Cheskin in *Education* Nov. 186/2 They are socially conscious, they study their society and interpret it, each in his own manner. **1951** M. McLuhan *Mech. Bride* (1967) 51/1 Panic enters the socially spotlighted host or hostess. **1955** *Sci. News Let.* 22 Jan. 56/1 Staphylococcus germs that are common even on 'socially clean' hands. **1961** D. Jenkins *Equality & Excellence* vi. 130 The great public schools and socially-privileged private schools. **1964** L. Woolf *Beginning Again* iii. 232 Socially it was the prehistoric era in which one still had servants living in one's house. **1964** *Language* XL. 92 A leading predecessor in socially-oriented thought. **1970** *Daily Tel.* 26 Nov. 9/3 One such smoker said: 'The claustrophobic atmosphere makes pot-smoking socially acceptable.' **1976** *Times* 20 Aug. 4/3 (*caption*) Socially deprived pupils from a West Berlin school. *Ibid.* 4/4 The Government is..deciding to spend £50,000 on job schemes for socially disadvantaged people. **1977** *Daily Tel.* 13 Oct. 10/4 In the past it has been opposed to any 'head counts' of this kind. They were considered socially divisive.

socialry. (Earlier example.)

1896 A. Small *Let.* 22 May in *Social Forces* (1932) Mar. 313/1 'Socialry' has an archaic sight sound & sense which will hardly get itself naturalized in modern society, and as to his division of the factors of life in society with 'economics' & 'socialry'—it is a classification of things that he [*sc.* F. H. Giddings] hasn't begun to correlate in his own thinking.

social science. [Social *a.* 9 b.] The scientific study of the structure and functions of society; any discipline that attempts to study human society, either as a whole or in part, in a systematic way. Also *attrib.*

[**1785** J. Adams *Let.* 10 Sept. in *Works* (1854) IX. 540 The social science will never be much improved, until the people unanimously know and consider themselves as the fountain of power. **1791** D.-J. Garat *Let. à M. Condorcet* 82 Ces vérités..qu'il etoit important de découvrir, de rendre incontestables, sont les premières données de la science sociale, mais elles ne sont point la science.] **1811** tr. *Destutt de Tracy's Commentary Montesquieu's Spirit of Laws* 4, I have no other ambition..than to contribute my effort to the progress of social science, the most important of all to the happiness of man, and that which must necessarily be the last to reach perfection, because it is the product and the result of all the other sciences. **1821** J. Bentham *Let.* 21 Apr. in J. H. Burns *J. Bentham & Univ. Coll.* (1962) 8 The minds of the ruling few in their growing state should be turned towards the science so aptly stiled by you *the social science*—that science, in the progress of which the allied powers of tyranny, corruption, and delusion have so long..beheld their final downfall. **1846** [in Dict. s.v. Social *a.* 9 b]. **1849** *Southern Lit. Messenger* XV. 77/2 On the Importance of the Social Sciences in the present day. **1874** [in Dict. s.v. Social *a.* 9 b]. **1908** W. McDougall *Introd. Social Psychol.* p. vii, I hope that the book may be of service to students of all the social sciences. **1949** M. Mead *Male & Female* 435 The relationship between our social-science skills and our world. **1966** G. N. Leech *Eng. in Advertising* i. 3 Linguistics..has so far been the least influential of the major social sciences. **1969** *Times* 7 Jan. 8/6 Students reading social science were more sceptical than either the arts students or the scientists. **1971** *New Scientist* 18 Mar. 591/1 It seems more difficult to present a programme of viable-looking research in the social sciences than in the natural sciences. **1977** A. Giddens *Stud. in Social & Polit. Theory* ix. 306 Such a view is founded upon an erroneous idea of the relation between lay and social-science concepts.

Hence **social scientific** *a.*, **social scientist.**

1875 R. J. Wright *Principia; or, Basis of Social Sci.* p. v, *As to Spencer*; we admit he is *the* King of the Social Scientists. **1882** W. James *Let.* 2 Nov. (1920) I. 211 As for Prague, *veni, vidi, vici.* I went there with much trepidation to do my social-scientific duty. **1920** J. M. Williams *Foundations of Social Sci.* p. xiii, The trend of thought of the psychological social scientists signifies an aim to arrive at truer assumptions, and to keep an open mind toward the psychological, as well as the other aspects of those assumptions. **1971** *Nature* 25 June 538/1 Why do social scientists, particularly American social scientists, murder the English language? **1977** J. M. Johnson in Douglas & Johnson *Existential Sociol.* v. 166 Investigations of..social scientific situations.

social security. [Social *a.* 7.] **1. a.** A system whereby the state provides financial assistance for those citizens whose income is inadequate or non-existent owing to disability, unemployment, old age, etc.

1908 [see sense 2 below]. **1933** *Old Age Security Herald* June 1/1 Transformed in the *American Association for Social Security*, the organization [*sc.* the American Association for Old Age Security] will continue to function. **1936** A. Epstein *Insecurity* (rev. ed.) p. vi, The Act bars the realization of the relief promised by social insurance even though the law is presented under the glittering title of 'Social Security'. **1941** *Atlantic Charter* (Messages of Presidents, U.S.) (1943) 5 They desire to bring about the fullest collaboration between all nations in the economic field, with the object of securing for all improved labour standards, economic advancement and social security. **1942** *Times* (Weekly ed.) 2 Dec. 2/1 Social security as envisaged in this report is a plan to secure to each citizen an income adequate to satisfy a national minimum standard. *Ibid.*, As regards unification, Sir William Beveridge suggests that there should be a Ministry of Social Security. **1959** G. Slatter *Gun in My Hand* 44 What in hell are ya doin in Christchurch anyway? Bludgin on the social security, I spose. **1969** N. W. Pirie *Food Resources* i. 31 The Ministry of Social Security..found that there are now a million children at or below the poverty line [in the U.K.]. *a* **1974** R. Crossman *Diaries* (1975) I. 23 For years I've been a specialist on social security and I know enough about it.

b. The money paid out under this system.

1959 in J. Reid *Kiwi Laughs* (1961) 217 'Use your brains,' said Father Christmas testily. 'When you get to my age you have to live on social security. There's not much over to buy racing cars for every kid that wants one.' **1971** *Sunday Times* (Colour Suppl.) 5 Dec. 28 He has seven of his children to support on social security and family allowances. **1975** J. Symons *Three Pipe Problem* xv. 140 And you draw social security? **1976** *National Observer* (U.S.) 2 Oct. 7/2 Ethel..takes in tourists to complement her Social Security.

2. *attrib.*, as *social-security benefit, legislation, policy*, etc.

1908 W. S. Churchill *Let.* 4 Jan. in R. S. Churchill *Winston S. Churchill* (1969) II. Compan. ii. 759 If we were able to underpin the whole existing social security apparatus with a foundation of comparatively low-grade state safeguards, we should in the result obtain something that would combine the greatest merits both of the English & the German systems. **1935** *N.Y. Times* 15 Aug. 1/4 The Social Security Bill, providing a broad program of unemployment insurance and old-age pensions..became law today. **1936** *U.S. Statutes* XLIX. 635 There is hereby established a Social Security Board..to be composed of three members to be appointed by the President. **1940** *Economist* 31 Aug. 282/1 The old social security tax and the new national security tax. **1941** J. S. Huxley *Uniqueness of Man* p. ix, Subsidized housing, free milk, social security legislation, health insurance, free education ..—these are all symptoms of the change. **1942** *Rep. Commissioners Insurance & Allied Services from Organisations* App. G. 35 in *Parl. Papers 1942–3* (Cmd. 6405) VI. 419 Post-war social policy should aim at establishing a *national Plimsoll line* of goods and services for all citizens. .. Such a social security policy grants the citizens new opportunities and freedoms. **1962** *Listener* 26 July 130/1 Poor people in Mexico City who can attend a social-security clinic. **1964** W. Markfield *To Early Grave* vii. 131 He spread out..his army discharge papers, his social security card and a B'nai B'rith newsletter. **1966** N. Freeling *Dresden Green* i. 16 Chemists' bills and a social security number. **1969** *Times* 13 Jan. 11/2 £250m. available for higher social security benefits in the very low income range. **1972** *Accountant* 21 Sept. 347/1 The social security structure of individual countries depends heavily on their political climate. *a* **1974** R. Crossman *Diaries* (1976) II. 587 As chairman of the Pensions Committee I just had to get down to thinking what to do about social security payments after devaluation. **1976** W. Trevor *Children of Dynmouth* iii. 80 She was tired of listening to Mrs Slewy complaining about the social security man. **1976** *Ilkeston Advertiser* 10 Dec. 2/2 The Social Security 'scroungers', some of whom deliberately swindle the taxpayers to the extent of £10 million per year. **1978** S. Sheldon *Bloodline* xxxix. 347 People were on record if they had a Social Security number, an insurance policy a driver's license or a bank account.

social service. [Social *a.* 7.] **1.** Service to society or to one's fellow-men, esp. as exhibited in work on behalf of the poor, the underprivileged, etc.

1851 J. S. Mill *Lett.* (1910) I. 169 Scientific inquiry into the production and distribution of wealth, as a branch of social service. **1890** W. James *Princ. Psychol.* I. xiv. 599 The other social affections, *Benevolence, Conscientiousness, Ambition*, etc., arise in like manner by the transfer of the bodily pleasure experienced as a reward for social service. **1921** R. H. Tawney *Acquisitive Society* x. 219 If medical officers of health, directors of education, and directors of the Co-operative Wholesale be assumed to be quite uninfluenced by any consciousness of social service. **1926** E. Hemingway *Sun also Rises* ix. 85 'I rather thought it would be good for him.' 'You might take up social service.' 'Don't be nasty.' **1977** R. L. Wolff *Gains & Losses* vii. 404 Sublimation of doubt in sex, social service among the poor as a substitute for faith.. we shall encounter them again and again in..novels of doubt.

2. With *a* and *pl.* A service supplied for the benefit of the community, esp. any of those provided by the central or local government, such as education, medical treatment, social welfare, etc.

1933 J. Buchan *Prince of Captivity* ii. iii. 230 He is not prepared to go back on our social services... All parties go on sluicing out..new benefits from the public funds. **1941** 'R. West' *Black Lamb & Grey Falcon* II. 506 This Cockney taxi-driver would be..able to rely on an amplitude of social services in any emergency. **1945** *Ann. Reg. 1944* i. 82 The basic principle that compensation of workmen for industrial injury should be made a public social service. **1959** *Times Lit. Suppl.* 10 Apr. 203/2 Not even the welfare state and social services, and certainly not the nationalized industries, are now viewed by the mass of adult Britons as immaculate, brought down from Sinai. **1976** *Times* 22 July 16/1 There is more demand to cut taxes than to expand social services.

3. *attrib.* **a.** *sing.* (senses 1 and 2), as *social-service cut, work*, etc.

1900 J. P. SMYTH (*title*) Social service ideals. **1911** J. B. HALDANE *Social Workers' Guide* 127/1 Diocesan Social Service Committees. **1921** *Daily Colonist* (Victoria, B.C.) 8 Apr. 9/4 Mrs. Hallam, secretary of the Social Service Committee, requested that Miss Thompson, now acting for the organization as a social worker, be recognized as a woman police officer. **1929** HUGHES & STUENKEL (*title*) The Social Service Exchange in Chicago. **1932** *Bombay Chron.* 20 Dec. 5 The work of the Social Service League has been good all round. **1937** M. HILLIS *Orchids on your Budget* iii. 57 She also does the marketing by car, does social-service work in it once a week. **1956** F. LAFITTE in A. Pryce-Jones *New Outl. Mod. Knowl.* 574 Britain's heavy heritage of obsolescent social-service buildings. *a* **1974** R. CROSSMAN *Diaries* (1976) II. 444 He made an immensely demagogic speech saying that we'd spent more on social services than the Tories in their last three years, denying there was any question of social-service cuts. **1975** *Language for Life* (Dept. Educ. & Sci.) xix. 279 They include the Social Service Departments, Youth Service Departments, probation officers, and officers of the L.E.A. Careers Service.

b. *pl.* (sense 2), as *social services department*, etc.

1973 *Guardian* 30 May 9/2 Croydon's social services department is setting up a special training programme for new foster parents. **1974** *Times* 13 Nov. 16/2 The whole social services structure leads to good fieldworkers being lost to the management side. *Ibid.*, Management training in the social services field is possible. **1976** *Derbyshire Times* (Peak ed.) 3 Sept. 1/1 The party was from a Social Services home in Wartsones Road, Wolverhampton.

social work. [SOCIAL *a.* 7.] Work of benefit to those in need of help, esp. professional or voluntary service of a specialized nature concerned with community welfare and family or social problems arising mainly from poverty, mental or physical handicap, maladjustment, delinquency, etc. Also (with hyphen) *attrib.*

1890 *Girl's Own Paper* 27 Dec. 197/3 'Stump oratory' may safely be regarded as quite beyond the limits of a woman's social work. **1892** S. M. LINDSAY in *Annals Amer. Acad. Pol. & Social Sci.* Nov. 76 The growth of the Krupp cast steel works and the motives of the firm in their social work. **1908** *Busy Man's Mag.* Jan. 88/1 Few who read Mrs. Humphrey Ward's interesting books know of her social work in London. **1914** *Lancet* 31 Jan. 345/2 (*heading*) The sixth international congress of social work and service. **1931** *Economist* 10 Jan. 57/1 For in spite of the very considerable development which organised social work has attained in the United States.. it is not capable of shouldering the responsibility of caring for the wreckage of a major industrial depression. **1964** *New Statesman* 10 Apr. 581/1 An experienced social work teacher from Canada. **1975** *Listener* 14 Aug. 212/1 By the use of social-work skills, probation officers seek to help the offender cope. **1979** G. WAGNER *Barnardo* xvii. 299 No teacher training colleges or social work courses existed. **1980** *Times Lit. Suppl.* 28 Nov. 1347/1 Notwithstanding the vagueness of its aims, social work became sanctified as a discrete discipline under the Social Services Act of 1970.

Hence **social worker**, one who undertakes social work, esp. someone professionally trained.

1904 *Ann. Reg. Univ. Chicago* 245 A training center for social workers. **1912** F. G. D'AETH in H. Bosanquet *Social Conditions in Provincial Towns* iv. 50 A Local Committee of Social Welfare..consists of clergy, ministers, and social workers. **1931** *Economist* 10 Jan. 57/1 Social workers in the United States are meeting an unusually 'hard winter' with feelings almost of despair. **1955** EARL WINTERTON *Fifty Tumultuous Years* 117 Few, if any, of the social workers of today are old enough to remember conditions then. **1964** [see *ALMONER[1] 4]. **1975** *New Yorker* 11 Aug. 27/1 Ma says her social worker will not permit her to move her furniture until the rent is paid for August. **1977** B. PYM *Quartet in Autumn* xxii. 201 A real bossy social-worker type.

sociation. Restrict † *Obs. rare* to sense in Dict. and add: (sōᵘʃiˌēⁱ·ʃən). **2.** *Ecol.* = *SOCIETY 11*.

1930 *Svensk Bot. Tidskrift* XXIV. 492 The most elementary units in the series of phytocoenoses, or the sociations, have until now been studied nearly only by the Scandinavian School of Ecologists (= Phytosociologists). Until 1928 they were called 'associations', but in order to facilitate an international agreement, Scandinavian ecologists have now agreed to accept this term in its Middle-European sense, following Rübel's proposition to apply the new term 'sociation' to the earlier Scandinavian 'associations' (or 'micro-associations'). **1936** *Jrnl. Ecol.* XXIV. 276 It is here proposed to call the aspect society a *sociation* and the layer society a *lamiation*, while the corresponding seral terms would be *socies* and *lamies*. **1973** P. A. COLINVAUX *Introd. Ecol.* v. 67 (*caption*) Hypothetical species area curve as used by the Uppsala school for determining both the number of species in the sociation and the minimum area of that sociation.

socies (sōᵘ·ʃiˌīz). *Ecol.* [mod.L., f. SOCIETY after *species* (cf. *ASSOCIES).] The term answering to *SOCIETY 11* in analyses of immature plant communities.

1916 F. E. CLEMENTS *Plant Succession* vii. 138 The socies bears exactly the same relation to consocies and associes that the society does to consociation and association... The term socies comes from the root *seq-* (*sec-, soc-*), *follow*. **1926** [see *ASSOCIES]. **1929** *Ecology* X. 133 Each group of seasonals plus the constantly present predominants make up a socies, that is a seasonal subdivision or aspect-phase of the presocies. **1964** [see *ASSOCIES].

‖**sociétaire** (sosyetɛ̄r'). [Fr., f. *société* society.] An actor who is a full member of the Comédie Française, Paris, and thereby has a share in its management and profits.

1881 W. H. RIDEING *Dramatic Notes, 1880–81* xii. 67 Of the three parts in which London audiences have now seen her [*sc.* Mme Modjeska], this of the gifted and passionate *sociétaire* of the Comédie Française [*sc.* Sarah Bernhardt] illustrates most fully the measure of her genius. **1901** *Scotsman* 16 Apr. 8/7 The vexed question of the distribution of rôles among sociétaires and pensionnaires—full members of the company and salaried aspirants. **1909** BEERBOHM in *Sat. Rev.* 30 Oct. 529/1 He, too, has schooled himself in the traditions of the Gaiety, and is a worthy sociétaire. **1923** G. ARTHUR *Sarah Bernhardt* iv. 66 To the Directors of the Français the *Sociétaires* ranked only by seniority. **1959** *Times* 23 Feb. 12/2 If we had a National Theatre properly based and founded, all of us could be Sociétaires as in the Comédie-Française and be called upon when required.

societal, *a.* Add: (Earlier and later examples.) Hence **soci·etally** *adv.*

1898 *Catal. Yale Univ. 1898–9* 204 A study of the evolution of the institutions of the democratic republic, of the societal organization, and of the history of the money of account. **1907** [see *MORES 1]. **1956** *Kenyon Rev.* XVIII. 411 Trager and Smith's results are amazingly coherent, both practically and societally. **1959** *Sunday Times* 22 Nov. 16/4 His [*sc.* Kipling's] passion..for the values of what D. H. Lawrence (borrowing the revolting word from Dr. Trigant Burrow) called 'societal man'. **1964** [see *EGOCENTRIC *a.*]. **1973** *Black World* Mar. 28 Educational systems are constructed to socialize individuals to perform societally defined and necessitated tasks. **1976** *Times Lit. Suppl.* 19 Nov. 1449/1 Leading educators believe that the schools must keep pace with broad societal changes. **1979** 'A. HAILEY' *Overload* IV. vii. 328 The Sequoia Club has been something we all needed—part of our societal system of checks and balances.

soci·etified, *ppl. a. rare.* [f. SOCIETY + -FY + -ED[1].] Of or made fitting for cultured or fashionable society.

1934 in WEBSTER. **1936** E. M. FORSTER *Abinger Harvest* 108 The societified lady and the obscure maniac are in a sense the same person.

societology (sosəiˌėtǫ·lŏdʒi). *U.S. rare.* [f. SOCIET(Y + -OLOGY.] The study of human society; sociology.

1895 *Catal. Yale Univ. 1895–6* 62 In connection with this is a course of lectures on systematic sociology (Societology). This course is strictly academical..and does not take up topics popularly classed under 'social science'. **1915** *Nation* (N.Y.) 14 Oct. 467 He has made a real contribution to the study of society, and has demonstrated (what some of us had begun to doubt) that there is such a subject as sociology—or at least societology. **1924** C. M. CASE *Outlines Introductory Sociol.* p. xxxvi, It [*sc.* sociology] probably *should* be, and more than probably will *not* be, known as 'societology'.

society. Add: **I. 3. e.** *alternative society*: the aggregate of (predominantly young) persons whose cultural values and habits of association purport to represent a preferable and cogent alternative to those of the established social order. Usu. with definite article.

1969 *It* 13–25 June 21/3 Brother Simon Tugwell is planning a 3-day talk-in on the alternative society. **1971** *Guardian* 16 Mar. 10/4 American cities seem full of young people wanting to 'drop out'—but what do they drop into? It is called 'The Alternative Society' and it is already becoming a vogue term. **1971** *Times Lit. Suppl.* 31 Dec. 1621/5 Sorel, like Nietzsche, preached the need for a new civilization of makers and doers, what is now called a counter-culture or an alternative society. **1975** D. LODGE *Changing Places* v. 164 A middle-aged parasite on the alternative society.

III. 9. c. *Zool.* A group of animals of the same species organized in a co-operative manner.

1902 *Encycl. Brit.* XXIX. 503/2 Perhaps the most remarkable fact as regards the higher societies of insects is that though the individuals composing a community are the offspring of one mother..yet they do not resemble their parents. **1925** A. D. IMMS *Gen. Textbk. Entomol.* 522 In certain species of the order [Hymenoptera] the individuals have acquired the habit of living together in great societies, as in the case of the ants. **1964** V. B. WIGGLESWORTH *Life of Insects* xiv. 237 All insect societies are overgrown families. **1971** E. O. WILSON *Insect Societies* ii. 6/2 Bird flocks, wolf packs, locust swarms, and groups of communally nesting bees are good examples of elementary societies.

11*. *Ecol.* A community of plants within a mature consociation characterized by one or more subdominant species.

1899 *Bot. Gaz.* XXVII. 111 A plant society is defined as a group of plants living together in a common habitat and subjected to similar life conditions. The term is taken to be the English equivalent of Warming's *Plantesamfund*, translated into the German as *Pflanzenverein*. **1905** F. E. CLEMENTS *Res. Methods in Ecol.* 296 For these areas controlled by principal species, but changing from aspect to aspect, the term *society* is proposed. **1916** —— *Plant Succession* vii. 130 The society is a community characterized by a subdominant or sometimes by two or more subdominants... The society comes next below the consociation in rank, but it is not necessarily a division of it, for the same society may extend through or recur in two or more consociations, *i.e.*, throughout the entire association. **1932** FULLER & CONARD tr. *Braun-Blanquet's Plant Sociol.* xiii. 306 The..'societies' of Clements and Weaver are based entirely upon the dominance of certain species; they are, thus, quite incapable of replacing our association in any system of classification. **1932** *Ecology* XIII. 118 A single pair of terms, society and socies (developmental), has been quite generally applied to subordinate assemblages within associes and associations. **1952** P. W. RICHARDS *Tropical Rain Forest* xi. 259 *Shorea curtesii*..dominates small societies on steep slopes in the hill rain forests of the Malay Peninsula.

IV. 12. b. With reference to cultured or fashionable society: further examples.

1875 MRS. STOWE *We & Our Neighbours* 205 My sisters ..are society girls in the best sense. **1880** J. C. HARRIS *Uncle Remus* viii. 203 'The old man's mind is wandering,' said the society editor. **1882** J. D. MCCABE *N.Y. by Sunlight & Gaslight* 228 An engagement..is promptly announced in one of the 'Society journals'. *c* **1884** (*title*) A society beauty. **1888** *St Louis* (Missouri) *Globe-Democrat* 29 Apr. 22/2 The brainy paragraphs thrown off by one society reporter. **1891** *Girl's Own Paper* 21 Mar. 385/1, I..said I was tired of society life, and..liked nursing better than anything. **1893** 'S. GRAND' *Heavenly Twins* I. xv. 109 You would not counsel a son of yours to marry a society woman of the same character as Major Colquehoun. **1895** T. K. GAVON *Fancy Notions by a Yankee Notion Clerk* 28 Already we have cattle kings, coal barons, merchant princes and society queens. **1910** E. M. FORSTER *Howards End* iii. 19 She did not..pretend that nothing had happened, as a competent society hostess would have done. **1910** CHESTERTON *G. B. Shaw* 152 A pleasant society lady, Lady Cicely Waynefleet. **1911** G. S. PORTER *Harvester* xx. 508 He scanned the society columns of the papers. **1924** GALSWORTHY *White Monkey* I. ix. 73 A society painter and his wife. **1947** 'N. BLAKE' *Minute for Murder* ii. 32 He had been a society photographer before the war. **1949** H. MACLENNAN *Precipice* I. 144 A picture I saw of her in the society page of *The New York Times*. **1950** *New Yorker* 8 Apr. 76/3 Hearst's society columnist, Cholly Knickerbocker. **1950** E. H. GOMBRICH *Story of Art* xxiii. 349 Vandyke had established a standard of society portraits. **1955** L. FEATHER *Encycl. of Jazz* x. 347 *Society band*,..band that plays innocuous commercial dance music. **1956** C. COCKBURN *In Time of Trouble* xvii. 228 The secretary was away attending some society wedding. **1957** D. PIPER *Eng. Face* viii. 199 Behind almost all society portraiture before Reynolds there is a basic, and dead, symmetry. **1959** G. D. PAINTER *Marcel Proust* I. vii. 85 In the name 'Le Gandare' Proust alludes to the society portraitist La Gandara. *Ibid.* xi. 181 A little bird..informed the society columnist of *Le Gaulois*. **1976** C. STORR *Unnatural Fathers* iii. 36 He had had a long liaison with a society beauty. **1977** *Time* 26 Sept. 36/1 The society columns buzzed regularly for years with accounts of their parties and travels aboard an assortment of yachts.

socio-. Add: Also with pronunc. (sōᵘ·sio). **2. socioce·ntric** *a.*, tending to focus one's interest on the community or one's own group; hence **socioce·ntrism**; **sociodyna·mic** *a.*, tending to produce change in a society or group; hence **sociodyna·mics** *sb. pl.*; **socio-eco·logy**, the study of the interactions both among the members of a species and between them and their environment; so **socio-ecolo·gic, -ecolo·gical** *adjs.*; **socio·geny**, the origin and development of society; hence **sociogeˑnic, socio·genous** *adjs.*, originating in society or social interaction; **so·ciogram** *Sociol.*, a diagrammatic representation of the ratings for popularity, leadership, etc., that members of a small group give each other; a sociometric diagram; **socio·graphy**, an empirical method of sociological analysis that makes use of both quantitative and qualitative data; such an analysis; hence **socio-gra·phic** *a.*; **so·ciogroup** *Sociol.*, a group of people who associate for some reason or purpose other than personal preference; **sociome·dical** *a.*, of or pertaining to the relations between medicine and society; **socio-no·mic**, relating to the environmental conditions affecting the formation and development of social groups, esp. as *socionomic sex ratio*, the ratio of females to males in relatively stable social groups; hence **sociono·mics** (*rare*).

1881 L. F. WARD in *Trans. Anthrop. Soc. Washington* (1882) I. 97 Those in consequence of which social progress tends to defeat itself—*anti-sociocentric facts*. **1930** [see *CEREBROCENTRIC *a.*]. **1970** J. D. CAUTE *Fanon* iv. 49 There was the Fanon who condemned such insularity as egocentric and sociocentric. **1947** G. MURPHY *Personality* xv. 386 Side by side with egocentrism there was sociocentrism. **1934** J. L. MORENO *Who shall Survive?* vii. 74 This demonstrates what we may call the process of slowing down of interest, the cooling off of emotional expansiveness, the sociodynamic decline of interest. **1977** R. HOLLAND *Self & Social Context* vii. 221 The hypothesis that there are psychodynamic and sociodynamic processes at work even in this relatively 'self-conscious' area of knowledge production. **1978** *Nature* 18 May 184/2 The number of administrators in an organisation expands irresistibly in response to the first law of sociodynamics. **1972** *Biol. Abstr.* LIV. 6370/2 Geographic vegetational zones are given, as are vegetational stages. Socioecologic groups are described. **1961** *Ibid.* XXXVI. 5947/1 (*heading*) A socio-ecological study of pastured domestic rabbits in Mae-sima. **1973** W. P. J. Dittus in R. H. Tuttle *Socioecol. & Psychol. Primates* 149 Its net reproductive rate is attuned to the availability of food, and is regulated through socioecological mechanisms. **1972** *Biol. Abstr.* LIV. 3830/1 (Index), Socio ecology. **1975** L. L. & D. J. Klein in R. H. Tuttle *Socioecol. & Psychol. Primates* 83 A dietary factor..that is generally overlooked in discussion of primate socioecology, was the degree to which specific primates are able to utilize.. varied substances in any single day. **1979** *Nature* 8 Feb. 433/3 The main aims are to study the socio-ecology of the lesser-known species such as the slow loris and the pig-tailed macaque. **1969** Zigler & Child in Lindzey & Aronson *Handbk. Social Psychol.* III. xxiv. 484 Two main types of interpretations have been employed to explain the cross-cultural findings, the sociogenic and the psychogenic. **1978** *Language* LIV. 228 His separation of cultures, making sociogenic interaction impossible. **1941** W. Dennis in *Genetic Psychol. Monographs* XXIII. 187 Prior to the second year of life sociogenous responses, those which are learned through the intercession of other persons, are few. **1967** C. L. Markmann tr. *Fanon's Black Skin, White Masks* (1968) 13 Besides phylogeny and ontogeny stands sociogeny. **1933** J. L. Moreno in *Proc. Amer. Assoc. Mental Deficiency* 236 To visualize how each individual is affected by the maze of attractions and repulsions coming from any individual or going out from any individual of a group we mapped these relations graphically into a *sociogram*. **1972** M. Argyle *Social Psychol. of Work* vi. 109 The choices may be plotted to form a sociogram, and this can show the affective structure of a group very clearly. **1954** *Encounter* Dec. 55/1 A sociographic study attempts to relate all the data concerning a given locality in a meaningful way. **1881** O. T. Mason in *Ann. Rep. Smithsonian Inst.* (1883) 501 Observing and descriptive stage..sociography. **1940** C. P. Loomis *Tönnies's Fundamental Concepts Sociol.* p. xxiv, (*heading*) Empirical sociology or sociography. **1966** *Listener* 12 May 677/1 We do not yet have a sociography of English Catholicism. **1968** *Internat. Encycl. Social Sci.* XV. 49/1 To this he [*sc.* Tönnies]..opposed his own notion of 'sociography', in which systematic observation, case studies, and other qualitative methods were included, together with statistics. **1950** H. H. Jennings *Leadership & Isolation* (ed. 2) xiii. 276 This collective, more or less formalized setting, where concerns must be shared and obligations held in common..might appropriately be called..the sociogroup. **1956** J. Klein *Study of Groups* 179 In sociometric theory a sociogroup is based on preferences involving work in the group. **1934** Webster, Sociomedical. **1961** *Lancet* 2 Sept. 549/1 Euthanasia..is more than a sociomedical problem. **1977** *Time* 10 Jan. 41/1 The flourishing condom market is only one sign of a growing sociomedical phenomenon in the U.S.: a back-to-basics movement in birth control. **1902** J. M. Baldwin *Social & Ethical Interpretations* (ed. 3) 3 The *Biogenetic* method is valuable mainly in investigating the *socionomic* forces (those which condition or limit social change, but are not themselves social in their character). **1935** *Jrnl. Mammology* XVI. 176 As yet..it is impossible to ascertain the central grouping tendencies and the characteristic socionomic sex ratio (ratio of males to females living within groups). **1976** *Nature* 12 Feb. 459/1 Most body weights..do not take into account interspecies differences in socionomic sex ratio. **1902** J. M. Baldwin *Social & Ethical Interpretations* (ed. 3) xi. 484 Socionomics—the science of the relation of social life to its environment, including other social groups.

3. Also in comb. with advbs., in the sense 'socially and..': *socio-critical, -cultural, -culturally, -demographic, -educational, -emotional, -environmental, -geographic, -geographical, -historical, -industrial, -literary, -politically, -psychological, -psychologically, -regional, -religious* (earlier example), *-scientific, -sexual, -technic* (hence *socio-technics* sb. pl.), *-technical.*

1963 *Cambr. Rev.* 4 May 401/1 The Leitmotiv of the 'socio-critical' movement [in literature] is 'human destiny and national destiny'. **1929** H. Schreuder *Pejorative Sense Devel. in English* II. vi. 65 (*heading*) The socio-cultural group. **1958** *New Biol.* XXVI. 123 In discussing human potentiality it is not useful to dissociate socio-cultural from biological factors. **1978** *Language* LIV. 188 Linguistics consists partly in an investigation of certain aspects of human socio-cultural behavior. **1980** *Times Lit. Suppl.* 19 Sept. 1044/4 For various socio-cultural reasons, the short story has always occupied a more central place in Australian fiction than in European literatures. **1968** C. A. Doxiadis *Betw. Dystopia & Utopia* 66 We are not in a position yet to define how far he [*sc.* man] is adjustable either biologically or socio-culturally. **1972** *Bankers Mag.* Winter 68/2 Socio-demographic characteristics of the population such as age, sex, income, occupation, race, [etc.]. **1961** *Times* 16 Sept. 9/3 There is here an old socio-educational dispute in a new context. **1974** *Times Lit. Suppl.* 31 May 580/5 While the mother's strategies correlate with the cognitive development of the child..this correlation is totally unrelated to social class—which effectively deflates some hoary socio-educational myths. **1973** *Word* 1966 XXII. 112 Interaction situations, with men preponderantly performing the task role, and women, the socioemotional. **1969** *Punch* 22 Jan. p. vi/2 Socio-environmental pressures on me had taken an entirely different turn: I had been seduced by advertising. **1962** in H. O. Beecheno *Introd. Business Stud.* p. iii, A condensed survey of the historical background of our present economy..and the more basic socio-geographic factors. **1945** *Archit. Rev.* XCVII. 70/1 The socio-geographical differentiation in our own cities is simple and peaceful compared with that of a newer country like the United States. **1949** *Sci. Amer.* Oct. 53/3 Their philosophical ideas stem from the same socio-historical conditions of our epoch. **1965** *English Studies* XLVI. 390 Melville embodies the concept of revolt in specific socio-historical frames. **1909** W. H. Tolman *Social Engineering* xii. 366 A new profession necessitated by the complexity of socio-industrial relations. **1933** A. Parry *Garrets & Pretenders* p. ix, Since Bohemianism is pre-eminently a socio-literary phenomenon, the periods of its rise and decay coincided fairly well throughout the world. **1980** *Times Lit. Suppl.* 7 Nov. 1249/2 He [*sc.* Edmund Wilson] acquired half a dozen languages that served as socio-literary tools. **1968** *New Left Rev.* Jan.–Feb. 63 Germany did not merely invent the *ersatz* industrially, it produced it socio-politically as well. **1899** *Amer. Jrnl. Sociol.* IV. 661 Such a theory can be developed only along socio-psychological lines. **1970** *Nature* 19 Dec. 1136/1 Too little work has been done on the socio-psychological aspects of spaceflight. **1971** J. J. Shapiro tr. *Habermas's Toward Rational Society* ii. 30 Insensitivity to what in more naive times philosophers called 'the good life' can only be broken through today under the socio-psychologically exceptional conditions of university study. **1964** M. A. K. Halliday et al. *Linguistic Sci.* iv. 86 Our dialects and accents are no longer simply regional: they are regional and social, or 'socio-regional'. **1871** *Aldine* Jan. 18/2 It is a prime merit of such writers as Mr. Keeler and Bret Harte to give a rousing nudge to the saintly self-complacency of our socio-religious 'priggishness'. **1891** *Nation* 3 Sept. 182 The current socio-scientific use of *environment* is first found in Carlyle (1827). **1932** S. Zuckerman *Soc. Life Monkeys & Apes* xiv. 215 Facts concerning sub-human primate socio-sexual responses. **1931** Sociotechnic [see *nuttery 3]. **1937** *Burlington Mag.* Nov. 246/1 The concreteness with which socio-technical problems are realized. **1975** *Times Lit. Suppl.* 28 Feb. 229/3 P. G. Herbst's *Socio-technical Design*.. explores the interaction between the social and technical parts of industrial, educational and scientific organizations. **1976** A. Cherns (*title*) Sociotechnics. *Ibid.* p. ix, Sociotechnics..is..a quest for a methodology of bringing the knowledge and concepts of the social sciences to bear on human and social issues.

sociobiological (sō^{u}:ʃiobəiˌolǫ·dʒikăl, sō^{u}:sio-), *a.* [f. Socio- + Biological *a.*] Of or pertaining to sociobiology. Hence **so:ciobiolo·gically** *adv.*

1921 Hannay & Collingwood tr. *Ruggiero's Mod. Philos.* v. 185 Espinas was one of the first to apply the socio-biological method to the treatment of social questions. According to him the instinct of sociability is found in all grades of being, and is shared by animals and men alike. **1948** *Amer. Scientist* XXXVI. 567 We may regard the mechanism, for sociobiological purposes, as given. **1978** M. S. Gregory et al. *Sociobiology & Human Nature* 3 Pure sociobiological theory, being independent of human biology, does not imply by itself that human social behavior is determed by genes. **1980** *Nature* 24 Apr. 682/1 Sociobiologically sophisticated readers.

sociobiology (sō^{u}:ʃiobəiˌǫ·lodʒi, sō^{u}:sio-). [f. Socio- + Biology.] The study of the biological, esp. the ecological and evolutionary, bases of social behaviour.

1946 J. P. Scott in *Minutes Conf. Genetics & Social Behaviour* 5 The central objective of the scientific method is the development of generalizations which are as nearly true as possible... The zoologists and psychologists who work with animals can do their part to help extend these generalizations by working toward the development of comparative sociology, or perhaps it may be called psychobiology or sociobiology. **1948** C. F. Hockett in *Amer. Scientist* XXXVI. 564 Since there is no generally accepted word for just what we mean, we can, for the purposes of the present discussion, coin one. On the analogy of *biophysics* we shall speak of *sociobiology*. **1950** J. P. Scott in *Ann. N.Y. Acad. Sci.* LI. 1004 An interdisciplinary science which lies between the fields of biology (particularly ecology and physiology) and psychology and sociology. Many names have been given to it, but perhaps the best and most descriptive is 'sociobiology'. **1975** E. O. Wilson *Sociobiology* i. 4/1 Sociobiology is defined as the systematic study of the biological basis of all social behaviour. **1976** *Ann. Rev. Microbiol.* XXX. 236 One of the most exciting aspects of this new field of sociobiology is the chemical control of behavioral responses. **1979** *Nature* 2 Aug. 427/1 The widespread identification of 'sociobiology' with a school of thought is an undeniable fact of current biological sociology.

Hence **so:ciobio·logist**, one who studies sociobiology.

1975 *Times* 29 Dec. 5/1 Interest is growing in the theories of sociobiologists who seek to prove that most human social behaviour has genetic origins. **1980** *Daily Tel.* 10 Mar. 12/8 Sociobiologists hope their theory of behaviour, which seems at present to apply only to individuals, can be expanded into a science which could analyse humanity as a whole.

so·ciodrama. *Sociol.* Also with hyphen. [f. Socio- + Drama.] An improvised play acted by or for those involved in a situation of social tension in order to portray different perceptions of the same situation and represent objectively what each experiences in his or her role; a form of psychiatric treatment based on this type of play. Hence **sociodrama·tic** *a.*, **sociodra·matist**, someone directing a sociodrama.

1943 J. L. Moreno in *Sociometry* VI. 331 Sociodrama which deals with inter-group relations and with collective ideologies. *Ibid.* 438 Let us consider first two broad fields of application of sociodramatic procedures. **1952** W. J. H. Sprott *Social Psychol.* ii. 36 The 'spontaneity training', from which the so-called 'Socio-drama' has been developed. **1958** —— *Human Groups* 188 The elaborate technique of training for foremanship, often employing the socio-drama technique in which foremen take the part of workers and act out a scene. **1964** *Telegraph* (Brisbane) 17 June 8 No one knew what to expect when Jean Jacques Lebel staged his 'sociodramatic event' the other night. **1972** H. J. Eysenck *Psychology is about People* i. 16 The psychiatrist asks, Is psychotherapy better than sociodrama? **1979** Glassner & Freedman *Clinical Sociol.* xiv. 326 In important respects all of the sociodramatic procedures are forms of spontaneity training. *Ibid.*, It is important to distinguish the sociodramatist's view of spontaneity from some others.

so:cio-econo·mic, *a.* Also as one word. [f. Socio- + Economic *a.*] That derives from both social and economic factors; that combines both factors to provide an indication of a person's or a group's effective social situation, esp. as *socio-economic class, status.*

1883 L. F. Ward *Dynamic Sociol.* I. vii. 525 It is not from an anthropological or ethnological stand-point that our treatise proceeds but rather from a strictly sociological or socio-economic one. **1937** L. B. Murphy *Social Behaviour & Child Personality* i. 32 Although the socio-economic status was important..it was by no means directly correlated with the educational stimulus which the children received. **1949** M. Mead in M. Fortes *Social Structure* 18 An account of Arapesh socio-economic life. **1966** Bereiter & Engelmann *Teaching Disadvantaged Children* i. 3 Studies of three- to five-year old children from lower socio-economic backgrounds have shown them to be retarded..in every intellectual ability. **1972** *Jrnl. Social Psychol.* LXXXVI. 207 The subjects were required to be from the same socioeconomic class, in this case the middle class. **1978** P. A. Cowan *Piaget: with Feeling* xii. 310 There are studies which compare infants and..children who differ in socioeconomic status.

Hence **socio-econo·mically** *adv.*

1955 *Social Problems* July 98 The strong influence of abortion law is seen in the refusal of hospitals to grant socio-economically indicated abortions. **1977** *Lancet* 30 Apr. 955/2 In socioeconomically advanced West Germany the vaccine is specifically recommended for infants with chronic diseases of the heart.

sociolect (sō^{u}·siolekt, sō^{u}·ʃio-). [f. Socio- + *-lect.] A variety of a language that is characteristic of the social background or status of its user. Also *attrib.* Hence **sociole·ctal** *a.*

1972 [see *-lect]. **1976** *Archivum Linguisticum* VII. 158 Here the functional shift from dialect to sociolect indicators is of particular interest. In fact, dialectal, sociolectal, and stylistic varieties will perhaps be the first 'partial features' which lend themselves to a more ambitious attempt at establishing a complex network of linguistic and social functional co-variation. **1978** *Language* LIV. 227 The book contains 491 pages, written in a highly academic sociolect of German which makes rich use of embedding devices, some sentences being over a page long. **1980** *English World-Wide* I. i. 129 A collection of twelve articles on a variety of sociolectal and dialectal phenomena in British English.

sociolinguistic (sō^{u}:sioliŋgwi·stik, sō^{u}:ʃio-), *a.* and *sb.* Also **socio-linguistic.** [f. Socio- + Linguistic *a.* and *sb.*] **A.** *adj.* Of or pertaining to the study of language in its social context.

1949 E. A. Nida *Morphology* (ed. 2) vi. 152 The reactions of language-users to the sociolinguistic environment. **1952** *Word* VIII. iii. 261 Therefore we may expect to come across socio-linguistic situations which we may hesitate to class in one or another of our four categories. **1959** *Amer. Speech* XXXIV. 118 Enumerating these sounds without giving clear indications of all the pertinent sociolinguistic facts can be dangerous. **1964** L. Kaiser in D. Abercombie et al. *Daniel Jones* 102 Ladefoged has discerned three kinds of information: linguistic, socio-linguistic, and personal. **1971** J. Spencer *Eng. Lang. W. Afr.* 7 Before we can understand the processes of stabilisation and change in the English of West Africa, we need a great deal more sociolinguistic evidence. **1978** *Verbatim* Feb. 10/1 Dillard organizes his work around 'socio-linguistic domains' and stresses the importance of discourse over sentence as the primary carrier of meaning.

B. *sb. pl.* (usu. const. as *sing.*). The study of language in relation to social factors. Also *attrib.*

1939 T. C. Hodson in *Man in India* XIX. 94 (*title*) Socio-linguistics in India. **1951** E. Haugen in *Language* XXVII. 213 If semantics should be an undesirable term, there is always 'ethno-linguistics' or perhaps 'socio-linguistics'. **1951** *Directory of American Scholars* 1061/2 Currie, Prof. Haver C(ecil)... History of American thought; socio-linguistics. **1952** H. C. Currie in *Southern Speech Jrnl.* XVIII. i. 28 This field is here designated *socio-linguistics*. *Ibid.* 36 The present projection of socio-linguistics proposes a fresh start toward researches into the social significance of language in all respects. **1964** *9th Internat. Congress Linguistics 1962* 1129 Those of us who work in the interdisciplinary area of 'socio-linguistics' may feel that we are here at this Congress on sufferance. **1967** *Language* XLIII. 586, I find that sociolinguistics connotes a branch of linguistics or, at best, a neutralization of the fruitful distinction between sociological linguistics and sociology of language. **1979** *London Rev. Bks.* 25 Oct. 4/3 (Advt.), Shows how social psychological theories and methods can increase the explanatory power of sociolinguistics. **1980** *English World-Wide* I. 179 Sociolinguistics intends to produce a linguistic description as its end result, although it uses social facts and methods to arrive at this end.

Hence **socio·li·nguist**, a student of or specialist in sociolinguistics; **so:ciolingui·stically** *adv.*

1960 *Amer. Anthropologist* LXVI. 86 Sociolinguists study verbal behavior in terms of the relations between the setting, the participants, the topic, the functions of the interaction, the form, and the values held by the participants about each of these. **1968** W. A. STEWART in J. A. Fishman *Readings in Sociol. of Lang.* 539 [Pidgins] and [Creoles] usually function sociolinguistically as special kinds of dialects of their lexical-source languages. **1972** J. L. DILLARD *Black English* v. 193 Men's dialects and languages as well as women's dialects and languages are well known to the sociolinguist. **1973** *Archivum Linguisticum* IV. 70 The following would seem most likely to be sociolinguistically of significance. **1979** *Amer. Speech 1976* LI. 118 Perhaps,..through the combined efforts of dialectologists, sociolinguists, and other observers of language, a more accurate picture will emerge.

sociologese (sōᵘ:siǫlǒdʒī·z, sōᵘ:ʃiǫ-). [f. SOCIOLOG(Y + -ESE.] A derogatory term used to describe the style of writing supposedly typical of sociologists; a style which is over-complicated or jargonistic and abstruse. Also *attrib.*

1963 *Times Lit. Suppl.* 29 Mar. 211/1 They are written ..not in Sociologese. **1965** E. GOWERS *Fowler's Mod. Eng. Usage* (ed. 2) 570/1 Sociologese, like Commercialese and Officialese, deserves an article to itself. **1969** R. BLACKBURN in Cockburn & Blackburn *Student Power* 184 The notion of structural contradiction emerges in Sociologese as 'lack of fit' between, for example, the economy and the 'core institutional framework'. **1973** *Times* 8 Nov. 16/3 His first chapter or two is marred by heavy sociologese. **1977** *New Statesman* 1 July 16/3 So, it's 'thwokk', is it? What a pity..for Mick Shepherd..that he was unable to find a better acoustic whizz-word than this in his dictionary of fifth-rate sociologese clichés. **1982** *Times Lit. Suppl.* 26 Mar. 356/5 *The Culture of Consent* contains, perhaps, too much sociologese for some tastes.

sociological, *a.* (Earlier example.)

1843 MILL *Logic* II. VI. x. 585 There are two kinds of sociological inquiry.

sociologism (sōᵘsiǫ·lǒdʒiz'm, sōᵘʃiǫ·-). [f. SOCIOLOG(Y + -ISM.] The tendency to ascribe a sociological basis to other disciplines. Hence **sociologi·stic** *a.*

1945 K. R. POPPER *Open Society* II. xxiii. 202 This theory of Hegel's..is sometimes called 'historicism'... The sociology of knowledge or 'sociologism' is obviously very closely related to or nearly identical with it. *Ibid.* 205 If scientific objectivity were founded, as the sociologistic theory of knowledge naïvely assumes, upon the individual scientist's impartiality,..we should have to say good-bye to it. **1958** W. STARK *Sociology of Knowledge* 331 We have to reject 'sociologism' (a pendant to psychologism). **1964** I. L. HOROWITZ *New Sociology* 17 The recent work in some quarters, ostensibly critical of excessive sociologism, seems to point precisely in the direction of the self-liquidation of sociology. **1965** E. E. EVANS-PRITCHARD *Theories Primitive Relig.* iii. 70 But, masterly though it was, its conclusions are an unconvincing piece of sociologistic metaphysics. **1977** *Language* LIII. 398 The fact that the autonomy principle underlies K's attack on Doroszewski is shown by the following remark on Saussure's alleged sociologism. **1978** E. A. TIRYAKIAN in Bottomore & Nisbet *Hist. Sociol. Anal.* vi. 212 Durkheim's 'sociologism' in this respect amounts to no less than an epistemological revolution.

sociologize, *v.* Add: Also *trans.*, to render sociological in character; to study from the standpoint of sociology. Hence **socio·logizing** *ppl. a.* and *vbl. sb.*

1924 *Amer. Jrnl. Sociol.* XXX. 302 (*title*) The sociologizing movement within political science. **1960** *20th Cent.* May 443 The 'sociologizing' of these disciplines [*sc.* economics and politics] in America..has increased their current vitality. **1971** *New Society* 7 Jan. 24/2 How many sociologists are there in Britain? We do not know, for the profession has not seriously sociologised itself. **1980** *Times Lit. Suppl.* 26 Sept. 1073/3 *The People's Choice* of 1944 is central to the beneficial sociologizing of more than one sector of the political science with which we now live.

sociology. Add: Also with pronunc. (sōᵘsi-). **1. a.** Also, the study of social organization and institutions and of collective behaviour and interaction, including the individual's relationship to the group; also *attrib.*

1897 L. F. WARD *Social Philos.* I. iv. 66 The nature of this being, man, whose associative habits form the chief subject of sociology. **1927** P. SOROKIN *Social Mobility* p. ix, Speculative sociology is passing over. An objective, factual, behavioristic, and quantitative sociology is.. superseding it. **1932** S. & B. WEBB *Meth. of Social Study* i. 3 Sociology is concerned not with the individual man, regarded as a living organism.., but with relations among men. **1951** SPAULDING & SIMPSON tr. E. Durkheim (*title*) Suicide. A study in sociology. **1965** HOWARD & WEAVER tr. *Aron's Main Currents in Sociolog. Thought* 8 Sociology may be said to be characterized by two specific aims which account for its nature. On the one hand, sociology lays claim to objective and scientific knowledge. On the other, what it claims to know objectively and scientifically is some vaguely defined thing we call society or societies or social phenomena. **1977** R. HOLLAND *Self & Social Context* ix. 260 A college would rather fall below its intake targets and lose revenue than take in sociology students. **1980** *Daily Tel.* 17 Apr. 10/8 He told me that he taught sociology and I told him straight that hogwash was not one of my subjects.

b. The application of sociological concepts and analysis to the social context of other disciplines or fields; a particular sociological system.

1916 E. EHRLICH in *Harvard Law Rev.* XXIX. 582 Mr. Justice Holmes has suggested a criticism of my book on the sociology of law..in that he finds therein no reference to Montesquieu. **1928** P. SOROKIN *Contemp. Sociological Theories* i. 40 It will be more convenient to discuss his [*sc.* Weber's] sociology in the chapters on the sociology of religion. **1936** WIRTH & SHILS tr. *Mannheim's Ideology & Utopia* ii. 69 The simple theory of ideology develops into the sociology of knowledge. **1947** J. WACH (*title*) Sociology of religion. **1965** HOWARD & WEAVER tr. *Aron's Main Currents in Sociological Thought* 7 The specialized sociologies—the sociology of science, the sociology of language, the sociology of art, the sociology of literature—are attempts to explain the evolution of human phenomena in relation to the social milieu. **1978** *Amer. N. & Q.* Feb. 92/1 The first volume.. contains seven essays on the sociology of reading. **1980** *English World-Wide* I. 179 The sociology of language.. uses linguistic information as a means of describing social phenomena.

2. The study of plant or animal communities. Cf. *PHYTOSOCIOLOGY.

1932 FULLER & CONARD tr. *Braun-Blanquet's Plant Sociol.* 1 We may divide all biology into (1) idiobiology: the science of individual organisms; and (2) sociology: the science of organic communities. The latter is divided into the social science of man (sociology in the usual sense), zoosociology, and phytosociology or plant sociology. **1932** S. ZUCKERMAN *Social Life Monkeys & Apes* i. 9 Mammalian sociology has developed without any real regard for questions concerning the validity of anecdotal and anthropomorphic evidence. **1953** D. A. BANNERMAN *Birds Brit. Isles* I. 35 We are learning more and more regarding what may be termed the sociology of birds. **1960** N. POLUNIN *Introd. Plant Geogr.* iii. 92 Plant sociology, where considerations of life-forms may help in the description of the structure of the communities.

sociometric (sōᵘsiome·trik, sōᵘʃio-). *a. Sociol.* and *Social Psychol.* [f. SOCIO- + *-METRIC.] Connected with or pertaining to sociometry or the assessment of relationships in groups. Hence **sociome·trically** *adv.*; **sociome·trics** *sb. pl.* = *SOCIOMETRY.

1933 J. L. MORENO in *Proc. Amer. Assoc. on Mental Deficiency* 224 An instrument to measure the amount of organization shown by social groups is called the sociometric test. **1943** —— in *Sociometry* VI. 316 How a community can be sociometrically tested. **1952** *Personnel Psychol.* V. 178 (*heading*) Sociometrically selected work teams increase production. **1956** C. W. VALENTINE *Normal Child* xi. 189 The 'sociometric' technique is flexible. **1964** D. F. DOWD in I. L. Horowitz *New Sociol.* 61 A mindless procession that moves from sociology to sociometrics. **1978** P. MARSH et al. *Rules of Disorder* iv. 86 Simply by looking at who meets whom and in what order we can begin to get some idea of the sociometric structure of the football fan culture.

sociometry (sōᵘsiǫ·mėtri, sōᵘʃiǫ·-). *Sociol.* and *Social Psychol.* [f. SOCIO- + -METRY.] The qualitative and quantitative analysis of the structure of groups, esp. through charting the relationships that exist between the members of small groups. Hence **socio·metrist.**

1908 W. DE MORGAN *Somehow Good* xi. 99 'I suppose you'd admit there *are* such things as social distinctions?' Sally wouldn't admit anything whatever. If sociometry was to be a science, it must be worked out without axioms or postulates. **1933** J. L. MORENO in *Proc. Amer. Assoc. on Mental Deficiency* 224 The mathematical study of psychological properties of populations, the experimental technique of and the results obtained by the application of quantitative and qualitative methods is called sociometry. **1937** *Sociometry* I. 219 The sociometrist has the task of breaking down..the misunderstandings and fears..in the group he is facing. **1956** J. KLEIN *Study of Groups* 180 The insistence of the sociometrist that the two kinds of criterion must be presented simultaneously now begins to sound suspicious. **1962** K. M. EVANS (*title*) Sociometry and education. **1976** *Times Lit. Suppl.* 26 Mar. 343/2 Mr Lucas deserves a loud cheer for writing a whole informative chapter on the way members of groups affect each other in communities without once using that dreadful word, beloved of educational theories, sociometry.

sociopath (sōᵘ·siopæþ, sōᵘ·ʃio-). *Psychol.* [f. SOCIO-, after PSYCHOPATH.] Someone with a personality disorder manifesting itself chiefly in anti-social attitudes and behaviour. Hence **sociopa·thic** *a.*; **socio·pathy.**

1930 G. E. PARTRIDGE in *Amer. Jrnl. Psychiatry* X. 55 A conspicuous number who..may justly be termed 'sociopathic'. *Ibid.*, We may use the term 'sociopathy' to mean anything deviated or pathological in social relations. *Ibid.* 56 We may exclude from the class of essential sociopaths those whose inadequacy is primarily related to physical weakness, fear, hypersensitiveness, shyness and self-blame. **1940** HINSIE & SCHATZKY *Psychiatric Dict.* 493/1 *Sociopathy*, this term has generally been used to designate an abnormal or pathological mental attitude toward the environment. **1962** L. YABLONSKY *Violent Gang* (1967) xii. 216 The violent-gang structure recruits its participants from the more sociopathic youths living in the disorganized-slum community. **1968** *Listener* 26 Sept. 408/1 In America 'psychopathy' has been replaced by 'sociopathy'. **1976** SMYTHIES & CORBETT *Psychiatry* iii. 29 Many sociopaths come from appalling backgrounds or from genetically afflicted families.

socius. Add: **3.** *Philos.* Applied to God, as the 'Great Companion' of man.

1890 W. JAMES *Princ. Psychol.* I. x. 316 The impulse to pray is a necessary consequence of the fact that whilst the innermost of the empirical selves of a man is a self of the *social* sort, it yet can find its only adequate *socius* in an ideal world. **1917** A. S. PRINGLE-PATTISON *Idea of God* xv. 297 The idea of a divine *socius* has been one of the most abiding inspirations of religious experience.

4. The individual person, considered as the unit of human society; the social self.

1895 J. M. BALDWIN *Mental Devel. Child & Race* xi. 338 Both *ego* and *alter* are thus essentially social; each is a *socius*, and each is an imitative creation. **1898** F. H. GIDDINGS *Elements of Sociol.* 10 What, now, is the unit of investigation in Sociology?... In its simplest form society exists whenever an individual has a companion or associate. The socius, then, is the unit of any social group or society. **1912** C. A. ELLWOOD *Sociol. in Psychol. Aspects* ii. 21 The *socius*, or associated individual,..the unit out of which all the simpler social groups are composed. **1963** S. KOCH *Psychol.* VI. p.v, (*title*) Investigations of man as socius: their place in psychology and the social sciences.

sock, *sb.*[1] Add: Pl. also **sox** (see as main entry). **2. a.** Slang and colloq. phrases: *in one's socks*, as a condition of measurement of stature; = *in one's stockings* s.v. STOCKING *sb.* 5 a (cf. *in one's shoes* s.v. SHOE *sb.* 2 c); *to knock the socks off* (someone), and varr. (*U.S.*): to beat thoroughly, to trounce; similarly *to rot the socks off*; *to pull one's socks up*: to make an effort, to pull oneself together; *to put a sock in it*: to stop speaking or making a noise, to shut up; to 'stop it'; usu. in *imp.*; *old socks* (orig. *N. Amer.*): a familiar form of address.

1835 DICKENS *Sk. Boz* (1836) II. 2 He..stood four feet six inches and three-quarters in his socks. **1913** T. H. S. ESCOTT *Anthony Trollope* x. 191 Those who knew Anthony Trollope in the flesh saw in him one who, at his prime, had stood some six feet in his socks. **1927** in C. J. Finger *Frontier Ballads* 69 This Floyd stood six feet in his socks and passed for mighty fly. **1977** *Horse & Hound* 14 Jan. 40/3 (Advt.), 11 hands in his socks... Smart, free-moving pony. **1845** C. BEECHER *Let.* in M. Rugoff *Beechers* (1981) xi. 212 'Beecher you must put in your best licks today!' 'You must knock the socks off those Old School folks!' And so they stood by to see me fight. **1964** J. PORTER *Dover One* vi. 65 This thick, fruity beverage..was guaranteed by one revolting old boozer as being strong enough to rot the socks off you. **1979** *Arizona Daily Star* 22 July D3/1 'Trucks have been beating our socks off,' said..a spokesman for the Atchison, Topeka & Santa Fe Railway in Chicago. 'But now we have a chance to get some of the business back.' **1893** H. F. MCCLELLAND *Jack & Beanstalk* 31 Pull up your socks! I'll see naught goes wrong with you. **1906** *Daily Mail* 14 Feb. 6/6 The 'smart set' have got hold of another neat expression. 'You must pull your socks up' is the latest form of saying 'Never mind', or 'Pull yourself together'. **1914** 'BARTIMEUS' *Naval Occasions* xi. 78 Pull your socks up, Ah Chee, an' think of something. **1936** M. KENNEDY *Together & Apart* IV. 294 There's hope for you if you pull your socks up. **1976** *Southern Even. Echo* (Southampton) 11 Nov. 17/5 The dismissal was unfair because Mr. Collier had not been given adequate warning and a chance 'to pull his socks up' before dismissal. **1919** *Athenæum* 8 Aug. 729/2 The expression 'Put a sock in it', meaning 'Leave off talking, singing or shouting'. **1930** J. B. PRIESTLEY *Good Companions* I. vi. 232 Two or three members of his audience laughed, but a young man in a green cloth cap was very annoyed. 'Oh, put a sock in it,' he said to the ripe gentleman, who immediately and very loudly asked him what he meant by it. **1933** M. LOWRY *Ultramarine* vi. 243 Aw, put a sock in it. Well, I'm going to sleep, chaps, and if you wake me again, the fellow that does it I'll slip him thirteen inches of saltpetre. **1944** 'N. SHUTE' *Pastoral* v. 107 'For Christ's sake put a sock in it,' he had said..'and tell them I want an ambulance down here.' **1978** A. PRICE *'44 Vintage* vi. 69 He..drew his finger across his throat, grinning horribly. 'Put a sock in it, Taf,' said Sergeant Purvis sharply. **1925** T. DREISER *Amer. Tragedy* I. II. iii. 185 Gee, it's good to have a look at you, old socks! **1934** H. G. RADCLIFFE in *Passing Show* 27 Jan. 5/4 Hey, Morrison, old socks. How's things! **1950** R. MOORE *Candlemas Bay* 19 Ninety..pounds, Jebby, old socks.

c. *colloq.* A sock used as a receptacle for storing one's money; hence, a store of money. Cf. STOCKING *sb.* 2 a.

1930 WODEHOUSE *Very Good, Jeeves!* x. 263 Her name was Maudie and he loved her dearly, but the family would have none of it. They dug down into the sock and paid her off. **1949** H. MACLENNAN *Precipice* III. 248 Once we've got enough put away in the sock I'm going to..go back to M.I.T. **1951** CUSACK & JAMES *Come in Spinner* 54 He just can't adjust himself to not having the best. And that's what marriage without a sock in the bank would mean. **1956** B. HOLIDAY *Lady sings Blues* (1973) x. 95, I opened Café Society as an unknown; I left two years later as a star. But you couldn't tell the difference from what I had in my sock.

d. *N.Z.* (See quot. 1965.)

1955 G. BOWEN *Wool Away!* iii. 45 Many sheepowners do not like socks taken off, as it puts hair in the wool. **1965** *N.Z. Listener* 26 Feb. 15/2 *Socks*, wool between the knee and the foot. In some sheds and competitions the instruction 'leave the socks on' means not to shear this wool, which usually contains a proportion of hair.

6. *attrib.* and *Comb.*, as **sock foot** *U.S.* =

STOCKING-FOOT c; hence **sock-footed** *a.*; **sock-suspender** = SUSPENDER 4 b. See also sense 2 in Dict.

1934 *Jrnl. Amer. Folk-Lore* XLVII. 52 No boots could he find. He was about to..go to his wedding in his sock feet, when a Voice told him to crawl out from under the bed. **1935** Z. N. HURSTON *Mules & Men* I. viii. 177 Pull off yo' shoes and set in yo' sock feet. **1981** *Nordic Skiing* Jan. 34/2 Chairback is for the making of memories... unforgettable skiing, bone-easing hot shower and sauna, a fine dinner, a tumbler of mulled wine, sock-footed by your woodstove. **1912** E. C. BENTLEY *Trent's last Case* iii. 36 He had on a complete outfit of underclothing, studs in his shirt, sock-suspenders. **1922** WODEHOUSE *Jill the Reckless* xviii. 268 Give me your share of the show for three dollars in cash and I'll throw in a pair of sock-suspenders and an Ingersoll. **1978** S. WILSON *Dealer's Move* ix. 185 One of his trousers had been dragged up to his knee... He was wearing sock suspenders.

sock, *sb.*[4] Add: **1.** Also in phr. *a sock in the eye* (also *fig.*).

1972 WODEHOUSE *Pearls, Girls, & Monty Bodkin* vi. 87 He's asked you to lunch in the hope of talking you into giving me the sock in the eye on which his heart is set. **1974** —— *Aunts aren't Gentlemen* xiv. 119, I knew that her name would be mud. I still wasn't sure she couldn't even be jugged, and what a sock in the eye that would give Uncle Tom's digestion. **1979** *Woman & Home* June 154/2 The return to tradition; a sock in the eye for the mechanisation that was creating unemployment.

2. *U.S. slang.* A strong impact, emphasis, a 'kick'.

1936 *Swing Music* Mar. 10/1, I used to get a terrific sock out of Rappolo riding high on his clarinet. **1937** B. GOODMAN *This Thing called Swing* 9 *Sock*, emphasis, usually referring to the last chorus. **1950** *Audio Engin.* Sept. 14/3 More low middles increase the *Punch* until the program is *solid*, and has *sock.* **1972** *Publishers' Weekly* 21 Aug. 15/1 (Advt.), Here's solid history with the sock of unforgettable fiction. **1979** *Arizona Daily Star* 22 July C3/2, I figure we have enough speed and sock in our lineup to score runs.

3. *attrib.* and *Comb.*, as **sock chorus** *Jazz* (see quot. 1936); **sock cymbal** *Jazz* = *HIGH HAT, HIGH-HAT 3; also *attrib.*

1936 *Delineator* Nov. 49/2 *Sock chorus*, last chorus of an arrangement. **1937** *Metronome* Mar. 31/1 The full sock chorus..hits you between the eyes. **1956** E. HUNTER *Second Ending* iv. 69 They rode into the sock chorus like a storm cloud of marauders. **1936** Sock cymbal [see *OFF-BEAT *a.* 1]. **1949** L. FEATHER *Inside Be-bop* III. 80 Kenny originally played the old Jo Jones sock cymbal style. **1972** *Jazz & Blues* Sept. 7/3 You wouldn't play your sock cymbal the same as your ride cymbal.

sock, *v.*[2] Add: **1. a.** (*a*) (Further examples.) (*b*) *fig.* To give a hard blow to; *esp.* to take large sums of money from (someone). *U.S.*

(*a*) **1870** R. B. MANSFIELD *School-Life at Wincheste College* 234 *Sock*, to hit hard at Cricket. **1916** [see *GAS *sb.*[2}]. **1926** *Variety* 29 Dec. 5/3 No craving for expression motivated me when I hung up the finger glove and sliding pads in favor of socking a typewriter. **1933** G. B. SHAW *Political Madhouse in America* 21 Why do you applaud these screen heroes who, when they are not kissing the heroine, are socking jaws? It is a criminal offence to sock a citizen in the jaw. **1982** B. CHATWIN *On Black Hill* xiv. 67 The porter had socked him on the jaw, and he now lay, face down on the paving.

(*b*) **1939** J. STEINBECK *Grapes of Wrath* xvi. 248 Find out how much they gonna sock ya for the lessons. **1941** B. SCHULBERG *What makes Sammy Run?* x. 191 When a moving picture is right, it socks the eye and the ear and the solar plexus. **1943** *Sun* (Baltimore) 8 Nov. 1/2 Cost rises are so precipitate..that one Congressman..suggested 'we're being socked everywhere in foreign countries.' **1973** J. CLEARY *Ransom* ii. 44, I don't know what sort of demands they're making. If they're socking the Mayor.. the price is gonna be high—he's a very rich man. **1978** *Detroit Free Press* 5 Mar. A.8/1 The township socked the company with a building permit violation.

c. Substitute for def.: orig. and chiefly *U.S.* (*a*) To drive or thrust *in* or *in(to)* something. (Earlier examples.) (*b*) Phr. *to sock it to* (one): to strike, deal a blow to (that person); to 'give it' to (one). *fig.* Freq. in imp., as catch-phrase *sock it to me* (*them*, etc.)*!*, used to express encouragement, sexual invitation, etc. Also in sb. phr. *sock-it-to-me*, a loud and violent style of music; a piece of such music. (Earlier and later examples.)

(*a*) **1843** *Spirit of Times* 15 July 234/1 About one hundred yards from home, Spicer pulled Beppo out, and 'socked in' his spurs. **1845** T. J. GREEN *Texian Exped.* xvii. 321 The corporal 'socked' it [*sc.* a shoe-maker's awl] in the thick of his back. **1878** J. H. BEADLE *Western Wilds* ii. 37 The very next day they put me in jail—socked me right in with them two Hodges.

(*b*) **1877** BARTLETT *Dict. Americanisms* (ed. 4) 623 Two loafers are fighting; one of the crowd cries out, '*Sock* it to him.' **1883** 'MARK TWAIN' *Life on Mississippi* xliii. 438 A rich man won't have anything but your very best; and you can..pile it on and sock it to him. **1889** —— *Connecticut Yankee* xxxiii. 422 'Well, observe the difference: you pay eight cents and four mills, we pay only eight cents.' I prepared, now, to sock it to him. I said: 'Look here..,what's become of your high wages you were bragging so about, a few minutes ago?'—and I looked around on the company with placid satisfaction. **1927** O. W. HOLMES in *Holmes-Laski Lett.* (1953) II. 975, I have heard an English judge sock it to the jury in a murder case. **1963** B. J. CHUTE *Shift to Right* 153 There was a shriek from the panting Trenton stands: 'Yea, Rusty. Sock it to 'em.' **1968** *Tel.* (Brisbane) 15 June 2/3 'Sock it to me' is a catch-phrase which is sweeping America... It's all due to Judy Carne,..who cheekily used the phrase in a weekly comedy show called 'Laugh In'. **1969** R. LOWELL *Notebook* 137 The little girl's bedroom, perfect with posters: 'Do not enter,' and 'Sock it to me, Baby.' **1969** *Times* 19 July 9/6 The black American phrase 'sock it to me' (with an obscene connotation). **1969** *Times* 29 July 1/3 If President Nixon is going to 'sock it' to anyone, the likeliest recipient is the South Vietnamese government. **1970** S. SHELDON *Naked Face* (1971) ii. 16 She reached between his legs and stroked him, whispering, 'Go, baby. Sock it to me.' **1970** *Melody Maker* 11 July 19/7 It's good to hear Pickett getting away from the sock-it-to-me and into gentler songs. **1971** *West Indian World* 12 Nov. 14/3 Back to the sock-it-to-me's with Jesse James's 'Don't Nobody Want to Get Married'..which storms breathlessly along complete with hard-hitting bass and wow-wow guitars. **1977** *New Yorker* 2 May 34/2, I can't afford a second divorce. Daphne would really sock it to me. **1978** *Railway Age* 25 Dec. 25/2 Does all this boil down to some kind of accounting legerdemain that, in the end, will be socking it to the taxpayers?

d. *Jazz.* To perform (music) in a swinging manner. Freq. in phr. *to sock it* (*out*).

1927 *Melody Maker* July 697 Sock out your last chorus on that, my friends. **1933** [see *GET *v.* 62 l]. **1935** *Vanity Fair* XLV. 71/3 Hot artists or bands that can put across their licks successfully are '*senders*';..they can '*sock it*'. **1955** SHAPIRO & HENTOFF *Hear me talkin' to Ya* vii. 79 'Blow it, kid. Sock it out,' Tig and Jones kept shouting, until I finally loosened up and did tricks with that slide that I probably never did before or since. **1968** *Radio Times* 28 Nov. 47/1 He's spent his evenings singing in pubs..'socking' out the rhythm and blues. **1976** *New Yorker* 12 Jan. 37 (*caption*) From the top—'Watermelon Man'. Let's sock it out and give Mrs. Ritterhouse a chance to really cook.

Hence **so·cking** *vbl. sb.*

1978 *N.Y. Times* 30 Mar. D 17/2 Harrelson played no part in all the socking because the Mets stopped scoring after four innings and the Phillies after five, and he didn't get into the game until the seventh.

sock, *v.*[3] **a.** (Earlier example.)

1842 *Eton Bureau* 162 Sock means prog, but when you sock a boy anything, he eats it, and you pay for it... I was asked by A— to sock him a verse the other day, and I had to sock him a construe of his lesson too.

sock, *v.*[5] Add: **2.** *colloq.* (orig. *U.S.*). To put (money) aside as savings. Also with *away.*

1942 BERREY & VAN DEN BARK *Amer. Thes. Slang* § 376/5 *Save*...sock one's money away. **1951** CUSACK & JAMES *Come in Spinner* 297, I bet he's socked a pretty packet away. **1962** E. LUCIA *Klondike Kate* iii. 97 Instead of gambling a fortune away at the wheels..[Kitty] was wisely socking it into the bank. **1963** C. D. SIMAK *They walked like Men* ix. 53 They've been busy for the last week scooping it in. People come in loaded and are socking it away. **1971** *Maclean's Mag.* Sept. 11/2 Now they seem to believe that a buck earned is a buck to be socked away. **1978** R. DOLINER *On the Edge* v. 84 He's got to have money... How much you figure he socked away?

3. *N. Amer.* Of fog, cloud, etc.: to close *in*, to enshroud.

1950 WEBSTER Add. Sock in. **1953** BERREY & VAN DEN BARK *Amer. Thes. Slang* (1954) § 761/2 *Socked in*, ceiling zero. **1955** *Sci. News Let.* 26 Feb. 136 Man-made ice-fog that 'socks in' Arctic airfields can now be licked by a new device developed by the Armour Research Foundation, Chicago. **1969** *Daily Tel.* 21 May 1/6 All of Europe, the Soviet Union,..are socked in cloud cover. **1975** *High Times* Dec. 70/3 Pilots..are often completely socked in by fog and haze. **1976** C. EGLETON *State Visit* iii. 25 Wednesday is always a busy day... As long as the airfield isn't socked in.

sockdolager. Add: Also **sock dologer, -doliger. 1.** (Earlier example.)

1830 *Virginia Literary Museum* I. 479 *Sock dologer*, a decisive blow.

3. (Earlier examples.)

1838 J. F. COOPER *Home as Found* II. 72 There is but one 'sogdollager' in the universe, and that is in Lake Oswego. **1842** *Knickerbocker* XIX. 223 This seemed to be a 'socdoliger' (which translated into Latin, means a ne plus ultra).

socked, *ppl. a.* (Later examples.)

1918 W. J. LOCKE *Rough Road* xxiii. 293 Her thoughts winged themselves back to an afternoon, remote almost as her socked and sashed childhood. **1937** L. DURRELL *Panic Spring* vii. 116 Her brown socked legs stretched out under the dashboard. **1976** 'J. Ross' *I know what it's like to Die* i. 7 Five feet and eight inches..in his socked feet.

socker. Add: Also **socca.** The form **soccer** is now usual. (Earlier and later examples.) Also in *Comb.* Hence **so·ccerite**, a player of soccer; also *attrib.*

1889 E. C. DOWSON *Let.* 21 Feb. (1967) 38, I absolutely decline to see socca' matches. **1916** BLANCROFT & PULVEMACHER *Handbk. Athletic Games* (1922) 429 Soccer football, as it is called in America, is the English Association Football. **1924** H. DE SELINCOURT *Cricket Match* iv. 83 However any sane person could prefer soccer to cricket the good little Horace totally failed to comprehend. **1935** *Punch* 24 Apr. 476/2 No one more thoroughly qualified to write the history of 'soccer'..can be imagined. **1945** *Gen* 13 Jan. 30/1 Many Soccerites..took to Rugby. **1951** R. CAMPBELL *Light on Dark Horse* 69 My father had founded the Technical College, a 'soccerite' school. **1951** *Sport* 7–13 Jan. 9/1 We had the F.A. scheme to bring the big professional clubs and the soccer-playing schools into closer contact. **1971** L. KOPPETT *N.Y. Times Guide Spectator Sports* xii. 193 All you need to play soccer is a ball, a field and players. **1976** *Field* 18 Nov. 989/2 They roar around, fighting and frolicking beneath like soccer hooligans. **1978** P. MARSH et al. *Rules of Disorder* iv. 97 The soccer terraces offer..a chance to escape from the dreariness of the weekday world.

sockeroo (sǫ:kĕrū·). *slang* (orig. *U.S.*). [f. SOCK *sb.*[4] + *-EROO.] Something with an overwhelming impact, a 'smash'.

1942 *Time* 9 Nov. 77/2 The act was an old-fashioned Hippodrome sockeroo. **1943** *Sat. Rev. Lit.* 18 Dec. 16/3 This program ..was a boff, a wham, a sockeroo. **1964** *Spectator* 7 Feb. 178 This latest box-office sockeroo also provides a modest example of the industry's throat-cutting activities. **1977** *Daily Tel.* 22 Apr. 13 The Royal Court's new régime opens with a great loud sockeroo of a play, a thumping American drama of a divided family, rich in purple prose and loaded with gutsy symbolism.

socket, *sb.* Add: **2. c.** An object in which the terminals of an electricity supply are inside holes made to receive the pins of a plug; *spec.* one that is fixed to a wall.

1885 C. J. WHARTON tr. *Hospitalier's Domestic Electr.* vii. 113 The whole [lamp-holder] is fitted to a wooden socket C, which may be screwed into an ordinary chandelier or in place of a gas burner. **1892** [see *PLUG *sb.* 1 c]. **1914** S. C. BATSTONE *Electric-Light Fitting* vi. 127 The wires come into the socket from behind the skirting. **1938** J. W. SIMS *Electr. Installations* 155 Apparatus requiring not more than 50 watts may be supplied from..one 15-amp socket. **1955** N. W. KAY *Mod. Building Encycl.* 637/1 The fuse can be renewed only when the plug-head is withdrawn from the socket. **1977** F. HALL *Building Services & Equipment* II. v. 35/2 The sockets will only accept plugs for 110V, single-phase, 50Hz supply.

d. *Golf.* That part of the head of a club into which the shaft is fitted; a shot made off the socket.

1887 W. G. SIMPSON *Art of Golf* I. iv. 22 Irons and cleeks ..have sockets instead of necks. **1922** C. LEITCH *Golf* 98 There is no bad shot in golf which flurries a player so much as a shot off the socket. **1927** *Daily Express* 12 Feb. 3/7 In the down stroke, the left hand and arm get ahead of the right, and that causes either a socket or a 'push out'. **1963** J. JACOBS *Golf* 78 The socket is simply explained—the club head is being brought down further away from the body than it should be.

7. a. For 'sense 1' read 'sense 2'. **socket outlet**, a socket (sense *2 c) fixed to a wall and connected to an electricity supply; cf. *OUTLET *sb.* 1 d, *POINT *sb.*[1] A. 19 e; **socket set**, a number of sockets for use with a socket wrench; **socket wrench**, a wrench equipped with a set of detachable sockets of different sizes.

1934 *Two-Pole & Earthing-Pin Plugs & Socket-Outlets* (Brit. Standards Inst.) 6 When the plug and the socket-outlet are in complete engagement no live parts shall be accessible. **1977** *Jrnl. R. Soc. Arts* CXXV. 119/2 There will probably be more storage space [in today's new house] and almost certainly more socket outlets. [**1918** A. L. DYKE *Automobile & Gasoline Engine Encycl.* 613/2 (*caption*) No. 12 combination socket wrench set.] **1935** *Gen. Catal. Tools & Supplies* (Buck & Hickman Ltd.) 270/2 'Ratchet handle' socket sets. **1976** *Star* (Sheffield) 29 Nov. 5/5 Hinds pleaded guilty to stealing an electric drill and a 52-piece socket set. **1905** W. ROGERS *Pumps & Hydraulics* II. 344 An interchangeable socket wrench is shown in Fig. 629. **1921** *Car* 31 Mar. 313/2 (Advt.), Your car will be kept in perfect tune if a socket wrench set is in your kit. **1977** *New Yorker* 9 May 34/3 Bicycling accessories for every contingency:..monkey wrenches, socket wrenches, wrench holders.

b. *socket-eyed* adj.

1964 F. WARNER *Early Poems* 76 Laws That rule this meaningless and cancered globe In socket-eyed, gigantic merriment. **1975** *New Yorker* 26 May 104/1 Raskolnikov ..is played by Georgi Taratorkin, a socket-eyed figure ransacked by self-inquiry and staring at us out of a very lonely desert.

socket, *v.* Add: **2.** *Golf.* To strike (the ball) inadvertently off the socket or heel of a club; to make (a shot) in this way. Also *absol.* Cf. *SHANK *v.* 4.

1911 C. LEITCH *Golf for Girls* 87 If you socket and don't want to, here's the cure. Keep your left elbow close to your side. **1920** *Isis* 27 Oct. 9/1 He socketed a couple of iron shots into the gorse. **1927** *Daily Express* 31 Jan. 8/2 A mashie that persists in socketing the ball. **1961** F. C. AVIS *Sportsman's Gloss.* 210/2 *Socket*, to hit the ball with the shank of the club; also known as Shank.

Hence **so·cketer**, one who sockets the ball.

1912 *New Bk. Golf* 341 Even the most confirmed socketer will find that with such a club socketing is a sheer impossibility. **1952** H. LONGHURST *Golf Mixture* 113 Frostick, of St George's Hill, tells the socketer to keep his head down.

socketed, *ppl. a.* Add: **2.** *Golf.* Of a ball or shot: that has been played off the socket.

1911 C. LEITCH *Golf for Girls* 86 At the finish of a socketted shot. **1963** P. CAMPBELL *How to become Scratch Golfer* v. 57 Tom's contribution is a socketed recovery shot out of the bushes.

socketing, *vbl. sb.* Add: **2.** *Golf.* The action of hitting the ball off the socket.

1911 C. LEITCH *Golf for Girls* 86 Socketting, that is, hitting the ball off the socket, or shank, as some call it, of the club. **1959** D. REES *Dai Rees on Golf* xxx. 126

Socketing is something which strikes suddenly, li tear poisonous adder.

sockette (sǫke·t). [f. SOCK *sb.*[1] + -ETTE.] A short sock.

1950 *Landfall* IV. 309 Tanned legs with neat navy sockettes. **1976** *Times* 26 Mar. 10/4 Sales of hosiery (which includes tights and sockettes etc) run at around 620,000,000 pairs a year.

socking (sǫ·kiŋ), *adv.* and *ppl. a. slang.* [? f. SOCK *v.*[2]: see also B below.] **A.** *adv.* As an intensive, esp. qualifying *big* or *great*: very.

1896 *Dialect Notes* I. 425 That was a socking big fish. **1942** *Tee Emm* (Air Ministry) II. 67 A socking great Wellington has just gate-crashed the range. **1951** J. B. PRIESTLEY *Festival at Farbridge* III. iii. 548 A teeny drink before lunch, and it turned out to be a socking great double gin and Dubonnet. **1958** M. DICKENS *Man Overboard* viii. 122 A socking great button-hole. **1976** D. FRANCIS *In Frame* iv. 65 A brooch I had..with a socking big diamond in the middle.

B. *ppl. a.* A euphemistic substitute for *FUCKING *ppl. a.*

1941 *Penguin New Writing* X. 114 That socking kid's playing a game with me. **1945** S. J. BAKER *Austral. Lang.* xiv. 257 *Socker* and *socking*, as synonyms for an old English vulgarism widely current in this country, are recent inventions.

sockless, *a.* (Later examples.)

1970 P. DICKINSON *Seals* vii. 145 His bruised feet slipping sockless in the unfamiliar boots. **1981** *Daily Tel.* 20 Feb. 17/1 Going sockless is the preferred style, 'to give the beachside look that is so desirable'.

socko (sǫ·ko), *int., a., sb. slang* (orig. and chiefly *U.S.*). [f. SOCK *sb.*[4] + *-O[2].] **A.** *int.* An interjection imitative of the sound of a violent blow.

1924 *Dialect Notes* V. 258 *Sock-o* (blow). **1931** E. LINKLATER *Juan in Amer.* II. i. 63 He hung a lullaby on the Frog's chin—socko! **1930** WODEHOUSE *Laughing Gas* xxi. 226 And then, as she stood there with the love-light shining in her eyes...socko! **1966** L. COHEN *Beautiful Losers* I. 71 We're fat, F.—Smack! Wham! Pow!—Fat.—Socko! Sok! Bash!

B. *adj.* Stunningly effective or successful, 'knock-out'.

1939 J. B. PRIESTLEY *Johnson over Jordan* II. 67 And now, friends, a new novelty act, the first time here, and I know it will be a socko number. **1942** *Photoplay & Movie Mirror* Mar. 6/3 Van Heflin..almost steals the show—and he must be good to rob Taylor of one iota of glory, Bob's that socko. **1960** *Sales Managem.* 6 May 96/1 Automated manufacture, sock-o selling and all-out advertising. **1961** *John o' London's* 14 Dec. 664/2 The religious plays which are at the moment filling our theatres, religion being Socko box office these days. **1972** T. P. MCMAHON *Issue of Bishop's Blood* vii. 83 The blue of the incense rising to the white gold of the altar..the soaring voices of the seventy or so nuns..provided a socko finish. **1981** *Underground Grammarian* Feb. 3/1 Their latest brochure starts *right off* with this absolutely socko bit of dialog: 'What is cooperative education? In it's simplist [*sic*] definition, it is learning by doing.'

C. *sb.* orig. *U.S.* A success, a 'hit'.

1937 *Amer. Speech* XII. 317/2 *Socko*, a success. **1942** BERREY & VAN DEN BARK *Amer. Thes. Slang* § 591/1 *Successful show hit...* socker,..socko, sock show. **1973** WODEHOUSE *Bachelors Anonymous* iii. 23 Triumph or disaster, socko or flop, he went on forever like one of those permanent officials at the Foreign Office.

Socratean (sǫkrǣtī·ăn), *a. rare.* [See -AN.] Pertaining to or resembling the celebrated Greek philosopher Socrates or his way of life; Socratic.

1930 BELLOC *Richelieu* I. vi. 114 Father Joseph was short, bullet-headed, of a vivacious Socratean ugliness. **1976** *S. Wales Echo* 26 Nov. 5/1 It's hardly the kind of job that Plato would have relished—and there's nothing Socratean about filling in a VAT return.

Socratist. Delete † *Obs.* and add later example.

1866 MILL in *Edin. Rev.* CXXIII. 337 There are..two complete Plato's in Plato—the Sokratist and the Dogmatist.

Socred (sōᵘ·kred). Abbrev. of *SOCIAL CREDIT, *SOCIAL CREDITER.

1955 *Pictou* (Novia Scotia) *Advocate* 24 Feb. 1/1 The addition of the British Columbia Socreds has given them just the monkey glands they needed to restore them! **1962** *Canada Month* Feb. 21/2 Social Credit has been badly damaged by the highhanded methods of B.C.'s Socred government. **1970** J. BLACKBURN *Land of Promise* xv. 191 It was a landslide for the Socreds, the name soon applied to members of the Social Credit Party. **1975** *Australasian Express* 24 Oct. 10/2 (*heading*) Socred fields more women.

sod, *sb.*[1] Add: **3. a.** Also *N. Amer.*, more generally, soil which is grass-covered; sward which has never been cultivated; the surface of a lawn.

1968 *Globe & Mail* (Toronto) 17 Feb. 47/1 (Advt.), 1st class sandy land with substantial buildings. This irrigated land would produce excellent sod. **1976** *National Observer* (U.S.) 12 June 5/2 Some Postal Service employes also think that 'a lot of people don't want us to cross their lawns, tear up yards, and stomp holes in the sod.' **1976** *Billings* (Montana) *Gaz.* 5 July 9-C/1 (Advt.), 761 Acres cropland; 600 Acres former cropland, grassed; 800 Acres sod to break.

Phr. *under the sod*: dead and buried; *to put under the sod*: to kill. *colloq.* and *dial.*

1847 TROLLOPE *Macdermots* III. vii. 286 I've heard the boys say that he would be undher the sod that day six months. *Ibid.* 288 A lot of boys swore together..to put him undher the sod. **1894** H. PEASE *Mark o' Deil* I. 19 'Fear-nowt Charlie,' who wes put under the sod, poor chap, a year come Michaelmas. **1972** K. BONFIGLIOLI *Don't point that Thing* xviii. 159 Happiness is..being alive and wonderful-for-his-age when old so-and-so is under the sod.

b. Restrict † *Obs.* to sense in Dict. and add: Also, the surface of a cockpit (sense 1); the institution, practice, or action of cock-fighting, the cock-fighting world.

1814 W. SKETCHLEY *Cocker* p. iii, The author having been attached to the sod at a very early period of life.. he flatters himself that..his attempt at writing 'The Cocker' will be found to contain..instruction. **1840** D. P. BLAINE *Encycl. Rural Sports* IX. i. 1208 His chief opponent was Potter, who was feeder for that veteran sportsman, the Earl of Derby, whose attachment for the sod continued unwearied. **1912** W. GILBEY *Sport in Olden Time* 41 So closely was the grass-covered pit associated with the sport, that 'the sod' bore to cocking the same significance as 'the turf' bears to racing. **1977** *Verbatim* Feb. 1/1 Although the cockpit is as remote from the lives of most of us as a brontosaurus wallow, our language has been richly endowed by The Sod, and few of us get through a single day without recourse to at least one phrase from the lexicon of cocking.

4. b. *spec.*, Ireland. Also without *old.*

1812 P. EGAN *Boxiana* I. 315 O'Donnel..was a native of Ireland, who left the *sod* at a very early period of his life. **1891** [in Dict.]. **1892** W. G. LYTTLE *Life in Ballycuddy* 12 (E.D.D.), A'll niver lee the auld sod again. **1939** JOYCE *Finnegans Wake* 19 To say too us to be every tim, nick and larry of us, sons of the sod. *Ibid.* 194 Dry yanks will visit old sod. *a* **1953** E. O'NEILL *Long Day's Journey into Night* (1956) II. ii. 80 Then before his father can react to this insult to the Old Sod, he adds dryly, [etc.]. **1955** J. P. DONLEAVY *Ginger Man* v. 35 I'll give you the jug to remember me when I'm gone from the ould sod, sacked in with some lovely French doll.

5. a. *sod cabin, -cloth, crop, ground, -house* (further examples), *-hut* (earlier and later examples), *land*; **sod widow** (see quot. 1946).

1932 W. FAULKNER *Light in August* xi. 232 He found the sod cabin. **1905** Sod-cloth [see *MUDWALLING *vbl. sb.*]. **1956** C. EVANS *On Climbing* viii. 128 Round the bottom of the tent, on the outside, a foot-wide strip of cloth should run, the 'sod-cloth', on which stones and snow can be put to anchor the tent. **1848** *Rep. U.S. Comm. Patents 1847* 539 This gave a sod crop without tending of thirty to forty bushels per acre. **1950** *Jrnl. Illinois State Hist. Soc.* Spring 37 They learned to plant a 'sod crop' by cutting upturned furrows with an ax, then dropping in a few kernels of corn. **1839** W. SEWALL *Diary* 23 Aug. (1930) 207/1 Broke up the sod ground in the prairie up the hollow for a yard in which to make brick. **1932** *Randolph Enterprise* (Elkins, W. Va.) 4 Feb. 4/2 Sod ground is about all ploughed and some stubble ground also. **1937** J. ISE (*title*) Sod-house days. Letters from a Kansas homesteader, 1877–78. **1948** B. SUNDKLER *Bantu Prophets* vi. 183 On the door of the sod house used as a church there is painted a green and white cross. **1977** *Westworld* (Vancouver, B.C.) May–June 6/2 There certainly was nothing like a sod house for being cool in summer and warm in winter. **1869** *Harper's Monthly* June 25/1 A warmer abode than the sod hut..he will never have. **1930** L. G. D. ACLAND *Early Canterbury Runs* 1st Ser. ii. 13 Ford built a six-roomed wooden cottage to replace the original sod hut. **1972** *Science* 19 May 747/2 While others were planning fancy facilities, Herzberg's helpers built a sod-hut similar to those used as homes by the early settlers of Saskatchewan. **1856** *Rep. U.S. Comm. Patents 1855: Agric.* 262 They were mostly sown upon sod-land. **1946** *Sun* (Baltimore) 11 Nov. 2/1 Anderson cautioned growers of wheat and flax not to break up sod or grass lands which are not adapted to continued cultivation and which would create erosion hazards in the future. **1927** *Amer. Speech* II. 278 *Sod* (widow), husband dead. **1946** G. STIMPSON *Bk. about Thousand Things* 349 A grass widow's husband was alive while a *sod widow*'s husband was under the sod. **1973** *Raleigh* (N.C.) *News & Observer* 12 Mar. 34/2 Last but not least is our large number of widows (sod). There are 70.

b. *sod-soaker*; **sod planting** *Agric.*, the sowing of seed in unploughed ground, herbicides being used to kill or control any existing vegetation; so **sod-plant** *v. trans.*, **sod-planted** *ppl. a.*

1965 *Proc. Southern Weed Control Conf.* XVIII. 146 A second screening test was conducted in 1963 in connection with a new sod planting research program. The aim.. was to develop a high producing summer grain or silage crop grown in a chemically controlled perennial sod which would return to productive pasture in the fall, winter and spring, maintaining a protective mulch cover at all times. **1967** *Agronomy Jrnl.* LIX. 549/1 Removal of the rye immediately before sod-planting corn in the stubble lowered yields as compared to mulched crops. *Ibid.* 548/1 Inclusion of the winter legumes..did not increase sod-planted corn yields. *Ibid.* 550/1 The moisture conserving aspect of sod planting is most pronounced for droughts of short duration. **1978** *McGraw-Hill Yearbk. Sci. & Technol.* 78/2 Various reduced tillage systems are referred to as direct drilling, minimum tillage, no-tillage, sod planting,..depending upon the operations used, the crops grown, and the locale. **1903** Sod-soaker [see *gully-washer* s.v. *GULLY *sb.*[1] 4]. **1953** *Manch. Guardian Weekly* 18 June 3/1 'Oh Lord, send us a sod-soaker and not a gully-drencher.' The prayer of the prairie farmer is specific.

c. *sod-built* (earlier example).

1805–6 WORDSWORTH *Prelude* (1959) VIII. 613 The Woodman languish'd Within his sod-built cabin.

sod, *pa. pple., ppl. a.*, and *sb.*[2] Add: **2. a.** Also as *sb.*: a damper (DAMPER 6) that has not risen. *Austral.*

1900–10 in G. A. Wilkes *Dict. Austral. Colloquialisms* (1978) 309/1. **1931** I. L. IDRIESS *Lasseter's Last Ride* v. 36 He made dampers so light that they were in danger of blowing away [and]..had not baked one 'sod' during the entire trip. **1957** R. S. PORTEOUS *Brigalow* 206 His dampers were leaden sods. **1975** X. HERBERT *Poor Fellow my Country* xvi. 838, I want to cook our own damper, too...don't want one of their sods.

sod (sǫd), *sb.*[3] [Short for SODOMITE.] **1.** One who practises or commits sodomy. *coarse slang.*

c **1855** *Yokel's Preceptor* 6 It is not long since, in the neighbourhood of Charing Cross, they posted bills in the windows of several respectable public houses, cautioning the public to 'Beware of Sods!' **1859** G. W. MATSELL *Vocabulum* 83 *Sod*, a worn-out debauchee, whom excess of indulgence has rendered unnatural. **1934** V. WOOLF *Let.* 24 Jan. (1979) V. 273, I am writing about sodomy at the moment and wish I could discuss the matter with you; how far can one say openly what is the relation of a woman and a sod? **1949** WYNDHAM LEWIS *Let.* ?8 Mar. (1963) 484 When you come to write your book, its scene our day to day life, I should put in the sods. Sartre has shown what a superb figure of comedy a homo can be. **1968** S. JAMESON *White Crow* xxxiv. 291 Homosexuals are always getting themselves assaulted. You read that some respectable middle-aged bachelor has been beaten insensible on the stairway of his Mayfair flat, and invariably it turns out that he was a sod.

2. a. Used as a vulgar term of abuse for (usu.) a male person. Also with weakened force, as the equivalent of 'fellow', 'chap', freq. affectionately or in commiseration; *odds and sods*: see *ODDS *sb.* 7 b.

1818 *Sessions* 17 June 283/2 As he passed me he said the other was a b—y s—d. **1931** K. O'BRIEN *Without my Cloak* III. xi. 380 That auld sod of a husband making her black and blue every night of his filthy life. **1931** W. V. TILSLEY *Other Ranks* 12 Lucky sods, getting this far and then going back. **1942** G. KERSH *Nine Lives Bill Nelson* x. 61 There are plenty of sods in this battalion that get their pleasure by exercising their two-penny-ha'penny authority. **1942** T. RATTIGAN *Flare Path* III. 164 Johnny, you old sod! Is it really you? **1957** I. MURDOCH *Sandcastle* xiii. 210 He thought to himself, what a sod I am, what a poor confused sod. **1958** 'E. O'CONNER' *Steak for Breakfast* 28 Good on yer, Martha, yer old sod! **1963** T. PARKER *Unknown Citizen* i. 40 Don't you call me a daft sod, you daft sod. **1968** J. BRAINE *Crying Game* i. 18 It's time he was dead... If you want to destroy the sod, Frank, I'll give you absolutely all the dirt. **1969** D. WALLACE *Turtle* xiv. 148 That's a shame, the poor little dawg, buf if that was moine I'd hev that put down. That can't help but make no end o' work, the poor little sod. **1974** N. FREELING *Dressing of Diamond* 201 Yes, now I remember him, cheeky young sod. **1978** *Globe & Mail* (Toronto) 16 Aug. 31/7 And when they do, these lucky sods will forget years of fish-fib training and head pell mell for shore, seeking, of all things, the truth.

b. Something difficult; a great nuisance. *slang.*

1936 'G. ORWELL' *Keep Aspidistra Flying* i. 11 'Bare' is a sod to 'rhyme'; however, there's always 'air'. **1950** C. MACINNES *To Victor Spoils* I. 84 It'd be a sod if they got through to the Meuse. **1971** V. CANNING *Firecrest* i. 3 At least..he'd seen them come back, though it was a sod he'd missed them going off. **1977** [see *SATIN *sb.* (and *a.*) 6 b].

c. *sod-all*, nothing, no. Cf. *ALL A. 8 f. *slang.*

1958 K. AMIS *I like it Here* i. 12 There's been sod-all since. **1961** I. JEFFERIES *It wasn't Me!* iii. 39 When I was at that pharmaceutical firm..I did sod-all for months on end. **1972** J. WAINWRIGHT *Requiem for Loser* viii. 167 Like the concert hall... A bit of a stage—and sod-all else. **1978** 'K. BLAKE' *Where Jungle Ends* iii. 37 Here he was in this cold chill room, and two maniacs sitting playing cards at the table and taking sod-all notice of him.

d. *not to give a sod* = *not to give a damn* s.v. *DAMN *sb.* 2. *slang.*

1961 B. ALDISS *Primal Urge* i. 29 Nobody gave a sod. Euphoria had its high tide. **1973** D. STOREY *Temporary Life* v. ii. 224, I don't give a sod for any of them, Phil.

e. *Sod's Law* = *Murphy's law* s.v. *MURPHY[2] 3.

1970 *New Statesman* 9 Oct. 460/1 Sod's Law..is the force in nature which causes it to rain mostly at weekends, which makes you get flu when you are on holiday, and which makes the phone ring just as you've got into the bath. **1978** *New Scientist* 7 Sept. 744/1 The great unshakeable list of interdisciplinary laws—Sod's Law, Newton's Fourth Law of Motion, the Inverse Midas Touch and their kin. **1980** *SLR Camera* July 56/2 Even if you're using a masking frame this can easily overbalance. According to Sod's Law, that's going to happen when you're halfway through exposing a sheet of 20 × 16in colour paper costing the best part of £1·30.

sod, *v.*[3] *slang.* [f. prec.] **1.** *trans.* = DAMN *v.* 5.

1904 *Eng. Dial. Dict.* V. 605/2 Phr. *sod him*, may mischief befall him. *w. Yks.* Sod him, he can go to —. **1942** G. KERSH *Nine Lives Bill Nelson* i. 3 Well, sod the Drill Pig. **1945** *Penguin New Writing* XXIII. 51 Sod that, chummie. **1953** P. SCOTT *Alien Sky* I. viii. 131 At seven-fifteen they had to go out to dinner. Sod it. **1958** —— *Mark of Warrior* II. 131 'Look, you'd better go sick.'

..'Sod you, Bob. I wouldn't miss it for the world.' **1967** J. WAIN *Smaller Sky* 170 'He'll come out,' said Swarthmore. 'And if he doesn't, we'll sit where we are and you'll get paid for a full day's work, with overtime if necessary, and you won't have to do a stroke.' 'I'd rather be at home,' said the chief cameraman, 'and sod the overtime. I'm definitely sickening for something.' **1971** B. W. ALDISS *Soldier Erect* 209 Quite a road! Sod me! I'll say it is! **1977** *Chainsaw* Sept./Oct. 3/2 Sod it! There goes my banner headline.

2. *intr.* With *off*: to go away, depart. Also = *get away* s.v. *GET *v.* 54 b, and *fig.* Usu. in imp.

1960 J. SYMONS *Progress of Crime* xv. 92 Now sod off and get your identification parade done. **1968** *Listener* 14 Nov. 650/3 It's good to learn what Mr Reed said to the vicar who complained that boys had damaged a valuable rose tree: 'I told him to sod off.' **1971** F. FORSYTH *Day of Jackal* xx. 335 The policeman asked for papers. The Jackal giggled seductively... 'Sod off,' said the policeman and withdrew. **1976** P. CAVE *High Flying Birds* ii. 16 'Sod off,' I said, 'How can you call a glider a vehicle?' **1977** *Observer* 4 Sept. 14/2, I am simply waiting for the day when I can say 'sod off' to your institution. **1978** I. MURDOCH *Sea* 168 That's right, sod off just when ..the light of understanding has dawned... Oh all right, sod off then!

soda[1]. Add: **4. a.** (Earlier example.)

1834 J. R. PLANCHÉ *Olympic Revels* in *Extravaganzas* (1879) I. 47 Make him sit down—give him some hock and soda.

b. A glass or drink of soda-water; also, an ice-cream soda.

1933 E. O'NEILL *Ah Wilderness!* II. 58 Ever drink anything besides sodas? **1962** A. LURIE *Love & Friendship* viii. 145 Vanilla sodas with strawberry ice-cream. **1973** 'E. MCBAIN' *Hail to Chief* vi. 94 Toy..put the straws between her lips, and busied herself with the soda.

4*. *Faro.* In full *soda card.* (See quot. 1975.) Phr. *from soda* (*card*) *to hock*: see *HOCK *sb.*[6] b.

1845 J. H. GREENE *Exposure of Arts & Miseries Gambling* (ed. 2) 135 The top card, when the deal is first commenced, is called the *deal card*; this card neither wins nor loses, and on that account is sometimes called the *soda card.* **1975** *Way to Play* 206/2 The exposed top card is called the 'soda'. It is ignored for betting.

4.** *Austral. slang.* Something easy to accomplish, a simple task; a 'pushover'.

1930 V. PALMER *Passage* I. i. 22 'Just one more guess.' ..'Umph, that's a soda! Must be the old doctor.' *Ibid.* x. 83 They're getting ready for the long dive now, and it ought to be a soda for you. If I hadn't rheumatics down the back of my leg, I'd give it a fly myself. **1943** G. H. JOHNSTON *New Guinea Diary* IV. 136 'The Middle East was a soda beside this,' one of them told me. **1955** A. MARSHALL *I can jump Puddles* 108 Swipe him on the knuckles if you can. If he's like his old man he's a soda. **1966** H. PORTER *Paper Chase* 74 The job, for which I have no really specialized training, is nevertheless a soda.

5. a. *soda pan* [PAN *sb.*[1] 5 a], *plain*; *soda-chapped* adj.; **soda-acid,** used *attrib.* to designate a fire extinguisher containing sulphuric acid and sodium bicarbonate (or sometimes the carbonate), which are mixed just before use to provide the gas for expelling the water; **soda cellulose,** a form of cellulose heavily impregnated with soda, produced by the action of caustic soda on wood-pulp esp. in the manufacture of paper or rayon; **soda glass,** glass containing a high proportion of soda; sometimes = **soda-lime glass*; **soda lake** (further examples); **soda-lime glass,** the standard form of glass in everyday use, manufactured essentially from silica, soda, and lime; **soda process,** a method of pulping wood by boiling with caustic soda; **soda pulp,** wood-pulp made by the soda process.

1928 R. NORTHWOOD *Fire Extinguishment & Fire Alarm Syst.* xxi. 185 (*caption*) Method of recharging 'The Conquest' soda-acid extinguisher. **1966** *McGraw-Hill Encycl. Sci. & Technol.* V. 279/1 In the small first-aid water fire extinguishers, a propellant must be provided. Usually this is carbon dioxide, which is either generated when needed (the soda-acid extinguisher) or stored in a cartridge. **1890** *Jrnl. Soc. Chem. Industry* 28 Feb. 225/1 Their production is estimated at 30,000 tons sulphite (wet) and 9,000 soda cellulose (dry). **1948** J. T. MARSH *Textile Sci.* ii. 19 Sheets of pulp are converted into soda-cellulose by steeping in caustic soda solution. **1973** *Materials & Technol.* VI. iv. 306 The swollen, and still further purified 'soda cellulose' so formed, is broken down into 'crumbs', and these are then transferred to reactor vessels. **1922** JOYCE *Ulysses* 59 Sodachapped hands. **1897** A. HARTSHORNE *Old English Glasses* 39 Venetian soda-glass is much lighter than that made in the Low Countries with potash. **1947** J. C. RICH *Materials & Methods of Sculpture* xi. 329 Sodium carbonate, calcium carbonate, and sand yield a soft or 'soda glass'. **1965** PHILLIPS & WILLIAMS *Inorg. Chem.* I. xiv. 553 Soda glass is conveniently worked at a lower temperature than borosilicate glass. **1937** *Discovery* Feb. 58/1 A new exhibit presented by the Magadi Soda Lake Co...at the Imperial Institute..illustrates..the exploitation of one of the most remarkable natural soda lakes in the world. **1976** K. THACKERAY *Crownbird* ix. 199 The road..ran steeply down beside a soda lake... The soda was firm near the edge. **1917** A. B. SEARLE in G. Martin *Industr. & Manufacturing Chem.* (*Inorg.*) II. 245 For soda-lime glasses the mean coefficient of expansion lies between 0·000023 and 0·000027 per 1°C. **1955** E. B. SHAND *Glass Engin. Handbk.* i. 2/1 Soda-lime glasses are commonly used for bottles, jars, window sheet and plate glass, electric lamp bulbs, and ophthalmic (sight-correcting) lenses. **1971** *Materials & Technol.* II. vi. 340 Soda-lime glasses in commercial use have devitrification temperatures in the region of 900 to 1000°C. **1976** K. THACKERAY *Crownbird* v. 82 The plane was flying..over one end of an enormous soda pan. **1946** D. C. PEATTIE *Road of Naturalist* i. 20 You find mariposas all over the West; they change height, change shape and colour, as you trace them from the mountains of Colorado, over the Utah soda plains. **1885** *Encycl. Brit.* XVIII. 226/1 The pulp produced by all those processes is of excellent quality; and, according to the statements of the patentees, it can be prepared at a cost greatly lower than by the soda process. **1907** *Jrnl. Soc. Chem. Industry* 15 June 561/2 In the period of 1865 to 1875 a large number of mills were erected throughout Canada and the United States, for the cooking of wood by the soda process. **1967** V. STRAUSS *Printing Industry* viii. 532/2 The soda process..has lower yields than the sulfate process..and the recovery of caustic soda is costly. For these and other reasons the soda process is losing ground fast to the sulfate process. **1893** *Jrnl. Soc. Chem. Industry* 30 Sept. 793/2 The product of 1892 included only 12,500 tons of soda pulp, the remaining 137,500 tons being produced by the sulphite process. **1962** F. T. DAY *Introd. Paper* ii. 20 Deciduous or broad-leafed trees such as the poplar are used in the production of soda pulp.

c. For 'minerals' read 'minerals and rocks'. (Further examples.)

1889 Soda-felsite [see *KERATOPHYRE]. **1913** Soda-amphibole, -richterite [see *IMERINITE]. **1926** *Proc. U.S. Nat. Mus.* LXVIII. Art. 17. 4 It may be chemically classed as a soda-rhyolite, but none of the calculated normative minerals of rhyolite are found in its mode. **1931** *Mineral. Mag.* XXII. 453 The brown augite has in places fringes of a green soda-augite. **1935** *Amer. Mineralogist* XX. 58 The high percentage of soda.. justifies the classification of the mineral as soda-alunite in the broad sense. **1965** G. J. WILLIAMS *Econ. Geol. N.Z.* xi. 167/1 Watters *et al.* (1961) noticed fergusonite in small water-worn grains from a restricted locality in the Canaan area where the Separation Point soda-granite invades Paleozoic marbles. **1966** *McGraw-Hill Encycl. Sci. & Technol.* XII. 407/2 Soda niter is by far the most abundant of the nitrate minerals. **1968** I. KOSTOV *Mineral.* 494 As 'alums' are denoted the following double sulphates:..Soda alum $NaAl(SO_4)_2.12H_2O$.

6. *soda-biscuit* (earlier example), *-bread* (earlier example), *-cake* (earlier example), *-cocktail*, *-cracker* (earlier example), *-fritter*, *-mint* (examples), *-powder*.

1830 *Albany Jrnl.* 25 Aug. 3/5 Fresh Soda Biscuit, just received from Treadwell's Bakery. **1850** N. KINGSLEY *Diary* 3 Aug. (1914) 134 They raised some bread with it, which he said was the best soda bread ever tasted. **1846** *Jewish Manual* vii. 155 (*heading*) A soda cake. **1818** *N.Y. Herald* 2 July 4/1 We have the Fourth of July thrown in with..its exhilarating associations so conducive of headaches and soda cocktails. **1863** *Harper's Mag.* Feb. 313/1 This repast, whatever its name might be, consisted of perhaps half a pound of soda crackers, two red herrings, and one red apple. **1837** M. R. WALKER *Diary* in C. M. Drury *Elkanah & Mary Walker* (1940) iii. 91 In the morning baked soda biscuit and fried soda fritters. **1895** *Montgomery Ward Catal.* Spring & Summer 261/2 Soda Mint tablets, for sour stomach, colic, flatulency, etc. **1928** D. L. SAYERS *Unpleasantness at Bellona Club* xv. 170 Suppose..somebody had dropped a poisoned pill into his usual bottle of soda-mints. **1975** C. MOTT-RADCLYFFE *Foreign Body in Eye* iv. 77 Joyce Britten-Jones asked me one evening whether I had any soda-mints. **1820** *Columbian Centinel* 1 July 3/6 Maynard & Noyes continue to prepare Soda Powders, of superior quality. **1843** MILL *Logic* I. III. xiii. 575 The old but not undisputed empirical generalization that soda powders weaken the human system.

7. Also, that dispenses soda water. *soda-clerk* (hence *soda-clerking* vbl. sb.), *-siphon*, *-straw*; **soda-counter,** the counter of a soda fountain; any counter or bar where soft drinks, ice cream, etc., are sold; **soda-fountain** (also † **-font, -fount**) orig. *U.S.*, (*a*) (see quot. 1875 in Dict.); (*b*) an apparatus for supplying ice-cream sodas, sundaes, etc.; a counter or an establishment of which this is a feature; **soda-jerk, -jerker** [*JERK *v.*[1] 7], one who mixes and sells soft drinks, etc., at a soda-fountain; **soda-pop,** flavoured soda-water.

1941 N. COWARD *Australia Visited* III. 16 That initial contact with the ordinary people [of New York]—the soda clerks, the cops, the struggling young theatre people. **1925** T. DREISER *Amer. Tragedy* I. II. iii. 180 He had wandered on..dishwashing in a restaurant, soda-clerking in a small outlying drug-store. **1846** *Dollar Newspaper* (Philadelphia) 19 Aug. 4/2 He..went up to the soda counter, and 'reckoned they'd take a little whisky'. **1939** A. HUXLEY *After Many a Summer* I. x. 135 Virginia was at the soda-counter, pensively eating a chocolate-and-banana split. **1976** J. LEE *Ninth Man* 31 A customer took a stool at the soda fountain... Dietrich..forced himself to..move..to the soda counter. **1848** *Knickerbocker* XXXI. 40 They had not a theatre, nor an oyster-saloon, nor a soda-font. **1848** in N. E. Eliason *Tarheel Talk* (1956) 296 My soda fount cost me in ninety dollars. **1908** *Home Herald* (Chicago) 13 May, Here is the popular soda-fount drink known as Coca-Cola. **1824** *Independent Chron.* (Boston) 9 Oct. 3/3 This luxury in a hot and dusty season, together with an ever-flowing Soda Fountain,.. he flatters himself will ensure a continuance of public patronage. **1876** *Napa* (California) *Reg.* 29 July 4/2 A Woodward avenue drug-store hired a new soda-fountain boy the other day. **1918** G. FRANKAU *One of Them* (1923) II. xv. 108, I loved thy daughters, daintiest as dowdiest; Cadby's tea'd Halls as Fuller's soda-fountain. **1955** R. BLESH *Shining Trumpets* (ed. 3) x. 232 A New Orleans Rhythm Kings' disc, playing in a soda fountain, gave these schoolboys the incentive. **1977** *New Yorker* 6 June 50/2 Afterward, at the soda fountain, they went over the day's movies. **1922** *Collier's* 17 June 4/1 You can tell a big-league head soda jerk by the way he picks up a glass, but the acid test is what kind of chocolate sirup he can make. **1958** *Daily Herald* 24 Mar. 3/7 This bustling little man never forgot his early years when he worked as a fairground barber and soda jerk. **1978** J. UPDIKE *Coup* (1979) iv. 132 The counter-boy, ingloriously dubbed the soda jerk... These 'soda jerks', I came to understand, were recruited from the adolescent ranks of the 'townies'. **1883** G. W. PECK *Groceryman & Peck's Bad Boy* 137 A sensitive soda jerker..feels that it is worse than three card monte. **1932** WODEHOUSE *Louder & Funnier* 48 He..is now a soda-jerker in a small town in Kansas. **1959** N. MAILER *Advts. for Myself* (1961) 35 The soda jerker.. from some outside compulsion had been forced to grow a beard. **1863** W. WHITMAN *Daybks. & Notebks.* (1978) III. 655 The continual soda-pop-like burstings of members calling 'Mr. Speaker! Mr. Speaker!' **1963** *Listener* 14 Feb. 301/3 The man who drove the soda-pop lorry. **1977** *Time* 11 Apr. 5/1 Were a visitor from another planet to read about the saccharin ban, he would conclude that earthlings' basic nutritional needs required large amounts of soda pop, jelly and chewing gum. **1926** *Daily Colonist* (Victoria, B.C.) 4 July 6/1 (Advt.), Warm Weather Supplies. Ice Cream Pails. Soda Straws. Lily Drinking Cups. **1911** *Ibid.* 21 Apr. 6/6 (Advt.), Soda Syphon Holder. This is a handsome silver plated stand into which the syphon fits. **1963** W. SOYINKA *Lion & Jewel* 24 The foreman..unpacks the usual box of bush comforts—soda siphon, whisky bottle and geometric sandwiches.

sodar (sōu·dāɹ). [f. SO(UND *sb.*[3] + *RA)DAR.] A system for investigating the state of the atmosphere, which works on the principle of radar but uses ultrasonic sound waves instead of microwaves.

1955 M. REIFER *Dict. New Words* 192/2 *Sodar*,..an instrument for detecting weather conditions by recording on an oscilloscope..the reflected sound waves which have been projected directly overhead. **1974** *Globe & Mail* (Toronto) 1 June 5/1 These new instruments, called lidar ..and sodar.., could be used for things like tracing and identifying particles in the atmosphere..and detecting dangerous wind patterns and turbulence around airport runways. **1976** *McGraw-Hill Yearbk. Sci. & Technol.* 402/2 The active network includes not only the standard pilot balloons and radiosondes with which meteorologists customarily measure wind, temperature, and humidity aloft, but also weather radars.., lidars..and sodars.

soda-water. Add: **1. b.** *soda-water-bottle* (earlier example), *manufacturer* (earlier example), *-room.*

1813 E. GERRY JR. *Diary* 4 July (1927) 168 We had not gone far, before the girls ordered the charioteer to stop at the soda water room. **1822** *Sunday Times* 20 Oct. 2/4 William Clarke..soda-water and ginger-beer manufacturer. **1852** DICKENS *Bleak Ho.* (1853) v. 35 Ginger-beer and soda-water bottles.

so·dbuster. *western N. Amer.* [f. SOD *sb.*[1] + BUSTER.] A term, chiefly opprobrious, for a farmer, farmworker, or homesteader in a cattle-grazing region, esp. one who ploughs virgin grassland. Hence **so·dbusting** *vbl. sb.*, ploughing virgin grassland; farming.

1922 R. STEAD *Neighbours* 126 Between your fine words I figger that you pick up a dollar now an' again by tottin' these tenderfoot sod-busters out over the bald-headed. **1927** C. SANDBURG *Amer. Songbag* 89 Its tune was familiar to the lonely 'sodbuster'. **1958** H. B. ALLEN in *Publ. Amer. Dialect Soc.* XXX. 11 The persistence of *sodbuster* and *soddy* as not necessarily opprobrious designations of the new settlers [in North Dakota]. **1965** G. SHEPHERD *West of Yesterday* x. 72 We owned cows and found that ranching was more attractive than sod-busting. **1970** [see *NESTER 2]. **1972** G. BEINE *Land of Coyote* 85 (*heading*) Sod busting a new field. **1979** *Guardian* 24 Mar. 12/1 The conflicts between sodbusters and cattlemen.

sod corn. *western N. Amer.* [f. SOD *sb.*[1] + CORN *sb.*[1]] **a.** Corn or maize planted in ploughed up grassland. **b.** Whisky made from sod corn. In full, *sod-corn whisky.*

1835 P. SHIRREFF *Tour* xxiv. 248 Indian corn is dropped into every third furrow..and covered with the next cut turf. This crop receives no farther cultivation of any kind, is termed sod corn, and said to yield fifty bushels per acre. **1838** *Bytown* (Ottawa) *Gaz.* 19 Sept. 1/3 The sod corn does not make up more than half a crop, and is..stacked for fodder stock. **1857** E. F. BEADLE *Diary* 2 Aug. (1923) 73 Found the family enjoying themselves over their 'Sod corn whiskey'. **1878** [see *BARE-FOOTED *a.* c]. **1913** W. CATHER *O Pioneers!* 27 John Bergson says to his boys, 'Try to break a little more land each year; sod corn is good for fodder.' **1927** K. EUBANK *Horse & Buggy Days* 94 They..ate their dinners,..munching cheese,.. which helped along on its onward course by a tumbler or so of sod corn, made in a moonshine still especially for the occasion. **1940** L. I. WILDER *Long Winter* iii. 29 He cut and shocked the sod corn.

so·ddenly, *adv.* [f. SODDEN *ppl. a.* + -LY[2].] In a sodden manner: heavily and dully; damply.

1901 KIPLING *Kim* xv. 390 Kim had reeled to a room with a cot in it, and was dozing soddenly. **1920** *Blackw. Mag.* Apr. 501/2, I slept, fitfully at first, soddenly later. **1939** JOYCE *Finnegans Wake* 514 Or (soddenly) Schott, furtivfired by the riots. **1976** *Church Times* 26 Nov. 5/1, I trudged soddenly along unfamiliar terrain.

soddenness. (Earlier example.)
1883 H. JAMES *Let.* 25 Nov. (1980) III. 14 Yes, I have read Trollope's autobiography and regard it as one of the most curious and amazing books in all literature, for its density, blockishness and general thickness and soddenness.

so·dding, *ppl. a.* and *adv. slang.* [f. *SOD *v.*³] A vague epithet expressing anger or contempt; freq. as a mere intensive.
1912 D. H. LAWRENCE *Let.* 3 July (1962) I. 134 The miserable sodding rotters..that make up England today. **1929** 'H. GREEN' *Living* iii. 25 'It [*sc.* Australia] am a grand country' 'e said to me, 'this [*sc.* England] be a poor sodding place for a poor bleeder', 'e said. 'I'm for goin'.' **1933** M. LOWRY *Ultramarine* 36, I don't know what you think you're doing idling round this sodding ship. **1950** R. GODDEN *Breath of Air* xix. 235 'That's my sodding business,' said McGinty. **1954** K. AMIS *Lucky Jim* xvii. 168 Cuts his own hair now, you see. Too sodding mean to pay out his one-and-six, that is what it is. My God. **1966** M. WOODHOUSE *Tree Frog* xxi. 155 Hundred and twenty two semiconductors in there, all radiating heat... What are we supposed to do, sodding blow on them? **1968** J. BRAINE *Crying Game* vi. 141 The bastard who was giving me dinner stood me up, and I shall sodding well ring him and tell him I'm going out with someone much nicer. **1976** C. STORR *Unnatural Fathers* ii. 27 My sodding brother got into hospital and then dropped out before his finals. **1980** D. BOGARDE *Gentle Occupation* i. 24 I'll remember this sodding day until the day I die.

so·ddish, *a.* [f. *SOD *sb*³.: see -ISH¹.] Awful, 'rotten', terrible.
1959 W. CAMP *Ruling Passion* xxvii. 237 What a bloody soddish thing to do.
So **so·ddishness** [-NESS], behaviour characteristic of a 'sod' (*SOD *sb.*³ 1, 2).
1938 L. MACNEICE *I crossed Minch* vi. 76 Charles Edward..sank into chambering and soddishness. **1970** 'D. CRAIG' *Young Men may Die* xvi. 121 Happily there was no opportunity for soddishness about whom I should go with.

soddite: see *SODDYITE.

soddy, *a.* and *sb.* **B.** *sb.* For *U.S.* read *western N. Amer.* and add: **1.** (Earlier and later examples.)
1877 H. RUEDE *Let.* 24 Apr. in J. Ise *Sod-Louse Days* (1937) 57 Many of the young bachelors..were building their own 'soddies'. **1970** *Islander* (Victoria, B.C.) 29 Nov. 10/4 It was a sort of soddy, the rear dug into a cutbank.
2. One who occupies or who has occupied a sod-house.
1958 [see *SODBUSTER]. **1977** *Westworld* (Vancouver, B.C.) May–June 6/2, I..received a nicely decorated certificate to the effect that I was a Soddy.

soddyite (sǫ·di,əit). *Min.* Orig. † **soddite.** [Coined in Fr. as *soddite* (A. Schoep 1922, in *Compt. Rend.* CLXXIV. 1067), f. the name of Frederick *Soddy* (1877–1956), English chemist and physicist: see -ITE¹.] A hydrated uranyl silicate found as yellow orthorhombic crystals.
1922 *Nature* 13 May 631/2 Soddite, a new radioactive mineral. This is a yellow crystalline mineral found associated with curite from Kasolo (Belgian Congo). **1927** *Mineral. Abstr.* III. 233 Soddyite (=soddite), $12UO_3.5SiO_2.14H_2O$. **1937** *Mem. Geol. Survey S. Afr.* No. 31. 108 Soddyite. This mineral occurs as an encrustation on quartz with malachite in the pegmatite at Norrabees. **1965** *Amer. Mineralogist* L. 919 Soddyite..occurs in blocky, fibrous, deep-yellow to yellow-green crystals which vein other uranyl minerals in the matrix.

sodian (sōᵘ·diăn), *a. Min.* [f. SOD(IUM + *-IAN 2.] Of a mineral: having a proportion of a constituent element replaced by sodium.
1930 W. T. SCHALLER in *Amer. Mineralogist* XV. 572 The adjectival endings thus formed for the names of all the chemical elements are given below... Sodium—sodian. **1951** C. PALACHE et al. *Dana's Syst. Min.* (ed. 7) II. 1022 On the dispersion of sodian and manganoan romeite ('atopite') from Brazil see Rose (1919). **1963** W. A. DEER et al. *Rock-Forming Minerals* II. 113 Titanaugites and sodian augites also have more ferric iron than most other pyroxenes.

sodic, *a.* Add: **b.** *Geol.* Of a mineral or rock: containing an appreciable or a greater-than-average quantity of sodium, often as compared with calcium or potassium. Also applied to a metamorphic process in which such minerals are formed.
1902 *Jrnl. Geol.* X. 574 The standard SO_3-bearing feldspathoid is therefore considered to be a purely sodic noselite. **1927** S. J. SHAND *Eruptive Rocks* xi. 200 More sodic types are also known, in which both orthoclase and quartz are present. **1952** T. F. W. BARTH *Theoret. Petrol.* 96 Plagioclases of gneisses and of crystalline schists, if zoned, usually show inverse order, that is, sodic core, calcic shell. **1967, 1971** [see *POTASSIC *a.* b]. **1978** *Nature* 7 Sept. 23/1 In addition to the phenocrysts appropriate to magmas of intermediate bulk composition, andesite and dacite contain both anomalously calcic and sodic plagioclase.

sodipotassic (sōᵘ:dipǫtæ·sik), *a. Geol.* Also **sodo-** (sōᵘ:do-). [Blend of SODIC and POTASSIC *adjs.*] Containing both sodium and potassium in appreciable quantities.
In quot. 1902 used to denote a specified compositional range in the classification scheme of Cross, Iddings, Pirsson, and Washington.
1902 *Jrnl. Geol.* X. 596 The minerals of the sodalite group are only present in the sodic or sodipotassic Subrangs of Classes I, II and III. **1927** S. J. SHAND *Eruptive Rocks* ix. 163 A typical example of the Quincy granite gave quartz 33, sodipotassic felspar 55, and ægirine and riebeckite 10 per cent. **1974** T. G. SAHAMA in H. Sørensen *Alkaline Rocks* 98/1 The rocks are mainly potassic to perpotassic, but sodopotassic to sodic varieties are known among the jumillites and fortunites.

sodium. Add: **2. a.** *sodium vapour* (freq. *attrib.*); **sodium Amytal** *Pharm.*, the sodium salt of *AMYTAL, used as a sedative and hypnotic; sodium 5-ethyl-5-isopropylbarbiturate, $C_{11}H_{17}N_2O_3Na$; **sodium Pentothal** (see *PENTOTHAL).
1929 *Proc. Soc. Exper. Biol. & Med.* XXVI. 709 Anesthesia has been produced in human beings by the intravenous injection of solutions of the anhydrous sodium amytal. **1937** [see *SECONAL]. **1938** [see *AMYTAL]. **1955** A. HUXLEY *Genius & Goddess* 9 One escapes into reminiscence as one escapes into gin or sodium amytal. **1933** *Discovery* Feb. 50/2 In the construction of sodium vapour lamps this difficulty is overcome by introducing a rare gas into the tube. **1968** M. S. LIVINGSTON *Particle Physics* iii. 39 A well-known example [of a multiplet] is the sodium D-line doublet which gives the yellow color to the light from a sodium-vapor lamp.
b. sodium-cooled *a.*, that employs liquid sodium as a coolant; *spec.* of (*a*) an aero-engine exhaust valve, or (*b*) a nuclear reactor; **sodium pump** *Physiol.*, a pump (*PUMP *sb.*¹ 1 e) which operates on sodium ions.
1934 *Jrnl. R. Aeronaut. Soc.* XXXVIII. 223 The Americans have attained and even exceeded [500 lbs. per sq. in.]..with a poppet valve (sodium cooled) engine. **1954** *Sci. Amer.* Dec. 38/3 A sodium-cooled reactor, which can be operated at very high temperatures, has greater thermal efficiency than a water-cooled system. **1956** E. MOLLOY *Automobile Engineer's Ref. Bk.* iii. 242 In engines where exhaust-valve cooling is a serious problem, the sodium-cooled valve has been adopted. **1971** *New Scientist* 11 Mar. 529/1 Rudzinski was mainly concerned about the immense complexity of the sodium-cooled technology. **1977** *Time* 15 Aug. 11/3 What worries them in particular is that Super Phénix will produce energy from a sophisticated sodium-cooled reactor eight times more powerful than smaller, water-cooled plants. **1951** *Jrnl. Physiol.* CXIV. 143 An active sodium pump cannot be ruled out on the grounds that it would require more energy than is available from the resting metabolism. **1964** [see *PUMP *sb.*¹ 1 e]. **1974** D. & M. WEBSTER *Compar. Vertebr. Morphol.* ix. 183 Instead of osmotically equilibrating, this imbalance of cations is maintained by the cell membrane's physical characteristics plus an enzyme system, called the sodium pump, which actively removes sodium from inside the cell.
c. Used *attrib.* and in *Comb.* with reference to (the intense yellow light emitted from) discharge tubes containing sodium vapour, used esp. for street lighting.
1888 Sodium light [in Dict., sense 2 b]. **1912** *Jrnl. Soc. Chem. Industry* 31 Oct. 1010/2 (*heading*) Polarisation; Sodium lamps for. **1933** *Discovery* Oct. 318/2 The electrical impulses corresponding to the television picture signals are converted into the light variations of a specially designed sodium tube. **1956** R. FULLER *Image of Society* viii. 195 The sodium lamps of the bypass. **1959** *New Statesman* 8 Aug. 152/2 Their fight is often associated with the campaign against concrete lamp-posts, sodium lighting and similar 'outrages' on our towns and cities. **1967** A. J. MARSHALL in L. Deighton *London Dossier* 138 Walking in the sodium-lit Kilburn High Road. **1973** J. MANN *Only Security* x. 132 Thea pressed the whole row of light switches and..the sodium strips flickered into brilliance. **1977** D. HARSENT *Dreams of Dead* 35 Midnight, bruised insomniacs, alive to the growing silence and opening to the sodium glare like flowers.
d. Objective, as *sodium-demanding*, *-retaining* adjs.
1977 J. L. HARPER *Population Biol. Plants* xxi. 655 The life cycle strategy is likely in such a case to be influenced by the optimal allocation of sodium between parents and offspring and between the various sodium-demanding activities. **1977** *Proc. R. Soc. Med.* LXX. 692/1 One of the hypotheses..has been that these patients fail to escape normally from the sodium-retaining effect of aldosterone.

sodoku (so·doku). *Path.* [Jap.] The form of rat-bite fever caused by *Spirillum minus.*
1926 *Trans. Soc. Tropical Med. & Hygiene* XIX. 183 Apert and his colleagues suggested the use of stovarsol or tréparsol by the mouth in the case of persons who had been exposed to the infection of sodoku **1955** W. L. JELLISON in T. G. Hull *Dis. transmitted from Animals to Man* (ed. 4) xxvii. 539 The term 'sodoku' is from the Japanese (*so*, a rat, *doku*, poison) and is being resorted to more commonly by American workers to avoid controversy and confusion over the correct application of the term rat-bite fever. Sodoku is primarily an infection of rats, mice, and other rodents. **1970** *Scand. Jrnl. Infectious Dis.* II. 71/1 Two aetiologically different but clinically similar diseases may occur as results of rat-bites: the Japanese Sodoku caused by Spirillum minus, and the bacillary form.

Sodom. Add: **1.** Also coupled with *Gomorrah* (see GOMORR(H)EAN *a.* and *sb.*), the name of the other of the two wicked cities of the plain in Gen. xviii–xix.
1862 QUEEN VICTORIA *Let.* 7 June in R. Fulford *Dearest Mama* (1968) 67 It was intended he should come home through Paris stopping only a day in order to have got over his visit to that Sodom and Gomorrah. **1864** TROLLOPE *Can you forgive Her?* I. xxiii. 179, I always regarded the States as a Sodom and Gomorrah, prospering in wickedness. **1972** I. HAMILTON *Thrill Machine* xv. 63 It wasn't exactly Sodom and Gomorrah—the ladies kept their clothes on. **1974** *Listener* 24 Jan. 121/3 Heliogabalus ..reduced Rome to a kind of post-Christian Sodom and Gomorrah.

sodomist. Add: (Example.) Also as *adj.* = SODOMITICAL *a.*
1948 *Rep. Native Laws Commission 1946–48* (Dept. Native Affairs, South Africa) 38/1 We may quote from a memorandum submitted by..the Reverend H. P. Junod:—'..He was the son of one of our Evangelists, and refused to submit to the sodomist suggestions and solicitations of old mine workers.' **1950** M. HAY *Foot of Pride* iv. 95 The inhabitants of Cahors..joined in the [money-lending] business, and Dante put them in Hell alongside the sodomists.

sodomize (sǫ·dəməiz), *v.* [f. SODOM(Y + -IZE.] *trans.* (occas. *absol.*) To practise sodomy upon (a man or a woman). Also **so·domized** *ppl. a.*, **so·domizing** *vbl. sb.*
1868 tr. *Index Expurgatorius of Martial* 89 You must give up sodomising and womanising. **1888** [see *IRRUMATION]. **1969** P. BARNES *Ruling Class* II. vi. 94 Earl of Gurney: You want two seconds of dripping sin to fertilize sodomized idiots. **1971** K. MILLETT *Sexual Politics* (1972) I. i. 13 Her gratitude at being sodomized is positively astonishing. **1972** *Times Lit. Suppl.* 2 June 622/4 Everything, animate and inanimate, appears to be either sodomizing, sodomized, ejaculating or bleeding. **1980** *Ibid.* 19 Sept. 1020/3 Cassady roughly sodomizing another man in a public lavatory.

sodopotassic, var. *SODIPOTASSIC *a.*

sody, *U.S. dial.* and *colloq.* var. SODA¹ (esp. in sense *4 b).
1900 *Dialect Notes* I. 241 *Soda.* Always *sōdi* in Kansas City. **1907** J. LONDON *White Fang* I. ii. 14 Swallow a spoonful of sody, an' you'll sweeten up wonderful. **1907** *Dialect Notes* III. 200 *Sody, n.*, soda; either bicarbonate of soda or soda water. 'Have a glass of sody with me?' The normal pronunciation seems affected. **1951** W. FAULKNER *Requiem for Nun* III. 267 She's usually got a bottle of sody pop in the icebox. **1975** B. GARFIELD *Hopscotch* viii. 86 There was even a sody-cracker barrel by the fountain.

soebak, var. *SUBAK. **soeju,** obs. var. *SHOYU.

soetkoekie (sutku·ki). *S. Afr.* Also **zoetekoekie, soet-koekie.** [Afrikaans, lit. 'a little sweet cake', f. Du. *zoet* sweet + *koek* cake + *-ie* dim. suff.] A traditional South African spiced biscuit.
1910 D. FAIRBRIDGE *That which hath Been* ix. 115 Juffvrouw wanted very bad to help hand zoete-koekies. **1949** L. G. GREEN *In Land of Afternoon* xii. 165, I have heard of a special ginger beer which is brewed during Christmas week and served with soetkoekies. **1939** 'D. RAME' *Wine of Good Hope* III. iii. 368 They ended their tea and the thin bread and butter and soet-koekies of Grim's ceremony. **1973** *Fair Lady* 7 Mar. 23 With visions of my Voortrekker ancestors embarking on hazardous journeys with tinfuls of 'mebos', biltong, and 'soetkoekies', I scratched through my recipe book.

sofa. Add: **3. a.** *sofa-cover, settee, -table* (earlier and further examples).
1805 *Times* 7 Nov. 4/2 Card, sofa, and Pembroke tables. **1807** JANE AUSTEN *Let.* 8 Feb. (1932) I. 49 There will then be the Window-Curtains, sofa-cover, & a carpet to be altered. **1848** MRS. GASKELL *Mary Barton* I. vii. 115 The dead body..which she was laying out on a board, placed on a sort of sofa-settee. **1861** C. M. YONGE *Young Stepmother* xxiii. 333 She felt the misfortune to the beautiful new sofa-cover as a most serious calamity. **1937** *Burlington Mag.* May 240/1 Attempts to introduce gothic ornament into a sofa-table, a bookcase or a chair. **1968** *Canad. Antiques Collector* Aug. 6/2 (Advt.), Exceptionally fine Rosewood Regency sofa table. **1978–9** *House & Garden* Dec./Jan. 78/2 Striped Welsh flannel chair and sofa covers.
4. sofa-back, (*a*) an antimacassar; (*b*) the back of a sofa; **sofa-bed** (earlier example).
1878 GEO. ELIOT *Let.* 27 June (1956) VII. 33 The sorrows of those who can afford..to think of anything better than sofa-backs. **1880** L. HIGGIN *Handbk. Embroidery* 63 Design for sofa-back cover. **1894** 'MARK TWAIN' in *Century Mag.* Jan. 338/2 Tom..hoisted a leg over the sofa-back. **1805** Sofa bed [see *chair-bed* s.v. *CHAIR *sb*¹. 15].
sofaed *ppl. a.*, (*b*) furnished with a sofa or sofas.
1802 T. CAMPBELL *Let.* 28 Aug. (1849) I. xv. 397 A lord's house, fashionable *strangers*, sofa'd saloons, and winding galleries. **1842** DICKENS *Let.* 3 Jan. (1974) III. 7 A comfortable room,..well-lighted, sofa'd, mirrored, and so forth. **1860** G. VANDENHOFF *Dramatic Reminiscences* vi. 104 A very good-sized room had been fitted up as my dressing-room, cleaned, carpeted, sofa'd, well lit. **1934** 'A. BRIDGE' *Ginger Griffin* ii. 22 The Grant-Howards sat in the green-sofa'd saloon.

Sofar (sōu·fɑɹ). Also **SOFAR**. [See quot. 1948.] A system in which the sound waves from an underwater explosion (either artificial or natural) are detected at a number of listening stations so that its position can be fixed; more generally, detection of deep explosions a great distance away.

1947 *Britannica Bk. of Year* 841/2 An underwater sound system, called 'Sofar'.., made possible the location of air and ship survivors as far as 2,000 mi. from shore. **1948** EWING & WORZEL *Long-Range Sound Transmission* 12 A network of four listening stations is being established in the Pacific by the Navy Department, and the name SOFAR, from the words SOund Fixing And Ranging, has been assigned to the system. **1961** H. H. KOELLE *Handbk. Astronaut. Engin.* XXVIII. 28 The missile must carry a Sofar bomb when a deep-water detection system is used, in order to provide a deep sound source. **1966** *McGraw-Hill Encycl. Sci. & Technol.* XIV. 429/2 Shock waves used in Sofar propagate long distances under water, being refracted by the isothermal layers in the oceans. **1979** *Nature* 20–27 Dec. 820/2 The deep ocean sound channel is used to obtain very long range (typically > 2,000 km) acoustic transmission via totally refracted propagation paths (SOFAR propagation).

soft, *sb.* Add: **2. b.** (Earlier and further examples.)

1821 [see *fancy-piece* s.v. *FANCY *sb.* and *a.* B. 2]. **1955** *Publ. Amer. Dialect Soc.* XXIV. 115 Paper money is known, in general, as *scratch* or *soft*.

d. *pl.* Soft commodities (see *SOFT *a.* 20 b (*b*)).

1979 *Financial Times* 28 Mar. 37/1 Will 'softs' boom next? **1981** *Times* 5 May 17/2 Softs are less homogeneous in outlook because crop conditions vary so much.

6. *Hist. rare.* A Menshevik.

1950 E. H. CARR *Bolshevik Revol.* I. ii. 30 But the withdrawal of seven delegates who had voted with the 'softs'..had the result of shifting the balance of votes in favour of the 'hards'. **1955** H. HODGKINSON *Doubletalk* 17 Lenin's group..was described as 'Iskraists'..or 'hards'... Its rivals were 'softs', because it approached the membership problem in the spirit of Martov's 'The more people there are called Party members, the better it will be'.

soft, *a.* Add: **I. 1. d.** Of a photographic film or paper: producing an image of low contrast.

1892 [in Dict., sense 1 c]. **1910** W. WALLINGTON *Chats on Photogr.* xiii. 113 The paper may be obtained in a number of speeds..the slower varieties being more suitable for printing soft negatives. **1937** *Amat. Photogr.* ix. 120 The 'soft' grade has the..merit of registering tone in dense high-lights without clogging shadows. **1966** D. G. BRANDON *Mod. Techniques Metallogr.* 15 An approximately linear dependence of the blackening is only obtained over a limited range of exposure times, and this range is far greater for 'soft' emulsions than for 'hard' ones. **1979** *SLR Camera* Jan. 59/1 If the photographic image shows a large number of tones between the extremes of light and dark, it is said to have soft gradation.

e. Of a lens: having low resolving power. Cf. *SOFT-FOCUS *a.*, *sb.*, and *v.*

1958 M. L. HALL *Newnes' Compl. Amat. Photographer* i. 26 Soft lenses. Some highly complex lenses are said to be 'soft' in definition. **1974** *Publishers' Weekly* 24 June 56/2 'Soft lens' photos well suited indeed to the muted inner dignity of these deeply religious black people. **1978** *SLR Camera* Sept. 37/3 How good is the lens on your camera? Is it a bit soft?

2. c. Applied in the Soviet Union and China to a class of railway carriage (esp. a sleeper) having soft, upholstered seats.

1928 *Cook's Continental Timetable* 15 May 102 Sleeping car of direct communication, soft and hard class. **1949** F. MACLEAN *Eastern Approaches* (1951) I. iii. 39 In the train I found myself in a 'soft' compartment with three senior and somewhat supercilious officers of the Red Army. **1954** KOESTLER *Invisible Writing* v. 61 It entitled me..to travel in the 'soft class' on trains. **1968** BETHELL & BURG tr. *Solzhenitsyn's Cancer Ward* I. xiv. 228 They found it quite unbearable, of course, to travel in ordinary railway carriages... The Rusanovs now travelled only in reserved compartments or 'soft class'. **1974** *Times* 1 Apr. 15/5 All the railways in Europe, and even those in China, have first and second class, although it may be wrapped up as 'hard' and 'soft' in USSR and China. **1978** G. E. NEWBY *Big Red Train Ride* ii. 22 We now took a closer look at our deluxe, 'soft-class' compartment. **1982** *Brit. Med. Jrnl.* 3 Apr. 1031/1 One end of our 'soft-class' carriage [in China].

III. 13. b. (Earlier example of *to have a soft spot in one's heart.*) Hence phr. *to have a soft spot for*, to have a tender regard for, be fond of.

1857 C. M. YONGE *Dynevor Terrace* I. xi. 160 Jane has a soft spot in her heart, and will not think true love is confined within the rank that keeps a gig. **1902** [see SPOT *sb.*[1] 10 b]. **1947** K. TENNANT *Lost Haven* i. 24 She always did have a soft spot for him. **1971** *New Scientist* 13 May 400/1 He won a scholarship advertised in New Scientist and has had a soft spot for the magazine ever since.

18. d. *to be* or *go soft on*: to be or become excessively lenient or partial to.

1883 'MARK TWAIN' *Life on Mississippi* xxxiv. 373 If he was soft on the Arkansas mosquitoes, he was hard enough on the mosquitoes of Lake Providence to make up for it. **1911** G. B. SHAW *Shewing-up of Blanco Posnet* 405 Why did He make me go soft on the child if He was going hard on it Himself? **1959** *New Statesman* 30 May 751 Why ..were we all 'going soft' on Dulles? **1971** *Guardian* 19 Nov. 13/7 In the eyes of the militants, the Guardian is still 'soft on the rebels'.

IV. 19. c. fig. *soft spot*, a weak or vulnerable place.

1933 [see *INFILTRATION 1 e]. **1956** A. L. ROWSE *Early Churchills* 239 The French..withdrew behind their fortifications... Marlborough was all for an assault on these; he had proved and found a soft spot opposite Ramillies. **1958** *Engineering* 21 Mar. 361/1 Even if the country as a whole was in the best of economic health, the local soft spots could not be ignored without serious political repercussions. **1965** H. I. ANSOFF *Corporate Strategy* vii. 126 If the problem appears as a minor 'soft spot' in an otherwise healthy product-market position, temporary *ad hoc* arrangement..may suffice. **1975** *Times Lit. Suppl.* 17 Oct. 1233/3 There is probably much truth in Mr Levison's analysis.., but his obvious sincerity and dedication mask a few soft spots in the argument.

d. *Mil.* Of a military vehicle: unarmoured. Of a missile base: vulnerable to a direct nuclear explosion because of its construction or location.

1944 A. JACOB *Traveller's War* vii. 129 The tanks crunch forward like a battle fleet: our 'soft' vehicles in the middle of the phalanx, with the armoured cars of the Dragoon Guards moving on both flanks. **1948** PARTRIDGE *Dict. Forces' Slang 1939–45* 175 *Soft-skinned vehicles; soft stuff*, unarmoured vehicles. (Army.) Both of these terms started as slang; the latter remained unofficial, although it did become colloquial; the former very rapidly became colloquial and then official. **1958** [see *HARD *a.* (*sb.*) 14 f]. **1961** E. BURGESS *Long-Range Ballistic Missiles* vi. 182 All forms of long-range missiles now appear to be developing towards the abandonment of the soft base, but there are..difficulties associated with the hardening concept. **1972** *Dict. Military & Associated Terms* (U.S. Department of Defense) 275/2 *Soft missile base*, a launching base that is not protected against a nuclear explosion.

e. *Physics.* Of a mode of vibration in a crystal lattice: such that its frequency decreases to zero as the temperature of the crystal approaches that of a phase transition.

1964 *Physical Rev.* CXXXVI. A. 429/1 Cochran proposed a theory which links the cause of ferroelectricity in the perovskites to the existence of a temperature-dependent 'soft' lattice vibrational mode. **1967** *Ibid.* CLVII. 396/1 The energy of this soft mode can be extracted from reflectivity measurements in the infrared region. **1973** G. R. WILKINSON in A. Anderson *Raman Effect* II. xi. 813 A number of 'soft' modes of vibration whose frequencies depend upon temperature have been found.

20. b. (*a*) (Earlier example.) Also *soft furnishing(s)*. (*b*) *Comm.*, designating relatively perishable consumer goods such as clothes, foods, and drugs; *spec.* in the commodity market, used of commodities produced from vegetables, such as textiles, rubber, and foodstuffs.

1833 *Chambers's Edin. Jrnl.* I. 385/3, I could occasionally hear a detached sentence on politics..the price of stocks—soft goods. **1925** *Daily Tel.* 13 May 20/6 Soft furnishing department. **1927** *Ibid.* 11 May 18/6 Manageress wanted... Must have thorough experience in the sale and scheme side of soft furnishings. **1946** *Sun* (Baltimore) 5 Oct. 2/6 These points stand out with respect to the production of 'soft' consumer goods (clothing, food, drugs and the like). **1961** *Ann. Reg. 1960* 502 The value of retail sales rose by 4 per cent, a higher demand for 'soft' goods more than offsetting the drop in purchases of durable household goods. **1967** E. SHORT *Embroidery & Fabric Collage* iii. 78 Probably the most useful and versatile object in soft furnishings is the cushion. **1976** L. DEIGHTON *Twinkle, twinkle, Little Spy* xvi. 169 She did nothing except sink lower in the soft furnishings and continue to drink. **1979** *Daily Tel.* 9 Oct. 21 While the metal markets continue their volatile course the 'soft' commodities, with the notable exception of sugar, have largely been untouched by the urge to get out of the dollar and currencies in general.

22. d. *Astronautics.* Of a landing made by a spacecraft: slow enough for no serious damage to be incurred. Chiefly in *SOFT LANDING *vbl. sb.*

1958 *Times* 28 Mar. 10/3 Next (in difficulty) would be a 'soft' (controlled) landing [on the moon] by an unmanned vehicle. **1966** E. BURGESS *Assault on Moon* v. 151 A soft lunar landing is the landing of a payload on the Moon with a small shock to that payload. **1975** *Daily Tel.* 11 Aug. 11/4 One vehicle will make a soft touchdown on Mars while the large spacecraft which carried it on its journey will remain in orbit.

e. Of a substance: readily magnetized by an ambient magnetic field but retaining no permanent magnetization in the absence of such a field.

1839, 1873 [see *soft iron*, sense 24 b in Dict.]. **1900** *Jrnl. Iron & Steel Inst.* LVII. 403 The author divides the different varieties of iron and steel into those which are magnetically 'soft' and those which are magnetically 'hard'. **1948** F. BRAILSFORD *Magnetic Materials* iv. 69 The most important source of internal strains in the higher grade soft magnetic materials is that due to the presence of impurities held in solution in the metal. **1976** *Nature* 5 Feb. 381/1 In a few cases large randomly directed magnetically soft components were removed in low alternating fields.

f. Of glass: softening at a relatively low temperature when heated.

1925 HODKIN & COUSEN *Textbk. Glass Technol.* vi. 51 A..vessel of soft soda-lime glass in which water is boiled, will liberate so much alkali in 15 minutes as to make impossible correct titrations with decinormal solutions. **1961** G. R. CHOPPIN *Exper. Nuclear Chem.* viii. 121 Since Pyrex glass contains boron..it is better to use a soft glass tube to hold the source. **1965** PHILLIPS & WILLIAMS *Inorg. Chem.* I. xiv. 545 Soft glasses are made by adding soda to the silica. About 25 per cent soda reduces the viscosity of a glass by a factor of 10^{10}.

g. Of a contact lens: made of a soft, yielding material.

1964 *Highlights Ophthalm.* VII. 252 (*heading*) The new hydrophilic gel, soft, contact lenses. **1971** *Time* 31 May 46, I intend using the soft lenses on every patient I possibly can. **1978** H. HAMAND in M. Ruben *Soft Contact Lenses* viii. 128 The thickness of cornea of a rabbit was found to increase by 20% with 17 h of hard lens wear and about 5% with soft lens.

24. b. *soft hammer, paste* (earlier examples), *porcelain* (earlier examples) (see PASTE *sb.* 3 b, PORCELAIN 1 a note).

1964 S. CRAWFORD *Basic Engin. Processes* i. 16 Hammers with heads made of lead, copper, rubber, or rawhide are known as soft hammers. The head is usually in the form of a cast tube with a recess at each end to locate the soft inserts. **1977** G. CLARK *World Prehistory* (ed. 3) v. 212 The introduction of the soft hammer technique resulted in the production of thinner bifaces. **1848** H. R. FORSTER *Stowe Catal.* 8 Chantilly Porcelain is a fine kind of 'soft paste'. **1879** Soft paste [see PASTE *sb.* 3 b]. **1819** A. REES *Cycl.* XXVIII. s.v. *Porcelain*, The porcelain is made of these substances [*sc.* porcelain clay and felspar]..but other materials are employed to give the required transparency at a lower temperature. This has received the name of soft porcelain. **1839** URE *Dict. Arts* II. 1025 The manufacture of soft porcelain is longer and more difficult than that of hard.

c. Applied to a coal of low rank, usu. a bituminous or a brown coal.

soft coal in sense 24 b in Dict. is coal that is easily cleft.

1857 J. B. JUKES *Student's Man. Geol.* iv. 133 All these minute varieties are commonly included under four principal heads:—1, Caking coal; 2, Splint or hard coal; 3, Cherry or soft coal, and 4, Cannel or parrot coal. **1903** *Bull. U.S. Geol. Surv.* No. 213. 265 By far the largest part of the coal mined [in the Eastern Interior field] is soft bituminous, making a good steam fuel. **1926** J. ROBERTS *Mining Educator* I. 677/1 American cities where the use of 'soft' or smoky coal is forbidden by law. **1958** I. C. F. STATHAM *Coal Mining Practice* (1960) I. ii. 77 Practically all black coals, such as are worked in British coalfields, show banding of soft bright and hard dull coal..parallel to the bedding. **1979** *Sci. Amer.* Jan. 28/3 Hard coal (anthracite and the various grades of bituminous coal) and soft coal (brown coal and lignite).

25. b. For *dial.* and *U.S.* read orig. *dial.* and *U.S.* Now usu. restricted to cold fruit drinks and the like. (Later examples.)

1911 *Chambers's Jrnl.* Feb. 111/2 In the matter of 'soft' drinks the chemist or druggist is not in it [in Canada]. **1919** P. B. CLAYTON *Tales Talbot House* 29 The House was always what the Canadians called a 'soft drink' establishment, but no one resented this, lapping up tea or cocoa or Bovril with thanksgiving. **1936** G. B. SHAW *Simpleton of Unexpected Isles* Prol. iii. 27 A feast of fruit and bread and soft drinks is spread on the ground. **1944** AUDEN *For Time Being* (1945) 113 Soft drinks and sandwiches may be had in the inns at reasonable prices. **1960** KOESTLER *Lotus & Robot* I. i. 36 A soft-drink cocktail party in the house of a leading Parsee politician. **1964** I. MURDOCH *Italian Girl* iii. 36 You haven't anything soft, ginger beer? All right, tomato juice. **1966** 'A. HALL' *9th Directive* xii. 116 The sun was hot..soft-drinks men worked their way through [the crowd]. **1978** R. LUDLUM *Holcroft Covenant* xviii. 203 They had proceeded to a second hotel on the rue Chevalle, where a soft-drink sign provided him with a name for the registry: N. Fresca.

c. Of a detergent: biodegradable.

1963 *New Scientist* 27 June 716/1 A soft detergent is one that is biologically soft; that is, readily oxidised in a modern sewage plant. *Ibid.* 717/1 In most western countries the consumption of soap, which is a soft detergent, remains fairly steady or is falling. **1966** *Economist* 23 July 385/1 Replacing this branched chain with a straight chain makes the detergent 'soft'—that is, easily munchable by the hard-working bugs. **1971** *Daily Tel.* 16 Oct. 10/6 The detergent industry switched over to 'soft', biodegradable detergents.

26*. a. *Electronics.* Of a thermionic valve or discharge tube: (*a*) having had an inert gas introduced into it at the time of manufacture in order to modify or enhance its performance; (*b*) containing gas at low pressure as a result of a leak or of outgassing by component parts. [tr. G. *weich*, used in sense (*a*) by W. C. Röntgen 1897, in *Sitzungsber. d. K. Preuss. Akad. d. Wissensch. zu Berlin* 584.]

1899 [see *HARD *a.* (*sb.*) 16* b]. **1901** *Phil. Trans. R. Soc.* CXCVI. 42 The value of λ obtained..for a much 'softer' bulb was ·001, or about four times the absorption of the bulb employed in these experiments. **1921** *Wireless World* 6 Aug. 288/2 One 'soft' triode will give as much amplification as two 'hard' valves. **1931** [see *HARD *a.* (*sb.*) 16* b]. **1932** *Discovery* July 216/1 These hard valves were found to be very much more reliable and uniform in their action than earlier 'soft' valves. **1948** *Electronic Engin.* XX. 384/1 In recent years the soft valve (thyratron) counter has been replaced by the hard valve counter. **1956** G. A. MONTGOMERIE *Digital Calculating Machines* ix. 178 The soft valves are usually beam-switching tubes of the multicathode type.

1919 R. D. BANGAY *Oscillation Valve* 203 There are several indications which enable one to tell when a valve is going 'soft'. The first is loss of power in the oscillatory circuit. **1929** DUNCAN & DREW *Radio Telegr. & Teleph.* xi. 214 The degree of vacuum in the tube would change and some tubes became soft (having less vacuum) while others became hard (having a higher vacuum, with little or no gas present). **1958** W. F. LOVERING *Radio Com-*

munication viii. 173 A valve in which the vacuum is poor is said to be soft; the presence of a small number of molecules of gas adversely affects the performance.

b. *Physics.* Of X-rays and gamma rays: of relatively long wavelength and low penetrating power. Of sub-atomic particles: of relatively low energy.

Orig. so called because soft X-rays are emitted by a soft tube (see prec. sense).

1901 *Phil. Trans. R. Soc.* CXCVI. 516 The radiation from the barium compound is enormously reduced by the interposition of so thin a screen as an ordinary piece of tinfoil; these 'soft' rays accordingly form much the greater part of the whole. **1925** *Proc. Cambr. Philos. Soc.* XXII. 834 The soft γ-radiation gave a well-marked spectrum containing two strong lines. **1940** *Nature* 20 July 94/2 The beryllium oxide was tested inside a counter so designed that even very soft particles could be detected. **1950** D. H. WILKINSON *Ionization Chambers & Counters* vi. 160 The use of a proportional counter for counting extremely soft electrons which give very few ion pairs, has been proposed. **1960** *Lebende Sprachen* V. 163/2 The soft X-rays emitted from television screens cause great concern among radiologists. **1978** *Nature* 30 Mar. 396/3 There are several isotopes..which emit radiation sufficiently soft to be shielded even by the syringe wall but which can be presented in a form such that all the tissues of an animal become labelled a short time after injection.

26.** Miscellaneous *transf.* and *fig.* uses. **a.** Of facts, information, etc.: insubstantial, impressionistic, imprecise (opp. *HARD *a.* 7 b, c). Of a science or its method: not amenable to precise mathematical treatment or to experimental verification or refutation; *esp.* in *soft science.*

1923 *Sci. Amer.* Feb. 77/2 Its functions and its limitations are to get the facts from the bottom to the top of the coal industry, both hard and soft. **1966** *Time* 3 June 43 Project SIMILE Director Hall T. Sprague says these games are 'to the soft sciences what a laboratory is to the hard sciences of physics, chemistry and biology'. **1968** *Physics Bull.* Oct. 351/2 One of the striking features of the present time is the penetration of 'hard' methods (quantitative, physical analyses) into subjects which were hitherto 'soft' (descriptive, non-numerical). **1970** *Publishers' Weekly* 8 June 154 Hardscience is science (physics, math, chemistry), softscience is the humanities, sociology in particular. **1972** *Lancet* 25 Nov. 1138/1 Clinical departments..must learn a new respect for the 'soft' data of sociology. **1976** *National Observer* (U.S.) 10 Apr. 20/5 *All the President's Men* is what reporters call a 'soft' story—breezily entertaining but short on hard facts. **1976** *Times Lit. Suppl.* 25 June 766/2 The soft areas in evolutionary theory, which he sorts into a series of Hegelian opposites: adaptive versus nonadaptive traits, [etc.]. **1980** *Dædalus* Spring 94 One might view these various expressions.. spanning (from the 'hard' end) science, history and anthropology..to (at the 'soft' end) dreams and personal fantasy. **1982** *Daily Tel.* 23 Apr. 22 Most academic articles in all the sciences (hard and soft) are read by very few people.

b. *Comm.* Of markets, commodities, etc.: depressed, characterized by falling prices or excess supply. (Cf. FIRM *a.* 7 a.)

1930 *Morning Post* 19 Aug. 3/4 Oils were generally soft, while Coppers were far from being buoyant. **1935** *Commercial & Financial Chron.* 7 Sept. 1488/2 Gold mining stocks were soft, and international issues were neglected. **1968** *Globe & Mail* (Toronto) 13 Feb. B1/2 At the end of last year, the fish industry in Newfoundland was reeling from the effects of the extremely soft U.S. market. **1981** *Times* 8 May 26/5 Disappointing trading news also left.. Francis Sumner 1p softer at 9p. **1982** *Times* 6 May 17/1 Britain must cease being the soft market for the so-called developing world and action was needed against countries which blocked imports of British goods by crippling duties while having free access to the United Kingdom.

c. *Econ.* Of currency: (see quot. 1949). (Cf. also sense 20 c in Dict. and *hard currency* (*b*) s.v. *HARD *a.* (*sb.*) 22 b.)

1940 *Economist* 6 Apr. 609/1 There are some currencies—the 'soft' currencies, notably the lira and the yen—for which no official rates are fixed. **1949** *Times* 10 Sept. 5/7 Soft currency..is a relative rather than an absolute term. It means a currency of which other countries (or some other countries) have earned more than they can willingly spend in the country whose currency it is... A soft currency is by definition, non-convertible—*i.e.*, cannot be converted into gold or dollars... A currency may, however, be 'transferable' (within limits) and yet remain a soft currency in relation to some other currencies. **1960** *Economist* 15 Oct. 241/1 The United States now 'sells' abroad each year surplus farm products worth more than $1 billion, taking in exchange soft currencies—as one bureaucrat calls them, 'clam shells, coloured buttons and other forms of local currency'. **1967** A. DIMENT *Dolly Dolly Spy* vii. 97, I had changed some of my hard Swiss francs into soft pesetas. **1980** *Times* 23 May 14/6 Some African countries can only make ends meet in Moscow by smuggling in soft roubles bought abroad... This is categorically forbidden by..most..western embassies.

d. Designating a kind of technology that uses renewable resources such as wind or solar power and human or animal exertion and is not harmful to the natural environment. Also, of energy employed in or derived from this technology.

1974 *Harper's Mag.* Apr. 6 The term 'soft technology' was coined amid the British counter-culture in 1970. Technology which is soft is gentle on its surroundings, responds to it, incorporates it, feeds it. A nuclear power-generating station doesn't qualify. A wooden windmill with cloth sails grinding local grain does. **1977** A. LOVINS *Soft Energy Paths* ii. 38, I shall call them 'soft' technologies: a textural description, intended to mean not vague, mushy, speculative, or ephemeral, but rather flexible, resilient, sustainable, and benign. Energy paths dependent on soft technologies..will be called 'soft' energy paths. **1978** *Dædalus* Summer 188 The Progressives.. have tended to emphasize economics and technology, yet they have been 'soft' technological determinists in a way that maintains..Rousseau's fascination with the potential..of human autonomy. **1978** *Internat. Relations Dict.* (U.S. Dept. State Library) 2/1 Other terms used synonymously with appropriate technology are alternative technology, intermediate technology, and soft technology.

V. 27. (Special combinations, corresponding in formation to those (undefined) under senses 28–30, are included here.) *softback* attrib., (of books) bound in paper or limp covers; *U.S.*; *soft-board* sb., a relatively soft form of fibreboard (see also sense 30 in Dict.); *soft cancer,* a cancer in which the affected tissue is soft and yielding; now *rare* or *Obs.*; *soft chancre,* a venereal disease caused by local infection with *Hæmophilus ducreyi*; chancroid; also, one of the characteristic lesions of this disease; *soft copy,* a legible but transient presentation of information, as on a VDU screen; information so displayed; *soft-core* attrib. [after *hard-core* (*pornography*): see *hard core* (*b*) s.v. *HARD *a.* 22 b], (of pornography) less obscene than hard-core pornography; also *absol.*; *soft corn* (examples); *soft-cover* attrib., of, pertaining to, or designating a book bound in a limp or paper cover; also (usu. as two words) *ellipt.* for some such phrase as *soft-cover edition*; hence *soft-covered* adj.; *soft drug,* a drug that is held to be comparatively non-addictive and safe to use; also *fig.*; *soft food,* the partly digested food which pigeons regurgitate to feed to their young; = PIGEON'S MILK 1 in Dict. and Suppl.; *soft-foot* vb. intr. (N. Amer.), to go with quiet footsteps, to tiptoe; *soft fruit* = *small fruit* s.v. *SMALL *a.* 21; *soft ground,* a sticky covering of wax mixed with grease for an etching plate; also = next; *soft ground etching,* a process of print-making using plates covered with a soft ground, producing prints with softened lines resembling chalk or pencil drawings; also, a print produced by this process; *soft hail,* precipitation of snow pellets (see *SNOW *sb.*[1] 9 a); *soft line,* a flexible or conciliatory policy; freq. (with hyphen) *attrib.*; hence *soft-liner, soft-lining* adj.; *soft loan* orig. *U.S.*, a loan, esp. one to a developing country, made on especially favourable terms; † *soft meat* = *soft food* above; *soft money,* (*a*) (see sense 20 c in Dict.); (*b*) (see quot. 1976); *soft-nosed* adj., (of a bullet) expanding; *soft option*: see *OPTION *sb.* 1; *soft palate*: see PALATE *sb.* (*a*) 1 b; *soft porn*(*ography*): see *PORN, PORNO *sb.* 2, *PORNOGRAPHY 2 a; *soft rock,* a type of rock music which is less strident than hard rock; hence *soft-rocker*; *soft rot,* any of various bacterial or fungal diseases of vegetables, fruit, and herbaceous plants in which the tissue becomes soft and pulpy; also, a condition of timber in which a fungus renders it soft and brittle; freq. *attrib.*; *soft sculpture* (Pop Art, etc.), a form of sculpture in cloth, foam rubber, or other pliable materials; *soft second* (Bowls) (see quot. 1905); *soft sell* orig. *U.S.*, advertising or salesmanship that is subtly persuasive rather than aggressive (opp. *hard sell* s.v. *HARD *a.* 22 b); also *transf.*, *fig.*, and *attrib.*; *soft-sell* vb. trans.; *soft-selling* ppl. adj.; *soft-shoe* attrib. (orig. *U.S.*), designating, of, or pertaining to a kind of tap-dance performed in soft-soled shoes without metal taps; also *fig.*; hence as *sb.*, a dance of this kind, and as *vb.*; *soft-shoulder* orig. *U.S.* [*SHOULDER *sb.* 6 j], an unmetalled strip of land at the side of a road; *soft silk,* silk from which the gum has been removed; *soft-skinned* adj., (*a*) having a soft skin (see sense 29 in Dict.); (*b*) *Mil.*, of a military vehicle, unarmoured (cf. sense 19 d above); *soft snap* U.S. (earlier example); *soft solder*: see SOLDER *sb.*[1] 4 a; *soft sore* = *soft chancre* above; *soft tissue,* body tissue other than bone and cartilage; also *attrib.*; *soft-top,* a roof of a motor vehicle that is made of soft material and can be opened; a car so fitted, a convertible; freq. *attrib.*; *soft touch*: see *TOUCH *sb.* 20 c; *soft toy,* a toy animal stuffed with a soft material; *soft wart,* a small, soft, pedunculated growth of skin occurring most frequently on the neck.

1958 B. MALAMUD *Magic Barrel* 141 He had got some of his softback books read. **1966** *Time* 8 July 60/2 Shimkin and three other men in 1939 founded his Pocket Books, Inc., the world's most voluminous soft-back-book producer. *Ibid.* 60/3 Pocket books will be better able to assure authors of bonuses for softback reprint rights. **1966** C. SWEENEY *Scurrying Bush* v. 68 The sagging soft-board ceiling. **1976** P. HILL *Hunters* v. 43 The inside wall was partially covered by a large sheet of soft-board pinned to which was a large-scale map. **1804** J. ABERNETHY *Surg. Observ. containing Classification of Tumours* 51 The sarcoma which is..generally found in the testis, and is distinguished by the name of the soft cancer of that part. **1834** [see SPONGOID *a.* 1]. **1871** *Med. Times & Gaz.* 20 May 568/1 A soft cancer of the uterus. **1894** R. QUAIN *Dict. Med.* (new ed.) I. 269/2 Encephaloid, medullary, or soft cancer, so named from its usually brain-like appearance and consistence, is softer and grows more rapidly..than scirrhus. **1961** A. S. MACNALTY *Brit. Med. Dict.* 247/2 *Soft cancer,* medullary carcinoma. [**1965** I. MACDONALD in T. F. Nealon *Managem. Patient with Cancer* xvii. 451 The designation of medullary (soft) is less than ideal, but is not of significance unless it refers to bulky, pseudo-encapsulated tumors.] **1859** C. F. MAUNDER tr. *Ricord's Lect. Chancre* 9 Numerous examples of the soft chancre. **1887** H. RAPHAEL tr. *Zeissl's Path. & Treatm. Syphilis* ii. 116 In the female the soft chancre is most frequently met with upon the labia majora and minora. **1917** *Act* 7 & 8 *Geo. V* c. 21 § 4 In this Act the expression 'venereal disease' means syphilis, gonorrhœa, or soft chancre. **1961** R. D. BAKER *Essent. Path.* ix. 157 Chancroid (soft chancre), a venereal sore on the genital organs, resembles the chancre of syphilis in location but differs in being the starting point of a purely regional process and never a systemic disease. **1968** *Internat. Solid-State Circuits Conf. Digest Technical Papers* 76/1 This scheme permits one to share the same phone link for both hard and soft-copy output. **1982** *New Yorker* 17 May 34/2 'Soft copy and hard copy' (words on a television screen and words on a piece of paper in hand). **1966** *N.Y. Times* 25 Sept. D 15/4 The soft-core pornography of advertisements like 'Have you had any lately?' **1971** *Guardian* 9 Mar. 8/2 The market for pure pornography is insatiable, while soft-core porno is waning in appeal. **1973** *Publishers Weekly* 6 Aug. 67/3 Lots of softcore sex scenes as Bertha finds revenge. **1977** *Time Out* 17–23 June 47/2 Borowczyk's slightest and most commercial offering has provoked wildly different responses: great pagan art or ultimate soft-core? **1979** *Listener* 5 July 21/3 The soft-core entertainment end of the television spectrum. **1834** W. A. CARRUTHERS *Kentuckian in N.Y.* I. 98 He's feeding me on soft corn, thought I. **1948** *Antioch Rev.* Autumn 161 He was all soft corn.., but you couldn't be sure, not with a man like Malcolm. **1958** *Times* 12 Feb. 9/4 Earnings from soft-cover rights, movie rights, etc. **1961** *Guardian* 20 Oct. 17/5 Creative fiction will eventually prove itself in soft cover in this mass market. **1965** *Amer. N. & Q.* Sept. 13/1 Olms has also initiated an important new series of 'Paperbacks', soft-cover reprints of important scholarly works. **1975** *Bookseller* 16 Aug. 1306/1 What makes a paperback publisher pay nearly two million dollars for the softcover privilege of a book? **1977** *Time* 17 Jan. 54/2 In 1976 U.S. softcover publishers issued more than 150 historical novels, many of them as paperback originals. **1960** *Times* 15 Oct. 7/4 Now British presses also are producing 'soft-covered' volumes that can cost anything up to a guinea. **1959** *Oxford Mail* 14 Jan. 4/4 Dr. D. C. M. Yardley of Oxford found that of about 50 university users of soft drugs (mostly marihuana) about 20 were regular takers, and that although the latter were convinced they could give it up at any time, in fact they hardly ever did so without professional help. **1968** *Sunday Mail Mag.* (Brisbane) 7 July 6/1 Some 300,000 people in Britain are estimated to be using some form of 'soft drug' such as marijuana, amphetamines or barbiturates. **1969** *Punch* 12 Mar. 376/2 For most of my life I've thought flattery was only a soft drug. It was nice; but I could take it or leave it. **1976** J. ARCHER *Not Penny More* i. 11 He was a sly, smart little boy, unloved by the school authorities..for his control of the underground school market in soft drugs and liquor. **1876** R. FULTON *Bk. Pigeons* iv. 39 This 'soft food'..is pumped up by the old ones with a sort of vomiting action. **1969** C. R. HILL *Pigeon Guide* vi. 91 At first, the parents will feed the youngsters on soft food (pigeons' milk). **1939** *Ottawa Jrnl.* 22 July 12/8 He softfooted to the window and looked inside. **1972** J. MOSHER *Adultery* III. xiv. 133 As he soft footed it through the kitchen, father began to whistle a tune she liked. **1918** W. P. SEABROOK *Mod. Fruit Growing* vii. 60 In the case of..soft (or bottom) fruit cutting back at once may be done. **1956** H. H. CRANE *Fruit* i. 9 If the area is very small, it may be possible to grow only soft fruits. **1981** *Observer* 26 Apr. (Colour Suppl.) 47/3 It's obviously much easier to fit soft fruit into a small garden. **1840** S. FULLER *Let.* 31 Jan. in N. N. Solly *Mem. Life David Cox* (1873) iv. 57 We propose to republish... The plates have been proved, and found to be in good condition, particularly the soft ground, which I consider as good as ever. **1925** E. S. LUMSDEN *Art of Etching* xiii. 113 Soft-ground (*vernis mou*) is nearly allied to etching proper. **1965** ZIGROSSER & GAEHDE *Guide Coll. Orig. Prints* iv. 56 A soft ground is prepared from hard ground by the addition of tallow or Vaseline. *Ibid.*, Both linear and textured or tonal effects can be created by soft ground. **1868** P. G. HAMERTON *Etching & Etchers* v. xi. 340 In some books on engraving, ordinary etching is called soft-ground etching, to distinguish it from etching done in a hard ground, by the old masters. This old hard ground now being disused, a modern writer may call common etching hard-ground etching, and reserve the title of soft-ground etching for that to which it is here applied. **1873** N. N. SOLLY *Mem. Life David Cox* iii. 36 Cox had been employed..to make soft ground etchings on copper from his own drawings. **1914** G. T. PLOWMAN *Etching & Other Graphic Arts* xiii. 111 For soft ground etching melt together lard or tallow and an equal amount of etching ground. **1976** P. COKER *Etching Technique* 70 The principle of soft ground etching is that the ground adheres to anything that is brought into contact with it. **1881** W.

MARRIOTT *Hints Meteorol. Observers* 16 International symbols... Soft hail *Δ*. **1894** [see GRAUPEL]. **1945** F. A. BERRY et al. *Handbk. Meteorol.* iii. 257 Soft hail usually accompanies the less severe winter or spring storms. **1970** R. M. LONGLEY *Elem. Meteorol.* iv. 91 At the tops of these clouds pellets of soft hail are formed by the collision of the snowflakes found there. **1966** *Sunday Times* 5 June 4 But Canada, Norway, Denmark and Italy prefer a 'soft' line and want to leave the Council where it is to minimise the rupture with France. **1975** *New Left Rev.* Nov.–Dec. 70 The ambassador..may have been part of the soft-line American faction. **1977** *Time* 30 May 20/2 They scorn labor unions and the Communist Party as soft-line collaborators. **1967** *Economist* 18 Feb. 614/2 Life is made even more difficult for the guerrillas, hard-liners by definition, because of their open conflict with the soft-liners in the Venezuelan communist party. **1980** *N.Y. Times* 17 Jan. A23 Soft-liners will say that the Huyser mission prevented a bloodbath, with the Iranian Army battling the mobs. **1977** *Time* 28 Mar. 13/2 They accuse it [*sc.* the Communist Party] of betraying the revolution and joining the Establishment with its soft-lining tacit support of Premier Giulio Andreotti's minority government. **1958** *N.Y. Times* 2 Mar. IV. 5/6 The fund is authorized to make some 'soft loans', that is with long maturity and partly repayable in local currency. **1958** *Washington Post* 8 Oct. A12/2 The..American proposal for a new International Development Association, equipped to make softer loans to supplement the 'bankable' advances of the World Bank, is vitally important. **1965** [see I.D.A. s.v. *I III]. **1979** *Financial Times* 11 Sept. 9/1 'Hidden subsidies' to the paper industry provided by most European governments—in the form of tax incentives, soft loans and regional employment schemes—will continue. **1765** *Treat. Pigeons* 22 Soft meat then is a kind of liquid pap, prepared as it were by instinct by the parents, by a dissolution of the hard grains in their craw. **1822** 'B. MOUBRAY' *Pract. Treat. Poultry* (ed. 4) xii. 185 Soft meat is a sort of milky fluid or pap secreted in the craw of pigeons, by the wise providence of nature. **1879** Soft meat [see *SICK *a.* 1 f]. **1971** Soft money [see *PENNY 9 l]. **1976** *Daily Tel.* 13 Dec. 8/5 'Soft money' is the research money which charitable foundations give to research workers to sponsor two-year or three-year research projects... Scientists who have depended on soft money are now beginning to worry... As the period of the sponsorship runs out, they are starting to be concerned about where the next money is coming from. **1979** *Bull. Amer. Acad. Arts & Sci.* Mar. 8 Research and teaching units that..tend to live on 'soft money' from grants and contracts. **1898** W. S. CHURCHILL *Let.* 5 Aug. in R. S. Churchill *Winston S. Churchill* (1967) I. Compan. II. 957 My thoughts are more concerned with swords—lances—pistols—& soft-nosed bullets—than with Bills—Acts & bye elections. **1899** [in Dict., sense 29 a]. **1922** JOYCE *Ulysses* 327 Mark for a softnosed bullet. **1979** J. BLACKBURN *Sins of Father* xviii. 155 Dumdums; soft-nosed bullets... Banned by the Geneva Convention. **1969** *Harper's Mag.* Sept. 24 Some soft-rock groups..have invaded the middle-of-the road market themselves. **1971** *Time* 11 Jan. 40 His songs delve ingeniously into hard and soft rock. **1980** *Washington Star* 31 July C1 Forget the sleek Hollywood production..and try to overlook the soft rock theme. **1977** *Time Out* 21 Jan. 43 (*caption*) David Bedford..who regularly set the classical fraternity wondering if one of their boys is turning irredeemably into a soft-rocker. **1901** *Ann. Rep. Vermont Agric. Exper. Station* No. 13. 299 A rapid soft rot of carrots caused by a bacillus (*B. carotovorus*). **1937** F. D. HEALD *Introd. Plant Path.* iv. 47 Storage and transportation losses may be heavy..in vegetables such as asparagus,..lettuce, etc. by bacterial soft rots (*Bacillus carotovorus*),..in sweet potatoes by soft rot (*Rhizopus nigricans*). **1961** J. S. BOYCE *Forest Path.* (ed. 3) xvi. 356 This type of decay, known as soft rot, is usually in the surface layers of wood in service. **1969** G. N. AGRIOS *Plant Path.* x. 355 Cruciferous plants and onions,..when infected by soft rot bacteria, almost always give off an offensive sulfurous odor. **1976** B. K. BAKSHI *Forest Path* III. 306 Treated wood which may show complete freedom from attack from decay fungi may exhibit soft rot attack. **1969** C. OLDENBURG in G. Baro *Claes Oldenburg* 18 Drawing in space required an emphasis on volume. This was stimulated by pieces made as props..for the Ray Gun Theatre performances—which led to the 'soft' sculptures. **1982** L. KALLEN *No Lady in House* xiii. 121 Soft Sculpture..large squashy objects made of patterned cloth..artfully shaped into human or animal caricatures. **1905** *Harmsworth Encycl.* II. 884/1 Usually a side [in flat-green bowling] is composed of four players, each with a distinct function... The second has to do as he is told. A captain will play his weakest man here (hence the phrase, the 'soft second'). **1955** *Life* 25 July 21/1 Sometimes they ran into the 'soft sell'—'Sit down, we don't want you to order anything, just get acquainted.' **1961** C. COCKBURN *View from West* iii. 24 Dons anxious to 'soft sell' ancient Greek culture to the modern world. **1967** V. S. NAIPAUL *Mimic Men* III. v. 260 Their soft-sell advertisements in the newspapers. **1970** G. F. NEWMAN *Sir, You Bastard* i. 15 Terry Sneed was a sceptic, no soft sell ever bought him. **1970** *Daily Colonist* (Victoria, B.C.) 26 Sept. 15/4 Now Broadway is lucky to have those masters of the softsell gag and casual comedy. **1978** LD. DROGHEDA *Double Harness* vi. 58 He..was a master of convincing overstatement whereas my gift was more for what is known in advertising jargon as soft sell. **1982** *Times* 19 Jan. 18/8 We have abandoned the softsell approach and become very aggressive. **1960** *New Left Rev.* Jan./Feb. 3/1 The 'society of equals' is better than the best soft-selling consumer-capitalist society. **1927** P. DUNNING *Broadway* 9 They were a brother act, a team of soft-shoe dancers. **1935** D. N. CROPPER *Dance Dict.* 76 *Soft-shoe*, generally acknowledge[d] to be dancing of the star type and containing certain ballet steps. Any tap dancing done without metal taps or clogs. **1941** *Life* 25 Aug. 74/2 George Primrose was famed as an exponent of 'soft-shoe' dancing 35 years ago. *Ibid.* 77/1 The misleading phrase 'soft-shoe' was applied to an increasingly popular form of mobile, eccentric step dance in rolling 4–4 time. **1962** J. D. SALINGER *Franny & Zooey* 180 Les and Bessie did a lovely soft-shoe on sand swiped by Boo Boo from the urn in the lobby. **1965** P. O'DONNELL *Modesty Blaise* xviii. 190 We'll make a soft-shoe job of it if we can... Straight for the diamonds..and away. *Ibid.* 197, I don't want to use the gun, not while there's any chance of keeping this soft-shoe. **1967** M. STEWART *Gabriel Hounds* x. 139 He..beckoned. I soft-shoed after him. **1975** W. MCILVANNEY *Docherty* I. xvi. 115 Only a few couples still soft-shoed around the floor. **1981** *Daily Tel.* 27 Jan. 12/6 They [*sc.* Adele and Fred Astaire] rapidly soft-shoed their way to acclaim in musical comedies on Broadway. **1939** *Time* 20 Feb. 28/3 Driving toward his home on the outskirts of Indianapolis..he got off the road on a soft shoulder. **1978** J. IRVING *World according to Garp* xii. 231, I run in the stuff of the soft shoulder, in the hot sand and gravel. **1862** M. MERRYWEATHER *Experiences of Factory Life* (ed. 3) iii. 31 In 1847, Messrs. C—— had 195 soft-silk looms at work in this town. *a* **1877** KNIGHT *Dict. Mech.* III. 2180/2 Silken thread..is called..if the natural gum is..removed, *soft silk*. **1921** C. SALTER tr. *Ganswindt's Dyeing Silk* i. 155 The bath temperature must..be modified..being lukewarm for soft silk and hard silk. **1942** *Hutchinson's Pictorial Hist. of War* 10 June–1 Sept. 129/1 That is the protection of all this paraphernalia of supply and maintenance, all what may be called the 'soft-skinned stuff', from air attack. **1980** *Times* 18 Jan. 14/6 Many of the 'soft-skinned' vehicles [brought into Afghanistan] have been civilian trucks, which is normal Russian practice in wartime. **1841** *Spirit of Times* 9 Oct. 378 One of them, however..suddenly lamed herself, and another..'found a softer snap,' so they paid forfeit to The Heiress. **1884** A. COOPER *Syphilis & Pseudo-Syphilis* iv. 33 There are two principal theories with regard to the relations existing between the hard and the soft sores. **1940** E. T. BURKE *Venereal Dis.* xx. 508 The term 'soft sore' or '*ulcus molle*' should, since they lead to much confusion, be discarded and the term 'chancroid' should be used. **1974** PASSMORE & ROBSON *Compan. Med. Stud.* III. xiii. 13/2 Chancroid or soft sore..is a venereal infection with *Haemophilus ducreyi*..causing genital ulceration and enlarged, tender inguinal lymph nodes. **1892** G. M. GOULD *Pocket Med. Dict.* 272 *Soft*, not bony, cartilaginous, etc., as the soft tissues. **1964** L. MARTIN *Clinical Endocrinol.* (ed. 4) iii. 113 Soft-tissue radiographs of the limbs. **1977** *Proc. R. Soc. Med.* LXX. 256/2 Advocates of early soft-tissue surgery..have reported successful results in a significant number of patients subjected to this method. **1959** *Motor* 23 Sept. 177/2 First soft-top model in the so-called compact car size. **1967** *Guardian* 3 Oct. 5/3 The soft top now costs £1,212. **1976** *Milton Keynes Express* 18 June 39/6 (Advt.), L registration Triumph Spitfire yellow, 33,000 miles, hard and soft-tops. **1979** *Tucson* (Ariz.) *Mag.* Mar. 25/1 A removable forward hardtop and a convertible softtop rear window. **1917** E. A. HICKMAN *Soft Toys & how to make Them* 1 The object of this book is to bring instruction in the art of making stuffed or soft toys. **1950** *Dryad Handicraft Catal.* 93 Soft toy making. **1964** M. LASKI in S. Nowell-Smith *Edwardian England* iv. 203 The named soft toy was now starting its long run of popularity..Golliwog..Teddy Bear..Caesar. **1970** *Guardian* 24 Sept. 11/1 Wendy Boston, pioneers in safe soft toys. **1887** *Jrnl. Cutaneous & Genito-Urinary Dis.* V. 50 The lesions known by the laity as moles, mothers'-marks..and by the profession as acrochordon, ecphyma mollusci-forme,..and among English-speaking physicians sometimes as soft warts. **1967** Soft wart [see *MOLLUSCUM 1 a].

b. *soft corn*, a variety of maize *Zea mays* var. *amylacea*, whose seeds are rich in soft starch; also, maize containing a high quantity of moisture, making it unlikely to keep well; *soft maple*, one of several maples with less durable wood, esp. the red maple, *Acer rubrum*, or the silver maple, *A. saccharinum*; also, the timber of these trees; *soft wheat*, one of several varieties of wheat having a soft grain rich in starch.

1751 J. BARTRAM *Observations* 60 Last of all was served a great bowl full of Indian dumplings, of new soft corn, cut or scraped off the ear. **1868** *Mich. Agric. Rep.* VII. 160 Early frosts made considerable 'soft corn'. **1902** A. S. HITCHCOCK in L. H. Bailey *Cycl. Amer. Hort.* IV. 2004/2 Brazilian Flour Corn sold by seedsmen is a type of the Soft Corn. **1947** *Chicago Tribune* 23 July 9/4 The state must prepare for a soft corn crop this fall. **1778** J. CARVER *Trav. N. Amer.* 496 The Maple. Of this tree there are two sorts, the hard and the soft. **1806** P. GASS *Jrnl.* 6 Apr. (1807) 195 The timber is mostly of the fir kind, with some..soft maple. **1810** [see *MAPLE TREE]. **1855, 1891** [in Dict.]. **1948** H. A. JACOBS *We chose Country* 25 We..saw the farm buildings, clustered behind a great row of soft maples. **1969** T. H. EVERETT *Living Trees of World* xxii. 221/1 The most important American soft maples are the red or swamp maple..and the silver maple. **1812, 1843** Soft wheat [see *hard wheat* s.v. *HARD *a.* (*sb.*) 22]. **1875** *Encycl. Brit.* III. 251/1 In commerce the grain is distinguished as white and red, or as hard and soft wheats. **1944** *Sun* (Baltimore) 5 Jan. 13/5 The Office of Price Administration..boosted the maximum prices for soft wheat. **1973** *Times* 3 Dec. 14/2 Soft wheat is cheaper for us thanks to being in the Community.

c. *soft-back*, a soft-shelled turtle of the genus *Trionyx*; (earlier example); *soft clam* = *LONG-NECK 2 b; (earlier examples); *soft crab*, a crab that has shed its shell and is awaiting the hardening of the new one; (earlier examples); *soft tick*, a tick of the family Argasidæ, lacking a dorsal shield.

1859 P. H. GOSSE *Lett. Alabama* 99 Another Tortoise of even greater size and equal ferocity is the Soft-back (*Trionyx ferox*). **1806** D. ROE *Jrnl.* 27 Feb. (1904) 25 Got Sum Soft Clams. **1855** *Knickerbocker* XLVI. 222 Along the strand..these great delicacies, 'soft clams' and sand-crabs may be found. **1772** L. CARTER *Jrnl.* 10 Oct. in *William & Mary Coll. Q.* (1906) 1st Ser. XIV. 38 Like the shell of a soft crab, the body of the crab after the shell is off seems by much too large for the shell. **1805** R. PARKINSON *Tour Amer.* 315 Soft crabs..are reckoned great dainties. **1932** R. MATHESON *Med. Entomol.* iii. 40 The family Argasidae contains those ticks which lack a scutum and hence have been called the soft ticks. **1974** *Nature* 25 Jan. 226/1 This is the first proven example of transmission of a mammalian piroplasm by an Argasid ('soft') tick.

28. a. *soft-foot* (later examples); *-ground*, *-top*.

1916 D. H. LAWRENCE *Amores* 73 When I carried my mother downstairs..at the beginning Of her soft-foot malady. **1959** *Listener* 8 Jan. 60/2 The soft-foot priest. **1916** *Daily Colonist* (Victoria, B.C.) 26 July 5/5 Muckers, sewermen, blacksmiths, softground workers, and timbermen are specially needed. **1977** P. GEDDES *Hangman* xi. 98 She carried everything she owned in the soft-top suitcase.

29. a. *soft-balled*, *-bellied*, *-chaired*, *-edged*, *-fleshed* (later example), *-grained*, *-horned*, *-minded* (later example; hence *soft-mindedness*), *-palmed*, *-sandalled*, *-skirted*, *-soled*, *-topped*, *-worded*.

a **1930** D. H. LAWRENCE *Last Poems* (1932) 42 Kisses of the soft-balled paws. **1923** —— *Birds, Beasts & Flowers* 113 He..trailed his yellow-brown slackness soft-bellied down. *a* **1918** W. OWEN *Poems* (1931) 98 Comforted years will sit soft-chaired In rooms of amber. **1970** *Jrnl. General Psychol.* Apr. 183 The other two paintings were non-representational 'soft-edged' geometric abstractions. **1928** D. H. LAWRENCE *Woman who rode Away* 113 If a woman looked pleasant and soft-fleshed..they were ardent and generous. **1848** J. R. LOWELL *Poems* 2nd Ser. 167 The red-oak, softer-grained yields all for lost. **1966** *Listener* 3 Mar. 329/1 Souzay..is..now able to make his beautiful soft-grained voice cover a wide range of human experience. **1868** G. M. HOPKINS *Jrnls. & Papers* (1959) 175 Beauty of the sycamores here, native to the soil, soft-horned, and falling apart like ashes. **1919** E. O'NEILL *Moon of Caribbees* 189 It's soft-minded she is, like I've always told you, an' stupid. **1925** F. SCOTT FITZGERALD *Great Gatsby* vi. 120 The transactions in Montana copper ..found him physically robust but on the verge of soft-mindedness. **1848** J. R. LOWELL *Uncoll. Poems* (1950) 59 The soft palmed tradesman coming home at eve. **1978** *Time* 3 July 1/3 Hooray for higher food prices... The American farm worker and farmer have subsidized the American dinner table long enough... There will be the usual soft-palmed protesters. **1886** KIPLING *Departmental Ditties* (ed. 2) 53 From rockridge to spur Fly the soft-sandalled feet. **1923** D. H. LAWRENCE *Birds, Beasts & Flowers* 201 Now that in England is silence, where before was a moving of soft-skirted women. **1933** J. BUCHAN *Prince of Captivity* III. ii. 287 The soft-soled shoes of the pursuit did not slip. **1976** *Milton Keynes Express* 23 July 39/1 Heavy rain during the day provided a soft-topped, damp wicket which gave a lot of help to the bowlers. **1916** JOYCE *Portrait of Artist* iv. 180 It was only amid soft-worded phrases..that he dared to conceive of the soul or body of a woman moving with tender life.

30. *soft-boil* (later examples), *-talk*. See also *SOFT-LAND *v.*

1903 G. B. SHAW *Let.* 21–2 Dec. (1972) II. 384 Mrs Robertson..would have had to get her brains extracted and her face soft-boiled to play the poor pitiful creature Judith [in *The Devil's Disciple*]. **1970** H. MCLEAVE *Question of Negligence* (1973) xxii. 170 The pressure in number-two boiler room is hardly high enough to soft-boil an egg. **1968** *Daily Progress* (Charlottesville, Va.) 15 Apr. 21/2 Young Gentry used artificial bait and said he also had to soft talk the fish as he pulled him in. **1968** B. MATHER *Springers* x. 100 He asked peevishly when the hell we would be moving—and where? I soft-talked him and said any minute.

31. With ppl. adjs., as *soft-looking*.

1860 C. M. YONGE *Hopes & Fears* I. ii. 33 Honora thought her the prettiest child she had ever seen..such a soft-looking little creature. **1924** 'R. CROMPTON' *William —the Fourth* vi. 87 He said he'd rather be killed than go to an ole dancing class anyway, with that soft-looking kid.

soft, *adv.* Add: **I. 1. c.** ellipt. for *soft class* (in travelling by train in China or the U.S.S.R.). Also *transf.*, first-class.

1939 'M. INNES' *Stop Press* I. ii. 44 As a matter of fact, he's on the train now. But of course travelling soft. **1976** *Times* 13 Nov. 11/1 Trains in China are made up of classless coaches but you travel *hard* or *soft* according to your position.

II. 9. a. *soft-falling*, *-flaming*, *-going*, *living*.

1845 F. W. FABER *Let.* 29 Jan. in R. Chapman *Father Faber* (1961) vi. 103 When I know how miserably sinful and soft-living I have been, I ought never to have stepped out in the way that I have done. *a* **1918** W. OWEN *Poems* (1963) 103 And through those snows my looks shall be soft-going. **1925** E. SITWELL *Troy Park* 45 Like curd soft-falling. **1944** E. BLUNDEN *Shells by Stream* 49 The cloud soft-flaming past the mountain wall.

b. *soft-falling*, *-living*, *-sailing*, *-speaking*.

1829 D. JERROLD *Black-Ey'd Susan* I. i. 13 That pretty piece of soft-speaking womanhood. **1888** W. WHITMAN *November Boughs* 33 And who art thou? said I to the soft-falling shower... I am the Poem of Earth, said the voice of the rain. **1916** D. H. LAWRENCE *Amores* 24 Soft-sailing waters where fears No longer shake. **1965** F. SARGESON *Memoirs of Peon* iv. 73 The shapely soft-speaking Maori girl..brought me a plate of sandwiches. **1975** *New Yorker* 5 May 109/1 He hit a great, soft-falling shot seven feet beyond the flag. **1977** *Times* 17 Mar. 18/6 A soft-living Mayfair clientele.

10. b. *soft-tinted*; **soft-spun**, loosely twisted in spinning; also *transf.*; opp. *hard-spun* s.v. HARD *adv.* 8 e. See also *SOFT-LANDED *ppl. a.*

1869 'MARK TWAIN' *Innoc. Abr.* xxx. 324 A lace-work of soft-tinted crystals of sulphur. **1902** W. DE LA MARE *Songs of Childhood* 96 As if it were a perfect jewel in the morning's soft-spun hair. **1906** Soft spun [see *hard spun* s.v. *HARD *adv.* 8 e]. **1940** E. BLUNDEN *Poems 1930–40* 193 Choose this soft-tinted willow tree. **1964** H. HODGES *Artifacts* ix. 129 Excessively twisted, or *hard-spun*, yarns may kink..while *soft-spun* threads with little twist may untwist further.

softball (sǫ·ftbǭl). Also **soft-ball, soft ball.** [f. Soft *a.* + Ball *sb.*[1]] **1.** *Confectionery.* (As two words or with hyphen.) A soft globule of sugar formed (e.g. by dropping into water) as a means of testing that the mass of sugar being boiled has reached a certain stage; hence used *attrib.* and *absol.* to designate this stage.

1894 E. Skuse *Compl. Confectioner* 70 Add the cocoanut slices and allow the whole to boil, for say ten minutes, or until the sugar comes to a soft ball. **1907** J. Kirkland *Mod. Baker, Confectioner & Caterer* IV. iv. 13 The *soft-ball* or full-feather degree is tested by making a small bulb of sugar between the fingers while cooling in cold water. **1921** [see *panoche 2]. **1980** T. Stobart *Cook's Encycl.* 404/1 Soft ball—116°C (240°F). The sugar clinging to the skimmer will now, when shaken, produce a feathery, downy effect. The syrup is now beginning to thicken and will form a soft ball if a little of it is dropped into cold water.

2. orig. *N. Amer.* **a.** A game resembling baseball but played on a smaller field with a larger ball that is pitched underarm.

1926 *Daily Colonist* (Victoria, B.C.) 2 July 5/3 The remainder of the morning was occupied by the younger members of the party in playing soft ball and other less strenuous games. **1947** J. Steinbeck *Wayward Bus* 54 A big and muscular young woman who taught ice hockey and softball and archery at the university. **1977** F. F. Fixx *Compl. Bk. Running* p. xvi, Someone who all his life had played tennis, touch football and Saturday-afternoon softball shouldn't be thus laid low.

b. A ball of the kind used in the game of softball.

1914 *Vanity Fair* Feb. 49 (*caption*) Soft ball, soft hands and a soft game. **1918** *Playground* Sept. 223 Suffice it to say that *Playground Baseball*..differs from ordinary baseball in four ways, namely: (1) A big *soft* ball is used [etc.]. **1974** [see *softball throw*, sense c below]. **1975** R. Kroetsch *Badlands* 136 Lumps of ice the size of softballs.

c. *attrib.*, as *softball court, field, game, team*; **softball question**, a question that is easy to answer; **softball throw**, an athletic event in which a softball is thrown as far as possible.

1943 J. S. Huxley *TVA* ix. 73 The playground is floodlit to give the adults a soft-ball court after their day's work is over. **1958** J. Kerouac *On Road* iii. i. 180 A softball game was going on under floodlights. **1974** *News & Press* (Darlington, S. Carolina) 25 Apr. 11/1 Beverly Robinson won first-place in the long jump and the softball throw. **1976** *New Society* 28 Oct. 209/3 'Why Switzerland?' may seem the ultimate softball question, its answer to be found behind those discreet name-plates along Zurich's Bahnhofstrasse. **1977** J. Cheever *Falconer* 4 There was a softball field where the gallows had stood. **1977** *Sci. Amer.* Nov. 15/2 He has also collaborated with Groth 'on a number of double plays for the physics department softball team'.

3. Tactical slow and gentle play in lawn tennis. Also *attrib.* So **soft-balling** *ppl. a.*, **soft-ball** *v. trans.* and *intr.*

1961 *Times* 18 May 5/2 Not only did Sangster adapt his game to the slow court and a soft-balling opponent. **1962** *Times* 25 Apr. 4/7 It was the Chilean's soft ball game that ruffled his opponent's feathers. *Ibid.* 26 June 4/2 Playing soft ball, and apparently resigned to defeat, he was offered a reprieve by a casual opponent. **1976** *Observer* 2 May 23/2 Miss Mottram, who was being made to run hard and dig deep on the dusty red court to stay in the game, decided to soft-ball her, to slow the pace. **1980** *Amer. Speech 1976* LI. 294 *Softball*, play slow soft shots.

soft-boiled, *a.* [f. *soft-boil* vb. s.v. Soft *a.* 30.] **1.** Of an egg: boiled but not hard-boiled. Also *transf.*

1889 Kipling in *Macmillan's Mag.* Dec. 153/1 You niver had a head worth a soft-boiled egg. **1906** *Woman's Home Companion* Nov. 5/3, I have plenty of towels and soap and soft-boiled eggs. **1948** W. Stevens *Let.* 2 Apr. (1967) 582 How good grated Parmesan is on soft-boiled eggs. **1954** —— *Let.* 23 July (1967) 841 The weather has been all sparkle with a hot day and soft-boiled night thrown in now and then. **1975** J. McClure *Snake* iii. 37 His big, soft-boiled eyes, with pouches beneath them like black egg-cups.

2. Of a person: mild, easy-going; naïve, impractical; opp. *hard-boiled *a.* 2.

a **1930** D. H. Lawrence *Last Poems* (1932) 258 O you hard-boiled conservatives and you soft-boiled liberals Don't you *see* how you make bolshevism inevitable? **1942** E. Waugh *Put out More Flags* iii. 191 Father's friends were all hard-boiled and rich... And then I met Cedric who was poor and very, very soft-boiled. **1963** *Times* 26 Feb. 16/4 But, say the T.V.A. enthusiasts, there is a psychological stimulus in receiving a rebate as opposed to merely not paying tax from the start. Is the British businessman really so soft-boiled? **1978** D. Grylls *Guardians & Angels* iv. 142 Dickens['s]..pantheon is crammed with a soft-boiled array of credulous infantile adults.

soft centre. Also **soft-centre.** [f. Soft *a.* + Centre *sb.*]

1. a. A soft filling inside a chocolate. Also *attrib.*

[**1930** H. W. Bywaters *Mod. Methods of Cocoa & Chocolate Manuf.* xxv. 251 During recent years chocolates containing soft creme centres..have increased in popularity.] **1947** 'G. Orwell' in *Tribune* 7 Mar. 11/3 The same kind of charm as belongs to a pink geranium or a soft-centre chocolate. **1959** [see *centre *sb.* 11 e].

b. *transf.* A chocolate with a soft filling.

1970 H. McLeave *Question of Negligence* (1973) ii. 18 Every time Lord Blye turned nasty..her consumption of *petit fours* and soft centres soared. **1974** P. Haines *Tea at Gunter's* xiv. 149 Me..lying about on the settee eating soft centres, and Mantovani on the radiogram.

2. A soft heart, esp. in contrast with a tough exterior; a vulnerable or weak core. Also *attrib.*

1955 E. Blishen *Roaring Boys* iv. 194 The fierceness and roughness of the boys was of the surface... The longer I stayed there, the more aware I became of this soft centre. **1973** M. Amis *Rachel Papers* 148, I gathered from the female novelists I had been reading..that the malleable, soft-centre syndrome was no longer considered attractive. **1974** *Bookseller* 20 July 197/1 Most of the publishers I've known have had soft centres. They love to be loved, especially by their authors.

soft-centred, *a.* [f. prec.] **1.** Of a person or his attitudes: soft-hearted; of works of literature, art, music, etc.: having a weak, vulnerable, or sentimental core.

1957 *Times Lit. Suppl.* 8 Nov. 674/4 Like his attack on the Monarchy his attachment to Socialism is essentially emotional and soft-centred. **1960** *Listener* 3 Mar. 425/2 The fact that the catalyst is a woman friend..does not make the play any less soft-centred. **1963** *Times* 7 Mar. 15/3 Like all nice Cockney Jewish characters, Harryboy is soft-centred. **1973** *Art Internat.* Mar. 57/1 His resulting paintings..proved to be simply a murky, soft-centered brand of Cubism. **1977** *Broadcast* 10 Oct. 17/2 Michael Arlen..[was] a writer of immense but somewhat soft-centred sophistication.

2. Of a chocolate: having a soft centre.

1970 C. Wood *'Terrible Hard', says Alice* viii. 110 A soft-centred milk chocolate. **1978** *Times Lit. Suppl.* 21 Apr. 438/3 Diamond Jim Brady..regularly ate a twelve-course dinner..ending with five pounds of soft-centred chocolates.

Hence **soft-ce·ntredness.**

1967 *Guardian* 10 Apr. 6/6 The critics..began to note..a soft-centredness about Britain, a complacency, a reluctance to scrap and build. **1981** *Economist* 28 Nov. 47/1 A mixture of Saudi soft-centredness, Arab pettiness and Syrian bloody-mindedness has led the Arabs to miss a rare opportunity.

soften, *v.* Add: **I. 4. c.** Usu. with *up.* To reduce the strength of (a defensive position) by bombing or other preliminary attack; also *transf.* Hence *fig.*: to undermine the resistance of (a person). *colloq.* (orig. *U.S.*).

1940 W. L. Shirer *Berlin Diary* (1941) 378 Stuka dive-bombers are softening the Allied defense positions, making them ripe for an easy attack. **1942** *Sun* (Baltimore) 3 Feb. 1/5 Japanese air raiders engaged in a grand-scale effort to soften up the stronghold for a final invasion thrust. **1949** F. Maclean *Eastern Approaches* iii. xv. 490 United States Army Air Force Mustangs had 'softened up' the target. **1950** J. Dempsey *Championship Fighting* 89 They will enable you to knock out or at least 'soften up' an opponent. **1951** *Here & Now* (N.Z.) May 8/2 These fellowships are part of the general system of 'softening up' overseas journalists and persuading them to see the advantages of the American way of life. **1952** S. Kauffmann *Philanderer* (1953) xii. 193 'You make me feel pretty cruel,' he said... Then in a moment she smiled. 'You said that just to soften me up.' **1962** *Listener* 1 Nov. 706/1 The farming industry is being softened up by the clear indications from ministers that changes are coming in the whole support system, whether or not we go into Europe. **1974** *Daily Tel.* 21 Sept. 15 A man who had told police of goings on in Soho was kidnapped in broad daylight, tied to a chair and softened up to find what he had said. **1980** G. B. Trudeau *Tad Overweight*, 'Over there's my Soviet-made Makarov mortar.' 'Mortar? What do you use the mortar for?' 'Deer hunting. I like to soften up an area before I hunt it.'

II. 7. (Later examples in sense *26** b of *soft *a.*)

1947 *Kiplinger Washington Let.* (Kiplinger Washington Agency) 5 Apr., Consumers are not buying quite enough to take up all production. Luxury markets began to soften last fall. **1982** *Daily Tel.* 6 July 15 American rates might soften following the publication of reassuring money supply figures on Friday evening. **1982** *Times* 17 Aug. 12 The shares softened 2p to 168p after announcement of the results.

softener. 1. (Further examples.)

1954 A. J. Hall *Stand. Handbk. Textiles* (ed. 4) iv. 265 It is important not to use softeners which reduce the fastness of coloured goods to light. **1973** *Times* 1 June 11/5 It tests the water every night, working its little two-inch square brain-box attached to the softener.

softening, *vbl. sb.* Add: **1.** Also, the action or process of becoming soft. (Later examples.)

1919 R. D. Bangay *Oscillation Valve* 203 Any serious 'softening' of the valve will entirely upset its characteristics and action. **1945** *Electronic Engin.* XVII. 338/3 A high grid leak may very rapidly cause softening of the valve. **1946** *Ann. Reg. 1945* 214 The constant harping on the subject [of Turkish Armenia] in the Soviet Press, accompanied by attacks on the régime in power in Turkey, conveyed the impression that the familiar process of softening would in due course be followed by a formal demand. **1957** *Economist* 30 Nov. 809/1 The recent softening of the markets for petroleum products. **1960** N. Mitford *Don't tell Alfred* xx. 216 When some softening up on these lines had been delivered the campaign settled down to its real objective. **1968** *Globe & Mail* (Toronto) 13 Jan. B1/2 It was too early to tell whether this marked a reversal of the softening trend in these important loans to businesses. **1977** P. Strevens *New Orientations Teaching Eng.* ii. 24 The integration of prior 'softening-up' with initial presentation and subsequent consolidation and repetition.

3. b. With *up*, in sense *4 c of the vb., as *softening-up period, process, raid, technique, trick.*

1951 *R.A.F. Rev.* Apr.–May 32/3 They helped to cover Allied bombers on 'softening-up' raids on the European fortress. **1953** L. P. Hartley *Go-Between* x. 127 The softening-up process, as we should call it now, which he had put me through had been enough. **1954** J. Stein *Basic Everyday Encycl.* 558/1 This 'softening-up' technique broke communications, disrupted production, disorganized civilian existence, destroyed the German air force. **1971** B. W. Aldiss *Soldier Erect* 229 After a softening up period, another attack was launched. Our attack! **1976** B. Lecomber *Dead Weight* viii. 90 Leaving the suspect to stew..is the oldest softening-up trick in the book.

soft-fo·cus, *a.* and *sb.* Also **soft focus.** [f. Soft *a.* + Focus *sb.*] **A.** *adj.* **a.** *Photogr.* Characterized by or producing a deliberate slight lack of clarity and definition in a photograph.

1917 P. L. Anderson *Pictorial Photogr.* ii. 42 It should be noted that the soft-focus lens..has greater apparent depth, both of field and of focus. **1940** A. L. M. Sowerby *Wall's Dict. Photogr.* (ed. 15) 600 It is generally considered that the most pleasing soft-focus effects are obtained by superposing a diffused image upon a more sharply-defined one, this giving a kind of 'halo' round the lights. **1958** [see sense *B]. **1975** *Publishers Weekly* 13 Jan. 58/1 Aided by lovely soft-focus photographs.., Miss Bailey tells the story of a little seedling blown away from its mother tree too soon. **1977** J. Hedgecoe *Photographer's Handbk.* 31 The design of soft focus lenses leaves one pronounced optical error, 'spherical aberration'. This gives halos to highlights and a general softness of outline. **1978** P. Theroux *Picture Palace* ix. 71 Photographs looked freckled and corpse-like, soft-focus poses that might have been painters' instant fossils.

b. *fig.* Diffuse, blurred, unclear, imprecise.

1961 W. T. Jones *Romantic Syndrome* viii. 227 We might begin..by making a count of soft-focus imagery in the works of various poets. **1965** *Punch* 17 Nov. 712 You will see the advantage of reviewing single instalments. It allows elbow-room to savour the glittering detail. Handle the whole book and you fall back on soft-focus generalities, the tiny individual flavours lost. **1975** *New Yorker* 24 Feb. 127/1 The voice is soft-focus, not keenly projected, but of pleasant quality in the middle ranges. **1979** *Listener* 16 Aug. 214/4 This [play]..was full of winsome Irishness and soft-focus sentimentality.

B. *sb.* A deliberate slight lack of clarity and definition in a photograph. Also *fig.*

1958 P. Pollack *Picture Hist. Photogr.* xx. 261 Dr. P. H. Emerson held that soft focus corresponded to natural vision and that soft-focus photography was an art superior to all other graphic arts. **1961** W. T. Jones *Romantic Syndrome* viii. 235 Once the critic replaces a vague liking for 'romantic qualities' with a preference for 'soft-focus'..he is much more likely to make an adequate assessment of the work of the poets and painters. **1977** *Practical Photogr.* Jan. 23/4 To suggest that this method of obtaining soft-focus costs 1p is ridiculous.

Hence **soft-fo·cus** *v. trans.*, **soft-fo·cused** *ppl. a.* (both *fig.* in the examples).

1957 *Archit. Rev.* CXXI. 319 The whole effect is to blur and 'soft-focus' the precision-made look which has been one of the chief qualities of the curtain wall. **1977** *New Yorker* 27 June 35/1 Rose did not like to look at them, at their soft-focussed meekly smiling gratitude.

soft-footed, *a.* (Later *fig.* example.)

1947 Auden *Age of Anxiety* (1948) ii. 47 In the soft-footed Hours of darkness.

soft-la·nd, *v. Astronautics.* Also **softland.** [Back-formation from next.] *trans.* and *intr.* To land slowly without serious damage, esp. on another planet or a satellite.

trans. **1960** *Aeroplane* XCIX. 540 (*caption*) The Surveyor-type probe..should be capable of soft-landing between 100 and 300 lb. of scientific equipment on the Moon. **1960** *Times Mag.* (Seattle) 29 May 22 The first lunar vehicle may be a small robot to be soft-landed on the moon within the next five years. **1966** *Times* 7 Apr. 9/3 This was to have been the final test flight before the United States attempts to softland a real Surveyor spacecraft on the moon. **1967** *New Scientist* 1 June 549/3 The balloon itself was constructed of fine polythene and helium-filled... It was soft-landed and recovered for further use. **1970** *Guardian* 21 Sept. 3/7 Russia today soft-landed its Luna 16 unmanned spacecraft on the moon's barren Sea of Fertility.

intr. **1964** *Yearbk. Astron. 1965* 135 The LEM will detach from the orbiting parent and soft-land on the Moon. **1967** *New Scientist* 3 Aug. 242/2 *Surveyor III*, which soft-landed on 20 April this year returned over 6000 TV pictures. **1969** *Daily Tel.* 18 July 1 Reports from Moscow..say that Luna 15 is ready 'to soft-land on the moon today' and collect moon dust. **1975** *Times* 7 Apr. 6/1 A manned Soyuz spacecraft..soft-landed southwest of the western Siberian town of Gorno-Altaysk.

So **soft-la·nded** *ppl. a.*; **soft-la·nder,** a vehicle that is capable of making or has made a soft landing.

1958 *Proc. Lunar & Planetary Exploration Colloquium* July 13/1 Would you..talk about the design and weight distribution of this soft-landed payload? **1961** *Aeroplane* C. 510/3 Russia's long-range space programme is said to include sending two spaceships to the Moon by 1967. They would be preceded by unmanned 'soft-landers' depositing supplies and propellants. **1966** *Guardian* 28 Dec. 7/1 Luna-13..is returning more information than any other soft lander, whether Russian or American. **1969** *Nature* 12 July 123/1 Between 1966 and 1968, seven Surveyor softlanders were launched which among other things tested the surface strength [of the moon]. **1971**

Ibid. 26 Nov. 211/2 Such data will be of value in interpreting the findings of soft-landed spacecraft on other planets. **1977** A. Hallam *Planet Earth* 20/1 The surface panoramas transmitted back to Earth from the Soviet soft-landers Veneras 9 and 10 show a barren landscape that contains both angular and rounded rocks.

soft landing, *vbl. sb. Astronautics.* Also softlanding. [f. Soft *a.* + Landing *vbl. sb.*] **1. a.** A landing of a spacecraft that is slow enough for no serious damage to be incurred. Cf. *soft *a.* 22 d.

1958 *Proc. Lunar & Planetary Exploration Colloquium* July 13/1 With a soft landing on the moon one might put down a payload of 225 to 800 pounds, but..only about 10 to 25 percent of this would be usable for instruments. **1959** *Washington Post* 24 Mar. A6/4 He said the first 'soft landing' on the moon and return probably will be made with a multi-stage chemical-fueled vehicle. **1966** *Listener* 24 Mar. 427/1 The main events [of 1966] have been the soft landing on the Moon.., and the progress of the two Venus rockets. **1967** *New Scientist* 25 May 448/2 Each of these craft will consist of..an experimental capsule to enter the Martian atmosphere and..make a soft landing either by parachute or..by means of retro rockets. **1971** *Guardian* 1 July 1/5 The Soyuz made a normal re-entry and soft landing.

b. *fig.*

1969 *Sci. Jrnl.* Jan. 54/3 Should one bombard with excess energy or attempt..a 'soft landing' where the energy of the incoming particle is just enough to allow it to penetrate the barrier, be captured and form the compound nucleus. **1973** *Newsweek* 17 Sept. 65/2 Even if the President succeeds in pulling in the rampaging economy for a soft landing, of course, the arrival will be nonetheless bumpy for many.

2. *attrib.* or as *adj.*

1960 *Aeroplane* XCIX. 541/2 Mr. Stoller said that in 1962 three Ranger vehicles were planned to rough-land payloads on the surface of the Moon. These will be followed by the soft-landing mission. **1962** [see *landing-place 1 c]. **1965** *Guardian* 29 Dec. 3/7 The Apollo moon landing programme..depends on highly sophisticated soft-landing techniques. **1969** *New Scientist* 27 Feb. 439/2 The upshot of the planetary experiments should be to discover more about the suitability of Mars to support life; and to select possible sites for future soft-landing craft.

softly, *adv.* Add: **4. c.** *softly, softly, catchee monkey* (and varr.): proverbial phr. advocating caution or guile as the best way to achieve an end. Also *ellipt.* as *softly softly* and (with hyphen) *attrib.*

1907 G. Benham *Cassell's Bk. of Quotations* 849/1 'Softly, softly' caught the monkey.—(Negro.) **1942** N. Balchin *Darkness falls from Air* x. 176 Softly catch monkey... That's the answer. **1960** *Times* 1 Oct. 7/2 That colloquial adage—'softly, softly, catchee monkey'. **1962** P. Brickhill *Deadline* xiii. 152, I didn't pursue it any further then. Softly, softly, catchee monkey—and I hated that phrase. **1967** *Autocar* 28 Dec. 7/1 Softly, softly is our policy too, but not at such expense in time. **1970** *Sunday Times* 5 July 11 (*heading*) Ulster: end of 'softly, softly'. **1971** E. F. Schoeters in B. de Ferranti *Living with Computer* viii. 71 Users are naturally applying a 'softly-softly' approach. **1979** *Now!* 14 Sept. 53/2 Sadat and Begin..are both adopting a softly-softly' approach to the Palestinian problem.

11. a. *softly-featured.*

1922 Joyce *Ulysses* 342 This..lent to her softly-featured face at whiles a look..that imparted a strange yearning tendency to the beautiful eyes.

b. *softly-burning, -gliding* (earlier example), *-smiling, -stirring, -swaying.*

1864 W. C. Bryant *Thirty Poems* 38 The softly gliding, bashful stream. **1907** Joyce *Chamber Music* p. xv, Eastward the gradual dawn prevails Where softly-burning fires appear. **1918** D. H Lawrence *New Poems* 48 Ah, love, Could I but..remove Its softly-stirring, crimson welling-up Of kisses! **1923** —— *Birds, Beasts & Flowers* 38 Vicious, dark cypresses: Vicious, you supple, brooding, softly-swaying pillars of dark flame. **1924** E. Sitwell *Sleeping Beauty* xvii 68 To catch the softly-smiling wind.

softness. Add: **II. 4. e.** The state or property (of a material or device) of being soft, in extended technical usage.

1900 *Sci. Trans. R. Dublin Soc.* VII. 121 The addition of 2 to 5½ per cent. of silicon to steel..increases the magnetic softness. **1919** R. D. Bangay *Oscillation Valve* 204 [A blue glow] is produced by the energy expended by the electrons as they collide with the atoms, and if noticeable is a certain indication of the softness of a valve. **1945** *Electronic Engin.* XVII. 338 The maximum value [of the grid leak resistance]..is limited by the danger of causing softness to develop in the succeeding valve. **1980** *Sci. Amer.* Apr. 94/3 The magnetic 'softness' and high resistivity of glassy alloys also make them likely candidates for the 'read' and 'write' heads in magnetic tape recorders and magnetic disk memories.

f. *Econ.* With reference to commodities, prices, etc.: a state of or tendency towards depression. Cf. *soft *a.* 26** b.

1927 *Comm. & Financ. Chron.* 20 Aug. 961/1 When sterling is firmer a stronger tone develops in the entire European list. On the other hand when sterling reacts, softness develops in the rest of the list. **1930** *Economist* 27 Sept. 569/1 Apart from the recent weakness in grain and cotton prices, and softness in the copper market, the commodity price structure seems to be strengthening. **1970** *Globe & Mail* (Toronto) 25 Sept. B5/1 William S. Brewster, chairman, attributes the disappointing results to softness in the economy.

soft pedal, *sb.* [f. Soft *a.* + Pedal *sb.* 1 b (*b*).] A foot-lever on a pianoforte which softens the tone. Also *fig.* (in senses corresponding to those of the vb.: see next) and (with hyphen) *attrib.*

1856 M. C. Clarke *tr. Berlioz' Treat. Mod. Instrumentation & Orchestration* 79 A pedal much less used than that which raises the dampers..is the soft pedal (or one-string pedal). **1861** [see Pedal *sb.* 1 b]. **1880** Grove *Dict. Mus.* II. 723/1 He..thus produces something of the shifting soft pedal *timbre.* **1911** A. B. Reeve *Poisoned Pen* 255 But can't it be done with the soft pedal? **1936** *Times* 12 Oct. 8/5 Some people thought that the 'soft pedal' should be put on the entertainment factor of a zoo, but he [*sc.* J. S. Huxley] did not agree. **1958** *Times* 8 Oct. 6/1 What this particular play demands from a film director is a certain application of the soft pedal. **1961** *Sunday Express* 23 Apr. 1/2 President de Gaulle—whose soft-pedal policy ..has sparked off this third rebellion. **1973** Junkin & Ornadel *Piano can be Fun* 69/2 Calling the damper pedal the 'loud' pedal neatly distinguishes it from the left foot pedal which is called the 'soft' pedal.

soft-pedal, *v.* [f. prec.] *trans.* and *intr.* (freq. const. *on*). To reduce the loudness or volume of (a noise); to reduce in force or effect; to tone down, play down, go easy on.

1915 R. Wagner in *Sat. Even. Post* 16 Oct. 15/2 The scene was rehearsed time and again, but always the action looked faked because of the necessity of soft-pedaling such a blow. **1916** G. A. England *Pod, Bender & Co.* i. 6 Can that! Soft pedal on that chatter, Ben! **1926** R. H. Davis *Over my Left Shoulder* xxix. 204 'Captain Sam heap mad!' replied the Peacemaker, with no effort to soft pedal the announcement. **1927** *Daily Express* 19 July 3/4 Both parties are at present 'soft pedalling' on the world-revolution thesis. **1931** F. F. Bond *Mr. Miller of 'The Times'* 170 The leading educational centres tended to stress the utilitarian studies and soft-pedal those courses which sought merely cultural ends. **1932** K. S. Prichard *Kiss on Lips & Other Stories* 20 He soft-pedalled about Rose, and the skinflint of an aunt who threatened to take her away. **1944** Auden *Sea & Mirror* in *For Time Being* i. 8 Be frank about our heathen foe, For Rome will be a goner If you soft-pedal the loud beast. **1953** A. Upfield *Murder must Wait* v. 47 'We'll get something out of her.' 'You will soft-pedal,' Bony said quietly. **1957** W. H. Whyte *Organization Man* 52 Out of respect for the sense of the meeting you tend to soft-pedal that which would go against the grain. **1965** *Listener* 27 May 764/1 He must have the drug or endure the sheer agony which the romanticists soft-pedal: high-fever, shivering, fits of vomiting, [etc.]. **1978** R. Hill *Pinch of Snuff* vi. 55 You're noted for soft-pedalling on these squatters.

Hence **soft-pe·dalling** *vbl. sb.*

1952 G. Raverat *Period Piece* x. 197 Uncle Lenny was far too judicious to need soft-pedalling. **1979** *New Statesman* 6 July 3/3 The concern of homophile organisations to make homosexuality an acceptable alternative has led to a distinct soft-pedalling on ticklish issues like paedophilia and transvestism.

soft sawder, *sb.*: see Sawder *sb.*

soft-shell. Add: **1.** *soft-shell clam, crab* = *soft clam, crab* s.v. *soft *a.* 27 c; (earlier and later examples); **soft-shell turtle,** a freshwater turtle of the genus *Trionyx*; (earlier and later examples).

1805 J. Ordway *Jrnl.* 26 May in *Wisconsin Hist. Coll.* (1916) XXII. 218 Passed 2 creeks..in one of them saw Soft Shell Turtle. **1818** *Amer. Monthly Mag.* II. 296 Soft shell Clam. These animals..are excellent eating. **1844** J. E. DeKay *Zool. N.Y.* vi. 11 During this interval, they are known under the name of Soft-shell Crabs, or Shedders. **1847** *Knickerbocker* XXIX. 494 A battle between a soft-shell turtle..and a terrier puppy. **1887** Soft-shell crab [see *diamond-back *a.*]. **1977** E. Leonard *Unknown Man No. 89* xx. 202 Softshell crabs, very good fish, steak. **1980** *Washington Post* 27 June (Weekend Suppl.) 36/1 You mustn't rush through the throng, hoagie in one hand, soft-shell crab sandwich in the other.

2. (Earlier example.)

1845 *Knickerbocker* XXVI. 285 The 'Hard and Soft Shell Baptists'.

3. a. (Earlier example.)

1845 [see *hardshell *sb.* 2].

b. Also, a soft-shelled crab or turtle.

1830 R. C. Sands *Writings* (1834) II. 230 The soft-shell of the Red River. **1846** T. B. Thorpe *Myst. Backwoods* 156 It is Turtle Lake from its abundance of 'green, amphibious soft-shells'. **1935** Z. N. Hurston *Mules & Men* 1. iii. 79 Ah'm gointer prune a gang of soft-shells (turtles). **1941** *Louisiana* (Writers' Program) 227 'Soft-shells' and 'busters' (shedding crabs from which the old shell is pried off) are coated with cracker meal and fried. **1942** [see *hardshell *a.* 1]. **1958** R. Conant *Field Guide Reptiles & Amphibians* 70 The Florida Softshell lives chiefly in lakes; all the others are river turtles to a large degree.

soft-shelled, *a.* Add: **1.** Esp. of the soft-shell crab or turtle. (Further examples.)

1796 *Rec. Smithtown, N.Y.* (1898) 129 Any person not an inhabitant..taking Soft shelled clams within the limits of said Town shall pay six pence for every bushel. **1835** J. J. Audubon *Ornith. Biogr.* III. 239 He knows.. how to watch the soft-shelled turtle's crawl. **1856** *Rep. Comm. Patents 1855: Agric.* (U.S.) p. xviii, The 'soft-shelled' almond..is the variety recently introduced and distributed by this Office. **1948** [see *paper-shelled* adj. s.v. *paper *sb.* 12]. **1953** G. M. Durrell *Overloaded Ark* xiii. 223 It was a species known as the Soft-shelled Turtle: the shell is fairly smooth and domed, and it protruded round the edge in a great soft rim.

soft soap, *sb.* Add: **2.** (Earlier examples.) Also *attrib.* orig. *U.S.*

1830 *Reg. Deb. Congress U.S.* 12 Apr. 774, I will not use the vulgar phrase, and say he has been pouring soft soap down the backs of the New York delegation. **1842** *People's Organ* (St. Louis) 15 Apr. 2/2 The magnificent bombshell, rammed full of pride, aristocracy,..soft-soap, curiosity, folly, display, nonsense, man-worship and small-talk, was touched off. **1934** *Sun* (Baltimore) 6 Nov. 2/2 Assailing Governor Lehman for his 'soft soap' manner of campaign, the park commissioner..renewed his assault on the Lehman banking family. **1961** *Radio Times* 6 Apr. 21/2 'Nobody likes to watch a soft-soap interview. People *want* the facts and they can take them,' says Robin Day. **1977** *Irish Times* 8 June 9/6 The public would not be fooled by this 'crazy parade of soft-soap offers'.

soft-soaper. (Earlier example.)

1852 'Mark Twain' in *Hannibal Jrnl.* Sept. 16 He was narrowly watching this soft-soaper of Democratic rascality.

soft-soapy, *a. rare.* [f. Soft soap *sb.* + -y[1].] Flattering, ingratiating, unctuous.

1904 J. C. Lincoln *Cap'n Eri* iii. 36 The thing to do is to be sort of soft-soapy and high-toned.

soft-solder, *v.* Add: Also **soft-sodder. 2.** = Soft-sawder *v. U.S. colloq.* Cf. Solder *sb.*[1] 4 b.

1866 C. H. Smith *Bill Arp, so called: Side Show of Southern Side of War* 159 Wouldn't you think that as a matter of policy they would soft sodder us a little and quit their slanderin? **1905** J. C. Lincoln *Partners of Tide* vi. 111 He soft-soddered me till I felt slippery all over.

software (sǫ·ftwēᵊɹ). [f. Soft *a.* + Ware *sb.*[3], after *hardware 1 c.] **1.** *Computers.* **a.** The programs and procedures required to enable a computer to perform a specific task, as opposed to the physical components of the system (see also quot. 1961). **b.** *esp.* The body of system programs, including compilers and library routines, required for the operation of a particular computer and often provided by the manufacturer, as opposed to program material provided by a user for a specific task.

In early use, the word was interpreted widely to include program material written by a user, as well as systems programs, and also occas. the cards and tapes by means of which programs and data are read into the system. Popular usage, as represented by sense 2, is freq. wider in meaning than the current more restrictive technical usage (sense b).

1960 *Communications Assoc. Computing Machinery* June 381 Nearly every manufacturer is claiming compatibility with all other equipment via such software as Cobol. **1961** *Computer Bull.* June 42 The programming expertise, or 'software', that is at the disposal of the computer user comprises expert advice on all matters of machine code programming, comprehensive libraries of subroutines for all purposes, and the pegasus/sirius scientific autocode. **1962** D. S. Halacy *Computers* iii. 54 Punched cards, which fall into the category called computer 'software' are cheap, flexible, and compatible with many types of equipment. **1964** *Observer* 13 Dec. 1/1 The toughest problem was the 'software'—particularly the 'supervisory programme', the complex instructions which enable the machine to handle many tasks simultaneously. **1965** Hollingdale & Tootill *Electronic Computers* 192 The cost of developing and making the computer itself (the *hardware*) is matched by the cost of making programming schemes for it (often, regrettably, termed *software*). **1966** *New Scientist* 25 Aug. 433/3 The cost of providing 'software'—the programmes for operating the computer on a wide range of problems—is enormous... The user needs to find the bureau which has the appropriate software for his problems. **1967** Cox & Grose *Organization & Handling Bibl. Rec. by Computer* 1 About three years ago, it became clear..that the computer software which was provided and maintained by the manufacturers was not suited to some of the problems of handling and processing large files of data. **1969** P. Dickinson *Pride of Heroes* 187 A rather wet young man who sells software for computers. **1971** B. de Ferranti *Living with Computer* 89 *Software*, all computer programs, or that part of a computer system that is not hardware. **1972** *Computer Bull.* XVI. 85/1 In those days [*sc.* 1966] the term 'software' was still thought rather disreputable, and the concept was probably thought rather vague... More recently, 'software' has become more particularised and often seems to refer to what we might call 'system software', that is, excluding any programs written for specific applications. ..Thus we have 'software packages' and 'application packages', and people who write software consider themselves superior to mere programmers. **1977** K. Heggstad in P. G. J. van Sterkenburg et al. *Lexicologie* 163 The unit price of hardware is going down... On the other hand software costs are rising equally dramatically. **1978** J. McNeil *Consultant* i. 30 Hardware is what you can touch—the actual computer, all its peripheral devices... Without software all that is quite useless... Software, computer programs—they're the same thing... My software staff are very strictly monitored.

2. *transf.* and *fig.*

1963 *Flight International* LXXXIII. 186/1 To get at the total commitment one has to consider the 'software' aspect very closely: for every controller at the scope there may need to be five in the background. **1966**

National Observer (U.S.) 21 Feb. 8/3 This deal..is the latest..in a series of corporate marriages combining.. 'the software and the hardware' of education. **1967** *Punch* 24 May 770/3 This documentary was a refreshing change from most space-age reportage, dealing sympathetically with the families of the astronauts living outside the perimeter fence of the Manned Spacecraft Centre in Texas: the software rather than the hardware. **1969** *Guardian* 29 Mar. 4/8 The 'Talking Page'..is..being launched with a mass of matching software—a maths course, a reading course, an English course for immigrants. **1978** *Gramophone* June 136/3 They [*sc.* players for digitally recorded discs] will be usable with normal stereo amplifiers and speakers but, of course, they will be incompatible with existing software (records and cassettes). **1979** *Observer* 11 Nov. 33/2 It was phrased in terms of Israel giving the United States 'software'—a more flexible attitude on the Middle East—in return for 'hardware'—arms and military equipment.

3. Special Combs.: **software engineering,** the professional development, production, and management of system software; so **software engineer; software house,** a company that specializes in producing and testing software; also *fig.*

1969 NAUR & RANDELL *Software Engin.* (NATO) 81 Is it possible to have software engineers in the numbers in which we need them, without formal software engineering education? **1979** JENSEN & TONIES *Software Engin.* 14 The software engineer is not a theoretician as is the computer scientist. **1969** (*title*) Software engineering; report of a conference sponsored by the NATO Science Committee, Garmisch, Germany, 7th to 11th October, 1968. **1973** K. W. MORTON in F. L. Bauer *Adv. Course Software Engin.* i. A. 4 When we sit down at a console to write an Algol program, it is software engineering which determines how easy it is to achieve this end. **1982** I. SOMMERVILLE *Software Engin.* i. 3 Software engineering is now maturing into a fully fledged discipline. **1969** *New Scientist* 6 Nov. 285/1 Today there are just over 2000 software houses throughout the world, mostly in America. **1982** *Listener* 23–30 Dec. 31/1 If the world's wealth is maximised by specialisation, Britain should become its 'software house'.

soft wood. Also as one word. Add: **1.** Esp. coniferous trees or their timber. Also *attrib.* (Later examples.)

1905 *Terms Forestry & Logging* (U.S. Dept. Agric.) 48 Softwood..As applied to trees and logs, needle-leafed, coniferous... Softwood..A needle-leafed, or coniferous, tree. **1914** MOON & BROWN *Elem. Forestry* 218 Many of our hardwoods are much softer in their wood structure than certain conifers or so-called softwoods. **1930** *Observer* 26 Jan. 20/4 Every year in Finland, Sweden and Russia millions of pine trees are felled and shipped to London... The trade name for such timber is softwood. **1968** J. ARNOLD *Shell Bk. Country Crafts* xxxi. 321 Yew, though as hard and heavy as oak, is classified as a softwood. **1977** J. L. HARPER *Population Biol. Plants* iv. 94 In some hardwood and softwood forests in Maine the buried seed population diverges remarkably in species composition from that of the vegetation.

softy, *sb.* Add: **b.** A very soft-hearted person.

1886 *19th Cent.* Jan. 80 The sentimental softy..who loses his heart at seventeen, is a father at eighteen, and at nineteen is the husband of a dirty trollop. **1914** *Maclean's Mag.* July 88/3 'It's cruel,' said Steve... 'You're a softy!' he said. **1964** MRS. L. B. JOHNSON *White House Diary* 16 Jan. (1970) A trip that I fear will not meet with the approval of all the members of our family, but which I—maybe I am a softie—very much want her to have. **1970** 'D. HALLIDAY' *Dolly & Cookie Bird* v. 66 You didn't know Daddy like I did. He was an awful old softie inside.

c. One who is considered cowardly, weak, or unmanly; a weakling; an effeminate man.

1895 *Cent. Mag.* Oct. 943/2 If the well-initiated inmates discover that he is unwilling to enter into all their schemes and customs, they call him a 'sucker' or 'softy', and shun his company. **1912** BEERBOHM *Christmas Garland* 16 There was nothing of the softy about Smithers. **1924** J. M. MURRY *Voyage* xii. 227 'It's no go,' he said. 'I'm not going to bed to-night'. 'But'..She didn't know what to say. Was he a softy? Or was she his first? **1960** T. MCLEAN *Kings of Rugby* xi. 204 Mr Jenkins declared that the All Blacks of the morrow were 'softies' for wearing such impedimenta [*sc.* shoulder-pads]. **1975** *Liverpool Echo* (Football ed.) 11 Jan. 8/6 He never lost his temper, but he was no softie. **1979** *Beano* 2 June 20/3 (*caption*) Who did that? No-one to be seen except those softies playing soppy games.

so·fty, *a.* [f. SOFT *a.* + -Y[1].] *rare. N. Amer.* Characterized by softness.

1884 'MARK TWAIN' *Huck. Finn* xxvii. 272 When the place was packed full, the undertaker he slid around in his black gloves with his softy soothering ways. **1970** *Globe & Mail* (Toronto) 25 Sept. 16/2 (Advt.), Fringed shoulder pouches in softy suede.

sog, *sb.*[3] Delete *rare*$^{-1}$ and substitute ? *Obs.* Add earlier and later examples.

1839 *Knickerbocker* XIII. 379 He was a most extraordinary fish; or, in the vernacular of Nantucket, 'a genuine old sog', of the first water. **1851** H. MELVILLE *Moby Dick* II. xxxix. 261 Such a sog! such a sogger! Don't ye love sperm!

SOGAT, Sogat (sōᵘ·gæt). [Acronym f. the initial letters of *S*ociety *o*f *G*raphical and *A*llied *T*rades.] A trade union now composed of paper-workers, etc. (see below), in the printing industries.

The union was formed in 1966 by the amalgamation of the National Union of Printing, Bookbinding, and Paper Workers and the National Society of Operative Printers and Assistants. In 1972 this union was divided, with the paper workers retaining the acronym SOGAT. In 1982 SOGAT amalgamated with the National Society of Operative Printers Graphical and Media Personnel. The new union was called SOGAT 1982.

1966 *Paperworker* Mar. 3/1 Formation of SOGAT. The Registrar of Friendly Societies informed us today of his approval of the..establishment of the Society of Graphical and Allied Trades (SOGAT). **1967** *SOGAT* Feb. 6/1 Only one year ago the Society of Graphical and Allied Trades, now using the coined name SOGAT, came into being. **1969** *Times* 2 May 1/8 About 500 Sogat members ..stopped work..at the Stationery Office's printing plant. **1971** H. WILSON *Labour Government* xiii. 210 SOGAT rejected a multilateral meeting. **1977** in R. Crossman *Diaries* III. 723 Richard Briginshaw, General Secretary of the National Society of Operative Printers, Graphical and Media Personnel (as SOGAT became) 1951–75. **1982** *Times* 8 Nov. 2/4 Sogat '82 hopes that several hundred trade unionists will demonstrate.

Sogdian (sǫ·gdiăn), *a.* and *sb.* Also **Soghdian, Sughdian.** [ad. L. *Sogdiānus*, a. Gr. *Σογδιανός*, f. O. Persian *Suguda*, later *Sugud*.] **A.** *adj.* Of or belonging to Sogdiana, an ancient Persian province corresponding to the modern Samarkand and Bokhara in the Uzbek S.S.R. **B.** *sb.* **a.** A native of this province. **b.** The Middle Iranian language of this province. Also *attrib.*

1553 J. BRENDE tr. *Quintus Curtius' Hist.* VII. sig. Ui, When he had ordred all thinges amonges the Sogdians, he..remoued into Bactria. **1700** G. BOOTH tr. *Diodorus Siculus' Historical Libr.* 785 How the King led his Army against the Sogdians and Scythians. *Ibid.* 787 How the Sogdian Noblemen being led forth to be put to Death, were unexpectedly preserv'd. **1729** J. ROOKE tr. *Arrian's Hist. of Alexander's Exped.* I. IV. xvi. 24 He then, with part of his army, march'd straight into the country of the Sogdians. *Ibid.*, Spitamenes, at the head of a band of Sogdian exiles, who had fled into Scythia,.. attack'd a certain castle in Bactria. **1909** *Indogerm. Forsch.* XXV. 182 The Sughdian rendering of the Syriac version of the Greek. **1923** H. G. WELLS *Outl. Hist.* (rev. ed.) xxx. 295/2 A very considerable literature..in Sogdian and another Aryan language has been discovered. **1947** C. P. SNOW *Light & Dark* I. iv. 47 It was written in an unknown variety of Middle Persian called Early Soghdian. **1954** I. GERSHEVITCH (*title*) Grammar of Manichean Sogdian. **1973** R. L. FOX *Alexander the Great* III. xxii. 309 Heavy drinking is the corollary of survival for a traveller in a Sogdian summer. *Ibid.* 314 By now, Sogdians and Bactrians were serving in Alexander's army.

sogged (sǫgd), *ppl. a.* [f. SOG *v.* + -ED[1].] Soaked, saturated.

1860 [see SOG *v.* 2]. **1929** H. WILLIAMSON *Beautiful Yrs.* xxiii. 237 A weary, misty dawn dispelled the phantasms and presented a reality of sogged ground and wet drippings from the trees. **1947** K. TENNANT *Lost Haven* iii. 53 Ground's too cold, everything's too sogged for the feed to grow. **1966** S. HEANEY *Death of Naturalist* 23 For days I sadly hung Round the yard, watching the three sogged remains Turn mealy and crisp as old summer dung.

soggily (sǫ·gili), *adv.* [f. next + -LY[2].] In a soggy manner.

1939 AUDEN & ISHERWOOD *Journey to a War* 222 The bastard, I thought soggily, he's sneaking off. **1960** *Times* 1 Nov. 16/4 The result [*sc.* a film]..rather soggily directed by Mr. Peter Brook. **1975** C. WESTON *Susannah Screaming* (1976) xxii. 118 'You can see what happened,' Haynes said soggily, mopping his nose. **1981** M. KENYON *Zigzag* xx. 131 Three slabs of still soggily magnificent date cake.

soggy, *a.* Add: Now common in standard English in the U.K. **2.** (Earlier example.) Also of persons.

a **1852** F. M. WHITCHER *Widow Bedott Papers* (1856) xxix. 375 Oh yes, to be sure it needs sugar, the best o' sugar, too; not this wet, soggy, brown sugar. **1964** [see *plastic-macked* s.v. *PLASTIC *sb.*[2] 5].

4. b. Of things, in various *transf.* and *fig.* uses: dull, lifeless, lacking in vigour, sluggish; (of steering) unresponsive.

1928 [see *DAWK *sb.*[2] b]. **1932** [see *BLIMEY *int.*]. **1957** J. BRAINE *Room at Top* xxv. 205 The steering [of a car] was low-geared and more than a trifle soggy. **1965** G. MCINNES *Road to Gundagai* v. 79 The poor fellow found the evening hanging pretty soggy on his hands. **1966** WILLIAMS & FLEMING *Spectrosc. Methods in Org. Chem.* iii. 44 The soggy vibrations of the molecule as a whole give rise to a series of absorption bands at low energy, below 1500 cm.$^{-1}$ **1977** *Gramophone* Dec. 1080/1 The brass fanfares at the start of the finale are hardly of the brightest in sound—but then tuttis show the general orchestral sound to be pretty soggy.

Soho (sōᵘ·hoᵘ, soᵘhōᵘ·), *sb.*[2] **a.** The name of a district in the West End of London, noted for its foreign population, prostitutes, and restaurants, and latterly for its night clubs, striptease shows, pornography shops, etc. Freq. *attrib.* of things connected with or characteristic of Soho.

1818 KEATS *Let.* 14 Mar. (1931) I. 127 Then who would go Into dark Soho, And chatter with dack'd hair'd critics. **1890** E. DOWSON *Let.* 10 or 11 June (1967) 153 The two artists—with some other artistic & Bohemian types might meet in the early part of the book in a Soho restaurant based on Poland. **1905** CHESTERTON *Club of Queer Trades* iv. 165 Some dirty Soho restaurant. **1913** W. WHITTEN *Londoner's London* vi. 140 He had always a nice Soho taste in wine. **1930** W. S. MAUGHAM *Cakes & Ale* i. 12 You drive away wondering whether when he comes he will think you are swanking if you ask him to Claridge's or mean if you suggest Soho. **1937** L. MACNEICE in Auden & MacNeice *Lett. from Iceland* 129 To pore on picture catalogues and Soho menus. **1959** *Good Food Guide* 221 There is now a good Soho restaurant in Birmingham with a wide menu properly cooked. It is also resolutely described in Soho French. **1964** *Times Lit. Suppl.* 12 Nov. 1019/4 [Frank] Harris..wrote about sex in the manner and style of the cheapest Soho trash. **1976** *Listener* 26 Feb. 239/2 Sex was..a mean..sleezy, Soho-type thing.

b. *Hist.* Used *attrib.* to designate a type of tapestry produced in England after 1685, usu. in Soho.

[**1914** W. G. THOMSON *Tapestry Weaving in England* xvii. 139 At Christmas 1685 the arras-workers and tailors employed in the Great Wardrobe changed the scene of their labours to offices in Great Queen Street, Soho, which lies between the northwest corner of Lincoln's Inn Fields and Drury Lane.] **1930** H.-C. MARILLER *Eng. Tapestries of Eighteenth Cent.* p. xvii, In the absence of records it would be impossible to say which Soho tapestries were executed in the late seventeenth and which in the eighteenth century. *Ibid.* p. xx, There is no clear line of demarcation between the later Mortlake and the earlier Soho tapestries. **1963** *Times* 18 Jan. 10/6 An anonymous purchaser secured four early-eighteenth-century walnut chairs covered in Soho tapestry, for 450 gns. **1978** *Country Life* 13 Apr. 973/1 The Soho tapestries which now line the room were originally bought..in 1720.

‖ **soigné** (swanʸe), *a.* Fem. **soignée.** [Fr., pa. pple. of *soigner* to take care of, f. *soin* care.] Dressed, adorned, tended, or prepared with great care and attention to detail; well-groomed.

1821 M. EDGEWORTH *Let.* 27 Nov. (1971) 281 Which would become me best..to pin or not to pin it. I think rather *not to pin*. It looks less soignée but then I may lose the frill. **1900** G. ARTHUR *Let.* 25 July in *Letters from Man of No Importance* (1928) 123 The Boers may not be particularly *soigné* in their habits, but the Japanese who are, use very little soap, and swear by vapour baths. **1907** E. GLYN *Three Weeks* xii. 137 This lady was so intensely *soignée*. **1927** A. E. W. MASON *No Other Tiger* xi. 98 As she stood there in that flood of radiance, *soignée*, polished from head to foot. **1936** *Punch* 24 June 710/2 William Powell is of course William Powell—suave and *soigné* and perfectly poised. **1959** *Good Food Guide* 35 The prices remain fairly high but the cooking is genuinely *soigné*. **1978** J. GARDNER *Dancing Dodo* xxxv. 276 The soignée women and immaculate men..who could afford places like the Hilton.

soil, *sb.*[1] Add: **II. 7. a.** (Further examples.) Usu., but not always, such material as will support the growth of plants, as contrasted with subsoil.

1906 E. W. HILGARD *Soils* viii. 120 Universal experience has long ago recognized and established the distinction between soil and subsoil: by which are ordinarily meant, respectively, the portion of the soil-material usually subjected to tillage, and what lies beneath. **1932** G. W. ROBINSON *Soils* i. 2 Soil consists essentially of (a) mineral matter,..(b) organic matter,..(c) soil moisture,..and (d) soil air. **1952** L. M. THOMPSON *Soils & Soil Fertility* i. 3 Soil is the mixture of mineral and organic material at the land surface of the earth that is capable of sustaining plant life. **1976** D. STEILA *Geogr. Soils* 2 Soil serves as an anchorage for plants and as their nutrient reservoir.

b. *Engin.* Fragmentary or unconsolidated material occurring naturally at or near the earth's surface, regardless of its suitability for plant life. Cf. *REGOLITH.

1934 L. C. URQUHART *Civil Engin. Handbk.* VIII. 632 The earth consists of various rock formations covered with a mantle of unconsolidated products of rock disintegration, called the regolith or, more commonly, the soil, although agriculturists use the term soil in a somewhat different sense. **1967** A. SINGH *Soil Engin.* i. 1 Soil is considered to include all naturally occurring loose or soft deposit overlying the solid bedrock crust. **1972** C. B. HUNT *Geol. Soils* i. 5 In engineering, 'soil' refers to the ground that can be excavated by earth-moving equipment without blasting.

c. Friable or powdery material occurring naturally on another planet.

1967 *Sci. Amer.* Nov. 43/1 Some of the objects observed on the lunar surface were clodlike clumps of soil. **1970** *Nature* 28 Nov. 795/2 (*caption*) Lunakhod-1 tracks in the lunar soil. **1976** *Daily Tel.* 4 Aug. 10/6 The mechanical digging arm on the Viking I lander was activated again yesterday, scooping up fresh soil to explore for basic life forms on Mars. **1977** J. M. PASACHOFF *Contemporary Astron.* III. xiii. 336 The Venera landers also made measurements of the soil, determining that its chemical composition and density correspond to that of basalt, in common with the Earth, the Moon, and Mars.

8. b. *Engin.* A particular kind of fragmentary material (sense 7 b above).

1913 BLANCHARD & DROWNE *Text-bk. Highway Engin.* vi. 127 Some of the more common soils encountered in highway work are classified as gravel, sand, clay, loam, marl, peat and muck. **1966** *McGraw-Hill Encycl. Sci. & Technol.* XII. 450/1 Soils range from deep-lying geologic deposits to agricultural soils.

9. *soil aggregate, amelioration, bacterium* (usu. *pl.*), *characteristic, classification, compaction, condition, cover, depletion, development, drainage, fertility, formation, genesis, geography,* *geology, layer, management, material, micro-biology, micro-organism, mineral, moisture, nutrient, organic matter, organism, particle, population, pore, restoration, -restorer, sterilization, structure, study, temperature, test, texture; soil-binding, -borne, -building, -depleting, -dwelling, -forming, -inhabiting, -restorative* adjs.; *soil-testing, -warming* sbs. and adjs.

1934 *Discovery* July 198/2 Important chemical properties are indicated by the form of the soil aggregates. **1967** Soil aggregate [see *Krilium]. **1969** *Gloss. for Landscape Work* (*B.S.I.*) v. 20 Soil amelioration. **1972** Edwards & Lofty *Biol. Earthworms* vii. 171 (*heading*) Soil amelioration by earthworms. **1900** *Knowledge* 2 July 161/2 In removing from the land his annual crop, the farmer carries off the greater part of the year's supply of potential humus whence the soil looks to be provided with Nitrates—by the action of the soil-bacteria—for the coming season. **1973** R. G. Krueger et al. *Introd. Microbiol.* xxx. 743/1 Two groups of aerobic soil bacteria are in large part responsible for the conversion of ammonia to nitrate. Representatives of the *Nitrosomonas* group oxidize ammonia to nitrite; those of the *Nitrobacter* group oxidize nitrite to nitrate. **1913** *Bull. Bureau of Soils U.S. Dept. Agric.* No. 96. 19 This wasteful wash can be checked..by seeding the land to soil-binding grasses. **1943** J. S. Huxley *TVA* vi. 42 Protective, soil-binding crops. **1946** *Nature* 9 Nov. 661/2 *Verticillium Malthousei* is the causal fungus; it may be soil-borne, or carried by flies. **1968** *Times* 16 Dec. 7/2 The soil-borne diseases, take-all and eyespot. **1977** J. L. Harper *Population Biol. Plants* v. 139 It is..not particularly easy to discriminate between direct toxic action of soil chemical conditions and indirect effects due to soil-borne pathogens which are themselves determined in distribution by the chemical conditions. **1920** W. W. Weir *Productive Soils* i. 9 Because of the source of soil building materials, the nature of soil formation, [etc.]..all soil can not be the same. **1938, 1962** Soil-building [see *soil-depleting* adj. below]. **1902** P. McConnell *Elem. Agric. Geol.* iv. 122 (*heading*) Soil characteristics. **1954** W. D. Thornbury *Princ. Geomorphol.* iv. 73 No geomorphologist today is adequately trained who lacks an appreciation of the soil-forming processes and a basic understanding of soil characteristics. **1923** *Soil Sci.* XVI. 95 On the basis of this concept of soils and soil classification, field and laboratory studies of soils in Michigan have been undertaken. **1946** L. D. Stamp *Britain's Struct. & Scenery* xi. 92 The basis of the soil classification used for these maps is a textural one:..broadly the purpose was to separate sands, light, medium and heavy loams, clays and peats. **1972** J. G. Cruickshank *Soil Geogr.* i. 23 Senior members of the national soil surveys such as G. W. Robinson (1932) and B. W. Avery (1956) have been responsible for soil classifications which developed from the work of soil survey in Britain. **1933** *Engin. News-Record* 31 Aug. 245/2 The basic principles of soil compaction..apply to all types of earthfills and to foundation design. **1971** *Power Farming* Mar. 80/1 (Advt.), The Salo [harrow] produces a fine, level, shallow bed with only one or two tractor passes. Soil compaction is reduced to the minimum. **1905** *Jrnl. Agric. Sci.* I. 78 The clover crop feels the effect of the changed soil conditions to a much greater extent. **1966** Soil condition [see *soil survey*, sense *10 below]. **1964** W. C. Putnam *Geology* x. 249/1 Soil cover serves to alleviate the starkness of a rock-dominated landscape. **1938** *Sun* (Baltimore) 14 Sept. 4/8 Payments will be made for keeping within soil-depleting acreage allotments and for attaining soil-building goals. **1962** *Times* 12 Oct. (Stand. Bank Suppl.) p. vii/5 The ability to overcome..problems by applying research findings such as..soil-building rotations as opposed to soil-depleting rotations and harmful practices such as monoculture. **1925** Soil depletion [see *mosaic *a.*[1] 6]. **1921** *Proc. 41st Ann. Meeting Soc. Promotion Agric. Sci., 1920* (U.S.) 118 A great deal of fundamental work has been done in Russia. It has been concerned..with the working out of the principles and the formulation of the laws of soil development. **1972** J. G. Cruickshank *Soil Geogr.* ii. 57 The origin of parent materials is not significant for soil development except as an indication of the soil properties that may be expected. **1946** L. D. Stamp *Britain's Struct. & Scenery* xi. 100 The relationship between vegetation cover and soil drainage is far from being sufficiently realised. **1970** Gay & Calaby in Krishna & Weesner *Biol. Termites* II. ix. 440 Soil-dwelling colonies commonly build radiating gallery systems on the soil surface to adjacent grass tussocks. **1901** *Proc. 22nd Ann. Meeting Soc. Promotion Agric. Sci.* (U.S.) 62 The subject of humus in its relation to soil fertility. **1968** R. W. Fairbridge *Encycl. Geomorphol.* 1235/2 Deposition of fine dust (obvious in the case of thick loess) has occurred in very thin mantles..over broad areas. The latter is a vastly underrated factor in the maintenance of soil fertility in wide regions. **1912** *Bull. Bur. Soils U.S. Dept. Agric.* No. 85. 14 The most important agency of soil formation is moisture. **1963** [see *pedogenesis]. **1967** M. J. Coe *Ecol. Alpine Zone Mt. Kenya* 69 The processes of soil formation are also very evident. **1902** P. McConnell *Elem. Agric. Geol.* iii. 66 (*heading*) List of the principal soil-forming minerals. **1936** [see *pedogenesis]. **1972** J. G. Cruickshank *Soil Geogr.* ii. 34 Climate was regarded as the principal and dominant soil-forming factor for the greater part of the short history of pedological thought. **1927** C. F. Marbut in tr. *Glinka's Great Soil Groups* p. i, The development of the first and only comprehensive theory of soil genesis. **1946** S. A. Wilde *Forest Soils & Forest Growth* iii. 20 An essential factor of soil genesis, the composition of vegetative cover. **1972** Soil genesis [see *pedocal]. **1927** C. F. Marbut tr. *Glinka's Great Soil Groups* 7 The study of the soil geography of North America has..enforced the recognition of the close relationship between the soil and climatic conditions. **1972** J. G. Cruickshank *Soil Geogr.* i. 30 Pedology is, by this definition, very close to soil geography except that the latter is concerned with all kinds of distributions involving soil, from those of natural genesis to limitations for soil cultivation. **1907** J. R. Kilroe (*title*) A description of the soil-geology of Ireland, based upon Geological Survey maps and records. **1972** J. G. Cruickshank *Soil Geogr.* i. 16 A further distinction differentiating soil from weathered rock was subsequently made.., but nevertheless the view of soil science as soil geology prevailed for the rest of the nineteenth century in Western Europe and America. **1939** Melhus & Kent *Elem. Plant Path.* vii. 97 Mercuric chloride in dilute solution has been used in the control of..certain soil-inhabiting pathogens, etc. **1969** W. L. Nutting in Krishna & Weesner *Biol. Termites* I. viii. 274 There is even less information on the wood- and soil-inhabiting Hodotermitidae. **1911** *Encycl. Brit.* XXV. 351/2 The general evidence indicates that the specific bacteria of cholera discharges are capable of a much longer existence in the superficial soil layers than was formerly supposed. **1964** W. C. Putnam *Geology* x. 249/2 Soil layers and particles may be lifted up by the expansion of freezing water. **1968** Soil layer [see *pedosphere]. **1909** *Bull. Bur. Soils U.S. Dept. Agric.* No. 55. 26 This is borne out by the experience of farmers, who testify as to differences in soil management. **1979** W. L. Pritchett *Properties & Managem. Forest Soils* p. v, Significant advances have been made in silviculture, especially in reforestation technology and soil management of short rotation forests for fiber production. **1912** *Bull. Bur. Soils U.S. Dept. Agric.* No. 85. 23 Numerous kinds of rocks or soil material, subjected to the action of many agencies and processes,..have resulted in the formation of many varieties or types of soil. **1971** A. R. Jumikis *Foundation Engin.* vii. 179 The soil materials to use for building earth cofferdams are sandy clay and clayey sand. **1925** *Soil Sci.* XIX. 201 Agricultural practice has hardly been modified as a result of the development of soil microbiology. **1972** J. G. Cruickshank *Soil Geogr.* i. 15 We are not concerned with the foundation or the history of soil chemistry, soil physics, soil microbiology, soil mineralogy, and other member parts of soil science, but rather with the inception and growth of pedology within the last century. **1916** *Soil Sci.* I. 99 The study of soil microörganisms has attracted the attention of many investigators. **1972** J. G. Cruickshank *Soil Geogr.* 170 Easily attacked by a wide variety of soil microorganisms are substances like protein, sugars, and pectins. **1913** *Phil. Trans. R. Soc.* B. CCIV. 181 The soil solution may not be of constant concentration, because the soil minerals may not be so similar as is supposed, especially after the application of fertilizers. **1980** *Amateur Gardening* 4 Oct. 23/3 Grass needs potassium.., but it is extraordinarily efficient about extracting it from naturally-occuring soil minerals. **1926** *Phytopathology* XVI. 582 Soil temperature and soil moisture were believed by many writers to be responsible in part for the variation in potato mosaic symptoms. **1980** *Amateur Gardening* 4 Oct. 23/1 Nitrogen..applied in the form of a fertiliser dissolves in the soil moisture and is very rapidly lost. **1926** *Phytopathology* XVI. 583 Some attempt has been made to modify the symptoms of mosaic by varying the soil nutrients. **1915** T. L. Lyon et al. *Soils* viii. 126 The source of practically all soil organic matter is plant tissue. **1971** *Gloss. Soil Sci. Terms* (Soil Sci. Soc. Amer.) 17/1 *Soil organic matter*, the organic fraction of the soil; includes plant and animal residues at various stages of decomposition, cells and tissues of soil organisms, and substances synthesized by the soil population. **1979** W. L. Prichett *Properties & Managem. Forest Soils* xvi. 290 While soil organic matter can be increased by use of green manure crops and the additions of composts.., such increases are temporary due to the decomposition of these materials by soil organisms. **1901** H. M. Ward *Dis. Plants* xv. 143 Cuttings..stuck into ordinary soil in dirty boxes covered with equally dirty glass, present every chance for infection by soil organisms. **1967** M. J. Coe *Ecol. Alpine Zone Mt. Kenya* 70 On account of the low temperature..and the consequent puacity of soil organisms, there is a marked inhibition of the chemical breakdown of parent materials. **1900** R. Warington *Lect. Physical Properties Soil* i. 11 Any group of particles obtained by subsidence will not be entirely of the same size in cases where the soil particles consist of substances having different specific gravities. **1914** [see *crumb *sb.* 1 c]. **1964** W. C. Putnam *Geology* x. 245/1 The C-horizon..is a mixture in varying proportions of altered and unaltered rock fragments and soil particles. **1927** Soil population [see *edaphon]. **1971** *Gloss. Soil Sci. Terms* (Soil Sci. Soc. Amer.) 17/1 Soil pores. **1976** *Physics Bull.* Aug. 342/3 Marshall's equation..implies a certain connectivity of soil pores which may not always be justified. **1946** *Nature* 2 Nov. 605/1 A combination of cereal agriculture and tree-fruit crops, with subsidiary pasturage, hunting, and fishing, as an approximately stable regime,..presumes a cycle of soil-restoration. **1962** E. Snow *Red China Today* (1963) lxvii. 508 Many of these toy dams are already used for local power, irrigation and soil-restorative purposes. **1910** *Chambers's Jrnl.* Aug. 560/1 The new alfalfa..is expected to yield an ideal forage and act as a soil-restorer. **1913** L. C. Corbett *Garden Farming* ii. 23 Soil sterilization has for its direct object the treatment of soil in such a way as to render it free from injurious enemies. **1923** W. F. Bewley *Dis. Glasshouse Plants* viii. 154 The practice of soil sterilization is now an accepted method of increasing the fertility of infertile soils. **1920** W. W. Weir *Productive Soils* ii. 13 Texture should not be confused with soil 'structure' which means the arrangements of the soil grains..or..the relation of the soil particles to each other. **1954** W. D. Thornbury *Princ. Geomorphol.* iv. 87 Not all soil structures are..solifluction features, for downslope movement may be either lacking or of minor importance. **1976** *Physics Bull.* Aug. 343/3 This amount of tillage..can also be harmful to the stability of the soil structure. **1927** C. F. Marbut tr. *Glinka's Great Soil Groups* 10 Natural exposures..can be utilized as aids to soil study but artificial exposures, such as dry wells,..are better. **1972** Soil study [see *soil profile*, sense *10 below]. **1923** W. F. Bewley *Dis. Glasshouse Plants* ii. 37 Investigations upon the *Verticillium* wilt of tomatoes..illustrate the importance of air and soil temperatures in conditioning the progress of disease. **1976** L. F. Curtis et al. *Soils in Brit. Isles* xii. 221 Another effect of good drainage is that it allows the soil temperature to rise more quickly in the spring. **1926** *Public Roads* VII. 153 (*heading*) Simplified soil tests for subgrades and their physical significance. **1978** Friedman & Sanders *Princ. Sedimentol.* xiii. 417/1 It suffices for most engineering purposes to put the samples from a soil-test boring into small jars. **1934** *Proc. Amer. Soc. Testing Materials* XXXIV. ii. 693 (*heading*) Subgrade soil testing methods. **1979** S. Smith *Survivor* vi. 74 A local horticulturist giving a demonstration of soil testing. **1980** *Amateur Gardening* 4 Oct. 23/3 Home soil-testing kits can be purchased at quite reasonable prices at garden centres. **1912** R. L. Watts *Vegetable Gardening* iii. 25 (*heading*) Soil texture. **1971** *Arable Farmer* Feb. 62/1 Soil texture is an important factor in determining the equilibrium of organic matter level. **1938** C. P. Quarrell *Intensive Salad Production* vi. 72 Before undertaking any system of electrical soil warming the grower should consult the cable manufacturers. **1954** A. G. L. Hellyer *Encycl. Garden Work* 97/1 Electric soil-warming cables may be buried in the soil.

b. *attrib.* in *pl.*

1925 P. Emerson *Soil Characteristics* i. 22 The soils student should become acquainted with the common soil-forming minerals and rocks. **1945** P. Work *Vegetable Production & Marketing* x. 164 See soils textbooks for discussions of the principles and practices of land drainage. **1969** *Civil Engin.* June 43/2 The stratum, our soils consultant recommended, could be used for safe bearing pressures of 1,200 and 1,800 psf, for dead load and total load respectively. **1973** [see *pedology].

10. soil air, air present in the soil; **soil amendment,** a substance added to the soil to improve its properties, esp. its physical properties; also, the use of such substances; **soil analysis,** the scientific investigation of the composition and structure of soil or soil samples; **soil association,** a group of soils that are related geographically or topographically, esp. ones derived from a common parent material; **soil auger,** a rotary tool (either powered or operated manually) for boring into or taking samples of soil; **soil bank,** (*a*) land taken out of use for agricultural production (? *temporary*); (*b*) the soil as a continuing store of seeds, pathogens, nutrients, etc.; **soil biology,** the study of soil organisms and their life; **soil catena:** see *catena c; **soil-cement** *a.* and (also without hyphen) *sb.*, (material) composed of soil or a soil substitute that has been strengthened and stabilized by the admixture of cement; **soil chemistry,** the branch of soil science concerned with the chemical properties and reactions of soil; so **soil chemist; soil class,** a group of soils similar to one another in texture or (in mod. use) some other physical property; **soil climate,** the prevailing physical conditions in the soil, esp. as they affect soil organisms and plant life; **soil colloid,** a substance present in the soil as a colloid, i.e. in the form of very small particles; **soil conditioner,** a substance added to the soil to improve its physical characteristics, *esp.* one made synthetically for the purpose; **soil conservation,** the protection and safeguarding of the soil against erosion, loss of fertility, and damage; **soil deficiency,** an insufficiency in the soil of some substance necessary for the proper growth of plants; **soil erosion,** the removal of soil by the action of wind or running water; **soil exhaustion,** the disappearance of fertility from the soil; **soil extract** (see quot. 1971); **soil group,** a group of soils; *spec.* in *Soil Sci.* (also *great soil group*), each of the relatively small number of groups into which the world's soils are divided on the basis of their profiles and the climate in which they exist; **soil horizon** = *horizon *sb.* 5 b; **soil mantle,** the soil as a covering of the underlying rock; **soil map,** a map showing the location and nature of the various kinds of soil in a region; so **soil mapping** *vbl. sb.*; **soil mark** *Archæol.*, a trace of a levelled or buried feature indicated by differences in the colour or texture of the soil, usu. on ploughed land; **soil mechanics,** the science concerned with the mechanical properties and behaviour of soil as they affect its use in civil engineering; **soil phase,** each of a number of soils that belong to the same soil type or soil series but differ in some feature such as stoniness, slope, etc.; **soil physics** (see quot. 1976); hence **soil physicist; soil polygon** = *polygon *sb.* 2 b; **soil profile** = *profile *sb.*[1] 4 d; **soil province:** see *province 6 d; **soil resistivity,** the electrical resistivity of the soil; usu. *attrib.*; **soil sample,** a sample of soil taken for scientific investigation; **soil sampler,** any device for taking soil samples; so **soil sampling** *vbl. sb.*; **soil science** = *pedology; so **soil scientist** = *pedologist; **soil separate,** a separate (sense *6) obtained from soil; **soil series,** a group of soils similar in profile, origin, and other characteristics but varying in the texture of the surface horizon; **soil sickness,** a condition of soil in which it has become unable to support the healthy growth of a crop; so **soil-sick** *a.* (*rare*); **soil solution,** the water present around and between soil particles as a dilute solution of mineral salts; **soil stabilization,** the treatment of soil to give it increased resistance to movement, esp. under load, and erosion; **soil stripe** *Geomorphol.*, one of the low ridges of stony soil which occur in cold environments and form parallel, evenly spaced lines; **soil survey,** a systematic examination and mapping of the different kinds of soil present in a region or on a site; a report of the results so obtained; a body of people engaged in such work; so **soil surveyor; soil type,** a particular kind of soil; *spec.* in *Soil Sci.*, a subdivision of a soil series made according to the texture of the surface horizon, and representing the lowest unit in the system of classification; (see also quot. 1928); **soil wash,** the movement of soil by ground water; **soil water,** the water present in soil.

1920 *Mem. Cornell Univ. Agric. Exper. Station* No. 32. 326 Before seeding, some preliminary studies were made in order to ascertain the best method of obtaining the sample of soil air for analysis. **1972** J. G. Cruickshank *Soil Geogr.* iii. 81 Differences between the composition of soil air and atmospheric air become greater with depth.. provided organisms remain present. **1915** T. L. Lyon et al. *Soils* xxiv. 542 Gypsum..was a popular soil amendment in this country before the common commercial fertilizers were used to any great extent. **1967** *Boston Sunday Globe* 28 Apr. B. 67/4 Whenever the garden has to be in a new housing development, liming is particularly needed and all the other additions of manure, peat and fertilizer. This is now called 'soil amendment' by the more technical. **1978** R. C. Oelhaf *Organic Agric.* iii. 37 Many 'organic' soil amendments are now on the market which are mainly crushed rock, selling at prices as high as 200 times the price of the ingredients. **1873** *Amer. Jrnl. Sci.* CVI. 289 In soil analysis special importance attaches to these finer sediments. **1891** R. Wallace *Rural Econ. Austral. & N.Z.* x. 169 No analyst, using the ordinary processes for soil analysis, can determine whether or not such infinitesimal amounts [of minerals] as are required by the crop are present or are not present in an available form in a soil. **1946** R. J. C. Atkinson *Field Archaeol.* ii. 62 Another technique which is becoming increasingly valuable to the excavator is that of soil-analysis. **1939** *Yearbk. Agric. 1938* (U.S. Dept. Agric.) 1163 *Soil association,* group of soils, with or without common characteristics, geographically associated in an individual pattern. **1952** L. M. Thompson *Soils & Soil Fertility* vi. 87 The most important grouping of series, in so far as the farmer is concerned, is that of the soil association. **1970** E. M. Bridges *World Soils* v. 34/1 The Scottish soil scientists have grouped topographically related soils developed on one geological parent material into a soil association. **1927** E. L. Worthen *Farm Soils* vi. 224 A soil auger, if available, should be used instead of a spade for sampling both surface soil and subsoil. **1975** *Sci. Amer.* May 93/1 The oak-hickory-tulip stand and the bigtooth aspen stand are on coarse, well-drained soil, which is aerated to as great a depth as I can reach with a two-meter soil auger. **1955** *Sun* (Baltimore) 26 Nov. 8/2 'Soil bank' is the current farm bloc slang for a scheme by which farmers are paid by the Government for taking acreage out of the production of surplus crops. **1958** J. K. Galbraith *Affluent Society* xx. 221 Wherever possible euphemisms were employed—as this is written, instead of taking acres out of production they are being put into a soil bank. **1977** J. L. Harper *Population Biol. Plants* iv. 95 In a sense there is a circular argument here; species which have pioneered the succession are strongly persistent in the soil-bank and so appear as pioneer species in the next succession on the area. Do they persist because they are pioneers or do they become pioneers because they have persisted. **1928** *Proc. & Papers 1st Internat. Congr. Soil Sci.* III. 325 Soil biology is essentially a science of observation and experimentation. **1967** Burges & Raw *Soil Biol.* p. vi, One of the stimulating developments in soil biology in recent years has been the general recognition that the soil cannot be studied solely from a chemical, microbiological, botanical or zoological stand-point. **1936** *Proc. Highway Res. Board* (U.S.) XVI. 324/2 Tests were conducted to determine the moisture-density relations of the raw soil and the soil-cement mixtures. *Ibid.* 348/2 Would the mixtures of soil-cement when compacted at optimum moisture to maximum density, maintain these characteristics under natural weathering conditions. **1950** *N.Z. Jrnl. Agric.* May 481/1 Soil cement (silty material mixed with cement) ..gives a building material which has a definite structural strength, besides being resistant to the action of water and frost. **1966** R. Ashworth *Highway Engin.* ix. 161 By far the greatest proportion of soil–cement construction has been carried out in the U.S.A. **1979** R. J. Salter *Highway Design & Constr.* i. 28 Soil cement may be formed by the addition of cement to a wide range of materials, including natural soils, chalk, pulverised fuel ash..and processed granular material. **1927** N. M. Comber *Introd. Scientific Study Soil* xiii. 130 Soil chemists and agriculturists frequently speak about soil 'types', and yet the definition of the various types is a matter which presents very considerable difficulty. **1959** J. D. Clark *Prehist. Southern Africa* ii. 36 It should be possible..to amass information concerning the main vegetation patterns..and for this we need the help of the..soil chemist. **1971** *Power Farming* Mar. 54/1 That handbook..is a chemical engineer's handbook and a 'natural' for all contractor services. Soil chemists have played only a minor role in assembling it. **1927** C. F. Marbut in tr. *Glinka's Great Soil Groups* p. ii, In the more detailed study of the soil profile, the clearer recognition of the nature of soil horizons, soil structures, soil colors and in the relation of soil chemistry to the processes of soil development in Nature, this book will be of great suggestive value. **1941** J. S. Huxley *Uniqueness of Man* vi. 103 What began as a study of local cattle diseases has turned into a problem of the soil chemistry of grasslands. **1972** J. G. Cruickshank *Soil Geogr.* i. 15 In this discussion we are not concerned with the foundation or the history of soil chemistry, soil physics,..and other member parts of soil science, but rather with the inception and growth of pedology within the last century. **1913** *Bull. Bur. Soils U.S. Dept. Agric.* No. 96. 8 A soil class..includes all soils having the same texture, such as sands, clays, loam, etc. **1951** *Soil Survey Man.* (U.S. Dept. Agric. Handbk. No. 18) 135 Soil class is observed in the field by feeling the soil with the fingers. **1900** R. Warington *Lect. Physical Properties Soil* p. xii, If seeds are to germinate in a soil,.. there must be a suitable soil climate. **1976** A. Young *Tropical Soils & Soil Survey* i. 7 The factor which directly influences soil-forming processes is soil climate rather than air climate. **1915** *Chem. Abstr.* IX. 1084 R. discusses the importance of soil colloids for agriculture. **1935** *Nature* 24 Aug. 307/2 Much attention was directed.. towards the base-exchange properties of soil colloids, particularly from the mineralogical point of view. **1970** J. A. Daji *Textbk. Soil Sci.* xiii. 120 Soil colloids are of two kinds: (1) inorganic and (2) organic... The organic colloid..is more commonly known as humus. **1952** *Sci. News Let.* 5 Jan. 8/2 The new soil conditioner changes the structure of clay making it porous and crumbly. **1976** L. F. Curtis et al. *Soils in Brit. Isles* xv. 285 Soil conditioners may be applied to add stability. **1978** Friedman & Sanders *Princ. Sedimentol.* v. 141/2 Zeolites..are mined from sedimentary deposits for use as fillers in the paper industry; as soil conditioners; [etc.]. **1932** *Yearbk. U.S. Dept. Agric.* 349 The national plan for soil and water conservation calls for the establishment of experiment stations. **1935** *U.S. Laws, Statutes* XLIX. I. 164 The Secretary of Agriculture shall establish an agency to be known as the 'Soil Conservation Service'. **1944** Auden *For Time Being* (1945) 90 The Committees on Fen-Drainage and Soil-Conservation. **1952** W. L. Miner *World of W. Faulkner* ii. 61 Since 1933 the various soil conservation programs..have done much for Lafayette county. **1971** *E. Afr. Standard* (Nairobi) 13 Apr. 2/1 The committee stressed that unlike in the colonial era, farmers in the rural areas should now take great pains in soil conservation. **1925** J. F. Cox *Crop Production & Soil Managem.* vii. 116 (*heading*) The elements of fertility, common soil deficiencies, and fertilizers carrying nitrogen, phosphorus and potassium. **1935** *Discovery* Oct. 294/1 Non-parasitic diseases of plants, due principally to soil deficiencies. **1896** *Nat. Geogr. Mag.* Nov. 368 (*heading*) The economic aspects of soil erosion. **1944** J. S. Huxley *Living in Revolution* iii. 30 It neglected conservation and amenities: the result was deforestation, soil erosion, the dust bowl. **1980** *Sci. Amer.* Sept. 114/2 Major problems related to land use, soil erosion and water pollution are likely to place further limits on the recovery of these nonconventional oil resources. **1920** W. W. Weir *Productive Soils* vii. 84 In some instances soil exhaustion may be attributed largely to the removal, mainly through cropping and leaching, of some one or all of the three named elements. **1934** A. Toynbee *Study of Hist.* I. 126 As regards the possibility of soil-exhaustion, an observation of latter-day native agriculture in the area..seems to show that a repeated clearing and burning-off of the tropical forest..does tend..to exhaust the soil. **1946** J. S. Huxley *Unesco* II. 28 It is possible to exploit new agricultural methods in a way that is..disastrous to agriculture itself, by causing soil exhaustion or erosion. **1957** G. E. Hutchinson *Treat. Limnol.* I. xvii. 896 The vitamins and accessory growth substances in soils and soil extracts. **1971** *Gloss. Soil Sci. Terms* (Soil Sci. Soc. Amer.) 15/2 *Soil extract,* the solution separated from a soil suspension or from a soil by filtration, centrifugation, suction, or pressure. **1921** Soil group [see *soil surveyor* below]. **1927** C. F. Marbut tr. *Glinka's Great Soil Groups* p. iii, Some of the great soil groups have not been studied by Russian investigators. **1954** W. D. Thornbury *Princ. Geomorphol.* iv. 76 Mature and old soils in areas that are climatically alike are strikingly similar, and it is possible to classify them in soil groups that developed under similar climatic conditions. **1972** J. G. Cruickshank *Soil Geogr.* iv. 110 There is only limited regional association in the world distribution of type profiles or great soil groups. **1976** A. Young *Tropical Soils & Soil Survey* xiii. 241 Although many of the soil groups [of the FAO classification of 1974] are natural soil types, this is structurally an artificial classification. **1923** *Soil Sci.* XVI. 97 The relative amount of silica in the gray horizon appears to be higher than in the soil horizons below. **1964** W. C. Putnam *Geology* x. 245/1 The C-horizon is essentially a transitional zone between the true soil horizons above and the unaltered parent material below. **1972** J. G. Cruickshank *Soil Geogr.* iii. 93 All soil horizons have a three-dimensional form, but those that have a clearly visible colour and texture..are perhaps the most convincing examples. **1961** *Listener* 12 Oct. 559/1 The changes that it [*sc.* soil science] recognizes in soil mantles and geological solids are termed 'weathering'. **1972** J. G. Cruickshank *Soil Geogr.* i. 28 Although the soil body or soil mantle obviously has a three-dimensional form, it has been represented traditionally by a so-called 'two-dimensional' section or slice called the soil profile. **1898** *Yearbk. U.S. Dept. Agric.* 43 One of the first necessities in the development of a new district or in the improvement of an established district is an accurate soil map of the locality. **1927** N. M. Comber *Introd. Scientific Study Soil* xiii. 132 Two important bases of classification..have been invoked in the attempts to prepare soil maps of agricultural significance. **1975** J. G. Evans *Environment Early Man Brit. Isles* vi. 138 W. F. Grimes was one of the first archaeologists to appreciate the importance of detailed soil maps in studying the settlement distribution of early man. **1920** W. W. Weir *Productive Soils* ii. 22 (*heading*) Soil mapping. **1928** *Proc. & Papers 1st Internat. Congr. Soil Sci.* IV. 34 In the soil survey of the United States the term Soil Type has been applied to the unit of soil mapping. **1972** J. G. Cruickshank *Soil Geogr.* i. 24 These men and many others, who have been responsible for selective soil mapping in countries like France..and Yugoslavia, have a history of soil research behind them going back to the nineteenth century. **1939** G. Clark *Archæol & Society* ii. 38 In chalk regions subjected to heavy ploughing, soil-marks, especially when seen from the air, preserve the sites of ancient monuments. **1950** *Oxoniensia* XV. 7 The best results of an air-survey of Celtic field-systems may be expected from photographs taken during the winter months... Soil-marks..will be more evident. **1963** E. S. Wood *Collins Field Guide to Archæol.* III. i. 284 Another type of mark is the soil-mark. When earthworks or barrows are levelled, or when grass is stripped, or on bare (ploughed) land, differences in soil-colour become apparent. **1920** *Engin. News-Record* 30 Sept. 630/1 (*heading*) Research in soil mechanics. **1965** A. B. Carson *Foundation Constr.* iii. 70/1 Despite the relative youth of the science of soil mechanics, the literature on the subject is extensive, particularly that relating the foundation structure to the..soil or rock formation upon which it will be built. **1977** A. Hallam *Planet Earth* 104 The engineering geologist works with experts in the related fields of soil mechanics and rock mechanics. [**1928** C. F. Marbut in *Proc. & Papers 1st Internat. Congr. Soil Sci.* IV. 51 *Phase,* a subdivision of the soil type covering departures from the typical soil characteristics, insufficient to justify the establishment of a new type, yet worthy of recognition.] **1939** *Yearbk. Agric. 1938* (U.S. Dept. Agric.) 1174 Soil phase. **1946** Lutz & Chandler *Forest Soils* xii. 424 Soil phases as currently recognized appear to have more significance for the agriculturist than for the forester. **1972** J. G. Cruickshank *Soil Geogr.* viii. 235 Soil phase..can only be shown in detail and with precision on maps of 1:10,000 scale or larger. **1937** C. A. Hogentogler et al. *Engin. Properties Soil* p. vii, Publications by the soil scientist, the soil physicist, the agronomist, the pedologist, and the geologist have been drawn upon. **1976** *Physics Bull.* Aug. 341/2 Soil physicists around the world are researching into an incredibly diverse range of phenomena, of which the diffusion of gases to and from plant roots..and the break-up of soil by tillage implements are just a few examples. **1900** R. Warington *Lect. Physical Properties Soil* p. xi, The only early investigation on soil physics is that of Schübler, made more than sixty years ago. **1935** *Nature* 24 Aug. 307/1 In the Soil Physics Section, the main interest centred round problems of soil moisture. **1972** [see *soil chemistry* above]. **1976** *Physics Bull.* Aug. 341/2 Soil physics is the branch of soil science that is concerned with the physical constitution and geometrical structure of soil, with the potentials and movements of water, gases and heat in soil, and with the deformation of soil in response to mechanical stress. **1927** *Q. Jrnl. Geol. Soc.* LXXXIII. 190 Soil-polygons are divided into (*a*) 'mud-polygons', containing few or no stones, and (*b*) 'stone-polygons', in which stones are arranged in curious patterns over the surface of the mud. **1963** D. W. & E. E. Humphries tr. *Termier's Erosion & Sedimentation* iv. 86 The periglacial zones are equally rich in detrital material and display phenomena completely comparable with those of hot deserts: loess, reg, soil polygons, 'dreikanters' and dunes. **1967** M. J. Coe *Ecol. Alpine Zone Mt. Kenya* 71 On ridge tops, which are usually scattered with boulders and small stones, soil polygons are particularly common. **1906, 1923** Soil profile [see *profile *sb.* 4 d]. **1928** *Forestry* II. 15 A natural basis for the classification of soils..resulted from a study of what have come to be known as soil profiles, vertical exposures of sections of soil down to the unaltered parent rock. **1954** W. D. Thornbury *Princ. Geomorphol.* iv. 76 A mature soil profile exhibits well-developed horizons. **1972** J. G. Cruickshank *Soil Geogr.* i. 28 Sometimes the soil profile is accepted as the basic unit of soil study. **1940** C. A. Heiland *Geophysical Explor.* x. 646 As an example of the galvanic application of intermediate frequency methods, the soil resistivity bridge..is illustrated. **1964** R. F. Ficchi *Electrical Interference* viii. 153 Probably the biggest stumbling block in such analytical calculations is the vaguely defined soil-resistivity measurements. **1967** *Gloss. Terms Gas Industry* (*B.S.I.*) 68 *Soil resistivity survey,* the determination of the electrical resistivity of the soil at intervals along the route of a main to assist in designing a cathodic protection system. **1902** *Bull. U.S. Fish Commission 1901* XXI. 58 For taking soil samples an instrument was made after drawings in Delbecque. **1975** *New Yorker* 28 Apr. 112/2 District-level officials are now collecting soil samples, so that in the future they can advise the co-ops on the most productive way to use their land. **1902** Soil sampler [see *sampler *sb.*[2] 2]. **1950** *N.Z. Jrnl. Agric.* June 553/3 Holes may be dug with a spade, sunk with a post-hole borer, or cored with a soil sampler [in order to examine the structure of the soil]. **1927** E. L. Worthern *Farm Soils* 409/1 (Index), Soil sampling. **1958** J. Blish *Case of Conscience* (1959) iv. 41 We will start a soil-sampling programme. **1960** *Farmer & Stockbreeder* 9 Feb. 97/3 Soil-sampling for ectoparasitic eel-worms may be worth a thought. **1915** *Chem. Abstr.* IX. 1084 (*heading*) The development of soil science from the earliest attempts to the beginning of the twentieth century. **1916** (*periodical title*) Soil science. **1935** *Nature* 24 Aug. 308/1 The very large number of papers dealing with the practical side of soil science..emphasised the dominating influence exerted on the development of soil science by modern economic conditions. **1938, 1958** [see *pedology]. **1972** *Nature* 28 Jan. 231/2 The most characteristic Russian contribution to science was soil science. **1979** W. L. Pritchett *Properties & Managem. Forest Soils* p. v, Most of the basic principles of soil science apply to forest soils as well as to agricultural soils. **1921** *Proc. 41st Ann. Meeting Soc. Promotion Agric. Sci., 1920* (U.S.) 117 The soil scientist must be concerned primarily with the accumulation or assimilation of knowledge concerning the soil without reference to the use to be made of that knowledge. **1958** *Times* 1 July (Agric. Suppl.) p. ii/2 The plant breeder and the soil scientist have worked hand in hand; together they are responsible for disproving the gloomy prophecies of increasing world hunger so commonly heard only 10 years ago. **1928** *Proc. & Papers 1st Internat. Congr. Soil Sci.* IV. 54 *Soil separate,* one of the several grain-size groups into which the soil is separated by mechanical analysis. **1951** *Soil Survey Man.* (U.S. Dept. Agric. Handbk. No. 18) 207 (*heading*) Size limits of soil separates from two schemes of analysis. **1972** J. G. Cruickshank *Soil Geogr.* ii. 55 These categories of particle size—sometimes called the soil separates—are mixed in any soil into what is called its texture. **1905** *Field Operations of U.S. Bur. Soils, 1904* 35 Whenever there is a general relationship between these two classes of soils, due either to their geological origin, their method of formation, or their location within an area, a common distinctive locality name is used, and the soils thus grouped together are called a soil series. **1946** L. D. Stamp *Britain's Struct. & Scenery* xi. 95 Within each soil series there may be a considerable range of texture which is important ecologically. **1972** J. G. Cruickshank *Soil Geogr.* i. 29 A soil series is a composite unit, but being the basic unit of soil mapping it is expected to be predominantly composed of one named soil profile type and confined to one parent material. **1962** *Listener* 25 Jan. 174/2 The ground beyond the filter-bed is what we call soil-sick. **1934** Webster, Soil sickness. **1938** *Encycl. Brit. Bk. of Year* 111/1 Among more recent concepts is that of the possibility of beneficial root-excretions, to which the older view ascribed toxic properties and the responsibility for soil-sickness. **1960** *Farmer & Stockbreeder* 9 Feb. 97/1 We have long been familiar with the potato root and sugar-beet eelworm..but other types are now known to cause 'soil sickness'. **1901** *Bull. Div. Soils U.S. Dept. Agric.* No. 17. 5 Soil solutions from which plants draw their food are for the most part aqueous solutions of the mineral components of the soil. **1957** G. E. Hutchinson *Treat. Limnol.* I. viii. 556 The over-all composition of soil solutions is in fact very similar to that of average river water. **1973** *Sci. Amer.* May 48/2 Perhaps 5 percent of a plant's dry weight is minerals. Eight elements account for the bulk of this amount... All are normally present in the 'soil solution', as the water of the soil is called, at very low concentrations. **1934** *Proc. Amer. Soc. Testing Materials* XXXIV. ii. 737 Investigations along the line suggested by Mr. Housel are also considered in our soil stabilization work. **1950** *Engineering* 13 Jan. 44/3 They were used in conjunction with processes of soil stabilisation in which the stability of the soil under traffic load is improved by adding clay, sand or gravel. **1969** Capper & Cassie *Mech. Engin. Soils* (ed. 5) xi. 234 An important method of soil stabilization is by the use of resins. **1910** *12th Rep. Michigan Acad. Sci.* 52 A comparison of the Asulkan and Greenland soil stripes with the great barrancas, suggests that the width of ridge..is in some way a function of the viscosity of the rock paste. **1954** W. D. Thornbury *Princ. Geomorphol.* iv. 89 Earth stripes or soil stripes are similar to stone stripes except that they have finer textures. **1900** *Yearbk. U.S. Dept. Agric. 1899* 26 A detailed soil survey has been undertaken of the soils of Maryland. **1924** [see *separate *sb.* 6]. **1966** R. Ashworth *Highway Engin.* iii. 49 The soil survey involves an exploration of the soil conditions along the proposed road alignment by means of boreholes or trial pits. **1972** J. G. Cruickshank *Soil Geogr.* i. 23 Some of the later private surveys have..introduced soil terms and definitions adopted later by the national soil surveys. **1921** *Proc. 41st Ann. Meeting Soc. Promotion Agric. Sci., 1920* (U.S.) 119 Before the soil surveyor had mapped textural soil units over any considerable area he discovered that these units are not all alike, that they are not ultimate soil units therefore but soil groups. **1902** *Instructions to Field Parties & Descr. Soil Types* (U.S. Bur. of Soils) 15 The selection of a provisional name for each soil type should be made, and in all correspondence and reports this name should be used when speaking of the type. **1928** *Proc. & Papers 1st Internat. Congr. Soil Sci.* IV. 41 The soil type is a subdivision of the soil series based primarily and almost wholly on the texture of the surface soil... The term Soil Type has been used by some writers with a more inclusive meaning, sometimes to indicate the general characteristics of the soils of a region. **1954** W. D. Thornbury *Princ. Geomorphol.* iv. 78 A common soil series in the middle western states is the Miami series... Included in this series are such soil types as the Miami fine sandy loam, Miami loam, Miami silt loam, and Miami silty clay loam. **1967** M. J. Coe *Ecol. Alpine Zone Mt. Kenya* 71 Soil movement and deformation are of great significance in governing the distribution of soil types and in their effect on vegetation. **1972** J. G. Cruickshank *Soil Geogr.* i. 26 In 1904 the soil series was introduced to include all soil types developed on the same parent material. **1926** *Sci. Amer.* Feb. 97/3 Erosion or soil wash is impoverishing our sloping farm lands. **1962** Soil wash [see *sailab]. **1892** J. M. H. Munro *Soils & Manures* i. 25 What this soil water contains we may see by examining the water running from the drain-pipes of any arable field when no crop is growing on it. **1921** *Discovery* Feb. 47/1 Plants require moisture, and in taking this up by the root-hairs, they also take up their food, consisting of salts dissolved in the soil water. **1976** *Physics Bull.* Aug. 343/3 One of the main obstacles to progress in the physics of soil water is the lack of quantitative methods for describing adequately the geometrical structure of soil at its various levels of organization.

soil, *sb.*^{3} Add: **II. 3. c.** Dirt or discolouring matter on cloth.

1959 Meredith & Hearle *Physical Methods Investigation Textiles* xiv. 376 Both the soiling of textiles and the removal of dirt from them can be investigated by using soils containing radioactive materials. **1968** E. R. Trotman *Textile Scouring & Bleaching* iii. 74 It [*sc.* the material] is then scoured under controlled conditions with the detergent under investigation, and the amount of soil removed is measured. **1975** J. Labarthe *Elem. Textiles* vii. 325 Soil may be deposited on and be made to cling to some of these fabrics as the result of static electricity.

IV. 7. (Further examples.) In *techn.* use, liquid matter likely to contain excrement. Cf. *waste *sb.* 12 c.

1928 E. T. Swinson *Sanitation of Buildings* xiv. 246 Lead pipes used for soil, ventilating, and waste purposes in London must be of *drawn* lead. **1973** H. King *Do your own Home Plumbing* ix. 87 Many older houses have a two-pipe plumbing system consisting of separate waste and soil services. **1977** E. Hall *Home Plumbing* vii. 57/1 From the point of view of drainage, bidets are regarded as being 'waste', not 'soil' fittings.

9. soil-pipe, *spec.* (see quot. 1928); (further examples); **soil-release** *a.*, causing the loosening of dirt from cloth during washing; also as *sb.*, such a substance.

1876 W. P. Buchan *Plumbing* xiv. 90 When soil-pipes and waste-pipes are put up *inside* the house, great care should be taken that they are properly fitted up. **1928** H. E. Babbitt *Plumbing* ix. 156 A soil pipe is any drainage pipe which carries human excrement... A waste pipe carries waste water which does not include human excrement. **1962** *New Statesman* 21 Dec. 897/3 Any fit man, given a certain amount of practice, can climb a soil pipe up to the first floor. **1978** T. Pettit *Home Plumbing* x. 53/2 Other waste pipes can be run into the soil pipe by means of a range of solvent-welded bossed fittings. **1969** A. J. Hall *Stand. Handbk. Textiles* (ed. 7) v. 340 To overcome such difficulties..'soil-release' agents have become available. These can be applied to the textile materials..during their production, or immediately before washing. **1969** [see *Oxford cloth* s.v. *Oxford]. **1977** D. S. Lyle *Performance Textiles* v. 219 Soil release finishes permit relatively easy removal of soils (especially oily soils) in laundering.

soil, *v.*^{1} Add: **2.** Also *spec.*, of a child or patient: to make foul by defecation (esp. when involuntary). Freq. *absol.*, to defecate involuntarily. Hence **soi·ler.**

1943, etc. [implied in *soiling *vbl. sb.*^{1} 1 b]. **1943** *Our Towns* (Women's Group on Public Welfare) iii. 85 The mother of the enuretic and the soiler does not teach her child..control of its natural functions. **1956** *Brit. Med. Jrnl.* 15 Dec. 1390/1 The mother or other adults show no resentment or disgust when the child soils the floor or the body of the person caring for it. *a* **1961** in Webster, s.v. ^{1}*soil*, Patients also showed infantile reactions..continually wetting and soiling. **1977** *New Society* 17 Feb. 333/1 When she started school she still wet and soiled by day and night.

soilage. Restrict † *Obs.* to senses in Dict. and add: **3.** The act or process of soiling; the condition of being soiled. *U.S. rare.*

1926 *Publishers' Weekly* 22 May 1679/2 One of the practical problems of retail bookselling is the depreciation of stock due to soilage.

soile: the variation also occurs in Newfoundland English (see *Dict. Newfoundland Eng.*). Cf. *swile.

soiled, *ppl. a.*^{1} Add: *Comb.* (Earlier and later examples); **soiled dove** *Austral.* and *N. Amer. slang.*, a prostitute.

1882 *Sydney Slang Dict.* 8/1 *Soiled doves*, the 'midnight meeting' term for prostitutes and 'gay' ladies generally. **1897** 'S. Grand' *Beth Book* xvi. 140 A white sheet filched from the soiled-clothes bag. **1907** *Yesterday's Shopping* (1969) 325/3 Soiled Linen Bags..Sack shape. **1929** Soiled dove [see *hustler 2 c]. **1939** M. Allingham *Mr Campion & Others* 181 He's only over here for four days and yet he's brought..a neat little soiled-linen bag embroidered with his monogram. **1962** E. Lucia *Klondike Kate* iii. 95 The line between the dance-hall girls and those of Lousetown was a thin one..because the soiled doves from across the river intermingled in the variety halls to pick up customers.

soiling, *vbl. sb.*^{1} Add: **1. b.** Defecation (usu. when caused by incontinence or stress in a patient or child).

1943 *Our Towns* (Women's Group on Public Welfare) iii. 83 Some evacuated children were guilty of deliberate wetting and soiling. **1960** I. Bennett *Delinquent & Neurotic Children* iii. 113 Faecal incontinence, and soiling episodes. **1980** *Jrnl. R. Soc. Med.* LXXIII. 217 The affected children themselves are liable to behavioural problems such as temper tantrums, soiling and school refusal.

soilless, *a.*^{1} Add: **a.** (Further example.)

1971 *Daily Tel.* 2 Oct. 8/3 Put each young plant in a pot of its own..using..one of the peat-based soilless mixtures.

b. Applied to methods of growing plants without soil. Cf. *hydroponics.

1938 *Sat. Even. Post* 20 Aug. 14/2 Having caught the public imagination, soilless farming has the trappings of another 'bubble'. **1946** *Soil Sci.* LXII. 71 Artificial or soilless cultures have been used very extensively during the last 30 years in plant nutrition studies. **1974** D. Harris *Hydroponics* ii. 45 Although called variously 'aggregate culture', 'soil-less culture', 'nutriculture', or 'chemiculture', Dr Gericke's term is so universally used that all forms of growing plants without soil are loosely referred to as 'hydroponics'.

soirée, *sb.* Add: (Earlier examples.) *soirée dansante*: see *dansant *a.*

1793 F. Burney *Jrnl.* 8 Apr. (1972) II. 58 He asked how my Mother did? I said if he came any *soiree*, he would probably see. **1802** C. Wilmot *Let.* 3 Jan. in T. U. Sadleir *Irish Peer on Continent* (1920) 22 We have had abundant specimens of Plays, Balls, Soirées, Thé's, &c.

‖**soit** (swa), *int.* [Fr., third pers. sing. pres. subj. of *etre* to be.] So be it.

1889 E. Dowson *Let.* 16 Nov. (1967) 116 Your letter greatly cheered me—especially by the hope it held out of a meeting at Philippi. Soit! **1912** T. E. Lawrence *Let.* 23 June (1954) 217 It seems the Turks suffered a defeat the other day somewhere: *soit*: it won't hurt Turkey. *a* **1935** —— *Mint* (1955) 141 The R.A.F. claims to order our sitting and standing, our lying down and our going forth. *Soit*: but let its direction be extremely good. **1958** L. Durrell *Mountolive* iv. 90 Well, *soit!*

‖**soixante-neuf** (swasant nöf). [Fr., lit. 'sixty-nine'.] Simultaneous cunnilingus and fellatio. Cf. *sixty-nine* s.v. *sixty *a.* 2 b.

1888 P. Perret *Tableaux Vivants* xiii. 109 In familiar language this divine variant of pleasure is called: *faire soixante neuf* (literally, to do '69'). **1970** E. M. Brecher *Sex Researchers* iv. 98 By a delicate turn of phrase, van de Velde awards his post-Victorian *nihil obstat* to the practice of *soixante-neuf*. **1973** M. Amis *Rachel Papers* 53 The other couple were writhing about still, now seemingly poised for a session of fully robed soixante-neuf.

sôk, var. *souk.

Soka Gakkai (sōka gakai). Also **Sōka-gakkai, Sokagakki.** [Jap. f. *so* to create + *ka* value + *Gakkai* (learned) society.] In Japan, a lay religious group whose teachings are based on Buddhism.

1958 *Jap. Christian Quarterly* Apr. 104 (*title*) Sōka Gakkai, strange Buddhist sect. **1964** *Asia Mag.* 18 Oct. 3/2 'Let us propagate Buddhism with high and bright spirit to save the world!' The dynamic society with such a transcendental goal is Sokagakkai—the startling new Japanese society. **1964** *Listener* 24 Dec. 998/2 The Soka Gakkai—a kind of mixture of Moral Rearmament and Goldwater republicanism. **1968** P. S. Buck *People of Japan* xiv. 174 The Soka Gakkai philosophy is an ancient one based on the only Buddhist sect which was, like Christianity, intolerant of all other religions. **1974** *Encycl. Brit. Micropædia* IX. 328/2 The Sōka-gakkai follows an intensive policy of conversion..which increased its membership within a seven-year period (1951–57) from 3,000 families to 765,000 families.

Sokol (so·kol). [Czech, lit. 'falcon'.] A Slav gymnastic society first formed in Prague in 1862 (and disbanded in Czechoslovakia in 1952), bearing the falcon as its ensign, and aiming to promote a communal spirit and physical fitness. Also, (a member of) a club in this society.

1910 W. S. Monroe *Bohemia* x. 189 The organization of the Sokols in 1862 has undoubtedly been the most forceful factor in the social unification of the Bohemian people. *Ibid.* 194 A great gathering of all the Sokol unions of the world was called at Prague in 1887. **1915** *Scotsman* 10 Feb. 10/1 The gymnastic volunteer organizations ('sokols') which are popular among all the Slav nationalities of Austria. **1920** *Public Opinion* 2 July 17/2 Over 100,000 Sokols have responded to the call and of that number 50,000 have been selected—27,000 men and 23,000 women. **1925** E. I. Robson *Wayfarer in Czecho-Slovakia* viii. 126 It is a fine sight to see a really big Sokol exhibition, hundreds of men or girls moving like one. **1941** *Ann. Reg. 1940* 200 The systematic arrest of leading Czechs..teachers, and Sokol workers. **1966** *Inland* (Inland Steel Co., Chicago) Autumn 15/2 In Czech settlements the athletic club might still be a *sokol*. **1978** *Chicago* June 56/2 The program will include folk dancing as well as calisthenics and apparatus work. Sponsored by the Central District of the American Sokol Organization.

sol (sǫl), *sb.*^{6} *Physical Chem.* [Orig. a suffix f. the first syllable of *solution* (as in *alcosol, *hydrosol).] **1.** A liquid solution or suspension of a colloid. Cf. *gel *sb.*

1899, etc. [see *gel *sb.*]. **1936** W. Stiles *Introd. Princ. Plant Physiol.* ii. 16 If the ability to flow is our criterion of the sol state, then protoplasm is usually, but by no means always, a sol; but there are other indicators of the colloidal state such as elasticity, rigidity, and inhibition, and these are gel characteristics. **1940** Glasstone *Textbk. Physical Chem.* xiv. 1213 The characteristic colors shown by many sols are related in some degree to the particle size; in the course of coagulation, for example, the color of a gold sol changes from red to violet and then to blue. **1970** Ambrose & Easty *Cell Biol.* xv. 479 When two hydrophilic sols carrying opposite charges are mixed, viscous drops known as coacervates often form instead of a continuous liquid phase.

2. *Comb.*: **sol–gel**, used *attrib.* with reference to the interconversion of sol and gel.

1915 W. W. Taylor *Chem. Colloids* i. 10 (*heading*) Sol-gel transformation. **1922** *Jrnl. Amer. Chem. Soc.* XLIV. 1313 (*heading*) The sol-gel equilibrium in protein systems. **1951** *New. Biol.* X. 14 These interchanges, the so-called sol-gel transformations, are constantly going on in the amoeba. **1967** *Oceanogr. & Marine Biol.* V. 191 Cytoplasmic movement results from sol-gel reactions within cells.

sol (sǫl), *sb.*^{7} [f. L. *sōl* sun: cf. Sol *sb.*^{1}] A solar day on the planet Mars (24 hours 39 minutes).

1976 *Times* 22 July 1/8 The squat little lander seemed to get through its first sol (as the Martian day..is called) without any problems. **1977** *Sci. Amer.* Nov. 58/3 The release of gas tapered off soon after the first sol. **1979** *New Yorker* 5 Feb. 41 On sol 8..the craft's sampler arm extended straight out and then dropped to the ground.

-sol, an ending [f. L. *solum* floor, ground, soil] used to form the names of different kinds and states of soil, as *lithosol* s.v. *litho-, *pergelisol.

sola, *a.* **2.** (Earlier Amer. examples.)

1737 W. Stephens *Jrnl.* 27 Oct. in *Jrnl. Proc. in Georgia* (1742) I. 5 He brought a small Box with sola Bills for a large Sum. **1750** *Colonial Rec. Georgia* (1906)

VI. 323 The last Issue of Sola Bills was not sufficient to defray the Estimate to Michaelmas.

Solacet (sǫ·lăset). Also **solacet.** [f. SOL(UBLE *a.* + ACET(ATE.] A proprietary name for any of a range of azo-dyestuffs which contain sulphate ester groups and were formerly much used for direct dyeing of artificial fibres.

1938 *Times* 11 Jan. 9/5 Another is the 'solacet' range, produced within the last half of 1937, for giving bright fast colours to acetate rayons. **1939** *Trade Marks Jrnl.* 17 May 647/1 *Solacet*.. Water soluble dyes for cellulose acetate silk. British Dyestuffs Corporation Limited. **1952** K. VENKATARAMAN *Chem. Synthetic Dyes* I. xxi. 646 The Solacets undergo no chemical change during the dyeing process. **1955** *Official Gaz.* (U.S. Patent Office) 7 June TM 7 *Solacet*.. For water soluble dyes for cellulose acetate silk. **1964** E. R. TROTMAN *Dyeing & Chem. Technol. of Textile Fibres* (ed. 3) xxiii. 515 The Solacet dyes..show little redistribution of colour on continued boiling. **1971** R. L. M. ALLEN *Colour Chem.* vi. 71 In consequence of the development of dispersed dyes with improved dyeing and fastness properties the Solacet range has now been superseded.

solapsone (sǭlæ·psōᵘn). *Pharm.* [f. SOL(UBLE *a.* + *d*)*apsone*, name of a drug of which solapsone is a more soluble derivative (f. *di*(*p*-*amino*ph*enyl*)*sul*ph*one*).] A white powder given as tablets or by injection of an aqueous solution for the treatment of leprosy; the hydrated tetrasodium salt of di(*p*-3-phenyl-1, 3-disulphopropylamino)phenylsulphone, $C_{30}H_{28}N_2O_{14}S_5Na_4.xH_2O$.

1952 *Brit. Pharm. Codex* Suppl. 66 Solapsone consists mainly of the tetrasodium salt. **1959** R. G. COCHRANE *Leprosy in Theory & Practice* xvii. 212 The following sulphone drugs are those most commonly employed in the treatment of leprosy: (*a*) the parent sulphone.. Dapsone (B.P.)..(*b*) Sulphetrone (Solapsone (B.P.)) administered orally or parenterally; [etc.]. **1974** R. M. KIRK et al. *Surgery* ii. 23 Specific treatment [of leprosy] is with dapsone..or solapsone (Sulphetrone) given orally, or by injection,..twice weekly. **1977** *Martindale's Extra Pharmacopoeia* (ed. 27) 1505/1 In general, the results with solapsone have not been impressive and it has been superseded by more active drugs.

solar, *a.* and *sb.*[1] Add: **A.** *adj.* **1. d.** (Further examples.)

1876 J. ERICSSON *Centennial Exhibition* xlv. 561 The solar engine..is composed of three distinct parts—the engine, the steam-generator, and the mechanism by means of which the..energy of the sun's rays..is increased. **1880** J. P. MAUZEY *U.S. Patent* 227,028 27 Apr. 1, I..have invented a new and Improved Solar Heater. **1914** *Metal Worker, Plumber & Steam Fitter* LXXXII. 758/2 Ordinarily a solar heater is mounted upon the roof of the house. **1929** C. G. ABBOT in *Smithsonian Sci. Ser.* II. ix. 222 The solar cooker is a delightful luxury. **1955** E. BURGESS *Frontier to Space* viii. 150 The system envisaged is a solar engine which would intercept a relatively minute portion of the 92,000 calories which each square centimetre of the Sun's surface radiates every minute. **1962** A. SHEPARD in *Into Orbit* 83 There is a solar distiller in the kit which will help you convert salt water into the pint of water you need a day to stay alive. **1967** *Daily Tel.* 30 Jan. 10/6 Cooking food at practically no cost has been achieved by scientists at the Hebrew University by the use of a 'solar cooker'. **1979** *Tucson Mag.* Apr. 62/3 A solar heater costs between $2000 and $2600 to buy and install.

e. Concerned with or pertaining to the utilization of the sun's rays as a source of energy.

1972 *Guardian* 17 Oct. 15/6 Ambitious schemes..are under study—including a huge solar farm on earth feeding heat to power stations. **1979** *Washington Star* 8 May A14/2 The crowd wasn't sure how well it liked *him*, impeccably solar though he is when it comes to energy. **1979** *N.Y. Rev. Bks.* 17 May 15/1 It will take a long time for solar energy to become the dominant source of world energy. It will first be necessary to eliminate inefficiencies in solar technologies. **1979** *Guardian* 6 Sept. 4/4 Solar systems were immediately viable.

4. a. (Further examples.)

1884 *Nature* 3 Jan. 217/2 This heater..contains the acting medium, steam or air, employed to transfer solar energy to the motor. **1939** A. HUXLEY *Many a Summer* I. x. 130 It's a gadget..for making use of solar energy. **1976** *National Observer* (U.S.) 21 Feb. 8/3 He's living in a house heated mostly by solar energy.

7. solar battery, a solar cell, or an assembly of such cells; **solar cell,** a photovoltaic device which converts solar radiation into electrical energy; **solar collector,** a device which absorbs solar radiation as heat or reflects it to a focus; **solar flare** = *FLARE *sb.*[1] 1 b; **solar furnace,** an apparatus in which high temperature reactions are carried out at the focus of a system which concentrates the sun's radiation, usually by reflection; **solar glass,** tinted glass for large windows; **solar house** orig. *U.S.*, a solar-heated house; **solar neutrino unit,** a unit used in expressing the detected flux of neutrinos from the sun, equal to 10^{-36} neutrino captures per target atom per second; abbrev. SNU s.v. *S 4 a; **solar paddle,** a large, flat array of solar cells projecting from a spacecraft like a paddle; **solar panel,** a panel designed to absorb the sun's rays for the purpose of generating electricity (by means of solar cells) or heating; **solar pillar** = *sun-pillar* s.v. SUN *sb.* 13; **solar plasma** = *solar wind* below; **solar pond, pool,** a pool or lake of very salty water in which convection is inhibited, allowing considerable heating of the bottom water by solar radiation; **solar power,** power derived more or less directly from solar radiation; **solar sail,** a surface designed to utilize the pressure of solar radiation to provide the propulsive force for a spacecraft to which it is attached; so **solar sailing** *vbl. sb.*; **solar salt,** salt obtained by allowing sea water to evaporate in sunlight; **solar still,** a still, often portable, in which solar radiation is employed to evaporate salty or impure water and produce fresh water; **solar wind,** the stream of ions and electrons which constantly emanates from the sun and which permeates the solar system.

1954 *N.Y. Times* 26 Apr. 1/2 A solar battery, the first of its kind, which converts useful amounts of the sun's radiation directly and efficiently into electricity, has been constructed. **1962** SIMPSON & RICHARDS *Physical Princ. Junction Transistors* iv. 73 Most of the radiation from the sun is in the region of 1·0eV and above so that 'solar batteries' can be made from germanium or silicon. The efficiency of the process is greater when silicon is used and commercial solar batteries (sometimes called 'solar cells') are at present made from this material. **1978** W. PALZ *Solar Electr.* iii. 179 The direct conversion of sunlight into electric power is achieved by means of solar batteries, made up of solar cells. **1955** G. L. PEARSON in *Bell Lab. Rec.* July 241/1 The Bell Solar Battery consists of a number of individual silicon solar cells. **1962** [see *solar battery* above]. **1967** *New Scientist* 25 May 463/2 The *Mariner IV* solar cell surface..provided power for the first close photographs of the planet Mars. **1980** *Solar Energy* XXIV. facing p. 1 (*caption*) The world's largest solar cell electric power generation station... The 60kW system consists of nearly 98,000 individual silicon solar cells. **1955** *Trans. Conf. Use of Solar Energy* (Tucson, Ariz.) II. I. vi. 75 For optimum performance a solar collector should face true south (north in the southern hemisphere). **1976** *Toronto Star* 24 Jan. E1/4 A well-insulated detached house requires about 35,000 kilowatt hours of energy per year to heat it. A solar collector of the size on the Mississauga house would be able to supply about half of the heat needed. **1980** *Solar Energy* XXV. facing p. 1 (*caption*) Giant parabolic dish solar collectors ..have produced efficiencies of 71 per cent at 750°F operating temperature. **1938** *Nature* 17 Sept. 500/2 It would..scarcely be permissible to deduce from the single observation of Carrington..that the three phenomena, solar flare, radio fade-out and..magnetic disturbance, were associated. **1957** *Practical Wireless* XXXIII. 722/1 Solar flares are shortlived, sudden increases in the intensity of the surface brightness in the neighbourhood of sunspots. **1979** C. KILIAN *Icequake* vii. 120 Your plane's electronics go bonkers now and then when another solar flare hits. **1924** M. E. MOREAU *U.S. Patent 1,479,923* The primary object of the present invention is to provide a new and improved solar furnace for producing an intense heat to be used for scientific purposes. **1951** *Bull. Amer. Ceramic Soc.* XXX. 163/1 A new and important instrument for high-temperature research is the recently developed solar furnace, which, by using the radiant energy of the sun, is able to produce extremely high temperatures in a small area. **1974** *Encycl. Brit. Micropædia* IX. 330/3 Because of its unique ability to heat materials for long periods without contamination, the solar furnace has become an important tool in high-temperature research. **1979** J. F. KREIDER *Medium & High Temp. Solar Processes* vi. 232 (*caption*) White Sands solar furnace showing the single heliostat on the right, the concentrator on the left, and flux control shutters in the center. **1977** *Whitaker's Almanack 1978* 1058/1 The window wall was designed to contain outer sheets of brown solar glass. **1978** J. MCNEIL *Consultant* iii. 55 The Waterman building soared in dark grey metal and matching tinted solar glass. **1946** *Fortune Mag.* Apr. 166 Solar houses will be erected in forty-eight states. **1957** *Economist* 28 Sept. 1027/1 The Massachusetts Institute of Technology is building a series of 'solar houses'. **1976** *Toronto Star* 24 Jan. E1/2 At Provident House, another experimental solar house now being built in King Township, the storage tank contains 60,300 gallons of water. **1970, 1976** Solar neutrino unit [see SNU s.v. *S 4 a]. **1980** *McGraw-Hill Yearbk. Sci. & Technol.* 397/1 The low rate, if attributed to solar neutrinos, would correspond to a neutrino capture rate in the tank of 0·41±0·07 per day. To compare this rate to [*sic*] the theory, one expresses the neutrino capture rate in solar neutrino units... The rate corresponds to 2·2±0·4 SNU. **1962** *Listener* 29 Nov. 902/1 The probe was first instructed to 'find the Sun'—by means of sun-sensors on the bottom of the vehicle and on the 'solar paddles'. **1968** *New Scientist* 2 May 230/2 An even greater increase in power can be obtained by adding solar paddles to the stabilised platform. **1964** *IEEE Trans. Aerospace* II. 770/1 The solar panel was set on a surface plate with a piece of frosted glass flush against the end of the panel. **1968** *Times* 16 Oct. 8/8 The spacecraft has large solar panels. **1974** P. DICKINSON *Poison Oracle* i. 13 The roof offered the widest possible expanse to the solar panels that provided much of the energy for the palace's gadgetry. **1976** *Pract. Householder* Nov. (Heating Suppl.) 23/2 The past summer..produced astonishingly high air temperature and sunshine hours so that reservoir temperature and storage tank levels rose and solar panels heated the water quickly. **1978** *Sci. Amer.* Apr. 149/1 The solar pillar, a commoner phenomenon, is a vertical shaft of light extending upward from the sun. **1962** *Listener* 29 Nov. 902/1 The solar plasma (commonly called 'solar wind'), which consists of low-energy charged particles which continually stream outward from the Sun. **1972** A. HEWISH in C. P. Sonett et al. *Solar Wind* vii. 477 Radio waves traversing the solar plasma are scattered by irregularities of plasma density. **1961** *Sci. News Let.* 12 Aug. 106/2 Instead of using vast expanses of expensive mirrors, a solar pond traps heat in shallow water. **1971** *Sci. Amer.* June 127/1 The hot, salty water is selectively withdrawn from the solar ponds and used to drive a generator. **1979** *Nature* 11 Jan. 91/2 A solar pond is a water-filled pond, 1–2 m deep, with a blackened bottom for greater heat absorption and a gradually increasing salt concentration towards the base to eliminate convection, which is the main cause of heat loss. **1960** *Daily Tel.* 18 Aug. 16/2 (*heading*) Solar pools as rival to nuclear power stations. **1975** *Globe & Mail* (Toronto) 15 Dec. 2/8 Scientists have failed to find a way of releasing the potential energy at the bottom of solar pools where water approaches the boiling point. **1979** *Arizona Daily Star* 5 Aug. (Advt. Section) 20/2 Featuring solar pool, putting green, horse facilities & country atmosphere. [**1908** *Sci. Amer.* 8 Feb. 97/1 (*heading*) A new solar power plant.] **1915** *Jrnl. R. Soc. Arts* LXIII. 564/1 Solar power was quite within the range of practical matters. **1956** *Sci. Amer.* July 97/2 Any attempt to produce solar power means collecting the energy falling on a large area. **1976** *Times* 26 Mar. (Energy Suppl.) p. vi/4 If an equal number of existing houses were converted, domestic solar power could then substitute for about 4 per cent of Britain's energy needs. **1960** *Aeroplane* XCIX. 693/1 Another interesting concept which has not yet really undergone feasibility determination is that of the solar sail. With this device, a space 'ship' may some day be able literally to sail through interplanetary space. **1978** *Listener* 6 July 13/3 The 'solar sail' makes space travel in the inner solar system very cheap. **1960** *Aeroplane* XCIX. 744/1 The subject of solar-sailing. **1973** C. SAGAN *Cosmic Connection* xxiii. 162 Solar sailing, the use of the pressure of sunlight and of the protons and electrons in the solar wind for tripping through the solar system. **1861** J. S. MUSPRATT *Chem., Theoret., Pract., & Analytical* II. 906/1 This Onondaga solar or coarse salt is unsurpassed..in the world. **1950** *Thorpe's Dict. Appl. Chem.* (ed. 4) X. 844/2 Some solar salt-factories produce high-quality table-salt by re-dissolving solar salt in water, purifying the resultant brine, and then evaporating it. **1972** *Times* 16 Oct. 19/7 Ventures ranging from solar salt to uranium. **1946** W. R. P. DELANO *U.S. Patent 2,413,101* (*heading*) Solar still with nonfogging window. **1970** *Guardian* 15 Jan. 11/2 At the end of 1969..the Clan McIlwraith sailed..for Mombasa, carrying a prefabricated solar still for Aldabra, a lonely coral atoll in the Indian Ocean. **1979** *Solar Energy* XXIII. 271/1 The basin-type pitched roof solar still is the commonest and cheapest. **1958** *Physical Rev.* CX. 1448/1 The geomagnetic field can be penetrated to a considerable depth by tongues of ionized gas from the solar wind. **1969** *Times* 22 July (Moon Rep.) p. iii/6 Buzz is erecting the solar wind experiment now. **1977** D. HARSENT *Dreams of Dead* 21 Unimaginable, the solar winds roared through space, putting the earth awry. **1978** PASACHOFF & KUTNER *University Astron.* viii. 227 (*caption*) The solar wind causes the wavy streaming of the tails of comets.

8. *solar-charged, -generated, -terrestrial* adjs.; **solar-heated** *a.*, heated by means of the sun's rays; equipped with a solar heating system; also **solar-heat** *v. trans.* (also *absol.*); **solar heating,** heating by means of the sun's rays, esp. when utilized for water or space heating; also *attrib.*; **solar-powered** *a.*, using power derived directly from the sun's rays.

1968 G. M. B. DOBSON *Explor. Atmos.* (ed. 2) xi. 195 The effect of the earth's magnetic field on the solar-charged particles is to deflect them back, away from the earth. **1978** *N.Y. Times* 30 Mar. A-14/6 The costs of solar-generated electric power currently did not 'stand up' in comparison with other energy sources. **1952** AYRES & SCARLOTT *Energy Sources—Wealth of World* xv. 208 Houses can be solar-heated completely without fuel when the mean atmospheric transmissivity is above 55 percent. **1977** *National Observer* (U.S.) 8 Jan. 8/4 When solar heating a house, the calculations become more complex. **1979** *Sunset* Apr. 132/1 (Advt.), The *Poolsaver* Automatic Solar Pool Cover solar heats and thermal insulates. By day *Poolsaver* absorbs solar energy. **1950** *Heating & Ventilating Engineer* XXIV. 148/1 The practicability of employing solar-heated air as a source of heat in removing moisture from a dehumidifying agent. **1956** *World Symposium on Applied Solar Energy* 107/2 The first solar-heated house was built in 1939 at M.I.T. as part of the Godfrey L. Cabot Solar Energy Conversion Research Project. **1977** *Time* 24 Jan. 19/1 Carter and Mondale will watch the parade in front of the White House from a 60-ft. by 40-ft. solar-heated reviewing stand. **1903** C. H. POPE *Solar Heat* i. 43 Another patent for solar-heating devices was obtained..from the British Government. **1951** *Archit. Rev.* CIX. 291/1 A limited supply of hot water is provided by solar heating systems on the roof of each ward block. **1958** *Times Rev. Industry* Feb. 94/1 The chief advantage claimed for solar heating, compared with other methods, is that the region of high temperature is localized, and contamination of material, while in the molten state, can thus be avoided. **1968** R. A. LYTTLETON *Mysteries Solar Syst.* v. 175 No serious effects of solar heating could be expected at such a distance from the sun, though some intense local heating on [*sic*] the particles through collisions could occur. **1977** 'E. TREVOR' *Theta Syndrome* iii. 43 David Pryor, a solar heating engineer. **1959** *Time* 26 Oct. 58/2 The satellite is shaped like a gyroscope... It squeals like a bagpipe as it signals from two transmitters—one powered by a chemical battery, the other solar-powered. **1978** *Illustr. London News* Nov. 19/2 The Administration succeeded in gaining agreement for..conservation measures, including tax relief for householders insulating their homes or for installing solar-powered systems. **1946** *Nature* 7 Sept. 329/1 Study of precise solar-terrestrial relationships has been a major Smithsonian activity for many years. **1966** *McGraw-Hill Encycl. Sci. & Technol.* I. 619/2 Solar physics..overlaps with geophysics in the consideration of solar-terrestrial relationships.

B. *sb.*[1] **2.** A solar lamp.

1853 M. J. McIntosh *Lofty & Lowly* i. 9 The astral lamp—solars were not yet invented—..throws its rays on cases filled with richly gilded volumes. **1976** H. R. F. Keating *Filmi, Filmi, Inspector Ghote* iii. 29 We are using a great number of different lights for different purposes in filming, Five-Ks, Two-Ks, Sunspots, Solars, Babies.

3. *U.S.* Solar radiation as a source of domestic or industrial energy.

1976 *National Observer* (U.S.) 17 July 9/2 What one is trying to do is go out and demonstrate for the building industry that solar is here for heating buildings. **1978** *Tucson* (Ariz.) *Mag.* Dec. 77 Passage of the solar tax credits by Congress will result in the rapid growth of solar in Southern Arizona.

solarimeter (sǝ͡ʊlări·mĭtəɹ). [f. Solari- + -meter.] A device for measuring the total intensity of radiation incident upon a surface.

1926 L. Gorczyński in *Monthly Weather Rev.* LIV. 381/2 To these direct-reading instruments, designed for both solar and sky radiation, we propose to give the name of 'Solarimeters' in order to distinguish them from pyrheliometers, which serve generally for radiation intensity of the sun at normal incidence. **1940** *Sci. Abstr.* XLIII. 383 The radiative properties of the snow cover were investigated... Two solarimeters were employed. **1969** McIntosh & Thom *Essent. Meteorol.* vii. 105 A solarimeter..detects both direct and diffuse solar radiation. *Ibid.*, An inverted solarimeter detects the short-wave radiation reflected by the surface.

solarium. Delete ‖ and add: **2. a.** Also, a sun-parlour. Chiefly *N. Amer.*

1911 G. W. James *Grand Canyon* iii. 20 It is called the solarium or sun-parlor. **1968** *Globe & Mail* (Toronto) 17 Feb. 45 (Advt.), Separate dining room with adjoining solarium—both overlook ravine. **1978** *Morecambe Guardian* 14 Mar. 25/1 (Advt.), Large..working kitchen, frontal solarium, porches [etc.].

b. A room equipped with sun-lamps.

1960 *Playboy* Mar. 70/2 There's a poolside soda fountain, as well as bar, massage rooms, steam cabinets, solaria, and Finnish baths. **1972** *Homes & Gardens* Sept. 20/2 The uncertain perils of the British climate..have finally induced one of our hotels to install a solarium. **1978** *Cornish Guardian* 27 Apr. 16/3 (Advt.), Heated swimming pool, sauna, solarium.

solarization. Add: **1. a.** More generally, the progressive reduction in the developable density of an emulsion (corresponding to a progressive darkening of the picture) following initial exposure beyond a certain light intensity. (Further examples.)

1948 James & Higgins *Fund. of Photogr. Theory* iv. 59 The curve representing developable density as a function of exposure passes through a maximum. If the exposure is increased beyond that which produces the maximum density, a decrease in developable density will occur... This effect is known as solarization. **1956** *Focal Encycl. Photogr.* 1079/1 Strictly speaking, solarization is the reversal of the image on a film or plate by an extreme amount of over-exposure... The term has by this time almost lost its original meaning. Nowadays it is applied.. to the technique for producing a partly reversed image by exposing the negative to unsafe light during development —actually, the phenomenon known as the Sabattier effect. **1961** *Jrnl. Photogr. Sci.* IX. 195/1 Solarization.. is usually attributed to a reduction in the number of developable grains. **1973** *SPSE Handbk. Photogr. Sci. & Engin.* vi. 427 The addition of halogen acceptors..to the emulsions prevents solarization.

b. *Photogr.* = *Sabatier effect* s.v. *Sabatier. Also called *pseudo-solarization.

1937 *Photogr. Jrnl.* LXXVII. 21/1 If the original negative consists of a well-exposed object on an unexposed background, the fogging of the background with the second exposure does not come right up to the edge of the image, but leaves a clear white line... This line was formerly only of academic interest. Recently, however, it has been used as the basis of the so-called 'Solarization Process'. **1939** [see *Sabatier effect* s.v. *Sabatier]. **1956** [see sense a above]. **1969** M. J. Langford *Adv. Photogr.* xi. 233 The image exposure relative to solarisation fogging exposure makes decisive changes in tone rendering. **1977** J. Hedgecoe *Photographer's Handbk.* 278 The solarization, below, was produced by the black and white method, but with the solarized positive printed onto color negative film, using a colored light source.

c. *Plant Physiol.* [a. G. *solarisation* (A. Ursprung 1913, in *Ber. d. Deut. bot. Ges.* XXXV. 57).] The inhibition of photosynthesis as a result of prolonged exposure to high light intensities.

1925 W. Stiles *Photosynthesis* vii. 97 Solarization appears to have no permanently injurious effect on the activities of the leaf. **1960** B. S. Meyer et al. *Introd. Plant Physiol.* (1963) xi. 219 Solarization effects appear to result principally..from the phenomenon of photo-oxidation, in which leaves consume oxygen in the light, and use it in the oxidation of certain cell constituents. **1974** R. G. S. Bidwell *Plant Physiol.* vii. 170 Very high light intensity may be damaging to plants—solarization is the photodestruction of chlorophyll by excessive illumination. Shade plants are more susceptible to solarization than are sun plants.

d. The alteration of the light transmission characteristics of glass as a result of prolonged exposure to visible or ultraviolet light.

1928 W. W. Coblentz *Let. Circular U.S. Bureau Standards* No. 235 (3rd revision) 4 A sample [of glass] which had been in a hospital window..for a year was found to have a transmission of 25 per cent at 302 mμ... Further exposure to the quartz mercury arc reduced the transmission but little, showing that solarization was complete. **1955** E. B. Shand *Glass Engin. Handbk.* xvi. 145/2 Mercury-vapor lamps utilize a number of glasses of different properties... Because of their exposure to strong ultra-violet radiations, the glasses must be capable of resisting solarization effects to a large degree. **1972** F. L. Harding in L. D. Pye et al. *Introd. Glass Sci.* 422 Long term exposure to the ultraviolet radiation in sunlight can result in another type of coloring phenomenon known as solarization. If certain multivalent ions..are present in the glass, their valence can be changed by ionizing radiation.

solarize, *v.* Add: **1.** More widely, to affect by solarization of any kind. (Earlier and later examples.)

1853 C. Goodyear *Gum-Elastic* I. vii. 114 Another effect yet more remarkable in the treatment of gum-elastic, is that of the sun's rays upon it. When combined with sulphur, and exposed to the action of the sun..it becomes solarized, or divested of its adhesive quality. **1950** *Jrnl. Amer. Ceramic Soc.* XXXIII. 257/2 From the general appearance of the glasses that were solarized in the mercury arc it became obvious that the depth of color change was slight. **1966** LaCow & Lathrop *Photo Technol.* xix. 229/2 To solarize a negative the developing process is carried on in a normal manner for about 2/3 to 3/4 of the developing time [etc.].

2. (Further examples.)

1955 E. B. Shand *Glass Engin. Handbk.* xvii. 159 Some glasses will discolor perceptibly, or 'solarize' when exposed to ultra-violet radiations. **1977** *Jrnl. Photogr. Sci.* XXV. 103/2 The emulsion investigated..was a chlorobromide, halide-exchange emulsion which had a low surface/internal speed ratio and which solarized readily.

solarized, solarizing *ppl. adjs.* (further examples); also **so·larizing** *vbl. sb.*

1853 C. Goodyear *Gum-Elastic* I. vii. 112 The use of acid gas in connection with the solarizing process. **1923** B. D. W. Luff *Chem. of Rubber* i. 18 Articles made with such a composition, when exposed to the sun's rays, a process termed solarising, were said to lose their adhesive nature. **1969** *Focal Encyl. Photogr.* (rev. ed.) 1415/2 The solarizing exposure itself must also be sufficient. Too little leads to..only a partially solarized image with weak border outlines. **1977** Solarized [see *solarization 1 b]. **1977** R. Hattersley *Photogr. Printing* ii. 20 It involves exposing a print twice: once in the usual way and once with a solarizing light source after development has gone about halfway.

solation[2] (sǝlē·ʃən). *Physical Chem.* [f. *sol *sb.*[6] + -ation.] The change of a gel into a sol. So **sola·te** *v. intr.*, to undergo solation; *trans.*, to convert into a sol.

1915 [see *gelation[2]]. **1926** *Jrnl. Morphol. & Physiol.* XLI. 351 Locomotion in Amoeba is associated with gelation and solation. **1951** *New Biol.* X. 16 The plasmagel must presumably contract at the hind end, as well as solating. **1958** *Jrnl. Cellular & Compar. Physiol.* LII. 270 The plasmagel system of the intact *Amoeba* undergoes complete solation under suitably high pressure. **1977** *Jrnl. Cell Biol.* LXXIV. 909/1 The gel solated slowly at room temperature after forming. *Ibid.* 921/1 Elevated KCl concentrations that solate the *Dictyostelium* gel.

sold, *ppl. a.* Add: **3.** *slang.* Tricked, deceived. Cf. Sell *v.* 9.

1876 'Mark Twain' *Tom Sawyer* xvii. 147 As the 'sold' congregation trooped out they said they would almost be willing to be made ridiculous again.

4. *sold-out.* **a.** *colloq.* Bankrupt; exhausted, 'finished'.

1859 Hotten *Dict. Slang* 98 *Sold up, or out,* broken down, bankrupt. **1958** F. C. Avis *Boxing Ref. Dict.* 104 *Sold out:* said of a boxer who is nearly exhausted. **1973** *Observer* 3 June 25/6 At the end of last season he was physically and mentally sold out. **1977** *New Yorker* 4 July 24/1 A pool player who was vaguely associated with the big-money barracudas and sold-out types hanging back in the pool-hall shadows.

b. That has sold all its stock, seats, etc.

1903 Kipling *Five Nations* 191 The sold-out shops and the bank And the wet, wide-open town. **1960** *Farmer & Stockbreeder* 8 Mar. 60/1 (*heading*) Sold-out at Bath. All available stand space at the Bath and West Show..has been sold. **1975** *High Times* Dec. 21/1 They..are a sold-out attraction wherever they perform. **1976** *Early Music* Oct. 447/2 Bodies whose present idea of an 18th-century orchestra is a group playing Haydn and Mozart badly to a sold-out Festival Hall.

solder, *sb.*[1] Add: **4. b.** (Earlier example.)

1845 J. R. Planché *Golden Fleece* ii. 23 Begone, I charge you, none of your soft solder: Your downy words don't weigh with me a feather.

6. *solder-pin*; *solder-coated, -sealed* adjs.

1964 R. F. Ficchi *Electr. Interference* x. 193 A third method of connecting bus bars is by bolting two solder-coated bus bars, and applying heat to make a continuous connection. **1965** *Wireless World* Sept. 464/2 This unit.. is available with either solder pins for direct connection.. or with valve base pins. **1964** R. F. Ficchi *Electr. Interference* v. 72 (*caption*) Input and output connections ..are solder-sealed terminals and an A–N connector.

so·lderable, *a.* [f. Solder *v.* + -able.] Able to be joined by means of solder. So **solderabi·lity,** the property of being solderable.

1949 *Iron Age* 8 Dec. 96/2 The solderability of electro-deposited lead-tin alloy remains excellent for at least 9 months under normal operating conditions. **1959** *Trans. Inst. Metal Finishing* XXXVI. 203 The solderability of various coatings of tin with lead, zinc, cadmium, and of cadmium and silver has been compared. **1961** Webster, Solderable. **1967** E. R. Wells in C. R. Martens *Technol. Paints, Varnishes & Lacquers* xiii. 214 The urethane single-package low solids..enamels..had the unique advantage of being solderable without removal from the ends of the wires to be joined. **1976** *Wireless World* Nov. 52/1 The transistor terminal pad was quite easily solderable. **1978** *BSI News* Mar. 7/1 The test methods included in the BS 9760 series cover solderability..of surface conductors.

soldered, *ppl. a.* Add: **1. b.** *soldered dot* (Building), a means of fastening sheet lead to woodwork, consisting of a mass of solder put in a depression in the lead after the latter has been fitted into a corresponding depression in the wood and a screw fixed through the bottom of it.

1893 J. W. Clarke *Lect. Plumbing* 70/1 Soldered dots never last for any great length of time and the lead invariably breaks away from them. **1930** P. Manser *Plumbing & Gasfitting* VII. xxii. 1606 Soldered dots are not quite satisfactory as they hold the lead too rigidly, and where the load on them is heavy the screws work through due to the strain on them. **1966** G. E. Evans *Pattern under Plough* iii. 51 A circle of plumber's black is painted round the outside of the hollow, partly to confine the soldered dot, and partly to give the whole a neat decorative finish.

so·lderless, *a.* [f. Solder *sb.*[1] + -less.] Made without solder; that does not require solder.

1920 C. T. Schaefer *Motor Lorry Design* iii. 43 A solderless copper radiator is obtained,..which..withstands severe vibration without failure. **1957** '*Motor Cycling' Workbench Wisdom* 75/2 A particularly neat type of solderless nipple. **1974** *Sci. Amer.* Apr. 79/1 The Logic Lab utilizes a solderless, plug-in connection technique for components and wires.

soldier, *sb.* Add: **1. d.** A member of the Salvation Army.

1876 W. Booth *Salvation Soldiery* (1882) 70 Get fixed in your mind the ungainsayable truth that every soldier can do something. **1890** —— *In Darkest England* ii. v. 168 Emma Y.—Now a Soldier of the Marylebone Slum Post. **1935** *Chambers's Encycl.* IX. 64/2 In some of the jails there is now a regularly organised corps of Salvation Army soldiers. **1978** *Lochaber News* 31 Mar. 3/2 At the evening service four young soldiers..were enrolled by Major Holstead.

e. *to play* (*at*) *soldiers*: said of children; also derisively of volunteers.

1911 in *Conc. Oxford Dict* s.v. *Soldier.* **1969** I. & P. Opie *Children's Games* xii. 338 There is a noteworthy difference between playing at 'Soldiers' and playing at 'War' with two opposing sides. *Ibid.*, If they [*sc.* the boys] were playing soldiers, she took it as a warning that it was time for her to arm. **1977** *Daily Mirror* 16 Mar. 10/2 (Advt.), I can tell you that digging a trench in pouring rain when you've had no kip is hardly playing at soldiers.

f. A rank-and-file member of the Mafia.

1963 *Organized Crime & Illicit Traffic in Narcotics* (Comm. Govt. Operations, U.S. Senate) i. 80 Then we had what we call a caporegima which is a lieutenant, and then we have what we call soldiers. **1970** L. Sanders *Anderson Tapes* lxxii. 218 The organization variably known as Cosa Nostra, Syndicate, Mafia, etc., even has military titles for its members—don for general or colonel, *capo* for major or captain, soldier for men in the ranks, etc. **1974** J. Gardner *Corner Men* xv. 248 Vescari was coming to him. There were several men around him, the don's soldiers. **1977** *Time* 16 May 35/3 Since then scores of new soldiers have signed up [in the Mafia].

2. c. *old soldier*: one practised or experienced in a thing, or one who pretends to be so. (See also quot. 1912.) Also *attrib.* Cf. senses 2 b in Dict. and *2 d.

1722 [see Old *a.* 5 b]. **1858** Geo. Eliot *Lett.* (1954) II. 511 He..will be as much interested as I shall be in knowing about the vicissitudes of Coventry journalism, when any new phase or crisis comes of which you can tell us. He is an old soldier, and cares for battles of that sort. **1912** R. A. Freeman *Singing Bone* ii. 119 Poor Pratt was what you'd call an old soldier—sly, you know, sir—and a bit of a sneak. **1949** [see *head *sb.* 49**]. **1950** N. Cardus *Second Innings* 93 The umpire (an old soldier) confidentially tells you he could see it all coming.

d. *Naut. slang* (orig. and chiefly *U.S.*). A worthless seaman; a loafer, a shirker. Also *old soldier.* Cf. Soldier *v.* 1 d.

1840 R. H. Dana *Two Yrs. before Mast* xvii. 154 The captain called him a 'soger', and promised to 'ride him down'. **1849** [see *soldiering *vbl. sb.* 2]. **1850** H. Melville *White Jacket* II. xxx. 205 Off Cape Horn some 'sogers' of sailors will stand cupping, and bleeding, and blistering, before they will budge. **1898** A. J. Boyd *Shellback* ii. 28 Some are good men, some mere 'sojers' (useless as seamen—loafers). **1933** E. P. Mitchell *Deep Water* xxi. 184, I hear that you have shipped as an A.B. You don't look like one, and if you're a soldier you'll get soldier's jobs and be disrated. **1958** B. Hamilton *Too Much of Water* vi. 140 He's a bit of an old soldier, but a first-rate seaman, and a hundred per cent reliable at sea.

e. *dead soldier* (*U.S. slang*): an empty bottle. Cf. (*dead*) *marine* s.v. Marine *sb.* 4 d.

1917 in *Dialect Notes* IV. 322. **1929** *New Yorker* 9 Feb. 42/3 His aim with a dead soldier was..unerring. **1940** R. Chandler *Farewell, my Lovely* v. 33, I held up the dead soldier and shook it. Then I..reached for the pint of bonded bourbon. **1979** R. B. Gillespie *Crossword Mystery* ii. 50 There weren't any prints on that bottle... That dead soldier was as clean as a whistle.

f. *colloq.* A strip or finger of bread or toast.
1966 N. FREELING *Dresden Green* I. 73 Potato soup with fried onions and 'soldiers' of fried bread. **1971** J. GRIGSON *Good Things* 120 First dip the asparagus into the butter, then into the runny egg yolk, as if it were a child's bread 'soldier'. **1979** *Woman's Own* 21 Apr. 8/3 Our medical writer..advises: 'Bread, butter and milk is a good idea, but you can't really beat a boiled egg and "soldiers".'

3. f. Substitute for def.: One of several deep-water fishes with reddish skins, esp. one of the genus *Hoplostethus*. (Later examples.)
1935 'R. M.' *Trawler* x. 51 By far the most plentiful animals in all the catch were the 'soldiers'. **1953** [see *DAGERAAD]. **1971** *Grocott's Mail* (Grahamstown, S.Afr.) 28 May 3 Mrs. E. Birch took both the ladies' awards with a soldier of 0·963 kg, another unusual fish and decidedly a deep sea species. **1974** *Nature* 22 Mar. 306/3 The berycoid fishes comprise a mixture of deepwater 'soldiers', *Hoplostethus*, and other genera.

6*. In allusion to the resemblance to a line of soldiers on parade. **a.** *Carpentry.* Each of a series of short vertical pieces of wood to which a skirting-board is fixed.
1927 T. CORKHILL in R. Greenhalgh *Building Educator* II. 817/2 The vertical grounds, or soldiers.., are plugged to the wall about every 3 ft. apart. **1950** M. T. TELLING *Carpentry & Joinery* v. 200 The skirting is fixed with nails to the horizontal ground and to the short vertical grounds called 'soldiers'.

b. *Building.* (See quot.) Cf. *soldier arch, course*, sense 8 below.
1929 W. C. HUNTINGTON *Building Constr.* iv. 130 Belt courses and flat arches may be formed of brick[s] set on end with the narrow side exposed. Such bricks are called soldiers.

c. *Building.* Each of a series of vertical members of timber or metal used to hold formwork in position or support the lining of an excavation.
1932 DOWSETT & BARTLE *Practical Formwork & Shuttering* ii. 19 The ribs are held in position by uprights made from 3″ × 6″ material; these uprights—frequently referred to as 'soldiers'—are in turn held by 3″ × 6″ horizontal timbers called 'walings'. **1932** T. CORKHILL *Conc. Building Encycl.* 197 *Soldiers*,..heavy vertical timbers placed across several walings and strutted. This is done in stages, to remove the lower struts for a deep excavation, as the wall is built. **1961** *Engineering* 8 Dec. 739/1 Aluminium 'soldiers' are being used..to support the shuttering for the concrete shields of the reactors. **1970** W. G. NASH *Brickwork Three* viii. 175 When a sufficient depth has been supported in this way the whole system is held back by soldiers which are secured by the permanent struts.

7. a. *soldier-boy, -poet, -servant* (earlier example).
1861 in *Rebellion Rec.* (1862) I. III. 91 My hungry soger-boys shall soon have meat and drink. **1978** J. BARNETT *Head of Force* viii. 72 This was his field. The soldier-boy was out of his depth. **1912** D. H. LAWRENCE in *Eng. Rev.* Jan. 373 Liliencron is well represented. But this soldier poet is so straight, so free from the modern artist's hyper-sensitive self-consciousness, that we would have more of him. **1958** BLUNDEN *War Poets 1914–18* i. 13 The number and the activity of the soldier-poets of Britain in the First World War were bewildering. **1794** W. B. STEVENS *Jrnl.* 13 Feb. (1965) 135 Stables has displayed a boisterousness of temper..to his Soldier-Servant..which I cannot palliate.

b. *soldier-settlement, -suit.*
1921 *Daily Colonist* (Victoria, B.C.) 25 Mar. 1/5 The opening for soldier settlement of about two townships from the Riding Mountain, Manitoba, reserve, will be held at the Dominion land office in Dauphin, Manitoba, in about two weeks. **1930** W. K. HANCOCK *Australia* vii. 141 It would..be not altogether unfair to separate soldier settlement from closer settlement, and to consider the former as part of the cost of the war. **1977** *Weekly Times* (Melbourne) 19 Jan. 39/2 The property remained in the Bell family until taken up under Soldier Settlement by Mr J. Smedley after World War 2. **1944** S. BELLOW *Dangling Man* 182 I d murder him, soldier suit or no soldier suit. **1977** H. FAST *Immigrants* II. 141 If you have to put on that lousy soldier suit to live with yourself, then for Christ's sake become a medic or a clerk or something like that.

8. soldier arch *Building*, a soldier course serving as a lintel; **soldier bean** *N. Amer.*, the mottled kidney-shaped seeds of certain varieties of *Phaseolus vulgaris*; **soldier-bug**, a predacious North American bug of the genus *Podisus* of the family Pentatomidæ, esp. *P. maculiventris*, which is yellowish brown and has a spine on the under-side of its head; **soldier course** *Building*, a course of bricks set on end with their narrower long face exposed; **soldier-fish**: delete *U.S.* and add: = SQUIRREL 4 and *squirrel-fish* s.v. SQUIRREL 7 b; (later examples); **soldier fly**: for *U.S.* read orig. *U.S.* and add: [tr. mod.L. *Stratiomys*], an often brightly coloured fly of the family Stratiomyidæ, the larvæ of which damage the roots of certain grasses; (earlier and later examples); **soldier orchid** = *military orchid* s.v. *MILITARY *a.* 3 b; **soldier-termite** = sense 3 e in Dict.
1963 SEAKINS & SMITH *Practical Brickwork* xiv. 174 (*caption*) Flexible D.P.C. behind soldier arch. **1972** S. SMITH *Brickwork* xiv. 73 A method of supporting a soldier arch by means of wire ties built into a concrete lintel at the rear, is shown. **1931** W. G. MCGREGOR *Field Beans in Canada* 8 In Nova Scotia..four leading varieties ..are Navy Ottawa 711, White Marrowfat, Soldier, and Yellow Eye. **1968** E. R. BUCKLER *Ox Bells & Fireflies* vi. 101 Yellow-eyed soldier beans to be threshed on the barn floor with the leather-jointed flail. **1868** *Mich. Agric. Rep.* VII. 175 [I] found [them] to be soldier-bugs, with their long harpoon bills thrust into a fine fat slug. **1946** *Richmond* (Va.) *Times-Dispatch* 4 Feb. 4/1 More than two tons of it [*sc.* an insecticide made from sabadilla] was used this year to kill..the soldier bugs in Illinois. **1948** DALZELL & TOWNSEND *Masonry Simplified* I. vii. 268 Soldier courses are used mainly as a water table around a building at the level of the first floor. **1979** *Arizona Daily Star* 1 Apr. (Advt. Section) 22/3 Burnt adobe hacienda with Soldier Course on parapet. **1905** D. S. JORDAN *Guide to Study of Fishes* II. xv. 253 The soldier-fishes (*Holocentridæ*) also known as squirrel-fishes ..are shore fishes very characteristic of rocky banks in the tropical seas. **1931** J. R. NORMAN *Hist. Fishes* iv. 69 Soldier-fishes..of the coral reefs of tropical seas derive their name from the stout and sharply pointed spines with which the fins are provided. **1961** E. S. HERALD *Living Fishes of World* 157/1 Squirrelfishes or soldier-fishes..tend to hide in crevices and cracks. **1842** T. W. HARRIS *Treat. Insects New England Injurious to Vegetation* 408 Most of the soldier-flies..are armed with two thorns or sharp spines on the hinder part of the thorax. **1905** V. L. KELLOGG *Amer. Insects* xiii. 329 The soldier-flies, Stratiomyidæ, are unfamiliar insects... Many of the species have bright yellow or green markings, and most of them have the abdomen curiously broad and flattened. **1952** J. CLEGG *Freshwater Life Brit. Isles* xiv. 238 The Soldier-flies are the first of the stouter, short-horned flies to be considered. **1975** *N.Z. Jrnl. Agric.* Sept. 7/1 Infestations of grassgrub and soldier fly..have the effect of inducing a clover-strong pasture which increases the danger of bloat. **1934, 1969** Soldier orchid [see *military orchid* s.v. *MILITARY *a.* 3 b]. **1963** Soldier-termite [see *NASUTE *a.* 3].

9. soldier's breeze = *soldier's wind*; **soldier's farewell** *slang*, an abusive farewell (cf. *sailor's farewell* s.v. *SAILOR 5 c); **soldier's heart** (further examples); = **irritable heart*; **soldiers' home**, a place of stay for soldiers.
1894 STEVENSON & OSBOURNE *Ebb-Tide* II. vii. 125 The *Farallone* made a soldier's breeze of it. **1909** J. R. WARE *Passing Eng.* 229/1 *Soldier's farewell*, 'Go to bed', with noisy additions. **1936** J. CURTIS *Gilt Kid* viii. 82 'Good-bye. I hope they'll poke you into the Lock Hospital.' 'Soldier's farewell to you.' **1938** F. D. SHARPE *Sharpe of Flying Squad* xviii. 184 As you pass through the door, you'll sometimes hear a raspberry... No one wants to accept responsibility for that soldier's farewell. **1979** *Guardian* 12 Nov. 2/5 One school of thought within ITN.. is that..the darling [newsreader] of millions then decided to say a soldier's farewell. **1967** *Punch* 29 Mar. 458/3 World War One produced, besides Trench Foot, a syndrome called Soldier's Heart, caused by great anxiety coupled with severe physical strain. **1971** Soldier's heart [see *IRRITABLE *a.* 2 b]. **1860** MRS. GASKELL *Let.* 10 Dec. (1966) 640 This autumn [I]..helped Florence Nightingale ..in establishing a Soldier's [*sic*] Home in Gibraltar where they can have cheap refreshments, can read, play games, write letters, &c. **1866** J. C. GREG *Life in Army* xxvi. 224 The idea of a Soldiers' Home is, I believe, original with the American people... It is said to have been first instituted in the city of Baltimore in 1861. **1900** *Congress. Rec.* 19 Jan. 1001/1 Part of his [*sc.* the veteran's] meager pension [is] confiscated at Soldiers' Homes.

soldier, *v.* Add: **1. f.** *to soldier on*: to persevere, to carry on doggedly.
1954 K. AMIS *Lucky Jim* vii. 77 The eeriness..disconcerted him..but he soldiered pluckily on to his objective. **1959** *Times* 20 Aug. 3/6 Lomax soldiered on and at tea had made 68. **1963** *Times* 21 Feb. 13/2 To give the maximum increase to the new recruits..and to offer a much smaller percentage to men and women who have soldiered on into the thirties and forties is a division hard to justify. **1978** *Jrnl. R. Soc. Med.* LXXI. 648 The alternatives are to let the patient soldier on, or to take the radical approach of abdominoperineal resection.

soldiering, *vbl. sb.* **2.** (Earlier examples.)
1840 R. H. DANA *Two Yrs. before Mast* xii. 91 '*Sogering*' was the order of the day. **1849** H. MELVILLE *Redburn* I. xii. 118 Sailors were always bitter against any thing like *sogering*..though this Jackson was a notorious old *soger* the whole voyage.

sole, *sb.*[1] Add: **8. d.** *Geol.* The underlying or lowest thrust plane of a thrust.
1889 H. M. CADELL in *Trans. R. Soc. Edin.* XXXV. 347 This experiment shows that underneath a series of beds, repeated and heaped together by small thrusts, inclined perhaps at considerable angles, there runs..a major thrust or 'sole', inclined at a lower angle, along which the whole mass may have travelled for considerable distances. **1907** J. HORNE in B. N. Peach et al. *Geol. Struct. N.W. Highlands Scotland* xxxii. 464 Owing to..the friction along the unyielding lower plane or 'sole' of the thrust, there was a tendency in the materials to fold over and curve under. **1965** A. HOLMES *Princ. Physical Geol.* (ed. 2) ix. 225 Along the sole of a major thrust severe crushing and grinding of the rocks is to be expected.

e. *Geol.* The lowest layer of ice in a glacier, containing rock debris.
1930 *Amer. Jrnl. Sci.* CCXIX. 13 A rock fragment subjected to the abrasion processes in action on the sole of a glacier. **1952** *Jrnl. Glaciol.* II. 128 This deposit is then pulled along in a continuous manner by the movements of the glacier, thus forming the sole. **1977** A. HALLAM *Planet Earth* 87 In the roofs of these cavities we see the rock-studded glacier sole.

f. *Geol.* The under-side of a sedimentary stratum.
1957, etc. [see *sole marking*, sense 9 below]. **1972** H. BLATT et al. *Origin Sedimentary Rocks* v. 170 Such structures are normally observed in the field on the sandstone sole. **1972** F. J. PETTIJOHN et al. *Sand & Sandstone* iv. 114 The flute..preserved as a raised structure or flute cast on the underside or sole of the overlying sand bed.

9. a. sole-bar (also **solebar**), *spec.* a longitudinal member forming part of the underframe of a railway carriage or wagon; (further examples); **sole mark, marking** *Geol.*, a feature that is found on the undersurface of sedimentary strata which overlie softer beds, and is the cast of a depression originally formed in the surface of the lower bed; **sole-plate** (also **soleplate**), *spec.* the metal plate forming the base of an electric iron; (further examples).
1930 *Engineering* 24 Jan. 102/2 The main frame.. consists of two longitudinals or solebars. **1977** *Modern Railways* Dec. 486/1 Current new stock..has an all-aluminium underframe with the solebars made from continuous extrusions. **1961** J. CHALLINOR *Dict. Geol.* 185/1 Sole-marks. **1972** J. F. PETTIJOHN et al. *Sand & Sandstone* I. iv. 113 Although they occur in almost all sands, sole marks are particularly abundant in turbidites where they provide the best means of determining current flow. **1978** FRIEDMAN & SANDERS *Princ. Sedimentol.* iv. 110/2 (*caption*) Sole mark assemblage dominated by counterparts of flutes..and transverse scour marks. **1957** P. H. KUENEN in *Jrnl. Geol.* LXV. 231/1 In a number of papers..mention is made of the occurrence of various types of markings on the sole of the graywackes. The present paper aims at presenting a coherent record of these sole markings. **1976** R. C. SELLEY *Introd. Sedimentol.* vii. 211 Flutes, grooves and tool marks are three of the commonest sole markings found as interbed sedimentary structures. **1960** *Housewife* Apr. 86/2 The sole-plate, being extra thin, heats quickly. **1974** *Spartanburg* (S. Carolina) *Herald* 24 Apr. (Sears Advts. Suppl.) 2 Has a 21-vent soleplate. Steams up to 30 minutes at a low setting.

sole, *sb.*[2] Add: **1. c.** In the names of various dishes, as *sole bonne femme* [*bonne femme* s.v. *BONNE C]; *sole (à la) Colbert* (see quot. 1877); *sole (à la) meunière* [*MEUNIÈRE *a.* and *adv.*]; *sole Véronique* (see quot. 1960).
1846 A. SOYER *Gastronomic Regenerator* 115 *Sole à la Colbert*,..sole..butter..chopped parsley..chopped tarragon and chervil..lemon juice. *Ibid.*, *Sole à la Meûnière*,.. sole..chopped onions..butter..lemon..cayenne pepper. **1877** E. S. DALLAS *Kettner's Bk. of Table* 136 The sole of Colbert..is a fried sole which after being cooked is boned and then filled with maître d'hôtel butter and with lemon-juice. **1928** D. L. SAYERS *Unpleasantness at Bellona Club* vii. 71 He..had a sole Colbert very well cooked. **1930** R. LEHMANN *Note in Music* v. 205 He..ordered sole *bonne femme*, a mixed grill, salad, trifle, a welsh rarebit. **1960** *Good Housek. Cookery Book* 95/2 *Sole Véronique*,.. sole..mushrooms..wine..cream..grapes..butter. **1966** *Harper's Bazaar* Sept. 87/3 She..does *sole Véronique* with lichees instead of grapes. **1967** G. GREENE *May we borrow your Husband?* 185 For a while the *sole meunière* gave them an excuse not to talk. **1978** F. MULLALLY *Deadly Payoff* xi. 142 The two burly men would..plough through a hearty meal of sea-food, sole *meunière* and Stilton. **1979** 'L. BLACK' *Penny Murders* iv. 38 Kate.. declared she would make it a fish day..a sole. Should it be *Véronique* with white grapes, or *à la Dugléré* [*sic*], cooked in white wine with tomatoes and shallots?

sole, *a.* Add: **10. c. sole-charge** *attrib.* *N.Z.*, (*a*) of a teacher: that has sole charge of a school; (*b*) of a school: having only one teacher; also *absol.*
1941 A. CURNOW *Island & Time* 12, I am the sums the sole-charge teachers teach. **1944** H. WILSON *Moonshine* ii. 21 It's [*sc.* the school's] a sole charge. **1955** D. O. W. HALL *Portrait of N.Z.* ix. 171 Small country settlements have their 'sole charge' or single-teacher schools.

Soledon [sǫ·lĕdǫn]. Also **soledon.** [Blend of SOLUBLE *a.* and *Caledon*, proprietary name of an earlier range of dyes.] A proprietary term for a range of water-soluble vat dyes derived mainly from anthraquinones. Freq. *attrib.*
1924 *Trade Marks Jrnl.* 24 Dec. 2898 *Soledon*... Dyes and dyestuffs,..Scottish Dyes Ltd. **1929** *Textile Colorist* XLVII. 568/1 Considerable interest has been expressed.. regarding another water-soluble vat dye, Soledon Jade Green. **1938** *Times* 11 Jan. 9/5 A third important recent advance was represented by the 'soledon' colours for cotton fabrics and linens and for rayons. **1952** K. VENKATARAMAN *Synthetic Dyes* II. xxxiv. 1050 About 35 Indigosols and 25 Soledons have been marketed. **1964** *Official Gaz.* (U.S. Patent Office) 22 Dec. TM153 Imperial Chemical Industries Limited... *Soledon*... For dyes and dyestuffs. **1970** *Times* 30 Apr. 12/7 A limited edition of Shaw's works was bound in his [*sc.* J. E. G. Harris's] Soledon jade green cloth. **1971** R. L. M. ALLEN *Colour Chem.* x. 179 The water-soluble sulphuric ester salts were marketed as Soledon dyes by Scottish Dyes Ltd, and are now produced under the same name by ICI.

solemn, *a.* (*adv.* and *sb.*). Add: **10. b.** *solemn-eyed.*
1889 W. B. YEATS *Wanderings of Oisin* 59 Away with us he's going, The solemn-eyed. **1930** M. MEAD *Growing up in New Guinea* ix. 151 A tiny curly grass skirt is fashioned.., and the solemn-eyed baby arrayed in it for a feast day.

solemncholy, *a.* Add: **A.** *adj.* (Earlier example.)

1772 P. V. FITHIAN *Jrnl.* 18 Dec. (1900) 27 Being very *Solemncholly* and somewhat tired, I concluded to stay there all night.

B. *sb. pl.* A solemn or serious mood. *rare.*

1834 W. A. CARRUTHERS *Kentuckian in New York* I. 214 It drives away the solemncholies, and makes a fellow feel so good-natured, and so comfortable.

solemnify, *v.* (Earlier example.)

1780 J. MAINWARING *Sermons on Several Occasions* p. xxv, Some divines delight to sadden and solemnify their sermons with Scripture passages.

solemnsides (sǫ·ləmsəi:dz), *a.* and *sb.* [f. SOLEMN *a.* + *-sides* as in SOBERSIDES.] **A.** *adj.* Excessively solemn or serious. **B.** *sb.* An excessively solemn or serious person.

1922 J. M. BARRIE *Courage* 36 Courage. I do not think it is to be got by your becoming solemnsides before your time. **1957** J. KIRKUP *Only Child* ii. 50 People who are 'solemn-sides' cannot account for self-mockery. **1959** I. & P. OPIE *Lore & Lang. Schoolch.* ix. 155 Sobersides, solemnsides.

solenoglyph (solī·noglif). *Zool.* [ad. F. *solénoglyphe*, mod.L. *Solenoglypha* (A. H. A. Duméril 1853, in *Mém. Acad. Sci.* XXIII. 417), f. SOLENO- + Gr. γλυφή carving.] A venomous snake belonging to a group characterized by extra venom glands and grooved fangs which can be retracted. Also as *adj.* Hence **solenogly·phous** *a.*, of or pertaining to a snake of this kind.

1913 G. A. BOULENGER *Snakes of Europe* v. 56 The Proteroglyphs (Cobras, Coral-snakes, Sea-snakes) and the Solenoglyphs (Vipers, Pit-vipers, Rattlesnakes) may be regarded as the diverging extremes in the development of the poison apparatus. **1965** R. & D. MORRIS *Men & Snakes* viii. 177 With the vipers, pit vipers and rattlesnakes, we come to..the Solenoglyphous forms... These are the so-called 'folding-fang' snakes. **1968** R. D. MARTIN tr. *Wickler's Mimicry in Plants & Animals* xii. 112 The vipers have the most specialised tooth-form,..a longitudinal canal that functions as a poison syringe. This condition is called solenoglyph. **1969** A. BELLAIRS *Life of Reptiles* I. v. 195 If the skull of a poisonous snake is examined, whether it be a proteroglyph or a solenoglyph, it very often appears that there are two fangs in each maxilla, set side by side.

solenoid. Add: Also with pronunc. (sǫ·lĕnoid); the pronunc. (solī·noid) is no longer current. **1.** (Earlier example.)

1827 J. CUMMING *Man. Electro Dynamics* 240 In the case of a straight solenoïd (an electro-dynamic cylinder) θ is the angle between the axis of the solenoïd and the extremity of the cylinder.

3. *attrib.* and *Comb.*, as *solenoid-operated* adj.; **solenoid brake,** a brake actuated by the movement of a core into or out of a solenoid when an electric current is passed through the latter; similarly **solenoid lock.**

1914 *Machinery* Dec. 328/1 A new automatic solenoid brake for crane, hoist, lift bridge and similar service has recently been developed. **1963** JONES & SCHUBERT *Engin. Encycl.* (ed. 3) 1168 One type of solenoid brake adapted for mill, crane and hoist motors and similar classes of service, is so arranged that the brake mechanism is held in the off or release position by a coil and plunger. **1976** L. DEIGHTON *Twinkle, twinkle Little Spy* iv. 41 The glass door..had an electric solenoid lock. I had to push the override. **1956** *Nature* 14 Jan. 84/2 Two solenoid-operated valves are incorporated in the flow line. **1971** *Jrnl. Gen. Psychol.* LXXXIV. 325 The four match stimuli were presented by the second projector through a solenoid operated shutter which varied exposure duration.

solenoidal, *a.* Add: *spec.* of a vector field: having no divergence anywhere, and hence expressible as the curl of another vector field. (Further examples.)

1873 J. C. MAXWELL *Electr. & Magnetism* I. 23 The whole space can be divided into tubes of this kind provided $d\mathbf{X}/dx + d\mathbf{Y}/dy + d\mathbf{Z}/dz = 0$, a distribution of a vector quantity consistent with this equation is called a Solenoidal Distribution. **1909** J. G. COFFIN *Vector Anal.* vi. 154 (*heading*) Separation of a vector point-function **W**, which has a vector-potential, into solenoidal or rotational and lamellar or irrotational components. **1933** H. PHILLIPS *Vector Anal.* viii. 195 If two vectors satisfy these conditions their difference, being irrotational, solenoidal, piecewise continuous, and zero at infinity, is zero. **1972** A. G. HOWSON *Handbk. Terms Algebra & Anal.* xxxv. 175 A vector field satisfying div $\mathbf{f} = 0$, i.e. div $\mathbf{f}(\mathbf{x}) = 0$ for all $\mathbf{x} \in S$, is said to be solenoidal.

solenoidally *adv.* (earlier example).

1851 *Phil. Trans. R. Soc.* CXLI. 270 The distribution of magnetism in it is said to be solenoidal, and the substance is said to be solenoidally magnetized.

solera. Add: **1.** Also *attrib.*, as *solera wine*; **solera system** (see quot. 1965).

1961 *Times* 16 Jan. 13/5 Sherry is made on the solera system. **1965** A. SICHEL *Penguin Bk. of Wines* III. 227 The solera system is..a..method of refreshing delicately flavoured old wines still in cask with small quantities of slightly younger wine of the same character in order to keep a continuous stock of mature wine of one type and character always available. **1972** *Times* (Spain Suppl.) 11 May p. iii/2 The sherries are *solera* wines.

‖ **solfège** (solfɛ̄ʒ). *Mus.* [Fr.] **a.** = SOLFEGGIO *sb.* **b.** (See quot. 1954.) Also *attrib.*

1912 E. INGHAM in J. W. Harvey *Eurhythmics Jaques-Dalcroze* 52 The solfège lessons are chiefly for ear-training and practical harmony. **1914** M. GIBB *Chassevant Method of Musical Educ.* ii. 19 In the 'First Solfège' there are no dots used, though there are many examples of tied notes. **1921** H. F. RUBINSTEIN tr. *Jaques-Dalcroze's Rhythm, Music & Educ.* v. 78 One of these groups confined itself to studying solfège, the other commenced pianoforte lessons... The solfège students were then initiated into the study of the piano. **1936** *Times Educ. Suppl.* 13 June 218/2 The course [of Eurhythmics] will consist of daily lessons in rhythmic movement and *solfège*. **1954** *Grove's Dict. Mus.* (ed. 5) VII. 877/2 *Solfège*... Although derived from the Italian *solfeggio*, and originally confined to the same meaning, the French word is now much more comprehensive. It stands for the teaching of the rudiments of music, which includes ear-training as an important factor. **1970** W. APEL *Harvard Dict. Mus.* (ed. 2) 786/1 Extensive courses in solfège..were first introduced in France and Belgium.

solicit, *v.* Add: **4. d.** More recently, also with a homosexual (or a pimp) as subj. Also *intr.*

1956 *Act* 4 & 5 *Eliz. II* c. 69 § 32 It is an offence for a man persistently to solicit or importune in a public place for immoral purposes. *Solicitation by men.* **1962** *Law Rep.* 13 Mar. 666 The appeal of the appellant..against his conviction..that he, being a man, persistently solicited in a public place for immoral purposes..contrary to s. 32 of the Sexual Offences Act, 1956. **1983** J. GARDNER *Elephants in Attic* xvii. 153 She was soliciting to cover her air fare.

solicitancy. (Later example.)

1890 W. JAMES *Princ. Psychol.* II. xxvi. 551 Those persons obey a curiously narrow teleological superstition who think themselves bound to interpret them [*sc.* the impulsions] in every instance as effects of the secret solicitancy of pleasure and repugnancy of pain.

solicitor. Add: **3. c. Official Solicitor** (see quot. 1977).

1875 *Minutes of Evidence taken by Commissioners appointed to inquire into Administrative Departments of Courts of Justice* 344/1 in *Parl. Papers* (C. 1245) XXX. 163, I hold the office of official solicitor to the Court of Chancery. **1896** *Law Rep. Chancery Div.* I. 368 We have an officer of this Court who is called the Official Solicitor. **1961** [see *AD LITEM]. **1977** *Jowitt's Dict. Eng. Law* (ed. 2) II. 1281/2 The Official Solicitor of the Court of Chancery was an officer whose functions consisted of protecting the Suitors Fund... He is now known as the Official Solicitor of the Supreme Court... He acts for persons suffering under a disability; he acts generally as solicitor in cases in which the Chancery Division requires his services as solicitor; he visits persons in custody for contempt.

7. *U.S.* One who solicits business orders, advertising, etc.

1897 *Scribner's Mag.* Oct. 463/2 A small army of solicitors is despatched to a neighborhood to go from house to house telling people about the features of the paper. **1903** E. L. SHUMAN *Practical Journalism* 200 Have as many good solicitors out as necessary and make your rates low enough to invite this form of advertising. **1916** *John Bull* 13 May 10/2 He called himself a grocer's solicitor, meaning a canvasser for orders. **1926** *Publishers' Weekly* 15 May 1589 Why can't he leave it to the judgment of the printers? Or to the advertising solicitor? **1952** S. EISENBERG *How to earn Income selling Products & Services by Phone* i. 4/2 If you can handle the English language..you can be a telephone solicitor. **1976** D. BARNES *Yesterday is Dead* (1977) II. 207 'No Solicitors', a sign on the glass double doors announced.

solicitrix. Restrict ? *Obs.* to sense 2 and add: **1.** (Later example.) *rare.*

1961 L. P. HARTLEY *Two for River* 48 When accosted I had not, as some men have, a polite formula of refusal ready: I swerved or..walked straight on. But one evening I couldn't, for my solicitrix..planted herself in front of me and blocked my way.

solid, *sb.*[1] Add: **4. a.** (Earlier and later examples.)

1786 J. WOODFORDE *Diary* 18 July (1926) II. 258, I..could eat no solids all day long. **1973** *Jrnl. Genetic Psychol.* CXXIII. 103 It can be seen also in Table 4 that infants did not eat solids at two weeks, but did at five weeks. **1977** W. H. MANVILLE *Good-bye* iv. 40 Junior just began eating solids.

f. Special Comb.: **solids-not-fat** *Dairying*, the components of milk other than water and fats and other lipids (being largely lactose and proteins); the proportion of such components in a sample of milk; **solids pump,** a machine for forcing lumpy or granular material, or liquid containing it, through a pipe or chamber against the force of gravity.

1874 J. A. WANKLYN *Milk-Analysis* ix. 38 The effect of skimming is to diminish the proportion of fat, and to leave the proportion of 'solids not fat' unaltered. **1930** *Analyst* LV. 543 The resulting curves..do not indicate that the highest proportion of solids-not-fat is contained in the bottom part of the milk. **1960** *Farmer & Stockbreeder* 5 Jan. 99/1 Changes in solids-not-fat were small, and nearly 19 per cent of the tests in Friesian herds and 7 per cent of those in Ayrshire herds were below the legal minimum standard of 8·5 per cent. **1957** T. G. HICKS *Pump Selection & Application* xiv. 313 Solids pumps..are designed to handle solutions containing large percentages of suspended abrasive materials. **1966** *McGraw-Hill Encycl. Sci. & Technol.* XII. 474/2 The solids pump has found its principal application in the operation of oil-shale retorts. Here it is used to feed crushed shale into the bottom of a conical vessel.

5. A solid rubber tyre. (No longer current.)

1919 *Brit. Manufacturer* Nov. 38/1, 50,000 pneumatic tyres a week, in addition to solids. **1924** A. W. JUDGE *Mod. Motor Cars* II. 178 Both ordinary and Giant Solids.

solid, *a.* Add: **I. 3. e.** *Astronautics.* Using solid fuel.

1949 G. P. SUTTON *Rocket Propulsion Elem.* i. 10 Long duration solid rocket units require an excessively heavy and large combustion chamber. **1961** *Flight* LXXX. 650/2 A study of the requirements associated with the transport, handling, checkout, assembly, and launch of extremely large solid boosters. **1967** *Technology Week* 20 Feb. 13/1 The program will cover the design, development and demonstration of a controllable solid propulsion system using integral propulsion. **1979** J. W. CORNELISSE et al. *Rocket Propulsion* ix. 169 Solid rockets find widespread military and civil applications.

II. 7. e. *Cards.* (See quot. 1927.)

1927 M. C. WORK *Contract Bridge* 145 *Solid suit*, one of such length and strength as to be practically sure of winning every trick in that suit. **1959** *Listener* 12 Feb. 309/1 The jump after a forcing opening bid shows a solid suit. **1976** *Country Life* 1 Apr. 846/2 Even when your trump suit is solid, it may still be fatal to touch it too early.

8. b, c. (Earlier and later examples.) *solid South*, the politically united southern States of America; the unanimous vote of the white electorate in these States for the Democratic party.

1855 in P. S. Foner *Business & Slavery* (1941) 114 We are now beaten by the solid vote of the City of New York. **1858** S. COLFAX *Let.* in O. J. Hollister *Life Schuyler Colfax* (1887) 137 We have fallen on strange times when the solid South in the House and a score of Northern Democrats dare to vote '*No*' on a resolution approving existing laws against the African slave trade. **1872** *Chicago Tribune* 14 Oct. 1/3 The Democrats are solid for Greeley in this county. **1876** *Harper's Weekly* 26 Aug. 691/2 We must recognize the solid South as the core of the Democratic party... The solid South is the Southern Confederacy seeking domination of the United States through the machinery of the Democratic party. **1880** *Sen. Rep. 46th U.S. Congress 2 Sess.* No. 693. 326 Q. These gentlemen..are both good Democrats? A. Yes, sir; they are solid Democrats. **1884, 1890** Solid South [in Dict.]. **1974** *Socialist Worker* 23 Nov. 16/5 With the exception of a handful of white scabs on one shift all four shifts are solid. **1977** *Chicago Tribune* 2 Oct. II. 2/5 It is possible for the GOP to revitalize itself by becoming the necessary counterweight to the newly reconstituted Solid South.

d. For *U.S.* read orig. *U.S.* and add earlier and later examples.

1882 G. W. PECK *Peck's Sunshine* 161, I was pretty solid with him. **1951** E. PAUL *Springtime in Paris* iv. 80 He..went back to his native village in the Ain, where there are plenty of unregenerate Pétainists to this day, quite solid with the bishop and the anti-Jewish provincial administration.

10. a. (The 'material' is not necessarily pure: the implication is of homogeneity rather than purity, so that, e.g., articles made of plate are excluded but not those made of an alloy.) (Further examples.)

1910 *Jrnl. R. Soc. Arts* LVIII. 260/2 There remained a mere film..like silver foil... That is, I believe, a fair example of the so-called 'solid silver' sold in our swell shops, with the aid of much electric light and many bowing salesmen. **1926** J. P. DE CASTRO *Law & Practice of hall-marking Gold & Silver Wares* I. 138 Though often legitimately used to differentiate between sterling silver and electro-plated silver, the expression 'solid silver' is frequently a much-abused term. **1962** L. S. SASIENI *Optical Dispensing* i. 3 Solid gold is not necessarily pure gold, but is an alloy of pure gold with other metals. The unalloyed pure metal is known as fine gold. *Ibid.*, The colour of solid gold can be varied by altering the proportions and the metals in the alloy. **1970** CHOATE & DE MAY *Creative Gold- & Silversmithing* ii. 10 Any karat gold is called solid gold to distinguish it from gold-filled metals. **1981** *Daily Tel.* 24 Sept. 17 (Advt.), An absolutely perfect solid gold neckchain... These are not seconds or plated gold—but sound 9 carat gold!

III. 18*. *Austral.* and *N.Z. slang.* Severe, difficult; unfair.

1916 C. J. DENNIS *Moods of Ginger Mick* 155 *Solid*, severe; severely. **1943** N. MARSH *Colour Scheme* ii. 35 You'd think it was royalty. They've been making it pretty solid for everybody down there. Hauling everything out and shifting us all round. **1948** R. PARK *Harp in South* v. 62 After all, Auntie Josie's got all them kids to look after. It must be pretty solid for her with Grandma as well. **1959** E. LAMBERT *Glory thrown In* 66 They'll be solid on him for that, won't they?

18.** *U.S. slang.* In the language of jazz: excellent, first-rate, 'great'; (see also quot. 1937). Also as *int. solid sender*: see *SENDER d.

1935 *Vanity Fair* (N.Y.) Nov. 38/1 He puts a solid man like Joe on suitcase. **1937** *Amer. Speech* XII. 182/2 *Solid*, describes a player whose improvisation indicates that he is en rapport with the rhythm of the band... A band that is solid has a psychic unanimity of feeling. **1943** *N.Y. Times* 9 May II. 5/4 There has [*sic*] been some solid trumpet players who can really send. **1959** 'F. NEWTON' *Jazz Scene* xii. 220 The hipster classifies what other people would call good as 'solid' or 'in there'. **1978** W. HJORTSBERG *Falling Angel* (1979) xii. 54 'Park your axe and have a drink.' 'Solid.' He placed his saxophone case carefully on the table.

IV. Quasi-*adv.* **19. a.** (Later U.S. dial. and colloq. examples.) Also, certainly, surely.

1937 *Amer. Speech* XII. 232/2 'Are you taking Amelia

to the Charcoal Dance?' 'I solid am.' **1944** *Richmond* (Va.) *Times-Dispatch* 5 Oct. 6/3 Dowdy [said] he was going to leave, whereupon the Bayer woman said she'd kill him if he did.. Dowdy told her that 'You'll solid have to kill me.' **1946** MEZZROW & WOLF *Really Blues* xii. 226 Not looking for trouble but solid ready for it. **1950** L. HUGHES *Simple speaks his Mind* xx. 108 Man, if I had a rocket plane, I would rock off into space and be solid gone. Gone. Real gone! I mean gone!

c. *to book solid*: to sell all the tickets of (a theatre, cinema, etc.). Usu. in *pass.* Also *absol.*

1916 *Variety* 27 Oct. 12/1 The Boston opera house is booked solid until March. **1921** *Kinematograph Monthly Rec.* Feb. 4 So many individual exhibitors are refusing to book 'solid'. **1955** M. ALLINGHAM *Beckoning Lady* vii. 105, I told him the show was booked solid. **1967** N. MARSH *Death at Dolphin* ix. 234 We're booked out solid for another four months.

d. Of time: consecutively, without a break.

1938 M. ALLINGHAM *Fashion in Shrouds* xx. 379 I've had forty-eight hours solid and I'm no longer intelligent. **1964** L. DEIGHTON *Funeral in Berlin* xlii. 270 He'll be out for eight hours solid.

20. *solid angle* (Math.), † (*a*) a vertex of a three-dimensional body; (*b*) a quantity associated with a vertex or the like in three dimensions, being proportional to the fraction of a sphere centred on it which would subtend it, and conventionally measured in steradians, of which 4π make up the whole sphere; *solid circuit* (Electronics) = *integrated circuit* s.v. *INTEGRATED *ppl. a.* b; *solid diffusion*, migration of atoms within the crystal lattice of a solid; *spec.* in *Geol.*, considered as a possible mechanism for a metasomatizing process in rock masses; *solid fuel*, fuel that is solid, rather than liquid or gaseous; *spec.* (*a*) coal, coke, etc., as opposed to oil, gas, or electricity for domestic heating; (*b*) as used in rocketry; freq. *attrib.*; hence *solid-fuelled* adj. (esp. of rockets); *solid geology*, the geological features of a given region specifically excluding superficial deposits such as clay, sand, etc.; opp. *drift*; *solid injection*, in diesel engines, the use of a mechanical pump to spray fuel into the cylinder at high pressure, without the use of compressed air; = **airless injection*; *solid solution*, a solid phase consisting of two or more substances uniformly mixed in proportions that can be varied; also, the state of being a constituent of such a phase; *solid stowing* (Coal Mining), the process of filling abandoned workings with solid material, esp. spoil; *solid system* (Electr. Engin.), a system of cable-laying in which insulated cables are laid in a trough which is then filled with bitumen; *solid tyre*, a tyre made of solid rubber, with no pneumatic cavity; so *solid-tyred* adj., fitted with such tyres.

1704 Solid angle [in Dict., sense 2 a]. **1798** C. HUTTON *Course in Math.* I. 327 Similar Solids, contained by plane figures, are such as have all their solid angles equal..and are bounded by the same number of similar planes. **1814** P. BARLOW *New Math. & Philos. Dict.* s.v., Solid angles may be computed and compared with each other, as to quantity, by considering the angular point as the centre of a sphere, and the portion of its surface intercepted between the bounding planes as the measure of the angles. **1820** N. J. LARKIN *Introd. Solid Geom.* 5 [The tetrahedron] differs from every other solid, whose faces are all equal, by having a solid angle opposite to each face. **1928** *Bureau Standards Jrnl. Res.* (U.S.) I. 34 The integrals are to be evaluated..over the surface of a hemisphere (solid angle 2π). **1948** *Research* I. 394/2 Substances..similar to a black body radiating in a solid angle of 2π. **1958** *Proc. Internat. Symp. Electronic Components, Malvern, 1957* 4 The increasing tempo of work on solid state physics may result in solid circuits of another form. **1961** *Solid-State Electronics* II. 20/1 Work on solid circuits was begun in the United Kingdom in 1956... The objective is..the fabrication of working circuits using doping, shaping and other techniques in single crystals of silicon. **1966** *New Scientist* 30 June 846/3 (*caption*) Solid-circuit amplifier. The chip measures 0·075 × 0·075 in and contains 30 resistors and 30 transistors. **1913** *Rep. Brit. Assoc. Adv. Sci. 1912* 367 The question whether true solid diffusion ever occurs in minerals is very difficult to answer. **1947** *Geol. Mag.* LXXXIV. 218 More recent work has shown that such transformations are most easily explained as a result of solid diffusion. **1965** P. C. BADGLEY *Structural & Tectonic Princ.* ix. 346 The advocates of solid diffusion propose.. large-scale granitization of country rocks without the presence of contemporary magmatic granites in the district. **1891** H. J. PHILLIPS *Fuels* 1 Determining the value of a solid fuel such as coal, coke, or patent fuel. **1936** *Archit. Rev.* LXXX. 45/1 In electric fires, Tudor and Adam surrounds flourished, and some characteristics of the traditional solid-fuel fireplace were introduced into the designs. **1952** E. BURGESS *Rocket Propulsion* ii. 38 Most British war rockets employed cordite, whereas America used ballistite for their solid-fuel rockets. **1960** *Which?* Jan. 7/2 In general..the most economic fuels are solid fuel and oil. **1971** P. J. MCMAHON *Aircraft Propulsion* x. 295 The most important factors which have led to the increase in interest in solid fuel rockets in recent years..have been concerned with the convenience and ease of storage of the solid propellants. **1979** H. MCLEAVE *Borderline Case* xiv. 145 Who had cached these ..boots, solid-fuel heater, and two sleeping bags? **1958** *Economist* 13 Dec. 985/2 Work is likely to continue on the Titan as a reinforcement for the Atlas..until the solid-fuelled Minuteman is ready some years hence. **1972** *Nature* 21 Apr. 368/3 The decision to use a solid fuelled disposable booster for the proposed space shuttle effectively limits the number of possible launch sites to Cape Kennedy and Vandenberg Air Force Base. **1937** J. S. FLETT *First 100 Yrs. Geol. Survey Gt. Brit.* v. 113 Many maps of north Yorkshire were issued only with 'Solid' geology. **1946** L. D. STAMP *Britain's Structure & Scenery* iv. 30 Following the practice of the Geological Survey in some of their detailed maps, there are to be two maps—one to show the 'solid' geology as it would appear if superficial deposits such as boulder clay, glacial sands and gravels and clay-with-flints..were removed and the other to show the 'drift' geology with all those surface deposits indicated. **1970** *Watsonia* VIII. 171 A map of the 'drift' as well as the solid geology would have been valuable. **1915** A. P. CHALKLEY *Diesel Engines for Land & Marine Work* (ed. 4) iii. 122 Solid injection is now being employed with a large number of engines installed in British submarines. **1936** [see *cold starting* s.v. *COLD *a.* 19]. **1969** J. FLACK et al. *Marine Combustion Practice* II. v. 154 Airless or solid injection superseded the blast system... Mechanically operated injectors have given way in their turn to automatic injectors. **1890** *Jrnl. Chem. Soc.* LVIII. 1044 As instances of solid solutions, we have isomorphous mixtures and mixed crystals, amorphous solutions, as in the case of the glasses and certain minerals; and then such cases as the solution of hydrogen by palladium and other metals. **1900** *Proc. R. Soc.* LXVII. 109 Silver and copper are each capable of holding a small percentage of the other in solid solution, but..if both metals are present in considerable amounts, the two solidified solutions exist side by side. **1964** H. HODGES *Artifacts* xix. 215 In brasses containing less than 36% zinc a solid solution, the α-phase, is formed in which the zinc atoms enter the space lattice of the copper. **1977** A. HALLAM *Planet Earth* 119 Such a series is called a solid solution series, and all members have the same crystalline structure. **1929** *Trans. Inst. Mining Engineers* LXXVI. 258 Solid stowing of the goaf is universal, and in most cases consists of dry stowing done by hand. **1964** *Times Rev. Industry* Feb. 48/3 The industry in this area has pioneered a method of dealing with subsidence known as 'solid stowing' in which colliery spoil is dampened and blown under pressure into abandoned seams. **1977** DOWN & STOCKS *Environmental Impact of Mining* xii. 313 Solid stowing reduces *a* [*sc.* the 'subsidence factor'] to about 0·4–0·5. **1891** *Electr. Engineer* 30 Jan. 121/2 In the Callender Solid system the insulated cables are laid in an iron trough and the whole filled in solid with melted bitumen. **1898** [see *BUILT *ppl. a.* 1 b]. **1920** *Whittaker's Electr. Engineer's Pocket-bk.* (ed. 4) 352 The B.O.T. raise no objection to the omission of the copper tape on unarmoured cables laid on the solid system; a great deal of such cable is in use without any leakage trouble. **1953** C. C. BARNES *Power Cables* xv. 154 The solid system is more expensive than burying cables direct in the ground and requires a greater measure of skilled supervision and favourable weather conditions... For the above reasons the solid system is seldom used today. **1891** *Bicycling News* 31 Jan. 77/1 Given a solid tyre..it will be found that about one half of its diameter is available for tractive and cushioning purposes. **1895** G. B. SHAW *Let.* 6 Aug. (1965) I. 540 It would be a bad machine even of its own kind, the art of building for solid tyres being a decaying one. **1946** W. H. CROUSE *Automobile Engin.* xxvii. 572 Solid tires have very limited usage, their use being confined largely to specialized industrial applications. **1891** Solid-tyred [see PNEUMATIC *sb.* 3 a]. **1963** BIRD & HUTTON-STOTT *Veteran Motor Car* 17 A horizontal-engined, twin-cylinder, chain-driven, solid-tyred 'dog-cart' was in production by the end of the year.

21. a. *solid-fuelled* (see sense *20), *-tyred* (see sense *20).

b. *solid-looking* (earlier example); **solid-drawn** *a.*, made or shaped by deep drawing (see *DEEP *a.* IV. c).

1888 *Lockwood's Dict. Mech. Engin. Terms* 335 The copper piping for feed, bilge, blow-off, and similar purposes in connection with marine engines..are all solid drawn. **1909** F. W. RAYNES *Domestic Sanitary Engin. & Plumbing* vii. 167 Solid drawn lead pipes have many advantages as soil pipes. **1966** A. W. LEWIS *Gloss. Woodworking Terms* 47 Best-quality brass hinges are 'solid drawn' because they are made by the leaf and the tube for the knuckle being drawn out in a long solid strip which is then cut off into lengths. **1840** POE in *Graham's Mag.* Dec. 268/1 These were known by their coats and pantaloons of black or brown..with white cravats and waistcoats, broad solid-looking shoes, and thick hose.

c. *solid-propellant*, *-stem*; **solid-shot** *U.S.* (see quot. 1949).

1946 *Jrnl. Brit. Interplanetary Soc.* VI. 45 The missile is driven by a solid-propellant rocket unit. **1961** Solid-propellant [see *APOGEE 4]. **1982** *Navy News* Mar. 18/3 The missiles would be accelerated from rest by two solid-propellant boosters. **1935** *Daily Progress* (Charlottesville, Va.) 25 July 1/5 'Solid shot' votes are within the law in primaries as well as in general elections. **1949** *Richmond* (Va.) *Times-Dispatch* 25 Nov. 4/5 Under the 'solid-shot' method a voter casts his ballot for a single candidate when two or more persons are to be elected to the same office. **1906** E. JOHNSTON *Writing and Illuminating* xii. 213 A solid-stem pattern cuts up the ground into small pieces. **1961** *B.S.I. News* July 23/2 Solid-stem calorimeter thermometers.

‖ **solidaire** (sǫlidēᵊ·ɹ), *a.* [Fr.] = SOLIDARY *a.* 2.

1845 MACAULAY *Let.* 1 Mar. (1977) IV. 244, I certainly did suppose that you considered yourself as solidaire for doctrines which the cabinet has repeatedly and emphatically proclaimed. **1877** W. R. ALGER *Life of Edwin Forrest* I. i. 25 When volition put rigidity into his muscles the centre was solidaire with the periphery. **1942** WYNDHAM LEWIS *Let.* 27 Jan. (1963) 316 But one cannot help feeling *solidaire* with the nation to which one belongs. **1962** *Times Lit. Suppl.* 3 Aug. 556/2 They must be made not 'solidaire' (to use M. Neveux's words) in a shared, superior understanding of the plight of the figure on the stage, but made 'solitaire' as they realize that they each, alone, share his fate.

solidarist. (In Dict. s.v. SOLIDARIC *a.*) Add: Also *attrib.* or as *adj.* Hence **solidari·stic** a.

1957 [see *PERSONALISM b]. **1968** *Economist* 28 Dec. 27/3 Further evidence of an 'instrumental collectivism' as opposed to a traditional 'solidaristic collectivism'. **1969** P. WORSLEY in Ionescu & Gellner *Populism* 224 These independent commodity-producers..were not simply 'petty-bourgeois' individualists, as..their solidarist political associations demonstrate. **1974** B. JESSOP *Traditionalism, Conservatism & Brit. Pol. Culture* ii. 32 The distinctive attribute of secular voters is an absence of solidaristic class consciousness rather than commitment to deferential norms.

solidarity. Add: **1.** (Earlier and further examples.) Also, *spec.* with reference to the aspirations or actions of trade-union members. Also *attrib.* and *Comb.*

Also the English rendering of Polish *Solidarność*, the name of an independent trade-union movement in Poland, registered in September 1980 and officially banned in October 1982.

1841 H. DOHERTY *False Assoc. & its Remedy* 24 Solidarity, Solidary. Collective responsibility. Collectively responsible. **1885** *To-day* III. 83 [Strike manifesto] But if, on the contrary, you design this strike as a step toward a final and definite solution of the great labour question, if you would make it the means of teaching the worker the absolute necessity of combination and of unity, if having secured the adoption of Solidarity you will build upon this a superstructure of Education, if you will learn why you are poor, [etc.]. **1962** *Listener* 31 May 935/1 These gangs have group-cohesiveness (in our present jargon) or solidarity (in socialist jargon), but they are against society. **1963** *Daily Tel.* 5 Feb. 10/2 Twice as many countries are attending this conference as were at the Afro-Asian States conference in Bandung in 1955; but the great difference is that those now meeting are merely 'solidarity organisations'. **1968** *Listener* 6 June 713/1 Well before the last election, sociologists were telling us that an increasing number of working-class people were beginning to look at politics instrumentally rather than in terms of class solidarity or ideological allegiance. **1969** *Ibid.* 30 Jan. 131/3 Afro-Asian Peoples Solidarity Committees display predictable signs at airports. **1971** I. DEUTSCHER *Marxism in our Time* (1972) v. 109 The perennial conflict between national egoism and international solidarity becomes more and more visible. **1974** *Socialist Worker* 9 Nov. 6/4 The building workers called a solidarity strike. **1977** *Time* 4 July 7/3 In the months since then, Soviet ideologues have opened a campaign to increase 'fidelity to the principles of internationalist solidarity'—party jargon for rallying round Moscow's flag. **1979** *Time* 13 Aug. 12/3 'Solidarity' marchers arrived from Sanandaj, the Kurds' provincial capital. **1980** *Times* 26 Sept. 6/4 The Warsaw daily *Zycie Warszawy* quoted members of the Solidarity free trade union movement as rejecting reforms of the old unions as mere name-changing. **1980** *Economist* 18 Oct. 46/1 Over 20 unions, including Mr Lech Walesa's Gdansk-based Solidarity (an umbrella organisation representing 50 small unions, and claiming a total membership of over 4m), have applied to register with the courts in Warsaw. **1982** *Times* 9 Oct. 1/5 The Polish Parliament..yesterday voted..for a new trade union law that sounds the death knell of Solidarity. *Ibid.*, In broad outline, the bill dissolves all registered trade unions including Solidarity.

solidary, *a.* **2.** (Earlier example.)

1841 [see *SOLIDARITY 1].

solidity. Add: **3. c.** The ratio of the area of the blades of a propeller (counting one side only) to the area of the circle they turn in.

1926 H. GLAUERT *Elements Aerofoil & Airscrew Theory* xvi. 213 This quantity σ represents the ratio of the area of the blade elements to the area of the annulus at the radial distance *r*, and may be termed the solidity of the blade element. **1953** D. O. DOMMASCH *Elem. Propeller & Helicopter Aerodynamics* ii. 61 As far as propeller operation is concerned, increasing solidity has much the same effect as decreasing the aspect ratio of the wing. **1980** *Sci. Amer.* July 114/2 The twin screws of the 31-knot *Queen Elizabeth 2*, each of which absorbs 55,000 h.p., are appreciably smaller, turn much faster and have an even greater solidity than the screws of the largest tankers.

solid state. [f. SOLID *a.* + STATE *sb.*] **1.** The condition or state of being solid rather than fluid.

1866 E. ATKINSON tr. *Ganot's Elem. Treat. Physics* (ed. 2) VII. iv. 425 A metallic salt is introduced either in a solid state or in a state of solution. **1908** *Chem. Abstr.* II. 1654 The electrical conductivity of a series of natural silicates was measured in the solid and liquid states. *Ibid.* 2757 (*heading*) The solid state. **1959** *Cambr. Rev.* 6 June 597/1 The section on nuclear magnetic resonance is almost entirely concerned with wide-line studies on the solid state.

2. *attrib.* (Usu. with hyphen.) **a.** Concerned with the structure and properties of solids, esp. with their explanation in terms of atomic and nuclear physics; as *solid-state physics* (hence *solid-state physicist*).

1953 C. KITTEL (*title*) Introduction to solid state physics. **1956** *Electronic Engin.* XXVIII. 63/1 Research in solid-state physics in recent years has yielded much information on the relations between the electrical magnetic and elastic properties of metals. **1964** *New Scientist* 4 June 595 In his studies, the solid-state physicist must have some means of knowing what compounds are likely to be semi-conducting if he makes them. **1973** *Sci. Amer.* Jan. 98/3 Solid-state physics is currently faced with the problem of constructing an effective theory of noncrystalline, amorphous substances. **1974** *BP Shield Internat.* Oct. p. iii/3 He graduated as an applied physicist and subsequently as a solid state physicist. **1975** *Nature* 20 Nov. 274/2, I think that the solid-state theorist will enjoy this part of the monograph particularly.

b. (Employing devices) utilizing the electronic properties of solids (as in transistors and other semiconductor devices, in contrast to the partial vacuum of valves). Occas. *absol.*, such devices collectively.

1959 *Economist* 23 May 769/2 The transistor, best known of the 'solid-state' devices that employ these materials [*sc.* semiconductors], can do most of the jobs of a valve while taking far less space. **1961** *Times* 30 June 9/2 In this system solid-state electronic circuits.. will replace conventional devices for interlocking signals and points. **1965** *Wireless World* July 350/2 Marconi's.. showed their new solid-state 4½-inch image orthicon. **1968** *Times* 1 Nov. 23/4 In [computer] hardware, solid-state electronic devices have completely transformed the reliability, cost, speed and size of central processors. **1970** *New Scientist* 15 Oct. (Suppl.) 13/2 Solid state radars are required for airborne applications where size and weight are of prime importance. **1971** *Hi-Fi Sound* Feb. 40/1 (Advt.), All silicon solid state circuitry using 20 transistors and 2 diodes provides a full 20 watts r.m.s. output. **1975** G. J. King *Audio Handbk.* ix. 202 A high-gain solidstate amplifier. **1978** *Broadcast* 5 June 21/2 The system's information is stored in solid state, not (as one might expect) on floppy disc.

solidungular, *a.* For *rare*$^{-1}$ read *rare* and add later example.

1922 Joyce *Ulysses* 699 Smart phaeton with good working solidungular cob.

solidus[1]. Add: **2.** Also, such a mark used in writing fractions and for other separations of figures and letters. Cf. *oblique *sb.* 5.

1891, etc. [in Dict.]. **1923** N. Shaw *Forecasting Weather* i. 35 A solidus (/) such as occurs in the combination 'bc/r' separates weather at the time of observation from the preceding weather, bc/r thus indicating 'fine or fair after rain or drizzle'. **1947** [see *non-linear *a.* b]. **1971** *Archivum Linguisticum* II. 4 Johnson/Jenkinson's 'oblique dash'.., which is otherwise called a 'solidus' or 'virgule'.

solidus[2]. Add: [Adopted in this sense in Ger. by H. W. B. Roozeboom 1899, in *Zeitschr. f. phys. Chem.* XXX. 387.] Substitute for def.: A line or surface in a binary or ternary phase diagram respectively, or a temperature (corresponding to a point on the line or surface), below which a mixture is entirely solid and above which it consists of solid and liquid in equilibrium. Freq. *attrib.*, as *solidus curve, temperature*, etc. (Earlier and later examples.)

1901, etc. [see *liquidus]. **1933** Liddell & Doan *Princ. Metall.* iii. xvi. 501 The solidus plane of the system..lies at a lower temperature than do any of the binary eutectics concerned. **1935** [see *homogenized *ppl. a.* 1]. **1959** B. Chalmers *Physical Metall.* iii. 85 For a ternary alloy the liquidus and solidus are surfaces. **1965** G. V. Raynor in R. W. Cahn *Physical Metall.* vii. 325 The solidus temperature for a given alloy composition. **1967** A. H. Cottrell *Introd. Metall.* xv. 230 This gives a phase diagram with a retrograde solidus curve,..with the striking property that alloys of certain compositions.. can become completely solid and then melt again on cooling.

solificatio (sǒᵘ:lifikā·tiǫ). *nonce-wd.* [An invented Latin word, formed on Solific *a.*: see -fication.] A radiating warmth as of sunshine.

1941 Auden *New Year Letter* iii. 74 Who on the lives about you throw A calm solificatio.

soliflual (sǭli·flᶦŭăl), *sb.* and *a. Physical Geogr.* [f. *soliflu(ction + -al.] **A.** *sb.* Material that has moved by solifluction. *rare.* **B.** *adj.* = *solifluctional *a.*

1941 *Trans. R. Soc. Edin.* LX. 376 Generally the layers basal to an aggradational series, following production of an erosion scarp, are re-sorted soliflual. **1965** B. T. Bunting *Geogr. of Soil* xii. 144 Sørensen classified higharctic soliflual soils into those of inhomogeneous material ..and those of stoneless fines.

solifluction (sǒᵘ-, sǫliflʌ·kʃən). *Physical Geogr.* Also **-fluxion.** [f. L. *sol-um* ground, earth + -i- + *fluction*, Fluxion.] **1.** The gradual movement of waterlogged soil or other surface material down a slope, esp. where the subsoil is frozen and acts as a barrier to the percolation of surface water.

1906 J. G. Andersson in *Jrnl. Geol.* XIV. 96 This process, the slow flowing from higher to lower ground of masses of waste saturated with water.., I propose to name *solifluction.* **1916** T. G. Taylor *With Scott* 115 These symmetrical polygons are due to a slow movement of half-frozen soil, which has been noted in polar lands, and is called solifluxion or soil-creep. **1936** *Geogr. Jrnl.* LXXXVII. 449 Solifluction also is known from the Alps, as for instance in the flysch region of the Segnas Pass. **1938** C. F. S. Sharpe *Landslides & Related Phenomena* iii. 35 The definition given by Andersson..does not limit solifluction to cold climates. From the cases he mentions, however, and from subsequent usages by Eakin.., Nichols.., and others, the word solifluction has come to be intimately associated with frost action. **1957** G. E. Hutchinson *Treat. Limnol.* I. i. 144 The presence of such ponds can lead to striking solifluction if the pressure of the water on the down-slope wall is great enough. **1965** M. Fieldes et al. in G. J. Williams *Econ. Geol. N.Z.* xx. 364/2 This solifluxion is thought to account for the emplacement of plastic clays occurring at..localities in the Wellington area. **1974** C. Taylor *Fieldwork in Medieval Archaeol.* iv. 85 Deep hollows on the faces of chalk scarps in Wessex are usually the result of periglacial action and solifluction.

2. *attrib.*

1946 F. E. Zeuner *Dating Past* 119 Solifluction deposits..are a conspicuous feature of sections from the periglacial zone. **1968** C. R. Twidale *Geomorphol.* ix. 274 Small solifluxion terraces and lobes are typical of slopes in periglacial regions. **1970** R. J. Small *Study of Landforms* i. 2 Our knowledge of the vital role of periglaciation..is based almost wholly on analysis..of the distribution and character of solifluxion gravels.

Hence **soliflu·ctional** *a.*, pertaining to or produced by solifluction; also (as a backformation) **so·liflucted** *a.*, that has moved by solifluction.

1924 *Geogr. Jrnl.* LXIII. 225 On well-developed solifluctional slopes of mixed material, the different-sized stones move downwards at different rates. **1954** *Sci. News* XXXIII. 70 On the continent, the task of dating soliflucted material is aided by interbedded sheets of loess. **1956** *Antiquity* XXX. 99 Weathered carboniferous sandstones (whose upper solifluxional levels are in several places separated by multi-coloured clays). **1971** J. N. Jennings in Jennings & Mabbutt *Landform Studies from Australia & New Guinea* xii. 271 Their hummockiness and the way they spread out distally with a bulging lower margin are features in favour of an end-moraine rather than a solifluctional origin. **1977** *Antiquaries Jrnl.* LVII. 187 Some sarsens..could be derived from chalk or Greensand as could the soliflucted spread in the Vale of Pewsey.

solifuge. Restrict † *Obs.*$^{-0}$ to sense in Dict. and add: **2.** = Solpugid in Dict. and Suppl. Also **soli·fugid** (-dʒid) [-id[3]], in the same sense.

1925 R. W. G. Hingston in E. F. Norton *Fight for Everest, 1924* iii. 286 Solifugids occur up to 15,000 feet. **1935** *Discovery* Sept. 282/2 The dread of a Spider or a Solifuge is due to the speed of its movement. **1964** J. Hillaby *Journey to Jade Sea* 182 The total bag was one grasshopper, one dead beetle..and a spider-like animal called a solifuge. **1968** R. D. Barnes *Invertebrate Zool.* (ed. 2) xiii. 399/2 Solifugids possess voracious appetites and feed on all types of small animals, including vertebrates.

Solignum (sǫli·gnǝ̆m). Also **solignum.** Proprietary name for a preservative for timber. Hence **soli·gnumed** *a.*, treated with this material.

1900 *Trade Marks Jrnl.* 17 Oct. 1105 *Solignum*... Preparations for the destruction of weeds, vermin, and insects. Major and Co. Ltd. Chemical manufacturers. **1909** *Chambers's Jrnl.* 27 Feb. 204/1 The preparation known as 'solignum'..is a fluid composition, applied.. with a brush, possesses great covering capacity, and.. improves with age both in appearance and resistant qualities. **1925** *Glasgow Herald* 19 June 8/8 One [way of dealing with white ants] is to keep painting the wood with solignum, and breaking down the trails whenever they appear. **1932** 'Dane' & Simpson *Re-enter Sir John* xx. 270 His neat little dressing-room, matchboard, solignumed [*sic*], sham-antique in the film-studio manner. **1969** *Observer* (Colour Suppl.) 12 Jan. 17/3 The walls continue with a cladding of weatherboarding, solignumed black, to the 12-ft level of the eaves.

soliloquacity (sǫlilǭkwæ·siti). [Blend of Soli(loquy *sb.* and Loquacity: cf. Soliloquacious *a.*] Soliloquizing at great length.

1895 *World* 30 Oct. 25/1 As he is soliloquising to this effect (he out-Hamlets Hamlet in soliloquacity), enter a letter from Mexico. **1967** *Time* 31 Mar. 40/3 Stephen's soliloquy on the beach, Bloom's trip to Paddy Dignam's funeral... Molly Bloom's magnificent end-spurt of soliloquacity.

solion. *Electronics. temporary.* [f. Sol(ution + Ion.] An electrochemical device consisting of two or more electrodes sealed in an electrolyte in which a reversible electrochemical reaction is monitored, versions of which are used as amplifiers, integrators, and as pressure transducers which also sense low-frequency sound and changes in temperature or acceleration. Freq. *attrib.*

1957 *N.Y. Times* 23 June 24/4 It has been nicknamed 'solion', which is short for ions in solution. *Ibid.*, The laboratory [*sc.* the U.S. Naval Ordnance Laboratory] expects that the solion will make possible cheaper, smaller and simpler electronic control systems. **1962** *New Scientist* 2 Aug. 254/1 The solion tetrode..is used as an integrator or as a low-frequency amplifier. **1966** *McGraw-Hill Encycl. Sci. & Technol.* XII. 482/2 The solion diode uses platinum electrodes in an aqueous solution that may be iodine and potassium iodide. *Ibid.* 483/1 The solion pressure transducer..measures fluid flow through an orifice separating two electrolyte chambers.

solipsism. Add: (Earlier and later examples.) Also, = Egoism 1, and in weakened sense.

1874 A. C. Fraser *Sel. from Berkeley* 47 Ueberweg suggests that Berkeley's reasoning implies that we can know only *our own* notions of what we call *other* spirits—thus leading, by a *reductio ad absurdum*, to Egoism or Solipsism. **1978** *Poetry* Aug. 298 The deep underlying motive of Mark Strand's poetry is solipsism or loneliness of the individual imagination.

solipsist. Add: **B.** *adj.* Favouring or characterized by solipsism; also in weakened sense.

1903 A. E. Taylor *Elements of Metaphysics* iii. ii. 202 Why..did Berkeley..accept neither the solipsist nor the sceptical conclusion? **1927** V. McNabb *Cath. Ch. & Philos.* iii. 101 His [*sc.* Kant's] own words are ingenuously solipsist! **1972** *Last Whole Earth Catalog* 16/2 Solipsist tyrants, believing that their will, like their eyeballs, could move mountains, have come to believe that it should trample over these small annoying figures in their visual field.

solipsistic, *a.* Add: (Earlier and later examples.) Also in weakened sense.

1885 W. James in *Mind* X. 37 Men who see each other's bodies sharing the same space..will never practically believe in a pluralism of solipsistic worlds. **1952** A. Wilson *Hemlock & After* ii. iii. 145 His intense, solipsistic world of personal ambition. **1958** I. Murdoch *Bell* xiv. 184 But now, driven by this fit of solipsistic melancholy one degree more desperate, she felt the need of an act. **1968** A. Storr *Human Aggression* xi. 104 Psychopaths share with the schizophrenic the characteristic of living in a world which is predominantly solipsistic; that is, in which people and events are not valued in and for themselves, but only in so far as they affect the subject. **1971** E. Shorris *Death of Great Spirit* iv. 66 The vision of Western man—seeing himself in the central role—might have been considered solipsistic only two hundred years ago. **1977** *Dædalus* Summer 42 It expanded, not by conflicts and deals with equals, but by short spurts of solipsistic exuberance at the expense of much weaker neighbors.

Hence **solipsi·stically** *adv.*

1898 W. James in R. B. Perry *Tht. & Char. of W. James* (1935) II. 370 Take me solipsistically if you will. My talk is merely a description of my present field of experience. **1923** *Times Lit. Suppl.* 23 Aug. 549/2 There are traits of experience which almost all of us are accustomed to explain solipsistically—our dream-worlds. **1952** *Mind* LXI. 10 We each solipsistically confined ourselves to statements which we may properly claim to know to be true directly. **1981** *Times Lit. Suppl.* 8 May 512/3 The real tramps aren't..made miserable by self-consciousness. For the most part, they seem solipsistically content, boozily quarrelling.

solitary, *a.* Add: **1. e.** *solitary wave*, a travelling, non-dissipative wave which is neither preceded nor followed by another such disturbance.

[**1837** J. S. Russell in *Trans. R. Soc. Edin.* (1840) XIV. 61 This accumulated mass..appeared to roll forward alone along the surface of the quiescent fluid, a large, solitary, progressive wave.] **1838** Russell & Robison in *Rep. Brit. Assoc. Adv. Sci. 1837* 418 This wave had been called the great solitary wave of the fluid. **1876** *Phil. Mag.* I. 262 The very different behaviour of solitary waves according as they are positive or negative... In the former case, the wave has a remarkable permanence, being propagated to great distances without much loss. **1899** [see *equivoluminal *a.*]. **1952** Russell & Macmillan *Waves & Tides* i. ii. 44 The velocity of solitary waves of small height is: √[g(depth of water + wave height)]. **1976** *Nature* 8 Apr. 510/2 Figure 2*a* and *b* shows typical streamline patterns for waves corresponding to solitary waves of elevation (E solitons) and of depression (D solitons).

3. c. (Later examples.)

1916 J. Buchan *Greenmantle* v. 62 There was nothing the Boche liked so much as an excuse for sending a poor devil to 'solitary'. **1924** W. M. Raine *Troubled Waters* xxvi. 262 'He's been in solitary for a week,' explained the warden. **1963** M. Duggan in C. K. Stead *N.Z. Short Stories* (1966) 101 Bread and water and solitary and take that writ on his eyeballs. **1978** T. Allbeury *Lantern Net* xi. 164, I visited prisoners in solitary every other day.

soliton (sǫ·litǫn). *Physics.* [f. Solit(ary *a.* + *-on[1].] A solitary wave (see *Solitary *a.* 1 e); a quantum or quasiparticle propagated in the manner of a solitary wave.

1965 Zabusky & Kruskal in *Physical Rev. Lett.* XV. 240/1 Each such 'solitary-wave pulse' or 'soliton' begins to move uniformly at a rate..which is linearly proportional to its amplitude. **1967** *Ibid.* XIX. 1096/1 The solitons exhibit a remarkable stability in that their identity is preserved through nonlinear interactions. This property of solitons..was discovered numerically and justifies the name suggestive of particles. **1968** *Trans. Amer. Geophysical Union* XLIX. 209/2 Steep waves in shallow water have nonlinear properties similar to those exhibited by interacting 'solitons', nonlinear dispersive wave entities that arise in solutions of the Korteweg-de-Vries..equation. **1976** [see *solitary wave* s.v. *solitary *a.* 1 e]. **1979** *Physica Scripta* XX. 306/1 Solitons appear in many fields of our life ranging from classical fluids, solid state and elementary particle physics to biophysics.

solitudinous, *a.* (Earlier example.)

1803 S. Pegge *Anecdotes of Eng. Lang.* 312, *-ous* is a termination which carries weight with it, and might be admitted, as in *multitudinous*, and other similar words in which it has obtained a situation; as,—magnitudinous, gratitudinous, solitudinous, plenitudinous, &c.

soljanka, var. *SOLYANKA.

sollar, *sb.*[1] Add: The form *solar* is now usual in sense 1 a, esp. when used *Hist.*

sollicker (sǫ·likəɹ). *Austral. slang.* Also **soliker.** [Of unknown origin.] Something very big, a 'whopper'. Hence **so·llicking** *a.*, 'whopping'.

1898 R. GRAEME *From England to Back Blocks* 82 Who was it I heard that in cutting-out some cattle on one of the Methvin plains, did come down a soliker and broke his horse's knees? **1899** 'S. RUDD' *On our Selection* 64 He kicked Farmer what he afterwards called 'a sollicker on the tail'. **1939** FRANKLIN & CUSACK *Pioneers on Parade* 168 She gave me a sollicker of a dose out of a blue bottle. **1946** K. TENNANT *Lost Haven* (1947) x. 155 It was a great big sollicking stitch if ever there was one. **1956** P. WHITE *Tree of Man* I. vii. 91 'You can jump down, can't you? You're quite big, you know.' 'Of course he can... He's a sollicker.'

sol-lunar, *a.* Delete *Med.* and add: Also **solunar.** (Further examples.)

1936 J. A. KNIGHT *Mod. Angler* xviii. 198 It is well to use a descriptive term or word instead of referring to 'inland tides' or 'the conditions which cause tides'. For this purpose the word 'Solunar' has been coined. Solunar ..may be defined as follows: The time at which the conditions which cause ocean tides (*i.e.* the pull of the sun and the moon) pass the longitudinal meridian of any given point is the Solunar period at that point. **1962** E. BRUTON *Dict. Clocks & Watches* 162 *'Solunar' dial*, daily tidal times, as shown on some wrist-chronographs and used in conjunction with 'solunar tables' (J. Alden Knight) to forecast feeding times of fish and game for sportsmen. **1971** *Nature* 31 Dec. 537/2 The phase lag in the incidence of large earthquakes with respect to overhead position of the Sun and Moon is coincident with the imposition of horizontal force in such a direction and sense as to increase accumulated shear strain if this is due to the solunar torque.

solo, *sb.*[1] and *a.* Add: **A.** *sb.* **III. 6. a.** (Earlier examples.)

1814 C. JONES *Hoyle's Games Improved* 189 The quotient shews the number of fish to be paid to each of the successful players by the other two; or in event of a Solo to be paid him by each of the three others. **1875** W. B. DICK *Mod. Pocket Hoyle* (ed. 7) 144 *Solo.*—This is an announcement to accomplish the same ends as in bidding to play in 'suit', but without the aid of the Scat cards.

b. *Solo Whist* (earlier example); also *ellipt.*; *Heart Solo* (earlier example).

c **1875** W. B. DICK *Mod. Pocket Hoyle* (ed. 6) 146 Thus a player announcing Heart Solo (worth six counters), and having in his hand four Matadores, can bid Heart Solo *with* four Matadores, equal to ten counters, [etc.]. **1888** WILKS & PARDON (*title*) How to play solo whist. **1907** [in Dict.]. **1972** C. DRUMMOND *Death at Bar* v. 129 They had looked forward to a cosy evening of cocoa and solo with..the other boys.

7. Solo flying; a solo flight.

1911 *Flight* 16 Sept. 805/1 Capt. Watt made a very good solo round Fargo and Stonehenge, landing exceptionally well. **1928** T. E. LAWRENCE *Let.* 20 Jan. (1938) 569 All decent birds hop it when their infants have done their first solo. **1942** R. HILLARY *Last Enemy* iii. 74 The flight immediately following our first solo was an hour's aerobatics. **1976** B. JACKSON *Flameout* iii. 44 'How long to get your license?' 'Thirty-five hours to solo, if you're good.'

B. *adj.* **1. a.** *spec.* with reference to flying.

1914 H. ROSHER *In R.N.A.S.* (1916) 15 Hope to be flying solo by Thursday or Friday. **1928** *Daily Mail Year Bk.* 24/1 They can obtain the use of a machine in which to fly solo for £1 an hour. **1934** *Sun* (Baltimore) 22 Oct. 2/1 Lieut. M. Hansen,..who is flying solo, left Athens at 9.11 A.M. for Baghdad. **1946** *Happy Landings* July 4/1 The sergeant-pilot..had amassed the considerable sum of two hours solo on Oxfords. **1955** *Times* 24 Aug. 6/4 Eight years later Colonel Lindbergh took 33hr. 30min. in his monoplane to fly solo non-stop from New York to Paris. **1977** 'J. HERRIOT' *Vet in Spin* x. 113 'I said take her up.' 'You mean, on my own?.. Go solo?'

b. Acting alone or without assistance (*spec.* in *N.Z.* of single parents).

1934 *Sun* (Baltimore) 2 Mar. 19/8 The sportsman pilot ..is variously designated as 'private', 'solo' and 'student' pilot. **1965** A. BLACKSHAW *Mountaineering* 19 The risks to the inexperienced *solo* rock climber or snow-and-ice climber are very great. **1966** P. O'DONNELL *Sabre-Tooth* vii. 100 She wondered..if an army of mercenaries was being assembled..But no—he was very much a solo man. **1977** *N.Z. Herald* 8 Jan. II. 2/7 So far, the research has shown that few solo mothers are out to skin the welfare state by claiming a domestic purposes benefit and living on boyfriends.

2. (Later example.)

1927 *Glasgow Herald* 18 Mar. 11 London..has only two 'solo' machines. Its members, nevertheless, contrived to put in a total of 84 hours flying during..January.

3. (Earlier example.)

1862 [see *EUPHONION].

4. That is achieved or performed unaccompanied or unassisted.

1909 *Flight* 18 Sept. 576/2 After making a short 'solo' flight he came down. **1914** *Daily Express* 22 Sept. 7/4 A solo effort by Cantrell, who weaved his way prettily through the defence, brought the winning goal. **1927** *Glasgow Herald* 30 Sept. 11 He has made the longest solo flight so far achieved by an airman. **1940** *Daily Progress* (Charlottesville, Va.) 25 Jan. 9/4 Police claim she admits one solo holdup, made to prove her nerve. **1944** *Ibid.* 12 Sept. 6/6 The trends within medicine which make solo practice no longer..the best..kind of service for the physician or for the patient. **1955** *Times* 22 Aug. 8/5 Lord de L'Isle and Dudley, V.C., Secretary of State for Air,..has logged 13 hours' solo flying. **1974** *Times* 6 Dec. 5/5 (*caption*) The Prince of Wales after making his first solo deck landing of a Royal Navy Wessex helicopter.

Solo (sōᵘ·lo), *sb.*[2] The name of a river in Java, used *attrib.* with reference to a neanderthaloid fossil hominid, *Homo soloensis*, known from skulls discovered at Ngandong in the valley of the Solo river in 1931.

1932 *Discovery* Aug. 240/2 A new type of early man..is to be called 'Solo Man' from the name of the river in the Pleistocene gravels of which the skull was found. **1951** *Anthrop. Papers Amer. Mus.* XLIII. 205 (*title*) Morphology of Solo Man. **1973** B. J. WILLIAMS *Evolution & Human Origins* xi. 185/1 The Solo skulls..appear to be more primitive than Neandertal. *Ibid.*, Solo Man tends to have an occipital torus higher on the skull than did the African Neandertals. **1978** B. G. CAMPBELL *W. E. Le Gross Clark's Fossil Evidence for Human Evolution* (ed. 3) iii. 120 The main problem in this connection lies in the status of the Solo population.

solo (sōᵘ·lo), *v.* [f. SOLO *sb.*[1] and *a.*] **1.** *intr.* To perform an action on one's own; *spec.* (*a*) to perform a vocal or instrumental solo (now usu. in jazz); (*b*) to fly solo; *spec.* to make one's first solo flight; (*c*) *Mountaineering*, to climb without a partner.

1886 W. BOOTH *Orders & Regul. Salvation Army* III. ii. 96 All cannot solo or speak eloquently. **1917** J. M. GRIDER *War Birds* (1927) 57, I have been flying for three days and Capt. Harrison says I can solo to-morrow if it's calm. **1931** V. W. PAGÉ *ABC of Gliding* 164 In training glider pilots the student usually 'solos' from the very start. **1932** *Daily Progress* (Charlottesville, Va.) 25 Feb. 4/3 The most magnificent bodega was recently ordered to remove its enormous bar and is now trying to solo to prosperity as a restaurant only. **1942** R. HILLARY *Last Enemy* iii. 72 Here for the first time was a machine in which there was no chance of making a dual circuit as a preliminary. I must solo right off. **1956** B. HOLIDAY *Lady sings Blues* (1973) vi. 60 Whenever Basie had an arranger work out something for me, I'd tell him I wanted Lester to solo behind me. **1958** P. GAMMOND *Decca Bk. of Jazz* xx. 249 With Reinhardt and Grappelly soloing over the pulsating guitars—bass rhythm section. **1962** E. SNOW *Red China Today* (1963) xxiv. 183 All the items I have mentioned are primary sinews of a modern industrial civilization, the development of which enables a nation to 'solo' as a major industrial power. **1964** J. E. B. WRIGHT in Murray & Wright *Craft of Climbing* v. 35, I solo-ed up the Slab Climb. **1971** M. TAK *Truck Talk* 148 *Solo*, 1. to drive a tractor without a trailer... 2. to drive a rig alone when the driver in question is usually part of a two-man operation. **1972** D. HASTON *In High Places* iv. 57 But what to do? Thoughts of soloing down and alerting a rescue party, but that would have meant a major operation. **1977** *National Observer* (U.S.) 1 Jan. 13/3 If the river is easy, it's fun to solo. But on a formidable stream you need a partner.

2. *trans.* To perform (a piece of music) as a solo. *rare.*

1858 *Punch* 8 May 184/2 The sweetness of his oratory would be completely wasted on the air of '*Keemo Kimo*' soloed by the ophicleide.

3. *Mountaineering.* To climb (a mountain, etc.) without a partner.

1962 *Listener* 8 Nov. 758/2 Not that you climb alone; only very talented fanatics or complete fools 'solo' hard routes. **1975** G. MOFFAT *Miss Pink at Edge of World* xiv. 194 Solo-ing steep rock at Clive's age is just not on.

Hence **so·loing** *vbl. sb.*; also *attrib.*

1929 *Papers Mich. Acad. Sci., Arts & Lett.* X. 324/2 *Soloing*, flying alone. **1971** C. BONINGTON *Annapurna South Face* 324 *Soloing*, climbing without the security of a rope. **1973** —— *Next Horizon* v. 90 Dick..was unaccustomed to fast soloing, and eventually they had turned back before even reaching the foot of the climb proper. **1977** *Rolling Stone* 24 Mar. 66/2 His guitar style combines Hendrix-inspired production technique with virtuoso soloing ability.

Solochrome (sōᵘ·lŏkrōᵘm). Also **solochrome.** A proprietary name for a range of synthetic dyestuffs used esp. in chemical analysis in colour tests for various metals, notably aluminium. Usu. *attrib.* in names of particular dyes.

1924 *Trade Marks Jrnl.* 23 Apr. 910 *Solochrome*... Chemical substances used in dyeing... British Dyestuffs Corporation Limited. **1938** *Analyst* LXIII. 266 A test for aluminium..has been based on the vivid orange-red fluorescence obtained with aqueous alcoholic solutions of Solochrome Red ERS and Solochrome Violet RS. **1960** A. G. E. PEARSE *Histochem.* (ed. 2) xxiv. 693 Other Solochrome dyes give coloured, non-fluorescent complexes with aluminium hydroxide. **1976** *Lancet* 4 Dec. 1209/2 Undecalcified 6μm sections were prepared and stained with toluidine blue, pH 2·8, and solochrome cyanin.

solod (sǫ·lət). *Soil Science.* Also **soloth.** Pl. (sometimes const. as *sing.*) **solodi, soloti**; also **solods.** [a. Russ. *sólod'*, f. *sol'* salt.] A type of soil derived from a solonetz by leaching of saline or alkaline constituents, having a pale, leached subsurface horizon, and occurring characteristically under grass or shrub vegetation in semi-arid and desert regions.

1925 S. A. WAKSMAN tr. *K. K. Gedroits's Soil Absorbing Complex & Absorbed Soil Cations* (U.S. Dept. Agric.) 13 The process of forming a new type of soil from an alkali soil as a mother soil leads to secondary soils ('soloti'), which are distinguished from primary podsol soils both in origin and in the properties of the formation. **1933** *Soil Sci.* XXXVI. 181 The solodi profiles of the semiarid short grass plains zone. *Ibid.* 184 (*caption*) A well-developed solodi. **1934** *Ibid.* XXXVIII. 484 After the complete formation of Soloth with the removal of the mobile colloids, the continued growth of the native grasses again changes the soil to that normal for the region. **1953** *Proc. Soil Sci. Soc. Amer.* XVII. 287 Solod soils ordinarily occur in the lowest local position in the landscape, usually a deep depression, while Solonetz and solodized Solonetz soils develop on level areas or in slight depressions. **1963** D. W. & E. E. HUMPHRIES tr. *Termier's Erosion & Sedimentation* xv. 324 The soloti are the degraded alkaline soils derived from solonetz soils by solotization, a process analogous to podsolization. *Ibid.* 325 Solotis are known in the U.S.S.R. and in the western United States. **1974** E. A. FITZPATRICK *Introd. Soil Sci.* vii. 119 Solods can be regarded as leached solonetzes in which the upper horizons are strongly bleached becoming pale grey or white.

Hence **solo·dic** *a.*, being, resembling, or characteristic of a solod; **so·lodize** *v. intr.*, to change into a solod; **solodiza·tion** (also **solot-**), the formation of a solod by the leaching of salts from a solonetz; **so·lodized (solot-)** *ppl. a.*, altered by this process.

1925 S. A. WAKSMAN tr. *K. K. Gedroits's Soil Absorbing Complex & Absorbed Soil Cations* (U.S. Dept. Agric.) 14 Just as the carbonates of calcium and magnesium protect the soil of forest zone from podsolization, these salts protect alkaline soils from 'solotization'. *Ibid.* 15 The question of the presence of absorbed hydrogen in solotized soils is still not clear. **1932** E. J. RUSSELL *Soil Conditions & Plant Growth* (ed. 6) iv. 269 In this process of solodisation, the percolating water continues to remove sodium and other products of decomposition from the soil complex, replacing the exchangeable sodium by hydrogen, and depositing the products of decomposition lower down. **1934** *Soil Sci.* XXXVIII. 484 As soon as solonetz forms it immediately begins to solotize with the development of a profile approaching the soloth. **1964** *Jrnl. Soil Sci.* XV. 176 The absence of solodized-solonetz from the deep sands is related to the coarser texture of the material of which they are composed. **1968** H. C. T. STACE et al. *Handbk. Austral. Soils* vi. 153 In the solodized solonetz, solodic soils and red-brown earths the topsoil is acid.., but all..contain secondary carbonate in the deeper horizons. **1978** FANIRAN & AREOLA *Essent. Soil Study* viii. 183 Salinization, solonization, and solodization..resulting in the formation of solonchaks, solonetz, and solodic soils respectively.

solograph. For *rare*⁻⁰ read *rare* and add *attrib.* example.

1851 C. CIST *Sketches & Statistics of Cincinnati in 1851* 187 Hawkins, in addition to his daguerrotypes, produces what he terms a *solograph* picture.

soloistic (sōᵘlo,i·stik), *a.* [f. SOLOIST + -IC.] Of, pertaining to, containing, or of the nature of, soloists or solo parts. Also *transf.* Hence **solo,i·stically** *adv.*

1947 A. EINSTEIN *Music in Romantic Era* xvi. 285 Three acts..: each one in two parts, the first part 'soloistic', the second always uniting all the figures of the farce, as the tradition of *opera buffa* demanded. **1952** B. ULANOV *Hist. Jazz in Amer.* (1958) xiv. 165 Edward Inge an alto, and Horace Henderson and Don Kirkpatrick on piano were other soloistic assets of the band. **1961** *Times* 9 June 17/1 The cellos are strung out in front of the basses, which..can cause the cello tone to be diffused when the section is used soloistically. **1974** *Daily Tel.* 11 Feb. 10/4 Every member of the choir seems to command a soloistic projection yet the overall sonority is magnificently blended. **1975** *Gramophone* Aug. 316/3 Above all, the position of the solo viola is too soloistic. **1977** *Country Life* 2 June 1494/3 The commitment, enthusiasm, and general lack of soloistic egotism of almost all involved was delightful to observe. **1980** *Early Music* Jan. 19/1 Soloistic music needs a more generous portion of personal sound.

Solomon Islander (sǫ·lŏmǫn əi·lændəɹ). [f. *Solomon Islands* (see below) + -ER[1].] A native or inhabitant of the Solomon Islands in the southwest Pacific.

1864 in C. M. Yonge *Life John Coleridge Patteson* (1874) II. ix. 96 Two of the Solomon Islanders distinguished themselves by jumping off the foreyard, and diving under the ship. **1911** F. COOMBE *Islands of Enchantment* III. i. 239 Perchance it is as well that the Solomon Islanders had about 300 years in which to forget the first Christian emissaries before the next visited them! **1951** R. FIRTH *Elements of Social Organization* iii. 92 The Solomon Islander is no less sensitive to the appellation of country bumpkin than is his European counterpart. **1968** *World Book Encycl. Australasia* II. 323 In 1896, Solomon Islanders killed five Austrian scientists who were attempting to climb their sacred mountain.

Solon. Add: Also (with small initial) in the *U.S.*, in weakened sense: a legislator, congressman.

1903 'O. HENRY' *Art & Bronco* in *Ainslee's* Feb. 59/1 The season of activity and profit that the congregation of the solons bestowed. The boarding houses were corralling the easy dollars of the gamesome lawmakers.

1948 E. POUND *Pisan Cantos* (1949) lxxxiv. 128 Thus the Solons, in Washington. **1959** *New Scientist* 29 Jan. 230/3 Congress was not in session at the time of the AAAS meeting... But the solons are back in the Capitol now. **1976** *National Observer* (U.S.) 21 Aug. 11/2 The great national political community of solons, scribes, policemen, [etc.].

solonchak (sǫ·lǫ̆ntʃæk). *Soil Science.* Also **solontschak**, etc. [a. Russ. *solonchák* salt marsh, salt lake, f. *sol′* salt.] A type of salty, alkaline soil that has little or no structure, is characteristically pale in colour, and occurs typically under salt-tolerant vegetation in poorly-drained semi-arid or desert regions.

1925 S. A. WAKSMAN tr. *K. K. Gedroits's Soil Absorbing Complex & Absorbed Soil Cations* (U.S. Dept. Agric.) 9 The stage of formation of a saline soil (solontshak) will in this case always take place before the stage of formation of an alkaline soil (solonetz). **1927** C. F. MARBUT tr. *Glinka's Great Soil Groups of World* 40 There is no word in English carrying the same meaning conveyed by the expression 'alkali soils with definite structure'. To avoid the use of so long a phrase the Russian word Solonetz will be used in the following pages while the word Solontschak will be used for 'alkali soils without pronounced structure'. **1939** *Agric. in 20th Cent.* 177 Where the soil water tended to move upwards, as in parts of the hot, dry countries, and especially where it contained salts in solution, another set of changes took place and the resulting soils were called 'solontchaks'. **1963** D. W. & E. E. HUMPHRIES tr. *Termier's Erosion & Sedimentation* xv. 325 At the research station at Hamadena, the soils are dominantly solonchak, secondarily characterized by being sodic, magnesian and calcic. **1972** J. G. CRUICKSHANK *Soil Geogr.* iv. 145 Where sodium salts exceed 2 per cent of the mineral matter, a salic horizon is produced which may even be a salt crust on the soil surface under extremely dry conditions and high groundwater table. The soil is called a solonchak.

solonetz (sǫ·lǫ̆nets). *Soil Science.* Also **-nez, -nietz.** [ad. Russ. *solonéts* salt marsh, salt lake, f. *sol′* salt.] A type of alkaline soil that is rich in carbonates, consists characteristically of a hard, dark, columnar subsoil overlain by a thin, friable surface layer, and occurs in conditions similar to those associated with solonchaks but having better drainage.

1924 S. A. WAKSMAN tr. *K. K. Gedroits's Ultramechanical Composition of Soils* (U.S. Dept. Agric.) 17 These are soils which have become saline with sodium salts (saline soils) and alkaline soils ('solonez' soil) formed from these as a result of removal of the salt. **1925, 1927** [see *SOLONCHAK]. **1932** E. J. RUSSELL *Soil Conditions & Plant Growth* (ed. 6) iv. 268 The last stage, when the solonietz has been exposed to prolonged leaching, is the solod of the Russians. **1938** [see *PLANOSOL]. **1968** H. C. T. STACE et al. *Handbk. Austral. Soils* vi. 153 The essential features of solonetz are prominent texture differentiation with an abrupt boundary between loamy A horizons and clay B horizons, neutral to alkaline surface soil and strongly alkaline subsoil [etc.]. **1972** J. G. CRUICKSHANK *Soil Geogr.* iv. 127 (*caption*) A solonetz profile in South Australia showing strong prismatic structure in the B horizon.

Hence **solone·tzic** *a.*, being, resembling, or characteristic of a solonetz.

1935 *Soil Sci.* XL. 465 A strongly solonetzic soil from Chongar. **1974** E. C. STACEY *Peace Country Heritage* ii. 74 If the parental material has a high salt content, a hard-pan solonetzic soil will result.

solonization (sǫ:lǫ̆nəizēɪ·ʃən). *Soil Science.* [f. *SOLON(ETZ + -IZATION.] The formation of a solonetzic soil by the leaching of salts from a solonchak. So **so·lonized** *ppl. a.*

1934 *Soil Sci.* XXXVIII. 483 This process is called solonization and might be said to consist of desalinization plus alkalinization. **1945** *Ibid.* LIX. 420 The physical and morphological feature is the compactness of the solonized section of the profile. **1948** *Queensland Jrnl. Agric. Sci.* V. 19 These solonized patches are comparatively widespread throughout the habitat of 'sandalwood'. **1963** D. W. & E. E. HUMPHRIES tr. *Termier's Erosion & Sedimentation* xv. 324 In a region of saline soils, the areas undergoing solonization become depressions where structural change brings about compaction of the soil.

soloth, var. *SOLOD.

solpugid. (Earlier and later examples.)

1869 A. S. PACKARD *Guide to Study of Insects* 655 Under the term Pedipalpi we would embrace.. the Solpugids and Phalangids. **1912** J. H. COMSTOCK *Spider Bk.* i. 34 Most solpugids spend the day under stones or other rubbish.. and come forth at night. **1954** BORROR & DELONG *Introd. Study of Insects* xxx. 787 The body of a solpugid is about ½ inch long and is somewhat constricted in the middle, and the chelicerae are very large.

solubility. Add: **4.** Special Combs.: **solubility curve** *Chem.*, a curve showing how the solubility of a substance varies with temperature; **solubility product** *Chem.*, the product of the concentrations (*spec.* the activities) of each of the component ions present in a saturated solution of a sparingly soluble salt.

1892 *Jrnl. Chem. Soc.* LXII. 1384 (*heading*) Solubility curves of pairs of salts. **1933** A. K. GOARD *Physical Chem.* ii. 36 A break in a solubility curve always indicates that the composition of the solid in equilibrium with the saturated solution has changed. **1971** Solubility curve [see *INVARIANT *a.* b]. **1899** J. WALKER *Introd. Physical Chem.* xxvi. 307 The solubility product of silver chloride in water is very small, corresponding to the very slight solubility of the salt. **1978** P. W. ATKINS *Physical Chem.* xii. 361 The magnitude of K_S, the solubility product, can be predicted from a knowledge of standard electrode potentials.

solubilization (sǫ:liŭbiləizēɪ·ʃən). [f. next + -ATION.] The process of making something (more) soluble.

1930 *Brit. Chem. Abstr.* B. XLIX. 1061/1 (*heading*) Solubilisation of a perylenetetracarboxylic di-imide dye and dyes produced thereby. **1946** *Industr. & Engin. Chem.* June 642 (*heading*) Solubilization of insoluble organic liquids by detergents. **1977** *Jrnl. Protozool.* XXIV. 17/2 The selective solubilization of protein C permitted us to determine its source.

solubilize (sǫ·liŭbĭləiz), *v.* [f. L. *solūbil-is* SOLUBLE *a.* + -IZE.] *trans.* To increase the solubility of; to convert into a soluble form. Also *absol.*

1926 [implied at SOLUBILIZING *vbl. sb.* below]. **1930** *U.S. Patent 1,776,971* (*title*) Process of solubilizing a perylenetetracarboxylic di-imide dyestuff. **1947** *Jrnl. Soc. Chem. Industry* Jan. 4/2 Free lauryl sulphonic acid solubilises slightly, even in chloroform. **1970** *Jrnl. Neurobiol.* I. 331 The tissue segments were solubilized. **1977** *Nature* 17 Nov. 272/1 After adding hydroxylamine to complex the excess retinal, the rhodopsin was solubilised by adding.. octyl glucoside.

So **so·lubilized** *ppl. a.*, **so·lubilizing** *vbl. sb.*; also **so·lubilizable** *a.*, capable of being solubilized.

1926 *Brit. Pat.* 275,267 3/2 The use of products.. as emulsifying agents or solubilising agents for organic solvents. *Ibid.* 280,647 1 (*title*) Manufacture of a solubilised vat dye and process of dyeing therewith. **1949** E. CHAIN in H. W. Florey et al. *Antibiotics* II. xviii. 748 A solubilizing effect of impurities on other salts of benzylpenicillin.. was observed. **1955** *Times* 1 July 16/2 The therapeutic advantages of solubilized aspirin are as much appreciated in a compound including phenacetin and codeine as they are in Disprin itself. **1978** *Nature* 6 Apr. p. xxv/3 Bio-Rad introduce a new solubilisable gel for polyacrylamide gel electrophoresis. **1979** *Experientia* XXXV. 280/2 For the various thicknesses of sections, the ratio of radioactivity level of the intact section to that of the solubilized one was expressed in percent.

solubilizer (sǫ·liŭbiləizəɹ). [f. prec. + -ER[1].] A solubilizing agent.

1963 *Chem. Abstr.* LIX. 6203 As solubilizers, Tween 20, 60, 80, Carbowax 1500, and Myrj 52 were used. **1979** *Experientia* XXXV. 280/2 The solubilizer.. was added to yield the same concentration of scintillator molecules as in the section undergoing solubilization.

soluble, *a.* Add: **2. b.** (Further examples.) *soluble blue* (also *Soluble Blue*), any of a class of water-soluble dyes that are di- and trisulphonic acid derivatives of aniline blue and are now used chiefly in papers and inks. In *Biochem.* applied to those species of RNA now usu. known as *transfer RNA.*

[**1862** E. C. NICHOLSON *Brit. Patent 1857* 3 A colourless solution is obtained which, when neutralized.., developes the improved soluble blue dye.] **1879** *Jrnl. Chem. Soc.* XXXVI. 418 In preparing the soluble blues, the monosulphonic acids and higher-substituted acids must be of great purity. **1893** T. E. THORPE *Dict. Appl. Chem.* III. 562/1 Perhaps the readiest way of preparing soluble starch is that recommended by Zulkowski.., who finds that starch dissolves in hot glycerin and is converted into the soluble modification. **1952** K. VENKATARAMAN *Chem. Synthetic Dyes* II. xxiii. 723 Sulphonic acids of phenylated Rosanilines, which are old dyes (Nicholson Blue, Soluble Blue, Water Blue, Alkali Blue; CI 703–707) continue to be extensively used. **1958** M. B. HOAGLAND et al. in *Jrnl. Biol. Chem.* CCXXXI. 256 Evidence is presented that a soluble ribonucleic acid.. binds amino acids in the presence of adenosine triphosphate. **1961** *Nature* 13 May 582/1 The other principal (10–15 per cent) form of RNA in *E. coli* is soluble RNA (now more appropriately called transfer RNA), which functions in the movement of activated amino-acids to the ribosomes. **1964** G. H. HAGGIS et al. *Introd. Molecular Biol.* xii. 306 Because of its special function this RNA is now generally called transfer-RNA, although it is also sometimes referred to as soluble-RNA, or as acceptor-RNA. **1971** R. L. M. ALLEN *Colour Chem.* viii. 115 A marked bathochromic effect is obtained by phenylation of the amino groups in rosanilines... These Soluble Blues are now little used for textile coloration, but are applied to leather, paper and.. in printing inks. **1973** *Times* 18 Oct. (Brazil Suppl.) p. v/2 Soluble (instant) coffee exports have grown at a remarkable pace. **1974** E. AMBLER *Doctor Frigo* III. 185, I gave her some soluble aspirin and left. **1977** *Whitaker's Almanack 1978* 914/1 The chief exports are cotton, coffee, beef, gold, sugar, cottonseed, bananas, copper and soluble coffee.

5. b. *Math.* = *SOLVABLE *a.* 3 b.

1902 *Encycl. Brit.* XXIX. 140/1 A group defines uniquely the set of factor-groups that occur in its composition series... When the orders of all the factor-groups are primes the group is said to be soluble. **1940** *Trans. Amer. Math. Soc.* XLVII. 393 A group may be termed soluble, if it may be swept out by an ascending (finite or transfinite) chain of normal subgroups such that the quotient groups of its consecutive terms are abelian groups of finite rank. **1972** [see *QUOTIENT 1 b].

B. *sb.* A soluble constituent, esp. of a foodstuff.

1952 *Poultry Sci.* XXXI. 937/1 There was no change in the hatchability of eggs from the hens receiving condensed fish solubles. **1962** M. N. HILL *Sea* I. vi. 305 (*heading*) Solubles. **1972** *Brit. Jrnl. Nutrition* XXVIII. 221 The main growth-promoting effect of fish solubles has been shown to be mediated through the intestinal microflora of the chick.

solum. Delete ‖ and add: **2.** *Soil Science.* (Pl. **solums, sola.**) The upper part of a soil profile, in which the soil-forming processes predominantly occur; *spec.* the A and B horizons. [Introduced (as G. *solumhorizont* solum horizon) by B. Frosterus 1922, in *Compt. Rend. de la Conf. Extraordinaire (IIème Internat.) Agropédologique* (1924) 361.]

1928 *Proc. & Papers 1st Internat. Congr. Soil Sci.* IV. 7 To the soil body has been given definitely the status of a well defined concept by the application to it of a name consisting of a single term, the *Solum*, by Frosterus. **1942** *Technical Bull. U.S. Dept. Agric.* No. 834. 49 All but small quantities or traces [of carbonates] are leached from the solums of all but the Clyde profile. **1956** *Soil Sci.* LXXXII. 451 In the coarser sand fractions (0.5–2mm.) weatherable mineral material such as granite, diorite, and basalt is abundant in all horizons of the sola. **1972** J. G. CRUICKSHANK *Soil Geogr.* ii. 41 The minimum moisture storage in the solum will be equivalent to between 10 and 15 cm water per unit area.

solunar, var. SOL-LUNAR *a.* in Dict. and Suppl.

solus, *a.* Add: **1. b.** *solus cum sola* [L.]: alone with an unchaperoned woman; *solus cum solo* [lit. 'alone with (oneself) alone']: all on one's own.

1611 CORYAT *Crudities* 404 They sing merily together, but especially that sweet & most amorous song of *solus cum solâ.* **1700** DRYDEN *Fables* 226 Stretching his Neck, and warbling in his Throat, *Solus cum Sola*, then was all his *Note.* **1742** R. NORTH *Life of Francis North, Ld. Guilford* 242 But he was in the midst of all the court, *solus cum solo*, alone by himself. **1818** LADY MORGAN *Florence Macarthy* II. iv. 202, I shall have the honour to drink your ladyship's health, *solus cum solo.* **1831** [see *CHAPERONLESS *a.*]. **1940** H. H. HENSON *Jrnl.* 24 Mar. in *Retrospect* (1950) III. ii. 88 In the afternoon I had tea with Mrs. Carnegie *solus cum sola.*

3. Of things. **a.** *Advertising.* Of an advertisement: that stands alone; sometimes, that deals with one item (e.g. one book) only. Also, pertaining to such advertisements. Also *transf.* and *absol.*

1937 PARTRIDGE *Dict. Slang* 800/1 *Solus*, an advertisement on a page containing no other advertisement. **1952** *Economist* 5 Apr. 18/2 The advertiser would no doubt be charged varying rates equivalent to 'solus position'. **1958** *Times Lit. Suppl.* 5 Dec. 699/1 Within four days of publication *The Middle Age of Mrs. Eliot* had received solus feature reviews in *The Observer, The Sunday Times*, [etc.]. **1974** *Bookseller* 4 May 2154 (Advt.), Massive promotion. 10 giant solus advertisements in the National Press. **1980** *Financial Rev.* (Sydney) 18 Apr. 42/3 Rod Muir's station does have a rate card which concentrates on selling solus spots—60 seconds to two minutes. Mr Muir thinks radio has lost a lot of its effectiveness with the clutter of 30 second ads.

b. *Comm.* Of an outlet for the sale of oil and petrol: that sells the products of one company only. Also, of or pertaining to such an arrangement.

1957 *Economist* 7 Dec. 836/2 Whether a solus site offering three grades of one brand of petrol provides less choice than a mixed site offering three brands of the same grade is a question for chemists and advertising men to answer. **1958** *Spectator* 11 July 62/3 The Government had struck a blow against monopoly.. by banning 'solus' petrol stations from the new motorways. **1965** *Economist* 7 Aug. 542/1 The major companies selling petrol in Britain have been sure for many months now that the Monopolies Commission would not find the 'solus' or 'tied garage' system, in itself, to be against the public interest. **1976** *Drive* Jan.–Feb. 10/1 One of the busiest solus sites (where only one brand of petrol is sold) in the country.

solute, *sb.* Add: Now usu. with pronunc. (sǫ·liŭt). **2.** (Earlier and later examples.)

1893 F. G. DONNAN in *Nature* 27 Dec. 200/2 Corresponding to the words 'solvent' and 'solution', some word is very badly wanted to express 'the dissolved substance'. The analogous word is evidently 'solute', and it is as short and euphonious as the others. **1978** P. W. ATKINS *Physical Chem.* viii. 216 When a solute is present there is an extra randomness present in the solution that was not present in the pure solvent.

solution, *sb.* Add: **II. 6. b.** = *rubber solution* s.v. *RUBBER *sb.*[1] 14.

1897 A. C. PEMBERTON *Complete Cyclist* vii. 190 The edges of the cut must be well cleaned and coated with solution. **1930** F. GARDNER *How to repair your Cycle* 20 Spread a thin layer of solution over the part that has been rubbed. **1974** S. TOWNROE *How to mend your Bike* 44 Never put on the patch until the solution has dried.

8. b. *Physical Geogr.* Denoting features and phenomena resulting from the solvent action of water, as *solution basin, depression, subsidence*, etc.

1894 Solution lake [in Dict., sense 8 a]. **1931** *Jrnl. Geol.* XXXIX. 641 (*heading*) Solution depressions in sandy sediments of the coastal plain in South Carolina. **1934** C. R. LONGWELL et al. *Outl. Physical Geol.* iv. 73 In some regions sinks, caverns, and solution valleys are so numerous that they give rise to a peculiar and characteristic topography with many surface depressions, irregular drainage patterns, and disappearing streams. **1939** A. K. LOBECK *Geomorphol.* iv. 145 Very large sinks or areas of depression are known as solution basins. **1954** *Geol. Mag.* XCI. 225 A lowering of surface by solution subsidence has been proceeding more or less continuously since Triassic times on this high moorland terrain. **1957** E. E. EVANS *Irish Folk Ways* ii. 18 The lowland of which it is the centre is..diversified by occasional low hills, by intricate solution lakes and by glacial eskers. **1977** *Antiquaries Jrnl.* LVII. 189 Three large masses..recovered from red clay-with-flints filling a solution pipe at Aston Rowant (Oxon.).

IV. 12. Special Combs.: **solution heat treatment** = *solution treatment* below; **solution set** *Math.*, the set of all the solutions of some equation or condition; **solution treatment** *Metallurgy*, a process designed to render an alloy susceptible to age-hardening, by which it is first heated to make a particular constituent enter into solid solution and then quenched; so **solution-treat** *v. trans.*, **solution-treated** *ppl. a.*

1935 G. E. DOAN *Princ. Physical Metallurgy* vi. 192 This heating and quenching is called the 'solution heat treatment'. **1979** J. NEELY *Pract. Metallurgy & Materials of Industry* xiv. 187/2 Successful solution heat treatment depends on putting the copper into solid solution and trapping it there. **1959** ALLENDOERFER & OAKLEY *Fund. Math.* vi. 102 Given a universal set X and an equation $F(x) = G(x)$ involving x, the set $\{x|F(x) = G(x)\}$ is called the solution set of the given equation. **1963** WEBBER & BROWN *Basic Concepts Math.* viii. 166 The truth set of an equation is often called the solution set, and members of the solution set are called solutions of the equation. **1972** A. G. HOWSON *Handbk. Terms Algebra & Anal.* i. 5 Those objects of a given set which satisfy an open statement form the solution set of the statement relative to that set. Thus the solution set of $x^2 = 2$ relative to the real numbers is the set $\{+\sqrt{2}, -\sqrt{2}\}$. Relative to the rational numbers.., the solution set of $x^2 = 2$ is empty. **1940** J. D. JEVONS *Metall. of Deep Drawing & Pressing* xv. 577 Rolled sheet could be 'solution-treated' to place it in a ductile condition. **1977** R. B. ROSS *Handbk. Metal Treatment & Testing* 207 Components which have been correctly Solution treated and aged are very often joined by [welding]. **1952** *Jrnl. R. Aeronaut. Soc.* LVI. 235/1 With highly tapered spar booms it is advisable to machine in the solution-treated condition in order that any correction..may be made before precipitation. **1931** *Metallurgist* VII. 12/2 The age hardening..of duralumin and a number of other alloys of similar type requires a previous heat treatment, which is frequently termed the 'solution' treatment. **1970** P. C. VARLEY *Technol. of Aluminium & its Alloys* v. 62 All solution treatment is carried out in forced air circulation furnaces.

solutioned (sŏlⁱū·ʃənd), *ppl. a.* [f. SOLUTION *v.* + -ED[1].] Treated or covered with solution.

1898 G. L. HILLIER *Cycling for Everybody* 81 The solutioned surface should be left alone for some minutes, which allows of the evaporation of the naphtha. **1909** 'R. ANDOM' *On Tour with Troddles* 264 We strengthened the cover with strips of rubber and solutioned canvas.

solutionist (sŏlⁱū·ʃənist). [f. SOLUTION *sb.* + -IST.] One who solves problems or puzzles; *spec.* an expert solver of crossword puzzles.

1885 *Liverpool Mercury* 24 Oct. 5 A large proportion belong to the party of the Right... M. Paul de Cassagnac calls them 'Solutionists'. **1915** *Competition Prize-Winner* I. 1 Our supporters may rest assured that no solutionist will be permitted to use our advertising space unless.. his methods are absolutely fair. **1926** *Weekly Dispatch* 29 Aug. 3/3 The insertion of clues capable of alternative solutions..gives the ordinary reader an equal chance with the professional solutionist. **1930** *Aberdeen Press & Jrnl.* 3 May 8/2 If you are keen on winning one of the big cash prizes..for competition enthusiasts, why not avail yourself of the help of expert solutionists?

solutionizing (sŏlⁱū·ʃənaiziŋ), *vbl. sb.* [f. SOLUTION *sb.* + -IZE + -ING[1].] The process of forming a solution; *spec.* = *solution treatment* s.v. *SOLUTION *sb.* 12. So **solu·tionized** *ppl. a.*

1950 *Chambers's Jrnl.* Mar. 189/2 A recently evolved solutionising system, which is used in conjunction with an overhead irrigation plant, allows the soluble plant-foods to be added at any desired rate. **1977** R. B. ROSS *Handbk. Metal Treatment & Testing* 206 The hardening of steel, where [solution treatment]..is occasionally referred to as 'Solutionizing' or 'Austenizing'. **1978** *Jrnl. R. Soc. Arts* CXXVI. 690/2 An aluminium alloy containing 6 per cent copper, Hid54, set in a freshly solutionized condition, was proposed as the rivet material.

solutizer (sǫ·liutəizəɹ). [f. L. *solūt-*, ppl. stem of *solvere* SOLVE *v.* + -IZE + -ER[1].] = *SOLUBILIZER.

1939 *Refiner & Natural Gas Manufacturer* XVIII. 171/2 It was found that the addition of suitable organic solvents or salts ('solutizers') to an aqueous alkaline solution increased the solubility of the resulting solution for mercaptans. **1957** VAN DER HAVE & VERVER *Petroleum & its Products* v. 197 In the so-called solutizer process the extracting medium is an alkaline solution to which substances have been added for promoting the solubility and reducing the hydrolysis of the alkali mercaptides in water. In one form of such a method, the 'solutizers' are the sodium and potassium salts of certain organic acids.

Solutrian, Solutrean, *a.* Add: [ad. F. *solutréen* (G. de Mortillet *c* 1867).] **B.** *sb.* **a.** The Solutrean culture.

1928 C. DAWSON *Age of Gods* i. 14 The Aurignacian culture of Europe..was replaced by the sudden intrusion of a new culture—the Solutrean—which originated in Eastern Europe or Asia. **1946** F. E. ZEUNER *Dating the Past* ix. 289 When the loess phase of this glacial phase was at its climax, Solutrian appeared, north of the Alpine mountain chains, and in Spain. **1969** G. CLARK *World Prehistory* (ed. 2) iii. 61 During the time of the late Solutrean and Early Magdalenian the artists ceased to engrave limbs as though they were hanging from their back-bones. **1975** J. G. EVANS *Environment Early Man Brit. Isles* ii. 49 The French Solutrean, an industry of unsurpassed elegance in its flint work.

b. A person of the Solutrean period. *rare.*

1944 H. G. WELLS *'42 to '44* 178 The distribution of the Solutreans gives a range quite in accordance with the ideas of W. H. Riddell.

solvable, *a.* Add: **3. b.** *Math.* Of a group: that may be regarded as the last of a finite series of groups of which the first is trivial, each being a normal subgroup of the next and each of the quotients being Abelian.

1892 E. NETTO *Theory of Substitutions* xiv. 267 We may carry over the expressions 'transitive', 'primitive' and 'non-primitive', 'simple' and 'compound' from the group to the equation... Conversely, we apply the term 'solvable', which is taken from the theory of equations, also to groups, and speak of solvable groups as those whose equations are solvable. **1898** *Amer. Jrnl. Math.* XX. 277 The necessary and sufficient condition that a group is solvable is that its αth derivative (derived group) is unity. **1929** *Ibid.* LI. 494 The total number of groups of order 72 is 50. Each of these groups is obviously solvable. **1971** D. GORENSTEIN in Powell & Higman *Finite Simple Groups* ii. 66 The celebrated Feit–Thompson theorem that groups of odd order are solvable implies that every nonabelian simple group has even order. **1982** *Sci. Amer.* Apr. 120/3 An equation is solvable by radicals if and only if the Galois group of the equation is a solvable group.

solvate (sǫ·lvēⁱt), *sb. Chem.* [f. SOLV(E *v.* + -ATE[1].] A more or less loosely bonded complex formed between a dissolved species and the solvent.

1905 *Amer. Chem. Jrnl.* XXXIV. 489 The existence of hydrates or solvates (in the case of non-aqueous solvents) in one form or another is an old conception. **1922** A. W. STEWART *Physico-Chem. Themes* 269 Another form of explanation is arrived at by assuming that solvates are formed on the addition of the salt. **1969** T. C. WADDINGTON *Non-Aqueous Solvents* ii. 18 Because of its ability to donate its lone pair of electrons to form a covalent coordinate link, as well as by ion-dipole attraction, ammonia forms many solvates.

solvate (sǫlvēⁱ·t), *v. Chem.* [f. SOLV(E *v.* + -ATE[3].] *trans.* To form a solvate with (a dissolved species). Usu. as **solva·ted** *pa. pple.* and *ppl. a.* Also (*rare*) *intr.*, to undergo solvation. Hence **solva·ting** *ppl. a.*

1909 *Publ. Carnegie Inst.* No. 110. 104 When a salt of one of these elements is dissolved in a solvent both the molecules of the salt and the ions formed from them become solvated. **1913** H. C. JONES *New Era Chem.* ix. 165 Non electrolytes solvate very slightly. The electrolytes combine with large amounts of the solvent. *Ibid.*, It is the ions which are the chief solvating agents. **1932** PHILBRICK & HOLMYARD *Text Bk. Theoret. & Inorg. Chem.* xi. 312 Hydrogen chloride is a strong acid only in solvents in which it is solvated. **1958** *Proc. Nat. Acad. Sci.* XLIV. 429 Strongly hydrogen-bonding organic solvents have been found to solvate polypeptides and proteins completely. **1968** V. GUTMANN *Coordination Chem. in Non-Aqueous Solutions* ii. 34 With increasing donor properties of the solvent its solvating properties become stronger. **1971** *Nature* 1 Jan. 13/2 The study of the solvated electron has its origins in the work begun by Kraus at the beginning of this century on the blue solutions formed by dissolving alkali metals in liquid ammonia and amines. Electrical conductivity and other measurements have established that the solvated electron is responsible for the blue colour of these solutions. **1976** J. DAINTITH *Dict. Physical Sci.* 4/2 In solution the hydrogen ion, H^+, is solvated by water and often considered to be a hydroxonium ion, H_3O^+. **1977** *Sci. Amer.* July 95/1 The solvated electrons in an alkali-metal-ammonia solution should behave like unpaired electrons in an atom and hence should make the solutions paramagnetic. *Ibid.* 98/3 The entire complex can then readily be solvated by a polar liquid such as an amine or an ether.

solvation (sǫlvēⁱ·ʃən). *Chem.* [f. SOLV(E *v.* + -ATION.] The process of becoming, or state of being, solvated. Freq. *attrib.*

1909 *Amer. Chem. Jrnl.* XLI. 41 The theory of solvation in solution. **1917** M. H. FISCHER tr. *Ostwald's Introd. Theoret. & Appl. Colloid Chem.* 51 These colloids are characterized by their great hydration or solvation. Their particles have taken up a large amount of the dispersion media. **1936** R. W. GURNEY *Ions in Solution* i. 4 If a free gaseous ion enters a solvent..energy is liberated. This is known as the Solvation Energy, and has a characteristic value for each ion in each solvent. **1948** *Nature* 31 Jan. 170/1 When the concentration of organic solvent is increased beyond 50 ml. per cent, organic solvent molecules begin to predominate in the medium and eventually replace the aqueous solvation shell. **1967** MARGERISON & EAST *Introd. Polymer Chem.* v. 239 The questions associated with solvation, its extent, the type of chemical bonding, the number of solvent molecules involved,..are largely unanswerable. **1976** *Nature* 3 June 435/1 Relaxation rates for ^{17}O in monosaccharides have been used to study solvation, the revised estimate of the solvation number being 5 ± 1 water molecules for D-glucose and $2{\cdot}5 \pm 1$ for D-ribose at 5 °C.

Solvay (sǫ·lvēⁱ). *Chem.* [The name of Ernest *Solvay* (1838–1922), Belgian chemist, who developed the process.] *Solvay* (or † *Solvay's*) *process*: a method of making sodium carbonate using brine, ammonia, and carbon dioxide (which is usu. made as part of the process, by calcining limestone); also called *ammonia-soda process*. Hence *Solvay plant*, etc.

1879 *Sci. Amer. Suppl.* 12 Apr. 2719/3 From these injurious impurities the Solvay soda is almost absolutely free. **1884** *Jrnl. Soc. Chem. Industry* 29 Dec. 633/1 In the Solvay process there have been introduced important improvements. **1888** C. L. BLOXAM *Chem.* (ed. 6) 262 (*heading*) Ammonia soda process, or Solvay's process. **1947** KIRK & OTHMER *Encycl. Chem. Technol.* I. 402 A 500-ton-per-day soda plant requires gas compressors of about 3000 to 4000 horsepower to handle the suction on the kilns and to compress the gas into the Solvay precipitating towers. **1950** *Thorpe's Dict. Appl. Chem.* (ed. 4) X. 835/1 The earliest Solvay plants used solid salt and dissolved it in a recycled alkaline water obtained from the scrubbing of calciner gases. **1966** *McGraw-Hill Encycl. Sci. & Technol.* II. 399/2 Calcium chloride, obtained as a waste product in the Solvay process. **1974** *Encycl. Brit. Micropædia* IX. 320/1 Its anhydrous form, soda ash (Na_2CO_3),..is now manufactured chiefly by the ammonia–soda (Solvay) process.

solvent, *sb.* **5.** *attrib.* and *Comb.*, as *solvent abuse, recovery, -sniffing*; *solvent-thinned* adj.; **solvent extraction,** the partial removal of a substance from a solution or a mixture of liquids by utilizing its greater solubility in another liquid or its greater permeability through a membrane; so **solvent-extract** *v. trans.*, to purify by means of solvent extraction; also as *sb.*, a fraction extracted from a mixture by this process; a spell of solvent extraction.

1977 Solvent abuse [see *SNIFFING *vbl. sb.*] **1949** *Our Industry* (Anglo-Iranian Oil Co.) (ed. 2) iv. 116 The kerosine fraction may..be solvent extracted by means of liquid sulphur dioxide. **1956** *Nature* 4 Feb. 224/2 When insulin was added to an acidic solvent-extract of liver..the recovery of the insulin varied between 92 and 93 per cent. **1963** A. J. HALL *Textile Sci.* iii. 122 Another system of purifying wool is to solvent extract it with an organic solvent such as trichloroethylene. **1978** *Nature* 23 Mar. 298/2 Subsequent solvent extract in mixer settlers will separate plutonium nitrate solution. **1920** *Chem. Trade Jrnl.* LXVI. 103 Quantities of oil for edible purposes were being produced by solvent extraction processes. **1949** *Our Industry* (Anglo-Iranian Oil Co.) (ed. 2) iv. 119 Solvent extraction processes are to-day used extensively in the petroleum industry for refining light distillates, kerosines and lubricating oils. **1978** *Sci. Amer.* July 97/3 Solvent extraction across membranes has been known at least since 1913, when Fritz Haber and Reinhardt Beutner showed that a thin film of oil could be employed as a membrane in two kinds of extraction process. **1947** KIRK & OTHMER *Encycl. Chem. Technol.* I. 231 Activated carbon is used on a large scale for solvent recovery. **1977** *Lancet* 8 Jan. 82/1 Cardiac arrhythmias,..neuropsychiatric disorders, and hepatorenal failure have all been reported after solvent sniffing. **1960** *McGraw-Hill Encycl. Sci. & Technol.* IX. 493/1 Solvent-thinned paints, which dry essentially by solvent evaporation, rely on a fairly hard resin as the vehicle.

solventless (sǫ·lvĕntlės), *a.* [f. SOLVENT *sb.* + -LESS.] Without a solvent.

1936 O. W. ESHBACH *Handbk. Engin. Fund.* XII. xxxiii. 70 (*heading*) Solventless varnishes. **1945** *Jrnl. Applied Physics* XVI. 584/2 A thin film of solventless varnish was applied to each sheet. **1970** *Financial Times* 13 Apr. 9/1 A feature of this two-component solventless coating..is that it can be applied cold.

‖ **solvitur ambulando** (sǫ·lvitǝ̆ɹ æmbiulæ·ndo). [L. phr., lit. '(the problem) is solved by walking'.] An appeal to practical experience for the solution of a problem or proof of a statement. Also as *sb. phr.* Also in shortened form **ambulando,** by experience; in the course of things.

Originally an allusion to the reported proof by Diogenes the Cynic of the possibility of motion: see Diogenes Laertius VI. 39.

[**1814** *Artis Logicæ Rudimenta. Accessit Solutio Sophismatum* 67 Ineptum est hoc Sophisma 1. Quia solvitur ambulando; quod fecit Diogenes.] **1852** A. H. CLOUGH *Let.* Mar. in *Poems & Prose Remains* (1869) I. 174 It is not..simply one's business in life to 'envisager' the most remarkable problems of humanity... Still we may be assured that only time can work out any sort of answer to them for us. '*Solvitur ambulando.*' **1863** J. CONINGTON *Horace's Odes* p. xxv, How easily the '*solvitur ambulando*' of an artist like Mr. Tennyson may disturb a whole chain of ingenious reasoning on the possibilities of things. **1863** C. READE *Hard Cash* I. viii. 226 To the à priori reasoners ..he replied by building an engine..hooking on eight carriages, and rattling off up an incline. 'Solvitur ambulando,' quoth Stephenson the stout hearted. **1876** W. JAMES in *Nation* 8 June 369/1 The ultimate decision of which side is right and which wrong shall only be reached *ambulando* or at the final integration of things, if at all. **1906** F. W. MAITLAND *L. Stephen* xvii. 366 He knew that he would have to proceed empirically. *Solvitur ambulando*—the motto of the philosophic tramp—had also to be the motto of the editor. **1930** J. LAIRD *Knowl., Belief & Opin.* iv. 103 Perfectly convincing evidence might turn up, so to say, *ambulando*, when we are engaged in something irrelevant. **1934** A. TOYNBEE *Stud. Hist.* III. 182 A modern Western philosopher applies the historic *solvitur ambulando* to the ancient sophism of the Eleatics. **1955** *Times* 30 Aug. 9/2 To what extent and for what purposes is it justifiable to transform personality by surgery, psychological techniques, or the administration of drugs? In so far as matters of this kind have been the subject of conscious policy in the past solvitur ambulando has been the motto. **1957** G. RYLE in C. A. Mace *Brit. Philos. in Mid-Cent.* 256 The assimilation of language to chess reminds us of what we knew *ambulando* all along.

solvolyse (sǫ·lvǫləiz), *v. Chem.* Also (*U.S.*) **-lyze.** [f. *SOLVOLYSIS after *analyse, analysis*, etc.] **a.** *trans.* To bring about the solvolysis of (a solute); usu. in *pass.* **b.** *intr.* To undergo solvolysis.

1916 *Chem. Abstr.* X. 2349 A table of salts is given which are 'solvolyzed' by C_6H_6. **1921** *Jrnl. Physical Chem.* XXV. 550 Lead chromate solvolyzes. **1965** PHILLIPS & WILLIAMS *Inorg. Chem.* I. xv. 569 In sulphuric acid nearly all inorganic salts are solvolysed in the dissolution process. **1974** *Nature* 19 Apr. 671/1 Tosylate..solvolysed in formic acid at 75°C to give an olefin as the major product. **1977** *Lancet* 24–31 Dec. 1298/1 The bile samples were solvolysed (which ensures that bile-acid sulphate esters are included), and individual acids were measured by gas chromatography.

solvolysis (sǫlvǫ·lisis). *Chem.* Pl. **-lyses** (-lisīz). [ad. G. *solvolyse* (P. Walden 1910, in *Sammlung chem. und chem.-techn. Vorträge* XV. x. 447), f. *solvens* SOLVENT *sb.*: see *-LYSIS.] The decomposition or dissociation of a solute brought about by the action of the solvent.

1916 *Chem. Abstr.* X. 2349 Most probably other indifferent, *i.e.*, non-ionizing solvents are also capable of dissociating salts into base and acid. This general property of solvents, which is independent of electrolytic dissociation, is designated 'solvolysis' or solvolytic dissociation. **1922** *Jrnl. Physical Chem.* XXVI. 567 The solvolyses were performed simultaneously in porcelain crucibles in an oven at 225°–230°. **1940** L. P. HAMMETT *Physical Org. Chem.* vi. 171 The product of the solvolysis is not completely racemized. **1972** R. A. JACKSON *Mechanism* iv. 56 Solvolysis of the diester 63 has been postulated to involve the intermediate carbonium ion 64.

So **solvoly·tic** *a.*, pertaining to or of the nature of solvolysis; **solvoly·tically** *adv.*

1916 [see *SOLVOLYSIS]. **1931** *Chem. Rev.* VIII. 199 Goldschmidt and Mathiesen..report the solvolytic constants for a variety of bases in ethyl and methyl alcohols. **1965** PHILLIPS & WILLIAMS *Inorg. Chem.* I. xv. 556 Solvolytic reactions are often of synthetic value, but they also severely limit the range of reactions which may be conducted in a particular solvent. **1974** GILL & WILLIS *Pericyclic Reactions* vi. 148 With a monohalogeno carbene a mixture of *endo-* and *exo*-halogenobicycloalkanes is formed, only one of which will usually be solvolytically reactive. **1975** *Nature* 21 Aug. 681/1 Overberger and Podsiadly have demonstrated the importance of polymeric chain aggregation on the rate of solvolytic reaction.

solvus (sǫ·lvŭs). Pl. **solvi.** [mod.L., f. L. *solvere* to dissolve, after *LIQUIDUS, SOLIDUS².] A line or surface in a phase diagram delimiting the region of stability of a solid solution.

1950 *Jrnl. Geol.* LVIII. 499/2 Now we have a means of establishing the position of the unmixing curve or solvus. **1956** *Amer. Mineralogist* XLIII. 877 In Fig. 4 three solvi are shown. **1963** W. A. DEER et al. *Rock-Forming Minerals* II. 127 If the liquidus minimum passes beyond the intersection with the solvus..the calcium-poor phase would cease to crystallize as a separate phase. **1968** R. A. HIGGINS *Engin. Metall.* (ed. 2) I. ix. 170 The only new feature of the system..is that we have phase boundaries occurring below the solidus, indicating that phase changes can take place in the solid. On the tin-lead thermal-equilibrium diagram..such phase boundaries.. are indicated by the lines *BC* and *FG*. A line such as *BC* or *FG* is often termed as [*sic*] solvus. **1975** *Nature* 3 Apr. 406/2 At 1,450°C a further solvus was reported between the pigeonite and a more calcic diopside.

‖ **solyanka** (sŏlya·nkă). Also **soljanka.** [Russ.] A soup made of vegetables and meat or fish.

1958 W. BICKEL tr. *Hering's Dict. Classical & Mod. Cookery* 113 *Soljanka is riba*, fish soup. **1970** 'J. MORRIS' *Candywine Devel.* xxv. 280 He..heaped the big serving-spoon with *solyanka* from the dish. **1972** M. GLENNY tr. *Solzhenitsyn's August 1914* xlii. 422 'Well, now, young men—what is it to be? *Solyanka*, meatballs, scrambled eggs?' said the old man invitingly.

‖ **sol y sombra** (sol *i* so·mbra). [Sp., lit. 'sun and shade'.] A drink of brandy mixed with anisette or gin.

1930 W. T. BOOTHBY *'Cocktail Bill' Boothby's World Drinks* (rev. ed.) 148 *Sol y Sombra* (*Sun & Shadow*) Brandy (Spanish) ½ jigger Gin ½ jigger. **1966** C. ROUGVIE *Gredos Reckoning* v. 76 'What's that you're drinking?' '*Sol y sombra*: a mixture of anis and brandy.' **1979** D. SERAFIN *Saturday of Glory* 17 A *sol y sombra*, an explosive mixture of brandy and anisette.

soma¹. Add: Also 8 som.

1. b. In Aldous Huxley's novel *Brave New World*, a narcotic drug which produces euphoria and hallucination, distributed by the state in order to promote content and social harmony. Also *transf.* and *attrib.*

1932 A. HUXLEY *Brave New World* iii. 66 There is always *soma*, delicious *soma*, half a gramme for a half-holiday, a gramme for a week-end, two grammes for a trip to the gorgeous East, three for a dark eternity on the moon. *Ibid.* v. 95 The *soma* had begun to work. Eyes shone, cheeks were flushed, the inner light of universal benevolence broke out on every face in happy, friendly smiles. *Ibid.* vi. 107 Bernard swallowed four tablets of *soma* at a gulp. *Ibid.* xv. 246 The two Groups..were served by the Deputy Sub-Bursar with their *soma* ration. **1959** *Times Lit. Suppl.* 27 Feb. 105/2 The forecast [in *Brave New World*] of a pain-killing, pleasure-giving pill called *soma*, at once the perfect substitute for alcohol, opium and benzedrine, has not yet been wholly fulfilled. **1968** 'J. LE CARRÉ' *Small Town in Germany* ix. 155 If I smoked I'd smoke one of your cigars. I could do with a bit of soma just now. **1976** *Interdisciplinary Sci. Rev.* I. 178/1 Suppose there was national agreement on the need for a 'good' psychoactive drug, one which would be as universally used as the ubiquitous *soma* of *Brave New World*.

2. (Earlier and later examples.)

1785 C. WILKINS tr. *Bhăgvăt Gēētā* ix. 80 The followers of the three *Vēds*, who drink the juice of the *Sōm*.. address me. *Ibid.* 143 *Sōm*—is the name of a creeper, the juice of which is commanded to be drank at the conclusion of a sacrifice. **1972** R. G. WASSON *Soma* ii. 10 My candidate for the identity of soma is *Amanita muscaria*.., in English the fly-agaric.

soma². Add: **1.** Also *fig.*

1914 W. R. INGE *Outspoken Ess.* (1919) 238, I can see no other fate in store for the *soma* of Catholicism; the germ-cells of true Christianity live their own life within it.

2. *Anat.* The compact portion of a nerve-cell, excluding the axon.

1947 R. LORENTE DE NÓ in *Jrnl. Cellular & Compar. Physiol.* XXIX. 211 The word 'soma' will be used to denote the body and all the dendritic branches of the neuron. **1970** *Jrnl. Neurobiol.* I. 340 The somas are likely to be the site of protein synthesis. **1974** *Nature* 8 Nov. 155/1 Studies with a few invertebrate preparations have suggested different ionic mechanisms for spike generation in the soma and axon of the same neurone.

3. The body in contrast to the mind or the soul. Opp. *psyche*.

1958 A. WILSON *Middle Age of Mrs Eliot* I. 72 He says that between Else fussing with his soma and me with his psyche, all he really wants is a complete rest and he wishes he were travelling with you. **1969** *Listener* 26 June 881/2 A score of youths and girls intent on exploring each other honestly and sincerely in psyche and soma can't help generating some degree of excitement. **1976** *Lancet* 30 Oct. 946/2 No personal physician, at any time, has been able to operate successfully without using substances, as symbols of healing of the soma and the psyche.

somaar, var. *SOMMER *adv.*

somæsthetic (sōᵘmīsþe·tik), *a. Physiol.* Also **-esthetic.** [f. Gr. σῶμα body + αἰσθητικ-ός perceptive.] Pertaining to or designating those sensations (as of pressure, pain, or warmth) which can occur anywhere in the body, in contrast to those that depend on highly localized sense organs (as sight, balance, or taste).

1899 L. F. BARKER *Nerv. System* xlvii. 667 The region of the cortex in which the axones of the general sensory conduction path here considered terminate, I have designated as the somæsthetic area of the cortex. [*Note*] I wish to thank Prof. Gildersleeve, of the Johns Hopkins University, for suggesting this term as a suitable English equivalent for Munk's *Körperfühlsphäre*. **1922** R. S. WOODWORTH *Psychology* iii. 63 There is a large and important area called the 'somesthetic', connected with the body senses generally, i.e., chiefly with the skin and muscle senses... Destruction of any part of this somesthetic area brings loss of the sensations from the corresponding part of the body. **1949** *Psychosomatic Med.* XI. 338/2 The thalamus probably participates in a crude awareness of somesthetic sensations. **1968** PASSMORE & ROBSON *Compan. Med. Stud.* I. xxiv. 51/1 The sensory or postcentral gyrus contains areas 1, 2 and 3 which are often considered together as the somaesthetic cortex, receiving sensations from the opposite side of the body. **1972** *Sci. Amer.* Apr. 82/3 The patient cannot name objects held in his left hand because the somesthetic sensations cannot reach the verbal centers in the left hemisphere. **1977** R. K. DAVENPORT in D. M. Rumbaugh *Language Learning by Chimpanzee* iii. 75 In the brain of nonhuman primates as compared with the human brain, the auditory, visual, and somesthetic association areas are relatively independent.

Hence **somæsthe·sis**, the somæsthetic senses.

1928 *Funk's Stand. Dict.*, Somesthesis. **1950** *Ann. Rev. Psychol.* I. 71 (*heading*) Somesthesis and the chemical senses. **1968** [see *KINÆSTHESIS]. **1977** H. G. BURGER in B. Bernardi *Concept & Dynamics of Culture* 423 It [*sc.* the angular gyrus] lies between the association cortices of three non-limbic sensation modalities: vision, audition, and internal sensibility (somesthesis).

Somaj, var. *SAMAJ.

somal, *a.* Add: **2.** Of or pertaining to the soma of a neurone.

1967 *Jrnl. Neurochem.* XIV. 329 Instead of a somal site of synthesis, an alternative possibility was considered; namely, a local axonal synthesis after entry from Schwann cells or a diffusion of precursor from the soma down into the axon. **1978** *Nature* 27 July 381/1 We compared the values of unit conductances activated by acetylcholine (ACh) applied to the somal membranes with values reported for other molluscan neurones.

Somali (somā·li), *sb.* and *a.* Also **Somal, Somauli,** etc. [Native name.] **A.** *sb.* **1. a.** A Hamitic people, adherents of Islam, living in the Horn of Africa, esp. in the Somali Democratic Republic (Somalia); a member of this people. **b.** The language of this people which belongs to the Cushitic sub-family and existed until recently in spoken form only. **B.** *adj.* Of or pertaining to the Somalis or their country.

1814 Somauli [see SWAHILI]. **1842** *Jrnl. R. Geogr. Soc.* XII. 241 There are also smaller kalifas that trade to Amin, Ugadin, and other parts of the Somauli country. **1850** *Trans. Bombay Geogr. Soc.* IX. 129 The country inhabited by the Somal is very extensive. *Ibid.* 130 Since the occupation of Aden by the English, the Somaulies have continued to cross over in considerable numbers. *Ibid.* 136 The article in Somauli is expressed by ka, ki or ga, gi. **1856** R. F. BURTON *First Footsteps E. Africa* 89 In the latter sense it is the polite address to a Somali. *Ibid.* 644/2 Tale of a Somal chief. **1888** F. L. JAMES *Unknown Horn of Africa* 30 'Hubla' (Somal for 'virgin'). **1878** [see *GALLA]. **1921** H. RAYNE *Sun, Sand & Somals* 5 The Somali has deeply religious tendencies. **1930** C. G. SELIGMAN *Races of Africa* v. 124 The early history of the Somali is obscure; that they are essentially Hamitic is certain. **1933** [see *CUSHITE *a.* and *sb.*]. **1937** K. BLIXEN *Out of Africa* II. iv. 137 The immigrant Somalis..are severe Mohammedans. *Ibid.* III. iii. 188 The circle of Somali women in my household. **1948** D. DIRINGER *Alphabet* II. iv. 300 This script, called..'the Osmanya script'..has been created recently for the Somali language by 'Isman Yusuf. **1978** *Encounter* Feb. 52/2 It may be that Cubans using Russian weapons saved Ethiopia from defeat by the Somalis in November 1977. **1978** *Language* LIV. 453 The status of Somali (no official orthography; 184, 201) has changed drastically (Romanization adopted).

Hence **Soma·lian** *a.* = *SOMALI *a.*

1948 D. DIRINGER *Alphabet* II. iv. 300 The origin of the Somalian alphabet. **1976** *Guardian* 23 Aug. 7/1 Her father was Christian and disapproved of the general Somalian habit of infibulation. **1981** *Sci. Amer.* Mar. 29/3 The other [skull] found more recently in a fertilizer factory near Mogadishu, where fishermen who had picked it up on a Somalian beach had sent it.

Soman (sōᵘ·mæn). Also **soman.** [Ger., of unknown origin.] The name of an odourless organophosphorus nerve gas.

1951 *Acta Physiol. Scandinavica* Suppl. No. 90. 106 (*table*) Pinacoloxy-methyl-phosphoryl-fluoride (SOMAN). **1953** *Proc. R. Soc. Med.* XLVI. 801 We found..that 3,4 dihydroxyphenylalanine..and other *o*-dihydroxybenzene derivatives were able to protect both true and pseudo ChE's [*sc.* cholinesterases] against, not only Sarin, but also against Tabun and Soman. **1968** [see *SARIN]. **1969** B. FORD *German Secret Weapons* (1970) 109 Soman has the most terrible effects on soldiers: within seconds they would have been reduced to a state of convulsive collapse and death would be relatively certain. **1980** *Sci. Amer.* Apr. 35/3 Soman, first prepared in Germany in 1944, is believed by Western officials to be the standard Russian nerve gas. **1982** *Guardian* 8 Mar. 12/3 The use of Soman and Tabun gases by the Soviet-directed Ethiopians.

somar, var. *SOMMER *adv.*

Somaschian, *sb.* and *a.* Add: More frequently **Somaschan, Somascan. a.** *sb.* (Further examples.)

1882 T. A. POPE tr. *Capecelatro's Life of St. Philip Neri* II. III. x. 153 He..co-operated in the erecting of a house of Somaschans for orphan boys. **1936** L. CHRISTIANI in E. Eyre *European Civilization* IV. II. i. 162 The immense achievements of Capuchins,..Somascans, and Barnabites. **1940** E. GRAF tr. *Pastor's Hist. of Popes* XXX. iv. 177 In 1647 Innocent dissolved the union between the Doctrinarians and the Somaschans.

So **Soma·schi** *sb. pl.*

1883 *Encycl. Brit.* XVI. 716/2 Clerks regular of St Majolus of Pavia, or 'Somaschi'. **1978** D. H. FARMER *Oxford Dict. Saints* 211/1 [St. Jerome Emiliani] founded orphanages, hospitals, and houses for repentant prostitutes. To look after them he also founded a small congregation of clerks regular, called the Somaschi after their place of origin.

somasteroid (somæ·stěroid), *a.* and *sb. Zool.* Also **Somasteroid.** [ad. mod.L. *Somasteroidea* (W. K. Spencer 1951, in *Phil. Trans. R. Soc.* B. CCXXXV. 87), f. Gr. σῶμα body + mod.L. *Asteroidea*, name of a subclass or class of echinoderms, f. Gr. ἀστεροειδής (see ASTEROID *a.* and *sb.*) + L. *-ea*, neut. pl. of *-eus* -EOUS.] **A.** *adj.* Belonging or pertaining to the subclass or class Somasteroidea, which belongs in the subphylum Asteroidea of star-shaped echinoderms and comprises extinct forms having broad, petal-like arms with a pinnate structure. **B.** *sb.* A somasteroid echinoderm.

1955 L. H. HYMAN *Invertebrates* IV. xv. 700 The arrangement recently adopted by palaeontologists.., according to which asteroids and ophiuroids derive from a common somasteroid..ancestor.., must be somehow wrong. **1962** D. NICHOLS *Echinoderms* iii. 40 The fossilized remains of these ossicles have even been found in the earliest asteroids, the Somasteroids. **1963** *Phil. Trans. R. Soc.* B. CCXLVI. 383 The Asterozoa, or star-shaped echinoderms, may be regarded as a natural taxon, comprising the somasteroids, asteroids and ophiuroids. **1964** [see *PHANEROZONE *a.* (*sb.*)]. **1979** W. D. RUSSELL-HUNTER *Life of Invertebrates* xxxiv. 607 The smallest class, Somasteroidea, which arose in the Ordovician, was never an extensively diversified group, being relegated by many neontologists to the status of a subclass of the Asteroidea. (The living genus, *Platasterias*, is no longer regarded as a somasteroid.)

Somastic (sǒmæ·stik). Also **somastic.** [Prob. f. initials of *S*tandard *O*il (see quot. 1930) + MASTIC *sb.*] A proprietary term in the U.S. for asphalt-based materials used in coating oil pipelines.

1930 *Official Gaz.* (U.S. Patent Office) 8 July 365/1 Standard Oil Company of California... *Somastic.* For asphalt, asphalt mastic, and pipe coatings. Claims use since May 8, 1930. **1974** *Petroleum Rev.* XXVIII. 634/1 A 40-ft long pipe..emerges from a somastic coating machine at Bredero Price's mill in Leith. **1976** *Offshore Platforms & Pipelining* 131/1 Field joints in the overbend are coated with flexible somastic.

‖ **somaten** (somate·n, somā·ten). Pl. **somatenes.** [a. Catalan (and Sp.) *somatén* an alarm bell; an armed body of citizens.] In Catalonia, a body of civilians armed for the protection of a town or district; a member of this body. Hence **soma·tenist** [Catalan *somatenista*], a member of a somaten.

1845 R. FORD *Hand-bk. Spain* I. 493/1 Thus time was given for the *somaten*, or tocsin, to be rung, and the armed peasantry collected... The Catalan *guerrilleros* were called *Somatenes*, from this bell. **1905** R. THIRLMERE *Lett. from Catalonia* I. v. 60 In Olot and other Catalan towns they have what they call *El Somaten*, an armed, local, volunteer force—which closes all the highways at the sound of an alarm bell. **1911** *Encycl. Brit.* XVIII. 566/2 *Miquelets* ..were irregular local troops in Catalonia... They were maintained by the several parishes..and as they had to turn out for duty on sound of the village alarm-bell (*somaten*) they are frequently called *somatenes.* **1928** *Daily Tel.* 29 May 9/5 A member of the 'Somaten' (Militia) to-day succeeded in finding the young man who ran amok with a rifle last Monday... As he refused to surrender the 'Somatenist' fired and killed him. **1929** A. F. G. BELL in E. A. Peers *Spain* 275 A more efficient city-police, together with the Somatenes and the Civil Guard, maintained order throughout Spain.

somatism. For † *Obs.* read *rare* and add later example.

1955 *Mind* LXIV. 495 Reism as such is not yet somatism, but somatism finds its place in the framework of reism as a particular case. Every soul is a body—this is the thesis of somatism.

somatization (sōᵘmătəizēⁱ·ʃən). [f. Gr. σῶμα, σωματ- body, SOMA² + -IZATION.] The occurrence of bodily symptoms in consequence of or as an expression of mental disorder. Hence **so·matizing** *a.*, pertaining to or exhibiting such symptoms.

1925 J. S. VAN TESLAAR tr. *Stekel's Peculiarities of Behav.* II. 341 *Somatization*, conversion of emotional states into physical symptoms. **1943** E. & C. PAUL tr. *Stekel's Interpretation of Dreams* I. iii. 25 Cases where the disorder—through somatization—secures bodily expression. **1954** GRINKER & ROBBINS *Psychosomatic Case Bk.* v. 74 In the narrower sense of the word, psychosomatic disturbances are differentiated from those neuroses in which somatization occurs through innervation of the voluntary nervous system. **1966** *McGraw-Hill Encycl. Sci. & Technol.* XI. 501/1 What characterizes the psychosomatic reaction in contrast to the other somatizing patterns is that there is an involvement of specific organs under the control of the autonomic nervous system. **1970** *Psychol. Rep.* XXVII. 756 One aspect of the stress and somatic reaction problem that has not received attention is the relationship between physiological reactions under laboratory-stress conditions and the tendency for individuals to develop somatic complaints under life stresses, as indicated by a personality characteristic of 'somatization'. **1978** *African Jrnl. Med.* VII. 209/2 Somatisation of psychological disorder..is common in the Nigerian population. **1980** I. G. & B. R. SARASON *Abnormal Psychol.* (ed. 3) viii. 202/1 The complaints of somatizing patients often lead to unnecessary surgery.

somato-. Add: **so·matocœl** *Zool.* [a. G. *somatocœl* (K. Heider 1912, in *Verhandl. d. deutsch. zool. Ges.* XXII. 241), f. Gr. κοιλία cavity of the body], each of a pair of cavities in an echinoderm embryo that develop into the main body cavity of the adult; hence **somatocœ·lic** *a.*; **somatome·tric -me·trical** *adjs.*, of or pertaining to the measurement of the body; hence **somato·me·trically** *adv.*; **somatopsy·chic** *a. Psychol.* [ad. G. *somatopsychisch* (C. Wernicke 1892, in *Path. des Nervensystems* (1893) 166], (*a*) of or pertaining to awareness of one's own body (? *obs.*); (*b*) arising from or pertaining to the effects of bodily illness on the mind; **somato-se·nsory** *a. Physiol.* = *SOMÆSTHETIC *a.*

1955 L. H. HYMAN *Invertebrates* IV. xv. 692 The inner walls of the somatocoels meet above and below the intestine to form the primary mesentery. **1962** D. NICHOLS *Echinoderms* x. 120 Almost as soon as the primary coelomic sacs have been formed, they bud off posteriorly another pair of sacs, the somatocoels, later to form the main coelom of the adult body. **1976** *Nature* 20 May 228/1 All this suggests that the new coelomocytes in the general body cavity can have come only from the somatocoelic epithelium. **1939** *Ibid.* 11 Nov. 807/1 By what somatometric method, which is both reliable and convenient of application, is it possible to assess nutritional status? **1951** *Proc. Sect. Sci. Koninkl. Akad Wetensch. Amsterdam* C. LIV. 480 (*heading*) The quantitative expression of resemblance in the somatometric study of relationship. *Ibid.*, Somatometrical data of different age-groups are not directly comparable. *Ibid.*, Training and interest will mostly induce the anthropologist to restrict himself to the study of properties than can be demonstrated somatometrically. **1902** *Buck's Handbk. Med. Sci.* (rev. ed.) V. 27/1 Consciousness is a function of the associative mechanism and may be considered in its threefold relationship to the outer world, the body and self—allopsychic, somatopsychic, and autopsychic. **1927** HENDERSON & GILLESPIE *Text-bk. Psychiatry* II. 13 His division of concepts into those of the outside world, of the personality, and of the body—'allopsychic', 'autopsychic', and 'somatopsychic'. **1955** *A.M.A. Arch. Neurol. & Psychiatry* LXXIII. 403/2 With the increasing severity in the lesion and the growing disability of the patient, much may be learned about the somatopsychic problem, i.e., about the manner in which the increasingly morbid process affects the state of mind of the patient and his relation to himself and his environment. **1961** *Guardian* 17 May 8/5 We should not allow a preoccupation with psychosomatic illness..to blind us to the advances ..in the treatment of somato-psychic disorders. **1978** F. MANN *Acupuncture* (ed. 3) x. 160 Modern medicine might use the word 'psychosomatic' to describe the diseases considered in this section, as they are physical results of uncontrolled emotion; those in the previous section might be given the label 'somatopsychic', being mental diseases resulting from outer or physical causes. **1952** *Federation Proc.* XI. 5/2 Responses from stimulation of arm and leg subdivisions of somatosensory area I were similar in location but differed in shape. **1975** *Nature* 30 Oct. 738/1 Axons carrying visual, auditory and somatosensory information converge on the tectum and interlace with tectal neurones. **1978** *Sci. Amer.* Sept. 82/2 In the somatosensory area of the cortex the cells in a column respond to the same type of stimulus (pressure, touch, heat, cold) at the same point on the body surface.

somatogamy (sōᵘmătǫ·gămi). *Biol.* [ad. G. *somatogamie* (O. Renner 1916, in *Biol. Centralbl.* XXXVI. 349): see SOMATO- and *-GAMY.] = *PSEUDOGAMY b. So **somato·gamous** *a.*

1949 I. F. & W. D. HENDERSON *Dict. Sci. Terms* (ed. 4) 403/2 *Somatogamy*, pseudogamy; pseudomixis. **1950** W. B. BRIERLEY tr. *Gäumann's Princ. Plant Infection* iii. 20 The nuclear association, initiated by somatogamous fusion, constitutes..the pre-condition for transition from the saprophytic to the parasitic mode of life. **1962** G. DALLDORF *Fungi & Fungous Diseases* x. 136 In fungi that undergo somatogamy, such as yeasts.

somatomedin (sōᵘmătomī·din). *Physiol.* [See quot. 1972.] Any of several peptides present in serum which are thought to act as intermediates in the stimulation of growth by growth hormone.

Quots. 1971, 1972 have no author in common.

1971 J. M. TANNER et al. in *Arch. Dis. Childhood* XLVI. 761/2 A few patients with short stature have the ability to secrete immunoreactive GH..; but their GH fails to stimulate the production of somatomedin, a substance found in the blood, and previously named 'sulphation factor'. **1972** W. H. DAUGHADAY et al. in *Nature* 14 Jan. 107/2 After consideration of many alternatives to the operational terms 'sulphation factor' or 'thymidine factor', we propose the more general term, 'somatomedin'; the prefix, 'somato', connotes both a hormonal relationship to somatotropin and, also, to the soma which is the target tissue of this agent. 'Medin' is included in the name to indicate that it is an intermediary in somatotropin action. **1978** VAN WYK & UNDERWOOD in G. Litwack *Biochem. Actions Hormones* V. iii. 102 It is.. generally agreed that to belong in the somatomedin group of peptides, a substance must fulfil three criteria: its concentration in serum must be growth-hormone dependent, it must possess insulin-like actions in skeletal tissues, and it must promote the incorporation of sulfate into proteoglycans of cartilage. **1978** F. L. STRAND *Physiology* xix. 360/1 Growth hormone, the somatomedins, insulin, and thyroxine have important anabolic effects that promote wound healing.

somatostatin (sōᵘmătostæ·tin). *Physiol.* [See quot. 1973.] A peptide secreted in the hypothalamus and elsewhere whose actions include the inhibition of the release of various hormones, esp. from the anterior pituitary.

1973 P. BRAZEAU et al. in *Science* 5 Jan. 79/3 We propose to name the peptide described here *somatostatin*, from somato(tropin), a pituitary factor affecting statural growth, and stat(in), from the Latin 'to halt, to arrest'. **1976** *Nature* 10 June 511/2 Somatostatin inhibits the release of growth hormone, thyrotropin and prolactin from the pituitary, of glucagon and insulin from the pancreas, and also of gastrin. **1977** *Lancet* 23 July 166/2 Somatostatin, a tetradecapeptide first isolated from the hypothalamus.., has been demonstrated in large quantities in the gastrointestinal tract and pancreas.

Hence **so:matostatino·ma** *Path.*, a tumour secreting excessive quantities of somatostatin.

1977 *Lancet* 26 Mar. 668/1 Measurements of insulin and glucagon responses during a glucose-tolerance test in somatostatinoma patients may help to explain this apparent association. **1978** *Jrnl. R. Soc. Med.* LXXI. 173 This somatostatinoma gave rise to the clinical abnormalities of hypochlorhydria, steatorrhoea, and a diabetic glucose tolerance curve.

somatotonic (sōᵘmătǒtǫ·nik), *a.* and *sb.* [f. SOMATO- + TONIC *a.*] **A.** *adj.* Designating or characteristic of a type of personality which is extroverted and aggressive, classified by Sheldon as being associated with a mesomorphic physique. **B.** *sb.* One having this type of personality. So **somatotonia** (-tōᵘ·niă), somatotonic personality or characteristics.

1937 [see *CEREBROTONIC *a.* and *sb.*]. **1938** H. G. WELLS *Apropos of Dolores* iv. 214 The classification of main human types and temperaments from Hippocrates' down to the cerebrotonics, somatotonics and viscerotonics of to-day. **1940** W. H. SHELDON *Varieties Human Physique* i. 8 Somatotonia is the motivational pattern dominated by the will to exertion, exercise and vigorous self-expression. It is the drive toward dominance of the functions of the soma. **1950** A. HUXLEY *Let.* 16 Mar. (1969) 621 We are fortunate to-day in possessing, at long last, a genuinely scientific method for describing physique, temperament and their interrelations..—viscerotonia, somatotonia and cerebrotonia for temperament. **1950** —— *Themes & Variations* 28 The viscerotonic and somatotonic extraverts who are at home in the world. **1969** V. DE SOLA PINTO *City that Shone* iii. 68, I suppose that in modern psychological jargon, as a child in those distant Edwardian days, I could be described as an introvert and cerebrotonic living in a world of extroverts, somatotonics and viscerotonics.

somatotopic (sōᵘmătotǫ·pik), *a. Neurol.* [f. SOMATO- + Gr. τοπικ-ός in respect to place (see TOPIC *a.* and *sb.*).] Characterized by or being a relationship between the locations of neurones in the central nervous system and in the tissues they serve. Also **somatoto·pical** *a.*, in the same sense.

1945 *Federation Proc.* IV. 31/1 Liminal faradic excitation of the cerebellar cortex reveals somatotopic localization in the anterior lobe and lobulus simplex of decerebrate animals. **1958** A. BRODAL *Neurol. Anat.* iii. 42 Here again is an example of a somatotopical arrangement of a fibre system. **1965** *Jrnl. Anat.* XCIX. 761 (*heading*) Correlation between nuclear morphology and somatotopic organization in the ventro-basal complex of the raccoon's thalamus. **1969** TRUEX & CARPENTER *Human Neuroanat.* (ed. 6) xvii. 423/1 In the cat there is evidence that corticopontine fibers arising from the sensorimotor cortex project in a somatotopical manner onto two longitudinally oriented cell columns within the pontine nuclei. **1976** *Nature* 20 May 190/3 Physiologists have revealed a strict somatotopic map of the skin in the spinal cord.

Hence **so:matoto·pically** *adv.*, in a manner which preserves such a relationship; **so·matotopy** (*rare*), somatotopic relationship.

1948 A. BRODAL *Neurol. Anat.* vi. 161 They have mapped out the areas giving response when different parts of the skin are stimulated, and established a pattern which mainly corresponds to that gained from study of human cases. The body is represented somatotopically, with a certain overlapping between adjacent dermatomes. **1961** *Lancet* 2 Sept. 546/2 Discriminative sensation travels by the lemniscal pathway and is relayed somatotopically via the thalamus to the cortex. **1976** *Progress in Sci. Culture* (E. Majorana Centre) Spring 48 The analysis of the properties, of these two inputs, in terms of somatotopy, frequency of discharge, sensory modality, timing and interaction between them suggests that integration of the information channelled through the two inputs on the same Purkyně cell is a basic mechanism of cerebellar operation.

somatotroph (sōᵘ·mătotrōᵘf). *Physiol.* [Back-formation from next.] A cell of the anterior pituitary which synthesizes somatotrophin (growth hormone).

1968 *Annales de Biologie Animale, Biochimie, Biophysique* VIII. 22 (*heading*) Cytological characteristics of gonadotroph, thyrotroph, corticotroph, somatotroph cells and of prolactin cells in the anterior lobe of the cattle pituitary. **1978** *Jrnl. R. Soc. Med.* LXXI. 434 There are several sera under study where the antibodies react neither with lactotrophs or somatotrophs.

somatotrophic (sōᵘmătotrōᵘ·fik), **-tropic** (trōᵘ·pik, -trǫ·pik), *a. Physiol.* [f. SOMATO- + *-TROPHIC, * -TROPIC.] Pertaining to or having the property of stimulating body growth; *spec.* applied to the hormone somatotrophin.

1938 H. L. WIEMAN *Gen. Zool.* (ed. 3) x. 206 The somatotropic hormone is necessary for the normal growth and development of the body. **1952** *Amer. Jrnl. Physiol.* CLXXI. 381 Some of the most striking effects of..cortisone..are directly opposed to the actions of the 'growth hormone' or somatotrophic hormone (STH). **1960** *Biol. Abstr.* XXXV. 1154/2 The somatotropic activity of the plasma was evaluated. **1977** *Lancet* 23 July 198/1, HG.H. secretion from another somatotrophic adenoma..was inhibited..by bromocriptine.

Hence **somatotro·phin, -tro·pin,** a hormone secreted by the anterior pituitary which promotes the release of somatomedin; growth hormone.

1947 H. Selye *Textbk. Endocrinol.* iii. 217/2 Denaturation of somatotrophin by treatment with urea does not influence its growth-promoting potency. **1952** *Endocrinol.* LI. 300 Growth hormone (somatotropin) can produce a growth-promoting and diabetogenic response in the developing chick embryo. **1965** Lee & Knowles *Animal Hormones* ii. 21 The growth hormone, also referred to as somatotrophin (STH), not only controls the rate of growth, but also the metabolism necessary for this growth. **1973** *Sci. Amer.* Sept. 41/3 (*caption*) Somatotrophin, acting with other hormones, regulates the normal growth of children. **1974** D. & M. Webster *Compar. Vertebr. Morphol.* xiii. 307 The growth hormone, somatotropin, produced by acidophilic cells, is a branched protein with about 200 amino acids.

somatotype (sōu·mătotəip), *sb.* [f. Somato- + Type *sb.*¹] The physique of an individual as expressed numerically in terms of the extent to which it exhibits the characteristics of each of three extremes (the endomorph, mesomorph, and ectomorph).

1940 W. H. Sheldon *Varieties Human Physique* i. 7 The patterning of the morphological components, as expressed by the three numerals, is called the somatotype of the individual. After examining..4,000 physiques we were able to describe..76 different somatotypes. **1944** A. Huxley *Let.* 19 July (1969) 508 From these a good draughtsman could turn out true representations of the various somatotypes. **1971** *Nature* 12 Mar. 113/2 An analysis of the somatotype data showed that there was a tendency for the twelve individuals to fall into two groups: a mesomorphic group (seven cases—wide heavy—typical somatotype 4,5,2) and an ectomorphic group (five cases—tall thin—typical somatotype 3,2,6). **1978** G. A. Sheehan *Running & Being* ii. 28, I dug into his [*sc.* Sheldon's] *Atlas of Men* and there I was. Somatotype 235... The number 235 is somatotype shorthand for little or no fat (2); a moderate amount of muscle (3); and a predominance of skin, hair, nervous tissue and thin bones (5). (The limits being one to seven.)

somatotype (sōu·mătotəip), *v.* [f. prec.] *trans.* To assign to a somatotype.

1940 W. H. Sheldon *Varieties Human Physique* vii. 220, 400 northern Negroes whom we have photographed and somatotyped. **1951** Auden *Nones* (1952) 47 Lovers of big numbers go horribly mad, Would have..all of us Well purged, somatotyped, baptised, taught baseball. **1954** W. H. Sheldon *Atlas of Men* 16/2 By the time I had somatotyped the 12,000 men who made up this total series the foundations were well laid.

So **so·matotyping** *vbl. sb.*, the assignation of somatotypes.

1940 W. H. Sheldon *Varieties Human Physique* i. 8 The criteria and the procedure for somatotyping..provide a practicable, objective method for segregating and classifying the varieties of human physique. **1959** A. Huxley *Let.* 15 Oct. (1969) 880 Have you found in your hospital work that somatotyping along Sheldonian lines has helped? **1978** *Nature* 12 Jan. 193/1 Sheldon is the man who invented somatotyping—a classification of variations in human body structure, to which he related variations in temperament, in physical and mental illness, and in patterns of growth and aging.

sombrero. Add: **3.** *Microbiol.* A bacterial plaque in which a ring of partial lysis surrounds a clear central area.

1971 Cunningham & Sercarz in *European Jrnl. Immunol.* I. 414/1 Plaques which were clear in the middle but with a variable concentric zone of partial lysis at the periphery (christened 'sombreros'), were scored as clear. **1975** *Nature* 20 Feb. 639/1 Those which started as sombreros..always grew into larger sombreros.

sombre·roed, *a.* [f. Sombrero + -ed².] Wearing or covered by a sombrero.

1899 F. Remington *Sundown Leflare* 51 Sombreroed and moccasined, Sundown pattered along on his roan pinto. **1906** *Out West* Jan. 49 'Oh, no, you never make it. Too mucho arena!' with an emphatic, disapproving shake of sombreroed head. **1912** D. H. Lawrence *Let.* 17 Sept. (1962) I. 147 Black sombrero'd Italians. **1966** H. W. Yoxall *Fashion of Life* xii. 120 A sombreroed, bearded, cloaked individual.

some, *indef. pron., a.*¹, *adv.*, and *sb.*¹ Add: **A.** *indef. pron.* **I. 4. e.** *to get some*: to have sexual intercourse; to succeed in finding a sexual partner. *U.S. slang.*

1889 W. H. Herndon *Let.* 5 Jan. in E. Hertz *Hidden Lincoln* (1940) 233 Speed about 1839–40 was keeping a pretty woman in this city, and Lincoln, desirous to have *a little*, said to Speed: 'Speed, do you know where I can get *some*?' **1971** E. E. Landy *Underground Dict.* 88 *Get some*.., obtain sexual intercourse with someone. **1978** J. Krantz *Scruples* vi. 173 Since his last visit she was getting some, somewhere, he'd bet his life on it.

f. *and then some*: and (plenty) more in addition. *colloq.* (chiefly *U.S.*).

1908 'Yeslah' *Tenderfoot in Southern California* ii. 22 It rains in sheets, in blankets, and in comforters, and then some. **1914** D. O. Barnett *Lett.* (1915) 19, I picked them out with those glasses, and let them have it, and then some! **1931** T. E. Lawrence *Let.* 10 June (1938) 724 It ..will be 12 guineas and then some! **1958** J. Cannan *And be Villain* i. 24, I waited till the train had gone out and then some. **1976** D. Clark *Dread & Water* ii. 51 People have got to talk... Tell us everything they know and then some.

B. *adj.*¹ **I. 4. e.** (Earlier and later examples.)

1844 *Spirit of Times* 30 Nov. 474/1 Many people have an idea that the 'big mare' will be 'some' in the race. **1876** 'Mark Twain' *Tom Sawyer* i. 8 Smarty! You think you're *some*, now, don't you. **1890** *Dialect Notes* I. 70 To say of a woman that 'she looks *some*', with emphasis on the *some*.., is equivalent to saying that she looks remarkably well.

f. Quite a; a remarkable. Used meiotically, often ironically, to suggest that something or someone is worthy of consideration. *some hope(s)!*: see *hope *sb.*¹ 4a. orig. *U.S.*

1808 J. Mackintosh in R. J. Mackintosh *Mem. Life Sir J. Mackintosh* (1835) I. viii. 448 You know that Bossuet and Arnauld believed their innocence—some authority. **1855** 'Q. K. P. Doesticks' *Doesticks, what he Says* iv. 28 It was 'some' bridge, in fact, a considerable curiosity, and a 'considerable' bridge. **1914** G. Atherton *Perch of Devil* i. 80 They're some geologists, he added with unwilling admiration. *Ibid.* 108 Butte is some education, believe me. **1925** F. Scott Fitzgerald *Great Gatsby* iii. 60 He smiled with jovial condescension, and added 'some sensation!' Whereupon everybody laughed. **1931** Brophy & Partridge *Songs & Slang Brit. Soldier* (ed. 3) 359 *Some hopes!*, it is most unlikely! **1941** W. S. Churchill *Unrelenting Struggle* (1942) 345 When I warned them [*sc.* the French Government] that Britain would fight on alone whatever they did, their Generals told their Prime Minister and his divided Cabinet: 'In three weeks England will have her neck wrung like a chicken.' Some chicken! Some neck! **1958** 'J. Byrom' *Or be he Dead* v. 69 'I gather you have Miss Canning as your assistant sleuth!' .. 'Some hope!..a good secretary always has to be in love with her boss!' **1976** A. Price *War Game* i. 66 'David has us to console him.'.. 'Some consolation!' murmured Frances. **1977** J. Wainwright *Do Nothin' till you hear from Me* x. 176 'Some band,' murmurs Ted—and there is suppressed excitement in his voice. I say, 'Ted—believe me—this is going to *be* some band.'

II. 9. a. Also following a numeral. *U.S.*

1968 *Time* 19 Jan. 7/2 Twenty-some years ago, when I was a nurse on the U.S.S. *Hope*. **1971** R. A. Carter *Manhattan Primitive* (1972) xi. 104 He's thirty years old, with..a master's degree and forty-some hours towards a doctorate. **1980** in S. Terkel *Amer. Dreams* 2 There were sixty-some contestants from all over the place.

C. *adv.* **2. b.** (Earlier examples.)

1745 J. Emerson *Jrnl.* 8 Apr. in *Mass. Hist. Soc. Proc.* (1911) XLIV. 74, I read some in Watson. **1785** *Massachusetts Spy* 28 Apr. 2/3 (Advt.), A tall stout looking fellow,..stammers some in his speech. **1817** *Essex Inst. Hist. Coll.* (1866) VIII. 228 The material of which it is built looks some like marble.

d. *to go some*: to go well or fast; to do well; to work hard. *slang* (orig. *U.S.*).

a **1911** D. G. Phillips *Susan Lenox* (1917) II. ii. 24 He had evidently been 'going some' for several days; the sour, worn, haggard face..suggested a moth-eaten jaguar. **1912** J. Sandilands *Western Canad. Dict. & Phrase-Bk.* s.v. *Some, That's going some* may mean great speed or excellence of workmanship, or it may even be used in reference to the speed at which a person races to his ruin. **1915** Wodehouse *Psmith, Journalist* x. 71, I guess we're making a hit. *Cosy Moments* is going some now. **1966** 'J. Hackston' *Father clears Out* 173 He had the easy movements of the retriever, and for a big dog could go some. **1973** J. Wainwright *Touch of Malice* 8 A uniformed inspector..with..less than five years service under his belt. Jesus—that was going some! **1982** H. Lieberman *Night Call* viii. 47 He'd known the girl for two months; for Daughtry that was going some.

3. (Earlier and later examples.)

c **1780** in *Amer. Speech 1969* (1973) XLIV. 304 Until it gets some darker. **1913** [see *gun-play]. **1940** W. Faulkner *Hamlet* i. ii. 31 We had done been feeding it [*sc.* a horse] for two–three days now by forced draft..and it looked some better now than when we had brung it home. **1956** G. E. Evans *Ask Fellows who cut Hay* xxv. 231 An old worker..turned the handle and tried it with a few roots. Asked what he thought of it he said with conviction: 'It's some stiff, maaster.' **1976** M. Machlin *Pipeline* iv. 44 He's going to be some pissed off when he finds out about this.

-some, *suffix*⁴, f. Gr. σῶμα body; (*a*) used with this sense, as in *ectosome* s.v. *ecto- *trophosome* s.v. Tropho-; (*b*) used to form words denoting an intracellular particle, as in *acrosome, *chromosome, *lysosome; (*c*) used to repr. *chromosome*, as in *disome, *monosome i.

1921 [see *hexasome* s.v. *hexa-].

somebody, *sb.* Add: **1. b.** Also with sense 'a rival for the affections' in phr. *there* (or *it*) *is somebody else.*

1911 G. B. Shaw *Getting Married* 200 You have never given me a real reason for refusing me yet. I once thought it was somebody else. There were lots of fellows after you. **1935** D. L. Sayers *Gaudy Night* xii. 260 'I suppose,' he said in a savage tone, 'there's somebody else.' **1946** 'Brahms' & 'Simon' *Trottie True* iii. 37 'I know what it is.' Joe tried to stop himself but he couldn't. 'There's somebody else.'

d. Also *somebody-or (-the) -other.*

1935 D. L. Sayers *Gaudy Night* xii. 255 Mr. Somebody-or-the-other had undertaken..to climb every tree in St. Giles. **1976** 'L. Black' *Healthy Way to Die* iii. 29 The two girls..were the Daughters of Lord Somebody-or-other.

3. (Later example.) *Somebody up there*, God; a supernatural controlling power.

1972 *Dict. Contemp. & Colloq. Usage* 27/3 *Somebody up there loves (hates) me*, an expression attributing one's good or bad luck..upon being in the good or bad graces of an unseen power above. **1975** J. Updike *Month of Sundays* xxx. 225 In the land of my parish, the shortest day of the year is approaching, and somebody's birthday, I think. **1977** R. Perry *Dead End* i. 9 All I could do was..pray that somebody up there loved me. **1980** *Times* 10 June 10/1 (*heading*) Somebody up there cares for me.

so·meday, *adv.* [f. Some *a.*¹ 2 + Day *sb.*] At some future time. Cf. Day *sb.* 7 b.

Earlier examples of *some day* as a two-word phrase will be found s.v. Some *a.* 2 b (*b*).

1898 G. B. Shaw *Candida* i, in *Plays Pleasant* 94 Theyll ave to give you somethink someday, if it's honly to stop yore mouth. **1902** W. B. Yeats *Cathleen ni Hoolihan* 13 220 We might be put in the way of making Patrick a priest someday, and he so good at his books. **1921** G. B. Shaw *Back to Methuselah* v. 221 Something or other must make an end of you someday. **1939** Joyce *Finnegans Wake* 119 A tea anyway for a tryst someday. **1940** W. Faulkner *Hamlet* ii. i. 110 He could almost see the husband which she would someday have. **1958** [see *Murphy³ 3]. **1966** *Punch* 24 Aug. 294 Won't someday a three-minute montage provide a more significant aesthetic treat than a sonnet? **1978** *Amer. Poetry Rev.* July/Aug. 31/3 It will clutch at a heart it did not seem to know, and someday die.

some one, someone, *pron.* (and *sb.*). Add: (Examples of *pl.*) *someone else*, used pregnantly to mean 'a rival for the affections'. Cf. *somebody else* s.v. *somebody *sb.* 1 b.

1914 'Bartimeus' *Naval Occasions* xxv. 261 It had become necessary to tell Selby that she couldn't love him any longer... Further, by her creed, it was only right that she should tell him about Someone Else as well. **1936** J. Curtis *Gilt Kid* xviii. 178 There's someone on that roof all right. Two someones. **1941** M. Allingham *Traitor's Purse* xi. 129 'She broke the engagement.'.. 'Why? 'As she seen someone else?' **1977** A. Hunter *Gently Instrumental* i. 14 Walt half-choked: There's—someone else!'.. 'You dirty old queen, that's just what you'd think.' **1978** P. Porter *Cost of Seriousness* 30 To whom someones in the city must pay homage.

somepin, var. *sump'n.

so·meplace, *adv.* and *sb. dial.* and *U.S.* Also **some place.** [f. Some *a.*¹ + Place *sb.*] **A.** *adv.* Somewhere; (at, in, to, etc.) a particular or unspecified place.

1880 *N. & Q.* 24 Apr. 340/2 'No place' in Devonshire is the usual form of 'nowhere', 'no place else' and 'some place else' being the commonest forms of 'nowhere else' and 'somewhere else'. **1896** *Dial. Notes* I. 425 *Some place*, somewhere. **1922** Joyce *Ulysses* 639 Lodging some place about the pit of the stomach. **1933** *Punch* 8 Nov. 511/3 Is there no' a nicer toon some place else? **1937** J. Steinbeck *Of Mice & Men* i. 18 Some place I'd find a cave. **1948** H. L. Mencken *Amer. Lang.* Suppl. II. 394 The long-awaited grammarian of vulgar American..will have a gaudy time anatomizing such forms as..'It was some place *else*', [*etc.*]. **1959** M. Dolinsky *There is no Silence* v. 78 She's here some-place. **1966** T. Pynchon *Crying of Lot 49* iii. 63 Tony Jaguar decided he could surely unload his harvest of bones on some American someplace... He was right. **1978** *Detroit Free Press* 16 Apr. E.7/4 I've always been able to get a room someplace, but this year I'm struggling.

B. *sb.* Somewhere; a particular or unspecified place.

1922 Joyce *Ulysses* 758 That drunken little barrelly man that bit his tongue off falling down the mens WC drunk in some place or other. **1940** W. Faulkner *Hamlet* iii. ii. 190 There will be some town, some place close where I can live. **1971** B. Patten *Irrelevant Song* 37 (*title*) In someplace further on. **1976** *National Observer* (U.S.) 7 Feb. 15/3 Next the Navy tried Texas, where defense-minded Sen. John Tower said it was a fine idea—for someplace else. **1977** H. Fast *Immigrants* iii. 165 His father came to America from someplace in Poland in eighteen sixty-nine.

somer, var. *sommer *adv.*

som'ers (sʊ·məɹz), *adv. U.S.* Also **somers.** Repr. colloq. pronunc. of *somewheres.*

1876 'Mark Twain' *Tom Sawyer* xxiii. 182 It keeps me in a sweat, constant, so's I want to hide som'ers. **1884** —— *Huck. Finn* xxiv. 241 It's reckoned he left three or four thousand in cash hid up som'ers. **1896** —— in *Harper's Mag.* Aug. 344/2 His aunt Polly wouldn't let him..go traipsing off somers wasting time. **1909** *Dial. Notes* III. 404 *Som'ers*, adv., somewhere. 'He's *som'ers* around.'

Somervillian (sʊməɹvi·lian), *a.* and *sb.* [f. the name of *Somerville* College (founded as a women's college in 1879 and named after Mary Somerville) + -ian.] **A.** *adj.* Of or pertaining to Somerville College, Oxford. **B.** *sb.* A member of the college.

1896 A. D. Godley in *More Echoes from Oxford Mag.* 64 Ye Somervillian students. **1904** R. Bridges *Let.* 26 May (1940) 50 The Somervillians might object. **1922** Byrne & Mansfield *Somerville College 1879–1921* iii. 38 The War Office was granted the use of the Somerville Buildings for the duration of the war..[which] overshadowed the situation of the young Somervillians. **1934** R. Macaulay *Going Abroad* xxix. 254 The two Somervillians..passed most of the afternoon and evening with the Josefs. **1966** E. H. Jones *Margery Fry* v. 35 'They were beautiful, in their Liberty dresses,' said an old Somervillian..remembering the leaders of College society in the 'nineties. **1976** 'A. Cross' *Question of Max* ix. 113 In 1918 Somervillians were still being housed in..Oriel College.

somesthesis, -esthetic varr. *SOMÆSTHESIS, *SOMÆSTHETIC *a.*

something, *sb.*, (*adj.*,) and *adv.* Add: **A.** *sb.* **1. a.** Phrases *something for everybody* (or *everyone*), *something for nothing.* Also used *attrib.*

1869 P. T. BARNUM *Struggles & Triumphs* viii. 132 When people expect to get 'something for nothing' they are sure to be cheated. **1924** G. B. SHAW *Saint Joan* iv. 41 The Jews generally give value. They make you pay; but they deliver the goods. In my experience the men who want something for nothing are invariably Christians. **1938** E. AMBLER *Cause for Alarm* vii. 115 A something-for-nothing proposition always has a string to it. **1955** R. MACAULAY *Let.* 20 Aug. in *Last Lett. to Friend* (1962) 206, I personally think it all to the good, as giving something for every one, however different their minds, backgrounds, and religious temperaments. **1960** *N.Y. Times Bk. Rev.* 17 Jan. 1 There's something for everybody. **1971** *Engineering* Apr. 129/2 Something-for-everyone entertainment. **1976** *Glasgow Herald* 26 Nov. 6/2 But human nature dictates that most people..are liable to take advantage of an opportunity to get something for nothing.

e. (Earlier and later examples.)

c **1863** T. TAYLOR *Ticket-of-Leave Man* II. 32 If Mr. Gibson would only give you employment. He's something in the City. **1907** E. GOSSE *Father & Son* ii. 21 My uncles ..earned a comfortable living, E. by teaching, A. as 'something in the City'. **1951** [see *SLINKY *a.*]. **1962** [see *COMMUTE *v.* 4 b]. **1978** P. FITZGERALD *Bookshop* ii. 20 He was known to drive up to London to work, and to be something in TV. **1979** R. BARNARD *Posthumous Papers* iv. 37 He was something in insurance.

f. *or something* (colloq.), used to express an indistinct or unknown alternative.

1814 JANE AUSTEN *Mansfield Park* I. xi. 223 There were generally delays, a bad passage or *something.* **1899** [see *MITTAGESSEN]. **1913** 'S. ROHMER' *Mystery of Dr. Fu-Manchu* i. 4 What, are you moved to London or something? **1926** I. MACKAY *Blencarrow* v. 49 Yet undoubtedly this man was drunk or ill, or something. **1938** *Chatelaine* Oct. 25/3 *Our* things must have tattle-tale gray or somethin' 'cause they never shine like *this.* **1951** M. KENNEDY *Lucy Carmichael* II. iii. 100 'Aren't they engaged or something?' 'I don't know what you mean by *or something*... It's a vulgar, slipshod phrase.' **1958** *N.Z. Listener* 4 July 7/1 Jarden was off the field—had hurt his foot or something—and it seemed that we might be hard up against it. **1969** N. FREELING *Tsing-Boum* viii. 54 She might have a police record or something. **1978** P. MARSH et al. *Rules of Disorder* iii. 69 You have to fight or else people..think you're a bit soft or something.

2. c. (Later examples.)

1931 R. CAMPBELL *Georgiad* iii. 55 Even the devil dwindles to a duiker, Who prides himself as something of a spiker. **1939** R. G. COLLINGWOOD *Autobiogr.* iv. 27, I had become something of a specialist in Aristotle. **1959** *Listener* 17 Dec. 1083/3 It had been, I admit, something of a party. **1978** *Lancashire Life* Sept. 51/1 During the last war he became something of a legend, working incredible hours and doing general and orthopaedic surgery, as well as obstetrics.

3. c. *something* (*good* or *special*), a useful racing tip.

1907 *Racing Expert* 9 July 3 For the benefit of those who care to wait and act upon the best information. 'The Expert' will occasionally wire when he knows Something Special. **1908** *Racing Judge* 6 June 4 Owing to Bank Holiday this Letter will be sent out on Tuesday Evening. ..Something good at Manchester will be given. **1937** PARTRIDGE *Dict. Slang* 800/2 *Something good*, a good racing tip.

4. b. (Later examples.)

a **1902** S. BUTLER *Way of all Flesh* (1903) liv. 249 When Christina pointed out to him that it would be cheap he replied that there was something in that. **1977** B. PYM *Quartet in Autumn* i. 7 'Cheerful, aren't you,' said Edwin, 'but perhaps there's something in it. Four people on the verge of retirement, each one of us living alone.'

d. *something to see* (or *look at*): an impressive sight.

1808 J. MACKINTOSH in R. J. Mackintosh *Mem. Life Sir J. Mackintosh* (1835) I. ix. 501 It was something to see children clinging round the necks of their fathers, and sons carrying their infirm parents in pursuit of health. **1942** T. BAILEY *Pink Camellia* i. 2 In khaki breeches, sitting her horse like a boy, her white shirt open at the throat, she was something to look at. **1957** E. B. WHITE *Let.* June (1976) 440 Martha is really something to see now.

e. *to have* (*got*) *something*, to have an idea or attribute of value or worthy of consideration.

1938 'E. QUEEN' *Four of Hearts* iv. 57 Say..the screwball's got something. Only I got a better idea. **1940** G. GREENE *Power & Glory* I. ii. 25 'I would take..a hostage.'..'You know,' the chief said, 'you've got something there.' **1948** POWYS & BOLTON *Don't listen, Ladies!* in *Plays of Year* (1949) 586 The Crusaders, gentlemen, they *had* something. The husband ordered his clothes from the blacksmith, and his wife's from the locksmith. **1960** *Times* 14 Sept. 12/6 Yet that girl 'had something', as any visitor to the United States will find out. **1973** L. COOPER *Tea on Sunday* i. 20 'I'm not at all the nice little wife she wanted for you.' 'She may have something there.'

f. Used in various phrases expressing admiration, as *isn't* (*that, he*, etc.) *something?*, *to be really something*; *quite something*: see *QUITE *adv.* 5 d.

1958 B. NICHOLS *Sweet & Twenties* ii. 42 The Ritz Bar, in those days, really was something. **1967** M. KENYON *Whole Hog* vii. 81 Isn't that something? So if they [*sc.* pigs] don't know you they're like interested? **1969** WIDDOWSON & HALPERT in Halpert & Story *Christmas Mumming in Newfoundland* 161 Mummers were really something when I was a boy. If you wasn't afraid of them, you wasn't afraid of nothing when you was four or five. **1973** A. CHRISTIE *Postern of Fate* III. x. 213 Perhaps it's something important... And so if they..tried to get whatever it was—that really would be something! **1977** 'A. YORK' *Tallant for Trouble* xi. 163 P. C. Abrahams presented arms..decked..out in full-dress white... 'Oh, isn't he something,' Jennie Kamm exclaimed.

g. *to have something going* (with *someone*), to have an 'understanding' or an affectionate relationship (with someone).

1971 V. CANNING *Firecrest* iii. 32 It didn't need any semaphore signals to tell her that there was something going between Mrs. Pilch and Major Cranston. **1973** *Philadelphia Inquirer* (Today Suppl.) 7 Oct. 7/2 Is it true that Sammy Davis Jr. has something going with Linda Lovelace. **1977** E. LEONARD *Unknown Man No. 89* xx. 200 She smiled..like they had something going.

5. a. Also in phr. *a little something*: some food or drink; a snack; refreshments. Cf. sense 1 c in Dict.

1866 GEO. ELIOT *Felix Holt* I. xi. 237 Like the shrill biting talk of a vixenish wife, it..compelled you to 'take a little something' by way of dulling your sensibility. **1926** A. A. MILNE *Winnie-the-Pooh* vi. 77 It was..as if somebody inside him were saying, 'Now then, Pooh, time for a little something.'..So he sat down and took the top off his jar of honey. **1950** J. CANNAN *Murder Included* vii. 146, I wonder if a little something could be provided to pacify the inner man? **1958** WODEHOUSE *Cocktail Time* xix. 159 Butlers always like to keep their strength up with a little something in the middle of the morning. **1977** P. D. JAMES *Death of Expert Witness* IV. iii. 192, I cook a little something for everyone in the evenings.

6. b. Also *slang* (orig. *N. Amer.*), a different matter; an exceptional or extraordinary (person, event, sight, etc.).

1909 R. E. KNOWLES *Attic Guest* 87 But when a lover comes across a couple of states, leaving behind him a big city—and all the girls are sorry to see him go, that's the best of it—that is something else, as we used to say in the South. **1940** W. FAULKNER *Hamlet* I. ii. 33 But when cash money starts changing hands, that's something else. **1949** R. HARVEY *Curtain Time* 67 Getting the small performer dressed for a public appearance was something else again. **1957** E. HORNE in *N.Y. Times Mag.* 18 Aug. 26/3 Something else—A phenomenon so special it defies description. Thus, when asked if the music is great..a cat may reply, 'No, man, not that; it was something else.' **1960** *Melody Maker* 31 Dec. 5/5 *Philly Joe Jones:* Aside from being a fabulous drummer, he could be a great comedian. He has people lying on the floor, he's so funny. Philly's something else. **1968** *Crescendo* Jan. 27/1 The one I rave about more than any other is the band of 1947... That was something else. It was a dream. **1973** R. L. SIMON *Big Fix* (1974) vii. 50 Dillworthy was something else again. **1977** *O.D.* No. 3, 12/1 (*caption*) Oh, wow, these guides are..something else man!

B. *adv.* **2. a.** (Further examples.)

1851 E. RUSKIN *Let.* 25 Nov. in M. Lutyens *Effie in Venice* (1965) II. 218 Nani makes them a great dish of Fish seasoned strongly with Garlic and the smell is something too dreadful if one happens to pass by the door. **1856** G. MEREDITH *Let.* 15 Dec. (1970) I. 38 The *dulness* is something frightful. **1918** C. MACKENZIE *Sylvia Scarlett* I. vii. 208 'These paths are something dreadful, Emmie,' said Mrs. Horne, as the three of them scrambled up through the garden. **1932** L. GOLDING *Magnolia Street* II. ii. 299 The way the razor trembled..now and again was something cruel.

c. Also, with *adj.* used for *adv.* in dial. and colloq. usage.

1898 G. B. SHAW *You never can Tell* in *Plays Pleasant* 211 *Gentleman*: Did you howl? *The Young Lady*: Oh, something awful. **1909** A. WOOLLCOTT *Let.* 24 Sept. (1944) 20 She gads around something fierce, as your friend Bert would say. **1915** J. WEBSTER *Dear Enemy* 300 When he was drunk..he smashed the furniture something awful. **1932** R. LEHMANN *Invitation to Waltz* I. iii. 58 Her husband drinks something shocking. **1963** W. H. MISSILDINE *Your Inner Child of Past* xv. 221, I was taken into the assembly hall. And beat up something terrible. **1978** D. CLARK *Libertines* ii. 41 'I'll put a plaster on that cut for you.'..'Thanks, doctor... It does sting something chronic.'

so·mething, *v.* Hence **so·methinged** *ppl. a. rare.*

1922 E. WALLACE *Valley of Ghosts* xiii. 120 You called me..a fool, and a somethinged fool, almost the first time we met.

so·methingth, *a.* (Earlier example.)

1854 MRS. GASKELL *Lett.* (1966) 302, I am very poor; which eases my cares wonderfully, see somethingth satire of Juvenal.

sometime, *adv.* (and *a.*). Add: **1. d.** Passing into adj. Freq. in phr. *a sometime thing*: something which is occasional or transient.

1935 G. GERSHWIN (*song-title*) A woman is a sometime thing. **1959** *Times Lit. Suppl.* 6 Nov. p. xxxi/1 Going to the movies still entailed leaving home and paying money, so that..the movies were a 'sometime thing' and a reward. **1964** 'E. MCBAIN' *Axe* vi. 115 The game..ain't regular, like you said it was. It's a sometime thing, whenever the urge strikes. **1967** *Observer* 19 Nov. 21/2 Money is a sometime thing for Simon Dee, here today and just possibly gone tomorrow. **1969** *Jrnl. Eng. & Gmc. Philol.* LXVIII. 214 Poetic propriety is a sometime thing. **1980** *Newsweek* 17 Nov. 12/2 Political parties are weaker, the Federal bureaucracy has grown unwieldy and party discipline in Congress is a sometime thing.

sometimes, *adv.* Add: **1. c.** Used adjectivally to denote 'occasional'. Cf. *SOMETIME *adv.* (and *a.*) 1 d.

a **1945** E. R. EDDISON *Mezentian Gate* (1958) I. v. 44 Nor did they find wholesome nor comfortable..his sometimes flashings into unforeknowable violence. **1974** *Publishers Weekly* 11 Feb. 56/3 Brando's sometimes generosity, his idealism. **1977** *Rolling Stone* 13 Jan. 36/2 Srouji confessed her entire FBI history, starting with her role in the Sixties as a sometimes informant.

sometimey (sʌ·mtəiːmi), *a.* *U.S. Black* and *Prison slang.* [f. SOMETIME *adv.* (and *a.*) + -Y¹.] Variable, unstable.

1946 MEZZROW & WOLFE *Really the Blues* 378 *Sometimey*, unstable, unpredictable, neurotic. **1969** R. PHARR in A. Chapman *New Black Voices* (1972) 62 She's the evilest and sometime-iest woman I ever shacked up with. **1977** *New Yorker* 24 Oct. 114/2 Men who have transferred to Green Haven from more rigorous but more consistent prisons..say that Green Haven's officers are 'sometimey'.

someway. *adv.* For Now *rare* exc. *dial.* read Now chiefly *U.S. colloq.* and add: **1.** (Later examples.)

1892 B. POTTER *Jrnl.* 8 Oct. (1966) 278 They are related someway to Neil Gow. **1902** W. B. YEATS *Where there is Nothing* (1903) v. 106, I thought he would have had half Ireland with him by this time with his great preaching, but someway when he preaches to the people, they don't seem to mind him much. **1922** JOYCE *Ulysses* 180 Pity of course: but somehow you can't cotton on to them someway. **1930** W. FAULKNER *As I lay Dying* 115 It's like he had got into the inside of you, someway. **1938** M. K. RAWLINGS *Yearling* xiv. 140, I hate the hawks eatin' the quail, but I don't someway mind the 'coons eatin' the grapes. **1978** *Washington Post* 22 July A8, I keep the windows open and run my box fan. I figure the Lord will take care of me somehow, someway.

somewhat, *sb.* and *adv.* Add: **B.** *adv.* **6.** *more than somewhat*, very, extremely; very much.

1930 D. RUNYON in *Collier's* 13 Sept. 7/3, I am now more nervous than somewhat. **1938** D. WHEATLEY *Uncharted Seas* xi. 190, I thought my nerve was pretty good, but this scares me more than somewhat. **1945** *Tee Emm* (Air Ministry) V. 40 Citizens have been known to leave the premises.., being more than somewhat apprehensive of future developments. **1964** WODEHOUSE *Frozen Assets* viii. 143 She said quite a number of things that wounded my sensitive nature more than somewhat. **1974** V. GIELGUD *In such a Night* vii. 67 It burned me up more than somewhat.

somewhen, *adv.* Add: Still found occas., esp. coupled with *somewhere* or *somehow*, but no longer common. (Earlier example in the recent use and later examples alone or coupled with *somehow.*)

1833 J. S. MILL *Let.* 5 July in *Wks.* (1963) XII. 163, I shall write out my thoughts more at length somewhere, and some*when*, probably soon. **1920** H. G. WELLS *Outl. History* (rev. ed.) viii. 37/1 Somewhen about 50,000 years ago..appeared *Homo Neanderthalensis.* **1934** J. L. MYRES in E. Eyre *Europ. Civilization* I. 87 Such accommodation between means and ends, resources and wants, is found to have been achieved, somewhen and somehow, [etc.]. **1975** J. C. MASTERMAN *On Chariot Wheel* v. 40, I cherished the belief that somehow and somewhen I should find my way to Oxford.

somewhere, *adv.* and *sb.* Add: **A.** *adv.* **1. e.** *somewhere in* (*France*, etc.), phr. orig. used during the war of 1914–18 in referring to some locality in the theatre of war without identifying it (because of the restrictions of censorship); hence, in extended use, somewhere unspecified for reasons of security or because one's stay there is temporary.

1915 *Illustr. London News* 20 Feb. 233 (*caption*) The War Area as seen by the Airman: 'somewhere in Flanders' photographed from a reconnoitring Aeroplane. *Ibid.* 241 For the moment 'Victoria' looks like 'Somewhere in France'. **1915** *Daily Sketch* 17 Aug. 12/1 None of these soldiers a year ago expected to be snapped one day..—somewhere in Egypt. **1918** *Wireless World* VI. 390 A Wireless Section 'Somewhere in England'. **1939** JOYCE *Finnegans Wake* 21 There was a brannewail that same sabboath night of falling angles somewhere in Erio. **1939** *War Illustr.* 14 Oct. 144 From 'Somewhere in England' to 'Somewhere in France': 1939 Echoes the Story of 1914. **1943** J. B. PRIESTLEY *Daylight on Saturday* viii. 52 If our lads was fightin' like 'ell somewhere in France, why yer'd see them production figures take a high jump. **1943** *Gramophone* Sept. 63/3 From Mr. Tony Puddy, Somewhere-in-England. **1973** *Jewish Chron.* 9 Feb. 15/2 The girls I visited recently on a training course 'somewhere in Israel' were not all bunched together in one group. **1977** 'J. LE CARRÉ' *Honourable Schoolboy* xvii. 400 The Somewhere-in-England sense of makeshift habitation..of every exiled correspondent.

B. *sb.* (Later examples.)

1914 R. BROOKE *Let.* 7 Mar. in *Coll. Poems* (1918) p. cxiii, I shall be glad to be back among you all, and tied to somewhere in England. *Ibid. Let.* Mar. p. cxvii, I want somewhere I needn't always be spick and span in, and somewhere I don't have to pay a vast sum. **1928** W. B. YEATS *Tower* 8 And I myself created Hanrahan And drove him drunk or sober through the dawn From somewhere in the neighbouring cottages. **1930** G. B. SHAW *Apple Cart* II. 69 All their people came from Scotland or Ireland or Wales or Jerusalem or somewhere. **1942** W. FAULKNER *Go down, Moses* 139 A big dog, a hound with a strain of mastiff from somewhere. **1958** B. W. ALDISS *Non-Stop* II. ii. 79 The ship..has come *from* somewhere and is going *to* somewhere. These somewheres are more important than the ship.

somma (sǫ·mă). *Physical Geogr.* Also **Somma.** [a. It. (*Monte*) *Somma*, proper name of the feature of this kind associated with Vesuvius.] A remnant of an older volcanic cone which partly or wholly encircles a younger cone; the rim of a caldera. Freq. *attrib.*, as *somma ring*.

c **1910** H. R. Mill *Dict. Geogr. Terms* in L. D. Stamp *Gloss. Geogr. Terms* (1961) 426 *Somma*, originally, the rampart remaining from the old crater of Vesuvius and forming an arc around one side of the new one. The name is sometimes extended to similar formations in other volcanoes. **1917** T. G. Bonney *T. Anderson's Volcanic Studies* 2nd Ser. vii. 39 This [ridge], according to Dr. Anderson, forms a Somma ring within which rises a smaller and a larger crater, both intermittently active. **1940** *Bull. Volcanologique* VI. 217 The older volcanic mass on the eastern side may be a continuation of the Somma. **1944** C. A. Cotton *Volcanoes as Landscape Forms* xi. 167 An example of a large cumulo-dome which has been built within a wide caldera or 'Somma ring' is the Soufrière of Guadeloupe, in the Lesser Antilles. **1975** Fielder & Wilson *Volcanoes of Earth, Moon & Mars* vii. 88/1 The so-called somma-type of nested cone..is named after Mount Somma, a residual portion of the encircling volcanic rim unit which was the precursor of the present, centrally disposed, Vesuvius. **1979** *Nature* 1 Nov. 24/1 It [*sc.* Soufrière volcano, St. Vincent] is a strato-volcano 1,220 m high with an open summit crater 1·6 km in diameter located in the southern part of a 2-km wide somma crater.

‖ **sommelier** (somǝlye). [Fr.: see Somler.] A wine waiter.

1889 *Harper's Mag.* Apr. 698/1 The 'sommelier', or butler, who runs from table to table, laden with bottles, and distributes here and there strange liquids. **1923** E. P. Oppenheim *Inevitable Millionaires* xiv. 146 Harold ..making cryptic signs with his fingers which intimated to the sommelier his urgent need of a cocktail. **1955** M. Allingham *Beckoning Lady* v. 77 He poured the awkward liquid with the skill of a *sommelier*. **1966** *Punch* 20 July 113/2 Although we've still got some cooks to shoot and many sommeliers to educate, our standards have improved beyond all recognition. **1974** *Times* (Wines & Spirits Suppl.) 2 Dec. p. iii/2 An awe-inspiringly stately *sommelier* and long wine lists..can often discourage the sale of wine.

sommer (sǫ·maɹ), *adv. S. Afr. colloq.* Also **somaar, 9 somar, somer.** [a. Afrikaans *somaar, sommer.*] Just, simply, for no specific reason, without further ado.

1835 T. Bowker *Jrnl.* 12 May (MS.), Bowkers party gone out on patrole *somer* heard from the third Division, they have been shooting some Kafirs, & taking Cattle & Goats. **1850** R. G. Cumming *Five Yrs. Hunter's Life S. Afr.* I. 27 The Dutch word *somar*..is also a word to which I think I could challenge the most learned schoolmaster in the Colony to attach any definite meaning. It is used by both Boers and Hottentots in almost every sentence. **1920** S. Black *Dorp* 174 'Ach, Oom Kaspar, can't I go back to look for my pipe and put it somaar in the box?' 'Nay, kerel, they won't let you go again inside the ballot-box.' **1959** *Cape Times* 15 Aug. (Weekend Mag.) 10/6 Too dangerous to sommer leave it like that with a child about the place. **1969** A. Fugard *Boesman & Lena* 15 Sannie who? Sommer Sannie Somebody. **1975** *Daily Dispatch* (E. London) 13 June 12 My father was a trader, who sold both blankets and ochre, and to my question as to why the tribesmen didn't sommer buy red blankets instead of going through all the trouble of dyeing white blankets with ochre, he replied that this was for hygienic reasons.

‖ **sommité** (som*i*te). [Fr., lit. 'summit, top, tip'.] A person of great eminence or influence.

1856 *Sat. Rev.* 19 Apr. 496/1 We observe the name of numerous *sommités* of the architectural profession. **1859** [see Collectionize *v.*]. **1900** W. James *Let.* 2 Apr. (1920) II. 121 We must go in for budding genius, if we seek a European. If an American, we can get a *sommité*! **1938** A. Huxley *Let.* 12 Apr. (1969) 434, I thought him [*sc.* Dr. Gerald Webb] a most remarkable old man, and they all say he's one of the *sommités* in the matter of TB. **1965** *Punch* 24 Nov. 752/1 A High Table is an institution; it is not merely a collection of what the French used to call *sommités*.

Somogyi unit (sǫ̆mō^u·gi). *Biochem.* [The name of Michael *Somogyi* (1883–1971), Hungarian-born U.S. biochemist who proposed the unit in 1948 (see quot.).] A unit in terms of which the effectiveness of a solution at catalysing the hydrolysis of starch can be stated (see quot. 1948).

[**1948** M. Somogyi in *Ann. Surg.* CXXVIII. 676 One unit is that amount of enzyme which hydrolyzes 1 mg. of starch in 1 hour at 37° and pH7 in phosphate buffer, provided that not more than 44% of the starch is hydrolyzed.] **1956** E. King *Micro-Anal. in Med. Biochem.* (ed. 3) iv. 92 Amylase activity... Somogyi units per 100ml. of plasma. **1961** *Lancet* 12 Aug. 373/1 A new amyloclastic technique which yields results in the equivalent of Somogyi units has been used to measure amylase activity in sera from..patients with diabetes mellitus. **1974** R. M. Kirk et al. *Surgery* vi. 110 The concentration of serum amylase is normally less than 200 Somogyi units.

son, *sb.*[1] Add: **1. a.** (Later example referring to an animal.)

1974 *New Yorker* 29 Apr. 102/2 A son of..a Thoroughbred, and..a quarter-horse brood mare.

3. b. Also, as a term of familiar address without implication of affection. Cf. *old son* s.v. *Old *a.* 8 a.

1914 G. B. Shaw *Misalliance* 5 *Bentley*:.. I should like to wring your damned neck for you. *Johnny* (*with a derisive laugh*): Try it, my son. **1959** E. H. Clements *High Tension* vii. 121 No good brooding, son. **1967** *Listener* 22 June 807/2 He was then asked to accompany the police to the police-box in order to confirm his identity. He replied, 'Look, son, I am not moving from this spot. If you want me you will have to arrest me.' **1974** S. Marcus *Minding Store* (1975) ix. 188 Mr. Seeligson said, 'Son, you've done me a great favor. I appreciate all the trouble you've gone to.'

6. d. *son of* ——: at one time a common formula for the title of a sequel to a book or film; hence used *joc.* to designate a programme, product, institution, etc., that is a derivative *of* its predecessor.

1929 E. R. Burroughs (*title*) Son of Tarzan. **1934** *Picturegoer* 23 June 20/3 *Son of Kong*... By no means a second *King Kong* this picture, nevertheless, has some clever technical qualities. **1941** 'B. Graeme' (*title*) Son of Blackshirt. **1965** [see *horror film* s.v. *Horror *sb.* 6]. **1966** 'O. Mills' *Enemies of Bride* iv. 47, I produced a scintillating piece of non-fiction called..*Elizabethan Domestic Drama*... I got a sequel—Son-of-Elizabethan-Domestic-Drama..—into print as well. **1971** R. Petrie *Thorne in Flesh* iii. 45 We don't want you playing Son of Sexton Blake... You could get hurt. **1976** *Gramophone* Nov. 910/1 The XSV/3000 is recognizably a 'son of' the XUV/4500Q: it has the same slim-line body and light-weight fixing wings. **1979** *Daily Tel.* 29 Mar. 6/3 (*heading*) Cheaper seats likely if 'Son of Concorde' flies. **1981** *Times* 19 Nov. 13/1 President Reagan..has now formally endorsed..negotiations..on strategic arms reductions (now known as 'Start', son of Salt).

7. d. Also used *ellipt.* for *Son of a bitch.

1951 W. Faulkner *Collected Stories* 171 Are you going to sit there and let a black son rape a white woman on the streets of Jefferson?

e. *Son of Heaven* († *Heaven's Son*) [tr. Chinese *tiānzǐ*], the Emperor of China; loosely, any Chinese. Cf. Celestial *a.* 4 and *sb.* 2.

1613 Purchas *Pilgrimage* IV. xvi. 369 The King's Title is, *Lord of the world, and Sonne of Heaven.* **1838** Gutzlaff & Reed *China Opened* II. xxvii. 541 To gain such honours as the Mongol princes pay to Heaven's Son, requires a well-stored treasury. **1850** *North-China Herald* 9 Nov. 58/4 One of the common appellations of the Emperors of China has been and still is *T'ien Tsze*, 'the Son of Heaven!' **1923** S. Merwin *Silk* (1924) 136 It is now my privilege to serve him who is in all but official style the Son of Heaven. **1938** *Foreign Affairs* XVI. 201 A dignity which the 'Sons of Heaven' consider has belonged to them for thousands of years. **1973** J. Leasor *Mandarin Gold* i. 1 The Emperor, Tao Kuang, the Son of Heaven, who ruled his celestial empire from..Peking, the forbidden city.

f. (*horny-handed*) *son of toil*, a manual labourer. Now often *ironically*.

1873 *Q. Rev.* CXXXV. 543 The peculiar virtues of the horny-handed sons of toil received a severe shock in 1848, and finally collapsed in 1871. **1902** 'Mark Twain' in *N. Amer. Rev.* Apr. 441 A crowd of ten thousand.. proud, untamed democrats, horny-handed sons of toil.. and fliers of the eagle. **1933** Wodehouse *Heavy Weather* xvii. 298 You look like one of those Sons of Toil Buried by Tons of Soil I once saw in a head-line. **1976** *Times* 23 Mar. 19/4 There won't be any room for your actual horny-handed sons of toil in the TUC; there'll be too many sharp-suited managers.

9. *son-lover*, a son who is his mother's lover.

1913 D. H. Lawrence *Let.* Jan. (1932) 102 The old son-lover was Œdipus.

son (sō^un), *sb.*[2] Also **sone.** [a. Sp. *son*, lit. 'sound'.] A slow Cuban dance and song in $\frac{2}{4}$ time; *son Afro-Cubano*, a form of the son influenced by Negro dances.

1934 S. R. Nelson *All about Jazz* vii. 167 The Son is far more refined than the Rumba, and when properly danced, is plaintively alluring. The Son is always danced in very slow tempo. This Cuban music is particularly characterized by the continual recurrence of singing. **1939** [see *Macumba]. **1954** *Grove's Dict. Mus.* (ed. 5) III. 215/1 When Afro-Cuban dances penetrated the port towns of Cuba they were assimilated by Spanish–Cuban folk music... The hybrid forms are then designated by such titles as *son afro-cubano*. **1956** M. Stearns *Story of Jazz* (1957) iii. 26 The Rhumba, Conga, Son Afro-Cubano, Mambo, and Cha-Cha are predominantly African. **1958** E. Borneman in P. Gammond *Decca Bk. Jazz* xxi. 270 The sone itself usually consisted of an eight-bar theme for solo voice, followed by an improvised four-bar tag, called montuno, that was sung in choir and repeated twice. Whereas the themes of the sones were usually lilting tunes of obviously Spanish descent, the montunos were unmistakably African. **1964** W. G. Raffé *Dict. Dance* 469/2 As a ballroom dance, the *Son* remained very popular until about 1950, when the *Mamba* began to supersede every other dance in *Cuba*. **1973** [see *rumba dancer* s.v. *Rumba *sb.* 2.]

‖ **so-na** (sō^u·na). *Mus.* Also **so na.** [Chinese *suǒnà*.] A Chinese wind instrument (see quots.)

1908 *Jrnl. North-China Branch R. Asiatic Soc.* XXXIX. 87 At Peking the *So Na* is regularly made of two sizes... The similarity of sound between *So Na* and *Zourna*, the name of a Persian oboe, is pointed out by M. Mahillon. **1954** *Grove's Dict. Mus.* (ed. 5) II. 236/1 *So-na* (S.W. *so-la*), conical oboe (wrongly, 'clarinet'). Its name connects it with the Persian *surna*... A wooden pipe with 7 + 1 holes terminated at one end by a copper bell and at the other end by a small reed mouthpiece. **1968** tr. *Hsia Hsiang* in Gray & Cavendish *Chinese Communism in Crisis* 165 A number of people regularly used to crowd into a small cave and listen to an old poor peasant playing the *So-na*. **1975** C. P. Mackerras *Chinese Theatre in Mod. Times* 23 Reed instruments are not of great significance in Chinese drama. The only one that need be mentioned here is the *so-na*, which has eight finger-holes and a double reed. Though in this way similar to the Western oboe, the *so-na* is rather shrill and piercing in tone.

sonagram, -graph, varr. *Sonogram, *Sonograph 1.

sonant, *a.* and *sb.* Add: **A.** *adj.* **b.** Syllabic; capable of forming a syllable, or constituting the essential element of a syllable.

1876 [see Diphthong *sb.* a]. **1932** W. L. Graff *Language & Languages* 56 The sound that possesses the highest degree of sonority in a syllable is called syllabic or sonant. **1957** C. L. Wrenn in *Wiener Beitrage zur Englischen Philologie* LXV. 255 The metrical value of a sonant or vocalic *n* in words like *forbidd'n*..and *heav'n*.

B. *sb.* **1.** (Earlier example.)

1849 J. R. Logan in *Jrnl. Ind. Archipel.* III. 229 (*heading*) Surds into sonants differing both in their organic and aspirate classes.

2. A syllabic sound; now usu., a syllabic consonant.

1893 *N.E.D.* s.v. *Consonant* sb., The use of the liquids and nasals as vowels or sonants. **1942** K. Malone in *Mod. Lang. Q.* Mar. 5 Traces of sonant-consonant opposition may be found in English liquids and nasals: thus *Gardner/Gardiner*. **1949** *Trans. Philol. Soc. 1948* 146 Nasals such as *m, n,* ŋ are often sonants—that is to say, have syllabic function.

3. A consonant that can be either syllabic or non-syllabic, i.e. a liquid, nasal, or semi-vowel.

1933 L. Bloomfield *Language* vii. 121 In most languages there is a third, intermediate group of *sonants*, phonemes which occur in both syllabic and non-syllabic positions. **1976** *Archivum Linguisticum* VII. 93 It [*sc.* *stød*]..can fall on sonants as well as vowels (for example, [hwal'b], [sdɔr'g]; *hvalpe, storke*).

sonantal (sonæ·ntăl), *a.* *Phonetics.* [f. Sonant *sb.* + -al.] **1.** Syllabic; = *Sonant *a.* b.

1891 A. L. Mayhew *Synopsis O.E. Phonol.* 36 The Indg. sonantal liquid l. **1897** *N.E.D.* s.v. *Diphthong*, The combination of a sonantal with a consonantal vowel. *Ibid.*, When these sounds [sc. *y* or *w*]..follow the sonantal vowel, the combination is called a 'falling diphthong'.

2. That is or contains a sonant (*Sonant *sb.* 3). *rare*.

1976 *Archivum Linguisticum* VII. 93 The discussion is divided into sections dealing with developments before geminates, in 'diphthongal groups' (vowel + sonant), with 'sonantal finals' (sonant preceded by another consonant) and before two consonants.

sonar (sō^u·nāɹ). orig. *U.S.* [f. initial letters of *so*und *na*vigation (*and*) *r*anging, after *radar*.] A system for use under the sea in which the audible or high-frequency sound reflected or emitted by an object in the sea is used to ascertain its position, nature, or speed; (an) apparatus used for this; also in extended use, a system in which the position of an object in air or water is ascertained by reflected ultrasound, e.g. as used by bats and in diagnostic medicine. Freq. *attrib.* Cf. *Asdic (see quot. 1963).

1946 *U.S. Navy Press Release* 6 Apr. 1 The word 'sonar' was coined from abbreviations for sound, navigation and ranging, and includes various types of underwater sound devices used in detecting submarines and other submerged objects and in obtaining water depths. **1952** [see *Asdic]. **1961** W. N. Kellogg *Porpoises & Sonar* (1962) iv. 48 The idea that sonar is systematically used by the great whales and porpoises is..a new and intriguing thought. **1963** *Times* 2 Feb. 5/2 In order to conform with NATO practice, the name Asdic..has been superseded by the word Sonar, the Admiralty announced yesterday... In future Asdic ratings will be known as Sonar operators. **1968** M. Woodhouse *Rock Baby* xiii. 129 Bats swooped past my head, bouncing their tiny high-pitched sonar echoes off me. **1971** *Hi-Fi Sound* Feb. 63 (Advt.), The photograph shows Ferrograph recorders at work in the Sonar Room aboard the Hunter Killer nuclear-powered Submarine H.M.S. 'Churchill'. **1971** *New Scientist* 3 June 568/1 The standard method of detecting submerged submarines is by sonar, either active or passive. **1973** *Brit. Med. Jrnl.* 6 Oct. 28/1 The 'in utero' crown-rump length of the fetus may be determined by sonar in the first trimester of pregnancy. **1974** *Sci. Amer.* Mar. 120/2 Frequency-modulation sonars..can exploit a Doppler signal to measure speed. **1979** *Ibid.* Feb. 67/1 (Advt.), These unique sonar cameras send out an inaudible sound signal that bounces off the subject and returns to the camera, in milliseconds—and the lens automatically rotates to perfect focus.

sonata. Add: Also with pl. ‖ **sonate** (sonā·te).

1. c. *sonata da camera*, a sonata suitable for performance in a room smaller than a concert-hall; *sonata da chiesa*, a sonata suitable for performance in a church.

[**1789** C. Burney *Gen. Hist. Music* (1935) III. ix. 548 Among the most early of these productions may be ranked the *Suonate per Chiesa*, of Legrenzi, published at Venice 1655; *Suonate da Chiesa e camera*, 1656.] **1801**

Busby *Dict. Mus.* s.v. Sonata, There are several kinds of *Sonatas*. The Italians, however, reduce them principally to two: the *Sonata da Camera*, or *Chamber Sonata*; and the *Sonata de Chiesa*, or *Church Sonata*. **1883** Grove *Dict. Mus.* III. 556/2 There are twenty-four 'Sonate da Chiesa' for strings, lute, and organ, twenty-four 'Sonate da Camera' for the same instruments, and twelve Solos or sonatas for violin and violoncello, or 'cembalo'. **1938** *Oxf. Compan. Mus.* 879/2 These may be said to close the period of the Sonata da Chiesa or abstract type of the contrapuntal period. Nearly all these composers also wrote works of the Sonata da Camera (or dance) type. **1968** *Listener* 20 June 813/3 The extent to which purely instrumental pieces were demanded during the services seems altogether extraordinary. This was the cradle of the *sonata da chiesa* and the *concerto grosso*. **1974** *Early Music* July 185/2 Adriano Banchieri was so smitten with the aria..that he set it..as a *sonata da camera* for two violins and bass.

3. *sonata movement.*

1942 *Ann. Reg. 1941* 295 Mr. T. S. Eliot's new poem, *The Dry Salvages*..had a sonata movement, the recurring theme being the timelessness of experience. **1947** A. Einstein *Music in Romantic Era* xviii. 350 The musical construction of a sonata or a sonata-movement does not follow real or idealized feelings.

sondage (sondā·ʒ). *Archæol.* [a. Fr. *sondage* sounding, borehole.] A deep trench dug to investigate the stratigraphy of a site.

[**1923** *Glasgow Herald* 13 Sept. 9/5 What is taking place in Berlin now is what the French call 'sondage'... The Chancellor is really endeavouring to see how the land lies.] **1930** *Discovery* Aug. 259/1 Against the south angle of the northern harbour a fairly prominent mound invited a sondage, and it proved to conceal a temple more perfectly preserved than any hitherto found in Mesopotamia. **1952** K. M. Kenyon *Beginning in Archaeol.* v. 102 The method of *sondage* is sometimes employed, in which a shaft of comparatively limited area is sunk..with the avowed object of establishing what is the succession of cultures. **1955** L. Woolley *Alalakh* i. 6 In 1948 and 1949 Mr. Sinclair Hood made *sondages* at Tabara al Akrad. **1977** P. Barker *Techniques Archaeol. Excavation* 76 We have seen that holes dug into extensive layers can be disastrous for their subsequent interpretation, and anyway the information gained by a 'sondage', however small, relates only to the area of the sondage.

sonde (sǫnd). [Fr., 'sounding-line, sounding'.] **a.** A radiosonde or similar device that is sent aloft to transmit or record information on conditions in the atmosphere. Orig. only as the second element in Combs. (as *ballon-sonde, ionosonde, radiosonde*, etc.).

1901 [see *ballon-sonde]. **1937** [see *radiosonde]. **1943** P. A. Anderson et al. *Captive Radiosonde & Wired Sonde Techniques* (U.S. Nat. Defense Res. Council Project P.D.R.C.-647, Rep. No. 3) 4 When the sonde is moved to a new altitude, a pause of 10–30 seconds is adequate to establish equilibrium readings on the meters. **1949** *Sci. Progr.* XXXVII. 490 A direct method of sounding may provide information on solar spectra from which data on the atmosphere above the highest level reached by the sonde may be derived. **1969** McIntosh & Thom *Essent. Meteorol.* vii. 111 More recently, ozone sondes have been used to measure the vertical distribution of ozone. **1975** *Nature* 1 May 20/2 A seventh aircraft was used to drop sondes from 40,000 feet and obtain additional vertical profiles of wind and temperature.

b. An instrument probe for transmitting information about its surroundings underground or under water.

1952 *Bull. Amer. Assoc. Petroleum Geologists* XXXVI. 310 The application of the limestone sonde log to the determination of the porosity profile of wells. **1962** *Research* XV. 298/1 This deflection increases as the sonde continues to enter the [coal] seam. **1962** [see *re-entry 2 d]. **1975** G. Anderson *Coring* vii. 124 The SP log is a measurement of the electrical potential energy in the mud around the sonde as compared with a reference electrode grounded at the surface.

sonder (zǫ·ndəɹ), *a.* and *sb.* *U.S.* [f. G. *sonderklasse* special class.] **A.** *adj.* Of, pertaining to, or designating a class of small racing yachts. **B.** *sb.* A yacht of this class.

1909 *N.Y. Even. Post* 9 Sept. 3/3 The Sonder yachtsmen, both victors and vanquished, were received by President Taft today. **1913** C. W. Ernst *Letter* (MS.), Our yachtsmen, since 1907, talk of 'sonder-boats', sonder class, sonder race,—meaning certain boats recognised by the International Yacht Racing Union. **1917** *Rudder* Apr. 328/1 Fred M. Hoyt is to have a Marconi rig put upon his sonder boat Skeezix. There are a few sonders left at Marblehead and the innovation will be watched with much interest. **1948** R. de Kerchove *Internat. Maritime Dict.* 695/2 *Sonder*, a class of small yacht originated in Germany, in which the sum of the waterline length, extreme beam, and extreme draft must not be greater than 32 ft.

Sonderbund (zǫ·ndəɹbunt). [a. G. *Sonderbund* special league, separate association.] A league formed by the R.C. cantons of Switzerland in 1843 and defeated in a civil war in 1847. Also *attrib.*

1847 G. Grote *Seven Lett. Politics Switzerland* i. 17 The invasion..in..1844..by bands of volunteers..called the Corps Francs—and the separate league of Seven Cantons, called the Sonderbund. **1887** *Encycl. Brit.* XXII. 795/1 The seven Catholic cantons—Uri, Schwyz, Unterwalden, Lucerne, Zug, Freiburg, and Wallis—formed (September 7, 1843) a 'Sonderbund' or separate league... In December 1845 the Sonderbund turned itself into an armed confederation. **1922** E. & C. Paul tr. *Oechsli's Hist. Switzerland* xxxiv. 396 The Sonderbund war. **1952** E. Bonjour et al. *Short Hist. Switzerland* x. 262 The founders of this Sonderbund, as it was soon aptly named. **1973** Howat & Taylor *Dict. World Hist.* 1465/1 The outnumbered Sonderbund expected Austrian and French help, but the swift victory of the Diet's troops under Dufour forestalled its arrival.

‖ **Sonderkommando** (zo·ndəɹkoma:ndo). [G. *Sonderkommando* special detachment.] In Nazi Germany, a detachment of prisoners in a concentration camp responsible for the disposal of the dead; also a member of such a detachment. Also *fig.*

1951 Moyse & Stenhouse tr. *Rousset's World Apart* v. 27 The *Sonderkommando*, totally isolated from the world, condemned to live every second of its eternity with tortured and charred bodies. **1960** S. Becker tr. *Schwarz-Bart's Last of Just* (1961) viii. 422 The team of *Sonderkommando* responsible for burning the Jews in the crematory ovens. **1976** *Times Lit. Suppl.* 2 July 815/1 A four-legged Sonderkommando who betrays his fellows to starvation. **1979** J. Gardner *Nostradamus Traitor* xxxv. 165 The womenfolk prepared a great spread of food... 'Enough food to feed the whole of a Sonderkommando.'

sone. Restrict † *Obs.*$^{-1}$ to sense in Dict. and add: **2.** (sōᵘn). A unit of subjective loudness such that the number of sones is proportional to the loudness of a sound: a tone of frequency 1000 Hz and 40 dB above the listener's audibility threshold produces a loudness of one sone.

1936 S. S. Stevens in *Psychol. Rev.* XLIII. 416 It is proposed that the unit of the scale be the loudness of 1000 cycle tone 40db above threshold heard with both ears, and that it be called a sone. **1952** *Sci. News Let.* 28 June 411/2 The field studies..used the 'sone' as a unit of loudness. The decibel..measures only the intensity of a noise. It is the loudness that is most objectionable to the human ear. **1958** *Times* 18 July 7/6 The sone scale is..based on the averaged impressions of supposedly normal individuals in identifying the relative loudness of different sounds, *i.e.*, that they are two, three or four times, &c., as loud as a sound of one sone. **1960** *New Scientist* 25 Feb. 454/1 The American Automobile Manufacturers' Association adopted in 1954 a noise specification for new vehicles of 125 sones measured at 50 feet. **1970** [see *noy].

sone, var. *son *sb.*²

Soneryl (sǫ·nĕrịl). *Pharm.* Also **soneryl.** A proprietary name (orig. French) for butobarbitone (5-butyl-5-ethylbarbituric acid, $C_{10}H_{16}N_2O_3$), given in tablet form as a sedative and hypnotic.

1923 *Pharmaceutical Jrnl.* LVI. 170/2 An interesting preparation which Messrs. May and Baker are shortly to issue is 'Soneryl'... Compared with veronal, Soneryl is twice as active. **1923** *Official Gaz.* (U.S. Patent Office) 18 Sept. 395/2 Etablissements Poulenc Frères, Paris... *Soneryl*... Claims use since Apr. 18, 1922. **1933** *Trade Marks Jrnl.* 3 May 510/2 *Soneryl*... A derivative of barbituric acid prepared for use in medicine and pharmacy. May and Baker Ltd... Manufacturing chemists. **1948** J. H. Burn *Lect. Notes Pharmacol.* 44 Tablets of Soneryl (butobarbitone) are used to ensure a good night's sleep either for a patient in hospital or for a normal person travelling by night train. **1959** D. du Maurier *Breaking Point* 115, I would sleep on it—if I could sleep, which seemed very doubtful. I took two soneryl tablets, and passed out. **1979** L. Brown *Encounters With Nature* vi. 79 By taking three Soneryl and four aspirin tablets, I suffered through the night in fitful drowsiness.

‖ **son et lumière** (sǫn eⁱ lū·miēᵊɹ, son *e* lümyęr). Also with capital initials. [Fr., lit. 'sound and light'.] **1.** A form of entertainment using recorded sound and lighting effects, usu. presented at night at a historic building and giving a dramatic narrative of its history. Also *attrib.*

1957 *Times* 1 Aug. 10/1 A dinner party..on the occasion of the preview of the *Son et Lumière* spectacle. *Ibid.* 13 Aug. 11/1 In the five years since M. Paul Robert-Houdin first introduced the technique at..Chambord, *son et lumière* has been adopted at..buildings of historic interest in France. **1959** *Times* 30 June 12/4 Son et lumière performances are being given this week, starting to-night at Greys Court, Henley-on-Thames. **1969** V. Rowe *Loire* 33 At Chambord, in 1952, a new kind of entertainment was born, *son-et-lumière*, a combination of sound and light effects. **1970** N. Fleming *Czech Point* (1971) xvi. 205, I felt as visible as a statue in a Son et Lumière display. **1977** J. I. M. Stewart *Madonna of Astrolabe* i. 19 A few years ago we had *son et lumière* in aid of some building project.

2. *fig.* Writing or behaviour resembling a *son et lumière* presentation, *esp.* in its dramatic qualities.

1968 *Punch* 16 Oct. 557/3 The effects are produced by a literary *son et lumière*—by liberal direct quotation of anecdotes, poetry, hymns and music, and a series of splendid photographs, rather than words about palaces. **1969** *Listener* 9 Jan. 41/1 Old Mr Seddeby's performance, from 11 o'clock to one daily, as an elder statesman in decline, an illusion which involved a lot of business with a monocle and a cigar-cutter, was pure *son et lumière*. **1978** *Times Lit. Suppl.* 24 Mar. 336/3 It would have been all too easy to end this biography in *son et lumière* and to paint a Tiepolo ceiling on which Forster is floating up to Olympus.

song, *sb.* Add: **2. d.** *song without words*, an instrumental composition in the style of a song (after Mendelssohn's title 'Lieder ohne Worte'); also *transf.*

1871 S. Smiles *Character* viii. 219 Cheerfulness..gives harmony of soul, and is a perpetual song without words. **1883** R. Prentice *Musician* II. 95 The second movement [of a Beethoven sonata] is a veritable Song without Words. **1938** *Oxf. Compan. Mus.* 885/1 *Song without words*, a term introduced by Mendelssohn to cover a type of one-movement pianoforte solo, throughout which a well-marked song-like melody progresses, with an accompaniment. **1974** *Encycl. Brit. Macropædia* XI. 902/1 She [*sc.* Fanny Mendelssohn] had herself written some of the *Songs Without Words* attributed to her brother.

4. d. *a song in one's heart*, a feeling of joy or pleasure.

1930 L. Hart *With a Song in my Heart* 4 With a song in my heart;—I behold your adorable face. **1946** *Hansard Commons* 9 Apr. 1807, I will find, and find with a song in my heart, whatever money is necessary to finance useful and practical proposals for developing these areas. **1978** *Times* 9 Jan. 13/1 Does the lending rate come down? Then every conservative owner-occupier has a song in his heart.

e. *on (full) song*, in good form, performing well. *colloq.*

1967 *Autocar* 27 Dec. 10/1 The close and even spacing of the ratios..make it easy to keep the engine 'on full song' during hard driving. **1971** *Daily Tel.* 21 Aug. 16/1 As the table reveals, most of the leading unit trust managers have at least one fund that is 'on song'. **1974** *Observer* 3 Feb. 24/5 Really on song since beating Manchester City in the Cup, Forest won 5–1. **1981** *Radio Times* 11 Apr. 23/2 If you are on song nothing will break your concentration.

5*. *song and dance.* **a.** A form of entertainment (*spec.* a vaudeville act) consisting of singing and dancing. Freq. *attrib.* orig. *U.S.*

[**1628** F. Drake *World Encompassed* 76 They yet continued their song and dance a reasonable time.] **1872** S. Hale *Let.* 16 Jan. (1918) iii. 78 He did a 'Song and Dance', two, in fact. **1872** *Chicago Tribune* 13 Oct. 5/6 First week of the distinguished song and dance artists. **1895** *N.Y. Dramatic News* 23 Nov. 13/3 The first double song and dance team was comprised of Wash Norton and Ben Cotton. **1940** *Chatelaine* Apr. 36/2, I practiced my song-and-dance act for weeks. **1959** R. Longrigg *Wrong Number* iv. 58 So up she pops from hell or wherever, just the time for a bit of song and dance. **1968** *Radio Times* 28 Nov. 53/1 The song-and-dance patter comedian. **1977** *Time Out* 17–23 June 47/2 Pleasant Nilsson-like song 'n' dance numbers.

b. *fig.* A rigmarole, an elaborately contrived story or entreaty, a fuss or outcry. Also *attrib.* *colloq.* (orig. *U.S. slang*). Cf. sense 4 c in Dict.

1895 E. W. Townsend *Chimmie Fadden* 6 Den, 'is whiskers gives me a song an' dance. **1900** B. Matthews *Confident To-Morrow* 9 And it ain't a song-and-dance I'm giving you either. **1913** Kipling *Diversity of Creatures* (1917) 292, I don't see how this song and dance helps us any. **1922** S. Lewis *Babbitt* xxxii. 375 George, what's this I hear about some song and dance you gave Colonel Snow about not wanting to join the G.C.L.? **1949** *Time* 5 Sept. 2/3 Labor Leader Preble..was not impressed by 'the song and dance about [Stefan's] mother and sister being persecuted and murdered'. **1958** 'E. Dundy' *Dud Avocado* III. vi. 266 If only he hadn't felt obliged to make such a song and dance about it. **1967** 'S. Woods' *And Shame Devil* 118 ''Appen tha means well,' he said, his speech suddenly broadened almost out of all recognition, 'and 'appen tha's joost making a song and dance.' **1980** J. Ditton *Copley's Hunch* II. ii. 132 The Prime Minister wants to make a song and dance about it.

6. a. *song-lyric, -sequence, -sheet, -strain, -tune* (earlier and later examples).

1944 C. Day Lewis *Poetry for You* vi. 61 The chief thing which poets took over from the song-lyric and preserved in the new lyrical poetry was..'singleness of mind'. **1947** A. Einstein *Music in Romantic Era* xiv. 187 With Op. 24, the Heine song-sequence, he [*sc.* Schumann] began to write lieder. **1930** P. Geddes et al. (*title*) Song-sheet and welcomes. **1967** A. L. Lloyd *Folk Song in England* i. 29 The countless Sorrowful Lamentations of hanged men did not become anchored in tradition ..perhaps because the song-sheets bearing these effusions are of late appearance. **1876** G. M. Hopkins *Poems* (1967) 176 So tiny a trickle of song-strain. **1809** E. Cutler *Diary* 28 Aug. in J. P. Cutler *Life & Times E. Cutler* (1890) v. 98 Very soon a man began to sing a hymn in a familiar song-tune. **1967** A. L. Lloyd *Folk Song in England* iii. 139 As feudal society gives way to capitalism..recitative melodies are replaced by songtunes.

b. *song-composer, -composition, -singing* vbl. sb. (earlier example), *-writing* vbl. sb. (earlier examples), *-writing* ppl. a.

1947 A. Einstein *Music in Romantic Era* xiv. 184 There were no Italian song-composers. *Ibid.* 191 The procession of musicians who contributed to Romantic song-composition. **1848** W. Allingham *Diary* 26 Sept. (1907) ii. 43 Dine at Peter Kelly's,..much song-singing afterwards. **1772** J. Aikin (*title*) Essays on song-writing. **1809** *Belfast Monthly Mag.* Mar. 164/2, I promise.. method in my handling the theory and practice of song-writing. **1947** A. Einstein *Music in Romantic Era* iv. 35 The song-writing Berlin purists.

c. *song-rapt, -wild* adjs.

1885 W. B. Yeats in *Dublin Univ. Rev.* July 137 A wandering song-rapt bird. **1937** Blunden *Elegy* 15 The flight of one small song-wild lark Finds heaven.

7. song-ballet, (*a*) *U.S. dial.*, a ballad; (*b*) a theatrical work combining songs and ballet; *song-cycle* [cf. G. *liederzyklus*], a series of songs intended to form one musical entity, and having words dealing with related subjects; **song-flight,** (a) flight of a characteristic pattern made by a bird as it sings, in a territorial display; **song-form** *Mus.*, a form used in the composition of songs; *spec.* [tr. G. *liedform*] the form of a simple melody with simple accompaniment, or that of a work in three sections of which the third is a repetition of the first; **song-fowl** *poet.* = SONG-BIRD 1; **song-hit** *colloq.*, a song which is a popular success; **song-motet,** a simple type of motet; **song-perch,** a place where a bird perches to sing, so as to establish its territory; **song period,** the part of the year during which the birds of a species sing; **song-plugger** orig. *U.S.*, a person employed to popularize songs, esp. by performing them repeatedly; hence **song-plugging** *vbl. sb.*, **song-plug** *v. trans.*, **song-plugged** *ppl. a.*; **song-post** = *song-perch* above; **song stylist,** a singer admired for his or her style.

1915 *Dialect Notes* IV. 190 *Song-ballet, n.*, a song or ballad. **1938** *Sun* (Baltimore) 15 June 6/7 Visitors will join the mountaineers to sing their 'song ballets'. **1962** AUDEN *Dyer's Hand* (1963) 484 We have translated.. Brecht's text for the song-ballet *Die sieben Todsünden* with music by Kurt Weill. **1899** Song-cycle [in Dict., sense 6 a]. **1942** E. BLOM *Music in England* x. 168 Arthur Somervell's settings of poems from Tennyson's 'Maud', which have remained among the world's few great song-cycles. **1978** *Listener* 30 Mar. 412/4 A mature song-cycle by Dallapiccola. **1936** NICHOLSON & KOCH *Songs of Wild Birds* 9 Song-flight is an extra means of making the singer temporarily as conspicuous as possible. **1961** A. J. BERGER *Bird Study* vi. 186 Song, song flights, and other special displays serve an orientation function: they attract a female to the male's territory or to a nest site. **1884** R. PRENTICE *Musician: Grade 3* 4 The simplest song-form is constructed on two or three sentences only. **1902** H. C. BANISTER *Mus. Anal.* i. 2 There is a term now in vogue to designate the simplest of all plans or forms: 'Song-Form' or 'Aria-Form'. **1946** R. BLESH *Shining Trumpets* (1949) v. 109 The blues are essentially a song form. **1954** *Grove's Dict. Mus.* (ed. 5) VII. 962/2 The term 'song form,' derived from the German, has unfortunately been used by different writers with different significations. The vagueness which results and the fact that the term is not happily chosen gives rise to doubts whether it had not better be entirely abandoned. **1877** G. M. HOPKINS *Poems* (1967) 71 Not that the sweet-fowl, song-fowl, needs no rest. **1914** 'HIGH JINKS, JR.' *Choice Slang* 18 *Song hit*, a popular song. **1918** [see *HIT *sb.* 4]. **1959** 'F. NEWTON' *Jazz Scene* 9 *Pop, pop music*, popular entertainment music as typified by the 'song-hit'. **1942** H. HEWITT *Harmonice Musices Odhecaton* vi. 69 A few 'song-motets' find a place in the Odhecaton. **1974** *Early Music* Oct. 219 Some of his [*sc.* Dufay's] most elegant Latin compositions.. are dedicated to the Virgin Mary, and their treble-dominated texture and lyrical charm—they resemble chansons in many ways—explain why they are called song-motets. **1934** *British Birds* XXVIII. 15 If a male is on his song perch when his hen quits her eggs, he usually follows her.. to her feeding ground. **1975** I. ROWLEY *Bird Life* v. 61 The kookaburra defends a large area, but in particular a number of song perches. **1908** *British Birds* I. 367 In the middle of the song-period all the individuals of a species found in any locality sing every day. **1961** A. J. BERGER *Bird Study* vi. 171 Many species have a short song period (post-breeding) after the molt has been completed. **1927** *Daily Express* 22 Sept. 9/3 'Clap Yo' Hands' must have been song-plugged for ten minutes right off... 'Do-Do-Do' is another song-plugged number. **1923** *N.Y. Times* 7 Oct. IX. 2/1 *Song plugger*, a retiring representative of a song publisher planted in the audience to call for songs, whistle refrains and applaud. **1927** *Melody Maker* May 437/1 Song pluggers are.. vocalists lent by the music publishers to the dance bands just for the nights on which these bands are due to broadcast, and, of course, sing only their employer's numbers. **1976** R. SANDERS in D. Villiers *Next Year in Jerusalem* 208 Gershwin.. embarked upon his musical career at sixteen as a Tin Pan Alley song plugger and composer. **1927** *Melody Maker* May 433 (*heading*) Song-plugging thro' the ages. **1972** P. BLACK *Biggest Aspidistra* I. iii. 29 The song-plugging wave did not recede until 1948, when the BBC and the publishers managed to draw up an agreement. **1938** *British Birds* XXXI. 320 The habitat was on open grassy ground with stones and sallow bushes as 'song posts'. **1938** *Sun* (Baltimore) 15 June 6/7 Special guests will be.. Miss Florence Clark, of Detroit, noted song stylist. **1973** *Black Panther* 24 Mar. 7/1 Elaine Brown, community activist.. is also a musician, composer, lyricist and song stylist.

Song, var. *SUNG.

songfest (sǫ·ŋfest). orig. and chiefly *N. Amer.* [f. SONG *sb.* + *FEST: cf. G. *sängerfest.*] An informal session of group-singing; a festive sing-song.

1912 J. SANDILANDS *Western Canad. Dict.* 9/1 *Songfest*, a feast of song. **1916** *Dialect Notes* IV. 354 *Songfest.* 'There's to be a *songfest* at the church Friday night.' **1953** *Manch. Guardian Weekly* 12 Nov. 9/1 According to the 'New York Times':..Their problem has been greatly complicated by the fact that each time they have tried to speak to the prisoners through the camp public address system the P.O.W. bosses have organised song fests, thrown rocks.. or set up a deafening clamour. **1961** 'I. Ross' *Old Students Never Die* (1963) viii. 109 The image of Jackie and Alison, holding hands and bowing to us after their little songfest. **1979** *Yale Alumni Mag.* Apr. 30/2 Fifty members of the two groups gathered for a gay, impromptu songfest in Pushkin Square.

Songhai (sǫŋgai·). Also **Songhay, Songhoi,** † **Sungai.** [Native name.] A people of West Africa, living mainly in Niger and Mali; the Nilo-Saharan language of this people. Also *attrib.*

1738 F. MOORE tr. *Leo the African's Geographical Hist. Afr.* in *Trav. Inland Parts Afr.* II. 28 The Negroes have a good many languages amongst them, of which.. Sungai is spoken in a great many of their kingdoms. **1858** H. BARTH *Travels & Discoveries in North & Central Afr.* IV. lix. 237 All the huts in these Songhay villages consist merely of reeds. *Ibid.* 238 The Songhay in general are among the most inhospitable people I ever met. **1911** *Encycl. Brit.* XXV. 414/1 According to the *Tarik é Sudan* ..the first king of the Songhoi was called Dialliaman (Arabic *Dia min al Jemen*, 'he is come from Yemen')... The Songhoi emigration must have begun towards the middle of the 7th century... The Songhoi language.. is often known as Kissur. **1930** C. G. SELIGMAN *Races of Afr.* iii. 60 Only in 1500, when Melle was captured by the Songhai king, Omar Askia, did the Melestine Empire cease to exist. *Ibid.* 62 The Songhai are moderately tall, with a stature of about 67 inches. **1957** W. M. HAILEY *Afr. Survey 1956* iii. 86 All languages which are known not to be attached to any of the above Units (e.g. Songhai). **1963** [see *SAHARAN *sb.*]. **1966** [see *NILO-]. **1977** H. GREENE *FSO-1* xviii. 161 The Republic of Mali.. with Bambara and Fulani tribes in the east, the Songhai and the Malinke and the wandering Tuaregs in the west.

Songish (sǫŋgī·ʃ). Also **Songeesh, Songhees,** 9 **Songhies, Songhish.** [Native name.] An American Indian people of Vancouver Island, British Columbia; the language of this people, a dialect of Straits Salish. Also *attrib.*

1860 [see *KLOOCH]. **1862** R. C. MAYNE *Four Years in Brit. Columbia & Vancouver Island* ii. 30 The road ascends a little hill, on the summit of which lies the Indian village of the Songhies. *Ibid.*, This village of the Songhies presents one of the most squalid pictures of dirt and misery it is possible to conceive. **1865** M. MACFIE *Vancouver Island & Brit. Columbia* xvi. 430 The Songhish tribe, resident near Victoria, hold a general merry-making annually in.. October. **1875** H. H. BANCROFT *Native Races of Pacific States* III. xii. 522 The Songhies said the hunter was transformed into a deer. **1911** *Encycl. Brit.* XXIV. 80/1 *Salishan*, the name of a linguistic family of North American Indian tribes, the more important of which [include] the Salish.., Skokomish, Songeesh, Spokan and Tulalip. **1911** [see *POTLATCH *v.*]. **1973** L. C. THOMPSON in T. A. Sebeok *Current Trends in Linguistics* X. 1010 The rest of the dialects extend from Lummi.. across to Songish (Lkungen) around modern Victoria, on Vancouver Island, and on northward to include Saanich.

songket (sǫ·ŋket), *a.* Also 9 **sungkit.** [Malay.] Of cloth: decorated by interweaving short lengths of gold or silver thread into the material. Also *ellipt.* as *sb.*

1894 N. B. DENNYS *Descr. Dict. Brit. Malaya* 107 Silk *sarongs*.. woven with silk and gold thread are termed *kain sungkit*. **1953** *Exhib. Malayan Arts & Crafts* (Malayan Agri-Horticultural Assoc.), Hand-woven cloths. The other important category of Malay cloths is that of the *kain songket*. **1963, 1971** [see *KAIN]. **1972** M. SHEPPARD *Taman Indera* 100 (*caption*) The gift is a piece of silk *songket* hand woven cloth, folded in the shape of a bird. *Ibid.* 120 The body of a *songket* sarong is silk, of a single plain colour. The decoration is carried out with gold or silver thread... The songket sarong is worn today by Malay men of all levels of society when attending social functions, and it is therefore in constant demand. **1972** *Malay Mail* 27 May 9/7 (Advt.), We are offering a very wide range of genuine Malaysian songket.

‖ **songkok** (sǫ·ŋkǫk). Also 9 **songko.** [Malay.] A cap worn by Malays, resembling a skull-cap.

1894 N. B. DENNYS *Descr. Dict. Brit. Malaya* 108 The skull-cap, *kopia* or *songko*, is worn by some. **1960** S. HARVESTER *Chinese Hammer* i. 8 An affable Indonesian official with his black *songkok* tilted at a rakish angle above his chubby face. **1966** D. FORBES *Heart of Malaya* xiv. 193 The bridegroom wears his *songkok*, the round brimless hat. **1977** P. THEROUX *Consul's File* 38 'This is serious,' he said, glowering and putting on his *songkok*.

songlessness (sǫ·ŋlėsnės). [f. SONGLESS *a.* + -NESS.] The state or condition of being songless.

1924 J. R. HARRIS *As pants Hart* viii. 85, I have often deplored the songlessness of the modern Evangelical and Protestant Churches. **1958** *Times* 9 Sept. 10/5 Another very common bird begins now to sing again after a period of songlessness.

songster. Add: **1. b.** *U.S.* (See quot. 1980.)

1925 ODUM & JOHNSON *Negro & his Songs* i. 1 Anyone hearing him sing day in and day out, together with thousands of others like him, must agree.. with the oft-repeated song claim of the 'musicianer', 'music-physicianer' and 'songster', that 'All don't see me goin' to hear me sing.' Not only does he sing, but he sings much and sings long with richness and variety. **1964** *Amer. Folk Music Occasional* I. 61 And if you describe the artist with accuracy, it will be with his own apt word: songster. The term suggests a musician who is both performer and inventor and harks back to the time when every Southern town had its songster, a man who was virtually in charge of the community's social life. **1968** P. OLIVER *Screening Blues* ii. 82 The 'songster' generation of singers. **1970** —— *Savannah Syncopators* 7 The instrumental techniques and traditions of the blues singers, the songsters, the ragtime banjoists and guitarists. *Ibid.* 86 Many of the older blues singers and songsters recall playing for white functions. **1980** *New Grove Dict. Music & Musicians* XVII. 17/1 *Songster*, a black American musician of the post-Reconstruction era who performed a wide variety of ballads, dance-tunes, reels and minstrel songs, singing to his own banjo or guitar accompaniment.

sonic (sǫ·nik), *a.* [f. L. *son-us* sound + -IC.] **1. a.** Employing or operated by sound waves; used esp. with reference to devices and techniques which make use of the reflected echo of a sound pulse.

1923 *Sci. Amer.* May 330/2 Sonic sounding is rendered possible by the fact that sound vibrations, passing through water and striking a solid surface, are returned as an echo to the source from which they originated. **1924** *Telegr. & Telephone Jrnl.* X. 172/2 The United States destroyers *Hull* and *Corry*, equipped with sonic depth sounders.. have been ordered to survey the ocean bed. **1933** *Geogr. Jrnl.* LXXXI. 572 The exploration of the Maldive ridge by sonic sounding should be interesting. **1952** *Chambers's Jrnl.* June 364/2 After the War a sonic gun was actually found in a German laboratory. **1961** *Flight* LXXIX. 249/2 In addition to the display system, the RH-1 was fitted with Ryan APN-97 Doppler and the sonic altimeter .**1965** *Punch* 17 Mar. 390/1 'That thing [*sc.* a torpedo] live?' I asked. 'Very,' said the Lieutenant-Commander, 'but it's only an antiquated sonic-homing job.' **1967** *Jane's Surface Skimmer Systems 1967–68* 94/1 It receives craft motion input from a sonic height sensor in the bow. **1976** B. BOVA *Multiple Man* (1977) i. 11 If anyone tried to fire a shot.. the scanning lasers would pick up the bullet... Sonic janglers would paralyse everyone in the auditorium.

b. Of or pertaining to sound or sound waves, esp. within the audible range.

1936 *Jrnl. Amer. Chem. Soc.* LVIII. 1071/2 In order to avoid any possible sonic action directly on a test reagent. **1939** [see *sonoluminescence* s.v. *SONO-]. **1942** *Jrnl. R. Aeronaut. Soc.* XLVI. 83 The guiding intention will be, to avoid.. the formation of sonic waves, and practical elimination of compression shocks, in order to obtain a minimum of the so-called wave-making resistance. **1947** *Aircraft Engin.* XIX. 180/1 The design of the VG-70 experimental monoplane.. was begun as a determined effort in the field of sonic research. **1962** F. I. ORDWAY et al. *Basic Astronautics* viii. 345 Since the flow often speeds up when passing over a body it is possible for sonic flow to exist over parts of a body which is moving at speeds somewhat less than Mach 1. **1969** L. F. YERGES *Sound, Noise, & Vibration Control* 1. 1 There is no essential difference between the sonic and vibratory forms of sound energy. **1972** *Observer* (Colour Suppl.) 22 Oct. 53/2 It is this *depth* of sound which stereophony failed to capture, or so the sonic engineers believed when they looked around for their next breakthrough. **1975** *Sci. Amer.* Oct. 135/1 The ultrasonic world is quieter than the sonic, mainly because its sounds are more local. **1977** *Gramophone* Dec. 1016/1 Sonic beauty abounds in *The Triumphs of Oriana*..: 64 minutes of music packed with admirable clarity.. on a single disc.

2. Special collocations: *sonic bang* = *sonic boom* below; *sonic barrier* = *sound barrier* s.v. *SOUND *sb.*[3] 7 a; *sonic boom,* the sudden loud noise heard when the shock wave from an aircraft travelling faster than sound reaches the ears; *sonic speed, velocity,* the speed at which sound waves travel in a particular medium, esp. air.

1953 *Sci. News* XXX. 118 Subsequently two sonic bangs were heard of the same intensity with a small time interval apparently the same as that between the vapour puffs. **1955** *Times* 20 June 8/7 As the new fighters showed their considerable paces the programme was punctuated with 'sonic bangs' as the speed of sound was exceeded in dives. *a* **1974** R. CROSSMAN *Diaries* (1976) II. 169 Next came the Minister of Aviation, Mr Mulley, who had put in a request for urgent legislation on sonic bangs. **1946** *Jrnl. R. Aeronaut. Soc.* L. 445/2, I do not imagine for one moment that man will be happy until he has conquered the 'sonic barrier'. **1955** *Sci. News Let.* 24 Sept. 195 (*caption*) By giving the aircraft a 'wasp waist', engineers ..made it slip more smoothly through the sonic barrier. **1952** *Times* 2 Sept. 4/5 Aircraft travelling at about the speed of sound cause a loud bang, which has become known as the 'sonic boom'. **1966** *Guardian* 2 May 8/6 Mr Amery, Minister of Aviation, told Parliament that damage from the Concord's sonic booms would be 'negligible'. **1969** *Times* 17 Nov. 4/7 Their home collapsed after another sonic boom. **1977** *New Yorker* 24 Oct. 36/2, I heard the explosion even inside the manuscript room... It sounded like a sonic boom. **1946** *Jrnl. R. Aeronaut. Soc.* L. 436/1 The problems of aerodynamics at speeds well in excess of that of sound are in some respects much simpler than those quite near the sonic speed. **1950** *Sci. News* XV. Plate 7 (*caption*) This model aeroplane.. was designed to investigate the forces acting on an aircraft reaching sonic speed. **1962** F. I. ORDWAY et al. *Basic Astronautics* viii. 344 At this point the body is moving at sonic speed and transonic conditions exist. **1942** *Jrnl. R. Aeronaut. Soc.* XLVI. 64 The local 'sonic velocity' *a* is then defined by the expression:—$a^2 = dp/d\rho$. **1949** *Jrnl. Appl. Physics* XX. 638/1 A slowly varying pressure change or signal is transmitted through the mixture with a definite critical or 'sonic' velocity.

Hence **so·nically** *adv.*, by means of sound waves; as regards sound.

1936 *Jrnl. Amer. Chem. Soc.* LVIII. 1070/2 A quantitative study of certain oxidation reactions sonically activated in the audible range. **1959** *Brookhaven Symp. in Biol.* XII. 11 A sonically fragmented sample. **1975** *Gramophone* June 36/1 Sonically the record is obviously to be preferred to Menuhin's earlier recording with Furtwängler. **1981** *Popular Hi-Fi* Mar. 21/2 The Crimson is a better pre-amplifier sonically.

sonicate (sǫ·nikēit), *sb.* and *v.* [f. prec. + *-ate*, after *filtrate, precipitate.*] **A.** *sb.* A sample which has been subjected to ultrasound so as to fragment the macromolecules and membranes in it.

1958 M. LITT et al. in *Proc. Nat. Acad. Sci.* XLIV. 144 The production of sonicates (degraded samples) covering more than a tenfold range in molecular weight. **1958** NISHIHARA & DOTY in *Ibid.* 412 Eight 30-cc. aliquots of a stock solution..were exposed to 9-kilocycle sonic waves in a 50-watt Raytheon magnetostriction generator... The samples produced in this way, termed 'sonicates', are listed. **1979** *Nature* 25 Jan. 314/2 (*caption*) Calvaria were washed again, sonicated, and the sonicate ultracentrifuged.

B. *v. trans.* To subject to such treatment.

1960 *Biochem. & Biophys. Res. Communications* III. 471 Tumor mitochondria were sonicated at maximum intensity (1·3 amps) for two 2·5-minute periods. **1974** *Nature* 20 Dec. 655/1 (*caption*) The DNA fragments were prepared by sonicating calf thymus DNA to a molecular weight of 5·4 × 10^6. **1978** [see below].

Hence **so·nicated** *ppl. a.*; **sonica·tion**, treatment with ultrasound; **so·nicator**, an apparatus for treating samples in this way.

1958 *Proc. Nat. Acad. Sci.* XLIV. 150 The loss in activity due to sónication occurs only as a result of reduction in molecular size below that required for attachment. **1959** *Brookhaven Symp. in Biol.* XII. 11 The variance due to any change in compositional heterogeneity of the sonicated sample, can be obtained. **1964** *Jrnl. Cellular & Compar. Physiol.* LXIV. 153/1 Washed ghosts were sonicated for ten minutes using an MSE 60 W sonicator. **1969** *Nature* 20 Dec. 1164/2 The supernatant contains the polymerase, which may then be assayed simply by adding sonicated calf thymus DNA. **1970** *Sci. Jrnl.* Apr. 42 Cleaning these parts is a major branch of ultraclean technology involving the application of special solvents, the use of 'sonication'—ultrasonic vibration—to jar the dirt loose,..and many other highly specialized procedures. **1978** *Jrnl. Protozool.* XXV. 492/2 Other aliquots of *E*[*ncephalitozoon*] *cuniculi*..were sonicated using a Bronson sonicator.

sonics (sǫ·niks), *sb. pl.* [f. *SONIC *a.*: see -IC 2.] Sonic techniques and equipment generally or collectively.

1955 HUETER & BOLT *Sonics* p. v, The multiplicity of concepts and techniques could be designated by the name *sonics*. *Ibid.*, Sonics encompasses the analysis, testing, and processing of materials and products by the use of mechanical vibratory energy. **1974** 'G. BLACK' *Golden Cockatrice* vi. 102 All three corvettes were now almost motionless..obviously listening on sonics.

Sonifier (sǫ·nifəi,əɪ). Also **sonifer.** [f. as prec. + -FY + -ER[1].] The proprietary name of a make of sonicator.

1961 *Official Gaz.* (U.S. Patent Office) 1 Aug. TM 10/1 Branson Instruments, Inc., Stamford, Conn... *Sonifier.* For electrical generators of ultrasonic energy, ultrasonic energy transducers and electrically powered processing systems for the same. First use Oct. 19, 1960. **1963** *Biochim. & Biophys. Acta* LXXI. 232 A suspension of ghosts..was treated with ultrasonic waves generated by a Branson Model S-75 Sonifier for 15 secs. **1965** *Trade Marks Jrnl.* 16 June 809/2 *Sonifier.* 875,310. Ultrasonic apparatus and instruments included in Class 9. Branson Instruments Incorporated..Connecticut, U.S.A.; manufacturers.—8th Feb. 1965. **1980** *European Jrnl. Biochem.* CV. 164/2 Sonication at 4°C with a Branson B-12 sonifier.

Soninke (sǫni·ŋke). [Native name.] A member of a people living in Mali and Senegal; the people itself; the Mandingo language or dialects spoken by this people. Also *attrib.* Cf. *MALINKE.

1886 *Encycl. Brit.* XXI. 662/2 The Mandingoes.. comprise the Mandingo proper, occupying Manding, and the Malinkés and Soninkés, scattered about Bambuk, Buré, and Fuladugu. **1911** [see *MALINKE]. **1939** C. G. SELIGMAN *Races Afr.* (rev. ed.) iii. 61 The Mandingo.. constitute one of the most important groups of Senegal and West Sudan..and include such large and important tribes as the..Soninke, Malinke, and Vei. **1971** N. LEVTZION in Ajayi & Crowder *Hist. W. Afr.* I. iv. 124 They are united by..their pride in having once been part of the ancient Soninke kingdom of Wagadu. **1974** *Encycl. Brit. Macropædia* XI. 382/2 Soninke and Dogon are also related to Bambara; Dogon includes many dialects.

Sonne (sǫ·nə). *Bacteriol.* The name of Carl Olaf *Sonne* (1882–1948), Danish bacteriologist, used *attrib.* and formerly in the possessive with reference to the Gram-negative bacterium *Shigella sonnei*, which causes a mild form of dysentery in man. [Described by Sonne in 1915 (*Zentralbl. f. Bakteriol.* LXXV. 408, *Zeitschr. f. klin. Med.* LXXXI. 73).]

1922 *Jrnl. Path. & Bacteriol.* XXV. 393 (*heading*) The Sonne dysentery bacillus in Australia. *Ibid.*, Thjötta.. recovered the Sonne bacillus from cases of dysentery in Norway. *Ibid.* 394 A culture of Sonne's bacillus. **1927** *Jrnl. Hygiene* XXV. 456 So far, none of the cases of Sonne dysentery confirmed bacteriologically have died. **1930** *Jrnl. Infectious Dis.* XXVII. 468 This experiment was repeated with another strain of the Sonne organism with essentially the same results. **1947** *Ann. Rev. Microbiol.* I. 314 Milder cases are more often caused by the Sonne bacillus than by other *Shigellae*. However, it would be erroneous to conclude from this that infections with *Sh. sonnei* are always light. **1972** *Times* 14 Dec. 2/3 Tests were ordered..after an outbreak in the lines of what was believed to have been Sonne dysentery, a mild form of the disease.

sonnet, *sb.* Add: **3.** *sonnet-like* adj., *-thought, -writing* (earlier example); **sonnet-sequence,** a set of sonnets with a common theme or subject.

1874 G. M. HOPKINS *Jrnls. & Papers* (1959) 259, I looked at some delicate flying shafted ashes—there was one especially of single sonnet-like inscape. **1881** D. G. ROSSETTI *Ballads & Sonnets* 161 (*title*) The House of Life: a sonnet-sequence. **1929** WODEHOUSE *Mr. Mulliner Speaking* v. 141 The poet who was spending the summer at the Anglers' Rest had just begun to read us his new sonnet-sequence. **1973** *Listener* 21 June 830/2 Ever since Shakespeare the sonnet-sequence has grouped itself lightly. **1929** BLUNDEN *Near & Far* 59 All that deep-sighing elegy might mourn, Glad lyric hail, and sonnet-thought adorn. **1871** D. G. ROSSETTI *Let.* 2 Aug. (1967) III. 964 A little sonnet-writing gets done.

sonny. Add: **1. b.** A small boy.

1850 *Knickerbocker* XXXVI. 288 'Pa' returned towards the cars; when 'sonny', quickly drawing his pocket-pistol, took a drink. **1939** JOYCE *Finnegans Wake* 335 How Holispolis went to Parkland with mabby and sammy and sonny and sissy and mop's varlet de shambles. **1967** [see *MUMMY *sb.*[2] 2].

2. *Comb.* **sonny boy,** from the title of a popular song, a boy; a man younger than the speaker or writer; freq. as a term of address and with disparaging sense; also *attrib.*; **sonny Jim:** see *sunny Jim* s.v. *SUNNY *a.* 5 c.

1928 A. JOLSON et al. *Sonny Boy* (song) 3 Climb upon my knee, Sonny Boy; You are only three, Sonny Boy. **1937** [see *OVER-COMPENSATE *v.*]. **1942** *Gen* 15 June 36/2 So you lay off taking the mike out of women, sonny-boys. **1955** W. GADDIS *Recognitions* III. iv. 850 Lie back and don't try to remember everything now, sonny boy. **1956** H. GOLD *Man who was not with It* (1965) x. 79 A sonnyboy trust that I had the right to be helpless. **1970** *Washington Post* 30 Sept. D1/6 When you're the youngest of four children, 'you know, folks call you like you're a sonny boy, and it stuck to me'. **1978** T. ALLBEURY *Lantern Network* xii. 191 What do you want, sonny boy?.. I don't trust you, you English bastard.

sono- (sōu·no), comb. form of L. *sonus* sound: **sonoche·mistry,** (the study of) the chemical action of sound waves; so **sonoche·mical** *a.*, of or pertaining to sonochemistry; **so:nolumine·scence** *Chem.*, luminescence excited in a substance by the passage of sound waves through it; hence **so:nolumine·scent** *a.*; **sono·lysis** *Chem.* [*-LYSIS 1], the decomposition by ultrasound of a liquid, esp. water, as a result of the high temperatures generated within the cavities formed; also, the secondary reactions between the unrecombined decomposition products and the liquid itself or compounds dissolved in it; hence **sonoly·tic** *a.*; **sonoly·tically** *adv.*; (as a back-formation) **so·nolyse** *v. trans.*, to subject to sonolysis; **so·nolysed** *ppl. a.*

1953 *Jrnl. Acoustical Soc. Amer.* XXV. 655/1 In view of the frequent attributing of sonochemical reactions to the concomitant heating effect, it is curious that higher temperatures give smaller yields. **1966** *New Scientist* 12 May 367/1 (*caption*) It now seems that a substantial part of the 'fixed' nitrogen available to marine plants and animals is due to sonochemical processes in waves. **1953** A. WEISSLER in *Jrnl. Acoustical Soc. Amer.* XXV. 651 (*heading*) Sonochemistry: the production of chemical changes with sound waves. **1958** *New Scientist* 25 Sept. 926/3 These conditions give rise to many remarkable effects which are now being studied such as sonoluminescence, ultrasonic cleaning and sonochemistry. **1966** *Ibid.* 12 May 367/1 It might well be said that an understanding of sonochemistry is the key to the understanding of numerous chemical changes which take place around us in everyday life. **1939** *Jrnl. Amer. Chem. Soc.* LXI. 2392/1 The luminescence which appears when sound waves pass through liquids has been called acoustic or sonic luminescence, for short, sonoluminescence. **1958** Sonoluminescence [see *sonochemistry* above]. **1976** *Jrnl. Acoustical Soc. Amer.* LX. 103/2 The sonoluminescence from a gas dissolved in water is inversely proportional to the thermal conductivity of the gas. **1974** *Ultrasonics* XII. 25/1 Chemical and sonoluminescent effects occur in gaseous (pseudo) cavitation but never in vaporous cavitation. **1964** *Jrnl. Chem. Physics* XL. 608/2 Water and dilute (0·1*M*) sodium formate solutions of different isotopic composition were subjected to sonolysis under argon... Hydrogen peroxide was produced. **1976** *Canad. Jrnl. Chem.* LIV. 1114/1 In aqueous solution..the lifetime of chemically active radicals produced by sonolysis is larger than the lifetime of the cavitation bubble. **1964** *Jrnl. Chem. Physics* XL. 608/2 In analogy to radiation chemistry of aqueous solutions, 'molecular' and atomic hydrogen are apparently produced under sonolytic conditions. **1966** *New Scientist* 12 May 367/2 Sonolytically induced polymerization may..compete with chemically induced processes. **1976** *Canad. Jrnl. Chem.* LIV. 1118/2 The mechanism whereby H_2O_2 is produced sonolytically has been the subject of some controversy. **1964** *Jrnl. Chem. Physics* XL. 609/1 DCO_2Na·0·1*M*, 98%D (pH = 5·5), was sonolyzed in H_2O. **1964** *Jrnl. Physical Chem.* LXVIII. 1460/1 The analogy between the behaviour of radiolyzed and sonolyzed aqueous solutions has been pointed out in several studies. **1966** *New Scientist* 12 May 366/1 We may thus envisage a sonolysed system as a heterogenous process wherein small centres of very high temperature exist in transient gas bubbles dispersed in a liquid medium.

sonobuoy (sōu·noboi). Also **sono-buoy, Sono-.** [f. *SONO- + BUOY *sb.*] A buoy equipped to detect underwater sounds and transmit them automatically by radio.

1945 *Washington Post* 26 Oct. 1/4 The Sonobuoy, a small buoy tossed overboard from plane or ship in the vicinity of a submarine. This device, in use since 1942, gets the sub's location by sound waves and automatically transmits the information to plane or ship by radio. **1950** *Engineering* 29 Sept. 269/3 There is provision for carrying sono-buoys and military stores on the wings. **1969** *New Scientist* 28 Aug. 420/2 Passive detection, that is, listening devices such as sono-buoys, can also be used. **1972** *Sci. Amer.* July 16/3 A hydrophone, dangling from each sonobuoy at a substantial depth, picks up pressure signals that are then relayed by radio to the aircraft. **1973** *Daily Tel.* 24 July 2/7 An RAF Nimrod maritime reconnaissance aircraft will lay Sonobuoys used to detect submarines.

sonofa, sonofer. Colloq. shortening of such phrases as *SON OF A BITCH, *son of a gun* s.v. GUN *sb.* 6 c, etc. Cf. SON *sb.* 7 d.

1951 W. SANSOM *Face of Innocence* i. 1 'Why!' Harry said. 'If it isn't you, you old sonofer!' **1968** 'G. BAGBY' *Another Day—Another Death* iii. 45 You wouldn't have found one man around here who hadn't threatened..this Clancy sonofa.

son of a bitch. *slang.* Also **son-of-a-bitch, sonofabitch, sonuvabitch,** etc. In pl., **sons of bitches.** [Cf. SON *sb.* 7 d.]

Now more common in the U.S. than elsewhere.

1. a. A despicable or hateful man. Also *attrib.* Cf. *S.O.B.* s.v. *S. I. 4 a.

[*c* **1330** *Of Arthour & of Merlin* (1973) 333 Abide þou þef malicious! Biche-sone þou drawest amis þou schalt abigge it ywis! **1605** SHAKS. *King Lear* II. ii, One that.. art nothing but the composition of a Knave, Begger, Coward, Pandar, and the Sonne and Heire of a Mungrill Bitch.] **1707** J. SHIRLEY *Triumph of Wit* (ed. 5) 203 There stands Jack Ketch, that Son of a Bitch, that owes us all a grudge. **1744** A. HAMILTON *Itinerarium* (1907) 229 It was the landlord ordering his negroes, with an imperious and exalted voice. In his orders the known term or epithet of *son of a bitch* was often repeated. **1762** L. STERNE *Let.* 8 Apr. in *Times Lit. Suppl.* (1965) 8 Apr. 284/4 Phelps is a son of a Bitch for saying I was worse than when I left You for I am ten, nay 15 per Cent better. **1800** J. SAPPINGTON in T. Jefferson *Notes on Virginia* 52 Logan's brother..attempted to strike him, saying, 'White man, son of a bitch'. **1823** BYRON *Don Juan* XI. xli. 123 Pray ask of your next neighbour, If he found not this spawn of tax-born riches, Like lap-dogs, the least civil sons of b—s. **1833** [see BITCH *sb.*[1] 2 a]. **1924** M. KENNEDY *Constant Nymph* III. xvi. 217 You think I ought to want to please every son of a bitch who can pay for a sixpenny ticket. **1929** E. POUND *Let.* 1 Feb. (1971) 224 The stinking sons-of-bitches who rot the country. **1939** S. SPENDER tr. *Toller's Pastor Hall* II. 77 Here, you fat-bellied son of a bitch, hand me some of your margarine. **1945** L. SAXON et al. *Gumbo Ya-Ya* iii. 65 The old woman looked at her for a minute, then she said, quiet-like, 'Well, I'm a son of a bitch!' **1951** J. D. SALINGER *Catcher in Rye* iii. 30 Boy, I can't stand that sonuvabitch. **1959** *Times* 25 Sept. 9/1 Hume..said..that a Scotland Yard report must have been prepared by 'some son-of-a-bitch inspector who wants to blacken my name'. **1963** R. SEAVER tr. *Beckett's End* in *Writers in Revolt* 357 He went bustling along..bowing and scraping and flourishing his hat... The insufferable son of a bitch. **1977** I. SHAW *Beggarman, Thief* II. iii. 139 Arrogant Hollywood sonofabitch.

b. With weakened force and neutral or friendly overtones: a fellow, a man.

1951 E. PAUL *Springtime in Paris* xv. 294 'The son of a bitch is crazy,' said, in soft English, but completely without malice or disapproval. **1958** J. CAREW *Wild Coast* ix. 124 He was a drinking, whoring, kindly savage son-of-a-bitch. **1979** 'A. HAILEY' *Overload* III. xiii. 258 Besides, the son-of-a-bitch had guts and was honest.

2. Applied to animals, etc., as a term of abuse.

1771 SMOLLETT *Humph. Cl.* I. 167 Damn the nasty son of a bitch, and them he belongs to! **1954** C. ODETS *Big Knife* in *Famous Plays 1954* 434 Our story is that the dog—a big son of a bitch—yanked the leash and threw her to the floor. **1958** J. KEROUAC *On Road* iv. 24 We been riding this sonofabitch since Des Moines. **1977** *New Yorker* 27 June 78/3, I figured that that grouse wouldn't be a meal for me... I..went over to the tree, shook it, and yelled, 'Get outa there you son of a bitch.'

3. Applied to a woman as a term of abuse. *rare.*

1936 H. MILLER *Black Spring* 250 He got to working overtime in order to lay aside the little bribe which would make the frigid son of a bitch come across like a nymphomaniac.

4. Used as an expletive.

1953 W. BURROUGHS *Junkie* (1972) ii. 28 'Sonofabitch!' she snarled. 'They can tell when a woman isn't looking for a pickup.' **1957** M. MILLAR *Soft Talkers* iii. 33 Sonuvabitch, I don't get it. What's the matter? What did *I* do?

5. Used in comparisons to suggest strength, ferocity, speed, etc.

1953 W. BURROUGHS *Junkie* (1972) viii. 75, I hit Philly sick as a sonofabitch. **1976** *New Yorker* 15 Mar. 32/3 Well, I hit that bastard with my white fist and ran out of there like a sonuvabitch.

Hence **son-of-a-bitching** *a.*, a general epithet of abuse.

1930 J. DOS PASSOS *42nd Parallel* I. 101 Every sonofabitchin yellerleg in the State of Nevada. **1941** E. P. O'DONNELL *Great Big Doorstep* vii. 98 Tayo put his bag down, and shed his coat uncertainly. 'Son of a bitchin pole-vaulter,' he muttered. **1960** J. KIRKWOOD *There must be a Pony!* (1961) i. 12 The meanest son-of-a-bitching parrot you could ever run up against. **1979** 'A. HAILEY' *Overload* IV. xiv. 370 'People!' Paulsen exploded. 'Son-of-a-bitching, stupid people!'

sonogram (sǭᵘ·nǫgræm). Also **sonagram.** [f. *SONO- + -GRAM.] A graphical representation, produced by a sonograph, of the distribution of sound energy among different frequencies, esp. as a function of time.

1956 *New Biol.* XX. 71 (*caption*) Sonograms of songs of two male chaffinches from different 'dialect areas'. **1957** *Jrnl. Acoustical Soc. Amer.* XXIX. 108/1 (*caption*) Sonagrams of the words 'tack' 'task' 'tact'..illustrating the role that transitions and bursts play in the perception of stops. **1969** R. STENUIT *Dolphin* v. 73 Analysis of the sonogram of a conversation shows click exchanges and whistle exchanges. **1978** *Country Life* 28 Dec. 2225/1 By comparing the sonograms differences can be isolated between the call patterns of individual birds. **1980** *Times* 19 Aug. 12/6 Dr Silver used a hydrophone to record the sounds under water and obtained a visual record in the form of a sonogram.

sonograph (sǭᵘ·nǫgrɑf). [f. *SONO- + -GRAPH.] **1.** Also **sonagraph** and with capital initial. An instrument which analyses sound into its component frequencies and produces a graphical record of the results.

Sonagraph is registered as a proprietary term in the U.S.

1951 *Official Gaz.* (U.S. Patent Office) 14 Aug. 345/2 Kay Electric Company, Pine Brook, N.J... *Sona-graph*... For instrument which is a sound spectrograph which produces permanent visual records showing distribution of energy vs. both frequency and time. Claims use since October 1948. **1953** J. B. CARROLL *Study of Lang.* vii. 206 The 'visible-speech' machine developed in the Bell Telephone Laboratories..produces the same type of record as does the Sonagraph, but on a continuous, transitory basis. **1954** *Nature* 13 Mar. 465/1 All this was changed by the invention of the sound spectrograph, now known commercially as the 'Sonograph'. **1956** *New Biol.* XX. 78 The structure of Chaffinch calls has been studied by making recordings on discs or magnetic tapes, and then analysing them on a sound spectrograph, or sonograph. **1976** J. M. BROWNJOHN tr. *Kirst's Time for Payment* v. 108 The Sonograph can pick up voice frequencies and record them. **1979** *New Scientist* 17 May 537/2 The sonagraph acts as a sonic prism.

2. An image of a tract of seabed obtained by means of side-scan sonar.

1970 *Sci. Jrnl.* Dec. 56/2 By 1964 the geological and economic value of obtaining sonographs of the continental shelf and uppermost continental slope was so evident that the National Institute of Oceanography decided to explore the possibility of adapting the same method for examination of the deeper lying ocean floors. **1974** *Nature* 15 Feb. 453/2 Between this trench and the Italian coast alongslope tectonic trends are seen on sonographs. **1976** *Physics Bull.* Sept. 381/3 Figure 1a..shows a sonograph of a portion of the seabed in the Bristol channel.

Sonoran (sǫnōᵊ·răn), *a.* [f. *Sonora*, the name of a state in North-west Mexico + -AN.] **1.** Of or pertaining to a biogeographical region including desert areas of the south-western United States and central Mexico.

1880 E. D. COPE in *Proc. Amer. Philos. Soc.* XVIII. 263 This collection..is of interest as serving to fix the extension of the Sonoran fauna to a point further south. **1892** *Proc. Biol. Soc. Washington* VII. 15 The term 'Sonoran Region' has been applied by Cope and others to an important life area which enters the southwestern part of the United States from the table-land of Mexico. **1902** *Nature* 14 Aug. 374/1 It is somewhat regrettable to find that the author is unable to convince himself of the necessity of a Sonoran region. **1937** *Discovery* July 206/1 This sub-region has much in common with the Sonoran sub-region of the Nearctic Region. **1979** *Tucson* (Ariz.) *Mag.* Feb. 79/1 There are more than 350 varieties of live animals and plants of the Sonoran desert on exhibit.

2. Of, pertaining to, or characteristic of a grouping of related Indian languages spoken in southern Arizona and northern Mexico.

The nineteenth-century classification of some Uto-Aztecan languages into a Sonoran sub-group is now discarded.

[**1875** H. H. BANCROFT *Native Races of Pacific States* III. 670 Sound-shunting..has..been found by Mr Buschmann in the languages of his Sonora family.] **1891** D. G. BRINTON *Amer. Race* 123 The Sonoran branch [of the Uto-Aztecan stock] begins on the north with the Pimas, who occupied the middle valley of the Gila, and the land south of it quite to the Rio Yaqui. I continue for it the name of *Sonoran* given by Buschmann, although it extended far beyond the bounds of that province. **1909** A. F. CHAMBERLAIN in *Amer. Anthropologist* XI. 535 A number of Shoshonean languages, from Ute to Nahuatl and some of the Sonoran tongues. **1935** B. L. WHORF in *Ibid.* XXXVII. 606 In times past some of us hoped that the stock could be classified in such a way that we could summarize the situation by stating generalized reflexes for sub-groups such as 'Shoshonean', 'Piman', 'Sonoran', from which the reflexes of the individual tongues in these groups could be derived as a second step. The hope is vain. No such groups exist. **1964** S. M. LAMB in *Univ. Calif. Publ. Ling.* XXXIV. 121 Further investigation of the northern Mexican languages, which Brinton had..put into a single group called Sonoran, revealed a high degree of diversity among them. **1977** C. F. & F. M. VOEGELIN in T. A. Sebeok *Native Languages of Americas* I. 482 The traditional major branches of the Uto-Aztecan family (Shoshonean, Sonoran and Aztec).

sonorant (sǫnōᵊ·rănt). *Phonetics.* [f. SONOR(OUS *a.* + -ANT[1].] A resonant; a sound produced with the vocal tract so positioned that spontaneous voicing is possible; a vowel, a glide, or a liquid or nasal consonant. Also *attrib.* or as *adj.*

1934 in WEBSTER. **1943** [see *RESONANT *a.* 1 b]. **1956** JAKOBSON & HALLE in Saporta & Bastian *Psycholinguistics* (1961) 349/2 It is advantageous to range these two related classes of phonemes under a common heading of sonorants. **1963** [see *OBSTRUENT *sb.* c]. **1968** CHOMSKY & HALLE *Sound Pattern Eng.* 302 Vowels, glides, nasal consonants, and liquids are sonorant. **1978** *Language* LIV. 327 Among these are:..; reduction of palatalized sonorants to simple yod, and of *č š* to *s.* **1981** *Publ. Amer. Dial. Soc.* LXVIII. 30 The major sonority distinction is between sonorants (i.e. nasals, liquids and all vocoids) on the one hand and obstruents (stops, affricates and fricatives) on the other.

sonorous, *a.* Add: Also with pronunc. (sǫ·nǫrəs). (Example concerning pronunc.)

1934 G. B. SHAW *Let.* in *Times* 2 Jan. 11/5 An announcer who pronounced decadent and sonorous as dekkadent and sonnerus would provoke Providence to strike him dumb.

‖ **sons bouchés** (soṅ buʃe), *sb. pl.* [Fr., lit. 'blocked sounds'.] In horn-playing, notes stopped by the insertion of the hand into the bell of the instrument; a direction indicating this. Also *attrib.* Cf. *CUIVRÉ, *a.*

1907 T. S. WOTTON *Dict. Mus. Terms, Sons bouchés,* closed notes on a horn. [**1927** *Grove's Dict. Mus* (ed. 3) II. 666/2 The composer's intentions should be indicated by the placing of a small cross over the note with the word stopped (Fr. *cuivré* or *sons bouchés*).] **1961** R. M. PEGGE in A. Baines *Musical Instruments through Ages* xi. 302 The hand in the bell..serves for a certain type of muting demanded when the part is marked 'stopped', 'sons bouchés', 'gestopft', or 'chiuso'. **1977** *Early Music* July 427/2 When one closes the bell fully and blows hard, the *sons bouchés* notes are a *whole tone* and not a semitone above the next lower harmonic.

sont (sǫnt), *v.* *U.S.* Sometimes used to represent *sent* in the written form of Black speech.

1890 *Dialect Notes* I. 71 *Sont,* sent. Used mainly by negroes. **1893** H. A. SHANDS *Some Peculiarities of Speech in Mississippi* 58 *Sont*.., Negro for *sent.* **1929** W. FAULKNER *Sound & Fury* 337, I sont dat boy up dar half hour ago. **1942** —— *Go down, Moses* 16 'What for?' he said. 'She just sont hit to you,' the nigger said. *Ibid.* 106 Ah went to yo house last night, but you want dar. She sont me.

sont, var. SUNT in Dict. and Suppl.

sontag (sǫ·ntæg, zo·ntak). The name of Henriette *Sontag* (1806–54), German singer, used to designate a type of knitted or crocheted jacket or cape, with long ends which are crossed in front of the body and tied behind, worn by women in the second half of the 19th century.

1862 *Harper's Mag.* Oct. 607/1 Constant relays of arrivals were successively denuding themselves of 'Clouds', 'Sontags', 'Mariposas', and other dainty feminine wraps. **1863** A. D. WHITNEY *Faith Gartney's Girlhood* xviii. 161 Faith brought quickly, sontag, jacket and cloak. **1900** E. A. DIX *Deacon Bradbury* 45 Did you hear what she said to Mrs Delane about that worsted sontag she brought?

Sonthal, Sonthali, varr. *SANTAL[2], *SANTALI.

soo·dling, *ppl. a. poet. rare.* [f. SOODLE *v.*] That flows or moves slowly.

1951 AUDEN *Nones* (1952) 39 The baltering torrent Shrunk to a soodling thread.

soogan, var. SUGGAN in Dict. and Suppl.

soogee (sū·dʒī). Also **soogie, soujie,** etc. = next.

1944 *Time* 10 Jan. 4/3 A bucket of 'soujge'. **1945** *Seafarers' Log* 7 Sept. 4/4 The old soogee bucket and paint brush will be working plenty overtime. **1953** J. MASEFIELD *Conway* (rev. ed.) II. 124 The recipe for the liquid used to clean 'holy ground' was one handful of soft soap, one of 'soojie' (soap powder). **1963** M. LOWRY *Ultramarine* iv. 198 Steamflies..are stealthily prowling over.. the limp bags of caustic soda and soogie.

So as *v. trans.*, to clean (wood and paintwork) with *SOOGEE-MOOGEE; **soog(ie)ing** *vbl. sb.*

1903 A. SONNICHSEN *Deep Sea Vagabonds* iii. 37 There was soodgee-moodgee. Soodgee is a sailor's horror; it means to wash paint-work with a strong solution of soda and water. **1945** *Seafarers' Log* 29 June 12 Soogieing, chipping, painting, etc., shall not be considered an emergency. **1947** *Ibid.* 14 Mar. 5/2 The messhalls were sougeed out, the gallery cleaned. **1950** R. BISSELL *Stretch on River* vii. 75, I was sooging down the walls in his [*sc.* the captain's] cabin. **1963** M. LOWRY *Ultramarine* v. 217, I had to do a bit of soogeing in the petty officers' washhouse.

soogee-moogee (sū·dʒī,mū:dʒī). *Naut. slang.* Also **soogie-moogie, soojee-moojee, souji-mouji, sugi-mugi,** etc. and without hyphens. [Origin unknown.] **a.** A mixture containing caustic soda used for cleaning paintwork and woodwork on ships and boats. Also *attrib.*

1882 D. KEMP *Yacht & Boat Sailing* (ed. 3) 579 *Soojee Moojee,* a caustic composition sold by yacht fitters for cleaning off old paint, varnish, &c. **1894** R. C. LESLIE *Waterbiography* xiii. 248 A certain caustic composition, known to yachtsmen by the mysterious name of 'skewgy-mewgy'. **1900** F. T. BULLEN *Men of Merchant Service* xiii. 120 No tramp second mate can hope to keep his hands out of the paint pot or the soogee-moogee bucket. **1903** [see *SOOGEE *v.*]. **1907** M. ROBERTS *Flying Cloud* xxiv. 229 She was as clean as a new pin with sand and canvas and souji-mouji. **1913** A. W. NELSON *Yankee Swanson* 57 He had a good scrubbing down with 'sudje mudje'. **1924** P. BLUNDELL *Confessions of Seaman* xii. 164 With a bucket containing hot soap and soda water—sougi-mougi sailors call it—he ascended ladders in the swaying engine-room and washed paint work. **1934** J. HANLEY in *Spectator* 26 Jan. 131/1 'There are no sailors to-day,' says [Conrad], 'only Sugi-Mugi men'... Mere washers of paint. Deck-hands on modern ships wash and chip paint, morning, noon and night. **1938** W. E. DEXTER *Rope Yarns* 82 In all the sailing ships I was in I never came across a long-handled holystone, or caustic soda, or 'soogy-moogy'. **1939** H. HUGHES *Through Mighty Seas* ii. 36 All hands wallowed in *soogie moogie.* **1962** A. G. COURSE *Dict. Naut. Terms* 182 *Soogee moogee,* a liquid used for cleaning paintwork and woodwork consisting of soda and water or soap and water.

b. A cleaning operation which involves the use of soogee-moogee.

1935 *Sea Breezes* Jan. 60 The equipment, particularly the sails, would be so perfect that my crew wouldn't mind the 'sooje-mooje' such perfection entailed. **1945** *Time* 31 Dec. 96/3 Soon Sailor Slobodkin..found himself loading cargo, eating slop and doing soogie moogie (scrubbing paint work) with a crew.

soojee. Add: Also **sooji.** (Later examples.) **sooji halwa** [*HALWA], a kind of dessert made with soojee.

1955 R. P. JHABVALA *To whom she Will* xxi. 157 O she is such a clever girl, kheer she makes,..and sooji halwa [etc.]. **1971** *Femina* (Bombay) 16 Apr. 57/2 *Sooji Halwa.* 220 gms. sooji (fine semolina); 60 gms. fat; 110 gms. sugar; 30 gms. peanuts; 2 gms. salt.

sook[1] (suk). *Austral.* and *N.Z. slang.* Also **sookie.** [perh. from Eng. dial. *suck*: see *Eng. Dial. Dict.* s.v. *suck* 19, a 'duffer', a stupid fellow.] A stupid or timid person; a coward; a 'softy'.

1933 N. SCANLAN *Tides of Youth* xv. 155 He looked a big sookie and wouldn't say a word. **1941** BAKER *Dict. Austral. Slang* 69 *Sook,* a coward, a timid person. **1950** 'B. JAMES' *Advancement of Spencer Button* 9 If he nervously declares he can't fight, and shows that he doesn't want to fight, then he is a 'sook' or a 'sissy'. **1970** G. GREER *Female Eunuch* 79 She may be reviled as a cissy, a sook. **1970** P. WHITE *Vivisector* 11 He wasn't a sook. He could run, shout, play, fight, had scabs on his knees, and twice split Billy Abrams's lip, who was two years older. **1975** *Courier-Mail* (Brisbane) 2 Jan. 9/4 The tough specimen might appear as somewhat of a myth by fearing to be different from his mates in case they might think him a bit of a sook.

Hence **soo·key, sooky** *adjs.*, cowardly, 'soft', stupid.

1953 D. CUSACK *Southern Steel* 328 Get along with you: you're getting real sookey. **1964** *Weekly News* (Auckland) 18 Mar. 58/3 The boys say they feel sooky wearing caps. **1970** *N.Z. Listener* 12 Oct. 13/5 Their attitude of tolerant resignation toward the sooky Maoris who are always getting into trouble.

sook[2] (sŭk). *U.S.* [Origin unknown.] A mature female blue crab, *Callinectes sapidus*, of the eastern coast of the United States.

1950 *Sun* (Baltimore) 10 Oct. 32/2 'Sooks' are female blue crabs. Their annual migration..has been under way for a month. **1978** J. A. MICHENER *Chesapeake* 647 He [*sc.* a blue crab] forgot his own preoccupations in order to swim among the grasses, looking for sooks which had been by-passed in the earlier mating periods. These overlooked females, on their way south to spend the winter near the entrance of the bay, where fertile sooks traditionally prepared to lay their eggs, sent out frantic signals to whatever males might be in the vicinity, for this was the final period in which they could be fertilized.

sook, var. *SOUK.

sool (sūl), *v.* Chiefly *Austral.* and *N.Z.* [var. SOWL *v.*[3]] **1.** *trans.* Of a dog, to attack or worry; freq. in command *sool* (*him,* etc.) Also *absol.* and *transf.*

1890 [see SOWL *v.*[3] 1]. **1896** MRS. K. L. PARKER *Austral. Legendary Tales* 90 She went quickly towards her camp, calling softly, 'Birree gougou', which meant 'Sool 'em, sool 'em', and was the signal for the dogs to come out. **1904** 'S. RUDD' *Sandy's Selection* 60 'Sool 'im, sool 'im!' the girls were shouting, and the blind dog sooled in moderation. **1935** *Bulletin* (Sydney) 6 Feb. 21/2 A pair of these birds will sometimes 'sool' a hare. **1959** A. UPFIELD *Bony & Black Virgin* xv. 135 'Sool 'em, Bluey,' Bony pleaded, and the dog nosed about and finally went down under the scrub by a hole made by the foxes. **1960** B.

CRUMP *Good Keen Man* 24 Another young dog would have been better encouragement than a man lumbering about trying to bark like a dog, and noisily skitching and sooling.

2. To urge or goad. Freq. with advbs., esp. *on*.

1898 *Bulletin* (Sydney) 30 Apr. 31/4 The rest of the company came out and 'sooled' on the twelve [arguers]. It was a glorious scrimmage. **1898** E. E. MORRIS *Austral English* 426/2 Sool.., used colloquially—(1) to excite a dog or set him on. **1911** *Chambers's Jrnl.* Mar. 222/2 Don't 'sool' the dogs to an unwise assault. **1911** L. STONE *Jonah* 31 The Push gathered round, grinning from ear to ear, sooling the women on as if they were dogs. **1916** C. J. DENNIS *Moods of Ginger Mick* 39 The bugles East and West sooled on the dawgs o' war. **1921** E. O'FERRALL in Murdoch & Drake-Brockman *Austral. Short Stories* (1951) 158 Served him right if I sooled th' dog on him! **1942** G. CASEY *It's Harder for Girls* 52 'Sool the dogs after him,' someone called out. **1960** B. CRUMP *Good Keen Man* 23, I ran over and sooled the dog after the trotting sow. **1963** B. PEARSON *Coal Flat* xii. 227 We'll get an Alsatian and sool it outa you. **1970** G. GREER *Female Eunuch* 190 The hero may..like a lion-tamer sool her on to his enemies. **1977** C. MCCULLOUGH *Thorn Birds* iv. 80 Father Ralph worked like a man in the grip of some obsession, sooling the dogs after unsuspecting bands of sheep.

Hence **soo·ler**, one who incites; an agitator.

1935 H. R. WILLIAMS *Comrades of Great Adventure* 35 Here, as chief 'sooler', he was urging the passing soldiers to patronize the eating-house. **1938** X. HERBERT *Capricornia* viii. 98 Then a war-monger, or Sooler, as such people were called in the locality, made his voice heard in the land. **1963** —— *Disturbing Element* 141 She had been sending white feathers round... She had become what her former comrades of the I.W.W. called a Sooler.

soon, *adv.* Add: **I. 4. e.** Also *dial.* and *colloq.*

1907 W. P. RIDGE *Name of Garland* ii. 33 Get out of my kitchen soon as you can. **1930** J. B. PRIESTLEY *Angel Pavement* ii. 91 We want another man for London and district, soon as we can get one. **1930** W. FAULKNER *As I lay Dying* 58, I done put supper on and I'll be there soon as I milk. **1940** —— *Hamlet* I. ii. 26 Jody came in last night. I knowed it soon as I saw him.

8. a, b. (Later examples.) Also *just as soon*; *as soon as look at you*: see *LOOK *v.* 1 a.

1913 W. B. YEATS *Hour-Glass* in *Mask* V. 328 I'd as soon listen to dried peas in a bladder as listen to your thoughts. **1930** A. P. HERBERT *Water Gipsies* xvii. 254 I'd as soon have stone-ginger any day. **1966** D. FRANCIS *Flying Finish* x. 133 He waved me to join him, which I would just as soon not have done. **1974** C. HAMPTON *Savages* (1976) vii. 45 Because Chico well He'd cut your head off soon as say good morning. **1974** M. HEBDEN *Pride of Dolphins* I. iii. 34 I'd just as soon you dropped me..and let me make my own way home.

9. *soon-arriving, -coming*; *soon-come, -dropped, -finished, -forgotten.* With infin., as *soon-to-be*.

a. 1886 E. G. WHITE *Historical Sketches* 164/2 The end so near, the warning of a soon-coming Judgment yet to be given to all nations, tongues, and peoples. **1930** AUDEN *Poems* 17 Hear something of that soon-arriving day.

b. 1901 G. B. SHAW *3 Plays for Puritans* p. xviii, An hour's soon-forgotten fuss. **1902** W. B. YEATS *Where there is Nothing* (1903) II. 44 Not the fighting of men in red coats, that formal, soon finished fighting, but the endless battle, the endless battle. **1925** BLUNDEN *Eng. Poems* 18 And hyacinth-eyes beneath soon-dropt lids. *Ibid.* 36 That now, this soon-come spring, goes slow and sere.

c. 1961 *Daily Tel.* 30 Aug. 10/2 He wants to appear in Belgrade at the neutralists' conference as the leader at least of a soon-to-be apparently united country. **1975** *Publishers Weekly* 10 Nov. 51/3 Often the dying are 'released' by the knowledge of their soon-to-be end.

II. 11. b. Phr. (*I'd*) *sooner* (*it should be*) *you than me*, and varr. Cf. *RATHER *adv.* 9 f.

1864 TROLLOPE *Can you forgive Her?* I. xiv. 108 You are going down to Cheltenham. are you?..I'd sooner it should be you than me; that's all I can say. **1905** H. A. VACHELL *Hill* iii. 53 Phew-w-w!..I'd sooner it was you than me, Verney. **1937** A. THIRKELL *Summer Half* vi. 181 'Good old Mr. Lorimer,' said Swan, 'sooner he than I.' **1973** 'J. STURROCK' *Wicked Way to Die* iii. 35 'Talk to her I must.' He shook his head. 'Sooner you than me.'

III. 14. a. (Later examples.) Now freq. (orig. *telegraphese*), as soon as possible.

1815 A. CONSTABLE *Let.* 29 Jan. in *J. Constable's Corr.* (1962) I. 113 The picture you request shall be sent per soonest. **1950** C. M. KORNBLUTH in *Mag. of Fantasy & Sci. Fiction* I. 4 They needed a bright and sparkling little news item..'soonest'. **1962** J. HAY in *E. Queen's 16th Mystery Annual* 163 'Bjornsson and whale to proceed soonest to Regensburg and await further orders,' Twenty-penny cabled Hawker. **1977** 'E. CRISPIN' *Glimpses of Moon* xiii. 262 Come back to London soonest prepare leave for Libya soonest terrorists blowing up all the oil-wells there. **1977** J. DIDION *Book of Common Prayer* II. xiv. 119 I'm getting you together soonest, that's definite.

soon, *a.* Add: **1.** (Later U.S. dial. examples.) Freq. in phr. *a soon start* (*in the morning*).

1913 H. KEPHART *Our Southern Highlanders* xiii. 296 Spell is used in the sense of while..and soon for early ('a soon start in the morning'). **1930** G. B. JOHNSON in B. A. Botkin *Folk-Say* VII. 357 *Soon*, early, quick, alert. 'A soon breakfast', 'a soon man'. **1949** H. HORNSBY *Lonesome Valley* ii. 21 People must have got a soon start, because the place was full up already. **1951** L. CRAIG *Singing Hills* iii. 18 The furrin woman wanted to get a soon start, come morning.

soon (sūn), *sb. rare.* [Substantival use of prec.] The near future.

1940 W. FAULKNER *Hamlet* III. i. 166 They are moving not toward a destination in space but a destination in time..; the sleight hand of May shapes them both, not in the immediate, the soon, but in the now.

sooner[1]. Add to def.: Chiefly with ref. to the settlement of the territory now known as Oklahoma before the official opening of the area to settlers on 22 April 1889. (Further examples.) Hence (with capital initial), an Oklahoman. Also *attrib.*; **the Sooner State**, Oklahoma. Hence **soo·nerism**, the practice of the unlawful and premature settlement of Oklahoma.

1890 *Congress. Rec.* 17 Jan. 657/2 We have recognized the fact that there are 'sooners' there. **1894** *Columbus* (Ohio) *Dispatch* 19 Mar., An important case growing out of the 'soonerism' at the Oklahoma opening will be given a hearing. **1904** *N.Y. Even. Post* 13 June 7 White 'sooners'..were trying to rob them [*sc.* Indians] of some of the most valuable mineral deposits on their reservation. **1930** *Sat. Rev. Lit.* (U.S.) 22 Mar. 841/3 She has done excellent reporting, has constructed a ripping yarn, has given us novel incidents, novel characters, a fresh setting, has created a strange new Sooner mythology. **1939** *New Yorker* 14 Oct. 73 Oklahoma uses on its road signs a phrase which I first heard in Kansas and never again except in the Sooner State. **1945** J. L. MARSHALL *Santa Fe* 232 They watched the line through telescopes and, congratulating themselves on their success in checkmating 'Soonerism', figured it would take the first settlers on the fastest horses, about ninety minutes to reach Oklahoma. **1948** *Okla. Cotton Grower* 15 May 2/2 For the Sooner State planter that is perhaps the first major theorem of the business. **1948** [see *OKIE]. **1976** *Billings* (Montana) *Gaz.* 30 June 4-E/2 University of Oklahoma quarterback Joe McReynolds was dropped from the Sooners football roster Tuesday.

sooner[2]. *slang* (chiefly *Austral.*). [perh. as prec.] An idler, shirker; applied as a term of abuse to an ineffectual or obstructive person, object, etc. Also *attrib.* in *sooner dog*.

1892 K. LENTZNER *Dict. Slang-English of Australia* 117 *Sooner*, a weak idler, a lazy good-for-nothing. **1919** E. DYSON *Hello, Soldier!* 31 He slugged a tubby Hun, Then choked a Fritzie with his dukes, 'n' pinched the sooner's gun! **1936** F. CLUNE *Roaming round Darling* xxv. 270 *Onlookers*: Tongue-tied Joe, a sooner dog, a Scotch dog, a dog of all nations, a hungry goat. **1937** PARTRIDGE *Dict. Slang* 801/1 *Sooner dog*, one that would sooner feed than fight. **1948** V. PALMER *Golconda* xix. 159 'The dirty sooners!' he burst out. 'They don't know a man when they find one, those heads down south.' **1969** P. A. SMITH *Folklore of Austral. Railwaymen* 117 This was an old sooner of an engine. She'd had it. On a stiff climb in a tunnel she began to slip.

soonish, *adv.* (Earlier example.)

1890 S. S. BUCKMAN *John Darke's Sojourn in Cotteswolds & Elsewhere* vii. 58 Good, honest drink..made a man knaow soonish as he wur a-getting nicely forrud.

soop, *v.* Add: **3.** Also without *up*.

a **1822** A. BOSWELL *Poet. Wks.* (1871) 195 Soop the rink, lads, wide enough, The *hog-scores* mak', and mak' ilk *brough*. **1885** J. STRATHESK *More Bits from Blinkbonny* (ed. 2) xiv. 270 Soop weel when I tell ye. **1963** *Times* 17 Jan. 12/5 Rob Roy's country today echoed not with the war cry of the MacGregors but with strange shouts of 'Yes, yes' and 'Soop, soop' as the great bonspiel of the curling game was staged for only the second time in 37 years.

sooping *vbl. sb.* (later examples in sense 3 of the vb.).

1937 T. HENDERSON *Lockerbie* ix. 57 The ice being keen it required little soopin'. **1976** *Alyn & Deeside Observer* 10 Dec. 5/2 Part of the fun of the game comes in 'sooping'. This is when the players sweep the ice with special brooms in front of a moving stone to help it go further.

soopie, soopje, varr. SOPIE in Dict. and Suppl. **soopolallie,** var. *SOAPOLALLIE.

soor[2] (sūᵊɹ). *Anglo-Indian slang.* [ad. Hindi *sūar* pig, f. Pali *sūkara-*, Prakrit *sūara-*, *suara-* pig.] A term of abuse for a person: pig, swine.

1848 J. H. STOCQUELER *Oriental Interpreter*, Soor, soor-ka-butcha, abusive terms of which the Hindostanee language is fertile. *Soor* is a pig, and *soor-ka-butcha* the offspring of a pig. **1864** HOTTEN *Slang Dict.* 240 *Soor*, an abusive term... *Anglo-Indian.* **1919** 'BOYD CABLE' *Old Contemptibles* vi. 92 'Why don't the *soors* come on an' fight it out?' said Corporal Smedley. **1926** *Blackw. Mag.* July 78/1 *'Soors!'* he cursed. 'They won't give me one of their Union Jacks.' **1936** F. RICHARDS *Old-Soldier Sahib* iv. 74 You black soor, when I order you to do a thing I expect it to be done at once.

soot, *sb.*[1] Add: **5. c.** *soot-blackened, -bleakened, -clogged, -coated, -roughened, -suffused.*

1894 'MARK TWAIN' in *Century Mag.* XLVIII. 17/1 It rained all day..apparently trying its best to wash that soot-blackened town [*sc.* St. Louis] white. **1916** JOYCE *Portrait of Artist* (1969) 115 The soot-coated packet of pictures which he had hidden in the flue of the fireplace. **1921** W. DE LA MARE *Veil* 68 Slow wreathed the grease adown from soot-clogged wick. **1932** W. FAULKNER *Light in August* vi. 111 Memory..knows remembers believes a corridor in a big long garbled cold echoing building of dark red brick sootbleakened by more chimneys than its own. **1947** W. DE LA MARE *Coll. Stories for Children* 122 Chapped, soot-roughened hands. **1956** D. GASCOYNE *Night Thoughts* 23 The soot-suffused sky-canopy. **1977** H. FAST *Immigrants* I. 29 The still half-naked citizens, soot-blackened and homeless, greeted the ruin as they had always greeted their city.

6. soot-blower, a device for clearing soot from the flues of a boiler, furnace, etc.; **soot house** (see quots.).

1930 *Engineering* 16 May 627/1 Steam driers had met with little success while soot-blowers had been widely introduced. **1967** *Trans. Inst. Engineers & Shipbuilders in Scotland* CX. 36 Naval boilers, up to the end of the last war, were not normally provided with sootblowers. **1957** E. E. EVANS *Irish Folk Ways* ix. 120 The soot-houses..whose roofs..were stripped in spring in the days when the whole family migrated to the summer pastures. At any rate the soot-house season runs from October to May... In the Hebrides it was customary to strip the soot-laden thatch of the black-houses annually for use as manure, and the roof was left without a smoke-hole to encourage the deposit of soot. **1966** *Daily Tel.* 21 Apr. 4/7 On Achill Island off the west coast of Ireland are the remains of some small buildings... They are called 'soot houses' and were used for the production of soot for fertilising the potato crop.

soot, *v.* Add: **3.** Sometimes with *up*: to fill or choke with a sooty deposit. Also *fig.*

1903 [implied at *sooting* vbl. sb. s.v. SOOT *v.*]. **1925** *Morris Owner's Manual* iv. 46 Bad plug insulation is sometimes caused through sooting. **1929** W. E. COLLINSON *Spoken Eng.* 84 The engine is knocking. One of the [sparking] plugs is probably sooted up. **1959** M. PUGH *Chancer* i. 9 London was sooting me up and I couldn't shed it, layer by layer, like the plane-trees in the park.

soothe, *v.* Add: **7. c.** With direct speech as object: to say in a soothing manner.

1934 N. MARSH *Man lay Dead* xii. 206 'You shall have every opportunity,' soothed Alleyn. **1976** I. LEVIN *Boys from Brazil* iii. 77 'I agree, Josef, I agree,' the colonel soothed.

soothe (sūð), *sb. rare.* [Back-formation f. the vb.] A soothing feeling or effect.

1947 *Landfall* (N.Z.) I. iv. 267 They felt the soothe of the darkness. **1971** J. GARDNER *Every Night's a Bullfight* vii. 170 Close whispering, kissing; the soothe of flesh against flesh.

soothering, *ppl. a. dial.* and *U.S.* [f. SOOTHER *v.* + -ING.[2]] Blandishing, cajoling.

1866 E. L. LINTON *Lizzie Lorton* II. i. 13 Thee 'se gitten a soothering tongue in thee head, lad. **1884** [see *SOFTY *a.*]. **1898** G. BARTRAM *White-Headed Boy* 5 A kind of gentle look in them—a 'soodherin' ' look, as we say in Ireland—the way a horse looks at you when he loves you. **1953** *Scots Mag.* Aug. 418 The mither sings a sootherin tune til a waukrif loon.

soothing, *ppl. a.* Add: **2. b.** (Earlier and later examples.) spec. *soothing powder* (in example *fig.*); *soothing syrup*, a medicinal preparation supposed to calm fretful children; freq. *fig.*, flattery; empty reassurance; merely palliative remedies; mawkish or sentimental music, emotion, etc.; hence *soothing-syrupy* adj.

1839 *Spirit of Times* 27 Apr. 87/2 Then comes an ague from Canady, vich can't be cured by American Soothing Syrup nor Durham Mustard. **1861** *N.Y. Tribune* 26 Dec. 2/5 Don't fail to procure Mrs. Winslow's Soothing Syrup for children teething. **1896** [in Dict.]. **1901** W. CHURCHILL *Crisis* II. ix. 193 Senator Bell was their candidate, and they proposed to give the Nation soothing-syrup. *Ibid.* xiv. 246 When the worst comes, the Soothing Syrup men will rally for the Union. **1902** G. H. LORIMER *Lett. Self-Made Merchant* xviii. 261 A lady..in a soothing-sirupy way asked if I would lend it to her. **1914** G. B. SHAW *Translations & Tomfooleries* (1926) 243, I really cannot earn two hundred and fifty guineas by playing soothing syrup to you. **1917** R. FRY *Let.* 20 July (1972) II. 415 My first soothing powder..was to have been a preface but got printed separately. **1926** E. GLYN *Love's Blindness* xvi. 183 If he dispelled..all alarm in Vanessa's imagination, it might possibly be only temporary soothing syrup. **1928** E. O'NEILL *Strange Interlude* VIII. 305 Here are passion and hatred and regret and joy and pain and ecstasy, and these are men and women..whose blood is blood and not soothing syrup! **1945** *Richmond* (Va.) *Times-Dispatch* 26 Oct. 5/1 The race between Russia and the United States to obtain strategic bases is fooling no one but the American people—who are still being doped with soothing syrup that differences between ourselves and Russia are those of language and inexperience in foreign affairs. **1963** *Times* 21 Jan. 9/2 Mr. Macmillan and his colleagues must put away the soothing syrup that nothing is really as bad as it seems, that even if all is not quite for the best it automatically will be in the end. **1978** O. WHITE *Silent Reach* xxvi. 268 That's a personal assurance, not official soothing syrup.

sooty, *a.* Add: **2. a.** (Later examples.)

1964 L. DEIGHTON *Funeral in Berlin* xvii. 105 The girl..fluttered her big sooty eyes. **1976** 'A. HALL' *Kobra Manifesto* ii. 23 Black hair and a grey face and sooty bags under his eyes.

e. In the names of plant diseases, as *sooty blotch*, a fungal disease of apples, pears, and citruses which is caused by *Glœodes pomigena* and gives rise to darkish blotches on the skin of the fruit; *sooty mould*, any of several fungal diseases of trees and shrubs which cause a dark discoloration of their fruit.

1901 H. M. Ward *Disease in Plants* xxv. 232 [Honey-dew] serves as nutritive material for various epiphytic fungi—*e.g.* sooty mould, *Capnodium*, *Fumago*, and *Antennaria*. **1902** *Ann. Rep. Secretary Connecticut Board Agric. 1901* 132 Among the diseases in this class which prey upon either the fruit or the foliage of the apple..are the bitter rot..and the sooty blotch. **1939** Sooty blotch [see *fly-speck* s.v. *fly *sb.*[1] 11]. **1939** *Ann. Bot.* III. 401 The distinction between parasitic and saprophytic 'sooty moulds'..appears to be valid. **1952** E. Ramsden tr. *Gram & Weber's Plant Diseases* ii. 126/2 Sooty mould can be avoided by keeping the tree free from aphides. *Ibid.* 127/1 Associated with *Leptothyrium pomi* is usually the fungus of sooty blotch, *Gloeodes pomigena*. **1969** G. N. Agrios *Plant Path.* ii. 19 Certain fungi, e.g., those causing sooty molds, can cause disease by growing on the surface of the plant and feeding on insect excretions rather than by parasitizing the plant.

5. *sooty-eyed*, *-mossed*.

1874 G. M. Hopkins *Jrnls. & Papers* (1959) 247 Sooty-mossed boulders in foreground. **1964** L. Deighton *Funeral in Berlin* xvii. 106 The sooty-eyed girl laughed.

sop, *v.* Add. **1. d.** With *up*: to soak up, absorb. Also *fig.*

1888 S. O. Addy *Gloss. Words Sheffield* 229 Come sop up that gravy. **1914** J. Galsworthy *Let.* in *Times* 28 Feb. 5/3 The admission or rejection of Tariff Reform, the Disestablishment or preservation of the Welsh Church, I would almost say than the granting or non-granting of Home Rule—questions that sop up *ad infinitum* the energies, the interest, the time of those we elect and pay to manage our business. *a* **1922** T. S. Eliot *Waste Land Drafts* (1971) 5 Blew in to the Opera Exchange, Sopped up some gin. **1951** D. Riesman *Individualism Reconsidered* in A. W. Loos *Religious Faith & World Culture* 73 The everpresent threat of war..used as a rationalization to sop up our 'excessive' comforts. **1962** S. Carpenter in *Into Orbit* 57 The nose [of the capsule] would sop up much of the friction we were running into and would become quite warm. **1973** J. G. Farrell *Siege of Krishnapur* ii. 25 The ladies discovered that while sitting in the boat the hems of their dresses had sopped up a certain amount of bilge water. **1977** A. Carter *Passion of New Eve* x. 158, I sopped up the sauce from the beans with a hunk of bread.

sopelalee, var. *soapolallie.

sophianic (sōufiæ·nik), *a. Theol. rare.* [f. Sophi(a[1] + *-anic* as in Messianic *a.*] Of or pertaining to wisdom.

1936 *Theology* XXXIII. 317 Karl Pfleger says of this Sophianic mysticism that it is 'extraordinarily profound'. **1970** R. Manheim tr. *Corbin's Creative Imagination Ṣūfism* 136 (*heading*) The sophianic poem of a *Fedele d'amore*. *Ibid.* 160 This sophianic intuition is perfectly in keeping with that of the extreme Shī'ites.

sophiology. Add: **1.** (Earlier example.)

1892 J. W. Powell in *Amer. Anthropologist* July 270 For the science of opinions I propose the name *Sophiology*.

2. *Theol.* The doctrine of the Divine Wisdom, as serving to explain the relations between God and the world.

1934 *Theology* XXVIII. 23 In his Christology the author [*sc.* Bulgakov] deliberately and openly relies on Sophiology, the doctrine of the eternal and created Wisdom. **1943** E. L. Mascall *He who Is* x. 135 The 'sophiology', or teaching concerning the Divine Wisdom, which looks back to the fourteenth-century mystic of Mount Athos, St Gregory Palamas, and which became prominent in Russian theology in the last century through ..Vladimir Solovyev. **1970** R. Manheim tr. *Corbin's Creative Imagination Ṣūfism* 98 From this idea of Creation as theophany..arises the idea of a sophiology, the figure of *Sophia aeterna*.

Hence **sophiolo·gical** *a.*; **sophio·logist.**

1933 *Theology* XXVI. 337 This has been related to modern categories of thought by the Russian sophiological school in Paris, especially by Professor S. Bulgakoff. **1937** *Ibid.* XXXV. 92 Such Sophiologists as Bulgakov, Berdyaev, and Solovive.

sophisticate (sŏfi·stikēit), *sb.* orig. *U.S.* [Back-formation from the vb.] One who is sophisticated or who has sophisticated tastes. Cf. *sophisticated *ppl. a.* 2 b.

1923 G. Atherton *Black Oxen* i. 1 All the Sophisticates (as Clavering had named them, abandoning 'Intellectuals' and 'Intelligentsia' to the Parlor Socialists) were present. **1930** H. S. Walpole *Rogue Herries* I. 163 Then Louis of France, making rude gestures, fingers at nose, that he may irritate, polished sophisticate that he is, the barbarian Stanislaus. **1936** 'J. Tey' *Shilling for Candles* xix. 208 Murder and that brittle insincere sophisticate were poles apart. **1942** *Scrutiny* X. 349, I think it is more than an accident that Copland, who started..as a sophisticate of the Big City, should in his mature work have come to express the loneliness..that lies back of all big cities. **1959** *Encounter* Sept. 52/1 For sophisticates, there is a touch of abnormal psychology. **1971** *Hi-Fi Sound* Feb. 25 (Advt.), The simple sophisticate. The Goldring-Lenco GL 69/2 transcription unit..with much more than 'the basics' for enthusiasts who don't require extreme sophistication of design. **1976** *UCT Stud. in English* (Univ. of Cape Town) Oct. 38 To the sophisticate it is a send-up of the genre in the vein of Chaucer's tale of Sir Thopas.

sophisticate, *v.* Add: **1. d.** *trans.* To render sophisticated (in senses in Suppl.; in quot. 1947 with weakened sense). Also *refl.*

1947 C. Morgan *Judge's Story* iv. 17 'But if you have reached the age of twenty-seven without ever having heard of Combined Metallurgical Industries, I am justified.'..'Now sophisticate me.' **1956** M. Stewart *Wildfire at Midnight* iii. 33 Three years of my great friend Nicholas ..would sophisticate a Vestal Virgin. **1978** J. I. M. Stewart *Full Term* xxii. 250, I..took to buying..all the paperbacks I could lay my hands on concerning espionage... It was a field that had sophisticated itself since the distant time when Patullo Minor, the Secret Service Boy, had enthralled his school-fellows with his hazardous escapades.

sophisticated, *ppl. a.* Add: **2. a.** Also, of a literary text: altered in the course of being copied or printed.

1948 *Studies in Bibliogr.* I. 112 This copy is only a sophisticated version of Stow. **1963** *N. & Q.* Mar. 101/1 We know..that F [of *King Lear*] is a sophisticated text, and it seems..possible that we have an example of sophistication here.

b. Of a person: free of naïvety, experienced, worldly-wise; subtle, discriminating, refined, cultured; aware of, versed in, the complexities of a subject or pursuit. Also *transf.* of a play, place, etc., that appeals to a sophisticated person.

Occas. (as in quot. 1952), *Biol.* and *Psychol.* used as opp. *naive *a.* 2.

1895 Hardy *Jude* iv. v. 303 Though so sophisticated in many things she was such a child in others that this satisfied her. **1904** J. C. Lincoln *Cap'n Eri* xii. 230 The only scoffer was the bored Josiah, who, being a sophisticated New Yorker, sat in the best chair and gazed contemptuously upon the entire proceeding. **1915** *New Republic* 13 Feb. 51/2 It is one of those sophisticated melodramas in which a glamor is thrown about the underworld... The dope-fiend, the thief's mistress, the crooked detective, are all exhibited to an audience that apparently prides itself on being 'knowing'. **1933** H. S. Walpole *Vanessa* iii. 531 Here in these pages was life, the life that so many polished sophisticated writers missed altogether. **1952** *Arch. Opthalmol.* XLVIII. 607 The sophisticated subject could always distinguish this illusion from the oculogravic illusion. **1954** *Word* X. 236 This conception has cropped up again and again. Even sophisticated thinkers have bent their ingenious efforts to preserving it. **1957** D. Robins *Noble One* vii. 71 She preferred smooth sophisticated young men like Keith who amused and flattered *her*. **1962** P. D. Strevens *Study of Present-Day Eng. Lang.* (1963) 23 The teaching of either language or literature in less educationally and linguistically sophisticated parts of the world. **1969** *Daily Tel.* 18 Oct. 11/5 Its nightclub-restaurant with an 'international' menu and Caribbean band is as sophisticated as you'd find anywhere. **1971** *Ibid.* 17 June 3/3 To the police he showed 'promise' of becoming a sophisticated criminal.

absol. **1952** G. Sarton *Hist. Sci.* I. xvi. 425 It is probable that pederasty was more common in Athens among the aristocrats, the idle rich, and the sophisticated than among the simpler people.

c. Of equipment, techniques, theories, etc.: employing advanced or refined methods or concepts; highly developed or complicated.

1945 C. S. Lewis *That Hideous Strength* xiv. 384 The man was so very allusive and used gesture so extensively that Mark's less sophisticated modes of communication were almost useless. **1952** G. Sarton *Hist. Sci.* I. xi. 289 He represents a second (or third) and more sophisticated stage in the evolution of Pythagorean astronomy. **1956** *N.Y. Times* 1 Apr. 19/1 Navy scientists are virtually exploring multidimensional space in a time machine in the search for what they call 'sophisticated' high-yield weapons. **1960** *Washington Post* 16 June 20/6 Soviet experts are said to have assisted the Peking regime with advanced nuclear reactors of a sophisticated type. **1966** *Times* 28 Mar. (Austral. Suppl.) p. v/4 Victoria now has many sophisticated industrial complexes. **1970** H. Braun *Parish Churches* xvii. 206 The High Gothic font was a sophisticated piece of furniture. **1970** *Daily Tel.* (Colour Suppl.) 28 Aug. 16/4 Laser beams..are useful to scientists as a sophisticated light-source. **1972** L. Alcock *By South Cadbury* viii. 182 The Breiddin had been refortified in the late fourth century with a sophisticated timber defence, in the form of a raised fighting platform and look-out towers. **1972** *Sci. Amer.* Sept. 53/2 One of the most sophisticated of all animal communication systems, the celebrated waggle dance of the honeybee. **1979** *Now!* 14 Sept. 78/1 When they raided the flat the police found two-way pocket radios, explosive substances and what were described as 'sophisticated' timing devices.

3. b. Of a printed book, containing alterations in content, binding, etc. which are intended to deceive.

1862 J. H. Burton *Book-Hunter* i. 25 His experience.. rendered him the most merciless detector of sophisticated books. Nothing, it might be supposed on first thought, can be a simpler or more easily recognized thing than a book genuine as printed. But in the old-book trade there are opportunities for the exercise of ingenuity. **1952** J. Carter *ABC for Book-Collectors* 168 Sophisticated..as applied to a book, is simply a polite synonym for doctored or faked-up.

4. *Comb.*, as *sophisticated-looking*.

1925 T. Dreiser *Amer. Tragedy* (1926) I. i. iv. 31 A brisk..and decidedly sophisticated-looking person.

sophi·sticatedly, *adv.* [f. prec. + -ly[2].] In a sophisticated manner.

1956 A. Wilson *Anglo-Saxon Attitudes* i. i. 27 He smiled sophisticatedly to show his superiority to congresses. **1960** E. Davies *Beyond Old Bone Trail* i. 2, I was very shy and self-conscious, suffering from what I later found out to be generally and more sophisticatedly known as an inferiority complex. **1971** *Daily Tel.* 1 May 10/2 The work skated sophisticatedly between pastoral musing and a more swinging, jazzy style.

sophistication. Add: **2. a.** Also, the alteration of a literary text in the course of copying or printing.

1956 *Studies in Bibliogr.* VIII. 10 The paucity of '*em's* in the pages set by Compositor B represents the compositor's sophistication of copy. **1963** [see *sophisticated *ppl. a.* 2 a]. **1981** *Times Lit. Suppl.* 10 July 793/2 It [*sc.* the Folio] also makes numerous minor alterations, many of them literary sophistications.

c. Also, the quality or fact of being sophisticated (sense *2 b): (*a*) worldly wisdom or experience; subtlety, discrimination, refinement; (*b*) knowledge, expertise, in some technical subject.

1915 *New Republic* 16 Jan. 27/1 As to semi-education, the assumption is sound enough, and Dr. Burton's chapters on method and structure, on development and climax and ending, are honest first aids to sophistication. **1934** C. Lambert *Music Ho!* ii. 112 In spite of his dazzling and outward sophistication Stravinsky is essentially primitive and naïve. **1951** R. Firth *Elem. Social Organization* v. 163 When we talk..of primitive Greek art.. we are referring..to art that is distinguished primarily by being earlier in time, though it..also bears the character of lack of sophistication. **1964** E. Bach *Introd. Transformational Gram.* vii. 145 The reader of the standard linguistic journals is apt to find articles..that demand considerable mathematical sophistication on his part. **1971** J. B. Carroll et al. *Word Freq. Bk.* p. xxi/1 Complete understanding of the lognormal model requires considerable mathematical sophistication. **1977** R. Williams *Marxism & Lit.* ii. iv. 99 Mediation, in this range of use, then seems little more than a sophistication of reflection.

d. (*a*) The property or condition (of a thing) of being highly developed or complicated; technical refinement.

1959 *Time* 12 Oct. 67/3 In the past the usual comment was that Russian space vehicles are big and brawny because of more powerful launching rockets, but that U.S. space vehicles, small and elegant, made up for the Russians' gross size by their sophistication. **1972** L. Alcock *By South Cadbury* viii. 195 Elaborate arrangements to maintain the defences and their garrisons demonstrate the administrative sophistication of Late Saxon England. **1972** *Practical Motorist* Oct. 162/1 On more modern cars, sophistication is now so far advanced that the linkage would virtually require specialist attention!

(*b*) *concr.* An instance of this; a technically advanced characteristic.

1973 *Nature* 9 Nov. 109/2 The range stretches from relatively simple systems such as bacterial flagella and plant viruses..towards bacterial spores and the more complex sophistications of ribosomes, cell walls and mitochondria. **1976** *Early Music* Oct. 451/2 Instamatics cost..over £50 with built-in light meter and other sophistications.

sophomoric, *a.* Add: **b.** Also *ellipt.* as *sb.*

1946 Auden in *Harvard Alumni Bull.* 15 June 707/1 The sophomoric Who face the future's darkest hints With giggles or with prairie squints.

sophrosyne (sōufrǫ·zini). Also **sophrosune.** [ad. Gr. σωφροσύνη prudence, moderation, f. σώφρων of sound mind, prudent.] Soundness of mind, moderation, prudence, self-control.

1889 *Cent. Dict.*, Sophrosyne. **1944** Auden *For Time Being* 89, I am that star most dreaded by the wise, For they are drawn against their will to me, Yet read in my procession through the skies The doom of orthodox sophrosyne [1945 *U.K. ed.* suphrosyne]. **1947** *Mind* LVI. 363 Lord Russell gives us to understand that he has no use for *sophrosyne*. *a* **1963** C. S. Lewis *Poems* (1964) 3 Thus with magistral hand the Puritan Sophrosune Cooled and schooled and tempered our uneasy motions. **1970** J. Gardner *Wreckage of Agathon* 153 Even when his ideas were crazy, the man had sophrosyne, as they used to call it in the old days.

sopie. Add: Also 9 **soopie, soopje, sopi, sopje. soupie, soupje, supje.** (Further examples.)

1790 E. Helme tr. *Le Vaillant's Trav. Afr.* I. v. 90 Those who enter a house are always presented with a *sopi*, that is to say, a glass of rack or gin, or rather of French brandy. **1812** A. Plumptre tr. *Lichtenstein's Trav. S. Afr.* I. ii. xii. 167 Whatever Mr. Barrow may say of the *Soopje* as the favourite drink of the colonists, I can very safely affirm, that I never..saw three Africans born, in liquor. **1824** W. J. Burchell *Trav. S. Afr.* II. x. 287 Muchunka..was..stopped from drinking it all off at once as he had seen the others drink their *sopje* (sópy) or dram. **1827** G. Thompson *Trav. & Adventures S. Afr.* i. iii. 33, I alighted and partook of a cup of coffee or a dram (*soopie*) with the hospitable boors. **1835** C. L. Stretch *Jrnl.* 13 May in *Voorloper* (1976) 743 The glass or cup..was presented to the Chief who previously to giving it to the person intended sipped out some portion and as several soupies were given in this way Macamo naturally became quite overcome with the strength of the Brandy. **1849** E. E. Napier *Excursions Southern Afr.* I. vii. 115 A 'Totty', to this day, will share his last sixpence,..or his last 'soupje', with a comrade. **1861** in *Life at Cape* (1973) 37 We ordered a halt to rest a bit, to take a 'soopie', [etc.]. **1862** L. Duff Gordon *Let.* 2 Mar. in *Lett. from Cape* (1925) 131 Though he declined wine or Cape smoke 'soopjes' (drams) with aversion. **1876** F. Boyle *Savage Life* 277 After a while, from his lonely cottage by the ford, came to us the boer farmer in quest of supje (Mercian suppy), of raw spirits and a gossip. **1939** F. B. Young *City of Gold* i. iii. 95 'Come along, Peruvian,' he shouted. 'Just in time for a sopie.' **1981** A. Paton *Towards Mountain* xv. 117 Part of the remuneration of the ['Cape Coloured'] farm workers is the 'sopie', the draught of sour inferior wine that is given them three or four times a day... The sopie has been condemned by generation after generation of social workers, teachers, and ministers of religion.

soppily (sǫ·pili), *adv.* [f. SOPPY *a.* + -LY².] In a soppy or sentimental manner.

1977 *Listener* 21 Apr. 527/1 This soppily indulgent account of..shallow suburbanites. **1980** *N.Y. Times* 15 June VII. 14/1 Caroline thinks Ivan is arrogant, which he is; he thinks she is soppily emotional, which she is.

soppiness. Add: **2.** Mawkish sentiment, facile emotion.

1974 I. MURDOCH *Sacred & Profane Love Machine* 202 Harriet was..fearing tears, a kind of soppiness which might embarrass her dignified friend. **1978** *Times Lit. Suppl.* 1 Dec. 1392/4 Soppiness vies with winsomeness in an exhibition of these postcards at the Bethnal Green Museum.

soppy, *a.* Add: **5.** Full of mawkish sentiment; foolishly affectionate; inane, indulgent; occas. used affectionately. Also *to be soppy on,* to be infatuated with (a person). *colloq.*

1918 H. G. WELLS *Joan & Peter* xi. 369 What Joan knew surely to be lovely, Highmorton denounced as 'soppy'. 'Soppy' was a terrible word in boys' schools and girls' schools alike, a flail for all romance. **1920** H. G. HIBBERT *Playgoer's Mem.* xxxi. 257 The music halls were filled up with the precipitated baseness of pantomime—the puns, the 'unprincipalled' boy, the soppy-sentimental heroine. **1923** C. MACKENZIE *Parson's Progress* x. 121 Everyone will be singing for ever and ever and waving palms and playing harps and all that... I reckon Heaven's soppy, I do. **1929** H. WILLIAMSON *Beautiful Years* xx. 139 'Isn't fair, is it, man?' 'Hush, don't let 'em hear us. They'll think us soppy.' **1930** 'E. BRAMAH' *Little Flutter* xix. 218, I may as well make up my mind that I'm soppy on the blighter. **1935, 1959** [see *DATE *sb.*¹ 1 b]. **1961** *Daily Tel.* 2 Dec. 1/5 Lord Parker, Lord Chief Justice, said yesterday he deplored the tendency towards 'soppy and sentimental' treatment of children in juvenile courts. **1974** J. COOPER *Women & Super Women* 16 Being photographed for the *Tatler* with a soppy expression on her face. **1977** *New Yorker* 8 Aug. 11/1 Side benefits include a Chinese Legionnaire who sings soppy Irish ballads.

sopra bianco: see *BIANCO SOPRA BIANCO.

sopranino (soprānī·no), *sb.* and *a.* [a. It. *sopranino,* dim. of SOPRANO *sb.* (and *a.*).] **A.** *sb.* An instrument (usu. wind) of higher pitch than a soprano (see SOPRANO 3 b). **B.** *adj.* Of or pertaining to such an instrument, as a recorder.

1907 T. S. WOTTON *Dict. Mus. Terms* 185 *Sopranino,* the diminutive of Soprano, a term applied to an instrument of higher pitch than that defined as soprano. **1938** *Oxf. Compan. Music* 785/2 The 'Flauto Piccolo' of Handel in *Acis and Galatea* is the little sopranino recorder, an octave above the treble one (or possibly the flageolet was used). *Ibid.* 832/1 *Sopranino Saxhorn in E Flat* (*or F*): also called *Soprano Saxhorn*; also often miscalled *Soprano Flügelhorn* or *Flügelhorn Piccolo.* **1939** A. CARSE *Musical Wind Instruments* xiii. 177 Each group [of saxophones] was in seven sizes... 1. Sopranino..2. Soprano [etc.]. **1954** [see *PARDESSUS 2]. **1964** S. MARCUSE *Mus. Instruments* (1966) 485/2 *Sopranino clarinet,* clarinet pitched between the ordinary C clarinet and the piccolo clarinet in high A♭. *Ibid.*, The sopranino in D was in use in 18th- and 19th-c. orchestras. **1968** *Observer* (Colour Suppl.) 19 May 40/5 His nice Irish wife..warms up the sopraninas (very small recorders) by cradling them inside her blouse. **1977** *Times* 27 May 16/4 A new type of violin, the 11¼ in sopranino, with strings of such high tension that when they were first used in the United States, the player wore protective goggles in case they snapped.

soprano, *sb.* (and *a.*). Add: **1. b.** Also *fig.*

1848 GEO. ELIOT *Let.* 8 Mar. (1954) I. 253, I should have written a soprano to your Jubilate.

3. b. *spec.* **soprano saxophone,** the second highest member of the saxophone family, usually pitched in B flat. Abbrev. **soprano sax.**

1859 C. MANDEL *Treat. on Instrumentation Military Bands* 18 The Saxophone. This instrument is made in various keys, viz.:- 1. The B flat soprano-saxophone. **1961** J. A. MACGILLIVRAY in A. Baines *Mus. Instruments* x. 261 The *Tarogato* is a Hungarian instrument resembling a soprano saxophone of wood. **1971** *Guardian* 28 Sept. 10/6 The music is for..flute, trumpet, soprano sax, two basses, and percussion.

5. *ellipt.* = *soprano saxophone,* sense 3 b above.

1876 [see *BARITONE]. **1934** S. R. NELSON *All about Jazz* ii. 57 The other saxophones in common use in the band are the tenor, baritone, soprano and bass. **1967** *Sat. Rev.* (U.S.) 15 Apr. 55/2 Bechet, adjusting the reed of his soprano, looked at him.

sops-in-wine. Add: **1.** (Later examples in revived use.)

1918 'K. MANSFIELD' *Let.* 11 Mar. (1928) I. 152 There is a certain little white pink, striped with dark red, called 'sops-in-wine'. **1972** J. METCALF *Going down Slow* v. 102 What a garden there was at the back of this..inn... Sops in Wine and Floramer, Widow Wail..and deep red damask roses. **1981** T. MCLEAN *Medieval Eng. Gardens* v. 150 Its English name, gillyflower, may be a corruption of July flower, one of its medieval names, others of which were sops-in-wine, queen of delights and..carnation.

sor, sorr, repr. Ir. pronunc. of SIR *sb.* (sense 7 a).

1889 KIPLING *Life's Handicap* (1891) 15 Indirectly, sorr, you have rescued..the peasanthry av a numerous village. **1901** M. FRANKLIN *My Brilliant Career* xix. 162 'How are you enjoying yourself?' 'Treminjous intoirely, sor.' **1914** [see *PHWAT]. **1933** E. O'NEILL *Ah, Wilderness!* II. 66 No harm done. Only careful, Norah, careful... Yes, sorr. **1977** M. KENYON *Rapist* v. 54 A fine figure y'are so, if ye'll pardon the unsolicited estimation, sor.

soralium (sorēⁱ·liŏm). *Bot.* Pl. **-alia.** [mod.L., f. SORAL *a.* + L. *-ium,* neut. sb. ending.] A well-defined area of the thallus in which soredia occur, characteristic of certain lichens.

1921 A. L. SMITH *Lichens* iii. 144 In lichens of foliose and fruticose structure, and in a few crustaceous forms, the soredia are massed together into the compact bodies called soralia. **1938** G. M. SMITH *Cryptogamic Bot.* I. xiv. 518 They [*sc.* the soredia] may develop over the entire surface of a thallus or in localized pustule-like areas (soralia). **1970** *Sci. Jrnl.* Mar. 32/1 Many lichens have small powdery areas called soralia, the shape and location of which are characteristic for each species. The individual grains of powder in the soralia consist of an algal cell surrounded by fungal hyphae, and it is believed that they have a reproductive function. *Ibid.*, Lichens which have abundant fungal fruit bodies rarely form soralia, and vice versa.

sorb (sǭɹb), *v. Physical Chem.* [Back-formation from *SORPTION, after *absorb, absorption.*]

a. *trans.* To collect by sorption. Also *absol.*

1909 J. W. MCBAIN in *Phil. Mag.* XVIII. 918 An idea of the quality of the carbon employed may be obtained from the amount of gas sorbed by it in actual experiment. **1938** *Proc. R. Soc.* A. CLXVII. 407 The two zeolites in the form of three-dimensional networks sorb ammonia copiously without ammoniate formation. **1954** ALEXANDER & HUDSON *Wool* viii. 261 When wool is immersed in hydrogen peroxide, some is initially sorbed by the amino and imino groups without reaction. **1970** *New Scientist* 2 July 9/3 Papers with inked designs sorb best on the inked areas. **1972** *Physics Bull.* Oct. 583/1 This has the advantage that exhausted water vapour is not sorbed by the trap on the fine side of the pump.

b. *intr.* for *pass.*

1970 *New Scientist* 2 July 9/3 The SO_2 sorbs strongly to these sweat patches.

Hence **sorbed, so·rbing** *ppl. adjs.*; also **so·rbate²** [after *distillate, filtrate,* etc.], that which is sorbed.

1909 *Phil. Mag.* XVIII. 923 The total amount of sorbed gas is 67·70 c.c. **1921** *Jrnl. Chem. Soc.* CXIX. 454 Experimental results have always been obtained by shaking a certain volume of a solution of known strength with a known amount of sorbing material such as charcoal, and analysing a sample of the remaining solution. **1928** *Phil. Mag.* V. 749 A revised conception of the mutual relations of sorbent and sorbate in cases where the 'power' time-equation holds. **1946** *Nature* 5 Oct. 475/1 Compact, nonporous sorbing media such as wool. **1949** *Discussions Faraday Soc.* VII. 136 Gmelinite and chabazite occlude a still greater variety of sorbates. **1975** *Nature* 28 Aug. 719/1 The Mg ion of dehydrated offretite should have a strong electrostatic field around it, and sorbed molecules should be strongly attracted to form a complex.

sorbent (sǭ·ɹbĕnt), *sb.* (*a.*) *Physical Chem.* [f. *SORB *v.*, after *absorbent.*] A material having the property of collecting molecules of a substance by sorption; that which sorbs. Also (and orig.) as *adj.*, having this property.

1909 J. W. MCBAIN in *Phil. Mag.* XVIII. 918 My results show that it [*sc.* a specimen of carbon] is highly sorbent towards hydrogen. **1922** *Chem. Abstr.* XVI. 3017 The sorption isotherms were det[ermine]d..with animal charcoal as the sorbent. **1954** *Trans. Faraday Soc.* L. 981 Montmorillonite has already found various large scale uses as a sorbent. **1973** *Nature* 12 Jan. 92/2 The use of a zirconium oxide sorbent may be an economically realistic method of recovering boron from the sea. **1975** *Petroleum Rev.* XXIX. 239/1 In addition CGA maintains equipment to generate foam having a high sorbent capacity.

Sorbian, *a.* and *sb.* Add: (Examples referring to the language.)

1877 [see *LUSATIAN *sb.* and *a.*]. **1889** *Cent. Dict.*, *Sorbian*... *a.* Pertaining to the Sorbs or to their language. **1908** [see *LECHISH *sb.* and *a.*]. **1933, 1972** [see *LUSATIAN *sb.* and *a.*]. **1977** *Language* LIII. 479 Soviet linguists talk about two Sorbian languages (Upper and Lower Sorbian), Western scholars about two Sorbian dialects.

sorbitan (sǭ·ɹbitæn). *Chem.* [f. SORBIT(OL + AN(HYDRIDE.] Any of a number of cyclic ethers which are monoanhydrides of sorbitol; *spec.* the 1,4-anhydride, $CH_2OH{\cdot}CHOH{\cdot}\underline{CH{\cdot}(CHOH)_2{\cdot}CH_2O}$, a colourless crystalline solid. Freq. *attrib.* in names of fatty-acid esters of these compounds, which are used as emulsifiers and surfactants.

1938 *Industr. & Engin. Chem.* Nov. 1222/2 The inner ether hypothesis was further tested by substituting a mixture of preformed sorbitol inner ethers, or sorbitans, for the sorbitol. **1950** KIRK & OTHMER *Encycl. Chem. Technol.* V. 688 Anhydrides of certain hexahydric alcohols and their derivatives, such as sorbitan and polyoxyethylene sorbitan esters of fatty acids, are used as emulsifiers and also possess emollient properties. **1958** *Martindale's Extra Pharmacopœia* (ed. 24) 696 The ether-esters, such as sorbitan oleate, are active water-in-oil emulsifying agents, while the polyoxyethylene derivatives mostly produce oil-in-water emulsions. **1969** tr. *Schönfeldt's Surface Active Ethylene Oxide Adducts* iv. 607 A composition containing glycine, phosphoric acid, and, e.g...ethoxylated sorbitan monolaurate as adduct, or sorbitan mono-oleate, is recommended as an antioxidant for fats. **1976** *Nature* 26 Aug. 777/2 By use of surfactants such as sorbitan stearates, water can be emulsified in hydrocarbon solvents and then readily supercooled.

sorbite². Substitute for def.: † **1.** A nitride and carbide of titanium found as red microscopic crystals in pig iron. *Obs.*

Quots. 1902, 1904 in Dict. belong with the next sense.

1888 H. M. HOWE in *Engin. & Mining Jrnl.* 18 Aug. 132 (*table*) Minerals which compose iron. Name suggested here..Sorbite. *Ibid.* 1 Sept. 177/1 Sorbite has been detected by Sorby in many cast-irons..as beautiful triangles, rhombs, hexagons and complex crosses. **1919** *Mineral. Mag.* XVIII. 376 It [*sc.* cochranite] is formed under the same conditions [as], and sometimes together with, the copper-red cubes of titanium cyano-nitride, $Ti(CN)_2{\cdot}3Ti_3N_2$. This was named sorbite.., a term afterwards withdrawn, as the same name was given..for one of the transition conditions in carbon-steel.

2. A constituent of steel consisting of microscopic granules of cementite in a ferrite matrix, produced esp. when hardened steel is tempered above about 450°C. [a. F. *sorbite* (F. Osmond 1895, in *Bull. de la Soc. d'Encouragement pour l'Industrie Nationale* X. 491).]

1900 *Metallographist* III. 196 The crystallites represent the solid solution of first solidification, from which, during cooling, plates of cementite separated first, then the eutectic, pearlyte or sorbite (the latter if the melting of the cementite was sufficiently complete). **1924** GREAVES & WRIGHTON *Pract. Micros. Metallogr.* vii. 57 Sorbite is the essential constituent of hardened and tempered steels intended for constructional purposes. **1964** H. HODGES *Artifacts* xix. 218 The effect of gently heating a quenched steel is that at low temperatures any martensite present forms troostite, while at higher temperatures..sorbite is produced. **1967** A. H. COTTRELL *Introd. Metallurgy* xx. 384 Above about 500°C the cementite particles grow competitively..into larger rounded particles dispersed through the B.C.C. iron matrix, giving a spheroidized structure (sorbite).

sorbitic *a.*² (earlier and later examples).

1902 *Jrnl. Iron & Steel Inst.* LXI. 140 Osmond said that probably in future all our steel rails will be made sorbitic. **1927** *Min. Proc. Inst. Civil Engineers* CCXXIV. 319 Photographs indicating the difference between sorbitic and ordinary steel. **1975** *Metals Abstr.* VIII. 1. 298/1 The production of reinforcing wire from grade 80 steel rod with a uniform sorbitic structure is described.

sorbitize (sǭ·ɹbitəiz), *v. Metallurgy.* [f. *SORBIT(E² + -IZE.] *trans.* To convert (steel) into a form containing sorbite. Hence **so·rbitized** *ppl. a.*, **so·rbitizing** *vbl. sb.*; **sorbitiza·tion,** the process of sorbitizing.

1918 D. K. BULLENS *Steel* (ed. 2) viii. 167 It required four quenchings to entirely sorbitize the steel. **1927** *Jrnl. Iron & Steel Inst.* CXVI. 582 Conditions of working which tend to keep the oxide content of the bath at a minimum favour the production of sorbitised rails free from hair cracks. **1928** C. J. ALLEN *Steel Highway* I. viii. 97 Another popular means of toughening the steel is by heat treatment, the process known as 'sorbitising' adding considerably to the wearing capacity with but a moderate addition to the cost of the rails. **1930** *Chem. Abstr.* XXIV. 3740 (*heading*) Method of 'sorbitization' of rails used at Nadezhdinsky iron and steel works. **1968** *Metals Abstr.* I. 1266/2 (*heading*) Sorbitizing of rolled wire from the rolling heat. **1975** *Ibid.* VIII. 298/1 (*heading*) Wire-rod sorbitized from its temperature at the end of rolling. **1975** *Chem. Abstr.* July–Aug. 215/1 (*heading*) Sorbitization of carbon steel wire rod during continuous rolling.

sorbitol. Add: It is a hexahydric alcohol, $CH_2OH{\cdot}(CHOH)_4{\cdot}CH_2OH$, found as a dextrorotatory isomer and crystallizing as colourless needles. (Further examples.)

1928 HAAS & HILL *Introd. Chem. Plant Products* (ed. 4) I. 70 Sorbitol occurs in the berries of *Pyrus aucuparia* and also in apple juice. **1955** *Sci. News Let.* 29 Jan. 70/1 A sugary substance called sorbitol..is used to 'entrap' the essential oils and esters that carry the citrus fruit flavor and fragrance. **1964** [see *hexahydric* adj. s.v. *HEXA-]. **1975** *Sci. Amer.* Dec. 80 In response to the raised level of glucose in the aqueous humour (as in the blood) that is characteristic of diabetes..the enzyme catalyzes the reduction of glucose to form the sugar alcohol sorbitol.

Sorbo (sǭ·rbo). Also **sorbo.** [Invented name: cf. ABSORB *v.*] The proprietary name of a make of sponge rubber. Usu. *attrib.*, esp. as *sorbo rubber.* Also *fig.*

1917 *Trade Marks Jrnl.* 15 Aug. 799 Sorbo..Sponge substitutes (India Rubber). Leeson Sponge and Rubber Co. Ltd. **1919** *Ibid.* 7 May 575 Sorbo Rubber-Sponge Products Ltd. **1926–7** *Army & Navy Stores Catal.* 104/2 Sorbo sponges—each 1/3. **1939** *Archit. Rev.* LXXXV. 251 (*caption*) The smaller sketch shows the large rounded sorbo strips fixed to door edges. **1940** *Amat. Radio Handbk.* (ed. 2) 134/1 Most microphones will tend to pick up floor vibrations if rested directly on the table. For this reason they should preferably be placed on a piece of sorbo rubber. **1941** C. KIRKUS *Let's go Climbing* ix. 132, I..put the sorbo mattress underneath my outer clothes, donned gloves and balaclava, and prepared to spend the night. **1941** 'R. WEST' *Black Lamb & Grey Falcon* I. 319 Astra..bounced from the platform like a great sorbo ball to say good-bye. **1942** M. Dickens *One Pair of Feet* viii. 159 Toots pursed her sorbo lips over the result. **1963** G. Freeman *Campaign* vii. 102 Boat-like red slippers with thick, white sorbo soles. **1976** *Lancet* 9 Oct. 801/2 The endangered areas, trochanters and sacrum, are kept free of pressure by placing the patient on a pillow or, better, sorborubber packs.

sorbose (sǭ·ɹbōᵘz, -s). *Chem.* [f. Sorb *sb.*[1] + -ose[2].] A ketohexose sugar obtained esp. from rowan berries as a fermentation product of sorbitol.

1889 *Jrnl. Chem. Soc.* LVI. 480 Sorbose ferments more slowly and less completely. **1913** Haas & Hill *Introd. Chem. Plant Products* 63 Sorbose is a ketanic sugar produced by the fermentative oxidation of the alcohol sorbite contained in the sap of the mountain ash..; this sugar probably does not exist as such in the plant. **1962** *New Scientist* 5 Apr. 804/2 The fermentations already mentioned, with the less difficult fermentations producing ..sorbose (a key intermediate in the synthesis of vitamin C).., more or less cover the extent of the British fermentation industry. **1970** *Ibid.* 5 Mar. 462/2 The possible non-nutritive sugars include sorbose (found in Mountain Ash berries), xylose (from oat husks), arabinose [etc.].

sorcerer. Add: *sorcerer's apprentice* [tr. F. *l'apprenti sorcier*, the title of a symphonic poem by Paul Dukas (1897), after *der zauberlehrling*, a ballad by Goethe (1797)], one who, like the apprentice in the ballad with his spells, instigates processes which he is unable to control. Also *attrib.*

1952 E. Coxhead *Play Toward* iii. 24 Of course there was always a sorcerer's-apprentice element in teaching: but of all their creations, Lance was surely not the one who should be getting out of hand. **1966** J. Aiken *Trouble with Product X* vi. 115, I wondered if his disciples, like the sorceror's [*sic*] apprentice, had not got out of control. **1967** *Sunday Times* 26 Feb. 2/3 The CIA is not a sorcerer's apprentice that has run wild, but..is under strict government control. **1974** Hawkey & Bingham *Wild Card* xiii. 116 Our first priority should be learning to live with the technology we have already, not acquiring more. Because, like the Sorcerer's Apprentice, we just *ain't* going to be able to handle it.

sorcerize, *v.* For *rare*[−1] read *rare* and add later U.S. example.

1972 M. Mead *Blackberry Winter* xv. 202 The threatening sorcerers of the plains..blackmailed our mild-mannered mountain people by promising temporarily not to sorcerize their relatives, providing they were given food and an adequate supply of trade goods.

sordid, *a.* Add: **II. 7.** Also with ppl. adj., as *sordid-seeming.*

1920 D. H. Lawrence *Lost Girl* xiv. 329 The dreary, to her sordid-seeming Campagna.

B. *sb. rare.* One who is sordid.

1959 C. MacInnes *Absolute Beginners* 13 All the old tax-payers know of this because, of course, for one thing, the poor old sordids recollect their own glorious teenage days. *Ibid.* 184 It doesn't seem possible such sordids as this lot could frighten you. **1960** N. Mitford *Don't tell Alfred* ix. 97 My children regarded everybody over the age of thirty as old sordids, old weirdies, ruins, hardly human at all.

sordidity. Delete † *Obs.* and add: **a.** (Later examples.)

1917 V. Woolf *Diary* 22 Nov. (1977) I. 80 Hearing women abuse each other & at the noise others come running with delight—all this sordidity made me think him rather likely to be right. **1923** *Times Lit. Suppl.* 23 Aug. 554/1 His [*sc.* Defoe's] very precise and solid account of licence, adventure, and sordidity [in Roxana]. **1964** A. Swinson *Six Minutes to Sunset* viii. 150 Carson then switched his attack to the political manœuvring, condemning it for its duplicity and sordidity. **1978** *Times Lit. Suppl.* 1 Dec. 1382/2 Empson seems to insist that one cannot truly admire him without agreeing with him about the sordidity of Englit.

b. (Later examples.)

1927 V. Woolf *Let.* 7 Feb. (1977) III. 326 Here it is pouring; rain coming through the roof; the sordidity too much for me even. **1936** S. Smith *Novel on Yellow Paper* 152 The lovely deep rich olive green and brown and yellow sordidity of Sickert's London interiors. **1958** *Times Lit. Suppl.* 30 May 291/1 As the inevitable midnight flittings required less and less transport for the furniture and a large family grew up in an atmosphere of increasing poverty, sordidity and even occasional violence, James observed the domestic scene with the eye of an artist.

sordine, *sb.* and *a.* Add: **A.** *sb.* **2.** (Examples of the form *sordino*, pl. *sordini*.) Also, = Damper 2 a (see also quot. 1907). See also *con sordino.

1883 Grove *Dict. Mus.* III. 636/2 The musical terms 'Senza sordini' and 'Con sordini' applied to the damper-stops were used exclusively by Beethoven in his earlier sonatas. **1888** Stainer & Barrett *Dict. Mus. Terms* (ed. 3) 406/2 *Sordini*... (3) Dampers of a pianoforte. **1894** G. du Maurier *Trilby* I. i. 42 Gecko..played..in minor, in pizzicato, and in sordino. **1907** T. S. Wotton *Dict. Mus. Terms* 185 *Senza sordini* is..an indication open to misconstruction in piano music of a certain date, since it may mean 'without dampers' i.e. raising the dampers by means of the damper pedal, or it may mean 'without using the mutes'. **1959** *Collins Mus. Encycl.* 617/2 *Sordino*... (2) Damper (in the piano)... (3) Also applied in the late 18th and 19th cent. to a strip of leather (later felt) used to mute the strings of a piano and controlled by a pedal.

sordor. (Later examples.)

1929 *Oxford Poetry* 28 The world..rises and falls On a wave of confetti and funerals And sordor and stinks and stupid faces. **1934** T. S. Eliot *After Strange Gods* i. 17 The sordor of the half-dead mill towns of southern New Hampshire and Massachusetts. **1982** *Observer* 10 Oct. 30/8 Budd, as a kid, knew the sordor behind the glamour.

sordume (sǭ·ɹdium). *rare.* [Alteration of *sordun.] = next.

1955 Auden *Shield of Achilles* iii. 76 There I stand in Eden again, welcomed back by the krumhorns, doppions, sordumes of jolly miners.

‖ **sordun** (zordū·n). Also **sordune.** [Ger.] An early form of bassoon, having a cylindrical bore with double reeds.

1876 Stainer & Barrett *Dict. Mus. Terms* 406/2 *Sordun, Sordono* (It.) (1) An old form of wood wind instrument, having a double reed, with twelve ventages and two keys. **1943** B. Miall tr. *K. Geiringer's Mus. Instruments* 133 An extremely rare variant of the Bassoon was the *Sordune*... This consisted of a gracefully turned wooden billet containing not merely two but sometimes three parallel cylindrical bores. **1977** *Early Music* Apr. (Advt., recto rear cover), The Sordunes which Praetorius ..illustrates in Syntagma Musicum 1619 show a controlled reed instrument of two parallel bores with a bocal tapering towards the end of its length. The Sordune is a useful bridge between the windcap range of instruments, and the controlled reed instruments. **1978** A. Baines in J. M. Thomson *Future of Early Music in Britain* 22 Once people have spent money on manufactured sorduns and cornamuses, they want their money's worth from them.

sore, *a.* Add: **II. 9. b.** Also, *a sight for sore eyes*: see *sight *sb.*[1] 1 d.

e. Colloq. phr. *dressed* (or *done*, etc.) *up like a sore finger* (or *toe*) and varr., overdressed. *Austral.* and *N.Z.*

1919 W. H. Downing *Digger Dialects* 46 *Sore finger*, an overdressed person (e.g. 'dolled up like a sore finger'). **1939** K. Tennant *Foveaux* 430 You ought to a seen us in the ole days when we 'ad a procession every year—done up like a sore toe with banners and floats. **1943** J. A. W. Bennett in *Amer. Speech* XVIII. 91 'All done up like a sore toe' describes someone dressed over-elaborately; many New Zealand children go barefoot much of the time, and it is with this circumstance in mind that we must interpret the simile. **1958** H. D. Williamson *Sunlit Plain* 10 Get an eyeful of him! Done up like a sore toe. **1965** P. White *Four Plays* 168 I'm gunna get out of this suit. Dressed up like a sore finger.

f. Colloq. phr. *to stick* (or *stand*) *out like a sore thumb*, to be very conspicuous or obvious.

1936 E. S. Gardner *Case of Sleepwalker's Niece* xiii. 128 'No,' he said, 'that's the one thing in the case that stands out like a sore thumb, now that I stop to think of it.' **1941** —— *Case of Haunted Husband* (1942) xvi. 126 A private detective in that atmosphere would stick out like a sore thumb on a waiter serving soup. **1958** *Spectator* 8 Aug. 187/1 A bad officer will stick out like a sore thumb. **1977** *New Yorker* 15 Aug. 42/3 In the strong late-afternoon light the twelve white houses stood out like twelve sore thumbs.

12. a. Also, angry, resentful. Also const. *about, on,* and *at.* Now colloq. (chiefly *N. Amer.*).

1852 Dickens in *Househ. Words* V. 307/1 The people were very sore about the French marriage. **1884** G. C. Davies *Peter Penniless* xxxii. 230 Everybody was greatly amused at the incident, except Quadling, who was sore about it for a long time. **1904** *N.Y. Even. Post* 13 June 1 Kelly denied the charges and said the patrolman was 'sore' on him. **1923** R. D. Paine *Comr. Rolling Ocean* xiv. 252 All hands were sore on him, but he couldn't take a hint. **1927** [see *high-hat *v.*]. **1932** Wodehouse *Hot Water* xvi. 257 But surely you aren't going to get sore at a little thing like that? **1946** *Sunday Dispatch* 8 Sept. 2/7 They were sore about the decision that had deprived them of complete victory. **1954** [see *nah[1]]. **1975** D. Lodge *Changing Places* iii. 120 Nobody believed him of course, and this made him sore as hell. **1980** *Amer. N. & Q.* Jan. 71/1 Jonson is likely to have been sore about Shakespeare..styling himself gentle.

c. (Earlier example.)

1803 C. Wilmot *Jrnl.* 6 Mar. in T. U. Sadleir *Irish Peer on Continent* (1924) 170 This however is a sore subject, as..there is scarcely any one that one sees who is not a living victim.

13. *sore-footed, -hearted* (later examples; hence *sore-heartedness*), *-rimmed*; **sore-back** *attrib.*, (of horses) having a sore back; so **sore-back** *v.* to give (a horse) a sore back, **sore-backed** *a.*

1835 J. E. Alexander *Sketches in Portugal* x. 224 It [*sc.* a hunting-saddle] sore-backs strange horses, is hard and smooth to the rider, and one can't carry any thing on it in the shape of arms or baggage. **1923** in 'Mark Twain' *Speeches* 9 They have always got a sore-back horse lying around somewhere to sell to the stranger. **1901** Kipling *Five Nations* (1903) 163 A top of a sore-backed Argentine, with a thirst that you couldn't buy. **1933** J. V. Allen *Cowboy Lore* iv. 131 But he went to see the gals on a sore-backed hoss. **1814** Jane Austen *Mansfield Park* II. x. 234 She had only to rise and..pass quietly away..sore-footed and fatigued. **1927** T. S. Eliot *Journey of Magi*, And the camels galled, sore-footed, refractory. **1884** D. Boucicault *Shaughraun* iii. i. 20/1 Blessings on your path; it always leads to the poor and to the sore-hearted! **1923** D. H. Lawrence *Birds, Beasts & Flowers* 55 Open ..And red at the core with the last sore-heartedness, Sore-hearted-looking. **1915** —— *Rainbow* xiii. 371 He lifted his face, the sore-rimmed eyes half smiling.

sore, *v.*[1] Add: **b.** With *up*. To annoy. *colloq.* (orig. *U.S.*). *rare.*

1929 D. Runyon in *Hearst's Internat.* July 56/1 It is a sure thing he will get sored up at the second peek. **1963** 'R. East' *Pin Men* vi. 162 He sored me up once for all and I left him flat.

sore-head, *a.* and *sb.* Add: Also **sorehead. B.** *sb.* **b.** *slang* (chiefly *N. Amer.*). A discontented, dissatisfied person, a malcontent; a mean, niggardly person.

1848 *Weekly Argus* (Albany, N.Y.) 12 Aug. 253/3 As no other selection could be supposed so well to represent such a conventicle of 'sore heads', it is perhaps quite as well it sho'd take that direction as any other. **1912** J. Sandilands *Western Canad. Dict. & Phrase-bk.*, *Sore-head*, a person who sees trouble and wickedness in everything. **1916** C. J. Dennis *Songs of Sentimental Bloke* 130 *Sore-head*, a curmudgeon. **1934** J. T. Farrell *Young Manhood of Studs Lonigan* iv. 61 'You damn Kike, you got too many horseshoes,' a sore-head said as Davey raked in the pot. **1939** T. Wolfe *Web & Rock* ii. 36 We thought he was a man, but he turns out to be just a little sore-head. **1964** L. Nkosi *Rhythm of Violence* ii. i. 23 *Mary*..You two are not to drink until the others arrive! *Jimmy* Rubbish! We have priority claims! *Mary*.. Soreheads! What makes you think you have priorities over others! **1978** M. Puzo *Fools Die* xx. 226, I was holding court with a lot of my customers, who were all telling me what a bunch of shit the whole business was, caused by a few soreheads.

sore-headedness (earlier example).

1860 *Marysville* (Calif.) *Appeal* 31 Mar. 2/2 The patriots of the Customs House [are] suffering from the sore-headedness which so often follows an unsuccessful attempt at ascendency in the political scale.

Sorelian (sǒre·liăn, -ī·liăn), *a.* [f. the name of Georges *Sorel* (1847–1922), French political philosopher + -ian.] Of, pertaining to, or characteristic of Sorel or his views on the regeneration of society through proletarian or syndicalist violence.

1921 N. Angell *Fruits of Victory* v. 165 The Sorelian philosophy of violence and instinctive pugnacity..gives us the tendency to an infinite splitting of the Labour movement. **1931** R. Soltau *French Pol. Thought in Nineteenth Cent.* xiv. 460 Sorelian philosophy can be examined from two aspects. **1936** Wirth & Shils tr. *Mannheim's Ideology & Utopia* iii. 125 This attitude takes many forms—appearing first in the anarchism of Bakunin and Proudhon, then in the Sorelien [*sic*] syndicalism, and finally in the fascism of Mussolini. **1970** H. Arendt *On Violence* iii. 73 The strange revival of the life philosophies of Bergson and Nietzsche in their Sorelian version. **1979** *Dædalus* Winter 19 Pragmatic proposals have replaced the Sorelian myth.

sorely, *adv.* Add: **5.** *sorely-battered, -needed, -sweated.*

1900 W. S. Churchill in *Morning Post* 1 Jan. 6/1 The engine was soon crowded and began to steam homewards —a mournful, sorely-battered locomotive. **1917** —— in M. Gilbert *Winston Churchill* (1977) IV. Compan. i. 87 A mere bluff designed to induce him to dissipate sorely-needed forces on coastal defence. **1952** R. Campbell tr. *Baudelaire's Poems* 129 Who come to waste their sorely-sweated pittance.

Sörensen (sö·rənsən). *Chem.* Also **Sorensen.** The name of Søren P. L. *Sørensen* (1868–1939), Danish biochemist, used *attrib.* and in the possessive to denote a titration method employed in the estimation of amino-acids, consisting in treating the sample with formaldehyde, which combines with the amino groups, and then titrating the carboxylic acid groups against base.

Sørensen first described the method in 1907 (*Compt.-Rend. des Travaux du Lab. de Carlsberg* VII. 1).

1914 J. A. Mandel tr. *Hammarsten's Text-bk. Physiol. Chem.* (ed. 7) ii. 166 On this behaviour is based Sörensen's formoltitration which serves for the estimation of amino-acids in the urine. **1916** A. P. Mathews *Physiol. Chem.* ix. 363 The capacity of the digestive products of combining with formaldehyde steadily increases, as is shown by the Sorensen titration. **1934** W. R. Fearon *Introd. Biochem.* vii. 100 Sörensen's method of formaldehyde titration..is applicable to many amino compounds, including ammonium salts in urine. **1973** Biggs & Woodson *Clin. Biochem.* iii. 40 The Sörensen formol titration technique can be used..to obtain accurate titration values.

Soret (so·re). *Chem.* [The name of Jacques-Louis *Soret* (1827–90), Swiss physicist, who first detected the absorption in a study of blood (*Bibliothèque univ. et Rev. suisse: Arch. des Sci. phys. et nat.* (1878) LXI. 347).] *Soret* (also † *Soret's*) *band*, a characteristic intense band at a wavelength of approximately 400 nanometres which occurs in the ultraviolet absorption spectra of porphyrins and their derivatives.

1899 W. D. Halliburton *Essent. Chem. Physiol.* (ed. 3) 148 Oxyhæmoglobin shows a band (Soret's band) between the lines G and H. **1959** *Lancet* 2 May 912/2 The most effective wavelength would be expected to lie in the region of the Soret band, 390–410 mμ, where light absorption is maximal. **1977** *Jrnl. Amer. Chem. Soc.* XCIX. 4191/1 The wavelength of irradiation corresponded to a region of intense Soret band absorption (in tetraarylporphine dications) or to the region of near minimal.. absorbance on the long wavelength side of the Soret band (in other species).

‖ **soroban** (sǫ·rǫban). [Jap., f. Chinese *suàn-pán* SWAN-PAN.] A kind of abacus used in Japan, adapted from the swan-pan.

1891 A. M. BAKER *Japanese Girls & Women* x. 266 Crowds of clerks sitting upon the matted floors, each with his *soroban*, or adding machine, by his side. **1903** W. DEL MAR *Around World through Japan* xiii. 133 The addition of seven and six presented difficulties unless he had an abacus (*soroban*). **1958** HOSOI Sō in *Japan* xxii. 612/1 In the beginning of the Edo Era, the *soroban* (abacus) was used by Japanese merchants and engineers for their calculations. The *soroban* was introduced from China. **1965** *Australian* 23 Nov. 12 The appearance of a low-cost, small-type, locally-made electronic computer..has driven a wedge under the four-century reign of the soroban.

‖ **soroche** (sorōᵘ·tʃe). [Sp., ad. Quechuan *surúči*, name of some mineral to which mountain sickness was attributed, and hence 'mountain sickness'.] A name in the Andes for mountain sickness.

1878 I. L. BIRD *Lady's Life in Rocky Mountains* (1879) iv. 48, I feel a singular lassitude... This is said to be the milder form of the affection known on higher altitudes as *soroche*, or 'mountain sickness'. **1891** E. B. CLARK *Twelve Months in Peru* 104 A headache with a weighty feeling on the brow, vomiting, and breathlessness are the usual symptoms of *sorroche*. **1922** *Glasgow Herald* 4 Jan. 4 In order to minimise the effects of soroche, or mountain sickness, on persons suffering from weak heart the company provide cars with compartments equipped with oxygen. **1963** *Times* 7 June 13/6 Faced with another presidential election this Sunday, the Peruvian people have apparently succumbed to some political equivalent of the *soroche*, the mountain sickness that shortens the breath, softens the will, and enfeebles the body. **1970** *Sci. Amer.* Feb. 56/1 Even mountain natives sometimes lose their acclimatization to high altitude and incur *soroche* (chronic mountain sickness), which is characterized by extreme elevation of the relative number and mass of red cells in the blood..and ultimately congestive heart failure if the victim remains at high altitude. **1981** L. LEAMER *Assignment* ix. 129 It's great to breathe some real air again... No more *soroche*.

Soroptimist (sǒrǫ·ptimist), *a.* and *sb.* [f. L. *sor-or* sister + OPTIMIST *sb.* (*a.*) (prob. after the *Optimist* Club, founded in 1911).] **A.** *adj.* Chiefly in *Soroptimist Club*, an international service club for professional and business women, founded in California in 1921. Also *Soroptimist International*. **B.** *sb.* A member of a Soroptimist club.

1921 *Charter* (Soroptimist Club, Oakland, California), Whereas, the persons who [*sic*] names appear at the foot hereof..having enrolled themselves as Charter Members of the Soroptimist Club (Oakland), [etc.]. **1924** *Glasgow Herald* 8 Mar. 6 The woman publisher who represents her profession in the Soroptimist Club (i.e., women Rotarians). **1924** *British Weekly* 14 Aug. 431/4, I know now what a Soroptimist is. **1930** M. BRADBURY *Cook Bk.* 2 The Soroptimist Club Code of Ethics... As a Soroptimist I pledge my untiring efforts to understand life, my true and right relation to sister Soroptimists and humanity at large, [etc.]. **1955** L. P. HARTLEY *Perfect Woman* iv. 39 Would it be easy, with possibly some Tablers and Soroptimists listening in? **1977** *Times* 6 Apr. 18/7 Among her many activities, Marina devoted a great deal of time to the Soroptimist International organisation. She was president of the National Union of Soroptimist Clubs (Italy) from 1969–1971, when their international golden jubilee was celebrated in Rome.

sororal, *a.* Add: **3. b.** *sororal polygyny* (Anthrop.), in some polygamous kinship systems, the custom whereby the first wife's sister(s) are preferred as secondary wives.

1952 A. R. RADCLIFFE-BROWN *Struct. & Funct. in Primitive Soc.* iii. 67 Sororal polygyny (marriage with two or more sisters). **1971** P. B. HAMMOND *Introd. Cultural & Soc. Anthrop.* vi. 159/2 Sometimes the desirability of a man's marrying his wife's sister is stressed, a usage referred to as sororal polygyny. **1977** C. R. & M. EMBER *Cultural Anthrop.* (ed. 2) viii. 154/2 Jealousy.. seems to be lessened if one man is married to two or more sisters (sororal polygyny). *Ibid.*, The Crow Indians practice sororal polygyny, and co-wives usually share the same tepee.

sororate (sorōᵊ·rět). *Anthrop.* [f. L. *soror* sister + -ATE¹, after LEVIRATE.] In some kinship systems a custom whereby, on the death of his wife, a man is expected to marry her (unmarried) sister; also occas. = *sororal polygyny* s.v. *SORORAL *a.* 3 b; also *attrib.* Hence **sorora·tic** *a.*, characterized by such a custom.

1910 J. G. FRAZER *Totemism & Exogamy* IV. 140 The other [custom] is the rule which allows or requires a man to marry the younger sisters either of his living or of his deceased wife... The latter custom..has no distinctive name, but on analogy I propose to call it the *sororate*. **1921** E. WESTERMARCK *Hist. Human Marriage* (ed. 5) xxxi. 263 The sororate, like the levirate, can be..interpreted as the outcome of existing conditions. **1947** CHAPPLE & COON *Princ. Anthrop.* xiii. 311 The sororate occurs when a man marries two or more sisters. **1952** M. N. SRINIVAS *Relig. & Society among Coorgs* v. 148 As sororatic unions are preferred among the Coorgs, a mother's younger sister steps into the mother's shoes in the event of the mother's death. **1963** W. N. STEPHENS *Family in Cross-Cultural Perspective* i. 27 In many primitive societies broken homes are automatically 'mended' by means of the sororate and levirate. **1970** *Internat. & Compar. Law Q.* XIX. I. 139 The levirate and sororate institutions could perpetuate the inter-kin tie.

sorority. 2. (Further *attrib.* examples.)

1911 *Daily Colonist* (Victoria, B.C.) 1 Apr. 2/5 All of the girls lived at a sorority house, 4522 Eighteenth avenue, Northeast. **1948** A. N. KEITH *Three come Home* xiii. 229, I had my sorority pin, which had been specially set in my college days with a diamond. **1977** [see *RAT *sb.*¹ 2 e].

sorosilicate (sorosi·likẹ̄t). *Min.* [a. F. *sorosilicate* (V. Billiet 1945, in *Bull. de la Soc. belge de Géol.* LIII. 182), f. Gr. σωρός heap: see SILICATE.] Any of the group of silicates characterized by isolated pairs of SiO^4 tetrahedra that share an oxygen atom at a common apex.

1947 [see *PHYLLOSILICATE]. **1960** *Amer. Mineralogist* XLV. 1 Perrierite is a sorosilicate, with a high number of O-atoms not bonded to silicon. **1972** R. W. FAIRBRIDGE *Encycl. Geochem. & Environmental Sci.* 101/1 In the sorosilicates (two isolated tetrahedra which share one oxygen atom) calcium is present mainly in the epidote group.

sorosis. 2. (Examples.)

1869 GEO. ELIOT *Jrnl.* 16 Feb. in *Lett.* (1956) V. 14 The Ladies of the 'Sorosis' at New York..proposed to make me an honorary member of their society—I declined. **1902** *Out West* May 557 The founding of the first woman's club, Sorosis of New York, was almost simultaneous with the union of the Atlantic and Pacific by the completion of the first transcontinental railway in 1869. **1942** C. MORLEY *Thorofare* xxiii. 98 I've promised to read a paper on my trip abroad to our literary sorosis.

sorption (sǭ·ɹpʃən). *Physical Chem.* [Extracted from *absorption* and *adsorption*.] The combined or undifferentiated action of absorption and adsorption. Freq. *attrib.*

1909 J. W. MCBAIN in *Phil. Mag.* XVIII. 916 The non-committal name 'sorption' may be coined to designate the sum of the phenomena, while 'absorption' and 'adsorption' should be restricted to proven cases of the solution or surface condensation respectively. **1932** *Trans. Faraday Soc.* XXVIII. 182 The rate of sorption at constant temperature was very nearly directly proportional to the pressure. **1945** *Electronic Engin.* XVII. 325/1 M. Francis—dealing mainly with the sorption effects of the walls—gives a detailed account of the use of the McLeod gauge with non-permanent gases. **1954** *Thorpe's Dict. Appl. Chem.* (ed. 4) XI. 33/1 In its practical aspects, the term 'sorption' is usually applied to the concentration at solid surfaces of gases and vapours, and of dissolved substances and colloids, and is therefore largely synonymous with adsorption. **1969** *McGraw-Hill Yearbk. Sci. & Technol.* 342/1 Sorption pumping, a process for producing a vacuum in a closed system by the capture and holding of gases by certain solids or liquids, has recently been developed into a practical technique. **1971** [see *ROUGH *v.*¹ 7 d]. **1973** *Nature* 12 Jan. 92/1 New work on the sorption of boron compounds may provide a way of isolating the element from seawater. **1978** *Ibid.* 16 Mar. 230/1 It is important in the field of forest products science to know the sorption of water in wood.

Hence **so·rptive** *a.*, of, pertaining to, or exhibiting sorption.

1921 *Jrnl. Chem. Soc.* CXIX. 928 After each heating, the density was determined and then the sorptive capacity at each of the three temperatures. **1938** *Proc. R. Soc.* A. CLXVII. 392 The paper describes an attempt to relate the sorptive properties [of zeolites] towards permanent gases..and towards ammonia..to the structure and properties revealed by the X-ray method.

sorr: see *SOR.

sorrel, *sb.*¹ Add: **7. b.** *sorrel soup* (earlier example).

1797 J. WOODFORDE *Diary* 20 Apr. (1931) V. 28 We had for Dinner to day, some Haddocks..Sorrell Soup, a boiled Tongue & Veal Cutlets.

sorrel, *a.* and *sb.*² Add: **A.** *adj.* **d.** *Comb.*, as *sorrel-coloured* adj.; **sorrel-top** *colloq.* (orig. *U.S.*), a red-haired person.

1887 W. B. YEATS *Let.* 13 Aug. in *Lett. W. B. Yeats to Katherine Tynan* (1953) 37, I enclose these trivial verses... The Fairy Doctor. The fairy doctor comes our way Over the sorrel-coloured wold. **1863** 'E. KIRKE' *My Southern Friends* iv. 58 'Har, you lousy sorrel-top,' said the trader to the red-faced and red-headed bar tender. **1904** 'O. HENRY' in *Everybody's Mag.* Feb. 187/1, I guess they don't raise 74-inch sorrel-tops with romping ways down in his precinct. **1918** G. FRANKAU *One of Them* xix. 145 Once more released to lavish wealth and name On head or blonde or sorrel-top or raven.

sorrow, *sb.* Add: **8. sorrow song**, a lament; *spec.* a song expressing the sorrows of the American Black people.

1903 W. E. B. DU BOIS *Souls of Black Folk* xiv. 250 (*heading*) The sorrow songs. *Ibid.*, They that walked in darkness sang songs in the olden days—Sorrow Songs—for they were weary at heart. **1936** A. LOCKE *Negro & his Music* iii. 25 These 'sorrow songs' are more than a priceless heritage from the racial past, they are promising material for the Negro music of the future. **1943** J. COLERIDGE-TAYLOR *Memory Sketch* v. 35 On her return from a South African tour, she [*sc.* Ada Crasby] gave a recital,..asking my husband to accompany her in his 'Six Sorrow Songs'. **1962** R. E. POOL *Beyond Blues* 18 Marcus Garvey headed a movement of a 'back to Africa' Zionism which was a symptom of race consciousness and of the Negro's awakening discovery of the land of long, long ago: 'All the way from Africa to Georgia, I carried my sorrow songs.'

sorry (sǫ·ri, sɒ·ri), *sb. Midlands* and *north dial.* Also **sorrey**. [Var. SIRRAH: cf. SIRREE.] A term of address (now expressing familiarity) for a man or boy.

a **1796** S. PEGGE *Derbycisms* (1896) 65 *Sorry*,..sirrah; in speaking to a boy or lad. **1913** D. H. LAWRENCE *Sons & Lovers* ii. 31 'Shall ter finish, Sorry?' cried Barker, his fellow butty. **1965** BROPHY & PARTRIDGE *Long Trail* 183 *Sorry*, mate, pal, chum. Usually in vocative and chiefly among Yorkshire and Lancashire troops. **1977** SCOLLINS & TITFORD *Ey up, mi Duck!* II. 56 *Sorrey*, the local version of the traditional term 'sirrah'... Nowadays, a term of familiarity, as in: 'Eh up, *sorrey*! Aah's it gooin?' Towards Nottingham the pronunciation sometimes approximates more to 'Surrey'.

sorry, *a.* Add: **7.** *sorry-looking* (earlier example): **sorry-go-round** [after MERRY-GO-ROUND: cf. †MERRY-GO-SORRY], a depressing cycle of events.

1872 'MARK TWAIN' *Roughing It* v. 48 The cayote is a..sorry-looking skeleton. **1959** V. NABOKOV *Nabokov's Dozen* 1 The blurred Mount St. George..on the picture postcards which since 1910..have been courting the tourist from the sorry-go-round of their prop, among.. lumps of rock and..sea shells. **1964** *Punch* 29 Apr. 630/1 It was time to stop the 'sorry-go-round' of inflation.

sort, *sb.*² Add: **I. 4. b.** Also without marked disparagement: of some (untypical or unusual) kind, not having the usual characteristics, equipment, facilities, etc.

1946 D. GWYNN *Bishop Challoner* x. 155 In the Midlands the Franciscans had a school of sorts at Edgbaston. **1959** N. MARSH *False Scent* (1960) i. 21 There's a party of sorts at half-past which I hope may amuse you. **1972** *Times Lit. Suppl.* 4 Aug. 909/4 (Advt.), He is a poetic eye, a visionary of sorts. **1973** *Times* 18 May 22/7 During the Second World War he was a soldier of sorts (he even rose from the ranks).

8. c. (*b*) Hence passing into use as a parenthetic qualifier expressing hesitation, diffidence, or the like, on the speaker's part; also (only in the full form *sort of*) following the statement it qualifies.

1903 G. B. SHAW *Man & Superman* II. 67 I'll sort of borrow the money from my dad until I get on my own feet. **1930** A. BENNETT *Imperial Palace* lxiii. 509, I don't believe they sort of understand English people, Italians don't. **1949** *Granta* Christmas 43/2 One of us had to do a big strong man to sort of separate them. **1958** [see *BUGGER *v.* 2 c]. **1973** *Art Internat.* Mar. 68/1, I sort of use music as a connection to more of the things I want to be about. **1976** *National Observer* (U.S.) 25 Sept. 17/1 He calls it the 'Icarus Human-Powered Aircraft.' 'It's sort of a cumbersome name.'

1923 J. MANCHON *Le Slang* 283 They hung back in their breeching sort-of, ils s'appuyaient sur l'avaloir, si je puis dire. **1952** M. LASKI *Village* xv. 206 It just happened, sort of, and we couldn't either of us help it. **1959** *Psychiatry* XXII. 293/1 Except I feel like, well, what you're doing anyway is just sitting here and saying all these things just to tease me and to taunt me, sort of. **1976** *National Observer* (U.S.) 28 Feb. 21/4 And it *is* all those things, sort of; and yet it is a really fine book.

10. b. *sort of thing*, used adverbially to indicate the inexactness or indefiniteness of the preceding words. Cf. sense 8 c (*b*) above. *colloq.*

1935 E. RAYMOND *We, the Accused* v. ii. 572 What he doesn't know about the law isn't worth knowing, sort of thing. **1968** *Guardian* 24 Apr. 9/2, I don't just give him a sharp slap in temper, sort of thing. **1979** A. FOX *Threat Warning Red* xi. 161 A dummy run. Only go through the motions, sort of thing.

11. b. Also (in phr. *the right sort*) with ref. to one person.

c **1863** T. TAYLOR *Ticket-of-Leave Man* III. 43 But don't look glum, Bob, you're the right sort, you are. **1914** G. B. SHAW *Fanny's First Play* I. 173 But hes the right sort: I can see that. **1936** [see *RIGHT *a.* 8 d].

c. (Earlier examples.)

c **1869** TAYLOR & DUBOURG *New Men & Old Acres* I. 10 Fanny Bunter—in spite of her Ruskinism-run-mad—isn't half a bad sort. **1875** W. READE *Outcast* 202 Our host told us the old woman was his mother, and we musn't [*sic*] mind her being cross, she being a real good sort all the same.

d. Proverb. *it takes all sorts to make a world*; also ellipt. *it takes all sorts*.

[**1620** T. SHELTON tr. *Cervantes' Hist. Don Quixote* II. vi. 34 In the world there must bee of all sorts. **1767** JOHNSON *Let.* 17 Nov. (1952) I. 194 The World, says Locke, has people of all sorts.] **1844** D. W. JERROLD *Story of Feather* xxviii. 161 Click can't get off this time?..Well, it takes all sorts to make a world. **1908** K. GRAHAME *Wind in Willows* iv. 89 The Wild Wood is pretty well populated.. with all the usual lot, good, bad, and indifferent... It takes all sorts to make a world. **1940** [see *COIN *v.*¹ 5 d].

1951 E. Coxhead *One Green Bottle* i. 35 'I daresay it takes all sorts—' conceded Harry vaguely. **1965** J. Fleming *Nothing is Number when you Die* II. iii. 68 She shrugged. 'It takes all sorts, you know.' **1975** J. I. M. Stewart *Young Pattullo* iii. 71 'My father's a banker during the week and a country gent at week-ends. Takes all sorts you know.' 'Takes all sorts?' 'To make a world.'

e. A girl or young woman; a girl-friend. (Predominantly in male use.) *slang* (orig. *Austral.*).

1933 F. Clune *Try Anything Once* 93 'Look here, George,' I said. 'Lend me a suit of civvies. I've got to meet a great little sort, and her father has a dead nark on soldiers.' **1953** T. A. G. Hungerford *Riverslake* 144 Felix came in after tea and said that his sort could come. **1968** K. Denton *Walk around my Cluttered Mind* 137 They'd told me, 'Don't worry about bringing anything except a bottle. The sorts are laid on.' Even after only ten months I understood this to mean that there would be feminine company. **1970** *Daily Progress* (Charlottesville, Va.) 7-c/3 He [*sc.* a skinhead in the U.K.] wants only to drink, go out with 'sorts', another word for girls, perhaps take pep pills or marijuana. **1972** A. Draper *Death Penalty* ii. 13 Ben..drove..to pick up Jeannie—his 'sort' or 'gimpy'. For that was how he described his girl friend.

12. b. *all-sorts*, as *sb.*: see *all E. 13.

sort (sǫɹt), *sb.*[4] *Computers.* [f. Sort *v.*[1] II.]

a. The action of arranging items of data in a prescribed sequence.

1956 *Jrnl. Assoc. Computing Machinery* III. 156 Seven passes will effect a complete sort but an eighth pass will be required to collect the items back on to one reel of tape. **1964** C. Dent *Quantity Surveying by Computer* vi. 79 The effect of this sort..will be to arrange the narrative items under their proper headings. **1973** *Computers & Humanities* VII. 202 We decided to remove the umlauts before performing the sort.

b. Special Comb.: **sort key**, a characteristic feature of items of data according to which the data may be arranged; **sort program,** a program written to perform a sort; **sort routine,** a routine written to perform a sort.

1967 D. G Hays *Introd. Computational Linguistics* x. 171 The sort has brought together all the contextual spans with a common sort key. Print the first sort key in some obvious place... Then begin printing the contextual spans with that sort key, one after another. **1969** *Computers & Humanities* III. 137 Each letter group, plus the word from which it was derived and the frequency of occurrence of that word..is then sorted in alphabetical order using the letter group as the first sortkey and the position of the first letter of each group.. as the second sortkey. **1963** *Communications Assoc. Computing Machinery* VI. 266/2 The tape merging program initially determines an optimum number of merge passes for merging the sorted files produced by the sort program. **1973** *Computers & Humanities* VII. 203 The IBM sort program..handled eight fields of character or numerical data. **1964** C. Dent *Quantity Surveying by Computer* vi. 79 If we rearrange the keyword so that the trade and heading numbers occupy the most significant position, a standard sort routine with four decks will sort the blocks into the order specified by the trade number plus the heading number. **1969** *Computers & Humanities* III. 137 The letter concordance program accepts the keyword output of the concordance program and generates sort records. These are then sorted by a standard sort routine.

sort, *v.*[1] Add: **II. 11. e.** To reprimand (a person); to deal with (a person) by means of force, repression, etc. *colloq.*

1941 Baker *Dict. Austral. Slang* 69 *Sort someone out, to,* to reprove a person, put him in his place. **1943** Hunt & Pringle *Service Slang* 61 To pick a quarrel and use force is to 'sort out' someone. **1958** J. Blackburn *Scent of New-Mown Hay* ii. 24 Get this fellow Kirk sorted out and don't overdo it. **1965** P. Arrowsmith *Jericho* ix. 92 Let's all go down and sort out that peace pickets' camp. **1974** *Times* 25 Feb. 10/7 Richards came in to sort Willis out and, although Willis prevailed in the end, it was not before Richards had hit him several times for four.

f. To separate out and resolve the complexities of (a problem); to clear up (a confusion or difficulty); to put to rights, deal with. Also, with a person as object: to solve the problems of (someone), 'put (him) straight'. Also *refl.*

1948 'N. Shute' *No Highway* v. 128 Will you see if you can get that one sorted out? **1954** J. Masters *Bhowani Junction* vi. 51 If I send a message, sort it out between Macaulay and that depilated Sikh assistant of Taylor's. **1962** *Woman's Own* 15 Sept. 69/2 Perhaps you haven't yet decided, assuming this is something which will sort itself out when the time comes. **1963** [see *favour *sb.* 2 b]. **1963** A. Ross *Australia 63* 17 The two Perth matches ..allow the visiting side to sort themselves out. **1973** M. Amis *Rachel Papers* 46 No, don't tell me she's the very girl to show me what egotistical folly it is to compartmentalize people in this sad way; don't tell me she's going to sort me out, take me on, supply the *cognitio* and comic resolution.

12. a. (Later example, of a thing.)

1925 E. F. Norton *Fight for Everest, 1924* 51 Nearly 300 yak-loads of provision boxes, rolls of bedding and stores of all sorts, dumped higgledy-piggledy off the yaks, began to sort themselves into orderly lines and piles.

16. a. For *Sc.* and *north.* read orig. and chiefly *Sc.* and *north.* and add later examples (corresponding in meaning to sense *11 f).

1950 'D. Divine' *King of Fassarai* x. 82 Take her along to Sergeant Marker. Let him sort it. **1975** M. Bradbury *History Man* xiii. 220 'Tomorrow will sort itself, Barbara,' says Felicity, 'you'll manage.' **1976** L. Henderson *Major Enquiry* ix. 57 They're the boys to get it sorted, all young, keen, and raring to go.

sorta, sorter (sǭ·ɹtə), repr. a colloq. pronunc. of the phr. *sort of* (see Sort *sb.*[2] 6, 8).

Formerly also *sort a, sort o'*.

1790, etc. [see Sort *sb.*[2] 8 c]. **1853** [see *jack-leg, jackleg *a.* and *sb.*]. **1898** J. D. Brayshaw *Slum Silhouettes* 1 Bloomfiel'—never yeard the nime. Wot sorter covey? **1952** B. Malamud *Natural* 126, I hoped she would straighten him out and sorta hold him in the team. **1967** E. & M. A. Radford *No Reason for Murder* xvii. 115 'He ain't a'goin' to come to life agin, guv'nor.'..'I dunno... Mebbe he might—in a sorta way.' **1978** J. Wainwright *Jury People* xxxv. 106 A funny sorta bloody joke. **1981** H. R. F. Keating *Go West, Inspector Ghote* vii. 85 Come on in here. We got some sorta kook.

sortable, *a.* Restrict *Obs.* exc. *dial.* to senses in Dict. and add: **4.** Capable of being sorted or arranged.

1972 *Computers & Humanities* VI. 188 *Description*: Creates sortable tape from card or card-image input, sorts tape, adds..other information to sorted tape.

sortal, *a.* Delete † *Obs.*$^{-1}$ and add later examples. Also as *sb.*

1959 P. F. Strawson *Individuals* v. 168, I shall draw a rough distinction..between two kinds of non-relational tie which bind particulars and universals. This is the distinction between *sortal* and *characterizing* universals. **1975** *Times Lit. Suppl.* 28 Feb. 215/3 The orthodox Fregean and Russellian view that the sortals 'man', 'woman', 'cat' are predicables and not names. **1980** D. Wiggins *Sameness & Substance* 7 Any predicate whose extension consists..of all the particular things or substances of one particular kind, say horses, or sheep, or pruning knives, will be called here a sortal predicate.

sorted, *ppl. a.* Add: **2.** Also *sorted-out.*

1927 Haldane & Huxley *Animal Biol.* ii. 64 Each sorted-out pack will be complete in having one card of each kind.

3. *Physical Geogr.* Said of shapes and other features displayed on patterned ground, where the stones forming the patterns are distributed in a way suggesting their having been sorted according to size.

1950 A. L. Washburn in *Rev. Canad. de Géogr.* IV. 9 In order to standardize the terminology for the purpose of this paper, the broad classification of patterned ground indicated below has been adopted... Patterns on horizontal ground. Sorted circles. Sorted polygons... Patterns on sloping ground. Sorted stripes. *Ibid.* 13 The stones of sorted stripes range in size from gravel in the narrow stripes to boulders in the largest ones. **1956** —— in *Bull. Geol. Soc. Amer.* LXVII. 830/1 A sorted net is patterned ground whose mesh is intermediate between that of a sorted circle and a sorted polygon and has a sorted appearance commonly due to a border of stones surrounding finer material. **1968** R. W. Fairbridge *Encycl. Geomorphol.* 374/2 In contrast to circles, sorted polygons.. apparently never develop singly. **1977** A. Hallam *Planet Earth* 89 The forces generated by freezing and thawing tend to segregate particles of different grain size in the soil to produce sorted polygons, whose margins are outlined by the coarser soil fragments.

sorter. Add: **3.** A machine that can sort punched cards into a prescribed order by means of a code punched on selected columns of the cards.

1917 L. R. Dicksee *Office Machinery* ii. 16 Beyond all question, the most notable..Sorting Machine is the Hollerith Sorter. **1940** W. J. Eckert *Punched Card Methods Sci. Computation* 10 The sorter automatically sorts the cards into groups according to the information punched in any chosen column of the cards. The cards to be sorted are placed in the hopper..and the sorted cards fall into the various receptacles. **1949** [see *interpreter 5 a]. **1956** G. A. Montgomerie *Digital Calculating Machines* viii. 146 The second basic piece of equipment is the sorter... A pack of punched cards can be fed into this machine and each card will be automatically examined in turn. **1970** O. Dopping *Computers & Data Processing* iv. 68 If a deck of cards is to be ordered according to a multi-digit number..by means of a sorter, it is necessary to let the cards pass through the sorter as many times as the number field has digits.

‖ **sortes** (sǭ·ɹtīz, sǭ·ɹtēⁱz), *sb. pl.* [L., pl. of *sors* lot, chance.] In phrases *sortes Virgilianae, Homericae, Biblicae*: divination, or the seeking of guidance, by chance selection of a passage in Virgil, Homer, or the Bible. Also *ellipt.* and *transf.*

a **1586** Sidney *Apol. Poet.* (1595) sig. B4, Whereupon grew the worde of *Sortes Virgilianæ*, when by suddaine opening *Virgils* booke, they lighted vpon any verse of hys making. **1646** T. Browne *Pseud. Ep.* v. xxi. 272 The first an imitation of *sortes Homericæ*, or *Virgilianæ*, drawing determinations from verses casually occurring. **1700** J. Welwood *Memoirs* 100 Lord Falkland, to divert the king, would have his Majesty make a trial of his fortune by the *Sortes Virgilianæ*, which..was an usual kind of augury some ages past. **1740** H. Walpole *Let.* 25 Sept. (1974) XXXVII. 79 In three words I will give you her picture as we drew it in the *Sortes Virgilianæ*—Insanam vatem aspicies. I give you my honour, we did not choose it. **1801** M. Edgeworth *Belinda* II. xiii. 25 Several volumes of French plays and novels were lying there, and Clarence Hervey raking up one of them, cried: 'Come, let us try our fate by the sortes Virgilianæ.' **1845** G. E. Jewsbury in A. Ireland *Sel. Lett. G. E. Jewsbury to J. Welsh Carlyle* (1892) 179, I send it you by way of a 'sortes', and the Bible has as much virtue—that way—as Virgil! **1886** D. C. Murray *Cynic Fortune* xv. 183 In the practice of the *sortes* (which was a favourite occupation of his) [he] was elevated or depressed by the text he fell upon. **1897** A. C. Benson *Diary* June in D. Newsome *On Edge of Paradise* (1980) ii. 63, I took a Sortes Biblicae before refusing. **1947** H. Nicolson *Diary* 11 Dec. (1968) 118, I consult *sortes Biblicas.* My Bible opens at Ezekiel XL 22. **1969** G. Greene *Travels with my Aunt* I. xvi. 170 The Sortes Virgilianae—a game my mother considered a little blasphemous unless it was played with the Bible. **1975** V. Canning *Kingsford Mark* vi. 105 He acknowledged the encouragement of the *sortes.* All the omens were right.

sortie, *sb.* Delete ‖ and add: **2. a.** (Earlier example.)

1778 H. Walpole *Let.* 8 Oct. (1967) XXIV. 413 Before their last *sortie*, one heard nothing but *What news of the fleets?*

d. An operational flight by a military aircraft.

1918 B. Hall *En l'Air* viii. 76 My machine was a single-seated Nieuport biplane... I carried 1,000 rounds of ammunition... An air sortie at dawn! **1941** *Hutchinson's Pictorial Hist. War* 19 Mar.–13 May 64/2 The main target of the R.A.F.'s night sorties is the industrial centre of Emden. **1955** *Times* 29 June 10/3 In the five active days of the test the two sides flew 12,347 sorties and simulated the dropping of over 300 atomic bombs. **1969** G. Macbeth *War Quartet* 37 Then Waking..we were up.. for New sorties. **1977** *R.A.F. News* 27 Apr.–10 May 11/3 The Phantom has an average sortie capability of more than 1½ hours.

e. *Photogr.* A series of aerial photographs taken during one flight; *transf.*, a photographic session. Also *attrib.*

1953 R. J. C. Atkinson *Field Archaeology* (ed. 2) i. 24 The unit of classification of prints is the *sortie*, that is, a series of prints taken on a single flight. Each sortie consists of one or more strips of prints, running approximately in an East–West direction, each print overlapping the next to East and West by about two-thirds of its width. *Ibid.*, Each print..is labelled at the top with the sortie-number. *Ibid.* 25 Sortie plots may be bought separately at the same charge per plot. **1959** N. Mailer *Advts. for Myself* (1961) 229 One sortie when she was photographed sipping a soda she shaped the second straw into a heart. **1963** W. K. Kilford *Elem. Air Survey* x. 226 When the sortie is complete the film is processed... The relative position of each photograph.. of the sortie is plotted. **1969** G. C. Dickinson *Maps & Air Photographs* xv. 246 A set of photographs taken during one flight is usually known as a *sortie*. *Ibid.* 247 More detailed information about coverage is contained on index diagrams, known as sortie plots.

3. b. (Earlier example.)

1809 D. Thompson *Jrnl.* 18 Aug. (1950) II. 31 The Sortie of the [stream] that falls into the [stream] at Deer's Horns Plains.

4. *attrib.* in *Astronautics*, designating spacecraft designed to return to earth after a period; so *sortie mission.*

1972 *National Observer* (U.S.) 27 May 6/4 NASA also plans a 'sortie module', a laboratory for six scientists and engineers that would be carried in the orbiter's cargo bay for earth-orbit missions lasting from one to four weeks. **1972** *New Scientist* 6 July 3 NASA has offered Europe the 'sortie can'—a pressurised laboratory module that is to swing out from the cargo bay of the orbiting shuttle. **1973** *Times* 15 June 27/7 Here the proposal is that Europe would develop a 'sortie lab' or 'spacelab' module. **1976** Lohman & Lee in L. G. Napolitano *Space Activity Impact on Sci. & Technol.* 108 In a series of flights, these aircraft duplicate the observations which would be conducted in a single sortie mission.

‖ **sortie de bal** (sort*i* də bal). [Fr., lit. 'departure from (the) ball'.] A woman's evening cloak with a quilted lining, popular in the late nineteenth century.

1864 M. B. Chesnut *Diary* 29 Dec. in C. V. Woodward *M. Chesnut's Civil War* (1981) xxxix. 696 Mary was wrapped in a snowy swansdown *sortie de bal.* **1895** [see *dove *sb.* 1 d]. **1908** A. Bennett *Old Wives' Tale* III. ii. 296 It was a tall and mature woman who wore over a dress of purplish-black silk a vast flowing *sortie de bal* of vermilion velvet, looped and tasselled with gold.

sorting, *vbl. sb.* Add: **4. a.** *sorting-out operation, process*; **sorting code** *Banking*, a code number which identifies a branch office in the banking system, and is used to facilitate the processing of cheques and credit transfers.

1959 D. S. Travers in *Electronics in Banking* (Institute of Bankers) 50 The cheque of the future... The code appears in five blocks... Block 2—Bank and branch sorting code. **1965** Perry & Ryder *Thomson's Dict. Banking* (ed. 11) 524/2 *Sorting code numbers*, a system devised to assist customers of banks who make considerable use of the Credit Transfer system... The number is placed in the box provided on the credit by the customer before passing the credit to the bank. It consists of three groups of two figures each, eg. 20-03-92, the first digits denoting the bank, and the remainder identifying the branch. **1977** *Canad. Jrnl. Linguistics 1976* XXI. II. 149 In (44) the criterion of the sorting-out operation is P_1. **1960** E. H. Gombrich *Art & Illusion* II. iv. 144 Classical art also underwent an evolution, a sorting-out process after its heroic period.

b. *sorting table*; with *adv.*, as *sorting-out centre.*

1952 S. Spender *Learning Laughter* vii. 97 The reader should be able to visualize them going to the sorting-out centre near Haifa. **1881** A. BATHGATE *Waitaruna* xii. 172 The 'pickers-up' were busy gathering the fleeces..and carrying them to the sorting table.

sort-out. [f. vbl. phr. *to sort out*: see SORT *v.*[1] II in Dict. and Suppl.] **a.** The action or an instance of sorting out (of things or situations that are in disarray). **b.** A fight or dispute.

1937 PARTRIDGE *Dict. Slang* 802/1 *Sort-out*, a fight, a mellay. **1961** *John o' London's* 25 May 591/2 An enlightened attempt at a black-and-white sort-out. **1964** C. WILLOCK *Enormous Zoo* i. 14 Beaton himself had a sort-out with a buffalo bull that tried to overturn his Land-Rover. **1972** *Tel.* (Brisbane) 18 May 18/4 He was the most cantankerous character I have met. I had only been here two days when we had our first sort-out. **1981** G. HAMMOND *Revenge Game* vii. 65 You folk finish the first sort-out downstairs.

S.O.S. (eːs,ōᵘ,eˑs), *sb.* Also **SOS.** [The letters *s*, *o* and *s*, chosen because easily transmitted in Morse code.] **1. a.** The international wireless code-signal of extreme distress, used esp. by ships at sea.

1910 J. A. FLEMING *Princ. Electr. Wave Telegr. & Teleph.* (ed. 2) 882 This signal, S,O,S, has superseded the Marconi Company's original high sea cry for help, which was C,Q,D. **1910** E. LAWTON *Boy Aviators in Nicaragua* 263 S.O.S. is now the wireless distress call. **1924** *Mod. Wireless* III. 310/3 The famous signal 'SOS' was adopted officially by the International Radio Telegraph Convention in July, 1908. **1930** 'SAPPER' *Finger of Fate* 245 The S.O.S. had been picked up by three other boats... The last S.O.S. had broken off abruptly in the middle of the message. **1942** [see *DASH *sb.*[1] 7 f].

b. *transf.* An urgent message or appeal for help.

1918 *Punch* 13 Mar. 176 S.O.S. at Suburban Pictures. (In cases of emergency affecting any of the audience messages are sometimes thrown on the screen by the courtesy of the management.) **1931** E. F. BENSON *Mapp & Lucia* iii. 80 There was nothing but helpful sunny cordiality in response to this S.O.S. **1965** D. FRANCIS *Odds Against* xix. 235 You'd sent him to me as a sort of S.O.S.

2. As an abbrev. of var. jocular phrases. **a.** 'same old story, stuff', etc. **b.** 'shit on a shingle': chipped beef on toast. *U.S. Mil. slang.*

1918 *Sat. Even. Post* 27 Apr. 62 'What have you got this morning, Thompson? SOS?' 'Yes sir,' returned the striker. 'Same old slum.' **1926** MAINES & GRANT *Wise-Crack Dict.* 14/2 *S.O.S.*, same old story. **1959** I. & P. OPIE *Lore & Lang. Schoolch.* ix. 162 The possessors of young and healthy appetites are lyrical about their food. School dinners are 'muck', 'pig swill'..'S.O.S.' (Same Old Slush). **1963** *Amer. Speech* XXXVII. 271 Haskell students do employ the standard American slang initials *S.O.S.*, but..Girls use them to mean 'same old stuff'... Boys..refer more specifically to creamed beef on toast.. and this abbreviation stands for either 'same old shit' or 'shit on a shingle'. **1974** *News & Observer* (Raleigh, N. Carolina) 8 July 23/2 The troops still sometimes get S.O.S. for breakfast, whether they want it or not.

3. *attrib.* and *Comb.*, as *S.O.S. call, message, signal*; **S.O.S. redouble** *Bridge* (see quot. 1926[2]); also *ellipt.*

1915 *Daily Mail* 10 May 4/5 The Marconi operators showed magnificent coolness in that hour of trial. They made the 'S.O.S.' call, and they had to make it quickly. **1938** *Encycl. Brit. Bk. of Year* 122/1 S.O.S. and police messages broadcast from all transmitters during the year reached a total of 1,213. **1978** J. THOMSON *Question of Identity* vii. 70 I'd've heard if he was dead... They'd've put it on the radio; an S.O.S. message. **1926** M. C. WORK *Auction Bridge Compl.* x. 134 The No Trumper resorts to a recently invented signal of acute distress and makes the 'S.O.S. Redouble'. *Ibid.* 498 *S.O.S.* (*redouble*), redouble made to indicate weakness rather than strength. **1939** N. DE V. HART *Bridge Players' Bedside Bk.* 135 If the strong opening No Trumps..is being played, a redouble by a player who has opened with One No-Trump is not an SOS. **1967** R. L. FREY *Bridge Players' Encycl.* 470/2 In rare circumstances a player may redouble his partner's bid as an SOS instead of his own bid. **1977** C. H. GOREN *Bridge Compl.* (ed. 3) 684 *Redouble*, a call that further increases the scoring value of tricks and penalties after an opposing double; sometimes also used as a request for partner to rescue (S.O.S. redouble). **1917** 'SAPPER' *No Man's Land* 71 A row of grey-painted rockets with a red top, which in case of emergency send up the coloured flares that give the S.O.S. signals to those behind. **1927** H. A. VACHELL *Dew of Sea* 257 He received a letter from the gentleman, regarded (and rightly) by the McCullough as an S.O.S. signal. **1929** C. H. SMITH *Bridge of Life* iv. 83 When one gave an SOS signal all the rest came to his assistance.

S.O.S., *v.* Also **SOS.** [f. prec.] **1.** *intr.* **a.** To make an S.O.S. signal or signals. **b.** *Bridge.* To execute an S.O.S. redouble.

1918 KIPLING *Land & Sea Tales* (1923) 114 Then..this Baxter-man got busy with his wireless and SOS'ed like winkie. **1926** M. C. WORK *Auction Bridge Compl.* x. 135 In the event of a business pass, the No Trumper can S.O.S. if in need of help. **1975** G. HOWELL *In Vogue* 75/1 We have been passing through the awkward age, when instead of conversing we 'S.O.S.ed' in monosyllabic slang.

2. *trans.* To send an urgent message requesting (someone) *to* do something.

a **1936** KIPLING *Something of Myself* (1937) viii. 221 One of the Captains S.O.S.-ed me to give him 'something to tell these somethinged tourists about it'.

so's: see *'s 5.

‖ **sosatie** (sǫsāˑti). *S. Afr.* Also **sas(s)atie, sas(s)atje, sosaartje,** etc. [Afrikaans, f. S. Afr. Du. *sasaatje*, f. Mal. (Javanese) *sesate* skewered meat.] Curried or spiced meat grilled on a skewer.

1833 *Cape Good Hope Lit. Gaz.* 2 Sept. 138 (Pettman), *Sasaitie*, or cabobs, is really no despicable eating. **1870** *Cape Monthly Mag.* Oct. 224 '*Sosaartjes*', '*smoor-picklaar*', and all sorts of vegetable '*breedies*', are importations from India. **1883** 'R. IRON' *Story Afr. Farm* II. ii. iv. 67, I got the Hottentot girl to show me how to make 'sar-sarties' this morning. **1885** L. H. MEURANT *Sixty Years Ago* 29 There existed in those days what we termed 'Sasaatje and Rice' houses, places where a favourite Dutch dish called 'Sasaatjes' was served in the evenings...two sassaatjes (diamond-shaped inch-sized pieces of mutton, curried and about half a dozen stuck upon a bamboo skewer, and then roasted upon a gridiron). **1894** *Cape Argus* 22 Dec. (Pettman), A Hittite..with a long spear and a very pronounced intention to spit you on it, like a sassatje. *a* **1920** [see *BOBOTIE]. **1939** S. CLOETE *Watch for Dawn* xxi. 310 A woman had so much to do with food. Sassaties, bobotee, snysels. **1948** H. V. MORTON *In Search of S. Afr.* 293 Sosaties..are a popular and delicious grill which can be as simple as veal or mutton cutlets sprinkled with curry powder and roasted on a skewer over a clear wood fire, or as complex as pieces of mutton or pork soaked in wine or vinegar, spiced with coriander, turmeric, pepper, tamarind and grilled in the same way. **1953** *Cape Times* 21 Mar. 3/3 These [South African recipes] are destined for Holland, where they will be needed to prepare *braaivleis* and *sasaties* when the South African *volkspele* team visits Culemborg and holds a *braaivleisaand* there. **1973** *Farmer's Weekly* (S. Afr.) 25 Apr., At a braaivleis the sosaties are eaten straight from the grill.

‖ **soshi** (sōᵘˑʃi). Pl. **soshi.** [Jap., lit. 'strong man', a Chinese *suǒshì*, f. *suǒ* lusty, valiant + *shì* warrior.] A mercenary political agitator or intimidator, a terrorist; a bodyguard.

1891 B. H. CHAMBERLAIN *Things Japanese* (ed. 2) 128 Since 1888, there has sprung up a class of rowdy youths, called *soshi* in Japanese—juvenile agitators who have taken all politics to be their province. **1894** G. N. CURZON *Probl. Far East* ii. 33 The *soshi* or professional rowdies, who are ready, for a consideration, to let out their services to either party in Japan. **1896** L. HEARN *Kokoro* vi. 95 Soshi form one of the modern curses of Japan. They are mostly ex-students who earn a living by hiring themselves out as rowdy terrorists. **1910** LADY LAWSON *Highways & Homes of Japan* xxv. 284 At one time this extraordinary man was a *soshi* or political bully, one of the turbulent class who suffer from too much education and too little to eat. **1930** M. D. KENNEDY *Changing Fabric of Japan* vii. 121 In 1923, meetings in favour of Manhood Suffrage were broken up by gangs of *soshi*. **1977** G. M. BERGER *Parties out of Power in Japan 1931–1941* iv. 147 Nakamizo Tamakichi, a former seiyūkai bodyguard (*sōshi*), organized a group of several hundred toughs.

so-soish, *a.* (Earlier examples.)

1819 KEATS *Let.* 15 *Apr.* (1931) II. 353 Do you and the miss Birkbecks get groggy on any thing—a little so so ish so as to be obliged to be seen home with a Lantern[?]. **1826** M. WILMOT *Let.* 13 Jan. (1935) 231 Major F[alconer] goes on so, so, ish, and poor dear Bessy out of spirits.

soss, *v.*[1] **2.** (Later *poet.* example.)

1951 AUDEN *Nones* (1952) 39 The three wise Maries come, Sossing through seamless waters.

sostenuto, *a.* and *sb.* Add: **A.** *adj.* **1.** (Later examples.)

1955 *Times* 27 July 5/6 Mr. Thomas Matthews, the soloist,..missed some of its finest effects, chiefly because he under-emphasized its sostenuto spaciousness. **1976** *Gramophone* Sept. 410/1 The *sostenuto* opening and eager staccato continuation are both beautifully judged.

2. (Earlier example.)

1826 M. KELLY *Reminisc.* I. 114 He had been the first cantabile singer of his time, and his sostenuto singing was still admirable.

B. *sb.* Delete *rare*[−1] and add later examples. Also *fig.*

1933 N. DOUGLAS *Looking Back* II. 460 It was September, that wonderful month when the melodies of summer linger on..in a tranquil *sostenuto*. **1934** C. LAMBERT *Music Ho!* v. 309 His [*sc.* Sibelius's] use of the brass is sparing, concentrating far more on its sostenuto than on its percussive qualities. **1943** D. GASCOYNE *Poems 1937–42* 14 The heart's receptive chalice in pure hands upheld Towards the sostenuto of the sky.

sot, *sb.*[1] **3. sot-weed**: for † read *Obs.* exc. *Hist.* and add earlier and later examples.

1698 E. WARD *London Spy* I. 9 We had each of us Stuck in our Mouths a lighted Pipe of Sotweed. **1708** E. COOK (*title*) The sot-weed factor; or, a voyage to Maryland. **1961** J. BARTH (*title*) The sot-weed factor. **1965** E. TUNIS *Colonial Craftsmen* iii. 52 Early Americans not only grew a lot of 'sot weed' they also consumed a lot of it.

sotalol (sōᵘˑtălǫl). *Pharm.* [Etym. unkn.: see -OL.] The compound, $CH_3.NH(SO_2).C_6H_4.CH(OH).CH_2.NH.CH(CH_3)_2$, a beta-adrenergic blocking agent used (in the form of its hydrochloride) in the treatment of cardiac arrhythmias.

1968 *Jrnl. Pharmacol. & Exper. Therapeutics* CLX. 231 The antiinflammatory action of morphine is reversed by nalorphine but not by a *beta* adrenergic blocking agent, sotalol (MJ 1999; 4-(2-isopropylamino-1-hydroxylethyl)-methanesulphonalinide hydrochloride). **1974** R. G. SHANKS et al. in A. G. Snart *Adv. in Beta-Adrenergic Blocking Therapy—Sotalol* I. 24 Sotalol is the only drug which blocks all adrenergic β-receptors and has no membrane stabilizing activity or intrinsic sympathomimetic activity. **1978** *Nature* 19 Oct. 596/2 In contrast, β-adrenergic antagonists lacking the hydrophobicity of propranolol, such as atenolol, practolol and sotalol, are not able to induce meiosis.

sotch (sǫtʃ). *Physical Geogr.* Pl. **sotchs, sotches.** [Fr. dialectal word of pre-Latin origin (Robert).] A doline, esp. one in the Causses region of France.

1910 H. R. MILL *Dict. Geogr. Terms* in L. D. Stamp *Gloss. Geogr. Terms* (1961) 426/2 *Sotch*, dolines (*q.v.*) (Causses, France). The term 'cloup' is used in Aquitaine. **1922** *Geol. Mag.* LIX. 394 The only fertile and habitable regions on these barren plateaus are the 'sotches' or hollows, where the red earth formed by the denudation of the limestone is preserved in large funnel-shaped hollows. **1937** *Georgr. Jrnl.* LXXXIX 63 A detailed study of the karst landscape, showing the important part played by the dolinas or 'sotchs' in the dissection of the surface. **1972** M. M. SWEETING *Karst Landforms* iv. 48/2 The sotchs are both circular and elongated, their diameters and depths variable and their topographic situations diverse.

Sotho (sūˑtu). Also **Suthu, Suto,** etc. [Native name.] **A.** *sb.* A subdivision of the Bantu people which includes the Basuto and various other tribes chiefly found in Botswana and the Transvaal; also, the languages spoken by these people. **B.** *adj.* Of or pertaining to this group of peoples or their languages. Cf. *SESOTHO.

1928 G. P. LESTRADE *Bantu Tribes S. Afr.* I. i. 14 There has..been..intermarriage between the Bavenda and the Basotho (there was a Sotho invasion of Bavendaland). **1928** *Africa* I. 481 In reality there are two main branches of this group, Chwana spoken in Bechwanaland and the Western Transvaal, and Suto with its main dialects. **1929** [see *NGUNI *sb.* and *a.*]. **1936** [see *hill-culture* s.v. *HILL *sb.* 4 d]. **1948** M. GUTHRIE *Classification Bantu Lang.* iv. 69 These radicals from Suthu. **1957** C. G. SELIGMAN *Races Afr.* (ed. 2) viii. 120 The Sotho..includes the Southern Sotho of Lesotho..the Tswana..of Botswana and western Transvaal, and the Northern Sotho..of central and northern Transvaal. **1977** *Times* 7 Sept. 7/4 [The South African] Secretary for Information..gives the population..as..whites,..Coloureds,..Indians,..Zulus, ..Xhosas,..Tswanas,..North Sothos,..South Sothos, [etc.]. **1979** *Listener* 25 Oct. 545/1 The text Modimo o Lerabu—'God is Love' in the Sotho language. Both Zulu and Sotho are used in the worship.

‖ **Soto** (sōᵘˑtōᵘ). [Jap.] One of the three sects of Zen Buddhism. Freq. *attrib.*

1893 S. KURODA *Outlines Mahâyâna* vi. 24 Dôgen introduced the Sôtô sect, 2176 after Buddha, or 1227 A.D. **1894** *Trans. Asiatic Soc. Japan* XXII. 430 The Zen sects.. are divided..into three divisions. The *Rinzai*..from 1168 A.D., the *Sōtō* from 1223 A.D. and the *Obaku* from 1650 A.D. **1917** A. K. REISCHAUER *Stud. in Japanese Buddhism* iii. 117 The chief difference between the Soto and the Rinzai branches of the Zen Sect is that the former puts more weight upon book learning as a subsidiary aid to silent meditation. **1949** C. HUMPHREYS *Zen Buddhism* v. 91 It is in Japan that Zen can best be studied, and although there are three sects of Zen, the Rinzai, Soto and Obaku, there is little difference between them. **1977** 'E. V. CUNNINGHAM' *Case of One-Penny Orange* (1978) iii. 29, I am Zen. The Soto School.

sotol (soˑtol). [Amer. Sp., f. Nahuatl *tzotolli*.] A plant of dry regions belonging to the genus *Dasylirion* of the family Agavaceæ, native to south-western North America and bearing linear leaves and small white flowers; also, the fibre from the leaves of this plant or the beverage made from the sap.

1881 *Amer. Naturalist* XV. 874 The home of the sotol is Western Texas, Southern New Mexico and Northern Chihuahua. **1908** D. T. MCDOUGAL *Bot. Features N. Amer. Deserts* 9 This is the typical sotol region. **1942** CASTETTER & BELL *Pima & Papago Agric.* 213 The mature leaves were dried by the Papago in the sun on a sotol mat. **1964** F. O'ROURKE *Mule for Marquesa* 72 The scorched grey of candelilla and guayule, Spanish daggers, sotol with the crowns burned a dirty white by sun and wind. **1976** *Hortus Third* (L. H. Bailey Hortorium) 364/1 An alcoholic beverage, sotol, is extracted from the trunks. **1976** F. A. & D. L. LATORRE *Mexican Kickapoo Indians* iii. 44 Two benches..are built and covered with dyed sotol or cattail mats. *Ibid.* v. 64 The favored material used today for basketmaking is sotol.

sotter, *v.* Add: **b.** To bubble. Also *poet.*

1834 J. GALT *Lit. Life* III. 51 The blood was sottering out of his shoe mouth. **1886** W. S. MCINTOSH in D. H. Edwards *Mod. Sc. Poets* IX. 70 This wee burnie sae sottered an' sang. **1951** AUDEN *Nones* (1952) 64 The sharp streams and sottering springs of A commuter's wish.

sottise. Add: (Later examples.) Also *transf.*

1952 J. BIGGS-DAVISON *Tory Lives* ii. 48 Tact and flexibility were not often exhibited by the Monarch of whose *sottise* his predecessor was wont to speak. **1963** N. MACRAE *Sunshades in October* iii. 39 The Conservative Government..dismantled two-and-a-half of these three *sottises*. **1977** *Times* 23 Mar. 16/8 The *Daily Mail* Diary.. is not slow to criticize errors and *sottises* in rival newspapers.

‖ **sottisier** (sotīzye). [Fr.] A collection of *sottises*; esp. a list of written stupidities. Also *transf.* and *fig.*

1929 E. POUND *Let.* 1 Feb. (1971) 224 The simplest and briefest form of attack is by a sottisier... Make your sottisier from *Poetry* and the main literary reviews, Sunday supplements, etc. **1944** *Horizon* Sept. 187 Nor is it [sc. *Finnegans Wake*] a mere *sottisier*. **1959** *Observer* 30 Aug. 13/7 A cast-iron certainty for the September *Sottisier* Stakes. **1969** J. GROSS *Rise & Fall of Man of Letters* ix. 238 It would be easy to compile a fair-sized sottisier of such remarks, but not very amusing. **1976** *Times Lit. Suppl.* 26 Mar. 345/5 The sloppy editing and the *sottisier* of an index, with its general confusion of names, styles, titles and sexes. **1978** *Times* 22 Mar. 11/8 Ginger Rogers..under-rehearsed commentary is a *sottisier* of all the awful things Americans are supposed to say.

soubrette. Add: **1.** (Later examples.) In extended use, a woman playing a role or roles in light entertainment, e.g. on television or at a seaside variety show, with implications of pertness, coquetry, intrigue, etc.

1905 R. BEACH *Pardners* (1912) i. 33 Variety house, with..two-ton soubrettes, with Barrios diamonds and hand-painted socks. **1951** *Sunday Pictorial* 21 Jan. 6/3 Harriet Cohen has the vivacity and femininity of a soubrette. **1956** *Ann. Reg. 1955* 360 Adele Leigh scored a special success in the soubrette part of Bella. **1958** *Time* 8 Oct. 6/3 His 'wife', Miss Rosita Segovia, takes too soubrette-like a view of this role. **1977** *Listener* 27 Jan. 111/1 By the time she was 18, she was a soubrette at the Gaiety. **1978** *TV Times* 28 Jan.–3 Feb. 26/2 Television's most resilient soubrette, Una Stubbs, can talk about love, marriage and happiness with a twinkle in her eye.

soubrettish *a.* (later example).

1979 J. CROSBY *Party of Year* (1980) xiv. 156 The soubrettish face darkened.

soucar: see also *SAHUKAR (now the more usual spelling).

Soudan. Add: Also = SOUDANESE *sb.* and *a.*

1867 'OUIDA' *Under Two Flags* I. xiii. 297 Chasseurs, Zouaves..mingled with jet-black Soudans. **1889** W. F. BUTLER *Charles George Gordon* iii. 58 Some of his old Soudan soldiers.

Soudanese *a.* (earlier example).

1884 E. W. HAMILTON *Diary* 13 May (1972) II. 615 In the House of Commons yesterday there was an abnormal display of excitement..on the occasion of the Soudanese or Gordonese vote of censure moved by Sir M. H. Beach.

soufflé, *sb.* and *a.* Add: **A.** *sb.* **a.** (Earlier and later *fig.* examples.)

1888 [in Dict., sense b]. **1916** E. POUND *Let.* 27 July (1971) 89 Sometime, certainly, you must have the soufflé of contemporary French poets. **1964** *New Statesman* 1 May 675/3 A girl, her yellow hair in a sort of lacquered soufflé, ran from the police court, crying black tears from the cosmetics of her child's eyes. **1980** T. MORGAN *Somerset Maugham* viii. 202 [The play] *Caroline* was a soufflé whipped up..out of boredom.

b. (Earlier example.)

1845 E. ACTON *Mod. Cookery* xix. 491 A common soufflé-pan may be purchased for four or five shillings.

B. *adj.* (Later example.)

1972 *Trans. Oriental Ceramics Soc.* XXXVIII. 141 The entire vessel covered with *soufflé* gilding.

‖ **souffrante** (sūfrant), *a.* [Fr., fem. sing. pres. pple. of *souffrir* to suffer.] Of women: delicate, indisposed or ill; prone to anxiety or depression.

1827 E. GROSVENOR in G. Huxley *Lady Elizabeth & Grosvenors* (1965) vii. 141 She is a very interesting person, very handsome, but pale and 'souffrante'. **1877** GEO. ELIOT *Let.* 10 July (1956) VI. 392, I have been *souffrante*, but am content to bear my share of such trouble. **1938** A. THIRKELL *Let.* in M. Strickland *A. Thirkell: Portrait of a Lady Novelist* (1977) vii. 120, I have been so *souffrante* this summer with perpetual headaches. **1977** *Times Lit. Suppl.* 28 Jan. 94/4 A tearful, tortured female, forever *souffrante*, forever worried, forever hoarding and cherishing her sufferings.

‖ **souffre-douleur** (sūfr,dūlör). Also **souffre douleur.** [Fr., lit. 'suffer sorrow'.] One who is in a subservient position and must listen to or share another's troubles; also *spec.* a woman who acts as a paid companion to an older woman.

1845 M. GARDINER *Strathern* II. xvii. 17 The woman on whose arm she leans is her *dame de compagnie*, her *souffre douleur*. **1864** C. M. YONGE *Trial* II. iii. 55 A younger brother and legitimate *souffre douleur*. **1907** M. E. BRADDON *Dead Love has Chains* i. 3 She had her maid and her *souffre-douleur*, a dowerless kinswoman of six-and-twenty. **1962** *Punch* 7 Nov. 684/1 Josephine, employed as Aunt March's *souffre-douleur*. **1981** W. GÉRIN *Anne Thackeray Ritchie* xx. 240 When away from home he always wrote regularly to his 'souffre douleur'.

soufrière (sūfriēᵊr). [Fr., f. *soufre* SULPHUR *sb.* + *-ière* -IER.] = SOLFATARA.

1879 J. W. BODDAM-WHETHAM *Roraima & Brit. Guiana* vi. 53 How pleasant it would be to spend a few days on each of these West Indian islands! To visit their *souffrières*, their mountain forests, their wild hills, and their cultivated estates! **1902** *Pop. Sci. Monthly* July 273 The warm springs and solfataras (or souffrieres [*sic*]) on Martinique and other islands displayed unwonted activity. **1939** *Nature* 14 Oct. 677/1 The soufrières of Montserrat are considered as having been caused mainly by the penetration of meteoric water to a subterrain of sulphided limestone that had been reheated intensively by uprising magma. **1972** *Whitaker's Almanack 1973* 786/2 Montserrat..contains three active soufrières and several hot springs.

sougee, var. *SOOGEE.

sough, *v.*[1] **1. b.** (Later example.)

1975 W. MCILVANNEY *Docherty* I. xviii. 124 Trees were brooding presences, soughing incantations. Every bush hid an invisible force, frequently malevolent.

sought, *ppl. a.* Add: **b.** *sought-after* (later examples).

1944 AUDEN *For Time Being* (1945) 32 Her famous, memorable, sought-after evenings. **1978** *Lancashire Life* Apr. 45/2 Foulridge took umbrage,..continuing to build on its [*sc.* Foulridge's] reputation of being a sought-after spot to live.

sougi-mougi, var. *SOOGEE-MOOGEE. **soujge, souji-mouji,** varr. *SOOGEE, *SOOGEE-MOOGEE.

‖ **souk** (sūk). Also **sok, sook, soug, suk(h, suq.** [Fr., ad. Arab. *sūḳ* market-place.] An Arab market or market-place, a bazaar (sense 1 a).

1826 DENHAM & CLAPPERTON *Narr. Trav. N. & Cent. Afr.* II. 51 The soug, or market, is well supplied with every necessary and luxury. **1829** J. L. BURCKHARDT *Trav. Arabia* 54 In a row of eight or ten shops are sold rice, onions, butter, dates, and coffee-beans... This is what the Arabs call a *souk*, or market. **1855** R. F. BURTON *Personal Narr. Pilgrimage to El-Medinah* I. 333 There is a large 'Suk', or market-place in the usual form, a long narrow lane darkened by a covering of palm leaves, with little shops let into the walls of the houses on both sides. **1899** A. E. W. MASON *Miranda of Balcony* ii. 24 Every evening he comes down to the Sôk, buys milk and bread. **1909** G. W. FURLONG *Gateway to Sahara* i. 21 One afternoon, I was passing here from the *Suk*..when a ragged, unkempt fellow appeared in the caravan road there, acting most strangely. **1921** *Glasgow Herald* 20 Oct. 4 The suqs or covered streets, which, being screened from the glare of the sun, afford fine shelter for shops and markets. **1926** D. BYRNE *Brother Saul* v. 64 When Anna went abroad.. to the sook of the perfumers. **1931** *Observer* 6 Sept. 13 The sun-smitten pavement of the *sukh*. **1959** W. THESIGER *Arabian Sands* xiii. 258 Behind the..houses which lined the water-front were the *suqs*, covered passageways, where merchants sat in the gloom, cross-legged in narrow alcoves among their piled merchandise. **1968** R. HARGREAVES *Bloodybacks* iii. 74 The importation of assorted consignments of *filles du roi*, nubile but dowerless wenches willing to marry anyone in a position to provide them with a home... Their distribution was reminiscent of nothing so much as the disposal of Christian slaves in an Oriental *Sok*. **1978** L. HEREN *Growing up on The Times* iii. 91 The assassins escaped into the souks of the city [*sc.* Damascus], and no more was heard of them. **1981** *Financial Times* 12 Dec. 7/2 The lust for gold..grabs most visitors to Sharjah and Dubai, where the gold souks gleam with the stuff.

soul, *sb.* Add: **I. 2. c.** Also in Naut. phr. *soul and body lashing* (see quot. 1962).

1903 C. PROTHEROE *Life in Mercantile Marine* 150 The best method of arranging his oil-skins to keep the water out,..known as a 'soul and body lashing'. **1936** B. ADAMS *Ships & Women* iv. 87 All wore rope yarns tightly tied about wrists and ankles... We call those rope yarns 'soul and body lashings'. **1962** A. G. COURSE *Dict. Naut. Terms* 182 *Soul and body lashings*, rope yarns tied round the waist and sleeves of oilskin jackets, and round the bottom of oilskin trousers, to prevent the water, from seas crashing on board, getting under the oilskins. They also prevented the wind from ballooning up inside the oilskins.

d. *soul and conscience*: in *Sc. Law*, the formula by which medical testimony in writing is authenticated; also *attrib.* (see quot. 1976).

1892 A. M. ANDERSON *Criminal Law of Scotland* v. xiii. 252 Medical reports are made on soul and conscience, read at the trial, and sworn to as true. **1925** W. J. LEWIS *Manual of Law of Evidence in Scotland* III. ii. 84 Medical certificates on soul and conscience, apparently holograph, appear, in non-contentious matters, to be generally accepted without further evidence. **1976** L. KENNEDY *Presumption of Innocence* III. 147 There was a soul and conscience certificate in relation to Mrs Carmichael; this meant that a doctor had sworn on his soul and conscience that she was unfit to attend the court.

3. b. Also in somewhat weakened use, deep feeling, sensitivity.

1823 BYRON *Don Juan* XIV. lxxi. 150 But there was something wanting on the whole—I don't know what, and therefore cannot tell—Which pretty women—the sweet souls!—call *Soul*. **1853** LYTTON *My Novel* III. IX. iii. 22 Oh, no! no picture of miserable, vicious, Parisian life. This is beautiful; there is *soul* here. **1904** F. H. JACKSON *Mural Painting* 21 Benozzo Gozzoli..filled his long life with the production of the most charming wall-paintings, which, if he had had what is often called 'soul', would have placed him very near the summit of the Palace of Art.

3*. a. The emotional or spiritual quality of Black American life and culture, manifested esp. in music (see quot. 1973).

1946 *Ebony* Sept. 34/2 He uses a bewildering, unorthodox technique and his playing is full of what jazzmen refer to as 'soul'. **1954** *Grove's Dict. Mus.* (ed. 5) IV. 600/2 Louis Armstrong declared that 'Anything played with beat and soul is jazz.' **1964** *Amer. Folk Music Occasional* I. 17 It's just really rough what the colored entertainers have to go through sometimes... That's why the colored people sing the blues; that's why they sing with soul. **1973** S. HENDERSON *Understanding New Black Poetry* 74 In the late 1950's the word 'Soul' surfaced in the musical community and quickly spread to the wider Black Community, where it came to mean not only a special kind of popular music..but also..'racial spirit' and 'racial flavor'... The word is losing some of its popularity now.

b. *ellipt.* for *soul music*, see sense 25 below.

1961 [see *FUNK *sb.*[2] 2]. **1968** P. OLIVER *Screening Blues* ii. 46 The distinction between gospel music and the most recent development of blues and rock 'n roll—soul—is one of content rather than style. **1975** *New Yorker* 28 Apr. 6/3 She's lately been branching out from a strict regimen of blues and folk songs..to include some rock, soul, and Nashville-inspired ditties. **1979** *Radio Times* 19 July 60/1 The word 'soul' probably originated with Ray Charles... Soul is the music of experience... It's one person's heart speaking to another person's.

c. *attrib.* passing into *adj.* (*a*) Characteristic of or pertaining to Black people or culture; (*b*) of or pertaining to soul music.

1962 *John o' London's* 1 Feb. 113/3 Feldman is not really a soul-merchant. **1968** *N.Y. Times* 17 June 46 Sonny Charles, the organist, took over, singing with a soul appeal that caught up even this predominantly white audience. **1969** C. HIMES *Blind Man with Pistol* xxi. 231 The big white man thought they were talking about him in a secret language known only to soul people. **1971** B. MALAMUD *Tenants* 63, I swear to myself I will be the best writer, the best Soul Writer. *Ibid.* 121 From across the street..Bill spied him and whooped, 'Lesser, man, for Christ's sake, cross on over here. I got some soul people with me.' **1972** *Sat. Rev.* (U.S.) 27 May. 18/1 You'll be surprised how many soul folk speak Dutch and work and play in surprising Amsterdam. **1975** D. PITTS *Target Manhattan* (1976) xxvi. 105 They had.. listened to a group of black soul singers. **1976** *Drum* (E. Afr. ed.) June 10/2 Soul language is a language of protest, a language of self-assertion, a language that rejects the white man's values. **1981** *Westindian World* 28 Aug. 5/6 The Crusaders are among the finest exponents of the art of making a good listenable soul record.

4. f. *to have no soul*: to be lacking in sensibility or right feeling.

1704 SWIFT *T. Tub* II. 64 That Fellow, cries one, has no Soul; where is his Shoulder-knot? **1850** 'L. LIMNER' *Christmas Comes* 9 He seeks refuge in his organ, much to the annoyance of a little tailor in the attic who has no soul in him. **1919** G. B. SHAW *Inca of Perusalem* in *Heartbreak House* 209 You have no soul for fine art.

g. *to have a soul above* (something): to be superior to or have higher aspirations than (something).

1795 G. COLMAN *New Hay at Old Market* 10 My father was an eminent Button-maker..but I had a soul above buttons... I panted for a liberal profession. **1834** F. MARRYAT *Peter Simple* I. i. 2 My father, who was a clergyman..had..a 'soul above buttons'. **1889** E. DOWSON *Let.* 27 Oct. (1967) 112, I have still a soul above tractlets. **1899** G. B. BURGIN *Bread of Tears* I. iii. 51 Miss Mercy Tressock evidently wrote a very bad hand, and she hadn't a soul above blots: they were dotted copiously about on every page. **1909** 'O. HENRY' *Rus in Urbe* in *Hampton's Mag.* Aug. 160/1 She had a soul above ducks—above nightingales.

h. *to make one's soul*: see MAKE *v.*[1] 47.

6. b. (Later example.)

a **1902** S. BUTLER *Way of All Flesh* (1903) xiii. 56 He had stuck to his post... He had said to himself: 'I..am the very soul of honour. **1976** R. LEHMANN *Sea-Grape Tree* 30 He's the soul of courtesy but he can be a wee bit difficult.

III. 12. d. In Tsarist Russia, a serf. Also *transf.*

1806 M. WILMOT *Jrnl.* 17 Aug. in *Russ. Jrnls.* (1934) III. 271 One..often hears two Ladies..talking to each other about the sale of Lands, purchase of *Souls* (slaves). **1895** C. GARNETT tr. *Turgenev's Fathers & Children* i. 2 Nikolai Petrovitch Kirsanov..had..a fine property of two hundred souls, or, as he expressed it—since he had arranged the division of his land with the peasants..of nearly five thousand acres. **1943** E. M. ALMEDINGEN *Frossia* iv. 169 The good Boyarin made it known that her dowry would be..five hundred souls, all under the age of fifty. **1969** V. G. KIERNAN *Lords of Human Kind* vi. 225 Africans were being disposed of as Europeans were by their princes not long before, when the Congress of Vienna ..distributed them in lots of so many thousand 'souls'. **1977** V. S. PRITCHETT *Gentle Barbarian* i. 5 Spasskoye was..a self-sufficient feudal community..an empire numbering 5,000 'souls'.

14. b. *The Souls*, a late nineteenth-century aristocratic coterie with predominantly cultural and intellectual interests.

1890 B. POTTER *Jrnl.* 31 Dec. (1982) I. 349 Balfour.. would crush them in the intervals between a flirtation with one of the 'Souls' and the reading of a French novel. **1934** H. G. WELLS *Exper. Autobiogr.* II. ix. 766 The 'Souls', the Balfour set. **1980** D. NEWSOME *On Edge of Paradise* ii. 47 The young and wealthy aspirants to public eminence and the eligible daughters of leading families... The group to be christened by Lord Charles Beresford in 1888 'the Souls'.

V. 19. *soul-food, -minster, -music, -power, -work* (later example).

1920 W. R. LETHABY in *London Mercury* Mar. 575 The history that can be seen and touched is a strong and stimulating soul-food, entirely different from vague and wearying written history. **1937** BLUNDEN *Elegy* 16 Foremost of all a matin hymn From these soul-minsters leaps aloft. **1900** W. JAMES *Let.* 20 July (1920) II. 133, I..sit *thinking* *of letters*, and of the soul-music with which they might be filled if my tongue could only utter the thoughts that arise in me to youward. *a* **1930** D. H. LAWRENCE *Phoenix* (1936) v. 607 They combine with their soul-power some great technical skill. **1927** —— *Let.* 9 Jan. (1932) 679 Painting is more fun and less soul-work than writing.

20. *soul-brother* (later examples), *-mate* (later examples), *-thief*, *-twister*.

1970 R. LOWELL *Notebook* 151 We were an empire, soul-brothers To Babylon and China. **1978** *Listener* 20 July 90/1 Baudelaire recognised in Poe a soul brother and mirror image. **1915** F. M. HUEFFER *Good Soldier* III. v. 202 He thought that Mrs Basil had been his soulmate. **1976** BOTHAM & DONNELLY *Valentino* ix. 71 Convinced that he had found the woman who would be his life's soulmate. **1889** W. B. YEATS *Lett. to New Island* (1934) 195 Perhaps they are evil-spirits, these soul-thiefs, and not fairies at all. **1928** D. H. LAWRENCE *Phoenix II* (1968) 284 Dmitri Karamazov doesn't go half the lengths of the other Russian soul-twisters. **1956** D. GASCOYNE *Night Thoughts* 33 This soultwister blisters the paint of the set.

21. *soul-making, -mating, -prompting, -transfiguring.*

1819 KEATS *Lett.* (1958) II. 102 Call the world if you Please 'The vale of Soul-making'. **1922** JOYCE *Ulysses* 138 If aught that the..hand of sculptor has wrought in marble of soultransfigured and of soul-transfiguring deserves to live. *a* **1930** D. H. LAWRENCE *Phoenix* (1936) v. 605 Man just doesn't know how to interpret his own soul-promptings. **1939** A. HUXLEY *After Many a Summer* x. 140 Love, Passion, Soul-mating—all in upper-case letters. **1958** *Times Lit. Suppl.* 21 Feb. 101/2 The mid-Victorian novelists..thought of it [*sc.* Oxford] as a moral testing-ground or 'a vale of soul-making'.

22. *soul-awakening, -deadening, -destroying* (later examples), *-inspiring, -satisfying* (later examples), *-searing, -shattering, -stirring* (later example), *-testing.*

a **1822** SHELLEY *Posthumous Poems* (1824) 320 Soul-awakening music, sweet and strong. **1926** C. BARRY *Detective's Holiday* iv. 33 Suddenly a soul-awakening boom behind him smote his ears. **1909** MRS. H. WARD *Daphne* viii. 186 This dull, soul-deadening English life. **1937** *Atlantic Monthly* CLIX. 57/1 Exact information which really can be taught is despised as soul-deadening. **1898** G. B. SHAW *Candida* II, in *Plays Pleasant* 123 What dreadful—what soul-destroying cynicism! **1930** *Engineering* 25 July 111/3 A common indictment against modern conditions is that machine tending is 'soul-destroying'. **1976** J. SNOW *Cricket Rebel* 40 It was often soul destroying. On wet wickets or slow ones, I was expected to charge up and down and let it go when I knew I had no earthly chance of getting anything out of the wicket. **1794** J. TRUMBULL in *Columbian Muse* 58 And damp'd, alas! thy soul-inspiring ray, Where Virtue prompted and where Genius soar'd. **1979** 'A. HAILEY' *Overload* II. i. 106, I guess it's real soul-inspiring to work in a ritzy layout like this. **1890** KIPLING *Life's Handicap* (1891) 151 He was afraid for the sake of another—which is the most soul-satisfying fear known to man. **1939** F. SCOTT FITZGERALD *Lett.* (1964) 48 It is not very soul-satisfying because it [*sc.* the cinema] is a business of telling stories fit for children. **1936** *Times Lit. Suppl.* 21 Mar. 242/3 We are..given a soul-searing account of a Russian pogrom. **1979** 'A. HAILEY' *Overload* III. xii. 253 A week and a half had passed since the soul-searing night when he learned that Ruth's life was endangered by cancerous cells at large in her body. **1899** KIPLING *From Sea to Sea* II. xxv. 5 The result is soul-shattering. **1974** R. HARRIS *Double Snare* xi. 73 She and I had a soul-shattering row, and weren't on speaking terms. **1927** *Granta* 14 Oct. 9/1 He rapidly composed and delivered a few soul-stirring orations. **1932** WODEHOUSE *Louder & Funnier* 212 The unmistakable look of a man who has passed through some soul-testing experience. **1965** J. A. MICHENER *Source* (1966) 192 Captain Epher's plan of battle required daring from all the Hebrews and soul-testing courage from a few.

23. *soul-struck, -transfigured.*

1949 BLUNDEN *After Bombing* 3 The child soul-struck with the yellow flag's new fire. **1922** Soul-transfigured [see *soul-transfiguring*, sense 21 above].

25. soul-bearer, among the Akan peoples of West Africa, a person deemed to carry within him the external soul of a ruler or important person; **soul-body** *Spiritualism*, a spiritual body (see SPIRITUAL *a.* 4 a); **soul-bolts** *pl.*, 'the bolts which fasten the soul in place', used in var. slang phrases expressive of surprise or shock; cf. *soul-case* below; **soul brother** orig. *U.S. Blacks*, a fellow Black man; cf. *soul sister* below; **soul-candle,** (*b*) [tr. Yiddish *neshome licht*, f. *neshome* soul (Heb. *nešāmā*) + *licht* LIGHT *sb.* (G. *licht*)] in Judaism, a candle lit on the eve of the anniversary of a parent's death, and also on the eve of Yom Kippur (the custom is said to derive from Prov. xx. 27); **soul-case:** restrict † to sense in Dict. and add: (*b*) *U.S.* and *Austral. slang*, 'the casing of the soul', chiefly used in slang phrases expressive of hardship or suffering; cf. *soul-bolts* above; **soul-catcher,** among various tribes of North American Indians, a hollowed bone tube used by a medicine man to contain the soul of a sick person (see also quot. 1976); **Soul City,** an epithet applied to the Harlem area of New York city; also *transf.*; **soul-doctor** *slang*, (*a*) a clergyman; (*b*) a psychiatrist; † **soul-driver,** (*a*) a clergyman; (*b*) *U.S.*, a person who trades the services of convicts, indentured servants, or slaves; **soul food** orig. *U.S. Blacks*, the kind of food typically eaten by Black people, *spec.* those foodstuffs originating in the southern states of America; **soul-force** = *SATYAGRAHA; **soul-friend:** also in extended use (see quots.); **soul kiss** = *deep kiss* s.v. *DEEP *a.* IV. c; so **soul-kiss** *v. trans.*; hence **soul-kissing** *vbl. sb.*; **soul music,** a type of music popularized by Black singers which incorporates elements of rhythm and blues and gospel music; also *ellipt.*: see sense *3*b; **soul sister** orig. *U.S. Blacks*, a fellow Black woman; cf. *soul-brother* above; **soul-sleeper** (later U.S. examples); **soul stuff** = next; **soul-substance,** a hypothetical immaterial substance believed to form the 'spirit' or 'self' of each person (in some cultures also of animals and objects), and which is independent of the material body and outlives it.

1951 E. L. R. MEYEROWITZ *Sacred State of Akan* ii. 51 Like every king.., the queenmother has her elders, among whom are several spokeswomen, female *akrafo* or soul-bearers. **1967** *Times* 14 Nov. 17/2 (Advt.), A Baga wood nimba shoulder mask,..an important large Ashanti gold soul-bearer's disc,..a large New Ireland Uli. **1961** Soul body [see *EXTERIORIZE *v.*]. **1971** *Spiritualist* Oct.–Dec. 6/2 Help each other that your soul-body may rise in beauty and can be admired when you reach the World of Spirit. **1850** H. MELVILLE *White Jacket* II. xliv. 296 Start my soul-bolts, maties, if any more Blue Peters and sailing signals fly at my fore! **1902** J. BURGESS *Some Shetland Folk* 77 If du has, I'll knock the bloomin' sowl-bolts out of him. **1903** 'T. COLLINS' *Such is Life* vi. 234 'Wouldn't think that horse had a devil in him as big as a bull-dog,' observed the horse-driver. 'Shake the soul-bolt out of a man, s'posen you *do* stick to him.' **1959** *Jazz* Fall 291 It's one of those type LPs. I had all 'soul brothers'. **1969** *Listener* 4 Sept. 319/3 And if you think the main feeling being expressed is self-pity (and the self-generated violence and frustrations of self-pity), then so what? This is strictly for soul-brothers. **1973** H. NIELSEN *Severed Key* xiv. 144 I've got some soul brothers hustling baggage at LAX. **1978** I. B. SINGER *Shosha* viii. 141 Toward the evening meal, she lit a large candle stuck in a pot of sand—a 'soul candle'—and put on a silk holiday dress. **1835** A. B. LONGSTREET *Georgia Scenes* 109 When you come to the last half mile of each heat, run his heart, liver, lights, and soul-case out of him. **1896** J. C. HARRIS *Sister Jane* 277 The way that hoss flung around wi' you was enough to jolt your soul-case loose. **1901** F. J. GILLEN *Diary* 15 Apr. (1968) 34 Flies were celebrating some festival all night and worried the very soul cases out of us. **1962** R. TULLIPAN *March into Morning* 13 Then he got the bright idea of bringin' in orphan kids and working the soulcase off them until they turn eighteen and have to be paid more money. **1932** D. JENNESS *Indians of Canada* 333 Peculiar to the medicine-men of the Haida, Tlinkit, and Tsimshian was the use of a special 'soul-catcher', a bone tube, generally carved, for capturing the wandering souls of the sick and restoring them to their bodies. **1969** *Times* 22 Sept. 14/2 One invariably sees a face in the centre of a soul-catcher, a tube of hollowed bone into which the shaman [of the Tsimshian Indians] sucked the soul of a sick man—to keep it safe from harm while the illness lasted. **1976** *Times* 10 Nov. 18/4 A nine-inch bone soul catcher of the Tsimshian tribe reached £12,000... A soul-catcher is a tube within which a medicine man would catch the imp that caused a sickness. **1964** *N.Y. Times Mag.* 23 Aug. 62/3 *Soul City*, Harlem. **1971** B. MALAMUD *Tenants* 89 Lesser descended..into Soul City by himself. **1977** M. HERR *Dispatches* (1978) 196 Danang was Soul City for many of us, it had showers and drinks. **1785** GROSE *Dict. Vulgar Tongue*, *Soul doctor*, or *driver*, a parson. **1962** D. LESSING *Golden Notebook* I. 202 Anna Wulf is sitting on a chair in front of a soul-doctor. **1699** B. E. *New Dict. Canting Crew*, *Soul-driver*, a Parson. **1774** in *Amer. Hist. Rev.* (1900) VI. 77 Among them there was two Soul drivers. They are men who..drive them [*sc.* servants and convicts] through the Country..untill they can sell them to advantage. **1818** *Massachusetts Spy* 4 Nov. (Th.), Two men, in the character of soul drivers, lodged in the jail for safe keeping, five negros. **1846** *Swell's Night Guide* 132/2 *Soul driver*, a methodist parson. **1973** A. DUNDES *Mother Wit* 230 Individuals who speculated in the purchase and sale of slaves were called 'Negro-drivers' or 'soul-drivers'. **1964** *N.Y. Times Mag.* 23 Aug. 62/3 *Soul food*, chitterlings, collard greens, ham hocks, grits, black-eyed peas and rice, and the like. **1969** L. SANDERS *Anderson Tapes* (1970) xxviii. 71 This soul food crap—knuckles and hocks and greens. **1972** *Times* 15 Nov. 10/5 *Soul food.* Professional chef with knowledge of American Southern food..wanted for a new restaurant..in Chelsea. **1978** *Broadcast's Programme Edinburgh TV Festival* 8/3 The social centre of the series is a soul-food grocery owned by a West Indian entrepreneur. **1969** *It* 4–17 July 10/4 With soul force we'll look to the needs of our brother In a world that's our universal home. **1977** *Arab Times* 14 Dec. 2/5 'The voice of women..is a special soul-force in the struggle for a non-violent world,' the 36-year-old pacificist leader from strife-torn Northern Ireland declared. **1929** I. M. CLARK *Church Discipline in Scotland* i. 29 Columba had a method of entrusting those who had sinned to the spiritual care of individual monks of his community, who were termed soul-friends and whose duty it was to restore the souls of those penitents. **1979** *Church Times* 11 May 2/3 A special sort of job is being offered to spiritually gifted women in the diocese of Truro. The Bishop..wants them to train to be 'soul friends'—so that they may give spiritual guidance and direction with his formal backing and recognition. **1953** H. WAUGH *Last seen Wearing* 55 She calls him exciting and lets him soul-kiss her. **1960** WENTWORTH & FLEXNER *Dict. Amer. Slang* 504/1 *Soul kiss*, a long passionate open-mouthed kiss, during which a lover's tongue licks, caresses, or explores the tongue and mouth of the beloved. **1970** R. DAVIES *Fifth Business* ii. 130 Some of them were experts in what were then called French kisses or soul kisses, which the irreverent called 'swapping spits'. **1973** E. JONG *Fear of Flying* 82, I had the distinct sensation of kissing my own mouth—like when I was nine and used to wet a piece of my pillow with saliva and then kiss it to try to imagine what 'soul-kissing' was like. **1961** *Commonweal* 24 Mar. 658 It's called 'soul music' because its practitioners have incorporated some of the backbeat, rhythms, and exclamatory melodic lines of Negro gospel music. **1968** P. OLIVER *Screening Blues* 9 Soul music, which exploits the intensity of expression of religious song, the form and instrumental character of the blues and the maudlin sentiments of pop music. **1974** *Black World* Mar. 57/2 Soul music belched from windows where Black women wearing tired faces gazed impassively down at the hopeless street. **1980** *Oxford Times* 8 Feb. 15/1 They get really close to the style and spirit of American soul music. **1967** WENTWORTH & FLEXNER *Dict. Amer. Slang* Suppl. 705/1 *Soul sister*, a female Negro. *Negro use only.* **1968** *N.Y. Times* 17 June 24 Plate glass in Negro-owned establishments remained intact and displayed the words, 'Soul Brother' or 'Soul Sister'. **1976** *Drum* (E. Afr. ed.) June 10/3 African girls have always plaited their hair, and it was the soul sisters in America who were copying the girls in Africa. **1860** *Southern Enterprise* (Thomasville, Georgia) 13 June 2/5 Soul Sleepers is the name of a new religious sect which has recently made its appearance at Fairfield, Iowa... They..think that the soul is a mortal substance, and sleeps within the body until resurrection. **1887** J. KIRKLAND *Zury* 65 He and Peddicomb had both been connected with the little sect of Christians called 'Soul-sleepers'. **1889** *Cent. Dict.*, *Soul-stuff*.., the hypothetical substance of the soul; psychoplasm. **1909** W. JAMES *Mem. & Stud.* (1911) viii. 202 If there were in the universe a lot of diffuse soul-stuff, unable of itself to get into consistent personal form..it might get its head into the air, parasitically, so to speak, by profiting by weak spots in the armour of human minds. **1972** D. DAVIES *Dict. Anthropol.* 165/2 *Soul-stuff*, marna. The spiritual power with which every male in primitive societies seeks to enhance his prowess and standing in the tribe. It can only be gained by special feats... It is also thought to be found in the hair. **1890** W. JAMES *Princ. Psychol.* I. x. 318 But what is this abstract numerical principle of identity..? May it be the indivisible Soul-Substance, in which, according to the orthodox tradition, my faculties inhere? **1924** W. B. SELBIE *Psychol. Relig.* ii. 28 Anthropologists are..fairly generally agreed that underlying all religions is what they call animism, or belief in a soul substance discoverable not merely in men but in things. **1972** H. J. EYSENCK *Encycl. Psychol.* II. 57/2 Heraclitus..considered fire as the primary force and 'soul-substance' because it moved and transformed matter.

‖**soulagement** (sūlaʒmaṅ). [Fr. Cf. SOLACE *sb.*[1] and SOLAGEMENT.] Solace, relief.

1777 EARL OF CARLISLE *Let.* 18 Feb. in J. H. Jesse *Geo. Selwyn & Contemporaries* (1844) III. 171, I know our house might be a *soulagement* to you. **1949** H. NICOLSON *Diary* 17 Apr. (1968) 169 All this calm reflects my deep *soulagement* at Vita's improvement in health. **1968** A. COATES *Myself Mandarin* xvii. 245 One of my Secretariat colleagues telephoned me..to remind me..to return my instrument... With a certain *soulagement* I learned that he was referring merely to a piece of paper—the frightening document on the basis of which it all began.

soulful, *a.* Add: **1.** (Earlier example, and later examples of extended sense.)

1860 PRINCESS VICTORIA *Let.* 6 Feb. in R. Fulford *Dearest Child* (1964) 232 The dear Princess said to Fritz Karl while they were singing something of Mozart 'You are looking soulful.' **1931** A. HUXLEY *Music at Night* 18 When the great obvious truth is affirmed..in a series of soulful close-ups..the sensitive can only wince. **1951** *Sunday Pictorial* 21 Jan. 6/4 His eyes become deceptively soulful.

3. Expressive of Black feeling; characteristic of Black music. Also as quasi-*adv.*

1964 *Amer. Folk Music Occasional* I. 46, I sing my song more soulful. **1973** *Black Panther* 15 Sept. 15/1 The audience is encouraged to join hands with their neighbors and all standing sway with the soulful music. **1973** *Black World* Apr. 9/1 'Soul' is a highly valued concept among Afro-Americans. Soulful behavior may be called something else by some Afro-Americans, but its value remains.

soulfully, *adv.* (Later examples.)

1922 JOYCE *Ulysses* 279 Bronze, listening by the beerpull, gazed far away. Soulfully. **1979** *Daily Tel.* 23 Apr. 15/2 Her two daughters,..one bitter and promiscuous, one soulfully virginal, appeared as remote from everyday living as folklore princesses.

soulhood. (In Dict. s.v. SOUL *sb.*) (Later examples.)

1933 S. SASSOON *Traveller to his Soul* in *Satirical Poems* (ed. 2) 68 The problem which concerns me most..Is, bluntly stated, 'Have I got a soul?' And, soulhood granted, while millenniums roll, Will it inhabit some congenial clime..Anonymous in what we name 'the Whole'? **1940** C. S. LEWIS *Problem of Pain* ix. 129 Supposing, as I do, that the personality of the tame animals is largely the gift of man—that their mere sentience is reborn to soulhood in us as our mere soulhood is reborn to spirituality in Christ—I naturally suppose that very few animals indeed, in their wild state, attain to a 'self' or *ego*.

soul-search, *v.* [Back-formation f. SOUL-SEARCHING *ppl. a.*] **a.** *trans.* To examine penetratingly and thoroughly; to make a soul-searching analysis of. *nonce-use.* **b.** *intr.* To engage in examination of one's thoughts, to reflect deeply.

1966 *Economist* 29 Jan. 421/2 Trotsky writing in exile, Mr Alistair Cooke soul-searching the trial of Mr Alger Hiss, Adlai Stevenson eulogising Robert Frost. **1968** A. MARIN *Clash of Distant Thunder* (1969) xv. 114 When we tried Eichmann people used to argue and discuss and soul-search. We Jews are very good at that. **1972** *Daily Tel.* 30 Aug. 11/4 Last week there was the heart-rending case of a man in public life soul-searching about the reasons his son took to drugs.

Also as *sb.*, an act of soul-searching; hence **soul-searched** *ppl. a.*

1966 *Guardian* 8 July 3/5 (*heading*) Soul-search by the Liberals. **1970** E. M. BRECHER *Sex Researchers* ix. 255 More prolonged eye-contacts, or 'soul-searches'. **1978** *Times* 9 Oct. 18/4 The most honest and soul-searched response of the conclave.

soul-searching, *ppl. a.* Also in extended and trivial use. Hence **soul-searchingly** *adv.*

1938 PARTRIDGE *World of Words* ix. 309 The following sextette, ultimately selected from a much longer list of words that had been soul-searchingly gathered for your delectation. **1959** *Economist* 17 Jan. 203/1 After a 'soul-searching' parliamentary debate, an openly penitent Belgian government has announced its plan for dealing with the suddenly agitated Congo. **1960** *News Chron.* 13 Oct. 3/2 The deeply soul-searching: 'What do you think of modern jazz?'

soul-searching, *vbl. sb.* [f. prec.] Examination of one's soul or conscience, deep reflection; penetrating consideration of a state of affairs.

1948 'E. CRISPIN' *Buried for Pleasure* xvii. 145 The announcement..is not made without a good deal of preliminary soul-searching. **1953** *Time* 6 July 6/3, I would suggest some honest soul-searching for these unrealistic fathers, and orchids to Father Gerald Murphy and the increasing number of his prototypes among the younger Jesuits. **1974** *Country Life* 18 Apr. 926/2 What has been the subject of..agitated soul-searching is whether rector and churchwardens..had any right whatsoever to sell it. **1978** P. G. WINSLOW *Coppergold* 39 It's causing a bit of soul-searching at the Yard.

souly, *a.* Restrict † *Obs.* to senses in Dict. and add: **1. b.** = SOULFUL *a.* 1 in Dict. and Suppl. *colloq. rare.*

1911 D. H. LAWRENCE *White Peacock* vii. 131 I'm not one of your souly sort.

Soumak (sū·mak). Also **Soumac, Sumac,** etc. [Orig. uncertain, perh. a corruption of the Azerbaijan place-name *Shemakha.*] A type of rug or carpet made in the neighbourhood of Shemakha in Azerbaijan, distinguished by a flat, napless surface and loose threads at the back. Freq. *attrib.* Cf. *KASHMIR 2.

1904, etc. [see *KASHMIR 2]. **1932** D. C. MINTER *Mod. Needlecraft* 228/2 *Knitting Stitch*..sometimes called Sumac or Kelim Stitch..is..a long diagonal stitch. It gives a surface effect like those of various traditional woven rugs. **1959** *Chambers's Encycl.* III. 135/2 There are two main varieties of smooth-faced carpets: Kilim, woven like tapestry, and Soumak, where the pattern weft passes over four and under two warp threads. **1960** H. HAYWARD *Antique Coll.* 261/1 *Soumac rugs*, Caucasian rugs in a tapestry weave with conventional designs. **1974** *Times* 9 Mar. 23/5 Specialists in Kelims, Soumaks and Tribal Rugs.

sou markee (sū mā·ɹkī·). Also **sou marquee, sumarkee,** etc. [ad. Fr. *sou marqué*, lit. 'marked sou'.] A small French coin of the eighteenth century issued for the colonies and circulating esp. in the West Indies and North America. Hence *loosely*, something of little value.

1665–7 J. LAUDER *Jrnls.* in *Publ. Scottish Hist. Soc.* (1900) XXXVI. 92 On the place wheir they make it its sold for a sous marky la livre. **1826** *Massachusetts Spy* 5 July (Th.), Who the d—l would give a sumarkee to read the newspapers after breakfast? **1896** H. G. PARKER *Pomp of Lavilettes* 54 I'll bet he's got nothing more than what he went away with, and that wasn't a sou markee! **1903** A. H. LEWIS *Boss* 181, I don't pony for a sou markee. **1936** J. A. MCKENNA *Black Range Tales* 268 Marshall drifted from one settlement to another, and he likewise died without a sou marquee. **1952** R. M. HAMILTON *Canad. Quotations* 138/2 It's not worth a sou marquee. Phrase common in the Maritime provinces meaning, of trifling value; a reference to French Guiana sous which, counterstamped by other West Indian colonies, were sometimes carried north to Canada. **1977** F. LEIBER *Swords & Ice Magic* 80 'By the beats of Titchubi,' the former breathed, 'this is no *sou marque*, black dog no *chien noir*.'

sound, *sb.*[3] Add: **1. a.** Also, pressure waves that differ from audible sound only in being of a lower or a higher frequency. Cf. *INFRASOUND, *ULTRASOUND.

1967 I. M. FREEMAN *All about Sound & Ultrasonics* xiii. 99 Sonar is just one of the many uses that engineers and scientists have found for ultrasonic sound, which is often called ultrasound. These are names for sound that is too high in frequency to be heard. **1973** D. ENSMINGER *Ultrasonics* i. 6 Perhaps the animal that is best known for its use of ultrasonics is the bat. Many scientists have studied these interesting animals and their use of sound to find food. **1978** R. B. MINNIX in Lipscomb & Taylor *Noise Control* i. 30 Infrasound is concerned with very low frequency (below about 20 Hz) longitudinal mechanical waves where sound is felt rather than heard.

c. *sound-on-film* (Cinemat.), the incorporation of the sound track with the film. Freq. *attrib.* Cf. *married print* s.v. *MARRIED *ppl. a.* 3.

1931 B. BROWN *Talking Pictures* 270 Sound-on-film recording may be monitored direct from a photo-electric cell in the recording machine. **1957** MANVELL & HUNTLEY *Technique Film Music* ii. 27 The true arrival of the sound film was the arrival of sound-on-film. **1976** *Oxf. Compan. Film* 450/1 In the Vitaphone process the sound came from a disc precariously synchronized with the picture. The limitations of this system were quickly recognized and 'sound-on-film' became standard.

d. *Physics.* Applied to various kinds of wave motion (designated *zero, second, third,* etc., *sound*) that are predicted or observed to occur in superfluids and physically bear some resemblance to ordinary ('first') sound.

1944, etc. [see *second sound* s.v. *SECOND *a.* 7 a]. **1957** tr. L. D. Landau in *Soviet Physics JETP* V. 102/1 It is shown..that in a Fermi liquid at absolute zero other waves can be propagated; these differ in nature from ordinary sound, and we shall call them waves of 'zero sound'. **1959** K. R. ATKINS in *Physical Rev.* CXIII. 962 This article discusses the possible existence of two hitherto undetected types of wave propagation in liquid helium II. Third sound is a surface wave of long wavelength on a liquid helium film... Fourth sound may exist in narrow two-sided channels. *Ibid.*, To discuss wave propagation in liquid helium II, it is necessary to write down two separate hydrodynamical equations, one for the superfluid component and the other for the normal component. In first sound the two components move in the same direction in phase, and there is a first-order oscillation of the density but only a second-order oscillation of the temperature. In second sound the two components move in opposite directions out of phase, and the temperature oscillation is then first-order while the density oscillation is only second-order. **1969** W. E. KELLER *Helium-3 & Helium-4* vi. 203 (*caption*) Attenuation and propagation velocity of sound in liquid He^3 showing the characteristics associated with the transition from first sound to zero sound for two frequencies. **1974** D. J. BERGMAN in K. D. Timmerhaus et al. *Low Temperature Physics—LT 13* I. 507 Following our experience with third sound, we may expect that in fourth sound, too, when the channels that hold the helium are sufficiently small so that the normal fluid motion is completely locked out, the only important source of attenuation will be conduction of heat into the walls of the helium channels. **1974** *Nature* 15 Mar. 194/3 The report..that they have observed the propagation of fourth sound in the two newly discovered phases of liquid ^{3}He amounts to the first unequivocal evidence that both of these new phases are superfluids. **1976** *Physics Bull.* Aug. 351/2 'Zero sound'..corresponds to oscillations in shape of the Fermi surface. **1981** *Nature* 2 Apr. 359/2 Second sound is an unusual type of propagating wave mode, which can occur in superfluids, involving fluctuations in the local temperature and entropy of a medium rather than in the local density and pressure as found in a conventional sound wave.

e. *sound and light* = *SON ET LUMIÈRE 1. Used *attrib.*

1960 *Woman* 23 Jan. 35/3 The pretty little town of Buxton, one of the first in England to stage a 'sound and light' production for summer visitors. **1966** J. PHILIPS *Wings of Madness* (1967) i. i. 9 The Sound and Light program put on..every night..kept tourists in town. **1979** *United States 1980/81* (Penguin Travel Guides) 548 On weekend evenings, a multimedia sound-and-light show using laser beams.

2. a. (Examples with reference to a television set: cf. *PICTURE *sb.* 2 f.)

1928 *Television* Oct. 10/2 A one-act play was..televised ..and receiving televisors within a range of four miles tuned in both sight and sound. **1960** [see *PICTURE *sb.* 2 f]. **1979** R. JAFFE *Class Reunion* (1980) III. iii. 322 Emma was..watching television, but she had the sound..low.

3. a. Also, a phenomenon identical to an audible sound except that it is inaudible by reason of its frequency (cf. sense *1 a).

1950 *Sci. Amer.* Aug. 52/2 The English physiologist H. Hartridge..watched bats flying through darkened rooms and advanced the theory that they might be orienting themselves by means of ultrasonic sounds too high in frequency for human ears to hear. **1976** L. H. SCHAUDINISCHKY *Sound, Man, & Building* i. 8 Above 20 000 Hz extends the 'infinite' supersonic range, the ultrasound. Man is not equipped with an organ capable of directly responding to sounds in that range, but where infrasound is concerned it may be picked up with the aid of a special sense of touch. **1978** J. GOLDSTEIN in P. M. Lipscomb *Noise & Audiol.* i. 6 In order to be heard, a sound must be within a certain frequency range because there are limitations in the frequencies the human ear can perceive.

d. *pl.* Popular music; also in *sing.*, a tune or record. *slang* (orig. *U.S.*).

1955 *Amer. Speech* XXX. 304 Kenton's music is round sounds. **1961** RIGNEY & SMITH *Real Bohemia* p. xvii, *Sounds*, music, mainly jazz. **1968** *Daily Mirror* 27 Aug. 7/5 Together cats don't buy records, they buy *sounds*, and they never blow their cool.

e. A characteristic style of (usu. popular) music indicated by a defining word or words. Cf. *Mersey sound* s.v. *MERSEY.

1963 [see *GEAR *sb.* 5 e]. **1967** *Radio Times* 21 Dec. 55/4 *The Greek Sound*... Tonight's programme is about the new genre, which in the last eight years has given a new impetus and vitality to Greek popular music. **1970** *Guardian* 15 June 9/5 Steel Bands and the Reggae Sound beloved of skinheads. **1974** *Listener* 13 June 767/1 In 1927, there was an inimitable Ellington sound, and so there was at the end.

4. f. The impression produced by a statement or report, freq. in phr. *to like the sound of* (some person or thing). (See note at sense 4 d in Dict.)

1859 MRS. GASKELL *Let.* 21 Mar. (1966) 543, I like the 'sound' of him extremely, and I hope he will like me when we come to know each other. **1965** R. SHECKLEY *Game of X* (1966) xxii. 155 'You take care of the piloting, and we will handle the navigating.' Somehow I didn't like the sound of that.

5*. In elliptical uses. **a.** *Cinemat.* and *Broadcasting.* The department in charge of recording sound. Also, an engineer in this department; the equipment used by him.

a **1940** F. SCOTT FITZGERALD *Last Tycoon* (1941) iii. 30 Call sound, and if he's been heard from, call him. **1969** M. STEINBECK *On Stage* 165 The voice track on a film is called the sound track. The engineer in charge and the whole unit is referred to simply as 'sound'. The director may call out before a take, 'Is sound ready?' **1972** *Listener* 21 Dec. 852/1 Sequence of calls before a shot. Production Assistant: 'Quiet. Going for a take. Standing by.' Director: 'Right.' Sound: 'Sound running.'

b. = *RADIO *sb.* 2 b. Cf. *sound radio*, sense 7 b below. Also *attrib.*

1949 *Times* 17 Feb. 5/3 The first hundred thousand mark is about to be reached in..television licences..compared with the 11 m. for sound. **1955** *Times* 29 June 11/2 So far not even B.B.C. television has found the way to transfer the aura of the 9 p.m. sound news to television. **1967** 'M. HUNTER' *Cambridgeshire Disaster* iv. 28 If necessary he would give up television, ask for a transfer to Sound, anything to get more time at home. **1972** P. BLACK *Biggest Aspidistra* III. iii. 171 The most obvious effect of the Coronation for television was the demand for sets... Though the BBC still regarded sound as the senior service..the sound audience never again exceeded television's.

6. a. *sound-aspect, -association, -change* (later examples), *-clause, -colour, -combination, -complex, -development, energy, event, -feature, -gesture, -group, -history* [tr. G. *lautgeschichte*], *-image, -intensity, -language, level, -mark, -output, -pattern, -picture, poem, power, -quality, -sentence, -sequence, -structure, -symbol, -system* (earlier and later examples), *-type, -unit, -value, -wave* (earlier example), *-word, -world.*

1936 H. MULDER *Cognition & Volition in Lang.* 46 The life of the language as regards its sound-aspect. **1954** A. H. GARDINER *Theory of Proper Names* (ed. 2) 73 Even logicians..overlooked the importance of the sound-aspect. **1924** MAWER & STENTON *Introd. to Survey of Eng. Place-Names* ix. 174 Its chief weakness is the remoteness of the sound-association between the original compound name and the suggested simple derivative. **1912** L. BLOOMFIELD in *Jrnl. Eng. & Gmc. Philol.* XI. 623 S[heffield] confuses the factors—sound-change and analogy—that constitute change in language. **1939** [see *PALATAL *a.* 2 b]. **1962** W. NOWOTTNY *Lang. Poets Use* i. 5 Calling in alliteration's aid and that of a sound-change. *a* **1889** G. M. HOPKINS *Jrnls. & Papers* (1959) 273 We may now say of rhythm i.e. verse that it is the recasting of speech into sound-words, sound-clauses and sound-sentences. **1890** G. B. SHAW in *Star* 9 May 2/5 Marlowe's line was not 'mighty'..but it was tuneful, exquisitely emphasized, and sometimes gorgeous in its sound color. **1962** *Listener* 9 Aug. 225/1 Schönberg's 'melody of sound-colours' (*Klangfarbenmelodie*). **1924** MAWER & STENTON *Introd. to Survey of Eng. Place-Names* v. 100 An unfamiliar English sound or sound-combination was altered to suit the Norman pronunciation. **1965** *Language* XLI. 93 First a child learns a sound-combination and then he attaches meaning to it! **1931** G. STERN *Meaning & Change of Meaning* 31 If the sound-complex is to be apprehended as meaning something..a mental content must accrue to it. **1900** E. BJÖRKMAN *Scand. Loan-Words in M.E.* I. 30 There are some tests of form which are not based on differences of sound-development between Scandinavian and English. **1965** *English Studies* XLVI. 141 Surnames, like Johe *Le Roper*..reflect the spoken dialect, but do not necessarily prove indigenous sound-developments. **1931** G. O. RUSSELL *Speech & Voice* iv. 21 (*heading*) Sound-energy not air motion. **1962** A. NISBETT *Technique Sound Studio* 239 They readily remove sound energy from the air at their resonant frequency, and this is then mopped up within the absorber. **1962** P. STREVENS *Papers in Lang.* (1965) xii. 146 When sound events are recorded, the technical standard of recording is important. **1939** *Word Study* Mar. 2/1 Linguistics..deals with the use of a limited number of definable events—the significant sound-features of a language—occurring in certain definable sequences. **1964** W. R. LEE in D. Abercrombie et al. *Daniel Jones* 292 Sounds and sound-features which belong to neither language. **1938** I. GOLDBERG *Wonder of Words* iv. 55 Sound-gesture, such as Paget draws upon in this etymology, is precisely what it is called. **1956** J. LOTZ in L. White *Frontiers of Knowl.* xiv. 219 Marginal sound-gestures like the bilabial trill used when shivering: *Brrr!* **1928** O. JESPERSEN in *Proc. Brit. Acad.* XIV. 352 There are no other words than *switch* and *stretch* beginning and ending with exactly these sound-groups. **1964** J. VACHEK in D. Abercrombie et al. *Daniel Jones* 199 If followed by a vowel, the same sound-group was preserved unimpaired. **1933** O. JESPERSEN *Essentials Eng. Gram.* vi. 62 The sound-history of French also serves to explain some striking peculiarities concerning the use of the letter *g* in English spelling. **1964** *English Studies* XLV. 422 A detailed knowledge of sound-history..and sound-substitutions. **1943** tr. M. Buber in H. Read *Educ. through Art* ix. 279 Sound-image after sound-image.. emerges from vibrating throat..into the surrounding air. **1951** A. GARDINER *Theory of Speech & Lang.* 70 It is only the sound-image connected with the words which can be reproduced in a physical copy. **1973** S. HEATH in *Screen* Spring/Summer 108 A *langue* is defined by Saussure as a system of signs, a sign being the union of *signifiant* ('sound-image') and *signifié* ('concept'). **1982** *Listener* 16 Dec. 26/3 There's something wrong with the way a taped sound-image remains fixed in eternity. **1934** *Discovery* Dec. 346/1 Noise is a subjective phenomenon and cannot be directly measured. The stimulus causing this impression of sound is a sound-intensity which can be defined and measured objectively. **1952** *Mind* LXI. 215 It is impossible to imagine a sound-intensity divorced from any definite sound-pitch. **1969** *Gloss. Acoustical Terms* (*B.S.I.*) 16 *Sound intensity*,..the sound energy flux through unit area. **1918** *Amer. Jrnl. Philol.* XXXIX. 89 A Dakota Indian..would not understand a Neapolitan, even though he would sooner understand the gestures than the sound-language. **1937** R. A. Wilson *Birth of Lang.* 160 The twenty-six already differentiated elements of sound-language. **1931** S. K. Wolf in L. Cowan *Recording Sound for Motion Pictures* xx. 301 It is necessary to have some means of varying sound levels in theatres. **1974** *Physics Bull.* June 227/1 Leeds City Council, decided to use its licensing laws to limit sound levels in ballrooms, discotheques and similar places of entertainment. *a* **1892** W. Whitman *Daybks. & Notebks.* (1978) III. 671 One of the first desiderata..is a set of..sound-marks attached to letters..each mark belonging to that specific sound. **1978** *Sci. Amer.* Jan. 29/3 We cannot shut our earlids; awake, we are always open to..the old soundmarks we remember and cherish. **1937** Sound output [see *control engineer* s.v. *control *sb.* 5]. **1947** Crowther & Whiddington *Science at War* 175 It was found that the sound-output was mainly due to propellers. **1925** *Language* I. 41 One must ascertain if the sound is a typical form or one of the points in its sound pattern, or is merely a variant of such a form. **1977** P. Strevens *New Orientations Teaching of English* xii. 154 Accent features are manifested in sound-patterns of various kinds. **1903** A. W. Patterson *Schumann* xvi. 186 The whole forms a kind of sound-picture representing the various personages in the dance. *Ibid.* xvii. 203 What if the tone poet..knew infinitely better than his..advisers what was or was not fitting in the great sound-poem to which his genius gave birth? **1971** *Guardian* 18 Feb. 10/6 Artaud wrote sound poems. **1947** Crowther & Whiddington *Science at War* iii. 155 A transmitter producing about 50 watts of sound-power in water was adequate. **1950** D. Jones *Phoneme* 12 An alphabetic system of phonetic transcription consists of letters representing sound-qualities. **1977** *Broadcast* 28 Nov. 14/2 The singles we get are so badly pressed that we get complaints from listeners about the sound quality. *a* **1889** Sound-sentence [see *sound-clause* above]. **1914** L. Bloomfield in *Trans. Amer. Philol. Assoc.* XLV. 69 The various parts of this sound-sequence..have been heard and uttered by the speaker (or the hearer). **1962** F. Behre *Contrib. Eng. Syntax* 134 The sound-sequence.. must correlate with certain extra-lingual elements to be inferred from the context. **1959** D. Cooke *Lang. Mus.* v. 234 Music..has now become pure sound-structure, an intellectual and aesthetic delight. **1936** *Science & Society* I. 38 Certain sound-symbols are universally attached to the same referent by all members of the community. **1975** *Language for Life* (Dept. Educ. & Sci.) xxvi. 521 The learning of sound-symbol correspondences should take place in the context of whole word recognition and reading for meaning. **1879** H. Sweet in *Trans. Philol. Soc. 1877–9* 544, I am fully conscious that mine is a very inadequate study of an exceptionally difficult sound-system. **1897** *Mod. Lang. Notes* XII. 244 Least understood..is the historical development of the sound-systems of modern dialects. **1949** J. R. Firth in *Trans. Philol. Soc. 1948* 132 More detailed notice of 'h' and the *glottal stop* in a variety of languages will reveal the scientific convenience of regarding them as belonging to the prosodic systems of certain languages rather than to the sound systems. **1977** *Canad. Jrnl. Linguistics 1976* XXI. 177 No information about how they work in the sound system of a language is gained. **1941** Sound-type [see *allophone]. **1964** J. C. Catford in D. Abercrombie et al. *Daniel Jones* 29 The laryngologists have no tradition of systematic..description of phonologically pertinent sound-types. **1934** J. J. Logan *Outl. Eng. Philol.* 24 A syllable, thus, is a sound-unit. **1920** T. S. Eliot *Sacred Wood* 133 It is an arrangement and choice of words which has a sound-value and at the same time a coherent comprehensible meaning. **1964** W. R. Lee in D. Abercrombie et al. *Daniel Jones* 288 There is a tendency to give them [*sc.* letters] the sound-values they possess in the learner's mother tongue. **1848** *Trans. R. Irish Acad.* XXI. 65, I proceed now to explain..the circumstances of the great sea wave and of the aërial sound wave, attending most great earthquakes. *a* **1889** Sound-word [see *sound-clause* above]. **1953** H. Read *True Voice of Feeling* I. viii. 144 The caesura is..the breaking of the rhythm into sense words of different length from the sound marks. **1961** *Times* 19 June 9/6 Its sound-world is the old sound-world —parts of it exult in the manner of Richard Strauss. **1976** *Gramophone* Aug. 319/3 Decca and DG engineers help their artists to create a much more limpid and crystalline soundworld.

b. (Also in other objective combinations.) *sound-detector, -locator; sound-deadening, -reflecting; sound-absorption, -production; sound-absorbent, -absorptive, -imitative* adjs.

1961 P. Strevens *Papers in Lang.* (1965) xi. 137 The upper surface..is hard, and therefore probably less sound-absorbent. **1935** *Discovery* May 126/2 The latest designs and materials for sound-proofing and sound absorption. **1972** *Lebende Sprachen* XVII. 37/1 *Sound absorption*, 1) the process of dissipating..sound energy. 2) The property possessed by materials..of absorbing sound energy. **1937** *Archit. Rev.* LXXXI. p. lxxii/1 The complete unit is also lined with sound-absorptive material. **1977** *Chicago Tribune* 2 Oct. VI. 9/2 Rehearsals with empty seats are one thing, performances with every seat ..filled with sound-absorptive bodies quite another. **1945** Nelson & Wright *Tomorrow's House* iii. 16/2 The existence of walls lined with books constitutes an excellent sound-deadening treatment. **1962** A. Nisbett *Technique Sound Studio* ii. 48 Of the various possible sound-deadening systems, it is best to try to avoid those which give a padded-cell effect. **1878** *Chambers's Jrnl.* 29 June 413/1 An extremely delicate sound detector. **1942** W. Simpson *One of our Pilots is Safe* 54 Chances of escaping detection would be good, either by enemy fighters high above or sound detectors on the ground. **1921** E. Sapir *Language* 4 The interjections and sound-imitative words. **1956** J. Lotz in L. White *Frontiers of Knowl.* xiv. 223 Even sound-imitative words vary: thus the English *splash* corresponds to Hungarian *loccsan.* **1919** Sound-locator [see *locator 4]. **1941** D. Masters *So Few* ix. 106 Human ears listening at the sound locators to detect the course [of the aircraft]. **1977** *Jrnl. R. Soc. Arts* CXXV. 419/2 The Sound Locator..greatly assisted the anti-aircraft personnel to plan their defences in advance. **1925** P. Radin tr. *Vendryès's Language* 20 The study of sound-production, that is to say,..phonation. **1933** *Archit. Rev.* LXXIII. 232 Only a small area of the walls has a sound-reflecting surface. **1962** A. Nisbett *Technique Sound Studio* 44 A 'bathroom' acoustic would be provided by a small room with strongly sound-reflecting walls.

7. a. sound-attribute *Linguistics*, a prosodic feature; **sound barrier,** the obstacle to supersonic flight posed by such factors as increased drag and reduced controllability, which occur when aircraft not specially designed for such flight approach the speed of sound; also *fig.*; *to break the sound barrier*, to travel faster than sound; **sound channel** *Oceanogr.*, a layer of water in which sound is propagated over long distances with minimum energy loss, usu. because of refraction back into this layer from above owing to the temperature gradient, and from below owing to the pressure gradient; **sound-conditioned** *a.* [*condition *v.* 9], sound-insulated; having improved acoustic qualities; hence **sound conditioning; sound effect,** (*a*) orig. *U.S.* (usu. in *pl.*), a sound typical of an event or evocative of an atmosphere, produced artificially in a play, film, etc. (cf. *effect *sb.* 3 c); also *attrib.* and *transf.*; (*b*) the effect produced by the sound of a word; **sound-insulated** *a.*, insulated against sound; also **sound insulation; sound-law** *Philol.* [tr. G. *lautgesetz*], a rule stating the regular occurrence of a phonetic change in the history of a language or language family; **sound meter,** an instrument for measuring the intensity of sound; **sound moderator,** a device fitted to a firearm which reduces the noise of report, a silencer; **sound pressure,** the difference between the instantaneous pressure at a point in the presence of a sound wave and the static pressure of the medium; **sound print** = *sonogram; **sound-proofed** *a.*, that has been made sound-proof; **sound-ranging** *Mil.* (see quot. 1973); hence **sound-ranger,** one trained in sound-ranging; **soundscape** [Scape *sb.*[3]], (*a*) a musical composition consisting of a texture of sounds; (*b*) the sounds which form an auditory environment; **sound-shift,** *Philol.* = *shift *sb.* 14 c; **sound-shifting** [tr. G. *lautverschiebung*]; **sound spectrogram** = *sonogram; **sound spectrograph** = *sonograph 1; hence **sound-spectrographic** *a.*; **sound spectrography; sound-substitution** *Linguistics*, the replacement of one phoneme by another; hence (as back-formation) **sound-substitute** *v. trans.*, to replace (one phoneme) by another (*rare*); **sound-symbolism** *Linguistics*, the (partial) natural representation of the sense of a word by its sound; hence **sound-symbolic** *a.*, pertaining to or manifesting such symbolism; **sound-tight** *a.* = *sound-proof* adj.

1932 D. Jones *Outl. Eng. Phonetics* (ed. 3) i. 2 The student of spoken English..must learn the proper usage in the matter of the 'sound-attributes' (length, stress, and voice-pitch). **1945–9** *Acta Linguistica* V. 88 The phonemes of a given language are realized in concrete sounds and sound-attributes. **1939** *Jrnl. R. Aeronaut. Soc.* XLIII. 818 It is noteworthy that the curve, which at first is flat, rises gradually for a while, without the enormous increases which other experimenters have found between M.n. 0·6 and 0·8, and which have made them speak of a concrete 'sound barrier'. **1952** *Times* 8 Sept. 5/2 Their moment of triumph after breaking once more through the sound barrier. *a* **1955** in T. H. Pear *Eng. Social Differences* (1955) iii. 112 Is there a Sound Barrier against your Son? **1955** *Times* 7 July 8/3 The bang that shook London early on Tuesday morning was caused..by a Gloster Javelin breaking the sound barrier. **1963** *Listener* 14 Mar. 457/1 The African rhythmic element is not part of the Asian musical heritage, and there are totally different tonal systems which constitute a kind of 'sound-barrier' which jazz has had to crash. **1973** A. Price *October Men* xvi. 231 When the General whispered, people moved..when he growled, they broke the sound barrier. **1976** *Lancs. Evening Post* 7 Dec. 1/4 When we went through the sound barrier I only felt a very slight judder. **1946** *Bull. Geol. Soc. Amer.* LVII. 928 The velocity of propagation of sound decreases, due to the temperature decrease, from the surface to 4000 feet and then increases, due to pressure increase, from there to bottom. This type of velocity pattern is known as a sound channel. **1972** M. G. Gross *Oceanogr.* vii. 200 This sound channel is a typical feature of the open ocean at depths of around 1000 meters at mid-latitudes to near the surface in polar regions. **1947** *Sun* (Baltimore) 5 Aug. 6 (Advt.), You travel all the way by the same luxurious Panagra DC-6..air-conditioned and sound-conditioned for your comfort! **1972** *Fortune* Jan. 8E/2 Sound conditioning assures privacy in these garden apartments. **1909** *Moving Picture World* 10 July 56/1 (Advt.), Yerkes & Co... Manufacturers of high grade sound effects for moving pictures. **1911** D. S. Hulfish *Cycl. Motion-Picture Work* II. 191 The orchestra comprises pianist and drummer, and a 'sound effect' man. **1928** *Exhibitor's Herald & Moving Picture World* 28 Apr. 21/2 The experts of Victor..will..arrange for the synchronized orchestration and sound effects for this picture, in which airplane battles will have an important part. **1942** Partridge *Usage & Abusage* 298/1 Passing over such obviousness as *bang, crash, hiss*..we see that imitation is most effective when the echoism and sound-effects extend over a succession of words. **1951** W. Empson *Structure of Complex Words* 412 *Rebuke* is prim, apparently from the sound-effect. **1958** *Listener* 25 Dec. 1091/3 The studio managers who twiddle the knobs and the sound-effects engineers. **1966** *Ibid.* 24 Feb. 284/1 A meteorite passed across the sky and produced a brilliant light, together with sound effects. **1972** P. Black *Biggest Aspidistra* I. iv. 36 Producers deplored the attention their ingenuities received, but the public was and is fascinated by sound effects. **1933** Sound-insulated [see *air-conditioning *vbl. sb.*]. **1970** Sound-insulated [see *insulated *ppl. a.* 3]. **1932** *B.B.C. Year Bk. 1933* 365 (*caption*) Eel grass for sound-insulation sandwiched in walls of pumice concrete. **1969** *Gloss. Acoustical Terms* (*B.S.I.*) 49 *Sound insulation*, means taken to reduce the transmission of sound. **1874** H. Bendall tr. *Schleicher's Compar. Gram.* 12 *Vowel sound-laws* (*i.e.* influence of vowels and consonants on vowels) were not existent in the original Indo-European language. **1911** L. Bloomfield in *Jrnl. Eng. & Gmc. Philol.* X. 629 Synonymous words might be collected to prove almost any desired sound-law. **1974** R. Quirk *Linguist & Eng. Lang.* i. 3 There are good historical reasons..for our firmly associating it [*sc.* 'language'] with..'sound-laws'. **1928** *Sci. Abstr.* A. XXXI. 39 Discusses the differences between physical and physiological intensity of sound and describes a form of sound meter for technical use. **1974** *Physics Bull.* Oct. 481/2 Dawe Instruments..has introduced the type 1400H sound-meter which uses a ceramic microphone... Sound levels as low as 24 dB can be measured. **1934** *Rep. Departmental Comm. Statutory Definition & Classification of Firearms & Ammunition* 44 in *Parl. Papers 1934–5* (Cmd. 4758) VIII. 871 There is procurable an appliance known as a silencer or sound moderator which can be fitted to almost all types of firearms for the purpose of reducing the noise of the explosion of the cartridge. **1953** W. G. B. Allen *Pistols, Rifles & Machine Guns* xiii. 172 Silencers are not permitted by law on privately owned weapons, but a 'sound moderator' may be used providing the appropriate endorsement is made on the..Certificate... The only sound moderators on sale are for .22 in. weapons. **1976** *Shooting Times & Country Mag.* 16–22 Dec. 47/1 (Advt.), Erma Emi semi-automatic carbine,..sound moderator, 'scope. **1916** *Sci. Abstr.* B. XIX. 514 (*heading*) Sound pressure. **1930** *Jrnl. Sci. Instruments* VII. 113 The response at a particular frequency is measured by the E.M.F. developed by the microphone per unit sound pressure per unit area. **1976** *Acustica* XXXV. 255/1 The transfer function is subtracted from the harmonic analysis of sound pressure to produce the source spectrum. **1969** R. Petrie *Despatch of Dove* I. iv. 64 Have you ever seen a soundprint of your own voice? **1932** *Times Educ. Suppl.* 20 Aug. 321/4 The divisions between class-rooms are soundproofed with eelgrass quilting. **1956** N. Mailer *Man who studied Yoga* in *New Short Novels* II. iv. 19 Scream my little one. It will do you no good. The walls are soundproofed. **1978** C. Tomlinson *Shaft* 39 The sighs that in a giant building rise up trapped between its sound-proofed surfaces. **1978** J. B. Hilton *Some run Crooked* ii. 17 They've learned to be radio mechanics, asdic operators, sound-rangers and flash-spotters. **1919** *Sci. Amer.* 17 May 509/1 Both parties to the late conflict excited their ingenuity..to improve methods of sound-ranging, on land and in the air and at sea. **1934** T. E. Lawrence *Let.* 19 Mar. (1938) 793 Research..to develop the art of sound-ranging, and anti-aircraft gunnery. **1973** J. Quick *Dict. Weapons & Mil. Terms* 407/3 *Sound ranging*, a method of locating the source of a sound, such as that of a gun report or a projectile burst, by calculations based on the intervals between the reception of the sound at various previously oriented microphone stations. **1968** *Time* 4 Oct. 6 In this collection, he proved his mastery of the subtle colors, treacherous rhythms, and delicate contrapuntal lines that fashioned Debussy's impressionistic soundscapes. **1973** *Daily Colonist* (Victoria, B.C.) 22 Sept. 5/5 The world soundscape project..counted horn blasts at intersections around the world. **1977** *Times Lit. Suppl.* 11 Feb. 144/3 A small number of jazz musicians have..gravitated towards the soundscapes of Varèse and Stockhausen. **1977** *Guardian Weekly* 18 Sept. 18/1 The 'soundscape', Schafer's word to describe our sonic environment, the day-to-day background of our auditory experience. **1911** L. Armitage *Introd. Study Old High German* II. iii. 57 OHG is distinguished from all other W. Gmc. languages by a series of Sound-changes affecting its consonant system, which are usually grouped together under the name of the Second or HG. Sound-Shift. **1922** O. Jespersen *Language* ii. 43 The first book in the 1822 volume [of Grimm's *Grammatik*] contains..his exposition of the 'sound shift' (lautverschiebung), which it has been customary in England since Max Müller to term 'Grimm's Law'. **1965** C. F. Hockett *Sound Change* 192 What then of the neat discrete 'speech sounds' of the comparativists? Even more, what of their 'sound shifts'? **1880** A. H. Sayce *Introd. Sci. Lang.* I. iv. 324 Practically the sound shiftings [in the Semitic dialects] are confined to the sibilants. **1908** J. Wright *O.E. Grammar* 100 The first sound-shifting, popularly called Grimm's Law, refers to the changes which the Indo-Germanic explosives underwent in the period of the Germanic primitive community. **1945** R. K. Potter in *Science* 9 Nov. 470/2 The beat of the heart may be recorded slowly and converted to the sound spectrogram form by high speed reproduction. **1974** *Sci. Amer.* Mar. 86/3 The sound spectrograms of Infant A's cries looked exactly like what we have come to regard as being typical of a normal infant. **1945**

Science 9 Nov. 465/1 The patterns..were made by an instrument that we have called the sound spectrograph. **1977** *Time* 21 Mar. 64/3 The most striking evidence came from a sound spectrograph, a machine that reduces speech to electronic 'pictures' called spectrograms or voiceprints. **1947** R. K. Potter et al. *Visible Speech* i. 4 A sound spectrographic record of the words '*Visible Speech*' is shown in Fig. 3. **1976** *Word 1971* XXVII. 57 Sound-spectrographic and cineradiographic analysis of neonatal cry and crysound. **1948** *Language* XXIV. 4 That we have reached a crucial point in the development of phonemics is clear from the first published results of sound spectrography. **1962** *Amer. Speech* XXXVII. 67 Surgical study..using synchronized cineradiography and sound spectrography. **1953** K. Jackson *Lang. & Hist. in Early Britain* II. 558 A possible case of pre-lenition *b* sound-substituted by AS. *ƀ*. **1898** *Trans. Amer. Philol. Assoc.* XXIX. 38 It is not always easy to say where sound-substitution ceases and natural speech begins. **1926** L. Bloomfield in *Language* II. 164 Whoever speaks a foreign language or dialect may in it substitute resemblant features of his native speech... Linguistic substitution of phonemes is *sound-substitution*. **1959** A. Campbell *O.E. Gram.* 200 In early loan-words this would arise by the operation of native sound-changes, but in later ones sound-substitution might produce similar results. **1964** R. H. Robins *Gen. Linguistics* 14 The onomatopoeic and 'sound-symbolic' part of language is of great significance. **1977** *Word 1972* XXVIII. 318 A new polar response pair with no relevance to the sound to be considered for membership in one of the sound-symbolic semantic clusters in a phonetic-symbolism experiment. **1901** H. Oertel *Lect. Study Lang.* 328 It would..embrace the attempts at word-painting and sound-symbolism. **1922** O. Jespersen *Language* 396 The idea that there is a natural correspondence between sound and sense, and that words acquire their contents and value through a certain sound symbolism, has at all times been a favourite one with linguistic dilettanti. **1957** R. W. Zandvoort *Handbk. Eng. Gram.* II. ii. 111 Thus *a man's club* by the side of *a men's club*; *a woman's college* by the side of *a women's college*. This seems to be to some extent a matter of 'sound-symbolism': the singular forms are preferred because they have a more 'manly' sound. **1977** G. W. Hewes in D. M. Rumbaugh *Language Learning by Chimpanzee* i. 48 Sound-symbolism may be explicable on the basis of mouth-gesture. **1932** Kipling *Limits & Renewals* 81 The door was shut; and it's sound-tight for reasons connected with the last nights of the condemned.

b. In combinations referring to the mechanical or electrical transmission, broadcasting, or reproduction of sound, as *sound boom, broadcasting, -crew, engineer, man, negative, programme, radio, record, recorder, recordist, source, studio, system, transmission*; *sound-recording* vbl. sb. and ppl. adj.; *sound-reproducing* ppl. adj.; **sound archive,** a library in which sound recordings are preserved; **sound-book** *disused*, a book supplied with gramophone records to supplement the text; **sound camera** *Cinemat.* (see quot. 1959); **sound check** *colloq.*, a test of sound equipment before a musical performance to ensure that the sound production is correct; **sound-film** *Cinemat.*, a cinematic film with accompanying recorded sound (see also quots. 1923, 1929); **sound gate** *Cinemat.*, the part of a sound head where the sound track is scanned as the film passes through it; **sound head** *Cinemat.*, the part of a film projector concerned with producing an electrical signal from the sound track (see also quot. 1959); **sound-mix**: see *mix *sb.*[2] 2; **sound mixer** see *mixer 1 c; hence **sound-mixing** *vbl. sb.*; **sound picture** = *sound-film* above; also, any recording of an auditory event; **Soundscriber,** a machine for the recording and subsequent reproduction of the spoken word (a proprietary term in the U.S.); **sound shop,** a shop which sells equipment for playing, reproducing, or recording music; **sound stage,** a stage having acoustic properties suitable for the recording of sound (*spec.* one used for filming); **sound stripe** *Cinemat.*, a narrow band of magnetic material on the edge of a film, which contains the sound track; **sound-thief** *slang*, an expert in 'bugging' or the installation and operation of concealed microphones; **sound track** *Cinemat.*, the sound constituent of a film, recorded on the edge of the film stock as either an optical or a magnetic band; also, such a record independent of the film; freq. *attrib.*; also *fig.*; hence **sound-track** *v. trans.*, to provide with a sound track; to serve as a sound track for; **sound truck,** (*a*) = *loud-speaker van* s.v. *loudspeaker 2; (*b*) (see quot. 1959[2]).

1962 (*title*) BBC sound archives recorded programmes library World War 1939–1945. **1977** *Times* 16 May 7/5 In July the Sound Records Department of the Imperial War Museum will be opening to the public... Some have been acquired from..the..BBC sound archives. **1937** *Discovery* Feb. 61/2 *Songs of Wild Birds.* By *E. M. Nicholson* and *L. Koch.* With gramophone records... It is the first sound-book published in Britain. **1938** *Times Lit. Suppl.* 17 Dec. 805/2 The sound-book..seems to be catching on. **1975** *Country Life* 13 Feb. 390/2 Ludwig Koch..conceived the idea of a sound-book—'a combination of text, picture and sound, the last supplied by gramophone records attached to the book'. **1961** G. Millerson *Technique Television Production* i. 14 Another camera and sound boom have taken over. **1929** *Television* Jan. 10/3 (*caption*) The Baird Company's Concert Party and Engineers, photographed in the sight and sound broadcasting studio in Long Acre. **1940** R. S. Lambert *Ariel & all his Quality* vii. 183 The coming of War, which would make sound broadcasting..indispensable..would sound the death-knell of television. **1958** *Listener* 21 Aug. 260/1 One must not imagine that sound broadcasting will fail to be of value to the community for many years to come. **1977** Sound broadcasting [see *television broadcasting* s.v. *television 3 b]. **1904** *Science Siftings* 26 Mar. 353/1 A wonderful camera that will photograph noises... With this sound camera, all noises..can be realistically reproduced. **1958** *New Statesman* 26 July 106/1 ITN's roving reporter, Robin Day, roved as far as Egypt with sound-cameras. **1959** W. S. Sharps *Dict. Cinematogr.* 130/2 *Sound camera.* (1) A film picture camera that makes no external noise in operation and is therefore suitable for use when sound is being recorded. (2) A camera that records sound on film. **1976** *Oxf. Compan. Film* 646/1 Optical sound cameras are now used only to produce negatives for making married prints of finished films. **1977** *Rolling Stone* 13 Jan. 10/1 He runs his hands through his straw-thatched hair as his new band kicks off the sound check with 'You Wear It Well'. **1961** K. Reisz *Technique Film Editing* xii. 185 Having chosen his topics, the producer must get together his unit—cameraman, editor, script-writer and the sound-crew. **1974** A. Morice *Killing with Kindness* ii. 14 It was some American production they were recording over here... He and the rest of the sound crew had been given Tuesday off. **1937** *Amer. Speech* XII. 101 Sound effect..refers to the diabolical work of the sound man or, with greater dignity, the sound engineer. **1973** J. Porter *It's Murder with Dover* iv. 34 The TV cameraman..lowered his camera... A nearby sound engineer agreed. **1923** *Mod. Wireless* I. 418/2 The successful production of such a sound record upon a separate film, the sound-film and the picture-film being run simultaneously. **1927** *Daily Mail* 2 July 8/2 The sound-film of the Walker-Milligan fight which was made by the British Phonofilm Co. **1929** *Times* 30 July 13/2 Contrasting 'dialogue films', which, in imitation of the stage, depend principally on dialogue to tell their story, with 'sound films', which use sound as a supplement to silent technique. **1957** Manvell & Huntley *Film Music* 9 We have tried to show how the first principles of sound film music composition were developed through the imaginative collaboration of composers and film-makers. **1964** N. Marsh *Dead Water* vi. 162 A badly-synchronised sound-film. **1975** G. Howell *In Vogue* 65/2 Sound came in 1927, and by the end of 1928 the worst sound film could outdraw the best silent movie. **1931** G. F. Jones *Sound-Film Reprod.* 12 The film must pass through the sound gate at a uniform speed, in order that the pitch of the music or speech shall not vary. **1960** O. Skilbeck *ABC of Film & TV* 61 The sound gate is the corresponding point—though here the film is in constant flow—in a sound camera or head. **1931** S. K. Wolf in L. Cowan *Recording Sound for Motion Pictures* xx. 289 (*caption*) Schematic diagram of Western Electric sound head. **1959** W. S. Sharps *Dict. Cinematogr.* 131/1 *Sound head,*..the mechanism in a film printing machine that is concerned with the printing of the sound track. **1979** *Amat. Photographer* 10 Jan. 88/1 The sound heads are well screened to reduce hum level and are only brought into contact with the film when the projector is set to 'forward, sound'. **1929** *N.Y. Times* 20 Oct. ix. 8/5 *Playback*..provides a means for the director, the actors and the sound men to determine in general how a scene will sound immediately after it has been taken. **1935** S. W. Pring tr. *L. Sabaneev's Music for Films* vi. 93 The volume of sound emitted is regulated, not by the conductor, but by the soundman in the monitor room. **1971** D. E. Westlake *I gave at Office* (1972) 12 At noon the engineer and the sound man and the director and I would all leave The Hub. **1932** Sound-mix [see *mix *sb.*[2] 2]. **1971** *Sat. Rev.* (U.S.) 25 Dec. 44/1 It was necessary to add quite a lot of traffic noise on the final sound mix. **1938** Sound mixer [see *cut *v.* 21 e]. **1972** D. Francis *Smokescreen* i. 9 The sound mixer took off his ear-phones..and fiddled ..with the knobs on his Nagra recorder. **1977** *Times* 18 Apr. (Gramophone Suppl.) p. iv/6 The controls of the sound-mixing console. **1929** *N.Y. Times* 20 Oct. ix. 8/6 *Soup*, the developing bath in which a sound negative is developed. **1928** *Times* 24 Dec. 28/1 Either British acoustics or the Anglo-German mechanism will presumably be installed in the Gaumont houses, to the exclusion of U.S. sound pictures. **1955** *Radio Times* 22 Apr. 47/3 A recorded sound picture of the Dutch people's struggle to win new land from the sea. **1979** J. Gardner *Nostradamus Traitor* xi. 37 There was a clean sound picture from almost every part of the flat. **1955** *Radio Times* 22 Apr. 1 Radio Times..BBC Sound and Television Programmes. **1966** R. Williams *Communications* (ed. 2) iii. 68 There are more emphatic differences in the distribution of interests in the various BBC sound programmes. **1938** K. Baily in *Radio Times* 21 Oct. 12/2 With a sound radio system that is chiefly a utility service, and in which listeners are participating, the ultimate fusion of vision with sound will be easily achieved. **1952** *Times* 1 Jan. (Rev. of 1951) p. v/2 Sound radio (wireless declined farther towards archaism) has done much during the year. **1971** M. Lee *Dying for Fun* xxiii. 107 The sound radio producer was supervising the recording of an interview. **1900** R. S. Baker *Boy's Bk. Inventions* vii. 258 The cylinder on which the sound pictures or records were to be made was covered with tin foil. **1977** Sound record [see *sound archive* above]. **1957** J. S. Huxley *Relig. without Revelation* (rev. ed.) vii. 171 The invention of the gramophone and the sound-recorder. **1961** L. van der Post *Heart of Hunter* I. i. 30 Charles Leonard, the mechanic who was also our sound recorder..would like nothing better than to go on recording Bushman music and folklore. **1871** *Eng. Mechanic* 17 Nov. 233/1 In sound-recording, I do not think that electro-magnetism would be of much service. **1931** *Electronics* Apr. 587/1 (*heading*) Effects of optical slits in variable area sound recording. **1933** *Chem. Abstr.* XXVII. 50/3 (*title*) Discharge lamp for use with sound-recording apparatus. **1967** A. L. Lloyd *Folk-Song in Eng.* i. 64 [Cecil] Sharp made the notations by ear without the controlling help of sound-recording. **1975** *Language for Life* (Dept. Educ. & Sci.) xv. 234 Another facility of value to the English department..is a sound recording studio. **1958** *Times* 18 Feb. 5/2 Thomas Arthur Howell.., sound recordist.., Twickenham. **1977** *Broadcast* 4 Apr. 25/3 BBC contract news cameramen and sound recordists spelled out their growing concern over pay and conditions. **1931** L. Cowan *Recording Sound for Motion Pict.* 387 *Sound head,* compartment on the projector which contains sound-reproducing systems and mechanisms for guiding and driving film. **1958** M. Kelly *Christmas Egg* iii. 105 Displays of perfectionists' sound-reproducing equipment. **1969** *Gloss. Acoustical Terms* (*B.S.I.*) 41 *Sound reproducing system,* an apparatus for re-creating sound which has been recorded. **1946** *Sun* (Baltimore) 6 Feb. 13/1 The Soundscriber is a recording device which enables observers to describe the position and actions of their assigned horses during a race. The description can be played back immediately..and compared with the pictures of the race. **1950** *Official Gaz.* (U.S. Patent Office) 24 Oct. 1011/2 *Sound Scriber*...for electric sound recording and reproducing machines... Claims use since Feb. 15, 1936. **1968** C. M. Vines *Little Nut-Brown Man* iv. 73 He dictated into the soundscriber, and handed to me the papers referred to in his dictation. **1972** *Daily Colonist* (Victoria, B.C.) 24 May 21/8 Phil Barker tuning a hi-fi set (he's a salesman in a sound shop). **1962** A. Nisbett *Technique Sound Studio* 247 *Crossfade,* a gradual mix from one sound source or group of sources to another. **1931** L. Cowan *Recording Sound for Motion Pict.* 243 Special buildings—sound stages—had to be constructed in which recording could be carried on. **1958** [see *bank *sb.*[2] 10 a]. **1978** S. Sheldon *Bloodline* xvii. 205 Rhys brought Elizabeth to a sound stage, where they made motion pictures for research and for their world-wide advertising and products divisions. **1965** *Focal Encycl. Photogr.* (rev. ed.) I. 1418/1 Recording live sound effects or commentary..may be done on the film actually exposed in the camera (usually containing a magnetic sound stripe) or on a tape recorder. **1979** *Amat. Photographer* 10 Jan. 88/1 One of the main criticisms of sound stripe reproduction has been background hiss and hum picked up at the recording stage. **1929** *Morning Post* 24 May 12/7 There are now 17 sound-studios in New York and Long Island. **1962** A. Nisbett *Technique Sound Studio* 272 *Sound studio,*..any room or hall which is primarily used for microphone work. Its most important properties lie in its size and its acoustics—the way in which sound is diffused and absorbed, and the reverberation time. **1964** M. McLuhan *Understanding Media* xxix. 296 Everyone has at some time wished he were equipped with his own sound system during a movie performance. **1977** 'J. le Carré' *Hon. Schoolboy* iii. 56 Where it was operable, he ran moles and sound-thieves in tandem..[that is], Karla had liked to back up his agent operations with microphones. **1929** *Photoplay* Apr. 31/2 *Sound track,* the narrow band of space along the left side of picture film on which is printed the ribbon-like strip of light and dark lines which constitute the record from which sound is projected. **1946** G. Millar *Horned Pigeon* xiv. 191 He made rude sucking noises with his lips, an exaggerated sound-track for the scene he witnessed through the window. **1949** Sound-track *v.* [see *kinescope *v.*]. **1957** Wodehouse *Over Seventy* xvi. 154 This is not always the laughter of a real studio audience. Frequently, it is tinned or bottled. They preserve it on sound tracks, often dating back for years. **1968** *Radio Times* 28 Nov. 57/5 Excerpts from the sound-track album of Finian's Rainbow. **1977** *New Statesman* 2 Sept. 314/1 The mindlessly self-pitying lyrics were just about swallowable if used to soundtrack shots of Kingston's corrugated iron shanty towns. **1982** *London Review Bks.* IV. xxiv. 8/1 When M. Hulot's author balances a soundtrack, the human voice plays a small and outclassed part in the din of the inanimate. **1935** *Discovery* Sept. 278/2 The ultra-short wave sound transmissions will stimulate further perfection of sound-reproducing apparatus. **1969** *Gloss. Acoustical Terms* (*B.S.I.*) 11 *Sound transmission,* the transfer of sound energy from one medium to another. **1936** P. Rotha *Documentary Film* iv. ii. 208 Sound-trucks are essentially large and cumbersome objects. **1940** *Nation* 30 Mar. 432/3 Forbidding..the operation of their own sound trucks, and the presentation of their own movie. **1959** *Economist* 2 May 433/1 In the cities, towns and villages of Japan over the past three weeks, the days..have been rendered hideous by 'sound-trucks' rumbling through the streets. **1959** W. S. Sharps *Dict. Cinematogr.* 132/1 *Sound truck,* a mobile sound recording unit, usually with its own power supply. **1971** *Black Scholar* Dec. 56/1 The first time we went out on the soundtrucks, I was on the soundtrucks, the first leaflet we put out, I wrote, the first demonstration, I made up the pamphlets.

sound, *a.* Add: **I. 3. c.** Also *spec.* of currency: having a fixed or stable value, esp. based on gold. Freq. as *sound money*. orig. *U.S.*

1841 J. Tyler in J. D. Richardson *Messages & Papers of Presidents 1789–1897* (1897) IV. 85 The idea..of furnishing a sound paper medium of exchange may be entirely abandoned. **1895** *Nation* 19 Dec. 438/1 He has astonished the friends of sound money. **1903** R. T. Ely *Studies in Evol. Industrial Society* 482 The Fabians have been in favour of what is called with us sound currency. **1938** H. V. Hodson *Slump & Recovery* vii. 217 The 'sound-money' provision that only unquestionably strong banks should be allowed to reopen. **1958** *Spectator* 8 Aug. 198/2 Are they now Sound Money men, after thirteen years of Tory-Socialist inflation?

sound, *v.*[1] Add: **I. 2. c.** *to sound off.* (*a*) Of a band: to strike up (see also quot. 1909). Also *imp. U.S. Mil.*

1909 Webster s.v. *sound, to sound off. Mil.,* at a certain point in the ceremony of parade or guard mounting in the United States army, to play, usually marching in quick time from right to left of the line and back;—said of the band or field music. **1919** *Review* (N.Y.) 30 Aug. 350/3 The organization of all possible 'errors' in the use of language into categories and hierarchies, and parading them before classes with all the pomp of 'Sound off!' and 'Pass in review!'. **1936** *Amer. Speech* XI. 61 The adjutant commands, 'Sound off!' and the band marches, playing, back and forth before the stationary troops... And so,..when a man talks loud and long, playing the tune of his own thoughts before uninterested comrades, he is said to be *sounding off*.

(*b*) to speak out, to speak loudly; to complain, protest; to brag; to put forward one's opinion, esp. forcefully and at length. *colloq.* (orig. *U.S.*).

1918 G. E. GRIFFIN *Ballads of Regiment* 39 You low-down, dirty rookey! What in blazes do you mean By sounding off and beefing, not a rag upon you clean. **1920** *Amer. Legion Weekly* 13 Aug. 28 (*caption*) *Sounding off.* But he is sounding off before inspection. You can't blame him because he has been hoping and waiting for the *Weekly*..but it hasn't come. **1935** C. G. FINNEY *Circus of Dr. Lao* 63 Kate, don't go sounding off that way in front of all these people. **1939** J. STEINBECK *Grapes of Wrath* xiii. 174, I didn' mean to sound off at ya, mister. It's the heat. **1943** *Amer. Mercury* Nov. 554 A guy who *sounds off* (talks too much) is told to *knock it off*. **1951** *Sunday Pictorial* 21 Jan. 10/2 The 'Pic' cites a few examples with the sincere wish that someone will shut them up the next time they sound off. **1960** L. COOPER *Accomplices* II. i. 80 He used to sound off about the chap and blackguard him all ends up. **1972** 'E. LATHEN' *Murder without Icing* (1973) xxii. 195 We thought he was just sounding off. **1979** 'A. HAILEY' *Overload* IV. ix. 340 It adds up to him being an exhibitionist with a need to 'sound off' constantly, even in small ways.

3. d. *Black English.* = *to play the dozens* s.v. *PLAY *v.* 16 e; *to sound on* (someone): to taunt, to criticize (someone). Cf. sense 13 below.

1962 R. D. ABRAHAMS in *Jrnl. Amer. Folklore* LXXV. 215 When men do 'sound'..it provides a very different kind of release than when adolescents do. **1971** B. MALAMUD *Tenants* 73 I'm not soundin on you, Lesser, but how can you be so whiteass sure of what you sayin if my book turns out to be two different things than you thought? **1972** W. LABOV *Language in Inner City* p. xxii, Johnny..had a curious bald spot on the top of his head several months ago, since grown over, and he is still sounded on regularly by reference to this bald spot. **1973** E. BULLINS *Theme is Blackness* 107 Hey..baby..why you got to sound on me like that? **1974** H. L. FOSTER *Ribbin', Jivin', & Playin' Dozens* iv. 160 He knows how to 'run a game', to 'signify', to 'woof'..and to 'sound'.

6. (Later examples of legal use with reference to other types of action.)

1918 *Law Rep. Appeal Cases* 289 Whether it sounds in debt or in damages such a cause of action implies a present obligation to pay simultaneous with its coming into existence. **1947** *Law Rep.*.23 Aug. 466 An action against a salvor for negligence or misconduct sounds in tort. **1964** *Mod. Law Rev.* XXVII. III. 264 To juggle with the language of the forms of action and say that the plaintiff's action sounds in tort not contract, cannot alter the fact that the line between liability and non-liability is drawn by seeing whether the act..is, or is not, a breach of contract between two other persons. **1972** *N.Y. Law Jrnl.* 24 Oct. 20/4 While the action sounds in contract, the complaint sets forth two causes of action for unliquidated amounts.

II. 12. (Example.)

1817 LD. SEFTON *Let.* 30 Dec. in *Creevey Papers* (1903) I. xii. 268 It was put into my hand while a surgeon was sounding my bladder..to ascertain whether I had a stone or not.

13. To taunt. Cf. sense 3 d above. *U.S. slang. rare.*

1958 H. SALISBURY *Shook-up Generation* iv. 63 He had heart. He would do things no other boy would dare. He would sound a cop on the beat and run away laughing.

sound, *v.*[2] Add: **2. a.** (Later *transf.* example.)

1972 *Science* 5 May 464/1 Lightweight ionosondes have been placed in satellites, and these sound from the height of the satellite..*down* to the peak of the F layer.

6. a. Also with *out*.

1944 E. S. GARDNER *Case of Careless Kitten* ii. 21 He..wants someone to sound out Aunt Matilda on how she'll feel. **1956** A. H. COMPTON *Atomic Quest* 230 Japan was sounding out Russia for her help in negotiating a conditional surrender. **1960** *News Chron.* 25 Feb. 1/2 He had sent a three-man mission to Madrid to sound-out the Spanish.

sound-alike. [f. SOUND *v.*[1], after *look-alike*.] A person or thing that closely resembles another (or others) in sound or name. Also *attrib.* or as *adj.*

1970 *Sat. Rev.* (U.S.) 31 Oct. 59/1 It is another of those more-of-the-same pieces, like the sound-alikes of another era, written by all those minor contemporary imitators of Haydn and Mozart. **1972** *Eye, Ear, Nose & Throat Monthly* Apr. 142/1 When a pharmacist takes a prescription over the telephone..there is always the possibility that a drug not intended by the prescriber is likely to be dispensed. Such an error could be the result of a 'sound-alike' or a 'read-alike' drug. **1975** *Verbatim* May 12/1 The lost *r* may one day ruin my professional reputation —by converting the word that's meant into an unrelated sound-alike. **1977** *Rolling Stone* 5 May 66/2 Hire a Pendergrass soundalike—David Ebo. **1979** *Logophile* II. v. 10/2 *The Encyclopedia of Homonyms*..claims to be 'the only complete comprehensive collection of 'sound-alike' words ever published'.

Soundex (sau·ndeks). *Information Sci.* [f. SOUND *sb.*[3]] Used, usu. *attrib.*, with reference to a phonetic coding system intended to suppress spelling variations, used esp. in *Med.* to encode surnames for record linkage. Also *absol.*, material encoded using the Soundex code. Hence **Soundex-code** *v. trans.*, to encode (a name or other data) using this code; **Soundex-coded** *ppl. a.*; **Soundex coding** *vbl. sb.*

1959 *Science* 16 Oct. 955/3 The surnames were first reduced to phonetic codes, consisting in each case of the first letter of the name followed by three numeric digits and known as the Russell Soundex Code. *Ibid.* 958/1 The family names on all cards in both files were Soundex coded by means of the computer. **1967** *Amer. Jrnl. Human Genetics* XIX. 340 The usefulness of surname information in its Soundex coded form can be shown to be considerably greater than that of the full alphabetic surnames. **1968** *Brit. Med. Bull.* XXIV. 207/2 The master file of identities of patients is held on magnetic tape in a quasi-alphabetical sequence, based on the Soundex code of surnames. **1970** *Jrnl. Interdisciplinary Hist.* I. 116 Our data are apparently twice as resistant to Soundex coding as Nitzberg's. *Ibid.* 117 No simple strategy such as 'search one Soundex pocket before and one after' will enable us to effect more linkages. *Ibid.*, We..first applied our pretreatments to all surnames in our test file ..and then applied the files of Soundex to the pretreated surnames. **1972** *Computers & Humanities* VI. 190 In the first attempt a quasi-alphabetic sequence known as the Soundex code, which has been used in the field of medical record linkage, was utilized. The Soundex system sets aside the least reliable portions of Anglo-Saxon surnames, thus Smith/Smyth/Smythe all are codified the same.

sounding, *vbl. sb.*[1] Add: **2. b.** *Black English.* Playing the dozens (*PLAY *v.* 16 e).

1962 R. D. ABRAHAMS in *Jrnl. Amer. Folklore* LXXV. 209 The dozens are commonly called 'playing' or 'sounding'. **1965** *Ibid.* LXXVIII. 343 Sounding, especially Mother-Sounding, demonstrates the second place given to the mother-son bond in comparison to the primary place assigned the clique. **1972** W. LABOV *Language in Inner City* p. xviii, The setting was essentially that of a party..with card games, eating and drinking, singing and sounding. **1974** H. L. FOSTER *Ribbin', Jivin', & Playin' Dozens* v. 183 In Pottsville, Pennsylvania, the term is sounding... In a Brooklyn, New York, secondary school the terms ranking and sounding are still used.

sounding, *vbl. sb.*[2] Add: **1. a.** Now usu. by means of echo.

1966 *McGraw-Hill Encycl. Sci. & Technol.* XIII. 216/1 Since about the middle of the 1920s, virtually all deep-sea soundings have been made by echo sounding.

b. Also with *out*.

1969 *Daily Tel.* 11 Nov. 21/4 The secret sounding-out by Plessey and BSR was an effort to clear the hurdle before breathing a word, but a share jump precipitated events.

c. *transf.* The determination of any physical property at a depth in the sea or at a height in the atmosphere; an instance of this.

1875 *Proc. R. Soc.* XXIII. 249 Temperature-soundings were taken on the 28th of September and on the 3rd of October, at depths of 2800 and 1420 fathoms respectively. **1947** *Sci. Progr.* XXXV. 88 These soundings have also shown exceedingly dry layers..to exist from time to time in the troposphere. **1955** E. BURGESS *Frontier to Space* iii. 24 The use of the rocket for altitude sounding is by no means a new idea. **1974** *Physics Bull.* Jan. 11/3 Further instrumental developments are bound to follow and it may be that balloon and rocket soundings of the atmosphere will soon become obsolete.

d. *Archæol.* A trial boring made on a site to gain preliminary information. Cf. *SONDAGE.

1957 K. KENYON *Digging up Jericho* 170 Our excavation at the highest point on the central ridge..was only a restricted sounding. **1967** *Amer. Anthropologist* LXIX. 401/2 At Chagar Bazar, Huwaish (at which only a seven-day sounding was carried out), and in the rest of Mesopotamia 'religious responsibilities rested with the local secular chiefs'.

5. *sounding-pole*; **sounding balloon** = *BALLON-SONDE; **sounding rocket,** a rocket designed to carry scientific instruments into the upper atmosphere in order to make measurements during its flight.

1902 Sounding balloon [see *BALLON-SONDE]. **1937** C. G. PHILP *Stratosphere & Rocket Flight* v. 33 By the aid of 'sounding' balloons..data has been obtained of the earth's atmosphere at a height of over 23 miles. **1965** R. A. CRAIG *Upper Atmosphere* ii. 17 Sounding balloons are most commonly made of neoprene and inflated with helium or hydrogen. **1875** 'MARK TWAIN' in *Atlantic Monthly* May 569/1 You can go and get the sounding-pole. **1975** *Islander* (Victoria, B.C.) 23 Feb. 13/2 Tying themselves together like mountain climbers, sounding poles in hand, they forded the river. **1947** *Amer. Jrnl. Physics* XV. 139/1 (*caption*) The WAC Corporal sounding rocket, which reached 43 mi altitude. **1962** F. I. ORDWAY et al. *Basic Astronautics* iv. 121 Data obtained from the sounding rockets were correlated with readings from the Explorer 4 artificial satellite. **1978** PASACHOFF & KUTNER *University Astron.* xxviii. 710 (*caption*) The ultraviolet spectrum of 3C 273, taken with a 40-cm telescope, the largest ever flown on a sounding rocket.

sounding, *ppl. a.*[1] Add: **1. d.** *sounding sand* = *singing sand* s.v. *SINGING *ppl. a.* 4 b.

1884 *Proc. Amer. Assoc. Adv. Sci. 1883* 251 The sounding sand is near the surface only, at the depth of one or two feet the acoustic properties disappear. **1897** G. P. MERRILL *Treat. Rocks, Rock-Weathering & Soils* II. ii. 143 On certain Hawaiian beaches, such sands [*sc.* shell sands] give out a distinct note..when walked over, or even when shaken in a closed vessel, and are popularly known as sounding, or singing, sands. **1976** *Nature* 5 Feb. 368/2 Hardly surprisingly in view of their weird effects, sounding sands are incorporated into folklore and legends going back at least 1,500 years.

soup, *sb.* Add: **1.** (Further *fig.* examples.) Phr. (*from*) *soup to nuts* (U.S. colloq.), from beginning to end, completely; everything.

1876 GEO. ELIOT *Let.* 2 May (1956) VI. 244 Are you not sometimes made rather desponding by the reading of newspapers and periodicals?.. All information is given in a soup of comment. **1910** C. MATHEWSON *Won in Ninth* 143 He knew the game from 'soup to nuts'. **1938** H. ASBURY *Sucker's Progress* 16 For many years a common expression was 'from soda to hock', meaning the whole thing, from soup to nuts. **1946** E. O'NEILL *Iceman Cometh* I. 79, I know all about that game from soup to nuts. **1964** F. O'ROURKE *Mule for Marquesa* 42 'Everything here we asked for?' 'Soup to nuts... Nothing but the best.' **1977** *Undercurrents* June–July 9/1 The twelve page Corruption Supplement is a rich soup of sex, planning scandals, corruption trials, housing fiddles, [etc.].

b. *Biol.* A solution rich in organic compounds which, it is believed, formerly made up the oceans or lakes of the earth and was the environment in which cellular life originated. Freq. as *primordial soup*.

[**1929** J. B. S. HALDANE in *Rationalist Ann.* 8 When ultra-violet light acts on a mixture of water, carbon dioxide, and ammonia, a vast variety of organic substances are made... Before the origin of life they must have accumulated till the primitive oceans reached the consistency of hot dilute soup.] **1956** *Amer. Scientist* XLIV. 356 One plausible explanation is that spontaneous resolution of an *early* biosynthetic intermediate from the primordial nutritional 'soup' of the first organisms led to a monoconfigurational world. **1971** I. G. GASS et al. *Understanding Earth* ix. 126/1 This primitive soup provided a nutrient 'broth' for the first living organisms which finally arose within it. **1976** R. DAWKINS *Selfish Gene* xi. 211 Floating chaotically free in the primeval soup. **1977** *Vole* No. 4. 13/2 We both [*sc.* humans and plants] have common ancestors..in that pool of organic nutrients known as the primordial soup.

2. b. For *U.S.* read 'orig. *U.S.*' and add further examples.

1915 J. BUCHAN *Thirty-Nine Steps* ii. 37, I was in the soup—that was pretty clear. **1917** LLOYD GEORGE *Let.* 31 July (1973) 184 Henderson has now put us into the soup & there is no knowing what will happen. **1925** [see *EYEBROW 1 d]. **1939** H. G. WELLS *Holy Terror* I. ii. 38 We're in the soup... We've got to do 1914 over again. **1968** *Listener* 23 May 660/3 You find you may want to move a group of pictures..to a different part of the building, and if the rooms over there are designed for quite a different kind of picture, you're rather in the soup. **1977** C. MCCULLOGH *Thorn Birds* xvii. 455, I do feel very sorry for her, and it makes me more determined than ever not to land in the same soup she did.

d. Fog; thick cloud. Cf. *PEA-SOUP a.

1901 [see sense 2 c]. **1941** F. H. JOSEPH *Let.* 7 Apr. in *Britain at War* (1942) 4 It wasn't long..before we were in the soup again. **1966** E. WEST *Night is Time for Listening* iii. 107 Over the North Sea the soup was dense and threatening; turbulence was marked. **1972** J. GORES *Dead Skip* (1973) xxiii. 161 Ballard watched the taillights recede into the soup.

e. Nitro-glycerine or gelignite.

1902 *N.Y. Tribune* 22 Oct. 8/4 Dynamite or nitro-glycerine is called 'soup'. **1903** I. K. FRIEDMAN *Autobiogr. of Beggar* vii. 218 Louis learned how ter make de 'soup' from a gang of 'yeagers' dat used ter blow de doors off country banks. **1905** [see sense 2 c]. **1920** 'SAPPER' *Bull-Dog Drummond* x. 265 I've got the soup here—gelignite. **1930** D. L. SAYERS *Strong Poison* xiii. 169 Sam put the soup in at the 'inges and it blowed the 'ole front clean off. **1960** *Observer* 24 Jan. 5/1 The American petermen had started it long before the First World War by using soup, nitro-glycerine in liquid form, to pour through a little plasticine channel to blow the fashionable combination lock safes.

f. *Photogr.* and *Cinemat.* A processing chemical, esp. the developer.

1929 *N.Y. Times* 20 Oct. IX. 8 *Soup*, the developing bath in which a sound negative is developed. **1934** *Tit-Bits* 31 Mar. 12/3 The chemicals in which the film is developed are known as 'soup'. **1969** GISH & PINCHOT *Lilian Gish* ix. 102 Joe showed me how film was developed in the 'soup'. **1978** L. DEIGHTON *SS-GB* xxiii. 220 Any special instructions? Over or under development? Fine grain soup? **1979** *SLR Camera* Dec. 60/1 When you've mixed the soup remember to keep it in a well stoppered dark bottle which has been thoroughly cleaned.

g. *Surfing.* (See quot. 1962.)

1962 T. MASTERS *Surfing made Easy* 65 *Soup*, the foam or broken portion of a wave. **1966** *Weekly News* (N.Z.) 19 Jan. 6/2 When going through waves, point the board directly into the oncoming 'soup'. **1968** *Surfer Mag.* Jan. 24/3 By standing feet parallel, you can float over breaking soup. **1977** *Surfing World* (Austral.) XVII. II. 88 Plow through miles of soup.

3. *soup-plate* (earlier example; also *fig.*), *-pot* (earlier example), *-tureen* (earlier example).

1726 D. EATON *Let.* 16 Feb. (1971) 46, I..left directions in writing..what to pack up. I wrote down all manner of herbes, and the soop plates, &c. **1924** E. M. FORSTER *Passage to India* I. iii. 28 A sunk soup plate of a lawn. **1939** H. HODGE *Cab, Sir?* 217 The badge itself..is called a 'soup-plate'. **1964** C. WILLOCK *Enormous Zoo* v. 80, I shone my torch..and found a couple of large pink soup-plates glaring back at me—a hippo. **1751** H. GLASSE *Art of Cookery* (ed. 4) App. 331 Put them with the Fins and Head in a Soop-pot. **1834** DICKENS *Sk. Boz* (1836) 1st Ser. I. 160 Delighted to screen himself behind a soup tureen.

b. soup-and-fish *slang*, men's evening dress, a dinner suit.

1918 WODEHOUSE *Piccadilly Jim* i. 26 He took me to supper at some swell joint where they all had the soup-and-fish on but me. **1945** 'A. GILBERT' *Black Stage* xi. 149 What do you do about dinner here? Soup-and-fish or just a clean collar? **1970** H. MCLEAVE *Question of Negligence* (1973) xviii. 141 Get him to take off his soup-and-fish and show us his scar.

4. soup bunch *U.S. dial.* (see quot. 1923); **soup-fin (shark),** a brown or grey shark with large teeth, *Galeorhinus zygopterus*, found off the Pacific coast of North America and once hunted for the value of its liver and fins; **soup gun** *U.S. Mil. slang*, a mobile army kitchen (? *obs.*); **soup-kitchen** (earlier example); hence **soup-kitchener,** one who accepts food from a soup-kitchen; **soup line** *U.S.*, a queue of people waiting to be fed at a soup-kitchen; **soup man** *Criminals' slang*, an expert user of nitro-glycerine, etc.; **soup-shop,** (*a*) (earlier example); **soup-strainer (moustache)** *colloq.*, a long moustache; **soup-ticket** (earlier example).

1923 *Dialect Notes* V. 244 *Soup bunch*, a small bundle of vegetables for soup. **1938** *Mississippi* (Federal Writers' Project) 286 The grocery stores and the fruit and vegetable stands sell 'soup bunches' which provide the base for home-cooked vegetable soup. **1905** D. S. JORDAN *Guide to Study of Fishes* I. xxx. 541 The soup-fin shark.. is found on the coast of California, where its fins are highly valued by the Chinese. **1941** *Sun* (Baltimore) 25 Nov. 5/3 Tales of big profits in soupfin shark liver fishing sent E. Smith..hustling..to get his share. **1961** E. S. HERALD *Living Fishes of World* 27/2 In 1942 and 1943 about five thousand soupfins were caught..west of Los Angeles. **1975** *Daily Colonist* (Victoria, B.C.) 22 Aug. 16/5 In San Diego the markets call it shark or 'soupfin'. **1975** *Islander* (Victoria, B.C.) 30 Nov. 10/2 One shark hunted to near extinction because of its liver..is the soup fin shark. **1918** C. J. SWAN *My Company* 72 The cooks took the 'soup gun', as they immediately nicknamed the kitchen, all apart. **1928** A. C. HAVLIN *Hist. Company A* 37 In spite of being accompanied by our 'soup gun', we frequently charged the trenches assisted only by coffee and a strip of bacon between two slices of bread. **1839** C. SINCLAIR *Holiday House* xi. 255 We never had a drop of broth from the soup-kitchen all winter. **1907** G. B. SHAW *Major Barbara* II. 220 You lie, you old soup-kitchener, you. **1938** C. HIMES *Black on Black* (1973) 167 The panic which he had prophesied was on hand and already soup lines had come into existence. **1980** *TWA Ambassador* Oct. 69/3 We had soup lines and the Depression because men lost confidence in themselves. **1961** B. KNOX *Die for Big Betsy* ii. 44 'Denby's a "soup" man,' he said. 'Specializes in second-rate safe-blowings.' **1799** *Manch. Mercury* 8 Jan. 4/5 The plan of the soup shops at Birmingham might be advantageously followed at Manchester. **1932** WODEHOUSE *Hot Water* viii. 153 He did not propose to have a valet hanging around him festooned with fungus and snorting at him all the time from behind a great beastly soupstrainer. **1962** E. LUCIA *Klondike Kate* iii. 86 A soulfully humming male quartet in soup-strainers and sideburns. **1968** *Listener* 1 Aug. 140/1 At the telegraph office we aroused with great difficulty an elderly man with a large grey soup-strainer moustache. **1839** E. HALL *Diary* 29 Jan. in O. A. Sherrard *Two Victorian Girls* (1966) i. 11 Our poor house was besieged by a host of people come for soup tickets.

soup, *v.* Add: **2.** [cf. SOUP *sb.* 2 b.] To place in difficulties, to bring to grief. Usu. in pa. pple. *colloq.*

1895 W. C. GORE in *Inlander* Dec. 114 *Soup*. v., to cause to fail; to bring to grief. **1922** JOYCE *Ulysses* 160 Luck I had the presence of mind to dive into Manning's or I was souped. **1964** *Daily Tel.* 16 Jan. 26/4 Admitting that he earned £3,000 a year, Lord Taylor said that if he accepted a junior Ministry he would be 'souped'.

3. [cf. quot. 1911 s.v. SOUP *sb.* 2 c; perh. infl. by SUPER-.] Orig. and chiefly with *up*. To modify (an engine, aircraft, motor vehicle, etc.) to increase its power and efficiency. Also *transf.* and *fig. colloq.* (orig. *U.S.*).

1931 [implied at *SOUPED(-UP) *ppl. a.*] **1933** C. K. STEWART *Speech Amer. Airman* 92 *Soup Up*, to super-charge. **1939** *Sun* (Baltimore) 3 Aug. 1/6 We have done this without 'souping up' our engines, without putting alcohol in our gasoline,..or flying with motors which last only five hours. **1949** A. HYND *We are Public Enemies* i. 22 Dillinger..bought two new Fords. He souped up the motors... Now he was ready to act as his own getaway driver. *Ibid.* 29 John Dillinger and five other public enemies arrived in three souped-up Ford cars. **1959** *Spectator* 17 Apr. 557/1 The collection is souped up with frantic editorial comments. **1962** *John o' London's* 8 Feb. 140/2, I don't think Mr. Hauser was at his most perceptive in souping-up what was already very funny. **1965** L. WHITTEN *Progeny of Adder* (1966) 31 The quintet, souped up on sets—tranquilizers and pep pills taken together. **1972** F. WARNER *Lying Figures* III. 35 The coffee soups her up so that she has to take a tranquillizer. **1976** K. BENTON *Single Monstrous Act* v. 152 He had lovingly souped up the Escort's engine, and now gave it full throttle. **1979** J. GARDNER *Nostradamus Traitor* xxxix. 188 A German car: Opel Kadett, souped, and probably reinforced.

So **sou·ped(-up)** *ppl. a.*; **sou·ping(-up)** *vbl. sb.*

1931 *Automotive Industries* 30 May 826/1 Ray Keech's run at Daytona Beach in the White Triplex powered with three 'souped-up' Liberty engines. **1941** *Time* 18 Aug. 76/2 Its hero, Slave Trader Matthew Flood, is built like a souped-up Abraham Lincoln. **1949** [see *SOUP *v.* 3]. **1956** D. WALKER *Harry Black* xiii. 196 You're like a souped-up version of my mother. **1957** *New Yorker* 2 Nov. 95/2 Their superb High Fidelity components reproduce all the sounds of the original..with no 'souped-up' tones, squeaks or other distortions. **1960** *News Chron.* 16 June 4/6 Without any souping at all, the Mini-Minor..produces a very useful performance. *Ibid.* 4/7 A specially cast manifold for the souped version of the Mini-Austin. **1961** *Times* 7 Nov. 19/1 In Britain a thriving business has grown up in tuning and modifying the engines of existing models to give more performance. So widespread has this practice (referred to by enthusiasts as 'brewing up', 'souping up', or merely 'hotting up') become, particularly with 'Minis' that the B.M.C. introduced an 'officially hotted up' version last September. **1965** *Listener* 18 Nov. 795/1 As if lacking confidence in his own directorial inventiveness, Visconti takes recourse during one sequence to a modulated version of Fellini's style, and at another juncture provides his audience with souped-up..Antonioni. **1975** B. GARFIELD *Death Sentence* (1976) ii. 11 A souped-up car with enormous rear tires growled past him. **1980** *SLR Camera* July 7/1 News from the Colonies tells us that Ilford have introduced a 'souped-up' ID-11 for processing black and white film in the USA.

‖**soupe** (sūp). The French word for SOUP *sb.*, usu. used with defining addition, as *soupe à l'oignon* (onion soup), etc.

1767 'CORIAT JUNIOR' *Another Traveller!* I. II. xx. 196, I well remember that the good father supt up his *Soupe a l'Oignon.* **1777** P. THICKNESSE *Year's Journey* II. xliv. 98 A Frenchman eats his *soupe* and *bouille* at twelve o'clock. **1794** [see SOUP MAIGRE *attrib.*]. **1863** G. MEREDITH *Let.* 9 Feb. (1970) I. 210 Soupe, à la sage femme. **1865** M. EYRE *Lady's Walks* xxxi. 330 They..dine, except on fête days, on *soupe aux choux*, or *aux haricots.* **1883** 'WYVERN' *Culinary Jottings for Madras* (ed. 4) xxx. 321 '*Soupe à l'oignon*':—Slice a couple of Bombay onions; powder them well with flour... Grated Parmesan should accompany. **1904** A. BENNETT *Great Man* xxvi. 306 The host's first spoonful of *soupe aux moules.* **1952** D. AMES *Murder, Maestro, Please* xvii. 126 She insisted on making *soupe à l'oignon* to go with the contents of the bar. **1975** *New Yorker* 6 Oct. 135/1 Good pastries are still sold, along with such popular dishes as *soupe Chinoise*, a pungent concoction containing shrimp, meat, and vegetables. **1980** E. LEATHER *Duveen Letter* xiv. 163 The waiter brought the *soupe à l'oignon.*

soupé, var. *SOUPER *sb.*[2]

souper, *sb.*[1] (Earlier example.)

1854 *Tablet* 11 Nov. 713/4 Every Souper, every tyrannical agent, every sworn Orangeman, will be a friend to this new order of things.

‖**souper** (supe), *sb.*[2] Also **soupé.** [Fr.] Esp. in France: an evening meal, supper; *souper intime* (æ̃ntīm) ['intimate']: for two, in privacy.

1787 H. MATY tr. *Riesbeck's Trav. Germany* I. xx. 238 But, alas! so soon as the body is satisfied here, so soon does the mind long for the friendly *dines* and *soupés* of Paris. **1834** *Baboo* I. i. 10 Those soupers are inestimable, and must not cease. **1851** E. RUSKIN *Let.* in W. James *Order of Release* (1948) ix. 169 The monk received us very kindly and soon after we had souper, milk, macaroni, salt fish, fritters and very bad wine. **1967** J. RICHARDSON *Courtesans* iii. 37/2 (*caption*) A courtesan bound for a *souper intime.* **1970** *Guardian* 30 Jan. 9/1 The *souper intime* with..low lights, and music. **1976** *New Yorker* 26 Jan. 40/3 By the time she returned, to give Joey a *souper* of boiled-liver chunks, macaroni, pig's maw, beef kidney, and rice, it was almost midnight.

soupie varr. *SOPIE, *SOUPY *sb.*

‖**soupirant** (sūpiraṅ). [Fr., = sighing (lover), pres. pple. of *soupirer* to sigh.] A male admirer, a suitor.

1849 THACKERAY *Pendennis* I. x. 93 And is Sir Derby Oaks..another *soupirant*?.. Another admirer of Miss Fotheringay? **1969** J. FOWLES *French Lieutenant's Woman* lxi. 443 But he no sooner saw that than he saw the reality of such an arrangement—how he would become the secret butt of this corrupt house, the starched *soupirant*, the pet donkey.

soupje, var. *SOPIE.

souple. Add: Also *souple silk.* Hence **sou·pling** *vbl. sb.*, the act or process of partially degumming raw silk which is to be made into souple silk.

1888 A. SANSONE *Dyeing* I. viii. 159 *Souple Silk*, silk which only loses 5 to 8 per cent of its weight, and is consequently not completely deprived of its gum. *Ibid.* 160 *Soupling*: Work 1½ hours in water, containing 3 to 4 grains of cream of tartar per litre. **1927** HORSFALL & LAWRIE *Dyeing Textile Fibres* x. 283 In the case of degumming for souple silk, the object is to remove only a portion of the gum... An operation called 'soupling' then follows, when the silk is treated for one and a half hours in a solution containing three to four parts tartar per 1,000. **1964** S. R. CROCKETT *Dyeing & Printing* ii. 23 Varying grades of degumming are exemplified by ecru silk..souple silk..and boiled-off silk.

soupy, *a.* Add: **1.** (Earlier example.)

1869 DICKENS *Uncomm. Traveller* (1958) xxxiii. 333 The dirty table-cloths, the stuffy, soupy, airless atmosphere.

2. Sentimental; mawkish.

1953 R. CRAWSHAY-WILLIAMS *Let.* 1 Aug. in B. Russell *Autobiogr.* (1969) III. ii. 92, I was glad to see..your emphasis..upon the role of power politics rather than ideologies—and also your re-emphasis upon the way in which science and scientific method have conditioned (all that is 'best' in) Western Values. It is maddening the way in which the opposite 'soupy' belief is accepted even by most unsoupy people. **1976** *National Observer* (U.S.) 20 Nov. 24/5 He has included them in the autobiography, along with..a series of sincerely affectionate, if soupy, tributes to Daddy from family and friends. **1977** *New Yorker* 4 July 82/3 There is the silliness of the movie's plangency: hard to feel soupy about a talented couple giving up their love because of the stardust in their eyes.

Hence **sou·piness,** sentimentality.

1963 WODEHOUSE *Stiff Upper Lip, Jeeves* v. 40 That squashy soupiness of hers, that subtle air she had of being on the point of talking baby-talk. **1977** *Gramophone* Jan. 1153/1 The slow movement brings a hint of soupiness in the tone.

soupy (sū·pi), *sb. U.S. Mil. slang.* Also **soupie.** [f. SOUP *sb.* + -Y[6], -IE.] (A summons to) a meal.

1899 J. R. SKINNER *Hist. Fourth Illinois Volunteers* 26 Answered the familiar call of 'soupy, soupy, soupy,' at 5:30 o'clock. **1918** *Stars & Stripes* 5 July 4, I say 'Yum yum' when 'soupie' blows. **1939** *Amer. Speech* XIV. 30/2 *Soupy*, n., mess call (general U.S. Army usage).

sour, *a.* and *sb.*[1] Add: **A.** *adj.* **I. 1. b.** (Later examples.)

1865 C. F. BROWNE *Artemus Ward: his Travels* 151 A Vigilance Committee, which hangs the more vicious of the pestiferous crowd to a sour apple-tree. **1922** JOYCE *Ulysses* 160 We'll hang Joe Chamberlain on a sourapple tree.

2. b. Esp. in *to go* (or *turn*) *sour* (*on* a person).

1928 *Daily Tel.* 20 Mar. 11/5 Sir Victor Sassoon.. advised the House to pass the bill, as there was a danger of the Government, in racing parlance, 'going sour'. **1952** C. DAY LEWIS tr. *Virgil's Aeneid* IX. 194 Let only my luck stay good And not turn sour on me. **1957** A. MACNAB *Bulls of Iberia* XV. 214 He cannot afford to ease up in one or two bulls, or the whole afternoon may go sour on him. **1964** L. NKOSI *Rhythm of Violence* 50 What is a cynic but a romanticist turned sour? **1971** A. SAMPSON *New Anatomy of Britain* 278 It is at the meetings with Treasury men that so many political ideals have been defeated, so many bold promises gone sour. **1981** P. NIESEWAND *Word of Gentleman* i. 14 Moorhouse and his party had wiped the floor with the opposition... Then suddenly everything went sour.

3*. Of petroleum, natural gas, etc.: containing a relatively high proportion of sulphur. Opp. *sweet.*

1919 E. W. DEAN *Motor Gasoline Properties* (U.S. Bureau of Mines Techn. Paper No. 214) 24 There is a possibility that gasoline 'sour' to the doctor test may have been the cause of certain reported corrosion of metal parts of carburetors. **1925** *Petroleum Age* 1 Jan. 16/2 Sour oils also have a distinctively unpleasant odor which is absent in sweet oils. **1936** W. L. NELSON *Petroleum Refinery Engin.* xxiv. 527 For 'sour' sulfur-bearing light distillates, the doctor treatment must be used. **1967** *Wall St. Jrnl.* 31 Jan. 32/2 Recovery of elemental sulphur from 'sour' gas is expected to materially increase available supplies. **1979** *Economist* 11 Aug. 67/1 There is a sour gas formation under the country's best oil field, Yibal.

II. 4. b. Of music: out of tune.

[**1593** SHAKS. *Richard II* v. iv. 42 How sowre sweet Musicke is, When Time is broke, and no Proportion kept?] **1937** *Amer. Speech* XII. 48/2 *Sour*, out-of-tune playing. **1976** *Gramophone* Feb. 1356/1 String tone is wirey, even a bit sour in the G minor, especially during loud passages.

III. 9. a. *sour-favoured, -tongued* (later example).

1916 JOYCE *Portrait of Artist* iv. 187 The face was eyeless and sourfavoured. **1930** BLUNDEN *Summer's Fancy* 22 And black-capped and gowned The sour-tongued master stared and hovered nigh.

10. sourball, sour-ball *U.S.*, (*a*) a peevish or sour-tempered person; also *attrib.* or as *adj.*; (*b*) a boiled sweet with an acid taste; **sour beef** *U.S. local* = *SAUERBRATEN; **sour bread,** restrict † to sense in Dict. and add: (*b*) *U.S.*, sourdough bread; **sour cream,** *spec.* fresh cream soured by the addition of lactic acid; **sour crop** *Vet. Sci.*, oidiomycosis of chickens, turkeys, or other poultry, producing a crop filled with foul-smelling liquid and often thickened and ulcerated; **sour grapes:** see GRAPE *sb.*[1] 1 a in Dict. and Suppl.; hence **sour-grapeism,** the action or practice of disparaging something because it is out of one's reach; **sour-grapey** *a.*, disparaging because something is out of reach; **sour-grapiness; sour-mash** *U.S.*, (whisky made from) fermenting grain mash; also *attrib.*; **sour orange,** the Seville orange, *Citrus aurantium* distinguished by its thick skin and bitter pulp; also, the tree bearing this fruit; also *attrib.*; **sourpuss, sour-puss** *slang* (orig. *U.S.*) [*PUSS *sb.*[2]], a sour-faced person; a grumbler; a killjoy; also *attrib.*; so **sour-pussed** *a.*, sour-faced, miserable; **sour veld(t)** *S. Afr.*, grassland covered with coarse grass lacking nutritive value.

1900 *Dialect Notes* II. 62 *Sour-ball*, a chronic grumbler. 1933 *Manufacturing Chemist* Nov. 41/1 Assorted Sour Balls (purchased in a railroad depot, Boston, Mass.)... Balls had a coating of grain. 1935 J. O'Hara *Appointment in Samarra* iv. 123 My God, you're sourball tonight. 1962 E. Lacy *Freeloaders* vi. 113 You think Gil is nuts? He's been acting the sourball all day. 1964 [see *halva]. 1976 *N.Y. Rev. Bks.* 15 Apr. 33/1 The witness from those years is overwhelming, and not just from snobbish intellectuals and sourball novelists. 1935 *Evening Sun* (Baltimore) 2 Mar. 18/3 Mrs. Haberkorn was 'a world champion' sour beef cooker. 1947 *Sun* (Baltimore) 3 Nov. 11/8 (Advt.), Old fashioned sour beef & dumplings. 1968 E. Staebler *Food that really Schmecks* 36 Sauerbraten (Sour Beef Pot Roast). 1884 H. A. Dwight *Bread-Making* 46 Sour bread is such a common evil that a special chapter should be given to it... Sour bread follows..as a consequence of sour yeast. 1902 W. Faulkner *Go down, Moses* 196 Then for two weeks he ate the coarse, rapid food—the shapeless sour bread, the wild strange meat. 1977 H. Fast *Immigrants* iii. 201 Lunch was homemade sausage meat..and fresh milk as thick as cream, and with it Mary Gallagher's home-baked sour bread and home-churned butter. 1855 E. Acton *Mod. Cookery* (rev. ed.) vi. 143 'Sour cream' is an ingredient not much approved by English taste, but it enters largely into German cookery. 1961 'E. Lathen' *Banking on Death* (1962) iii. 22 Roast beef, baked potato—'For God's sake, no sour cream!' 1978 D. Francis *Trial Run* iii. 45 The object of her curiosity..spooned sour cream into his borsch. 1951, 1975 Sour crop [see *oidiomycosis]. 1975 B. Meyrick *Behind Light* xv. 199 'Sour crop,' he announced..as he gently felt the chicken's full crop. 1853 Mrs. Gaskell *Cranford* i. 5 There, economy was always 'elegant', and money-spending always 'vulgar and ostentatious'; a sort of sour grapeism which made us very peaceful and satisfied. 1957 R. W. Zandvoort *Handbk. Eng. Gram.* ix. ii. 307 The suffix is added to syntactic word groups..in such formations as *sour-grapeism*, [etc.]. 1962 *Punch* 11 Apr. 579/1 It may have sounded a silly and sour-grapey sort of thing to say. 1980 *Good Housekeeping* Nov. 15/3 Perhaps I'm being a tiny bit sour grapey. 1970 *Guardian* 30 July 9/4 One Amsterdam camp site owner who..almost moulded away with sour grapiness. 1885 'C. E. Craddock' *Prophet of Gt. Smoky Mountains* 150 Him an' me run a sour mash still on the top o' the mounting. 1892 'Mark Twain' *Amer. Claimant* i. 23 Over-confidence and gaiety induced by over-plus of sour-mash. 1958 'W. Henry' *Seven Men at Mimbres Springs* 216 The reservation doctor..was definitely given to a rigorous regimen of sourmash Kentucky bond taken internally for pain as self-directed. 1976 T. Stoppard *Dirty Linen* 65 Big bellied, red-eyed men in white crumpled suits swig from medicine bottles of two-year-old sour mash bourbon. [1890 E. Bonavia *Cultivated Oranges & Lemons* pl. vi, The Seville Orange of Kandy..known there by the name of *Amool Dódan* (sour round orange).] 1920 H. J. Webber in *Bull. Calif. Agric. Exper. Station* No. 317. 268 An examination of sweet and sour orange seedling stock..showed the presence of many widely different types. 1926 H. H. Hume *Cultivation of Citrus Fruits* iv. 45 Sour oranges, or bigarades, are distinguished from the sweet varieties by their broadly winged petioles. 1938 M. K. Rawlings *Yearling* i. 12 There were..sour orange biscuits. 1973 *Advocate-News* (Barbados) 26 Feb. 5/1 A virus of unknown nature..was found to be infecting sour orange seedlings. 1937 *Sun* (Baltimore) 28 May 14/7 Hadley doesn't look like the kind of sour-puss who would do that. 1942 *Penguin New Writing* XV. 92 He pretends to be more interested in the antics of his birds than in the puffings an' blowings of a sourpuss of a council clerk. 1960 *Guardian* 15 Mar. 7/3 It's about time we got away from sourpuss champions. 1966 'H. MacDiarmid' *Company I've Kept* i. 34 All the Moral Rearmers and other sour-pusses in Scotland. 1980 *Logophile* IV. i. 45/2 He had always been henpecked by his wife, a sourpuss with a waspish temper. 1952 J. Steinbeck *East of Eden* xlvii. 520 Henry was a man who liked fun—needed it. A sour-pussed associate could make him sick. [1801 Sour veldt: see *sour grass 3.] 1863 J. S. Dobie *S. Afr. Jrnl.* (1945) 76 On across the Little Tugela ..over rank sour-veldt grass. 1894 T. R. Sim *Sk. Flora Kaffraria* 14 The sour veld..is composed of rank strong growing grasses. 1948 *Star* (Johannesburg) 20 Oct. 3/7 Sourveld management presents formidable problems. 1978 *Jrnl. Afr. Hist.* XIX. 479 Seasonal loss of nutrition of the plateau grasses (i.e. the presence of sourveld).

B. *sb.*[1] **3.** (Earlier example.)

1862 J. Thomas *How to mix Drinks* 59 The brandy sour is made with the same ingredients as the brandy fix, omitting all fruits.

sour, *v.* Add: **4. b.** In pa. pple., also const. *on* (the source of embitterment, etc.). *U.S.* and *Austral. colloq.*

1898 E. N. Westcott *David Harum* xli. 346 He's kind o' soured on the hull thing. 1906 E. Dyson *Fact'ry 'Ands* xvii. 225 'Fact is,' said the packer, 'we're gettin' er bit soured on wimmin.' 1907 *St. Nicholas* XXXIV. 601/2 Maybe if I get any more soured on Hammond I'll skate over with my trunk and try Ferry Hill.

source, *sb.* Add: **4. e.** Also, a person supplying information, an informant, a spokesman.

1934 Webster s.v. *source n.*, one who or that which supplies information. 1940 W. Faulkner *Hamlet* ii. i. 131 The Varners would know by now from the one incontrovertible source, the girl herself, that two of them were not guilty. *a* 1961 E. M. Mills in *Webster* s.v. [1]*source*, Sources close to the chief executive report he is planning to request the Legislature to approve state purchase. 1973 *Atlanta* (Georgia) *Jrnl.* 19 Apr. 17A/1 Deputy White House press secretary Gerald Warren issued the following statement: 'The White House is not prepared to react to a story based on sources.' 1979 E. Newman *Sunday Punch* i. 3 He had pointed me in the direction of a couple of stories—he was a kindly man and, as a source, needed no special motivation.

f. *attrib.*, as (sense 4 e) *source book, data, document, material, study.*

1899 A. B. Hart (*title*) Source-book of American history. *Ibid.* p. xvii, The Source Book is meant to supplement, not to supplant the text-book. 1900 [in Dict., sense 4 e]. 1948 L. MacNeice *Holes in Sky* 43 We rarely read their poems, Mere source-books now. 1961 J. D. Rosenberg *Darkening Glass* (1963) v. 101 'The Nature of Gothic'..is the source book for *Unto This Last.* 1974 *Education & Community Relations* Jan. 3 The researchers also included a question on what support teachers would welcome from external sources and seven ideas were suggested, i.e. in-service courses, teachers guides or source books, pupils books, films, TV lessons, radio lessons and visiting speakers. 1982 *N. & Q.* Dec. 535/2 *Le Menagier de Paris* has long been known as an invaluable sourcebook for practical details of everyday life in a reasonably prosperous middle-class household in France in the 1390s. 1971 J. Howlett in B. de Ferranti *Living with Computer* ii. 17 The general principle is to..use it..as source data for a whole series of studies. 1920 A. J. Grieve in A. S. Peake *Commentary on Bible* 725 It has therefore been surmised that the writer has here incorporated an Aramaic (possibly Greek) source-document. 1977 *New Yorker* 29 Aug. 35/2 Source documents, once put into computer-readable form, tend to become relatively inaccessible, and in some computer systems are even eliminated. 1936 *Time* 21 Sept. 47/1 For most of their source material the editors relied on second-rate writers. 1955 W. Moore *Bring Jubilee* xix. 182 It is not easy to see behind source material, to visualise state papers, reports, letters, diaries as written by men. 1978 *Early Music* Oct. 597/3 The discussion of the music combines a flair for words with great attention to stylistic interactions and the lessons to be learned from study of the source material. 1964 *English Studies* XLV. 252 Even those readers least interested in source-study are likely to have their notions of Shakespear's work made altogether more accurate. 1979 *Studies in Eng. Lit.: Eng. Number* (Tokyo) 3 Source study—by this is meant here not a mere source-hunting but a comparative study between words and their sources—is certainly rewarding so far as *Confessio Amantis* is concerned.

5. a. More widely, any point where, or process by which, energy or some material component enters a physical system; opp. Sink *sb.*[1] 8 in Dict. and Suppl. (Earlier and further examples.)

Freq. without const., but otherwise not really distinct from sense 4 d in Dict.

1855, etc. [see *sink *sb.*[1] 8]. 1926 H. Glauert *Elem. Aerofoil & Airscrew Theory* iii. 21 A sink is a negative source or a point at which fluid is disappearing. 1956 E. H. Hutten *Lang. Mod. Physics* iv. 139 The engine is in contact with two heat reservoirs (the boiler and condenser, or the source and sink of energy) at different temperatures. 1971 I. G. Gass et al. *Understanding Earth* xix. 263/1 Boundaries at which the net effect of motion is to generate surface area are here termed sources.

b. *Electronics.* (The material forming) the part of a unipolar transistor which corresponds in function to the cathode of a thermionic valve.

1952 [see *gate *sb.*[1] 8 h]. 1962 Simpson & Richards *Physical Princ. Junction Transistors* viii. 173 The source and drain..are ohmic electrodes attached to the *n*-type body of the device [*sc.* a field-effect transistor]. 1977 *Sci. Amer.* Sept. 74/3 The inversion creates a continuous *n*-type channel from source to drain and large currents can flow.

6. *Comb.*, as (sense 4 e) *source-hunter, -hunting*; **source-criticism** *Theol.*, analysis and study of the sources used by the authors of the biblical text; hence **source-critical** *a.*; **source program** *Computers*, a program written in a language other than machine code, usu. a high-level language (cf. *object program* s.v. *object *sb.* 10); **source rock** *Geol.*, a rock formation in which a particular mineral material originates; *spec.* a deposit in which petroleum is formed.

1977 J. L. Houlden *Patterns of Faith* iii. 26 This is particularly true of the gospels of Matthew and Luke, where, according to the source-critical orthodoxy.., visible alterations of the Markan basis could be observed. 1901 J. Moffatt *Historical New Testament* App. 677 No method which neglects source-criticism can satisfactorily explain the doublets [in the Apocalypse]. 1931 K. E. Kirk *Vision of God* 498 An elaborate source-criticism which must be adjudged..to be in the main based upon the theory, and therefore to involve a vicious circle. 1977 G. W. H. Lampe *God as Spirit* iv. 102 The Jesus whom historical research tries to reconstruct through the laborious processes of source criticism, form criticism, and redaction criticism. 1964 D. Daiches *Eng. Lit.* iv. 82 An attempt to rescue literary study from the philologists and source-hunters. 1956 *Canad. Forum* June 67/1 His treatment of sources and analogues lacks the rigorous testing which we require of source-hunting in literary studies after twenty years of sniping by new critics and old scholars alike. 1979 Source-hunting [see *source study*, sense *4 f]. 1959 M. H. Wrubel *Primer of Programming for Digital Computers* vi. 129 The program can be corrected or modified at the source program stage and reassembled. 1970 O. Dopping *Computers & Data Processing* xix. 304 Instead of machine instructions, the source program contains statements or symbolic instructions, which the computer then translates to an object program by means of a special program. 1973 C. W. Gear *Introd. Computer Sci.* iv. 158 A language compiler accepts as input a set of statements called a source program. 1931 *Bull. Amer. Assoc. Petroleum Geologists* XV. 161 Source rocks of petroleum include carbonaceous or 'bituminous' sedimentary deposits, containing aquatic plant and animal remains..and the products of their biochemical and geochemical alterations. 1965 G. J. Williams *Econ. Geol. N.Z.* xix. 352/1 Early borings at Kotuku..left little doubt that the oil at Kotuku comes from the Oligocene Cobden Limestone—though this does not necessarily mean that the Limestone is the source rock. 1971 I. G. Gass et al. *Understanding Earth* xxii. 323/2 The concentration of diamond source-rocks in the older cratons.

source, *v.*[1] Restrict † *Obs.* to senses in Dict. and add: **4.** *trans.* **a.** In pass., *to be sourced in*, to originate in, to be based in; to mention as a source.

1941 W. C. Handy *Father of Blues* xxii. 298 Affinities that may be sourced in a common ultimate Oriental origin. 1972 'J. Godey' *Three Worlds of Johnny Handsome* ii. 23 Mitchell became aware of a rumbling sound vaguely sourced in the floor. 1978 *Maledicta 1977* I. 326 Over twenty of Mr. Tamony's scripts are sourced in H. L. Mencken's *American Language, Supplements* 1 and 2. 1982 *Times Lit. Suppl.* 17 Dec. 1394/1, I also drew on a scientific paper discussing Vittoz's work by the Chicago psychoanalyst, Dr Harry Trosman, which is sourced in my notes.

b. To obtain from a specified source; *spec.* of components (for a vehicle). Chiefly in pa. pple.

1972 *Wall St. Jrnl.* 24 Feb. 1/5 Ford works on stripped-down cars, called 'Asian Model Ts' that could be sourced and assembled anywhere in Asia. 1980 *Times* 20 Mar. 27/5 One component manufacturer said last night: 'Our indications are that less than 10 per cent of the Bounty [*sc.* a new car] will be sourced in the United Kingdom.' 1981 *Times* 6 Feb. 18/2 Counterfeited goods, largely sourced from south east Asia..have mainly been finding their way into British export markets. *Ibid.* 15 Aug. 15/4 British manufacturers..have stressed that Nissan should source at least 80 per cent of the contents of the cars it plans to make in the United Kingdom in Europe.

Hence **sou·rcing** *vbl. sb.*, *spec.* the obtaining of goods and components from a specified or understood source.

1960 *Business Week* 2 Jan. 67/3 Businessmen now refer to imports from foreign plants as 'sourcing'—a term that until recently referred to company purchases from a domestic supplier. 1960 *Wall St. Jrnl.* 15 Mar. 14/5 There is a growing tendency toward foreign 'sourcing', the purchase or production of finished goods or components abroad. 1970 *Daily Tel.* 1 Oct. 2/2 Ford, British Leyland and other manufacturing companies has had to resort to 'dual sourcing' for some components because of this year's unprecedented run of major supplier strikes. 1972 *Wall St. Jrnl.* 24 Feb. 1/5 Experience under the U.S.-Canadian auto pact and in the Common Market has emboldened Detroit to expand multi-national sourcing of parts and components.

source language. [f. Source *sb.* + Language *sb.*] **1.** A language from which a translation is made.

1953 *Philos. Sci.* XX. 217 One of the decisive steps in certain methods of machine translation is the determination of the syntactic structure of any given sentence in the source-language (i.e., the language from which we translate). 1964 M. A. K. Halliday et al. *Linguistic Sciences* 123 Translation as activity faces only one way; the translator observes an event in one language, the 'source' language, and performs a related event in another, the 'target' language. 1974 R. Quirk *Linguist & Eng. Lang.* vi. 97 The difficulties vary profoundly according to the manifold combinations of source- and target-languages involved.

2. *Computers.* The programming language in which a program or procedure is written. Cf. *object language 3.

1959 *Communications Assoc. Computing Machinery* Feb. 9/2 Sections 2 and 3 give a formal description of the Fortran source language, insofar as arithmetic type statements are concerned. 1963 *Ibid.* VI. 430/1 The debugging system has been implemented for Fortran as the source language and could be easily adapted to other problem-oriented languages. 1975 T. Bartee *Introd. Computer Sci.* xiii. 377 For high-level compiler languages such as Fortran, PL/I, and Algol, there is an attempt to make the source language machine-independent.

sourceless, *a.* (Later examples.)

1908 *Punch* 25 Sept. 436/1 The unnoticed, sourceless wound. 1981 *Washington Post* 8 July c1 Talent—this sourceless asset that one cannot command to be born.

sourdine, *sb.* Add: **a.** *Early Mus.* (Later examples.)

1891 C. R. Day *Descr. Catal. Mus. Instruments recently exhibited at R. Mil. Exhibition* v. 96 The combination of a double reed with a cylindrical bore..presents certain theoretical difficulties... During the 14th, 15th, and 16th centuries instruments thus constructed were in common use. Those most generally met with were the *krumhorn* ..and the *sourdine*. 1941 N. Bessaraboff *Anc. Europ. Mus. Instruments* 80 There were several families of instruments, such as the cromornes, the racketts ('the sausage bassoons'), the sourdines. 1976 D. Munrow *Instruments Middle Ages & Renaissance* vi. 45/3 The tone is much softer and more muffled, however, and very similar to that of a rackett; hence the other name given to the instrument..*sourdine* (French).

b. A mute or damper.

c 1779 W. Waring tr. *Rousseau's Dict. Mus.* 384 *Sourdine*, a small instrument of copper or silver, which is applied to the bridge of a violin or violincello, to render the sounds weaker. 1959 *Collins Mus. Encycl.* 618/2 *Sourdine*... (1) Mute (of a string or wind instrument). (2) Damper (in the piano). (3) A device for muting the strings of the piano.

sour-dough, *sb.* Add: **1. c.** *N. Amer.* Fermenting dough, esp. that left over from a previous baking, used as leaven; bread made from this. Also *attrib.*

1868 J. ANDERSON *Sawney's Lett.*, Gie my respecks to your guid wife; If ever I get hame to Fife, I'll teach her hoo to mak loaf bread, Wi' sour dough. **1922** G. C. F. PRINGLE *Tillicums* 156 In every old prospector's cabin.. you would see a bowl which contained sour dough from the previous making. This was used as yeast to be mixed in with the dough at the next baking. **1931** *Sun* (Baltimore) 5 Mar. 12/3 [Maryland] might be thought wanting in pride in the culinary art for which the State enjoyed well-earned fame when Indiana was eating sour dough and jerked meat. **1959** M. SHAND *Summit & Beyond* xi. 197 There was good old sourdough bread, too. **1966** MRS. L. B. JOHNSON *White House Diary* 3 Apr. (1970) 380 They had sour-dough biscuits too—although they had trouble making them rise in this high altitude. **1971** *Daily Colonist* (Victoria, B.C.) 23 Apr. 4/7 In early America, a pot of sourdough starter was part of a bride's dowry. **1976** *National Observer* (U.S.) 26 June 8/3 San Francisco sourdough has a character all its own, because there are microscopic organisms in the air here that do funny things to the starter. Some say it's the same wild yeasts that work on the nearby vineyards. **1979** *United States 1980/1* (Penguin Travel Guides) 370 Two-pound Porterhouses..served with sourdough bread and pinto beans.

2. Substitute for def.: An experienced prospector in Alaska, the Yukon, or the Northwest territories. (Earlier example.)

In quot. 1904 in Dict. for '[of frost]' read '[below zero]'.

1898 *Klondike Nugget* (Dawson, Yukon Terr.) 20 July 1/4 The usual strong expletives had been used expressive of their meeting and Mr. Chee Chaco was not looking for information from his old friend Mr. Sour Dough.

sour grass. Add: **3.** *S. Afr.* The coarse grass characteristic of sour veld (see *SOUR *a.* 10).

1801 J. BARROW *Acct. Trav. S. Afr.* I. iii. 110 That division of the district called the *Zuure-veldt*, or Sour Grass plains. **1852** M. B. HUDSON *S. Afr. Frontier Life* I. 236 About Graham's Town and Lower Albany is 'the Zuurveld or Sour Grass Country'.

soursob (sau·ɹsɒb). *Austral.* [Alteration of SOUR-SOP, perh. in reference to the acid sap.] A bulbous plant, *Oxalis cernua*, of the family Oxalidaceæ, native to South Africa and widely naturalized as a weed elsewhere, bearing divided leaves and clusters of bright yellow bell-shaped flowers; also called the Bermuda buttercup.

1907 *Jrnl. Dept. Agric. S. Austral.* X. 802 Can anyone tell me to destroy a weed called by some 'Soursob'? **1909** J. M. BLACK *Naturalised Flora S. Austral.* 41 *Oxalis cernua*, Thunb. Soursob. **1961** *Times* 23 May 3/1 (Advt.), Biological control of several important weeds and pests of South African origin, such as cape tulip, spiny emex, soursob,..white wax scale and black beetle. **1972** *Advertiser* (Adelaide) 2 Sept. 5/7 Never have I met an Englishman who actually grew soursobs or oxalis or whatever they are properly called at home.

sour-sop. Add: **2*.** = *SOURSOB.

1885 *Garden & Field* (Adelaide) Aug. 29/3 'Amateur' wants to know a remedy for 'soursops', and if gas lime would do. *Ibid.* Sept. 41/1 Now there's a fellow who wants £500 to tell farmers how to kill the Soursops or oxalis. **1930** A. J. EWART *Flora of Victoria* 687 O[*xalis*] *cernua*..Soursop. A perennial with a brown bulb and a tapering root... A troublesome weed, native to South Africa, originally a garden escape.

sous-, *prefix.* Add: **sous-chef, -officier** (further examples), **-préfecture, -préfet.**

1825–40 F. BURNEY *Jrnls. & Lett.* (1980) VIII. 49 M. d'Arblay continued in his humbler office, of *sous chef* to one of the *Bureaux de l'Interieur.* **1902** A. BENNETT *Grand Babylon Hotel* xxi. 238 We have found in our second sous-chef an artist. **1973** *New Society* 15 Nov. 412/2, I gradually pieced together the hierarchy. After the chef..came Jacko, the sous-chef. **1980** N. FREELING *Castang's City* i. 1 Lasserre was a Commissaire... He was the sous-chef, the Chief of Staff. **1895** E. DOWSON *Let.* 2 Oct. (1967) 316 Owing to a great demand for lodgings by officiers and sous-officiers, we found it..impossible to find what we wanted. **1972** G. BELL *Villains Galore* vi. 68 He had been a *sous-officier* in the [Foreign] Legion. **1940** J. JOYCE *Let.* 16 Sept. (1966) III. 487 Our applications.. passed through the sous-préfecture of this department this morning. **1976** N. FREELING *Lake Isle* viii. 43 Soulay was a sous-préfecture, and sub-prefects are small beer. **1865** L. BOOTH in S. Pakenham *Sixty Miles from England* (1967) v. 67 Etiquette expects yearly residents to leave cards on the Sous-Préfet. **1944** H. NICOLSON *Let.* 27 June (1967) 382 They went to the *souspréfecture.* The *sous-préfet*..had been secretary to Pucheu. **1974** E. AMBLER *Dr Frigo* III. 186 The sous-Préfet assured me of his most distinguished sentiments.

sousaphone (sū·zăfōᵘn). Also **Sousaphone.** [f. the name of John Philip *Sousa* (1854–1932), American bandmaster and composer, after *saxophone*, etc. (see also quot. 1939).] A large bass wind instrument of the helicon type. Also *attrib.*

1925 *Punch* 27 May 561/3 An instrument called the Sousaphone weighs eighteen pounds and is twenty feet long. **1935** *Ibid.* 23 Oct. 470/2 As it was removed from its case he saw that it was a sousaphone—the instrument that plays the 'oom' in Viennese waltzes while the rest of the orchestra follows with the 'wump wump'. **1939** *Internat. Cycl. Mus.* 1772/2 The first sousaphone was made by C. G. Conn in 1899 expressly for Sousa's band and its bell opened directly upward. The present bell-front type was first made in 1908. **1958** [see *EXOTICA]. **1974** P. DE VRIES *Glory of Hummingbird* i. 4 The sousaphone tuba he played in the local marching band.

souse, *sb.*[1] Add: **1.** (Examples in W. Indies.)

1929 W. J. LOCKE *Ancestor Jorico* viii. 108 We were given..souse, which is the gelatinous parts of a pig pickled in lime-juice. **1952** S. SELVON *Brighter Sun* ii. 23 They make souse—boiled pork, seasoned with lime and pepper and cucumber. **1958** B. HAMILTON *Too Much of Water* iv. 74 A real Barbadian breakfast. 'Maan,' he said, 'I give you flying fish an' pepper-pot, an' pudding and souse.' **1974** *Sunday Advocate-News* (Barbados) 10 Mar. 8/1 She is selling a popular Barbadian delicacy—pudding and souse.

3. *souse meat.*

1972 E. WIGGINTON *Foxfire Bk.* 20 Souse meat. Boy, that's the best stuff I ever eat. **1976** *Washington Post* 7 Nov. K1/5 We will try to re-create the atmosphere of a country store. Sardines,..souse meat and soda crackers.

souse, *sb.*[5] Add: **1. b.** A heavy drinking-bout. *U.S. slang.*

1903 G. ADE *People you Know* 13 (*heading*) The periodical souse. **1930** E. WALLACE *Calendar* xviii. 244 If ever a man had an excuse for a souse, you've got it. **1946** E. O'NEILL *Iceman Cometh* III. 199 Bejees, we'll go on a grand old souse together.

3. A drunkard. *slang* (chiefly *U.S.*).

1915 J. LONDON *Jacket* 213, I remember you mentioned playing chess with that royal souse of an emperor's brother. **1936** WODEHOUSE *Laughing Gas* i. 11 The lad.., who is pretty generally recognized as London W.1's most prominent souse. **1953** R. CHANDLER *Long Good-Bye* v. 27 Sylvia is not a souse. When she does get over the edge it's pretty drastic.

souse, *v.*[1] Add: **I. 3. d.** To intoxicate thoroughly. Chiefly in pa. pple. Now *slang.*

1613 [see SOUSED *ppl. a.* 2]. **1902** H. L. WILSON *Spenders* ix. 87, I could see then that he was good and soused. **1953** K. TENNANT *Joyful Condemned* xxxi. 306 Grandma used to get a bit soused sometimes, but she fed me O.K. **1976** M. RUSSELL *Double Deal* vi. 46 Ralph's a pro. He's soused every night, and I don't recall an edition going astray yet.

II. 6. c. To drink so as to become intoxicated, to carouse. *slang.*

1921 E. O'NEILL in *Theatre Arts Mag.* V. 32 Ain't you sousin' with 'em most every day? **1923** M. WATTS *Luther Nichols* 43 Just as they're middling honest and don't souse.

soused, *ppl. a.* **2.** (Later example.)

1932 J. T. FARRELL *Young Lonigan* i. 34 Coming home, he had almost gotten into a mixup with some soused mick.

‖**sous-entendu** (suzɑ̃tɑ̃dü). [Fr.] Something not expressed but left to be understood by the hearer or reader.

1865 MILL *Exam. Hamilton's Philos.* xxii. 442 No shadow of justification is shown for thus..adopting into logic a mere *sous-entendu* of common conversation in its most unprecise form. **1907** W. DE MORGAN *Alice-for-Short* xxxii. 332 She knew well enough that the unheard portions of the conversation were worse than what had reached her ears, and the *sous-entendus* probably still worse than they. **1972** *Times Lit. Suppl.* 31 Mar. 374/3 It is satisfyingly like other such duets, though embellished at least once with an erotic *sous-entendu.*

‖**souteneur** (sūtənör). [Fr., = protector, f. *soutenir* to sustain.] A man who lives on the earnings of a prostitute or prostitutes under his protection. Also *transf.*

1906 tr. *Weininger's Sex & Character* II. x. 234 The souteneur is always a criminal, a thief, a fraudulent person, or sometimes even a murderer. **1920** A. HUXLEY *Limbo* 38 After midnight he would write novels with a feminine pen, earning the money that would make his unproductive male labours possible. A kind of spiritual *souteneur.* **1927** *Observer* 11 Dec. 20/2 The souteneur.. extends some shadowy kind of patronage and protection over the girl in return for a 50 per cent or still higher share of her earnings as prostitute. **1969** *Punch* 26 Mar. 469/1 The death-knell of revolution in Britain was the football match between strikers and the police in 1926. It was the moment when the Russian *souteneurs* of the British Communist Party realised with disgust that revolutions can't be made, they have to happen. **1977** M. T. BLOOM *13th Man* viii. 147 The underworld of traffickers, *souteneurs*, and prostitutes..at Buenos Aires.

‖**soutenu** (sūtənü), *a.* and *sb. Ballet.* [Fr., pa. pple. of *soutenir* to sustain.] **A.** *adj.* Of a movement: sustained, performed slowly. **B.** *sb.* A sustained or slowly-performed movement, *spec.* a complete turn on point or half point.

1930 [see *PLIÉ]. **1947** N. NICOLAEVA-LEGAT *Ballet Educ.* IV. 63 After *en dedans*, the opposite *soutenu* is performed and the *port-de-bras* executed with the active foot extended in front. **1978** *N.Y. Times* 29 Mar. C19/1 The faint sounds of a tune to dance by are drifting out, then a louder shout. 'All you have there is a little soutenu... You did six counts, she did seven.'

south, *adv.*, *prep.*, *sb.*, and *a.* Add: **A.** *adv.* **1. b.** Also, in or into the southern states. *U.S.*

1852 MRS. STOWE *Uncle Tom's Cabin* I. x. 142 To appreciate the sufferings of the negroes sold south. **1936** M. MITCHELL *Gone with Wind* iii. 51 The air was always thick with threats of selling slaves south and of direful whippings. **1976** M. G. EBERHART *Family Fortune* (1977) vii. 77 'Suppose Mr Jeff sell me south?'.. 'He can't sell you... You and all the slaves..were set free.'

B. *sb.* **2. a.** (Further examples, of Ireland.) *spec.* The Republic of Ireland.

1913 R. KIPLING *Let.* Dec. in Ld. Birkenhead *Rudyard Kipling* (1978) xvi. 257 Which is the most [*sic*] dangerous enemy? The South playing a game it has not got its heart in, or the North in a blind rage? **1974** D. SEAMAN *Bomb that could Lip-Read* vii. 60 The whole attitude of the South baffled and angered him. Irish politics were beyond him. **1978** D. MURPHY *Place Apart* ii. 33 In Northern Ireland one has a wide choice of names for the rest of the island: the Twenty-six Counties, the Free State, Southern Ireland, the South, Eire and the Republic of Ireland.

3. *South of England*, also (freq. with hyphens) *attrib.* (earlier and later examples); *South of France, spec.* the French Riviera; also *attrib.*

1741 M. W. MONTAGU *Let.* 29 July (1966) II. 245 They are gone to Marseilles and design passing some months in the South of France. **1815** E. FREMANTLE *Diary* 8 Sept. in *Wynne Diaries* (1952) xxxi. 533 We determined to take the former Road, particularly as the South of France is not quite quiet. **1847** C. BRONTË *Jane Eyre* III. iv. 106 A large, fashionable, south-of-England city. **1872** C. M. YONGE *P's & Q's* ii. 10 At the time of her death, Elspeth and Persis had been in the South of France. **1922** M. ARLEN *Piracy* III. v. 183 We are going to the south of France to-morrow. **1922** E. SITWELL in *New Age* 6 July 120/1, I liked..the warm, South-of-France feeling about her, and her faded hair that was like dry, powdery mimosa. **1940** 'G. ORWELL' *Inside Whale* 42 Dickens..is a south-of-England man, and a cockney at that. **1971** J. BRUNNER *Honky in Woodpile* ii. 14 I'll start on the Sunday papers and catch their South of England editions. **1980** I. MURDOCH *Nuns & Soldiers* i. 83 Soho in summer was his South of France.

6. *Bridge.* The player sitting opposite and partnering north: occas. in conventional printed representations of the game, the player who wins the bidding and plays the hand.

1926 [see *EAST *sb.* 4]. **1933** C. VANDYCK *Contract Contracted* iii. 31 South deals and bids 1 Diamond. North seeing the possibilities of a Slam gives a Slam Invitation by bidding 5 Spades. **1958** *Listener* 2 Oct. 541/1 One would expect South to pass. **1964** FREY & TRUSCOTT *Official Encycl. Bridge* 514/2 In bridge writing for general reading, South is, conventionally, the declarer... However, in reporting International Matches, the actual positions at the table are used. **1978** *Country Life* 14 Dec. 2098/2 Most Souths without further thought would bid Three No Trumps.

7. A collective name for the industrially and economically less advanced countries of the world, typically situated to the south of the industrialized nations.

1975 *Economist* 18 Oct. 103/2 North-south dialogue... This week's preliminary get-together [between] the west and the oil and non-oil developing nations..illuminated the snake pit ahead. **1977** *N.Y. Times* 22 Sept. 43 Today, any regional struggle over who is to become managing director of the I.M.F. is far less likely to be one between the United States and Western Europe as between the 'North' and the 'South'—that is, the developed, industrial countries and the so-called developing countries, some oil-rich and others oil-poor; some well on the way to industrialization, and others desperately poor. **1978** *New Internationalist* May 6/1 Present patterns of technology transfers from North to South vindicate Bertrand Russell's view..that 'I am compelled to fear that science will be used to promote the power of dominant groups rather than to make men happy.' **1979** *Newsweek* 19 Nov. 144 The turbulent years of the 1970s have witnessed an uneasy confrontation between the North and the South, and a largely unresolved debate on a whole series of specific economic problems.

C. *adj.* **1. b.** (Further examples.) Also, denoting the southern part of a city, town, district, ocean, etc.; *South Kensington* (colloq. *Ken*), a district of London noted esp. for the museums and other cultural and scientific institutions located there; also *ellipt.*, any of these institutions; *South-Spain* attrib., designating or pertaining to a South Spainer (see sense 1 c below).

1835 *Penny Cycl.* III. 25/2 The South Atlantic Ocean does not offer any other peculiarity in its formation, but the Northern is distinguished by several. **1845** *Encycl. Metrop.* VIII. 600 (*heading*) South London. **1862** A. J. MUNBY *Diary* 18 Jan. in D. Hudson *Munby* (1972) 114, I walked past the South Kensington Museum and along the Cromwell Road. **1882** *Girl's Own Paper* 1 Apr. 432/2 We advise your going direct to the British Museum or South Kensington, and make a study of one gallery after another. **1885** A. EDWARDES *Girton Girl* I. iii. 59 There was no South Kensington, and we never called ourselves art students. **1885** *Encycl. Brit.* XVIII. 119/1 When the 'Challenger' was cruising in the South Pacific..the water was found to be uniformly warmer than the air. **1924** J. BUCHAN *Three Hostages* iii. 50 He was M.P. for a South London division. **1924** W. RUNCIMAN *Before Mast* III. ii. 78 A visit was paid to a very fine South Spain barque. *Ibid.*, As it was a Friday we had presented to us a real South Spain meal, pea soup and pork. **1933** M. ALLINGHAM *Sweet Danger* xiv. 172 If we get away with this we might start on the South Ken. There's a large-size model of a flea there I've always had my eye on. **1933** J. MASEFIELD *Bird of Dawning* 98 All South-Spain ships pass where we pass, going or coming. **1944** W. TEMPLE *Church looks Forward* ii. 17 That, broadly speaking, is the aim of the South India Scheme. **1946** *Whitaker's Almanack 1947* 783/2 South Georgia is permanently inhabited and is an important seat of the whaling industry. **1948** *Times* 11 May 3/3 The Communists continued with their campaign to keep the population of South Korea from voting in today's elections. **1949** O. HAMMERSTEIN (*title of musical*) South Pacific. **1950** *Times* 28 Apr. 5/4 The Federal Government has decided to send a mission.. to the island of Amboyna, where the revolt which resulted in the proclamation yesterday of the 'independent Republic of the South Moluccas' originated. **1954** *Times* 21 July 6/1 There will probably be two other enclaves for Viet-minh troops now in south Viet Nam. **1965** M. ALLINGHAM *Mind Readers* i. 22 Her drawl, which Peggie had known when it was pure South London, was now very Mayfair. **1966** *Times* 22 Jan. 7/1 Both the Yemen Government and the Arab League have welcomed the N.L.F.–O.L.O.S. merger into the new anti-British militant 'Front for the Liberation of Occupied South Yemen' (F.L.O.S.Y.). **1972** F. MACCARTHY *All Things Bright & Beautiful* ii. 44 Lethaby..retired from the Central [School] to concentrate on the South Kensington professorship. **1972** H. KURATH *Studies in Area Linguistics* 54 The South Atlantic States—the Southern and South Midland dialect areas. **1975** *Times* 11 Mar. 13/2 Little girls with South Ken accents. **1982** *Daily Tel.* 11 Oct. 18/4 Spinks of St. James's tell me..that the South Atlantic Medal will be seen.

c. (Further examples.) *South Spainer*, formerly, a ship engaged in trade with Spain; a sailor on such a ship. See also *SOUTH AFRICAN *sb.* and *a.*, *SOUTH AMERICAN *sb.* and *a.*

1821 A. ROYALL *Lett. from Alabama* (1830) 137 She married a South Carolinian. **1839** *Dublin Rev.* May 449 'Read Mr. James's book,' said a South Australian colonist to the writer of this article. **1842** *Penny Cycl.* XXII. 270/2 South Polar countries. **1856** C. NORDHOFF *Merchant Vessel* viii. 97 They hold all manner of foreign vessels, or 'south Spainers', in supreme contempt. **1877** *Encycl. Brit.* VII. 188/2 *South Slavic* [dictionary]—Richter and Ballman, Wien, 1839–40. **1881** *Ibid.* XII. 755/2 The South Indian [railway line] (the only one on the narrow gauge), in the extreme south, from Cape Comorin to Madras city. **1889** *N.Y. Semi-Weekly Tribune* 6 Dec. 13/4 Three ballots were put in the box for the South Dakotans to draw from. **1903** H. HOLMES *Life & Adv. on Oceans* 8 There may be truth in the saying that a South Spainer, bound for a warm climate, can put his clothes in a stocking. **1924** W. RUNCIMAN *Before Mast* II. iii. 46 Never a cargo vessel looked cleaner or better cared for than this little South-Spainer. **1936** A. W. CLAPHAM *Romanesque Archit.* iv. 81 The system of barrel-vaults without direct lighting of the aisled nave is general in the south-French school. **1939** South Caucasian [see *LAZ]. **1941** C. S. FORESTER *Captain from Connecticut* iii. 57 Hubbard's South Carolinian speech. **1949** *Britannica Bk. of Year* 380/1 An interim agreement was signed calling for some U.S. troops to remain in Korea until South Korean military forces could be well organized. **1950** 'P. WOODRUFF' *Island of Chamba* ii. 43 There will be food in the Persian style as well as Moghul and South Indian. **1951** *Britannica Bk. of Year* 342/2 In East Indonesia some prominent Ambonnese people..on April 25 [1950] seceded and proclaimed a South Moluccan independent republic. **1958** T. HICKINBOTHAM *Aden* xii. 196 The South Arabian League which originally advocated union between the Colony and the Protectorate. **1963** E. HUMPHREYS *Gift* II. i. 207 'No thanks, Stel, love.' With her I tended to talk as if I were a South Walian. **1966** J. CLEARY *High Commissioner* i. 20 The Americans will accuse the Chinese and vice versa. The same with the South Vietnamese and the Viet Cong. **1971** *Guardian* 12 July 7/2 Guiding bewildered Irishmen and rooted South Londoners through the intricacies of Notting Hill Gate. **1972** 'E. PETERS' *Death to Landlords!* ix. 135 You are a South Indian yourself, Mr. Narayanan. **1975** *Amer. Speech 1973* XLVIII. 60 A South Dakotan holds that a wet bituminous road is slippery but an icy road is slick. **1975** *Times* 3 Dec. 1/6 The hijackers, all South Moluccans who demanded the return of the islands. **1977** *Trans. Philol. Soc. 1975* 176 *Cuillem* looks possible, *c* presumably representing South Walian phonetics. **1978** *Amer. Speech* LIII. 41 Three areas of the eastern states provided the bulk of the English-speaking settlers for the North Central states: South Midlanders from the Upland South, [etc.]. **1979** *Guardian* 5 Nov. 11/6 The marvellous Tipi cover by South Dakotan Sioux braves.

2. c. *South Bank*, *spec.* the southern bank of the Thames and the areas adjacent to it, (*a*) noted esp. for the cultural complexes and public gardens developed between Westminster and Blackfriars bridges for and since the Festival of Britain in 1951; also *attrib.* and *ellipt.*, any of these complexes; (*b*) used (freq. *attrib.* and as *adj.*) with reference to the policy of the Anglican diocese of Southwark to re-express traditional beliefs and practices in ways that would make them better suited to contemporary life.

1951 H. NICOLSON *Diary* 4 May (1968) 206 Viti and I go to the South Bank Exhibition. We are entranced. **1961** *Guardian* 19 May 22/5 A glass-and-wood pavilion in best South Bank style. **1963** M. FRAYN in Sissons & French *Age of Austerity* xv. 329 The South Bank site—a derelict slum, low-lying, marshy, and heavily blitzed. *Ibid.* 330 A model of the South Bank made out of toilet rolls. **1963** *Guardian* 8 July 14/3 The problems of the South Bank parishes which this so-called South Bank religion is trying to tackle. **1965** LUNN & LEAN *Cult of Softness* iv. 44 The new predestination exercises a certain attraction on South Bank theologians. **1967** A. LASKI *Seven Other Years* xiii. 179 It may be that I am going a little far in calling it atheism; it might, I suppose, be regarded as an effusion of so-called South Bank Christianity. **1968** J. TURNER *Requiem for Two Sisters* i. 5 The vicar..had never thought it part of his duty to dress in a black suit and dog-collar all the time. Indeed, his opinions were to a great extent South Bank. **1977** 'E. CRISPIN' *Glimpses of Moon* vi. 88 No one takes any notice of the clergy nowadays, except for Humanists waiting to welcome South-Bank bishops into the fold. **1977** *Skateboard Special* Sept. 3/4, I do a lot of riding on the South Bank. **1980** *Times* 22 Oct. 13/7 The National have given us many fine productions... This one lapse of quality does not justify the witch-hunt on the South Bank.

3. (Later examples.) Also *fig.*

1917 N. DOUGLAS *South Wind* ii. 16 For Nepenthe was famous not only for its girls and lobsters, but also for its south wind. **1937** C. MACKENZIE (*title*) The south wind of love. **1946** L. B. LYON *Rough Walk Home* 28 Ask that for these may blow The hot south rage of life again.

4. (Later example.)

1973 *Express* (Trinidad & Tobago) 1 Feb. 17/1 Behind the move to promote female calypsonians is well-known south businessman, Mr. Lall Parsotan.

south-[1]. Add: **1.** *south-facing.*

1961 *Times* 23 Dec. 3/4 The aspect is right, that is south-facing. **1978** 'J. BELL' *Swan-Song Betrayed* ii. 16 Her workroom, small but south-facing.

2. Also in *Comb.* with advbs., as **south-about** *adv.*, by a southerly route; also *attrib.*; **south-away** quasi-*sb.*, somewhere to the south.

1958 *Times* 20 Dec. 3/3 Bass frequent the coast from Suffolk south-about to Cheshire. **1961** *Times* 24 Nov. 14/6 So it was decided..to send the ship by the south-about route via Cape Horn. **1954** J. R. R. TOLKIEN *Fellowship of Ring* 16 The folk of the Marish..came..up from south-away.

South African, *sb.* and *a.* [f. *South Africa*: see SOUTH *a.* 1, -AN.] **A.** *sb.* **1.** A native or inhabitant of South Africa (see below).

This area of southernmost Africa consisted in the 19th century of a group of British and Boer territories; in 1910, following the British victory in the Boer war (1899–1902), these united to form the Union of South Africa; in 1961 the Republic of South Africa was established.

1806 J. W. JANSSENS *Let.* 17 Jan. in G. M. Theal *Rec. Cape Colony* (1899) V. 298 The interest of the few unfortunate Men who I have the Honor to command, that of the brave and good Dutch South Africans.., put me under the necessity to accept the painful conditions. **1871** J. MACKENZIE *Ten Years North of Orange River* p. v, I would specially direct attention to that part.. which describes the results of the past contact of Europeans with South Africans. **1897** G. A. PARKER *S. Afr. Sports* p. xiii, I am glad of this opportunity of dedicating this, the first compilation relating to South African sports, to the foremost South African [*sc.* Cecil Rhodes], and one who has for many years encouraged outdoor games with characteristic liberality. **1913** C. PETTMAN *Africanderisms* 3 As South Africans our lot is cast in a country which..is quite young. **1949** E. POUND *Pisan Cantos* lxxx. 92 And persuaded an Aussie or Zealander or S. African To kneel with him in prayer. **1978** J. BRANFORD *Dict. S. Afr. Eng.* p. xiii, This text..has been written for South Africans of all racial groups.

2. *absol.* uses of the adj.

1930 *Economist* 8 Nov. 866/2 South Africans [*sc.* shares] remained firm. **1969** *Guardian* 24 Oct. 9/5 You will need some medium-dry sherry... You could go for a good South African at about £1.

B. *adj.* Of or pertaining to South Africa or its inhabitants.

1824 (*title of newspaper*) The South African Commercial Advertiser. **1838** W. B. BOYCE *Notes on S. Afr. Affairs from 1834 to 1838* p. xv, Much of the misrepresentation of South African affairs, arises from the fact, that the Colonists labour under the..disadvantage of being..unconnected with the powerful interests, which in England press the claims of the Colonists of other British dependencies upon the attention of Parliament and the Public. **1876** in J. Flint *Cecil Rhodes* (1976) iii. 39 Lord Carnarvon's South African policy. **1894** [see SOUTH *a.* 1 c (*b*)]. **1913** C. PETTMAN *Africanderisms* 8 The words of Portuguese, Indian, and Malay origin, still current in South African Dutch. **1921, 1925** [see *AFRIKAANS *sb.*]. **1949** A. WILSON *Wrong Set* 41 Everyone was anxious to know what Harry thought of the South African hock. **1967** L. MEYNELL *Mauve Front Door* v. 64 South African sherry was absolutely right on that evening. **1978** J. BRANFORD *Dict. S. Afr. Eng.* p. xi, South African English ..is in every sense, culturally, lexically, grammatically and phonologically, a 'mixed bag'.

Hence **South Africanism**, (*a*) distinctive South African quality; (*b*) a word or idiom peculiar to or characteristic of South Africa.

1959 *Listener* 29 Oct. 714/2 South Africans..were lulled into thinking the essential South Africanism of General Smuts permanently secure. **1961** *Personality* 16 May 27, I think my favourite South Africanism is 'Bioscope'. **1978** J. BRANFORD *Dict. S. Afr. Eng.* p. xiii, These South Africanisms include..a number of English phrases or usages.

South American, *sb.* and *a.* [f. *South America*, the name of the southern part of the continent of America, excluding Central America: see SOUTH *a.* 1, -AN.] **A.** *sb.* A native or inhabitant of South America.

1775 [see SOUTH *a.* 1 c (*a*)]. **1826** F. B. HEAD *Rough Notes Journeys Pampas & Andes* 306 The Spanish South Americans have certainly become independent of the government of Spain. **1863** T. W. HINCHLIFF *S. Amer. Sk.* viii. 173 Spaniards, Italians and South Americans have a vile habit of using the knife. **1913** A. S. PECK *S. Amer. Tour* xxxiii. 361 The manufacturer..should understand that the South Americans in general are not eager to trade with us. **1943** H. F. ARTUCIO *Nazi Octopus in S. Amer.* I. i. 7 This book is a summing up of experiences and observations which might have been those of any South American who believed in the principles of democracy. **1979** *Guardian* 23 Oct. 28/5 The race got off to a bad start, blamed on Europeans and South Americans surging forward before the signal went off.

B. *adj.* Of or pertaining to South America or its inhabitants.

1820 *Times* 11 Mar. 3/5 (*heading*) South-American affairs. **1833** [see SOUTH *a.* 1 c (*b*)]. **1869** *Month* Jan. 82 The same operation could be carried on in the South American plains. **1950** T. D. MCCOWN in J. H. Steward *Handbk. S. Amer. Indians* VI. i. 2 The osseous human remains and the artifacts of human manufacture..have been accumulated mainly by European and South American scientists over a period of about 100 years. **1976** 'A. HALL' *Kobra Manifesto* xi. 153 Half the people in the queue were South American Indians.

sou·thbound, *a.* (*sb.*) Also south-bound. [f. SOUTH-[1] + BOUND *ppl. a.*[1]] **A.** *adj.* **1.** Bound or directed southwards; travelling south.

1885 H. M. JACKSON *Zeph.* vi. 227, I am going on the south-bound train. **1960** 'E. MCBAIN' *Killer's Payoff* ix. 88 A southbound trip that eventually led back to the city. **1976** W. GREATOREX *Crossover* 170 He ran wildly across the south-bound traffic. **1980** K. FOLLETT *Key to Rebecca* xxvi. 276 Southbound trains are less in demand.

2. Intended for traffic travelling south.

1971 *Daily Tel.* 29 Dec. 1/5 Most of the pile-ups were on the southbound carriageway near the junction of the M1 and M10. **1980** *West Lancs. Even. Gaz.* 1 Mar. 3 Sections of north and southbound carriageways of the M6 near Preston will be closed for at least four hours.

B. *ellipt.* as *sb.* A southbound train.

1903 'O. HENRY' in *Everybody's Mag.* Feb. 173/1 Passengers on the south-bound saw them seated together. **1932** W. FAULKNER *Light in August* xv. 340 Folks.. begun to come in and buy tickers for the southbound.

South Devon. [f. SOUTH *a.* 1 + *DEVON.] A bull or cow belonging to the breed so called, characterized by its large size and light red or fawn colour, and used for both milk and beef production; also, the breed itself.

1897 W. HOUSMAN *Cattle* ii. 59 A breed of cattle, now called the South Devon breed, but long known by the local name of 'South Hams', has sprung up. *Ibid.* 61 The 250 animals of 1893..give the aggregate of 2,961 entries of South Devons. **1946** F. H. GARNER *Brit. Dairying* iii. 161 At maturity the South Devon is..heavier than any other breed. Quite commonly South Devon cows weigh 15 or 16 cwt. **1977** 'E. CRISPIN' *Glimpses of Moon* v. 69 Then came the cows, fourteen-hundredweight yearling South Devons.

southdown. 3. (Earlier example.)

1826 B. R. HAYDON *Let.* 18 Aug. in *Autobiogr. & Mem.* (1927) xxiv. 331 His sly hints as I passed his shop that he had 'a bit of South Down, very fine'.

south-east, *adv.*, *sb.*, and *a.* Add: **B.** *sb.* **3.** (Later examples.)

1968 *Radio Times* 28 Nov. 20/5 A look at some non-broadcast music events taking place in London and the South East. **1972** P. JOHNSON *Offshore Islanders* III. 146 There was an enormous bias in favour of the south-east. Clergymen did not want to serve in the wilder and poorer districts of the north and west.

C. *adj.* **1. b.** With proper names, denoting the south-eastern division of a continent, race, etc., and with sbs. and adjs. derived from them.

1893 *Geogr. Jrnl.* Nov. 474 Travel and Adventure in South-east Africa: being the narrative of the last eleven years spent..on the Zambesi. **1909** *Prospectus* (South-East Borneo Rubber Plantations Ltd.) 2 This Company has been formed for the purpose of acquiring and working the Rubber Plantation known as Tanah-Intan..situated in South-East Borneo. **1946** F. OWEN *Campaign in Burma* vii. 44 To complete the picture of South-East Asia Command we must reintroduce Lieutenant-General Joseph Stilwell. **1959** 'M. DERBY' *Tigress* ii. 86 Young South-East Asians at play. **1964** *Whitaker's Almanack 1965* 71/1 South-East England Development Proposals. **1968** O. WYND *Sumatra Seven Zero* v. 57 The South-east Asian male is never turned out burly. **1971** H. TREVELYAN *Worlds Apart* xvii. 193 The Deputy Minister in charge of South-East Asian affairs spoke to me..about the responsibilities of the co-chairman for Vietnam.

south-easter. (Earlier example.)

1797 A. BARNARD *Let.* 15 Oct. in *S. Afr. a Century Ago* (1901) 100 What a bold south-easter we have had these two days!

south-ea·sterner. [f. SOUTH-EASTERN *a.* + -ER[1].] An inhabitant or native of the south-eastern part of a country.

1960 G. ASHE *From Caesar to Arthur* v. 115 The resulting cleavage between Vortigern and the south-easterners whom he aspired to govern was widened by the Pelagian heresy. **1964** *New Society* 26 Mar. 3/2 At present two out of three southeasterners live within 40 miles of Charing Cross.

souther, *sb.* (Earlier example.)

1851 *Austral. & N.Z. Gaz.* XXX. 483 During the night a 'stiff souther' put [the *Pauline*] again on shore.

southerly, *a.* Add: **2.** For '*Southerly buster* (see BUSTER 3)' read '*southerly burster, buster* (see BURSTER 2, BUSTER 3 a in Dict. and Suppl.)'. (Earlier example.)

1850 B. C. PECK *Recollections of Sydney* viii. 132 It is almost a corollary, that the evening of a hot-wind day brings up a 'southerly buster', as we have heard the vulgar call it, very chill indeed..as this wind comes from the southerly region of the Australian Alps.

B. *sb.* A wind blowing from the south; a southerly buster. *Austral.* and *N.Z.*

1943 K. TENNANT *Ride on Stranger* viii. 79 When the Southerly blew, the stiff leaves..twisted rim-on to the blast. **1964** R. BRADDON *Year Angry Rabbit* xiv. 123 What use is it being able to guarantee fine weather, or rain, or a cool southerly only on the coast? **1973** P. WHITE *Eye of Storm* i. 65 How exotic, how naked her body felt when the southerly began to blow at the end of a sticky summer's day, caressing her inside her dresses.

southern, *a.* and *sb.* Add: **A.** *adj.* **1. b.** (Earlier and further examples.) *Southern Baptist*, a Baptist who is a member of a church belonging to the Southern Baptist Convention, first organized in 1845; also *attrib.*

1789 *Deb. Congress U.S.* 28 Apr. (1834) 215 Suppose a member from Massachusetts was to propose an impost on negroes, what would you hear from the Southern gentlemen, if fifty dollars was the sum to be laid? **1846** J. SOULE in *Jrnls. Gen. Conf. Methodist Episcopal Church, South* (1851) I. 105 Southern Methodists were able so far to conciliate public opinion, and quiet popular apprehension, as to carry on..the ordinary operations of church enterprise and discipline. **1866** in W. L. Fleming *Documentary Hist. Reconstruction* (1907) II. 247 In 1845, when the Southern Baptist Convention was organized,..in proportion to the population there were more negroes than white people who were members of our churches. **1932** *N.Y. Times* 3 Nov. 19/3 The Southern Baptist handbook for 1932 declares Southern Baptists are 'still wasting money in riotous living'. **1936** M. MITCHELL *Gone with Wind* ix. 195 A delicately nurtured Southern belle with her Irish up. **1964** 'E. MCBAIN' *Ax* ii. 32 A simpering smile on her lips, as though she were a Southern belle waiting to be asked for a dance. **1978** N. LONGMATE *Hungry Mills* i. 21 The 'Southern gentlemen', a breed already famous for their independence and arrogance, owned the large plantations. **1979** *Arizona Daily Star* 1 Apr. E7/4 Television station WFAA, which aired his program, said Robison's remarks crossed over from religious to political proselytizing and then canceled the half-hour program. The result has been a wave of support for the popular Southern Baptist evangelist.

3. b. *Southern Cross*: also *transf.*, the Australian national flag.

1855 R. CARBONI *Eureka Stockade* xxxvii. 50 There is no flag in old Europe half so beautiful as the 'Southern Cross' of the Ballaarat miners. **1917** 'H. H. RICHARDSON' *Richard Mahoney* II. i. 96 The 'Southern Cross' hoisted—a blue bunting that bore the silver stars of the constellation after which it was named.

4. c. *U.S. spec.* Pertaining to or belonging to the southern States of America (cf. SOUTH *sb.* 2 c). *Southern Comfort*, the proprietary name of a brand of alcoholic drink, based on whisky and orig. manufactured in the U.S.

1819 D. THOMAS *Trav. through Western Country* 100 The mistress..treated us to milk, in the true spirit of southern hospitality. **1836** *Southern Lit. Messenger* II. 111/2 We have known a New Englander laugh at the Southern use of the word clever. **1860** *Charleston* (S. Carolina) *Mercury* 15 Nov. 2/5 The 'Lone Star' was very suggestive of the additions which may hereafter be made to the Independent Southern Confederacy. **1877** C. HALLOCK *Sportsman's Gazetteer* 96 The Southern Fox Squirrel inhabits the Southern States from North Carolina to Texas. **1880** 'MARK TWAIN' *Tramp Abroad* xlix. 574 Hot wheat-bread, Southern style. **1925** G. P. KRAPP *Eng. Lang. in Amer.* I. 40 It is..much easier for an American to call up in his mind a kind of image of the Eastern and Southern types of American speech than of the Western or General type. **1934** *Official Gaz.* (U.S. Patent Office) 24 July 786/2 Midland Distilleries, Incorporated, St. Louis, Mo... Southern Comfort. For Cordial. **1947** *Trade Marks Jrnl.* 12 Nov. 707/1 *Southern Comfort* B647,105. Wines, spirits (beverages) and liqueurs. Southern Comfort Corporation.., 2121, Olive Street, St. Louis,..Missouri, United States of America; Manufacturers. **1962** A. LURIE *Love & Friendship* iv. 60 He had a slight Southern accent. **1978** M. G. EBERHART *Nine O'Clock Tide* i. 21 I'll take a little drink..Southern Comfort. **1979** *United States* 1980/81 (Penguin Travel Guides) 280 The corn bread, fried chicken..and the like are served buffet-style in a big Southern-style mansion. **1980** *Blair & Ketchum's Country Jrnl.* Oct. 142 (Advt.), Grandma Johnston's southern fruit cake.

5. b. southern beech = *NOTHOFAGUS.

1914 W. J. BEAN *Trees & Shrubs Hardy in Brit. Isles* II. 97 The southern beeches are only adapted for the milder parts of the country. **1957** M. HADFIELD *Brit. Trees* 189 The so-called 'southern beeches'..represent the beech family in South America, south-east Australia, and New Zealand. **1974** [see *NOTHOFAGUS].

9. *southern-shaped*; **southern-fried** *U.S.*, cooked in a manner characteristic of the southern states; also *fig.*

1972 *St. Louis Post-Dispatch* 5 Nov. C1/4 'Ah sure thought we were gonna win,' he said in his Southern-fried drawl. 'Ah really did.' **1973** *Sat. Rev. World* (U.S.) 6 Nov. 43/1 Southern-fried chicken..with bananas, sweet corn, and tomatoes. **1976** N. THORNBURG *Cutter & Bone* vi. 142 Not hillbilly really. Just a good ole boy, southern fried. **1982** *Times* 19 June 7/5 Southern fried chicken really is a speciality. **1922** D. H. LAWRENCE *Aaron's Rod* xiv. 195 There was..something inhuman and possessed-looking in their foreign, southern-shaped faces, so much more formed and demon-looking than northern faces.

B. *sb.* **3.** *U.S.* The dialect of English spoken in the southern states.

1935, 1951 [see *NEW ENGLAND a]. **1975** *New Yorker* 21 Apr. 33/3, I listened to the Governor's lady talking for some minutes to some of her South Delaware friends, and they *were* talking Southern. **1981** J. SCOTT *Distant View of Death* x. 147 Saying in her comedy Southern: 'Why, *Colonel*..you jest *spoil* lil' ol' me.'

southernism. Add: **1. b.** An idiom, expression, or word peculiar to a more southerly part of Britain, esp. to the South of England.

1967 P. J. BAWCUTT *Shorter Poems of Gavin Douglas* p. lxxv, The absence of the southernisms and archaic verbal inflections that are found in Douglas, side by side with the regular Middle Scots forms. **1978** *Trans. Yorks. Dial. Soc.* LXXVIII. 9 More definitely attributable to error is the intrusion of Southernisms such as *hond* for hand, *darter* for daughter and, grammatically, *she* for her as object pronoun.

2. (Earlier example.)

1861 *N.Y. Tribune* 15 July 6/4 Southernism has raised the standard and gage of social condition absolutely; and those who are so unfortunate as not to be high-born—i.e., born at the South—are given to feel that they must eke out their shortcomings with an extra amount of Southern ardor and Pro-Slavery talk.

southernization (sʊːðəɹnəizēⁱ·ʃən). [f. SOUTHERNIZE *v.*: see -ATION.] The act of making southern in respect of character.

1976 *Time* 27 Sept. 98/2 These developments helped to modify the old stereotypes and mitigate fear of Southernization in the North. **1976** *National Observer* (U.S.) 6 Nov. 14/2 Great pains were taken to ensure the success of this historic occasion, otherwise known as 'The Southernization of Central Park'.

sou·thernness. Delete *rare* and add later examples.

1931 BLUNDEN *Votive Tablets* 210 The weaknesses of his verse,..the exuberant southernness of so much of it might be effeminate. **1966** *Listener* 10 Mar. 357/3 Cleanth Brooks's recent book on the Southernness of Faulkner. **1973** D. AARON *Unwritten War* vii. 118 Charleston, the hatchery of rebellion and quintessence of Southernness. **1980** T. HOLME *Neapolitan Streak* 10 He had never shown ..prejudice against Peroni's southern-ness as most northerners invariably did.

Southeyan (sʊ·ðiăn), *a.* [f. the name of the English poet and prose writer Robert *Southey* (1774–1843) + -AN.] Of, pertaining to or characteristic of the writings of Southey. Hence **Southeya·na** [ANA *suff.*], writings, etc., relating to Southey.

1817 KEATS *Let.* 11 May (1931) I. 32, I am very near agreeing with Hazlitt that Shakespeare is enough for us. By the by what a tremendous Southean [*sic*] article his last was. **1931** BLUNDEN *Votive Tablets* 191 A modern house would not contain a collection of Southeyana. *Ibid.* 198 The last sentences of the extract show the Southeyan good sense. **1974** R. HOLMES *Shelley* ix. 207 The prose notes are constantly more powerful and effective than the long-drawn Miltonic or Southeyan rhetoric of the verse.

southland. Restrict 'Now *arch.* or *poet.*' to sense 1 and add: **2.** (Further examples.)

1849 J. G. WHITTIER in *National Era* 1 Nov. 174/4 The South land hath its fields of cane, The Prairie boasts its heavy grain. **1905** *Florida Times-Union* 7 May II. 8/1 Yet is this place rich in its treasured holdings of art, its clustered memories and traditions of the Old South or the southland of ante-bellum days. **1956** G. P. KURATH in A. F. C. Wallace *Men & Cultures* (1960) 153 The Charleston, after seething in the Southland as a Negro round dance, was discovered in 1923. **1974** P. MCCUTCHAN *Call for Simon Shard* iv. 32 He entered the Southland.. unofficially, no fanfares, no men from Canberra. **1978** *Guardian Weekly* 1 Oct. 9/1, I believe in the Southland... I believe in the people from South Carolina..and I believe in the people of Georgia.

3. Southland beech = *silver beech* s.v. *SILVER *sb.* and *a.* 21 e, in reference to the region of New Zealand on the west coast of the South Island.

1947 J. C. S. BROUGH *Timbers for Woodwork* xvi. 138 Imported beeches are..Red beech..and Southland, or 'Silver' beech. **1966** G. W. TURNER *Eng. Lang. Austral. & N.Z.* viii. 166 The Southland beech is not really a beech.

southpaw (sɑu·þpǭː), *sb.* (*a.*) *colloq.* (orig. *U.S.*, in *Baseball*). [f. SOUTH *a.* + PAW *sb.*[1]]

1. A person's left hand. (In quot. 1848, a punch or blow with the left hand.)

1848 *Democratic B-hoy*, 'I say, Lewy, give him a sockdologer!' 'Curse the Old Hoss, what a south-paw he has given me!' **1885** *Sporting Life* 14 Jan. 4/3 They had always been accustomed to having their opponents hug their bases pretty close, out of respect for Morris' quick throw over to first with that south-paw of his. **1942** BERREY & VAN DEN BARK *Amer. Thes. Slang* § 121/53 *Southpaw, wrong hand* or *fist*, the left hand or fist. **1948** *Chicago Tribune* 20 Apr. I. 20/5 He waved his big southpaw and ducked under the roof.

2. One who pitches or throws with the left hand; a left-handed person.

In *Boxing*, a southpaw leads with his right hand.

1891 *Chicago Herald* 24 July 6/1 The new south-paw.. came to town yesterday. **1911** *Daily Colonist* (Victoria, B.C.) 15 Apr. 8/5 Davis came up to bat... He faced the twirler right-handed. He always does with southpaws. **1932** *Ring* Apr. 5/2 McCoy was a slow southpaw who had proved just a good workout for Joe Chip. **1942** BERREY & VAN DEN BARK *Amer. Thes. Slang* § 430/10 Left-handed person,..*south-paw*. **1947** J. GUNTHER *Inside U.S.A.* xl. 657 Ah won't even go to the Polo Grounds unless a southpaw's pitchin'. **1951** *Sport* 6–12 Apr. 8/2 On the same bill, Joe Lucy, the young southpaw, meets South African lightweight Gerald Dreyer. **1955** *Sci. News Let.* 14 May 310/2 The family cat may have a preferred paw.., and pussy is most often a southpaw when she is not ambidextrous. **1959** *Sunday Times* 8 Nov. 32/6 In the ball parks all over the United States the so-called 'diamond', formed by the track between the bases, is always oriented to the same points of the compass, so that in whatever park a team is playing the pitcher on his mound will always have his right hand on the north side of his body; hence a left-hander is a 'southpaw'. **1967** *Boston Sunday Herald* 26 Mar. II. 7/1 Rocket Rod Laver leads the greatest tennis show on earth into Boston Garden Monday night... The freckle-faced southpaw is the top-seeded player. **1970** H. MCLEAVE *Question of Negligence* (1973) vi. 48 'Nobody told me he was a southpaw.' Even the psychiatrist had.. forgotten that the surgeon cut with his left hand. **1976** *Billings* (Montana) *Gaz.* 26 June 1-B/2 The 6-0 lefthander, the only southpaw listed on the Angels' roster, struck out six and walked the same number. **1976** 'A. BURGESS' *Beard's Roman Women* (1977) v. 110 Donatella, a southpaw, animated this [*sc.* her left shoulder-blade] while lifting the one remaining chair from the front room. **1978** M. KENYON *Deep Pocket* ix. 103 He wore shorts and boxing gloves. ''E's a southpaw,' Peckover said.

3. *attrib.* or as *adj.* Left-handed; also *transf.*, left-footed, and *fig.*

1891 *Cricket* 29 Oct. 463/1 The Germantown man returned the ball like a flash to the wicket, and the 'south-paw' batsman was run out. **1932** J. T. FARRELL *Young Lonigan* iii. 126 It was swell for Studs to play,.. knowing he had made that good kick,..to run back and pick one of Helen's southpaw kicks out of the air. **1949** *Sun* (Baltimore) 3 June 18/8 They would have been bunched against southpaw pitching. **1957** R. WATSON-WATT *Three Steps to Victory* xliii. 245 This was, however, a south-paw kind of compliment. **1969** *New Scientist* 6 Nov. 277/2 Jack Bodell has just become the first southpaw heavyweight champion in British boxing history.

Hence **sou·thpaw** *v. trans.*, to pitch with the left hand; **sou·thpawing** *vbl. sb.*, the action of pitching with the left hand.

1928 *Daily Ardmoreite* (Ardmore, Okla.) 12 Apr. 8/1 Herb Pennock southpawed his way the route for the Yankees. **1938** *Chicago Tribune* 4 Apr. 21/1 The White Sox positively refused to be awed today by the southpawing of Larry French. **1951** *Sun* (Baltimore) 23 Aug. 20/1 Jim Burns southpawed his eighth straight triumph.

southron, *sb.* Add: **2. b.** (Earlier examples.) Also *transf.*

1828 *Free Press* (Tarboro, N. Carolina) 9 Nov., I am a Republican in principle, and a Southron in feeling. **1831** J. J. AUDUBON *Ornith. Biogr.* I. 110 When those [mocking birds] which had gone to the Eastern States..have returned, they are instantly known by the 'southrons' who attack them on all occasions.

South Sea. Add: **5. c.** *South Sea Islander*.

1832 A. EARLE *Narr. Residence N.Z.* (1966) 58, I am persuaded that these South Sea islanders, though so nearly of the same complexion, still are not of the same race. **1913** C. MACKENZIE *Sinister Street* I. II. ii. 173 That belt of yours, Michael, would give a South Sea Islander a headache. **1974** J. POPE-HENNESSY *R. L. Stevenson* xi. 211 Louis..was as brown as a South Sea Islander.

south-side. Add: **a.** Also *attrib.*

1869 *Bradshaw's Railway Man.* XXI. 58 The railway.. joins the Glasgow and South Western and the Caledonian (southside branches), on the south side of the city. **1937** H. G. WELLS *Star Begotten* vi. 105 The Punic Wars..he presented as a gigantic necessary struggle between noble north-side soldiers and revengeful, obdurate but extremely competent south-side loanmongers. **1955** KEEPNEWS & GRAUER *Pict. Hist. of Jazz* iii. 43 Pianist Blythe, who died in 1930, was..in the forefront of the 'South Side style', which meant small-band recordings and jobs at small, rough clubs. **1979** *Irish Times* 28 Sept. 12/6 If the northside area described here is compared with a southside suburb the differences become more marked.

South Suffolk. [f. SOUTH(DOWN + SUFFOLK.] A sheep belonging to the breed so called, developed in New Zealand by crossing Suffolk and Southdown sheep and used to produce lean meat and short, fine wool.

1950 *N.Z. Jrnl. Agric.* Feb. 144/3 Two instances of fresh development with sheep breeds may be mentioned: First, the aim of some breeders in the South Island '..to establish a new breed by crossing Suffolk and Southdown with a view to producing a sheep having Southdown characteristics with a maximum of lean meat'—the South Suffolk. **1956** G. BOWEN *Wool Away!* (ed. 2) xii. 148 South Suffolk. This is a New Zealand type derived from crossing Southdowns with Suffolks, and is being very widely used..in Canterbury and is spreading rapidly to other parts of New Zealand. **1977** *N.Z. Herald* 8 Jan. 4-8/6 (Advt.), 23 South Suffolk ewes.

south-west, *adv.*, *sb.*, and *a.* Add: **B.** *sb.* **1. b.** *U.S.* The south-western states.

1835 J. H. OTEY in W. M. Green *Mem. J. H. Otey* (1885) 15 Connected with my journey to the South-West, was an ardent desire to forward..a projected plan of a *Literary and Theological Seminary*, to meet the wants of Episcopalians in Tennessee and Mississippi and Louisiana. **1897** *Sears, Roebuck Catal.* 342/2 The best specimens of broad burlesque for which the Southwest is so distinguished. **1925** C. F. LUMMIS (*title*) Mesa, cañon and pueblo; our wonderland of the Southwest. **1935** A. G. MACDONELL *Visit to America* ix. 142 It must have been from the Spanish south-west..that the first prospectors came..into Montana. **1976** 'R. MACDONALD' *Blue Hammer* xv. 83 Mildred was the most beautiful woman in the South-west. **1979** G. MACDONALD *Camera* ix. 130/2 In the South-West the pueblo Indians..were..much photographed.

c. *ellipt.* for South West Africa (now Namibia).

1976 J. MCCLURE *Rogue Eagle* i. 22 Ma..said she'd write to her family in South West, but he said that was just another Bantustan these days. **1978** S. NAIPAUL *North of South* II. vi. 245 Abraham had been in Namibia ('South-West')... It was in South-West..that he and Tessa had met.

C. *adj.* **2. b.** With proper names, denoting the south-western division of a city, country, continent, etc.

1858 *1st Rep. South-West London Protestant Inst.* 3 *Rules.* I. That this Society be called 'The South-West London Protestant Institute'. **1899** *Geogr. Jrnl.* May 563 A notice of Dr. Rehbock's work on irrigation in German South-West Africa. **1946** *Whitaker's Almanack 1947* 789 The *Orange*..is the principal river of the south,..flowing into the Atlantic between the Protectorate of South-West Africa and the Cape of Good Hope. **1950** H. BRIERCLIFFE *Southern England* p. iii, There is necessarily some overlapping with..South-west England and the Midlands. **1968** *Ann. Reg. 1967* 326 The South African Government remained completely unmoved by United Nations' efforts to plan the implementation of the 1966 General Assembly resolution that South West Africa be removed from South African control. **1980** *Times* 14 June 1/8 The Middle East, or south-west Asia as the Americans now call it.

south-wester, *sb.* Add: **2.** (Earlier example.)

1836 R. S. SURTEES *Let.* in A. Mathews *Mem. Charles Mathews* (1839) IV. ix. 193 Throwing aside his hat, he put on one of the boatman's 'south-westers'.

3. A (white) inhabitant of Namibia (formerly known as South West Africa).

1976 *Times* 21 Aug. 13/3 South Africa's original plans to break up South West Africa into eight or nine ministates, of which the only viable ones would be a 'ranchistan' containing the 99,000 rich German, Afrikaans and English-speaking 'Southwesters', and Ovamboland. **1978** *Guardian Weekly* 7 May 6/2 The Teutonic calm of Windhoek... Like their White Rhodesian counterparts most 'Southwesters' as they call themselves have yet to grasp the dimension of the change.

south-western, *a.* Add: **2. b.** *U.S.* Of, pertaining to, or characteristic of the south-western states.

1806 *New Eng. Palladium* (Boston) 30 July 2/1 The President appoints the Legislative Councils in our South-western Territories. **1832** *Jrnl. Gen. Convention Prot. Episc. Church* 51 Delegates have been chosen to co-operate with Alabama and Louisiana in organizing the contemplated South-Western Diocese. **1973** J. M. WHITE *Garden Game* 150 The walls were whitewashed in simple, South-Western style.

south-westward, *a.* (Later example.)

1972 *Science* 19 May 791/1 The southwestward flow of cold drier air is suggested to account for two aspects.

souvenir, *sb.* Delete ‖ and add: **2. c.** *Mil. slang.* In the 1914–18 war, a jocular term for a bullet or shell.

1915 D. O. BARNETT *Let.* 17 May 140 They kept sending their big black souvenirs over. **1929** *Papers Mich. Acad. Sci. Arts & Lett.* X. 324 *Souvenirs*, shells.

3. *souvenir-hunter, programme, shop.*

1923 KIPLING *Irish Guards in Gt. War* I. 131 Being a hardened souvenir-hunter, he is reported to have removed the official German name-board of the establishment. **1976** B. JACKSON *Flameout* (1977) iii. 40 Souvenir hunters were a menace..stealing bits of metal that could, if left in position, help determine the cause of the crash. **1962** L. DEIGHTON *Ipcress File* ii. 22 A cigarette-girl..tried to sell me a souvenir programme. **1950** J. FLANNER in *New Yorker* 25 Feb. 84/2 The best souvenir shops for the pilgrims are in the Via della Conciliazione. **1980** J. GARDNER *Garden of Weapons* III. iii. 246 From the souvenir shop the coach party went ..for a drink.

souvenir (sūvĕnīᵊ·ɹ), *v.* [f. the sb.] **1.** *trans.* To pierce with a bullet or shell. Cf. sense *2 c of the sb. *Mil. slang* (in the war of 1914–18).

1915 *Chambers's Jrnl.* Oct. 663/1 Our periscope was 'souvenired' later on with a rifle-bullet clean through the tin sides.

2. To provide with or constitute a souvenir of (something). *rare.*

1917 W. OWEN *Let.* 25 Nov. (1967) 510 How much better than a photograph does it [*sc.* a poem] souvenir that day! **1976** *Vogue* Jan. 7/2 The Tate..is issuing a special Constable diary..and a Constable paper-weight. So the exhibition will be fully souvenired.

3. To take as a 'souvenir'; to appropriate; to pilfer, steal. Also *absol. slang* (orig. *Mil.*).

1919 W. H. DOWNING *Digger Dialects* 46 *Souvenir*,..to steal, find, capture, etc. **1920** *Punch* 28 Jan. 65/1 The Major..set the ladies souveniring among old water-tin stoppers, which he alleged to be the plugs of hand-grenades. **1944** F. CLUNE *Red Heart* 19, I dug up his body, souvenired his false teeth. **1956** S. HOPE *Diggers' Paradise* ix. 83 But early, too, numbers of youngsters show that tendency to 'souvenir' which is the euphonious term for pilfering. **1969** I. BROWN *Rhapsody of Words* 120 Silver spoons and jewellery souvenired from rooms with open windows. **1975** J. I. M. STEWART *Gaudy* vii. 116 It's possible that people sometimes souvenir such things.

Hence **souveni·ring** *vbl. sb.*

1969 'M. INNES' *Family Affair* xiii. 145 It had been lifted much as somebody might lift a china gnome..from a suburban garden. Souveniring, as they say. **1972** *Guardian* 15 May 1/4 The House of Commons is determined to end the 'souveniring' of cutlery... All crests will be removed from the cutlery in some of the visitors' cafeterias.

‖**souvlaki** (su-, suvlā·ki). Pl. **souvlakia.** [mod. Gr. σουβλάκι, f. σοῦβλα skewer.] A Greek dish consisting of pieces of meat grilled on a skewer. Also *attrib.* Cf. *KEBAB.

1958 R. LIDDELL *Morea* II. vii. 171 They had bought *souvlakia* or bread and cheese at every halt. **1963** J. M. STUBBS *Home Bk. Greek Cookery* vii. 97 The best *souvlakia* I have eaten in Greece are those sold..at Antirhion. **1972** J. AIKEN *Butterfly Picnic* i. 19 Lamb grilled on skewers, souvlakia, and all the different forms of mince that the Greeks delight in. **1979** M. A. SHARP *Sunflower* iii. 30 The building..was..sandwiched between a *souvlaki* stand and a tiny hotel.

souzalite (sū·zăləit). *Min.* [f. the name of A. J. A. de *Souza*, 20th-c. Brazilian mining administrator: see -ITE¹.] A hydrated basic phosphate of aluminium, iron, and magnesium, found in association with scorzalite as fibrous masses of green crystals.

1947 PECORA & FAHEY in *Bull. Geol. Soc. Amer.* LVIII. 1217 The new minerals are named in honor of Dr. Evaristo Scorza and Dr. Antonio José Alves de Souza... Souzalite is a fibrous, green hydrous iron magnesium aluminum phosphate. **1951** C. PALACHE et al. *Dana's Syst. Min.* (ed. 7) II. 911 Scorzalite is known from the Corrego Frio pegmatite, Minas Geraes, Brazil, where it occurs with souzalite and brazilianite. **1970** *Amer. Mineralogist* LV. 152 Souzalite is a hydrothermally reworked product of scorzalite and occurs as bluish-green aggregates of polysynthetically twinned prismatic crystals.

sov. (Earlier examples.)

1829 P. EGAN *Boxiana* 2nd Ser. II. 492 'Come,' said an old ring-goer, 'here's my *sov.* to begin.' **1846** *Swell's Night Guide* 101 But of whatever size if a known gentleman and some liberality (as nothing less than five sovs would be any inducement) you may perhaps get admittance in the absence of her keeper.

Sov² (sǫv), colloq. abbrev. of *SOVIET *sb.* 2. Usu. in *pl.* with *the.*

1967 [see *CHICOM *sb.* and *a.*]. **1969** H. H. COOPER *Cave with Two Exits* II. 163 Their only worry would be that Washington might think the Sovs had done it. **1977** *Time* 28 Feb. 23/3 Certainly in every case I know of, the opposition—usually the Sovs but sometimes the Chicoms —were involved up to their eyeballs on the other side. **1981** P. FOX *Satan's Messenger* ix. 68 'Comeback from the Sovs?' 'Never heard of you.'

sovereign, *sb.* and *a.* Add: **I. 2.** δ. **suffering** (later dial. and slang examples). Now *rare.*

1836 [see *BLANK *sb.* 12]. **1914** E. PUGH *Cockney at Home* 221 I've..played..till twelve at night, and then not made half a suffering.

II. A. *sb.* **1.** † **d.** A free citizen or voter of America. *U.S. Obs.*

1846 in *Indiana Hist. Soc. Publ.* (1905) III. 412 Thousands of children in our state have not received even the trifling aid which these [public] funds afford... This fact illustrates the situation of thousands of the future sovereigns of our beloved State. **1861** *Harper's Mag.* Mar. 570/1 Deacon E— lived out West... The 'sovereigns' of that section met in caucus to appoint delegates to a County Convention. **1869** 'MARK TWAIN' *Innoc. Abr.* xi. 110, I am a free-born sovereign, sir, an American.

4. b. *attrib.* Also *sovereign purse.*

1907 *Yesterday's Shopping* (1969) 402/1 Gentlemen's sovereign purses, Russia leather.. 4/6. **1977** *Lancashire Life* Dec. 59/1 Years afterwards I showed him a sovereign purse containing a solitary half sovereign.

B. *adj.* **5. d.** *Banking.* Of or pertaining to a commercial loan made to a sovereign state.

1977 *47th Ann. Rep. Bank Internat. Settlements* 102 This..may have improved the quality of the banks' loan portfolio..but what about the corresponding rise in the country of 'sovereign' risks? **1982** *Daily Tel.* 8 Dec. 21/4 Only £26 million was set aside as a general provision, which is where the bank is believed to take account of sovereign loans. **1983** *Times* 3 Mar. 17/3 The report calls for much greater availability of information about sovereign lending.

Soviet (sōᵘ·viet, sǫ·viet, -y-, -ĕt), *sb.* and *a.* Also **soviet.** [a. Russ. *sovét* council.] **A.** *sb.* **1. a.** In the U.S.S.R.: one of a number of elected councils which operate at all levels of government, having legislative and executive functions.

The term was also applied to various revolutionary councils set up prior to the establishment of socialist rule in 1917.

1917 *Times* 27 July 6/4 (*heading*) Hostile vote against the Soviet. *Ibid.* 8 Sept. 6/4 A meeting of the Central Committee of the Soviet was held..at which the situation on the front was considered. **1920** *Edin. Rev.* July 59 Soviets, *i.e.*, councils or committees of workmen's and soldiers' delegates, are elected in every township, village or rural district for the purpose of local administration. **1930** *Times Lit. Suppl.* 30 Oct. 880/1 The chairman of the village soviet..may in theory be master in his own limited sphere; in practice he is the servant of a Communist 'cell'. **1941** E. STRAUSS *Soviet Russia* iv. 33 Workers and soldiers ..organized their own Councils or Soviets. **1953** B. MIALL tr. *Delbars's Real Stalin* vii. 48 The first Soviets of working-class deputies were formed. The president of the Soviet of St. Petersburg was a Menshevik. **1965** B. PEARCE tr. *Preobrazhensky's New Economics* 191 No more workers and office-workers are employed by the state, the local soviets, and the co-operatives than are employed in private industry, private trade, and agriculture. **1979** O. SELA *Petrograd Consignment* 20 During the 1905 uprising in St. Petersburg, together with Rakovsky and Trotsky he [*sc.* Helphand] had led the Soviet.

b. In other countries: a similar council organized on socialist principles.

1918 *Daily Mirror* 12 Nov. 2/4 (*heading*) Berlin Soviet Meets... The first sitting of the Workers' and Soldiers' Council in Berlin was held..this evening in..the Reichstag. **1934** *Fundamental Laws Chinese Soviet Republic* vi. 79 The First All-China Congress of Soviets of Workers ..calls upon the Chinese workers and peasants..to fight resolutely against Sun Yat-Sen. **1977** J. CLEARY *High Road to China* ii. 45 The Bolshevists..in Saxony..have taken over some of the towns, declared soviets.

c. *transf.* and *fig.*

1945 *Tee Emm* (Air Ministry) V. 40 Pistons, connecting rods, and other vitals cease to follow the paths their designer intended and form a sort of Soviet of miscellaneous salvage. **1947** CROWTHER & WHIDDINGTON *Science at War* 86 Owing to their character of complete equality and outspokenness, these meetings were called 'Sunday Soviets'. **1972** *History Workshop Pamphlet* No. 6. 26 The cavilling system..was an embryo of workers' control... It was a little Soviet which had grown up within the capitalist system.

2. A citizen of the U.S.S.R. Chiefly in *pl.* (hence *loosely*, = Soviet Union or its leaders).

1920 *Commercial & Financial Chron.* 24 Jan. 288/1 He [*sc.* Clemenceau] insisted upon writing the final paragraph, 'affirming that the Allies had not changed their attitude towards the Soviets'. **1930** *Amer. Speech* VI. 121 (*heading*) Jailed Soviets go on hunger strike. **1943** W. S. CHURCHILL *End of Beginning* 221 The Soviets had to repel the terrific onslaught of Germany. **1959** *Daily Tel.* 7 Feb. 11/4 President Eisenhower, seeking one word to cover citizens of the Soviet Union, has braved the criticism of purists and adopted the term 'Soviets'. **1964** R. A. BUTLER in *Listener* 13 Aug. 222/2, I am sure that the Soviets are not plotting a war against us, or anything like that, at the present time. **1977** C. MCCARRY *Secret Lovers* iii. 34 'Who did Bülow meet in Dresden?'.. 'A Soviet, an Army captain named Kalmyk.'

B. *adj.* **1.** Of, pertaining to, or having, a system of government based on soviets; *Soviet Union*: the Union of Soviet Socialist Republics.

1918 *Decrees issued by Revolutionary Peoples Govt.* I. 11 The Soviet Government does not look backward, but forward. **1920** *Glasgow Herald* 9 Mar. 8 The [American] Government has virtually decided to permit the resumption of trade relations with Soviet Russia. **1925** A. J. TOYNBEE *Survey Internat. Affairs 1920–3* 369 The new 'Red' Army of Soviet Armenia. **1928** H. N. BRAILSFORD *How Soviets Work* vii. 99 What the Soviet Union has done on a small scale for backward races like the Tartars and Bashkirs may one day have immense significance for.. Central Asia. **1946** *Ann. Reg. 1945* 193 It was agreed that the Soviet Union's claims for reparations should be met by removals from the Russian zone in Germany. **1965** M. MICHAEL tr. *J. Myrdal's Rep. Chinese Village* I. 4 In the early 1930s the peasants of northern Shensi..set up their own soviet republic. **1974** tr. *Sniečkus's Soviet Lithuania* 16 The congress called for a socialist revolution in Lithuania and the establishment of Soviet power.

2. Of, pertaining to, under the influence of, or living in the U.S.S.R.

1920 *Russian Economist* I. 89 This is the secret of 'bourgeois' diplomacy, and this riddle is being solved by Soviet diplomacy and with it by all the Russian-speaking people. **1932** *Sun* (Baltimore) 27 Jan. 12/7 If what is Russia is now known as the Soviet Republic, we should have some adjective similar to 'French', 'American', etc... 'Soviet'..has been regularly used—Soviet literature, Soviet morals, and so on. **1935** A. HUXLEY *Let.* June (1969) 397 The thing simply turned out to be a series of public meetings organized by the French Communist writers..and by the Russians as a piece of Soviet propaganda. **1961** *Ann. Reg. 1960* 499 New trade agreements were negotiated also with several countries in the 'Soviet block'. **1964** V. NABOKOV *Defence* xiv. 223 She.. bought the latest numbers of émigré magazines and—for comparison—several Soviet magazines and newspapers. **1977** *Times* 14 June 16/7 He is a Soviet Jew whose family has been refused an exit visa to go to Israel.

Comb. **1920** *Glasgow Herald* 3 Nov. 13 Fifty-two French citizens..reached Paris yesterday from Sovietland. **1945** *Salt* July 17/2 A Jap–Russian conflict would encourage the Soviet-hating 'Nationalist' (formerly 'isolationist') group. **1962** *Times* 1 Jan. 11/6 The Albanian party lacks the intellectual conditioning of a Soviet-trained leadership. **1964** T. B. BOTTOMORE *Elites & Society* vi. 111 The unified elite in Soviet-type societies is contrasted with the plurality of elites in Western-type societies. **1978** *Detroit Free Press* 5 Mar. (Parade Suppl.) 14/4 Romanov would crack down on the mishmash of more than 100 government ministries and independent agencies that create confusion in Sovietland.

3. In combination with adjs. designating another country or people in the sense 'Soviet and..', as *Soviet-American, -Chinese, -German,* etc.

1939 W. S. CHURCHILL in *Daily Mirror* 24 Aug. 14/2 In view of the Soviet–German intrigue and all other information to hand it is becoming increasingly difficult to see how war can be averted. **1958** *Listener* 28 Aug. 295/2 The theme of Soviet–Arab friendship. **1965** H. KAHN *On Escalation* xiii. 249 The U.S. in fact was carefully concerned to limit, if not avoid direct Soviet–American confrontations. **1971** H. TREVELYAN *Worlds Apart* xvi. 177 In Moscow we saw little prospect of any new initiative being successful at that moment when Soviet–Chinese relations were in an uncertain phase of manœuvre. **1978** F. MACLEAN *Take Nine Spies* iv. 158 The Soviet–German Pact of August 1939.

Hence **Sovie·tic** *a.* (now *rare*), of or pertaining to the (Russian) Soviet system; **So·vietism**, the (Russian) Soviet system; **So·vietist** *rare* an adherent of the Soviet system; **Sovie·tophile** *a.*, that loves the Soviet Union; **So:vietopho·bia**, fear of the Soviet Union (cf. *Russophobia* s.v. RUSSO- b in Dict. and Suppl.); hence **Sovie·tophobe.**

1919 E. E. CUMMINGS *Let.* 7 Nov. (1969) 62 All N.Y.'s radicals are throwing up their hats in celebration of the anniversary of Sovietism. **1920** W. T. GOODE *Bolshevism at Work* 68 The order existing in Sovietic Moscow. **1920** *Glasgow Herald* 19 Aug. 7 All Russia, apart from the Sovietists, bears no ill to Poland. **1934** Sovietic [see *dope-dream* s.v. *DOPE *sb.* 5]. **1950** *Sun* (Baltimore) 4 Jan. 1/8 Controversy over what the Truman Administration..can do to keep Sovietism in China from engulfing Formosa, the last refuge of the Nationalists. **1955** *Bull. Atomic Sci.* Jan. 35/3 The strong wine of Sovietophobia on which most of the contributors had dined was just milk for babes at the Burnham table. **1957** V. NABOKOV *Pnin* iii. 71 Only another Russian could understand the reactionary and Sovietophile blend presented by the pseudo-colorful Komarovs. **1966** *Listener* 3 Mar. 325/1 This bloody love..which must go on vitiating all our attempts at Sovietophobia. **1976** *Survey* Summer–Autumn 237 After 1968 Sartre discovered that ultimately his philosophy was more likely to culminate in anarchy than in Sovietism. **1980** *Daily Tel.* 8 July 14 Should not the British media sort out this phobia? Otherwise 'Sovietophobes' might well be in danger of alienating the most convinced of their potential allies, i.e. the Russians.

Sovietize (sǭu-, sǫ·viĕtəiz), *v.* Also **sovietize.** [f. *SOVIET *sb.* and *a.* + -IZE.] *trans.* To convert to a Soviet system of government; to bring into conformity with soviet, communist or Marxist principles; to subject to the influence or control of the Soviet Union.

1920 *Glasgow Herald* 18 Aug. 7 Lenin's attempt to Sovietise the..countries possessed by the Cossacks of the Don, Terek, and Kuban. **1922** *Ibid.* 29 July 8 Not long since the Bolshevists succeeded in Sovietising Bokhara. **1928** *Daily Express* 1 Nov. 9 The izvoschiks (cabdrivers) of Moscow are to be organised, their hours of work regulated, and..their cabs equipped with meters. The task of 'Sovietising' the izvoschik will not be an easy one. **1936** *Sun* (Baltimore) 15 Sept. 13/8 Owners of Lille textile mills, fearful lest their factories 'be Sovietized', tonight defied Government efforts to grant a forty-hour week to labor. Owners of the mills..demanded the right to prevent 'establishment of Soviets' in their plants. **1954** A. KOESTLER *Invisible Writing* 138 Bokhara the noble was being sovietised more ruthlessly than any other Asiatic town. **1968** J. M. WHITE *Nightclimber* xvi. 108 [He] assisted Panchevski, the Defence Minister, to Sovietize the army. **1980** *English World-Wide* I. 1. 20 Yiddish spelling was proletarianized, declericalized, and 'Sovietized' in the U.S.S.R.

Hence **So:vietiza·tion**; also, more *rarely*, **So·vietizer; So·vietized** *ppl. a.*; **So·vietizing** *vbl. sb.* and *ppl. a.*

1920 *Glasgow Herald* 12 Aug. 7 A Sovietised Poland subject to the Moscow Government. **1921** *Ibid.* 17 Jan. 11 It remains to be seen how the Persian Court will take to the idea of Sovietisation. **1922** *Ibid.* 29 July 8 The Amir..cannot but view the Sovietising of this region with great disfavour. **1925** *Ibid.* 26 Mar. 8 The principal virtue of wireless is its sovietising power. **1939** *Sun* (Baltimore) 29 May 13/2 An effort by the medical profession to brand socialized medicine, 'Sovietized medicine' has failed. **1939** *War Illustr.* 9 Dec. 392/3 In Russian Poland conditions were on the whole rather better... The process of Sovietization was carried out gradually. **1948** J. TOWSTER *Political Power in U.S.S.R.* I. iv. 70 The People's Commissariat for the Affairs of the Nationalities..operated as watchdog, organizer, sovietizer, and protector of the nationalities. **1949** F. MACLEAN *Eastern Approaches* I. vi. 70 At Talgar we boarded a lorry full of highly Sovietized Kazakh girl students. **1955** *Times* 16 Aug. 9/7 As constituent units of the U.S.S.R., the process of sovietization has been applied to the Baltic States without mercy. **1968** V. V. ASPATURIAN in A. Kassof *Prospects for Soviet Society* vii. 159 Sovietization is here defined as the process of modernization and industrialization within the Marxist-Leninist norms of social, economic, and political behavior. **1974** V. NABOKOV *Look at Harlequins* III. i. 132 The President of Quirn..timorously sympathized with the fashionable Sovietizers. **1982** *Daily Tel.* 30 July 12 If the Western alliance splits and the Russians establish military supremacy in Europe,..we should fear..'Sovietisation'.

Sovietology (sǭu-, sǫ:viĕtǫ·lǒdʒi). Also **sovietology.** [f. *SOVIET *sb.* and *a.* + -OLOGY.] The study and analysis of affairs and events in the U.S.S.R. So **So:vieto·logist**, a student of Soviet affairs; **So:vietolo·gical** *a.*; **So:vietolo·gically** *adv.*

1958 *Spectator* 3 Jan. 10/2 The Sovietologist really can help his listeners by explaining what has happened. *Ibid.* 13/3 A complete service with serious Sovietological analysis. **1958** *Times Lit. Suppl.* 17 Oct. 595/2 Many works of fuller and more detailed scholarship are..already becoming available as 'Sovietology' develops more and more into a major industry. **1963** *Ibid.* 4 Jan. 3/1 Mr. Dudinstev's brief excursion into fantasy may be sovietologically significant. **1968** *Soviet Studies* XIX. 467 The change in the function of Soviet ideology..could then be matched by a change in the function of Sovietology, at least in the field of theoretical-ideological controversy. **1971** H. TREVELYAN *Worlds Apart* xx. 237 The Sovietologists of the Western press, working on the documents in London or Washington, were forced by the nature of their occupation to draw conclusions, not always justified by the facts. **1976** *Daily Tel.* 21 Oct. 16/6 A newspaper photograph showing the arrival of President Tsedenbal of Mongolia at Moscow Airport has been examined in detail by the 'Way of the World' Sovietological department. **1979** *Dædalus* Winter 121 There are cracks in sovietology as well as in the Soviet monolith itself.

‖ **sovkhoz** (sǫ·vkǫz). Also **sovhoz, sovkhos,** etc. Pl. **sovkhoz, sovkhozes, sovkhozy.** [Russ., f. *sov(étskoe khoz(yáĭstvo* Soviet farm.] In the U.S.S.R.: a state-owned farm. Also *attrib.* Cf. *KOLKHOZ.

1921 *Russian Economist* I. 385 Sovkhoses, i.e., Soviet farms, that include agriculture of industrial workmen as well as the States' farms proper. **1926** *Spectator* 29 May 922/1 In Soviet Russia any estate is liable to be turned into a *Sovkhos*, a government model farm. **1932** H. G. WELLS *Work, Wealth & Happiness of Mankind* iv. 184 The Sovkhoz is a state plantation, a really scientifically planned and directed modern large-scale organization of production... The Sovkhozy have to take up lands hitherto uncultivated. **1938** *Nature* Mar. 453/2 The 'organization of the sovkhozes' (large-scale State agricultural enterprises). **1943** E. M. ALMEDINGEN *Frossia* v. 219 New tractors..meant help for thousands of our Sovhoz farms. **1953** O. CAROE *Soviet Empire* xi. 175 Land and water had been nationalized and, after taking a large share for the *Sovkhozes* or state farms, redistributed in an arbitrary fashion. **1955** H. HODGKINSON *Doubletalk* 28 The collective farms are not to be confused with the State farms or *sovkhoz*..which are owned by the State and worked by government employees. **1967** *Bull. Inst. Study USSR* (Munich) June 15 A wave of sovkhoz development followed which, beginning in 1954, did not recede until 1964. **1977** tr. *Le Monde* in *Guardian Weekly* 27 Nov. 12/5 They..lay siege to the stores in search of rare or common articles which cannot be found in their *kolkhoz* or *sovkhoz* (state farm) general stores.

‖ **sovnarkhoz** (sǫ·vnāɹkǫz). Also **Sovnarkhoz.** Pl. **sovnarkhozy, sovnarkhozie.** [Russ. *sovnarkhóz*, abbrev. of *sovét naródnovo khozyáĭstva*, council of national economy.] In the U.S.S.R.: a regional council for the local regulation of the economy.

These councils were introduced in 1957 and abandoned in 1965.

1958 *Ann. Reg. 1957* 207 The country was split into 105 'economic regions', in each of which an 'economic council' (*sovnarkhoz*) was established, responsible to the Republican Government. **1962** *Economist* 3 Mar. 788/3 The 107 smaller economic sub-divisions and their councils, or *sovnarkhozy*. **1964** *Ann. Reg. 1963* 211 The most important decisions were now taken by the Party's new Central Asian Bureau or the single regional *sovnarkhoz*. **1964** *Times Rev. Industry* Mar. 90/1 The programme included visits to the Moscow and Leningrad Sovnarkhozie (Councils of National Economy). **1964** *Economist* 12 Dec. 1242/2 The system of regional councils, or Sovnarkhozy, introduced by Mr Khrushchev in 1957.

Sovnarkom (sǫ·vnāɹkǫm). [a. Russ. *sovnarkóm*, abbrev. of *sovét naródnykh komissárov*, council of people's commissars.] The highest executive and administrative organ of government of the U.S.S.R. (renamed the Council of Ministers in 1946). Also, a council having analogous functions in one of the republics of the U.S.S.R.

1938 *Ann. Reg. 1937* 196 The Sovnarkom ordered the Gosplan to finish the schedule for the third five-year period. **1939** G. B. SHAW *Geneva* I. 21, I am Commissar Posky of the Sovnarkom and Politbureau, Soviet delegate to the League Council. **1948** J. TOWSTER *Political Power in U.S.S.R.* 248 The central executive committees and sovnarkoms of the constituent republics. **1959** *Times Lit. Suppl.* 2 Oct. 553/3 His [*sc.* Trotsky's] refusal of an offer by Lenin in 1922, twice repeated, that he should be appointed a vice-president of Sovnarkom. **1959** E. H. CARR *Socialism in One Country* II. IV. xx. 244 Even in the domain of treaty-making Sovnarkom acquired independent constitutional powers.

sow, *sb.*[1] Add: **8. a.** *sowcunt* (coarse *nonce-wd.*), *-feeder*; *sow-dugged adj.*; **sow-belly** *U.S. slang*, (salted) side of pork.

1867 W. L. GOSS *Soldier's Story of his Captivity* 205 My captor presented to me a generous slice of 'sow-belly'. **1945** B. MACDONALD *Egg & I* (1946) III. viii. 97 Tits fed this baby pickles, beer, sow-belly and cabbage. **1976** G. EWART *No Fool* III. 69 To go into your South, a different life. Sow-belly and cornbread with syrup poured over it. **1922** JOYCE *Ulysses* 541 (*Her sowcunt barks.*) Fohracht! **1960** AUDEN *Homage to Clio* 55 Steatopygous, sow-dugged and owl-headed. **1960** *Farmer & Stockbreeder* 16 Feb. (Suppl.) 37/2 Such an arrangement with individual sow-feeders, allows for better attention to each sow.

c. Also *sow beaver, grizzly bear.*

1959 E. COLLIER *Three against Wilderness* xxi. 210 She was an old sow beaver who could be reckoned upon to give birth to four or five sturdy kits. **1976** *Telegraph-Journal* (St. John, New Brunswick) 12 Aug. 12/4 A sow grizzly bear that..mauled him..was only trying to protect her young.

sow, *v.*[1] Add: **2. a.** Also, *to sow* (land) *to* (a crop). Cf. PUT *v.*[1] 26 b, *PLANT *v.* 6 a.

1939 *Sun* (Baltimore) 4 July 16/2 There will be no possibility of spreading the galls to land that is sown to wheat or rye. **1972** *Morning Star* 4 Jan. 4/1 This was cattle-breeding country, with a dairy produce industry and with only about 75,000 acres sown to grain.

4. c. *transf.* in *Mil.* To lay or 'plant' (an explosive mine); *spec.* to drop (mines, etc.) by aircraft into the sea or otherwise. Also *absol.*

1939 *Sun* (Baltimore) 20 Nov. 8/2 In the last conflict the Germans sowed 44,000 mines, 11,000 of them in British home waters. **1943** *Ibid.* 26 Nov. 1/5 After they have dropped their first flares they remain over the target area, keeping it marked by sowing more flares. **1944** K. DOUGLAS *Alamein to Zem Zem* (1946) xiv. 82 Mines were sown in the tracks of vehicles, where other vehicles might be expected to follow. **1974** *Times* 18 Apr. 1/3 A lot of anti-personnel mines sown on the canal banks have slipped into the water. **1979** J. BARNETT *Backfire is Hostile!* xiii. 135 Twenty-four Tu-16 Badgers began..sowing at forty-two thousand feet.

sowlth (sault). [ad. Ir. *samhailt* likeness, apparition.] A formless, luminous spectre. Chiefly in the writings of W. B. Yeats.

1829 G. GRIFFIN *Collegians* II. xxviii. 289 The Sowlth was seen upon the Black Lake last week. **1892** W. B. YEATS *Countess Kathleen* iii. 54 Call hither now the sowlths and tevishes. **1895** —— *Poems* 79 Pooka, sowlth, or demon of the pit. **1963** *Times Lit. Suppl.* 1 Feb. 78/4 In the first version [of *The Countess Kathleen*]..there is a naive elaboration, in which 'sheogues', 'tevishies', 'sowlths', and other rustic spirits appear.

sown, *ppl. a.* Add: **2.** (Later *absol.* examples contrasted with *desert.*)

1926 T. E. LAWRENCE *Seven Pillars* (1935) v. lviii. 328 The difference between Hejaz and Syria was the difference between the desert and the sown. **1940** J. BUCHAN *Memory Hold-the-Door* i. 22 We had for our playground both the desert and the sown. **1957** K. KENYON *Digging up Jericho* 29 The age-long struggle of the Desert and the Sown.

sox (sǫks), commercial and informal spelling of *socks*, pl. of SOCK *sb.*[1]

Also used as the final element in the names of some sports teams, esp. in *U.S. Baseball.*

1905 H. G. WELLS *Kipps* I. ii. 37 He abbreviated every word he could; he would have considered himself the laughing-stock of Wood Street if he had chanced to spell *socks* in any way but 'sox'. **1912** G. FRANKAU *One of Us* v. 41 To dollars deaf, impervious to invective, They plunged profaning hands in shirts and sox. **1942** Z. N. HURSTON in *Amer. Mercury* July 88 Dat broad couldn't make the down payment on a pair of sox. **1948** *Richmond* (Va.) *Times-Dispatch* 11 June 27/1 The Boston Red Sox today socked the Cleveland Indians 15–7. **1965** *Liberator* Aug. 20/1 And Sweet Mac was there; legs crossed, showing his..two-fifty sox. **1977** *West Briton* 25 Aug. 17/7 (Advt.), Assorted nylon plain & fancy short sox.

Soxhlet (sǫ·kslĕt). *Chem.* Also **soxhlet.** The name of Franz *Soxhlet* (1848–1926), Belgian chemist, used *attrib.* (and † in the possessive) to denote an apparatus and method which he devised for the continuous solvent extraction of a solid.

1889 *Jrnl. Chem. Soc.* LV. 359 When using the ordinary form of Soxhlet extractor, there is always a doubt as to the exact time when the substance is completely extracted, unless the whole apparatus is taken to pieces. **1899** *Jrnl. Physiol.* XXIV. 319, I used casein which had been extracted for a week in Soxhlet's apparatus. **1945** M. F. GLAESSNER *Princ. Micropalaeont.* x. 239 Space and equipment for..simple porosity and permeability tests, soxhlet extraction of bituminous rock samples, and gas analysis may be provided. **1950** *Jrnl. Org. Chem.* XV. 256 The salt-like product was extracted with butyl alcohol in a Soxhlet apparatus for 6 hours. **1968** R. O. C. NORMAN *Princ. Org. Synthesis* vii. 224 Barium hydroxide is placed in the thimble of a Soxhlet extractor over a flask of boiling acetone.

soy[1]. **1, 2.** For Latin names substitute *Glycine max.*

3. Equivalent to *SOYA 2: *soy bottle, jam, oil, protein*; **soy frame**, an ornamental stand with a ring frame used for holding a soy bottle; **soy-sauce** = sense 1 (earlier and later examples). See also *SOY-BEAN.

1960 Soy bottle [see *soy frame* below]. **1970** *Canadian Antiques Collector* Oct. 18 (*caption*) Four 12-sided soy bottles with shoulder bands of diamonds cut in high relief. **1788–1815** *Watson & Bradbury Pattern Bk.* in F. Bradbury *Hist. Old Sheffield Plate* (1912) IX. 197 Soy frames... Sugar Tongs... Snuffers. **1912** F. BRADBURY *Hist. Old Sheffield Plate* IX. 271 The soy frames and cruet frames..are sufficiently illustrated here to give a very fair general idea of the different fashions. **1931** E. WENHAM *Domestic Silver* x. 142 Snuffer-trays and soy-frames can be..made into attractive inkstands. **1960** H. HAYWARD *Antique Coll.* 261/2 *Soy frame*, silver or plated oblong or oval stand with ring frame for holding soy or sauce bottles. **1956** B. Y. CHAO *How to cook & eat in Chinese* I. iii. 50 Similar to soy sauce is a *soy jam*, which is much thicker in consistency. **1976** *Billings* (Montana) *Gaz.* 30 June 4-B/1 Soy oil lost some 25 points. **1974** *Sci. Amer.* Feb. 19/1 Soy protein is nutritionally somewhat less complete than meat. **1795** Soy sauce [see *SOY-BEAN a]. **1959** R. KIRKBRIDE *Tamiko* vii. 54 They had hors d'oeuvres of raw wild vegetables, sashimi, thin slices of raw tuna and sea bream with soy sauce. **1978** *Nagel's Encycl.-Guide: China* 380 The seven sauces used in the stew are replaced by soy sauce, into which the meat is dipped before being cooked.

soya. Add: **1.** (Later examples.)

1905 [see *MISO]. **1970** *Times* 20 Apr. 4/5 Liveweight gains in turkeys and pigs..were as good as those with fishmeal or soya.

2. *attrib.*, as *soya flour, meal, milk, oil*; **soya-burger,** a hamburger made with (beef and) soya beans; also, a mixture of minced beef and soya beans; **soya link** [LINK *sb.*[2] 2 c] = next; **soya sausage,** a sausage made with minced soya beans. Cf. *SOYA BEAN.

1953 POHL & KORNBLUTH *Space Merchants* ii. 14 When real meat got scarce, we had soyaburgers ready. **1974** *Globe & Mail* (Toronto) 29 Oct. 15/9 The federal government decided to allow soyaburger products to be marketed. **1930** *Times Lit. Suppl.* 27 Feb. 167/2 Soya flour prepared by the ordinary methods soon turns rancid. **1951** *Good Housek. Home Encycl.* 333/1 Stir in the soya flour. **1965** B. SWEET-ESCOTT *Baker Street Irregular* vii. 200 That unspeakable dish, the soya link, the staple diet of the British in the Mediterranean campaign. **1968** J. W. PURSEGLOVE *Trop. Crops: Dicotyledons* I. 265 Soya meal, the residue after the extraction of the oil, is a very rich protein feeding stuff for livestock. **1977** C. MCFADDEN *Serial* (1978) viii. 22/2 Harvey..drank his soya milk without complaint. **1917** H. A. GARDNER *Paint Researches* xxiii. 316 A series of tests were conducted to determine the rate of drying of soya oil. **1982** *Times* 14 Apr. 11/1 Sunoil, linoil and soyaoil prices appeared to be rising. **1971** D. MEIRING *Wall of Glass* xxiii. 195 They went to the counter. It was soya sausages, potatoes, cabbage.

soya bean. Also † **soja bean; soyabean.** [f. SOYA + BEAN.] **a.** = SOY[1] 2. Cf. also next entry.

1897 *Publ. Georgia Dept. Agric. 1896* 64 A display of soja beans..a legume of exceptionally fine quality for stock feed. **1905** *Chambers's Jrnl.* Mar. 220/2 Soya beans ..are grown all over Japan and in Manchuria. **1930** *Times Lit. Suppl.* 27 Feb. 167/2 The high nutritive value of the soya bean has long been recognized. **1958** *Times Rev. Industry* Apr. 92/2 The 1957 increase was well spread; there were..good crops of soyabeans in the United States. **1968** J. W. PURSEGLOVE *Trop. Crops: Dicotyledons* I. 265 Soya beans are one of the world's most important sources of oil and protein. **1973** *Saint Croix Courier* (St. Stephen, New Brunswick) 26 July 1 Canada is not a big user of soya beans.

b. *attrib.*

1911 *Daily Colonist* (Victoria, B.C.) 6 Apr. 14/2 In the cargo for Victoria was a shipment of 500 tubs of soya bean oil. **1944** V. HODGSON *Diary* 7 May in C. Driver *British at Table* (1983) ii. 16, I have an order with the Dairy for a pound of sausage..of soya bean flour. **1966** GETTENS & STOUT *Painting Materials* 62 Soya Bean Oil... A typical analysis of soya bean oil gives 14 per cent of palmitic acid. **1977** G. SCOTT *Hot Pursuit* iii. 26 Drinking glass after glass of..soya bean milk bought from little carts at every corner.

soy-bean. (In Dict. s.v. SOY[1] 3.) Add: **a.** (Earlier and later examples.)

1795 tr. *C. P. Thunberg's Trav.* IV. 121 Soy-sauce, which is every where and every day used throughout the whole empire,..is prepared from Soy Beans..and salt, mixed with barley or wheat. **1970** *N.Y. Times Encycl. Almanac* 259/2 [Iowa] ranks first in popcorn and oats, and is second in soybeans. **1975** *New Yorker* 26 May 50/3 He said that in the nineteen-sixties the United States 'had excess capacity in corn and soybeans'. **1978** J. IRVING *World according to Garp* xv. 300 A field of corn and a field of soybeans.

b. *attrib.*, esp. as *soybean oil.*

1935 *Cereal Chemistry* XII. 442 It is only within the last decade that the use of soybean flour for food purposes in this country has been seriously considered. **1938** A. A. HORVATH *Soybean Industry* xiv. 97 Quantities of soybean oil have been used in the manufacture of foundry cores. **1956** B. Y. CHAO *How to cook & eat in Chinese* I. iii. 49 The most important flavourer of Chinese food is *soy-bean sauce* or soy sauce for short. **1967** D. & E. T. RIESMAN *Conversations in Japan* 58 Delicacies such as fresh ginger root, soybean soup, meat and vegetables. **1973** P. THEROUX *Saint Jack* v. 52 Over in an armchair drinking soy-bean milk..sat old Mr. Tan Lim Hock. **1979** C. MACLEOD *Luck runs Out* vii. 76 Her successful campaign to have soybean cutlets put on the menu.

Soyer (soi·əɪ). The name of Alexis Benoît *Soyer* (1809–58), French-born cook to fashionable society in England, subsequently working for Irish famine-relief and with the British army in the Crimea, used *attrib.* and formerly in the possessive, as **Soyer('s) stove,** to designate a table-top cooking-range (the *Magic stove*) developed by him in 1849, or his Field stove invented in 1857. Also *absol.*

1856 A. SOYER *Mod. Housewife* (new ed.) 513 (Advt.), Soyer's Magic Stove and Lilliputian Apparatus, specially adapted for out-door cooking. **1857** —— *Culinary Campaign* 524 These receipts are also applicable for barracks, in camp, or while on the march, by the use of Soyer's New Field Stove, now adopted by the military authorities. **1858** VOLANT & WARREN *Mem. Alexis Soyer* xiii. 157 M. Soyer at once perceived the importance of this little apparatus, and..it was brought out..as 'Soyer's Magic Stove', to which was added the 'Camp Kitchen'. **1878** *Instructions to Mil. Cooks in Prep. Dinners* 9 The field cooking apparatus in use in the Army are Feetham's and Soyer's stoves... Soyer's stove..is fitted with a boiler only, and will cook for 50 men. **1941** *Jrnl. R. Army Med. Corps* LXXVII. 274 Soyer stoves or other improvised water heaters. **1981** J. BARNETT *Firing Squad* II. 116 Blackened cauldrons, known in the Army as Soyer stoves, spew thick smoke from tall thin chimneys... The men are offered soup from the Soyers.

sozzle, *sb.* Add: Also † **sossle. 2.** (Earlier example.)

1848 BARTLETT *Dict. Americanisms* 321 *Sossle,* or *sozzle,* a lazy or sluttish woman.

sozzle, *v.* Add: **3.** *intr.* [Back-formation f. *SOZZLED *ppl. a.*] To imbibe intoxicating drink. *slang.*

1937 G. FRANKAU *More of Us* xv. 160 Then Sophie called; and brooding, 'Nice schemozzle If that lot stays to feed as well as sozzle.' **1953** N. FITZGERALD *Midsummer Malice* xx. 242 We can sit here and sozzle gently and enjoy ourselves.

sozzled (sǫ·z'ld), *ppl. a. slang.* Also † **sosselled.** [f. SOZZLE *v.*] Intoxicated, drunk; drunken.

1886–96 in Farmer & Henley *Slang* (1903) VI. 301/2 She was thick in the clear, Fairly sosselled on beer. **1904** ADE *True Bills* 26 It was customary to mix Tea,..Egg-nog,..and Straight Goods until..the last Caller was Sozzled. **1921** *Blackw. Mag.* Feb. 157/1, I wasn't what you'd call sozzled. I might have been lit up a bit, but sozzled—no. **1935** D. L. SAYERS *Gaudy Night* xx. 414 He was beautifully sozzled last night. **1951** 'J. WYNDHAM' *Day of Triffids* i. 23 'Gin, blast it! T'hell with gin!'.. The voice gave a sozzled chuckle. **1963** N. MARSH *Dead Water* (1964) i. 13 'She'm sozzled,' said Wally, and indeed, it was so. **1972** E. STAEBLER *Cape Breton Harbour* xiv. 130 With a sozzled smile he began to sing about a little yellow dory.

spa, *sb.* Add: **2. b.** Also *spa bath, pool.* A health bath containing hot, aerated water. *U.S.*

1974 *Los Angeles Times* 13 Oct. III. 8 (Advt.), The Original Santa Barbara Hotub is a superbly-engineered spa that is beautiful furniture. **1976** *Outdoor Living* (N.Z.) I. II. 59/1 A spa pool is a large, hot bath with aerated water, bubbling softly around, massaging your body. **1977** *Times* 29 Oct. 11/5 The latest craze [in Los Angeles] is bathing with your friends..in a jacuzzi or spa-bath. **1979** *Arizona Daily Star* 8 Apr. J1/5 Spas in or next to the pools are also a hot item. Ragel says he sells spas with about 50 percent of his pools.

3. b. A commercial establishment which offers health and beauty treatment (esp. for women) through steam baths, exercise equipment, massage, and the like. *U.S.*

1960 *Life* 8 Feb. 111/1 The submerged specter above.. is getting a hydraulic underwater massage at a plush health spa near San Diego called the Golden Gate beauty resort whose customers are usually female. **1976** *Vogue* Dec. 214/1 Most American spas are designed exclusively for women. **1981** W. SAFIRE in *N.Y. Times Mag.* 21 June 10/2 Only fuddy-duddies go to the *gym*,..the upscale..crowd goes to the *spa*.

space, *sb.*[1] Add: **II. 6. d.** For *U.S.* read orig. *U.S.* and add earlier and later examples.

1894 E. L. SHUMAN *Steps into Journalism* 83 Articles by the beginner are nearly always submitted 'on space'. **1933** E. WAUGH *Scoop* III. i. 259 I've only been on the paper three weeks... It is the first time I've drawn any money... I'm 'on space', you see. **1971** D. AYERST *Guardian* xxv. 357 Williams represented the *Guardian* in St Petersburg at first on a small salary..and then..on space.

e. Room in a newspaper, periodical, etc., or on some other medium, which may be acquired for a specific purpose, esp. advertising.

1930 *Economist* 29 Nov. 1003/2 In advertising Britain is far behind America in buying space. **1940** R. S. LAMBERT *Ariel & All his Quality* vii. 168 Selling 'space'.. breeds a very different outlook from providing programmes. **1950** *Times* 7 Feb. 5/5 In the last election, one company gave space to the Communist Party and the Commonwealth Party, but the main newsreels adhered to the general agreement that space should be given only to the main parties.

8. a. (Later examples.)

1901, etc. [see *outer space* s.v. *OUTER *a.* 3]. **1924** R. GRAVES *Mock Beggar Hall* 40 May not Space be housing and sheltering millions of other beings like us, or different from us? **1959** *Daily Tel.* 23 Feb. 11/6 For the human body, space begins about 12 miles up, where there is not enough air left to burn a candle. **1961** 'C. E. MAINE' *Man who owned World* vii. 86 Such is human psychology that a living man returning from space attracts less attention than a dead man not returning. **1962** F. I. ORDWAY et al. *Basic Astronautics* ii. 26 On April 12, 1961, a 27-year old Russian air force pilot Yuri Gagarin..whirled once around the earth in an orbit at an average altitude of 158 miles. Some 108 minutes after launching, he had returned to earth the first man to travel in space.

9. e. = *living space* (a) s.v. *LIVING *vbl. sb.* 7 a. *slang* (chiefly *N. Amer.*).

1976 *New Times* 19 Mar. 36 Werner Erhard through est, has created the 'space' for them to 'be' and given them the 'opportunity' to 'take responsibility' for their lives. **1977** C. MCFADDEN *Serial* (1978) iii. 13/2 Leonard had a lot going for him otherwise, and Kate liked the space he was in. **1980** G. B. TRUDEAU *Tad Overweight,* Seriously, I think I know where you're coming from, and I'd like to share that space. **1981** *Gossip* (Holiday Special) 31/3 The reason why I can say that so boldly is because they give me my space. They let me be me.

10. d. A portion of a page (in a newspaper, etc.) available for a specific purpose, esp. advertising; a period or interval of broadcasting time available to or occupied by a particular programme or advertising 'slot'. Esp. in injunction *watch this space!* (freq. *transf.*). Cf. sense 6 e above.

1917 *B.E.F. Times* 20 Jan. 15/2 (Advt.), Watch this Space. **1956** *B.B.C. Handbk. 1957* 78 Plays from the West End..are often heard in the more 'popular' programme spaces. **1972** *Sci. Amer.* Feb. 114/1 Kant's own book was discussed in this space a couple of years ago from the paper-back edition issued by the University of Michigan Press. **1979** J. RATHBONE *Euro-Killers* iv. 44 Where is he? Watch this space for exciting revelations in the next few days.

15. c. *Telecommunications.* An interval between consecutive marks in a mark–space signalling system such as telegraphy. Opp. *MARK *sb.*[1] 13 e.

1859, etc. [see *MARK *sb.*[1] 13 e]. **1906** A. E. KENNELLY *Wireless Telegr.* xi. 153 A dash has the length of three dots, and the space separating dots or dashes in a letter are [*sic*] of dot length... The space separating adjacent letters is three dots long and the space separating words, six dots long. **1954** *Electronic Engin.* XXVI. 230/1 The principle..is to explore the centre of each received signal element..to determine whether it is 'mark' or 'space', and use the information so obtained to initiate new signals of correct length. **1968** D. C. GREEN *Radio & Line Transmission (A)* xvi. 292 [In the Murray code] each character is represented by a combination of five signal elements that may be either a mark or a space. In Great Britain a mark is represented by a negative potential or the presence of a tone and a space is represented by a positive potential or the absence of a tone.

16*. *Math.* An instance of any of various mathematical concepts, usu. regarded as a set of points having some specified structure; cf. **metric space,* **topological space,* **vector space.*

1911 *Trans. Amer. Math. Soc.* XII. 287 It is not always necessary to set up a definition of distance for the Hilbert space; for other domains of objects to do so might be very difficult or even impossible. **1927** *Bull. Amer. Math. Soc.* XXXIII. 14 The Hilbert space of infinitely many dimensions in which the coordinates $x_1, x_2, x_3, \ldots, x_n, \ldots$ of each point are subject to the condition that the sum of their squares be a convergent series is a metric space in which distance is defined by the formula [etc.]. **1932** M. H. STONE *Linear Transformations in Hilbert Space* i. 1 The word 'space' has gradually acquired a mathematical significance so broad that it is virtually equivalent to the word 'class', as used in logic. **1964** A. P. & W. ROBERTSON *Topological Vector Spaces* i. 5 A topological space is a set provided with a structure that enables convergence and continuity to be considered. **1968** P. A. P. MORAN *Introd. Probability Theory* i. 2 The experiment can turn out in one of a..number of exclusive ways which we denote as $E_1, E_2, E_3, \ldots,$ and which we call the 'elementary events'. The set of all such events is called the 'space' of elementary events.

III. 17. a. *space-band, -bar, -gauge.*

1888 J. HARRISON *Man. Type-Writer* 18 In front of the four banks of keys there is a narrow strip of wood which is called the 'space-bar'. *Ibid.* 25 The 'space-gauge' is a little thumb-piece at the extreme right of the carriage. **1895** E. COLLYNS *Typists' Man.* 17 The space between the lines is regulated by the 'Space Gauge'. **1904** C. T. JACOBI *Printing* (ed. 3) x. 132 A stationary box..contains a series of space-bands. **1919** B. DE BEAR *Typewriting* 22 You depress the space-bar whenever you want to leave a space in a line of the work. **1930** *Daily Express* 23 May 4/6 Spacebands are pushed up to fill out the line to the required width, and then the whole line is automatically conveyed to the face of a mould and filled with molten metal. **1957** *Encycl. Brit.* XVIII. 502/2 By touching another key, a double wedge spaceband is placed between the words. **1962** *Which?* Dec. 359/2 The space bar.. moved the carriage exactly half a space when depressed, the other half when released.

b. *space continuum, harmony, music, -occupancy* (earlier example), *-perception, -relation* (earlier example), *-sensation, -sense, -symmetry, -value.*

1865 S. HODGSON *Time & Space* ii. 65 Their space-relations are not capable of analysis into relations of time. *Ibid.* 75 The space-senses sight and touch..are brought into play simultaneously with the other senses. **1875** G. H. LEWES *Probl. Life & Mind* II. 278 What is signified in speaking of material extension is space-occupancy. **1886** W. JAMES *Let.* 12 Sept. in R. B. Perry *Tht. & Char. W. James* (1935) I. 604 Of already written things I have a long-finished article on space-perception, [etc.]. **1890** —— *Princ. Psychol.* II. xx. 195 Let the movement *bc*, of a certain joint, derive its absolute space-value from the cutaneous feeling it is always capable of engendering. *Ibid.* 219 We must..seek to discover *by what means* the circumstances can so have transformed a space-sensation. **1911** —— *Some Probl. Philos.* xi. 182 God, as the orthodox believe, created the space-continuum, with its infinite parts already standing in it, by an instantaneous *fiat.* **1924** R. M. OGDEN tr. *Koffka's Growth of Mind* 72 Psychology of space-perception. **1932** F. L. WRIGHT *Autobiogr.* II. 145 Freedom of floorspace and elimination of useless heights worked a miracle in the new dwelling place... An entirely new sense of space values in architecture came home. **1933** H. READ *Art Now* ii. 78 At our period the artist..had to infer the extension of plane surfaces..the placing of all objects in a space continuum. **1957** —— *Tenth Muse* xxxi. 279 A distinction between an aesthetic consciousness determined by time-sense (music and poetry) and an aesthetic consciousness determined by space-sense (the plastic arts). **1963** *Times* 30 Apr. 15/1 A 'poème plastique', written in 1918, uses the very up-to-date idea of instrumental units separated in space; a kind of early stereophonic, space music. **1965** W. LAMB *Posture & Gesture* iv. 56 The process of variation, sometimes under the heading Narrow-Wide, is recognized and figures as a component in 'Space Harmonies'. **1977** 'J. LE CARRÉ' *Hon. Schoolboy* xix. 467 Jerry..walked into the reception room... Space music was playing and there was even conversation under it. **1979** *Nature* 11 Oct. 433/1 Depending on the symmetry of the lattice and of the arrangement of the atoms within each cell, a crystal is assigned to one of the 230 possible space-symmetry groups.

c. *space-coordinate, -derivative, -inversion.*
1888 *Rep. Brit. Assoc. Adv. Sci. 1887* 507 Certain relations which held between the fluid velocities *u, v, w*, and their space-derivatives at any point of a rigid boundary. **1967** CONDON & ODISHAW *Handbk. Physics* (ed. 2) II. vi. 41/1 The Minkowski matrix η is a Lorentz matrix which defines the space-inversion transformation $x' = -x, y' = -y, z' = -z, t' = -t$. **1968** M. S. LIVINGSTON *Particle Physics* vii. 137 Scientists, philosophers, and others have been interested in the significance of space-inversion invariance. **1970** G. K. WOODGATE *Elem. Atomic Struct.* iii. 41 And r_i is the space-co-ordinate of the incident wave at the position of the *i*th electron.

d. For *U.S.* read orig. *U.S.* *space-writer* (later example); *space rate* (examples); relating to the purchase of (advertising, etc.) space, as *space-buyer, salesman.*
1902 E. BANKS *Autobiogr. Newspaper Girl* 207 [By] the 'guarantee space' system..a member of the staff is guaranteed a stipulated sum of money every week, and as much over that amount as he or she makes by writing at ordinary or special space-rates. **1934** S. BECKETT *More Pricks than Kicks* 92 'Well' insisted the space-writer. **1939** F. M. FORD *Let.* 14 Mar. (1965) 316 You can be certain of occupying a certain space in the pages of the Review and being paid at the usual..space rates. **1948** G. V. GALWEY *Lift & Drop* i. 11 Mrs Lawson, the space-buyer of Rooster's. **1954** KOESTLER *Invisible Writing* iv. xxxv. 377 Dr. Magnus..was now space-salesman for an obscure little Polish gazette. **1972** G. BROMLEY *In Absence of Body* iii. 41 He's the chief space buyer. **1979** *Amer. Film* July–Aug. 55/1 'Now who in the audience will know what a space salesman is?' quizzed Jaffe; a space salesman sells advertising space in a magazine.

e. In sense 8 a, outer space regarded as a field for human activity; (many of these formations are modelled on analogous uses of *air, air-*): *space agency, biology, bus, conquest, -crew, doctor, exploration, explorer, journey, law, lifeboat, liner, museum, navigation, navigator, pilot, relay, research, science, scientist, taxi, technology, travel, traveller, tug,* etc.
1958 *Science* 11 Apr. 807/2 Herbert F. York..has been named chief scientist of the Defense Department's new space agency. **1970** *Times* 15 Apr. 1/5 This firm decision was taken today by the space agency in preference to the much riskier feat of attempting a landing a day earlier after a faster return. **1960** *IRE Trans. Military Electronics* IV. 284/2 To gain some insight into the problems.. ultimately to be studied in space biology, using these missiles as experimental tools. **1977** J. TODD in S. Brand *Space Colonies* 49/2 During the hey-day of interest in space exploration (summer 1962) a symposium on the ecological aspects of space biology was convened. **1961** *New Scientist* 27 July 216 Ultimately, the space bus named *Ranger* will find its way to the moon, running on electric power drawn from the sun. **1967** *Boston Sunday Globe* 23 Apr. 1/4 Komarov, 40, spent 24 hours 17 minutes in space Oct. 12–13, 1964, aboard the Voshkod 1 'space bus'. **1949** E. F. RUSSELL in 'E. Crispin' *Best SF* (1955) 209 The biped tribes..need all their unity to cope with space-conquest. **1951** A. C. CLARKE *Sands of Mars* x. 126 Visiting space-crews..soon got bored if they had nothing to do between trips. **1974** *Sci. & Technical Aerospace Rep.* XII. 1600/2 Aeromedical problems of weightlessness and the transfer of spacecrews between Soyuz and Apollo spacecrafts are discussed. **1953** J. N. LEONARD *Flight into Space* xi. 103 Using the scientific method of dissecting a many-sided problem into its separate parts, the space doctors discuss and study the dangers of space individually. **1964** *Skylights* Mar. 1 Pulmonary atelectasis—collapse of the small lung sacs—was feared by space doctors, but did not appear during the 17-day test span. **1957** *IRE Trans. Mil. Electronics* I. 43 (*heading*) Space exploration—the new challenge to the electronics industry. **1969** *Guardian* 7 June 2/8 Russia was spending a significantly higher percentage..on space exploration. **1959** K. VONNEGUT *Sirens of Titan* i. 30 The state of mind on Earth with regard to space exploration was much like the state of mind in Europe..before Christopher Columbus set out... The monsters between space explorers and their goals were not imaginary. **1975** *New Yorker* 21 Apr. 108/2 It has turned out that our real space explorers have necessarily been practical men. **1901** H. G. WELLS *First Men in Moon* xx. 248 All through the major portion of that vast space journey I hung thinking of such immaterial things. **1961** *Daily Tel.* 6 May 8/2 Cdr. Shepard's successful space journey is an immense relief not only to the Americans but the entire free world. **1955** A. G. HALEY in *Jet Propulsion* (1956) XXVI. 951/1 We have about as clear a vision of the space law that will prevail one or two centuries from now as Hammurabi in the 22nd century B.C. **1960** *Daily Tel.* 17 Aug. 13/3 Mr Shawcross also announced that he would resign as chairman of the organising committee on space law, recently set up in London. **1980** *Oxf. Compan. Law* 1165/2 *Space law*, principles of law accepted by nations as binding on them and their nationals in engaging in activities in outer space..and in relation to celestial bodies. **1966** *Observer* 4 Dec. 2/7 American scientists are planning 'space lifeboats' to rescue the crews of disabled spaceships. **1944** E. COLLINS *Mariners of Space* i. 14 Earth's new Space Liner..leaves Croydon to-day at noon. **1982** A. HEMINGWAY *Pzyche* i. 16 The castaway..was a former waiter on a spaceliner. **1977** SACHS & JAHN *Celestial Passengers* xxxii. 190 A new space museum is being developed a mile from Disneyland in Anaheim, California. **1931** J. M. WALSH *Vandals of Void* iv. 40 A ticklish job..is this of space navigation. **1976** *Internat. Aerospace Abstr.* XVI. 23/2 Time intervals in problems of space navigation and communication are often obtained by determining the phase of binary signals. **1936** *Forum & Century* July 36/2 Suppose that a breed of space navigators has begun to appear on earth. **1951** A. C. CLARKE *Exploration of Space* 82 His position is, clearly, only one of the things a space-navigator would want to know. **1962** *Amer. Speech* XXXVII. 43 Before April 12, 1961, the concept expressed by *cosmonaut*, in reference to both American and Soviet space flights, was rendered in the American press by such terms as *astronaut, spaceman,..space navigator.* **1944** E. COLLINS *Mariners of Space* iii. 21 Space pilots and their mechanics buzzed bee-like in and out of their quarters. **1978** *Space Picture Library Holiday Special* 6 The man who rushed forward.. could do little more than break the space-pilot's fall. **1958** *Listener* 4 Dec. 910/1 The result implied that the moon could be used as a space relay for transatlantic radio communication. **1957** *IRE Trans. Mil. Electronics* I. 43/1 The development of a system to control remotely a space-research vehicle. **1982** M. DUKE *Flashpoint* xv. 108 We've already had benefits from space research. **1957** D. J. ENRIGHT *Apothecary's Shop* 232 At least one writer, Robert Conquest, is exploring space-science as a subject for his poetry. **1978** *Nature* 16 Feb. 599/1 If the future facing space science 20 years ago lay full of hope and promise, the symposium indicated how confused and uncertain the picture is today. **1953** M. O. HYDE *Flight Today & Tomorrow* 100 Space scientists look to the rocket to carry them beyond the earth. **1969** *Times* 2 May 16/4 Space scientists have discovered six concentrations of dense material below the surface of the moon. **1952** W. LEY in C. Ryan *Across Space Frontier* 114 The space station..is always spinning, and obviously it cannot be stopped just to enable a space taxi to enter one of the turrets. **1970** N. ARMSTRONG et al. *First on Moon* xiv. 369 An orbiting space station and the 'space taxi'..to take astronauts there and back. **1958** *Science* 11 Apr. 803/1 To be strong and bold in space technology will enhance the prestige of the United States among the peoples of the world. **1972** *Guardian* 10 July 11/7 France..and West Germany [are] eager to embrace the most advanced of space technologies. [**1929** Space travel: see *space station*, sense 19 below]. **1931** J. M. WALSH *Vandals of Void* i. 23 In the early days of space travel more than one ship was pirated. **1951** 'J. WYNDHAM' in *Best of John Wyndham* (1973) 196 The question of continued space-travel ships of the present types becomes grave. **1978** I. WATSON in C. Priest *Anticipations* 13 What kind of space travel..? Well, they can only be going to the stars. **1930** *Science Wonder Q.* Spring 342/2 (*caption*) Illustrating the journey of the space travelers from Astropol to Venus. **1949** 'M. INNES' *Journeying Boy* iv. 39 So might the earth's first space-traveller exclaim as his rocket took off for the moon. **1976** *Listener* 22 July 83/3 A journey of merely five light years would take about 500,000 years... 15,000 generations of men and women..would successively replace the original crew of stellar space-travellers en route. **1961** *Aeroplane* C. 184/1 The one-man 'space tug' would be used for assembling a large space-station in orbit. **1970** *Physics Bull.* Apr. 145/2 A manned moon station is foreseen, as are..a 'space shuttle' for commuting between the earth and vehicles in low earth orbit, and a 'space tug' for transport to Mars in the 1980s.

f. Applied to sprays designed to produce droplets that will remain suspended in the air for a long period.
1956 *Aerosol Age* June 70/2 This opens up some interesting possibilities in the lower cost, non-toxic pressurized space sprays. **1958** HERZKA & PICKTHALL *Pressurized Packaging* xiv. 271 Although it is possible to produce a space deodorant which employs only deodorant perfume and propellant..it is better to use the perfume in conjunction with glycols. **1973** J. B. WILKINSON et al. *Harry's Cosmeticology* (ed. 6) xliv. 764 A good example of the functional use of space sprays is the aerosol room deodorant. **1974** M. O. JOHNSON in Sciarra & Stoller *Sci. & Technol. Aerosol Packaging* xx. 541 (*heading*) Air fresheners and space bactericides.

18. a. *space-based, -dependent, -spanned.*
1931 C. DAY LEWIS *From Feathers to Iron* 45 Space-spanned, God-girdled, love will keep Its form, being planned of bone. **1958** I. ASIMOV *Naked Sun* viii. 107 Try getting rid of me against my will and you'll be looking down the throats of space-based artillery. **1962** CORSON & LORRAIN *Introd. Electromagn. Fields* 534 Space-dependent functions can also be represented with the exponential notation. **1972** *Guardian* 9 Feb. 3/8 The US is evolving..an entire space-based defence network.

b. *space-devouring, -travelling, -wasting.* Also with (formally identical) vbl. sbs.
1907 W. JAMES *Let.* 14 Feb. (1920) II. 265 The magnificent space-devouring Subway roaring me back and forth. **1934** C. LAMBERT *Music Ho!* II. 108 His time travelling is like the space travelling of a character like Douglas Fairbanks. **1938** *Times Lit. Suppl.* 1 Oct. 625/3 The space-travelling itself forces a more direct comparison with..'The First Men in the Moon'. **1949** E. MUIR *Coll. Poems* (1960) 177 Its space-devouring eyes Pass me and hurry on. **1962** F. W. HOUSEHOLDER in Householder & Saporta *Probl. Lexicogr.* 281 Others objected to them as (a) space-wasting, (b) often irrelevant and unhelpful. **1979** J. PATON *Sea of Rings* xv. 122 We've never encountered any other space-travelling civilisation.

c. In adjectival phr., as *space-to-ground.*
1958 C. C. ADAMS *Space Flight* 144 Whether bombing or space-to-ground missile attacks would be any more effective from such a [space] station has not been established. **1967** *Economist* 29 Apr. 479/1 A Soviet space ship that, according to some reports, was having a variety of troubles with attitude control, power consumption and space-to-ground communication.

19. space age, the period of human exploration and exploitation of space; freq. *attrib.*, applied to products supposed to be characteristic of this age; hence (*nonce-wds.*) **space-ager,** one living in this age; **space-agey** *a.*, characteristic of this age; **space-averaged** *a. Physics*, averaged over a region of space; **space blanket,** a light metal-coated plastic sheet designed to retain heat; **space-borne** *a.*, carried through space; also, carried out in space or by means of instruments in space; **space-bound** *a.*, bound or limited by the properties of space; **space cabin,** a chamber designed to support human life in space; **space cadet,** a trainee spaceman; also *transf.*, esp. a (young) enthusiast for space travel; **space capsule,** a small spacecraft containing the instruments or crew relating to the purpose of a space flight; **space chamber,** a chamber in which conditions in space or a spacecraft can be simulated; **space charge** *Electronics*, a collection of particles with a net electric charge occupying a volume, either in free space or in a device; freq. *attrib.* and in *Comb.*, as *space-charge-limited* adj.; **space club,** a group of nations that has launched or intends to launch spacecraft; *spec.* a consortium of European nations formed to co-operate in space research and development; **space colony,** a large group of people imagined as living and working in a space station or on another planet; **space curve** *Geom.*, a curve that is not confined to any one plane; **space density** *Astr.*, frequency of occurrence per specified volume of space; **space fiction,** science fiction set in space or on other worlds, or involving space travel; so **space-fictional** *a.*; **space-filler,** something that serves to occupy an otherwise vacant space; *spec.* a brief or insignificant item in a newspaper or magazine; **space fleet** *Science Fiction*, a fleet of spacecraft; **space flight,** a journey or travel through space; **space flyer,** (*a*) a spacecraft; (*b*) an astronaut; **space frame** *Engin.*, a three-dimensional structural framework which is designed to behave as an integral unit and to withstand loads applied at any point; **space gun,** (*a*) a large gun which projects a spacecraft into space; (*b*) a hand-held gun whose recoil is used by an astronaut or spaceman to propel himself; **space heater,** any self-contained appliance for heating an enclosed space within a building; also **space heating; space helmet,** a helmet worn in space to protect the head and provide air; also *transf.*; also **space-helmeted** *a.*; **space industry,** the sector of industry which manufactures goods and materials in connection with space flight; **Space Invaders,** the name of an animated computer game in which a player attempts to defend himself against a fleet of enemy spaceships; also, the attacking force itself; **space lab, spacelab** = next; *spec.* (with capital initial(s)) as a proper name (see quot. 1980); **space laboratory,** a laboratory in space, esp. a spacecraft equipped as a laboratory; **space lattice** *Cryst.*, substitute for def.: a regular, indefinitely repeated array of points in three dimensions in which the points lie at the intersections of three sets of parallel equidistant planes and every point is surrounded by the same pattern of points in the same orientation; a three-dimensional Bravais lattice; (examples); **space launcher,** a rocket used to lift spacecraft into space; **space lift, spacelift** [after *AIR-LIFT 2], an act of transporting goods or personnel in space; **space medicine,** the branch of science concerned with the medical effects of being in space; **space myopia** (see quot. 1973); **space needle,** a small rod or fibre of conducting material in orbit about a planet; **space observatory,** an astronomical observatory in space; **space-occupying lesion** *Path.*, a mass, freq. a tumour, which has displaced brain tissue; **space opera** chiefly *U.S.* [cf. **horse opera*, *SOAP OPERA], space fiction, esp. of a primitive and extravagant kind; an example of this genre; **space-order,** an ordering of points or events in space; **space physics,** the physics of extraterrestrial phenomena and bodies, esp. within the solar system; **space-plane,** (*a*) (see quot. 1961); (*b*) = *SHUTTLE *sb.*[1] 8 c; **space platform** = *space station* below; **space-port,** a base from which spacecraft are launched; (in fiction) a base at which spaceships take off and land; **space probe,** an unmanned spacecraft for research or reconnaissance; **space programme,** a programme of exploration of space and development of space technology; **space race,** the competition between nations to be first to achieve various objectives in the exploration of space; **space-reddening** *vbl. sb. Astr.*, the reddening of starlight as a result of wavelength-dependent absorption and scattering by interstellar dust; also **space-reddened** *ppl. a.*; **space rocket,** a rocket designed to travel beyond the earth's atmosphere; **space satellite** = *SATELLITE *sb.* 2 c; **space-saving** *a.*, that uses space economically or tends to the better use of available room; also as *sb.* and **space saver,** a device or appliance designed to this end; **space shot,** the launch of a spacecraft and its subsequent progress in space; **space shuttle** see *SHUTTLE *sb.*[1] 8 c; **space sick, space-sick** *a.*, sick from the effects of space flight; hence **space sickness; space simulator,** a device which simulates the conditions of space, or of the interior of a spacecraft; **space-speak** [*-SPEAK], the jargon of space technologists, considered as a corruption of standard English; **space stage** *Theatr.*, a modern stage on which the significant action alone is lighted, the rest remaining in darkness; hence **space staging; space station,** a large artificial satellite used as a base for operations in space; **space suit,** a garment designed to protect the wearer against the conditions of space; so **space-suited** *a.*, wearing such clothing; **space vehicle,** a spacecraft, esp. a large one; **space velocity** *Astr.*, the velocity in space of a star relative to the sun, equal to the vector sum of its proper motion and its radial velocity; **spacewalk, space walk,** an act or spell of physical activity undertaken in space outside a spacecraft; also as *v. intr.*; hence **spacewalking** *vbl. sb.* and *ppl. a.*; also **spacewalker; space warp,** an imaginary distortion of space-time that is conceived as enabling space travellers to make journeys that would otherwise be contrary to the known laws of nature; **space wave** *Radio* [tr. G. *raumwelle* (A. Sommerfeld 1911, in *Jahrb. der drahtl. Telegr.* IV. 166)], the radio wave that passes from a transmitter to a receiver either directly through space without reflection or with reflection from the ground; **spaceway** *Science Fiction*, an established route of space travellers; usu. *pl.*

1946 H. HARPER *Dawn of Space Age* I. i. 5 We have had an age of steam-power, an age of electricity and of the petrol engine, and an age of the air, and now with the coming of atomic power the world should, in due course, find itself in the space age. **1960** K. AMIS *New Maps of Hell* iii. 80 The outset of the space age and the immense technological effort involved in it are obviously the propelling force of much science fiction today. **1963** *New Yorker* 8 June 96 The space-age, space-tested material that makes possible this smart, new look in luggage. **1980** *Times Lit. Suppl.* 7 Nov. 1258/4 Our space-age Palace of History—the new computerized Public Record Office at Kew. **1959** *Times* 9 Mar. 13/5 One of the rockets, the space-ager firmly believes, will have him aboard. **1962** *Punch* 28 Nov. 781/1 A modern caravan..trying to look zippy and space-agey. **1946** *Nature* 26 Oct. 582/2 Such time- or space-averaged statistical structures are becoming increasingly familiar to X-ray crystallographers. **1962** CORSON & LORRAIN *Introd. Electromagn. Fields* iii. 91 (*caption*) To find the space-averaged field intensity produced by the dipoles, we calculate the field intensity at *O*..and then repeat this calculation for many other points *O′*. **1972** *Brit. Med. Jrnl.* 29 Jan. 293/2 The body temperature should be slowly raised to normal, using a 'space blanket' and heating pads if necessary, in a warm room. **1953** J. N. LEONARD *Flight into Space* 157 Undoubtedly one of the great preoccupations of the space-borne astronomers will be to study the moon and the planets. **1965** *New Scientist* 26 Aug. 485/1 One would have thought that the bugs could have been eliminated from the fuel cell system before it ever became space-borne. **1968** *Ibid.* 28 Mar. 680 In spite of considerable lobbying to make optical astronomy a space-borne science, many practising observers show little enthusiasm for the idea. **1975** *Nature* 22 May 287/1 With the shuttle taking up an ever-increasing share of the space budget, there is likely to be little money to spare for expanding space-borne astronomy. **1960** *Analog Science Fact & Fiction* Nov. 14/2 He banged it shut behind him and, feeling that he might as well continue with his spacebound existence, walked all the way to the elevator. **1958** D. G. SIMONS in M. Alperin et al. *Vistas in Astronautics* I. VI. 301 The systems and controls required to establish a space cabin capsule. **1961** *Guardian* 10 Mar. 1/5 As on previous occasions in this series of Russian experiments, the space cabin, as it is called, weighed 4·5 tons. **1974** *Sci. & Technical Aerospace Rep.* XII. 1013/1 (*heading*) Survival of infectious microorganisms in space cabin environments. **1952** *Newsweek* 13 Oct. 39/2 (*caption*) Test pilot A. M. 'Tex' Johnston..resembles a space cadet in the new high-altitude helmet and suit designed to protect pilots in the upper air. **1957** P. MOORE *Science & Fiction* i. 18 Lucian's seamen are the logical ancestors of the rocketeers and space-cadets of to-day. **1958** C. C. ADAMS *Space Flight* p. vii, There have been space books for children—our present space cadets and future rocket pilots. **1979** *Harvard Mag.* May–June 15 How can I be one of the first to see these new worlds in detail and not be crawling with gooseflesh? Me, an original space cadet? **1959** *Listener* 15 Jan. 118/1 An American firm is given a contract to build a space-capsule designed to put a man into orbit round the earth. **1963** *Ann. Reg. 1962* 398 The larger two-man Gemini space capsules, orbiting for a fortnight on end. **1977** G. SCOTT *Hot Pursuit* x. 88 It starts..with the space capsule... A Russian satellite, one of the Cosmos series. **1959** *Daily Tel.* 23 Feb. 11/7 Col. Steinkamp and his colleagues have been carrying out interesting tests, lasting from four hours to a week, in a sealed 'space chamber'. **1966** *Science World* 7 Jan. 10 The Air Force has been testing the ability of men to live for long periods in a new gas mixture that may be used in space ships... There have been two short tests in 'space chambers'. **1913** *Physical Rev.* II. 450 (*heading*) The effect of space charge and residual gases on thermionic currents in high vacuum. **1921** *Ibid.* XVIII. 56 The maximum space-charge limited current was the same for each [tube]. **1956** *Nature* 11 Feb. 285/2 The corresponding current..for maximum space-charged-limited pulsed emission from the surface of the oxide coat is 8 amp. per sq. cm. **1962** SIMPSON & RICHARDS *Physical Princ. Junction Transistors* iv. 54 For this reason the region AB is often referred to as the space-charge or depletion region. **1980** J. W. HILL *Intermediate Physics* xxii. 210 In the Maltese cross tube and the deflection tube, the space charge formed by the filament is attracted towards the positively-charged anode and accelerated. **1961** *Economist* 14 Jan. 116/2 West Germany agreed by the 1954 treaties not to manufacture long-range missiles. Participation in a space club with a military potential would take the erosion of the treaties a stage further. **1970** *Daily Tel.* 3 Sept. 5 Britain failed to join the 'space club' yesterday because of a fault in the second stage of the Black Arrow rocket fired from Woomera, Australia. **1974** *N.Y. Times* 19 May IV. 6 The space colonies..would provide an alternative to earth if the earth's resources ever reach the point of depletion. **1971** *Proc. Nat. Acad. Sci.* LXVIII. 815/1 Our interest here is in space curves that are the central curves of elastic rods. **1931** *Astrophysical Jrnl.* LXXIV. 268 (*heading*) A numerical method of determining the space density of stars. **1978** *Nature* 10 Aug. 569/1 *RS Canum venaticorum* systems are the most plentiful binary stars known, having a space density of at least 10^{-6} systems pc^{-3}. **1952** *Space Science Fiction* May 2/1 We like good space fiction, and we intend to bring you the best of it... The space-opera of flashing rayguns and invincible heroes has long since been overdone. **1960** *Guardian* 19 Aug. 5/4 A frantic urge for escape, but where to? Astrology, necromancy, space-fiction? **1979** *Daily Tel.* 14 Dec. 13/3 Star Trek is the latest in an increasing number of space fiction films which..tend to find individuality. **1963** V. GIELGUD *Goggle-Box Affair* xviii. 191 Space-fictional horrors. **1911** H. S. HARRISON *Queed* xviii. 232 There's a little squib about the college that may serve as a space-filler. **1956** *Nature* 17 Mar. 530/2 Into the large centre well 3–4 drops of anti-serum are deposited and a glass or aluminium plug... The latter serves merely as a space-filler to spare anti-serum. **1972** *Sci. Amer.* July 13/3, I have written some poetry, mostly nonserious, that has found its way into medical journals as space-filler. **1944** E. COLLINS *Mariners of Space* iii. 25 Space-Captain Jan Marthus of the Martian Space Fleet steered his friend into the restaurant. **1979** J. PATON *Sea of Rings* 23 William Robert Mahony, ex-Captain, Space Fleet, aged 46. **1931** *Wonder Stories* Jan. 900/1 We know now what conditions are necessary for a space flight... After all space flying is too great a matter to be limited by national pride and jealousy. **1949** A. C. CLARKE *Across Sea of Stars* (1959) 76 There is a timelessness about space-flight..unmatched by any other experience of man. **1978** J. UPDIKE *Coup* (1979) v. 183 The hollow head with which a mummified Pharaoh is helmeted for *his* space-flight. **1911** *Mod. Electrics* Nov. 516/1 He knew now that Fernand 60O 10 had carried off his sweetheart in a space-flyer and that the machine by this time was probably far out from the earth's boundary. **1931** *Wonder Stories* Feb. 958 To old and seasoned space-fliers like Professor Galloway and myself, there was something ludicrous in all this emotional bustle..over a little hop to the Moon. **1962** M. V. GLENNY tr. *Gartmann's Space Travel* 130/1 The space flyer will..encounter two opposed physical conditions: pressure and weightlessness. **1962** *Listener* 1 Mar. 368/2 All three American space-fliers had had to be landed in the sea. **1912** A. MORLEY *Theory of Structures* xiii. 380 (*heading*) Space frames. **1967** *Jane's Surface Skimmer Systems 1967–68* 48/1 The craft is of lightweight space-frame construction in marine aluminium. **1974** *Times Lit. Suppl.* 4 Jan. 14/4 The debased standards of theatre design today and..artists who think 'empty space, lighting, and maybe an aluminium space frame' are enough. **1935** H. G. WELLS *Things to Come* 12 The stormy victory of the new ideas as the Space Gun fires and the moon cylinder starts on its momentous journey. **1954** K. W. GATLAND *Devel. Guided Missile* (ed. 2) 197 All the propellant could be consumed in the first second of take-off—as Jules Verne proposed in his famous 'space-gun'. **1968** *Amer. Speech* XLIII. 166 *Space gun*, a handheld instrument used to propel an astronaut outside the capsule. **1970** N. ARMSTRONG et al. *First on Moon* viii. 180 This was where I had to use the little space gun. **1976** P. MOORE *Next Fifty Years in Space* i. 16 It is not impossible that the space-gun principle may have its uses in the future, but it will be confined to firing non-fragile payloads off airless worlds. **1925** *Sci. Amer.* Mar. 162/3 Space heaters. **1951** *Good Housek. Home Encycl.* 203/1 The stove..is primarily designed as a boiling ring but it will also serve as a space heater. **1980** *Amat. Gardening* 25 Oct. 9/1 Electrical space heaters are extremely expensive to run at high temperatures. **1934** *Jrnl. Inst. Heating & Ventilating Engineers* XIII. 234 The open fire is still..the most widely-used domestic space-heating appliance. **1973** *Guardian* 17 Mar. 12/5 What is especially intolerable..is that..electricity with a starting efficiency of only 20 per cent or so is allowed to be sold for space heating, a role particularly suitable for the 80 per cent of low grade heat that has been thrown away. **1954** *Newsweek* 6 Dec. 108/1 It is significant, too, that the American kid of 1954, dazzled by space helmets and death-ray guns, has time in his daily make-believe for the mustang and the six-shooter. **1973** *Times* 29 Aug. 3/2 Scientists are developing a 'space helmet' respirator to protect miners against dust. **1979** R. JAFFE *Class Reunion* (1980) II. ii. 191 Her blonde, teased, sprayed bubble hairdo..looked like a space helmet. **1957** *Time* 22 July 52/1 From a sealed chamber like the cabin of a rocket ship, and from space-helmeted human guinea pigs who live in it, medical researchers..hope to learn answers to some fundamental questions about the body's consumption of fuel and oxygen. **1982** D. MACKENZIE *Raven's Revenge* x. 94 A space-helmeted motorcyclist. **1962** M. V. GLENNY tr. *Gartmann's Space Travel* 9 The space industry ..has plans for huge multi-purpose earth satellites. **1972** *Guardian* 10 July 11/2 The unhappy fragmental European space industry. **1979** *Los Angeles Times* 23 Sept. VII. 17/1 Nobody likes to be a loser, but when playing Space Invaders, most gamesters don't seem to mind. **1980** *Guardian* 2 Feb. 8/3 Driven out of the BR station buffet by bleeping Space Invaders. **1980** *Washington Post* 2 Sept. B1 A world-class Space Invaders player can keep the machine going for an hour. **1982** *London Rev. Bks.* IV. XXIV. 7/1 The advent of the Space Invaders can't mean anything except that new inventions bring new possibilities. **1966** *Electronics* 31 Oct. 134 Although the Gemini computers are highly flexible.., they are not versatile enough for space labs. **1975** K. GATLAND *Missiles & Rockets* xv. 246 Hatches on top of the cargo compartment will open to permit Space Lab to be hinged out into space. **1979** *Fortune* 29 Jan. 77 In the microgravity of an orbiting spacelab, NASA will make crystals, alloys, and medicines never seen on earth. **1980** T. FURNISS *Space Satellites* 30/2 One of the payloads the Shuttle carries is the Spacelab research station. Spacelab is built in Europe by the member countries of the European Space Agency. **1960** Space-laboratory [see *meteor bumper* s.v. *METEOR]. **1973** *Guardian* 28 May 2/2 The battered American space laboratory, Skylab, cooling parasol now clutched tightly over her gold-foiled head. **1895** Space-lattice [see *LATTICE *sb.* 3* a]. **1923** GLAZEBROOK *Dict. Appl. Physics* IV. 18/2 In the crystals of very simple chemical compounds..the space-lattice is directly formed by the chemical atoms. In the more complicated crystalline substances..the space-lattice points are surrounded or replaced by groups of atoms. **1973** J. G. TWEEDDALE *Materials Technol.* I. iii. 59 Although there are countless varieties of crystals, there can be only 14 types of space lattice. **1961** *Daily Tel.* 1 Feb. 16/4 (*heading*) Joint effort for space 'launcher'. **1963** *Guardian* 9 Nov. 7/7 The Soviet Union has now apparently agreed that Governments should be allowed to license private space-launchers. **1954** 'J. CHRISTOPHER' *22nd Cent.* 65 As many as possible would be got away to those planets by a full space lift. **1964** *Yearbk. Astron. 1965* 142 What then might be realized is a joint use of the nationally developed space hardware in a space-lift of supplies to obtain the first firm footholds on the Moon in the shape of a scientific base. **1949** *Time* 12 Sept. 29/2 The U.S. Air Force's School of Aviation Medicine..has set up an interplanetary research section, [and] named it the Department of Space Medicine. **1962** F. I. ORDWAY et al. *Basic Astronautics* xiii. 539 This centrifuge is unique among those used in space medicine research. *Ibid.* xii. 474 Other visual phenomena associated with space flight include space myopia... Looking out into the darkness of space, the astronaut would not know whether his eyes were focused at infinity or only a few feet from his ship. **1973** *Gloss. Aeronaut. & Astronaut. Terms* (*B.S.I.*) XVII. 1 *Space myopia*, the tendency of the human eye to accommodate for a distance commonly of the order of six feet when in a featureless environment, resulting in potential failure to perceive objects at considerably greater distance. **1961** *Daily Tel.* 23 Oct. 1/3 (*heading*) Space needles begin to form radio band. **1964** Space needle [see *DIPOLE 2]. **1952** F. L. WHIPPLE in C. Ryan *Across Space Frontier* 136 Our space observatory can give us vital information as to how some stars die in a spectacular blaze of glory. **1972** *Guardian* 22 Aug. 2/4 A space observatory, Copernicus, was launched here today, the fourth to be put in orbit. **1961** *Lancet* 9 Sept. 570/1 The patients reported in this paper had small pretectal space-occupying lesions demonstrated both clinically and radiologically. **1978** *Jrnl. R. Soc. Med.* LXXI. 226 These cases illustrate some atypical presentations of tuberculosis—as epilepsy, cranial nerve palsy,..or space-occupying lesion. **1949** *Sat. Rev. Lit.* (U.S.) 24 Dec. 7/3 No less than eight of this year's crop of science-fiction novels are what is known in the trade as 'space operas'—books built round the theme of interplanetary travel. **1952** [see *space fiction* above]. **1960** K. AMIS *New Maps of Hell* ii. 44 In space-opera, Mars takes the place of Arizona with a few physical alterations, the hero totes a blaster instead of a six-gun. **1969** H. WARNER *All our Yesterdays* ii. 41 [Wilson] Tucker is responsible for the use of 'space opera', which he proposed in the January, 1941, *Le Zombie* as a name for the 'hacky, grinding, stinking, outworn space-ship yarn'. **1978** *Broadcast* 31 July 24/1 The Seven-Up [TV advertisement] series..is meant as a space opera send up. **1890** W. JAMES *Princ. Psychol.* II. xx. 276 The obvious objection is that mere serial order is a *genus*, and space-order a very peculiar species of that *genus*. **1927** B. RUSSELL *Outl. Philos.* iv. 50 A written word is a series of pieces of matter, having an essential space-order. **1961** *Adv. Astronaut. Sci.* VI. 779 Space physics. **1962** F. I. ORDWAY et al. *Basic Astronautics* iv. 117 An important characteristic of space physics is that it is closely related to two aspects of geophysics, namely atmospheric physics and ionospherics. **1980** *Jrnl. R. Soc. Arts* May 357/1 The College has now built more instruments..making thereby vast additions to space–physics knowledge. **1961** *Aeroplane* C. 597 A spaceplane is an aircraft capable of entry into orbit, using for propulsion purposes the atmosphere through which it has passed. **1978** *N.Y. Times Mag.* 29 Jan. 26 Designed to take off like a rocket, fly in orbit like a spacecraft, and return to a runway landing like a glider, these huge spaceplanes are expected to make the near reaches of space more accessible than ever before.

1958 F. A. Warren *Rocket Propellants* xi. 196 Thought of space platforms, space ships, satellite stations, and high-altitude exploratory rockets overshadows consideration of other rocket uses. **1980** M. Babson *Dangerous to Know* vii. 47 She'd crashed like a chunk of rubble from an abandoned space platform. **1935** *Amer. Speech* X. 54/1 Spaceport. **1943** *Astounding Science-Fiction* Feb. 9/1 Carew had landed him at one of the less expensive spaceports. **1962** *Daily Progress* (Charlottesville, Va.) 23 Feb. 11 After these few words, Glenn set out for the ride through brilliant sunshine to this space port—where it all began—and his meeting with President Kennedy. **1977** *Time* 30 May 45/2 For one scene, set in a brawling space-port bar, the casting director went to a London firm called Uglies, Ltd. **1977** *Daily Tel.* 28 July 1/6 The small spaceport at Kagoshima, at the southern tip of Japan, looked more like a station for amateur rocketry than a serious rival to Cape Canaveral. [**1955** E. Burgess *Frontier to Space* viii. 152 We would then have the deep-space probe.] **1958** *Listener* 20 Nov. 822/1 Direct contact between some form of space probe and the moon..must be close at hand. **1977** *Whitaker's Almanack 1978* 158/2 A Russian space probe has revealed that the lower layers [of Venus] are extremely dense. **1958** *New Statesman* 6 Sept. 263/2 It was Congress, rather than the President, that took the initiative in pushing a space programme. **1977** B. Langley *Death Stalk* ii. 23 A number of senators had a vested interest in seeing that the space programme continued. **1959** *Listener* 29 Jan. 226/2 The possible nature of Britain's contribution to the space-race. **1967** M. Kenyon *Whole Hog* iii. 31 If you've got something which could keep the same men..in the capsules..the space race would be won. **1978** *Nature* 9 Mar. 119/2 Czechoslovakia has won the 'little space race' for the third nation to put a citizen into orbit. **1959** *Listener* 24 Dec. 1111/2 The stars are said to be space-reddened. In the same way atmospheric dust causes the sun to appear red at sunset. **1931** *Astrophysical Jrnl.* LXXV. 392 The differential absorption or space reddening at 1000 parsecs in the galactic plane is unquestionably real. **1937** Space reddening [see *interstellar *a.*]. **1928** *Discovery* June 190/1 The arguments used in regard to objections so far raised meet the case in respect of space-rocket machines. **1936** 'J. Beynon' *Planet Plane* iv. 36 You can be sure that if they were building a space rocket anywhere we'd have heard of it. **1958** *Listener* 16 Oct. 606/1 A space-rocket, aimed towards the moon, is successfully launched from Cape Canaveral. **1977** 'J. Fraser' *Hearts Ease in Death* vii. 76 Mark Dunton's bed..looked like some sort of space rocket, with tubes connecting various parts of Mark's body to pieces of apparatus. **1954** *Jrnl. Brit. Interplanetary Soc.* XIII. 165 Since it is theoretically possible today to design and build instrumented rocket vehicles for both orbital and escape missions, one is often asked whether there is not justification for a space-satellite programme, such as the Americans suggested in 1948. **1962** E. Snow *Red China Today* (1963) lxxxvi. 723 The development of space satellite espionage and electronic detection devices had so far advanced that all essential information needed to guarantee against surprise attacks would soon be in possession of both sides. **1974** P. Cattermole *All about Space Exploration* vi. 74 Unmanned space satellites had been approved by the U.S. Government. **1970** *Toronto Daily Star* 24 Sept. 5/2 (Advt.), Just out on sale!.. New.. Space-saver Consolette [television]. **1921** *Sci. Amer.* 30 July 79/1 Home Building..Many unique space-saving devices are now being used. **1934** Webster, *Spacesaving*, n. **1936** *Punch* 11 Mar. 287/1 For space-saving reasons, [I] have exchanged the old edition of the D.N.B. for its India paper form. **1964** E. Bach *Introd. Transformational Gram.* ii. 17 The latter notation is useful as a space-saving device. **1978** M. & N. Ward *Home in Twenties & Thirties* 23 Cost saving was one necessity, space saving another. **1961** *Guardian* 29 Mar. 1/6 Russia did not give advance notice of space shots. **1969** *Times* 19 Feb. 13/4 Between now and April, Mars lies in a favourable position for space shots. **1977** D. Bagley *Enemy* xxxii. 259 Designing a trajectory for a space shot to Pluto. **1949** A. C. Clarke *Across Sea of Stars* (1959) 93, I was sure I'd never be space sick. **1971** *New Yorker* 27 Feb. 32 If an astronaut were made to move his hand repeatedly in the wrong direction in relation to the spin, he could easily get spacesick. **1951** A. C. Clarke *Sands of Mars* i. 3 Space-sickness was a thing of the past. **1969** *New Scientist* 2 Oct. 28/1 The Russian cosmonaut Titov was the first to complain of space sickness in 1961. **1959** *IRE Trans. Mil. Electronics* III. 96/1 For the first space simulator, it is proposed to use a combination of visual references and cabin motion to give a hint or illusion of 'g' forces. **1974** *Sci. & Technical Aerospace Rep.* XII. 37 (*heading*) Radiometer for measuring a wide range of irradiances in space simulators. **1966** *Science* 13 May 875/1 We read of 'space speak' on every hand. Newspapers and magazines discuss it in their science columns, and popular fancy seems to have been captured by it. The belief is that the space effort has given us, in addition to the possibility of going to the moon, a new linguistic phenomenon. **1982** M. Leapman *Yankee Doodles* iii. 175 Transiting is a typical piece of spacespeak in that it makes a verb out of a noun. **1928** J. Dolman *Art of Play Production* xviii. 397 Three types of modern stages have..been reasonably successful in accomplishing the true purpose of formalism. One is..the so-called 'space stage', the essential feature of which is light, so controlled as to reveal only the significant action and to suppress the background altogether in a void of darkness. The methods of the space stage are.. adaptable to the purposes of expressionism. **1961** *Twentieth Cent.* Feb. 121 A space stage..a broad platform with no barrier between audience and performer. **1959** *Listener* 9 July 73/1 A television equivalent to Brechtian 'space staging'. [**1929** *Science Wonder Stories* Sept. 365 (*heading*) The spatial station as a basis for spatial travel.] **1936** P. E. Cleator *Rockets through Space* vi. 141 So great are the possibilities of the space-station that von Pirquet is of the opinion that the achievement of interplanetary travel..must depend upon the construction of such a station. **1956** J. G. Porter in A. Pryce-Jones *New Outl. Mod. Knowl.* 135 We are to visualize a space station, a sort of artificial satellite of the earth which is to act as a landing stage for all space ships. **1969** *Sci. Jrnl.* Feb. 66/1 Although any manned satellite might literally be called a manned space station, the term is usually restricted to spacecraft which remain in orbit for long periods and which carry relatively large crews. **1929** *Science Wonder Stories* July 175/1 Normal communication by speech would be impossible. Of course, this is not true of enclosed, air-filled rooms... But it is true when one is out 'in the open' (in the space suit). **1962** J. Glenn et al. in *Into Orbit* 244 G-suits are not to be confused with pressure suits (or, now, spacesuits) which the Astronaut wears during space flight to maintain atmospheric pressure at high altitudes. **1979** D. Adams *Hitch-Hiker's Guide to Galaxy* iii. 25 He will automatically assume he is also in possession of a toothbrush,..space suit etc., etc. **1951** Coggins & Pratt *Rockets, Jets, Guided Missiles & Spaceships* v. (*caption*) Switching off the electromagnets in his boots, the space-suited chief engineer kicks off for a look at his project. **1977** *Daily Mirror* 10 May 19/2 A Staffordshire housewife..saw two Space-suited people with long blonde hair looking down at her from a craft above her house. **1946** *N.Y. Times* 29 July 1/2 They are to serve as pioneers for the long-range guided missiles and 'space' vehicles. **1959** *Daily Tel.* 23 Feb. 11/7 Protective clothing..will be needed to help guard a man against the heavy G forces imposed on him because of the great thrust upwards that a space vehicle will develop. **1959** *Times* 15 Sept. 11/3 In putting a space vehicle on to the moon the Russians have provided the most complete.. proof of the length of the lead that they now hold. **1977** 'M. Underwood' *Fatal Trip* xx. 117 We can often track a load of porn..as successfully as the Americans track a space vehicle..to Mars. **1921** *Bull. Nat. Res. Council Nat. Acad. Sci.* II. 196 Average space velocities vary from 10 to 30km/sec., there being a well-marked increase in average space velocity as one proceeds from the blue to the redder stars. **1927** H. N. Russell et al. *Astronomy* II. xix. 652 The space velocity, being found from the proper motion, parallax, and radial velocity, demands for its determination the combination of observations made in very different ways. **1978** Pasachoff & Kutner *University Astron.* iii. 62 We can combine the values of velocity in the plane of the sky and in the radial direction to find the actual velocity of the star in space, the space velocity. **1965** *Newsweek* 14 June 30/3 Thirteen new layers had been added [to his spacesuit]..to protect his torso and legs against micro-meteorites and the extreme temperatures on his spacewalk. **1969** *Daily Tel.* 17 Jan. 1/2 The link-up was controlled manually by the cosmonauts. The two who made the space 'walk' reported 'feeling fine' after their feat. **1970** *Guardian* 8 July 20/7 Astronaut figures, 12 ft high, will 'space walk' over a quarter-mile section of Blackpool promenade in this autumn's illuminations. **1978** *Nature* 19 Jan. 201/3 The work aboard Salyut-6 is more interesting than his previous mission on Salyut-4, since the cosmonauts can now go for spacewalks. **1979** M. Collins *Flying to Moon* vi. 44 We would fly alongside the second Agena, and I would space walk over to it. **1965** *Newsweek* 14 June 30/1 Spacewalker White had trouble sleeping, due to the excitement. **1965** *Ibid.* 21 June 24/1 He was firmly convinced that spacewalking is an easily mastered art. **1970** *Daily Tel.* (Colour Suppl.) 10 Apr. 9/4 Theoretically we could now send a space-walking astronaut as an electric repair man to one of these satellites if anything went wrong. **1947** *Jrnl. Brit. Interplanetary Soc.* VI. 138 The next step is to explain that matter and energy are mutually convertible..and from this it is an easy process to pass to the 'invention' of a plausible device which produces a 'space-warp' in the opposite sense to the normal one, by means of the expenditure of energy in some form. Bodies in the region of this artificial 'space-warp' therefore acquire a negative weight—what could be simpler? **1953** *Galaxy Sci. Fiction* Nov. 53/2 He read the next one ..about a star-ship that hit a space warp and got hurled into another universe. **1974** G. Butler *Coffin for Canary* ix. 108 Don't unnerve me, boss. *You* don't believe in space-warps and voyagers back from another age. **1913** *Rep. Brit. Assoc. Adv. Sci. 1912* 403 His theory leads to the conclusion that there are not only space-waves (*Raumwellen*) in these media, but also surface-waves (*Oberflächenwallen*) at the boundary surface. **1943** F. E. Terman *Radio Engineers' Handbk.* x. 674 The ground wave can conveniently be divided into two components, a surface wave and a space wave. **1974** Harvey & Bohlman *Stereo F.M. Radio Handbk.* vii. 145 The range of the space-wave is chiefly determined by the height of the transmitting and receiving aerials. **1947** *Astounding Sci. Fiction* Sept. 171 You can't believe..your eyes... It was a platitude of the spaceways. **1979** *Daily Tel.* 1 Feb. 15/2 Everyone loves Harry Harrison; the genre would be poorer without this Monty Python of the spaceways.

space, *v.* Add: **4. d.** *intr.* With *out.* To experience a drug-induced state of euphoria; to become disoriented by the use of narcotic stimulus. Cf. *spaced *ppl. a.* 4. *U.S. slang.*

1968–70 *Current Slang* (Univ. S. Dakota) III–IV. 116 *Space out, v.* To achieve an euphoric state because of drug use... To lose one's train of thought while under the influence of a drug. **1970** *New York* 16 Nov. 48/3 Karenga ..looks like he's going crazy or spacing out on dope.

spacearium (spē^{i}sē^{ə}·riɒm). [f. Space *sb.*^{1} + Planet)arium.] A large room arranged so that scenes representing space may be projected on to its interior; a planetarium.

1962 *Times* 18 Apr. 11/7 Five separate exhibits..will include such things as the 'Spacearium'. **1976** *Nature* 16 Sept. 180/1 At his disposal is a team of 250, a vast archive, a huge 'spacearium', an enormous theatre with a 55-foot high screen, scores of audio-visual aids and, of course, hundreds of artefacts—which means aircraft and spacecraft.

spacecraft (spē^{i}·skraft). Also **space-craft, space craft.** Pl. spacecraft. [Space *sb.*^{1}] Any vehicle designed to travel in space.

1930 *Sci. Amer.* Aug. 142/1 Valier was the principal proponent of working toward the space craft from the known forms of surface or air craft. **1932** D. Lasser *Conquest of Space* xvii. 279 Our experience with cosmic speeds and distances is not equal to the task of guiding a space-craft on its perilous journey. **1946** [see *artificial *a.* 1 c]. **1959** *Observer* 2 Aug. 11/5 In the next few days, 40,000 ft. above the Californian desert, the world's first manned spacecraft will switch on its rocket engines for the first time. **1960** *New Statesman* 13 Feb. 214/2 One.. complains bitterly of the 'world-wide conspiracy in operation throughout this planet which has succeeded in suppressing *almost all* knowledge of, and discussion of the space-craft known to terrestrials as "Flying Saucers"'. **1960** *Guardian* 15 Dec. 9/5 An American attempt to put a 388 lb spacecraft into orbit around the moon. **1968** *Times* 12 Oct. 18/6 They suggest that the altitude measurement made by the Russian space craft as it approached the surface of Venus was almost exactly half what it should have been. **1976** A. Davis *Television: First Forty Years* 47 There are graphics departments..and props departments that can build models of, say, spacecraft.

spaced, *ppl. a.* Add: **2. a.** (Examples in *techn.* contexts.)

1920 *Wireless World* 12 June 200 (*heading*) Spaced loop aerial. **1949** G. A. Briggs *Sound Reproduction* iii. 35 Sound is picked up by 3 spaced microphones, recorded on separate channels, and played back through 3 spaced speakers. **1959** K. Henney *Radio Engin. Handbk.* (ed. 5) xxvi. 27 Analysis..indicates that, regardless of the value of the incident and polarization angles, the spaced-loop output voltage goes through a null when the directions of propagation are contained in the planes of the loop antennas. **1968** *Times* 29 Nov. (Sound of Leisure Suppl.) p. vi/5 The spaced microphone technique (using microphones a few inches or several feet apart, according to taste) relies both on volume and time of arrival differences. **1978** *Geophysical Research Lett.* V. 917/1 Observations of the troposphere with a VHF radar using a large antenna for transmission and small spaced antennas for reception.

b. With *out.*

1937 'M. Innes' *Hamlet, Revenge* iii. v. 295 The number of spaced-out acts committed by the criminal. **1952** C. Day Lewis tr. *Virgil's Aeneid* ix. 200 Where the ring of defenders was thinnest and daylight showed Between their spaced-out bodies. **1976** 'J. Ross' *I know what it's like to Die* xxxi. 203 The spaced-out drops of water from the tap.

c. Of children: born or conceived at intervals (of a kind denoted by qualifying advb.).

1939 [see *expect *v.* 4 e (b)]. **1965** M. Stewart *Airs above Ground* i. 10 She acquired a wealthy London banker..the kind of man..safely ensconced in the Jaguar belt with three carefully spaced children away at carefully chosen schools. **1976** *Times* 25 Feb. 16/5 The advantages of a smaller or adequately spaced family.

4. In a state of drug-induced euphoria, 'high'; removed from actuality or disoriented, by narcotic stimulus. Also *transf.* Freq. with *out. slang* (orig. *U.S.*).

1968–70 *Current Slang* (Univ. S. Dakota) III–IV. 116 *Spaced out*, adj., mentally deficient; strange; absent-minded. **1969** *Negro Digest* Sept. 10 Spaced poems say that our ancestors are in the air and will communicate with us. **1969** *Time* 26 Sept. 41 The culture has its own in-group argot:..'straights' (everyone else), 'heat' (the police)..and being 'spaced out' (in a drug daze). **1971** J. Mandelkau *Buttons* v. 68, I remember being really spaced out and someone handing me a ladybird—telling me how nice they tasted. **1974** A. Lurie *War between Tates* vi. 131 'You look exhausted.' 'I am sorta spaced out.' **1975** *New Yorker* 5 May 6/1 Vibraharpist Mike Mainieri and pianist Warren Bernhardt play some heavily lyrical and spaced-out duets. **1977** C. McFadden *Serial* (1978) xx. 47/1 She just sort of stood there, feeling totally spaced, because the whole number was nothing short of *unreal*.

spacefaring (spē^{i}·sfē^{ə}riŋ), *vbl. sb.* and *ppl. a.* [f. Space *sb.*^{1}, after *seafaring*.] **A.** *vbl. sb.* Space travel. **B.** *ppl. a.* That engages in space travel.

1959 P. Anderson *Virgin Planet* (1969) iii. 20 Who had ever begun the idea that spacefaring was one long wild adventure? **1962** *New Scientist* 1 Mar. 489 The leaders of the two spacefaring countries. **1973** *Sci. News* 3 Nov. 283 My own view..was that they [*sc.* pulsars] were perfect interstellar navigation beacons, the sort of markers that an interstellar spacefaring society would want to place throughout the galaxy. **1978** D. R. Mason *Mission to Pactolus R* i. 11 A long session in a Fingalnan brothel would set them up for another stint of spacefaring.

Also **spa·cefarer,** one who travels in space.

1974 *New Scientist* 27 June 772 Such an asteroid-ark might one day encounter spacefarers of another civilisation, members of an intellectual brotherhood of the stars.

space group. *Cryst.* [f. Space *sb.*^{1} + Group *sb.*, tr. G. *raumgruppe* (A. Schoenflies 1891, in *Krystallsyst. und Krystallstruct.* II. iv. 359).] Any of the 230 sets of symmetry operations, derived from the point groups by the inclusion of translations, glide planes, and screw axes, which are used to classify crystal structures.

1901 *Rep. Brit. Assoc. Adv. Sci. 1901* 322 [Schoenflies] calls the groups of operations, whether those of Jordan or those added by himself, 'space-groups' (*Raumgruppen*). **1903** H. Hilton *Math. Crystallogr.* xvii. 159 Every space-group is isomorphous with one of the thirty-two point-groups consistent with the law of rational indices. **1934** W. P. Davey *Study of Crystal Struct.* viii. 240 The 230 space-groups are listed..giving..the Schoenflies code for the derivation of the space-group. **1974** *Nature* 11 Jan. 85/2 Dark-field observation could establish the presence of centres of symmetry, glide planes and screw axes, which could lead to the establishment of the space group.

spaceless, *a.* Add: Hence **spa·celessly** *adv.*; **spa·celessness,** the quality or condition of being unbounded by space, or of lacking space.

1895 G. MacDonald *Lilith* xxxix. 286 We were not in the outer darkness; had we been, we could not have been *with* her; we should have been timelessly, spacelessly, absolutely apart. **1920** S. Alexander *Space, Time, & Deity* I. 342 To possess spacelessness or timelessness (eternity). **1981** M. Spark *Listening with Intent* v. 91 The spacelessness of this room where I lived..with..a bed for sitting and sleeping on.

spa·ce-like, *a. Physics.* [f. Space *sb.*[1] + -like.] Resembling or having the properties of space; *spec.* being or related to an interval between two points in space-time that lie outside one another's light cones (so that no signal or observer can pass from one to the other).

1914 [see *four-vector* s.v. *four C. 2]. **1920** A. S. Eddington *Space, Time & Gravit.* iii. 60 Even if the discovery of a new ray led us to modify the reckoning of time and space, it would still be necessary in the study of material systems to preserve the *present* absolute distinction of time-like and space-like intervals. **1934** A. Huxley *Beyond Mexique Bay* 215 It may be possible to think of vast durations as composed of space-like fragments. **1955** L. Rosenfeld in W. Pauli *Niels Bohr* 87 An arbitrary family of space-like surfaces. **1964** *Cambr. Rev.* 24 Oct. 51/2 The commutativity..of the field operators at spacelike distances. **1978** Pasachoff & Kutner *University Astron.* xxvii. 694 The distance between the events is greater than the distance that light can travel in the time between the events. Such an interval is called spacelike.

spaceman (spēi·smæn). Also **space-man.** [Space *sb.*[1]] **1.** (In Dict. s.v. Space *sb.*[1] 17 d.) (Later example.)

1935 G. Greene *England made Me* ii. 80 He's News... I'm a space man... I can't afford to miss a thing.

2. One who travels in space or comes from another planet.

1942 *Thrilling Wonder Stories* Apr. 110/1 Maybe Lambert was a spaceman. Maybe he wasn't, but if he knew anything at all about spaceman's lingo he'd have to give now. **1944** F. Brown in B. Aldiss *Introducing SF* (1964) 69 Earth's armada, all ten thousand ships and half-million fighting spacemen. **1956** 'J. Wyndham' *Seeds of Time* 81 Whither thou goest, I will go... It was all right for a tribe of nomads, but nowadays the wives of soldiers, sailors, pilots, spacemen—. **1962** A. Lurie *Love & Friendship* xiii. 250 Amateur experts..Visitors from another world... They think they're space men. **1977** P. Carter *Under Goliath* iv. 21, I was reading a good book all about spacemen.

Hence **spa·cemanship.**

1957 *Economist* 2 Mar. 400/1 Dr von Braun has always entertained, and shared with the public, the most ambitious ideals of spacemanship. **1966** *Life* 7 Jan. 32 (*caption*) Down from adventure and spacemanship, Stafford and Schirra pop out for an eye-level look at the sea.

spacer[1]. Add: **1. a.** (Later examples.)

1916 *Chambers's Jrnl.* July 480/1 A new unit in roofing called a spacer allows of ordinary plain tiles or slates being laid wider apart than usual. **1943** *Sun* (Baltimore) 15 Apr. 26/3 She figured out a way to save countless man-hours in the manufacture of spacers—small rubber rings used in Rolls Royce airplane engines. **1954** *Automobile Engineer* XLIV. 508/3 A tubular spacer and two thrust washers round the shaft separate the roller bearings. **1962** *Which?* July 197/2 The second type [of life-jacket]..used *sealed-in air* between inner and outer coverings..which are held apart by 'spacers' of absorbent foam plastic. **1976** *Shooting Mag.* Dec. 12 (Advt.), It's a quality production gun, with one major difference. You can adjust the stock and insert various 'spacers' to achieve the perfect cast and drop.

b. *Archæol.* In full, *spacer plate.* A flat bead perforated with several holes in the same plane, by which the threads of a primitive multi-strand necklace are held apart.

1924 D. Randall-MacIver *Villanovans & Early Etruscans* vi. 173 Fusiform and spherical gold beads, white and blue glass cylinders and small perforated spacers of amber formed the other elements of the necklace. **1940** V. G. Childe *Prehist. Communities of British Isles* vii. 124 In Ireland..the crescentic necklace was translated into a crescentic collar, cut out of a sheet of native gold and relieved with designs in panels, imitating the spacer-plates of the necklaces. **1958** *Antiquity* XXXII. 209 The complex-bored amber spacers from Hagenau. **1980** J. J. Taylor *Bronze Age Gold Work* iii. 41 The spacer-plate motif can be found in the Beaker repertoire pre-dating Wessex, to which the earliest dated spacer-plate is likely to belong.

3. *Biol.* A section of DNA which is not represented in the final RNA transcript, separating two sections which are.

1970 O. L. Miller et al. in *Cold Spring Harbor Symp. Quantitative Biol.* XXXV. 505/2 Non-matrix segments of varying lengths (spacers) are intercalated between matrix units. **1974** *New Scientist* 9 May 329 Chemists..have succeeded in synthesising a nucleotide complementary to a definite part of a small bacteriophage.., a part regarded as a spacer. **1982** W. I. P. Mainwaring et al. *Nucleic Acid Biochem. & Molecular Biol.* vii. 258 There are spacer regions between genes which *may or may not* be transcribed. If transcribed, their contribution to the RNA transcript is removed by an excision process during the maturation of the RNA.

4. Special Comb.: **spacer gel,** a part of the gel used in electrophoresis (see quot. 1975).

1968 J. R. Sargent *Methods in Zone Electrophoresis* vii. 90 It is possible to eliminate the sample gel and the spacer gels..and to apply the sample directly on top of the main gel. **1975** Davis & Simpkins in Williams & Wilson *Biologist's Guide to Princ. & Techniques Pract. Biochem.* iv. 115 The upper third of the gel consists of a large pore 'stacking' or 'spacer' gel, and the lower portion of smaller pore 'running' or 'separating' gel. The function of the stacking gel is to concentrate the sample as it moves through the gel, so that on entering the running gel it is an extremely narrow band.

spacer[2] (spēi·səɹ). *Science Fiction.* [f. Space *sb.*[1] + -er[1].] **1.** = *spaceman 2.

1955 C. M. Kornbluth *Mindworm* 59 'I'm a spacer,' he said... 'Venus.' **1958** I. Asimov *Naked Sun* i. 11 The Galaxy was closed to Earthmen. It was pre-empted by the Spacers, whose ancestors had been Earthmen centuries before.

2. A spaceship, spacecraft.

1962 *New Worlds Sci. Fiction* Sept. 50 The spacer broke through the low hanging layer of clouds above. **1978** D. R. Mason *Mission to Pactolus R* i. 5 A Fingalnan voice spoke into the quiet command cabin of the hurrying spacer.

spaceship (spēi·sʃip). Also **space ship, space-ship.** [Space *sb.*[1]] **1.** A spacecraft; esp. a manned one under the control of its crew.

1894 J. J. Astor *Journey in Other Worlds* I. vi. 93 'What sort of space-ship do you propose to have?' asked the vice-president.

1929 *Sci. Wonder Q.* I. 65/2 Since the space ship.. was circling freely in space..the proximity of the moon was no hindrance to leaving the ship. **1936** *Jrnl. Brit. Interplanetary Soc.* III. 26 It is essential that the spaceship should be in constant communication with its base station. **1938** C. S. Lewis *Out of Silent Planet* iv. 38 All he ever remembered of his first meal in the space-ship was the tyranny of heat and light. **1948** 'N. Shute' *No Highway* ix. 226 Designs for a rocket-propelled Space Ship, I think he called it, for a projected journey to the moon. **1951** A. C. Clarke *Sands of Mars* i. 9 Sleek, streamlined spaceships..had been the dream of the early twentieth century. **1962** F. I. Ordway et al. *Basic Astronautics* i. 2 The spaceship is stimulating the study of space navigation. **1970** N. Armstrong et al. *First on Moon* xiv. 338 If you're going to run a spaceship you've got to be pretty cautious about how you use your resources. **1977** P. Carter *Under Goliath* vi. 29 It's from Mars... It's a spaceship from Mars.

2. *spaceship earth* (also with capital initials), a phr. used to draw attention to the finite nature of the earth's resources.

1966 B. Ward (*title*) Space ship earth. **1969** R. B. Fuller *Operating Man. Spaceship Earth* iv. 52 We have not been seeing our Spaceship Earth as an integrally-designed machine which to be persistently successful must be comprehended and serviced in total. **1976** *Conservation News* Sept./Oct. 12/1 There is a growing awareness of the need to conserve the life-support systems of spaceship earth. **1981** *Nature* 5 Nov. 41/3 All species on 'Spaceship Earth' have an equal right to exist.

space-time (spēi·s,tai·m), *adj. phr.* and *sb.* Also **spacetime, space time.** [Space *sb.*[1]] **A.** *adj. phr.* Pertaining to or situated in both space and time.

1905 R. B. Perry *Approach to Philos.* 131 An experimentally verifiable system must contain space–time variables. **1938** *Harper's Mag.* Jan. 151/2 If you denounce him as a 'Jew', apart from his space-time characteristics, you perform a monstrous act. **1965** *Math. in Biol. & Med.* (Med. Res. Council) v. 227 For many years leukaemia has been alleged to occur in clusters, though the evidence has been largely anecdotal and its interpretation intuitive because of the difficulties..of formulating the hypothesis of space-time clustering in precise and testable terms. **1973** *Nature* 27 July 214/2 The projection of the most recent seismic migration wave to the latitude of maximum recurrence of earthquakes provides the basis for setting the space–time bounds on the next earthquake greater than magnitude 5.

B. *sb. Physics.* [tr. G. *raumzeit.*] Time and three-dimensional space regarded as fused in a four-dimensional continuum containing all events. Also *attrib.*

1915 E. Cunningham *Relativity* 9 (*heading*) The space-time transformations. *Ibid.* 10 Newtonian Relativity consists in the fact that either (x, y, z, t) or (x', y', z', t') are equally valid as space-time coordinates. **1927** S. Ertz *Now East, now West* viii. 117 I've got quite drunk on theories about the space-time continuum. **1930** *Morning Post* 17 June 13/1 The 'metrical structure' of space-time now adopted by Einstein is based on the assumption that there is a meaning in saying that two short lines are equal in length, that they are parallel, and that the angle between them is not altered when they are moved so as to remain parallel to themselves. **1934** E. Muir *Coll. Poems* (1960) 44 Lengthening league by league The ghastly thin anatomy of Space Time Stripped to the nerve. **1940** W. Empson *Gathering Storm* 18 But if it parts Into uncommunicable spacetimes. **1956** *Nature* 10 Mar. 458/1 He [*sc.* H. Weyl] discovered the first 'unified field theory' in which the Maxwell field appears along with the gravitational field as a geometrical property of space-time. **1967** G. Steiner *Lang. Silence* 283 We are imprisoned in the unexamined assumption or unconscious illusion of a homogeneous, forward-flowing space-time continuum. **1978** Pasachoff & Kutner *University Astron.* xxvii. 695 The basic conclusion of the general theory [of relativity] is that gravitational fields change the geometry of spacetime. We say that in the presence of gravitational fields, spacetime becomes curved.

spacewoman (spēi·swumăn). [f. Space *sb.*[1], after *spaceman.] A female traveller in space; a woman who comes from another planet.

1962 N. Mitchison (*title*) Memoirs of a spacewoman. **1963** *Daily Tel.* 18 Oct. 23/3 (*caption*) Russia's first space woman, Valentina Tereshkova, 26, waving at Prestwick yesterday when her plane made a two-hour refuelling stop. **1978** G. Household *Last Two Weeks of Georges Rivac* i. 14 It doesn't matter which way up I'm put. I ought to be a spacewoman.

spaceworthy (spēi·swɒ̄ɹði), *a.* [f. Space *sb.*[1] + Worthy *a.*] In a fit condition for space travel. Also **spa·ceworthiness.**

1959 'Wyndham' & Parkes *Outward Urge* iv. 156 She reclaimed the damaged Satellites, and made three of them spaceworthy again. **1959** J. Blish *Clash of Cymbals* ii. 39 The unending demands of the city's spaceworthiness. **1960** *New Statesman* 30 Jan. 146/2 Apparently no other proofs were needed to demonstrate the efficacy of their measures to ensure the space-worthiness of the cosmic vehicle. **1968** *Daily Tel.* 16 Dec. 1/8 Russia's unmanned Zond 5 and 6 made successful 'boomerang' flights round the moon, and Soyuz 3 has been proved space-worthy for four days.

spacey, var. Spacy *a.* in Dict. and Suppl.

spacing, *vbl. sb.* Add: **1. b.** *attrib.* Also, *spacing collar, washer.*

1916 *Automobile Engineer* VI. 92/2 (*caption*) Adjustable spacing collar for milling cutters. **1923** *Popular Wireless* 27 Oct. 294/1 (Advt.), Spacing washers, large ... per doz. 2½d. **1971** *Buck & Hickman Tool Buyer's Guide* 96 Spacing Washers also supplied 1½ in. bore × 2¼ in. dia. *Ibid.*, Spacing collars and washers for milling machine arbors.

spacistor (spēi·si·stəɹ). *Electronics.* [f. Space *sb.*[1] + *trans)istor.] A kind of semiconductor device (see quot. 1957).

1957 Statz & Pucel in *Proc. IRE* XLV. 317/1 New devices are considered in which electrons or holes are injected directly into space-charge regions of reverse-biased junctions avoiding the diffusion of carriers through field-free regions. The case considered is one in which the junction is biased at a voltage such that the injected carriers are multiplied by the avalanche process. A device of this type shall be called a spacistor. **1962** Simpson & Richards *Physical Princ. Junction Transistors* viii. 175 The spacistor can have input and output impedances of the order of tens of megohms and the coupling between input and output terminals is almost purely capacitative. **1969** A. Marcus *Electronics for Technicians* viii. 160 There is not, as yet, general agreement upon a symbol for the spacistor transistor.

Spackle (spæk'l). *N. Amer.* Also **spackle.** [Cf. Sparkle *v.*[2] 4 b and G. *spachtel* putty knife, mastic, filler.] A proprietary name for a compound used to fill cracks in plaster and produce a smooth surface before decoration.

1928 *Official Gaz.* (U.S. Patent Office) 7 Feb. 17/1 *Spackle*... A surfacing compound for filling imperfection so as to bring up to a smooth and level surface areas that are to be painted or decorated. Claims use since Aug. 1, 1927. **1951** *Home Painting, Wallpapering & Decorating* ii. 34 You must be sure there is paint on the surface upon which you are going to put the spackle. **1971** *Black World* Mar. 65/2 After he did that he mixed the spackle with water and spread it as evenly as he could over the crack. **1975** *Amer. Speech* 1969 XLIV. 26 *Spackle, n.*, a prepared paste that, when mixed with water, is used to repair cracks and holes in plaster or gypsum wallboard.

Hence as *v. trans.*, to repair or fill with Spackle (see also quot. 1940); **spa·ckling** *vbl. sb.*

1940 R. Mayer *Artist's Hand-bk. Materials & Techniques* xii. 506 *Spackling* or *Sparkling* (probably from the German *spachteln*, to putty up). The rectifying of a defect in plaster or a mural painting by digging out the defective spot and filling it in with a plastic gesso, plaster of Paris, Keene's cement, or other similar material. **1941** *Pop. Science* July 149 In addition to patching plaster, other prepared powders or so-called 'spachtling [*sic*] compounds' are sold for patching, filling, and smoothing purposes. **1971** H. Smith *View from Chivo* vii. 69 Then he coated each wire with a spackling compound. **1971** *Black World* Mar. 67/1 People who could watch for him if Death came suddenly sweeping through the crack in the kitchen wall that he hadn't spackled properly. **1980** *Redbook* Oct. 58/3 She cooked better than I and it was a fact that I Spackled the walls better than she.

spacy, *a.* Add: Also **spacey. 2.** In a heightened state of consciousness; disoriented from reality, = *spaced *ppl. a.* 4. *slang* (chiefly *U.S.*).

1968–70 *Current Slang* (Univ. S. Dakota) III–IV. 117 *Spacey*, adj, appearing to be functioning on a level higher than normal. **1972** *Last Whole Earth Catalog* (Portola Inst.) 67/3 Her expression was very spacy... Her eyes were so weird it was hard to read anything very definite in her face... She..sat on the curb in the lotus posture and stared off into the east. **1975** *Globe & Mail* (Toronto) 12 July 32/6 'You get pretty spacey after doing a lot of interviews,' she said. 'One time someone asked me if Dylan had changed a lot and I was so spacey I said, "Well, he doesn't bum drinks any more."' **1977** C. McFadden *Serial* (1978) ii. 10/2 She spotted Martha's ex-husband-once-removed with his spacy new old lady. **1980** J. A. Carver *Panglor* (1981) viii. 138 His head felt large, and a little spacey, and he felt a heightened sense of geometry, of perspective.

3. Of, pertaining to, or purportedly characteristic of (conditions in) outer space; esp. used in connection with electronic music.

1971 *It* 2–16 June 19/2 A good studio-produced album sounding very live and certainly spacey. **1977** *Rolling Stone* 13 Jan. 62/5 Terje Rypdal,..spun spacey riffs clothed in lots of distortion. **1980** *Radio Times* 27 Sept.–3 Oct. 89/3 For 18 years Ron Grainger's tune gave the programme [*sc.* 'Dr. Who'] an eerie, spacey feel.

spad[1] (spæd). orig. *U.S.* [Var. of SPUD *sb.*] A spike with a flattened end containing a hole to support a plumb-line, so that it can be driven into a tunnel roof to provide a marker.

1908 L. W. TRUMBULL *Man. Underground Surveying* iii. 93 A majority of the mines of the United States are using punched horseshoe nails known as 'spads'. The head of the horseshoe nail..is hammered flat and a hole punched through it. **1957** R. C. A. HOOPER *Winiberg's Metalliferous Mine Surveying* (ed. 4) ix. 186 Some surveyors prefer to have the width of the spad along the longitudinal axis of a drive rather than at right angles. **1973** B. A. BARRY *Construction Measurements* xvi. 220 Line is carried forward in tunneling by tape and theodolite to marks placed either on the floor or side or roof of the tunnel. Driving plugs and spads into the roof to serve as horizontal control (traverse) points keeps them free from traffic damage or disturbance.

Spad[2] (spæd). [f. the initials of *Société pour Aviation et ses Dérivés*, the designers.] Any of several types of French aircraft, esp. a biplane fighter much used in the war of 1914–18. Also *attrib.*

1917 *Sci. Amer.* 6 Oct. 249/1 Still faster is the 'Spad', a tiny biplane. **1918** J. M. GRIDER *War Birds* (1927) 60 They have Pups and Spads and Avros. *Ibid.* 88 There were three Spads so Capt. Foggin asked for Spad pilots. **1920** A. J. L. SCOTT *Hist. Sixty Squadron, R.A.F.* ii. 15 Foot..was given a 'Spad', on which he did great execution during the autumn. **1926** J. L. PRITCHARD *Bk. Aeroplane* xii. 230 Spad machines were recognised as among the fastest..used by the Allies during the war. **1929** HALL & NILES *One Man's War* 170 In very high, thin air the Nieuports manœuvred very well, better perhaps than the Spads did, because the Spad was a heavier machine. **1970** *Word Watching* Apr. 7/1 *Spad*, A-1 fighter-bomber escort for rescue helicopters. **1973** D. LEES *Rape of Quiet Town* vi. 101 Vague memories of anti-aircraft drill from the days of Spads and Fokkers.

spadaite (spā·dă,ɔit). *Min.* [ad. G. *spadait* (F. von Kobell 1843, in *Jrnl. für prakt. Chem.* XXX. 467), f. the name of Lavinio *Spada* de Medici (1801–63), Italian writer, politician, and mineralogist: see -ITE[1].] A hydrated magnesium silicate, $MgSiO_3.2H_2O$, found as an alteration product in lavas, and occurring as amorphous masses coloured red by impurities.

1848 J. D. DANA *Man. Mineral.* 149 Spadaite. A flesh-red mineral, near Schiller spar. **1931** *Amer. Mineralogist* XVI. 232 Spadaite occurs only in the ore shoots, associated with the silicates mentioned, quartz, various sulphides (chiefly chalcopyrite and bornite) and their oxidation products, and small quantities of native gold. **1968** I. KOSTOV *Mineral.* 334 Spadaite, $MgSiO_3.2H_2O$,.. corresponds to hydrated enstatite.

spaddle. For *Obs.*⁻¹ read *Obs. rare* and add: **a.** (Later example.) **b.** = SPATTLE *sb.*[2] 1.

1835 H. C. TODD *Notes upon Canada & U.S.A.* 8 Jonathan..[uses] *spaddle*, for spade. **1861** MRS. BEETON *Bk. Househ. Managem.* 760 The principal utensils required for making ice-creams are ice-tubs, freezing-pots, spaddles, and a cellaret. The use of the spaddle is to stir up..the cream.

spade, *sb.*[1] Add: **2. c.** More forcefully, in colloq. phr. *to call a spade a* (*bloody*) *shovel*: to speak with great or unnecessary bluntness.

1919 W. S. MAUGHAM *Moon & Sixpence* iii. 12 We did not think it hypocritical to draw over our vagaries the curtain of a decent silence. The spade was not invariably called a bloody shovel. **1945** N. BALCHIN *Mine Own Executioner* ii. 34 Sometimes..I get so fed up with all the mumbo-jumbo and abracadabra and making of holy mysteries about simple things that I like to call a spade a shovel. **1978** CADOGAN & CRAIG *Women & Children First* ii. 48 As a literary starting-off point, the determination to call a spade a bloody shovel has imposed a fundamental limitation... Outspokenness..is simply not enough.

4. a. *spade-type* adj.

1960 *Farmer & Stockbreeder* 29 Mar. 57/2 Most impressive do I find these new spade-type rotary cultivators which have been imported from the Continent. **1967** *Jane's Surface Skimmer Systems 1967–68* 31/1 The steering gear comprises twin balanced spade-type rudders.

b. *spade-armed, -footed* (earlier example), *-handed, -proud.*

1782 J. TRUMBULL *M'Fingal* III. 61 Till looking back he spied in rear The spade-arm'd chief. **1962** E. SNOW *Red China Today* (1963) lxvii. 508 Battalions, whole divisions, of spade-armed peasants in this general area have been working on a plan. **1867** *Amer. Naturalist* I. 108 The Spade-footed Toads..are more uncertain in their appearance, being governed entirely by the dampness or dryness of the season. **1934** DYLAN THOMAS *18 Poems* 25 When blood, spade-handed, and the logic time Drive children up like bruises to the thumb. **1941** L. B. LYON *Tomorrow is Revealing* 24 It hurt me, the efficient, spade-proud hole, That earth-room with its tapestry of boughs.

5. spade lug *Agric.*, each of a number of metal lugs that are bolted to the rim of a tractor wheel so as to project radially outwards and give an improved grip; hence **spade-lugged** *a.*; **spade terminal** *Electr.*, a flat, spade-shaped piece of metal having a slot or hole in it for fixing under a nut or bolt to make an electrical connection; **spade-work,** (*a*) work done with a spade for the preparation of ground; (*b*) *fig.*, preliminary work, difficult or laborious preparation, pioneering research; hence (*rarely*) **spade-worker.**

1921 *Trans. Amer. Soc. Agric. Engin.* XV. 175 The tri-spade lugs were cast with three spades on each casting.. and were staggered on the wheel when in place similar to the bolt on spade lugs. **1950** *Engineering* 5 May 506/1 The use of spade lugs in place of plain steel rims and strakes gradually reduced the tractor weight per drawbar-horsepower. **1967** J. OATES *Farm Machinery* xi. 77 Spade lugs and strake bars are used to bite more deeply into the ground. **1945** H. J. HINE *Tractors on Farm* (ed. 2) iv. 38 With spade-lugged steel wheels the spaces between the lugs must be cleaned out from time to time with a paddle. **1968** *Wireless World* Feb. 133/1 (Advt.), Heavy duty terminals... Black only will take spade terminals and wander plug. **1976** *Gramophone* May 1841/1 A twin phono-plug low capacitance signal cable is supplied, plus a green spade terminal earth wire. **1778,** etc. Spade-work [in Dict., sense 4 a]. **1912** H. G. ALDIS in *Cambr. Hist. Eng. Lit.* IX. xiii. 346 Brian Twyne, a diligent Oxford antiquary who had done much pioneer spade-work in the same field. **1927** *Daily Tel.* 12 July 9/1 The discovery of a helpful blood-test for cancer may be placed among the important advances the near future may give us as a result of spade-work already carried out. **1931** E. F. BENSON *Mapp & Lucia* iv. 93 Lucia..had insisted that all the credit was due to Drake's wife, who had planned everything (or nearly) and had done all the spade-work. **1951** *Sport* 27 Apr.–3 May 8/3 Ernie's crafty spadework has been responsible for many of the goals netted by Jack Milburn and George Robledo. **1977** A. CLARKE *Letter from Dead* ix. 105, I did a bit of spadework on him yesterday..and he seemed to be thawing a little. **1912** 'SAKI' *Chron. Clovis* 267 'Where I think you political spade-workers are so silly,' said the Duke, 'is in the misdirection of your efforts.'

spade, *sb.*[2] Add: **1. b.** *attrib.* in *sing.*

1904 'O. HENRY' *Cabbages & Kings* vi. 105 The invitations to the musicale came sliding in by pairs and threes and spade flushes. **1973** *Country Life* 10 May 1331/1 West led the Spade Knave, which I took with dummy's Ace.

c. *fig.* in advb. phr. *in spades*, very much, in abundance, extremely. (Spades is the highest ranking suit in Bridge.) *colloq.* (chiefly *U.S.*).

1929 D. RUNYON in *Hearst's International* Oct. 62/2, I always hear the same thing about every bum on Broadway, male and female, including some I know are bums, in spades, right from taw. **1964** WODEHOUSE *Frozen Assets* i. 19 'It's the law I'm beefing about. You didn't make the law.' 'But I administer it.' 'I'll say you do. In spades.' **1972** R. NIXON *Diary* in *Mem.* (1978) 619 Anybody who gets to the top in the Communist hierarchy and stays at the top has to have a great deal of political ability and a great deal of toughness. All three of the Soviet leaders have this in spades.

3. a. A Black person, a Negro, esp. male: freq. in White use, as a term of contempt or casual reference. Formerly among U.S. Blacks, a very dark-skinned Negro. *slang* (orig. *U.S.*).

1928 C. MCKAY *Home to Harlem* vi. 56 Jake is such a fool spade. Don't know how to handle the womens. **1929** W. THURMAN *Blacker the Berry* I. 34 Wonder where all the spades keep themselves? **1945** L. SHELLY *Jive Talk Dict.* 17 *Spade*, colored person. **1957** C. MACINNES *City of Spades* II. ii. 118 A British lady with a wild love of Spades, and a horrid habit of touching you on the shoulder because she says 'to stroke a darkie brings you luck.' **1969** [see *DINGE *sb.*[3]]. **1971** N. SAUNDERS *Alternative London* xxviii. 263 On Saturdays try Brixton market—nearly as big, more genuine, lots of spades. **1978** J. A. MICHENER *Chesapeake* 678 The four Turlocks hated Negroes and never hesitated in voicing their disgust. 'Goddamned spades killed my cousin Captain Matt—one of them gets out of line with me, he's dead.'

b. *attrib.* or as *adj.*

1928 C. MCKAY *Home to Harlem* vi. 56 She was of the complexion known among Negroes as spade or chocolate-to-the-bone. **1952** C. BROSSARD *Who walk in Darkness* x. 61 These spade intellectuals really think they've made it when they get a white girl. **1964** *Negro Digest* Feb. 55/1, I can't see why no colored man'd want to marry no white chick... Not when there's so many fine spade chicks around. **1978** M. PUZO *Fools Die* liv. 568 Two spade hookers went gliding by arm in arm.

Hence **spa·delet** *nonce-wd.* [-LET], a Black child.

1959 C. MACINNES *Absolute Beginners* 62, I passed a crocodile of infants, and among them a number of little Spadelets.

spade, *v.*[1] **2. b.** (Earlier example.)

1785 G. WASHINGTON *Diary* 5 Sept. (1925) II. 410 Began to spade up the Lawn in front of the Court yard.

spadger. Add: **2.** *transf.* A boy. *colloq. rare.*

1899 *Captain* II. 273/2 If we've got to take these three young spadgers..we shall want something bigger'n this here gig. **1978** K. BONFIGLIOLI *All Tea in China* I. iii. 29 'See here, young spadger,' he said..'if you should be a little short of tin..come and spend a night or two at Great Coram Street.'

Hence as *v. intr.* (*rare*), (*a*) to catch sparrows or other small birds, to go sparrow-netting; (*b*) *fig.*, to play or frolic *about* in the manner of a sparrow.

1939 F. THOMPSON *Lark Rise* ix. 171 In winter in the 'eighties the youths and big boys of the hamlet would go out on dark nights 'spadgering'. For this a large net upon four poles was carried... When they came to a spot where a flock of sparrows or other small birds was roosting, the net was dropped over the hedge..and the birds enclosed were slaughtered. **1967** *Listener* 7 Sept. 315/2 Tommy Steele spadgered larkily about among the zoomorphs.

spadgers, var. *SPAGGERS.

spadona (spădōu·nă). *S. Afr.* [ad. It. *spadone* large sword.] An imperfectly developed feather taken from a young ostrich in its first year.

1881 in A. Douglass *Ostrich Farming in S. Afr.* xiv. 91 Light Spadona..white Boos. **1896** R. WALLACE *Farming Industries of Cape Colony* xi. 235 Spadonas..are pointed like a sword, hence the name, which comes from the Italian. **1955** G. ARCHMAN in Saron & Hotz *Jews in S. Afr.* vii. 130 The different types of feathers that the ostrich produces—chicks, wings, bodies, tails, spadonas.. bloods, and female bodies.

Spaetlese, var. *SPÄTLESE.

spag (spæg). Slang abbrev. of *SPAGHETTI 1 a. Also **spag bol** (bǫl), spaghetti Bolognese.

1948 PARTRIDGE *Dict. Forces' Slang* 176 *Spag*, spaghetti. (Italian front.) **1969** *Southerly* XXIX. 308 'I'll shout you a plate of steak and spag,' I said. 'It's only a buck.' **1970** D. CLARK *Deadly Pattern* iv. 86 To eat oxtail and spag bol properly, you've got to be stripped to the waist.

spaggers (spæ·gəɹz). Also **spadgers.** Slang abbrev. of *SPAGHETTI 1 a. Cf. *-ER[6] and prec.

1960 I. JEFFERIES *Dignity & Purity* v. 96 Thinking of the spaggers I would have rustled up, left to myself. **1980** I. MURDOCH *Nuns & Soldiers* ii. 127 'You said you were tired of spaghetti and potatoes and —' 'Spuds and spadgers fill you up at least.'

spaghetti (spăge·ti). [It., pl. of *spaghetto* thin string, twine.] **1. a.** A variety of pasta made in strings intermediate in thickness between macaroni and vermicelli. Occas., a dish of spaghetti.

1849 E. ACTON *Mod. Cookery* (ed. 8) p. xxxii, *Sparghetti* [sic]—Naples vermicelli. **1888** MRS. BEETON *Bk. Househ. Managem.* § 2952 Maccheroni, or Spaghetti, a smaller kind of macaroni,..generally follows the soup. **1921** F. SWINNERTON *Coquette* II. xvi. 175 The waitress approached, bearing two large plates piled high with spaghetti. **1931** B. STARKE *Touch & Go* iv. 51 A..school-teacher took us to lunch in Avon and showed us how to manage yards of spaghetti by rolling it up on our forks. **1949** J. MORE *Land of Italy* 4 A capacity to eat..*pasta* is an essential requirement... The principal varieties.. are the rope-like spaghetti of Naples, the pipe-like macaroni,..and the omelet-like cannelloni. **1956** N. DE LA FÈRE *Italian Bouquet* vi. 66 He slipped the menu under my eyes... I..refused to admit that the only recognisable word was 'spaghetti'. **1965** C. K. STEAD in *N.Z. Short Stories* (1966) 337 Julian came into Gomeo's and asked for a spaghetti. **1981** M. NABB *Death of Englishman* II. iii. 97 Old men..munching slowly at their *spaghetti* with toothless gums.

b. *fig.* and *transf.*

1935 A. HUXLEY *Let.* 17 Feb. (1969) 391 Orlo Williams ..has read every inch of spaghetti that has ever emerged from the Italian presses. **1940** O. NASH *Face is Familiar* 195 And they give you a look that implies that your spine is spaghetti and your soul is lard. **1946** F. HAMANN *Air Words* 50 *Spaghetti*, (1) electric wiring; (2) strings of sealing compound. **1960** COOKE & MARKUS *Electronics & Nucleonics Dict.* 446/2 *Spaghetti*, insulating tubing used over bare wires or as a sleeve for holding two or more insulated wires together. The tubing is usually made of varnished cloth or a plastic. **1973** C. WILLIAMS *Man on Leash* (1974) viii. 119 He was always..experimenting and lashing up nutty pieces of electronic spaghetti. **1981** T. BARLING *Bikini Red North* xiii. 276 His vasectomy could be reversed. 'New techniques... We can join up all that miniature spaghetti with incredible accuracy.'

2. An Italian: usu. contemptuous. *slang.*

1931 'D. STIFF' *Milk & Honey Route* iii. 38 Italian hobos are equally rare. They are the 'wops' or 'spaghettis'. **1977** *New Society* 29 Sept. 651/1 When the war criminal, Herbert Kappler, who served a life sentence for having commanded an execution squad that massacred 335 Italian civilians, was spirited out of a military hospital in Rome by his wife, this was generally welcomed [in Germany] with an almost racialist feeling of superiority vis-a-vis those doting spaghettis.

3. Complex roadways forming a multi-level junction, esp. on a motorway. *colloq.*

1963 *Lebende Sprachen* VIII. 166/1 Driver talk..Plenty of spaghetti. **1966** *Guardian* 4 June 14/2 Details of one of the biggest pieces of motorway spaghetti so far designed in Britain were published... It is the Gravelly Hill interchange on the M6. **1972** *Daily Tel.* 19 June 19/3 The transport profession has produced its own jargon... Multi-level motorway-junctions are 'plates of spaghetti'. **1976** *Times Lit. Suppl.* 20 Feb. 184/5 The best-known examples [of three-dimensional mazes] are motorway spaghetti, aesthetically unpleasing and disturbing to drive through.

4. *attrib.* and *Comb.* *spaghetti house, joint,*

sauce, tongs; *spaghetti-like* adj.; **spaghetti Bolognese,** spaghetti served with a sauce of which the principal ingredients are beef and tomato; **spaghetti bowl,** a network of pipelines constructed to carry materials between petrochemical companies on the Gulf Coast of the U.S.; also *transf.*; **spaghetti junction** *colloq.*, a complex junction of roads at different levels; applied *spec.* to a major interchange on the M6 near Birmingham; also *fig.*; **spaghetti (shoulder) strap,** a thin cord-like shoulder strap for a dress or the like; **spaghetti tubing** *colloq.*, tubular insulation for electrical wire; **spaghetti Western,** a 'Western' (*WESTERN *sb.* 4) or film set in the U.S. 'old west', but made in Italy or by Italians, esp. cheaply.

[**1947** L. P. DE GOUY *Gold Cookery Bk.* 760 (*heading*) Spaghetti alla Bolognese.] **1950** E. DAVID *Bk. Mediterranean Food* 93 If you are serving the classic spaghetti *Bolognese*..see that it is highly flavoured. **1973** 'M. UNDERWOOD' *Reward for Defector* vii. 56 [He] reached out for everything he needed to make himself a plateful of spaghetti bolognese. **1958** *Houston* Apr. 16/1 The mighty petrochemical industry today is feeding from an overflowing 'Spaghetti Bowl'. *Ibid.* 16/3 Industrial Sales Engineer G. R. Walton of the Houston Pipe Line Company (the man who coined the term 'Spaghetti Bowl' about two years ago). **1970** *Chem. & Engin. News* 26 Oct. 30 Mention 'the spaghetti bowl' and most West European petrochemical producers would probably think of the pipeline system in the Gulf Coast of the U.S. rather than the maze being developed in their own back yard. **1962** I. FLEMING *Spy who loved Me* I. ii. 34 Derek took me right across London to a spaghetti house called 'The Bamboo'. **1900** ADE *Fables in Slang* 158 He knew his Works were good, because all the Free and Untrammeled Souls in the Spaghetti Joint told him so. **1982** H. ENGEL *Murder on Location* (1983) ix. 87, I could see a spaghetti joint across the street. **1971** *Evening News* (Worcester) 15 Nov. 7/4 Worcester will have its own 'spaghetti junction' if the big multi-level interchange is ever constructed in the Arboretum. **1978** *Listener* 5 Jan. 25/4 We pass abruptly from the *proprium* to the *ordinarium*—from the winding country road into a great spaghetti junction of criss-cross melodies. **1980** S. BRETT *Dead Side of Mike* xi. 125 He got held up..under the spaghetti junction between the M23 and M25 because of road works. **1979** K. BONFIGLIOLI *After You with Pistol* vi. 25 We parted in a spaghetti-like tangle of insincere matiness. **1953** A. BONI *Talisman Italian Cook Bk.* xiii. 222 (*heading*) Spaghetti sauce home style. **1968** C. DRUMMOND *Death & Leaping Ladies* v. 111 He was neatly avoiding spilling spaghetti sauce over a very snappy jacket. **1980** B. FREEMANTLE *Charlie Muffin's Uncle Sam* vii. 73 The man hadn't changed his shirt... There was spaghetti sauce on the collar. **1972** *New Yorker* 30 Sept. 81/1 Black cocktail dresses with sparkling spaghetti straps. **1977** *Lancashire Life* Dec. 104/3 The demure look from Elizabeth Hayes consists of a lace-trimmed polyester satin bedjacket which, when taken off, reveals a sexy nightdress with spaghetti shoulder straps. **1980** *Times* 12 Feb. 7/5 A natty little camisole top with spaghetti shoulder straps topped with an amazing sort of opened up tube of knitting which seals your arms and then blossoms into a shrug for the back and shoulders. Do not ask me how it is done. **1972** *House & Garden* Feb. 78/1 Spaghetti tongs, 85p. **1977** 'E. MCBAIN' *Long Time no See* iii. 32 Knives and forks piled haphazardly..paper napkins, spaghetti tongs, a corkscrew. **1922** *Science & Invention Mag.* May (Advt., rear cover), Spaghetti Tubing, black or yellow in 2½-ft. lengths..18 cents per length. **1969** M. PEI *Words in Sheep's Clothing* (1970) iii. 22 'Spaghetti Western' and 'Sukiyaki Western' are terms applied to cheap Westerns produced in Italy and Japan. **1973** J. SUSANN *Once is not Enough* i. 34 It started with the flop of Melba's picture... When your kid is busted into pieces, you can't worry about a spaghetti western. **1977** G. MARTON *Alarum* 56, I wanted to see a Spaghetti Western movie.

‖ **spaghettini** (spagetī·ni). [It.] A thin variety of spaghetti.

1953 A. BONI *Talisman Italian Cook Bk.* ix. 156 Bring water and salt to boil, add spaghettini and cook 12 minutes. **1974** *Encycl. Brit. Micropædia* VII. 789/3 Among the popular cord forms [of pasta] are spaghetti ('little string'), a finer type called spaghettini, and the very fine vermicelli. **1977** D. E. WESTLAKE *Nobody's Perfect* (1978) II. v. 120 You can buy me spaghettini with clam sauce.

spake (speɪk), *sb. S. Wales.* [Of unknown origin: perh. var. SPOKE *sb.*] A string of rail-mounted wagons or trolleys used in coal mines to transport men.

1935 *Trans. Inst. Mining Engineers* LXXXVIII. 384 In mines where the men are brought out in spakes, provision should be made for their protection from the cold intake air. *Ibid.* XC. 140 A spake is composed of a number of flat trolleys fitted with wooden seats placed at intervals at right angles to the length of the trolley, and consequently at right angles to the slant. **1971** *Guardian* 6 July 1/5 A colliery accident in which an underground train ran out of control... It was remarkable the train—known as a spake—did not leave the rails. **1979** *Times* 29 Dec. 12/5 The seams lay, in places, three miles below ground. To reach them by 'spake', the man-carrying wagons, entailed a journey of half an hour.

spall, *v.*[1] Add: **1. b.** (Later example.)

a **1925** F. S. ANTHONY *Follow Call* (1936) ii. 22, I landed..on a patch of broken stone I had spalled up.. for metalling in front of the stand.

2. a. (Further examples.) Also, to detach as small fragments or particles.

1971 *Sci. Amer.* June 29/2 As the shock wave traversed a gas bubble some of its energy would go into spalling liquid from the inner surface of the bubble and projecting it through the void to strike the bubble wall at the other side. **1973** J. G. TWEEDDALE *Materials Technol.* II. vi. 154 Thermal fracturing is a somewhat crude way in which material may be 'spalled' off the surface of a brittle material which has low thermal-shock resistance. **1980** M. NAPIER *Blind Chance* xii. 109 She looked at the huge chip of stone spalled off by a bullet.

b. *Nuclear Physics.* To cause spallation of (a nucleus).

1976 *Nature* 16 Sept. 201/1 Stronger shock waves.. spall nearly all the nuclei to free nucleons.

3. (Later examples.) Also without *off.*

1940 K. REXROTH *In what Hour* 33 Novelty emerges after centuries, a rock spalls from the cliff. **1968** *Engineering* 26 July 171/3 These alloys would spall after enamelling. **1977** *Sci. Amer.* Feb. 35/1 High-energy impacts cause large pieces of the target to spall off. **1980** *National Trust* Autumn 14/2 Damp has penetrated the stone..and the corners have broken off or spalled.

spallation (spǫlēɪ·ʃən). [f. SPALL *v.*[1] + -ATION.] **1.** *Nuclear Physics.* The detachment of a number of nucleons or small nuclei from a larger nucleus, esp. as a result of the impact of an energetic nucleon or other particle. Freq. *attrib.*, as *spallation product.*

1948 LAPP & ANDREWS *Nuclear Radiation Physics* xiii. 305 When a high-energy neutron strikes a target nucleus, a reaction known as spallation may occur. **1950** GLASSTONE *Sourcebk. Atomic Energy* x. 259/2 They do not undergo fission and break up into two, more or less equal, parts. Instead, such nuclei emit various numbers ..of nucleons, leaving a series of products of lower mass and atomic number. The name *spallation* has been proposed for reactions of this kind. [*Note*] This term is based on the verb 'to spall', meaning to break up by chipping off small fragments, which was suggested as appropriate by W. H. Sullivan. **1953** *Ann. Rev. Nuclear Sci.* II. 401 O'Connor & Seaborg..bombarded uranium with 380-Mev α-particles and then analyzed radiochemically for spallation and fission products. **1962** B. G. HARVEY *Introd. Nuclear Physics & Chem.* ix. 183 Reactions in which several particles are emitted are often called 'spallation', regardless of the mechanism by which they take place. **1979** *Nature* 15 Feb. 519/1, ^{18}C can be produced fairly readily in heavy ion collisions, or as a spallation product of heavy nuclei.

2. *gen.* Spalling.

1971 *New Scientist* 8 Apr. 72/3 An outer spallation zone due to the interaction of shock waves with the rock surface. **1974** HAWKEY & BINGHAM *Wild Card* xv. 133 The crash guys..look for recrystallization at micro-promontories, Neumann banding, parallel banding, spallation.

spalled, *ppl. a.* Add: **1.** More widely, broken off or chipped by spalling. Also *spalled-off.*

1931 G. W. TYRRELL *Volcanoes* ii. 67 Such rocks..may be distinguished from agglomerate by the..occurrence of fragments of spalled-off scoria in the interstices between the blocks. **1971** *Ann. Rep. Delegates Sci. Area Univ. Oxford* 67 Coke ash slag on spalled ends of Steetley tarred dolomite blocks. **1975** *Country Life* 9 Oct. 924/3 Spalled and fractured brickwork was cut out and replaced.

spalliard, dial. form of ESPALIER *sb.* (Simple and attrib. examples.)

1886 F. T. ELWORTHY *W. Somerset Word-Bk.* 696 *Spalliard* (spaal·yurd), *sb.*, espalier, a trained fruit tree. I think, sir, we must dig up that *spalliard* plum. **1920** [see *PLEACH *sb.*].

Spam (spæm). Also **spam.** [App. blend of SP(ICED *ppl. a.* + H)AM *sb.*[1], but see also quot. 1937[1].] **1.** The proprietary name of a type of tinned meat consisting chiefly of pork; also (with small initial) applied *loosely* to other types of tinned luncheon meat.

1937 *Squeal* 1 July 1/2 In the last month Geo. A. Hormel & Co...launched the product *Spam*... The 'think-up' of the name [is] credited to Kenneth Daigneau, New York actor... Seems as if he had considered the word a good memorable trade-name for some time, had only waited for a product to attach it to. **1937** *Official Gaz.* (U.S. Patent Office) 26 Oct. 750/2 Geo. A. Hormel & Company, Austin, Minn... Spam..For Canned Meats—Namely, Spiced Ham. Claims use since May 11, 1937. **1939** J. STEINBECK *Grapes of Wrath* v. 49 The tractor driver stopped..and opened his lunch: sandwiches wrapped in waxed paper, white bread, pickle, cheese, Spam. **1942** *Yank* 28 Oct. 8 There, arrayed in all their glory, were slices of ham, spam, bologna and potato salad. **1951** 'A. GARVE' *Murder in Moscow* xiii. 127, I received..four tins of meat—spam, I think it was called. **1957** H. ROOSENBURG *Walls came tumbling Down* ix. 199 We were offered Spam sandwiches. **1971** C. BONINGTON *Annapurna South Face* xi. 134 That night he made supper, a magnificent concoction of fried Spam and fried new potatoes. **1981** G. MACBETH *Kind of Treason* iv. 41 A plate of Molly's best Spam sandwiches.

fig. **1958** *Listener* 6 Nov. 750/2 An actor can only turn the quite unconscious richness of it [*sc.* the Hoxton voice] into—spam.

2. *Comb.* **Spam can** *slang*, a streamlined steam locomotive formerly used on the Southern Region of British Rail; **Spam Medal** *Mil. slang*, a medal awarded to all the members of a force (see also quot. 1962).

1967 G. F. FIENNES *I tried to run Railway* v. 54 We borrowed from the Southern for trials two Battle of Britain class engines. We took these Spam Cans out. **1971** D. J. SMITH *Discovery Railwayana* x. 59 *Spam can*, streamlined locomotive of the SR. **1945** PARTRIDGE *Dict. R.A.F. Slang* 40 Naffy gong 1939–45 star (medal). Since late 1943... It is also called *the spam medal.* **1959** *Legionary* Mar. 11/1 As all of us overseas at the time were volunteers, it meant that everybody wore one and so, in patronizing fashion, we tagged it [*sc.* the Canadian Volunteer Service Medal] the Spam Medal. **1962** GRANVILLE *Dict. Sailors' Slang* 110 *Spam medal*, 1939–45 star whose ribbon has the same colours as the NAAFI girls' arm flash. As *spam*, a kind of *sp*iced-*ham*, was sold in the NAAFI canteen, what more obvious term could suggest itself?

Hence **spa·mmy** *a.*, consisting or tasting chiefly of (bland) luncheon meat; also *fig.*, commonplace, mediocre, unexciting.

1959 *Observer* 11 Jan. 18/3 Skipton is toned down to scale with our spammy age. **1960** J. STROUD *Shorn Lamb* i. 13 We got a spammy sort of meal.

span, *sb.*[1] Add: **5. c.** *Psychol.* Mental extent; the amount of information that the mind can be conscious of at a given moment, or the number of items it can reproduce after one presentation; esp. const. *of*, as *span of apprehension, attention, consciousness*, etc. Cf. *memory span* s.v. *MEMORY 12.

1887 *Mind* XII. 76 The highest number correctly reproduced is to be regarded as the limit which we wish to find, and which we term here the *span. Ibid.* 79 We might expect that 'span of prehension' should be an important factor in determining mental grasp. **1890** W. JAMES *Princ. Psychol.* I. xi. 405 The question of *the 'span' of consciousness* [*sc.* to how many things can we attend at once] has often been asked and answered. **1922** R. S. WOODWORTH *Psychol.* xi. 262 The 'span of attention' for objects..is measured by discovering how many such objects can be clearly seen, or heard, or felt, in a single instant of time. Measurement of this 'span' is one of the oldest experiments in psychology. **1945** *Mind* LIV. 165 She reduced the number of choices to a range lying within or just within the 'span of attention' of her subjects. **1971** *Jrnl. Gen. Psychol.* Jan. 129 No matter how high the level of luminance, the span of apprehensions will not exceed eight items during the critical interval. **1979** R. JAFFE *Class Reunion* (1980) III. ii. 312 The child was very bright and had a long attention span.

d. The maximum lateral dimension of an aircraft, or of a wing, from wing tip to wing tip.

1909 R. KENNEDY *Flying Machines* ii. 34 It will be difficult to get a monoplane of sufficient span for heavy lifts, together with a strong construction. **1927** C. L. M. BROWN *Conquest of Air* vii. 98 It was a biplane, the two main wings being 32 ft. in frontal width (span) and 5 ft. in depth (chord). **1953** *New Biol.* XIV. 73 A vulture has a broad wing of large surface area as well as large span. **1968** MILLER & SAWERS *Technical Devel. Mod. Aviation* v. 137 For the first time Douglas made a basic change in the wing..and increased the span by 10 feet to give greater lift and fuel capacity.

e. A range of numerical values; the difference between the highest and lowest values in a range.

1962 *Gloss. Terms Automatic Data Processing* (*B.S.I.*) 13 *Range.* 1. All the values which a quantity may have. 2. The difference between the highest and lowest of these values (in mathematics often called the span). **1974** *Physics Bull.* Jan. 31/3 The series covers the temperature range 223 to 573 K in eight spans.

f. *span of control*: in Business Studies, the area of activity, number of functions or subordinates, etc., for which an individual or organization is responsible.

1937 L. GULICK in Gulick & Urwick *Papers on Sci. of Administration* i. 7 Span of control. Just as the hand of man can span only a limited number of notes on the piano, so the mind and will of man can span but a limited number of immediate managerial contacts. **1956** E. BRIDGES in A. Dunsire *Making of Administrator* 5 He will look to see that too many people are not reporting to any one head—that the 'span of control' or of management as they call it, is not too wide. **1962** *Rep. Comm. Broadcasting 1960* 226 in *Parl. Papers 1961–2* (Cmnd. 1753) IX. 259 Since there might well be some scores of companies, it is highly unlikely that a corporation could exercise its responsibilities effectively; the 'span of control' would be too great. **1976** P. R. WHITE *Planning for Public Transport* i. 20 Operation of private party coach hire or excursions may require frequent decisions on pricing and scheduling, and hence a small span of control for each manager is desirable.

6*. *Math.* That which is generated by the elements of some set. Cf. *SPAN *v.*[1] 5*.

1968 D. PASSMAN *Permutation Groups* ii. 155 We define the span of A, Span A, to be the subspace of FG spanned by all the functions a_{ij}. We list some basic properties of the span. **1981** *Sci. Amer.* Oct. 153 (*caption*) Their [*sc.* vectors'] span is a plane because any point in the plane can be reached by vectorially adding some scalar multiple of *A* to some scalar multiple of *B*.

7. (sense 5 c) *span test*; (poet.) *spanlong, -wide* adjs.; **span loading** *Aeronaut.*, the gross weight of an aircraft divided by its wing span or, more commonly, by the square of the wing span; also *transf.*, of a bird; **span wire,** each of the series of wires suspended across the route of a tram or trolleybus to carry the overhead electric wire; **span-worm** *U.S.* = LOOPER[1] in Dict. and Suppl.

1929 *Jrnl. R. Aeronaut. Soc.* XXXIII. 359 This.. depends primarily on 'span loading' that is weight/(span)^2.

1953 *New Biol.* XIV. 72 The sinking speed is a function of the 'span loading', i.e. weight/wing span. A low sinking speed can only be achieved by having a wing span which is large relative to the weight of the bird. **1983** D. STINTON *Design of Aeroplane* iv. 120 In straight and level flight the lift loading across the span..is equal to..the weight of the aircraft divided by the wingspan. Both are referred to collectively as the span loading. **1957** BLUNDEN *Poems of Many Years* 281 Spanlong rabbits quite forget danger's eye. **1971** *Jrnl. Gen. Psychol.* Apr. 238 We have here a well-defined figural-span measure which does *not* link with other span tests. **1943** E. MUIR *Narrow Place* 7 Was this the ground That stretched beyond the span-wide world-wide ditch. **1891** *Electr. World* 21 Mar. 225/1 In the case of side pole and span wire, construction poles should be placed at the points represented and a span wire run between them. **1963** A. T. DOVER *Electric Traction* (ed. 4) xxiii. 358 At curves the span wire must be on a level with the trolley wire, otherwise the hangar will be pulled out of the vertical. **1820** *Amer. Farmer* I. 375/3 What can our obliging correspondents tell us about the..best method of destroying that dreadful plague of our orchards, the span worm. **1903** [see *MEASURING *ppl. a.* b]. **1972** SWAN & PAPP *Common Insects N. Amer.* xix. 293 The Bruce spanworm is a major defoliator of aspen in the prairie regions.

span, *v.*[1] Add: **I. 5*.** *Math.* To generate. Cf. *SPAN *sb.*[1] 6*.

1941 BIRKHOFF & MACLANE *Survey Mod. Algebra* vii. 170 This subspace is evidently the smallest subspace containing all the given vectors; hence it is called the subspace generated or spanned by them. **1964** A. P. & W. ROBERTSON *Topological Vector Spaces* i. 3 If L is a linearly independent subset of a vector space E and if S is a subset containing L and spanning E, there is a base B of E with L ⊂ B ⊂ S. **1981** *Sci. Amer.* Oct. 156/2 For example, the *u*–*v* plane is a vector space that can be spanned by two vectors directed along the positive *u* and *v* axes.

II. 6. (Further example.)

1976 *Offshore Platforms & Pipelining* 151/1 Any relatively stiff pipeline laid in a wavy seabed will span in places.

span, *v.*[2] Add: **1. a.** Also *absol.* (Earlier example.)

1793 J. BAXTER *Jrnl.* 2 Feb. in *Amer. Speech* XL. (1965) 199, I and John Schenck spaned in together.

spanandry (spæ·nændri). *Zool.* [ad. F. *spanandrie* (P. Marchal 1913, in *Ann. des Sci. Nat.*: *Zool.* XVIII. 268), ad. Patristic Gr. σπανανδρία scarcity of population, f. Gr. σπάνις scarcity + ἀνήρ, ἀνδρ- man: see -Y[3].] Lack or extreme scarcity of males in a population. Hence **spana·ndric** *a.*

1924 *Nature* 14 June 880/1 A. Vandel: Geographical spanandry in a Branchiopod Crustacean, *Lepidurus apus*. **1967** *Science* 28 Apr. 483/3 Polygamy is extreme, but, since this follows from the fact that males are produced in much smaller numbers than females, *spanandry* seems a better term, and is used here. **1976** *Bull. Entomol. Res.* LXVI. 179 (*heading*) The identity of the greenhouse thrips *Heliothrips haemorrhoidalis* (Bouché) (Thysanoptera) and the taxonomic significance of spanandric males. **1976** *Entomol. Meddelelser* XLIV. 60 The major types of parthenogenesis: thelytoky, cyclical parthenogenesis,..and spanandry are reviewed.

spancelled, *ppl. a.* and *pa. pple.* Add: Also *fig.*

1910 J. M. SYNGE *Deirdre of Sorrows* II. 35 You're seven years spancelled with Naisi and the Pair. **1965** *New Statesman* 26 Nov. 848/1 In England it is the wives who regard themselves as the spancelled party. **1980** *Times Lit. Suppl.* 20 June 688/4 He was..spancelled by a lack of money that meant he could never be apprenticed to a leading London surgeon.

Spandau (spæ·ndau). Also **spandau.** [f. *Spandau*, name of a district of (West) Berlin.] **a.** A German machine-gun used during the war of 1914–18 (see quot. 1966). **b.** Applied to other machine-guns of German design, esp. the MG34 and MG42 of the war of 1939–45. Freq. *attrib.* as *Spandau* (*machine*) *gun*.

a **1918** J. T. B. MCCUDDEN *Five Years in Royal Flying Corps* (1919) v. xii. 241, I distinctly noticed the red-yellow flashes from his parallel Spandau guns. **1929** E. W. SPRINGS *Above Bright Blue Sky* 221 He was suddenly cold as he awaited the crack of the spandaus. **1938** G. S. HUTCHINSON *Machine Guns* xii. 333 The British were armed with Vickers, the Germans with Spandaus. **1944** K. DOUGLAS *Alamein to Zem Zem* (1946) iv. 29 In their pit lay a Spandau machine-gun. **1966** T. R. FUNDERBURK *Fighters* 27 The Maxim gun was manufactured in England..as a Vickers gun. The same gun was manufactured under license by the German Weapons and Munitions Factory, a state arsenal at Spandau, Berlin, and was known as a Spandau gun. A light version ..was developed by the Germans for the use of aerial gunners and known as a Parabellum. **1968** A. DIMENT *Bang Bang Birds* vi. 97 Vitconne is crouched behind a Spandau lent to him by a friendly German officer. **1971** F. W. A. HOBART *Pictorial Hist. Machine Gun* 228 (*caption*) First German Airborne Corps defending Cassino... The MG-42 was a very effective dual purpose machine gun. The Germans used it a lot on a tripod to produce fixed line fire. The British troops called it the 'Spandau'.

Spandex (spæ·ndeks). orig. *U.S.* Also **spandex.** [Arbitrarily f. EXPAND *v.*] **a.** A synthetic elastomeric fibre composed largely of polyurethane. **b.** A proprietary name for certain fabrics made from this fibre.

1959 *Federal Register* 10 Feb. 981/3 The following generic names for manufactured fibers..are hereby established... *Spandex*, a manufactured fiber in which the fiber-forming substance is a long chain synthetic elastomer comprised of at least 85 percent of a segmented polyurethane. **1962** *New Scientist* 22 Mar. 697/1 As materials classified as spandex may have 15 per cent of some other compound to be introduced with the polyurethane, wide variations in fibre properties are possible. **1968** *Trade Marks Jrnl.* 7 Feb. 176/2 *Spandex*... All goods included in Class 22 made wholly or substantially of spandex fibres. Monsanto Chemical Company..U.S.A.; manufacturers.—4th Sept. 1964. **1972** *Brazilian Bull.* (Brazilian Trade Centre, London) Apr. 3 The Brazilian subsidiary of the U.S. Du Pont company is to build a factory at Paulínia..for the production of Lycra Spandex fibre. **1973** *Materials & Technology* VI. iv. 334 The illustration shows cross-sections through three well-known brands of spandex fibre, these being 'Lycra'.., 'Spanzelle'.., and 'Vyrene'. **1978** *Neiman-Marcus Christmas Bk.* 26 Nylon and spandex maillot.

spandite (spæ·ndəit). *Min.* [Blend of SPESSARTITE and ANDRADITE.] A manganiferous garnet resembling spessartine but containing more iron and calcium.

1907 *Rec. Geol. Survey India* XXXV. 22 The garnet is intermediate in composition between spessartite and andradite, and..Mr. Fermor proposes to introduce the term spessart-andradite, which may be shortened for convenience in general use to spandite. **1955** BROWN & DEY *India's Mineral Wealth* (ed. 3) 606 Spandite, a garnet intermediate in composition between spessartite and andradite, occurs in the Kodurite series of the Srikakulam district of Andhra. It varies in colour from deep orange to brown orange-red and blood-red and never displays the lighter orange shades of the true spessartite. **1972** *Mineral. Abstr.* XXXIII. 121/1 X-ray data for hiddenite diopside, [etc.]..and a probable spandite are given.

spandrel. Add: **1. c.** On oriental patterned rugs or carpets: one of the spaces between the central field and the border, or between an arch motif and its frame.

1900 J. K. MUMFORD *Oriental Rugs* x. 147 In the spandrels over the arch of the prayer rugs there is a repetition of the pear patterns. **1931** A. U. DILLEY *Oriental Rugs & Carpets* iii. 63 Large central medallions, brilliant pendants, traceried spandrels and graceful floral scrolls. **1962** C. W. JACOBSEN *Oriental Rugs* II. 264 Mudjars have a definite prayer arch design... Many of these have panels above the spandrel with van dykes designs. **1967** *Times* 26 Jan. 22 (Advt.), A *Silk Heriz* with all over blue spandrels on an old mellowed field, classical rust medallion, floral border.

spandrelled, *a.* (Earlier example.)

1813 M. EDGEWORTH *Let.* 1 May (1971) 37 The beauty of the spandrilled ceiling with all its rich, and light ornaments.

spandy, *a.* Delete *rare* and add earlier example. Also *spandy-bright, spandy new.*

1838 'T. TITTERWELL' *Yankee Notions* 116, I have heard of a ghost that always came in a new coat..and a spandy clean dickey. **1903** K. D. WIGGIN *Rebecca of Sunnybrook Farm* i. 14 The trouble is to get the shoes... These are spandy new I've got on. **1968** J. UPDIKE *Couples* iii. 227 Ben's lank hairs ran together to make black seams, like sores downrunning into the tops of his comically new topsiders, cup-soled, spandy-bright. **1973** E.-J. BAHR *Nice Neighbourhood* ii. 23 Don has this very definite fixation that I am going to bang up our spandy new car.

spang, *v.*[2] For '*Sc.* and *north.*' read 'orig. *Sc.* and *north.*' and add: **1.** (Later examples.) Also *fig.*

1966 *If, Worlds of Sci. Fiction* Dec. 39/2 [He] kneed the screen door open so that it spanged against the outside wall. **1976** L. SANDERS *Hamlet Warning* (1977) xix. 165 A stream of bullets spanged off the metal around him. **1979** *Observer* 4 Feb. 4/7 We shared champagne and Coke with the nurses. Thank God spanged out on all sides.

spang, *adv.* For *U.S.* read 'orig. and chiefly *U.S.*' and add later examples.

1921 D. CANFIELD *Brimming Cup* I. v. 65 The brooks were..all running spang full to the very edge with snow-water. **1925** WODEHOUSE *Sam the Sudden* xiii. 91 If he thinks a young bride's going to stand for that sort of conduct right plumb spang in the middle of what you might call the honeymoon, [etc.]. **1936** M. MITCHELL *Gone with Wind* xxxii. 547 So you needs a spang new pretty dress. **1962** *Punch* 26 Dec. 943/1 With its superb flair for the nostalgic and traditional the BBC has put this year's Christmas spang in the middle of its dramatised version of The Old Curiosity Shop. **1971** 'D. CORY' *Sunburst* xiii. 212 Will you *look* at that?.. Spang in the middle of the bloody road.

spangle, *sb.*[1] Add: **4. c.** A fowl or pigeon belonging to a variety distinguished by speckled plumage.

1854 *Poultry Chron.* II. 66/1 Eighteen pens of beautiful silver spangles added to the old laurels of Mr. Vivian. **1855** *Ibid.* III. 175/2 The Toys [*sc.* pigeons] are as follows: Suabians or Spangles, [etc.]. *Ibid.* 355/2 The third kind is what the old breeders of Game fowls call 'Spangles'. The cock is red and white in the hackle and saddle, and black and white in the tail and breast. The hens are partridge-colour, spotted with white. **1948** G. O. RICKWOOD *Constable's Country* 14 The..'King's Arms'..was a rendezvous of cock-fighters in days when the 'feeders' of the birds—Shropshire reds, Staffordshire jet-blacks,.. spangles and other noted breeds—were..important personages in the hierarchy of the sport.

spangled, *ppl. a.* **1.** (Later *fig.* examples.)

1920 E. SITWELL *Wooden Pegasus* 13 Flickered down the street together In the spangled weather. **1943** L. B. LYON *Evening in Stepney* 17 By spangled weirs we pass the gas-works. **1977** [see *RHINESTONE b].

Spanglish (spæ·ŋgliʃ). [Blend of SPANISH *sb.*[1] + ENGLISH *sb.*] A type of Spanish contaminated by English words and forms of expression, spoken in Latin America.

[**1954** S. Tío *A Fuego Lento* 62 Esta lengua nueva se llamará el 'Espanglish'. La etimología es clara. Viene de español y de english.] **1967** *Time* 7 Apr. 12 A historical pageant known as a 'Texas Fandangle'—border-country Spanglish for fandango, the frenetic Mexican dance. **1972** *Daily Tel.* 28 Nov. 13/8 Argentina is not alone in falling victim to 'Spanglish'. Chilean housewives who have problems with the plumbing call for el gasfitter. **1974** *Amer. Speech 1970* XLV. 230 Spanglish may be characterized as a gradual relexification of Puerto Rican Spanish through borrowings, adaptations, and innovations. **1976** M. MILLAR *Ask for me Tomorrow* (1977) vi. 43 A mixture of Spanish and English slang sometimes called Spanglish.

spangolite (spæ·ŋgŏləit). *Min.* [f. the name of Norman *Spang*, 19th-cent. U.S. mineral collector + *-ol-* + -ITE[1].] A hydrated basic sulphate and chloride of copper and aluminium, $Cu_6AlSO_4(OH)_{12}Cl\cdot 3H_2O$, which is a secondary mineral found as pale green, prismatic or tabular, rhombohedral crystals.

1890 S. L. PENFIELD in *Amer. Jrnl. Sci.* CXXXIX. 371, I take pleasure in not only expressing at this time my thanks to Mr. Spang for his kindness but also in naming the mineral..Spangolite after him. **1949** *Amer. Mineralogist* XXXIV. 182 A few months ago, Mr. Hatfield Goudey..found a new occurrence of spangolite at Majuba Hill, Pershing County, Nevada. **1968** I. KOSTOV *Mineralogy* 514 Spangolite is ditrigonal-pyramidal.., also with perfect {001} cleavage.

Spaniard, *sb.* (and *a.*); Add: Hence **Spaniarde·ss**, a Spanish woman; **Spa·niardly** *adv.*, in a manner typical of the Spanish.

1909 KIPLING *Rewards & Fairies* (1910) 42 De Avila.. very Spaniardly hung them all for heretics. **1931** O. NASH *Hard Lines* 93 The bashful Spaniardess apparently finds the amorous Spaniard..menacing to her virtue.

spaniel, *sb.*[1] (and *a.*). Add: **3. a.** *spaniel eye*; *spaniel-eyed* adj.

1958 M. KELLY *Christmas Egg* III. 125 Brett could well imagine his assumed spaniel eyes of reproach. **1975** T. ALLBEURY *Special Collection* xi. 79 Felinski wondered what women would make of those liquid, spaniel eyes. **1963** P. FLEMING *Kolchak* vii. 84 A plump, spaniel-eyed, ineffective little man.

spaniel, *v.* **a.** (Later examples.)

1924 GALSWORTHY *Forest* II. i. 33 Devoted to him; spaniels round him all the time. **1958** 'W. HENRY' *Seven Men at Mimbres Springs* vii. 80 With that reference to the gun, Sparhawk began spanielling again, obsequious as ever.

Spanish, *a.* (*adv.*) and *sb.*[1] Add: **A.** *adj.* **1. d.** Of a Jew or Jewish institution: of or belonging to the Sephardim. Also *Spanish-Hebrew, Spanish* (*and*) *Portuguese* (cf. *PORTUGUESE *a.* a.) Hence **Spanish-Jewish** *a.*

1817 M. EDGEWORTH *Harrington* iv. 88 This Spanish Jew must..be a most accomplished and amiable person. **1851** [see SEPHARDI]. **1876** GEO. ELIOT *D. Deronda* VII. lv. 238 His mind went to the synagogue..and heard the Spanish–Hebrew liturgy. **1892** [see *ASHKENAZIM]. **1894** I. ZANGWILL *King of Schnorrers* v. 105 The Mahamad..administered the affairs of the Spanish–Portuguese community. **1902** G. E. MITTON *Hampstead & Marylebone* 80 In Bryanston Street there is a synagogue which was built for the Spanish and Portuguese Jews. **1932** C. ROTH *Hist. of Marranos* xii. 315 On his death in 1762, he left..a legacy of £1,000 to the Spanish and Portuguese community. **1949** 'R. WEST' *Meaning of Treason* I. vi. 122 That slender and distinguished old gentleman of Spanish Jewish descent, Mr Salzedo. **1977** *Early Music* Apr. 262 Basil Douglas Ltd. presents.. Sephardic Romances from before the expulsion of the Spanish Jews (1492). **1981** *Times* 16 Oct. 9/1 Elias Canetti..was born in Bulgaria, of Spanish–Jewish descent. **1982** *Times* 26 Jan. 11/5 Sir Moses Montefiore ..was an intensely loyal Englishman. The Spanish Portuguese Jewish Congregation..refused a request to transfer the remains to Israel.

2. a. *Spanish saddle.*

1821 S. F. AUSTIN *Jrnl.* 8 July in *Texas Hist. Assoc. Q.* (1904) VII. 287 Swapped away Wilsons Horse & an old Grey..for a mule, & exchanged a french saddle for a Spanish one. **1897** E. HOUGH *Story of Cowboy* 67 The Spanish saddles of the Southwest were often heavily decorated with silver. **1945** *Elk Mountain Pilot* (Crested Butte, Colorado) 19 July 3/1 (Advt.), For Sale... A Spanish Saddle, excellent condition.

c. *Spanish shawl.*

1925 G. GREENE *Babbling April* 17 And the night was so hot, And no one can see in the dark, And a rent in the Spanish shawl. **1967** A. WILSON *No Laughing Matter*

II. 92 A grand piano on which [is] a white Spanish shawl with red and green embroidered roses. **1975** 'R. PLAYER' *Let's talk of Graves* iii. 77 The year '54..the year of the largest crinolines... Thrown over them..were..large Spanish shawls.

e. (*a*) Denoting a style of art or architecture native to or characteristic of Spain; (*b*) denoting a style of decoration or architecture imitative of that of Spain. Also *Spanish-style* adj.

1927 *Sunset Mag.* May 87/1 Many builders and real estate men are masquerading whole city blocks of houses under the name of Spanish. **1931** S. SITWELL (*title*) Spanish Baroque art. **1937** J. LAVER *Taste & Fashion* xviii. 258 The style of his interior decoration may be shortly described as Spanish 'baroque'. **1950** A. WILSON *Such Darling Dodos* 159 There were Regency bedrooms, a Spanish Baroque dining room. **1953** S. BEDFORD *Sudden View* I. i. 20 The dining-car..turned out to be..decorated with machine-carved Spanish Renaissance woodwork of astonishing gloom. **1960** *Encounter* Apr. 3/2 There is something ancient and unfamiliar about its [*sc.* a skyscraper's] situation among Spanish-style San Francisco homes. **1970** H. BRAUN *Parish Churches* xi. 148 It [*sc.* the arch] is often four-centred or, in some of the more opulent examples, the three-centred 'Spanish' arch. **1976** *Liverpool Echo* 22 Nov. 14/2 (Advt.), Hall, lounge, Spanish arch to dining room, [etc.]. **1977** *N.Z. Herald* 8 Jan. 4-3/1 (Advt.), $5000 deposit will secure this charming Spanish bungalow in New Windsor. **1979** *Arizona Daily Star* 1 Apr. (Advt. Section) 19/5 Enter this custom Spanish territorial home over a wooden bridge. **1979** N. HARTLEY *Quicksilver* vi. 77 Several Spanish-style interior patios.

3. b. *an old Spanish custom*: phr. used *joc.* to justify a long-standing practice which is unauthorized or otherwise irregular.

1932 *N. & Q.* 13 Feb. 122/1 Could any reader tell me the origin of the phrase, 'An old Spanish custom,' as applied, in a jocular sense, to any unauthorised practice? **1966** M. TORRIE *Heavy as Lead* x. 115 Giving Sir Ganymede lunch at the pub..appeared by this time to have become an old Spanish custom. **1982** *Listener* 25 Nov. 13/2 The December issue of *Encounter*..lifts some lids on the 'old Spanish customs' of Fleet Street print unions.

6. *Spanish-American* (earlier example), *-Indian* (earlier example), *-Mexican*.

1705 R. BEVERLEY *Virginia* 51 By their Accounts, we suppose him to have come from the Spanish Indians, some-where near Mexico, or the Mines of St. Barbe. **1727** E. DORRINGTON *Hermit* I. i. 1, I accidentally fell into Discourse with a Spanish Mexican Inhabitant, named Alvarado. **1811** *Niles' Reg.* I. 14/2 The Creoles—Spanish Americans—i.e. the descendants of Spaniards born in this country. **1935** E. FARJEON *Nursery in Nineties* II. iii. 91 A beautiful Spanish-Mexican girl who smoked cigarettes. **1980** *Amer. Speech* LV. 39 Geographic names of Spanish linguistic origin [are] utilized..to determine the sphere of Spanish-Mexican influence in California.

7. Spanish bowline (see quot. 1968); **Spanish Civil War,** the civil war in Spain (1936–9), espoused on both sides as a popular 'cause' throughout Europe and America, in which Nationalist rebel forces, with Fascist support, overcame the Republican Government and its anti-Fascist allies (cf. *International Brigade* s.v. *INTERNATIONAL *a.* 2); **Spanish-Colonial** *a.*, designating a style of architecture characteristic of the former Spanish colonies in the Americas; also *absol.*; **Spanish comb,** a decorative comb having a deep top, worn in the hair; **Spanish dance,** the traditional dance form of Spain, of gypsy origin and characterized by elaborate heel-work and freq. involving the use of castanets; hence **Spanish dancer, dancing; Spanish flu** *colloq.* = *Spanish influenza* below; **Spanish foot,** a foot (of a chair or other piece of furniture) of a scroll form with vertical ribs; **Spanish guitar,** the standard six-stringed (orig. five-stringed) non-electric guitar, used for both folk and classical music; **Spanish hat** (see quot. 1960); **Spanish influenza,** a popular name for influenza caused by an influenza virus of type A; *esp.* that of the pandemic which began in 1918; **Spanish omelette,** an omelette containing a selection of tomatoes, onions, potatoes, and other vegetables; **Spanish tile** *Building*, (*a*) a roofing tile that is curved cylindrically and slightly tapered, to be laid alternately convex and concave so as to overlap at both sides; (*b*) *U.S.*, a curved roofing tile that is laid convex upwards and overlaps at one side only by means of a straight projection; **Spanish tummy** *colloq.*, a stomach upset of a type freq. experienced by visitors to Spain; **Spanish War** = *Spanish Civil War* above.

1968 E. FRANKLIN *Dict. Knots* 26 *Spanish bowline*, a double loop knot that is tied in the bight in which the two loops are splayed. **1974** *Maclean's Mag.* May 10/2 Spanish bowlines to make slings for scaffolding. **1936** C. PRIETO *Spanish Front* xi. 80 It is hardly necessary in this book to give a detailed description of the Spanish Civil War. **1981** A. PRICE *Soldier no More* xi. 144 He'd subscribed to all sorts of causes, from the Spanish Civil War onwards. **1927** *Sunset Mag.* May 15/2 The popular desire seems to be to call this architecture Spanish. Architects are inclined to call it Spanish-Colonial. **1937** R. NEWCOMB *Spanish-Colonial Archit. in U.S.* viii. 37 Many in these states have wished to build in the Spanish Colonial rather than in the American Colonial. **1973** G. SIMS *Hunters Point* xiii. 114 It's what they call Spanish Colonial style with wooden columns and a roof of heavily twisted tiles. **1977** H. FAST *Immigrants* I. 39 There was much substance if little taste all through the dining room,..a curious and uninspiring marriage of Spanish Colonial and Victorian. **1873** *Young Englishwoman* Mar. 131/2 Diadem plaits or torsade, fastened with a Spanish comb. **1923** M. KENNEDY *Ladies of Lyndon* iv. 234 Could you find my Spanish comb? And..that black lace shawl. **1975** *Times* 23 Aug. 7/2 She hoped her mother would let her wear a Spanish comb she had rashly bought. **1931** K. BOYLE *Plagued by Nightingale* xvi. 137 He was doing a lively Spanish dance to the piercing screams of their laughter. **1974** W. FOLEY *Child in Forest* 20 Our elder sister..once did a 'Spanish' dance on the end of the bed, with a cracked soap-dish for a castanet. **1948** 'LA MERI' *Spanish Dancing* i. 1 There are great Spanish dancers, male and female, who are not Spanish. *Ibid.* 4 Hermetic Spain is that promised land to which we go to find..the greatest..Spanish dancing in the world. **1980** A. CORNELISEN *Torregreca* vi. 129 At *Carnevale*..Maria made "Spanish dancers'" dresses for herself and her little brother. **1918** W. OWEN *Let.* 24 June (1967) 560 About 30 officers are smitten with the Spanish Flu. **1937** K. BLIXEN *Out of Africa* II. v. 161 When we had the Spanish Flu on the farm, Farah was..shivering with fever. **1979** D. WILLIAMS *Genesis & Exodus* xi. 213 Those who had survived 1914–18 and the plague of Spanish flu that followed. **1902** F. C. MORSE *Furnit. of Olden Time* vi. 151 The chair..is of the style called Queen Anne. It has Spanish feet. **1923** J. C. ROGERS *English Furnit.* II. ii. 56 Legs also were given a sudden broadening like an inverted cup... In some cases there was the carved 'Spanish' foot. **1975** *Country Life* 29 May (Suppl.) 40h (Advt.), Early 16th century Virginia walnut gateleg table with..Spanish feet. **1862** G. BORROW *Wild Wales* i. 10 Playing remarkably well on the guitar—not the trumpery German thing so called—but the real Spanish guitar. **1934** S. R. NELSON *All about Jazz* ii. 54 The Spanish Guitar, with its resonant tone and range, has created a minor revolution in the ranks of the fretted instrument players. **1961** A. BIRCH in A. Baines *Mus. Instruments through Ages* vii. 168 At some point during the sixteenth century a fifth course became standard for guitar in Spain... It was this new five-course instrument which was to carry the name of 'Spanish guitar'. **1784** E. SHERIDAN *Jrnl.* 1 Oct. (1960) 26, I found a Spanish hat was what I must bye... Even silk Balloons are almost out—I have not seen a Cap since I came. **1840** THACKERAY in *Fraser's Mag.* XXI. 688/1 A ricketty lay-figure, in a Spanish hat and cloak. **1882** C. M. YONGE *Unknown to History* II. iv. 47 Captain Fortescue..a long plume in his Spanish hat. **1960** C. W. CUNNINGTON et al. *Dict. Eng. Costume* 201/2 *Spanish hat*,..a large hat of velvet, satin or sarcenet, the brim evasé, trimmed with feathers. **1980** A. CRAWLEY *Dial 200–200* xi. 119 Maria, looking fabulous in her white satin bolero, tight trousers and black Spanish hat. **1918** *Policeman's Monthly* Oct. 4/2 The members of the Hartford department comprise the motor-cycle squad, one of whom was a victim of Spanish influenza this week. **1940** *N. & Q.* 30 Mar. 218/1 The ravages of the 'Spanish influenza' which, between 1918 and 1922, caused four times as many deaths as those caused by the last war. **1976** BOTHAM & DONNELLY *Valentino* viii. 64 The worst Spanish influenza epidemic since the turn of the century had swept through California. **1886** S. T. RORER *Mrs. Rorer's Philadelphia Cook Bk.* 260 (*heading*) Spanish omelet. **1935** S. LEWIS *It can't happen Here* xxv. 270 One eye was..so surrounded with bruised flesh that..it looked like a Spanish omelet. **1974** A. WILLIAMS *Gentleman Traitor* xv. 248 He..had the African cook prepare him a Spanish omelette. [**1904** F. E. KIDDER *Architect's & Builder's Pocket-bk.* (ed. 14) III. 1430 Galvanized-iron tiles of the 'Spanish' pattern.] **1913** —— *Building-Construction & Superintendence* (ed. 9) II. iv. 278 The rafters..are covered with Ludovici interlocking Spanish tiles set on the 'shiplap' roof-boarding. **1956** E. MOLLOY *Builders' & Decorators' Ref. Bk.* XVII. 3 The English pantile..is a descendant of the Spanish tile.., also called the over-and-under tile. **1979** *Tucson* (Arizona) *Citizen* (Advt. Suppl.) 28 Apr. 16/4 High beamed ceilings, brick floors, French doors, and Spanish tile all help in adding southwestern flavor to a contemporary look. **1967** *Sunday Times* (Colour Suppl.) 21 May 39 They never seem to get Spanish tummy, and their children are never overtired brats. **1968** A. BROWN *Slay me Suddenly* ix. 129 'Where's Herbert?' 'Vomiting... Spanish tummy, I suppose.' **1937** H. NICOLSON *Diary* 27 July (1966) 310 He [*sc.* Anthony Eden] thinks that the Spanish War will last another year. **1977** C. MCCARRY *Secret Lovers* x. 130 Is it a good book? You said you were in the Spanish war.

8. a. (*c*) **Spanish Merino** = MERINO 1; **Spanish sheep,** (i) = MERINO 1 (earlier example); (ii) = *JACOB 4.

1788 W. B. CONYNGHAM *Let.* 28 June in H. B. Carter *His Majesty's Spanish Flock* (1964) iii. 60 In answer to what Evidence I have relative to the success of my Cross from the Spanish sheep I have..the greatest Reason to believe that the Breed may be greatly improved. **1802** F. L. HUMPHREYS *Life D. Humphreys* II. 346 A Gold Medal..is presented to you..for your patriotic exertions in introducing into New-England one hundred of the Spanish Merino breed of Sheep. **1891** R. WALLACE *Rural Economy Austral. & N.Z.* xxvi. 357 The Spanish Merino is a sheep of large size, producing a superior quality of strong combing wool. **1913** Spanish sheep [see *JACOB 4]. **1964** H. B. CARTER *His Majesty's Spanish Flock* p. x, These were the men who..transformed the Spanish Merino from an envied monopoly of one nation into the essential foundation of the modern world trade in wool. **1974** *Times* 25 Nov. 3/3 There are now about 150 registered flocks [of Jacob sheep] in Britain, comprising 3,000 spotty sheep, also known as Spanish or piebald.

9. Spanish beard (earlier example); **Spanish bluebell** = *Spanish squill* below; **Spanish cedar,** a species of Central American cedar, esp. *Cedrela mexicana*, or its timber; **Spanish dagger:** also more generally, one of several species of *Yucca*, esp. *Y. gloriosa*; (earlier and later examples); **Spanish harebell** = *Spanish squill* below; **Spanish moss** (earlier example); **Spanish squill,** a bulbous plant, *Endymion hispanicus* (formerly *Scilla hispanica*), bearing loose racemes of blue, pink, or white bell-shaped flowers; (earlier and later examples); **Spanish stopper** = *gurgeon stopper* s.v. *GURGEON; cf. STOPPER *sb.* 8.

1763 tr. *La Page du Pratz's Hist. Louisiana* II. iv. 37 The other excrescence is commonly found upon trees near the banks of rivers and lakes. It is called Spanish beard. **1924** L. H. BAILEY *Man. Cultivated Plants* 164 Spanish Bluebell..fl[ower]s blue to rose-purple, usually a dozen or more, ascending or nodding in an open raceme. **1979** *Guardian* 5 June 10/1 Large white butterflies..thrusting their long tongues into the Spanish bluebells. **1907** Spanish cedar [see *cigar-box* s.v. *CIGAR 2]. **1947** J. C. RICH *Materials & Methods of Sculpture* x. 287 Spanish cedar is not a true cedar variety, but the wood is favored by some sculptors for carving. **1972** *Handbk. of Hardwoods* (Forest Prod. Res. Lab.) (ed. 2) 53 'Central American cedar' is sometimes called 'Spanish cedar' in reference to the former Spanish colonies. **1859** A. VAN BUREN *Sojourn in South* 108 A tall 'Spanish dagger' stood leaning its crested head. **1939** G. B. PICKWELL *Deserts* 25/1 Spanish daggers bloom in deserts. **1975** *Islander* (Victoria, B.C.) 3 Aug. 3/4 The Spanish Dagger, with fruits that are eaten raw, baked on hot stones, made into jelly or dried for winter use. **1808** *Curtis's Bot. Mag.* XXVIII. 1102 (*heading*) Spanish Harebell. **1823** E. JAMES *Acct. Exped. Rocky Mts.* III. 220 The Spanish moss disappears northwardly of the 33d degree of north latitude. **1790** *Curtis's Bot. Mag.* IV. 128 (*heading*) Spanish Squill. **1977** *Chicago Tribune* 2 Oct. XI. 13/2 Late—Spanish squill..and double late tulips. **1883** G. O. SHIELDS *Rustlings in Rockies* xxi. 195 Within the space of this five acres may be found ..Spanish stoppor [*sic*]. **1908, 1921** Spanish stopper [see *GURGEON].

10. *Spanish-looking, -surnamed* adjs.

1944 N. COWARD *Star Quality* (1951) 85 Rather a good Spanish-looking sideboard. **1976** *Billings* (Montana) *Gaz.* 20 June 2-A/1 In what was called the first tabulation of Latino 'segregation trends', the study also said segregation of Spanish-surnamed pupils increased in the 1970s in all regions of the nation. **1981** R. RENDELL *Put on by Cunning* vii. 65 A dark, Spanish-looking girl.

B. *sb.* or *ellipt.* **2. a.** Delete *rare*$^{-1}$ and add later examples.

1832 W. IRVING in P. M. Irving *Life & Lett. Washington Irving* (1863) III. 43 The levee..presents the most whimsical groups of people of all nations, castes, and colors—French, Spanish, half-breeds, [etc.]. **1880** *News & Press* (Cimarron, New Mexico) 24 June 2/2 The famous Pecos Church, built by the Spanish in 1680. **1932** [see *MOMENT *sb.* 1 d]. **1962** *Amer. Speech* XXXVII. 207 English speakers [in northern Colorado] refer to Spanish speakers as *Spanish*. The word *Spaniard* is not used.

Hence **Spa·nishness, Spa·nishry,** the quality of being Spanish; **Spa·nishy** *a.*, of a Spanish type or character.

1922 JOYCE *Ulysses* 273 Big Spanishy eyes goggling at nothing. **1957** *American Anthropologist* LIX. 818 Spanish-speaking Venezuelans and 'Spanishy' local-born people. **1960** L. DURRELL in *N.Y. Times Bk. Rev.* 12 June VII. 1/1 We travel really to try and get to grips with this mysterious quality of 'Greekness' or 'Spanishness'. **1963** *Times Lit. Suppl.* 17 May 356/5 This intense 'Spanishry' of Unamuno's..may be a reason..for his comparative neglect in this country. **1965** *Listener* 25 Nov. 873/2 In the company of the desolate *Gigues*, even Iberia takes on a less obvious Spanishry. **1977** V. S. PRITCHETT *Gentle Barbarian* iii. 41 Her Spanishness had its Islamic roots. **1979** B. MALAMUD *Dubin's Lives* vii. 228 She's been reading Spanish love poems... Her voice sounds Spanishy.

Spanisher (spæ·nɪʃəɪ). *colloq. rare.* [f. SPANISH *a.* + -ER[1].] A Spaniard.

1910 KIPLING *Rewards & Fairies* 293 The Spanishers had shut down all their Dutch ports against us English. **1940** [see *AIM *v.* 5 b].

spank, *v.*[1] Add: **1. d.** *N.Z. colloq.* To milk (a cow).

1897 I. SCOTT *How I stole 10,000 Sheep* ii. 8 We got on pretty well and spanked, *i.e.* milked, his cows for him night and morning. **1948** D. W. BALLANTYNE *Cunninghams* II. ix. 199 They spanked cows and built fences.

spanker[1]. Add: **3. b.** In full *spanker mast.* The fourth (or fifth) mast of a ship with four or more masts.

1853 D. MCLEAN *Great Republic* 17 The ship has 4 masts, the after one named the spanker mast. **1892** *Nautical Mag.* June 546 During the first four years of the four-posters, the 'after mizzen' and 'spanker mast' were sometimes heard of. **1902** [see *PUSHER 2 b]. **1946** *Amer. Neptune* VI. 138/1 Mr. Bush called the fourth mast the 'jigger' and the fifth the 'spanker', the reverse of the usual nomenclature. **1970** H. CHEVALIER *Last Voyage of Rosamond* 37 We soon not only learned the names of the four masts—the foremast, the mainmast, the mizzen and the spanker.

spanker[2]. (Later example.)

1931 K. BOYLE *Plagued by Nightingale* iv. 28 Washerwomen bending over the stream..and with wooden spankers beating the life out of dish-cloths.

spanking, *vbl. sb.* Add: Also *fig.*
1922 H. CRANE *Let.* 25 Feb. (1965) 80 Your translations amuse me without interesting me as thoroughly as your nicely administered spanking of McAlmon. **1978** *Times Lit. Suppl.* 1 Dec. 1393/1 A. A. Milne's Winnie-the-Pooh stories receive a monstrous spanking for their promotion of snobbery and imperialist values.

spanking, *ppl. a.* Add: **5.** Used as *adv.* Very, exceedingly; esp. as *spanking new*, brand-new. Cf. SPAN-NEW *a. colloq.*
1886 H. BAUMANN *Londinismen* 188/2 A spanking fine dinner. **1905** *Dial. Notes* III. 71 *Bran spankin' new*,.. absolutely new. **1925** F. SCOTT FITZGERALD *Great Gatsby* i. 6 The [house]..on my right was a colossal affair.. spanking new under a thin beard of raw ivy. **1959** *Weekly Times* (Melbourne) 30 Sept. 1 (Advt.), Imagine that great day..when you take delivery of your new working partner: a spanking new Ferguson 35. **1972** *Newsweek* 10 Jan. 34/2 The spanking new city of Brasília was carved painfully out of the wilderness. **1977** *Time* 19 Dec. 12/1 The spanking-white train chugged into Reading station. **1979** *Radio Times* 5–11 May 4/1 Luxurious surroundings at Lewisham's spanking new leisure centre. **1979** W. STYRON *Sophie's Choice* vii. 164 On the driveway there now rested a spanking clean and polished Cadillac sedan.

spankled, *ppl. a.* (Later example.)
1866 G. M. HOPKINS *Jrnls. & Papers* (1959) 143 Carnations..have their tongue-shaped petals powdered with spankled red glister.

spanned (spænd), *a. Biol.* [f. SPAN *sb.*[1] + -ED[2].] Of a culture of cells or micro-organisms: having a restricted lifespan; unable to propagate asexually without limit.
1968 *Exper. Cell Res.* XLIX. 116 To produce 'spanned' amoebae the nutritional state of amoebae must be altered for a protracted period. **1971** J. Z. YOUNG *Introd. Study Man* xxii. 293 Transfer of a normal nucleus into spanned cytoplasm produced resumed logarithmic growth, and a spanned nucleus in normal cytoplasm produced the spanned condition. **1973** *Nature* 22 June 444/1 The switch from a 'spanned' culture to one that is 'immortal' does not necessarily signify a qualitative change in other cellular properties.

spanner[1]. Add: **2. b.** Colloq. phr. *to throw a spanner in the works* and varr.: to cause disruption, to interfere with the smooth running of something. Cf. *monkey-wrench* s.v. *MONKEY *sb.* 17 a.
1934 WODEHOUSE *Right Ho, Jeeves* xi. 142 He should have had sense enough to see that he was throwing a spanner into the works. **1939** A. RANSOME *Secret Water* i. 18 We can't go. It's all off. The First Lord's chucked a spanner in the works. **1946** D. L. SAYERS *Unpopular Opinions* 111 She was in love with Leicester—why didn't she marry him? Well, for the very same reason that numberless kings have not married their lovers—because it would have thrown a spanner into the wheels of the State machine. **1959** *News Chron.* 10 July 4/1 Mr. Cousins has thrown a spanner into the Labour Party's works. **1960** R. EAST *Kingston Black* ix. 90 My department might be able to throw a spanner into the works—if necessary. **1977** *Time Out* 17–23 June 5/4 Either way, the 60 workers occupying the factory have put a spanner in the works.
4. *attrib.* and *Comb.*, as **spanner tight** *a.*, of a nut: as tight as can be secured manually with a spanner; **spanner wrench** *U.S.*, a non-adjustable spanner.
1925 *Morris Owner's Man.* 53 The nuts should always be kept (small) spanner tight. **1931** *Daily Express* 31 Jan. 3/6 Even where the nut was absolutely spanner tight. **1940** *Sun* (Baltimore) 30 Mar. 20/1 The fuel door..was bolted closed the night before the ship sank, but was found open with a spanner wrench beside it when salvagers examined the sunken vessel. **1969** *Publ. Amer. Dial Soc.* LII. 35 *Spanner wrench*,..a wrench having a fixed distance between its jaws which fits on the hose couplings and is used to tighten or loosen connections.

spanners (spæ·nəɪz), *sb. pl.* Chiefly *dial.* [Pl. of *spanner*, f. SPAN *sb.*[1] or *v.*[1] + -ER[1]: cf. SPANNER[3].] A game of marbles (see quot. 1881). Also **spa·nnims.**
1847 J. O. HALLIWELL *Dict. Archaic & Provinc. Words* II. 779/1 *Spannims*, a game at marbles played in the eastern parts of England. **1881** *Cassell's Bk. Sports & Pastimes* 250 Spanners. This is a good simple game for two players. Player No. 1 shoots off his taw, player No. 2 following suit, it being his object either to hit his opponent's taw with his own, or to place his own within a span of it. **1903** *J. Strutt's Sports & Pastimes of People of England* (new ed.) IV. iv. 304 The following is a list of the present (1902) best known marble games:—Bounce About,..Handers,..Pyramid,..Spanners. **1948** J. L. BAILES *Vocab. Marbles* in *Trans. Yorks. Dial. Soc.* VIII. 23 *Spannims*, sb., E. Ang., the game of hundreds.

spanning, *ppl. a.* Add: **2.** *Math.* Of a subgraph, esp. one that is a tree: that includes and connects every vertex of a graph.
1956 *Proc. Amer. Math. Soc.* VII. 49 The set of edges eventually chosen must form a spanning tree of *G*, and in fact it forms a shortest spanning tree. **1965** BUSACKER & SAATY *Finite Graphs & Networks* i. 20 A spanning tree is a maximal subgraph of a connected graph which contains no circuits and is a minimal subgraph which joins all vertices. **1972** R. J. WILSON *Introd. Graph Theory* iv. 46 Given any connected graph *G*, we can choose a circuit and remove one of its edges, the resulting graph remaining connected... We repeat this procedure with one of the remaining circuits, continuing until there are no circuits left. The graph which remains will be a tree which connects all the vertices of *G*; it is called a spanning tree of *G*... More generally, if *G* now denotes an arbitrary graph with..*k* components, we can carry out the above procedure on each component of *G*, the result being called a spanning forest (or skeleton).

spanspek (spa·nspek). *S. Afr.* Also **spanspec, sponspe(c)k.** [ad. Afrikaans *spaanspek* sweet melon, f. Du. *Spaans(ch)e* Spanish + *spek* bacon.] = CANTALOUP in Dict. and Suppl.
[**1731** G. MEDLEY tr. *Kolb's Descr. Cape Good Hope* II. 277 *Melo Hispanicus.* i.e. The Spanish or Musk-Melon. The Musk Melons, produc'd at the Cape, are as good as those produc'd in Spain. The Cape-Europeans call 'em Spanish Bacon.] **1886** G. A. FARINI *Through Kalahari Desert* v. 61 Mr. Barlett came and asked if I would like to buy any musk-melons (*spanspeck*). **1913** J. J. DOKE *Secret City* 78 The ground was cumbered by water-melons and spanspeks. **1951** R. CAMPBELL *Light on Dark Horse* iv. 70 The district is..scarcely excelled for the size and succulence of its..spanspec, watermelons, strawberries, [etc.]. **1958** *Cape Times* 12 Dec. 11/4 The always-popular sweet melon—spanspek—is not expected in quantities till the New Year. **1971** *Fair Lady* 10 Nov. 111 Baked egg custard/or Medium slice sponspek melon. **1975** *Cape Times* 13 Jan. 2 A Paarl spanspek exporter said in an interview at the weekend that these prices.. were paid only at the beginning of the season.

Spansule (spæ·nsiūl). Also **spansule.** [f. SPAN *sb.*[1] + CAP)SULE.] A proprietary name for a capsule that when swallowed releases a drug steadily for several hours, or that releases various drugs at prearranged times. Cf. *sustained-release* s.v. *SUSTAINED *ppl. a.* 1 c.
1954 *Official Gaz.* (U.S. Patent Office) 2 Mar. 18/2 Smith Kline & French Laboratories, Philadelphia... *Spansule*... For capsules containing multiples of specially coated globules..and providing for the gradual release of a medicament in the gastro-intestinal tract. **1954** *Trade Marks Jrnl.* 6 Oct. 1000/1 *Spansule*... Pharmaceutical preparations... Smith, Kline & French International Co. **1955** OSOL & FARRAR *Dispensatory of U.S.A.* (ed. 25) 89/1 Dexedrine Sulfate Spansules contain 15 mg. of the dextro salt in the form of tiny pellets, of which there are over a hundred in each capsule, having varying disintegration times so as to release the drug uniformly over a period of 8 to 10 hours. **1971** C. WILLIAMS *And Deep Blue Sea* (1972) ix. 102 Our labs came up several years ago with a timed-release spansule; the opiate takes effect in about twenty minutes and then an aphrodisiac eight hours later. **1974** 'J. BLACK' *Oil* (1975) IV. viii. 349 The two men had stayed up the remainder of the night, swallowing Dexamyl spansules while they meticulously went over all that Needham would have to do.

spanwise (spæ·nwəiz), *a. Aeronaut.* [f. SPAN *sb.*[1] + -WISE.] Following the direction of the span of a wing or other aerofoil.
1946 *Jrnl. Brit. Interplanetary Soc.* VI. 95 The phenomenon of tip stall is brought about by spanwise drift in the boundary layer over a swept wing. **1955** J. SHAPIRO *Princ. Helicopter Engin.* vi. 360 Spanwise mass distribution in uniform section blades..gives rise to considerable bending moments when the blade is stiff. **1967** *Jane's Surface Skimmer Systems 1967–8* 121/2 A drive pad.. enables the engines of a multi-engined aircraft to be coupled together by spanwise shafting. **1977** *Jrnl. R. Soc. Arts* CXXV. 350/1 A swept wing was made with narrow spanwise slots on the surface.

spar, *sb.*[1] Add: **4. b.** *Aeronaut.* Each of the main members of a wing on older aircraft, which run transversely to the fuselage and carry the ribs.
1866 *1st Rep. Aëronaut. Soc.* 35 But with all such arrangements the apparatus must fail—*length of wing is indispensable!* and a spar thirty feet long must be strong, heavy, and cumbrous. **1895** *Amer. Engineer & Railroad Jrnl.* Aug. 387/2 Being caught by a side puff, the machine was blown over, and the front starboard spar was too much broken to mend on the field. **1919**, etc. [see *RIB *sb.*[1] 11 e]. **1930** NAYLER & OWER *Aviation of To-Day* vii. 154 The modern steel spar of an aeroplane wing..can be treated by calculation. **1960** C. H. GIBBS-SMITH *Aeroplane* xiii. 96 In 1919, he [*sc.* Adolph Rohrbach] started building smooth-skinned metal surfaces, combined with metal box-spar construction in the wings, thus allowing more stresses to be borne by the surfaces.
4*. *Oil Industry.* Also **Spar, SPAR.** An installation intended to float above a submarine well-head and provide large storage tanks and various service facilities, esp. for loading tankers.
1973 *Times* 31 Oct. (Offshore Supply Suppl.) p. iii/2 The concrete spar is anchored above a submarine manifold with pipelines from production platforms. The lower part of the spar is a 300,000-barrel capacity storage chamber. **1975** *Offshore Progress—Technol. & Costs* (Shell Briefing Service) 18 One of the newest deep water concepts is the Spar—floating storage and loading terminal all in one. **1976** *Offshore Platforms & Pipelining* 218 The SPAR has been designed to maintain a constant draft in both the loaded and ballasted conditions. **1979** *North Sea Progress* (Shell Internat. Petroleum Co.) 8 Other methods involve ..the use of custom-built SPAR-type semi-submersible production units.
6. spar tree *Forestry*, a tree or other tall structure to which cables are attached for hauling logs.
1925[see *high lead* s.v. *HIGH *a.* 21]. **1965** [see *high line* s.v. *HIGH *a.* 21]. **1980** *Beautiful Brit. Columbia* Fall 40 Atop the cliff stands a long-disused spar tree; close by the bay are the broken bricks, cement and tile that testify to a long-abandoned project here.

spar, *sb.*[3] Add: **5.** *Comb.*, as **sparmate** *U.S.*, a sparring partner.
1937 *Sun* (Baltimore) 30 Aug. 15/2 Ten days ago one of his sparmates opened up a deep cut under his eye with a punch. **1950** J. DEMPSEY *Championship Fighting* 15, I found plenty of kid sparmates. **1974** *Los Angeles Times* 13 Oct. III. 13/3 Chartchai, three-time world flyweight champion, has been staying at a Tokyo hotel,..with his wife and his manager and his wife, sparmate and trainer.

spar, *v.*[3] Add: **2. c.** (Earlier examples.) Also with *off.*
1843 T. TALBOT *Jrnls.* (1931) 4 [We became] finally the prey of an insidious sand-bar, where after hours of sparring,..we again resume the slow ascent. **1875** 'MARK TWAIN' in *Atlantic Mag.* May 568/1 Maybe she 'strikes and swings'. Then she has to while away several hours (or days) sparring herself off.

sparagmite (spæ·răgməit). *Geol.* [ad. G. *sparagmit* (J. Esmark *Reise von Christiania nach Drontheim*, etc. (1829) 25), f. Gr. σπάραγμα fragment, piece torn off: see -ITE[1].] A generic term for the feldspathic sandstones (chiefly arkoses), conglomerates, and other fragmental rocks which occur in late Pre-Cambrian formations in Scandinavia.
[**1866** *Geol. Mag.* III. 384 (*table*) 'Spragmitic' strata—conglomerates, Schists, Dolomitic beds.] **1882** A. GEIKIE *Text-bk. Geol.* 657 In central and northern Norway the Archæan gneiss is overlaid by reddish and grey sandstones and conglomerates (Sparagmite), with schists, quartzites, and limestones. **1930** PEACH & HORNE *Geol. Scotland* iii. 72 The Sparagmite of Scandinavia is an arkose resembling the dominant type of the Torridon Sandstone. **1979** *Nature* 25 Jan. 290/1 Micaceous meta-arkoses (sparagmites) have, in places, a basal conglomerate resting unconformably on the Basal gneisses.

‖ **sparagmos** (spăræ·gmǫs). [a. Gr. σπαραγμός tearing, rending.] The tearing apart of a hero, or his ritualized death in an analogous manner as represented in some tragedies or myths when it symbolizes part of the cycle of death and rebirth. Also *fig.*
1949 F. FERGUSSON *Idea of Theater* i. 32 The ritual had ..its *Sparagmos*, in which the royal victim was literally or symbolically torn asunder. **1957** N. FRYE *Anat. of Criticism* iii. 192 The disappearance of the hero, a theme which often takes the form of *sparagmos* or tearing to pieces. Sometimes the hero's body is divided among his followers. **1961** J. HOLLOWAY *Story of Night* vii. 130 The death of Coriolanus is almost as much a *sparagmos* of the ritual victim by the whole social group as was possible on the stage. **1977** *Dædalus* Summer 62 Not that conferences alone can do this, but they are signals that the reconstitution of anthropology at a higher level under the aegis of processualism is under way. Otherwise the centrifugal drift, indeed, the suicidal sparagmos, will go on and on.

spare, *sb.*[1] Add: **3. a.** (Later examples.) Also *spec.* in *pl.*, spare parts.
1907 C. W. BROWN *Petrol Engine* i. 11 The manufacture is simplified and the number of 'spares' which the owner of a car is called upon to carry considerably reduced. **1914** *Vanity Fair* Jan. 95/1 Some ingenious modifications have been devised for taking care of the 'spare'. **1930** A. P. HERBERT *Water Gipsies* xxiii. 334 I'll put you to bed in the spare, and let nobody come near you. **1957** *Practical Wireless* XXXIII. 701/2 A suitable piece of aluminium can probably be found in almost any spares box. **1976** M. MAGUIRE *Scratchproof* v. 66 Did it usually take him an hour to put on the spare? Would he mind if I looked at the punctured tyre? **1979** B. PARVIN *Deadly Dyke* v. 23 A small room with a single bed..had never been used... It would have been thought of as the spare.
b. *slang.* An unattached woman, esp. one available for casual sex. Freq. in phr. *a bit of spare.*
1969 J. BOLAND *Shakespeare Curse* xxi. 169 Kelley was a man whose wife was in an advanced state of pregnancy. You think he'd turn down a bit of spare if it was offered to him? **1974** P. CAVE *Dirtiest Picture Postcard* x. 61 The men would not have to bother with the married girls anyway. There's plenty of spare about. **1978** R. BUSBY *Garvey's Code* iv. 44, I..got the impression Maurice was ..on the look-out for a bit of spare... Some of the girls we get in here..don't leave much to the imagination.
4. For *U.S.* read orig. *U.S.* and add earlier and later examples. Also in skittles.
1843 *Knickerbocker* XXII. 327 His bowling at nine-pins was the very perfection of carelessness. He was never guilty of a 'spare'. **1976** *Bridgwater Mercury* 21 Dec., Keith Pollard, whose top-of-the-board 84 included four spares, led Alleycats to a runaway home win..in a first division Puriton and District Skittles League Game.

spare, *a.* and *adv.* Add: **I. 1. a.** (*a*) *spare tyre*, (i) an extra tyre carried in a motor vehicle for emergencies; similarly, *spare wheel*; also (ii) *transf.*, a roll of fat around the stomach (*colloq.*).
1917 KIPLING *Diversity of Creatures* 162 The policeman laid his hand on the rim of the right driving-door (Woodhouse carries his spare tyres aft). **1920** 'O. DOUGLAS' *Penny Plain* xxiii. 267 It was a tyre gone... Stark

put on the spare wheel and they started again. **1961** *Harper's Bazaar* Dec. 43/1 The deep diaphragm section slims you... That 'spare-tyre' has vanished! **1971** D. DEVINE *Dead Trouble* v. 48 My spare tyre keeps me warm. You're too skinny. **1972** *Country Life* 7 Dec. 1592/3 The luggage boot is..fairly well filled by the spare wheel. **1977** *Lancashire Life* Nov. 153/1 There is no need for a spare tyre to clutter up the Mini's limited boot space.

(*d*) *spare room*, a room not regularly used, esp. a bedroom reserved for visitors.

1814 JANE AUSTEN *Mansfield Park* I. iii. 54 The absolute necessity of a spare-room for a friend was now never forgotten. **1837** *Southern Lit. Messenger* III. 333 One of the third-story rooms we must keep for a spare room. **1855** *Knickerbocker* XLVI. 380 They have stolen away into the spare-room, otherwise, parlor. **1904** A. DALE *Wanted: a Cook* 332 The wine-cellar was under the bed in the spare-room. **1928** GALSWORTHY *Swan Song* III. ix. 280 He spied a spare-room window open at the top. **1953** E. SIMON *Past Masters* III. 169 The spare room, newly done up, was frequently inhabited by..distinguished visitors. **1977** J. PORTER *Who the Heck is Sylvia?* ix. 79 Her habit of knocking on the spare-room door before entering.

e. *colloq.* Of persons: off-duty, idle (cf. sense 1 a (*c*) in Dict.). Also, useless, superfluous.

1919 *Athenæum* 1 Aug. 695/2 'To be spare' is to be temporarily off duty. **1925** FRASER & GIBBONS *Soldier & Sailor Words & Phrases* 266 *Spare, to look*, to be idle: not engaged on any particular job. **1936** J. CURTIS *Gilt Kid* xv. 154 We can't stand around here spare... Come on. **1970** 'D. HALLIDAY' *Dolly & Cookie Bird* viii. 117 Janey stayed there with her manicured hand on his brow..and I felt a bit spare.

f. Phr. *to go spare*: (*a*) to be unemployed; (*b*) to become infuriated or distraught. *colloq.*

c **1942** R. DIMBLEBY *Let.* in J. Dimbleby *Richard Dimbleby* (1975) vii. 163 I'd be grateful if your team would remember an at least practised broadcaster who appears to be 'going spare'! **1958** F. NORMAN *Bang to Rights* 169 When he saw what I had done he went spare. **1969** J. N. SMITH *Is he Dead, Miss ffinch?* xv. 95 The train had just gone. His lordship nearly went spare. **1975** T. HEALD *Deadline* iv. 68 What's the time? Monica will be going spare.

II. 4. e. Of style: unadorned, bare, simple.

1965 *Listener* 7 Oct. 552/2 The narrative..was spare, precise, almost a little cold, and made its tale of muddle and butchery thereby the more devastating. **1966** *Ibid.* 12 May 702/2 We feel the participants to be in agony and it is impossible to remain indifferent to them. This achievement has something to do with the spare, angular dialogue. **1977** *Times* 23 May 25/1 Tom Courtenay gives a frighteningly spare performance in One Day in the Life of Ivan Denisovich.

III. 8. *spare-bodied* (later example); **spare-time** *a.*, that is done in one's spare time; operating in or occupying spare time.

1936 'M. INNES' *Death at President's Lodging* ii. 39 The spare-bodied man that he was. **1931** Spare-time [see *PART-TIME *a.*]. **1955** BLUNDEN *Addresses on General Subjects* 24 This poet [*sc.* Shelley] almost achieved, as one of his spare-time labours, the establishment of the first steamship service in the Mediterranean. **1973** A. HOLDEN *Girl on Beach* 143 He really is a professional lawyer after all, and merely a spare-time amateur art critic. **1978** *Nagel's Encycl.-Guide: China* 320 The 'Spare Time Industrial University' at Shanghai.

spare, *v.*[1] Add: **I. 1. b.** *spare me* (or *my*) *days!* an exclamatory ejaculation. *Austral.* and *N.Z. colloq.*

1916 C. J. DENNIS *Songs of Sentimental Bloke* 16 The music of the sorft an' barmy breeze... Aw, spare me days! *c* **1926** 'MIXER' *Transport Workers' Song Bk.* 13 Yet you'll find when work is busy, Spare me days, we're slipping back. **1967** *Coast to Coast 1965–6* 134 Spare me days, you go and toil your guts out [etc.]. **1970** K. GILES *Death in Church* iv. 101 He..gave me one and, spare me days, I almost certainly have it.

spare part. [f. SPARE *a.* + PART *sb.*] **1.** A duplicate of a part of a machine kept in readiness to replace a loss, failure, or breakage. Freq. *pl.*

1888 J. G. HORNER *Lockwood's Dict. Mech. Engin.* 336 It is customary to include spare parts with work which is despatched to the colonies and with sea-going engines. **1904** *C. B. Fry's Mag.* June 294/2 In addition to the actual trying of the racing car..there is a great deal of detail work in connection with supplies of..spare parts. **1931** *Proc. Inst. Automobile Engineers* XXV. 106 In some cases spare-part lists hardly exist, very largely due no doubt to rapid change of design. **1936** E. WAUGH *Waugh in Abyssinia* v. 182 We would not take the lorry until it was fully equipped... He could not get the spare parts on credit. **1971** *Engineering* Apr. 31/1 Quick and easy overhaul and spare-part replacement. **1972** *Guardian* 18 Oct. 14/2 Some agent for British cars abroad is heard complaining..that he can make no profit because he sells no spare parts.

2. *transf.* A visceral organ or other bodily part from a donor, or a prosthetic device, which is to be used to replace a defective organ, etc., in a person. Freq. *attrib.*, as *spare-part(s) surgery*. *colloq.*

1944 [see *BANK *sb.*[3] 7 f]. **1960** S. PLATH *Colossus* 87 The storerooms are full of hearts. This is the city of spare parts. **1963** *Daily Tel.* 21 Sept. 9/5 Spare part surgery is still in its infancy. **1967** *New Scientist* 25 May 449/1 With the technique of kidney transplantation now firmly established..spare-part surgeons are now turning their attention to other organs in the body. **1968** *Guardian* 6 May 8/1 Spare parts surgery is too important to be left to the surgeons alone. **1970** D. J. MARLOWE in *Mystery Writers' Choice 1977* (1977) 4 'Well, what about your body?' I still didn't care for the idea about being used for spare parts. **1977** B. PYM *Quartet in Autumn* ii. 20 She could donate certain organs to assist in research or spare-part surgery.

sparganosis. Add: **3.** Infection with larval tapeworms of the genus *Sparganum.* (The only current sense.)

1928 *Proc. Soc. Exper. Biol. & Med.* XXVI. 254 Sparganosis results from applying frogs infected with these spargana to inflamed and ulcerated areas of the body. **1954** *Amer. Jrnl. Tropical Med. & Hygiene* III. 123 It is probable that human sparganosis is acquired in Korea by the consumption of raw snake, which is a fairly common practice in this area. **1976** EDINGTON & GILLES *Path. in Tropics* (ed. 2) iii. 210 Sparganosis has been reported in man from many tropical countries such as South East Asia, Africa, Madagascar, China, and South America.

sparge, *sb.* Add: **3.** *attrib.*, as **sparge arm** *Brewing*, a sparge pipe used to sprinkle hot water over the malt, usu. arranged to rotate above the tun; **sparge pipe**, a horizontal perforated pipe used to sprinkle or spray water or other liquids, esp. one used to flush a slab urinal.

1947 *Brewing* (ed. 2) ii. 23 The holes in the actual sparge arms have to be made much larger. **1971** J. S. HOUGH et al. *Malting & Brewing Sci.* x. 261 Other rotating machinery within the mash tun comprises sparge arms (which are moved by water pressure) for spraying liquor evenly over the goods. **1910** MAXWELL & BROWN *Encycl. Municipal & Sanitary Engin.* 444/2 *Sparge pipe*, a pipe having fine holes drilled throughout its length so as to deliver a spray of water as is required for flushing. **1948** *Archit. Rev.* CIV. 289 A sparge pipe on the sky-light ridge cools the glass by water spray in summer. *c* **1972** *Shanks* (Barrhead) *Catal.* 93 Chromium plated flush and sparge pipes with clips.

sparge, *v.* Add: **4. b.** To aerate (a liquid) with air (in quot. *absol.*).

1973 *Nature* 23 Feb. 534/1 The *p*H was adjusted to 3·8 with concentrated HCl and aeration and mixing accomplished by sparging with air.

sparger. Add: Also, an appliance for sprinkling a liquid other than water, or for aerating a liquid with air.

1949 E. CHAIN in H. W. Florey et al. *Antibiotics* II. xvii. 700 The fermenters..were made of steel; they contained a sparger for air distribution. *Ibid.*, The air sparger consisted of a ⅜-in. stainless steel pipe bent to form a 12-in. square. **1963** ECKENFELDER & MCCABE *Biol. Waste Treatment* 183 Spargers, each with four 5/16 in. diameter holes radiating horizontally from the center were checked for oxygen absorption efficiency. **1976** *IEEE Spectrum* May 54/2 An early example of..fatigue failure was that of the liquid boron, or 'poison', sparger at the Garigliano Plant of Ente Nazionale per l'Energia Electrica..in Cessa Aurunca, Italy, in 1964.

spargosis. Add: Also *fig.*

1934 'H. MACDIARMID' *Stony Limits & Other Poems* 23 In open country..watching an aching spargosis of stars.

spark, *sb.*[1] Add: **1. f.** Phr. *sparks fly* and varr.: heated words are spoken, friction or excited action occurs.

[**1732** T. FULLER *Gnomologia* 244 When the Heart is a fire, some Sparks will fly out of the Mouth.] **1929** *Amer. Speech* V. 124 It was also said of an angry woman that she will 'make the sparks fly'. **1950** F. STARK *Traveller's Prelude* 182 My sister never hurried and never scolded..while the effect of 'sparks flying' in the next ward reacted on all the men. **1977** *Western Morning News* 1 Sept. 10/3 Robertson scored from the spot, and then sparks really began to fly.

2. d. A trace or dash of spirit, courage, etc. (cf. sense 6 b in Dict.). *to get a spark up* (N.Z. colloq.): to fortify one's spirits with alcohol.

1939 C. BELTON *Outside Law in N.Z.* 50 Today young men who intend going to a dance drink until closing time ..just to get a spark up, they say. **1942** *Sun* (Baltimore) 30 Nov. 15/4 Navy had a spark plug in Hamberg and another in Hume that Army lacked. There was no man on Army's squad able to supply this needed spark. **1949** J. R. COLE *It was so Late* 15 Can't get a spark up on beer tonight. **1977** *Sniffin' Glue* July 11 The estates are dismal but anyone who's got any spark is alive enough to get active and out.

3. b. *divine spark:* a trace of the divine nature in man. Also in trivial use.

1853 LYTTON *My Novel* II. VI. xxi. 180 The divine spark had fled from the human face; the Beast is everywhere growing more and more out of the thing that had been Man. **1920** H. J. LASKI *Let.* 15 May in *Holmes–Laski Letters* (1953) I. 263 They may be stupid, lazy, what you will; but ninety-nine out of every hundred have a divine spark in them somewhere which sympathy and enthusiasm is sure to light. **1932** *Week-End Rev.* 9 Jan. 46/2 She felt she had not got into touch, had not given herself, had not transmitted the divine spark. **1957** *Oxf. Dict. Chr. Ch.* 1218/1 As originally formed, man was a powerless entity who wriggled on the ground like a worm ..until a Divine spark set him on his feet. **1968** F. LUNDBERG *Rich & Super-Rich* xv. 632 (*heading*) The divine spark among the rich.

6. c. *pl.* usu. const. as *sing.* One who works with electrical equipment: a radio operator, an electrician, etc. *slang.*

1914 *Dialect Notes* IV. 151 *Sparks*, wireless operator. **1917** *Wireless World* V. 37 In the Service the regular nickname for wireless telegraphists is graphically expressed as 'Sparks'. **1922** P. F. WESTERMAN *Wireless Officer* iii. 25 A burly, jovial-featured man..greeted Mostyn as he stepped off the gang-plank. 'Hello, you're our Sparks, aren't you?' **1934** *Sun* (Baltimore) 31 Jan. 20/3 'Sparks', the radio operator, was busy at his key. **1938** H. BORUST *In Plain Clothes* xii. 184 Scene shifters, 'sparks' (light men), wardrobe-keepers. **1971** *Guardian* 24 Sept. 12/4, I went to Manchester as a spark's mate—an electrician's mate. **1975** *Listener* 10 Apr. 461/3 Lord Sneaker tells his sparks to wrap up the lights. **1977** M. BABSON *Murder, murder, Little Star* viii. 56 The Technical Crew were called by the names of the jobs they did... Sparks was the electrician, Props was the property master, Camera the cameraman. **1980** R. MITTON *Master & Son* i. 9 Meet Ulrica Halsted..the sexiest Spark that ever went to sea.

d. Short for *spark telegraphy* (cf. senses *7 b, d).

1921 *Wireless World* 2 Apr. 21/1 Commencing by pointing out the advantages and disadvantages of various circuits for the reception of Spark, C. W. and Telephony, Captain Tingey gave many useful hints. **1922** *Ibid.* 15 Apr. 76/2 One ought to..switch that connection on to different places when one is receiving spark or telephony. **1925** *Weekly Dispatch* 22 Nov. 8/2 If the Government were to replace spark by continuous wave the loss on old apparatus could be set aside by the revenue from wireless licences.

7. b. More widely, as *spark discharge(r)*, *frequency*, *-gap* (later examples; also *attrib.*), *source*, *station*, *tester*, *transmitter*.

1848 *Patent Jrnl.* 5 Aug. 266/1 In frictional spark discharges, the consequent shock, light, and other peculiarities are in part owing to waves of..polarization. **1973** L. R. LENTZ et al. in *Automotive Electr. Equipment* (Inst. Mech. Engineers) 63/2 The fuel mixture is ignited prior to the occurrence of the normal spark discharge. **1921** E. E. BUCHER *Pract. Wireless Telegr.* 101 Spark dischargers for radio-telegraphy. **1906** J. A. FLEMING *Princ. Electric Wave Telegr.* ii. 157 The author has..devised the following appliances for measuring spark frequency. **1925** W. GREENWOOD *Wireless Telegr. & Teleph.* iv. 75 If a low spark frequency is required the alternator circuit can be tuned to the alternator frequency, and the spark gap lengthened. **1905** *Electrician* Feb. 614/1 Measurements of spark-gap resistance in wireless telegraph senders. **1935** *Discovery* Aug. 226/1 There are two different types of short-wave generator in actual use, the valve and the spark-gap oscillators. **1967** *New Scientist* 14 Dec. 671/1 The operator closes the discharge switch, and the electric charge in the capacitors leaps across the spark gap. **1944** *Jrnl. Optical Soc. Amer.* XXXIV. 773/2 A type of interrupted spark source involving no mechanical parts has been developed for use in quantitative spectrographic analysis. **1956** *Nature* 4 Feb. 222/1 A high-precision spark source and an optical arrangement containing a rotating mirror are needed. **1913** *Year-Bk. Wireless Telegr. & Teleph.* 401 It does not follow..that a continuous-wave station is immune from interference by a spark station. **1925** *Sci. Abstr.* B. XXVIII. 232 (*heading*) International measurements of the wave-lengths of spark stations. **1925** *Morris Owner's Man.* 84 The motorist should try each plug in turn with the aid of a 'spark tester'. **1916** J. A. FLEMING *Princ. Electric Wave Telegr.* (ed. 3) 671 The types of transmitter employing such condenser discharges are called spark transmitters. **1934** A. L. ALBERT *Electr. Communication* xv. 426 The reception of damped waves from a spark transmitter..is very simple.

c. In other uses, as *spark guard*, *-pistol*, *-shower*, *-storm*; *spark-gushing*, *-sprayed* adjs.

1916 *Daily Colonist* (Victoria, B.C.) 11 July 13/5 (Advt.), Furniture and furnishings..including..fender and spark guard. **1972** *Oxford Times* 14 Jan. 2 A spark guard—of close wire mesh—will prevent sparks from flying out. **1938** S. LESLIE *Film of Memory* 131 The spark-gushing engine passed underfoot. **1938** S. BECKETT *Murphy* ix. 171 Firing a spark-pistol with a kind of despair. **1938** S. SPENDER *Trial of Judge* I. 16 We..motored out..Skidding—spark-showers at corners. **1950** D. GASCOYNE *Vagrant* 28 Till all night's spark-sprayed dome is stunned with quick air-quakes of gold. **1969** G. MACBETH *War Quartet* 47 Here, unspilled, The blood of London lay enchaliced, rich Over the spark-storm.

d. Special Combs.: **spark ball**, a sphere forming one side of a spark gap; **spark chamber** *Physics*, a form of spark counter in which many closely spaced electrodes are used to enable the path of an ionizing particle to be determined; **spark coil**, an induction coil that generates high-voltage pulses from an interrupted low-voltage source, used esp. to energize the sparking plugs in an internal-combustion engine; **spark counter** *Physics* [tr. G. *funkenzähler* (H. Greinacher 1935, in *Helv. Physica Acta* VIII. 266)], a detector for charged particles consisting of two charged electrodes separated by a gas that is ionized by the passage of the particle; **spark erosion** *Engin.*, a method of machining metal in which a series of electric sparks is used to remove droplets from the piece; freq. *attrib.*; hence **spark-erode** *v. trans.*, to machine (a piece) by spark erosion; **spark line**, a spectral line corresponding to an atom in a given state of ionization; **spark machining** *Engin.* = *spark erosion* above; **spark-prop** *Criminals'* *slang*, a diamond pin, a tie-pin; **spark spectrum**, a spectrum produced by an atom in a given state of ionization, commonly excited under laboratory conditions by an electric spark; **spark telegraphy**, an early method of radio-telegraphy in which high-frequency oscillations are set up in a transmitting aerial by the discharge of a highly charged capacitor through a spark gap in series with an inductance connected to the aerial; hence **spark telegraph**.

1902 *Encycl. Brit.* XXXIII. 230/2 The distance at which the effects of the oscillatory spark could be perceived by the aid of the coherer was closely connected with the height of this air-wire or aerial connected to the spark balls and coherer. **1924** O. LODGE *Harmsworth's Wireless Encycl.* III. 1864/2 The object of replacing the pointed ends of the wires by spark balls is to prevent the gradual leaking discharge. **1961** *Rev. Sci. Instruments* XXXII. 482/1 The spark chamber is a direct outgrowth of an older detector called the spark counter. **1974** FRAUENFELDER & HENLEY *Subatomic Physics* iv. 56 Spark chambers have many of the advantages of bubble chambers, and they can be triggered. [**1868** Spark coil: see *SPRENGEL.] **1900** G. D. HISCOX *Horseless Vehicles* vii. 121 The Edison spark coil..is a short, thick coil, which will give a hot, bright spark, and yet will have an instantaneous discharge. **1902** [in Dict., sense 7 b]. **1922** [see *jump-spark, jump spark* s.v. *JUMP-]. **1971** *Sci. Amer.* May 86/2 The ordinary automobile spark coil..is the commonest version of the induction coil. **1935** *Sci. Abstr.* XXXVIII. 718 The general name 'spark counter' is proposed for the new counters devised by the author. **1970** *Nucl. Instruments & Methods* LXXXVII. 181/1 Cylindrical spark counters have been designed that employ boron nitride disks as converters. **1980** J. W. HILL *Intermediate Physics* xxiii. 220 (*heading*) The spark counter. **1960** *Metal Treatment* XXVII. 206/1 When a die showed signs of wear, one must be able to take it out, spark-erode it and replace it. **1955** *Aircraft Production* XVII. 421/1 The process of spark-erosion machining is becoming widely used for special purposes, such as machining holes in tungsten-carbide. **1977** R. B. ROSS *Handbk. Metal Treatments & Testing* 360 Spark erosion is extremely useful where shapes are required in hardened or difficult to machine materials. **1980** *West Lancs. Evening Gaz.* 4 Jan. 10 (Advt.), Familiarity with close tolerance machining and bench work is essential and some experience of spark erosion machining would be an advantage. **1879** *Proc. R. Soc.* XXX. 27 The spark lines are in the sun, but the less refrangible member of the wide triplet and the blue line seen in the flame are absent. **1932** *Ibid.* CXXXIV. 611 It is proposed to give a complete catalogue of the spark lines of arsenic. **1950** *Jrnl. Optical Soc. Amer.* XL. 180/1 By adjusting the conditions of discharge either arc or spark lines may be made to predominate. **1954** *Engineer* 2 July 12/2 Although spark machining may, in theory, be carried out with electrode and workpiece separated only by air, in practice a liquid dielectric is used. **1973** J. G. TWEEDDALE *Materials Technol.* II. vi. 152 Spark machining is applicable only to electrically conducting materials. **1879** *Macmillan's Mag.* Oct. 506/1 My pal said, 'Pipe his spark prop' (diamond pin). **1923** J. C. GOODWIN *Sidelights on Criminal Matters* iii. 32 To steal a tie-pin, or 'spark prop' as it is termed in the slang of thieves, [etc.]. **1873** *Phil. Trans. R. Soc.* CLXIII. 266 (*table*) The spark-spectrum of the chloride. **1905** E. C. C. BALY *Spectroscopy* 374 The induction coil is used..for the production of the so-called spark spectra of substances. **1970** G. K. WOODGATE *Elem. Atomic Struct.* vi. 105 Na I is also called the arc spectrum of sodium, Mg II the first spark spectrum of magnesium and Al III the second spark spectrum of aluminium. **1934** A. L. ALBERT *Electr. Communication* xv. 426/1 (*caption*) The generation of damped waves with a spark telegraph set. **1898** *Ludgate* VII. 78/1 Mr. Marconi, in July, 1897, came to England to introduce his new plan of 'Spark Telegraphy'. **1908** *Rep. Brit. Assoc. Adv. Sci. 1907* 730 A movement which much more nearly corresponds with the actual current in the vertical wire as used in spark telegraphy.

spark, *v.*^{1} Add: **1. a.** *spec.* in *Electr.* To produce or emit an electric spark or sparks by ionization of the medium separating two conductors at different potentials. Also *fig.* in phr. *to spark on all cylinders* = *to function* (etc.) *on all cylinders* s.v. *CYLINDER *sb.* 6.

1884 S. P. THOMPSON *Dynamo-Electr. Machinery* 60 Any dynamo in which the curve of potentials at the commutator presented such irregularities..would probably spark excessively at the collector. **1905** T. H. HAWLEY *Motor Ignition Appliances* iv. 20 If our charge fails to explode or the plug to spark, the fault must usually be sought for elsewhere. **1926** R. W. HUTCHINSON *Wireless* 112 The spark gap consists of two small spheres sparking across the diameters of two larger ones. **1967** L. BACON in L. Holmes *Odhams New Motor Man.* iii. 81 One simple check can clear the whole of the ignition circuit—are the plugs sparking? **1977** M. HINXMAN *One-Way Cemetery* viii. 55 John realized his inspector was sparking on all cylinders. He looked a damned sight fresher than Waller felt.

c. With *over*. To be crossed or connected by a spark as a result of a breakdown in insulation. Also *fig.*

1915 *Standardization Rules Amer. Inst. Electr. Engineers* 48 The voltage at which a given gap sparks over is found by taking the voltage corresponding to the spacing..and multiplying by the correction factor. **1966** R. ARDREY *Territorial Imperative* iii. 88 When antagonists face each other..inhibited from further attack..their energy..'sparks over'—another ethologist's term—into a third instinctual channel which will cause no damage. **1974** *Sci. Amer.* Feb. 78/2 Since the magnets were not designed to work under water many of them sparked over and failed when power was fed into them.

3. d. *fig.* To fire, to inspire; to kindle, to set in motion; *to spark off*, to be the immediate cause of (something hard to control). orig. *U.S.*

1912 L. J. VANCE *Destroying Angel* ii. 21 Abrupt inspiration sparked the imagination of Peter Stark, and he began to sputter with enthusiasm. **1941** *Sun* (Baltimore) 24 Apr. 15/2 He is the type [of ballplayer] that sparks an infield and hustles all of the time. **1947** *Richmond* (Va.) *Times-Dispatch* 1 Dec. 10/1 We hope that circumstances which might well spark another world conflict will not rise in Palestine. **1957** *Economist* 26 Oct. 287/2 Any encroachment on vital western interests is liable to spark off the sort of war that would incinerate communism along with communists. **1962** *Listener* 4 Oct. 501/1 A story has come out of California and sparked the November election campaign, which is now beginning to smoulder and crackle. **1964** *Ann. Reg. 1963* 100 The final decision to end Federation sparked off immediately a new constitutional controversy. **1970** S. L. BARRACLOUGH in I. L. Horowitz *Masses in Lat. Amer.* iv. 158 The more widely distributed post-reform incomes help spark development by changing propensities to invest. **1978** *Dumfries Courier* 20 Oct. 5/1 The club has taken no stand against this sort of behaviour, which can spark off bad behaviour among the spectators. **1979** *IEEE Trans. Professional Communication* XXII. 70/1 Man has always been intrigued by the elusive nature of the brain mechanisms which spark new and unexpected ideas to solve problems. **1981** *Times* 24 July 23/1 Stocks on the New York Stock Exchange closed higher due to a late afternoon rally, sparked by bargain hunting among oil stocks and blue chip issues.

sparker. Add: **3.** A powerful form of sonar apparatus used to investigate solid structures underlying sediment on the sea bed.

1961 *Ann. Reg. 1960* 406 The whole area was surveyed by the newly developed 'sparker' technique, an extension of the echo-sounding method used for charting the sea-bottom. The sparker used an intense sound source (a spark) which enabled the sound wave to penetrate the sea bottom. The sound waves were reflected from the interfaces between different kinds of rock. **1969** J. MAVOR *Voyage to Atlantis* II. iii. 84 The 'sparker' and line hydrophone for listening to the reflected sound signals were the most powerful in the world but required a depth of 60 feet and 150 yards of towline astern. **1974** *Nature* 26 Apr. 745/1 An 8 kJ sparker was also used.

sparking, *vbl. sb.*^{1} Add: **b.** Special Combs.: **sparking coil** = *spark coil* s.v. *SPARK *sb.*^{1} 7 d; **sparking plug,** a device that is fitted to the cylinder head of an internal-combustion engine and used to ignite the explosive mixture in the cylinder by the discharge of a spark between two electrodes at its end.

1897 G. D. HISCOX *Gas, Gasoline, & Oil Vapor Engines* x. 74 The sparking coil..consists of a bundle of iron wire, insulated and wrapped with insulated copper wire. **1929** *Proc. Inst. Automobile Engineers* XXIII. 252 If the sparking coil and plug gap be so balanced that the spark is just able to pass without a following arc, then the least widening of the gap will result in a failure of the spark to pass. **1902** Sparking plug [in Dict.]. **1908** tr. *Lieckfeld's Oil Motors* v. 85 A further improvement in electric ignition was introduced by the French firm [*sc.* de Dion et Bouton] when they brought out the sparking plug. **1929** E. LINKLATER *Poet's Pub* xxvi. 279 The life of a sparking-plug is a fierce tropical existence. **1970** K. BALL *Fiat 600, 600D Autobook* iii. 35/2 For the best performance, sparking plugs should be renewed every 10,000 miles.

sparkle, *v.*^{1} **3. b.** (Later example.)

1981 *Times* 10 June 20 Banks and insurances sparkle. An initial flurry of activity was seen in banks and insurances.

sparkler. 5. (Later examples.)

1975 *Country Life* 2 Oct. 839/3 Other sparklers made by the champagne method can be excellent: notably Sparkling Saumur and Seyssel from Savoy. **1981** *Times* 6 Mar. (Bride & Home Suppl.) p. vi/4 There are lots of good sparkling wines..Blanquette de Limoux or the Spanish sparklers.

sparklessly, *adv.* (Example.)

1906 H. M. HOBART *Elem. Princ. Continuous-Current Dynamo Design* iv. 106 Prior to coming into the position of short-circuit under the brush, it has been carrying a current of, say, 100 ampères in one direction. Immediately after emerging from the position of short-circuit, it will be carrying a current of 100 ampères in the opposite position. The change must take place sparklessly.

sparklet. Add: **3.** Properly **Sparklet,** with capital initial. The proprietary name of a metal capsule containing carbon dioxide under pressure, used to carbonate the water in a siphon; the siphon or bottle containing such a capsule; the carbonated water produced by this device. Freq. *attrib.*

1896 *Trade Marks Jrnl.* 23 Dec. 1102 *Sparklets.* 198134. Metal capsules to contain compressed gases. Aerators, Limited,..London; Manufacturers. **1902** KIPLING in *Collier's* 6 Dec. 8/1 Captain Mankelton..fed me canned beef and biscuits and give me a cigar—a Henry Clay—and a whiskey and sparklet. **1903** M. A. STEIN *Sand-Buried Ruins Khotan* ix. 158 The water from the well..tasted extremely brackish, and neither filtering nor the lavish use of 'Sparklets' could make it palatable. **1905** [see *AERATE *v.* 3]. **1911** *T. Eaton & Co. Catal.* Spring & Summer 175/2 Fresh soda water at a minimum cost with a Sparklet Bottle and a Sparklet Bulb. **1920** *Blackw. Mag.* Apr. 542/2 His particular fancy in drinks—usually whisky and sparklet. **1929** J. BUCHAN *Courts of Morning* II. xii. 271 A mess-servant brought him a long drink of lime-juice and sparklets. **1933** J. CARY *American Visitor* v. 51 He bustled to fetch glass and sparklet bottle. Bewsher was famous for his hospitality. **1971** R. DENTRY *Encounter at Kharmel* iii. 54 He squirted soda water from the sparklet syphon into the generous measure of whisky.

sparkly (spā·ɹkli), *a.* [f. SPARKLE *sb.* or *v.*^{1} + -Y^1.] Sparkling; that sparkles. Also *fig.*, lively.

1922 *Glasgow Herald* 18 Dec. 8 Among the shiny, sparkly rings. **1957** J. FRAME *Owls do Cry* 124 Evening bags covered with sparkly beads. **1978** *Detroit Free Press* 5 Mar. 14 (Parade Suppl.) 14E/3 (Advt.), A wee bouquet—jewel-bright & sparkly as springtime! **1979** *Rescue News* Sept. 8/3 The shop needs a good facelift and more positive selling policy with a wider range of goods and a sparklier range of staff.

spark out, *predic. a.* (and *adv.*) *dial.* and *colloq.* [perh. f. SPARK *sb.*^{1} + OUT *adv.*; cf. SPARK *v.*^{1} 2 c.] **a.** Utterly extinguished. **b.** *fig.* Forgotten; (completely) unconscious. Also as *adv.*

1880 J. HARTLEY *Halifax Clock Almanack* 17 Th' fire wor spark aght. **1882** NODAL & MILNER *Gloss. Lancs. Dial.* 249 He'll goo spark-out—*i.e.* be entirely lost or forgotten. **1936** J. CURTIS *Gilt Kid* v. 51 Eileen..was drunk, proper lit up and had passed spark out. **1952** M. ALLINGHAM *Tiger in Smoke* xi. 172 He's spark out, only just breathin'. Bin like that two days. **1966** A. PRIOR *Operators* xvi. 264 When she goes out, she's spark out. For three hours at least. **1977** *Zigzag* Aug. 5/1 If she tried to physically stop me doing something I would knock her spark out. **1971** F. NORMAN *Dodgem-Greaser* iii. 32 He keeled over like a felled tree and crashed to the canvas, spark out.

spa·rkover. Also **spark-over.** [f. vbl. phr. *to spark over*: see *SPARK *v.*^{1} 1 c.] = *FLASH-OVER.

1915 *Standardization Rules Amer. Inst. Electr. Engineers* 48 The Spark-over voltage, for a given gap, decreases with decreasing barometric pressure and increasing temperature. **1936** *Nature* 19 Sept. 509/1 The crackling sound of more or less prolonged duration finishes with a loud crack coincident with the final sparkover. **1942** [see *ACCELERATING *vbl. sb.*]. **1946** *Nature* 2 Nov. 603/2 The sparkover voltage of different electrode arrangements in air.

spark plug, *sb.* Also (chiefly in *fig.* use) **spark-plug, sparkplug.** [f. SPARK *sb.*^{1} or *v.*^{1} + PLUG *sb.*] **1.** = *sparking plug* s.v. SPARKING *vbl. sb.*^{1} b in Dict. and Suppl. Cf. *PLUG *sb.* 2 m.

1903 *Motor* 3 June 376/1 A small stiff bristle tooth brush..is very convenient for cleaning the porcelain of a spark plug. **1914** F. STRICKLAND *Petrol Motors* (ed. 2) 55 The high-tension leads and spark plug. **1920** J. D. MORGAN *Electr. Spark Ignition* iv. 43 A natural starting point for the study of spark plugs..is the voltage required to produce sparking. **1931** J. A. POLSON *Internal Combustion Engines* xii. 250 Deposits of carbon on spark plugs may cause failure by providing a path from the central electrode to the shell. **1973** V. CANNING *Flight of Grey Goose* ix. 171 He can't use ours [*sc.* a boat]... I got the spark plug in me pocket.

2. *fig.* One who or that which initiates or is the driving force behind any activity or undertaking. *colloq.* (chiefly *U.S.*).

1941 *Sun* (Baltimore) 24 Aug. 15/2 Introducing Hal Sieling... He's sparkplug of infield. **1953** M. MCCARTHY *Groves of Academe* viii. 159 In an experimental college like our own..a teacher's excitement is the spark-plug behind the whole system. **1958** [see *LIQUIDITY 1 d]. **1977** *Time* 14 Mar. 53/3 Lillee is the Australian sparkplug.

Hence **spa·rk-plug** *v. trans.*, to inspire, encourage, or lead (some activity). *U.S. colloq.*

1945 *Sun* (Baltimore) 22 Sept. 4-0/2 Our own reconversion directors have just taken the lid off the construction industry with the hope..that a boom here will help sparkplug a general re-employment drive over the reconversion badlands. **1956** A. H. COMPTON *Atomic Quest* 322 It is important that our government spark-plug the advance of nuclear power. **1961** *Time* 7 July 63/2 Ray Stevens, 67, who sparkplugged the company's diversification, was president from 1956 to 1960.

sparky, *a.* **2.** (Further *fig.* examples.)

c **1865** G. M. HOPKINS *Poems* (1967) 147 Thus he.. Gilds with some sparky fancies his black night. **1928** D. H. LAWRENCE *Lady Chatterley's Lover* x. 134 Pure, sparky, fearless new life! **1979** *Daily Tel.* 6 Apr. 15/2 If they [*sc.* the films] are all as sparky as these larks they deserve support.

sparmannia (spāɹmæ·niă). [mod.L. (Linnæus filius *Supplementum Plantarum* (1782) 41), f. the name of Andres *Sparrman* (1748–1820), Swedish traveller + -IA^1.] A large hairy shrub of the genus *Sparmannia* (family Tiliaceæ) native to southern Africa, and bearing toothed heart-shaped leaves and clusters of white flowers, esp. *S. africana*.

1801 *Curtis's Bot. Mag.* XV. 516 African Sparmannia... This beautiful shrub is a native of the Cape of Good Hope. **1818** M. EDGEWORTH *Let.* Sept. (1971) 101, I wish I could get a Sparmania [*sic*] for Lady Lansdowne. **1885** T. BAINES *Greenhouse & Stove Plants* 317/2 Most of the insects that are troublesome on indoor plants will live on this Sparmannia. **1956** X. FIELD *Housewife Bk. House Plants* III. 84 The sparmannia likes plenty of elbow room and is inclined to swamp its neighbours. **1976** *Homes & Gardens* Aug. 75/3 Bold foliage plants that will fill out your glass-enclosed jungle include..sparmannia.

sparrer² (spæ·rəɹ), repr. dial. pronunc. of SPARROW; also as first element of SPARROW-GRASS.

1884 [see NEGRO I d]. **1935** in Z. N. Hurston *Mules & Men* I. vii. 153 He seen a sparrer sittin' on a dead limb of a tree. **1961** *John o' London's* 19 Oct. 447/1 Cloak-and-dagger intellectuals, or game little cockney sparrers. **1970** N. STREATFEILD *Thursday's Child* xxiii. 156 That Ebeneezer we 'ave to 'elp..'asn't got no more brains than a sparrer. **1979** R. CASSILIS *Arrow of God* III. ix. 78 A dark-skinned..dhoti-clad cockney sparrer.

sparring, *vbl. sb.* Add: **3. sparring partner,** a boxer employed to practise with another in training for a contest; also *transf.* and *fig.*, esp. a person with whom one enjoys arguing.

1908 *Captain* Sept. 530/2 Jack was the best sparring partner he could have. **1930** *Daily Express* 8 Sept. 2/3 Cal Barton (Birmingham), Jack Hood's sparring partner. **1958** *Victorian Studies* I. 248 Mill..is used with the utmost disrespect as a sort of punch-drunk sparring-partner. **1971** H. WILSON *Labour Govt.* xxv. 493 Mr Mikoyan, my old sparring-partner and friend of the 1947 trade talks, now in honourable retirement, was waiting for us. **1977** 'E. MCBAIN' *Long Time No See* iv. 60, I was workin [*sic*] with Warren and a sparring partner... Warren's got a fight Tuesday night.

sparrow. Add: **1. d.** A chirpy, quick-witted person; used *spec.* of a Londoner, in *cockney sparrow*, etc.

1861 C. M. YONGE *Stokesley Secret* iv. 62 'A cock-sparrow for her London manners.'..'A London-bred sparrow; a pert forward chit.' **1892** —— *That Stick* I. ix. 95, I care about my neighbours..after a sort, but the jolly city sparrows of the slums for me! **1961** [see *SPARRER²]. **1969** J. GARDNER *Compl. State of Death* vi. 116 'Your mother's English?' 'Yes. Ma's a little cockney sparrow.' **1969** G. BUTLER *Coffin's Dark Number* xii. 151 She recognized her for what she was, one of those sharp little London sparrows. **1977** *Zigzag* Aug. 4/1 There are never any low class twits, only cockney sparrows and 'characters'.

3. *sparrow-shot*; *sparrow-legged* adj.

1965 F. SARGESON *Memoirs of Peon* vi. 173 Two young sparrow-legged ruffians. **1761** STERNE *Tr. Shandy* III. x. 33 Small curses..upon great occasions..are but so much waste of our strength... They are like sparrow shot.. fired against a bastion. **1955** L. DURRELL *Tree of Idleness* 48 Under rain, that rattles down the leaves like sparrow-shot.

4. sparrow-brain *colloq.*, (a person with) a tiny brain, (a person of) limited intelligence or perception; **sparrow-bub** *dial.*, a fledgling sparrow; **sparrow cop** *U.S. slang* (see quots.); **sparrow-fall** *poet.* (cf. SHAKES. *Ham.* v. ii. 233), a sparrow's death; hence *gen.* mortality; also *attrib.*; **sparrow-fart,** (*a*) *dial.* and *slang*, break of day, very early morning; also *pl.*; (*b*) *rare*, a person of no consequence.

1930 V. SACKVILLE-WEST *Edwardians* v. 241, I don't suppose it satisfies anyone, except perhaps a sparrow-brain like mother. **1975** H. FLEETWOOD *Picture of Innocence* iii. 45 She didn't actually *care* about her, and even, with her sparrow brain, despised her. **1917** D. H. LAWRENCE *Look! We have come Through!* 159 Curious long-legged foals, and wide-eared calves, and naked sparrow-bulbs. **1896** *Harper's Mag.* June 104/1 The boys do call a park policeman a sparrow-cop, don't they? **1935** A. J. POLLOCK *Underworld Speaks* 111/1 *Sparrow cop*, police or motorcycle officer who patrols parks and boulevards (petty thefts and petting parties). **1960** WENTWORTH & FLEXNER *Dict. Amer. Slang* 506/2 *Sparrow cop*, a policeman in disfavor with his superiors and assigned to a park to guard the grass. **1946** DYLAN THOMAS *Deaths & Entrances* 40 Mammoth and sparrowfall Everybody's earth. **1970** T. HUGHES *Crow* 32 An old man..Gazed towards the nearby polished shoes And slowly forgot the deaths in Homer The sparrowfall natural economy Of the dark simple curtain. **1886** R. HOLLAND *Cheshire Gloss.* 331 *Sparrowfarts*, very early morning 'Tha mun be up by *sparrowfarts* or tha'll be too late.' **1922** JOYCE *Ulysses* 747 Miss This Miss That Miss Theother lot of sparrowfarts skitting around talking about politics they know as much about as my backside. **1947** D. M. DAVIN *Gorse blooms Pale* 194 There we were as usual this morning at Sparrowfart, me with the jeep pulled up in front of the General's caravan. **1974** H. MCLEAVE *Only Gentlemen can Play* (1975) II. i. 92 It was important enough to bring you out here at sparrow fart.

sparrowy *a.*, (*b*) characteristic of or resembling a sparrow; so *sparrowy-looking* adj.

1926 S. SITWELL *All Summer in Day* I. i. 18 The sun, also, was very sparrowy in voice, and both sun and birds seemed satisfied for the moment. **1948** I. BROWN *No Idle Words* 31 Were they [*sc.* buntings] bunters in the perky.. sparrowy sense. **1953** D. A. BANNERMAN *Birds Brit. Isles* I. 300 The female is a sparrowy-looking little bird at all seasons. **1955** R. GRAVES *Greek Myths* I. lxxiv. 252 Castor and Polydeuces..come darting on 'sparrowy wings' through the upper air. **1976** A. J. RUSSELL *Pour Hemlock* vii. 63 She clutched steno pad to sparrowy chest.

sparse, *a.* **4.** *Comb.* (earlier and later examples).

1870 J. R. LOWELL in *Atlantic Monthly* Jan. 8 And thrust far off The Heaven..To voids sparse-sown with alienated stars. **1923** D. H. LAWRENCE *Birds, Beasts, & Flowers* 172 What would they do, those..sparse-haired elephants slowly following? **1924** J. MASEFIELD *Sard Harker* III. 201 He held on across the foothills through the sparse-growing sage.

Spartacist (spā·ɹtăsist, -kist). Also **Spartakist.** [ad. G. *Spartakist*, f. *Spartakus* *SPARTACUS, the name of a Thracian slave-leader in the Gladiatorial War (73–71 B.C.) against Rome, adopted as a pseudonym by K. Liebknecht (see below) in his political tracts: see -IST.] A member of a German radical socialist group formed in 1916 by Karl Liebknecht (1871–1919), Rosa Luxemburg (1870–1919), and Franz Mehring (1846–1919) and dedicated to ending the war of 1914–18 through revolution and to establishing a socialist government. Also *attrib.* or as *adj.*

1919 W. R. INGE *Outspoken Ess.* i. 18 The 'Spartacist' scoundrels who have betrayed and ruined their country. **1920** *19th Cent.* Mar. 560 The extreme Left wing of the Independents, known as Spartacists. **1925** *Contemp. Rev.* Dec. 715 The movement which a few Spartakists originated in the hope of establishing Soviet rule in Germany. **1965** *Listener* 4 Nov. 700/2 Otto Neurath..had been a member of the short-lived revolutionary Spartacist government in Munich. **1974** J. WHITE tr. *Poulantzas's Fascism & Dictatorship* IV. ii. 168 The process followed particular steps...1918–19. Failure of the German revolution and defeat of the Spartakist militants.

So **Spa·rtacan** (-kăn) *rare* = *SPARTACIST; **Spa·rtacism** (-siz'm, -kiz'm), the policy and principles of the Spartacists.

1918 *N.Y. Times* 15 Dec. I. 3/5 Spartacism appeared in Munich openly..when 'the bloody events in Berlin and the guilt of the Government' were discussed. *Ibid.*, Premier Eisner visited the meeting and defied the Spartacan leaders. **1919** *Nation* (N.Y.) 19 Apr. 632 The Programme of the Spartacans. **1919** J. M. KEYNES *Econ. Conseq. Peace* 271 A victory of Spartacism in Germany might well be the prelude to Revolution everywhere. **1920** *Glasgow Herald* 9 Apr. 9 Spartacism in Germany is a domestic matter for the German Government to deal with.

Spartacus (spā·ɹtăkŏs). [See prec.] Used *attrib.* in *Spartacus group, league* [tr. G. *Spartakusbund*], the Spartacists.

1918 *Spectator* 30 Nov. 607/1 The Spartacus group—the wild adherents to Liebknecht and Rosa Luxemburg. **1974** *Encycl. Brit. Macropædia* XI. 205/2 Rosa Luxemburg..in an alliance with Karl Liebknecht and other like-minded radicals..formed the..Spartacus League.

Spartakist, var. *SPARTACIST.

spartina (spāɹtəi·nă, -ī·nă). [mod.L. (J. C. D. Schreber *Linnæus' Genera Plantarum* (ed. 8, 1789) I. 43), ad. Gr. σπαρτίνη rope.] = *RICE-GRASS c.

1836 W. J. HOOKER *Compan. Bot. Mag.* II. 258 Distinguishing characters of both our British Spartinas. **1867** M. PLUES *Brit. Grasses* vii. 192 *Spartina stricta*, Smith. Cord Spartina. **1907** *Bull. Misc. Inf. R. Bot. Gardens Kew* 191 Others regard the three recognisable English Spartinas as varieties. *Ibid.* 193 These Spartina-swamps extend along each side of the river [Beaulieu]. **1925** *Jrnl. Ecol.* XIII. 83 *Spartina* is eagerly devoured by beasts of all kinds. **1934** [see *GLYCERIA]. **1943** J. W. DAY *Farming Adventure* xxi. 241 Spartina grass will live and grow in salt water on mud where no other plant could exist. **1965** *Times* 31 Aug. 10/6 Spartina grass.. thrives on tidal marshes. **1977** *Birds* Autumn 42/3 The fields of spartina have shrunk to spiky islands which are vanishing fast.

spartum. (Later example.)

1841 H. H. WILSON *Trav. Moorcroft & Trebeck in Himalayan Prov.* I. I. i. 10 A..swinging bridge..of the construction common in these mountains. The ropes used in its formation are made of a variety of spartum or star-three grass.

spas, var. *SPAZ.

spasm, *sb.* Add: **4.** Special Combs., as **spasm band** *U.S.* (now *Hist.*), a group, freq. of children, playing jazz on home-made musical instruments; **spasm music** *U.S.* (now *Hist.*), music played by spasm bands; **spasm war,** a war in which the combatants use their complete thermo-nuclear capabilities.

1926 WHITEMAN & MCBRIDE *Jazz* xiii. 267 When the last fearful note died, he turned to the leader. 'Stale Bread,' said he [*sc.* a judge], 'you may be a band, but you're a spasm band. Discharged.' The name stuck and the spasm band went on playing. **1943** I. LANG *Background of Blues* 4 Then there were the spasm bands... The saloons and sidewalks where spasm music and street singers found their most generous audiences were those of the French Quarter and particularly those in Storyville. **1964** HALL & WHANNEL *Pop. Arts* x. 297 In the early decades of the century the 'spasm bands' played a kind of home-made jazz on improvised instruments. **1943** Spasm music [see *spasm band* above]. **1965** H. KAHN *On Escalation* i. 14 But we need alternatives other than all-out spasm war or peace at any price. **1967** M. H. HALPERIN *Contemp. Mil. Strategy* (1968) ii. 15 The assumption that a general nuclear war between the United States and the Soviet Union would be an all-out, or 'spasm' war.

spasm (spæ·z'm), *v.* [f. the sb.] **1.** *trans.* To afflict with spasms (only in *pass.*); to cause to move convulsively. *rare.*

1790 J. BYNG *Jrnl.* 27 Aug. in *Torrington Diaries* (1935) II. 284 Otherwise I feel myself very low, and enfeebled, relaxed by day, and spasm'd by night. **1962** J. D. MACDONALD *Key to Suite* (1968) ix. 152 He spasmed his body inward, dropped the few remaining inches and landed on the railing.

2. *intr.* To twitch convulsively; to suffer a spasm.

1900 W. D. HOWELLS *Lit. Friends & Acquaintances* viii. 269 Of a person who had a nervous twitching of the face..he [*sc.* Henry James Sr.] said 'He *spasmed* to the fellow across the room and introduced him.' **1958** 'W. HENRY' *Seven Men at Mimbres Springs* xii. 142 Frank's gun fell from his spasming fingers. **1970** J. HANSEN *Fadeout* ix. 74 The boy's fine head did its slow, neck-straining roll while the unexpectedly deep voice spasmed and his mouth labored. **1978** J. IRVING *World according to Garp* xv. 304 The prostrate pig..squealed, its short legs spasmed.

spasmodic, *a.* **5.** (Earlier example.)

1832 CARLYLE *Let.* 28 Aug. (1977) VI. 211 Were I of the spasmodic School, I could gnash my teeth, now and then, over such a banishment: but..I reflect rather what deluges of Folly and Falsehood I stand safe from.

spasmogen (spæ·zmodʒĕn). *Pharm.* [Back-formation from next.] A spasmogenic drug.

1952 *Brit. Jrnl. Pharmacol. & Chemotherapy* VII. 91 There was little differentiation between the degrees of inhibition of..the 'direct' acting spasmogens, as compared with that shown by atropine. **1961** *Jrnl. Pharm. & Pharmacol.* XIII. 446 Common spasmogens such as histamine and 5-HT. **1974** *Nature* 4 Oct. 427/2 The response of the ileum to spasmogens varied widely at different times of the year.

spasmogenic (spæzmodʒe·nik), *a.* [f. SPASM + -O + *-GENIC.] † **1.** *Med.* (See quot.) *Obs.*

1899 CHURCH & PETERSON *Nervous & Mental Dis.* VII. vi. 546 If such a hyperesthetic zone arises from or becomes associated with some mental storm, pressure upon it may serve to revive the memories in question and provoke a hysterical fit. It is then denominated a spasmogenic or hysterogenic point or zone.

2. *Pharm.* Of a drug or other substance: promoting the contraction of smooth muscle.

1913 *Chem. Abstr.* VII. 3163 KCl has definit[e] spasmogenic properties in children. **1942** *Jrnl. Pharmacol. & Exper. Therapeutics* LXXIV. 275 Papaverine antagonizes the spasmogenic agents equally. **1975** *Nature* 13 Mar. 151/2 It can block the spasmogenic effects of 5-HT on the smooth muscle of isolated guinea pig ileum.

spasmolytic (spæzmŏli·tik), *a.* and *sb.* *Pharm.* [f. SPASM + -O + *-LYTIC.] **A.** *adj.* That relieves spasm of smooth muscle.

1937 *Jrnl. Pharmacol. & Exper. Therapeutics* LX. 13 The spasmolytic action of Syntropan exerted through the nerve endings on the isolated rabbit intestine is only about 20 times less than that of Atropine. **1953** [see *SERPASIL]. **1964** W. G. SMITH *Allergy & Tissue Metabolism* iv. 56 The effects of high dosage include ganglionic blockage and spasmolytic activity. **1982** *Jrnl. Med. Chem.* XXV. 1358/2 Some of these compounds have intensive spasmolytic activity for colonic motility.

B. *sb.* A spasmolytic drug.

1937 *Brit. Med. Jrnl.* 11 Sept. 560/1 The employment of spasmolytics in obstetrics is useful. **1978** *Acta Neurol. Scandinavica* LVII. 65 The drug is..capable of depressing distressing clonus, and it is concluded that it deserves further testing as a spasmolytic.

Hence **spasmo·lysis**, the action of such drugs.

1946 *Biol. Abstr.* XX. 1122/1 Although the compounds ..have some papaverine-like action on smooth muscle. spasmolysis results largely from their anticholinergic action. **1964** *Jrnl. Amer. Geriatric Soc.* XII. 1083 (*heading*) Spasmolysis: a new technique for treatment of spasticity. **1977** *Scandinavian Jrnl. Respiratory Dis.* Suppl. No. 98. 47 (*heading*) Sensitization of contracted tracheal smooth muscle to β-adrenergic spasmolysis by subthreshold doses of papaverine.

spasmoneme (spæ·zmonīm). *Zool.* [ad. G. *spasmonem* (G. Entz 1892, in *Math. und naturwissensch. Berichte aus Ungarn* X. 27), f. Gr. σπασμό-ς pulling, convulsion + νῆμ-α thread.] One of the three strands in the stalk of a vorticellid whose sudden contraction causes the stalk to coil tightly, withdrawing the animal from possible danger.

1901 [see *AXONEME]. **1941** BEAMS & KING in Calkins & Summers *Protozoa in Biol. Res.* ii. 94 The spasmoneme does not function like a true muscle but like a modified flagellum. **1978** *Jrnl. Cell Biol.* LXXVII. 358/2 Within the stalk is the contractile organelle, often referred to as the myoneme, though the term spasmoneme is preferable since recent studies indicate that the organelle is biochemically distinct from the myosin- and actin-based contractile systems.

spasmophilia (spæzmofi·liă). *Path.* [f. SPASM + -O + *-PHILIA.] Undue tendency of the muscles to contract, *esp.* as caused by a deficiency of systemic calcium.

1859 R. G. MAYNE *Expos. Lex. Med. Sci.* 1177/2 *Spasmophilia*, an epithet by Jos. Frank applied to erratic, spasmodic affections. **1892** D. H. TUKE *Dict. Psychol.*

Med. II. 843/1 Hyperæsthesia, with the corresponding hyperkinesis, spasmophilia or convulsions, is the principal symptom of spinal irritation. **1907** *Brit. Jrnl. Children's Dis.* IV. 448 J. Zahorsky includes tetany, carpal spasm, carpopedal spasm, laryngospasm and eclampsia, under the name of spasmophilia. **1953** J. H. Ebbs in Gaisford & Lightwood *Paediatrics* I. xxxix. 436 Spasmophilia can be defined as an increased excitability of the neuro-muscular junction. **1976** *Roumanian Jrnl. Med. Endocrinol.* XIV. 249 Normocalcemic spasmophilia is not recognized as a morbid entity but as a minor symptom often associated to neurosis.

Hence **spa·smophile** *rare*⁻¹, one who suffers from spasmophilia; **spasmophi·lic** *a.*, of, pertaining to, or suffering from spasmophilia.

1908 *Med. Rec.* (N.Y.) 30 May 903/1 The theory..that spasmophilic diathesis is a form of latent tetany. **1930** *Jrnl. Amer. Med. Assoc.* 22 Feb. 525/1 The calcium and inorganic phosphate tended toward spasmophilic levels. **1938** S. Beckett *Murphy* 49 That schizoidal spasmophile. **1941** *Amer. Jrnl. Dis. Children* LXI. 376 (*heading*) Presentation of a spasmophilic newborn infant.

spastic, *a.* Add: **1. b.** (Further examples.) *spastic paralysis*, a condition in which some muscles undergo tonic spasm (sometimes resulting in abnormal posture) and resist passive displacement, so that voluntary movement of the part affected is difficult and poorly coordinated.

1877 tr. W. Erb in *London Med. Rec.* V. 435/1 (*heading*) On spastic spinal paralysis (tabes dorsal spasmodique, Charcot). **1879** *Glasgow Med. Jrnl.* XI. 147 (*heading*) Paraplegia, with great muscular rigidity (Erb's spastic paralysis?). **1889** [see *palsy *sb.* (*a.*) 1 b]. **1903** Tubby & Jones *Surg. Paralyses* II. 203 Examples of Little's disease or spastic paralysis. **1937** E. Kenny *Infantile Paralysis & Cerebral Diplegia* viii. 92 In spastic paralysis, if the patient is asked to do something with the fingers, all the muscles controlling the fingers, as well as all the other muscles of the forearm and those of the arm and shoulder girdle, go into spastic contraction. **1938**, etc. [see *Little's disease]. **1954** S. Duke-Elder *Parsons' Dis. Eye* (ed. 12) xxix. 586 Spastic entropion is due to spasm of the orbicularis. **1973** W. Barlow *Alexander Principle* ix. 141 The diagnosis of 'spastic colon' is very often accompanied by such unnoticed abdominal misuse. **1977** *Lancet* 22 Oct. 844/2 He was hypertonic, with mild spastic diplegia.

3. a. Affected with spastic paralysis.

1903 Tubby & Jones *Mod. Methods Surgery of Paralyses* II. 228 Transformation of the pronator radii teres and transplantation of the carpal flexors were effected in spastic children. **1937** P. M. Girard *Home Treatment Spastic Paralysis* i. 10 As a spastic child later learns to walk, a typical 'scissors gait' is frequently observed. **1977** *Whitaker's Almanack 1978* 26 (Advt.), Jonathan has been severely spastic since birth, and is unable to walk unsupported. He also has difficulty with speaking and writing.

b. In weakened use: uncoordinated, incompetent; foolish, stupid. *slang.*

1981 [see sense b of the sb., below]. **1982** Barr & York *Official Sloane Ranger Handbk.* 159/3 *Spastic*, temporarily unintelligent. Sloanes don't consider lack of intelligence should be insulted; one, they are basically kind; two, they are unintellectual themselves.

B. *sb.* **a.** A person with spastic paralysis.

1896 *Pediatrics* II. 194 The staggering, uncertain gait of the spastic, often with knees striking or actually crossed, with knees flexed and heels raised, is well known. **1937** E. R. Carlson in P. M. Girard *Home Treatment Spastic Paralysis* p. xix, Through repeated exercises..the spastic gradually acquires muscular coordination. **1953** M. McCarthy *Groves of Academe* ii. 22 The male part of the college included an unusual number of child prodigies,..as well as some spastics and paraplegics. **1976** *National Observer* (U.S.) 25 Sept. 21/1 Christy Brown, you will remember, is the Dubliner..and almost total spastic who, a few years ago, with his left foot tapped out a novel. **1978** R. B. Scott *Price's Textbk. Pract. Med.* (ed. 12) XVI. 1347/2 Even with the most skilled and sympathetic management, the emotional needs and problems of the 'spastic' and of the immediate family may present insoluble problems.

b. In weakened use, esp. contemptuously: one who is uncoordinated or incompetent; a fool. Cf. *spaz. *slang.*

Although current for some fifteen years or more, it is generally condemned as a tasteless expression, and is not common in print.

1981 R. A. Spears *Slang & Euphemism* 369 *Spastic*, (1) a jerk; a giddy person..; (2) pertaining to a blunderer.

Hence **spa·stically** *adv.*, in a spastic manner.

1862 A. Meadows *Man. Midwifery* VI. ii. 217 The longer it [*sc.* the placenta] is allowed to remain the more spastically does the uterus contract upon it. **1978** R. Ludlum *Holcroft Covenant* iii. 39 He arched his back spastically, as if gasping for air.

spasticity. (Further examples.)

1964 *Proc. R. Soc. Med.* LVII. 715/2 Spasticity is said to be present when a paretic limb involuntarily resists passive displacement, particularly in one direction of movement. Anti-gravity muscles are often affected, but spasticity is by no means restricted to these muscles. **1974** *Times* 23 Jan. 9/7 Spasticity is the end result of pathological changes which disturb the physiology of the central nervous system.

spat, *sb.*¹ Add: **3.** *Comb.*: **spat fall, spatfall,** the settling of the planktonic larvæ of bivalves at the sites where they will develop as adults; the extent of such settling.

1925 *Nature* 26 Sept. 486/2 The spat falls in the three years 1922–24 were failures. **1963** *Washington Post* 2 Oct. B-2 The 1963 fall of spat (young oysters) in the James River seed area has been inadequate to maintain seed stocks for the third successive year. This contrasts sharply with the above average spatfall throughout the rest of Virginia's Chesapeake Bay system. **1972** *Aquaculture* I. 258 The possibility of spatfalls must be recognized if the harbour were heavily stocked with this species.

spat, *sb.*⁵ Add: **2.** *Aeronaut.* A streamlined covering for the upper part of the wheel of an aircraft, usu. one with fixed landing gear.

1931 *Flight* 16 Oct. 1047/1 (*caption*) The way in which the radius rod and axle are faired into the 'spat' is shown very clearly in these pictures. **1938** *Jrnl. R. Aeronaut. Soc.* XLII. 442, I have noticed that wheels which have spats covering all but the lower portion often spin quite fast in flight. **1943** [see *spatted *ppl. a.* b].

spat, pa. t., pa. pple., and pa. ppl. adj. of Spit *v.*² (q.v.). As ppl. adj. also with preps. and advbs., as *spat-on*, *-out*.

1922 Joyce *Ulysses* 167 His gorge rose. Spat on sawdust, warmish cigarette smoke..the state of ferment. **1948** T. A. M. Nash *Anchau Rural Devel. & Settlement Scheme* 6 Ankle deep in spat-out sugarcane fibre. **1968** *Listener* 11 July 40/1 It was generally conceived in the Labour movement that that old-fashioned and now spat-out word, 'comradeship', mattered an awful lot. **1978** A. J. Huxley *Illustr. Hist. Gardening* i. 10 Presumably growing from spat-out seeds, they [*sc.* wild fruits] were nearly always found close to the dwellings.

spatial, *a.* Add: **2. b.** *spatial-temporal* = *spatio-temporal *a.*

1903 A. E. Taylor *Elem. Metaphysics* III. iv. 249 We can..confine our attention to the spatial-temporal system of positions. **1925** *Mind* XXXIV. 44 The spatial-temporal order..is and must be taken for granted as ultimate by common sense and science. **1979** *Amer. Pol. Sci. Rev.* Mar. 157/2 Our language is filled with words whose original reference was to the position of one's body in the spatial-temporal world.

4. (Further examples.) *spatial ability* (Psychol.), the measured aptitude for perceiving and comprehending relations involving space or extension.

1940 R. S. Woodworth *Psychol.* (ed. 12) iii. 77 Spatial ability is the ability to grasp and use spatial relations. **1952** M. K. Wilson tr. *Lorenz's King Solomon's Ring* vii. 72 Only a few small passerines..possess enough 'spatial intelligence' to find their way through the windows and doors of a house. **1962** J. Tiffin *Industr. Psychol.* (rev. ed.) v. 158 The spatial ability tests showed the highest relative validity indexes for structural workers..and for some jobs for which such indexes would not be expected. **1964** M. Argyle *Psychol. & Social Probl.* xi. 141 Although spatial and non-verbal intelligence tests do not give a good prediction to success at grammar school, they do predict well to success at technical colleges. **1977** *Psychol. Abstr.* LVIII. 813/2 Factor analysis of the intercorrelation matrices for 14 variables yielded the same 4 factors in each group for space perception and spatial ability.

spatialism (spē¹·ʃăliz'm). [f. Spatial *a.* + -ism; in sense 2, ad. Fr. *spatialisme.*] **1.** *Philos.* (See quot.) *rare.*

1935 *Mind* XLIV. 363 Pure Spatialism which asserts that matter has only spatial, temporal and causal properties.

2. The name of a movement in experimental French poetry led by Pierre Garnier.

1964 *Times Lit. Suppl.* 3 Sept. 827/2 Les Lettres..is Pierre Garnier's organ for a new 'spatialist' conception of poetry... No. 29 (janvier 1963) contains a preliminary manifesto for Spatialism. **1971** J. Sharkey *Mindplay* 12 *Les Lettres*..in 1963..tried to bring together all of these [modern poetry movements] under a new term—Spatialism—which would include concepts of time, structure and energy.

spatialist (spē·ʃălist), *sb* .and *a.* [f. as prec. + -ist]. **A.** *sb.* **1.** An adherent of spatialism, in either sense.

1934 J. Wisdom *Problems of Mind & Matter* II. x. 168 The Pure Spatialist. The language of some scientists..when they are trying to do philosophy, suggests that they believe that the internal characters of material things consist wholly of spatio-temporal characters—say size, shape and speed. **1964** *Times Lit. Suppl.* 6 Aug. 696/5 Pierre Garnier's review *les lettres* aims at centering spatialists everywhere.

2. One who is concerned with spatial qualities or relations. *rare.*

1940 J. Joyce *Let.* 13 Mar. (1966) III. 469, I did not wish to inflict temporal art on a spatialist in asking you to go to the concert.

B. *adj.* Of, pertaining to, or characteristic of spatialism.

1964 *Times Lit. Suppl.* 6 Aug. 697/1 Synthesis of the eye-ear-cybernetic trinity of spatialist manifesto. **1967** S. Bann *Concrete Poetry* 19 Yet there is at least one significant point of contact between Goeritz and Garnier. This lies in their common concern with the wider possibilities of the Concrete (or, in Garnier's case, 'spatialist') idiom. **1971** Taylor & Lucie-Smith *French Poetry Today* 24 Its legitimate offspring thus include genuinely international movements such as Concrete Poetry and Spatialist Poetry.

spatialize (spē¹·ʃăləiz), *v.* [f. Spatial *a.* + -ize.] *trans.* To make spatial; to think of as spatial; to invest with spatial qualities or relations. So **spa·tialized** *ppl. a.*, **spa·tializing** *vbl. sb.*

1906 S. S. Laurie *Synthetica* I. 24 There could be no spatialising or localising at all. **1911** A. Mitchell tr. *Bergson's Creative Evolution* iii. 225 Deduction is an operation governed by the properties of matter... As long as it turns upon space or spatialized time, it has only to let itself go. **1925** A. N. Whitehead *Science & Mod. World* vii. 177 Thus a duration is spatialised; and by 'spatialised' is meant that the duration is the field for the realized pattern constituting the character of the event. **1934** A. Huxley *Beyond Mexique Bay* 220 The time that Vaughan perceived..was not real time..; it was the acceptably spatialized, circular duration of the calendar-makers. **1946** R. G. Collingwood *Idea of History* 188 It is the clock-time of the external world, a spatialized time in which different times exclude one another, just like parts of space. **1949** *Mind* LVIII. 493 By our substantialising of events and our consequent spatialising of time we make this syntactical similarity still closer. **1973** M. Hollington in R. Fowler *Dict. Mod. Critical Terms* 183 The contribution of structuralism to the analysis of individual literary works has been hampered by its extreme tendency to spatialize the object of contemplation.

spatio-temporal (spē¹:ʃio,te·mpŏrăl), *a.* [f. *spatio-*, used as comb. form of L. *spatium* Space *sb.*¹ + Temporal *a.*¹] Belonging to both space and time.

1900 B. Russell *Leibniz* v. 57 Two things could not co-exist in one spatio-temporal point. **1920** A. N. Whitehead *Concept of Nature* viii. 173 The spatio-temporal structure of events. *a* **1931** G. H. Mead *Philos. of Act* (1938) II. xv. 232 Physical identity with distant objects gives functional contemporaneity, while the acts that are going on involve the actual concrete spatiotemporal happenings. **1954** A. J. Ayer *Philos. Ess.* i. 3 Spatio-temporal points are individuals,..but not everyone would allow it to be said that they existed. **1975** I. Stewart *Concepts Mod. Math.* xiv. 208 Depress your foot, and move slightly forward in time, thereby dragging a small loop of string with you in the time direction, though leaving most of the knot in its original spatio-temporal state. **1979** A. R. Peacocke *Creation & World of Science* I. i. 24 A more general view that reality consists of two orders..: the natural/the supernatural; the spatio-temporal/the eternal; [etc.].

Hence **spa:tio-tempora·lity,** the quality or fact of being spatio-temporal; **spa:tio-temporaliza·tion,** the fact of making or investing with spatio-temporal qualities or relations; **spa:tio-te·mporalized** *a.*; **spa:tio-te·mporally** *adv.*, in space and time, with reference to both space and time.

1920 S. Alexander *Space, Time, & Deity* I. 250 Relation..which unites things, is outside each of them spatially (or rather spatio-temporally). *Ibid.* 269 A category which arises not so much out of the whole of spatio-temporality taken as a whole..as out of the 'relation'..between the spatial and the temporal elements in any space-time. **1923** C. D. Broad *Sci. Thought* x. 403 Science regards the ultimate scientific objects as being spatio-temporally homogeneous. **1940** *Mind* XLIX. 185 The qualitative content must vanish with the abstraction of its spatio-temporality. *Ibid.*, It remains possible to take the quality as the spatio-temporalized appearance of the real action of the 'other' with the 'self'. *Ibid.* 324 Evidently the qualification is a function of the spatio-temporalization. **1959** P. F. Strawson *Individuals* I. i. 34 Since spatio-temporally continuous existence is..observed *neither* in the case where we are inclined to speak of qualitative identity *nor* in the case where we are inclined to speak of numerical identity, by what right do we suppose that there is a fundamental difference between these cases? **1964** P. Meadows in I. L. Horowitz *New Sociol.* xxviii. 446 They sought to discern in the sweeping spatio-temporalizations of historic experience..the unfolding 'form'..beyond appearance. **1980** A. Quinton *Francis Bacon* vii. 62 Causes may be spatio-temporally remote from their effects.

‖ **Spätlese** (ʃpę·tlēzĕ). Also **Spaetlese,** and with small initial. Pl. **-lesen.** [Ger., f. *spät* late + *lese* picking, vintage.] A white wine made (esp. in Germany) from grapes gathered later than the general harvest.

[**1926** P. M. Shand *Bk. of Wine* vi. 185 Where the wine is a selected one..the inscription should terminate with the word *Auslese*.., or *Spätlese*.] **1935** H. R. Rudd *Hocks & Moselles* ii. 24 The grower may..leave some..grapes hanging for a week or two longer... He will make with them casks of 'Spätlese', or 'late gathered'. **1951** S. F. Hallgarten *Rhineland Wineland* 52 Sweet white wines, Spaetlesen and Auslesen, are very suitable. **1963** *Times* 8 Feb. 12/5 We shall consider three main groups—the lesser wines; the Spätlesen (made from grapes gathered later than the general harvest) and Auslesen (gathering of selected bunches). **1967** K. Giles *Death & Mr Prettyman* i. 37 My husband sent back a case of Spätlese, six years old, light on the tongue as Epsom salts, just the thing with a bit of smoked fish. **1977** *Times* 2 Apr. 14/8 In such a [good] year all the grapes are..upgraded..so that the simple Qualitätswein..would be as great as a Spätlese, and so on.

spatted, *ppl. a.* Add: **b.** Of an aircraft or its undercarriage: equipped with spats.

1936 R. Brenard in J. Hammerton *War in Air* XIX. 606 (*caption*) The latest version..has its three 350 h.p. Gnome-Rhone engines enclosed in low-drag cowlings and faired into a 'spatted' undercarriage. **1943** Hunt & Pringle *Service Slang* 61 If the wheels of a 'spatted' plane do not retract, it is said to have 'permanent spats'. **1960** C. H. Gibbs-Smith *Aeroplane* I. xi. 78 This remarkable three-seater had fully cantilevered wings..and spatted' undercarriage.

spattee (spæti·). [f. SPAT *sb.*[5], after *puttee.*] Formerly, an outer stocking or legging worn by women for protection against wet and cold.

1926 *Bulletin* 17 Aug. 4/3 The invention is called the 'Highland spattee' and is a Highlander's stocking made spat-fashion to allow the wearer to slip it easily over her shoes and silk stocking. **1928** *Daily Tel.* 10 Jan. 6 The knitted spattee. **1939** JOYCE *Finnegans Wake* I. 11 All spoiled goods go into her nabsack: curtrages and rattlin buttins, nappy spattees and flasks of all nations.

spatter, *sb.*[2] Add: **2.** *Geol.* Magmatic material emitted as small fluid fragments by a vent or fissure associated with a volcano; also, a fragment of this.

1953 *Bull. U.S. Geol. Survey* No. 994. 23 Small steep-sided cones composed very largely of spatter are common on the rift zones of Hualalai volcano. **1969** [see *DRIBLET *sb.* 4]. **1971** *New Scientist* 10 June 611/1 Irregular explosions threw bright orange lumps of spatter as high as 20 metres. **1976** G. B. OAKESHOTT *Volcanoes & Earthquakes* vi. 49 Activity had concentrated on the building of a combined cinder-and-spatter cone made up of hardened lava fragments and congealed blobs or spatters.

spatter, *v.* Add: **7. spatter rampart** *Geol.*, a wall or ridge formed of spatter along the edge of a fissure in a volcanic area; **spatterware, spatter ware** (see quots. 1959, 1977[2]).

1953 *Bull. U.S. Geol. Survey* No. 994. 6 The common basalts of Hawaii erupt quietly, building only low spatter ramparts and diminutive spatter-and-cinder cones. **1967** G. MACDONALD in Hess & Poldervaart *Basalts* I. 53 Spatter ramparts may be several kilometers long, although generally they are not continuous over the entire distance. **1977** A. HALLAM *Planet Earth* 96 Spatter cones and spatter ramparts form around parasitic vents and fissures when eruptions are less violent and the magma more fluid. **1935** *N.Y. Times* 9 June x. 9/2 'Gaudy Dutch' was the name given to some of the spatterware made in the shape of peacocks and tulips for this area many years ago. **1959** L. GROSS *Guide to Antiques* viii. 97 Spatterware is a fairly heavy earthenware with characteristic decoration of color applied with a sponge or spattered on to give a stippled effect. **1977** FLEMING & HONOUR *Penguin Dict. Decorative Arts* 751/1 *Spatter ware*, C19 wares decorated with bright colours applied with a sponge through a stencil, usually giving a blotchy effect. **1980** *Times* 4 Oct. 14/3 On the Staffordshire 'spatterware', in particular, Sotheby's American experts were out by a factor of 10 on some of their estimates.

spatulate (spæ·tiŭlĕ[i]t), *v.* [f. SPATUL(A + -ATE[3].] *trans.* To stir or mix with a spatula. Also *absol.*

1923 in L. P. ANTHONY *Dict. Dental Sci.* 269/1. **1954** O. C. APPLEGATE *Essentials of Removable Partial Denture Prosthesis* 261 Spatulate thoroughly to free the mix of contained air. **1956** J. N. ANDERSON *Appl. Dental Materials* xviii. 216 The difficulty of spatulating such a mixture..usually results in overspatulation. **1957** *Jrnl. Amer. Ceramic Soc.* XL. 254/1 The fine powders were spatulated intensively with either pine oil or a commercial screen oil. **1981** *Scand. Jrnl. Dental Res.* LXXXIX. 100/2 Dentists often spatulate for too short a time.

2. *Surg.* To give a spatulate form to (a tubular vessel).

1976 *Ann. Thoracic Surg.* XXII. 235/2 The end of the divided subclavian artery was then spatulated. **1977** *Urologia Internat.* XXXII. 369 The..terminal ureter is amputated as needed and the ureter is spatulated for about 10 mm on its anterior surface.

Hence **spa·tulating** *vbl. sb.*

1966 *Brit. Jrnl. Urol.* XXXVIII. 525 An atraumatic catgut suture is then inserted..at the apex of the spatulating incision. **1977** *Urologia Internat.* XXXII. 368 The main differences are the way the submucosal tunnel is prepared, the resection and spatulating of the terminal ureter, [etc.].

spatulated, *a.* Add: Also as *ppl. a.*, given a spatulate form.

1957 *Jrnl. Urol.* LXXVII. 413 The technique of anastomosing the spatulated ends of the ureter was used without the ureterotomy above the site of anastomosis. **1977** *Urologia Internat.* XXXII. 369 The spatulated end of the ureter is spread over the trigonal mucosa.

spatulation. Restrict *rare* to sense in Dict. and add: **III.** [f. *SPATULATE *v.*] **2.** Chiefly *Dentistry.* The process of stirring or mixing with a spatula.

1939 J. OSBORNE *Dental Mechanics* i. 5 (*heading*) Spatulation time. **1940** E. COVINGTON *Efficient Dental Assistant* iii. 71 Rapid and longer spatulation accelerate [*sic*] setting time with most plasters. **1957** V. J. KEHOE *Technique Film & Television Make-Up* xii. 147 Mix by spatulation until a smooth cream is obtained. **1977** *Jrnl. Biomed. Materials Res.* XI. 863 The spatulation was conducted at approximately 150 rpm, but that rate was difficult to maintain throughout the mixing interval. **1981** *Scand. Jrnl. Dental Res.* LXXXIX. 97/2 Twelve fillings with diameters of 6 mm were made.., varying the spatulation time from 5 to 60 s at 5 s intervals.

3. *Surg.* The procedure of spatulating a tubular vessel; also, the spatulated portion.

1977 *Urologia Internat.* XXXII. 372 We advocate spatulation of the terminal end of the ureter. **1979** *Brit. Jrnl. Urol.* LI. 105/2 The stitch is continued around the upper ends of the spatulations.

‖ **Spätzle** (ʃpę·tslĕ, ʃpe·ts'l), *sb. pl.* Also Spatzle, spätzle, and (anglicized) -s. [Ger. dial., lit. 'little sparrows'.] Noodles of a type made in southern Germany.

1933 E. E. AMIET *Palmer House Cook Bk.* 247 Spatzles. Into 3 soup-spoonfuls of flour, beat 1 egg and 3 soup-spoonfuls of milk. Add a pinch of salt, a pinch of pepper and a little ground nutmeg. Set a colander over boiling water and squeeze this mixture through, boil for a minute and pour into a sieve and serve. **1959** M. CROSLAND tr. *Rovan's Germany* 179 The *Spätzle*, a kind of fresh pasta from Swabia. **1978** J. IRVING *World according to Garp* viii. 155 Garp had cooked an elegant Paprika Chicken and spätzle.

spaug (spǭg). *Anglo-Irish.* [Ir. *spág.*] A clumsy, awkward foot.

1910 P. W. JOYCE *English as we speak it in Ireland* 331 *Spaug*, a big clumsy foot:— 'You put your ugly spaug down on my handkerchief. **1922** JOYCE *Ulysses* 128 Taking off his flat spaugs and the walk.

spaulty (spǭ·lti), *a. dial.* Also **spoalty, spoulty.** [f. SPALT *a.* + -Y[1].] Dry and brittle.

1895 J. J. RAVEN *Hist. Suffolk* xix. 266 When turnips are hard and brittle..they are said to be *spoalty*, which William Ellis (1750) spells *spalt*, and Professor Skeat notes as a Cambridge-Shire word. **1904** *Eng. Dial. Dict.* V. 643/1 Them turnips is spoulty. **1906** KIPLING *Puck of Pook's Hill* 238 Did he promise me a set of iron cramps or ties for the roof? They never came to hand, or else they were spaulty or cracked.

spawn, *sb.* Add: **3.** (Later *fig.* example.)

1920 D. H. LAWRENCE *Touch & Go* 6 The plays of A People's Theatre are—oh heaven, what are they?—not popular nor populous nor plebeian nor proletarian nor folk nor parish plays. None of that adjectival spawn.

8. *spawn-like* adj.

1938 S. BECKETT *Murphy* 249 The iris was reduced to a thin glaucous rim of spawnlike consistency.

spawn, *v.* Add: **2. b.** (Later example.)

a **1930** D. H. LAWRENCE *Last Poems* (1932) 198 Oh I have loved the working class Where I was born, And lived to see them spawn into machine-robots.

6. (Further examples, *spec.* of tornadoes or the like.)

1955 *Sci. News Let.* 18 June 394/1 The general atmospheric conditions in which hurricanes are spawned are known. **1965** *Listener* 21 Oct. 610/1 Every summer the violent climate of the central United States spawns a series of devastating storms—tornadoes—twisters they call them here. **1976** *Bay City* (Michigan) *Times* 12 July 1/5 Powerful thunderstorms roamed much of the East Sunday spawning tornadoes and flash floods.

spawned *ppl. a.* **b.** Also with *out.*

1972 *Trout & Salmon* June 41/1 Unripe fish as well as spawned-out carcasses and unused roe..are sold in the market. **1972** L. HANCOCK *There's a Seal in my Sleeping Bag* vi. 132 Birds congregated on the salmon river to feed on the spawned-out salmon.

spaz (spæz). *slang.* Also **spas.** [Abbrev. of *SPASTIC *sb.*] = *SPASTIC *sb.* b (see also quot. 1977[1]).

1965 P. KAEL *I lost it at Movies* III. 259 The term that American teen-agers now use as the opposite of 'tough' is 'spaz'. A spaz is a person who is courteous to teachers, plans for a career..and believes in official values. A spaz is something like what adults still call a square. **1975** M. AMIS *Dead Babies* viii. 47, I know how long, you little spaz. **1977** *Amer. Speech* 1975 L. 67 *Spas*,..1: Uncoordinated, clumsy person 2: Person regarded as dull, foolish, or stupid 3: Friend (jocular use) 'Hey spas, do we have any homework?' **1977** J. WAMBAUGH *Black Marble* (1978) viii. 117 The man's a spaz! A total spaz! **1982** *Guardian* 26 Oct. 8/4 Come onnnnn—bag your face, you geek, you grody totally shanky spaz.

speak, *sb.* Add: **4.** (Earlier example.)

1811 *Lexicon Balatronicum* s.v. *Speak*, He has made a good speak; he has stolen something considerable.

5. = *SPEAKEASY.

1930 *Bookman* (U.S.) LXXII. 398/1 Better grade speaks in Times Square are dispensing with femme shills and hangers-out. **1952** [see *OPEN *a.* 2 c]. **1977** H. FAST *Immigrants* IV. 242 We're just lucky it happened in a speak, because maybe no one will bring any charges.

speak, *v.* Add: **I. 1. c.** *spec.* To speak to another by means of a telephone; —— *speaking* (where —— is a speaker on a telephone), phr. used by the speaker to announce his identity.

1885 *List of Subscribers* (United Telephone Co.) p. xiv, 'Who speaks?' came distinctly from the wires into the office. '2577,' was the reply—it was the hotel number. **1925** F. SCOTT FITZGERALD *Great Gatsby* ix. 200 But the connection came through as a man's voice, very thin and far away. 'This is Slagle speaking.'.. 'Yes?' The name was unfamiliar. **1933** 'SAPPER' *Knock-Out* i. 9 Standish.. took the receiver from the other's hand. 'Hullo! Sanderson,' he said. 'Yes—Standish speaking. What now?' **1973** J. WAINWRIGHT *Pride of Pigs* 166 'Quince?' said the voice. 'Speaking.' Quince hooked his fingers through the carrying handle of the Trimphone, telephone hand set... He said: 'Who's that?.. Who's speaking?' **1977** L. MEYNELL *Hooky gets Wooden Spoon* xiii. 151 C.I.D. here..who is it speaking, please?

g. *spec.* To propose marriage. Cf. sense *13 d.

1604 SHAKS. *Othello* I. iii. 166 She thank'd me, And bad me, if I had a Friend that lou'd her, I should but teach him how to tell my Story, And that would wooe her. Vpon this hint I spake. **1803** G. COLMAN *John Bull* III. i. 31 *Lady Caroline.* Lard, Mr. Shuffleton!.. You never spoke anything to—that is—to justify such a—. *Shuffleton.* (Aside.) That's as much as to say, speak now. **1858** TROLLOPE *Doctor Thorne* II. vi. 81, I think you may speak now, Frank... She is very fond of you. **1904** H. JAMES *Golden Bowl* I. I. xii. 213 He liked..to feel that he should be able to 'speak'..the word itself being romantic. **1932** S. GIBBONS *Cold Comfort Farm* xiv. 195 Flora did not dare to imagine what would happen if they returned from the ball and he had not spoken. He *must* speak! **1964** M. LASKI in S. Nowell-Smith *Edwardian England* iv. 198 An interval might have been found—perhaps in the conservatory, perhaps on a sofa in a dark nook under the stairs—when *he* had spoken and *she* accepted.

4. a. (*b*). (Earlier example.)

1824 LONGFELLOW *Let.* 2 Mar. in S. Longfellow *Life H. W. Longfellow* (1886) I. iii. 37 If this were not another building, I should have imagined I occupied the same chamber that you did in former times, for it seemed to be the very highest point of the dwelling, the very *apogee*, so to speak.

II. 10. speak for —. a. *speak for yourself*: expressing a desire to dissociate oneself from what another has just said or the assumptions behind it.

1738 SWIFT *Polite Conversation* I. 16 Pray, sir, speak for yourself. **1778** BOSWELL in *London Mag.* Feb. 58/1, I remember hearing a late celebrated infidel tell that he was not at all pleased when the infidel wife of his friend, a poet of some eminence, addressed him in a company in London, 'we Deists'.—Speak for yourself, Madam, said he abruptly. **1824** SCOTT *Redgauntlet* III. x. 292 'Speak for yourself, friend,' said Peter, scornfully. **1916** G. B. SHAW *Androcles & Lion* Prologue 3 *Megaera*: Everybody knows that the Christians are the very lowest of the low. *Androcles*: Just like us, dear. *Megaera*: Speak for yourself. **1946** L. P. HARTLEY *Sixth Heaven* ii. 46 'Speak for yourself,' said Barbara defiantly. **1976** *Times Lit. Suppl.* 30 Apr. 508/4 We learn that 'when viewing serials..we feel we know these characters well enough, for example, to say hello to in the street.'.. My reaction to this is to say: speak for yourself!

c. (Later examples.)

1943 *Sun* (Baltimore) 25 Feb. 6/1 (Advt.), We hope to preserve even more food this year. But well over half of this season's pack is already spoken for by the Government. **1971** *Petticoat* 17 July 29/2 He's not married, but he's involved, as they say, spoken for, and has lived with his girlfriend in London for the last few years.

12*. speak past —. To talk at cross-purposes with; to speak incomprehensibly to. Cf. G. *vorbeireden.*

1952 G. HIMMELFARB *Lord Acton* i. 2 This historian.. ended his life..as a lecturer doomed to speak past his audience. **1975** *United Church Observer* Nov. 15/1 The most important issue..is whether we can speak together and converse together, not *at* each other or *past* each other.

13. speak to —. d. *spec.* To propose marriage to. Cf. sense *1 g.

1809 LD. GRANVILLE *Let.* 14 Nov. in B. Askwith *Piety & Wit* (1982) iv. 64, I spoke to Harriet last night; she was very nervous and so was I... She consented to my speaking to the Duke [her father]. **1840** THACKERAY in *Fraser's Mag.* XXII. 230/1 'Will you marry me?' In fact, this very speech had been taught him by cunning Gann, who saw well enough that Swigby would speak to one or other of his daughters. **1863** MRS. GASKELL *Dark Night's Work* iv. 46 He had some discussion with himself as to whether he should speak to her, and so secure her promise. **1977** G. BUTLER *Brides of Friedberg* i. 12 Next day someone I would *much* rather have accepted spoke to me riding in the Row. But it was too late.

III. 17. speak out. b. *to speak out in meeting* (examples).

1830 *Mass. Spy* 23 June 4/1 O dear, I spoke out in meeting. **1906** *Springfield* (Mass.) *Weekly Republic* 13 Sept. 8, I do not think the president will think any the less of me for speaking right out in meeting and saying that I am not for it.

IV. 21. c. *to speak one's piece*: see *PIECE *sb.* 17 g.

27. c. For † *Obs.*$^{-1}$ read *rare* and add later example.

1936 J. STEINBECK *In Dubious Battle* vi. 97 If the bitch ever whelps, I'd like to speak a pup.

VI. 36. speak-back = **talk-back*; **speak-box,** an intercom device by a (usu. outside) door which allows a caller to speak to someone elsewhere in the building (cf. *voice-box* (*b*) s.v. *VOICE *sb.* 14); **speak-easy**: delete and see *SPEAKEASY; **speak-out,** an occasion on which people can speak freely and unreservedly; **speak-your-weight machine,** a weighing machine which announces one's weight in spoken words.

1940 *Chambers's Techn. Dict.* 788/1 *Speak-back*, the subsidiary microphone-amplifier-reproducer in a motion-picture studio, by which the remote recordist can speak to the director on the sound-stage. **1960** *Guardian* 14 Apr. 8/3 His most recent hero..attempts to teach speak-your-weight machines to sing. **1962** N. FREELING *Love in Amsterdam* II. 106 The buzzer went, and he heard Sophia's voice on the speakbox. **1966** *Illustr. London News* 30 July 11 Kidbrooke has its own T.V. studio which incorporates a 'speak-back'. **1966** L. DEIGHTON *Billion-Dollar Brain* xv. 146 His voice was..like a speak-your-weight machine. **1968** *Guardian* 19 Aug. 14/5 Americans Abroad for McCarthy held a 'speak out' near the Speakers' Corner in a sunlit but swampy Hyde Park yesterday. **1970** W. J. BURLEY *To kill a Cat* ix. 152 He rang the bell. Almost at once he was startled by a woman's voice from close at hand. A speak-box which he hadn't expected. He found the little metal grille and spoke into it. 'Come up, please.' **1977** *Daily Tel.* 25 Oct. 11/4 At the New York 'speak out', women were invited to tell anonymously of abuse suffered from promiscuous or sexually taunting male employers or superiors.

-speak (spīk), *suffix.* The verb SPEAK used, after Orwell's *Newspeak* and *Oldspeak*, as a substantival suffix (cf. SPEAK *sb.* 1) to denote a particular variety of language or characteristic mode of speaking.

1949, etc. [see *NEWSPEAK]. **1949**, etc. [see *OLDSPEAK]. **1960** K. AMIS *Take Girl Like You* xi. 140 Charlton, his creep-speak effectively silenced, had departed in protest-march style. **1966** *Science* 13 May 875/1 We read of 'space speak' on every hand. Newspapers and magazines discuss it in their science columns... The belief is that the space effort has given us, in addition to the possibility of going to the moon, a new linguistic phenomenon. **1972** *College English* Jan. 439 (*heading*) Doublespeak: dialectology in the service of Big Brother. **1980** *Times* 27 Feb. 14/2 Such emphasizers as *undoubtedly* (Ponderoso Speak: *indubitably*)..diminish, if they do not actually destroy the assurance of a statement. **1981** *Times* 28 Jan. 7/1 (*heading*) Haigspeak rewrites the grammar. **1981** *Guardian* 1 May 2/4 'I am very sorry that I cannot be with you today... I am most grateful and touched that you have decided to name a locomotive after me,' it [*sc.* a telegram] said in classic royalspeak.

speakable, *a.* Add: **3.** Able or fit to be spoken *to.*

1956 'C. BLACKSTOCK' *Dewey Death* x. 227 I'm simply not speakable to this morning. **1979** *Daily Tel.* 20 Sept. 18/3, I don't think he is speakable to at the moment... Could you ring back in 20 minutes?

speakeasy (spī·kīzi). *slang* (orig. and chiefly *U.S.*). Also **speak-easy.** [f. SPEAK *v.* + EASY *adv.*] A shop or bar where alcoholic liquor is sold illegally. Also *attrib.*

1889 [see SPEAK *v.* 36]. **1895** L. PENDLETON *Corona of Nantahalas* iv. 45 A sort of rural 'speak easy', where the colourless liquid was poured into the purchasers' bottles from a new and innocent-looking kerosene can. **1903** A. H. LEWIS *Boss* xiii. 162 That..no side-doors or speak-easy racket [should be] stood for. **1922** JOYCE *Ulysses* 418 In the speakeasy. Tight. I shee you, shir. **1946** [see *creep joint* s.v. *CREEP *sb.* 6]. **1958** S. TRAILL in P. Gammond *Decca Bk. Jazz* vi. 75 Every cheap speakeasy had its resident piano player. **1961** W. VAUGHAN-THOMAS *Anzio* vii. 138 Inevitably some of these underground caves became 'speak-easy' dens where the local black-marketeers sold *vino* to the troops. **1968** [see *prohibition era* s.v. *PROHIBITION 6]. **1982** *Age* (Melbourne) 3 Feb. 6/6 Unable to find a respectable job, she first became a bootlegger during the Prohibition era and ran a speakeasy.

speaker. Add: **7.** (Earlier example.)

1875 W. D. WHITNEY *Life & Growth of Lang.* iv. 72 The difficulty is one which English-speakers can hardly realize.

8. = *LOUD-SPEAKER.

1926 *Jrnl. Franklin Inst.* CCII. 436 This speaker employs a six-inch cone driven by an electromagnetic power unit. **1954** R. DAHL *Someone like You* 66 Maybe the great radio engineer doesn't know how to connect the mike to the speaker? **1978** *Hi-Fi News* Sept. 15 (Advt.), High Fidelity speakers for the discerning ear.

9. *attrib.* and *Comb.*, as (sense *8) *speaker grille, system*; **speaker-hearer,** a person regarded as a user of language; **speaker-key,** a key fitted to a wind instrument to enable the playing of notes an octave or a twelfth higher (cf. *octave key* s.v. *OCTAVE *sb.* (*a.*) 8); **speaker-listener** = *speaker-hearer* above; **speaker-phone** *U.S.*, a telephone receiver which need not be held in the hand; **Speaker's Conference,** a conference, first set up in 1916, whose purpose is to examine electoral law and reform under the chairmanship of the Speaker of the House of Commons; **Speakers' Corner,** the north-east corner of Hyde Park, near Marble Arch, noted as a place where soap-box orators traditionally air their views; also *transf.*

1979 P. WAY *Sunrise* iv. 44 There was a bell push and a speaker-grille just above it. **1965** N. CHOMSKY *Aspects of Theory of Syntax* i. 4 To study actual linguistic performance, we must consider the interaction of a variety of factors, of which the underlying competence of the speaker-hearer is only one. **1982** *Amer. Speech* LVII. 16 He must ultimately be willing to make claims about this base with respect to a speaker-hearer's capabilities. **1890** D. J. BLAIKLEY *Acoustics in Relation to Wind Instruments* 31 In one direction advantage is taken..to aid the player in producing certain notes, notably on the clarinet; the thumb,—or speaker-key of which is designedly used to open a small air-way, thereby introducing a weak place, by which means certain sub-divisions of the air column are aided, and certain others are hindered. **1972** S. RICHMOND *Clarinet & Saxophone Experience* vi. 104 By pressing the speaker key for the second harmonic all notes will sound an octave higher. **1965** N. CHOMSKY *Aspects of Theory of Syntax* i. 3 Linguistic theory is concerned primarily with an ideal speaker-listener, in a completely homogeneous speech-community. **1978** *Archivum Linguisticum* IX. 10 The ideal speaker-listener of generative theory. **1955** *Sun* (Baltimore) 29 July 8/6 The new 'hands-free' Speakerphones enable you to take notes, refer to records, have others in the room with you join in the telephone conversation. **1968** *Time* 5 Apr. 54 Emerson, a municipal court judge in Downey, Calif., finds the speakerphone invaluable for getting a brief piece of testimony from a policeman, parole officer or technical expert. [**1916** *Times* 16 Dec. 9/5 The Speaker's Electoral Reform Conference is for the moment in suspense.] **1917** *Times* 18 Jan. 9/5 The recommendations of the Speaker's Conference on Electoral Reform. **1974** *Times* 5 Mar. 2/3 Electoral reform has always been a matter for Parliament itself, expressing its view by means of free votes on recommendations by a Speaker's Conference. **1980** *Guardian* 18 Feb. 3/7 The last Speaker's Conference on electoral law, which met between 1972 and 1974, recommended.. that the minimum age for standing for Parliament should be reduced. **1936** J. C. GOODWIN *One of Crowd* xix. 271 Speakers' Corner is a mixed grill of apostles and propagators, of oddities and crudities, of fanatics and eccentrics. **1953** EARL WINTERTON *Orders of Day* xxii. 313 'Speakers' Corner' in Hyde Park. **1982** *Times* 16 Mar. 10/2 The crypt of St Paul's cathedral is regaining some of its historical reputation as an ecclesiastical Speakers' Corner. **1938** C. HIMES *Black on Black* (1973) 172 A speaker system was installed to throw his powerful voice even farther. **1974** *Times* 4 Mar. 1/8 At about 4.40 pm the hijacker in the cockpit announced over the speaker system that the aircraft would be landing at Amsterdam.

speakerine (spīkərī·n). [a. Fr. *speakerine*, f. *speaker* announcer (f. SPEAKER) + fem. suff. *-ine.*] A woman announcer on radio or television; a television hostess.

1957 *Manch. Guardian* 19 Dec. 5/3 B.B.C. television viewers will see a programme..in which ten European countries will take part... The British contribution is to be the 'finale', in which Sylvia Peters is to introduce the women announcers—known as 'speakerines'—of Europe. **1973** D. MAY *Laughter in Djakarta* v. 97 We're going to hear the news from this lovely speakerine? **1979** J. RATHBONE *Euro-Killers* ix. 96 He..turned on the television. A speakerine was announcing the programme.

speakie (spī·ki). *temporary.* [f. SPEAK *v.* + -IE, after *MOVIE, *TALKIE.] A stage play in contrast to a (silent) film; rarely, = *TALKIE. Usu. *pl.*

1921 J. M. BARRIE *Let.* 18 Sept. (1942) 192 The ordinary stage drama he [*sc.* Charlie Chaplin] called the 'Speakies'. **1927** *Observer* 24 Apr. 15/1 She prophesied the downfall of the 'speakies' and the triumphant survival of the 'movies'. **1927** *Daily Tel.* 11 Oct. 6 An innovation last night was the introduction of a real stage set in the middle of the film... Whether this mixture of 'movie' and 'speakie' is desirable may be questioned. **1928** *Sunday Dispatch* 15 July 14 'Talkies' or 'speakies' as they are calling them in Hollywood, have very definitely arrived.

speaking, *vbl. sb.* Add: **2. b.** Now chiefly *U.S.* (Further examples.) *at this* (or *the*) *present speaking*, at this moment.

1835 J. P. KENNEDY *Horse-Shoe Robinson* I. vi. 78 If I suspicioned a bamboozlement, which I am not far from at this present speaking. **1863** C. C. HOPLEY *Life in South* I. 57 Then came the 'speaking', as the sermon was called. **1891** M. E. RYAN *Told in Hills* III. v. 205 At the present speaking the days are not picnic days. **1895** 'C. E. CRADDOCK' *Mystery Witch-Face Mt.* 206 Thar war a big crowd at the cross roads ter hear the speakin'. **1942** J. THOMAS *Blue Ridge* v. 155 Men..will travel miles to a speaking—which may be a political gathering or one for.. discussing road building.

3. b. (Later example.)

1920 D. H. LAWRENCE *Lost Girl* iv. 54 She began to hate outspokenness and direct speaking-forth of the whole mind.

5. a. *speaking engagement, order, part* (later examples), *tour, trip, voice* (examples).

1870 O. LOGAN *Before Footlights & behind Scenes* iii. 37 By and by I got into 'speaking parts', such as the Duke of York in Richard the Third. **1879** *Law Rep. Appeal Cases* IV. 40 If the Court of Quarter Sessions stated upon the face of the order, by way of recital, that the facts were so and so, and the grounds of its decision were such as were so stated, then the order became upon the face of it, a speaking order. **1908** E. TERRY *Story of My Life* xiv. 355 Melba..had a bad cold, and therefore a frightful *speaking* voice for the moment. **1924** W. HOLTBY *Crowded Street* xxxvi. 270 Delia..departed northwards on a speaking tour. **1931** F. L. ALLEN *Only Yesterday* ii. 32 He would win them to his cause, making a speaking trip through the West. **1944** N. STREATFEILD *Curtain Up* viii. 99 Mime..she loved. Then there were her speaking parts. **1973** 'E. MCBAIN' *Hail to Chief* vi. 109, I have a speaking engagement... I'm talking at a women's college. **1977** *Rolling Stone* 5 May 15/4 White, a big man with a rich, resonant speaking voice which turned into a tough growl when he sang. **1978** M. DICKENS *Open Book* xix. 173 On this speaking tour, my engagements fell roughly into two main categories. **1979** LD. DENNING *Discipline of Law* II. i. 66 It was possible to extend it to include not only the order of the Tribunal itself—when it was a 'speaking order'—but in addition all the documents properly before the Tribunal and considered by them.

c. (Example with *upon.*)

1801 M. EDGEWORTH *Belinda* I. xii. 370 Lady Delacour is not upon speaking terms with this Mrs. Margaret Delacour; she cannot endure her.

speaking, *ppl. a.* Add: **1.** *speaking clock*, a telephone service giving the correct time in words (cf. *talking clock* s.v. *TALKING *ppl. a.* 2); *speaking stop*, a stop key on an organ which permits or prevents the sounding of a rank of pipes.

1934 *P.O. Electr. Engineers' Jrnl.* XXVII. 142/1 For some time past a speaking clock has been installed in Paris. **1938** *Oxf. Compan. Mus.* 660/2 An organ of 168 actual 'speaking stops' (we so call the stops which really sound, as distinct from other devices.) **1977** *Gramophone* Mar. 1444/2 This is a very large Compton organ indeed, with 37 speaking stops on the pedal. **1978** 'H. CARMICHAEL' *Life Cycle* xiii. 139 If nobody at Scotland Yard has a watch you could've dialled the Speaking Clock.

speakingness. (Later example.)

1957 E. BOWEN in K. Mansfield *34 Short Stories* 15 Words had but one appeal for her, that of speakingness.

speako (spī·ko). *U.S. slang.* [f. *SPEAK(EASY + *-O[2].] = *SPEAKEASY.

1931 *Amer. Mercury* Dec. 415/2 There's only one thing in the world that puts a speako over, and that's good will. **1932** *Ibid.* Jan. 11 A brewery which supplied every other speako between Fourteenth and Canal streets. **1941** J. M. CAIN *Mildred Pierce* (1943) i. 29 Making the grand tour of all the speako's he knows.

spear, *sb.*[1] Add: **I. 2. a.** (Later examples.)

1930 R. CAMPBELL *Adamastor* 60 A starved mongrel.. From where he crouched, a thrilling spear of pain, Hurled forth his Alleluia to the sky. **1934** T. S. ELIOT *Rock* ii. 78 Encompassed with enemies armed with the spears of mistaken ideals.

b. The 'sack'; dismissal. *Austral. slang.*

1912 in Stewart & Keesing *Old Bush Songs* (1957) 273 I've been many years a shearer and I fancied I could shear, I've shore for Rouse of Guntawung and always missed the spear. **1941** BAKER *Dict. Austral. Slang* 69 *Get the spear*, to be dismissed from a job.

II. 8. *spear-tip*; *spear-forest, -print, surge.*

1946 S. SPENDER *European Witness* xiv. 217 A country of clustered spear-forests and gloomy heaths. **1911** E. POUND *Canzoni* 4 Deep in my heart that spear-print stays, That wound I got beyond the waters. **1900** CHESTERTON *Wild Knight & Other Poems* 103 The crest of the spear-surge. **1930** T. S. ELIOT tr. *St.-J. Perse's Anabasis* 43 The horsemen..feeding on their spear-tips the pure disasters of sunshine.

9. a. *spear-fisher, -fisherman.*

1951 T. C. ROUGHLEY *Fish & Fisheries of Australia* ix. 309 Members will not..seek quarrels with line-fishermen or other spear-fishermen regarding priority rights of fishing at any place. **1962** *Underwater Swimming* ('Know the Game' Ser.) 19/1 The spearfisherman should always carry a knife. *Ibid.*, An added safety device is to have a float anchored in the diving area to which the spearfisher can go to rest or leave his catch. **1982** *Times* 21 July 3/3 Dr Paul Cragg, a biologist, was in favour of resuming grants for spearfishermen.

b. *spear-fishing* (later examples; hence, as a back-formation, *spear-fish* vb. intr. and trans.); also similative, as *spear-flashing.*

1962 *Times* 6 Apr. 7/2 Sail, snorkel, skin-dive, spear-fish in tropical Florida. **1963** *Harper's Bazaar* Jan. 65/1 On the Côte d'Azur, many of the big fish have been.. spear-fished out of sight. **1973** J. JONES *Touch of Danger* xix. 106, I spearfished... Sonny..was no adept with flippers or speargun. **1945** Spear-fishing [see *FLIPPER *sb.*[2] 1 b]. **1960** M. A. GABRIELSEN et al. *Aquatics Handbk.* xiv. 102/1 Spear fishing is becoming a popular competitive as well as recreational sport. **1973** J. JONES *Touch of Danger* xix. 107 Sonny was against spearfishing for sport. **1937** BLUNDEN *Elegy* 78 Against high blue Spear-flashing white the spire.

c. *spear-shaken, -stuck, -tipped.*

1947 S. SPENDER *Poems of Dedication* IV. 56 Above the destroyed city reborn city..Tower of wings climbing spear-shaken skies. **1943** D. GASCOYNE *Poems 1937–42* 5 Whose are these hollow red-filmed eyes And thorn-spiked head and spear-stuck side? **1954** W. FAULKNER *Fable* 132 The spear-tipped iron fence beyond which the three sentries flanked the blank door beneath the three morning-windy flags.

d. *spear-straight* adj.

1848 J. R. LOWELL *Poems* 2nd Ser. 69 A stem.. Standing spear-straight in the waist-deep moss. **1919** J. MASEFIELD *Reynard the Fox* II. 107 With spear-straight stern.

10. spear-carrier, a carrier of a spear, a spearman: used *transf.* as (*a*) orig. *Theatr. slang*, an actor with a walk-on part; hence, an unimportant participant; (*b*) *U.S. colloq.*, a proponent or 'standard-bearer' (cf. *SPEARHEAD 1 b); **spear gun,** a type of weapon used in spearfishing which operates by firing a detachable harpoon; also *attrib.*; hence **spear-gunner; spear tackle** *Austral.*, an illegal tackle in rugby football in which a player is lifted and thrust to the ground head first; hence as *v. trans.*

1960 *New Yorker* 13 Aug. 97/1 The 'Quartet' is full of characters who in one novel may seem irritatingly superfluous spear-carriers,..but who in the 'Quartet' turn out to be members of a literary repertory company. **1963** *Times* 20 May 12/5 Most of those spear-carriers not only don't know where the United States is but they don't know where they are themselves. **1967** *N.Y. Times* 21 May 26/1 Dr. King had 'emerged as the public spear-carrier of a civil disobedience program'. **1976** *Times* 18 Mar. 10 In Wisconsin on the same day Representative Morris Udall, the 'liberal-progressive' spear carrier, will have to win to stay in the race. **1981** N. MARSH *Black Beech & Honeydew* (rev. ed.) x. 215 The students.. would begin to accept the enormous challenge of a Shakespeare play and their own real importance, if only as spear-carriers, in doing so. **1982** *Sunday Sun-Times* (Chicago) 20 June 100/1 By the time Breakfast at Wimbledon telecasts are beamed into the United States on Fourth of July weekend, American tennis pros Davis, Dunk and Hardie will have vacated their present lodging and be long gone from the venerable tournament that they graced momentarily as spear-carriers. **1951** T. C. ROUGHLEY *Fish & Fisheries Austral.* ix. 303 The sport of fishing with spears or spear-guns under water..has had only a brief history. *Ibid.* 304 Most Australian spear-gun fishermen use a gun with rubber as the motive power. **1979** J. LEASOR *Love & Land Beyond* i. 7 The..five-pronged fork of an underwater spear gun. **1951** T. C. ROUGHLEY *Fish & Fisheries Austral.* ix. 308 Those responsible for such an attitude know little of the spear-gunner's activities. **1969** *Sun-Herald* (Sydney) 13 July 36/2 Canterbury were penalised for a spear tackle on Cavanagh. **1977** *Telegraph* (Brisbane) 8 Nov. 3/3 He was injured after he was allegedly spear-tackled... A player is spear-tackled when an opponent tackles low, lifts the man with the ball high, turns him over and thrusts him into the ground head first.

spear, *sb.*² Add: **2. d.** The edible shoot, including stem and tip or head, of asparagus or of sprouting broccoli (esp. calabrese).

1952 *Quick Freezing* Jan. 9/1 At a Birds Eye press conference held recently it was stated that three new products have been added to that range. These are: (1) Chicken livers... (2) Broccoli spears, broccoli cuts... (3) Pineapple slices in syrup. **1966** *Harrod's Food News* Sept. 2/1 Brocolli Spears—8 oz. 2/11 *Ibid.* 5/1 Asparagus spears Spanish (5½ in. long)—17 oz. tin 4/9. **1969** *Oxf. Bk. Food Plants* 162/1 Asparagus..is usually considered to be a luxury vegetable. The part eaten is the young shoot or 'spear'. **1974** P. WESTLAND *Taste of Country* ii. 37/2 Cover with the cooked broccoli spears and then the cheese sauce. **1979** *Sunset* Apr. 178/2 A light entrée, it's especially good when accompanied with sliced ham..and additional spears of freshly cooked asparagus.

spear, *v.*³ Add: **1. b.** To dismiss. *Austral. slang.* Cf. *SPEAR *sb.*¹ 2 b.

1911 'S. RUDD' *Dashwoods* 13 If I was the boss here I would. I'd spear him without warnin'.

c. To cause to move like a spear; to spear-head.

1920 W. CAMP *Football without Coach* v. 85 The ball should be held in the hand and speared through the air by giving the hand a twist as the ball leaves it. **1951** *Daily Progress* (Charlottesville, Va.) 11 Feb. 1/6 The Second Division at the end of its eight-day battle had set the pattern of the Eighth Army's new hunt-and-kill offensive with aggressive tank forces spearing the way. **1969** G. MACBETH *War Quartet* 46 So when I Speared the first squadron in the dawn assault Over the cliffs, that wool..Warmed the heart's beating.

d. To beg; to obtain by begging. *U.S. slang.*

1912 *Railroad Man's Mag.* Apr. 493/1 They had mooched the stem and threw their feet, And speared four-bits on which to eat. **1926** *Amer. Speech* II. 390/1 To *make the grade* or *connect* is to get the amount of money one is after. *Spear* is another word for connecting. **1942** BERREY & VAN DEN BARK *Amer. Thes. Slang* § 370/3 Beg; request a loan or gift,..*spear.*

2. b. To move like a spear. *rare.*

1944 *Times* 14 Apr. 4/2 Yesterday the tanks handed over to the infantry, and speared south-east and south-west towards the Crimean mountains.

spear-head, *sb.* Add: **1. b.** The leading part or element (of a thrust, movement, etc.); a person or group leading an attack.

1929 *Times* 12 Nov. 17/3 The Belfast members of the society..were made the spearhead of a thrust for an advance of wages for shipyard joiners alone. **1932** *Times* 12 July 6/3 Afterwards they [*sc.* Yorkshire] broke down before the Nottinghamshire attack, with Larwood as its spearhead, and lost seven wickets for 53 runs. **1940** *Hutchinson's Pictorial Hist. War* 10 Apr.–11 June 176 Synchronizing their Blitzkrieg attack with dive-bombers, German tanks acted as the spearhead in the rapid Nazi advance through the Low Countries and Northern France. **1945** L. MUMFORD *City Development* xii. 130 The park system is thus the very spearhead of comprehensive urban planning. **1946** *R.A.F. Jrnl.* May 168 He was called upon to organize the new spearhead for Bomber Command. **1951** 'J. WYNDHAM' *Day of Triffids* xii. 223 When they found that we represented only a group similar to their own, and were not the spearhead of a rescue party on the grand scale their interest would lapse. **1958** *Manch. Guardian* 20 Aug. 4/2 Lord Cameron and his colleagues do not think that the dockers' claim can be fairly regarded as the spearhead of a new national wage movement. **1962** *Times* 27 Nov. 13/2 Mr. W. P. Tapley..told me of..preparations to..keep traffic flowing regardless of the weather. 'Salt,' he said, 'is still the spearhead.' **1970** A. TOFFLER *Future Shock* iii. 40 America, as the spearhead of superindustrialism, represents a new, quicker, and very much unwanted tempo. **1977** 'J. LE CARRÉ' *Honourable Schoolboy* xviii. 442 The spearhead of the operation will be handled by ourselves. If supportive action is required, Martello will supply it.

3. *spear-head army, forces, group.*

1931 W. S. CHURCHILL *World Crisis* VI. xx. 301 Amid these varying schemes one plain question stood forth. Should Mackensen with the 'spear-head army' go on or stop? **1978** R. V. JONES *Most Secret War* xlix. 486 The enthusiasm of its members was such that they were sometimes ahead of our spearhead forces. **1977** M. WALKER *National Front* ii. 39 During 1961, the Special Branch had been aware that the Spearhead group had been formed.

Hence **spea·r-head** *v. trans.*, to act as the spear-head of, to lead (a movement, attack, etc.).

1938 *Daily News* (Los Angeles) 27 July 8/1 Liberal leader who spearheaded the debate. **1943** *Sun* (Baltimore) 9 July 1/6 He also disclosed that the Marines spearheaded the direct invasion of New Georgia by landing at Segi. **1944** *Times* 19 Feb. 4/7 Spearheaded by our fleet, we have been able to drive the enemy from these bases. **1957** K. A. WITTFOGEL *Oriental Despotism* 8 Those nonbureaucratic groups and strata which, in feudal Europe and Japan, spearheaded the rise of a commercial and industrial society. **1968** P. OLIVER *Screening Blues* ii. 88 Spearheaded by singers like Little Richard Penniman, Ray Charles or B. B. King.., the musical forms which had been held at a distance for so long were allowed to merge. **1980** M. FONTEYN *Magic of Dance* 289 She was such an intelligent artist and fine dancer that she was able to spearhead the ballet reforms, still advancing rather slowly. **1983** *Times* 21 Jan. 16/5 Furniture sales appear to be spearheading the upturn in consumer spending.

Spearman² (spiə·ɹmæn). *Statistics.* The name of Charles Edward *Spearman* (1863–1943), English psychologist, used *attrib.* and in the possessive to designate a coefficient he devised as a measure of the degree of agreement between two rankings, being their product-moment correlation coefficient; symbol ρ or *R.*

1907 *Drapers' Company Res. Mem.* (Biometric Ser.) IV. 22 There is a further very serious indictment to be made against Spearman's R... R retains a constant value for wide variations in ρ_{12}. **1942** *Biometrika* XXXII. 277 The Spearman coefficient ρ may be regarded as a sample grade correlation. *Ibid.* 278 The error involved in using Spearman's ρ from a small sample. **1970** *Jrnl. Gen. Psychol.* LXXXIII. 91 A Spearman rank correlation coefficient.. between the median latency scores on the last day of training and the mean of the median latencies over the three days of testing produced a value of —·3.

spearmint. Add: **1. c.** *ellipt.* A piece of chewing-gum flavoured with the oil extracted from this plant.

1920 'SAPPER' *Bull-Dog Drummond* ix. 240 A grim-faced man at the wheel..had apparently felt the seriousness of the occasion so acutely, as to deposit his third piece of spearmint on the underneath side of the steering-wheel for greater safety. **1945** J. STEINBECK *Cannery Row* i. 9 No Abbeville child..knew the lack of a stick of spearmint ever afterward.

spear-point. Add: **1.** (Later *Comb.* example.)

1930 BLUNDEN *Poems* 55 Like stars in frost as spear-point-bright.

2. Also *fig.*

1937 R. WARNER in C. Day Lewis *Mind in Chains* 37 Let us utilise this weight without blunting the spearpoint of our advances. **1963** *Times* 15 Jan. 8/4 The spearpoint of aggression has been blunted in Vietnam.

spec, *sb.*¹ Add: **1. b.** In recent use more generally, as a gamble, on the off chance.

1928 R. CAMPBELL *Wayzgoose* ii. 36 Some came on spec and others came on bikes. **1938** F. D. SHARPE *Sharpe of Flying Squad* xxv. 256 He never tries anywhere on spec., and never does more than two houses a night. **1970** G. GREER *Female Eunuch* 178 The third book bought on that same day was bought on spec. **1978** *New York* 3 Apr. 36/3 Franklin Thomas remembers starting the center on spec with an analysis that projected a 50–50 chance of succeeding. **1981** B. HINES *Looks & Smiles* 197 'Is he expecting you?' 'No, we just came on spec.'

spec, *sb.*² *U.S. slang.* [Short for SPECTACLE *sb.*¹ or SPECTACULAR *sb.*] **a.** In a circus: (see quot. 1926). **b.** An elaborate and expensive television show.

1926 *Amer. Speech* I. 283/1 *Spec.*, the opening spectacle, or grand entry. **1949** *New Yorker* 5 Nov. 61 Mrs. Webster rode an elephant in the 'spec'. **1959** G. MARX *Let.* 7 Dec. in *Groucho Lett.* (1967) 268 Our little play..could possibly be done as a TV spec.

spec, *sb.*³ *colloq.* [Short for SPECIFICATION.] A detailed working description; a standard of manufacture or construction. Also *transf.* Freq. *pl.*

1956 *Mag. Fantasy & Sci. Fiction* Oct. 20/2 Belle was not only a perfect secretary.. she also had personal specs which would have delighted Praxiteles. **1966** *Aviation Week & Space Technology* 5 Dec. 5/3 (Advt.), The reliability requirements are, in many cases, virtually unbelievable. Seemingly, a unit built to these kinds of specs would almost have to work perfectly forever. **1976** J. CARROLL *Madonna Red* (1977) i. 30 The 707 spec sheets she had memorised..at the Black September training camp. **1979** *Amat. Photographer* 30 May 99/1 The basic specs of these two new OMs remain the same. **1979** *Truck & Bus Transportation* July 20/2 Leyland Australia is basically working within the U.K. spec. to keep costs down.

spec, *sb.*⁴ Colloq. abbrev. of *SPECIALIST 2 c. *U.S.*

1958 *Army–Navy–Air Force Register* 14 June 7 Grade E7. Title, Old: Master Spec. New: Specialist-7. **1969** I. KEMP *Brit. G.I. in Vietnam* iii. 43 Specialist Fourth Class—or Spec. Four—Much, a small man..who talked in a continuous monotone. **1977** 'E. MCBAIN' *Long Time no See* xii. 200 These are designations of rank. An E-3 is a Pfc., a Spec 4 is Specialist 4th Class, a corporal. An E-5 is a three-striper, and so on.

spec, *a. colloq.* [Short for SPECULATIVE *a.*] Of or pertaining to the practice of building houses without prior guarantee of sale, esp. in estate developments. Also as *adv.* Cf. SPECULATIVE *a.* 7 a in Dict. and Suppl.

1958 *Observer* 2 Mar. 8/4 As 'developers' and L.P.T.B. leap-frogged over each other..far into the Home Counties, we created the vast paradise of spec' building and hire-purchase. **1958** *Spectator* 4 July 13/1 Builder-designed 'spec' houses. *Ibid.* 8 Aug. 193/2 A film snippet of 'spec.' housing. **1962** D. TENCH *Law for Consumers* vii. 100 Where the buyer buys a completed new house from the builder or developer (what is sometimes called a 'spec' built house). **1965** *New Society* 11 Nov. 6/3 How seldom local authorities and spec builders use any research at all. **1970** J. BETJEMAN *Ghastly Good Taste* (new ed.) p. xxv, Spec. builders and advertisement hoardings and litter droppers. **1978** J. WAINWRIGHT *Jury People* iii. 191 That estate..contains..'high density' housing... 'Spec building'—that is, or was, the term used for such estates. **1978** *Listener* 14 Sept. 337/3 The new, spec-built, often neo-Georgian houses.

special, *a.*, *adv.*, and *sb.* Add: **A.** *adj.* **3. a.** (Further examples.)

1854 GEO. ELIOT tr. *Feuerbach's Essence Christianity* iii. 44 God as God..has no more significance for religion than a fundamental general principle has for a special science. **1859** BARTLETT *Dict. Amer.* (ed. 2) 432 *Special deposit*, a deposit made in a bank subject to the control of the depositor, and which is not made a part of the funds of the bank to be used by it in its business. **1866** *Weekly New Mexican* (Santa Fe) 22 Dec. 2/2 One of the senators from San Miguel county having resigned, a special election was held. **1886** I. M. RITTENHOUSE *Jrnl.* 3 Feb. in *Maud* (1939) xi. 368 Eliza brought me a special delivery letter from my good boy. **1904** *Harper's Mag.* Feb. 462/2 And what a lucky chance that brought me a 'special delivery'. **1907** R. HERMON-HODGE *Let.* 20 Jan. in R. S. Churchill *Winston S. Churchill* (1969) II. Compan. I. 641, I am sure you will agree that while the class of men which provides the Yeomanry with officers must often present 'special cases' such as yours, it would never do to make them precedents. **1908** Special school [see *DEFECTIVE *sb.* 2 c]. **1911** W. JAMES *Some Probl. Philos.* i. 4 Limited by the omission of the special sciences, the name of philosophy has come more and more to denote ideas of universal scope exclusively. **1921** *Handicapped Children* (Connecticut Board of Educ.) 6 Let us consider those children who are in need of special education because of some degree of mental abnormality. **1929** E. C. THOMAS *Lay Folks' Hist. Liturgy* I. xiv. 62 In addition to the missions mentioned above, there seems to have been a special relationship between Britain and Galicia. **1944** *Act* 7 & 8 *Geo. VI* c. 31 § 228 In fulfilling their duties under this section, a local education authority shall, in particular, have regard..to the need for securing that provision is made for pupils who suffer from any disability of mind or body by providing, either in special schools or otherwise, special educational treatment. **1944** H. A. HODGES *Wilhelm Dilthey* 110 At the close of the Middle Age the emancipation of the special sciences began. **1945** *Hansard Commons* 7 Nov. 1299 We should not abandon our special relationship with the United States and Canada about the atomic bomb. **1957** LD. HAILEY *African Survey 1956* xvii. 1160 The academic standards to be adopted in the new University College in the first instance were to be those of the University of London, and an application to enter into 'special relationship' with the University of London was accepted. **1958** *Times* 4 July 15/1 The new scheme of 'special deposits' to be introduced by the Bank of England will in effect be kept in reserve in case of need. **1961** *Yale Review* LI. 21 If Britain enters 'Europe', the possibly illusory 'special relationship' with the United States will lose much of its plausibility. **1963** *Sunday Express* 7 July 1 There is a faction in Washington which does not share the official United States policy of friendship for Britain, and which dislikes the 'special relationship' between the two countries. **1968** Special class [see *PREEMIE]. **1974** *State* (Columbia, S. Carolina) 15 Feb. 22-A/6 The beleaguered Republican candidate in the February 5 special election to replace the late Rep. John Saylor of Pennsylvania. **1974** Special vote [see *OVERALL, OVER-ALL *adv.* 1 c]. **1976** *Pacifist* Jan. 4/1 The Secretary of State for Defence insists that defence is a special case—housing, social services, education are not? **1977** Special delivery [see *RECORDED *ppl. a.* 1 b]. **1977** *Times Educ. Suppl.* 21 Oct. 47/3 A teacher with experience in Special Education to teach basic subjects to groups of slow-learning children. **1978** *London Clearing Banks* (Committee London Clearing Bankers) 68 From 1958 onwards the Bank was able to supplement its open-market operations with calls for special deposits from the clearing banks; when a call was made, each bank had to lodge at the Bank of England a cash deposit of a specified percentage of its total deposits. **1979** R. JAFFE *Class Reunion* (1980) III. iv. 333 The baby had been sent to a special school because she had been born with a kind of sickness. **1980** *Encounter* May 41/2 The encounters took on a peculiarly symbolic significance at a time when various signs point to the possible demise of Israel's 'special relationship' with West Germany and the United States.

c. *special edition* (earlier and later examples).

1872 B. JERROLD *London* xx. 177 The news-boy would deliver the special edition. **1939** L. MACNEICE *Autumn Jrnl.* v. 23 They are selling and buying the late Special editions snatched and read abruptly. **1957** V. BRITTAIN *Testament of Experience* iv. 162 Newsvendors calling special editions ran up and down.

d. Special collocations: *Special Air Service*, a special section of the armed forces trained in commando techniques of warfare; cf. *S.A.S.* s.v. *S 4 a; *special area*, a depressed area of high unemployment designated in 1934 (see quot.) for development and improvement; cf. *development area* s.v. *DEVELOPMENT 11; *Special Branch*, a section of the C.I.D. which deals with police matters relating to political security; *Special Drawing Right*, an additional drawing right allocated to member countries of the International Monetary Fund, allowing them extra powers to purchase foreign currency from the Fund, and so increase their foreign exchange reserves; usu. *pl.*; cf. SDR s.v. *S 4 a; *special effect* (Cinematogr.), a scenic illusion created by props and camera-work (see quot. 1951); usu. *pl.*; *special interest* (U.S.), a group or corporation which seeks special advantages for itself, usu. by political means; *special paper*, an extra advanced examination of the General Certificate of Education, formerly known as a scholarship paper; *Special Reserve*, special units formed in peacetime to furnish a reserve for the regular army in time of war; *special stage* (see quot. 1967).

1942 *We speak from the Air* (Ministry of Information) xvii. 53 There is no better example of co-operation between the services than in the organisation and training of the Special Air Service troops that has been quietly taking place for some time. **1977** *Proc. R. Soc. Med.* LXX. 504/1 Major I. T. Houghton discussed first aid in the Special Air Service Regiment. This was formed in 1941 by David Stirling for operations behind the enemy lines in North Africa. **1980** *Jrnl. R. Soc. Arts* July 491/1 The Special Air Service..is trained for special tasks and it therefore represents the ready-made anti-hijacking force. **1934** *Act* 25 *Geo. V* c. 1 § 8 (1) This Act may be cited as the Special Areas (Development and Improvement) Act, 1934. **1945** *Archit. Rev.* XCVII. 109/1 The former Special Areas, now renamed (with adjustments) the Development Areas, are not necessarily economic and social entities. **1979** G. Pottinger *Secretaries of State for Scotland 1926–76* xiv. 148 The modest incentives dating originally from the Special Areas Acts of 1934 and 1937, and modified by post-war legislation, to persuade firms to move to depressed districts were no longer considered adequate. **1894** J. G. Littlechild *Reminiscences* i. 8 The later years of my service at Scotland Yard were spent in connection with the 'special' branch of the Criminal Investigation Department. **1936** 'N. Blake' *Thin Shell of Death* ix. 159 Scotland Yard had got into touch with the Special Branch in Dublin. **1962** *Listener* 15 Mar. 459/2 Warrants of this kind would be normally executed by special branch officers acting under the directions of the Director of Public Prosecutions. **1979** J. Wainwright *Duty Elsewhere* vii. 30 The Special Branch... Originally, it was the Special *Irish* Branch. Terror met by terror. **1982** *Listener* 16 Dec. 4/1 It is held by those in Special Branch that contact with Security Service is already so close that SB ought to take over primary responsibility for counter-espionage. **1967** *Bankers' Mag.* CCIV. 216 The scheme for creating new 'reserve units'.. had already been abandoned for a plan for establishing new special automatic drawing rights with the IMF... The special drawing rights will be shown as part of the reserves in Britain and the US... The special drawing rights are to be administered by the IMF, but kept separate from its other assets. **1971** H. Wilson *Labour Govt.* xxxv. 726 The IMF Special Drawing Rights scheme..had come into effect on 28 July [1969]. **1978** *Internat. Relations Dict.* (U.S. Dept. State Library) 23/2 The IMF has created its own international unit of account—the Special Drawing Right (or SDR or 'paper gold'). **1937** Special effects [see *editor *sb.* 5]. **1951** *Jrnl. Soc. Motion Picture & Television Engineers* LVII. 53/1 Studio terminology combines under 'special effects' a large variety of items, materials, equipment and processes which..aid in realistically imitating natural phenomena..which otherwise could be considered only at prohibitive expense or with impossible hazards. **1978** R. Hill *Pinch of Snuff* vii. 65 The special effects department must be getting better. **1910** G. Pinchot *Fight for Conservation* 134 The people of the United States believe that..the Senate and the House no longer represent the voters by whom they were elected, but the special interests by whom they are controlled. **1980** *Outdoor Life* (U.S.) (Northeast ed.) Oct. 21/2 It is a measure of the arrogance of the special interests that 53 of the new lease applications are for tracts inside the proposed wilderness area. **1963** *Times Educ. Suppl.* 1 Feb. 197/4 In your issue of November 23 a letter was published concerning the restriction imposed by the S.S.E.C. that no A level candidate may offer more than two of the special papers which are to replace the scholarship papers. **1976** *Bridgwater Mercury* 21 Dec. 1/5 Karen..passed all of her A level subjects, English, Economics and History at Grade A, as well as gaining a Distinction on the Special Paper in the last subject. **1908** *Times* 11 Apr. 8/2 The second order details the precise conditions of the transfer of all Militia units, except those disbanded, to the Special Reserve. **1908** *Regs. for Officers of Special Reserve* 1 The Special Reserve of Officers is a branch of the Reserve of Officers, established by Royal Warrant dated the 3rd April, 1908. *Ibid.*, The Special Reserve. Special reservists form part of the first class of the army reserve. **1909** *Army & Navy Gaz.* 19 June 589/2 Mr. Haldane stated that bayonets are now being issued to all infantry units of the Special Reserve which are being armed with the short rifle. **1931** [see *cadre 2]. **1935** *Regs. for Officers & Airmen of Special Reserve serving in R.A.F. Squadrons* (Amendment 5) 1 Applications for the attendance of Special Reserve personnel to give evidence in private lawsuits will be reported at once through the usual channels. **1967** P. Moss *Story so Far* vi. 65 A lot of international rallies..have special stages, or tests, over the worst bits of road they can find. Not all big rallies have to do this but on those which do it is on these special stages that the rally is won and lost. **1977** *Belfast Tel.* 27 Jan. 25/4 The other two members of the team have elected him to drive all the competitive sections—or special stages—along the 18,000 mile route.

4. a. (Further examples.)

1843 N. Simons *Statutes at Large, U.K.* XVI. 131 Commissioners for General Purposes to execute all Matters with respect to the Duties under all the Schedules except such as are directed to be executed by Special or other commissioners. **1926** *Daily Chron.* 13 May 1/3 Measures must be taken to demobilise the special constabulary.. and to ensure the speedy return to normal conditions. **1932** Auden *Orators* i. 36 Jokes about special constables and conscientious objectors. **1956** in J. Biggs-Davison *Hand is Red* (1973) x. 134 Members of the R.U.C. and B Special Constabulary. **1970** *Britain 1970: an Official Handbk.* (Central Office of Information) 105 All police forces have an attachment of special constables, who are volunteers willing to perform police duties without pay in their spare time. In England and Wales the function of special constables is to act as auxiliary to the regular force when required. In Scotland they are employed only in emergencies, although they may be assigned for duty for training purposes. **1970** P. Laurie *Scotland Yard* 294 *Special patrol group*, a unit of uniform policemen, about 130 strong, attached to no particular area. They are available for intensive patrolling, searches, guards, raids, etc. **1971** *Halsbury's Statutes England* (ed. 3) XXXIV. 1252 Unlike the General Commissioners..the Special Commissioners are civil servants, and their powers and duties are not limited to any particular area... They do, however, act independently of the Crown. **1980** P. G. Winslow *Counsellor Heart* xx. 215 Men were sent to saturate the area. The Special Patrol Group was called in.

c. *special buyer*, the bill-broker of the Bank of England in the discount market; *special partner* (U.S.) = *limited partner* s.v. *limited *ppl. a.* 2 b.

1941 *Economist* 1 Feb. 149/1 The help given to the market last week by the special buyer has made itself more felt. **1965** Seldon & Pennance *Dict. Econ.* 311 In Britain open market operations in Treasury Bills are conducted through a firm of discount brokers (the 'Special Buyer') on instructions from the Bank of England. **1822** *Laws of State of New-York* ccxliv. 259 That partnerships, to be formed under this act, shall consist of one or more partners, jointly and severally responsible..who shall be called general partners; and one or more partners, who furnish certain funds or capital to the common stock, whose liability shall extend no further than the fund which he or they have furnished to the partnership stock, and who shall be called special partners. **1839** Marryat *Diary Amer.* 1st Ser. II. 251 In America, if a person wishes to become a special partner (a sleeping partner) in any concern, he may do so to any extent he pleases. **1889** *Cent. Dict.* 4309/1 If the statute governing partnerships is violated the special partner becomes liable as a general partner.

5. a. (Further examples.)

1790 F. Burney *Diary* Jan. (1842) V. III. 85 Mr Fairly's marriage..was by special licence, and at the house of Sir R— F—. **1825** Special licence [see *droit[1] 1 b]. **1849** *Rep. Sel. Comm. Public Libraries* 138 in *Parl. Papers* XVII. 1 The second description of libraries would be those destined to represent special branches of literature; for instance the Commercial Library, or the Library of Fine Arts, at Hamburgh, would be a most perfect instance of those special libraries. **1908** H. Cecil *Let.* 20 Aug. in R. S. Churchill *Winston S. Churchill* (1969) II. Compan. II. 808 A special licence costs a lot of money..so you had better go for an ordinary one or for banns. **1937** *Discovery* June 192/2 At the request of the British Council, the Association of Special Libraries and Information Bureaux has undertaken the compilation of a short list of standard and technical books by British authors. **1954** K. Amis *Lucky Jim* iii. 27 Have you got that syllabus together.. the list of stuff for your special subject next year? **1966** A. Battersby *Math. in Management* ix. 232 The appeal to elasticity is evident in any retail outlet with price reductions, 'special offers' or trading stamps. **1971** P. D. James *Shroud for Nightingale* vii. 243 He might well have told his special nurse or blurted it out in his delirium. **1973** *Scotsman* 7 Aug. 6/2 The 'wedding' in the registrar's office at Dumfries took place after the couple were granted a special licence in the courthouse only 50 yards away. **1976** *Gloss. Documentation Terms* (*B.S.I.*) 62 *Special library*, a library maintained by an association, government agency, parliament, research institution, learned society, professional association, museum, business firm, industrial organization, chamber of commerce, etc. or other organized group, the greater part of its collection being in a specific field or subject. **1977** *Western Morning News* 1 Sept. 1/1 Instant coffee is to be on 'special offer' in various shops and supermarkets for the next six months.

c. *special* (*theory of*) *relativity*: see *relativity 2.

7. *special magistrate, order, prosecutor, term.*

1852 *Alabama Reports* XX. 446 The Court of Commissioners of Roads and Revenue in this State has no power to hold special terms, except in cases expressly authorized by law. **1859** *Indiana Reports* XI. 562 The indictment was signed by James F. Suit, as prosecuting attorney; but it appears that he was a special prosecutor elected by the people. **1889** *Cent. Dict.*, *Special orders*, in *law*, those orders which are made only in view of the peculiar circumstances of the case, and require notice to the adversary and a hearing by the court. **1919** *Act* 9 & 10 *Geo. V* c. 100 § 26 Anything which under the Electric Lighting Acts may be effected by a provisional order confirmed by Parliament may be effected by a special order made by the Electricity Commissioners and confirmed by the Board of Trade. **1934** *Northeastern Reporter* CXC. 270/2 'Special term of court' is one not fixed by general statute establishing court terms, but ordinarily called pursuant to power granted by statute. **1936** *Panel* Mar. 3/3 Several thousand additional witnesses have been examined in the office of Mr. Dewey, the Special Prosecutor. **1966** Tacheron & Udall *Job of Congressman* vii. 198 Special orders are designed primarily to authorize the House to disregard the regular rules of procedure so that a particular matter can be handled with dispatch. **1973** *N.Y. Law Jrnl.* 25 July 12/8 The sole question raised on this appeal is whether or not Special Term erred when it concluded that a 1960 Pontiac convertible ..was covered under an automobile insurance policy issued with respect to a 1960 Buick sedan. **1974** *Greenville* (S. Carolina) *News* 22 Apr. 1/3 'The special prosecutor has already indicted and is preparing to try' seven former Nixon campaign or administration aides. **1975** J. P. Morgan *House of Lords & Labour Govt.* ii. 64 Orders are known in the Lords as Special Orders. **1979** *Internat. Jrnl. Sociol. of Law* VII. 279 The function of the Special Magistrate was 'to represent in his own person the whole policy of Britain'.

7*. *Math.* Of a group: that can be represented by matrices of unit determinant.

1903 J. E. Campbell *Theory Continuous Groups* i. 17 This group is called the special linear homogeneous group; it is a sub-group of the general linear homogeneous group. **1955** B. Higman *Appl. Group-Theoretic & Matrix Methods* xii. 181 The rotation group in three dimensions is isomorphic with a factor group of the special unitary group in two dimensions containing half the number of elements. **1955, 1967** [see *SU* s.v. *S 4 a]. **1968** M. S. Livingston *Particle Physics* xii. 212 Special unitary group theory based on two fundamental states (known by the symbol SU(2)) leads to the prediction of a multiplet structure in the spectrum of substates. **1971** D. Gorenstein in Powell & Higman *Finite Simple Groups* ii. 68 The latter group is the projective special unitary group.

8. *special agreement, -interest, -occasion, -procedure, -purpose, -range.*

1944 *Act* 7 & 8 *Geo. VI* c. 31 § 236 If at any time the managers or governors of an aided school or a special agreement school are unable or unwilling to carry out their obligations..it shall be their duty to apply to the Minister for an order revoking the order by virtue of which the school is an aided school or special agreement school. **1945** Nelson & Wright *Tomorrow's House* vii. 80/1 The living-room..is..turning into a special-purpose room like the study. **1952** *Times* 4 Feb. 2/3, £250,000 for grants in aid towards a new 'special agreement' secondary school, and for works at four aided polytechnics. **1956** Abraham & Hawtrey *Parliamentary Dict.* 188 *Special procedure order*, a term applied by the standing orders of both Houses to an order, made or confirmed by a minister, in relation to which the Statutory Orders (Special Procedure) Act, 1945, applies. **1957** *Times Lit. Suppl.* 8 Nov. 678/5 Instruction covers everything from the regular features of the dinner table to special-occasion items for the buffet or the hors-d'œuvre tray. **1959** W. K. Richmond *British Birds of Prey* p. xi, How far, if at all, was it safe to rely on a phraseology which enjoyed no common currency, however acceptable it might be to this or that special-interest group? **1961** *Act* 9 & 10 *Eliz. II* c. 62 2nd Schedule § 2 Where a trust fund includes special-range property,..the special-range property shall be carried to a separate part of the fund. **1964** D. Foulkes *Introd. Admin. Law* i. 6 The first part of the procedure provides for the proper publication of the order (known as a 'special procedure order') and the making of objections, and the second part for parliamentary scrutiny. **1982** *Time* 8 Nov. 92/2 The special-interest slangs generated then were interminably publicized.

C. *sb.* **5. a.** (Further examples.)

1833 W. H. Breton *Excursions in New South Wales* ii. 51 A Government Establishment formerly existed at Wellington Valley..and it was to this place that all the principal convicts, or those called *specials* were sent: that is to say, those of good connections. **1867** J. Morison *Australia* ix. 220 A laudable consideration was shown by the Government to a class of convicts belonging to..'the upper classes of society', and who were known by the name 'specials'. **1939** *War Illustr.* 9 Dec. 393/3 Accompanied by German police, bands of Sudeten 'specials' raided the University and the Czech societies, and many persons were taken to the Gestapo headquarters. **1955** *Times* 20 July 4/3 There were only two police constables on St. Mary's, reinforced for the occasion by four 'specials'. **1972** *Times* 7 Apr. 5/2 (*heading*) Specials platoon fired into crowd.

b. Also, a special article, dish, edition, offer, programme.

1867 *Oregon State Jrnl.* 19 Jan. 2/3 A Washington special says that [etc.]. **1899** J. F. Fraser *Round World on a Wheel* xiv. 162, I described..the London evening papers..the 'specials', 'extra specials', and 'second extra specials'. **1914** Joyce *Dubliners* 115 They went into the parlour at the back and O'Halloran ordered small hot specials all round. **1933** E. Waugh *Scoop* II. iv. 212 Make up the Irish edition with his morning cable... If the follow-up comes in..run a special. **1939** J. B. Priestley *Let People Sing* ii. 44 What about ordering the *Ninepenny Special*—steak-and-kidney pudding and peas? **1952** *Hist. Times* IV. 1. ix. 415 The leading articles and 'specials' exposing the exaggerations of the 'yellow peril' school published during the year. **1958** *Punch* 1 Jan. 60/3 Accepting one of his hostess's 'specials' at one of her now-famous 'get-together' parties. **1961** *Listener* 28 Dec. 1135/2 There have, however, been single performances and 'specials' worthy to be recalled. **1966** T. Pynchon *Crying of Lot 49* i. 14 Pink flyers advertising specials at the markets. **1977** B. Pym *Quartet in Autumn* ii. 24 I'll do one of my specials—baked beans on toast with a poached egg on top. **1979** *Tucson* (Arizona) *Citizen* 20 Sept. 7B/6 NBC made a deal with the studio to make a few two-hour 'Buck Rogers' movies, to be shown occasionally as specials. **1980** *Redbook* Oct. 46/1 Before you go to the supermarket, check your newspaper for sales. Watch for patterns; 'specials' usually occur toward the beginning of the month, when supplies are highest.

spe·cial, *v. slang.* [f. the sb.] **1.** *intr.* To work as a special correspondent for a newspaper.

1915 T. Burke *Nights in Town* 318, I have worked on six newspapers... I have done everything, from subbing to specialling.

2. *trans.* Of a member of the staff of a hospital: to attend continuously to (a single patient).

1961 'K. Norway' *Waterfront Hospital* vii. 130 She seems determined to special Emlyn Roberts. **1967** *Nursing Times* 27 Jan. 111/1 A nurse will have to 'special' the patient to make the necessary observations. **1978** L. Isenberg in D. Abse *My Medical School* 207 One night we were asked if someone would 'special' a lady who might require surgery during the night for suspected abdominal trauma.

specialism. Add: **2.** Also, a specialized area of knowledge or work; a professional or academic field.

1937 L. MUMFORD in F. Mackenzie *Planned Society* p. vii, Specialists..cannot plan: for planning involves the job of coordinating specialisms, focussing them in common fields of knowledge, and canalizing them in appropriate channels of common action. **1950** [see *EXPERTISE]. **1967** *Times Rev. Industry* May 125/2 These [*sc.* technical specifications] can be prepared in a fashion likely to impress a group of people of different specialisms, including operating managers, engineers, finance officers and scientists. **1977** *Antiquaries Jrnl.* LVII. 342 But why did the Americanist W. M. Bray find it so difficult to extract a subject from his own specialism?

specialist. Add: **2. b.** [tr. Russ. *spetsialist.*] In Communist parlance, a person with a specialist knowledge in some area of science, engineering, or culture; an engineer, scientist.

1929 V. M. MOLOTOV *Communist Party Soviet Union* 39 Of course there cannot be many among the ranks of the old specialists who could be taken into the Party... The Shakhty case revealed clearly enough that we have some of the most bitter enemies among the specialists, whose skill we must nevertheless use. **1974** T. P. WHITNEY tr. *Solzhenitsyn's Gulag Archipelago* I. I. ix. 334 The Case of Glavtop—May, 1921. This case was important because it involved *engineers*—or, as they had been christened in the terminology of the times, 'specialists', or spetsy. **1977** 'S. LEYS' *Chinese Shadows* (1978) ii. 101 It [*sc.* the Tower of the Six Harmonies] is such a sturdy building that an army of 'specialists' would have been necessary to demolish it.

c. An enlisted man in the U.S. army employed on specialized duties. Cf. *SPEC *sb.*[4]

Freq. prefixed to the name of a soldier. The grades of specialists are modelled on the ranks, from corporal to master sergeant, but do not correspond to them in other respects.

1955 *Army–Navy–Air Force Register* 14 May 1/1 Army personnel in the top four enlisted grades will be separated into two groups, non-commissioned officers and specialists... Those who perform non-leadership duties of a technical or administrative nature will be designated 'Specialists'.. and will rank among themselves as Master Specialists (E-7), Specialist First Class (E-6), Specialist Second Class (E-5), and Specialist (E-4). **1969** I. KEMP *Brit. G.I. in Vietnam* iii. 67, I got on particularly well with the new crew chief, Specialist Fifth Class Jaycelon. **1974** *Encycl. Brit. Micropædia* VII. 406/2 *Specialist*, military, any of four enlisted ranks in the U.S. Army corresponding to the grades of corporal (Specialist 4) through sergeant first class (Specialist 7).

2*. *Ecol.* A species which is closely adapted, and largely restricted, to a particular mode of life.

1966 *Amer. Naturalist* C. 607 When the gain to a jack-of-all-trades in reduced travelling time makes up for his lower hunting efficiency compared to the patch specialists, then the jack-of-all-trades will outcompete both specialists. **1973** P. A. COLINVAUX *Introd. Ecol.* xli. 576 Animals become specialists in eating particular plants; the plants, on an evolutionary time scale, respond with new poisons. **1978** *Nature* 5 Jan. 56/2 *K*-selected species (or 'specialists') exhibit conservative strategies for survival in predictable environments, and are adapted against pressures from predators and interspecific competition.

‖ **spécialité** (spesialite). Also **specialité.** [Fr.: see SPECIALITY.] A special or distinguishing feature, characteristic, etc.; a speciality. Also *specialité de la maison*, a dish which a restaurant considers its speciality, or one for which it is particularly noted. Cf. SPECIALITY 5 c in Dict. and Suppl.

1839 W. A. SHEE *Jrnl.* Sept. in *My Contemporaries* (1893) iii. 79 The jousts..are..the *specialité* of such a meeting. **1857** GEO. ELIOT *Let.* 1 Sept. (1954) II. 379 Every new or renovated journal should have a specialité —do something not yet done, fill up a gap. **1861** K. STANLEY *Let.* 1 Feb. in B. & P. Russell *Amberley Papers* (1937) I. iii. 114 Mr. Oliphant..is very anxious that Japan should not be thought his spécialité so he will not learn the language. **1893** SOMERVILLE & 'ROSS' *Vine Country* ix. 167 The *spécialité* of the town, ordered expressly for us by Monsieur A., the macaroons made at the convent according to an ancient recipe known to the nuns. **1914** 'SAKI' *When William Came* xiv. 242 Iced mulberry salad, my dear, it's a *spécialité de la maison*, so to speak; they say the roving husband brought the recipe from Astrakhan, or Seville, or some such outlandish place. **1935** A. E. W. MASON *They wouldn't be Chessmen* xii. 137 He would take his luncheon at a famous restaurant on the Quai which had a specialité de la maison. **1956** R. MACAULAY *Towers of Trebizond* xi. 119 We got several good trout, and two odd-shaped fishes which must have been a specialité of that lake, as we had never seen them before. **1957** 'P. PORTOBELLO' *Deb's Mum* 18 Old Lady Dolgelly, who made a *spécialité* of housekeeping. **1962** 'R. SIMONS' *Killing Chase* v. 68 'How about *Specialité de la Maison*?' 'What's that?' 'Cod roes on toast.' **1976** 'M. INNES' *Gay Phoenix* iii. 42 These Paphians, like the restaurants, had their *spécialités*.

speciality. Add: **5. c.** (Later examples.) Cf. *SPÉCIALITÉ.

1977 T. HEALD *Just Desserts* i. 16 Bognor chose..a speciality of the house called Pollo Sophia Loren. **1980** F. KING *Indirect Method* 161 You must try these profiteroles. Speciality of the *maison*. **1982** J. MIDGLEY *Stone Killer* iii. 23 They dined on the restaurant speciality, Sicilian-style macaroni.

6. b. *attrib.*

1930 E. FERBER *Cimarron* xxiii. 373 Fascinating little speciality shops..just like those..on Madison Avenue. **1938** [see *BACK *sb.*[1] 25 a]. **1959** *Times* 9 Mar. (Britain's Food Suppl.) p. xiv/4 Dishes produced in the speciality restaurant often surpass..those of establishments that attempt to run the full range. **1967** *Times Rev. Industry* Feb. 31/1 The newly-created group was thus firmly based in three different markets—household and pharmaceutical products and speciality foods. **1979** N. FREELING *Widow* iii. 10 A gigantic supermarket, with a covered gallery of speciality shops all around.

7. *Theatr.* Used *attrib.* to designate a performer or performance, esp. in variety entertainments, of an unusual or specialized character.

1933 P. GODFREY *Back-Stage* xv. 187 The next important subdivision of the chorus consists of the speciality dancing troupe. *Ibid.*, A few speciality solo steps. **1952** W. GRANVILLE *Dict. Theatrical Terms* 166 *Speciality artiste*, a vaudeville artiste who specializes in impersonations, juggling, etc. **1962** A. NISBETT *Technique Sound Studio* iii. 69 It is also possible to balance most dance bands and speciality groups on a single microphone provided that sufficient trouble is taken. **1967** *Stage* 2 Mar. 21/4 (Advt.), Wanted for long summer season speciality act, strong male vocal..and two girl dancers. **1970** W. J. BURLEY *To kill Cat* iii. 58 We had a cabaret artiste of that name... She was a speciality dancer and her art possessed great artistic merit.

specialization. Add: **2.** *Biol.* A specialized character or adaptive feature in an organism.

1918 F. W. JONES *Probl. Man's Ancestry* 30 Pithecoid specializations vary so much in their manifestations in the different groups of monkeys. **1978** *Nature* 26 Jan. 353/1 It seems that both intermuscular and subcutaneous lipid accumulation and a reduction in skeletal ossification have evolved as specialisations to reduce density in *Pleuragramma*, a pelagic Antarctic fish without a swim bladder.

specialty. Add: **9.** *N. Amer.* = SPECIALITY 6, *7, and 8.

1888 G. O. SEILHAMER *Hist. Amer. Theatre* II. 118 Dr. Bayley, a specialty performer..gave entertainments in this country as early as 1752. **1901** *Daily Colonist* (Victoria, B.C.) 3 Nov. 12/3 These expensive attractions in conjunction with a big specialty company of no mean pretensions will go to make up an excellent show. **1915** in S. Marcus *Minding Store* (1974) ii. 23 Twenty-five specialty shops in one building. **1919** [see *FOLLY *sb.*[1] 5 b]. **1936** J. STEINBECK *In Dubious Battle* i. 3 Department stores and specialty shops. **1961** BOWMAN & BALL *Theatre Lang.* 338 *Specialty number*, a song not intended to be fully integrated with the rest of the entertainment—Musical comedy. **1968** *Globe & Mail* (Toronto) 17 Feb. B4 Roblin Steel Corp..., maker of specialty steel forgings and castings.., plans to buy privately owned Washburn Co., maker of specialty household products. **1978** *Language* LIV. 189 M & M apparently prefer to leave these rich but page-devouring matters to specialty works.

speciate (spī·ʃiēit), *v. Biol.* [Back-formation from *SPECIATION.] *intr.* Of a population of plants or animals: to exhibit evolutionary development leading to the recognition of a new species. Hence **spe·ciating** *ppl. a.*, showing or inducing speciation.

1964 *Oceanogr. & Marine Biol.* II. 206 *C[odium] fragile* appears to be speciating as it moves into waters where these two subspecies are present. **1970** *Watsonia* VIII. 67 The lack of flower-constancy and of other speciating factors in the visitors. **1973** P. A. COLINVAUX *Introd. Ecol.* xli. 579 Man alone can change his niche without speciating. **1981** *Nature* 26 Feb. 743/2 Only rarely will members of the small speciating population be fossilized, so that the lineage will show what are known as 'punctuated equilibria'—a long series of unaltered fossil forms followed by a rapid shift to a new type.

speciation (spīʃiēi·ʃən). *Biol.* [f. SPECI(ES + -ATION.] The formation of new and distinct species in the course of evolution.

1906 O. F. COOK in *Science* 30 Mar. 506/2 Speciation.. is the origination or multiplication of species by subdivision, usually..as a result of environmental incidents. **1926** *Nature* 21 Aug. 271/1 Thus *speciation* through continuity stands in contrast with *mutation* through discontinuity. *Ibid.* 272/1 Isolation is the most important factor in the speciation of birds. **1953** J. S. HUXLEY *Evolution in Action* iii. 71 Much of speciation represents a frill of mere diversity. **1978** *Nature* 21 Sept. 255/1 Speciation involves the splitting of a single evolutionary lineage into two or more genetically independent ones.

specie. Add: **7. b.** For 'Now *rare* or *Obs.*' read 'Now *Obs.* exc. as erron. sing. of SPECIES *sb.* 10'. (Later examples.)

1974 A. SCOTT-JAMES *Sissinghurst* vi. 74 There are.. thickets of specie roses in many odd corners. **1974** *Country Life* 25 Apr. 1033/2 (Advt.), We specialise in Roses (specie & old-fashioned). **1980** *Daily Tel.* 22 Jan. 11/2 Castrated rats and other animals live longer than normal creatures of the specie. **1980** *Pan Am Clipper* Oct. 48/1 Is he [*sc.* man] descended directly from apes, or is he a specie that evolved from an entirely new.. branch of the primate tree?

8. specie jar, a large glass or china jar formerly used for storage in chemists' shops and now used only for display; **specie point** = *gold point* s.v. *GOLD[1] 10; **specie-room**, a strong-room on a ship in which gold coin was deposited.

1914 *N. & Q.* 14 Feb. 127/1 The well-known 'specie jars' of chemists' shops. **1929** C. J. S. THOMPSON *Myst. Apothecary* xix. 257 The large cylindrical vessels called 'specie jars', with metal or gilded lids, that still decorate some of the chemists' shop-windows. **1861** G. J. GOSCHEN *Theory Foreign Exchanges* iv. 50 There would have existed a certain competition..to buy at a heavy discount, much below specie point, in order subsequently to realize at least the specie value. **1966** A. GILPIN *Dict. Econ. Terms* 190 *Specie points or Gold points*, the extreme points of variation in a rate of exchange under the gold standard. **1891** *Scribner's Mag.* Nov. 603/2 In these days of heavy gold shipments, the specie-room on the steamship is a very important institution. *a* **1929** R. BEDFORD in Murdoch & Drake-Brockman *Austral. Short Stories* (1951) 100 I'll bring dynamite..and blow the specie-room open..and haul out the gold-boxes.

species, *sb.* Add: **9. f.** *Chem.* and *Physics.* A particular kind of molecule, ion, free radical, etc.; a distinct kind of atom (esp. a radioactive one) or sub-atomic particle.

[**1857** W. A. MILLER *Elem. Chem.* III. 45 Other remarkable species of compounds which are obtained by substitution, are those in which a portion of the hydrogen of the original body is displaced by chlorine.] **1895** C. S. PALMER tr. *Nernst's Theoret. Chem.* IV. ii. 521 We will select as a further..example of complete heterogeneous equilibrium, a system composed of H_2O and SO_2, i.e. two molecular species. **1948** *Nature* 28 Feb. 291/2 The use of tracer materials, radioactive species, and radiations. **1962** COTTON & WILKINSON *Adv. Inorg. Chem.* xiv. 427 Pure sulfuric acid contains a number of species in equilibrium. **1967** M. CHANDLER *Ceramics in Mod. World* vi. 179 Natural uranium is not a single nuclear species. It contains two isotopes. **1971** *Physics Bull.* Dec. 720/3 Using the techniques of flash photolysis..he has identified the spectra of many new species, like CH_2, CH_3 and NH_2. **1974** *Nature* 13 Dec. 538/1 Whether *n* is considered to be the total number of particles in the Universe or the number of a given species, such as electrons or nucleons, is not important within the accuracy considered here.

14. *species-cross*, *diversity*, *-evolution*, *-formation*, *group*; **species being**, a term [tr. G. *Gattungswesen* (P. C. Reinhard, 1797)] used by Marx to denote man's objective consciousness of life and the mastery of the natural world through work which characterize the human species; man considered in respect to these qualities; **species pair**, a pair of species which are similar, sympatric, and closely related, but distinct; **species-poor, -rich** *adjs.*, having a small, or large, number of species; so **species richness**; **species rose**, a rose belonging to a distinct species and not to one of the many varieties produced by hybridization; cf. *OLD ROSE; **species sanitation** *Med.*, measures taken against a particular species of mosquito in order to reduce the incidence of malaria; **species-specific** *a.*, found in or characteristic of the members of one species only; hence **species specificity**; **species-uniform** *a.*, consistent throughout a species.

1959 M. MILLIGAN tr. *Marx's Econ. & Philos. MSS of 1844* 75 Conscious life-activity directly distinguishes man from animal life-activity. It is just because of this that he is a species being. *Ibid.* 76 It is just in the working-up of the objective world, therefore, that man first really proves himself to be a *species being*. **1979** GLASSNER & FREEDMAN *Clinical Sociol.* iv. 95 Workers are alienated from..their 'species being', or from their human capacity for conscious and creative activity. **1926** J. S. HUXLEY *Ess. Pop. Sci.* 25 Where the offspring of species-crosses are perfectly fertile, [etc.]. **1967** *Oceanogr. & Marine Biol.* V. 257 An intuitive character referable to any natural population or assemblage of individuals is species diversity or biotic diversity. **1972** Species diversity [see *species richness* below]. **1946** F. E. ZEUNER *Dating Past* xii. 355 This genus experienced an episode of abundant species-evolution from the Eocene to the Miocene, or roughly for 50 million years. **1977** R. HOLLAND *Self & Social Context* viii. 246 Mead's concept of the social-self.. never clarifies the relation between species-evolution and individual development. **1941** J. S. HUXLEY *Uniqueness of Man* vi. 155 Chromosome-doubling after crossing is a method of species-formation in which the isolation is not spatial but genetic. **1975** *Nature* 24 Jan. 290/3 Some hakes, especially the western South American species-group (*M[erluccius] gayi*), might support a greater fishery than at present. **1942** J. S. HUXLEY *Evolution* vi. 284 Overlapping Species Pairs. Numerous puzzling cases are presented by extremely similar species which overlap over much of their range and yet remain distinct. **1959** *New Biol.* XXVIII. 70 Of some sympatric species-pairs, one member releases pollen in the morning and the other in the evening, and the stigmas of each species are receptive only at the appropriate times, so considerably reducing the chances of receiving foreign pollen. **1964** V. J. CHAPMAN *Coastal Veg.* ix. 225 In the absence of grazing a luxuriant and species-poor Festucetum rubrae develops. **1976** *Jrnl. R. Soc. Arts* CXXIV. 640/1 The Southern Ocean is characterized by a species-rich, productive ecosystem which contrasts sharply with the species-poor, relatively barren terrestrial and freshwater ecosystems of the islands and continental landmass. **1973** *Nature* 30 Mar. 344/2 In maintaining or reconstructing types of herbaceous vegetation in which the density of flowering plants exceeds 20 species/m²—the so-called 'species-rich' communities, success is often frustrated by competitive exclusion. **1981** *Country Life* 12 Feb. 376/3 Species-rich hedges were treated sympathetically. **1972**

Ecology LIII. 279/2 The pattern of bird species richness (mean number of species per census) was quite similar to the pattern of bird species diversity. **1930** J. N. HART *Rose Growing* ix. 57 The species roses are actually wild roses, either native..or imported. **1935** N. MITCHISON *We have been Warned* II. 196 There were Penzance briars, and species roses growing unpruned. **1976** LD. HOME *Way Wind Blows* xiv. 200 A very attractive garden to the south and front of the house..had been filled with a wide variety of species roses. **1930** M. F. BOYD *Introd. Malariol.* vi. 418 'Selective control', 'species control' or 'species sanitation', as it is variously designated, *i.e.*, limiting efforts to the control of one species. **1945** *New Biol.* I. 107 The disease can be controlled by applying anti-mosquito measures to these kinds [*sc.* malarial vectors] only. This method of control, species sanitation, was first used, with spectacular results, by Watson in Malaya. **1959** A. A. SANDOSHAM *Malariology* i. 19 The increased knowledge of the systematics and bionomics of local anopheline fauna made it possible to evolve the more scientific and more economic method of mosquito control referred to as 'species-sanitation'. **1924** *Jrnl. Exper. Med.* XL. 106 The question arises whether these antigens are simple species-specific proteins. **1956** *Nature* 21 Jan. 133/1 The reduction in oxygen consumption appears to be caused by a species-specific antibody in the N'Dama serum. **1980** A. KENNY *Aquinas* iii. 76 Chomsky has argued that it is impossible to explain the rapidity with which children acquire the grammar of a language from the..utterances of their parents unless we postulate a species-specific innate language-learning ability. **1925** *Jrnl. Exper. Med.* XLII. 141 Species specificity of cells is of a different order as opposed to species specificity of proteins. **1964** M. HYNES *Med. Bacteriol.* (ed. 8) vii. 76 The differences that make a protein molecule a specific antibody are only minor; in chemical structure and species-specificity..it is still a γ-globulin molecule. **1968** R. W. LANGACKER *Lang. & its Structure* ix. 247 The view that linguistic experience serves more to activate language than to shape it accounts for the fact that language is species uniform and species specific. **1976** *Word* 1971 XXVII. 225 If a sign language is treated on a par with an oral language, then language is neither species-specific nor species-uniform, because other species are now known to be capable of learning a sign language.

speciesism (spī·ʃīziz'm). [f. SPECIES *sb.* + -ISM.] Discrimination against or exploitation of certain animal species by human beings, based on an assumption of mankind's superiority.

1975 R. D. RYDER *Victims of Sci.* 16, I use the word 'speciesism' to describe the widespread discrimination that is practised by man against other species... Speciesism and racism both overlook or underestimate the similarities between the discriminator and those discriminated against. **1976** *New Society* 3 June 544/1 If racism and sexism are wrong, what about speciesism? Peter Singer apologises for using this graceless term. **1979** *Listener* 7 June 777/1 'Speciesism' is intended to convey the idea that one animal species, human beings, supposes that it has the right to exploit other species. **1982** *Times* 8 Apr. 13/1 Animals have rights... There are forms of 'speciesism' as corrupting as 'racism' or 'sexism'.

Hence **spe·ciesist** *a.* and *sb.*

1975 R. D. RYDER *Victims of Sci.* 21 The main speciesist defence of cruelty to animals is that mankind benefits—in terms of knowledge, economy or sport, for example. **1977** *Daily Tel.* 5 May 16 A demonstrating mob of anti-speciesists, perhaps accompanied by species even odder than themselves, may soon be..cawing, roaring and singing..at your door. **1978** *Nature* 9 Nov. 122/2 Gould is, in general, rather good at puncturing human speciesist vanity, and in particular he will have nothing to do with the myth that evolution represents progress toward man.

specific, *a.* and *sb.* Add: **A.** *adj.* **2. d.** *Physics.* (i) Of or designating a dimensionless number equal to the ratio of the value of a property of a given substance to the value of the same property of some reference substance (as water) or of vacuum under the same conditions, so providing a relative value for comparison with different substances, as *specific gravity* (see GRAVITY 4 c); *specific heat* (see HEAT *sb.* 2 d); *specific inductive capacity* = *dielectric constant* s.v. *DIELECTRIC *a.* 2 b; *specific viscosity*, the difference between the viscosity of a solution of a given concentration and that of the pure solvent, divided by the viscosity of the pure solvent.

1838 M. FARADAY in *Phil. Trans. R. Soc.* CXXVIII. 33, I feel satisfied that the experiments altogether fully prove the existence of a difference between dielectrics as to their power of favouring an inductive action through them; which difference may..be expressed by the term specific inductive capacity. **1918** *Physical Rev.* XII. 50 One arm was then filled with water, and the other with a mixture of water and ethyl alcohol, the specific inductive capacity of which was known. **1935** *Jrnl. Physical Chem.* XXXIX. 157 Staudinger later adopted the term 'specific viscosity', for the quantity $\eta_r - 1$. **1944** [see *PERMITTIVITY]. **1959** K. HENNEY *Radio Engin. Handbk.* (ed. 5) iv. 2 The dielectric constant *K* of an insulating material is the ratio of the capacitance C_x of a capacitor using the material as the dielectric to the capacitance C_a using air as the dielectric... This property of the material is sometimes called inductivity or specific inductive capacity. **1966** M. L. MILLER *Struct. Polymers* v. 206 At the highest rate of shear used in these experiments, the reduced specific viscosity was independent of concentration.

(ii) Of or designating a physical quantity that is referred to a unit of mass, volume, or other measure in order to form a number independent of the properties of the particular system studied, and so measuring an inherent property or characteristic that can be scaled to describe a given system or used as an indicator of the effect of an action or process, as *specific acoustic impedance* (see *IMPEDANCE 2); *specific activity*, the activity of a given radioisotope per unit mass; *specific charge*, the ratio of the charge of an ion or sub-atomic particle to its mass; *specific conductance, conductivity*, the conductivity of unit length of a material of unit cross-sectional area; the reciprocal of resistivity (see *RESISTIVITY 1); *specific* (*fuel*) *consumption*, the weight of fuel consumed by an engine per unit time per unit of power or thrust developed; the reciprocal of specific impulse; *specific impulse* (see *IMPULSE *sb.* 2 c); *specific ionization*, the number of ion pairs produced by an ionizing particle per unit path length; *specific refraction, refractive constant*, a constant relating the refractive index (n) of a material to its density (ρ), given by $(n^2 - 1)/(\rho(n^2 + 2))$; *specific resistance, resistivity* = *RESISTIVITY 1; *specific rotation, rotatory power*, the angle through which the plane of polarization of light of a specified wavelength is rotated by passage through a column of an optically active substance of given length (usu. 10 cm.) and at unit concentration; *specific surface*, the surface area per unit volume of a finely-divided substance; *specific thrust* = *specific impulse* above; *specific volume*, the volume of a substance per unit mass; the reciprocal of density.

In mod. use, there is a tendency to restrict the application of *specific* to quantities that are referred to unit mass. Accordingly, alternative terms are being advocated to replace those that do not conform to this narrow definition, as ***conductivity*** for ***specific conductance*** and ***specific conductivity***, ***relative density*** for ***specific gravity***, ***specific heat capacity*** (which is referred to unit mass) for ***specific heat***, ***dielectric constant*** or ***relative permittivity*** for ***specific inductive capacity***, and ***resistivity*** for ***specific resistance*** and ***specific resistivity***.

The examples follow in alphabetical order.

1938 *Nature* 18 June 1098/1 The specific activity of phosphatide P extracted from human blood corpuscles 24 hours after administration of labelled sodium phosphate was found to be 40 times less than that of plasma inorganic P. **1961** G. R. CHOPPIN *Exper. Nuclear Chem.* xi. 186 Much higher levels of specific activity may be counted with no resolving time losses. **1926** R. W. LAWSON tr. *Hevesy's Man. Radioactivity* i. 6 From the magnitude of the deflexion, combined with similar deflexion experiments in an electric field, we can determine the magnitude of the specific charge (e/m). **1971** D. F. JACKSON *Concepts of Atomic Physics* ii. 18 The specific charge of the lightest known ion, that of hydrogen, is $9{\cdot}579 \times 10^7$ C. kg^{-1}. **1885, 1886** Specific conductance [see *CONDUCTANCE]. **1924** J. R. PARTINGTON in H. S. Taylor *Treat. Physical Chem.* I. xi. 517 In such cells conductivity water with a specific conductance of $0{\cdot}21 \times 10^{-6}$ ohm^{-1} can be kept 12 hours without change. **1958** CONDON & ODISHAW *Handbk. Physics* IV. ix. 141/1 In terms of Ohm's law, the defining equation..for specific conductance reduces to $\kappa = I/E$..where I is the current and E the potential applied to a centimeter-cube sample of the conductor. **1898** C. L. SPEYERS *Text-bk. Physical Chem.* ix. 166 A 5% aqueous solution of KCl at 0° has a specific conductivity of $0{\cdot}0_56617$ mhos. **1957** G. E. HUTCHINSON *Treat. Limnol.* I. viii. 558 (*caption*) Composition of standard bicarbonate waters of varying specific conductivities. **1931** *Automotive Industries* 9 May 726/2 Fig. 10 shows the variation in specific consumption, power and head temperature of the A70 cylinder, with change in fuel flow. **1946** J. W. VALE *Aviation Mechanic's Engine Man.* ix. 271 At any altitude the specific fuel consumption increases with the increase of power output. **1966** J. H. HORLOCK *Axial Flow Turbines* viii. 214 For the high by-pass ratios..the specific fuel consumption drops rapidly with increasing turbine temperature. **1932** *Physical Rev.* XXXIX. 884 The specific ionization thus determined does not exceed 32 ion-pairs per cm, in water-saturated air at 68 cm pressure. **1961** G. R. CHOPPIN *Exper. Nuclear Chem.* iii. 23 This specific ionization is a measure of the rate of energy loss. **1940** GLASSTONE *Textbk. Physical Chem.* viii. 524 The difference between the specific refractions for two wave lengths, e.g., the Hα and Hγ lines, is called the specific dispersivity. **1899** J. WALKER *Introd. Physical Chem.* xiv. 138 Another specific refractive constant is given by [etc.]. **1899** J. MCCRAE tr. *Reychler's Outl. Physical Chem.* III. ii. 197 In order to determine the specific resistance of a solution in ohms, we consider a cubical mass of the solution, the length of whose side is 1 centimetre. **1935** WILSON & DOWSE tr. *Holzer's Foundations Short Wave Therapy* 74 The specific resistance is not..a constant, independent of frequency. **1978** P. W. ATKINS *Physical Chem.* xxv. 820 The resistance of a material increases with its length l but decreases with its cross-section A... The proportionality coefficient is called the resistivity, or specific resistance. **1958** *Chambers's Techn. Dict.* 716/1 *Resistivity*, a term denoting volume resistivity, i.e. the resistance of a block of the material in question having unit length and unit cross-sectional area; also called specific resistivity. **1964** R. F. FICCHI *Electrical Interference* viii. 133, ρ is the specific resistivity of the conductor. **1899** J. WALKER *Introd. Physical Chem.* xv. 150 The specific rotation of lævorotatory oil of turpentine is 37·01°. **1940** GLASSTONE *Textbk. Physical Chem.* viii. 585 The optical rotatory power of a pure substance, particularly in the liquid state, is generally expressed in terms of its specific rotation or specific rotatory power. **1958** CONDON & ODISHAW *Handbk. Physics* VI. vi. 120/1 The molecular rotation is the product of the specific rotation by the molecular weight M of the active material. **1876** *Jrnl. Chem. Soc.* I. 667 It is proposed to substitute α_D for the specific rotatory power obtained by means of the sodium ray. **1899** J. WALKER *Introd. Physical Chem.* xiv. 139 The specific rotatory power is usually denoted by the symbol [α]. **1924** *Chem. Abstr.* XVIII. 3507 The specific surfaces of several varieties of charcoal were measured. **1951** A. E. ALEXANDER *Surface Chem.* i. 4 Colloidal materials such as charcoal and clays show adsorption phenomena very markedly owing to their large specific surfaces.. which arises [*sic*] from their fine state of subdivision. **1977** ROWELL & FARINATO in L.-H. Lee *Characterization of Metal & Polymer Surfaces* II. 399 The specific surface of a monodisperse colloid becomes independent of the number concentration and refractive index of the spherical particles. **1949** D. G. SHEPHERD *Introd. Gas Turbine* iii. 78 The curves for specific thrust are in general of similar shape.., increasing with T_{max} and having in an optimum value at a certain pressure ratio. **1966** J. H. HORLOCK *Axial Flow Turbines* viii. 211 A high value of specific thrust means that small engine weight is required. **1868** JONES & WATTS *Fownes's Man. Chem.* (ed. 10) II. 250 The numbers obtained.., representing the specific volumes of the various solid and liquid elementary substances, present far more cases of discrepancy than of agreement. **1957** *Amer. Inst. Physics Handbk.* II. 117 Many tables and other aids have been prepared for the routine calculation of density and specific volume of sea water.

4. c. Of a duty or tax: assessed on an article or goods according to quantity or amount without reference to value.

1789 *Deb. Congress U.S.* 9 Apr. 107, I shall not pretend to say that there ought not to be specific duties laid upon every one of the articles enumerated. **1845** J. K. POLK *Diary* 1 Nov. (1929) 23, I had recommended..the abolition of the minimum principle and specific duties. **1901** J. S. NICHOLSON *Pol. Econ.* III. 348 If the tax is specific and not *ad valorem*. **1930** M. CLARK *Home Trade* III. xxii. 187 Specific duties are those which are based on the quantity of the imported produce, i.e. they are so much per lb. or so much per gallon, etc. **1959** *Chambers's Encycl.* V. 512/2 Specific duties are expressed as an amount of money on the unit amount of the product while *ad valorem* duties are expressed as a percentage addition to the selling price.

5. *specific epithet* (chiefly *Bot.* and *Microbiology*), the second (adjectival) element in the Latin name of a species according to the binomial system, which follows the generic name and serves to distinguish a species from others in the same genus; *specific name*, (*a*) (now chiefly *Zool.*) = *specific epithet* above; (*b*) (now chiefly *Bot.* and *Microbiol.*), the Latin name of a species, which in the binomial system comprises a generic name and a specific epithet.

1753, etc. Specific name [in Dict.]. **1871** *Nature* 20 July 221/1 The mistake Cotteau is accused of making of assigning to Desor instead of Agassiz the specific name of *Pseudodiadema hemisphæricum* is entirely unfounded. **1905** *Règles Internat. Nomencl. Zool.* (Congrès Internat. de Zool.) 31 A specific name becomes a subspecific name when the species so named becomes a subspecies. **1906** *Internat. Rules Bot. Nomencl.* 1905 47 When a..species is moved into another genus..the first specific epithet.. must be retained. **1926** *Rep. Brit. Assoc. Adv. Sci.* 1925 75 A species [of animal] is a community, or a number of related communities, whose distinctive morphological characters are..sufficiently definite to entitle it, or them, to a specific name. **1945** *Rhodora* XLVII. 274 Binomial nomenclature was not intended by Linnaeus to supersede the polynomial specific name. **1964** *Internat. Code Zool. Nomencl.* ii. 7 The name of a species consists of two words (binomen)..;..the first word is the generic name, the second word is the specific name. **1966** *Internat. Code Bot. Nomencl.* iii. 27 *Tuber*..was accompanied by binary specific names, e.g. *Tuber cibarium*, and is therefore admissible. *Ibid.* 30 The name of a species is a binary combination consisting of the name of the genus followed by a single specific epithet. **1970** *Watsonia* VIII. 156 The specific epithet *racemosa* is..not applicable in the genus *Amelanchier*. **1974** *Encycl. Brit. Macropædia* II. 1019/2 Gaspard Bauhin, a Swiss botanist of the late 16th and early 17th centuries, designated plants by a generic and a specific name. **1982** ARMS & CAMP *Biology* (ed. 2) xx. 310 Specific epithets..are adjectives, and the same one may be combined with different generic names and used for a number of unrelated organisms; for example, *Erythronium americanum*, the trout lily; *Euarctos americanus*, the American black bear.

B. *sb.* **2.** Usu. *pl.* Also *loosely*, details, particulars.

1966 *New Statesman* 9 Sept. 350/2 The latter [*sc.* journalism]..considers the specifics of an event, using implicit general principles of behaviour out of necessity. **1972** G. BROMLEY *In Absence of Body* iii. 30 Let's get down to specifics. What can we actually do to help? **1975** *N.Y. Times* 11 Sept. 8/1 Placing this tragedy of a woman's sexual obsession with her stepson within the arresting specifics of this strange setting does at least remove it from the fury-bestrewn never-never-land of the antique Greek drama. **1977** F. BRANSTON *Up & Coming Man* xii. 125 He told us he had been investing in property in London, but he was a bit vague about the specifics. **1980** *Jrnl. R. Soc. Arts* Feb. 152/1 Planning should start..with specifics rather than concepts.

3. A specific word, name, etc., *spec.* in taxonomy or toponymy.

1962 BURRILL & BONSACK in Householder & Saporta *Probl. Lexicogr.* 195 The elements in geographic names that indicate the class of the entity, e.g., in *Red Hill*..

or *Lake Erie*.., *Hill* and *Lake*, are the generic elements (or 'generics'). The elements that identify the particular entity, in the above instances *Red* and *Erie*, are called the specific elements (or 'specifics'). **1969** J. FOWLES *French Lieutenant's Woman* viii. 50 Although many scientists of the day gratefully used her [*sc.* Mary Anning's] finds to establish their own reputation, not one native type bears the specific *anningii*. **1977** *Word 1972* XXVIII. 133 Most of the specifics, or second elements, in such names are demonstrably of Gaelic and not of Pictish origin.

-specific. The adj. used as the final element in combination with sbs. to designate phenomena peculiar to the category indicated by the precedent element: specific to or that specifies (something).

1924, etc. [see *species-specific* adj. s.v. *SPECIES *sb.* 14]. **1936**, etc. [see *organ-specific* adj. s.v. *ORGAN *sb.*[1] 8]. **1949** K. DAVIS *Human Society* xxi. 600 Age-specific fertility trends show that a stationary or a declining population will soon eventuate. **1965**, etc. [see *language-specific* adj. s.v. *LANGUAGE *sb.* 6 b]. **1971** J. Z. YOUNG *Introd. Study Man* v. 84 Study of some brain-specific proteins. **1978** *Dædalus* Fall 7 Herodotus' report..refracts into intensely age-specific opinions. **1979** *Nature* 25 Jan. 251/1 But there is a far less trivial, and far more nation-specific way in which intellectual resources may be used or squandered.

specificity. Delete 'Chiefly *Med.* and *Path.*' and add: **1. a.** (Later examples.)

1922 [see *DIRECTEDNESS]. **1946** *Scrutiny* XIV. 109 George Eliot's genius appears in the specificity with which she exhibits the accomplishments in Gwendolen of the kind of conscious advantage she resembles Isabel in enjoying. **1977** J. F. FIXX *Compl. Bk. Running* vii. 89 Few runners had supposed it could possibly be so hot on a mid-April day in Massachusetts, so practically nobody had trained properly. As a result, most people's times were terrible. The same specificity principle applies to terrain.

b. The narrowness of the range of substances with which an antibody or other agent acts or is effective.

[**1896**: in Dict., sense 1.] **1904** G. H. F. NUTTALL *Blood Immunity & Blood Relationship* ix. 381 Wassermann.. brought the question of specificity into greater prominence. *Ibid.* 443/1 (Index), Specificity of precipitins. **1935** N. P. SHERWOOD *Immunol.* xii. 274 Two kinds of specificity can be demonstrated by immune reactions, one that applies to species and the second to type variation within a species. **1971** *Sci. Amer.* July 26/1 The specificity, or narrow spectrum, of vaccines is a limitation; it means that a different vaccine is required for each virus or strain of virus.

c. *Biol.* The degree to which a parasite or symbiote is restricted in its range of hosts.

1924 *Rep. Brit. Assoc. Adv. Sci. 1923* 453 They [*sc.* parasitic nematodes] may be divided broadly into a section with more or less strict 'specificity' and a section with members occurring in various hosts, often of quite distantly related groups. **1955** *Sci. Amer.* July 77/1 It is also known that the protein coat determines the specificity of the virus, i.e., whether or not it will attack a certain bacterium. **1965** B. E. FREEMAN tr. *Vandel's Biospeleology* xv. 245 This is more a case of parasitic or symbiotic specificity than cavernicolous specialisation.

2. (Later examples.)

1928 HARTSHORNE & MAY *Studies in Deceit* II. xii. 221 (*heading*) Specificity of attitudes. **1958** R. WILLIAMS *Culture & Society* III. iii. 231 A principal virtue was always the specificity, not only of definition, but of illustration. **1981** *Times* 16 July 6/1 They also want to avoid 'specificity' because they have not yet formulated fully-fledged policies.

specificness. (Later examples.)

1905 W. STEVENS *Let.* 31 Dec. (1967) 85 Reflections.. on Japanese life, on specificness,..on my future. **1966** J. ELLIS in C. E. Bazell *In Memory of J. R. Firth* 83 By *register-choice* is meant the particular register out of the performer's range to which the utterance may be assigned ..the specificness of the assignment depending on the delicacy of the analysis.

specifier. Add: **b.** That which specifies.

1954 A. J. AYER *Philos. Ess.* iii. 61 Let us say of any two singular referential statements S and S'..that S is a specifier of S' if and only if S' is not a component of S, S entails S', and S' does not entail S. **1964** E. A. NIDA *Toward Sci. Transl.* xii. 258 As the data are analyzed both semantically and structurally, certain 'specifiers' can be associated with the elements in question, as tags of identification. In the comparison stage, the specifiers of the source-language text are matched with specifiers of the receptor language, so that the corresponding semantic and structural elements are properly identified. **1971** [see *INTENSIFIER].

specimen. Add: **8. b. specimen-book** (earlier example); **specimen page**, a page submitted by a printer as a sample setting for a book; **specimen tree**, a tree planted on its own, away from other plants of a similar size.

1871 W. BLACKWOOD *Let.* 19 Sept. in *Geo. Eliot Lett.* (1956) V. 190, I also send you by Book Post a specimen Book from which you will..be able to select the colour for the paper cover. **1835** DICKENS *Let.* 9 Dec. (1965) I. 102, I have received neither specimen page nor proofs. **1877** W. PATER *Let.* 30 Jan. (1970) 27 Dear Mr. Macmillan..Of the two specimen pages, I enclose the one I think preferable. **1926** S. UNWIN *Truth about Publishing* ii. 37 As soon as the printers' estimate and specimen page are received and have been checked, the estimate has to be completed by the addition of the cost of paper, binding and other items. **1975** J. BUTCHER *Copy-Editing* ii. 13 Specimen pages are intended to show solutions to all the general typographical problems that the printers will meet in the book. **1933** A. OSBORN *Shrubs & Trees for Garden* xxiv. 119 Weeping trees are unsuitable for grouping, but very valuable for planting as specimen trees on the lawn. **1961** E. WAUGH *Unconditional Surrender* III. ii. 230 Guy took to walking..in the public gardens... There were winding paths, specimen trees, statuary. **1980** *Amat. Gardening* 25 Oct. 15/1 It makes a shapely specimen tree as well as being good for making a hedge or screen.

speck, *sb.*[1] Add: **2. c.** Also *the Speck* (Austral. colloq.), Tasmania.

1930 *Bulletin* (Sydney) 11 June 21 N.S.W., V., Q., S.A., W.A. and the Speck. **1949** *Geogr. Mag.* Feb. 373 *Tassie* and *The Speck*, meaning Tasmania. **1963** *Times* 12 Mar. (Austral. Suppl.) p. v/4 Tasmania—affectionately known as 'the speck'.

d. (Later example.)

1936 M. MITCHELL *Gone with Wind* xl. 719 You're smart enough about dollars and cents... But you..aren't a speck smart about folks.

5. *Comb.*, as *speck-like* adj.

1917 J. MASEFIELD *Lollingdon Downs* 56 No spark of him is specklike in his glass. **1965** E. BISHOP *Questions of Travel* I. 11 A specklike girl and boy, Alone, but near a specklike house.

speck, *v.*[1] Add: **5.** *Austral.* [Both this and sense 1 of the vbl. sb. below may properly repr. abbrev. of SPECULATE *v.*: cf. SPEC *sb.*] **a.** *intr.* To search for small particles of gold or opal on the surface. **b.** *trans.* To search the surface of (the ground) for traces of gold or opal; to discover (particles of gold, etc.) in this manner.

1888 H. LAWSON *His Father's Mate* in *Stories* (1964) I. 139 A pick and shovel, and a gold dish..with which he used to go 'a-speckin'' and 'fossickin'' amongst the old mullock heaps. **1903** R. BEDFORD *True Eyes* lviii. 305 With little cries of delight he 'specked' a four-ounce slug of the red gold. *Ibid.* lx. 315 They had sieved and dry-blown and 'specked' the little tongue of auriferous soil. **1926** *Spectator* 14 Aug. 240/2 Went 'specking' in nearby creeks. Got colours of gold but no nuggets. **1936** I. L. IDRIESS *Cattle King* xxiv. 211 Next morning they picked up gold. In trembling excitement they 'specked' piece after piece. **1969** E. WALLER *And there's Opal out There* 116 A couple of tourists specking for bits of potch and opal.

specking, *vbl. sb.* [f. SPECK *v.*[1] + -ING[1].] **1.** *Austral.* The action of searching for surface gold or opal. Cf. sense 5 of the vb. above.

1901 M. VIVIENNE *Travels in W. Australia* 171 Almost everyone in the camp went out for an afternoon's specking (looking on the ground for nuggets). **1945** *Walkabout* (Melbourne) 1 Mar. 14 Most of the residents of Lightning Ridge are experts at the art of 'specking'.

2. The discoloration of pottery through contamination of the glaze, or this effect contrived for decoration.

1967 M. CHANDLER *Ceramics in Mod. World* iii. 96 In the case of a glaze mix, it is particularly important to avoid contamination and specking. *a* **1977** *Harrison Mayer Ltd. Catal.* 22/3 Ilmenite...can be used in glazes to obtain specking effects.

speckle, *sb.* Add: **2. b.** A granular appearance seen in images formed by originally coherent light as a result of the interference of waves that have been reflected at a rough surface or have passed through an inhomogeneous medium; also, each of the light or dark areas giving rise to this appearance. Freq. *attrib.*

1965 *Jrnl. Optical Soc. Amer.* LV. 247 Exposing photographic film directly to the backscattered radiation confirms the independent existence of the speckles. *Ibid.* 252/2 Both speckle pattern and diffraction pattern were recorded (photographically) at the same distance from the aperture. **1970** A. LABEYRIE in *Astron. & Astrophysics* VI. 85/1 'Speckle' refers to the grainy structure observed when a laser beam is reflected from a diffusing surface... In large telescopes, the image of point stars also features a speckle pattern, due to seeing induced phase fluctuations on the wavefront. **1975** T. S. MCKECHNIE in J. C. Dainty *Laser Speckle & Related Phenomena* iv. 126 We may reduce speckle by simply reducing the coherence of the illumination. **1976** *Physics Bull.* Aug. 357/2 Objects viewed in highly coherent light acquire a peculiar granular appearance. This is the laser speckle phenomenon. **1977** *McGraw-Hill Encycl. Sci. & Technol.* 397/1 The size of the speckles is equal to the diffraction-limited resolution limit of the telescope, regardless of the resolution limit determined by the turbulent atmosphere. **1979** *Nature* 5 July p. vii/2 A double laser speckle camera which is used for non-destructive stress, vibration, and flaw analysis of engineering components.

3. speckle interferometry, the analysis of speckle in two or more images, differing only in the instant of exposure, as a means of obtaining information about the source of light or the agent that caused the speckle; so **speckle-interferometric** *a.*

1973 *Astrophysical Jrnl.* CLXXXII. L139 Speckle interferometric techniques are an effective way of obtaining information about small solar features without the problems of lifting large telescopes above the Earth's atmosphere. **1970** A. LABEYRIE in *Astron. & Astrophysics* VI. 85 Key words: speckle interferometry. **1972** *Sci. Amer.* Feb. 106 The technique, known as speckle interferometry, can also be used to map local deformations in stressed mechanical parts. **1973** *Astrophysical Jrnl.* CLXXXII. L139 Speckle interferometry is potentially more powerful than two-aperture Michelson stellar interferometry because the entire aperture is used. **1978** PASACHOFF & KUTNER *University Astron.* II. vi. 148 The speckle interferometry technique involves taking photographs of the speckle pattern with very short exposures—on the order of 1/100 second—or using electronic detection devices and then using mathematical techniques and computer assistance to deduce the properties of the starlight that entered the telescope.

speckle, *v.* Add: **2.** (Earlier and later examples.) Also, to become speckled.

1703 tr. *H. van Oosten's Dutch Gardener* IV. ix. 218 If you water them in the Heat of the Sun, the leaves will speckle, and so often lose their Spindel. **1973** R. ADAMS *Watership Down* ix. 36 As the plants moved in the breeze, the sunlight dappled and speckled back and forth over the brown soil.

speckled, (*ppl.*) *a.* and *pa. pple.* **1.** (Later examples.)

1965 *Jrnl. Optical Soc. Amer.* LV. 247 When a diffuse surface is illuminated by a coherent monochromatic source such as a laser, the illuminated area appears speckled. **1978** PASACHOFF & KUTNER *University Astron.* II. vi. 148 At any one instant, the image of a star through a large telescope looks speckled because different parts of the image are affected by different small turbulent areas in the earth's atmosphere.

3. a. (*b*) *speckled hen, perch*: (earlier examples).

1877 C. HALLOCK *Sportsman's Gazetteer* 276 Locally they are..severally known as yellow perch,..speckled hen, etc. *Ibid.* 378 Silver Perch, or Speckled Perch.

b. speckled wood, (*b*) a brown butterfly with yellowish spots, *Pararge egeria*, found in lightly shaded places in Britain, much of continental Europe, and North Africa.

1766 M. HARRIS *Aurelian* 132 Speckled wood... It flies in woods. The caterpillar feeds on grass. **1974** [see *meadow brown* (*butterfly*) s.v. *MEADOW *sb.* 4 b].

c. speckled yellows, a disease of sugar beet characterized by distorted and discoloured leaves, caused by a deficiency of manganese.

1938 *Brit. Sugar Beet Rev.* XII. 77/2 Fields affected with 'Speckled Yellows' can be recognised from a considerable distance. **1959** *New Biol.* XXX. 91 Diseases such as 'grey speck' of oats, 'speckled yellows' of sugar beet and 'marsh spot' of peas are caused by the low availability of manganese in the soil. **1960** *Farmer & Stockbreeder* 15 Mar. 149/2 (*caption*) Sugar Beet leaf—illustrating deficiency of manganese ('speckled yellows').

speckling, *vbl. sb.* (Later examples.)

1965 *Jrnl. Optical Soc. Amer.* LV. 247/1 Speckling has ..been observed when viewing a translucent material which is backlighted by a cw [*sc.* continuous wave] laser. **1973** *Astrophysical Jrnl.* CLXXXII. L139 Small, high-contrast features such as umbral dots and faculae near the limb [of the sun] show the speckling most clearly.

spe·cky, *a.*[1] *colloq.* [f. SPEC(S + -Y[1].] Bespectacled.

1956 R. JENKINS *Guests of War* IV. i. 167 The unbraw unlovable puke married to yon specky gasping smout of a barber. **1959** I. & P. OPIE *Lore & Lang. Schoolch.* ix. 172 A girl or boy with spectacles is known as 'Four-eyes', 'Specky four-eyes', '*Annie* four eyes'... Occasionally he is 'Eye balls'..and 'Specky Jock' (Scotland).

Speclette (spekle·t). [f. SPEC(S + *-lette* (refashioned on Fr. model after -LET): cf. -ETTE.] A pair of spectacles that folds at the bridge (see quot. 1962[1]).

1931 *Illustr. London News* 31 Oct. 707/3 (Advt.), Speclettes the delightful and fashionable folding spectacles. **1962** L. S. SASIENI *Optical Dispensing* viii. 182 In the 'Speclette' the sides are folded in halves on to the lenses and the two halves of the front folded over each other in the plane of the lenses, the one sliding across the other. *Ibid.* 183 (*caption*) 'Speclette' folding spectacles.

spect, *v.* Also **spec, speck, 'spect,** etc. Repr. (chiefly U.S.) non-standard pronunc. of (*I*) *expect* or *suspect*.

1839 F. A. KEMBLE *Jrnl. Residence Georgian Plantation* (1863) xii. 118 Good for colored folks, missis; me 'spect not good enough for white people. **1852** MRS. STOWE *Uncle Tom's Cabin* II. xx. 38, I spect I grow'd. Don't think nobody never made me. **1893** H. A. SHANDS *Some Peculiarities of Speech in Mississippi* 59 Speck (spec). Used by negroes for both *expect* and *suspect*. **1914** 'BARTIMEUS' *Naval Occasions* xx. 182 'Spect's you wants yer breakfus'—same's me! **1927** A. P. RANDOLPH in A. Dundes *Mother Wit* (1973) 200 What's th' matter wid you? 'Specks you got dat Randolph fever, too, eh? **1976** *Washington Post* 7 Nov. K2/2 We'll teach them..how to say: I SPEC (as in 'I spec I will do that.'). **1976** C. DEXTER *Last seen Wearing* xix. 151 'Has the wife got the chips on, Lewis?' 'I 'spect so.' **1977** F. PARRISH *Fire in Barley* x. 106, I 'speck you want me to feed the zoo.

spectacle, *sb.*[1] Add: **II. 7. c.** (Earlier and later examples.) † Also (*rarely*) in sing., a score of zero in one innings. Cf. *PAIR *sb.*[1] 2 b.

1835 *Bell's Life* 13 Sept. 3/4 Good put a spectacle on him first ball. **1865** *F. Lillywhite's Guide to Cricketers* 27 The ominous 'spectacles' have been worn by the best sighted men. **1907** E. V. LUCAS *Hambledon Men* 230 It is believed he never made two noughts, or 'a pair of spectacles', in any match of note! **1979** *Wisden Cricket Monthly* Dec. 21/3 Who got a 'pair of spectacles' for Yorkshire on his first appearance?

9. a. *spectacle-blurred* adj.

1932 W. FAULKNER *Light in August* (1933) xiii. 291 Misshapen, with his gray stubble and his dark spectacle-blurred eyes.

spectacular, *a.* and *sb.* Add: **1.** Also *fig.*

1934 J. B. PRIESTLEY *Eng. Journey* ix. 316 Both my companions knew about this yard, which had been a spectacular failure in which over a million of money had been lost.

4. (Later examples.) Also *spec.* a radio or television programme, entertainment, etc., produced on a lavish or spectacular scale.

1953 *N.Y. Times* 3 Jan. 8/5 Thirteen 'spectaculars' will be affected, including the giant British Overseas Airways sign, Cunard and Canadian Pacific Lines displays and advertisements for gin, wine, radio and television. **1954** *Ibid.* 28 Mar. x13/1 Its [*sc.* NBC's] big feature..will be a series of costly and lavish ninety-minute 'spectaculars'—opera, drama, musical comedy, circuses, ice shows, etc. **1958** *Times* 28 Mar. 3/4 A television 'spectacular' transmitted by the National Broadcasting Company. **1966** *Punch* 8 June 858/2 *The Disorderly Knights*, a historical novel of the sixteenth century by Dorothy Dunnett, is a five hundred page spectacular: enormous in every possible way. **1969** *Listener* 20 Feb. 249/3 Radio drama may miss its former purse-power, and the multi-studio 'spectacular' is a fashion of the past. **1971** *Scope* (S. Afr.) 19 Mar. 4/2 It was a golfing spectacular the old pros will talk about for years. **1978** S. BRILL *Teamsters* x. 391 The ceremony and dinner party were followed by an entertainment spectacular put on by.. Barbara McNair, Billy Daniels, Ed McMahon and Frank Sinatra.

specta·cularism. [f. SPECTACULAR *a.* and *sb.* + -ISM.] Spectacular character or quality.

1888 G. B. SHAW in *Star* 18 July 2/4 These are but details, only to be noted at Covent Garden, because so much is there sacrificed to spectacularism on the highest scale. **1931** *Aberdeen Press & Jrnl.* 14 Oct. 6/4 The spectacularism of Noel Coward.

spectate, *v.* Add: **2.** *intr.* [Back-formation from SPECTATOR.] To be a spectator rather than a participant, esp. at a sporting event.

1929 *Amer. Speech* IV. 501 An advertisement in an Iowa paper reads: 'Ladies Only at the Promenade Roller Rink Thursday afternoon, 2:30 to 5. No men will be allowed to skate or to spectate.' **1971** H. C. RAE *Marksman* II. iii. 118 On Sunday afternoons..the boys meet and play soccer... Occasionally Gordon went there, to play or to spectate. I'm not sure which. **1974** 'P. B. YUILL' *Bornless Keeper* xiii. 125 He enjoyed spectating at a good snarling-match. **1980** L. BIRNBACH et al. *Official Preppy Handbk.* 90/2 They..provide entertainment for the Prep women who spectate when they're not flinging a ball about themselves.

spectating *ppl. a.* (later example). Also as *vbl. sb.*

1942 *Amer. Speech* XVII. 24 'Tackle the shoe problem —shoes for *spectating*' was the heading of an advertisement of a Department Store, Oct. 11, 1941. **1966** *Listener* 12 May 697/2 Only a gigantic comic talent..could.. communicate the comic grandeur to a spectating, as opposed to a reading, audience. **1978** D. FRANCIS *Trial Run* xix. 234 I'd ridden in races in that state..so why fret at some gentle spectating.

spectation. Delete † *Obs.* and add later example.

1940 R. G. COLLINGWOOD *Ess. Metaphysics* xxxi. 307 The mere act of spectation could in time generate the idea of a cause.

spectator. Add: **2. b.** *spectator sport*, a sport which affords good entertainment for spectators as well as for participants. Also *transf.* and *fig.*

1943 *Amer. Speech* XVIII. 95 The American 'spectator-sports' (of clothes) has been mistranslated in at least one advertisement [in New Zealand] as 'spectacular-sports'. **1944** M. LASKI *Love on Supertax* xi. 109 Burn all those clothes you've got on..and get back into a decent unpretentious spectator-sports-suit. **1954** *Encounter* Feb. 57/1 The fascination of the great spectator-sports—soccer, athletics, cricket, lawn tennis—is partly due to the effect of the game on its audience. **1969** A. GLYN *Dragon Variation* ix. 268 Well, call this [*sc.* chess] a spectator sport, twenty goddam minutes and nobody's moved a thing. Give me tennis! **1975** *New Yorker* 10 Feb. 110/3 With hard times upon us there may be a question in the minds of even the least dedicated office-holders both here and in Albany about how long their hard-pressed constituents will let them get away with treating representative government as a minor spectator sport. **1979** *Guardian* 12 June 8/1 Watching election coverage all through the night is a great spectator sport.

spectatorial, *a.* Add: Hence **spectato·rially** *adv.*

1930 A. HUXLEY *Brief Candles* 14 People think I'm an excellent psychologist. And I suppose I am. Spectatorially. But I'm a bad experiencer. **1973** *Times Lit. Suppl.* 14 Dec. 1536/5 Our Londoner applauds not a murder, but a representation; and he himself is spectatorially present at a representation, not at a murder. **1980** D. NEWSOME *On Edge of Paradise* vi. 211 Arthur was invited to a number of spectatorially promising occasions.

spectatory. 2. (Earlier and later examples.)

1829 H. FOOTE *Compan. to Theatres* 135 Such as do not wish to mix in their frolics, may witness them from the spectatory of the theatre. **1881** P. FITZGERALD *World behind Scenes* I. ii. 21 One of the most difficult questions is how is the *salle* or 'spectatory', as old writers call it—not a bad word either—to be effectively lighted.

spectinomycin (spe:ktinǒmǝi·sin). *Pharm.* [f. mod.L. *spect-ābilis* visible, remarkable (see SPECTABLE *a.*), + *-MYCIN.] An antimicrobial substance obtained from the fungus *Streptomyces spectabilis* and used esp. to treat gonorrhœa that is resistant to penicillin.

1964 *Antimicrobial Agents & Chemotherapy* 438/1 The in vitro activity of spectinomycin..was tested against routine gonococcal isolates and against resistant strains isolated from penicillin therapy failure cases of gonorrhea. **1976** *Lancet* 25 Dec. 1379/2 Spectinomycin succeeded in 21 (95%) of 22 patients treated. **1977** *Maclean's Mag.* Feb. 54 The only cure so far for the new strain is spectinomycin, a drug four times as costly as penicillin and hence not widely applicable in the Far East.

spectral, *a.* Add: **5. a.** Also applied to a property or parameter which is being considered as a function of frequency or wavelength, or which pertains to a given frequency range or value within the spectrum. (Later examples, which also illustrate the extended use of 'spectrum'; cf. *SPECTRUM 3 a, b.)

1919 *Sci. Abstr.* A. XXII. 563 Section 2 considers the definition of temperature. This is based upon thermal radiation and spectral distribution. **1950** *Audio Engin.* Aug. 14/2 A knowledge of the spectral characteristics of sound sources will indicate the regions in the frequency scale to which particular attention must be paid in assessing the effect of response changes in the sound system. **1951** *New Biol.* XI. 34 A spectral absorption curve, in which the proportion of light absorbed is plotted against wavelength. **1957** G. E. HUTCHINSON *Treat. Limnol.* I. vi. 376 The spectral composition of the total reflected light when the sun is high is little different from that of the incident. **1964** *Oceanogr. & Marine Biol.* II. 13 The turbulent fluctuations of velocity or of some other property of the water..may be observed directly, and the spectral distribution of energy..derived from the observations. **1966** *McGraw-Hill Encycl. Sci. & Technol.* IV. 582/2 Any spectral emissivity value is valid only for a narrow wavelength interval. **1971** *Physics Bull.* July 385/2 Spectral intensity is intensity per unit bandwidth ($W\ sr^{-1}\ Hz^{-1}$). *Ibid.* Nov. 653/3 An investigation of the spectral content, vibrato, attack and sound pressure of vowels sung by male and female students under technical and performing conditions. **1977** I. M. CAMPBELL *Energy & Atmosphere* viii. 272 The spectral absorption characteristics of alkyl nitrates are rather similar to those of nitric acid.

d. *Math.* Of or pertaining to the spectrum of a transformation (*SPECTRUM 5*).

1948 P. R. HALMOS *Finite Dimensional Vector Spaces* ii. 80 The characteristic equation, and consequently every other spectral concept such as the proper values and their multiplicities, is invariant under replacing A by BAB^{-1}. **1968** P. A. P. MORAN *Introd. Probability Theory* iii. 118 Hence *U* and *V* are non-singular matrices, and we have $P = U^{-1}\Lambda U = V\Lambda V^{-1}$, which is a 'spectral' decomposition of *P*.

6. Special collocations: *spectral analysis*, chemical analysis of substances by means of their spectra; analysis of light or another oscillating system into a spectrum; *spectral index* (see quot. 1956); *spectral series* = *SERIES *sb.* 16; *spectral term*: see *TERM *sb.* 11 d; *spectral type* (Astr.), any of the types used to classify stellar spectra, each being associated with stars of a characteristic range of temperatures and compositions and designated by a letter or letters.

1862 Spectral analysis [in Dict., sense 5 b]. **1888** *Phil. Mag.* XXV. 343 (*heading*) Mathematical spectral analysis of magnesium and carbon. **1930** *Proc. IRE* XVIII. 1199 Expression (9) lends itself to spectral analysis into its component frequencies by the following process. **1978** *Nature* 16 Mar. 232/2 As a further step, we carried out a spectral analysis according to the techniques of Blackman and Tukey on the time series for each of our latitude bands. **1956** *Observatory* LXXVI. 181 The usual terminology is adopted, where the flux density *S* from a discrete source refers to the flux in both polarizations, and the spectral index *x* refers to the index in the relationship $S \propto (\text{frequency})^x$. **1967** *Astrophysical Jrnl.* CL. 5 The average spectral index of twenty-six spirals between 40 and 21 cm is −0·83. **1974** *Nature* 4 Oct. 398/2 The spectral shape of the pulsed emission..can be approximated by a power law with an energy spectral index of $\alpha \sim 1$ to about a GeV. **1900** *Sci. Abstr.* III. 465 A most useful review of the present state of knowledge respecting spectral series. **1974** G. REECE tr. *Hund's Hist. Quantum Theory* iv. 61 Several attempts were made to give a theoretical interpretation of the spectral series. **1890** A. M. CLERKE *System of Stars* iii. 37 About eleven-twelfths of all the stars show linear spectra of absorption. They fall into two great divisions, corresponding to Father Secchi's first and second spectral types. **1924** *Proc. Amer. Acad. Arts & Sci.* LIX. 217 If the stellar density for any spectral type were uniform throughout space, the number of stars visible should double with every increase of half a magnitude in brightness. **1973** SMITH & JACOBS *Introd. Astron. & Astrophysics* x. 268 Since we will have occasion to refer to specific spectral types in the following paragraphs, we give the spectral sequence from hot to cool stars (40,000 K to 3000 K) here: O, B, A, F, G, K, and M. Each spectral class is further divided into ten subclasses 0 to 9.

spectrally, *adv.* Add: **2.** In the form of a spectrum; as regards, or in terms of, the spectrum.

1914 S. E. SHEPPARD *Photo-Chem.* viii. 325 Spectrally dispersed rays. **1971** *Jrnl. Gen. Psychol.* LXXXIV. 95 Spectrally pure stimuli are being produced by passing the output of a xenon arc through narrow-band interference filters. **1973** *Sci. Amer.* Nov. 77/1 The results of this experiment suggest that noise spectrally adjacent to the signal is most effective in masking recognition. **1980** *Ibid.* Oct. 123/1 The light..is spectrally pure and monochromatic.

spectre, *sb.* Add: For '7–8 **specter**' read '7– **specter** (now *U.S.*)' and add: **6. b.** *spectre-faint, -pale.*

1924 R. GRAVES *Mock Beggar Hall* 5 The exiled Alcibiades Beheld him in the Chersonese, Yet spectre-faint. **1928** V. WOOLF *Orlando* v. 233 The spectre-pale beech trees.

spectrin (spe·ktrin). *Biochem.* [f. SPECTR(E *sb.* + -IN[1]; so called because it was isolated from 'ghosts' (sense *11 e) of red blood cells.] A fibrous protein constituent of the membranes of red blood cells, forming a network on the inside of the plasma membrane.

1968 MARCHESI & STEERS in *Science* 12 Jan. 204/2 Because this protein appears to be a new molecular species and is extractable from erythrocyte ghost membranes, we suggest that it be called Spectrin. **1974** *Sci. Amer.* Mar. 27/3 The two heaviest polypeptide components, with molecular weights of 255,000 and 220,000, are collectively known as spectrin. **1978** *Bio Systems* X. 98/1 A variety of proteins other than actin can form filaments (e.g., flagellin, spectrin, spasmoneme filaments, skeletin).

spectro-. Add: **spectrohe·liogram,** a photograph obtained with a spectroheliograph; **spectroheliograph,** add def.: (*a*) an instrument which photographs the sun using light of a particular wavelength, *esp.* that of the Balmer α emission line of hydrogen; † (*b*) a spectroheliogram; (later examples); hence **spe:ctroheliogra·phic** *a.*; **spe:ctrohelio·meter,** a spectrophotometer for use in studying the sun; **spectrohe·lioscope,** an instrument which provides a directly observable monochromatic image of the sun by means of a rapidly scanning device which transmits light of only one wavelength (which may be modified so that Doppler shifts can be observed); **spectrophone,** add def.: a device in which a body of gas may be caused to emit sound waves when illuminated by a periodically interrupted beam of electromagnetic radiation (usu. visible or infra-red); (later examples); **spe:ctrophosphori·metry,** the spectrometric study of phosphorescence; so **spe:ctrophosphori·meter,** a spectrometer designed for this; **spe:ctrophosphorime·tric** *a.*; **spe:ctrophotofluoro·meter,** a spectrophotometer designed for the study of fluorescence; hence **spe:ctropho:tofluorome·tric** *a.*, **-fluorome·trically** *adv.*; **spe:ctropolari·meter,** an instrument designed to measure rotation of the plane of polarized light as a function of wavelength; so **spe:ctropolarime·tric** *a.*; **spe:ctropolari·metry**; **spe:ctroradio·meter,** a combination of a spectroscope and a radiometer, designed to measure the intensity of electromagnetic radiation over a range of wavelengths; so **spe:ctroradiome·tric** *a.*; **spe·ctroradio·metry**; **spe·ctrotype** *Immunol.*, the range of antigens to which a given antibody is reactive.

1905 *Astrophysical Jrnl.* XXI. 354 Spectroheliograms were obtained showing detail in the centre of the disk. **1968** *New Scientist* 11 Jan. 97/1 (*caption*) X-ray spectroheliograms of solar plages obtained with *OSO*-4. **1973** Spectroheliogram [see *RASTER *sb.*[2] a]. **1903, 1915** Spectroheliograph [see *FLOCCULUS 3 b]. **1965** P. WYLIE *They both were Naked* iv. 152 Big gadgets—telescopes, spectroheliographs, particle accelerators and the like. **1905** *Astrophysical Jrnl.* XXI. 279 Our new explanation of the spectroheliographic results will be founded on the hypothesis that the sun is an unlimited mass of gas in which convection currents..are continually forming. **1973** *Sci. Amer.* Oct. 76/2 The major experiments of Skylab include a spectroheliometer from the Harvard College Observatory that is mapping the sun at wavelengths of from 300 to 1,350 angstroms with a resolution of five seconds of arc. **1976** *New Yorker* 6 Sept. 40 The spectroheliometer showed that they extended up from the chromosphere..into the transition region between the chromosphere and the corona. **1906** *Astrophysical Jrnl.* XXIV. 42 This instrument..constitutes a spectrohelioscope, and was intended for the visual study of prominences. **1929** G. E. HALE in *Encycl. Brit.* XXI. 179/2 The spectrohelioscope renders visible to the eye many of the phenomena of the solar atmosphere photographed with the spectroheliograph and also permits their velocities in the line of sight to be measured. **1955** *Sci. Amer.* Sept. 194/2 In 1890 George Ellery Hale and Henri Deslandres independently invented the spectrohelioscope. This instrument utilized the red light of hydrogen to produce an image of the entire disk of the sun. **1948** *Chem. Abstr.* XLII. 1467 An app. was constructed for the detn. of gases absorbing in either the infrared or the visible region, on the principle of Bell's spectrophone. **1965** *New Scientist* 21 Oct. 199/3 The collisional phenomenon has recently been investigated.. using a device named the 'spectrophone', in which a sample of gas is subjected to a sequence of pulses of infrared (140 a second) during which the molecules acquire vibrational energy. If they lose that energy by collision, the increase in molecular velocities, and therefore in pressure, is detected by a microphone in the gas, which accordingly registers a 140 c/s note. **1961** *Nature* 8 Apr. 166/1 The measurements with our spectrophosphorimeter set an upper limit to the lifetime of the pyrene dimer. **1978** *Ibid.* 19 Jan. 236/1 The weak afterglow spectrum is also shown in Fig. 1*a*, at a gain factor of 20 for 100% solid crystalline carbazole at an identical setting of the spectrophosphorimeter. **1968** M. Zander *Phosphorimetry* iii. 136 The quantitative spectrophosphorimetric analysis of mixtures. *Ibid.* 138 The qualitative and quantitative analysis of a mixture is possible by spectrophosphorimetry. **1974** *Nature* 30 Aug. 763/1 Analysis of the fluorescent material (by chromatography on the adsorbent *in situ* by spectrofluorimetry *in situ*, and by the latter technique and by spectrophosphorimetry after solvent extraction from the adsorbent). **1956** *Rev. Sci. Instruments* XXVII. 664/2 Spectrophotofluorometer. Continuous activation of compounds and measurement of the resulting fluorescence throughout the visible and ultraviolet regions is provided by this instrument. **1974** *Nature* 1 Feb. 291/1 The continuous formation of NADH:NADH was measured fluorometrically at 37°C with an Aminco Bowman spectrophotofluorometer using an excitation wavelength of 340 nm and an emission wavelength of 460 nm. **1964** *Jrnl. Exper. Med.* CXX. 509 The spectrophotofluorometric technique of Shore *et al.*.. was used with slight alterations. **1975** *Nature* 17 Apr. 636/1 Cells were centrifuged and the histamine released into the supernatant..was determined spectrophotofluorometrically. **1926** *Sci. Abstr.* A. XXIX. 310 (*heading*) A spectro-polarimeter for the ultra-violet. **1971** *Nature* 16 July 192/1 Circular dichroism was measured at 25°C with a JASCO ORD/UV-5 spectropolarimeter equipped with a CD attachment. **1960** C. Djerassi *Optical Rotatory Dispersion* iii. 28 These refractive index gradients.. account for the 'blanking-out' phenomenon noted in the spectropolarimetric examination of ketal formation. *Ibid.* 18 The single most important factor responsible for the renewed interest in rotatory dispersion has been recent advances in ultraviolet spectropolarimetry. **1927** *Jrnl. Optical Soc. Amer.* VII. 439 The essential parts of a spectroradiometer consist of (1) a suitable spectrometer for dispersing thermal radiation into a spectrum, and (2) suitable radiometric instruments for measuring the spectral radiation intensities. **1975** *Nature* 10 Apr. 512/2 Measurements of the spectral energy distributions..of natural radiation between 400 and 800 nm were made using a spectroradiometer. **1922** *Jrnl. Optical Soc. Amer.* VI. 1021 The transmission screen method should prove useful in supplementing the spectroradiometric measurements..on fainter stars. **1951** *Electronics* Jan. 81/3 This is a spectroradiometric curve of a particular color, obtained by measuring..the number of watts radiated by the source at each wavelength. **1921** *Jrnl. Optical Soc. Amer.* V. 133 The fiducial line in this Bureau's spectroradiometry is the yellow helium line. **1945** R. A. Sawyer *Exper. Spectroscopy* xi. 277 The methods used in the investigation of the infrared radiation..are essentially the methods of spectroradiometry. **1974** *Nature* 16 Aug. 532/2 The A5A idiotype has been found to be associated with a particular antibody spectrotype. **1981** *Exper. Parasitol.* LII. 216/2 When a clone of S1 spectrotype was allowed to establish a relapsing infection on two separate occasions, two variants of different spectrotypes were produced.

spectrochemical (spektroke·mikăl), *a.* [f. Spectro- + Chemical *a.*] Of or pertaining to spectrochemistry; *spectrochemical series*, a series of ligands arranged in order of magnitude of the ligand field splitting that they cause in the electronic orbitals of a central atom.

1896 *Jrnl. Chem. Soc.* LXX. I. 553 The results of a spectrochemical investigation..establish the formula. **1938** R. Tsuchida in *Bull. Chem. Soc. Japan* XIII. 393 Arranging in the ascending order of *P* [*sc.* 'the work which would be done by the system if the ligand were to approach from infinity to the seat of co-ordination'], we obtain a spectrochemical series for the first band: viz., NH_3, H_2O, F^-, Cl^-, Br^-, I^-. **1960** *Jrnl. Iron & Steel Inst.* CXCV. 375/1 The most satisfactory boron line for spectrochemical use is at 2497·73 Å. **1966** Phillips & Williams *Inorg. Chem.* II. xxviii. 396 Now when the [crystal-field splitting] energies, △, obtained from spectra ..are compared for a large number of different cations, it is found that there is an approximately constant ligand series, the Fajans–Tsuchida spectrochemical series: $CO > CN^- > NO^- > ..S^{2-} > Br^- > I^-$. **1975** P. S. Braterman *Metal Carbonyl Spectra* i. 3 Electronic spectra contain *d-d* bands that place CO in the spectrochemical and nephelauxetic series.

Hence **spectroche·mically** *adv.*, as regards spectrochemistry; by spectrochemical methods.

1905 *Nature* 15 June 160/2 Several simple molecules of this kind may be combined into one crystallised particle of the spectrochemically normal diamond. **1966** P. W. J. M. Boumans *Spectrochemical Excitation* i. 4 Alloys containing more than two elements..were investigated spectrochemically.

spectrochemistry (spektroke·mistri). [f. Spectro- + Chemistry.] The branch of chemistry dealing with the chemical application of spectroscopy, esp. in analysis, and with the interpretation of spectra in chemical terms.

1893 *Jrnl. Chem. Soc.* LXIV. I. 254 (*heading*) Spectrochemistry of nitrogen. **1905** *Nature* 15 June 162/1 It is of course of the greatest value to be able to examine the constitution of the bodies without affecting them chemically; and spectrochemistry..gives us the means of doing so. **1957** *Technology* Sept. 258/2 In the department of applied science..radio-chemistry, spectro-chemistry and metallurgy are all prominent. **1966** P. W. J. M. Boumans *Spectrochemical Excitation* p. viii, This book will..contribute to further progress in the field of theoretical spectrochemistry.

spe:ctrofluori·metry. Also **-fluoro-.** [f. Spectro- + *fluoro-, fluorimetry.] The spectrometric study of fluorescence. So **spe:ctrofluori·meter (-fluoro-)**, a spectrometer designed for this; **spe:ctrofluorime·tric (-fluoro-)** *a.*, **-me·trically** *adv.*

1957 *Analyst* LXXXII. 611 The sensitivity of the spectrofluorimeter depends not only on the sensitivity of the detector and the intensity of the exciting light, but also on the slit width and aperture of the analysing monochromator. **1961** *Analytical Chem.* XXXIII. 1362/1 The spectrofluorometer has a sensitivity equivalent to 0·01 p.p.m. of quinine sulphate. **1962** *Lancet* 26 May 1130/1 The plasma was analysed spectrofluorometrically for the pharmacologically active spirolactone. **1965** *Analytical Chem.* XXXVII. 137/1 (*heading*) Spectrofluorometric determination of submicrogram amounts of aluminium and beryllium. **1965** *Jrnl. Clin. Path.* XVIII. 375/1 (*heading*) A device for spectrofluorimetry. **1971** *Nature* 2 July 24/2 All the chromosomes in the human complement can be paired by these patterns, which can be analysed most accurately by a quantitative spectrofluorimetric method. **1975** D. H. Burrin in Williams & Wilson *Biologist's Guide to Princ. & Techniques Pract. Biochem.* v. 147 Spectrofluorimetry is most accurate at very low concentrations. *Ibid.*, Spectrofluorimeters enable the utilization of great spectral selectivity since.. two monochromators may be used. **1957** *N.Y. Times* 8 Nov. 33/4 In the meantime, using spectrofluorometry, thin-layer chromatography and a third technique with iodine, the Coast Guard and the E.P.A. conducted 741 tests at its laboratories in Georgia and Connecticut. **1976** *Nature* 16 Sept. 242/2 The amine was isolated by ion-exchange chromatography..and estimated spectrofluorimetrically.

spectrogram. Add: More widely, a visual representation of a spectrum of any kind. (Later examples.)

1939 *Amer. Speech* XIV. 313/2 Examination of eleven subjects singing the vowel 'ah' normally and after hydrogen inhalation... Illustrated with acoustic spectrograms. **1961** *Brit. Birds* LIV. 388 The original spectrograms have a frequency scale from 0 to 10 kilocycles per second. **1975** *Nature* 25 Sept. 295/1 Spectrograms obtained with a Carnegie image tube on the 2·1-m telescope at the Kitt Peak National Observatory have been used to complete the determination of radial velocities for 50 of the 52 galaxies. **1978** *Hi-Fi News* Sept. 175/1 None of these, however, exceeded −70dB ref. 36 V RMS across the load (shown in spectrogram *fig. 2*). **1981** *Amer. Speech* 1977 LII. 237 The degree of centralization was determined by the use of a bilogarithmic scale in measuring the spectrograms of eighty instances of /aɪ/.

spectrograph. Add: **1.** (Later examples.) More widely, any apparatus for producing a visual record of a spectrum (optical or otherwise). Cf. *mass spectrograph* s.v. *mass *sb.*[2] 10 d, *sound spectrograph* s.v. *sound *sb.*[3] 7.

1940 *Geogr. Jrnl.* XCV. 276 My own work was research on the Ozone Layer with a Dobson Spectrograph. **1955** *Times* 15 June 5/5 Such spectrographs are used in laboratories to examine the ions existing in ionized gases, and an American version has been used in rockets. **1967** M. Schlauch *Language* v. 102 There is an instrument called the spectrograph which can record and photograph the complex series of vibrations of the air which convey a sequence of spoken sounds. **1974** *Encycl. Brit. Macropædia* XI. 605/1 The most noteworthy observation made with the parabola spectrograph was the spectrum of rare gases present in the atmosphere... There was a line corresponding to an ion of mass 22 that could not be attributed to any known gas.

spectrographic *a.*, **-graphically** *adv.* (examples relating to spectra other than of light); also **spectro·grapher,** one who uses a spectrograph.

1946 *Nature* 20 July 79/1 The result of this selection is a volume from which spectrographers may derive helpful guidance in the correct choice of analytical methods. **1959** E. Pulgram *Introd. Spectrography of Speech* i. 20 The position, which I have at least in part adopted in consequence of learning to view language spectrographically. *Ibid.* ii. 27 The experimental linguist.., like the spectrographer of speech, is interested in the cultural *and* the physical values of the phenomena at the same time. **1962** *Amer. Speech* XXXVII. 62 Phonemic analysis of the stress-intonation system based on spectrographic analysis of a specific corpus. **1974** *Sci. Amer.* Mar. 86/3 Another promising diagnostic technique for detecting abnormalities in infants, in addition to the spectrographic analysis of the cry, is the measurement of..changes in brain waves in response to sounds. **1981** *Amer. Speech* 1977 LII. 269 A carefully developed argument, supported with spectrographic evidence.

spectrology. 2. (Later example; still *rare.*)

1969 James & Sternberg *Design of Optical Spectrometers* p. x, Spectroscopy (or *spectrology*, to introduce here a word coined by Fellgett) belongs to this branch of physics.

spectrometer. Add: Now in extended use, any of a wide range of instruments for producing spectra and measuring the positions, etc., of spectral features. Cf. *mass spectrometer* s.v. *mass *sb.*[2] 10 d.

1901 *Sci. Abstr.* IV. 930 Universal spectrometer... This instrument can be used for studying any portion of the spectrum, either visually, photographically, or photometrically, with two different dispersions. **1950** *Sci. News* XV. 19 Monochromatic light of chosen wavelength, from a spectrometer, is now used in order to stimulate the retinal receptors. **1958** *Antiquity* XXXII. 124 The characteristics of the trace-elements present are detected by a special Gamma-ray Spectrometer. **1978** P. W. Atkins *Physical Chem.* xix. 616 The centre of the e.s.r. spectrum of the methyl radical occurs at 329·4 mT when the spectrometer is using 9·233 GHz microwaves.

spectrometric *a.* (later example); **spectrometry** (examples); also **spectrome·trically** *adv.*; **spectro·metrist,** an expert in spectrometry; a person employed to operate a spectrometer.

1948 *Physical Rev.* LXXIV. 1222/1 By extending the method..a higher order mass resolution is obtained which is generally usable in the mass spectrometry of positive ions. **1953** G. P. Barnard *Mod. Mass Spectrometry* 286 A different method was used..to determine the half-life of ^{85}Kr mass spectrometrically. **1954** Powell & Ross in *Appl. Mass Spectrometry* (Inst. Petroleum) 7 In Raman spectrometry, the material is irradiated with monochromatic light..and the light scattered at right angles to the incident beam is examined spectrometrically. **1958** *Antiquity* XXXII. 124 The staff consists now of two Senior Scientific Officers, two Research Assistants, three technicians, a secretary and two part-time workers (optical spectrometrist and statistician). *Ibid.*, In Optical Spectrometry, a programme of analysis of prehistoric European bronzes..is being carried out. **1962** *Oxf. Univ. Gaz.* 9 Mar. 775/2 Continuing his research on the history of British Bronze Age metallurgy, he completed a programme of spectrometric analyses of Early Bronze Age material. **1971** *Nature* 27 Aug. 646/2 Some 3,3-diaryl oxetanes which could not be isolated but only detected spectrometrically in solution. **1973** *Physics Bull.* Feb. 108/1 The term chemi-ionization has unfortunately taken on a different meaning amongst mass spectrometrists. **1975** *McGraw-Hill Yearbk. Sci. & Technol.* 193/1 Flame spectrometry, traditionally a single-element technique, has been advanced recently to include multielement analysis.

spectrophotometer (spe:ktrŏfotǫ·mĭtəɹ). [f. Spectro- + Photometer.] An instrument designed to measure the relative intensity of light (usu. transmitted or emitted by a substance under study) at different wavelengths in a particular region of the spectrum.

1881 [in Dict. s.v. Spectro-]. **1938** *Jrnl. Optical Soc. Amer.* XXVIII. 18 This spectrophotometer was designed specifically to measure in the visible region the absorption spectrum of visual purple. **1948** *Nature* 21 Feb. 285/2 Total penicillin may be assayed non-biologically with the aid of the..ultra-violet spectrophotometer. **1966** *McGraw-Hill Encycl. Sci. & Technol.* II. 594 d/1 The split-beam spectrophotometer..measures the difference in absorption at any given wavelength between two nearly identical cell suspensions. **1976** C. Skegg tr. *Welz's Atomic Absorption Spectroscopy* v. 84 In modern spectrophotometers a logarithmization of the signal takes place within the instrument, so that the readout on the display is already in absorbance and no conversion is required.

Hence **spe:ctrophotome·tric** *a.*, of, pertaining to, or employing a spectrophotometer; **spe:ctrophotome·trically** *adv.*; **spectrophoto·metry,** the technique of using a spectrophotometer.

1884 Spectrophotometric [in Dict. s.v. Spectro-]. **1897** Spectrophotometrically [in Dict. s.v. Spectro-]. **1899** *Phil. Mag.* XLVIII. 421 In direct comparisons of white light this latter principle has been successfully applied; but in spectrophotometry the optical difficulties in the way of its use have prevented the obtaining of corresponding results. **1942** *Astrophysical Jrnl.* XCVI. 451 Spectrophotometric observations of the light of the night sky have been made for the stronger lines of the visual region of the spectrum. **1961** *Times* 9 Jan. 2/3 (Advt.), The Physical Assay Division..is concerned..with..application of industrial methods of analysis including ultraviolet and infra-red spectrophotometry. **1972** R. A. Jackson *Mechanism* iv. 76 If the reaction is followed spectrophotometrically the presence or absence of stable intermediates is often indicated from the changes in the spectrum as the reaction proceeds. **1976** G. Thurston *Coronership* i. 13 Methods of analysis by chromatography and spectrophotometry enable accurate results to be produced with speed. **1977** I. M. Campbell *Energy & Atmosphere* ix. 307 (*caption*) Concentration profile of O_2.. versus altitude in the upper mesosphere, measured by rocket-borne spectrophotometric detection.

spectroscopic, *a.* Add: **2. b.** *spectroscopic binary* (Astr.), a star whose binary nature is revealed only by a study of its spectrum.

1896 *Circular Harvard Univ. Observatory* No. 11, Professor Solon I. Bailey has found that the star μ^1 Scorpii is a spectroscopic binary. **1930** R. H. Baker *Astron.* viii. 338 Some examples of spectroscopic binaries among the bright stars are: Capella, Spica, Castor, β Aurigae and Algol. **1975** *Sci. Amer.* Mar. 28/2 The normal star associated with Cygnus X-1 is a single-line spectroscopic binary with a period of 5·6 days. The term spectroscopic here means that the presence of two stars is indicated by a periodic Doppler shift of the spectral lines of at least one of the stars as they revolve around a common center of gravity. **1978** Pasachoff & Kutner *University Astron.*

vi. 134 (*caption*) Alcor and Mizar provide examples of both visual and spectroscopic binaries.

spectroscopy. Add: In mod. use, the investigation of spectra by any of various instruments.

1955 *Sci. Amer.* Sept. 144/2 The faintness of the aurora and the rapidity with which it changes make spectroscopy difficult, but development of the technique..has produced beautiful spectrograms of auroras extending..into the near ultraviolet and the near infrared. **1966** *McGraw-Hill Encycl. Sci. & Technol.* XII. 589/1 The important instruments that are used in spectroscopy include spectroscopes, spectrometers, spectrographs, interferometers, and spectrophotometers. **1978** *Nature* 21 Sept. 199/2 We intend carrying out further spectroscopy on the object, providing that it does not fade too quickly, to monitor spectral variations.

spectrum. Add: **3. a.** Also, a dark band containing bright lines produced similarly; such a (coloured or dark) band, or the pattern of lines in it, as characteristic of the light source; hence, the pattern of absorption or emission of light or other electromagnetic radiation over any range of wavelengths exhibited by a body or substance.

1824 *Edin. Philos. Jrnl.* X. 39 Lines are also seen in the spectrum of other fixed stars of the first magnitude. **1879** *Encycl. Brit.* X. 215/1 When the light of a burning metal is examined with a properly-arranged prism, it is seen to give a dark band or spectrum which is traversed by certain vertical bright lines. **1900** *Proc. R. Soc.* LXVI. 45 The expected argon spectrum was almost entirely absent. **1925** G. A. Lindsay tr. *Siegbahn's Spectroscopy of X-Rays* vi. 195 X-ray spectra afford one of the most direct sources of information concerning the inner structure of the atom. **1966** *McGraw-Hill Encycl. Sci. & Technol.* VIII. 420/2 Microwave spectra of atoms can be used to measure..nuclear electric and magnetic moments. **1971** *Physics Bull.* July 401/1 The laser spectrum extends from the vacuum ultraviolet to the far infrared. **1978** Pasachoff & Kutner *University Astron.* xxviii. 709 All the lines in the spectrum of 3C 48 were shifted by 37 per cent, a still more astounding redshift.

b. The entire range of wavelengths (or frequencies) of electromagnetic radiation, from the longest radio waves to the shortest gamma rays of which the range of visible light is only a small part; any one part of this larger range.

1888 *Encycl. Brit.* XXIII. 142/1 When a telescope is to be constructed for photographic purposes the aim should be to unite..the rays near that portion of the spectrum which act most powerfully on the photographic plate. **1923** Glazebrook *Dict. Appl. Physics* IV. 891/1 Beyond the photographic limit, investigation of the infra-red spectrum by means of the heating effect of the rays has been carried on. **1947** *Sci. News* IV. 54 The wave lengths of the visible spectrum, from red over yellow, green, blue to violet, lie between 700 and 350 millionths of a millimetre. **1962** *Rep. Comm. Broadcasting 1960* i. 5 in *Parl. Papers 1961–2* (Cmnd. 1753) IX. 259 The division by international agreement of the frequency spectrum into bands allocated to particular services forms part of the International Radio Regulations. **1978** Pasachoff & Kutner *University Astron.* ii. 21 The new ability that astronomers have to study parts of the electromagnetic spectrum other than light waves enables us to increase our knowledge of celestial objects manyfold.

c. An actual or notional arrangement of the component parts of any phenomenon according to frequency, energy, mass, or the like. Cf. *mass spectrum* s.v. *MASS *sb.*[2] 10 d, *power spectrum* s.v. *POWER *sb.*[1] 18 f.

1887 *Science* 11 Mar. 238/1 It is proposed to analyze a composition by forming what may be called a 'word-spectrum', or 'characteristic curve', which shall be a graphic representation of an arrangement of words according to their length and to the relative frequency of their occurrence. **1897** J. J. Thomson in *Phil. Mag.* XLIV. 297 When the cathode rays are deflected by the electrostatic field, the phosphorescent band breaks up into several bright bands separated by comparatively dark spaces; the phenomena are exactly analogous to those observed by Birkeland when the cathode rays are deflected by a magnet, and called by him the magnetic spectrum. **1933** *Proc. R. Soc.* A. CXLII. 347 A large number of experiments was made to determine the distribution of α-particles over the whole of the spectrum, which includes α-particles of ranges between 7 cm. and 12 cm. **1939** *Psychol. Rec.* III. 60 Fig. 1 shows the acoustic spectra of three tones of the same singer and vowel, sung at the three different intensity levels at approximately the same frequency. **1962** A. C. Gimson *Introd. Pronunc. Eng.* iii. 21 The spectrum above 4,000 cps would appear to be largely irrelevant to the recognition of our vowels. **1971** *Nature* 3 Sept. 2/2 The idea..is that even quite small explosions can be distinguished from earthquakes of comparable size by the high frequency parts of their seismic spectra. **1973** Williams & Fleming *Spectrosc. Methods in Inorg. Chem.* (ed. 2) iv. 181 In many cases, convenient starting points for counting the spectrum are the peaks at m/e 28 (N_2^+) and m/e 32 (O_2^+).

d. *fig.* The entire range or extent of something, arranged by degree, quality, etc.

1936 R. Campbell *Mithraic Emblems* 20 Their sistered stridences ignite The spectrum of the poets' lyre. **1952**, etc. [see *broad-spectrum* a. s.v. *BROAD D. 2]. **1958** *Listener* 28 Aug. 308/2 At the other end of the political spectrum Lloyd Warner has used similar methods in his nostalgic account of the status system of old New England. **1964** G. L. Cohen *What's Wrong with Hospitals?* i. 18 Theoretically, students remain long enough on each type of ward to give them a spectrum of experience. **1971** *Sci. Amer.* July 25/2 At the polar ends of the age spectrum—children and 'senior citizens'—the trends at the moment are following different courses. **1979** *Practical Woodworking* Mar. 42 P— hand tools embrace a wide spectrum of products.

5*. *Math.* (See quots.)

1948 P. R. Halmos *Finite Dimensional Vector Spaces* ii. 79 The set on n proper values of A, with multiplicities properly counted, is the spectrum of A. **1972** A. G. Howson *Handbk. Terms Algebra & Anal.* xvii. 83 The set of all eigenvalues of a linear transformation t of a finite-dimensional vector space V is known as the spectrum of t.

6. b. *spectrum allocation.*

1960 *McGraw-Hill Encycl. Sci. & Technol.* XI. 260/1 (*caption*) Radio spectrum allocations. **1980** *Sci. Amer.* Feb. 32/1 The control of interference lies at the heart of spectrum allocation, which entails the development of systematic plans for the use of frequencies in radio communication.

7. Special Comb.: **spectrum analyser,** a device which analyses a system of oscillations into its spectral components.

1942 *Radiation Lab.* (Mass. Inst. Technol.) *Man.* No. M-115 (*title*) Spectrum analyzer (Type 103) for pulsed oscillators at 3,000 Mc/sec. **1973** *Times* 14 Dec. 8/8 So far they had spent 150 man-hours in preliminary work, setting up 'spectrum analysers, computers, graphical displays and other advanced equipment'.

specular, *a.* **3. c.** Add def.: Designating or pertaining to reflection by a surface in which incident light is reflected as in a mirror. (Later examples.)

1927 *Jrnl. Optical Soc. Amer.* XIV. 371 The instrument is so constructed that the identical areas employed in the measurement of specular density may be used without change for the measurement of the diffuse density. **1940** *Chambers's Techn. Dict.* 789/2 *Specular density*, the photographic density in an image measured with parallel light, as contrasted with diffuse density, when the total light passed is measured, including that dispersed. **1967** E. Chambers *Photolitho-Offset* vii. 76 Some surfaces have both specular and diffuse reflection—such as varnished wood. **1974** *Jrnl. Optical Soc. Amer.* LXIV. 546/2 Conventional definitions of reflectance treat the road as a *Ultrasound Diagnosis* II. 10 Only echoes specularly component of reflectance.

specularite (spe·kiŭlărəit). *Min.* [f. Specular *a.* + -ite[1].] = *specular iron ore* s.v. Specular *a.* 3 b.

1892 E. S. Dana *Dana's Syst. Min.* (ed. 6) 213 Specular iron; Red Hematite, Red Ocher. Specularite. **1959** Berry & Mason *Mineralogy* x. 364 In the variety called specular hematite or specularite the color is black and the luster metallic and splendent. **1959** J. D. Clark *Prehist. Southern Africa* ix. 244 Specularite (specular iron) was apparently an often sought-after medium for paint in the Later Stone Age. **1970** *Prof. Papers U.S. Geol. Survey* No. 700-C. 103/1 A specularite-bearing conglomeratic sandstone containing minor malachite was noted about 1 mile southeast of the copper locality.

specularly, *adv.* Delete *rare*$^{-1}$ and add later examples.

1930 *Jrnl. Optical Soc. Amer.* XX. 23 The smoother the surface, the greater is the intensity of the specularly reflected light and the greater..is the lustre or gloss. **1978** D. N. Lapedes *McGraw-Hill Dict. Physics & Maths.* 920 *Specular reflection factor*, the ratio of the specularly reflected light to the incident light. **1980** *Rec. Advances Ultrasound Diagnosis* II. 10 Only echoes specularly reflected could be identified with any certainty.

speculative, *a.* and *sb.* Add: **A.** *adj.* **7. a.** *speculative builder*, a builder who has houses erected without securing buyers in advance. Hence *speculative-built* adj. Cf. *SPEC *a.*

1868 *1st Rep. Comm. Employment Children, Young Persons, & Women in Agric.* 35 in *Parl. Papers 1867–8* XVII. 95 Cottages..have been put up by speculative builders of the flimsiest materials. **1902** G. K. Chesterton *Twelve Types* 13 The colossal diagram of streets and houses is..the opium dream of a speculative builder. **1933** *Archit. Rev.* LXXIV. 120 There is a possibility, of course, that the speculative builder who has bought this estate is an intelligent man. **1960** Pidgeon & Crosby *Anthology of Houses* 94, 2-storey, speculative-built terrace houses. **1973** *Listener* 25 Jan. 118/1 The idiocies and crudities permitted to the developer—or, as I prefer to call him, the speculative builder.

8. Special collocations: *speculative fiction* (see quot. 1953); *speculative grammar*, a late medieval scholastic grammatical system in which the structure of language is interpreted through scholastic philosophy in terms of our perception and representation of the world by the 'modes of signification' (*modi significandi*) (cf. *MODISTÆ); any one of the grammatical theories arising from this analysis.

1953 R. A. Heinlein in *Library Jrnl.* July 1188/1 The term 'speculative fiction' may be defined negatively as being fiction about things that have not happened. **1978** Speculative fiction [see *SCI-FI]. **1951** R. H. Robins *Anc. & Mediaeval Gram. Theory in Europe* iii. 80 Most of these philosophical or 'speculative' grammars were entitled *De Modis Significandi* (whence the name 'Modistae'), or, as we might put it to-day, 'On Semantics'; they covered a great deal more ground than would now be included in 'grammar' narrowly considered. **1968** J. Lyons *Introd. Theoretical Linguistics* i. 15 It was the task of scientific, or 'speculative', grammar to discover the principles whereby the word, as a 'sign', was related on the one hand to the human intellect and on the other to the thing it represented, or 'signified'. **1972** Hartmann & Stork *Dict. Lang. & Linguistics* 139/1 New in these universal speculative grammars [were]..the refinements in syntactic analysis, e.g. the function of prepositions, the formal criteria of grammatical acceptability, and the concepts of dependency, government and transitivity. **1975** *Canad. Jrnl. Linguistics* XX. 134 Speculative grammar attempted to show how the 'modes of existence' of objects were apprehended by the 'modes of understanding' of the human intellect.

speculum. Add: **4*.** = *speculum metal* (in Dict., sense 5 a).

1912 *Phil. Mag.* XXIV. 321 The gold surface was brought into closer proximity to the speculum surface. **1929** *Bureau of Standards Jrnl. Res.* (U.S.) II. 343 Data are presented on the ultra-violet reflecting power of various metals—beryllium, chromium,..speculum, stellite, and stain-less steel. **1941** *Proc. Physical Soc.* LIII. 263 It is not without interest to note that speculum has not such a good reflecting power as the three former materials. **1966** *McGraw-Hill Encycl. Sci. & Technol.* XIII. 650/1 Among special cast bronzes are bell metal..and speculum.

speech, *sb.*[1] Add: **I. 1. d.** *spec.* in *Linguistics*. = *PAROLE *sb.* 2*.

[**1924**: see *speech-utterance*, sense 12 a below.] **1935** [see *PAROLE *sb.* 2*]. **1937** J. R. Firth *Tongues of Men* 16 De Saussure's famous lectures..in which the speech-language distinction is regarded as fundamental. **1953** U. Weinreich *Languages in Contact* ii. 9 The question of merging vs. unmerged coexistence is a problem *par excellence* in speech-language relations. **1964** *English Studies* XLV. (Suppl.) 35 A second aspect of no less importance is the distinction between 'language' (*langue*) and 'speech' (*parole*). **1974** M. Taylor in *Metz's Film Lang.* p. ix, *Speech* (parole) is the antithesis, or, rather, correlative, of language system: language system is the social aspect of language, whereas speech is the utterance, the actual practice, of a language system.

III. 8. d. Also † *His Majesty's Speech, Speech from the Throne, King's* (or *Queen's*) *Speech*: a speech delivered by the sovereign (in person or by commission) at the opening or prorogation of Parliament; now *spec.* the speech delivered by the sovereign at the opening of Parliament, written by his or her ministers and setting forth the policies and legislative programme of the Government. Also, a speech delivered by the representative of the sovereign at the opening of the legislative assembly of a member of the Commonwealth.

1603 in *Jrnls. House of Commons 1547–1628* I. 146/2 His Majesty's Speech ended, Mr. Speaker..presented himself to his Majesty. **1641** *Diurnall Occvrrences of Parliament 20th Jan.–10th Mar. 1628* 1 M. Selden reported to the House that his Majesties Speech made the last day of the Parliament, in the upper House, is also entred by his Majesties command. *Ibid.* 5 (*heading*) The Kings Speech. **1751** *Parliamentary Hist.* V. 279 Nor, like the former Speech from the Throne, is it mention'd by any Historian. **1771** [in Dict.]. **1792** J. Woodforde *Diary* 15 Dec. (1927) III. 395 The Kings Speech in the House of Lords, a very long one. **1844** Erskine May *Law of Parl.* vii. 142 The session is opened at once by the Queen's speech. *Ibid.* xxi. 326 On the opening of Parliament, the Queen, in her speech from the throne, addresses the commons. **1897** [in Dict.]. **1906** *Daily Colonist* (Victoria, B.C.) 11 Jan. 4/1 The opening [of the Legislative Assembly] will be attended with the usual ceremonies, and in the King's Speech will be indicated some of the salient points of the government policy. **1923** J. C. W. Reith in *Radio Times* 23 Nov. 290/3 At the opening of Parliament..our proposal to broadcast the King's Speech was..declined. **1964** Abraham & Hawtrey *Parliamentary Dict.* 165 A Queen's speech is read by the Lord Chancellor on proroguing Parliament, but this is never debated... This speech reviews the session which it concludes. **1971** *Guardian* 17 Aug. 2/1 The traditional Speech from the Throne read in Maltese by the new Governor-General. *a* **1974** R. Crossman *Diaries* (1975) I. 508 As a backbencher I never dreamed of attending the Queen's Speech debates, regarding them as the most boring occasions.

IV. 12. a. *speech-acoustics, act, area, -behaviour, -breathing, -correctionist, -energy, -event, -feeling, -group, -habit, -material, -melody, -movement, -organ, -pattern, -response, -rhythm, science, -situation, -sound* (earlier example), *-stuff, -style, -system, -unit, -utterance, -way.*

1949 *Archivum Linguisticum* I. 1. 42 Philologists are beginning to turn away from phonetics to speech-acoustics. **1961** *Amer. Speech* XXXVI. 222 A treatment of speech acoustics up to spectrography. **1946** C. Morris *Signs, Lang. & Behavior* ii. 37 There is no language..without the production of sign-vehicles, and it is such production which constitutes a speech-act. **1955** J. L. Austin *How to do Things with Words* (1962) iv. 40 Here there is an obvious parallel with one element in *lying*, in performing a speech-act of an *assertive* kind. **1974** D. Hymes *Foundations of Socio-Linguistics* ii. 52 A party (speech situation), a conversation during the party (speech event), a joke within the conversation (speech act). **1982** *Papers Dict. Soc. N. Amer. 1977* 86 Speech acts are not predictable from code characteristics either. **1933** Speech area [see *DIALECT 2 b]. **1961** *Amer. Speech*

XXXVI. 95 Speech areas can be delineated and subdivided on the basis of heteroglosses. **1931** T. H. PEAR *Voice & Personality* ii. 22 There is the person whose speech-behaviour adumbrates what would develop if at this point the speaker received encouragement. **1980** *English World-Wide* I. 283 Seven of the essays are by German-writing authors on linguistic problems of German, ranging from urban speech (Vienna) to the speech behaviour of accused in court. **1955** *Brit. Jrnl. Psychol.* XLVI. 54 Measures of speech-breathing activity promised to be more immediately relevant to the changing states of tension and affect during interview. **1977** D. FRY *Homo Loquens* iii. 23 An interesting feature of speech breathing is that the moments at which we breathe in are far from being arranged haphazard. **1972** J. L. DILLARD *Black English* vii. 267 Speech correctionists and educators... One Negro speech correctionist–psychologist..went so far as to indulge in a little too-elementary learning theory: language, being a learned activity, can be learned badly. **1943** Speech energy [see *audio frequency* s.v. *AUDIO-]. **1933** L. BLOOMFIELD *Language* ii. 24 We have yet to examine B, the speech-event in our story. **1948** J. R. FIRTH in *Lingua* I. 400 A *speech event* in a context of situation is therefore a technical abstraction from utterances and occurrences. A *speech event* may be sub-divided into *speech items*. **1976** *Word 1971* XXVII. 197 In my analysis, the communicative process is divided into the threefold gradation proposed by Hymes of *speech situation*, *speech event*, and *speech act*. **1916** L. BLOOMFIELD in *Trans. Amer. Philol. Assoc.* XLVII. 13 Our speech-feeling seems to distinguish quite clearly between predicating and non-predicating utterances. **1979** *Amer. Speech 1976* LI. 135 The double negative is both a part of our speech-feeling and a sensible way to strengthen a negative statement. **1925** L. P. SMITH *Words & Idioms* 245 Linguistically considered, England, the Dominions, and the United States may almost be regarded as one speech-group. **1964** C. BARBER *Present-Day Eng.* v. 124 There are phase-differences between different speech-groups, and it would be unsafe to assume that the words currently fashionable in a Birmingham rock-and-roll club were simultaneously fashionable in a West End night-club, or that the picturesque phrases used by schoolboys were still fashionable in R.A.F. messes. **1928** O. JESPERSEN *Internat. Lang.* I. 26 Everybody will necessarily transfer some of his speech-habits to the international language. **1979** M. MILLAR *Murder of Miranda* II. 72 It's a speech habit I picked up from all the teenagers. **1912** A. D. SHEFFIELD *Grammar & Thinking* vii. 188 Sentence-study..can profitably keep in view the diverse speech-material that the pupil meets in his work with foreign languages. **1962** A. J. BLISS in Davis & Wrenn *Eng. & Med. Studies presented to J. R. R. Tolkien* 29 Either a fragment of speech-material has one of the rhythms which are acceptable, in which case *ictus* and stress inevitably coincide; or else it cannot be used in verse at all. **1934** *Essays & Studies* XIX. 141 This speech-melody of ordinary intercourse. **1970** *English Studies* LI. 278 This latter feature, also known as intonation or speech melody, is of course almost a subject in itself. **1918** R. BRIDGES in *Poems of G. M. Hopkins* 96 It was at one time the author's practice to use a very elaborate system of marks, all indicating the speech-movement. **1957** C. E. OSGOOD et al. *Measurement of Meaning* i. 12 Little or no correspondence between thought-movements and speech-movements was found. **1925** GRATTAN & GURREY *Our Living Lang.* p. xxi, Sounds are produced and modified by the position of speech-organs. **1961** *Amer. Speech* XXXVI. 217 Theory of the syllable must be based on the articulatory movements of speech organs. **1936** G. K. ZIPF *Psycho-Biology of Lang.* v. 195 One infers the nature of speech-patterns from the exemplifications of the patterns, i.e. the configurations of speech-elements. **1969** M. PUGH *Last Place Left* xxix. 207 His speech patterns were as elaborate as ever, but his voice was no longer so well modulated. **1974** *Howard Jrnl.* XIV. 80 The restricted and elaborate codes which characterize the speech patterns of the lower and middle classes respectively. **1927** G. A. DE LAGUNA *Speech Development* ii. 36 The correlation between the speech-response and its objective conditions is a correlation between independently variable elements of response and independently variable elements of the external situation. **1910** G. SAINTSBURY *Hist. Man. Eng. Prosody* IV. iii. 316 The presence of closely allied forms [of the alliterative line], in the different Scandinavian and Teutonic languages, assumes..a natural rise from some speech-rhythm or tune-rhythm proper to the race and tongue. **1976** J. LEE *Ninth Man* 275 His poor father with the snicker-provoking Germanic speech rhythms. **1933** *Amer. Speech* VIII. 37/1 Graduate curricula in speech science, phonetics, speech psychology, and rhetoric. **1977** *Whitaker's Almanack 1978* 530 First degrees..are awarded..in *Speech Science* by the University of Sheffield. **1953** *English Studies* XXXIV. 258 'Man' and 'garden' in this context denote..definite, individualized concepts... Taken out of the context (or of the speech-situation) they are semantically colourless. **1980** *English World-Wide* I. I. 99 This is still used..if at least one of the participants in a speech situation has not been educated in English or..Bahasa Malaysia. **1840** GEO. ELIOT *Let.* 21 Dec. (1954) I. 77 Pray bring Phonarthron—speech–sound is a boon that I often need—I shall expect from it..a key to the classic Oriental and Sclavonic tongues. **1934** JOYCE *Let.* 9 Aug. (1966) III. 316 Also why for you make me big speechstuff about Frankee Doodles? **1936** J. KANTOR *Objective Psychol. Gram.* xi. 156 As a test of the validity of the speech-style conception we may inquire into its applicability to speech studies. **1978** *Amer. Speech* LIII. 66 Samarin notes that speech styles of glossolalia are socioculturally determined, as are speech styles of English prayers. **1946** H. JACOB *On Choice of Common Lang.* II. ii. 96 Inflected systems are highly resistant to simplification... However, most of the European speech-systems have progressed considerably in the right direction. **1964** *English Studies* XLV. (Suppl.) 37 Whereas Aristotle started from..'speech' (*parole*), these philosophers had the speech-system (*langue*) in mind. **1936** G. K. ZIPF *Psycho-Biology of Lang.* 233 A sentence is a speech-element, or a speech-unit. **1949** C. E. BAZELL in *Travaux du Cercle Linguistique de Copenhague* V. 77 This succession of speech-units need not answer to anything in the system. **1924** L. BLOOMFIELD in *Mod. Lang. Jrnl.* Feb. 319 Actual speech-utterance, *la parole*, varies not only as to matters not fixed by the system..but also as to the system itself. **1956** J. WHATMOUGH *Language* 42 There is an inverse relationship between frequency of occurrence and the comparative perspicuity that accompanies the utilization of a speech-utterance. **1931** H. SHENTON *Internat. Communication* I. 46 This approach to the problem might well be called a study of the speech-ways of mankind. **1955** *English Studies* XXXVI. 17 Current Elizabethan usage, harking back to much older, popular speechways. **1972** H. KURATH *Studies in Area Linguistics* i. 12 Any native speaker's usage is in a large measure representative of the speechways of a social or age group in his community.

b. *speech analyser, -trainer, -writer; speech-training.*

1973 *Canad. Jrnl. Linguistics* XVIII. 90 Using the speech analyzer..we then recorded an intonation curve (in Hz) for each sentence on photo-sensitive paper. **1955** T. H. PEAR *Eng. Social Differences* 99 Many people.. flare up at any suggestion (except from a speech-trainer consulted voluntarily) of possible improvements in their speech. **1933** *Amer. Speech* VIII. 11/1 To complete any gaps there may be in the speech training of the members. **1977** P. STREVENS *New Orientations Teaching of Eng.* vii. 86 Young learners will learn best through mimicry with speech training games for interest and for special points of difficulty, but with little or no use of phonetics. **1834** J. S. MILL in *Monthly Repos.* VIII. 419 One of our politicians..reproached him..with being a λογογράφος, or speech-writer. **1976** H. WILSON *Governance of Britain* iv. 88 The transatlantic custom of using speech-writers, recently imported into Britain for the use of certain eminent politicians and others, is only to be deplored.

13. speech area, a region of the brain involved in the comprehension or production of speech, a speech-centre; **speech chain** *Linguistics*, an utterance regarded as a sequence of elements; **speech clinic**, a centre for the treatment of speech defects; **speech code** *Cryptology*, a simple verbal code formed by the regular substitution of secret words; **speech coil**, a coil that drives the cone of a loud-speaker according to the signal current flowing in it; **speech-community** *Linguistics*, a group of persons sharing a language or variety of a language; **speech island** *Linguistics*, a small area inhabited by speakers of a language or dialect other than that spoken in the surrounding areas; **speech pathology**, the study and treatment of defective speech; hence **speech pathologist**; **speech physiology**, the study of the physical production of speech sounds; **speech-prefix**, in the text of a play: the name or description of the speaker(s) of a line or lines, set at the head of each speech; **speech psychology**, the study or application of psychological methods and techniques useful in learning to speak a language; also **speech psychologist**; **speech recognition**, the process of identifying and interpreting or responding to the sounds produced in human speech; **speech recognizer**, a machine capable of responding to the content of speech; **speech-song** = *SPRECHGESANG; **speech stretcher** *Phonetics* (see quot. 1972); **speech synthesizer**, a machine designed to generate sounds imitative of the human voice and recognizable as meaningful speech; **speech therapy**, the training of patients in the production of a full range of speech sounds; hence **speech therapist**, one who practises this; **speech-to-noise ratio**, the signal-to-noise ratio of speech.

1885 *Harper's Mag.* Mar. 638/2 (*in figure*) Speech area. **1913** *Q. Rev.* Jan. 124 Over a large portion of the highest level of the brain the special work of each group of cells or 'area' is now known. If our speech-areas are diseased we cannot speak. **1968** PASSMORE & ROBSON *Compan. Med. Stud.* I. xxiv. 52/1 (*caption*) The three speech areas [*sc.* Broca's area, superior area, Wernicke's area] shown on the left cerebral cortex. **1950** D. JONES *Phoneme* i Nearly every utterance, or 'speech chain', is made up of a large number of small elements. **1953** C. E. BAZELL *Linguistic Form* i. 5 But the smaller the number of choices, at any one point of the speech-chain, the smaller the probability of open juncture. **1963** DENES & PINSON (*title*) The speech chain: the physics and biology of spoken language. **1963** R. I. MCDAVID *Mencken's Amer. Lang.* 320 The spread of technical medical terminology to education, as *clinic* (yielding *reading clinic* and *speech clinic*). **1976** *New Yorker* 15 Nov. 146/2 A young man.. who took a Ph.D. in speech pathology at Iowa in 1936 and then left to set up a speech clinic and research centre. **1973** 'A. HALL' *Tango Briefing* xviii. 221 Fred was the standard speech-code name for any third member of an active cell. **1928** *Wireless World* 6 June 603/2 (*caption*) Various gauges of wire for speech coil. **1934** *Discovery* Oct. 301/2 The 2-in. speech coil attached to the 11-in. cone works in a flux density of 11,500. **1975** G. J. KING *Audio Handbk.* vi. 132 The speech coil is composed of inductance, distributed capacitance and resistance. **1894** G. E. KARSTEN in *Publ. Mod. Lang. Assoc.* IX. 327 It is pre-eminently the speech-community which moulds the individual's language. **1911** L. BLOOMFIELD in *Jrnl. Eng. & Gmc. Philol.* X. 629 A language is formed (i.e., a new speech-community is segregated) by definite changes in the outer surroundings of a group of people. **1950** R. A. HALL *Leave your Language Alone!* x. 153 Theoretically, it might be possible to keep an otherwise-normal speech-community hermetically sealed off from all outside sources of borrowing. **1978** K. HUDSON *Jargon of Professions* 10 Speech communities are no longer as self-contained as they were. **1888** M. D. LEARNED in *Amer. Jrnl. Philol.* IX. 65 We are to seek the causes which have contributed to the formation of this important speech-island in the domain of German dialects. **1933** [see *LUSATIAN *sb.* and *a.*]. **1957** *Publ. Amer. Dial. Soc.* XXVII. 5 In one instance, that of *stone boat*, there is an additional speech island along the Mississippi, opposite St. Louis. **1978** *Amer. Speech* LIII. 44 A large speech island appears in the German-settlement area of Missouri and Illinois. **1972** J. L. DILLARD *Black English* vii. 267 A linguistically sophisticated speech pathologist like Joan Baratz. **1982** *Amer. Speech* LVII. 213 Speech pathologists, audiologists,..and many others have had some introduction to formal linguistic analysis. **1931** L. E. TRAVIS *Speech Path.* p. vii, Speech pathology is in its growing pains. **1976** *New Yorker* 15 Nov. 148/2 One of his advisers suggested that he sign up instead for the graduate program in speech pathology at the University of Iowa. **1936** G. K. ZIPF *Psycho-Biology of Lang.* iii. 96 The experimental phoneticist..attempts to determine by his laboratory study of speech-physiology what changes [in a language] are possible. **1961** *Amer. Speech* XXXVI. 222 A treatment..of speech physiology by means of X-ray stills and films. **1959** *N. & Q.* June 213/1 It is therefore recommended that for the last speech of 'Elder Worthy' on I, 60..the speech-prefix 'Young Worthy' be substituted. **1978** *Studies in Eng. Lit.: Eng. Number* (Tokyo) 12 There are eleven Latin speech-prefixes. The first five are '*Omn.*' for all the characters on the stage. **1937** PALMER & HORNBY *Thousand-Word Eng.* i. 21 It is in the nature of a designed *plateau* (as speech-psychologists call it), that is..a given stage..at which the learner may pause. **1921** H. E. PALMER *Princ. Lang.-Study* 19 A logical order of progression in accordance with principles of speech-psychology. **1933** *Amer. Speech* VIII. IV. 37/1 There are graduate curricula in speech science, phonetics, speech psychology, and rhetoric. **1953** FRY & DENES in W. Jackson *Communication Theory* xxx. 426 (*heading*) Mechanical speech recognition. *Ibid.* 427 The reasons for the failure of these..systems becomes clear when the mechanism of human speech recognition is considered. **1970** *New Scientist* 30 Apr. 216/2 Research on speech-recognition devices is still in its extreme infancy. **1980** *TWA Ambassador* Oct. 25/1 A second went to Bell Telephone Laboratories for a computerized speech-recognition system that can respond to human sentences. **1953** W. JACKSON *Communication Theory* 431 Any mechanical speech recognizer requires for its operation a considerable amount of linguistic information. **1970** O. DOPPING *Computers & Data Processing* xi. 162 A 'normal' speech recognizer would recognise words regardless of the speaker. **1909** *Cent. Dict.* Suppl., Speech-song. [**1925** Song-speech: see *SPRECHGESANG.] **1946** E. BLOM *Everyman's Dict. Mus.* 580/1 *Speech-song*,..a term for a kind of singing that approximates to speech and touches the notes, indicated by special signs, without intoning them clearly at the proper pitch. **1959** *Listener* 17 Dec. 1093/2 The Roman practice of narrating during Holy Week the Evangelists' accounts of the Passion in a stylized speech-song (*tonus lectionis*). **1976** P. STADLEN in D. Villiers *Next Year in Jerusalem* 324 The Bible's casual hint at Moses' 'heavy tongue'..[is] realized, by having Moses engage in speech song while..Aaron is made to sing. **1948** M. JOOS *Acoustic Phonetics* (Lang. Monogr. No. 23) 129 The usefulness of the speech stretcher for phonetic demonstration is immense. **1972** HARTMANN & STORK *Dict. Lang. & Linguistics* 216/2 *Speech stretcher*, a device used in phonetic research to slow down recorded speech without changing the pitch or distorting it in any other way. **1953** *Jrnl. Acoustical Soc. Amer.* XXV. 735/1 A speech synthesizer would be required to simulate..closely the actual dimensions of the vocal tract. **1970** *Times Lit. Suppl.* 23 July 787/4 If the zealous phoneticist is dissatisfied with the acoustics of a real human voice he can nowadays, it seems, ring down for a speech synthesizer, couple it up to his computer, and manufacture ideal vowel sounds. **1933** S. M. STINCHFIELD *Speech Disorders* i. 10 A clinician, psychologist or speech therapist might suspect that one of the following conditions would be found in such a case. The child may be deaf, or some childhood illness may have slowed up his rate of development. **1975** M. KENYON *Mr Big* ii. 21 A speech therapist..who'd insisted that correct speech being a matter of breath control for six months he would simply have to learn to breathe. **1933** S. M. STINCHFIELD *Speech Disorders* vii. 141 It is worthwhile to spend some time in reviewing the more important types of nervous disorders, in order to better understand their implications, in undertaking speech therapy. **1976** E. WARD *Hanged Man* xl. 267, I took the speech therapy and the office-boy jobs. **1951** *Engineering* 23 Feb. 226/3 Those concerned with the telephone apparatus..have paid much attention to questions of speech intelligibility, but in its broad aspects the matter is of direct interest to most shop executives. It is not their business to design loud speakers, but they are certainly concerned with the speech-to-noise ratio in workshops. **1981** *Amer. Speech* XXXVI. 221 Monosyllabic, bisyllabic, and trisyllabic words presented for identification in seven different speech-to-noise ratios.

speechful, *a.* **b.** (Earlier example.)

1820 C. R. MATURIN *Melmoth the Wanderer* IV. xxviii. 228 No form of Guido's, hovering in exquisite and speechful undulation between earth and heaven.

speechless, *a.* Add: **2. b.** Also (*dial.*) as *adv.*

1915 D. H. LAWRENCE *Rainbow* i. 34 The woman's not speechless dumb. She's not clutterin' at the nipple. She's got the right to please herself.

speechment. (Earlier example.)

1826 J. O'KEEFE *Recoll.* I. ix. 341 After this grand speechment, it was thought advisable not to let her have any thing at all to say.

speed, *sb.* Add: **II. 5. c.** (Later examples.) Freq. in sense d below; also *ellipt.*, a bicycle having the number of gears indicated.

1955 *Radio Times* 22 Apr. 30/1 (Advt.), 6-valve, 3-speed, autochange table radiogram. **1970** 'D. Halliday' *Dolly & Cookie Bird* iii. 26 A runaway self-propelled two-speed-gear lawnmower. **1975** *Sat. Rev.* (U.S.) 3 May 44/1 Then they'll hop onto their sleek 3-, 5-, or 10-speeds and..explore America's city streets.

d. Any of the possible gear ratios of a machine, esp. a bicycle or motor vehicle; the equipment associated with this; = *GEAR *sb.* 7 b.

1866 *English Mechanic* 22 June 263/1, I think in velocipede construction it is necessary to have two speeds... By pulling the lever A it throws the small wheels out of gear, and the driver can use the large wheels for level ground and the small ones for ascending hills. **1904** Kipling *Traffics & Discoveries* 304, I was on the point of reversing and working my way back on the second speed ere I ended in some swamp, when I saw sunshine through the tangle ahead and lifted the brake. **1907** G. B. Shaw *John Bull's Other Island* iv. 80 The pig..put in the fourth speed with its right crubeen. **1926** T. E. Lawrence *Seven Pillars* (1935) ix. cii. 560 The armoured car was too heavy for the flints, and always she sank in a little, making heavy going on third speed. **1951** N. Mitford *Blessing* ii. ii. 170 I'll get you a bike with three speeds. **1974** *Encycl. Brit. Macropædia* II. 522/2 The simplest automobile transmission is the sliding-spur-gear type with three or four forward speeds and a reverse. **1980** P. Lively *Judgement Day* x. 129 A shiny new bike with three speeds.

6. b. (Later examples.)

1935 S. C. Johnson *Foulsham's Compl. Photographer* iii. 26 The last of the four factors which must be considered in determining the length of an exposure is the speed of the plate or film. **1977** 'J. le Carré' *Hon. Schoolboy* vi. 123 Loading a cassette into the camera, he set the film speed.

c. *Photogr.* = *shutter speed* s.v. *SHUTTER *sb.* 3 b.

1917 P. L. Anderson *Pictorial Photogr.* v. 95 Of course these high speeds are not necessary for indoor work, where an exposure of less than 1/8 second is practically never desired. **1947** A. Ransome *Great Northern?* xxiii. 286 He set the aperture at f.11, the speed at a twenty-fifth of a second. **1977** J. Hedgecoe *Photographer's Handbk.* 162 Speeds of 1/500–1/2000 sec allow you to freeze subject action beyond the perception of the eye.

d. The rate, measured in words per minute, at which a person can write shorthand or can type; *spec.* (freq. in *pl.* of both skills) applied to the capacity of a particular person.

1886 *Encycl. Brit.* XXI. 840/2, 180 or 200 words a minute is no uncommon speed in certain styles of speech such as the conversational,—a speed which many [short-hand writers]..would never acquire. **1933** Smith & Munro *Guide to High Speed Writing in Pitman's Shorthand* i. 10 It is well within the capacity of the majority.. to reach a speed of, say, 160 words a minute, and..all writers of the system should make up their minds that that is to be their *minimum* speed. **1957** C. Smith *Case of Torches* xi. 137 He..said there wouldn't be much shorthand or typing. So I thought—well, I don't want to lose my speeds, then I heard about this job. **1976** H. Tracy *Death in Reserve* i. 14 I'm a sort of secretary... I've got high speeds in shorthand and typing.

6*. An amphetamine drug, esp. methamphetamine, freq. taken intravenously. Cf. *SPEEDBALL 1 a. *slang* (orig. *U.S.*).

1967 [see *FREAK *sb.*[1] 4 c]. **1967** [see *METHEDRINE]. **1969** Fabian & Byrne *Groupie* viii. 66 Now he was on speed the paranoid fantasies were really beginning. **1970** N. Saunders *Alternative London* xxii. 175 Amphetamines ('speed') are stimulants which can temporarily reduce fatigue, increase mental activity and give you a general feeling of well-being. **1975** J. Symons *Three Pipe Problem* ix. 65 'What was he on?'.. 'Speed mostly. Sometimes acid.' **1978** G. Vidal *Kalki* v. 109 Dr Lowell produced a hypodermic needle. I let him shoot me up... I assumed that he had given me speed.

9. c. *to be one's speed*: to suit one's tastes, interests, or abilities; to be one's 'cup of tea' (*CUP *sb.* 12 b (ii)). *colloq.* (chiefly *U.S.*).

1923 E. L. Rice *Adding Machine* v. 77 'Did you ever carve a leg of lamb?'.. 'No, corned beef was our speed.' **1954** R. Bissell *High Water* iii. 36 'I'm gonna buy you an Uncle Wiggly book,' I said. 'He'd be just your speed.' **1970** J. Sangster *Touchfeather, Too* i. 11 Lesbianism.. isn't really my speed at all. I'm a normal type girl.

11. a. *speed-meter.*

1938 *Times* 14 Oct. 15/4 The driver of the omnibus.. traversed the evidence of the speed-meter by pleading that his omnibus was so constructed as to be incapable of travelling at the alleged illegal speed. **1958** *Manch. Guardian* 21 Jan. 6/3 The use of radar speedmeters to enforce the law on the roads promises to be more successful than most efforts to reduce..road accidents.

11. b. *speed-bike, bowler, launch.*

1904 *Trans. Inst. Naval Archit.* XLVI. 161 The American speed launches. **1950** W. Hammond *Cricketers' School* v. 52 No one exemplified better than Larwood the true speed-bowler's action. **1955** S. Spender *Coll. Poems 1928–1953* ii. 74 Speed-bikes and tracks are real. **1977** *Arab Times* 3 Dec. 10/5 West Indian speed bowlers Andy Roberts and Michael Holding helped bring about the collapse of the Australian 'super test' cricket team.

11. c. *speed-law, record, trial* (earlier example); *speed-time, -torque* adjs.; **speed-boat,** a high-speed motor boat; hence **speed-boating,** riding in a speed-boat; **speed bug** [*BUG *sb.*[2] 4 a] *slang*, one who enjoys travelling at high speed; an addict of speed sports; **speed bump** *colloq.* = *sleeping policeman* s.v. *POLICEMAN 1 e; **speed cop** *slang*, a policeman or official detailed to enforce traffic laws, esp. a motorcycle patrolman; **speed demon** [*DEMON 2 e] *slang*, one who likes to travel at great speed, a 'speed bug'; also *transf.*; **speed freak** (orig. *U.S.*), a person addicted to an amphetamine drug (cf. sense 6* above); **speed gun,** a hand-held device for estimating the speed of a moving vehicle (proprietary name in U.S.); **speed hog** [*HOG *sb.*[1] 7 c] *slang*, one who causes annoyance by exceeding the normal or legal speed limit; **speed king** *slang* (orig. *U.S.*), a motor-racing champion; **speed limit,** (*a*) the maximum speed a vehicle is capable of achieving (quot. in Dict.); (*b*) the maximum speed permitted by law on certain types of road or to specified classes of vehicle; **speed merchant** *colloq.*, one whose 'business' concerns the use of speed; *spec.* (*a*) *Cricket*, a fast bowler; (*b*) one who enjoys driving or riding at high speed (cf. *MERCHANT *sb.* 3); **speed-read** *v. trans.* and *intr.*, to read rapidly by assimilating several phrases or sentences at once; so **speed-reader,** one who speed-reads; **speed-reading** *vbl. sb.*; **speed shop** *slang* (see quot. 1954); **speed trap,** a system operated by the police for detecting motorists exceeding the speed-limit; **Speed-walk** *U.S.*, a proprietary term for a moving walkway for conveying passengers; also (with small initial) in general use; cf. *TRAVOLATOR; **Speedwriting** orig. *U.S.*, the proprietary name of a form of shorthand which uses the letters of the alphabet; hence **speedwriter.** See also *SPEEDBALL, *SPEEDWAY.

1911 *New Fry's Mag.* May 224/1 The number of speed-boats, pure and simple, has grown greatly. **1929** 'Seamark' *Down River* i. 6 Hillary Kittredge..had fallen under the lure of speed-boat racing. **1940** R. Chandler *Farewell, my Lovely* xxxvii. 280 The speedboat scuffed the *Montecito's* ancient sides. **1976** H. Kemelman *Wednesday the Rabbi got Wet* liii. 311 There are houses all around this little lake and each..must have a speedboat or an outboard. **1928** *Sunday Dispatch* 5 Aug. 11/3 The heavy demand for petrol, created by the new sport of 'speed' boating. **1975** *Country Life* 30 Oct. 1129/1 A useful side effect of the speed-boating..was the weed being cut by the propellers of the boats. **1914** *Automobile Topics* XXXIV. 191/1 The trials..were crowded with excitement for the speed bugs who filled the grandstands. **1928** Speedbug [see *AQUAPLANE]. **1975** *Public Works* Aug. 73/1 Speed bumps had been installed in many apartment complexes and shopping center parking lots. **1978** T. L. Smith *Money War* (1979) i. 59 As he approached the speed bumps, Hogan slowed... They took the bumps gently and then pulled off the road. **1924** *Cape Argus* 12 Jan. 20 These 'speed cops', however, wear uniform and are not got up to appear like ordinary motor-cyclists. **1933** *Amer. Speech* VIII. 72/2 His Grace, on being stopped, demanded 'Are you a speed-cop?' The patriotic magistrates fined him £10. 10s. and suspended his license for three months. **1948** *Sat. Even. Post* 3 July 77/3 Speed cops still speak politely to me. **1941** Speed demon [see *DICE *v.* 1 a]. **1962** A. Lurie *Love & Friendship* vii. 113 Helen, the regular cashier, was a speed demon. **1971** *Black Scholar* Jan. 35/1 Jack Johnson.. has been called many things, e.g. show off, fool, speed demon. **1967** Speed-freak [see *FREAK *sb.*[1] 4 c]. **1973** R. Mills *Young Outsiders* ii. 63 In the summer of 1970 Jimmy would have been labelled a 'speedfreak' within the circles in which he moved. **1972** *Official Gaz.* (U.S. Patent Office) 1 Aug. TM 29/1 CMI, Incorporated, Minturn, Colo. Filed Feb. 1, 1971. *Speed Gun* for Traffic Radar..First use Dec. 10, 1970. **1972** *Tuscaloosa* (Ala.) *News* 14 Dec. 32/4 The hand-held Digital Doppler, a new tool police are using to catch speeders... The police purchased eight of the devices—also known as 'speed guns'. **1976** *Tel.* (Brisbane) 24 June 1 The speed guns are being used by traffic police mainly in areas of potential traffic hazard. **1928** *Daily Express* 23 Aug. 9/4 The scheme to limit 'speed-hogs'. **1974** *Country Life* 30 May 1360/1, I join issue with the RYA on their objection to..boat registration... Without it the speed hog..will often continue to go undetected. **1913** *Illustr. Technical World Mag.* June 493/1 (*caption*) Ralph De Palma. The 'speed king' of 1912. **1938** C. Graves *Swiss Summer* 108 German princes, English speed-kings..are usually to be found here. **1976** *Western Mail* (Cardiff) 22 Nov. 3/2 Yesterday's event was held to raise money for the memorial fund to the Welsh speed king who died in a rally incident in the summer. **1926** *Scribner's Mag.* Aug. 152/1, I hear you break speed-laws as recklessly as hearts. **1902** *To-day* 13 Mar. 648 The Automobile Club urges that the existing speed limit should be abolished. **1909** *Chambers' Jrnl.* Mar. 225/1 A speed-limit sometimes as low as..four and three-quarter miles per hour. **1926** *Motor* 26 Oct. 561/1 (*heading*) The speed limit. 35–40 m.p.h. or none at all? **1970** P. Laurie *Scotland Yard* v. 113 Fifty mph..is only ten mph above the speed limit there. **1973** H. McCloy *Change of Heart* i. 6 As for my mother, I can't make her drive ten miles over the speed limit. **1913** J. B. Hobbs *How to make Century* xi. 80 The speed merchant was now sending up such hot samples that his every delivery was more likely to take a wicket than offer a chance of runs. **1923** *Daily Mail* 15 Feb. 6 The goggled 'speed merchant' cannot see so well as usual. **1951** *Ithaca* (N.Y.) *Jrnl.* 9 Aug. 21/1 [He] had a glass arm and he certainly was no speed merchant. **1982** J. B. Hilton *Sunset Law* i. 11 A County Court judge..drove at reckless speed about the highways, menacing speed-merchants with a Smith & Wesson. **1960** *Time* 24 Nov. 21 Bagwell taught himself to speed-read, gulping whole paragraphs at a glance. **1973** *Sat. Rev. World* (U.S.) 20 Nov. 64/2 (*caption*), I speed-read your last book in two minutes and twenty seconds. **1965** *N.Y. Times* 5 June 22 The Evelyn Wood Reading Dynamics Institute..teaches prospective speed-readers to see every word on the page—but to read three words at once, not one word out of three. **1975** 'S. Marlowe' *Cawthorn Jrnls.* xix. 162 He wished he had something to read... He was a speed-reader. He had an IQ of 140. **1983** *Listener* 20 Jan. 25/2 A library for an extra-terrestrial speed-reader cruising above the British Isles. **1965** G. Jackson *Let.* 3 Oct. in *Soledad Brother* (1971) 89 Be sure to look into the course on speed reading. **1977** *Time* 3 Jan. 13/3 Having promised to read every bill brought up before the state senate, he ran into 2,300 of them. So he took a speed-reading course and read them all. **1935** P. Frankau *I find Four People* iv. 235 About this time the copywriter accomplished a speed-record for journalism. **1942** E. Paul *Narrow St.* xvii. 132 The *Bremen* made her maiden trip to New York and set a speed record. **1954** *Amer. Speech* XXIX. 102 *Speed shop*, a parts house, where engine parts and equipment are sold, and sometimes where hot rods are built. **1962** *Punch* 17 Oct. 561/1 Engineering firms and speed shops supply every beefed or stripped refinement. **1977** *Hot Car* Oct. 49/3 You can often pick up reasonable headers off the shelf from a good speed shop. **1917** A. T. Dover *Electric Traction* ii. 8 A speed-time curve, for a run between two stations, is usually made up of periods of—(1) acceleration; (2) constant speed, or 'free running'..; (3) coasting..; and (4) retardation or braking. **1976** P. R. White *Planning for Public Transport* x. 216 In urban areas, higher rates of acceleration followed by a period of coasting can enable a given schedule to be covered using less energy (this is illustrated with reference to speed-time curves in Chapter 4). **1920** *Whittaker's Electr. Engineer's Pocket-bk.* (ed. 4) 544 For electric traction on railways and tramways, a motor possessing a variable speed-torque characteristic is preferable to one possessing a constant speed-torque characteristic. **1962** G. A. T. Burdett *Automatic Control Handbk.* i. 2 The motor must often have a speed/torque characteristic to match that of the driven machine. **1927** U. Sinclair *Oil!* 9 'Sit still,' said the man. 'Don't look round. A speed-trap!' **1980** G. M. Fraser *Mr American* xviii. 344 She had been caught in a police speed trap on the way to Brighton. **1883** W. H. Maw *Rec. Pract. Marine Engineering* I. 286/2 It was not found possible to take indicator diagrams on the full speed trials, but a considerable number of trials were run at lower speeds progressing up to 11·74 knots per hour. **1955** *Britannica Bk. of Year* 490/1 *Speedwalk*, a moving sidewalk. **1956** *Official Gaz.* (U.S. Patent Office) 4 Sept. TM 9 Passenger Belt Conveyors, Inc., Akron, Ohio... Speedwalk..For Passenger Belt Conveying Apparatus. First use Mar. 29, 1954. **1960** *Times Rev. Industry* Apr. 28/1 A twin-track passenger-carrying conveyor belt..is being constructed in London... Known as speed-walks..and travolators, at least two dozen installations are already in use in the United States. **1978** *Jrnl. R. Soc. Arts* CXXVI. 431/1 We can expect to see improvements in short-haul feeder and ancillary systems such as speedwalks, travelators and escalators. **1955** W. Gaddis *Recognitions* iii. ii. 740 You didn't send me a speedwriter down. **1925** *Speedwriting* (Brief Eng. Systems, Inc.) 7 (*caption*) Speedwriting, the wonderfully efficient new system of shorthand, developed by Miss Emma B. Dearborn, can be written after a few weeks' study, either by pencil or on any make of typewriter. **1927** *Official Gaz.* (U.S. Patent Office) 8 Aug. 242/1 *Speedwriting*... Printed Lessons and Examination Sheets Issued from Time to Time. Claims use since Dec. 29, 1924. **1929** *Radio Times* 8 Nov. 439/2 Speedwriting (The Universal Shorthand). **1938** E. B. White *Quo Vadimus?* 24 They sell a new kind of shorthand course, called the Quigley Method of Intensive Speedwriting. **1962** *New Scientist* 5 July 11/1 Part of the Speedwriting method is to cut out most of the vowels and unnecessary movement in making other letters. **1976** T. Stoppard *Dirty Linen* 24 You do speedwriting I suppose?.. Yes, if I'm given enough time. **1982** Barr & York *Official Sloane Ranger Handbk.* 84/1 Every Sloane secretarial college has a nimbus of girls with their shorthand books or red speed-writing books.

e. *Photogr.* In names for an electronic flash-gun, as *speed flash, gun, lamp, -light.*

1940 A. L. M. Sowerby *Wall's Dict. Photogr.* (ed. 15) 315 Externally, a speed-gun takes the form of a box or casing that can be attached to the camera to make the whole a single unit. **1950** W. F. Berg *Exposure* 339 A special kind of flash lamp is the speed flash, also known as multiple or electronic flash... One of the most important advantages of speed lamps is their exceedingly short flash time. **1953** *Sun* (Baltimore) 10 Jan. 5 (*caption*) A photo snapped of Prime Minister Winston Churchill..showed five-sided 'spots'. It was raining at the time and was attributed to reflections from a speedlight. **1969** A. Feininger *Compl. Colour Photographer* ii. 45 Electronic flash or speedlight has..advantages over conventional flashbulbs. **1979** *SLR Camera* Jan. 36/1 The AE-1 is.. an automated system camera. It includes a power winder for auto film transport, a speedlite for auto flash photography and an automatic exposure control.

speed, *v.* Add: Also *Pa. pple.* 8— **speeded.**

II. 11. d. Also *fig.*

1909 C. F. G. Masterman *Condition of England* ii. 23 When life has become 'speeded up' to the motor-car level. **1931** *Times Lit. Suppl.* 3 Dec. 979/3 He brought youth to the theatre; he speeded it up. **1974** A. Lurie *War between Tates* xiv. 277 He has the sense of being slowed down and speeded up alternatively.

13. e. To drive a motor vehicle fast, esp. at an illegal speed; to break the speed limit in a motor vehicle.

1931 Galsworthy *Maid-in-Waiting* xiii. 118 'I'm going to speed,' said Jean, looking back. The speedometer rose rapidly. **1941** M. Halsey *Traffic Accidents & Congestion* v. 41 The very word *speed* has come to mean *speeding* or going too fast. **1949** R. A. BYRD *Driving to Live* xi. 156 It becomes ridiculous, in the light of this new discovery [*sc.* road-stare phenomenon], for any driver to brag about his ability to speed. **1954** B. PRESTON *Focus on Road Accidents* II. 63 If the motorist continued to speed and was caught, several times a day, every day, then he would soon stop speeding. **1969** *New Yorker* 14 June 29/2 If you speed, we'll charge you the same amount we charge anyone. **1979** D. ANTHONY *Long Hard Cure* viii. 72, I..went back to my car. I sped a little on the way back to town.

f. To be addicted to or under the influence of an amphetamine drug. Also *fig.* Usu. as *pres. pple.* Cf. sense *6* of the sb. *slang.*

1973 R. MILLS *Young Outsiders* ii. 60 If you are speeding you go out and do more things. **1977** *Rolling Stone* 7 Apr. 47/1 'The best diet for the road,' he says, 'is soup for lunch and candy for supper. It keeps the weight off and you're speeding on all that sugar by show time.' **1978** S. GEORGE *Screen Test* ii. 18 'You speeding?' He shrugged. 'Yes. Cancels the alcohol.'

spee·dball. Also **speed-ball, speed ball.** [SPEED *sb.*] **1. a.** A dose of a drug, esp. a mixture of cocaine and morphine or of cocaine and heroin. *slang* (orig. *U.S.*).

1909 R. BEACH *Silver Horde* v. 58 You must have fed him a speed-ball, for I never saw a guy gear up so fast... He's developed a remarkable burst of speed. **1935** N. ERSINE *Underworld & Prison Slang* 69 *Speedball,* a mixture of *coke* and *morph* which is much in demand among drug addicts. **1953** W. BURROUGHS *Junkie* xiv. 139 A shot of morphine would be nice later when I was ready to sleep, or, better, a speedball, half cocaine, half morphine. **1964** *Guardian* 18 Apr. 6/3 To give a nobbler eighteen months for slipping a speedball in a greyhound's breakfast is like tossing up a ball and then punishing it for having the effrontery to bounce. **1974** M. C. GERALD *Pharmacol.* xv. 291 The 'speedball', a mixture of cocaine and heroin, is frequently employed to modulate the extreme feelings of excitement.

b. A glass of wine, *spec.* when strengthened by additional alcohol or spirits. *U.S. slang.*

1926 *Amer. Speech* I. 653 *Speed-balls,* wine. **1931** 'D. STIFF' *Milk & Honey Route* 215 *Speed balls,* sherry wine. These days it may be any wine, even *dago red.* **1931** G. IRWIN *Amer. Tramp & Underworld Slang* 178 *Speedball,* a glass of wine, more especially when 'doped' or made stronger by the addition of some alcohol, ether or strong spirits.

2. a. A ball-game resembling soccer, but in which a ball caught in the air may be passed by hand (see quot. 1976). *U.S.*

1923 *Amer. Boy* Jan. 24 (*heading*) Speedball—a new boys' game. *Ibid.* 25/1 Rychener..called out to Coach Mitchell, 'This is certainly a speedy game. Let's call it speedball.' **1928** *Sportswoman* Oct. 22/2 Speedball furnishes exercise for the whole body—legs, trunk, arms. **1933** *Jrnl. Health & Phys. Educ.* Oct. 38/1 Speedball has gained popularity until it is now used by high schools, private schools, teachers' colleges, and universities from coast to coast. **1946** E. D. MITCHELL in Fox & Davies *Official Soccer-Speedball Guide* It is fitting that this particular year should be a reminder to me to see what has been happening to Speedball... It was twenty-five years ago in the Fall of 1921, at the University of Michigan, that it was first played. **1961** J. S. SALAK *Dict. Amer. Sport* 413 The conversion of a ground ball to an aerial ball is the essential difference between speedball soccer. **1976** *Webster's Sports Dict.* 410/1 *Speedball,* a game played between 2 teams of 11 players on a football field with the object of kicking a ball between the uprights of the goal or passing the ball over the end line to score and preventing the opposing team from scoring.

b. *Boxing.* A type of small, fast punch-ball.

1955 F. MILLS *Learn Boxing with Me* v. 72 The platform pear ball is not an easy ball to punch... The ball to use is the small-type speedball, weighing about nine to ten ounces. The heavier kinds are too slow to be beneficial. **1975** OLIVER & RILEY *Boxing* ix. 46 Gyms vary in..the amount of equipment..available. Essentially what is needed is a ring, punch-balls, speed-balls, heavy bags and punching-pads.

speeded-up, *ppl. a.* [f. SPEED *v.* + -ED[1] + UP *adv.*]

a. Of a film: giving the appearance of rapid motion usu. as a result of being projected at a speed greater than that of original shooting. Cf. SPEED *v.* II d.

1931 J. S. HUXLEY *What dare I Think?* ii. 54 It is one of the most astonishing spectacles to see, on the speeded-up film, the processes of cell-division, of organization of growth. **1951** A. C. CLARKE *Sounds of Mars* xi. 143 You've all seen the films we made—especially the speeded-up colour one showing a complete cycle of Saturn's phases. **1968** A. DIMENT *Bang Bang Birds* viii. 146 Everything was happening like a speeded up holiday movie. **1976** *Listener* 25 Mar. 381/2 A speeded-up film of a flower opening and closing.

b. *transf.* Having an increased speed.

1962 M. MCLUHAN *Gutenberg Galaxy* 47 The new institutes for speeded-up reading. **1980** U. CURTISS *Poisoned Orchard* vii. 65 Sarah went to meet her at a speeded-up saunter.

speeder. Add: **3.** (Earlier example.)

1847 *Knickerbocker* XXX. 517 A few [girls] tend the 'warpers', the 'spoolers', and the 'speeders'.

4. Also *spec.* one who exceeds the speed limit in a vehicle.

1974 R. B. PARKER *God save Child* i. 6 [The police] have to arrest drunks and flag down speeders and break up fights.

5. *N. Amer.* A small vehicle running on railway tracks used for line maintenance, etc., orig. only manually propelled.

1905 J. OUTRAM *In Heart of Canad. Rockies* 152 The top of a box car is the choicest of propelling methods, unless one can get a ride on a hand-car or a speeder, with opportunity to slacken speed or stop whenever one desires. **1934** *Sun* (Baltimore) 6 Aug. 2/1 One hour in advance of the pilot train section men went over the President's route in gasoline 'speeders'. **1947** A. SAUNDERS *Algonquin Story* xi. 128 The husband, apparently a section man, had rushed up the tracks on a three-wheeled 'speeder' to bring Molly back to help. **1960** J. J. ROWLANDS *Spindrift from House by Sea* ii. 107 They had taken him out with pneumonia..fifty miles on a gasoline speeder..at twenty below zero. **1970** R. & J. PATERSON *Cranberry Portage* xxiii. 152 For days I travelled by locomotive, trolley, speeder, anything moving my way.

speeding, *vbl. sb.* Add: **4. b.** The act of driving a motor vehicle fast, esp. at an illegal speed. Also *transf.*

1908 *Evening Star* (Washington) in *Daily Chron.* 7 Oct. 4/7 Baby carriages are required to carry lights at night in Chicago. That rapid city may yet find it necessary to provide special police to keep the baby carriages from speeding. **1911** *Daily Colonist* (Victoria, B.C.) 2 Apr. 2/4 It was decided that everything possible would be done to assist the authorities in enforcing reasonable regulations regarding speeding. **1922** J. A. DUNN *Man Trap* ii. 24 Driving a car about the countryside at the expense of many fines for speeding. **1977** E. W. HILDICK *Loop* xvii. 115 The copper... He's been trying to get you all afternoon... I hope you haven't been doing no speeding.

5. *Comb.* **speeding citation, ticket** *U.S.*, a summons given to a motorist who has violated a speed regulation.

1974 *Marlboro Herald-Advocate* (Bennettsville, S. Carolina) 18 Apr. 1/4 Out of the 228 speeding citations..there was only one request for a jury trial. **1960** 'E. MCBAIN' *Heckler* v. 70 He had flatly refused to square any raps for them, raps ranging from speeding tickets to disorderly conduct. **1978** R. LUDLUM *Holcroft Covenant* ix. 114 If it'll get you out of Rio..I'll go like a greased pig in a slaughterhouse and pay the speeding tickets from my per diem.

speeding, *ppl. a.* Add: **2. d.** Of motor vehicles, motorists, etc.: travelling fast, esp. at an illegal speed.

1957 R. MATHESON *Shores of Space* 156 People who had ..been struck down by speeding cars. **1960** *Daily Tel.* 16 Jan. 1/5 Now the speeding motorist will find things more difficult. **1978** 'M. YORKE' *Point of Murder* xiii. 125 A speeding Mini, in the small hours, might attract notice if a police patrol car were around.

speedo (spī·do), colloq. abbrev. of SPEEDOMETER.

1934 *Passing Show* 21 July 19/3 The puzzled eyes of his scarlet face went hopelessly to the speedo. The needle was steady at fifty-five. **1938** L. MACNEICE *I crossed Minch* vi. 81 Lever..stepped on the gas, He said,..'Just you watch the speedo climb.' **1960** *News Chron.* 10 Oct. 6/6 The speedo needle does not obscure the mileage indicator. **1969** M. CALTHORPE *Defectors* 140 He glanced at the speedo... He'd driven almost five miles. **1976** P. HILL *Hunters* vii. 93 The car [was as] steady as a rock.. as the speedo reached up towards its limit.

speedometer. Add: **1. a.** (Later examples.)

1912 *Motor Man.* (ed. 14) 115 (*caption*) Details of system of friction drive for shaft of speedometer. **1932** *World Today* Feb. 261/1 The noisiest thing about this car was its speedometer, which maintained a noise something between a click and a swish. **1955** L. G. PRINGLE *Driving Lessons* 35 Chancing to glance at his speedometer, he discovered he was travelling at 45 m.p.h. through a built-up area! **1978** K. JOLLY *Driving made Easy* 35 The speedometer shows your speed in miles per hour... It should be checked frequently quickly when on the move.

b. The distance-indicator that is often incorporated in the speed-indicator of a motor vehicle; an odometer. *U.S.*

1929 *Collier's* 12 Jan. 8/2 Don't believe the speedometer of that magnificent limousine. It could have been fixed for sale purposes in twenty minutes. **1938** PALMER & CROOKS *Millions on Wheels* v. 87 Several courts have decided..that setting speedometers to indicate lower than actual mileage is a fraudulent practice... The buyer of a used car should therefore not even bother to look at the speedometer mileage. **1942** R. W. RIIS *Repairmen will get You* ii. 19 The car has gone at least 20,000 miles, although I think the speedometer doesn't register all the miles.

2. *attrib.*, as *speedometer needle.*

1909 *Quarterly Rev.* Jan. 148 Men are tempted to feel as if they must be acting rightly when the speedometer needle hovers below the figures 10. **1977** N. SLATER *Crossfire* iv. 77 The speedometer needle [was] jumping erratically around the 50 mph mark.

speedster (spī·dstəɹ). [f. SPEED *sb.* + -STER, after *roadster.*] **1.** A fast motor vehicle; a speed-boat.

1918 WEBSTER Addenda, *Speedster,*..a high-speed roadster, usually with low seats, accommodating two persons seated side by side. **1928** *Daily Express* 3 Sept. 5/5 But I'm not telling everyone who comes up in a swell speedster [*sc.* a speed-boat]. **1977** 'J. GASH' *Judas Pair* vi. 72 He lived about fifteen miles off the trunk road... I patted my speedster and swung the handle.

2. a. A motorist who drives fast.

1921 *Daily Colonist* (Victoria, B.C.) 16 Oct. 25/3 As a means of checking up on the speedster, a device has been invented. **1930** *Aberdeen Press & Jrnl.* 17 May 8/5 Lochiel criticised the making of trunk roads for the use of south speedsters. **1974** J. CLEARY *Peter's Pence* vii. 197 McBride drove fast: in Rome slow drivers got more attention..than speedsters.

b. More generally, a person who moves or acts very quickly, a fast runner. Also applied to animals.

1947 *Richmond* (Va.) *Times-Dispatch* 9 Nov. B7/7 The 175-pound speedster from Bridgeton, N.J., never quit running until he was across the goalline. **1966** D. VARADAY *Gara-Yaka's Domain* iv. 48 The four speedsters made a sudden concentrated rush at the meat-rich tycoon. **1977** *Time* 13 June 21/2 An American track-meet promoter, anxious to lure a top dash man to his indoor meet to increase the gate, called a speedster and promised him $800 plus expenses for joining the field.

speed-up. [f. vbl. phr. *to speed up*: see SPEED *v.* II d.] **a.** The act or process of increasing the speed or working rate of a thing. Also *attrib.*

1923 *Daily Mail* 3 Mar. 7 Train Speed-up..The speeding up of all services. **1944** *Sun* (Baltimore) 18 May 18/6 (*heading*) Assembly speedup law is planned. **1953** J. S. HUXLEY *Evolution in Action* i. 33 With a hundred-thousand-fold speed-up [of the film]..the overall processes of evolution became visible. **1970** R. LOWELL *Notebook* 158, I too in the end will see the things like this, Whatever I've lived assumed in one bright glance Like speed-up reading. **1977** P. SOMERVILLE-LARGE *Eagles near Carcase* v. 102 'Go on,' I said, 'not too fast.'.. The last thing I wanted was a speed-up.

b. The act or process of increasing productivity, esp. without raising rates of pay. orig. and chiefly *U.S.*

1935 *Sun* (Baltimore) 9 Feb. 2/1 Labor unrest..flows from..inequitable hiring and rehiring methods, espionage, speed-up and displacement of workers at an extremely early age. **1938** *Reader's Digest* May 55/2 There is no piecework, no speedup. **1943** *Sun* (Baltimore) 14 June 10/7 The extreme manifestation of management is the ruthless speedup or stretch-out, where production is increased without thought of the health of the workingman. **1959** N. MAILER *Advts. for Myself* (1961) 184 The productive speed-up tends to be replaced by..'featherbedding'. **1962** E. SNOW *Other Side of River* xxxi. 235 In 1955, for example, the *Workers Daily* revealed that alleged gains made in 'speed-up' drives by shocking overuse of labor were more than offset by heavily increased losses in man-power output. **1974** *Time Out* 22 Nov. 64/3 It's a depressing and probably accurate picture of a failure of consciousness in a barely unionised community where speed-ups, piece-work and cheap labour are rife.

spee·dway. [SPEED *sb.*] **1. a.** *U.S.* A track or road prepared for fast horse-driving. Now *Hist.*

1894 [in Dict. s.v. SPEED *sb.* II c]. **1968** *N.Y. City* (Michelin Tire Corp.) 97 Trotters were in fashion, and they whipped through the Park to the speedways of Harlem.

b. A road on which motor vehicles may travel fast. Also *gen.*, a motorway. Also *fig.* orig. *U.S.*

1903 *N.Y. Times* 16 Aug. 24/7 The numerous owners of rapid roadsters are devoting no inconsiderable portion of their Summer leisure to spirited brushes on the new speedway. **1919** *Public Opinion* 14 Nov. 471 (*heading*) The Speedway to Prosperity. **1927** [see *AUTOSTRADA]. **1946** J. W. DAY *Harvest Adventure* xiv. 247 The traffic on that concrete speed-way, the Great West Road. **1976** J. VAN DE WETERING *Tumbleweed* xx. 176 Their car..was joining the main traffic on the speedway.

2. *Sport.* **a.** A racing track for motor vehicles. Also *transf.*

1925 *Kansas City* (Missouri) *Star* 31 May 1/1 Here is how they finished..in the thirteenth annual 500-mile motor classic on the Indianapolis speedway yesterday. **1968** D. BRAITHWAITE *Fairground Architecture* 170/1 *Speedway,* a loose term which could refer either to an Ark —mounted with *motor-cycles,* or to a Monte Carlo Rally. **1979** *Arizona Daily Star* 1 Apr. c 12/2 USAC's 200-mile race at the Ontario Motor Speedway last weekend turned out better than a lot of people figured.

b. *transf.* A sport in which motorcyclists race several laps about a short oval dirt track. Freq. *attrib.*

1930 S. ELDER *Romance of Speedway* i. 9 Now that Speedway Racing has taken its place as one of our national pastimes. *Ibid.* ii. 27 In the first rank among Speedway riders. *Ibid.* 33 Habitual frequenters of Speedway gatherings. **1937** D. W. HARDING in *Scrutiny* VI. III. 254 When we have passed..from the state of idly watching men..and have accepted the invitation to form part of an audience for jugglers, acrobats..or speedway riders..we may speak of display entertainment. **1950** *Sport* 22–8 Sept. 21/2 The Wembley crowds shot up and speedway in general benefited. **1961** K. REISZ *Technique Film Editing* (ed. 9) ii. 77 Bill Fox (Dirk Bogarde) had been an ace speedway rider before the war. **1977** *Western Morning News* 30 Aug. 12/3 Exeter gave themselves a tremendous boost in their challenge for the Gulf British League speedway title when they snatched a precious point from title rivals Reading.

speedy, *a.* Add: **5. b.** Also *speedy trial* (U.S. Law), a criminal trial held after a minimum of delay, considered to be a citizen's right. Also *attrib.*

[**1776** G. MASON *Virginia Decl. Rights* in *Virginia Gaz.* (Williamsburg) 1 June 2/2 In all capital or criminal prosecutions a man hath a right to demand the cause and nature of his accusation, to be confronted with the accusers or witnesses, to call for evidence in his favour, and a speedy trial by an impartial jury. **1789** J. MADISON in T. Lloyd *Congress. Reg.* 4 June 428 In all criminal prosecutions, the accused shall enjoy the right to a speedy and public trial. **1807** J. OVERTON *Tennessee Reports* (1813) I. 253 The 9th section of the bill of rights secures to the citizen a speedy, public trial, and to demand the cause of accusation against him. **1878** *Michigan Reports* XXXVIII. 739 The right to a speedy and public trial in criminal cases by an impartial jury cannot be taken away by legislation.] **1893** *Southeastern Reporter* (1894) XVIII. 284/1 The 'speedy trial', and the policy of the law to expedite the trial of criminal cases, forbid that the person accused of crime shall be detained in prison beyond any term of the court at which he can lawfully be tried. **1901** *Daily Colonist* (Victoria, B.C.) 22 Oct. 1/6 Robt. Cameron, a penitentiary convict, before Judge Bole in the Speedy Trial court today, pleaded guilty to attempting to escape. **1926** J. BLACK *You can't Win* xviii. 262, I..decided to go before the court under the Speedy Trials Act. A defendant electing for a speedy trial dispenses with a jury and saves time and money for the community. **1951** F. H. HELLER *Sixth Amendment* iv. 60 The right to a speedy trial may not be asserted merely in order to forestall the ends of public justice. **1976** *Billings* (Montana) *Gaz.* 30 June 1-c/3 Judge Sorte rejected defense motions to dismiss the charges against the couple on grounds of prejudicial pretrial news coverage and lack of a speedy trial.

speel, *v.*² For entry substitute:

† **speel,** *v.*² *dial.* and *slang. Obs.* Also spiel. [Origin obscure: perh. f. SPEEL *v.*¹] **a.** *intr.* To go fast; to run *away*, make off.

a **1818** W. MIDFORD *Cappy* in T. Thompson *Coll. Songs* (1827) 49 Owre his airm hung a basket—thus onward he speels, And enter'd Newcassel wi' Cap at his heels. **1829** *Sessions Papers at Old Bailey* 9 Apr. 329 The blake come, i speld away. **1882** *Sydney Slang Dict.* 9/2 Shake this mob, Bill, and speel to the den, and let our lushy shicksters bring the ruin in. **1905** in A. B. Paterson *Old Bush Songs* 56 No more shall we muster the river for fats, Or spiel on the Fifteen-mile plain. *a* **1921** G. H. GIBSON in *Penguin Bk. Austral. Ballads* (1964) 207 With a turn o' speed..As can spiel like a four-year brumby. **1945** S. J. BAKER *Austral. Lang.* 70 Horses are said..*to speel* when they travel fast.

b. *trans.* Phr. *to speel the drum* (see quots.). Cf. *DRUM *sb.*¹ 9 d.

1839 H. BRANDON in W. A. Miles *Poverty, Mendicity & Crime* 167/2 *To speel the drum*, to run away with the stolen property. **1859** [in Dict.].

Speenhamland (spī·nămlænd). The name of a village near Newbury, Berks., used *attrib.*, esp. as *Speenhamland system*, and (rarely) *absol.* of a system of poor relief adopted by the magistrates there in 1795, and subsequently established throughout most of rural England.

[**1797** F. M. EDEN *State of Poor* I. ii. 577 This shews.. what should be the weekly Income of the industrious poor, as settled by the Magistrates for the County of Berks, at a meeting held at Speenhamland, May the 6th, 1795.] **1835** R. HALL *Let.* 10 July in *1st Ann. Rep. Poor Law Commissioners* 208 It is singular that the provisions of the Speenhamland Act of Parliament, as the Berkshire table is called,..contemplate only the case of the *industrious* poor. **1854** G. NICHOLLS *Hist. Eng. Poor Law* II. xii. 139 The famous Berkshire bread-scale, locally known as the 'Speenhamland Act of Parliament'. **1902** *Encycl. Brit.* XXVI. 665/2 The well-known Speenhamland scale (1795), by which a larger or lesser allowance was given to a family according to its size and the prevailing price of corn. **1925** C. M. WATERS *Econ. Hist. England 1066–1874* vi. i. 332 The enclosures and Speenhamland had quadrupled the poor-rate. **1934** B. RUSSELL *Freedom & Organization 1814–1914* vi. 78 An important step in the development of the Poor Law was taken by the inauguration of what is called the 'Speenhamland' system in 1795. **1959** *Chambers's Encycl.* VII. 550 The 'Speenhamland' system of poor relief..remained in force until the Poor Law Amendment Act of 1834. **1973** *Listener* 19 Apr. 500/3 Bill Jordan, a sociologist,..sees the social security system..as a modern Speenhamland system, deepening the division between the rich middle classes and the 'pauperised' poor.

Speeton (spī·tən). *Geol.* The name of a village on the North Yorkshire coast, used *attrib.* with reference to a series of clays of Lower Cretaceous age which outcrop there.

1829 J. PHILLIPS *Geol. Yorkshire* I. iii. 74 From the termination of the white cliffs the coast bends to the northward, and exhibits in succession, rising from beneath the chalk, the Speeton clay and the coralline oolite series. **1882** A. GEIKIE *Text-bk. Geol.* 816 The marine Neocomian strata of England are well exposed on the cliffs of the Yorkshire coast at Filey, where they occur in a deposit long known as the 'Speeton Clay'. **1946** L. D. STAMP *Britain's Structure & Scenery* xviii. 204 In the northern basin the Lower Greensand is represented by the Speeton Clays, with 'carstone', succeeded by marls and the famous Red Chalk of Hunstanton and Lincolnshire. **1969** BENNISON & WRIGHT *Geol. Hist. Brit. Isles* xiv. 323 On the north side of the Yorkshire Wolds a narrow outcrop of clays is found and it extends to the coast near Speeton. These clays, some 300 feet thick and known as the Speeton Series, range in age from the Ryazanian to the Albian.

‖ **Speisesaal** (ʃpəi·zəzāl). [Ger.] In German-speaking countries: a dining room, dining hall.

1871 *Monthly Packet* Christmas 57 The gentlemen betook themselves to the Speise saal, about which a cheerful bustle prevailed. **1929** E. M. BRENT-DYER *Rivals of Chalet School* v. 61 'No walk *this* day!' said that young person, looking sadly out of the window of the *Speisesaal* while they were having hot coffee and biscuits. **1969** J. EASTWOOD *Come die with Me* (1970) ii. 20 She..went down to the Speisesal [*sic*].

spelæology. Add: The form **speleo-** is now usual. Also, the hobby of exploring caves.

1937 *Caves & Caving* I. 7/1 The objectives of the British Speleological Association... 1. The promotion of friendship and the exchange of ideas amongst those who are interested in speleology. 2. The study of the geological, hydrological, archaeological and 'sporting' aspects of speleology. **1974** *Islander* (Victoria, B.C.) 8 Dec. 15/4 Press reports..have promoted public interest in the sport and science of speleology.

spelæologist (later examples); also, an explorer of caves.

1955 *Times* 20 Aug. 5/3 A team of Spanish speleologists from Pamplona..have completed a 10-day exploration of the Larra region of the Pyrenees. **1971** *Daily Tel.* 1 May 11/4 Speleologists (or cavemen) should explore the Dove's Nest in Borrowdale.

speleothem (spī·li,oþem). *Geol.* [f. Gr. σπήλαιον cave + θέμα that which is laid down, deposit.] Any structure which is formed in a cave by the deposition of minerals from water, e.g. a stalactite, stalagmite, etc.

1952 G. W. MOORE in *Nat. Speleol. Soc. News* June 2/1 In an effort to relieve the ambiguities of 'formation', the term speleothem is proposed... It is suggested that the word be used as a general term for secondary mineral deposits formed from water in caves, such as stalactites, helictites, rimstone terraces. **1968** *Nature* 6 July 49/1 Temperature dependent fluctuations in the $^{18}O/^{16}O$ composition of calcite deposited on speleothems could be used to fill this gap in the present understanding of past climates. **1976** W. B. WHITE in Ford & Cullingford *Sci. of Speleology* viii. 271 There is a competition between shapes guided by the flow path of the solution and shapes guided by the particular mineral and its crystal habit. This gives rise to two broad classes of speleothems, dripstone and flowstone forms and erratic forms. **1980** *Cambr. Encycl. Archaeol.* 53/1 Methods involving the measurement of different isotopes are being widely applied to derive long climatic records from ice cores, cave deposits like stalagmites (speleothems) and tree rings.

spell, *sb.*¹ Add: **4. a.** *spell-enslaved, -soaked.*

1938 DYLAN THOMAS *Let.* 14 Oct. (1966) 210 A still room in a spellsoaked house. **1955** J. R. R. TOLKIEN *Return of King* VI. iv. 227 The creatures of Sauron, orc or troll or beast spell-enslaved, ran hither and thither.

spell, *sb.*³ Add: **3. b.** For *Austr.* read *dial.* and *Austral.* and add earlier and further examples.

Examples from 1863 to 1975 may be found in *Dict. Newfoundland English* (1982).

c **1845** J. TUCKER *Ralph Rashleigh* (1929) xi. 146 Both men took a hoe and gave the children a spell. **1847** J. O. HALLIWELL *Dict. Archaic & Provincial Words* 781/2 *Spell*,..pleasure; relaxation. *Somerset.* **1862** J. S. DOBIE *Jrnl.* 10 Sept. in *S. Afr. Jrnl.* (1945) 23 Invited to stay and give my horse a day's spell. **1867** M. A. BARKER *Station Life in N.Z.* 128 We were all so breathless that a 'spell' (do you know that means 'rest'?) would have been most acceptable. **1931** G. L. NUTE *Voyageur* 96 Every five miles or so a halt was made to rest the dogs and to allow the men to smoke. These stops were termed 'spells' or 'pipes', and the voyageurs spoke of a day's journey as being so many spells or pipes. **1940** F. SARGESON *Man & his Wife* (1944) 30 About half-way back to the shore he took a spell. **1954** B. MILES *Stars my Blanket* xix. 141 We stopped for a 'spell' in the sandy bed, spreading out ground-sheets in the shade of the trees that lined the centre of it. **1972** *Regional Lang. Studies Newfoundland* May 9 *Spell*, a period of rest or a short sleep. Used..in Newfoundland and in Anglo-Irish. **1977** *N.Z. Herald* 8 Jan. 1-9/2 Marie Kay has been back racing only a little over a month following a long, enforced spell.

4. d. (*b*) (Earlier example.)

1745 D. GIDDINGS *Jrnl.* 27 May in *Essex Inst. Hist. Coll.* (1912) XLVIII. 299, I..continued in ye Trench a Spell.

e. *N.Z.* One of the periods into which a game of rugby is divided.

1900 *N.Z. Illustr. Mag.* III. 237/1 Usually in the second spell, when play is getting more exciting. **1934** A. E. MULGAN *Spur of Morning* I. iii. 23 The school won a hard game by six to nil, a try in each spell.

f. *Cricket.* A period or series of overs during a session of play in which a bowler bowls unchanged.

1976 J. SNOW *Cricket Rebel* 77 On that last afternoon at Colchester I took three quick wickets in my first spell. **1977** *World of Cricket Monthly* June 27/3 He was brilliantly caught by Richards at second-slip off Croft's first ball of a new spell.

spell, *v.*² Add: **3. e.** *U.S. to spell* (someone) *down*: to defeat (someone) in a spelling-contest. **† f.** *U.S.* To put to the test in spelling. *Obs.*

1854 B. F. TAYLOR *Jan. & June* 259 They all stand in solid phalanx by schools, and the struggle is, to spell each other down. **1866** C. H. SMITH *Bill Arp* 171 He then spelt him right straight along on all sorts of big words, and little words. **1871** E. EGGLESTON *Hoosier Schoolm.* (1872) iv. 47 Ralph dreaded the loss of influence..if he should be easily spelled down. **1932** *Randolph Enterprise* (Elkins, W. Va.) 18 Feb. 4/5 He was fairly spelled down at close of my school at Job, spring 1882, by a little girl not 7 years old. **1952** T. PYLES *Words & Ways of Amer. Eng.* (1954) v. 82 He who misspelled had to take his seat; the master's purpose was to 'spell down' the pupils.

g. *fig. to spell out* (orig. *U.S.*): to explain (something) step by step; to state explicitly or in detail.

1940 *San Francisco News* 31 Dec. 11 In the interest of clarifying public opinion, these opponents should spell out their position fully. **1952** B. WOLFE *Limbo '90* (1953) xxiv. 390 Spelling out the bald verities to a retarded child. **1956** J. POTTS *Diehard* xiii. 196 If you weren't such a fool you'd know it too. You want me to spell it out in words of one syllable for you? **1960** *Guardian* 1 Nov. 8/5 Dr. Kaldor would apparently have us spell all these things out. But..there really is a limit to the amount of detail ..to which a party in Opposition can commit itself. **1973** G. W. TURNER *Stylistics* vi. 171 An electrician asking which of three wires is 'the earth' clearly means 'the earth(ed) wire' or 'the wire connected with the earth', but hardly needs to spell it out. **1978** J. A. MICHENER *Chesapeake* v. 239 With studied care Thomas Janney spelled out the terms of the deal he had arranged.

spellbinder. For *U.S.* read orig. *U.S.* and add later examples. Also *gen.*

1906 *Calgary* (Alberta) *Eye Opener* 6 Oct. 1/3 He is a spell-binder all right. **1932** [see *flesh-creeper* s.v. *FLESH *sb.* 12 b]. **1939** *English* II. 245 Coleridge..would seem to have been something of a spell-binder: we have many witnesses..to the potency of the fascination he exerted over those with whom he came in contact. **1969** *N.Y. Rev. Books* 2 Jan. 15/2 'The books of all three are products of men who do not necessarily believe in their thoughts.' The risk is obvious of course—the false prophet, the spellbinder. **1974** P. DE VRIES *Glory of Hummingbird* (1975) ii. 11 A ministry replete enough with intimations..that he was less than a spellbinder.

spe·llbinding *ppl. a.*; **sp·ell-bindingly** *adv.*

1977 *Gramophone* Dec. 1121/3 A group of songs with orchestra..sounded so spellbindingly lovely. **1978** K. J. DOVER *Greek Homosexuality* iii. 164 Philosophy..was not the product of solitary meditation, to be communicated by a spell-binding orator.

spelldown (spe·ldaun). *U.S.* [f. vbl. phr. *to spell down*: see *SPELL *v.*² 3 f.] An eliminating contest in spelling.

1943 *Nat. Geogr. Mag.* Dec. 755 Among cherished memories of 'the days of real sport', the old-fashioned 'spelldown' takes high rank. **1951** E. GRAHAM *My Window looks down East* xv. 131 Mrs. Rowen decided to give him another chance and started the 'spelldown' over, but the children were consulted first. They agreed. The spelling started again. **1958** *Time* (Atlantic ed.) 23 June 38/1 In the..19th round of the spelldown, 13-year-old Betty Morgan,..choked up on *chiaus.*

spelling, *vbl. sb.*² Add: **1. b.** *U.S.* A spelling-bee, spelling-test. *rare.*

1860 O. L. JACKSON *Colonel's Diary* (1922) 23 The boys were anxious for a spelling in the evening. **1889** J. W. RILEY *Pipes o' Pan at Zekesbury* 45 How her face used to look in the twilight As I tuck her to spellin'. **1975** *Budget* (Sugarcreek, Ohio) 20 Mar. 14/3 The young folk are having german spellings once a week.

3. *spelling card, match, mistake, reform* (earlier example), *reformer* (later examples); **spelling pronunciation**, the pronunciation of a word according to its written form; **spelling school**, † (*a*) a building in which spelling is taught; (*b*) *U.S.*, a contest in spelling.

1850 C. M. YONGE *Langley School* xviii. 166 'Nobody' left the gate open,..tore the spelling cards, scratched the slates. **1974** 'J. LE CARRÉ' *Tinker, Tailor, Soldier, Spy* xxii. 186 Spelling cards lay spread over the floor. **1845** H. GREELEY in *Publ. Mod. Lang. Soc. Amer.* (1941) LVI. 501 It used to be the custom that the head of the first class and the next should choose sides for a 'spelling match'. **1967** B. BANFILL *Pioneer Nurse* xiii. 146 An invitation for all of us to an old-fashioned Spelling Match. **1966** N. MARSH *Black Beech & Honeydew* iii. 74, I won a Navy League Empire Prize..with an essay containing thirty-one spelling mistakes. **1901** E. KOEPPEL (*title*) Spelling-pronunciations. **1927** L. BLOOMFIELD in *Amer. Speech* II. 438/1 This last feature is a fairly close parallel to our 'spelling pronunciations', such as the full form *fore-head* for *forrid* and the now perhaps accepted *waist-coat* and *seam-stress* for *weskit* and *semstress*. **1944** [see *pronunciation-spelling* s.v. *PRONUNCIATION 6]. **1977** P. STREVENS *New Orientations Teaching of English* xii. 153 One further characteristic of American pronunciation that contrasts with British speech is the frequency of 'spelling pronunciations' in both place-names and proper names. **1848** A. J. ELLIS (*title*) A plain statement of the objects and advantages of the spelling reform. **1908** G. K. CHESTERTON *All Things Considered* 220 Some spelling-reformers..do spell his name phonetically. **1936** *Discovery* May 164/2 Unlike many spelling reformers, he respects tradition and the 'look' of a word. **1704** SWIFT *Tale of Tub* 16 There is also, the Spelling School, a very spacious Building. **1832** E. M. CHAMBERLAIN *Jrnl.* 25 July in *Indiana Mag. Hist.* (1919) XV. 241 In the evening I appointed a spelling school at which I invited all the parents to attend. **1948** E. N. DICK *Dixie Frontier* 138 Backwoods debating societies, spelling schools, story telling, and singing helped to while away the time.

spelling, *vbl. sb.*³ Add: (Later *attrib.* example.) *rare.*

1939 DYLAN THOMAS *Map of Love* 15 Endure burial under the spelling wall.

spelling (spe·liŋ), *vbl. sb.*⁴ [f. SPELL *v.*³] **1.** *Sc.* The practice of acting as a substitute for another or taking turns at some work or labour.

1920 *Glasgow Herald* 16 Apr. 7 The Sheriff finds that the custom known as 'spelling' is recognised in the West of Scotland, and in this case the defender's stevedore assented to the pursuer 'spelling' for the regular employee. **1955** *Times* 17 Aug. 5/4 Organized 'spelling'—that is to say, arrangements between members of a gang that they shall take it in turns to leave their work—is still to be found in Glasgow and Liverpool, in spite of many attempts to stamp it out. **1965** *Daily Express* 6 Aug. 4/5 'Spelling' in Glasgow is the same as 'welting' in Liverpool.

2. *Austral.* Resting from work. Also *attrib.*
1911 *Chambers's Jrnl.* Aug. 591/2 Old Davy..settled down on a selection near Grassmere which the Cornet Scrubber,..used as a spelling-place in his spare hours. **1926** B. Cronin *Red Dawson* ii. 36 There was need for their spelling before they sat in on the game in real earnest.

spelter, *sb.* Add: **1.** Also *locally* applied to various ores; (later example).
1912 *Trans. R. Geol. Soc. Cornwall* XIV. 153 In some of the deeper levels..an intimate mixture of chalcopyrite and garnet, which sometimes contains cassiterite also, locally known as 'spelter', has been met with in considerable quantities.

speltoid (spe·ltoid), *a.* and *sb.* *Bot.* [a. G. *speltoid* (H. Nilsson-Ehle 1917, in *Botaniska Notiser* 305), f. *spelt*: see Spelt *sb.*[1] and -oid.] **A.** *adj.* Of a wheat: resembling or having certain characteristics of spelt. **B.** *sb.* A speltoid wheat.
1920 *Hereditas* I. 116 A distinctive character of these speltoids..is the short outer glumes, abruptly cut off at the top as in *Triticum spelta*... Speltoid heterozygotes are also characterized by longer straws and longer and more lax spikes than the mother sort. **1932** *Proc. 6th Internat. Congr. Genetics* I. 286 Speltoid and dwarf types ..are found in the progeny of treated plants of *Triticum vulgare*. **1939** Sansome & Philp *Recent Adv. Plant Genetics* vii. 212 The speltoids differ from the parental type in having lax ears, thick keeled glumes which can only be pulled away from the grain with difficulty, and by the presence of awns. **1975** *Proc. R. Soc.* B. CLXXXVIII. 149 Reasonably uniform lines were available for test crosses with *vulgare* and speltoid tester stocks. *Ibid.* 156 *Spelta* and speltoid cannot be distinguished phenotypically... The low frequency of defectives in F_2's with base-sterile speltoids indicates a high degree of buffering by the polygenic system.
Hence **spe·ltoidy**, speltoid character.
1944 *Genetics* XXIX. 233 Speltoidy (so called because of the resemblance to *T. spelta*) has been shown..frequently to be due to the effects of a particular monosome. **1958** *Nature* 28 Jan. 1813/1 Okamato..has shown that chromosome IX is in the A genome, and has thus reduced the historical importance of speltoidy and compactoidy.

spelunker (spelʌ·ŋkəɹ). *N. Amer. slang.* [f. as Spelunk + -er[1].] One who explores caves, esp. as a hobby; a caver, a speleologist.
1942 A. F. Harlow *Weep no More, my Lady* xxiii. 407 A young man named Floyd Collins, a native of the hills a few miles north of the Mammoth, had long been a confirmed 'spelunker', or cave bug. **1946** *Life* 4 Nov. 143 Cave exploring,..which bears the scientific name of speleology, has a group of amateur followers who like to call themselves 'spelunkers'. **1965** P. Ordway *Night of Reckoning* (1967) 131 Not being a spelunker at heart, let's hope..there aren't too many bats. **1971** G. G. Luce *Body Time* ii. 54 A courageous spelunker and geologist, Michel Siffre, who spent two months on a subterranean glacier in the French Alps in 1962. **1980** 'E. McBain' *Ghosts* viii. 155 The cave seemed not in the least bit inviting. He had always considered spelunkers the choicest sorts of maniacs.
Hence (as a back-formation) **spelu·nk** *v. intr.*, to explore caves as a hobby; **spelu·nking** *vbl. sb.*, the practice or hobby of exploring caves.
1946 *Life* 4 Nov. 143 (*heading*) Life goes spelunking. **1959** *Weekend* 12 Sept. 77/2 To take a second look at Cadomin caves *Weekend* organized another spelunking expedition. **1965** R. McDowell *Hound's Tooth* vii. 105 They had no legitimate complaint if he chose to take Jenny spelunking in Hunter's Cave. **1974** *Islander* (Victoria, B.C.) 8 Dec. 15/3 Spelunking..is a sport which has become popular within our time. **1979** *United States 1980/81* (Penguin Travel Guides) 563 You can see these on..walks through the cave,..and on spelunking tours where you do your own locomoting on all fours.

Spencer, *sb.*[2] Add: [In sense *5, from the name of Christopher Miner Spencer (1833–1922), U.S. inventor and manufacturer.]
2. a. (Earlier examples.)
1795 *Sporting Mag.* V. 324/2 Spencers. These fashionable coatlets. *Ibid.* VI. 41/2 A young gentleman then approaching, dressed in a light coat, and a blue spencer.
b. (Earlier example.)
1799 J. Woodforde *Diary* 19 June (1931) V. 200 Very cold indeed again today, so cold that Mrs. Custance came walking in her Spenser with a Bosom-friend.
c. (Earlier example.)
1831 J. Brown *Let.* 26 Oct. (1912) 27 Then there is the odd dress of the sailors, with bright yellow worsted spencers and large slouched hats.
d. A type of under-bodice (usu. made of wool) worn esp. by women and girls to provide extra warmth in winter.
1881 in A. Adburgham *Shops & Shopping* (1964) xvii. 189 Light, elastic, inexpensive [hand-knitted clothes], including Jerseys, Cardigans, Vests, Spencers, Combinations, etc. **1924** [see *hug-me-tight 1]. **1953** 'P. Wentworth' *Ivory Dagger* xvii. 69 Miss Silver stood revealed in a slip petticoat of grey artificial silk and a neat white spencer whose high neck and long sleeves had..a narrow crochet edging. **1972** L. Hancock *There's a Seal in my Sleeping Bag* viii. 204, I wore two spencers (Australian item of thermal underwear).
5. A type of rim-fire repeating rifle or carbine used esp. during the U.S. Civil War. Freq. *attrib.*
1866 'F. Kirkland' *Pictorial Bk. Anecdotes & Incidents* 660/1 Harris ordered the skirmish line forward,..with orders to silence the troublesome battery..with the aid of the Spencer rifle. **1873** J. H. Beadle *Undeveloped West* 545 My horse, bridle, saddle, lariat, gun (a Spencer) and two Navajo blankets cost me two hundred dollars. **1904** *Kynoch Jrnl.* Apr.–June 96 The second repeater—and the one most prominent in the war—was the Spencer, having a magazine in the butt containing seven cartridges. **1923** J. H. Cook *Fifty Yrs. on Old Frontier* 5, I had traded a pistol..for a Spencer carbine. **1949** *Exciting Western* May 36/2 The .52 Spencer he kept under the bunk was a souvenir of Malvern Hill. **1974** *Encycl. Brit. Micropædia* IX. 412/1 *Spencer carbine*, military rifle with a magazine in the buttstock that contained seven cartridges. The cartridges were fed into the chamber by means of a trigger-guard operating lever.

Spencerian, *a.* and *sb.* Add: Also † **Spencerean. A.** *adj.* **1.** (Earlier examples.)
1865 *N.Y. Social Science Rev.* I. 70 Spencerean philosophy will permeate and penetrate the world of thought. **1878** W. James in *Jrnl. Speculative Philos.* XII. 9 This explicit acknowledgement..seems, after all, to bring back unity and simplicity into the Spencerian formula.
2. [f. the name of the U.S. calligrapher Platt Rogers *Spencer* (1800–64).] **a.** Designating a system of handwriting developed by Spencer.
1863 *Amer. Jrnl. Educ.* XIII. 876 (Advt.), Spencerian system of penmanship. **1865** *21st Ann. Rep. Board of Trustees Public Schools Washington D.C.* (1866) 19 The committee recommend that the Spencerian System of Penmanship be substituted for that of Potter and Hammond. They deem the Spencerian superior. **1906** *Mod. Writing Master* Sept. & Oct. 5/1 The condemning of the old Spencerian penmanship by the educators..marks the first point at which one can detect sober and serious thought on the subject. The old Spencerian had many faults as a system.
b. Of, pertaining to, or characteristic of the cursive script developed by Spencer and used in his system.
1883 G. A. Gaskell *Penman's Handbk.* 21/2 Spencerian, by P. R. Spencer, 1848. **1892** Howard & Brown *Lessons in Rapid Writing* 8 Use an elastic steel pen with fine and well tempered point. Gillott's No. 604..and Spencerian No. 1, are as good as any pens manufactured. **1895** *Montgomery Ward Catal.* Spring & Summer 118/1 Spencerian Script Ruler, a heavy maple ruler.., copies of penmanship printed on both sides of ruler. **1911** G. S. Porter *Harvester* xix. 479 That is where Uncle Henry showed his fine Spencerian hand. **1966** H. Nielsen *After Midnight* (1967) iv. 60 On the sheet of paper one line was written in a severe Spencerian script. **1972** J. Mosedale *Football* ii. 16 A document in Spencerian script faded by the years. **1982** 'W. R. Duncan' *Queen's Messenger* xii. 153 His script was close to Spencerian at times.
B. *sb.* (Earlier example.)
1878 W. James in *Jrnl. Speculative Philos.* XII. 7 Whether any Spencerian would hail with hearty joy their advent is another matter.

Spencerite. (Earlier example.)
1871 J. McCosh *Christianity & Positivism* vii. 182 There is a..set of youths in our day who will become Comtists, or Millites, or Spencerites, or even Huxleyites.

spencerite[2] (spe·nsərəit). *Min.* [f. the name of L. J. *Spencer* (1870–1959), British mineralogist + -ite[1].] A hydrated basic zinc phosphate, $Zn_4(PO_4)_2(OH)_2{\cdot}3H_2O$, found as colourless or white monoclinic crystals, freq. in stalactitic masses, in a zinc mine near Salmo, British Columbia.
1916 *Nature* 29 June 375/1 Prof. T. L. Walker: Spencerite, a new zinc phosphate from British Columbia. **1918** *Univ. of Toronto Studies* (*Geol. Ser.*) No. 10. 13 The spencerite forms the central part of the stalactitic growths and would appear to have been sealed up by the later shell of calamine. **1972** *Mineral. Mag.* XXXVIII. 690 Spencerite is an example of a mineral containing Zn in both octahedral and tetrahedral co-ordination.

spencite (spe·nsəit). *Min.* [f. the name of Hugh S. *Spence* (1885–1978), Canadian mineralogist + -ite[1].] A metamict borosilicate of rare-earth and other elements (chiefly yttrium and calcium), which is closely related to tritomite and occurs as brownish- or greenish-black grains and irregular masses.
1961 C. Frondel in *Canad. Mineralogist* VI. 576 Spencite is a new borate-silicate of calcium and yttrium, $(Ca,Fe)_2(Y,La)_3(B_3Si_{4\cdot3}Al_7)_8(O,OH,F,Cl)_{20}$ ... This new mineral was collected by Hugh S. Spence in 1934 from a prospect pit in Cardiff township..and was tentatively identified as thalenite. **1968** I. Kostov *Mineral.* 319 Spencite, $Y_3(CeTh)CaBSi_2O_{13}$, is another member [of the tourmaline group] occurring as black grains. **1973** *Canad. Mineralogist* XII. 71/1 Spencite varies widely in its physical properties and chemical composition. **1976** *Mineral. Abstr.* XXVII. 246/2 Spencite (tritomite-Y) is described from nepheline syenite pegmatites in the Dugdu and Kadyros Palaeozoic alkaline massifs.

spend, *sb.*[1] Add: **1. a.** (Further examples.) Also, the amount spent.
No longer restricted to the phrases in Dict.
1976 *Computers in Higher Education & Research: Next Decade* (Dept. Educ. & Sci.) 22 About £21 million should be spent for universities on new machines, buildings and operating costs..with a spend of about £10 million for research councils for similar purposes. **1982** *ICL News* Oct. 4/1 On the hardware side customer spends are relatively high—typically around £3 million for an installation. **1983** *Observer* 16 Jan. 8/4 The battle for advertising spend.
b. *ellipt.* for 'spending money'. Freq. in *pl.* *colloq.* and *dial.* (chiefly northern).
1970 *Guardian* 9 Dec. 9/2, I can remember when Lancashire children..turned over their unopened wage packet to Mum, who gave them back very modest 'spends'. **1976** *West Lancs. Even. Gaz.* 13 Dec. 6/2 What do other OAPs get for 'spends'. **1977** P. Carter *Under Goliath* xxiii. 127 Nearly everyone I knew got their spends on Friday night so they would all be at the pictures.
† **2.** *Obs. slang.* Semen, vaginal secretion; ejaculation. Cf. *spend *v.*[1] 15 c.
1879–80 *Pearl* (1970) 13, I felt her crack deluged with a warm, creamy spend whilst my own juice spurted..in loving sympathy. *Ibid.* 217 You dissembling, bleeding, rotten..lump of shit, rubbed over with a little spend. *c* **1888–94** *My Secret Life* III. 143, I could always go on pushing after a spend in those days, my prick would not loose its stiffness for minutes afterwards. **1891** *Simple Tale of Suzan Aked* (1898) iii. 100 Then, of course, not a drop of spend can get into me, because it is all caught by the letter.

spend, *v.*[1] Add: **I. 1. b.** (Later examples with *for*.)
1971 *Publishers' Weekly* 4 Oct. 42/2 Countless people.. have longed to own the Oxford dictionary and could not afford to spend $300 for it. **1977** H. Fast *Immigrants* 6 Anna persuaded him..to spend two dollars for a heavy jacket.
II. 15. c. To ejaculate; to have an orgasm. *slang.*
1662 Pepys *Diary* 7 Sept. (1970) 191, I went up to her and played and talked with her and, God forgive me, did feel her; which I am much ashamed of, but I did no more, though I had so much a mind to it that I spent in my breeches. **1714** *Cabinet of Love* 19 For at one instant both together spent. **1763** Wilkes & Potter *Essay on Woman*, Oft when we spend we propagate unknown. **1868** *Index Expurgatorius of Martial* 1 When you say, Hedylus, 'I shall spend, finish if you mean to finish', my flame languishes. **1922** Joyce *Ulysses* 739 He made me spend the 2nd time tickling me behind with his finger. **1980** R. L. Duncan *Brimstone* vii. 163 He felt himself spending at the very moment she contracted around him.

spending, *vbl. sb.* Add: **4.** † **b.** *Obs. slang.* An orgasm; an ejaculation. Cf. *spend *v.*[1] 15 c.
1856 W. Whitman *Leaves of Grass* 242 The babes I beget upon you are to beget babes in their turn, I shall demand perfect men and women out of my love-spendings. **1879–80** *Pearl* (1970) 15 She came again in another luscious flood of spendings.
7. b. In the sense 'of or pertaining to expenditure or disbursement', as *spending -power, spree, tax.*
1930 *Economist* 13 Sept. 477/1 Economy appeared to be denounced as a 'policy of stagnation' and the dangerous line of 'increased spending-power' once more held out as a remedial policy. **1942** *Time* 7 Sept. 94/3 The Senate Finance committee..pondered a new Treasury proposal for a 'spending tax' designed to encourage war savings. **1956** A. Huxley *Adonis & Alphabet* 140 We are now squandering the capital of metallic ores and fossil fuels... How long can this spending spree go on? **1968** *Punch* 23 Oct. 563/1 At the back of my mind there is a tiny doubt about the feasibility of the Spending Tax. **1980** 'R. B. Dominic' *Attending Physician* xvi. 144 You're not going on a spending spree with all that loot, are you?

spe·ndsavour, *a.* *nonce-wd.* [f. Spend *v.*[1] + Savour *sb.*] That has lost its savour.
1879 G. M. Hopkins *Poems* (1967) 81 Are you beam-blind, yet to a fault in a neighbour deft-handed? are you that liar And, cast by conscience out, spendsavour salt?

spe·ndthri:ftiness. *rare.* [f. Spendthrifty *a.* + -ness.] The act or quality of being spendthrifty.
1950 H. J. Massingham *Curious Traveller* iv. 76 For such spendthriftiness no honest word can be said. **1959** *Times* 29 June 12/6 The feeling of pleasurable spendthriftiness.

Spenglerian (ʃpeŋglīə·riăn), *a.* [f. the name of the German philosopher Oswald *Spengler* (1880–1936) + -ian.] Of, pertaining to, or characteristic of the philosophy of Spengler, esp. as expressed in his work *Der Untergang des Abendlandes* ('The Decline of the West').
1922 *Contemp. Rev.* July 52 Here the Spenglerian antithesis between Apollonian and Faustian is apparent. **1933** *PMLA* XLVIII. 608 It is hardly necessary to refer to Spenglerian pessimism. **1948** A. Toynbee *Civilization on Trial* 12 We do here seem to find a certain measure of Spenglerian uniformity. **1964** P. Worsley in I. L. Horowitz *New Sociology* 373 Spenglerian-cycle schemas. **1978** H. Wouk *War & Remembrance* xvi. 165 They sometimes played chess, and Hesse gloomed over the board in Spenglerian tones about the collapse of European man.

Also (now *rarely*) **Spe·nglerism**, the philosophy of Spengler or views in accordance with his; **Spe·nglerist** *a.* and *sb.*

1922 *Contemp. Rev.* July 50 There is no doubt in the minds of the Spenglerists that..from the ruins of Russia will arise a new culture. *Ibid.* 51 He will not have 'Spenglerism' dismissed as mere materialist determinism. *Ibid.* 52 The Spenglerist philosophy has not so far been exploited in the interests of German chauvinism. **1931** *Times Lit. Suppl.* 5 Feb. 93/2 His criticism of Pragmatism, Behaviourism, Spenglerism..are..intellectually acute.

Spenserian, *a.* (Earlier example.)

1817 COLERIDGE *Biog. Lit.* I. iv. 84 The Spencerian stanza, which always..recalls to the reader's mind Spencer's own style.

spent, *pa. pple.* and *ppl. a.* Add: **II. 5. b.** Also *ellipt.* as *sb.*, a spent herring.

1957 W. C. HODGSON *Herring & its Fishery* ii. 18 In this area [of the North Sea] there are large shoals of small immature herrings of low fat-content mixed with recovered spents that are just beginning to fatten. **1975** *New Yorker* 22 Dec. 55/1 April and May are the slack months, since the spring spawning has by then completed itself, and the herring are what are known as 'spents'—thin, indolent, not worth the catching.

spergula. (Earlier example.)

1829 [see *CERASTIUM].

sperm, *sb.* Add: **I. 4. a. sperm bank** = *semen bank* s.v. *SEMEN 2; hence **sperm banking; sperm count,** the number of spermatozoa in the ejaculate or in one millilitre of it; **sperm morula,** a ball of spermatozoa.

1963 B. RUSSELL *Let.* 10 Mar. in *Autobiogr.* (1969) III. iv. 173 If a sperm-bank, such as you envisage, had existed during the régime of Hitler, Hitler would have been the sire of all babies born in his time in Germany. **1977** M. SOKOLINSKY tr. *Merle's Virility Factor* vi. 130 Suppose you've had a vasectomy done... The men kept the sperm..in a sperm bank, in case their wives wanted to be fertilized. **1972** *Science* 7 Apr. 32 Biologist Mark Lappé..is disturbed that commercial outfits are the first to introduce large-scale sperm banking. **1941** *Endocrinology* XXVIII. 783 For approximately 18 days after the fever, the human total sperm counts remain at a relatively normal level. **1979** *Daily Tel.* 29 Nov. 19/1 Her twin was told she was unlikely to have children because of her husband's low sperm count. **1889** *Cent. Dict.*, Sperm morula. **1921** *Nature* 7 July 586/1 The occurrence of developing sperm-morulæ in microscopic sections of.. oysters has..been already observed. **1936** *Mem. Musée Royal d'Histoire Naturelle de Belgique* (2nd Ser.) III. 1003 Since females on English [oyster] beds nearly always carry some sperm morulae amongst the eggs, self-fertilisation will nearly always be possible.

b. *sperm-producing* adj.

1927 HALDANE & HUXLEY *Animal Biol.* ii. 52 Their walls are composed of germ-cells (sperm-producing cells).

II. 5. b. (Earlier examples.)

1775 in *Essex Inst. Hist. Coll.* (1887) XIII. 202 He heard sperm candles were 3s. **1839** C. F. BRIGGS *Adventures Harry Franco* II. 143 Mrs. Brown's house was brilliantly illuminated with a sperm candle in each side light.

spermacetic (spɜːmăsī·tik), *a.* *rare*⁻¹. [f. SPERMACET(I + -IC.] Of or pertaining to spermaceti; *spermacetic oil* = *spermaceti oil* s.v. SPERMACETI 2 a.

1922 JOYCE *Ulysses* 393 They..rubbed him all over with spermacetic oil.

spermacide (spɜ̄·ɹmăsəid). *rare*⁻¹. [f SPERMA- + -CIDE.] = *SPERMICIDE.

1908 *Chem. Abstr.* II. 3128 Reports upon Dr. Bamberger's lupina powder, spermacide, and choleysin are given.

spermalege (spɜ̄·ɹmălėdʒ). *Ent.* [ad. F. *spermalège* (J. Carayon 1959, in *Rev. de Zool. et de Bot. Africaines* LX. 82), f. L. *sperma* SPERM *sb.* + *legere* to gather, collect.] In female bedbugs, an organ in which sperm are received and stored.

1964 H. E. HINTON in K. C. Highnam *Insect Reproduction* (Symp. R. Entomol. Soc. Lond. No. 2) 101 These cells constitute the mesodermal part of the organ of Ribaga (or Berlese), or, as it is now aptly called by Carayon, the mesodermal part of the spermalege. **1978** H. V. DALY *Introd. Insect Biol.* iv. 62/2 In some bedbugs a spermalege, or specialized organ of the integument, is developed where the puncture normally is made.

sperm-aster (spɜ̄·ɹmˌæstəɹ). *Biol.* Also **spermaster, sperm aster.** [f. SPERM *sb.* + *ASTER 4.] A star-shaped configuration which in some species forms ahead of the sperm nucleus as it enters the egg in fertilization, and which develops into the amphiaster.

1904 *Biol. Bull.* VI. 226 One is the growth and division of the sperm aster, the other the growth of the nucleus. **1925** E. B. WILSON *Cell* (ed. 3) v. 400 In almost all cases the sperm-nucleus, as it advances within the egg, is typically preceded by a sperm-aster which sooner or later divides to form an amphiaster that is the forerunner of the cleavage-amphiaster. **1946** *Nature* 17 Aug. 239/1 Colchicine treatment..inhibits spindle formation as well as the appearance of the spermaster in fertilized eggs and of the monaster in parthenogenesis. **1977** *Jrnl. Embryol. & Exper. Zool.* XL. 194 It would be of the utmost interest to establish whether a causal relationship does also exist between sperm aster formation and the movement and directionality of the female pronucleus.

spermatic, *a.* **5.** (Earlier example.)

1685 J. LOCKE *Jrnl.* 22 June in Ld. King *Life & Lett. John Locke* (1830) I. 309, I saw, at Mr. Lewenhook's, several microscopical observations..but the best of all his glasses, and those by which he describes his spermatic animals, we did not see.

spermaticide (spəɹmæ·tisəid). Now *rare*. [f. SPERMATO-: see -CIDE.] = *SPERMICIDE. Hence **sperma·ticidal** *a.* = *SPERMICIDAL *a.*

1923 M. C. STOPES *Contraception* v. 104 Of all the chemical substances used as spermaticides, undoubtedly quinine is in the most general use. **1931** Spermaticide, spermaticidal [see *SPERMICIDE]. **1934** J. ELLISON et al. *Sex Ethics* v. 93 The spermaticidal effect of these pessaries is not very high, and many failures have resulted. *Ibid.*, The use of lactic acid jelly ointment, as a lubricant, will assist in ensuring that all parts of the vagina are covered with spermaticide.

spermatid. Add: *spec.* one that is formed by the meiotic division of a secondary spermatocyte and develops into a spermatozoon without dividing again. (Later examples.)

1924 E. W. MACBRIDE *Study of Heredity* ii. 46 In the case of the male cell each secondary spermatocyte divides into two precisely equal cells called spermatids. **1959** [see *spermatogonium* s.v. *SPERMATO- 1]. **1968** *New Scientist* 2 May 218/2 It now appears that the X and the Y chromosomes become genetically inert before the spermatids (the cells from which the spermatozoa develop) are formed.

Hence **sperma·tidal** *a.*

1975 *Biochem. & Biophysical Res. Communications* LXVII. 183 Proteins extracted from elongated spermatids..reveal the presence of a new spermatidal basic protein fraction.

spermatize, *v.* Restrict † *Obs.* to sense in Dict. and add: **2.** [Back-formation f. *SPERMATIZATION.] *trans. Mycology.* To effect spermatization upon. *rare.*

1932 *Mycologia* XXIV. 347 Apothecia are produced only when the isolate from the crocus is used as a source of microconidia to spermatize any of the other six.

Also **spermatiza·tion** (see quot. 1932); **spe·rmatizing** *ppl. a.*

1932 F. L. DRAYTON in *Mycologia* XXIV. 346 The development of apothecia by *Sclerotium Gladioli*..has been induced by means of placing the microconidia of one thallus on certain structures which develop on another thallus. This process may be called 'spermatization', and it will be so designated throughout this paper. **1945** *Ibid.* XXXVII. 635 He attempted to intercross these four races by the spermatization method. **1967** M. E. HALE *Biol. Lichens* iii. 42 The spermatizing element may be any hypha that can contact the ascogonium. **1970** *Cytologia* XXXV. 427 The mechanism of spermatization in this fungus..is of a type not so far reported.

spermato-. Add: **1. spermatocyte,** a cell which gives rise to spermatids by meiosis; the *primary spermatocyte* gives rise in meiosis I to two *secondary spermatocytes,* which each give rise in meiosis II to two spermatids; (later examples); **spermatogonial** *a.* (examples); **spermatogonium,** (*a*) *Bot.* (see quot. 1957); (*b*) *Zool.*, a primordial male reproductive cell which undergoes mitosis and gives rise to primary spermatocytes; (later examples).

1920 Spermatocyte [see *OOGONIUM 2]. **1959** [see *spermatogonium* below]. **1970** Spermatocyte [see *OOCYTE]. **1902** *Biol. Bull.* III. 44 In the case of the accessory chromosome, it has been found advantageous to trace its course through the spermatogonial divisions in *Brachystola*, and through the spermatocyte changes in *Hippiscus*. **1976** *Nature* 22 Jan. 209/1 After 600 rad of X rays, the mean spermatogonial mutation rate was one-third that of the 7-locus mean. **1957** SNELL & DICK *Gloss. Mycol.* 144/2 *Spermatogonium*, the proper form for what is called 'spermogonium'.., but seldom used. **1959** W. ANDREW *Textbk. Compar. Histol.* xii. 490 [In fishes] spermatogenesis consists of the same general cytological stages as in the invertebrates: namely, spermatogonia, spermatocytes, spermatids, and spermatozoa. **1968** PASSMORE & ROBSON *Compan. Med. Stud.* I. xxxvii. 27/2 Spermatogonia show little sign of activity until puberty when they begin to multiply rapidly. **1970** [see *OOGONIUM]. **1974** *Sci. Amer.* Sept. 56/3 In the course of spermatogenesis the two important objectives are reduction of the chromosome number from the diploid number (46) of the spermatogonium to the haploid number (23) of the spermatozoon and the preparation of the spermatozoon for its role in fertilization.

2. spermatoci·dal *a.* = *SPERMICIDAL *a.*; **spe·rmatocide** = *SPERMICIDE; **spermatoge·nically** *adv.*, as regards the production of sperm; **spermatogenesis,** the formation and development of spermatozoa (cf. *SPERMIOGENESIS); (later examples); **spermatology,** † (*a*) a treatise on sperm; (*b*) the scientific study of sperm; (examples).

1928 *Funk's Stand. Dict.* 2337/3 *Spermatocidal*, checking or killing the motor-power of spermatozoa. **1937** Spermatocidal [see *CHINOSOL]. **1949** *New Gould Med. Dict.*, Spermatocide. **1980** *Nature* 10 Apr. 548/1 Spermatogenically active testes. **1978** P. J. HOGARTH *Biol. Reproduction* ii. 11 The final phase of spermatogenesis in the testes is known as spermiogenesis.., and consists of the progressive conversion, without division, of the spermatids into functional spermatozoa. **1980** Spermatogenesis [see *SPERMIOGENESIS]. **1833** DUNGLISON *Dict. Med. Sci.* II. 312/2 *Spermatology*, a treatise on sperm. **1970** B. A. AFZELIUS in B. Baccetti *Compar. Spermatol.* 568 In spite of the great efforts to solve the problems in comparative spermatology we find ourselves confronted with more questions than answers. **1976** T. SHARPE *Wilt* iv. 32 He got the Nobel prize for spermatology.

spermatophore. Add: Hence **spermatopho·ric** *a.*

1959 W. ANDREW *Textbk. Compar. Histol.* xii. 475 [In the common squid] peculiarly complicated organs, the spermatophoric organs and sacs, receive the sperm from the vas deferens, pack them into bundles, and cover them with a tunic..before their ejection as spermatophores by the penis. **1977** M. J. & J. WELLS in Giese & Pearse *Reproduction Marine Invertebrates* IV. vi. 297 In..the wider initial section of the first spermatophoric gland, the sperm are embedded in a mucin secretion.

spermatozoan, *a.* (Example.)

1954 G. I. M. SWYER *Reproduction & Sex* ii. 24 The spermatozoan content of the ejaculate.

spermicide (spɜ̄·ɹmisəid). [f. SPERMI- + -CIDE.] Any substance which kills spermatozoa, esp. one used as a contraceptive. So **spermici·dal** *a.* Cf. *SPERMACIDE, *SPERMATICIDE, and *spermatocide* s.v. *SPERMATO-.

1929 *Jrnl. Hygiene* XXIX. 323 The spermicidal powers of the various chemical contraceptives sold to the public have never previously been compared, and no one has been in a position to say that one spermicide is preferable to another. **1931** *Ibid.* XXXI. 190 The words 'spermicide' and 'spermicidal' are preferred, on grounds of euphony, to 'spermaticide' and 'spermaticidal'. **1936** *Discovery* Sept. 277/2 Baker has shown that soap solution is more spermicidal than most chemical contraceptives. **1962** A. HUXLEY *Island* vi. 84 Before the age of rubber and spermicides. **1977** V. COLEMAN *Paper Doctors* ix. 93 There were 15 different types of spermicidal contraceptive waiting to be prescribed. **1977** E. J. TRIMMER et al. *Visual Dict. Sex* (1978) xiv. 135/3 Spermicides..should not be used alone as a contraceptive method.

spermidine (spɜ̄·ɹmidīn). *Biochem.* [f. SPERM(IN + *-IDINE.] A colourless liquid triamine, $H_2N(CH_2)_3NH(CH_2)_4NH_2$, which is found very widely in living tissues, in company with spermine, and has a number of metabolic functions.

1927 H. W. DUDLEY et al. in *Biochem. Jrnl.* XXI. 97 This base has been given the name spermidine since it not only occurs in association with spermine but also has been found to be structurally related to the latter substance. **1964** A. WHITE et al. *Princ. Biochem.* (ed. 3) xxvi. 538 Spermine and spermidine are present in significant amounts in ribosomes and appear to be essential to their structure and function. **1974** *Nature* 17 May 250/1 The polyamines spermine spermidine and their precursor putrescine occur ubiquitously and in high concentrations in animals and plants.

spermin. Add: The spelling *spermine* (-īn) is now usual. (Later examples.)

1927 [see *SPERMIDINE]. **1937** *Thorpe's Dict. Appl. Chem.* (ed. 4) I. 315/1 The polyamino-compounds are of little interest with the exception of spermine, a tetra-amino derivative of the constitution $NH_2{\cdot}[CH_2]_3{\cdot}NH{\cdot}[CH_2]_4{\cdot}NH{\cdot}[CH_2]_3{\cdot}NH_2$, first isolated from human semen by Schreiner, and occurring in many mammalian organs. **1964, 1974** [see *SPERMIDINE].

spermiogenesis (spɜ̄ɹmiˌodʒe·nėsis). *Biol.* [f. SPERMI- + -O + -GENESIS.] The development of spermatozoa; *spec.* the maturation of spermatids into spermatozoa (the last phase of spermatogenesis).

1920 *Biol. Bull.* XXXIX. 333 The general topography of spermiogenesis has been worked out on *Murgantia*. **1956** *Nature* 25 Feb. 387/2 A study of spermiogenesis in the bandicoot..has shown that an acrosome is indeed present. **1980** D. J. BEGLEY et al. *Human Reproduction* iii. 30/2 Following spermatogenesis and spermiogenesis, which take about 64 days in man, sperm pass through the rete into the epididymis.

spe·rmy, *a.* For *rare*⁻¹ read *rare* and add later examples. Also, full of sperm. (In quot. 1851, with reference to spermaceti.)

1851 H. MELVILLE *Moby Dick* II. xxxviii. 253 If you unload the skull of its spermy heaps..you will be struck by its resemblance to the human skull. **1973** M. AMIS *Rachel Papers* 31, I decided I would ring her when I got back. It would be intelligent to do it while I still felt tolerably spermy and Joycean after my night with Gloria.

speromagnetic (spiᵊ:rŏmægne·tik), *a.* *Physics.* [f. Gr. διασπείρειν to scatter + *ANTIFERR)OMAGNETIC *a.*] Applied to an amorphous magnetic material in which the individual electron spins are aligned more or less anti-parallel to their closest neighbours but overall there is a statistical distribution of orientations with no preferred direction. Also **speroma·gnetism.**

The form *sperimagnetic* occurred throughout the 1973 coinage paper. This was corrected by Coey et al. in *Physical Rev. Lett.* (1976) XXXVI. 1062.
1973 *Nature* 21–28 Dec. 445/2 The new phenomenon of speromagnetism (or amorphous superparamagnetism) adds a further delectable layer of complexity to what is already a highly elaborate network of phenomena. **1973** COEY & READMAN in *Ibid.* 477/2 Such a configuration, with the spins fixed relative to each other but possessing no overall preferred direction, is illustrated in Fig. 2*c*. It is termed 'sperimagnetic' [*sic*]..and..is probably a fairly common phenomenon in amorphous compounds. **1976** *Physical Rev. Lett.* XXXVI. 1062/1 Speromagnetism may also occur where the anisotropy dominates the exchange, in pure amorphous rare-earth metals, for example. **1976** *Physics Bull.* July 294/3 Speromagnetic ordering may also result when the exchange is distributed about zero with a range of positive and negative values.

sperrylite (spe·rilǝit). *Min.* [f. the name of Francis L. *Sperry* (*c* 1862–1906), U.S. chemist + -ITE¹.] Platinum arsenide, $PtAs_2$, found as opaque greyish-white isometric crystals.
1889 H. L. WELLS in *Amer. Jrnl. Sci.* CXXXVII. 67 (*heading*) Sperrylite, a new mineral. **1902** H. A. MIERS *Mineral.* II. 332 Sperrylite, the only natural compound of platinum, occurs as brilliant microscopic crystals..in a nickeliferous ore consisting of various sulphides, at Sudbury in Ontario. **1926** *Mineral Mag.* XXI. 94 A very fine and unusual crystal of sperrylite..came from a new adit on the Tweefontein farm..about 10 miles NNW. of Potgietersrust, Waterberg district, Transvaal. **1975** *Canad. Mineralogist* XIII. 327/2 Sperrylite is a common mineral in many platinum-bearing deposits.

‖ **spes** (spēⁱz). *Law.* [L.] A hope or expectancy, esp. of some future benefit. Also in various Latin phrases (see quots. 1959).
1815 *Decisions First & Second Divisions Court of Session* (Faculty of Advocates) 28 Feb. 258 There is a *jus crediti* conferred on the heir of a marriage-contract. It is not a mere *spes successionis*, but a *jus crediti*. **1945** *Law Rep.* 10 May 363 *Sine spe recuperandi*, in the sense of abandoning all hope of his owner recovering the ship. **1952** *Ibid.* 10 July 486 The taxpayer's answer to that is, first of all, that this is not property at all but a mere *spes* or hope of getting something. **1959** JOWITT *Dict. Eng. Law* II. 1664/2 *Spes recuperandi*, the hope of recovery. If it is entertained by a person in danger of death, it makes a declaration by him inadmissible in evidence... *Ibid.*, *Spes successionis*, an expectation of succession, as distinct from a vested right. **1977** JOHNS & GREENFIELD *Dymond's Capital Transfer Tax* ii. 40 The fiction of *Re Scott* does not go so far as to require one to suppose that the beneficiary had more than an interest in expectancy ..or indeed a mere *spes*, when he died.

speshul (spe·ʃǎl), repr. supposed colloq. pronunc. of SPECIAL *a.* and *sb.*
1900 *Times* 7 July 10/1 Boys..trample continually on your toes and screech everlastingly into your ears 'Cigarettes, cigars, chocolates'..'Speshul 'dition—latest cricket scores.' **1979** *Jrnl. Lancs. Dial. Soc.* Jan. 5 His first *buzz* was a *football speshul* to Maine Road.

spessartine. Now usu. with pronunc. (-īn). Substitute for def.: Garnet containing manganese in place of calcium; manganese garnet. (Later examples.)
1910 *Encycl. Brit.* XI. 471/1 Spessartite, or spessartine, ..is a fine aurora-red garnet, cut for jewelry when sufficiently clear. **1977** A. HALLAM *Planet Earth* 128 An individual [garnet] can be regarded as an intimate mixture of two or more of the following end-members: pyrope (magnesium-aluminum garnet), almandine (iron-aluminum garnet), spessartine (manganese-aluminum garnet), grossularite (calcium-aluminum garnet), andradite (calcium-iron garnet), and uvarovite (calcium-chromium garnet).

spessartite (spe·sǎɹtǝit). [f. as SPESSARTINE: see -ITE¹.] **1.** *Min.* = SPESSARTINE in Dict. and Suppl. Chiefly *N. Amer.*
1868 J. D. DANA *Syst. Mineral.* (ed. 5) 268 Manganese-Aluminagarnet; Spessartite. **1910** [see *SPESSARTINE]. **1934** G. L. ENGLISH *Getting acquainted with Minerals* II. 228 Some of the fine garnets of Delaware County, Pennsylvania are spessartite. **1953** F. H. POUGH *Field Guide to Rocks & Minerals* II. 296 Spessartite is less common and not often properly identified when it is in a schist. **1971** R. PURVIS *Treasure Hunting in Brit. Columbia* i. 21/2 Spessartite is pink to dark brown.
2. *Petrogr.* [ad. G. *spessartit* (H. Rosenbusch *Mikrosk. Physiogr.* (ed. 3) (1896) II. 529).] A porphyritic lamprophyre in which the feldspar is sodic plagioclase and the phenocrysts consist of an amphibole or pyroxene, usu. green hornblende.
1908 P. MACNAIR *Geol. & Scenery of Grampians* II. x. 64 Dykes and sills of lamprophyre, including kersantites, vogesites, and spessartites, are..to be met with throughout the Highlands. **1930** PEACH & HORNE *Chapters Geol. Scotland* iv. 108 The dark basic sills in the dolomites of the Assynt region..include representations of vogesites and spessartites. **1966** [see *lamprophyre* s.v. *LAMPRO-]. **1970** *Jrnl. Geol.* LXXVIII. 742/1 The dikelets probably formed during later stages of crystallization of the spessartite.

spew, *sb.* Add: **1. c.** Surplus material exuded between the halves of a mould during the manufacture of plastic objects. Freq. *attrib.*
1933 *Industr. & Engin. Chem.* June 647/1 The degree of flow can be readily controlled by the location, size and placement of the spew hole. **1945** A. T. BIRKBY *Phenolic Plastics* iv. 43 Provision should be made for air venting, and, in the case of compression moulds, for spew-ways. *Ibid.* viii. 93 'Flash' or 'spew' soon begins to appear round each press, and unless swept up and removed becomes a nuisance. **1964** WORDINGHAM & REBOUL *Dict. Plastics* 165 *Spew groove*, in moulding operations, the groove in a mould which permits the escape of surplus material.
4. Special Comb.: **spew frost** = *needle ice* s.v. *NEEDLE *sb.* 14.
1938 C. F. S. SHARPE *Landslides & Related Phenomena* iii. 27 Growths of frost crystal of this sort are known as spew frost.., feather-ice, or needle-ice..and on the European continent as Pipkrake or Kammeis. **1939** [see *needle ice* s.v. *NEEDLE *sb.* 14].

sphacelia. Add: Hence **sphace·lial** *a.*
1909 B. M. DUGGAR *Fungous Dis. Plants* xi. 245 The surface mycelial areas are thrown into folds and numerous short conidiophores arise, bearing small ovate conidia. This is known as the sphacelial stage. **1938** G. M. SMITH *Cryptogamic Bot.* I. xii. 453 This is followed by a progressively upward metamorphosis into compact tissue until the whole mycelium has been changed into a sclerotium that is capped with remnants of the sphacelial tissue. **1976** G. C. AINSWORTH *Introd. Hist. Mycol.* vii. 187 The major contribution of L. R. Tulasne in his classic paper in 1853..was to demonstrate that the sphacelial phase, the sclerotia, and the ascocarps were all stages of one fungus, *Claviceps purpurea*.

sphaerite (sfīᵊ·rǝit). *Min.* [ad. G. *sphärit* (V. von Zepharovich 1867, in *Sitzungsber. der K. Akad. der Wissensch.* (*Math.-Nat. Classe*) LVI. 24), f. *sphärisch* spherical: see -ITE¹.] A hydrous aluminium phosphate now identified with variscite.
1886 J. D. DANA *Syst. Mineral.* (ed. 5) 587 Sphærite... In globular concretions with a drusy faceted surface, without a distinct fibrous or concentric structure. **1921** *Bull. U.S. Geol. Survey* No. 679. 135 Sphaerite... Spherical masses of white fibers. **1950** *Amer. Mineralogist* XXXV. 1059 It appears that sphaerite is wholly identical with variscite.

sphæro-. Add: **sphærocobaltite** (earlier example); cf. *spherocobaltite* s.v. *SPHERO-; **sphæ·rocone** *Palæont.*, an ammonoid with a very involute shell in which the outer whorl conceals the inner one and the whole has a globular form; **sphærosome**, var. *SPHEROSOME; **sphærolite**, obs. var. SPHERULITE in Dict. and Suppl.
1877 *Mineral. Mag.* I. 267 Sphœrocobaltite [*sic*].. occurs in spheroidal forms with roselite at Schneeberg, Saxony. **1923** Sphærocone [see *SERPENTICONE]. **1970** R. M. BLACK *Elements Palaeont.* viii. 89 Sphaerocones occur repeatedly during ammonoid history.

sphagnum. For 'mod.L.' read 'mod.L. (J. J. Dillenius *Hist. Muscorum* (1741) 240)' and add: **1.** (Earlier example.)
1741 J. J. DILLENIUS *Hist. Muscorum* 240 The larger soft and hollow-leaf'd Bog Sphagnum.
3. Special Comb.: **sphagnum bog, swamp,** a bog in which the plant-life consists chiefly of mosses of the genus *Sphagnum*.
1911 C. B. CRAMPTON *Vegetation Caithness* iv. 51 In recent times..*Sphagnum* bogs have been reduced to their present small proportion in the moorland associations. **1951** V. NABOKOV *Conclusive Evidence* iv. 47 Beyond the lower course of the river..the vast expanse of a misty-blue sphagnum bog. **1972** DEAN & SMITH *Wisconsin* 78/2 Sphagnum bogs are one stage in the succession from open-water lake to conifer swamp. **1890** Sphagnum swamp [in Dict., sense 1]. **1941** J. BUCHAN *Sick Heart River* II. 124 A bottomless half-frozen sphagnum swamp ..heaved under his tread.

sphairistike (sfēᵊri·stikĭ). *Obs.* exc. *Hist.* [ad. Gr. σφαιριστική (τέχνη) (skill) in playing at ball, f. σφαιριστικός: see SPHAIRISTIC *a.* Cf. STICKÉ.] A type of tennis first played in 1873 which was later developed into and renamed lawn-tennis.
1874 G. D. FITZGERALD in *Field* 21 Mar. 270/2 Sir, I have lately seen a new game played which will be a great acquisition as an out-of-door amusement at country houses. The game is called Sphairistike, or Lawn Tennis. **1874** F. KILVERT *Diary* 27 July (1969) III. 55 We began to play 'sphairistike' or lawn tennis. **1927** *Times* 10 June 10/4 Badminton quickly got a certain popularity in England, and from it Major Wingfield invented sphairistike. The net of sphairistike was practically the badminton net, 5 ft. high at the sides, with the same, if a broader, red tape along the top. *Ibid.*, The name 'sphairistike', however, was impossible (if only because people would pronounce it as a word of three syllables to rhyme with 'pike'), and it was soon rechristened. **1965** *Punch* 16 June 895/2 The British invented lawn tennis, though the original name for it, 'sphairistike', didn't catch on. *Ibid.* 896/3 Arthur Balfour..mildly suggested that a better name for 'sphairistike' would be 'lawn tennis'! **1982** 'J. GASH' *Firefly Gadroon* v. 62 My eyes lit upon a genuine old Sphairistike racquet.

sphalerite. (Examples.)
1871 *Jrnl. Chem. Soc.* XXIV. 312 (*heading*) On the occurrence of thallium in sphalerite from Geroldseck (Breisgau). **1925** A. S. ALEXANDER *Tramps across Watersheds* v. 235 Some of these minerals and ores are:—gold, silver bloom, galena or lead ore, blende or sphalerite or zinc ore..and a great variety of quartz. **1952** [see *ROBINSONITE]. **1969** BENNISON & WRIGHT *Geol. Hist. Brit. Isles* x. 247 The later, mesothermal, lodes..carry such minerals as galena and sphalerite with a little uranium ore as well. **1973** *Times* 1 Dec. 11/3 'This piece', he said, indicating a toffee-coloured chunk of sphalerite from Picos de Europa, Santander, Spain, 'was brought up from the mine for me by a local dealer'.

sphecid (sfe·sid), *sb.* and *a.* *Ent.* [f. mod.L. family name *Sphecidæ*, f. *Sphex* SPHEX (Linnæus *Systema Naturæ* (ed. 10, 1758) I. 569): see -ID³.]
A. *sb.* A fossorial wasp of the family Sphecidæ. **B.** *adj.* Of or pertaining to an insect of this kind.
1895 J. H. & A. B. COMSTOCK *Man. Study of Insects* xxii. 650 The Sphecids or the Thread-waisted Wasps.. are the most commonly observed of all our digger-wasps as certain species build their mud nests in the attics of our houses. **1926** E. O. ESSIG *Insects Western N. Amer.* xxviii. 871 Sphecid or Thread-Waisted Wasps..are solitary, nest in the soil, and provision the nests with spiders or insects. **1966** C. SWEENEY *Scurrying Bush* v. 75, I saw a handsome, inch long, metallic blue-black wasp fly out from behind the row of books. It was a sphecid or mud dauber. **1976** R. M. BOHART et al. (*title*) Sphecid wasps of the world. *Ibid.* 1 Adult sphecids feed on a variety of food.

spheno-. Add: **1. spheno-mandi·bular.**
1893 H. MORRIS *Human Anat.* ii. 190 The spheno-mandibular ligament (long internal lateral)..is a thin, loose band, situated some little distance from the joint. **1967** G. M. WYBURN et al. *Conc. Anat.* iv. 112/2 The sphenomandibular ligament runs from the spine of the sphenoid to the lingula at the mandibular foramen.

sphenochasm. (sfī·nokæz'm). *Geol.* [f. SPHENO- + Gr. χάσμ-α CHASM.] (See quot. 1958.)
1958 S. W. CAREY in *Continental Drift* (Geol. Dept., Univ. of Tasmania, Hobart) 193 A Sphenochasm..is the triangular gap of oceanic crust separating two cratonic blocks with fault margins converging to a point, and interpreted as having originated by the rotation of one of the blocks with respect to the other. **1965** A. HOLMES *Princ. Physical Geol.* (ed. 2) xxix. 1086 The Gulf [of California] sphenochasm appears to have been filled with rheid mantle material in much the same way as the Red Sea. **1971** *Nature* 2 July 21/2 As the Gulf of Honduras sphenochasm completed its opening, the Yucatan and Nicaraguan cratons assumed their modern positions relative to North America.

sphere, *sb.* Add: **I. 7. d.** Read 'orig. esp. in Africa or Asia' and add later examples.
1950 L. FISCHER in R. H. S. Crossman *God that Failed* 223 It provided for a spheres-of-influence division of the areas accessible to Soviet–Nazi aggression. **1973** A. BROINOWSKI *Take One Ambassador* iv. 43 The Japanese themselves are told they can't resort to force, even in what they see as their own sphere of influence. **1981** *Times* 21 Feb. 13/5 A programme of reform [in Poland] sufficiently limited to reassure the Russians that their sphere of influence is safe.
II. 8. a. Esp. in *Math.*, the set of all points at a specified distance from a specified point. (Later examples.)
1934 C. C. KRIEGER tr. *Sierpiński's Introd. Gen Topology* vi. 77 The set $K(p,r)$ (where $p \in M$, and $r > 0$) is called an open sphere of centre p and radius r. **1959** E. M. PATTERSON *Topology* i. 3 Since all spheres are homeomorphic, we speak of *the* sphere, rather than *a* sphere. **1968** E. T. COPSON *Metric Spaces* iii. 32 If we impose on the set..of all ordered pairs of real numbers the metric $\rho(\mathbf{x},\mathbf{y}) = \max\{|x_1 - y_1|, |x_2 - y_2|\}$ the spheres are squares.
12. sphere gap *Electr.*, a form of spark gap with two spherical electrodes, used esp. in devices for measuring high voltages.
1913 *Trans. Amer. Inst. Electr. Engineers* XXXII. 739 The sphere gap has been suggested as a standard instrument to be used in the measurement of high voltage. **1962** *Newnes Conc. Encycl. Electr. Engin.* 767/2 The measurement and recording of testing voltages requires either a voltage divider..or a sphere gap..capable of measuring the peak voltage.

-sphere, *suffix.* [f. the sb., after *atmosphere.*] Used in names of more or less spherical structures or regions forming part of or associated with the earth (or any celestial object), as *BARYSPHERE, *BIOSPHERE, *IONOSPHERE, *MAGNETOSPHERE, etc.

spherical, *a.* and *sb.* Add: **A.** *adj.* **4.** *spherical wave*: a wave in which the wave fronts are concentric spheres.
1907 *Chem. Abstr.* I. 1470 The spherical wave of explosion is propagated in a fluid medium according to formulas analogous to those derived for plane waves. **1976** D. ROSS *Mechanics of Underwater Noise* ii. 35 The intensity of a spherical wave is proportional to the square of the pressure.
5. Forming parasynthetic adjs., as *spherical-bodied, -roofed, -surfaced*.
1804 Spherical-bodied [in Dict., sense 1 *a Comb.*]. **1946** *Nature* 26 Oct. 26 583/2 The aberrations of a spherical mirror are corrected by a single spherical-surfaced meniscus lens. **1977** *N.Y. Rev. Bks.* 13 Oct. 16/1 The

spherical-roofed auditorium at CIA headquarters in Langley.

spherics, occas. var. *SFERICS *sb. pl.*

spherify, *v.* For *rare*⁻¹ read *rare* and add: Also, to turn *into* a spherical body. Also **spherifica·tion.**

1848 POE *Eureka* 74 Several fragments..were..spherified into a moon. *Ibid.* 75 Three moons..having been formed..by the rupture and general spherification of as many distinct ununiform rings.

spheristerion. For *rare*⁻¹ read *rare* and add earlier example in literal sense (in the Latinized form **spheristerium).**

1764 R. ADAM *Ruins Palace Spalatro* 11 On the other side of the Cella Media was a Spheristerium.., a room alotted for the different exercises of the ball.

sphero-. Add: **spheroco·baltite** *Min.* = *sphærocobaltite* s.v. SPHÆRO-; **sphero-cyli·ndrical** *a.*, (of a lens) having a spherical and a cylindrical surface; **sphe·roplast** *Biol.* [-PLAST], a bacterium or plant cell bound by its plasma membrane, the cell wall being deficient or lacking and the whole having a spherical form; hence **sphe·roplasting** *vbl. sb.*, treatment (as with an enzyme) that converts cells to spheroplasts; **sphe·roplasted** *a.*; **spherosymme·trical** *a.*, spherically symmetrical.

1889 *Cent. Dict.*, Spherocobaltite. **1924** *Amer. Mineralogist* IX. 61 Spherocobaltite. **1975** *Soviet Physics—Crystallogr.* XX. 74/1 The reaction involved in the synthesis of $CoCO_3$ has been studied in connection with the problem of growing single crystals of spherocobaltite. **1881** Sphero-cylindrical [see *ASTIGMATIC *a.* 2]. **1962** L. S. SASIENI *Optical Dispensing* x. 264 A toric lens is a curved sphero-cylindrical lens. **1958** C. HURWITZ et al. *Jrnl. Bacteriol.* LXXVI. 612/2 Lederberg (1956) has referred to these forms as protoplasts. In view of current uncertainty as to the fate of the cell wall in this case, we shall use 'spheroplasts' (McQuillen, 1958, personal communication) as a neutral term. *Ibid.* 613/2 Spheroplasts are osmotically fragile in a hypotonic environment. **1976** *Ann. Rev. Microbiol.* XXX. 42 Conversion of these cells to spheroplasts results in the release of periplasmic proteins into the supernatant. **1973** *Jrnl. Bacteriol.* CXVI. 491/1 Spheroplasted cells were found to lose endonuclease I from periplasm to surrounding medium. **1965** *Acta Path. Microbiol. Scand.* LXIII. 412 The mechanism of the ..spheroplasting effect of the incubation temperature is not obvious. **1973** *Jrnl. Bacteriol.* CXVI. 493/2 Spheroplasting does not affect gamma-ray induced DNA degradation in *E. coli CRthy*⁻. **1964** *Progress Reaction Kinetics* II. 299 The ions SO_4^{-} and F^-..both can be considered as fairly spherosymmetrical.

spherocyte (sfe·rosəit, sfīᵊ·ro-). *Med.* [f. SPHERO- + -CYTE.] A red blood cell which is biconvex instead of biconcave.

1908 CHRISTOPHERS & BENTLEY in *Sci. Mem. Officers Med. & Sanitary Dept. Govt. India* XXXV. 77 As such cells..are a sign of most important pathological changes, we have thought it desirable to have a name to designate the condition and have termed them spherocytes. **1947** *Amer. Jrnl. Med. Sci.* CCXIV. 255/1 The increased hemolysis seems due to the fact that spherocytes and ovalocytes are removed by the spleen more readily than are normal biconcave disks. **1977** *Lancet* 12 Nov. 1025/2 The blood smear showed many fragmented red blood-cells and some spherocytes.

Hence **spherocy·tic** *a.*, of, pertaining to, or characterized by the presence of spherocytes; **spherocyto·sis,** any spherocytic condition.

1933 F. W. PRICE et al. *Textbk. Pract. Med.* (ed. 4) XI. 775 Acholuric jaundice. Synonyms.—Spherocytosis; congenital hæmolytic anæmia. **1937** E. B. KRUMBHAAR in R. L. Cecil *Textbk. Med.* (ed. 4) 1266 Hemolytic Jaundice. (Congenital, Familial,..Spherocytic Anemia, [etc.]). **1947** *Amer. Jrnl. Med. Sci.* CCXIV. 255/1, 2 families which have a characteristic history and the clinical findings of hereditary spherocytic hemolytic icterus but show no spherocytosis. **1970** PASSMORE & ROBSON *Compan. Med. Stud.* II. xxxi. 3/2 The specific abnormality underlying spherocytic haemolytic anaemia is unknown. **1977** *Lancet* 6 Aug. 305/1 Repeated phagocytosis in lymphoreticular tissues is a feature of many hæmatological disorders, of which hereditary spherocytosis is an example *par excellence.*

spheroidal, *a.* Add: **2. c.** *Metallurgy.* = *NODULAR *a.* 4.

1920 *Jrnl. Iron & Steel Inst.* CII. 261 The present experiments were undertaken to clear up the cause of the formation of the spheroidal cementite. **1957** *Technology* July 172/3 To-day, nodular or spheroidal graphite cast iron is an article of commercial manufacture. **1977** *Metals Abstr.* X. 1801/1 Tests were made on boronizing spheroidal graphite cast iron (SGCI) to improve surface hardness and wear resistance.

spheroidize (sfīᵊ·roidəiz), *v. Metallurgy.* [f. SPHEROID *sb.* + -IZE.] **a.** *intr.* Of grains, esp. of graphite in cast iron or steel: to undergo conversion into spheroids.

1912 in A. Sauveur *Metallogr. Iron & Steel* App. II. 6 On long heating the pro-eutectoid and pearlitic cementite spheroidize slowly, and neighboring particles merge. **1936** G. F. C. GORDON *Elem. Metallurgy* (ed. 2) ix. 125 The effect of annealing hyper-eutectoid steel, if done with great care, is to cause the network of free cementite to 'spheroidise'. **1939** E. C. ROLLASON *Metallurgy for Engineers* viii. 112 Prolonged annealing induces greater ductility at the expense of strength, owing to the tendency of the cementite in the strained pearlite to 'ball-up' or spheroidize.

b. *trans.* To convert (grains) into spheroids.

1918 *Jrnl. Iron & Steel Inst.* XCVII. 433 The cementite is completely spherodised [*sic*] into round-shaped globules. **1958** *Times Rev. Industry* July 48/3 The high carbon chrome tubes..have to be 'spheroidized' to get them into a good machinable condition. **1978** *Nature* 20 July 237/1 One hypothesis is that the BeO particles were spheroidised (grain refining agents should be angular and sharp-cornered) either during the hot isostatic pressing or during the time when molten.

Hence **sphe·roidized** *ppl. a.*, **sphe·roidizing** *vbl. sb.*; **spheroidiza·tion,** the process of converting to spheroids.

1912 A. SAUVEUR *Metallogr. Iron & Steel* xii. 15 It may well be asked whether..the spheroidizing of pearlite is due to excessively slow cooling. *Ibid.*, Spheroidized pearlite is softer, less tenacious, and more ductile than lamellar pearlite. **1920** *Jrnl. Iron & Steel Inst.* CII. 267 The temperature interval of spheroidisation in low carbon steels is very small, extending only to about 20°. **1923** GLAZEBROOK *Dict. Appl. Physics* V. 341/1 Pearlite which has undergone spheroidising is known as granular pearlite. **1939** E. C. ROLLASON *Metall. Engineers* viii. 118 During subsequent hardening operations the time required to dissolve fine spheroidised cementite is less than for the lamellar type. **1944** GREGORY & SIMONS *Heat-Treatment of Steel* xv. 181 The reheating temperature is below the lower critical or transformation point, as in the spheroidization of the carbide particles in high carbon tool steels. **1958** *Times Rev. Industry* July 48/3 To soften them they are heat treated in spheroidizing furnaces. **1967** A. H. COTTRELL *Introd. Metallurgy* xx. 384 Above about 500°C the cementite particles grow competitively ..into larger rounded particles dispersed through the B.C.C. iron matrix, giving a spheroidized structure (Sorbite). **1977** *Industr. & Engin. Chem. Process Design & Development* XVI. 108/1 The process involves the melting and spheroidization of 44–125-μ magnetite grit.

spherosome (sfīᵊ·rosōᵘm). *Biol.* Also **sphæro-.** [ad. F. *sphérome* (P.-A. Dangeard 1919, in *Compt. Rend.* CLXIX. 1008): see SPHERO- and *-SOME⁴.] A cytoplasmic liquid droplet or cell organelle found in plant tissues, often associated with hydrolytic enzymic activity; the plant structure answering to the lysosome in animal tissues. Hence **spheroso·mal** *a.*

1954 *Biol. Abstr.* XXVIII. 2398/1 The sphaerosomes are real and permanent cytoplasmic structures, and..are neither artifacts nor temporary storage droplets of fat or other lipoids. **1958** *Exper. Cell Res.* XV. 611 The spherosomes are seen as opaque white globules 0·7 μ in diameter, or as dark-rimmed spheres. **1966** *Protoplasma* LXII. 220 In the cells studied..spherosomal motion is rapid during the first 24 hr. **1976** BELL & COOMBE tr. *Strasburger's Textbk. Bot.* (rev. ed.) 16 The nucleus, plastids, mitochondria, spherosomes and golgi bodies remain throughout within the cytoplasm.

spherule. Add: **3.** Special Comb. **spherule cell** *Ent.*, a kind of cell in the hæmolymph of certain insects (see quot. 1969).

1935 R. E. SNODGRASS *Princ. Insect Morphol.* xiv. 394 The spherule cells of caterpillars differ in many ways from those of Coleoptera, but they appear to be cells of the same type. **1969** R. F. CHAPMAN *Insects* xxxiii. 677 Spherule cells, found in Lepidoptera and Diptera, are round or oval cells with large, non-refringent, usually acidophilic inclusions filling the whole cell. **1974** Spherule cell [see *œnocytoid* s.v. *ŒNO-].

spherulite. Add: Formerly also **sphærolite, spherolite.** [ad. G. *sphærolit* (now *sphärolit*) (A. G. Werner, *a* 1816: see W. G. W. Becker *Journal einer Bergmännischen Reise* (1816) II. p. vi).]

1. a. Now *Obs.*

b. Substitute for def.: *Geol.* A small spheroidal mass found in rock; *spec.* one consisting of many crystals which have grown radially from a point. (Earlier and later examples.)

1829 *Trans. Geol. Soc.* II. 202 A previous separation had taken place of the feldspathose spherolites. **1844** C. DARWIN *Geol. Observations on Volcanic Islands* iii. 58 The sphærulites are either white and translucent, or brown and opaque. **1856** *Q. Jrnl. Geol. Soc.* XII. 340 The multiplication and confusion of these crystallites or sphærulites ultimately destroy the glassy character of the substance altogether. **1868** *Mem. California Acad. Sci.* I. 52 Small globular grains, from the size of a pin-head to that of a rifle bullet, called 'sphærolites' by Beudant. **1909** J. P. IDDINGS *Igneous Rocks* I. vi. 230 Such spherulites..consist of radiating prisms of alkali feldspar with submicroscopic graphic intergrowths of quartz. **1931** [see *ORBICULE]. **1939** W. H. TWENHOFEL *Princ. Sedimentation* xv. 570 Spherulites with radiate structure are evidently a form of crystal aggregate, whereas those with amorphous internal structure are either excremental particles or colloidal aggregates as glauconite, greenalite, or chamoisite. **1974** A. C. TENNISSEN *Nature of Earth Materials* v. 280 Spherulites have a radial type of internal structure.

c. A small spheroidal mass of crystals or fibrils of any substance, esp. a polymer.

1893 *Mineral. Mag.* X. 97 (*table*) $LiNaSO_4$... Spherulitic... Some of the spherulites have a radial structure. **1911** *Chem. Abstr.* V. 1052 The author describes the peculiar structure of spherulites obtained in cholesterol and β-naphthalene benzoate. **1933** *Bureau of Standards Jrnl. Res.* (U.S.) X. 488 The microscopical examination of the crystals of rubber hydrocarbon indicates that they are spherulites composed of many fine needles. **1963** *New Scientist* 7 Nov. 334/1 Some polymers, like nylon and polystyrene are highly crystalline. They do not normally form single crystals, however, but produce so-called spherulites which are clusters of plate-like or needle-like individual crystals. **1975** *Sci. Amer.* Dec. 99/1 The spherulite, or 'sunburst' microstructure normally results from crystallization under quiescent conditions.

spherulitic, *a.* Add: Also † **spherolitic. 1.** Also of other substances. Cf. *SPHERULITE 1 c. (Later examples.)

1893 [see *SPHERULITE 1 c]. **1975** *Sci. Amer.* Dec. 100/2 The microstructure of spherulitic polymers is also significantly affected by the phenomenon of secondary crystallization.

2. (Earlier and later examples.)

1829 *Trans. Geol. Soc.* II. 202 Even where no traces of spherolitic structure are visible, the ribboned arrangement of the rock is owing to the mass of matter having been drawn out in the direction of the zones while still liquid. **1945** *Trans. Faraday Soc.* XLI. 321 One of the clearest demonstrations of the spherulitic structure was provided by a specimen of polythene. **1962** F. W. BILLMEYER *Textbk. Polymer Sci.* v. 149 The point of initiation of spherulitic growth, its nucleus, may be a foreign particle..or may arise spontaneously in the melt.

3. (Earlier and later examples.)

1844 C. DARWIN *Geol. Observations on Volcanic Islands* iii. 64 The little brown sphærulitic globules of the rocks of Ascension. **1933** *Bureau of Standards Jrnl. Res.* (U.S.) X. 486 The appearance and properties of the spherulitic clusters did not depend upon the sample of ammoniated latex from which they had been prepared.

Hence **spheruli·tically** *adv.*

1975 *Sci. Amer.* Dec. 104/2 A spherulitically crystallized polymer.

sphincter. Add: **2. a.** *sphincter control.*

1949 M. MEAD *Male & Female* v. 115 They [*sc.* Samoan children] do not need to fear that they themselves, by their unsteady sphincter control,..will endanger the normal order of existence. **1957** *Psychoanal. Rev.* XLIV. 121 The attainment of anal sphincter control in childhood is so fundamental in human socialization that the surgical destruction of anal sphincter control must result in a severe emotional and social disruption.

Hence **sphincte·rial** *a.*; also **sphi·nctered** *a.*, possessing a sphincter (of a specified kind).

1889 *Cent. Dict.*, Sphincterial. **1963** R. P. DALES *Annelids* i. 32 A terminal bladder or vesicle closed by means of a sphinctered nephridiopore. **1965** AUDEN *About House* (1966) 27 A second childhood, petulant, weak-sphinctered In a cheap hotel. **1976** R. POUND *A. P. Herbert* xxvi. 298 Its equability, with or without the reinforcement of vitamins, deep breathing, and the eccentric sphincterial discipline, may have added to his length of days.

sphincterotomy (sfiŋktěrǫ·tŏmi). *Surg.* [f. SPHINCTER: see -TOMY.] The surgical cutting of or into a sphincter.

1890 in BILLINGS *Med. Dict.* **1892** A. DUANE tr. *Fuchs's Textbk. Ophthalm.* IV. iii 726 Stellwag's operation is called oblique blepharotomy or sphincterotomy. **1922** J. JOYCE *Let.* 4 Oct. (1966) III. 67 He says that..a slight operation —not iridectomy or iridotomy but sphincterotomy will probably restore a great part of former vision. **1977** *Proc. R. Soc. Med.* LXX. 160/2, I do not think this particular technique is suitable for simple procedures such as cholecystectomy or sphincterotomy.

sphingid (sfi·ndʒid), *sb.* and *a. Ent.* [f. mod.L. family name *Sphingidæ*, f. *Sphinx* SPHINX, adopted as a generic name by Linnæus (*Systema Naturæ* (ed. 6, 1748) 63): see -ID¹.] **A.** *sb.* A hawk-moth of the family Sphingidœ. **B.** *adj* Of or pertaining to an insect of this kind.

1911 *Trans. Zool. Soc. London* XX. 85 Almost the entire surface is thinly coated with fine, short, white hair, an exceptional feature with Sphingid larvæ. *Ibid.* 95 *Erinnyis ello*... The commonest Sphingid of tropical America. **1930** *Proc. Entomol. Soc.* V. 24 The caudal horn was movable in many Sphingid caterpillars. **1933** *Discovery* Apr. 125/1 Eye-spots..occur particularly in sphingids. **1973** *Nature* 16 Mar. 205/2 Recently internal ocelli have been reported in several adult sphingids. **1981** G. KEYNES *Gates of Memory* iii. 41 A boy in another House had been fortunate enough to catch a specimen of an extremely rare immigrant sphingid moth.

Sphingine (sfi·ndʒəin), *a. rare*⁻¹. [f. *sphing-* stem of SPHINX + INE¹.] Sphinx-like; characteristic of a Sphinx; enigmatic, inscrutable.

1925 A. HUXLEY *Those Barren Leaves* II. i. 86, I would put on..my most Sphingine smile.

sphingo- (sfi·ŋgo). *Biochem.* Comb. form of Gr. Σφίγξ, stem Σφιγγ- SPHINX (see quot. 1881 for *sphingosin*), used in the names of a number of related compounds isolated from the brain and nervous tissue, as **sphingoli·pid(e,** any naturally occurring fatty acid derivative of a sphingosine; hence **sphi:ngolipido·sis** (see quot. 1962); **sphingomy·elin** [MYELO-], any of a number of complex phospholipids which are phosphoryl choline derivatives of *N*-acyl sphingosines; **sphi·ngosine** (formerly -in), a colourless crystalline base, $C_{18}H_{37}NO_2$, or any of various homologues and derivatives of this, which combined as sphingolipids occur widely in brain and nervous tissue.

1947 H. E. CARTER et al. in *Jrnl. Biol. Chem.* CLXIX. 77 Among the lipide constituents [of nerve tissue] there are at least three, the cerebrosides.., sphingomyelins.., and gangliosides.., which are derivatives of the organic base sphingosine. Sphingosine may also be present in other compounds... As a matter of convenience it is proposed that the term sphingolipide be used to designate these substances. **1978** J. R. HOLUM *Org. & Biol. Chem.* xi. 225 The acyl units in the acylamido parts of the sphingolipids are not the usual fatty acids found in neutral fats. **1962** KNUDSON & KAPLAN in Aronson & Volk *Cerebral Sphingolipidoses* 395 The sphingolipidoses are hereditary diseases in which there is an accumulation of sphingolipids in one or more tissues of the body... There are at least three enzyme defects among the sphingolipidoses. **1976** *Adv. Exper. Med. & Biol.* LXVIII. 9 (*caption*) Examples of early prenatal diagnoses carried out with the present microtechniques in pregnancies at risk for sphingolipidoses. **1883** J. L. W. THUDICHUM in *12th Ann. Rep. Local Govt. Board 1882–3: Rep. Med. Officer 1882* App. B. No. 3. 221, I have for the purposes of the present research isolated and analysed two representatives of this remarkable class of bodies, one *amidomyelin*..another *sphingomyelin*, which was found to be ..a genuine educt and principle of the brain. **1920** [see *CEPHALIN[2]]. **1946** *Biol. Rev.* XXVI. 285 Sphingomyelins are phosphatides in which the sphingosine or a closely related base is bound by an NH—CO linkage to a fatty acid..and by an ester linkage to choline phosphoric acid. **1973** Sphingomyelin [see *LECITHIN]. **1881** J. L. W. THUDICHUM in *Ann. Chem. Med.* II. 18 A body remained insoluble which was of an alkaloidal nature, and to which, in commemoration of the many enigmas which it presented to the inquirer, I have given the name of *Sphingosin.* **1908** HALL & DEFREN tr. *Abderhalden's Text-bk. Physiol. Chem.* ii. 20 On being subjected to hydrolysis this substance took up two molecules of water and formed one molecule of cerebronic acid, one of sphingosine and one of galactose. **1957** [see *CEREBROSIDE]. **1968** A. WHITE et al. *Princ. Biochem.* (ed. 4) iv. 73 Although the above C_{18} sphingosines are most abundant in sphingolipids, other homologous C_{16}, C_{17}, C_{19}, and C_{20} sphingosines also are found among the naturally occurring sphingolipids.

Sphinx. Add: **5. a.** *sphinx-look.*

1923 D. H. LAWRENCE *Ladybird* 230 The queer, blank, sphinx-look with which he gazed out beyond himself.

c. sphinx moth (later examples).

1939 DUNCAN & PICKWELL *World of Insects* x. 168 The caterpillars of the family of sphinx moths..have earned their name of 'sphinx' by their habit of rearing up their front ends, drawing in their heads, and thus assuming a threatening attitude. **1972** *Sci. Amer.* June 73/1 The larger sphinx moths weigh from two to six grams.

sphygmo-. Add: **sphygmographic** *a.* (earlier example); **sphygmogra·phically** *adv.*; **sphygmomanometer**: delete 'or rate'; **sphy:gmomano·metry**, the use of a sphygmomanometer; **sphy:gmomanome·tric** *a.*; **spyhgmometer**, substitute for def.: an instrument for exhibiting or measuring the force or rate of the pulse (earlier and later examples); **sphygmo·metry; sphygmoscope** (earlier example).

1867 *Brit. Med. Jrnl.* 20 July 40/1, I refer to pulse No. 10 principally for the purpose of shewing how completely the sphygmographic form may be modified by merely functional, that is to say nervous, disorder. *Ibid.* 13 July 20/1 The full pulse (sphygmographically, that in which the second event is well marked or developed). **1885** J. B. YEO tr. *M. J. Oertel's Respiratory Therapeutics* II. 472 When..inspiration is slow and cautious,.. sphygmographically the pulse waves altered by the rise of blood pressure immediately succeed to the average normal ones. **1902** *Amer. Jrnl. Physiol.* V. 205 For sphygmomanometric work it was found necessary to pack the small space between this collar and the forearm with soft muslin to prevent a distention of the reflected bands when the pressure within was raised. **1905** *Johns Hopkins Hosp. Rep.* XII. 69 Points of interest in sphygmomanometry. **1962** *Lancet* 15 Dec. 1225/2 Many of the difficulties inherent in clinical sphygmomanometry of the newborn infant have been overcome by the latest development in photoelectric methods. **1834** *Ibid.* 20 Sept. 936/2 At the meeting of the French Academy of Sciences on the 1st inst, M. Magendie read a report on an instrument invented by a Dr. Herisson, called the 'sphygmometer', and intended to measure the state of the pulse... The bottom of the instrument is placed over the radial artery, each pulsation of which elevates the mercury, and thus discloses to the eye the minutest variation of the circulation. **1890** *Practitioner* June 421 (*caption*) Upper curve, radial pulse obtained from healthy adult male by air modified sphygmograph (sphygmometer). **1867** *Med. Rec.* (N.Y.) 15 July 243/2 Herrison's and Blundell's ideas on sphygmometry were sunk in oblivion. **1908** G. OLIVER *Studies in Blood-Pressure* (ed. 2) ii. 42 Writers on sphygmometry have always grouped together all the instruments which derive their readings of the arterial pressure from a single artery. **1856** *Lancet* 8 Nov. 510/1 The numerous cases of disease of the heart which have come under the care of Dr. Scott Alison..have afforded abundant means of applying..the new sphygmoscope, or cardioscope, (contrived by that physician).

sphygmology (sfigmǫ·lŏdʒi). *Med.* [See SPHYGMO- and -LOGY.] The study of the pulse. Hence **sphygmolo·gical** *a.*

1890 BILLINGS *Med. Dict.* II. 570/1 Sphygmology. **1931** G. SARTON *Introd. Hist. Sci.* II. 75 Sphygmology is even older than urology and more universal. *Ibid.* 87 The Shang-han-lun is divided into ten books of which the first is a sort of scientific (sphygmological) introduction to the others. **1941** *Bull. Hist. Med.* X. 210 It seems probable that some Aegimius may be credited with being the founder of sphygmology. **1973** C. R. S. HARRIS *Heart & Vascular System Anc. Greek Med.* v. 255 The supposed perception of fullness is a typical feature of post-Herophilian sphygmology from which only the Empirics apparently dissented. *Ibid.* vii. 409 But enough of these sphygmological conundrums.

spic (spik), *sb.* and *a.* *U.S. slang.* Also **spick, spig, spik,** and with capital initial. [Shortened f. *SPIGGOTY *sb.* (and *a.*)] **A.** *sb.* **a.** A contemptuous and offensive name for a Spanish-speaking native of Central or South America or the Caribbean; a spiggoty.

1913 H. A. FRANCK *Zone Policeman 88* i. 10 It was my first entrance into the land of the *panameños*, technically known on the Zone as 'Spigoties', and familiarly, with a tinge of despite, as 'Spigs'. **1916** E. PEIXOTTO *Our Hispanic Southwest* 102 The Mexican men they despise and call 'spicks'. **1928** S. LEWIS *Man who knew Coolidge* II. 116 We need a supply of cheap labour, and where get it better than by encouraging these Wops and Hunks and Spigs and so on to raise as many brats as they can? **1936** *Opportunity* Aug. 239/1 Frank was just a 'huerco' to his mother, 'spick' to his white schoolmates in Queensville, Texas. **1949** W. FAULKNER *Knight's Gambit* 137, I don't intend that a fortune-hunting Spick shall marry my mother. **1953** F. SCOTT FITZGERALD *Tender is Night* ix. 275 'He's a spic!' he said. He was frantic with jealousy. **1964** E. LACY *Pity Honest* iii. 48 This is becoming a tough neighbourhood, full of Spics. **1977** D. E. WESTLAKE *Nobody's Perfect* (1978) 39 You'd put your kid in a school with a lotta niggers and kikes and wops and spics?

b. The Spanish language; *spec.* Spanish-American.

1933 E. HEMINGWAY *Winner take Nothing* (1934) 200, I wish I could talk spik... I don't get any fun out of asking that spik questions. **1977** *Amer. Speech 1975* L. 67 *Spic n,* 1: Spanish language 2: course in the Spanish language 'I've had two years of Spic.'

B. *adj.* = *SPIGGOTY *sb.* (and *a.*) 3. *derog.*

1919 *Ladies' Home Jrnl.* Sept. 27 The Marines had been..silencing the elusive 'spick' bandit in Santo Domingo. **1950** R. MOORE *Candlemas Bay* 29 Jerry Canneri. Or Carnoodle. Some such damn spik name. **1976** N. THORNBURG *Cutter & Bone* iii. 74 A nigger fag and two spic girls with a pet monkey.

‖ **spiccato** (spikā·to), *a.* (*adv., sb.*) *Mus.* [It., detached, distinct.] Of a style of staccato bowing, esp. on the violin: detached, *i.e.* with short breaks between notes caused by controlled bouncing of the bow; of music played in this manner. Also used *advb.*, as a direction to the performer and as *sb.*, an instance of spiccato playing; a passage in this style.

1724 [see STACCATO *a.* (*adv., sb.*)]. **1740** J. GRASSINEAU *Mus. Dict., Spiccato,* signifies to separate, divide, part,.. that is, to give every note its distinct sound, and is the contrary of what we call slurring. **1883** GROVE *Dict. Mus.* III. 650/2 *Spicato* [sic].., a term applied in violin-playing to a particular vibratory style of bowing. *Ibid.* 682/2 The Spicato [sic] is marked by dots over the notes. **1938** *Oxf. Compan. Mus.* 891/2 *Spiccato,*..in music..implying staccato effect. **1955** *Times* 12 May 5/6 The scherzo, which incidentally allowed Mr. Campoli to unfold long stretches of the most prodigious *spiccato* bowing. **1964** *Listener* 25 June 1043/1 Paganini's innovations in violin technique—the big bouncing *spiccato,* for instance. **1978** *Gramophone* Aug. 355/3 The lyrical grace of Norbert Brainin's playing in the Adagio and his *spiccato* triplets in the finale.

spice, *sb.* Add: **2. e.** A medicated preparation added to cattle or horse feed. ? Now only *Hist.*

1707 J. MORTIMER *Whole Art of Husbandry* 157 Take a quart of Ale, half an ounce of Diapente.., Horse-spice two Ounces. **1928** E. P. OPPENHEIM *Chron. Melhampton* 143 A retired dealer in cattle spices. **1961** M. W. BARLEY *Eng. Farmhouse & Cottage* v. i. 253 Thomas Morrison kept a much more interesting shop, in the last years of the seventeenth century... There was ironmongery.. 'horse spice and jollop' for the farmer.

7. a. *spice-cabinet, jar*; *spice-bazaar.*

1924 R. GRAVES *Mock Beggar Hall* 6 Scepticos heard this popular Figment in the spice-bazaar. **1893–4** *T. Eaton & Co. Catal.* Fall & Winter 120/3 Spice cabinets, 90c. **1908** *Sears, Roebuck Catal.* 359/3 German china cereal and spice jars..with names of spices or cereals on each jar. **1977** C. WATSON *One Man's Meat* iii. 25 The dining enclosure..was screened from cook top and sluice unit by rubber plants and rows of spice jars.

b. *spice-enrichened, -sweet* adjs.

1940 C. DAY LEWIS tr. *Virgil's Georgics* II. 39 Nor all Arabia's acres of spice-enriched soil. **1953** W. DE LA MARE *O Lovely England* 51 The spice-sweet gorse.

8. spice-berry: for *U.S.* read *N. Amer.* and add earlier example; **spice-bush** (earlier example); **spice-isle**, one of the spice-islands (*poet. rare*); **spice-wood,** (*a*) (earlier example).

1792 G. IMLAY *Topogr. Descr. N. Amer.* 216 There is a variety of shrubs in every part of the country, the principal of which are the myrtle and spice berry. **1770** G. WASHINGTON *Jrnl.* 15 Oct. (1925) I. 409 The Soil.. being as black as Coal and the Growth, Walnut, Cherry, Spice Bushes. **1885** W. B. YEATS in *Dublin Univ. Rev.* Sept. 121 Where spice-isles nestle on the star-trod seas. **1756** P. KALM *Resa til N. Amer.* II. 204 Spicewood. (Laurus æstivalis. *Spec.* 370).

spice, *v.* Add: **1. b.** Also with *up*, to enliven, to make more interesting or racy. *colloq.*

1927 *Scribner's Mag.* Apr. 390/1 The brazen forgery in *The Gentlemen's Magazine* seems to have been a facetious attempt to spice up a sober-toned, political news-letter. **1979** *Arizona Daily Star* 8 Apr. (Wedding Suppl.) 15/2 One Tucson couple spiced up a wedding with circus performances, complete with a juggler and unicyclist.

spicing *vbl. sb.*: also with *up*.

1934 C. LAMBERT *Music Ho!* II. 127 There is no instance ..of the spicing up of a simple harmonic basis.

spick, *sb.*[4] *dial.* Also **spic.** [Var. of dial. *speak*: see *E.D.D.*] A withy or rod, usu. pointed and doubled, used to secure thatch; a spar (SPAR *sb.*[4]).

1890 J. D. ROBERTSON *Gloss. Words County of Gloucester* 147 *Speeks* or *spicks*, the pieces of wood used for holding together the thatch on a rick. **1893** DARTNELL & GODDARD *Gloss. Words Wiltshire* 152 *Spick*.., in thatching, the same as *spar.* **1934** *Times Lit. Suppl.* 1 Feb. 71/3 The thatcher's tackle of 'spicks' or 'spars' (pointed hazel-rods) which fix the bands to hold down the thatch. **1939** D. HARTLEY *Made in England* ii. 57 A bundle of the doubled withies split and bent into a twisted hook or double prong... These, when used in stack work, are called 'spics' or 'speks'. **1949** K. S. WOODS *Rural Crafts Eng.* III. vii. 109 *Thatching Spics.* The riving, or rending of the wood, which is the basis of a number of crafts, is illustrated.

spick, *a.* (Later example.)

1920 D. H. LAWRENCE *Lost Girl* vi. 99 He liked to have his clothes neat and spick.

spick, var. *SPIC *sb.* and *a.*

spick-and-spanness. (Examples.)

1911 MRS. H. WARD *Case of Richard Meynell* II. viii. 174 [He] was himself a model of spick-and-span-ness. **1931** *Times Lit. Suppl.* 21 May 407/1 The ancient houses..had a touch of mysterious romance that the bright spick-and-spanness of the new architecture misses. **1975** *New Yorker* 28 Apr. 52/2 A life that, in spite of its inferior neatness and spick-and-spanness, was essentially more serious and finer than our own.

spiculation. (Earlier example.)

1868 G. M. HOPKINS *Jrnls. & Papers* (1959) 185 Spiculation in a dry blot in a smooth inkstand.

spicule. Add: **5.** (Earlier examples.)

1835 J. PAGET *Let.* 16 Apr. in S. Paget *Mem. & Lett. Sir J. Paget* (1901) 57 The same appearances have been noticed in our dissecting-rooms, where they have been attributed to the deposition of small spicules of bone (which, indeed, they somewhat resemble). **1865** MILTON & CHEADLE *N.-W. Passage by Land* xv. 301 The fallen timber lay as thickly and entangled as the spiculæ in the children's game of spelicans.

6. *Astr.* Any of numerous short-lived, relatively small radial jets of gas observed to occur in the sun's atmosphere in the chromosphere and lower corona.

1945 W. O. ROBERTS in *Astrophysical Jrnl.* CI. 136 Small spikes of chromospheric material, observed in Hα with the coronagraph and quartz-polaroid monochromator are described. These spicules, seen in polar regions of the sun, have very brief lifetimes, amounting on the average to 4 or 5 minutes. **1948,** etc. [see *JET *sb.*[2] 4 c (ii)]. **1974** BRAY & LOUGHHEAD *Solar Chromosphere* ii. 60 Spicules in the polar regions of the sun tend to follow the direction of the overlying coronal rays. **1978** PASACHOFF & KUTNER *University Astron.* viii. 191 Spicules are best seen when we are looking off the edge of the sun, beyond the limb.

spider, *sb.* Add: **3. a.** (Earlier example.)

1807 in *Austin Papers* (1924) I. I. 132, 2 Spiders with Covers.

4. Also, an alcoholic drink of similar ingredients (see quots. 1861, 1888); a soft drink with ice-cream floating in it.

1861 H. EARLE *Ups & Downs* 283 They are..up to unlimited 'spiders', or lemonade and sherry. **1888** E. FINN *Chron. Early Melbourne* ii. 548 The favourite tipple of the bushman was mixed brandy and ginger beer—a 'spider', as it was called. **1941** *Coast to Coast* 229 'You've had your drink, so now you've got to buy us all a spider at Smith's'... I didn't want to go back and sit in Smith's and drink silly coloured muck with ice-cream floating in it. **1965** G. MCINNES *Road to Gundagai* 14 She reached for a thick yellow glass and poured in the ginger beer.. an enormous dollop of ice-cream which she dropped into the ginger beer. 'There's your spider.' **1974** BUCKLEY & HAMILTON *Festival* 127 You used to strut into the milk bar as though you owned the place. 'A lime spider, Harry.'

6. a. Also, similar parts of instruments and other apparatus. (Earlier and later examples.)

1860 CLARK & COLBURN *Recent Practice Locomotive Engine* 52/1 In driving wheels, the centre, or 'spider', for a 5-feet wheel to carry 4½ tons, will weigh 1800 pounds and upwards. **1935** A. G. INGALLS *Amateur Telescope Making* (ed. 4) 371 Another interesting diffraction phenomena [*sic*]..known to most able telescope designers, is the fact that there will be fewer diffraction lines from a four-legged diagonal support spider than from one having only three legs. **1961** MICZAIKA & SINTON *Tools of Astronomer* iii. 75 Diffraction of light by the spider supporting the secondary mirror is a frequent complaint. **1966** L. A. H. EASTMAN tr. *Schenkel's Plastics Extrusion Technol. & Theory* xi. 326 The melt is..fed via a 90° bend into a distributor spider, which may have four to eight symmetrically arranged radial channels.

d. *Austral. Opal-mining.* (See quot. 1912.)
1912 *Empire Mag.* Nov. 281/2 *Spider*, a small iron instrument which serves the double purpose of holding the candle, and 'lifting' the seam of opal. **1940** I. L. Idriess *Lightning Ridge* xxiii. 158, I gouged around and under, then pryed it out with the spider point. **1958** M. D. Berrington *Stones of Fire* iii. 33 A candle in a 'spider' that queer, spiked holder that is used below ground. **1967** *Sunday Mail Mag.* (Brisbane) 10 Dec. 3/5 The candle in its spider dropped to the floor and went out.

e. *Engin.* A metal sleeve within which an object may be gripped by screws or wedges.
1920 *Bull. U.S. Bureau of Mines* No. 182. 7 *Spider*, tool that encircles and holds the pipe by means of steel wedges. *Ibid.* 17 The swinging spider..is probably one of the most useful inventions..for the handling of casing in drilling oil wells. **1940** [see *cat-head *sb.* 3 c]. **1950** A. W. Judge *Centre, Capstan & Automatic Lathes* II. iii. 135 The short end of the hub faces outwards, and the spider is gripped between the arms by three chuck jaws. **1977** R. D. Langenkamp *Handbk. Oil Industry Terms & Phrases* (ed. 2) 159 The spider is manually locked around a length of tubing just below the tool joint. Some advanced types of elevator spiders are air operated.

f. *Electronics.* A flexible linkage formerly placed between the moving cone and the fixed magnet assembly of a loudspeaker.
1928 *Wireless World* 6 June 608/1 A centring device in the form of a brass spider attached to the pin is supplied. **1948** G. A. Briggs *Loudspeakers* vi. 20 The bakelised spider gives a sharply defined bass response to the cone, resulting in a crispness in the tone. **1959** N. H. Crowhurst *Basic Audio* I. 49 To prevent the coil rubbing against the magnet poles, a centering 'spider' or suspension is used, which allows free movement in the direction of vibration, while preventing the coil from moving against the pole faces.

7. a. Also, a trotting gig. *Austral.*
1945 S. J. Baker *Austral. Lang.* ix. 175 *Spider* or *junker*, a trotting gig. **1955** A. Ross *Australia 55* 34 The drivers, dressed in silks like jockeys, sit behind their animals in tiny carriages known as spiders. **1969** *West Australian* 5 July 32/5 Causing Pyraket to strike and badly buckle the inside wheel of Master Flame's spider.

b. An early bicycle with the benefit of steel wheels, as opp. to those of wood. Cf. *spider-wheel*, sense 10 a below. Now only *Hist.*
1874 *Bicycling* 4 Had he lived in the days of the 'Coventry Spiders'. **1908** E. M. Sneyd-Kynnersley *H.M.I.* ix. 82 Safety bicycles were not yet: the Boneshaker was not tempting, and the Spider was perilous.

8. d. A spider-nævus.
1942 *Amer. Jrnl. Med. Sci.* CCIV. 251 The well known increase in excretion of estrogenic substances in pregnancy coincides with the period during which vascular spiders and palmar erythema tend to appear. **1948** D. Ballantyne *Cunninghams* iii. 15 Winter weather gave her the blue spiders. **1969** *Daily Colonist* (Victoria, B.C.) 9 Jan. 2/3 Does wearing a 'pants-type' girdle cause broken blood vessels in the thighs?..These little vessels are called 'spiders'... These spiders are commonest in women; hence the hormone (estrogen) level is thought to have a bearing. **1974** R. M. Kirk et al. *Surgery* vi. 107 Hepatic failure causes weakness,..vascular spiders (named from the spider-like appearance of dilated arterioles), palmar erythema..and encephalopathy.

8*. *Cards.* A variety of patience played with two packs.
1890 'Cavendish' *Patience Games* 186 The Spider.. requires quite sufficient exercise of thought to render it very interesting. **1901** 'Tarbart' *Patience* 49 Spider. Played with two full packs of cards. **1930** W. S. Maugham *Gent. in Parlour* xv. 78, I knew seventeen varieties of patience. I tried the Spider and never by any chance got it out.

9. a. *spider-cloth, floss, -form.*
1916 D. H. Lawrence *Amores* 86 Great grey spider-cloths hanging Low from the roof. **1978** C. Tomlinson *Shaft* 13 Finer than the lines Of spider floss. **1954** J. R. R. Tolkien *Two Towers* 332 There agelong she had dwelt, an evil thing in spider-form.

d. *spider-tongued; spider-spruce, -thin.*
1948 C. Day Lewis *Poems 1943–1947* 82 But look at her parlour, all lighted and spider-spruce! **1928** V. Woolf *Orlando* vi. 257 The Serpentine..was a bronze colour; spider-thin boats were skimming from side to side. **1939** G. Greene *Confidential Agent* I. ii. 48 A..cotton bedspread, clean and faded and spider-thin. **1934** Dylan Thomas *18 Poems* 24 Some let me make you of autumnal spells, The spider-tongued, and the loud hill of Wales.

e. Instrumental, as *spider-curtained* adj.
1925 Blunden *English Poems* 40 The spider-curtained darkness in the attic of black Jacob's farm.

10. a. spider angioma *Path.*, a spider-nævus; **spider-man,** one employed to work on high structures; a steeple-jack; **spiderveil,** a kind of veil; **spider veins,** small dilated superficial veins around varicosities on a leg; **spider-wheel,** (*c*) a metal wheel with wire spokes (formerly applied *spec.* to a bicycle-wheel); hence **spider-wheeled,** *a.*, fitted with spider-wheels; **spider-work,** also *spec.* in *Needlework* = *opus araneum.
1956 *New Gould Med. Dict.* (ed. 2) 77/1 Spider angioma. **1961** R. D. Baker *Essent. Path.* xvi. 412 At autopsy one notes ascites and subcutaneous edema of the legs, often with hydrothorax. Spider angiomata are frequently observed on the skin. **1955** *Britannica Bk. of Year* 489/2 *Spiderman*, an erector of building structures. **1958** *Radio Times* 25 July 3/1 These spider-men and steel-erectors work at great heights, often where there are no means of protection. They walk along girders at dizzy heights as though they were strolling along Piccadilly. **1962** *B.S.I. News* July 11/1 Safety harness worn by window-cleaners and spidermen. **1972** J. Wainwright *Night is Time to Die* 8 They used an expression familiar to all working policemen. 'Sudden Death.' It covers everything; from.. the spiderman who takes that one chance too many..to the hippy who spins into permanent orbit. **1922** Joyce *Ulysses* 441 In smart Saxe tailormade, white velours hat and spiderveil. **1976** *Vogue* Jan. 20/4 The treatment of broken and spider veins on legs. **1875** *Eng. Mechanic* 23 Apr. 146/2 With the spider-wheels I found that there was rather a tendency to get loose. **1882** *Bicycle* 15 The Spider-Wheel, invented by the Coventry Machinists Company and now almost universal. **1906** *Chambers's Jrnl.* Oct. 735/1 The introduction of the free spider-wheel, pneumatic-tired cycle. **1969** *West Australian* 5 July 32/5 On the turn out of the back straight in the last lap Majestic Scott's spider wheel was badly buckled. **1977** *Weekly Times* (Melbourne) 19 Jan. 57/4 (Advt.), Semi-tipper, 10–1 spread bogey... Hercules body and hoists.. 900 × 20 tyres, spider wheels. **1886** *Century Mag.* July 338/2 There may be a crowd of onlookers in every kind of trap, from a four-in-hand drag to a spider-wheeled buggy drawn by a pair of long-tailed trotters. **1943** J. W. Day *Farming Adventure* iii. 40 A high spider-wheeled dogcart. **1865** Spider-work [see *opus araneum]. **1874, 1883** Spider-work [in Dict.].

b. spider beetle, a long-legged beetle of the family Ptinidæ.
1954 Borror & DeLong *Introd. Study of Insects* xxii. 379 The Ptinidae, or spider beetles, are small long-legged beetles..somewhat spiderlike in appearance. **1979** P. L. G. Bateman *Household Pests* II. 106 Spider beetles are basically scavengers and infestations often originate in old birds' nests.

c. spider flower, an annual herb of the genus *Cleome* of the family Capparaceæ, esp. *C. hasslerana,* which has clusters of pink or white flowers with long stamens (cf. *cleome); **spider lily,** a bulbous plant belonging to the genus *Hymenocallis,* native to North and South America, or *Crinum,* native to tropical regions, both of the family Amaryllidaceæ, and bearing clusters of white or pink flowers, often fragrant; **spider plant,** (*b*) a perennial herb, *Chlorophytum comosum,* of the family Liliaceæ, native to South Africa, of which forms bearing variegated linear leaves and clusters of white flowers are much cultivated as house plants.
1861 A. Wood *Class-Bk. Bot.* (ed. 10) 240 Spider Flower...Herbs or shrubs. **1909** A. E. Mack *Bush Calendar* 4 Faded by the excessive rain were the red spider-flowers. **1931** W. N. Clute *Common Names Plants* 101 The spiderflower (*Cleome*) named from the long and sprawling stamens like spider's legs. **1968** Peterson & McKenny *Field Guide Wildflowers* 230 Spider-flower... Note the extraordinarily long stamens projecting beyond the 4 narrow-stalked pink or white petals. **1887** *Harper's Mag.* Feb. 351/1 The exquisite white spider-lily, nodding in clusters on long stalks. **1908** E. J. Banfield *Confessions of Beachcomber* I. i. 21 Along the deltas of the creeks are fragrant, gigantic 'spider lilies' (*Crinum*). **1946** D. C. Peattie *Road of Naturalist* v. 58 The cypress woods around Charleston with sudden spider lilies. **1980** A. Desai *Clear Light of Day* i. 7 They went slowly up the wide stairs between the massed pots of spider lilies and asparagus fern. **1946** M. Free *All about House Plants* xv. 126 That plant with striped leaves known to many as spider-plant..increases by means of plantlets produced on the ends of its flower stalks. **1979** S. Rifkin *McQuaid in August* vii. 48 Three enormous spider plants hung..in front of the window.

spi·derish *a.*, resembling a spider; hence **spi·derishness.**
1935 O. Stapledon *Odd John* i. 3 Strangers were often revolted by his uncouth proportions. They called him spiderish. **1944** G. B. Shaw *Everybody's Political What's What?* xxxvi. 320 Commercial ability is often really mere spiderishness.

spider, *v.* Add: **2. a.** *intr.* To move in a manner suggestive of a spider. **b.** *trans.* To cause to move or appear thus.
1938 G. Greene *Brighton Rock* vi. i. 236 Ida Arnold had been trained by the Board. Queerer things than that had spidered out under her fingers and old Crow's. **1975** *New Yorker* 26 May 39/3 It is impossible to resist a post-script at the bottom of that august form, though no doubt it would have to be spidered up the margin. **1976** 'F. Clifford' *Drummer in Dark* vi. 27 His fingers spidered over the map, stressing a detail here, a field of fire there.

Hence **spi·dering** *ppl. a.* and *vbl. sb.*
1973 T. Pynchon *Gravity's Rainbow* I. 55 His little bureau is dominated now by a glimmering map,..written names and spidering streets. **1975** *New Yorker* 12 May 141/1 He wishes only, with his nimble, sinister spidering amid the complexities of our cultural situation, to give us —one of his favorite words—*frissons.*

spider-web, *sb.* Add: **2. a.** (Later examples.)
1923 G. H. McKnight *English Words* iv. 53 The early years of the war were productive in slang language among the British troops... Wire entanglements were *fly traps* and *spider webs.* **1957** O. Nash *You can't get there from Here* 61 This is the most enticing spiderweb of a tarradiddle ever spun. **1978** J. Carroll *Mortal Friends* II. v. 187 He was running his finger along the cold pane of the window, making spiderwebs in the fog.

b. A variety of turquoise characterized by a network of fine dark lines running through it. Also *spider-web turquoise.*
1936 M. Bedinger *Navajo Indian Silver Work* 18 There is another famous variety, of exceptionally good quality... It is a dark blue with black tracery all through it, which gives it the name of 'Spider Web' turquoise. **1968** J. Sinkankas *Van Nostrand's Standard Catalog Gems* iv. 202 Persian spiderweb is similar except that a network of fine black lines divides the surface of the gem into a mosaic of even patches. **1975** R. Webster *Gems in Jewellery* xiv. 79 The turquoise and the matrix of dark brown limonite or fawn-coloured sandstone are then cut together to give stones known as turquoise matrix or, if the veins are fine, spider web turquoise.

spider-web *v.*, (*b*) *intr.* in various fig. uses (see quots.); **spider-webby** *a.*, resembling a spider-web.
1823 L. Hunt in *Liberal* II. 369 'What the devil's here? To bring my stockings home at last undone?'.. 'Undone... They so spider-web, it's a despair.' **1864** Spider-webby [in Dict. s.v. Spider *sb.* 9 d]. **1884** 'Mark Twain' *Huck. Finn* ix. 74 The rain would thrash along by so thick that the trees off a little ways looked dim and spider-webby. **1936** I. L. Idriess *Cattle King* iv. 34 He and others have spider-webbed from around the Australian coasts far into the inland. **1974** M. Hoyt *Thirty Miles for Ice Cream* x. 110 The deciduous trees, without their leaves, show at that distance as gray or a spider-webby black.

spidery, *a.* **1. b.** (Earlier example.)
1825 Coleridge *Let.* 21 Feb. (1971) V. 414 As we advance in years, the World, that spidery Witch, spins it's threads narrower and narrower, still closing in on us.

spiel (spīl, ʃpīl), *sb.*² *slang* (orig. *U.S.*). [a. G. *spiel* play, game; see also next.] **1.** Talk, a story; a speech intended to persuade or advertise, patter. Also *transf.*
1896 Ade *Artie* xi. 100 There was a long spiel by the high guy in the pulpit. **1906** *Daily Colonist* (Victoria, B.C.) 25 Jan. 6/1 We appointed him mayor at five minutes' notice and gave him the job of giving the Chinks the right kind of a spiel. **1925** Wodehouse *Sam the Sudden* xiii. 92 He pulled this long spiel about having had a letter from a guy he used to know named Finglass. **1926** J. Black *You can't Win* ii. 9 Your capable beggar on the street does not say 'please'. He rips off his spiel in such exact and precise language that you get your dime without it. **1931** 'D. Stiff' *Milk & Honey Route* 189 In the missions, to make him lonely and the more susceptible to the 'righteous spiel', they sometimes sing *Where is my wandering Boy Tonight?* **1937** *Printers' Ink Monthly* May 42/2 *Spiel*, the advertising copy. **1944** D. Burley *Orig. Handbk. Harlem Jive* 59, I latched on to this hard, mad spiel. **1953** H. Miller *Plexus* I. iii. 137 Flatter the pants off him! Then go into a little spiel—you know what I mean. Give him some pointers on how to launch the magazine. **1959** *New Statesman* 19 Sept. 344/1 At the end of these flights the poor bored hostess is still compelled to repeat her antique *spiel*; 'We hope you have enjoyed your flight.' **1962** J. Wain *Strike Father Dead* 59, I gave her just the Christian name, and she gave me the spiel about never having met anybody called that before, and its being a nice name, and so forth. *a* **1974** R. Crossman *Diaries* (1975) I. 82 Then Callaghan started off with a long spiel which he read aloud from a Treasury brief on pale blue paper, describing the extreme gravity of the economic situation. **1980** *Listener* 13 Nov. 665/3 A long spiel..from a tart about how much horrider Soho has become.

2. A swindle, a dishonest line of business.
1901 'J. Flynt' *World of Graft* iv. 169 I've been shut up a number of years..but I didn't mind them as much as you would; I took them as part of the spiel. **1921** P. & T. Casey *Gay Cat* 303/1 'What's your spiel?' asks one hobo of another. **1932** W. Hatfield *Ginger Murdoch* 175, I reckon you were thinking you had shaken me off, and could go about your spiel, whatever it is. **1954** T. A. G. Hungerford *Sowers of Wind* 174 This isn't a spiel, Colonel... I know this bloke, and he's on the level.

spiel (spīl, ʃpīl), *v. slang* (orig. *U.S.*). Also † **speel, speil.** [ad. G. *spielen* to play, gamble].
1. a. *intr.* To gamble. Also rarely *trans.*
1859 [implied at *spieling *vbl. sb.*]. **1882** *Sydney Slang Dict.* 8/1 *Speel*, to gamble. **1892** I. Zangwill *Childr. Ghetto* I. iv. 124 They played loo, 'klobbiyos', napoleon... Old Hyams did not *spiel*, because he could not afford to. **1931** [see *half *sb.* 6 i]. **1953** W. Mankowitz *Bespoke Overcoat* xiv. 21 You go to the dog tracks in the evening? Not for me... Horses? No horses, neither. You must spiel something. Poker, shemmy?

b. To play music.
1870 *Territorial Enterprise* (Virginia City, Nevada) 16 July 3/1 The new 'circus' is to be seen at the corner of D street and Sutton avenue—down var der orkan goes a spielin'. **1871** *Nassau Lit. Mag.* Feb. 179 Come now, old fellow, 'speil'. **1947** G. S. Perry *Cities of Amer.* 187 Denver's Symphony chooses to spiel only when winter's winds doth blow.

2. To talk, esp. volubly or glibly; to patter. Also with *away.*
1894 *Mid-Winter Appeal* (San Francisco) 10 Mar. 1/3 Tell [the barker] to stop spieling now and then. **1904** 'O. Henry' *Cabbages & Kings* xiii. 220 If you can borrow some gent's hat in the audience, and make a lot of customers for an idle stock of shoes come out of it, you'd better spiel. **1914** [see *ballyhoo *sb.*]. **1920** Wodehouse *Coming of Bill* I. v. 60 Spiel away, ma'am... The floor's yours. **1946** Mezzrow & Wolfe *Really Blues* (1957) vi. 70 One of the funniest things I ever heard was Mac spieling in Yiddish. **1966** R. Sheckley *Mindswap* vii. 49 Silent and disdainful, scorning to spiel, the little man stood with arms folded as Flynn walked up to the booth.

3. *trans.* To tell, to reel *off*; to announce; to perform.
1904 'O. Henry' *Cabbages & Kings* iii. 58 I'll come right back and hear you spiel the rest before bedtime. **1936** W. A. Gape *Half a Million Tramps* v. 139 When my

turn came I was not ready to 'spiel' off the answers. **1962** *Coast to Coast 1961–62* 81 Garish neons had spieled, in Latin letters, the delights of innumerable honkeytonks. **1970** A. Toffler *Future Shock* xviii. 378 Each participant spieled off his reason for attending. **1977** *Time* 28 Nov. 64/1 In a few hours he would be on a..stage singing his songs and spieling his narrative jazz poetry to an audience of college kids.

Hence **spie·ling** *vbl. sb.*

1859 G. Matsell *Vocabulum* 84 *Speiling*, gambling. **1898** A. M. Binstead *Pink 'Un & Pelican* ix. 190 A raid upon a 'spieling' club by the police. **1904** 'O. Henry' in *McClure's Mag.* July 353/2 It was just what Buck wanted —a regular business at a permanent stand, with no open air spieling..on the street corners every evening. **1937** G. Frankau *More of Us* vii. 78 Nor think this spieling shames our British blood. **1959** T. H. White *Godstone & Blackymor* 47 There was no patter now, no fair ground spieling. **1981** *Observer* 9 Aug. 3/2 'Pitching', or spieling, is how traders sell by a kind of inverted auction: prices start out sky-high, and buyers leap into the breach as the pitcher brings them tumbling down.

spiel, var. *speel *v.*[2]

spieler. For *Austr. slang* read *slang* (orig. *U.S.*) and add: Also † **speiler. 1.** (Earlier and later examples.) Now chiefly *Austral.*

1859 G. Matsell *Vocabulum* 83 *Speiler*, a gambler. **1885** [see *Murrumbidgee]. **1911** W. H. Koebel *In Maoriland Bush* xxii. 283 The professional sharper or 'spieler'..wings his periodical flights from Sydney or Melbourne. **1929** *Detective Fiction Weekly* 13 July 731/2 Hard on their trail would come all the 'magsmen', the 'spielers', the dips, the 'broadsmen', and the 'pickers up'. **1935** H. R. Williams *Comrades of Great Adventure* 234 The spielers worked the three-card trick on the 'mugs'. **1957** J. Waten *Shares in Murder* 156 You could match your wits against smart con-men and spielers.

2. One who spiels (*spiel *v.* 2); a 'barker'; a voluble speaker.

1894 *Mid-Winter Appeal* (San Francisco) 19 May 15/1 Some spielers for the Midway who attempted to lick the Camp gate keeper were sent up for 24 hours. **1901** [see *ballyhooer]. **1936** J. L. Hodson *Our Two Englands* vi. 109 The public..are as fascinated by a good spieler or barker on the show front as they were then. **1937** *Printer's Ink Monthly* May 42/3 *Spieler*, a radio commentator. **1956** *Time* 11 June 42 Mary Costa..agrees that a girl spieler should be 'good-looking but not too flashy to detract from the product'. **1976** *National Observer* (U.S.) 8 May 16/1 His style is all style, a curious amalgam that incorporates at its corniest Dare to Be Great spieler Glenn Turner.

3. A gambling club.

1931 *Police Jrnl.* IV. 502 A cardsharper (broadsman) met a confidence trickster (con-head) and a thief (tea-leaf) in a gaming house (speiler). **1945** P. Cheyney *I'll say she Does* iii. 57 It's a gamblin' *spieler*... There's big play there every night. **1955** D. Webb *Deadline for Crime* iv. 88 Throughout Soho and Mayfair there are a number of what are known as speilers, illicit gambling dens run by the underworld mainly for the underworld, or wealthier mugs of the racecourses. **1962** [see *kite *sb.* 4 c]. **1976** J. O'Connor *Eleventh Commandment* iv. 62 A well-known boxing referee who used to run a dirty low-down dive of a spieler.

‖ **Spielraum** (ʃpī·lrɑum). *Philos.* Pl. **Spielräume.** [Ger. (J. von Kries *Die Principien der Wahrscheinlichkeitsrechnung*, 1886), f. *spiel* play + *raum* room.] The range of possibilities (orig. in probability theory) within which the probability of an outcome or likelihood of a hypothesis is to be assessed.

1921 J. M. Keynes *Treat. Probability* vii. 88 Briefly.. he [*sc.* von Kries] may be said to hold that the hypotheses for the probabilities of which we wish to obtain a numerical comparison, must refer to 'fields' (Spielräume). **1937** *Mind* XLVI. 486 In this connexion he criticises von Kries's '*Spielraum*'-theory of probability. **1944** *Horizon* IX. 235, I propose to borrow from a theory of probability the concept of a *spielraum*. In connection with the judgments we make about freedom, this metaphor of a playing-space can be applied in three ways. **1961** J. N. Findlay *Values & Intentions* iii. 111 The image of a *Spielraum* or space of possibilities seems..indispensable to the full development of partial belief. **1969** P. Geach *God & Soul* vii. 97 There has to be this element of chance in things if human choices are to have any *Spielraum*.

spiff, *v.*[2] Add: Also with *up*.

1979 *Arizona Daily Star* 22 July J 3/2 The man doing it was an interior decorator, not an art conservator, and he did what he felt was best—he went in and spiffed up the church.

spiffy, *a.* (Earlier and later examples.)

1853 D. G. Rossetti *Let.* 2 Nov. (1965) I. 161 The frame for my water-colour has just come in and is spiffy cheesy jammy nobby [etc.]. **1958** T. Stanwell-Fletcher *Clear Lands* 24 This was with the comparatively new, very spiffy Canadian government's *C. D. Howe*. **1978** H. Wouk *War & Remembrance* viii. 86 She's turned into quite the spiffy New York gal.

spiflicate, *v.* (Earlier example.)

1749 *Gentl. Mag.* Dec. 563 Whence the term *spifflicated*? **spiflicating** *ppl. a.* (earlier example).

1852 [see *rowdy-dow *sb.*].

spiflicated (spi·flikēⁱtėd), *ppl. a. slang* (orig. *U.S.*). Also **spifflicated.** [f. prec. + -ed[1].] Intoxicated, drunk.

1906 'O. Henry' *Four Million* 114 He uses Nature's Own Remedy. He gets spifflicated. **1910** [see *pie-eyed *a.*]. **1927** *New Republic* 9 Mar. 71/2 The following is a partial list of words denoting drunkenness now in common use in the United States..spifflicated. **1931** *Sun* (Baltimore) 6 Jan. 6/7 Almost every name you could think of to describe the state of being drunk was given, but one splendid one that I know of was omitted—'spifflicated'. *a* **1966** 'M. na Gopaleen' *Best of Myles* (1968) 338 Drunk; jarred;..spiflicated. **1971** H. A. Smith *View from Chivo* i. 5, I do not believe..that I was spifflicated last night.

spig, var. *spic *sb.* and *a.*

spiggoty (spi·gǫti), *sb.* (and *a.*). *U.S. slang.* Also **spiggity, spigotti, spigoty.** [Orig. uncertain: prob. repr. broken English (see sense 1, quot. 1938): now generally superseded by *spic *sb* and *a.*] **1.** A contemptuous name for a Spanish-speaking native of Central or South America.

1910 'W. Lawton' *Boy Aviators in Nicaragua* 331 Ring..steamed down here on his gunboat just in time to fire that shell and throw a scare into the spiggotys at the very physicky moment. **1913** H. A. Franck *Zone Policeman 88* 10 It was my first entrance into the land of the panameños, technically known on the Zone as 'spigoties'. **1916** *Recruiter's Bull.* (U.S. Marine Corps, N.Y.) Jan. 10/1 Well, we did not get to Haut de Cap—we ran into a 'nest' of Spiggoties and things were pretty warm for about three hours. **1934** R. Stout *Fer-de-Lance* xv. 248 'He's a dirty spiggoty.' 'No, Archie, Mr Manuel Kimball is an Argentine.' **1938** *Amer. Speech* XIII. 311/1 'Spiggoty' originated in Panama during Construction Days, and is assumed to be a corruption of 'spikee de' in the sentence 'No spikee de English', which was then the most common response of Panamanians to any question in English. **1959** R. Campbell *I would do it Again* xxvi. 196, I learned that the young ladies were mostly Spigoties, a name applied to those of mixed Spanish and Indian blood.

2. Spanish-American; more generally, a foreign language.

1914 E. O'Neill *Movie Man* in *Lost Plays* (1950) 37 Say, you're getting to be a regular talker of spigoty! Slip me the answer to that word 'basta', will you? **1922** H. L. Foster *Adventures Trop. Tramp* ix. 132 Just stood around the dock and jabbered a lot of spiggoty talk at me, like I could understand spiggoty! I don't know a word of this damned Spanish, and I'm glad of it! **1923** *Amer. Legion Weekly* 27 Apr. 12 Yer S.O.L. kid!! All I can dope out is the date—I can't get this frog spiggity a 'tall!!

3. *attrib.* passing into *adj.* Central or South American; foreign.

1918 W. S. Poague *Diary* 1 Feb. (? 1919) 28 We repaired to the town and had a white man's dinner with some spigotti liquor. **1937** H. Klemmer *Harbor Nights* 197 *Marijuana* is a popular spiggoty drug which has spread rapidly into the North during recent years.

spigot, *v.* Add: Also (*lit.*), to insert in the manner of a spigot.

1910 *Automobile Engineering 1911* 19/3 Single separate cylinders..are spiggotted deeply into the crankcase. **1954** *Automobile Engineer* XLIV. 507/2 This cover is spigoted into the housing and bolted to the front wall of the box.

spik, var. *spic *sb.* and *a.*

spike, *sb.*[2] Add: **2. d.** Usu. in *pl.* One of a number of sharp-pointed metal studs driven into the sole of a cricket boot, running shoe, etc., to give a surer foothold. Also (*pl.*) by metonymy, a pair of spiked shoes.

1832 P. Egan *Bk. Sports* 348/2 And all in spikes and jackets clad, Elate for vict'ry came. **1898** *N.Y. Tribune* 23 Apr. 9/3 He was in collision with Jennings and McGann and his foot and legs were injured with their spikes. **1955** R. Bannister *First Four Minutes* ii. 16, I suddenly noticed that my best pair of spikes had split along the side. **1976** J. Wainwright *Who goes Next?* 29 'Footprints.. Spiked. Now *he* isn't wearing spikes.' Enfield nodded towards the corpse. 'The two Herberts who found him—I doubt if *they'll* have spiked shoes.'

e. *fig.* A prickly resentment; anger, venom. Freq. in phr. *to have* (or *get*) *the spike*, to be (or become) angry or offended.

1890 J. D. Robertson *Gloss. Words County of Gloucester* 147 'To have the *spike*' is to be out of temper, or offended. **1895** *Daily News* 4 Jan. 3/7 Of course Chris gets the spike (in a temper) because Sullivan had shopped him. **1922** Joyce *Ulysses* 388 He had in his bosom a spike named Bitterness. **1960** N. Hilliard *Maori Girl* ii. xi. 141 But you don't have to get the spike with me just for that. **1978** *Chicago* June 166/3, I had located the spike inside him, the one that Arabs get hooked on when they detect a Jewish émigré.

f. (*a*) A quantity of alcohol, esp. spirits, added to a drink. *U.S. slang.*

1906 *Dialect Notes* III. 157 *Spike, n.*, alcohol, an alcoholic beverage. 'This punch has a good big spike in it.' **1969** J. Cheever *Bullet Park* xiv. 189 She..returned with a bottle of whiskey and spiked her coffee... The spike steadied her hand. **1974** *Times-Picayune* (New Orleans) 14 Aug. iii. 2 It's like chips without dips, or punch without the spike.

(*b*) A small quantity *of* a radioisotope or other substance added to a material in order to act as a tracer, reference, etc.

1959 R. E. Tate in Hausner & Schumar *Nucl. Fuel Elements* viii. 110 Spike enrichment, in which some of the fuel elements..contain plutonium dispersed in an inert matrix, requires a high through-put of the enriched elements. **1962** *Analytical Chem.* XXXIV. 709/2 The U^{233} plus U^{236} isotopic dilution spike is added to an unknown uranium sample. **1965** *Jrnl. Geophysical Res.* LXX. 1844/1 Five to twenty grams of sample was dissolved in 1 *N* HCl, Th^{234} and U^{232} spike added, and the solution evaporated to dryness. **1976** *Nature* 24 June 685/2 After ensuring that the spike and sample were well mixed, the cadmium was chemically extracted by ion exchange.

g. A bayonet. *Mil. slang.*

1928 E. Blunden *Undertones of War* 270 The cowman now turned warrior measured out His up-and-down *sans* fierce 'bundook and spike'.

h. A hypodermic needle or syringe used for the injection of an intoxicating drug; hence, the drug itself or an injection of this. *slang* (orig. *U.S.*).

[**1923** J. Manchon *Le Slang* 285 *Spike, s*... 30 *V*[*ulgaire*] une aiguille.] **1934** *Detective Fiction Weekly* 21 Apr. 107/2 Both me and the twist was on junk and when they fanned us they found a spike on me but no stuff. **1953** Anslinger & Tompkins *Traffic in Narcotics* 315 *Spike*, a drug. *Also* a hypodermic needle, an injection of a drug. **1959** 'E. McBain' *Pusher* viii. 383 'You say you shot up together? Did you both use the same syringe?' 'No, Annabelle had his spike, and I had mine.' **1964** *Daily Tel.* 25 Nov. 22/6 Among the terms used by addicts are..'blast parties', for groups of marijuana smokers, and 'spikes' for hypodermic needles. **1974** J. Wainwright *Evidence I shall Give* xxxvii. 211 It was a mounting yearning. A craving... He needed a spike—badly! **1979** P. Driscoll *Pangolin* xvii. 139 This punk kid, shooting amphetamines, can't find enough spikes.

i. (*a*) *Electr.* A pulse of very short duration in which a rapid increase in voltage is followed immediately by a rapid decrease; (*b*) a burst of electromagnetic radiation marked by short duration or great intensity, esp. one from space.

1935 *Arch. Neurol. & Psychiatry* XXXIV. 1140 Sharp negative spikes in the record often seem to be associated with motor movements of a clonic sort. **1957** *Wireless World* Jan. 10/2 Some of the output-signals have the form of sharp spikes, each pulse of ignition interference producing two spikes of the same polarity. **1969** J. J. Sparkes *Transistor Switching* iv. 109 Noise-voltage spikes in the earth line or at the input have to exceed about 600 mV before significant signals appear at the output. **1973** T. Pynchon *Gravity's Rainbow* i. 146 He's been under Rollo Groast's EEG countless times since first he came to 'The White Visitation', and all's normal-adult except for, oh once or twice perhaps a stray 50-millivolt spike off a temporal lobe.

1969 *Astrophysical Jrnl. Lett.* CLVII. L73 Four out of five consecutive optical spikes, each reaching in some 10 days a peak of luminosity that is a factor of 2–3 above a varying background level,..have been observed for the single QSS 3C 345. **1974** *Nature* 8 Nov. 113/1 Well known transient phenomena such as supernovae, galactic radio noise spikes. **1975** D. G. Fink *Electronics Engineers' Handbk.* xi. 13 The typical output of an optical laser consists of a series of spikes. **1977** *Sci. Amer.* Oct. 53/2 Grindlay and Gursky suggested that the X-ray photons of a burst are released in a two-second 'spike'. **1980** *Nature* 7 Feb. 551/1 There are no clear spikes in the Kavalur bursts.

j. *Journalism.* A spindle on which recent newspaper stories are filed, *spec.* when rejected for publication.

1936 B. Brooker *Think of Earth* ii. iii. 141 The editor picked up a spike-file from the top of the desk. **1942** W. Faulkner *Go down, Moses* 374 He took the press association flimsy from its spike and handed it to Stevens. **1962** [see *copy-taster* s.v. *copy *sb.* C]. **1974** D. Seaman *Bomb that could Lip-Read* vii. 58 The P.A. copy was neatly pierced by a spike, Fleet Street's time-honoured way of giving the thumbs-down to a story.

4. Also *spec.* the casual ward of a workhouse (see Casual *a.* 9) (earlier and later examples); an institution affording more or less temporary accommodation for the homeless.

1866 *Temple Bar* XVII. 184 Let the 'spikes' be what they may they were a great deal better than the 'padding-kens'. **1903** J. London *People of Abyss* viii. 78 On asking him what the 'spike' was, he answered, 'The casual ward. It's a cant word.' **1933** 'G. Orwell' *Down & Out* xxvi. 189 D'you come out o' one o' de London spikes (casual wards), eh? **1949** C. Graves *Ireland Revisited* viii. 125 At first we did not understand thieves' slang, or that a 'spike' meant a workhouse. (We were told to avoid the Portsmouth 'spike'.) **1972** *Times* 27 Dec. 2/8 'If this place was not here,' a proud articulate Glaswegian 'dosser' said, 'we'd be on the road or in the reception centre, the spike. I have been in the spike for the past 11 months.' **1980** *Guardian* 2 Oct. 18/1 A generation ago there were half a dozen lodging houses in the town..as well as the 'spike' or casual ward of the workhouse.

5. c. *spike-heeled*, *-helmeted*, *-tailed* (earlier example).

1953 D. Dodge *To catch Thief* i. 11 She was dressed for the evening; a long gown, fragile, spike-heeled slippers, a fur wrap. **1981** A. Lurie *Language of Clothes* iv. 106 French-speaking Canadians..negotiating the icy snow-heaped streets..in nyloned legs and spike-heeled boots. **1916** R. Graves *Goliath & David* 6 And look, spike-helmeted, grey, grim, Goliath straddles over him. **1870** *North Alabamian* (Tuscaloosa, Ala.) 12 Jan. 1/2 'Who's that gentleman, my little man?' was asked of an urchin. 'That one with the spike-tailed coat?'

6. spike-fiddle *Mus.* = *rebab; **spike heel,** a fashionable narrow high heel of a woman's shoe, tapering towards a point (cf. *stiletto heel* s.v. *stiletto *sb.* 5); hence, a spike-heeled shoe; **spike microphone,** (*colloq.*) **mike** (see quot. 1962).

1940 C. SACHS *Hist. Mus. Instruments* (1942) xii. 242 Most Islamic instruments..have no place in art music, with the exception of the Persian *spike fiddle* (called *rabâb* or *kamânga a'gûz* in the Near East)... Malay fiddles, which have preserved the old Persian name in the form *rebab*, are much simpler. **1974** SCHACHT & BOSWORTH *Legacy of Islam* (ed. 2) x. 500 Al-Fārābī also provides the first description of a bowed instrument, the *rabāb*. This was later known in two forms, one with a separate neck, the other a spike-fiddle with a hemispherical sound-chest. **1929** D. L. MOORE *Pandora's Letter Box* xi. 205 The 'spike' heel now popular is disgustingly difficult to balance on. **1950** 'S. RANSOME' *Deadly Miss Ashley* xi. 136 A pair of sandals..featured spike heels decorated with brilliants. **1971** D. C. BROWN *Yukon Trophy Trails* ii. 31, I wanted to live in a log cabin, shoot my own steaks and never wear another pair of spike heels. **1962** *Symposia of Zool. Soc.* VII. 8 There is also the 'spike' microphone, which is extremely small, and can be driven through hard material to record sounds in an inner chamber. **1966** *Economist* 3 Dec. 1029/2 Though there is no federal law against bugging or wire-tapping *per se*, the Supreme Court held that the spike microphone driven through the wall of Mr Black's hotel room constituted physical trespass. **1950** *Washington Post* 20 Mar. D1/4 Police had slipped the 'spike mike' into a wall common to the adjoining premises. **1973** 'D. HALLIDAY' *Dolly & Starry Bird* xvi. 248 *No one* in sneakers with spike mikes and tapes and transmitters?

spike, *sb.*[4] *slang.* [Back-formation f. *SPIKY *a.*[2] 4: a use of SPIKE *sb.*[2]] An Anglican who advocates or practises Anglo-Catholic ritual and observances.

1902 *Church Times* 14 Mar. 320/2 A priest is wanted for this parish. A hard-working Catholic. Not a 'spike'. **1914** J. W. LEGG *Eng. Church Life* 159 It would seem that there were spikes (as Dr. Bright of Christ-church used to call them) in 1768. **1922** E. RAYMOND *Tell England* II. iii. 204 My altar has generally been two ration boxes, marked 'Unsweetened Milk', but the spike has surrounded it. And look here.., the spike knows how to die. He just asks for his absolution and his last sacrament, and—and dies. **1930** SAYERS & 'EUSTACE' *Docs. in Case* i. 37 He turned out to be an earnest and cultivated middle-aged spike from Keble. **1952** R. MACAULAY *Let.* 23 May (1961) 318 Is she one who would be shocked at seeing communicants at High Mass? There have always been those there, I gather; and 'spikes' don't like it. **1963** C. MACKENZIE *My Life & Times* II. 203 In that summer of 1897 Sandys Wason was still a deacon... It was he who started using 'spike' for an extremist... One can still be spiked up; one can still talk of spikiness, and in Anglican circles be understood. **1980** A. N. WILSON *Healing Art* iv. 47 There were several other effigies of famous spikes, including the legendary Father Tooth.

Hence as *v.*[2] *trans.* with *up*: to make (more) 'spiky' or High Church; to enliven with ritual; also **spi·kery,** 'spiky' character or behaviour.

1923 C. MACKENZIE *Parson's Progress* xvi. 214 Was it really worth while trying to spike up the Rector and his services and his flock? **1958** B. PYM *Glass of Blessings* iii. 48 A new vicar trying to spike things up a bit. **1965** C. E. POCKNEE *Parson's Handbk.* (ed. 13) vii. 85 There is no ancient authority for the custom of sitting for the psalms. This is a slovenly piece of modern 'spikery'. **1972** C. STEPHENSON *Merrily on High* ii. 35, I was encouraged by the high church ladies who would listen with amusement and interest to my plans for 'spiking' up the church. **1980** A. N. WILSON *Healing Art* ix. 110 For all her spikery, there would always be a part of herself which found it impossible to shake off the freedoms of scepticism.

spike, *v.*[1] Add: **2.** *fig.* (Earlier and later examples, esp. in phr. to *spike* (*some*)*one's guns*.)

1823 T. CREEVEY *Let.* 11 Mar. in *Creevey Papers* (1903) II. iii. 66 He has himself entirely spiked his guns in the House of Commons. **1862** E. HALL *Jrnl.* 9 Mar. in O. A. Sherrard *Two Victorian Girls* (1966) II. 291 He proceeded to kiss her forehead... She should have spiked the first gun instead of leaving it to clear the way for the advance of others. **1927** *New Republic* 21 Sept. 122/2 They have flitted from one foolish suggestion to the other. The silliest of these was that, to spike the third-term objection, Mr. Coolidge would agree, if elected in 1928, to resign at the expiration of his eighth year of continued occupancy. **1953** L. P. HARTLEY *Go-Between* 16 My enemies would be off their guard, they would never suspect danger from a gun they had so thoroughly spiked. **1971** S. E. MORISON *European Discovery Amer.: Northern Voy.* xiv. 469 It remained for Samuel de Champlain to spike the legend of a City of Norumbega, storied like a New Jerusalem.

5. c. To lace (a drink) with alcohol; to fortify (beer, etc.) by the addition of spirits. Also *transf. slang* (orig. *U.S.*).

1889 L. PENDLETON *In Wiregrass* xviii. 201 Water from biled hops an' poke root, an' 's sweetened wi' 'lasses and spiked wi' good strong whiskey. **1900** *Dialect Notes* II. 63 *Spike*, to fortify a drink by adding wine or spirits. **1915** *Ibid.* IV. 229 *Spike*, to flavor with wine or whiskey, as 'She spikes her cakes.' **1941** J. SMILEY *Hash House Lingo* 52 *Spike*, (bar) add liquor to a drink. **1952** B. MALAMUD *Natural* 24 A crushed cocoanut [*sic*] drink which he privately spiked with a shot from a new bottle. **1962** *Sunday Times* (Colour Suppl.) 14 Oct. 24/1 Spike a *béchamel* sauce with Parmesan cheese. **1980** G. THOMPSON *Murder Mystery* (1981) xxii. 175 She made tea, which he spiked with bourbon.

d. Of a newspaper editor: to reject (a story or part of one) as by filing it on a spike (*SPIKE *sb.*[2] 2 j).

1908 A. S. M. HUTCHINSON *Once aboard Lugger* v. vii. 263 Tiny little scrap of news..copied out a dozen times by Mr. Issy Jago and left..at the offices of as many newspapers. Seven sub-editors 'spiked' it, [etc.]. **1940** W. P. CROZIER *Jrnl.* 9 Dec. in D. Ayerst *Guardian* (1971) xxxiv. 539 E.A.M. disgruntled because I spiked pars (for London letter) on last night's bombing. **1950** C. M. KORNBLUTH in *Astounding Science Fiction* July 150/2 The M[anaging] E[ditor]..decided nobody would believe it. He spiked the story on the 'dead' hook. **1961** B. WELLS *Day Earth caught Fire* vii. 115 This is the newsroom, the place where all the best stories are spiked. **1978** L. HEREN *Growing up on The Times* viii. 283, I discovered that my story had been spiked. It was the first and only time the paper had questioned my judgment, and I felt badly about it.

e. *intr.* To inject another or (for *refl.*) oneself with an intoxicating drug. Also *trans.* and *fig.*

1935 N. ERSINE *Underworld & Prison Slang* 69 *Spike*, to take a shot of dope. 'He spiked about an hour ago.' **1971** J. MANDELKAU *Buttons* v. 68 Almost immediately I was spiked with wine and acid. **1973** T. PYNCHON *Gravity's Rainbow* I. 47 Kevin Spectro will take his syringe and spike away a dozen times tonight..to sedate Fox (his generic term for any patient). **1974** *Guardian* 28 Jan. 11/5 The addicts..'ll sometime try and spike you, try and get you mainlining too. **1977** 'J. LE CARRÉ' *Honourable Schoolboy* ii. 46 The girl..alone and spiked with tiredness.

f. To enrich (a nuclear reactor or its fuel) *with* a particular isotope; to add a small proportion of some distinctive material to.

1956 *Ann. Rev. Nucl. Sci.* VI. 330 A natural uranium power reactor of this size might not become critical, so that the reactor will be 'spiked' with a few enriched elements. **1959** F. G. FOOTE in Hausner & Schumar *Nucl. Fuel Elements* v. 78 The uranium can be spiked with either plutonium or U^{233}. **1971** *New Scientist* 13 May 386/2 Early work in Britain on spiking enriched uranium with plutonium as a possible fuel for Advanced Gas-cooled Reactors. **1974** *Nature* 1 Feb. 310/2 The homogenised mixture was spiked with a known volume of a solution containing 1 $\mu g\ ml^{-1}$ of the N-nitroso compound. **1976** *Lancet* 4 Dec. 1223/1 Concentrations were measured against cadmium standards..prepared from blood spiked with cadmium chloride standard solution. **1977** *Rolling Stone* 13 Jan. 31/2 Silkwood had slipped a vial of plutonium into her vagina or rectum, then used a syringe to spike her samples at home.

7. *intr.* To rise in a spike; to protrude angularly.

1958 *Listener* 18 Sept. 418/2 High mounds of rubble and tangled, bombed machinery which spiked into the air like the legs of dead animals. **1975** N. NICHOLSON *Wednesday Early Closing* i. 21 St. George's steeple spikes up against the sky, graceful as a larch tree and bold as Blackpool Tower.

spike-bozzle (spəikbǫ·z'l), *v. slang* (orig. *Mil.*). Now *rare*. Also **spike-boozle.** [f. SPIKE *v.*[1] 2: the second element is obscure (but see quot. 1962).] To render (an enemy plane, etc.) unserviceable; to destroy; to upset. Also *transf.*

1915 H. ROSHER *In R. Naval Air Service* (1916) 123 Last night 'old man Zepp' came over here... Two machines went up to spike-bozzle him, but..never even saw him. **1923** *Blackw. Mag.* July 5/1 Piffers used to wear them..until the clothing department spike-bozzled them. **1942** BERREY & VAN DEN BARK *Amer. Thes. Slang* § 759/10 Spike bozzle, to chase an enemy plane. **1962** W. GRANVILLE *Dict. Sailors' Slang* 110/2 *Spike boozle*, render ineffective; sabotage, blow up or otherwise destroy a ship or upset a plan. A merging of *spike*, a gun and bam-*boozle*, cheat, mystify, bemuse.

spiked, *a.*[2] Add: **3. a.** Laced or fortified with alcohol. Also *transf.* and *fig.*

In some examples parsable as pa.pple. of the verb.

1909 *Dialect Notes* III. 374 *Spike, v.tr.* 1. To mix an alcoholic with a non-alcoholic beverage. Chiefly in the *pp.* 'This lemonade is heavily spiked.' **1929** *Detective Fiction Weekly* 23 Mar. 161/2 'I can ditch a drink that I suspect of being spiked.' This word 'spiked' was that year [*sc.* c 1899] the very newest slang, signifying 'doped'. **1942** E. PAUL *Narrow St.* i. 2 Some of the early risers huddled round the counter to swallow their coffee, often spiked with cheap, watered rum or cognac. **1960** J. MCNAMEE *Florencia Bay* 52 Then the promoter who, on the strength of spiked assays, had floated a company. **1974** P. CAVE *Mama* (new ed.) xi. 95 The babble of conversation was liberally spiked with laughter, merriment and enthusiasm.

b. *transf.* Containing a small addition of a radioactive or otherwise distinctive material; enriched.

1959 F. G. FOOTE in Hausner & Schumar *Nucl. Fuel Elem.* v. 78 The best use of plutonium-spiked uranium fuels would be in fast neutron reactors. **1962** *Analytical Chem.* XXXIV. 709/2 Separate spiked and unspiked analyses must be made of the unknown uranium sample. **1975** *Sci. Amer.* Oct. 27/2 The idea is to add about half a gram of plutonium 239 to each kilogram of uranium. Since a kilogram of natural uranium contains 7·2 grams of U-235, the 'spiked' fuel would contain a total of 7·7 grams of fissionable material.

spikey: delete 'obs.'

spikily, *adv.* (Later examples.)

1959 *Times* 18 June 15/4 Higo Harada's Music for Piano and Violin, Op. 12,..was spikily intellectual music, rarely visited by any spirit of delight. **1976** J. COOPER *Harriet* (1977) xiii. 81 Her spikily mascara'd eyes softened.

spikiness. (Later examples.)

1962 *Listener* 3 May 788/3 The curious spikiness of the quartet writing. **1977** D. BAGLEY *Enemy* i. 10 Her comments were acute... I found her spikiness of mind very agreeable. **1979** E. H. GOMBRICH *Sense of Order* viii. 200 Does it make sense, therefore, to diagnose the spikiness of Gothic shapes by the same standards we might adopt when seeing such spiky forms in a contemporary hand?

spiking, *vbl. sb.* Add: **3.** The action of adding a spike (*SPIKE *sb.*[2] 2 f (*b*)).

1962 *Newnes Conc. Encycl. Nucl. Energy* 772/2 Spiking was first carried out in the NRX reactor in 1951. **1974** *Sci. Amer.* Feb. 121/1 The use of isotope-spiking and mass spectrometry. **1979** *Liquefied Petroleum Gas* (Shell Internat. Petroleum Co.) 4 In some instances LPG can also be transported by 'spiking'—that is, enriching crude oil with small quantities of LPG.

spiky, *a.*[2] For 8 **spikey** read 8— **spikey** and add: **3.** (Later examples.)

1930 M. KENNEDY *Fool of Family* xv. 147 'How spikey you are!' protested Fenella mildly. 'Oh yes. Keep your temper when I'm rude. You would.' **1955** *Times* 4 Aug. 10/5 What matter that the melodic line is as seductively curved as that of any of the great operatic romanticists of the near past, instead of being spiky and angular in the contemporary fashion? **1964** CRYSTAL & QUIRK *Prosodic & Paralinguist. Features in Eng.* iv. 47 Pitch variation, with extremes in a 'spiky' movement on the one hand..and in a 'glissando' movement..on the other. **1981** N. J. CRISP *Festival* vii. 176 He seemed more relaxed ..not as spiky and difficult as he had been.

4. Of a particularly ritualistic or High-Church Anglican character. *slang.*

1893 W. BRIGHT *Let.* 20 Oct. (1903) 348 The ultras, as they might be called, on the Catholic side, present Church ideas, too often, in a form altogether too hard to be attractive; I believe I am said to have called it 'spiky', in a letter to my friend the Principal of Ely College. **1921** *Church Times* 12 Aug. 147/3 We wonder what would be thought of some of his sayings if they were uttered by a spiky young curate to-day. **1950** A. WILSON *Such Darling Dodos* 34 She became a daily communicant and delighted the more 'spikey' of her neighbours. **1962** *Times Lit. Suppl.* 13 July 505/1 Her story is of the American priest, Charles Phillips, whose churchmanship would in England be rated high-to-spiky. **1977** B. PYM *Quartet in Autumn* xxiv. 212 He had been a server at the spikiest Anglo-Catholic church.

spile, *sb.*[2] Add: **2. b.** Also *Canad.* (Earlier and later examples.)

1844 *Knickerbocker* XXIII. 444 The spiles you see sticking from sugar-holes in every maple. **1868** *Amer. Naturalist* Mar. 39 He remembers very distinctly making 'spiles' of its [*sc.* elder] stems when tapping sugar-trees. **1947** K. M. WELLS *Owl Pen* 89 It is time..to get the rusty spiles and sap buckets down from the beams in the woodshed. It is maple syrup time. **1973** L. RUSSELL *Everyday Life Colonial Canada* xi. 144 The operator drilled a hole into the side of the [maple tree] trunk..and set into this a small wooden spout called a spile.

spile, *sb.*[3] **1. d.** *spile-driver* (earlier example).

1865 *Atlantic Monthly* Apr. 393/1 By means of a spile-driver, an iron pipe..is driven down until it rests upon the solid rock.

spilikin, var. SPILLIKIN, SPELLICAN in Dict. and Suppl.

spilite. Add: Also with pronunc. (spi·ləit). [orig. formed as F. *spillite* (Al. Brongniart: see A. H. de Bonnard in *Nouveau Dict. d'Hist. nat. appliquée aux Arts* (rev. ed.) (1819) XXIX. 371), f. Gr. σπίλος spot, stain.] In mod. use, an altered basalt, commonly amygdaloidal in structure, which is characterized by the albitization of its constituent feldspars and the presence of numerous secondary minerals, and is exemplified by many pillow-lavas. (Earlier and later examples.)

Brongniart did not use *spilite* in its usual modern sense, applying it to amygdaloidal diabase, and much variation in usage has occurred subsequently. There is a comprehensive review by T. G. Vallance in *Proc. Linnean Soc. New South Wales* (1960) LXXXV. 8–52.

1834 *Jrnl. Geol. Soc. Dublin* I. 119 In adopting the term spilites in preference to that of amygdaloid,..I have been induced to do so because the English names were.. irrelevant to the variable nature of the mineral substances. **1893** *Geol. Mag.* Decade III. X. 59 Prof. de Lapparent.. refers to these 'spilites' as amydaloidal melaphyres. **1911** *Ibid.* Decade V. VIII. 203 In addition to the pillow-structure there are certain characteristics that mark the spilites of Great Britain. The first of these is that they are as a rule very completely decomposed, and the second that their felspars are always rich in soda. **1937** A. JOHANNSEN *Descriptive Petrogr. Igneous Rocks* III. 300 The British Geological Survey uses spilite 'to designate the Carboniferous, Devonian, and Ordovician pillow-lavas of Devon and Cornwall...' This variation from the original usage apparently still persists, for Holmes in 1920, defined them as basaltic rocks whose feldspars have been albitized. The term should be dropped. **1960** *Proc. Linnean Soc. New South Wales* LXXXV. 10 English-speaking geologists made little or no use of the term during the 19th century. Rocks which would have been called spilites by the French were usually known as greenstones. *Ibid.* 12 There appear to be four main criteria used in the recogniton of spilites, namely, fabric, mineralogy, chemical composition and geological occurrence. Much of the confusion associated with the name spilite derives from the fact that various workers have emphasized different features. **1974** F. FIALA in G. C. Amstutz *Spilites & Spilitic Rocks* 18 Spilites are abundant in pillow lavas. Nevertheless, both terms are not synonymous, as has been assumed by many workers. **1981** F. J. TURNER *Metamorphic Petrol.* (ed. 2) 223 (*heading*) Spilites as metamorphic rocks.

Hence **spilitiza·tion**, alteration into spilite; **spi·litized** *a.*

1946 *Amer. Jrnl. Sci.* CCXLIV. 313 During spilitization the ferro-magnesian minerals were broken down, and.. the manganese, with other constituents, migrated to the tops of the flows. **1960** *Q. Jrnl. Geol. Soc.* CXVI. 388 Dewey and Flett.. came to the right conclusion in attributing a large proportion of spilitization of pillow-lavas to reactions quickly achieved under submarine volcanic conditions. **1962** E. A. VINCENT tr. *Rittmann's Volcanoes & their Activity* viii. 225 In thick submarine basalt flows.. it is often to be observed that only their upper layers consist of spilitized pillow lavas. **1974** F. FIALA in G. C. Amstutz *Spilites & Spilitic Rocks* 19 The association of spilitized diabases and spilites with keratophyres is.. marked in the initial Devonian volcanism of northern Moravia. **1978** *Nature* 8 June 459/1 Due to the vitric nature and widespread secondary alteration (incipient spilitisation and weathering) the exact petrologic character and petrogenetic affinity of these rocks have not been clearly defined.

spilitic (spəil-, spili·tik), *a. Geol.* [f. SPILITE in Dict. and Suppl. + -IC.] Of, pertaining to, or of the nature of spilite; characterized by the presence of spilite.

1911 *Geol. Mag.* Decade V. VIII. 205 The basic felspar can be traced in every stage of development as we follow the spilitic lavas from the outer precincts of the aureoles to the actual contacts with the granite. *Ibid.* 243 The spilitic suite of igneous rocks. **1965** A. HOLMES *Princ. Physical Geol.* (ed. 2) xxx. 1126 The volcanic rocks interbedded with eugeosynclinal sediments are characteristically submarine lavas of the spilitic suite.., including pillow lavas. **1974** D. S. COOMBS in G. C. Amstutz *Spilites & Spilitic Rocks* 377 Augite was thus *unstable* relative to chlorite.. during the production of the diagnostic spilitic mineralogy. **1977** A. HALLAM *Planet Earth* 201 The geosynclinal belt across Europe, with its associated zones of spilitic volcanics and serpentines, has been interpreted as site of an old ocean.

spill, *sb.*[1] Add: **1. b.** (Later examples.)

1904 *Kynoch Jrnl.* Oct.–Dec. 204 The reader will observe.. a flaw technically termed a 'spill', the result of a small hollow or depression near the surface of the ingot, which, in the process of rolling has been closed, but which, in the extending process of pressing the metal into a case has again been opened & made manifest. **1954** A. R. BAILEY *Text-bk. Metallurgy* xi. 377 Cavities near the surface.. are likely to become opened up during working, become oxidised and fail to weld up, thus forming surface oxide laminations, sometimes known as spills.

2. a. (Earlier example.)

1821 M. EDGEWORTH *Let.* 14 Nov. (1971) 268 Harriet performed to admiration as Fire eater—I held lamp.. and lighted *spills* which she seemed to devour.

b. *spill-holder* (earlier example), *-jar, vase.*

1851 *Parker's Jrnl.* 5 Apr. 185/2 The mantelpiece is probably painted to imitate marble, and on it are placed two 'spill-holders' of perforated card, with bouquets worked in silk on each. **1868** C. L. EASTLAKE *Hints on Household Taste* v. 134 Chimneypiece spill-vases, made of brass,.. decorated with a pattern in encaustic colour. **1903** A. BENNETT *Leonora* x. 282 Reaching a second spill from the spill-jar on the mantlepiece. **1978** *Country Life* 13 Apr. (Suppl.) 38/1 (*caption*) A Pair of English Porcelain Spill Vases.

spill, *sb.*[4] Add: **2. a.** *spec.* = *oil spill* s.v. *OIL *sb.*[1] 6 e.

1972 L. M. HARRIS *Introd. Deepwater Floating Drilling Operations* xvii. 178 Equipment and practices designed for safety and reliability are the first line of defense against oil spills and pollution. Should a spill occur, however, advance planning can reduce its severity. **1975** *Petroleum Rev.* XXIX. 237/3 The ability of present-day booms to contain a spill is limited to good weather conditions.

4. A diffusion of light, esp. beyond the area intended to be illuminated.

1952 [see *BAFFLE *sb.*[1] 5]. **1972** T. COE *Don't lie to Me* (1974) i. 4 Her features.. hard to read in the dim spill from a nearby streetlight. **1977** P. SCUPHAM *Hinterland* 9 A spill Of light poured off rough drapery As blacks and whites and ochre tones Work shifts about the curtain wall.

5. *Austral. Pol.* A vacating of other posts after one important change of office.

1956 J. T. LANG *I Remember* 311 There had to be an annual election of leader. That made it inevitable that someone would intrigue against the leader hoping for a Cabinet spill. **1974** *Courier-Mail* (Brisbane) 6 July 3/1 After Mr. Tucker's election as new party leader, Mr. Dean (Sandgate) moved for a 'spill' of all other Opposition front bench positions. **1975** *Australian* 18 Mar. 1 It will be left to Mr Fraser's supporters to force the issue and move against Mr Snedden through either a spill of leadership positions or a motion of no confidence.

6. *attrib.* and *Comb.*, as *spill-proof* adj.; **spill burner**, a form of burner used in some gas turbines which allows excess fuel to be re-circulated; **spill valve**, a valve which serves to allow the escape of surplus fluid.

1945 *Proc. Inst. Mech. Engineers* CLIII. 464/2 (*caption*) o Indicates the condition giving a mean particle size of 200μ: On the spill burner this limit is not attained. **1972** H. COHEN et al. *Gas Turbine Theory* (ed. 2) vi. 177 A second practical method of obtaining good atomization over a wide range of fuel flow: the spill burner. It is virtually a simplex burner with a passage from the vortex chamber through which excess fuel can be spilled off. **1920** E. BUTLER *Internal Combustion Engine Design & Pract.* (ed. 2) viii. 138 When used on an automobile, owing to vibration, they [*sc.* accumulator cells] should be occasionally examined for scaling or other damage, and also for loss of solution, if not spill proof. **1944** W. A. KOEHLER *Princ. & Applications Electrochem.* (ed. 2) II. iv. 69 A portable radio battery with a transparent plastic case and spill-proof cover. **1963** *Glamour* Oct. 12/1 (Advt.), New spray mist! Unbreakable. Spill-proof... Intimate by Revlon. **1922** *Trans. Inst. Engineers & Shipbuilders Scotland* LXV. 421 This spill valve opens from the discharge chamber of the pump and is worked by the same lever as actuates the pump plunger. **1959** *Motor Manual* (ed. 36) ii. 30 At a predetermined moment, this outlet is closed and fuel is then forced to the engine cylinder until a second outlet (commonly called a spill valve) is opened so as to release the pressure and return the surplus oil to the supply side of the system. **1975** T. D. MORTON *Reed's Motor Engin. Knowledge for Marine Engineers* iii. 77 A fuel spill valve (pneumatically loaded) maintains rail pressure as decided at the controls.

spill, *v.* Add: **II. 12. a.** (Further example.)

1918 D. H. LAWRENCE *New Poems* 30 In the street spilled over splendidly With wet, flat lights.

13. b. Also from a parachute.

1925 *Literary Digest* 11 July 25/1 Used as a dividing mark in folding the parachute, and also to 'spill' the wind out of it after a landing. **1942** A. M. LOW *Parachutes in Peace & War* iii. 48 The parachute might 'spill air' & drop faster. **1976** A. WHITE *Long Silence* vii. 59 Spill air, ride the motion down as rapidly as is safe. Look around .. trying to make out the other parachutes.

15. a. (Later *transf.* and *fig.* examples.)

1920 H. CRANE *Let.* 14 Apr. (1965) 37 A mood which rose and spilled over in a slightly cruder form than what you see. **1962** *Amer. Speech* XXXVII. 17 The metropolitan area of New York City.. has spilled into the surrounding countryside, engulfing cities and communities which had their own economic and cultural centers. **1962** A. NISBETT *Technique of Sound Studio* iv. 84 Where a tape has spilled and wound round the spindle and become crumpled, speech recordings are often still playable. **1972** B. MOORE *Catholics* i. 17 An anchor spilled like entrails from its bow, falling deep into the sea. **1976** *Times* 10 Sept. 1/6 Cape riots spill into white zones. The anti-apartheid rioting spilled out of Cape Town and spread into white areas of Cape Province. **1976** P. & W. PROCTOR *Women in Pulpit* vii. 124 Although Connie Parvey is primarily a campus chaplain, her work in this case spilled over into the role of hospital chaplain.

16. a. *trans.* To utter (words); to confess or divulge (facts). *slang* (orig. *U.S.*).

[**1574**: in Dict., sense 10 b.] **1917** R. W. LARDNER *Gullible's Travels* 213 'Go ahead and spill it,' I says. **1920** C. SANDBURG *Smoke & Steel* 44 Men at tables spill Peloponnesian syllables. **1923** 'B. M. BOWER' *Parowan Bonanza* iv. 47 Maybe he taught the parrot that lingo just to have her spill it in town and start a rush. **1925** E. WALLACE *King by Night* xxxi. 143 Spill it quick, Goldy. **1944** [see *OIL *sb.*[1] 3 j]. **1953** K. TENNANT *Joyful Condemned* xxiv. 233 She was going to spill everything to him.. She would have pooled you, too. **1973** 'B. MATHER' *Snowline* vi. 70 You didn't come down here.. just to tempt me.. with a beer. Spill it. **1977** I. SHAW *Beggarman, Thief* II. i. 119 He picked up the phone to call the Colonel, spill everything.

b. *to spill the beans*: to reveal a secret. *slang* (orig. *U.S.*).

1919 T. K. HOLMES *Man from Tall Timber* xxviii. 355 'Mother certainly has spilled the beans!' thought Stafford in vast amusement. **1921** R. D. PAINE *Comr. Rolling Ocean* viii. 136 The beans are spilled, and that is what Maddigan guessed the moment he set eyes on you. **1928** [see *CLEAN *a.* 3 d]. **1929** E. LINKLATER *Poet's Pub* vii. 91 'Tell me the truth,' she says. 'Spill the beans, Holly, old man!' **1945** *Sun* (Baltimore) 28 Nov. 1/1 A Government publication in this country spilled the beans concerning our urgent interest in experiments with uranium. **1958** E. DUNDY *Dud Avocado* I. vi. 93 Spilling beans of shattering truths or equally shattering lies. **1966** D. VARADAY *Gara-Yaka's Domain* vii. 82 Wilson in an indulgent moment of weakness 'spilt the beans'. **1979** G. HAMMOND *Dead Game* vii. 83 You asked me to trust you... So now I think you'd better spill the beans. **1982** *Listener* 23–30 Dec. 3/1 Julian Critchley spills the beans about El Vino and says why he likes it.

c. *to spill one's guts* (*out*): to divulge as much as one can, to confess. *slang* (chiefly *U.S.*).

1927 C. F. COE *Me—Gangster* iv. 78 'Throw him out, eh?' the old man snarled... 'Throw him out an' have him spill his guts about the whole gang?' **1945** S. J. BAKER *Austral. Lang.* vii. 140 *To hold one's guts*, to be silent, and *to spill one's guts*, to talk, reveal a secret. **1973** *Black Panther* 8 Sept. 10/3 Mistakenly believing that Haldeman and another assistant had told the truth during previous questioning, Butterfield spilled his guts out. **1979** 'A. HAILEY' *Overload* III. viii. 226 The kid—he was eighteen, by the way, and not long out of trade school—broke down and spilled his guts.

spill-. Add: **3. spillbank** (see quot. 1961).

1909 H. M. WILSON *Irrigation Engin.* (ed. 6) xix. 560 The material brought up by these [buckets] is deposited on one of two endless belt-carriers running on booms which dump it on either spillbank. **1961** L. D. STAMP *Gloss. Geogr. Terms* 427/2 Spill-bank is the term used by British and Indian engineers engaged in river training for the bank of coarse alluvium spilled over by a river in flood (C. C. Inglis).

4. In the sense 'that empties by spilling', as *spillbucket.*

1938 L. MACNEICE *Earth Compels* 20 Bric-a-brac Pick-a-back Spillbucket Splits.

spillage (spi·lėdʒ). [f. SPILL *v.* + -AGE.] The action or fact of spilling; that which spills or is spilt. Also *attrib.*

1934 WEBSTER, *Spillage*.., the act of spilling; that which spills or is spilled over; as, a trough to divert any *spillage.* **1937** *Times* 9 Oct. 9/6 A miner.. was trapped underground by a fall of rock and completely buried. Dr. Saunders arrived at 3.15 p.m., by which time the rescue party had removed most of the spillage from the imprisoned man's body. **1947** *Sun* (Baltimore) 26 June 8/1 Recent oil spillages in and near Baltimore harbor have resulted in great annoyance to bathers. **1962** A. NISBETT *Technique of Sound Studio* vii. 128 Remember also when handling music tapes that any damage due to spillage or stretching, etc., will be more noticeable than on speech tapes. **1963** *Daily Mail* 15 May 4/4 On every bottle of brandy sold in the Hilton, two and two-thirds ounces are written off for 'spillage'. **1969** *Gloss. Aeronaut. & Astronaut. Terms* (*B.S.I.*) IV. 3 *Spillage drag*, the difference between the drag at a given intake flow and the drag at some specified intake flow. *Ibid.* 4 *Spillage*, the amount by which the intake flow is less than some specified intake flow. **1969** *Daily Tel.* 30 Aug. 12/6 A pesticide spillage has killed 11,000 fish in the South Holland Drain. **1972** *Ibid.* 14 Apr. 19/3 A glass is often placed beneath the tap as a substitute for the drip tray and used for topping up... The patron should ensure that he rejects any beer which contains a mixture of this spillage. **1973** *Times* 30 July 11/2 If you spill anything you simply move your saucepan to another burner, lift off the support, and underneath there is a spillage bowl which has collected what has boiled over and which has only to be taken out and rinsed. **1976** *Washington Post* 23 Jan. A 14/4 Accidents are caused by drivers trying to avoid rock spillage.. on the Beltway. **1976** *Offshore Platforms & Pipelining* 222/1 The utmost attention was given to reducing the risk of oil spillage during operations. **1976** *Cambridge Independent Press* 16 Dec. II. 7 (Advt.), Family-size oven with 'Cook Clean' panels... Hob light, auto-timer, slide-out spillage trays. **1977** *R.A.F. News* 27 Apr.–10 May 3/4 Allegations that excessive 'spillage' drag from the engine intakes will seriously impair Tornado's performance, particularly at high angles of incidence in the transonic speed range, were refuted.

spiller, *sb.*[3] **2.** (Earlier example.)

1884 *Bull. U.S. Nat. Museum* No. 27. 998 Mackerel pocket or spiller... The pocket was introduced into the mackerel-seine fishery in 1878 for holding the surplus catch which would otherwise spoil before being cleaned and salted.

spiller (spi·ləɹ), *sb.*[4] [f. SPILL *sb.*[1] + -ER[1].] = SPILL *sb.*[1] 2 a.

1936 M. MITCHELL *Gone with Wind* 71 Pork took a long spiller from the mantelpiece, lit it from the lamp flame and went into the hall.

spillikin, spellican. Add: **3.** (Further examples.) Also in sing.

1907 E. GOSSE *Father & Son* ii. 50 My nerves were a packet of spilikins. **1940** W. DE LA MARE *Pleasures & Speculations* 71 No fine shades of psychology, or ethical spellicans are here. **1945** —— *Burning-Glass* 44 To ponder upon a moth.. A spelican from his palm.

spilling, *vbl. sb.*[1] Add: **3. c.** The action of causing air to escape from a parachute; also such an escape of air.

1930 *Flight* 11 July 784/2 As usual, he judged his distance perfectly, and by judicious 'spilling' landed right in front of the club enclosure. **1951** *Gloss. Aeronaut. Terms* (*B.S.I.*) III. 15 *Spilling*, the escape of air, with local partial collapse, at the periphery of a parachute canopy, caused either by the instability of the parachute or by side-slipping.

spillover (spi·lōᵘvəɹ), *sb.* and *a.* Also **spill-over.** [f. SPILL- + OVER *adv.*] **A.** *sb.* That which spills over; the process of spilling over; (an) incidental development; a consequence, a repercussion, a by-product.

1940 [see *KAROK]. **1949** *Richmond* (Va.) *Times-Dispatch* 6 Oct. 26/1 A rush to buy got under way as soon as the opening bell sounded. This was evidently a spillover from yesterday when the market established a new high for the year. **1957** J. I. M. STEWART *James Joyce* 10 This has no relevance to the action, and is a spill-over from Joyce's more openly autobiographical writing in the history of Dedalus. **1957** P. WORSLEY *Trumpet shall Sound* 269 Weber.. looks for the source of change in social tensions..; the danger of resentment of disciplinary authority..; or the spill-over into irrational channels of affect which is not absorbed by the rational order. **1962** *Lancet* 12 May 1009/1, 32 patients had pulmonary disease preoperatively, presumably owing to 'spill-over', and only in those with chronic pulmonary suppuration did this fail to clear up. **1970** *Daily Colonist* (Victoria, B.C.) 11 Nov. 3/5 The threat to Canadian security possibly being greater from a spillover of violence and the potential of anarchy in the streets. **1971** *Gloss. Electrotechnical, Power Terms* (*B.S.I.*) III. ii. 27 *Spill-over*, in a.c. signalling on multi-link connections, that part of a signal which passes from one section to another before the connection between the sections is split. **1973** 'D. HALLIDAY' *Dolly & Starry Bird* vii. 97 The revolver was pointed straight at my head... I wasn't keen on the spillover into small arms. **1977** *New Yorker* 26 Sept. 66/3 The continuing rise in crime, its increasing spillover into the white community, and the failure of our criminal justice system.. have created apprehension. **1979** *United States 1980/81* (Penguin Travel Guides) 309 Soho is a very livable combination of 19th-century cast-iron buildings, spillovers from Little Italy. **1980** *Times Lit. Suppl.* 5 Sept. 965/5 What economists call 'spillovers'—those unwanted side-effects, incidental to the legitimate production and use of man-made goods, that are familiar to the public as pollution, noise, congestion and other pervasive hazards and disadvantages.

B. *attrib.* or as *adj.* That results from spilling over; incidentally developed.

1953 J. S. HUXLEY *Evolution in Action* iv. 96 The nervous excitation spills over and is discharged into another channel, that of digging a nest hole. Such irrelevant spill-over activities are called displacement activities. **1961** *Listener* 2 Nov. 692/2 It is always experimental (and exciting) to work on the basis of 'spillover' audiences, and place a known 'difficult' programme immediately after a known winner. **1967** *Spectator* 14 July 44/1 With the postwar growth of technology and population these disservices or 'spillover effects'..have become too conspicuous to be ignored. **1971** *Physics Bull.* Nov. 654/2 The tilting of the subreflection of a Cassegrain antenna with the object of redirecting spillover radiation away from warm earth regions, has considerable geometric optical consequences. **1981** *Times* 31 July 19/1 If the United States slips into recession the spill-over effect could hamper what appears to be a slow recovery in the world chemical industry.

spillspilling (spi·lspiliŋ), *ppl. a. nonce-wd.* [Redupl. f. SPILL *v.*: see -ING².] Repeatedly spilling.

1922 JOYCE *Ulysses* 439 Advances with a tilted dish of spillspilling gravy.

spillway (spi·lwēⁱ). Also **spill-way.** [f. SPILL- + WAY *sb.*¹] **1. a.** A channel or slope built to carry away surplus water from a reservoir.

1889, 1892 [in Dict. s.v. SPILL- 3]. **1943** J. S. HUXLEY *TVA* xi. 83 The road bridge across the spillway..became part of a bold composition finishing on a strong horizontal line and broken only by the small scale tower of the lift shaft. **1962** R. B. FULLER *Epic Poem on Industrialization* 133 It was but a warning trickle down the spillway Of the cosmic power dam. **1979** *United States 1980/81* (Penguin Travel Guides) 611 The world's largest concrete dam..has a spillway twice as high as Niagara Falls.

b. *Physical Geogr.* A natural feature providing a channel for the overflow or escape of water from a lake.

1914 DAVID & PRIESTLEY *Brit. Antarctic Exped. 1907–9 Rep. on Sci. Investigations* I. i. 5 At intervals the horst is breached by valleys..which form outlets, 'by-washes', or 'spillways' for the surplus inland ice and snow. **1929** C. R. LONGWELL *Pirsson's Textbk. Geol.* (ed. 3) I. vii. 156 Each of the lakes..has streams or springs flowing into it, and an outlet or spillway determined by the lowest point in the rim of the containing basin. **1957** G. E. HUTCHINSON *Treat. Limnol.* I. i. 80 When the ice had fully retreated, spillways to the west were established. **1971** *Nature* 3 Sept. 34/2 The latter [*sc.* a gorge] may have operated for a time as a spillway from a glacial lake covering the upper part of the Chew valley.

2. *attrib.*, as *spillway dam.*

1913 P. A. M. PARKER *Control of Water* vii. 415 We find in spillway dams, that such damage as occurs is apparently due to a partial vacuum induced by the flowing water. **1951** W. F. HEALD *Scenic Guide Oregon* 11 The spillway dam, 1450 feet long crosses the north channel.

spilt, *ppl. a.* Add: **2. a.** (Further examples.) Also with *out.*

1881 O. WILDE *Poems* 149 The heart of the lotus drenched..With the spilt-out blood of the rose-red wine. **1939** DYLAN THOMAS *Map of Love* 11 Carved birds blunt their striking throats on the salt gravel, Pierce the spilt sky with diving wing in weed and heel An inch in froth.

b. (Earlier examples.)

1738 SWIFT *Polite Conv.* i. 27 'Tis a Folly to cry for spilt Milk. **1828** J. NEAL *Rachel Dyer* xx. 248, I pity you both, but there's no help for you now—never cry for spilt milk.

spin, *sb.*¹ Add: **1. b.** The product of a machine which rotates and twists toffee.

1913 D. H. LAWRENCE *Sons & Lovers* i. 4 She..went to get Annie a spin of toffee.

2. a. (Examples with reference to spin-drying.)

1966 D. V. DAVIS *New Domestic Encycl.* (ed. 2) iii. 127 Each spin should be restricted to about 15 seconds. **1969** K. J. MILLS *Washing Wisdom* vi. 97 If a spin has been selected, then this will happen for the required time.

c. (Earlier and further examples.) Also, the ability to impart such a motion to the ball; spin-bowling.

1851 J. PYCROFT *Cricket Field* ix. 174 The more spin you give the ball, the better the delivery; because then the ball will twist, rise quickly, or cut variously, the instant it touches the ground. **1855** *F. Lillywhite's Guide to Cricketers* 81 A bowler with a great spin. **1861** *Bell's Life* 10 Nov. 6/3 But however good their trundling, pitch or pace, or break or spin, Still the monarch of all bowlers, to my mind was Alfred Mynn. **1951** *Sport* 27 Apr.–3 May 12/1 Wardle's left-arm slows and the rapid advance of Eddie Leadbetter, the 23-year-old leg-break and googly bowler, offer spin enough to check the best opponents. **1955** *Times* 5 July 4/1 Silk was probably right in thinking that his seamers would get more out of it than his spinners, but what he did not know was that Oxford were likely to lose their composure against spin. **1958** *Times* 19 July 3/5 Even if we are to be short of spin in Australia our pace attack will be as formidable as it was four years ago. **1977** *World of Cricket Monthly* June 32/3 It was left to the spin of Holford to separate the dangerous pair.

d. *Aeronaut.* A steep descent in which an aircraft describes a helix at an angle of attack greater than the stalling angle; *flat spin*: see s.v. *FLAT *a.* 15.

1915 *Aeroplane* 10 Nov. 578/2 Several times their aeroplane got into a 'spin'. **1930** NAYLER & OWER *Aviation To-Day* 324 To come out of the spin the pilot pushes his stick forward so as to unstall the wings. **1939** [see *SPIRAL *a.*¹ 1 b]. **1953** *Aeroplane* 30 Jan. 140/2 Apart from spins that resulted in fatal accidents, there were also quite a number before 1914 which had less drastic consequences. **1977** *New Yorker* 27 June 62/1 The Liberator..went into a spin, dived toward the earth.

e. The continued revolving of the clutch of a motor after being disengaged.

1919 B. H. DAVIES *Motor Driving* 129 The disc A is pressed against the disc B, which damps out the 'spin'. **1948** A. W. JUDGE *Mod. Motor Engineer* (ed. 4) II. 305 If the car is fitted with a clutch stop, or brake, this will effectively obviate clutch spin on disengagement. **1977** J. H. HAYNES *Ford Fiesta Owners Workshop Man.* v. 95/2 Clutch spin is a condition that occurs when there is an obstruction in the clutch.

f. *colloq.* The act of playing a gramophone record, esp. on the air; a session of playing gramophone records.

1977 *Broadcast* 28 Nov. 10/1 Records not receiving maxiplay but likely to get at least one daytime spin. **1977** *R.A.F. News* 11–24 May 20/6 Disc jockey SAC 'Duke' Bedford set off on a record non-stop spin of 72½ hours.

4. a. Now freq. a ride or run in a motor vehicle or aircraft.

1907 G. MEREDITH *Let.* 7 Sept. (1970) III. 1606 To vary my growls..I hire a motor and have a spin of 100 miles, a way of ensuring appetite and prolonged sleep. **1942** A. CHRISTIE *Body in Library* xi. 102 He took his car and went for a spin down to the front. **1960** M. SPARK *Ballad of Peckham Rye* vii. 164 'I called for you last Saturday,' Mr. Druce said. 'I thought you would care for a spin.' **1976** *Southern Even. Echo* (Southampton) 12 Nov. 14/5 A 15-year-old boy..took his father's car, and went in it for a spin around Basingstoke. **1978** G. VIDAL *Kalki* iii. 59 'We'll go for a spin,' said Kalki... First we had to get through to the Katmandu airport. That took an hour... It was five o'clock before we were able to take off.

c. *Austral.* and *N.Z. slang.* A (good, bad, etc.) experience or piece of luck.

1919 in W. H. DOWNING *Digger Dialects* 47. **1929** K. S. PRICHARD *Coonardoo* xix. 188 Mollie had had a crook spin when the children were little. **1934** T. WOOD *Cobbers* xi. 134 People generally said they were having a bad spin. **1948** D. BALLANTYNE *Cunninghams* 132 What a miserable bloody spin he was having. **1960** N. HILLIARD *Maori Girl* IV. iii. 261 Give her a decent spin now and she'll turn out all right. **1964** H. P. TRITTON *Time means Tucker* 113 When I remarked that he'd had a tough spin he grinned, 'Served me right for being such a blanky fool.'

6. *Math.* The local rotation of a continuous medium, as expressed by the curl of the local velocity; vorticity.

1878 W. K. CLIFFORD *Elements of Dynamic* I. II. ii. 123 The velocity-system due to a definite angular velocity about a definite axis is spoken of as the rotation-velocity. To specify it completely we must assign its magnitude and the position of the axis... A rotation-velocity, so denoted, shall be called a spin. **1878, 1882** [in Dict., sense 2 a]. **1937** S. L. GREEN *Hydro- & Aero-Dynamics* ii. 14 There is an essential difference between motions with and without spin, i.e. between rotational and irrotational motion. **1958** *Science* 4 Apr. 731/3 The arrow, which points along the axis of spin and has length equal to the angular speed, is the 'vorticity'... The case of no spin is appropriate to some applications, particularly for waves on water and for aeronautics.

7. *Physics.* An intrinsic property of certain elementary particles which is a form of angular momentum and is usu. pictured as a rotation (it is distinct from angular momentum possessed by virtue of occupation of an orbital); a vector representing this in the case of a particular particle.

1926 UHLENBECK & GOUDSMIT in *Nature* 20 Feb. 264/1 To start with, we shall consider the effect of the spin on the manifold of stationary states which corresponds to motion of an electron round a nucleus. **1938** R. W. LAWSON tr. *Hevesy & Paneth's Man. Radioactivity* (ed. 2) viii. 83 The electrons exhibit a rotation proper to themselves and generally referred to as 'spin', and this confers upon them the property of small magnets. **1943** *Ann. Reg. 1942* II. 365 Mesons are of two types—the more usual with the longer life and zero spin and another of shorter life having a spin 1*h*. **1955** *Sci. News Let.* 19 Feb. 117/3 They have passed proton beams through two hydrogen filled chambers to get atoms whose spins are all in the same direction. **1966** C. R. TOTTLE *Sci. Engin. Materials* i. 13 Beryllium..can have two electrons in the 2s state, since they can have opposite spin. **1974** P. W. ATKINS *Quanta* 223/1 The spin is the intrinsic, characteristic, and irremovable angular momentum of a particle. A convenient fiction is to suppose that the spin is the angular momentum arising from the rotation of a body about its own axis.

8. *Austral. slang.* [Perhaps a different word.] Five pounds in money.

1941 *Coast to Coast 1941* 225 'How'd you go at the two-up?' I asked. 'Aw, I got a spin,' said Tom. **1949** L. GLASSOP *Lucky Palmer* 15 'Not five bob. A spin,' said the carpenter, fishing a five pound note out. **1962** S. GORE *Down Golden Mile* 261 Backed Sweet Friday for a spin... But it never run a drum.

9. *attrib.* and *Comb.*, as *spin axis*; (sense *7) *spin angular momentum, multiplicity* (= *MULTIPLICITY 1 e (*a*)), *quantum number, state*; **spin-allowed** *a. Physics,* consistent with the selection rules describing changes in spin quantum number; **spin bowler** *Cricket,* a slow bowler who imparts spin to the ball on delivery; also **spin-bowling; spin-dye** *v. trans. Textiles,* to dye (textiles) by a process which incorporates the colouring matter before the filament is formed; so **spin-dyed** *ppl. a.*, **spin-dyeing** *vbl. sb.*; **spin echo** *Physics,* a radio-frequency signal induced in a coil surrounding a system of (esp. nuclear) spins in a static magnetic field in the plane of the coil following the application of two radio-frequency pulses to the coil; freq. *attrib.*; **spin flip** *Physics,* the quantum jump of a particle from one spin state to another; **spin glass,** a dilute solid solution of a magnetic substance in a non-magnetic host; **spin-labelling** *Chem.*, the technique of labelling (*LABEL *v.* 2) with stable paramagnetic radicals which can be studied using electron spin resonance techniques; so **spin-label** *v. trans.*; also as *sb.*, a radical or compound used in spin-labelling; **spin-labelled** *a.*; **spin-lattice** *Physics,* used *attrib.* with reference to the interaction between a crystal lattice and a particle possessing spin; **spin-orbit** *Physics,* used *attrib.* with reference to the interaction between spin and orbital motion, esp. of an electron in an atom; **spin polarization** *Physics* = *POLARIZATION 1*; so **spin-polarized** *a.*; **spin-spin** *Physics,* used *attrib.* with reference to the interaction between two or more particles possessing spin; **spin-stabilized** *a. Astr.*, (of a rocket, spacecraft, etc.) stabilized in a desired orientation by being made to rotate about an axis; so **spin-stabilization; spin tunnel** *Aeronaut.* = *spinning tunnel* s.v. *SPINNING *vbl. sb.* 8 c; **spin vector** *Math.* and *Physics,* a vector representing rotation; *spec.* one which by its magnitude and direction represents the intrinsic angular momentum of a particle; **spin wave** *Physics,* a cooperative oscillation in the alignment of electron spins, propagated through a magnetic material in the form of a wave.

1972 DEPUY & CHAPMAN *Molec. Reactions & Photochem.* iii. 34 Electronic transitions between states of the same multiplicity, i.e., singlet-singlet and triplet-triplet transitions, are spin-allowed. **1973** Spin-allowed [see *PHOSPHORESCENCE]. **1928** *Proc. R. Soc.* A. CXVII. 610 Goudsmit and Uhleenbeck have introduced the idea of an electron with a spin angular momentum of half a quantum and a magnetic moment of one Bohr magneton. **1977** *Dædalus* Summer 27 Some quantum numbers, such as electric charge and spin angular momentum, refer to physical, measurable attributes of the particle. **1922** GLAZEBROOK *Dict. Appl. Physics* I. 421/2 A true circular disc, mounted eccentrically on a spin-axis normal to its plane, illustrates the state of bad static balance. **1926** *Nature* 20 Feb. 264/1 This couple will cause a slow precession of the spin axis. **1977** *Dædalus* Fall 48 The spin axis of this satellite could be oriented at will by command from the Earth. **1920** D. J. KNIGHT in P. F. Warner *Cricket* 42 Let any player who does not believe in this dictum go and face such spin bowlers as Barnes, Hearne, [etc.]..on a sticky wicket. **1955** *Times* 14 July 3/5 One has doubts as to just how much the spin bowlers approve of these pitches. **1976** DEXTER & MAKINS *Testkill* 90 A book he was planning on the history of the great spin bowlers. **1955** *Times* 5 July 4/6 They are clearly a useful team, well equipped with stroke-players but perhaps a little short of spin bowling. **1963** *Times* 7 June 4/3 Mushtaq Mohammad, Pakistan's Test batsman, amply confirmed his ability against spin bowling. **1975** *Cricketer* May 20/1 Critics of the English cricket scene often bemoan the lack of spin bowling. **1948** *Jrnl. Soc. Dyers & Colourists* LXIV. 291/2 Dyes suitable for spin-dyeing..are those of nitrodiarylamine, azo, and anthraquinone types. **1961** F. D. LEWIS *Chem. & Technol. Rayon Manufacture* xii. 148 Lack of space precludes more than a cursory consideration here of the spindyeing of viscose rayon yarns. *Ibid.* 149 It would not seem possible to spindye thread with a single organic pigment. **1963** A. J. HALL *Textile Sci.* iii. 132 Generally, by this use of pigments instead of dyes it is possible to produce coloured fibres and yarns having the maximum fastness properties; they are often designated 'spin-dyed' yarns. **1949** *Bull. Amer. Physical Soc.* XXIV. VII. 13/2 Spin Echoes. E. L. Hahn, University of Illinois. **1963** *Times* 8 May 2/7 (Advt.), Post-Doctoral Research Fellowship..for work on relaxation time measurements by spin-echo techniques. **1979** *Nature* 22 Nov. 367/1 Experiments using the weakly inelastic scattering of neutrons have also become feasible; they give similar information [about the motion of polymer chains in a liquid], but for higher frequencies: from $10^{11}s^{-1}$ with 'back scattering spectrometers' down to $2 \times 10^{8}s^{-1}$ with the most recent 'spin echo' method. **1955** *Physical Rev.* C. 1505/1 The special form of the dispersion relations depends on the high-frequency behavior of the spin-flip amplitude. **1971** *New Scientist* 1 Apr. 6/2 Light..from a Q-switched carbon-dioxide laser is the 'pumping' source for the spin-flip laser. **1975** *Sci. Amer.* May 89/2 Units of time and distance are specified in terms of the frequency of the hydrogen spin-flip at 1,420 megahertz. **1970** P. W. ANDERSON in *Materials Res. Bull.* V. 549 (*heading*) Localisation theory and the Cu-Mn problem: spin glasses. **1976** *New Scientist* 2 Dec. 533/1 The essential feature of the spin glass transition is that below some critical temperature, the magnetic atoms are locked or frozen into random orientations (hence the analogy with a glass). **1979** *McGraw-Hill Yearbk. Sci. & Technol.* 247/2 The transition from the paramagnetic to spin glass phase occurs as the material is cooled through a certain temperature point. **1965** T. J. STONE et al. in *Proc. Nat. Acad. Sci.* LIV. 1010 (*heading*) Spin-labeled biomolecules.

Ibid. 1785 Stone..obtained a measure of the rotational mobility of the region of the macromolecule to which the spin labels were bonded. *Ibid.* 1791 It appears likely that the spin-labeling method will be useful in studies of the interaction of haptens, coenzymes, inhibitors, and substrates with proteins and other macromolecules. **1969** *New Scientist* 30 Oct. 224/2 The use of spin-labelled substrate analogues shows clearly..the subtle changes in protein conformation that occur during the enzymic process. **1974** *Nature* 12 Apr. (verso rear cover), The most commonly used spin labels are molecules which contain a nitroxide moiety. **1975** D. H. Burrin in Williams & Wilson *Biologist's Guide to Princ. & Techniques Pract. Biochem.* v. 161 By spin labelling glycerophosphatides with a stable nitroxide free radical, the lateral diffusion of the labelled molecules in a membrane.. may be studied. **1976** *Tetrahedron Lett.* June 2180 Spin labelling with carbonyl compounds was carried out for 1–2 days in pH 7·5 aqueous phosphate buffer. **1938** *Physica* V. 502 The period of the alternating field must be of the order of magnitude of the relaxation time τ of the spin-lattice equilibrium. **1978** P. W. Atkins *Physical Chem.* xix. 629 The motion of nuclei can affect the shapes and widths of lines in n.m.r. just as it does in e.s.r., and the spin-lattice and spin-spin relaxation times can be discussed in precisely the same way. **1956** *Nature* 18 Feb. 306/1 The 'electronegativity' of all the cations is not that of their ground states, for several of them are in states of lower spin-multiplicity. **1977** I. M. Campbell *Energy & Atmosphere* viii. 219 Radiative transitions between states of the same spin multiplicity are easy in the absence of contravention of other selection rules. **1932** Bacher & Goudsmit *Atomic Energy States* 14 The interaction between the two electrons is smaller than the spin-orbit interaction of the 3*p* electron. **1963** G. Troup *Masers & Lasers* (ed. 2) 185 Because of spin-orbit coupling..the 'spin' S in the Hamiltonian is not necessarily equal to the true spin of the ion, but is rather an 'effective spin' related to the multiplicity of levels actually found. **1978** W. J. Kaufmann *Exploration of Solar System* xi. 396 This means that Mercury rotates three times about its axis while circling the sun twice. This phenomenon is known as spin-orbit coupling. **1966** *Proc. Physical Soc.* LXXXIX. 587 The fundamental spin polarization (**P**) is typically represented by $\mathbf{P}(x) = P_0 \hat{\varepsilon} \cos Qx$ where **Q** is the spin-density wave vector and is a unit vector along the direction of polarization. **1970** I. E. McCarthy *Nuclear Reactions* i. i. 7 They [*sc.* the proton and the neutron] may be identified separately by measuring the spin polarization of the beams. **1977** *New Scientist* 24 Feb. 455/2 The process is called 'spin polarisation by optical pumping'. **1968** M. S. Livingston *Particle Physics* vii. 138 If parity is not conserved in other weak interactions, it could lead to an asymmetry in the direction of emission of β rays from spin-polarized radioactive nuclei. **1980** *Nature* 17 Jan. 248/1 One way of producing spin-polarised electrons is to take a storage ring, fill it with electrons or positrons, and leave for an hour or so. **1930** Pauling & Goudsmit *Struct. Line Spectra* iv. 53 It seems to be sufficient to give all electrons the same rotation, so that they have the angular momentum $sh/2\pi$, with *s*, the spin quantum number, always 1/2. **1964** J. W. Linnett *Electronic Struct. Molecules* i. 9 Since each spatial orbital is defined by the three quantum numbers *n*, *l* and *m*, this is equivalent to saying that each orbital can accommodate two electrons, and these only if they have different spin quantum numbers. **1934** H. E. White *Introd. Atomic Spectra* xii. 186 (*heading*) Spin-spin-, or ss-coupling. **1936** *Proc. R. Soc.* A. CLV. 641 This degeneracy can only be removed by an external magnetic field or by the spin-spin interaction between the ions. **1978** Spin-spin [see *spin-lattice* above]. **1961** *Planetary & Space Sci.* IV. 262/2 Spin stabilization turned out to be one of the more difficult design problems encountered in the program. **1976** M. H. Kaplan *Mod. Spacecraft Dynamics & Control* iv. 124 The use of spin stabilization in this orbit..was seen as a means of achieving the..mission at an early date. **1956** *Spaceflight* I. 19/1 The satellite..was intended to be spin-stabilized so that one hemisphere..always faced the Sun. **1976** M. H. Kaplan *Mod. Spacecraft Dynamics & Control* iv. 124 The concept of a spin-stabilized, 24-hour satellite was first proposed by the Hughes Aircraft Company in the fall of 1959. **1956** *Physical Rev.* CIV. 488/1 If the two spin states are equally abundant, this indication implies that the average neutron width is not the same in each state. **1947** A. Pope *Wind-Tunnel Testing* i. 11 The vertical tunnels for testing parachutes differ from the spin tunnels in that they require an even velocity front instead of the dish-shaped front required for the spin tunnel. **1959** F. D. Adams *Aeronaut. Dict.* 158/1 The air speed in the spin tunnel may be kept equal to the rate of descent of a tested model, causing the model, while spinning, to remain at a given height relative to the observer. **1882** Spin-vector [in Dict., sense 2]. **1899** C. J. Joly in W. R. Hamilton *Elem. Quaternions* (ed. 2) I. III. ii. 492 This vector γ has been called the spin-vector of the function ϕ. **1948** *Physical Rev.* LXXIII. 415/1 The integral Lorentz transformations are represented by exactly those spin transformations which, together with their inverse, map integral spinvectors into integrals pinvectors. **1981** *Sci. Amer.* Apr. 47/3 A particle with one-half quantum of intrinsic spin can have only two possible orientations; in the simplest case, where the particle is in motion, the spin vector can point either in the same direction the particle is moving or in the opposite direction. **1936** *Proc. R. Soc.* A. CLV. 644 For long waves one can carry out the transition to a continuum in the same way as Bloch did in his theory of 'spin waves'. **1953** *Rev. Mod. Physics* XXV. 235/2 The rf magnetic field excites spin waves with wave numbers in the range 1 to 10^6 cm^{-1}. **1973** *Sci. Amer.* Jan. 88/3 Waves produced by oscillations of magnetic moment in ferromagnetic and antiferromagnetic materials (spin waves) generate quasiparticles called magnons.

spin, *sb.*[2] (Earlier example.)

1842 C. Ridley *Let.* Mar. in *Cecilia* (1958) vii. 90 Mrs. Dixon, a good lady..who was sitting in a very tidy, very hot room with two old spins as companions.

spin, *v.* Add: **I. 2. a.** (Examples relating to man-made fibres.)

1899 *Jrnl. Soc. Arts* 8 Dec. 62/2 The solution of gelatine must be coloured to the required shade before being spun. **1921** T. Woodhouse tr. *Foltzer's Artif. Silk* 23 This solution..is conducted or spun through special capillary tubes. **1974** *Encycl. Brit. Macropædia* VII. 258/2 Acetate is dry spun by extruding acetone solutions of cellulose acetate into hot air.

c. (Examples relating to man-made fibres.)

1899 *Jrnl. Soc. Arts* 8 Dec. 63/2 If too much water is present the collodion will not be tenacious and therefore will not spin. **1963** A. J. Hall *Textile Sci.* ii. 50 If a suitable proportion of opaque white titanium dioxide pigment is added to the viscose solution just before it is spun into filaments, these can be produced with a lower lustre or even be matt.

3. a. (Examples relating to man-made fibres.)

1891 *Jrnl. Soc. Chem. Industry* 30 Apr. 359/1 This invention relates to the process and apparatus for spinning artificial silk from nitro-cellulose. **1973** *Materials & Technol.* VI. iv. 292 Dry spinning. This method is used to spin filaments from syrups which can be prepared by dissolving the fibre-forming materials in a suitable solvent.

II. 10. c. *Cricket.* Of a ball: to travel through the air with spin (Spin *sb.*[1] 2 c).

1851 J. Pycroft *Cricket Field* ix. 174 Clarke is not conscious of any attempt to make his ball spin or twist: a certain action has become habitual to him. **1970** N. Cardus *Full Score* 120 Mailey would tell me how much he revelled in the 'feel' of a ball spinning from his fingers. **1980** *Cricketer International* Apr. 83/3 Hollies..came up to bowl the next ball. It neither spun nor twisted in the air but drifted up and then down in a graceful parabola.

d. *Aeronaut.* Of an aircraft or its pilot: to perform or undergo a spin (*spin *sb.* 2 d).

1914 *Aeroplane* 1 July 17/2 If a 'scout' started to spin round its own nose it would never come into control again. **1918** J. M. Grider *War Birds* (1927) 66, I am going up to ten thousand [feet] and shut off and spin down and see what happens. **1931** C. D. Barnard *Learning to Fly* 151 Only a stalled aeroplane will spin—in other words when the machine is no longer airborne. **1952** *Technical Rep. Aeronaut. Res. Committee 1943* II. 755 The model usually spins more steeply and recovers from the spin more easily than the aeroplane.

e. Of a motor clutch: to continue to revolve after being disengaged.

1918 *Dyke's Automobile Encycl.* (ed. 7) 662/1 When a clutch spins, when thrown out of engagement, it is difficult to shift gears. **1928** *Motor Man.* (ed. 27) 57 The flange..is brought into contact with the stop, which acts as a brake and prevents the cone or plate spinning. **1965** D. Kaberry *Ford Corsair* viii. 53/1 If the clutch is spinning, difficulty will be experienced in engaging gear, particularly from a standstill.

11. a. Fig. phr. *to spin one's wheels* (U.S. colloq.), to mark time, to do nothing productive.

1960 *Wall St. Jrnl.* 15 Mar. 1 'We're just sitting here spinning our wheels,' says a disgruntled Naval aviator in California. **1974** *Evening Herald* (Rock Hill, S. Carolina) 19 Apr. 4/1 The Selective Service System has, in fact, done little but spin its wheels for the past 14 months.

e. *Cricket.* Of a bowler: to impart spin to (a ball) on delivery; to cause (the ball) to break after pitching.

1904 *Westm. Gaz.* 21 May 3/1 He can spin the ordinary left-hander's break-back. **1920** D. J. Knight in P. F. Warner *Cricket* 49 Rhodes and Woolley..seem to spin the ball in such a way that it gets straight up from the pitch in quite a different manner. **1960** [see *cut *v.* 31 a].

f. To make (an aircraft) perform a spin (*spin *sb.* 2 d).

1918 J. M. Grider *War Birds* (1927) 87 Then Ortmeyer ..spun a Camel into the ground and killed himself. **1928** O. Stewart *Aerobatics* 13 Machines fitted with Handley-Page automatic slots are extremely difficult to spin. **1952** *Technical Rep. Aeronaut. Res. Committee 1943* II. 766 The aircraft was spun from 28,000 ft., one 2½-turn spin to the left being carried out and two 2½-turn spins to the right.

g. = *spin-dry *v.* Also *absol.*

1959 *Which?* Aug. 92/1 Tumbler driers are intended to take washing that has either been wrung or spun to a half-dry state. **1966** D. V. Davis *New Domestic Encycl.* (ed. 2) iii. 127 If you spin a minimum-iron fabric while it is hot you are much more likely to press in creases. **1969** K. J. Mills *Washing Wisdom* vi. 98 Hook the outlet pipe over the sink. Spin for 15–20 seconds.

h. To play (a gramophone record).

1965 *Listener* 23 Dec. 1036/3 If he will dust off his old Plum Label HMV 78..and spin it, he will hear Gertrude Lawrence very distinctly saying to Noël Coward: 'Strange how potent cheap music is!' **1966** T. Pynchon *Crying of Lot 49* v. 140 She sat alone..listening to Mucho's colleague Rabbit Warren spin records.

13*. spin down: a. *trans. Biol.* To centrifuge so as to cause the separation of components.

1947 Ackerman & Regato *Cancer* xiv. 817 The fluid is spun down and sectioned. **1965** *Proc. Nat. Acad. Sci.* LIV. 400 A unit of blood was drawn into a heparin receiving pack and spun down slowly for 15–20 min. **1978** *Sci. Amer.* Dec. 30/2 If the unbonded cells are then spun down into a mixed-up mass and given fluid containing antibiotics and the right salts, new hydras form in a few days.

b. *intr. Astr.* Of a rotating body, esp. a star: to rotate more slowly, usu. because of decreasing angular momentum. Also *trans.*

1967 *Nature* 24 June 1297/2 The boundary layer suction causes a slow internal motion which stretches vortex lines and spins down the solar interior. *Ibid.* 1299/1 The region itself spins down quickly. **1976** *Sci. News* 30 Oct. 280 This pulsar is spinning down so slowly that when the effects of its motion across the sky on its apparent (to us) spin rate are considered, it may actually be spinning up from the point of view of someone riding along with it. **1979** *Nature* 29 Feb. 602/2 Any loss of radiation from the region will transport vast quantities of angular momentum away from the rotating body. The reaction back on the body itself will cause it to spin down.

13. spin off: a.** *trans.* To throw off by or as if by centrifugal force in spinning; freq. *fig.*, esp. (*a*) *U.S. Comm.*, to distribute (stock of a new company) to shareholders of a parent company; to create (a company) in this way; (*b*) to produce as a by-product, side-effect, or indirect benefit.

1957 *N.Y. Times* 9 June F1/3 Right now, there is considerable speculation that du Pont will 'spin off' its G.M. stock—that is, give it to its own stockholders in the form of a dividend. **1959** *Wall St. Jrnl.* 20 May 1/5 A subsidiary set up in early 1950 to rent out space in an engineering firm's new building was spun off in December, 1954. **1964** *Science* 29 May 1113 The Systems Development Corporation (SDC) was 'spun off' by RAND in 1956 to help specifically with design and programming for the first computerized air defense system. **1969** *Physics Bull.* June 215/2 If..pulsars are neutron stars,..then these could rotate at up to 10^3 Hz; they would 'spin off' electrons (or plasma) which would be accelerated in the star's magnetic field. **1969** *Wall St. Jrnl.* 3 July 4/2 The publicly owned company then 'spins off' those shares to its holders, who, in turn, often sell the shares to other traders. **1972** *Real Estate Rev.* Winter 5/2 A black who has invested his savings in a commercial or residential venture is not permitted..to parlay small investments into big ones by spinning them off through refinancing vehicles. **1972** *Publishers Weekly* 4 Dec. 35/1 From the file, the publisher can now produce updated editions with minimum effort, and can spin off subsidiary products as well. **1974** *Nature* 29 Mar. 459/2 Several papers have already been spun off from discussions and presentations at the CETI conference. **1977** *Time* 10 Jan. 47/3 Tandy Corp. has spun off most of its other businesses into separate companies chaired by Charles Tandy. **1979** *Daily Tel.* 15 Jan. 5/6 'Softly, Softly' was spun off 'Z Cars' and no one complained about that.

b. *intr.* To be thrown or move off by or as if by centrifugal force in spinning; usu. *fig.*

1969 *N.Y. Rev. Books* 16 Jan. 33/2 (Advt.), More interesting, however, is the way in which the material is organized to allow the class or individuals to spin-off into the study of related problems. **1969** *Sci. Jrnl.* Nov. 74 People have claimed..that space is a great thing because all the technology evolved will ultimately spin-off to the commercial market place. **1971** *New Scientist* 4 Mar. 488/1 These small companies specialising in technologically advanced products have 'spun off' largely from powerful local universities. **1971** *Daily Tel.* (Colour Suppl.) 6 Aug. 12/4 This prestige spins off to make Europeans more and more rail conscious.

13*. spin out:** *intr.* Of a vehicle: to skid round out of control. *N. Amer. slang.*

1954 *Amer. Speech* XXIX. 102 Last Sunday some car spun out and hit five parked cars. **1971** M. Tak *Truck Talk* 150 *Spin out*, to lose traction on a slippery road.

13**. spin up:** *Astr.* Of a rotating body, esp. a star: to rotate more quickly because of a gain in angular momentum or a redistribution of matter. Also *trans.*

1967 *Nature* 24 June 1299/1 If the interior were rotating at the rapid rate suggested by Dicke, the convective envelope would be spun up to this rate in a very short time. **1974** *Ibid.* 29 Nov. 366/1 As the Sun evolves, its rotating core gets smaller while its outer part spins up. **1976** [see sense 13* b above]. **1978** *Nature* 16 Feb. 635/1 Before the neutron star starts to accrete and spin up..it spends a comparatively long time being spun down in the weak stellar wind of its companion. **1979** *Ibid.* 11 Jan. 116/1 The neutron star would be spun up in the process.

spina. 1. *spina bifida*: substitute for def.: A congenital malformation of widely varying severity in which there is a failure of one or more vertebræ to surround completely the meninges and spinal cord, usu. with effects on spinal cord function. (Further examples.) [mod.L. (N. Tulpius *Observationes Medicæ* (1641) III. 233, 235).]

1853 J. Erichsen *Science & Art of Surgery* xliv. 631 Spina bifida may be met with in any part of the vertebral column. **1885** *Trans. Clin. Soc. London* XVIII. 361 Lastly, this examination serves to complete the refutation of the view..that spina bifida in the great majority of cases is due to a dropsy of the central canal of the cord. **1887** *Lancet* 2 July 4/2 The term 'spina bifida occulta' is applied to a defect in the arches of the vertebræ such as occurs in the commoner forms of spina bifida, but no tumour or cyst appears externally. The deformity is, however, accompanied by some remarkable external conditions. **1965** E. D. Smith *Spina Bifida* i. 5/1 In 1875, Virchow, who introduced the term 'spina bifida occulta', used it to describe a spina bifida in association with lumbosacral hypertrichosis. **1966** [see *meningo-myelocele* s.v. *meningo-]. **1974** Passmore & Robson *Compan. Med. Stud.* III. xxxvi. 9/1 Spina bifida is an incomplete vertebral arch. When this bony defect is covered with skin and fascia it is usually symptomless, and is called spina bifida occulta.

spinach. Add: Now also with pronunc. (spi·nėtʃ). **3. b.** Nonsense, rubbish. *U.S. colloq.* (now *rare*).

[**1928** C. Rose in *New Yorker* 8 Dec. 27/2 (*caption*) 'It's broccoli dear.' 'I say it's spinach, and I say the hell with it.'] **1929** J. P. McEvoy *Hollywood Girl* xiii. 205 It's a flop and then I says to him, in other words I say it's spinach and I say to hell with it. **1933** E. Hawes (*title*) Fashion is spinach. **1934** A. Woollcott *While Rome Burns* 304 This..reticence..will..be described by certain temperaments as..good taste.'.. I say it's spinach. **1950** R. Bissell *Stretch on River* xxi. 207 'It's a transferral of intent. It's a result of childhood trauma. It's Oedipus denial,' said my sister-in-law, who was beautiful, thank god, so you could put up with this spinach.

4. spinach beet = *silver beet* s.v. *silver *sb.* and *a.* 21 e; (later examples); **spinach-green,** (*a*) a dark green vegetable dye made from spinach; (*b*) a dark green colour; also *attrib.* or as *adj.*; **spinach jade** (see quot. 1964); also *attrib.*

1885 W. Robinson tr. *Vilmorin-Andrieux's Veg. Garden* 279 The leaves of the Common White Leaf-Beet, or Spinach Beet, may be cut for use even earlier. **1978** *Times* 17 July 14/3 The experts recommend growing Swiss chard, otherwise known as spinach beet. **1845** E. Acton *Mod. Cookery* xx. 508 (*heading*) Spinach green, for colouring sweet dishes. **1861** Mrs. Beeton *Bk. Househ. Managem.* 250 (*heading*) Spinach green for colouring various dishes... Pick and wash the spinach free from dirt, and pound the leaves in a mortar to extract the juice; [etc.]. **1896** [in Dict.]. **1937** *Burlington Mag.* June 300/2 A fine example of the bold relief of the K'ang-hsi period is a bowl of spinach-green nephrite. **1943** R. Godden *Rungli-Rungliot* 4 The engine..was painted a spinach-green. **1968** 'J. Ross' *Diminished by Death* xvii. 163 A figured silk confection in spinach green. **1975** *Times* 31 May 7/2 His former employers ought to be spinach-green with envy. **1980** *Catal. Fine Chinese Ceramics* (Sotheby, Hong Kong) 210 A spinach-green jade covered censer, raised on tripod supports. **1958** W. Willetts *Chinese Art* I. ii. 61 Siberian jade has a rather distinctive appearance owing to the presence of small particles of black graphite embedded in the stone, which leads the Chinese to call it 'spinach jade'. **1964** M. Medley *Handbk. Chinese Art* 108/2 *Spinach jade*, in Chinese *po-ts'ai-yü*; a nephrite from Siberia characterised by black flecks of graphite. **1976** 'M. Delving' *China Expert* xii. 158 Mei was wearing a *ch'i pao* of dark grey silk..fastened up to the neck with spinach jade buttons.

spinachy (spi·nedʒi, -ɛtʃi), *a.* [f. Spinach + -y¹.] Characteristic or suggestive of spinach.

1950 O. Nash *Family Reunion* (1951) 18 So spinach was too spinachy For Leonardo da Vinaci. **1981** P. Theroux *Mosquito Coast* xv. 191 Tiptoeing through this spinachy swamp on duckboards.

spinal, *a.* Add: **1. b.** *spinal puncture* or *tap*: the insertion of a needle into the subarachnoid space of the spine, usu. in the lumbar region, so that cerebrospinal fluid may be withdrawn or something introduced.

1896 *Brit. Med. Jrnl.* Suppl. 4 Jan. 1/3 Only a few drops of fluid could be obtained by spinal puncture. **1919** A. Levinson *Cerebrospinal Fluid* i. 25 Corning, who was the first to use spinal puncture, employed an operation that was fraught with danger to the cord. **1972** Noback & Demarest *Nervous System* iv. 35 Some CSF is withdrawn and replaced by air which acts as a contrast medium. The air is introduced by passing a needle either directly into the ventricle or between the lower two lumbar vertebrae (spinal tap) into the lumbar cistern. **1979** *Sci. Amer.* Aug. 66/3 He underwent at least 48 spinal taps, three air encephalograms and numerous myelograms. **1980** K. E. Moyer *Neuroanatomy* xii. 36/2 In a spinal tap, or spinal puncture, the needle is always introduced into the subarachnoid space below the termination of the spinal cord itself.

3. (Further examples.)

1884 *Queen* 9 Feb. 132/2 (Advt.), Partial paralysis. Spinal curvature,..constipation, corpulence, &c. **1976** J. Blackburn *Face of Lion* viii. 54 A cripple with one leg longer than the other and a pronounced spinal curvature.

5. b. *spinal reflex*, a reflex involving the spinal cord but not the brain.

1898 *Phil. Trans. R. Soc.* B. CXC. 141 In the Dog and Cat the spinal reflex movements are more forcible. **1924** *Jrnl. Physiol.* LVIII. 411 Shivering to cold cannot be produced as a spinal reflex. **1978** *Brain Res.* CXLII. 431 Stimulation of all three segmental nerves simultaneously produced up to a 100% increase in size of the spinal reflex.

6. Also of a seat or carriage: designed to support the spine. Now *Hist.*

1884 *Queen* 16 Feb. 189/2 (Advt.), Leveson's Improved Invalid's Carriage... Adjustable Spinal Couches. **1900** *Illustr. London News* 25 Aug. 291/2 (Advt.), Adjustable Bath Chair or Spinal Carriage. **1917** *Harrods Gen. Catal.* 1038 A very easy and comfortable Bath Chair and Spinal Carriage Combined, enabling a person to take outdoor exercise in a sitting, reclining, or horizontal position. **1973** *Times* 7 May 17/7 Many years ago I travelled in a spinal carriage every few weeks from Selby to Leeds and back in the guard's van.

6*. *Physiol.* **a.** Involving the spine as containing a major part of the central nervous system: *spinal anæsthesia, analgesia,* anæsthesia, analgesia induced by an injection into the spine (see quot. 1938); *spinal block* (*a*) an obstruction to the flow of the cerebro-spinal fluid; (*b*) spinal anæsthesia or analgesia; *spinal shock*, a temporary flaccid paralysis and loss of reflexes in some muscles that may follow an injury to the spine, the ones affected being those whose nerves come from a point in the spinal cord below the site of the injury.

1885 *N.Y. Med. Jrnl.* XLII. 483/2 (*heading*) Spinal anaesthesia and local medication of the cord. **1912** *Jrnl. Amer. Med. Assoc.* 23 Nov. 1859/1 There are practically no contraindications to the employment of spinal analgesia. **1938** Maxson & Babcock *Spinal Anesthesia* i. 1 Spinal anesthesia is the term most commonly used... It is technically correct when all the sensory faculties—touch, temperature and muscle sense, as well as pain—are abolished in the affected region. Spinal analgesia is the correct technical term when pain sense alone is abolished without the loss of the epicritical faculties. The distinction between the two terms, however, is rarely made. **1974** Lichtiger & Moya *Introd. Pract. Anesthesia* xv. 152 Tetracaine is the most commonly used drug for spinal anesthesia. **1976** D. D. Moir *Obstetric Anaesthesia & Analgesia* vii. 209 Low spinal analgesia is eminently suited to the performance of forceps delivery. **1928** *Arch. Neurol. & Psychiatry* XIX. 613 The compression of the veins of the neck..is used most often in spinal lesions with level symptoms in order to determine whether a 'spinal block' is present. **1976** D. D. Moir *Obstetric Anaesthesia & Analgesia* vii. 215 A low spinal block creates a tranquil patient, free of all pain and operating conditions are excellent. **1898** *Phil. Trans. R. Soc.* B. CXC. 134 Goltz's descriptions of spinal shock are masterly, but they refer entirely to the Dog, and to transection below the middle of the back. **1962** D. D. Bonnycastle in Keele & Smith *Assessment of Pain in Man & Animals* 235 It was felt that these animals might still be exhibiting some degree of spinal shock, and therefore we prepared a colony of chronic spinal rats. **1978** *Exper. Neurol.* IX. 16 Spinal shock is caused by the lack of excitatory input from the brain.

b. Used to describe an animal whose spine has been severed from its brain.

1900 C. S. Sherrington in E. A. Schäfer *Text-bk. Physiol.* II. 818 The spinal frog, when placed on its back, does not, as a rule, right itself. **1917** *Brain* XL. 230 'Spinal man' cannot stand, and shows no primary extensor activity. **1962** [see prec. sense]. **1971** *Sci. Amer.* Aug. 75/2 Sherrington found for example, that a spinal dog would withdraw a leg that received a sharp poke and would simultaneously brace the opposite leg to assume the weight removed from the withdrawn leg.

spinar (spi·nāɹ). *Astr.* [f. *spin*(*ning st*)*ar*, after *quasar, *pulsar.] A hypothetical, supermassive, rapidly rotating celestial object which may be located in the nuclei of some active galaxies and quasars, and which could help to account for the huge energy output of quasars.

1971 Morrison & Cavaliere in D. J. K. O'Connell *Nuclei of Galaxies* 487 By spinars we mean a class of bodies storing a considerable fraction of their total energy in a single, continuous degree of freedom—rotation... Pulsars are a very special subclass of spinars. **1977** *Astron. & Astrophysics* LVI. 166/2 We will consider..a supermassive oblique rotator (SOR) having solid-body rotation and quasi-dipole magnetic field. In the 'cold' version such a rotator coincides with a 'spinar' or a 'giant pulsar' proposed by Morrison. **1978** *Nature* 28 Sept. 282/1 The nonthermal radiation of a spinar can in some circumstances far exceed the thermal (Eddington-limited) component.

spindle, *sb.* Add: **I. 4. b.** Delete latter part of def., and transfer quot. 1899 to sense 4 d below.

c. *Cytology.* A bipolar configuration of fibres to which the chromosomes become attached by their centromeres at metaphase of mitosis before being pulled towards its poles; cf. *spindle fibre*, sense 17 below.

1878 *Q. Jrnl. Microsc. Sci.* XVIII. 114 The portion of the spindle which remains in the egg after the formation of the second polar cell reconstitutes itself into a nucleus. **1927** Haldane & Huxley *Animal Biol.* ii. 58 A star-shaped figure of radiating fibres is seen in the cell. This divides into two, forming a spindle-shaped set of fibres with a radiating 'star' at each end, and the chromosomes arrange themselves where the fibres from the two stars meet, in the centre of the spindle. **1971** *Sci. Amer.* Oct. 77/3 The action of the mitotic spindle in pulling the chromosomes apart when a cell divides.

d. *Anat.* [tr. G. *spindel* (W. Kühne 1863, in *Arch. f. path. Anat. u. Physiol.* XXVII. 520).] = *muscle spindle* s.v. *muscle *sb.* 3 d.

1894 *Jrnl. Physiol.* XVII. 238 The spindles have been studied by Golgi (1880); Golgi's definition of them is 'bundles of incompletely developed muscle-fibres, surrounded by a special sheath, and to be found in muscles at every period of growth'. **1930** Maximow & Bloom *Text-bk. Histol.* xiv. 276 The muscle fibers of the spindle are approximately half as thick as the ordinary muscle fibers. **1962** *Phil. Trans. R. Soc.* B. CCXLV. 82 All spindles contain two distinct types of intrafusal muscle fibre, 'nuclear bag fibres' and 'nuclear chain fibres', which differ in structure and innervation. **1974** [see **muscle spindle*].

e. *Anat.* Any of numerous small sensory organs within tendons and aponeuroses which consist of a spindle-shaped bundle of tendon fibres containing the branching endings of a nerve and enclosed in a capsule; a neurotendinous spindle; = *tendon organ, spindle* s.v. *tendon c.

1896 E. L. Bilstein tr. *Stöhr's Text-bk. Histol.* ii. 115 The medullated nerves of tendons terminate in part in a close plexus of gray nerve-fibers, and in part in tendon-spindles. **1901**, etc. [see *neurotendinous* adj. s.v. *neuro-]. **1905** J. S. Ferguson *Normal Histol.* ix. 138 Nerve fibres enter the spindle and give off several medullated branches which run between the tendon bundles near the axis of the spindle. **1954** T. L. Peele *Neuroanat. Basis Clinical Neurol.* xix. 420/1 Neurotendinous spindles are usually present near the musculotendinous junction. **1966** T. S. & C. R. Leeson *Histology* xx. 440/2 Neuromuscular spindles lie in muscle... Neurotendinous spindles are similar and are located in tendons and aponeuroses near their junctions with muscle.

f. *Med.* A configuration seen in an electroencephalogram (see quot. 1935).

1935 A. L. Loomis et al. in *Science* 14 June 597/2 The amplitude [of the waves] builds regularly to a maximum and then falls regularly so that we have designated these 'spindles', because of their appearance in the record. **1952** *Confinia Neurologica* XII. 73 Spindles are most prominent in the thalamus of cats under barbiturates. **1965** *Math. in Biol. & Med.* (Med. Res. Council) iv. 171 Often exact identification of the maxima and minima of the spindles can be difficult. **1983** *Brit. Med. Jrnl.* 12 Nov. 1401/1 A slowing of the alpha, concurrent alpha and theta, and beta spindles are found during relaxation and on the borders of sleep.

II. 7. c. A spindle moulder (see sense *17).

1920 F. T. Hill *Pract. Aeroplane Constr.* 108 This is known as a French spindle, and its cutting action, in order to form the recesses, is shown in the enlarged view on the right. **1925** W. J. Blackmur *How to work Spindle Moulder* iii. 29 In working a spindle there are three kinds of cutters—those used on the square block, those used with the slotted cutters, and those used on the French spindle.

9. a. (Further examples.)

1824 'A. Singleton' *Lett. from South & West* 82 They [*sc.* Virginians] also call, what we [*sc.* New Englanders] call the spindle, the tassel. **1871** *Amer. Naturalist* V. 245 The corn..sent forth a new tassel or spindle.

12. a. (Later example.)

1904 *Hartford* (Connecticut) *Courant* 19 Aug. 13 What this man was really doing was simply placing a spindle on Magazine Rock.

III. 16. *spindle-shaped.*

1859 D. Bunce *Travels with Dr. Leichhardt* 15 Blue spindle-shaped fruits or berries. **1927** [see sense 4 c above]. **1966** J. S. Cox *Illustr. Dict. Hairdressing & Wigmaking* 141/2 Spindle-shaped curler, a rounded rod, tapering towards each end.

17. spindle-back, used *attrib.* to designate a chair with a back consisting of framed cylindrical bars; **spindle-berry,** the bright red fruit of the spindle-tree, *Euonymus europæus*; **spindle cell** *Med.* and *Biol.*, a narrow, elongated cell; *spec.* one in the blood of some lower vertebrates analogous to the platelet in mammals; freq. *attrib.* (cf. *spindle-celled,* sense 16 in Dict.); **spindle fibre** *Cytology*, any of the microtubular strands which form the visible structure of a spindle (sense 4 c above); **spindle hour,** an hour during which a spindle is involved in spinning, used as a unit of measurement; **spindle machine, moulder,** a woodworking machine used to shape mouldings, in which one or more cutters are carried on a spindle; so **spindle moulding; spindle oil,** a light distillation product of petroleum, used for lubrication esp. of high-speed machinery.

1896 *Heal & Son Catal.: Bedroom Furnit.* 156 Solid Oak Spindleback Rush-Seat Chair..£0 19 6. **1918** *Ibid.: Cottage Furnit.* 18 'Spindle Back' Arm Chair, stained oak colour..28/–. **1937** *Times* 15 Nov. 19/4 One could repeat this story in respect of the spindleback chairs made in the West of England from the Solway Firth to Herefordshire. **1959** G. Savage *Antique Collector's Handbk.* 126 The Lancashire spindle-back chair is similar in many ways to the ladder-back. **1921** *19th Cent.* June 1039 The dying glory of bracken, oak, birch, mountain-ash and spindle-berry. **1923** *Daily Mail* 12 Sept. 15/4 Pink spindle berries are lovely in a pewter mug. **1950** J. Brooke *Goose Cathedral* viii. 167 The hedges were hung with a multitude of spindleberries—lurid purple bursting into fiery orange. **1878** Spindle-cell [in Dict., sense 15 b]. **1901** A. P. Ohlmacher in Hektoen & Riesman *Text-bk. Path.* I. 200 It [*sc.* round-celled sarcoma] grows more rapidly, and is generally softer and more malignant than the spindle-cell sarcoma. **1905** J. S. Ferguson *Normal Histol.* iii. 34 In the denser forms of mature connective tissue..the connective tissue cells lose their typical embryonal stellate form and become somewhat fusiform; they are then known as the spindle cells of connective tissue. *Ibid.* vi. 81 Confusion..has arisen from the supposed analogy of the true blood platelets of human blood with certain other structures found in the blood of the lower vertebrates, especially the 'spindle-cells' of amphibians. **1949** A. S. Romer *Vertebrate Body* xiii. 427 In most nonmammalian vertebrates the thrombocytes take the form of spindle cells—small, oval, pointed structures with a central nucleus. **1959** W. Andrew *Textbk. Compar. Histol.* ix. 371 Spindle cells are conspicuous and probably should be thought of as fusiform lymphocytoid cells rather than platelet-forming elements. **1971** T. J. Hara in Hoar & Randall *Fish Physiol.* V. iv. 88 Aside from the taste buds, specialized epidermal 'spindle' cells were found on the head and body of minnows and various teleost fishes. **1976** *Path. Ann.* XI. 214 (*caption*) Spindle cell variant of thymic carcinoid tumor. **1878** *Q. Jrnl. Microsc. Sci.* XVIII. 229 The spindle-fibres are identical with the stellate rays. **1974** *Encycl. Brit. Micropædia* VI. 946/1 In anaphase the chromatid pairs separate and are pulled to opposite ends of the cell by the spindle fibres. **1930** *Times* 24 Mar. 23/5 Mill activity in the cotton growing states, measured by spindle hours, established a high record. **1970** P. R. Lord *Spinning in '70's* 11 Production per spindle hour has been increased by raising spindle speeds. **1902** G. Ellis *Mod. Pract. Joinery* xxiii. 364 *Spindle machine*, an irregular moulding machine in which the cutters are fixed at the end of a vertical spindle which projects through the table. **1915** *Machine Woodworker* 15 Nov. 15/2 Running moulds from thicknessed boards on spindle machine may do if it is a special type of mould. **1912** *Ibid.* 15 July 17/2 A spindle moulder being a machine that has to do a large variety of work, the stock of cutters should be large. **1925** W. J. Blackmur *How to work Spindle Moulder* i. 11 As the spindle moulder is used for working regular sections upon edges of various shaped pieces of wood it is best to place it close to the band saw. **1965** F. L. Dunsmore *Technique Woodworking Machinery* II. i. 14 No machine has a greater selection of cutter heads than the spindle moulder. **1979** *Building* Dec. 105/3 Planing, thicknessing, sawing, routing and spindle moulding. **1887** B. J. Crew *Pract. Treat. Petroleum* ix. 316 Spindle oils. Distillers of residuum usually divide their products into three classes... The third..product constitutes the stock for spindle and machinery oils. **1931** *Engineering* 2 Jan. 1/2 Oil PL will be recognised as a 'spindle oil', used only for lightly loaded high speed journals. **1977** *Lubricants Business* (Shell Internat. Petroleum Co.) 1 Refining of the distillates, which removes unsuitable components, produces lubricating oil fractions of the desired properties ranging from thin spindle oil to heavy cylinder oil.

Hence **spi·ndleless** *a.*, having no spindle or spindles.

1964 *Gloss. Letterpress Rotary Printing Terms (B.S.I.)* 7 *Spindleless reel stand*, a reel stand supporting the reel on free-running cones at each side of the reel. **1967** *Economist* 29 Apr. 459/3 There [*sc.* in Czechoslovakia] the BD 200 spindleless spinning unit has been developed; by next year it will be modified to run at 40,000 rpm as against the conventional spindle's 10,000.

spindle, *v.* Add: **5.** To recess and taper (a spar for an aeroplane's wing); to cut *out* (a recess) in a spar.

1918 *Aeronaut. Jrnl.* Feb. 44 Jigs for small parts should be so constructed that several pieces may be spindled at the same time. **1919** Pippard & Pritchard *Aeroplane Struct.* 201 Questions of strength determine the amount which can safely be spindled out. **1920** F. T. Hill *Pract. Aeroplane Constr.* v. 106 Having drilled the spar, the next operation will be to spindle out the recess. **1928** *Technical Rep. Aeronaut. Res. Committee 1926–7* 466 These specimens were first formed..with a length of 2 inches spindled to give a cross section geometrically similar to the fractured portion of the spar.

spindleage (spi·nd'lėdʒ). [f. Spindle *sb.* + -age.] The total number of cotton spindles in use at a given time and in a specified area.

1921 A. S. Wade *Cotton Spinning* 15 The loss o[f] spindleage due to the reduction of the working week. **1954** R. Robson et al. in A. F. W. Coulson *Man. Cotton Spinning* I. i. 6 By 1928 the number of spindles had risen to just over 165 million but this was to represent the peak world spindleage. **1972** C. H. Lee *Cotton Enterprise* ii. 16 The spindleage of the trade grew from 1·7 million to four or five million between the early 1780's and 1812.

spindled, *ppl. a.* Add: **3. b.** Of a spar or strut for an aeroplane wing: having been recessed and tapered. Also with *out*.

1919 S. Camm *Aeroplane Construction* iii. 23 This [steel] strut..is superior to the solid spindled strut..which possesses a tendency to buckle laterally. **1928** *Technical Rep. Aeronaut. Res. Committee 1926–7* 467 The fracture ran through part of the bolt hole and tended to follow a 'zig-zag' course on its way into the spindled portion. **1930** *Flight* 17 Jan. 119/1 The wing is of equally simple construction with two spindled-out spruce spars and light girder ribs.

spindling, (*vbl.*) *sb.* Add: **4.** The process of recessing and tapering a spar for an aeroplane wing. Also *attrib.*, as *spindling jig, machine.*

1918 *Aeronaut. Jrnl.* Feb. 40 In the spindling of spars the job should be placed in a jig having stops upon it. **1920** F. T. Hill *Pract. Aeroplane Constr.* v. 108 The base of the spindling jig. *Ibid.* 110 The only marking out required for spindling is the end of the recess. *Ibid.* 116 Flanges are grooved on the spindling machine with a jig.

5. *Med.* The occurrence of fairly regular alternating increases and decreases of amplitude in an electroencephalogram.

1963 *Electroencephalogr. & Clin. Neurophysiol.* XV. 766/2 This randomness can account for such characteristics as spindling without involving concepts of beating between alpha patterns. **1968** *Brit. Med. Bull.* XXIV. 257/1 Barnet and Lodge (1966) have averaged responses to 100 clicks or pure-tone bursts during deep sleep (high-voltage spindling in the EEG) in 22 infants.

spindly, *a.* Add: **3.** *Comb.*, as *spindly-legged, -stemmed* adjs.

1951 J. Cleary in Murdoch & Drake-Brockman *Austral. Short Stories* 434 The other boy and the two girls, the freckle-faced, spindly-legged..girls, are all working now. **1971** *Flying* Apr. 71/2 It was a big, spindly-legged beast. **1897** Spindly-stemmed [in Dict., see sense 1 a].

spin-down (spi·ndaun), *sb.* [f. Spin *v.* + Down *adv.*] A decrease in the speed of rotation of something.

1963 *Jrnl. Fluid Mechanics* XVII. 402 The initial angular velocity $\Omega_0 = 3{\cdot}668\ \text{sec}^{-1}$, and the final angular velocity $\Omega_1 = 3{\cdot}033\ \text{sec}^{-1}$. (This was a case of 'spin-down'.) **1967** *Astrophysical Jrnl. Lett.* CXLIX. L121 The 'spin-down' time of a cup of tea is approximately $(R^2/\nu\Omega)^{\frac{1}{2}}$, where R is the radius of the cup and Ω is the angular velocity of the tea. **1971** *New Scientist* 26 Aug. 452/2 The favourite explanation that decreases in period, or 'spin-ups', occur when starquakes take place in the deformed crust of the star seems to fall flat on its face when confronted with the discovery that the Crab pulsar, at least, also undergoes 'spin-downs'. **1977** *Astron. & Astrophysics* LX. 85/1 Braking by tidal torques and possibly magnetospheric friction can account for a spin-down of Venus within some 10^9 years.

spin-down (spindaun), *a.* *Physics.* [f. Spin *sb.*[1] + Down *a.*] Being or pertaining to a particle whose spin points downwards.

1965, etc. [see *spin-up *a.*].

spin-drier, -dryer (spindrəi·əɹ). Also without hyphen and as two words. [f. *spin-dry *v.*: cf. Drier, dryer.] A machine which removes excess water from washing by spinning it rapidly in a rotating perforated drum.

1939 *Archit. Rev.* LXXXV. 76/3 The laundry is all electric, and is equipped with a Rotary Washer and Spin Dryer, and Rotary Ironer, in which all the laundry of the house can be done without resort to clothes lines. **1948** *Sun* (Baltimore) 15 July 8 (Advt.), Be among the first to see the amazing new easy spindrier with automatic spin-rinse! **1958** *Observer* 2 Mar. 10/3 Spin-driers liberate housewives from the effort of wringing and pegging out clothes. **1959** G. Freeman *Jack would be Gentleman* vi. 114 We didn't have a spin dryer like you've got, only racks in the kitchen. **1967** *Spectator* 30 June 758/1 A canny Scot who salvaged Vat 69 filter pads and extracted whisky from them in his spin-drier was found to have done nothing illegal. **1972** J. Aiken *Died on Rainy Sunday* 12 The spin-dryer whirred to a halt.

spindrift. Add: **a.** Also *fig.* (example *attrib.*).

1946 Dylan Thomas *Deaths & Entrances* 36 Not for the proud man apart From the raging moon I write On these spindrift pages.

b. *transf.* Driving snow, sand, etc. Also *attrib.*

1961 Webster, *Spindrift*,..sand, dust, or snow driven before the wind like sea spray. **1971** C. Bonington *Annapurna South Face* xii. 147 At Camp V, the spindrift avalanches swished down all night, filling the platform, burying the tent. *Ibid.*, Cataracts of spindrift kept pouring over the cliffs above. **1972** D. Haston *In High Places* vii. 90 A spindrift avalanche had come right down the chute, filling up the tent sack and covering everything. ..This wasn't the first time we'd been buried in spindrift.

c. *Comb.*, as *spindrift-laden, -streaming* adjs.

1971 D. Haston in C. Bonington *Annapurna South Face* xvii. 214 Once again it was cold with snapping spindrift-laden wind. **1916** Blunden *Harbingers* 7 Or green and spindrift-streaming shelf of stone.

spin-dry (spindrəi·), *v.* Also **spin dry.** Inflected both as for Spin *v.* (*dry* taken as adj.) and Dry *v.* [f. Spin *v.* + Dry *v.* or Dry *a.*] *trans.* To remove excess water from (washing) by spinning it rapidly in a rotating perforated drum; to dry partially in a spin-drier. Also *absol.*

1927 *Sat. Even. Post* 19 Mar. 135 It takes the Savage [Washer & Dryer] just one-tenth the time to *spin-dry* the entire load *in its own tub.* **1951** *Good Housek. Home Encycl.* 304/1 The automatic type..will..spin-dry the clothes at a turn of the switch. **1958** *Observer* 2 Mar. 10/3 If clothes are spin-dried after soaking, much of their dirt goes out with the water. **1958** *Times* 2 June p. ix/5 Thus clothes can be boiled and then spun-dry ready for ironing. **1960** *Guardian* 15 Feb. 4/4 Finally, it [*sc.* a washing-machine] spins-dry. **1976** *Country Life* 22 Jan. 211/2 Give it a cool wash, however and spin dry if you like.

So **spi·n-dry** *sb.*; **spin-dry·ing** *vbl. sb.*

1932 *House Beautiful* Jan. 50/2 The newest models [of washing machines] include a drying feature known as the 'spin dry' or 'extractor'. *Ibid.* 51/1 If the 'spin dry' is to work efficiently, it must not be overloaded, and clothes should be evenly distributed. **1956** *Archit. Rev.* CXX. 346/1 Spin-drying considerably reduces the line-drying time as opposed to wringing. **1962** *Which?* Aug. 238/1 Too much spin drying can set creases in drip dry cottons. **1978** P. Porter *Cost of Seriousness* 36 When I start an allegro It's planned like those washing programmes Right through to the spin-dry.

spine, *sb.*[1] Add: **I. 5. c.** A tall mass of lava projecting upwards from the mouth of a volcano.

1903 *Amer. Jrnl. Sci.* CLXVI. 270 The ancient summit of the mountain [*sc.* Mont Pelée] has lost most of its former prominence above the rim of the crater, but within the old Caldera a cone has risen which overtops the surrounding walls and terminates in a spine rising hundreds of feet above the main mass of the new cone. **1954** W. D. Thornbury *Princ. Geomorphol.* xix. 500 The rapid growth of plug domes is further illustrated by one on Santa Maria volcano on Guatemala... It had a spine which attained a height of 66 meters. **1976** P. Francis *Volcanoes* iii. 124 Evidence of just how viscous the lavas are,..was provided by the great spine which was pushed up out of the vent of Mt Pelée, reaching over 300 metres in height.

II. 6. b. Also *fig.*

1912 Galsworthy *Inn of Tranquility* 189 The vice of drawing these distorted morals has permeated the Drama to its spine. **1977** *New Yorker* 9 May 126/2 A beauty called Laura..who is the spine of the place. **1977** P. Scupham *Hinterland* 44 Doors shake on their jambs: the spine of the house Thrills as the sprung wood quivers, and goes still. **1979** *Tucson Mag.* Mar. 8/2 No one cares or has the spine to sound off. **1981** F. Inglis *Promise of Happiness* i. 3 We try to say what some of the best books are like, so that we can hand them on... This expression of the gift relationship..gives spine and structure to this study.

9. b. The back of a book, that is, the part bearing the title, etc., which is visible when the book is standing on a shelf; also, the corresponding part of a dust-jacket or a shallow box.

1922 M. Sadleir *Vict. Bibliogr.* 14 Be wary of books in cloth which bear no publisher's imprint on the spine. **1931** *Publisher & Bookseller* 20 Feb. 345/2 The utility of having the selling price printed on the spine of a book jacket. **1952** V. Canning *House of Seven Flies* i. 24 He stared at the coloured spines of the books in the rack. **1962** A. Nisbett *Technique Sound Studio* vi. 113 Programme details are written..on the spine of the box in which it [*sc.* a tape] is kept. **1976** S. Brett *So much Blood* i. 16 Brown velvet upholstery and the leather spines of books gave the quality of an old sepia photograph.

III. 10. a. *spinebreaker*; *spine-wise* advb.

1851 H. Melville *Moby Dick* III. xlviii. 281 Launch me, spine-wise, on the sea. **1947** Dylan Thomas *Let.* 11 June (1966) 314 The hill to the nearest village is a spinebreaker.

11. spine-basher *Austral. slang*, a loafer; so **spine-bashing** *vbl. sb.* (and *pres. pple.*); **spine-bill**, insert after 'honey-eaters': of the genus *Acanthorhynchus*; (later examples); **spine-chiller, -freezer,** something (*rarely* someone) that inspires excitement and terror; *esp.* a horror or suspense story, film, etc.; **spine-chilling** *ppl. a.* and *vbl. sb.*, **-freezing** *ppl. a.*, inspiring excitement and terror, horrifying; **spine road**, a major road linking other important routes or points; **spine-thriller, -tingler**, something pleasurably frightening; *esp.* an exciting story, etc.; **spine-tingling** *ppl. a.*, pleasurably frightening or disturbing; spine-chilling; **spine wall** *Building* (see quot. 1963).

1946 R. Rivett *Behind Bamboo* 399 *Spinebasher*, one always on his back, always resting. **1976** *Sydney Morning Herald* 20 Mar. 14 The elbow-benders, spine-bashers, eternal babblers keep one ear to the loudspeakers, an ear to the ground. **1941** *Argus* (Melbourne) *Week-End Mag.* 15 Nov. 1/4 *Spine bashing*, having a rest; loafing. **1944** L. Glassop *We were Rats* 208 'She's sweet,' I said. 'Go and do some spine bashing.' **1966** G. W. Turner *Eng. Lang. in Austral. & N.Z.* vi. 135 Lying down and doing nothing, what the Australian calls *spinebashing*. **1911** A. E. Mack *Bush Days* 52 Spine-bills flashed by. **1977** *Daily News* (Perth, Austral.) 19 Jan. 11/2 Weighing only 10 grams the spinebill can put on an extra 10 per cent body weight in one day. **1940** *Amer. Speech* XV. 205/1 *Spine-chiller*, a mystery film or play. **1942** Berrey & Van den Bark *Amer. Thes. Slang* § 202/4 *Sensational story or book*,..spine chiller *or* tingler. **1957** *London Mag.* Aug. 59 *Elective Affinities* is a far more important novel than Walpole's *Castle of Otranto*, and yet there has only been one edition of it in the past hundred years, compared to the dozen or so of Walpole's unreadable spine-chiller. **1969** E. Lemarchand *Alibi for Corpse* xv. 189 Even now the idea of her..gives me the willies. And Twentyman was a spine-chiller. **1976** *Listener* 21 Oct. 509/2 The arrival of a mysterious stranger, murder, a dumb-struck child, suicide. This was a spine-chiller, and no mistake. **1946** 'M. Innes' *From London Far* i. ii. 20 A sweet and—as he hoped—wholly spine-chilling smile. **1958** *New Statesman* 25 Jan. 103/1 With unerring instinct H. G. Clouzot, the spine-chilling specialist of *The Wages of Fear* and *The Fiends*, has sought a new tension in Picasso. **1958** *Times Lit. Suppl.* 11 July 389/3 As an exercise in spine-chilling and blood-curdling, *Caves of Night* is masterly. **1960** H. Agar *Saving Remnant* v. 127 'What, still so many Jews?'—that spine-chilling comment. **1983** *Listener* 10 Feb. 16/3 She realised that I was retailing an antiquarian donnish history instead of the mildly spine-chilling ghost story she expected. **1960** Wodehouse *Jeeves in Offing* iii. 41 Mrs. Cream..worked in her room every afternoon on her new spine-freezer. **1961** —— *Ice in Bedroom* i. 9, I dipped into one of her products once, misled by the title into supposing it to be a spine-freezer. **1937** *Discovery* Dec. 373/1 The spine-freezing howl of the *kiret*. **1961** *Guardian* 3 Apr. 5/4 The spine-freezing wail of sirens. **1961** *New Left Rev.* July/Aug. 56/1 A spine road runs east–west between these blocks. **1971** *Guardian* 12 Oct. 28/4 Oxford city's consultants drew up an alternative for a spine road feeding into large car parks. **1912** *Maclean's Mag.* Nov. 135 (*heading*) Producing spine thrillers. How successful melodramas are furnished—some confessions about art of capitalizing spines. **1962** *Listener* 21 June 1085/3 It ranges over the whole field of spine-thrillers, from puppets to poisons. **1942** Spine tingler [see *spine-chiller* above]. **1978** *TV Times* 28 Jan.–3 Feb. 19/1 This week's *The South Bank Show* homes in on ..the best Shakespearian actor alive today. Also on view: little spine-tinglers from his *Henry V*, *Henry VI* and *Coriolanus*. **1955** E. Caldwell *Love & Money* 206 A spine-tingling historical romance. **1968** *Blues Unlimited* Dec. 4 John Lee's spine-tingling guitar. **1978** J. B. Hilton *Some run Crooked* xi. 118 He spoke the words quietly..and there was something spine-tingling about them. **1949** *Archit. Rev.* CV. 236 Construction is box-frame with continuous reinforced concrete slabs, and with load-bearing spine walls of reinforced concrete. **1963** *Gloss. Gen. Building Terms (B.S.I.)* 22 *Spine wall*, an internal loadbearing wall running in the direction of the main axis of a building or structure.

spinel. Add: **2. a.** The formula of the typical species is $MgAl_2O_4$. (Further examples.)

1953 F. H. Pough *Field Guide Rocks & Minerals* II. 141 Spinel, like corundum, is a mineral of metamorphosed limestones and low-silica pegmatites, and consequently it is commonly associated with corundum. **1977** A. HALLAM *Planet Earth* 137 The name spinel broadly refers to a group which includes the minerals magnetite and chromite. In a narrower sense, spinel is the magnesium aluminum oxide member of the group.

b. The general formula of the minerals is $A^{2+}B_2^{3+}O_4$, *spec.* where *B* is Al. The name is also applied to any of a large number of artificial minerals having similar structures. (Further examples.)

1944 C. PALACHE et al. *Dana's Syst. Min.* (ed. 7) I. 688 In addition to the natural spinels a considerable number of artificial spinels have been described, where *A* = Co, Cd, Cu and *B* = Co, Ti, Sn, V, Ga, In, Mn. One of the further complexities of composition in the artificial spinels is a tendency for substitution of *A* atoms for part of the *B* atoms of the formula, i.e., the formula may be written $BABX_4$ (as in the compounds $GaMgGaO_4$, etc.). **1967** D. H. MARTIN *Magnetism in Solids* i. 39 The two crystal types to which the most fully investigated ferrimagnetics belong are those known as 'spinels' and 'garnets'. **1974** D. M. ADAMS *Inorg. Solids* iii. 69 The structure of a spinel is conveniently described by a parameter γ which equals the fraction of A^{2+} in octahedral sites. Thus, for a 'normal' spinel, γ = 0, for an 'inverse' spinel, γ = 1. A random distribution of A^{2+} amongst the two groups of sites gives γ = 2/3.

c. *spinel structure*.

1944 C. PALACHE et al. *Dana's Syst. Min.* (ed. 7) I. 688 Another chemical feature of interest is the ability of artificial Mg, Al spinel to contain considerable excess of Al_2O_3 without impairment of the spinel structure. **1967** M. CHANDLER *Ceramics in Mod. World* vi. 178 Today most ferrites have spinel structures.

spineless, *a.* Add: Hence **spi·nelessly** *adv.*, **spi·nelessness.**

1920 *Chambers's Jrnl.* 18 Dec. 35/2 His spinelessness and low tastes. **1948** A. L. ROWSE *End of Epoch* 186 The spinelessness, the disastrous disunity of the liberal elements in Germany. **1960** *Middlesex Hospital Jrnl.* Jan.–Feb. 12/1 At interviews, the salesman applicant has to steer a course between spinelessness and cockiness. **1977** J. PORTER *Who the Heck is Sylvia?* xii. 110 Capitulating as spinelessly as usual, Miss Jones..unfastened her seat belt. **1981** CRAIG & CADOGAN *Lady Investigates* xi. 214 Gregory's vacillation..seems to be an example of the kind of spinelessness that he usually condemns in others.

spinet[1]. Add: **2.** *U.S.* In full *spinet piano.* A type of small piano.

1936 *Arts & Decoration* Jan. 30/1 The spinet pianos are inviting musical instruments. Their design, suitable to the modern apartment or small house, delights the decorator and the owner. **1937** *Étude* Dec. 803/3 In a few months manufacturers had worked out many refinements in the popular vertical pianos, which came to be known under the generic terms of 'consoles' or 'spinets'. **1970** W. APEL *Harvard Dict. Mus.* (ed. 2) 804/2 *Spinet,*..a piano with strings perpendicular to the keyboard (as in an upright piano) but with an indirect action. **1977** J. PHILIPS *Five Roads to Death* (1978) I. ii. 31 There was a little spinet piano in one corner.

spinifex. Insert in etym. after mod.L.: (Linnæus *Mantissa Plantarum* (1771) II. 163). **1.** For *Tricuspis* substitute '*Triodia* or *Plectrachne*'.

spinkie (spi·ŋki). *dial.* [f. SPINK *sb.*[1] + -IE.] = SPINK *sb.*[1] I.

1911 D. H. LAWRENCE *White Peacock* II. vii. 316 There are two or three robins' nests, and a spinkie's.

spinks (spiŋks). *Austral.* [f. SPINK *sb.*[1] + *-S[2].] = *Jacky Winter* s.v. *JACKY 3.

1945 BAKER *Austral. Lang.* xii. 211 The Brown Flycatcher is called..spinks. **1969** [see *Jacky Winter* s.v. *JACKY 3].

spinless (spi·nlės), *a.* [f. SPIN *sb.*[1] + -LESS.] Having no spin, or no tendency to spin.

1936 *Aeroplane* 22 Jan. 116/2 The plane must be totally different from anything on the market to-day. It must.. be spinless and viceless. **1951** *Physical Rev.* LXXXI. 282/2 (*heading*) On the Lamb shift for spinless electrons. **1966** *Nucl. Sci. Abstr.* XX. 1931/1 (*heading*) A fortran code for computing angular distributions, polarizations and transport cross sections of neutrons scattered by spinless targets. **1981** M. GELL-MANN in J. H. Mulvey *Nature of Matter* viii. 184 That theory should include.. the spinless particles we believe we need for spontaneous symmetry breaking.

spinnable, *a.* Add: (Further examples.)

1926 *Chambers's Jrnl.* 16 Oct. 726/1 The cotton fibres of spinnable length are removed..by machines called 'gins'. **1927** M. H. AVRAM *Rayon Industry* 186 Not every solution which possesses sufficient viscosity and is capable of being drawn into filaments is spinnable. **1967** A. ZIABICKI in H. F. Mark et al. *Man-Made Fibers* I. 6 There are known many spinnable liquids, such as honey and high-mineral oils, which nobody would consider fiber-forming.

Hence **spinnabi·lity**, the capacity for being spun; applied esp. to a solution from which a synthetic fibre may be drawn.

1939 *Chem. Abstr.* XXXIII. 4493 (*heading*) The relation between elasticity, streaming anomalies and spinability of solutions with particular reference to fibrinogen. **1953** R. J. W. REYNOLDS in R. Hill *Fibres from Synthetic Polymers* v. 91 Spinnability occurs at only a moderately high molecular weight. **1979** TADMOR & GOGOS *Princ. Polymer Processing* xv. 637 The problems of draw resonance and spinnability are not fully understood.

spinnaker. Add: Also carried on other sailing vessels. (Further examples.) Also *fig.*

1912 E. K. CHATTERTON *Fore & Aft* vii. 233 She [*sc.* a Thames barge] has all her canvas tanned with the exception of her jib staysail, which her skipper calls a 'spinnaker'. **1925** H. W. SMYTH *Sea-Wake* 179 The spinnaker hand, young and unspoiled in eye or thought, kept looking round him. *Ibid.* 191 'Hooroo,' began the spinnaker man, and no one interrupted him now; he had done the best day's spinnaker work of his life. **1927** G. BRADFORD *Gloss. Sea Terms* 168/1 Large jibs on English coast craft are sometimes called spinnakers. **1949** *Sun* (Baltimore) 9 Aug. 8/5 The big China-built cutter..carried a huge sky-blue Nylon spinnaker across the finish line. **1957** R. CAMPBELL *Coll. Poems* II. 253 The spring with rosy spinnaker outfanned Comes curling silver fleeces through the land. **1959** *Yachting World Annual* 9/2 *Columbia's* combination of a small, flat spinnaker and small short-luffed spinnaker staysail seemed to be pulling more effectively. **1963** G. MILLAR *Oyster River* 60 We put the nine-foot dinghy in the river (easily done with a short boom fitted into a spinnaker cup set low on the aft side of the mainmast). **1967** J. HOWARD-WILLIAMS *Sails* xii. 164 The spinnaker-staysail..sets under the spinnaker on a reach, in order to fill a slight gap forward. **1972** *Sail* May 100 A typical low aspect ratio spinnaker staysail.

‖ **spinnbar** (ʃpi·nbāɹ), *a.* [Ger.] Of a viscous liquid: capable of being drawn into strands; spinnable.

1944 G. W. S. BLAIR *Survey Gen. & Appl. Rheol.* v. 68 Many spinnbar materials show flow-elasticity. **1945** *Proc. R. Soc. Med.* XXXIX. 8 Curves cannot be directly obtained for spinnbar materials because the ratio of pressure (stress) to rate of flow not only falls with rising stress but increases with increasing deformation (work-hardening).

‖ **spinnbarkeit** (ʃpi·nbāɹkəit). Also **Spinnbarkeit.** [a. G. *spinnbarkeit* (H. Erbring 1936, in *Kolloid-Beihefte* XLIV. 173), f. *spinnbar* (see prec.).] The capacity of a viscous liquid, esp. the cervical mucus, for being drawn into strands; spinnability.

[**1938** G. W. S. BLAIR *Introd. Industr. Rheol.* x. 108 Erbring, studying this property in detail, calls it 'Spinnbarkeit', which perhaps is best translated as 'fibrosity'.] **1944** —— *Survey Gen. & Appl. Rheol.* v. 69 Both tack and 'Spinnbarkeit' are often associated with adhesive properties. **1954** G. I. M. SWYER *Reproduction & Sex* iv. 47 During the two or three days immediately prior to ovulation, the healthy cervix pours forth a copious flow of clear, almost watery mucus which flows out over the vaginal surface of the cervix... At this time it possesses in marked degree the rheological property variously called 'spinnbarkeit', 'fibrosity' or, perhaps better, 'ductility', that is, the ability to be drawn out into a fine thread (or to be blown up into a sizeable bubble). **1975** *Acta Endocrinologia Suppl.* CXCIX. 242 The amount, spinnbarkeit and ferning of the cervical mucus correlated well with the estradiol concentration.

spinner. Add: **II. 7. c.** The person who tosses the coins in the game of two-up; *come in spinner*: the cry commonly used to start the game. Chiefly *Austral.*

1911 L. STONE *Jonah* II. vi. 215 The spinner placed the two pennies face down on the kip, and then, with a turn of the wrist, the coins flew twenty feet into the air. **1945** T. RONAN *Strangers on Ophir* 119 Cries of 'Another quid to see him go. Get set on the side. All set, come in Spinner.' **1948** V. PALMER *Golconda* iv. 25 Step in, spinner... I'm backing heads... They're up. Fair go. **1958** 'N. CULOTTA' *They're a Weird Mob* viii. 117 He began to play... 'Come in, spinner'..I sang softly. **1964** [see *KIP *sb.*[5]]. **1975** L. RYAN *Shearers* 97 'All set?' Lofty asked. 'Set!' Sandy said. 'Come in, spinner!'

d. *Agric.* A rotating device for lifting potatoes out of the ground.

1923 J. R. BOND *Farm Implements & Machinery* xi. 164 The old high-speed spinner did considerable damage to the tubers. **1943** J. W. DAY *Farming Adventure* xvii. 197 Another machine with a great future is the potato digger or spinner. **1960** *Times* 5 July (Agric. Suppl.) p. viii/2 Spinners are still by far the most universal lifting appliances. **1973** M. PARTRIDGE *Farm Tools through Ages* v. 154/2 An iron share..preceded the spinner as the machine was hauled forward, serving to break down the soil.

e. *Cricket.* A spin bowler.

1951 *People* 3 June 7/5 Jim Sims, Middlesex spinner, tells me that he's never felt fitter than he does this season. **1963** A. ROSS *Australia 63* 13 Since the departure of Laker and Wardle no class spinner of any kind had emerged. **1976** DEXTER & MAKINS *Testkill* 78 The spinner, Flinders,..hit Ackroyd for two staggering sixes into the Mound Stand.

f. *Surfing.* (See quot. 1970.)

1962 *Surfer* (1962–3) Dec.–Jan. 52/2 (Advt.), One beautiful turn can't make a good movie, but...1286 beautiful turns, nose rides, spinners..can. **1968** *Surfer Mag.* Jan. 73/2 He showed them skeg-first takeoffs, spinners. **1970** *Studies in English* (Univ. of Cape Town) I. 31 Another popular hot dogging stunt is the *spinner*, in which the surfer turns himself in a full circle on the board, preferably while he is on the nose.

10. *Aeronaut.* A metal fairing that is attached to and revolves with the propeller boss of an aircraft in order to streamline it.

1918 *Flight* 11 July 767/2 The airscrew..had its boss enclosed in the usual 'spinner'. **1944** *R.A.F. Jrnl.* Aug. 287 Peter looked at..the starboard engine cowling, and the spinner revolving at high speed, yet so perfectly made that it seemed to be a motionless dome. **1969** K. MUNSON *Pioneer Aircraft 1903–14* 159/1 The 2-blade propeller had a shallow, bowl-shaped spinner similar to that fitted to the Bristol M.1C.

11. Comb.: **spinner magnetometer**, a magnetometer used to measure the remanent magnetism of rocks, baked clay, etc., in which a sample is spun between coils and induces in them a current dependent on the strength and direction of the magnetic field; see also *spinning magnetometer* s.v. *SPINNING *vbl. sb.* 8 d.

1955 *Jrnl. Geophysical Res.* LX. 332 Spinner magnetometer. This magnetometer is a further development of the type first pioneered by Johnson. **1963** *Jrnl. Sci. Instruments* XL. 162/1 The sensitivity of the spinner magnetometer is proportional to the speed at which the specimen is rotated. **1973** *Nature* 4 May 28/2 The remanent magnetizations were measured with a spinner magnetometer.

spinneret. Add: Also **spinnerette. 1.** (Further example.)

1926 T. H. SAVORY *Brit. Spiders* 8 Now it raises its abdomen..and secretes a drop of silk from its spinnerettes.

2. A cap or plate having a number of small holes through which a spinnable solution is forced in the production of man-made fibres; an individual hole or channel in such a plate.

1894 *Work* 7 July 391/2 The resultant..substance..is next forced..through minute holes in a glass spinneret. **1927** M. H. AVRAM *Rayon Industry* viii. 197 Glass spinnerettes are now produced with 66 holes. **1957** D. C. HAGUE *Economics of Man-Made Fibres* iii. 93 Nylon is a truly synthetic fibre... In fact, it is a plastic which has been forced through a spinnerette to form a textile fibre. **1973** *Materials & Technology* VI. iv. 291 The number of holes in a spinneret will determine the number of filaments which will be present in the yarns; this usually varies between 15 and 100.

spinning, *vbl. sb.* Add: **I. 1. c.** The process or action of drawing into a thread; *spec.* the process of forming a man-made fibre by drawing or extruding a melt or viscous solution of a polymer through a spinneret; *dry, melt, wet spinning*: (see quots. 1974).

1883 [in Dict., sense 1 b]. **1896** *Jrnl. Soc. Chem. Industry* 30 May 317/2 The production of a lustrous thread of cellulose in continuous length, by the process of drawing or 'spinning' is..an accomplished fact. **1910** A. F. BARKER *Textiles* iii. 59 Vanduara silk is obtained by using gelatine as a basis, the threads, after spinning, being treated with formaldehyde to render them insoluble in water. **1927** T. WOODHOUSE *Artificial Silk* v. 37 Coagulation may be effected in warm air by so called 'dry-spinning', when the solvents can be vaporized by such air. **1963** A. J. HALL *Textile Sci.* ii. 75 With the introduction of nylon an entirely new method of fibre spinning was established—so-called melt-spinning in which the polymer..is melted in a novel device above the spinneret so that it can..be extruded through the multi-holed spinneret into cold air. **1974** *Encycl. Brit. Macropædia* VII. 258/2 In wet spinning, the solution of fibre-forming material is extruded into a coagulating bath that causes the jets to harden. *Ibid.*, In dry spinning the fibre-forming substance is dissolved in a solvent before the solution is extruded. As the jets of solution emerge from the spinneret, a stream of hot air causes the solvent to evaporate from the spinning solution, leaving solid filaments. *Ibid.*, In melt spinning the fibre-forming material is melted and extruded through spinnerets, and the jets harden into solid filaments as they cool on emerging from the spinneret.

4. b. Of a motor clutch: the fault of continuing to revolve after being disengaged.

1913 W. E. DOMMETT *Motor Car Mech.* 125 The clutch shaft has a coned brake which prevents 'spinning' when gear changing. **1948** A. W. JUDGE *Mod. Motor Engineer* (ed. 4) II. 305 In some cases the use of a thicker lubricant in the gear-box will prevent clutch spinning.

c. *Aeronaut.* The action of an aircraft when in a spin (*SPIN *sb.*[1] 2 d).

1915 *Aeroplane* 10 Nov. 578/2 It is always possible to avoid spinning or side-slipping in fog or cloud. **1930** NAYLER & OWER *Aviation To-day* 324 Spinning..was first started in the War as a means to bewilder, or escape from, the enemy. **1977** *R.A.F. News* 27 Apr.–10 May 11/4 The Phantom pilots go up with an instructor for a twice-yearly check-out in the trials and tribulations of spinning.

6. (Further examples.) Also *concr.*

1927 *Daily Tel.* 11 May 18/6 To place orders for general metal spinnings. **1964** H. HODGES *Artifacts* iv. 74 The method of shaping bronze vessels known as spinning is virtually a mechanical form of raising. **1973** J. G. TWEEDDALE *Materials Technol.* II. iv. 86 Spinning has certain similarities to panel-beating.

II. 7. b. *spinning-machine* (later examples), *nozzle*; also in terms denoting substances that are spun to form man-made fibres, as *spinning dope, solution, syrup.*

1959 *Times Rev. Industry* Sept. 5/3 There has been an expansion in the production of man-made fibres, already coloured during their spinning by the addition of pigments to the spinning dope. **1899** *Jrnl. Soc. Arts* 8 Dec. 63/2 The filtering is to eliminate every particle of suspended matter which may exist in the collodion before it arrives at the spinning machines. **1975** J. KASPAREK in E. Dyson *Rotor Spinning* x. 161 (*heading*) Processing of man-made staple fibres on the..rotor spinning machine. **1914** *Chem. Abstr.* VIII. 258 A process and device for perforating and cleaning the capillary tube of spinning nozzles for artificial silk manufacture. **1921** T. WOODHOUSE tr. *J. Foltzer's Artificial Silk* xix. 192 The spinning nozzles or spinnerets, from which separate threads..issue. **1931** S. E. & E. R. Trotman *Artificial Silks* 49 The spinning nozzle consists of a head or rose containing a number of capillary apertures through which the spinning solution enters the coagulating bath or evaporating chamber. **1921** T. Woodhouse tr. *J. Foltzer's Artificial Silk* vi. 40 When the solution of the cotton is complete, the spinning solution begins to decompose, unless it is kept at a low temperature. **1973** O. Steinerová tr. *B. Piller's Bulked Yarns* xi. 434 The latter [*sc.* viscose staple fibres] were made dyeable by acid wool dyes due to addition of protein particles to the spinning solution. **1973** *Materials & Technology* VI. iv. 290 The spinning syrup has to be extruded through very tiny holes in the spinneret.

c. *spinning gallery.*

1956 R. W. McDowell in W. A. Singleton *Stud. Archit. History* II. 133 Reference must be made to the 'spinning galleries'..an attractive feature of some.. ..Lakeland villages. **1976** G. Moffat *Short Time to Live* xi. 115 'What's brought you to Sandale?'.. 'Vernacular architecture, sir... Interiors too: spice cupboards, stone stairways, spinning galleries.'

8. c. *spinning tunnel,* a wind tunnel with a vertical air flow for testing the behaviour of model aircraft in simulated spins. Also *free-spinning tunnel.*

1934 *Rep. & Mem. Aeronaut. Res. Committee* No. 1578. 2 Tests in the Free Spinning Tunnel were accordingly projected as a check upon the validity of the results which could be obtained with small dynamical models. *Ibid.* 12 In the spinning tunnel the models are usually about 1/25 scale, and thus the rate of rotation is about five times that of the full scale spin. **1937** *Technical Rep. Aeronaut. Res. Committee 1936* I. 452 The R.A.E. Free Spinning Tunnel was brought into use in 1932 to examine the spinning properties of various existing and projected designs of aeroplanes. **1939** *Ibid. 1937* I. 552 The effect of mass distribution has been explored as a matter of routine on all designs tested in the spinning tunnel. **1947** A. Pope *Wind-Tunnel Testing* i. 10 The NACA has two free-spinning tunnels, one 15 ft in diameter, the other 20 ft.

d. *spinning magnetometer* = *spinner magnetometer* s.v. *Spinner 11.

1960 *Archaeometry* III. 47 The great advantage that a spinning magnetometer has over the astatic type is that it can be used in a normal laboratory in the presence of a relatively large amount of local magnetic interference. **1963** R. M. Cook in Brothwell & Briggs *Science in Archaeol.* I. v. 64 In the spinning magnetometer the sample is rotated continuously to produce an alternating current.

spinning, *ppl. a.* Add: **3.** *spinning reserve* (Electr. Engin.), reserve power-generating capacity which is available to meet sudden increases in load.

1932 *Rep. Proposed Amer. Stand. Defs. Electr. Terms* (Amer. Inst. Electr. Engineers) 62/2 Spinning reserve is that reserve generating capacity connected to the bus and ready to take load. **1974** *Times* 21 Jan. 15/6 These 'spinning reserves' are carried on plant which is generating power, but not fully loaded. **1979** 'A. Hailey' *Overload* I. i. 5 GSP & L's last spinning reserve had been brought to full load.

Hence **spi·nningly** *adv.*

1923 *Daily Mail* 19 May 6 The ball is cracked spinningly through the gap between point and third man.

spinning-jenny. Add: **2.** Also, the whole of such an apparatus. (Earlier example.)

1879 H. A. Simmons *Ernest Struggles* iv. 72 To the ceiling of the taproom was fixed what the men called a 'spinning jenny', which was a revolving hand, like that on a clock, with a number of figures round it. It was with this that the customers won and lost pots of beer.

spino-. Add: **spino-cerebe·llar, -tha·lamic** *adjs.*

1900 E. A. Schäfer *Text-bk. Physiol.* II. 806 Another spino-cerebellar system, mainly crossed (heteromeric), lies in the ventro-lateral edge of the lateral column. **1975** *Sci. Amer.* Jan. 71/2 They found that one of the main afferent tracts leading to the cerebellum, the ventral spinocerebellar tract, conveys information not about the state of the body or the external environment but about the activity of inhibitory interneurons in the spinal cord. **1900** E. A. Schäfer *Text-bk. Physiol.* II. 807 Others [*sc.* spinal cells], it is said..enter the diencephalon, ending in the ventro-lateral nucleus of the optic thalamus, forming a spino-thalamic system. **1974** D. & M. Webster *Compar. Vertebr. Morphol.* xii. 278 Like the ventral spinothalamic tract, with which it is confluent, the lateral spinothalamic tract joins the medial lemniscus in the brainstem.

spinodal (spəinōᵘ·dăl), *a.* and *sb. Physical Chem.* [f. Spinod(e + -al.] **A.** *adj.* Being or pertaining to a spinodal; involving a metastable condition described by such a curve. **B.** *sb.* A curve which is the locus of stationary points in a system of curves; *spec.* such a curve in a pressure-volume diagram or the like which delimits a region of thermodynamic metastability from one of instability.

1956 *Nature* 3 Mar. 419/2 A single kinetic law did not apply at all temperatures, which suggests that the spinodal curve may have some influence. **1961** *Acta Metallurgica* IX. 536/2 The spinodal is the locus of points within a miscibility gap where $\partial^2F/\partial x^2 = 0$. F is the free energy of mixing and x the composition. *Ibid.* 801/2 Au–Ni thin foils decompose by what is almost certainly a spinodal mechanism. **1969** *Trans. Metallurg. Soc. AIME* CCXLV. 1707 Just above and just below the spinodal, we expect the reaction to proceed along a path which is not necessarily the energetically most favorable one. **1973** *Physics Bull.* Apr. 230 Spinodal decomposition of equimolar NaCl–KCl mixed crystals. **1974** *Nature* 29 Nov. 381/2 The locus of all the tangent points *c* defines a metastability limit (spinodal).

spin-off (spi·nǫf), *sb.* and *a.* orig. *U.S.* Also **spinoff.** [f. vbl. phr. *to spin off*: see spin *v.* 13**.]

A. *sb.* **1.** *Comm.* A distribution of stock of a new company to shareholders of a parent company; a company so created.

1951 Stanley & Kilcullen *Federal Income Tax* 182 Sec. 112 (*b*) (11), added by the 1951 Act, permits the distribution of stock in a spin-off without recognition of gain to the stock-holders, subject to certain restrictions designed to prevent the use of spin-offs to distribute earnings and profits. **1956** *Sun* (Baltimore) 30 May 15/1 The proposed 'spin-off' was to be on the basis of three shares of Bestwall Gypsum for each share of Certain-Teed. **1969** *Daily Tel.* 4 June 3 Many had been anticipating a complete spin-off by B P of its United States subsidiary with a United States quotation and a chance of more direct public participation in the group's Alaskan activities. **1974** *Telegraph* (Brisbane) 8 May 46/4 Spea is a subsidiary of the Italstrade Company. Italstrade, in turn, is a subsidiary, or spin-off, of Italstat. **1981** *Observer* 4 Oct. 21/1 A growing phenomenon in British business life: the hive-off, spin-off or demerger—the management buy-out, in fact. **1981** *Times* 28 Oct. 19/5 Even split into four separate companies, the spin-offs would be equal fifteenth in the league table.

2. A by-product, an incidental development, side-effect, or benefit; the production or accrual of side-effects or indirect benefits; *spec.* (*a*) a business, organization, etc., developed out of or by (former) members of another larger business, etc.; (*b*) a show, television programme, etc., developed from an idea or character in another.

1959 *Wall St. Jrnl.* 12 May 1/4 Numerous firms have been organized by M.I.T. scientists who decided to strike out on their own—'spin-offs from M.I.T.', one research official terms them. **1961** *Guardian* 10 Oct. 6/6 'Technological fall-out' or 'technological spin-off'..are the terms used to denote the desirable social byproducts of the plan to send men to the moon. **1963** *Listener* 7 Nov. 735/2 The development out of (or 'spin off', as the Americans call it) magazines [*sc.* magazine programmes] must not be interpreted as any lack of conviction in their continuing role. **1967** *Technology Week* 23 Jan. 75/2 There were to be spin-offs in the form of a series of assist devices for emergency, temporary or permanent assistance to cardiac function. **1967** *Daily Tel.* 15 May 9/8 The close season is also the signal for another series of BBC Comedy Playhouse 'try-outs'. It produced 'Steptoe'; and last season, to use the current jargon, the 'spin-offs' in series form were 'The Whitehall Worrier', [etc.]. **1968** *Economist* 13 Jan. 55/2 It was flatly denied that the huge military and space programmes had been of any advantage, in terms of technological spin-off, to industry. **1968** P. McKellar *Experience & Behav.* xv. 398 In this connexion we encounter the notion of 'spin off', the term used for other applications of findings that have emerged from space research. **1969** *Daily Tel.* (Colour Suppl.) 28 Mar. 7/3 A car..is a means of transport with a horrifying spin-off of death and injury. **1975** *Lady* 17 July 97/1 One of the spin-offs of our affluent society is that more people can afford to keep dogs. **1976** *TV Times* (Brisbane) 22 May 7/2 There is a tradition in American TV—if a show is a success, do a spin-off. In other words, take one or two characters from the parent series and build another series around them. **1977** Sachs & Jahn *Celestial Passengers* xxxii. 198 Space spinoffs have resulted in many new products to improve the quality of our recreational activities. *Ibid.* 193 Probably the best-known space spinoff to health is the cardiac pacemaker. **1979** *Jrnl. R. Soc. Arts* CXXVII. 626/1 If we can improve our productivity ..then there will be all sorts of spin-offs from this in the way of leisure industries and service industries.

B. *attrib.* or as *adj.* That develops or is created as a spin-off.

1966 *National Observer* (U.S.) 18 July 7 Although the column hasn't been as successful churning up front-page news stories as some editors had hoped, it does develop an occasional 'spin-off' story. **1967** *Boston Globe* 18 May 35/6 Shares of the spin-off company will be distributed tax free to United Fruit stockholders. **1969** *Physics Bull.* July 268/2 Many of the successful 'spin-off' firms in the United States were based on a transfer of technology by individuals from large and continuing programmes in government and university laboratories. **1974** *Financial Times* 8 Apr. 23/7 Hardly anyone earns less than the proposed new minima, which would therefore raise only a few earnings and so would hit employers' wage bills and eat into Stage Three allowances only through the spin-off effect on holiday and sick pay. **1979** *Amer. Jrnl. Trop. Med. & Hygiene* XXVIII. 1043/2 No attempt was made to document 'spinoff' costs, notably losses of tourism revenue. **1980** J. Wainwright *Man of Law* xi. 64 With hindsight..I *knew*... But honesty demands that I ask spin-off questions. How much did I know?

spinone (spinōᵘ·ni). [It.] A wire-haired gun-dog of an Italian breed, usually white with tan or brown markings, drooping ears, and a docked tail.

1945 C. L. B. Hubbard *Observer's Bk. Dogs* 188 The Spinone..has for centuries been the Italian all-purpose shooting dog. **1964** E. F. Dalglish tr. *Schneider-Leyer's Dogs of World* xvi. 219 Spinone... A big, squarely built, rough-coated dog with long ears and docked tail. **1972** *Daily Tel.* 5 Dec. 7/7 Breeds of dog whose docking is permitted by the Kennel Club are: sporting spaniels,.. Italian spinones,..Weimaraners, [etc.].

spinor (spi·nəɹ). *Physics.* [a. G. *spinor* (B. L. van der Waerden 1929, in *Nachr. von d. Ges. d. Wissensch. zu Göttingen* 100), f. Spin *v.* + -or, after Tensor, Vector.] Any quantity existing in a space and having the property that rotation through 360° reverses its sign and leaves it otherwise unchanged; also, applied to quantities constructed from two or more of these in the way that tensors may be constructed from vectors.

1931 *Physical Rev.* XXXVII. 1022 With the spinor analysis developed by B. Van der Waerden.., which comprises all representations of the Lorentz group, even those not contained in ordinary tensor calculus, one is able to write all derivations and equations in an automatically covariant form. **1952** *Amer. Jrnl. Physics* XX. 253/2 The available literature on spinors is exceedingly hard to understand. **1974** P. A. M. Dirac *Spinors in Hilbert Space* ii. 4 Spinors, like tensors, are geometrical objects embedded in a space and have components that transform linearly under transformations of the coordinates of the space. Spinors differ from tensors in that they change sign when one applies a complete revolution about an axis, while tensors are unchanged. **1974** G. Reece tr. *Hund's Hist. Quantum Theory* xv. 200 It was soon seen that the four-component Dirac ψ was a particular kind of entity... It was called a spinor. **1977** K. O. May tr. *Iyanaga & Kawada's Encycl. Dict. Math.* I. 216/2 Although $SO(n)$ ($n \geq 3$) is a connected Lie group, it is not simply connected. The simply connected Lie group which is locally isomorphic to $SO(n)$ is called the spinor group and is denoted by $Spin(n)$.

Hence **spino·rial** *a.*, involving spinors, decribed by means of spinors.

1968 *Physics Bull.* Nov. 381/1 The wavefunction must have four components which transform according to the 'spinorial' transformation encountered by Pauli. **1978** *McGraw-Hill Yearbk. Sci. & Technol.* 356/1 A spinorial gauge field with spin 3/2.

spin-out (spi·naut). *N. Amer. slang.* [f. vbl. phr. *to spin out*: see spin *v.* 13***.] A skidding spin by a vehicle out of control.

1957 *Daily Progress* (Charlottesville, Va.) 28 Oct. 14/6 A spin-out in the last 10 minutes of the race may have cost Tony Briggs of Charlottesville top honors in the first preliminary race before the President's Cup automobile race. **1971** *Maclean's Mag.* Oct. 39/3 He had trouble eliminating his spin-outs, those heart-stopping moments when the car slithers in circles and semi-circles on the track.

Spinozism, Spinozist. Add: Also **Spino·zaism, Spino·zaist.**

1852 H. Melville *Pierre* xx. ii. 381 Why, lad, I have received propositions from the Editors of the Spinozaist to contribute a weekly column to their paper, and you know how very few can understand the Spinozaist. **1912** *Q. Rev.* Oct. 393 Modern Spinozaism is inclined to identify ethics with religion. *Ibid.* 398 He no longer speaks as a Spinozaist.

Spinozite: for *rare*⁻¹ read *rare* and add later example.

1946 *Mind* LV. 101 Some of these assumptions..are often confidently made by others than professed Spinozites.

spin-rinse (spi·nrins). [f. Spin *v.* + Rinse *sb.*] A rinsing of washing in a rotating perforated drum which draws off water; a combined rinse and partial spin-dry.

1948 [see *spin-drier, -dryer]. **1961** *Guardian* 22 Mar. 8/3 A powerful spin-dryer.., to which a crafty bit of design has given a built-in spin-rinse percolating downwards through the clothes to give an effective rinse, hitherto lacking in the conventional spinner.

spin-scan (spi·nskæn), *a.* and *sb.* [f. Spin *v.* + Scan *sb.*] **A.** *adj.* Applied to devices whose scanning motion is provided by the rotation of the craft carrying them.

1967 *Electronics* 6 Mar. 73 (Advt.), SB RC also built the spin-scan camera that has been sending back high-resolution black-and-white photos of the earth's cloud cover. **1979** *Sci. Amer.* Nov. 21 (Advt.), The satellite's 'camera' is a visible-infrared spin-scan radiometer.

B. *sb.* A scan performed or produced by such a device. Also *attrib.*

1972 *Space Research* XII. 1768 Television would have taken a shorter exposure (a fraction of a second, compared with several minutes for a spin scan). **1974** *Science* 25 Jan. 318/2 A 2·5 centimeter telescope aboard Pioneer 10 is capable of making two-dimensional spin-scan maps..at high resolution. **1974** *Nature* 6 Sept. 18/1 The most striking early results were the hundreds of photographs that resulted from the spin-scans of the planet, giving higher resolution pictures of the planet than had previously been possible.

So **spi·n-scanning** *a.*

1972 *Space Research* XII. 1765 A summary description is made of spin-scanning devices for various space missions.

spinster. Add: **3.** (Sense 2 b) *spinster-baiting.*

1938 L. MacNeice *Mod. Poetry* 191 Merely a piece of rather cruel spinster-baiting.

spi·nsterishness.

1913 R. West *Let.* June in G. N. Ray *H. G. Wells & Rebecca West* (1974) 23 Your spinsterishness makes you feel that a woman desperately and hopelessly in love with a man is an indecent spectacle. **1930** R. Macaulay *Staying with Relations* iii. 44 The elegant spinsterishness of Claudia and Benet had turned, in Julia,..to something more sensuous.

spinstry. 2. For *Obs.*[-1] read *rare* and add later example.

1894 *Wales* Aug. 192/1 The local gossips..watched the progress of events from the heights of maternity and spinstry.

spintrian. For † *Obs.* read *rare* and add later examples.

1887 L. C. SMITHERS tr. *Forberg's Man. Class. Erotol.* viii. 166 More than three may enjoy themselves together; this is what we call after Tiberius, the spintrian kind. **1913** C. MACKENZIE *Sinister St.* I. II. ix. 287 My library ..holds as many secrets as the Spintrian books of Elephantis, long ago lost and purified by the sea.

spinulosin (spəiniu̇lōᵘ·sin). *Biochem.* [f. mod.L. *spīnulōs-us*, specific epithet of the fungus from which it was first isolated (see SPINULOSE *a.*): see -IN[1].] A purple-black crystalline benzoquinone derivative, $C_8H_8O_5$, which is produced in cultures of the moulds *Penicillium spinulosum* and *Aspergillus fumigatus*.

1938 ANSLOW & RAISTRICK in *Biochem. Jrnl.* XXXII. 689 Birkinshaw & Raistrick (1931) reported the isolation from cultures of strains in the *Penicillium spinulosum* Thom series of a new mould metabolic product which was unnamed at that time, but for which the name *spinulosin* is now proposed. **1946** [see *FUMIGATIN]. **1950** L. F. & M. FIESER *Org. Chem.* (ed. 2) xxxii. 770 Spinulosin..has been prepared from fumigatin by Thiele addition of acetic anhydride, hydrolysis of the resulting tetraacetate, and oxidation. **1979** *Biol. Abstr.* LXVII. 6332/2 A strain of *A. fumigatus* (Fresenius)..was grown on a culture medium with added saccharose. The synthesis of..spinulosin was studied under many different temperature, pH and inoculum conditions.

spin-up (spi·nʌp), *sb.* [f. SPIN *v.* + UP *adv.*[1]] An increase in the speed of rotation.

1960 *Jrnl. Geophysical Res.* LXV. 2994 (*caption*) Increased stability of both the theoretical and observed motion is seen after spinup. **1968** *New Scientist* 3 Oct. 8/2 The particular merit of the autogyro is that its rotor does not depend on engine power, except for the spin-up before take-off. **1969** *Nature* 29 Nov. 873/1 The time scale for the cracking and initial spin up is of the order of 0·01 to 0·1 s, the time for a shear wave in the crust to propagate a stellar radius. **1971** [see *SPIN-DOWN *sb.*] **1977** *Astron. & Astrophysics* LX. 85/1 Subsequent retrograde spinup via thermally driven atmospheric tides can explain the present slow retrograde motion of the planet.

spin-up (spinʌ·p), *a. Physics.* [f. SPIN *sb.*[1] + UP *adv.*[2]] Being or pertaining to a particle with a spin pointing upwards.

1965 *Sci. Amer.* Jan. 106/3 The electrons' magnetic field at the nucleus is produced by..the net spin density, or the 'spin up' density minus the 'spin down' density. **1970** *Nature* 25 July 372/2 Four spin-up electrons at the corners of a tetrahedron and four spin-down electrons at the corners of an interpenetrating tetrahedron pointing the opposite way are arranged around each oxygen centre. **1973** *McGraw-Hill Yearbk. Sci. & Technol.* 287/1 With this technique, it is possible to calculate the difference between the spin-up and the spin-down populations in each electron shell. **1980** RUDDEN & WILSON *Elem. Solid State Physics* ii. 41 The first available electron is placed in the 1s spin-up state, the second in the 1s spin-down state.

spiny, *a.* Add: **3. b. spiny rat,** a rodent of the family Echimyidæ, found in tropical South and Central America and distinguished by bristly fur.

1876 A. R. WALLACE *Geogr. Distrib. Animals* II. xvii. 238 The Echimyidæ, or spiny rats, are a family, chiefly South American. **1924** W. B. SCOTT *Hist. Land Mammals Western Hemisphere* v. 184 The spiny rats (*Echimys* and *Loncheres*) are so called from their appearance, not because they are related to the true rats. **1974** H. MACINNES *Climb to Lost World* ix. 147 A spiny rat, a rare creature: Mike Atherley and I both saw it more than once and thought that it had no tail.

Spion Kop: see *KOP 2.

spiral, *sb.* Add: **2. c.** *U.S. Football.* A kick or pass in which the ball in flight spins round its long axis.

1896 CAMP & DELAND *Football* vi. 61 *Spiral*, a kick similar to the twister, in which the ball maintains a true course while revolving on its long axis. **1910** W. CAMP *Book of Foot-Ball* viii. 308 Long passes are best made by holding the ball like a spear and sending a spiral. **1972** J. MOSEDALE *Football* v. 69 Fourteen times his soft spirals connected, for 216 yards.

d. *fig.* A progressive movement in one direction (esp. upwards or downwards, and marking a relentlessly deteriorating state of affairs), considered to take the form of a spiral; *spec.* one caused by the interaction or alternate overtaking of interdependent quantities; *vicious spiral*: see *VICIOUS *a.* 9.

1897 P. GEDDES *Let.* 10 Feb. in P. Boardman *Worlds of P. Geddes* (1978) vi. 155 New money = new crime = new report.. = new police and so on, in downward spiral. **1931**, etc. [see *INFLATIONARY *a.*]. **1939** *Economist* 16 Dec. 405 The fear of an accelerating spiral of wages and prices. **1958** *Spectator* 15 Aug. 211/1 Steps to avoid a new arms race spiral. **1965** *Listener* 23 Sept. 439/2 We have got to get rid of the endless spiral, price increases and pay claims. **1975** *Physics Bull.* Aug. 345/1 The tendency for departments with the highest demand for undergraduate places to take the largest slice of the UGC cake has meant that engineering and physical science departments have fallen into a spiral of fewer students resulting in lower grants. **1980** *Times* 15 Jan. 14 Price of antique silver follows the gold spiral.

e. *Aeronaut.* A descent (or, rarely, a climb) made by an aircraft in the form of a helix; a continuous banking turn accompanying a descent or ascent.

1910 *Sphere* 30 July 103/2 This descent..was composed of several high-speed dives and short spirals. **1918** E. M. ROBERTS *Flying Fighter* 272 When I came out of my spiral,..my engine would not start again. *Ibid.* 301 The Hun machine started upward in a spiral. **1941** POPE & OTIS *Elements of Aeronaut.* ix. 85 The spiral, usually done with power off, is merely a gliding turn, continued to make several complete turns, gradually descending. **1975** G. H. SAUNDERS *Dynamics of Helicopter Flight* v. 178 A neutrally stable spiral would require the pilot to take back out his cyclic input once his desired bank angle has been achieved.

3. c. (Earlier example.)

1850 LD. ROSSE in *Phil. Trans. R. Soc.* CXL. 511 Night excellent, a spiral seen in an oblique direction, resolved well, particularly towards the centre, where it is very bright.

spiral, *a.*[1] and *adv.* Add: **1. b.** Also, of a descending course or path. (Further examples, from *Aeronaut.*)

1908 F. W. LANCHESTER *Aerodonetics* vii. 180 The aerodrone..loses its equilibrium and comes rapidly to earth with a kind of spiral dive. **1912** *Flight* 31 Aug. 787/1 The machine at once started a spiral nose-dive. **1939** *Aircraft Engin.* XI. 40/3 There are many references to spiral or corkscrew descent in the literature..but this always implies a fully controllable motion at an angle of incidence below the critical angle; very different to the spin proper. **1961** C. B. SMITH *Testing Time* 53 To their horror, the men on the ground saw the aircraft drop out of control into a whirling dive, the 'spiral dive' which they knew meant almost certain death.

d. *Surg.* Of a fracture: curving round a long bone lengthwise.

1897 *Lippincott's Med. Dict.* 955/2 Spiral fracture. **1934** *Practitioners Library Med. & Surg.* V. ii. 301 Fractures of the Shaft of the Femur... Nonunion may occur... This is likely to happen in the oblique or spiral types. **1950** *Brit. Encycl. Med. Pract.* (ed. 2) IV. 369 (*caption*) Spiral fracture of tibia in boy aged 8 years, three weeks after accident; no clinical signs or symptoms except his refusal to use his leg. **1976** M. MACHLIN *Pipeline* xlii. 455 At the Medical Center Hospitals in Houston they had told him that the spiral break would take at least six months to heal to the point where the cast could be removed.

3. a. *spiral bevel gear*, a bevel gear that is also a spiral gear; *spiral binding*, a book binding in which a helical wire passes through a closely spaced row of holes near the inside edge of each leaf; so *spiral-bound* adj.; *spiral divergence* (Aeronaut.) = *spiral instability* below; *spiral gear*, a gear wheel whose teeth are cut obliquely to the axis of the wheel and are curved to form part of what is approximately a spiral or helix; *esp.* a skew gear of this kind; so *spiral gearing*; *spiral instability* (Aeronaut.), an instability in which an aeroplane undergoing a banked turn tends to enter a descending spiral as a result of sideslipping and reduction of the radius of turn; *spiral stability* (Aeronaut.), the capacity of an aeroplane not to enter a spiral while executing a banked turn, or to recover from a steeply-banked spiral path.

1915 V. W. PAGÉ *Automobile Repairing* ix. 767 The advantages of the spiral bevel gear are mainly due to the shape of the teeth which roll into engagement more smoothly than the ordinary form of bevel gears. **1973** *Transmission & Rear Axle—Bedford Trucks & Coaches* (Vauxhall Motors) 168 The differential, spiral bevel gear and pinion can be serviced without removing axle from vehicle. **1949** MELCHER & LARRICK *Printing & Promotion Handbk.* 280/2 *Spiral binding*, see *mechanical bindings*. **1968** F. H. HOLLIDAY *Man. Stationery, Office Machines & Equipment* II. viii. 440 The sheets..are fed on to a conveyor to be trimmed, knocked up and punched to receive the spiral binding. **1961** *Lebende Sprachen* VI. 104/1 Spiral-bound stenographer's notebook. **1969** D. FRANCIS *Enquiry* iii. 37 He stood..holding a spiral bound notebook. **1976** E. WARD *Hanged Man* xxxi. 200 A thick spiral-bound document. **1949** *Jrnl. R. Aeronaut. Soc.* LIII. 541/1 There are two common kinds of aircraft instability which usually would be judged tolerable according to the above criterion. These are the phugoid oscillation (longitudinal-symmetric motion) and the spiral divergence (lateral-antisymmetric motion). **1970** T. HACKER *Flight Stability & Control* vii. 159 The possibility of eliminating spiral divergence by design can be made to stand out by means of stability diagrams. **1888** J. G. HORNER *Lockwood's Dict. Mech. Engin.* 338 *Spiral gear*, includes helical, stepped, and worm gearing. **1914** —— *Gear Cutting* v. 48 Since the special gear-cutting machines have come into general use, the manufacture of spiral gears has been established on a better commercial basis than hitherto. **1971** B. SCHARF *Engin. & its Lang.* xii. 155 In some types of multiple gear train, the same gear drives a helical gear (with parallel axis) as well as a spiral gear (with skew axis). *a* **1877** KNIGHT *Dict. Mech.* III. 2275/1 *Spiral gearing*, a gear-wheel having meshing spiral ribs and grooves. The teeth run around the periphery of the gear-wheel, and meet in an angle on a line midway from either edge of the wheel. **1930** *Engineering* 2 May 559/2 Spiral gearing has been found to have many valuable applications. **1914** L. BAIRSTOW et al. *Rep. & Mem. Advisory Comm. for Aeronautics* No. 77. 168 A machine which is liable to spiral instability when gyroscopic actions are eliminated, cannot become stable owing to gyroscopic action of the propeller and engine. **1970** T. HACKER *Flight Stability & Control* vii. 162 The elimination of spiral instability..is achieved by the constraint of the angle of bank ϕ, obviously in addition to correcting the heading. **1947** C. F. TOMS *Introd. Aeronautics* v. 222 The use of a certain amount of dihedral..is essential for both directional and spiral stability. **1978** M. SIMONS *Model Aircraft Aerodynamics* xi. 126 If the model is primarily a thermal soarer..effort should be concentrated on spiral stability.

b. *spiral thickening*.

1933 *Trop. Woods* XXXVI. 4 Spiral Thickenings.—Helical ridges on the inner face of, and a part of, the secondary wall. **1953** K. ESAU *Plant Anat.* xi. 228 Such secondary thickenings [of the xylem] are called, respectively, annular, spiral or helical, and reticulate.

c. Also *spiral cleavage*, a pattern of embryogenesis characteristic of certain invertebrate groups, in which the third cell division is asymmetrical and destroys all but four-fold rotational symmetry.

1892 E. B. WILSON in *Jrnl. Morphol.* VI. 377 The events of the cleavage fall into three very marked periods which I shall designate respectively as the (1) spiral, (2) transitional, and (3) bilateral periods. *Ibid.* 441 The third spiral cleavage of the primary micromeres gives rise to four apical cells. **1948** *New Biol.* V. 113 The same fundamental pattern (called spiral cleavage because of the oblique direction of many of the divisions; the actual pattern of cells resulting is not a spiral) is found also in other groups, such as the flatworms. **1967** L. A. BORRADAILE et al. *Invertebrata* i. 2 The annelid superphylum has eggs that develop by means of spiral cleavage. When the blastula divides from the four-cell stage to the eight-cell stage the second quartet lie on top of and between the cells of the first quartet.

e. *Astr.* Special collocations in sense 2, as: *spiral arm*, an arm of a spiral galaxy; *spiral galaxy*, a galaxy in which bright stars and gas clouds tend to be located along arms that appear to spiral from a central nucleus; *spiral nebula*, a spiral galaxy (now chiefly *Hist.*).

1914 A. S. EDDINGTON *Stellar Movements & Struct. of Universe* xi. 243 The star clouds of the Milky Way form its [*sc.* our galaxy's] spiral arms. **1978** PASACHOFF & KUTNER *University Astron.* xxiii. 582 The interstellar extinction prevents us from studying parts of the spiral arms farther away from the sun. **1913** *Astrophysical Jrnl.* XXXVII. 112 The stellar accumulations might be arranged so as to produce the phenomenon of the Milky Way—on the supposition of a spiral galaxy. **1944** H. SHAPLEY *Galaxies* i. 26 The subclassifications of bright spheroidal and spiral galaxies..are possible only for those systems near enough for large-scale photography. **1980** *Sky & Telescope* July 25 By studying star formation in spiral galaxies, we can do more than test theories of spiral structure. **1850** LD. ROSSE in *Phil. Trans. R. Soc.* CXL. 505 The other spiral nebulæ discovered up to the present time are comparatively difficult to be seen. **1920** A. S. EDDINGTON *Space, Time & Gravitation* x. 160 The most remote objects known are the spiral nebulae, whose distances may perhaps be of the order a million light years. **1978** PASACHOFF & KUTNER *University Astron.* xxiii. 572 Another class of objects was once known as 'spiral nebulae'... However, these spiral nebulae are now known to be galaxies in their own right.

4*. = *spiral-bound* adj., sense 3 a above.

1977 H. GREENE *FSO-1* ix. 83 [He] whipped out large black reading glasses, and peered downward at a spiral pad. **1978** R. THOMAS *Chinaman's Chance* xiii. 135 Durant was seated on the couch..a secretary's spiral notebook in his lap.

spiral, *v.* Add: **1. b.** To fly an aircraft in a spiral path. Also with *down, downwards*.

1916 E. C. MIDDLETON *Aircraft* iii. 33 The pilot either 'spirals' or glides down, until he is able to ascertain the direction of the prevailing wind. **1922** H. L. FOSTER *Adventures of Tropical Tramp* xi. 173 The aviator spiraled downwards towards his landing place. **1941** POPE & OTIS *Elements of Aeronautics* ix. 85 Practice is required.. to spiral over a fixed spot when the wind is blowing. **1978** M. SIMONS *Model Aircraft Aerodynamics* iv. 37 Even better rates of climb would result if the model did not have to spiral.

c. *fig.* To move rapidly in one direction (usu. upwards), in a manner considered to resemble a spiral; to increase or decrease in response to the same movement of another quantity or other quantities. Cf. sense 2 d of the sb. above.

1922 H. CRANE *Let.* *c* 18 June (1965) 91 Under the influence of aether and *amnesia* my mind spiraled to a kind of seventh heaven of consciousness. **1941** *Time* 20 Oct. 35/1 Even if import and farm prices resist all controls, processors' and retailers' prices will rise but not spiral with them. **1942** E. W. KEMMERER *ABC of Inflation* 156 If wages and the prices of farm products are not adequately restricted but are permitted to spiral upward..the whole price situation will get out of control. **1959** *Listener* 18 June 1052/1 The cost of living has spiralled. **1977** *Milestones* Summer 19/1 A similar table published in the Autumn 1974 issue of *Milestones* shows how much the cost of spare parts has spiralled. **1979** *Tucson* (Arizona) *Citizen* 20 Sept. 1A/4 The dollar spiraled downward on European money markets today. **1979** *Daily Tel.* 5 Dec. 21 The..risks of sending demand, output and tax revenue spiralling down again while the cost of spending programmes such as unemployment benefit..spiral up.

Hence **spi·ralling** *ppl. a.* and *vbl. sb.*

1944 AUDEN *For Time Being* (1945) 90 Even the problems of Trade Cycles And Spiralling Prices are regarded by the experts As practically solved. **1958** *Spectator* 18 July 92/3 The twin threat of a renewed world currency crisis and a spiralling of trade restriction. **1965** [see *OH-SO *adv.*]. **1969** H. PERKIN *Key Profession* iv. 138 The post-war situation of spiralling prices and incomes. **1979** E. H. GOMBRICH *Sense of Order* vi. 160 Spiralling terminations suggest the curling of elastic matter. **1979** *Nature* 14 June 622/1 Viscous drag on the planet's orbital motion would then lead to a spiralling into the stellar core. **1980** *Oxf. Diocesan Mag.* June 7/2 The failure of extrinsic motivation to fill the need is evident from the spiralling demands of frustrated materialists.

spiralism (spəiə·răliz'm). *Sociol.* [f. SPIRAL *sb.* + -ISM.] A term for mobility in career and place of residence as part of individual success in an industrial economy. So **spi·ralist** *sb.* and *a.*

1957 W. WATSON in M. Gluckman *Closed Systems & Open Minds* (1964) vi. 147 The progressive ascent of the specialists of different skills..forms a characteristic combination of social and spatial mobility which may be called 'spiralism'. *Ibid.* 148 A spiralist's possible range of activity is the total number of fields within which his education qualifies him to compete. *Ibid.* 149 The generic spiralist culture. **1962** A. SAMPSON *Anat. of Britain* xxviii. 461 The career of a corporation manager cuts across traditional societies and local communities; he is a 'spiralist'—moving towards the top in narrowing circles, from one community or country to another, gathering local experience before he settles in the head office as a senior executive. **1969** C. BELL *Middle Class Families* ii. 40 There were 13 'blocked' spiralists who admitted they were not at the top. **1971** —— & NEWBY *Community Stud.* v. 158 Social mobility in Franza proceeds by a kind of spiralism. Individuals must 'get out' in order to 'get on'.

spiralization (spəiə:răləizē·ʃən). [f. SPIRALIZE *v.* + -ATION.] The acquisition of spiral form; (in quot. 1851, a spiral coil).

1851 H. MELVILLE *Moby Dick* II. xviii. 141 The whale-line..is spirally coiled away in the tub..so as to form..layers of concentric spiralizations. **1910** J. A. FLEMING *Princ. Electr. Wave Telegr.* (ed. 2) 127 The increase in resistance of a solenoid due to the spiralization. **1928** T. C. CHAMBERLIN *Two Solar Families* xvii. 159 The propulsion of solar bolts into planetary space and the drawing of these into orbits by the joint action of the sun and the passing star (the spiralization) was only the beginning of the process of..nebularization. **1941** *Cold Spring Harbor Symp. Quantitative Biol.* IX. 15/2 The outstanding question is whether or not this amount of 'contraction' can all be accounted for by spiralization. **1969** I. B. RAIKOV in T. T. Chen *Res. in Protozool.* III. 75 Shortly before nuclear division, the chromosomes undergo spiralization and become longitudinally split. **1980** *Macromolecules* XIII. 799/2 Since..spiralization of the chain cannot be invoked for steric control, the stereoregularity can only result from the asymmetric spatial arrangement around the metal atom of the catalytic complexes.

spiralize, *v.* Add: Also *intr.*, to move in a spiral. Hence **spi·ralized** *ppl. a.*, formed into a spiral shape; **spi·ralizing** *ppl. a.*

1851 H. MELVILLE *Moby Dick* I. xxxv. 265 Drink and pass!.. Short draughts—long swallows, men; 'tis hot as Satan's hoof. So, so; it goes round excellently. It spiralizes in ye. **1928** T. C. CHAMBERLIN *Two Solar Families* 145 A group of bodies already separated may respond to the spiralizing whirl of two centers of gravity even more freely than an eruptive body from which the spiralized matter must be shot forth. **1940** *Jrnl. Genetics* XL. 67 The suggestion has been made..that whereas all non-heteropycnotic regions have a spiral structure the heteropycnotic regions are not spiralized at all. **1977** *Nucl. Instruments & Methods* CXLV. 258/2 A new extrapolation is computed to associate track segments. In this way a spiralizing track can be followed. **1980** *Macromolecules* XIII. 798 Neither a chiral carbon nor a spiralized chain participates in the first two addition steps.

spiramycin (spəirămǝi·sin). *Pharm.* [ad. F. *spiramycine*, f. *spira-* (of unkn. origin): see *-MYCIN.] A mixture of macrolide antibiotics obtained from the fungus *Streptomyces ambofaciens.*

1955 *Antibiotics Ann.* *1954–5* 724 A new antibiotic, spiramycin, has been extracted from the culture filtrates of a previously undescribed species of streptomyces. **1974** *New England Jrnl. Med.* CCXC. 1110/2 Treatment with spiramycin during pregnancy reduced the overall frequency of the fetal infections.

spirane (spəiə·rēin). *Chem.* Also **spiran** (-æn). [ad. G. *spiran*: see *SPIRO- 2 and -ANE.] Any organic compound having two rings in the molecule with a single atom (usu. of carbon or nitrogen) common to both; a spiro-compound.

In quot. 1919 used *attrib.* of the shared atom.

1911 *Jrnl. Chem. Soc.* C. I. 497 Spirans or dispirans are homo- or hetero-cyclic compounds containing two rings with a carbon atom common to both. **1919** *Ibid.* CXV. I. 323 Strains existing in one ring of a *spiro*-compound could not possibly make themselves felt in the second ring unless communicated by a spirane carbon atom, which itself is in a state of strain. **1950** E. DE B. BARNETT *Stereochem.* iv. 55 Any spirane in which the rings are identical but unsymmetrical should be enantiomorphic. **1972** NATTA & FARINE *Stereochem.* iv. 113 A class very similar to the allenes consists of the spirans—bicyclic compounds whose rings are attached to only one atom. **1978** R. L. BAUMGARTEN *Org. Chem.* xvii. 289 Biphenyls substituted with bulky ortho substituents, substituted allenes, and spiranes are among the classes of compounds that exhibit optical activity although there is no asymmetric carbon atom present.

spirant, *sb.* (Earlier example.)

1862 W. D. WHITNEY in *Jrnl. Amer. Oriental Soc.* VII. VII. 319 The labial series has no sibilants; for its pair of fricatives, surd and sonant..so lack the hissing quality which distinguishes the..sibilants, that it seems preferable to put them in another class; which..we will call the spirants.

spirantal (spəiræ·ntăl), *a.* [f. SPIRANT *sb.* + -AL.] = SPIRANT *a.*

1893 J. CLARK *Man. Linguistics* iii. 41, kį, ghį, k į, ghʷį give for result a sort of geminated spirantal sound. **1928** J. & E. M. WRIGHT *Elem. Middle English Gram.* (ed. 2) vi. 131 The palatal spirantal element began to disappear in pronunciation from about the end of the fourteenth century in the south Midland and southern dialects. **1965** [see *CHIPEWYAN].

spirantization (spəiə:răntəizēi·ʃən). [f. next: see -IZATION.] Making into a spirant; development of a spirantal pronunciation. Also *attrib.*

1911 *Amer. Jrnl. Philol.* XXXII. 37 Breath stress was weaker here than in Germanic, where spirantization took place in spite of the escape of breath in a preceding nasal. **1939** *Language* XV. 64 The second point..is the problem of the spirantization of ungeminated non-emphatic stopped consonants. **1973** J. M. ANDERSON *Structural Aspects Lang. Change* 209 A second spirantization rule converted [ǧ] → [ž] through loss of occlusion. **1977** *Trans. Philol. Soc. 1975* 11 There is no principled way to separate a rule like the spirantization of intervocalic /b d g/ in Spanish from German obstruent devoicing or OE verbal ablaut.

spirantize, *v.* (In Dict. s.v. SPIRANT *sb.* and *a.*) Add: *trans.* To pronounce as a spirant, to make into a spirant. So **spi·rantizing** *ppl. a.* and *vbl. sb.*

1911 *Amer. Jrnl. Philol.* XXXII. 36 The former [*sc.* Iranian] is a spirantizing language, like the old Germanic. *Ibid.*, The spirantizing of voiceless aspirates in Iranian. **1936** *Language* XII. 247 If with the vowels we may include the semivowels, we note here the Balto-Slavonic palatalizations,..[and] the spirantizing of Latin *c* (that is, [k]) as it develops into the Romance languages. **1964** S. K. CHATTERJI in D. Abercrombie et al. *Daniel Jones* 411 In Bengali, the aspirates *ph, bh*, are normally spirantized to [ɸ, β]. **1977** *Word 1972* XXVIII. 252 It cannot be argued that early Guarani might have had an occlusive [d] in initial position and that it would have been a simple matter to spirantize it.

spire, *sb.*[1] Add: **10. b.** *spire-passion.*

1944 BLUNDEN *Cricket Country* v. 64 There is only one person known to me who quite equals my spire-passion.

c. *spire-straight* adj.

1933 C. DAY LEWIS *Magnetic Mountain* 26 There, as a candle's beam Stands firm and will not waver Spire-straight in a close chamber.

† **spireme.** *Cytology. Obs.* Also **spirem.** [ad. G. *spirem* (W. Flemming *Zellsubstanz, Kern und Zelltheilung* (1882) xx. 195), f. Ionic Gr. σπείρημ-α coil, convolution.] The tangled strands of chromosomal material seen in the early stages of cell division, formerly believed to be a single continuous strand (or two in a diploid cell, etc.); = *SKEIN *sb.*[1] 2 c.

1889 *Q. Jrnl. Microsc. Sci.* XXX. 171 We call this stage, with Flemming, the 'Knäuel-Stadium' (skein stage), or 'spirem', or 'mother-skein'. **1905** *Amer. Naturalist* XXXIX. 484 During synapsis the reticulum becomes transformed into a definite spirem. **1910** *Encycl. Brit.* VII. 714/1 As the spireme thread contracts, it segments into a number of short, and usually U-shaped, segments —the 'chromosomes'. **1936** *Discovery* May 161/1 The hypothesis of the continuous spireme, long given up by cytologists, is resurrected, and entirely inaccurate statements are made.

spirit, *sb.* Add: **II. 6. c.** (Further examples.) In Christian charismatic groups: *baptism in* (*of*, etc.) *the Spirit* (and similar phrases), an experience subsequent to conversion and water-baptism, usually evidenced by speaking in tongues (see quot. 1972[2]): in allusion to Mark i. 8 and parallel passages; *to receive the Spirit*, to experience conversion, evidenced by speaking in tongues; *to sing in the Spirit*, to sing in a language apparently unknown to the singer (cf. I Cor. xiv. 15); so *song in the Spirit; the spirit moves me*: see MOVE *v.* 11.

1865 T. T. CARTER in *Oxford Lent Sermons* xiii. 198 Within this new dispensation of the Spirit there is a specially sacred Presence of our Lord. **1896** R. A. TORREY *Baptism with Holy Spirit* i. 20 The Baptism with the Holy Spirit is the Spirit of God coming upon the believer,..imparting to him gifts not naturally his own, but which qualify him for the service to which God has called him. **1902** *Christian* 11 Dec. 13/1 If we are born again, we have received the Spirit once for all. **1903** R. C. MORGAN *Outpoured Spirit* viii. 53 By coming unto Jesus ..as members of the Spirit-baptized Church. **1909** T. B. BARRATT *In Days of Latter Rain* 98 One who is filled with the Spirit..gets visions, prophesies, sings in the Spirit, staggers under the overwhelming weight of the Glory. **1932** C. E. RAVEN *Creator Spirit* iv. 113 It is just as much within this one order that the Spirit works in creation as in those fuller manifestations which we call the Incarnation and Atonement. **1941** D. GEE *Pentecostal Movement* i. 7 For the individual recipient of the baptism in the Spirit it is subsequent to..regeneration. **1948** L. W. BROWN in M. Warren *Triumph of God* vi. 154 There are.. those who maintain that no man has truly received the Spirit unless he has spoken with tongues. **1964** N. BLOCH-HOELL *Pentecostal Movement* ii. 28 Mrs. Arthur.. gives a striking account of angel visions and singing in the Spirit in perfect Latin followed by correct translation into English. *Ibid.*, With regard to the 'song in the Spirit' and the testimony of the nuns it must be remembered that the latter was no first-hand evidence. **1972** S. TUGWELL (*title*) Did you receive the Spirit? **1972** R. A. WILSON tr. *Hollenweger's Pentecostals* ii. 22 In a Bible school in Topeka, Kansas, run by Charles Parham, speaking in tongues was recognized as a distinguishing characteristic of the baptism of the Spirit. **1977** G. W. H. LAMPE *God as Spirit* iii. 91 Perhaps the most original and significant insights of Paul are that the Spirit's inspiration makes men Christlike and, ideally, makes the community a visible re-embodiment of Christ.

8. b. *that's the spirit:* exclamatory phr. used in commendation of someone's courage, determination, etc.

1923 *Spectator* 21 Apr. 657/2 'That's the spirit!' has been the immediate comment of the country. **1930** M. ALLINGHAM *Mystery Mile* xxvii. 272 'I was ashamed that he should be..in my service.' 'That's the spirit,' said Campion. **1963** *Mad Mag.* July 47/1 Good! Good! *That's* the spirit! **1974** G. F. NEWMAN *Price* ii. 70 'I'm absolutely certain I'll be completely vindicated.' 'That's the spirit.'

9. a. *moving spirit* (MOVING *ppl. a.* 2 b).

1902 [see MOVING *ppl. a.* 2 b]. **1926** S. BALDWIN *On England* 66 In a city like this, where the intelligence and the moving spirits of industry meet round this table, what an opportunity you have! **1954** N. MITFORD *Madame de Pompadour* xix. 242 The state papers still passed through her hands and the work was done in her room, but she ceased to be the moving spirit.

10. a. *spirit of place* [tr. L. *genius loci*], the characteristic atmosphere and influence of a particular place.

1918 D. H. LAWRENCE in *Eng. Rev.* Nov. 319 All art partakes of the Spirit of Place in which it is produced. **1955** G. MURCHIE (*title*) The Spirit of Place in Keats. **1980** P. LIVELY *Judgement Day* iii. 26 It was as though the spirit of place, nowadays, exerted its power only over the young. **1981** *Sunday Tel.* 25 Jan. 30/2 Of even the great cathedral of Canterbury Hilaire Belloc wrote with deep sadness for a spirit of place sought but not found.

c. (Further examples.)

1880 *Church Times* 7 May 295/1 Anything in more flagrant violation of the spirit and letter of the Prayer Book can hardly be conceived than to send the Elect out of the choir to put on 'the rest of the Episcopal habit'. **1926** G. M. TREVELYAN *History of England* II. iii. 172 Radicals appealed to the letter and the spirit of 'Magna Charta' against gagging acts, packed juries and restrictions of the franchise. **1961** [see *protectorate law* s.v. *PROTECTORATE *sb.* 4]. **1982** *Church Times* 15 Jan. 20/2 It is..neither in the letter nor spirit of these resolutions for anyone..to act in a way which has the effect of forcing one view upon those who hold the other.

III. 11. b. (Further examples, with reference to Matt. xxvi. 41.)

1666 G. TORRIANO *Piazza Universale di Proverbi Italiani* 268/2 The *spirit* is ready, but the body is lame. **1925** A. HUXLEY *Those Barren Leaves* III. xiii. 269 The spirit is willing, but the flesh is weak. Weak in pain, but weaker still,..more inexcusably weak, in pleasure. **1935** C. ISHERWOOD *Mr. Norris changes Trains* ix. 138, I really must apologize for my shortcomings as a correspondent... The spirit was willing, dear boy. I hope you'll believe that. **1938** W. S. MAUGHAM *Summing Up* x. 30 Though ceasing my methodical study of the old masters (for though the spirit is willing, the flesh is weak), I have continued with increasing assiduity to try to write better.

c. Also (with reference to John iv. 23), *in spirit and in truth*, spiritually and sincerely.

1920 GALSWORTHY *In Chancery* III. xiv. 328 At this moment he knew with certainty that he would never be near to her in spirit and in truth, nor she to him. **1953** A. J. TOYNBEE *World & West* vi. 96 Our hearts are hungry for a divinity that we can worship in spirit and in truth.

IV. 17. d. *out of spirits* (later examples).

1907 G. B. SHAW *John Bull's Other Island* IV. 94 You seem rather out of spirits... You havnt got neuralgia, have you? **1966** G. GREENE *Comedians* I. v. 140 He seemed tired and out of spirits.

VI. 23. a. *spirit-call, -communication, -doctor, -harmony, -house, -land* (earlier example), *-medium, -mischief, -nature, -possession, -stream, thing, tower, -visit, -voice* (earlier example), *-wall, -world* (earlier example).

Some of these are used in sense 23 g but now have a wider use in Anthropology.

1949 BLUNDEN *After Bombing* 17 For young, for old, a spirit-call Even now, bright music, stirs the air. **1869** GEO. ELIOT *Let.* 11 July (1956) V. 48 'Spiritualism' (by which I mean, of course, spirit-communications). **1960** W. NAYLOR *Silver Birch Anthol.* 7 The uncertain art of continuous spirit communication. **1936** *Discovery* June 187/1 The would-be spirit-doctor, who must have what the African regards as a faculty for 'seeing spirits'—we might term it clairvoyancy. **1928** BLUNDEN *Undertones of War* xvii. 177 The flush and abundance of antique life and memorial and achievement, such as blend into the great spirit-harmony of the cities in that part of Europe. **1856** Spirit-house [see *CIRCLE *sb.* 21 b]. **1966** MRS. L. B. JOHNSON *White House Diary* 27 Oct. (1970) 437 There were 'spirit houses' everywhere—brightly decorated little houses..about the size of a bird house, standing on stilts—one beside almost every residence. These houses are to entice the spirits so they will leave *your* house to you. **1973** P. BERTON *Drifting Home* vi. 89 In Little Salmon, the graves are as numerous as the houses. Indeed they are like small cabins—a village of spirit houses with sloping roofs, glass windows and curtains, containing dead flowers and teapots and plates for the use of the deceased. **1841** E. A. POE in *Graham's Mag.* May 241/2 A traveller from the spirit-land. **1853** *Theatr. Jrnl.* 22 June 190/1 A celebrated 'spirit-medium'..advertises a *seance* for the demonstration of spiritual communications. **1979** P. NIESEWAND *Member of Club* vii. 50 We've..got..to enlist the support of spirit mediums. The ancestral spirits are supposed to speak through them. **1915** W. B. YEATS *Reveries over Childhood & Youth* xiv. 70 Somnambulistic country girls..become mediums for some genuine spirit-mischief, surrendering to their desire for the marvellous. **1962** AUDEN *Dyer's Hand* (1963) 135 The greatest of spirit-nature pairs and the most orthodox is, of course, Don Quixote-Sancho Panza. **1909** W. JAMES in *Proc. Soc. Psychical Research* XXIII. LVIII. 35 The whole record of spirit-possession in human history. **1950** BLESH & JANIS *They all played Ragtime* x. 188 The incalculable power generated by the ring-shout rhythms brings about 'spirit-possession', referred to in jazz as being 'sent out of this world'. **1964** GOULD & KOLB *Dict. Soc. Sci.* 638/2 *Spirit possession* seems too broad a term to specify the social functions and active controlling role characteristic of the shaman. **1925** BLUNDEN *English Poems* 93 The time will come when, at the point to die I'll wish a spirit-stream as cool and clear. **1886** W. B. YEATS in *Dublin Univ. Rev.* Jan. 75 Two spirit things a man hath for his friends: Sorrow that gives for guerdon liberty, And joy. *a* **1957** Spirit-thing [see *root-sensation* s.v. *ROOT *sb.*[1] 20]. **1955** E. POUND *Classic Anthol.* III. 158 When he planned to begin a spirit tower Folk rushed to the work-camp and overran All the leisure of King Wen's plan. **1936** E. SITWELL *Victoria of England* i. 20 According to Mr Owen's account, the Duke returned.., after death,..in order to confide matters of importance to him... These spirit-visits must, one imagines, have been the result of the Duke's interest in minor details. **1844** E. A. POE in *Graham's Mag.* Mar. 142/1 During the swell of the organ, the spirit-voice of the deceased addresses itself to the murderer. **1937** *Burlington Mag.* Oct. 162/1 These walls are now generally called *ying pi*—shadow- or spirit-walls... They are often found in front of the street-door, but sometimes also inside the enclosure behind the entrance in order to shut out a view of the interior. They served too as a protection against demons. The idea is current that demons are stupid and therefore only walk straight forward. **1948** G. H. JOHNSTON *Death takes Small Bites* ii. 47 Alongside the road, protecting the big houses from wandering devils, were spirit-walls, blank and forbidding. **1847** W. SMITH tr. *Fichte's Present Age* 62 So does the Spirit-World not indeed *flow* together at the breath of Love, for in it there is no Winter, but there all *is* and *abides* in eternal communion with the mighty Whole.

b. *spirit-bride, -wind* (further examples).

1904 W. H. HUDSON *Green Mansions* xxi. 306 Nor did my mournful spirit-bride come to me. **1917** G. FRANKAU *City of Fear* 26 My Soul would bide with its spirit-bride At the Inn of a Thousand Dreams. **1894** *Wales* May 38/2 Lord, round me then with weeping clouds, And let my mind In quick blasts sigh beneath those shrouds, A spirit-wind. **1934** BLUNDEN *Choice or Chance* 3 (*heading*) Spirit-Wind.

d. *spirit-dazzling, -giving, -lifting, quelling* (earlier example), *-quenching, -strangling, -up-lifting.*

1946 R. S. THOMAS *Stones of Field* 12 Deadly as a falcon brooding over its prey In a tower of spirit-dazzling and splendid light. **1946** BLUNDEN *Shelley* xvi. 199 The spirit-giving blue sky of spring. **1841** E. A. POE in *Gift 1842* 161 Spirit-lifting ecstasy of adoration. **1812** Spirit quelling [see *nerve-racking* s.v. *NERVE *sb.* 11 b]. **1601** DONNE *Progresse of Soule* in *Poems* (1633) 3 Spirit-quenching sicknesse, dull captivitie. **1948** F. R. LEAVIS *Great Tradition* v. 232 Coketown (the spirit-quenching hideousness of which is hauntingly evoked). **1930** BLUNDEN *Summer's Fancy* 49 Of sloughs, of sleepless pangs, of Golgothas, of spirit-strangling. **1951** L. MACNEICE tr. *Goethe's Faust* 299 Here is the prospect free, Spirit-uplifting.

e. (*a*) *spirit-baptized, -filled;* (*b*) *spirit-rotten.*

1903 R. C. MORGAN *Outpoured Spirit & Pentecost* 53 How are we to be filled with the Spirit? By drinking; by coming unto Jesus, and as members of the Spirit-baptized Church. **1974** Spirit-baptized [see *PENTECOSTAL *sb.* b]. **1895** J. MACNEIL (*title*) Spirit-filled life. **1936** J. BRICE *Pentecost* xiii. 226 The prayer-life of the Spirit-filled believer is transformed through his new apprehension of the Father. **1977** *Belfast Tel.* 17 Jan. 2/8 (Advt.), Full Gospel Bible College at Millmount, Randalstown... We can promise you dynamic spirit-filled Ministry with David Hathaway. **1922** D. H. LAWRENCE *Fantasia of Unconscious* v. 75 We are sympathy-rotten, and spirit-rotten, and idea-rotten.

g. *spirit guide, healer, healing, photograph, photography* (earlier example), *-writing* (earlier example).

1856 *Spiritual Herald* Feb. 3 Spirit hands, spirit voices, spirit healing. **1864** BROWNING *Dram. Pers.* 179 David.. peeps in the glass ball, Sets to the spirit-writing, hears the raps. **1872** *Spiritualist* 15 Apr. 25/1 Within the last six weeks in London, spirit photography has set in like a flood. **1877** H. P. BLAVATSKY *Isis Unveiled* II. ii. 118 A medium must be *passive*; and if a firm believer in his 'spirit-guide' he will allow himself to be ruled by the latter. **1909** W. JAMES in *Amer. Mag.* Oct. 585/2 Rappings, apparitions, poltergeists, spirit-photographs, and materializations. **1956** R. M. LESTER *Towards Hereafter* x. 124 My husband and I visited a trance medium, and a spirit healer we now know as Dr Light spoke through her. **1960** *Spectator* 28 Oct. 649 One of their [*sc.* Spiritualists'] chief interests is 'spirit healing'; that is, any healing that is brought about by a non-human agency. **1982** E. JENKINS *Shadow & Light* xxii. 172 A matter between him and his spirit-guides, not one with which human beings had anything to do.

i. Special *Comb.*: **Spirit baptism** = *baptism in the Spirit,* sense 6 c above.

1964 N. BLOCH-HOELL *Pentecostal Movement* vii. 142 Glossolalia, in connection with the Spirit baptism, was generally believed to be a permanent Gift of Grace. **1977** G. W. H. LAMPE *God as Spirit* vii. 199 It [*sc.* Pentecostalism] is very emphatic in its assertion of a two-stage relationship to God, reception of the Spirit, or Spirit-baptism, being sharply differentiated from the state of being a Christian without that added gift of God.

24. b. *spirit-flask* (earlier and later examples); *spirit-shop* (earlier example), *vault* (earlier example).

1829 G. GRIFFIN *Collegians* II. xxix. 302 The assault made by Danny on her spirit flask, which she now.. discovered to be empty. **1961** L. G. G. RAMSEY *Connoisseur New Guide to Antique English Pott., Porc. & Glass* 73 Other manifestations of Early Victorian work..were the ..spirit flasks formed into the shapes of human figures. **1835** *Mirror of Parliament* 20 May 983/2, I would willingly, if there was any chance of succeeding, include spirit-shops. **1848** MRS. GASKELL *Mary Barton* II. iv. 57 The rest was taken in a spirit vault, and the refreshment was a glass of gin.

c. *spirit-merchant* (earlier example).

1822 *Sunday Times* 20 Oct. 3/4 *Bankrupts*... James Cayne, jun. and Thomas Bullock Watts, of Yeovil, Somersetshire, spirit-merchants.

e. *spirit duplicator, kettle.*

1958 *Daily Mail* 24 July 6/6 We came to the spirit duplicators... These machines *were* rather magical. They duplicated in seven different colours. **1890** *Girl's Own Paper* 4 Jan. 213/3 An Etna or small spirit kettle, and a bottle of spirits; some tea and a little sugar. **1923** M. BEERBOHM *Peep into Past* 10 His portly form..may be seen bending over the little spirit-kettle. **1960** C. DAY LEWIS *Buried Day* vii. 137 Cake-stand,..heavy silver teapot, spirit-kettle and all.

spiriting, *vbl. sb.* Add: **3. b.** The application of a spirit, as a finishing process in french polishing. Also with *off.*

1933 C. CRAMPTON *Canework* (ed. 6) iii. 36 The last operation in french polishing, which gives the final gloss, is known as 'spiriting off'. **1960** C. H. HAYWARD *Staining & Polishing* ix. 55 Purpose of spiriting. The idea of this process is gradually to burnish the surface of semi-soft shellac.

spiritism. (Earlier example.)

1856 *Spiritual Herald* July 203 Witchcraft was an unfriendly form of spiritism, and calculated to produce fear.

spirit-lamp. (Earlier example.)

1767 J. PRIESTLEY *Hist. & Present State of Electricity* VIII. xii. 700 The bar was heated by a spirit lamp placed underneath it.

spirit-rapper. (Earlier example.)

1853 H. PAUL *Rappings & Table Movings* 9 A rival spirit rapper! A genuine Medium.

spirit-rapping. Add: **1.** (Earlier example.)

1852 *Harper's Mag.* Dec. 129/1 The spirit-rappings are again engrossing a lion's share of the talk.

2. (Earlier example.)

1853 H. MATTISON (*title*) Spirit rapping unveiled!

spiritual, *a.* and *sb.* Add: **A.** *adj.* **I. 1. a.** (Further *Comb.* examples, in apposition.)

1916 JOYCE *Portrait of Artist* (1969) v. 252 Turned off that valve at once and opened the spiritual-heroic refrigerating apparatus, invented and patented in all countries by Dante Alighieri. **1929** D. H. LAWRENCE *Paintings of D. H. Lawrence* A4[v] This no doubt is all in the course of the growth of the 'spiritual-mental' consciousness.

c. (Later examples.) See sense 5 of the sb. in Dict. and Suppl.

1905 [see *gospel song* s.v. *GOSPEL *sb.* 9]. **1964** *Amer. Folk Music Occasional* I. 15 Q. What kind of music did you like best at this time, spiritual music or blues or what? R. I always liked the spiritual music the best.

e. *spiritual home* (with no religious connotation), a place or milieu, other than one's home, which seems especially congenial or in harmony with one's nature, or to which one feels a sense of belonging or indebtedness.

1932 *Week-End Rev.* 7 May 586/1 If they write about it at all they make it clear that Europe is their spiritual home. **1941** A. CHRISTIE *Evil under Sun* iii. 52 A man like you would be at Deauville or Le Touquet... That's your—what's the phrase?—spiritual home. **1962** WODEHOUSE *Service with Smile* xi. 164 He disliked Lord Ickenham, considering him a potty sort of feller whose spiritual home was a padded cell in some not too choosy lunatic asylum. **1967** [see *PAPER *sb.* 8 b]. **1977** [see *RASTAFARIAN *a.* and *sb.*].

3. a. (Further examples.)

1843 *Quincy* (Illinois) *Herald* 15 Dec. 3/1 Hyram Smith has had a revelation confirming the spiritual wife system. **1901** KIPLING *Kim* v. 111 The comfort..of being properly ..respected as her spiritual adviser by a well-born woman. **1925** *Ladies' Home Jrnl.* Apr. 38/1 It is considered by the elderly women of Utah a great and sacred privilege to be the spiritual wife of Brigham Young or the Prophet Joseph Smith in the world to come. **1951** J. T. MCNEILL *History of Cure of Souls* iii. 42 Among ancient civilizations, that of India seems to have given the greatest prominence to the spiritual director. **1980** *Tablet* 26 Jan. 8/2 He.. cited..divorced Catholics in second marriages who, after prayer and consultation with a spiritual director, have returned to the sacraments. *Ibid.* 95/3 A letter I wrote in reply to my spiritual children was produced.

4. c. *spiritual healing,* cure or healing attributed to the agency of (a) spirit; faith-healing.

1899 H. W. DRESSER *Spiritual Healing* vi. 54 How can I live according to the principles of spiritual healing among people who have no sympathy with the new principles. **1926** W. T. WALSH *Sci. Spiritual Healing* iii. 30, I announced a service of spiritual healing to be held in the church every Thursday morning after the celebration of the Holy Communion. **1980** *Spiritual Healer* XXVIII. 131 We have known many instances of migraine..being overcome through spiritual healing.

B. *sb.* **5.** Substitute for def.: = *Negro spiritual* s.v. *NEGRO 7. (Earlier and later examples.)

1866 *Harper's Mag.* May 775/1 Maum Rina flavored all her dishes with these 'spirituals', as they are called among the negroes. **1926** A. NILES in W. C. Handy *Blues* 9 These songs [*sc.* the blues] were woven of the same stuff as the other overlapping items in the long list,—the work-songs, love-songs..; yes, and decidedly the spirituals. **1947** S. BELLOW *Victim* iv. 39 Harkavy and a girl he had brought to the party were singing spirituals and old ballads. **1981** M. DOODY in Martin & Mullen *No Alternative* iv. 53 'Oh! Sometimes it causes me to tremble, tremble, tremble' as the spiritual goes.

spiritualism. Add: **2.** (Earlier example.)

1796 [see *IDEAL *sb.* 1].

3. (Earlier example.)

1853 J. DIX *Transatlantic Tracings* xiv. 244 Every two or three years the Americans have a paroxysm of humbug—..at the present time it is Spiritual-ism.

4. (Earlier examples.)

1850 J. R. LOGAN in *Jrnl. Indian Archipelago* IV. 552, I would proceed at once to facts illustrative of the different forms of spiritualism which prevail in Eastern Asia and Asianesia. **1867** E. B. TYLOR in *Proc. R. Inst.* V. 90 A slight acquaintance with the spiritualism of the savage has sometimes led to its being considered as the result of a degeneration from the opinions of more cultured races.

spiritualist. Add: **3.** (Earlier example.)

1796 F. A. NITSCH *Kant's Princ. concerning Man* 153 The Spiritualists having discovered immaterial objects convert the mind into a spirit, and so on.

4. (Earlier example.)

1852 E. B. BROWNING *Let.* 13–14 May in *Lett. Brownings to George Barrett* (1958) 181 Lady Elgin is a great spiritualist with a leaning to Irvingism & a belief in every sort of incredible thing.

5. (Earlier example.)

1837 J. S. MILL in *Westm. Rev.* XXVII. 17 Many sterling thoughts are..disguised in phraseology borrowed from the spiritualist school of German poets and metaphysicians.

spiritus (spi·ritus). [L., = breath, aspiration, spirit.] **1.** *Gr. Gram.* = BREATHING *vbl. sb.* 9; *spiritus asper*: see ASPER *sb.*[1]; *spiritus lenis* (lī·nis), smooth breathing; the sign (') placed over an initial vowel to show that it is not aspirated.

[**1470** PRISCIANUS *Grammatici* (1855) I. II. 51 In dictione tenor certus, absque ea incertus, non potest tamen sine eo esse. Similiter spiritus asper vel lenis.] **1867** MAX MÜLLER *Chips from German Workshop* II. 87 Sanskrit v is generally represented in Greek by the Digamma, or the spiritus lenis. **1878** W. G. RUTHERFORD *First Gr. Gram.* 3 This sign (') is called *spiritus asper,* or rough breathing. **1888** KING & COOKSON *Princ. Sound & Inflexion Gr. & Latin* viii. 171 An initial *i̯* becomes the spiritus asper, sometimes changed to spiritus lenis. **1936** G. K. ZIPF *Psycho-Biol. of Lang.* iii. 84 In Greek..the aspiration of the first aspirate was lost, even though the first aspirate was only an *h* (spiritus asper), that is, a phoneme which consisted exclusively of the aspiration. **1948** D. DIRINGER *Alphabet* viii. 458 By adopting this system of rough and smooth breathing (*spiritus asper* and *spiritus lenis*) for the vowel sounds,..the Greek alphabet helped to preserve flexibility in the Greek speech. **1976** *Archivum Linguisticum* VII. 170 Thus Schmalstieg does not give a clear explanation of..other initial aspirations like the *spiritus asper* in Greek.

2. *spiritus rector* (re·ktǫɪ), a ruling or directing spirit.

1911 W. JAMES *Some Probl. Philos.* i. 16 Thus a '*spiritus rector*' would be a metaphysical,—a 'principle of attraction' a theological,—and a 'law of the squares' would be a positive theory of the planetary movements. **1935** A. REVUSKY *Jews in Palestine* xii. 202 The leader and *spiritus rector* of this movement, Vladimir Jabotinsky. **1942** D. D. RUNES *Dict. Philos.* 300/1 *Spiritus rector,*.. some sort of subtle natural force in corporeal beings. The alchemists applied the expression to some substance..said to be capable of transmuting metals into gold, and also an elixir which was supposed to prolong life indefinitely. **1959** R. F. C. HULL tr. *Jung's Aion* in *Coll. Wks.* IX. 167 It [*sc.* the self]..is older than the ego, and..is the *spiritus rector* of our fate. **1977** *Times* 20 Dec. 13/6 It has often been reported that the international oil companies were the real *spiritus rector* for the explosion of oil prices during the winter of 1973–74. **1980** *Encounter* May 35/1 More than fifteen years ago he was the *spiritus rector* of the *European Journal of Sociology*.

spiro-. Add: **1. spirochæte** (also **-chet-** in this word and its derivatives): now with pronunc. (spəi·rəkīt); in mod. use, any bacterium of the order Spirochætales, comprising actively motile non-spore-forming organisms having a helical form; (later examples); hence **spirochæ·tal** *a.*, that is a spirochæte; caused by spirochætes; **spi:rochætici·dal** *a.*, lethal to spirochætes; **spirochæ·ticide** a spirochæticidal substance; **spirochæto·sis,** infection with or a disease caused by spirochætes.

1916 *Jrnl. Exper. Med.* XXIII. 377 We discovered a spirochætal microorganism which is now believed to be the cause [of Weil's disease]. **1922** *Encycl. Brit.* XXXI. 906/1 It is best described as spirochætal jaundice rather than by the older name of Weil's disease. **1969** Edington & Gilles *Path. in Tropics* vii. 298 Leptospirosis is caused by infection with spirochaetal organisms. **1908** *Practitioner* Oct. 549 The treponema, or, as they are usually designated in this country, the spirochaetes. **1919** *Chambers's Jrnl.* June 415/2 This organism belongs to the class known as spirochaetes, of which the spirochaete of syphilis and that of relapsing fever are other members. **1939** R. Campbell *Flowering Rifle* II. 47 The fierce spirochete. **1973** R. G. Krueger et al. *Introd. Microbiol.* iii. 59/1 The order is subdivided into two families: Spirochaetaceae for the larger..spirochaetes, which are free-living or parasitic in shellfish; and Treponemataceae for spirochetes that are only about 0·2–0·3 μm in diameter and do not exceed 16 μm in length. **1913** *Jrnl. Exper. Med.* XVIII. 435 (*heading*) A study of the spirochæticidal action of the serum of patients treated with Salvarsan. **1949** M. A. Jennings in H. W. Florey et al. *Antibiotics* II. xxxi. 1037 Penicillin possessed some spirocheticidal activity. **1920** *Jrnl. Amer. Med. Assoc.* 25 Dec. 1768/1 The efficacy of..spirocheticides in the so-called chemical prophylaxis of syphilis is limited to a period of not more than eight hours after the spirochete has had the opportunity of invading the healthy person. **1906** *Jrnl. Hygiene* VI. 580 (*heading*) Spirochaetosis of mice due to *Spirochaeta muris* n.sp. in the blood. **1951** Whitby & Hynes *Med. Bacteriol.* (ed. 5) xxi. 350 Spirochætes and fusiform bacilli of Vincent's type may be found in large numbers in various conditions, particularly of the lung, known as spirochætosis. **1981** *Brit. Med. Jrnl.* 21 Nov. 1362/1 A review of 100 consecutive rectal biopsy specimens obtained from patients with rectal bleeding or diarrhoea showed that 10 had spirochaetosis.

2. *Chem.* Formative element used in the names of organic compounds whose molecular structure includes two rings with a single atom (usu. of carbon or nitrogen) common to both. Also in *Comb.* or as quasi-*adj.*, as *spiro-compound*. [Introduced in Ger. (A. Baeyer 1900, in *Ber. d. Deut. Chem. Ges.* XXXIII. 3771).]

1908 *Chem. Abstr.* II. 75 (*heading*) Spirocyclane. *Ibid.*, The term 'spiro' is applied by the author to systems of two cycloids, having only one carbon atom in common. **1909** *Jrnl. Chem. Soc.* XCVI. I. 652 The product, decomposed by cold water, yields the spirocyclane derivative. **1915** *Ibid.* CVII. II. 1080 (*heading*) The formation and stability of *spiro*-compounds. **1932** *Proc. R. Soc.* A. CXXXIV. 359 The anhydrous crystals of racemic *spiro*-dihydantoin have a density of 1·94. **1960** *Jrnl. Amer. Chem. Soc.* LXXXII. 5560/1 According to the number of spiro atoms present, the compounds are distinguished as monospiro, dispiro, trispiro compounds *etc.* **1976** A. L. Ternay *Contemp. Org. Chem.* vii. 185 A spiro compound results when two rings share one atom. **1978** *Nature* 5 Jan. 44/2 During irradiation of spiropyrans, in non-polar solvents dimer and charge-transfer complexes are formed. **1978** *Further Perspectives Org. Chem.* (CIBA) 40 Evidence for the possible spiro intermediate would give enormous support and we are seeking it.

spirograph (spəiə·rəgraf). *Med.* [f. Spiro- + -graph.] An instrument which provides a continuous tracing of the movements of the lungs during respiration.

1890 in Gould *New Med. Dict.* **1934** *Publ. Mod. Lang. Assoc. Amer.* XLIX. 1168 The air pressure and vibrations taken back of the point of contact with the spirograph. **1977** *Bull. Exper. Biol. & Med.* LXIV. 1662 The investigation is stopped when changes in the helium concentration in the spirograph decrease to a certain small value.

Hence **spi·rogram,** the tracing produced by a spirograph; **spirogra·phic** *a.*, pertaining to or observed by means of a spirograph; **spirogra·phically** *adv.*; **spiro·graphy,** the study of respiration by means of a spirograph.

1946 L. N. Gay *Bronchial Asthma* i. 7 (*caption*) Spirographic tracings of Hofbauer. **1956** Hinshaw & Garland *Dis. of Chest* vi. 89 Tracings of respiration, sometimes called spirograms, are readily made by means of a calibrated spirometer equipped with a writing device. **1959** *Presse Médicale* No. 47. Suppl. 2/1 Having studied clinically and spirographically a population of 232 patients, authors make first a distinction between three groups according to the intensity of dyspnea. *Ibid.*, Spirography allows effectively to make a distinction between three groups of patients. **1977** *Lancet* 22 Jan. 156/1 (*caption*) Spirogram of habitual hyperventilator showing irregular amplitude and frequency of respiration and sighing tendency. *Ibid.* 26 Mar. 709/1 Their diagnosis of hyperventilation is based on..a spirographic pattern for which criteria of abnormality are lacking. **1977** *Bull. Exper. Biol. & Med.* LXXXIII. 3 On the basis of indices obtained by the motion-picture spirography method, a definite idea can thus be obtained of the functional state of the apparatus for controlling respiration under different conditions.

spirogyra (spəirodʒəi·rā). Also **Spiro-**. [mod.L. (H. F. Link in C. G. D. Nees von Esenbeck *Horæ Physicæ Berolinensis* (1820) i. 5), f. Spiro- + Gr. γῦρός, γῦρά round.] A green filamentous fresh-water alga of the genus of this name.

1875 Bennett & Dyer tr. *Sachs's Text-bk. Bot.* II. 220 Each single cell of Spirogyra, like an isolated cell of Closterium, &c., constitutes an individual. **1906** G. F. S. Elliot *First Course Pract. Bot.* 57 The joint protoplasm, called the 'zygospore',..begins to divide and form a new Spirogyra. **1937** E. E. Stanford *Gen. & Econ. Bot.* xiii. 346 Spirogyra..is so abundant, so characteristic, and so readily studied that it commonly passes as a 'characteristic' chlorophyte, which decidedly it is not. **1962** *Listener* 16 Aug. 240/1 There are many other kinds of microscopic organisms,..the desmids, the green strands of Spirogyra, and the rest. **1971** P. Crampton tr. *Heyerdahl's Ra Expeditions* iii. 50 A shallow pool about as big as a wash-basin, but completely covered with green spirogyra.

spiroidal (spəiroi·dăl), *a.* [f. Spiroid *a.* + -al.] = Spiroid *a.*

1928 T. C. Chamberlin *Two Solar Families* xiv. 143 If a series of projected bolts were shot forth from a sun in succession toward the star while all were being pulled forward by the star but in different degrees, the train they formed would obviously be curved in a spiroidal manner. **1972** *Nature: Physical Sci.* 6 Nov. 22/1 The majority of the crystals were acicular or whisker-like although a few were spiroidal.

spirolactone (spəirolæ·ktōun). *Chem.* and *Pharm.* [f. *spiro- 2 + *lactone 2.] Any spirane in which one of the rings is a lactone; *spec.* any of the series of steroid derivatives to which spironolactone belongs.

1958 *Canad. Med. Assoc. Jrnl.* LXXIX. 883/1 The administration of Spirolactone results in a persistent and significant increase in sodium excretion. **1959** *Jrnl. Org. Chem.* XXIV. 743/1 The spirolactone side chain was built onto a steroid nucleus containing an aromatic A ring. **1961** *Lancet* 16 Sept. 618/2 With the development of the 17-spirolactones, which are aldosterone antagonists, a new method has become available for investigating possible cases of primary aldosteronism. **1970** Passmore & Robson *Compan. Med. Stud.* II. xi. 10/1 The main reason for believing that spirolactones are aldosterone antagonists is that they reverse all the renal effects of aldosterone.

spironolactone (spəiə:rŏnolæ·ktōun). *Pharm.* [f. *spirolactone.] A steroid spirolactone derivative, $C_{24}H_{32}O_4S$, which is an aldosterone antagonist, increasing sodium excretion, and is used esp. in the treatment of œdema and hypertension associated with hyperaldosteronism.

1960 *Austral. Ann. Med.* IX. 188/1 In the present paper we describe the use of a similar drug, spironolactone ('SC 9420', 'Aldactone', Searle). **1961** *Lancet* 2 Sept. 528/2 Spironolactone 100 mg. four times daily definitely improved six out of seven myasthenic patients. **1974** R. M. Kirk et al. *Surgery* vii. 146 Treatment with diuretics or spironolactone, and dietary salt restriction, help to reduce the accumulation of fluid. **1977** *Lancet* 17 Sept. 600/2 Spironolactone relieved muscle fatigue in paramyotonia congenita—an effect possibly mediated by the accompanying hyperkalæmia.

spiroplasma (spəiə·roplæzma). *Biol.* [mod. L., f. Spiro + Plasma.] Any of a group of pathogenic prokaryotes lacking a cell wall and related to the mycoplasmas, but characterized by their helical structure and rotatory movement.

1973 Davis & Worley in *Phytopathology* LXIII. 407/1 In order to distinguish the organism from previously described species and to avoid possible inappropriate use of the term 'mycoplasmalike',..we are coining the term spiroplasma. **1976** *Ann. Rev. Microbiol.* XXX. 181 More recently, spiroplasmas have been cultivated from corn plants infected with corn stunt disease.

spit, *sb.*[1] Add: **4. b.** An instrument used by Customs officers for probing and examining cargo.

1925 *Chambers's Jrnl.* 19 Sept. 668/1 A barbed 'spit' is used for examining cotton, wool, and various coarse goods, so that a portion of the interior may be drawn out. A flat, wooden 'spit' is used in the examination of rolls of carpet, cloth, linoleum... A short, fine 'spit' is used for probing the stuffing and packing in and around furniture. **1970** M. Greener *Penguin Dict. Commerce* 310 *Spit*, a weapon used by Customs authorities to discover whether dutiable goods are hidden in other cargo.

7. spit-jack, a spit with a turning mechanism (see quot. 1967).

1967 *Antique Finder* Aug. 11/3 *Spit jacks...* These mechanisms were fitted on the wall at the side of the fireplace in order to rotate the carcass in front of the fire. A heavy weight was suspended from a cord and wound over the cylinder. The power was conveyed by a series of cogged wheels to another cylinder connected by a cord with a grooved disc on the end of the spit itself, which it slowly turned. **1971** R. Howe *Mrs Groundes-Peace's Old Cookery Notebk.* 65 There was the 'spit-jack', a weight-driven spit, considered in the sixteenth century as a labour-saving device.

spit, *sb.*[2] Add: **1. c.** *spit and sawdust*: the floor covering (esp. formerly) typical of the general bar of a public house (see quot. 1937); hence, the bar itself. Freq. *attrib.* (also *transf.*). Cf. *sawdust *sb.* 3 b.

1937 Partridge *Dict. Slang* Add. 995/1 *Spit and sawdust*, a general saloon in a public-house: C. 20. Ex the sawdust sprinkled on the floor and the spitting on to the sawdust. **1969** D. Clark *Death after Evensong* ii. 40 Where shall I start? In the spit and sawdust? I take it you'll do the saloon bar yourself. **1971** R. Busby *Deadlock* x. 158 The Porter's Arms, a spit and sawdust public house near the markets. **1972** *Guardian* 24 Feb. 10/2 Pub styles polarize into 'Spit and Sawdust'..and 'Architects' Fanciful'. **1976** *Rhyl Jrnl. & Advertiser* 9 Dec. 1/1 He thought that a 'rough and ready, spit and sawdust affair' could be produced and made available for consideration at the council's estimates meetings. **1977** *Lancashire Life* Mar. 58/2 They also convert buildings into billiard clubs, where the decor is attractive and the spit-and-sawdust era is just a memory.

2. c. *to go for the big spit*: to vomit. *Austral. slang.*

1967 F. Hardy *Billy Borker yarns Again* 40 Don't tell me the Gargler went for the big spit. **1970** *Private Eye* 10 Apr. 16 He goes for the big spit and accidentally entombs a nice old lady and her dog in tepid chuck. **1975** R. Beilby *Brown Land Crying* 225 Goin' for the big spit, was I? I don't remember.

3. a. Also, *the* (*dead*) *spit of. colloq.*

1885 Hall Caine *Shadow of Crime* II. xxvi. 129 A brother..the spit of hissel'. **1901** E. W. Hornung *Black Mask* 37 I'll chance you having another ring..the dead spit of mine. **1921** 'K. Mansfield' *Let.* Sept. (1977) 232 One of his [*sc.* Cézanne's] men gave me quite a shock. He's the *spit* of a man I've just written about, one Jonathan Trout. **1936** M. de la Roche *Whiteoak Harvest* v. 98 Easy for a boy to look like his grandmother. There was Renny—the spit of old Gran! **1953** A. Upfield *Murder must Wait* xvii. 154 The son's the dead spit of the old man. **1966** [see *gramp].

b. *spit and image*: see also *image *sb.* 4 a. Also *spit image* and absol. *spit.* Cf. the (later) forms *spitten image, spitting image* s.v. *spitten *a.*, *spitting *ppl. a.* 3 respectively.

1929 J. B. Priestley *Good Companions* I. v. 166 That's theirs... It's the spit image o' yours, too. **1949** *Penguin New Writing* XXXVI. 35 My husband saw a man that was the spit-image of King no further away than Jackson. **1966** *New Statesman* 18 Feb. 235/1 For most of the last two acts he's catapulted in and out of doors, changing on the way into the cheerfully sodden porter of the bordel who happens to be his spit.

5. spit-curl: for *U.S.* read orig. *U.S.*; (earlier and later examples); **spit-insect,** restrict † to sense in Dict. and add: (*b*) the cuckoo-spit insect, *Philænus spumarius*; cf. *spittle-bug* s.v. *spittle *sb.*[2] 4.

1831 *Boston* (Mass.) *Transcript* 9 Sept. 2/1 What would the reverend Doctor say of the 'spit curls', and Chinese precision of a modern dandyzette's head gear? **1857** [see *beau-catcher* s.v. *beau *sb.* 3]. **1903** Farmer & Henley *Slang* VI. 314/1 *Spit-curl, subs. phr.* (costers').—A curl lying flat on the temple; a *soap-curl*. **1957** L. Durrell *Justine* I. 37 A spitcurl at each temple. **1968** J. Ironside *Fashion Alphabet* 198 *Spit curls*, small curls brought forward on to the cheek, often moistened with 'spit'. **1950** J. Brooke *Goose Cathedral* iv. 82 Little green spit-insects dropped out of the tamarisks into one's cup. **1917** Kipling *Divers. Creatures* 9 There's a nice little spit-kitten for you!

Spit, *sb.*[4] Colloq. abbrev. of *Spitfire* (in full *Supermarine Spitfire*), a British fighter aeroplane produced between 1936 and 1947.

1941 *Saturday Rev. Lit.* (U.S.) 4 Oct. 9/3 A pilot 'aviates'..a Wimpy or Spit (Spitfire). **1948** G. V. Galwey *Lift & Drop* ii. 25 From time to time Miss Procter..said 'Here come the jet jobs,' or 'The Spits are lovely.' **1965** *New Statesman* 7 May 718/2 'Look, Ron,' he cried, 'my old Spit!' **1980** J. McClure *Blood of an Englishman* vi. 64, I was flying Spits, Hurricanes, while Bonzo..was in Bomber Command.

spit, *v.*[1] Add: **1. c.** Of a Customs officer: to examine with a 'spit'.

1925 *Chambers's Jrnl.* 19 Sept. 668/1 The officer.. selects a number of bales for inspection. These he 'spits' —that is, he inserts a special iron instrument, which is capable of penetrating to the interior of a large bale and extracting a small piece of the commodity.

spit, *v.*[2] Add: **I. 2. b.** (Later *fig.* example.)

1915 T. S. Eliot *Love Song J. Alfred Prufrock* in *Poetry* (Chicago) June 132 How should I begin to spit out all the butt-ends of my days and ways.

c. Also, to *spit blood*, (*a*) to express vehement anger, to rage (*colloq.*); (*b*) *slang*, of a spy, etc.: to fear exposure; *to spit chips* (Austral. slang), (*a*) to feel extreme thirst; (*b*) to manifest acute anger or vexation.

1901 *Bulletin Reciter* (Sydney) 108 While you're spitting chips like thunder... And the streams of sweat near blind you. **1946** A. Marshall *Tell us about the Turkey, Jo* 142, I was spitting chips. God, I was dry! **1947** J. Morrison *Sailors belong Ships* 189 Old Mick Doyle's with them. He's spitting chips because they're not using sea water. **1954** P. GLADWIN *Long Beat Home* 17 It's enough to make you spit chips when you think of Sydney—movies and vaudeville comedies and a decent musician once in two years. **1963** J. JOESTEN *They call it Intelligence* I. iv. 45 When a resident agent is forced to lie low, because counter-espionage is on his trail, it is said of him that he is 'spitting blood'. **1963** WODEHOUSE *Stiff Upper Lip, Jeeves* ix. 72 If there's one thing that makes a collector spit blood, it's hearing about another collector getting a bargain. **1965** I. SOUTHALL *Ash Road* 77 Not when I saw Mr Fairhall last. He was spittin' chips because Peter had gone away. **1966** L. DEIGHTON *Billion-Dollar Brain* x. 90 A man tailed or suspected is said to be 'spitting blood'. **1966** 'L. LANE' *ABZ of Scouse* 102 When I think of it I could spit blood.

3. a. (Further Amer. examples.)

1773 *Let.* 26 Aug. in *Maryland Hist. Mag.* (1920) XV. 280 The wind is strong at N:E. & it spits Rain. **1803** B. HUNT *Diary* 16 Apr. in *Chester Co.* (Pa.) *Hist. Soc. Bull.* (1898) 7 Continues cold and Spiting snow. **1835** N. WYETH *Jrnl.* 12 Jan. in F. G. Young *Sources Hist. Oregon* (1899) I. 243 Spit snow all day at night set in to snow.

4. Freq. in phr. *to spit it out*: to reveal, confess, disclose something.

1855 MRS. GASKELL *North & South* I. xxv. 313 I'm easier in my mind for having spit it out. **1904** [in Dict.]. **1920** GALSWORTHY *Skin Game* I. 31 Don't be so mysterious, mother. If you know something, do spit it out! **1935** AUDEN & ISHERWOOD *Dog beneath Skin* II. v. 115 Go on, then, spit it aht! **1950** J. CANNAN *Murder Included* vi. 123 'I've gotta clue.'.. 'Spit it out, for mercy's sake, boy.' **1981** A. PRICE *Soldier No More* 43 'Well—spit it out, man! Don't just stand there,' Willis exhorted him.

II. 7. b. Also *spec.* with *out*, of ceramic glazes: to form blisters which burst during firing.

1904 *Trans. Eng. Ceramic Soc.* IV. 30 The china vase.. with the Seger porcelain glaze..has no sign of blister.., and does not spit out in the kiln. *Ibid.* 32 The earthenware trials that have spit out are not verified by the china trials.

c. (Later examples with *on*.)

1949 H. L. MENCKEN *Mencken Chrestomathy* xxx. 626 Is it hot in the rolling-mill? Are the hours long? Is $15 a day not enough? Then escape is very easy. Simply throw up your job, spit on your hands, and write another 'Rosenkavalier'. *a* **1975** WODEHOUSE *Sunset at Blandings* (1977) ii. 20 There was a time when you had to employ wild horses to drag me from London, and they had to spit on their hands and make a special effort.

10. *spit and polish*: also in extended use, precise correctness, smartness; freq. as a derogatory expression in contrast with purposeful work or utility. Also *attrib.*, smart in appearance; hence *spit-and-polished* adj.

1914 C. BERESFORD *Mem.* I. 120 From that day onwards I set myself steadily against bright-work and spit-and-polish. **1920** *Q. Rev.* Jan. 196 Gunnery had been neglected in pursuit of 'spit and polish'. **1949** 'J. TEY' *Brat Farrar* xiii. 116 He had understood Brat's distrust of the [stables'] spit and polish. **1950** *Daily Progress* (Charlottesville, Va.) 23 Sept. 1/7 Officially Pretzer was.. part of the spit and polish First Infantry Division. **1958** *Times* 12 Nov. 3/3 Holst's suite, 'The Planets', was very, very much better..thanks to..the orchestra's ever-increasing spit-and-polish. **1977** L. MEYNELL *Hooky gets Wooden Spoon* xiii. 172 Some nice chubby-faced spit and polish Sandhurst type. **1977** *Times* 8 Nov. 4/3 The spit-and-polished toecaps of his boots. **1979** *United States 1980/81* (Penguin Travel Guides) 614 The 4,300 spit-and-polished midshipmen have a 3:45 PM dress parade on Warden Field.

III. 11. The vb. stem in combination as **spit-cat, kitten** *colloq.* = SPITFIRE *sb.* 2.

1898 A. OLLIVANT *Owd Bob* v. 51 Eh, but art' a tearin' spit-cat surely! **1912** KIPLING *Divers. Creatures* (1917) 9 There's a nice little spit-kitten for you!

Spitalfield(s). Add: Also applied to silk and velvet made up there into furnishings, etc., or to the weavers (orig. Huguenot refugees) involved in this trade. Occas. *absol.*

1812 H. & J. SMITH *Rejected Addresses* 120 Spital-fields with real India vies... Old calico, torn silk, and muslin new. **1819** M. EDGEWORTH *Let.* 24 Mar. (1971) 185 Mr. Buxton very plain sense and admirable facts about Newgate and Spitalfield weavers and all that. **1861** C. M. YONGE *Young Step-Mother* iii. 26 He was..of the Protestant French sort, that..ran away from the Sicilian vespers, or the Edict of Nantes, I don't remember which; only the Spitalfields weavers have something to do with it. **1894** *Country Gentleman's Catal.* 155/2 Umbrellas.. very best Spitalfields twill silk. **1952** M. COST *Hour Awaits* 89 The small red drawing-room, its damask hangings of Spitalfields silk. **1955** R. FASTNEDGE *Eng. Furniture Styles* iii. 86 Queen Anne's state bed, at Hampton Court, is hung, with Spitalfields velvet, patterned in rich colours on a cream ground. **1972** P. ROGERS *Grub Street* ii. 115 Such persistant troublemakers as the Spitalfields weavers. **1976** T. JEAL *Until Colours Fade* ii. 30 The Red Drawing Room..its walls were lined with faded crimson Spitalfields' silk. **1980** J. ROSE *Elizabeth Fry* iv. 68 The Spitalfields weavers, thrown out of work by the powerlooms.

spi·tball. *N. Amer.* Also **spit-ball, spit ball.** [f. SPIT *sb.*[2] + BALL *sb.*[1]] **1.** A spittle-ball (see SPITTLE *sb.*[2] 4), esp. one thrown as a missile by a schoolchild.

1846 *Knickerbocker* XXVII. 410 They..crooked pins, made pop-guns, ejected spit-balls. **1899** W. JAMES *Talks to Teachers* 92 The spitballs that Tommy is ready to throw. **1939** L. M. MONTGOMERY *Anne of Ingleside* xi. 71 Bertie Shakespeare Drew threw a spit-ball at her. **1956** M. STEARNS *Story of Jazz* (1957) xix. 252 Gillespie was also perfecting his spitball-throwing technique while in the Calloway band. **1977** I. SHAW *Beggarman, Thief* II. iii. 143 They [*sc.* the teachers] spend most of the time trying to keep the kids from..throwing spitballs.

2. *Baseball.* A ball moistened on one side with saliva or sweat before pitching, so that it acquires a swerve. (Illegal in the official game.)

1905 J. J. MCGRAW *Official Baseball Guide* 13 The perfect 'spit' ball drops from a batter's hips to his knees or below in perhaps two feet of forward motion. **1912** C. MATHEWSON *Pitching in Pinch* 20 Some spit-ball pitchers announce when they are going to throw a moist one by looking at the ball as they dampen it. **1928** G. H. RUTH *Baseball* vi. 75 All spit balls break down, but by turning the wet spot one way or the other the pitcher can make the ball break in or out as he desires. **1946** MEZZROW & WOLFE *Really the Blues* (1957) viii. 125 His arms [were] pumping like he was a pitcher winding up to shoot a spitball over the plate. **1976** *Billings* (Montana) *Gaz.* 7 July 4–A/2 That's what I can do for the Cubs. I guarantee that they will be snarling and swearing, gouging, spiking, mauling. They'll be throwing beanballs and spitballs.

3. *transf.* and *fig.*

1888 *Judge* 10 Nov. 68/1 All statements to the opposite effect are spit-balls at the moon. **1925** FRASER & GIBBONS *Soldier & Sailor Words* 266 *Spit ball*, hand-grenade. (U.S. Army.) **1931** W. G. MCADOO *Crowded Years* xv. 225 Their vitriolic comments..consisted chiefly of mere verbal spitballs thrown in a..mood of..sabotage. **1933** E. O'NEILL *Days without End* I. 33 They'd turned naughty schoolboys and were throwing spitballs at Almighty God. **1960** I. WALLACH *Absence of Cello* 58 She also thought that their impulse to outrage was over-developed. 'You all sit around and throw spitballs at the world,' she said. **1981** T. BARLING *Bikini Red North* xii. 263 It doesn't make a spitball of difference. The deadline stands.

Hence **spi·tball** *v. intr.*, to throw out suggestions for discussion; **spi·tballer,** one who throws spitballs.

1928 *Chicago Tribune* 7 June 19/4 The Giants..made only three hits off..Clarence Mitchell, the southpaw spitballer. **1955** H. KURNITZ *Invasion of Privacy* (1956) viii. 64 I'm just thinking out loud... Spitballing we call it in the movie business. **1961** J. B. PRIESTLEY *Saturn over Water* iv. 52 No, don't tell me we're not talking about painting. I'm only spitballing while I try to think. **1976** C. LARSON *Muir's Blood* xvii. 98 'Are you serious?' Blixen asked. 'I'm spitballing,' Schreiber replied. **1977** *New Yorker* 2 May 100/3 The spitballer won't grow into His father's jacket.

spitchered (spi·tʃəɹd), *a. slang* (orig. *Naut.*). [f. Maltese *spicca* finished, ended, perh. ult. f. It. *spezzare* to break into pieces, fragment.] Rendered inoperative, ruined.

1920 *Blackw. Mag.* Mar. 340/2 'Cease firing!' screamed the C.O. 'He's spitchered.' **1946** J. IRVING *Royal Navalese* 163 *Spitcher'd*, finished, done. **1970** P. DICKINSON *Seals* i. 14 That damned gadget might..be functioning right as rain in thirty seconds, or it might be spitchered for ever.

spite, *sb.* Add: **2. d.** *spite fence*, a wall, fence, etc., erected with the intention of causing annoyance. orig. and chiefly *U.S.*

1899 *Everybody's Mag.* I. 70/2 Meanwhile an ordinance was passed making the building of spite fences illegal. **1928** *Hearst's Internat.* Aug. 89/2 For the full depth of the boundary ran a tall fence of unpainted boards set upright. This fence was fully eighteen feet high. It was what is known as a spite-fence. **1957** R. F. V. HEUSTON *Salmond on Torts* (ed. 12) v. 201 An occupier of land is free to erect a wall or fence with the sole object of blocking his neighbour's view, or preventing him from acquiring an easement of light—a 'spite-fence' as it is sometimes called. **1977** *New Yorker* 23 May 50/3 To gain privacy from the street, he put up a nine-foot wall, which one of his neighbors, interpreting it as a spite fence, sued unsuccessfully to have removed.

spitfire, *a.* **2.** (Earlier example.)

1858 MAYNE REID *Ran away to Sea* (1859) xii. 93 Even under such a wind she still continued to carry most of her sail..while her storm, spit-fire, and third jibs were still kept bent to the breeze.

Spi·thead. The name of an anchorage and a strait which lie off Portsmouth, used *attrib.* in *Spithead nightingale* (see quots.) and *Spithead pheasant* (*a*) a bloater; (*b*) a kipper. *Naut. slang.*

1890 BARRÈRE & LELAND *Dict. Slang* II. 283/1 *Spithead nightingales* (naval), boatswains, and boatswains' mates, on account of their calls. **1948** PARTRIDGE *Dict. Forces' Slang* 177 *Spithead pheasant, a*, a bloater. (Navy.) **1954** *News Chron.* 4 Nov. 1/4 He had to produce: 1. a cat; 2. a Spithead Pheasant (a kipper); 3. a Sick Bay Shackle (a safety-pin). **1963** *Times* 26 Feb. 12/6 Spithead pheasant—slang for a kipper—still appears on the Navy's menu, but Spithead nightingales—bo'sun's mates and call boys are 'off'.

spi·t-out. *Ceramics.* [f. vbl. phr. *to spit out*: see *SPIT *v.*[2] 7 b.] Accidental blistering of a glaze when fired, caused by air or gas bubbles; the blisters so caused.

1909 *Trans. Engl. Ceramic Soc.* VII. 1 'Spit-out' is one of a number of 'mysterious' faults which occur in the manufacture of pottery. **1930** A. B. SEARLE *Encycl. Ceramic Industries* III. 199/1 'Spit-out' is most abundant when the atmosphere in the kiln is alternately reducing and oxidising. **1964** H. HODGES *Artifacts* ii. 52 Pin-holes ..and spit-out (fine, broken blisters) are most commonly due to the evolution of gases from the body during firing puncturing the molten glaze. *a* **1977** *Harrison Mayer Ltd. Catal.* 19/2 Spit-out. This is a common fault which occurs during the decorating fire and consists of the formation of minute blisters or bubbles in the glaze... Spit-out occurs at the higher enamel kiln temperature.

spi·t-roast, *v.* [f. SPIT *sb.*[1] + ROAST *v.*] *trans.* To cook (meat or fish) on a spit, either over a fire or in an oven. Freq. as *vbl. sb.* and *ppl. a.*

1954 J. A. BEARD *Compl. Bk. Barbecue & Rotisserie Cooking* 39 (*heading*) Rotisserie & spit roasting. **1959** *Good Food Guide* 27 The new landlord has already succeeded in astonishing the locality by spit-roasting a whole calf in the open for a Church festival. **1961** *House & Garden* Feb. 45 A spit-roasted chicken bought from the supermarket. **1961** S. BECK et al. *Mastering Art French Cooking* vi. 240 Spit roasting, when the chicken is wrapped in fat and continually rotated, is far less exacting than oven roasting. **1973** *Country Life* 13 Dec. 2024/2 Pike is particularly delicious when spit-roasted whole. **1976** *Times* 14 Feb. 11/5 Spit roasted is how these birds are served... Baste them frequently while spit roasting..you can check whether your spit roasted chicken is ready. **1978** *Lancashire Life* Nov. 150/2 John explains how the spring chicken will be spit roasted.

‖ **spitskop** (spi·tskǫp). *S. Afr.* Also **spitzkop,** and in dim. forms **spitzkopje, -koppie.** [Afrikaans *spitskop*, f. Du. *spits* pointed + *kop* *KOP.] A sharp-pointed hill; also (with capital initial) used as a proper name.

1872 C. A. PAYTON *Diamond-Diggings S. Afr.* 3 He has the tabular mountains and 'spitzkops' (sharp pointed hills and peaks)..till he arrives within a few hours' distance of the Vaal. **1889** [see *RANDJIE]. **1905** G. W. STOW *Native Races S. Afr.* xx. 396 The headquarters of 'Kousopp were at the two spitzkopjes to the left of the 'Gumaap. **1937** A. J. H. GOODWIN in I. Schapera *Bantu-Speaking Tribes S. Afr.* ii. 33 The flat-topped and 'spitzkop' hills so typical of the Karroo country and other parts. **1974** *Standard Encycl. S. Afr.* X. 221/2 The Spitskoppies group is a collection of gigantic granite rocks or 'island' mountains rising out of the Namib plain... It is a broken range dominated by the Great Spitskop (.. 1742 metres).

spit-sticker. Add: Also in shortened form **spit-stick.**

1909 in WEBSTER. **1920** R. J. BEEDHAM *Wood Engraving* 3 The spit-sticks..are tools by which the cut can be easily broadened by gradually pressing the point deeper into the wood. **1960** G. LEWIS *Handbk. of Crafts* 187 The Spitstick, like the graver, is made in several thicknesses. Its section is triangular, with sides tapering gently down to a point.

spitten (spit'n), *a. dial.* Repr. corrupted pronunc. *spit and* (*image, picture*) s.v. SPIT *sb.*[2] 3 b in Dict. and Suppl. Cf. *spitting image* s.v. *SPITTING *ppl. a.* 3; *splitting image* s.v. *SPLITTING *ppl. a.* 5.

1878 W. DICKINSON *Gloss. Dial. Cumberland* (ed. 2) 92/1 *Spitten picter*.., a strong likeness. **1887** HALL CAINE *Deemster* II. xxvi. 233 He looked the spitten picture of my ould father. **1910** A. BENNETT *Clayhanger* I. ii. 17 A nice-behaved young gentleman, and the spitten image of his poor mother. **1928** *Eng. Jrnl.* Dec. 819 Hit's the spitten image of you, Jilson. Your likeness, pint blank... Thar you are a-settin' in your cheer, a-holdin' your fiddle; thar's your basket. **1936** W. HOLTBY *South Riding* v. iv. 313 Spitten image of his dad, little Alf is, isn't he, Reg? **1941** J. FAULKNER *Men Working* vi. 105 Ifen hit ain't the spitten image of that church acrost the street.

spitter[2]**.** Add: **3.** *U.S. Baseball.* = *SPITBALL 2.

1908 *Baseball Mag.* July 7/2, I found by holding the ball with my finger tips and steadying it with my thumb alone I could get a peculiar break to it... It is not a 'spitter'. **1975** *New Yorker* 14 Apr. 98/2 The next pitch broke down sharply over the plate, and everyone cried, 'Spitter! Hey, a spitter!'

spitting, *vbl. sb.*[2] Add: **4. c.** Also *spitting distance.*

1959 P. BULL *I know Face, but..* iv. 70 One of the reasons I had closed with the Chatham offer was that it was within spitting distance of London. **1965** *Listener* 3 June 841/3 All this the spectators can see at spitting distance. **1977** *Western Mail* (Cardiff) 5 Mar. 6/1 More than doubled pre-tax profits has taken the Midland Bank to within spitting distance of its two giant High Street rivals—National Westminster and Barclays.

spitting, *ppl. a.* Add: **1.** (Later *poet.* examples.)

1910 W. B. YEATS *Green Helmet* 33 With my spitting-cat heads, my frenzied moon-bred band. **1953** DYLAN THOMAS *Under Milk Wood* (1954) 48 And in Willy Nilly the Postman's dark and sizzling damp tea-coated misty pygmy kitchen where the spittingcat kettles throb and hop on the range.

2. spitting cobra, the African black-necked cobra, *Naja nigricollis.*

1931 R. L. DITMARS *Snakes of World* xiii. 167 The Spitting Cobra or Black-necked Cobra..comes close to being the most dangerous snake of Africa. **1976** G. DURRELL *Stationary Ark* ii. 28 This [word] was expectorated with a venom that would have done credit to a spitting cobra.

3. *spitting image*, alteration of *spitten image* (see *SPITTEN *a.*). Cf. *splitting image* s.v. *SPLITTING *ppl. a.* 5.

1901 A. H. RICE *Mrs. Wiggs* vii. 94 He's jes' like his pa —the very spittin' image of him! **1917** A. W. BLUE *Quay Head Tryst* 70 He's the spittin image o' a thrawn fechter. **1929** H. S. WALPOLE *Hans Frost* III. v. 370 In another twenty years..she would be her mother's spitting image. **1938** N. COWARD *Operette* I. vii. 58 Believe it or not, she was the spitting image of Princess Ena! **1960** H. PINTER *Caretaker* II. 33 Your spitting image he was. *a* **1974** R. CROSSMAN *Diaries* (1975) I. 243 Far from adapting himself to his new position he is adapting his new position to himself (No. 10, as I saw the other day, is the spitting image of his little house in Hampstead).

spittle, *sb.*^{2} Add: **4. spittle bug** *U.S.* = *froghopper* s.v. FROG^{1} 8; cf. CUCKOO-SPIT^{2} I.

1882 *Vermont Agric. Rep.* VII. 77 Dr. Cutting spoke of the frog hopper, usually known as the spittle bug on grass. **1948** *Sun* (Baltimore) 9 June 26/8 Spittle-bug infection has damaged alfalfa fields. **1972** SWAN & PAPP *Common Insects N. Amer.* xiii. 136 Spittlebugs are named for the sticky, bubbly mass of froth with which the nymphs surround themselves.

spi·ttled, *a.* [f. SPITTLE *sb.*^{2} + -ED^{2}: cf. SPITTLE *v.*^{1}] Covered with spittle.

1926 *Scots Observer* 1 Jan. 5/1 The tangled, insect-spittled vetches. **1939** DYLAN THOMAS *Map of Love* 12 The spittled eyes, the salt ponds in the sleeves.

spittly, *a.* Delete † *Obs. rare*$^{-0}$ and add: Also **spittley.** (Examples.)

a **1861** [see *BOXY *a.*^{2} 1]. **1935** E. R. EDDISON *Mistress* xxi. 434 Spittly and slimy..from the beast's mouth I plucked it out. **1949** L. A. G. STRONG *Maud Cherrill* ix. 47 Once again would come the sly leer and the spittly whisper. **1980** J. O'FAOLAIN *No Country for Young Men* iv. 71 'God blosht the wet turf,' she whispered and blasted it herself with spittly breath.

spitty (spi·ti), *a.* [f. SPIT *sb.*^{2} and *v.*^{2} + -Y^{1}.] Resembling spit; spitting or inclined to spit. Also *fig.*

1742 W. ELLIS *Mod. Husb.* June x. 73 They believe the Grass-hopper will breed from this spitty Matter. **1865** H. J. DANIEL *Muse in Motley* 43 He wud spet, Iss, spetty like a toad. **1909** *Chambers's Jrnl.* June 388/1 It took longer to get acquainted with the Major, who..spoke in such a spitty, hissy, foreign kind of way. **1945** B. MACDONALD *Egg & I* vi. 99 Great winds came bounding down..; blew rain at us in spitty gusts. **1950** *Audio Engin.* Sept. 32/2 The program material sounds *ragged* and *spitty*, and the *whisker* at the main peak can sometimes be detected. **1976** U. HOLDEN *String Horses* ii. 26 Lavender..smiled her spitty smile.

Spitz. Substitute for def.: A dog belonging to one of a group of northern breeds distinguished by thick fur, a pointed muzzle, pricked ears, and a tail curled over the back. Also *attrib.*, as *Spitz dog.* (Earlier and further examples.)

1842 H. STANLEY *Let.* 18 July in N. Mitford *Ladies of Alderley* (1938) 38 In this town [*sc.* Ems] wherever you go you see a white Spitz dog with a curly tail & black eyes. **1897** *Private Life of Queen* xviii. 147 The perky little tan-coloured German Spitz-dog, 'Marco'. *a* **1910** 'O. HENRY' *Rolling Stones* (1912) 181 Six burglars..bore away..a five-hundred-dollar prize Spitz dog. **1948** [see *LAIKA]. **1978** *Times* 11 Feb. 2/4 The Japanese spitz, a small, white prick-eared creature like an undernourished Samoyed, appeared at Crufts for the first time.

Spitzenberg (spi·tsənbɜːɡ). Also **spitzenberg, Spitzenbergh, Spitzenburg.** [Origin unkn.; cf. quot. 1795.] An apple with a red and yellow skin, belonging to the North American variety so called, developed from a seedling first found at Esopus, N.Y.; also, the tree bearing this fruit.

1795 J. JAY *Let.* 12 Dec. in *Columbia Library Columns* (1970) XIX. 43 Ten are what we call Spitzenberghs, from the Name of the Man in whose orchard the first tree of the kind was found. **1809** 'D. KNICKERBOCKER' *Hist. N.Y.* I. III. i. 122 Mottled and streaked with dusty red, like a spitzenberg apple. *a* **1817** T. DWIGHT *Trav. New-Eng.* (1821) I. 45 The varieties of apple-trees are:.. Spitzenberg, Holden Sweeting, Fall pippin. **1869** *Rep. Comm. Agric. 1868* (U.S. Dept. Agric.) 482 [He] names the Baldwin for dessert and cooking, the Spitzenburg for cooking. **1894** H. FREDERIC *Copperhead* 71 He..picked out another apple—a spitzenberg this time. **1921** *Daily Colonist* (Victoria, B.C.) 8 Oct. 19/1 (Advt.), 320 Boxes of Apples..from our own ranch..Spitzenberg at $3.23. **1949** J. B. HERRICK *Memories* 5 Father laid in..a barrel each of Spitzenburgs and Baldwins.

Spitzflöte (spi·tsflötə). Also with small initial and anglicized **Spitz-flute, spitz flute,** etc. [Ger., f. *spitz* pointed, acute + *flöte* flute.] An organ stop of the type of the gemshorn, yeilding a tone resembling that of the flute.

1855 E. J. HOPKINS *Organ* 118 The pipes of the Spitzflute are slightly conical. **1884** *Encycl. Brit.* XVII. 831/1 The 8 spitzflöte may be regarded as a variety of open diapason. **1894** T. ELLISTON *Organs* 119 *Spitz flute*, 8 ft. pitch. **1923** N. A. BONAVIA-HUNT *Mod. Organ Stops* 31 The spitzflöte differs in having a more graduated taper. **1925** W. L. SUMNER *Organ* x. 301 In British organs the stop is usually called spitzflöte or spitz flute... The spitzflöte has an interesting..and attractive tone with more harmonic development than the usual English gemshorn. **1966** H. & J. NORMAN *Organ Today* xi. 120 The Spitzflute (or more accurately Spitzflöte) is a large-scale open flute, the taper giving it blending qualities that would otherwise be lacking.

spitzkop, var. *SPITSKOP.

spitzy (spi·tsi), *a.* [f. SPITZ + -Y^{1}.] Resembling or pertaining to a Spitz dog. Also *fig.*, pointed.

1937 AUDEN & MACNEICE *Lett. from Iceland* xii. 185 A sort of little sheepdog, black and white with a thick but not very long coat, a broad forehead and a spitzy foreface. **1952** C. L. B. HUBBARD *Pembrokeshire Corgi Handbk.* i. 14 The extremely sharp-pointed tips to the ears prevalent in the more Spitzy Pembrokeshires. **1968** *Sunday Truth* (Brisbane) 3 Nov. 58/4 He had a 'spitzy nose'—a sharp nose—a scar on his left arm where he had been hurt by machinery.

spiv (spiv), *sb. slang.* [Origin obscure: perh. from SPIFF *v.*^{2}, SPIFFY *a.*] A man who lives by his wits and has no regular employment; one engaging in petty blackmarket dealings and freq. characterized by flashy dress.

1934 A. BRACEY *School for Scoundrels* 336 *Spiv*, petty crook who will turn his hand to anything so long as it does not involve honest work. **1937** *Even. News* 12 Mar. 15/6 (Advt.), With the Lincoln and the Grand National in the offing, the twisters, the welshers, the 'spivs' and the 'boys' are getting ready for a profitable session of the gentle sport of rooking the racegoer. **1939** [see *BARROW *sb.*^{3} 4]. **1945** [see *LAIRY *a.*^{2} 1]. **1947** *Times* 13 Aug. 6/1 If spivs meant men living by their wits, the nets could be thrown very wide indeed. **1948** I. BROWN *No Idle Words* 107 It is queer that its opposite [of *deep*], wide, should have replaced it in Spiv-English. **1952** 'J. HENRY' *Who lie in Gaol* viii. 123 In appearance, he resembled the typical spiv; with coat-hanger shoulders, and pointed shoes, and a smile that would have been an asset to any confidence man. **1958** *People* 4 May 1/4 Who was responsible for letting the spivs hi-jack the crowds at Wembley? **1965** *New Statesman* 26 Nov. 851/1 The emergence of Robert Stephens, once a type-cast West End performer of small, seedy spiv-roles, as a major heroic actor in the making. **1978** *Cornish Guardian* 27 Apr. 3 Metrication will be an open invitation for every spiv and racketeer to cheat the British public.

Hence as *vbs.*, (*a*) *intr.*, to make one's living as a spiv; (*b*) *trans.*, to spiff, to spruce (oneself) *up*; **spivved** (spivd), *ppl. a.*; **spi·v(v)ery,** behaviour characteristic of a spiv or the state of being a spiv; **spi·vvish, spi·v(v)y** *adjs.*, characteristic of a spiv; **spi·vishly** *adv.*

1945 B. NAUGHTON in C. Madge *Pilot Papers* 99 See his Spivy coat—the width of the lapels, the padded-out shoulders? **1947** *Times* 18 Nov. 2/4 Instead of that brave new Britain all they had left was a land fit for bookies to spiv in. **1948** *Chambers's Jrnl.* Oct. 547/1 That is their focus, their touchstone—recognition of a unique quality in him, not to be obliterated by the sordid elements in his story, his obvious shiftiness of character, his spivery attributes or his too frequent lapses. **1948** C. DAY LEWIS *Otterbury Incident* ii. 18 Tilting his hat at an even more spivvish angle. **1951** KOESTLER *Age of Longing* I. i. 7 Surrounded by relatives and friends, a spivvy son and an insipid daughter,..he would have to meet the ultimate ordeal. **1952** A. WILSON *Hemlock & After* I. v. 96 I've spivved along on my own steam as far as I can go. **1956** D. M. DAVIN *Sullen Bell* 87 There were few people in the restaurant, spivvish-looking and absorbed. **1957** R. HOGGART *Uses of Literacy* ix. 225 Where domestic or personal roots are weak or have been forcibly broken, these attitudes can quickly lead to an extensive moral 'spivvery'. **1959** I. JEFFERIES *Thirteen Days* iii. 37 Scruffy lot. They'll get spivved up quick enough for a Naafi girl. **1965** *New Statesman* 19 Mar. 463/1 The spivvish businessman. **1966** J. GLOAG *Sentence of Life* ii. 30 The inspector's jacket was sharply, spivishly waisted. **1971** B. W. ALDISS *Soldier Erect* 177 We spivved ourselves up, put on clean shirts, and strolled out of camp. **1976** *Times* 5 Feb. 21/5 Willott..has no time for spivvery within or without the law. **1976** *Listener* 26 Feb. 245/4 The pelvic lead singer, spivved, moustached, sharp. **1978** *Time Out* 18 Aug. 55/5 Hoffman, spivvy and moustached for maximum seediness, is an ex-con on parole who can't go straight.

splack, *adv. rare*$^{-1}$. [Echoic.] With a sound suggestive of splashing and smacking.

a **1960** E. M. FORSTER *Maurice* (1971) xxxviii. 182 Mr London and Mr Featherstonhaugh dived splack into the water lilies.

splake (splēɪk). *N. Amer.* [f. SP(ECKLED (*ppl.*) *a.* + LAKE *sb.*^{4}] A trout produced by crossing the lake trout, *Salvelinus namaycush*, and the speckled trout, *S. fontinalis.*

1954 *Sun* (Baltimore) 27 May 2/7 Biologists of the Ontario Department of Lands and Forests have completed the first step of an experiment in producing a new variety of game fish. The 'splake' has resulted. It is a hybrid, the result of crossing speckled and lake trout. **1968** *Globe & Mail* (Toronto) 5 Feb. 6/4 A hardier type of trout called splake..is being introduced. **1979** *Whig-Standard* (Kingston, Ontario) 9 Feb. 26/1 Splake from inland waters are highly colored compared to those from the great lakes which are usually silvery.

splanchno-. Add: **splanchnocra·nium,** those lower and anterior bones and cartilages of the head and face that are derived from visceral arch elements; opp. *neurocranium* s.v. *NEURO-; hence **splanchnocra·nial** *a.*; **splanchnome·galy** [Gr. *μεγαλ-*, *μέγας* large], an enlarged condition of the viscera.

1907 W. N. PARKER tr. *Wiedersheim's Compar. Anat. Vertebrates* (ed. 3) 75 A series of cartilaginous arches arise in serial order on the ventral side of the brain-case; these encircle the anterior part of the alimentary tract like hoops, incomplete dorsally, and are distinguished as the visceral portion of the skull (splanchnocranium). **1931** SAUNDERS & MANTON *Man. Pract. Vertebr. Morphol.* xii. 121 The brain-box and sense capsules form the neurocranium, while the jaws and visceral arches form the splanchnocranium. **1974** D. & M. WEBSTER *Compar. Vertebr. Morphol.* iv. 58 Of the splanchnocranial cartilages, the most anterior pair is the mandibular arch. *Ibid.* 59 (*caption*) Lateral view of the splanchnocranium of an acanthodian. [**1900** DORLAND *Med. Dict.*, Splanchnomegalia.] **1910** *Practitioner* Jan. 34 There is sometimes also a general increase in the size of the various internal organs, a condition of splanchnomegaly. **1970** N. G. SCHNEEBERG *Clin. Endocrinol.* v. 70/2 Generalized marked splanchnomegaly occurs, though enlargement of the liver is most common.

splash, *sb.*^{1} Add: **1. e.** A small quantity of liquid, *spec.* a dash of soda-water or tonic, etc., added to spirits as a drink.

1922 JOYCE *Ulysses* 551 Here, to buy yourself a gin and splash. **1935** G. GREENE *England made Me* v. 243 The atmosphere of..the week-end jaunt, the whisky and splash. **1965** 'J. LE CARRÉ' *Looking-Glass War* xv. 173 Woodford's wife added a little soda to her Scotch, a splash: it was habit rather than taste. **1977** *Rolling Stone* 30 June 81/3, I walked to the bar, ordered a double vodka with a splash of tonic no fruit.

2. a. *to make a splash* (earlier example).

1804 G. COLMAN *Let.* 9 Jan. in A. Mathews *Mem. Charles Mathews* (1838) I. xx. 434 A vile part, surely, for the *début* of a man who is to make a *splash.*

b. Also *attrib.*

1832 J. ROMILLY *Diary* 6 May (1967) 12 Missed Hearing Roze's Sermon..:—hear it was poor: tho with a splash passage against the wickedness of manufactures.

d. *colloq.* The prominent display in a newspaper of an advertisement, headline, or story; the material so displayed, usu. of a dramatic or sensational character. Freq. *attrib.*

1922 JOYCE *Ulysses* 638 The usual splash page of letterpress about the same old matrimonial tangle. **1932** H. NICOLSON *Public Faces* xi. 288 We must get the news back here before to-night—time for full splash in tomorrow's papers. **1933** W. MOSS *Polit. Parties Irish Free State* iii. 127 'Splashes', i.e. full-page advertisements using the most effective appeals and backed with extensive and detailed argument. **1948** *Manch. Guardian Weekly* 1 July 2 The perfect 'splash' story in the lull after the Republican Convention. **1960** J. ROBB *Front Page Story* 46 Percy tossed the latest copy over to Bert, the 'Splash' sub. 'Splash' sub was the title given to the man who normally handled only the page-one lead. He was usually..the best sub-editor in the office. **1966** *New Statesman* 13 May 680/3 The paper had reverted to its old jittery habit of lifting other people's splashes and exclusives. **1974** *Globe & Mail* (Toronto) 23 Oct. 12/7 'Anything could happen,' said..Michael Wilson after the London papers gave splash play to his announcement. **1977** *New Yorker* 24 Oct. 55/2 The violent crimes.., if they occur in New York City, get a one-day splash in the *News.* **1979** P. NIESEWAND *Member of Club* iv. 31 Coutrney turned back to the paper ..to look at the front page. The splash story was the row over the death of a young South African commando. **1982** *Chicago Sun-Times* 2 Dec. 67 Speakes gave a thorough briefing on the Cabinet Council study, providing the rest of the nation a Page 1 splash the next day.

4. b. *Med.* Also *splash sound.* A sound produced by a mixture of air and liquid in the stomach or other cavity when it is sharply disturbed. Cf. *SPLASHING *vbl. sb.*^{1} 1 b.

1890 F. TAYLOR *Pract. Med.* 435 The presence of air and liquid together in the pleural cavity may be demonstrated by the test known as Hippocratic succussion, or splash sound. **1908** HUTCHISON & RAINY *Clin. Methods* (ed. 4) 66 It should be remembered..that a splash may be elicited over even a normal stomach shortly after a meal containing much fluid,..and care should also be taken not to mistake a splash produced in the transverse colon for a stomach splash. **1938** N. L. ECKHOFF in H. Rolleston *Brit. Encycl. Med. Pract.* VII. 226 A splash may be heard in cases of pyloric obstruction, and in some cases of obstruction in the colon. **1971** [see *SPLASHING *vbl. sb.*^{1} 1 b].

6. b. Amphetamines. *U.S. slang.*

1969 J. GARDNER *Complete State of Death* ix. 166 The American..addicts..call most of the amphetamines 'speed', in the same way as they talk of others as 'bennies', 'splash', 'cartwheels'. **1974** M. C. GERALD *Pharmacol.* xvii. 332 Amphetamines (Benzedrine),..*Bennies, Peaches, Splash.*

splash, *v.*^{1} Add: **I. 2. a.** Also, to pour *out* with a splash.

1908 E. F. BENSON *Blotting Bk.* ii. 51 Mills..splashed himself out a liberal allowance of brandy into his glass.

c. *colloq.* To present (news, etc.) ostentatiously, or as a 'splash' (*SPLASH *sb.*^{1} 2 d).

1930 *London Mercury* Feb. 317 All the evening papers have 'splashed' the story. **1934** A. P. HERBERT *Holy Deadlock* 210 She was 'splashed' in the newspapers as a sort of modern St. Joan. **1946** J. W. DAY *Harvest Adventure* xvi. 272 London and provincial newspapers 'splashed' this first organized revolt against a tyranny and waste of public money. **1958** *Punch* 1 Jan. 59/3 The story was splashed over the front page. **1969** [see *PAR *sb.*^{4}]. **1979** A. BRINK *Dry White Season* II. vi. 138 The photograph of Emily embracing Ben was splashed on the front page of an English newspaper.

d. *colloq.* To spend (money) extravagantly or ostentatiously. Freq. const. advbs., esp.

in phr. *to splash* (money) *out on* (something). Also *intr.*

1934 *Times* 7 Mar. 7/5 Public money ought not to be splashed about in this manner without grave and searching examination by the House of Commons. **1938** S. Beckett *Murphy* 79 He thought for a second of splashing the fourpence. **1946** F. Sargeson *That Summer* 82 After we'd splashed on a talkie we went home. **1960** S. Barstow *Kind of Loving* II. ii. 170, I splash eight-and-six on a pound box of chocolates and send them with a little note. **1973** *Courier & Advertiser* (Dundee) 1 Mar. 2/2 Allied now plan to splash out an extra £150,000 on advertising. **1973** E. Lemarchand *Let or Hindrance* xiv. 170 They..splashed the lolly around when the pay packets came in. **1978** *Morecambe Guardian* 14 Mar. 17/2 Splash out on something new to wear; the result will be worthwhile.

II. 5. d. Const. *down*. Of a spacecraft: to alight on the sea after a space flight. Also *transf.* Cf. *splashdown.

1962 *Daily Tel.* 4 Oct. 1/7 Cdr. Walter Schirra.. 'splashed down' safely in the Pacific at 10.28 (BST) last night. **1965** *Economist* 4 Sept. 873/1 By the time they splashed down on Sunday Lieutenant-Colonel Cooper and Lieutenant-Commander Conrad had completed the longest-ever manned flight in space. **1969** *Times* 3 June (Suppl.) p. iii/4 Apollo 11 is due to splash down at 5.52 on July 24. **1978** *Times* 1 Aug. 2/1 The ill-fated [balloon] Zanussi in which they splashed down.

splash-. Add: **1. splashback,** a panel fastened to and protecting the wall behind a sink, cooker, etc., from splashes; **splash cymbal,** a small, light cymbal; **splashguard,** a guard fitted to an object to prevent splashing; **splash party** *U.S.*, a party at which the guests engage in swimming and other water sports; **splashplate,** a metal splashback on a cooker; **splash pool,** a shallow paddling pool for children; **splash-proof,** *a.*, impermeable to splashes; **splash zone,** that area adjacent to the sea, a waterfall, etc., that is continually splashed by water.

1926–7 *Army & Navy Stores Catal.* 295/3 *Bathroom accessories*... White opal Splash Back with fitted 5-in. shelf. **1961** *Which?* Dec. 317/1 Oven, grill and hotplate controls were either on the front of the cooker or on the splash-back. **1971** *Ideal Home* Apr. 52/1 Plain blue tiles form a splashback panel round the back. **1982** *Daily Tel.* 3 Aug. 9/1 Cast iron washstand.., with tiled splashback and mirror, is rare and costly at £1,000. **1961** Splash cymbal [see *crash cymbal* s.v. *crash *sb.*[1] 7]. **1964** Splash cymbal [see *choke *v.* 10 b]. **1917** *Harrods Gen. Catal.* 516/1 The 'Reliance' Splash Guard. Solid Red Rubber... When ordering please state outside diameter of tap. **1962** *Which?* Mar. 87/1 All the continuous feed models [of waste-disposers]..had a splashguard, a slotted rubber cover across the entrance to the grinding chamber which allows you to push waste through but prevents water and scraps from being flung out. **1930** *Amer. Speech* VI. 121 *Splash*.., swimming: Splash Party of Girls' Club Lively Affair. **1956** W. H. Whyte *Organization Man* xxii. 291 'Splash' parties (all you can eat for a dollar). **1967** *Gloss. Terms Gas Industry* (*B.S.I.*) 89 *Splashplate*, a panel above and behind a hotplate. **1970** *Which?* June 175/1 Many of the stoves had splash plates—usually of painted metal. **1971** *Sunday Express* (Johannesburg) 28 Mar. 16/3 (Advt.), Beautiful 3 bedroomed home with really lovely garden... Splash pool for children. **1976** *Billings* (Montana) *Gaz.* 16 June 5-D/4 (Advt.), Keep kids cool all summer. 8′ × 18″ splash pool with vinyl liner. **1929** *Radio Times* 8 Nov. 451/2 A 20 amp-hour accumulator... Vent is large, splash-proof and spray-tight and screws in. **1965** *Wireless World* July 36 (Advt.), Dustproof and splashproof. **1933** *Jrnl. Marine Biol. Assoc.* XVIII. 453 During the winter, continued storms will keep the height of the splash zone at five feet or more. **1956** F. W. Adams in D. L. Linton *Sheffield* 330 [*Scapania undulata*.] Common in waterfalls, 'splash zones', reservoir-overflows, and just below the water line on stones in non-calcareous streams. **1976** *Offshore Platforms & Pipelining* 30/1 A central shaft..will permit divers to go 50 m below sea level when there is rough water in the splash zone.

2. Used (usu. without following hyphen) with reference to a system of lubrication in which oil is distributed throughout an engine in the form of drops initially splashed from a reservoir by the working of certain moving parts. So *splash lubrication*.

1906 *Evening Express* (Liverpool) 9 Mar. 7/4 If the splash system of lubrication were more generally adopted by the makers there would be no trouble on this score. **1907** F. Strickland *Man. Petrol Motors & Motor Cars* xvi. 247 The difficulty in splash lubrication is to provide enough oil for the various parts, without having so much in the crank chamber that it works up into the cylinder and produces smoke. **1924** A. W. Judge *Mod. Motor Cars* I. iv. 119 A low speed engine, an over-cooled one, or a splash-lubricated one would require a low-viscosity or 'thin' grade [of oil]. **1939** J. I. Clower *Lubricants & Lubrication* xiv. 358 Splash oiling is widely used on small, vertical and horizontal single-acting machines [*sc.* compressors]. **1963** [see *fly-wheel]. **1966** *McGraw-Hill Encycl. Sci. & Technol.* VII. 607/1 In splash lubrication, the oil entering the engine flows to troughs into which extensions of the connecting rods dip.

splash-board. Add: **1.** (Earlier example.)

1826 Disraeli *Vivian Grey* II. iii. viii. 121 By dint of rattling the whip against the splash-board.

4. A splashback; a protective panel attached to a wall.

1868 C. L. Eastlake *Hints on Household Taste* viii. 183 The common bed-room wash-stand..has a splash-board to protect the wall against which it is placed. **1976** *Billings* (Montana) *Gaz.* 16 June 11-A/4 Even a minimal remodeling job can cost $2,500 before the flower-print wallpaper is stuck on the splashboard.

splashdown (splæ·ʃdaun). Also **splash-down.** [f. Splash- + Down *adv.*] The alighting of a spacecraft on the sea. Also *transf.*

1961 *Washington Post* 5 May B2 They [*sc.* several warships] are strung out about 60 miles apart, and their mission is to retrieve Shepard after 'splashdown'. *Ibid.* 6 May A1 The perfect flight, from lift-off to splash-down, lasted only 15 minutes. **1968** [see *recovery fleet* s.v. *recovery 10]. **1968** *Guardian* 28 Dec. 8/2 From launch to splashdown the Apollo-8 mission went entirely without hitch. **1970** N. Armstrong et al. *First on Moon* xiv. 347 The Navy's weathermen had predicted acceptable splash-down conditions. **1978** *Times* 1 Aug. 2/2 (*caption*) He [*sc.* a member of the crew of a balloon] hears the recording of their splashdown transmission.

splasher[1]. Add: **3.** A piece of cloth or the like hung behind a washstand to protect the wall from splashes. *U.S. Obs.* exc. *Hist.*

1895 *Montgomery Ward Catal.* Spring & Summer 123/1 Stamped Splashers, white cotton duck; size, 18 × 28 inches. *Ibid.* 577/2 Toilet Splasher for protecting wall above washstand, etc., waterproof, made of sewed wood splints, to roll up. **1905** D. Belasco in M. J. Moses *Representative Amer. Dramas* (1925) II. 73/1 A washstand, backed by a 'splasher' of white oilcloth, is near the bed. **1945** *Sun* (Baltimore) 20 June 4-0/3 The furnishings of the Victorian style bedroom were simple linen scarfs... They were used on the flat surfaces, and 'splashers' of linen were fastened to the wall back of the washstand.

splashily, *adv.* (Later example.)

1978 D. Francis *Trial Run* vi. 87, I watched some horses..their feet plopping splashily in the wet.

splashiness. For *rare*$^{-0}$ read *rare* and add: Also, the quality of being splashy.

1978 *Listener* 30 Mar. 412/4 There is a certain wayward splashiness about some of its more 'texturising' sections —all bells, string glissandi and chattering winds.

splashing, *vbl. sb.*[1] Add: **1. b.** *Med.* Noisy motion of air and liquid inside the body.

1890 F. Taylor *Pract. Med.* 344 In cases of hydro- or pyo-pneumothorax, shaking the patient will elicit a splashing sound. **1897** Hutchison & Rainy *Clin. Methods* 62 If 'splashing' be elicited it will be partly heard and partly felt. Distinct splashing elicited three hours after a meal..is very suggestive of a dilated stomach. **1971** R. B. Cole *Essent. Respiratory Dis.* iii. 29 The presence of air and fluid in the pleural space (hydropneumothorax) is indicated if a splash can be heard on auscultation when the thoracic cage is gently shaken. It should not be confused with the splashing of gastric contents.

3. splashing-board = Splash-board 1.

a **1817** Jane Austen *Northanger Abbey* (1818) I. vii. 87 Seat, trunk, sword-case, splashing-board, lamps, silver moulding, all you see complete; the iron work as good as new, or better. He asked fifty guineas.

splashy, *a.*[2] Add: **3.** (Later examples.) Cf. *splash *sb.*[1] 2 d.

1972 'T. Coe' *Don't lie to Me* ix. 87 The killing had originally gotten a pretty splashy play in the newspapers. **1976** *Scotsman* 25 Nov. 14/2 A preposterous miracle has rescued the 'Observer'. It was the sort of last-minute, cliff-hanging rescue which the 'Observer' would hesitate to make a big, splashy story out of.

splat, *sb.*[2] [f. *splat *v.*[2]] **1.** *colloq.* A slapping and splashing sound; a smack.

1958 S. A. Grau *Hard Blue Sky* vi. 375 Annie was throwing the mud by handfuls and listening to the splat and sizzle. **1974** *Publishers Weekly* 11 Nov. 48/1 She tosses her head as she thinks how superior she'll be and, of course, the basket of eggs falls with a 'Splatt!' [*sic*]. **1976** 'Trevanian' *Main* (1977) iv. 72 A spoiled child dangles from her free hand... She gives it a good shake and a splat on the bottom. **1979** D. Gurr *Troika* xxiv. 176 The dough hit him across the face with a vicious slapping *splat*.

2. *Metallurgy.* **a.** Used *attrib.* and in *Comb.* with reference to a method of cooling hot liquid metal extremely rapidly by causing droplets of the metal, propelled by a shock wave, to strike and spread out upon a (usu. rotating) metal surface; so *splat-cool* vb., *-cooled* ppl. adj., *-cooling* vbl. sb., *splat-quench* vb., etc.

1960 *New Scientist* 28 July 286/2 Known as 'splat cooling', it consists in melting about 25 mg of metal in a shock tube by inductive heating. The resultant liquid drops are shot out of the tube by the shock wave and, travelling at high speed, impinge on the inside rim of a fast-revolving copper wheel. Because the splattering drops spread into a very thin film and the centrifugal force imparted by the spinning wheel ensures good thermal contact, the metal or alloy cools at something like a million degrees a second. **1965** *Trans. Metall. Soc. AIME* CCXXXIII. 1584/1 Heat-transfer coefficients.. for aluminum and silver splat cooled essentially on a nickel substrate. **1968** *Acta Metallurgica* XVI. 1204/2 Alloys from 5 to 95% Sn in approximately 5% steps were splat cooled. **1968** *Jrnl. Chem. Physics* XLVIII. 1911/1 No stacking disorder was observed in splat-quenched two-phase alloys between α-Pb and ϵ [*sc.* a Pb–Bi alloy]. **1972** *Materials Sci. & Engin.* X. 343/1 Small pieces of the homogenized ingots were splat quenched at a rate of approximately 10^6 deg per sec. **1974** *Nature* 8 Nov. 100/2 He [*sc.* Pol Duwez] conceived the idea of blasting a small molten drop of alloy by means of a gaseous shock wave against a sloping piece of copper: the technique soon acquired..the onomatopoeic designation 'splat-cooling'. **1976** *Ibid.* 29 Jan. 271/3 A technique for splat-quenching and compaction of Al–Fe alloys.

b. A thin, localized film of metal produced in splat-cooling.

1965 *Trans. Metall. Soc. AIME* CCXXXIII. 1581/1 Upon impact the metal spread into a thin nonuniform film called a splat, about 10^{-4} cm thick. **1976** *Materials Sci. & Engin.* XXIII. 101/2 Chemical analyses of splats ..indicated that some Cr was lost.

splat, *v.*[2] (*int.* and *adv.*) *colloq.* [Shortening of Splatter *v.*]

1. *intr.* To land with a sharp smacking sound, or with a sound as of slapping and splashing. Also as *adv.*, as *to go splat*, and *int.*

1897 'H. S. Merriman' *In Kedar's Tents* v. 55 A bullet went 'splat' against a rock. **1922** J. A. Dunn *Man Trap* xvi. 226 A bullet whistled by Jimmy's head, *splatting* on the lava crust. **1937** J. Steinbeck in *Esquire* Sept. 200/3 His fist splatted into Johnny Bear's smiling mouth. **1970** R. D. Abrahams *Positively Black* iv. 101 This here bird flies over head and really lets go, right splat on her head. **1976** J. Grady *Great Pebble Affair* (1977) 96 I'll jump out of the window... I hope I splat and spoil all the upholstery on those goddamn jalopies. **1977** *Undercurrents* June–July 34/3 Picked up the tap and splat! It leapt across the room.

2. *trans. Metallurgy.* To cause droplets of (a metal) to strike a surface and form a film in the process of splat-cooling.

1965 *Trans. Metall. Soc. AIME* CCXXXIII. 1583/1 Two metals, aluminum and silver, were selected to be splatted because of their high thermal conductivities and lack of oxidation problems.

Hence **spla·tted** *ppl. a.*, **spla·tting** *vbl. sb.*

1976 *Phil. Mag.* XXXIV. 236 The average energy loss ..was determined..from specimens immediately after splatting. *Ibid.*, Prior to performing microanalysis it was necessary to calibrate the variation of energy loss E_p with copper concentration for splatted material.

splather (splæ·ðəɪ), *v. dial.* [Perh. var. of Splatter *v.*] *intr.* To splash; to sprawl.

1877 F. Ross et al. *Gloss. Words Holderness* 134/2 *Splather*,..to splash water or mud. **1886** R. Holland *Gloss. County of Chester* 333 A procumbent plant which spreads over the ground would be said to '*splather* about'. **1887** T. Darlington *Folk-Speech S. Cheshire* 365 *Splather*, ..to sprawl. 'He had bu' just spokken th' word, an' o'er he went *splatherin*' 'i' th' middle o' th' bruk.' **1936** F. Clune *Roaming round Darling* xiv. 118 The closed Experiment Farm, now profusely splathered with flora and fauna animate and inanimate.

Also as *sb.* (see quot. 1877); hence **spla·thering** *ppl. a.*

1877 E. Peacock *Gloss. Words Manley & Corringham, Lincolnshire* 235/1 *Splather*, (1) a splash. (2) Noisy talk. **1879** *Dewsbre Olmenac* in *Eng. Dial. Dict.* (1904) V. 673/2 Matters hev gotten squared up efter a deeal o' conflab an splather. **1929** J. B. Priestley *Good Companions* I. v. 188 She sends a long splathering telegram and never puts her address in it. **1937** Partridge *Dict. Slang* 811/2 *Hold your splathers!* be silent!

splatter, *v.* Add: **1. c.** Of objects.

1931 W. G. Carr *By Guess & by God* 91 A salvo of shells splattered around the periscope. **1976** 'E. McBain' *Guns* (1977) iii. 66 It had certainly been traumatic pulling the trigger of the .38 and watching the back of that cop's head come off and splatter onto the Seagrim's poster. **1978** *Amer. Poetry Rev.* July/Aug. 4/1 His deep brown feces splatter over Queen Anne's Lace and the waving sedge Of the pond.

2. b. To beat or batter.

1881 J. Sargisson *Joe Scoap's Jurneh through Three Wardles* 31 If it wasn't for that oald grey heid o' thine Ah wud splatter thee. **1897** W. Beatty *Secretar* xiv. 110, I would have splattered his harns on the causey. **1959** I. & P. Opie *Lore & Lang. Schoolch.* x. 198 Recommendations by boys in East and South-East London: 'Bash him up.' 'Beat him up.'.. 'Splatter him.'

splattered, *ppl. a.* (Later example.)

1979 E. Newman *Sunday Punch* i. 1 The prize being, for some of the fighters, fame and fortune, often accompanied by splattered noses.

splay, *sb.* Add: **1. d.** A tapered widening of the carriageway at a road intersection or corner provided in order to increase visibility for motorists.

1956 *Proc. Inst. Civil Engineers* V. ii. 356 The splay provided in the boundary line of the minor road approaching the intersection should remove any possible restriction on vision at the point where the vehicle turning right-in has to cross the right-out stream from the minor road. **1963** W. F. Cassie in E. Davies *Traffic Engin. Practice* x. 280 A minor road intersecting a major road. There are three possibilities..: (*a*) right-angled intersection; (*b*) right-hand splay; and (*c*) left-hand splay. **1968** J. L. Paisley in *Ibid.* (ed. 2) iv. 99 At uncontrolled junctions visibility splays should be provided to give full visibility to right and left. **1977** *Cornish Times* 19 Aug. 5/2 The Cornwall Surveyor..offered no objections subject to the formation of a suitable access with visibility splays of 30 by 500 feet in each direction along the adjoining highway.

splay, *a.* Add: **1.** (Later examples.)
1895 R. L. STEVENSON *Amateur Emigrant* 38 We had a fellow on board, an Irish-American, for all the world like a beggar in a print by Callot; one-eyed, with great, splay crow's-feet round the sockets. **1952** DYLAN THOMAS *Coll. Poems* p. viii, Though song Is a burning and crested act, The fire of birds in The world's turning wood, For my sawn, splay sounds.

2. splay fault *Geol.*, a subsidiary fault diverging at an acute angle from a larger dislocation.
1942 E. M. ANDERSON *Dynamics of Faulting* vii. 150 Splay faults may..be expected to diverge from the main fracture at about this angle [*sc.* 22½°]. **1969** BENNISON & WRIGHT *Geol. Hist. Brit. Isles* vii. 147 These structures continue across into Northern Ireland but are much less strongly developed there and are replaced by series of en-echelon and splay faults. **1971** *Nature* 19 Feb. 538/1 North and south of the Gregory rift..the periclinal ends of the uplifted area are broad transverse depressions traversed by splay-faults.

splay foot, splay-foot. 2. For † *Obs.* read '*Obs.* or *rare*' and add later example.
1922 JOYCE *Ulysses* 690 A slender splayfoot chair of glossy cane curves.

spleen, *sb.* Add: **9. c. spleen index, rate,** the proportion of the population having enlarged spleens (as determined by palpation), useful as indicating the incidence of malaria.
1969 EDINGTON & GILLES *Path. in Tropics* ii. 13 The former [methods] determine parasite rates in random blood samples and spleen indices... A close correlation exists between parasite and spleen rates. **1903** STEPHENS & CHRISTOPHERS *Pract. Study Malaria* xxiii. 261 Above ten years, the spleen rate is usually considerably in excess of the parasite rate. **1935** *Discovery* Jan. 11/1 In these districts today the spleen rate, indicating the incidence of malaria amongst the inhabitants, is very low. **1963** E. PAMPANA *Textbk. Malaria Eradication* iv. 72 The spleen rate underestimates the true percentage of enlarged spleens.

spleen, *v.* Add: **1. c.** (Later examples.) *U.S.*
1889 R. T. COOKE *Steadfast* xviii. 198 [It] makes me spleen to think on't! **1902** H. L. WILSON *Spenders* x. 110 Well, I knew Dan'l J. purty well, and I spleened against some of his ways, but that's done fur.

spleenical (splī·nikăl), *a. rare*⁻¹. [f. SPLEEN *sb.* + -ICAL.] Spleenful.
1818 KEATS *Let.* Oct. (1931) I. 262 You see there is nothing spleenical in all this. The only thing that can ever affect me personally..is any doubt about my powers for poetry.

‖ **splendeurs et misères** (splandöɹ e mizɛ̄r'). [Fr., lit. 'splendours and miseries', from the title of Balzac's novel sequence *Splendeurs et Misères des Courtisanes* (1839–47).] The glories and degradation of life set side by side; hence, applied to other co-existent extremes of conditions. Cf. *splendours and miseries* s.v. *SPLENDOUR *sb.* 5.
1952 *Observer* 13 Jan. 7/5, I don't seem to have read any piece of criticism in the past month that doesn't speak of *splendeurs et misères*, so I'd better jump on the band-waggon. **1977** *N.Y. Rev. Bks.* 15 Sept. 42/4 *Mario Puzo Inside Las Vegas*..seems to me one of the liveliest testimonials to the *splendeurs et misères* of gaming fever I've read.

splendid, *a.* Add: **6.** *splendid isolation*, phr. used with reference to the political and commercial uniqueness or isolation of Great Britain; also *transf.* Cf. ISOLATION a (quots. 1896[1,2]).
[**1896** G. E. FOSTER in *Official Rep. Deb. H. Com. Canada* 16 Jan. 176 The great mother Empire stands splendidly isolated in Europe.] **1896** *Times* 22 Jan. 10/1 Splendid isolation... A few weeks ago England appeared to stand alone in the world, surrounded by jealous competitors and..unexpected hostility. **1898** [in Dict.]. **1902** J. CHAMBERLAIN in *Times* 7 Jan. 4/4 It is the duty of the British people to count upon themselves alone... I say alone, yes, in a splendid isolation, surrounded and supported by our kinsfolk. **1912** *Review of Reviews* July 63/1 The abandonment by Great Britain of her splendid isolation. **1933** *Times* 21 Feb. 12/3 A Nazi band played in splendid isolation in the square. **1976** *National Observer* (U.S.) 13 Nov. 1/2 In a little while Williams and his bodyguard will be leaving this splendid isolation (we are in a hotel suite 30-odd floors above Central Park South) and going to the Ambassador Theatre.

splendidness. (Later example.)
1980 *N.Y. Times* 5 Oct. VII. 33/5 Miss Leffland at her best is extraordinarily good; indeed, there is not a contemporary writer of short stories from whom truth of feeling, splendidness of insight, and a human beauty both aching and real can more confidently be expected.

splendi·ferously, *adv. joc.* [f. SPLENDIFEROUS *a.* + -LY².] Splendidly; magnificently.
1900 J. VAIZEY *About Peggy Saville* viii. 57 If you weren't so fat, you would do splendiferously for Ophelia. **1930** D. H. LAWRENCE *Apocalypse* (1932) i. 22 And nowhere does this happen so splendiferously as in Revelation. **1959** *Good Food Guide* 292 This splendiferously-named hotel. **1982** *Country Life* 28 Jan. 251/4 It is almost impossible to use *Brewer* to look up what you want to find..and this goes as splendiferously for the new edition as ever in the past.

splendi·ferousness. *joc.* [f. SPLENDIFEROUS *a.* + -NESS.] Splendour; magnificence.
1934 in WEBSTER. **1971** J. H. GRAY *Red Lights on Prairies* v. 103 The splendiferousness of the new schools, warehouses.

splendour, *sb.* Add: **5.** *splendours and miseries* = *SPLENDEURS ET MISÈRES.
1943 S. SITWELL (*title*) Splendours and miseries. **1971** A. MORICE *Death of Gay Dog* iv. 44, I took in a survey of the room, to see what further splendours and miseries were in store for us. **1981** *Times* 1 Apr. 11/2 *Omnibus* looked at the splendours and miseries of acting.

spleniculus (splĭni·kiulŏs). *Med.* [mod.L., f. L. *splen* SPLEEN *sb.* + *-iculus*, diminutive ending.] A detached portion of the spleen, a small accessory spleen.
[**1848** QUAIN & SHARPEY *Elem. Anat.* (ed. 5) II. 1089 These are commonly named accessory or supplementary spleens (splenculi [*sic, bis*], lienculi).] **1897** *Brit. Med. Jrnl.* 16 Jan. 145/2 A spleniculus was left [after splenectomy], and that patient did not suffer from any of these symptoms. **1939** MCNEE & MCMICHAEL in H. Rolleston *Brit. Encycl. Med. Pract.* XI. 402 In the neighbourhood of the spleen there are usually some small haemolymph glands or splenicul... Their enlargement may cause persistence of clinical symptoms after splenectomy. **1973** A. I. S. MACPHERSON et al. *Spleen* iii. 97 Splenicul or accessory spleens are found in 10 to 20 percent of all post-mortem examinations.

splenium (splī·niǝm). *Anat.* [a. L. *splēnium* (see SPLENIAL *a.*¹ and *sb.*).] The thick posterior part of the corpus callosum of the brain.
1845 W. J. E. WILSON *Anatomist's Vade Mecum* (ed. 3) viii. 411 Posteriorly [the corpus callosum]..forms a thick rounded fold (splenium), which is continuous with the fornix. **1902** D. J. CUNNINGHAM *Text-Bk. Anat.* 529 The massive posterior end [of the corpus callosum]..lies over the mesencephalon... It is called the splenium, and it consists of an upper and a lower part. **1968** PASSMORE & ROBSON *Compan. Med. Stud.* I. xxiv. 44/2 The corpus callosum forms a prominent feature and its divisions into the rostrum, genu, body and splenium can be readily recognized. **1977** *Neurology* XXVII. 688/2 If we infer that inferior splenium has a significant functional role in relaying visual verbal codes from the right to left cerebral hemisphere, a plausible corollary may be that color-valuing tends to use superior or dorsal splenium.

spleno-. Add: **sple·nocyte** [-CYTE], one of the mononuclear leucocytes formerly thought to be characteristic of the spleen; **sple:nohepato-me·galy** [HEPATO-; cf. next] = *hepatosplenomegaly* s.v. *HEPATO-; **splenomega·lia, -me·galy** [Gr. μεγάλ-, μέγας large], enlargement of the spleen; hence **splenome·galic** *a.*; **sple·no-pexy** [-*PEXY], surgical fixation of a wandering spleen; **sple:noporto·graphy** [ad. F. *splénoportographie* (G. Sotgiu et al. 1952, in *La Presse Médicale* LX. 1295/1)], radiography of the hepatic portal system following the introduction of a contrast medium into the spleen to make the system detectable; so **splenopo·rtogram,** a radiograph obtained in this way; **splenore·nal** *a.*, connecting the spleen and a kidney; **splenotomy** (earlier example).
1900 DORLAND *Med. Dict.* 621/1 Splenocyte. **1925** STRONG & ELWYN *Bailey's Text-bk. Histol.* (ed. 7) iv. 82 They are..free mesenchymal elements..aggregated in enormous numbers in the mammalian splenic pulp (splenocytes). **1979** *Nature* 18 Jan. 218/2 Some of these IFC were..cultured..in the presence of irradiated syngeneic splenocytes or thymocytes as feeder layer. **1900** DORLAND *Med. Dict.* 621/1 Splenohepatomegaly. **1936** Splenohepatomegaly [see *LIPOIDOSIS]. [**1898** *Allbutt's Syst. Med.* V. 539 Splenic anæmia is the name by which the disease is best known in this country; but it has also been called..*spleno-megalie primitive*; under the last name chiefly it is described in French literature.] **1900** DORLAND *Med. Dict.* 621/2 *Splenomegalia, splenomegaly*, enlargement of the spleen. **1952** COLE & ELMAN *Textbk. Gen. Surg.* (ed. 6) xxiv. 679 The typical case of hemolytic jaundice or anemia is diagnosed without difficulty. Cardinal manifestations are slight to moderate jaundice, splenomegalia, and anemia of the spherocytic, reticulocytic type. **1900** *Guy's Hosp. Rep.* LIV. 1 Splenomegalic cirrhosis of the liver. **1900** Splenomegaly [see *splenomegalia* above]. **1903** T. K. MONRO *Man. Med.* 316 (*heading*) Splenic anæmia (primary splenomegaly). **1974** *Trypanosomiasis & Leishmaniasis* (Ciba Foundation) 207 Symptoms like marked general lymphadenopathy and splenomegaly should be considered as signs of activation of the immune apparatus. **1897** *Brit. Med. Jrnl.* 16 Jan. 133/2 The great difference between splenectomy and splenopexy is that in the former case the individual is deprived of an organ, and, although we do not know with any degree of precision what its real use is, we are nevertheless bound to display caution in dealing with it. **1923** POOL & STILLMAN *Surg. Spleen* v. 88 Although the immediate results of splenopexy are claimed to be favorable, the late results are uncertain. **1955** R. T. SHACKELFORD *Surg. Alimentary Tract* II. vi. 996 The fixation (splenopexy) of a 'wandering spleen'..has been abandoned. Splenectomy rather than splenopexy is indicated. **1953** *Ann. Surg.* CXXXVIII. 583/2 The splenoportogram for this patient..demonstrated a well functioning portacaval shunt in the three-second film which was taken during the injection of the last 5 cc. of the opaque media. **1969** S. I. SCHWARTZ *Princ. Surg.* xxix. 1052/1 (*caption*) Normal splenoportogram. Note site of injection in spleen and diffusion of radiopaque material through organ. **1953** *Ann. Surg.* CXXXVIII. 582/2 It employs the visualization of the splenic and portal veins by roentgenographic examination. This is accomplished by injecting contrast media directly into the spleen... Sotgiu, Cacciari and Frassineti, working in Bologne, reported favorable results in four patients. It is from these authors that we have borrowed the term 'Splenoportography'. **1980** *Rec. Adv. Surg.* X. 5 Pre-operative determination by means of..splenoportography..and selective arteriography..are important. **1945** *Ann. Surg.* CXXII. 479 It is undesirable..to resort to the use of a vein graft in the performance of a splenorenal anastomosis. **1974** R. M. KIRK et al. *Surgery* vi. 108/1 (*caption*) Portal venous hypertension is reduced by portacaval or splenorenal shunt. **1976** *Lancet* 11 Dec. 1300/2 Our results suggest that hypergastrinæmia is more likely to follow portacaval than splenorenal anastomosis. **1868** *Guy's Hosp. Rep.* XIII. 416 The operation of splenotomy as a means of cure [for leucocythæmia] is physiologically unsound.

splenosis (splĭnōᵘ·sis). *Med.* [f. SPLEN(O- + -OSIS.] The presence in the body of numerous separate pieces of living splenic tissue.
1939 BUCHBINDER & LIPKOFF in *Surgery* VI. 933 A case is reported of autotransplantation of splenic tissue throughout the abdominal cavity following trauma of the spleen... We offer the term splenosis to describe this condition. **1947** *Canad. Med. Assoc. Jrnl.* LVI. 376/2 A case of splenosis is reported, in which seeding occurred after splenectomy for non-traumatic reasons. **1973** A. I. S. MACPHERSON et al. *Spleen* ix. 224 The seeding of viable cells from the ruptured spleen throughout the peritoneal cavity and their subsequent growth to form numerous tiny nodules of histologically normal splenic tissue has been described and has been given the name 'Splenosis'.

splenunculus (splĭnɒ·ŋkiŭlŏs). *Med.* [mod.L., f. L. *splēn* SPLEEN *sb.* + *-unculus*, diminutive ending.] = *SPLENICULUS.
[**1848**: see *SPLENDICULUS.] **1897** [see LIENCULUS]. **1909** ADAMI & NICHOLLS *Princ. Path.* II. x. 222 Nearly 400 of these splenunculi were found scattered throughout the abdominal cavity. **1962** *Lancet* 26 May 1104/1 After the removal of the splenunculus there was remission. **1974** W. A. SODEMAN *Pathologic Physiol.* (ed. 5) xxiii. 680/2 Such a hemolytic relapse has been documented..in a splenectomized patient with hereditary spherocytosis; at surgery a splenunculus was found to weigh 217 grams.

splib. *U.S. Blacks.* [Origin obscure.] A Negro.
1964 *N.Y. Times Mag.* 23 Aug. 62/2 *Soul brother*, Negro; also referred to as *scobe, blue, splib*. **1969** A. YOUNG *Dancing* 5 Nobody want no nice nigger no more... They want an angry splib A furious nigrah.. **1970** *Atlantic Monthly* Jan. 38 Any other terms such as 'boy', 'spook', 'splib',..or 'colored' carry connotations of prejudice. **1976** *Amer. Speech 1974* XLIX. 184 *Splib*,..liberal black who looks angry but will not upset the status quo.

splice, *sb.* Add: **1. b.** Also, a joining of metal girders or rails, concrete beams, etc. (Examples.)
1877 *Rep. & Awards Group XVIII U.S. Centennial Comm. Internat. Exhib. 1876* 66 (*caption*) Rails and splices used on Pennsylvania Railroad and branches. **1892** L. DE C. BERG *Safe Building* II. x. 113 In locating the rivets of a splice care should be taken not to weaken the original plate. **1934** RELF & JOHANSEN *Handbk. Aerodynamics* (ed. 2) I. ix. 638 In splicing built-up or box spars the splices in the flanges should come at the points of inflection. **1951** R. D. CHELLIS *Pile Foundations* xi. 271 If piles are restrained throughout their full length in firm soil..a splice consisting of a full butt weld or single web and flange plates welded on in the field suffices. **1977** J. P. COOK *Composite Construction Methods* x. 209 In the usual steel frame, column sizes are normally kept constant for a height of two stories, with the column splice about 3 or 4 ft above the floor level.

c. *Cricket.* The v-shaped tang of a bat-handle, which forms a joint with the blade; the joint itself. Also in slang phr. *to sit* (*on* or *upon*) *the splice,* to play a cautious defensive game.
1906 A. E. KNIGHT *Compl. Cricketer* 44 The spliced handle was a later development, and some of the earliest splices were of ash. *Ibid.* 352 To sit upon the splice.—To play with too much caution, to deliberately refrain from scoring. **1912** *Daily Mirror* 9 July 14/2 Vidler sat icily on the splice, playing the right game and keeping up an end while Crutchley got runs. **1927** *Punch* 26 Jan. 108/1 'I don't think you're helping the score at all,' I protested. 'You're just sitting on your splice and leaving it all to me.' **1935** *Encycl. Sports* 195/1 Cricketers who bought a new bat treated it almost with reverence... They oiled every part of it, except the handle and splice. **1963** A. ROSS *Australia 63* iii. 79 Dexter, hooking at him, nearly returned a gentle catch off the splice. **1968** L. FREWIN *Best of Cricket's Fiction* II. 267 There was a business-like look about him, the air of one who without being the least downhearted or inclined to sit upon the splice, was yet determined to take no foolish risks.

d. A joint made in editing or repairing film or magnetic or paper tape.
1923 F. A. TALBOT *Moving Pictures* (ed. 3) viii. 100 In making the splice care has to be observed to introduce the two pieces true to frame-line, gauge and marginal perforations. **1931, 1936** [see *BLOOP *v.*]. **1949** FRAYNE & WOLFE *Elem. Sound Recording* xxix. 603 A program can be edited in advance by cutting out portions or inserting

other portions, since splices in the tape cannot be heard. **1973** *Screen* Spring/Summer 43 Montage in the narrow sense (ie as an editing splice) has a diminishing importance in certain modern films.

splice, *v.* Add: **I. 2. a.** Also, to fasten together (metal girders and rails, concrete beams, etc.).

1892 L. de C. Berg *Safe Building* II. x. 113 If any part of a girder..is spliced, made of two parts, the number of rivets each side of splice..should be made sufficient to transfer the full strength of original plate across the joint. **1913** W. H. Sellew *Steel Rails* iv. 263 The stiffness of the rail that is to be spliced. **1951** R. D. Chellis *Pile Foundations* ix. 201 (*caption*) Exposing reinforcing preparatory to splicing a large precast concrete pile. **1976** R. Chudley *Construction Technol.* III. vii. 75 Where members of the frame are joined or spliced together the connections are generally mechanical (nut and bolt).

c. Also *spec.* in *Biol.*, to join or insert (a gene or gene fragment).

1975 *Nature* 18 Dec. 563/1 The genes to be cloned would first be spliced on to either a bacterial plasmid.. or on to the DNA of bacteriophage lambda which would then infect the bacterium. **1977** *Sci. News* 29 Jan. 70 The controversial research in question is a class of experiments that..include splicing the genes of a virus or bacteria to partially purified DNA from mammals or birds..known to produce potent toxins or pathogens. **1979** *Newsweek* 4 June 64 One valuable product has already resulted from the work: human insulin, manufactured by splicing fragments of DNA that manufacture the hormone in humans into an intestinal bacterium.

e. To make a splice or joint in (a length of film or magnetic or paper tape); to join (film or tape) *in, on* or *up*. Occas. *intr.* (or *absol.*).

1912 F. A. Talbot *Moving Pictures* xii. 137 Occasionally when a film is being run through the projector it becomes severed by some means or other. Before it can be used again the break must be repaired by splicing the two parts together. **1931** Wilkinson & Reis in L. Cowan *Recording Sound for Motion Pictures* xiv. 200 When film is spliced on a standard splicing machine, the splice crosses the sound track at right angles to its length. **1958** W. E. Stewart *Magn. Recording Techn.* ii. 42 The wire, still useful in some applications, cannot be spliced so easily as tape. **1962** L. Deighton *Ipcress File* xxiv. 156 The film lab had been very thorough, they had spliced on to the end of the film the incident of my arrest. **1973** A. Broinowski *Take One Ambassador* x. 140 The odd *faux pas*..would have to be cut; splice in a bedroom scene there. **1974** N. Freeling *Dressing of Diamond* 174 Snip a bit off this [tape] and splice it up. **1978** L. Davidson *Chelsea Murders* xxiii. 141 He put in six solid hours at the editing... He compared and cut and spliced till two in the morning. **1978** [see *splicer 2 b]. **1980** S. Hockey *Guide Computer Applic. Humanities* ii. 25 Sections of corrected [paper] tape can be spliced or glued into the original.

f. *Cricket.* To strike (the ball) with the splice of the bat, as a mishit.

1982 *Guardian* 19 Feb. 22/2 Botham went for a swinging pull shot, and spliced it tamely but safely to mid-wicket.

3. b. *intr.* To get married. Also const. *with*.

1874 E. Eggleston *Circuit Rider* xxiii. 216, I heerd say as he was goin' to splice with a gal that could pray like a angel afire. **1875** J. G. Holland *Sevenoaks* xii. 155, Jim, be ye goin' to splice? **1981** T. Heald *Murder at Moose Jaw* xii. 114 If the old flapper spliced with the colonel she stood to lose a million dollars.

spliced, *ppl. a.* (Earlier and later examples.) Also, reinforced by splicing.

1859 T. P. Shaffner *Telegraph Man.* xli. 597 Fig. 13 is the two ends spliced, having first been cleaned. **1867** G. H. Selkirk *Guide to Cricket Ground* iii. 44 A new handle can be inserted..and the 'spliced bat' will be quite as good as before—indeed, many players have their bats spliced at first, thinking it a great improvement. **1891** W. G. Grace *Cricket* ii. 42 This one [*sc.* a bat] had a spliced handle with a strip of whalebone down the centre of it, and was very much prized. **1897** *Sears, Roebuck & Co. Catal.* 243/3 Men's Seamless Cotton Half Hose... Spliced heels and toes. **1931** Wilkinson & Reis in L. Cowan *Recording Sound for Motion Pictures* xiv. 201 A similar section of silent track, matching the average density of the spliced tracks, is..cemented into the hole. **1968** J. Ironside *Fashion Alphabet* 69 *Spliced heel*, heel reinforced with the same fabric as the stocking. **1970** E.-O. Libuda tr. *Heinhold's Power Cables & Application* xlvi. 457 Brazing is necessary for spliced connections [in copper conductors].

splicer. Add: **2. a.** A tool or implement used in splicing.

1923 J. H. Cook *Fifty Years on Old Frontier* 114 A wire cutter, splicer, and staple-puller combined.

b. A mechanical device used to splice film or tape.

1927 E. G. Lutz *Motion-Picture Cameraman* xi. 243 (*caption*) B. & H. 16 mm. rewinder and splicer. **1931** Wilkinson & Reis in L. Cowan *Recording Sound for Motion Pictures* xiv. 202 A diagonal splicer has been evolved to produce a silent splice. **1953** K. Reisz *Technique Film Editing* 274 The two reels, one of sound track, one of picture, both provisionally held together by paper clips, are joined on a splicer. **1978** G. McDonald *Fletch's Fortune* xxx. 201 'I need one of those cassette tape recorders. You know, with a tape splicer. I need to splice some tape.' 'Mine doesn't have a splicer.'

splicing, *vbl. sb.* Add: **I. 1. a.** (Later examples.)

1912 F. A. Talbot *Moving Pictures* xii. 138 To facilitate..splicing a small clamping device is used. **1931** L. E. Clark in L. Cowan *Recording Sound for Motion Pictures* ix. 144 In splicing a certain amount is lost at each end. **1973** *Screen* Spring/Summer 42 The montage in question is not..necessarily montage in the narrow sense (ie splicing). **1980** *Daily Tel.* 18 Jan. 14/6 The scientists.. have modified common laboratory bacteria by 'gene splicing' to produce human interferon.

b. *splicing-block, machine, -tape.*

1927 E. G. Lutz *Motion-Picture Cameraman* xi. 241 Joining films is made with the aid of a splicing-block which has as its main feature series of teeth over which the film-perforations fit. **1931** Splicing machine [see *splice *v.* 2 e]. **1958** J. Tall *Techniques of Magnetic Recording* x. 161 The splicing tape should be laid down.. at an angle. **1974** H. Bursten *Questions & Answers about Tape Recording* xviii. 246 The leading edge of the splicing tape presents a resistance.

spliff (splif). *slang* (orig. *W. Indies*). Also **splif.** [Origin unknown.] A cannabis cigarette, *spec.* one rolled in a conical form; a smoke of cannabis.

1936 *Daily Gleaner* (Kingston, Jamaica) 3 Oct. 35 Here is the hot-bed of ganja smoking..and even the children may be seen at times taking what is better known as their 'spliff'. **1953** R. Mais *Hills were Joyful Together* I. xi. 111 He took the spliff and lit up, dragged long at it, drawing the smoke deep down into his lungs. **1959** C. MacInnes *Absolute Beginners* 76 A third just said, 'Great', with a soft dream in his eyes—but that may have been because he'd just been dragging on a splif inside the toilet. **1969** Fabian & Byrne *Groupie* (1970) i. 9 He showed me how to roll spliffs—as he called them—so that I could roll for him. **1972** J. Brown *Chancer* ii. 30 They might be going ..to meet a pusher or they might be going just for a few spliffs and to catch the party feeling. **1975** *High Times* Dec. 137/1 Like Marley, he's a spliff-toking Rastafarian. **1977** *Transatlantic Rev.* LX. 192 Coon rolled a massive splif and blew clouds of ganja gremlins through the hatch.

spline, *sb.* Add: **1. b.** (Examples.)

1904 *Drapers' Co. Res. Memoirs* XIII. 12 The curves.. were plotted with our coordinatograph for a series of values of *k* or *r* on a large scale, drawn in with a spline and integrated with a Coradi compensating planimeter. **1953** A. H. Robinson *Elements Cartogr.* v. 83/1 For larger curves, the defining points of which are far apart, a flexible curve or a spline with weights is more satisfactory.

2. Now *esp.* such a key that is formed integrally with the shaft; also, a corresponding recess in a hub along which the key may slide.

1909 Kimball & Barr *Elements Machine Design* viii. 196 Sometimes it is desirable to have the hub free to slide axially along the shaft, but constrained to rotate with it. In such cases a feather or spline is used. **1932** R. C. H. Heck in C. E. O'Rourke *Gen. Engin. Handbk.* xviii. 532 Often a gear has to slide along its shaft. The key in this service is called a spline or feather. **1952** F. J. Camm *Newnes Engineer's Ref. Bk.* (ed. 5) 854 The efficiency of a spline for driving purposes is measured by the amount of contact made by the male and female splines. **1966** G. W. Michalec *Precision Gearing* vii. 324 Generally, involute internal and external teeth are mated, but non-involute splines are also suitable. **1979** *Industrial Fasteners Handbk.* I. 318 There are two basic forms of spline—straight-sided splines which may number 4, 6, 10 or up to 16 splines equally distributed around the circumference of a shaft, and serrated splines which are in the form of adjacent triangular teeth.

3. *Math.* Also *spline curve.* A continuous curve constructed so as to pass through a given set of points and have continuous first and second derivatives.

1946 I. J. Schoenberg in *Q. Appl. Math.* IV. 48 For $k = 4$ they represent approximately the curves drawn by means of a spline and for this reason we propose to call them spline curves of order *k*. **1966** *Notices Amer. Math. Soc.* XIII. 140 This paper extends and strengthens convergence properties previously published..for periodic splines and for nonperiodic splines satisfying general end conditions. **1978** *Nature* 1 June 407/2 Cubic spline interpolation was applied at standard depths to 800 m.

spline, *v.* Add: (Examples.) Also, to secure (a part) by means of a spline. **splining** *vbl. sb.* (examples).

1901 *Shop & Foundry Practice* II. § 15. 14 Fig. 13 shows a jig designed for holding shafts for key-seating or splining, plain cutters being used for the purpose. *Ibid.* 15 The shafts..which are to be splined or key-seated, are laid into these grooves and are clamped. **1920** *Autocar Handbk.* (ed. 10) x. 125 In order to allow the gear wheels to drive the shaft on which they are placed, or vice versa, the latter is often grooved or 'splined'. **1926** *Motor Man.* (ed. 26) v. 82 The worm-wheel spindle emerges from the off side of the steering box, and splined thereto is a short lever, generally known as the drop arm. **1953** *Straight-Sided Splines & Serrations (B.S.I.)* 5/2 If two shafts are splined to different fits by the same cutter.. the radius of the arc at the root..will vary slightly from the designed arc.

Hence **splined** *ppl. a.*, provided with a spline or splines.

1909 N. Hawkins *Mech. Dict.* 529/2 *Splined shaft*, a shaft provided with a long feather way; as a splined feed rod on a lathe. **1952** P. S. Houghton *Gears* ix. 156 The length of bearing in an involute splined hub will depend upon the chosen materials. **1967** [see *knock-off *a.* 2 b]. **1979** *Industrial Fasteners Handbk.* I. 318 British Standard 3550:1963 specifies dimensions of involuted splined shafts and splined holes with a 30° pressure angle.

splint, *sb.* Add: **3. b.** *S. Afr.* A fragment or broken piece of diamond.

1872 C. Rhodes *Let.* in B. Williams *Cecil Rhodes* (1921) iv. 29 You must not however think that every diamond one finds is a beauty, the great proportion are nothing but splints. **1887** J. W. Matthews *Incwadi Yami* xxvii. 415 Faithfully carrying out their master's behests, and never robbing him of a single splint. **1903** W. R. Cattelle *Precious Stones* 79 Beyond the small pieces resulting from cleavages, other fragments are saved which cannot be cut to jewels. Some of these are called 'splints', and are used for mechanical purposes or ground to powder.

4. a. Also, an object used to fasten or immobilize teeth or the jaws.

1948 *Brit. Dental Jrnl.* LXXXV. 223/1 Removable acrylic bite blocks or splints with clasps were constructed.., so that the bite was opened..and the mandible moved forward. **1962** Blake & Trott *Periodontology* xiv. 144 The main object of periodontal splint design is to make use of sound teeth to give stability to mobile teeth.

9. b. (sense 2) *splint-bottom; splint-bottomed* adj.

1850 *Knickerbocker* XXXVI. 73 She wiped out the seats of some splint-bottomed chairs with her calico apron. **1876** 'Mark Twain' *Tom Sawyer* vi. 68 The master, throned on high in his great splint-bottom arm-chair, was dozing. **1919** T. K. Holmes *Man from Tall Timber* iv. 36 A comfortable armchair with splint-bottom. *Ibid.* v. 46 Their splint-bottomed armchairs.

splintage. Delete *rare*$^{-0}$ and add examples. For 'surgical' read 'surgical or dental'.

1956 H. & A. J. Kazis *Complete Mouth Rehabilitation* vii. 88 As a result of splintage there is a reduction of the stress load on the supporting bone. **1970** R. D. Muckart in G. Murdoch *Prosthetic & Orthotic Pract.* xi. 471 Maintenance of mobility and the prevention of deformity or contracture is by far the most important function of upper-limb splintage. **1978** *Jrnl. R. Soc. Med.* LXXI. 186 The wrist fixation device is designed to control Colles' fracture by internal splintage.

splinter, *sb.* Add: **1. f.** A splinter group (see sense 7 b below). orig. and chiefly *U.S.*

1948 *Sun* (Baltimore) 20 Aug. 1/2 The Republican party and its Dewey-Warren ticket, without 'leftist or extreme right splinters', is the nation's only hope 'to put an end to disunity'. **1972** D. E. Westlake *Bank Shot* viii. 56 Probably a new splinter... They keep fractionalizing, makes it extremely difficult to keep proper surveillance. **1977** *New Yorker* 9 May 67/2 The old-guard splinter of the Congress which Mrs. Gandhi had routed in 1969. **1981** *Listener* 1 Jan. 24/1 A newly imaginative use of a Red Brigade splinter.

7. a. splinter bid *Bridge*, an unusual jump bid showing a singleton or void in the suit bid; **splinter-deck,** an armour-plated deck on a ship (see also quot. 1909); **splinter hæmorrhage,** a narrow, elongated hæmorrhage resembling one produced by a splinter.

1977 *Oxf. Times* 11 Feb. 8/7 The bidding went: One Heart—pass—Three Spades (splinter bid showing a singleton or void together with a heart fit). **1978** *N.Y. Times* 29 Mar. c 25/2 For slam purposes, the splinter bid, or unusual jump to show a singleton or a void, solves many problems. **1909** *Cent. Dict.* Suppl. 346/2 A deck worked for protective purposes below a protective deck is called the splinter-deck. **1933** *Jane's Fighting Ships* 171 Above again is a $1\frac{1}{15}''$ splinter deck against aerial attack. **1973** J. Quick *Dict. Weapons & Mil. Terms* 416/3 *Splinter deck*, a deck fitted with armor. **1931** W. Boyd *Path. Internal Dis.* i. 40 There may be small 'splinter hemorrhages' under the nail—a linear track as if a sliver had been run in. **1971** Robbins & Angell *Basic Path.* ix. 274/2 Seeding of the nail beds and of the skin produces small petechial hemorrhages known as 'splinter hemorrhages' or microabscesses.

b. *attrib.* or as *adj.* Of or pertaining to a group, party, etc., which splits itself off as an independent entity from a larger political or social group, esp. as *splinter group*. orig. *N. Amer.*

1935 *Economist* 19 Oct. 742/2 The new 'splinter parties', it will be observed—the Co-operative Commonwealth Federation (farmer-labour), Mr. H. H. Stevens's 'Reconstructionists', and the Social Credit League—have hardly succeeded in making a scratch on the traditional surface of Canadian politics. **1948** *Manch. Guardian Weekly* 15 Jan. 5/2 He challenges the Republicans to dodge the stigma of reaction and encourages the Wallace 'splinter groups' to hold firm. **1948** *Sun* (Baltimore) 23 Feb. 8/3 While splinter minorities may have a voice in the legislature, they cannot extend that voice beyond their own minority base. **1950** *Times* 27 Feb. 5/3 The Cabinet is made up of an uneasy coalition of splinter parties. **1958** *Spectator* 17 Jan. 73/2 The formation of superior-minded splinter groups which have no wish to become part of the main body of the Church. **1898** Middleton & Tait *Tribes without Rulers* 209 Splinter-segments of a clan do not form cores of tribes. **1964** R. Braddon *Year Angry Rabbit* v. 43 The fourteen new splinter nations now beginning to flake off the edges of a ripely rich Soviet Russia. **1968** *Guardian* 17 June 8/1 The ineffective splinter-group politics of the Fourth Republic. **1975** *N.Y. Times* 8 Nov. 26/2 The women's movement has increasingly allowed itself to be dominated..by radical splinter groups and issues which lack support among the majority of women. **1978** L. Heren *Growing up on The Times* ix. 293 Malcolm X formed a splinter movement, the organization of Afro-American unity. **1979** D. Sanders *Queen sends for Mrs Chadwick* 82 Supposing..the two main parties are deadlocked... They would have to turn to whatever splinter party happened to be closest to their own line.

splinter, *v.* Add: **3. c.** *fig.* To break off to

form a splinter group or groups; *loosely*, to divide or split. Also with *off*.

1967 M. L. King *Trumpet of Conscience* iii. 49 Under the impact of social forces unique to their times, young people have splintered into three principal groups, though of course there is some overlap among the three. **1972** *Guardian* 11 Jan. 9/1 Later Frank Ashbourn joined them ..and in May 1970 he and Mersh splintered off to form South Sea Bubble. **1976** *Oxford Diocesan Mag.* July 11/1 But the village's young people, distressed at seeing the parishioners splinter off to other towns for church, asked to hold the new prayer assembly in place of Mass.

splintering, *vbl. sb.* Add: Also *fig.*

1958 *Listener* 11 Sept. 366/2 He [*sc.* Ben-Gurion] is.. haunted by a well-nigh perverse splintering of political parties at home. **1968** P. Oliver *Screening Blues* ii. 62 The distinctions in the names [of Negro Churches] were indicative of the splintering of the churches into separate factions.

splinterless (spli·ntəɹlės), *a.* [f. Splinter *v.* + -less.] Of glass: guaranteed not to break into splinters; = *splinter-proof *a.* 2 (now the more usual term).

1928 *Sunday Express* 15 Jan. 6 The manufacture of splinterless glass. **1928** *Daily Express* 19 June 3 A splinterless shock-proof safety glass.

splinter-proof, *sb.* and *a.* Restrict *Mil.* to senses in Dict. and add: **B.** *adj.* **2.** That does not break into splinters; designed so as not to splinter.

1941 *AWA Techn. Rev.* V. 214 The control panel is mounted..below a re-entrant window of splinter-proof glass. **1964** *Economist* 19 Sept. 1124/3 A perfect mirror. It is unbreakable, splinterproof, lightweight.

splinting, *vbl. sb.* **2.** For 'surgical' read 'surgical or dental', and add later example.

1960 W. L. McCracken *Partial Denture Construction* xiv. 270 Splinting should not be used for the purpose of retaining a tooth that would otherwise be condemned for periodontal reasons.

split, *sb.*[1] Add: **2. d.** *Canad.* (chiefly *Newfoundland*). A piece of kindling-wood. Usu. in *pl.*

1858 R. T. S. Lowell *New Priest in Conception Bay* I. 74 The fire, where the round bake-pot stood, covered with its blazing 'splits'. **1919** W. T. Grenfell *Labrador Days* 198 'Get a few more splits, then, boy,' she replied, 'and I'll be cutting t' pork t' while.' **1976** Taylor & Horwood *Beyond Road* 55 Well, one time I was only a small boy gettin' in the splits—that's kindling.

e. *Anglo-Irish.* A piece of bogwood burned for illumination.

1892 *Ballymena Observer* 29 Apr. 6/1 *Splits*, long thin pieces of bogwood used for giving light. **1957** E. E. Evans *Irish Folk Ways* xiv. 185 Considerable use was made of buried timber dug from the bogs, of oak for roofing beams and..resinous 'splits' to give light.

4. d. *U.S.* = *split-up* s.v. *split-.

1972 *N.Y. Law Jrnl.* 10 Oct. 3/2 Tacking is permitted for stock dividends and splits, recapitalizations, [etc.]. **1976** [see *split-down* s.v. *split-].

6. Also, a policeman.

1932 'G. Orwell' *Coll. Essays* (1968) I. 89 He would.. exclaim 'Fucking toe-rag!'..meaning the 'split' who had arrested him. **1935** G. Ingram *Cockney Cavalcade* xiii. 202 'Here's the 'splits', boys!' A young lad who had been at the entrance with some others, had seen a police-car draw up and risked his liberty by dashing in to warn the hall occupants. **1966** W. Merrilees *Short Arm of Law* 140 At this point a destination board attendant asked another railway employee what the splits were after.

7. b. Also *spec.*, a half-bottle of champagne.

1973 T. Pynchon *Gravity's Rainbow* i. 5 All that's keeping him up there is an empty champagne split in his hip pocket, that's got hooked somehow. **1980** *N.Y. Times* 6 Nov. c2/3 To uncork a split of Champagne, some of which froths to the ground.

e. A sweet dish consisting of sliced fruit (esp. banana, split open lengthways), with ice-cream, syrup, etc. orig. *U.S.*

1920, etc. [see *banana split* s.v. *banana 3]. **1936** [see *parfait]. **1938** G. Greene *Brighton Rock* i. i. 17 That's what I want, a sundae. Delia likes splits best. **1939** A. Huxley *After Many a Summer* i. x. 135 Virginia was at the soda-counter, pensively eating a chocolate-and-banana split. **1979** M. Denny *Fruit in Season* 33 Banana splits... Place one banana per person in a dish with a portion of ice-cream in the centre... Pour a little chocolate sauce over.

f. *N. Amer.* A split-level house.

1970 *Toronto Daily Star* 24 Sept. 28/7 Back splits, side splits, bungalows. **1976** *Billings* (Montana) *Gaz.* 6 July 5-d/7 (Advt.), This gorgeously decorated 4 level split. **1980** *Times* 7 Apr. 5/6 French-speakers [in Montreal] would buy 'side halls, split levels, back splits'.

g. A split shift (see *split *ppl. a.* 3 a).

1973 R. Busby *Pattern of Violence* iii. 41 I'm working the split today. Get that boss of yours to give you a couple of hours off. **1977** P. Carter *Under Goliath* xxvi. 145 She..went moaning on... They were still at it at nine o'clock when Mr Black came back from his split.

8. *slang.* **a.** A division or share of the proceeds of a legal or illegal undertaking.

1889 Clarkson & Richardson *Police!* xxiii. 321 A share... Regular, split, drop. **1916** *Variety* 27 Oct. 12/1 W. S. Campbell..would not accept the 55–45 division of the receipts offered by the management, Campbell wanting a 50–50 split. **1934** J. T. Farrell *Young Manhood of Studs Lonigan* xiii. 206, I wasn't working for a long time, and then I got me this job, and now I'm also lined up with a can-house, and get my split on anybody I bring there. **1964** J. P. Clark *Three Plays* 121 Both thieves Will certainly be content to settle For an even split. **1973** J. Leasor *Host of Extras* i. 24 'I'll give you five thousand cash, the pair.' I must know *someone* who could advance this on the promise of a fifty per cent split down the middle of the selling price?

b. *N. Amer.* A girl, a woman.

1935 A. J. Pollock *Underworld Speaks* 111/2 *Split*, a girl. **1975** *Globe & Mail* (Toronto) 16 Dec. 9/5 An announcement was posted that the force's first female officer Constable Jacqueline Hall, had been hired. 'He's gone and hired another split, as if we don't have enough whores and splits in the department already,' Mrs. Nesbitt quoted the sergeant as saying.

9. *Croquet.* (See quot. 1961.)

1896 *Cassell's Bk. Sports & Pastimes* 305 The Split is a stroke used when you desire in taking croquet to move both balls some distance. **1961** *Croquet* ('Know the Game' Ser.) 36/1 *Split*, a croquet stroke in which the balls go in different directions.

10. *U.S. Sports.* A draw; a drawn series of matches.

1967 [see *double-header c]. **1974** *Cleveland* (Ohio) *Plain Dealer* 13 Oct. c1/1 The loss evened the C's exhibition slate to 2–2 and gave them a split in the two-game series with the Toros. **1976** *Springfield* (Mass.) *Daily News* 22 Apr. 40/2 With the VL getting only a split in six battles.

split, *v.* Add: **I. 5. e.** *to split one's* (or *the*) *ticket* or *ballot*: to vote for candidates of more than one party in an election. Also *ellipt.* *U.S.*

1842 *Spirit of Times* (Philadelphia) 14 July 2/1 The cry is raised of 'Vote the whole ticket! Don't split your ticket!' **1848** J. J. Hooper *Widow Rugby's Husb.* (1851) 23 Never split in my life. **1905** *N.Y. Even. Post* 17 Oct. 1 Plenty of talk is heard about intentions to split ballots. **1946** *Chicago Daily News* 20 Nov. 18/5 Democrats..decided the country did need a change, and split their ticket. **1975** R. Stout *Family Affair* (1976) xiii. 141 He asked if I had split the ticket, and I said yes, I had voted for Carey but not for Clark. **1980** *Times* 8 Oct. 8/4 To persuade electors to 'split the ticket'—to vote for a Republican President and for a Democratic senator.

f. *to split the atom*, to cause atomic nuclei to undergo fission. Also *fig.*

1909 *Busy Man's Mag.* Oct. 44/2 He [*sc.* Professor J. J. Thomson] is known both as 'The Man of Ion', and as the man 'who split the atom'. **1930** Sayers & 'Eustace' *Documents in Case* ii. 262 If anyone goes quietly away into a corner to experiment with high-voltage electric currents, they start a lot of ill-informed rubbish about splitting the atom. **1932** *Discovery* Mar. 69/2 The problem of splitting the atom is briefly this: given..that at the centre of every atom there is a minute nucleus whose electrical charge fixes the elementary nature of the atom, can we by any agency detach a part of this charge? **1935** J. Guthrie *Little Country* xxi. 335 With the blast of his cornet, Archibald Packer had split the Temmian atom. **1964** M. Gowing *Britain & Atomic Energy 1939–1945* 18 They bombarded a foil of the metal lithium, disrupting the lithium nuclei which, after combining with incident protons, split into two alpha particles. The experimenters had 'split' atoms by artificial means. **1981** *Daily Tel.* 24 Sept. 16/4 The first scientists to work on 'splitting the atom'.

6*. *slang* (orig. *U.S.*). To depart from, to leave. Freq. in phr. *to split the scene*: cf. *scene 8 e.

1956 O. Duke *Sideman* iii. vii. 272 Naw, man—I split that scene. **1963** *Freedomways* III. 522 Evil Indians sink feathered arrows into the good guys, who kicked a couple of times and then split the scene. **1968** Busby & Holtham *Main Line Kill* vi. 66 Where you bin? We thought you split the scene without giving us the word. **1971** *Sunday Sun* (Brisbane) 26 Sept. 3/3 When he split the Brisbane scene he left behind documents that could be incriminating to the drug gangsters. **1973** *Black Panther* 27 Oct. 17/2 We'll be splitting this place soon and once the book is written we won't have to come back. **1978** S. Wilson *Dealer's Move* i. 12 He and Miranda split Scotland for good and came down to London.

II. 10. c. *U.S. Sports.* To draw, to tie; *spec.* in *Baseball*, to win one game of a double-header, or to win half of the games in a series. Also *trans.*

1975 *Cleveland* (Ohio) *Plain Dealer* 31 Mar. 1-d/5 If Houston loses both of its remaining games and the Cavs split, the Cavs..have a better record against other division teams than Houston does. **1979** *Tucson* (Arizona) *Citizen* 20 Sept. 10d/1 He split two decisions this season in hookups with Gaylord Perry.

11. c. *slang* (orig. and chiefly *U.S.*). Of a couple: to become divorced; to separate.

1942 Berrey & Van den Bark *Amer. Thes. Slang* § 360/2 *Divorce*...split. **1951** E. Coxhead *One Green Bottle* x. 267 'Why did Chris go off early? Is anything wrong?' 'We've split,' Cathy answered. **1976** *National Observer* (U.S.) 14 Aug. 1/4 They had to split. If they don't love each other, what else can they do? **1978** *Detroit Free Press* 2 Apr. 19a/2 The [divorce] suit ended months of speculation that the TV sportscaster and film producer were splitting. **1982** 'J. Gash' *Firefly Gadroon* i. 13 Women are always unreasonable... We split after a terrible fight.

13*. *slang* (orig. *U.S.*). To depart, to take one's leave.

1954 *Time* 8 Nov. 42 *Split*,..depart. **1956** O. Duke *Sideman* iii. ix. 294 But that's why the cat split. **1956** B. Holiday *Lady sings Blues* (1973) iii. 38, I grabbed him and told him to do something because I had to split for the bathroom again. **1962** *Radio Times* 17 May 43 After the gig, dad, let's split to your pad for some suds. **1967** W. Murray *Sweet Ride* viii. 128 Since nobody asked you over, why don't you just split so we can finish our lunch? **1977** *Sounds* 1 Jan. 21/4 In the main hall Roger Scott from London's Capital Radio arrived, took one look at the wasteland and split.

III. 14. a. With *out*: also *slang* (now *Obs.* or *rare*), to separate or disentangle from another.

1924 G. C. Henderson *Keys to Crookdom* 419 *Splitting out*, separating pickpocket from his victim in case of trouble. The stall splits out the wire. **1931** *Collier's* 16 May 66/2 Everybody else is busy trying to split out Regret and the bloodhounds.

b. With *out*: also *slang*, to quarrel; to part company; to take one's leave (cf. sense 13* above). With *up*: also *colloq.*, to break up a relationship (esp. of a couple); *spec.* to become divorced.

1850 G. W. Matsell *Vocabulum* 84 *Split out*, no longer friends; quarrelled; dissolved partnership. **1879** *Macmillan's Mag.* Oct. 505/2 There is a reeler over there which knows me, we had better split out. **1903** G. H. Lorimer *Lett. from Self-Made Merchant to his Son* viii. 104 He and his father split up, temporarily, over it, and, of course, it cost me the old man's trade and friendship. **1927** J. Black *You can't Win* x. 132 'Where are you going, kid?'..'If you are going to split out, I'll go to San Francisco for a while.' **1942** Berrey & Van den Bark *Amer. Thes. Slang* § 360/2 *Divorce*...split up. **1956** B. Holiday *Lady sings Blues* (1973) xxii. 176 Even if I could have split out I'd have been in a snowstorm of lawsuits. **1959** 'E. Peters' *Death Mask* i. 15 When we split up..I felt it was all my fault. I had to be free of him. **1976** M. Machlin *Pipeline* xlvii. 491 You just split out like a streak of blue lightning, without saying nothing to nobody. **1976** W. Corlett *Dark Side of Moon* i. i. 29 'He thought his parents were..splitting up?' 'Divorce?.. he thought it was on the cards.'

split-. Add: **split-down** *U.S. Stock Exchange* (see quot. 1976); cf. *split-up* below; **split-off,** an act of splitting off; something that splits off or that has become split off; **split-up,** an act of splitting up; *spec.* in the U.S. Stock Exchange: the division of a stock into two or more stocks of the same total value; cf. *split-down* above.

1932 *Sun* (Baltimore) 16 Apr. 15/8 The whys and wherefores of the 'split-down' movement in the capital structures of various corporations, in contrast with the stock 'split-ups' popular in the boom days of 1928–29 are now being explained in Wall Street. **1976** D. W. Moffat *Econ. Dict.* 257/2 The reverse split, or split-down in which a corporation reduces the number of shares into which its ownership is divided. The single word split usually refers to a split-up. **1935** Z. N. Hurston *Mules & Men* i. ii. 40 Ah knowed one preacher dat was called to preach at one of dese split-off churches. De members had done split off from a big church... He come and preached at dis split-off for two whole weeks. **1964** *New Statesman* 14 Feb. 248/1 The split-off of science into a separate culture. **1878** H. Sweet tr. H. Paul in *Trans. Philol. Soc.* (1879) 390 Even in the parent Indogermanic language long before its split-up, there were no longer any roots, stems and suffixes, but only ready-made *words*. **1908** G. H. Lorimer *Jack Spurlock* iv. 76, I should have told her then about my split-up with the Governor. **1928** E. S. Mead *Corporation Finance* (ed. 6) I. xxx. 358 We may note finally the difference between a stock 'split-up' and a stock dividend. In the first case two or three shares are issued for one share of existing stock, and when this is par-value stock the par value is reduced. **1944** *Sun* (Baltimore) 9 Sept. 11/1 Pepsi-Cola added $\frac{7}{8}$ to its brisk upturn of the previous day in response to the three-for-one splitup proposal. **1975** *High Times* Dec. 51/2 Last year I was still spinning from my split-up with a man. **1976** Split-up [see *split-down* above].

split, *ppl. a.* Add: **2. a.** *split-ring* (earlier example); *split bearing* (Mech.), a bearing for a shaft in which the housing and bush are each split laterally into two parts for ease of assembly; *split flap* (Aeronaut.), a flap occupying only the lower part of the wing thickness.

1902 R. Grimshaw *Mod. Workshop Hints* xiv. 268 (*heading*) Filling split bearings with babbitt. **1973** O. S. Nock *Gresley Pacifics* I. vii. 91/2 The inside big end.. necessarily had split bearings. **1929** *Techn. Notes U.S. Nat. Advisory Comm. Aeronaut.* No. 324. 1 It is known that..a suction exists between the parts of a split flap located at the trailing edge. **1968** Miller & Sawers *Technical Devel. Mod. Aviation* iii. 84 The adoption of retractable undercarriages, which increased drag when they were lowered for landing, made it less important to use flaps which increased drag as greatly as the split flap. **1853** C. M. Yonge *Heir of Redclyffe* II. xxi. 340 It was locked, but the key was on her own split-ring.

b. *split-face, skirt, stitch* (earlier example); *split baluster* (see quot. 1969); *split end* (Amer. and Canad. Football), an end (*end *sb.* 3 g) positioned at some distance from the rest of the formation; *split falls* (see quot. 1960); *split graft* (Med.) = *split-skin graft*, sense 5 a below; *split jump* (Figure-skating), a jump during which the legs are momentarily kicked out into the splits position; *split pea*, rhyming slang for 'tea' (*obs.*); cf. *Rosy Lee; *split shot, stroke* (Croquet) = *split *sb.*[1] 9; *split-turn*, a sharp turn.

1904 P. Macquoid *Hist. Eng. Furnit.* ix. 228 The split baluster ornament..has been variously named split baluser, cannon, or mace decoration. 1934 *Burlington Mag.* Sept. 125/1 An extensive use of relief decoration in the form of turned 'split balusters' is also rather characteristic of many of these pieces. 1969 J. Gloag *Short Dict. Furnit.* 635 *Split baluster*, a turned baluster split centrally, and applied ornamentally to a surface. 1955 C. V. Mather *Winning High School Football* vii. 187 (caption) The halfback splits half the distance with the split end. 1968 *Globe & Mail* (Toronto) 10 July 27/5 Adkins will be the split end with underrated Jay Roberts, a tough blocker, remaining at tight end. 1977 *New Yorker* 10 Oct. 177/2 Using only two backs..and sending four split ends..downfield, Restic had Harvard throw fifty-seven passes that afternoon, thirty-one of them valid. 1923 D. H. Lawrence *Birds, Beasts & Flowers* 182 And white teeth showing in your dragon-grin as you race, you split-face. 1939 *Country Life* 11 Feb. p. xxxiii/1 (Advt.), Made in Cavalry Twills..Sheppards Checks, Split falls or fly front. 1960 C. W. Cunnington et al. *Dict. Eng. Costume* 75/2 *Falls*, a buttoned flap to the front of breeches and..of pantaloons and trousers... 'Small' or 'Split Falls' was a narrow central flap. 1929 *Surg., Gynecol. & Obstetrics* XLIX. 96/2 In lining a contractile cavity with a split graft allowance should always be made for contraction. 1958 *New Biol.* XXVII. 40 Split-grafts are prepared by enzyme digestion of the fibres joining the epidermis to the dermis, which frees the epidermis for use as the graft. 1961 J. S. Salak *Dict. Amer. Sports* 416 *Split jump*,..a variation of the jump from the back edge with the free toe assisting. 1968 Split jump [see *lay-back 2 b]. 1857 'Ducange Anglicus' *Vulgar Tongue* 20 *Split-Pea*, tea. 1931 S. Kaye-Smith *Hist. Susan Spray* iii. 296 I'll make you a nice cup of split pea. 1975 *Oxf. Compan. Sports & Games* 218/2 When the balls travel in different directions the stroke is also known as a split shot. 1976 *Scotsman* 20 Nov. (Weekend Suppl.) 4/1 The look of clothes today suggests country more than town... Capes and ponchos, loose knits and split skirts, are more at home on town birds than country cousins. 1880 L. Higgin *Handbk. Embroidery* iii. 22 *Split Stitch* is worked like ordinary 'stem', except that the needle is always brought up *through* the crewel or silk, which it splits. 1897 *Encycl. Sport* I. 254/1 *Split stroke*, taking croquet so as to drive the balls on courses nearly at right angles to one another. 1932 W. Faulkner *Sartoris* iii. 252 The damn thing zoomed past and did a split-turn and came back at me again.

c. Phr. *to keep on a split yarn* and varr.: to keep in a state of alert. *Naut. slang.*

1929 *Papers Mich. Acad. Sci., Arts & Lett.* X. 298/2 *Having everything on a split yarn*, ready to start at once. 1958 W. King *Stick & Stars* 73 All submariners had to be kept on a split yarn in case England was invaded.

3. a. *split beam*, a beam (of radiation, etc.) that has been split into two or more components, *spec.* as used in a radar technique in which a single aerial transmits alternately two beams slightly displaced from each other in order accurately to obtain the direction of a target; freq. *attrib.*; *split beaver* (slang) (see quots.); *split decision* (Boxing), a decision made on points in which the judges and referee are not unanimous in their choice of a winner; *split entrance, entry* adj. (N. Amer.), designating a house in which the entrance is half-way between the levels of the two floors; also *absol.* as *sb.*; cf. *split-level *a.*; *split-field* = next; usu. *attrib.*; *split-image*, (*a*) an image in a rangefinder or focusing system that has been bisected by optical means, the halves of which are displaced when the system is out of focus, used esp. in various types of camera; usu. *attrib.*; (*b*) = *splitting image* s.v. *splitting *ppl. a.* 5; *split instant, minute, moment*, an extremely small space of time; cf. *split-second *a.* and *sb.*; *split page* (U.S. Journalism) (see quot. 1970); *split-phase* (Electr.), used *attrib.* with reference to devices, esp. induction motors, that utilize two or more voltages at different phases produced from a single-phase supply; also *transf.*; *split rail* (orig. U.S.), a fence rail split from a log; freq. *attrib.*, as *split-rail fence*; *split run*, a press run of a newspaper in which some portions contain certain copy, advertisements, etc., not carried by other portions; *split screen* (Cinemat., Television, and Computing), a screen on which are projected simultaneously two or more images; *split shift*, (*a*) a working shift split into two or more periods separated by an interval or intervals of several hours; (*b*) a shift overlapping the times of two other shifts; *split ticket* (earlier and later examples); *split trial* (U.S. Law), a trial conducted in two stages of which the first will establish facts necessary to the impartial or swift conducting of the second; *split week*, (*a*) *Theatr.* (see quot. 1948); (*b*) a working week in which days off occur other than at the weekend.

1947 Crowther & Whiddington *Science at War* 25 This 'split-beam' method of direction-finding gives very accurate results. 1966 D. Taylor *Radar* ii. 24 Special stations..with facilities for 'split-beam' d.f. [*sc.* direction finding] were provided for accurate tracking of ships and fire-control purposes. 1966 [see *spectrophotometer]. 1978 R. V. Jones *Most Secret War* xlii. 397 The method was to set a Freya station on the coast of France so that its split-beam pointed over the target in London. 1972 *New Society* 7 Dec. 591/1 The business has evolved its own jargon; full frontals are 'beavers', becoming 'split-beavers' if the legs are parted. 1976 Lieberman & Rhodes *Compl. CB Handbk.* vi. 137 *Split beaver*, stripper. 1977 E. J. Trimmer et al. *Visual Dict. Sex* (1978) xxiv. 270 In the further stages of frankness 'beaver' and 'split beaver' shots show the hairy vulva. 1978 J. Irving *World according to Garp* xiii. 241 Pictures of naked women... If you could see the sex parts..that was a beaver... If the parts were *open*, that was called a *split* beaver. 1970 *Times* 28 Sept. 13/4 Buchanan, the British lightweight champion, gained a 15 round split points decision over Ismael Laguna of Panama. 1976 *Daily Times* (Lagos) 8 Oct. 30/3 The 29-year-old Panther..then said he had already petitioned the Nigerian Boxing Board of Control over the decision which gave Billy Savage the title by a split decision on September 24. 1968 *Globe & Mail* (Toronto) 13 Feb. 31/2 (Advt.), Beautiful split entrance bungalow. 1967 *Boston Sunday Globe* 23 Apr. B42/5 (Advt.), Keep that city job and enjoy country living in these unusually attractive split entry ranches. 1976 *Laurel* (Montana) *Outlook* 23 June 19/1 (Advt.), You will never regret buying this new 4 bdrm split entry. 1941 *Amateur Photographer's Handbk.* (ed. 2) vi. 121 Some people find this split-field type of range finder difficult to use. 1976 C. Reynolds *Photoguide to Filters* 156 One special accessory is the split-field lens. 1950 R. A. McCoy *Pract. Photogr.* ii. 15 To operate the split image type [of rangefinder] it is necessary to look through the finder and observe that the image seems to be broken in the center and offset. 1960 *Focal Encycl. Photogr.* (rev. ed.) 946/2 The parallax effect appears as a split image which joins up across a dividing line when the lens is set to maximum sharpness. 1977 J. Hedgecoe *Photographer's Handbk.* 15 As a focusing aid a 'split image' or focusing screen rangefinder may be sunk into the center of the underside of the screen. 1981 'M. Innes' *Lord Mullion's Secret* 179 He was by a strange freak of heredity the split image of one commemorated by Nicholas Hilliard some centuries ago. 1936 M. Mitchell *Gone with Wind* xx. 348 'Rain,' she thought... But, in a split instant: 'Rain? No!... Cannon!' 1931 W. G. Carr *By Guess & by God* 27 Using his one periscope for split-minute looks. 1957 I. Asimov *Naked Sun* ii. 31 For one fleeting split moment he bent his head back and stared directly at Solaria's sun. 1953 B. Westley *News Editing* 419/1 *Split page*, same as 'second front page'. 1957 J. Steinbeck *Pippin IV* 58 Colour photographs filled the split-page of every newspaper. 1970 R. K. Kent *Lang. Journalism* 26 *Split page*, the front page of a newspaper's second section; second front page. 1895 S. P. Thompson *Polyphase Electric Currents* ix. 175 This is a form of split-phase motor having two or more sets of coils placed at different angles. 1921 W. S. Ibbetson *Motor & Dynamo Control* vi. 174 This split-phase winding has a very high resistance and induction, so that the current in it lays nearly 90° behind that in the running coils. 1953 *Pedestrian* Summer 26 Sometimes the policeman is operating what is known as a split phase; pedestrians may cross half the road in front of halted traffic and not realize that the traffic on the other half has the right of way. 1976 C. G. Grolle *Compl. Guide Electr. Repairs* viii. 120 All split-phase motors have a centrifugal switch that drops out the contacts on the start winding after full speed is attained. 1826 T. Flint *Recollections of Last Ten Years* 206 Scarcely has a family fixed itself, and enclosed a plantation with the universal fence,—split rails [etc.]. 1897 *Essex Antiq.* (Salem, Mass.) Feb. 27/2 The split-rail fence is also old. Logs, generally of ash, about nine feet in length, and a foot or more in diameter, split the entire length into about sixteen equal parts, formed the rails, which were chamfered at each end. Of such split sections posts were also made, having holes cut in them in the proper places to receive the ends of the rails. 1934 *Bulletin* (Sydney) 14 Feb. 30/2 A new post or a new set of rails has to be put in a split-rail fence. 1976 Scott & Koski *Walk-In* (1977) xxx. 216 A weathered split-rail fence..announced the boundary. 1961 Webster, Split run. 1963 D. Ogilvy *Confessions Advert. Man* (1964) vi. 110 In split-run tests, long copy invariably outsells short copy. 1977 D. Grossman *Samson Management Lexicon* ii. 19 Split-run copy testing. 1979 *Austral. Financial Rev.* 15 Aug. 22/6 The commission's investigations cover practices known in some sectors of the trade as 'split runs' and 'blowing'. A split run involves several print runs of the same editorial content, but with different advertising content. 1953 R. Bretz *Techniques Television Production* xi. 206 In the case of the phone conversation the split screen might appear in a direct cut after a single shot of the person making the call. 1958 *Times* 20 Jan. 3/2 Attempts to quicken the action [of a film] by a split screen device fail lamentably in their object. 1970 W. Wager *Sledgehammer* (1971) xv. 91 As if in some film.. Williston's neatly typed dossiers..jumped into focus... Actually they appeared side by side in a split-screen effect, hung there for a long moment and vanished. 1977 *Time* 26 Sept. 42/2 Alvy and Annie, on a split screen, talking to their shrinks about the frequency with which they have sex. 1955 M. Reifer *Dict. New Words* 196/1 *Split shift*,..a work schedule or shift in which there is a break in the working hours. 1960 *Guardian* 30 June 10/4 Split shifts (e.g. 4–9 a.m. and 5–8 p.m.) and split days off. 1964 G. L. Cohen *What's Wrong with Hospitals?* ii. 39 Wards operating a three-shift system, instead of the generally abhorred 'split shift' which gave nurses a useless afternoon break. 1970 F. McKenna *Gloss. Railwaymen's Talk* p. v, The footplate crew has an even worse cycle—what is called the 'split shift' system. 1978 *Detroit Free Press* 16 Apr. F5/3 (Advt.), We have psychiatric nursing positions available on all shifts. No split shifts. 1836 J. Hoyt *Let.* 21 Nov. in W. L. Mackenzie *Life M. Van Buren* (1846) 262, I was reproached by you for having voted a 'split ticket'. 1964 *Economist* 31 Oct. 482/2 A 'split-ticket' group..to urge voters to support Mr Johnson and Mr Keating, the Republican senatorial candidate. 1960 *Annals Amer. Acad. Pol. & Soc. Sci.* CCCXXVIII. 52/1 Of all the time-saving remedies, the split trial should prove the most powerful. 1967 *North-Western Reporter* 2nd. Ser. CL. 323/1 In that year [*sc.* 1878] secs. 4697–98–99, R.S. 1878, were enacted and provided a split trial in which the insanity issue was tried first and if the accused was found sane he was then tried on his plea of not guilty before the same jury. 1926 Split week [see *ham *sb.*[1] 5]. 1948 H. L. Mencken *Amer. Lang.* Suppl. II. 691 *Split week*, a week on the road divided between two or more towns. 1974 P. Wright *Lang. Brit. Industry* ix. 81 *Split weeks* have also become fashionable instead of unvarying Saturday-to-Saturday weeks.

d. *fig.* With reference to division or dissociation affecting a person's mental life or the self. In special collocations, as *split consciousness, man, mind, -mindedness, personality*; *split-minded* adj.

1958 R. F. C. Hull tr. *Jung's Undiscovered Self* v. 74 The rupture between faith and knowledge is a symptom of the split consciousness which is so characteristic of the mental disorder of our day. 1944 H. Read *Educ. Free Men* x. 32 We divide the intelligence from the sensibility of our children, create split-men (schizophrenics, to give them a psychological name), and then discover that we have no social unity. 1962 M. McLuhan *Gutenberg Galaxy* 51 (*heading*) The Homeric hero becomes a split-man as he assumes an individual ego. 1938 Split mind [see *schizoid *a.* a]. 1945 Koestler *Yogi & Commissar* iii. i. 121 Typical examples of socially approved split-mind patterns are the Astronomer who believes both in his instruments and in Christian dogma [etc.]. *a* 1974 R. Crossman *Diaries* (1977) III. 372 The fact is that Jim is absolutely split-minded. 1976 *Jrnl. R. Soc. Arts* CXXIV. 630/2, I must admit to being rather split-minded on this subject. 1947 S. O'Faolain *Irish* i. 23 A delightful dualism—the moderns would call it splitmindedness. 1963 R. F. C. Hull tr. *Jung's Mysterium Coniunctionis* in *Coll. Wks.* XIV. iii. 248 The surprisingly common phenomenon of masculine split-mindedness, when the right hand mustn't know what the left is doing. 1919 M. K. Bradby *Psycho-Anal.* x. 129 The split personalities of hysterics and mediums..have a subjective meaning. 1931 E. Wilson *Axel's Castle* ii. 40 A theory which makes one's poetic self figure as one of the halves of a split personality. 1966 'H. MacDiarmid' *Company I've Kept* xiii. 259 In my view, he [*sc.* Walter Elliott] was a split personality. 1974 *Listener* 31 Jan. 131/1 Every nation becomes a bundle of contradictions and paradoxes—practically a split personality.

5. a. *split-site comprehensive* (*school*), *school*; *split-brain*, used with reference to a person or animal whose corpus callosum has been severed or is lacking, so that there is no direct connection between the two halves of the brain; *split-dose* (Med.), applied to the technique of administering a given quantity of ionizing radiation in several exposures so as to reduce its harmful effects in relation to its therapeutic ones; *split-half* (Statistics), used *attrib.* with reference to the technique of splitting a body of supposedly homogeneous data into two halves and calculating the results separately from each to assess their reliability; also *absol.*; *split-skin graft* (Med.), a skin graft which involves only the superficial portion of the thickness of the skin; cf. *split graft*, sense 2 b above.

1958 R. W. Sperry in Harlow & Woolsey *Biol. & Biochem. Bases Behavior* 418 In recent efforts to learn more about connectivity principles in perceptual integration, we have been putting to use the demonstrated functional independence of the two hemispheres in what we have come to call the 'split-brain' preparation... In these split-brain animals one can leave intact a whole hemisphere to maintain generalized background function. 1968 Passmore & Robson *Compan. Med. Stud.* I. xxiv. 94/2 At times, the non-dominant hand may 'go off on its own' and have to be restricted by the dominant hand. One begins to doubt whether a split brain man is singular or plural. But in no sense does he resemble a schizophrenic, in spite of the layman's interpretation of that word. 1972 R. E. Ornstein *Psychol. of Consciousness* ii. 55 In day-to-day living, these 'split-brain' people exhibit almost no abnormality. 1947 *Radiology* XLIX. 321/1 In this study the split-dose technic was applied to recovery as tested by lethal effects. 1968 *Brit. Med. Bull.* XXIV. 246/2 Young..has written a program to synthesize the results of split-dose experiments from survival curves at various phases of the cycle. 1935 *Psychol. Rev.* XLII. 158 This conception of split-half or comparable-form reliability as simply inter-item correlation can and should be brought into relationship with Kelley's concept of reliability as adequacy of sampling. 1946 *Jrnl. Educational Psychol.* XXXVII. 473 Since any test may be split in a large number of ways, the split-half method of estimating test reliability fails to give a unique result. 1971 *Computers & Humanities* V. 260 Because 0101 and 0410 had high internal reliability (split half), we did not cut, Xerox, and translate further samples from these books. 1972 *Guardian* 8 Mar. 12/6 Since they are..formed from a merger of two or three existing schools, the split-site comprehensive schools have some attraction for local educational authorities. 1973 *Times* 11 Apr. 8/6 A minibus is used in one of our split-site comprehensives. 1975 *Times* 30 Dec. 3/2 The survey of 18 split-site schools, most of them divided by one or two miles across cities and industrial roads, concludes that they are 'the unfortunate by-products of imposing a comprehensive system too quickly'. 1981 *West Lancs. Evening Gaz.* 11 Nov. 9/8 But in 24 of the 63 cases, the authority would have to create either a split-site school, or a school with more than 490 pupils. 1929 *Surg., Gynecol. & Obstetrics* XLIX. 82 (*heading*) The use and uses of large split skin grafts of intermediate thickness. **1977** *Proc. R. Soc. Med.* LXX. 480/1 Excision and split-skin graft undertaken in 5 patients was successful in the 3 who were traced.

split-arse, -ass, *a. slang.* [f. SPLIT *ppl. a.* + ARSE *sb.*] **1.** *split-arse mechanic* (see quot.).

1903 FARMER & HENLEY *Slang* VI. 317/1 *Split-arse mechanic*,..a harlot.

2. *Forces' Slang* (orig. *Air Force*). **a.** Classy, showy; (of an airman) reckless, that performs stunts; (of aircraft) having good manœuvrability.

1917 F. T. NETTLEINGHAM *Tommy's Tunes* 49 The expression 'a splitass merchant' is applied indiscriminately to a reckless individual or to a really good flyer capable of executing stunts with a modicum of safety. **1919** W. H. DOWNING *Digger Dialects* 47 *Split-ass*, unusual. **1934** V. M. YEATES *Winged Victory* II. xii. 288 They were sufficiently splitarse and did all the stunts, but there was nothing like a Camel for lightness of touch. **1946** J. IRVING *Royal Navalese* 163 Split-ass, showy. **1966** A. LA BERN *Goodbye Piccadilly* vi. 67 The Royal Air Force and the Fleet Air Arm used to describe certain flyers as 'split-arse types'. This coarse expression was reserved for outstandingly reckless airmen.

b. *split-arse cap* (see quots.).

1931 BROPHY & PARTRIDGE *Songs & Slang Brit. Soldier* (ed. 3) 360 *Split-arse cap*, the old R.F.C. cap, rather like a Glengarry. **1945** C. H. WARD-JACKSON *It's a Piece of Cake* (ed. 2) 56 *Split-arse cap*, the field service cap as distinct from the peaked dress service cap.

Hence as *sb.*, a flying stunt (see also quot. 1919); as *v. intr.*, to make a sudden turn in an aircraft; to perform stunt flying; **spli·t-arsing** *vbl. sb.* and *ppl. a.*

1917 F. T. NETTLEINGHAM *Tommy's Tunes* 49 So won't you splitass back Along the track To my dear old Omer Town. **1919** W. H. DOWNING *Digger Dialects* 47 *Split-ass*, an aeroplane on its side in banking for a sharp turn. **1929** *Papers Mich. Acad. Sci., Arts & Lett.* X. 325/2 *Splitass*, to do stunt flying, or to fly in a reckless manner. **1931** BROPHY & PARTRIDGE *Songs & Slang Brit. Soldier* (ed. 3) 360 *Split-arsing*,..stunting low and flying near the roofs of..huts. **1934** V. M. YEATES *Winged Victory* III. iv. 326 The triplanes had come down..and did some diving at the splitarsing Camels but didn't hit anyone. *Ibid.* vi. 347 Something fired at him. He splitarsed and nearly hit an SE. **1945** C. H. WARD-JACKSON *It's a Piece of Cake* (ed. 2) 56 *Split-arse*, stunt.

spli·t-level, *a.* [f. SPLIT *ppl. a.* + LEVEL *sb.*] **1. a.** Designating a house or other building which has a floor between the floor-levels of two adjoining storeys (see quot. 1957); applied to this type of design. Also, designating a room having a floor on two levels. Also *absol.* orig. *U.S.*

1952 *N.Y. Times* 7 Sept. VIII. 1/1 A community of 129 split-level houses. **1955** *New Yorker* 1 Oct. 102/2 In the majority of the ads for new houses, 'split-level' is the big word, the selling word. There are, it appears, a good many kinds of split-levels. **1957** *Times* 12 Nov. (Canada Suppl.) p. xv/2 A visit to one of the new planned communities will convince the stranger that Canada has gone split-level mad, provided he knows what split-level means. This is the house originally designed for a sloping site, with entrance midway between upper and lower floors. **1958** *Spectator* 18 July 116/2 It is the first split-level church building in America. **1959** [see *MULTILEVEL *a.*]. **1960** *Guardian* 3 Feb. 6/6 The split-level £2,000 room. *Ibid.* 24 Feb. 12/5 The house is on a sloping site, so this split-level treatment makes sense. **1963** J. N. HARRIS *Weird World Wes Beattie* (1964) ii. 20 One split level was much like another to him, but the general arrangements of Mrs. Ledley's house showed quiet good taste. **1968** P. ABLEMAN *Vac* xvii. 91 There was a spiral staircase leading to split-level bedrooms. **1980** *Times* 29 Feb. 23 (Advt.), Luxury individually designed modern split level detached house.

b. Of a cooker: having the oven and hob in separately installed units.

1960 *Times* 4 Jan. 13/1 British manufacturers are at last taking advantage of the experience of the Americans. .. Now, in England, a number of manufacturers are producing standard units incorporating split level cookers with the oven at waist level, the hob fixed into the working surface, [etc.]. **1976** *S. Wales Echo* 25 Nov. 27/4 (Advt.), Extended kitchen, including Creda split-level oven and hob. **1978** *Cornish Guardian* 27 Apr. 16/3 (Advt.), Large kitchen, split level cooker etc.

2. *transf.* and *fig.*

1955 *N.Y. Times Mag.* 30 Oct. 4/4 Mr. Spectorsky has looked on a community..and seen only what he planned to see—the fieldstone houses and the split-level personalities, the couples who cannot make ends meet on forty or fifty thousand a year. **1959** *N.Y. Times* 23 Aug. I. 66/4 (Advt.), Urban and suburban fashion-seekers find the split-level dress a good investment. **1960** *Washington Post* 14 Jan. D 1/2 The migrant worker leads a split-level life... One state may provide adequate housing and other services. But as soon as he steps across a state line he may find himself in an area with no program to meet his needs. **1965** *New Statesman* 19 Mar. 456/3 George is the natural man drawn to pubs and barmaids, Arbuthnott the conscience that natters at him. This sort of split-level Englishman seems to belong with Mr Pooter. **1968** *Language* XLIV. 501 Morphologically conditioned sound change (analogical change) is normally of such a nature that no new phoneme arises in a 'split-level' analysis. **1973** *Irish Times* 2 Mar. 13/4 We Irish are now inured to a split-level morality: we react in low key and circumspection when one of 'our own people' murder or maim; but vehemently when the slayer is 'one of them'.

split-second, *a.* and *sb.* Also **split second(s).** [Abbrev. of *split second(s) hands*: see SPLIT *ppl. a.* 2 a and SECOND *sb.*[1] 3.] **A.** *adj.* **1.** Designating a stop-watch having two seconds hands, one underneath the other and one of which may be stopped independently of the other. Also *absol.*

1884, 1888 [in Dict. s.v. SPLIT *ppl. a.* 2 a]. **1897** *Sears, Roebuck Catal.* 377/2 This is the best cheap Split Second Horse Timer made. **1916** H. L. WILSON *Somewhere in Red Gap* ix. 379 When I left 'em Jake was holding a split-second watch on the waiter he'd just given an order to. **1971** T. C. COLLOCOTT *Dict. Sci. & Technol.* 1106/1 *Split-seconds chronograph*,..a chronograph with two independent centre seconds hands, one underneath the other.

2. Occurring, executed in, or lasting a fraction of a second; timed or calculated to a fraction of a second; sudden, instantaneous.

1946 'M. INNES' *From London Far* III. v. 206 The issue of modern naval conflicts depends upon split-second decisions. **1951** *People* 3 June 2/4 Watch for the two split-second appearances of twenty-one-years-old Audrey Hepburn. **1957** *New Yorker* 2 Nov. 68/2 He pictures himself as being locked in a death struggle with ringing telephones, split-second appointments, and traffic jams. **1959** W. GOLDING *Free Fall* iv. 82, I was..sitting my bike, willing them to die..because this demanded split-second timing. **1975** R. L. DUNCAN *Dragons at Gate* iv. 125 An instant pressure on the trigger, sound dispersed by a silencer, split-second work. **1978** *Poland* May 50/2 A player who cannot report punctually..cannot be counted on to carry out complex tactical maneuvers requiring split-second decisions when he is under a great mental strain.

B. *sb.* A fraction of a second.

1912 CHESTERTON *Manalive* I. iv. 97 Mr. Moon stood for one split second astonished. **1935** S. LEWIS *It can't happen Here* iv. 40 Typed revelations timed to the split-second. **1940** [see *RECEIVER[1] 1 c]. **1950** *Sport* 22–28 Sept. 12/1 (*caption*) Racing in, a split second too late for the tackle, is home centre-half, Tommy Cummings. **1978** J. WAINWRIGHT *Jury People* xl. 141 For a split second, she'd known pain she'd never dreamed existed..then she'd passed out.

splitter, *sb.*[2] Add: **1. d.** An auxiliary set of gears that provides a set of ratios between those of the main gearbox. Freq. *attrib.*

1963 *Automobile Engineer* LIII. 228/2 An overdrive in front of the gearbox can be used as a splitter gear..to provide intermediate ratios between any two of the gearbox. These can be engaged without operating the clutch. **1967** *Economist* 8 July (Commercial Vehicles Suppl.) p. xxx/1, Even when there are enough speeds in the splitter box (which may be either in front or behind the normal box) rear axles are getting more complicated. **1977** *Belfast Tel.* 27 Jan. 21/8 (Advt.), 1969 Leyland Super Commet, 6-wheel Tipper, fitted with p.a.s., splitter box, 401 engine. **1977** 'D. RUTHERFORD' *Return Load* ii. 32 'How many gears have you got?' 'Thirteen forward and two reverse.'..'It's got a splitter.' Sally said..'You don't have to move the gear lever thirteen times.'

5. *Hunting slang.* A first-rate hunt.

1843 *Ainsworth's Mag.* III. 219 'What a fine country before us!' observes a third; 'what a splitter we shall have!' says a fourth. **1976** *Shooting Times & Country Mag.* 16–22 Dec. 25/2 There was more than a holding scent and..we were in for a splitter.

splitting, *vbl. sb.* Add: **2. c.** *spec.* in *Psychol.* The process of division or dissociation affecting the mind or self. Also with *off.*

1890 W. JAMES *Princ. Psychol.* I. ix. 227 According to M. Janet these secondary personalities are always abnormal, and result from the splitting of what ought to be a single complete self into two parts. **1910** tr. *Freud's Orig. & Devel. Psycho-Anal.* in *Amer. Jrnl. Psychol.* XXI. 191 We followed his [*sc.* Janet's] example when we made the mental splitting and the dissociation of personality the central points of our theory. *Ibid.*, I soon came to another view of the origin of hysterical dissociation (or splitting of consciousness). **1927** HENDERSON & GILLESPIE *Text-Bk. Psychiatry* v. 101 The most extensive, and at the same time the most profound, of all personality changes is the 'splitting of the personality' that occurs in advanced schizophrenia. **1945** M. KLEIN *Contributions to Psycho-Analysis* (1948) 346 The early splitting of the mother figure into a good and bad 'breast mother' as a way of dealing with ambivalence had been very marked. **1967** J. A. HADFIELD *Introd. Psychotherapy* xviii. 134 A severe shock such as a car accident or even a severe illness can result in a splitting off of some part of consciousness.

5. *splitting mill* (earlier example); **splitting field** *Math.*, the least field which includes all roots of a specified polynomial.

1841 H. SCRIVENOR *Hist. Iron Trade* vi. 120 All below that size were cut in the splitting-mill. **1942** E. ARTIN *Galois Theory* ii. 22 A splitting field is of finite degree since it is constructed by a finite number of adjunctions of algebraic elements, each defining a field of finite degree. **1971** E. C. DADE in Powell & Higman *Finite Simple Groups* viii. 256 If F is algebraically closed, then it is a splitting field for any simple F-algebra.

splitting, *ppl. a.* Add: **4.** (Earlier examples.)

1828 *Oscotian* I. 461 Felt a splitting head-ache under my night-cap. **1835** DICKENS *Let.* 18 Dec. (1965) I. 109 The noise and confusion here..is so great that my head is actually splitting.

5. *splitting image*, an exact likeness. Also (*dial.*) *splitten image.* Cf. *spitting image* s.v. *SPITTING *ppl. a.* 3.

1880 T. CLARKE *Specimens Westmoreland Dial.* II. 36 Soa t'kersmas up i't'fells Et just be t'splitten image Ov a kersmas 'mang yersells. **1939** D. HARTLEY *Made in England* i. 3 Evenness and symmetry are got by pairing the two split halves of the same tree, or branch. (Hence the country saying: he's the 'splitting image'—an exact likeness.)

splittism (spli·tiz'm). [tr. Chinese *fēnliè zhǔyì*: see SPLIT *v.* and -ISM.] In Communist use: the pursuance of factional interests in opposition to official party policy. Also *transf.* Hence **spli·ttist,** one who practises splittism; also as *adj.*

1962 *Guardian* 15 Dec. 7/1 That dread word, 'Splittism', which has never before darkened a page of the Sino-Soviet polemic, broke through to the surface of the Peking 'People's Daily' yesterday in the first open discussion of the possibility of a split. This term, taken from the translation of the Chinese document into English by the official New China News Agency, appears from the context to be identical with the Russian Communist concept of 'fractionalism'. **1964** *Economist* 8 Feb. 490/3 In Peking's view splittism means opposing and betraying Marxism–Leninism, usually in the interests of the bourgeoisie. **1968** *Ibid.* 5 Oct. 22/3 It is no longer the 'splittists' in Peking who are on trial before the majority of the world's communist parties, but the hard-liners in the Kremlin. **1969** *Daily Tel.* 11 Feb. 19/7 Frelimo and the Organisation of African Unity Liberation Committee are aware of the dangers of 'splittist'—as Peking calls it—tendencies. **1976** *Times* 20 Oct. 10 We must..repudiate all those who betray Marxist–Leninist–Mao Tse-tung thought, tamper with Chairman Mao's directives, practise revisionism and splittism, [etc.]. **1978** *Peking Rev.* 10 Mar. 9/2 The 'gang of four'..once again indulged in splittist activities and devised all kinds of schemes and plots. **1980** *Economist* 31 May 9/1 One challenge to western unity..had been compounded by another..and the danger of splittism was evident.

splodgily (splǫ·dʒili), *adv.* [f. SPLODGY *a.* + -LY[2].] In a splodgy manner. Also *fig.*

1963 *Times* 16 Feb. 4/1 This matches the dancing not wisely but too well, and her imaginative splodgily-splashed costumes looked ill-cut. **1978** R. HILL *Pinch of Snuff* xiv. 141 'Your girl's got two minutes, missus,' he said splodgily.

splosh (splǫʃ), *sb. colloq.* and *dial.* [Echoic: cf. SPLASH *sb.*[1] and SLOSH *sb.*] **1.** The dull, splashing sound of the impact of a hard object striking or struck by something wet and soft; the impact itself. Also, a quantity of liquid suddenly dashed or dropped.

1857 C. E. DELONG in *Calif. Hist. Soc. Q.* (1930) IX. 133 Storming like fury..a mixture of snow and rain.. splosh almost knee deep. **1895** E. M. STOOKE *Not Exactly* xi. 280 Arter all 'tis but dree minutes or zo of acoot zufferin' in th' grip o' Bill Brooks, then a bit of a splosh, an' hout the beggur comes. **1916** J. K. BANGS *From Pillar to Post* xii. 235 The committee hustled me into the hall with no more damage than one rather slush splosh of snow. **1919** W. DEEPING *Second Youth* xii. 112 The roof had dropped a splosh of water on Uncle Reginald's new hat. **1936** A. G. STREET *Gentleman of Party* i. 11 An hour of steady splosh, splosh, splosh, of their horses' feet in thick batter of mud which creamed over the road. **1954** L. M. BOSTON *Children of Green Knowe* 64 A [snow]flake landed on his cheek... He felt the splosh. **1983** 'F. PARRISH' *Bait on Hook* ii. 35 'At splosh o' paint on the mudguard. Got reason to remember 'at, I 'ave.

2. *slang.* Money.

1893 G. ELEN *'E dunno where 'e Are* (*song*) Since Jack Jones come into that little bit o' splosh. **1916** 'TAFFRAIL' *Pincher Martin* vi. 100 The show's orf 'less I kin raise some splosh some'ow. **1924** *Westm. Gaz.* (weekly ed.) 30 Aug. 526/3 The gentleman in the Old Kent Road who came into a little bit of splosh. **1950** WODEHOUSE *Nothing Serious* 216 The jolliness of having all that splosh in the old sock. **1967** A. WILSON *No Laughing Matter* II. 82 Intentions need a bit of splosh to back em up.

splosh, *v.* (*int.* and *adv.*) *colloq.* and *dial.* [f. prec.] **a.** *trans.* To splash (something); to cause (something) to move with a splashing sound. **b.** *intr.* To move with a splash. Also *int.* and as *adv.*

1890 *Harry Fludyer* 47 Such larks when you heard the ball go splosh on a man's hat. **1901** J. PRIOR *Forest Folk* xi. 111 Nell continued to turn the handle of her old barrel churn. Splash! splosh! went the cream. **1904** *Eng. Dial. Dict.* V. 678/2 (S. Not.), What are yer sploshin the watter about for? **1923** WODEHOUSE *Inimit. Jeeves* iii. 30, I began to sing like a bally nightingale as I sploshed the sponge away. **1924** GALSWORTHY *White Monkey* II. ix. 194 Down came death—splosh!—and a creature wiped out, like a fly on a wall. **1926** *Somerset Year Bk.* 54 She brought down th' liddle shutter again splosh-bang. **1930** R. CAMPBELL *Poems* 10 Jack Squire through his own teardrops sploshes. **1931** W. FAULKNER in *Amer. Mercury* Mar. 261/2 She made the sound into the cup and the coffee sploshed out on to her hands and her dress. **1941** W. FORTESCUE *Trampled Lilies* v. 61, I sploshed through the morass of mud and manure. **1966** M. WOODHOUSE *Tree Frog* iii. 24 He was sploshing around in a quicksand. **1978** S. RADLEY *Death & Maiden* i. 6 He sploshed on down the muddy track.

Hence **splo·shing** *vbl. sb.*

1929 W. DEEPING *Roper's Row* xxx. 334 The sound of debate would cease suddenly. Boards creaked. Sploshings and sandpaperings recommenced. **1974** P. DICKINSON *Poison Oracle* v. 115 The awkward sploshings of his paddle..had been the loudest sounds in the marsh.

sploshy, *a.* Add: **a.** (Earlier example.) Also, characterized by splashing or sploshing.

1838 *N.Y. Advertiser & Express* 28 Mar. 1/4 On Tuesday it was muggy and sploshy. **1972** [see *PLASTICIZED *ppl. a.* 2].

b. = SPLOTCHY *a.*

1942 E. WAUGH *Put out More Flags* iii. 199 Cedric turned from the portrait of Angela... 'Is it finished?' 'Yes. It was very hard to make the man finish it, though.' 'It hardly looks finished now, does it Daddy? It's all sploshy.'

c. = SPLASHY *a.*[2] 3.

1966 [see *coffee-table book* s.v. *COFFEE *sb.* 5 b].

spludge (splʌdʒ). *U.S. dial.* [Echoic: cf. next.] A 'splurge' or ostentatious display; *to cut a spludge* = *to cut a splurge* s.v. *SPLURGE *sb.* 1 a.

1831 *Essayist* II. 80/2, I was naturally anxious to see a little more of Tennessee life, and inasmuch as it was said there was to be a great *spludge* at the shooting, I went with him. **1856** F. M. WHITCHER *Widow Bedott Papers* ix. 89 She tries to cut a spludge and make folk think she's a lady. **1913** *Dialect Notes* IV. 113 [Kansas words] *Spludge*, splurge.

splurge, *sb.* For *U.S.* read orig. *U.S.* and add: **1. a.** (Later examples.) Also in phr. *to cut a splurge*, to make an ostentatious display.

The first quot. in Dict. should be cited from 'F. Herbert', *The Talisman for 1829* (1828), II. 107.

1860 BARTLETT *Dict. Amer.* (ed. 3) 112 *Cut a splurge*,.. to make a show or display in dress. **1895** *Punch* 1 June 258/2 My anti-gambling old Gaffer 'as spiled the whole splurge. **1897** *Chicago Tribune* 19 Sept. 37/1 Two shrewd young Hoosiers..came to Chicago in 1891 and cut a big splurge in monetary and real estate circles. **1977** *Daily Tel.* 19 Jan. 4/3 Presidential inauguration ceremonies.. will go on for the rest of the week in a $3 million (about £1,700,000) splurge of dances, parties and celebrations.

b. A sudden extravagant indulgence, esp. in spending.

1928 *Publishers' Weekly* 16 June 2429 The Sales Force hadn't the courage to urge big splurges. **1929** W. DEEPING *Roper's Row* xxx. 342 He was not to be the slave of other people's animal appetites, their sex splurges. **1937** M. HILLIS *Orchids on your Budget* iv. 74 For years she has been putting something aside—not for a rainy day, but for a splurge. **1957** M. MILLAR *Soft Talkers* 193 A chicken salad which she looked at ravenously but barely touched, as if she knew too well the penalties of such a splurge. **1976** *National Observer* (U.S.) 27 Mar. 12/6 The Air Transport Association predicts a 6 per cent increase in air travel this year. 'We don't see any tremendous splurge,' a spokesman said.

c. *spec.* in *Journalism*, a large or showy advertisement, feature, etc.

1960 E. PARTRIDGE *Charm of Words* 31 A full-page advertisement..is usually called either a *splash* or, if showy, a *splurge*. **1971** 'L. BLACK' *Death has Green Fingers* x. 109 We've got..quite a splurge about the rose industry generally.

splurge, *v.* For *U.S.* read orig. *U.S.* and add: **1. b.** To spend money extravagantly. Freq. const. *on*. Also *trans.*

1934 in WEBSTER. **1947** *Chicago Sun* 28 Jan. 17/2 When I got around to furnishing my office, I thought I'd splurge on a good 18th Century English armchair. **1961** *Observer* 19 Mar. 3/3 The cigarette manufacturers splurged [on advertising], in spite of or because of cancer fears. **1975** *High Times* Dec. 130/1 If you really get into omelettes, you should splurge and procure a good copper or stainless steel omelette pan. **1977** *Spare Rib* June 6 So what does Bhagwan offer which is so compelling that feminists will splurge this sort of money? **1979** R. JAFFE *Class Reunion* (1980) II. v. 229 You don't have to splurge on Maxim's now—we can go somewhere simple.

splurgy, *a.* For *U.S.* read orig. *U.S.* and add earlier and later examples.

1852 *Yale Tomahawk* May 4/3 They even pronounce his speeches splurgy. **1937** *Sunday Times* 20 Feb. 6/1 Diana is equally obviously one of those big splurgy actresses who have been successes up to the word Gone.

splutteringly (splʌ·tərɪŋli), *adv.* [f. SPLUTTERING *ppl. a.* + -LY[2].] In a spluttering manner.

1941 *Penguin New Writing* X. 21 The rifles volleyed splutteringly three times and the funeral was over. **1969** *Listener* 16 Jan. 85/3 This is often a splutteringly funny book, but the humour seems to me to spring from an underlying sadness and spiritual discomfort. **1978** P. MASON *Shaft of Sunlight* iii. 47 He..made me try—splutteringly—to explain why the whole of the Rhondda valley could not be sentenced to transportation for life without having even poached a hare.

spoalty, var. *SPAULTY *a.*

Spock-marked (spǫ·kmāɹkt), *a. joc.* [f. the name of Benjamin McLane *Spock* (b. 1903), U.S. physician and specialist in child care + MARKED *ppl. a.*, after *pock-marked.*] (Adversely) affected by an upbringing held to be in accordance with the principles of Dr. Spock, esp. as set forth in his *Common Sense Book of Baby and Child Care* (1946).

1967 A. COMFORT *Anxiety Makers* vi. 186 Liberal and sane advice can still leave the children of anxious parents permanently Spock-marked. **1974** J. COOPER *Women & Super Women* 10 Permanently Spock-marked, they believe the world owes them a living.

Spode[2]. (Earlier examples.)

1869 C. SCHREIBER *Jrnl.* 16 Sept. (1911) I. 37 The only thing the small shops at Exeter presented was a little Spode basket. **1875** L. TROUBRIDGE *Life amongst Troubridges* (1966) 106 We fished out several things—a blue Spode plate, for which we gave a shilling, [etc.].

spodic (spǫ·dik), *a. Soil Science.* [f. Gr. σποδ-ός wood ashes, embers + -IC.] Of a soil horizon: that is an illuvial deposit rich in aluminium oxide and organic matter and usu. also contains iron oxide.

1960 *Soil Classification (7th Approximation)* (U.S. Dept. Agric., Soil Survey Staff) v. 46/2 The spodic horizon is an illuvial accumulation of free sesquioxides accompanied by appreciable amounts of organic carbon, an illuvial accumulation of free iron not accompanied by roughly equivalent amounts of illuvial crystalline clay, or an illuvial accumulation of organic carbon usually if not always accompanied by an accumulation of aluminum combined in some form other than that of the crystalline silicate clays. **1972** J. G. CRUICKSHANK *Soil Geogr.* iii. 91 Podsolisation involves the translocation downward or laterally of iron and aluminium compounds from silicate clays, and their concentration in a specific lower horizon (B_2, Bf, or spodic horizon). **1979** *Nature* 4 Oct. 366/2 Soils in this forest are histosols (peat soils) with some spodic (podzolic) characteristics.

spodiosite (spǫ·d-, spōᵘ·diǒsəit). *Min.* [ad. Sw. *spodiosit* (H. V. Tiberg 1872, in *Geol. Förening. Stockholm Förhandl.* I. 84), f. Gr. σπόδιος ash-grey: see -ITE[1].] A phosphate and fluoride of calcium, Ca_2PO_4F, found as orthorhombic crystals; also, any of a series of artificial minerals having similar crystal structures but containing other elements.

1887 *Jrnl. Chem. Soc.* LII. I. 346 In consequence of the chemical and crystallographical resemblance between spodiosite and kjerulfine, the author suggests that the two minerals may be isomorphous compounds. **1911** *Jrnl. Physical Chem.* XV. 469 The spodiosite found at Nordmark in Sweden occurs in orthorhombic crystals. **1953** *Mineral. Mag.* XXX. 167 These orthorhombic cell dimensions provide some justification for the inclusion by Dana of spodiosite in the wagnerite group. **1970** *Inorg. Chem.* IX. 2264/2 Spodiosites with the general formula Ca_2XO_4Cl, with X = P, V, Cr, and As have been prepared. **1974** *Jrnl. Amer. Ceramic Soc.* LVII. 102/1 Spodiosite analogs, a class of compounds related to apatites, are used in phosphors and have possible future industrial applications as laser hosts and bioceramic materials.

Spodosol (spǫ·dosǫl). *Soil Science.* [f. Gr. σποδός wood ashes, embers + *-SOL.] Any soil belonging to an order characterized by the presence of a spodic horizon and including most podzols and podzolic soils.

1960 *Soil Classification (7th Approximation)* (U.S. Dept. Agric., Soil Survey Staff) xiii. 192/1 The Spodosols include primarily the soils that have been called Podzols, Brown Podzolic soils, and Ground-Water Podzols. Not all soils called Podzols, however, are in this order. **1969** BUCKMAN & BRADY *Nature & Properties of Soils* (ed. 7) xii. 317 The low native fertility of most Spodosols makes them uncompetitive for tilled crops. **1978** R. W. SIMONSON in W. C. Mahaney *Quaternary Soils* 15 Direct evidence for transfers of organic matter within profiles has been obtained by measuring amounts moving down from A horizons of Spodosols.

spoewslang, var. *SPUUGSLANG.

spoil, *sb.* Add: **III. 11. a.** (sense 10) *spoil heap* (later examples), *tip.*

1927 F. B. YOUNG *Portrait of Clare* I. iii. 34 The black dome of the Mawne Road spoil-heap fell away on her left into the tree-softened contours of Mawne Bank. **1973** *Times* 18 May 4/5 Above them towered the 300ft Eppleston spoilheap, started in the 1820s and at its peak containing well over 1,500,000 tons of red shale, dwarfing the houses. **1967** *Times Rev. Industry* May 58/1 Around it [*sc.* Doncaster] stretches a flat, ill-drained corner of Yorkshire's West Riding, pockmarked with colliery spoil tips. **1972** *Times* 4 July 3/2 A devastated landscape of abandoned slurry ponds and spoil tips.

b. spoils system (earlier example).

1839 R. MAYO *Political Sk. Eight Years in Washington* 40 Mr. Jefferson..authorized a friend to compromise with the federalists for..a guarantee against the spoils system.

spoil, *v.*[1] Add: **III. 10. d.** (Later examples.) Also *transf.*

1847 *Sporting Life* 16 Oct. 106/2 Hudson returned some heavy hitting; but Cannon would not be denied, although he met with a stopper that would have spoiled the upper works of the best chancery lawyer in the kingdom. **1866** *Chambers's Jrnl.* 20 Jan. 33/1 Come on, you beggar!..I'll spile your pretty face for you.

11. e. To render (a ballot paper) invalid, as by improper marking, deliberate defacement, etc.; to invalidate (a vote) in this manner.

1872 *Act* 35 & 36 *Vict.* §33 If the voter inadvertently spoils a ballot paper, he can return it to the officer, who will, if satisfied of such inadvertence, give him another paper. ?**1886** *Truth About Irish Election 1885* (Irish Loyal & Patriotic Union) 24 He clearly informed him that he would *spoil his vote.* **1953** *Ann. Reg. 1952* 235 The pro-Germans had been urged to abstain or to spoil their ballot papers. **1978** G. HERMET et al. *Elections without Choice* i. 3 The difference between free and controlled elections is indicated by the opportunity a voter has..to have his franchise recognised through registration..to decide how to vote, even to spoil his ballot, without external pressure.

14. b. Also const. *inf.*

a **1960** E. M. FORSTER *Maurice* (1971) vii. 42 Durham.. would be found at all hours curled up in his room and spoiling to argue.

spoilage. Add: **2. b.** The deterioration or decay of foodstuffs and perishable goods. orig. *U.S.*

1928 *Mineral Water Trade Rev.* 18 Jan. 16/1 The question of spoilage is not thoroughly dealt with in this country. Spoilage is an American term denoting any kind of deterioration found in a bottled carbonated beverage. **1958** *New Scientist* 24 July 481/1 The time that elapses between the killing of a whale and its arrival at the processing plant is often long enough for serious bacterial spoilage to develop, impairing both the yield and quality of the oil and the flesh itself. **1976** *National Observer* (U.S.) 27 Mar. 3/1 Israel has relied on subtler tactics to control the West Bankers. These have included detaining farmers' produce trucks to cause spoilage.

spoiled, *ppl. a.* Add: **3. c.** Of a vote or ballot paper: rendered invalid.

1944 *Federal Reporter* (U.S.) CXXXVIII. 248/1 In the election..201 [employees] cast ballots, with the result 39 unchallenged votes for United, 51 for International.. 7 votes were challenged spoiled, or blank. **1958** W. MACKENZIE *Free Elections* xv. 131 Even if there is compulsory voting, this general dissent may express itself through the proportion of 'spoiled papers' handed in. *Ibid.* 136 Administrative difficulties arise not over papers that are clearly 'spoiled' but over marginal cases. **1973** *Irish Times* 2 Mar. 8/1 Electorate, 37,299... Spoiled votes, 488. **1976** *Guardian* 17 Apr. 24/3 There was only one spoiled paper in the 94 per cent poll.

d. *spoiled nun, priest*, a nun or priest who has repudiated her or his vocation.

1904 S. JOYCE *Dublin Diary* (1962) 26 He is the spoiled priest to his finger tips. **1916** J. JOYCE *Portrait of Artist* (1969) i. 35 He had heard his father say that she was a spoiled nun. *c* **1932** F. SCOTT FITZGERALD in A. Mizener *Far Side of Paradise* (1951) 307 The novel should do this. Show a man who is a natural idealist, a spoiled priest. **1977** *Times Lit. Suppl.* 13 May 593/1 Romantic wickedness (or, in O'Flaherty's own spoiled-priest phrase, 'romantic sin').

spoiler. Add: **2. b.** *Boxing.* An inferior fighter who sets out to disrupt his opponent's style.

1948 *Sun* (Baltimore) 29 June 15/2 Walcot is only a timid defensive heavyweight to whom the words 'offense' and 'attack' are abhorrent. In the language of the ring he is known as a 'spoiler', the type of fighter who can make an opponent look bad but who can never look good himself. **1959** *Times* 14 Oct. 16/5 Carroll, a 'spoiler' when at close quarters, has a good left jab.

c. *U.S.* One who mars the chance of victory for an opponent, while not being a potential winner. Also, applied to a thing. Esp. in *Sport* and *Pol.*

1950 *Sun* (Baltimore) 9 June 20/4 In meeting San Francisco here..the Colts will get a crack at their biggest 'spoiler' of the past two seasons. **1965** *N.Y. Times* 1 Nov. 40 It seems clear that William Buckley will poll enough votes to be a 'spoiler', though it is not yet certain for whom. **1967** CONNABLE & SILBERFARB *Tigers of Tammany* iv. 117 Van Buren was the 'spoiler' in a three-way race. **1968** *N.Y. Times* 25 Jan. 19 Mr. Javits..described the six-year-old Conservative party as 'a faction' that had been set up as 'a spoiler' party. **1971** *Ibid.* 22 Aug. IV. 3/4 What he [*sc.* George Wallace] is doing these days is laying the premise for another 'spoiler' campaign in 1972. **1976** J. V. O'BRIEN *William O'Brien* viii. 194 It was felt that the Protestant vote had gone not to O'Brien but to the spoiler candidate and ex-Lord Mayor. **1979** *N.Y. Post* 20 Aug. 44 It looks like we're out of it now, so we'll just have to be spoilers from here on. *Ibid.* 46, I suppose you can't have a 'spoiler' in soccer. **1980** *Washington Post* 11 Sept. 1/1 Not that Anderson is yet seen as a serious challenger for the presidency... But he is now perceived as a genuine factor in the presidential election, a certified political spoiler.

3. a. *Aeronaut.* A flap or the like that can be made to project from the upper surface of an aircraft wing to break up a smooth airflow and so increase drag.

1928 DE PORT & BORDEN *Rep. U.S. Air Corps Materiel Div. Airplane Branch* No. 2878. 2 The 'spoiler' or 'lift destroyer' described in this report causes a decrease in lift by a 'burbling' action. **1932** *Rep. U.S. Nat. Advisory Comm. for Aeronautics* No. 439. 3/1 When ailerons and spoilers are used together the full effect of both is not obtained if the spoilers are located directly in front of the ailerons. **1947** A. C. DOUGLAS *Gliding & Advanced Soaring* iii. 84 When the spoilers are raised a certain amount of the lift of the wing is destroyed and the machine must glide at a steeper angle in order to keep the speed constant. **1978** R. JANSSON *News Caper* xiii. 115 Thackaray trimmed once more, and briefly pulled on the spoilers to reduce our air speed.

b. A structure on a motor vehicle intended to reduce lift and so increase the pressure on the wheels at high speed; also, one located so as to reduce the drag caused by components on the underside of a car.

1963 *Times* 8 Mar. 3/7 A special feature..is the tail, which is sharply cut-back in Ferrari style, the roof sweeping down to end in a 'spoiler' or raised lip. This treatment eliminates turbulence and wind drag by killing low-pressure over the tail, and keeping weights on the rear wheels at high speed. **1965** *Observer* 10 Oct. 5/1 It has retractable spoilers which can be pushed up to increase high-speed stability. **1974** L. Deighton *Spy Story* i. 10 His car..was..all dressed up in black vinyl, Lamborghini-style rear-window slats, and even a spoiler. **1979** *Time* 2 Apr. 6 (Advt.), The front spoiler is there to give you increased tyre adhesion at high speeds.

spoiling, *vbl. sb.*[1] Add: **3.** *Rugby Football.* The act or process of disrupting the opposing side's play; usu. *attrib.* Also *transf.*

1937 C. W. Jones *Rugby Football* i. 1 Experiments are being made with a new rule affecting the spoiling around the scrummages. **1959** *Times* 19 Oct. 14/2 Some dazzling moves started by breaks by Mulligan, who throughout found Jeeps in fine spoiling form. **1967** J. Potter *Foul Play* ix. 111 A finer display of spoiling tactics and spectacular bouleversements had probably never disgraced a hockey field. **1978** *Rugby World* Apr. 43/3 It was a very interesting game, but I thought the criticism by the Barbarians of spoiling tactics after the game was unjustified.

spoil-sport. Add: (Earlier example.)

1801 M. Edgeworth *Belinda* I. iii. 97 Harriot swore at the colonel, for the veriest *spoil-sport* she had ever seen.

Hence **spoil sport** *v. intr.*, to behave as a spoil-sport.

1869 Taylor & Dubourg *New Men & Old Acres* iii. 72 *Brown.* I'm locked in... Let me out. *Lilian.* (Unlocking door...) What was that for? *Brown.* (*Laughing.*) For fear I might spoil sport. **1946** K. Tennant *Lost Haven* (1947) xvii. 285 He did not want to spoil sport; he wanted the whole gang.

spoilt, *ppl. a.* Add: (Earlier and later examples.)

1816 Jane Austen *Emma* III. xvii. 312, I am losing all my bitterness against spoilt children. **1935** W. G. Gillings *Handbk. for Presiding Officers* 25 The spoilt ballot paper shall be at once cancelled by the presiding officer. **1983** *Times* 5 July 10/7 *We* are not protesting like spoilt children.

spoilure (spoi·liŭɹ). *rare.* [f. Spoil *v.*[1], after *failure.*] The act of plundering or despoiling.

a **1918** W. Owen *Poems* (1931) 77 Be slowly lifted up.. Great gun..about to curse... Be not withdrawn, dark arm, thy spoilure done. **1928** *Daily Sketch* 7 Aug. 19/2 Lion, my Lord, this camp was left in your charge. You made a big spoilure of it, so I am taking your work away.

Spokane (spōᵘkæ·n), *sb.* (and *a.*) Also 9 **Spokan, Spokein.** [Native name.] A tribe of the Salish group of North American Indians; the language of this people. Also *attrib.* or as *adj.*

1831 R. Cox *Adventures on Columbia River* I. ix. 197 The Spokans we found to be a quiet, honest, inoffensive tribe. **1838** S. Parker *Jrnl. Exploring Tour beyond Rocky Mts.* 284 We passed to-day several small villages of the Nez Percé and Spokein nations. **1875** H. H. Bancroft *Native Races Pacific States* III. iii. 615 The northernmost Salish language is the Shushwap.., then there are the.. Pend d'Oreille, the Spokane, the Soaiatlpi, and the Okanagan, which with others spoken on the Columbia show close affinities. **1894** *Messenger Sacred Heart Jesus* Apr. 273 Colonel George Wright gained a general victory over the..Spokanes. **1933** V. F. Ray *Sanpoil & Nespelem* 9 The Sanpoil spoke a dialect of Interior Salish and were surrounded by other Salish speaking peoples. All of the neighboring dialects were intelligible to them except Columbia and Spokane. **1944** N. W. Ross *Westward Women* 71 She had to learn the Spokane language... This was a difficult task, as the sounds the Spokanes made in speech were like nothing so much as the sounds of husking corn. **1965** *Canad. Jrnl. Linguistics* Spring 78 Languages of sure affiliation..Spokan. *Ibid.* 159 In Spokane, one of the Interior Salish languages showing the greatest contrast, there are four terms that are generation-reciprocal. **1974** J. Fahey *Flathead Indians* ii. 22 Flatheads married freely among contiguous Pend Oreilles, Nez Percés, and Spokanes.

spoke, *sb.* Add: **1. d.** *Basket-Making* = Stake *sb.*[1] 5 d.

1897 A. Firth *Cane Basket Work* ii. 17 *Spokes*, the coarser canes used as the foundation, and round which the weavers are placed. **1925** A. A. Gill *Practical Basketry* 39 After the spokes are arranged for weaving, take a short strand. **1958** O. R. Scott *Basketry Step by Step* 8 The uprights of a basket are called stakes or spokes.

b. spoke-wood (earlier example).

1851 J. Brown *Forester* (ed. 2) iv. 362 Young oaks, of the size generally termed spoke-wood, sell well.

spoken, *ppl. a.* Add: **2. d.** *the spoken word*, speech (as opp. to written language, etc.), esp. in the context of radio broadcasting.

1832 Carlyle in *Fraser's Mag.* Apr. 257/1 Whether man *can* any longer be so interested by the spoken Word, as he often was in those primeval days. **1929** *Radio Times* 29 Nov. 432 Poetry..has its roots in the spoken word: the written word is only a means of saving poetry from the oblivion of time. **1940** R. S. Lambert *Ariel & All his Quality* iii. 60 The 'spoken word' is the most contentious and most closely scrutinised part of the broadcast programme. **1944** *Ann. Reg. 1943* 62 Training..in understanding of the written and spoken word. **1961** *Listener* 28 Sept. 456/1 One criticism that has been made of spoken-word material in the Third is that it has sometimes been too esoteric. **1972** *Ibid.* 2 Nov. 574/2 It was the treatment of the spoken word that seemed to fox the early fathers of broadcasting.

spokenness (later example).

1947 L. MacNeice *Dark Tower* 10 But when no character can be presented except through spoken words, whether in dialogue or soliloquy, that very *spokenness* makes this distinction between subjective and objective futile.

spokeslady (spōᵘ·kslēⁱdi). [Cf. Spokeswoman.] = Spokeswoman.

1936 *Richmond* (Va.) *Times-Dispatch* 23 June 7/4 'Don't you quote us, though,' the spokeslady hastened. **1969** *Guardian* 31 July 9/5 'It came out like that, and they decided to leave it like that,' a spokeslady said. **1972** *Daily Tel.* 25 Sept. 7/1 Our most clamorous spokeslady for censorious opinion.

spokesman. 2. (Later examples.)

1976 *Times* 21 May 2/4 Mary Whitehouse, spokesman for the campaign. **1976** *Daily Tel.* 30 June 2/1 A spokesman for the British Medical Association.

spokesmanship. Add: **b.** [Cf. *-manship.] Skilful use of the position of spokesman.

1960 *Encounter* May 27 Such spokesmanship underplays the potential excitement of the work itself. **1963** *Times* 19 Apr. 8/5 Official explanations about why there is no such sign at the chief bookshop of all in Kingsway are simply an exercise in spokesmanship.

spokespeople (spōᵘ·ks,pī:p'l). [Cf. Spokesman.] Two or more 'spokespersons'.

1974 *Black Panther* 27 Apr. 8/4 Spokespeople for several leftist groups feel the murders are being carried out by a terrorist organization called 'The Black Hand'. **1977** *Undercurrents* June–July 5/2 Each group of ten or twenty had elected a 'spokesperson' who met in plenary with other 'spokespeople'. **1983** *Listener* 18 Aug. 27/2 The BBC spokespeople were obliged to come back with efforts to explain that the comparison..was not as clear as it might seem.

spokesperson (spōᵘ·ks,pəɹs'n). [f. Spokesman, after *chairperson* (see *person *sb.* 2 f).] A manufactured substitute for 'spokeswoman' or 'spokesman'.

One of numerous words formed to avoid alleged sexual discrimination in terminology.

1972 *Guardian* 18 Feb. 11/3 The spokesperson (non-sexist term) for UCWR complained that she had been 'physically assaulted by a university administrator'. **1976** *New Yorker* 29 Nov. 172/2 One's heart and imagination.. were repelled by the ascetic, sexual, Christian woman who recurs in Mrs. Spark's novels so often as to suggest, if not an alter ego, a spokesperson. **1978** J. Irving *World according to Garp* xviii. 402 A 'spokesperson' for the Ellen Jamesians. **1981** *Economist* 28 Nov. 30/1 As a feminist fillip Miss Joan Lestor..has been made spokesperson for women's rights and welfare.

spokeswoman. (Later examples.)

1974 *Sunday* (Charleston, S. Carolina) 28 Apr. 5-A/8 A hospital spokeswoman said Mrs. Agnew had scheduled her visit and was receiving routine care. **1976** *Film & Television Technician* Nov. 7/4 'The arguments against racism have to take place at a local level, they can't be imposed from above,' said a spokeswoman from Transport House. **1979** *Guardian* 23 Jan. 1/8 A spokeswoman..said the response from members yesterday was 'phenomenal'.

spondulicks. Add: (Further examples.) Also as quasi-*sing.* **spondoolick, spondulick,** etc. Also, a piece of money, a coin.

1864 [see *dingbat 1]. **1868** *All Year Round* 19 Sept. 354/1 A restaurant..where the tallest sort of feeding may be had at all hours at the lowest possible cost to the spondoolics. **1889** E. Sampson *Tales of Fancy* 36, I was instructed to allow my opponent to gain a lap in advance ..in order to draw out the spondoolicks. **1902** W. N. Harben *Abner Daniel* 58 The one with the spondoolix wonders harder than the one who has none. **1912** W. Owen *Let.* 23 Apr. (1967) 131, I shall do nothing until Father brings me some 'spondoolick'. **1923** E. P. Oppenheim *Inevitable Millionaires* xi. 121 'Do I understand that the young man..has dissipated the whole of his patrimony, in twelve months?' he inquired. 'Every bean,' Harold assented. 'Not a spondulik left.' **1966** *Courier-Mail* (Brisbane) 9 Aug. 1/10 (Advt.), *Spondooliks.* Dollars, pounds or call it what you like, you'll save plenty at Direct Disposals. **1980** *Private Eye* 29 Feb. 13/1 No one seemed very anxious to come up with the spondulicks.

spondylitic (spǫndili·tik), *sb.* and *a.* *Path.* [f. Spondylit(is + -ic.] **A.** *sb.* A person suffering from spondylitis.

1898 *N.Y. Med. Jrnl.* 8 Oct. 510/1 A comparison shows that the spondylitics are far below the average height for age. **1973** *Nature* 9 Feb. 367/2 Such people are the ankylosing spondylitics and the children originally irradiated *in utero.*

B. *adj.* Of spondylitis; caused by or associated with spondylitis.

1900 in Dorland *Med. Dict.* **1949** F. Hernaman-Johnson et al. *Ankylosing Spondylitis* i. ii. 16 Russian surgeons, and later, American surgeons, began to operate on spondylitic cases. *Ibid.* iii. 26 The patient with a commencing spondylitic arthritis of the hip may show some of the classical early signs of tuberculosis. **1977** *Lancet* 17 Sept. 591/2 Clinical investigation of first-degree relatives of patients with classic ankylosing spondylitis will reveal spondylitic symptoms in approximately 15%. **1980** *Jrnl. R. Soc. Med.* LXXIII. 65 Views of the cervical spine showed minor spondylitic changes.

spondylolisthesis (spǫ:ndilolisþī·sis). *Path.* [mod.L. (H. F. Kilian *Spondylolisthesi* (1853) 33), f. Gr. σπόνδυλ-ος, var. σφόνδυλος vertebra + ὀλίσθησις dislocation, slipping.] The forward displacement of the body of the lowest lumbar vertebra (but not the posterior lamina and spine) relative to the bones of the pelvis, or of any other lumbar vertebra relative to the one below it.

1858 *Brit. & Foreign Med.-Chir. Rev.* XXII. 177 (*heading*) The nature and origin of spondylolisthesis. **1885** *Trans. Obstetr. Soc.* XXVI. 187 Neugebauer considers that the predisposing cause of spondylolisthesis is either a congenital deficiency between the superior and inferior articular process on both sides, or a fracture of the same parts. **1932** *Brit. Jrnl. Surg.* XIX. 374 There are two types of spondylolisthesis... In [the first]..the entire 5th lumbar vertebra slips forwards upon the sacrum and carries the rest of the spine with it. The second type.. consists in the separation (or spondylolysis) of the 5th lumbar vertebra into two portions.., in such a way that the part bearing the spinous process and inferior articular surfaces moves backwards and the rest of the vertebra slips forwards upon the sacrum. **1977** *Proc. R. Soc. Med.* LXX. 421/1 In a proportion of patients the spondylolysis progresses to spondylolisthesis and may then cause symptoms and signs. **1981** *Church Times* 4 Sept. 12/4 As one born with congenital spondylolisthesis (a dangerous defect of the spine linkage requiring bone grafts chiselled off my hip), I am delighted with my restricted life.

Hence **spo:ndylolisthe·tic** *a.*

1884 *Amer. Jrnl. Med. Sci.* LXXXVIII. 600 Neugebauer's description of spondylolisthetic subjects applied exactly to this case. **1932** *Brit. Jrnl. Surg.* XIX. 380 That the supports of the spondylolisthetic 5th lumbar vertebra are very insecure is obvious.

spondylolysis (spǫndilǫ·lisis). *Path.* [f. as prec. + *-lysis.] The splitting or partial disintegration of a vertebra.

1885 *Trans. Obstetr. Soc.* XXVI. 188 A specimen of spondylolisthesis upon one side, a hemiolisthesis of the fourth lumbar vertebra caused by a similar spondylolysis. **1932** [see *spondylolisthesis]. **1959** *Jrnl. Bone & Joint Surg.* XLI. A. 311 A preceding bone abnormality or defect of the isthmus need not be necessarily present for the development of spondylolysis. **1977** [see *spondylolisthesis].

Hence **spondyloly·tic** *a.*

1959 *Jrnl. Bone & Joint Surg.* XLI. A. 312 In the spondylolytic cases..the articular processes above and below the affected vertebra were free to reach and compress the isthmus.

spondylosis (spǫndilōᵘ·sis). *Path.* [ad. F. *spondylose* (P. Marie 1898, in *Bull. de la Soc. Méd. des Hôp.* 11 Feb. 121), f. as prec.: see -osis.] Ankylosis of the spine, or of a vertebral joint.

1900 *Jrnl. Nerv. & Mental Dis.* XXVII. 558 (*heading*) A case of rhizomelic spondylosis. **1942** *Jrnl. Bone & Joint Surg.* XXIV. 827 The apparatus and routine used in twenty-two cases of rhizomelic spondylosis treated by roentgenotherapy combined with well-established orthopaedic measures. **1949** F. Hernaman-Johnson et al. *Ankylosing Spondylitis* i. iv. 40 (*heading*) 'Old man's spine' (spondylosis). *Ibid.*, The radiograph of a case of spondylosis shows a general curvature of the spine. **1977** *Brit. Med. Jrnl.* 26 Mar. 822/1 The local and root symptoms of cervical spondylosis are usually well controlled by non-operative methods.

Hence **spondylo·tic** *a.*

1964 *Amer. Jrnl. Roentgenol.* XCII. 1268/1 Spondylotic changes in the cervical and lower thoracic spinal column sometimes affect the spinal cord. **1972** *Lancet* 8 July 71/2 Patients with spondylotic myelopathy.

spondylus. Add: Also *attrib.*, as *spondylus shell.*

1932 R. F. Fortune *Sorcerers of Dobu* v. 189 The groom and his kin..must accumulate..a spondylus shell necklace or two. **1979** *Archaeology* July 11/2 Many Precolumbian ornaments and beads were manufactured from the rosy-colored rims of spondylus shells.

sponge, *sb.*[1] Add: **I. 1. c.** (Further examples.)

1872 'Mark Twain' *Roughing It* xlvii. 333 One of the boys has gone up the flume..throwed up the sponge.. kicked the bucket..he's dead! **1874** Trollope *Phineas Redux* I. xxxix. 325 When..Thursday afternoon came, Mr. Daubeny 'threw up the sponge'.

II. 6. d. (Earlier examples.)

1747 H. Glasse *Art of Cookery* (ed. 2) xvii. 297 To make White Bread..when your Spunge has stood its proper Time clear the Oven, and begin to make your Bread. **1796** A. Simmons *Amer. Cookery* 38 *Butter biscuit.* One pint each milk and emptins, laid into flour, in sponge.

g. With defining word: a type of thick jelly eaten as a dessert.

1859 J. H. Walsh *Eng. Cookery Bk.* 275 Lemon sponge. .. Take half an ounce of isinglass..the juice of eight lemons. **1907** *Yesterday's Shopping* (1969) 55/1 Sweets.. Lemon Sponge, Raspberry Sponge (in copper moulds, 10/0 extra, returnable). **1978** E. Lothian *Country House Cookery from West* 19 Orange sponge. 1 oz (30 g) gelatine. 4 oranges.

h. A sponge-cake; the mixture from which such a cake is made.

1877 *Cassell's Dict. Cookery* 920/1 *Sponge, Savoy*,.. pour the batter gently into a mould. **1907** *Yesterday's Shopping* (1969) 55/2 Golf Sponge, iced chocolate, coffee, pink or white..each of 0/11. **1917** *Harrods Gen. Catal.* 1269/2 Sponge Swiss Roll..per lb. 1/8... Caracas Roll (Rich Chocolate Sponge)..per lb. 1/10. **1948** *Good Housek. Cookery Bk.* II. 447 Steamed sponge puddings. *Ibid.* 579 Genoese Sponge (basic recipe) 3 oz. butter $2\frac{1}{2}$ oz.

flour ½ oz. cornflour 3 large eggs 4 oz. caster sugar. **1960** R. DANIEL *Death by Drowning* v. 54 A jam sponge, please. **1975** *Times* 10 May 13/4 The mixture can be baked..as a sponge flan.

IV. 11. a. *sponge box.*

1895 *Army & Navy Co-op. Soc. Price List* 191/2 Sponge box for travelling, patent aluminium. **1970** *Canadian Antiques Collector* Oct. 18/2 Similar trifles for feminine use included snuff boxes, sponge boxes and bodkin cases.

13. sponge-bag trousers, a pair of men's checked trousers, patterned in the style of many sponge-bags; **sponge biscuit** (later examples); **sponge cloth,** (*b*) a thin piece of spongy material used for cleaning; (*c*) a type of cotton fabric (see quot. 1957); **sponge mixture,** (*a*) a packet of prepared dry ingredients for making a sponge-cake; (*b*) the ingredients of a sponge-cake mixed together ready for baking; **sponge rubber** liquid rubber latex processed into a sponge-like substance; freq. *attrib.*; **sponge sandwich** a sponge-cake consisting of two halves sandwiched together with a filling; in earlier use, covered with custard and eaten as a pudding.

1915 V. WOOLF *Voyage Out* xxiii. 376 Can't you imagine him—bald as a coot with a pair of sponge-bag trousers? **1977** A. J. AYER *Part of My Life* ii. 35 The members of Pop also had the privileges..of wearing coloured waist-coats, sponge-bag trousers, braid on their tail-coats, flowers in their button-holes and sealing wax on their top-hats. **1837** MRS. GASKELL *Let.* 18 Mar. (1966) 10 Aunt L. has..expressed a strong wish to hear 'her dear little voice once again' and has a spunge biscuit behind her pillow this 4 days to give her. **1892** T. F. GARRETT *Encycl. Pract. Cookery* 147/1 *Sponge Biscuit.*—Beat ten eggs very thick and smooth. **1954** D. HARTLEY *Food in England* vii. 218 (*heading*) Egg and lemon jelly (using sponge biscuits). **1902** D. SALOMONS in A. C. Harmsworth *Motors & Motor Driving* vi. 93 Sponge cloths are a desirable accessory for cleaning and for polishing up. **1919** *Queen* 26 July 138 White sponge cloth is the thing for this new coat and skirt. **1957** M. B. PICKEN *Fashion Dict.* 318/2 *Sponge cloth*... Cotton fabric of coarse yarn woven in honeycomb weave to produce open spongy effect. **1976** W. TREVOR *Children of Dynmouth* iii. 58 Timothy rinsed the sponge-cloth he was using, squeezing it out in his bowl of dirty water. He wiped the inside of the oven..and closed the door. **1926–7** *Army & Navy Stores Catal.* 50/1 Sponge mixture..pkt. -/5½. **1962** 'O. MILLS' *Headlines make Murder* x. 119 She..poured boiling water on her sponge mixture. **1975** *Times* 10 May 13/4 A sponge mixture that you bake yourself tastes very much nicer than a shop bought one. **1932** *New Yorker* 9 Apr. 56/3 A luxurious soft pile combined with a sponge rubber back. **1934** G. F. CHARNOCK *Mech. Technol.* (ed. 2) xxii. 278 Sponge rubber, such as is sometimes used for upholstery, and in which the pores are many times larger than the cells of expanded rubber, is not such an effective insulator. **1951** *Archit. Rev.* CIX. 164 (*caption*) A sponge rubber overlay is fitted over the springs. **1967** N. FREELING *Strike out where not Applicable* 20 Metal furniture, upholstered in sponge rubber, covered with grey plastic. **1884** *Myra's Cookery Bk.* xiv. 309 Sponge sandwiches... Sponge cakes 6—cut in half lengthways. **1917** *Harrods Gen. Catal.* 1269/2 Sponge Sandwiches..each 1/6. **1967** A. LASKI *Seven Other Years* iii. 30, I want you to go..and get a sponge sandwich for tomorrow. A chocolate sponge with cream.

sponge, *sb.*² **2.** (Later examples with *down.*)

1954 M. STEWART *Madam, will you Talk?* vii. 60, I hadn't time for a bath, but I took a quick cool sponge down. **1960** *House & Garden* Mar. 63/1 All the paper will need will be a sponge down. **1977** W. GOLDING *Moving Target* (1982) 66 Ann has just had a sponge-down in the beastly bath.

sponge, *v.* Add: **I. 4.** Also *intr.*

1962 M. E. MURIE *Two in Far North* II. vii. 171 The [bread] sponge didn't sponge in spite of red damask tablecloth and fur parka I had lovingly wrapped it in.

Hence **spo·ngeable** *a.*, able to be wiped with a sponge.

1971 *Ideal Home* Apr. 75/2 Spongeable wallpaper. **1976** *Milton Keynes Express* 23 July 22/5 (Advt.), Roller blind kits and dozens of fabulous spongeable fabrics at Bedford Wednesday Market behind statue.

sponge-cake. Add: Now usu. made without milk. (Earlier example.) Also *fig.*

1808 JANE AUSTEN *Let.* 15 June (1952) 191 You know how interesting the purchase of a sponge-cake is to me. **1902** W. JAMES *Var. Relig. Exper.* xiv. 364 Naturalistic optimism is mere syllabub and flattery and sponge-cake in comparison. **1909** W. S. CHURCHILL *Let.* 15 Sept. in R. S. Churchill *Winston S. Churchill* (1969) II. *Compan.* II. xii. 911 It appears to me to belong to the whipped cream and sponge cake style of painting.

Hence **spo·nge-cakey** *a.*

1858 MRS. GASKELL *Let.* 1 Oct. (1966) 896 Some little sponge cakey puddings. **1971** B. W. ALDISS *Soldier Erect* 15, I flung my sexual emotions into gear by imagining sponge-cakey vulvas.

sponged, *ppl. a.* Add: **3. b.** Of colour, paint, design, etc.: applied with a sponge. Hence *sponged ware*, pottery decorated by being dabbed with a sponge impregnated with colour. Cf. *spatterware* s.v. *SPATTER *v.* 7.

1925 *Heal & Son Catal.: Table Wares* (1972), A sponged design in clear blue under-glaze on white ground. **1957** MANKOWITZ & HAGGAR *Conc. Encycl. Eng. Pott. & Porc.* 101/1 Mocha was made here [at Greens] as well as sponged and lined wares. **1971** L. A. BOGER *Dict. World Pott. & Porcelain* 323/1 *Sponged Ware.* In American ceramics; decorating the surface of pottery by dabbing with a sponge or something of the sort.

sponging, *vbl. sb.* Add: **4.** *Cookery.* The action or process of setting a sponge of flour, yeast, water, and salt.

1895 J. GOODFELLOW *Elem. Princ. Breadmaking* xiv. 93 The golden rules to follow in sponging are..Work at as low a temperature as possible... Use as little yeast as possible. **1929** E. B. BENNION *Breadmaking* 250 Sponging and doughing. **1949** A. R. DANIEL *Baker's Dict., Sponging*, the baker's term for setting a sponge of flour, yeast, or barm, water, and salt.

spongio-. Add: **spongioplasm** (later examples); now † *Obs.*; [ad. G. *spongioplasma* (F. Leydig *Zelle und Gewebe* (1885) vii. 173)].

1891 [see *RETICULUM 4 b]. **1896** [see *ENCHYLEMA]. **1933** M. FERNÁN-NÚÑEZ tr. *Ramón-Cajal's Histology* xvii. 299 The chromatic granules offer in their interior a vacuolated spongioplasm. **1936** W. SEIFRIZ *Protoplasm* xv. 266 The older workers in cytology held similar opinions, expressed in the 'spongioplasm' (framework) and 'hyaloplasm' (intervening fluid) of Leydig and the 'ground substance' and 'reticulum' of Carnoy and others.

spongioblastoma (spɒːndʒioblæstōᵘ·mă). *Path.* [ad. G. *spongioblastom*: see *spongioblast* s.v. SPONGIO- and *-OMA.] A malignant tumour, usu. of the brain or optic nerve, believed to be derived from spongioblasts.

1918 *Neurol. Bull.* I. 276/2 He [*sc.* Kaufmann] suggests the name *columnar cell glioma* and provisionally the term *spongioblastoma.* **1925** *Arch. Neurol. & Psychiatry* XIV. 145 They are both—neuroblastomas and spongioblastomas—richly cellular, very proliferative and rapidly growing. **1967** *Nursing Times* 27 Jan. 108/2 The highly malignant spongioblastoma multiforme which can kill within a month or two of its first symptom.

spongiosa (spɒndʒiōᵘ·ză). *Anat.* [L. *spongiōsa* (sc. *substantia*): see SPONGIOSE *a.*] **a.** The tissue constituting the bulk of the posterior grey column of the spinal cord. Now *rare.* **b.** Cancellous or spongy bone tissue, such as that found within the ends of the long bones.

1947 H. C. ELLIOTT *Textbk. Nerv. System* xiii. 157/1 Like the dorsal gray column, the spinal V nucleus has a dorsolateral substantia gelatinosa, the relay nucleus for pain fibers, and a more central spongiosa for touch fibers. **1949** *New Biol.* VI. 73 If we take a bone such as the thigh-bone (femur) and saw it in two lengthways, we find that the two ends near the joints consist of a spongy lattice (spongiosa) while the shaft is a hollow tube of dense bone (compacta). **1954** T. L. PEELE *Neuroanat. Basis Clinica Neurol.* v. 79/1 The 'body', or spongiosa, is subdivided into a ventrally placed basal part adjoining the intermediate gray columns, a dorsally placed 'cervix' or neck, and a 'caput' or head. **1966** *Lancet* 31 Dec. 1430/1 Histological sections..confirmed the increase in trabecular bone in experiment 11. The increase was striking in both primary spongiosa..and secondary spongiosa. **1982** *Calcified Tissue Internat.* XXXIV. 425/2 Osteoclasts in the primary spongiosa near the growth plate were the first to incorporate ³H-TdR.

spongiosis (spɒndʒiōᵘ·sis). *Path.* [f. SPONGIO- + -OSIS.] † **a.** (See quot. 1907.) *Obs.* **b.** Accumulation of fluid between the cells of the epidermis.

1907 A. WHITFIELD *Skin Dis. & their Treatm.* xi. 172 Some of the epithelial cells become swollen from the imbibition of the plasma, and the condition thus produced is known as spongiosis. **1932** R. L. SUTTON *Introd. Dermatol.* iv. 30 Intercellular edema, or spongiosis, is shown by widening of intercellular spaces. **1966** WRIGHT & SYMMERS *Systemic Path.* II. xxxix. 1461/2 Spongiosis, separation of cells of the prickle cell layer by an accumulation of fluid between them—in other words, oedema of the epidermis. Sometimes referred to tautologically as 'intercellular oedema' to distinguish it from so-called 'intracellular oedema' (which is hydropic degeneration of the cytoplasm of epidermal cells, as seen, for example, in certain viral infections). **1976** *Lancet* 27 Nov. 1168/2 The epidermis showed several areas of basal vacuolation and spongiosis with many eosiniphilic bodies.

spongo-. Add: **spongolite** *Geol.* [ad. F. *spongolithe* (L. Cayeux 1897, in *Mém. Soc. géol. du Nord* IV. 99)], a rock formed almost entirely of sponge spicules.

1945 M. F. GLAESSNER *Princ. Micropalaeont.* ii. 23 Some rocks known as spongolites are largely formed of siliceous sponge spicules. **1963** *Geol. Mag.* C. 296 The Ardagh spongolites appear to have been laid down as a biohermal deposit. **1968** R. W. FAIRBRIDGE *Encycl. Geomorphol.* 780 In rare cases, sponge banks accumulate quite extensive deposits of siliceous spicules (spongolite or sometimes 'spiculite').

spongy, *a.* Add: **1. e.** Of suspension and braking systems in motor vehicles: deficient in firmness.

1952 FRADZEE & BEDELL *Automotive Maintenance & Trouble Shooting* x. 396 A spongy pedal on hydraulic brake systems may be due to excessive clearance between the shoes and the drum. **1954** I. FLEMING *Live & let Die* xiii. 134 All the fun of driving had been taken out of them ..with hydraulic-assisted steering and spongy suspension. **1962** *Which? Car Suppl.* Oct. 123/1 The Fiat 1500..had one disconcerting point [*sc.* in its braking system]—the long pedal travel necessary, which always felt 'spongy' and gave the impression that there was less power available in the brakes than in fact was the case. **1967** B. C. MACDONALD *Car Doctor A to Z* iii. 19 (*heading*) Pedal has 'spongy' feel.

sponson, *sb.* Add: **3. a.** *Canad.* An air-filled buoyancy chamber in a canoe, intended to reduce the risk of sinking even if the canoe becomes filled with water; so *sponson canoe.*

1911 *Daily Colonist* (Victoria, B.C.) 14 Apr. 19/1 (Advt.), Don't fail to see the safety sponson canoes that cannot sink. **1917** P. L. HAWORTH *On Headwaters of Peace River* i. 6 The craft in question were really Chestnut sponson canoes, seventeen feet long... It had never been my intention to take a sponson canoe on the trip. **1968** R. M. PATTERSON *Finlay's River* 109 This proved to be a seventeen-foot Chestnut 'Pleasure Model' canoe fitted with sponsons—that is, with air-chambers along the gunwales so designed that the canoe, with an average load in it, would float even when swamped and full of water.

b. A projection from the hull or body of some kinds of aircraft, intended to increase its lateral stability in the water; also, a stabilizer in the form of a float at the end of a wing.

1928 V. W. PAGÉ *Mod. Aircraft* xvi. 668 It is a braced monoplane type, the hull being supplemented by sponsons of aerofoil section at each side. **1930** *Flight* 31 Oct. (Aircraft Engineer Suppl.) 1192b/2 Design of wing-tip floats or sponsons. **1935** [see *AERODYNAMICS]. **1965** [see *HYDROPLANE *sb.* 2]. **1971** *Maclean's Mag.* Oct. 70/2 Only part of the propeller, some of the rudder, and pieces of the sponsons at the front actually cut into the water. **1983** *Times* 5 Aug. 2/8 The helicopter hit the sea... The impact ripped open the bottom of the fuselage and removed the sponsons containing emergency flotation gear.

sponsor, *sb.* Add: **4.** One who pays, or contributes towards, the cost of a broadcast programme or other spectacle, *spec.* in return for commercial advertisement.

1931 P. DIXON *Radio Writing* 18 The sponsor wants a dramatic type of program and is willing to spend one thousand dollars a week for the program. **1953** *Manch. Guardian Weekly* 2 July 15/2 United States broadcasting started as a service of information and entertainment for the family accompanied by restrained acknowledgements to the sponsor before and after each programme. **1956** AUDEN & KALLMAN *Magic Flute* (1957) 57 To name a sponsor or to praise a brand. **1972** 'E. LATHEN' *Murder without Icing* (1973) vii. 67 It is axiomatic in all sports coverage that the sponsor's time should never intrude on the action.

sponsor, *v.* Add: **1. b.** To promote and support (a resolution, bill, etc.), esp. in a legislative assembly.

1961 *Time* 14 July 25/3 The U.A.R. forthwith sponsored a Security Council resolution. **1964** *Ann. Reg. 1963* III. ii. 152 Virtually the same resolution as had been vetoed in the Security Council was sponsored in the General Assembly by 44 nations. **1973** *Daily Tel.* 19 Nov. 3/3 Sir Gerald Nabarro..successfully sponsored legislation on clean air, coroners, oil burners, and thermal insulation.

2. To pay, or contribute towards, the expenses of a radio or television programme, a performance or other event or work, *spec.* in return for advertising space or rights.

1931 F. A. ARNOLD *Fourth Dimension* x. 78 The travelogue type of program, sponsored by a tourist agency or a steamship company. **1931** P. DIXON *Radio Writing* 25 When an advertiser decides that the program's worth sponsoring. **1963** *Amer. N. & Q.* I. 67/1 Ohio State University and its Press deserve great credit for sponsoring the work through the English Department, the University Libraries, and the Graduate School. **1976** *Jrnl. R. Soc. Arts* June 364/2 But a lot of them are sponsoring these concerts now, which are being broadcast regularly with the names of the sponsors.

3. To support (someone) in a fund-raising activity by pledging a certain sum for each unit completed. Cf. *SPONSORED *ppl. a.* 2.

1967 *Oxfam News* Jan. 2/3 Over £35,000 was raised by young people..sponsored by friends at a penny a mile or more. *Ibid.* June 6/2 Marathon marches..are a big money-spinner... Everyone who walks collects threepence per completed mile from a friend who has sponsored them.

spo·nsored, *ppl. a.* [f. SPONSOR *v.* + -ED¹.] **1.** Financially supported or promoted; freq. of radio or television programmes, etc., having (a portion of) their expenses paid by a commercial interest in return for granting advertising space or rights.

1931 F. A. ARNOLD *Fourth Dimension* 31 Sponsored programs are those that are prepared for advertisers or organizations that pay for their time on the air and also pay for the program that is broadcast. **1932** *B.B.C. Yearbk. 1933* 35 The danger to Press interests that would be involved in changing over from public-service to sponsored broadcasting. *1953* O. LANCASTER in *Daily Express* 28 Nov. 1/4 (*caption*) Will sponsored TV help Miss Cheesecake in her career? **1973** *Ann. Rep. Curators Bodl. Libr. 1971–2* 54 The OSTI-sponsored experiment with MARC tapes was completed in 1971.

2. Of a fund-raising activity (orig. a walk), usu. organized on behalf of a charity, in which each participant obtains pledges from sponsors to donate a certain sum for each unit completed.

[**1966** *Oxfam News* Apr. 1/4 There were Oxfam-sponsored walkers..in the..annual Margate to Maidstone 50-mile walk. Sponsors paid 3d. for each completed mile.] **1967** *Ibid.* Jan. 2/3 Teenage support for Oxfam increased. ..The 'sponsored walk' caught on. **1970** *Times* 11 May 10/4 (*caption*) People taking part in a sponsored walk along the Grand Union Canal..to raise funds for the British Council for Rehabilitation of the Disabled. **1973** [see *SLIM-IN]. **1977** *R.A.F. News* 11–24 May 8/4 Flt Lt O'Doherty..organised a sponsored team ride from Lands End to John O'Groats.

sponsorship. (Later examples.)
1931 P. DIXON *Radio Writing* 25 The sponsorship of the Philadelphia Symphony Orchestra by Philco. *Ibid.* 26 The men who do 'Amos 'n' Andy'..worked for years without sponsorship and at very small salaries. **1955** *Bull. Atomic Sci.* Mar. 104/3 Will sponsorship, however, be forthcoming soon enough and on a sufficient scale? **1966** *Oxfam News* Oct. 4/1 A contingent..from Oxfam House took part in the walk and faces..became..winning and chatty as sponsorships were sought. **1978** 'D. RUTHERFORD' *Collision Course* 20 Regent have decided to put some sponsorship money into motor racing.

spontaneity. Now freq. with pronunc. (spǫntănē̆·iti).

spoof, *sb.* Add: **1.** (Earlier example.)
1884 *Topical Times* 13 Dec. 3/2 The revival of Spouf in Great Britain and America is..wholly due to private enterprise, and..Monsieur Arthur Roberts.

2. a. (Earlier example.)
1889 E. DOWSON *Let.* 19 May (1967) 80 We sat dejectedly in the office but were obliged to admit finally that it was a case of 'spoof'.

b. A skit or 'send-up'; *spec.* a film, play, or other work that satirizes a particular genre.
1958 *Oxf. Mag.* 13 Mar. 374/2 This..programme.. proved to be an experimental double-dose of theatrical spoof. **1958** *Films in Review* May 254/1 There had been a few films which foreshadowed the screwball pattern, particularly the hilarious Hollywood spoof *Bombshell*. **1975** D. LODGE *Changing Places* ii. 61 Even the weather forecast seemed to be some kind of spoof. **1977** *Time* 3 Jan. 71/1 The prolific Gardner sets a spoof of pulp fiction inside a philosophical monologue on good and evil.

3. (Earlier and later examples.) Also as *adj.*
1884 *Topical Times* 13 Dec. 3/2 At Byzantium many Spouf Courts were; but when it became the capital of the Greek empire the game fell into disuse. **1914** G. B. SHAW *Fanny's First Play* 229 How am I to know how to take it? Is it serious, or is it spoof? If the author knows what his play is, let him tell us what it is. **1927** [see *SPOOF *v.* b]. **1946** V. TEMPEST *Near Sun* iii. 27 The spoof-feint raid that has been put on to make Jerry think that we are going to central Germany. **1978** K. GREGORY *First Cuckoo* 25 [Readers] are invited to spot the 'spoof' letter whose apparent erudition hoaxed the editor into printing it.

spoof, *v.* Add: **a.** (Earlier and later examples.) Also, † to avoid by means of a ruse. Also *absol.*
1889 E. DOWSON *Let.* 10 Mar. (1967) 48 It is the 'après' wh. spoofs us. *Ibid.* 11 Nov. 115 The Lord Mayorlet's Tom Foolery was a nuisance. I spoofed it successfully by going from Limehouse to Bloomsbury by tram. **1933** *Sun* (Baltimore) 8 July 6/7 It will be found necessary to handle our Doctor with much circumspection if he is not spoofing. **1977** 'J. LE CARRÉ' *Honourable Schoolboy* i. 31 The story had everything... It spoofed the British.

b. To make (something) appear foolish by means of parody; to 'send up'. Also *absol.*
1927 *Observer* 20 Nov. 20/5 This is a spoof piece which fails, through sheer clumsiness, to spoof. **1953** [see *GOOGOL]. **1981** W. SAFIRE in *N.Y. Times Mag.* 29 Mar. 10/3 'Urbababble'..spoofs the lingo of those urbane people in the city business.

c. To render (a radar system, etc.) useless by providing it with false information.
1972 *Sci. Amer.* July 18/3 The opposition need not even destroy the installation; by sampling the pulses emitted by the system it can contrive to 'spoof' or jam it. **1977** *R.A.F. News* 27 Apr.–10 May 20/4 They were, however, 'soft spots' in a defensive system. They would have to be attacked again and again and they would have to be spoofed by the considerable number of methods now available.

Hence **spoofed** (spūft) *ppl. a.*; **spoo·fer**, one who spoofs; **spoo·fery**, † (*a*) *pl.*, a low sporting club; also *spec.* the Adelphi (cf. SPOOF *sb.*, quot. 1889) (*obs. slang*); (*b*) trickery, hoaxing; **spoo·fing** *vbl. sb.* and *ppl. a.*
1895 *People* 6 Jan. 13/4 About half-past one this morning I was in the 'Spooferies'—Where? In the 'Spooferies'—the Trafalgar Club they call it now—in Maiden-Lane. **1903** A. M. BINSTEAD *Pitcher in Paradise* x. 227 'And when it comes to comparing the Spooferies with the House of Lords,' the missive concluded, 'it is a million to one on the Spooferies.' The other name of the Spooferies was the Adelphi Club. **1914** *Conc. Oxf. Dict.* Addenda, *Spoofer.* **1920** *Quill* Dec. 9 The after-dinner speeches..were brilliant impromptu spoofings directed at the guest of honor. **1926** A. H. GODWIN *Gilbert & Sullivan* 219 Bunthorne..is, in common language, a spoofer. **1926** K. GRAHAME in G. Sanger *Seventy Years a Showman* 20 The whole thing was unabashed 'spoofery' —clumsy fakes, dried fish, abortions in bottles,..and so on. *a* **1936** KIPLING *Something of Myself* (1937) iii. 48 There were..'spoofing'-letters from subalterns to be guarded against. **1958** P. SCOTT *Mark of Warrior* II. 176 He's got me spoofed in terms of the exercise. **1965** H. KAHN *On Escalation* v. 86 If the super-ready status is accompanied by limited 'spoofing' or 'jamming' or other hostile acts. **1975** *New Yorker* 19 May 22/3 It's an atrocity, of course, and one of the most spoofed of all the Jeanette MacDonald–Nelson Eddy operettas. **1976** *Time* 20 Dec. 53/3 Gardner has set himself two roles..: the hilarious spoofer of pulp fiction [etc.]. **1978** G. MITCHELL *Wraiths & Changelings* xv. 147 Ghosts are part of my stock-in-trade..so..I'm up to most of the dodges... The plainsong..was the only artistic effort..attempted in any of the spoofery.

spoogslang, var. *SPUUGSLANG.

spook, *sb.* Add: **2.** *slang* (orig. and chiefly *U.S.*). An undercover agent; a spy.
1942 BERREY & VAN DEN BARK *Amer. Thes. Slang* § 458/16 'Spotter.' (One who spys upon employees.).. *Silent eye, spook, spotter. Ibid.* § 765/7 *Rat, rubber heel, spook, spotter*, a person employed to detect irregularities. **1954** *People* (Austral.) 3 Nov. 24/1 The *spooks* were senior constables who wore no uniform, worked in pairs and followed constables about the city and suburbs to see if they did their work properly. **1961** *John o' London's* 20 Apr. 434/1 The idea of making a living as a spy— 'spook' in current Washington slang—is repugnant to most of us. **1966** R. THOMAS *Spy in Vodka* (1967) vi. 50 I'd like him to get out of the spook business. **1979** L. PRYOR *Viper* i. 9 'My training was also in espionage at the CIA farm.'.. 'A spook,' I said in wonder.

3. *slang* (orig. and chiefly *U.S.*). A derogatory term for a Black person.
1945 L. SHELLY *Hepcats Jive Talk Dict.* 17/2 *Spook* (n), frightened negro. **1953** K. TENNANT *Joyful Condemned* xxvii. 262 The boss of the ward..was doing time for going with 'spooks'—negroes. **1966** *New Statesman* 25 Nov. 778/1, I find a disturbing minority of my English contemporaries..pointedly tossing off inconsequential remarks about spades and spooks in my company. **1977** E. LEONARD *Unknown Man, No. 89* xxiii. 235 We almost had another riot... The bar-owner..shoots a spook in his parking lot.

spook, *v.* Add: **1. a.** (Later example.)
1976 *Publishers Weekly* 21 June 88/1 The ghost of the highwayman Black Charlie who spooks Flora with regular visitations.

b. To frighten or unnerve; *spec.* (of a hunter, etc.) to alarm (a wild animal). *slang* (chiefly *N. Amer.*).
1935 E. HEMINGWAY *Green Hills Afr.* I. i. 13 We spooked one [kudu]... No chance of a shot. **1944** *Nat. Geogr. Mag.* June 669/1 To get photographs of the herds Williams took to the saddle, since a man on foot is liable to 'spook', or stampede them. **1959** W. FAULKNER *Mansion* ix. 222 Pupils and teacher both who were already spooked..by the sudden presence of the unexplained white woman. **1973** A. GARNER *Red Shift* 12 You're spooking me. You're too quiet. **1980** M. GORDON *Company of Women* (1981) II. iv. 187 You always act like you're waiting for something... It spooks me.

2. a. (Earlier examples.) Also *fig.*
1871 *N.Y. Tribune* 24 Feb. 1/5 Once he saw Toussaint L'Ouverture spooking about with an air of mournful majesty. **1886** [see *ASTRALLY *adv.*]. **1973** E.-J. BAHR *Nice Neighbourhood* xviii. 190 A free-wheeling teen-ager.. [who] seems to be spooking around half-shot all the time.

b. To take fright; to become alarmed. *N. Amer. slang.*
1928 R. SANTEE *Cowboy* xvii. 250 As luck would have it I got a throw, for the cattle spooked an' run. **1941** E. HEMINGWAY *For whom Bell Tolls* xxii. 272 He'll probably leave tracks like an old bull elk spooking out of the country. **1957** W. FAULKNER *Town* i. 14 The old dug-in city fathers..spooked to the desperate expedient of.. exhuming..the story of the Cuban dice game. **1974** R. M. PIRSIG *Zen & Art of Motorcycle Maintenance* III. xx. 245, I spook very easily these days... *He* never spooked at anything.

spooked, *ppl. a. U.S. slang.* [f. SPOOK *v.* + -ED[1].] **a.** Frightened; nervy; dogged by ill-fortune.
1937 E. HEMINGWAY *To have & have Not* I. iii. 50 He would get to worrying and get so spooked he wouldn't be any use. **1952** B. HARWIN *Home is Upriver* xiii. 128 The cattle backed away to the far side, a skittish, spooked mass of bristling horns and rolling eyes. **1969** L. SANDERS *Anderson Tapes* (1970) li. 137 Don't get spooked when something comes up you didn't figure on. **1970** E. TIDYMAN *Shaft* (1971) x. 132 There were still some people.. staring into the night. The spooked, the stoned and the sleepless. **1977** E. LEONARD *Unknown Man, No. 89* xxi. 214 He was running for town, spooked good now, in a panic.

b. *spooked up*, excited, pepped up.
1939 WODEHOUSE *Uncle Fred in Springtime* iii. 43, I saw one of those Western pictures at our local cinema last night, in which a character described himself as being all spooked up with zip and vinegar. That is precisely how I feel. The yeast of spring is fermenting in my veins, and I am ready for anything. **1969** C. BURKE *God is Beautiful, Man* (1970) 85 Well this makes her pretty happy and she gets so spooked up about it that she ran into the city and forgot her jar of water.

spookery. (In Dict. s.v. SPOOK *sb.*) (Later examples.)
1927 [see *PSYCH *sb.* 2 a]. **1935** *Times Lit. Suppl.* 3 Jan. 10/4 The author does not exclude provincial and foreign spookeries. **1960** *Times* 20 Aug. 3/7 *Der Freischütz*..the quintessence of early romanticism with its naive spookery. **1973** E. PACE *Any War will Do* (1974) I. 23 Taking corners too quickly seemed to be another sign of the immaturity..that makes a man opt for the profitless thrills of 'spookery' in the first place.

spoo·king, *vbl. sb.* [f. SPOOK *v.* + -ING[1].] **1. a.** The action of calling spirits; a séance.
1919 E. H. JONES *Road to En-Dor* i. 2 'What's the suggestion?' Alec asked. 'Spooking,' said I. 'Cripes!' said Alec... Matthews brought in the..table... Little wrote a letter of the alphabet on [squares] and arranged them in a circle... I polished the tumbler... We had constructed our first 'Ouija'. **1930** H. G. WELLS *Autocracy of Mr. Parham* II. iv. 135, I will not relax one jot or one tittle in these precautions until I have demonstrated forever the farcical fraudulence of all this solemn spooking.

b. Haunting, frightening.
1961 *Amer. Speech* XXXVI. 224 The use of *spook* can extend to the frightening of people; it is not limited to physical *spooking* but can indicate mental frightening. **1966** T. PYNCHON *Crying of Lot 49* v. 106 Oedipa wondered what hangups, crises, spookings in the middle of the night might be developed from the shadowed subtleties of his mouth, hidden under a full beard. **1979** *Angling* July 19/3 The spooking of fish by striking at line bites.

2. The action of spying.
1977 M. HERR *Dispatches* (1978) 51 The romance of spooking started to fall away..leaving the spooks on the beach.

spoo·kist. [f. SPOOK *sb.* + -IST.] A spiritualist or medium.
1902 G. W. E. RUSSELL *For Better? For Worse?* xi. 171 A man whom I knew well was taken suddenly and seriously ill, and his relations, who were enthusiastic spookists, telegraphed for the celebrated clairvoyante Mrs Endor. **1920** M. ASQUITH *Autobiogr.* I. v. 72 If he could 'get through'—to use the orthodox expression of the spookists—he would find all his opinions on this subject more than justified. **1959** *Listener* 9 Apr. 645/1 This eminent spookist had such a look of the slim operator.

spooky, *a.* (In Dict. s.v. SPOOK *sb.*) Add: **1. a.** Of, pertaining to, or characteristic of spirits or the supernatural; frightening, eerie. (Earlier and later examples.)
1854 *Wide West* (San Francisco) 16 July 1/5 After treading many dark passages, the guide, having unlocked all sorts of 'spooky' looking iron doors,..ushered us before the tomb. **1906** E. DYSON *Fact'ry 'Ands* xviii. 239 There was somethin' spooky 'n' soopernatural erbout er pertickler weird 'n' unaccountable erfluvium. **1929** T. WOLFE *Look Homeward, Angel* xxvii. 378 Don't start that ..spooky stuff! It makes my flesh crawl. **1948** *Time* 1 Nov. 90/2 Shakespeare's *Macbeth* is a turbulent melodrama, full of spooky claptrap. **1960** R. DAHL *Kiss, Kiss* 187 This..is really beginning to get interesting—a trifle spooky, too. **1977** J. F. FIXX *Compl. Bk. Running* viii. 104, I had the spooky feeling that I was dressed up in somebody else's body. **1980** G. MITCHELL *Whispering Knights* ix. 98 'It's a spooky-looking place,' said Capella nervously.

b. *Surfing.* Of a wave: dangerous or frightening.
1966 *Surfer* VII. iv. 48 Morne Plage features a left breaking over a coral reef and tapering into a big black deep spooky pass a half a mile from the coast. **1970** *Studies in English* (Univ. Cape Town) I. 34 Waves, especially the bigger and more powerful ones, are often dangerous and frightening, and can sometimes be referred to as *spooky*... *Spooky* might indicate the difficult or the unpredictable, as in: 'Things get a little spooky when you're faced with fifteen feet of soup.'

2. Of a person (or animal): nervous; easily frightened; superstitious. *N. Amer. slang.*
1926 D. BRANCH *Cowboy & his Interpreters* 12 There were times when the steer would get spooky and mad. **1932** L. GOLDING *Magnolia St.* II. v. 354 I'm not a spooky person but I sometimes think he was the Devil. **1947** *Westerners Brand Bk.* (Denver Posse) 51 Range cattle.. were too 'spooky' in those days for man-made bridges. **1962** G. MACEWAN *Blazing Old Cattle Trails* i. 4 Attendants knew that the nervous and spooky longhorns were easily alarmed and would stampede at the slightest provocation. **1979** *Fortune* 26 Mar. 24/2 Even those spooky about coping with Italian traffic can easily find the well-marked way to Monza, about ten miles northeast of Milan.

3. Of or pertaining to spies or espionage. *U.S. slang.*
1975 *Times* 12 June 18/4 The Central Intelligence Agency spooks are the most spooky spooks. **1979** L. PRYOR *Viper* iv. 79 They're tough, crusading terrorists... That isn't going to make your job..any easier... Keep your spooky friends out of my life. **1980** J. MELVILLE *Chrysanthemum Chain* 120 Somebody on the spooky side of the Embassy might have a view.

Hence **spoo·kily** *adv.*, in a spooky manner.
1955 R. HOBSON *Nothing too Good for Cowboy* xviii. 186 These wild ones [*sc.* steers] were held in one bunch and slithered spookily along immediately behind my saddle horse. **1959** 'P. QUENTIN' *Shadow of Guilt* xiv. 126 We both stood looking at the shirt... It had a spookily human quality.

spool, *sb.*[1] Add: **1. d.** (Later examples.)
1955 R. HOBSON *Nothing Too Good for Cowboy* xviii. 186 Two spools are attached in a light-tight box to the top of the instrument. **1936** *Discovery* Aug. 238/2 The film..is mounted in a supply spool on the top part of the camera. It is carried around guide spools and across the focal plane to the take-up spool. **1967** *Tape Recording Mag.* July 260/1 The..conventional, spool-to-spool machines. **1977** W. MARSHALL *Thin Air* v. 58 Feiffer watched the twin spools on the tape recorder winding in Number Two's words.

2*. The sliding member of a spool valve.
1960 LEE & BLACKBURN in J. F. Blackburn et al. *Fluid Power Control* ix. 239 The spool valve must be very

accurately made since it depends upon closeness of fit between spool and sleeve to hold the leakage down. **1974** *Encycl. Brit. Micropædia* X. 344/3 In the mid or neutral position of the spool, ports A and B are blocked. The movement of the spool may be manually or electrically controlled.

3. a. spool valve, a valve in which a shaft with channels in its surface slides inside a sleeve with ports in it, the flow between which depends on the position of the shaft in the sleeve.

1908 R. PEELE *Compressed Air Plant for Mines* xx. 248 The throw of the spool valve..is produced indirectly by the introduction of a system of small, auxiliary ports, connecting the ends of the valve chest with the cylinder. **1926** R. M. EVANS in J. Roberts *Mining Educator* I. 618/2 There are two forms..: the air-thrown or spool-valve drill for use with compressed air, and the tappet drill for use with steam. **1971** *Farmers Weekly* 19 Mar. 82/4 Three hydraulic spool valves were fitted on the side of the trailer. One lifted and lowered the trailer. **1976** D. E. TURNBULL *Fluid Power Engin.* vi. 172 The spool valve was originally developed..more than a century ago when it was used for controlling the flow of steam to steam engine cylinders at the famous Gorton locomotive works in Manchester.

b. Designating (an article of) furniture popular in N. Amer. during the second half of the 19th cent. and decorated with spool-shaped turnery.

1928 JOHNSON & SIRONEN *Man. Furnit. Arts & Crafts* I. xiii. 79 The first and most noticeable product of the [powered wood-working] machine was a type [of furniture made up almost entirely of turned posts, frames, legs and arms and became known as spool furniture. **1931** S. GLASPELL *Ambrose Holt & Family* xxvii. 263 She went up to the bed, a walnut spool bed. **1946** *Sun* (Baltimore) 16 July 10/3 The spool rack..had nice roomy shelves, which were used to store many back copies of the *Sunpapers*. **1969** J. GLOAG *Short Dict. Furnit.* 636 *Spool Furniture*, an American style, introduced in the 1850s, and based on the use of spool turning on the members of chairs, beds, tables, and wash stands. This form of decoration with its string of spools was an attenuated variation of the more robust bobbin turning..of the mid- and late 17th century. **1974** R. B. PARKER *God save Child* (1975) xxii. 153 There was a spool bed with a gold-patterned spread. **1981** *Times Lit. Suppl.* 20 Feb. 210/1 Jane Carlyle sitting in her spool chair.

spool, *v.* Delete *rare* and add: **a.** (Later examples.) Also with advbs. and *transf.*

1976 S. BRETT *So Much Blood* x. 126 I'll spool through and see if there's anything relevant.'.. Gerald busied himself spooling on and playing snatches of the tape. **1976** B. LECOMBER *Dead Weight* iii. 46 The Boeing's engines spooled up to a keening howl. **1977** *Time* 10 Jan. 6/1 Poised at the gate. Once more the course spools through the mind. Now the Starter's signal. **1978** J. CARROLL *Mortal Friends* IV. iv. 433 His fear unraveled itself and then spooled quickly around his winch of a throat.

b. Also, to wind (film, etc.) on (to) a spool. Also *transf.*

1979 G. SCOTT *Hot Pursuit* ix. 80, I began to spool the film of what had happened through my mind. **1980** S. BRETT *Dead Side of Mike* x. 116 Shall I spool it [*sc.* a cassette] back and see if there's something we missed?

spooled *ppl. a.* (later example); **spoo·ling** *vbl. sb.*

1897 *Sears, Roebuck Catal.* 333/1 Spooled Wire for Tissue Paper Work. **1969** *Listener* 13 Feb. 193/3 There is no lacing or spooling. The films in the cassette are sealed. **1976** *Offshore Platforms & Pipelining* 209/1 Studies show that this method of spooling between flanges can be used on lines and risers.

spoon, *sb.* Add: **2. c.** A spoonful of sugar or other substance.

1922 JOYCE *Ulysses* 69 He scalded and rinsed out the teapot and put in four full spoons of tea. **1944** C. HIMES *Black on Black* (1973) 200 By the time I find they was gettin' up for breakfast all the breakfast was gone but a spoon of grits. **1968** P. DICKINSON *Skin Deep* vii. 142 How many spoons shall I put in?.. Bob likes six. **1980** R. HILL *Spy's Wife* iv. 22 Aspinall came in with a tea tray. 'Three spoons for me,' said Monk.

d. A dose or measure of an intoxicating drug, *spec.* two grammes of heroin. *U.S.*

1968–70 *Current Slang* (Univ. S. Dakota) III–IV. 118 *Spoon*, a level teaspoon of heroin. (Drug users' jargon). **1977** J. CHEEVER *Falconer* 46 Two spoons had been found, hidden in Farragut's toilet bowl.

e. *pl.* A pair of spoons held in the hand and beaten together as a simple percussion instrument.

1972 *Jazz & Blues* Nov. 27/1 'Main line' has added interest in that Shorty accompanies himself on spoons. **1977** P. CARTER *Under Goliath* xxvii. 147 It was a terrific party... Mr Mitchell played the spoons and Mr Gannon brought out his accordion and we had a singsong.

4. c. Delete quot. 1814 and add earlier and later examples. Also, a lofted stroke played with this club.

1790 C. JONES *Hoyle's Games Impr.* 288 The Spoon.. [is used] when in a Hollow. **1858** [see *GUTTA² 1 b]. **1927** *Daily Mail* 8 July 14/4 The 3 at the difficult twelfth, where he was five yards from the pin with a drive and a spoon and holed the putt, would have shaken any youthful rival. **1962** *Times* 9 June 3/2 He struck a spoon, which ran pleasingly up on to the ninth green. **1971** L. KOPPETT *N.Y. Times Guide Spectator Sports* vi. 128 The No. 3 wood, or the 'spoon', provides distance with more loft.

f. *Cricket.* A ball lofted by a soft or weak shot; a stroke which 'spoons' the ball. Cf. SPOON *v.*² 2 b.

1871 'THOMSONBY' *Cricketers in Council* 3 A ball hit into the air is a 'spoon', unless it goes a long way, when it becomes a 'skyer'. **1906** A. E. KNIGHT *Compl. Cricketer* 353 *Spoon*, a badly mistimed hit.

g. *Surfing.* = *ROCKER¹ 5 e.

1963 *Pix* 28 Sept. 62/4 *Spoon*, the slight upward slope in a surfboard. **1970** *Studies in English* (Univ. Cape Town) I. 28 *Rocker*, or *banana*,..indicates the curvature of the surfboard along its length; in other words, the surfboard, when viewed from the side, is higher at both ends than in the centre. More specific is the word *spoon*, which applies to the upturn of the nose of the surfboard.

8. a. (Earlier example with *about*.)

c **1859** J. S. COYNE *Everybody's Friend* I. i. 7 It was one of my nonsensical effusions, when I was spoons about you... Mrs. F. Spoons! Feath. Well, when I was dying in love with you, my dear.

b. (Earlier and later examples.) Also in *sing.* (*rarely*), an instance of sentimental love-play; a fond lover.

1846 *Spirit of Times* 18 Apr. 92/2 The girls are beautiful, with a very liberal allowance of 'the spoons', as our friend Smith would say. *c* **1921** D. H. LAWRENCE *Mod. Lover* (1934) 188 A young chap goes out on Sunday night for a bit of a spoon. What is it but natural? *Ibid.* 195 Yes, his reputation as a spoon would not belie him. He had lovely lips for kissing. **1939** JOYCE *Finnegans Wake* 115 Some softnosed peruser might mayhem take it up erogenously as the usual case of spoons, *prostituta in herba*.

9. a. *spoon-case* (later example), *-tray*, *-victuals* (earlier and *fig.* examples).

1922 JOYCE *Ulysses* 30 And snug in their spooncase of purple plush, faded, the twelve apostles. **1765** J. WEDGWOOD *Let.* 17 June (1965) 34 The articles are..teapot and stand, spoon-tray, Coffeepot, [etc.]. **1977** FLEMING & HONOUR *Penguin Dict. Decorative Arts* 751/1 *Spoon tray*, a small oval or oblong dish used in mid-C18 England to hold tea-spoons. **1777** *Pennsylvania Even. Post* 11 Feb. 73/2 Philip Clark..has a remarkable way of throwing his head back when he eats spoon victuals. **1877** C. BOX *Eng. Game Cricket* 461 *Spooning*, getting under the ball. In derision, it is called 'spoon victuals', especially at Cambridge.

b. *spoon-seat.*

1922 JOYCE *Ulysses* 653 He..drew two spoonseat deal chairs to the hearthstone.

11. spoon-back, the back of a chair (of a type esp. popular in the late-18th and 19th cent.) curved concavely to fit the shape of the occupant; a chair of this style; hence *attrib.*, as *spoon-back chair*; also **spoon-backed** *a.*; **spoon-bait** (earlier *fig.* example); **spoon-bending,** the distortion of a spoon-handle by apparently psychokinetic means; also **spoon-bend** *v. intr.* and **spoon-bender; spoon bow,** a ship's bow having full round sections reminiscent of the bowl of a spoon; so **spoon-bowed** *a.*; **spoon bread** *U.S.* (chiefly *Southern*) = *egg bread* s.v. *EGG *sb.* 7 (of such a consistency that it is usu. served with a spoon); **spoon canoe** *Canad.*, a spoon-bowed canoe; **spoon drain** *Austral.*, a shallow drain across a street.

1909 G. O. WHEELER *Old Eng. Furnit.* (ed. 2) v. 167 In our illustration..we see one of those transitional specimens with cane-panels and spoon-back. *Ibid.* v. 156 (*caption*) Queen Anne cabinet, and spoon-backed chair showing early cabriole legs. **1936** *Burlington Mag.* July 42/2 Half-way between the spoon-back chair and the strapwork back of the George II period. **1969** J. GLOAG *Short Dict. Furnit.* (ed. 2) 636 *Spoon back*, sometimes used in America for the banded back chair, of the Queen Anne period, the term may have been suggested because the profile of the back resembles the curve of a spoon. In England a comparatively rare early 19th century chair with an open concave back and semi-circular top rail is called a spoon-back... Mid-Victorian single chairs with oval, waisted backs are also described as spoon-backed. **1979** A. SCHOLEFIELD *Point of Honour* 40 We sat down in two Victorian spoon-back chairs. *c* **1878** J. ALBERY *Crisis* in *Dram. Works* (1939) II. 321 She has thrown away her heart..on..young Denham. Any cold, glittering thing does for spoon-bait. **1975** *Nature* 2 Oct. 354/3 Some of the children still claimed they could spoon-bend without cheating. **1977** *Times* 3 Nov. 6/1 Britain and Japan have a higher proportion of spoon-benders a head than any other country..people who can distort cutlery simply by thinking about it. *Ibid.* 6/4 The military implications of spoon-bending. **1979** J. WAINWRIGHT *Duty Elsewhere* i. 7 He was ready to give E.S.P. the benefit of a man-sized doubt. He even claimed to have an open mind concerning the spoon-bending gag. **1909** *Cent. Dict. Suppl.*, Spoon-bow. **1927** [see *bulb-keel* s.v. *BULB *sb.* 5]. **1969** *Islander* (Victoria, B.C.) 23 Nov. 11/2 She is still under construction, a 54-foot fishing schooner with the same spoon bow as the famous Bluenose and the Lunenburg schooners. **1900** Spoon-bowed [in Dict., sense 10 a]. **1932** *Scribner's Mag.* June 364/3 It was time for me to speed back to the spoon bread and young broiled turkey that were being prepared for me now in Edith's kitchen. **1941** W. A. PERCY *Lanterns on Levee* i. 11 Oh, the poor little boys..never put a lump of butter into steaming batter-bread (spoon-bread is the same thing). **1960** J. J. ROWLANDS *Spindrift* iii. 176 Spoon-bread made from coarse water-ground corn-meal. **1979** M. G. EBERHART *Bayou Rd.* i. 17 We can have some flour and spoon bread and chicken. **1907** T. CROSBY *Among An-ko-me-nums of Pacific Coast* 141 The canoes of the Pacific coast are of the type usually called 'dugouts'..[including] a 'spoon canoe', flat-bottomed and nearly straight with hardly any bow or stern. **1976** *Islander* (Victoria, B.C.) 13 June 5/3 Their graceful spoon canoes, hand hewn, 30 feet long, 3 feet 6 inches wide..were only used on the shallow draft, northern rivers. **1934** *Bulletin* (Sydney) 7 Mar. 21/1, I saw your ropes fly off when you went over the spoon drain. **1972** *Advertiser* (Adelaide) 13 June 5/8 To lessen level crossing accidents, a double spoon drain at the approaches to all level crossings may help.

spoon, *v.*² Add: **I. 1.** *fig.* and *transf.* (Earlier example.)

1840 M. EDGEWORTH *Let.* 30 Dec. (1971) 574 At Coffee time she spooned out a fine compliment to Miss E about Frank and Rosamond.

2. b. (Earlier example.) Also, to hit (a simple catch).

1836 E. JESSE *Angler's Rambles* 296 She had a perfect knowledge of what was a *bad hit*; and when her lover *spooned* a ball up into the air, which was of course caught, he generally walked off to a distant part of the field. **1912** A. BRAZIL *New Girl at St. Chad's* vii. 115 She played too soon at a short-pitched ball, and spooned a catch to mid-on. **1976** J. SNOW *Cricket Rebel* 113 Soon afterwards he spooned a simple catch from a stroke ringsiders described as a 'protective jab'.

spooner². (Later examples.)

c **1921** D. H. LAWRENCE *Mod. Lover* (1934) 195 Emmie ..cuddled into his arms. He was famous as a spooner, and she was famous as a sport. **1976** *Times* 24 Mar. 13/3 A wilderness of forms for the convenience of spooners.

spoonerism. (Later examples.)

1923 [see *MARROWSKY b]. **1976** *Oxford Diocesan Mag.* July 15/1, I am *not* going to put on any weight until I'm fifty, when I shall allow myself to become matronly, ready to be a follower of 'soda and gobbly matrons', as enjoined by the marriage service. (A good Spoonerism that, created quite involuntarily by my mother some years ago.)

Hence **Spooneri·smus** [nonce mock-German], a spoonerism; **spoo·nerize** *v. trans.*, to alter (a word or phrase) by a spoonerism; hence **spoo·nerized** *ppl. a.*

1923 A. HUXLEY *Antic Hay* xx. 284 When pain and anguish wring the brow, an interesting mangle thou, as we used to say in the good old days when the pun and the Spoonerismus were in fashion. **1927** *Daily Express* 22 July 7 Zoojolical Gardens... But why not let the misprint stick? The Zoo gardens are 'jolical' gardens, and probably the London Zoological Society would have no objection to them being spoonerised as such. **1972** D. W. BAHLMAN in E. W. Hamilton *Diary* p. xxv, The Herbert family, Hamilton, and other friends..called themselves the Bilton Waggers, a Spoonerized version of Wilton Baggers. **1974** V. NABOKOV *Look at Harlequins* (1975) II. v. 101 Only a lunatic would have chosen a pair of third-rate publicists to write about—spoonerizing their names in addition!

spoon-feed, *v.* Add: Hence **spoon-feeding** *vbl. sb.* (in quots., *fig.*).

1905 M. F. REANY *Medical Profession* i. 21 'Spoon-feeding'..is excellent for obtaining good examination results, but is it quite so productive of good practioners? **1978** *Listener* 19 Jan. 87/2 The mixture of spoonfeeding and stimulation is..the essential quality of the lectures on scientific themes given..to an audience of children.

spooniness. 2. (Earlier example.)

1856 D. G. ROSSETTI *Let.* June (1965) I. 303, I fear tin is out of question, as I think *all* contributors write for love or spooniness.

spoony, *a.* **1. b.** (Earlier example.)

1834 C. MATHEWS *Let.* 13 Mar. in A. Mathews *Mem. Charles Mathews* (1839) IV. xiii. 280 It [*sc.* misreporting a speech] has such a *spoony* appearance, breaking out in a fresh place with such a phrase.

sporadic, *a.* Add: **2. a.** (Earlier example.)

1813 T. YOUNG in *Quarterly Rev.* Oct. 255 All the Asiatic and European languages..which may be subdivided into five orders, Sporadic, Caucasian, Tartarian, Siberian, and Insular.

d. *Astr.* Applied to a meteor that is isolated and does not appear to belong to a shower. Also *absol.*, a sporadic meteor.

1929 C. HOFFMEISTER in *Astrophysical Jrnl.* LXIX. 167, I have developed some methods..to find out..which portion of meteors..may be regarded as 'sporadic', i.e., the directions of motions being distributed in an irregular way without indication of radiation in currents... Meteors emanating from a real radiant are mostly of cometary character and sporadic meteors are mostly of interstellar origin. **1954** A. C. B. LOVELL *Meteor Astron.* xxi. 429 A good deal of attention has been given..to the problem of the velocity of sporadic meteors, and the conclusion now seems inescapable that they must be contained in the solar system as distinct from the interstellar view which has prevailed for so long. **1961** D. W. R. MCKINLEY *Meteor Sci. & Engin.* i. 3 The number of sporadics greatly outweighs the total number of meteors belonging to the well-known showers. **1978** V. F. BUCHWALD *Iron Meteorites* I. i. 11/1 It is commonly inferred that all meteors—including the sporadic—are fragments of comets.

3. b. *sporadic E-layer, -region*: a discontinuous region of ionization that occurs from time to time in the E-layer of the ionosphere and results in the anomalous reflection back to earth of VHF radio waves. Also *ellipt.* as *sporadic E, sporadic-E*, used *attrib.* and *absol.*

1937 *Terrestrial Magnetism* XLII. 76 No relation between the sporadic *E*-region ionizations and magnetic disturbances of widespread character is apparent so far. **1949** *Nature* 2 Apr. 528/2 The usual measure of sporadic *E*-layer ionization is the so-called 'critical frequency', that is, the highest reflected frequency for this layer. **1955** *Sci. Amer.* Sept. 129/1 One of the outstanding mysteries of the ionosphere is a type of irregularity called 'sporadic E'. **1967** *Economist* 22 July 280/1 UHF is virtually immune to sporadic-E problems which so beset VHF. **1974** E. HARNISCHMACHER in F. Verniani *Struct. & Dynamics of Upper Atmosphere* 272 The Sporadic E layer, Es, is the most irregular and the thinnest layer of the ionosphere.

4. *Math.* Being a finite simple group that does not fall into any of the infinite classes into which most finite simple groups fall. Also *absol.* as *sb.*

1968 *Proc. Nat. Acad. Sci.* LXI. 398 (*heading*) A perfect group of order 8,315,553,613,086,720,000 and the sporadic simple groups. **1968** *Manifold* I. 12 Apart from the Mathieu groups, no other sporadic simple groups were known until Zvonomir Janko discovered one in Australia ..in 1965. **1973** *Amer. Math. Monthly* LXXX. 1028 Still, some hardy souls felt a thorn in their side. For the five groups of Mathieu all reason defied; Not A_n, not twisted, and not Chevalley, They called them sporadic and filed them away. **1980** *Sci. Amer.* May 68/1 There is good reason to believe the number of sporadic groups is finite, and indeed many mathematicians believe the sporadics that have already been identified, a total of 26, complete the list of finite simple groups.

sporangiole: see SPORANGIOLUM in Dict. and Suppl.

sporangiolum. (Examples of the form *sporangiole*.)

1895 F. W. OLIVER tr. *Kerner's Nat. Hist. Plants* II. 673 In *Thamnidium* the sporangial branch ends in a large sporangium, and in addition bears laterally a number of tiny sporangia (sporangioles) containing four spores each. **1928** C. W. DODGE tr. *Gäuman's Compar. Morphol. Fungi* ix. 105 Under favorable conditions of nourishment, however, they are continued through several generations when the sporangioles become as large and multispored as the sporangia. **1953** J. RAMSBOTTOM *Mushrooms & Toadstools* xviii. 209 In this common form..the fungus usually shows finely-branched endings (arbuscules) with characteristic granular masses (sporangioles) when they are being absorbed by the host plant. **1969** F. E. ROUND *Introd. Lower Plants* iv. 67 No flagellate cells have ever been found in the class [*sc.* Zygomycetes]..; the spores germinate directly into a germ tube and are formed either in a large spherical sporangium or in various reduced few-spored 'sporangioles' or even singly.

sporangiospore (sporæ·ndʒiǒspōəɹ). *Bot.* [f. SPORANG(IUM + -O + SPORE.] A spore produced in a sporangium.

1889 in *Cent. Dict.* **1899** *Ann. Bot.* XIII. 477 Léger [in 1897] distinguishes three types of spores in the Mucorineae: sporangiospores, chlamydospores and zygospores. **1930** H. M. FITZPATRICK *Lower Fungi* vii. 149 In *Geolegnia* the encysted sporangiospores are thick-walled and remain quiescent in the sporangium until freed by the disintegration of its wall. **1974** *Encycl. Brit. Macropædia* XII. 761/2 The lower fungi (*i.e.*, more primitive) produce spores in sporangia, which are saclike sporophores whose entire cytoplasmic contents cleave into spores, called sporangiospores. Sporangiospores are either naked and flagellated (zoospores) or walled and nonmotile (aplanospores).

spore. Add: **3. a. spore print,** a permanent image of the spore-producing structures of a fungal fruiting body, made by allowing spores to fall a short distance on to a surface where they adhere.

1900 MCILVAINE & MACADAM *Thousand Amer. Fungi* p. xxx, When a spore-print is to be taken, select a fully-grown specimen, remove the stem, place the spore-bearing surface upon the gummed paper, cover tightly with an inverted bowl or saucer, and allow to stand undisturbed for eight or ten hours. **1969** F. E. ROUND *Introd. Lower Plants* vi. 85 Spore colour is a valuable aid to identification and is easily detected by placing a mature 'mushroom' head on a piece of white paper and leaving overnight to produce a 'spore print'.

sporeling (spōə·ɹliŋ). [f. SPORE + -LING[1], after *seedling*.] A young plant (e.g. a fern) developed from a spore.

1910 C. T. DRUERY *Brit. Ferns* iv. 27 Given improved seedlings (we prefer seedling to sporeling, even in Ferns, since practically a seed precedes the young Fern) of this class, the probability is that their offspring will vary still more. **1914** *Plant World* Feb. 31 Both tetraspores and carpospores..were sown on oyster shells... In about twenty-four hours, when the resulting sporelings were firmly attached, the shells were clamped to boards. **1946** *Nature* 19 Oct. 536/1 Ontogeny was also illustrated by living sporelings and beautiful microscope preparations from fronds of different ages of the fern-royal. **1970** R. CARSON *Rocky Coast* i. 38 The algal spores swarming in the water, ready to settle down and become sporelings.

Spörer (ʃpǒ·rəɪ). *Astr.* Also **Spoerer, Sporer.** The name of Gustav-Friedrich Wilhelm *Spörer* (1822–96), German astronomer, used *attrib.* and in the possessive, as **Spörer's law,** an empirical relationship noticed by Spörer according to which the mean latitude of sunspots tends to decrease as a sunspot cycle progresses; **Spörer minimum,** the interval between about A.D. 1400 and 1510 during which little activity is thought to have taken place on the sun.

1922 *Monthly Notices R. Astron. Soc.* LXXXII. 536 Each cycle begins with an activity in high latitude; each cycle ends with the last remnants of activity transferred to a low one. This is what is known as 'Spoerer's Law of Zones'. **1968** P. MOORE *Sun* v. 52 Spörer's law is undoubtedly significant, and if we could explain it we should obtain a valuable clue as to the cause of the solar cycle. **1976** J. A. EDDY in *Science* 18 June 1196/1 The earlier minimum, which we might call the Spörer Minimum, persisted by our 10-parts-per-mil criterion from about 1460 through 1550... We can presume that the Spörer Minimum was probably as pronounced as the Maunder Minimum and that during those years there were few sunspots indeed. *Ibid.* 1199/3 The Spörer Minimum of the 16th century is coincident with the other severe temperature dip of the Little Ice Age. **1978** *Daily Tel.* 8 May 11/8 The 15th century..marked the Sporer Minimum of sunspots..and was cold.

sporidesmin (spǫride·zmin). *Biochem.* Also **sporo-.** [f. mod.L. *Sporidesmium*, generic name of the fungus from which the first such substance was isolated (H. F. Link 1825, in D. C. L. Willdenow *Linnæus' Species Plantarum* (ed. 4) VI. II. 120), f. SPORID(IUM (or *spori-*, comb. form of Gr. σπορά SPORE) + Gr. δεσμ-ός band, bundle: see -IN[1].] Any of a class of toxins that are produced by fungi and cause various diseases of animals, esp. sheep, when ingested.

1959 SYNGE & WHITE in *Chem. & Industry* 5 Dec. 1547/1 We propose the name 'sporidesmin' for the substance now described. **1963** *Jrnl. Chem. Soc.* 3172 On alkaline degradation ammonia, methylamine, and a red ketone were isolated from both sporidesmins. **1969** EDINGTON & GILLES *Path. in Tropics* xi. 486 Various toxic substances have been isolated from moulds contaminating animal foodstuffs during this century, sporodesmin isolated from *Pithymyces chartarum* and causing liver necrosis and cirrhosis in sheep being an example. **1975** *N.Z. Jrnl. Agric.* Sept. 17/1 Very high zinc intakes protected against sporidesmin, the fungal toxin causing facial eczema. **1981–2** *Deer Farmer* (N.Z.) Summer 11/1 The susceptibility of both Red and Fallow deer to sporidesmin, the facial eczema toxin.

Spork (spǭɹk). Also **spork.** [Blend of SP(OON *sb.* + F)ORK *sb.*] A proprietary name for a piece of cutlery combining the features of a spoon, fork, (and sometimes, knife).

1909 in *Cent. Dict.* Suppl. **1970** *Official Gaz.* (U.S. Patent Office) 11 Aug. TM 65 Van Brode Milling Co., Inc., Clinton, Mass... *Spork* for Combination Plastic Spoon, Fork and Knife. **1971** P. J. R. NICHOLS *Rehabil. Severely Disabled* II. iii. 117 Spoons or spoons with fork ends (sporks), either fitted with a swivel or shaped to a child's needs, are the commonest aids supplied. **1975** *Equipment for Disabled: Home Managem.* (ed. 4) 50/1 The spork can be adapted by bending and/or lengthened by rivetting on an extension. **1976** *Trade Marks Jrnl.* 22 Dec. 2628/1 *Spork*... Cutlery, forks and spoons, all included in Class 8. D. Green and Company.., Sutton, Surrey..; manufacturers and merchants.

sporo-. Add: Also with pronunc. (spōəro). **sporoge·nesis,** the formation of spores; **sporophy·tically** *adv.*; **spor·oplasm,** the protoplasm of a spore.

1890 WEBSTER, *Sporogenesis*, reproduction by spores. **1905** *Bot. Gaz.* XL. 93 The events of sporogenesis in *Pallavincia Lyellii* present..no fundamental differences from those of other liverworts and higher plants. **1969** A. M CAMPBELL *Episomes* xiv. 166 It was suggested.. that activation of an episome might play a causative role in sporogenesis. **1970** *Bot. Gaz.* CXXXI. 139/2 The incompatibility system of the family is of the homomorphic, sporophytically controlled type. **1893** R. R. GURLEY in *Bull. U.S. Fish Comm. 1891* 413 *Cystodiscidae*... A bivalve shell..: condition of sporoplasm unknown. [*Note*] *Sporoplasm.* Protoplasm of the spore. **1947** *Ann. Rev. Microbiol.* I. 6 Typically each spore results from the cooperative activity of six cells, two giving rise to the valves of the sporocyst, two producing the polar capsules, ..and two being sporoplasm cells each with a gamete nucleus. **1979** *Jrnl. Protozool.* XXVI. 448/2 Mature spores are short-lived and within 12–24 h begin to extrude their sporoplasms in all directions.

sporodesmin, var. *SPORIDESMIN.

sporodochium (-dōᵘ·kiǒm). *Bot.* Pl. **-dochia.** [ad. mod.L. *sporidochium* (H. F. Link 1824, in D. C. L. Willdenow *Linnæus' Species Plantarum* (ed. 4) VI. II. 1), f. Gr. σπορά SPORE + δοχή receptacle + L. *-ium*. neut. suffix.] A fungal fructification composed of an exposed mass of conidia overlying a cushion-like layer of short conidiophores.

1913 *Phytopathology* III. 24 The chief contrast to pionnotes lies in the Tubercularia-like hemispherical form of the sporodochia. **1947** *Ann. Rev. Microbiol.* I. 66 Miller.. presented good evidence that the sporodochia produced by isolates of *Fusarium* growing on agar media are in reality patch mutants. **1971** P. H. B. TALBOT *Princ. Fungal Taxonomy* x. 143 A sporodochium..is a compound sporophore of pulvinate (cushion-shaped) form, composed of a stromatic base giving rise to closely grouped erect conidiophores.

Hence **sporodo·chial** *a.*, of or pertaining to a sporodochium.

1913 *Phytopathology* III. 36, I find it very easy to produce cotton, tomato, and cowpea wilt with the young pionnotes and sporodochial stage of the 3-septate conidia which the vascular parasites freely form in pure culture. **1973** *Ibid.* LXIII. 831/1 Sporodochial development counts were made at full bloom.

sporonin (spǫ·rǫ̆nin). *Biochem.* [a. G. *sporonin* (Zetsche & Huggler 1928, in *Ann. der Chem.* CDLXI. 94): see SPORO- and -IN[1].] An inert substance forming the resistant outer covering of spores. Cf. *SPOROPOLLENIN.

1928 *Chem. Abstr.* XXII. 2949 This, after prolonged digestion with HCl, followed by boiling with 5% alkali, affords a new brownish yellow substance, sporonin, $(C_{10}H_{16}O_3)x$. **1964** *Grana Palynologica* V. 247 According to Zetsche the membranes consisted of cellulose and a specific substance called sporonin, or pollenin if derived from pollen, which was responsible for the chemical stability of the membranes. **1974** STANLEY & LINSKENS *Pollen* ix. 138 Because of the similarity of spore wall sporonin to pollen wall pollenin they [*sc.* Zetsche et al.] subsequently used the word '*sporopollenin*'.

sporont (spǫ·rǫnt, spǒr-). *Zool.* [f. SPORO- + Gr. ὀντ-, ὤν, pres. pple. of εἶναι to be, exist.] A protozoan cell at a stage of the life cycle following syngenesis and preceding the formation of spores.

1885 [see *CEPHALONT]. **1900** *Jrnl. R. Microsc. Soc.* 337 The macrogametes are fertilised by microgametes, and in each case an oocyst is formed round the conjugates. The new nucleus (sporont-nucleus) divides, the daughter-nuclei also divide, and later the protoplasm, so that four sporoblasts are formed within the oocyst. **1912** [see *GAMONT]. **1947** *Ann. Rev. Microbiol.* I. 7 Fusion of these gametes in pairs produces eight zygotes which become sporonts. **1977** *Jrnl. Protozool.* XXIV. 55/1 Binucleate and quadrinucleate sporonts..were observed.

Hence **spoронtici·dal** *a.* [-CIDE], lethal to sporonts.

1970 W. PETERS *Chemotherapy & Drug Resistance in Malaria* iv. 123 Pyrimethamine alone at a dose of 0·078 mg/kg had no sporontocidal action. **1977** *Martindale's Extra Pharmacopoeia* (ed. 27) 343/2 The biguanides.. have..a rapid sporonticidal action against some strains.

sporopollenin (-pǫ·lěnin). *Biochem.* [a. G. *sporopollenin* (Zetsche & Vicari 1931, in *Helv. Chim. Acta* XIV. 64): see *SPORONIN and POLLENIN (in Dict. and Suppl.).] An inert substance, consisting largely of polysaccharides, that forms the resistant outer coating of spores and pollen grains.

1931 *Chem. Abstr.* XXV. 2455 The crude sporopollenin, *i.e.* mixt. of spore and pollen membranes, obtained was purified as previously described. **1966** *Jrnl. Chem. Soc.: C* 16/2 A major problem in the study of sporopollenins is their degradation by sufficiently mild methods to give relatively large molecular species. **1978** HOYLE & WICKRAMASINGHE *Life Cloud* x. 91 The first possibility..was that it might be a rather exotic material, sporopollenin. This substance forms a major component of the protective coatings in pollens and spores and is chemically and thermally extremely stable.

sporotrichosis (-trikōᵘ·sis). *Med.* [f. mod.L. *Sporotrich-um* (orig. *Sporothricum*), former name of the genus *Sporothrix* (H. F. Link 1809, in *Mag. für die neuesten Entdeckungen in der ges. Naturkunde* III. 12), f. Gr. σπορά SPORE + τριχ-, θρίξ hair: see -OSIS.] A disease caused by the chronic presence in the tissues of the fungus *Sporothrix schenckii*, common in soil and wood and freq. introduced by a superficial scratch, typically producing nodules and ulcers in the lymph nodes and skin.

1908 *Brit. Jrnl. Dermatol.* XX. 301 Sporotrichosis is not incompatible with the presence of syphilis or tuberculosis. **1939** *Yearbk. Dermatol. & Syphilol. 1938* 57 The most common type of sporotrichosis reported is the cutaneous or localized form with secondary regional lymphangitis. **1976** EDINGTON & GILLES *Path. in Tropics* (ed. 2) v. 284 Sporotrichosis..assumed almost epidemic proportions in miners in South Africa due to splinters infecting the skin.

sport, *sb.*[1] Add: **I. 1. e.** In proverbial phr. *the sport of kings* (latterly, influenced by sense 5), orig. applied to war-making, but later extended to hunting and horse-racing (also surf-riding).

[*a* **1668** DAVENANT *Soldier going to Field* in *Works* (1673) 322 For I must go where lazy Peace, Will hide her drouzy head; And, for the sport of Kings, encrease The number of the Dead. **1691** DRYDEN *King Arthur* II. 19, I count not War a Wrong: War is the Trade of Kings, that fight for Empire; And better be a Lyon, than a Sheep.] **1735** W. SOMERVILE *Chace* I. 14 My hoarse-sounding Horn Invites thee to the Chace, the Sport of Kings, Image of War, without its Guilt. **1843** R. S. SURTEES *Handley Cross* I. xiii. 253 'Untin', as I have often said, is the sport of kings—the image of war without its guilt, and only five-and-twenty per cent. of its danger. **1918** G. FRANKAU *Poet. Works* (1923) II. xxi. 130 Weep for the King of Sports, the Sport of Kings;..On thousand tracks, unridden, desolate, Hay waves from winning-post to starting-gate. **1935** T. BLAKE *Hawaiian Surfboard* iii. 66 News reels and still cameramen will be on hand to shoot the thrilling rides that always accompany big surf, so the rest of the world may see the 'sport of kings' by picture. **1961** L. MUMFORD *City in History* ii. 44 With concentration on war as the supreme 'sport of kings', an ever larger portion of the city's new resources..went into the manufacture of new weapons. **1968** W. WARWICK *Surfriding in N.Z.* 1 Surfriding was practised almost exclusively by members of Hawaiian royal families: hence surfriding's now anachronistic title, 'Sport of Kings'. **1978** *N.Y. Times* 29 Mar. B4/7 The track plans to feature rhinoceroses thundering down the homestretch in the next novelty of the sport of kings.

II. 6. b. *fig.* (Later examples.)

1954 N. R. KER in R. M. Wilson *Ancr. Riwle* p. xii, If the whole method of writing and the orthography of the Caius manuscript were typically English the aberrant *r* could be explained..as a 'sport' by an English scribe in a period of experiment and change. **1971** *Lancet* 9 Oct. 811/1, I found myself immersed in a tangle of phys- words... Except for a few sports like 'physbuttock' (from fizz) they all come from two roots.

8. d. A good fellow, a lively, sociable person (applied to men or women); one who behaves in a 'sportsmanlike' fashion. Also *good sport*; *old sport* (freq. as a familiar term of address, more usually of men than women); *be a sport*, act in a generous and sportsmanlike spirit.

1881 LD. RHONDDA *Let.* 30 Oct. in *D. A. Thomas Viscount Rhondda* ii. 24 X— didn't make herself particularly unpleasant to me, though no doubt she was annoyed about something. I think she is rather a sport because she is such a good type of a certain class of character. **1905** *Punch* 22 Mar. 199, I shouldn't mind, Old Sport. **1913** *Ibid.* 21 May 405, I say, old chap, I've not had a smoke for half-an-hour, so I think I'll go on top. Be a sport and go inside with the women, will you? **1915** R. H. DAVIS *With Allies* viii. 159 All that was asked of the stranded Americans was to keep cool and, like true sports, suffer inconvenience. **1917** M. B. OWEN *Secret of Typewriting Speed* 85 It is better to be known by everyone as a 'fine girl' than a 'good sport'. **1918** C. MACKENZIE *Sylvia Scarlett* I. ii. 64 You're no sport, Maudie. You've got the chance of your life and you're turning it down. **1920** W. J. LOCKE *House of Baltazar* xvii. 208 The old man must be a good sport. *a* **1922** T. S. ELIOT *Waste Land Drafts* (1971) 5 Myrtle was always a good sport. **1923** GALSWORTHY *Captures* 145 'Let me go, mister!' came the hoarse voice again. 'Be a sport!' **1925** F. SCOTT FITZGERALD *Great Gatsby* iii. 57 Want to go with me, old sport? **1931** W. FAULKNER *Sanctuary* vi. 57 'Come on,' Temple said. 'Be a sport. It wont take you any time in that Packard.' **1932** J. FARRELL *Young Lonigan* ii. 65 He told himself Bertha was a pretty good sport, all things considered. **1933** E. O'NEILL *Ah, Wilderness!* III. i. 83 He's a hot sport, can't you tell it? **1942** A. CHRISTIE *Body in Library* ix. 85, I did like her. I thought she was a good sport. **1952** M. LASKI *Village* ii. 48 People turned to slap Roy on the back and say 'Well done, old sport.' **1973** *Guardian* 2 Mar. 15/8 The North Vietnamese.. walked out of a drafting committee in protest against.. one of Waldheim's men... Waldheim is being a good sport and going round explaining that he is not the least offended. **1982** P. MCGINLEY *Goosefoot* viii. 114 Will you come out..this evening?..Come on, be a sport.

e. Chiefly *Austral.* A familiar form of address, esp. used to a stranger. Occas. *sports*.

1935 [see *JOLT *sb.* 4 a]. **1943** K. TENNANT *Ride on Stranger* v. 48 The small boy rose and said rapidly: 'Fair go, sports.' **1952** E. LAMBERT *Twenty Thousand Thieves* I. 29 'Have a swig, sport.' He took the bottle..and helped himself to a mouthful. 'Thanks, sport.' He handed the bottle back and idly he noted that he had never called a man 'sport' before. **1962** L. DAVIDSON *Rose of Tibet* ii. 48 Houston introduced himself. 'Glad to know you, sport. You've caught me at a busy moment.' **1975** R. BEILBY *Brown Land Crying* 80 'Come on, sport,' the doorman was saying patiently. 'You can't stop here. You've had a skinful.'

8*. *colloq.* † **a.** A film about athletic sports (*obs.*). **b.** *ellipt.* or in *pl.* The sports section of a newspaper. *U.S.*

1913 [see *feature picture* s.v. *FEATURE *sb.* 4 c]. **1923** *Nation* (N.Y.) 17 Oct. 25/1 Crime and comic strips, sports and 'columns'—the *Leader* provides them all. **1955** W. TUCKER *Wild Talent* v. 65 He asked, 'Can I have the sports?' Conklin pulled the section from the paper.

c. A sports car; a sports model of a motor car.

1948 M. LASKI *Tory Heaven* ix. 123 Rupert..was driving her down in his own super-charged super-sports Bentley. **1952** A. R. D. FAIRBURN *Strange Rendezvous* 50 Epicene Sir Giles..plays at Walton Heath, and drives a sports. **1974** R. RENDELL *Face of Trespass* xviii. 168 The powerful purr of a Jaguar sports.

III. 9. a. *sport-lover*; *sport-minded* adj.

1929 *Daily Express* 12 Jan. 3 To-day the thoughts of sport-lovers will be spread over thirty-two battle-grounds, where the third round of the F.A. Cup competition will be fought. **1960** V. JENKINS *Lions down Under* vii. 103 The people of Christchurch are extremely sport-minded.

b. *sports centre, club, complex, day, deck, department, desk, edition, editor* (later example), *equipment, field, girl, ground, hall, news, page, pavilion, programme, section, shop, stadium, -writer*; *sports-mad, -minded* adjs.

1973 *Times* 27 July (Leisure Suppl.) p. i/2 The Sports Council..claimed that England and Wales need 842 indoor multi-purpose sports centres built by 1981 to supply the leisure demands of the public. **1965** 'J. LE CARRÉ' *Looking-Glass War* xii. 145, I got the knife at cost.. through the sports club. **1976** *Globe & Mail* (Toronto) 30 Jan. 4 (*caption*) Metro says university to pay 50%-plus to use sports complex. **1940** F. SARGESON *Man & his Wife* (1944) 54 When the last war ended I was at the High School. We got the news of the armistice on our annual sports day. *a* **1936** KIPLING *Something of Myself* (1937) viii. 229 The new three-deckers..hellishly noisy from the sports' deck to the barber's shop. **1981** J. M. BRINNIN *Beau Voyage* (1982) 59 The sports deck echoing with the click of the discs used in shuffleboard. **1975** G. HOWELL *In Vogue* 80/1 Jean Patou's new sports department sells jersey and marocain bathing suits. **1968** D. FRANCIS *Forfeit* viii. 101 The sports desk is a big asset to the paper. **1959** M. SHADBOLT *New Zealanders* 75 Mr Jackson lay belly-upwards on an unshaded part of the baked-brittle back lawn. The Saturday sports edition covered his face. **1969** Sports editor [see *night-editor* s.v. *NIGHT *sb.* 13 c]. **1969** H. MACINNES *Salzburg Connection* iv. 50 He had opened a sports-equipment shop in Salzburg. **1931** *What is Fascism & Why?* 174 You must give houses, schools, baths, gardens, and sports fields to the working Fascist people. **1938** J. BETJEMAN in *New Statesman* 12 Nov. 777/1, I adore you, Pam, you great big mountainous sports girl. **1933** J. BUCHAN *Prince of Captivity* IV. i. 325 The aeroplane..had landed in the sports ground of the factory. **1972** G. BROMLEY *In Absence of Body* ix. 119 'Where's the match played?' 'At their sports ground.' **1943** Sports hall [see *SIPOREX]. **1976** *Dumfries & Galloway Standard* 25 Dec. 18/6 (Advt.), Sports Hall Area £3.00 per hour. **1963** *Times Lit. Suppl.* 24 May 370/2 Australians..are sports-mad. **1960** I. CROSS *Backward Sex* iii. 76 She was not exactly sports-minded. **1928** *Radio Times* 27 Apr. 149/2 (*caption*) Bert simply puts up with [the radio set]..for the sake of the sports news. **1967** Sports news [see *city page* s.v. *CITY 9]. **1930** J. B. PRIESTLEY *Angel Pavement* ii. 57 Mr. Smeeth.. arrived at the sports page, where the prospects of certain women golfers were discussed at considerable length. **1976** L. HENDERSON *Major Enquiry* ii. 11 Milton glanced only briefly at the headlines of the newspaper before he turned to the sports pages. **1931** 'G. TREVOR' *Murder at School* ii. 42 The pair had reached the sports pavilion. **1938** J. JOYCE *Let.* 6 June (1966) III. 424 The director who has charge of the singing almost resents even a friendly introduction from the director, say, who controls the sports programme. **1973** J. PORTER *It's Murder with Dover* vi. 60 He sat in front of the television watching that sports programme. **1940** G. MARX *Let.* in *Groucho Lett.* (1967) 46, I picked up the paper Tuesday morning, nervously turned to the sports section. **1926** S. LEWIS *Mantrap* xxv. 288 Joe and he would..found a sports-shop of their own. **1971** C. WHITMAN *Death Suspended* iv. 80 Alec was at his sports shop. **1973** *Times* 5 Dec. 16/3 Those responsible for the conduct and management of any designated sports stadium. **1932** Sportswriter [see *QUARTERBACK *sb.* 2 b]. **1972** J. MOSEDALE *Football* ii. 21 The principal address at the Philadelphia Sportswriters Association banquet.

c. Used (chiefly *pl.* in U.K. and *sing.* in U.S.) to designate articles of attire suitable for outdoor sports or for informal wear, as *sport(s) clothes, coat, jacket, shirt, shoe, skirt, suit, wear*, etc.; also *sport(s)-coated, -jacketed, -shirted* adjs.

(*a*) **1912** *Sphere* 17 Aug. p. ii/1 The shirts I can also specially commend for holiday as well as for..sports wear. **1914** *Queen* 4 July 15 (Advt.), Smart fitting mercerised Sports Coat. **1922** *Moving Picture Stories* 23 June 23/2 A great many of the new sports clothes are shown with the divided skirt and pantalette cuff. **1925** *Eaton's News Weekly* 2 May 10 The sports shirt above, of fine white Oxford material. **1927** 'C. BARRY' *Mouls House Mystery* xx. 178 In an hour, Gilmartin was at his home, clad in an old sports jacket. **1930** J. BUCHAN *Castle Gay* xii. 191 At a small draper's..a jacket of rough tweed was purchased—what is known in the trade as a 'sports' line. **1948** 'J. TEY' *Franchise Affair* x. 110 The male with the sports jacket and the pin-striped trousers. **1952** B. HAMILTON *So Sad, so Fresh* ii. 22 These sports-coated, bepiped, sophisticated young bloods. **1955** N. FITZGERALD *House is Falling* vii. 107 Brigadier Poodle Poole-Casey, hatless and sports-jacketed. **1962** J. D. SALINGER *Franny & Zooey* 132 And there was old Dick..Sitting at a table in blue jeans and a gruesome sports jacket. **1967** N. FREELING *Strike out where not Applicable* 70 She was the kind of woman that would not look her best in sports clothes. **1973** 'S. HARVESTER' *Corner of Playground* III. i. 173 The sports-shirted wrestler. **1975** G. V. HIGGINS *City on Hill* ii. 34 His silver-blue double-knit sportscoat was too large. **1982** 'M. INNES' *Sheiks & Adders* vii. 61 An English youth..in a very commonplace sports-shirt and dark trousers.

(*b*) **1916** H. L. WILSON *Somewhere in Red Gap* v. 188 Beryl Mae Macomber in her sport shirt. **1925** *Eaton's News Weekly* 2 May 10 Sport shoes of smoked elk and tan calf, with crepe rubber sole and heel. **1927** P. BOTTOME *Belated Reckoning* iv. 57 The happy princess.. beautiful in her English 'sport suit' and crushed felt hat. **1946** *Reader's Digest* July 85/1 Found in addition were an Army blouse..and a sport jacket. **1946** *Chicago Daily News* 17 May 35/8 And to think I've been afraid to be seen outside in my new sport coat! **1950** M. HUXLEY *Let.* 21 June in A. Huxley *Lett.* (1969) 625 When you order shirts please ask whether they have an Airtex blue with sport collar, long sleeves; that is a collar which at will is worn with or without tie. **1966** H. KEMELMAN *Saturday Rabbi went Hungry* (1967) xiv. 89 The local chief of police was wearing a sport shirt and chinos. **1972** J. MOSEDALE *Football* ii. 21 He arrived resplendent in a new sport jacket. **1977** R. E. HARRINGTON *Quintain* xi. 120 Atlas had changed from his plaid dinner jacket into a sport coat.

d. *pl.* Applied to fast, low-built motor cars of a racing type. Freq. as sports car. Also *transf.* and occas. in *sing.*

(*a*) **1925** *Correct Lubrication* 52 Lea-Francis (sports models). **1928** *Proc. Inst. Automobile Engineers* XXII. 316 With regard to the acceleration of 'sports' cars, I agree that rough running and noise are taken for power development. **1932** G. WINN *Unequal Conflict* xviii. 350 She nourished a wild hope that..she would find Derek's silver sports car standing outside. **1936** 'N. BLAKE' *Thou Shell of Death* iii. 46 A Lagonda sports-tourer. **1955** E. POUND *Classic Anthol.* I. 60 His sports-car leads with the iron-grays, Six reins are in his hand. **1963** BIRD & HUTTON-STOTT *Veteran Motor Car* 73 One of the pleasantest sports-touring cars of the pre-war era. **1967** N. FREELING *Strike out where not Applicable* 39 It is not far.. especially for the fast sports coupé. **1971** 'D. SHANNON' *Murder with Love* iv. 68, I don't somehow think Mrs. Franks drives a Mercedes sports model. **1977** C. MCCULLOUGH *Thorn Birds* xviii. 484 He pushed on, gunned the red sports car up..the Domokos Pass.

(*b*) **1927** U. SINCLAIR *Oil!* iv. 80 But that didn't trouble Mr. Bankside, who had already..bought himself..a big new limousine, also a 'sport-car'. **1927** *Scribner's Mag.* Feb. 159/1 Laban, furious, mounts his Sport-model Camel and takes after the elopers. **1955** *Amer. Speech* XXX. 238 The best known writer on the subject, Tom McCahill, calls his most recent book *The Modern Sports Car* (New York, 1954); but a volume by Raymond F. Yates and Brock W. Yates..is named *Sport and Racing Cars* (New York, 1954). Of the two, *sports car* is unquestionably the more commonly used. **1978** J. IRVING *World according to Garp* xiv. 280 The man's sport car still chugged like an animal.

10. a. sportcast(er, sportcasting = *sportscaster*, etc., sense 10 b below; **sportfest** [*FEST], a festival of sport; a meeting for athletics or other competitive sports; **sport-fisherman,** a sea-going boat equipped for sportfishing; **sportfishery; sportfishing** orig. *U.S.*, fishing by rod and line for sport or recreation; hence (as a back-formation) **sportfish,** a fish caught thus for sport rather than (primarily) for eating.

1939 *Amer. Speech* XIV. 6 Newspaper and magazine columns..'Sportorial', 'Sportcast', 'Sportlight'. **1938** *Variety* 28 Dec. 30/4 Jim Britt, WBEN sportcaster, promised a copy of a set of health rules to any listeners who would write in. **1941** *Time* 31 Mar. 50/1 Adam has sponsored the sportcasting of big-time bouts. **1937** AUDEN in Auden & MacNeice *Lett. from Iceland* xi. 147 The sport-fest was a primitive affair. Some part singing ..and a swimming race. **1950** E. BRADNER *Northwest Angling* III. i. 172 As a sport fish, the salmon is highly valued by the anglers of the Pacific Coast. **1971** *Nature* 18 June 422/3 The billfishes of the family Istiophoridae, which include several well known sportfish such as the sailfish, the marlins, and spearfishes. **1954** *Field & Stream* Jan. 72 (*caption*) *Miss Chevy IV*, unique 34-foot, V-bottom, twin-engine sport fisherman. **1967** *Jane's Surface Skimmer Systems 1967–68* 107/2 Sportfisherman is a luxury fishing yacht with living and sleeping accommodation for four. **1955** (*title*) Sport fishery abstracts. I. 1. **1910** C. G. HOLDER in *Proc. 4th International Fishery Congress* I. 201 (*heading*) Sport fishing in California and Florida. **1926** *Daily Colonist* (Victoria, B.C.) 15 July 5/3 Something had to be done in order to save the sport fishing of Vancouver Island. **1978** A. GILCHRIST *Cod Wars* v. 36 The Icelandic government (well aware of the amount of money which sport-fishing brings into the country) takes care of the availability of salmon in two important ways.

b. *pl.* **sportscaster** *N. Amer.* [after *broadcaster*: cf. *newscaster*, etc.] one who presents a sports broadcast on radio or television; a broadcasting sports commentator; hence **sportscasting**; also **sportscast,** a sports broadcast; **sportsfest** = *sportfest*, sense 10 a above; **sports finder** *Photogr.*, a direct-vision viewfinder usu. consisting of a simple frame which allows action outside the field of view of the camera to be seen, fitted esp. to twin-lens reflex cameras; **sports medicine,** the branch of medicine dealing especially with the consequences of engaging in sports.

1961 WEBSTER, Sportscast. **1976** N. NIELSEN *Brink of Murder* i. 11 The sportscast on the portable TV was in progress. **1938** *Amer. Speech* XIII. 239 Note that newscaster and sportscaster are now common terms in *Variety*. **1952** B. WOLFE *Limbo* xx. 323 With each passing day the sportscaster's voice lost a few more decibels of its professional bounce. **1964** M. MCLUHAN *Understanding Media* xxx. 303 A sportscaster had just begun his fifteen-minute reading from a script. **1981** 'E. MCBAIN' *Heat* iii. 51 The sportscaster read off the baseball scores. **1969** C. ARMSTRONG *Seven Seats to Moon* xii. 125 J sat all the way through the sportscasting. **1976** *Listener* 5 Aug. 151/1 Television caught both aspects of this mammoth *sportsfest* [sc. *The Olympic Games*] very well. **1953** A. MATHESON *Leica Way* 100 The sports finders are an earlier version of the brilliant finders. **1977** J. HEDGECOE *Photographer's Handbk.* 165 Most twin lens reflexes have a 'sports finder' which folds out of the hood. **1961** (*title*) Journal of sports medicine and physical fitness. **1973** *Times* 13 Dec. 7/2 Britain is far behind some European countries, America and Australia in her attitude to sports medicine, Dr Ian Adams, medical officer to Leeds United Football Club, said. **1977** J. F. FIXX *Compl. Bk. Running* xxii. 248 The general physician is not interested in sportsmedicine.

sport, *v.* Add: **I. 2. e.** (Earlier example.)

1789 *Loiterer* 20 June 9 The Squire of the Parish..will ..give him unlimited leave to sport over his Manor.

II. 11. a. Restrict ? *Obs.* to *to sport timber*; *to sport* (usually *one's* or *the*) *oak*: (later examples).

1911 BEERBOHM *Zuleika D.* xii. 187 The man who now occupied my room had sported his oak—my oak. **1932** R. ALDINGTON *Soft Answers* 72 My bell rang again...

Had they come back to make my flat the battleground for another Idiot scene? It was no use sporting the oak with the lights in my windows. **1951** S. SPENDER *World within World* ii. 50 If one arrived early one was liable to find the heavy outer door of his room, called 'the oak', sported as a sign that he was not to be disturbed. **1974** J. I. M. STEWART *Gaudy* viii. 145 The light on the little landing was extinguished, but Ivo Mumford's oak had not been sported.

13. (Later example.)

1894 A. MORRISON *Tales of Mean Streets* 41 There was a milliner's window, with a show of..hats... 'Which d'yer like, Lizer?—.. I'll sport yer one.'

‖ **sportif** (sportīf), *a.* (*sb.*) [Fr.] Of a sporting character, sportive; interested in or pursuing athletic sports. Also, of a garment: suitable for sporting or informal wear. Also *absol.* and as *sb.*

1934 C. LAMBERT *Music Ho!* IV. 242 The musical equivalent of this obsession with the mechanical, the *sportif* and the soi-disant contemporary, is provided by the naïvely realistic orchestral pieces of Honegger, such as *Pacific 231* and *Rugby*. **1938** E. HEMINGWAY *Fifth Column* (1939) 171 There were two kinds: the drunkards and the sportifs... The sportifs took it out in exercise. **1958** *Manch. Guardian* 4 Aug. 3/6 Last year it was..the man who played boogie-woogie on a gramophone all night in the next room and when I complained said I wasn't *sportif* and made a bigger row than ever. **1963** *Times* 1 May 9/6 Elegance is the word that immediately comes to mind—elegance with more than a touch of the *sportif*, for the performance is a good bit better than you might expect from a car of less than 1-litre capacity. **1966** *Listener* 30 June 936/1 All nations are now *sportif*, although they do not necessarily acclaim the same sports as we do. **1977** *Times* 30 July 10/1 The hooded sweat-shirt is..casual and sportif yet neat and warm.

sporting, *vbl. sb.* Add: **3. b.** *sporting column, page, paper; sporting event; sporting goods, jacket.*

1901 *Bookman* Oct. 123/2 Americans..have noted the peculiarities of the diction of the writers of the sporting columns. **1920** *Times* 14 June 15/3 Among the sporting events which follow each other in..June, Royal Ascot.. is unique. **1869** *Boyd's Business Directory* 500 John H. Mann, importer and dealer in guns, fishing tackle, gun powder, and all sporting goods. **1978** R. B. PARKER *Judas Goat* xxii. 135 'Picked up a new shotgun at a sporting goods store,' he said. **1837** DICKENS *Sk. Boz* 2nd Ser. 53 A brown coat, something between a great-coat and a 'sporting' jacket, on his back. **1915** *Lit. Digest* 21 Aug. 360/3 Bozeman Bulger..contributes to the sporting page of the New York *Evening World*. **1961** P. WHITE *Riders in Chariot* ix. 259 He would..go away, or reach for the sporting page. **1849** C. BRONTË *Shirley* III. iv. 75 He reads only a sporting paper. **1907** M. E. BRADDON *Dead Love has Chains* vi. 130 Slang has to be forgiven in a man, like smoking, and sporting papers, and motors.

c. sporting editor *U.S.*, a sports editor; **sporting print**, a print of a scene taken from the field-sports; also *transf.*

1857 *Spirit of Times* 1 Aug. 340/2 We see exactly, where the 'sporting editor' of *The Times* has made his fatal mistake about handicaps and handicappers. **1899** T. HALL *Tales* 128 The somewhat intellectual-looking sporting editor of the aforesaid *Universe*. **1849** THACKERAY *Pendennis* I. xviii. 168 Six sporting prints, and four groups of opera-dancers..formed the late occupant's pictorial collection. **1964** R. JEFFRIES *Embarrassing Death* viii. 84 Two thousand men eager to pay five or ten shillings for a 'sporting print' every month. **1973** G. GREENE *Honorary Consul* II. iii. 81 A corridor hung with Victorian sporting prints: riders falling into a stream, checked at a bullfinch, rebuked by the master.

sporting, *ppl. a.* Add: **2. a.** Also *spec.* in phr. *sporting parson.*

1826 F. REYNOLDS *Life & Times* I. iii. 99 The family consisted of the Dowager Lady Grandison,..an old Irish Major—a sporting parson—the house apothecary—my father, my aunt, and myself. **1901** *Daily Tel.* 23 July 10/6 Those who imagined that the last 'sporting parson' had disappeared from the Church of England are quite mistaken. **1982** M. YOUNG *Elmhirsts of Dartington* ii. 21 His mother..meant him to be a priest, not a sporting parson..but a proper God-fearing priest.

b. *sporting man* (earlier example). Also used in other collocations referring to low gaming and betting.

1824 R. HUMPHREYS *Mem. J. Decastro* 206 Bob Todrington, a sporting man (caricatured by Old Dighton). **1857** *Household Words* 12 Sept. 264/1 With its sparring snobs, and flashing satins, and sporting gents and painted cheeks. **1902** G. B. SHAW *Mrs Warren's Profession* p. xxix, Well, does anybody who knows the sporting world really believe that bookmakers are worse than their neighbors? **1946** K. TENNANT *Lost Haven* (1947) ii. 40 Her mother was entertaining some sporting friends who had dropped in to settle up certain transactions. **1967** S. BECKETT *Stories & Texts for Nothing* III. 84 Thronged already with sporting men fevering to get their bets out of harm's way before the bars open.

c. *N. Amer.* Used *spec.* to denote a prostitute or loose woman, as *sporting girl, woman.* Cf. SPORTSWOMAN b.

1925 *Amer. Speech* I. 151/2 The woman of the underworld is spoken of as a 'sporting woman'. **1938** A. J. LIEBLING *Back where I came From* 152 Most of the women..go out by the day as house-workers. There may be a few sporting girls, but if so they don't work their own block. **1951** E. PAUL *Springtime in Paris* iv. 89 The *place* Xavier Privas, where the former sporting girls and their male friends congregate. **1971** J. GRAY *Red Lights on Prairies* vi. 143 The existence of a colony of sporting women at Nose Creek was prejudicially affecting the morals and welfare of the Community.

3. a. (Earlier and later examples.) Also, of or characterized by conduct consonant with that of a sportsman or 'good sport'.

1799 *Times* 1 June 4/3 Hunting Box, pleasantly situate in a sporting part of the Country. **1920** 'O. DOUGLAS' *Penny Plain* xi. 115 'Isn't it awful..about our minister marrying..a girl twenty years younger than himself.' 'But how sporting of him,' Pamela said. **1923** WODEHOUSE *Inimitable Jeeves* x. 112, I had..got as far as the lift before I remembered what it was that I had meant to do to reward Jeeves for his really sporting behaviour in this matter of the chump Cyril. **1962** S. RAVEN *Close of Play* III. xv. 186 By declaring when they did, they left Baron's Lodge with three-hundred and twenty-two runs to make in two hours... It was, on the whole, a sporting declaration.

b. Also, an opportunity that a sportsman might consider. (Later examples.)

1913 *Granta* 7 Mar. 255/2 If bad shows are booked for this theatre the *actors* are not the people to be blamed; they are, naturally, trying to do their best—give them a sporting chance. **1977** M. ALLEN *Spence in Petal Park* xxxi. 146 All that rubbish they learnt on the rugger field about giving the other fellow a sporting chance... The world just doesn't work like that.

sportive, *a.* Add: **6. a.** (Later example.)

1969 *Daily Tel.* 13 Mar. 18 Sportive readers of this paper's report yesterday on the pay talks of 90 Tonbridge cricket ball makers are puzzled..that these craftsmen should be represented by the National Union of Furniture Trade Operatives.

b. Of clothes: suitable for sporting or informal wear. Cf. *SPORTIF *a.*

1935 *Amer. Speech* X. 193/2 Combinations like *smoothly sportive, fetchingly feminine*..are numberless. **1963** C. BEATON *Diary* 15 Feb. (1979) 358 In his yachting jacket and sportive shoes, he has something about his swashbuckling style that reminds me of Douglas Fairbanks, Senior.

sportster (spōᵊ·ɹtstəɹ). [f. SPORT *sb.*¹ + -STER.] **a.** A sports coat. *rare.* **b.** A sports car. Cf. *ROADSTER 2 d.

1963 *N.Y. Times* 20 Dec. 11 Sportster. Made of cotton Safari cloth, lined with wool alpaca. **1971** *New Scientist* 6 May 324/1 (*heading*) Spark speeds sportsters. **1974** P. J. FILBY *Specialist Sports Cars* 90/1 The 803, which was an open sportster with a ladder frame chassis bonded to its fibreglass body.

sportswoman. Add: **1.** Also *transf.* in recent use, a woman who displays the typical good qualities of a sportswoman. Cf. note at SPORTSMAN 1 a.

1906 KIPLING *Puck of Pook's Hill* 148 She'd say she'd get us whipped. She never did, though... Aglaia was a thorough sportswoman. **1925** F. SCOTT FITZGERALD *Great Gatsby* iv. 86 Miss Baker's a great sportswoman... She'd never do anything that wasn't all right. **1948** F. THOMPSON *Still glides Stream* ii. 42 If I can't bear a bit of pain at my time of life I'm no sportswoman.

sporty, *a.* Add: **2.** Of a motor car: of a racing type; resembling a sports car in appearance or performance.

1962 A. LURIE *Love & Friendship* xii. 228 Traded in his Pontiac got him one of those new Valiants,..kind of sporty for a man his age. **1966** *Economist* 9 July p. xvii/2 Chevrolet's Corvair only began to sell when the Monza version was introduced after a few months, with bucket seats and a 'sporty' reputation, but precious little else for the extra $250. **1972** *Sunday Express* 9 Jan. 5/1 Performance is distinctly sporty. Its top gear acceleration of 40–60 in 9 seconds beats anything else in the class.

‖ **sposa** (spǭ·să). Now *rare.* [It.] A wife; a bride. Also as **cara** (cā·ră) **sposa**, 'dear wife'; a devoted female companion. Cf. *SPOSO.

1624 J. CHAMBERLAIN *Let.* 4 Dec. (1939) II. 589 Tom Cary a privado of the Princes bedchamber was dispatcht ..into Fraunce with a love letter and some rich and rare jewell to the Sposa. **1781** N. MUNDY *Let.* 15 Oct. in A. E. Newdigate-Newdegate *Cheverels* (1898) iii. 48 Adieu my dear Sr Roger, may you and yr Cara Sposa meet in health & spirits. **1793** W. B. STEVENS *Jrnl.* 13 Mar. (1965) I. 72 His Wife..handsome enough for a Cara Sposa. **1797** E. WYNNE *Jrnl.* 22 Jan. in A. Fremantle *Wynne Diaries* (1952) xx. 265 The *sposa* received so many fine compliments of congratulation that she was quite at a loss. **1821** SHELLEY *Let.* 22 Oct. (1964) II. 363 La Guiccioli his [*sc.* Byron's] cara sposa who attends him impatiently.

s'pose (spōᵘz), *v.* Also **spose, 'spose, spoze.** Repr. an informal pronunc. of SUPPOSE *v.*

1852 R. S. SURTEES *Mr Sponge's Sporting Tour* xvii. 84 Law, ma! but you don't 'spose pa would ever allow such a thing. **1873** TROLLOPE *Harry Heathcote* (1874) i. 12 'I s'pose the poor must live somewheres,'..said Mrs. Growler, the old maid-servant. ? **1912** R. FRY *Let.* (1972) I. 358, I 'spose women weren't artists enough. **1936** L. DURRELL *Let.* in *Spirit of Place* (1969) 40, I no longer care... A new phase I spoze. **1945** A. KOBER *Parm Me* 44 If you're not enjoying yesself, Max, spose you sit with them. **1968** D. O'GRADY *Bottle of Sandwiches* (1969) i. 7 'And s'posin' it rains in the meantime?' 'See what you mean. Small marquee, eh?' **1971** *Black World* June 72/1, I paid them out of receipts I was sposed to turn in. **1980** H. R. F. KEATING *Murder of Maharajah* iii. 37, I s'pose we're not strictly his guests. We're the Maharajah's guests.

sposhy, *a.* (Earlier example.)

1842 *Yale Lit. Mag.* VIII. 96, I can't always decipher quail tracks—specially in *sposhy* weather.

‖ **sposo** (spǭ·so). Now *rare.* [It.] A husband. Also as **caro** (cā·ro) **sposo**, 'dear husband'. Cf. *SPOSA.

1778 F. BURNEY *Diary* Aug. (1940) I. 12 Hetty, who, with her *sposo*, was here to receive us. **1792** —— *Let.* 2 Oct. (1972) I. 229 Her caro sposo has continued very tolerably well. **1816** JANE AUSTEN *Emma* III. vi. 88 The thing would be for us all to come on donkies, Jane, Miss Bates, and me—and my caro sposo walking by. **1858** TROLLOPE *Three Clerks* III. xviii. 328 The gentleman who has the honour of being her intended sposo. **1887** *Athenæum* 21 May 670/2 Italian girlhood..has two sole points of interest, the *sposo* and the fashion plate. **1976** *Times Lit. Suppl.* 30 Jan. 103/1 Nor was her husband.. a mere *caro sposo*: their devotion was total.

spot, *sb.*¹ Add: **II. 4. c.** (Earlier and later examples.) Now usu. without the definite article.

1856 *Spirit of Times* 22 Nov. 196/1 Addison County leads the van (or 'knocks the spots off', as we say here) in Vermont, and is celebrated over the world for its fine horses. **1861** *Atlantic Monthly* June 747/1, I wish I had control of chain-lightning for a few minutes;..I'd make it come thick and heavy and knock spots out of Secession. **1903** A. BENNETT *Truth about Author* xiii. 171 'We will write a play together... We can do something that will knock spots off—' etc., etc. We determined upon a grand drawing-room melodrama which should unite style with those qualities which make for financial success on the British stage. **1943** A. L. ROWSE *Cornish Childhood* 186 They [*sc.* the Nazis]..have at any rate been intelligent, and knocked spots off those public-school gentlemen.

d. A pip on a playing-card. Also, a playing-card having a specified number of pips (cf. sense 5 d). In recent use *U.S.*

1578 J. STOCKWOOD *Sermon preached..24 Aug.* 142 They perfectlye can tell howe manye spottes there be in a payre of Cardes..when as they scarce reade a leafe of the Bible twice in a Moneth. **1844** 'J. SLICK' *High Life N.Y.* II. xxx. 215 'Jest so,' sez I, a fli[n]gin down the ten spot o' clubs and the ace-o' diamonds. **1873** J. H. BEADLE *Undevel. West* iv. 92 The ace is your winning card. The eight and ten spot win for me. **1976** *Washington Post* 19 Apr. B8/3 South won the opening trump lead with his ten-spot. **1977** D. ANTHONY *Stud Game* xix. 118, I had a poker game... I played mechanically, counting spots and backing the odds.

5. d. (Earlier example.)

1846 DURIVAGE & BURNHAM *Stray Subjects* 135, I moved towards the money, but he prevented my raising it, by covering it with a *twenty*-spot.

e. Substitute for def.: Either of two marine food fishes of the family Sciænidæ, *Leiostomus xanthurus* or the channel bass, *Sciænops ocellata.* (Earlier and later examples.)

1877 C. HALLOCK *Sportsman's Gazetteer* 396 Spot.—*Liostomus obliquus.* **1961** E. S. HERALD *Living Fishes of World* 192/1 The spot, *Leiostomus xanthurus*, found from Cape Cod to Texas, is easily recognized by the spot above the base of the pectoral fin.

f. = *spot board* in sense 14 below.

1922 E. J. EVANS *Building Contracts* xviii. 81 It is essential that all plant, such as Derby's sieves, cornice moulds..spots, scaffolding, etc.,..be on site in readiness. **1927** A. H. TELLING *ABC of Plastering* 195 It is part of the labourer's business to see that the 'spot' is supplied with 'stuff' for the plasterer's use. **1964** [see *spot board*, sense 14 below].

III. 7. a. (Further examples, esp. *colloq.* with *of* and abstract nouns.)

1915 H. ROSHER *In R.N.A.S.* (1916) 117 Pity I'm not due for another spot of leave yet. **1924** D. B. W. LEWIS *At Sign of Blue Moon* 272 What about a spot of lunch? **1933** M. ALLINGHAM *Sweet Danger* ii. 21 Since the spot of bother last year, the tunnel is no longer a tunnel. **1951** *People* 3 June 5/6 A dead-broke barrister who turns burglar following a spot of light coaching from a retired cracksman. **1959** H. HAMILTON *Answer in Negative* iv. 52 The police will be coming..to deal with a spot of trouble. **1976** F. MUIR *Frank Muir Book* 43 The first major French ballet company visited New York in 1827. They had a spot of bother with their tights.

d. Also preceded by a defining word and *absol.*

1924 LAWRENCE & SKINNER *Boy in Bush* vi. 85 Y' slog t' th' nearest pub t'cadge a beer spot. **1930** J. DEVANNY *Butcher Shop* 200 The 'spot' she craved, or failing that a cup of tea. **1936** WODEHOUSE *Laughing Gas* ix. 90 May I offer you a spot?.. I can recommend the Scotch. **1950** G. GREENE *Third Man* viii. 63 'Have another drink, Mr. Martins?' 'No, I don't think I will.' 'Well, I'd like another spot.'

e. *slang* (orig. and chiefly *U.S.*). A term of imprisonment. Usu. preceded by numeral, designating a term of the specified number of years. Cf. sense 5 d.

1901 'J. FLYNT' *World of Graft* 220/2 *Spot*, term in prison. A 'one spot' means a sentence of one year. **1907** J. LONDON *Road* 84 He had never been in the particular penitentiary to which we were going, but he had done 'one-', 'two-', and 'five-spots' in various other penitentiaries (a 'spot' is a year). **1966** M. BREWER *Man against Fear* x. 105 He was serving a three spot for cunning... He got into a row with one of the warders.

8. d. = *SLOT *sb.*² 5*, esp. in a performance, show, or programme; *spec.* in *Broadcasting*, a short interval for an advertisement or announcement; an advertisement or announcement occupying such an interval. orig. *U.S.*

1923 *N.Y. Times* 7 Oct. IX. 2 *Spot*, an act's position on a bill. **1926** *Amer. Mercury* Dec. 465/1 Fields and Fink moved in to a homer in the next to closing spot. **1937** *Amer. Speech* XII. 101 *Spot* or *spot announcement* refers to a brief announcement, usually commercial, spotted at various times. **1950** *Sport* 22–28 Sept. 18/2 Jack..continued to fill the centre-half spot in the Celtic line-up. **1958** *Listener* 25 Sept. 462/2 Occasional spectacular successes may please advertisers who happen to have 'spots' next to them. **1958** *Manch. Guardian* 29 Sept. 4/4 Spots, unlike full-length programmes, would reach people not already prejudiced in favour of the candidate. **1960** *Twentieth Cent.* Apr. 357 Dons..will do anything for a television spot. **1962** H. E. Beecheno *Introd. Business Stud.* ix. 81 They [*sc.* TAM ratings] also help to determine, on the commercial channel, the prices of advertising 'spots'. **1967** *Technology Week* XX. 95/2 (Advt.), Your spot? Perhaps operating a ground computer complex. **1972** *Newsweek* 10 Jan. 9/2 Among these super-rich, two families contend for the No. 1 spot in the financial pecking order. **1972** G. Durrell *Catch me a Colobus* vii. 139 He appeared on the local television as 'Uncle Ambrose', doing a children's spot in which he always had an animal of some sort to show them and talk to them about. **1976** *Southern Even. Echo* (Southampton) 17 Nov. 21/3 The 125cc solo class provides a championship medal for yet another Italian, Pietro Bianchi, with Spain's Angel Nieto in second spot. **1977** J. Wainwright *Do Nothin' till you hear from Me* x. 177 Tricks to get the tempo moving... Tricks to introduce a solo spot. **1978** S. Brill *Teamsters* iii. 98 What pervaded Fitzsimmons' union..was a generally low level of competence in the top-paying spots. **1980** *Times* 5 Feb. 19/4 At present rates £44,300 would buy 49 30-second spots on each [radio] station during day-time shows.

e. *colloq.* With preceding adj.: a situation of the (unpleasant or difficult) kind specified; *in a spot*, in difficulties, in trouble.

1929 C. F. Coe *Hooch* v. 103 Jimmie Daust is in a bad spot, too. **1932** Wodehouse *Hot Water* xvi. 257 If that guy's in a spot, I'm glad of it. **1940** A. Christie *One, Two, buckle my Shoe* 160 It's the sort of business that might land him in a tight spot. **1967** E. S. Gardner *Case of Queenly Contestant* vii. 84 He was afraid his father would find out. He was in a spot. So he turned to the troubleshooter. **1978** A. Price *'44 Vintage* xviii. 200 She'd probably only been humouring him, like any nice girl in an awkward spot might do.

f. *colloq.* A place of entertainment; *spec.* = *night spot* s.v. *night *sb.* 14.

1954 G. Greene *Twenty-One Stories* 205 I should be taken to plenty of Spots if I wasn't with a husband. **1956** B. Holiday *Lady sings Blues* (1973) iii. 32 It was jumping with after-hour spots, regular-hour joints, restaurants, cafés, a dozen to a block. **1970** C. Major *Dict. Afro-Amer. Slang* 108 *Spot*, usually a nightclub but also any popular place.

9. b. In phr. *the man on the spot.* See also *on-the-spot *a.*

1897 I. Malcolm in R. S. Churchill *W. S. Churchill* (1967) I. Compan. II. xii. 848, I write like the 'man on the spot' The most inconceivable rot. **1922** M. Asquith *Autobiogr.* II. i. 21, I took my host aside and asked him if 'the man on the spot'—generally a favourite with the stupid—had given him his views on South Africa. **1955** G. Greene *Quiet American* I. ii. 21, I always like to know what the man on the spot has to say. **1978** *Listener* 26 Jan. 119/3 If the man on the spot senses paralysis on the field, he ought to be able to abdicate.

d. *to put* (a person) *on the spot*: (*a*) *colloq.* (orig. *U.S.*), to place (someone) in a particular location; to put in a difficult or embarrassing position; (*b*) *U.S. slang*, to arrange for the murder of (someone), to kill; also *fig.* Cf. sense 8 e above.

1928 *Detective Fiction Weekly* 11 Aug. 735/2 We learned that the State still had one reliable witness, who could 'put us on the spot'. **1929** *Amer. Speech* IV. 343 *Put-on-the-spot*, left waiting at an appointed meeting place. **1929** M. A. Gill *Underworld Slang* 9/2 *Put on the spot*, killed. **1930** *Punch* 16 Apr. 442 You get rid of inconvenient subordinates..by 'putting them on the spot'—that is deliberately sending them to their death. **1930** *Sun* (Baltimore) 31 Oct. 1/3 Confident that America's prohibition law is about to be 'put on the spot', enterprising English vintners are already preparing for a resumption of their happy relations with their American clientele. **1934** G. Ade *Let.* 24 June (1973) 184 The Democrats have put every independent voter on the spot by nominating [Sherman] Minton at the dictation of Paul McNutt. **1937** *Sunday Express* 21 Feb. 1/3 (*heading*) Englishman 'put on the spot'. **1951** M. Lowry *Let.* 5 June (1967) 244 The last thing we'd want to do is to put you on the spot or embarrass you. **1960** H. Innes *Doomed Oasis* II. iii. 145, I couldn't exactly say it in my report of the search. It would have put the Company on the spot, if you see what I mean.

10. c. *Cricket.* (*a*) The point at which a ball should pitch for optimum length and direction; (*b*) an irregular place on the pitch from which the ball, when bowled, may move in an unexpected direction.

1855 F. Lillywhite *Guide to Cricketers* 29 The second day, however, Dean and Nixon found out the 'spot', and seemingly deposited every ball..on the precise place. **1859** *All Year Round* 23 July 305/2 The wicket..had no dead spots, no lively ones; no chance for 'shooters', none for 'bumpers'. **1901** *Encycl. Sport* I. 247/1 To bowl 'on the spot' is to bowl a good 'length'. **1908** W. E. W. Collins *Leaves from Old Country Cricketer's Diary* ix. 145 Their fast bowler found a spot on which the ball shot dead instead of bumping. **1950** F. N. S. Creek *Teach yourself Cricket* vi. 111 A mere mechanical ability to pitch the ball on some regular spot called a 'good length' is of little value. **1980** *Wisden Cricket Monthly* Apr. 31/1 He was heartened by the presence of an awkward spot—a pretty large one, right on his length—from which the ball flew viciously from the very start.

d. Phr. *to hit* (or *go to* or *touch*) *the spot*: to be exactly what is required, 'to fit the bill' (said esp. of food or drink). *colloq.* (chiefly *U.S.*).

1868 *Putnam's Mag.* I. 670/1 'I hope that last corjul set you up?' 'Yes, Mr. Plunkitt, it went right to the spot.' **1897** *Strand Mag.* May 500/2 Then percussion or detonation was tried, and that 'touched the spot'! **1908** 'O. Henry' *Voice of City* 235 Oh, pass the bottle... That hits the spot... My first drink in three months. **1923** W. Nutting *Massachusetts Beautiful* 241 Did ever a dish of apple dowdy go to the spot like that? **1949** F. P. Keyes *Dinner at Antoine's* xvii. 268 That hot chocolate and those big chunks of roast beef certainly hit the spot. **1974** P. de Vries *Glory of Hummingbird* xviii. 275 'They haven't got a name for it [*sc.* a pancake] yet.'.. 'Batter Up. It hits the spot.' **1976** 'E. McBain' *Guns* (1977) vii. 194 Colley would love a drink... A gin and tonic would hit the spot.

e. *Stock Exch.* With preceding adj.: a share in which dealings are of the specified kind.

1928 *Daily Sketch* 10 Aug. 20/3 Courtaulds' shares remain a firm spot at $4\frac{1}{2}$. **1981** *Times* 23 Apr. 18/3 Another dull spot was Danish Bacon, which gave up 2p to 104p after results.

f. *Assoc. Football.* With *the*: the penalty spot (see *penalty 5).

1970 *Liverpool Daily Post* 26 Sept. 5/5 *Smith made no mistake from the spot*: Smith scored a penalty. **1976** *Ilkeston Advertiser* 10 Dec. 19/5 Penalty expert Alan Crisp gave the goalkeeper no chance from the spot. **1977** *Guardian* 9 Mar. 20/3 Amid strong protests from several Forest players, the referee pointed to the spot.

11. b. (Earlier example.) Also in *sing.*

1881 *Harper's Mag.* Apr. 734/2 'Spots', 'futures', 'longs' and 'shorts' were unknown terms. **1930** *Sunday Times* 12 Oct. 2/4 Raw Rubber prices became easier, and spot was dealt in down to 3 11-16d. **1976** *Scotsman* 25 Nov. 2/8 Silver fluctuated with sterling and ended about 2p down at 262.50p for spot and 273p for three-month.

11*. *ellipt.* for *spotlight *sb.* (*a*).

1920 Wodehouse *Jill the Reckless* xvi. 231 Another debate on the subject of blues, ambers, and the management of the 'spot'. **1930** [see *flood *sb.* 6*]. **1960** J. Symons *Progress of Crime* xl. 218 We cut off our engines after putting the spots on first to make sure this was the right show. **1968** K. Weatherly *Roo Shooter* 40 While the kangaroo shooter swings the spot in wide-reaching sweeps, the rabbit shooter uses it at about thirty-five yards and shoots into the sidelight. **1977** *Times* 24 Sept. 22/4 Wall spots are just over £6, table and standard lamps at reasonable prices.

IV. 12. b. *spot-development, -group, -zone.*

1909 G. Forbes *Hist. Astron.* 105 During the sun-spot maximum the corona seems most developed over the spot-zones—*i.e.*, neither at the equator nor the poles. **1926** H. Macpherson *Mod. Astron.* iii. 41 The regions where the bombs are likely to appear are around and among active spot-groups. *Ibid.* 45 A relation between high-rotation speeds and spot-development.

d. *spot market, rate.*

1939 *Sun* (Baltimore) 12 Dec. 17/6 As the price of tin for future delivery advanced..local cash or spot market prices declined slightly. **1956** *Ann. Reg. 1955* 436 Dealings in lire were restricted to the spot market. The Bank of England began the publication of official spot T.T. rates for lire. **1982** *Daily Tel.* 3 Aug. 13/2 Saudi oil is being traded on the spot market at up to $3 a barrel discount. **1933, 1971** Spot rate [see *premium 3 c].

e. In sense 9: = 'made on the spot', as *spot decision, fine*, etc. See also *spot test* (*b*), sense 14 below, and *spot check *sb.*

1921 Z. Cope *Early Diagnosis Acute Abdomen* i. 3 Spot-diagnosis is impressive but unsafe. **1934** *Amer. Speech* IX. 113/1 One man may make a *spot count*, for eight or nine hours. **1953** *Times* 29 July 6/6 He said that the 'spot scrutiny' of vehicles such as has been carried out in Bedfordshire was one of the best ways of identifying those which should not be on the roads. **1959** *Economist* 21 Mar. 1047/1 He may now be obliged to make spot decisions with inadequate notice in highly controversial circumstances. **1976** *Wymondham & Attleborough Express* 17 Dec. 2/1 Prosecution is a waste of time of already crowded courts, so what about spot fines for these moronic motor maniacs. **1979** H. S. Kent *In on Act* xxii. 247 Although..I would often be glad of a 'spot opinion' on one of my new problems, it was never quite the same again.

14. spot ad, advertisement *Broadcasting*, an advertisement occupying a short break during or between programmes; so **spot advertising** *vbl. sb.*; **spot announcement** *Broadcasting*, an announcement occupying a short break during or between programmes; **spot board** *Plastering* (see quot. 1964); **spot cash** orig. *U.S.*, money paid on the spot; **spot commercial** = **spot advertisement*; **spot dance**, a competitive dance in which a spotlight plays on the dancers until the music stops, at which time the couple on whom the spotlight rests wins; **spot effect** *Broadcasting*, a sound effect created in the studio (see quots. 1941 and 1976); also *attrib.* in *pl.*; **spot-fish** = sense 5 e in Dict. and Suppl.; **spot height** *Surveying*, the height of a point above mean sea level, usu. as marked on a map; **spot kick** *Assoc. Football*, a penalty kick; also *attrib.*; **spot lamp** = *spotlight *sb.*; **spot level** *Surveying* = **spot height*; also *fig.*; **spot-list** *v. trans.*, to place (a building) on a list (*list *sb.* 6 a (*b*)) as the result of special consideration; so **spot-listing** *vbl. sb.*; **spot map**, a map in which spots or points indicate individual locations or occurrences of something; **spot meter**, a photometer that measures the intensity of light received within a cone of small angle, usu. 2° or less; **spot news** *Journalism* (orig. *U.S.*), news reported of events as they occur; also *attrib.*; **spot plate** *Chem.*, a plate having several small depressions in which spot tests can be performed; **spot-proof** *a.*, (of a fabric) that is not susceptible to small stains; **spot-reducing** *vbl. sb.*, reduction of fat in selected areas of the body; **spot test**, (*a*) a chemical test performed using a single drop of sample; (*b*) = *spot check *sb*; also **spot-test** *v. trans.*, to subject to a spot test; **spot testing** *vbl. sb.*; **spot welding** *Engin.*, a form of resistance welding in which one or more small, localized welds are produced on the overlapping surfaces to be joined; so **spot weld** *sb.*, a weld of this kind; also (with hyphen) as *v. trans.*, to join by spot welding; **spot-welded** *ppl. a.*; **spot welder**, an apparatus that carries out spot welding; **spot wobble** *Television* (now *disused*), small periodic oscillation of the scanning spot, formerly used to render the scanning lines less noticeable; **spot zoning** *U.S.*, the special rezoning (see *zoning *vbl. sb.*) of an area to meet a particular interest.

1934 J. Rorty *Our Master's Voice Advertising* 269 Canada prohibits the broadcasting of 'spot ads'. **1962** *Rep. Comm. Broadcasting 1960* 82 in *Parl. Papers 1961–2* (Cmnd. 1753) IX. 259 The principle of the control of advertising time applied only to 'spot' advertisements, and not in any analogous way to advertising magazines. **1961** *Ann. Reg. 1960* 452 The amount of 'spot' advertising in the clock hour was to be reduced to $7\frac{1}{2}$ minutes. **1979** *Guardian* 4 Aug. 8/7 This danger [of competition] can.. be avoided..if only a different kind of advertising is permitted on the new commercial channel: if it may show only *block* not *spot* advertising. **1937** Spot announcement [see sense 8 d above]. **1949** *Consumer Reports* May 236/2 A 'spot announcement'..can..be inserted between the close of one commercial program and the opening of the next. **1976** *National Observer* (U.S.) 3 July 13 To defend his position, Mr. Reagan taped a $1\frac{1}{2}$ minute 'spot' announcement. **1931** W. Verrall in T. Corkhill *Brickwork, Concrete & Masonry* VIII. XXXI. 1940 The spot board, as it is sometimes called, is made of floor boards, about 3 ft. long, nailed together with cleats at the back. **1939** *Archit. Rev.* LXXXV. 213 Where hand-mixing [of plaster] is carried out the mess and waste that are inevitable when plaster is mixed on 'banker-boards' and then transferred to 'spot-boards' should be avoided where possible. **1964** J. S. Scott *Dict. Building* 307 *Spot board* or *gauge board* or *spot*, a plasterer's board about 3 ft square on which he works up the plaster before he puts it on. It rests on a stand about 27 in. high. **1879** *Bradstreet's* 8 Oct. 4/3 A business Utopia where credit shall be unknown and 'spot cash' an unvarying rule. **1909** A. N. Lyons *Sixpenny Pieces* ii. 12 The spot-cash practitioners of Mile End Road are rather strange..to us. **1957** V. Packard *Hidden Persuaders* xii. 131 After the car went on sale reports from dealers stated that 90 per cent of the people buying paid spot cash. **1978** *Dumfries & Galloway Standard* 21 Oct. 21/3 (Advt.), Caravans wanted, spot cash, any size, any make. **1955** *Times* 28 July 9/7 Television uses many old pictures to fill less valuable time, mainly as vehicles for strings of 'spot' commercials that effectively break any thread they may possess. **1962** A. Nisbett *Technique Sound Studio* i. 18 He [*sc.* the announcer] also presents programme trailers and (in many countries outside Britain) spot commercials. **1976** *National Observer* (U.S.) 10 Apr. 2/5 The networks have said they will make regular prime-time spot-commercial time available. **1944** M. Laski *Love on Supertax* iii. 40 Such refinements as 'spot-dances' and..jazz superbly played. **1947** *Daily Gleaner* (Kingston, Jamaica) 4 Nov. 15/1 Spot dances, raffles, games and a grand floor show. **1941** *B.B.C. Gloss. Broadcasting Terms* 31 *Spot effects*, effects created in a studio where the performance of which they form part is taking place. **1944** L. MacNeice *Christopher Columbus* 17 'Effects'..are of two kinds—records on a gramophone or spot effects in the studio. **1961** G. Millerson *Telev. Production* i. 14 A spot-effects man sounds the horn of an 'approaching car'. **1976** B. Armstrong *Gloss. TV Terms* 84 *Spot effect*, a brief sound—door closing, bell ring—added during the dub. **1875** *Fur, Fin & Feather* 122 You are always welcome to a seat in his boat, if disposed for snipe or duck, or spot-fish. **1913** A. R. Hinks *Maps & Survey* i. 23 There is a strong tendency to give spot heights for summits, and not for the bottoms of depressions. **1928** E. D. Laborde *Pop. Map Reading* iii. 65 In actual practice, it is often difficult to find the exact height of ground: small areas of high ground are not always marked with spot heights. **1977** D. Beaty *Excellency* vi. 74 He drew his track on the maps and charts..and memorized the spot-heights over the Alps. **1950** *Sport* 22–28 Sept. 4/4 He has handed over the responsibility of taking penalty kicks to left-back 'Jock' Ferrier, who converted a spot-kick last Saturday. **1971** *Post* (S. Afr., Cape ed.) 9 May 23/5 Dumile Melane never faltered with the spot-kick amid cheers from jubilant Cubs supporters. **1977** *Belfast Tel.* 22 Feb. 30/6

Magee remains the Blues' spot kick expert and, if a penalty is awarded.., he will be the man to take it. **1937** *Motor Catal.* (East London Rubber Co.) 151 'Raydyot' Spot Lamp... Universal movement. **1962** H. C. Weston *Sight, Light & Work* (ed. 2) vi. 197 A low voltage 50 watt spot-lamp unit..can be mounted at a distance of 6 ft. from the work and yet provide an illumination upwards of 300 lm/ft.² **1976** *Liverpool Echo* 22 Nov. 14/3 (Advt.), Daimler Sovereign 1973, automatic, power steering,.. spotlamps, [etc.]. **1908** N. F. Mackenzie *Methods of Surveying* x. 118 From these 'spot levels' the actual contour lines are sketched in by interpolation. **1920** J. K. Finch *Topographic Maps & Sketch Mapping* I. i. 19 The exact height of the ground is only shown at important points on hachure maps. This is done by means of 'spot levels' or 'spot heights' scattered over the map. **1958** *Listener* 20 Nov. 813/1 As the polls attempt a nationwide cross-section one would expect them to reflect the gradual development and movement of political opinion ..more steadily and consistently than the spot-levels, so to speak, which are taken at by-elections, with all their variations of locality, candidate, and so on. **1974** W. H. Irvine *Surveying for Construction* iii. 12/1 At present spot levels are shown to the nearest foot but with metrication the levels will be to the nearest 100 mm. **1974** *Country Life* 31 Jan. 197/3 After representations by the Victorian Society, the building was recently spot-listed. **1977** M. Binney in Binney & Burman *Change & Decay* 188/1 If a church is of any merit yet still not listed it is worth asking the Department of the Environment to consider spot-listing it. **1973** *Times* 8 Jan. 3/3 Widespread 'spot listing' to save buildings threatened by development may be counter-productive. **1901** Parkes & Kenwood *Hygiene & Public Health* xi. 666 'Spot maps'—maps of a district, on which the deaths or cases of various infectious diseases are spotted out—furnish valuable graphic expressions of any grouping. **1973** J. J. McKelvey *Man against Tsetse* ii. 81 In three months the commission acquired 460 collections of flies and made a spot map of tsetse locations. **1979** *Dictionaries* I. 36 The spot maps will be effectively utilized to show the distribution of a single [dialectal] term. **1955** J. Lipinski *Miniature & Precision Cameras* vi. 240 The incident light meter may measure the light incident upon the scene. Or the spot meter may measure it from a white card. **1976** *Physics Bull.* Sept. 395/3 A range of luminance (brightness) spotmeters and illuminance meters will be displayed. **1912** S. Washburn *Cable Game* 9 The other type, the 'cable men', are collectors of what might be called 'spot' news. **1936** E. Waugh *Waugh in Abyssinia* 82 There were demands from Fleet Street for daily items of 'spot news'. **1976** *National Observer* (U.S.) 15 May 2/3 Other Pulitzer winners were: Sydney Schanberg of the New York Times, international reporting;..and the staff of the Chicago Tribune, spot-news reporting. **1928** *Chemist-Analyst* XVII. I. 18/2 Spot plate for outside indications. **1937** J. W. Matthews tr. *Feigl's Spot Tests* ii. 5 Spot plates are made from glazed porcelain, and usually contain 6–12 adjacent depressions of equal size that hold 0·5–1 c.c. of liquid. **1981** *Sci. Amer.* Feb. 128/1 The aluminum compound responsible for the buffering effect of buffered aspirin can be detected with filter paper or a spot plate. **1950** Spotproof [see *habutai]. **1958** *Times* 6 Oct. 13/1 Leather and suède jackets and coats many of which are treated to be spot-proof against rain. **1960** *Sunday Express* 27 Nov. 14/3 Gymnasia with spot-reducing and general slimming equipment. **1970** *Harrod's Catal.* May 14/1 Spot reducing 'Faradic' and 'G.5' from £2. 2. 0. **1921** *Chem. Abstr.* XV. 2599 Spot tests which depend upon the formation of $PbCrO_4$ or of $AgCrO_4$ are fairly sensitive. **1948** *Ann. N.Y. Acad. Sci.* XLIX. 268 Prior to quantitative analysis.. the fractions are spot-tested on paper impregnated with ninhydrin. **1955** *Times* 16 June 9/3 'Spot tests' could be extended, and it would be well if the Minister were to declare his intention with regard to them. **1960** *Jrnl. Iron & Steel Inst.* CXCIV. 285/3 For Cu, a spot test is suggested which allows estimation in the range 0·1–0·5 p.p.m. **1969** *Listener* 28 Aug. 287/1 Miss Atwood's Toronto heroine works for Seymour Surveys, spot-testing consumer products. **1942** *Industr. & Engin. Chem.* (Analytical Ed.) 15 Apr. 278/2 (*heading*) Application of infrared radiation to spot-testing. **1908** *Engineering* 9 Oct. 486/1 The pedal of one of the machines on view had been made..by attaching a piece of angle iron on each side of the lever by two 'spot welds'. **1951** *Ibid.* 13 Apr. 439/1 The shear strength of an individual spot weld was nearly twice that of a rivet. **1977** *Modern Railways* Dec. 488/1 The main handicap..was the high labour cost which resulted from the 50,000 rivets and 60,000 spot-welds involved in the construction of one vehicle. **1909** *Engineering* 15 Jan. 69/3 We have seen three thicknesses of 3/16-in. iron spot-welded together, the spot being about ⅛ in. in diameter. **1958** *Ibid.* 14 Mar. 344/2 The panels are..automatically seam-welded before being spot-welded to the framing. **1973** A. Parrish *Mech. Engineer's Ref. Bk.* vi. 34 Aluminium is readily spot welded but the welding parameters must be closely controlled because the metal has a short plastic temperature range. **1921** *Automobile Engineer* Mar. 106/3 (*caption*) A spot welded bonnet. **1969** J. G. Tweeddale *Welding Fabrication* II. iii. 87 In a spot welded assembly the joint is comparatively rigid. **1914** *Proc. Inst. Mech. Engineers* 167 An attempt was made to put down one small machine, a spot welder or a contact welder. **1963** H. R. Clauser *Encycl. Engin. Materials & Processes* 573/2 Semi-portable spot welders are..available for assemblies such as automotive structures, housings and cases that cannot be handled by permanently placed..machines. **1976** Spot welder [see *seam welder* s.v. *seam *sb.*¹ 10]. **1908** *Engineering* 9 Oct. 486/1 The method of spot-welding appears cheaper, quicker, and as good as riveting. **1912** *Automobile Engineer* 30 Oct. 387/3 In the spot-welding machine the sheets are joined at spots instead of rivets. **1970** K. Ball *Fiat 600, 600 D Autobook* xii. 141/1 The body structure is made up from nine separate assemblies joined together by spot welding. **1951** *Sun* (Baltimore) 19 Oct. (B ed.) 5/7 First sets to incorporate 'spot wobble' are 15-inch home receivers. Focusing is by the normal line-pattern method, but the flick of a switch converts to 'spot wobble'. **1956** *B.B.C. Engin. Monogr.* No. 1. 5/2 The obliteration of the line structure by carefully adjusted spot wobble is of course essential in any telerecording system if beat patterns are to be avoided when the film is scanned. **1932** *Sun* (Baltimore) 6 May 14/2 All cities which have zoning laws go through a period of attacks that aim to break them down for private as opposed to public interests. The practice is called 'spot' zoning. **1933** *Ibid.* 16 Nov. 12/1 The Board of Zoning Appeals has disapproved a proposed 'spot-zoning' ordinance in the interest of the promoters of a distillery. **1946** *Amer. Home* Sept. 96/3 There is..one very deplorable habit among the creators and administrators of Zoning Laws which was, to permit what is known as 'spot zoning'. This may allow a small 'spot' of business to establish itself in an exclusively residential area. **1976** *Tulane Law Rev.* L. 357 The term 'spot zoning'..may mean rezoning not in accordance with a comprehensive plan, rezoning in the absence of a mistake or change, or rezoning which is arbitrary and improper.

spot, *v.* Add: **I. 3.** (Earlier example.)

1850 *Rep. Comm. Patents: Agric. 1849* (U.S.) 456 These varieties spot better, and produce a finer leaf than any I have ever seen.

II. 4. d. (Earlier examples.)

1856 E. M. Curr *Waste Lands of Province of Wellington* 30 The practice of which I speak is called in New Zealand '*spotting*' or '*spoiling*' country. **1864** E. Muter *Trav. & Adv. Officer's Wife* II. xiii. 260 'Cockatoos', as the station-owners call the other [class of land-purchasers], who 'spotted' his run all over with fifty and one hundred acre sections.

e. To moisten *with* a drop of liquid; to place a drop of (liquid) *on* (*to*) a surface, etc.

1954 R. E. Oesper tr. *Feigl's Spot Tests* (ed. 3) II. iv. 158 The moist reagent paper is spotted with the test solution. **1972** *Sci. Amer.* June 34 (*caption*) The mixture is spotted at one corner (X) of a square of filter paper; the fragments are separated by chromatography in one direction and by electrophoresis in another. **1977** *Lancet* 26 Nov. 1140/2 Blood is spotted on to filterpaper. **1978** *Nature* 9 Feb. 577/2 Even concentrated lysates did not result in killing or lysogenisation when spotted on a lawn of Mu-sensitive bacteria.

7. Also without *out*.

1915 B. E. Jones *Cinematograph Bk.* 176 Having cleaned and spotted the film, attention may be given to any torn portions or broken perforations. **1937** *Discovery* Feb. p. xiv/1 This book [*sc.* J. Deschin *New Ways in Photography*]..contains many suggestions and practical methods for getting better results in..spotting prints. **1979** *Amateur Photographer* 7 Feb. 4 (Advt.), A custom hand print, cropped, hand printed, spotted, dry mounted and heat sealed.

7*. *N. Amer.* To place (something) in a particular location; *esp.* to place (a railway car) in the proper place for loading or unloading.

1917 *Dial. Notes* IV. 329 *Spot*, to stop (a car) at the proper place on a railroad track. **1936** B. Brooker *Think of Earth* I. iii. 38 It was a wilderness of rusting steel and rotten ties where old dump-cars were 'spotted' for repairs. **1937** *Liberty* 25 Dec. 20/1 Already strategically spotted throughout..our population are sergeants and lieutenants and chiefs of police of the new 'supertrained' school. **1947** *Sun* (Baltimore) 13 May 6/3 Passengers would walk.. under cover to their planes spotted alongside the pier. **1956** T. Raddall *Wings of Night* (1957) xii. 106 You might phone the railway people and tell 'em to spot four or five boxcars on the Hall's Creek siding not later than Tuesday. **1962** J. Onslow *Bowler-Hatted Cowboy* xiv. 136 When I arrived at the yards the cars were ready spotted opposite the loading-chutes. **1970** J. H. Gray *Boy from Winnipeg* 55 The rest of us spotted our lunch kits, towels, and swimming things at a convenient table. **1979** *Arizona Daily Star* 22 July I. 6/4 If you're playing a Nevada audience, you can't give them all new stuff, and you have to be careful how you spot it.

III. 9. b. (Earlier examples.)

1848 E. Z. C. Judson *Mysteries & Miseries of New York* I. 116 To spot is to recognize—to mark. **1849** G. G. Foster *New York in Slices* 15 The expertness acquired by the keepers of these shops in 'spotting' their man is truly wonderful.

d. *Mil.* To locate (an enemy position). Also *intr.* and const. *for*.

1914 *Aeroplane* 11 Nov. 425/2 He poised..for a spell to spot the lurking place of the battery. **1915** D. O. Barnett *Let.* 23–25 Jan. 51, I had a man with a periscope spotting for me, and he registered some near things for the Bosch's face. **1916** 'Boyd Cable' *Action Front* 135 'Stand by for trouble. That brute is spotting for his gun.' The aeroplane dropped a light, turned, and circled round to the left. **1918** C. Bright *Telegraphy, Aeronautics & War* 51 While he is spotting he is continually subjected to tremendous shelling. **1942** *Hutchinson's Pictorial Hist. War* 18 Mar.–9 June 62 (*caption*) Men of a Cypriot company..spotting for enemy aircraft. **1973** R. Dentry *Encounter at Kharmel* ix. 152 I'll come in low. You spot. I'll be busy.

e. To watch out for and observe (a certain class of objects) as a hobby. See also *train-spot *v.*

1919 G. B. Shaw *Inca of Perusalem* in *Heartbreak House* 212 Chips keeps owls and rabbits. Spots motor bicycles. **1957** *Times Lit. Suppl.* 8 Nov. 675/2 As other boys spot railway engines, Alan Villiers as a child in Melbourne spotted and studied the big sailing ships lying at anchor in Port Phillip bay.

spot check, *sb.* orig. *U.S.* Also hyphened. [f. Spot *sb.*¹ + Check *sb.*] A check made on the spot; a quick check made on a random sample. Also *attrib.*

1933 *Sun* (Baltimore) 15 Aug. 8/1 The spot check made on bread prices from February 15 to August 2 in sixteen representative cities. **1946** *N.Y. Times* 30 June L-25/2 Spot checks are made but many of these slaughter houses go as long as five weeks without a check. **1947** *Sun* (Baltimore) 3 Apr. 5/1 Troops and police made a surprise spot-check of identities in the center of Jerusalem today, hastily erecting roadblocks while they examined the papers of pedestrians and persons in trucks and automobiles. **1963** *Language* XXXIX. 465 A survey of the vast..literature of ethology, supplemented by repeated spot checks of ongoing research projects, reveals that the study of signaling behavior in animals has, by and large, been taxonomically parochial. **1972** *Daily Tel.* 1 Mar. 2 A spot check by the Inner London Education Authority last autumn showed that 17,000 out of 165,000 secondary school pupils were absent that day. **1978** L. Deighton *SS-GB* iv. 37 They saw the soldiers doing the spot-check. Parked across the roadway there were three Bedford lorries. **1980** *Sunday Times* 24 Aug. 1/1 Six French paratroopers have also been charged after spot-checks on kitbags revealed stolen electrical goods.

Hence **spo·t-che·ck** *v. trans.*, to subject to a spot check; also *absol.*; **spo·t-che·cking** *vbl. sb.*

1944 U. Sinclair *Presidential Agent* I. ii. 43 Robbie Budd lived and breathed and ate and talked aeroplanes: cat-walks and bulkhead segments, stabilizers and de-icers, sub-assemblies and spot-checking—a whole new vocabulary. **1955** *Times* 5 July 10/7 They had decided.. not to make vehicle tests compulsory and they were considering falling back on the proposal..to extend 'spot checking' to private vehicles. **1962** *Guardian* 15 Jan. 3/4, I recently saw vehicles being spot-checked by the Ministry of Transport. **1962** E. Snow *Red China Today* (1963) xxxviii. 277 We spent another forty days spot-checking all over the county. **1972** *Accountant* 14 Sept. 314/1 He'd spot-checked them against actual orders. **1976** C. Weston *Rouse Demon* (1977) xix. 90 By spot-checking instead of monitoring each complete tape, Adrian had managed to go through seven. **1980** P. Moyes *Angel Death* i. 9 Once in a while, a Customs Officer will..do a certain amount of spot-checking on visiting private yachts.

spo·tlight, *sb.* Also spot light, spot-light. [f. Spot *sb.*¹ + Light *sb.*] A source of artificial light casting a narrow and intense beam; *esp.* (*a*) *Theatr.*, a lamp used to cast intense illumination on a small area of a stage; also, the light cast by such a lamp; also *fig.* (cf. *limelight); (*b*) an auxiliary lamp on a motor vehicle.

1904 *Minneapolis Times* 1 Aug. 4 In the drama that was enacted Mr. Galvin was not in the spotlight at any time, but it cannot be denied that his was an important part. **1916** *Lit. Digest* (N.Y.) 8 Jan. 89/1 It will put the magnates and the self-styled fighters..into the background and give the players the spot-light. **1920** *T. Eaton Catal.* Spring & Summer 395/5 Spotlights are very necessary accessories, especially in country driving. **1921** *Daily Colonist* (Victoria, B.C.) 11 Oct. 7/4 (Advt.), These new Spot Lights constitute the most remarkable improvement in the history of the flashlight business. This flashlight is capable of throwing a beam 300 feet or more. For motoring, picking out road signs, boating,..or for night flash signalling, nothing can equal them. **1922** C. Aiken *Jig of Forslin* 25 While in the warm dark seats, we watch the spot-light Dazzle upon the singer's hair and eyes. **1922** M. B. Houston *Witch Man* xiv. 193 He has a nice baritone, but he's the sort of man who gravitates to the centre of the floor and deliberately absorbs all the spotlight. **1928** *Daily Express* 7 July 5/2 Ahead of him was the professor's spot-light, making a little glow upon the ground... Charlie..dared not approach within serviceable distance of the professor's torch. **1930** J. B. Priestley *Good Companions* II. ii. 295 He comes to me and asks all about curtains and footlights and spot-lights and props, and he goes about looking so important when he's anything to do. **1931** H. F. Pringle *Theodore Roosevelt* I. xi. 135 The spotlight focused on Roosevelt, a spotlight so white and continuous that the other..commissioners found themselves in..shadow. **1937** *Motor Catal.* (East London Rubber Co.) 151/1 'Bosch' Spotlight... Gives a brilliant, long beam, which can be trained upon the kerb, on the road ahead, or signposts. **1946** D. C. Peattie *Road of Naturalist* ii. 24 Some sixty years ago the spotlight fell upon Pronuba. **1949** 'P. Wentworth' *Spotlight* xxviii. 175 He wanted the hall to be dark, with the single lamp on the mantelpiece arranged to be as much like a spotlight as possible. **1957** *Encycl. Brit.* XXI. 285/2 The spot-light—in contrast to the flood light—which can be controlled and focussed accurately upon one particular spot. **1964** L. Deighton *Funeral in Berlin* xix. 113 A V.W. saloon with blue flasher and spotlight full on. **1967** N. Freeling *Strike out where not Applicable* 129 It was a kind of altar. No spotlights, thank heaven, but a decided feeling of stiffly-bunched-madonna-lilies. **1972** *Times* 30 Nov. 23/8 A strong consumer and governmental spotlight on food prices. **1973** 'R. MacLeod' *Nest of Vultures* ii. 40 A half-dozen blinding spotlights were trained on a postage-stamp stage. **1978** R. Ludlum *Holcroft Covenant* vi. 79 Several passengers were reading under the beams of tiny spotlights, but most were asleep. **1980** M. Booth *Bad Track* i. 18 On the front of the radiator grille was mounted a pair of very large Cibie spotlights that dwarfed the standard headlamps.

spo·tlight, *v.* Also spot-light. [f. the sb.] *trans.* **a.** To illuminate with a spotlight. Also *fig.*

1923 [implied at *spotlighted *ppl. a.*]. **1926** H. T. Wilkins *Marvels Mod. Mechanics* 234 These panorama lamps can be swung round in a circle, and, along with flood lights, be concentrated in a beam of rays to 'spotlight' the stage stars. **1935** *Amer. Speech* X. 192/2 A dress that scarfs and sleeves itself with stripes will *spotlight* her and *outsmart* her neighbors. **1942** *Sun* (Baltimore) 1 Jan. 22/8 He hoped that the publicity in connection with the measure has 'spotlighted' the abuse of charity racketeers. **1955** *Radio Times* 22 Apr. 15/3 Each programme in the series will spotlight a particular breed of dog. **1963** *Listener* 21 Feb. 353/3 His understanding of the jazz idiom spotlighted the 'bluesy' features of the Concerto beautifully. **1973** R. Perry *Ticket to Ride* i. 11 The standard lamp..was softly spot-lighting her from behind. **1975** J. Cleary *Safe House* ii. 73 An elderly motorbike.. the weak beam of its headlamp spotlighting them as they stood at the back of the truck. **1976** C. Blackwood *Stepdaughter* i. 56, I feel that my future career as a painter stands spot-lit and exposed. **1977** F. Young in J. Hick *Myth of God Incarnate* ii. 29 Too often the so-called outdated substance-categories have been spotlighted and criticized.

b. Chiefly *U.S.* To hunt (game) by spotlight. Cf. Jack-light *v.*

1934 in Webster. **1968** *Daily Progress* (Charlottesville, Va.) 26 Jan. 3/4 After illegally spotlighting and killing a deer [etc.].

So **spo·tlighted, -lit** *ppl. a.*; **spo·tlighter,** one who hunts by spotlight; **spo·tlighting** *vbl. sb.*, (*a*) illumination by spotlight; (*b*) hunting by spotlight; also *attrib.*

1923 B. Hecht *Florentine Dagger* v. 72 A crowd.. stood watching officials and the spotlighted figures of mystery enter. **1932** *Observer* 26 June 13/4 The spotlit nocturne that follows..is starred by Spessiva's solos. **1934** Webster, Spotlighter, Spotlighting. **1952** *New Yorker* 4 Oct. 119/1 With insufficient spotlighting, the spectacle was like a succession of obscure museum paintings in need of cleaning. **1953** E. Simon *Past Masters* II. 110 Everyone returning from the spotlighted centre was surrounded. **1961** *Daily Progress* (Charlottesville, Va.) 27 Jan. 3 (*heading*) Deer 'spotlighting' convictions hit 14. *Ibid.*, The deer 'spotlighters' were ordered to pay a total of $3,250 in fines. **1972** L. Hancock *There's a Seal in my Sleeping Bag* i. 13 He was surprised to learn in Australia that pit-lamping or spotlighting not only is legal but the accepted way of hunting.

spot on, -on, *adv.* and *a.* (*phr.*) [f. Spot *sb.*[1] + On *adv.*] Completely accurate(ly), precise(ly), exactly right.

1920 E. H. Young *By Sea & Land* i. 56 All these X-chasing instruments make my head go round. You can overdo all that, I say; shoot quick and spot on—that is the best way in the long run. **1956** C. Willcock *Death at Flight* iii. 34 'What a spot for a front tyre to choose to burst,' he said. 'Funny thing, sir, the outer casing looks as though it was in spot-on condition.' **1961** *Punch* 18 Jan. 130/3 'Self-discipline and self-restraint', to use the P.M.'s spot-on terms, become minimal requirements in the ordinary citizen. **1962** L. Davidson *Rose of Tibet* vii. 134 Our oracle here warned that you would be coming... The time was fixed fairly spot-on. **1966** M. Woodhouse *Tree Frog* xxv. 182 Neither the altimeter nor the compass is one hundred per cent spot on, because we didn't have time for an instrument check. **1969** W. Garner *Us or Them War* i. 14 'I'm still getting things right?' The plain-clothes man said, 'Spot on, Mr Morton.' **1973** *Times* 14 May 9/1, I moved my run-up back from 109ft to 114ft and fitted in 18 strides so that I was hitting the board spot on. **1976** *Courier-Mail* (Brisbane) 2 June 4/5 It's about time somebody with influence said the sort of things Mr. Colin Lamont..said about education. He is spot on. **1977** *Sounds* 9 July 8/1 Pristine production and spot on playing, A.R.S. could be up there alongside the L.A. crowd if they concentrate more on albums full of songs of this quality. **1978** R. Perry *Dutch Courage* vii. 82 Although the sarcasm was overdone, the cynicism was spot on. **1981** T. Barling *Bikini Red North* ix. 194 Getting here..with a day to spare is spot-on timing. **1982** *N. & Q.* Oct. 472/2 His thesis is provocative, its evidences spot-on, and his conclusions pretty convincing.

spotted, *a.* and *ppl. a.* Add: **3. a.** (Further examples.) Also, = *Rocky Mountain* (*spotted*) *fever* s.v. *Rocky *a.*[1] 1 b.

1902 Wilson & Chowning in *First Biennial Rep. Montana State Board of Health* 27 Enough was accomplished to warrant the formation of a working hypothesis ..that the so-called 'Spotted Fever' is due to the presence in the patient's blood of the above mentioned haematozoan..; and that the parasite is conveyed to man through the bite of a tick. **1903** *U.S. Hygienic Lab. Bull.* XIV. 7 (*heading*) Spotted fever (tick fever) of the Rocky Mountains. *Ibid.*, I have suggested as a name for the disease 'Tick Fever', as there are already two diseases sometimes called 'spotted fever'.

6. spotted dog, (*a*) a white or light-coloured dog with black or dark spots, esp. a Dalmatian; (*b*) *fig.* = *Spotted Dick* in Dict.; also *attrib.*; **spotted wilt,** a virus disease of herbaceous plants, esp. tomatoes, in which it causes curling and necrotic spotting of the leaves.

1854 C. M. Smith *Working-Men's Way in World* xii. 288 For supper come smoking sheep's-heads..and 'spotted dog', a very marly species of plum-pudding. **1910** F. W. Hackwood *Inns, Ales, & Drinking Customs* 288 The 'Talbot' readily became known among the vulgar as the 'Spotted Dog'. **1930** E. C. Ash *Pract. Dog Bk.* 47 The Spotted Dog [*sc.* the Dalmatian] became the dog of the Circus. *a* **1936** Kipling *Something of Myself* (1937) i. 18 An enormous currant roly-poly—a 'spotted dog' a foot long. **1974** *Country Life* 25 Apr. 990/1 The other hound ..reminded me of a spotted dog pudding at school. **1919** C. C. Brittlebank in *Jrnl. Dept. Agric. Victoria* XVII. 231 It is well to have a common name for every tomato disease, and I propose that of 'Spotted Wilt' for this latest one, from the spotting and subsequent wilting of the attacked plants. **1950** *N.Z. Jrnl. Agric.* June 587/1 Iceland poppies should be inspected regularly from now on for symptoms of the virus disease known as spotted wilt. **1979** *Ann. Appl. Biol.* XCIII. 173 Chlorotic ringspots.., leaf specking, terminal bud necrosis,..and severe stunting of groundnut (*Arachis hypogaea*) were shown to be caused by tomato spotted wilt virus.

spotter. Add: **2. a.** (Earlier example.)

1876 *Scribner's Monthly* Apr. 911/2 The stockholders and directors, the 'car-starters' and 'spotters'.

c. A look-out, an observer; a scout; one who identifies or looks out a target; *spec.* (Mil.), an aviator who locates enemy positions and directs fire.

1903 A. M. Binstead *Pitcher in Paradise* v. 127 So vigilant and observant was that solitary optic that its owner was the chosen 'spotter' of a most relentless band of racecourse pickpockets. **1914** *Illustr. London News* 29 Aug. 320/3 Electric contrivances for communicating messages between the 'spotter' aloft and the gun-layer below. **1918** E. M. Roberts *Flying Fighter* 108 The fire was being directed from the ground from what the battery commander called the O.P., or observation post. He sent me up to that post with one of the spotters. **1925** J. C. Goodwin *Queer Fish* xvi. 153, I surmise that they are 'spotters', posted where they are to warn the proprietor of the card-room should the police or their informers put in an appearance. **1935** A. J. Cronin *Stars look Down* I. ix. 70, I heard the Tynecassel spotter was coming down to watch ye at the next Sleescale match. **1935** A. J. Pollock *Underworld Speaks* 112/1 *Spotter*, an accomplice who sizes up the victim and surroundings for the purpose of robbery, murder, kidnaping or a beating. **1939** *Illustrated* 16 Dec. 28 The 'spotter' sweeps the sky with his powerful telescope in search of aircraft. **1940** *Sun* (Baltimore) 13 Aug. 1/7 The Germans..have mounted long-range guns between Calais and Boulogne..but they will be simply shooting into the blue unless they have effective spotters aloft. **1940** *Times* 13 Nov. 3/1 Spotters with machine-guns man the roofs. **1943** *Times* 9 Oct. 2/5 The spotters 'tell' every outgoing or incoming aircraft by direct telephone line to the nearest R.O.C. centre. **1949** *Times* 5 Jan. 4/5 Aircraft from Kuala Lumpur carried spotters for the naval gunners. **1955** *Times* 21 June 9/4 One spotter aircraft to each forest operating company is the minimum requirement for efficiency. Such spotters can ask for..'bulldozer' rights for a patrol on a hot scent to pass through the areas of other units without being shot in error. **1959** I. & P. Opie *Lore & Lang. Schoolch.* xvii. 373 The sentinel may..be called a guard, spotter, scout, [etc.]. **1963** T. & P. Morris *Pentonville* 353 Crime or crimes are to a great extent planned in gaol..then the necessary men (i.e. safe blower, drivers, spotters, con men, fence,) are found in here and given the word. **1976** *Globe & Mail* (Toronto) 11 June 9/8 Once Mr. Drmbie or his spotter sight a fire, they circle, swoop in at treetop level and note the size of the blaze. **1976** *Eastern Even. News* (Norwich) 13 Dec. 4/3 Chic is heavily involved in all forms of entertainment and is the local 'spotter' for television's 'New Faces'. **1977** 'O. Jacks' *Autumn Heroes* vii. 96 'Spotter plane, boss.'.. 'I don't like the idea of a spotter.' **1980** J. O'Faolain *No Country for Young Men* i. 23 The Tans came in shooting... At the barracks, 'spotters' with bags over their heads and slits for their eyes identified known activists.

d. One who spots (*spot *v.* 9 e) trains, etc. See also *train-spotter.

1950 *Oxf. Jun. Encycl.* IX. 400/1 The main activity of spotters' clubs is the collecting of locomotive numbers. **1957** *Railway Mag.* Dec. 887/2 (*heading*) Necktie for spotters. **1958** *Times* 6 Dec. 7/4 As a young 'spotter' [of car registration numbers in Egypt] I quickly noticed that the Arabic face was always legible at a considerably greater distance than the Western face. **1973** *Times* 27 July (Leisure Suppl.) p. iv/4 Steam railway enthusiasts seem to grow in number each year as spotters young and old rue the passing of steam.

3. *attrib.*, as (sense *2 c) *spotter aircraft, pilot, plane.*

1942 *Daily Tel.* 1 Jan. 1/8 Three enemy fighters..and a 'spotter' aircraft were shot down. **1959** *Times* 18 May 6/1 From Marks Tey, Essex, on the main Colchester road, spotter aircraft yesterday radioed a report of a 20-mile queue of close-packed traffic. **1976** *Globe & Mail* (Toronto) 11 June 9/8 A second source of fire information—three Cessna spotter aircraft flying 3,000 feet overhead signalling radio reports into the fire control room. **1967** *Listener* 21 Sept. 355/3 The radio in the company HQ chatters with constant news from the ground control and the spotter pilots. **1958** *Observer* 3 Aug. 1/4 Floating 1,000 ft. over Southern England in the Automobile Association's spotter plane..I watched the holiday traffic streaming out of London yesterday. **1977** *Time* 22 Aug. 10/1 Israeli batteries—sometimes directed by observers in spotter planes—fired 16 times at Palestinian forces. **1981** E. Clark *Send in Lions* v. 53 Spotter planes searched the vastness of the Sahara.

spotting, *vbl. sb.* Add: **1. c.** Also without *out.*

1940 *Amer. Speech* XV. 360/1 *Spotting*, eliminating spots from negatives. **1951** *Good Housek. Home Encycl.* 269/2 *Spotting*,..the term applied to a process in the cleaning of a garment such as a suit. **1958** *Spectator* 4 July 15/3 The store or small cleaner will deal with finishing such as spotting and pressing. **1977** J. Hedgecoe *Photographer's Handbk.* 267 Spotting is the filling in of clear specks (which would otherwise print black) until they match the surrounding tone, and so vanish.

4*. A slight discharge of blood via the vagina, *esp.* as a side-effect of oral contraceptives; light staining due to this.

1900 Dorland *Med. Dict.* 624/2 *Spotting*, a slight menstrual show upon a woman's napkin. **1944** Miller & Bryant *Gynecol. & Gynecol. Nursing* iv. 57 A faint spotting noted on the underclothing or nightclothing may be the only symptom of an early carcinoma of the cervix. **1962** *Lancet* 22 Dec. 1315/2 The clinical criterion of adequate dosage most commonly used was absence of break-through bleeding and spotting. **1977** *Ibid.* 5 Nov. 947/1 According to Islamic precepts, intercourse is prohibited during menstruation, and spotting is interpreted as a prolonged menstrual period.

4.** The action of observing, acting as a look-out; *spec.* (Mil.), the action of locating enemy positions from an aircraft and directing fire.

1914 A. Hurd *Fleets at War* iv. 136 Jellicoe did all that was possible..to instal a fire-control set of instruments in each ship for 'spotting' and controlling at long-range shooting. **1918** W. H. Berry *Aircraft in War & Commerce* vi. 77 At the Dardanelles..some of the 'spotting' [by seaplanes] for the battleship guns..was not beaten later. **1928** C. F. S. Gamble *Story of North Sea Air Station* viii. 113 The duties of this air station were:..(*f*) Spotting for coastal batteries.

5. *spotting scope* [*scope *sb.*[3] b].

1960 C. E. Chapel *Art of Shooting* xv. 147 The shooter may have a spotting scope. This is a telescope of comparatively high power, which may be mounted on a tripod and placed near the shooter..and used to observe the location of shot holes on the target. **1970** R. A. Steindler *Firearms Dict.* 238/2 With the help of a spotting scope.., the spotter informs the shooter as to the exact point of bullet impact on the target. **1980** *Hunting Ann. 1981* 62/2 If you are serious about trying for a trophy, use a spotting scope.

spotty, *a.* Add: **2. c.** *gen.* Unsteady, uneven; patchy; sporadic, intermittent. orig. and chiefly *U.S.*

1932 *Sun* (Baltimore) 25 Feb. 19/6 The advance [of the curb market] was somewhat spotty, but on the whole, the list developed a firm tone. **1934** *Ibid.* 17 Sept. 8/1 Business conditions..are..'spotty'. One section may flourish,..while another suffers. **1937** R. S. Morton *Woman Surgeon* i. 21 My grown brothers played whist with my father before dinner... His luck was spotty. **1937** E. B. White *Let.* 31 May (1976) 155 My attendance at meals may be a little spotty—for a twelvemonth I shall not adjust my steps to a soufflé. **1957** K. A. Wittfogel *Oriental Despotism* 55 The spotty distribution of his administrative centers. **1970** A. Toffler *Future Shock* v. 72 Available statistics, unfortunately, are spotty. **1977** H. Fast *Immigrants* I. 57 Clair's schooling was spotty, but she learned to read. **1979** *Dictionaries* I. 97 Philosophers' general interest in dictionaries has been spotty.

spoulty, var. *spaulty *a.*

spouse-breach[1]**.** Add: *transf.* (Later *arch.* example.)

1922 Joyce *Ulysses* 47 He [*sc.* a dog] rooted in the sand,..a pard, a panther, got in spousebreach.

spout, *sb.* Add: **I. 4. a.** (Earlier example.)

1834 W. H. Ainsworth *Rookwood* II. III. v. 345 To the spout with the sneezers in grand array.

b. *up the spout* (earlier *fig.* examples).

1829 P. Egan *Boxiana* 2nd Ser. II. 351 At the expiration of thirty-five minutes, and seventeen rounds, the *flue faker* acknowledged he was '*up the spout*'. **1846** *Swell's Night Guide* 64 And when she saw all hope was up the spout, She spouted everything a spout would take.

c. *to put* (someone) *up the spout*: to make pregnant (esp. out of wedlock); also simply *up the spout*, in the womb; pregnant. Cf. *up the pole* s.v. *pole *sb.*[1] 1 b. *slang.*

1937 Partridge *Dict. Slang* 815/2 *Spout, up the*,.. pregnant with child...Often in form, *to have been put up the spout*. **1949** *Landfall* III. 234 Well, they say he put her up the spout. **1956** P. Scott *Male Child* II. i. 95 All these years taking every possible care and suddenly there's one up the spout. **1970** 'S. Troy' *Blind Man's Garden* viii. 100 Up the spout, isn't she? I thought Michel would have had more bloody savvy.

d. A gun barrel. Usu. in phr. *up the spout*, of a bullet or cartridge: in the barrel and ready to be fired. *slang.*

1943 C. H. Ward-Jackson *Piece of Cake* 55 *Spout*, a gun barrel. **1943** *R.A.F. Jrnl.* Aug. 12 He'd a round up the spout from being on this guard..and when he pulled the trigger there was a bang and a flash. **1969** M. Gilbert *Blood & Judgement* vii. 70, I can count six here in the clip... There's probably one up the spout. **1966** D. Varaday *Gara-Yaka's Domain* xi. 128 The pin failed to fire the dud cartridge in the chamber. There was no time to pump another into the spout. **1976** G. Seymour *Glory Boys* xv. 191 The Uzi was concealed there. Wonder if he's put the catch off, thought Jimmy, put one up the spout.

III. 11. spout-bath *N.Z.*, a natural douche-bath; **spout cup,** (*a*): for † in Dict. read 'Now only *Hist.*' and add later examples.

1929 C. C. Martindale *Risen Sun* 164 There are things in New Zealand that they call 'spout-baths'. A solid shining stream thuds on to your back from a height, and you feel as strong as it does. **1977** *N.Z. Herald* 5 Jan. 2-20/11 (Advt.), Rotorua Boulevard Motel, New units, sleep 1–6, restaurant adj, TV, putting green, hot swimming pool, 6 pvte spa and spout baths. **1956** G. Taylor *Silver* iv. 80 *Spout Cups.* Found also in faience, they are no more than a tankard or two-handled cup..ending in a curved spout. **1970** *Canadian Antiques Collector* June 28/2 What were spout cups? Used to feed invalids and children. Popular in the 18th century. Bulbous body, domed cover, duck-neck spout with handle generally at the right angle to the spout.

spouting, *ppl. a.* Add: **2. c.** *spouting well* = Spouter 3 b.

1861 *Chem. News* 28 Sept. 164/2 At about 325 feet in depth, there is about 40 feet of white sandstone, near the top of which 'spouting wells' are found. **1898** *Knowledge* 1 June 124/2 The 'spouting' wells of Russia entirely eclipse those of America in output. **1912** Tower & Roberts *Petroleum* v. 83 On the basis of the general character of the yield wells are divided into two classes, the flowing, spouting, or gushing wells, and the pumping wells.

spoze, var. *s'pose *v.*

‖ **Sprachgefühl** (ʃprā·χgĕfül). [Ger., f. *sprache* speech + *gefühl* feeling.] The intuitive feeling of a speaker for the essential character of a language; linguistic instinct. Also *loosely*, the character or genius of a language.
1902 GREENOUGH & KITTREDGE *Worlds & their Ways* ix. 127 Men of genius may take great liberties with their mother tongue without offence; but..let them violate its *Sprachgefühl*, and their mannerism becomes, as it were, a foreign language. **1914** *Pedagogical Seminary* June 256 If there is to be instruction in modern foreign languages the age of about ten is for most children the best to begin it. If it comes before this the child has not developed sufficient *Sprachgefühl* for his *own* language, has not developed sufficient idiomatic sense of it to avoid the danger of interference. **1938** E. PARTRIDGE *World of Words* II. vi. 163 The *Sprachgefühl*, feeling for speech, exercises a pervasive influence in a language so long cultivated as English. **1953** K. JACKSON *Lang. & Hist. in Early Britain* 682 It may be thought that the language was in some way committed by its *Sprachgefühl* to a penultimate accent. **1976** *Amer. Speech* 1973 XLVIII. 224 Whether this development is associated with the loss of sprachgefühl in a community where the use of a language is declining is a possibility to be considered.

spraddle, *v.* Add: **2.** *trans.* To spread or stretch (one's legs, etc.) wide apart. Also *transf.*
1913 J. LONDON *Son of Sun* vii. 241 He stood with legs spraddled over a large grass basket. **1928** 'BRENT OF BIN BIN' *Up Country* xv. 264 As she walked she spraddled the off hind hoof. **1929** 'SEAMARK' *Down River* i. 6 Let this decrepit tub of yours spraddle her old legs a little faster.
3. The vb.-stem in combination with ppl. adjs., to form adjs., as *spraddle-footed*, *-hipped*, *-legged*. *U.S.*
1935 Z. N. HURSTON *Mules & Men* I. viii. 177 Don't set there all spraddle-legged. **1974** D. SEARS *Lark in Clear Air* ii. 33 They were big, old, spraddle-hipped, spavined bays with a lot of Clyde in them. **1975** J. GORES *Hammett* (1976) xiv. 102 The boy stood spraddle-footed on the porch.

spra·ddled *ppl. a.* (also with *out*: see also quot. 1927); **spraddling** *ppl. a.* (later examples).
1898 H. S. CANFIELD *Maid of Frontier* 89 He rode with the spraddling seat of a man more accustomed to the plow than to the scout's saddle. **1926** E. HEMINGWAY *Sun also Rises* xviii. 230 They held him and lifted him. It was uncomfortable and his legs were spraddled. **1927** *Amer. Speech* Dec. 169 To put on airs or be dudishly dressed was to be 'all spraddled out'. **1930** D. RUNYON in *Collier's* 1 Feb. 46/2 Down he comes all spraddled out. **1935** L. A. G. STRONG *Tuesday Afternoon* 83 Between his spraddling knees he had spread a clean white napkin. **1940** *Harper's Mag.* Oct. 513/2 Every now and then a nigger would come flying out and go sailing through the air..spraddled like a flying squirrel. **1975** J. GORES *Hammett* (1976) xxxii. 221 Laverty's right knee pumped, twice, up between Lynch's spraddled legs.

sprag, *sb.*[3] Add: **2. a.** More widely, any of several devices formerly fitted to motor vehicles to prevent them from running backwards down a hill (see quots.).
1902 A. C. HARMSWORTH et al. *Motor & Motor-Driving* xv. 332 The Sprag..is an adjunct fitted to most cars... The sprag should be dropped before the car actually starts to run backwards. *c* **1915** *Autocar Handbk.* (ed. 6) xiv. 216 The sprag is normally held up clear of the ground by a cord, but when the car is likely to stop on a hill the driver should release the cord in good time, and let the 'devil' drag on the ground. Then directly the car stops, the pointed end of the bar digs into the ground. *Ibid.* 217 Another good form of sprag consists of a strong pawl, which is allowed to trip over ratchet teeth out on a revolving part of the gear... Even with good brakes the one great advantage of a sprag is that it permits the car to be restarted on the steepest hill with both brakes off. **1933** *Motoring Encycl.* 723/2 The sprags often fitted on horse-drawn vehicles..have been revived in a new form on motor vehicles. *Ibid.*, The sprag is arranged at the rear of the gear-box, and consists of a roller and wedge adapted to produce a gripping motion on a drum..which turns with the transmission shaft.
b. *fig.* Cf. SPOKE *sb.* 4 a.
1914 'HIGH JINKS, JR.' *Choice Slang* 21 A sprag in the wheel of progress. **1973** R. DENTRY *Encounter at Kharmel* vii. 111 If you were in the President's shoes, how would you put a sprag in Ziauddin's wheel?

sprag, *v.* Add: **3.** To accost truculently. *Austral. slang.*
1916 C. J. DENNIS *Songs of Sentimental Bloke* 130 *Sprag*, to accost truculently. **1935** L. LUARD *Conquering Seas* iii. 41 'Twas only to save you from getting spragged. *a* **1938** C. J. DENNIS in *Penguin Bk. Austral. Ballads* (1964) 236 A tug named Tyball..Sprags 'em an' makes a start to sling off dirt.

Sprague–Dawley (sprēⁱg,dǭ·li). The names of R. W. *Dawley* (1897–1949) U.S. physical chemist who established the strain, and of his wife, née *Sprague*, used *attrib.* to designate an inbred strain of rat much used in laboratories.
A proprietary name in the U.S.A.
1951 *Proc. Soc. Exper. Biol. & Med.* LXXVII. 635/2 Weanling rats of the Sprague-Dawley (SD) strain have a lower choline requirement..than was observed in rats of the Alabama Experiment Station (AES) strain. **1967** B. S. WOSTMANN et al. in M. L. Conalty *Husbandry Lab. Animals* 195 Germfree rats were of the Sprague-Dawley or Lobund Wistar strains. **1970** *Jrnl. Gen. Psychol.* LXXXIII. 88 The *Ss* were 70 male albino rats of the Sprague Dawley strain. **1978** *Official Gaz.* (U.S. Patent Office) 3 Jan. TM 67/1 Sprague-Dawley. The Mogul Corporation... Pub. 10–11–77. Filed 6–9–77.

sprain, *v.*[1] Add: **2.** *to sprain one's ankle*: (of a woman) to be seduced (and become pregnant); to lose one's virginity. *euphem. Obs.* exc. *Hist.*
1785 F. GROSE *Classical Dict. Vulgar Tongue* s.v. *Ankle*, a girl who is got with child, is said to have sprained her ankle. **1940** M. SADLEIR *Fanny by Gaslight* I. 286 'I suppose you are still—still a ——.'..'I suppose you mean, have I sprained my ankle yet?'

spraing, *sb.* Restrict *Sc.* to sense in Dict. and add: **2.** Also † **sprain.** A disease of potatoes in which they appear sound on the outside but show curved lines of discoloration when cut.
1909 *Jrnl. Board Agric.* XVI. 33 Several complaints have reached the Board respecting the losses caused to potato growers from the ailment known as sprain in potatoes, and it is asserted that cases of it..are causing some anxiety in Scotland and elsewhere. **1929** *Trans. Brit. Mycol. Soc.* XIV. 150 Spraing. (Sprain, Internal Rust Spot.)... Internal brown spot. **1980** F. HOPE in E. Gram et al. *Recognition & Control of Pests & Diseases of Farm Crops* (ed. 3) 155/1 Spraing is thought to be caused by a virus. **1980** *Amat. Gardening* 4 Oct. 12/1 The [potato] crop is affected with a physiological disorder known as spraing.

spraints, *sb. pl.* **b.** Delete *rare* and add: in *sing.* or *collect.* sense. (Later examples.)
1960 G. MAXWELL *Ring of Bright Water* xi. 155 There is a lavatory at every other holt, and the excrement (which is known as 'spraint', and has no offensive odour..) often forms a high pyramidal pile. **1979** *Guardian* 16 Mar. 11/3 A spraint is a blackish smear of digested fishbone and otter-lunch which the animal tends to leave.

sprangly, *a.* (Earlier examples.)
1840 C. F. HOFFMAN *Greyslaer* II. III. i. 103 His great sprangly beard. **1886** *Leslie's Pop. Monthly* XXII. 503/1 We can command a view through their sprangly branches.

spraser, sprasy, varr. *SPRAZER.

sprauncy (sprǭn·(t)si), *a. slang.* Also **sprauntsy, spróncy.** [Of uncertain origin: perh. related to dial. *sprouncey* cheerful (*Eng. Dial. Dict.*).] Smart or showy in appearance or sound of voice.
1957 L. P. HARTLEY *Hireling* xi. 90 She's bought new sprauncy clothes for the children. **1959** H. HOBSON *Mission House Murder* viii. 57 That sprauncy Girton voice of hers. **1969** *Guardian* 4 Feb. 7/2 The 'sprauntsy' (showy) antique dealers. **1971** G. EWART *Gavin Ewart Show* I. 21 Two sprauncy birds inhibit the parkway. **1976** 'P. B. YUILL' *Hazell & Menacing Jester* xiii. 142 They pay sixty grand to live in a sproncy little street like this.

sprawl, *sb.* Add: **1. d.** The straggling expansion of an indeterminate urban or industrial environment into the adjoining countryside; the area of this advancement. Freq. with defining adj. (see *suburban* and *urban sprawl* at first element in Suppl.).
1955 *Times* 23 Aug. 10/2 It is sad to think that London's great sprawl will inevitably engulf us sooner or later, no matter how many 'green belts' are interposed in the meantime between the colossus and ourselves. **1958** *Listener* 23 Oct. 641/1 As the new industrial zones came to life on the edges of the built-up areas, they frequently appeared to be no more than an extension of the old industrial sprawl. **1967** *Ibid.* 3 Aug. 147/2 Planning so far has failed to contain sprawl. **1971** P. GRESSWELL *Environment* 122 Green Belt policy stopped sprawl in crucial places at a crucial time. **1977** *Listener* (N.Z.) 15 Jan. 9/2 It's a sad reflection on our society that 'suburban' has become a dirty word, synonymous with 'subtopia' and responsible for many urban problems from neurosis to sprawl.

spraw·lingly, *adv.* [f. SPRAWLING *ppl. a.* + -LY².] In a sprawling manner.
1921 *Spectator* 7 May 585/2 Gauntly outlined, white and still, Three haystacks peer above the hill; Three agèd rakes thrust sprawlingly Fantastic tendons to the sky. **1980** *Economist* 15 Mar. 104/1 Several books of sociology, history, politics and literary criticism uneasily brought together into one weightily erudite but sprawlingly inconclusive survey.

spray, *sb.*[1] **1. c.** Delete † and add later examples.
1870 HARDY *Satires of Circumstance* (1914) 20 When I set out for Lyonnesse, A hundred miles away, The rime was on the spray. **1893** F. THOMPSON *Poems* 66 Oh, there were flowers in Storrington On the turf and on the spray. **1921** W. DE LA MARE *Veil* 19 Thrush and robin perched mute on spray.
2. d. A brooch or clip fashioned in imitation of a bouquet of flowers, or of a twig with fruit or foliage. In full, *spray brooch.*
1803 C. WILMOT *Jrnl.* 6 Mar. in T. U. Sadleir *Irish Peer on Continent* (1920) 142 Necklaces, sprays of brilliants, towering on the head like feathers, diamond nets, combs. **1863** MRS. GASKELL *Dark Night's Work* v. 64 Your pearls..were..handsome..but we must have them re-set; the sprays are old-fashioned. **1939** P. WENTWORTH *Lonesome Road* viii. 50, I should love to give her a diamond spray from Woolworth's. *Ibid.* xii. 73 The oak spray..two diamond oak-leaves and three acorns. **1951** *Catal. of Exhibits, South Bank Exhib., Festival of Britain* 39/1 Ruby and diamond spray brooch. **1966** *Harper's Bazaar* Sept. 76 A pair of Victorian diamond sprays in the hair..£900. **1979** *Country Life* 11 Oct. Suppl. p.v., Modern diamond and emerald spray brooch.

spray, *sb.*[2] **2.** For *Med.* read orig. *Med.* and add: **a.** (Earlier and further examples.) Now applied to any jet of (esp. liquid) particles emitted by an atomizer or similar device.
1870 *Brit. Med. Jrnl.* 2 July 21/1 The value of sprays in the treatment of affections of the throat and windpipe ..is much hindered by the inconvenience attending the use of the apparatus... Clarke's [apparatus] produces a fine spray. **1891** KIPLING *Light that Failed* viii. 146, I haven't any spray, and I never leave charcoal unfixed overnight. **1963** R. CARSON *Silent Spring* iii. 23 There were cockroaches in the house..and..a spray containing endrin was used. **1974** A. J. HUXLEY *Plant & Planet* xxviii. 337 Temperate fruit growers may apply fifteen different sprays in a season.
3. b. *spray-based, -clouded, -dabbled, -haired.*
1895 W. B. YEATS *Poems* 210 With blown, spray-dabbled hair. **1930** R. CAMPBELL *Adamastor* 74 The rocks, spray-clouded, are your signal guns. **1939** DYLAN THOMAS *Map of Love* 4 Spray-based and rock-chested sea. **1956** P. LARKIN *Less Deceived* 38 Rain patters on a floor that tilts and sighs. Fast-running floors, collapsing into hollows, Tower suddenly, spray-haired.
c. *spray booth, can, job, nozzle, pump*; **spray-gun**, an apparatus for applying a liquid substance in the form of spray; an atomizer; **spray irrigation**, a form of irrigation in which water is sprayed from pipes running along or above the ground and reaches the surface in the form of droplets; **spray line**, a perforated pipe used in spray irrigation; **spray pond**, a pool over which water is sprayed in a chamber through which air is passed, so as to cool the air or humidify it; **spray refining, steel-making**, a continuous method of making steel in which molten iron falling in a stream is atomized by jets of oxygen and flux that combine with impurities in the droplets; hence **spray steelmaker**, an installation in which spray steelmaking is carried out; **spray tower**, a hollow tower in which a liquid is made to fall as a spray, e.g. to cool it or to bring it into contact with a gas.
1959 *Times* 17 Feb. 2/3 The manufacture of Industrial Equipment such as Ovens, Spraybooths. **1975** 'R. BUTLER' *Where all Girls are Sweeter* vi. 63 A man was spraying a car in a spray booth. **1972** *Times* 14 Dec. 9/5 A higgledy-piggledy mixture of colours..all laid on with spray cans and felt-tipped marker pens. **1980** *Times Lit. Suppl.* 5 Sept. 972/4 Not only are felt-pens and spray-cans rare in Africa, but so is literacy. **1920** *Brass World* Dec. 343 (*caption*) A new spray gun invention. **1944** R. CHANDLER *Five Murderers* 31 A woman..was popping at aphis [*sic*] with a spray-gun. **1956** 'B. BUCKINGHAM' *Three Bad Nights* xiv. 122 Battered old spray-guns with which they were sprinkling the plants. **1974** 'S. WOODS' *Done to Death* 29 Mr Gillespie was pottering about in his garden with a green spray-gun in his hand. **1931** *Circular U.S. Dept. Agric.* No. 195. 1 Recently spray-irrigation equipment, designed for the irrigation of general farm crops, has been developed in Germany. **1950** *N.Z. Jrnl. Agric.* LXXX. 520/1 Centrifugal pumps are most commonly used for spray irrigation. **1974** WITHERS & VIPOND *Irrigation* ii. 55 Spray irrigation..is suitable for use in temperatures down to −9°C (16°F). **1963** L. DEIGHTON *Horse under Water* xvii. 69 The last rays of the sun did a spray job on one side of da Cunha's bony head. **1971** *Engineering* Apr. 95/2 (Advt.), Your problem will be solved by an enthusiastic team well versed in the study of Spray Characteristics and Patterns for any particular Sprayjob. **1961** H. J. HINE *Dict. Agric. Engin.* 130 It is possible to divide up the methods of overhead application to field soil into spray lines, sprinklers and rainers. **1974** WITHERS & VIPOND *Irrigation* ii. 54 A more elaborate spray line consists of a water pipe, about 30 mm diameter, perforated in one quadrant along its length, and mounted on light tressles. **1919** FRASER & JONES *Motor Vehicles & their Engines* viii. 65 The suction created by the rush of air past the spray nozzle causes the gasoline to be delivered to the mixing chamber in a fine spray. **1966** GURNEY & COTTER *Cooling Towers* iii. 62 (*caption*) Typical sections of cooling tower timber distribution system showing header, lateral and porcelain spray nozzle. **1924** L. C. LICHTY *Measurement Natural Gas* III. iv. 349 Two general methods are used to cool the water, namely, the spray pond or cooling tower method. **1951** J. JACKSON *Cooling Towers* ii. 7 Spray ponds are only suitable where a close approach to the wet-bulb temperature is not required; their main use lies in cooling water prior to discharge into a river. **1913** *Chambers's Jrnl.* Jan. 61/2 The stamps are moistened within the machine by a tiny spray pump. **1950** *N.Z. Jrnl. Agric.* May 470/1 A spray pump [for a garden]..may be of bucket or knapsack type according to personal preference. **1967** A. H. COTTRELL *Introd. Metallurgy* xi. 141 Very recently a new steel-making process, spray-refining, has been developed by the British Iron and Steel Research Association. A stream of molten iron from a blast furnace falls through a ring of jets, which breaks it up into droplets,..and a second ring of jets which inject powdered lime and other fluxes. **1975** *Steel USSR* V. 493 The optimum working pressure in the

chamber for carrying out spray refining of pig iron in a vacuum is 150 mmHg. **1965** *Economist* 25 Dec. 1437/2 (*heading*) Spray steelmaking. **1966** *Ibid.* 15 Oct. 293/3 As operated at present, the spray steelmaker is far from continuous: it only runs during part of a blast furnace tap and its capacity is limited by the size of the ladle that is pushed underneath. **1966** *Observer* 16 Oct. 9/1 The revolutionary 'spray' steel-making process, developed by the British Iron and Steel Research Association in Sheffield,..has all the makings of a major technological advance. **1976** *Metals Abstr.* IX. 1750/2 (*heading*) An investigation into oxidation processes occurring during spray steelmaking using naturally alloyed pig iron. **1937** T. K. SHERWOOD *Absorption & Extraction* vi. 168 Spray towers are best suited to the absorption of very soluble gases. **1951** J. JACKSON *Cooling Towers* ii. 7 Like the cooling pond and the spray pond, the spray tower is probably suitable only for easy cooling duties. **1979** A. L. LYDERSEN *Fluid Flow & Heat Transfer* vi. 155 Spray towers are the simplest type of gas scrubbers.

d. Special Comb. relating to natural spraying or the production of spray, as **spray region,** the region at the top of the atmosphere where molecules are so far apart that their paths are determined by gravity and upward moving ones are likely to escape into space; **spray zone,** that area near the sea or a waterfall that is often moistened by spray.

1949 *Jrnl. Brit. Interplanetary Soc.* VIII. 255A While it is generally believed that the Zodiacal Light is due to extra-terrestrial particles, it is possible that the scattering particles are molecules in the 'spray' region, very high up in the Earth's atmosphere. **1963** G. M. B. DOBSON *Exploring Atmosphere* i. 8 The top of this spray region, which is the top of the atmosphere, is quite indefinite. **1946** *Ecology* XXVII. 321/1 These communities of the spray zone are present only in situations either exposed directly to spray or very well protected from desiccation. **1976** *New Phytologist* LXXVI. 361 Two contrasting coastal habitats which create salinity problems for species occupying them are the spray zone and the salt marsh.

spray, *v.*[4] Add: **1. b.** *fig.*

1923 H. G. WELLS *Men Like Gods* III. iv. 284 From some slope above a lark had gone heavenward, spraying sweet notes. **1924** R. CAMPBELL *Flaming Terrapin* ii. 23 The trees came crashing down lengthwise, And sprayed their flustered birds into the skies. **1976** E. DUNPHY *Only a Game?* iv. 125 They were giving us space to come further forward, and giving us room to turn and spray it about.

2. b. *transf.* To subject to a rapid succession or shower of bullets, shot, etc.

1926 T. E. LAWRENCE *Seven Pillars* VI. lxxvii. 404 Wood..got the Indians ready to spray the guard tent. **1977** C. FORBES *Avalanche Express* xv. 152 The man behind the gun..sprayed the Wagon-Lit... A hail of bullets thudded into their compartment.

3. b. Of a male cat: to mark its environment with the smell of its urine, as an attractant to the female.

[**1949** M. C. GAY *How to live with a Cat* xi. 175 A tomcat sprays whiffs of cat smell about in the hope of luring a maiden feline to his moon-bespattered lair.] **1954** L. F. WHITNEY *Compl. Bk. Cat Care* xvi. 199 The males specifically lose their potent and..obnoxious odour, stop spraying and use their pans or boxes. **1967** A. LEWIN *Unaltered Cat* II. iv. 117 If he's frustrated, he'll begin to spray. It's an unpleasant odour, except, of course to a female cat.

sprayable (sprē^i·ăb'l), *a.* [f. SPRAY *v.*[4] + -ABLE.] Capable of being sprayed.

1957 B. A. DOMBROW *Polyurethanes* iv. 67 Heaters.. are necessary to reduce the initial viscosity of the prepolymer to a sprayable consistency. **1972** D. G. SHEPHERD *Aerospace Propulsion* iv. 108 Another possible fuel is powdered metal, for example magnesium or aluminium, mixed with a liquid hydrocarbon to form a pumpable and sprayable slurry.

spray drying (stress variable). Also **spray-drying.** [SPRAY *sb.*[2] or *v.*[4]] A method of drying foodstuffs, ceramic materials, etc., by spraying finely-divided particles of the substance into a current of hot air or another gas, the water in the particles being rapidly evaporated.

1921 *Jrnl. Industr. & Engin. Chem.* May 448/2 Spray drying is comparatively expensive, mainly because it is impossible to utilize all the heat going through the drying chamber. **1946** [see *flash-drying* vbl. sb. s.v. *FLASH *sb.*[2] 14 b]. **1968** *Economist* 15 June 64/3 The dried milk market, so far dominated by Cadbury's 'Marvel' which is the product of an improved spray drying technique, is worth around £3 million a year.

Hence (as a back-formation) **spray-dry** *v. trans.*; **spray-dried** *ppl. a.*; **spray drier,** a machine or installation that performs spray drying.

1921 *Jrnl. Industr. & Engin. Chem.* May 448/2 It is very difficult to give the cost of operating a spray dryer either in dollars or in heat units. **1932** *Bull. Hannah Dairy Res. Inst.* No. 3. 134 Rancidity appeared less frequently in roller-dried than in spray-dried powders. **1945** *Biochem. Jrnl.* XXXIX. p. xxvi, We have examined ..the biological value of the proteins (nitrogen) of a sample of spray dried milk manufactured in 1939. **1950** *Thorpe's Dict. Applied Chem.* (ed. 4) x. 197/2 The essential features in spray-drying eggs are the avoidance of scorching..and the production of a powder containing not more, and preferably less, than 5% moisture. **1961** M. HYNES *Med. Bacteriol.* (ed. 7) xii. 196 More than 10 per cent of imported spray-dried egg contain live *Salmonellæ*. **1967** M. CHANDLER *Ceramics in Mod. World* ii. 62 The spray dryer consists of a cylindrical drum..with a conical outlet at the bottom. **1971** *Sci. Amer.* Oct. 5/3 (Advt.), Our engineers solved the..problem..by spray-drying it [*sc.* powdered ceramic] in a blast of hot air. **1979** A. L. LYDERSEN *Fluid Flow & Heat Transfer* vi. 167 A spray dryer for detergent containing 45 weight% water.

sprayman (sprē^i·mæn). Also **spray-man.** [f. SPRAY *v.*[4] + MAN *sb.*[1]] A person who sprays crops with insecticide or the like.

1959 *Bull. World Health Organization* XX. 23 No clinical symptoms of dieldrin poisoning have been observed among the teams of spray-men. **1969** W. F. DURHAM in Miller & Berg *Chem. Fallout* xxiii. 439 Both respiratory and dermal exposure of spraymen were greater for day than for nocturnal spraying. **1973** J. J. MCKELVEY *Man against Tsetse* iii. 190 The spraymen walked along the outer margins of the vegetation on each river bank.

spray-on (sprē^i·ǫn), *a.* [f. SPRAY *v.*[4] + ON *adv.*] Of a liquid substance: that is applied in the form of spray. Also of the container.

1959 *Wall St. Jrnl.* 3 July (Eastern ed.) 13/4 The company also reports brisk sales of its new aerosol package spray-on cans of enamel. **1965** *Harper's Bazaar* Dec. 89/1 Spray-on fragrance flacons combine luxury with efficiency of application. **1976** R. RENDELL *Demon in my View* ii. 19 Arthur still felt guilty about using spray-on polish instead of the old-fashioned wax kind.

spray-painting (stress variable). [SPRAY *sb.*[2] or *v.*[4]] The application of paint in the form of spray.

[**1902**: see *painting-machine* s.v. *PAINTING *vbl. sb.* 6.] **1921** C. W. TERRY *Practical Motor Body Building* xliii. 310 Spray painting by compressed air is a system followed by many of the large modern motor car builders. **1934** *Archit. Rev.* LXXV. 12/2 As a constructivist painter Moholy-Nagy was the first to..employ spray-painting to secure more exact chromatic effects. **1968** J. IRONSIDE *Fashion Alphabet* 229 *Flocking.* This is a method of applying patterns or dots to fabric... The method is rather similar to spray-painting. **1978** *N.Y. Times* 30 Mar. C13/3 (Advt.), French polishing and spray painting for piano refinishing.

Hence (as a back-formation) **spray-paint** *v. trans.*, to paint (a surface) by means of a spray; also as *sb.*, paint that is applied thus; **spray-painted** *ppl. a.*

1928 *Daily Express* 5 Oct. 2/1 A new base-material with which the car is covered, and which can be spray-painted to any finish desired by the customer. **1973** 'E. MCBAIN' *Hail to Chief* iv. 51 The decrepit brick building..had been spray-painted with graffiti. **1975** B. GARFIELD *Hopscotch* x. 97 He spent the next hour buying..automobile spray-paint. **1975** *Listener* 16 Oct. 491/3 Political posters and spray-painted slogans on every square inch of stone.

sprazer (sprā·zəɪ). *slang.* Also **spraser, sprasy, sprazey,** etc. [ad. Shelta *sprazi.*] Sixpence; a sixpenny piece. Cf. *SPROWSIE.

1931 [see *HALF *sb.* 6 i]. **1934** [see *HOLE *sb.* 2 d]. **1936** J. CURTIS *Gilt Kid* xvii. 175 I'll..let you have the odd twenty-seven [pounds] and a sprazer. **1939** J. B. PRIESTLEY *Let People Sing* x. 257 See if we can't take another spraser or two from the punters. **1961** *John o' London's* 30 Nov. 610/3 Sixpence—*tanner, spraf, sprarsy.*

spread, *sb.* Add: **I. 2. e.** *Diamond-cutting.* The width of a stone considered in proportion to its depth.

1813 J. MAWE *Treat. Diamonds* i. 47 The artist..has to examine carefully, in what direction the stone may be cut, so as to afford the greatest breadth, or *spread* as it is technically termed. **1930** W. R. CATTELLE *Precious Stones* 62 Since the trade have found how important it is to have a proper 'spread' to the stone..there has been a tendency to demand stones too shallow for the best results.

† **f.** *Aeronaut.* = *SPAN *sb.*[1] 5 d. *Obs.*

1894 *To-Day* II. 171/2 The wings have a spread of twenty yards square. **1909** A. BERGET *Conquest of Air* 188 The spread of the wings is 10·20 metres. **1912** C. B. HAYWARD *Pract. Aeronaut.* 262 The ratio of spread to depth (aspect ratio) of the monoplanes is usually less than that of biplanes.

g. *Econ.* The difference between two rates or prices.

1919 A. C. WHITAKER *Foreign Exchange* xii. 369 The spread between the local and the foreign money rates. **1928** *Britain's Industr. Future* (*Liberal Industr. Inquiry*) IV. xxiv. § 7.331 The Linlithgow Committee..came to the conclusion that 'the spread between the producer's and the consumer's prices is unjustifiably wide'. **1938** *Sun* (Baltimore) 8 June 6/1 Charges of price-cutting came into the open at a hearing May 19 on distributors' request for a wider 'spread' between the prices they paid for milk and those for which they sold it. **1978** *N.Y. Times* 29 Mar. B2/1 But adding to the rise in farm beef prices is the widening spread between what a cattle raiser gets for a steer and what a roast costs in the supermarket.

h. The degree or manner of variation of a quantity among the members of a population or sample.

1929 *Jrnl. du Conseil* IV. 219 It has hitherto been the practice to employ such statistical methods as finding the mean length, median length, or semi-inter-quartile range in dealing with the 'spread' of length frequency groups. **1957** *Practical Wireless* XXXIII. 696/2 The current gain of the first stage transistor has been quoted as about 50 times, but it could be as low as 30 times, due to manufacturing spread. **1974** *Listener* 7 Nov. 595/2 Now there is a more even spread of intelligence and the skew in the graph is at both ends.

i. The expansion of a person's girth, esp. at middle age; paunchiness. Also, an example of this. Usu. in phr. *middle-aged spread*: see *MIDDLE-AGED *a.* 1 b. *colloq.*

1930 *Field* 29 Nov. 775/2 An older woman..middle-aged, with, possibly, a 'spread'. **1931,** etc. [see *MIDDLE-AGED *a.* 1 b]. **1976** N. THORNBURG *Cutter & Bone* iv. 86 Swanson could have passed for a decade older, having already achieved a comfortable middle-aged spread.

3. c. A ranch, esp. for raising cattle; a large farm. Also *fig.* orig. and chiefly *U.S.*

1927 W. JAMES *Cow Country* 67 He'd paid a big price for the said spread, and he was lord and master there sure enough. **1947** *Trail Riders Bull.* Feb. 20/1, I wuz top bronc buster for the Tumblin' L spread. **1963** R. D. SYMONS *Many Trails* iii. 25 So he had a few dollars coming in, and could see his way, as he would have said, to running a 'spread'. **1966** G. DURRELL *Two in Bush* vi. 186 Harry, together with Bevan Bowan, took us out to a 'spread' not far from Canberra (a tiny little smallholding of some 200,000 acres) on which they were investigating another facet of the kangaroo's biology. **1973** J. WAINWRIGHT *Devil you Don't* 30 'The Ponderosa' was his spread and no cheap, jumped up, fiddle-foot was gonna muscle in. **1981** J. BEECHING *Death of Terrorist* iii. 34 He thought of his ranch up in Texas. 'Not a big spread,' he said modestly.

d. *Geol.* A relatively thin sedimentary deposit.

1956 A. L. ARMSTRONG in D. L. Linton *Sheffield* vi. 90 It is from these beds that the sands and gravels of the lower terraces and valley spreads were mainly derived. **1977** *Antiquaries Jrnl.* LVII. 187 Some sarsens..could be derived from chalk or Greensand as could the soliflucted spread in the Vale of Pewsey.

e. *Cytology.* A microscopic preparation (as a smear or a squash) in which material is spread for observation rather than thin-sectioned, esp. for the purpose of showing chromosomes at metaphase.

1963 *Stain Technol.* XXXVIII. 284 Heteroploidy was not observed in any of the spreads, unlike those observed in long term cultures of rabbit endothelial cells. **1968** *Brit. Med. Bull.* XXIV. 261/2 Typical spreads produced in her laboratory show metaphase material in about one of every 50 fields of 100 × 100 µ. **1978** *Nature* 23 Mar. 325/1 Figure 2 shows the distribution of silver grains in autoradiograms of human metaphase chromosome spreads.

4. d. *Billiards.* A rebound of a cue ball from the object ball at a considerable angle from its former course. *U.S.*

1858 M. PHELAN *Game of Billiards* (ed. 3) 102 To effect a 'spread' it is not necessary to hit the object-ball so far off from the centre as would appear at the first glance. **1913** M. DALY *Daly's Billiard Bk.* iii. 46 Try the same plan for the dead follow and the dead 'spread' (wide angle carom).

II. 6. b. Any substance suitable for spreading on bread to make it tasty, such as paste or jam. orig. *U.S.*

1866 *Hours at Home* III. 507/2 A late rebel told me that, while with Lee upon the Gettysburgh campaign, he went to a farm-house one day and demanded some 'spread', as they call marmalade in that matter-of-fact country. **1886** F. R. STOCKTON *Casting away of Mrs. Lecks* 40 There was some sort of jam left at the bottom, so that the one who gets the last biscuit will have somethin' of a little spread on it. *c* **1938,** etc. [see *sandwich spread* s.v. *SANDWICH *sb.*[2] 3]. **1962** M. DUFFY *That's how it Was* xiii. 107, I had to..mix up some chocolate spread from cocoa, sugar and a little milk. **1972** *Daily Tel.* 11 Nov. 2/7 There were increases of 3·41 per cent in the prices of jams, honey, and spreads.

9. An article or advertisement displayed prominently in a newspaper or periodical; *spec.* printed matter occupying two facing pages. Also *fig.* orig. *U.S.*

[**1858** O. W. HOLMES *Autocrat of Breakf.-Table* 131 One gives a 'spread' on lines, and the other on paper—that is all.] **1877** *Harper's Mag.* Dec. 50/1 His remarkable ability is best seen when occasion arises for a 'spread'. **1924** in WEBSTER. **1931** *Week-End Rev.* 7 Nov. 563/2 The inclusion of a four-page 'spread', printed in two colours. **1940** [see *centre spread* s.v. *CENTRE *sb.* 19]. **1951** M. MCLUHAN *Mech. Bride* (1967) 61/1 Another full-page spread shows a threesome in a panic. **1956** H. KURNITZ *Invasion of Privacy* xviii. 117 The afternoon papers, and the late radio broadcasts..had given the Morley case a big spread. **1969** A. GLYN *Dragon Variation* viii. 238 You'll give the match a good spread in your papers, won't you, Paul? **1972** D. LEES *Zodiac* 7 Get a centre page spread with pictures.

10. *U.S. Stock Exchange.* A contract combining the option of buying shares of stock within a specified time, at a specified price above that prevailing when the contract is signed, and the option of selling shares of the same stock within the same time, at a specified price below that prevailing when the contract is signed. Cf. *SPREAD EAGLE *sb.* 3* b, STRADDLE *sb.* 2 a.

1879 in WEBSTER. **1885** *Harper's Mag.* Nov. 844/1 A 'straddle'..differs from the 'spread' in that the market price at the time of purchase is filled into the latter, while in the 'straddle' the price may vary from that of the market, by agreement or otherwise. **1900** S. A. NELSON *ABC of Wall St.* 160 *Spread.* This is a double stock privilege which entitles the holder to the right to deliver or demand a certain amount of stock on specified terms, or grain price differences between different options, or between the same option in different cities, or between the put and call price. **1957** Clark & Gottfried *University Dict. Business & Finance* (1967) 332/1 If a stock is selling at 100, a speculator may buy a *spread* option for $5 per share, with a *spread* in the buying and selling prices of 5 points up or down. Thus, if the stock later goes below 90 (including the 5 point *spread* and the 5 point cost of the option), it can be sold at a profit. **1970** Sloan & Zurcher *Dict. Econ.* (ed. 5) 412 *Spread*, as applied to security trading, two separate options, a *put*..specifying a price below the prevailing market, and a *call*..specifying a price above the prevailing market, both options applying to the same security and expiring on the same date.

11. *Bridge.* (See quot. 1929.) Cf. *spread *v.* 19.

1929 M. C. Work *Compl. Contract Bridge* 245 *Spread*, a hand which Declarer can show in proof of his ability to win all thirteen tricks. **1977** *Field* 13 Jan. 65/1 Only the duplication of values prevented the contract from being a spread.

12. a. *Geol.* An array of seismometers used simultaneously to detect and record disturbances resulting from a single shot in a geophysical survey.

1942 *Geophysics* VII. 138 The problem of the wide shot spread is much more complicated than that of the vertical shot. **1945** *Ibid.* X. 351 To correct for these weathering variations a series of short refraction shots was taken at each recording spread. **1962** *Jrnl. Geophysical Res.* LXVII. 2852/2 The method used was to keep the geophone spread fixed and to move the shot away from the spread. **1977** A. Hallam *Planet Earth* 29/1 Large spreads of seismometers have recently been set up, one of the largest being in Norway.

b. *Oil Industry.* The total assemblage of men and equipment needed for a particular job, esp. laying a pipeline.

1974 *Petroleum Rev.* XXVIII. 765/1 The prospect of lay barge spreads capable of operating in depths of up to 1,000 feet certainly posed problems. **1975** *North Sea Background Notes* (Brit. Petroleum Co.) 32 The land line was laid in three spreads, two working between the Tay and Cruden Bay and the third from the Tay to Grangemouth. **1976** *Offshore Platforms & Pipelining* 175/3 Two of the pipeline spreads will use automatic welding.

spread, *v.* Add: **I. 1. g.** *Mus.* To play (the notes of a chord or a chord itself) in rapid succession instead of simultaneously.

1873 [in Dict., sense 1 a]. **1938** *Oxf. Compan. Mus.* 48/1 *Arpeggiare* (It.), to play harpwise, i.e. (on the piano, etc.) to spread the notes of a chord, from the bottom up. **1953** W. Emery *Bach's Ornaments* 102 On the harpsichord or clavichord, a chord is often very much more effective when spread than when played *sec.* **1977** *Gramophone* June 68/2 The violinist also spreads some of his two-note chords.

4. e. To record or enter *on* a documentary record. *U.S.*

1845 J. F. Cooper *Chainbearer* II. iv. 44 It will greatly aid the reader..if I spread on the record the language that passed between my late agent and..his confidant. **1894** T. F. Robley *Hist. Bourbon County, Kansas* 184 Councilmen Dimon, White and Drake caused the following order to be spread upon the minutes. **1910** *Atlantic Monthly* Feb. 231 Achievements in that field are naturally not spread on the record as are exploits in railway financiering. **1931** *Randolph Enterprise* (Elkins, W. Va.) 26 Mar. 1/5 Resolved that a copy of these resolutions be sent to the family, a copy spread on the minutes of the lodge, [etc.].

7. b. (Earlier *absol.* examples.)

1860 J. G. Holland *Miss Gilbert's Career* x. 173 He sort o' stands round, and spreads, and lets off all the big talk he hears. **1884** 'Mark Twain' *Huck. Finn* xxi. 206 He howled, and spread around, and swelled up his chest.

19. *Bridge.* (See quot. 1964.) Cf. *spread *sb.* 11.

1929 M. C. Work *Compl. Contract Bridge* 245 *Spread*, to 'claim the rest'. **1964** Frey & Truscott *Official Encycl. Bridge* 520/1 *Spread*,..verb: to spread the hand, either as a claim or as a concession of the remaining tricks.

spread, *ppl. a.* Add: **1. d.** *Phonetics.* Pronounced with the lips drawn out rather than rounded; unrounded.

1902 [see *fan consonant* s.v. *fan *sb.*[1] 11]. **1965** *Language* XLI. 26 The spread phonemes /ī/ and /ẽi/ are realized in the back allophones.

3. spread head *U.S. Journalism*, a display heading; hence **spread-headed** *a.*

1907 *Everybody's Mag.* XVI. 321 There is no such thing as fashion in dogs, despite the frequent 'spread heads'. **1923** O. G. Villard *Some Newspapers & Newspapermen* 152 It has not been able to rise without the vulgar comic section or the Sunday pictorial, and the usual spread-headed Sunday features.

4. In parasynthetic combinations, as *spread-kneed, -legged, -lipped, -winged* adjs.

1932 W. Faulkner *Light in August* vii. 140 McEachern lowered himself stiffly to the top of a feed box, spread-kneed, one hand on his knee and the silver watch in the other palm. **1969** L. Michaels *Going Places* 21, I stood spread-legged, bolt naked. **1973** G. W. Turner *Stylistics* ii. 63 If Australians tend to use spread-lipped vowels.., they perhaps seem matey fellows. **1936** R. Campbell *Mithraic Emblems* 89 A spread-winged phœnix from its ash The Cross remained against the sky. **1972** R. Adams *Watership Down* xlv. 375 Four partridges..sailed down, spread-winged, into the field.

Hence **sprea:dou·tness** *rare*, the quality or condition of being spread out.

1879 W. James in *Mind* IV. 339 Since the essences of things are as a matter of fact spread out and disseminated through the whole extent of time and space, it is in their spread-outness and alternation that he [*sc.* the entire man] will enjoy them. **1915** G. F. Stout *Man. Psychol.* (ed. 3) II. i. 214 There is another inseparable character belonging to many kinds of sensation, though, probably, not to all, which may be called Extensity or extensiveness or diffusion or 'spreadoutness'.

spreadable (spre·dăb'l), *a.* [f. Spread *v.* + -able.] That can be easily spread: esp. of butter, etc. So **spreadabi·lity.**

1940 'Plastes' *Plastics in Industry* xi. 165 The easy spreadability of animal and vegetable glues is a very important property. **1962** P. Bracken *I hate to housekeep Bk.* vi. 65 The moisture in the onion turns this into a good spreadable spread for sandwiches or canapés. **1971** *Nature* 26 Nov. 238/1 The causes of cracks in cheese, poor spreadability in butter. **1979** J. Rathbone *Euro-Killers* i. 10 The butter was..cool but spreadable.

spread eagle, *sb.* Add: **3*. a.** *U.S. Stock Exchange.* An operation by which a broker agrees to buy shares of stock within a specified time at a specified price, and sells the option of buying shares of the same stock within the same time at a higher price. **b.** = *spread *sb.* 10. Cf. Straddle *sb.* 2 a.

1857 *Merchants' Mag.* XXXVII. 136 The buyer can call when he pleases, which would compel the 'spread eagle' operator to deliver. **1870** J. K. Medbery *Men & Myst. Wall St.* 86 One modification of this is the Spread Eagle, formerly a highly popular style of speculation with capitalists who had plenty of money and a wide-awake broker. **1910** *Encycl. Brit.* V. 55/1 A combined option of either calling or putting is termed a 'straddle', and sometimes on the American stock exchange a 'spread-eagle'.

6. quasi-*adv.* Like a spread eagle, with arms and legs outstretched.

1922 Joyce *Ulysses* 492 A blond feeble goosefat whore ..lolls spreadeagle in the sofacorner. **1954** *Sun* (Baltimore) 16 Jan. 12/2 He told the two men to stand 'spread eagle' against the wall of a building while Joseph L. Klingenberg..frisked them. **1973** W. H. Hallahan *Ross Forgery* iv. 59 Ross stripped the klutz of all his clothes and staked him spread-eagle to the ground under a tropical sun.

spread-eagle, *v.* Add: Also **spreadeagle.**

2. b. (Earlier and later examples.)

1887 *N. & Q.* 1 Oct. 278/2 Cod—as well as haddock and ling..may be seen spread-eagled across transverse sticks to dry. **1955** J. P. Donleavy *Ginger Man* xxvi. 252 The kangaroo fell spread-eagled to the floor. **1976** 'D. Halliday' *Dolly & Nanny Bird* v. 65 He spreadeagled a broad, powerful hand and clenched Johnson's in it.

c. (Earlier and later examples in *Cricket.*)

1887 *Cricket* 24 Nov. 460/2 A high one from Miss Tompkins spread-eagled Miss White's wicket. **1955** *Times* 15 June 6/3 McDonald added only 12 runs in 65 minutes before his stumps were spreadeagled by Worrell.

Hence **spread-eagled** *ppl. a.*

1940 L. MacNeice *Last Ditch* 21 Light on her feet and gentle with her fingers; Put on a little flesh, became an easy Spreadeagled beauty for Renaissance painters. **1982** B. Fantoni *Stickman* xxiii. 161 Stepping over Lonnie's spread-eagled body, I lit a cigarette.

spreader. Add: **I. 4. d.** = *lifting beam* s.v. *lifting *vbl. sb.* 2 b. Also *spreader beam.*

1960 S. P. Oppenheimer *Erecting Structural Steel* vii. 88 Slings having a center ring and known as spreaders or bridle slings are used. *Ibid.*, When a long, thin piece, which might buckle under compression, is to be lifted, an additional heavy spreader beam is used above separate single slings placed at the ends. **1968** W. G. Rapp *Construction of Structural Steel Building Frames* vi. 175 To choke the load with a sling around it one eye is passed through the other, the free eye is then hooked or shackled into the hoisting spreaders on the main load hook. **1970** *Specification for Flat Lifting Slings* (*B.S.I.*) 20 Use a spreader beam or other suitable arrangement to ensure that the slings are as nearly as practicable vertical.

II. 7. A surfactant.

1918 *Jrnl. Econ. Entomol.* XI. 67 The surface tension and specific gravity are probably factors of importance in determining the value of a spreader. **1941** *Nature* 12 Apr. 438/2 The efficiency of..'spreaders' in a given oil may be gauged by the direct measurement of their spreading power against surface contamination in the Adam-Langmuir surface pressure trough. **1963** H. Martin *Insecticide & Fungicide Handbk.* iii. 57 Where high or medium volume is used, the addition to the spray of surface-active 'wetters' or 'spreaders' may be recommended in order to increase the cover obtained.

III. 8. *Comb.*, as **spreader-bar** = Spreader 3; **spreader light,** a light attached to the spreader of a yacht.

1927 C. A. Lindbergh *We* iii. 44 The wheels touched earth..rolled.., sank into the spreader bar and we nosed over. **1954** W. Faulkner *Fable* 222 When they sat up it was together as though a spreader bar connected them. **1968** J. Arnold *Shell Bk. Country Crafts* xi. 166 Between the two horses, the trace-chains were kept steady by a spreader-bar. **1947** *Sun* (Baltimore) 3 July 15/5 The practice of a flashlight on sails as something approaches in the darkness is a good one, the authorities say, and the spreader lights now carried by many sailing yachts is [*sic*] an even better idea. **1977** G. V. Higgins *Dreamland* ix. 96 With the spreader lights on the main-mast on, I took down the mizzen sail.

spreading, *vbl. sb.* Add: **2. spreading-board,** (*a*) a board on which sheep are laid while being shorn (*rare*); (*b*) a setting-board for insect specimens; **spreading factor** *Biol.* = *hyaluronidase.

1874 Hardy *Far from Madding Crowd* I. xxii. 247 The issue of their dialogue was the taking of her hand by the courteous farmer to help her over the spreading-board into the bright May sunlight outside. **1909** in Webster. **1963** V. Nabokov *Gift* ii. 111 To drive a pin smoothly through the insect's thorax, stick it in the cork groove of the spreading board. [**1930** *Science* 14 Nov. 508/2 The ink particles were..spread through a wider area under the influence of the factor.] **1939** *Nature* 9 Dec. 978/2 The occurrence of spreading factor in bacterial filtrates has so far been found to go parallel with their mucinase content. **1978** *Exper. Cell Res.* CXV. 227 Techniques previously developed for the purification of the fetal calf adhesion and spreading factor were directly applied to human serum.

spreading, *ppl. a.* **2. b.** *spreading adder*, substitute for def.: the hog-nosed snake, *Heterodon contortrix*, a harmless snake which characteristically inflates its body, flattens its head, and hisses loudly. Cf. Hog-nose. (Examples.)

1842 J. E. DeKay *Zool. N.Y.* III. 52 The Hog-nosed Snake..is also called Dead Adder, Spreading Adder, Hog-nose and Buckwheat-nose. **1904** R. Stuart *River's Children* 91 Rattlers and copperheads, spreading-adders, moccasins, and conger-eels come up to the island. **1931** W. Faulkner in *Amer. Mercury* Mar. 261/2 Her mouth pursed out like a spreading adder's, like a rubber mouth. **1972** E. Wigginton *Foxfire Bk.* 295 Spreading adder. They tell me they're an awful poisonous snake.

sprea·d-over. Also **spreadover.** [f. Spread *v.* 4 c + Over *prep.*] A system of distributing work or holidays over a period of time; *spec.* an arrangement by which a fixed number of work-hours may be performed at varying times within a given period. Also *attrib.* Cf. *split shift* (*a*) s.v. *split *ppl. a.* 3 a.

1923 *Westm. Gaz.* 14 Apr. 1/2 A 'spread-over' of 44 hours. **1924** *Ibid.* 7 Mar. 1/2 The 'spread-over' system—the performance of eight hours' work any time within twelve hours. **1930** *New Statesman* 27 Dec. 350/2 The Lancashire miners resolved..to work the spreadover. **1963** *Times* 1 June 12/2 There is in most Coventry factories no observance of the Whitsun holiday, the period having been moved to September to allow a better spread-over of holidays. **1976** P. R. White *Planning for Public Transport* v. 104 A substantial number of bus crews.. work 'split' or 'spreadover' shifts, covering both morning and evening peaks. **1978** *Daily Tel.* 21 Mar. 2/8 Supplementary payments bus crews may qualify for, such as spread-over duties, unsocial hours, [etc.].

spreadsheet (spre·dʃīt). *Computers.* [f. Spread *ppl. a.* + Sheet *sb.*[1]] A program that allows any part of a rectangular array of positions or cells to be displayed on a VDU screen, with the contents of any cell able to be specified either independently or in terms of the contents of other cells.

1982 *Micro Software Mag.* May-June 4/1 Software designers have used two distinct methods in their attempt to provide the perfect package for financial modelling on a microcomputer: dynamic on-screen spreadsheet calculations, and the more traditionally processed logic file. **1983** *Daily Tel.* 13 Aug. 18 A good spreadsheet will let you put in all your figures, then just press one specified key and do all the calculations at once producing your completed accounts.

spready, *a.* For † *Obs.*$^{-1}$ read *rare* and add:

1. (Later example.)

1924 R. Hall *Unlit Lamp* v. 30 She looks like a tree... A beech tree? No, that's too spready—a larch tree.

2. Of a meal: plenteous, lavish. Cf. Spread *sb.* 7.

1962 G. Avery *Greatest Gresham* ix. 165 Nice to have a spready tea for once.

3. Spreadable, easily spread.

1974 J. E. Underhill *Wild Berries Pacific Northwest* 19 With a jelly..we..have a product that is very smooth and 'spready'.

‖ **Sprechgesang** (ʃpre·χ^y^gĕza:ŋ). *Mus.* Also **sprechgesang.** [Ger., lit. 'speech song'.] A style of dramatic vocalization intermediate between speech and song. See next.

1925 W. H. Kerridge tr. *Wellesz' Arnold Schönberg* 138 The *Dreimal sieben Gedichte* (*Thrice seven songs*), from Albert Giraud's *Pierrot Lunaire*..are written for a *Sprechgesang* (song-speech), piano, flute.., clarinet.., violin.., and violoncello. **1938** *Oxf. Compan. Mus.* 883/1 'Sprechgesang', the older term, is properly singing tinged with a speaking quality, whereas 'Sprechstimme' is rather speech tinged with a singing quality. **1947** E. Newman *Life Richard Wagner* IV. xxii. 437 There used to be much talk, a generation or so ago, about the so-called *Sprechgesang*—a term apparently designed to make more acceptable to us the canine sounds emitted by some Wagnerian singers. **1959** *Listener* 11 June 1039/3 The Stravinsky sounded tense and its Sprechgesang (or was it perhaps just ordinary muttering) very dramatic. **1978** P. Griffiths *Conc. Hist. Mod. Music* iii. 36 *Pierrot lunaire* is an ambiguous work in many senses. The soloist is required to use Sprechgesang, a mode of vocalization lying between song and speech.

‖ **Sprechstimme** (ʃpre·χʸʃti:mə). *Mus.* Also **sprechstimme.** [Ger. (Grimm, 1871), lit. 'speech voice'.] A term used by Schoenberg to describe the voice of a performer singing according to the principles of *Sprechgesang*; also *loosely*, = prec.

1922 *Music & Lett.* III. 83 *Pierrot Lunaire*..represents the zenith of Schönberg's powers... In a foreword the composer explains that the voice part is to be what he calls a 'Sprechstimme', neither song nor speech, but something in between. **1938** [see *SPRECHGESANG]. **1954** *Grove's Dict. Mus.* (ed. 5) VIII. 26/2 *Sprechstimme*.., a human voice written for by a composer who requires from the performer a delivery according to the principles of *Sprechgesang*. **1961** *Listener* 17 Aug. 257/3 The *Gurrelieder* provided Schönberg with the first occasion to make use of a speaking part that anticipates the *Sprechstimme* of *Pierrot Lunaire* in being in strict rhythms and with a fixed pitch. **1968** *Ibid.* 31 Oct. 591/2 Berg's strict distinction between Schoenbergian *sprechstimme* and half-sung phrases frequently receives cavalier treatment. **1982** *Times Lit. Suppl.* 25 June 693/2 His words are shared out among the whole company, cowled and carrying candles, like a coven going in for *sprechstimme*.

spree, *sb.* Add: **1. a.** *transf.* (Later examples.) Cf. also *shopping, spending spree* under the first element in Suppl.

1955 *Times* 29 Aug. 11/1 What has been described as a profit boom and a dividend spree is being used to foster the idea that wage claims can be advanced one after the other without respite. **1976** J. Snow *Cricket Rebel* 21 A six-hitting spree by Jim Pressdee who..made 115. **1983** *Times* 22 Feb. 17/2 (*heading*) Kellock joins own shares buying spree.

spree *v.* (earlier example); also *trans.*, to spend (money) recklessly; **spreeing** *vbl. sb.* (earlier examples).

1845 in N. E. Eliason *Tarheel Talk* (1956) iv. 137 They both had been spreeing it the evening before with some members of Congress. **1860** Spreeing [see *BUMMING *vbl. sb.*]. **1885** 'Mark Twain' *Let.* 11 Sept. (1917) II. 457 The drunkenness (and sometimes pretty reckless spreeing) ceased before he came East. **1897**——*Following Equator* i. 33 It was the remittance-man's custom to..spree away the rest of his money in a single night. **1907** G. B. Shaw *Let.* 27 July (1972) II. 703 The guarantee fund shall not be drawn upon for current expenses at the Savoy (Barker would spree it on a single scene in Peer Gynt). **1928**——*Intelligent Woman's Guide Socialism* lxiv. 296 They destroy the sense of security which induces the possessors of spare money to invest it instead of spreeing it.

spreeu, var. *SPREW^2.

‖ **spreite** (ʃprəi·tə). *Palæont.* Also **Spreite.** Pl. **spreiten.** [Ger., a layer or lamina, esp. something extending between two supports.] A banded pattern of uncertain origin found in the infill of the burrows of certain fossil invertebrates.

1962 W. Häntzschel in R. C. Moore *Treat. Invertebrate Paleont.* W. 182/2 The vast majority of trace fossils remain unchanged through the geologic eras. This is true for nondescript, smooth furrow-like crawling trails and cylindrical burrows, as well as for more distinctive U-shaped burrows with *Spreite*. *Ibid.* 200/1 *Gyrophyllites*.., vertical shaft from which rosettes of short, simple (feeding) tunnels radiate at different levels, as in a mine; 'leaves' with sculpture of *Spreiten* burrows. **1976** *Nature* 17 June 576/2 The burrow walls are laminated parallel to the long axis of the burrow, and the infill exhibits a cuspate ('spreite') structure.., probably indicating active backfilling by the animal responsible.

sprekelia (sprekī·liă). [mod.L. (L. Heister *Systema Plantarum Generale* (1748) 5), f. the name of J. H. von *Sprekelsen* (d. 1764) who sent bulbs of the plant to Linnæus + -IA^1.] A bulbous plant of the monotypic genus so called, belonging to the family Amaryllidaceæ, native to Mexico, and bearing linear leaves and large crimson flowers; = *jacobæa lily* s.v. *JACOBÆA 2.

1840 *Edwards's Bot. Reg.* XXVI. 33 (*heading*) The Tumbler Sprekelia, shorter-flowered variety. **1962** *Amateur Gardening* 10 Mar. 33/2 Sprekelia..takes us to.. Mexico... The oddly shaped flowers with three erect and three drooping petals are deep crimson. **1975** *Country Life* 16 Jan. 158/3 Dormant sprekelia bulbs will be.. replanted.

Sprengel (ʃpre·ŋ'l). The name of Hermann Johannes Philip *Sprengel* (1834–1906), German-born English chemist, used *attrib.* and in the possessive to denote devices developed by him, as **Sprengel('s) (air, mercury) pump,** a vacuum pump in which exhaustion is produced by trapping bubbles of gas between short columns of mercury falling down a narrow vertical tube; also *absol.*; **Sprengel('s) tube,** a glass U-tube that narrows to a capillary at each end, used to determine the specific gravity of a liquid by weighing the tube when filled with the liquid and then with water at the same temperature.

1868 *Chem. News* 7 Feb. 73/2 Could any one give me information about the dimensions for a Sprengel air pump, and the quantity of mercury required. I wish to use it for exhausting vacuum tubes for a 4-inch spark induction coil. **1868** E. Atkinson tr. *Ganot's Physics* (ed. 3) 144 Sprengel's air pump. **1879** *Jrnl. Chem. Soc.* XXXVI. 197 The use of Sprengel's tube..has given much better results [than a specific gravity bottle]. **1883** *Encycl. Brit.* XVI. 31/1 One [improvement]..is to pass the mercury, before it enters the 'falling' tube, through a bulb in which a good vacuum is maintained, by means of an ordinary air-pump or a second 'Sprengel'. **1890** *Rep. Brit. Assoc. Adv. Sci. 1889* 232 The density of ice and of water at various temperatures may then be determined, a Sprengel tube—which is easily made—being used for warm water. **1906** *Chem. News* 19 Jan. 28/2 It is by the well-known Sprengel mercury pump that his name will be best remembered. **1932** *Proc. R. Soc.* A. CXXXV. 514 A continuously operating Sprengel pump..removed the gas from that part of the apparatus..and delivered it, without loss, into the Töpler pump. **1934** *Analyst* LIX. 172 The under-surface of the arms of the Sprengel tube is made of white enamel glass. **1962** J. Thewlis *Encycl. Dict. Physics* V. 715/1 The Sprengel pump was used extensively in the early days of vacuum experimentation. It is now obsolete, because its rate of working is very low and the ultimate vacuum reached only of the order of 10^{-5} mm mercury.

sprew^2. Add: Also **spreeu, spreo, spreuw.** (Earlier and later examples.)

1795 C. R. Hopson tr. *C. P. Thunberg's Trav. Europe, Africa & Asia* (ed. 2) II. 48 A kind of *Corvus*, (or crow) called *Spreuw*, was found..in great plenty. **1801** [see *FISCAL *sb.* 3]. **1867** E. L. Layard *Birds S. Afr.* 173 The red-wing spreo, aided by finches,..would soon pick the crop [of grapes]. **1913** J. J. Doke *Secret City* 229 'Jolly fine birds, spreeuws,' he said. **1939** S. Cloete *Watch for Dawn* 106 A spreeu dug its beak into some half-dried dung for the fly-worms that were in it. **1961** B. C. Tait *Durban Story* 69 Blue-black sprews flash above incredibly green lawns.

‖ **sprezzatura** (spre:tsatū·ra). [It.] Ease of manner, studied carelessness; the appearance of acting or being done without effort; *spec.* of literary style or performance.

1957 N. Frye *Anat. Criticism* 93 The quality that the Italian critics called *sprezzatura*. **1960** E. H. Gombrich *Art & Illusion* III. vi. 193 *Sprezzatura*, the nonchalance which marks the perfect courtier and the perfect artist. **1960** *Spectator* 14 Oct. 569 The style governed by *sprezzatura*, dash and mandarin neoclassicism. **1973** *Times Lit. Suppl.* 14 Sept. 1063/2 Literary fashion and his own aristocratic *sprezzatura* demanded that he affect an unconcern.

sprig, *sb.*^{1} Add: **2.** Also *spec.* (*N.Z.*), a stud or spike attached to the sole of a boot, esp. in *Sport.*

1930 [implied at *SPRIG *v.*^{1} 1]. **1949** D. M. Davin *Roads from Home* I. ii. 27 John hammered the last tack into a sprig of his football boots. **1972** *Guardian* 11 Nov. 21/5 You look at Sid [Going] when we're changing, he's got sprig (stud) marks all over him. **1981** I. A. Gordon in *N.Z. Listener* 2–8 May, The *sprig* (though it has acquired a new meaning on the football field), was originally a short headless nail.

sprig, *sb.*^{2} Add: **6.** *sprig mould, -muslin.*

1922 Hardy *Late Lyrics & Earlier* 1 And maids come forth sprig-muslin drest. **1951** J. B. Kenny *Compl. Bk. Pottery Making* vii. 123 A sprig mold is a block of plaster with a depression shaped like the ornament in reverse. **1956** G. Heyer (*title*) Sprig muslin. **1976** *Canadian Antiques Collector* (Toronto) Mar.–Apr. 20/1 There were over 22 sprig moulds for making applied decorative relief to pots.

sprig, *v.*^{1} Add: **1.** Also *spec.* (*N.Z.*), to equip (a boot) with sprigs. Cf. *SPRIG *sb.*^{1} 2.

1930 C. V. Grimmett *Getting Wickets* v. 105 Had his boots been properly sprigged, it is probable that he would easily have taken the catch.

sprig, *v.*^{2} Add: **2.** Also *absol.*

1960 H. Powell *Beginner's Bk. Pottery* II. ii. 21 When sprigging, you may find that the small, thin sprigged shapes dry too quickly.

sprigged, *ppl. a.* Add: **1. c.** Of ceramic ware: adorned with, or forming, sprigs or other ornaments in applied relief. Cf. Sprig *sb.*^{2} 4 b.

1756 J. Bowcocke *Acct. Bk.* in L. Jewitt *Ceramic Art Gt. Brit.* (1878) I. vii. 209 Mr. White: 1 imag'd cup and 7 sprig'd chocolates. **1906** R. L. Hobson *Porcelain of All Countries* xx. 190 The 'sprigged' pattern..consists of sprays of Chinese plum. **1960** [see *SPRIG *v.*^{2} 2]. **1971** L. A. Boger *Dict. World Pott. & Porc.* 323/2 *Sprigged ware*, in English ceramics; a contemporary English name given to 18th century wares decorated in applied reliefs principally of flowers, foliage, and stems.

sprigging, *vbl. sb.* Add: **3.** The process of decorating ceramic ware with sprigs or other ornaments in applied relief.

1928 W. B. Honey *Old Eng. Porc.* iii. 63 'Sprigging' is the Staffordshire name for the process of applying these reliefs. **1961** L. G. G. Ramsey *Connoisseur New Guide Antique Eng. Pott., Porc. & Glass* 35 The ornament was obtained by 'luting' to the surface of the pot previously moulded relief-motifs, and by connecting these with 'stems' formed of threads of clay rolled out thin between the hands. This whole process was known as 'sprigging'. **1969** G. Wills *Eng. Pott. & Porc.* 102 What is known to potters as 'sprigging'..was done by using a patterned mould made of plaster. The soft clay was pressed into it and the surplus scraped carefully away.

sprightle (sprəi·t'l), *v. Midland dial.* [Back-formation f. Sprightly *a.*] *intr.* With *up*: to become lively or alert.

1896 G. F. Northall *Warwickshire Word-bk.* 224 *Sprightle up! excl.*, be lively, alert (sprightly). **1920** D. H. Lawrence *Lost Girl* ix. 206 Oh but she sprightles up a bit sometimes.

spring, *sb.*^{1} Add: **I. 4. spring branch** (earlier example); **spring hole, house**: for *U.S.* read *N. Amer.* (later examples).

1823 *Amer. State Papers: Public Lands* (U.S. Congr.) (1834) III. 811 One hundred [acres] on Sweet spring branch, St. Mary's river. **1956** K. M. Wells *By Jumping Cat Bridge* xiv. 83 We followed it, up to the spring hole on the edge of the flat land, a no-good bit of bog hole on the edge of arable land. **1933** H. Allen *Anthony Adverse* ii. 26 A fresh cheese cool from the spring house, and a firm, white loaf caught in a silver clamp provided with a small steel saw in the shape of a dragon's head with teeth amused Maria. **1972** E. Wigginton *Foxfire Bk.* 207 Roll the sausage into balls, pack them in a churn jar..and set in the water trough in your spring house. **1980** *Knoxville* (Tennessee) *News-Sentinel* 6 Apr. c4/5 He also said, 'Milk kept in the *springhouse* will blink and sometimes clabber during a severe thunderstorm or toad-strangler.'

II. 6. h. *ellipt.* A spring salmon (see sense 7 c below).

1913 *Chambers's Jrnl.* Oct. 729/2 Next in value comes the 'spring', the largest fish often weighing sixty-five pounds. **1921** *Daily Colonist* (Victoria, B.C.) 12 Mar. 9/4 In May it [*sc.* the largest cannery in the North] will commence to pack springs. **1975** H. White *Raincoast Chron.* (1976) 222/1 Some men hand trolled springs during the winter.

7. a. *spring-broidery, crop, fever* (earlier example), *fret, shoot* (later example), *-song*; **spring cabbage,** a variety of cabbage that matures in the spring; a cabbage of this variety; **spring greens,** the leaves of young cabbage plants, used as a vegetable; also, a cabbage of a variety that matures in spring; **spring roll,** a Chinese snack consisting of a pancake filled with vegetables and fried in the shape of a roll; **spring training** *Baseball*, pre-season fitness and skills training taking place in spring.

1862 G. M. Hopkins *Vision of Mermaids* (1929), Until it seem'd their father Sea Had gotten him a wreath of sweet Spring-broidery. **1842** J. C. Loudon *Suburban Horticulturist* III. v. 629 This [*sc.* tying up the leaves] may be usefully practised with the earliest spring cabbages. **1900** W. D. Drury *Bk. Gardening* 1196/1 (Index), Spring cabbages. **1979** P. J. Salter et al. *Know & grow Veg.* iv. 104 Spring cabbage..may be short of nitrogen. **1834** *Chambers's Edin. Jrnl.* III. 255/1 The remainder may be ready for spring crop with very little labour. **1962** E. Snow *Red China Today* (1963) xxiii. 174 In July, on a visit to the Agricultural Exhibition Building, I was told by the director that, the spring crop having failed, only phenomenally good weather during August could save the autumn harvest. **1978** *Biol. Abstr.* LXVI. 2091/2 (*heading*) Effect of gibberellic acid..sprays on a spring crop of artichoke. **1843** Lytton *Last of Barons* II. vi. vii. 256 The love of Sibyll was no common girl's spring-fever of sighs and blushes. **1897** Kipling in *Scribner's Mag.* Dec. 679 'Send your road is clear before you when the old Spring-fret comes o'er you. **1969** in *Current Trends in Linguistics* (1972) X. 155 *Spring fret*, animals' feeling of restlessness in the spring. (Ga.). **1919** C. S. Peel *Daily Mail Cookery Bk.* (ed. 2) vii. 134 Vegetables which can be cooked in this manner—cauliflowers, brussels sprouts, spring greens, broccoli tops, [etc.]. **1937** Middleton & Heath *From Garden to Kitchen* iii. 52 Every alternate one can be pulled out and used as spring greens. **1972** Y. Lovelock *Veg. Bk.* I. 69 Spring greens, either hearted or leafy, are gradually superseding the tougher British coleworts. **1943** M. P. Lee *Chinese Cookery* i. 21 Spring rolls... After having made all the rolls, fry them in..hot lard. **1972** D. Bloodworth *Any Number can Play* xxii. 219 Helping himself to a spring roll from a trolley of hot Chinese delicacies. **1946** Dylan Thomas *Deaths & Entrances* 41 Tell his street on its back he stopped a sun And the craters of his eyes grew spring-shoots and fire. **1857** J. W. Davidson *Mendelssohn's Six Bks. Songs without Words* p. ii/1 The *Allegretto Grazioso*, in A major..to which he is believed to have given the name of *Frühlingslied* (Spring Song). **1889** O. Wilde in *Woman's World* II. 111/2 However, if the 'Songs of the Inner Life' are not very successful, the 'Spring Songs' are delightful. **1958** *Anglia* LXXVI. 55 The well-known Spring-song..'Lencten is come wiþ love to toune'. **1897** *Sporting News* 27 Mar. 5/3, I am on my way to join the Boston team at Savannah where the players have all been ordered to report for spring training. **1928** G. H. Ruth *Babe Ruth's Own Book of Baseball* i. 17 In 1925 when I collapsed in Asheville, during the spring training trip, a lot of people figured I'd never put on a uniform again. **1976** *National Observer* (U.S.) 12 June 14/3 Randolph was hardly awed at becoming a Yankee... I came to spring training looking for a job.

c. spring peeper, a very small tree frog, *Hyla crucifer*, of eastern North America; **spring salmon** *N. Amer.*, a Pacific coast salmon that returns from the sea to the river in spring, esp. the chinook, *Oncorhynchus tshawytscha.*

1906, etc. Spring peeper [see *PEEPER^1 2 b]. **1950** *Chicago Tribune* 28 Mar. 14/3 Then there are those who listen for choruses of spring peepers. **1977** *Globe & Mail*

(Toronto) 11 Apr. 8/3, I don't know how many people other than those who live in the country are familiar with one of our prime sounds of spring: the spring peeper. **1850** G. Hines *Voy. round World* 331 In this country [*sc.* America] they are generally distinguished by the names of spring-salmon and fall-salmon. **1905** D. S. Jordan *Introd. Study of Fishes* II. 80 The economic value of any species depends in great part on its being a 'spring salmon'. **1964** G. C. Carl *Some Common Fishes Brit. Columbia* 28 A few mature [Chinook salmon] may enter the larger rivers in late spring or early summer (hence the name 'spring salmon').

8. *spring-filled, -impassioned, -scented.*

1932 W. Faulkner *Light in August* (1933) vii. 138 Into the bleak, clean room the springfilled air blew in fainting gusts. **1881** O. Wilde *Poems* 178 Each spring-impassioned tree Flames into green. **1925** G. Greene *Babbling April* 25 She waits without fear that spring-scented day.

IV. 14. e. *slang* (orig. *U.S.*). An escape or rescue from prison.

1901 'J. Flynt' *World of Graft* ii. 32 It is comparatively easy to make a 'spring' out of the clutches of the law when there is sufficient money to hand around to the various persons with 'pull'. **1923** A. Stringer *Diamond Thieves* xx. 385, I *did* wait. But his swell friends didn't come across wit' any spring. **1968** 'B. Mather' *Springers* xv. 161 We just..waited for what we knew would eventually come. A spring. **1977** F. Ross *Dead Runner* i. 41 Springing some bugger from the Scrubs—O.K. Not easy. ..You can't pull a spring like that without help on the inside.

21. c. *Bootmaking.* The raising or rise of the toe of a last above the ground-line. Also, arch or curvature in the instep.

In quot. 1885 *spec.* applied to the steel support which gives the desired curvature to the boot or shoe.

1885 J. B. Leno *Art of Boot & Shoemaking* viii. 54 The patterns for the springs of large size boots should have a good quarter of an inch left on at sides and bottom. *Ibid.* xix. 145 The spring is attached to the inner sole... Care should be taken in..fixing the metal shield... Instances have occurred in which the spring, through being inadequately shielded, has pierced through the inner sole to the foot. **1902** F. Y. Golding *Manuf. Boots & Shoes* 107 *Spring* is the term used to denote the elevation of the toe of the last... If the substance of the sole be light very little spring is required. *Ibid.*, Sometimes the term 'spring' is used to describe the hollowness or arch of the waist. **1905** E. J. C. Swaysland *Boot & Shoe Design* 20 For light dress work the spring of the toe should be half an inch. **1916** F. Plucknett *Boot & Shoe Manuf.* ii. 17 It is advisable to put spring into the forepart of the last, equal to the amount which the boot would probably acquire in wear. **1935** J. Ball in F. Y. Golding *Boots & Shoes* VI. xi. vi. 39 Spring is the amount of *curve* from the joint to the point of the toe, and whereas a light flexible shoe requires very little, the stouter and stiffer the sole the greater the amount of spring.

V. 24. b. (Later *attrib.* examples.)

1916 *Daily Colonist* (Victoria, B.C.) 23 July 4/6 The mate was on the forecastle head, but outside the rail, when the spring line parted. One end of the big hawser flicked up and smashed the mate's leg. **1975** H. White *Raincoast Chron.* (1976) 156/1 A deck-hand expertly heaves a throwing-line ashore. Somebody catches it, pulls in the steel spring-line from amidships.

25. a. *spring bell* (earlier example), *blind, clip* (earlier example), *heel, mattress* (earlier example), *roller, seat* (earlier example), *stay* (earlier example), *tab, tine, washer.*

1847 *Illustr. London News* 13 Mar. 165/1 There is..a spring-bell, which the Prisoner is to sound when he requires the attendance of an officer. **1835** Dickens in *Evening Chron.* 18 June 3/4 Spring blinds were fitted to the windows. **1889** *Cassell's Bk. Househ.* I. 250/2 Spring blinds, though very nice when they work well, are subject, as an old housekeeper once said, to 'tempers'. **1934** *Cassell's Home Encycl.* 86/2 Automatic or spring blinds are made with a hollow roller. **1871** Spring clip [see Release *sb.*[1] 6 b]. **1897** *Sears, Roebuck Catal.* 194d/2 Chocolate Goat Button, made with spring heel, new opera toe with tip. **1952** M. Allingham *Tiger in Smoke* viii. 140 'He's got nerve.'..'Likewise spring heels and rubber bones.' **1850** Spring mattress [see Mattress[1] 1]. **1821** P. Egan *Life in London* (1822) II. iv. 266 A fine collection of maps, concealed by the cornices of the book-cases, on spring rollers, can be referred to without the least trouble. **1971** *Habitat Catal.* 86/2 Roller blinds ..come complete with spring roller and fixing brackets. **1853** *Heal & Son Catal.: Bedsteads*, Sofas and Couches.. with squab or spring seats. **1745** in J. S. McLennan *Louisbourg* (1918) 177 Ye fore Spring Stay was Shott away. **1942** *Rep. & Memoranda Aeronaut. Res. Committee* No. 2029. 9 Notes on the Spring Tab. R.A.E. Report No. B.A. 1665. (5058.) April, 1941. (Unpublished.) **1969** *Gloss. Aeronaut. & Astronaut. Terms* (*B.S.I.*) v. 10 *Spring tab*, a balance tab, the angular movement of which is geared to the compression or extension of a spring embedded in the main control circuit. **1923** J. R. Bond *Farm Implements & Machinery* v. 49 The simple spring tine as first introduced on the Canadian cultivator had not sufficient strength. **1971** *Farmers Weekly* 19 Mar. 84 The RCM firm offers a choice of tines to fit one basic frame—a normal spring tine..or subsoiler tines. **1912** *Motor Man.* (ed. 14) 206 Spring washers are less effective, but answer well enough for the less vital parts of the mechanism. **1929** *Ibid.* (ed. 26) 20 *Spring washer*, a tempered steel washer cut through at one place and given a 'set' to provide a certain amount of spring. Used under a nut to keep it secure.

c. (Further examples.)

1948 *Penguin Music Mag.* June 54 Sir Henry Wood.. recommended the use of spring-clip mutes which fastened on the music desks. **1972** *Times* 23 Sept. 9/1 These spring-clip pans..spring open when a clip at the side is released. **1897** *Sears, Roebuck Catal.* 192/1 The most handsome and up-to-date spring heel shoe ever placed on the market. **1934** *Heal & Son Catal.: Better Furnit.* 2 'Chassis'..(to fix to spring-mattress frame). **1973** *Sun* 4 Sept. 20/2 (Advt.), Spring roller blinds from £2.94... Inc. all fittings, fringe and pull cords. **1907** Spring-side safety iron [see *Iron *sb.*[1] 4 i]. **1921** W. de la Mare *Memoirs of Midget* viii. 48 She, too, was in black, with a long, springside boot. **1923** J. R. Bond *Farm Implements & Machinery* v. 54 (*caption*) Canadian spring-tine cultivator with corn and grass seed boxes. **1960** *Farmer & Stockbreeder* 15 Mar. 98/3 The spring-tine rake to the rear..is provided to meet necessary safety regulations. *Ibid.* 134/1 It's a Spring-tine Cultivator—Spring-tine Harrow..all in one.

26. c. *spring-doored, -driven, -heeled, -mattressed, -mounted, -tailed, -tined.*

1978 J. Irving *World according to Garp* xv. 311 In a Laundromat... They had opened one of the big spring-doored dryers. **1928** J. E. Haswell *Horology* vii. 78 In the category 'spring-driven' clocks are placed the numerous types which derive their motive power from the energy of a coiled mainspring. **1958** *Times* 20 Aug. 2/6 Zhukov, Pudov, and Ozog all flashed past the now weary Eldon in pursuit of the fleeing, spring-heeled Pole. **1977** *Vogue* Dec. 11/2 'Colleagues' has something inert and passive about it, compared with the spring-heeled activity of 'work mates'. **1920** Galsworthy *In Chancery* ii. vi. 236 His spring-mattressed bed. **1960** E. L. Delmar-Morgan *Cruising Yacht Equipm. & Navigation* 37 If the compass is of the spring-mounted type [etc.]. **1952** Dylan Thomas *Coll. Poems* 174 No springtailed tom in the red hot town. **1938** C. Culpin *Farm Machinery* vii. 95 The spring-tined harrow is a really light cultivator that can be adjusted to produce very variable effects.

d. Special Combs.: **spring bows** = Bow-compass 1; **spring collet** *Engin.*, a tapered collet that is slotted along much of its length, so that when moved in a similarly tapered seat the separate parts are pressed against the stock inside the collet; **spring line**, a line where the water table reaches the surface and along which springs are numerous; **spring-loaded** *a.*, containing a compressed or a stretched spring pressing one part against another; **spring rate** = *rate *sb.*[1] 8 c; **spring sail** (see quot. 1931); **spring sweep** = prec.; **spring-tree**, a saddle-tree with two springs.

1895 *Army & Navy Co-op. Soc. Price List* 686 Spring Bows, set of three, Ink, Pencil, and Divider, in case. **1964** G. Baker *Scale Drawing* 31 Spring-bows do not have knee-joints because the angle of working is so small as not to matter. **1932** W. P. Turner *Machine Tool Work* xiii. 290 The clamping lever..is pushed back, which moves the hollow push sleeve..against the end of the spring collet, forcing it into the nose cap, thus closing the collet on the stock and holding it firmly. **1971** B. Scharf *Engin. & its Lang.* viii. 61 The bore (internal diameter) of the spring collet matches the size and shape of the bar to be gripped. **1932** *Geol. Mag.* LXIX. 407 West of the spring line, thin outcrops of hard ferrugineous sandstone occur in the clays. **1963** L. F. Chitty in Foster & Alcock *Culture & Environment* vii. 181 Other finds suggest an alternative route by the present hillside road over Clee Hill, with its far-extending outlook, keeping above the spring-line to Doddington. **1975** J. G. Evans *Environment Early Man Brit. Isles* vii. 159 Stream courses have a similar effect.., and the well known phenomenon of 'spring-line settlement' is an extreme example of this form of geographical determinism. **1904** *Engin. Rev.* XI. 418/2 Delivery valves..of the mushroom spring-loaded type. **1938** *Brit. Jrnl. Psychol.* XXIX. 40 A spring-loaded pencil..made a record on a sheet of graph paper. **1979** J. Wainwright *Tension* v. 21 The door is spring-loaded. **1957, 1959** Spring rate [see *rate *sb.*[1] 8 c]. **1931** S. P. B. Mais *England of Windmills* p. xxiv, [Andrew] Meikle was ..the inventor of the spring sail. *Ibid.*, The spring sail is made up of wooden shutters, or a canvas-covered wire frame, hinged at one edge and connected to a common sail-rod so that they all open or shut simultaneously. **1971** S. Freese *Windmills & Millwrighting* iv. 58 The framework of spring sails consists of eight or ten sail bars, spaced 3 ft. apart and forming a series of bays, in each of which are three shutters 4 or 5 ft. by 11 in., wood or metal framed, and covered by wood or canvas. **1919** *Jrnl. Franklin Inst.* CLXXXVII. 178 In some cases these shutters worked against the tension of a spring instead of the pull of a weight, and such were known as Meikle's 'spring sweeps'. **1924** *Trans. Newcomen Soc. 1922–3* III. 50 It was desired to fit patent sail regulation instead of 'spring' or 'sail' sweeps. **1963** E. H. Edwards *Saddlery* xiv. 97 In the modern spring tree of correct design..the necessity for a cut-back head is largely obviated by the fact that the head itself is set back at an angle of 45 degrees. **1976** *Horse & Hound* 3 Dec. 31 (Advt.), Parzival all purpose/jumping [saddle]. Again built on the same spring tree, finished in Stubben's special dark brown Sella leather.

spring, *v.*[1] Add: **I. 3. e.** Phr. *Where did you spring from?* and varr., used when someone appears unexpectedly. *colloq.*

1892 I. Zangwill *Childr. Ghetto* III. ii. vi. 109 'Hullo! where did *you* spring from?' It was Raphael who had elicited the exclamation. He suddenly loomed upon the party. **1924** Wodehouse *Leave it to Psmith* ix. 181 'Wherever,' she inquired, 'did you spring from, Ed?' **1932** G. Heyer *Devil's Cub* ix. 141 Several persons hailed him, demanding to know whence he had sprung. **1971** 'S. Woods' *Serpent's Tooth* 154 She was, perhaps, the last person he had expected... 'Where did you spring from?'

f. *U.S. slang.* To escape or be released from arrest or imprisonment.

1904 H. Hapgood *Autobiogr. of Thief* ix. 188 Soon after I was transferred from Sing Sing..a friend..said '..If you can get on Keeper Riley's gallery I think you can spring (escape).' **1926** *Clues* Nov. 162/2 *Spring*, to be released, as from jail or prison. **1955** *Publ. Amer. Dial. Soc.* xxiv. 184 You get snatched in the neck and it costs you twelve hundred to spring. **1962** 'K. Orvis' *Damned & Destroyed* xii. 82 When I sprung..Moss was standing by the prison door.

g. *Austral.* and *U.S. slang.* To pay *for* a treat. Also without const.

1906 E. Dyson *Fact'ry 'Ands* xviii. 250 Feathers..said reproachfully to the Aberdeen engineer..whose turn it was to 'spring': 'Blime, cobber, er yer givin' ther barmaid er perpetual 'oliday 'r what?' **1973** W. McCarthy *Detail* iii. 163 I'm springing for chow tonight and charging it to the Service. **1976** M. Machlin *Pipeline* ix. 107 We'll spring for the booze.

IV. 21. d. Also const. *on* and without following prep.

1876 'Mark Twain' *Tom Sawyer* xxxiv. 265 Old Mr. Jones is going to try to spring something on the people here to-night. **1895** Roberts & Morton *Adventures of Arthur Roberts* xi. 145 'Dinner!' ejaculated Johnson. 'Yes, we shall have to spring the landlady for that at once. That's where she will want a bit of the ready money on account.' **1922** *Ladies' Home Jrnl.* July 72/1 But one day she sprang a surprise; she sprinkled the salad with Dromedary [Shredded Coconut]—*father actually smiled.* **1943** K. Tennant *Ride on Stranger* i. 1 'One I didn't mind,' he admitted. 'Two's plenty. But to spring it on a man like this.' His tone was one of outrage. **1969** *Listener* 14 Aug. 204/1 The official French government spokesman sprang the wholly unexpected news: the franc was to be devalued. **1979** D. Eden *Storrington Papers* xiii. 149 She's a bit upset. I did rather spring it on her.

22. c. Also *fig.*

1930 D. Hammett *Dain Curse* xv. 165 'All right, spring it,' I said, as we sat down in his..living room. 'Any trace of Gabrielle yet?' he asked. 'No. But spring the puzzle. Don't be literary with me, building up to climaxes and the like... Just spread it out for me.' **1980** J. Barnes *Metroland* iii. iv. 161, I started again, more seriously this time, masochistically trying to spring that familiar trigger for panic and terror.

22*. To release (a person) from custody or imprisonment, esp. to contrive such a release by means of bail. Also, to contrive an unlawful escape from prison. *slang* (orig. *U.S.*).

1900 'Flynt' & 'Walton' *Powers that Prey* 62 It cost his push a thousand plunks to spring him from the coppers. **1911** C. B. Chrysler *White Slavery* ix. 70 If you get nicked..you can 'raspberry' the 'bull' and get 'sprung'. **1929** *Sun* (Baltimore) 15 Nov. 1/6, I got sick of him [*sc.* the lawyer] and I started examining the jury myself. They sprung me in five minutes. **1936** J. Steinbeck *In Dubious Battle* iii. 24 They'll give him the works if George doesn't get busy. Tell George to try to spring him for a drunk... If a sanity board ever gets hold of that poor devil, he's in for life. **1963** *Security Gaz.* V. 187/3 Those who may be preparing to 'spring' an inmate. **1967** *Punch* 15 Mar. 375 In the main the British bail system works better than the American one. Over there a professional bondsman..'springs' the accused man for roughly ten per cent of the bail fixed. **1974** *Daily Tel.* 2 Sept. 3 Miss Mary Tyler, the English school-teacher who has spent more than four years in Indian jails awaiting trial, is to be returned to a high security prison this week in case militant Maoists try to 'spring' her. **1977** J. Cheever *Falconer* 13 I'm in cellblock F... Last Tuesday they forgot to spring us for supper. **1980** *Observer* 3 Apr. 9/5 What the Minister has in mind is the 'springing' of the dockers in 1972 following the intervention of that hitherto mysterious figure, the Official Solicitor.

23. c. *Naut.* To move, haul, or swing (a vessel) by means of a spring or cable. Cf. Spring *sb.*[1] 24.

a **1865** W. H. Smyth *Sailor's Word-bk.* (1867) 646 *Sprung*..the ship slued round by means of guys. **1898** S. B. Luce *Text-bk. Seamanship* 217 Ships may be sprung broadside to the wind..for the purpose of better ventilation; or in engagements at anchor, to bring the guns to bear on various points. **1922** C. C. Soule *Naval Terms & Definitions* 69/2 *Spring*, to turn a vessel with a line.

d. *Bootmaking.* To raise (the toe or waist of a last) above the ground-line (see also quot. 1953).

1905 E. J. C. Swaysland *Boot & Shoe Design* iii. 21 An upward curve in the waist of about an eighth of an inch... This is very much less than lasts are usually sprung in the waist. **1916** F. Plucknett *Boot & Shoe Manuf.* ii. 16 Provision should be made for alteration in shape which would be likely to take place in wear.., *e.g.* springing the toe of the last. **1953** A. V. Goodfellow in J. H. Thornton *Textbk. Footwear Manuf.* ii. vii. 89 The effect of springing a pattern, or changing the relationship between one part and another of the same pattern is to lengthen one line and shorten another.

springal(d[1]**.** *β.* (Later example.)

1909 W. Deeping *Red Saint* xl. 340 The King's men who still held the castle, had thrown springalds of fire down upon the houses, setting the thatch ablaze.

‖ **springar** (spri·ŋgăɪ). [Norw.] A Norwegian country-dance in three-four time; also, the music for this dance.

1947 [see *halling]. **1959** *Listener* 2 July 37/1 To achieve the truly national in Norwegian music they should not rest content to quote *springars* and *hallings*, and other dances. **1964** W. G. Raffé *Dict. of Dance* 474/1 *Springar* has nine different steps, and is a dance in which partners show their individual qualities—the man his virility and accomplishment, the girl her skill and grace.

spri·ng-back. Also spring back, springback. **1.** [f. Spring *sb.*[1] 22.] **a.** A folder with a spring clip incorporated in the spine to hold the papers placed in it; also, the clip itself. **b.** = *loose back* s.v. *loose *a.* 9. Also *attrib.*

1895 *Montgomery Ward. Catal.* Spring & Summer 247/1 Music Folio, imitation leather, spring back. **1919** 'ETIENNE' *Strange Tales from Fleet* 64 The stupendous and well-filled 'spring-back', replete with bills, a few receipts, and reams of official correspondence. **1923**, etc. [see *loose back* s.v. *LOOSE *a.* 9]. **1948** G. V. GALWEY *Lift & Drop* vi. 162 Bourne opened the spring-back correspondence file. **1982** P. D. JAMES *Skull beneath Skin* xli. 332 The archives were bound in springback folders.

2. [f. SPRING *v.*^{1}] The capacity to spring flexibly back into position after subjection to pressure. Freq. *attrib.* or as *adj.* Also *fig.*

1945 *Richmond* (Va.) *Times-Dispatch* 2 Mar. 19/3 It [*sc.* a type of compressed wood] can be made..with negligible springback tendencies. **1970** *Motoring Which?* July 116/1 All the arm-type mirrors we included were either spring-back or collapsible. **1972** A. AMIN tr. *Ahmad's No Harvest but Thorn* x. 98 She leapt over the spring-back wooden fence like a young mouse-deer startled by a *pulut* fox. **1973** J. G. TWEEDDALE *Materials Technol.* II. iv. 87 Whenever a material possesses significant elasticity, as in cold working, there is difficulty with spring back. **1975** *N.Z. Jrnl. Agric.* Sept. 55/2 The finished fence..has a feeling of controlled flexibility and springback to true that augurs well for its stock-holding qualities. **1977** *Time* 31 Jan. 40/1 Charles Schultze agrees that the first quarter 'will show a pretty good springback' from the recent economic pause.

spring-board. Add: **2.** (Earlier examples.)

1799 *Times* 1 June 3/4 He positively leaps over a large tilted waggon and four horses..and does not make use of a spring board or trampoline. **1841** THOREAU *Jrnl.* 23 Jan. (1906) I. v. 174 Like the spring-board on which tumblers perform and develop their elasticity.

3. Also *Austral.* and *Canad.*

1934 *Bulletin* (Sydney) 19 Sept. 20/1 Nerves of steel are needed day by day By those who on the springboard stand, while forest monarchs sway. **1972** *Daily Colonist* (Victoria, B.C.) 16 July 6/5 He captured first place in the springboard chop open competition to become Canadian champion. **1975** H. WHITE *Raincoast Chron.* (1976) 102/2 Metal-tipped springboards set in notches were used by the early fallers to climb above the butt-swell [of a tree].

springbok. Add: **2.** *pl.* (usu. with capital initial). **a.** A nickname for a South African national sporting team or touring party. Also *sing.*, one who represents South Africa in international sport.

1906 *S. African News Weekly* 3 Oct. 24/1 A crowd of 9,000..accorded the springboks a great reception as they walked on the field. **1932** *Grocott's Mail* (Grahamstown, S. Afr.) 2 Jan. 3 It cannot be said that many English rugby critics strongly favour England's chance against the Springboks on Saturday. **1959** *Cape Argus* 23 Jan. 19/6 (*heading*) Hockey Springboks train. **1970** *Times* 5 Feb. 9/3 Such an admission would be a natural sequel to our recent failure to protect our Springbok guests from repeated insult and persecution. **1975** *Country Life* 16 Jan. 137/3 The French, who lost both their matches against the Springboks..are often underestimated.

b. A nickname for a contingent of South African troops. Also *sing.*, a South African soldier.

1916 'CAPTAIN' (*title*) With the Springboks in Egypt. **1925** FRASER & GIBBONS *Soldier & Sailor Words* 267 *Springboks*.., the South African contingent in the war. From their badge, the Colonial emblem of a springbok antelope. **1943** J. BURGER *Black Man's Burden* 236 The Springboks (Union troops) are spoken of as the successors to the pioneer Voortrekkers. **1944** *Eastern Province Herald* 25 Aug. 1 The company is doing urgent tank maintenance and repair work for the Fifth and Eighth armies; and the Marshall said that he was impressed by the efficiency of the Springbok 'backroom boys'.

spring chicken. [f. SPRING *sb.*^{1} 6 b.] **1.** A small chicken (esp. a roasting bird); *spec.* one aged between eleven and fourteen weeks and weighing around one and a half kilograms (see also quot. 1958).

1780 J. WOODFORDE *Diary* 13 June (1924) I. 285 We had for dinner..three nice Spring Chicken rosted. **1849** [in Dict. s.v. SPRING *sb.*^{1} 7 a]. **1892** [see *ON *prep.* 20 f]. **1917** *Harrods Gen. Catal.* 1267 Poultry... Chickens (Spring). **1943** L. I. WILDER *These Happy Golden Years* xxi. 191 Ma finished frying a spring chicken while the new potatoes and the peas were cooked. **1958** *Times* 18 Aug. 11/2 The term 'spring chicken' has come to be something of a misnomer for the small bird now available at poulterers...all the year round. It is the product of a specialist industry which has developed this particular type of bird to come to maturity in about 10 weeks only. **1974** *Times* 7 Mar. 13/5 Spring chickens are also in the shops, these are a little older [than *poussins*]—from eight weeks to four months.

2. *fig.* A young person. Freq. in phr. *to be no spring chicken* and varr., to be no longer young. *colloq.* (orig. *U.S.*).

1910 *National Police Gaz.* (U.S.) 6 Aug. 3/1 She wasn't a Spring chicken, by any means, yet she wasn't old. *a* **1911** D. G. PHILLIPS *Susan Lenox* (1917) II. ii. 20 Miss Hinkle was showing her age—and she was 'no spring chicken'. **1964** 'E. MCBAIN' *Axe* vii. 125 I'm not a spring chicken any more... I'm fifty-two years old. **1973** G. BEARE *Snake on Grave* iv. 23 She was no spring chicken any more, she was pushing forty. **1977** *New Yorker* 10 Oct. 131/1 Americans were impressed by Dr. White's prescription whenever they saw a photo of President Eisenhower swinging a golf club or of Dr. White, no spring chicken himself, bent low over the handlebars of his bicycle. **1981** D. M. THOMAS *White Hotel* IV. i. 145 You're just a spring chicken, Lisa dear!

spring-cleaning. (Earlier examples.)

1857 E. M. STONE *Life J. Howland* i. 28 At the annual 'spring cleaning', they discovered a bundle of manuscripts. **1873** H. MARTINEAU *Let.* 6 Mar. in *Autobiogr.* (1897) III. 416 This will be a busy month, with the spring cleaning and whitewashing.

spring-clean *v.*: also *intr.* and as *sb.*, the act of spring-cleaning. Also *transf.* and *fig.*

1849 C. BRONTË *Shirley* I. xi. 289 Very handsome.. these shining brown panels are..but—if you know what a 'Spring-clean' is—very execrable and inhuman. **1908** in *Englische Studien* (1935) Apr. 119 He was helping his wife to 'spring-clean'. **1926** *Socialist Rev.* Dec. 14 House to house inspections [should be] made in the worst areas; in fact, a regular spring-clean of the whole town organised. **1957** L. DURRELL *Justine* I. 23 It was thrown away by Hamid in the course of a spring-clean. **1961** *Countryman* Autumn 515 The exhausted hound awoke and started a relentless spring-clean of his dusty coat. **1978** N. MARSH *Grave Mistake* i. 36, I was helping springclean at the time. **1979** *Guardian* 19 July 14/5 If, early next week, the Carter White House has truly been spring-cleaned..then the Presidency will be much strengthened.

springer^1. Add: **3. a.** (Earlier example.)

1727 J. G. SCHEUCHZER tr. *Kæmpfer's Hist. Japan* I. 137 Tobiwo is what the Dutch call a Springer (Flying-fish) because it leaps out of the water.

4. c. *Naut. slang.* A physical-training instructor in the navy.

1935 *N. & Q.* 29 June 465/1 The officer in charge of physical training was known in my ship..as 'Bunje'. The modern term is 'Springer', both words being descriptive of the acrobatic nature of these duties. **1964** J. HALE *Grudge Fight* vi. 93 The springers all fancy their chance in the training line.

11. *slang.* A racehorse on which the betting odds suddenly shorten (see quot. 1961).

1922 E. WALLACE *Flying Fifty-Five* xi. 67 The 'springer' in the market, the horse that opened at ten to one and came rapidly to five to two. **1961** J. PRESCOT *Case for Hearing* iv. 61 Plenty of punters like to know how the market's moving so that they can go for the 'springer', the horse that suddenly shortens in price because someone in the know slaps a lot of money on at the last possible moment.

Springfield (spri·ŋfīld). The name of *Springfield*, Mass., used *attrib.* and *absol.* to designate firearms produced at the U.S. government armoury located there.

1813 *Niles' Reg.* IV. 87/2 [The] gun..is but one pound and a half heavier than the common Springfield gun. **1849** *Knickerbocker* XXXIII. 3 They carried slung from their saddles the excellent Springfield carbines, loading at the breech. **1866** *Harper's Mag.* Aug. 407/1 'Puss' had been doing his best with his 'Springfield', but all at once he stopped firing. **1904** *Kynoch Jrnl.* Apr.–June 95 The Government of the United States had adopted in 1855 the Springfield rifle—a muzzle-loader, calibre .58 bore, with which a 500 grain bullet & 60 grains of powder were used. **1933** F. B. WILLOUGHBY *Alaskans All* 3 His flannel shirt, high laced boots, the hunting-knife in his belt, and the Springfield by his side, made it difficult for me to realize he was a priest. **1964** M. MCLUHAN *Understanding Media* xxxii. 341 The old-timers who backed the Springfield rifle against perimeter fire. **1976** 'O. JACKS' *Assassination Day* (1978) v. 81 The rifle..was an old World War II American Springfield.

spring garden. Restrict † *Obs.* to senses in Dict. and add: **d.** A garden containing many plants that bloom early in the year.

1883 W. ROBINSON *Eng. Flower Garden* I. p. l/1 What we should counsel those who care for their spring gardens is this: To begin and always to work with a series of nursery beds. **1914** E. A. BOWLES *My Garden in Spring* xvii. 295 If you have enjoyed strolling round the spring garden with me..I hope later on you will accompany me on a second journey to review the summer aspect of the place and plants. **1947** H. NICOLSON *Diary* May (1968) 97 Sissinghurst is lovely The spring-garden has lost its early bloom.

‖**springhaas** (spri·ŋhās). *S. Afr.* Also (with hyphen) **spring-haas.** [Afrikaans, f. Du. *spring* jump, leap + *haas* hare.] The jumping hare, *Pedetes capensis*, a nocturnal rodent with large and powerful hind legs and a hopping gait.

1785 G. FORSTER tr. *Sparrman's Voy. Cape Good Hope* II. 195 By the colonists it [*sc.* the *jerbua Capensis*] is called *berg-haas*, or *spring-haas* (the mountain or bounding hare). **1837** J. E. ALEXANDER *Narr. Voy. W. Afr.* I. 347 One of the party shot a *spring-haas*, or jumping hare, formed like the kangaroo, with very short fore-legs and long hind ones. **1890** A. MARTIN *Home Life on Ostrich Farm* xi. 225 Most uncanny of all the hares is the springhaas. This creature..is never seen in the daytime, and can only be shot on moonlight nights. **1942** S. CLOETE *Hill of Doves* 145 His pulse..is fast and jumping like a springhaas.

spring-hare (spri·ŋhēᵊɹ). Also **springhare, spring hare.** [Partial tr. Afrikaans *spring-haas*: see prec.] = *SPRINGHAAS.

1822 W. J. BURCHELL *Trav. Interior S. Afr.* I. 343 Besides the holes of the Aardvark, those of the Springhaas (Springhare)..were very frequent. **1853** F. GALTON *Trop. S. Afr.* ix. 281 The spring-hare..is a creature about two feet long, shaped like a kangaroo in body and in tail, but with a different head; it burrows and lives in holes all day, but at night frisks about and grazes. **1912** J. STEVENSON-HAMILTON *Anim. Life Afr.* xvi. 253 The Spring Hare..is found locally through Africa south of the Equator. **1937** K. BLIXEN *Out of Africa* ii. 96 The little spring-hares were out on the roads..jumping along. **1966** E. PALMER *Plains of Camdeboo* x. 179 All around us in their roomy burrows were springhares, those kangaroo-like creatures with their enormous hind legs that go hoppity-hoppity over the veld at night.

springing, *vbl. sb.*^{1} **III. 13. c.** *springing-board* (earlier example).

1846 GEO. ELIOT *Let.* 29 Oct. (1954) I. 224, I do not know whether I can get up any steam again in the subject. ..I must have the book as a springing-board.

springing, *vbl. sb.*^{2} Add: Also, the state or quality of a set of springs; hence, the suspension of a vehicle.

1952 *Times* 19 Aug. 11/6 The springing gives a comfortable ride for the passengers. **1978** *Lancashire Life* Apr. 141/1 The springing is quite soft, so it soaks up the bumps.

springing, *ppl. a.* **10.** (Earlier example.)

1725 D. EATON *Let.* 13 July (1971) 30 Mr. Joseph Lynwood..considering..that he had better mind other business than shooting (for they were all springing spaniels), hang'd three of them of his own accord.

springless, *a.* **5.** (Literal example.)

1927 E. SITWELL *Rustic Elegies* 82 Delivered from that springless frost.

springy, *a.* Add: **1. b.** Characteristic of the season of spring; spring-like.

1860 S. WARNER *Say & Seal* II. xviii. 229 It was April now, and a soft springy day. **1936** N. COWARD *To-night at 8.30* III. 85 Quite Springy out, isn't it?

sprinkler. Add: **4.** *attrib.* and *Comb.*, as (sense 1 c) *sprinkler installation, system*; **sprinkler irrigation** = *spray irrigation* s.v. *SPRAY *sb.*^{2} 3 c.

1935 *Jrnl. R. Aeronaut. Soc.* XXXIX. 164 Sprinkler installation for air defence. **1967** *Guardian* 24 May 1/6 The store had no sprinkler installation. **1950** O. W. ISRAELSEN *Irrigation Princ. & Pract.* (ed. 2) vi. 142 Sprinkler irrigation systems may be divided into three groups according to the purpose for which they are used. **1955** MCCOLLY & MARTIN *Introd. Agric. Engin.* xxxvii. 531 Horizontal centrifugal pumps and turbine pumps are the common types used for sprinkler irrigation, as they give a steady flow of water. **1980** *Jrnl. R. Soc. Arts* Mar. 175/1 There are sophisticated forms of sprinkler irrigation..whereby the optimal nutrient content is fed to the crops at just the right moment. **1930** *Engineering* 28 Feb. 279/2 Sprinkler systems in various store rooms. **1973** *Scottish Sunday Express* 5 Aug. 1/2 Why was no sprinkler system installed in the Isle of Man Summerland entertainment centre in which 51 people died in one of Britain's worst-ever fires?

Hence **spri·nklered** *a.*, of or pertaining to a sprinkler system; *spec.* (chiefly *N. Amer.*), provided with or watered by a sprinkler system.

1930 F. E. WOLFE *Princ. Property Insurance* ix. 151 In Great Britain the principle is commonly applied to plural risks, to sprinklered and other fire-resisting risks. **1968** *Globe & Mail* (Toronto) 13 Feb. B11/6 (Advt.), 16,500 sq. ft. on second floor, vinyl tile floors, fully sprinklered, oil and steam heated,..air-conditioned offices. **1975** J. MONTAGUE *Slow Dance* 48 Our true Catholic world, a graveyard..water sprinklered grass, collapsing wreaths. **1978** *N.Y. Times* 29 Mar. D12/6 (Advt.), Over 50,000 sq. ft. now available in prime industrial location Complete burglar & fire alarm systems ...Totally sprinklered.

sprinkling, *vbl. sb.*^{1} Add: **4. sprinkling irrigation** = *spray irrigation* s.v. *SPRAY *sb.*^{2} 3 c.

1927 *Bull. New Jersey Agric. Exper. Station* No. 453. 3 Three general methods of irrigation, known as surface, sub-, and sprinkling irrigation have been developed. *Ibid.*, Sprinkling irrigation, also known as overhead or Skinner irrigation, from the name of the inventor, is the method of watering crops by means of spray from small nozzles.

sprint, *sb.*^{1} Add: **3. sprint car** orig. *U.S.*, a type of racing car (see quot. 1969).

1954 *Motorsport* June 19/2 Sprint cars were drawing big crowds at the half-mile speedways. **1955** *Sun* (Baltimore) 14 Apr. (B ed.) 18/7 Drivers for the latest entries are two Speedway veterans..and two rookies from the sprint-car circuit. **1961** [see *DRAGSTER]. **1969** *Britannica Bk. of Year 1968* 801/1 *Sprint car*, a rugged racing automobile that is midway in size between midget racers and ordinary racers, has about the same horsepower as the larger racers, and is usually raced on a dirt track. **1981** *Telegraph* (Brisbane) 27 Nov. 18/3 The Queensland Bomber and National Sprintcar champion, Bob Kelly also will be having a crack at tonight's title.

sprit, *v.*^{1} Add: Hence **spri·tted** *ppl. a.*

1911 D. H. LAWRENCE *White Peacock* II. viii. 335 We.. went along the wet furrows, sticking the spritted tubers in the cold ground.

sprite, *sb.* **1. a.** (Later *arch.* example.)

1928 R. CAMPBELL *Wayzgoose* ii. 53 As she bent above her chosen Knight A lovely fragrance ravished all his sprite.

spritely, *a.* and *adv.* Add: Still found as a variant of SPRIGHTLY *a.* and *adv.*

1898 G. B. SHAW in *Sat. Rev.* 21 May 683/1 The younger generation is knocking at the door; and as I open it there steps spritely in the incomparable Max. **1927** *Daily Tel.*

21 June 14/7 The programme was the usual compound of items serious and spritely—mostly spritely of course—and from time to time dancers and comedy cyclists flashed across the stage. **1977** *Monitor* (McAllen, Texas) 9 Jan. 5c/1 Instantly the room is filled with the spritely, bubbling sound of ragtime. **1981** *N.Y. Times* 10 May XI. 23/1 The clams Casino..covered with a spritely seasoned well-blended onion-garlic topping.

spritty (spri·ti), *sb. colloq.* Also **spRittie.** [f. SPRIT(SAIL + -Y[6].] A spritsail barge.

1948 H. BENHAM *Last Stronghold of Sail* ii. 27 The ketch barge skipper had no doubt of his superior status as compared with the sprittie sailorman... He admitted that in their own weather the spritties were faster. **1952** W. G. ARNOTT *Alde Estuary* vi. 46 The last spritties to visit Snape were the *Una* and *Beatrice Maud* about 1928. **1960** *Guardian* 1 July 7/5 The Cambria, the last 'spritty' to trade under sail as a coaster.

spritz (sprits, ||ʃprits), *v. U.S.* [f. G. *spritzen* to squirt.] *trans.* To sprinkle, squirt, or spray.

1917 *Dialect Notes* IV. 339 *Spritz*,..to sprinkle. 'Look out, I'll *spritz* you.' **1948** MENCKEN *Amer. Lang.* Suppl. II. 202 *Spritz*, to sprinkle or squirt. **1950** T. SHANE *Bar Guide* 156 Spritz seltzer over lemon juice, lime juice, grape juice, and sugar. **1976** N. THORNBURG *Cutter & Bone* i. 15 The dog, a male, was spritzing a dwarf palm tree. **1978** *Detroit Free Press* 16 Apr. D10/1 Pierre de France..maintains the stars tell which fragrances men and women should be spritzing on their bodies.

Hence **spritz** *sb.*; **spri·tzing** *vbl. sb.*

1935 H. R. RUDD *Hocks & Moselles* x. 125 Light wine.. often..possesses that natural sparkle or spritz that is so attractive in the Moselle wines. **1975** *High Times* Dec. 89/3 (Advt.), This spray will make any room smell like a candy store... A one-second spritz will mask any odour. **1976** *National Observer* (U.S.) 21 Aug. 12/3, I found myself inexplicably caught up by the nonsense..the inevitable spritzing of the seltzer bottle.

spritzer (spri·tsəɹ, ||ʃpri·tsəɹ). Chiefly *N. Amer.* [a. G. *spritzer* a splash.] A mixture of wine and soda water; a drink of this mixture.

1961 in WEBSTER. **1964** *Vogue* Apr. 71/1 Drink *Spritzer* (dry white wine and soda). **1972** G. BAXT *Burning Sappho* iii. 50 Flo's [drink] was a white wine spritzer. **1979** *Toronto Star* 7 Apr. G1/6 Order a spritzer and never look at who you're talking to—something better could be walking in the door.

||**spritzig** (ʃpri·tsig), *a.* [Ger.] Of wines: sparkling, *pétillant*. Also as *sb.*

1949 T. A. LAYTON *Choose your Wine* (ed. 2) vii. 66 Sometimes the wines are shipped so that there is a delightful natural sparkle in them..called by the Germans *spritzig*. **1959** *Times* 21 Sept. 13/3 This is a wine that is *spritzig*, as the Germans say, or what the French call *pétillant*—that is, it has a slight prickle or sparkle. **1968** *Vogue* Dec. 141/1 A young moselle is a perfect aperitif, especially if it has that rare characteristic *spritzig*: an almost imperceptible touch of effervescence. **1972** *House & Garden* Feb. 100/4 KWV Late Vintage..is slightly *spritzig*, and has a very fresh taste. **1980** *Times* 9 Aug. 8/8 The wine is very big, with..a slight touch of spritzig on the palate.

s-process: see *S II. 9.

sprocket, *sb.* Add: **2. b.** *sprocket hole*, each of a line of holes along film or paper tape with which sprockets can engage to propel it or keep it correctly aligned.

1910 F. H. RICHARDSON *Motion Picture Handbk.* 101 Old, dry films jump because..the sprocket holes are shrunken. **1931** B. BROWN *Talking Pictures* viii. 182 Bad tracking produces a loud hum due to either the picture or the sprocket holes running across the light beam. **1960** M. G. SAY et al. *Analogue & Digital Computers* ix. 263 A row of holes across the tape consists of one sprocket hole, 0·043 in. diameter.., and up to five information holes, 0·072 in. diameter. **1971** *Southerly* XXXI. 138, I could print those four or five with the sprocket holes still on the film. **1980** S. HOCKEY *Guide Computer Applic. Humanities* ii. 25 It is normally necessary to leave a foot or so of blank tape with only the sprocket holes punched at each end of a paper tape.

c. (Later examples.) Also *Cinemat.*, a sprocket-wheel that propels film by engaging with perforations along its edge.

1910 F. H. RICHARDSON *Motion Picture Handbk.* 110 The intermittent sprocket..should be watched and promptly renewed when there are signs of serious wear. **1925** R. V. JOHNSON *Mod. Picture Theatre Electrical Equipment & Projection* 67 The intermittent sprocket pulls the film through the gate, and the bottom sprocket carries the film to the lower spool box. **1953** L. J. WHEELER *Princ. Cinemat.* vi. 181 It is reasonable to expect the sprocket dimensions to be different to those in the camera mechanism. **1977** D. MACKENZIE *Raven & Kamikaze* vi. 77 Slade unwound the film from the sprockets and put it back in the can.

attrib. **1910** F. H. RICHARDSON *Motion Picture Handbk.* 102 A machine with worn intermittent sprocket teeth. **1935** *Discovery* Nov. 325/2 Disturbances such as sprocket-tooth ripple.

sprocketed, *a.* Add: Also, furnished with sprocket holes.

1967 P. GROSSET *Compl. Bk. Amateur Film Making* viii. 143/2 You will need to use..sprocketed tape (which cannot slip, shrink or stretch). **1978** [see next].

sprocketless (sprǫ·ketles), *a.* [f. SPROCKET *sb.* + -LESS.] Not employing or requiring sprockets.

1967 *Boston Sunday Herald* 26 Mar. VI. 2/8 The smooth, quick operation results from the projector's sprocketless film drive. **1978** *Broadcast* 23 Apr. 24/2 Synchronising sprocketed film..with sprocketless video tape.

sprog (sprǫg). [Cf. SPRAG *sb.*[2]] **1.** *Services' slang.* A new recruit; a trainee; a novice. Also *occas.*, one of inferior or ordinary rank. Freq. *attrib.*

1941 *New Statesman* 30 Aug. 218/3 *Sprog* (R.A.F.), a tyro. **1942** *Word Study* Dec. 6/2 'Hey, *sprog*,' said the corporal, 'how about us gettin' another *cliner*?' **1943** J. HILLIER in *Penguin New Writing* XVI. 23 Never mind, Wendy, you sprogs of 'B' flight will learn to fly yet—if you live long enough! **1946** J. IRVING *Royal Navalese* 164 *Sprog*, a new entry. **1949** J. R. COLE *It was so Late* 62 Each time a new course of pilots arrived the sprog officers among them used to fall over themselves after her. **1970** C. WOOD *'Terrible Hard' says Alice* ii. 31 Pasty-faced sprog subalterns. **1978** F. BRANSTON *Sergeant Ritchie's Conscience* i. 12 Some sprog copper, so new he did not even recognize him.

2. *slang* (orig. *Naut.*). A youngster; a child, a baby.

1945 'TACKLINE' *Holiday Sailor* vii. 75, I can't deny him nothing. Always giving the sprog a tanner to nip off and buy himself some nutty. **1949** in Partridge *Dict. Slang* (ed. 3) Add. 1181/2 Nobby Clark's gone on leave, his wife's just had a sprog. **1968** 'O. MILLS' *Sundry Fell Designs* x. 115 All those sprogs, and that ghastly earth-mother missus. **1973** M. AMIS *Rachel Papers* 64 Here I attempted a few minutes' work, not easy because the fifty bawling sprogs had classes there in the afternoon. **1981** D. CLARK *Longest Pleasure* ii. 14, I don't think he's been really with us since the sprog came along.

sproncy, var. *SPRAUNCY *a.*

sprosser (sprǫ·səɹ). [Ger.] The thrush-nightingale, *Luscinia luscinia*, of the family Turdidæ, found in eastern Europe and Asia.

1871 NEWTON & SAUNDERS *Yarrell's Hist. Brit. Birds* (ed. 4) I. 320 A second species of Nightingale occurs.. long known to German bird-fanciers as the sprosser. **1912** BAXTER & RINTOUL *Rep. Scott. Ornithol. 1911* 3 Curiously enough, both the Common Nightingale..and the Northern Nightingale or Sprosser..were added in spring to the Scottish list. **1954** D. A. BANNERMAN *Birds Brit. Isles* III. 304 This [*sc.* the thrush-nightingale] is the 'sprosser' of Germany, inhabiting the same type of cover as its better known relative.

sprottle (sprǫ·t'l), *v.* dial. [Cf. SPARTLE *v.*[2], SPRATTLE *v.*[2]] *intr.* To sprawl, to struggle helplessly. Hence **spro·ttling** *ppl. a.*

1829 J. HUNTER *Hallamshire Gloss.* 85 *Sprottle*, to struggle with inefficacious vehemence. **1839** A. BYWATER *Sheffield Dial.* 15 An we sprottlin abaht to ger up. **1917** D. H. LAWRENCE *Look! We have come Through!* 97 Why do you spurt and sprottle like that, bunny? **1921** —— *Tortoises* 19 It goes right through him, the sprottling insect. **1937** A. UTTLEY *Ambush of Young Days* iv. 65 The lamb suddenly gave a tiny wailing 'Baa', and tried to struggle to its feet. 'It's sprottling. It'll be all right,' cried Josiah, our old manservant.

sprount (spraunt), *v. rare*[−1]. [App. altered form of SPROUT *v.*[1]; but cf. SPROUNTING *vbl. sb.*] *intr.* To sprout.

1939 DYLAN THOMAS *Map of Love* 64 The half-liquid plants sprounting from the bog.

sprouse, var. *SPROWSIE.

sprout, *sb.*[1] Add: **3. b.** *U.S. colloq.* and *slang*. A young person, a child.

1934 *Jrnl. Amer. Folk-Lore* Jan./Mar. 51 One time she was getting ready to go to a play-party. Some of the young sprouts were waiting for her. **1942** BERREY & VAN DEN BARK *Amer. Thes. Slang* § 383/2 Child..(little or young) sprout. **1950** R. MOORE *Candlemas Bay* 24 I'm going to beat the living pickle out of this goddam sprout of mine. **1951** *Harper's Mag.* July 36/1 A girl out your way has married..and is coming home with a sprout. **1983** *Verbatim* IX. III. 23/2 The young sprouts and broths of lads who feel their oats and are full of beans.

6. sprout-land (earlier and later examples).

1851 THOREAU *Jrnl.* 12 Feb. in *Writings* (1906) VIII. 156 It is refreshing to walk over sprout-lands, where oak and chestnut sprouts are mounting swiftly up again into the sky. **1914** R. FROST *North of Boston* 87 A rock-strewn town where farming has fallen off, And sprout-lands flourish where the axe has gone.

sprouter. Restrict *rare* to sense in Dict. and add: **2.** A container in which seeds (esp. of mung beans) are sprouted.

1971 *Health Food Age* June 33/2 (Advt.), Get more vitamins daily with a seed sprouter. *Ibid.*, Be one of the first to get a Miracle Seed Sprouter. **1977** C. MCFADDEN *Serial* (1978) xvii. 41/2 She was starting mung beans in her sprouter.

sprowsie (sprau·zi). *slang.* Also **sprouse, sprowser.** [Prob. var. of *SPRAZER.] Sixpence; a sixpenny piece.

1931 'G. ORWELL' in *Coll. Essays* (1968) I. 70 *Sprowsie*, *a*, a sixpence. **1933** —— *Down & Out in Paris & London* xxxii. 236 These..are some of the cant words now used in London... A hog—a shilling. A sprowsie—sixpence. **1960** A. PRIOR in *Pick of Today's Short Stories* XI. 180, I walked across to the record player and took some silver out of my pocket... 'Half-Nelson, do me a favour and put a sprouse in there for me... I've got no change.' **1966** F. SHAW et al. *Lern Yerself Scouse* 34/2 *Sprowser*, sixpenny piece.

spruce, *sb.* Add. **5.** *spruce green*; **spruce budworm,** the brown larva of a tortricid moth, *Choristoneura fumiferana*, which damages the foliage of spruce trees in North America; **spruce grouse,** also Franklin's grouse, *Canachites canadensis*; (earlier and later examples); **spruce hen,** a female spruce grouse; **spruce partridge** (earlier and later examples); **spruce pine,** one of several North American conifers, formerly esp. the bog or black spruce, *Picea mariana*, but now usually *Pinus glabra*; **spruce tea,** an infusion of tender spruce shoots.

1884 *Rep. Comm. Agric.* (U.S. Dept. Agric.) 378 The Reddish-Yellow Spruce-Bud Worm..was found to be very injurious to the white spruce. **1925** [see *BIOCŒNOSIS]. **1976** *Maclean's Mag.* 3 May 56/3 Except for its larva..the spruce budworm is an unexceptional creature. **1939** *Sun* (Baltimore) 11 Feb. 20/2 Enrollees of the Civilian Conservation Corps will be attired in new uniforms.. of 'forest' or 'spruce' green. **1844** J. E. DEKAY *Zool. N.Y.* II. 206 The Spruce Grouse... The flesh is bitter, and has a peculiar taste as if boiled in turpentine. **1946** T. M. STANWELL-FLETCHER *Driftwood Valley* 13 Several times we've scared up coveys of spruce grouse along the trail. **1966** *Kingston* (Ontario) *Whig-Standard* 21 Jan. 11/1 The spruce grouse is so retiring..that few people get to see one. **1902** W. D. HULBERT *Forest Neighbors* 87 Spruce hens and partridges. **1959** W. A. LEISING *Arctic Wings* 31, I had not seen the spruce hen until the shot bird came tumbling out of the tree. **1971** A. FRY *Long Journey* vii. 41 We came on half a dozen spruce hens. **1771** W. RICHARDSON *Jrnl.* in *Canad. Hist. Rev.* (1935) XVI. 57 There are more spruce Partridges in the woods than I have seen anywhere in this country. **1917** T. G. PEARSON *Birds Amer.* II. 15/1 There is no such bird as the Spruce Partridge. It is the Spruce Grouse. **1963** *Calgary Herald* 4 Oct. 27/7 Spruce partridge and Franklin's grouse season has been open since Aug. 31. **1765** J. BARTRAM *Jrnl.* 25 Sept. in *Trans. Amer. Philos. Soc.* (1942) XXXIII. 30/2 Ye 2 leaved or spruice pine grows very large in swamps. **1842** M. CRAWFORD *Jrnl.* 10 Sept. (1897) 19, I noticed the White Pine and the Spruce Pine. **1886** *Outing* VIII. 60/2 One morning I entered a clump of bushes near a spruce-pine thicket. **1913** H. KEPHART *Our Southern Highlanders* xiii. 295 The hemlock tree is named spruce-pine. **1949** *Boston Globe Mag.* 4 Dec. 11/2 He went up to the white 'Honor Roll' board nailed to a big spruce pine. **1967** N. T. MIROV *Genus Pinus* iii. 183 *Pinus glabra* (spruce pine) is the least common pine of the southeastern United States. **1783** in *New Brunswick Mag.* (1899) II. 320 Some chocolate is wanted for our Masting Camp for at present we use Spruce Tea which causes sum murmuring. **1936** *Discovery* Jan. 31/1 That unpalatable beverage, spruce tea. **1956** *Beaver* Summer 18, I lashed out strong laxatives all round and ordered spruce tea to be brewed and administered constantly.

spruce, *v.*[2] *slang* (orig. *Mil.*). [Of unknown origin.] **a.** *intr.* To lie, practise deception; to evade a duty, malinger. Also with quasi-obj. **b.** *trans.* To deceive.

1917 W. MUIR *Observ. Orderly* xiv. 230 To spruce is to dodge duty or to deceive. A man who contrived to slip out of the ranks of a squad when they were performing some distasteful task would be said to 'spruce off'. **1919** *Athenæum* 8 Aug. 728/1 *Spruce*, deceive. **1925** FRASER & GIBBONS *Soldier & Sailor Words* 267 *Spruce*.., to lie. To deceive. **1951** A. BARON *Rosie Hogarth* 222 Write your own cheque. It's yours for the asking..Go on! I ain't sprucing. **1967** G. M. WILSON *Cake for Caroline* vi. 71 Dr. Meunier's no fool, he'd have known if she was sprucing..Malingering. Faking tummy trouble. **1969** H. CARVIC *Miss Seeton draws Line* ix. 172 Them two old tarts at the Nut House, they spruced you proper. **1970** A. HUNTER *Gently with Innocents* xiii. 166 The coin is damning. He can't spruce his way round that. **1978** *Daily Tel.* 26 May 16 A kipper..by inference, should cost more than the untreated fish. Who is sprucing whom?

Hence **spru·cer,** one who tells tall stories, a trickster.

1917 W. MUIR *Observ. Orderly* xiv. 230 He would be denounced as a 'sprucer' if he managed to arrive late for his meal and yet, by a trick, to secure a front place in the waiting queue at the canteen. **1919** *Athenæum* 15 Aug. 759/1 'A sprucer' is a man who tells tall stories. A man who is 'ticked off' for wrong doing by his officer may escape further punishment by 'sprucing him up a yarn'. **1930** P. MACDONALD *Link* ix. 194 This is where the G.D. begins to show up for the sprucer that he is. **1968** *Listener* 25 Jan. 111/2, I suspect Peter Eckersley was pulling Cutforth's leg. He was a good 'sprucer', as they used to say in Swadlincote.

sprue, *sb.*[2] Add: **a.** A channel through which molten metal or plastic flows into a mould cavity or the runner supplying it. (Further examples.)

1939 J. OSBORNE *Dental Mechanics* xvi. 173 Sprues are necessary to convey the gold to the denture base. In order that this may be accomplished as quickly as possible it is usual to use three, four or even five sprues. **1943** SIMONDS & ELLIS *Handbk. Plastics* xv. 593 In a single-cavity mold, the sprue usually leads directly to the cavity, and there is no runner. **1979** L. J. BOUCHER *Comprehensive Rev. Dentistry* xxiii. 640/2 The sprues should be large enough that the molten metal in them will not solidify until after the metal in the casting has solidified.

b. A piece of metal or plastic attached to a casting, having solidified in the mould channel; *spec.* a stem joining a number of toys or other small items of moulded plastic.

1875 [in Dict.]. **1911** G. H. Wilson *Dental Prosthetics* ix. 353 The investment is broken and brushed away from the casting... The sprues are snipped away and the edges filed. **1940** M. G. Swenson *Complete Dentures* xxxiii. 576 The sprues..are removed by cutting with a carborundum disc or a jeweler's saw. **1966** *Airfix Mag.* June 308/1 Stretched sprue comes in very useful for numerous jobs. It is exceptionally rigid as compared with wire. **1971** W. R. Matthews *Plastic Scale Model Aircraft* 72 Some practice is needed to master the technique and initially the failure rate is high—the plastic sprue just pulls in two. **1977** *Vole* I. 16/1 The sprue is the little plastic tree to which the functional bits of plastic are attached as in an aeroplane modelling kit.

c. An object used to form such a channel, e.g. by being withdrawn or by melting.

a **1877** Knight *Dict. Mech.* III. 2292/2 *Sprue*, a piece of metal or wood used by a molder in making the ingate through the sand. **1908** G. V. Black *Operative Dentistry* II. 353 The hole left connecting the mold with the little crucible by the removal of the sprue is too small for even the very highly heated gold to run through by its own weight. **1979** L. J. Boucher *Comprehensive Rev. Dentistry* xiv. 388/2 The wax sprue melts at the same time as the wax in the pattern.

2. *Comb.* **sprue former** *Dentistry*, (*a*) a wax channel for guiding moulding material into a mould; (*b*) = sense 1 c above; (*c*) a tube or syringe for producing a wax channel.

1911 G. H. Wilson *Dental Prosthetics* x. 344 The completed wax model is prepared for flasking by attaching gate or sprue formers. **1920** *Ibid.* (ed. 4) x. 406 To operate the sprue former remove the screw plunger and fill the barrel with the desired wax. **1930** S. S. Jaffe in I. G. Nichols *Prosthetic Dentistry* xxx. 537 Make five sprue formers about the size of matchsticks. **1936** E. W. Skinner *Sci. Dental Materials* xxix. 252 After obtaining the wax pattern, it is used for preparing a casting mold. A small length of wire, called the sprue former, is attached. **1961** J. N. Anderson *Applied Dental Materials* (ed. 2) xv. 141 The pattern may be removed by attaching a metal sprue former and then withdrawing the wax in a straight line away from the cavity. **1975** Brewer & Morrow *Overdentures* xiv. 197/1 The stainless steel sprue former is placed in the impression in the hydrocolloid formed by the cone attached to the master cast.

sprue, *v. Dentistry.* [f. Sprue *sb.*[2]] *trans.* To furnish with a sprue or sprues.

1943 F. A. Peyton *Restorative Dental Materials* vii. 246/2 (*heading*) Spruing the pattern. **1949** *Brit. Dental Jrnl.* LXXXVI. 114/1 The wax pattern is thoroughly cleansed... It is sprued, the reservoir added and mounted on a rubber crucible former. **1963** J. Osborne *Dental Mechanics* (ed. 5) xiv. 319 If the pattern has been sprued from above then the mixed investment is coated over the pattern and sprues. **1975** Brewer & Morrow *Overdentures* xiv. 201/1 After completion of the wax-up, the case is sprued.

So **sprue·ing** *vbl. sb.*, provision of sprues.

1930 S. S. Jaffe in I. G. Nichols *Prosthetic Dentistry* xxx. 537 This method of 'sprueing' is only suitable for a centrifugal casting machine. **1979** L. J. Boucher *Comprehensive Rev. Dentistry* xxiii. 640/2, 8 to 12 gauge round wax forms are usually used for multiple sprueing of removable partial denture castings.

sprued (sprūd), *a. Dentistry.* [f. Sprue *sb.*[2] + -ed[2].] Furnished with a sprue or sprues.

1930 S. S. Jaffe in I. G. Nichols *Prosthetic Dentistry* xxx. 538 Place the waxed and sprued model on the mix.. and allow it to set. **1963** C. R. Cowell et al. *Inlays, Crowns, & Bridges* v. 46 The sprued pattern must be invested immediately because delay increases the chances of distortion due to the release of strains in the wax. **1979** L. J. Boucher *Comprehensive Rev. Dentistry* xxii. 579/1 The sprued pattern should be placed one-quarter inch from the end of the casting ring.

spruik (sprūk), *v. Austral.* and *N.Z. slang.* [Of unknown origin.] *intr.* Esp. of a showman: to deliver a speech, hold forth, speak in public.

1916 C. J. Dennis *Songs of Sentimental Bloke* 42 'E'll sigh and spruik, an' 'owl a love-sick vow. **1934** V. Palmer *Swayne Family* 250 Wonder you didn't get a job spruiking for the pictures down there in town. **1941** K. Tennant *Battlers* xiii. 143 The ampster's is an easy job. He stands in the front row of the listening crowd registering intense interest and enthusiasm while the showman 'spruiks'. **1955** D. Niland *Shiralee* 106 Kelly was chanting the count, banging the big drum, lining the fighters up on the board again, spruiking to the crowd. **1963** *Truth* (Wellington, N.Z.) 15 Oct., Announcers who spruik just for the sake of hearing themselves need to be mighty sure of their facts. **1975** H. Porter *Extra* 244 Hollow-chested men.. who sell agitated toys on street corners or spruik outside strip-tease joints.

Hence **sprui·ker**, a speaker employed to attract custom to a sideshow, a barker; a public speaker.

1924 *Truth* (Sydney) 27 Apr. 6 *Spruiker*, a speaker. **1933** *Bulletin* (Sydney) 2 Aug. 10/4 General Blamey's somewhat ill-advised efforts to prevent political spruikers addressing the Friday-night crowds. **1952** J. Cleary *Sundowners* 154 Rupe sounds like a spruiker from the Domain. **1959** J. Wright *Generations of Men* xvi. 203 Spruikers dressed in red flannel shirts..shouted and gestured in hoarse invitation. **1977** C. McCullough *Thorn Birds* v. 93 'Come on, chaps, who'll take a glove?' the spruiker was braying. 'Who wants to have a go?'

spruit. (Earlier examples.)

1832 *Graham's Town Jrnl.* 13 Apr. 62 They were joined by Lieut. Warden and his party.., who had been ordered to come over the back of the mountains and rendezvous at the *Spruits* of the Keiskamma. **1850** N. J. Merriman *Jrnl.* in *Kafir, Hottentot & Frontier Farmer* (1854) 85 In two days more we found ourselves, just after sundown, at Carl Spruit, (a small stream,) about ten miles this side of Bloemfontein.

sprung, *ppl. a.*[1] Add: **5.** *sprung rhythm*, a term coined by Gerard Manley Hopkins (1844–89) for a poetic metre used by him which approximates to the rhythm of speech and in which each foot consists of one stressed syllable either alone or followed by a varying number of unstressed syllables; hence applied to verse, etc., using this metre.

1877 G. M. Hopkins *Lett. to R. Bridges* (1955) 43 The *Deutschland*, though in sprung rhythm, is marked with accents. *Ibid.* 45, I do not of course claim to have invented *sprung rhythms* but only *sprung rhythm*; I mean that single lines and instances of it are not uncommon in English. *Ibid.*, The choruses in *Samson Agonistes* are intermediate between counterpointed and sprung rhythm. In reality they are sprung. *Ibid.* 46 Why do I employ sprung rhythm at all? Because it is the nearest to the rhythm of prose,..the least forced, the most rhetorical and emphatic of all possible rhythms. **1879** —— *Let.* 27 Feb./10 Mar. in Hopkins & Dixon *Corr.* (1935) 23, I shd. add that the word Sprung which I use for this rhythm means something like *abrupt* and applies by rights only where one stress follows another running, without syllable between. *c* **1883** —— *Poems* 3 Sprung Rhythm, as used in this book, is measured by feet of from one to four syllables, regularly, and for particular effects any number of weak or slack syllables may be used. *Ibid.* 6 Sprung rhythm..has..ceased to be used since the Elizabethan age, Greene being the last writer who can be said to have recognized it. **1935** W. B. Yeats *Let.* 16 Dec. (1954) 844, I think of writing for the first time in sprung verse (four stresses) with a certain amount of rhyme. **1940** H. S. Walpole *Roman Fountain* xii. 169 'But the metre —' 'This is sprung verse and you can run as many syllables into a line as you please.' **1961** *Listener* 23 Nov. 863/1 The myth is created in strikingly personal terms—a kind of sprung verse, for example, developed [by Isaac Rosenberg] quite independently of Hopkins. **1977** J. Milroy *Lang. of G. M. Hopkins* v. 116 Many 'sprung' lines can be quoted in which some of the metric feet have only one strongly stressed syllable.

b. *transf.* in *Mus.*

1944 M. Tippett *String Quartet No. 2 in F sharp* (verso front cover), The 4th *movement* needs a decisively sprung rhythm on which virtually the whole movement is based. **1959** *Listener* 8 Jan. 80/1 *The Heart's Assurance* was the first work in which Tippett's long-breathed melody and sprung rhythm flowered into what one might call creative ornamentation. **1975** *Gramophone* Jan. 1313/3 Even an early work like the Double Concerto.. whose characteristic 'sprung-rhythm' style, derived from the Elizabethan and Jacobean madrigal,..demands from the string orchestra a litheness and an emancipation from the bar-line that were not common in those days.

6. Produced unexpectedly in order to disconcert (in quots., of an alibi which has been 'sprung' upon the prosecution in a court of law). Cf. Spring *v.*[1] 21 d.

1966 *Listener* 1 Sept. 301/1 The sprung alibi in which the defence suddenly at the last minute..produces an alibi which has not been heard of before. **1973** Smith & Keenan *Eng. Law* (ed. 4) ii. 22 The abuse of 'sprung' or late alibis had been so widespread in criminal trials that Sect. 11 of the Criminal Justice Act, 1967, provides that, in general, notice of alibi must be given in advance of a trial on indictment. This is not required in summary trials because of the ease with which the prosecution can ask for an adjournment where the defendant 'springs' an alibi on the prosecution at the last moment.

sprung, *ppl. a.*[2] [Irreg. f. Spring *v.*[2] by analogy with Spring *v.*[1], Sprung *ppl. a.*[1] The expected regular form, *springed*, is rare.] **1.** Provided with a spring or springs. Also *Comb.*, as *sprung-edge(d)* adj.

[**1884**: see Spring *v.*[2] 4.] **1909** *Westm. Gaz.* 11 Nov. 5/1 An entirely new form of suspension is to be introduced which is claimed not only to render the best sprung car extremely coarse in comparison, but which does away with springs altogether. **1916** 'Boyd Cable' *Action Front* 146 The longer but smoother journey in the sweetly-sprung motor ambulance. **1932** *Daily Tel.* 8 Oct. 19/6 (Advt.), 50 luxuriously sprung easy chairs in various coverings. **1948**, etc. [see *interior-sprung mattress* s.v. *interior *a.* 3]. **1976** *Star* (Sheffield) 29 Oct. 3/3 (Advt.), 3 piece 10 cushioned traditional suite in high quality Dralon, incorporating sprung-edged seating. **1976** *Evening Standard* 29 Dec. 6 (Advt.), Pocketed spring mattress. Sprung-edge base.

2. Of a floor, esp. a dance floor: constructed so as to be resilient. Cf. *spring floor* s.v. Spring *sb.*[1] 25 a.

1966 J. B. Priestley *Salt is Leaving* xv. 202 Lights all colours. Sprung floor. Five-piece band. **1972** G. Hale *Floors* ix. 91 *Spring floors*, floors intended for dancing should have a degree of resilience and for this reason ballroom floors..are often fully sprung. **1978** *Daily Tel.* 31 Oct. 19/5 The hotel's sprung dance floor still exists.

spud, *sb.* Add: **3. f.** *Forestry.* A chisel-like implement used to remove the bark from timber.

1914 Moon & Brown *Elem. Forestry* 383 *Spud*, a tool for removing bark. **1919** N. C. Brown *Forest Products* iii. 68 The spudder..proceeds to peel off the bark by inserting the spud between the bark and the wood, and gradually pries it off. **1966** A. E. Wackerman et al. *Harvesting Timber Crops* (ed. 2) viii. 198 Some [Redwood bark] is still removed by hand with spuds, but hydraulic methods are also in use. Mechanical power spuds are also used, as are tractors with spud attachments similar to dozer blades.

g. = *spade lug* s.v. *Spade *sb.*[1] 5.

1917 *Proc. Inst. Automobile Engineers* XII. 80 A machine with a 30 cwt. axle loading and short spuds pulls partly by adhesion and partly by grip. **1933** Watson & More *Agriculture* (ed. 3) 1. v. 157 A disadvantage of wheeled tractors is that the spuds or bars that are needed on the wheels for soft land are damaging to roads. **1950** C. Davies *Mechanized Agric.* vi. 39 There are many designs of this [skeleton wheel]—as, in fact, there are of wheel lugs, spuds and cleats.

h. *Thatching.* (see quots.)

1939 H. J. Massingham *Country Relics* i. 13 The equipment is the same when a roof is rethatched, except for the addition of a thatching spud still used by the older thatchers... It is a light, squarish slab of wood..with one end chamfered on both sides to an edge and an oblong slit cut out at the other end through which the fingers pass when the tool is grasped. It is thrust up into the old thatch at the eaves in order to make an opening for the new yealm to be made fast at its thin end. **1968** J. Arnold *Shell Book of Country Crafts* 185, I watched one man.. driving home his pegs with a flat oblong board: this had a spade-like handle and was called a 'spud'. **1972** [see *Legget].

5. (Earlier example.)

1845 E. J. Wakefield *Adventure in N.Z.* I. xi. 319 Pigs and potatoes were respectively represented by '*grunters*' and '*spuds*'.

b. = *Potato *sb.* 5 d.

1960 I. MacCormick *Small Victory* 86 Are you any good at darning socks, Sister? I got a *spud* in my spare pair. **1978** M. de Larrabeiti *Rose beyond Thames* 34 There were huge spuds in the heels of their socks.

6. Each of a number of poles that can be put out from a dredger and stuck into the bed or bank of the river so as to keep the vessel stationary.

1891 F. Wyatt *Phosphates of America* iv. 51 The boats are held in position at the four corners by 'spuds' or strong square poles with iron points, which are dropped into the water before dredging is begun. **1912** C. Prelini *Dredges & Dredging* xx. 166 The bow spuds are of great size, 43 in. square and 52 ft. long. **1925** G. W. Pickels *Drainage & Flood-Control Engin.* xiv. 397 Spuds are devices for holding the hull still while the dredge is working. There are three of them, one at the center of the stern and one on each side near the front end. The rear spud is always vertical and consists of a heavy timber with a pointed iron shoe at its lower end which moves in a box or guide frame attached to the hull. When lowered, the pointed end is forced into the bottom of the ditch or river and prevents the rear end of the hull from moving. The spud is raised by a cable operated by the spud engine. The side spuds may be either vertical or inclined. *Ibid.* 398 Inclined spuds are fastened to the A-frame and their lower ends rest on the banks, hence they are called bank spuds. **1969** R. Hammond *Mod. Dredging Pract.* iv. 136 The spuds are provided with sliding collars in order to allow for the wide range of dredging depths.

7. *Plumbing.* A short length of pipe used as a connecting piece between two components or taking the form of a projection from a fitting to which a pipe may be screwed.

1905 *Internat. Libr. of Technol.* LXXI. §15. 68 The end..of the spud is threaded iron-pipe size for screwing into the tapping of an ordinary iron kitchen boiler. **1907** R. M. Starbuck *Mod. Plumbing Illustr.* 123 Ventilation.. consists in connecting a pipe from the local vent spud on the water-closet bowl to a heated flue. **1908** A. G. King *Practical Steam & Hot Water Heating & Ventilation* xi. 105 The branches should be one size larger than the vertical pipe or 'spud' supplying the radiator valve, or one size larger than the riser which they feed. **1939** [see *spud wrench* in sense 8 below]. **1972** J. Hastings *Plumber's Compan.* 184 The 'spud connection' is a brass fitting comprising a socket on one end for receiving the nozzle and on the other end a male thread for connecting a pipe.

8. *attrib.* and *Comb.*, as **spud barber** *slang*, one who peels potatoes; **spud-bashing** *slang* (orig. *Mil.*), the peeling of potatoes; **spud can** *Oil Industry*, a structure that can be sunk into a soft sea-bottom by temporary ballasting and then used as the base of a tower platform extending above the surface of the water; **Spud Islander** *Canad. slang*, a native or inhabitant of Prince Edward Island, which is noted for its fine potatoes; **spud line**: in slang phr. *in the spud line*, pregnant; **spud wrench** (see quots. 1939, 1960[1]).

1935 A. J. Pollock *Underworld Speaks* 112/2 *Spud barber*, a potato peeler (prison). **1961** G. Foulser *Seaman's Voice* 48 The galley-boy [was] just a spudbarber after all. **1940**, etc. Spud-bashing [see *bashing *vbl. sb.* 3]. **1980** *Times* 13 Nov. 10/1 Between dashing home from the office..and having a bath, there is not much time for spud bashing. **1975** *Offshore* Sept. 49-04/3 Spud cans are designed for soft seabeds, giving minimum penetration. **1976** *Offshore Platforms & Pipelining* 53/3 The tower base consists of a truss-reinforced stiffened shell called a spud can... After the tower is uprighted, the spud can is artificially forced into the ocean bottom until the desired load-carrying capability is reached. **1957** *Globe Mag.* (Toronto) 29 June 4/2 (*caption*) Spud Islanders are known throughout Canada for the quality of their potatoes. **1962** G. MacEwan *Blazing Old Cattle Trail* xxxiii. 222 In 1900, the twenty-four-year-old 'Spud Islander' journeyed to the far Northwest. **1937** J. Curtis *There ain't no Justice* xxiv. 245 You mean she's in the spud line? **1967** H. W. Sutherland *Magnie* vi. 80 It couldn't have been himself that put Kathleen Ertall in the spud line. **1939** W. T. Walters *Steam & Hot Water Fitting* x. 145 Spud Wrenches. This type of wrench is another handy tool. It is made to fit the spuds of the different sizes of the union radiator valves and traps. **1960** S. P. Oppenheimer *Erecting Structural Steel* vii. 93 The open-end spud wrench ..is the most common... It is so called because the handle is formed into a long, heavy pin (or spud) that is thrust through and used by the erection men for matching up holes in connections to be fastened together. **1960** D. A. Halperin *Building with Steel* xii. 163/1 It is permissible to tighten the bolts with a long handled socket or spud wrench.

spud, *v.* **3. a.** Substitute for def.: To begin to drill (a hole for an oil well) by imparting an up-and-down motion to the drilling bit. Now usu. more widely, to drill (a well) through the upper part of the overburden; also *absol.* Freq. const. *in* and occas. written *spud-in.* Also with *out.* (Further examples.)

1913 V. B. Lewes *Oil Fuel* 64 If the hole is not deep enough, it has to be 'spudded out' to the necessary depth. **1924** *Bull. Amer. Assoc. Petroleum Geologists* VIII. 643 The driller, with his hand on the brake and familiar with the action of his machinery and pump since the well was 'spudded' in, is by far the best judge of the formation in which he is drilling. **1928** *Publ. Texas Folk-Lore Soc.* VII. 59 He had a 100,000 barrel gusher and was spudding in on another location. **1948** *Sun* (Baltimore) 16 Apr. 12/1 Drillers spudded in the first well of the big Leduc field in November, 1946. **1966** *Southern Reporter* CLXXX. 746/2 Substantial surface preparations to drill are sufficient to be considered 'commencement' of drilling operations for lease-clause purposes,..provided that such preliminary operations are continued..until well is actually spudded in. **1967** *Economist* 18 Nov. 788/2 The company has a world-wide business instrumentation for well-drilling.., whenever 'wildcats are spudded'. **1975** *BP Shield Internat.* May 1/2 BP's drilling contractors.. will spud and drill to completion the first Forties well. **1977** *Irish Times* 8 June 10/3 The Deminex consortium yesterday disclosed that it spudded-in its exploratory well in block 34/15, off the west coast, on Friday last.

spudder[2] (spʊ·dəɹ). [f. Spud *v.* + -er[1].] A small drilling rig used for spudding.

1922 L. C. Sands in D. T. Day *Handbk. Petroleum Industry* I. 250 These lighter outfits generally manipulate the drilling tools by the spudding principle and are often called 'spudders'. **1935** *Discovery* Apr. 119/1 The see-saw motion of the [rocking] 'beam'..transmits to the tool a motion very similar to that of the spudder. **1960** *Pacific Reporter* CCCLIV. 444/2 Plaintiff..purchased four small standard drilling rigs (commonly referred to as 'spudders') at an aggregate cost of $15,750. **1977** R. D. Langenkamp *Handbk. Oil Industry Terms & Phrases* (ed. 2) 160 Spudders are used in shallow-well workovers, for spudding in, or bringing in a rotary-drilled well.

spudding, *vbl. sb.* (In Dict. s.v. Spud *v.*) Add: **1.** *spec.* The preliminary drilling of a well-hole through the upper part of the overburden (see *spud *v.* 3 a). Freq. as *spudding in, spudding-in.* (Earlier and further examples.)

1885 *Engineering* 26 June 708/2 The bore is usually started by what is termed spudding—*i.e.*, working the tools direct from the Bull wheel, lifting and dropping by slacking or surging the rope on the wheel. **1922** A. Blum *Petroleum* III. i. 162 The hole is started with a bit, eight to twenty inches across the cutting edge, the size depending upon the proposed depth of the hole... This is called 'spudding in'. **1929** Babbitt & Doland *Water Supply Engin.* vii. 160 The well hole is usually started by 'spudding', which consists in drilling without the walking beam because of the shorter length of tools and the lack of 'stretch' in the rope. **1967** *Sun* 22 Sept. 8/5 Exploratory drilling starts this weekend with the 'spudding-in' of a well 15 miles off the Lincolnshire coast. **1974** *Bull. Amer. Assoc. Petroleum Geologists* LVIII. 1124/2 The present drilling program began in 1971 with the spudding of the Eider well.

2. Special Comb.: **spudding bit,** a drilling bit used in spudding.

1907 *Internat. Libr. Technol.: Rock Boring* 16 The spudding bit in Fig. 16 is for drilling earth down to solid rock. **1924** L. C. Uren *Textbk. Petroleum Production Engin.* v. 125 A special spudding bit is used which is shorter than the usual pattern. **1939** D. Hager *Fund. Petroleum Industry* ix. 225 With the Lucy spudding bit a cement plug is set at the bottom of the hole, and the bit, by being raised or lowered, digs a hole several feet deep into the side of the hole.

spugslang, var. *spuugslang.

spumante (spumæ·nti). Also erron. **spumanti.** [It., = 'sparkling'.] A sparkling (usu. sweet) white wine from Asti in Piedmont; in full, *Asti Spumante.*

1908 C. E. Hawker *Chats about Wine* 89 The Frenchman with his Sillery..The Italian with his Asti Spumante, all favour sweetness. **1938** C. Isherwood *Lions & Shadows* i. 37 To celebrate the achievement, Mr. Holmes has ordered Asti Spumanti. What a marvellous drink!..So cool and fizzy and sweet. **1945** *Comment from Italy* (Three Arts Club) 22 It was beer issue night, and most of the groups had reinforced it with bottles of vino, vermouth, and spumanti as well. **1958** L. Durrell *Balthazar* III. x. 206 Pursewarden was inveighing somewhat incoherently against the Cervonis for serving Spumante instead of champagne. **1971** *Country Life* 25 Nov. 1466/2 A dry spumante wine. **1982** *Sunday Tel.* (Colour Suppl.) 7 Mar. 38/3 The Spumanti was flowing in the officers' mess, everyone cheering.

spume, *sb.* Add: **3.** *spume-bow.*

1921 W. de la Mare *Veil* 15 With myriad spume-bows roaring ocean swills The cold profuse abundance of the rain.

spumed (spiūmd), *ppl. a.* [f. Spume *sb.* + -ed[2].] Flecked as with spume.

1923 D. H. Lawrence *Birds, Beasts & Flowers* 60 Cyclamen leaves..Frost-filigreed Spumed with mud.

spumoni (spŭmōu·ni). *U.S.* [ad. It. *spumone* (used in the same sense). f. *spuma* foam, Spume.] A kind of ice-cream dessert (see quot. 1950).

1929 M. Lief *Hangover* v. 83 Mogador picked up a spoon and helped himself to some of the star's spumoni ice-cream. **1936** J. dos Passos *Big Money* 126 After they'd had their spumoni Mr. Barrow ordered himself brandy. **1950** Fransden & Nelson *Ice Cream & Other Frozen Desserts* xvii. 177 A special spumoni cup should be used. Press one-fourth of a spumoni cupful of vanilla ice cream around the sides and bottom to line the cup. Add chocolate ice cream... Finish filling with a mixture of fruit and whipped cream. **1968** P. Durst *Badge of Infamy* iv. 37 In addition to the minestrone and pizza there was a green salad..spumoni and coffee. **1977** J. Wambaugh *Black Marble* (1978) xi. 246 Had her little two-year-old spumoni sucker *in the car* when I picked her up.

spun, *ppl. a.* Add: **1. a.** Also of normally rigid materials, as glass. Also Comb. *spun-dyed* adj., of materials coloured during spinning. (Further examples.)

1779 Spun glass [in Dict.]. **1899** *Jrnl. Soc. Arts* XLVIII. 62/1 Spun glass is probably the earliest production which resembles natural silk. **1936** H. Miller *Black Spring* 192 Suddenly like spun-glass under a blue flame, the street quickens into tongues of fire. **1940** *Engineering* 1 Nov. 343/3 The advantages of such spun-concrete products as pipes and poles are well known. **1947** J. C. Rich *Materials & Methods of Sculpture* iv. 64 Spun-copper bowls are highly recommended for use in mixing plaster of Paris. **1980** *Nature* 14 Feb. p. xiii/2 The body is a spun steel bowl and lid on die cast iron base.

Comb. **1955** Cockett & Hilton *Basic Chem. Textile Colouring & Finishing* i. 34 Spun-coloured or pigmented fibres. These are sometimes known as spun-dyed fibres, although the method of colouration is not a dyeing process in the usual sense. **1975** R. H. Peters *Textile Chem.* III. i. 4 Other ways of colouring with insoluble compounds are to introduce them in fibre manufacture, i.e. in the polymer solution prior to extrusion giving 'spun-dyed' filaments.

b. *spun gold* (later *attrib.* example). Hence *spun-golden* adj.

1966 T. Pynchon *Crying of Lot 49* i. 21 Frail girls with heart-shaped faces, huge eyes, spun-gold hair. **1978** S. Sheldon *Bloodline* ii. 40 She had spun-golden hair and skin as delicate as porcelain.

c*. Applied to vegetable protein, esp. soya, that has been spun into fibres so as to resemble meat and to the meat substitutes made from it.

1973 *Guardian* 21 Apr. 12/3 'Spun steak.' Looks like steak..only it is made of spun soya. **1976** T. Heald *Let Sleeping Dogs Die* v. 81 Canine comestibles... Doggy buckwheat..spun protein tripe.

2. (Earlier example.)

1869 K. H. Digby *Little Low Bushes* 244 Carheil is like a long and spun-out speech.

spunk, *sb.* Add: **5. c.** *coarse slang.* Seminal fluid.

For the sense development, compare the obs. slang *mettle,* which had the same meaning.

c **1888–94** *My Secret Life* I. 87 It seemed to me scarcely possible, that the sweet, well dressed, smooth-spoken ladies..could let men put the spunk up their cunts. **1896** A. Beardsley *Let.* 21 Dec. (1970) 236 She played dirty tricks... Till the spunk trickled right down her femur. **1923** J. Manchon *Le Slang* 289 *Spunk,*..2° courage, vivacité, feu; on dit de préférence *mettle,* parce que 3° O[bscène] (=*come, s.*). **1971** B. W. Aldiss *Soldier Erect* 196 By sprawling right back on the seat and ignoring the stink of the shit-pit below me, I managed in no time to lob some spurts of spunk over my stomach, with some relief. **1978** J. Irving *World according to Garp* ii. 32 The boys were beating off, in turn, and rushing with their hot spunk in their hands to the microscopes in the infirmary lab—to see if they were sterile.

6. spunk-water *U.S.,* rain-water that collects in hollow tree-stumps, popularly thought to be a cure for warts.

1876 [see *blame *v.* 7 d]. **1949** *Time* 29 Aug. 7/2 Spunk-water, spunk-water, wash away my warts!

spunkily, *adv.* Add: Also spiritedly, courageously. *U.S.*

1949 J. Flanner in *New Yorker* 9 Apr. 58/2 A hundred artists, from all over Italy,..are spunkily giving their first show this month. **1976** *Publishers Weekly* 21 June 88/2 Judith hurries out to be with her sister and spunkily unravels the mystery.

spun-yarn, spunyarn. Add: **2.** (Later *Comb.* examples.) *spun-yarn major, spun-yarn trick* (slang): see quots. 1929, 1925.

1916 *In Northern Mists* xvi. 63 The practice *has* been known of getting everything ready the night before and the proper fastenings replaced with pieces of spunyarn which can be cut with a sailor knife as soon as the signal is made. Of course, it is not playing the game: that's a 'spunyarn trick'. **1925** Fraser & Gibbons *Soldier & Sailor Words* 267 *Spun yarn tricks,* underhand dealing. **1929** F. Bowen *Sea Slang* 132 *Spun-yarn major,* a lieutenant-commander in the Navy. **1942** 'Sea Wrack' *Six Bells* 163 Above her head sounded the drumming footsteps of Tommy and his crew of spunyarn majors as they clattered round the decks securing stays.

spur, *sb.*[1] Add: **I. 2. d.** (Earlier example of (*a*).) Hence *spur-of-the-moment* attrib. phr.

1801 *Ann. Reg. 1799* II. 27/1 Volunteers, with a party of the Surrey cavalry, attended and prevented the populace in general from taking that step, which, perhaps, the best feelings of human nature had, upon the spur of the moment dictated. **1948** C. Day Lewis *Otterbury Incident* viii. 94 Toppy is tops at spur-of-the-moment tactics. **1958** C. Williams *Man in Motion* (1959) vii. 77 There's no such thing as a spur-of-the-moment suicide. **1978** M. Puzo *Fools Die* xv. 161 Junkies, alcoholics, amateur pimps, small-scale thieves and spur-of-the-moment rapists.

II. 6. d. (Later examples in calligraphy and typography.)

1912 E. M. Thompson *Introd. Greek & Latin Palaeography* xix. 521 Long strokes [of letters]..are occasionally provided with an ornamental spur near the top of the vertical stems. **1976** *Visible Language* X. 44 *Spur,* a small projection, usually pointed, from a stroke or terminal.

IV. 12. a. *spur-clink.*

1911 E. Pound *Canzoni* 43 The silken trains go rustling, The spur-clinks sound between.

14. spur blight, a fungus disease of raspberries and loganberries causing discoloured patches on the stems and the death of buds at the nodes, and weakening the laterals; **spur line,** a railway branch-line; **spur mark,** one of the marks left on the base of a glazed pot by the spurs (sense 8 c) on which it has rested during firing (see also quot. 1933); **spur road** (later examples); now applied to a connecting road that branches off from a motorway or main highway.

1915 *Bull. Colorado Agric. Exper. Station* No. 206 (*title*) Spur blight of the red raspberry caused by Sphaerella rubina. **1941** *Sun* (Baltimore) 18 Feb. 6/4 Anthracnose, spur blight on red raspberries and cane blight can be controlled by promptly removing and burning all old fruiting canes after harvest and spraying the new canes one to four times in the growing season. **1979** Scopes & Ledieu *Pest & Disease Control Handbk.* vi. 55 Some of the fungicides for spur blight will also control cane spot. **1924** Kipling *Debits & Credits* (1926) 166 'E 'ad us all screened in over in a cuttin' on a little spur-line. **1977** H. Fast *Immigrants* 8 This great railroad..has begun the construction of a spur line to connect its main line with the City of San Francisco. **1895** R. Mills *Catal. Blue & White Orient. Porc.* 52 'Spur marks' are little projections of the paste, apparently to prevent the bottom of the vessel touching the oven. They are peculiar to Japanese porcelain. **1933** *Burlington Mag.* Oct. 160/2 On the bottom of the interior of the bowl will be found five spur marks where the pontil was broken off. **1972** *Trans. Oriental Ceramics Soc.* XXXVIII. 23 A ring of spur marks usually is to be seen on the base of proto-Yüeh pieces. **1958** *Times* 19 Mar. 10/3 The spur road to London Airport will be served by a flyover junction. **1963** *Listener* 31 Jan. 198/2 Heavy trucks rumble along the spur roads from the Alaska Highway to mining camps deep in the frozen interior. **1977** *Jrnl. R. Soc. Arts* CXXV. 359/1 These needs could be met by a six-lane spur road connecting with adjacent motorways.

14. b. spur-dog, a small spiny shark, *Squalus acanthias,* found in the Atlantic and the Mediterranean; (later examples).

1921 [see *nurse-hound* s.v. *nurse *sb.*[2] b]. **1959** A. C. Hardy *Open Sea* II. ix. 179 The spur-dog can easily be distinguished by the prominent spine immediately in front of each of its dorsal fins. **1976** *Evening Post* (Nottingham) 13 Dec. 7/2 Other trophies for the best specimen fish went to..Eric Rawson for an 8½ lb. spur dog, [etc.].

spur, *v.*[1] Add: **I. 2.** Also occas., with an action or activity as object.

1951 *Newsweek* 27 Sept. 74/3 Much of this expansion has been spurred by the government. **1976** *National Observer* (U.S.) 17 Apr. 7/2 Mae Craig,..Liz Carpenter, and I spurred a move for the survivors of the Spruce Goose week end to entertain our millionaire host with an appreciation party.

spuria (spiūə·riă). *sb. pl.* [L., neut. pl. of *spurius* spurious: cf. *trivia *sb. pl.*] Spurious works, words, etc.

1918 E. Marsh *Rupert Brooke* 110, I hope this note will not start a vain hunt for *spuria* among the published poems. **1935** *Mind* XLIV. 105 There is a record of posthumously published remains and an interesting section on spuria. **1977** *Times Lit. Suppl.* 22 Apr. 496/4 The Platonic corpus (including spuria and doubtful works).

spurling[2] (spɒ̄·ɹliŋ). *Naut.* [Origin unknown.] Only in Combs., as **spurling gate** (see quot. 1927); **spurling pipe** (see quot. 1962). Cf. Spurling-line.

1927 G. Bradford *Gloss. Sea Terms* 169/2 *Spurling gate,* the iron casting set in the deck through which the anchor chain passes. **1938** F. A. Worsley *First Voyage* 217 The spurlingate pipes were now uncovered and the ends of the chain cables roused up. **1962** A. G. Course *Dict. Nautical Terms* 186 *Spurling pipe,* the pipe that encloses the anchor cable from windlass to cable locker.

‖ **spurlos versenkt** (ʃpū·rlōs fərze·ŋkt), *adj. phr.* [Ger., = sunk without trace.] Sunk without trace; usu. *fig.*, done for, lost from sight. Hence occas. (with partial translation) *sunk spurlos*. Cf. *to sink without trace* s.v. *SINK *v.* 1 a.

The phrase became widely known as a result of the publication in September 1917 of a secret telegram sent in May of that year by Count Luxburg, the German minister in Buenos Aires, to Berlin, advising that Argentine shipping should be either turned back or sunk without trace.

1918 W. H. ALLEN in *Stories of Americans in World War* 24 He was merely seeking an excuse for the inhuman conduct he planned. The order 'spurlos versenkt'—to be sunk without leaving a trace—was to be obeyed. **1922** A. HUXLEY *Mortal Coils* 92 You're done for..sunk—spurlos. **1928** H. CRANE *Let.* 23 Oct. (1965) 329, I haven't had a creative thought for so long that I feel quite lost and *spurlos versenkt*. **1930** W. F. SANDS *Undiplomatic Mem.* xv. 225 My plan for neutralization of Korea..was sunk without trace, completely *spurlos*. **1946** W. S. CHURCHILL in *Compl. Speeches* (1974) VII. 7337 He has departed '*spurlos versengkt*' [*sic*] as the German expression says—sunk without leaving a trace behind. **1963** *Oxf. Med. School Gaz.* XV. 23 Many distinguished research workers have ceased production when they have become professors and like submarines in dangerous waters have been *spurlos versenkt*.

spur-of-the-moment *attrib. phr.*: see *SPUR *sb.*[1] 2 d.

spurrite (spʊ̈·rəit). *Min.* [f. the name of Josiah E. *Spurr* (1870–1950), U.S. geologist + -ITE[1].] A monoclinic carbonate and silicate of calcium, $(Ca_2SiO_4)_2.CaCO_3$, which is a product of the contact metamorphism of limestone and usu. occurs as pale grey crystalline masses.

1908 F. E. WRIGHT in *Amer. Jrnl. Sci.* CLXXVI. 551 Spurrite occurs in the hand specimens either in pure, unaltered state, except for minute inclusions of magnetite, or together with yellow garnet, calcite and gehlenite. **1938** *Mineral. Mag.* XXV. 38 Spurrite is..a constituent not only of the silicated zone of the contact but also occurs isolated in calcite in the marbles derived from the chalk. **1968** I. KOSTOV *Mineralogy* 304 The minerals of the group are contact-metamorphic products in limestones, spurrite being a characteristic high-temperature mineral.

spurt, *v.*[3] Add: **1. b.** Of stocks and shares: to rise suddenly in price or value. Cf. SPURT *sb.*[1] 2 d.

1931 *Economist* 27 June 1385/2 Dunlops and Imperial Chemicals spurted on bear closing. **1977** *Belfast Tel.* 19 Jan. 4/1 Beecham 406p spurted 10p to 15p among top industrials. **1982** *Times* 27 Apr. 15/2 Building contractor J. Jarvis spurted 41p to 341p in response to a dawn raid.

spurtlet (spʊ̈·ɹtlėt). *rare*[−1]. [f. SPURT *sb.*[1] or *sb.*[3] + -LET.] A little spurt.

1921 E. M. FORSTER *Let.* 28 Sept. in *Hill of Devi* (1953) 132, I annoyed him.., and he had a spurtlet of temper and said I was not his friend.

sputnik (spu·tnik). Also **Sputnik.** [a. Russ. *spútnik*, lit. 'travelling companion', f. *s* with + *put'* way, journey + *-nik*, agent suffix (cf. *-NIK).] An unmanned artificial earth satellite, esp. a Russian one; *spec.* (usu. with capital initial) the proper name of a series of such satellites launched by the Soviet Union between 1957 and 1961.

The first Sputnik, launched on 4 October 1957, was the first artificial satellite.

1957 *Times* 9 Oct. 10/6 Pride in the launching of the *sputnik* ('fellow-traveller'), as the satellite is called, as well as the guided missile, were reflected in a speech by Mr. Krushchev..last night. *Ibid.* 30 Oct. 10/2 Mr. Khrushchev replied: 'To peace and to the *sputnik* as a symbol of peace!' *Ibid.* 4 Nov. 11/2 The régime which sends a second Sputnik girdling the earth has just emerged from another of its secretly contrived shifts of political power. **1958** A. HUXLEY *Let.* 15 Feb. (1969) 846 The technical advances in these psychological, physiological and bio-chemical fields are probably far more important.. than the physical and engineering advances which have put sputniks into the heavens. **1964** M. MCLUHAN *Understanding Media* iii. 44 When Sputnik had first gone into orbit a schoolteacher asked her second-graders to write some verse on the subject. **1971** *New Scientist* 10 June 638/1 China's remarkable progress in the field is underscored by the weight of its first sputnik (unmatched ..by any satellite launched by France or Japan). **1983** *N.Y. Times* 7 Jan. A1/4 It is not a dangerous situation.. and we have no worries about the fate of this sputnik.

b. *transf.* and *fig.*

1958 *Newsweek* 10 Feb. 25/1 We may find ourselves confronted with a sputnik in the chemical, biological, and radiological field, as we did in missiles. **1959** *Daily Tel.* 10 Dec. 16/7 Internal 'sputniks', pills containing miniature radio transmitters, which can travel around the intestines. **1963** *Punch* 17 Apr. 549/1 Such Hollywood *sputniks* as Frank Sinatra and Sammy Davis Jnr. **1968** [see *LOOP *v.*[1] 6].

2. *attrib.* and *Comb.*, as *sputnik diplomacy, race, town*; **Sputnik double** *Bridge*, a take-out double of a suit overcall of one's partner's opening bid; also *absol.* as *Sputnik*.

1957 *N.Y. Times* 20 Oct. IV. 4/1 Since the Soviet space satellite has been in its orbit, Moscow has been showing what many are now calling sputnik diplomacy. **1959** *Listener* 15 Jan. 96/2 The rocket would set the stage for a diplomatic offensive [in Russia] similar to the sputnik diplomacy a year ago. **1958** *Bridge World* July 33/2 We noticed that the negative double ('Sputnik') would fit. **1976** *Country Life* 1 Apr. 846/2 A Sputnik double, if played, will lead to the same final contract. **1957** *Times Lit. Suppl.* 27 Dec. 782/4 America's defeat in the sputnik race. **1959** *Daily Tel.* 27 Apr. 10/2 The political sensationalism of the sputnik race. **1958** *Daily Mail* 7 June 5/5 Russian planners will deal with overspill population from big cities... They are planning 'sputnik' towns. **1966** *Listener* 19 May 729/3 In preparation for the creation of Moscow's own ring of 'Sputnik towns'—though this development may not happen until after 1980.

Hence **spu·tnik(e)ry, sputniki·tis** (*nonce-wds.*).

1957 *Observer* 20 Oct. 14/2 We rang up Hamley's to see how Sputnikitis was hitting them... 'No, I'd not say our space toys were on the up... It's always in competition with cowboys and Red Indians, you see.' **1957** *Economist* 30 Nov. 762/1 The United States and the Soviet Union are pouring in money and scientists in an Antarctic form of sputnikitis. **1960** *Spectator* 10 June 826 The abnormal concentration of effort in such fields as 'sputnikery'. **1961** *New Scientist* 6 July 38/1 The narrower field of sputnikry.

sputter, *sb.* Add: **4.** Special Comb.: **sputter ion pump** *Physics* [perh. f. the vb.], a pump in which the gas is absorbed by a getter that is deposited by sputtering it from a cathode.

1962 *Sci. Amer* Mar. 82/1 (*caption*) Sputter ion pump works by ionizing gas molecules and removing them from the chamber..to be evacuated. **1980** J. F. O'HANLON *User's Guide Vacuum Technol.* ix. 221 The sputter ion pump has the advantage of freedom from hydrocarbon contamination and ease of fault protecting but does suffer from the reemission of previously pumped gases.

sputter, *v.* Add: **5. a.** Also with adv., to move *away*, come *in*, etc., with a sputtering sound; also *fig.*

1936 L. C. DOUGLAS *White Banners* ix. 200 The taxi sputtered away. **1977** N. SAHGAL *Situation in New Delhi* xii. 123 Thank God no one was around as they sputtered in. **1977** *Time* 11 Apr. 36/3 Terrorism sputters on, but Argentines have learned to cope with it, even ignore it.

b. Also with *out*, to sputter and die out (in quots., *fig.*).

1964 D. MACARTHUR *Reminiscences* VI. 162, I was certain that..his advance would sputter out as it ran ahead of its supply line. **1974** H. L. FOSTER *Ribbin'* v. 228 In most cases, if teachers would not interfere, these incidents would sputter out.

6. *Physics.* **a.** To remove atoms of (a metal) *from* a cathode by bombarding it with fast positive ions; to deposit (metal removed in this way) *on* another surface.

1910 *Phil. Mag.* XX. 337 A relatively thick film was sputtered on a 1 mm. quartz plate. **1924** *Science* 31 Oct. 392/2 The cathode drop sputters tungsten from the cathode in an amount..between 10^{-6} and 10^{-7} grams. **1949** S. FRANKEL in J. F. Blackburn *Components Handbk.* v. 182 A gold plating is sputtered on and is baked for at least one hour at 500°C. **1961** *Proc. IRE* XLIX. 1148/2 The gas is found in the metal which has been sputtered from the cathode. **1965** *Wireless World* Aug. 409/1 The positive plasma ions..impinge with sufficient energy to sputter atoms onto an adjacent substrate. **1974** *Sci. Amer.* Apr. 35/1 The film can be sputtered onto the substrate in a vacuum chamber.

b. To cover (a surface) with metal by sputtering.

1910 *Phil. Mag.* XX. 331 Two plates were sputtered simultaneously so as to insure the same thickness for both films. **1962** *Sci. Amer.* Mar. 86/3 The steady hail of ions 'sputters' the surface. **1971** *Physics Bull.* Sept. 554/2 Pure silica glass surfaces have been sputtered by 20 keV argon ions at 0° incidence to the general plane.

sputtered (spʌ·tənd), *ppl. a.* [f. prec. + -ED[1].] Formed by or resulting from sputtering (see *SPUTTERING *vbl. sb.* 2).

1910 *Phil. Mag.* XX. 337 A second blank quartz plate.. was now rigidly fastened to the blank side of the sputtered plate. **1921** *Physical Rev.* XVIII. 215 Sputtered films are crystalline. **1971** *Physics Bull.* Sept. 554/2 Redeposition of low energy sputtered particles on to adjacent surfaces.

sputterer. For *rare*[−0] read *rare* and add examples.

1881 *Punch* 15 Oct. 174/1 Whilst facts *be* facts, whilst truth its cold *douche* showers, Hydrants & squirts can ne'er be equal powers; One sturdy spout will spoil the sputterers all. **1935** A. J. POLLOCK *Underworld Speaks* 112/2 *Sputterer*, a person who has just begun opium smoking and smokes a small quantity daily, getting much satisfaction from the drug with the belief that he will never become addicted.

sputtering, *vbl. sb.* Add: **2.** The removal of atoms from a substance subject to bombardment, esp. from a metallic cathode bombarded by positive ions, and usu. with subsequent deposition on an adjacent surface.

1902 *Phil. Mag.* IV. 653 The metallic films..were obtained by sputtering from a cathode *in vacuo* on glass strips. **1930** *Rev. Mod. Physics* II. 186 'Sputtering', or disintegration of an electrode subjected to positive ion bombardment is a well known and often troublesome phenomenon. **1948** L. D. SMULLIN in Smullin & Montgomery *Microwave Duplexers* v. 210 Sputtering is a process in which the cathode is heated by positive-ion bombardment to the point where particles are boiled out of the cathode and finally condense on the anode or on the tube walls. **1952** [see *ion bombardment* s.v. *ION 2]. **1976** *Sci. Amer.* May 115/3 By the process known as sputtering, the impact of electrons and protons on the surface could chip away atoms and release them into the atmosphere, from which they would quickly escape.

sputum. Add: (See quot. 1973.)

1973 *Lancet* 24 Feb. 420/1 Bacteriologists and exfoliative cytologists often report on a specimen sent as sputum: 'No sputum present, saliva only.' *Ibid.*, Sputum is material brought up from the trachea by the actions of coughing or hawking, or the same material spat out with (usually) an admixture of saliva. (Material hawked up into the pharynx and swallowed is generally referred to as swallowed sputum, so the first half of this definition is necessary—sputum is sputum even if it is not spat out.)

‖**spuugslang** (spū̆·χslaŋ). *S. Afr.* Also **spoew-, spoog-, spug-, spuw-,** etc. [Afrikaans *spuugslang, spoegslang*, f. *spu(ug), spoe(g)* to spit + *slang* snake.] = *RINGHALS.

1789 W. PATERSON *Narr. Four Journeys Country of Hottentots* 165 The Spoog Slang, or Spitting Snake. **1812** A. PLUMPTRE tr. *Lichtenstein's Trav. S. Afr.* I. I. vii. 95 A very rare sort of serpent, called here the *spugslang* (the spurting snake)..is from three to four feet long, of a black colour, and..when attacked it will spurt out its venom. **1911** *Encycl. Brit.* XXV. 299/1 It shares with the cobra a third Dutch name, that of 'spuw slang' (spitting snake). **1923** KIPLING *Land & Sea Tales* 34 He gave us half-a-crown for a spuugh-slange—a kind of snake. **1931** R. L. DITMARS *Snakes of World* xiii. 172 Another name [for the ringhals] is Spoew-slang, applied from the reptile's 'spitting' its poison.

spy, *sb.* Add: **1.** Joc. phr. *one's spies*: one's private or unofficial sources of information.

1955 E. H. CLEMENTS *Discord in Air* iii. 32 He designed the engine... I got that from my spies. There's no secret about it, anyway. **1965** M. FRAYN *Tin Men* v. 31 The Queen's going to pay an official visit... So I'm told by my spies, anyway.

5. *spy-catcher, -catching, fever, -fiction, film, -government, mania* (earlier example), *movie, -net, network, novel, play, scandal, scare, school, series, story, system* (earlier example), *thriller, trial, work* (later example); **spy in the cab** *colloq.* = *TACHOGRAPH; **spy in the sky,** a satellite or aircraft used to gather intelligence; freq. *attrib.* (with hyphens); **spy-master,** the head of an organization of spies; **spy plane,** an aircraft used to gather intelligence; **spy ring** = *RING *sb.*[1] 11 c; **spy satellite,** a space satellite used to gather intelligence, usu. military; **spy-ship** (later examples).

1952 O. PINTO *Spy-Catcher* i. 7 There is indeed excitement at times in the life of a real spy-catcher. **1976** *Eastern Evening News* (Norwich) 13 Dec. 1/1 Spycatcher.. 'Jock' Wilson, head of London's C.I.D. **1978** CADOGAN & CRAIG *Women & Children First* x. 223 The most irresistible wartime subjects were evacuation and spy-catching. *Ibid.* 225 The spy-catching tales of Dorita Fairlie Bruce. **1973** 'D. HALLIDAY' *Dolly & Starry Bird* xvi. 234 The spy fever had spread like foot-and-mouth disease. **1963** *Times Lit. Suppl.* 8 Feb. 92/2 The famous heroes of British spy-fiction..have seldom been professionals. **1942** *N.Y. Times* 13 June 11/2 A tautly intriguing and sometimes hair-raising spy film. **1972** 'E. FERRARS' *Breath of Suspicion* iii. 46 It struck Richard, that this must be a spy film. **1929** D. H. LAWRENCE *Pansies* 127 The big, flamboyant Russia Might have been saved if a pair Of rebels like Anna and Vronsky Had blasted the sickly air Of Dostoevsky and Tchekov, And spy-government everywhere. **1968** J. KELSON in *Headlight* Sept. 15/3 The tachograph is a gadget that has been hotly argued over.. but..against all..obstacles to productivity and efficiency, the Spy in the Cab is the crowning irrelevancy of the age. **1980** *Daily Tel.* 30 Dec. 1/1 The new rules on drivers' hours and the use of tachographs, the so-called 'Spy in the cab', will come into force on Thursday. **1960** *N.Y. Times* 12 June IV. 6/2 The U-2 reconnaissance 'overflights' provided, by aerial photography and tape recording of Soviet radio and radar emissions, the most important intelligence gathered by the C.I.A. The 'spy in the sky' more than compensated for the very few spies on the ground that the United States has been able to infiltrate into Russia. **1961** *Time* 7 July 16 The spy-in-the-sky warning system. **1969** *Daily Tel.* 18 Apr. 24/8 The NSA..is responsible for ship, aircraft and 'spy-in-the-sky' satellite espionage. **1976** *Daily News* (N.Y.) 11 June (CB & Sound Suppl.) 2/1 *Spy in the Sky*, police aircraft. **1977** *Time* 23 May 33/2 A lot of the information is picked up by those spy-in-the-sky satellites. **1892** *Englishman in Paris* II. xii. 275 The spy mania..became positively contagious. **1943** *Time* 18 Jan. 38/2 The Nazi spymaster and Naval Attaché, Captain Dietrich Niebuhr. **1978** A. NEAVE *Nuremberg* xiii. 148 The older generation remembered him for his incompetence as a spy-master in the United States during the First World War. **1969** G. LYALL *Venus with Pistol* iii. 20 It's all a bit like something out of a bad spy movie. **1955** W. TUCKER *Wild Talent* xvi. 215 A master spy-net, efficiently directed. **1977** G. MARKSTEIN *Chance Awakening* xxv. 76 Hentoff is..a key figure in a British-based spy network. **1919** C. MACKENZIE *Sylvia & Michael* vi. 222 Our spy-novels and spy-plays must have been of priceless assistance to the Germans. **1979** *Guardian* 1 Mar. 7/2 Literaturnaya Gazeta..cast doubt on the value of spy novels. **1960** *Aeroplane* XCVIII. 627/1 That the U-2 'Spy-plane' operation is nothing new is evident from what I heard in America about three years ago. **1962** *Spectator* 14 Sept. 351 The Chinese..brought down an American spyplane. **1976** J. POYER *Day of Reckoning* iv. 21 Wasn't there something about a spy plane—yes..the U-2 incident. **1919** Spy-play [see *spy novel* above]. **1943** Spy ring [see *RING *sb.*[1] 11 c]. **1960** *Guardian* 22 July 1/2 The spy-ring members began checking on the habits of people working in radar..establishments. **1980** *Times* 22 Jan. 15/1 General Miyanaga, the leader of the spy ring, had been a Russian-speaking specialist working in intelligence for many years. **1960** *Washington Post* 29 Mar. A16 Much of the money..will go for additional Atlas intercontinental ballistic missiles in hardened sites and for acceleration of the Midas, or 'spy' satellite development. **1976** W. H. CANAWAY *Willow-Pattern War* xx. 204 There's a camouflaged installation... You couldn't see it from a spy satellite. **1977** *Arab Times* 14 Dec. 1/1 Georg Leber, defending his role in a burgeoning spy scandal. **1923** R. MACAULAY *Told by Idiot* III. xxi. 257 The German spy scare, the British spy scare, these fevers were worked up in the jingo press. **1976** J. LEE *Ninth Man* 74, I like an informed citizenry. Spy scares keep them alert. **1968** *Observer* 22 Dec. 11/2 New recruits..are sent for training to Group Four's headquarters... A large country house.. it conjures up all the spy-school images. **1975** *Listener* 28 Aug. 281/4 Drama..is supplied by *The Eiger Sanction* ..but only so far as the most standard of television spy series. **1962** *Daily Tel.* 13 June 1/4 (*heading*) Fourth Soviet spyship watching U.S. tests. **1977** C. FORBES *Avalanche Express* xxiii. 242 The 17,000-ton Soviet freighter..the new pride of Soviet..spy ships. **1923** Spy story [see *DAFFY *a.*]. **1978** F. MACLEAN *Take Nine Spies* 333 The well-known story of the Watchmaker of Orkney ..as neat a spy story as one could wish. **1823** T. BEWICK *Memoir* (1975) xi. 103 This happy society was however, at length broken up, at the time when the War on behalf [of] despotism was raging & the Spy system was set afloat. **1952** I. ASIMOV *Stars, like Dust* iv. 48 All young fools who get their notions of interstellar intrigue from the video spy thrillers are easily handled. **1977** *Amer. N. & Q.* XV. 76/2 Somehow, the categorization 'spy thriller'.. seems to diminish the 'classic' quality. **1972** K. BENTON *Spy in Chancery* xxi. 249, I don't hanker after another spy trial, thank you. **1915** J. BUCHAN *Thirty-Nine Steps* vii. 184 It is ordinary spy work.

spy, *v.* Add: **I. 1. b.** Phr. *to spy out the land*; freq. *fig.*

1535 [in Dict.] **1913** GALSWORTHY *Dark Flower* III. v. 230 What had Dromore come for? To spy out the land, discover why Lennan and his wife thought nothing of the world 'outside'. **1936** A. CHRISTIE *ABC Murders* xv. 112 This man must have been spying out the land beforehand and discovered your brother's habit of taking an evening stroll. **1958** P. H. NEWBY *Ten Miles from Anywhere* 124 Maybe you think I'm up to no good? A poultry thief spying out the land. **1979** A. BOYLE *Climate of Treason* i. 32 An unofficial representative of the new Soviet régime arrived in London to spy out the land not long after the 1918 Armistice.

4. d. In the names of children's games: (*a*) *hy-spy, I spy*: see HY-SPY in Dict. and Suppl.; (*b*) *I spy* (*with my little eye*), a game in which one player selects an object (visible to all) for the others to guess, giving them its colour or its initial letter with the words 'I spy with my little eye something (blue, etc.)' *or* beginning with —'.

1946 R. LEHMANN *Gipsy's Baby* 80 We remained below and played *I Spy*—with colours, not the alphabet, so that my brother could join in. **1969** I. & P. OPIE *Children's Games* x. 275 Their participation in intellectual guessing games, even of the humble order of..'I Spy With My Little Eye', is apt to be limited to occasions when they are restricted and unable to play anything else. **1975** *Language for Life* (Dept. Educ. & Sci.) vi. 85 Stories, and such verbal games as 'I-spy' and 'Knock-knock', encourage children to explore speech sounds and help them develop a better intuitive understanding of these sounds.

spy-. Add: *spy-camera, -microphone, -mike, -window* (earlier example).

1968 *Punch* 2 Oct. 495/1 Television spy-cameras, hooked to machines which will translate a visual image into patterns and templates, hooked to high-speed rotary presses, will start stamping out copies in all sizes. **1972** *Times* 14 Dec. 2/8 A Henry Moore bronze..disappeared from the Lefevre Gallery..although a television 'spy' camera was operating. **1977** J. HEDGECOE *Photographer's Handbk.* 21 Made in Czechoslovakia the Mikroma 'spy camera'..has a seven speed shutter and a f3.5 lens. **1960** *Sunday Express* 17 July 1 Tiny hidden spy-microphones planted by foreign agents. **1955** POHL & KORNBLUTH *Space Merchants* i. 4 Nothing but the usual State Department and House of Representatives spy-mikes. **1960** *Sunday Express* 17 July 1 (*heading*) Spy-mikes sensation. Arms firms checked for 'listening walls'. **1755** S. RICHARDSON *Let.* 15 Aug. in *Sel. Lett.* (1964) 321 My spy-window—Ay, that is the window of my vexation —workmen are—workmen... Only, that workmen I wish they were.

spying, *vbl. sb.* Add: **b.** *spyingpoint.*

1922 JOYCE *Ulysses* 254 What is it?..—Find out, Miss Douce retorted, leaving her spyingpoint.

sqn, abbrev. of SQUADRON *sb.* in Dict. and Suppl.

1914 W. S. CHURCHILL *Let.* 26 Aug. in M. Gilbert *Winston S. Churchill* (1972) III. *Compan.* I. 55, I am trying to get the 3rd Sqn (yours I hope) for the Infantry division I am forming from Marines and Naval reservists. **1942** PARTRIDGE *Dict. Abbrev.* 91/2 *Sqn.*, squadron, whether naval or aerial. *Sqn Ldr.*, Squadron Leader. **1977** *R.A.F. News* 22 June–5 July 5/1 Sqn Ldr Sean Maffett..has been a commentator for nearly ten years.

squab, *sb.* Add: **5. b.** In mod. use, the padded back or side of a car-seat.

1904 *Car* 15 June 114/2 Two extra seats..fold up underneath the back squab. **1924** *Motor* 28 Oct. 700/1 Several different methods have been invented to enable the angle of the squab to be varied. **1966** 'A. HALL' *9th Directive* vii. 62, I slid back and rested my head on the rear squab... It was a big car, comfortable. **1972** *Drive* Spring 147/3 The height, legroom and squab level of the driver's seat can be adjusted.

squad, *sb.*[1] Add: **3. b.** Also *transf.* and *fig.*

1914 JOYCE *Dubliners* 244 Three squads of bottles of stout and ale and minerals, drawn up according to the colours of their uniforms. **1940** T. S. ELIOT *East Coker* v. 14 The general mess of imprecision of feeling Undisciplined squads of emotion. **1979** *N. & Q.* Feb. 83/2 The only unforgiveable fault is the abbreviation of titles to unpronounceable squads of initials.

4. b. *Sport* (orig. *U.S.*). A group of players forming a team or from which a team is chosen.

1902 *Harvard Bull.* 19 Mar. 2/2 The rest of the squad will leave the cage as soon as the ground is dry enough. **1920** W. CAMP *Football without Coach* i. 17 A player should take the ball in his hands,..release it and pass it to the next player. This next man repeats the performance, and so it goes through the squad. **1950** *Daily Ardmoreite* (Ardmore, Okla.) 15 Jan. 14/3 It was the second loss of the season for the Tiger 'A' squad as the unbeaten Cougars took them 47 to 40. **1975** *Cricketer* May 4/1 Intikhab Alam ..has been omitted from the squad of 19 from which the 14 will finally be chosen. **1981** G. BOYCOTT *In Fast Lane* i. 7 Like everyone who has ever played or watched a cricket match I have my own views about the tour party —and I wouldn't have picked quite this squad.

c. A unit within a police force, organized to investigate or prevent a particular type of crime; freq. in ellipt. use for *flying squad* s.v. *FLYING *ppl. a.* 4 e (*b*). See also *fraud, murder, riot, vice squad* at first element in Suppl.

1905 *N.Y. Times* 22 June 8/6 Commissioner McAdoo selected yesterday the men for the special squad which will arrest women in the streets. **1928** E. WALLACE *Flying Squad* xv. 132 You do your best, eh? You did your best to put Bradley away, and draw the attention of the Squad to you and me! **1938** [see *GUY *v.*[4]]. **1939** 'N. WEST' *Day of Locust* xxvii. 221 A big squad of policemen was trying to keep a lane open between the front rank of the crowd and the façade of the theatre. **1962** *Daily Tel.* 15 June 22/5 Three detectives, two of them drug squad officers, flew to Gibraltar from London yesterday to investigate the haul of illegal drugs found in the cruiser Belfast. **1980** *Times* 24 Jan. 5/3 Serious crime squads throughout Britain are searching for the inventor and manufacturer of a black box which contains a device that can reverse electricity meter readings.

5. *squad car, drill* (earlier example), *leader, room.*

1938 F. D. SHARPE *Sharpe of Flying Squad* x. 120 A Squad car went down at once. **1956** D. G. BROWNE *Rise of Scotl. Yard* III. xxv. 339 Squad cars, area cars, and 'Q' cars..kept in touch by wireless with the Information Room at Scotland Yard. **1970** G. F. NEWMAN *Sir, You Bastard* iii. 109 Sneed parked behind the squad car, which had been directed via the information room. **1891** *Macm. Mag.* Oct. 466/1 The best thing for them to do would be to go back to squad drill. **1953** *Amer. Speech* XXVIII. 23 A special group is formed by these military words and phrases...squad, squad leader, and training. **1967** tr. *Quotations from Chairman Mao Tsetung* (ed. 2) 106 The secretary of a Party committee must be good at being a 'squad leader'. **1946** *Sun* (Baltimore) 3 July 15/4 John Moynahan, lockup keeper at the town hall police station, was puzzled as he watched Midnight, the seven-year-old station cat, leap madly around the squadroom. **1981** W. MARSHALL *Perfect End* 5 [He] went through the lobby and into the squadroom.

squaddie (skwǫ·di). *Services' slang.* Also **squaddy.** [f. SQUAD *sb.*[1] + -IE, perh. influenced by SWADDY *sb.*] A member of a squad; a private soldier; a recruit. Also *transf.*

1933 G. INGRAM *Stir* xvi. 254 You get the screws and squaddies to shoot at us! Why, you're—well mad, you are. **1943** HUNT & PRINGLE *Service Slang* 61 *Squaddie*, recruit—new to the squad. **1959** I. JEFFERIES *Thirteen Days* viii. 105, I had a motley but effective army of luckless squaddies who had been selected by orderly sergeants. **1970** *Daily Tel.* (Colour Suppl.) 30 Oct. 25/4 Most of the Beatles have been seen several times, as have Danny Cohn-Bendit, Jean-Jacques Lebel, the CIA, of course, and drug squaddies with joss sticks and beards. **1978** J. B. HILTON *Some run Crooked* xi. 114 'It needn't have been a squaddy who'd lost the knife.' 'It was a soldier's knife.'

‖ **squadra** (skwa·dra). *Hist.* Pl. **squadre.** [It.; cf. SQUADRON *sb.*] In Italy: a paramilitary squad organized to support and promulgate Fascism; a Fascist cadre.

1922 *English Rev.* XXXV. 558 When the Fascista army is mobilised..full authority is given to a secret military command. Their smallest unit is the 'manipolo'; then come the 'squadra', 'centuria', 'coörte', and 'legione'. **1924** K. L. ROBERTS *Black Magic* ii. 55 The smallest military unit of the Fascisti was the squadra of eight or ten or fifteen men—any small number. Three squadre made a manipolo. **1967** C. SETON-WATSON *Italy from Liberalism to Fascism* xiii. 571 As the *squadre* grew in strength and boldness, they held up socialist local councils at the pistol point [*sic*] and forced them to resign. **1974** J. WHITE tr. *Poulantzas's Fascism & Dictatorship* III. iii. 126 Para-military *squadre* were also formed outside the *fasci*, even if most fascists took part in them.

† **squadrilla** (skwǫdri·lă). *temporary.* [Blend of SQUADRON *sb.* and FLOTILLA. Cf. F. *escadrille.*] = *SQUADRON *sb.* 3 b.

1914 *Daily Mail* 28 Dec. 5/1 A squadrilla of five German aeroplanes caused a hundred casualties in the suburbs of Warsaw. **1916** *Glasgow Herald* 18 Aug. 8 Squadrillas of aeroplanes were sent forward to bring down or drive back the enemy aviators. **1917** *Daily Chron.* 11 Dec. 2/3 The strength of the German aviation services..rather more than 200 squadrillas.

squadrism (skwǫ·driz'm). [ad. It. *squadrismo* (also used), f. *SQUADRA.] The organization and activities of the *squadre*.

1926 B. B. CARTER tr. *L. Sturzo's Italy & Fascismo* ii. 46 The phenomenon of *arditismo* and *squadrismo*, or the use of armed irregular bands. **1932** H. R. SPENCER *Govt. & Politics of Italy* xii. 115 After the March on Rome the existence of the *squadra* and the guerilla habit known as *squadrismo* constituted a serious difficulty for a régime that was seeking to regularize itself. **1940** *Ann. Reg. 1939* 195 All the new office-holders are old Fascists from the period of 'squadrism' (the earliest Fascist formation). **1954** B. & R. NORTH tr. *Duverger's Pol. Parties* I. i. 39 Hitler reacted violently against the tendencies of Roehm, Mussolini against the excesses of squadrism. **1967** C. SETON-WATSON *Italy from Liberalism to Fascism* xiii. 571 At the end of 1920 *squadrismo* spread from its training ground in Venezia Giulia to Emilia.

squadrist (skwǫ·drist). Pl. ‖ **squadristi** (skwadri·sti); **squadrists.** [ad. It. *squadrista*, f. as prec.] A member of a *squadra*. Also *attrib.*

1938 E. AMBLER *Cause for Alarm* iv. 62 His father had been killed by the Squadristi in nineteen-twenty-three. **1957** *Encycl. Brit.* XII. 802/1 In the early years the *squadristi* had freely used rubber truncheons and castor oil. **1967** C. SETON-WATSON *Italy from Liberalism to Fascism* xiii. 571 In July 1920..youths of the Trieste Fascio..burnt down the headquarters of the Slovene organisations... This was the first appearance of *squadristi*. **1973** *Times Lit. Suppl.* 2 Mar. 226/1 The *ras* of Cremona could claim the support of the 'squadrists'. *Ibid.*, The ultimate limit to Farinacci's squadrist ethic was its dependence upon Fascism's capacity to retain power. **1977** M. WALKER *National Front* i. 19 They [*sc.* Mosley's army] had neither the numbers nor the organization of Hitler's *Sturmabteilung* or Mussolini's *Squadristi.*

squadrol (skwǫ·drǒᵘl). *U.S. slang.* [f. SQUAD *sb.* + PAT)ROL *sb.*] A small police van.

1961 in WEBSTER. **1965** J. MCCORMICK *Bravo* ii. 44, I sat between them in the front seat of the squadrol, stone faced, my arms crossed, as we drove off under the thin pealing of noontime bells from Loyalty Chapel. **1972** B. GARFIELD *Line of Succession* (1974) I. 38 The Plymouth..was a block ahead when the squadrol, its red and blue lights flashing, came in sight on a collision course. **1976** *Tel.* (Brisbane) 21 Dec. 36/5 No one got excited when the small van, called a 'squadrol', pulled up in front of the Starr Hotel at 617 West Madison.

squadron, *sb.* Add: **I. 3. b.** *Air Force.* A small operational unit in an air force, consisting of aircraft and the personnel necessary to fly them.

1912 *Times* 9 May 14/5 A party of officers and non-commissioned officers..are to leave the Aviation School at Farnborough on May 15... These will form the nucleus of two flying squadrons of the new Royal Flying Corps. **1919** *Daily Mail Year Bk.* 46/2 The range of such raiding squadrons..tends to grow constantly from day to day. **1939** [see *GROUP *sb.* 3 e]. **1942** T. RATTIGAN *Flare Path* I. 26 He was on a week's leave, and we were married before he went back to his Squadron. **1959** [see *FLIGHT *sb.*[1] I h]. **1978** R. V. JONES *Most Secret War* xliv. 420 The main point, though, was the esprit de corps, and this was what Hartley had meant with his 'last *squadron* in the Air Force'.

5. b. (Later examples.)

1930 T. S. ELIOT tr. *St.-J. Perse's Anabasis* 39 Squadrons of stars pass the edge of the world. **1978** J. A. MICHENER *Chesapeake* 759 What Steed did next, in the late 1950s, was to pension off his field hands and purchase a squadron of gigantic automatic corn harvesters.

8. *squadron commander, leader* (later examples), *officer.*

1907 R. HERMON-HODGE *Let.* 12 Jan. in R. S. Churchill *Winston S. Churchill* (1969) II. Compan. I. 640 In reporting on the Regiment in 1905 the GOC remarks 'I thought the Squadron Commanders exceptionally well qualified for their positions'. **1976** *Southern Even. Echo* (Southampton) 15 Nov. 9/2 If the junior NCO's are not doing their job properly it does not matter how good the squadron commander is. **1919** W. S. CHURCHILL *Let.* 8 Feb. in M. Gilbert *Winston S. Churchill* (1977) IV. Compan. I. 517 The ranks in contemplation are as follows:—Air Marshal: Air Commodore: Wing Commander: Squadron Leader: Flight Leader: Flying Officer or Observer. *a* **1944** K. DOUGLAS *Alamein to Zem Zem* (1946) ii. 13 He now found himself second in command of a squadron whose squadron leader had been a subaltern under him before. **1943** J. R. WILLIAMS *Aircraftwoman Grey* xiii. 146, I have asked Squadron Officer Hedley, the Group Officer, to call and see you. **1972** A. PRICE *Col. Butler's Wolf* i. 9 Squadron Leader Roskill is a colleague of mine at the Ministry of Defence. **1971** K. B. BEAUMAN *Partners in Blue* iv. 72 The Squadron Officer was one of six of this rank appointed on September 27th... She had joined the Directorate in August.

squalene (skwē̆ⁱ·līn). *Chem.* [f. SQUAL(US + -ENE.] A colourless, oily, liquid, triterpenoid hydrocarbon, $C_{30}H_{50}$, which in animals is an intermediate in the biosynthesis of cholesterol and occurs esp. in the liver oils of sharks and other elasmobranch fishes.

1916 M. TSUJIMOTO in *Jrnl. Industr. & Engin. Chem.* VIII. 896/2 From..the fact that the author has discovered the hydrocarbon first in the liver oils of the squaloid sharks, he proposes the name '*Squalene*' for the hydrocarbon. **1938** [see *ŒSTRIN]. **1964** *New Scientist* 22 Oct.

221/1 These rearrangements occur as part of a marvellously complicated, concerted enzymic process by which the long molecule of squalene is folded and formed into rings. **1978** *Sci. Amer.* Sept. 94/1 Sterols, such as cholesterol and the steroid hormones, are flat, platelike molecules derived from the compound squalene.

squall, *sb.*³ Add: **3.** Special Comb.: **squall line,** a line along which high winds and storms are occurring (see also quot. 1950).

1906 *Q. Jrnl. Meteorol. Soc.* XXXII. 264 From the Kew curves we might be led to suppose that the velocity in the squall was approximately of the same magnitude as the velocity of the squall line. **1923** N. SHAW *Air & its Ways* 75 The surface boundary of the polar front in this region is called the 'squall line'. **1950** *Jrnl. Meteorol.* VII. 21/1 The term *squall line* is among the oldest in meteorology and is perhaps the least clearly defined. Prior to the general adoption..of the frontal theory of cyclones, it was customary to designate as a squall line any line of storms projecting in a general southerly and easterly direction from a depression... With the advent of the frontal theory, some of these lines of storms were redesignated more descriptively as *cold fronts*... There remained the lines of storms which appear in general in the warm sector of cyclones, roughly parallel to the cold front, and along which there is intense convective activity. **1979** L. J. BATTAN *Fund. Meteorol.* ix. 187 Most often the storms regarded as being in the organized class are those that form in lines or bands of thunderstorms, sometimes called squall lines... They commonly are initiated along a cold front, or ahead of, and nearly parallel to it.

squally (skwǭ·li), *a.*¹ [f. SQUALL *sb.*² + -Y¹.] Of a child, etc.: that screams discordantly or shrilly; squalling, noisy.

1861 [see *mother's blessing* s.v. *MOTHER *sb.*¹ 15 a]. **1947** D. RIESMAN in *University Observer* Winter 24/2, I prefer sensitive and cultivated people to squally brats on trains. **1958** *Listener* 25 Dec. 1093/3 Maria Callas seemed right out of the picture, squally and weak at climaxes.

squalmish (skwā·miʃ, skwǫ·miʃ), *a. U.S. colloq.* Also **squamish, squawmish.** [Var. QUALMISH *a.*, perh. influenced by SQUEAMISH *a.*] Nauseous, qualmish, queasy.

1867 'MARK TWAIN' *Notebk.* (1935) vi. 59, I am..very tired of being seasick... All I take an interest in is being squalmish and getting to shore again. **1902** S. CLAPIN *New Dict. Americanisms* 381 *Squawmish,* in parts of New England, said for queasy. **1944** H. WENTWORTH *Amer. Dial. Dict.* 590/1 *Squalmish, squamish*.., squeamish, qualmish. **1948** *Daily Progress* (Charlottesville, Va.) 24 Jan. 4/4, I am not only not interested in food but maybe a little squalmish at the very thought of it.

squalor. Add: **1. b.** Also, the quality or state of being mentally squalid, or of lacking intellectual sensitivity and order.

1933 E. A. ROBERTSON *Ordinary Families* v. 88 The whole family is much the same. Lives Dangerously in mental squalor. **1941** A. HUXLEY *Grey Eminence* vi. 139 This strength and magnificence, so very different from our own weakness and mental squalor.

squaloro·logy. [f. SQUALOR + -OLOGY.] The study of squalor, esp. as a supposed science. So **squalorolo·gical** *a.*; **squaloro·logist,** a student of or a person particularly interested in squalor.

1956 *Observer* 7 Oct. 17/4 Toughish thriller about gigolo-adventurer smuggling between Venice and Yugoslavia. Distinguished by some sociological and squalorological realism. **1957** *Brittanica Bk. of Year* 814/1 *Squalorologist,* a writer stressing unpleasant matters. (1955). **1958** *Observer* 27 Apr. 14/7 To congratulate Dan Farson on two vivid squalorogical [*sic*] scoops; one of methylated-spirit drinkers on a bomb-site.., the other of Soho's afternoon nudist shows. **1961** *John o' London's* 6 July 57/4 This [*sc.* a film] is a piece of glamourised squalorology. **1973** *Observer* 29 July 31/7 Himself an Ohio policeman and expert squalorologist.

squame. Add: **4.** *Med.* **a.** A small flake of dead tissue shed from the surface of the skin in some disorders.

1911 M. MORRIS *Dis. Skin* (ed. 5) i. 16 The scale, or squame, is a dry and usually laminated exfoliation of the epidermis. **1953** S. BECKETT *Watt* 170 A..constipated man, covered with squames. **1975** *Sci. Amer.* Nov. 70/3 Finally they fuse into the flakes called squames, which are eventually shed from the surface.

b. A squamous cell (see *SQUAMOUS *a.* 8).

1949 in *New Gould Med. Dict.* **1954** *Jrnl. Obstetr. & Gynecol.* LXI. 156/2 Smears of patients with erratic or inactive curves consist mainly of intermediate squames and have a high proportion of basal cells. **1973** *Gray's Anat.* (ed. 35) 27/2 Squamous (pavement) epithelium. This is composed of flattened, interlocking, polygonal cells (squames).

Squamish (skwǭ·miʃ), *sb.* and *a.* Also † **Skwamish; Squawmish.** [a Comox cognate of Squamish *sqxʷúʔmiš*.] **A.** *sb.* **a.** A (member of a) North American Indian people of the Coast Salish group of southwestern British Columbia. **b.** The language of this people. **B.** *adj.* Of, pertaining to, or characteristic of this people or their language.

1846 R. B. SAGE *Scenes in Rocky Mountains* 221 The Indians principally consist of the following tribes: the Snakes,..Squamishes,[etc.]. **1884** *Ann. Rep. Canad. Dept. Indian Affairs 1883* 189 (*table*) Fraser River Agency..Squamish..Hon Sound..367. **1907** T. CROSBY *Among An-ko-me-nums* i. 10 The An-ko-me-nums..inhabit the valley of the Fraser River..and include the..Songees, Skwamish, Sumats. **1928** J. MOONEY *Aboriginal Population Amer. North of Mexico* 29 Squawmish tribes. **1934** WEBSTER, Squawmish. **1955** H. G. BARNETT *Coast Salish of British Columbia* 3 Aboriginally the Squamish made their homes on the river named after them at the head of Howe Sound. **1957** *Encycl. Brit.* XIX. 888/1 The principal [Salishan] groups or tribes are:..2, Coast Salish, ..Nanaimo, Squawmish, Lummi, [etc.]. **1967** A. H. KUIPERS (*title*) The Squamish language. **1969** P. SEDLAK in *Working Papers on Language Universals* I. 24 *Squamish* ..must be analyzed differently since the phonetic specification is not that indicated for the cases just discussed *Ibid.* 26 *Mandarin Chinese* involves two more features than those necessary to describe *Squamish.* **1977** H. LANDAR in T. A. Sebeok *Native Langs. of Americas* II. III. 356 Squamish. South Georgia Salish; 100 to 200 in British Columbia (1962).

squamish, var. *SQUALMISH *a.*

squamous, *a.* Add: **6.** (Earlier example.)

1829 *Glasgow Med. Jrnl.* II. 327 These eruptions may be exanthematic, vesicular..or squamous.

8. *Med.* Designating epithelium that contains (or consists of) a layer of very thin, flattened cells, and the cells themselves. Also *squamous-celled* adj.

1860, 1872 [in Dict., sense 5]. **1891** Squamous-celled [in Dict., sense 6]. **1908** *Practitioner* Sept. 355 Wherever the disease occurs, seeing that it is commonly a squamous-celled epitheliomatous ulcer, it is reasonable to suppose that it starts as the result of some previous lesion causing a denudation of the epithelium at one of these spots. **1937** E. E. HEWER *Text-bk. Histol.* ii. 9 Three types can be distinguished:—(1) Simple squamous epithelium...(2) Simple columnar and cubical epithelium...(3) Stratified epithelium. **1947** *Radiology* XLIX. 281/1 A variety of other tumors, such as..squamous-cell carcinomas of the vagina and fore-stomach..were observed. **1968** PASSMORE & ROBSON *Compan. Med. Stud.* I. xvii. 2/1 There are two varieties of stratified squamous epithelium, comified (keratinized) and non-comified (non-keratinized). **1978** *Jrnl. R. Soc. Med.* LXXI. 726 Metaplasis into stratified squamous-cell epithelium is very common in the middle ear.

squander-bug. *colloq.* Also **squander bug, squanderbug.** [f. SQUANDER *v.* + *BUG *sb.*² 4 a, after *jitterbug*, etc.] A symbol of reckless extravagance and waste, first used in government publicity campaigns to promote economy during the war of 1939–45 and represented as a devilish insect; a likeness of this. Also, one who is profligate with money or resources. Hence **squa·nderbugging.**

Introduced in 1943 by the National Savings Committee.

1943 *Times* 8 Jan. 8/1 (Advt.), Beware the treacherous Squander Bug! He's the prince of fifth-columnists—doesn't believe in a nest-egg for the future—doesn't believe in making money fight for Britain... Join a Savings Group to defeat the Squander Bug! **1943** O. LANCASTER *More Pocket Cartoons* 55 (*caption*) Oh, just look at this sweet little squander-bug in platinum and rubies that darling Boysy's just sent me. **1944** *Convoy* Feb. 26 A Government so dexterous, through its armies of Public Relations Depts., in persuading us to squash the squander bug or grow more onions or shave in tepid water. **1946** J. W. DAY *Harvest Adventure* xvi. 268 That is the question to ask these rural squander-bugs. **1966** *Punch* 26 Jan. 108/2 The more favoured nations continue to outdo each other in squanderbugging. The new Russian satellite will have showers, electric razors, fresh linen and a load of other luxury items. What a blow to American prestige. **1976** *Listener* 23 Dec. 843/3 No initiative could be broached..for fear of earning the name of Squanderbugs.

squa·nderlust. *U.S. slang.* [f. SQUANDER *v.*, after *WANDERLUST.] A strong desire to spend money or to waste assets; also *loosely* = next.

1935 *Amer. Speech* X. 155/1 Louis Ludlow, member of Congress and former Washington correspondent..is the author of *America Go Bust,* which 'focuses attention on the bureaucratic *squanderlust*' of our times. **1960** *Wall St. Jrnl.* 5 May 8/2 Politicians.., moved..by an any-year philosophy of squanderlust, lead the country down the road to economic trouble. **1977** *Time* 18 July 72/3 No longer the ultimate expression of corporate and personal squanderlust, the private plane is now a ubiquitous..means of air travel to smaller cities.

squanderma·nia. *colloq.* [f. SQUANDER *v.* + -MANIA.] An insane desire or obsession to spend money recklessly or to waste assets. Hence **squanderma·niac** *a.* and *sb.*

1920 *Public Opinion* 2 July 3/1 The public are deeply roused upon the Squandermania issue. **1921** *Glasgow Herald* 2 Apr. 7 The burden imposed upon him [*sc.* the tax-payer] by a 'Squandermaniac' Government. **1922** *Public Opinion* 10 Mar. 228/1 The real squandermaniac would be revealed in the man with an infinite capacity for standing at street corners. **1931** *Punch* 4 Nov. 481/1 The triumph of Reason over Squandermania. **1933** C. MACKENZIE *Water on Brain* vii. 85 There cheek by jowl sat the squandermaniac and the suicidal junior clerk. **1956** *Sun* (Baltimore) 14 June (ed. B) 16/2 They think that people who support the provision of some military aid to our allies are 'soft' and afflicted with 'squandermania'. **1976** *Times* 16 Aug. 11/5 Sheer 'squander-mania'..has currently invaded our society.

squantum (skwǫ·ntǝ̆m). *U.S. local.* Also **Squantum.** [f. *Squantum*, the name of a sea-coast village (now part of Quincy), in Norfolk Co., E. Mass: see also M. Mathews *Dict. Americanisms*.] In Massachusetts: a picnic, a 'clambake'; *spec.* an annual feast formerly held on the sea-shore at which sea-food was eaten.

1812 *Boston Gaz.* 24 Aug. 2/5 The Squantum Celebration Will be this day, (Monday) at the old celebrated spot... The Feast was postponed on Saturday on account of the weather... The antient Celebrators of the Squantum Feast, will be honored..with the presence of their illustrious friends. **1832** S. G. GOODRICH *Syst. Universal Geogr.* 106 The feast of *Squantum* is held annually on the shore to the E. of Neponset Bridge, at a rocky point projecting into Boston Bay. **1855** H. A. WISE *Tales for Marines* i. 21, I wish to all fired smash I was..hazin' round with Charity Bunker and the rest o' the gals at a squantum. **1890** E. BELLAMY *Six to One* vi. 60 The squantum was to be held at a point on the narrow peninsula.. that divides the ocean from the broad lagoon.

square, *sb.* Add: **II. 8. b.** *method* (or *principle*) *of least squares* [tr. F. *méthode des moindres quarrés* (A.-M. Legendre *Nouvelles Méthodes pour la Détermination des Orbites des Comètes* (1806) 74)], the technique of estimating a quantity, fitting a graph to a set of experimental values, etc., so as to minimize the sum of the squares of the differences between the observed data and their estimated true values; so *least square(s)* attrib., denoting estimates, regression lines, etc., obtained by this method, the method itself, and the processes which it involves.

[**1812** *Phil. Mag.* XXXIX. 242 M. Legendre had not in any way mentioned the method which he has denominated that of small squares, (*moindres carrées,*). *Ibid.* 243 The principle of the small squares.] **1825** *Ibid.* LXV. 10 The principle of least squares will hold good, whatever law of probability be adopted. **1830** POISSON in *Q. Jrnl. Sci., Lit. & Arts* VI. 96 This embarrassment..remained to the period when M. Legendre proposed a direct and uniform method of forming the final equations, which was generally adopted under the name of Method of least squares of the errors, which was assigned to it by its author. **1872** THOMSON & TAIT *Elem. Nat. Philos.* I. iii. 115 *A* and *B* are to be found by the method of least squares from values of *l* observed for different given values of *t.* **1916** L. D. WELD *Theory of Errors & Least Squares* v. 87 If more [observations] are made, least-square reduction may be applied to their adjustment. **1939** A. E. TRELOAR *Elem. Statistical Reasoning* iv. 59 'Least squares' solutions, or the minimizing of squared deviations to reach representative values, may be made with facility, whereas the minimizing of absolute deviations becomes so involved that the problems can rarely be solved that way. **1950** A. McF. MOOD *Introd. Theory Statistics* xiii. 311 The primary reason that the method of least squares is commonly used for curve fitting is merely that it leads to a simple linear system of equations for determining the coefficients. **1957** G. E. HUTCHINSON *Treat. Limnol.* I. vii. 469 *C* is determined from the distribution of temperatures by the method of least squares. **1970** *Jrnl. Gen. Psychol.* July 127 The principle of the method is to rotate one matrix (usually a principal-components matrix) as close as possible to a hypothesized factor matrix, in a least-square solution. **1974** *Encycl. Brit. Macropædia* VII. 967/1 Gauss developed a technique for calculating its orbital components with such accuracy that several astronomers late in 1801 and early in 1802 were able to locate Ceres again without difficulty. As part of his technique, Gauss used his method of least squares, developed about 1794.

10. e. A square piece of material used as a scarf or cravat.

1882 *Queen* 7 Oct. 334/2 Lace Bows... Lace Sets... Indian Muslin and Lace Squares, from 1s. 11d. to 12s. 6d. **1926** in C. W. Cunnington *Eng. Women's Clothing in Present Cent.* (1952) vi. 190 The latest scarf conceit is a square of chiffon caught round the neck. **1960** C. DALE *Spring of Love* iv. 94 Miss Burroughs [wearing]..a silk square over her shoulders against the draught. **1966** B. KIMENYE *Kalasanda Revisited* 60 Removing the georgette square which had been tightly binding her head. **1979** A. SCHOLEFIELD *Point of Honour* 142 Yellow knotted silk square at the throat.

11. b. *Cricket.* A closer-cut area at the centre of a ground, any strip of which may be prepared as a wicket.

1899 *Lawns* (Sutton & Sons, Reading) 32 The club purse must determine the extent of ground to be treated in the manner we recommend, but while the work is in progress it is worth while to strain the point to make the playing square sufficiently large, say, at the very least, forty yards in the line of the wickets, by thirty yards in width. **1924** H. DE SÉLINCOURT *Cricket Match* v. 110 As they reached the square, five Raveley men emerged, running, from the Pavilion, and called loudly for the ball. **1950** F. J. REED *Lawns & Playing Fields* xvii. 174 On established cricket squares mowing should commence as early as possible, setting the machine high and gradually lowering the cut as the season advances. **1976** J. SNOW *Cricket Rebel* 22 We were not to meet up as a side until we got on to the square.

c. *Mil. slang.* A parade ground.

1915 F. H. LAWRENCE in *Home Lett. T. E. Lawrence* (1954) 644 There were 10 officers on the square when I joined in September, and four of them are now dead, four wounded and one missing. **1925** FRASER & GIBBONS *Soldier & Sailor Words* 268 *Square,*..an army term for the drill or parade ground. In general, the Barrack Square.

1962 A. Wesker *Chips with Everything* I. iii. 17 This is the Square. We call it a square-bashing square. **1982** 'W. Haggard' *Mischief-Makers* ii. 21 He had failed to pass Sandhurst. He had failed to pass off the square and had been put back a term.

14. Delete † *Obs.* and add later examples.

1819 J. Wilson *Compl. Dict. Astrol.* 379 *Square*, the quartile aspect, containing a quadrant or right angle. **1861** R. J. Morrison *Hand-bk. Astrol.* I. I. iii. 8 When a sextile aspect or distance of *sixty* degrees falls in the latter, Ptolemy intimates that it has the effect of a square, or *ninety* degrees. And when a trine falls in signs of short ascension, he says that the effect is also that of a square aspect. **1929** V. E. Robson *Alan Leo's Dict. Astrol.* 188 The Square is the most critical and conflicting of aspects. *a* **1963** L. MacNeice *Astrol.* (1964) viii. 258 Sextiles..are supposed to be 'good'..aspects, while the square (90°) is considered 'bad'. **1975** I. M. Hickey *Astrol.* viii. 72 Squares represent the lessons we have failed to learn.

15. g. *Bookbinding.* Usu. in *pl.* The portion of the cover of a bound book which projects beyond the leaves.

1835 'J. A. Arnett' *Bibliopegia* 207 Squares.—That portion of the boards of a volume which projects over the edges. **1876** *Encycl. Brit.* IV. 43/2 The same processes are followed with the sides and the 'squares' when any ornamentation is tooled upon them. **1901** D. Cockerell *Bookbinding* ix. 131 If the book has been trimmed, or is to remain uncut, a little more must be allowed for the 'squares'. **1946** E. Diehl *Bookbinding* II. xi. 148 If the squares are too large when the boards have been laced on, it is a simple matter to cut them down.

h. A given space on the page of a newspaper, etc., considered as a unit of measurement for advertisements. *U.S.* (now *Hist.*).

1800 *Impartial Observer* (Natchez, Mississippi) 5 May 1/1 Advertisements..which exceed a square will be inserted at the same proportionate price. **1877** *Harper's Mag.* Dec. 111/1 These newspaper people set an extraordinary value on their squares, as they call them. **1943** C. Crow *Great Amer. Customer* 122 The standard space measurement [for advertising] was the 'square', which meant a space equal in depth to the width of a column—approximately two column inches.

15*. Slang uses. **a.** One who is square (*square *a.* 9 d); a person considered to hold conventional or old-fashioned views. orig. *U.S. Jazz.*

1944 *Sun* (Baltimore) 27 Jan. 10/5 *Square*, in musician's jargon, anyone who is not cognizant of the beauties of true jazz. **1944** D. Burley *Orig. Handbk. Harlem Jive* 70 Are you going to be a square all you days? **1947** [see *hip *v.*[8]]. **1952** 'E. Box' *Death in Fifth Position* (1954) i. 23 Though I might not be entirely a square I was..hopelessly ignorant of all that..mattered. **1959** H. Hobson *Mission House Murder* ii. 15 The odd fifty million citizens who don't dig them are dead-beats—squares. **1965** G. Hackforth-Jones *Storm in Harbour* ix. 142 You and I are what the up and coming generation call squares. We live in the past and we don't like what we see of the present. **1968** T. Wolfe *Electric Kool-Aid Acid Test* xxvii. 386 We're in two different worlds. You're a hippie and I'm a square. **1974** *Howard Jrnl.* XIV. 101 The 'square' are women who are basically pro-authority, in favour of law and order, and share the values of 'respectable' society. **1977** J. D. Douglas in Douglas & Johnson *Existential Sociol.* i. 42 Marihuana has been widely used for decades by artists and other groups, probably also as a way of expressing feelings against the squares.

b. A cigarette containing tobacco, rather than marijuana. *U.S.* (chiefly *Blacks'*).

1970 H. E. Roberts *Third Ear* 13/1 *Square*, a cigarette. **1971** *Black Scholar* Sept. 36/2 Why, why, he kept asking himself, as he lit a square.., why do I keep having that dream. **1974** *Black World* Nov. 57 Light me up a square, baby.

16. Also, a square meal. orig. and chiefly *U.S.*

1882 O. Merdian *Let.* 20 Sept. in *Frontier* (1930) X. 252/1, I went in..and had some dinner..ate a square & talked awhile. **1927** J. Barbican *Confess. Rum-Runner* xxiii. 260 We sure was hungry for the dough, for it was weeks since we had roped in our three squares a day. **1962** 'E. McBain' *Like Love* ii. 21 But he had had a clean bed to sleep in, and three squares a day, as the saying goes. **1979** 'H. Howard' *Sealed Envelope* x. 135 Mine was a lousy job. There must be a better way of making three squares a day.

IV. 20. *square one*: the beginning, the starting-point. Freq. as *back to* (also *in, on*) *square one.*

Often said to derive from the notional division of an association football pitch into eight numbered sections for the purposes of early radio commentaries (see *Radio Times*, 1927, 28 Jan.). This suggestion cannot be upheld with any certainty, and the phrase may simply come from a board-game such as Snakes and Ladders.

1960 *Times* 21 May 9/2 As far as building up a basis for profitable negotiations is concerned the two sides are back in square one. **1965** *Listener* 24 June 930/2 Let us drop the logical knot that twin studies have tied us in and go back for a moment to square one. **1965** *Guardian* 13 Oct. 2/7 The city's medical officer..said they were still in 'square one', and would stay there till they got some real facts. **1966** J. I. M. Stewart *Aylwins* x. 126 That he had seized a chance to break off our interview at that point seemed to argue a refusal to abide by this judgement of the matter. We were back, so to speak, in Square One. **1970** G. F. Newman *Sir, You Bastard* 279 A couple of wrong answers and Sneed knew he'd be right back on square one. **1973** G. Talbot *Ten Seconds from Now* (1974) viii. 111 After each of those successful essays it was 'back to Square One'. **1977** 'M. Innes' *Honeybath's Haven* x. 98 Honeybath broke off in these bold proposals, suddenly aware that Edwin was weeping. It was like being back on square one. **1980** D. Bogarde *Gentle Occupation* xii. 332 'Black is black, Moluccans.'..'Are coloured people. They are dark,' said Emmie with force. 'Well, don't let's *have* any blasted children'... 'But I do. I want.'..'Oh for God's sake. We're back to square one again.'

V. 21. *attrib.* and *Comb.*, as **square-bashing** *vbl. sb.* and *ppl. a. Mil. slang* [*bashing *vbl. sb.* 3], drilling; hence **square-basher; square-free** *a. Math.* [tr. G. *quadratfrei*], (of an integer) equal to the product of a set of different primes; not divisible by a perfect square; **square-pusher** *slang*, (*a*) a respectable girl; (*b*) a boyfriend; hence **square-pushing,** the act or practice of walking out with a girl (popularly associated with accompanying nursemaids, etc., about town squares); love-making; also as *pres. pple.*

1959 *Spectator* 21 Aug. 212/2 The transition away from the era of the square-basher and the char-and-wadder is painfully slow. **1943** Square-bashing [see *bashing *vbl. sb.* 3]. **1946** C. Fry *Phoenix too Frequent* 28 There, do you see her, you acorn-chewing infantryman? You've made her cry, you square-bashing barbarian. **1962** [see sense 11 c above]. **1975** 'G. Black' *Big Wind for Summer* ii. 20 Attached to a Malay regiment, supervising weapon training and square bashing. **1960** Niven & Zuckerman *Introd. Theory Numbers* xi. 226 The set of square-free integers has natural density $6/\pi^2$. **1971** G. Higman in Powell & Higman *Finite Simple Groups* vi. 209 All elements have square-free order. **1890** Barrère & Leland *Dict. Slang* II. 158/1 A square pusher is a girl of good reputation. **1922** Joyce *Ulysses* 425, I seen you up Faithful place with your squarepusher, the greaser off the railway, in his cometobed hat. **1918** W. J. Locke *Rough Road* x. 116 'Go "square-pushing"?' said Doggie contemptuously, using the soldiers' slang for walking about with a young woman. **1922** Joyce *Ulysses* 161 Squarepushing up against a backdoor. Maul her a bit. **1928** F. E. Baily *Golden Vanity* xii. 178 Left me cold in a strange place to go square-pushing with some forward young woman. **1930** J. B. Priestley *Good Companions* I. iv. 134 'E wouldn't bother, though, too busy square-pushing, taking the girls out, see.

square, *a.* Add: **I. 1. b.** *square mile*: also *spec.* a familiar term for the (heart of the) City of London.

1966 L. Southworth *Felon in Disguise* i. 13 Being a non-residential area, murders seldom occur in the square mile. **1971** *Guardian* 3 Mar. 18/4 Prince Charles was made a Freeman of the City of London yesterday... It was the kind of traditional occasion that the square mile does so well. **1975** *Times* 1 Mar. 12/2 The City Corporation hopes to have redeveloped 90 per cent of the square mile by 1980.

6. d. *Assoc. Football*, etc. Of a group of players: positioned in a line at right angles to the direction of play (*spec.* as a defensive weakness).

1972 G. Green *Great Moments in Sport: Soccer* x. 97 Often, too, Mullen and Hancocks would find each other with long, cross-field passes which travelled from one touchline to the other during the course of an attack, with the result that opposing defences were often caught square offering vital openings to the forwards in the middle. **1977** *Times* 28 Feb. 8/3 They were goals Middlesbrough always looked like taking against Arsenal's soft, square defence.

7. c. Also in other sports.

1955 *Times* 14 May 3/4 (*heading*) All square in Davis Cup.

7*. *Mus.* Of rhythm: simple, straightforward.

1958 *Times* 27 Oct. 12/3 Attempts have been made.. in recent years to get away from the square style of playing that arose out of the hymns and other purely vocal music. **1967** A. L. Lloyd *Folk Song in England* iv. 170 The earlier melodies are more vigorous, squarer, franker in cast. **1976** *Early Music* July 270 The opening sinfonia for strings and trombones is remarkably like several opera overtures of the time, with square rhythms [etc.].

II. 8. a. *square deal*: see *deal *sb.*[2] 4 c.

9. d. Designating one who is out of touch with the ideas and conventions of a particular popular contemporary movement (orig. *Jazz*); conventional, old-fashioned. Formerly opp. *hep *a.* Also of things. *slang* (orig. *U.S.*).

1946 B. Treadwell *Big Bk. Swing* 125/2 *Square*, not versed in Swing, puritanical. **1950** J. Vedey *Band Leaders* 175 Consummate performer that Ellington is, he put these numbers over to the delight of all types of audience, young and old, sophisticated and 'square'. **1953** W. Burroughs *Junkie* (1972) x. 110 The other patients were a pretty square and sorry lot. **1959** N. Mailer *Advts. for Myself* (1961) 264 They wish this newspaper to be more conservative, more Square—I wish it to be more Hip. **1959** *Punch* 2 Sept. 103/1, I..told her that the bang-opening was old-hat and a completely square method of writing these days. **1965** F. Raphael *Darling* i. 7 You know books. Those things with pages very square people still occasionally read. **1971** B. Malamud *Tenants* 80, I didn't expect it to be that good, not from the square dude you are. **1977** P. G. Winslow *Witch Hill Murder* II. xvii. 219 He wants to be in with the law. Square at heart.

10. e. (Earlier example.)

1825 H. Wilson *Mem.* (ed. 2) III. 360 As though I had been the Duchess's chosen daughter-in-law, for whom he was making all square.

III. 11. g. Having membership of the Freemasons; in accordance with the Masonic code.

1888 Kipling *Man who would be King* in *Phantom 'Rickshaw* 73, I am hoping you will give him the message on the Square. **1927** —— *Limits & Renewals* (1932) 172, I told him I was something else besides a G.P... From then on he told the tale on the Square. **1974** *Times Educ. Suppl.* 21 June 2/4 How many local councils..are riddled with freemasonry? At how many appointments are the best men..passed over because they are not on the square?

IV. 12. a. *square-bracketed, -ended, -faced* (earlier example), *-pupilled, -sectioned, -shaled*; *square-hung, -pied*; *square-looking* (earlier example); *square footage.*

1970 *Guardian* 26 Nov. 13/4 Attention is focussed on the heavy-typed and square-bracketed passages. **1923** *Trans. Scottish Ecclesiological Soc.* VII. 65 The Lady Chapel was ..removed and a long square-ended one substituted. **1936** W. Faulkner *Absalom, Absalom!* 369 He saw then the square-ended saw chunk beside the wall. **1978** A. & G. Ritchie *Anc. Monuments Orkney* 71 The church consisted of a rectangular nave with a porch at its W end and a square-ended chancel at the E end. **1872** Geo. Eliot *Middlemarch* II. III. xxiv. 32 She was of the same curly-haired, square-faced type as Mary. **1963** A. Smith *Throw out Two Hands* i. 16 One man sitting down in a thing 3 feet 11 inches by 2 feet 11 inches tends to occupy the bulk of the available square footage. **1874** G. M. Hopkins *Jrnls. & Papers* (1959) 255, I am not so sure of the tiles being squarehung—they may have been lozenges. **1845** Poe in *Godey's Lady's Bk.* Feb. 63/1 On the very tips of their heads were certain square-looking boxes. **1868** G. M. Hopkins *Jrnls. & Papers* (1959) 178 Like the skin of a white snake square-pied with black. **1957** T. Hughes *Hawk in Rain* 39 And looked down A square-pupilled yellow-eyed look. **1964** W. L. Goodman *Hist. Woodworking Tools* 99 Another jack..with a similar casting screwed to a square-sectioned wooden stock. **1917** E. Pound *Lustra* 183 Breaking the riven waves On square-shaled rocks.

14. a. square capital *Palæogr.*, a form of rectilinear capital letter, *spec.* characterizing a script used in early Latin manuscripts (cf. Rustic *a.* 5 b); **square cut** *Cricket*, a cut hit square on the off-side; hence **square-cut** *v. trans.*, to cut (a ball) thus; **square cutter; square dance,** a dance in which four couples face inwards from four sides; also *loosely*, a country-dance; hence **square-dance** *v. intr.*; **square dancer, -dancing** *vbl. sb.*; **square dinkum**: see *dinkum *a.*; **square drive** *Cricket*, a drive hit square on the off-side; hence **square-drive** *v. trans.*, to drive (a ball or bowler) in this manner; **square engine,** an internal-combustion engine in which the length of the stroke is approximately equal to the bore of the cylinders; **square-eyed** *a. joc.*, affected by or given to excessive viewing of television; **square Hebrew** *Palæogr.*, the standard Hebrew script which displaced the Aramaic form towards the end of the Biblical period, and has been adopted for use in printed texts; **square John** *N. Amer. slang*, an upright, respectable person; *spec.* one who is not a drug-addict; **square law** *Physics*, a law relating two variables one of which varies either directly or inversely as the square of the other (cf. *inverse square* (*law*) s.v. Inverse *a.* 3 a); also used *attrib.* of a device whose action obeys the square law; **square-lipped rhino(ceros** = *white rhino*(*ceros*) s.v. *white *a.* 11 a; **square motor** = *square engine* above; **square-mouthed rhino(ceros** = *white rhino*(*ceros*) s.v. *white *a.* 11 a; **square piano** = *square pianoforte;* **square pianoforte** (earlier example); **square pin**: on an electrical plug, a pin with a rectangular rather than a circular cross-section; **square-rig,** (*b*) *Naut. slang*, the uniform of a naval rating (see also quot. 1942); **square-rigger** (earlier example); **square serif** *Typogr.*, a type-face distinguished by straight serifs as thick as the other parts of the letters; **square-shooter** *slang* (orig. and chiefly *U.S.*), an honest, dependable, sound person; hence **square-shooting** *a.*, honest, respectable; **square thread** *Mech.*, a screw thread which in cross-section is castellated in form, with the width and height of the thread equal to the width of the valley between threads; **square wave** *Electronics*, (a voltage represented by) a periodic wave that varies abruptly in amplitude between two fixed values, spending equal times at each; **square well** *Nucl. Physics*, a potential well of square section; **square wheels,** used *joc.* of a set of wheels which give a jolting ride, as if they were square; also *fig.*

1699 M. Lister *Journey to Paris* 108 The same MS... is written in Square Capitals and very short Lines. **1883** [see Rustic *a.* 5 b]. **1906** E. Johnston *Writing & Illumin. & Lettering* I. i. 37 Square Capitals were formed, pen-made Roman Capitals, of the monumental type. **1897** K. S. Ranjitsinhji *Jubilee Bk. Cricket* iv. 164 A square-cut travels somewhere between point and third-man. It is the commonest form of cut. **1956** N. Cardus *Close of Play* 150 Those who saw him will cherish memories of his vehement hooking..his square-cuts. **1976** Dexter & Makins *Testkill* 167 Hunt let the first ball go by, then square-cut the second with great majesty. **1920** D. J. Knight in P. F. Warner *Cricket* 32 Another beautiful square cutter is J. T. Tyldesley. **1870** L. M. Alcott *Old-Fashioned Girl* vii. 132 I'm going to begin with a redowa, because..it's better fun than square dances. **1902** *Encycl. Brit.* XXVII. 375/2 'Dull Sir John' and 'Faine I would' were square dances popular in England three hundred years ago. **1955** *Times* 28 June 11/4 The term 'square dance' is the American equivalent of the English 'country dance'. **1959** *Manch. Guardian* 7 Aug. 6/4 The entire population turns out to square-dance in the main streets. **1976** *West Lancs. Evening Gaz.* 15 Dec. 1. 8/2 One woman square dancer had fallen on the polished floor of the hall. **1977** *Times* 24 Jan. 4/7 The mass free admission square dance..bore witness that square dancing is alive and well across the continent. **1900** W. J. Ford *Cricketer on Cricket* xii. 140 His strokes are limited to the off-side, chiefly cuts and square drives. **1954** J. Fingleton *Ashes crown Year* 271 May brilliantly square-drove him for 4. **1977** *Guardian* 3 Jan. 11/7 Amiss began the afternoon by square driving Bedi's first ball for four. **1930** *Engineering* 7 Mar. 303/2 He then analyses the main differences between a square engine and one with a stroke:bore ratio of 2. **1964** J. Braine *Jealous God* viii. 136 'Square-eyed sods,' he said. **1976** *Listener* 8 July 2/2 He called the television set 'the Devil's Box', claimed.. that it would turn the bronzed, outdoor-loving youngster into a round-backed, square-eyed weakling. **1915** Square Hebrew [see note in Dict., sense 14 a]. **1948** D. Diringer *Alphabet* 261 The Aramaic script therefore became the parent of the 'square Hebrew'. **1974** *Encycl. Brit. Micropædia* IV. 983/1 Between the 6th and 2nd centuries BC, Classical, or Square, Hebrew gradually displaced the Aramaic alphabet. **1934** *Detective Fiction Weekly* 21 Apr. 113/1 The man who works for a living..is generally referred to in terms of contempt such as working stiff, Honest John, Square John, sucker or scissor bill. **1935** A. J. Pollock *Underworld Speaks* 112/2 *Square John*, a dope peddler who is not addicted. **1962** 'K. Orvis' *Damned & Destroyed* ix. 62, I played it even safer with those uptown Square Johns. **1968** *Daily Colonist* (Victoria, B.C.) 2 Nov. 8/1 He kept saying that McWhirter was a 'square John'. 'What does a 'square John' mean? Does it mean an ordinary law-abiding citizen?' Mr. Owen-Flood asked. 'As far as I know,' Porter replied. **1921** *Physical Rev.* XVIII. 263 For the weaker [magnetic] fields there is a decided curvature in the lines which gradually smooth out into practically straight lines. It is in this lower region that the 'square law', proposed by Sir J. J. Thomson, holds. **1945** *Electronic Engin.* XVII. 734/2 The valve will work satisfactorily as a square law rectifier. **1958** W. T. O'Dea *Social Hist. Lighting* i. 8 A room forty feet by thirty could be lit quite cheerfully by the candles and would be dismal by the light of a single bulb. The reason is the 'square law' so well known to anyone who has studied physics. Ten feet away from a light source the illumination per unit area is only one-hundredth of what it is one foot away, and so on. **1976** *Nature* 29 Jan. 294/2 The vector voltmeters had a bandwidth of 1 kHz and employed a square-law detector following the narrow-band filter. [**1931** C. R. S. Pitman *Game Warden among his Charges* i. 3 There is the huge, square mouth—from which it derives its sobriquet of 'square-lipped'.] **1961** *New Scientist* 9 Nov. 340/2 A rare animal, the white or square-lipped rhino, is threatened by extinction. **1970** *Nature* 28 Mar. 1180/1 (*caption*) By 1966 ..there were about 800 southern square-lipped rhinoceroses in the Hluhluwe and Umfolozi reserves in Natal. **1912** C. B. Hayward *Pract. Aeronaut.* 349 Design in this field [*sc.* aircraft engines] has..gone back to automobile standards of several years ago when it was customary to build what are known as square motors, i.e. those in which the bore and stroke are the same. **1881** *Proc. Zool. Soc.* 726 The square-mouthed rhinoceros is a huge ungainly-looking beast. **1915** Roosevelt & Heller *Life-Histories Afr. Game Animals* II. xxi. 662 The square-mouthed rhinos..seemed to be of a perceptibly lighter gray. **1853** Dickens *Bleak Ho.* xxxviii. 379 A little jingling square piano. **1938** R. Field *All this & Heaven Too* (1939) I. xvi. 208 One of the girls went to a square piano and began trying the keys. **1980** *Early Music* July 377/2 Included in the sale was the Zumpe square piano of 1766 (£3,200) the earliest known piano to have been made in England. **1787** *Brit. Patent* specn. 1596 (*caption*) This figure represents the movement of a square Piano Forte. **1965** P. Honey *Planning Electricity in House* iii. 75 The 13-amp. plug has square pins (which are superior to round pins) and will not fit any other size of socket. **1942** Berrey & Van den Bark *Amer. Thes. Slang* § 791/10 *Square rig* or *rigger*, a double-breasted uniform. **1951** N. Coward *Star Quality* 24 Attired as they were in the usual 'Square-Rig' of British Ordinary Seamen, they caused a mild sensation. **1962** W. Granville *Dict. Sailors' Slang* 112/1 *Square rig*, uniform worn by 'men dressed as seamen', the jumper, flannel, jean collar and bell-bottomed trousers. **1979** *Navy News* Feb. 4/1 It is a once-only increase to enable these ratings to complete the replacement of old-pattern suits of square rig, without being out of pocket. **1855** C. Nordhoff *Merchant Vessel* 285 Our mate..had never before been in a 'square-rigger'. **1940** H. F. Lock *Basic Typogr.* iii. 30 The modern square-serif letters are derived from the 'Antiques' and 'Egyptians' of a century ago. **1967** E. Chambers *Photolitho-Offset* ii. 13 Leading the contemporary field are the square serif and the sans serif. **1978** S. Rice *Bk. Design* 214 *Sans serif*, typeface design not having the small bracketing accents at the ends of the letter strokes... Square serif letters do not properly belong to this grouping. **1914** Jackson & Hellyer *Vocab. Criminal Slang* 79 *Square-shooter*,..a dependable person; a reliable, compact-keeping person. **1928** S. Lewis *Man who knew Coolidge* 1. 51 There's a man that it's a pleasure to do business with, a square-shooter if ever there was one. **1937** Wyndham Lewis *Blasting & Bombardiering* 1. vi. 63 My friend..was somehow treacherous and not at all the good sport and 'square-shooter' I had supposed him to be. **1962** E. Lucia *Klondike Kate* ii. 24 Kitty was looked upon as a 'square shooter' in the rough give-and-take game of the Dawson gambling joints. **1922** Square shooting [see *animal A. 6]. **1932** J. Dos Passos *1919* 428 One of them made a speech in English and another one in Sicilian saying that this was a squareshooting concern that had always treated laborers square. **1908** E. Oberg *Handbk. Small Tools* i. 29 The Acme thread..has of late become widely used, having in most instances taken the place of the square thread on account of its better wearing qualities. **1939** S. E. Winston *Machine Design* iii. 72 The Square Thread..is probably the most typical transmission screw thread, as its mechanical efficiency is considerably higher than that of such threads as the V thread. **1975** Bram & Downs *Manuf. Technol.* iv. 120 In the square thread the sides are parallel and normal to the axis of the screw. **1944** *Jrnl. Scientific Instruments* XXI. 64 (*heading*) A simple variable 'square-wave' stimulator for biological work. **1965** *Wireless World* Sept. 460/1 One popular method of amplifier stability assessment is 'square-wave testing' in which a suitable square wave is applied to the input, and the output inspected on an oscilloscope screen. **1975** G. J. King *Audio Handbk.* v. 120 It is assumed that the input waveform is a true square wave of very small rise time. **1939** *Physical Rev.* LVI. 890/1 The square well fitting proton-proton scattering is not as deep as that fitting proton-neutron scattering. **1954** *Ibid.* XCVI. 461/1 The smoothing of the edges of the square-well potential was of significance for the interpretation of the elastic proton scattering with heavy nuclei. **1975** W. F. Hornyak *Nuclear Structure* iv. 242 Another simple potential well used to represent the average potential of the single-particle model is the three-dimensional square well. **1924** *Radio Times* 19 Dec. 594/1 (Advt.), Thousands of Wireless enthusiasts..are running their broadcasting reception on square wheels, enduring..distortion... Are *you* getting square wheel reception? **1977** 'O. Jacks' *Autumn Heroes* viii. 111 It was almost impossible to stand upright. The truck was operating on square wheels.

b. square flipper [app. a folk etymologizing of Newfoundland dial. *fipper, fripper*, etc. (also used), of uncertain origin], the bearded seal, *Erignathus barbatus*, native to Arctic regions (earlier and later examples); **square-tail**, (*b*) the char or brook trout, *Salvelinus fontinalis*, native to eastern North America.

1774 G. Cartwright *Jrnl.* 12 Dec. (1792) II. 38 A squarephripper was caught in a net to-day. **1784** T. Pennant *Arctic Zool.* 161 The Seal-hunters in Newfoundland have a large kind, which they call the Square Phipper, and say weighs five hundred pounds. **1832** J. McGregor *Hist. & Descr. Sk. Brit. Amer.* I. 108 The harp seal..the hooded seal..the square flipper, the blue seal, and the jar seal. **1842** J. B. Jukes *Excursions in Newfoundland* I. 312 The 'square fipper'..is, however, very rare. **1861** L. de Boilieu *Recoll. Labrador Life* 91 These seals are not like the Square Frippers. **1911** D. M. Lindsay *Voyage to Arctic* iii. 39 Square flippers..are also found on the coast [of Newfoundland]. **1957** *Beaver* Spring 49/1 They were immensely strong and could carry off a square-flipper seal single-handed. **1935** B. Perry *And gladly Teach* vii. 151 The lake was perfect for bathing and boating. There were big 'square-tails' in it then. **1972** *Trout & Salmon* Feb. 14/2 It brought to mind an experience I had in Labrador this past summer when I was up there fishing for squaretail trout.

square, *adv.* Add: **3. d.** *U.S. colloq.* Completely, exactly.

1862 E. S. Philbrick *Let.* 2 Nov. in E. W. Pearson *Lett. from Port Royal* (1906) 103 His heart failed him and he backed square out. **1880** 'Mark Twain' *Tramp Abr.* xvii. 152 He..shot the dragon square in the center of his cavernous mouth. **1903** A. D. McFaul *Ike Glidden* xxvi. 236 Hain't I bin a-runnin' my legs right square off this four days? **1921** R. D. Paine *Comr. Rolling Ocean* i. 8 It surely did hit me square between the eyes.

e. *Mus.* In a square fashion (*square *a.* 7*).

1960 L. Bernstein *Joy of Music* 105 Now that you've heard what syncopation is like, let's see what that same Blues we heard before would sound like without it... *Played 'square' by sax, no vibrato.*

4. b. *square on*: (*a*) *Cricket*, of a bowler: having one's body square to the batsman; (*b*) *fig.*, directly, honestly. Also as *adj. phr.*, straightforward.

1963 A. Ross *Australia 63* ii. 65 His actual delivery, a shade reminiscent of George Tribe's, is made more square-on than is classical. **1968** K. Weatherly *Roo Shooter* 145 Jim, we've got to look at this square on. We haven't given the game away. It's given us away. **1977** *Lancashire Life* Dec. 60/2 Some of his more ambitious attempts, however, don't quite 'come off', while others are 'square-on' to the point of suggesting a lack of imagination.

5. b. *Cricket.* At right angles to the line of the delivery.

1851 J. Pycroft *Cricket Field* vii. 154 Practise diligently with leg-balls, till balls..a little wide of leg-stump go nearly square. **1891** [see *fine *a.* 7 f]. **1909** W. Caffyn *Seventy-One not Out* viii. 90 He was a fine leg-hitter, generally hitting square. **1963** T. E. Bailey *Improve your Cricket* i. 38 (*caption*) The ball has been played behind square, but it can be played in front.

square, *v.* Add: **I. 1. d.** Also *fig.*

1930 T. S. Eliot tr. *St.-J. Perse's Anabasis* 53 The boundless unreckoned year, squared out with dawns and fires.

3. e. *refl.* To put oneself into a posture of defence. Also *fig.* Cf. sense 11 in Dict. and Suppl. orig. *U.S.*

1823 J. F. Cooper *Pioneers* II. xv. 223 Square yourself, you lubber,..and we'll soon know who's the better man. **1864** 'Mark Twain' *Celebrated Jumping Frog* (1867) 107 Caesar..squared himself to receive his assailants. **1893** *Harper's Mag.* Mar. 643/1 With a look of determination on his face, [he] squared himself to write. **1977** J. I. M. Stewart *Madonna of Astrolabe* i. 28, I was squaring myself to the necessity of telling him that I was no good for the purpose he had in mind when our walk came suddenly to an end.

f. *Assoc. Football*, etc. To pass (the ball) across the pitch, esp. towards the centre.

1972 G. Green *Great Moments in Sport: Soccer* viii. 85 Bloomfield made it 2–3 from a squared header by Groves. **1976** E. Dunphy *Only a Game?* iv. 113 Having to go round the back of the goal and square it back before you could score. **1978** *Times* 12 Jan. 10/3 Tait..squared the ball into the stride of Rafferty who hit in a first-time shot.

II. 4. e. *colloq.* With *away*: to put in proper order, to tidy up, to 'sort out'.

1909 R. A. Wason *Happy Hawkins* (1912) xvi. 203 She had a head on her, Barbie had, an' when she got squared away, she made 'em all get down an' scratch. **1947** *Seafarers' Log* 19 Dec. 10/1 Motion carried that Ship's Delegate contact all tripcard men who have not acted in a way becoming to a Union man and get them squared away. **1956** H. Kurnitz *Invasion of Privacy* xiv. 87 Let's get you squared away, Mr. Jarrold. You knew damn well what you were doing..didn't you? **1966** T. Pynchon *Crying of Lot 49* i. 20 He outlined what she was in for.. decide what to liquidate and what to hold on to, pay off claims, square away taxes, distribute legacies. **1980** 'R. B. Dominic' *Attending Physician* ii. 12 We've got Mrs Bertilucci squared away... Sorry about her yelling at you.

5. d. (Earlier examples.)

1821 J. A. Quitman *Let.* 4 Dec. in J. F. H. Claiborne *Life & Corr. J. A. Quitman* (1860) I. 69, I paid my $25, squared my bill, and departed. **1855** 'Q. K. P. Doesticks' *Doesticks, what he Says* xvii. 141 Damphool squared up his broad bill, and paid his washerwoman, which left him dead broke.

e. *Sport.* To make the scores of (a match, etc.) equal. Also *absol.*

1923 *Daily Mail* 8 May 12 The American captain missed his chance to square at the 17th, where he had a putt of 4 feet to win the hole. **1926** Wodehouse *Heart of Goof* ii. 66 Bradbury, driving another long ball, won the fifteenth, squaring the match. **1955** *Times* 26 July 3/1 England, in fact, if they are to win..must make 366 in six hours to-day, while South Africa, to square the rubber, have eight wickets yet to take. **1976** J. Snow *Cricket Rebel* 54 The last few tense and dramatic overs later on in the final Test in Georgetown when the West Indies were pressing for victory to square the series.

6. c. *Austral.* With *off*: to placate or conciliate (a person). Also *intr.*

1945 Baker *Austral. Lang.* vi. 134 *Square off, to*, to apologize, to produce a glib explanation for some lapse or misdeameanour. **1969** *Courier-Mail* (Brisbane) 15 Jan. 7/3 Moloney said..that he had been drinking at hotels... As they were driving home, he..decided..to buy beer to 'square off' with his wife. **1976** *Nature* 19 Feb. 519/2 Squaring off the proprietors of the three national chains of newspapers, whose unquestioning support he [*sc.* Mr. Fraser] enjoyed throughout the campaign.

III. 11. d. With *off*: to assume a fighting attitude. Also *fig.* orig. *U.S.*

1838 J. C. Neal *Charcoal Sketches* 41 If he 'squares off' at a big fellow, he is obliged..to hit his antagonist on the knee. **1856** 'Q. K. P. Doesticks' *Plu-ri-bus-tah* xi. 126 Then, at once, squared off at Cuffee, Instantly 'sailed into' Cuffee. **1873** J. H. Beadle *Undevel. West* xxxvi. 773 The bow appeared to be rearing up to square off at the midday sun. **1942** E. Paul *Narrow St.* xxix. 267 The rest of the world were squaring off for a life-and-death struggle. **1960** T. McLean *Kings of Rugby* 170 Wellington was still ahead, 6 to 3, as the two teams squared off for the second half. **1974** 'E. Lathen' *Sweet & Low* iv. 49 The yelling started... It sounded to me like they were going to square off.

12. c. (Earlier and later examples.) Also *fig.*, to get moving; to put oneself into shape; to make ready.

1849 N. Kingsley *Diary* 3 Sept. (1914) 57 The wind died away and soon sprung out from the South and [we] squared away before it. **1868** H. Woodruff *Trotting Horse Amer.* ix. 101 They must be wakened up from time to time, so as to make them get out of their sluggish habit and square away. **1889** 'Mark Twain' *Connecticut Yankee* xxxvii. 479, I didn't waste any time..but squared away for business. **1961** 'E. Lathen' *Banking on Death* (1962) xiii. 103 Miss Todd wasted no more time on idle chatter but squared away to her typewriter.

14. In Comb., as **square-up** *colloq.*, a quarrel.

? **1949** Dylan Thomas *Sel. Lett.* (1966) 339 Bert and I had a regular square-up, but he came over to my way of thinking.

squared, *ppl. a.* Add: **1. a.** Also with *off*.

1965 J. A. Michener *Source* (1966) 580 No square corners would be allowed, no neatly squared-off towers. **1973** D. May *Laughter in Djakarta* v. 83 Tapping some magazines into a squared-off pile.

c. (Earlier example.)

1887 *Science* 11 Mar. 240/1 The graphic representation of the results will be readily understood. It is only necessary to take a sheet of 'squared' paper, or paper ruled in two directions at right angles to each other.

2. (Later examples.) Also *fig.*

1964 J. W. Linnett *Electronic Struct. Molecules* vi. 92 There will be five squared-terms..and twenty cross-terms ..in the square of the total function. **1979** *Tucson* (Arizona) *Citizen* 20 Sept. 11A/1, I don't know if tarantulas are considered insects or just some form of spider.. squared.

squa·rehead. *slang.* Also **square-head.** [Square *a.* 9 c.] **1.** An honest person; one who is not a criminal (see quots.).

1890 Barrère & Leland *Dict. Slang* II. 293/1 'Honesty among thieves' is undoubtedly the production of a square-head or sham thief; a good thief will rob anybody. **1950** *Austral. Police Jrnl.* Apr. 119 *Square-head* (or *squarey*), one who has no convictions. **1977** *Courier-Mail* (Brisbane) 16 Feb. 5/1 Half an hour or so later a squarehead (criminal slang for someone who is going straight), who was minding the money in a bag for Blair, handed it over to one of the Toecutters.

2. A foreigner of Germanic extraction, esp. a German (spec. *Army slang* in the war of 1914–18) or Scandinavian.

1903 FARMER & HENLEY *Slang* VI. 333/1 *Squarehead*,.. a German or Scandinavian. **1906** *Soldier Slang* in C. McGovern *Sarjint Larry an' Frinds, Square-head*, a soldier of German birth and addicted to the use of German idioms. **1918** H. C. WITWER in *Collier's* 16 Mar. 21/2 The English call 'em 'Uns..we call 'em squareheads. **1932** J. DOS PASSOS *1919* 61 She started firing across the North Star's bows with a small gun that the squareheads manned. **1942** C. BARRETT *On Wallaby* v. 95 A bunch of Germans with this mob behaved very differently: the square-heads were sullen and surly. **1953** *Times Lit. Suppl.* 23 Oct. 678/2 Those of Swedish extraction in America, known as squareheads, suffer the reputation of being dull, heavy, stupid, simple. **1973** D. JONES *Let.* 15 Apr. in R. Hague *Dai Greatcoat* (1980) iv. 244 In the ranks we often used 'Squarehead' of old Jerry—'That poor old 'squarehead' they brought in from last night's raid looked pretty far gone to me.'

3. In misc. *transf.* and *fig.* uses.

1919 *Dialect Notes* V. 62 *Square-head*, a dull, stupid person. **1949** *Sun* (Baltimore) 26 Oct. 10/3 A real 'square-head' seaman, who knows what it is like to drift for days without food. **1958** 'CASTLE' & 'HAILEY' *Flight into Danger* i. 13 This plane is crammed with squareheads who are going to Vancouver..to root like hell for their boys.

square-headed, *a.* Add: **d.** Level-headed, sensible.

1896 H. G. WELLS *Let.* 24 Jan. in *Exper. Autobiogr.* (1934) I. vi. 402 He's a first rate, square headed, thoroughly honest man. **1922** JOYCE *Ulysses* 82 Squareheaded chaps those must be in Rome: they work the whole show.

e. Stolid, dull.

1936 C. S. LEWIS *Allegory of Love* iv. 172 To believe thus is to attribute to Chaucer a square-headed vulgarity of thought and feeling.

f. Describing one of a Germanic race.

1942 E. PAUL *Narrow St.* xxix. 268 The square-headed, owl-like Nazis. **1979** O. SELA *Petrograd Consignment* 35 A big, square-headed man.

Hence **square-hea·dedness.**

1930 *Times Lit. Suppl.* 10 Apr. 321/1 An underlying sanity and square-headedness about Huneker's critical judgments.

squareness. Add: **3. b.** *Assoc. Football*, etc. Of a defence: the condition of being square (*SQUARE *a.* 6 d) and lacking in depth.

1978 *Guardian Weekly* 19 Nov. 23/5 Taking full advantage of Manchester United's inadequacy in the air and punishing the squareness of their defence on the ground.

4. Conventionality, dullness. Cf. *SQUARE *a.* 9 d.

1961 *John o' London's* 16 Nov. 548/2 Where Squareness is the ultimate low, anything can get by if it proclaims itself Hip loudly enough. **1972** M. J. BOSSE *Incident at Naha* ii. 119, I was beginning to care about our Bostonian, even though he was capable of, like, ultimate squareness. **1977** P. USTINOV *Dear Me* xiii. 173 It is out of fear of what is known as squareness that we rarely say what we really think or feel.

squarer. Add: **4.** *Electronics.* A device that converts a sinusoidal or other periodic wave into a square wave of the same period.

1965 *Wireless World* Aug. 402/1 If the square wave output is integrated and used to bias the first transistor, and if the squarer is d.c. coupled throughout and has an odd number of stages, then the feedback maintains the mark-to-space ratio constant. **1971** *Physics Bull.* July 427/1 The basic module was an inverter and was demonstrated as a squarer, then two or more were joined together to produce various logic gates and multivibrators.

Squaresville (skwēᵊ·ɹzvil). orig. *U.S.* Also **Squareville**. [f. SQUARE *sb.* or *a.*: see *-VILLE.] An imaginary town characterized by dullness and conventionality. Also *attrib.* or as *adj.*

1956 'E. MCBAIN' *Cop Hater* (1958) viii. 75 This guy is from Squaresville, fellas, I'm telling you. He wouldn't know a ·45 from a cement mixer. **1961** *Times* 27 Apr. 17/2 To look round a crowded room and murmur 'Squareville' or 'Hicksville' may be elliptical, but is certainly more effective than the full form. **1967** P. WELLES *Babyhip* (1968) ii. 31 It's such squaresville talk. **1968** *Listener* 11 July 51/1 And they went away, more than ever convinced that the war between the generations was for real. And through the window there floated a querulous, puzzled voice. 'A queer fish, real squaresville.'

square-toed, *a.* Add: **1. b.** *transf.* in *U.S. Naut.* use. Now only *Hist.*

1851 H. MELVILLE *Moby Dick* I. xvi. 110 You may have seen many a quaint craft in your day, for aught I know: square-toed luggers, mountainous Japanese junks. **1886** *Forest & Stream* 13 May 316/3 Even the regular 'square-toed' schooner, supposed to be original to San Francisco, flourishes up the James. **1948** R. DE KERCHOVE *Internat. Maritime Dict.* (1958) 771/1 *Square-toed frigate*,..local name given in Quincy, Mass., to the scow sloops engaged in the granite trade. (Obsolete.)

squaring, *ppl. a.* Add: **3.** That multiplies a quantity by itself.

1961 *Technology* Feb. 44/2 An automatic neon overload indicator..detects signal peaks exceeding the range of the squaring unit. **1979** *Proc. London Math. Soc.* XXXVIII. 514 The squaring map $a \to a^2$, determined by this Jordan product, is the same as that determined by functional calculus.

squarish, *a.* Add: Occas. **square-ish.** (Later examples.)

1921 S. COLVIN *Memories & Notes* viii. 130 In spite of her squareish build she was supple and elastic in all her movements. **1950** M. PEAKE *Gormenghast* lxxvii. 417 A largish, square-ish room. **1981** *Times* 21 Apr. 14/5 Later, the mausoleum was superseded by a small squarish chapel.

squash, *sb.*[1] Add: **I. 3. a.** *squash-ball* (example), *-racket* (= the bat used in the game: examples), *-rackets* (= the game: later examples); **squash tennis** *U.S.*, a game similar to squash rackets, played with a lawn-tennis ball.

1901 E. MILES *Game of Squash* i. 16 Americans generally use a Lawn-Tennis ball..and a Squash-Tennis racket, which is like a miniature Lawn-Tennis racket. **1905** H. A. VACHELL *Hill* ii. 26 He bought..a 'squash' racquet, 'squash' balls, and a yard ball. **1917** *National Squash Tennis Assoc. Rules* 18 Description and specifications of a Squash Tennis Court, as adopted by the National Squash Tennis Association... The dimensions of a Standard Court shall be..Length 32 feet 6 inches Width 17 feet. **1928** *N.Y. Times* 12 Dec. 32/6 The success of the American players in the English squash racquets tournament... At the [American] colleges..squash racquets became more popular. **1930** A. DANZIG *Racquet Game* III. i. 157 The two varieties of squash—squash tennis and squash racquets—have so much in common that they may be called first cousins. **1973** *Times* 28 Sept. 5/6 There is a wide disparity between the international and American versions of squash rackets. **1975** *Oxf. Compan. Sports & Games* 985/1 The squash racket is not as strong as the rackets racket. *Ibid.* 992/2 Squash tennis was born in a school in Concord, New Hampshire,..but..was refined by Feron, of New York, who first wrapped netting round the ball.

b. *ellipt.* for *squash rackets* or occas. (*U.S.*), *squash tennis.*

1899 *N.Y. World* 8 Aug. 14/4 'Squash'..is a variation of the time-honored court tennis. **1902** E. MILES (*title*) Racquets, tennis and squash. **1930** [see *squash tennis*, sense 3 a above]. **1952** J. B. PICK *Phoenix Dict. Games* 183 Squash is played with a rubber ball on a four-walled court. *Ibid.* 185 Service in squash is not the deadly weapon it is in rackets. **1975** *Oxf. Compan. Sports & Games* 986/1 Squash is derived from, and has much in common with, the much older game of rackets, and originated at Harrow School.

II. 5. c. A social gathering; an informal religious or literary meeting.

1904 H. JAMES *Golden Bowl* I. III. xiv. 252 The intrinsic oddity of the London 'squash', a thing of vague, slow, senseless eddies. **1916** L. EINSTEIN *Let.* 31 July in *Holmes-Einstein Letters* (1964) II. 134 The season, however, which I loathe, was rendered nicer by the war..no more fat squashes but agreeable dinners and luncheons. **1938** M. WHITLOW *J. Taylor Smith* xi. 114 The Inter-varsity Christian Fellowship have a 'date' with him for a series of 'Squashes' at Oxford and Cambridge. **1977** L. GORDON *Eliot's Early Years* iii. 47 In 1912, Conrad Aiken took 'Prufrock' to a 'poetry squash' in London and showed it to Harold Monro. **1979** *PN Review 13* 19/1 Lord, you know that next week is the Freshers' Squash.

6. b. *Biol.* A preparation of softened tissue that has been made thin for microscopic examination by pressing or tapping.

1942 DARLINGTON & LA COUR *Handling of Chromosomes* v. 40 Sections have now been largely replaced by smears and squashes for all but the smallest masses of material. **1971** *Nature* 18 June 452/2 Fifty cells of three females and thirty-two cells of four males were examined. A testis squash was also made to give meiotic figures. **1981** *Japanese Jrnl. Genetics* LVI. 529 This method enables the observation of both C-banding patterns and the karyotypes by aceto-orcein squash technique in the same chromosome complement.

7. Also, a drink made from the juice of crushed fruit other than lemons; = *CRUSH *sb.* 4 e. Freq. as second element of combinations: see *lime-squash* s.v. *LIME *sb.*[2] 2, *orange squash* s.v. *ORANGE *sb.*[1] 7 a.

1914 C. MACKENZIE *Sinister Street* II. III. vii. 644 Will you have a squash and a biscuit? **1936** *Discovery* June 192/1 Fruit Squashes, containing the pulp of the fruit, were analogous to the well-known orange and lemon squashes. The blackcurrant squash was remarkable for its delicate flavour. **1939** A. P. HERBERT *Water Gipsies* (rev. ed.) x. 99 Jane suggested that they should..have a lemon-squash... Ernest did not want a squash. **1967** *Coast to Coast 1965–6* 185 'Come on in and I'll make you a squash.'..Meg squeezed a lemon for his drink. **1980** *Brit. Med. Jrnl.* 29 Mar. 913 Most fruit squashes are unsuitable for babies.

8. *attrib.* as **squash bite** *Dentistry*, an impression of the teeth made by biting the jaws together on a piece of plastic material.

1914 N. G. BENNETT *Sci. & Pract. Dental Surg.* xxxvii. 607/1 A 'squash bite' impression, or even one taken in the ordinary way in a tray, is very easily distorted in removing from the mouth. **1940** J. OSBORNE *Dental Mechanics* v. 47 It is usual if this type of block is used to have taken a 'squash bite' at the impression stage. **1963** C. R. COWELL et al. *Inlays, Crowns, & Bridges* ii. 10 The relationship of the prepared tooth to adjacent and opposing teeth must be recorded in the indirect technique with a wax or an alginate squash bite.

squash, *sb.*[2] Add: **4. squash-berry,** the red berry of *Viburnum pauciflorum*, a deciduous North American shrub; = *moose-berry* s.v. MOOSE[1] b; **squash blossom,** the flower of the plant on which squashes grow, applied *attrib.* to jewellery made by the Navajo which is characterized by designs (of Spanish, and ult. Moorish, derivation, representing pomegranates) resembling this flower.

1937 LADY ROCKLEY *Some Canadian Wild Flowers* 77 Its [sc. *Viburnum pauciflorum's*] berries known as the 'Squash-berry' are gathered and make an excellent preserve. **1966** A. R. SCAMMELL *My Newfoundland* 32 He even shook his head at bakeapple jam, squashberry jelly and 'meshberries'. **1974** J. E. UNDERHILL *Wild Berries Pacific Northwest* 23 Huckleberries, Blueberries, Squash-berries, and many others, may be made into delicious jams. **1923** D. H. LAWRENCE *Birds, Beasts & Flowers* 19 The fig, the horseshoe, the squash-blossom. Symbols. **1930** D. & M. R. COOLIDGE *Navajo Indians* xvi. 115 The beautiful squash-blossom pendants which the Hopis like so much. **1944** J. ADAIR *Navajo & Pueblo Silversmiths* v. 83, I watched Charie make other pieces. One of them was a squash-blossom bead. **1950** S. H. BABINGTON *Navajos, Gods & Tom-Toms* xv. 170 The pronged pieces in the beautiful so-called squash blossom necklace are the buttons which were sewed along the outside seams..of Spanish army officers' pants. **1977** C. MCFADDEN *Serial* (1978) ii. 10/2 Carol..had embellished it with her trademark jewelry: an authentic squash-blossom necklace.

squashed, *ppl. a.* (In Dict. s.v. SQUASH *v.*[1]) Add: **2.** Special collocations: **squashed fly (biscuit)** *colloq.* = *GARIBALDI 3; **squashed tomato** *slang*, a name given in different localities to various children's games (see quots.).

1900 J. S. FARMER *Public School Word-bk.* 85 *Squashed flies*,..biscuits with currants. **1909**, etc. [see *GARIBALDI 3]. **1931** C. LITHGOW *Simple Sailor* v. 49 In 'the break', they grappled for their milk and bun, or 'squashed-fly' biscuit. **1977** K. M. E. MURRAY *Caught in Web of Words* xvii. 321 Gwyneth remembered her anguish as a little girl at finding nothing in her parcel but a Garibaldi ('squashed fly') biscuit. **1959** I. & P. OPIE *Lore & Lang. Schoolch.* xviii. 381 There are more than sixty established names for the pursuit of illegally knocking at doors... *Squashed tomato.* Wolverhampton. **1963** S. MARSHALL *Exper. in Educ.* ii. 56 The new look given to the age-old playground game which for some unknown reason has become 'Squashed Tomato' in the language of today... A voice was giving orders to the players. 'John, three scissors south towards Cambridge. Carol, two pigeon steps towards Newmarket [on a map painted on a school playground].' **1969** I. & P. OPIE *Children's Games* iv. 157 The game is usually known as 'Sardines', but also..'Squashed Sardines', and 'Squashed Tomatoes'. *Ibid.* vi. 189 *Squashed Tomato.* Both caller and called run towards each other, with arms crossed in front of them. The one advancing remains at the spot where they squash into each other. The caller returns to his place in front.

squashily (skwǫ·ʃili), *adv.* [f. SQUASHY *a.* + -LY[2].] In a squashy or squelchy manner.

1922 *Blackw. Mag.* Oct. 485/2 A small damp object.. struck the ground squashily near where I was standing. **1924** 'L. MALET' *Dogs of Want* viii. 262 Upon the seat.. Mr. Noakes heavily, not to say squashily, subsided.

squat, *sb.*[1] Add: **6. a.** *spec.* in Gymnastics and Weight-lifting.

Earlier called *crouch.*

1954 M. FALLON *Muscle Building for Beginners* x. 56 Keep the head up and the back flat, and resist any temptation to lean forward, particularly at the lowest point of the squat. **1959** LOKEN & WILLOUGHBY *Compl. Bk. Gymnastics* iv. 35 *Squat Head Balance.* Start this stunt from a squat position with the hands on the mat and the inside of the knees resting on the elbows. **1964** G. C. KUNZLE *Parallel Bars* ii. 42 Simple squats on one bar. *Ibid.* 44 Complete the squat off by pushing away strongly with the arms and drawing the shoulders forwards. **1977** J. F. FIXX *Compl. Bk. Running* vii. 91 Some runners and coaches think weightlifting is essential to good performances. Emil Zatopek..used to do squats while holding his wife, Dana, on his shoulders.

b. *hot squat*: see *HOT *a.* 1 e.

8. a. The illegal occupation of an uninhabited building (esp. by a group of homeless people organized for this purpose); the period of such an occupation.

1946 *Daily Mail* 20 Sept. 2/3 The Great Squat is over... Today at 1200 hours the rearguards of Squat-Force will retire. **1963** S. COOPER in Sissons & French *Age of Austerity* 44 Early in September 1946 Londoners were startled by what was christened the Great Sunday Squat. **1969** *Guardian* 27 Sept. 9/2 The Diggers have decided not to take part in any more hippie squats. **1970** N. SAUNDERS *Alternative London* xvii. 122 They then organised the squatters in East London, which has developed into the longest squat ever, lasting over ten months, in Arbour Square. **1975** *Times* 8 Jan. 3/6 This is the biggest squat ever, a serious attempt to house homeless people. **1981** *Daily Tel.* 3 Mar. 2/1 This squat cost the ratepayer £46,700—money we need not have spent had the squat not taken place.

b. A house, flat, or building occupied by squatters; a squatter's place of residence.

1975 *Guardian* 26 Sept. 5/8 He's at 14 Algernon Road. It's a squat. **1977** M. DRABBLE *Ice Age* II. 211 They'd been hosed out of their last squat. **1980** *Daily Tel.* 28 Oct. 17/3 A whipround among punks from a squat near the police station raised £12.50.

squat (skwǫt), *sb.*⁴ *U.S. slang.* [Prob. f. slang *to squat* to void excrement.] Nothing at all; (following a negative construction) anything. Orig. as second element of phr. *doodly-squat* [prob. f. U.S. slang *doodle* excrement].

1934 Z. N. HURSTON *Jonah's Gourd Vine* xviii. 217 She ain't never had nothin'—not eben doodly-squat, and when she gits uh chance tuh git holt uh sumpin de ole buzzard is gone on uh rampage. **1946** MEZZROW & WOLFE *Really Blues* viii. 107 These cats weren't from doodlely-squat. *Ibid.* 373 *Doodlely-squat,* nothing, no more than the product of a child who squats to do his duty. **1967** WENTWORTH & FLEXNER *Dict. Amer. Slang* Suppl. 705/2 *Squat,*.. = zot. *Ibid.* 712/2 *Zot,*..a grade or a score of zero. **1975** G. V. HIGGINS *City on Hill* i. 18 A lot of people that didn't care squat about the war went with us on that point. **1977** *Rolling Stone* 30 June 82/1 Under no circumstances would I ask those..judges down in Oswego to give him back his shingle on the condition it doesn't mean doodly-squat. **1979** P. BENCHLEY *Island* ii. 26 It'll be another forecast-of-Armageddon cover that won't amount to squat.

squat, *pa. pple.* and (*ppl.*) *a.* Add: **2.** (Later examples.)

1956 G. E. EVANS *Ask Fellows who cut Hay* xxv. 228 Another feature of the dialect is the expressive vigour of many of the words and phrases:..*squat* (pronounced with a very broad *a*) hidden or quiet. **1962** M. PROCTER *Devil in Moonlight* xv. 155 We'll keep it squat and take a chance on having trouble later.

4. *squat-lobster*: for (see quot. 1902) read: a crab-like marine animal belonging to the family Galatheidæ, and add later examples.

1928 RUSSELL & YONGE *Seas* iii. 67 There are also squat-lobsters, which have long claws and broad, flattened bodies. **1978** *Sci. Amer.* Dec. 99/2 The galatheids (the squat-lobsters, a group intermediate between the macrurans and the true crabs) have reflecting superposition eyes with square facets.

squat (skwǫt), *adv. rare*⁻¹. [f. the (*ppl.*) *a.*] In a direct and straightforward manner, 'flat'.

1909 KIPLING *Songs from Books* (1913) 24 Tell old Winter, if he doubt, Tell him squat and square-a!

squat, *v.* Add: **II. 9. c.** To occupy an uninhabited building illegally (esp. said of a group of homeless people organized for this purpose); to live as a squatter (*SQUATTER *sb.*¹ 1 d).

An isolated early example of this sense is entered as *transf.* under sense 9 a in Dict. (its correct date, however, is 1880, not 1879 as given there).

1937 'G. ORWELL' *Road to Wigan Pier* v. 81 In one town I remember a whole colony of them who were squatting, more or less illicitly, in a derelict house which was practically falling down. **1946** *Daily Worker* 9 Sept. 4/3 We..decided to assist homeless people to squat in certain of these buildings. **1969** *Listener* 15 May 665/1 No one expects to see 40,000 people squatting this year as there were 23 years ago. **1969** *Peace News* 13 June 5/1 One startling realisation..is how few is the number of families that have had the courage to squat. **1980** *Oxf. Compan. Law* 1171/2 Persons may squat in buildings by reason of inability to find other accommodation and may do so deliberately as a protest against shortage of housing in the area.

d. *trans.* (*a*) To install (someone) as a squatter. (*b*) To occupy (a building) as a squatter.

1973 *Guardian* 23 Mar. 9/5 Shelter, the campaign for the homeless, has squatted a homeless family of six people in an Ealing council house..reserved by the council for a homeless widow with four children. **1975** *Daily Tel.* 22 July 12 Much has been made of cases in which occupied privately-owned property has been squatted in the temporary absence of the owner. **1976** *Milton Keynes Express* 28 May 11/7 He added that he squats dozens of homeless people in corporation or council houses. **1977** *It* June 5/1 By January '76 the place was squatted by Enrique Ahriman, self-styled Demon of Confusion.

squa·t board, squatboard. *Naut.* [f. SQUAT *v.* + BOARD *sb.*] (See quots.)

1905 *Rudder* Feb. 62/2 There is one institution on the St. Lawrence which, it is believed, is peculiar to it and but little known of elsewhere; the 'squat board'. This is an appendage in the form of a horizontal plane attached to the stern. **1953** M. V. BREWINGTON *Chesapeake Bay: Pictorial Maritime Hist.* vi. 167 The stern settled so badly when underway 'squatboards' were necessary. **1955** J.-O. TRAUNG *Fishing Boats of World* I. 8/2 To overcome the resulting 'squatting' or settling aft, 'squatboards' have been added. These are flat wooden fins or planes placed at and nearly parallel to the waterline under and abaft the stern, to hold the stern up when the boat is driven hard.

squat tag. *U.S.* [f. SQUAT *v.* + TAG *sb.*²] A version of the game of tag in which a player may gain temporary immunity by squatting on the ground.

1883 W. W. NEWELL *Games & Songs Amer. Children* xi. 159 In *squat-tag,* the fugitive is safe while in that position. **1960** V. WILLIAMS *Walk Egypt* 95 Half a dozen children played Squat Tag around a wagon.

squatted, *ppl. a.* Add: **4.** Occupied by squatters. Also with *in.*

1963 S. COOPER in Sissons & French *Age of Austerity* 46 The squatted-in camps were..a useful temporary stop-gap for the housing problem. **1973** *Guardian* 5 Mar. 6/4 Everyone dropped in on another squatted house. **1975** *Time Out* 25 July 5/4 Islington Council is currently threatening to have electricity and gas supplies cut off to dozens of squatted houses in Finsbury Park. **1981** *Times* 14 July 2/4 According to Mrs Jean Styles..only two flats are empty and two 'squatted'.

squatter, *sb.*¹ Add: **1.** (Examples of the early Austral. use indicated by the note to sense 2 in Dict.)

1830 J. BETTS in *Occas. Papers Univ. Sydney Austral. Lang. Res. Cent.* (1965) No. 4. 13 A clan of people called 'Squatters'. These were generally emancipated convicts, or ticket-of-leave men, who, having obtained a small grant, under the old system, or without any grant at all, sat themselves down in remote situations, and maintained large flocks, obtained generally, in very nefarious ways, by having the run of all the surrounding country. **1833** W. H. BRETON *Excursions in N.S.W.* 442 There are likewise in the colony certain persons called 'squatters' (the term is American) who are commonly..of the lowest grade. **1835** *Sydney Gaz.* 28 Apr. 2 In every part of the country squatters without any reasonable means of maintaining themselves by honesty, have formed stations, and evidently pursued a predatory warfare against the flocks and herds in the vicinity.

d. One who occupies an uninhabited building illegally (esp. as a member of an organized group).

1880 W. H. DIXON *Royal Windsor* IV. xxix. 269 The King's house was a wreck; the fanatic, the pilferer, and the squatter, having been at work. **1946** *Times* 12 Aug. 2/3 Doncaster Rural District Council has turned on the water supply for a colony of its 'squatters' in military huts at Sprotborough. **1952** M. LASKI *Village* xiii. 185 The London squatters had moved into their flats and their hotels, and triumphantly held the police and all the authorities at bay. **1968** *Guardian* 2 Dec. 1/3 The London Squatters Campaign—formed three weeks ago. **1973** LD. DENNING in *All England Law Reports* III. 395 [McPhail v. Persons unknown]. What is a squatter? He is one who, without any colour of right, enters on an unoccupied house or land, intending to stay there as long as he can. **1980** *Oxf. Compan. Law* 1171/2 A squatter is a trespasser and liable to criminal penalties if he forces entry against the opposition of the lawful occupier or if, having been warned, he fails to leave.

2. Also *N.Z.*

1872 M. A. BARKER *Christmas Cake in Four Quarters* IV. ii. 260 Amongst our most constant guests were the Scotch shepherds of a neighbouring 'squatter'. **1891, 1911, 1933** [see *COCKY *sb.*² 2]. **1959** P. R. STEPHENS in A. McLintock *Descr. Atlas N.Z.* 38 The squatters soon became the dominant political force in the new country.

3. b. Substitute for def.: A bronze-wing pigeon of the genus *Phaps,* either *P. elegans* or *P. chalcoptera.*

c. *Cricket.* A ball which remains low on pitching; a shooter.

1955 I. PEEBLES *On Ashes* 109 In Statham's first over to Miller there were three 'squatters'. **1959** *Times* 7 Aug. 4/4 Phelan failed by only a whisker to bowl Pataudi with a squatter.

4. squatter's (or **squatters'**; occas. †**squatter**) **right(s)** orig. *U.S.,* the right of a squatter to the land on which he has settled; also in extended and *fig.* use.

1854 H. D. THOREAU *Walden* i. 54 These are all the materials excepting the timber, stones and sand, which I claimed by squatter's right. **1857** T. H. GLADSTONE *Englishman in Kansas* 168 The 'squatter-right' to a lot of ground is bought and sold on the strength of the law.. which asserts its power by rifle and tomahawk. **1883** *Brandon* (Manitoba) *Daily Mail* 24 Feb. 4/2 The infernal row you are all making up there about grievances, monopolies, squatters' rights, etc. **1944** N. STREATFEILD *Curtain Up* xvi. 222 A talent once accepted acquired squatter's rights, as it were. **1958** B. HAMILTON *Too Much of Water* x. 209 They had, by constant use.., almost acquired squatters' rights over a small table in the aft corner. **1968** E. S. RUSSENHOLT *Heart of Continent* II. v. 76 Families already living along the Assiniboine, exercise 'squatter's rights', and lay claim to the newly-surveyed River Lots. **1973** 'TREVANIAN' *Loo Sanction* (1974) 207 The lone painter..had come to assume over the years that the space, the stove, and the tea were his by squatter's right.

‖ **squattez-vous** (skwǫ·tē^ɪ^ˌvū:), *imp. phr. slang.* [Joc. f. SQUAT *v.,* after Fr. *asseyez-vous* sit down.] Sit down.

1899 KIPLING *Stalky & Co.* 177 *Squattez-vous* on the floor, then!... I swear you aren't going to sit on *my* bed! **1959** R. POSTGATE *Every Man is God* xxiii. 216 'Squattez-vous' was an invitation to sit down—Captain Roddman offered it to tenants who called on him in his office.

squatting, *vbl. sb.* Add: **3.** Also in sense 9 c of *SQUAT *v.*

1946 *Times* 17 Aug. 2/5 A new form of 'squatting' is reported from Gravesend, Kent. **1969** *Guardian* 27 Sept. 9/2 The Diggers will continue to support squatting by genuinely homeless families. **1976** *Times* 21 May 2/3 We publicly would not yield to the left..on other issues, such as squatting.

squatting, *ppl. a.* Add: **1. b.** Occupying an empty building as a squatter.

1963 S. COOPER in Sissons & French *Age of Austerity* 44 One of the squatting families. **1970** *Guardian* 12 Sept. 5/7 Last October the first four squatting families moved into flats which..had been empty for up to two years.

squaw, *sb.* (and *a.*). Add: **5. a.** *squaw dance* (earlier example), *hitch* (earlier example); **squaw boot** (see quot. 1975); **squawman** (earlier examples); **squaw winter** (earlier examples); **squaw wood** (see quot. 1944).

1952 J. K. HOWARD *Strange Empire* 336 All the women had beaded ornaments and lavishly embroidered 'squaw boots'. **1975** C. CALASIBETTA *Fairchild's Dict. Fashion* 50/2 *Squaw boot,* below-the-knee boot made of buckskin with fringed turned down cuff at top, soft sole, no heel, worn by American Indian women and popular with young people in the 1960's. **1864** in *Beaver* (Winnipeg) (1963) Autumn 52/2 Oregon Jack gave a squaw dance at which everybody got very drunk, I believe. **1887** LEES & CLUTTERBUCK *British Columbia* 232 Other hitches there are of less fame than this, notably the 'Squaw Hitch', a comparatively simple affair. **1866** *Rep. Indian Affairs* (U.S.) 91 White men, who have located in the vicinity of the reservation, and are known as squaw men. **1877** R. I. DODGE *Hunting Grounds Gt. West* xliii. 427 Squaw men. This is the name given by Indians to those men, not of their tribe, who, by purchase of squaws (marriage), have been adopted by or are tolerated in it. **1861** *Amer. Agriculturist* XX. 321/2 The best authorities put them immediately after Squaw Winter, which is the first cold snap that destroys tender vegetation. **1871** *Lakeside Monthly* V. 4/2 Those single-minded, grand old fellows.. kicked the light snow of 'squaw winter' from their Spanish-leather boots. **1914** *Outing* June 191/2 The cooking fire is only the beginning of the possibilities of 'squaw wood'. **1944** R. F. ADAMS *Western Words* 153/1 *Squaw wood,* a slang name for dried cow chips; also used in speaking of small, dry, easily broken sticks when used for fuel. **1968** C. HELMERICKS *Down Wild River North* I. vi. 100 Anything is squaw wood that you don't have to chop.

b. squaw-berry, the edible berry of one of several shrubs, esp. the bear-berry, *Arctostaphylos uva-ursi,* an evergreen prostrate creeper; **squaw corn,** a variety of maize having soft grains of various colours.

1852 *Anglo-Amer. Mag.* I. 418/2 The partridge leads her young brood forth to feed upon the soft luscious fruits of the huckleberry and squaw-berry. **1884** M. G. C. HALL *Lady's Life on Farm in Manitoba* 162 We have had jelly made of squawberries. **1956** V. FISHER *Pemmican* (1957) 161 Dried elderberry, or squawberry or wild currant he did not care for. **1824** J. DODDRIDGE *Notes Settlement Virginia* 90 How widely different is the large squaw corn, in its size, and the period of its growth. **1914** E. STEWART *Lett. Woman Homesteader* 151 They had a small patch of land..on which was raised the squaw corn that hung in bunches from the rafters. **1975** *Daily Colonist* (Victoria, B.C.) 5 Oct. 22/5 Nowadays, squaw corn is grown purely for its highly ornamental, variegated ears with kernels in purple, mauve, red, yellow, cream and black, very nice for Thanksgiving..displays.

squawk, *sb.* Add: **1. b.** *fig.* A complaint, a protest, esp. in phr. *to set* (or *put*) *up a squawk. slang* (orig. and chiefly *U.S.*).

1909 C. B. CHRYSLER *White Slavery* ix. 70 'Snatchin' simps' is good enough for Little Willie, there is no 'fall', no squawk, all you have to do is to stall. **1914** JACKSON & HELLYER *Vocab. Criminal Slang* 79 *Squawk,*..a protest; a vociferous demonstration, as an indignant repudiation of an injustice...'If you don't put up a squawk they'll trim you.' **1948** M. LASKI *Tory Heaven* ix. 126 They was just told to shut down and shut down they did..there wasn't a squawk out of none of them. **1973** 'B. MATHER' *Snowline* ii. 25 Our starry-eyed bleeding-hearts and permissives at home set up a squawk. **1976** 'R. B. DOMINIC' *Murder out of Commission* xvi. 147 How in God's name can we set up a squawk? We don't know what's going on.

squawk, *v.* Add: **1. c.** *U.S. slang.* To turn informer, to 'squeal'.

1872 G. P. BURNHAM *Memoirs U.S. Secret Service* p. vii, *Play baby,* to whine; 'squawk'; or assume innocence. **1929** W. R. BURNETT *Little Caesar* VI. v. 251 You know.. Joe squawked. **1935** *Amer. Speech* X. 12/2 *Belch,* to confess or carry information to the police. Modern *to squawk.* **1937** *Times Lit. Suppl.* 25 Dec. 974/4 The thief who 'squawks' is expelled as professionally infamous; his occupation's gone.

d. *U.S. slang.* To complain, protest.

1875 J. G. HOLLAND *Sevenoaks* xvii. 239 He mustn't squawk an' try to git another feller to help 'im out of 'is bargain. **1926** J. BLACK *You can't Win* iv. 41 Usually the sucker is a married man and can't squawk. But when he does squawk..the only thing to do is to blow back his money. **1939** *Time* 23 Jan. 30/2 Since most Hummert ghosts are glad to add caviar to bread-&-butter from other jobs, they have seldom squawked. **1948** *Sun* (Baltimore) 7 Jan. 13/1 When you pass a law and hire somebody to enforce it, you can't squawk if your kids get pinched for violating it. **1951** E. PAUL *Springtime in Paris* vi. 121 The contractor had been getting away with plenty..and would not dare squawk, no matter how high a bill was presented. **1976** M. MACHLIN *Pipeline* xxvii. 319 If the EPA ever finds out and squawks, they'll just fight it out in the courts.

squaw·k box. *U.S. slang.* Also with hyphen or as one word. [f. SQUAWK *sb.* or *v.* + BOX *sb.*²] **a.** A loud-speaker or public-address system.

1945 *New Yorker* 17 Mar. 28/3 The squawk box became alive for that second before any message comes over. **1950** 'D. DIVINE' *King of Fassarai* xxv. 219 There was a radio blaring..its music was punctuated with the hoarse stridencies of the squawk-box. **1973** *New Scientist* 20 Sept. 684/2 The squawk box emits two marginally different frequencies, almost out of audible range, through separate speakers. **1978** W. F. BUCKLEY *Stained Glass* xi. 104 The whistle stopped blowing, the passengers were all in their seats, the coordinators stopped speaking into their squawk boxes.

b. A speaker or receiving device which forms part of an intercommunication system, esp. in an office.

1954 *Sun* (Baltimore) 16 Apr. 27/2 Office buildings were deserted or skeleton staffed as interoffice 'squawk-boxes' carried in the doings on Thirty-third street by radio. **1962** L. DEIGHTON *Ipcress File* i. 15 Even over the squawk-box I could hear the lift in Alice's voice. **1964** P. GALLICO *Hand of Mary Constable* 48 To the right of the desk, on a small table, there was a squawk box with some dozen switches for inter-office communications. **1970** N. ARMSTRONG et al. *First on Moon* p. xiii, *Squawk box*, a small speaker, connected by telephone line to Mission Control, for home or office reception of live conversation between the spacecraft and earth. **1976** P. HARCOURT *Dance for Diplomats* ix. 96 The buzzer on my intercom made frantic noises...'Coming,' I said into the squawk box.

squawker. Add: **2.** (Examples.)

1896 G. B. SHAW *Let.* 8 Dec. (1965) I. 712 Yes, Lena is a fascinating squawker. **1923** H. C. WITWER in *Collier's* 29 July 26/3 To show you what a cheap squawker this Rags is, Spence tells me he has just welshed on a bet with him.

3. A loudspeaker designed to reproduce accurately sounds in the middle of the audible range.

1959 N. H. CROWHURST *Basic Audio* I. 67 Many installations use two or more speakers of different sizes..: large speakers (woofers) for the low frequencies, medium-sized speakers (squawkers) for the mid-range, and small speakers (tweeters) for the high frequencies. **1975** G. J. KING *Audio Handbk.* vi. 150 The output..drives the middle-frequency unit (squawker) and the high-frequency unit (tweeter) via a 4 kHz frequency divider.

squawmish, var. *SQUALMISH.

squdge (skwɒdʒ), *v.* [Perh. blend of SQUEEZE *v.* or SQUASH *v.*^{1} and PUDGE^1; cf. next and *SQUSH *v.*] *trans.* To squash or squeeze; to hug tightly. Also as *sb.*

1870 R. H. D. BARHAM *Life & Lett. R. H. Barham* II. vii. 27 At last he got so terrible bad surely nothing would ease him, so that we was forced to *squdge* him under the blankets. **1909** KIPLING *Rewards & Fairies* (1910) 5 They've put us into boots..and my toes are squdged together awfully. **1928** J. M. BARRIE *Peter Pan* v. ii. 159 Oh, Peter, how I wish I could take you up and squdge you! **1975** *New Society* 13 Nov. 388/1 Why does a large tube of toothpaste have a large hole? It is by length we judge the squdge of our brush, not by girth.

squdgy (skwɒ·dʒi), *a.* [Perh. f. prec. + -Y^1, or blend of SQUASHY *a.* and PUDGY *a.*^{1}] Soft and moist or yielding, squashy.

1892 KIPLING *Barrack-Room Ballads* 51 Elephints a-pilin' teak In the sludgy, squdgy creek. **1919** W. DEEPING *Second Youth* xvii. 145 He made haste to shake Joseph Bluett's squdgy hand and escape. **1959** M. STEEN *Woman in Back Seat* I. v. 97 'Don't you like babies?' Lavinia shook her head... 'They're so squdgy, and they haven't got any shape!'

squeak, *sb.* Add: **2. a.** Also *fig.* in neg. contexts (*colloq.*). Cf. *PEEP *sb.*^{1} 2 d.

1977 *Spare Rib* July 10/1 We've hardly heard a squeak out of them since. **1982** S. BRETT *Murder Unprompted* iv. 41 'I'm surprised you haven't heard anything about it... You sure you haven't heard anything?' 'Not a squeak.'

3. b. (Later examples without qualifying adjs.)

1880 MRS. H. WOOD in *Argosy* XXIX. 191 At the last moment, when the ship was getting away, and I had given the captain up, he came on board... 'I've had a squeak for it, Johnny,' he laughed, as he shook my hand. **1939** A. RANSOME *Secret Water* x. 121 You oughtn't to have waited. It's going to be a squeak getting home across the Wade.

4. Restrict † *Obs.* to sense in Dict. and add: **b.** A piece of incriminating information offered to the police; *to put in the* (or *a*) *squeak*: to turn informer, to inform *against.*

1922 [see *FLATTY^2 3]. **1936** J. CURTIS *Gilt Kid* ii. 22 You'll..turn grass and put in the bleeding squeak against me. **1955** D. WEBB *Deadline for Crime* i. 14 Then the squeak goes in. A bent buyer grasses to the law. **1973** A. HUNTER *Gently French* iv. 33, I can see another villain putting a squeak in but knocking off Freddy would be just stupid.

squeak, *v.* Add: **4. b.** To cause (something) to squeak.

1913 C. MACKENZIE *Sinister St.* I. II. xv. 401 Michael solemnly regarded the fair-haired boy of two who was squeaking an indiarubber horse. **1977** 'J. GASH' *Judas Pair* xv. 177 Could he see the curtain? I'd moved it without squeaking its noisy runners.

5. *intr.* **a.** *to squeak through*: to get through by a narrow shave, to scrape through.

1938 H. NICOLSON *Diary* 1 Sept. (1966) 358 We may just squeak through. On the other hand, we may get into the same mess as in 1914. **1943** *Sun* (Baltimore) 22 Nov. 14/2 The Irish squeaked through to a 14-to-13 verdict over Iowa Pre-Flight. **1971** J. BISHOP *Days of Martin Luther King, Jr.* iv. 329 The President..said he was not optimistic about the passage of the civil rights bill. It would require strong bipartisan support to squeak through. **1977** *Time* 7 Mar. 24/2 Rabin only squeaked through by sweeping the votes allotted to Israel's conservative kibbutzim.

b. With preps.: to make one's way by a narrow shave, to scrape *by, into,* etc. Chiefly *U.S.*

a **1961** H. H. MARTIN in *Webster* s.v., By six months of hard cramming..he squeaked by the finals. **1966** *Economist* 27 Aug. 810/3 His Progressive Conservatives squeaked back into power with only 39 per cent of the votes. **1968** *Ibid.* 20 Apr. 20/3 The Bill squeaked out of the Rules Committee on a single vote. **1974** *Union* (S. Carolina) *Daily Times* 24 Apr. 1/4 Texaco..squeaked by Mobil last year to become the country's second biggest oil firm. **1977** *Monitor* (McAllen, Texas) 26 June 1B/5 Jimmy Connors squeaked past a valiant Stan Smith in five sets.

squeaker. Add: **1. d.** *Criminals' slang.* An informer. Cf. SQUEALER 2 b.

1903 FARMER & HENLEY *Slang* VI. 335/1 *Squeaker*, (1) a blab.., and (2) an informer. **1924** E. WALLACE *Room 13* vii. 171, I want to talk with you, you dirty squeaker! You're the fellow that told the deputy I was getting tobacco in through a screw. **1930** *Observer* 19 Oct. 17 The recent attempt to murder him..was not due to..the impulse to remove rivals or 'squeakers'. **1950** [see *GRASSER^2]. **1973** A. HUNTER *Gently French* ii. 14 Dutt had been brooding over the tip-off mystery... The squeaker must have been Rampant.

2. e. Also, esp. = CICADA.

1897 'NATALIAN' *S. Afr. Boy* viii. 76 The youthful genius who brought two squeakers—tree cicadæ—before school hours, and released one in each room. **1959** S. J. BAKER *Drum* 147 Squeaker: A type of cicada.

3. b. (Later examples.) Esp. as a party toy (see quot. 1980).

1930 [see *paper streamer* s.v. *PAPER *sb.* 12]. **1939** N. COWARD *To step Aside* 49 She was seated on the knee of an Argentine with a paper fireman's hat on her head, blowing a squeaker. **1980** J. W. HILL *Intermediate Physics* v. 45 The party 'squeaker', a paper tube containing a weak coiled spring which uncoils when it is blown, works on the same principle.

4. b. *N. Amer. colloq.* A game won by a very narrow margin.

1961 in WEBSTER. **1969** *Eugene* (Oregon) *Register-Guard* 3 Dec. 1D/1 Remember that 26–24 squeaker over Stanford, when the Indians kicked a field goal with 63 seconds left to 'win' the game. **1970** *Globe & Mail* (Toronto) 28 Sept. 18/8 Ottawa Rough Riders..lost a squeaker to Montreal.

squeaking, *ppl. a.* Add: **2. b.** *squeaking sand,* sand that gives out a short, high-pitched sound when disturbed.

1966 *Sedimentology* VI. 136 A 'squeaking' sand was found by the writer in Gower, S. Wales and this has been used for comparison with the 'booming' sand of the desert. **1976** *Nature* 5 Feb. 368/2 The most common of the musical sediments is probably squeaking (otherwise known as singing, barking or whistling) sand which produces a high frequency note in the range 500–2,500 Hz.

squeaky, *a.* Add: **a.** Proverbial phr. *the squeaky wheel gets the grease* (and varr.): the person who makes the most fuss or trouble gets the attention.

[**1937** in J. Bartlett *Familiar Quotations* 518/2 The wheel that squeaks the loudest is the one that gets the grease. **1948** in B. Stevenson *Home Bk. Prov.* 2883/2, I hate to be a kicker, I always long for peace, But the wheel that does the squeaking is the one that gets the grease.] **1969** J. LA MARSH *Mem. Bird in Gilded Cage* x. 291 Mrs. Kinnear did..put on a most relentless campaign over the years..in line with the best of political principles—'the squeaky wheel got the grease'. **1974** *Hansard* (Canada) 17 Oct. 502/1 It is the old story: the squeaky wheel gets the grease.

c. *Comb.* **squeaky clean** (also with hyphen), (of hair, etc.) washed and rinsed so clean that it squeaks; completely clean; freq. *fig.*, above criticism, beyond reproach.

1975 *Country Life* 8 May 1176/2 *No one*..is in a position to criticise... No one is, in the current idiom, that squeaky-clean. **1976** N. THORNBURG *Cutter & Bone* i. 24 Still towelling his hair, Bone returned to the living room. ..'Behold, the squeaky clean Richard Bone.' **1978** *Guardian Weekly* 13 Aug. 16/2 The [Ford Motor] company has denied making any illegal payments, claiming that it is 'squeaky clean' in this area. **1980** [see *SET-ASIDE *sb. phr.*]. **1981** L. DEIGHTON *XPD* xvii. 155 His..long dark hair was wavy and squeaky clean.

squeal, *sb.* **3. a.** *U.S. slang.* An act of informing against another.

1872 G. P. BURNHAM *Memoirs of U.S. Secret Service* 152 This 'squeal' among the 'queersmen' brings this foul business straight home to *you.* **1903** *N.Y. Sun* 5 Nov. 3 Ever since his so-called 'squeal' at the Lexow investigation he has been a marked man. **1907** 'O. HENRY' *Trimmed Lamp* 185, I always thought that Kike's squeal on his boss was about the lowest-down play that ever happened.

b. *U.S. Police slang.* A call for police assistance or investigation; a report of a case investigated by the police.

1949 S. KINGSLEY *Detective Story* I. 14 'This is Jim's squeal, ain't it?'..'Yeah, I'll take it... This is my partner's case.' *Ibid.* II. 86 Get me the old files on that Cottsworth squeal! **1960** 'E. MCBAIN' *See them Die* vii. 79 Parker's on the prowl, Hernandez is answering a squeal. **1972** B. GARFIELD *Line of Succession* (1974) I. 3 The first cop said, 'Do it. Send in a squeal—we'll want the wagon.' **1973** 'E. MCBAIN' *Hail to Chief* i. 6 The appearance of Homicide cops at the scene of a murder was mandatory, even though the subsequent investigation was handled by the precinct detectives catching the squeal.

squeal, *v.* **3.** (Earlier example.)

1846 *National Police Gaz.* (U.S.) 413/2 Some dozen of the infamous rogues, well known to them, who infest that city, will be 'pulled' until they find one that will 'squeal'.

squeamy (skwī·mi), *a.* orig. *U.S.* [f. SQUEAM(ISH *a.* + -Y^1.] = SQUEAMISH *a.*

1838 C. GILMAN *Recoll. Southern Matron* v. 44, I feel so squeamy-like at my stomach. **1863** 'E. KIRKE' *My Southern Friends* v. 76 Doan't be squeamy, gal; out with it. **1880** *Harper's Mag.* Sept. 582/1, I expect they'd eet so much sweet it kinder made 'em squeamy. **1908** H. G. WELLS *War in Air* v. 174 They're a bit squeamy now, but you wait till they've got their hands in.

squeegee, *sb.* Add: **1. b.** A similar implement for cleaning windows, windscreens, etc., or for other purposes requiring smooth application of pressure.

1918 L. E. RUGGLES *Navy Explained* 130 Squeegee—..used in civil life to clean windows. **1955** *Sci. News Let.* 2 Apr. 224/1 Resembling a window cleaner's squeegee, the sweeper is ribbed to fold gently back and forth when it is moved across the floor. **1955** *Sci. Amer.* Oct. 126/3 A small squeegee or an automobile windshield wiper will help in the cleaning job. **1962** *Which?* Oct. 314/1 The *Gnomist transfer* had to be stuck on with water and a squeegee, which the manufacturer provided. *a* **1977** *Harrison Mayer Ltd. Catal.* 15/1 The colour in paste form is forced by means of a squeegee through a fine mesh mounted on a frame.

3. *Comb.* **squeegee band** *Naut. colloq.*, an improvised band (see quots.). Cf. *WASH-BOARD 3 d.

1916 'TAFFRAIL' *Pincher Martin* x. 176 Before very long the 'squeegee band', composed of two drums, a dozen fifes, many mouth-organs, and an unholy number of mess kettles and other noisy utensils, was marching round the deck. **1979** A. C. HAMPSHIRE *Just Old Navy Custom* 225 *Squeegee band,* composed of instruments not usually found in a band, e.g. Jew's harp; mouth-organ; comb and paper, etc.

squeegee, *v.* Add: **3.** *intr.* To use a squeegee.

1972 *Times* 20 Sept. 3/3 He washes, then squeegees. **1977** *Centuryan* (Office Cleaning Services) Christmas 17/2 Eva squeegeed off as first of the guest shiners.

squeeze, *sb.* Add: **1. b.** (Further examples, esp. in *Pol.* contexts.) Colloq. phr. (orig. *U.S.*) *to put the squeeze on* (someone): to exert influence on (someone) to act in a particular way, to 'pressurize' someone. Also without indirect obj.

1777 J. WEDGWOOD *Let.* 13 Apr. (1965) 204 Mrs. Du Burk's assurance in asking us to pay her debts is very great... It is another squeeze, and I would not pay a stiver. **1941** E. B. WHITE *Let.* 24 June (1967) 210, I am writing you direct to put the old personal squeeze on you. **1942** R. CHANDLER *High Window* (1943) xxxiii. 220 She hired me to..put the squeeze on Linda for a divorce. **1949** *Ann. Reg. 1948* 6 The tension was not relaxed, for there now began the Russian 'squeeze' in Berlin. **1954** 'J. CHRISTOPHER' *22nd Century* 21 They're putting the squeeze on. But there's got to be an excuse before they can swallow us. **1969** A. G. FRANK *Latin Amer.* xxv. 394 The imperialist squeeze obliges them to react by squeezing their workers. **1978** S. BRILL *Teamsters* vi. 217 Spilotro's army of enforcers..put the squeeze on hard-pressed loan-shark victims.

d. (Earlier and later examples.) Also, a restriction in the supply of money, credit, goods, etc.; *spec.* in Stock Market usage, pressure applied to dealers in shorts to cause them to settle at a loss. Cf. *credit squeeze* s.v. *CREDIT *sb.* 14.

1872 *Chicago Tribune* 23 Oct. 1/5 The Gold Room was treated to a slight sensation to-day in the shape of a 'squeeze' in cash gold, which was made as high as 3/8 per cent per diem for borrowing. **1924** G. G. MUNN *Encycl. Banking & Finance* 523/1 A money squeeze refers to a temporary shortage in the supply of loanable funds accompanied by difficulty in borrowing and marking up of interest rates. **1927** W. H. HUBBARD *Cotton & Cotton Market* (ed. 2) 396 While we have never had a corner since 1910, we have had in recent years a succession of annoying premiums on the near deliveries. The trade calls these minor corners a 'squeeze'. **1937** *Sun* (Baltimore) 25 Sept. 15/8 'Longs' are traders who in recent months have been accumulating contracts specifying delivery of corn to them in September. 'Shorts' are those who have sold these contracts, many of them reportedly without having possession of the corn to deliver. The attempt to make these 'shorts' pay a comparatively high price either to buy back their contracts or to buy the corn to deliver on them is known as a 'squeeze' in market parlance. **1943** [see *ROLL BACK, ROLL-BACK, ROLLBACK 2]. **1958** J. K. GALBRAITH *Affluent Society* xvi. 184 A severe squeeze will ordinarily be placed on the capital requirements of smaller-scale firms. **1979** B. HINES *Price of Coal* I. 48 I'm talking about spending thousands of pounds of public money... I thought there was a squeeze on?

e. *Bridge.* A tactic used to force an opponent to discard or unguard a potentially winning card.

1926 *Work-Whitehead Auction Bridge Bull.* Jan. 117/1 The Squeeze is unquestionably the least understood of the several more or less rare plays arising from time to time in the proper play of Auction hands. **1933** *Sunday Times* 5 Feb. 5/1 The coup formerly only known as the 'Vienna Coup', but now, more appropriately, also termed the 'Squeeze'. **1959** *Listener* 5 Nov. 802/3 He played for a squeeze. **1976** *National Observer* (U.S.) 20 Nov. 21-A/2 Another 'cooked' story is behind this week's hand. It involved a refusal to finesse and ended with a very fancy squeeze.

6. c. (Earlier example in the sense 'plan' or 'work'.)

c **1863** T. Taylor *Ticket-of-Leave Man* III. 59, I owe him one for spoiling my squeeze.

7. b. *slang.* An impression of an object made for criminal purposes.

1882 *Sydney Slang Dict.* 8/2 *Squeeze*, an impression of a keyhole in wax. **1930** G. D. H. & M. Cole *Burglars in Bucks.* III. xxxiv. 135 Where did the dummy keys..come from?.. If they were forgeries it would be simpler, for Sir Hiram might remember if anyone had handled his keys long enough to take a squeeze. **1941** Baker *Dict. Austral. Slang* 71 *Squeeze*, an impression of a keyhole in wax.

9. a. (Earlier example.)

1848 J. F. Cooper *Oak Openings* II. v. 78 In one instance, however, a young Indian had a still narrower 'squeeze' for his life.

c. A difficult situation.

1905 *Dialect Notes* III. 22 *Tight squeeze*,..a difficulty. **1972** *National Observer* (U.S.) 27 May 1/1 The safest drivers are those who know what their cars can do and how to make them do it in a squeeze.

9*. *Baseball.* The use of squeeze play (*Squeeze play 1 a); a bunt made to try to bring home a runner from third base.

1908 *Spalding's Official Base Ball Guide* 279 Under Ned Hanlon the Cincinnati team worked the 'squeeze' nearly as well as the New York Americans. **1942** L. Fonseca *How to pitch Baseball* III. i. 93 Another play for which the pitcher—and catcher, too—must always be on guard is the squeeze, one of baseball's most spectacular plays. **1976** *Billings* (Montana) *Gaz.* 30 June 2-E/6 In the eighth inning, the Royals tried to salvage the game with a squeeze with the bases loaded.

10. a. squeeze bunt *Baseball*, the bunt (*Bunt *sb.*[8] 2) made in squeeze play (*Squeeze play 1 a); also as *v. intr.*; **squeeze-pidgin** *slang*, a bribe.

1952 B. Feller *Pitching to Win* viii. 108 During the 1951 season, we had a number of squeeze bunts, those which score a runner from third base, beat us in several important ball games. **1955** P. Richards *Mod. Baseball Strategy* xi. 130 Many managers make a big mistake asking pitchers to squeeze-bunt. **1974** *Cleveland* (Ohio) *Plain Dealer* 13 Oct. c. 1/2 The big run for the defending world champions came on a two-strike, suicide squeeze bunt by Bert Campaneris in the fifth inning. **1946** J. Irving *Royal Navalese* 165 *Squeeze-pidgin*, a tip: a bribe. **1970** 'B. Mather' *Break in Line* i. 11 'What's a squeeze-pidgin?'..'A bribe... Something you *squeeze* out of somebody.'

b. *attrib.* uses in *Bridge* (sense 1 e above).

1936 E. H. Downes *Squeezes, Coups & End Plays* 10 The Squeeze trick must always be won in the hand opposite the final entry card. **1947** J. Brown *Winning Tricks* xxi. 233 A long suit is not necessarily for a squeeze, although long suits have come to be associated with squeeze positions. **1954** G. S. Coffin *Bridge Play from A to Z* 328 Many types of preparatory squeezes occur..such as the squeeze long-suit..; the squeeze finesse, the squeeze strip, etc. **1964** Frey & Truscott *Official Encycl. Bridge* 526/1 The squeeze finesse is characterized by the presence of a symmetric menace which must be guarded with an equal number of cards by both opponents. **1974** *Times* 5 Jan. 8/7 The counter-attack by the declarer to keep one move ahead of the squeeze-breaking defence.

squeeze, *v.* Add: Also with *dial. preterite* and *pa. pple.* 9– **squoze,** *pa. pple.* 9 **squozen.**

1844 'J. Slick' *High Life N.Y.* II. 195, I sot down on a bench runnin over with harnsome gals, that squoze close together and squinched themselves up to make room for me. **1866** J. T. Staton *Rays fro' Loominany* 107 Awd welly as lief they'd squozzen my guts eawt as speighlt my bonnet. **1878** *Roger Plowman's Excursion to London* ii. 21, I gently squoze hur 'and. **1928** A. A. Milne *House at Pooh Corner* viii. 143 He squeezed and he sqoze [*sic*], and then with one last squze he was out. **1931** *Sun* (Baltimore) 1 Sept. 8/7 'Orange?' repeated Waitress No. 1. 'Do you want it squoze?' **1933** M. Lowry *Ultramarine* vi. 237 He just sort of *squoze* the rabbit. **1938** J. Agate *Diary* 17 Dec. in *Selective Ego* (1976) 115 Before going down to correct my proofs at the *S.T.* squeezed in a performance of the *Messiah*. Or, rather, Beecham squoze it in for me.

1. f. To fire *off* (a round, shot, etc.) from a gun. *colloq.*

1956 *Amer. Speech* XXXI. 192 A rifleman never fires a shot, he *squeezes off a round.* **1975** A. Price *Our Man in Camelot* vii. 136 He..got his gun clear just as Harry squeezed off his first shot.

g. To approach or 'push' (a certain age). *colloq.*

1976 *National Observer* (U.S.) 20 Nov. 24/1 But that takes a lot out of a man, particularly when he's squeezing 70. So sometimes he's pretty tired. **1978** *Guardian Weekly* 30 July 21/1 The original heroine, now squeezing forty.

3. e. To exert commercial or financial pressure on (someone); to restrict a supply of money, credit, goods, etc.; *spec.* in Stock Market usage, to force dealers in shorts to settle at a loss.

1885 *Harper's Mag.* Nov. 842/1 The bulls get a 'twist on the shorts' by artificially raising prices, and 'squeezing', or compelling the bears to settle at ruinous rates. **1900** S. A. Nelson *ABC Wall St.* 160 When shorts become frightened after having oversold and then are forced to violently bid up prices in competition with the owners of stocks they are said to have been squeezed. **1902** L. L. Bell *Hope Loring* xiv. 272 You squeezed me badly in '93. **1951** *Times* 3 Jan. 7/2 The domestic consumer of coal and coke is already being squeezed, but he often uses more gas and more electricity as a result. **1970** *Daily Tel.* 3 Sept. 3/2 The Government can scarcely ask banks to squeeze their customers when a State Corporation is advertising loans to attract business. **1978** *Jrnl. R. Soc. Arts* CXXVI. 390/2 Manufacturing industry's profits have been greatly squeezed.

5. e. *Bridge.* To force (an opponent) to discard a guarding or potentially winning card.

1926 *Work-Whitehead Auction Bridge Bull.* Jan. 118/2, I will give the three cards remaining in each of the four hands to show how South was squeezed by the lead of the Queen of Clubs. **1934** G. F. Hervey *Mod. Contract Bridge* xxi. 223 The Americans now call this coup [*sc.* the Vienna coup] Squeezing or Squeeze Play. The name is apt as the play of the declarer is such that he squeezes the opponents and forces them to discard and unguard a suit. **1949** H. G. Freehill *Squeeze at Bridge* i. 19 The essential features of the squeeze are three. First: there must be a squeeze-card. That is, a card to the lead of which the player who is squeezed has to discard. **1959** T. Reese *Bridge Player's Dict.* 209 Playing no trump, South lays down the ten of hearts and West is squeezed; he must either unguard spades or throw away the winning diamond. **1979** N. Squire *Squeeze Play Simplified* i. 4 The two menaces are on the left of the player to be squeezed, the squeeze card on his right.

6. a. (Later example.)

1974 J. Gardner *Corner Men* xiii. 188 The man in the rear of the Merc fired once... Wright squeezed twice.

squeeze-. Add: **squeeze bottle,** a bottle made of flexible plastic, squeezed to expel the contents; **squeeze-box** *slang*, † (*a*) *Naut.*, a ship's harmonium (*obs.*); (*b*) an accordion or concertina; **squeeze cementing** *Oil Industry* (see quot. 1938); **squeeze lens** *Cinemat.* (orig. *U.S.*), an anamorphic lens attachment (cf. *Anamorphic *a.* 2); **squeeze toy,** a child's doll or similar toy which sounds when pressed; **squeeze tube** = Tube *sb.* 2 d; a tube-shaped container which yields its contents when squeezed.

1953 *Wall St. Jrnl.* 16 Sept. 23/4 The principal addition to the product line will be polyethyline, best known in its form of 'squeeze bottles' and transparent packaging material. **1964** V. E. Yarsley et al. *Cellulosic Plastics* i. 5 To-day 'squeeze-bottles' in polythene are used in increasing quantities all over the world. **1976** 'E. McBain' *Guns* (1977) vii. 177 The doctor..takes a squeeze-bottle.. and then wets a piece of gauze. **1909** J. R. Ware *Passing Eng.* 232/1 *Squeeze-box*,..the ship harmonium—used in the hasty Sunday service. From the action of the feet. **1936** *Amer. Speech* XI. 280/1 *Squeeze-box*, an accordion. **1938** Auden & Isherwood *On Frontier* III. i. 99 Get yer squeeze-box. [*First Soldier begins to play the accordion.*] **1942** E. Paul *Narrow St.* x. 77, I told my Marseilles accordion teacher that the experience had disabled me from practising the squeeze-box for a week. **1963** *Times* 26 Jan. 11/1 They imagine everyone spends their time dancing to squeezebox music and living on Knackwurst and Apfelstrudel. **1973** C. Bonington *Next Horizon* vii. 105 He was already ensconced in the bar at the Clachaig, his squeeze box out, a dram of whisky at his side and a cigarette in his mouth. **1938** *Oil Weekly* 28 Feb. 36/1 Squeeze cementing means that cement slurry is forced, or 'squeezed', by pressure into or against a permeable formation or through perforations in casing and liners for the purpose of shutting off water or for reducing gas/oil ratios. **1974** D. K. Smith in P. L. Moore et al. *Drilling Practices Man.* xvi. 400 Squeeze cementing is necessary for many reasons, but probably the most important use is to segregate hydrocarbon producing zones from those formations producing other fluids. **1957** *Amer. Cinematographer* Mar. 149/1 Focal distortion is practically eliminated by a technique that adds a squeeze (anamorphic) lens to the system that produces partial scene compression in the camera, with the remainder being effected in the printing process. **1977** J. Hedgecoe *Photographer's Handbk.* 31 *Squeeze lens.* This is an 'anamorphic' supplementary lens system continuing cylindrical lens elements. When mounted on a normal lens it squeezes the image by reducing either its vertical or its horizontal size without affecting the other dimension. **1954** *Toys & Novelties* Mar. 421 (Advt.), A complete new line of unique squeeze toys by Alan Jay. **1976** *National Observer* (U.S.) 25 Dec. 6/4 He would also like to see a uniform law covering sound levels of toys... 'I have been responsible for manufacturing more than 35 million squeeze toys in my career, and I have never run into anything like this,' Young says. **1872** S. Hale *Let.* 1 Oct. (1919) iv. 86 We went to Rowney's,—delicious! —and I bought two squeeze tubes..; there were water-colours there. **1962** J. Glenn in *Into Orbit* 201, I pulled a squeeze-tube of apple sauce out of its receptacle and parked it in the air in front of me.

squeezed, *ppl. a.* Add: **1. b.** Also with *out*, *up* (earlier example).

1831 M. Edgeworth *Let.* 30 Apr. (1971) 533 A squeezed up poke bonnetted old mother. **1880** in I. M. Tarbell *Hist. Standard Oil Co.* (1904) II. 325 This constitutes the only foundation for the oft-repeated expressions 'crushed out', 'squeezed out', and 'bulldozing'. **1951** W. Faulkner *Requiem for Nun* 225 The long invincible arm of Progress ..released him, not flung him away like a squeezed-out tube of paint, but rather..merely opening its fingers.

squee·ze play. Also **squeeze-play.** [f. Squeeze *v.* + Play *sb.*] **1. a.** *Baseball.* A tactic whereby the batter bunts so that a runner at third base can attempt to reach home safely and score.

1905 *St. Louis Globe-Democrat* 2 July II. 8/5 Like the spit ball, the squeeze play is not strictly an invention of the present season. **1909** *Collier's* 15 May 29/2 The 'squeeze' play, of which we have heard so much in the past two or three years, is the method of scoring a man from third base on the hit-and-run system. **1949** *Chicago Tribune* 27 Sept. II. 1/8 The mighty sox..had to resort to the squeeze play to score their all-important victory. **1979** *Arizona Daily Star* 22 July c 4/4 Not many pitchers throw inside anymore. It's like the squeeze play. It's a lost art.

b. *transf.* and *fig.* An act of coercion or 'pressurizing'; the application of force or pressure to obtain an end. *colloq.* (chiefly *U.S.*).

1916 *Independent* (N.Y.) 5 June 410 (*heading*) The 'squeeze-play' at the capital. **1932** *Sun* (Baltimore) 14 Sept. 10/1 Mostly employers of relatively small numbers of workers, they appear to have been caught in an economic 'squeeze play' in which 'contract' shops..are played against each other in pursuit of the lowest bids. **1944** D. Wecter *When Johnny comes marching Home* IV. vii. 557 You perhaps mentioned the fact that Hitler was putting the squeeze play on Hindenburg a few years later. **1966** *Economist* 10 Sept. 1009/1 The real victims of the Franco government's squeeze-play—the Spaniards whose prospects of being allowed to go on crossing the border daily to work in Gibraltar are now in jeopardy. **1977** D. Anthony *Stud Game* xx. 122 She hinted that her partner had worked this squeeze-play once before, with..a pregnant girl..and a widow who paid off.

2. *Bridge.* The employment of a squeeze. Cf. *Squeeze *sb.* 1 e.

1926 *Work-Whitehead Auction Bridge Bull.* May 50 The squeeze play is made when running a suit, by forcing an opponent to discard a number of times. **1934** G. F. Hervey *Contract Bridge Dict.* 139 Squeeze Play is the basis of practically all double-dummy problems. **1959** T. Reese *Bridge Player's Dict.* 209 The technique of squeeze play is complicated, and even in the simplest three-card ending..certain basic elements have to be present, such as threat cards, entries, a squeeze card and correct timing. **1976** *Country Life* 19 Feb. 440/2 South did not understand squeeze play... When the Nine of Clubs falls from East, the squeeze against West is marked.

squeezer. Add: **4.** Usu. *pl.* A playing-card which has its value indicated in one or two corners, so that a player may ascertain his hand while holding the cards closely arranged. (App. orig. used in Poker, but now standard.)

1876 *Paper & Printing Trades Jrnl.* Sept. 8/1 The 'Squeezers' Playing Cards introduced by Messrs. Lawrence Brothers..are rapidly rising in popular estimation. **1888** *Amer. Humorist* 15 Sept. 3/1 The editor picked up his hand, slid the squeezers past his good eye, and began to softly whisper the 'Pirate King'. **1906** G. Frankau *X.Y.Z. of Bridge* 47 Horatius in a long frock-coat Rending two 'squeezer' packs. **1930** C. P. Hargrave *Hist. Playing Cards* xiii. 345 The New York Consolidated Card Company..issued indexed cards..under the name of 'Squeezers'.

squeezy, *a.* Add: Also, capable of being squeezed, esp. as *squeezy bottle*, squeeze bottle.

1971 R. A. Percy *Charlesworth on Negligence* (ed. 5) xviii. 732 Using a squeezy bottle to squirt coolant liquid into the interior of a workpiece on a centre lathe. **1972** *Guardian* 5 Dec. 16/6 Strong colours ready mixed in squeezy bottles, a boon for..young children.

squegger (skwe·gəɪ). *Electronics.* [Of uncertain origin: perh. a shortened respelling of *self-quench(ing* + -er[1].] An oscillator whose oscillations build up to a certain amplitude and then cease for a time before beginning again; also, the production of such oscillations.

1921 *Radio Rev.* May 248 The production of notes by a high-frequency oscillating valve making use of a grid leak and condenser, and the factors governing the pitch of this note, were discussed. The application of this arrangement (termed by Major Prince a 'squegger') to a receiver..was also described. **1932** *Admiralty Handbk. Wireless Telegr. 1931* xvi. 727 Receivers in which..self-oscillations alternately build up and are damped out without the necessity of a separate circuit to vary the reaction. These are called self-quenching receivers or squeggers. **1932** Ladner & Stoner *Short Wave Wireless Communications* viii. 147 The presence of audible modulation..may also be brought about by a high resistance in the grid circuit... This effect..was called originally a 'squegger'. **1932** *Wireless Engineer* IX. 186 In the super-regenerative class, two receivers were available, one of the self-quench (or squegger) type. **1946** C. A. Quarrington *Mod. Pract. Radio & Television* II. x. 156 Time bases employing the squegger principle are inclined to be affected unduly by working conditions.

Hence (as a back-formation) **squeg** *v. intr.*, (of an electrical circuit) to oscillate intermittently, to be self-quenching; † **sque·ggering** *vbl. sb.*; **sque·gging** *vbl. sb.* and *ppl. a.*

1933 *QST* Sept. 66/2 Coupling between this 'squegging' oscillator and the receiver is obtained. *Ibid.* Nov. 17/1 The receiver may be made..to operate as a super-regenerator, by increasing the screen voltage to the point where 'squegging' (low frequency oscillation) starts. **1938** *Television* XI. 540/3 The valve is allowed to oscillate continuously with pauses of quiescence ('squeggering'). **1939** *Radio Amateur's Handbk. 1940* (ed. 17) iv. 61/1 Too much feed-back will cause the oscillator to 'squeg', or operate at several frequencies simultaneously. **1942** *Electronic Engin.* XIV. 629/3 The great difficulty in ultra high frequency oscillators is to obtain sufficient oscillation amplitude without squeggering or dead-spots in the turning range. **1947** *Ibid.* XIX. 162 Increase of R_3 to successively greater values results in the oscillator squegging.

1959 K. Henney *Radio Engin. Handbk.* (ed. 5) xii. 22 The adjustment of the feedback to give oscillation without pulsing or squegging is very critical. **1973** *Simulation* XXI. 77/2 There are circumstances under which squegging is desirable, such as in a superregenerative receiver. *Ibid.* 79/2 A squegging oscillator is highly sensitive to the settings of certain parameters.

squelch, *sb.* Add: **1. c.** A devastating argument or retort; a crushing blow. *slang* (orig. *U.S.*).
1942 Berrey & Van den Bark *Amer. Thes. Slang* § 11/3 Something conclusive or decisive (as an argument, answer, blow, or the like),..squasher, squelch, squelcher. **1964** *Pix* (Australia) 4 Aug., *Pix* has added to its large collection of famous squelches with contributions from readers. **1977** *Amer. Speech 1975* L. 155 If I use *humdinger*, I have to face the derisive remark of my elder son, 'Nobody used that word since Theodore Roosevelt died'.., or the equally crushing squelch of the younger one, 'Papa, that is not even funny.'

4. *Electronics.* A circuit that suppresses all input signals except ones of a predetermined character; *spec.* in *Radio*, a circuit that suppresses the noise output of a receiver when the signal strength falls below a predetermined level. Freq. *attrib.*
1937 [see *quieting *vbl. sb.* 2 a]. **1945** *FM & Television* Apr. 31/1 The feature of this squelch circuit is that sharp pulses of interference do not open the squelch... It has been found that a 1-microvolt signal can open the squelch, but noise pulses of considerable amplitude do not. **1950** J. K. Henney *Radio Engin. Handbk.* (ed. 4) xvii. 822 A signal of 140 db (0·1 μu) is sufficient to open the squelch of a police receiver. **1959** [see *muting *vbl. sb.* b]. **1976** *CB Mag.* June 64/1 (Advt.), the transceiver is combined through a switchable standby circuit to interrupt the music when the adjustable squelch level is broken. **1981** *Daily Tel.* 5 Nov. 2 (Advt.), Ultra compact, yet has variable squelch to cut signal 'chopping'.

squelch, *v.* Add: **1. b.** (Later examples.) Now chiefly *U.S.*
1910 *Dialect Notes* III. 455 *Squelch, v. tr.*, to snub, to turn down. 'She *squelched* him.' **1936** L. C. Douglas *White Banners* vi. 135 An inquisitive maid-of-all-work who might try to be chummy unless promptly squelched. **1960** *Wall St. Jrnl.* 15 Mar. 14 Recent attempts by other domestic unions to hurtle national boundaries have been squelched. **1978** H. Wouk *War & Remembrance* xxv. 252 That'll squelch him, I assure you, and he'll be as quiet as a mouse.

3. *trans. Electronics.* = *quiet *v.* 2 d.
1950 J. K. Henney *Radio Engin. Handbk.* (ed. 4) xvii. 822 This voltage drop biases the first audio amplifier beyond cutoff, thus squelching the set. **1976** *S9* (N.Y.) May/June 107/1 The light..then remains on (although the receiver may be squelched, it will then pick up all calls on the channel until it is reset by the firefighter).

squelched *ppl. a.* (*fig.* examples).
1914 'High Jinks, Jr.' *Choice Slang* 18 *Squelched*, ignored, insulted, 'sat upon'. **1928** *Sat. Even. Post* 7 Jan. 20/2 Apparently squelched, she made no reply.

squelchy, *a.* **1.** (Examples in more general use.)
1914 [see *papaia]. **1928** *Daily Express* 12 June 10/5 What Will Woman Do Next?.. Start an agitation, I shouldn't wonder, for the suppression of the word 'women'. Sober and dignified once.., the over-work of the last ten years has made a sickening, squelchy mess of it.

squench, *v.* Add: **2.** (Later examples.) *rare.*
1865 *Punch* 20 May 200/2 Mr. Newdegate had a plan, whereof not much need be said, as it was squenched by 126 to 42. **1923** U. L. Silberrad *Lett. Jean Armiter* iv. 100 You are not easily squenching Art, with a capital A, when it is once fairly talking.

squib, *sb.* **4. a.** Delete † *Obs.* and add later examples in similar use; also, a short or thin person.
1898 *Leeds Mercury Suppl.* 26 Mar. (E.D.D.), Ah'll knock thee dahn, yo' little squib, if tha doesn't shut thi gob. **1979** *Courier-Mail* (Brisbane) 28 Apr. 17/2 We have numerous utility expressions for people such as..sparrow squib, nugget and streak, for men of varying sizes.

d. For def. read: *erron.* for *squil.

e. A horse lacking courage or endurance; hence, a coward. *Austral. slang.*
1908 [see *monty]. **1924** *Truth* (Sydney) 27 Apr. 6 *Squib*, a coward. **1933** *Bulletin* (Sydney) 15 Nov. 8/4 In the result stayers reproducing the old-time qualities of the Australian thoroughbred became rare; but speedy squibs abounded. **1936** A. Russell *Gone Nomad* 55 There's no place in this town for squibs. **1947** *Coast to Coast 1946* 217 'You're a bloody lot of squibs,' said Darky disgustedly. **1951** F. Hardy *Power without Glory* 160, I know these johnnys; they're all squibs. **1978** *Telegraph* (Brisbane) 8 Feb. 20/1 Don Ash is the sort of bloke who makes you feel a squib for crying off with some minor ache or pain from that daily canter around the block.

squib, *v.* Add: **I. 3. b.** With *on*: to betray or let down (someone). Also without const., to funk, to behave in a cowardly manner; to wriggle or squirm. *Austral. slang.*
1938 S. J. Baker in *Observer* 13 Nov. 11/3 Rat on = to betray, let down. Squib on = ditto. **1941** —— *Dict. Austral. Slang* 71 *Squib, to*, to funk, to be afraid of something. **1945** *Coast to Coast 1944* 5 I'll let him through; it's better to squib than to wreck old Dutch and myself, too. **1947** K. Tennant *Lost Haven* xvii. 292 You'll probably squib out of it at thel ast moment. **1962** *Coast to Coast 1961–62* 83 He could finish on a good wicket in anything. And never squib on a bloke.

II. 8. To avoid (a difficulty or responsibility); to funk, to shirk through fear or cowardice. *Austral. slang.*
1934 *Bulletin* (Sydney) 1 Aug. 46/4 He judges the dodger's done just what he'd do himself; squibbed it and dropped his load. **1936** F. Clune *Roaming round Darling* xv. 138 Oxley and Evans attempted to explore the Macquarie, but floundering about the marshes Oxley squibbed the job once more. **1940** N. Monks *Squadrons Up* i. 26 The censor..said that we should not let the enemy Command know their fighters were squibbing it [*sc.* avoiding combat]. **1955** D. Niland *Shiralee* 50 The rough-and-tumble doesn't worry me. I'm not squibbing the issue.

squibber. (Earlier example.)
1810 *Irish Mag.* Aug. 377/1 Nothing like a squibber writing of his own acquirements.

squid, *sb.* Add: **1. d.** Also with capital initial. A ship-mounted anti-submarine mortar with three barrels, developed in the war of 1939–45.
1947 Crowther & Whiddington *Science at War* iv. 160 A three-barrelled mortar for throwing three projectiles each was developed, and named the Squid... The expenditure of ammunition required to sink a U-boat with the Squid was very much less than with depth charges. The production of the Squid was ordered direct from the drawing board in the urgency of the situation in 1943. **1962** W. Granville *Dict. Sailors' Slang* 112/2 *Squid box*, housing of a *squid*, a triple-barrelled mortar for firing depth charges. It is placed on the sterns of destroyers and frigates. **1973** J. Quick *Dict. Weapons* 418/3 *Squid*, a British shipborne surface-to-sub-surface medium-range antisubmarine mortar system. A triple-barreled mortar fires a pattern of three mortar bombs which are programmed to give a three dimensional explosive pattern ahead of the target.

3*. A stable configuration of a parachute which is only partially extended.
1947 *Techn. Rep. Aeronaut. Res. Comm. 1946* II. 1465 If a parachute is released into an airstream and its speed relative to the air is greater than a certain critical speed, it will not open fully. Instead it will take up a dynamically-stable partly-open shape known as a 'squid'. **1949** *Jrnl. R. Aeronaut. Soc.* LIII. 1055/1 For a parachute in a steady squid state, the inflow to the canopy equals the outflow.

4. squid-hound (earlier example); also *attrib.*
1794 A. Thomas *Newfoundland Jrnl.* (1968) xiii. 183 Whenever Squids are found is also found a Fish called Jumpers, or Squid Hounds, from the avidity with which they pursue and eat squids. **1934** E. Reynard *Narrow Land* v. 250 Hut moved fast, almost as fast as the squidhound bass.

SQUID (skwid), *sb.*[2] *Physics.* Also **Squid, squid.** [Acronym f. the initials of *s*uper-conducting *qu*antum *i*nterference *d*evice.] A device consisting essentially of a superconducting ring containing one or more Josephson junctions, made the basis of a very sensitive magnetometer by utilizing the fact that a change in the magnetic flux linkage of the ring by one flux quantum produces a sharp change in the ring's impedance.
1967 W. S. Goree in *Proc. Symp. Physics of Superconducting Devices* (U.S. Naval Research Lab.) 9 One embodiment of this device is the SQUID originated by Mercerau and others, which is two Josephson junctions in a superconducting ring. **1972** *Cryogenics* XII. 28/1 SQUID magnetometers and related devices have been used to make quantitative measurements of thermal fluctuations at temperatures as low as 0·023 K. **1979** *Nature* 22 Feb. 643/1 The magnetisation was measured with a Squid magnetometer. **1979** *McGraw-Hill Yearbk. Sci. & Technol.* 379/2 The dc SQUID has recently been developed for fast switching applications, that is, as an electronic logic or memory element. **1982** *Economist* 3 Apr. 120/3 At the frontiers of R and D now being done into superfast computers..is a device that is known as a squid—which is short for superconducting quantum interference device.

squid, *v.* Add: **2.** Of a parachute: to achieve a stable configuration when only partially extended.
1943 *Rep. & Mem. Aeronaut. Res. Council* No. 2119. 4 A non-porous parachute will not squid. **1951** W. D. Brown *Parachutes* vii. 68 The mouth of the canopy will begin to collapse inward, and the parachute will squid. **1956** W. A. Heflin *U.S.A.F. Dict.* 148/1 *Critical closing speed*, in wind-tunnel tests, the airspeed at which an open parachute begins to squid, i.e. close or collapse into longitudinal shape.

Hence **squi·dded** *ppl. a.*; **squi·dding** *vbl. sb.*
1894 Squidding [in Dict., s.v. Squid *v.*]. **1943** *Rep. & Mem. Aeronaut. Res. Council* No. 2119. 1 Squidding obviously may be a source of trouble in applications of parachutes. *Ibid.* 5 If a parachute is taken in the squidded condition and the air-speed reduced, the effective permeability of the canopy falls. **1969** J. Gardner *Founder Member* viii. 132 A parachute training instructor went over all the elementary lessons..recalling things like critical speeds, oscillation and squidding.

squidge[2]. *U.S. slang. rare.* [Origin unknown.] One charged with performing troublesome duties for another (see quots.).
1907 Ade *Slim Princess* vii. 80 The squidge—that means the fellow who does all the worrying and gets nothing out of it. **1942** —— *Let.* 16 June (1973) 230 When Mr. and Mrs. Al Laflin and I traveled in distant countries, we always hired a 'squidge' the moment we arrived in a new town. His job was to stay with us and accept all the hardships and worries. **1953** [see *patsy *sb.*]

squidge, *v.* [Cf. Squidge *sb.*; sense 2 may represent an independent imitative formation.)] *trans.* **1.** To squeeze; to squelch or to mix roughly; to press together, so as to make a sucking noise. Also *intr. dial.* and *colloq.*
1881 H. & C. R. Smith *Isle of Wight Words* 34 *Squidge*, to squeeze. **1939** J. Steinbeck *Grapes of Wrath* x. 136 The children squidged their toes in the red dust. **1947** —— *Wayward Bus* iii. 33 His shoes squidged sloppily on the floor. **1952** —— *East of Eden* xxxvi. 427 Now spit in your palm... Squidge the spit all together. **1969** *Guardian* 16 Aug. 3/8 Waiting for the day when lunch will be a blob of something squidged out of a tube. **1971** B. W. Aldiss *Soldier Erect* 242 The leeches were at me... I squidged them underfoot. **1977** *Basildon Yellow Advertiser* 19 May 5/2 To clean very dirty nails make a thick lather in a sponge and then 'squidge' your nails in the sponge—the suction will draw out the dirt.

2. *Tiddlywinks.* To play (a wink) by snapping it with a larger counter.
1955 *Sci. of Tiddlywinks* (Cambridge Univ. Tiddlywinks Club) 8 If the tiddlywink is squidged on the floor it will not rise more than an inch or two. **1962** *Time* 14 Sept. 56 A squopped wink cannot be squidged again until it is de-squopped. **1977** Sharp & Piggott *Bk. Games* 165 No player may squidge another's wink.

squidger (skwi·dʒəɹ). *Tiddlywinks.* [f. prec. + -er[1].] **a.** The larger wink used to propel or flip a player's winks. **b.** One who propels winks with another wink of larger size. (*rare*).
1955 *Sci. of Tiddlywinks* (Cambridge Univ. Tiddlywinks Club) 6 The game is played with five variable factors..(3) The squidger (the instrument used to flick with; this is usually another round counter in normal games). **1958** *Sports Illustr.* 7 Apr. M5 Each tiddlywinker plays with two large and four medium-size winks and, to hoist them, uses a wink of suitable size. It is called a squidger. **1962** [see *squopper]. **1975** *Sunday Mail Color Mag.* (Brisbane) 28 Sept. 21/2 The *squidger* is the tiddly-winker's most valuable tool—the large wink, with which he flips the smaller counters. **1977** [see *squopped *ppl. a.*].

squidgy, *a.* Add: **1.** (Earlier and later examples.)
1891 Kipling *Life's Handicap* 30 There's a dale more in nature than your squidgy little legs have iver taken you to, Orth'ris, me son. **1942** G. Kersh *Nine Lives Bill Nelson* xi. 68 He..liked to get about with a few nice squidgy blondes. **1978** *Morecambe Guardian* 14 Mar. 6/2 (Advt.), Upholstery does not now rely on spectacular outlines to make its impact. Gone are the way-out 'squidgy' shapes that the Italians launched so successfully a few years ago, instead the line is neat and classical, with a strong accent on comfort.

2. Moist and pliant; squashy, soggy. Esp. of food. Cf. *sqUDGY *a.*
1973 *Times* 17 May 18/6 We settled for sandwiches. This was not a good idea. They were made of squidgy and tasteless bread of the wrapped and sliced variety. **1976** U. Holden *String Horses* vi. 69 Her kiddies spread ketchup on their bread, liking squidgy food. **1977** *Times* 28 May 11/6 A nice squidgy fruit cake.

Hence **squi·dgily** *adv.*
1933 E. A. Robertson *Ordinary Families* ix. 193 He turned out to be as squidgily repulsive as only an undersized Italian can be.

squiff[2]. *slang. rare.* [Of uncertain origin: perh. f. Squiffy *a.*] **1.** A contemptible person.
1939 E. Pound *Let.* Feb. (1971) 322 Yes, do better than that squiff, that femme ouistiti and lowest degree of animal life (apart from Cambridge Eng. profs).

2. The head. In phr. *off* (one's) *squiff* = *off* (one's) *head* s.v. Head *sb.* 34.
1960 H. Pinter *Room* 115 Mr. Kidd: I don't know what I think. (He sits.) I think I'm going off my squiff.

squiffed, *a. slang.* [var. Squiffy *a.*] Intoxicated, drunk.
a **1890** in Barrère & Leland *Dict. Slang* (1890) II. 295/1 He rolls home rather squiffed, just as the day is dawning. **1926** S. Howard *Lucky Sam McCarver* I. 36, I think I did meet you once before, though I was a bit squiffed at the time. **1961** [see *chumble *v.*]. **1977** B. Garfield *Recoil* ii. 28 I'm already a little squiffed. Ought to go on the wagon.

squiffer (skwi·fəɹ). *slang.* [Origin obscure.] A concertina; also, an organ-bellows or organ. Also *transf.* (see quot. 1934).
1914 G. B. Shaw *Fanny's First Play* I. 175 If you can get Holy Joe to sprint a hundred yards, I'll stand you that squiffer with the gold keys... What's a squiffer?..a concertina. **1934** 'I. Hay' *David & Destiny* v. 78 What exactly is a Squiffer... Strictly speaking, a concertina. By a process of excusable exaggeration, an organ-bellows, or even the organ itself. By a characteristic confusion of ideas, a person who blows an organ.

squiffy, *a.* Add: **1.** (Earlier example.)
?**1855** Mrs. Gaskell *Lett.* (1966) 375 Curious enough there is a Lady Erskine, wife of Lord E, her husband's eldest brother living at Bollington, who tipples & 'gets squiffy' just like *this* Mrs E.

2. Askew, skew-whiff.
1941 Baker *Dict. Austral. Slang* 71 *Squiffy*, askew. **1977** G. Melly *Rum, Bum & Concertina* vii. 85, I never associated it with an orgy, a term I felt to imply a Roman profusion of grapes, wine, buttocks, breasts, marble *chaises-longues*, and squiffy laurel crowns.

squiggle, *sb.*² Add: **1.** (Later examples.) Esp. a wavy or twisting line drawn on a surface.
1928 *Daily Express* 9 July 10/3 No hieroglyphics in timetables to be looked up, no particular squiggle to be remembered lest one is unhooked from the express at Dijon or goes to Rome instead of Florence. **1934** R. Fry *Let.* 3 Aug. (1972) II. 692 The squiggles in the foreground represent runnels of water flowing everywhere. **1957** V. S. Naipaul *Mystic Masseur* v. 78 The handwriting became a hasty, tired squiggle, and the note-book was abandoned. **1979** *Listener* 3 May 603/3 From time to time, squiggles appeared on the screen which were interpreted by some as subliminal instructions to vote labour.
2. *Comb.*, as **squiggle-eyed** *adv.*: in phr. *to look squiggle-eyed* (*at* someone), to view askance or unfavourably. Also as *adj.* (Only in P. G. Wodehouse.)
1927 Wodehouse *Meet Mr Mulliner* vi. 178 There is a certain stage in the progress of a man's love when he feels like curling up in a ball and making little bleating noises if the object of his affections so much as looks squiggle-eyed at him. **1941** —— *Berlin Broadcasts* in *Performing Flea* (1961) i. 265 The internee is always being told to show his passport, and if he has not got one, the authorities tend to look squiggle-eyed. **1960** —— *Jeeves in Offing* xii. 136 She's always been a bit squiggle-eyed about Phyllis, because in Switzerland she held the view that we were a shade too matey. **1972** —— *Pearls, Girls & Monty Bodkin* i. 9 He was very fond of her—in a brotherly way, of course, to which even Gertrude Butterwick, always inclined to look squiggle-eyed at his female friends, could not have taken exception.

squiggle, *v.* Add: **2.** (Later U.S. examples.) Also *fig.*
1922 W. Stevens in *Dial* July 91 Our bawdiness..Is equally converted into palms, Squiggling like saxophones. **1978** *Detroit Free Press* 16 Apr. D11/1 Snitman..drew from the water a thin, blackish-brown worm that squiggled in his palm, trying to sink tiny teeth into his flesh.
3. To write (something) in a squiggly manner, to scrawl. Also, to squeeze or daub (paint) from a tube thus.
1942 N. Balchin *Darkness falls from Air* vi. 108, I signed it. Lennox squiggled underneath, 'I foresee difficulties but the scheme is right in principle. J.L.' **1969** *Observer* 12 Jan. 8/5, I watched a little girl squiggle yellow and red paint on a piece of white paper. **1973** *Daily Tel.* 24 Oct. 17/2 It was the 15th tube [of paint], so I squiggled it on.

† **squil** (skwil). *Oxford University Slang. Obs.* exc. *Hist.* Also **squill.** [Curtailed form of L. *Esquilīnus* of or pertaining to the Esquiline Hill, one of the seven hills of Rome (see quots.). The Esquiline was largely inhabited by low persons; it was used as a cemetery, ult. for paupers (cf. Hor. *Sat.* I. 8).] A name formerly used by Christ Church men to designate opprobriously any member of the university not a member of Christ Church (see also quot. 1970).
1721 [see Hodman 3]. **1874** C. Wordsworth *Soc. Life Eng. Univ. 18th Cent.* 304 Ch. Ch. was unpopular:..the men gave themselves airs, with wonderful ignorance and conceit they claimed to belong to an House, not to a College; those of other Colleges were 'squils' and 'hodmen'. **1900** H. L. Thompson *Christ Church* vii. 151 The phrase 'Squils and Hodmen' needs some explanation. The first word is now happily forgotten, but was in use within the last twenty years, as a colloquial designation of members of other colleges. It was supposed to be a corruption of 'Ex-Collegees', or 'Esquilini'. **1921** S. Paget *H. Scott Holland* iv. 82 He belonged to us, not to 'out-college men', whom some of us called Squills, *i.e.* dwellers on the Esquiline. **1970** Bill & Mason *Christ Church & Reform* p. ix, We are both non-gremial members of Christ Church, and in the abusive word of an earlier day are therefore 'squills'.

squilgee, *sb.* Add: (Earlier example.)
1851 H. Melville *Moby Dick* III. viii. 66 Edgewise moved along the oily deck, it operates like a leathern squilgee.
squilgee *v.*: also *fig.*
1905 J. C. Lincoln *Partners of Tide* vii. 147 That doctor squilgeein' my maintop with his physic stuff has made me feel A1 again.

squill. 1. c. (Examples of *red squill* as a substance.)
1947 *Federation Proc.* VI. 333/1 The identity of the cardiac and the convulsant properties of red squill receives support from an experiment. **1963** *Times* 25 Jan. 13/7 The poisons are principally red squill, sodium fluoro-acetate, and rodenticides containing elemental phosphorus. **1974** M. C. Gerald *Pharmacol.* iii. 57 Strychnine and red squill have been used as rat poisons.

squinch, *v.* Add: **1.** (Later examples.)
1939 *Real Detective Mag.* Aug. 89 She squinched and twisted her too prominent nose in a way that was not at all becoming. **1956** R. Ellison in W. King *Black Short Story Anthol.* (1972) 263 Buster stopped and looked at me, squinching up his eyes with his head cocked to one side. **1974** *Gen. Systems* XIX. 65/2 Within a few hours, the palsy paralyzes the seventh cranial nerve, squinching half the victim's face. The eye cannot close and it waters excessively. The lips displace, and the mouth corner sags.
2. *intr.* To squeeze up so as to occupy less place; to crouch. Also with advbs., as *down*, *over*, etc.
1843 'J. Slick' *High Life in N.Y.* II. 195 Wal, she squinched a trifle and gin a leetle start. **1942** W. Faulkner *Go down, Moses* ii. 158 The old woman was kind of squinched down in one corner. **1972** M. J. Bosse *Incident at Naha* III. 144 Virgil..waited for me to move from the doorway, which I did not by rising but by squinching over.

squinch-owl. *U.S. local.* [Squinch *v.*] = *screech-owl 1 b.
1880 J. C. Harris *Uncle Remus* xix. 89 Word went roun' dat de man Squinch Owl done kotch nudder watziname. **1929** W. Faulkner *Sound & Fury* 48, I heard a squinch owl that night. **1966** *Publ. Amer. Dial. Soc. 1964* XLII. 23 *Screech* (or *scritch*, or *squeach*, or *squinch*, or *scrooch*) *owl*, *Otus asio*, each name of which suggests some characteristic of the little owl.

squint, *sb.* Add: **1. d.** *Radar.* Lack of alignment between the axis of a transmitting aerial and the direction of maximum radiation, deliberately introduced in some systems. Freq. *attrib.*
1947 L. N. Ridenour *Radar Syst. Engin.* vi. 197 'Squint', which results from improper installation or trimming of antennas, has the same operational effect as crabbing of the aircraft in a cross-wind. **1969** Barton & Ward *Handbk. Radar Measurement* ii. 31 The fall-off in energy ratio restricts the practical squint angles to about half the individual beamwidth. **1969** C. A. Wiley in Kayton & Fried *Avionics Navigation Syst.* viii. 370 (*caption*) Squint-mode window display.

squint, *v.* **6. b.** (Earlier example.)
1844 Queen Victoria *Jrnl.* 21 Sept. in D. Duff *Victoria in Highlands* (1968) I. 58 We then began our descent, 'squinting' the hill, the ponies going as safely..as possible.

squinted, *ppl. a.* Add: **2.** *Radar.* Of an aerial: having squint (sense *1 d).
1966 R. W. Bickmore in R. C. Hansen *Microwave Scanning Antennas* iv. 297 Resolution will suffer if a linear phase term is programmed into the processor to cause 'squinting' of the synthetic beam. This is due to the projected aperture effect and is true for all electrically squinted antennas. **1969** Barton & Ward *Handbk. Radar Measurement* ii. 31 The feeds required for generation of slightly squinted beams must overlap in the focal plane.

squinty, *a.* Restrict *Obs.*$^{-0}$ to sense in Dict. and add: **2. a.** Of persons: = Squint-eyed *a.* 1 a, b.
[**1819** Keats *Let.* 20 Sept. (1958) II. 204, I am like a squinti(n)g [squinty: 1931 ed.] gentleman who saying soft things to one Lady ogles another.] **1922** Joyce *Ulysses* 343 She knew right well..what made squinty Edy say that because of him cooling in his attentions. **1957** *Numbers* (N.Z.) Mar. 16, I was only a squinty little third-former.
b. Of the eyes: characterized by squint or oblique vision.
1925 T. Dreiser *Amer. Tragedy* II. I. ii. 174 The young girl with the yellow hair and squinty blue eyes. **1978** J. Irving *World according to Garp* ii. 37 The eyes..as red-lidded and squinty as a pig's.

squire, *sb.* Add: **5. d.** As a term of polite address to a gentleman not formally a squire. More recently, a jocular or familiar address to another man, not necessarily of different status.
1828 J. F. Cooper *Notions* I. 102 His usual address is 'friend', or sometimes he contemplates a stranger of a gentlemanly appearance, with the title of 'squire'. **1864** Trollope *Can you forgive Her?* (1865) II. i. 6 'Well, Squire,' said Scruby, 'how is it to be?' **1959** [see *long *a.*¹ 7 c]. **1962** C. Watson *Hopjoy was Here* x. 111 You see, squire, it's reasonable. **1968** *Listener* 22 Feb. 255/3 At a garage in Paddington I overheard a very sleek young man..ask the attendant to 'fill both tanks up'. 'Blimey, squire,' was the reply, 'you going all the way to Marble Arch?' **1977** N. J. Crisp *Odd Job Man* i. 6 'Good-night then, squire,' he said, to the barman. **1982** *Times* 15 May 14/6 (*caption*) Tell you what, squire—keep the pension and I'll take the cash!
6. Also, applied more widely to any local dignitary.
1848 *Knickerbocker* XVIII. 379 Every body is a squire in these days. **1873** 'Mark Twain' & Warner *Gilded Age* 17 'Squire' Hawkins got his title from being postmaster of Obedstown. **1935** H. W. Horwill *Dict. Mod. Amer. Usage* 301/1 In Am. the *squire* is primarily a justice of the peace, but the name is loosely given, most commonly as a title, to any prominent resident in a village. **1948** W. Faulkner *Intruder in Dust* ii. 34 He had already telephoned Squire Fraser.
7. (Earlier example.)
1874 [see *count-fish* s.v. *count *sb.*¹ 9].

squire, *v.* Add: **1.** Now more freq. in U.S. use. **a.** (Later examples.)
1901 G. B. Shaw *Cæsar & Cleopatra* III, in *Three Plays for Puritans* 148 Ftatateeta comes to her. Apollonius offers to squire them into the palace. **1949** N. Mitford *Love in Cold Climate* I. ix. 97 Squiring royal old ladies to the supper-room. **1967** *Boston Herald* 1 Apr. 20/5 You will squire Machree wherever she wants to go. **1977** I. Shaw *Beggarman, Thief* III. x. 334 The sight of his mother ..being squired..off the plane by a man who seemed not much older than himself had disturbed him.
b. (Later examples.)
1962 D. Lessing *Golden Notebk.* I. 120 That second night of dancing she was squired by Stanley while her husband drank in the bar until it closed. **1977** *Time* 31 Jan. 31/1 At least one of Carter's aides turned up: Pollster Pat Caddell, who squired Hugh Hefner's daughter Christie.

squirearchal, *a.* (Earlier example.)
a. **1833** J. S. Mill in *Jurist* IV. 15 Some stupid younger son of a squirearchal house.

squirearchy¹. **1. a.** (Earlier example.)
a. **1796** W. Tone *Autobiogr.* (1893) II. iii. 55 Such is the honesty of the Squirearchy of Ireland.

Squi·rearchy². [f. the name of Sir John Collings *Squire* (1884–1958), Eng. poet and man of letters, punningly after prec.] The influential literary circle, composed principally of critics and poets, which surrounded Squire, esp. during his editorship of the *London Mercury* (1919–34).
1930 J. Arrow *J. C. Squire v. D. H. Lawrence* 5 Mr. J. C. Squire has pronounced... The magnanimous verdict is that the work of which the 'Squirearchy' does not approve will be 'easily forgiven and even forgotten'. **1959** *Times Lit. Suppl.* 10 Apr. 210/1 When Dr. Leavis founded *Scrutiny* it was with the laudable intention of cleaning out the Augean Stables of the Squirearchy, and an academic Hercules indeed he proved to be. **1978** J. Pearson *Façades* viii. 146 The next encounter [of] the Sitwells.. was the battle with the group who called themselves..the 'Squirearchy'.

squirl (skwɜ̄ɹl). *dial.* and *colloq.* [Perh. blend of Squiggle *sb.*² and Twirl *sb.* or Whirl *sb.*] A flourish or twirl, esp. in handwriting.
1843 J. Ballantine *Gaberlunzie's Wallet* ix. 212 Look at the lang turns o' his L's, and the squirls o' his B's; he's been weel brought up. **1922** *Sunday at Home* Oct. 59/2 'What a squiggly handwriting,' she said... 'They would not let us write that way at school. But when I am grown up I shall make lots of squirls.' **1955** E. Bowen *World of Love* iii. 58 They are simply signed with a squirl. **1971** H. R. Loyn *Wulfstan MS.* 22, S2 three times uses a distinctive squirl, rather like a reversed *c*, to show the end of a section before a blank half-line. **1979** *PN Rev.* 10 7/1 The anterior reinforcing board..has a similar but not identical configuration of interlaced and interlocking squirls.

squirm, *sb.* Add: **c.** A twisting or curving form of decoration characteristic of *art nouveau*; hence *colloq.* (with *the*), the style itself.
1909 [see *art nouveau* s.v. *art *sb.* VI. e]. **1972** F. MacCarthy *All Things Bright & Beautiful* ii. 46 Art nouveau was called 'the squirm'. When 'the squirm' arrived in Britain..Lewis F. Day and Walter Crane were outraged.

squirm, *v.* Add: **2. b.** *trans.* To twist or contort (something) *into* a new form. *rare.*
1876 'Mark Twain' *Tom Sawyer* xxi. 171 A brain-racking effort was made to squirm it into some aspect or other that the moral and religious mind could contemplate with edification.

squirmer (skwɜ̄·ɹməɹ). [f. Squirm *v.* + -er¹.] One who squirms or writhes, esp. with embarrassment; an evasive person.
1951 O. Nash *Family Reunion* 109 Ho, squirmers and writhers, how long will ye suffer The medical tyrant, the social rebuffer! **1977** P. Dickinson *Walking Dead* iv. 59 He was anxious to pin the little squirmer down.

squirmy, *a.* **2.** (Later examples.)
1922 E. Raymond *Tell England* I. ii. 46, I felt a pleasing, squirmy excitement to think that we were to walk on to the..field in the company of the great Middlesex amateur. **1943** D. Powell *Time to be Born* viii. 182 It was a squirmy feeling and reminded Ken..that..the carapace should be a little thicker. **1982** Barr & York *Official Sloane Ranger Handbk.* 57/1 One would never talk about true feelings—excessive piety is rather squirmy.

squirrel, *sb.* Add: **1. b.** Also, squirrel-fur in fashionable use (in the 19th and 20th cent.). Also *ellipt.*, a coat of squirrel fur.
1827 *Manch. Guardian* 27 Oct. 1/2 (Advt.), A perfectly new, elegant..and fashionable assortment of Furs, consisting of Chinchilla, Russia Fitch,..Squirrel and Sable. **1895** *Army & Navy Co-op. Soc. Price List* 15 Sept. 1038 Cape, lined throughout with grey and white Squirrel. **1930** P. Hambledon *Straight Flame* iv. 169 A fur coat.. fashioned of the softest silvery squirrel from Manchuria. **1978** *Country Life* 31 Aug. 598/3 There are..squirrels and durable musquashes for the less well heeled.
6. b. Also, made of squirrel skin or fur, as *squirrel coat, hat, lining.*
1936 E. M. Delafield *Provincial Lady in Amer.* 235 Ella, elegant..in..grey squirrel coat. **1969** L. Hellman *Unfinished Woman* xi. 153 A little girl in a fine squirrel coat and hat. **1974** *Selfridge Xmas Catal.* 14 Leather coat with silvered racoon collar and squirrel lining, £330.00.
7. a. squirrel-cage: spec. *transf.* in *Electr.*, a form of rotor resembling a squirrel-cage,

used in small electric motors (usu. *attrib.*); **squirrel-headed** *a.* (later U.S. example); also **squirrel-headedness.**

1895 S. P. THOMPSON *Polyphase Electr. Currents* iv. 117 A solid cylinder of iron is improved [as a rotor] by surrounding it with a mantle of copper, or by a squirrel-cage of copper bars. **1920** *Whittaker's Electr. Engineer's Pocket-bk.* (ed. 4) 552 Motors with squirrel-cage rotors require special features in the rotor to obtain large starting torque without large losses at normal load. **1972** *Sci. Amer.* Oct. 114/2 The air is circulated and exhausted by a system of squirrel-cage blowers. **1953** *Sun* (Baltimore) 30 Jan. B4/1 Former President Harry S. Truman was quoted as saying..that action..to curb President Eisenhower's Government reorganisation powers 'was a squirrel-headed thing to do'. **1955** E. POUND *Section: Rock-Drill* lxxxv. 6 Not to pamper this squirrel-headedness.

b. squirrel briar, a name used in New England for either of two local species of *Smilax, S. glauca* or *S. rotundifolia,* deciduous prickly vines bearing blue-black berries.

1910 C. B. GRAVES et al. *Catal. Flowering Plants & Ferns Connecticut* 125 Smilax glauca..Saw, Cat or Squirrel Briar. Common. Dry or moist open woods and thickets. *Ibid.*, Smilax rotundifolia..Common Green Briar. Horse, Cat, Bull or Squirrel Briar. **1979** C. MACLEOD *Family Vault* viii. 53 Something grabbed her..but it was only a squirrel briar.

squirrel, *v.* Restrict † *Obs.* to senses in Dict. and add: **1. c.** *intr.* To go round in circles like a caged squirrel; to run or scurry (*round*) like a squirrel.

1921 *Sat. Westm. Gaz.* 29 Jan. 21/1 His deeply affectionate but explosive father inexhaustibly squirrelling round the cage of conventional ideas. **1953** A. CLARKE *Coll. Plays* (1963) 374 My soul was waiting for me, so small, It wriggled and squirrelled to my shoulder. **1966** D. FRANCIS *Flying Finish* xvii. 200 The useless thoughts squirrelled round and round, achieving nothing. **1983** 'M. YORKE' *Find me Villain* v. 39 Nina's mind went on squirrelling round unhappily.

2. *trans.* To store *away* in the manner of a squirrel; to save, hoard; to cache. Rarely with *up* and without advb.

1939 J. STEINBECK *Grapes of Wrath* xxviii. 569, I been squirrelin' money away. **1949** M. MEAD *Male & Female* vii. 145 Mouths first suck and later bite, and are capable of spitting, of squirrelling food in the cheek all night. **1953** J. BLISH *Case of Conscience* in *If. Worlds of Sci. Fiction* I. IV. 40 I've got more plans to that effect squirrelled away. **1959** J. BRAINE *Vodi* vi. 95 Dick felt somehow provident, squirrelling up at least one good event to remember in the winter. **1965** G. HOLDEN *Don't go it Alone* (1966) xvii. 141 He wasn't the type of person to squirrel away something and forget it. **1974** D. SMITH *Look Back with Love* viii. 68, I started a bottom drawer, but it petered out after I had squirrelled one tea-cosy and a pen-wiper. **1981** N. FREELING *One Damn Thing after Another* viii. 58 Arlette..was good at squirrelling away things in obscure places.

squirrelling, *vbl. sb.* Restrict † to sense in Dict. and add: **2.** Hoarding, saving up; storing *away*.

1960 *Listener* 31 Mar. 564/2 Surplus hours..used either to offset the effect of tight times, or as a safeguard against situations when..work became short, and time had to be booked at the 'lower' time rate. I have heard this practice described as 'squirrelling' in other industries. **1965** *Wall St. Jrnl.* 17 Feb. 1 Presumably, the worsening could result from public hoarding of the new coins or the squirreling away of old ones as keepsakes. **1969** *Daily Tel.* 31 July 15/1 We resolved to resist all temptations to lay in 1969 supplies of anything which remained in bulk from 1968's feverish squirrelling. **1972** *Guardian* 25 Sept. 8/1 The specialist's squirrelling of facts.

squirrelly (skwi·rĕli), *a.* Also **squirrely.** [f. SQUIRREL *sb.* + -Y[1].] **1.** Resembling or characteristic of a squirrel.

1925 D. H. LAWRENCE *Reflections on Death of Porcupine* 204 The chipmunks..were little squirrely things with stripes down their backs. **1965** H. GOLD *Man who was not with It* ii. 11, I saw that squirrelly look which says: 'Win it all back with the rent money.'

2. Inclined to rush this way and that, unpredictable. Of a person: demented, crazy; jumpy, nervy.

1928 O. ELTON *Survey Eng. Lit.* (1730–80) I. iii. 70 Lady Sarah Lennox's letters are 'at first squirrelly and girlish'. **1934** M. H. WESEEN *Dict. Amer. Slang* 198 *Squirrely,* abnormal; queer; crazy. **1960** *Spectator* 25 Mar. 438 Her description of contestants going 'squirrelly' (demented) with exhaustion..makes an unpleasant sociological document. **1970** K. PLATT *Pushbutton Butterfly* (1971) x. 117, I got all squirrelly after you left. I just couldn't sit around doing nothing. **1977** J. WAMBAUGH *Black Marble* (1978) viii. 108 Squirrelly dog, Pattie Mae... Squirrelly! Just like his goddamn owner. I never shoulda said I'd bring him today.

squirt, *sb.* Add: **2. d.** A jet-propelled aeroplane, punningly after *jet. Air Force slang. temporary.*

1945 L. R. GRIBBLE *Battle Stories of R.A.F.* xxiii. 59 To fly the squirts in combat meant the development of a new technique. **1948** *N.Y. World-Telegram* 30 Dec. 11/7 The plane itself is called a 'blow torch', a 'flame thrower', a 'squirt', [etc.].

3. c. *transf. spec.* in *Air Force slang,* a burst of gun-fire.

1942 BRENNAN & HESSELYN *Spitfires over Malta* i. 28, I gave him a squirt with the scatter guns. **1948** *Welsh Rev.* Winter 287 There was another squirt of song and then silence. **1978** K. AMIS *Jake's Thing* iv. 34 To be given the choice of two [buses]..was..certainly welcome in the increasing rain and squirts of cold wind.

d. A compressed radio signal transmitted at high speed. Cf. sense *9 of the vb.

1968 M. WOODHOUSE *Rock Baby* vii. 64 It can't transmit continuously, though, surely... What does it do, transmit in squirts? **1974** 'J. LE CARRÉ' *Tinker, Tailor, Soldier, Spy* vi. 50 Irina..boiled down the microdots and played radio for him on a high-speed squirt to beat the listeners.

5. a. For (Chiefly *U.S.* and *dial.*) read orig. *U.S.* and add: (Later examples.) Also *spec.* a child or young person.

1914 G. ATHERTON *Perch of Devil* I. 39 She had 'sized him up' as a 'squirt'.., but he was 'a long sight better than nothing'. **1924** KIPLING *Debits & Credits* (1926) 153 They both shook 'ands with the young squirt across the table. **1935** 'N. BLAKE' *Question of Proof* i. 17 It's about time that squirt Wemyss was suppressed. **1955** M. GILBERT *Sky High* iii. 46 Most people who send letters like that are cowardly little squirts. **1958** B. MALAMUD *Magic Barrel* (1960) 138 George..remembered him giving him nickels..when he was a squirt. **1967** [see *half-portion* s.v. *HALF- II. n]. **1977** J. BINGHAM *Marriage Bureau Murders* xi. 134 Sidney Shaw, the little squirt.. ought to be able to intercept a letter.

squirt, *v.* Add: **II. 4.** †**d.** Phr. *to squirt a mouldy,* to fire a torpedo. *Naut. slang. Obs.*

1916 [see *MOULDY *sb.*].

9. To transmit (information) in highly compressed or speeded-up form. Also *absol.*

1971 C. EGLETON *Last Post for Partisan* xii. 113, I should have been given the means to squirt... You prerecord the message and then push it through in a second, before they have a chance to find your frequency. **1977** P. VAN RJNDT *Blueprint* xiii. 231 The message is recorded on a separate tape which is then treated electronically in order to compress the message... The normal procedure is to 'squirt' it over radio transmission. **1979** C. MCCARRY *Better Angels* II. i. 106 Radio equipment..could squirt a million words from one continent to another via satellite in a droplet of electric energy that required less than a millisecond to send or receive.

squirter. Add: **4.** (Later examples.)

1966 *Punch* 3 Aug. 193 The advertisements inviting operators to take up space at forthcoming fairs, feasts, wakes and well-dressings are full of cavillings like..'No squirters or confetti.' **1983** 'F. PARRISH' *Bait on Hook* ii. 29 You squirt it [*sc.* paint] out of a tin... You can't do a thin line easily with a squirter.

5. *slang.* A revolver.

1935 G. INGRAM *Cockney Cavalcade* xvi. 260 There've been reports..of some of you..doing that film stuff with squirters and handkerchiefs over your faces.

squish, *sb.* Add: **3.** *Engin.* In some internal-combustion engines, the forced radial flow of mixture from the cylinder into the combustion chamber as the piston approaches the cylinder head at the end of a stroke. Freq. *attrib.*

1934 *Proc. Inst. Mech. Engineers* CXXVIII. 155 Satisfactory mixing was brought about largely by the 'squish'. **1953** *Proc. Inst. Mech. Engineers: Automobile Division 1951–2* 103/2 Since squish occurs late in the compression stroke, it is not likely to affect maximum-power spark timing. **1957** *Encycl. Brit.* XII. 505/1 The squish turbulence..feeds most of the charge that would otherwise have been last to burn into the flame front. **1979** R. H. WARRING *Know Your Model Aero Engines* xii. 72 With a squish head, the outer section of the head is flat, with a smaller hemispherical combustion chamber in the middle.

squish, *v.* Add: **1.** Also *colloq.*

1976 D. HEFFRON *Crusty Crossed* ix. 69 We squished our teeth into the berries in our mouths to stop giggling. **1977** G. DURRELL *Golden Bats & Pink Pigeons* v. 129 He [*sc.* an octopus] had wedged himself, or rather squished himself, into a small crevice.

2. b. Of a person, etc.: to proceed or make *one's way* with a squishing sound. *colloq.*

1952 *Sun* (Baltimore) 9 July 30/4 (*caption*) Soaked to the point of not caring, this waterlogged pedestrian squishes his way across a downtown street. **1963** M. BEADLE *These Ruins are Inhabited* iii. 40 We squished down a rutted lane. **1965** F. KNEBEL *Night of Camp David* ii. 50 Tires squishing through the slush and spraying muddy water from little pools at the edge of the pavement. **1978** *Chicago* June 72/2 The highlight of Day is to squish around in the foam spread in a contained area by the Village Fire Department.

squishy, *a.* Add: Also *fig.*

1953 *Freckles* in *News & Observer* (Raleigh, N.C.) 9 Mar. 15/7 Everyone knows you're squishy about Miss Springtime! **1973** *Times Lit. Suppl.* 26 Oct. 1310/5 The very delicacy and respect for words in themselves which are radio's chief strengths do tend to make it rather a squishy medium. **1981** *Sunday Tel.* 8 Mar. 13/3 All the lovely squishy feeling flowed over us when we waved and the driver waved and tooted.

squit, *sb.*[1] For *dial.* read *dial.* and *slang* and add: **1.** (Later examples.)

1909 G. B. SHAW *Let.* 4 Nov. in *Lett. to Granville Barker* (1956) 160 Some little squit of a nervous boy who can cry and scream like a burlesque of Eugene. **1928** A. HUXLEY *Point Counter Point* xxi. 389 Miserable scrofulous little squit! **1947** E. COXHEAD *Play Toward* iv. 102 It's impossible, darling. That—that little squit—and Peggy Jacques! **1976** J. SNOW *Cricket Rebel* 11, I was left in the hands of a second year prep boy, my 'nursemaid', to be introduced to the way of life of a new boy or 'squitt' as he was called.

2. (Later examples.)

1959 A. WESKER *Roots* I. 26 Love? I don't believe in any of that squit—we just got married. **1976** *Norwich Mercury* 19 Nov. 6/8 Dont talk squit.

squitter. 1. For Now *dial.* read Now *dial.* and *colloq.* and add later examples. Cf. *SKITTER *sb.*[1] 1.

1958 P. SCOTT *Mark of Warrior* II. 131 'Aren't you sleeping?' 'I get the squitters pretty regularly.' **1976** A. PRICE *War Game* 13, I reckon squitters was queen [of the battlefield]. More of the poor bastards crapped themselves to death than killed each other. **1981** LD. HAREWOOD *Tongs & Bones* ii. 37 We went incessantly to those over-public latrines... My squitters were at their worst.

2. *Radar.* Random pulses produced by a transponder in the absence of interrogating signals.

1958 *Proc. Inst. Electr. Engineers* CV. B. Suppl. No. 8. 299/2 An average of 2700 pulses/sec are produced by the trigger circuit. These pulses are of constant amplitude and shape, but entirely random in time spacing and are known as 'squitter'. **1976** P. HONOLD *Secondary Radar* i. 67 If the dynamic characteristics of the receiver are too low, the message transmitted may be falsified.., should the signal level be very high. This..will also cause additional dead times—if these are triggered by interference pulses (squitter).

squiz (skwiz), *sb. Austral.* and *N.Z. slang.* [f. QUIZ *sb.*[2], prob. blended with SQUINT *sb.*] A look or glance.

1916 C. J. DENNIS *Songs Sentimental Bloke* 130 *Squiz,* a brief glance. **1922** K. MANSFIELD *Garden Party* 72, I say Laura..you might just give a squiz at my coat before this afternoon. See if it wants pressing. **1948** V. PALMER *Golconda* xxx. 254 With one squiz at it [*sc.* the ore] he can tell how much it would crush to the ton. **1961** R. PARK *Hole in Hill* (1962) viii. 60 'All right, let's have a squiz.' They looked out very cautiously. **1972** J. MCCLURE *Caterpillar Cop* iv. 62 You won't find it there... I had a good squiz over the whole area.

squiz, *v. Austral.* and *N.Z. slang.* [f. prec.] *trans.* and *intr.* To look (at) or glance; to peer.

1941 BAKER *Dict. Austral. Slang* 71 *Squiz,* to look at, inspect. **1947** *Coast to Coast* 132 Kids, who used to slip up the lane behind our place and squiz through the cracks in the fence. **1948** D. W. BALLANTYNE *Cunninghams* (1963) xvi. 73 They walked down the passage and squizzed in the dining-room.

squizzed (skwizd), *a. U.S. slang. rare.* [Orig. unknown.] Drunk, tipsy.

1845 *Knickerbocker* XXV. 75 He was rescued from the pyre..looking like a squizzed cat. **1941** *Sat. Rev. Lit.* 22 Mar. 5/1 A judge of good whiskey, who is, for the purpose of this narrative, slightly squizzed.

squizzle (skwi·z'l), *v. colloq.* and *dial.* Now *rare.* [Imitative.] *intr.* To squirt *out,* to squish. Hence **squi·zzling** *ppl. a.*

1856 'J. PHŒNIX' *Phœnixiana* (ed. 11) xviii. 130 When the mouth is filled with the luscious fruit, and the.. sweet though embarrassing juice is squizzling out all over the chin, and shirt-bosom. **1872** HARDY *Under Greenw. Tree* I. ii. 19 Such a squizzling and squirting job as 'tis in your hands. **1901** *Westm. Gaz.* 27 Feb. 1/3 Boots squeak and squizzle in the mud.

squodgy (skwǫ·dʒi), *a. colloq.* Also **squodgey.** [Imitative: cf. SQUASHY *a.*] Soft and soggy; squelchy.

1970 *Daily Tel.* 15 June 11 Paper cups..tend to go squodgy and superimpose their own faint flavour to hot drinks. **1981** *Church of England Newspaper* 28 Aug. 10/3 One buries by pouring earth upon the deceased, rather than searching for squodgey ground in which to submerge the body.

squoggy (skwǫ·gi), *a. colloq.* [Prob. blend of QUAGGY *a.* and SOGGY *a.*] Wet and miry.

1950 J. CANNAN *Murder Included* vi. 121 'These heel-marks.'..'The ground's too squoggy to tell whether they're male or female.'

squop (skwǫp), *v. Tiddlywinks.* Also † **squallop** (pa. t. and pa. pple. † **squapt**). [Of unknown origin.]

1. *trans.* To cover and immobilize (another's wink) with one's own; also with another player as obj.

1956 *Minutes Cambr. Univ. Tiddlywinks Club* Mar. 12 in G. Consterdine *On Mat* (1967) 8 If both members of the team have all their winks either cupped or covered, then it shall be said that they are *squapt.* The verb shall be declined thus: *Present* I squallop..*Past* I squapt..*Past participle*—Squapt..*Noun*—squap. **1958** *Sunday Times* 2 Mar. 16/3 Mr. Harry Secombe squopted his own captain, who observed irritably that he was a Charlie. **1962** *Christian Sci. Monitor* 1 Oct. 13 In tournament play games are generally limited to 25 minutes, and a scoring system is instigated which takes account of how many winks a team has potted, squopped, etc. **1971** *Ottawa Citizen* 6 Feb. (Canadian Mag.) 24 You can't get something going for you if too many of your winks get squopped by an opponent's wink. **1978** *Boston Herald American* 25 Apr. 6

A gentle shot which either frees one of your winks or squops one of your opponent's winks is referred to as a 'piddle'.

2. *intr.* To cover an opponent's wink with one's own.

1963 *Observer* 22 Dec. 11/8 To squop is to cover an opponent's wink. **1971** *Philadelphia Evening Bull.* 13 Feb. 8 Squidgers in hand, the Hark Yon Tree Hath No Leaves But They Will Out Club is off to Toronto to squop and counter-squop for the North American Tiddlywinks Association Championship. **1977** *Cornell Alumni News* July 25 Sunshine tried to defuse the potential blitz by coming inside Drix's zone and threatening to squop.

Hence **squopped** *ppl. a.*, **squo·pping** *vbl. sb.* and *ppl. a.*; **squo·pper**, a player who squops.

1962 *N.Y. Times* 5 Aug. 23 It was in squopping that the British excelled. **1962** *Time* 14 Sept. 56 A squopped wink cannot be squidged again until it is de-squopped, either by the original squopper or by a squopped player's partner. **1962** *Life* 14 Dec. 122 Two-man units each with a powerful offensive squidger and a canny defensive squopper. **1971** *Ottawa Citizen* 22 Jan. 24/1 When it comes to squidging and squopping, Rosemary Wain and Andy Tomaszeuski are two of the best in the business. **1975** *Sunday Mail Color Mag.* (Brisbane) 28 Sept. 21/2 Squopping is the ability to flip one of your winks on top of your opponent's wink—and prevent him playing it. Then the squopped player tries to free his captive counter by squopping the counter on top. **1977** SHARP & PIGGOTT *Bk. of Games* 165 The owner of a squopped wink must wait until it is freed.. The owner of a squopping wink.. must ensure that his squidger first touched his own wink.

squop (skwǫp), *sb. Tiddlywinks.* [f. prec.] The act or achievement of covering an opponent's wink with one's own; a wink squopped in this way.

1962 *Time* 14 Sept. 56 The squop shot is entirely new to them. **1962** *N.Y. Times* 21 Oct. 83 The high point of the match was a septenary squop by Mr. Stein in which he immobilized seven winks with a single shot. **1979** *Harvard Mag.* May–June 40 The wink is shot into a key position, from which it can defend friendly squops, attack enemy squops, or set up a strategic zone.

squoze, squozen: see *SQUEEZE *v.*

sqush (skwɒʃ), *v. U.S. colloq.* and *dial. rare.* [Imitative: cf. SQUASH *v.*¹, *SQUDGE *v.*, SQUISH *v.*] **1.** *intr.* To collapse into a soft, pulpy mass.

1884 'MARK TWAIN' *Huck. Finn* xxix. 303 He'd a squshed down like a bluff bank that the river has cut under. **1955** E. POUND *Section: Rock-Drill* lxxxviii. 41 Belascio or Topaze, and not have it sqush, a 'throne', something God can sit on without having it sqush.

b. To squelch, squeeze messily.

1929 in H. Wentworth *Amer. Dial. Dict.* (1944) 592/1, I..'squshed' through many a weary mile of mud. **1949** H. HORNSBY *Lonesome Valley* xix. 249 He could take off his shoes and walk around in the mud and let the mud ooze and sqush between his toes.

Sr., abbrev. of: **1.** SIR *sb.* (q.v.).

‖ **2.** SEÑOR I a, SIGNOR I a.

a **1912** W. T. ROGERS *Dict. Abbrev.* (1913) 182/1 *Sr.*,.. Señor. **1973** *Listener* 3 May 582/3 Sr Bassetti felt that the Italian Communist Party is not the ogre it used to be. **1977** 'D. CORY' *Bennett* ii. 43 My instructions with regard to the search for Sr Bennett are..unequivocal. **1982** *Listener* 14 Jan. 8/3 Sr Fraga won the recent elections in his native Galicia.

3. SENIOR *a.* I a. Chiefly *U.S.*

1936 *N.Y. Herald Tribune* 5 June 2/2 (*heading*) Extradition of Ellis Parker Sr. to await Republican Convention. **1973** D. AARON *Unwritten War* (1975) III. vii. 108 James Sr., for all his geniality and charm, was an opinionated and strong-minded man. **1977** D. DELMAN *Nice Murderers* iv. 53 Horowitz felt..a stab of sympathy for Kennicutt, Sr. Fathers and sons, he thought.

Sranan (srā·nan). [Prob. Taki-Taki: in full *Sranan Tongo*, Surinam tongue (also used).] = *TALKEE-TALKEE. Also *attrib.*

1953 L. L. E. RENS *Hist. & Social Background of Surinam's Negro-Eng.* x. 135 The term NE was used simply because none of the other appellations (takki-takki, Krioro, sranang tongo) was adequate. **1957** *Lingua* VI. 374 (*heading*) The verbal system of Sranan. **1964** *English Studies* XLV. 423 'Phonetic Interpretation', by which term he [*sc.* Echteld] means the substitution of Sranan phonemes for the original English ones. **1974** R. A. HALL *External Hist. Romance Languages* 45 The Portuguese element in Sranan. **1980** *English World-Wide* I. I. 6 This argument is valid even for such cases as Krio, Tok Pisin or Sranan.

Sri: see *SHRI, SRI. **'sright**: see *'S I c.

Sri Lankan (ʃrī læ·ŋkăn, ʃrilæ·ŋkăn, s-), *sb.* and *a.* [f. Skr. *Srī Laṅkā* name of the island known in English until 1972 as Ceylon (f. *śrī* *SHRI, SRI, honorific prefix + *Laṅkā* name of (the chief town of) the island) + -AN.] **A.** *sb.* A native or inhabitant of Sri Lanka. **B.** *adj.* Of or pertaining to Sri Lanka or its people.

1973 *Advocate-News* (Barbados) 29 Dec. 7/2 (*heading*) Sri Lankan is world billiards champion. **1974** *Times* 9 Sept. 12/8 At the Edinburgh military tattoo, the Sri Lankan police reserve band have been giving a display. **1976** *Scotsman* 25 Nov. 3/5 BOC International are fighting the Sri Lankan plans to nationalise their Ceylon Oxygen offshoot. **1977** J. LAKER *One-Day Cricket* 66 The Sri Lankans rattled the score along. **1982** *Church Times* 29 Jan. 11/4 In all its life the Church there was both Anglican and totally Sri Lankan.

S-rope: see *S 2 c.

‖ **sruti** (ʃru·ti). *Mus.* [Skr. *śruti*, lit. hearing, listening.] A microtonal interval in Indian music.

1792 W. JONES in *Asiatick Researches* III. 69 They unanimously reckon twenty-two *srutis*, or quarters and thirds of a tone, in their octave. **1891** [see *GRAMA²]. **1954** *Grove's Dict. Mus.* (ed. 5) IV. 457/1 That disposes of the widely accepted view of the 'quartertone'—that it is half a semitone, and that Hindus have 22 of these *srutis* to make a melody with! What they have is five, six or seven notes to the octave, but 60 or more ways of disposing them. **1972** R. SHANKAR *Indian Music* iv. 135 The scale of twenty-two srutis is never sung chromatically, and the intervals are not important to one another but only as *groups* of intervals.

S-scroll(ed), -shaped, -sofa: see *S 2 c.

St. Add: **e.** (with small initial) for *stumped (by)* in *Cricket*. Cf. STUMP *v.*¹ 8.

stab, *sb.*¹ Add: **2. f.** In colloq. phr. *to make* (or *have*, etc.) *a stab at* (something), to try, attempt; to make a shot at. orig. *U.S.*

1895 W. C. GORE in *Inlander* Dec. 115 *Stab, to make a*, to make a blind attempt to answer a question. **1908** K. MCGAFFEY *Show Girl* 235, I..made a stab for the rail. **1915** WODEHOUSE *Something Fresh* xi. 315 'I *do* wish that this time you would endeavour..not to make a fool of yourself.'..'I'll have a jolly good stab at it, governor.' **1930** GALSWORTHY *Roof* vi. 96 D'you think you'll be able to travel the day after to-morrow?..I'll have a good stab at it, as my more genial colleagues say. **1940** 'N. SHUTE' *Old Captivity* x. 294 We may have to come back again... But I think we'll have a stab at it. **1961** *Press Jrnl.* Apr. 10/3 Let's say you're going to take a stab at writing up the annual office picnic. **1973** 'S. WOODS' *Enter Corpse* 113 'Now that,' said Nelson, 'I can't believe.' 'You might have a stab at it,' Maitland suggested, 'It happens to be true.' **1980** W. MAXWELL *So Long, see You Tomorrow* (1981) ii. 7 She may have made a stab at being a mother to my older brother and me.

g. In fig. phr. *stab in the back*, a treacherous deed. Cf. sense *1 g of the vb.

1922 JOYCE *Ulysses* 621 That stab in the back touch was quite in keeping with those Italianos. **1934** R. H. LUTZ *Causes of German Collapse in 1918* v. 132 (*heading*) The 'stab-in-the-back' question. **1934** —— tr. von Kuhl in *Ibid.*, Some maintain that we lost the war owing to the stab in the back administered to the Army by those at home... On the other side the 'stab-in-the-back legend' is rejected as 'one of the most malignant and..stupidest legends'. **1953** J. W. WHEELER-BENNETT *Nemesis of Power* I. i. 67 For several days before his political appearance..Hindenburg was closeted with..the extreme Nationalist leaders. In this brief period was crystallized the legend of the 'stab-in-the-back', in justification of which many innocent Germans were to suffer when the National Socialists came to power. *Ibid.*, The Marshal [*sc.* Hindenburg] testified..on November 18... He.. addressed himself to the German people. Their defeat, he told them, was not attributable to the Army but to the civilian demoralization and disunion. The irreproachable Army had received a 'stab-in-the-back' (*Dolchstoss*) from the Revolution. **1959** *Times* 21 Oct. 13/4 Professor Nordhoff, the managing director of Volkswagen, reacted as if he were the victim of another stab-in-the-back legend. **1971** A. BULLOCK *Twentieth Cent.* 25/1 Our knowledge of the recent past..will be based on hear-say, myths ('the Stab in the Back', for instance).

3*. *Oil Industry.* (See quot. 1975.)

1972 L. M. HARRIS *Introd. Deepwater Floating Drilling Operations* xii. 133 The integral marine-riser system has the choke and kill lines installed on the riser joints so that they are simultaneously stabbed and made up during the stab and make up of the marine-riser connector. **1975** L. CROOK *Oil Terms* 106 *Stab*, the operation of guiding one end of a pipe into the connection of another pipe to 'make up' a connection.

4. stab-and-drag *Archæol.*, a technique of ceramic decoration whereby a point is drawn along the surface of a pot and pushed in deeper at intervals (usu. *attrib.*); **stab-stitch** *Needlework* (see quot. 1964); hence as *v. trans.* and **stab-stitching** *vbl. sb.*

1931 V. G. CHILDE in *Archæol. Jrnl.* LXXXVIII. 47 Handles and flat bases first make their appearance in Fort Harrouard II. In the same levels the fine incision of the early Chassey style gives place to deep incision, or stab-and-drag. **1931** S. PIGGOTT in *Ibid.* 78 *Stab-and-drag* lines—made with a point that is drawn along the clay and pushed in deeper at intervals—occur only on certain Scottish pots, e.g., from Unstan. **1954** —— *Neolithic Cultures* vii. 204 Certain vessels with stab-and-drag motifs. **1978** *Proc. Prehist. Soc.* XLIV. 276 Decorated wall-sherd; fine vertical stab and drag lines. **1917** E. R. HAMBRIDGE *Simple Dressmaking* I. 7/2 Back stitches should be frequent in stab tacking... *Cf.* Fig. 28 for stab stitch, which is similarly worked. *Ibid.* 10/1 Stab-stitching..is back-stitching, but worked with the needle placed vertically through the material..instead of horizontally. *Ibid.*, Running, run-stitching, and half back-stitching can also be stab-stitched, but strong thread or silk should be employed. **1932** D. C. MINTER *Mod. Needlecraft* 159/2 Stab stitching..close to the fold of the felt..may be employed. *c* **1951** *Glovemaking* (Dryad Leaflet 31) 6 A hand-made glove..is almost always sewn on the right side, and various stitches can be used. The most popular of these is the 'prix' or stab-stitch. **1964** *McCall's Sewing* ii. 32/2 *Stab-stitch* a stitch in which the needle is brought in and out of the fabric at right angles. **1976** *Woman's Weekly* 6 Nov. 42/3 Stab-stitch the boots together in pairs.

stab (stæb), *sb.*⁵ *Med.* [a. G. *stab* rod, after V. Schilling's use of G. *stabförmig* rod-shaped, *stabkern* rod-nucleus (*Zeitscher. f. exper. Path. u. Therapie* (1911) IX. 691, 692): cf. STAFF *sb.*¹] Used *attrib.* and *absol.* to designate white blood cells characterized by a nucleus in the form of a single bent or twisted rod (orig. regarded as abnormal forms).

1929 R. B. H. GRADWOHL tr. *Schilling's Blood Picture* ii. 128 The neutrophilic degenerative stab or staff forms are not present in the normal blood picture. *Ibid.* 135 They [*sc.* degenerative forms] are practically insignificant, with the exception of the stabs..which deserve special mention as a degenerative phenomenon in the nuclear shift. **1938** W. MAGNER *Textbk. Hematol.* v. 79 Schilling divides the neutrophile leukocytes into the following classes. (1) Myelocytes. (2) Juvenile leukocytes or metamyelocytes. (3) Stab, staff or rod-nuclear cells. **1972** W. J. WILLIAMS et al. *Hematol.* iii. 27/2 (*heading*) Band form or stab cell. *Ibid.* lxvi. 562/2 The stab is the least mature cell of the granulocytic series found in the peripheral blood of normal persons.

stab, *v.* Add: **1. g.** In fig. phr. *to stab* (a person, etc.) *in the back*, to harm or damage in a treacherous manner. Cf. *BACK-STABBER.

1916 G. B. SHAW in *N.Y. Times Mag.* 9 Apr. 2/2 The cry that 'England's Difficulty Is Ireland's Opportunity' is raised in the old senseless, spiteful way as a recommendation to stab England in the back when she is fighting some one else. **1932** KIPLING *Limits & Renewals* 384 He makes my job ten times more difficult than it need be..stabs me in the back with his crazy schemes for betterment. **1956** N. NICOLSON *Diary* 4 Nov. in *Diaries & Lett. H. Nicolson* (1968) 315, I did not want to publish any letter until the crisis in Egypt had ended, as otherwise I might be accused of stabbing the troops in the back. **1979** F. OLBRICH *Sweet & Deadly* viii. 91 All these years with me he's been completely honest and now he stabs me in the back.

2. d. Delete *nonce-use* and add: Also *fig.*, to pierce like a pointed weapon.

1920 R. MACAULAY *Potterism* VI. v. 259 Gideon's fate pilloried on that placard had stabbed through him. **1946** D. C. PEATTIE *Road of Naturalist* ii. 33 Outside our mortal dusty sphere, Canopus must be a horrible, blinding searchlight stabbing through a black and icy void.

7. *Oil Industry.* To guide (a length of pipe) so as to connect it properly to another member.

[**1922**: implied at *STABBER 1 d.]. **1932** *Amer. Speech* VII. 271 *Stab*, to guide (pipe) in making connections so that the threads engage properly. **1948** *Petroleum Handbk.* (ed. 3) v. 85 As the empty elevator hook is hoisted the derrick man latches in a stand as it passes his level. The stand is picked up and 'stabbed' into the tool joint at the rotary table. **1976** *Offshore Platforms & Pipelining* 6/3 Only one pile add-on will have to be stabbed and welded to drive the sleeve piles.

stabber. Add: **1. d.** *Oil Industry.* One who stabs pipes (see *STAB *v.* 7).

1922 F. M. TOWL in D. T. Day *Handbk. Petroleum Industry* I. 410 The joint is lifted into place, and a man, the 'stabber', standing by the end of the joint with a handspike, moves the joint until it is straight with the last joint laid. **1976** M. MACHLIN *Pipeline* iv. 50, I worked as a stabber—that's the man who sits on the end of the walking beam and holds the pipe straight.

stabbing, *vbl. sb.* Add: **1. b. stabbing board** *Oil Industry* (see quot. 1932).

1932 *Amer. Speech* VII. 271 *Stabbing-board*, a board in the derrick at the height of one joint, from which the derrick man stabs pipe. **1974** R. D. LANGENKAMP *Handbk. Oil Industry Terms & Phrases* 126 The derrick man stands on the stabbing board and assists in guiding the threaded end of the casing into the collar of the preceding joint that is hanging in the slips in the rotary table.

stabilate (stēⁱ·bilēⁱt). *Biol.* [f. L. *stabil-is* STABLE *a.* + *-ate*, after *filtrate*, *precipitate*, etc.] A sample of biological material from a homogeneous source which is preserved by freezing on a single occasion to serve as a standard, portions of it being restored as desired.

1965 LUMSDEN & HARDY in *Nature* 6 Mar. 1032/2 A separate term is now required to convey this implication of the stabilization of biological characters in preserved material and to distinguish preserved from 'strain' material. The word 'stabilate' is now proposed for this purpose. A 'stabilate' may be defined as a population of an organism preserved in viable condition on a unique occasion. **1970** *Ibid.* 19 Sept. 1255/1 A stabilate of infected blood was frozen to −70° at the start of each experiment to ensure that a strict homologous challenge of vaccinated animals was subsequently made. **1976** *Ibid.* 24 June 698/2 All eight surviving cattle were challenged with a similar injection of stabilate.

Hence as *v. trans.*, to make into a stabilate.

1978 *Tropenmedizin und Parasitologie* XXIX. 443/2 The isolate was needle-passaged once in a goat and then stabilated.

stabile (stē̆ⁱ·bəil). [f. L. *stabil-is* STABLE *a.*, after *MOBILE *sb.*[3]] A rigid sculpture or similar construction of wire, sheet metal, etc., of a type first developed by Alexander Calder 1898–1976), Amer. sculptor and painter, opp. *MOBILE *sb.*[3] 1 a. (The name was suggested by Jean Arp.)

1943 J. J. SWEENEY *Alexander Calder* 30 The sculpture which was exhibited at the Galerie Percier shows a full assimilation of his experiences... It was to this type of stationary abstract sculpture that Arp. a few months later, gave the name 'stabiles'. **1949** [see *MOBILE *sb.*[3] 1 a]. **1957** [see *KINETIC *a.* 6]. **1967** *Times* 28 Feb. (Canada Suppl.) 31 This 46-ton 'stabile' is conceived and created in nickel stainless steel. **1977** P. LEACH *Baby & Child* iii. 179 Her stabile will still be useful when she is in her cot.

stabilimentum (stăbilime·ntŏm). *Ent.* Pl. **-menta.** [See STABILIMENT.] A conspicuous broad band of silk running across the web of certain kinds of spider.

1912 J. H. COMSTOCK *Spider Bk.* iv. 203 Some of the orb-weavers strengthen their webs by spinning a zigzag ribbon across the centre or below the hub (Fig. 188). This ribbon has been termed the *stabilimentum.* **1952** T. H. SAVORY *Spider's Web* iv, In addition to radii and spirals there are certain accessory structures which most webs possess. Of these the most conspicuous, when present, is the stabilimentum. **1983** *New Scientist* 10 Feb. 366/1 It seems that stabilimenta are really early warning landmarks for birds.

stabilimeter. Restrict *Aeronautics* to sense in Dict. and add: **2.** *Biol.* A device attached to or forming an animal's cage, the movement of which is recorded as a measure of the animal's activity.

1940 *Jrnl. Exper. Psychol.* XXVII. 91 A similar but smaller stabilimeter has been constructed for studies on spontaneous activity and conditioning in guinea pigs. **1954** *Jrnl. Compar. & Physiol. Psychol.* XLVII. 97 The basic apparatus unit was a stabilimeter-type activity recorder... It involves a circular living cage resting on a central pivot about which it can tilt slightly in any direction. **1972** A. K. BARTOSHUK in Kling & Riggs *Woodworth & Schlosberg's Exper. Psychol.* (ed. 3) xviii. 822/2 Stabilimeter activity increased markedly for the younger rats..but scarcely at all for 100-day rats.

stability. Add: **1. f.** Also of an atomic nucleus or sub-atomic particle.

1955 J. A. WHEELER in W. Pauli *Niels Bohr* 163 (*heading*) Nuclear fission and nuclear stability.

2. e. Also, of a physical property or the system possessing it.

1925 W. GREENWOOD *Text-bk. Wireless Telegr. & Teleph.* vi. 121 Stability is essential [in a receiver]. By this is meant that the sensitivity must be capable of being controlled by the operator, and must not be liable to be upset by the reception of very strong signals. **1962** J. H. & P. J. REYNER *Radio Communication* iv. 153 Modern conditions call for high stability, the capacitance being required to remain constant with time. **1963** B. FOZARD *Instrumentation & Control Nucl. Reactors* x. 122 For high quality equipments..requiring a gain stability of 0·1% both H.T. and heater supplies must be stabilised. **1975** D. G. FINK *Electronics Engineers' Handbk.* XVII. 50 The stability of feedback systems is of great importance since an unstable system will not be effective in maintaining the controlled variable at approximately the desired value.

stabilization. (In Dict. s.v. STABILIZE *v.*) Add: **a.** (Later examples.)

1922 *World's Paper Trade Rev.* 10 Mar. 767/1 Stabilisation of wages is an urgent necessity in order that the ndustry might enjoy continued peace. **1945** *Electronic Industries* Sept. 226 *Stabilization*, a system for maintaining a radar beam in a desired direction in space despite the roll and pitch of the ship or aircraft. **1963** B. FOZARD *Instrumentation & Control Nucl. Reactors* x. 122 Stabilisation of heater current is conveniently arranged by joining the valve heaters in series and supplying them with direct current from a regulated supply. **1975** *Petroleum Rev.* XXIX. 92/1 The stabilisation consists of the separation of light hydrocarbon components from the raw crude so that the 'stabilised' product is 'stable' in the sense that it can be stored and handled under atmospheric conditions.

b. *attrib.*

1940 *Times* 5 June 7/4 Inasmuch as the wage structure of the country has reached a stabilization point, the only justification for wage adjustments now will be in conditions common to all industry. **1958** *Spectator* 6 June 752/2 Sir Oliver Franks..called for a 'stabilisation' loan [from the U.S.] and the reinforcement of the IMF resources. **1969** *Advancement of Sci.* XXVI. 65/2 Management was thus seen as concerned primarily with stabilization policy and with the short-run, since stability is by definition a short-term affair. **1974** *Daily Tel.* 11 Mar. 18/5 The South African government may introduce a gold stabilisation fund.

stabilize, *v.* Add: **1.** Also with other objs. and *refl.*

1916 H. BARBER *Aeroplane Speaks* 71 If an aeroplane was not stabilized in this way. **1938** G. H. RICHTER *Textbk. Org. Chem.* xxix. 595 The majority of the reactions of naphthalene are..the formation of unstable 1,4 addition products..which then stabilize themselves by the elimination of two atoms. **1958** *Times* 30 Aug. 6/1 The rocket during the whole of its flight was stabilized, to prevent rotation. **1975** *Petroleum Rev.* XXIX. 89/3 The raw crude oil will be stabilised and the natural gas liquids recovered.

3. *intr.* To become stable; *esp.* to cease varying in value.

1961 in WEBSTER. **1971** *Timber Trades Jrnl.* 21 Aug. 16/1 Lumber stabilises at approximately 15% moisture content under normal use conditions. **1974** *State* (Columbia, S. Carolina) 26 Apr. 19-A/2 The Nixon administration contends the economy will stabilize in the second quarter. **1981** *Times* 4 Feb. 16/7 He was obliged with his pilot to eject from a Javelin which had stabilized in an unrecoverable spin.

stabilized, *ppl. a.* Made stable. **1. a.** (Later examples.) Prevented from oscillating or moving.

1958 *Times Rev. Industry* Sept. 96/1 The country's [*sc.* South Africa's] highways consist of gravelled or stabilized roads. **1968** R. W. FAIRBRIDGE *Encycl. Geomorphol.* 126/1 Sand-sized pellets from drying crusts of saline flats with 8% or more of clay..form stabilized dunes. **1977** 'D. RUTHERFORD' *Return Load* ii. 40 The modern, stabilized vessel provided good accommodation for the drivers.

b. Prevented from fluctuating in value or quality.

1918 *Nation* (N.Y.) Feb. 129/2 To give every farmer just returns and stabilized prices.

2. Of cloth: treated in order to prevent stretching or shrinking.

1960 *Textile Terms & Definitions* (Textile Inst.) (ed. 4) 140 *Stabilized finish*, treatment applied to a textile material to increase its resistance to dimensional changes in laundering and use. **1977** *Austral. Sailing* Jan. 41/1 Cheret, Banks and Fogh spinnakers..are made from either ¾ oz or ½ oz stabilised or zephylite cloth.

3. Made stable in character or behaviour; *spec.* of a drug addict, able to live more or less normally on a repeated constant dose.

1961 *Drug Addiction* (Min. of Health) 11 Arising also.. is the conception of a 'stabilised addict'... A careful scrutiny of the histories of more than a hundred persons classified as addicts reveals that many of them who have been taking small and regular doses for years show little evidence of tolerance and are often leading reasonably satisfactory lives. **1964** G. L. COHEN *What's Wrong with Hospitals?* vii. 152 They sit in one charabanc, and the stabilized male chronics in another. **1967** M. M. GLATT et al. *Drug Scene* vii. 81 The 'stabilized addict', i.e. a person who was able to maintain a fixed dose of the narcotic drug without the need for ever-increasing doses and who, at the same time, was able to follow his occupation. **1976** J. I. M. STEWART *Young Pattullo* viii. 188 Fish looked stabilized, at least until the following day, when I could take stock of his state again.

stabilizer. Add: **1. a.** (Later examples.)

1911 G. C. LOENING *Monoplanes & Biplanes* x. 136 A horizontal surface placed at the rear acts as a longitudinal stabilizer. **1918** J. M. GRIDER *War Birds* (1927) 221 He managed to land with his stabilizer wheel. **1920** *Discovery* Mar. 77/2 Captain Caquot solved the problem by fitting the peculiar large stabilisers, or tails, which give the balloon a conspicuous, almost an uncanny appearance. **1948** W. LEY *Rockets & Space Travel* vii. 180 Schaefer and I are inclined to believe that even a 1 *g* rocket might be able to do without a stabilizer. **1962** F. I. ORDWAY et al. *Basic Astronautics* ii. 17 The Dutch tried using small fins attached to the body of the rocket in order to do away with the unwieldy stabilizer stick. **1973** *Times* 21 Feb. 7/1 The stabilizer of the Soviet airliner..had jammed.

b. *Naut.* A device intended to reduce the rolling of a ship in heavy seas. Cf. *gyro-stabilizer* s.v. *GYRO- b.

1913 *Engineering* 13 June 820/1 The perfect stabiliser must act against the forces which are acting on the ship in such a way as to always resist the effect of the sea in producing motion. **1946** *Nature* 24 Aug. 250/2 A chapter follows on the sperry gyro ship-stabilizer, in which each gyro rotor weighs 100 tons and spins at 800 revolutions a minute. **1958** *Engineering* 28 Mar. 386/3 The installation of anti-roll Denny-Brown stabilisers in the Cunard Liner Queen Mary has now been finished. **1968** W. J. FOX *Marine Auxiliary Machinery* (ed. 4) xvi. 461 It is in the provision of this form of [flume] control that the main differences lie between the flume stabilization system and the older types of passive tank stabilizer. **1983** *Listener* 14 July 12/1 We abruptly lurched... 'Technical proving of the stabiliser,' said the announcement.

c. Chiefly *N. Amer.* A stabilizing device on a motor vehicle or tractor; *spec.* = *sway bar* (*b*) s.v. *SWAY-. Also *stabilizer bar*.

1931 *Automobile Engineer* Nov. 481/3 The stabiliser bar on the Panhard-Levassow..is fitted transversely at the rear end of the chassis. **1939** *Audel's New Automotive Guide* xxxii. 827 Practically all modern cars are provided with stabilizers as standard equipment. **1949** LANDON & HAFFERKAMP in Frazee & Bedell *Automotive Fundamentals* viii. 445 The stabilizer may be thought of as a third spring which connects the two individual suspensions. **1962** *Which? Car Suppl.* Oct. 138/1 Clamp bolts of stabiliser bar [were] slightly loose. **1966** SHIPPEN & TURNER *Basic Farm Machinery* I. viii. 94 *Stabilizers.* These are also used to prevent side to side movement of certain farm implements. They usually take the form of metal bars slightly cranked at each end and they fit between an anchorage point beneath the rear axle and the ends of the linkage bars. **1977** 'D. RUTHERFORD' *Return Load* ii. 32 She's got optional six-wheel drive with stabilizers operating on the front and rear axle.

d. *pl.* A pair of small supporting wheels fitted one at each side of the rear wheel of a child's bicycle, to keep it upright.

1960 A. L. PULLEN *Cycling Handbk.* (ed. 3) i. 10 (*caption*) Child's lightweight cycle with stabilizers. **1970** *Kay & Co.* (Worcester) *Catal.* 1970–71 Autumn/Winter 982/1 RSW 11 Cycle... It has a 12 inch frame, 11 inch pneumatic tyres, a spacious rear hold-all, and stabilizers. **1978** *Dumfries & Galloway Standard* 21 Oct. 21/7 (Advt.), Child's bicycle, with stabilisers, as new, to suit 3–6 years.

2. (Examples.) More widely, an additive which inhibits chemical or physical change in a substance, esp. one used to prevent the breaking of an emulsion.

1909 *Chem. Abstr.* III. 1342 Vaseline which was added originally to protect the gun has turned out to be a valuable stabilizer for the powder. **1932** *Discovery* Aug. 240/1 The coal was prevented from separating from the oil by the addition of a 'stabilizer'. **1940** *Thorpe's Dict. Appl. Chem.* (ed. 4) IV. 520/1 In the early days of smokeless powders a small amount of alkali was added as a stabiliser. **1948** J. OSBORNE *Dental Mech.* (ed 2) xi. 183 Since the monomer will polymerize by the action of heat or light, it is necessary to prevent this occurring... An inhibitor, or stabilizer, is therefore added to all dental monomers. **1963** W. J. WOOLGAR *Plastics in Plumbing* v. 57 A small proportion of stabilizer is added, to prevent the P.V.C. from decomposing at processing temperatures. **1966** *Punch* 5 Jan. 9/1 Mrs. Joyce Butler..has introduced a Labelling of Food Bill which calls for a detailed specification..of anti-oxidants, emulsifiers and stabilisers in foods. **1977** *Lancet* 15 Oct. 780/2 Because it increases the viscosity of solutions guar gum is widely used in the food industry as a thickener and stabiliser of fat emulsions.

3. *Electronics.* **a.** A circuit or device for preventing unwanted feedback. **b.** A circuit that holds the output voltage of a power supply at a constant level despite changes in supply voltage or load, by comparison with a fixed reference voltage. Also *stabilizer circuit.*

1924 MOYER & WOSTREL *Practical Radio* viii. 119 A common stabilizer for all the radio-frequency stages is generally sufficient. **1936** *Physical Rev.* L. 1094/2 (*heading*) Electronic voltage stabilizers. **1958** D. G. A. THOMAS in O. R. Frisch *Nuclear Handbk.* xv. 24 The principle of ..stabilisers is to compare the output voltage (or fraction of it) with that of a voltage reference source, amplify the difference, and use it to control the output. **1974** HARVEY & BOHLMAN *Stereo F.M. Radio Handbk.* v. 82 An amplifier is not essential but its use improves the regulation of the stabilizer circuit.

4. *gen.* Something that reduces variation in the condition or behaviour of anything.

1955 *Times* 15 July 9/2 These stabilizers included increased social service payments, agricultural price supports..an easy credit policy..and a tax system which made tax liabilities fall faster than income during the recession. **1958** *Manch. Guardian* 21 Jan. 6/1 The 'built-in stabilisers' of the American economy are beginning to grip.

5. *Math.* A subgroup of a permutation group, being the group of elements that map some subset of the permuted elements on to itself.

1965 J. J. ROTMAN *Theory of Groups* iii. 49 If $x \in X$, then the set of all $t \in G$ that fix x forms a subgroup H_x of G (called the stabilizer of x). **1979** *Proc. London Math. Soc.* XXXVIII. 200 Hence the stabilizer of e, Stab $(e) = \{g \mid ge = e\}$ is finite.

stabilizing, *ppl. a.* (Later examples.)

1935 H. A. L. FISHER *Hist. Europe* I. xii. 137 The Arabs were poets, dreamers, fighters, traders; they were not politicians. Nor had they found in religion a stabilizing or unifying power. **1954** P. MASON *Ess. Racial Tension* 141 Stabilizing devices are introduced to preserve the dominant position and genetic purity of the dominating race. **1960** C. DAY LEWIS *Buried Day* i. 18 For a rather rootless person like myself, there is something reassuring, if not stabilising, in the mere known existence of individual ancestors. **1981** *Sci. Amer.* Feb. 36/3 The ability to monitor Russian missile-carrying submarines could..be considered stabilizing in that it deters surprise attack.

Stabit (stæ·bit). *Engin.* [Arbitrary, suggested by STABILITY.] A large mass of concrete so shaped that when large numbers are placed together they tend to interlock and form a strong barrier that will act as a breakwater.

1962 *Dock & Harbour Authority* May 29/2 The Stabit is basically a hollow tetrahedron and, besides its use for breakwater construction, it is considered to be particularly suitable for beach and coast protection works. **1963** *Guardian* 30 Aug. 3/5 (*caption*) Six hundred concrete 'teeth' have been fixed in position to protect the root of Shoreham harbour's east breakwater from the pounding of heavy seas. The 'teeth'..are called Stabits, and are interlocking in a sloping, double layer. **1968** *Proc. 11th Conf. Coastal Engin.* II. 797 The number of 29 ton Stabits which have been used on the reconstructed moles at Benghazi is about 10,000.

stable, *a.* Add: **3. d.** *Nucl. Physics.* Of an isotope: not subject to spontaneous radioactive decay, or decaying only very slowly.

1904 F. SODDY *Radio-Activity* viii. 126 The elements known to the chemist are stable *because* they exist and have survived. **1924** O. LODGE *Atoms & Rays* ii. 30 Even uranium is not quite stable... The element with 82 active pairs [of electrons] would be fairly or perhaps quite stable, and would be indistinguishable from lead. **1942** J. D. STRANATHAN *'Particles' of Mod. Physics* v. 167 Those elements with the greatest number of stable isotopes are Sn with 10 and Xe with 9. **1956** *Nature* 28 Jan. 159/2 Long-lived aluminium-26 may easily be confused with the stable aluminium-27 as product nucleus. **1977** J. L. HARPER *Population Biol. of Plants* xi. 365 Small amounts of ^{15}N, a stable isotope, had been applied to the soil.

stable, *sb.*^{1} Add: **1. d.** *transf.* and *fig.* Also in phr. *straight from the stable* = *straight from the horse's mouth* s.v. *HORSE *sb.* 25 c.

1907 LADY MONKSWELL *Jrnl.* 13 July in *Victorian Diarist* (1946) II. 188 The beautiful Surrey landscape looks down into this purgatory of motor stables & everything that motors require. **1922** JOYCE *Ulysses* 145 Tell him that straight from the stable. **1949** A. CHRISTIE *Crooked House* iii. 14 My information..came from the stable itself... She dined with me.

2. b. *slang.* A group of prostitutes working for the same person or organization.

1937 [see *KNOCK-DOWN *sb.* 5]. **1940** 'J. CRAD' *Traders in Women* i. 26 He..now runs a 'stable' of white women for coloured seamen in Cardiff. **1973** C. & R. MILNER *Black Players* ii. 35 Many players [*sc.* pimps] have several ladies, who constitute their stable. **1979** N. HYND *False Flags* xi. 91 The consulate maintained a stable of young women..whose only purposes were those of sexual entrapment.

c. *transf.* (In quots., of motor vehicles.)

1949 *Sun* (Baltimore) 29 July 12/3 The man who owned a stable of bulldozers laughed and said, 'We'll do it tomorrow morning.' **1974** *Spartanburg* (S. Carolina) *Herald* 18 Apr. C1/2 John Greenwood, a self-made millionaire, announced Wednesday that his stable of Corvettes would be running out of John Green Automotive garage on highway 221 at I-85.

3. b. *transf.* An establishment where boxers are trained; a group of boxers under the same management.

1897 *Nat. Police Gaz.* (U.S.) 26 May 11/4 His boxing academy at..Dale End, Birmingham, is being largely supported, and some likely lads will shortly emerge from Anthony's stable. **1936** *Sun* (Baltimore) 16 Mar. 3/3 He insisted his occupation was manager of prizefighters, but the arresting detectives failed to recognize the pugilists he mentioned as his 'stable'. **1953** *Chicago Daily Sun-Times* 29 Dec. 40/5 Some years ago Rocky's hometown pal, Al Columbo, sent Marciano to New York as a candidate for membership in the Weill stable. **1976** *Scotsman* 24 Dec. 15/1 Maurice Hope..becomes the third member of the East London stable managed by Terry Lawless.

c. A team or organization which prepares motor cars for racing; a group of racing cars owned by the same enterprise.

1935 EYSTON & LYNDEN *Motor Racing & Record Breaking* ii. 20 The Italian term [*scuderia*] finds its equivalent in..our own 'stable', and the formation of such terms among racing men is a development of very recent years. *Ibid.* vii. 65 Every important Continental racing stable was represented. **1957** S. MOSS *In Track of Speed* v. 61 He returned to Europe at the head of a racing stable of mechanics. **1966** *Publ. Amer. Dial. Soc.* *1964* XLII. 8 *Scuderia*.., a stable of cars, usually privately entered.

d. More widely, an establishment which trains or produces persons, etc., esp. of a characteristic quality or type. Also, a group *of* persons (*spec.* in publishing) under the same management or trained at the same place.

1942 *Tee Emm* (Air Ministry) II. 137 Robert..takes the lead in the latest offering from the Air Ministry Instructional Film stables. **1951** *Sun* (Baltimore) 19 June 7/2 Best known in the SRP's stable of führers is Remer. **1963** *Listener* 14 Mar. 458/1 The now-famous group centred on George Webb..which used to meet at the 'Red Barn', Bexleyheath, the stable out of which Humphrey Lyttelton came, played, typically, for a small audience of each other. **1970** C. L. CLINE *Lett. George Meredith* I. 37 Lucas recruited the best staff of artists in the business..mainly from the *Punch* stable. **1977** 'J. LE CARRÉ' *Hon. Schoolboy* i. 17 Luke..had been the star turn in his magazine's Saigon stable of war reporters.

e. In colloq. phr. *from the same stable*, from the same source.

1950 *Sun* (Baltimore) 6 Jan. 5 (*caption*) This jet plane is from the same stable as the Comet. **1959** *Listener* 2 July 36/1, I would be interested to hear a play from the same stable. **1962** H. E. BEECHENO *Introd. Business Stud.* v. 42 We find many competing products are coming from the same 'stables'. **1972** G. BELL *Villains Galore* xiv. 213 No one was quite sure who Boote actually was, except that he was from the same stable as Stallion.

5. a. *stable-dog*, *-girl*, *-jacket* (earlier example), *jockey*, *slang*, *-theatre*.

1865 *Our Young Folks* I. 461 It began to be remarked that this was a stable-dog, educated for the coach-boy and stable. **1967** N. FREELING *Strike out where not Applicable* 36 He blusters..shouting at the stable-girls. **1852** C. M. YONGE *Two Guardians* i. 12 Edmund..seeing a boy in a stable jacket, asked Marian if he should not let him lead the ponies round by the drive. **1971** D. FRANCIS *Bonecrack* xvi. 215 'You can stay on..if you like.'. 'What as?' he said apprehensively... 'Stable jockey,' I said. **1894** Stable slang [see *LAD *sb.*^{1} 2 c]. **1903** SOMERVILLE & 'ROSS' *All on Irish Shore* 269 His speech, what there is of it, is ungarnished with stable slang. **1928** T. S. ELIOT *Dialogue on Poetic Drama* in *Dryden's Ess. Dram. Poesie* p. xxvi, We shall end with a..cosmopolitan little-theatre ... What is..more likely is that nothing will be done at all. We are all too busy..to prance about in a stable-theatre.

b. stable block, a building designed to house stables; **stable companion,** also *transf.*; **stable-craft,** the knowledge and skill involved in the proper maintenance of stables and stable animals; **stable manure** = *stable-dung*; **stable-mate** = *stable companion* in Dict. and Suppl.

1977 P. D. JAMES *Death of Expert Witness* II. i. 56 As she had come round the corner of the house from putting her bicycle in the old stable block, Inspector Blakelock had been standing at the front door. **1892** *Strand Mag.* July 36/1 Its stable companion was the Challenge tricycle. **1920** GALSWORTHY *Tatterdemalion* xii. 179, I used to like very much his attitude to the young 'stable-companion' who had arrived with him. **1968** 'J. LE CARRÉ' *Small Town in Germany* xiii. 214 'Praschko was up there, was he? In Berlin? With the Russians and Aickman?' 'Stable companions.' **1931** *Times Lit. Suppl.* 25 June 502/3 His remarks on stablecraft are also thoroughly sound. **1953** G. BROOKE (*title*) Introduction to riding and stablecraft. **1629** J. PARKINSON *Parad.* I. i. 2 Sandy loame..may soone be helped with old stable manure of horses. **1864** TROLLOPE *Small House at Allington* II. xxx. 306 There was..a vexed question between Hopkins and Joliffe the bailiff on the matter of—stable manure. **1973** 'I. DRUMMOND' *Jaws of Watchdog* vii. 95 Give it plenty of muck... Stable manure is the best. **1941** WYNDHAM LEWIS *Let.* May (1963) 288 The 'practical politicians' and ..their stable-mates the hardboiled business-men' have somehow or other to be tamed. **1958** *Daily Sketch* 2 June 15/3 Guersillus's stablemate, Paridel, will not now run in the Derby. **1979** J. LEASOR *Love & Land Beyond* i. 13, I run a stable mate of the Cord, an Auburn 851 cabriolet.

stable (stē^i·b'l), *sb.*^{2} *Coal Mining.* [Of uncertain origin: perh. the same word as prec.; cf. also STAPLE *sb.*^{4}.] An excavation in a face to accommodate a coal-cutting machine or loader working into it. Also *stable hole.*

1906 *Trans. Inst. Mining Engin.* XXXI. 401 Coal-cutters, which have a disc or a chain-jib fixed to their longitudinal centre, cannot cut close to the ends of the face, and require a stable-hole or heading to be driven in advance at each end. **1914** G. L. KERR *Practical Coal-Mining* (ed. 5) vi. 148 This avoids the necessity of making jib-holes or 'stables' at the start and finish of the cut. **1945** *Trans. Inst. Mining Engin.* CIV. 209 Stables to a depth of at least twice the depth of the cut are required at each end of the face. **1968** *Economist* 8 June 85/3 The great benefit of the machine is in avoiding the present concentration of men in the 'stable hole' the most dangerous part of the pit. **1973** L. J. THOMAS *Introd. Mining* vii. 278 A longwall face stable was necessary so that the face cutting and loading machinery could stand in it.. while the face conveyor was pushed over.

stable, *v.* Add: **1.** Also *transf.*

c **1957–8** E. M. FORSTER *Life to Come* (1972) 175 British officers are never stabled with dagoes, never, it was too damn awkward for words. **1962** *Daily Tel.* 8 Jan. 15/7 The possibility of 'stabling' Underground trains in the tunnels instead of in the open at depots during periods of severe icy weather..unfortunately is unworkable.

stabled, *ppl. a.*^{2} Add: Also *transf.*

1962 *Daily Tel.* 8 Jan. 15/8 No passenger service could start until the last stabled train had left.

stably, *a.*^{2} Add: (Earlier and later examples.) Also *Comb.*, as *stably-smelling* adj.

1851 E. WARD *Jrnl.* 20 June (1951) III. 196 Slept at Wortley's on the floor—rather stably. **1930** J. DOS PASSOS *42nd Parallel* I. 12 The musty stably smelling herdic cab. **1968** E. MCGIRR *Lead-Lined Coffin* iii. 100 The next [shed] had been a stable years ago: there was still a faint stably whiff attached to it.

stachybotryotoxicosis (stækibǫ:tri,otǫksi-kō^u·sis). *Vet. Sci.* [f. mod.L. *Stachybotrys* (A. C. J. Corda *Icones Fungorum* (1837) I. 21/1), generic name (f. Gr. στάχυς ear of corn + βότρυς cluster) + TOXICOSIS.] Toxicosis caused by toxins of the graminivorous fungus *Stachybotrys alternans*, affecting esp. horses and characterized by hæmorrhage and necrosis.

1945 V. G. DROBOTKO in *Amer. Rev. Soviet Med.* II. 238 *Stachybotryotoxicosis* is the name we have given to a new disease of horses, of unknown etiology, which appeared in the Ukraine several years ago. **1970** JUBB & KENNEDY *Path. Domestic Animals* (ed. 2) I. iv. 352/2 Stachybotryotoxicosis is caused by preformed toxins of *Stachybotrys alter[n]ans* (*atra*) growing on substances rich in cellulose. **1978** *Bio Systems* X. 193/1 A group of toxins ..produced by various species of *Fusarium*, *Trichoderma*,..and other genera [of fungi] are implicated in a number of mycotoxicoses. Among these are alimentary toxic aleukia and stachybotryotoxicosis.

stachyose (stæ·ki,ō^{u}z). *Chem.* [a. G. *stachyose* (Von Planta & Schulze 1890, in *Ber. d. Deut. Chem. Ges.* XXIII. 1693): see STACHYS and -OSE^2.] A tetrasaccharide first isolated from the Chinese artichoke, *Stachys affinis*, and found in a number of plants of this genus and in the seeds of most leguminous plants.

1890 *Jrnl. Chem. Soc.* LVIII. II. 1089 The carbohydrate, for which the authors propose the name *stachyose*, has a slightly sweet taste, and forms a neutral solution. **1937** *Thorpe's Dict. Appl. Chem.* (ed. 4) I. 497/1 The characteristic carbohydrate is stachyose, $C_{24}H_{42}O_{21}$, $4H_2O$, yielding on hydrolysis one molecule of glucose, one molecule of fructose, and two molecules of galactose from one molecule of the carbohydrate. **1977** *Jrnl. Nutrition* CVII. 1861/1 A 1:1 mixture of soybean flour and sucrose would contain 2% stachyose.

stachys. Add: **b.** (Earlier example.) Cf. *RABBIT'S EAR I.

1789 W. AITON *Hortus Kewensis* II. 300 Wood Stachys, or Hedge-nettle..Fl[owers] July and August.

stack, *sb.* Add: **1. b.** (Earlier and later examples.) Also in *pl.* and as *advb. ellipt.*, a pile of money. orig. *U.S.*

1870 'MARK TWAIN' in *Galaxy* Sept. 425/2 Never saw 'such a stack of them on one establishment'. **1892** —— *Amer. Claim.* xxiv. 236 Stacks of money had been placed in bank [*sic*] for him and Hawkins by the Yankee. **1904** W. N. HARBEN *Georgians* xxiii. 222 My boy, I had stacks an' stacks of fun on that trip. **1919** WODEHOUSE *My Man Jeeves* 15 I'm a bit foggy as to what jute is, but..Mr. Worple had made quite an indecently large stack out of it. **1952** E. F. DAVIES *Illyrian Venture* vii. 127 Chesshire had stacks of letters from a girl friend and decided to read one a day for a month. **1968** B. HINES *Kestrel for Knave* (1972) 81 I'm not that bad, I'm no worse than stacks o' kids, but they just seem to get away with it. *Ibid.* 83 It's stacks better than roamin' t'streets doin' nowt.

c. *to swear on a stack of Bibles* (see quot. 1909). *U.S. colloq.*

1866 M. REID *Headless Horseman* II. lvii. 287 I'll sware it on the crass—or a whole stack av Bibles if yez say so. **1909** *Dialect Notes* III. 378 *Swear on a stack of Bibles* (*a mile high*),..an exaggerated or emphatic form of oath. **1926** M. J. ATKINSON in J. F. Dobie *Rainbow in Morning* (1965) 82, I would not believe him if he swore to it on a stack of Bibles as high as his head. **1956** B. HOLIDAY *Lady sings Blues* (1973) ii. 24 Mom..swore on a stack of Bibles I was eighteen.

d. A set of shelving on which books are arranged for storage, esp. in a library (also *book-stack* s.v. *BOOK *sb.* 18); hence, a part of a library designed for the storage of books, and to which access by readers may be restricted. Freq. *attrib.* and in *pl.*

1879 C. A. CUTTER in *Library Jrnl.* IV. 235 The new wing..consists of a perfectly uniform series of book stacks arranged like a gridiron. **1884** Stack-room [in Dict., sense 8 b]. **1900** *Library Jrnl.* Nov. 679/2 Electric signals are also a part of the apparatus, and convenient elevators for passengers and freight are provided in the book-stacks. **1910** A. E. BOSTWICK *Amer. Public Library* 284 The relation of reading room to stack must be such as to make these [carriers] easily operable. **1933** *Times* 9 Nov. 9/2 Before leaving the building they paused to visit one of the new two-tier book-stacks on the ground floor. **1946** *Library Quarterly* Apr. 128/2 It is a modern brick building, five stories high, and contains, in addition to the stack space, a small reading room. **1956** 'C. BLACKSTOCK' *Dewey Death* i. 5 There were some seven thousand books. ..Barbara spent most of her spare time in the history section, wandering from stack to stack. **1966** C. POTOK *Chosen* (1967) II. viii. 152 Its stacks were filled mostly with bound volumes of scholarly journals and pamphlets. **1980** *Cosmopolitan* Dec. 221/1, I located a promising title for my Proust researches. 'Not on the open shelves.' I would have to order it to be fetched for me from the stacks of the library.

e. *Aeronaut.* A series of aeroplanes circling at different altitudes and awaiting landing instructions.

1947 *Britannica Bk. of Year* 841/2 As the bottom plane lands, each member of the stack drops 1,000 ft. and a new plane can then be brought in on top. **1952** *Jrnl. R. Aeronaut. Soc.* LVI. 615/2 Once an aircraft was in a stack it was difficult to bring it forward. **1965** *Observer* 31 Oct. 1/1 He came in for a third attempt after circling for a further 40 minutes in the Watford 'stack'. **1976** L. DEIGHTON *Twinkle, twinkle, Little Spy* x. 94 We joined the stack.. and circled to await landing permission.

f. In a computer or calculator, a set of registers or storage locations which store data in such a way that the most recently stored item is the first to be retrieved; also, a list of items so stored, a push-down list.

1960 E. W. DIJKSTRA in *Numerische Math.* II. 312 The basic concept of the method is the so-called stack. One uses a stack for storing a sequence of information units that increases and decreases at one end only. **1963** *Ann. Rev. Automatic Programming* IV. 183 A stack is merely an area of storage with an associated administrative quantity, the 'stack pointer', which controls the addressing of the stack. **1973** C. W. GEAR *Introd. Computer Sci.* viii. 359 We can choose a section of memory at execution time to store this stack. **1976** *Sci. Amer.* June 88/1 (Advt.), HP's special logic system with four-register stack almost completely eliminates the need to re-enter data.

5. c. In *fig.* phr. *to blow one's stack* = *to blow one's top* s.v. *BLOW *v.*^{1} 24 i. *slang* (orig. *U.S.*).

1947 BERREY & VAN DEN BARK *Amer. Thes. Slang* Suppl. § 48/1 *Blow one's stack*, to become angry or excited. **1952** R. BISSELL *Monongahela* 189 When Andrew [Carnegie] received the minutes and read them he blew his stack a mile high. **1965** F. KNEBEL *Night of Camp David* xi. 173 O'Malley looked startled. 'Well, he..he was goddam mad. Frankly, he blew his stack.' **1979** W. H. CANAWAY *Solid Gold Buddha* xxiv. 156, I ain't whingeing, honest... I'm sorry I blew me stack.

7. (Later examples.) No longer *dial.* Cf. *sea-stack* s.v. *SEA *sb.* 23 a.

1944 A. HOLMES *Princ. Physical Geol.* xiv. 287 Later the arch falls in, and the seaward portion of the headland then remains as an isolated stack. **1957** G. E. HUTCHINSON *Treat. Limnol.* I. ii. 173 Coastal islands formed by cutting behind promontories, so producing isolated stacks, occur along the margins of large lakes. **1975** [see *SEVERE *a.* 9 b].

8. a. (sense 2) *stack-shaped* adj.

1864 J. A. GRANT *Walk across Afr.* 62 Grain is housed under the eaves of stack-shaped huts. **1921** *Glasgow*

Herald 26 Mar. 7 About a dozen 18-pounder shell cases, some of which contained curious stack-shaped bombs.

b. **stack gas,** gas emitted by a chimney-stack.

1945 H. D. SMYTH *Gen. Acct. Devel. Atomic Energy Mil. Purposes* viii. 91 It became essential to know whether the stack gases (at Clinton and at Hanford) would be likely to spread radioactive fission products in dangerous concentrations. **1973** H. GRUPPE *Truxton Cipher* xiii. 135 The smell of stack gas lay heavy upon the destroyer's upperworks.

stack, *v.*[1] Add: **1. b.** *Aeronaut.* To order (aircraft waiting to land) at different flight levels and in landing sequence above an airport; to place (an aeroplane) in a waiting stack (freq. with *up*). Also *intr.* (of aircraft), to form a stack.

1941 K. HENNEY *Radio Engin. Handbk.* (ed. 3) xvii. 616 The present practice of 'stacking' airplanes..limits the number of landings..to about 4 per hour. **1943** M. FEIGEN *Pocket Aviation Quiz Bk.* 55 Planes cruising above an airport at varying assigned altitudes in order not to collide while awaiting their turns to land are said to be: stacked up. **1949** *Sun* (Baltimore) 4 Nov. 2/6 Planes 'stack up' over the range station near Mount Vernon. **1965** P. WYLIE *They both were Naked* I. i. 4 We'd spent that interval..'stacked up' and waiting for planes..to be called down for landings. **1975** D. LODGE *Changing Places* vi. 218, I hope to hell we aren't stacked for hours over Kennedy.

2. b. To pile *up* one's chips at poker. Now usu. *fig.*, to present oneself, measure up; to arise, build up. *colloq.* (chiefly *U.S.*).

1896 ADE *Artie* ii. 10 He'd stack up, you know, an' feel in his pockets and then he'd say: 'I'm forty-seven cents loser.' **1911** R. D. SAUNDERS *Col. Todhunter* xiii. 198 Old Bill Strickland, of Nineveh, somehow don't seem to stack up the right way against the Honourable Stephen K. Vancey. **1921** R. D. PAINE *Comr. Rolling Ocean* iv. 71, I wish this trouble hadn't stacked up between us. **1938** *Sun* (Baltimore) 6 Apr. 11/5, I think every one will agree my record stacks up favourably enough with that of any other pro. past or present. **1951** M. MCLUHAN *Mech. Bride* (1967) 48/1 See how you stack up with your fellow men on the following issues. **1965** WODEHOUSE *Galahad at Blandings* x. 169 I've never been a brainy sort of guy, and what I want is a wife with about the same amount of grey matter I have, and that's how Vee stacks up. **1977** R. E. MEGILL *Introd. Risk Analysis* xv. 170 Dougherty and Nozaki ranked knowing your competitors as of equal value to knowing how well your own estimate stacks up.

6. a. To shuffle or arrange (playing-cards) dishonestly. In *fig.* phr. *to stack the cards* (etc.) *against*: to reduce (a person or thing's) chance of success. Cf. PACK *v.*[2] 5, STOCK *v.*[1] 23 b. orig. *U.S.*

1825 in M. Bayard Smith *Forty Yrs. Washington Soc.* (1906) 186 John Randolph observed after counting the ballots, 'It was impossible to win the game, gentlemen, the cards were stacked.' **1896** J. F. LILLARD *Poker Stories* 54 The stranger got skinned right and left. The cards were stacked and marked on the back, so that he didn't have any chance at all to win. *c* **1926** 'MIXER' *Transport Workers' Song Bk.* 31 He'll know this when I stack the cards. **1941** B. SCHULBERG *What makes Sammy Run?* v. 81 You read the papers, you know how the cards are stacked against this nut. **1977** *New Yorker* 24 Oct. 37/1 He..confirmed our worst fear: the deck is stacked... He picked up a cardboard box containing several packs of cards. **1978** G. VAUGHAN *Belgrade Drop* x. 67 'Pin your ears back,' Yardly murmured. 'We've got a lot stacked against us.'

b. = PACK *v.*[2] 4 in Dict. and Suppl. Also *fig.*

1948 *Durant* (Okla.) *Daily Democrat* 2 July 1/5 His young polltaker detected no signs of 'stacking' the poll for any candidate. **1963** *Wall St. Jrnl.* 25 Jan. 16/3 The government is now stacked from top to bottom with men who reflect their President's prejudices. **1970** *New Yorker* 28 Nov. 104/2 Legally, marriage is still stacked in favor of the man. **1975** *N.Y. Times* 10 Apr. 29/1 Gov. George C. Wallace of Alabama charged today that.. efforts were being made..to stack delegate-selection procedures against him.

stackable (stæ·kăb'l), *a.* [f. STACK *v.*[1] + -ABLE.] Able to be stacked or piled up: esp. of chairs and other furniture. Hence **stackabi·lity.**

1958 *Archit. Rev.* CXXIII. 255 (*caption*) The chairs are stackable. **1960** *House & Garden* Oct. 80/2 Stackable Italian table..for use in large works canteens. **1969** *Jane's Freight Containers 1968–69* 490/3 Stackability... When the ends are folded down, five stacked together stand 8 ft high. **1973** J. ELSOM *Erotic Theatre* x. 209 Surrounded by a Brighton beach of stackable chairs. **1977** *Design Engin.* July 41/1 Stackable valves often introduce unacceptable pressure losses and fault finding often means dismantling the whole stack.

stacked, *ppl. a.* Add: **4.** Of a female figure: well-rounded and attractively shaped. Also of a woman: having a prominent bosom. Similarly, *stacked up, well-stacked. U.S. slang* (as a term of male approbation).

1942 BERREY & VAN DEN BARK *Amer. Thes. Slang* § 37/14 *Shapely*,..stacked up nicely. **1952** *Esquire* June 131/2 The singer ain't a bad-looking broad, she's well-stacked and sort of young. **1954** *Amer. Speech* XXIX. 234 There is a present fashion of referring to an attractively proportioned woman as well stacked, or simply, stacked, period. **1965** *Liberator* (N.Y.) Aug. 22/3 Two stacked broads approached. Everyone attained a hip position. It consisted of pulling pants high, rolling the Hi-Lo collar, [etc.]. **1975** D. LODGE *Changing Places* v. 154 What about your wife?.. Is she well-stacked? **1981** 'D. SHANNON' *Murder Most Strange* vii. 147 A cute little blond chick.. really stacked.

5. *stacked head*, in a tape recorder: a head (*HEAD *sb.* 11 g) in which the gaps corresponding to the tracks in multi-channel recording are located one above another.

1954 C. A. TUTHILL *How to service Tape Recorders* iv. 45 Typical individual or stacked heads, currently being released by The Brush Development Company, are cast in synthetic resin. **1962** A. NISBETT *Technique Sound Studio* 267 For stereo, the first and third tracks are recorded at the same time, using a stacked head (one with both gaps in line). *a* **1975** *Tape Talk* (Sony Corporation) 3 *In-line heads*, arrangement of stereophonic heads on a tape recorder in which the head gaps are mounted one directly above the other. Also called 'stacked heads'.

6. *stacked heel*, a heel built by stacking or appearing to stack thin layers of wood or other material. Also *stacked-heeled* adj.

[**1960** *Harper's Bazaar* Aug. 24 Stack-heeled moccasin in deep brown leather.] **1960** *Sunday Express* 11 Sept. 15/4 In Paris Dior..showed Cuban 'stacked' heels. **1964** in Hamblett & Deverson *Generation X* 13 Mod girls have a short back-and-sides hair cut like men used to, wear shift-style dresses with round collars... Stacked heeled shoes, white stockings. **1966** T. PYNCHON *Crying of Lot 49* vi. 177 She turned, pivoting on one stacked heel. **1977** J. WAMBAUGH *Black Marble* (1978) v. 62 Comfortable loafers with low stacked heels in colors to match wool-knit pants and jackets.

7. *stacked deck*, a pack of cards that has cheatingly been set in a prearranged order; also *fig.* Hence more widely (and without the implication of dishonesty), of odds. Cf. *STACK *v.*[1] 6 a. Chiefly *U.S.*

1964 A. WYKES *Gambling* 329/1 *Stacked deck*, a pack of cards that a cheat has prearranged for his own benefit. **1971** P. O'DONNELL *Impossible Virgin* vii. 144 They worked alone, without hirelings, and so often went in against stacked odds. **1976** *Honolulu Star-Bull.* 21 Dec. H-3/1 The Minnesota Vikings, shooting to become the first National Football League team to make four Super Bowl appearances, will be playing with a stacked deck Sunday. **1978** E. TIDYMAN *Table Stakes* II. vii. 345 You played the game with a stacked deck. You had his daughter, his trust, and his face.

stacker, *sb.*[1] Add: **2. a.** More widely, any machine for raising individual items or bulk material and depositing them on a stack or pile; also, a stacker crane. (Later examples.)

1922 G. F. ZIMMER *Mech. Handling & Storing* (ed. 3) xxxviii. 654 A similar stacker is illustrated in Fig. 954; it is composed of a slat conveyor, and is for handling cases. **1950** W. STANIAR *Plant Engin. Handbk.* xx. 1417 A number of different types of portable elevators, stackers, or tiering machines are made with the lifting mechanism either motor or hand operated... Portable stackers are made for the handling of smaller units. **1979** *Belt Conveyors for Bulk Materials* (Conveyor Equipment Manufacturers Assoc., U.S.) (ed. 2) i. 7 Belt conveyors, with their stackers and reclaimers, have become the only practical means for large-scale stockpiling and reclaiming of such bulk materials as coal, ore, and taconite pellets.

b. A part of a data-processing machine in which punched cards are deposited in a stack after having passed through the machine.

1962 in *Gloss. Terms Automatic Data Processing* (*B.S.I.*) 90. **1969** P. B. JORDAIN *Condensed Computer Encycl.* 82 A card stacker ensures the correct sequencing of emerging cards. **1971** J. T. MURRAY *Introd. Computing* vii. 126 The input hopper provides the cards which are sorted into any of the six available stacker pockets.

3. Special Comb.: **stacker crane**, a hoist running on a fixed horizontal track for stacking and retrieving pallets or the like.

1959 W. STANIAR *Plant Engin. Handbk.* (ed. 2) XXVIII. 32 The makers of the stacker crane claim that it may be employed for safe stacking of materials to greater heights than with other forms of equipment. **1979** *Computers in Shell* (Shell Internat. Petroleum Co.) 6 A computer-controlled stacker crane takes the pallet and places it in one of the thousands of pallet spaces in the racks, the location being recorded by the computer.

stacking, *vbl. sb.* Add: **a.** (Examples in sense *1 b of the vb.)

1942 H. L. SMITH *Airways* 365 Since speed is the commodity sold by the air-line operator, he is interested in any system that can solve the problem of stacking. **1969** *Daily Tel.* 14 Nov. 1/7 Stacking over a 'holding area' while waiting a turn to land, is not uncommon. **1979** C. WOOD *James Bond & Moonraker* i. 13 If there were no stacking positions at Heathrow..he would be home in time to.. eat supper with the family.

b. *stacking chair*; **stacking fault** *Cryst.*, a break in the regular order of stacking of layers of atoms in a crystal.

1939 MARTIN & SPEIGHT *Flat Bk.* 101 Stacking chair, by Alvar Aalto in natural birch or lacquered..20s od. **1951** *Catal. of Exhibits, South Bank Exhib., Festival of Britain* 87/2 Cantilevered all-purpose stacking chairs. **1982** E. DEWHURST *Whoever I Am* vii. 90 Motioning her niece to fetch up one of the stacking chairs. **1951** *Phil. Mag.* XLII. 815 The best-known examples of translation twinning are 'stacking faults' in the sphere-packing lattices, *i.e.* breaches of the stacking rules which lead to face-centred cubic or hexagonal close-packing. **1976** *Sci. Amer.* Nov. 105/2 In brass, bronze and certain stainless steels, for example, stacking faults extend over distances equivalent to many atomic diameters.

stack-up. [f. vbl. phr. *to stack up*: see *STACK *v.*[1] 1 b.] The arrangement of objects in a stack or pile; a build-up. *spec.* in *Aeronaut.* = *STACK *sb.* 1 e.

1945 F. WALTON *Airman's Almanac* 403 *Stack-up*, airplanes flying at different altitudes over an airport awaiting signal to land. **1948** *Jrnl. R. Aeronaut. Soc.* LII. 681/2 Once the diversion and 'stack up' problem is eliminated the plain jet..can become almost as cheap to operate as propeller-powered aircraft. **1950** *Daily Progress* (Charlottesville, Va.) 14 Dec. 1/8 The department has under study a plan for shifting first class surface mail to the air lines in order to avoid a stack-up of such mail. **1970** *Sci. Amer.* Mar. 86/1 Unsafe weather conditions at airports, forcing the stack-up and diversion of aircraft,.. take an immense annual toll in inconvenience. **1976** *Lebende Sprachen* XXI. 153/2 The failure was caused by a build-up/stack-up of adverse manufacturing tolerances.

stade[1]. Add: **3.** *Geol.* (See quot. 1961); = *STADIAL *sb.*, *STADIUM 5.

1961 *Bull. Amer. Assoc. Petroleum Geologists* XLV. 660/2 A stade was a climatic episode within a glaciation during which a secondary advance of glaciers took place. **1964** *Prof. Papers U.S. Geol. Survey* No. 501-D. 104/2 Currently, the oldest group of moraines define the early stade of Bull Lake Glaciation, and the middle and youngest groups together define the late stade. **1974** *Nature* 26 Apr. 752/2 The 'cold' water fauna [belongs] to the period of the Loch Lomond readvance stade.

stadial, *a.* Restrict † *Obs. rare*$^{-1}$ to sense in Dict. and add: **2. a.** *Geol.* Of or pertaining to a glacial stadium or stade; *stadial moraine* = *recessional moraine* s.v. *RECESSIONAL *a.* 3.

1937 WOOLDRIDGE & MORGAN *Physical Basis of Geogr.* xxii. 378 Retreatal stages of the ice in the valleys are marked by 'stadial moraines'. **1970** R. J. SMALL *Study of Landforms* xi. 388 If the ice is affected by episodes of retreat, separated by stillstands, a number of smaller, sub-parallel ridges ('recessional' or 'stadial' moraines) will be formed. **1971** S. C. PORTER in K. K. Turekian *Late Cenozoic Glacial Ages* xi. 320 In the Puget Lowland only two stadial episodes have been determined for the Puget lobe. **1979** *Nature* 19 July 199/2 The landforms produced by the stadial glaciers in the Highlands are often clear and abundant.

b. *Archæol.* Pertaining to or expressed in terms of a series of successive stages into which a culture or period can be divided.

1959 *Science* 6 Feb. 305/2 Willey and Phillips' stadial conception of New World prehistory. **1968** L. R. BINFORD in S. R. & L. R. Binford *New Perspectives in Archeol.* I. i. 15 The application of such a scale to innumerable empirical cases..can never provide us with an understanding of the processes operative in the past which resulted in the stadial sequence. **1977** G. CLARK *World Prehistory* (ed. 3) ii. 41 The use of the term 'Neolithic' in this connection in itself poses a problem. If stadial terms are rarely used in contemporary archaeological discourse, it seems all the more important to be clear about their meaning.

B. *sb. Geol.* = *STADE[1] 3.

1954 *Antiquity* XXVIII. 8 The tundra-like phase at the beginning of the third Würm stadial. **1964** K. W. BUTZER *Environment & Archeol.* xxvii. 395 It seems improbable that food-collectors at the Neanderthaler level would venture through thousands of kilometers of harsh environment at the height of any of the Würm stadials. **1979** SEYFERT & SIRKIN *Earth Hist. & Plate Tectonics* (ed. 2) xiv. 515/2 Glacial advances occurred during stadials.

stadiometer. Add: **2.** An apparatus for measuring a person's height.

1972 *Sunday Times* 22 Oct. 65/2 His product range does not end at anthropometers. There is a stadiometer for measuring height to a high degree of accuracy. **1980** *Brit. Med. Jrnl.* 29 Mar. 915 When the child is old enough to stand a special stadiometer can be used to measure height.

stadium. **2.** Add to final sentence: *spec.* an enclosed area for sporting events equipped with tiers of seats for spectators. (The pl. *stadiums* is usual in this sense.)

1928 *Times* 20 Apr. 6/6 It would be difficult to imagine a more impressive enclosure than the Stadium [*sc.* Wembley Stadium] for the holding of the greatest football festival of the year. **1938** L. MACNEICE *Earth Compels* 59 It's no go the picture palace, it's no go the stadium. **1972** G. GREEN *Great Moments in Sport: Soccer* iii. 44 As for Lenin Stadium itself, it was very much like Wembley before the cover went on, an elliptical concrete monster, liberally dotted with exits and entrances, and steeply tiered.

5. *Geol.* = *STADE[1] 3. Now *Obs.* or *rare.*

1910 *Zeitschr. für Gletscherkunde* IV. 246 The later stages of glaciation in the scheme proposed by Geikie.. may prove to correspond to the *stadia* of the Alpine region which are so clearly brought out by Penck and Brückner in their recent great work. **1914** W. B. WRIGHT *Quaternary Ice Age* vii. 156 An investigation of the stages of retreat in the Etsch district has shown that three main stadia can also be distinguished here. **1937** *Ibid.* (ed. 2) xi. 185 This stadium must..be dated back before the Swiss pile-dwellings, or in round numbers 7000 years ago.

staff, *sb.*[1] Add: **I. 9. f.** = *train staff* (*a*) s.v. TRAIN *sb.*[1] 22 b. Cf. *TOKEN *sb.* 7 b.

1885 E. B. IVATTS *Railway Managem. at Stations* 559 *Staff* (*train*), a piece of wood or metal used on single lines, which..confers the 'right of road' for an engine. **1902**

Encycl. Brit. XXXII. 147/1 The staff..is delivered to the engine-driver at station A, and constitutes his authority to occupy the main track between that station and station B. On reaching B he surrenders the staff, and receives another one which gives him the right to the road between B and C. **1931** D. L. SAYERS *Five Red Herrings* xxvii. 330 The station-master marched across, carrying the staff under his arm. **1974** J. S. HOLDEN *Watlington Branch* v. 87 One instance is recorded of the branch train being snowed up... A porter, despatched with the staff, had to make his way on foot.

III. 21. a. *General Staff*: hence *Chief of the General Staff*. *Chief of Staff*, the senior staff officer of a service or commander.

1904 *Rep. War Office (Reconstruction) Committee* II. 22 in *Parl. Papers* (Cd. 1968) VIII. 121 In accordance with our recommendations, a Chief of the General Staff of the Army has been appointed. **1937** H. NICOLSON *Diary* 21 Apr. (1966) 299 It is a man's dinner and consists mainly of the Cabinet and a few Chiefs-of-Staff. **1948** in M. McLuhan *Mech. Bride* (1951) 6/7 The artificial boundary line was decided upon by the joint chiefs of staffs during the war. *a* **1974** R. CROSSMAN *Diaries* (1975) I. 595 Couldn't we have officials there as well, like the Chiefs of Staff?

b. *ellipt.* (chiefly with initial capital) = *staff sergeant*, sense 25 in Dict.

1925 FRASER & GIBBONS *Soldier & Sailor Words & Phrases* 269 *Staff*, staff-sergeant. **1943** *Yank* 8 Oct. 15 If all staffs are as shallow minded as this one, buck privates at the front are worth 10 staffs back home. **1958** P. SCOTT *Mark of Warrior* I. i. 23 A sergeant..addressed them as 'Gentlemen' and told them to address him as 'Staff'. **1965** 'J. LE CARRÉ' *Looking-Glass War* xii. 136 'You call me "Staff",' the instructor said. **1978** J. BARNETT *Head of Force* x. 88, I worked with Staff Gredek... The Staff was in charge of the depot.

22. b. Construed as *pl.*: members of a staff, employees. *Rarely*, an employee.

1931 E. M. BRENT-DYER *Chalet School & Jo* xvii. 220 You're almost a Staff, so that'll be all right. **1955** *Times* 10 May 17/4 A continuing supply of higher technical staff. **1970** *Daily Tel.* 4 May 2/4 A Yorkshire factory with 250 staff, nearly all women. **1979** P. NIHALANI et al. *Indian & Brit. English* I. 166 The Director will introduce the new staff and ask him to say a few words.

c. *spec.* in a business organization: (*a*) the employees responsible for providing advisory and ancillary services to line managers and their subordinates; (*b*) salaried (as opp. to wage-earning) employees.

1915 C. E. KNOEPPEL *Installing Efficiency Methods* viii. 58 He [*sc.* the engineer] decides to create an organization to be known as the 'staff'—advisory in nature and without jurisdiction over any of the line officials. **1923** O. SHELDON *Philos. Managem.* iv. 114 A 'Staff and Line' organization..is based upon a strict demarcation between thinking and doing; between the actual execution of production, which is the 'Line', and the business of analysing, testing, comparing, recording, making researches, co-ordinating information, and advising, which is the 'Staff'. **1960, 1964** [see *LINE *sb.*[2] 19 d]. **1980** *Daily Tel.* 16 Feb. 25/3 Almost all the major companies pay more [in redundancy payments] than the statutory minimum and generally staff will enjoy more generous benefits than shopfloor workers.

IV. 25. a. *staff appointment* (earlier example), *car*, *duty* (example), *job*; **staff college** (later examples); **staff-wallah** *slang* [cf. WALLAH b], a disparaging term for a non-combatant army officer; **staff-work**, the supportive work of planning, organization, etc., done by staff officers for the commander; also in civilian contexts.

1802 J. ORROK *Let.* 22 July (1927) 23 I'm in hopes thro' his Interest to obtain a Staff appointment there. *a* **1944** K. DOUGLAS *Alamein to Zem Zem* (1946) i. 11 A few staff and liaison officers in jeeps and staff cars still passed. **1978** R. V. JONES *Most Secret War* xix. 155 Scott-Farnie himself would be going and would have a staff car. **1911** W. S. CHURCHILL in R. S. Churchill *Winston S. Churchill* (1969) II. Compan. II. xvi. 1283 You are authorized to apply to the War Office for the services of 25 Staff College Officers. **1974** A. PRICE *Other Paths to Glory* I. vi. 63 He had a lecture to give at the Staff College. **1913** R. MEINERTZHAGEN *Diary* 19 Dec. (1960) 57, I expected a better groundwork in staff duties. **1916** F. M. FORD *Let.* Aug. (1965) 67 Bridges..has written to Plumer to suggest that I ought to be given a staff job. **1951** R. CAMPBELL *Light on Dark Horse* xi. 145 A family connection who was only a staff-wallah, and jealous of my being a soldier. **1969** V. DE S. PINTO *City that Shone* viii. 161 She's chock full of bleeding staff-wallahs. **1923** KIPLING *Irish Guards in Gt. War* I. p. xi, Bad staff-work or faulty generalship. **1933** W. S. CHURCHILL *Marlborough* I. xxviii. 484 His private fortune was amassed upon the same principles as marked the staff-work of his campaigns. **1951** *Engineering* 2 Mar. 269/2 Consultations among..executives, linked by 'staffwork'. **1980** *Sunday Tel.* 23 Mar. 17/8 [The new Archbishop of Canterbury] will need good staff work: some of his appointments in the past have been questioned, and he is by all accounts a bad delegator.

b. Also in passenger ships.

1932 S. G. MCNEIL *In Great Waters* 136, I was to be the first holder of the newly created post of Staff-Captain. **1944** *New Yorker* 23 Dec. 26/1 One man who had this second feeling to a degree was Lemuel Watkins, staff captain and second in command to the *Marquette*'s master. **1957** D. G. O. BAILLIE *Sea Affair* 111 In ships carrying anything over a thousand passengers, there is usually a Staff Captain who devotes his entire activities to their proper entertainment.

c. (Later examples.) Similarly, *staff member*. Also in sense 'of, provided or reserved for, arranged by, the staff of an establishment', as *staff canteen*, *dance*, etc.

1940 R. S. LAMBERT *Ariel & all his Quality* i. 33 He fought shy of..social gatherings, except for appearances at occasional staff dances. **1942** WYNDHAM LEWIS *Let.* 27 Jan. (1963) 313 Your staff-member who has ended up a prisoner in Athens had an interesting journey. **1966** *Economist* 3 Sept. 888/1 The employers' habit of describing concessions of better pay and conditions to manual workers as creating 'staff conditions' for all has often meant that yet further concessions have been made to 'staff' employees, in order to preserve their differentials over the men on the shop floor. **1972** K. BENTON *Spy in Chancery* xvii. 192 She probably had lunch there. There's a staff canteen. **1977** F. BRANSTON *Up & Coming Man* xiv. 150 Freelancing..binds you to a tighter routine than a staff job.

26. staff and ticket (system) an elaboration of the staff system (below) allowing for the movement of several trains in one direction along a single line, whereby the last train carried the staff (sense 9 f above) and the preceding trains carried tickets pertaining to this (*Obs.* exc. *Hist.*); **staffholster** *nonce-wd.*, a holster for a watchman's staff; **staff-man,** (*c*) *Surveying* (see quot. 1940); (*d*) a member of a staff; **staff nurse,** a trained nurse in a hospital, ranking above a registered nurse and below a ward sister; **staff photographer,** a photographer on the staff of a newspaper or journal; **staff-room,** a common room for the use of the staff, as in a school; also *transf.*, the staff itself; **staff–student** *a.*, designating the relation between students and teaching staff; esp. in phr. *staff–student ratio* (cf. *pupil–teacher* adj. s.v. *PUPIL *sb.*[1]); **staff system,** a block system on railways according to which an engine-driver may not proceed along a single line without carrying the staff (sense 9 f above) authorizing him to do so; **staff ticket,** a ticket used on railways to operate the staff and ticket system (see above); **staff writer,** a writer employed on the staff of a newspaper, radio or television station, or the like.

1887 C. E. STRETTON *Safe Railway Working* iii. 64 All other single lines should be worked under the train staff and ticket system. **1889** W. M. ACWORTH *Railways of Eng.* x. 392 Single lines are commonly worked on what is known as the 'staff and ticket' system. **1927** E. T. MACDERMOT *Hist. Gt. Western Railway* I. II. xii. 611 The Wycombe Branch, on its extension to Thame in 1862, seems to have been the first on which the Train Staff and Ticket system was introduced. **1969** *Railway Mag.* Feb. 67 Up to 1892, all movement of trains was controlled by staff and ticket, which was replaced by the Webb-Thompson electric train staff. **1922** JOYCE *Ulysses* 423 At a corner two night watch in shoulder capes, their hands upon their staffholsters, loom tall. **1940** *Chambers's Techn. Dict.* 799/2 *Staffman* (Surv.), the surveyor's assistant whose duty it is to hold the levelling staff while the instrument is sighted upon it and readings are being taken. **1976** *Time* 27 Sept. 12/2 Says one Carter staffman: 'Jimmy has his good smiles and his bad smiles.' **1977** P. POLLACK *Pict. Hist. Photogr.* (rev. ed.) 138/1 The largest pool of talented recorders..unsurprisingly, was to be found among the staffmen of *Life* magazine. **1888** Staff nurse [in Dict., sense 25 c]. **1972** J. MCCLURE *Caterpillar Cop* xiii. 216 The staff nurse calls them from the other ward if she needs help. **1978** *Jrnl. R. Soc. Med.* LXXI. 401 This is presumably what the Briggs report implies when it recommends that staff nurses should be made head of ward teams whose teaching they themselves would undertake. **1941** *Times* (weekly ed.) 30 July 6/4 This special study was taken in the garden of 10, Downing Street by a staff photographer. **1977** P. POLLACK *Pict. Hist. Photogr.* (rev. ed.) 134/2 In the Israeli–Arab War of June 1967, the first casualty was Paul Schutzer, staff photographer of *Life* magazine. **1925** W. DEEPING *Sorrell & Son* xxx. 297 There is a vacancy at the Northern Free, a junior surgeonship. Sir Ormsby told me about it to-day in the staff-room. **1953** K. TENNANT *Joyful Condemned* xvi. 136 The staff-room was split over the sensational row between Miss Page and the Head. **1977** P. KEMP in *Winter's Tales* XXIII. 46 On the first day of the last term..she hurried to the staff-room. **1969** H. PERKIN *Key Profession* iv. 130 After the immediate post-war crush an improved staff–student ratio. *Ibid.* vi. 246 The A.U.T.'s policy on staff–student relations should stand firmly on the principle of a community of scholars. **1974** *Howard Jrnl.* XIV. 80 There is a good staff–student ratio as well as up-to-date teaching equipment. **1982** M. MILLAR *Mermaid* iv. 49 Staff–student romances..can be a problem. **1887** C. E. STRETTON *Safe Railway Working* iii. 64 (*heading*) The train staff system. **1902** *Encycl. Brit.* XXXII. 147/1 In the United Kingdom and in Australia the means for preventing collisions between trains running towards each other is the 'staff system'. **1966** K. MÖLLER *Amer. & Brit. Railway Eng.* 39 The..staff system is still in use in Britain; every engine running over a certain section of a line must carry the corresponding token or staff. **1885** E. B. IVATT *Railway Managem. at Stations* 559 Two or three trains may be passed forward by 'staff ticket' in this way, but ultimately either a train, an engine, or a messenger must convey the staff to enable trains being sent in the opposite direction. **1914** Staff writer [see *CREDIT *sb.* 13 f]. **1941** W. ABBOT *Handbk. Broadcasting* (ed. 2) xxvi. 322 Staff writers prepare commercial continuity, talks, announcements, interviews, special-occasion scripts, original plays, adaptations, and often station publicity. **1967** E. E. WILLIS *Writing Television & Radio Programs* i. 11 Writers who are permanently attached to the staff of a broadcasting organization and are paid on a regular weekly or monthly basis instead of being paid per script are known as *staff writers*. **1977** D. GREENE in Bond & McLeod *Newslett. to Newspapers* II. 89 Cave's other early 'staff writers'..were much more than Grub Street hacks.

staffelite (stæ·fĕləit). *Min.* [ad. G. *staffelit* (C. A. Stein 1866, in *Jahrb. des Vereins für Naturkunde im Herzogthum Nassau* XIX–XX. 57), f. *Staffel*, name of a locality in Hesse, W. Germany: see -ITE[1].] A carbonate-containing variety of apatite found as colourless or yellow masses; carbonate-fluorapatite; = FRANCOLITE.

1868 J. D. DANA *Syst. Mineral.* (ed. 5) 534 Staffelite of Stein..occurs incrusting the phosphorite of Staffel, in botryoidal, reniform, or stalactitic masses. **1939** *Mineral. Mag.* XXV. 401 Francolite and staffelite are identical, and the name francolite has priority. **1977** V. GISSING tr. *Kouřimský's Illustr. Encycl. Minerals & Rocks* viii. 256 Staffelite..is a stalactitic apatite and occurs in the Staffel deposits near Limburg, West Germany.

staffer[2] (stɑ·fəɹ). orig. and chiefly *U.S.* [f. STAFF *sb.*[1] + -ER[1].] A member of a staff.

a. Of a newspaper or journal: a staff writer.

1949 *Cavalier Daily* (Univ. of Virginia) 22 Oct. 4/2 Staffers of the Daily Pennsylvanian visited the Princetonian offices following the Penn–Princeton football game. **1952** G. REINHARDT *Crime without Punishment* 290 He knew..what confidential memos had been passed between the managing editor and publisher of the *New York Times*—a fact doubtless not known to most *Times* staffers. **1973** E. B. WHITE *Let.* 24 May (1976) 648 The story of *The New Yorker* has yet to be *well* told. Many staffers were indignant about parts of the Thurber book.

b. More widely, of a business or other organization.

1950 in WEBSTER Add. **1962** *Housewife* (Ceylon) Apr. 34 (*caption*) Mr. Neale talks to staffers of a local advertising agency. **1966** *Economist* 3 Sept. 888/1 Clerks, foremen and other staffers. **1972** M. GLENNY tr. *Solzhenitsyn's August 1914* xi. 108 The younger General Staffers of recent vintage all knew each other and stuck together like members of a secret order. **1980** *Information Retrieval & Library Automation* XVI. 11/2 The issue of April 1980 for example contains a brief but informative report on 'interlending' in Czechoslovakia, prepared by a BLL staffer who spent two weeks surveying the Czech scene.

c. *spec.* of the President of the U.S.; a member of the President's White House staff.

1969 R. NEUSTADT in A. King *Brit. Prime Minister* 145 The functional equivalence between a British Cabinet and our set of influentials—whether Secretaries, Senators, White House staffers, Congressmen or others. **1976** *National Observer* (U.S.) 14 Feb. 16/6 The letter was written by a Carter staffer who misrepresented Carter's position. **1981** W. SAFIRE in *N.Y. Times Mag.* 29 Mar. 10/2 Some of the White House staffers at the time looked for a way round it.

staffless, *a.* Add: **2.** Having no business or domestic staff; without employees. Also *transf.*

1957 'P. PORTOBELLO' *How to be Deb's Mum* 38 Her husband nursed the chef, a foreign refugee, back to health from influenza in an otherwise staffless but turreted castle. **1965** L. MEYNELL *Double Fault* II. iii. 126 In these almost staff-less days I can't tell you how comforting it is to lie awake in the morning and hear the gravel of the drive being raked. **1976** T. HEALD *Let Sleeping Dogs Die* ii. 46 You'll have to take pot luck... I'm staffless now..but I shall be able to rustle something up.

Staffordshire. Add: **a. Staffordshire bull terrier,** a small stocky terrier of the breed so called, first developed by crossing bulldogs and terriers, characterized by a fawn, blue, or brindle coat, often with white markings, and a short, broad head with dropped ears; **Staffordshire cone,** a kind of pyrometric cone; **Staffordshire knot**: also, a Stafford knot or half-hitch used as a craftsman's device or motif; **Staffordshire ware** (earlier example).

1765 J. WEDGWOOD *Let.* 17 June (1965) 34 An order from St. James's for a service of Staffordshire ware. **1901** *Our Dogs* 13 July 47/2 (Advt.), Old Staffordshire red brindled Bull-Terrier Dog Pup, five weeks, makes 20lbs. **1904** *Ibid.* 2 Jan. 24/2 (Advt.), Grand Litter Staffordshire Bull-terrier Pups, gamest strain. **1908** B. W. WATSON *Old Silver Platers & their Marks* 9/2 (*table*) 1808 Feb. 4 Josh Gibbs... Staffordshire Knott. **1950** A. C. SMITH *Dogs since 1900* xi. 174 In 1935 the Staffordshire Bull Terrier Club was founded. **1967** M. CHANDLER *Ceramics in Mod. World* i. 38 Cones used in continental Europe are still known as Seger cones, the slightly modified cones used in America are called Orton cones, and those used in England—also slightly modified—are called Staffordshire cones. **1968** J. ARNOLD *Shell Bk. Country Crafts* 280 The figures represented by [Corn] Dollies cover a considerable variety... We may name a few... The Horn of Plenty,..the Staffordshire Knot, [etc.]. **1971** *Vogue* 15 Oct. p. LS ii, The strikingly unusual motif features Staffordshire knots. *a* **1977** *Harrison Mayer Ltd. Catal.* 70/1 Staffordshire Cones..are slender, Trihedral pyramids made of ceramic materials and are so constituted as to deform when subjected to elevated temperature for a period of time. *Ibid.*, 'Staffordshire Cones', have been manufactured in England for nearly fifty years. **1977** J.

WAMBAUGH *Black Marble* (1978) viii. 126 Pattie Mae didn't do so well with the Staffordshire bull terrier.

b. (Earlier example in sense 'Staffordshire ware'.)

[**1770** H. WALPOLE *Let.* 6 May (1967) XXIII. 211 We have Etruscan vases, make of earthen ware in Staffordshire, from two to five guineas.] **1866** QUEEN VICTORIA *Let.* 16 May in R. Fulford *Your Dear Letter* (1971) 75, I send her a tea-set..which I hope she will often use. It is Staffordshire.

c. *ellipt.* = *Staffordshire bull terrier*, sense a above. Also *attrib.*

1903 *Our Dogs* 27 June 944/1 (Advt.), Pure-bred Staffordshire Bitch, good guard, and very game. **1943** H. N. BEILBY *Staffordshire Bull Terrier* i. 3 The Staffordshire will, by his intelligence and general usefulness, make a very strong appeal. **1968** [see *FILLED *ppl. a.* 2].

stag, *sb.*[1] Add: **1. b.** (Later example.)

1935 T. S. ELIOT *Murder in Cathedral* i. 29 Cabined in Canterbury, realmless ruler, Self-bound servant of a powerless Pope, The old stag, circled with hounds.

5*. *dial.* and *colloq.* A big, romping girl; a bold woman.

1684 G. MERITON *Yorks. Dialogue* 55 Nea, nea, great stags, what a durdum thou macks! **1790** GROSE *Provinc. Gloss.* (ed. 2), *Stag*,..a romping girl. **1877** F. Ross et al. *Gloss. Words Holderness* 135/2 *Stag*,..a rude, romping girl. **1922** JOYCE *Ulysses* 425 The likes of her! Stag that one is. Stubborn as a mule! **1922** D. H. LAWRENCE *Aaron's Rod* iii. 33 She too was a tall stag of a thing.

6. d. A spell of duty. (See also quot. 1881.)

1881 S. EVANS *A.B.E. Evans's Leicestershire Words* (new ed.) 255 A 'stag' is also one set to watch while his fellows are engaged in anything in which they wish not to be caught. **1931** BROPHY & PARTRIDGE *Songs & Slang Brit. Soldier: 1914–18* (ed. 3) 361 *Stag*, sentry-go. **1958** R. STOREY *Touch it Light* in J. C. Trewin *Plays of Year* XVIII. 341 There's seven stags in the hours o' darkness and only five of you to do 'em. Somebody has to do two. **1975** A. BEEVOR *Violent Brink* iv. 97 The films would be handed in for processing when they were relieved at the end of their two hour 'stag'.

e. *ellipt.* for *stag-dinner, -party*, etc. (sense 8 c in Dict. and Suppl.). *N. Amer.*

1904 *Brooklyn Eagle* 28 May 3 The Myrtle Fishing Club will have a stag at Hurman Hub's Park this evening. **1947** *Chicago Tribune* 19 Oct. (Comic Suppl.) 6 The marchin' and chowder club's throwin' a stag tonight. **1971** R. LEWIS *Fenokee Project* viii. 148 He's getting married tomorrow. Tonight he's holding his stag, and most of the men from the dam are going along.

f. *U.S.* A man who attends a social function without a female partner. Also quasi-*adv.* in phr. *to go stag.*

1905 N. DAVIS *Northerner* 213 'No man not escorting a lady'—a stag, you know—could go upon the floor. **1905** *Dialect Notes* III. 21 Are you going to the dance stag? **1924** P. MARKS *Plastic Age* xix. 210 True, he was not 'dragging a woman', but several of the brothers were going 'stag'; so he felt completely at ease. **1928** *Daily Express* 14 Dec. 19 A needy or avaricious 'stag'—as male dancers are called in the United States. **1948** *This Week Mag.* 1 May 16/3 The sign read: 'No Stags Allowed'. **1979** R. JAFFE *Class Reunion* (1980) I. viii. 117 A lot of boys went to the parties stag. Social life was easy for them, not the way it was for girls, who had to wait..until someone called. **1980** R. L. DUNCAN *Brimstone* iii. 59 They're not going to let you in by yourself. They have a rule against stags.

8. c. For *U.S. slang* read *slang* (orig. *U.S.*). *stag-night, -party* (later examples): freq. applied *spec.* to a celebration held on the eve of a man's marriage. Cf. *hen-party* s.v. HEN *sb.* 8.

1965 *Listener* 9 Sept. 373/2 On 'stag nights' it [*sc.* the entertainment] is pretty blue. **1973** in E. Dunphy *Only a Game?* (1976) iv. 110 We went out this evening for his stag night. **1923** 'BARTIMEUS' *Seaways* xii. 234 We don't want any women. We'll just have a stag party and talk Service shop and play pool afterwards. **1978** J. WAINWRIGHT *Thief of Time* 83, I know people... Class strippers. Stag-party hostesses. There's a real market.

9. a. stag film orig. *U.S.*, a pornographic film made for a male audience; **stag line** *U.S.*, the group of unattached young men at a social function; **stag movie** orig. *U.S.* = *stag film* above.

1968 *Wall St. Jrnl.* 11 Sept. 18/1 Pornography is not one of the nation's truly burning issues, and showing stag films is not our idea of how to run the world's greatest deliberative body. **1977** *Gay News* 7–20 Apr. 23/2 She.. made these very tame, anodyne stag films that she's always denying. **1934** J. O'HARA *Appointment in Samarra* i. 16 She would get twice around the dance floor with the same partner, then someone would step out of the stag line and cut in. **1977** G. V. HIGGINS *Dreamland* v. 47 As a member of Porcellian I had been invited to the stag line at a gathering on Beacon Hill. **1960** *Christian Herald* July 14/2 Teen-agers bought 'stag movies' for as much as $50 a reel. **1971** *Ink* 12 June 3/1 What he found was a hundred men having their mid-shift tea break and enjoying a stag movie.

stag, *v.*[3] Add: **2. b.** *trans.* To deal in (shares) as a stag.

1935 *Times* 27 Nov. 19/2 The loan was heavily stagged, for the total applications exceeded £14,000,000. **1966** *New Statesman* 23 Sept. 456/3 The gilt-edged market has now improved to the point where the new issue of *ICI* loan stock seems likely to be stagged even more heavily than the last. **1981** *Daily Tel.* 20 July 15/2 The offer is likely to be subscribed although the opportunities for stagging the issue will be limited.

4. *intr.* To go to or attend a social occasion unaccompanied. Also const. *it.* *U.S. slang.*

1900 *Dialect Notes* II. 64 *To stag it*, to go to a party without escorting a lady. **1941** *Sat. Even. Post* 10 May 74/3 If you won't go with me to the picnic, I'll stag. **1973** *Lebende Sprachen* XVIII. 38/1 He had planned to stag at the class dance.

5. *trans.* To cut (trousers or other articles of clothing) off short. Also with *off.* *N. Amer.*

1902 [implied at *stagged* ppl. a. below]. **1905** *Terms Forestry & Logging* (U.S. Dept. Agric. Bureau Forestry) 49 *Stag*, to cut off trousers at the knee, or boots at the ankle. **1942** L. RICH *We took to Woods* vii. 188 One stags one's pants, one's shirt sleeves, anything that needs to be abbreviated quickly, even one's hair. **1953** R. MOON *This is Saskatchewan* 215 They [*sc.* the lumberjacks] wore pants stagged off or rolled half way to the knee so as not to be confused with mere city dwellers. **1972** *Islander* (Victoria, B.C.) 30 Apr. 16/1 He was always dressed in the same way..heavy..underwear, tin pants stagged to the proper working length.

Hence **stagged** *ppl. a.*, (of trousers) cut off short; also with *off.* *N. Amer.*

1902 S. E. WHITE *Blazed Trail* xxvii. 190 A gigantic young riverman in the conventional stagged (*i.e.* chopped off) trousers. **1933** E. HEMINGWAY *Winner take Nothing* 29 He wore stagged trousers and lumbermen's rubbers and a mackinaw shirt. **1956** H. S. M. KEMP *Northern Trader* 114 He had the mackinaw shirt and stagged-off pants, [etc.].

stage, *sb.* Add: **I. 1. i.** (*a*) (Further examples.) In mod. use, a division of a stratigraphic series, composed of a number of zones and corresponding to an age in time; the rocks deposited during any particular age. [tr. F. *étage* (introduced in this sense by A. d'Orbigny 1841, in *Paléont. Française: Terrains Crétacés* I. 417).]

1898 [see *GROUP *sb.* 4 b (iii)]. **1915** C. SCHUCHERT *Text-bk. Geol.* II. xxx. 582 The epochs and series are further divided into ages (time) and stages (rocks), but these divisions have as yet no scientific precision. **1931** [see *SERIES 11 a (ii)]. **1960** J. M. WELLER *Stratigr. Princ. & Pract.* 443 Biostratigraphic zones are combined to form larger units termed stages. **1966** D. T. DONOVAN *Stratigraphy* vii. 160 Thus we speak of Ordovician System or Ordovician Period, Albian Stage or Albian Age, according to whether we are referring to the rocks themselves or the time occupied by their accumulation. **1976** H. D. HEDBERG *Internat. Stratigraphic Guide* vii. 71 Currently recognized stages are variable in time span, but on the average they range from 3 to 10 million years as indicated by isotopic age determinations.

(*b*) A glacial or interglacial period.

1895 *Jrnl. Geol.* III. 247 These [flood-loams] cannot always be separated from the similar deposits of later glacial stages which must obviously have been deposited over the same tracts. **1939** A. K. LOBECK *Geomorphology* ix. 314 The following names have been given to the several stages of glaciation [in America]: Nebraskan, Kansan, Illinoian, Iowan, and Wisconsin... The world may now be in an interglacial period, to be followed by another glacial stage. **1969** R. V. RUHE *Quaternary Landscapes in Iowa* ii. 26 Four of the major units of the standard glacial and interglacial stages were established in Iowa.

4. g. (Later example in sense 'landing-place'.)

1969 F. MOWAT *Boat who wouldn't Float* iii. 24 We emerged at the base of a spindly and unbelievably rickety stage (as fishermen's wharves are called) made of peeled spruce poles.

i. A boxing ring. Now *Hist.*

1829 P. EGAN *Boxiana* 2nd Ser. II. 44 He was carried upon the shoulders of several men, from the stage to a private room in the Stand. **1954** F. C. AVIS *Boxing Ref. Dict.* 106 *Stage*, the old name for the ring. **1982** S. B. FLEXNER *Listening to America* 105 *Broughton's rules* called for a 'stage' with a one-yard square chalked or scratched in the middle.

j. *Canad.* An erection on which meat is kept out of the reach of animals, or on which meat is dried.

1715 J. KNIGHT *Let.* 30 June in *Lett. from Hudson Bay* (1965) 51 Wee were all forcd to leave the factory & to take our Selves to ye Woods & to gett on trees & Stages for Six Days. **1800** A. HENRY *Jrnl.* 9 Sept. in E. Coues *New Light on Greater Northwest* (1897) I. iii. 91 We then arranged camp..and made a suitable stage near by, to hold fresh meat, etc. **1922** *Beaver* Mar. 39/2 Passing a considerable amount of jerked meat on a stage, I entered the wigwam. **1940** F. NIVEN *Mine Inheritance* 45 The erection of stages, platforms raised high on poles above the prairies on which food could be left beyond the reach of leaping wolves.

5. a. *to hold the stage*: see *HOLD *v.* 6 g; *to set the stage*: see SET *v.* 74.

f. *stage left* (or *right*): (on) the left (or right) side of a stage (as considered from a position facing the audience). Similarly, *stage centre.* Also *fig.*

1947 *Gloss. Techn. Theatr. Terms* (Strand Electr. & Engin. Co.) 28 *Stage left*, that half of the stage on the actor's left when facing the audience. **1961** BOWMAN & BALL *Theatre Lang.* 351 *Stage right*,..right stage, or right of stage. **1972** F. WARNER *Lying Figures* III. 16 Epigyne ..sits stage left in hanging basket chair. **1977** 'C. AIRD' *Parting Breath* vi. 79 The Devil always enters stage left. **1979** *Internat. Jrnl. Sociol. of Law* Feb. 26 There are three things that are very evident already: one is that he brought to a 20th century anthropological stage-center classic legal problems that preoccupied Maine in the 19th century.

IV. 8. a. More recently, as *fare stage*, one of the principal stops on an omnibus or tram route, which marks the start of a new step in the fare structure: see *FARE *sb.*[1] 9.

9. c. (Examples of sense 'an omnibus'.)

1853 'MARK TWAIN' *Let.* 26 Oct. (1917) I. 28 The Phila. 'bus drivers cannot cheat. In the front of the stage is a thing like an office clock. **1912** J. MILNE *John Jonathan & Co.* 92 A fleet of motor-buses, which the New Yorkers call 'stages', short for stage-coaches, meanders up and down it [*sc.* Fifth Avenue]. **1939** *Nat. Geogr. Mag.* Feb. 133/2 Mammoth sleeper buses (which they still call 'stages'). **1973** R. HAYES *Hungarian Game* iii. 30 Nearly a dozen standbys had taken the stage back to Mammoth village.

10. b. *stage-by-stage* adj. phr., that proceeds by stages; step-by-step.

1956 *Nature* 25 Feb. 391/1 Using the Townsend electron avalanche process in a gas in a stage-by-stage system. **1959** *Daily Tel.* 14 Apr. 22/3 (*heading*) Stage-by-stage atomic offer to Russia. **1962** E. SNOW *Red China Today* (1963) xix. 139 An accurate stage-by-stage itinerary prepared for me by the First Army Corps showed a main trek of some 6,000 miles.

11. a. (Later examples.)

1908 E. M. FORSTER *Room with View* x. 170 She was too great for all society, and had reached the stage where personal intercourse would alone satisfy her. **1940** J. BUCHAN *Memory Hold-the-Door* ii. 39, I have used the word politics, but at this stage I was no politician, being interested only to a small degree in theories, and not at all in parties. **1956** W. S. CHURCHILL *Hist. Eng.-Speaking Peoples* II. xx. 247 It was at this stage that a group of lawyers and gentry decided to offer Cromwell the crown. **1966** *Oxf. Univ. Gaz.* 23 Dec. 429/1 This legislation will.. come forward next term or in the following term, and it is at that stage that members of the House will be asked to take the responsibility of deciding [etc.]. **1977** J. THOMSON *Case Closed* i. 15 I'm not risking you making a balls-up of it at this stage in the game.

c. (Examples in *Ent.*)

1925, 1932 [see *INSTAR *sb.*]. **1974** *Nature* 18 Jan. 154/2 The term 'stage' is here used as equivalent to the French term *étape* and is composed of several 'stadia' separated by a moult.

d. *slang.* A period of imprisonment during which privileges are allowed.

1932 'JOCK OF DARTMOOR' *Dartmoor from Within* ii. 56 In his fourth year he [*sc.* the convict] enters the highest stage. In this stage he is permitted a tobacco and cigarette ration. **1958** F. NORMAN *Bang to Rights* 30 My punishment was three days bread and water..and twenty eight days stage.

11*. a. *Electronics.* A part of a circuit usu. comprising one transistor or valve, or two or more functioning as a single unit, and the associated resistors, capacitors, etc.

1920 *Jrnl. Inst. Electr. Engineers* LVIII. 65/1 This is the first attempt to deal comprehensively with the problems of the multiple-stage amplifier. **1930** *Proc. IRE* XVIII. 1715 It will be seen that there are two stages of push–pull high-frequency amplification. **1944** *Electronic Engin.* XVI. 392 A multivibrator functioning as a divider requires three valves per dividing stage. **1961** *Listener* 9 Nov. 776/2 The relatively poor amplifying stages..in even the most costly television sets [are] incapable of providing the full and almost distortion-free sound of a genuine 'high-fidelity' system. **1975** D. G. FINK *Electronics Engineers' Handbk.* XIII. 18 An amplifier may take the form of a single stage or a complex single stage or it may employ an interconnection of several stages... For a multistage amplifier, the individual stages may be essentially identical or radically different.

b. *Astronautics.* Each of two or more sections of a rocket that have their own engines and propellant and fall away in turn as their propellant becomes exhausted.

1935 C. S. PHILP *Stratosphere & Rocket Flight* xii. 62 The first method consists of a rocket built in two or more stages, the first stage being a relatively low-power engine for use in the lower parts of the earth's atmosphere, and the second stage, or subsequent multiple stages, of increased power for use in the higher and more rarefied regions. **1948** *Jrnl. Brit. Interplanetary Soc.* VII. 168 Into this section propellant from the 1st, 2nd and 3rd stage tanks is automatically transferred..so that as its own propellant is drawn off by the motor it is replaced and both the 4th and Final stages achieve 'release velocity' with tanks at capacity level. **1955** *Times* 4 Aug 6/2 We shall be limited to one-stage rockets at first, but afterwards we may work on two-stage rockets which will reach greater heights. **1963** *Ann. Reg. 1962* 445 The satellite, weighing 170 lb., was placed in orbit by a three-stage Delta rocket. **1975** K. GATLAND *Missiles & Rockets* viii. 185 The first stage engines burnt for about 2½ minutes, boosting the Apollo astronauts to an altitude of 36 miles.

12. a. *stage-carpenter* (earlier example), *-carpentering, crew, design, designer, -hand* (earlier example), *lighting, -picture, show, trick, version*; *stage army, aside, -dialect, -villain* (earlier example); similarly *stage Australian, Frenchman, Irishman*, etc.; *stage Irish* sb. and adj.

1922 C. S. CHURCHILL *Let.* 4 Jan. in M. Soames *Clementine Churchill* (1979) xiii. 203 All the sad events of last year culminating in Marigold passing and re-passing like a stage Army through my sad heart. **1957** A. C. L. DAY *Outl. Monetary Economics* xiii. 177 There was, therefore, a stage army of cash moving from bank to bank through each week, helping improve appearances. **1813** M. EDGEworth *Let.* 16 May (1971) 53 Lady Derby he says is always *acting*—that there is continually a stage *aside* which betrays her. **1945** *Essays & Studies 1944* XXX. 35 A dry unsympathetic comment delivered curtly like a stage-aside, 'Would he had blotted a thousand!' **1965** *Times Lit. Suppl.* 16 Sept. 812/1 Only the baggy trousers and the wide brimmed hat anchor him to the image of the 'stage' Australian, or the Boy from the Bush. **1826** O'Keeffe *Recoll.* I. iv. 146 Years after, some such enthusiastic spirit possessed the stage carpenters at Cork. **1899** 'Mark Twain' in *Cosmopolitan* Oct. 593/2 He had to retire from his profession of stage-carpentering. **1959** *Guardian* 13 Nov. 9/3 The Banana Boat song was booming on the telly in the stage-crew's room. **1975** *New Yorker* 21 Apr. 112/1 The theatre can devote all its resources—orchestra, singers, coaches, stage crews, lighting team—to the preparation and performance of the work. **1943** J. Leyda tr. *S. Eisenstein's Film Sense* ii. 77 This is an important law which can be found in painting, in stage design..of this period. **1977** J. Aiken *Last Movement* vi. 116 Is that your profession—stage design? **1938** L. Bemelmans *Life Class* II. iii. 141 An energetic hostess.. will often arrive with a squadron of orchestra leaders, architects..and stage designers. **1978** R. Ludlum *Holcroft Covenant* xiii. 151 There was a man in London, a stage designer, who'd had a brief vogue as a decorator among the wealthy on both sides of the Atlantic. **1927** *New Republic* 12 Oct. 218/2 Mr. Wiley has a further advantage over his fellow craftsmen in being master of two stage-dialects—pidgin English and Negro. **1966** G. N. Leech *Eng. in Advertising* viii. 78 A music-hall comedian adopts a 'stage-dialect'. **1824** in A. Mathews *Mem. Charles Mathews* (1839) III. xx. 453 Talbot is the stock Morbleu, which he makes a monkey—a ballet-master—in short, a stage Frenchman. **1885** F. Leslie in *Entr'acte Ann.* 22/1 The stage hands were non-expectorants, and the ladies were quite vexed at the clean condition of the stage. **1962** *Listener* 1 Mar. 387/3 These pages are littered with wild stage-Irish cries of 'Jasez', 'begod', and the like. **1962** A. Lurie *Love & Friendship* xi. 208 'That's a gra-and idea,' Charley said, stage Irish. **1977** A. J. Bliss in D. O'Muirithe *Eng. Lang. in Ireland* 9 At this early date a conventional 'stage Irish' had been established. **1980** J. O'Faolain *No Country for Young Men* v. 96 He must think he'd fallen into a stage-Irish household. **1860** *Players* I. 131 The dialect he assumed, though it may not have been so productive of laughter as that in which the 'stage Irishman' usually delivers himself. **1911** G. B. Shaw in *Evening Sun* (N.Y.) 9 Dec. 4/6 The stage Irishman of the nineteenth century, generous, drunken, thriftless, with a joke always on his lips and a sentimental tear always in his eye. **1973** J. Elsom *Erotic Theatre* ii. 33 A stage actress—as recognizable a type as a stage Irishman and more frequently seen. **1895** *New Budget* 4 Apr. 21/1 One would have practically to invent new methods of scene-painting and stage-lighting. **1908** G. B. Shaw *Let.* 2 Aug. (1972) II. 804 There were some very clever tricks of stage lighting in the second act of Siegfried. **1983** 'J. le Carré' *Little Drummer Girl* iii. 51 The stage lighting was too good, she couldn't penetrate the haze. **1920** W. B. Yeats *Poems* p. vii, When our stage-pictures were made out of poor conventional scenery and hired costumes. **1949** F. Fergusson *Idea of Theatre* i. 28 The contemplation of the final stage-picture or epiphany. **1980** *Times* 29 Feb. 13/2 The WNO *Onegin* is..a procession of stage-pictures far beyond the everyday purview of opera production. **1895** G. B. Shaw in *Sat. Rev.* 16 Feb. 217/1 Stage shows with nothing to redeem their obvious silliness but a promise of as much lewdness as the audience will stand. **1982** N. Frye *Great Code* v. 117 The Puritan and Jansenist prejudice against 'stage shows'. **1776** *St. James's Chron.* 19 Oct., Allowing reasonably for stage trick, this appears to us to be extravagantly over-done. **1895** G. B. Shaw *Let.* 28 Nov. (1965) I. 572 This is not one of my great plays..: it is only a display of my knowledge of stage tricks. **1856** A. C. Ritchie *Mimic Life* 105 Desdemona, according to the stage version (which omits her during the midnight brawl). **1955** *Radio Times* 22 Apr. 31/2 '*A Woman of No Importance*'.. Adapted for radio from the stage version. **1885** A. Edwardes *Girton Girl* II. xvii. 281 Dismissed as one occasionally sees the frustrated stage villain, long before the final falling of the curtain!

b. *stage-line* (earlier example), *-office.*

1830 *Williams's N.Y. Ann. Reg.* 115 Other principal Stage lines from Albany. **1812** J. McNab *Jrnl.* 4 Mar. in *Beaver* (1973) Summer 9/2 We..inquired at the stage office when the sleigh sets out for New York on Friday. **1872** 'Mark Twain' *Roughing It* 22 The first thing we did..was to hunt up the stage-office, and pay..for tickets per overland coach.

13. stage box (later examples); **stage direction,** (*b*) stage-management (also *fig.*); **stage director** orig. *U.S.*., a stage-manager; also, more recently, a director (sense *1 g); **stage-door,** (*a*) (earlier example of *stage-door keeper*); † (*b*) a door at the side of the proscenium arch (*obs.*); **stage-door Johnny** *slang* (chiefly *U.S.*), a (young) gentleman who frequents stage-doors for the company of actresses; **stage-entrance** = *stage-door*; **stage-fright** (earlier example); **stage name** (later examples); **stage presence,** the (forceful) impression made by a performer on an audience; **stage school,** an academy of drama; **stage-set** = Set *sb.*[1] 28 in Dict. and Suppl. (also *transf.*); **stage-setting** (earlier and later examples); also *fig.*; **stage-struck** *a.* (later examples); **stage-whisper** (earlier and later examples); hence as *v. trans.*, (*a*) to address (a person) in a stage-whisper; (*b*) with obj. as direct speech: to say (something) in a stage-whisper; **stage-whispered** *ppl. a.*, spoken in a stage-whisper; **stage-whispering** *ppl. a.*; **stage-worthy** *a.* (later examples); hence **stage-worthiness.**

1857 H. Martineau *Autobiogr.* I. IV. 388 [Mr. Macready] gave us the stage box, whenever we chose to ask for it. **1982** C. Castle *Folies Bergère* ii. 64 He was to be seen..accepting congratulations in a stage box. **1833** R. Dyer *Nine Years of Actor's Life* 78, I began a correspondence with the well-known Henry Lee, and finally agreed to take the stage direction of his theatres. **1962** V. Nabokov *Pale Fire* 55 When morning finds us marching to the wall Under the stage direction of some goon Political, some uniformed baboon. **1782** T. Hall in G. O. Seilhamer *Hist. Amer. Theatre* (1889) II. v. 55 Before you see one of your stage directors Or, if you please, one of those strange projectors. **1849** *Theatrical Mirror* 27 Aug. 101/1 Mr A. Harris, stage-director of the Royal Italian Opera, of Covent Garden, has been presented with a piece of plate. **1908** E. Terry *Story of my Life* xiv. 326 It was not as an actor but as a stage director that he wanted to work. **1979** A. Williamson *Funeral March for Siegfried* ix. 42 'We'll have to chase up the stage staff,'.. 'I can give you the stage director's address.' **1761** A. Murphy *Way to keep Him* (ed. 4) v. 101 Enter Lady Constant. *Lovemore* No way to escape?—[Attempts both stage doors, and is prevented]. **1776** R. Y. Walsingham *Let.* 6 Feb. in J. Boaden *Private Corresp. David Garrick* (1832) II. 134 That you will be so good as to pardon the stage-door keeper for admitting *me* last night. **1829** H. Foote *Companion to Theatres* 33 At this time, the proscenium was altered; stage doors were introduced, there having been none in the original building. **1883** D. Cook *On Stage* I. ix. 187 Of such stage-doors as are here described there is no London theatre in possession. **1912** *Out West* Feb. 139/1 No theater can hope to do business without stage door Johnnies. **1922** [see *rich *adv.* and *Comb.* 10 b]. **1952** Granville *Dict. Theatrical Terms* 169 *Stage-door Johnny*, the Victorian buck..who haunted the stage door of the Gaiety Theatre, London,..when some of the most beautiful women of the day were members of the chorus. **1976** Botham & Donnelly *Valentino* iv. 35 Two Ziegfield Follies girls who were doing the town with a pair of wealthy stage-door Johnnies. **1830** J. Bernard *Retrospections of Stage* II. ix. 273 He got the carpenter to fix a bucket on a swivel, over the stage-entrance of the Theatre. **1956** B. Holiday *Lady sings Blues* (1973) xii. 112 We were supposed to pick up all the cats at the Braddock Motel.., near the stage entrance of the Apollo. **1876** 'Mark Twain' *Tom Sawyer* xxi. 169 A ghastly stage-fright seized him. **1941** A. Christie *Evil under Sun* iv. 66 He doubted if Arlena Stuart, to give her her stage name, had ever wanted to be alone in her life. **1959** T. S. Eliot *Elder Statesman* II. 51 You know I meant my stage name. The name by which you knew me. **1977** *Sounds* 9 July 28/1 *Stooges*..headed by James Osterburg—stage name Iggy Stooge. **1929** *Melody Maker* Feb. 195/2 There was a wide gap between the stage presence of the cornet soloist and the stage presence of the other artists. **1959** R. Longrigg *Wrong Number* iv. 49 Mrs. Proctor, in the soubrette part of the kitchen-maid, made up for her vocal uncertainty with a racy and convincing stage presence. **1977** *Zigzag* Aug. 16/1 Syl's got a lot of what directors call 'stage presence'. **1936** N. Streatfeild *Ballet Shoes* iv. 55 She..ran an ordinary stage school where the children learnt all kinds of dancing. **1977** S. Brett *Star Trap* ii. 24 He came out of one of the stage schools... He may have been a child star in films. **1861** Stage set [see Set *sb.*[1] 28]. **1947** J. C. Rich *Materials & Methods of Sculpture* i. 13 In designing for a garden..an excellent and highly recommended procedure is first to make a small three-dimensional scale model of the garden and its immediate environs, and to use this small 'stage-set' actively as an aid in determining the nature and placing of the garden ornament. **1958** S. Spender *Engaged in Writing* i. 13 A large, bare room with faded nineteenth-century murals, like the back of an operatic stage-set. **1977** *Proc. R. Soc. Med.* LXX. 427/2 A collaborative effort in which satirical comedy is fused with the sort of music, dance, lavish costumes and stage-sets used in court ballets. **1881** C. C. Harrison *Woman's Handiwork* III. 152 All the little invisible wires that control the scenery and 'stage setting' of a home-interior. **1929** *Oxford Poetry* 10 For three-and-twenty years, he curled And drooped, on this stage-setting of the world. **1982** P. Raby '*Fair Ophelia*' iv. 48 Ciceri extended into the sphere of stage settings the reforms which Talma himself had introduced so far as historical accuracy of costume was concerned. **1911** Stage struck [see *rumble *sb.* 6]. **1976** *Southern Even. Echo* (Southampton) 6 Nov., Despite warnings of financial trouble in the theatre,..she has remained stage-struck throughout her life after deciding at the age of four to become an actress. **1864** H. Morley *Jrnl.* 17 Dec. (1866) 355 His bedroom scene, spoken throughout in an oppressively ostentatious stage whisper, is an intolerable blunder. **1927** J. N. McIlwraith *Kinsmen at War* xx. 198 Mrs. Secord spoke in a stage whisper. **1932** Kipling *Limits & Renewals* 80 Private Gillock, who poses as a wit, was stage-whispering me for leave to 'put a shot into his radiator'. **1941** B. Schulberg *What makes Sammy Run?* iii. 49 'What are you thinking about, honey?' Billie stage-whispered. **1960** J. Rae *Custard Boys* I. v. 52 'Who's your German friend?' he asked in a stage whisper. **1977** W. M. Spackman *Armful of Warm Girl* 38 A huge handsome white-haired classmate flung himself jovially upon them..to beg in a whooping and waggish stage-whisper. **1979** R. Littell *Debriefing* iii. 33 'Do you have the pouch?' she stage-whispers. **1978** G. Sims *Rex Mundi* iv. 26 The stage-whispered duet started again...I made out only odd words. **1883** 'Mark Twain' *Life on Miss.* xxxi. 342 'The captain's voice, by G—!' said the stage-whispering ruffian. **1973** *Times Lit. Suppl.* 19 Oct. 1272/4 The recent Jonathan Miller production of *The Malcontent* has demonstrated that play's stageworthiness. **1959** *Times* 4 Dec. 15/1 None of his [*sc.* Mussorgsky's] operatic undertakings is stageworthy. **1979** *Amer. N. & Q.* Nov. 40/1 In an effective and stageworthy central scene, the old miser's secrets..are discovered.

stage, *v.* Add: **3. d.** *transf.* To mount or put on (a spectacle). Also, to effect (a recovery); *to stage a comeback*: see *come-back *sb.*[2] 2.

1924 F. J. Haskin *Amer. Govt.* (rev. ed.) xxxvii. 437 In combating..bootlegging,..Federal agents staged raids that revealed..the widespread extent of Volstead Law violations. **1951** *Sport* 27 Apr.–3 May 5/1 It is grand to think that the event can be staged at Wembley. **1956** A. H. Compton *Atomic Quest* 122 His Nazi-trained students staged a protest. **1973** *Daily Tel.* 15 Feb. 1/4 More than 500 students staged a sit-in at Cambridge University yesterday. **1981** *Times* 9 May 19/4 A gradual return of confidence saw equities and gilts stage a rally yesterday.

6. b. Of a pilot or aircraft: to make a brief landing in the course of a long journey.

1971 P. Purser *Holy Father's Navy* I. iii. 17 The pilot [had]..staged in Iceland and was on his way to Norway. **1973** D. Kyle *Raft of Swords* (1974) I. iv. 32 The agent.. was in time to join the Air Canada Hawaii to Montreal flight when it staged at Vancouver.

7. *trans. Astronautics.* To separate (a section or stage) from the upper or remaining part of a rocket. Also *intr.* of the stage.

1957 *Collier's Encycl. Year Bk. 1956* 264/1 After launching, when the propellants in the booster tanks are nearly exhausted, the three motors and the rear tanks will be staged, or shut down and separated from the missile. **1962** J. Glenn et al. *Into Orbit* 246 When one section of it [*sc.* a multi-stage booster] separates and is jettisoned.., the section is said to have staged. **1966** H. O. Ruppe *Introd. Astronaut.* I. iii. 91 It is possible to 'parallel-stage' tankage or engines only . . . E.g., a three-stage vehicle can have its first and second stages parallel staged, and the second and third stages tandem staged.

8. To cause (a person) to pass through stages; to bring about (something) in stages.

1957 A. C. Clarke *Deep Range* ix. 83 We've got to haul him in around the hundred-and-fifty-foot level—no higher—and then start staging him in the air lock. **1962** E. Snow *Red China Today* (1963) III. xxxviii. 279 We staged them through quick courses of training and re-training in the Ningtu technique. **1980** *Daily Tel.* 15 Mar. 1/7 The Government will 'stage' the payment of the increases to stay within its cash limits.

stage-coach. b. (Earlier examples.)

1831 *Boston Transcript* 2 Aug. 2/3 The entertainment happened to be the 'Stage Coach', which was acted so wretchedly that it was impossible to make head or tail of it. **1872** 'S. Coolidge' *What Katy Did* (1873) v. 89 They all fell to playing 'Stage-coach'..in spite of close quarters and an occasional bump.

staged, *ppl. a.* Add: **4.** That proceeds by stages; = *phased *ppl. a.* 2.

1960 *Economist* 15 Oct. 255/3 A group of commissioners who disagree with these proposals favour a traditional policy of staged development. **1969** *Daily Tel.* 16 May 1 A mutual and staged withdrawal of all foreign troops from South Vietnam. **1973** *Ibid.* 13 Dec. 2/8 New wage rates which would be introduced, with staged pay rises, over 2½ years.

stage-manage, *v.* (In Dict. s.v. Stage-manager.) Add: (Later *fig.* examples.) Also *absol.*

1910 Wodehouse *Psmith in City* i. 3 My pater wants to jump in and stage manage. **1924** J. Buchan *Three Hostages* viii. 118 'Now wake.' I was puzzled to know how to stage-manage that wakening. **1958** *Washington Post* 26 June 1/7 The United States..accused the Russian Government of stage-managing a demonstration against the U.S. Embassy in Moscow. **1964** 'E. McBain' *Ax* ii. 36 We did it [*sc.* a play] in highschool... I stage-managed. **1980** D. Lodge *How Far can you Go?* vi. 218 The whole prank, she was now convinced, was being stage-managed..to get them all naked together.

Hence **stage-managed** *ppl. a.*

1930 *Times Lit. Suppl.* 1 May 359/3 In 1891 France and Russia had signalized their closer relations by the enthusiastic, though carefully stage-managed, reception given to the French fleet at Kronstadt. **1974** *Listener* 10 Oct. 461/3 These are not press conferences at all, but carefully stage-managed events, put on..for the audiences of BBC and ITV news.

stage-management. (In Dict. s.v. Stage-manager.) Add: (Earlier example.) Also *fig.*

1812 C. Mathews *Let.* 15 Jan. in A. Mathews *Mem. Charles Mathews* (1838) II. viii. 184 Mr Kemble is the proprietor. Whether he solely directs the stage management, or whether he does not at all interfere. **1949** M. Steen *Twilight on Floods* IV. i. 547 The sun, by one of the erratic tricks of Nature's stage-management, forced itself through the clouds. **1977** A. Giddens *Stud. in Social & Polit. Theory* ix. 329 Through the agency of Durkheim..the analysis of suicide became a critical issue in the struggle to establish sociology as a recognized academic discipline in France. This was, of course, largely due to Durkheim's own stage-management.

stage-manager. Add: (Earlier and later examples.) Also, in mod. usage, one who is in charge of the technical side of a production (see quot. 1961). Also *transf.* and *fig.*

1805 R. W. Elliston *Let.* 20 July in G. Raymond *Life & Enterprises of Robert William Elliston, Comedian* (1857) I. ii. 113 If to my office, as stage-manager, the term *officious* be applied. **1905** G. B. Shaw *Let.* in *Times* 3 July 8/2 My language was fairly moderate considering..the respectful ignorance of the dramatic points of the score exhibited by the conductor and the stage manager—if there is such a functionary at Covent Garden. **1906** E. Dyson *Fact'ry Ands* x. 121 Every woman in an astonishing frock is at heart a stage-manager. **1961** Bowman & Ball *Theatre Lang.* 349 *Stage manager*,..the head of the production staff, who assists the stage director, during rehearsals, in technical matters.., and who, once the production opens, takes complete charge of the stage, the actors.., and the crews. **1982** S. Brett *Murder Unprompted* ii. 21 The Stage Manager's calming voice came over the loudspeaker, 'Beginners, Act One, please.'

Hence as *v. trans.*, to stage-manage (*rare*); **stage-manageress**, a female stage-manager.

1900 M. Beerbohm *Let.* 11 Dec. (1964) 138 As stage-manageress she has been absolutely intelligent and sweet and charming. **1902** G. B. Shaw *Let.* 9 Aug. (1972) II. 281 It is..very important to get the last scene well stage managered, with a big surging crowd. **1926** E. F. Crosse *Let.* in *Times* 13 Apr. 15/5 There was no shyness and the stage manageress explained to me all details.

stager. Add: **5.** One who erects scaffolding in a shipyard. Cf. Stage *sb.* 4 e.

1927 *Dict. Occupational Terms* § 668 *Stager*,..erects staging on which workmen stand to work. **1974** *Socialist Worker* 26 Oct. 16/5 Management agreed that stagers in the Society of Boilermakers be made a skilled section with parity with packers and sheeters.

stagflation (stægflē·ɪʃən). *Econ.* [Blend of Stag(nation and In)flation: cf. *slumpflation.] A state of the economy in which stagnant demand is accompanied by severe inflation.

1965 I. Macleod *Hansard Commons* 17 Nov. 1165/1 We now have the worst of both worlds—not just inflation on the one side or stagnation on the other, but both of them together. We have a sort of 'stagflation' situation. **1971** R. Boyson *Down with Poor* 5 The result of all this extra state interference..has been..what might be called rampant stagflation, that is to say stagnation in production and raging inflation which..destroys belief in the future. **1974** W. Rees-Mogg *Reigning Error* iv. 75 So-called stagflation and slumpflation are the inevitable reflection of the progressive divergence between a rising nominal and a falling real supply of money. **1976** F. Zweig *New Acquisitive Society* ii. xi. 137 Even recession, stagnation, 'stag-flation' or steeply rising unemployment do not rule out wage explosions. **1979** *N.Y. Rev. Bks.* 25 Oct. 44/2 Stagflation ate away at prosperity. In 1975 industrial production fell.

staggeen. (Earlier example.)

1829 G. Griffin *Collegians* I. vii. 135 A parcel of ould *staggeens*, sir, that's running for a saddle, that's all the races they'll have.

stagger, *sb.*[1] Add: **3.** (Earlier example.)

1865 'Mark Twain' *Screamers* (1871) 149 He would make one more stagger at it anyway.

3*. A staggered arrangement or disposition; *spec.* in *Aeronaut.*, an arrangement of the wings of a biplane such that the leading edge of the upper wing is in front of or behind that of the lower wing.

1915 W. E. Dommett *Aeroplanes & Airships* 104 When the wings of a biplane are set with the upper one slightly ahead of, or abaft of the other, they are said to be staggered. The stagger is measured by the angle made by the line joining the leading edges with the normal to the fore and aft axis of the aeroplane. It is convenient to call the stagger positive if the upper wing is ahead of the lower. **1919** H. Shaw *Text-Bk. Aeronaut.* iii. 58 The effect of positive stagger on a biplane is to cause the lower plane to work in a slight downdraught from the upper plane, and so decreases its angle of incidence, giving the machine greater stability. **1937** *Times* 13 Nov. 13/5 All the footmarks lay on the same straight line with no 'stagger' right or left of it. **1950** R. G. Batson *Roads* v. 83 A stagger interrupts the passage of traffic from one branch of the minor road to the other. **1957** L. L. Beckford *A.B.C. of Aeronaut.* 95/2 When the upper wing is placed behind the arrangement is known as Back Stagger. **1972** *Times* 14 Nov. 15/7 The method of arranging the 'stagger' was one of the matters on which Customs and Excise consulted a wide range of trade bodies. **1980** M. Booth *Bad Track* i. 17 At the head of the small approach road was a T-junction... At a stagger from the slip-road was another, going down the other side to join the motorway.

4. a. stagger-juice: for *Austral. slang* read *slang* and add earlier example; **stagger tuning** *Electronics*, the tuning of different stages of an amplifier to slightly different frequencies so as to broaden the overall frequency response; so **stagger-tuned** *a.*

1905 *Chambers's Jrnl.* Oct. 730/1 A liquor labelled Scotch whisky, but commonly known as 'stagger juice'. **1947** F. E. Terman *Radio Engin.* (ed. 3) vii. 360 The behavior of such stagger-tuned pairs under conditions corresponding to maximal flatness..is of particular interest. **1975** D. G. Fink *Electronics Engineers' Handbk.* xiii. 57 The simple shunt-compensated stage has found extensive use in stagger-tuned pulse-amplifier applications. **1953** Fowler & Lippert *Television Fund.* vi. 121 Some of the later-model TV receivers make use of a single tuned inductance between tube sections of the i–f amplifier and obtain the necessary bandwidth by means of stagger-tuning. **1979** G. M. Miller *Handbk. Electronic Communication* ix. 285 The problem here is..how to get a wide-enough bandwidth but still have relatively sharp falloff at the pass-hand edges. Most TV IF amps solve this problem through the use of stagger tuning.

b. That involves the implementation of a staggered arrangement, as *stagger hours, schedule, plan.* Cf. sense *9 b of the vb. orig. *U.S.*

1918 *Dial* 2 Nov. 369/1 'Stagger' hours have been instituted—whereby one department goes to its work a half hour earlier than another, thus relieving the congestion of the street cars. **1933** *Sun* (Baltimore) 16 Aug. 4/2 The animals would be marketed..under a system of 'stagger' shipments to prevent swamping market and packing facilities. **1943** *Ibid.* 16 Nov. 11/3 State liquor stores went on a new 'stagger' schedule of hours..with doors opening at 9 a.m. and closing at 3 p.m. **1947** *News Chron.* 11 Apr. 4/6 (*heading*) Firms favour 'stagger' plan. **1960** *Wall St. Jrnl.* 7 Apr. 8 The stagger system is election of directors in classes for various terms of office.

stagger, *v.* Add: **II. 9. a.** Delete *Mech.* and add: Also, to position (things) at successively greater distances from the straight line they would otherwise form. (Later examples.)

1916 H. Barber *Aeroplane Speaks* 63 By staggering the top surface forward..it is removed from the action of the lower surface and engages undisturbed air. **1937** *Memo. Lay-out & Constr. Roads* (Min. of Transport) No. 483. 13 Where a minor road crosses a major road constructed with a single carriageway the minor road should be staggered, preferably to the left. **1959** *Listener* 6 Aug. 208/2 Then the road engineers got to work and staggered the cross-roads.

b. To arrange (holidays, times, etc.) so that they do not coincide; to arrange (an event or action) so that its implementation is spread over a period of time, or so that it is performed by different persons at different times. orig. *U.S.*

1918 *Daily Chron.* 23 Apr. 4/2 In order to maintain efficient service for industrial traffic, it is urged by the Tramways..Committee that factories and other places of business should 'stagger' their times of opening and closing. **1929** *Sun* (Baltimore) 27 Sept. 12/3 The days of rest will be staggered, one-fifth of the workers presumably laying off each twenty-four hours. **1934** *Ibid.* 3 Nov. 2/2 Omitting their national shows and staggering the introduction of new models. **1946** in P. N. S. Mansergh *Const. Rel. between Brit. & India* (1979) VIII. 211 Though the departure of officers on proportionate pension could be 'staggered', the right to retire could not be taken away. **1951** *Engineering* 7 Sept. 302/2 A scheme for staggering working hours, to ease the..load at..peak hours. **1962** E. Godfrey *Retail Selling & Organ.* xvii. 172 Many firms have found it better to stagger stock-taking, so that all departments are not disrupted at the same time. **1978** L. Davidson *Chelsea Murders* iii. xxi. 122 Lunch was being staggered, the six of them dashing out individually for a sandwich.

staggered, *ppl. a.* Add: **2.** *spec.* **a.** Positioned alternately on one side and the other of a line, or obliquely at successively greater distances from it; also, composed of parts so placed.

1875, 1905 [in Dict.]. **1909** V. Lougheed *Vehicles of Air* iv. 205 (*heading*) Staggered surfaces. **1930** *Engineering* 20 June 787/2 The removal of completely assembled portions of [railway] track would be awkward in the face of the general use of staggered joints. **1937** *Times* 13 Apr. (Motor Suppl.) p. x/1 Where this is not practicable staggered crossing or roundabouts are recommended. **1947** *Highway Engineers' Ref. Bk.* iv. 122/2 On straight roads side-mounted lanterns may be arranged either opposite to each other or in a staggered arrangement. **1960** C. H. Gibbs-Smith *Aeroplane* i. xi. 69 The Goupy had staggered biplane wings with pivoting wing-tip ailerons. **1961** F. C. Avis *Sportsman's Gloss.* 62/2 *Staggered start*, one in a race on an oval track..where the runner in the outside lane starts apparently in front of the runner in the inside lane, but only to compensate for the greater distance of the outside lane. **1968** Batson & Proudlove *Roads* (ed. 2) iv. 67 (*caption*) Layouts of T-junctions and staggered cross-roads on 2-way and divided roads. **1978** J. A. Michener *Chesapeake* xi. 654 From the woods came six doves, flying low in their wonderfully staggered fashion.

b. Arranged not to coincide in time; having starting and finishing times that overlap. Cf. *Stagger *sb.* 4 b.

1932 *Sun* (Baltimore) 8 Oct. 13/7 Severely curtailed appropriations, which necessitated recourse to a 'staggered' schedule of openings. **1940** *Ann. Reg. 1939* 358 A scheme of 'staggered' hours was evolved whereby some playhouses would be allowed to keep open till ten on condition that others still kept to the six o'clock rule. **1955** *Times* 12 Aug. 5/2 'Staggered' working hours for nearly 10,000 office workers in the West End of London may be introduced to ease the peak hour travelling problem. **1980** M. Babson *Dangerous to Know* iii. 15 The rest of the staff arrived at staggered hours.

staggering, *vbl. sb.* Add: **2. c.** See *stagger *v.* 9 b.

1955 *Times* 19 May 7/3 Difficulties had arisen by all the pool mail being received in the same week and as a result 'staggering arrangements' were made to spread the traffic. **1959** *Ann. Reg. 1958* 507 He undertook to consider whether the staggering of hours should be made compulsory. **1971** *Timber Trades Jrnl.* 14 Aug. 53/1 The reduction in productivity..due to the staggering of holidays. **1979** *Daily Tel.* 15 Dec. 2/3 The inquest had been told that the staggering procedure under which the 32 [parachute] troops left opposite doors of their Hercules had gone out of synchronisation.

staggering, *ppl. a.* Add: **1. d.** (Later examples.)

1922 Joyce *Ulysses* 413 Staggering bob in the vile parlance of our lower class licensed victuallers signifies the cookable and eatable flesh of a calf newly dropped from its mother. **1966** W. S. Ramson *Austral. Eng.* iv. 70 *Staggering bob*, a widespread dialect phrase used either of a very young calf which has not yet found its legs or of the veal from such a calf.

2. Also in trivial use: amazing, astounding; enormous.

1934 J. B. Priestley *Eng. Journey* vi. 202 He still controlled this staggering array of properties, extending from remote industrial villages in Yorkshire to Shaftesbury Avenue. **1939** [see *bally *a.* and *adv.*]. **1951** *Sport* 30 Mar.–5 Apr. 9/1 Staggering offers have been made for Twentyman, a half-back of immense promise. **1958** P. H. Gibbs *Curtains of Yesterday* iv. 53 Summoning two of his men he had the lorry filled up with a staggering amount of food—cheese, bread, bully beef, hams, tinned food. **1978** *Lancashire Life* July 55/4 Rich man though he was ..the High Sheriff must have faced a staggering bill.

staggeringly, *adv.* Add: Also in trivial use, amazingly; exceedingly.

1976 J. Cooper *Harriet* xvi. 131 She felt staggeringly untogether... She had a blinding headache. **1979** *PN Rev.* 9 60/2 It is the mark of staggeringly few of the great pulpiteers. **1979** *Guardian* 3 Nov. 11/3 What he is going to say in his six lectures..is staggeringly banal.

sta·ggerment. *nonce-wd.* [f. Stagger *v.* + -ment.] Great amazement, astonishment.

1933 J. R. R. Tolkien *Let.* 16 Mar., (MS.) I have actually been presented by a well-wishing old gentleman with a complete N.E.D., to my staggerment, as I had quite given up hope of possessing one. **1937** —— *Hobbit* xii. 221 To say that Bilbo's breath was taken away is no description at all. There are no words left to express his staggerment. **1975** *Church Times* 31 Jan. 11/1 As I lifted my arms for the quick frisk, I was conscious of unjournalistic feelings of staggerment. I had been through this process often enough at airports across the world, but never before, ever in a cathedral for goodness' sake.

staggy (stæ·gi), *a.* [f. Stag *sb.*[1] + -y[1].]

1. a. *N.Z.* and *N. Amer.* Of an animal or its meat: having the characteristics or appearance of a mature male (see quots.).

1933 *Press* (Christchurch, N.Z.) 9 Dec. 17/8 *Stag*, imperfectly, or late castrated male sheep or steer. Hence *staggy*. **1934** Webster, *Staggy*, having the appearance of a mature male animal;—said of female domestic animals. **1950** *N.Z. Jrnl. Agric.* Sept. 201/3 Complaints about the proportion of 'staggy' New Zealand wether lamb carcasses have been received recently from the United Kingdom. **1974** *Globe & Mail* (Toronto) 12 Dec. 8/2 The quality of beef within a grade can vary, depending on whether an animal is staggy or whether it weighs less than 550 pounds or more than 700. A staggy steer exhibits bull-like characteristics and has tougher meat.

b. *Austral.* (See quot.)

1891 R. Wallace *Rural Econ. Austral. & N.Z.* i. 30 Sometimes the [potato] sets remain fresh and do not decay in the soil after the haulms have developed; they remain 'staggy' or hard and woody.

2. a. Abounding in stags. *rare.*

1921 *Blackw. Mag.* July 34/2 Very staggy ground this. Indeed, a sambur grunted in covert which we watched.

b. *fig.* Of a tree, etc.: having bare branches. Cf. Stag-headed *a.* 2.

1933 R. Campbell *Flowering Reeds* 21 Bare trees.. Down the long avenue in staggy flight Are hunted by the hungers of the gale. **1961** P. White *Riders in Chariot* i. 13 Slapped by a staggy elder-bush..Whipped by the little sarsaparilla vine. **1973** —— *Eye of Storm* vii. 322 Under the staggy orange trees, amongst the hummocks, in the green haze of Noamurra.

stag-horn. Add: **3. b. stag('s) horn coral,** a branching coral of the genus *Acropora*.

[**1785** in G. H. Millar *New Syst. Nat. Hist.* iv. ii. 286 The coral plants..sometimes shoot out like trees without leaves in winter;..sometimes they are found to resemble ..the antlers of a stag, with great exactness and regularity.] **1884** R. Rathbun in G. B. Goode *Fisheries U.S.: Nat. Hist. Aquatic Animals* I. v. 841 Among the true stony corals are the Stag-horn Corals..and many others. **1928** Russell & Yonge *Seas* vii. pl. 59 (*caption*) Stag's Horn Coral. **1977** G. Durrell *Golden Bats & Pink Pigeons* v. 123 The predominant coral was Stag's horn,.. like a great graveyard of all the finest Victorian deer trophies, decked out in white and electric blue.

4. *Naut.* (See quot. 1961.)

1923 *Man. Seamanship* (Admiralty) II. 87 The 15-in. cordite whips..are either taken to the motor..or to the special staghorn for lowering. **1961** F. H. Burgess *Dict. Sailing* 196 *Staghorn*, a metal bollard with two horizontal arms.

5. *Path.* Used *attrib.* to designate a large calculus of the kidney having the branched form of the renal pelvis that it occupies.

1910 *Lippincott's New Med. Dict.* 924/1 Stag-horn calculus. **1926** Young & Davis *Young's Pract. Urol.* I. vi. 377 In some extreme cases the kidney is only a thin sheet of dense scar tissue in which no trace of tubules or glomeruli can be found, overlying a large stag-horn calculus. **1961** R. D. Baker *Essent. Path.* xvii. 441 (*caption*) The large staghorn calculus is a cast of the renal pelvis and of renal calyces. **1974** J. D. Maynard in R. M. Kirk et al. *Surgery* viii. 161 Renal calculi may be entirely symptomless, particularly the very large staghorn type filling most of the pelvicalyceal system.

staging, *vbl. sb.* Add: **1. a.** Also, *spec.* shelving for plants in a greenhouse.

1886 *Bk. Garden Managem.* 437 The great desideratum in the arrangement of staging of any kind, as far as the plants themselves are concerned, is to bring them as close to the light as possible. **1929** *Radio Times* 8 Nov. 417/2 Chrysanthemums are now displaying..bloom under glass. ..Be careful not to spill water on the floor and staging. **1974** *Country Life* 24 Jan. 150/2 *Tulipa humilis* and crocus ..have been moved to staging in an airy, unheated greenhouse.

3. To Chiefly *Anglo-Indian* add: and *U.S.* (Earlier and further examples.) Now *rare*.

1840 *Southern Lit. Messenger* VI. 381/2 He does not follow the sea nor staging. **1864** *Harper's Mag.* Oct. 563/1 In an ancient adobe building,..Mr. Banning carried on his staging and teaming operations. **1894** *Outing* XXIV. 399/2 Stagin' in them days, stranger, was *stagin'*.

4. *Astronautics.* The arrangement of stages (*STAGE *sb.* II* b) in a rocket; the separation and falling away of a stage from the remainder of the rocket when its propellant is spent.

1959 H. S. SEIFERT *Space Technol.* xix. 19 In the staging operation the uncoupling of the two sections must take place smoothly so as not to put asymmetric loads on the continuing part of the structure. **1962** D. SLAYTON in J. Glenn et al. *Into Orbit* 26 About thirty seconds after staging..the Atlas goes over into about a 14° pitch to get you headed into the precise angle for a good orbit. **1966** H. O. RUPPE *Introd. Astronaut.* I. iii. 88 In conventional 'tandem staging' or 'series staging' each complete stage burns and separates before the next stage ignites. In parallel staging, components (engines, tanks, or stages) operate simultaneously.

5. Used *attrib.* to designate a stopping-place or assembly-point at a place intermediate between a base and a destination, as *staging-area, -point, -post.* orig. and chiefly *Mil.*

1945 *Amer. Speech* XX. 259 Other terms are used metaphorically: some which are particularly adaptable are..*ration allowance, staging area.* **1971** *Fremdsprachen* XV. 45 The states in the U.S. Coastal Zone contain most of the nation's population and industry, the gateway for maritime trade of about $40 billion, the staging area for the $500 million fish and crustacean industry. **1976** *New Yorker* 24 May 29/1 Almost all the American athletes will be 'processed' at a staging area on the premises of the State University College at Plattsburgh. **1955** *Times* 25 Aug. 9/2 Egypt is the vital staging point in air routes for the reinforcing of the Far East. **1969** H. HORWOOD *Newfoundland* i. 2 The point that I had reached had once been a meeting place for Indian bands, a summer staging-point. **1952** *Times* 21 Aug. 5/6 The American base in England is one of a number of strategic strongholds developed by the S.S.A.F. since the war. There are air bases, staging posts, and other installations in widely scattered places all over the world. **1959** *Listener* 1 Jan. 8/1 Explorers have met and drunk tea at the South Pole, as if it were just any other staging post. **1970** H. TREVELYAN *Middle East in Revolution* 154 All that was left at the revolution was an R.A.F. staging post and technicians helping to train the Iraqi Forces.

‖ **stagione** (stadʒ¹ō·nĕ). *Opera* and *Ballet.* [It., lit. 'season'.] (See quot. 1978.) Freq. *attrib.* Also in *Comb.*, as ‖ **stagione lirica** [lit. 'lyrical season'], the opera season of an Italian theatre.

1946 E. BLOM *Everyman's Dict. Music, Stagione,*..the term is used esp. for an opera season. **1963** *Times* 19 Feb. 15/3 Como's Teatro Sociale..has opened its *stagione lirica* for 1963 with a work by Verdi. *Ibid.* 20 Feb. 16/7 The *stagione* and *abonnement* system (necessitating unvaried programmes on a subscription throughout the season), while working well for opera, is hard on the ballet. **1970** *Daily Tel.* 12 Oct. 11/5 He..examined the problems of opera in English and the 'stagione' versus repertory systems. **1978** LD. DROGHEDA *Double Harness* xxi. 289 The repertory system meant running a large number of different operas on consecutive nights, whereas *stagione* (literally 'season' in Italian) meant grouping a series of performances of one opera fairly closely together, performed with basically identical casts and conductor.

stagnant, *a.* Add: **2. a.** Also of (the ice of) a glacier or ice sheet.

1902 *Geol. Survey New Jersey* V. iii. 86 Such isolated bodies of ice doubtless preserved their motion..for a time. But when they became small, or when the local topography was unfavorable to motion, they became stagnant, and all the drift they held was let down on the surface as the ice melted. **1949** *Amer. Jrnl. Sci.* CCXLVII. 291 The lower 9 miles of this glacier are stagnant, but the upper part and most of the tributary ice streams are active; some receding and some advancing. **1973** R. J. PRICE *Glacial & Fluvioglacial Landforms* viii. 206 Examples of downwasting, stagnant valley glaciers are known to have existed in the Scandinavian mountains.. during the last of the Pleistocene glaciations.

stagnate, *v.* Add: **1. a.** Also of (the ice of) a glacier or ice sheet.

1924 *Bull. N.Y. State Mus.* No. 251. 159 If any general cause were to operate to deprive the whole glacier of a part of its pressure head, this part would be more likely to respond by stagnating. **1968** R. W. FAIRBRIDGE *Encycl. Geomorphol.* 1045/1 A variety of landforms have been interpreted as evidence that ice stagnated and melted over large areas during its retreat from various parts of Europe and North America.

stagnation. Add: **1. a.** Also of ice.

1929 *Geogr. Rev.* XIX. 256 (*heading*) The stagnation and dissipation of the last ice sheet. **1943** *Amer. Jrnl. Sci.* CCXLI. 97 When the ice finally disappeared, the gravel blanket..would be let down to form kames and hummocky gravel deposits such as have commonly been taken as indicators of general ice stagnation. **1973** R. J. PRICE *Glacial & Fluvioglacial Landforms* viii. 207 When stagnation of a valley glacier occurs, glacial erosion ceases.

2. Also *spec.* in *Econ.*, an absence or low rate of growth.

1938 A. H. HANSEN *Full Recovery or Stagnation* xx. 319 It ought to appear incongruous..to follow a chapter on secular stagnation with one on inflation. *Ibid.*, Paradoxical though it be, the more we sink into deep stagnation with vast unemployment of labor and resources, the more imminent is the danger of inflation. **1965** J. L. HANSON *Dict. Econ. & Commerce* 362/2 *Stagnation thesis*, the belief that in advanced economies saving might be so great as to make the maintenance of full employment difficult. **1972** *Oxf. Univ. Gaz.* CII. Suppl. No. 7 p. 4 Whereas the adoption of the I.M.F. prescriptions had apparently led to stagnation in Argentina. **1974** M. B. BROWN *Economics of Imperialism* ix. 224 Concentration..would be discouraged in periods of rapid economic growth and encouraged during stagnation or slump.

3. *Comb.* **stagnation point** *Aeronaut.*, a point on the leading edge of a moving aerofoil at which the air is at rest relative to the aerofoil.

1926 H. GLAUERT *Elements Aerofoil & Airscrew Theory* ii. 14 Consider first the pressure which occurs at a stagnation point, where the fluid is brought to rest at the nose of the body. **1955** *Sci. Amer.* Oct. 126/3 At what is called the 'stagnation' point, just in front of the model, the streamline splits in two, one half flowing around each side of the obstruction. **1979** BERTIN & SMITH *Aerodynamics for Engin.* vii. 269 We see that the temperature of the air at the stagnation point is sufficiently high that we could not use an aluminum structure.

stagnationist (stægnē¹·ʃənist), *a.* and *sb.* Chiefly *Econ.* [f. STAGNATION + -IST.] **A.** *adj.* Characterized by stagnation; promoting stagnation. **B.** *sb.* One who advocates or forecasts stagnation.

1951 A. KOESTLER *Age of Longing* v. 103 After some twenty million factory workers..had sent in resolutions calling for death to the 'stagnationist vermin', Edwards published another book. **1958** *Listener* 10 July 57/2 Mr. Nicholson..joins the ranks of the 'stagnationists'—those who would preserve forms when the functions have decayed. **1964** *Economist* 25 July 332/1 Consumption has moved into a stagnationist stage of the cycle. **1972** HUNT & SHERMAN *Economics* I. vi. 84 Marx..was not a 'stagnationist'—that is, he did not believe capitalism would suffer one long depression or that mass unemployment at high levels would last forever.

‖ **Stahlhelm** (ʃtā·lhelm). [Ger., lit. 'steel helmet'.] The Steel Helmet organization. Also *attrib.* Hence **Sta·hlhelmer,** a member of this organization. See *STEEL HELMET.

1927 *Daily Tel.* 16 Aug. 10/6 The Stahlhelm's boast that it mustered 80,000 members was grossly exaggerated. **1927** *Times* 29 Nov. 15/5 The Stahlhelm organization of ex-soldiers. **1928** *Times* 4 June 13/2 It is the Stahlhelmers' boast that they embody the traditions of the old Army. **1930** [see *MINORITY 3 b]. **1934** *New Republic* 18 July 249/2 The *Stahlhelm*, the Steel Helmets, is a voluntary organization of khaki-uniformed veterans..tending ..to be brought into semi-official relationship with the Nazi party. **1978** W. FEST *Dict. German Hist.* 150 *Stahlhelm*, association of ex-servicemen founded on 29 Dec. 1918... The Stahlhelm was anti-republican and from the late twenties it became militant in its demand for an authoritarian government... In 1934 it was converted into a 'National Socialist front-line fighters' union', but dissensions with the new Nazi members led to its dissolution in 1935.

stain, *sb.* Add: **7. stain painting,** a style of painting in which diluted acrylic paints are applied to unsized canvas; a painting executed in this style; hence **stain painter,** an exponent of this style; **stain-resistance,** resistance to staining; hence **stain-resistant** *a.*

1965 *New Statesman* 30 Apr. 693/2 Some of the hard-edge and stain painters are making matters worse by panicking themselves into the optical movement. **1965** Stain painting [see *hard-edge* s.v. *HARD *a.* (*sb.*) 22]. **1974** *Globe & Mail* (Toronto) 23 Oct. 14/8 Her big canvases.. are stain paintings (staining is a technique using acrylics mixed with water, on unsized canvas). **1959** *Times* 12 Jan. 11/5 For use on wool, cotton, or synthetic fibres to improve oil, grease, and water stain-resistance. **1960** *Farmer & Stockbreeder* Suppl. 12 Jan. 3/3 Casual coat by Salbry is in waterproof, stain-resistant Norzon and has a fleecy wool lining.

stainierite (stē¹·niərəit). *Min.* [ad. Du. *stainierit* (V. Cuvelier 1929, in *Natuurwetensch. Tijdschr.* XI. 177), f. the name of Xavier *Stainier* (b. 1865), Belgian geologist: see -ITE¹.] A hydrous oxide of cobalt which is usu. found as black needles forming microcrystalline crusts on cobalt ores, and is now regarded as the same as heterogenite.

1930 *Mineral. Abstr.* IV. 248 This is regarded as the crystalline equivalent of the colloidal heterogenite, and is named stainierite. **1941** *Ibid.* VIII. 86 X-ray powder photographs of heterogenite, stainierite, mindigite, and trieuite from Katanga..show identical patterns, and these minerals are to be regarded as varieties of the heterogenite group, differing in the relative amounts of Co_2O_3 and CuO. **1962** [see *HETEROGENITE]. **1968** I. KOSTOV *Mineralogy* 228 The last mineral [*sc.* heterogenite] is also known as stainierite.

stainless, *a.* (*sb.*). Add: **A.** *adj.* **2.** Highly resistant to staining or corrosion. See also *STAINLESS STEEL.

1897 *Sears, Roebuck Catal.* 244/1 Ladies' Fast Black Cotton Hose... Fast color and stainless. **1921** *Engineer* 11 Nov. 504/2 Stainless iron may be easily forged by hand into such difficult objects as spurs. **1932** *Discovery* May 145/1 Low carbon stainless steel, frequently called stainless iron, contains less than 0·12 per cent of carbon and from 11 to 12 per cent of chromium. **1945** *ABC of Cookery* (Ministry of Food) i. 8 Any cutlery which is not stainless should be kept well polished. **1960** *Good Housek. Cookery Bk.* (rev. ed.) 574/1 A sharp-pointed, stainless vegetable knife. **1979** T. MOTOGOSHI in M. Nurse *Stainless Steel* 19/1 The use of stainless tubes has been boosted by the increase in the erection of high rise buildings.

B. *ellipt.* for *STAINLESS STEEL; articles made of this.

1971 G. V. HIGGINS *Friends of Eddie Coyle* (1972) x. 64, I don't care whether it's the stainless or not... I got to have the stuff. **1975** *New Yorker* 26 May 111 (Advt.), Galax, a unique combination of solid brass and 18-8 stainless, is light-years ahead in function and design. **1977** C. McFADDEN *Serial* (1978) i. 8/2 They spent it rapidly on ..Dansk stainless and Rosenthal china.

stainless steel. [f. STAINLESS *a.* + STEEL *sb.*¹] **1.** A chromium-steel alloy, usu. containing about 14 per cent of chromium when used for cutlery, etc., that does not rust or tarnish under oxidizing conditions because of the formation of a film of oxide on its surface. Freq. *attrib.*

1917 *Sci. Amer.* 31 Mar. 329/3 A steel that does not stain or tarnish is one of the latest new materials... It is called 'stainless steel'. **1920** *Glasgow Herald* 4 Aug. 9 Since the Armistice there has been an enormous sale of stainless steel for cutlery purposes. **1926** J. H. G. MONYPENNY *Stainless Iron & Steel* i. 6 Stainless steel was first introduced to the public in 1914 in the form of table cutlery. *Ibid.* 13 The discovery of the non-corrosive properties of stainless steel by Brearley, in 1913, was something entirely new in the history of chromium steels. **1932** *Discovery* May 145/1 There are three principal types of stainless steel. Low carbon stainless steel, frequently called stainless iron, contains less than 0·12 per cent of carbon and from 11 to 12 per cent of chromium... Cutlery steel, so called because it was first used for knives, contains 0·3 per cent of carbon and from 12 to 15 per cent of chromium... Austenitic stainless steel has the highest resistance of all to corrosion and is the most generally useful of the stainless steels. **1958** *Times Rev. Industry* Apr. 73/1 There were..many worthy examples of..the application of newer materials, especially stainless steel and aluminium, to domestic requirements. **1979** V. S. NAIPAUL *Bend in River* v. 83 The stainless steel jug..had only a stale-looking trickle of powdered milk.

2. *fig.* or in fig. context: chiefly used *attrib.* with allusion to the qualities of brightness, hardness, coldness, etc., associated with stainless steel.

1963 *Times* 10 June 6/5 Miss Astrid Varney's Isolde has the hallmark of true greatness upon it, but sometimes the voice takes on a stainless steel quality that would be more suited to the role of Ortrud. **1964** G. LYALL *Most Dangerous Game* xxiii. 192, I was..searching for the stainless-steel glint of a river to fix my position. **1974** *Publishers Weekly* 25 Mar. 6/2 She is..married to Sir Alfred Ayer, the celebrated English philosopher, whom she describes affectionately as 'the man with the stainless steel mind'. **1978** R. DOLINER *On the Edge* (1979) ix. 142 His ego was gleaming hard, made of stainless steel.

stair, *sb.* Add: **1. d.** (Later examples.)

1928 T. S. ELIOT *Song for Simeon* 2 They shall praise Thee and suffer in every generation..Light upon light, mounting the saints' stair. **1930** R. CAMPBELL *Poems* 4 All the gifts my faith has brought Along the secret stair of thought.

5. a. *stair-carpet* (earlier example).

1817 M. HOLYOKE in G. F. Dow *Holyoke Diaries* (1911) 167 Began to mend Stair carpet.

b. stair dancer *slang*, a thief who steals from open buildings; cf. *DANCER 6; **stairlift,** a device that can be built into a domestic staircase for the conveyance of disabled or infirm people up and down stairs; **stair-rod** (earlier example); also (in *pl.*) a proverbial comparison for heavy rainfall), **stair-step** *sb.* (earlier and later examples); also *fig.* and as *adj.*, resembling a stair-step; **stair-step** *v.*: also *intr.*, to resemble stair-steps; hence **stair-stepper, stairstepping** *ppl. a.*; **stair-tread** = TREAD *sb.* 11; **stairwell,** the shaft containing a flight of stairs, a well (WELL *sb.*¹ 8 a).

1958 *Times* 10 Feb. 4/5 'Stair dancer' is..the name given by the police to the thief who walks in and out of City offices, looking for something to steal. **1977** 'E. CRISPIN' *Glimpses of Moon* xii. 235 Since he was a stair dancer, a walk-in thief, judges had been inclined to be lenient until the last occasion, when his offence had been said..to have been aggravated by his having broken a window to 'effect an entrance'. **1977** *Hansard Commons* 24 Jan. 472 Stairlift and personal passenger vertical lifts for the disabled. **1980** *BSI News* Aug. 13/1 Stairlifts and homelifts are now extensively used in domestic situations, where they can be an invaluable aid to the disabled or infirm person. **1843** DICKENS *Christmas Carol* iv. 130 The old man raked the fire together with an old stair-rod. **1963** *Times* 22 Apr. 4/6 During the morning the rain came down like stair-rods. During the match it turned to a swirling drizzle. **1977** D. MACKENZIE *Raven & Ratcatcher* i. 14 The rain was falling in stair rods. **1794** N. PARRY *Jrnl.* 26 June in *Kentucky Hist. Soc. Reg.* (1936) XXXIV. 386 Ky. hill on the south shore is exceeding bad, being long, steep, & broken with Limestone, somewhat resembling stair-steps. **1925** C. R. COOPER *Lions 'n' Tigers* iv. 76 This was the district of 'stair-steps', of thin, narrow-shouldered women, trailed by processions of children, five and six in a line. **1944** S. PUTNAM tr. *E. da*

Cunha's Rebellion in Backlands ix. 415 This position.. occupied a broad stairstep on the slope of the hill between Mount Mario..and the Vasa-Barris. **1959** *Wall St. Jrnl.* (Eastern ed.) 12 Aug. 19/2 The 'stairstep' plan in use in Nashville calls for integration classes starting with the first grades and adding one grade each year. **1961** WEBSTER, Stair-step *v. intr.* **1963** *Amer. Speech* XXXVIII. 203 Some of the English terms are literal equivalents of terms used by German-speaking skiers and might be called loan translations:..*stair step*, Treppenschritt. **1976** *Billings* (Montana) *Gaz.* 11 July 1-C/3 Yellow clover which carpets the banks smells sweet, grassy rims stair-step against the distant horizon. **1925** C. R. COOPER *Lions 'n' Tigers* iv. 77 Don't need many ladders aroun' this country... All they have t'do is line up the kids and walk on their heads. Ever see so many stair-steppers? **1972** *Nat. Geographic* Sept. 335 (*caption*) Stairstepping head-waters of the..river cascade out of a..bog. **1919** *Brit. Manufacturer* Nov. 34/1 Sections..such as are utilised for stair-treads, cornices, etc. **1931** DOUGHERTY & KEARNEY *Fire* vii. 99 Stair wells and other shafts extending from the first floor to the roof. **1958** 'W. HENRY' *Seven Men at Mimbres Springs* xiv. 164 Shortly, they heard his step on the stationhouse stairs, then saw his shadow rise out of the stairwell's greater blackness. **1977** B. BAINBRIDGE *Injury Time* xiii. 109 Lights burned on the stairwells of the flats and along the deserted balconies.

staircase. Add: **1. a.** *spec.*, at Oxford and Cambridge, a college staircase and the rooms accessible from it; in *transf.* use, the people living in those rooms. *moving staircase*: see *MOVING *ppl. a.* 3.

1762 [in Dict.]. **1861** T. HUGHES *Tom Brown at Oxford* I. i. 13 The rest is divided into staircases, on each of which are six or eight sets of rooms. **1914** C. MACKENZIE *Sinister St.* II. III. x. 699 'Alan, who are these mysterious creatures that come down for cocoa at ten?'.. 'They'd bore you rather... They're people who live on this staircase. I don't see them any other time.' **1974** J. I. M. STEWART *Gaudy* ii. 26 The corridor is not an Oxford institution. One lives on a staircase: commonly one set of rooms on either hand, storey by storey, from ground floor to attics. A hospitable man will give a party for the whole staircase. **1977** K. BENTON *Red Hen Conspiracy* xvi. 130 He was one of my pupils... Leader of a very rowdy staircase.

d. *spirit* (also *bravery*) *of the staircase*, phrases rendering Fr. *esprit de l'escalier* (see *ESPRIT 2 c). See also sense 4 below.

a **1906** J. MORLEY in H. W. & F. G. Fowler *King's English* (1906) i. 32, I thought afterwards, but it was *the spirit of the staircase*, what a pity it was that I did not stand at the door with a hat, saying, 'Give an obol to Belisarius.' **1906** [see *ESPRIT 2 c]. **1976** L. HELLMAN *Scoundrel Time* 110 Ah, the bravery you tell yourself was possible when it's all over, the bravery of the staircase.

e. *Electronics.* A voltage that alters in equal steps to a maximum or minimum value.

1956 *Electronics* Feb. 192/2 A..staircase generator which generates a negative-going staircase is shown in Fig. 1. **1959** *Ibid.* 23 Jan. 36/3 Each pulse in the train causes one step of the staircase. **1965** *Wireless World* Sept. 425/1 This signal..consists of a 12·5 μs bar, a sine-squared pulse..and a five-step staircase.

4. (sense 1 d) *staircase afterthought, thought, wit*; **staircase generator** *Electronics*, a signal generator whose output is a staircase (sense 1 e above).

1964 *Guardian* 17 Jan. 11/6 The Senator, having written this last passage, decided not to deliver it, a staircase afterthought that will cost him dear. **1956** Staircase generator [see sense *1 e]. **1976** *Pract. Electronics* Oct. 812/2 The output from the staircase generator is then fed into one input of a comparator. **1958** J. LODWICK *Bid Soldiers Shoot* II. vi. 210 'At what time did it start to snow that night, Lodwick?' He was referring..to the night of the parachutage... Staircase thought makes me wish that I had suggested that they have a look at my companion's boots, to which the virginal blanket fallen from Heaven might still..be clinging. **1920** A. DOBSON in *National Rev.* July 654 Staircase-wit. If you fail to understand a joke within twenty-four hours, your symptoms indicate sluggish apprehension... This is what the French call '*L'esprit de l'escalier*'.

stair-foot. b. (Later example.)

1914 D. H. LAWRENCE *Widowing of Mrs. Holroyd* I. ii. 22 At that instant the stairfoot door opens slowly, revealing the children.

stairway. Add: **b.** *spec.* in *Geomorphol.*, a series of abrupt changes of level in the floor of a glaciated valley.

1904 *Jrnl. Geol.* XII. 570 The tread of the steps in the long stairway..greatly lengthened in down-canyon order. **1957** J. K. CHARLESWORTH *Quaternary Era* I. xiii. 297 Cirques in almost all glaciated regions frequently occur in tiers, the 'tandem cirque' or 'cirque stairway'.., each step often with its rock-basin and tarn. **1974** [see *RISER 7 b].

stake, *sb.*[1] Add: **1. e.** *to pull up stakes* (earlier and later examples); also, *to pick up stakes*; *to set stakes* = *to drive stakes*; *to tie* (*someone*) *to the stake*: see TIE *v.* 2 in Dict. and Suppl.

1703 S. SEWALL *Diary* 15 Apr. (1879) II. 76 Went to my Bounds, asserted them,..then ordered Kibbe to pull up the Stakes. Told Mr. Lynde's Tenants what my Bounds were..; forwarn'd them of coming there to set any Stakes. **1817** J. K. PAULDING *Lett. from South* I. 83 When they have exhausted one hunting-ground, [the Indians] pull up stakes, and incontinently march off to another. **1924** 'R. DALY' *Outpost* xvii. 165 I've sometimes thought of pulling up stakes and pushing further into the mountains. **1949** *Boston Globe* 15 May (Fiction Mag.) 6/2 We'll set our stakes, an' I'll slip down to Dawson an' record the claim. **1974** M. ALLEN *Super Tour* (1975) i. 23 'I'm assuming you're in a position to pick up stakes in a hurry.' 'As long as it will take to pack two bags.' **1980** *Dallas Times Herald* 10 May (Week End Suppl.) 6/1 The economic incentive that Europeans once had to pull up stakes and move to America.

2. c. *stake and rider* (later *attrib.* examples); *stake and ridered* adj. (earlier example).

1846 *Knickerbocker* XXVII. 208 Already the 'stake and ridered' fence was beginning to enclose the cleared land. **1884** G. W. CABLE *Dr. Sevier* II. liv. 175 Again they followed him along a line of stake-and-rider fence. **1950** *Pennsylvania Dutchman* Jan. 3/3 He could do nothing better than to quickly place his gun behind him in a corner of a stake-and-rider fence.

5. c. Also *ellipt.* for *stake-body truck* (sense 7 below). *N. Amer. colloq.*

1968 *Globe & Mail* (Toronto) 17 Feb. 50/3 (Advt.), Immediate delivery on new pick-ups, panels, vans and stakes. *Ibid.*, Ford 2½ ton stake with covered compartment for carrying personnel. **1978** *Detroit Free Press* 16 Apr. F13/7 (Advt.), 1978 Chevy truck sale. Pickups. Elcaminos. Stakes. Stepvans.

d. (Examples.)

1903, 1910 [see *LEAGUE *sb.*[2] 3*]. **1959** D. WRIGHT *Baskets & Basketry* vi. 136 *Stakes*, rods driven in with the bottom sticks to form the foundation of the sides of a basket. **1964** H. HODGES *Artifacts* x. 146 Most baskets were made by first weaving a base, although solid wooden bases drilled to take the uprights, or stakes, were occasionally used.

6. (Further examples.) Also *Stake* (*in* or *of*) *Zion.*

1843 H. CASWALL *Prophet of 19th Cent.* 90 Other 'churches' established by 'revelations' given to Smith, are called 'Stakes of Zion', or simply 'Stakes'. **1857** *Southern Illinoisian* (Shawneetown) 1 May 1/3 Throughout the States and Territories, at various and convenient locations, the Mormons have what are termed 'stakes in Zion', and each stake is governed by a Presidency. **1870** J. H. BEADLE *Life in Utah* 124 All the wealthy members were to follow him to western Pennsylvania, and establish a new 'stake' for the others to gather to! **1905** *Out West* Sept. 246 The Stakes of Zion, I will explain, are those gathering places of the Saints that are outside of Zion proper—Jackson county, Missouri, where the holy city it is believed will yet be built. **1961** *Guardian* 23 Jan. 2/3 The share of the Manchester 'stake' (stake is roughly the Mormon for diocese) is £2 million. **1976** *Times* 18 June (Spec. Rep. Mormons) p. iii/7 A stake is administered by local lay members.

7. *stake-fence, -hole*; (sense 6) *stake centre, house, president*; **stake-boat** (earlier and later examples); also, a fixed boat to which other boats may be moored; **stake-body** *U.S.*, a body for a lorry, etc., which has an open, flat platform fitted with removable stakes (sense 5 c in Dict.) along the sides in order to retain the load; also *attrib.* in *stake-body truck*, a lorry fitted with such a body; **stake-net** (later examples); **stake-truck** = *stake-body truck* above.

1839 *Spirit of Times* 13 July 217/2 After a smart pull for it, she [*sc.* a boat] overhauled them one by one, passing the Washington about half way to the stake-boat. **1902** *Federal Reports* CXIII. 926 The tug left the tow in order to engage in other work, picking up light boats, and towing them down to a stake boat off Liberty Island. **1943** A. GIBBS *U-Boat Prisoner* 121 We went over to Jersey and took a motorboat to what he called a stake boat, where we found the barge. **1907** *Cycle & Auto. Trade Jrnl.* 1 Feb. 390 (*caption*) Studebaker 3½ ton paying load truck with stake body. **1913** *Hub* July 123 (*caption*) Universal Chain Drive Stake Body Truck. **1976** *Washington Post* 19 Apr. D3/5 (Advt.), Discount center for stake bodies, step vans, medium duty trucks, [etc.]. **1978** J. GORES *Gone, no Forwarding* (1979) 4 He..opened the door of his stake-body truck. **1976** *Times* 18 June (Spec. Rep. Mormons) p. iii/7 Twenty stakes are now functioning, most of them headquartered in new stake centre church buildings. **1882** W. D. HAY *Brighter Britain!* I. vii. 190 A stake-fence ought to be proof against both pigs and cattle. **1913** J. MASEFIELD *Daffodil Fields* 46 Beside the stake-fence Lion stopped. **1977** Stake-hole [see *POST-HOLE 1]. **1930** L. FOSTER *Larry* 131 Then we all paraded down to the Stake House (Mormon Districts are called 'Stakes'), where there was a pioneer's meeting. **1936** *Sun* (Baltimore) 17 Feb. 7/1 A number of Rock Hall fishermen walked from their homes over the ice in the Chesapeake Bay to their stake nets near Tolchester Beach the past week, cut out their nets, and landed three hundred pounds of rock fish. **1973** W. ELMER *Terminol. Fishing* ii. 73 The stake net is a fixed net now only found on the south-west coast of Scotland. **1947** G. S. PERRY *Cities of Amer.* iii. 39 Each stake president will parcel out the acreages he has agreed to accept among his bishops, and each bishop will divide his commitment among the Saints in his ward. **1907** *Cycle & Auto. Trade Jrnl.* 1 Jan. 346a (*caption*) Five-ton Imperial Stake Truck. **1975** C. WESTON *Susannah Screaming* xxvi. 137 An old stake truck passed him, the back jammed with long-haired college-age kids.

stake, *sb.*[2] Add: **1. c.** Hence *spec.*, a shareholding (*in* a company).

1955 *Times* 4 Aug. 12/1 Pilkington Brothers, famous the world over for plate and other kinds of glass, is proposing to increase its stake in another hardly less famous glass business. **1969** *Listener* 31 July 137/2 If the local paper has a stake in a local commercial station, this would tend to perpetuate the monopoly in local news and comment which has existed for too long in many provincial cities. **1981** *Times* 6 May 24/7 (*heading*) Trafalgar House buys 14.9 pc stake in French Kier.

3. b. *colloq.* Used *fig.* with defining words to denote a particular business or way of life in which success is attained through competition.

c **1885** A. W. PINERO *Magistrate* (1892) I. 24 You nominated yourself for the Matrimonial Stakes. Mr. Farringdon's The Widow, by Bereavement, out of Mourning, ten pounds extra. **1885** *Sat. Rev.* 7 Feb. 181/2 The hothouse kind of life..enabled this nervous, delicate, and curiously constituted competitor to win the Novel Stakes time after time. **1901** G. B. SHAW *Admirable Bashville* II. i. 309 Yet so threadbare as to accept these consolation stakes. **1926** GALSWORTHY *Silver Spoon* II. v. 145 He was not going to enter for the slander stakes. **1936** J. CURTIS *Gilt Kid* iii. 34 Both the men looked as if they might be on the Jo Roncing [i.e. poncing] stakes. **1969** *Listener* 3 Apr. 470/1 No music is more recuperative than Mozart's and, in the therapy stakes, none runs it as close as Webern's. **1977** *Spare Rib* May 37/1 Energy and money were spent outdoing other girls in the beauty stakes.

4. (Earlier and later examples.) Also *N. Amer.*, a grub-stake; a sum of money earned or saved; a store of provisions or sum of money necessary for survival during a certain period.

1738 W. BYRD *Hist. Dividing Line* (1901) 178 [We] recommended to the men to manage this, their last stake, to best advantage. **1853** 'P. PAXTON' *Yankee in Texas* 204 The horse is his last resource... When lost, the quondam owner is said to be flat broke or flat footed, and must beg, borrow, or steal, for a stake. **1873** J. H. BEADLE *Undeveloped West* 510 It is a splendid country to travel through; a miserable poor one to stop in to make a 'stake'. **1899** 'J. FLYNT' *Tramping* I. i. 20 It is usually immaterial to him what happens to society as such so long as he [*sc.* a thief] can make a 'stake'. **1931** 'D. STIFF' *Milk & Honey Route* xi. 117 A hobo may go to town with a stake and blow it in during two or three nights of slapping it up. **1946** E. O'NEILL *Iceman Cometh* I. 53 I'll make my stake and get my new gamblin' house open before you boys leave. **1966** *Islander* (Victoria, B.C.) 21 Aug. 5/1 They [*sc.* loggers] seldom worked more than a few months in one place, just long enough to gather a stake, which they spent in a few days in town. **1978** J. UPDIKE *Coup* (1979) vii. 279, I worked in that oil town in the Rift..and when I had a little stake I hitched back to Istiqlal.

5. *stake-race*; **stake-man** *U.S. slang*, a hobo, a tramp.

1899 'J. FLYNT' *Tramping* II. v. 310 He learns to travel merely for travel's sake, and develops into a 'stake-man', who only works long enough to get a 'stake' and then go off on a trip again. **1901** [see *BINDLE[2] a]. **1896** H. M. BLOSSOM *Checkers* ii. 20 Y' see, take a big stake-race like this, where every horse is a 'cracker-jack',..and they've all got a chance. **1968** *Globe & Mail* (Toronto) 17 Feb. 1/5 Deep in the bush you can have just about all the comforts of home as the great uranium stake race enters its final two days.

stake, *v.*[1] Add: **1. a.** Also *N. Amer.*, to claim (land) by marking it with stakes; also *absol.*

1908 M. A. GRAINGER *Woodsmen of West* 78 Now Billy Hewlitt was a 'timber-cruiser'—a man who sought for forest timber, to stake it. **1916** *Yukon Territory* (Canada Dept. Interior) 12 In a short time Bonanza was staked from end to end. **1945** *Clarke County Democrat* (Grove Hill, Alabama) 24 May 1/6 The California Oil Company.. has staked a location for the drilling of a test well. **1959** M. SHAND *Summit & Beyond* vii. 113 There was a report of a [gold] strike up White River. The men were talking of going to 'stake'. **1968** *Globe & Mail* (Toronto) 17 Feb. 1/7 It is land that was staked before in the madness of 1954, when it became known that one of the world's greatest concentrations of uranium ores had been uncovered.

c. Phr. *to stake* (*out*, † *off*) *a claim*, to make or register a claim (to land) by marking it with stakes; freq. *fig.* orig. *U.S.*

1851 *State Jrnl.* (San Jose, Calif.) 15 Mar. 2/1 It was estimated that ten thousand people were on the ground staking off 'claims'. **1876** [in Dict., sense 1 b]. **1904** J. LONDON *Daughter of Snows* xiii. 140 You staked that claim before he was dry behind the ears. **1928** H. CRANE *Let.* 17 Apr. (1965) 324 Skepticism may stop there.., but I am not exactly satisfied by that... I still stake some claims on the pertinence of the intuitions. **1939** WODEHOUSE *Uncle Fred in Springtime* xiv. 199 Up till now, he had regarded Lord Emsworth as the most promising claim that any prospector for ore could hope to stake out. **1949** *Nat. Hist.* Apr. 189/3 Sometimes when the bee hunter finds a nest that has not yet reached its peak of honey production, he will 'stake his claim' by marking the tree so that other hunters will know of his prior discovery.

8. *colloq.* (orig. *U.S.*). **a.** Usu. with adv. *out.* To maintain surveillance of (a place, etc.) in order to detect criminal activity or apprehend a suspect. Cf. *STAKE-OUT.

1942 BERREY & VAN DEN BARK *Amer. Thes. Slang* § 499/4 *Stake out*,..to surround a criminal retreat to spy upon or prevent escape. **1943** R. CHANDLER *Lady in Lake* (1944) xxix. 157 They had the house staked. **1962** L. DEIGHTON *Ipcress File* 221 When..the French police staked out the courier routes, they found..50,000 dollars of forged signed travellers' cheques. **1967** M. PROCTER *Exercise Hoodwink* xiii. 91 The house was 'staked out.'.. A man called Whipper Slade emerged. 'Coo, he's a real deadleg,' said a detective who recognised him. **1974** *Black World* June 28/1 Places that are so staked out with doormen and electronic gadgets that only god can enter the lobby. **1981** *Daily Tel.* 6 July 2/2 Police were tipped off that trouble might occur with skinheads at nearby Greenford. They staked out a likely disco there.

b. *to be staked out*: to be set, or to set oneself, to maintain surveillance of a place.

1951 M. Spillane *Big Kill* vi. 122 He's been a cop a long time. He's been staked out often enough to spot it when he's being watched himself. **1974** J. A. Michener *Centennial* iv. 162 The Pawnee reacted as had been expected, with a countercharge of their own, and their leaders had covered only a short distance when they spotted Lame Beaver staked out, his rifle at the ready. **1979** H. Kissinger *White House Years* xix. 756 David Bruce..came to the Embassy through the front door where the press was staked out.

stake, *v.*[3] Add: **5.** *colloq.* (orig. *U.S.*). To furnish with money or supplies, etc.; to grub-stake. Also with compl. introduced by *with* or *to* indicating the commodity, etc., supplied.

1853 'P. Paxton' *Stray Yankee in Texas* 219 The jo-fired mean whelp wouldn't stake me. **1894** 'Mark Twain' *Pudd'n-head Wilson* iv. 58 Tom staked him with marbles to play 'keeps' with. **1917** G. B. McCutcheon *Green Fancy* 25 He staked her to a ticket to New York. **1934** R. Graves *I, Claudius* xxiii. 333 He gave me a purse of money and muttered in my ear: 'Tell nobody that I'm staking you, but put this on Scarlet.' **1942** Z. N. Hurston in *Amer. Mercury* LV. 88 If Jelly really had had some money, he might have staked him..to a hot. Good Southern cornbread with a piano on a platter. **1969** *Coast to Coast 1967–68* 138 They would stake him, buy his grub, supply him with horses and packs, pay him a hundred pounds for her scalp. **1978** M. Puzo *Fools Die* ii. 38 He felt their happiness for him, and to repay it he said, 'Now let me stake you guys, you too, Diane. Twenty grand apiece.'

staked, *ppl. a.* Add: *staked and ridered* = *stake-and-ridered* adj. s.v. Stake *sb.*[1] 2 c.

1901 W. N. Harben *Westerfelt* xx. 271 The scarecrow in the cornfield beyond the staked-and-ridered rail fence looked like the corpse of a human being flattened against the yellow sky. **1852**, etc. [see *ridered *a.* 2].

stakement (stēɪ·kmĕnt). *Hist.* [f. Stake *v.*[1] + -ment.] The entitlement of tenants whose rents are in arrears to have their eviction delayed.

1904 M. Bateson *Borough Customs* I. ii. 297 The 'stakement' appears to be the equivalent of the Germanic 'wiffatio'. **1927** J. S. Furley *Ancient Usages City of Winchester* 22 The *Usages* closes with an account of 'stakement'. When a tenant was in arrears with his rent the landlord could take no steps till after year and day. *Ibid.*, Stakement is symbolic... At Exeter the custom was to carry away a stone..but the stake was used at Reading, at Fordwich, and the other Cinque Ports. **1927** *Contemp. Rev.* Aug. 261 The procedure of 'Stakement', a court process that delayed adverse possession, is very early and full of interest. **1935** K. M. E. Murray *Constitutional Hist. Cinque Ports* ii. 16 Such is the practice of 'stakement' for rent arrears.

sta·ke-out. *colloq.* (orig. *U.S.*). Also as one word. [f. vbl. phr. *to stake out*: see *stake *v.*[1] 8.] An act or period of surveillance of a place by police or investigative agents. Also *transf.* and *attrib.*

1942 Berrey & Van den Bark *Amer. Thes. Slang* § 499/2 *Stake-out*, a surrounding of a criminal retreat to spy upon or prevent the escape of criminals. **1943** R. Chandler *Lady in Lake* (1944) xl. 208 Somebody stood behind that green curtain..as silently as only a cop on a stake-out knows how to stand. **1955** *Sun* (Baltimore) (B ed.) 11 Jan. 26/8 Bergen was arrested..by..rookie policemen who were part of an extensive stakeout in the area which had been set up to trap the person or persons responsible for the large number of burglaries. **1960** *Washington Post* 15 Jan. A12 The success of the police in these instances has been largely due to the 'stake-out' system. **1966** J. Gardner *Amber Nine* viii. 95 He had enjoyed that time as stake-out man at London Central: lurking, watching (and watching for) people. **1972** *New Yorker* 16 Jan. 27/1 A group of agents..who were conducting a stakeout of a house in suburban Wilmette. **1979** *Daily Tel.* 19 Sept 36/5 Father Frederick Linale.. said police asked him last week if they could use the mission on a 'stake out'. **1983** *Times* 29 Jan. 6/8 President Reagan's impromptu visit to a Boston Irish pub for a quick beer broke up a stake-out by armed FBI agents.

staker[1]. Add: **c.** *Canad.* One who stakes a (mining) claim.

1898 *Yukon Midnight Sun* (Dawson, Yukon Territory) 15 Aug. 1/3 He also said that until after September 1st no one but the original staker has any business upon these claims. **1921** *Daily Colonist* (Victoria, B.C.) 13 Oct. 2/4 The original stakers are reported to be taking out $35 a day in coarse gold, some very large nuggets being found. **1954** *North Star* (Yellowknife, N.W. Territory) Aug. 2/1 Though a few stakers were 'made', it was generally the brokers and speculators who skimmed off the cream.

staker[2]. (Later examples.)

1975 J. Symons *Three Pipe Problem* vii. 45 Willie was a great staker of his reputation. **1976** *Sunday Times* (Lagos) 7 Nov. 21/3 (Advt.), Pools Magnet have won over ten million Naira for Stakers all over the world.

stakey (stēɪ·ki), *a.* *slang* (chiefly *Canad.*). Also **staky.** [f. Stake *sb.*[2] + -y[1].] Well provided with money; 'flush'.

1919 *Camp Worker* (Vancouver) 28 June 7/1 If they hold a job for a month they have done something out of the ordinary, and as a consequence, they are never very staky, and the question of funds comes first in most cases. **1927** *Amer. Speech* II. 392/1 When a *staky* worker comes to town, his giving money to his impecunious acquaintances is called the *pay-off*. **1960** *Weekend Mag.* (Montreal) 8 Oct. 28/1, I wasn't going to go in, because at the time I wasn't stakey. **1970** P. St. Pierre *Chilcotin Holiday* 31 On being assured that the prisoner was stakey, the mayor imposed a ten-dollar fine. **1973** B. Broadfoot *Ten Lost Years* xv. 172 Why, we was making 15 cents a glass... Both of us were getting stakey as hell.

Stakhanovite (stăkā·novəit), *sb.* and *a.* [f. the name of the Soviet coal-miner Alekséĭ Grigór'evich *Stakhánov* (1906–77) + -ite[1]; cf. Russ. *stakhánovets* sb., *stakhánovskiĭ* adj.

The Soviet authorities publicized the prodigious output achieved by Stakhanov in 1935 as part of a campaign to increase industrial output.]

A. *sb.* In the U.S.S.R. during the 1930s and 1940s, a worker whose productivity exceeded the norms and who thus earned special privileges and rewards; *transf.*, one who is exceptionally hard-working and productive. **B.** *adj.* Designating, pertaining to, or characteristic of such a worker or such workers collectively.

1935 *Time* 16 Dec. 25/3 In the coal mine at Stalino two assistant foremen, a checkweighter and an electrician were arrested for the murder of a fast-working Stakhanovite. **1936** W. Citrine *I search for Truth in Russia* 349 In the best building works the Stakhanovite builders have shown examples of high productivity of labour in brick-laying, beton work, plastering and excavating work. **1938** *Times Lit. Suppl.* 8 Jan. 18/4 The *udarnik* (or Stakhanovite, as he now is called) was 'curiously like the pep-it-up-team-work-factory-spirit fellows I knew at home, and equally detested by his clock-watching fellow-workers'. **1949** [see *shock *sb.*[3] 7 b]. **1952** [see *norm c]. **1959** *Times* 29 May 8/5 This conferring with East Anglian trade union leaders and stakhanovites of his party..has probably been the most useful thing to come out of his [*sc.* Hugh Gaitskell's] tour. **1961** C. T. Hsia *Hist. Mod. Chinese Fiction* xviii. 495 The application of Stakhanovite methods to literary production could only mean further deterioration in quality. **1977** *Time* 1 Aug. 5/3 Though U.S. workers have been regularly chided at home for goofing off on the job, they are veritable Stakhanovites compared with some of their European counterparts.

Hence **Stakha·novism**, a movement in the U.S.S.R. aimed at encouraging hard work and maximum output, following the example of Stakhanov; also *transf.*; **Stakha·novist** *a.* and *sb.* = *Stakhanovite *sb.* and *a.*

1936 V. M. Molotov (*title*) What is Stakhanovism? **1937** *Nature* 27 Feb. 364/2 He outlined the development of the principles of scientific management from the pioneer work..to such recent manifestations as 'Stakhanovism' in Russia. **1938** *Downside Rev.* LVI. 370 Before summing up the authors insert a valuable chapter on the Stakhanovist movement in Russia. **1940** *Manch. Guardian Weekly* 16 Feb. 130 News of what in the Soviet Union is called 'Socialist emulation' confirms again and again that certain 'Stakhanovists' accomplish 'norms' (their own normal production) of 260 to 400 per cent of normal. **1949** E. Fitzgerald tr. *Labin's Stalin's Russia* ii. 53 Stakhanovism (with all its serious industrial accidents) was introduced in Novosibirsk. **1954** *Encounter* Feb. 39/2 The tense, driving Stakhanovist atmosphere of Soviet Europe. **1957** *Times Lit. Suppl.* 25 Oct. 641/2 The romantic legend by which democracy lives, on the other hand, venerates Stakhanovism in high places. **1970** G. Greer *Female Eunuch* 123 Many others [*sc.* working wives] pride themselves on the way they manage to run a home and hold their own in a job at the same time, accepting the patronizing title of 'working wonders' in a kind of unofficial Stakhanovism. *Ibid.* 275 Women's literature is full of the trumpeting of female Stakhanovists.

staking, *vbl. sb.* Add: **a.** Also *N. Amer.*, the action of *stake *v.*[1] 1 a.

1952 *North Star* (Yellowknife, N.W. Territory) Nov. 3/2 There, the mineral claims map sheet is completely filled, so far as staking is concerned. **1968** *Globe & Mail* (Toronto) 17 Feb. 1/7 At noon on Monday, 100,000 acres of land beyond the geological formation that gave Elliot Lake 13 uranium mines in the 1950s, will be opened to staking. **1979** *Arizona Daily Star* 5 Aug. (Advt. Section) 4/3 You will be responsible for the acquisition of uranium mineral properties required through staking, bids,..joint ventures and/or purchase.

d. staking rush *Canad.*, a rush (Rush *sb.*[2] 4) to stake (mining) claims.

1953 *North Star* (Yellowknife, N.W. Territory) July 1/1 There are possibilities of an additional poll in the Marion River area, where a staking rush is now under way. **1964** *North* (Ottawa) May–June 14 A miniature 'staking rush' to the Pine Point area took place during the following winter.

staky, var. *stakey *a.*

stalactite. Add: **3.** (Earlier and later examples.)

1851 W. Irving *Alhambra* (rev. ed.) 76 The lofty ceiling was originally of the same favorite material, with the usual frostwork and pensile ornaments or stalactites. **1931** C. Hill *Moorish Towns in Spain* 147 We stand amid a small labyrinth of columns, under a roof of stalactites in stone. **1974** *Encycl. Brit. Micropædia* IX. 517/1 A peculiar type of faceted, crystal-shaped stalactite is found in Turkey; this form became the most common Turkish capital decoration.

4. (Earlier example in sense 3.)

1855 J. Fergusson *Illustr. Handbk. Archit.* I. ix. v. 463 Instead of the simple curves of the dome, the roofs are made up of honeycombed or stalactite patterns, which look more like natural rock-work than the forms of an art.

Stalag (stā·læg, ‖ tā·lag). [a. Ger., abbrev. of *stammlager* main camp.] In Nazi Germany: a prison-camp primarily for captured enemy private soldiers and non-commissioned officers. **Stalag Luft, Stalagluft** (-luft) [G. *luft* air], such a camp for Air Force personnel.

1940 *Times* 30 July 7/3 There are three types of camps for British prisoners known officially as Oflag, Stalag, and Dulag (contractions for Offizierslager, Stammlager, and Durchgangslager). **1941** [see *Ilag]. **1944** V. G. Garvin tr. *Gary's Forest of Anger* xxix. 141 The old man was sent to a Stalag in Poland. **1945** [see *Oflag]. **1947** *News Chron.* 24 Jan. 1/4 Scharpwinkel, who is believed to have ordered the murder of many of the 50 R.A.F., Commonwealth and Allied airmen after their escape from Stalagluft III in March 1944. **1959** W. Faulkner *Mansion* xiii. 295 If it had been a..book instead of a war..they would have escaped. But he..never knew anyone who ever actually escaped from a genuine authentic stalag, so they had to wait for regular routine liberation. **1974** *Times* 18 Oct. 16/6 On at least first sight Long Kesh *looks* like one of the *Stalags*. **1978** R. V. Jones *Most Secret War* xxxi. 265 While in Stalag Luft 3 he not only concealed his knowledge of our new radar devices, but built a radio transmitter.

stalagmometer. Add: (Further examples.) Hence **sta:lagmome·tric** *a.*

1910 *Chem. Abstr.* IV. 1765 (*heading*) The significance of the stalagmometric method. **1920** *Jrnl. Biol. Chem.* XLIV. 378 The amount of lipase in blood serum, determined by..the stalagmometric method. **1940** Glasstone *Text-bk. Physical Chem.* vii. 482 The weight of a definite number of drops is determined, or the number obtained from a given volume of liquid, as it flows between two marks on a stalagmometer, is counted. **1976** *Coll. Czech. Chem. Commun.* XLI. 1845 The dependence between the mass of the detached drop and the rate of its formation was determined by means of three stalagmometers with different sizes of the dripping area and with a different angle of the capillary edge.

stale (stēɪl), *sb.*[7] *colloq.* [Absol. use of Stale *a.*[1]] A stale cake or loaf of bread, etc.

1874 Hardy *Madding Crowd* II. iii. 39, I went to Riggs's batty-cake shop, and asked 'em for a penneth of the cheapest and nicest stales, that were all but blue-mouldy, but not quite. **1937** DeArmond & Graf *Route Sales Managem.* 4 The man who sells and delivers bread to the grocer must remove the stales each day. **1937** 'G. Orwell' *Road to Wigan Pier* i. i. 15 Frayed-looking sweet-cakes..bought as 'stales' from the baker.

stale, *a.*[1] Add: **3. c.** *Comm.* That has remained inactive for a considerable time; (of a cheque) out-of-date.

1889 Barrère & Leland *Dict. Slang* II. 297/2 *Stale bear*,..a man who has sold stock which he does not possess, and has not bought it back. A bear who has been short of stock for a considerable period... *Stale bull*, a man who has held stock for a long period without profit. **1901** C. Duguid *How to read Money Article* viii. 37 The time comes when the 'bull campaign' turns into a 'stale bull account', that is, when the bulls are anxious to sell, even at a loss. **1901** *Business Terms & Phrases* (ed. 2) 199 *Stale cheque*,..a cheque which has remained unpaid for some considerable time. **1930** M. Clark *Home Trade* 271 Stale bulls are those who come to the conclusion that they have waited long enough for a rise in price and who, therefore, sell out. **1939** F. Lee *City Page* iii. 61 Eventually every crossed cheque has to be paid into a banker's account, usually within a time limit of six months; otherwise the cheque is 'stale'. **1957** Clark & Gottfried *Dict. Business & Finance* (1967) 332/2 *Stale*,..in business, out of date, or outstanding for a long time. **1979** F. E. Perry *Dict. Banking* 11/2 A banker receiving a cheque antedated by six months or more for payment would regard it as 'stale'.

6. Also *stale-smelling* adj.; (in sense 3 c above) *stale-dated* adj.

1963 J. N. Harris *Weird World Wes Beattie* (1964) xv. 179 This check came along... It was stale-dated, see? I mean it had been drawn the previous September, and this was about May. **1936** E. Wilson *Travels in Two Democracies* 286 They carried me into a stale-smelling building. **1973** T. Pynchon *Gravity's Rainbow* i. 24 The city around them at once a big desolate ice-box, stale-smelling.

stalely, *adv.* Delete *rare* and add later examples.

1920 [see *class-jealousy* s.v. *class *sb.* 9]. **1938** G. Greene *Brighton Rock* vii. i. 279 She smelt faintly, stalely, of Californian Poppy. **1957** 'M. M. Kaye' *Shadow of Moon* xxi. 326 The drawing-room smelt stalely of cigar smoke.

stalemated, *ppl. a.* Add: Also *fig.*

1952 D. MacArthur *Reminiscences* (1964) x. 409 The terrible blood tribute exacted by this type of stalemated attrition. **1965** *Economist* 9 Jan. 104/1 The United States accepted a stalemated substitute for victory in Korea. **1977** *Time* 31 Jan. 7/3 The Vice President also wants to know just what allied or U.S. initiatives Europeans would welcome to get the stalemated talks..going once again.

Stalin (stā·lin). The name of Joseph *Stalin* (see *Stalinism) used *attrib.* to designate things instituted by him or developed during his leadership of the Soviet Union, as *Stalin Line, Prize, tank* (see quots.); **Stalin organ** *Mil. slang*, a type of Soviet multi-barrelled mobile rocket launcher.

1942 *Foreign Affairs* XX. 317 The Stalin Line, with Kiev as a strong base behind it, runs along the Dniester and then through very easily defensible country in the direction of Zhitomir and Korosten. **1942** *Nature* 25 Apr. 475/1 The following awards of Stalin Prizes for outstanding scientific work in 1941 have been made. **1945** *Times* 1 Jan. 4/1 The Russians are using an entirely new type of tank.. It is the super-heavy Stalin tank and has the biggest tank gun in the world. **1952** *Sun* (Baltimore) 16 May (B* ed.) 9/1 Eastern Germany, under Russian directions, is to help build a vast fortified 'Stalin line' defense belt across Eastern Europe, including V-2 rocket bases and bomber fields. **1954** KOESTLER *Invisible Writing* ii. 29 Those who survived have..become Stalin-prize court jesters. **1955** *Britannica Bk. of Year* 490/1 *Stalin organ*, a device for firing multiple rockets. **1977** *Time* 21 Feb. 21/1 Sakharov..won the Stalin Prize and was thrice awarded the country's highest civilian medal. **1982** *Daily Tel.* 5 Aug. 28/6 There was the characteristic, terrifying noise of 'Stalin organs' being fired—40 rockets going off within 10 seconds.

Stalinesque (stāline·sk), *a.* [f. as prec. + -ESQUE.] Of, pertaining to, or characteristic of Joseph Stalin, his policies, activities, etc.; Stalinist.

1943 L. ADAMIC *My Native Land* 129 When I quoted to him a rumor that he was engaging in Stalinesque hold-ups to procure money for revolutionary purposes, he did not deny it. **1979** *Times* 14 Nov. 12/4 Stalin rebuilt the city [*sc.* Minsk] in Stalinesque style: a grandiose central avenue with a trade union palace.

staling (stē^i·liŋ), *ppl. a. Bot.* [f. STALE *v.*² + -ING².] Of fungal products: diverting or inhibiting fungal growth.

1916 A. H. GRAVES in *Mem. N.Y. Bot. Gard.* VI. 326 The problem was now to obtain..this substance, which we may for convenience call the 'staling substance', free from mycelium. **1948** *Nature* Mar. 422/2 A similar effect is obtained when the metabolism of the latter [*sc.* a wound parasite of a plant] leads to the formation of substances ('staling substances') which by and by inhibit growth; hence the formation of lesions of limited size. **1979** *Experientia* XXXV. 200/2 This may possibly be due to reduction of growth of both interacting colonies caused by diffused staling products.

Stalinism (stā·liniz'm). [f. Joseph *Stalin* (Russ. Ióśif *Stálin*), the assumed name of Iosif Vissariónovich Dzhugashvíli (1879–1953), leader of the Soviet Communist Party and head of state of the Soviet Union + -ISM.] The policies pursued by Stalin, based on but later deviating from Leninism, esp. the formation of a centralized, totalitarian, objectivist government.

1927 *Daily Tel.* 22 Nov. 10/3 A violent denunciation of 'Stalinism' and its 'terrorising of the party'. **1941** KOESTLER *Scum of Earth* 23 We had realised that Stalinism had soiled and compromised the Socialist Utopia. **1947** C. MALAMUTH tr. *L. Trotski's Stalin* 422 On the theoretical plane every bit of 'Stalinism' has issued from the criticism of the theory of permanent revolution as it was formulated in 1905. **1955** *Times* 5 May 15/4 Indirectly the tenets of Stalinism and Trotskyism are being subjected in new tests at the conference tables of international diplomacy. **1958** *Times Lit. Suppl.* 7 Mar. 123/1 The Yugoslav system has relapsed into totalitarianism after a promising breakaway from Stalinism. **1968** *Russian Review* XXVII. 309 A formal definition of Stalinism would run something like this: a *one*-man dictatorship in which a single dictator ruling arbitrarily, uncontrolled by any party organs, is the sole interpreter of the Marxist–Leninist dogma, and is surrounded by the cult of his personality. A revised definition..would be the same as above, but the single personality clause would be replaced by the CC Politburo collective leadership. **1971** I. DEUTSCHER *Marxism in our Time* (1972) 86 In the end the nonviolent meaning of Marxism was suppressed under the massive, crushing weight of Stalinism. **1977** *Time* 21 Mar. 12/2 In a bitter statement, Gui accused the Communists of practicing 'Stalinism', calling himself the victim of the chamber's 'will for my political execution'.

Stalinist (stā·linist), *sb.* and *a.* [f. as prec. + -IST.] **A.** *sb.* A follower or supporter of Stalin or his policies. **B.** *adj.* Of, pertaining to, or characteristic of Stalin, his followers, or his policies.

1928 *Observer* 22 Jan. 14/5 Open calculations measured in advance by the Stalinists. **1930** *Times* 27 Mar. 13/3 The Stalinist group of Communist leaders. **1939** G. GREENE *Lawless Roads* iii. 107 The papers were full of a Stalinist plot. **1941** KOESTLER *Scum of Earth* 113 The sectarian hatred between Stalinists, Trotskists, and Reformists still existed. **1955** *Times* 3 Aug. 9/6 Khrushchev, the reputed Stalinist, goes on a mission to China. **1974** tr. *Wertheim's Evolution & Revolution* i. 70 In Stalinist Marxism ..there was no sign whatever that the Russian way was considered to be a deviation from the usual succession of phases. **1977** *Socialist Press* 2 Mar. 11/4 Their series of Conferences..were 'bureaucratically controlled' as was that called by the Stalinist-led BLMC Combine Committee. **1978** I. B. SINGER *Shosha* xiii. 229 The designation..as Fascist lackeys and agents of Hitler evoked protests even from sworn Stalinists.

Stalinite (stā·linait), *sb.* and *a. rare.* [f. as prec. + -ITE¹.] = *STALINIST *sb.* and *a.*

1927 *Daily Tel.* 6 Dec. 11 The struggle between the Trotskists and the Stalinites. **1938** R. H. S. CROSSMAN in *New Statesman* 7 May 780/2 Unlike the Stalinites, he has learnt nothing from the experience of Fascism, and so can greet it as a positive advance towards the millennium. **1945** KOESTLER *Yogi & Commissar* III. i. 134 The *New Statesman and Nation*'s interpretations of Stalinite policy display all the ingeniousness of the official Apologist. **1973** *Times* 19 Jan. 4/5 (*heading*) 'Almost Stalinite' to deny effective power to local parties.

Stalinize (stā·linaiz), *v.* [f. as prec. + -IZE.] *trans.* To transform, etc., in accordance with Stalin's policies and practices. Hence **Staliniza·tion.**

1949 I. DEUTSCHER *Stalin* 366 Even the spoken language became 'Stalinized' to a fantastic extent. **1954** KOESTLER *Invisible Writing* x. 110 The natives were drawn into the towns, educated, Russified and Stalinised. **1956** *Washington Post* 19 Nov. A21/1 Even today, after the unspeakable horror of the blood bath in Hungary, the betting is still somewhat against a 're-Stalinization'. **1959** *Manch. Guardian* 5 Aug. 10/3 Returning to Hungary ..in 1944 to take part in the 'Stalinisation' of his country. **1971** I. DEUTSCHER *Marxism in our Time* (1972) vi. 124 This was the first dangerous attack on the autonomy of the [Polish] Communist Party, the first act, as it turned out, of 'Stalinization'. **1979** *Dædalus* Winter 135 Mutual contamination or interpenetration between the Communist party (which had not been Stalinized in the first place..) and Italian society. **1981** *Guardian* 16 Feb. 4/5 Mr Gerald Kaufman..said he did not regard 'the Stalinisation of the Labour Party as democracy'.

Stalinoid (stā·linoid), *a.* (and *sb.*). [f. as prec. + -OID.] Resembling or having some characteristics of Stalinism; loosely Stalinist. Also as *sb.*

1941 *Amer. Mercury* Apr. 498/2 Years of careful reading of the Stalinoid literature of hallucination. **1947** *Sun* (Baltimore) 4 Nov. 10/3 Food prices have come down—to the consternation of the Stalinoid cohorts. **1952** *Manch. Guardian Weekly* 16 Oct. 7/3 It is Marxist, hostile to 'Stalinoids and to modern Trotskyites'. **1952** P. SELZNICK *Organizational Weapon* vii. 297 The term 'stalinoid' is usually employed as a rough synonym for 'fellow traveler'. **1961** *Guardian* 26 May 6/5 The Stalinist intellectuals and the Stalinoid 'liberals'. **1977** *Daily Tel.* 12 Oct. 18 The Nobel Peace Prize has gone to some rum customers in its time, including Le Duc Tho, the villainous Stalinoid secretary of the North Vietnam Communist party.

stalk, *sb.*¹ Add: **4. d.** *coarse slang.* A penis, esp. one that is erect.

1597 SHAKES. *Lover's Compl.* (1609) l. 147 My wofull selfe..Threw my affections in his charmed power, Reseru'd the stalke and gaue him al my flower. **1608** —— *Per.* IV. vi. 46 *Bawd.* Heere comes that which growes to the stalke, Neuer pluckt yet I can assure you. Is shee not a faire creature?

[**1939** JOYCE *Finnegans Wake* (1964) ii. 236 Just so stylled with the nattes are their flowerheads now and each of all has a lovestalk onto herself.] **1961** PARTRIDGE *Dict. Slang* Suppl. 1293/2 *Stalk*,..an erection. **1976** A. WHITE *Long Silence* iv. 37, I had a stalk on me long as my arm. A right handful, that one. **1978** J. UPDIKE *Coup* (1979) ii. 79 My stalk verged upon response, upon enlargement and erection. **1979** W. STYRON *Sophie's Choice* ii. 45 She..prepared to take between those lips unkissed by my own the bone-rigid stalk of my passion.

5. e. *colloq.* A lever mounted on the floor or on the steering column of a motor vehicle, which controls the gears or such devices as horn, indicators, lights, windscreen wipers, etc.

1964 *Road & Track* Jan. 22/2 The gears are selected by an odd curved floor stalk which fouls the passenger seat but they go in all right. **1972** *Country Life* 15 June 1577/2 Steering-column stalks look after the windscreen washer and wiper. **1977** *Daily Tel.* 19 Jan. 12/6, I liked the cloth-trimmed seats and the control stalks on the steering column in place of the old rocker switches on the fascia.

10. stalk switch, a switch in the form of a stalk or lever mounted on the steering column of a motor vehicle (see sense 5 e above).

1976 *Evening Post* (Nottingham) 15 Dec. 10/8 Stalk switches, within easy reach of fingers on the wheel, control the lights, wipers, wash and flasher, also horn and direction indicators.

stalking-horse. 2. a. Delete ? *Obs.* and add later examples.

1963 *Times* 12 Jan. 6/2 This meant that the Europeans would regard us as the stalking horse or paid hand of Uncle Sam and would not wish us to participate fully in European affairs. **1977** J. M. HARRISON in Bond & McLeod *Newslett. to Newspapers* III. 208 Zenger was actually a stalking horse for the group of wealthy politicians who owned the *New York Journal*. **1980** *Jewish Chron.* 15 Feb. 1/1 It raises the fear that the Irish may be acting as a stalking horse for the whole European Economic Community.

stall, *sb.*¹ Add: **3. c.** A parking space for a motor vehicle, usu. marked out but not partitioned off. *U.S.*

1940 *College Topics* (Univ. of Virginia) 4 Nov., These stalls will be painted to facilitate parking and a time limit of one hour has been ordered for both sides of the street in this area between 8 a. m. and 6 p. m. **1955** J. H. SCHMITZ in Aldiss & Harrison *Decade the 1950s* (1976) 17 Cord hurriedly flew the skipboat round the station and rolled it back into its stall. **1976** C. WESTON *Rouse Demon* (1977) xxiii. 110 Her car was in its stall in the subterranean garage.

d. One of a series of urinals separated by divisions, in a men's lavatory; also, a compartment in a wash-room. Also *urinal stall, toilet stall.*

1967 *Gloss. Sanitation Terms* (*B.S.I.*) 58 *Stall urinal*, a urinal having a back curved on plan to form a stall for the user... When stall urinals are fixed in ranges, divisions or cloaking pieces are provided between each stall. **1969** C. LOGUE *New Numbers* (1971) 62 Mechanical faucets drench a line of porcelain stalls. **1977** P. D. JAMES *Death of Expert Witness* II. vii. 90 The male washroom, apart from the urinal stalls, differed very little from the women's. **1978** R. LUDLUM *Holcroft Covenant* xxiii. 265 If they let the weapon through, he was to reassemble it immediately, in the toilet stall of a men's room.

5. d. *transf.* pl. Those who occupy the stalls in a theatre.

1901 G. B. SHAW *Three Plays for Puritans* Pref. p. viii, English influence on the theatre, as far as the stalls are concerned, does not exist. **1920** *Daily Mail* 17 Sept. 4/5 'I wonder whether we shall ever get our 'stalls' back,' a West End box-office manager remarked to me; the 'stalls' in the front-of-the-house vernacular signifying a particular class of playgoer. **1927** *Sunday Express* 10 Apr. 5/4 'Why should the stalls stand to oblige the pit?' asked a satellite near me.

12*. [f. *STALL *v.*¹ 9 d, e.] **a.** *Aeronaut.* The condition of an aircraft when the streamline flow over its wings breaks down, usu. owing to a low air speed or a high angle of attack; the sudden loss of lift (and height) associated with this.

1918 J. M. GRIDER *War Birds* (1927) 88 He went straight up three hundred feet and stalled and fell out of the stall right into the middle of the field. **1927** *Glasgow Herald* 31 Aug. 10 There is only one issue to the stall near the ground—a spin and a crash. **1928** [see *LEVEL *v.*¹ 5*]. **1966** M. WOODHOUSE *Tree Frog* xxv. 191 He couldn't slow down to my airspeed without..stalling and nobody..would risk a stall this close to the ground. **1976** W. GREATOREX *Crossover* 204 The big jet fell ten thousand feet..in a stall that would have turned into a spin..with a less-experienced captain.

b. The sudden stopping of an internal-combustion engine at low revolutions (see also quot. 1959).

1959 *Motor Manual* (ed. 36) iv. 83 The very simple torque converter..would work well only at one speed. It could, for instance, be designed to give quite high multiplication at 'stall' (the moment when the car is on the point of moving). **1973** R. ROSENBLUM *Mushroom Cave* (1974) 3 The [boat's] motor was finicky; tying off the cord had precipitated a coughing fit in the carburetor, followed by a stall.

13. a. (sense 12*) *stall warning* (usu. *attrib.*).

1958 *Chambers's Techn. Dict.* Add. 1016/1 *Stall-warning indicator*, a device fitted to aeroplanes which do not provide positive warning of the approach of a stall by buffeting. **1976** B. LELOMBER *Dead Weight* ii. 32 The stall-warning light blazed urgently as I tried to haul the shuddering nose up.

13. b. stall-holder, (*c*) one who occupies a seat in the stalls of a theatre, concert-hall, etc.; **stall-keeper,** (*c*) (earlier example); **stall plate:** also, a similar plate bearing the arms of a knight of another Order (earlier and later examples); **stall seat,** a seat in the stalls of a theatre; **stall shower,** a shower-bath enclosed in a cubicle; **stall turn** *Aeronaut.*, a turn achieved by stalling one wing of an aircraft, causing increased drag on that wing and reduction of the radius of the turn; hence **stall-turn** *v. intr.*

1849 *Theatr. Programme* 34/2 The Committee have the honor to announce the following Stall Holders:—The Duchess of Leeds, [etc.]. **1963** *Times* 10 Jan. 4/3 Last night's performance in the Albert Hall allowed stall-holders, at least, to hear more of that detail than ever before. **1842** *Ainsworth's Mag.* II. 157 Went to keep a stall at the fancy fair. Threw all the other stall-keepers into the shade. **1842** N. H. NICHOLAS *Hist. Order of Bath* 206 A copy of the Inscriptions on some of the Stall Plates of Knights of the Bath, will be found in the appendix. **1980** J. BROOKE-LITTLE *Royal Ceremonies of State* vii. 102/2 Henry VII's magnificent chapel at the East end of Westminster Abbey..makes a splendid setting for the installation of Knights Grand Cross who, like Garter Knights display banners and have stall plates. **1920** *Daily Mail* 17 Sept. 4/5 Before the war approximately 90 per cent. of the occupants of stall seats in a West End theatre of any repute were in evening dress. **1939** R. CHANDLER in *Dime Detective Mag.* Aug. 65/1 A glass stall shower, monogrammed towels on a rack. **1978** S. SHELDON *Bloodline* xvii. 202 She walked through a tiled bathroom that included a marble bathtub and a stall shower. **1942** *R.A.F. Jrnl.* 3 Oct. 30 How insecure the safety belt seemed when called upon to do stall turns in the back seat of a Hart. **1948** *Times* 9 Feb. 2/3 The aircraft.. climbed steeply, stall-turned, and..burst into flames. **1952** A. Y. BRAMBLE *Air-Plane Flight* 205 The 'stall turn' is a useful manœuvre for changing to a reciprocal course (heading altered through 180°) in less time and space than by normal turning.

stall, *sb.*² Add: **4. a.** More recently, without *off.*

1846 *Swell's Night Guide* 41 They are never at a loss for a stall. **1931** W. FAULKNER *Sanctuary* xvii. 156 If it was a stall, dont common sense tell you I'd have invented a better one? **1939** E. S. GARDNER *D. A. draws Circle* (1940) vii. 98 'Sometimes when he'd be working, I'd take meals up to him. I think that was just a stall.' 'You mean the meals were for someone else?' 'Yes.'

b. An act of stalling (for time) or prevarication. Cf. *STALL *v.*² 3 a. *colloq.*

1945 *Sun* (Baltimore) 21 Nov. 1/1 The 200 delegates termed the company reply 'a stall pure and simple'. **1963** J. N. HARRIS *Weird World Wes Beattie* (1964) iv. 49 It was a very good stall, if you know Edgar... So he left the whole matter in abeyance. **1977** D. E. WESTLAKE *Nobody's Perfect* (1978) 141 It'll take me a while to get the cash together... This isn't a stall... I do have the money.

stall, *v.*[1] **III. 9.** Restrict † *Obs.* to senses in Dict. and add: **c.** Of a draught animal: To come to a halt because of mud or other impediment.

1807 C. W. JANSON *Stranger in Amer.* 172 The last time he passed, his horses *stalled*, that is, they were for some time unable to drag the wagon through the worst places. **1857** W. CHANDLESS *Visit to Salt Lake* II. vi. 233 His team were none too strong, and twice he 'stalled' hopelessly, and had to send to the nearest farm for a yoke of cattle.

d. Of an aircraft or its pilot: to enter a stall.

1910 R. LORAINE *Jrnl.* Apr. in W. Loraine *Robert Loraine* (1938) vi. 106 The machine leapt higher, so did my heart, higher still—then—puff!—I came to earth, having stalled and crashed. **1917** *Flying* 21 Feb. 136/1 An aeroplane can only reduce its flying speed to a certain minimum, after which it will stall. **1931** *Statesman* (Calcutta) 5 Dec., It is claimed that the autogiro cannot 'stall', or lose flying-speed. **1958** D. PIGGOTT *Gliding* vii. 34 The actual speed at which the glider stalls will be raised when the glider is being turned or manœuvred.. or if a heavier load is being carried. **1975** L. J. CLANCY *Aerodynamics* v. 98 If a particular wing is such that it stalls too suddenly, it may be necessary to provide some artificial pre-stall warning device.

e. Of an engine or vehicle: to stop suddenly as if of its own accord. Also with the driver or the occupants of the vehicle as subj.

1914 R. & E. SHACKLETON *Four on Tour in Eng.* 204 A few miles beyond Chipping Norton we stalled near the foot of a hill—and found that it was because of an inexcusable forgetting of gasoline! **1932** *Birmingham Post* 17 Dec. 16/2 The men drove off in the van. A few minutes later the engine stalled. **1956** 'C. BLACKSTOCK' *Dewey Death* ix. 207, I share.. a car with a friend... She once stalled in the middle of Piccadilly Circus. **1973** R. ROSENBLUM *Mushroom Cave* (1974) 5 He let go of the throttle string, and the [boat's] motor stalled.

f. To loiter or linger *around* (also *along*); to 'hang about'. *U.S. colloq.*

1916 'B. M. BOWER' *Phantom Herd* i. 5 I've been stalling along and keeping the best of the bucks in the foreground. *Ibid.* xi. 194, I stalled around out there till my money gave out. **1976** P. G. WINSLOW *Witch Hill Murder* (1977) II. xv. 207, I hoped he might answer sort of friendly.. and I've been kind of stalling around.

g. *transf.* and *fig.*

1923 R. D. PAINE *Comrades of Rolling Ocean* ii. 22 When things happened too fast, his mind stalled on a dead center. **1953** N. TINBERGEN *Herring Gull's World* i. 1 It stalls, makes a sharp turn and dives down. **1971** C. BONINGTON *Annapurna South Face* xvi. 199, I immediately noticed the lack of oxygen; once again my progress stalled into a crawl with rests at almost every step.

11. b. Also *fig.*, of an assembly, plan, etc.: to be hindered or held up. Chiefly *U.S.*

1910 *Outlook* 2 July 473 Congress would have been stalled in its efforts to prepare certain legislation without their aid. **1953** *Times* 31 Oct. 3/6 General Thimayya said that 'explanations', which have been stalled for the past fortnight, were to be resumed to-morrow. **1970** G. F. NEWMAN *Sir, you Bastard* v. 143 Both their requests to make phone calls were stalled. **1978** *N.Y. Times* 29 Mar. A 8/3 The seventh session of the.. conference was stalled at its beginning here today over the question of who would preside.

c. Add def.: To cause (an aircraft, vehicle, engine, etc.) to stall.

1904 W. WRIGHT in M. McFarland *Papers Wilbur & Orville Wright* (1953) I. 442 He allowed the machine to turn up a little too much and it stalled it. **1918** BROKAW & STARR *Putnam's Automobile Handbk.* xxv. 167 Stalling the motor is the result of feeding too little gas with the accelerator. **1930** J. DOS PASSOS *42nd Parallel* iv. 266 He had to get out to crank the car as he had stalled the motor. **1947** F. S. HOLLIDGE *Driving Test Fully Explained* iii. 10 A timely change down will often prevent 'stalling' the engine. *c* **1965** A. CHRISTIE *Autobiogr.* (1977) VII. ii. 332, I stalled the engine once or twice.. and I was rather chary about passing things. **1973** *Daily Tel.* 11 July 2/5 There was no structural failure in the Russian TU-144 supersonic airliner until after the pilot had stalled it.

12. c. To weary or tire; to fatigue. Usu. in *pass.* Chiefly *Sc.* and *north dial.*

1816, etc. in *Eng. Dial. Dict.* s.v. STALL *v.* 19. **1948** I. BROWN *No Idle Words* 108 Stalled, applied to depressed human beings, is a good old usage. 'You look stalled' is Yorkshire for 'You look dull'. **1967** J. WAINWRIGHT *Talent for Murder* 133 He was.. cold, wet and fed-up—to use his own expression (as a Yorkshireman) he was 'stalled'.

stall, *v.*[2] Add: **1. b.** *intr.* To screen a pickpocket's operation; to act as a look-out during a robbery or burglary.

[**1839:** in Dict., sense 1.] **1882** *Sydney Slang Dict.* 9/2, I pinched a swell of a fawney and fenced it for a double finnip and a cooter. My jomer stalled. **1926** J. BLACK *You can't Win* xxi. 338 Coppers located 'work' for burglars and stalled for them while they worked.

3. a. *trans.* To put (someone) *off* for the time being. Now usu. without advb.

1829 P. EGAN *Boxiana* 2nd Ser. II. 345 He would not be '*stalled off*' by the most knowing of the knowing. **1930** *Sat. Even. Post* 26 July 26/1 We might be able to stall them for two or three days with the idea that Tony is in Washington tryin' to fix the rap against them. **1948** A. HYND *Pinkerton Case Bk.* 56 He kept stalling the woman off with one excuse or another. **1963** J. N. HARRIS *Weird World Wes Beattie* (1964) iii. 36 So I stalled him off. I said I couldn't remember meeting anyone at Mac's. **1977** J. CROSBY *Company of Friends* xx. 128 Elaine is in Paris. To bargain some more. It's the only way left to stall him. It's important to stall him.

b. *intr.* To prevaricate; to be evasive. Also, to play *for time* or temporize. Freq. in U.S. colloq. phr. *quit stalling* (usu. imp.). orig. *U.S.*

1903 A. H. LEWIS *Boss* 23 [If] Big Kennedy shows up to stall ag'inst you, why I should say [etc.]. **1932** W. FAULKNER *Light in August* ix. 202 'Quit stalling,' the stranger said. 'If you croaked the guy, say so.' **1934** D. RUNYON in *Collier's* 24 Nov. 52/2 All she can think of.. is to stall for time. **1953** J. HILTON *Time & Time Again* III. 220 He was stalling for time. **1959** F. HOBSON *Death on Back-Bench* viii. 101 Just quit stalling.. and come clean. **1969** *Listener* 9 Jan. 41/2 Suppose Mr Ransom suddenly seized Miss Gold and flung her down on the office table with a snarl of 'Quit stalling,' like one of her favourite film actors. **1980** S. NAIPAUL *Black & White* I. iii. 34 For more than a year the Guyanese courts had been stalling on the custody suit his parents had brought.

stalled, *ppl. a.* Add: **4. b.** Archæol. *stalled cairn*: on the Orkneys, a Neolithic cairn covering a burial-chamber which was divided into lateral cells by stone slabs projecting from the wall.

[**1934** J. G. CALLANDER in *Proc. Soc. Antiq. Scotl.* LXVIII. 320 (*heading*) A long stalled chambered cairn or mausoleum (Rousay type) near Midhowe, Rousay, Orkney.] **1937** C. S. T. CALDER in *Ibid.* LXXI. 117 (*caption*) Stalled cairn, Calf of Eday: plan and sections. **1954** S. PIGGOTT *Neolithic Cultures Brit. Isles* viii. 234 The *Camster* tombs.. are.. from the northern shores of the Moray Firth.. and thence up the coastal strip of Sutherland and Caithness. Their derivatives in Orkney, which include as the ultimate form the long 'Stalled Cairn' type .. are mostly concentrated in the islands of Rousay and Eday. **1963** *Field Archaeol.* (Ordnance Survey) (ed. 4) 31 Other peculiar features in Orkney are the 'stalled' cairns in which what is really a long and carefully-constructed cist is divided into as many as ten or more lateral cells. **1980** *Encounter* May 56/2 Renfrew and his team focused on the island of Rousay with its remarkable number of stalled cairns.

5. b. Of an aircraft or aerofoil: in an airflow that has ceased to be streamline. Also applied to flight in this condition.

1912 O. WRIGHT in M. McFarland *Papers Wilbur & Orville Wright* (1953) II. 1050 There is only one explanation that I can give and that is the one that you suggest, that the machine was 'stalled'. **1932** *Jrnl. R. Aeronaut. Soc.* XXXVI. 312 Two sensations are characteristic of stalled flying: first of all, a very noticeable increase in the rate of descent, and secondly the reversed effect of elevator control on the inclination of the gliding path. **1966** *McGraw-Hill Encycl. Sci. & Technol.* XIII. 228/2 For some wings, if the root section is placed at an angle near stall, the tip sections will probably be stalled. **1969** W. THOMSON *Thrust for Flight* 8 If the angle of attack is made too large.., flow becomes turbulent and the blade is said to be stalled.

c. Of a vehicle or engine: stopped through having stalled.

1966 B. H. DEAL *Fancy's Knell* (1967) x. 153 A man with a stalled pickup stood futilely beside it in the middle of the street. **1977** 'D. RUTHERFORD' *Return Load* i. 13 Sally restarted the stalled engine, engaged first gear and tentatively let in the clutch.

staller[2]. Add: **1.** (Recent example without *up.*)

1977 *New Society* 7 July 6/2 At first he was a staller. 'You get a woman trying to get on a train, someone goes in front of her, stalls her for ten to 15 seconds, and she's forgot about her bag.'

2. One who stalls or prevaricates; a person who gains time by obstructionism.

1937 PARTRIDGE *Dict. Slang* 823/1 *Staller*, a person constantly, or very good at, making excuses or playing for time. **1977** H. GREENE *FSO-1* ix. 76 You are.. one of the world's most transparent stallers... We are convened to talk about Larry. **1981** 'W. HAGGARD' *Money Men* vii. 74 He was an experienced staller. Postponing action was called good judgment.

sta·ll-in. *U.S.* [f. STALL *v.*[1] II c + *-IN[3].] A form of protest in which participants block the roads with immobilized vehicles.

1964 [see *lie-in* s.v. *LIE *sb.*[2] 6]. **1977** *Time* 14 Nov. 21/3 They need hardly fear the kind of traffic stall-ins staged by New York City residents to protest the arrival of the Concorde.

stalling, *vbl. sb.* Add: **5.** The event of coming to an unintended halt or stalling (*STALL *v.*[1] 9). In *Aeronaut.* freq. *attrib.*, as *stalling point, speed.*

1808 M. L. WEEMS *Let.* 17 May in E. E. F. Skeel *M. L. Weems* (1929) II. 377 Stalling of Waggons, sweeping away of Stages, drowning of Horses &c. &c. are dreadful. **1888** J. KIRKLAND *McVeys* 220 The occurrence —the 'stalling' of a wagon and team, was common enough in those early days. **1912** O. WRIGHT in M. McFarland *Papers Wilbur & Orville Wright* (1953) II. 1052 The liability of the machine to dive in case of 'stalling' is present in every one. **1916** H. BARKER *Aeroplane Speaks* 89 If it[*sc.* the engine] is throttled down, then the course must be one of a steeper angle than B, or there will be danger of stalling. **1917** 'CONTACT' *Airman's Outings* iv. 100 At times he varied this method by lifting the machine almost to stalling point, letting her down again, and repeating the process. **1928** C. F. S. GAMBLE *North Sea Air Station* v. 84 An inherently stable machine was.. found to be of little value for aerial fighting, as the possession of a high degree of manœuvrability, combined with a low 'stalling' speed, are some of the essentials for this work. **1932** H. H. PRICE *Perception* vi. 149 A short-eared owl flying at just above stalling-point. **1952** L. NATHAN *Car Driving in Two Weeks* iii. 21 To prevent stalling of engine the following procedure is invaluable. **1966** D. FRANCIS *Flying Finish* 129 We touched down.. at a fraction above stalling speed. **1976** 'A. HALL' *Kobra Manifesto* i. 15 He reached the stalling-point and dropped tail first and bounced and tilted and.. then bucked forward.

6. *Surfing.* (See quots.)

1962 T. MASTERS *Surfing made Easy* 65 *Stalling a board*, stepping or leaning back on a board to slow it down. **1968** W. WARWICK *Surfriding in N.Z.* 10/2 Step back on your board and put it out of trim, this will slow your board down... This manoeuvre is called stalling.

stalling (stǭ·liŋ), *vbl. sb.*[2] [f. STALL *v.*[2] + -ING[1].] **1.** The action of helping a pickpocket by distracting or jostling his victim. *Criminals' slang.*

1908 J. M. SULLIVAN *Criminal Slang* 24 *Stalling for a dip*, arranging [a pickpocket's] victims so that they can be successfully robbed. **1926** *Flynn's* 16 Jan. 638/1 The gay cat and spotters got 'em on location; then it was a case of palin', stick up, stallin' or rollin' in any way you please.

2. Prevaricating, temporizing; the action of being evasive or devious.

1927 *Vanity Fair* XXIX. 132/4 'The run-around' is stalling or failing to keep a promise. **1952** *Landfall* Sept. 227 Walk into a Saturday-afternoon bar and hear the noise; do you get the impression of *stalling*?

stallion. Add: **1. a.** Also *fig.*

1924 R. CAMPBELL *Flaming Terrapin* ii. 27 He would hear the whinnying stallions of the wind career. **1940** L. MACNEICE *Last Ditch* 15 The stallions of the soul—Eager to take the fences That fence about my soul.

2. b. Delete † *Obs.* and add: Now only in former sense.

1933 D. PARKER *After Such Pleasures* 138 Go answer it, you damned—you damned *stallion*! **1978** L. MEYNELL *Papersnake* v. 70 Barton amused himself by keeping a tally of Lasting's women; 'that insatiable stallion' he called him.

3. b. Among U.S. Blacks, a tall, good-looking girl or woman. *colloq.*

1970 C. MAJOR *Dict. Afro-Amer. Slang* 108 *Stallion*, a good-looking black woman. **1975** R. H. RIMMER *Premar Experiments* (1976) i. 148, I love you Samantha Brown. In black ghetto language, you're a lovely stallion.

Stamford (stæ·mfǝɹd). The name of a town in Cambridgeshire, used *attrib.*, as **Stamford ware** *Archæol.*, a kind of Saxo-Norman lead-glazed pottery made of estuarine clay from the vicinity of Stamford.

1956 G. C. DUNNING in D. B. Harden *Dark-Age Britain* III. 230 The term 'Stamford ware' may be proposed for the lead-glazed pottery of fine quality of the late Anglo-Saxon and Norman periods, provided it is clearly understood that this is a generic term for pottery made of.. specific clays but at more than one centre within the area. **1956** *Proc. Cambridge Antiquarian Soc.* XLIX. 48 Saxo-Norman glaze only occurs on this Stamford ware. **1962** [see *lead-glazing* vbl. sb. s.v. *LEAD *sb.*[1] 12]. **1974** M. INGATE *Sound of Weir* xx. 172 Stamford ware made from 900 to the 13th century from middle Jurassic esturine clay.

staminoid (stæ·minoid), *a. Bot.* [f. L. *stāmin-*, STAMEN + -OID.] Of the nature of or resembling a stamen.

1869 M. T. MASTERS *Vegetable Teratology* 301 The scales that are met with in some plants, either as excrescences from the petals, or as imperfect representatives of stamens or other organs, are occasionally staminoid. **1930** *Jrnl. Genetics* XXIII. 107 A collection.. in which the petals had become metamorphosed into stamens, showed every type of staminoid petal. **1974** *Flora* CLXIII. 405 (*heading*) Staminoid petals in *Geranium pratense* L. and their inheritance.

‖ **Stammbaum** (ʃta·mbaum). *Linguistics.* [Ger., family tree: the sense was introduced by A. Schleicher in *Darwinische Theorie u. die Sprachwissenschaft* (1863) 13.] A family tree of languages: see *family-tree* s.v. *FAMILY *sb.* 11. Hence **Sta·mmbaumtheorie** (-te:ori) (see quot. 1954).

1939 E. PROKOSCH *Compar. Gmc. Gram.* 21 August Schleicher conceived the Indo-European primitive language as the trunk of a linguistic 'Stammbaum'. **1954** M. A. PEI *Dict. Linguistics* 162 *Pedigree theory*, the theory (*Stammbaumtheorie*) formulated by August Schleicher in 1866, according to which a parent language split into two branches, each of which again bifurcated into two languages, etc. **1965** *Language* XLI. 106 Rodríguez stresses .. the ultimate reconcilability of the Stammbaumtheorie and the Wellentheorie. **1971** W. LABOV in W. O. Dingwall *Survey of Linguistic Science* 426 One of the classic unresolved dichotomies of historical linguistics is the opposition of the *Stammbaum* and *wave theories* of linguistic differentiation.

‖ **Stammtisch** (ʃta·mtiʃ). [Ger., f. *stamm* tree trunk, cadre + *tisch* table.] A table reserved for regular customers in a German restaurant, beer-hall, etc.

1938 L. Bemelmans *Life Class* (1939) II. vii. 197 Political discourses at his *Stammtisch*, the table regularly reserved for him and his group of friends, at the Löwenbräu. **1940** G. Frankau *Self-Portrait* xi. 62 We lunched, with others of the same ilk, at his 'Stammtisch' (perpetually reserved table) in the Hamburg Rathskeller. **1964** I. Fleming *You only live Twice* iv. 54 The quiet corner table that appeared to be his *Stammtisch*. **1970** L. Deighton *Bomber* xxi. 312 The three best tables were marked with *Stammtisch* flags, so that only regulars would dare to sit there.

stamp, *sb.*^{3} Add: **II. 9. b.** Maize that has been crushed or pounded with a wooden pestle. *S. Afr.* Cf. *stamp mealies*, sense 20 below, and Samp.

1923 *S. Afr. Pioneer* Dec. 143/2 All partook freely of the feast of meat and stamp. **1976** J. McClure *Rogue Eagle* vi. 112 The price of mealie *stamp* in Maseru.

III. 14. e. = *insurance stamp* s.v. *Insurance 5.

1912 [see *insurance stamp* s.v. *Insurance 5]. **1946** *Act* 9 & 10 *Geo. VI* c. 67. 720 Contributions..are payable by means of adhesive stamps. **1974** *Times* 6 Feb. 14/2 The qualification test has been simplified for the emergency: a declaration that 26 stamps have been paid within the previous 12 months is enough to entitle people to the full rate for a year.

f. = *trading stamp* s.v. *Trading *vbl. sb.* b.

1933 in *Parl. Papers 1932–33, Rep. Cttee on Gift Coupons & Trading Stamps* 12 (Cmd. 4385) XII. 387 The stamps are given to the customer in proportion to the amount spent and are stuck by him into a collecting book... When the book is full..the stamps may be tendered in exchange for a gift. **1963** J. T. Story *Something for Nothing* iii. 89 You get a grocer, you get a baker, you get a hairdresser and a chemist and a garage and a draper all giving stamps. **1976** A. Grey *Bulgarian Exclusive* I. i. 17 The two psychedelic gift mugs the garage.. had given them in exchange for seven Heron stamps.

IV. 19. *stamp-licker*; *stamp-licking* vbl. sb. and ppl. adj. (freq. with reference to menial office work).

1928 F. Le Gros Clark *Apparition* xiii. 176 You've never even held a commission. Bloody stamp-licker in an office. **1978** J. Updike *Coup* (1979) vii. 269 In the bureaucracy of Kush Amid so many posts for stamp-lickers and boot-lickers. **1913** *Punch* 14 May 382/3 There is something after all to be said for the Stamp-licking Act. **1973** G. Talbot *Ten Seconds from Now* (1974) ii. 22 At first the job was stamp-licking office boy on the commercial side. **1979** *Nature* 4 Jan. 7/1 A total paid staff of two people who do everything from typing, stamp-licking and driving to..producing scholarly catalogues.

20. stamp collection, a philatelist's collection of postage stamps; also *fig.*; **stamp machine,** (*b*) a vending machine which supplies postage stamps; **stamp mealies** *S. Afr.* [ad. Afrikaans *stampmielies*] = sense 9 b above; cf. *Stamped *ppl. a.* 1 b; **stamp war,** competition amongst retailers to attract custom by providing the best trading-stamp offer; an instance of this.

[**1865** *Stamp-Collector's Mag.* 1 Jan. 2/1 When we first saw a postage-stamp collection, more than ten years past, it contained about a hundred and fifty specimens.] **1884** *Stamp Collectors' Jrnl.* 15 Jan. 19/1 The value of a stamp collection does not depend entirely upon the amount of money expended for the album and the stamps. **1926** J. S. Huxley *Ess. Pop. Sci.* 164 This *corpus* of fact..is only a vast stamp-collection, no more than a lumber-room, unless each generation in its turn will make it live. **1978** S. Sheldon *Bloodline* iv. 62 He was basically a retiring man, content to make a modest living, reside in a little apartment in Passy and tend to his small stamp collection. **1944** J. D. Carr *Till Death do us Part* xviii. 191 There's no stamp machine at the post office... Anyone who wants stamps must buy 'em..over the counter. **1969** R. Thomas *Singapore Wink* xxvi. 250 Trippet and I went in search of a stamp machine. We fed dimes and nickels and quarters into it until we had almost three dollars' worth. He helped me lick them. **1952** L. Green *Lords of Last Frontier* 79 We now live well and keep strong on stamp mealies from Oorlog's place. **1963** *Daily Tel.* 14 Oct. 1/4 (*heading*) Stamp war challenge to Garfield Weston. **1972** *Guardian* 16 Oct. 9/5 In the early sixties the stamp war broke out. Different supermarket chains started offering different stamps, each one claiming to give better value and better gifts.

stamp and go. Add: **1.** Also, a shanty sung to accompany this action.

1929 F. Bowen *Sea Slang* 132 Stamp and Go. The shanty sung for a straight pull along the deck. 'What shall we do with the drunken sailor?' is probably the best known.

2. (Usu. with hyphens.) In the West Indies: a simple, quickly prepared codfish fritter (see also quot. 1893).

1893 C. Sullivan *Jamaica Cookery Bk.* 87 Stamp and go. These are rough cakes made with cornmeal and flour ..salt fish and a little butter... The country people as they travel stop at the way-side shops and buy them... Hence the name. **1953** *Caribbean Q.* III. i. 11 *Stamp-and-go*,..a kind of codfish fritter that is quickly made. **1970** *New Yorker* 10 Jan. 54/3 (Advt.), A chief who can water your mouth with a..native Stamp-and-Go.

stamped, *ppl. a.* Add: **1. b.** *stamped mealies* = *Stamp *sb.*^{3} 9 b. *S. Afr.*

1911 A. B. Lamont *Rural Reader for S. Afr.* 189 'Stamped mealies'—that is mealies from which the outer husk has been removed—are made by stamping the grain with a heavy wooden stick in a large bowl. **1937** C. R. Prance *Tante Rebella's Saga* 82 Oom Fanie and his family had just asked a blessing on their supper of pumpkin and stamped mealies.

2. c. Also *stamped (and) addressed envelope*: a self-addressed envelope with a postage stamp affixed, enclosed with a letter so that the recipient may reply at the sender's expense. Freq. required by an organization of a private enquirer and often abbrev. *S.A.E.*, *s.a.e.* (cf. *S 4 a).

In this sense the word may now be considered f. Stamp *sb.*^{3} + -ed^2.

1873 *Young Englishwoman* Apr. 208/1 We..will return your edging if you will send a stamped addressed envelope. **1949** N. Mitford *Love in Cold Climate* I. xiii. 131 The fella says here to enclose a stamped and addressed envelope but I don't think I shall pander to him. *a* **1953** Dylan Thomas *Under Milk Wood* (1954) 39 Here's a letter for you with stamped and addressed envelope enclosed. **1977** *Graduate* 9 Dec. 14/2 (Advt.), Enquiries and applications, with stamped addressed envelope, to Mr P Austin, DoE Archaeological Services, Carlisle Castle, Carlisle, Cumbria. **1981** M. Spark *Loitering with Intent* ii. 52 An unpublished poem..which..had been rejected eight times, returning to roost in my own stamped addressed envelope.

stampede, *sb.* For **a, b** read **1, 2** and add: Also † **stampado, stampido. 1. a.** *α.* (Earlier example.)

[**1826** T. Flint *Francis Berrian* I. ii. 46 Instantly this prodigious multitude..took what the Spanish call the 'stompado'. With a trampling like the noise of thunder,.. they [*sc.* the horses] took to their heels.] **1828** in *Missouri Hist. Rev.* (1914) VIII. 187 A little before daylight, the mules made an abortive attempt to raise a stampido.

b. In N. Amer., an exhibition of cowboy skills, a rodeo; *spec.* that held at Calgary, Alberta (usu. *Calgary Stampede*), for the first time in 1912 and annually since 1919.

1912 *Calgary* (Alta.) *Daily Herald* 31 Aug. 6/1 Calgary is on the eve of its Stampede festival. **1919** *Eye Opener* (Calgary, Alta.) 9 Aug. 4 Come to Calgary Stampede Week and have the time of your life. **1923** C. M. Barbeau *Indian Days* 5 Picturesque stampedes take place every summer in the July celebrations at Banff. **1948** *Ada* (Okla.) *Even. News* 2 July 1/5 A capacity crowd was on hand for the opening performance of the Hereford Heaven Stampede. **1950** B. Hutchison *Fraser* xvii. 251 Here the ranchers and Indians gather once a year for the innocent fun of the stampede. **1974** *Sat. Rev. World* 2 Nov. 30/2 The Calgary Stampede during the first two weeks of each July..offer[s] competition in matches ranging from wild-cow milking to buffalo riding.

2. a. Also *spec.* (N. Amer. Hist.), a concerted rush of prospectors to the goldfields.

1872 R. W. Raymond *Statistics of Mines* III. iv. 202 Rocky Bar..has suffered somewhat from the stampede to the bars of the Snake River. **1916** *Yukon Territory* (Canada Dept. Interior) 11 In the autumn of 1886 coarse gold was discovered in the Fortymile River, and ..the usual stampede occurred. **1937** C. L. Andrews *Pioneers & Nuggets of Verse they Panned* 17 The stampede to the gold fields of the Tanana Valley..caused an exodus from Dawson. **1965** *Canad. Geogr. Jrnl.* Apr. 119/1 Not only was it the last of the old-fashioned stampedes in which dog teams and men vied for space along the narrow trail, but it also ushered in the air age of prospecting.

b. (With initial capital.) An uproarious kind of dance. Also *Stampede Dance* (in quot., a dancing-party).

1856 *Spirit of Times* 13 Dec. 238/2 The following was the programme of dancing: Part the Fourth—Scotch Reel,..French Four, General Stampede. **1870** J. C. Duval *Adventures Big-Foot Wallace* xlii. 263, I see you haven't yet introduced the Texas national dance—the Stampede. **1950** *Chicago Daily News* 10 May 10/1 The annual 'Stampede Dance' of the Order of the Builders, State of Illinois, will be held May 20.

stampede, *v.* Add: Also † **stompede. 1. a.** *β.* (Earlier examples.)

1838 *Hesperian* Nov. 37/2 When we awoke, we found that the flies had *stompeded* our horses, to use the expression of the country, which means that they made them so restive that they broke loose from the hopples. **1844** J. Gregg *Commerce of Prairies* II. 35 A party of Mexicans..*stampeded* and carried away, not only their own horses, but those of the Texans.

b. Also, to cause (an individual) to take precipitate action.

1890 C. King *Sunset Pass* 56 Don't get stampeded. Just keep cool; watch and listen. **1912** R. Pocock *Man in Open* 104 The lady attracted attention by screaming, so the third shot stampeded poor Jones. **1924** *Machinists' Bull.* (Winnipeg) Oct. 3/2 Efforts are being made by various agencies to use the present condition as a club to stampede the men and disgust them with their Organization. **1950** *Time* 3 Apr. 20/2 A solid, grey, calm man, never rushed to a conclusion, impossible to stampede.

2. a. (Earlier example.)

1823 S. Williams in E. C. Barker *Austin Papers* (1924) I. 699 On the way..the Cavallada Stampeded and a part of the horses and mules were not recovered.

b. Also *spec.* of a prospector: to rush to the goldfields.

1877 R. W. Raymond *Statistics of Mines* VIII. v. 263 Among the miners who had 'stampeded' to Cedar were many of the best prospectors in the Territory. **1898** M. Landreville *Appeal of Yukon Miners* 23 Miners are prone to stampede to any district which has the appearance of greater richness than the one wherein they are at work. **1951** V. B. Angier *At Home in Woods* 41 The prospectors who stampeded through here around '98 on their way to the Yukon had a pretty good trick.

stampeder. (In Dict. s.v. Stampede *v.*) Add: *N. Amer.* **1.** One who takes part in a sudden or unreasoning rush of persons, esp. for gold. (Further examples.)

1859 E. H. N. Patterson *Jrnl.* 22 May in L. Hafen *Overland Routes to Gold Fields* (1942) 143 In anything that I may have heretofore written that might be deemed disparaging of the 'stampeders', I do not wish to be understood as intentionally unjust or uncharitable. **1884** *Century Mag.* Oct. 844/2 In the days of the stampeders and the toboggan trains, this was the only house on the trail. **1936** N. A. D. Armstrong *Yukon Yesterdays* 13 No wonder that hundreds of the weaker stampeders returned to the base to take the first steamer back home! **1963** *Beaver* (Winnipeg) Summer 42/2 Before the turn of the century, hordes of rushing stampeders..had reason to curse the savage stretch of water.

2. One who causes a stampede amongst cattle or horses.

1862 *Harper's Mag.* Sept. 450/1 Horses..which, having been 'hobbled' beside the fires of their respective owners, had..escaped the notice of the stampeders.

stamper, *sb.* Add: **3. e.** A matrix or copy of an original disc recording used to press other copies of a gramophone record.

1918 [see *Matrix 4 c]. **1935** [see *Master *sb.*^{1} 9* a]. **1952** [see *Mother *sb.*^{1} 10*]. **1975** G. J. King *Audio Handbk.* vii. 154 Most gramophone records start as very high quality tape recordings, the edited material then being recorded in disc form on to a lacquer blank, from which the stamper is ultimately derived.

stamping, *vbl. sb.* **3. stamping ground**: for *U.S.* read orig. *U.S.* and add earlier and further examples.

1821 D. Dunklin *Let.* 25 Dec. in E. C. Barker *Austin Papers* (1924) I. 456 It is unnecessary to undertake to give you any details of affairs in your old Stamping-ground. **1862** *Harper's Mag.* June 34/1, I found myself near one of these 'stamping grounds', and a simultaneous roar from five hundred infuriated animals gave notice of my danger. **1915** E. R. Burroughs *Return of Tarzan* xxiii. 326 The woman he loved was within a short journey of the stamping-ground of his tribe. **1955** *Times* 19 Aug. 2/5 Henry Wood used the Proms as a stamping ground for new music because there was little opportunity otherwise for making it known. **1977** J. I. M. Stewart *Madonna of Astrolabe* iv. 74 Tell Charles Atlas I'd have a go if asked —I suppose as Tutor for Admissions it's his stamping-ground.

stance, *sb.*^{2} Add: **1. c.** Also *spec.* in *Mountaineering*, a ledge or foothold on which a climber can secure a belay.

1920 G. W. Young *Mountain Craft* v. 218 It is..vital for a leader to know what character of stance he requires in order to bring up his following safely. **1933** G. D. Abraham *Mod. Mountaineering* viii. 154 The second man looped the rope behind him around the projection from a stance a few feet along the ledge. **1956** [see *Intilted *ppl. a.*]. **1971** C. Bonington *Annapurna South Face* xi. 127, I had to wait another hour while he safeguarded his stance with carefully placed pitons.

d. Also *transf.*, the position of the player's body in readiness or in playing a stroke. Similarly *gen.*, a standing attitude or way of positioning.

1929 M. Lief *Hangover* 234 At dinner Mogador's young bride was plainly worried about her fork-stance. **1936** M. Allingham *Flowers for Judge* v. 84 No one who saw him could have dreamed for a moment that he regarded himself as anything else but the Head of the Firm. His poise and stance proclaimed it. **1965** 'W. Trevor' *Boarding-House* ii. 19 Gallelty and Mrs Slape stood close together..humble in their stance. **1970** J. G. Farrell *Troubles* II. 220 Driscoll instantly dropped into a boxing stance, right fist guarding his chin, left fist pumping exaggeratedly back and forth.

e. *fig.* An attitude adopted in relation to a particular object of contemplation; a policy, 'posture'.

1960 *Amer. Speech* XXXV. 215 An 'unlinguistic' stance is evidenced in the view that some variants embody language 'corruption'. **1964** *Ann. Reg. 1963* 216 In general those Parties in economically more advanced countries adopted a pro-Soviet stance, although several had dissident pro-Chinese minorities. **1972** [see *Rhetoricize *v.*]. **1977** J. I. M. Stewart *Madonna of Astrolabe* xx. 277 Moderate regret and underlying unconcern established itself as our public stance.

3. b. *Sc.* The pitch of a showman or street-trader; a location for a fair or market. Cf. Stand *sb.*^{1} 15.

1814 *Farmer's Mag.* Nov. 466 If they are not in the market the night before, it is not often that a stance can be got after day-light in the morning. **1924** *Kelso Chron.* 25 July 4 This old-established Border fair was held on the usual stance on St Boswells Green on Friday. **1933** *Cases Court of Session* (Scotland) 65 A street trader shall not carry on business on any stance..unless he holds a permit from the chief constable for such stance. **1964** M. Banton *Policeman in Community* ii. 31 He..can attend to less pressing matters such as an application for a news-vendor's stance.

c. *Sc.* A standing-place for (a row of) public vehicles; a bus-stop or taxi-rank. Cf. STAND *sb.*[1] 17.

1926 *Edinburgh Corp. (General Powers) Order Confirmation* 25 in *Bills Public* I. 461 'Stance' means a place where omnibuses may stop a longer time than is necessary for the taking up and setting down of passengers. **1931** A. A. MACGREGOR *Last Voyage* 24 The erection of stance poles [for tram-cars] along Princes St. **1978** *Dumfries Courier* 13 Oct. 6/2 Travellers will find that early buses and taxis are temporarily sitting in different stances than is usual.

stand, *sb.*[1] Add: **I. 2. e.** Also, the place at which a halt is made; the performance itself; *transf.*, esp. in *one-night stand*: see *ONE *numeral a., pron.*, etc. 33.

1895 *N.Y. Dramatic News* 19 Oct. 11/1 Denver was the second stand of the week. **1931** *Amer. Speech* VI. 336 *Stand*, n., a town or city where a show stops to give performances. **1938** D. BAKER *Young Man with Horn* III. 149 He'd been making stands at moving-picture houses all over the country. **1959** *Times* 16 Dec. 3/2 A number of travelling road-shows do one or two-night stands at such unlikely places as the Constitution Hall. **1964** MRS. L. B. JOHNSON *White House Diary* 22 Apr. (1970) 115 Mrs. Eisenhower invited them in 1953, and had entertained around four thousand guests, about a four-hour stand. **1973** G. BEARE *Snake on Grave* ii. 12 When the Sands in Vegas offered her a stand she took Latch with her to play for her.

f. The mean sea-level at a given epoch in the past; also, the level of the sea at high or low tide.

1934 WEBSTER, *Stand*, the state of the tide at high or low water when there is no vertical movement. **1966** *Gloss. Oceanogr. Terms* (U.S. Naval Oceanographic Office) (ed. 2) 156/1 Where a double tide occurs, the stand may last for several hours even with a large range of tide. **1972** *Science* 13 Oct. 190/3 On Barbados, sedimentological considerations suggest that the high stand associated with the last interglacial (terrace III, 124,000 years ago) lasted no longer than about 5,000 years. **1978** *Nature* 18 May 185/3 At that time [*sc.* 22,000 years ago], sea-level was about 300 foot below its present stand because so much of the Earth's water was locked in glaciers.

4. c. (Earlier and later examples in *Cricket*.) Now *spec.* a partnership between two batsmen at the crease.

1851 J. PYCROFT *Cricket Field* x. 189 Then comes the time when your great gun tumbles down his men: and that is the time that some sure, judgmatic batsman.. comes calmly and composedly to the wicket and makes a stand. **1912** P. F. WARNER *Eng. v. Austral.* iv. 29 Barnes and Strudwick made a capital last wicket stand. **1980** *Wisden Cricket Monthly* Mar. 6/3 Charlie Davis..was then joined by..Garfield Sobers, in a stand of 254 in 363 minutes.

5. c. (The performance of) a stallion or bull at stud. Also, a stud or stud-farm. *U.S.*

1797 E. CHAMBERS *Let.* 29 Nov. in J. Steele *Papers* (1924) I. 151 As a covering horse I am of Opinion he would make a very good Stand. **1836** *Russellville* (Kentucky) *Weekly Advertiser* 21 Jan. 3/3 (Advt.), Merlin is now at this stand in Elkton... Books are opened for those who may wish to enter their mares. **1959** W. FAULKNER *Mansion* i. 9 He had to lead the cow the three miles back..to claim a second stand from the bull.

d. = ERECTION 4. *slang.*

1867, etc. [see *cock-stand* s.v. *COCK *sb.*[1] 23]. **1868** *Index Expurgatorius of Martial* 88 Maevius who while sleeping only gets A piss-proud stand that melts away on waking. **1903** FARMER & HENLEY *Slang* VI. 346/1 *Stand*,.. (venery).—1. An *erectio penis*.

9. (Later examples in *Gymnastics*.)

1956 KUNZLE & THOMAS *Freestanding* i. 26 Also try jumps from stand, both from half knee bend and with very little knee bend. **1964** G. C. KUNZLE *Parallel Bars* ii. 50 Push away from the bars with the left hand to land in side stand.

II. 11. †**e.** A degree of proficiency measured by achievement in school-work; a mark or grade awarded in assessment. *U.S. Educ. Obs.*

1900 *Dialect Notes* II. 64 *Stand*, degree of proficiency in college studies, as evidenced by marks and honors. **1904** *N.Y. Even. Post* 17 Mar. 7 The highest stand man of the non-elective scholastic period was Dean Wright of 1868, who attained a stand of 3·71 on a scale of 4·00. **1921** R. D. PAINE *Comrades of Rolling Ocean* i. 11, I had a rotten stand in your course.

12. b. The post or station of a sheep-shearer. *Austral.* and *N.Z.*

1893 S. NEWLAND *Paving Way* II. xviii. 339 As applicants for a 'stand' on the shearing-floor began to camp about, his audiences became more numerous. **1901** 'R. BOLDREWOOD' *In Bad Company* 21 It's hard on a chap, when he comes to a shed..to be told that all the stands is took up. **1922** C. G. TURNER *Happy Wanderer* 143 Four hundred men might answer the roll-call where only one hundred could 'get a stand'—i.e. a chance to shear. **1933** *Bulletin* (Sydney) 6 Sept. 20/2 They run a record long shearing, six stands being considered sufficient to cope with 60,000 sheep. **1949** D. WALKER *We went to Australia* 97 We watched them [*sc.* shearers] in the 'eight-stand' shed at Nareeb. **1956** G. BOWEN *Wool Away!* (ed. 2) x. 110, I have set out the plan of a three-stand shed..which should meet the needs of a large cross-section of sheep farmers.

15. b. (Later U.S. example.)

1929 [see *MEET *sb.* 1 b].

18. (Further examples.)

1885 *Daily Tel.* 11 Nov. 3/7 Many changes have taken place at Aintree, and, if the weather had permitted, the new stands would have been finished off. **1902** *Daily Mail* 7 Apr. 5/1 (*heading*) Stand collapses at a football match. **1977** *Evening Post* (Nottingham) 27 Jan. 20/4 There will be other rises with best seats in the stands going up to £1.40.

IV. 23. c. *Metallurgy.* A set of rolls and their auxiliary fittings which during any one pass provide one gap for the metal being rolled.

1874 *Jrnl. Iron & Steel Inst.* I. 349 Space is left at the end of the train for two stands of merchant roughing and finishing rolls. **1958** A. D. MERRIMAN *Dict. Metallurgy* 338/2 A stand is usually..described as 2-high, 3-high, [etc.].. A rolling-mill may consist of a single stand or of several stands in series. **1973** G. F. BRYANT *Automation of Tandem Mills* ix. 160 In 1968, a fifth stand was added to the BSC Abbey Works tandem cold-rolling mill.

d. *Oil Industry.* A number of lengths of drill pipe (usually from one to four) joined together, esp. when being unscrewed from a string or racked in a derrick.

1913 B. REDWOOD *Petroleum* (ed. 3) I. v. 317 The casing with which it is desired to shut off the water must admit of being moved quite freely in the bore-hole, so that it may be raised or lowered the full length of a 'stand', that is, for a distance of, say, three lengths or joints. **1949** [see *RACK *v.*[2] 4 a]. **1960** C. GATLIN *Petroleum Engin.* v. 52/2 Only two or three joints per stand will be pulled when using shorter derricks. **1973** J. W. JENNER in Hobson & Pohl *Mod. Petroleum Technol.* (ed. 4) iv. 120 The drawworks then hauls the blocks up the derrick until a stand of three joints of drill pipe is above the rotary table.

26. (Earlier U.S. example.)

1851 W. KELLY *Excursion to California* I. v. 83 A stand of prairie plover most opportunely made their appearance as we pulled up.

29. For *U.S.* read *orig. U.S.* and add: *spec.* one of trees; now also applied to natural assemblages of plants, esp. when only one species is present or considered. (Later examples).

1905 *Terms Forestry & Logging* (U.S. Dept. Agric. Bureau Forestry) 22 *Stand*, all growing trees in a forest or in part of a forest. Syn.: growing stock. **1912** HAWLEY & HAWES *Forestry in New England* i. 8 The term 'stand' is the unit of description applied to any definite portion of a forest having a definite distinguishing characteristic. Thus in a certain type we may have a stand of young growth; a stand of diseased and damaged trees; a stand of exceptionally tall specimens, etc. These stands may be extensive, covering many acres or they may be confined each to a small part of an acre. **1947** K. TENNANT *Lost Haven* xvii. 284 Nice stand of trees, brushwood, coachwood, white soapy box. **1967** M. J. COE *Ecol. Alpine Zone Mt. Kenya* 28 All the genera cited..are..obvious components of the alpine zone, with the megaphytic Senecios and Alchemilla scrub forming almost pure stands under suitable conditions. **1975** P. LIVELY *Going Back* i. 8 Old wooden chicken-houses half-submerged in grass and cow-parsley and stands of nettles. **1979** H. W. HOCKER *Introd. Forest Biol.* iv. 99 The stand is a basic unit of management and is important to planning silvicultural operations... In the terminology of plant ecology, a forest stand would be designated as a community, or an ecosystem... Foresters use the term stand to designate the tree portion of the ecosystem.

stand, *v.* Add: **I. 3. b.** Of a stallion: to be available as a stud-horse to serve mares (esp. *at* a certain place). Also, *to stand at stud* (cf. STUD *sb.*[2]). orig. *U.S.*

1766 *Virginia Gaz.* 4 Apr. 3/3 Merry Tom Stands at my house, and covers mares at a guinea the leap. **1788** W. LENOIR in N. E. Eliason *Tarheel Talk* (1956) 297 Whirligig will stand this season..& will cover Mares at Forty Shillings per season Twenty Shillings per cover. **1846** *Spirit of Times* 18 Apr. 94/1 Young Dread will stand this season at Watertown, Jefferson County, N.Y. **1891** J. L. KIPLING *Beast & Man in India* viii. 207 Importing English thoroughbreds, Arabs, and Norfolk trotters who stand as sires at the service of farmers. **1959** *Times* 31 Aug. 13/5 (*heading*) Shantung to stand in England. **1974** D. FRANCIS *Knock Down* xiv. 171 Nestegg is standing at stud in Ireland. **1974** *New Yorker* 29 Apr. 102/2 Go Man Go stands at stud at Buena Suerte Ranch. *Ibid.* 102/3 Tony B Deck's father, who stood in Perry, Oklahoma, was murdered in his stall. **1977** *N.Z. Herald* 5 Jan. 1–12/5 Aristoi is by Sir Gaylord from Attlea, by Mt Trouble from Athenia, by Pharamond II, and stands at the Preston Farm Stud.

6. c. Of the penis: to become or remain erect.

? **1508** DUNBAR *Tua Mariit Wemen* sig. b ii, And a stif standand thing staiffis in mi neiff. *c* **1593** NASHE *Choise of Valentines* (1899) 12 'Unhappie me,' quoth shee, and wilt' not stand? Com, lett me rubb and chafe it with my hand!' **1762** T. BRIDGES *Homer Travestie* I. IV. 189 She guides his weapon where she list;..a touch of her soft hand, If fallen down, will make him stand. **1868** *Index Expurgatorius of Martial* 82 That's the way to make your Martial stand. **1903** FARMER & HENLEY *Slang* VI. 346/2 Also (proverbial) 'Stand always, as the girl said.'

7. Also *to stand from under*: see *UNDER *adv.* 4 c.

14. to stand pat. For *U.S.* read Chiefly *U.S.* and add: (*b*) (earlier example). **stand-pat** *a.* (later examples); **stand-patter** (later examples); **stand-pattism** (later examples).

1890 *Stock Grower & Farmer* 29 Mar. 7/1 When it came to them two accomplishments he stood pat. **1920** W. A. WHITE *Let.* 4 Feb. (1947) 204 He also has on [the Republican Platform Committee]..a lot of old high-binder standpatters who haven't had an idea since the fall of Babylon. **1922** *Nation* 18 Nov. 271/1 The Bonar Law Government..remains in power, but probably on a minority vote..This deprives it of the right to pursue the standpat Toryism on which it made the elections. **1952** W. D. JACOBS *William Barnes* v. 79 A sobering realization is that a certain antagonism to a new credo of language is plain stand-pattism. **1975** G. V. HIGGINS *City on Hill* vii. 202 The mood of the country may be such that a stand-patter is the only candidate who can be elected. **1977** *Daily Tel.* 17 Feb. 14/7 He is highly critical of stand-pat, counter-reformation Catholicism.

II. 24. *all standing. to be brought up all standing*: also *actively*; *to gybe all standing* (see quot. 1976); (earlier *transf.* examples); also *fig.*

1837 *Southern Lit. Messenger* III. 178 This reflection brought me up, as the sailors say, 'all standing'. **1840** R. H. DANA *Two Years before Mast* xxxi. 231 The mate ..turned in 'all standing', and was always on deck the moment he was called. **1879** HARTIGAN & WALKER *Stray Leaves* 2nd Ser. 198 [They] gained their respective domiciles, and turned in 'regimental', or, as Jack has it, 'all standing', for their..last night's rest in Old England. **1884** [see GYBE *sb.*[2]]. **1903** A. BENNETT *Let.* 27 Mar. (1966) 35 The close of the book, as it stands, will 'bring him up all standing'. **1924** A. J. SMALL *Frozen Gold* i. 13 A spring..would take him from his chair, all-standing, sheer to the throat of the swaggering giant who held the gun. **1976** *Oxf. Compan. Ships & Sea* 365/2 To gybe without attending the runners, or to do so involuntarily, is known as to 'gybe all-standing', and is dangerous.

29. Also, of (a pot of) tea: to be left to draw.

1933 E. A. ROBERTSON *Ordinary Families* vii. 162 Well, I'll get Olive to bring some fresh tea, then. This has been standing rather a long time. **1935** G. SANTAYANA *Last Puritan* III. v. 333 Don't keep this tea standing any longer... It will be poison. Make some fresh for the boys when they come down. **1976** L. HENDERSON *Major Enquiry* xii. 76 It will be ready soon. I like tea to stand properly, don't you?

V. 59. b. (Later examples.)

1919 CONRAD *Arrow of Gold* IV. ii. 162 Captain Blunt jumped up. 'My mother can't stand tobacco smoke.' **1949** 'G. ORWELL' *1984* II. iii. 134 'I could have stood it if it hadn't been for one thing,' he said. **1964** I. MURDOCH *Italian Girl* iii. 39 Do turn that music off, would you? I can't stand music in the background. **1981** E. A. TAYLOR *Cable Car Murder* (1983) xxiii. 170 Don't get me started on her; I can't stand her.

61. b. Also, to put up or make a present of (a sum of money), esp. as part of a larger amount sought.

1844 DICKENS *Let.* 22 July (1977) IV. 157 If you should decide to come, I will very gladly stand £10 of this Thirty. **1914** G. B. SHAW *Fanny's First Play* I. 177, I cant pay the fine and get him out; but if youll stand 3 pounds I'll stand one; and thatll do it. **1970** G. F. NEWMAN *Sir, you Bastard* viii. 214 Friends able to stand five-thousand pounds surety for his bail.

VI. 71. stand for—. m. To endure, put up with, tolerate. Cf. sense 59 in Dict. *colloq.* (orig. *U.S.*).

1896 ADE *Artie* xii. 107 They say they can't stand for that kind o' work. **1911** R. W. CHAMBERS *Common Law* x. 282 It's going to be hard for her. She can't stand for a mutt—and it's the only sort that will marry her. **1916** E. V. LUCAS *Vermilion Box* lxvi. 72 So crabbed and odd and disagreeable that the store let him go... Two weeks ago he lost his position in the country store. Even that place could not stand for him. **1927** *Punch* 20 Apr. 428/1 The English public, it appears, will only stand for American films. **1952** M. LASKI *Village* xix. 265 Me and Dad have stood for a lot of things..but there's one thing we won't stand for and that's any hole-and-corner business. **1967** N. FREELING *Strike out where not Applicable* 77 Marguerite wouldn't have stood for being humiliated. **1973** E.-J. BAHR *Nice Neighbourhood* i. 6 He was a man who just purely couldn't stand for anyone..to be asleep when he was awake.

74. stand on—. m. In (chiefly imp.) phr. *stand on me*, (you may) rely on me, believe me. Cf. *stand upon* sense 78 c in Dict. *slang.*

1933 *Cornh. Mag.* June 697 'E'll finish like a crab—stand on me fer that. **1935** WALLACE & CURTIS *Mouthpiece* i. 17 If any of your clients ever want to go abroad.. in a hurry—never mind about passports, eh? Just stand on me. **1959** F. NORMAN (*title*) Stand on me, a true story of Soho. **1970** G. F. NEWMAN *Sir, you Bastard* i. 35 You'll be all right, stand on me.

75. stand over—. Also *transf.* in extended use; *Austral. slang*, to intimidate or threaten; to extort money from (someone).

1932 V. WOOLF *Pargiters* (1978) 31 Miss Edwards, the small dressmaker,..could cut out quite well, but one had to stand over her. **1939** K. TENNANT *Foveaux* 173, I just had Thompson in here and he stood over me for three quid. **1940** *Punch* 24 Apr. 449/2, I could *occasionally* leave her to wash up a few cups or something like that without actually standing over her the whole time. **1953** K. TENNANT *Joyful Condemned* iii. 21 There's many a man thought he was going to stand over some little lowie and now he's..looking through the bars. **1967** K. GILES *Death & Mr Prettyman* ii. 58 [Australian loq.] You could stand over—pardon, persecute me. **1978** D. FRANCIS *Trial Run* vii. 105, I should stand over them... Make yourself a bit of a nuisance, so they send it [*sc.* a Telex] to get rid of you.

76. stand to—. f. (Later *arch.* example.)

1935 T. S. ELIOT *Murder in Cathedral* i. 20 Do not ask us To stand to the doom on the house, the doom on the Archbishop.

s. [tr. Ir. *seasamh do.*] To be to one's advantage, to sustain. *Anglo-Irish.*

1907 YEATS *Deirdre* 34 Women, if I die, If Naoise die this night, how will you praise? What words seek out?

for that will stand to you; For being but dead we shall have many friends. **1914** JOYCE *Dubliners* 11 Why, when I was a nipper, every morning of my life I had a cold bath... That's what stands to me now. **1922** —— *Ulysses* 622 Through all those perils of the deep..there was one thing, he declared, stood to him..a pious medal he had that saved him.

VII. 91. stand by. c. Now, of a juror: to withdraw from the jury, esp. at the challenge of the prosecution. Also *trans.* with juror as obj. Cf. CHALLENGE *sb.* 3 a.

1828 *Act 9 Geo. IV* c. 54. 500 Nothing herein contained shall affect..the power of any court in Ireland to order any juror to stand by. **1890** T. BRETT *Comm. Present Laws of Eng.* II. XIII. viii. 1162 The names of those ordered to 'stand by' are called again. **1923** W. J. BYRNE *Dict. Eng. Law* 167/1 The Crown, although it can challenge for cause, has no peremptory challenge, but it may order any person to 'stand by', and need not show cause. **1969** *Sunday Tel.* 12 Jan. 4/6 The defence..could have called 'Challenge!' 70 times without offering reasons. The prosecution called 'Stand by for the Crown!' nine times. (In a British court the phrase 'I object' does not arise in this context.)

trans. **1927** A. M. SULLIVAN *Old Ireland* ii. 41 If this infamous creature attempts to 'stand by' a single Nationalist juror, you will ram it down his throat! **1960** V. T. H. DELANY *Christopher Palles* xi. 101 The Crown 'stood by' 96 jurors, while the defence challenged 36. **1979** *Criminal Law Rev.* May 273 The Crown's right to 'stand-by' jurors is a term which refers to the Crown's power of challenge.

e. (Examples of *gen.* use.)

1866 'MARK TWAIN' *Lett. from Hawaii* (1967) 117 Just as you take a sustaining breath and 'stand by' for the crash, his poor little rocket fizzes faintly in the zenith. **1917** 'CONTACT' *Airman's Outings* iv. 84 For thirty hours the flight had 'stood by' for a long reconnaissance... A slight but steady rain washed away all chance of an immediate job. **1943** *Ann. Reg. 1942* 28 The wastefulness of keeping so many men merely 'standing-by'. **1972** *Listener* 21 Dec. 852/1 Sequence of calls before a shot. Production Assistant: 'Quiet. Going for a take. Standing by.'

92. stand down. d. *Mil.* To come off duty; to relax after a state of alert (also *trans.*).

1916 I. GURNEY *Let.* 25 Oct. in *PN Review* 29 (1982) 32/1 Our last orders were as follows.—From Stand to 5.30. Stand Down, clean rifles... Stand to 5–5.30. Stand Down. **1918** E. S. FARROW *Dict. Mil. Terms* s.v. *Stand to*, Stand down is the order countermanding 'stand-to'. **1919** W. H. DOWNING *Digger Dialects* 47 *Stand-down*, the order by which the period of intense armed vigilance is ended at daybreak, nightfall, or after the alarm of a threatened enemy attack has passed over. **1931** F. TILSLEY *Other Ranks* 108 They religiously stood-to and stood-down every dawn and dusk. **1973** *Daily Tel.* 29 Oct. 30/3 Pres. Nixon ordered..troops in Europe..to remain on the alert..but elsewhere round the world American forces were stood down. **1983** *Times* 12 Feb. 1/1 Acas officials were fighting to keep alive the proposal for a third-party intervention to settle the water workers' strike. But a lull in the peace process is expected over the weekend after the Acas conciliation team was stood down.

94. stand forward. (Earlier example.)

1790 *Loiterer* 9 Jan. 7, I shall be happy to contribute my mite... I dare say his Lordship would stand forward [i.e. with a donation].

95. stand in. d. Also *rarely*, to fall in *with* (a proposal).

1911 M. BEERBOHM *Zuleika Dobson* viii. 138 'Dorset,' he said huskily, 'I shall die too.'.. 'I stand in with that,' said Mr. Oover [an American]. 'So do I!' said Lord Sayes.

f. To fill the place of another (usu. temporarily); to deputize *for* (a person). *spec.* in *Cinemat.*, to act as a substitute *for* a principal actor. Cf. *STAND-IN 2.

1904 in *Eng. Dial. Dict.* V. 725/2 *e. Ken.* Mrs. —— will stand in while Mrs. —— is ill. **1943** HUNT & PRINGLE *Service Slang* 62 *Stand-in*, a deputy; one who 'stands in' for you, or does your duty while you go out. **1955** *Times* 6 June 7/6 There is always a way, especially in Russia where queueing has had to be carried to a fine art. You can employ the willing services of an Armenian or Georgian or other agile-minded person who will stand in for you or will, in turn, get another to stand in for him. **1958** *Listener* 7 Aug. 210/2 The people who stand-in for the film stars when the rough stuff begins. **1978** 'B. GRAEME' *Double Trouble* ii. 20 She has to stand-in for the star while they are working out lighting, camera angles and so on... They try to have a stand-in as much like the star as possible.

96. stand off. f. (Earlier examples.)

1878 J. H. BEADLE *Western Wilds* ii. 38 He offered him fifty thousand for it, and the feller stood him off for seventy-five thousand. **1883** J. HAY *Bread-Winners* xvii. 274 Come, come, Sam, don't stand me off that way.

g. To lay (an employee) off temporarily. Also *intr.* of an employee. Cf. LAY *v.*¹ 54 f in Dict. and Suppl.

1918 [implied at *STAND-OFF *sb.* 5]. **1927** CARR-SAUNDERS & JONES *Soc. Struct. Eng. & Wales* 135 It is not uncommon for indentures to contain a clause enabling the employer to 'stand off' the apprentice without pay if there is no work for him. **1930** *Daily Express* 8 Sept. 11/4 Thirteen hundred Chislet miners..went on strike..as a protest against the standing-off of six men. **1940** H. G. WELLS *New World Order* §5. 58 A state of five million people with half a million of useless hands, will be twice as unstable as forty million with two million standing off. **1952** M. LASKI *Village* i. 17 It wasn't very nice me having to go out to work when Mr. Wilson was stood off, and him staying at home to keep an eye on the children. **1960** G. E. EVANS *Horse in Furrow* i. 22 The day-men were liable to be *stood-off* on wet days. **1976** *Eastern Daily Press* (Norwich) 16 Dec., He was later stood off but went back there to work from 1962 to 1975.

100. stand over. b. (Earlier example.)

1822 M. EDGEWORTH *Let.* 30 May (1971) 404 A beef and pigeon pie that had stood over from the preceding week.

101. stand to. c. *Mil. ellipt.* for *to stand to one's arms*, sense 76 d in Dict. Hence, to come or remain on duty. Cf. *stand-to*, sense 104 below.

1915 F. H. LAWRENCE *Let.* 7 Mar. in *Home Lett. T. E. Lawrence* (1954) 671, I thought the Germans were attacking us, so I passed the word along for all my men to stand to, as we call it. *a* **1918** W. OWEN *Poems* (1963) 60 Eh? What the 'ell! Stand to? Stand to! Jim, Give's a hand with pack on, lad. **1942** E. WAUGH *Put out More Flags* i. 22 She saw him as Siegfried Sassoon, an infantry subaltern in a mud-bogged trench, standing to at dawn,.. waiting for zero hour. **1977** J. B. HILTON *Dead-Nettle* xv. 120 After days of pointless standing-to in dew-drenched hedge-bottoms, there was a cleaning-up of uniforms.

103. stand up. e. Also, † to present oneself for marriage.

1842 *Amer. Pioneer* I. 314 They were married without any previous preparation..he standing up in a hunting dress, and she in a short gown and petticoat of homespun.

f. (Earlier example.)

1836 DICKENS *Sk. Boz* (1st Ser.) I. 252 Nobody thought of 'standing up' under doorways or arches.

g. (Later examples.) Also, freq. in extended phr. (*only*) *the clothes one stands up in.*

1937 'G. ORWELL' *Road to Wigan Pier* ix. 182, I.. planned..how one could..start out with no money and nothing but the clothes one stood up in. **1944** N. STREATFEILD *Curtain Up* vi. 71 Monsieur Manoff and most of his pupils..escaped to America... They had, of course, nothing but what they stood up in. **1981** E. LONGFORD *Queen Mother* v. 83 Queen Wilhelmina of the Netherlands ..brought only the clothes she stood up in plus a tin hat.

j. (Later *poet.* example.)

1896 A. E. HOUSMAN *Shropshire Lad* vii. 11 When smoke stood up from Ludlow And mist blew off the Teme.

p. Also with impersonal subj.: to endure or withstand.

1921 G. B. SHAW *Back to Methuselah* p. lxxxv, I had seen Bible fetichism, after standing up to all the rationalistic batteries of Hume, Voltaire, and the rest, collapse before the onslaught of much less gifted Evolutionists. **1940** *Punch* 11 Dec. p. xiii, Nylon tufts will stand up to an incredible amount of hard use.

q. To fail to keep an appointment with (someone), esp. a social engagement or 'date' with a member of the opposite sex. *colloq.* (orig. *U.S.*).

1902 O. V. LIMERICK *Billy Burgundy's Opinions* 57, I am awfully sorry I had to stand you up last night. **1906** 'O. HENRY' *Four Million* 122 Rosy's stuck to the affirmative this time for two whole days. But it's five hours yet till the time, and I'm afraid she'll stand me up when it comes to the scratch. **1936** J. CURTIS *Gilt Kid* xxv. 244 It must be getting along. He didn't want Maisie to think that he was standing her up. **1940** R. CHANDLER *Farewell, my Lovely* xxxii. 246 You stood me up for an hour the other night. **1952** J. CANNAN *Body in Beck* ix. 186 Time and again..I stood up the chaps so as to climb with him. **1959** *New Statesman* 11 Apr. 519/2 It isn't long, however, before she discovers the canker in the bud, in the person of William, a young smoothie from Madison Avenue, who stands her up. **1978** L. THOMAS *Ormerod's Landing* iii. 43 'What about the other agent, the lady?'.. 'Stood you up, I shouldn't wonder,' laughed Charles.

r. In colloq. phr. *to stand up and* (also *to*) *be counted*, to show one's political colours; also more widely, to display one's conviction or sympathy, esp. when this requires courage. orig. *U.S.*

1904 *Hartford* (Connecticut) *Courant* 12 Aug. 10 Another democratic paper, the 'Sacramento Bee', follows the example of the 'Chicago Chronicle' and stands up to be counted for Roosevelt. **1945** *Somerset News* (Princess Anne, Maryland) 22 Mar. 1/3 Why then weren't Shore delegates men enough to stand up and be counted? **1968** *Listener* 1 Aug. 134/2, I suppose in the end it was having to stand up and be counted as part of 'The New Establishment'; being forced to own up that I earn my living and have my being in that world. **1969** *Ibid.* 13 Nov. 658/3, I was a great one for demos in my youth... I can remember a good deal of self-righteousness, in standing up to be counted with the saints. **1973** 'M. INNES' *Appleby's Answer* iv. 38 A mild-mannered man. But he felt he must stand up and be counted. **1977** D. JAMES *Spy at Evening* xxiv. 199 People like you haven't stood up to be counted.

s. To sustain close examination, to be tenable: esp. of a charge or theory.

1948 in M. McLuhan *Mech. Bride* (1967) 6/3 Authorities here voiced doubt..whether such a charge would 'stand up'. **1962** *Listener* 10 May 814/3 It will be interesting to see if this conclusion stands up when more results become available. **1976** N. FREELING *Lake Isle* xxxii. 232 It won't stand up in law, I tell you.

t. *will the real — please stand up?*, a catch-phrase which requests that a person clarify his position or make himself known (often rhetorical). orig. *U.S.*

1971 *Black Scholar* June 32 (*heading*) Will the real black man please stand up? **1973** *Illustr. London News* July 76/3 Will the real Kate Brown please stand up and show herself? **1981** *Nature* 12 Mar. 89 (*heading*) Will the real Grenville Orogeny please stand up.

VIII. 104. stand-alone *a. Computers*, designating a part of a computer system that can be used independently; **stand-away** *a.*, (*a*) of a person: reserved, chilly, 'standoffish'; (*b*) of a collar, etc.: that lies or rises away from the neck of the wearer; also *absol.* as *sb.*; **stand-back** *rare*, (*a*) a source of reassurance or support; a dependable person; (*b*) one who holds back; **stand-down** *Mil.* (now esp. *Air Force*), the action or state of coming or remaining off duty or of relaxing from a period of vigilance; the end of a spell of duty; **stand-over**, (*b*) *Austral. slang*, used *attrib.* to designate the perpetrator of extortion by threat, a protection-racketeer, as *stand-over man*; or the process of such extortion; occas. *absol.* and *transf.*; **stand-to** *Mil., ellipt.* for *stand-to-arms*; also, the time of coming on duty, as at dawn or dusk, or in preparation for an attack; also *attrib.*; **stand-to-arms**: also, the period of standing to arms.

1966 C. J. SIPPL *Computer Dict. & Handbk.* 295/2 *Stand-alone capability*, a multiplexor designed to function independently of a host or master computer, either some of the time or all of the time. **1969** *Computers & Humanities* III. 137 A system for typing concordance output on an IBM Selectric typewriter is being developed for use with a stand-alone device which consists of a magnetic tape unit, keyboard, and heavy-duty selectric typewriter. **1977** *Sci. Amer.* Sept. 147/2 At the next level in the hierarchy of capability and function are the small computer systems that are prepackaged as stand-alone units... They have a self-contained power supply. **1938** J. CARY *Castle Corner* iii. 155 Rifty had Bridget for his partner but Bridget was even more standaway than usual. **1955** *Sun* (Baltimore) 3 Feb. (B ed.) 3/1 Most of Balenciaga's collars are simple turnover standaways. **1964** *McCall's Sewing* i. 12/1 Stand-away collars, collarless styles and V- or U-shaped necklines will make the neck seem longer. **1971** *Woman's Own* 27 Mar. 24/1 A stand-away collar is good for a thick neck. **1915** D. H. LAWRENCE *Rainbow* xii. 313 Gudrun was..a great comfort and shield to her... This was a great stand-back to Ursula, who suffered agonies when she thought a person disliked her. **1922** —— *Aaron's Rod* x. 122, I had a corporal called Wallace... He was my stand-back. **1946** J. W. DAY *Harvest Adventure* vi. 89 We've got a fine lot o' stand-backs to tell others to git forrad. **1919** W. H. DOWNING *Digger Dialects* 47 *Stand-down*, the hours at which the above orders [to go off duty] are regularly given each day. **1925** FRASER & GIBBONS *Soldier & Sailor Words* s.v. *Stand-to*, 'Stand-down' was the corresponding order at the end of the Danger Period, used in like manner as an expression for a definite point of time. **1945** C. H. WARD-JACKSON *It's Piece of Cake* (ed. 2) 57 *Stand-down*, time-off when flying is cancelled. **1949** W. S. CHURCHILL *Second World War* II. II. xvi. 297 On February 13, 1942, Admiral Raeder had his final interview on 'Sea Lion' and got Hitler to agree to a complete 'stand-down'. **1953** EARL WINTERTON *Orders of Day* xix. 270 Next morning at 'stand down', on a cold grey day, I went to have a look at where the place had been where I had spent so many years of my life [engaged in fire-watching]. **1978** H. WOUK *War & Remembrance* xxviii. 284 Then would come the bored wait, the stand-down, the recovery of aircraft, and the resumed plan of the day. **1939** K. TENNANT *Foveaux* 174 He didn't deserve to be a 'standover man' if he couldn't move quicker. **1941** BAKER *Dict. Austral. Slang* 71 *Standover (man)*, a criminal who exacts toll from other lawbreakers or innocents. *Ibid.*, *Standover, work the*, to act as a 'stand-over man'. Also, a door-to-door hawker's term for bullying tactics adopted to intimidate housewives. **1954** L. H. EVERS *Pattern of Conquest* 198 Don't come the stand-over tactics you used with Charlie. **1977** *Daily News* (Perth, Austral.) 19 Jan. 16/5 Detectives believe the shooting is part of a war that has broken out amongst stand-over men in the massage parlour industry in Melbourne. **1915** in W. Wood *In Line of Battle* (1916) 217 At stand-to, 6 a.m. Much shelling. **1928** E. BLUNDEN *Undertones of War* ii. 21 Let me take you..back now..into the stand-to billets in Festubert village. **1942** *R.A.F. Jrnl.* 3 Oct. 31 There was that stand-to in the small hours one day. **1954** W. K. HANCOCK *Country & Calling* vii. 195 In the quiet middle years of the war we were allowed to lie down after our training until stand-to at 6 a.m. **1975** T. ALLBEURY *Special Collection* xi. 78 They made a permanent stand-to situation with just six of their anti-missile missiles. **1915** A. D. GILLESPIE *Let.* 11 Mar. in *Lett. from Flanders* (1916) 43 As I write, during the evening 'stand to arms', the birds are all singing in spite of the sniping.

standard, *sb.* Add: **A. II. 10. b.** Also *double standard*: see *DOUBLE *a.* 6.

12. a. *standard of comfort* (examples); also *standard of life*.

1879 A. & M. P. MARSHALL *Econ. Industry* II. vii. 102 The Standard of Comfort which young people are prudent enough to secure for themselves before they marry, varies from place to place and from time to time. **1898** B. BOSANQUET (*title*) Standard of life, and other studies. **1907** G. B. SHAW *John Bull's Other Island* II. 41 He guesses Broadbent's standard of comfort a little more accurately than his sister does. **1936** J. M. KEYNES *Gen. Theory Employment, Interest & Money* xvi. 218 The position of equilibrium, under conditions of *laissez-faire*, will be one in which employment is low enough and the standard of life sufficiently miserable to bring savings to zero.

b. Also *transf.*, the form or class in which pupils are prepared for a particular standard.

1878 F. KILVERT *Jrnl.* 16 Jan. (1977) 300 Gave the upper standards at the school questions on paper on the Catechism. **1915** D. H. LAWRENCE *Rainbow* xiii. 353 She made friends with the Standard Three teacher. **1934** G. B. SHAW *On Rocks* Pref. 168 The likeliest outcome is an elaborate creed of useful illusions, to be discarded bit by bit as the child is promoted from standard to standard or from form to form. **1966** C. ACHEBE *Man of People* i. 2

Sixteen years or so he had been my teacher in standard three. **1973** *Express* (Trinidad & Tobago) 17 Mar. 7/1 He left Trinidad a Seventh standard pupil of the St. Helena C.M. School.

16. Short for: **c.** *standard lamp*, sense 30 in Dict.

1910 H. G. WELLS *New Machiavelli* III. iii, in *English Rev.* Sept. 292 The light of the big electric standard in the corner. **1939** O. LANCASTER *Homes, Sweet Homes* 10 All over Europe the lights are going out..olde Tudor lanthorns, standards and wall-brackets. **1974** M. INGATE *Sound of Weir* ix. 74 Tall lamps, 'they're Standards,' said Iris, had large coloured shades.

d. A standard form of a language (see *STANDARD *a.* 3 e). *Modified* (also *Received*) *Standard*: see the first element in Suppl.

1913 *Mod. Lang. Teaching* Dec. 262/2 While within the London sphere of influence..Received Standard goes on quite gaily, the London type of Modified Standard has won the day in this area, among those sections of the community who might otherwise speak a Kentish..or Surrey type of Modified Standard. **1972** HARTMANN & STORK *Dict. Lang. & Linguistics* 218/1 Deviations from the respective established standards are called non-standard or sub-standard.

III. 26. c. A tune or song of established popularity, esp. in *Jazz*.

1937 *Amer. Speech* XII. 184/1 *Standard*, a number whose popularity has withstood the test of time. **1938** 'JELLY ROLL' MORTON in *Downbeat* Aug. 31/1, I also transformed..*After the Ball, Back Home in Indiana*, etc., and all standards that I saw fit. **1947** R. DE TOLEDANO *Frontiers of Jazz* p. xii, Half a dozen ancient Melrose stock arrangements of jazz standards 'as played by King Oliver'. **1959** 'F. NEWTON' *Jazz Scene* ii. 29 The repertoire [of jazz] consists of so-called 'standards'—themes which for one reason or another, lend themselves to profitable jazz playing. They may be drawn from any source, the traditional blues and the current popular song being the most important. **1971** C. FICK *Danziger Transcript* 95 There was a Cuban quartet in the garden playing light standards. **1980** M. BOOTH *Bad Track* v. 84 For an hour or so, the band jammed,..before going into standards that they knew and admired.

IV. 30. standard-bred *a.* (earlier example); also *N. Amer.* as *sb.*, a horse of this breed, developed esp. for harness racing (contrasted with *thoroughbred*); **standard lamp** (earlier and later examples).

1888 G. W. CURTIS *Horses, Cattle, Sheep, & Swine* x. 56 When an animal meets the requirements of admission, and is duly registered, it should be accepted as a standard bred trotting animal. **1948** *Sun* (Baltimore) 20 Aug. 18/1 The standardbreds..make running horses look like sissies. **1976** *National Observer* (U.S.) 2 Oct. 7/2, I grew up in.. the western part of Illinois..and every farmer..had a standardbred, either trotter or pacer... They just tied sulky bikes to the backs of the nags and drove them around the track themselves. **1894** *Country Gentlemen's Catal.* 115/1 Wrought Iron Standard Lamp, with copper Oil Container, 70/-. **1932** R. LEHMANN *Invitation to Waltz* I. xi. 110 The light was very bright and white, coming from three brass standard lamps with white silk shades. **1980** A. N. WILSON *Healing Art* xvi. 195 By the fireplace..gas blazed, and a standard lamp shone dimly.

B. *adj.* **I. 1. a.** Also freq. in special scientific collocations, as *standard atmosphere*, (*a*) a unit of atmospheric pressure, equal to 760 torr or 1013·25 millibars; (*b*) a hypothetical atmosphere with defined surface temperature and pressure and specified profile of temperature with altitude, used esp. in aviation and space research; *standard cable*, a unit of attenuation formerly used in telephone engineering (see quot. 1963), now replaced by the *BEL; *standard candle*, a disused unit of luminous intensity, defined as the intensity of the flame of a spermaceti candle of specified properties (see quots.), now replaced by the *CANDELA; also *transf.*; *standard cell*, any of several forms of voltaic cell designed to produce a constant and reproducible electromotive force as long as the current drawn is not too large; *standard deviation*: see *DEVIATION 2 d; *standard error*, a measure of the statistical accuracy of an estimate, equal to the standard deviation which a large population of such estimates would have; *standard wire gauge*, one of the series of standard thicknesses for wire and metal plates in the United Kingdom; any specific measure in this series; abbrev. *s.w.g.*, *S.W.G.* s.v. *S 4 a.

1911 W. N. SHAW *Forecasting Weather* p. xi, The accepted normal pressure of the atmosphere, or 'standard atmosphere', is that of a column of mercury 76 centimetres high at the freezing-point of water under the conditions as to gravitation which are to be found in latitude 45°N. or S. **1924** *Official Bull. Internat. Comm. Air Navigation* VII. 34 The Commission decides: To adopt the Regulations set out hereunder concerning the definition of an international standard atmosphere. **1930** *Meteorol. Gloss.* (Met. Office) (ed. 2) 162 The International Standard Atmosphere which is used as the basis of graduation of altimeters assumes at mean sea level a temperature of 15°C., a pressure of 1,013·2 mb., and a lapse rate of 6·5°C. per kilometre from sea level up to 11 km., above which the temperature is assumed constant at −56·5°C. **1963** JERRARD & MCNEILL *Dict. Sci. Units* 130 One standard atmosphere corresponds to a barometric pressure of 29·9213 inches or 760 mm of mercury of density 13·595 g cm^{-3}, where the acceleration due to gravity if 980·665 cm sec^{-2}... The ICAO [*sc.* International Civil Aviation Organisation] standard atmosphere was introduced about 1940. **1977** I. M. CAMPBELL *Energy & Atmosphere* iii. 47 The origin of the rising temperature from 11 to 50 km in the standard atmosphere is the degradation of a portion of the solar irradiance to thermal energy through the agency of primary absorption by ozone. **1906** J. POOLE *Pract. Telephone Handbk.* (ed. 3) xxvi. 413 Standard Cable and Equivalents.—In the agreement entered into in February 1905 between the British Post Office and the National Telephone Co. certain standards of telephonic transmission were stipulated, and these were to be measured by comparison with the transmission results obtained with standard telephone instruments through certain lengths of standard test cable. **1924** *Trans. Amer. Inst. Electr. Engineers* XLIII. 797/1 The 'mile of standard cable' has been used in telephone engineering in this country for over twenty years..as the unit for expressing the transmission efficiency of telephone circuits and apparatus. **1963** JERRARD & MCNEILL *Dict. Sci. Units* 131 The unit compared the attenuation produced in the circuit under test with that in a standard cable which was defined as a theoretical cable one mile in length, resistance 88 ohms, capacitance 0·054 microfarad, inductance one millihenry and leakance 5× 10^{-6} mho. The standard cable produced an attenuation of about 20% for a 800 c/s input. **1879** Standard candle [in Dict.]. **1937** G. S. MONK *Light* v. 36 The standard candle was originally of sperm wax, weighing $\frac{1}{6}$ lb., $\frac{7}{8}$ in. diameter, and burning 120 grains per hr. **1959** *Listener* 2 July 14/2 By studying the period of a Cepheid, we can.. find out its real luminosity; its apparent magnitude is easy to measure, and hence its distance may be determined, so that these convenient variables act as our standard candles in space. **1976** *New Scientist* 2 Dec. 530/1 The new finding opens the way to calibrate a new standard candle, namely, the absolute brightness of a galaxy by means of an easy measurement in radio astronomy. **1872** L. CLARK in *Proc. R. Soc.* XX. 447 We have therefore the mean value of the electromotive force of the standard-cells, as determined by the electrodynamometer, 18 observations..1·45735 Volt. **1920** *Whittaker's Electr. Engineer's Pocket-bk.* (ed. 4) 100 The original standard cell devised by Latimer Clark is a mercury-zinc cell using zinc and mercurous sulphates as electrolyte and depolarizer respectively. **1980** J. P. BROMBERG *Physical Chem.* xvii. 315 The voltage of the unknown cell..can be determined from the calibrated slide wire and the known voltage of the standard cell. **1897** G. U. YULE in *Jrnl. R. Statist. Soc.* LX. 821 We see that $\sigma_1\sqrt{(1-r^2)}$ is the standard error made in estimating *x*. **1956** J. H. BURN *Lect. Notes Pharmacol.* (ed. 4) 129 The standard error of the mean is proportional to the standard deviation and inversely proportional to the number of animals used. **1962** J. H. KINOSHITA et al. in A. Pirie *Lens Metabolism Rel. Cataract* 409 The results are given as the mean ± standard error of the mean of 12 determinations. **1858** J. WHITWORTH *Misc. Papers Mech. Subjects* 68 (*caption*) Standard wire-gauge. **1884** *Rep. Board of Trade on Proc. & Business Weights & Measures Act, 1878* 3 in *Parl. Papers* XXVIII. 851 The new standard wire-gauge has been adopted by the War, Admiralty, and India Departments. **1941** *Trans Newcomen Soc.* XXI. 94 He [*sc.* Sir Joseph Whitworth] named it the 'Standard Wire Gauge'; it covered a range of 38 sizes of from 0·3 in. to 0·0018 in. diam. **1963** JERRARD & MCNEILL *Dict. Sci. Units* 151 The Standard Wire Gauge..classifies wire diameters in geometrical progression. **1971** B. SCHARF *Engin. & its Lang.* ix. 75 In Great Britain the main gauges are the Standard Wire Gauge (S.W.G., s.w.g.), and the Birmingham Gauge (B.G.).

b. Also *standard costs* Accountancy (see quot. 1959); freq. *attrib.*, as *standard cost card* etc. Hence *standard costing*. Also as parasynthetic adj., *standard-rated*.

1917 W. N. POLAKOV in *Trans. Amer. Soc. Mech. Engineers* XXXVIII. 587 Carrying out the analysis of the economy limit to its logical conclusion, the standard cost of the product is arrived at. **1918** G. C. HARRISON in *Industrial Managem.* LVI. 393/2 In the 'Standard Cost Card' shown in Form I it will be seen that the estimated or standard cost of the bolts is $11·079 per thousand. **1921** (*title*) Standard costing principles & practices for the plywood industry. **1935** C. M. GILLESPIE *Accounting Procedure for Standard Costs* iv. 62 The structure of standard cost cards becomes complex. **1959** *Chambers's Encycl.* I. 39/2 Two major developments in cost accounting must be briefly mentioned. Firstly the introduction of standard costing. Standard costs are estimates made in detail for operations, processes of articles on the basis of predetermined standards. **1974** *Terminol. Managem. & Financial Accountancy* (Inst. Cost and Managem. Accountants) 15 *Standard cost rate*, a rate calculated by dividing the expected overhead cost attributable to a cost centre by the predetermined quantity of the base to which the rate is applied.

Comb. **1972** *V.A.T.: Gen. Guide* (H.M. Customs) 30 Where an amount payable covers both standard-rated and zero-rated goods or services, the amount must be split in fair proportion. **1977** *Jrnl. R. Soc. Arts* CXXV. 440/1 The most sensitive systems might have legislation applied at a luxury rate whilst others could be standard rated.

e. Bridge. *Standard American*, the commonest system of bidding in the U.S.

1961 A. SHEINWOLD *Short Cut to winning Bridge* 13/1 Most of the hands in this book are bid according to the principles of 'Standard American'. **1963** H. SCHENKEN *Better Bidding* i. 16 The most popular system in this country is called Standard American... They all have one thing in common with Standard American: the opening bid of one in a suit is almost unlimited. **1968** ROTH & RUBENS *Mod. Bridge Bidding* p. xvi, Standard American is the most widely used although not..the best approach to bidding. **1976** *National Observer* (U.S.) 24 July 15/3 If you are playing under Precision's rules or by agreement in Standard American and you open light.., you can pass third hand with a subminimum count.

3. b. Also *standard work*.

1821 HAZLITT in *London Mag.* Aug. 179/2 Pictures are scattered like stray gifts through the world... There are plenty of standard works still to be found in this country. **1849** C. BRONTË *Shirley* I. v. 94 One should not be apathetic in studying standard works. **1922** JOYCE *Ulysses* 628 You know the standard works on the subject. **1969** J. GROSS *Rise & Fall Man of Lett.* iv. 115 He goes on to supply a list of standard works, English and European,..which would certainly keep most ordinary readers tied up for as far ahead as they could plan.

e. Applied to that variety of a spoken or written language of a country or other linguistic area which is generally considered the most correct and acceptable form, as *Standard English, American*, etc.; Received Standard; also, *standard pronunciation* = *received pronunciation* s.v. *RECEIVED *ppl. a.* 1 b.

1836 *Q. Rev.* Feb. 356 It is, however, certain that there were in his [*sc.* Higden's] time, and probably long before, five distinctly marked forms, which may be classed as follows:—1. Southern or standard English, which in the fourteenth century was perhaps best spoken in Kent and Surrey by the body of the inhabitants. **1859** *Proposal Publ. New Eng. Dict.* 3 As soon as a standard language has been formed, which in England was the case after the Reformation, the lexicographer is bound to deal with that alone. **1878** J. A. H. MURRAY in *Encycl. Brit.* VIII. 396/2 Chaucer's language is well known to be more southern than standard English eventually became. **1908** H. SWEET *Sounds Eng.* 7 Standard English, like Standard French, is now a class-dialect more than a local dialect: it is the language of the educated all over Great Britain. **1909** D. JONES *Pronunc. Eng.* i. 1 Standard Pronunciation. **1919** G. P. KRAPP (*title*) The pronunciation of standard English in America. **1925** —— *Eng. Lang. in Amer.* I. v. 296 The informal or local speech will often seem more penetrating, more genuine than the standard speech. **1947** PARTRIDGE *Usage & Abusage* 304/1 Standard English and Standard American are the speech of the educated classes in the British Empire and the United States. **1962** P. H. JOHNSON *Error of Judgment* ii. 5 Had spoken standard English varied by a few fancies such as 'crorss' for 'cross' and 'poyt' for 'poet'. **1975** *Times Lit. Suppl.* 7 Feb. 136/2 Local names pronounced in [Chinese] dialects widely different from 'Mandarin' or, as it must now be called, Standard Speech. **1978** *English Jrnl.* Dec. 7/1 There is also a kind of 'standard standard'. Some people call it 'broadcast' or 'publications' standard, because most newspapers and television news shows use it.

f. *standard time*: see *TIME *sb.* 27.

3*. *Math.* That does not involve infinitesimal quantities.

1961 A. ROBINSON in *Proc. K. Nederlandse Akad. v. Wetensch.* A. LXIV. 434 We consider in the first instance functions, relations, sets, etc. which are defined already in R_0 [*sc.* the set of all real numbers]... Such concepts will be called standard (functions, relations, sets, etc.). **1972** [see *NON-STANDARD *a.* b].

Hence **sta·ndardless** *a.* [-LESS], having no standard or standards; unprincipled; **sta·ndardness** [-NESS].

1912 GALSWORTHY *Inn of Tranquillity* 217 How can we help it, seeing that we are undisciplined and standardless, seeing that we started without the backbone that schooling gives? **1944** AUDEN *Sea & Mirror* in *For Time Being* iii. 29 On the shuddering edge of the bohemian standardless abyss. **1972** J. L. DILLARD *Black English* vi. 238 A combination of age-grading, status-grading, and peer group influence causes a special feature to operate among young males at about the age of puberty. At that time, their graph of standardness will actually swing 'downward' a bit. **1973** *N.Y. Law Jrnl.* 2 Aug. 4/8 Such a subjective determination as is proposed here lacks the necessary standards to insure a nondiscriminatory result. The danger of discrimination which inheres in such a standardless approval is..evidenced by the determination in question here.

standardizable (stæ·ndǎrdəizǎb'l), *a.* [f. STANDARDIZE *v.* + -ABLE.] That may be standardized.

1922 *19th Cent.* Feb. 185 The sale of the more standardisable profits. **1980** *U.S. News & World Rep.* 1 Dec. 45/1 Legal clinics offering adoptions, divorces, wills and other frequently cut-and-dried standardizable services at low cost are flourishing.

standardly (stæ·ndǎrdli), *adv.* [f. STANDARD *a.* + -LY².] In a standard manner; according to common practice; normally, generally.

1957 *Proc. Aristotelian Soc.* LVII. 237 Knowledge of a particular event will standardly give one knowledge only of the location of its witnesses. **1978** A. RYAN in Hookway & Pettit *Action & Interpretation* 75 A game in which we are standardly beset by something like Prisoners' Dilemma problems.

‖**Standartenführer** (ʃta·ndaɹtenfǖ:rəɪ). Ger., lit. 'leader of the standard'.] Under the Third Reich, a commanding officer of a unit of the Schutzstaffel or Sturmabteilung.

1943 W. NECKER *German Army of To-day* IV. 168 *Staff Officers*:.. *SS-Standartenführer* = colonel. **1971** BENDER & TAYLOR *Uniforms, Organization & Hist. Waffen-SS* II. 72 SS-Standartenführer, promoted on Nov. 4, 1944 to SS Oberführer, Wilhelm Mohnke. **1973** 'D. JORDAN' *Nile Green* xliv. 225 He was on the staff of the SS Hauptamt. He ended the war as Standartenfuhrer. **1978** *Detroit Free Press* 16 Apr. (Record) 12/2 These strips had been collected by a German doctor who was writing a treatise on tatooes, and also by the 28-year-old wife of the Standartenfuehrer or commanding officer.

stand-by. Add: **1. c.** The state of being immediately available to come on duty if required; readiness for duty. Also *transf.* Usu. in phr. *on stand-by*. orig. *Naut.*

1946 R. E. HIGGINBOTHAM *Wine for my Brothers* iv. 75 I'm on stand-by—take the wheel in fifteen minutes. **1959** WALLIS & BLAIR *Thunder Above* (ed. 2) ii. 13 With a full load we could use an extra stewardess. You're on stand-by, aren't you? **1960** *Times* 22 Mar. 12/1 Darkness brought peace to the riot areas, but an active citizen force was put on standby. **1971** W. KEENAN *Murder in Melancholy* v. 48 We'll use two of the vans every night, the other will be on standby. **1974** D. FRANCIS *Knock Down* iv. 45 I'm on stand-by from four this afternoon for twelve hours... Most stand-bys are just a bore.

d. *spec.* in civilian aviation, a stand-by passenger; *on stand-by*, waiting for a stand-by seat; in possession of a stand-by ticket. See sense 9 below.

1961 'E. LATHEN' *Banking on Death* (1962) xix. 156 Four stand-bys who were convinced that by keeping in motion their chances of getting on a plane were improved. **1962** J. D. MACDONALD *Key to Suite* (1968) ii. 31 'You got in real early.' 'Earlier than I wanted to. But all they could do for me on anything later was to put me on standby.' **1970** *Guardian* 8 Sept. 11/4 All the flights are full. They're likely to be on standby half the night for seats on any plane. **1973** [see *STAGE *sb.* 9 c].

4. *ellipt.* for: **a.** *stand-by credit, loan*, etc.; **b.** a stand-by fare or ticket.

1959 *Daily Tel.* 18 Dec. 20/5 It was in December, 1956, after the Suez crisis, that Britain drew $561 million from the Fund and arranged for a 'stand-by' of $738 million.. to be drawn upon if necessary. **1975** *Offshore* Aug. 42/1 The Smit tug was lounging around, lapping up stand-by at a thousand dollars a day. **1980** *Daily Tel.* 29 Aug. 7/2 The £20 Scottish standby, the airline claims, is more than £5 cheaper than the second-class rail fare.

II. *attrib.* or as *adj.* **5.** Of a charge for electricity: remaining constant, fixed; levied for the availability of an electrical supply in a given period, irrespective of the amount used; *stand-by losses*: (see quot. 1940). Also *transf.*

1900 *Jrnl. Inst. Electr. Engineers* May 680 What are called the Standing or Stand-by Charges. Other items which might fairly be added to the stand-by charges are the rent, rates and taxes, and part of the management expenses. **1907** *Chambers's Jrnl.* 1 June 432/2 What are called the stand-by losses are also much reduced in the gas system. **1933** *Discovery* Feb. 65/1 The 'standby charges' of internal combustion cars are negligible, and therefore running costs are extremely low. **1940** *Chambers's Techn. Dict.* 800/2 *Stand-by losses*, that part of the power expended in a generating station in order to maintain plant in instant readiness to take a sudden load. **1973** *Gloss. Electrotechnical, Power Terms* (*B.S.I.*) II. vii. 7 *Standby charge*, a demand charge for the availability of a supply under the conditions of a standby tariff, to be paid by the consumer irrespective of whether or not he makes use of the standby supply.

6. a. Of machinery or equipment: kept in a position of reserve, *spec.* in case of failure of a primary device or supply.

1908 *Sears, Roebuck Catal.* 205/2 The Stand-By Dry Batteries..will produce more current and last longer. **1930** *Engineering* 28 Feb. 295/1 A standby machine of this type is also useful. **1942** *R.A.F. Jrnl.* 3 Oct. 25 From the..roof, electric lights and stand-by hurricane lamps are suspended. **1954** 'J. CHRISTOPHER' *Twenty-Second Cent.* 122, I knew they would have the stand-by generators on in a minute or two. **1969** *Gloss. Terms Magnetic Compasses & Binnacles* (*B.S.I.*) 4 *Stand-by steering compass*, a magnetic compass which provides a secondary heading reference for steering a ship. **1972** *Daily Tel.* 1 Mar. 2/6 Stand-by electric generators kept for emergencies have been packed ready for transport.

b. Of (a body of) persons: on stand-by; available to come on duty. More generally, ready to stand in for another if required. orig. *Naut.*

1933 J. H. MCCULLOCH *Million Miles* iii. 59 It was the standby man from the other watch, dragging us out again for another four-hour battle on the deck. **1937** *Amer. Speech* XII. 100 The public is..not so accustomed to *stand by organist* or *pianist*, an artist who remains on call for emergency work. **1946** R. E. HIGGINBOTHAM *Wine for my Brothers* 178 Dane was stand-by man, and he started over the catwalk for the bridge. **1958** *Economist* 16 Aug. 507/2 When he asked the assembly to create a United Nations 'standby' peace force, he was making a gesture of conciliation. **1974** *Sumter* (S. Carolina) *Daily Item* 18 Apr. 6B/1 The White House has secretly appointed wealthy campaign contributors to the standby corps, which would help run the country in case of war. **1981** G. CLARE *Last Waltz in Vienna* (1982) II. 144 My role was that of stand-by boy-friend very much playing second fiddle.

c. Similarly, of a vehicle or craft held in reserve.

1959 *Economist* 14 Mar. 992/2 In case of breakdown a 'standby' vehicle can be hired from the manufacturers when needed. **1974** *BP Shield Internat.* Oct. 20/1 I'm keeping in touch with our standby vessel, *Otterburn*. **1976** P. R. WHITE *Planning for Public Transport* viii. 183 It may be cheaper to move to direct sale coupled with retention of standby vehicles and crews to duplicate workings if required. **1982** *Times* 3 June 8/5 Several of the smaller frigates have been pulled out of standby fleets.

7. Designating a state, condition, or position of readiness. Also *stand-by duty*.

1922 *Wireless World* X. 355/1 The receiving telephones are hung on a special rest, this automatically putting the call-receiver in a stand-by position. **1944** *Daily Progress* (Charlottesville, Va.) 25 May 4/1 Ammunition plants which were closed or placed on a standby basis..have been ordered reopened. **1959** *Times* 11 Sept. 7/2 This new cell is specially designed for standby duties. **1977** *Cornish Times* 19 Aug. 15/3 The present Saltash ambulance station is manned from 7 a.m. to 11 p.m. each day with a stand-by-basis operating during the remaining eight hours.

8. Applied to an economic or financial measure prepared for implementation should certain conditions obtain; spec. *stand-by credit*: an additional credit facility reserved at low interest which may be drawn upon at standard rates if needed; cf. *line of credit* s.v. *LINE *sb.*[2] 30 c. Hence of loan arrangements, etc.

1947 *Sun* (Baltimore) 26 Nov. 14/3 The President's proposals for stand-by price-wage ceilings and rationing authority. **1957** *Encycl. Brit.* III. 56/2 It is a common practice for banks to grant their regular customers a 'line of credit' under which the bank agrees to extend loans up to a certain maximum... Borrowers sometimes pay a small interest charge, amounting to perhaps ½% of the unused part of the line of credit, under so-called 'stand-by' agreements. **1957** *Times* 17 Dec. 13/1 The decision to ask for an extension of the $739 standby credit with the International Monetary Fund..is a logical one. **1962** *Economist* 9 June 996/2 Ways to stimulate business..preferably by winning from Congress stand-by authority to cut taxes across the board. **1973** 'D. JORDAN' *Nile Green* xi. 50 We'd have to have some sort of standby agreement for the remaining $45m. **1977** *Time* 8 Aug. 18/2 Italy has repaid on schedule an International Monetary Fund stand-by loan.

9. In civilian aviation: designating a system of seat allocation whereby a passenger does not book in advance, but may board at a cheaper rate the next flight with spare unbooked capacity; also *stand-by fare, passenger, ticket*, etc. Also as *adv.* Cf. sense 1 d above.

1963 *Guardian* 9 Feb. 12/2 BEA had proposed a one third cut in fares for stand-by passengers, namely, people prepared to chance obtaining a seat after booked passengers had boarded the plane. **1963** *Daily Tel.* 19 Feb. 1/8 Stand-by night tourist fares in April and May represent a rate of less than 2d a mile... The full cost of the stand-by ticket will be refunded to passengers who do not travel. **1968** 'A. YORK' *Predator* viii. 124, I had to come in as a standby tourist. But they've had a last-minute cancellation. **1970** D. HARPER *Hijacked* (1971) 6 We've been notified not to accept standby passengers for Flight 901. **1977** *Daily Tel.* 16 Sept. 1/3 The cost of travelling standby both ways is £149 as opposed to..the normal return fare between London and New York of £392. **1978** *Times* 28 July 2/6 The argument over where to buy stand-by tickets was causing much confusion... Pan Am and TWA handled many..stand-by passengers at their London offices.

standee. For *U.S.* read orig. and chiefly *U.S.* and add: **1.** (Earlier examples.) Also *transf.* in *Theatr. U.S.*

1831 *American* (Harrodsburg, Kentucky) 25 Mar. 1/5 'I say Cap'en, what have I got?' 'A standee,' roared a dozen voices... 'Captain, I demand a berth.' **1849** G. G. FOSTER *N.Y. in Slices* xxiv. 90 Some police reporter.. thus nobly earns the privilege of a seat in the dress circle.. or a standee in the lobby on full nights.

2. a. (Earlier and later examples.) Also *spec.* a standing passenger in a public vehicle.

1856 *Knickerbocker* Mar. 278 Occasionally the car is brought to a full stop, and the 'standees' are thrown against each other like alley-pins by a 'ten-strike'. **1934** WODEHOUSE *Right Ho, Jeeves* xvii. 211, I wedged myself in among the standees at the back. **1942** *Sun* (Baltimore) 12 Aug. 9/2 Mr. Maxwell admitted that the bus left the terminal at Overlea with fourteen standees. **1954** E. E. CUMMINGS *Let.* 8 Dec. (1969) 238 A 9 o'clock, all 'standees' had to be given the seats of all ticketowners who..hadn't appeared. **1964** N. MARSH *Dead Water* iii. 81 There were not enough chairs... Major Barrimore, Superintendent Coombe and Dr. Maine formed a rather ill-assorted group of standees. **1976** J. LEE *Ninth Man* 70 No seats were vacant, and standees stared angrily at the children for taking up so much space. **1982** S. B. FLEXNER *Listening to America* 109 The stands..seated 4,000 fans,..with over 20,000 added standees also watching.

b. *attrib.*, esp. of public transport vehicles, as *standee bus*.

1937 *Sun* (Baltimore) 27 Oct. 5/2 Spectators began storming the playhouse long before curtain time, and by the time the show began, there was a standee audience. **1952** *Public Transport Assoc. Jrnl.* July 336 Large capacity single deck motor buses of special construction... The Minister had under review the whole question of standing passengers (including standing passengers on 'Standee' type vehicles). **1959** KITCHIN & WENLOCK *Road Transport Law* (ed. 12) 124 Laden weight of p.s.v. is total of vehicle with water, oil and fuel, plus 140 lb per seat (and, in the case of 'standee' vehicles registered after December 31, 1954, an additional 140 lb for each standing passenger in excess of eight). **1962** *Daily Tel.* 5 Nov. 10/2 The introduction of 'standee' buses, carrying 35 standing passengers and 35 seated. **1970** *Commercial Motor* 25 Sept. 122/2 The stanchions which one would expect in a standee bus are absent..to enable operators to suggest where handrails and stanchions would best be fitted. **1976** P. R. WHITE *Planning for Public Transport* iv. 80 The pattern of three or four sets of sliding doors per car..is related to an interior layout of limited seating capacity, often arranged longitudinally, and a high proportion of standee space. **1983** *Buses* Feb. 56/2 This [bus] was fitted with a dual exit and a standee area on the lower deck.

stander. Add: **I. 1. d.** One who 'stands' another a drink: see STAND *v.* 61 b. *nonce-use.*

1922 JOYCE *Ulysses* 419 Will immensely splendiferous stander permit one stooder..to terminate one expensive ..libation.

sta·nd-in. [f. vbl. phr. *to stand in*: see STAND *v.* 95.] † **1.** A friendly or profitable understanding (*with* another), esp. a corrupt arrangement or 'put-up job'. *U.S. colloq. Obs.*

1870 *Food Jrnl.* 1 Nov. 523 The affair is settled amicably by a 'stand in', which means that the purchaser shall pay the other, or others, a certain sum not to bid against him. **1908** K. MCGAFFEY *Sorrows of Show Girl* 89 My heart went out to him the minute he said he had a stand in with three city editors. **1926** J. BLACK *You can't Win* iv. 41 The whole thing was a stand-in from the captain down. Everybody's satisfied. The sucker has his money, the girls are all out.

2. a. *Cinemat.* One who substitutes for a principal film actor while the cameras and lighting for a scene are set. Formerly, *stand-in man*. Chiefly *U.S.*

1928 *N.Y. Times* 11 Mar. VIII. 6/2 *Stand-in men*, substitute for the star used by the director while cameramen and electricians are testing the lights on a scene. **1935** *Evening Sun* (Baltimore) 21 May 16/2 Dorothy Granger, actress, and George Lollier, actor and 'stand-in' for Richard Dix, had a June wedding last year. **1937** *Daily Mirror* 16 Mar. 2/1 Frances is often described as Glenda's double, but 'I'm a good head taller,' she told me. 'Being a 'stand-in' does not necessarily mean that you must be exactly alike.' **1948** 'N. SHUTE' *No Highway* iv. 92 In Hollywood beauties were two a penny, and it was years before she got an inkling what it was that differentiated her from all the stand-ins and walkers-on. **1958** *People* 4 May 15/4 He won't use a stand-in for any of his roles. **1976** M. MAGUIRE *Scratchproof* ii. 22 The stand-ins were called for. The shot was lined up.

b. *gen.* One who fills the place of or substitutes for another. Also *transf.*

1937 D. RUNYON in *Collier's* 21 Aug. 32/1 Nobody cares much about this idea of a stand-in for Nicely-Nicely..and many citizens are in favor of pulling out of the contest altogether. **1940** *Punch* 7 Feb. 156/1 Easily bored by the polite functions that not even dictators can wholly avoid ..the German ruler has made..use of the 'stand-in' since he came to power. **1952** *Sun* (Baltimore) 19 Apr. (B ed.) 3/3 An absorbable gelatin sponge..may serve..as a stand-in for the liver when it becomes necessary to remove part of that organ. **1958** S. ELLIN *Eighth Circle* (1959) II. i. 32 His arrest was a fake; he was just a stand-in for the real culprit. **1968** T. STOPPARD *Real Inspector Hound* (1970) 11 An army of assistants and deputies, the seconds-in-command, the runners-up, the right-hand men.. stand-ins of the world stand up! **1981** 'A. HALL' *Pekin Target* v. 45 A decoy, a scapegoat, a stand-in for us at the show trial.

c. *attrib.*

1938 *N.Y. Times* 28 Dec. 11/1 'Stand-in' ruse jails 3... Policy game collectors, with previous convictions on which they might receive long jail terms, were using 'stand-ins' to receive new sentences for them. **1958** *Engineering* 11 Apr. 457/3 Preliminary experiments were made on 'stand-in' compounds, which it was hoped would simulate the behaviour of plutonium compounds in reduction to the element. **1976** *Southern Even. Echo* (Southampton) 15 Nov. 15/4 Stand-in goalkeeper, Les Northrop, stood between Tonbridge and a hammering at the hands of unbeaten Salisbury.

standing, *vbl. sb.* Add: **4. h.** *Law* (orig. *U.S.*). A position from which one has the right to prosecute a claim or seek legal redress; the right itself; = *locus standi* s.v. LOCUS *sb.*[1] 4. (See also quot. 1962.)

1924 *Chicago Junction Case* in *U.S. Reports* CCLXIV. 271 Mr. Justice George Sutherland, dissenting... The complainants have no standing, to vindicate the rights of the public. **1962** *Stanford Law Rev.* May 433 Defined generally, if not very helpfully, in the context of this article 'standing' is the word of art for an interest which the federal courts hold worthy of legal protection from the effects of unconstitutional governmental action. **1967** H. W. R. WADE *Administrative Law* (ed. 2) iv. 126 These remedies are not restricted by the notion of *locus standi*. Every citizen has standing to invite the court to prevent some abuse of power. **1972** *N.Y. Law Jrnl.* 24 Oct. 3/3 It is sufficient for purposes of standing that plaintiff establish a causal connection between the violations alleged, be they fraud or breach of fiduciary duty, and plaintiff's loss. **1982** *Law Reports* (Appeal Cases) June 639 The rules as to 'standing' for the purpose of applying for prerogative orders..are not to be found in any statute.

9. b. The position of a person or organization in a graduated table, esp. in *Sport* and *Educ.* Also, a score indicating this. Freq. *pl.* Chiefly *N. Amer.*

1881 *N.Y. Herald* 12 Sept. 11/5 The appended table will show the standing of the clubs up to date. **1904** *Spalding's Official Base Ball Guide* (ed. 28) 108 To find the Standing of the Clubs—Divide the number of games won by games played. Example: Pittsburgh, in 1903, played 140 games and won 91; 91 divided by 140 equals .650. **1917** R. EARLE *Life at U.S. Naval Academy* v. 113 Class standing is affected in some measure by conduct. **1938** K. BANNING *Annapolis Today* vii. 99 Their academic and conduct records..in combination with the aptitude marks..will become factors when their final class standings for the four-year course are computed. **1968** *Globe & Mail* (Toronto) 13 Feb. 8/1 The appointment leaves 10 vacancies in the 102-seat Senate. Standings now are: Liberal 60; Conservative 29; Independent 2; Independent Liberal 1. **1977** *Belfast Tel.* 24 Jan. 17/7 He now leads the world drivers' championship standings with 13 points.

11. standing point (earlier example); **standing room** (earlier *Theatr.* and later examples); also in phr. *standing room only*, esp. in a theatre or similar place of resort (abbrev. *S.R.O.* s.v. S 4 a).

1847 W. Smith tr. *Fichte's Characteristics Present Age* xvii. 254 A view taken from the standing-point of this Age itself. **1807** *Cabinet* I. 344 To be rewarded at last..by finding—'a little standing room'! **1889** G. B. Shaw *Fabian Ess. in Socialism* 11 The board is at the door, inscribed 'Only standing room left'. **1910** *National Police Gaz.* (U.S.) 5 Nov. 2/2 The Davenport Lady Minstrels opened their season in Asheville, N.C., recently, to standing room only. **1934** Wodehouse *Right Ho, Jeeves* ix. 101 The place being loaded down above the Plimsoll mark and standing room only as regarded tortured souls. **1964** Mrs. L. B. Johnson *White House Diary* 5 June (1970) 154 A standing-room rally in the Senate caucus room. **1981** G. Thompson *Murder Mystery* xix. 146 That bar is mobbed. Standing room only.

standing, *ppl. a.* Add: **I. 1. e.** *spec.* in *Sport* (esp. *Athletics*): performed from a standing position (cf. *crouch *sb.*[2] b). Also *standing start*, of a motor car, etc.: a start, esp. of a race or performance trial, from a stationary state.

1875 *Encycl. Brit.* III. 13/1 The running hop-step-and-jump, standing high-leaping, and standing wide-leaping. **1891** H. H. Griffin *Athletics* 85 The standing long and high jumps are rarely ever heard of. **1900** *Motor-Car World* Oct. 9/2 Jenatzy..covered..the first kilometre.. with a standing start in 57 seconds. **1933** *Illustr. London News* 9 Dec. 962/1 (Advt.), Speed up Brooklands Test hill from a standing start, 16 m.p.h. **1951** D. W. Maurer in *Publ. Amer. Dial. Soc.* xvi. 60 *Standing start*, a type of start in which the horses line up exactly at the pole marking the distance they are to run and break at the starter's command... No starting gate is used. **1960** E. S. & W. J. Higham *High Speed Rugby* vii. 63 When a long pass is needed, the 'dive' pass, done properly, has advantages over the 'standing' pass. **1973** 'D. Rutherford' *Kick Start* vi. 138, I was making a standing start... The Norton Commando accelerates from 0 to 100 m.p.h. in 13 seconds.

f. *standing ovation*: a rousing ovation conferred by an audience standing as a mark of enthusiastic approval, esp. after a speech.

1969 B. Russell *Autobiogr.* III. ii. 87, I was deeply touched by being given a standing ovation when I rose to speak. **1971** H. Wilson *Labour Govt.* xxvii. 564 At the end there was a spontaneous and wild standing ovation. **1981** S. Jackman *Game of Soldiers* ii. iii. 175 The men gave him a standing ovation, whistling and stamping as he stood there grinning and bowing.

2. c. *standing crop*, a growing crop; now used *spec.* in *Ecol.* to denote the total quantity of living things in an (esp. planktonic) ecosystem, or in some component of one.

1861 J. Brown *Forester* (ed. 3) vii. 477 There is great danger of having it [*sc.* the work] carelessly performed, and very often to the damage of a considerable portion of the standing crop. **1935** P. S. Welch *Limnol.* ix. 253 A quantitative measure of the production of a lake can be expressed in terms of (1) standing crop—the total amount of plankton present in the water on a selected date—and (2) annual crop. **1946** *Ecol. Monogr.* XVI. 324/2 The size of the standing crop at any time is the result of the summation of the excess of production over destruction from the beginning of the growth of the population to the moment of observation. **1957** G. E. Hutchinson *Treat. Limnol.* I. xii. 746 The addition of a large quantity of phosphorus in 1938 undoubtedly led to a considerable increase in the standing crop of plankton. **1979** R. Brewer *Princ. Ecol.* iv. 129 At any one time each trophic level contains some amount of energy stored as biomass, often referred to as the standing crop.

3. e. *standing iron*, a metal spike on the collar of a sledge dog, to which a ribbon or similar decoration may be attached. *Canad.*

1934 P. H. Godsell *Arctic Trader* 39 Bells jangled as the dogs proudly tossed their massive heads and shook their beribboned standing-irons in the gusty breeze. **1939** *Beaver* Sept. 23 Fox tails and coloured ribbons decorated the leather collars and standing-irons. **1959** J. W. Godsell *I was no Lady* iv. 64 The fluttering rainbows of ribbons on the standing-irons of the harness.

4. b. *standing salt*: in medieval and later times, a large, often ornate, salt-cellar placed in the middle of a dining-table. Cf. Salt *sb.*[1] 7 a, b. *Hist.*

1878 W. J. Cripps *Old Eng. Plate* x. 255 A cylindrical standing salt, of the year 1554. **1931** E. Wenham *Domestic Silver* v. 42 The imposing standing-salts.., from the Middle Ages to the third quarter of the seventeenth century, were the symbols of social distinction. **1956** G. Taylor *Silver* ii. 42 The most important and often the most elaborate piece of table plate during the Middle Ages was the standing salt. **1972** *Times* 28 Nov. 24/1 (Advt.), An Elizabeth I silver-gilt standing-salt.

II. 11. d. Also *standing matter, type.*

1875 J. Southward *Dict. Typogr.* (ed. 2) 129 *Standing matter*, composed matter remaining undistributed after it has been printed. **1916** *Estimating for Printers* 24 If a job repeats and the printer has kept it standing without ..rent, the job should be estimated as though it were reset, and the advantage of standing type kept by the printer. **1964** F. Bowers *Bibliogr. & Textual Crit.* i. v. 31 This homogeneity extended to the variants in the standing type..but not to their pages of reset type.

e. Physics. *standing wave*, a wave in which the positions of maximum and minimum oscillation remain stationary; = *stationary wave* s.v. *stationary *a.* 1 e.

1896 *Knowledge* 1 June 136/1 Each wave crest maintains its position relative to the stone, and from this comes the term *standing wave*. **1905** *Trans. R. Soc. Edin.* XLI. 592 The remarkable analogy between the sound-vibrations of an elastic body and the light-vibrations of a radiating atom is at least suggestive. Is it not, for instance, conceivable that the latter are caused by 'standing waves' in the elastic system which constitutes the atom? **1947** A. E. Slater in A. C. Douglas *Gliding & Adv. Soaring* i. 29 Similar 'standing waves' have now been found, and soared in, elsewhere. For instance, in an experimental flight to leeward of the Alps a sailplane has reached 30,000 feet above sea level. **1962** A. Nisbett *Technique Sound Studio* ii. 46 If there are two parallel screens on opposite sides of the microphone a standing-wave pattern will be set up. **1977** A. Hallam *Planet Earth* 55/2 Such features, called antidunes or standing waves, are often seen in streams running across beaches at low tide or in gutters during heavy rain.

III. 15. a. Also *standing order*, a written directive to a banker instructing that a regular payment be made from an account, usu. to another party; similarly, *transf.* in *Commerce.*

1913 Bagshaw & Hannaford *Pract. Banking* ix. 144 Executing Standing Orders... A customer may instruct his banker to pay a certain sum at a stated time, and the main instances of this are in the payment of annual subscriptions to clubs. **1937** A. F. Fergus *Pract. Branch Banking* xv. 207 All those regular periodical payments, such as rent, insurance premiums, club subscriptions.. which are made by the Branch on the instructions of customers, come under the general description of 'Standing Orders'. **1962** D. Francis *Dead Cert* xii. 134 I'll place a standing order with Interflora, for lilies. **1972** G. Lyall *Blame Dead* ix. 67 The standing orders were easy enough: they'd be payments to the life insurance companies and probably the rent on that flat.

17. b. *standing committee* (earlier and later examples).

a **1636** H. Elsynge *Expedicio Billarum Antiquitus* (1954) 23 Even this doth prove that there was one Standing Committee for all Bills in parlement. **1656** H. Scobell *Memorials* iii. 9 In Parliament there have usually been Five Standing Committees appointed in the beginning of the Parliament, and remaining during all the Session. **1868** Erskine May *Law of Parl.* (ed. 6) xiv. 379 There is further an exceptional class of committees, called standing committees. The only committee properly so termed is one whose appointment, being by standing order, is permanent, the nomination only being renewed from session to session. Such is the committee of public accounts, under a standing order of the 3rd April 1862. **1921** *Legislative Assembly Deb.* (Delhi) 1 Mar. 418 A Standing Finance Committee of this Assembly has been appointed. It is not proposed—at present at any rate—to appoint any other Standing Committee of the Legislature. **1967** J. D. Lees *Committee System U.S. Congr.* ii. 5 Standing committees..are permanent committees that continue from Congress to Congress... They are quite different from Standing Committees of the House of Commons which are not specialised and whose main purpose is to save time which would otherwise be spent by the House sitting as Committee of the Whole. **1978** *Nagel's Encycl.-Guide: China* 292 Out of session, the National People's Congress appoints a standing Committee. Theoretically at least, this committee (made up of a Chairman, 13 Vice-chairmen, 1 Secretary-general and 35 ordinary members) is all-powerful.

c. Also, *standing patrol.*

1923 Kipling *Irish Guards in Gt. War* I. 25 The Germans pushed a patrol through the wood and our standing-patrol went out and discovered one German under-officer..dead. **1941** P. Richey *Fighter Pilot* 35 Germans..maintained a standing patrol on their own side, only crossing over to our side occasionally, and always very high. **1959** P. Fleming *Siege at Peking* xiii. 202 General Lineivitch..sent forward an advance-guard of one battalion and half a battery..to act as what used to be called a standing patrol.

IV. 19. Naut. *all standing*: see Stand *v.* 24.

stand-off, *attrib. phr., a.* and *sb.* Add: **A.** *attrib. phr. and adj.* **3.** Of an object: that projects or is positioned a short distance away from a surface or another object; that serves to hold something in such a position.

1952 *Chambers's Jrnl.* Feb. 128/2 The well at the base of the shower-unit has a stand-off waste-pipe and the well can be used as a foot-bath. **1962** *Air-Cushion Vehicles* I. 58/2 On top of the trusses are secured box-section full-length longerons, known as 'stand-off booms', which are braced together and complete the primary structure. **1964** R. F. Ficchi *Electr. Interference* v. 52 Component manufacturers have developed the ceramic stand-off, or stud-type, capacitor in an effort to reduce the internal and lead-in inductance of the capacitor. **1977** *Gramophone* Oct. 743/1 The GC300..is finished with a..matt charcoal plastic base with four stand-off feet.

4. *Mil.* Of a guided missile: designed to be launched against its target from an aircraft at long range, esp. as *stand-off bomb*. Also *stand-off range.*

1957 *Times Survey British Aviation* Sept. 2/1 Improved marks of the V-class bombers will carry a powered guided bomb (the so-called stand-off bomb) and will form the foundation of our striking force for many years. **1960** A. Ball *Ballistic & Guided Missiles* iv. 62 Already there are short-range missiles.., often called 'stand-off bombs'. **1969** *Times* 30 Apr. 27/3 The Swingfire anti-tank weapon is now being delivered to the British Army, and we hope that the Division will shortly obtain a contract to develop Swingfire further by exploiting its ability to 'kill' armour from the air and at long stand-off range. **1971** E. Luttwak *Dict. Mod. War* 181/1 *Stand-off missile*, a missile, generally fitted with a nuclear warhead, which is launched by a bomber and substitutes for the latter in the final phase of the attack. **1978** R. V. Jones *Most Secret War* xlvi. 463 A long-range glider bomb, the BV 246.. was thus an early example of a 'stand-off' missile. **1982** *Navy News* Mar. 18/2 With its considerable 'stand-off' range, it is designed to destroy or disable enemy warships up to the largest-known size.

B. *sb.* For *U.S.* read Chiefly *U.S.* **1.** (Earlier U.K. example.)

1865 Trollope *Can You forgive Her?* II. xxiv. 183 There's a stand-off about some women—what the men call a 'nollimy tangere'.

2. b. *Mexican stand-off*, no chance to benefit (or *spec.* to defend oneself); hence, a general stalemate (cf. sense 3 in Dict. and Suppl.). *slang.*

1891 *N.Y. Sporting Times* 19 Sept. 4/3 'Monk' Cline, who got a Mexican stand-off from Dave Rowe has signed with Louisville. **1929** Hostetter & Beesley *It's a Racket!* 231 *Mexican stand-off*, to kill in cold blood. **1935** J. O'Hara *Appointment in Samarra* vii. 222 The men were the victims of the St. Valentine's Day massacre in Chicago, when seven men were given the Mexican stand-off against the inside wall of a gang garage. **1958** 'W. Henry' *Seven Men at Mimbres Springs* xvi. 189, I rightly and firmly believe we've taken some of the flap out of Mangas's shirttails and can turn this thing into a Mexican stand-off, given any luck at all. **1979** D. MacKenzie *Raven settles Score* 26 As things stood it was a Mexican standoff. He couldn't go to the law but..nor could the Koreans.

c. In *gen.* use, any uneasy stalemate or deadlock; an impasse. Freq. in *Pol.* contexts.

1958 *Spectator* 31 Oct. 588/2 On the Fuchs–Hillary standoff whether to continue to Scott Base or not..Sir Vivian tactfully writes: 'Unfortunately this exchange became known publicly.' **1971** T. W. Robinson *Cultural Revolution in China* i. 15 The standoff with Cambodia was precipitated by the propaganda activities of the Chinese embassy and the New China News Agency. **1974** *Spartanburg* (S. Carolina) *Herald* 19 Apr. A1/5 A 29-year-old Colombian..died in a hail of police bullets after a four-hour standoff. **1981** 'E. V. Cunningham' *Case of Sliding Pool* (1982) xii. 145 We can't do anything, neither can he. It's a standoff.

3. (Examples.)

1843 J. H. Greene *Exposure Arts Gambling* 187 Thus, if a man bets on the ace and deuce, and the ace comes to his side, and the deuce to the dealer's side, it is a stand-off, and neither wins. **1893** 'Mark Twain' in *St. Nicholas* Nov. 21/2 It was about a stand-off; so both of them had to whoop up their dangerous adventures, and try to get ahead *that* way. **1938** *Sun* (Baltimore) 17 May 14/5 Supreme Court decisions were about a standoff. There was a ruling against the General Electric in a patent suit... The High Court agreed to consider the validity of the TVA on an appeal by eighteen Southeastern utilities. **1964** F. Bowers *Bibliogr. & Textual Crit.* iv. iii. 115 But in *Old Fortunatus* the evidence is a stand-off... In the 11 extant copies, 5 contain the uncorrected state of A and 6 the uncorrected state of B. **1974** *Cleveland* (Ohio) *Plain Dealer* 26 Oct. 7-D/7 Cleveland Benedictine and Cambridge battled to a 0–0 standoff in a non-league football game here Friday night.

4. (Examples.) Also *fig.* *U.S.* Now *rare.*

1883 B. Harte *Carquinez Woods* 65, I reckon you'd better make it [*sc.* a bet] a stand-off for twenty-four hours, and I'll find out and let you know. **1891** M. E. Ryan *Told in Hills* iv. viii. 350, I got a stand-off on the hostilities—till your return. **1906** 'O. Henry' in *Everybody's Mag.* Aug. 166/2 I've negotiated a stand-off at a delicatessen hut down-town.

5. A rest; a temporary cessation from work. Cf. *stand *v.* 96 g. *rare.*

1918 *Jrnl. R. Naval Med. Service* IV. 181 He should have four months 'stand off'. **1930** C. R. Sansom *Fights & Flights* 100 He told me..to give my cars a stand-off for the rest of the day.

6. Rugby Football. *ellipt.* for *stand-off half.* Cf. *fly-half* s.v. Fly *sb.*[2] 8.

1922 *Daily Mail* 15 Nov. 11 Cassels at stand-off seeming to be able to take any sort of pass. **1939** *Daily Tel.* 18 Dec. 11/3 Their backs, with the exception of P. Hodgson, at stand-off, were disappointing. **1969** *Listener* 15 May 700/3 Castleford..are captained by their stand-off Alan Hardisty. **1980** *Sunday Times* 21 Sept. 29 Even now, 100 days later, it's still something of a whirl for the Lions stand-off.

7. Something serving to hold an object clear of a surface or another object.

1967 *Boston Sunday Herald* 26 Mar. I. 22/1 (Advt.), Two mast strap standoffs... Four 3½" wood screw standoffs. **1974** *Physics Bull.* Dec. 592/2 Two quartz blocks are positioned adjacent to the device, and a preformed gold tape is bonded across the quartz standoffs and the back contact of the diode. **1977** *Engin. Materials & Design* Aug. 56/2 The brochure details a selection of fasteners, from a plain self-clinching nut or stud, to standoffs, self-locking, floating and miniature types, having thread sizes from M2 to M12.

stand oil. Also **sta·ndoil.** [tr. G. *standöl*: see Stand *sb.*[1], Oil *sb.*[1] So called from its formerly being prepared by allowing linseed oil to stand.] Linseed oil or another drying oil that has been thickened by heating, used in paints, varnishes, and printing inks.

1908 Livache & McIntosh *Manuf. Varnishes & Kindred Industries* (ed. 2) II. vii. 153 Reb's Stock Mixing Varnishes.—... The different ingredients are prepared as follows. (1) Linseed oil, 'stand oil'.—Raw oil is heated without driers until it deposits mucilage and clarifies, after which it is tanked for three to four weeks before use. **1934** H. Hiler *Notes on Technique of Painting* iii. 234 A good varnish containing some standoil (and a hard resin). **1955** W. Gaddis *Recognitions* i. iii. 124 This Van Eyck,..how sharp the lines are, look how smoothly they flow, it's perfect painting in stand oil, isn't it. **1981** *National Gallery Report 1980–81* 69 The problem of distinguishing, in the dried state, between raw and heat-treated oils (stand oils) remains obstinately unresolved.

stand out. Add: Now usu. **standout** or with hyphen. **2. a.** One who stands out from the crowd; an outstanding or conspicuous person or thing. *N. Amer. colloq.*

1928 *Collier's* 29 Dec. 26/2 When the show opened, this girl had improved in her dancing so amazingly that she was a distinct 'standout'. **1936** *Sun* (Baltimore) 13 July 4/1 The smash-ups are staged realistically, the standout being that in which an apparently new..car hurtles over a parapet and arcs one hundred feet or so through the air. **1938** D. Baker *Young Man with Horn* iii. ii. 145 He was blessed above the run of band leaders. It isn't given to all organizers to have a stand-out in their organizations. **1944** *Sat. Rev. Lit.* (U.S.) 8 Jan. 14/3 John Hersey's novel about the AMG in Italy, 'A Bell for Adano', is likely to be one of the action stand-outs of the new season. **1958** *Times* 24 Nov. (Canad. Suppl.) p. xii/6, If they see a boy who is a standout,..they can't go wrong by putting him down as a good prospect. **1979** *Time* 8 Jan. 46/2 Another campus standout, Phyllis Wallace, now in her 50s, has been burdened by prejudice against blacks as well as women.

b. *attrib. phr.* or as *adj.*

1932 *Sun* (Baltimore) 15 Aug. 9/1 California's rowing triumph and Japan's first swimming conquest were the stand-out performances. **1955** Keepnews & Graver *Pictorial Hist. Jazz* xi. 117/2 Red Nichols and Miff Mole were the stand-out figures in this phase. **1978** J. Irving *World according to Garp* viii. 162 Robert Muldoon, a standout tight end for the Philadelphia Eagles.

standpoint. 2. (Earlier example.)

1854 Geo. Eliot tr. *Feuerbach's Essence Christianity* ix. 96 This abstraction..is determined by the essential standpoint of man.

stand-still, standstill, *a.* Add: **2. a.** Characterized by the absence or restriction of movement.

1829 P. Egan *Boxiana* 2nd Ser. II. 233 Jem had now reduced the 'big one' to his own weight, and had also placed him upon the stand-still system. **1852** J. Reynolds *Hist. Illinois* 266 The cotillions, or stand still dances, were not then known. **1927** *Daily Express* 27 Dec. 1 A 'standstill' order prohibiting all movements of cattle, sheep, pigs, or goats in thirteen counties. **1975** J. G. Evans *Environment Early Man Brit. Isles* ii. 46 Intervening organic horizons represent standstill phases when the climate ameliorated sufficiently for a continuous vegetation cover to form.

b. *Econ.* Of an agreement, etc.: that seeks to maintain the present state of affairs, esp. by deferring the necessity to repay an international debt. Also *transf.* and of the debt itself.

The original *standstill agreement* was concluded in 1931 between German and U.S. and other Allied banking and commercial concerns, and allowed for the postponement of German short-term credit repayments in the light of the country's severe economic plight.

1931 *Times* 17 Aug. 9/2 The agreements negotiated between the national 'standstill' committees and the German bankers will..be mentioned in the report. *Ibid.* 20 Aug. 9/1 The 'standstill' agreement for the prolongation of short-term credits to Germany was signed..today. **1932** *Sun* (Baltimore) 12 Sept. 7/4 The standstill agreement..was designed to lift the pressure of world creditors on Germany until that nation could nurse its financial affairs back into something like normal vigor. **1938** H. V. Hodson *Slump & Recovery* ix. 331 The story of Germany's 'standstill' debt in this period. **1940** *Economist* 10 Aug. 191/2 The new standstill agreement was signed on behalf of the British, American and Swiss Banking Committees. **1955** *Ann. Reg. 1954* 425 Although further 'reactivation' of standstill debts was effected during the war, the amount of standstill debts declined substantially. **1970** *Internat. & Compar. Law Q.* 4th Ser. XIX. ii. 270 Even an obligation of member States merely to abstain—a so-called standstill clause..must be clear enough as to permit its direct application. **1980** *Wall St. Jrnl.* 6 June 1/2 Diamond International disclosed that it is discussing several courses of action that include a 'standstill agreement' with Cavenham Holdings.

stand-up, *a.* and *sb.* Add: **A.** *adj.* **1. d.** *stand-up comic* (also *comedian*), a comedian whose act consists of standing before an audience and telling a succession of jokes.

1966 *Listener* 11 Aug. 194/1 In television complex sentences need to be eschewed, especially by stand-up comics. **1969** *Ibid.* 24 Apr. 588/2 The audience, used to jazz singers, satire companies or stand-up comedians, could make nothing of his work. **1969** *New Yorker* 14 June 92/2 Bruce had just begun to surface as a standup comic. *a* **1975** Wodehouse *Sunset at Blandings* (1977) vi. 44 I've known Home Secretaries who were as cheerful as stand-up comics. **1980** D. MacKenzie *Raven & Paperhangers* i. 9 Playing straight man to a stand-up comic in a Vegas night club.

2. a. Also, designating a cafeteria or other establishment at which patrons stand at a counter to eat or drink; also applied to the counter itself.

1920 H. G. Wells *Outl. Hist.* xviii. 130/2 A stand-up buffet for light refreshments. **1971** R. J. White *Second-Hand Tomb* v. 59 Jasper..took a peep into the stand-up bar. **1981** M. C. Smith *Gorky Park* i. vii. 87 A stand-up cafeteria next to the children's store.

B. *sb.* **4.** Also *rarely*, a counter at which stand-up refreshment can be obtained and consumed.

1897 'Mark Twain' *Following Equator* xiii. 143 He halted in front of the best restaurant, then glanced at his clothes and passed on, and got his breakfast at a 'stand-up'.

6. An act of failing to keep an engagement or 'date' with another; also, *to give* (someone) *the stand-up*. Cf. *stand *v.* 103 q. *slang* (orig. *U.S.*).

1921 A. G. Empey *Madonna of Hills* vii. 56, I wonder if that jane's double-crossed me and given me the stand-up? **1940** R. Chandler *Farewell, my Lovely* xxxix. 297 'It's a little late, but I've had a lot to do.' 'Another stand-up?' Her voice got cool. **1961** J. MacLaren-Ross *Doomsday Bk.* ii. vii. 172 Find out where he's ringing from if it's another stand-up. **1977** D. Ramsay *You can't call it Murder* i. 15 We made a dinner date... He didn't show up... I'd write it off as an ordinary stand-up, except that he left that ten-gallon job [*sc.* hat] behind.

7. A police identification parade. *U.S. slang.*

1935 A. J. Pollock *Underworld Speaks* 113/2 *Stand-up*, the police line-up; show-up. **1949** *Philadelphia Even. Bull.* 14 Apr. 2/4 Jackson was brought to City Hall last night to take a look at Norman in a police standup, but he could not positively identify the prisoner.

Stanford–Binet (stæ·nfǝɹd bi·ne). *Psychol.* The names of *Stanford* University and Alfred *Binet* (1857–1911), used *attrib.* and *absol.* to designate the revision and extension of the Binet-Simon intelligence tests (see *Binet-Simon) undertaken by L. M. Terman and first published in 1916, which established the concept of an intelligence quotient.

1918 Cuneo & Terman in *Pedagogical Seminary* Dec. 414 The purposes of this study were..to correlate the results of Stanford-Binet tests with school marks. *Ibid.* 428 The Stanford-Binet scale was given to 112 representative school children. **1937** Terman & Merrill *Measuring Intelligence* iii. 51 The old Stanford-Binet..yields mental ages slightly too high at the younger ages. **1939** *Brit. Jrnl. Psychol.* XXX. 8 The Stanford-Binet test gives a good estimate of general intelligence though it gives verbal ability undue weight. **1954** A. Anastasi *Psychol. Testing* i. 11 In America, a number of revisions were prepared, the most famous of which is..known as the Stanford-Binet. **1974** R. M. Pirsig *Zen & Art of Motorcycle Maintenance* (1976) i. vii. 80 His Stanford-Binet IQ, which is essentially a record of skill at analytic manipulation, was recorded at 170.

Stanhope. Add: **4.** The name of the historian Philip Henry *Stanhope* (1805–75), 5th Earl Stanhope, used *attrib.* and *absol.* to designate the historical essay prize founded by him at Oxford University in 1855, or essays associated with this prize.

[**1856** *Oxford Univ. Calendar* 273 Earl Stanhope's Prize. In a Convocation holden on Friday, December 14, 1855, the following Regulations for a Prize founded by the Right Hon. Earl Stanhope, with a view to the full development and the continued growth and welfare of the School of Law and Modern History, and accepted by Convocation on the 20th day of June, 1855, were agreed upon.] **1861** J. A. Symonds *Let.* 17 Apr. (1967) I. 285 Conington..declares the Stanhope to be about as much too long. *Ibid.* 1 June 296, I confess to being a little anxious myself about the Stanhope, though one ought never to be disturbed on account of Prizes. **1863** *Oxford Univ. Calendar* 105 (*heading*) Stanhope historical essay. **1896** J. Buchan in W. Buchan *John Buchan* (1982) iv. 81 Get the Newdigate. Get the Stanhope. **1915** A. Huxley *Let.* 8 June (1969) 71, I may come up here in September to do some reading in Bodley for the Stanhope Prize. **1916** *Ibid.* 18 June 101, I trust I don't have to read the Stanhope at the Encaenia. **1934** *Oxford Univ. Gaz.* 21 Nov. 140/2 Stanhope Essay Prize, 1935. The subject for 1935 is '*Edward, the Black Prince*.' **1976** M. Green *Children of Sun* ii. 51 John Buchan..went to Oxford, where he won the Stanhope Essay Prize, the Newdigate Poetry Prize..and a first-class degree.

stanhopea (stænhōᵘ·piă). [mod.L. (J. Frost 1829, in *Curtis's Bot. Mag.* LVI. 2948), f. the name of Philip Henry *Stanhope* (1781–1855), 4th Earl Stanhope, President of the Medico-Botanical Society.] An epiphytic orchid of the genus of that name, native to tropical America and bearing large, often fragrant, flowers.

1829 *Curtis's Bot. Mag.* LVI. 2948 (*heading*) Splendid Stanhopea. **1890** W. Watson *Orchids* lxi. 465 Some cultivators use nothing but sphagnum for Stanhopeas. **1917** L. H. Bailey *Stand. Cycl. Hort.* VI. 3222/2 Stanhopeas enjoy a shady, moist location. **1962** *Amateur Gardening* 7 Apr. 6/1 The stanhopeas have large highly scented wax-like flowers.

stanine (stæ·nǝin). *Psychol.* [Blend of Standard *sb.* and Nine *sb.*] A nine-point scale on which test scores can be grouped in descending order of achievement, first developed by the United States Air Force in 1942 (see quot. 1968); also, a score on such a scale. Freq. *attrib.*

1945 *Sun* (Baltimore) 1 Oct. 6/5 The result..was a 'stanine' rating (stanine being an invented word, from 'standard of nine'). **1957** E. R. Hilgard *Introd. Psychol.* (ed. 2) xvi. 400/2 A score of..650 on a Graduate Record Examination, or 8 on the Air Force stanine scale is above that achieved by 93 per cent of those on whom the test was calibrated. **1961** A. Anastasi *Psychol. Testing* (ed. 2) iv. 93 Raw scores can readily be converted to stanines by arranging the original scores in order of size and then assigning stanines in accordance with the normal curve percentages. **1968** *Internat. Encycl. Social Sci.* I. 38/1 Single-digit standard scores, ranging from 1 to 9, with a mean of 5 and a standard deviation of 2 are called *stanines* (*standard nines*). **1976** *Word 1971* XXVII. 330 The performance of the Experimental children placed them at the second stanine with respect to French-speaking children in Montreal. **1976** *Woman's Day* (U.S.) Nov. 62/2 But few educators use such simple terms anymore. Instead, we may be unnecessarily confused by a *stanine* score.

Stanislavsky (stænislæ·vski). *Theatr.* Also **Stanislavski.** The name of the Russian actor and director Konstantin *Stanislavsky* (1863–1938), used *attrib.* to designate the style and technique of acting practised and taught by him: see *method *sb.* 2 e.

1924 J. J. Robins tr. *Stanislavsky's My Life in Art* xxxiii. 351 Chekhov gave that inner truth to the art of the stage which served as the foundation for what was later called the Stanislavsky System. **1958** *Spectator* 22 Aug. 248/3 The success of the Bolshoi Theatre Ballet rests on the application to dancing of the Stanislavsky technique. **1972** *Village Voice* (N.Y.) 1 June 55/4 The Stanislavski approach may meet one of its greatest challenges in a Stein play. **1974** T. P. Whitney tr. *Solzhenitsyn's Gulag Archipelago* I. i. x. 387 Krylenko abandoned the Stanislavsky method, didn't assign the roles, relied on improvisation.

Hence **Stanisla·vskian, -yan** *a.*

1958 *Spectator* 20 June 813/1 Stanislavskyan acting was being practised by Schepkin fifty years before the genesis of the System. **1965** *New Statesman* 8 Oct. 537/1 Gielgud ..is the outstanding Stanislavskian actor in the West. **1979** A. Williamson *Funeral March for Siegfried* x. 50 He would have thought most [singers]..incapable of expressing so lucid a Stanislavskian principle.

Stanley (stæ·nli). The name of Edward Smith *Stanley* (1775–1851), 13th Earl of Derby, zoologist, used *attrib.* to denote birds named in his honour, as **Stanley bustard,** a large black and brown bustard, *Neotis denhami* (formerly *Otis stanleyi*), native to south-eastern Africa; **Stanley crane** = *paradise crane* s.v. *paradise *sb.* 8; (*Tetrapteryx paradisea*, formerly *Anthropoides stanleyanus*).

1831 J. E. Gray *Zool. Misc.* 12 Stanley Bustard. *Otis Stanleyi.* Above vermiculated, black and white. **1884** R. B. Sharpe *Layard's Birds S. Afr.* (ed. 2) 634 Stanley Bustard..is common in the northern portions of the colony. **1912** J. Stevenson-Hamilton *Anim. Life Afr.* xvii. 273 The Stanley bustard..is partial to..the high country of East and South Africa. **1979** K. B. Newman *Birdlife in S. Afr.* xii. 134/2 Both the Kori Bustard and the second largest, the Stanley Bustard, perform rather grand courtship displays. **1867** E. L. Layard *Birds S. Afr.* 303 The 'Stanley' or 'Blue' Crane is not abundant in any locality. **1937** *N. & Q.* 19 June 450/2 A Stanley Crane, elegant in dove-like grey. **1958** [see *paradise crane* s.v. *paradise *sb.* 8]. **1966** E. Palmer *Plains of Camdeboo* xi. 187 Our blue crane is also known as the Stanley crane. It belongs only to South Africa.

stannite. Add: **2.** (Earlier and later examples.) [ad. F. *stannine* (F. S. Beudant *Traité élémentaire de Minéralogie* (ed. 2, 1832) II. 416).]

1868 J. D. Dana *Syst. Mineral.* (ed. 5) 68 Stannite... Probably tetragonal, and hemihedral like chalcopyrite. **1976** [see next].

stannoidite (stæ·noidǝit). *Min.* [f. Stann(ite + -oid + -ite¹.] A sulphide of copper, tin, iron, and zinc, $Cu_8\ (Fe,Zn)_3Sn_2S_{12}$, found as yellow-brown orthorhombic crystals having a metallic lustre, superficially resembling those of stannite.

1969 A Kato in *Bull. Nat. Sci. Mus. Japan* XII. 165 (*heading*) Stannoidite,..a new stannite-like mineral from the Konjo Mine, Okayama Prefecture, Japan. **1975** *Econ. Geol.* LXX. 834 Mawsonite and stannoidite characteristically occur with bornite and chalcopyrite in xenothermal ore deposits in Japan. **1976** *Nature* 10 June 482/2 The Japanese ores, however, contain tin minerals other than cassiterite (for instance, stannite, stannoidite, and mawsonite).

stanol (stē̆ⁱ·nǫl). *Chem.* [f. *st(er)ol about -an(e, after *cholestanol*, *ergostanol*, etc. (the respective saturated derivatives of *cholesterol, *ergosterol, etc.).] Any fully saturated sterol.

1949 L. F. & M. Fieser *Nat. Products related to Phenanthrene* (ed. 3) iii. 93 Members of the sterol series that are fully saturated, like cholestanol, are conveniently described as stanols; those that contain one double bond are stenols. **1958** C. W. SHOPPEE *Chem. Steroids* ii. 78 The test is positive with stenols, negative with stanols. **1972** *Nature* 21 July 149/1 Although stanols have been shown to occur in *Sphagnum* moss and in a pollen mixture they are extremely rare in the rest of the contemporary plant kingdom. **1979** *Experientia* XXXV. 186/1 Saturated sterols (stanols) comprise 50–75% of the total sterols of this insect.

Stanton (stæ·ntən). [Name of Sir Thomas Edward *Stanton* (1865–1931), English engineer.] *Stanton number*, a dimensionless measure of heat transfer used in forced convection studies, equivalent to the ratio of the Nusselt number to the product of the Reynolds and Prandtl numbers, viz. $h/c_p\rho v$, where h is the heat transfer coefficient of the fluid, c_p is its heat capacity at constant pressure, ρ is its density, and v is its velocity.

Defined as the reciprocal of the Prandtl number in some dictionaries, but no textual evidence for this has been found.

1942 W. H. MCADAMS *Heat Transmission* (ed. 2) iv. 95 Stanton number. **1966** W. M. KAYS *Convective Heat & Mass Transfer* xi. 248 The decrease in Stanton number noted here occurs in what still seems to be essentially a turbulent boundary layer. **1978** *Internat. Jrnl. Heat & Mass Transfer* XXI. 282/2 From the results for the Nusselt number, the dimensionless heat transfer, expressed as the Stanton number, can be determined: $St = Nu/Re\ Pr$.

stanza. Add: **4.** *Sport.* A half or other session of a game.

1945 S. J. BAKER *Austral. Lang.* xvii. 299 In football news we find..*first* or *second stanza*, the first or second half of a game. **1974** *News & Reporter* (Chester, S. Carolina) 22 Apr. 10-A/5 Comfort Control warmed their bats up in the final three stanzas to gain the victory. **1981** *National Times* (Austral.) 25–31 Jan. 23/3 There is also a growing habit of describing the next half or quarter of a football match as a 'stanza'—perhaps because it is so poetic.

5. *Comb.*, as **stanza-form**, the form of a stanza (sense 1); arrangement in stanzas.

1927 E. V. GORDON *Introd. Old Norse* 293 There were variants of the normal stanza-forms. **1957** E. T. CONE in N. Frye *Sound & Poetry* I. 6 Zelter, keeping close to the unusual stanza-form..produces a top-heavy musical period. **1976** *Classical Q.* XXVI. 16 The catalectic effect in English or German is a function of the particular stanza-form. **1978** *Early Music* Oct. 629/1 A large number of 'wasted pages'..are taken up with setting out the poetic texts in stanza form.

stapelia. Add: Hence **stape·liad**, a plant belonging to one of a group of closely related genera including *Stapelia* and others formerly considered part of it.

1933 WHITE & SLOANE *Stapelieae* I The corolla of Stapeliads is usually fleshy. **1966** E. PALMER *Plains of Camdeboo* xvi. 261 Among the great plant travellers are the Stapeliads of the family Asclepiadaceæ. **1977** W. P. U. JACKSON *Wild Flowers Table Mt.* 48/2 *Orbea variegata*.. is the only Stapeliad in the Cape Peninsula.

staph (stæf). Colloq. abbrev. of mod.L. *Staphylococcus*, name of a genus of pathogenic bacteria.

1933 PARTRIDGE *Slang To-day & Yesterday* III. iii. 190 *Staph*, staphylococcus, one of the commonest types of bacteria. **1956** A. HUXLEY *Let.* 13 Aug. (1969) 804 The average mortality after surgery was twenty-nine per cent, with peaks, during epidemics of streps and staphs, of over fifty per cent. **1978** J. IRVING *World according to Garp* ii. 47 He later went through Harvard Business School, a staph infection, and a divorce.

staphylinid, *sb.* and *a.* (Examples.)

1925 A. D. IMMS *Gen. Textbk. Entomol.* III. 481 Staphylinid larvæ are typically campodeiform. **1965** B. E. FREEMAN tr. *Vandel's Biospeleology* xiii. 208 The staphylinids found in caves belong to three ecological categories. **1978** *Nature* 16 Mar. 209/1 Among the many other examples are various species of staphylinid beetles that march with army ants.

staphylorrhaphy. (Earlier example.)

1835 *Lancet* 31 Jan. 648/1 In the operation of staphyloraphy,..if care be not taken to leave the ends of the sutures rather long..the knots will readily untie.

staple, *sb.*[1] Add: **2. d.** A piece of thin wire (characteristically shaped in the form of three sides of a rectangle), driven through papers, etc., and clinched to bind them.

1895 *Army & Navy Co-op. Soc. Price List* 540/2 Patent Staple Presses (For Fastening Papers &c.)..Wire Staples. Size ¼ inch, per 1000 0/6. **1898** G. B. SHAW *Let.* 4 Mar. (1972) II. 11 Come along & bring some long staples (⅜" will do) with you. **1907** *Yesterday's Shopping* (1969) 349/1 The Self-Feeding Automatic Staple Press. Holds 25 staples which travel automatically. Staples are in strips of 25, as shown in illustration. **1926–7** *Army & Navy Stores Catal.* 369/3 The 'Longdon' Combined Stapler ..only one staple can pass at a time. **1940** *Brit. Stationer Ann.* 2 (Advt.), Ace Stapling Machines..Staples: ¼ in... 7/2 per box of 5,000. **1967** *New Yorker* 15 July 26/3, I.. dropped into a stationery store..looking for a mechanism of sorts with which to run a staple into my thumb. **1981** H. ENGEL *Ransom Game* (1982) iii. 21, I wondered how could I possibly discuss anything with a man who called staples Bostitch pins.

3. b. *Mus.* A metal tube on to which the double reed of a wind instrument is tied.

1880 GROVE *Dict. Mus.* II. 486/2 It [*sc.* the oboe] is usually made in three pieces, a top, bottom, and bell joints, to which is added a short metal tube, the staple, on which the reed..is attached by means of silk. **1908** *Ibid.* (ed. 2) IV. 42/2 The bassoon reed is placed directly upon the 'crook' of the instrument, but the oboe reed is built up upon a small tube or 'staple'. **1953** E. ROTHWELL *Oboe Technique* 49 The part of the cane from the tip downwards which has been scraped and thinned with the knife after tying the cane on the staple, is known as the 'scrape' (or sometimes as the 'lay'). **1976** D. MUNROW *Instr. Middle Ages & Renaissance* i. 8/4 The [shawm] player presses his lips against a metal disc at the base of the staple, taking the entire reed inside his mouth. *Ibid.* vi. 39/3 (*caption*) Set of modern rackett reeds mounted on their staples.

4. *staple-driver* (later example, in sense *2 d); **staple gun**, a hand-held device for driving staples home; hence (hyphened) as *v. trans.*; † **staple press** = *STAPLER[2].

1895 *Montgomery Ward Catal.* Spring & Summer 116/3 Staple Driver, for binding books, papers, pamphlets, etc. ..staple is placed in holder, driven to place. **1960** G. LEWIS *Handbk. Crafts* 350 A staple gun can be useful, but is not essential. **1975** *Harpers & Queen* May 128/3 Looks like some faggot decorator went nuts in here with a staple gun. **1977** J. FRASER *Hearts Ease* ix. 107 The heavy squad..had staple-gunned plastic sheets to cover the hole. **1895, 1907** Staple press [see sense 2 d above].

staple, *sb.*[2] Add: **3. b.** Also, the principal or basic food on which a community lives.

1970 C. FURTADO in I. L. Horowitz *Masses in Lat. Amer.* ii. 33 In the case of exported staples, there occasionally appeared competitive productive areas which were better situated geographically or which had access to protected markets. **1971** *Sci. Amer.* Sept. 113/1 Except for the staples and tea, tobacco and candy, there is no strong desire for non-Eskimo foods. *Ibid.* Oct. 21/1 It is only recently that human populations have come to depend heavily on a single cultivated plant staple for food. **1977** *N.Y. Rev. Bks.* 23 June 16/1 Much of this inflation can be attributed to a rise in the world price of oil and food staples.

staple, *sb.*[3] Add: **4.** *staple fibre, yarn.*

1928 E. FYLEMAN tr. *Hottenroth's Artificial Silk* i. 16 Staple fibre..consists of artificial silk, the thread of which is cut into sections of about the length of cotton or worsted staple. **1974** *Sci. Amer.* Apr. 57/3 The viscose-rayon process..regenerates pure cellulose..as a continuous filament or a staple fiber. **1955** *Times* 10 May 18/3 More inquiry continues to come forward for filament rayon and staple yarns. **1968** J. IRONSIDE *Fashion Alphabet* 209 The filaments are bunched together, cut into short lengths, combed, drawn and spun into spun or staple yarn, which is fuzzier and is made into fabrics.

staple, *v.*[1] Add: **b.** (Later examples in sense *2 d of the sb.).

1964 R. PETRIE *Murder by Precedent* vi. 87 At no time after stapling the copies did I move any sheets apart. **1975** D. RAMSAY *Descent into Dark* iv. 130 You were stapling that article on abortion together.

stapled, *a.*[2] Add: Also *spec.* of papers, fastened together with a staple or staples.

1956 S. BELLOW *Seize Day* (1957) i. 32 Several pages of blue hectographed script, stapled together. **1958** *N. & Q.* Jan. 46/2 The cost of this book by English standards ($1.50 for a text in stapled paper cover) is prohibitive. **1974** 'P. B. YUILL' *Bornless Keeper* xii. 113 He picked up the wad of stapled foolscap sheets.

stapler[2] (stē̆i·pləɹ). [f. *STAPLE *sb.*[1] 2 d + -ER[1].] A device for fastening together papers, etc., with a staple or staples.

1951 *Catal. of Exhibits, South Bank Exhib., Festival o Britain* 64 Office equipment..'Velos' plier stapler. **1969** 'C. KEITH' *Missing Book-Keeper* iv. 48 The shallow centre drawer..contained..some extra staples for the stapler on top of the desk. **1973** *Sci. Amer.* July 113/2 Edges of the foil can be fastened together with tape or with a stapler. **1978** *Detroit Free Press* 16 Apr. (Advt. Suppl.) 1/4 Full-size standard stapler with open-channel loading.

stapling (stē̆i·pliŋ), *vbl. sb.* [f. STAPLE *v.*[1] + -ING[1].] The action of the verb, esp. that of fastening papers together with staples; the fastening so made.

1898 G. B. SHAW *Let.* 4 Mar. (1972) II. 11 The plays.. require endless cutting & folding and stapling into brown paper covers. **1940** [see *STAPLE *sb.*[1] 2 d]. **1961** *Lebende Sprachen* VI. 104/1 Stapling machine, stapler. **1970** *Guardian* 5 May 4/5 He looked at his report again and noticed the stapling had been interfered with. **1973** D. MILLER *Chinese Jade Affair* xix. 190 The secretary came in with..official seals, a stapling gadget, sealing-wax.

star, *sb.*[1] Add: **I. 1. e.** (Earlier and later examples of phr. *to see stars.*)

1839 *Spirit of Times* 16 Nov. 434/1 She fetched me a slap in the face that made me see stars. **1924** GALSWORTHY *White Monkey* II. xi. 206 '*Per ardua ad astra,*' 'Through hard knocks we shall see stars.' **1966** D. VARADAY *Gara-Yaka's Domain* xiv. 160 Had it been daylight I would still have seen the stars caused by the searing pain I felt in my thumb! **1977** *Cleethorpes News* 27 May 32/3 Already three fighters have seen stars as they have been sent crashing to the canvas.

3. b. (Further examples.) *to thank* (or *praise*) *one's lucky stars*: see LUCKY *a.* 3.

1819 M. WILMOT *Let.* 24 Oct. (1935) 24 O ye stars and garters how often do I wish for Mary and a green Lawn!!! **1913** [see *BOBBY-DAZZLER]. **1931** F. L. ALLEN *Only Yesterday* ix. 237 In any café in Paris one might find an American expatriate thanking his stars that he was free from standardization at last. **1976** M. MILLAR *Ask for me Tomorrow* (1977) ix. 77 My stars, you needn't shout.

5. a. Also applied to celebrities in other spheres of entertainment. *film star*: see *FILM *sb.* 7 c; *movie star*: see *MOVIE b.

1919 G. B. SHAW *Annajanska* in *Heartbreak House* 265 You still want to be a circus star. **1941** *Picturegoer & Film Weekly* 6 Sept. 3/1 Barbara Mullen is no longer unknown. It would be an exaggeration to say *Jeannie* makes her a star. It needs more than one part to do that. **1946** *R.A.F. Jrnl.* May 175 The British Forces Network finds new stars of radio from the ranks of the R.A.F. **1969** *Oxf. Compan. Film* 468/2 Hayley..has been the more prominent in films, scoring a success as a teenage star, notably in *Tiger Bay*.

b. (Earlier and later examples.)

1829 G. GRIFFIN *Collegians* II. xx. 103 Anne Chute.. was, beyond all competition, the star of the evening. **1881** C. E. PASCOE *Everyday Life in our Public Schools* 218 The Torpid game is reserved as a sphere for young 'stars' who come up to Harrow with a reputation. **1973** *Art Internat.* Mar. 55/1 George Washington Wilson's *The Brig and Cliffs, Filey, From the North Landing*..was for me the star of the group [of photographs]. **1975** *Nature* 16 Oct. 531/3 It was supported by a galaxy of scientific stars, including 14 Nobel Prizewinners.

c. *Sport.* An outstanding performer.

1916 [see *clay court* s.v. *CLAY *sb.* 9]. **1928** E. O'NEILL *Strange Interlude* VI. 210 I'm going to start in training him..so he'll be a crack athlete when he goes to college... I want him to..be a bigger star than Gordon ever was. **1930** *Sun* (Baltimore) 26 Dec. 11/7 No player is now on the field more than half of that, so even a star averages only about a half hour's real work throughout the year. **1964** G. C. KUNZLE *Parallel Bars* ix. 407 The content of five difficulties and one superior difficulty was more than most international stars had at that time. **1979** R. JAFFE *Class Reunion* (1980) III. iii. 318 Emma..was the star of her gymnastics class.

6. c. A badge of rank, authority, or military service.

1890 [see *PACK *v.*[1] 9 a]. **1895** *Montgomery Ward Catal.* Spring & Summer 296/3 Policemen's regulation rubber coats..pocket for billy and shield for star. **1908** W. H. DAVIES *Autobiogr. Super-Tramp* 48 With that the marshal of the town stood before the open door, showing the star of his authority on his dark clothes. **1924** C. J. TOLLEY *Mod. Golfer* 6, I passed on from there in '16 with a second lieutenant's star in that regiment. **1942** [see *SAM BROWNE]. **1946** W. S. CHURCHILL *Victory* 143 Two new stars for operations in the East will also mark the service of those who have gone out..to finish the war against the Japanese. **1977** R. LUDLUM *Chancellor Manuscript* xxix. 312 My permanent rank is brigadier-general. I will undoubtedly receive my second star in June.

d. A small star of coloured paper, awarded to a (usu. primary) schoolchild for a good piece of work. (The star is often stuck alongside the work in an exercise book, or displayed on a wall-chart.)

1977 *Cleethorpes News* 6 May 17/2 The books were all very neat and dotted with gold stars on nearly every page. The stars are worth house points which build up over the term. **1978** *Jrnl. R. Soc. Arts* CXXVI. 351/1 If they get 80 per cent or over, they get a blue star, 90 per cent or over a gold star. And ten lessons with stars will win them a prize.

10. c. In guidebooks, one of a number of stars or asterisks against the name of a hotel, restaurant, resort, etc., indicating its rank in a grading system. Cf. **four-star*, **five-star*, etc., under the first elements.

[**1886** S. COOLIDGE *What Katy did Next* vi. 138 'Following a star', in their choice of a hotel..they had decided upon one of those thus distinguished in Baedeker's guide-book.] **1905** E. M. FORSTER *Where Angels fear to Tread* vi. 172 Giotto..has painted two frescoes... That is why Baedeker gives the place a star. **1939** J. B. PRIESTLEY *Let People Sing* v. 99 A bad inn that is given two stars in the Automobile Association's handbook. **1963** R. CARRIER *Great Dishes of World* 128 If one gave stars to the regions of France—as well as to their better restaurants—for the excellence of their cooking, Burgundy would have an unchallenged 'three'. **1974** *Guardian* 20 Mar. 1/1 The Michelin Guide..said that no [British] restaurants had been awarded two or three stars.

d. Used in various other grading systems, as for cognac, refrigerators, petrol, etc.

1922 JOYCE *Ulysses* 498 It was in consequence of a portwine beverage on top of Hennessy's three stars. **1951** R. POSTGATE *Plain Man's Guide to Wine* ix. 125 'Three Stars' indicates the standard and satisfactory degree of distillation... Five Stars should indicate a good brandy. **1968** S. E. ELLACOTT *Everyday Things in England 1914–68* ii. 42 Frozen foods and refrigerators were graded with stars according to the length of time they could be kept fresh. One star denoted a week, two stars a month, and three stars three months. **1971** *Homes & Gardens* Aug. 86/1 Two stars indicate that the temperature is about 10 deg. F. (−12 deg. C.) and frozen food will last for up to four weeks. **1982** *Sunday Tel.* 1 Aug. 6/1 My correspondent objects to the use of star petrol ratings in place of octane numbers.

11. d. *Physics.* A photographic image consisting of a number of lines emanating from a central point, which represent the paths of sub-atomic particles produced by the impact of a cosmic ray or other energetic particle.

1938 *Nature* 1 Oct. 613/1 After an exposure of five months the plates have now been developed and examined. They present singular tracks and stars like those reported in previous papers. **1948** *Science* 26 Nov. 588/2 Approximately 75% of the heavy negative mesons give rise to stars when they come to rest in the emulsion. **1957** G. E. HUTCHINSON *Treat. Limnol.* I. iii. 212 Reactions in which a number of particles are produced.., when they are recorded in a photographic emulsion, are recognized as cosmic ray 'stars'. **1974** *Encycl. Brit. Macropædia* V. 201/2 Interaction of the cosmic-ray particle with the constituents of the emulsion can often be observed as a 'star' in the emulsion; *i.e.*, a spot from which secondary particles are emitted.

12. i. *Electr. Engin.* A star-connected set of windings; *in star*, by means of a star connection.

1907 [see *NEUTRAL *a.* 4 f]. **1924** A. L. COOK *Elem. Electr. Engin.* xviii. 509 When starting, the three groups of coils are connected in star (or Y). **1962** *Newnes Conc. Encycl. Electr. Engin.* 709/1 A 4-branch star converts to a 6-branch mesh. **1974** HOWATSON & LUND *Princ. Heavy Current Engin.* 109 It is possible to connect star to delta but..no fourth wire can be used and so the calculations become tedious if the system is not balanced. **1976** F. DE LA C. CHARD *Electricity Supply* v. 147 Transformers for 3-phase duty..may have both primary and secondary windings connected in delta or star.

14. (Later examples of sense 'a prisoner of star-class'.)

1928 *Notes on Imprisonment* (Home Office) 11 Promotion to the Third Stage may be earned after 12 months, or by 'Stars' after six months. **1945** *Prisons & Borstals* (Home Office) ii. 18 An Ordinary Class prisoner comes into the Second Stage after 12 weeks, a Star after 4 weeks. **1962** 'J. BELL' *Crime in Our Time* vi. ii. 170 Nowadays, the 'stars' as a general rule are by no means first offenders. **1976** A. MILLER *Inside Outside* iv. 48 Several..said that if that was what one-time Stars became, they were cured of returning.

II. 15. a. *star-crowd, -distance, -field, -glimmer, -image, -rise.*

1870 T. W. HIGGINSON *Army Life in Black Regiment* ix. 209, I know moon-rise, I know star-rise, Lay dis body down. **1904** *Nature* 9 June 135/2 The error inherent in the star-images. *a* **1918** W. OWEN *Poems* (1963) 95 And tiring after beauty through star-crowds, Dared I go side by side with you. **1920** A. S. EDDINGTON *Space, Time & Gravitation* viii. 127 The measurement of the displacement of the star-image on the photographic plate. **1952** C. DAY LEWIS tr. *Virgil's Aeneid* iv. 82 Often as star-rise, the troubled ghost of my father, Anchises, Comes to me in my dreams. **1954** J. R. R. TOLKIEN *Fellowship of Ring* ii. ix. 402 In the star-glimmer they must have offered their cunning foes some mark. **1961** WEBSTER, *Star field*, a region of the sky containing stars either as seen in a telescope or recorded on a photograph. *a* **1963** S. PLATH *Crossing Water* (1971) 63 The pale, star-distance faces. **1968** P. MOORE tr. *E. L. Schatzman's Struct. Universe* i. 11 In 1838 F. W. Bessel..measured the first star-distance. **1976** *Houston* (Texas) *Chron.* 22 Sept. vii. 1/2 Sumner's first lecture covers the starfield, with the movements of the sun, moon, planets illustrated and explained.

c. *star-dusted, -filled, -guided, -powdered, -sown, -strewn, -studded, -taught* (earlier and later examples) adjs.

1786 T. DWIGHT *Amer. Poems* (1793) I. 39 Let every sage and seer, Dreamer of dreams, and star-taught prophet hear! **1868** J. R. LOWELL in *Atlantic Monthly* May 627 It is wider Than the star-sown vague of space. **1886** W. B. YEATS *Mosada* 2 For Azolar The star-taught Moor said thus it was decreed. **1895** M. H. KINGSLEY *Diary* 5 June in *Trav. W. Afr.* (1897) vii. 124 The hills silhouetted against the star-powdered purple sky. **1896** A. E. HOUSMAN *Shropshire Lad* 87 The star-filled seas are smooth to-night. **1901** H. G. WELLS *First Men in Moon* v. 62 That airless, star-dusted sky! **1915** G. FRANKAU *Tid'apa* v. 25 Blue-dark against star-strewn turquoise, rose the ramparts of Lallong Ridge. **1920** J. GREGORY *Man to Man* xxiv. 284 The field of star-strewn sky. **1930** J. MASEFIELD *Wanderer of Liverpool* 87 Star-lighted, star-guided, the sea-gleaming beautiful thing. *a* **1936** A. E. HOUSMAN *More Poems* (1936) 166 No star is lost at all From all the star-sown sky. **1945** W. DE LA MARE *Burning-Glass* 11 Ev'n happier in watch of..A star-strewn nightfall. **1958** *People* 4 May 19/5 Star-studded with ex-League players. **1962** *Daily Tel.* 28 Apr. 20 (*heading*) U.S. seeking 'star-guided' missile for NATO. **1977** *New Yorker* 29 Aug. 20/2 It's Mickey Mouse, imprisoned inside a star-dusted transparent balloon. **1978** *Listener* 16 Mar. 339/1 In an otherwise star-studded cast, the lead characters are not quite up to their role.

d. *star-eyed* (later example), *-glimmering, -tall* adjs.

1878 G. M. HOPKINS *Poems* (1967) 77 Star-eyed strawberry-breasted Throstle. **1900** W. B. YEATS *Shadowy Waters* 9 More shining winds, more star-glimmering ponds? **1943** S. SPENDER *Spiritual Exercises* 6 Outside, the eternal star-tall mountains gleam.

19. (Earlier and further examples.) Also in sense *5 c.

1839 F. MARRYAT *Diary in Amer.* II. ii. xiii. 121 They look for importations of star actors from this country. **1876** 'MARK TWAIN' *Tom Sawyer* iv. 50 He had been around among the star pupils inquiring. **1879** C. E. PASCOE *Dramatic Notes* 68 What is known as 'star-acting' usually forms the principal feature of the bills of this theatre. **1890** W. JAMES *Princ. Psychol.* I. xi. 453 The laws of stimulation and association..*may* at times simply form the background for a 'star-performer', who is no more their 'inert accompaniment' or their 'incidental product' than Hamlet is Horatio's or Ophelia's. **1909** *Times* 24 Aug. 15/6 The engaging of outside 'star' players to strengthen a county [cricket] side. **1917** T. E. LAWRENCE *Lett.* (1938) 219 The star film showed the Pyramids. **1927** *Melody Maker* Sept. 923/1 The all too few star performers in this country. **1933** J. CARY *Amer. Visitor* xiii. 169 Uli turned out one of the star pupils. **1943** N. COWARD *Middle East Diary* (1944) 23 He must possess ..what is described in the theatre as 'star quality'... Complete authority, a direct eye, and a compelling economy of gesture. **1950** *Sport* 22–28 Sept. 12/4 Have too many star players been allowed to drift away from the Swansea Town fold? **1961** *Ann. Reg. 1960* 446 Star acting was also the chief merit of *The Last Angry Man.* **1972** *Vogue* Feb. 89/3 Twiggy's got this rather mysterious presence. Star quality. **1977** *New Yorker* 19 Sept. 75/1 I'm sure Mme. Dorfmann is furious with the review, because he's her star pupil. **1978** J. GARDNER *Dancing Dodo* xxxii. 256 You're playing the star role—Hercule Poirot—and I've got to coach you. **1982** *London Review Bks.* IV. xxiv. 20/2 Star quality, however, was not at all what was looked for in those who played opposite a superstar like Kean.

20. star-back *slang*, an expensive, reserved seat at a circus; **star bill,** a poster advertising a theatrical star; **star billing** = *top billing* s.v. *BILLING *vbl. sb.*[3] b; also *transf.* and *fig.*; **star boarder** *U.S.*, a boarder, usu. of long standing, having or regarded as having special privileges; also used euphemistically of more complicated relationships; **starburst,** (*a*) an explosion of a star or stars, or an explosion producing an appearance of stars; (*b*) *Photogr.*, a lens attachment which causes a bright light source to appear in a photograph with added star-like rays; also, the effect so produced; usu. *attrib.*; **star cloud,** a region of the sky where stars appear to be especially numerous and close together; **star connection** *Electr. Engin.*, an arrangement in a polyphase system in motors and the like by which one end of each phase winding is connected to a common point; so **star-connected** *a.*; **star count,** a statistical survey of the stars in various directions in space to ascertain the numerical distribution across the sky of stars brighter than some given magnitude; **star-crossed:** delete † and add later examples, after quot. 1592 (Shakes.) in Dict.; **star-cut** *a.*: also in extended uses (see quots.); **star-delta** *Electr. Engin.*, used *attrib.* with reference to the use of star connection when an induction motor is started with a change to delta connection for continuous running; **star drag** *Angling* (see quot. 1960); **star network,** a data or communication network in which all terminals are independently connected to one central unit; **Star of David** = *MAGEN DAVID; **star point** *Electr. Engin.*, the common junction of the windings in a star-connected system; **star quad** *Telecommunications*, a quad (*QUAD *sb.*[6]) in which the four conductors are all twisted around a common axis, with members of each pair being diametrically opposite each other; usu. *attrib.*; **star stream,** † (*a*) a narrow band of the sky that is rich in stars; (*b*) each of the two groups of stars in star streaming; **star streaming,** the phenomenon (explained by the rotation of the galaxy) in which stars show a broad tendency to have proper motions in one or other of two opposite directions, thus falling approximately into two intermingled groups ('streams'); **star system,** (*a*) in the world of film and theatrical entertainment, the practice of promoting an eminent artiste in leading roles; (*b*) a large structured collection of stars, a galaxy; **star-tracker,** a self-regulating device which maintains its orientation relative to a star, used in the control systems of spacecraft; so **star-tracking** *vbl. sb.*; **star turn,** the principal or most important item in an entertainment; also *fig.*; **star-vehicle,** a play or film designed especially to show off the talents of a particular actor or actress; **star witness,** the principal or most important witness in a trial.

1931 *Amer. Mercury* Nov. 354/1 *Starbacks*, the reserved seat section. **1933** E. SEAGO *Circus Company* iii. 23 He sat with me in the 'star backs'. **1965** M. STEWART *Airs above Ground* vi. 72 Tim had no difficulty in getting what he called 'starback' seats... These, the best seats, were rather comfortable portable chairs..right at the ringside. **1901** A. CHEVALIER *Before I Forget* 157 Just ordered fresh stock of special printing, star bills, &c. **1956** H. KURNITZ *Invasion of Privacy* iii. 27 One picture a year.:. Star billing. **1959** *Listener* 5 Feb. 238/1 The Chinese still give credit to the Russians for their technical aid, but there has been a change in the star billing. Now they say these things were done by Chinese engineers with Soviet assistance. **1967** *Amer. N. & Q.* June 156/1 *Behind Spanish American Footlights* is the key reference tool in its field, and as such rates star billing. **1979** *Listener* 25 Oct. 547/3 The *Radio Times*..gives Ted Heath (1970–74) star billing. **1877** in H. Asbury *Gem of Prairie* (1940) iv. 135 Jessie Curtis, star boarder, is still at 519 State Street. **1897** *Boston Jrnl.* 16 Jan. 6/5 'I'm afraid you are about to be dethroned.' The Star Boarder —'Why?' **1908** J. M. SULLIVAN *Criminal Slang* 24 *Star boarder or lodger*, a boarder..in good financial standing who has all the privileges of a husband. **1922** N. B. TARKINGTON *Gentle Julia* 113 The pill-boxes [for insects] ..evidently contained star boarders, for they were pierced with 'breathing holes'. **1935** J. HARGAN *Gloss. Prison Lang.* 8 *Star-boarder*, a lifer. **1935** A. J. POLLOCK *Underworld Speaks* 113/2 *Star boarder*, the inmate of a house of prostitution, who earns the most money. **1976** 'O. BLEECK' *No Questions Asked* xii. 137 He lived here and we split expenses... He was sort of a star boarder. **1965** G. MCINNES *Road to Gundagai* iii. 56 Rockets whooshed skyward ending in great parabolic starbursts. **1977** G. MICHANOWSKY *Once & Future Star* i. 3 At the dawn of human history,..this starburst occurred and briefly became visible as a..second sun in our sky. **1977** J. HEDGECOE *Photographer's Handbk.* 181 A clear sky can be filled with diverging lines if the sun is spread by means of a starburst filter. **1978** *Amateur Photographer* 2 Aug. 110/1 Sparkling highlights are emphasized with a cross screen (star-burst). **1979** *Ibid.* 30 May 92/3 A very special filter which not only gives a star-burst effect, but rays of the starburst are tinged with the colours of the spectrum. **1924** *Proc. Amer. Acad. Arts & Sciences* LIX. 217 Fainter stars of division A reveal through their distribution the relative nearness of the star clouds in Cygnus. **1947** *Astrophysical Jrnl.* CV. 257 The regions of the star clouds in Sagittarius and Ophiuchus are rich in clearly marked globules. **1896** D. C. & J. P. JACKSON *Alternating Currents* II. viii. 395 If the armature is star connected, the pressure between rings is equal to the vector sum of the pressure developed in the two coils. **1976** F. DE LA C. CHARD *Electr. Supply* v. 145 A star-connected winding has only $1/\sqrt{3}$ times the line voltage across each phase but carries the full line current. **1894** G. KAPP *Electric Transmission of Energy* (ed. 4) xii. 418 The armature is drum wound with star connection. **1969** *Power System Protection* (Electr. Council) II. xi. 404 Busbar reactors. (b) Tie bar connected. Two methods are commonly adopted and may be classified as (i) the star connection.., and (ii) the ring connection. **1889** *Nature* 8 Aug. 345/1 For simple star-counts, we have only to substitute star-counts by magnitudes over selected areas of the sky. **1933** *Discovery* Feb. 41/2 The modern method employed for thus studying the distribution of stars is the statistical one of 'star-counts'. **1947** *Astrophysical Jrnl.* CV. 257 Stoddard has made star counts according to photographic and photovisual magnitudes for four large globules. **1962** C. OMAN *Mary of Modena* v. 172 Abbé Armand Jean de Bouthillier de Rancé of La Trappe had, according to rumour, well known star-crost love before he suddenly renounced the world at the age of thirty-six. **1973** *Alberta Hist. Rev.* Winter 12/1 But if Uncle Charlie's first motivation was star-crossed love, his second was certainly horses. **1977** W. M. SPACKMAN *Armful of Warm Girl* 18 She wailed in star-crossed despair. **1967** WODEHOUSE *Company for Henry* iii. 45 Clichy double overlay weight,.. the top flattened by a large window, star-cut base. **1972** J. HOWARD-WILLIAMS *Sails* (ed. 3) xii. 172 The genniker (or spanker, or star-cut spinnaker) is..a cross between a genoa and a spinnaker... It is primarily a racing sail... It is cut rather like a storm spinnaker, with full width foot tapering to the rule minimum 75 per cent at midgirth, with narrow shoulders from there up. **1976** *Yachting World* Oct. 72/1 Spinnakers are sewn in a special corner of Hood's loft with a five-step machine. This sews a unique five-stitch seam on star-cut spinnakers. **1908** W. B. HIRD *Elem. Dynamo Design* ix. 260 If the star-delta method of connection is used [in the starting of a squirrel-cage motor], the ratio must be 1 to 1·73, and no other choice can be made. **1962** *Newnes Conc. Encycl. Electr. Engin.* 517/1 Star-delta starting is one method of reducing starting current of 3-phase motors. **1976** F. DE LA C. CHARD *Electr. Supply* v. 148 A star-delta connection for a step-down transformer is normally used. **1950** *N.Y. Times* 30 Dec. 18/8 While you could stand a heavier bait rod and a reel with star drag, the regulation bait rod will suffice. **1960** C. WILLOCK *Angler's Encycl.*, *Star-drag*, adjustable tension device often built into big sea multiplying reels. Tension is varied by means of a star-shaped nut. **1979** *Angling* July 33/1 (Advt.), Rugged star drag design with white-oak leather washers for smooth line control. **1977** *Financial Times* 21 Feb. 13/1 Modern data networks have come a long way since the banks first started installing their enormous star networks, consisting of one or tv o very big computer centres serving several thousand simple terminals installed in branch back offices. **1979** T. HOUSLEY *Data Communications & Teleprocessing Systems* ii. 52 There are four basic network configurations that can be used: the star network, the ring network, the mesh network, and the hierarchical network. The star network..is probably the most common. **1941** M. SAMUEL tr. *Bein's Theodore Herzl* ii. vii. 229 At one side hung a flag: a white field with two blue stripes and the Star of David. **1979** *N.Y. Rev. Bks.* 25 Oct. 3/2 Jan Friedländer's book plates displayed a score by Chopin set within a Star of David. **1908** W. B. HIRD *Elem. Dynamo Design* vii. 186 The star point..is usually connected to earth, both at the generator and at the load end. **1969** *Power System Protection* (Electr. Council) II. xi. 404 Each section of busbar is connected via a reactor to a common star point, and if the feeders and generators are suitably arranged little or no current need flow through the reactors. **1930** *Gloss. Terms Telegraphs & Telephones* (*B.S.I.*) 31 *Star quad cable*, a cable containing a number of quads, each quad formed by twisting together four insulated conductors about a common axis. **1958** J. R. G. SMITH *Elem. Telecommunications Pract.* v. 73 Other features of star-quad cables are that in some cables certain of the pairs are screened by being wrapped in metallized paper..; they are placed in the centre of the core and used for music. **1970** P. NORMAN in T. L. Squires *Telecomm. Pocket Bk.* v. 53 Some 4,000 miles of these [balanced pair] systems are installed in this country, consisting mainly of 24-pair,

40 lb per mile conductors in star-quad formation. **1894** *Knowledge* 1 June 133/1 The streams are in most cases accompanied by narrow black channels in the general nebulosity, which run parallel to and alongside of the star streams. **1904** J. C. KAPTEYN in H. J. Rogers *Congress of Arts & Science* (1906) IV. 418 Here we have a clear indication that we have to do with two star-streams. **1925** *Ark. f. Mat., Astr. och Fysik* XIXA. XXI. 1, I have tried to find a clue to a possible connection between the star-streaming discovered by Kapteyn, 'the two star-streams', and the asymmetrical drift of high stellar velocities. **1968** W. M. SMART *Riddle of Universe* vi. 106 Kapteyn's star-streams are consistent with the phenomenon of galactic rotation and are indeed explained by it. **1906** *Rep. Brit. Assoc. Adv. Sci. 1905* 257 (*heading*) Star streaming. **1921** *Discovery* Feb. 36/1 In 1904 Professor Kapteyn..read at the Astronomical Congress at St. Louis, U.S.A., a paper of far-reaching importance, in which he announced the discovery of star-streaming. **1979** LANG & GINGERICH *Source Bk. Astron. & Astrophysics* lxxvii. 514 Karl Schwarzschild showed that it was unnecessary to think of two star streams and that the phenomenon of star streaming could be explained by assuming that the individual motions of the stars are distributed in an ellipsoid with the long axis in the direction of motion of Kapteyn's two star streams. **1832** *Rep. Sel. Comm. on Dramatic Lit.* in *Parl. Papers 1831–32* VII. 30 The star system that has been adopted by the two great theatres. **1870** R. A. PROCTOR *Other Worlds than Ours* 256 To return for a moment to fig. 2, it will be seen at once that an aperture extending laterally through a star system so shaped must have a particular direction and be perfectly straight in order to be visible to observers placed, as we are supposed to be, in the central opening. **1890** G. B. SHAW in *Star* 18 Apr. 2/3 The familiar star system trick of making the minor characters slur their work in order to leave plenty of time for the mock pregnant pauses..of the leading actor. **1928** A. S. EDDINGTON *Nature Physical World* viii. 167 The first partitions [of the gaseous nebulae] are the star-systems such as our galactic system. **1937** A. CALDER-MARSHALL in C. Day Lewis *Mind in Chains* 71 This tendency..has led to the star-system deplored by film critics almost without exception. **1967** P. MOORE *Amat. Astronomer's Gloss.* 89 *Nubeculæ* (or Magellanic Clouds), the nearest of the external star-systems, and so the brightest as seen with the naked eye. **1971** *Guardian* 5 June 9/4 Hollywood was devising the 'star system', the big solo buildup, the personality cult of the silent screen. **1962** *Aeroplane & Commercial Aviation News* CIII. 32/1 The main outstanding problem in the provision of such a system is the development of a suitable daylight star-tracker. **1978** *Nature* 5 Oct. 378/2 The star tracker in the scientific instrument can identify and guide on stars brighter than 14 mag. **1964** *Discovery* Oct. 7/3 A star-tracking ability can readily be developed from the same system. **1898** A. M. BINSTEAD *Pink 'Un & Pelican* ii. 44 The 'star turns' in the entertainment, which took place twice every day, were the then unknown Paul Cinquevalli, Batty, the natty horseman..the 'Beautiful Geraldine', and two savage and sullen brown bears. **1906** E. DYSON *Fact'ry 'Ands* vii. 78 In fact the packer soon found that waiting was Eric's 'star turn'. **1909** *Flight* 3 July 398/1 M. Bleriot..is the 'star turn' at the Brayelle aerodrome at Douai just now. **1915** H. G. WELLS *Boon* 328 'Inevitably,' said the Bishop, 'this theatricalism, this star-turn business, with its extreme spiritual excitements, ..leads to such a breakdown as afflicts you.' **1951** J. G. FENNESSY *Sonnet in Bottle* IV. iv. 116 You're our star turn, it's up to you. **1977** 'E. CRISPIN' *Glimpses of Moon* xii. 232 His normal chief recreation..is watching other people at work. And in this..it is the two workmen who are the star turns. **1932** *New Yorker* 9 Jan. 43/1 As a spectacle it is a typical star vehicle hitched up to a singer with..a weak larynx. **1953** K. REISZ *Technique Film Editing* i. 60 Many of the films built round the personality of Greta Garbo..are little more than ingeniously contrived star-vehicles, yet they cannot be dismissed as worthless. **1974** *Listener* 2 May 580/2 Few self-respecting dramatists want to construct star-vehicles nowadays, and so Robert Morley..has written one for himself. **1924** W. M. RAINE *Troubled Waters* xvii. 183 Haight [*sc.* a district attorney] was very gentle and considerate of his star witness. **1978** P. MOYES *Who is Simon Warwick?* xi. 137 The prosecutors were..satisfied with the evidence. Susan Benedict was to be their star witness.

22. a. star-anise, also, *Illicium verum*, a small evergreen tree found in southern China; the fruit of this tree, or the oil or spice obtained from it; (later examples); **star tulip**, a glabrous perennial bulbous plant belonging to any of several species of the genus *Calochortus* (family Liliaceæ), native to temperate western N. America; (formerly distinguished from Mariposa lilies, but now sometimes used synonymously for the whole genus).

1883 Star anise [see *coffin-wood* s.v. *COFFIN *sb.* 13]. **1972** K. LO *Chinese Food* I. 12 One or two pieces of star-anise and a sprinkling of cinnamon. **1895** W. ROBINSON *English Flower Garden* (ed. 4) II. 347/2 One of the most experienced growers of the Calochorti, Dr. Wallace, of Colchester, writes of the family thus:.. 'Other dwarf forms among the Star Tulips lasted well up to the end of June, when the beautiful Mariposa Lilies continued the display with their tall spikes.' **1921** M. HAMPDEN *Bulb Gardening* xvii. 185 Every garden should contain Calochorti... They consist of three groups, but I consider two only fit for the amateur gardener's patronage; these are known as Mariposa, or Butterfly Tulips, and Star Tulips. **1925** [see *MARIPOSA LILY]. **1974** H. G. W. FOGG *Compl. Handbk. Bulbs* vii. 49/2 Of those described as star tulips, *C*[*alochortus*] *benthami*, clear yellow with dark central blotch, and *C. maweanus* 'Major'..are among the finest.

23. (Later example.)

1976 *Sci. Amer.* Apr. 94/2 A type of opal new to us has recently been mined near Spencer, Idaho. It is a star opal that shows streaks of colour in symmetrically arranged angular patterns similar to the rays of a star sapphire.

star, *v.* Add: **7.** (Earlier example.)

1827 *Gardener's Mag.* II. 105, I wonder indeed that members of a (professedly) liberal society should quietly submit to be classed and regulated, and starred and scheduled, like the items in a paper of assessed taxes.

8. a. (Later examples.) Also in sport, to play a star role in a team.

1933 *Radio Times* 14 Apr. 73/1 There may have been two Zazels, one of whom..retired before 1890, when the other took over the name and 'starred' at the Westminster Aquarium. **1972** J. MOSEDALE *Football* viii. 116 Turner.. starred from 1940 through 1952. **1976** *Oxf. Compan. Film* 633/2 She returned to Britain to star in *Say Hello to Yesterday*. **1978** *Dumfries Courier* 20 Oct. 5/3 Carson starred on the right wing, and was the mainspring of a lively Queens side.

d. To advertise as a film or theatrical star; to give a star part to (an actor or actress); (with a film, etc., as subject) to present in a leading role.

1895 G. B. SHAW *Let.* 27 Mar. (1965) I. 508 It is good business to star Janet. **1922** *Encycl. Brit.* XXX. 699/2 He appeared in a minor rôle on the New York stage in 1901; later he was 'starred' in several comedies and musical pieces. **1929** A. C. & C. EDINGTON *Studio Murder Mystery* viii. 102 Already ve are going to star her! Already ve haff bought a story, just for her. **1936** [see *FEATURE *v.* 4 b]. **1951** 'N. SHUTE' *Lonely Road* (ed. 2) p. v, In 1936 a film was made..starring Clive Brook. **1962** E. ALBEE *Who's afraid of Virginia Woolf?* (1964) I. 5 *Chicago* was a 'thirties musical, starring little Miss Alice *Faye*. Don't you know *anything*? **1980** *Sunday Times* 21 Sept. 14 Since then he has earned an international reputation with plays..and The Faith Healer, which starred James Mason last year on Broadway.

starboard, *sb.* (and *a.*). Add: **A.** *sb.* **a.** Also used with reference to aircraft.

1909 F. T. JANE *All World's Air-Ships* 142 Motor–3–cylinder 10–12 h.p. Buchet, mounted directly on the lower plane, a little to starboard of centre line. **1977** J. CLEARY *High Road to China* ii. 65 The Bristol slid to starboard, kept sliding and I let it go, feeling I was getting it under control.

B. *attrib.* or as *adj.* Also used with reference to aircraft.

1917 [see *PORT *sb.*[6] (*a.*) 2 a]. **1948** 'N. SHUTE' *No Highway* iii. 61 The second pilot..came down into the cabin... Then he said: 'Which is the boffin?'..'Sitting on the starboard side, near the front.' **1976** B. LECOMBER *Dead Weight* iii. 45 The tailwheel lock had broken... The starboard prop had run away.

star-bright. Add: Also **star bright**. **b.** Delete '? *technical*' and add def.: Of wine and cider: perfectly clear and free from sediment (see quot. 1979). (Later examples.)

1923 A. L. SIMON *Supply, Care & Sale of Wine* xvi. 109 Before bottling any wine, you must make sure:–..That the wine is star-bright. *Ibid.* 110 These..conditions are, to my mind, rules without exception, but there are bottlers who make an exception to the 'star-bright bottling' rule when they bottle Vintage Ports. **1945** *Wine & Spirit Trade Rec.* 18 June 650/1 A device that helps the examination of Wines is to paint sheets of tin..with black pigment..and to fix it in an angle of the cellar walls where a short gas jet can be lit behind the bottle so that the Wine can be seen..under the best conditions for discovering whether the Wine is 'star bright' or not. **1973** *Times* 20 Oct. 14/2 Modern vinification makes the majority of wines 'star bright' but the presence of a little deposit in many fine wines means quality. **1979** TURNER & ROYCROFT *Winemaker's Encycl.* 167 Wines which are brilliantly clear and reflect highlights when in the bottle are said to be 'star-bright'. All wines that are entered in competitions or are otherwise exhibited publicly should be star-bright.

starch, *sb.* Add: **4.** Freq. in phr. *to take the starch out of* (a person or thing): to remove the stiffness, formality, or pompousness from (someone, etc.), esp. by ridicule; to deflate.

1840 *Spirit of Times* 25 Apr. 90/1 There is something in training in these parts that will be very apt to 'take the starch out' of any 'conceit' they may have. **1846** [in Dict.] **1889** G. B. SHAW in *Hawk* 13 Aug. 172/1 This is the sort of thing that takes the starch out of the most bumptious critic. **1922** *Daily Mail* 20 Nov. 12 The home forwards were unquestioned masters, and on the day's play would have taken the starch out of any other pack in the country. **1936** V. W. BROOKS *Flowering of New England* vi. 113 The British reviews were cold and formal. .. The great Romantic critics had not appeared, to take the starch out of their pompous manners.

5. a. *starch-free* adj.

1939 A. THIRKELL *Before Lunch* iv. 88 Miss Starter is on a diet and has to have a special bread called Kornog, which is practically starch-free. **1971** *Guardian* 29 June 13/2 Anyone on a starch-free diet should seek some other country [than Scotland].

b. starch blocker, a dietary preparation that supposedly affects the metabolism of starch so that it does not contribute to a gain in weight; **starch gel**, a gel made from starch and an aqueous buffer solution, used as the supporting medium in a method of zone electrophoresis; so *starch-gel electrophoresis*; **starch hyacinth**, a small bulbous plant, *Muscari neglectum*, belonging to the family Liliaceæ, native to Europe and western Asia, and bearing spikes of dark blue, strongly scented flowers; **starch-reduced** *a.*, processed so as to contain less than the normal proportion of starch.

1981 *Arizona Med.* XXXVIII. 848/1 A new product has appeared on the market... It is not a drug, but a processed food made from a certain type of bean. It is also called NBE (Northern Bean Extract) or The Starch Blocker. **1983** *Daily Tel.* 14 Apr. 6/5 Slimmers who use starch blockers..are wasting their money... Experts.. say they do not affect the quantity of starch digested and could have unpleasant effects if they did work. **1955** O. SMITHIES in *Biochem. Jrnl.* 630/1 A starch gel containing the desired buffer is prepared in a suitable plastic tray. *Ibid.* 635/1 α_1-Globulin does not appear as a definite band between α_2-globulin and albumin in starch gel electrophoresis. **1961** *Lancet* 5 Aug. 291/1 On electrophoresis in starch gel, no macroglobulin moved out from the point of insertion. **1978** *Jrnl. R. Soc. Med.* LXXI. 192 Investigations into this isoenzyme composition of the circulating CK using starch-gel electrophoresis. **1790** *Curtis's Bot. Mag.* IV. 122 We have thought it better to call this species the Starch Hyacinth, the smell of the flower in the general opinion resembling that substance. **1808** J. E. SMITH *Eng. Bot.* XXVII. 1931 Starch Hyacinth..is so abundantly wild in many places. **1900** G. BELL *Let.* 11 Jan. (1927) I. v. 61, I went there yesterday afternoon for starch hyacinths and cyclamen and had a tremendous scramble. **1927** F. B. YOUNG *Portrait of Claire* IV. iii. 372 In sheltered crevices gentian, starch-hyacinth and chionodoxa mocked with their living blue the surly Midland winter. **1939** A. THIRKELL *Before Lunch* iv. 89 Pepso is only starch-reduced. **1972** 'G. NORTH' *Sgt. Cluff rings True* ix. 76 Sugar substitutes, starch-reduced biscuits and breads, low-calorie soups.

Star-chamber, † starred chamber. Add: **2. b.** (Later examples.) Also *fig*

1896 W. C. GORE in *Inlander* Jan. 150 *Star chamber*, an oral examination given to a student privately. **1934** [see *GAY-PAY-OO]. **1958** M. KENNEDY *Outlaws on Parnassus* xiii. 208 A large group of [novelists]..will never allow that the novel can be subjected to legislation. If some Star Chamber has been set up, they..will have none of it. **1973** *Times* 4 Dec. 17/6 The constitutional propriety of the present industrial star chamber is dubious. **1975** 'S. MARLOWE' *Cawthorn Jrnls.* (1976) xviii. 150 Mexican law's based on the Code Napoleon... You could say the courtroom's a Star Chamber instead of a field of forensic battle.

starchy, *a.* Add: **2. b.** Of food: containing much starch.

1948 *Good Housek. Cookery Bk.* I. 12 *Carbohydrates.* These comprise starchy foods and sugars. **1977** C. MCCULLOUGH *Thorn Birds* i. 13 No one carried a pound of superfluous flesh, in spite of the vast quantities of starchy food.

4. Also *transf.*

1874 'MARK TWAIN' *Lett. to Publishers* (1967) 81 It will thus be a mighty starchy book. **1880** [in Dict.]. **1977** E. W. HILDICK *Loop* xxiv. 164 Maybe that's putting it a bit too formal, Ralph, just a bit starchy.

stardom. Delete *nonce-wd.* and add: (Later examples.) Also, the status of a celebrity or star performer in other spheres of activity. Also *fig.*

1901 C. MORRIS *Life on Stage* xxv. 203 At the curtain's fall her stardom was over. **1927** *Radio Times* 21 Oct. 143/2 From a clerkship in an insurance office to 'stardom' at a Royal Variety Performance is a long step. **1941** 'N. BLAKE' *Case of Abominable Snowman* xvi. 177 'I fancy lady Macbeth had put in a good deal of quiet work before the play opens, telling her husband what a worm he was.' 'Grooming him for evil stardom?' **1951** *Sport* 16–22 Mar. 13/3 Quietly plodding the hard road to stardom is Terry Webster, goalkeeper of Derby County. **1977** *New Yorker* 9 May 143/2 The media..impel a Prime Minister to seek stardom at the expense of the Cabinet. **1979** *Tucson* (Arizona) *Citizen* 20 Sept. 1D/3 Giangardella has been tackling opponents since he was a fourth grader at Mt. Carmel Elementary School back in Niles. He went on to stardom at Niles McKinley High School.

star-dust. Add: Also **stardust**. **3.** *fig.* That which is illusory or insubstantial. Freq. in phr. *to have stardust in one's eyes* and varr.

1933 E. SITWELL *English Eccentrics* iv. 116 Here comes the star-dust, the noisy chattering crowd of tipsters and smaller racing men. **1934** V. WOOLF *Walter Sickert* 20 His [*sc.* Sickert's] paint has a tangible quality; it is made not of air and star-dust but of oil and earth. **1967** WODEHOUSE *Company for Henry* iii. 45 Clichy double overlay weight..centred by a pink rose within a ring of white stardust canes. **1975** A. HUNTER *Gently with Love* xxii. 81 'You had a different opinion of her once.'..'I must have had some stardust in my eyes.' **1977** *New Yorker* 4 July 82/3 There is the silliness of the movie's plangency: hard to feel soupy about a talented couple giving up their love because of the stardust in their eyes.

stare, *v.* Add: **2. b.** Also (in *fig.* sense) to be apparently obvious but nevertheless overlooked.

1966 J. B. PRIESTLEY *Salt is Leaving* iii. 43 She found the Mahler album...'It must have been staring you in the face,' she added. **1972** 'G. NORTH' *Sgt. Cluff rings True* xvi. 120 'It was staring me in the face,' the Sergeant said, and he should have seen it sooner. **1979** A. BOYLE *Climate of Treason* viii. 236 The over-caution of Cowgill in fumbling for conclusions that stared him in the face demanded some patience.

d. *to stare* (someone) *down, out*: to stare at someone without being first to blink or lower one's gaze, usu. as an expression of resistance or hostility; to outstare. Also *fig.*

1856 DICKENS *Little Dorrit* (1857) I. xxiv. 215 'She looked at the Princess, and the Princess looked at her.' 'Like trying to stare one another out,' said Maggy. **1946** T. H. WHITE *Mistress Masham's Repose* xiv. 115 Miss Brown searched out her pupil's eyes and fixed them with her own. She had a..trick of staring Maria down. **1965** 'T. HINDE' *Games of Chance* I. iv. 110 That made me shout at Kenny a lot, and mimic him, and stare him out. **1972** R. THOMAS *Porkchoppers* (1974) xii. 107 He spent nearly a minute staring at Goff. Goff had stared back, thinking that he was damned if he'd let any pal of Cloke's stare him down. **1979** *Guardian* 12 Jan. 8/5 Some measure of fiscal 'mid-term adjustment'..is called for. So is a serious attempt to stare down the local government workers. **1979** G. SEYMOUR *Red Fox* iv. 56 The maid in the starched apron stared him out.

6. stare-you-out, the activity of staring someone out (see sense 2 d above), esp. as a children's game; also *attrib.*

1962 E. O'BRIEN *Lonely Girl* ix. 107 In the village.. people stopped to look..with savage stare-you-out eyes. **1972** J. QUARTERMAIN *Rock of Diamonds* xxvi. 140 She held her expression... I grinned and played 'Stare-you-out'. But I blinked first. **1977** D. MORRIS *Manwatching* 75 (*caption*) Such is the impact of the close-quarters gaze that the schoolboy game of stare-you-out is extremely difficult to maintain over a long period of time.

‖ **stare decisis** (stēᵊri dėsəizis, stāre dėsīsīs). *Law.* [L., lit. to stand by things decided.] The legal principle of determining points in litigation according to precedent; properly as *vbl. phr.*, to be bound by precedents.

1782 F. BULLER in E. H. East *Rep. King's Bench* (1801) I. 495 The rule *stare decisis* is one of the most sacred in the law. **1811** *Q. Rev.* Dec. 434 The learned judge..professes his anxiety 'stare decisis', and to abide by authorities. **1845** H. BROOM *Legal Maxims* ii. 61 It is..an established rule to abide by former precedents, *stare decisis*, where the same points come again into litigation. **1936** J. C. GARDNER *Judicial Precedent Scots Law* iii. 41 It probably cannot be said that the *stare decisis* doctrine had no part in the operation of precedent on the inferior Courts in Scotland. **1970** *Internat. & Compar. Law Q.* XIX. I. 145 A rigid adherence to *stare decisis*..is of little assistance where the law hopes to offer an answer to the people it serves. **1982** *Sci. Amer.* June 20/2 The doctrine of *stare decisis* (namely that precedents should be followed) may be imposed at the players' option, or it may arise without explicit amendment, as successive judges feel impelled to treat 'similarly situated' persons 'similarly'.

‖ **starets, staretz** (stā·ryets). Pl. **startsy, startzy** (stā·rtsi). [Russ., = (venerable) old man, elder.] In the Russian Orthodox Church, a spiritual leader or counsellor. Also *transf.*

1923 G. BUCHANAN *My Mission to Russia* I. xviii. 240 Rasputin..thus gradually acquired the reputation of a holy man, or elder (*staretz*), and was credited with the gifts of healing and prophecy. **1955** J. D. SALINGER in *New Yorker* 29 Jan. 36/2 He meets this person called a starets—some sort of terribly advanced religious person—and the starets tells him about a book called the 'Philokalia'. **1966** A. BLOOM *Living Prayer* v. 73 The Staretz Ambrose of Optina had the kind of vision which allowed him to see a person's real good. **1975** *Christian* III. 91 The Startsy became enormously influential in the last hundred years of Tsarism. **1976** *Ibid.* III. 150 She was meeting..a man who was himself the spiritual soul of one of the greatest *startzy* (spiritual fathers) of the nineteenth century West, the Abbé Huvelin. **1981** A. EDWARDS *Sonya* 492 Rasputin..'cured' Tsarevich Alexis's hemophilia in 1904. Thereafter, with each recurrence of her son's illness, the Tsarina grew more dependent upon this starets. **1983** *Church Times* 4 Feb. 7/1 They tell us of the hidden work of the *Startsy*, the 'elders' or spiritual fathers, whose counsel and prayer is an inspiration to many.

starey (stēᵊ·ri), *a.* Also **stary.** [f. STARE *v.* + -Y[1].] **1.** Inclined to stare; giving the appearance of staring.

1924 *Chambers's Jrnl.* Aug. 557 A bit flushed and starey about the eyes but still breathing. **1950** T. E. LAWRENCE *Mint* xiv. 50 Her eyes were starey, like a haddock's. **1960** P. COLERIDGE *Running Footsteps* 170 Did he go blind at the end? He was getting very stary, very vacant, like. **1975** *Listener* 9 Oct. 479/1 Vanessa Redgrave, very starey and earnest. **1980** S. KING *Firestarter* I. 57 There was something starey in her eyes that made him think about those combat-fatigue stories you heard during wartime.

2. = STARING *ppl. a.* 3.

1955 W. W. DENLINGER *Complete Boston* I. 94 They [*sc.* internal parasites] reflect themselves in a dull starey coat.

star-fish, starfish. Add: **3.** Special Comb.: **starfish bed** *Geol.*, a stratum rich in starfish fossils; (usu. with capital initial(s) as a proper name).

1863 *Q. Jrnl. Geol. Soc.* XIX. 289 Capping these, in Down Cliffs, is the Starfish-bed, above which begin the Middle Lias Sands. **1935** J. PRINGLE *South of Scotland* ii. 34 Near the head of the Lady Burn the mudstones are underlain by a hard greenish-grey calcareous sandstone, the well-known Starfish Bed. **1970** R. M. BLACK *Elements Palaeont.* x. 141 While, in general, they are rare fossils, in some horizons (referred to as 'starfish' beds) they are relatively numerous, e.g. in the Upper Ordovician, Girvan and in the Lower Ludlow in Herefordshire. **1977** J. W. PERKINS *Geol. explained in Dorset* xi. 138 The base of the Starfish Bed forms a strong spring-line, and hillsides below this level are often cut by deep wooded gullies as a result.

star-gazy, stargazy, stargazey (stā·ɹgēⁱzi), *a.* Also **star-a-gaze, starry-gazey, starry-gazy.** [f. STAR-GAZE *v.* + -Y[1].] *star-gazy pie*, a kind of fish pie traditionally made in Cornwall (see quots.).

1847 J. O. HALLIWELL *Dict. Archaic & Provinc. Words* II. 799/1 Starry-gazy-pie. A pie made of pilchards and leeks, the heads of the pilchards appearing through the crust as if they were studying the stars. *Cornw.* **1864** F. T. O'DONOGHUE *St. Knighton's Keive: a Cornish Tale* Gloss. 303 *Star-a-gaze pie*, a mackerel pie with the heads above the paste, gazing upwards, as it were. **1954** D. HARTLEY *Food in England* x. 246 *Stargazey pies.* These are properly made of pilchards... The cooks covered the body of the fish—but left the head sticking out. **1966** *Punch* 14 Sept. 385/1 To provide the dishes that one's forbears ate—roast saddle of hare,..or stargazy pie, or syllabub—would be to proclaim oneself madly affected. **1970** A. PASCOE *Cornish Recipes Old & New* 30 (*heading*) Stargazy pie. **1980** *ABMR* Feb. 75/1, I now believe that heavy cake, like starry-gazey pie, was originally made from pilchards.

stark, *adv.* Add: **2. b.** (Later examples of *stark raving mad.*) Also *stark ravers* (slang): see *RAVERS *a.*

1958 E. DUNDY *Dud Avocado* III. vi. 270 My first thought was that I had gone stark raving mad..and that I was now hallucinating in a looney bin. **1968** [see *COOL *v.* 5 b].

Stark (stāɹk). *Physics.* The name of Johannes *Stark* (1874–1957), German physicist, used *attrib.* with reference to an effect observed by him (*Sitzungsber. der k. Preuss. Akad. der Wissensch.* (1913) 20 Nov. 932) in which spectral lines of a gas are broadened, split, or shifted when the source is in an electrostatic field (either applied externally or due to charged particles within it). Cf. *ZEEMAN.

1914 *Science* 2 Oct. 493/2 The Stark-electric effect differs from the Zeeman effect in that the various lines of the same series are not equally affected. **1939** *Nature* 20 May 834/1 The spectroscopy team is drawn from an even wider area,..dealing..with atomic spectra, hyperfine structure, Stark effect and related phenomena. **1962** G. M. BARROW *Introd. Molecular Spectrosc.* v. 92 Some dipole-moment determinations that have been made using the Stark effect in rotational spectra. **1979** *Physical Rev.* A. XX. 504/2 Stark-broadening parameters for the brighter isolated tin lines are given in Table VI.

starkers (stā·ɹkəɹz), *a. slang.* [f. STARK *adv.*: cf. *-ER[6].] **1.** = STARK NAKED *a.*

1923 J. MANCHON *Le Slang* 292 *Starko*,..= *stark naked* = *starkers*, tout nu. **1952** M. ALLINGHAM *Tiger in Smoke* vi. 105 We was all starkers and painted black. **1963** *Guardian* 20 Apr. 12/6 There was no stripping... The girls were starkers all the time. **1972** 'D. DEVINE' *Three Green Bottles* 12, I dare you to go in starkers. **1981** *Times Lit. Suppl.* 11 Sept. 1046/3 There is also Rosemary Martin as the Art School model in David Storey's *Life Class*, and Cathy Kessler, similarly starkers in *Lay-By*.

2. Stark raving mad. Cf. STARK *adv.* 2 b in Dict. and Suppl.

1962 E. GRIERSON *Massingham Affair* v. i. 245 She's.. a bit starkers, poor soul, and driving Matron..up the wall. **1972** L. P. DAVIES *What did I do Tomorrow?* iii. 38 You belted out of that room... They thought you were starkers.

starko (stā·ɹko), *a. slang.* [f. STARK (NAKED + -O[2].] = STARK NAKED *a.*

1923 [see *STARKERS *a.* 1]. **1935** L. LUARD *Conquering Seas* iii. 40 They'll be stripping us starko next. **1946** B. MARSHALL *George Brown's Schooldays* iv. 16 Doing a bundle means getting dressed from starko in five minutes. **1961** J. PUDNEY *Thin Air* xv. 197 Leave him in his birthday suit. Miss bloody Garth can walk back to Midsomer starko and explain to the folks that she's been a man all the time. **1979** C. BRAND *Rose in Darkness* iv. 25 She opened the door, practically starko, and couldn't think what the lady was so surprised about.

starlet. Add: **3.** A young promising performer (usu. an actress) in the world of entertainment; also used in sport, etc. Cf. STAR *sb.*[1] 5 a, c in Dict. and Suppl.

1920 J. FERGUSON in *Northern Numbers* 97 Some 'starlet' sings, Into the footlights' glare. **1938** *Life* 29 Aug. 37 When Hollywood uncovers a starlet with a unique personality, like Marie Wilson, they turn her over to the still-picture department for a publicity 'build-up'. **1951** M. MCLUHAN *Mech. Bride* (1967) 24/1 As much time goes into the search for a title of some indigestible cold lard as in launching a starlet. **1959** ANON. *Streetwalker* iii. 48 A paragraph about a film starlet catches my eye. **1976** *Star* (Sheffield) 29 Oct. 28/1 Sheffield United manager Jimmy Sirrel produced another starlet from his club's youth policy today when he named Gary Hamson in his side. **1978** J. WAINWRIGHT *Thief of Time* 105 Very few 'starlets' end up as stars. They stay there—chocolate-box perfection with nil personality.

star-light, starlight, *sb.* and *a.* Add: **3. b.** Special Comb.: **starlight scope** *Mil.*, a device incorporating an image intensifier for use as a gun sight or telescope when there is little light.

1969 I. KEMP *Brit. G.I. in Vietnam* vii. 146 The North Vietnamese found two very valuable, expensive, and secret items of equipment, known as 'Starlightscopes'. The Starlightscope is an infra-red telescope for observation at night, which can also be fixed to a rifle for shooting in the dark. **1973** T. O'BRIEN *If I die in Combat Zone* iv. 28 Look at this... It's a starlight scope... Supposed to let you see in the dark. **1977** *Time* 23 May 33/2 There's the 90-mm. recoilless rifle with a 'starlight' scope for enhanced visibility.

‖ **starover** (stārŏvyḗ·r). Pl. **starovers, starovery.** [Russ.] = *OLD BELIEVER.

1861 A. P. STANLEY *Lectures on Hist. Eastern Church* xii. 471 The real force, the permanent interest, of the Rascolniks lies in the eight millions of souls who call themselves *Starovers*; that is, 'the Old Believers'. **1957** *Oxf. Dict. Chr. Ch.* 1287/1 *Starovery*, another name for the Russian sect of the Old Believers. **1963** N. V. RIASANOVSKY *Hist. Russia* xix. 220 The Old Believers or Old Ritualists—*starovery* or *staroobriadtsy*—rejected the new sign of the cross, the corrected spelling of the name of Jesus, the tripling instead of the doubling of the 'Hallelujah' and other similar emendations.

starquake (stā·ɹkwēⁱk). *Astr.* [f. STAR *sb.*[1] after EARTHQUAKE.] A sudden change of shape or structure undergone by a neutron star, pulsar, etc.

1969 *Nature* 9 Aug. 598/1 Neutron stars which satisfy the criterion, $\omega \geqslant 10^3\ s^{-1}$, should have starquakes as they slow up. **1970** *New Scientist* 4 June 465/3 After the starquake, the pulsar readjusts its shape and speeds up. **1976** *Sci. Amer.* Oct. 78/3 In still other neutron-star models the source of the gamma rays is ascribed to 'starquakes', volcanic activity or other sudden changes in size or shape. **1978** PASACHOFF & KUTNER *University Astron.* xi. 314 As a result of this 'starquake', the matter would then be distributed slightly closer to the center of the star.

starred, *ppl. a.* Add: **2. e.** *spec.* thus marked in order to indicate some special category or merit. (Later examples.)

1914 *Hansard Lords* 24 Nov. 459 My original arrangement with Lord Kitchener was that a starred man should neither be solicited for recruitment nor accepted for the Army if he offered himself. **1927, 1937** [see *NAP *sb.*[6] 2 c]. **1940** *Hansard Lords* 6 Aug. 148 As far as I remember, the starred question was introduced at the instance of the late Lord Curzon about twenty years ago, and the object was to enable noble Lords to put down questions which they would wish to see mentioned in the House, rather than dealt with by a written reply, but upon which no debate should take place. **1964** F. WHITE *West of Rhone* xxii. 233, I stopped at a starred hotel... It deserved its star, for it was very good. **1970** R. LOWELL *Notebk.* 104 Four stone inkfish, thrice stepped on, lifting the spout—Not starred in any guidebook. **1971** *Guardian* 19 July 8/2 Margaret Drabble..whom he much admires for..her starred first. **1974** R. QUIRK *Linguist & Eng. Lang.* xi. 158 American English items [in a dictionary] are prefixed by a warning asterisk (an unhappy emblem when we consider what a starred form means in linguistics). **1976** N. ROBERTS *Face of France* xix. 185 The starred items on the menu.

f. Also *spec.* of a shattered vehicle windscreen of splinterproof glass.

1960 *B.S.I. News* Mar. 8/2 A windscreen of laminated glass may crack under impact but it will hold together, though 'starred', and remain in one place except in the most violent of collisions. **1979** R. PERRY *Bishop's Pawn* ix. 153, I continued driving blind, unable to see through the starred windscreen.

starrer. Restrict *local* to sense in Dict. and add: **2.** *slang.* A play or film which provides an impressive leading role for an actor or actress.

1951 GREEN & LAURIE *Show Biz* 571/2 *Starrer*, starring vehicle. **1978** M. PUZO *Fools Die* xxvii. 311 A Kellino starrer would get the studio's two million back.

starrigan (stæ·rigăn). *Newfoundland.* Also **starigan.** [Perh. ad. Ir. *stairricín* stump, stick.] A young, stunted, or decayed evergreen tree (chiefly fir), esp. cut for firewood; a stick, branch, or stump of this.

1895 *Jrnl. Amer. Folk-Lore* VIII. 39 *Starrigan*, a young fir-tree, which is neither good for firewood nor large enough to be used for timber, hence applied with contempt to anything constructed of unsuitable materials. *c* **1900** in *Regional Lang. Stud. Newfoundland* (1978) VIII. 26 *Starrigan*, a green stick, especially a var of small dimensions. **1903** *Newfoundland Q.* Dec. 5 He could get nothin' there but a few green var starrigans. or dun boughs. **1920** GRENFELL & SPALDING *Le Petit Nord* 94 Light snow has fallen during the night, and every 'starigan', every patch of 'tuckamore' is 'decked in sparkling raiment white'. **1964** *Newfoundland Herald* 26 Jan., *Starrigans*, actually dry tree stumps which formed an important source of fuel in the depression days. **1977** *Decks Awash* Sept. 64 De bull would get de tacklin An off 'e'd go for starrigans Wid frosty snow acracklin. **1981** *Publ. Amer. Dial. Soc.* LXVIII. 43 *Starrigan*.., very sappy fir, this name usually applied only when cut for firewood.

starring, *vbl. sb.* Add: **1.** (Earlier and later non-*attrib.* examples.)

1841 *Punch* 17 July 12/1 We consider Mr. Phelps' opposition to this ruinous system of 'starring' as commendable and manly. **1849** *Theatrical Programme* 25 June 38 Queen's Theatre, Hull... Starring is the order of the day here. **1940** *Illustr. London News* CXCVI. 188/2 This kind of 'starring' I regard as a foolish departure at a theatre which has built up a reputation as a repertory with a first-rate team.

starry, *a.* Add: **2. d.** Of or pertaining to stars in the world of entertainment.

1907 G. B. Shaw *Let.* 24 May (1972) II. 690, I have.. utterly rejected the starry part of it [*sc.* a production of *Man & Superman*]. **1918** R. Wagner *Film Folk* 8 The starry firmament of Los Angeles. **1929** H. G. Wells *King who was King* i. 30 The film *entrepreneur*..has to secure the services of a starry lady. **1959** *Manch. Guardian* 30 Jan. 7/1 One of the most persistent critical complaints about Miss Dresdel has been her tendency to shine too brightly even in the starriest company. **1981** *Times* 24 Jan. 7/2 Gertrude Lawrence..needed something very big, something very starry.

starry-eyed, *a.* [f. Starry *a.* + Eyed *ppl. a.*] **a.** Of persons: idealistic, uplifted, romantic: ingenuous, naïve.

1936 M. Mitchell *Gone with Wind* xxix. 489 She had never stood starry-eyed when the Stars and Bars ran up a pole. **1945** Nelson & Wright *Tomorrow's House* xviii. 206/2 Starry-eyed prospective home builders. **1955** M. Dickens *Winds of Heaven* v. 130 Holding hands and being starry-eyed over bottles of Chianti in romantic little cafés. **1958** *Spectator* 10 Jan. 37/3 He can hardly be so starry-eyed as to suppose that a similar enterprise on a national scale would be blessed by the whole hierarchy. **1964** S. Brittan *Treasury under Tories* ii. vii. 208 He understood both businessmen and bureaucrats too well to be starry-eyed about either. **1979** *Dædalus* Summer 107 A starry-eyed bachelor woos the kitchen maid.

b. *transf.* and *fig.*

[**1928** 'Brent of Bin Bin' *Up Country* x. 163 She expressed starry-eyed sympathy with his loss, having a struggle to keep back the tears.] **1947** A. L. Rowse *End of Epoch* i. 14 The starry-eyed vacuity of the unteachable and the uneducable. **1958** *Listener* 25 Sept. 476/2 All too often United States policy-makers..tend to hover between a starry-eyed idealism and a dangerous brinkmanship. **1973** *Times Lit. Suppl.* 3 Aug. 891/4 Mr Grunberger's account is balanced, but..his conclusion is starry-eyed. **1978** *Jrnl. R. Soc. Arts* CXXVI. 345/2 It is just not possible to accomplish anything like so starry-eyed a concept.

starscape (stā·ɪskēip). [f. Star *sb.*[1], after Landscape.] A view or prospect of a sky filled with stars. Also *fig.*

1926 S. Leslie *Cantab* (ed. 2) xiii. 163 He stared through the window at the Sussex star-scape. **1947** *Horizon* Aug. 100 He [*sc.* Paalen]..leads us into 'starscapes', a happy nomenclature invented by him. **1958** L. Durrell *Balthazar* i. i. 13 Winter: freezing snow, cool sand. clear sky panels...magnificent starscapes. **1965** *Spectator* 1 Jan. 16/1 One of those golden, glittering Covent Garden starscapes which..are so fascinating to diagnose through opera glasses. **1968** A. C. Clarke *2001: Space Odyssey* xliv. 210 The scurrying flecks of light no longer moved across the redly-glowing starscape still thousands of miles below.

star-ship. Also **star ship, starship.** [f. Star *sb.*[1] + Ship *sb.*[1]] **1.** (In Dict. s.v. Star *sb.*[1] 20.)

2. *Sci. Fiction.* A large manned spacecraft designed for interstellar travel.

1934 *Astounding Stories* Dec. 9 To start the year we offer you *Star Ship Invincible*, by Frank K. Kelly. **1956** F. Pohl *Alternating Currents* 77 A particle of meteoric matter slammed into *Starship Terra II* in hyperspace. **1967** J. Blish *Star Trek* 40 Capt. James Kirk of the starship *Enterprise*..had seen more planets than most men knew existed. **1972** H. C. Rae *Shooting Gallery* iv. 242 Now he was to be..flung, like one of those plastic starships, out into a galaxy of worlds which didn't really exist. **1978** *Listener* 30 Mar. 405/1 Smaller monitor screens were scattered about. It could have been the bridge of a star-ship. **1980** *Daily Tel.* 14 Jan. 8/1 Could star ships ever be propelled by the violent mutual annihilation of matter and anti-matter?

star-spangled, *ppl. a.* Add: **2.** *star-spangled banner.* **a.** The national flag of the United States of America. Also *fig.* Cf. *Stars and stripes* s.v. Star *sb.*[1] 6 b.

1814 F. S. Key in *Baltimore Patriot* 20 Sept. 2/1 The star-spangled banner in triumph shall wave. **1843** Dickens *Martin Chuzzlewit* (1844) xxi. 261, I thank you, sir, in the name of the star-spangled banner of the Great United States. **1869** 'Mark Twain' *Innoc. Abr.* xlix. 515 A robe..that was a very star-spangled banner of curved and sinuous bars of black and white. **1887** —— *Let.* 18 Dec. (1917) II. 480 It had bought them of the star spangled banner Masterthief. **1949** *Chicago Daily News* 15 Dec. 3 Was the Star-Spangled Banner made in a brewery?

b. With capital initials: the name of the U.S. national anthem.

1814 [in Dict.] **1843** *Quincy* (Illinois) *Herald* 3 Mar. 1/1 It is a most beautiful history of that national ballad, 'The Star Spangled Banner'. **1899** Kipling *From Sea to Sea* ii. xxv. 15 When we had chanted 'The Star-Spangled Banner' not more than eight times, we adjourned. **1936** *Nation* 10 Oct. 419/2 As the band played the Star Spangled Banner at the end,..the President stood erect. **1977** G. Markstein *Chance Awakening* xliii. 128 He was on his feet..with 17,000 other people in the stadium as the Star Spangled Banner thundered out of the loudspeakers.

start, *sb.*[2] Add: **5. b.** Also *start-to-stop*, used (usu. *attrib.*) with reference to train journeys or their schedules.

1899 *Railway Mag.* IV. 375/1 They comprise one of the best start-to-stop runs I have ever had on a British line. **1931** *Times Educ. Suppl.* 19 Sept. (Home & Classroom Section) p. ii/2 (*caption*) The Great Western Railway Company regained this week the record for the fastest start-to-stop journey in the world. **1936** *Discovery* Nov. 356/1 Two or three runs booked, start-to-stop, at over 80 miles an hour. **1968** O. S. Nock *Railway Enthusiast's Encycl.* 279 The run of the 'Silver Jubilee' from King's Cross to Darlington is also tabulated; and finally that of the 'Coronation', introduced in 1937, with the fastest start-to-stop schedule ever tabled with steam in Great Britain.

g. *Sport.* By synedoche, a contest, race, or game. Chiefly *N. Amer.*

1944 *Sun* (Baltimore) 23 Feb. 12/3 Davis is a welter-weight... Davis isn't that good. At least he never has been in most of his previous starts. **1949** *Richmond* (Va.) *Times-Despatch* 10 Oct. 13/2 The Rebels, in gaining their third win in four league starts..won it as convincingly as the score would indicate. **1966** *Telegraph* (Brisbane) 22 Jan. 5/2 He [*sc.* a horse] started racing in November, and in five starts has tallied a win, second, and a third. **1970** *Globe & Mail* (Toronto) 25 Sept. 32/3 Winless in 14 previous starts this season, Miss Ella Cinders had little trouble with Sandy Hawley up last Saturday as she galloped to a 12-length win. **1970** *Washington Post* 30 Sept. D1/7 The hapless, helpless Nats..couldn't hold off the East Division champions, who have captured nine consecutive starts.

h. The act of beginning to build a house. Also *housing start.*

1946 *Sun* (Baltimore) 20 Aug. 8/2 The Wyatt office claims about 406,000 'starts' of dwelling units in the first five months of the year. **1955** *Times* 30 May 11/1 New housing 'starts' rose in April but by less than they usually do over March. **1966** *New Statesman* 25 Nov. 769/2 What is worrying is that the starts are falling in the private sector and, as a house takes an average of about a year to build, the effects will be projected into next year's figures. **1976** *National Observer* (U.S.) 22 May 8/3 Around 28 to 29 per cent of all single-family housing starts.

i. Phr. *for a start*: to begin with. *colloq.* Cf. *Starter 2*.

1951 E. Paul *Springtime in Paris* iii. 56, I..found Montherlant's *Les Célibataires*... 'That's a good one for a start.' **1971** *Radio Times* 21 Aug. 47/3 What makes Raven unusual? *For a start* he's 46, and..he was a ballet dancer a lieutenant of infantry, a classical actor and a television producer. **1978** L. Thomas *Ormerod's Landing* iii. 48 Everybody else knows... The submarine crew know for a start.

12. start button, a switch that is pressed in order to set a machine or process in action; **start-line** = *starting-line* s.v. *Starting *vbl. sb.* 2 b; chiefly *transf.* and *fig.*, esp. in *Mil.* use (see quot. 1961).

1964 Start button [see *control register* s.v. *Control *sb.* 5]. **1968** *Brit. Med. Bull.* XXIV. 190/1 When the start-button of the machine is pressed, it simply causes the programmed procedure to operate on the data, giving rise to an action which will depend entirely on the data and the procedure. **1977** D. MacKenzie *Raven & Kamikaze* iii. 40 He..plugged the cable into a wall-socket and thumbed the start button. **1945** E. Waugh *Brideshead Revisited* 224, I would..think at such and such a time.. I shall cross the start-line and open my attack for better or worse... With Julia there were no phases, no start-line, no tactics at all. **1946** G. Millar *Horned Pigeon* ii. 32 Rommel's Afrika Korps were on the start line of their long advance. **1961** W. Vaughan-Thomas *Anzio* v. 69 The concept of a start line—an essential part of infantry tactics—is simply a matter of applied common sense... Just as in a race in athletics all competitors must line up at a starting-point..so, in the infinitely more exacting race of an infantry attack, the unit—be it battalion, brigade or division—needs some feature on the ground along which the troops can be lined for the take off. **1982** J. Wainwright *Anatomy of Riot* 15 In Army parlance he was going to be the field commander when the war left the start-line.

start, *v.* Add: **I. 3. e.** Also with *forth* (*arch.* and *poet.*). Cf. sense 4 b in Dict.

1916 Joyce *Portrait of Artist* ii. 86 All day the stream of gloomy tenderness within him had started forth and returned upon itself in dark courses and eddies. *Ibid.* iv. 171 He seemed..to see the amount of his purchase start forth immediately in heaven..as a frail column of incense. **1939** C. S. Lewis in M. Black *Importance of Lang.* (1962) 37 A new metaphor simply starts forth, under the pressure of composition or argument.

11. a. Also const. *out.* orig. *U.S.* Cf. sense 12 d in Dict. and Suppl.

1925 E. O'Neill *Desire under Elms* in *Compl. Wks.* II. 170 We're free, old man..an' we're startin' out for the gold fields of Californi—a! **1933** —— *Ah, Wilderness!* ii. 71 He dared me to race him... So I said all right and we started out. We swam and swam and were pretty evenly matched. **1978** W. F. Buckley *Stained Glass* xii. 117 There are escort vessels, and it is quite a muddle if every boat decides for itself when to start out.

c. Of a motor vehicle or its engine: to begin to operate. Also with *up*.

1902 A. C. Harmsworth *Motors & Motor-Driving* ix. 165 A petrol engine will generally start most easily with all the cold-air inlets closed. **1904** J. F. Gill *How to build Petrol Motor* 57 When a speed of about four miles per hour has been obtained, the current may be switched on, after which, the motor should start. **1932** D. L. Sayers *Have his Carcase* xii. 145 The Morgan wouldn't start, not for toffee... On their..putting in a new one [*sc.* lead], the engine had started up at once. **1971** *Daily Tel.* 27 Oct. 13/5 The engine would start instantly from cold without using the choke control. **1973** L. Cooper *Tea on Sunday* iii. 44, I left early..because of the bad weather. I was afraid my car might not start.

12. d. *to start in*: for (U.S. colloq.) read colloq. (orig. *U.S.*); (later examples); also *to start in on*; *to start out*: also const. *prep.*; *to start over* (U.S.): to begin again.

1892 'Mark Twain' *Amer. Claimant* 138 He had started out on a high emprise. **1912** Wodehouse *Prince & Betty* iv. 53 Then we start in. **1924** F. Scott Fitzgerald *Let.* 27 Oct. (1964) 168 I'm tired of being the author of *This Side of Paradise* and I want to start over. **1925** J. Buchan *John Macnab* vii. 144 In this country, once you start in on politics you're fixed in a class and members of a hierarchy. **1929** D. H. Lawrence *Pansies* 20 Then I am willing to fight, I will roll my sleeves up And start in. **1951** M. McLuhan *Mech. Bride* (1967) 68/2 She started out as a Tillie the Toiler. **1957** O. Nash *You can't get there from Here* 84 Once they start in on ideas and ideals they'll end up spouting ideologies and isms. **1965** M. Bradbury *Stepping Westward* ii. 112 Now go back to the beginning and start over. **1976** *National Observer* (U.S.) 26 June 8/6 If it doesn't work, throw the whole mess out and start over, adding a teaspoon of active dry yeast and a few drops of vinegar at the beginning. **1978** T. Allbeury *Lantern Network* vii. 87 Chaland had started in straight-away. 'Bonnier your group is far too big.'

f. To begin to go *to* (school). *U.S.*

1836 W. Sewall *Diary* 10 Aug. (1930) 172/1 Henry and Catherine started to school. **1898** C. A. Bates *Clothing Bk.* No. 1279 That boy..will have to start to school soon. **1931** *Amer. Speech* VII. 20 *Start*, begin to go. Used mainly in the one expression, start to school. 'I started to school when I was five.' (Widespread.)

g. *to start* (*in*) *on*: to attack; to nag or bully. Cf. sense 12 d above. *colloq.*

1907 G. B. Shaw *Major Barbara* ii. 214 When trade is bad..and the employers az to sack arf their men, they generally start on me. **1953** K. Tennant *Joyful Condemned* iii. 23 I'll give you five minutes, and then I'll start in on you. So hand over the two quid. **1967** J. Morrison in *Coast to Coast 1965–6* 140 The minute I mentioned it she started on me. **1968** Bethell & Burg tr. *Solzhenitsyn's Cancer Ward* I. xxi. 32 The critics may start it on you.

h. Colloq. phr. *don't you start*, expressing exasperation at hearing sentiments (of praise, criticism, advice, etc.) repeated by another speaker.

1934 N. Marsh *Man lay Dead* x. 167 'You're a—a wonder,' finished Nigel seriously. 'Don't you start!' said Mrs North. **1956** P. Scott *Male Child* ii. v. 157 'She ought to get out more.' He grinned. 'Now don't you start.' **1974** 'S. Woods' *Done to Death* 129 'She's a spinster.'.. 'Don't you start!' said Hugh explosively.

13. d. Also *loosely*, to begin.

1979 *Southern Star* (Eire) 29 Sept. 3/4 Mr. McCarthy also told Mr. Coleman that £160,000 had been allocated for further work on the Cork–Brandon road and the Viaduct aided by the EEC Regional Development Fund and would start up in two weeks after the meeting. **1981** E. North *Dames* viii. 138 The music started up and played..a tango.

II. 18. Also const. *forth. rare.*

a **1817** Jane Austen *Northanger Abbey* (1818) II. xiii. 245 She took the first opportunity..to start forth her obligation of going away very soon.

23. c. Also with *up* (occas. *absol.*).

1910 *Marine Oil Engine Handbk.* 14 It is possible to start up from cold on petrol. *Ibid.* 57 There is little difficulty about starting up small engines. **1945** C. S. Lewis *That Hideous Strength* xiv. 383 He started his engine up and they drove away. **1979** D. Clark *Heberden's Seat* i. 8 A car with a set of jump leads to start me up would do it.

e. Also, to set *up* a business (occas. *absol.*). Cf. sense 12 c in Dict.

1974 McArthur & Atkins *Dict. Eng. Phrasal Verbs & their Idioms* 215 He has started up a new business. **1975** Cowie & Mackin *Oxf. Dict. Current Idiomatic Eng.* I. 305/2 He *started up* a successful car hire firm. *Ibid.*, They were thinking of *starting up* in the fruit and vegetable trade.

g. To conceive (a baby), to succeed in conceiving (a child). Also, *to start a family*.

1931 N. Mitchison *Corn King & Spring Queen* iii. vii. 306 She wanted to start another baby at once, but he was very anxious that she should be as strong and well as possible at Plowing Eve. **1934** H. G. Wells *Exper. Autobiogr.* II. viii. 638 We were now justified in starting a family. **1938** E. Bowen *Death of Heart* i. i. 24 Irene had started Portia. **1956** *Mademoiselle* Sept. 185/1 After the apple farm was started we were going to start a child. **1973** G. Greene *Honorary Consul* ii. iii. 96 'He wanted to marry... And if there's a child—' 'Have you started one?' 'No.' **1975** M. Babson *There must be some Mistake* xiv. 107 We would have married immediately, perhaps have started a family. **1977** *Listener* 25 Aug. 227/1 When a couple have become used to a two-wage standard of living, how do they give it up to start a family?

h. To begin to suffer from or succumb to an illness, esp. a cold.

1932 E. M. Delafield *Thank Heaven Fasting* i. i. 14, I think Cecily's starting a cold. **1943** J. B. Priestley *Daylight on Saturday* xi. 68 The very sight of her streaming face..had made him feel that at any minute he would start a cold too. **1958** P. Kemp *No Colours or Crest* vii. 147 He himself was recovering from the malaria he had started at Arborie, but was still very weak.

24. b. Phr. *to start something*: to cause some trouble, agitation, etc. *colloq.* (orig. *U.S.*).

1917 U. B. Sinclair *King Coal* 78 Either the man was an agitator, seeking to 'start something', or else he was a detective sent in by the company. **1917** Wodehouse *Uneasy Money* xvi. 179 You certainly did the wrong thing. You started something! **1924** E. O'Neill *Welded* i. 97 We're not 'starting something' now, are we—after our promise? **1943** F. J. Bell *Condition Red* 59 The Japs.. slunk by without starting anything.

III. 28. start-stop, used *attrib.* with reference to an electric telegraph system in which each group of elements transmitted is respectively begun and ended with signals activating and deactivating the receiving mechanism.

1922 *Electrician* 8 Sept. 265/2 The teletype..is a 'start-stop' printer. **1937** *Sci. Abstr.* B. XL. 48 A machine for correcting start-stop 5-unit signals. **1974** R. N. RENTON *Internat. Telex Service* iii. 12/2 In the start-stop system, although the driving motors may be running, the sending and receiving devices are normally held at rest in a zero-phase position.

startability (stɑ̄ɹtăbi·liti). [f. START *v.* + -ABILITY.] **a.** Of a fuel: the degree to which it facilitates the starting of an engine. **b.** Of an engine: the degree to which it can be readily started.

1933 *Petroleum Handbk.* (R. Dutch-Shell Group) viii. 131 The exact point in the distillation curve which controls 'startability' varies somewhat with the atmospheric temperature and the particular engine in which the gasoline is used. **1935** *Jrnl. R. Aeronaut. Soc.* XXXIX. 907 Experimental evidence has shown that until very low temperatures are reached the startability of a gasoline is roughly dependent upon the percentage distilling to 100°C. **1971** *Good Motoring* Sept. 4/3 Checking startability on steep hills. **1976** *Drive* Sept.–Oct. 114/2 The Beetle has a deserved reputation for..unfailing startability in all weathers.

starter. Add: **I. 2. a.** (Later *fig.* examples.) Also *transf. spec.* an idea that deserves initial consideration (only in neg. contexts: cf. *NON-STARTER).

1917 'I. HAY' *Carrying On* iv. 93 That exasperating race of bad starters but great stayers, the British people. **1947** G. B. SHAW in *Musical Times* Jan. 10/1 They can all sing passably in tune and are selected..because they are good readers and good starters. **1948** M. ALLINGHAM *More Work for Undertaker* xiii. 166 The tip about Brownies [*sc.* shares] was never even a likely starter. **1960** *Times* 7 July 13/2 'Bevanism' was never a starter as a political philosophy or programme. **1976** *Listener* 18 Nov. 641/2 The objections to it are so strong that it isn't a starter.

b. With qualifying adj.: a motor vehicle or engine which starts (well, slowly, etc.). Cf. sense *11 c of the vb.

1952 M. STEEN *Phoenix Rising* viii. 179 That's my car..; it's the easiest starter... Get in and start the engine. **1975** *Country Life* 27 Feb. 508/3, I found the Lancia a good starter with no need for choke.

2*. a. Phr. *as* or *for a starter, for starters*: to begin with, for a start. *colloq.* (orig. *U.S.*).

1873 J. H. BEADLE *Undeveloped West* xxii. 450 He gave me twenty drops of laudanum as a starter. **1902** G. H. LORIMER *Lett. Self-Made Merchant* v. 64 All that he ever needed was a few hundred for a starter. **1947** *Chicago Tribune* 3 Sept. 6/3 As a starter, agents have begun a canvass of small independent food wholesalers. **1950** *Manch. Guardian Weekly* 9 Nov. 7 He wired how many frogs' legs did they think they could handle. They told him ten thousand as a starter. **1969** D. FRANCIS *Enquiry* xii. 168, I fell with a crash. 'That's for starters,' he said. **1970** *New Yorker* 5 Dec. 142/1 (Advt.), For starters, here's the line-up of Knicks and Rangers games for the rest of the month. **1973** *Listener* 6 Dec. 767/3 The vehicles for enlargement could be found in new stations or wavelengths..but what happens is likely to require as a starter some change in current assumptions. **1978** *Globe & Mail* (Toronto) 11 Jan. 8/1 For starters, do not call us scalpers. We are ticket hosts.

b. A dish eaten as the first course of a meal, before the main course (also in *pl.*). *colloq.*

1966 [see *DESSERT 1 b]. **1966** *Sunday Express* 16 Oct. 18/3 You get a three-course dinner, with four 'starter' courses and seven main dishes to choose from, and a sweet. **1966** *Vogue* Nov. 154/3 Starters include fish soup, cock-a-leekie, duck-liver pâté. **1968** *New Society* 22 Aug. 266/1 The first course of a meal is sometimes called a 'starter', which is perhaps not so much non-U as jargon. **1969** P. HIGHSMITH *Tremor of Forgery* xvii. 155 'Try this Tunisian starter. Turns up on every menu.' He meant the antipasto of tuna, olives, and tomatoes. **1975** *Reveille* 20 June 2/2 They are equally good as a 'starter' or served with salad. **1979** V. CANNING *Satan Sampler* ii. 30 There was avocado pear for what some people disgustingly called 'starters'.

II. 4. b. *N. Amer. Sport.* The player in a team game who sta ts the game; in Baseball *spec.* the pitcher.

1967 *Boston Herald* 8 May 16/6 The victory gave Atlanta starter Pat Jarvis a 3–0 record. **1968** *Globe & Mail* (Toronto) 3 Feb. 35/2 Two of our starters are in Quebec City on an exchange visit, one player is away sick and Bill Edwards is still injured. **1974** *State* (Columbia, S. Carolina) 3 Mar. 3-D/4 Collins..led the way with 20 points as again all starters hit in double figures. **1976** *Billings* (Montana) *Gaz.* 16 June 3-C/7 The Phillies jumped on starter Ed Halicki and reliever Dave Heaverlo for an eight-run lead after two innings.

5. a. Freq. in phr. *under starter's orders* (Horseracing): subject to the instruction of the starter, ready to begin a race. Also *transf.* and *fig.* Cf. ORDER *sb.* 23 a in Dict. and Suppl.

1965 M. SPARK *Mandelbaum Gate* vi. 197 Freddy has said to tell you we are under starter's orders; what is starter's orders? **1973** P. MALLOCH *Kirkback* i. 10 'Drink it up, chum. I forgot we were under starter's orders.' Gilchrist drank it. Five minutes later they were on their way. **1974** *Times* 27 Jan. 10/5 With the first day of the £44,000 Philadelphia indoor tennis tournament only half over, six of the 16 seeds were already out of the running. Nastase, Newcombe and Orantes were all injured and, like five other entrants, did not even come under starter's orders. **1976** *Milton Keynes Express* 11 June 3/2 Show jumping commentator Dorian Williams put the horses under starter's orders. **1979** REESE & FLINT *Trick 13* 82 They're under starter's orders... They're off!

b. *U.S.* (*a*) One who directs the operation of lifts in a large building; (*b*) an employee of a hotel, station, etc., who organizes transport for patrons (see also quot. 1917).

1909 *Pacific Monthly* Feb. 123/1 Thanks to the crowd in the lobby, the uniformed 'starter' had not seen the bum and come over from the elevators to order him away. **1917** *Street Railway Employment in U.S.* (U.S. Bureau of Labor Statistics) 14 *Starters.*—See that cars leave terminal points on scheduled time..reroute cars to straighten schedules and perform duties of inspectors. **1922** S. LEWIS *Babbitt* 32 The little unknown people who inhabited the Reeves Building corridors—elevator-runners, starter..—were in no way city-dwellers. **1931** WODEHOUSE *Let.* 19 May in *Performing Flea* (1961) 66 A man standing in the crowd outside a movie theatre here after a big opening hears the carriage starter calling for 'Mr Warner's automobile'. **1932** *Making Bus Operations Pay* iv. 77 The station is kept open 24 hours a day by a force of eleven paid employees and three redcaps to handle baggage. Included in the paid force is a station manager, three ticket managers..and a special officer who also acts as a taxi starter. **1978** R. LUDLUM *Holcroft Covenant* 541 She was given a number on the twelfth floor, the top floor, but as it was the lunch hour, the starter doubted anyone was there. **1981** *Washington Post Mag.* 22 Mar. 8/4 'A *starter*,' she said. 'You know, the man who gets a guest a taxi.'

6. a. (Later examples.)

1926 W. FAULKNER *Soldiers' Pay* ii. 86 She turned the switch and tried to reach the starter with her foot. **1934** *Discovery* Nov. 324/2 A hand starter is provided on the engine, or it may be started from a car battery. **1969** G. MACBETH *War Quartet* 30 When we kicked the starters, drove On across other countries..I remembered all Who fought. **1970** K. BALL *Fiat 600, 600D Autobook* xi. 135/2 Dismantling of the starter is a simple task and is similar to that for the generator. **1977** [see *SHOCK *sb.*[3] 6*].

b. An automatic switch forming part of the auxiliary circuit of some fluorescent lamps, the purpose of which is to enable the electrodes to become hot enough for a discharge to occur after it becomes inactive. Also *starter switch.*

1942 C. L. AMICK *Fluorescent Lighting Man.* ii. 22 Each lamp requires a separate starter and a separate ballast. *Ibid.* 23 The heat from the discharge itself keeps the cathodes hot during normal operation, hence the starter switch can remain open. **1962** *Newnes Conc. Encycl. Electr. Engin.* 433/2 In place of the starter switch..a cathode-heating transformer can be used, so avoiding the need for replacement parts. **1967** P. HONEY *Household Electricity* 44 Fluorescent lamps..generally need a special circuit with what is called a starter, a device which heats up the electrodes for a second or two after the current is switched on.

7. Delete (See quot.) and substitute: A culture containing bacteria, yeast, or the like, used to initiate souring or fermentation in the making of butter, cheese, dough, etc. (Earlier and later examples.)

1896 *Vermont Agric. Rep. 1895* 67 This may be done..by using a 'starter' made from cream. **1935** *Discovery* Nov. 340/2 In the manufacture of butter 'starters' are employed to sour the cream under controlled conditions. **1939** K. PINKERTON *Wilderness Wife* vii. 74 At least sour dough bread was sure... Robert had sponsored it by making the 'starter', a mixture of flour and water which grabbed its yeast germs from the air. **1950** *N.Z. Jrnl. Agric.* Jan. 27/2 Quick granulation is achieved by the addition of a 'starter' and the storing of the packed honey immediately in a consistent temperature of about 56 degrees F. **1973** W. H. T. TAYLEUR *Home Brewing & Wine-Making* vii. 55 The optimum amount of starter in wine-making is about 1 to 15.

8. *attrib.* and *Comb.*, as (sense 6) *starter button, cord, motor, switch*; **starter home** orig. *U.S.*, a first home, usu. one bought by a young couple; also *ellipt.*; **starter set** orig. *U.S.*, a small set of china intended to be the basis of a larger collection; also *transf.*

1971 Starter button [see *starter motor* below]. **1977** D. BEATTY *Excellency* vi. 80 He primed the engines, pressed the starter button, heard the propeller creak round. **1971** *Scope* (S. Afr.) 19 Mar. 65/2 Damned engine doesn't have a starting handle, just a starter cord. **1976** *Billings* (Montana) *Gaz.* 27 June 5-D/7 (Advt.), Also a fenced back yard makes it a great starter home. **1979** *Arizona Daily Star* 5 Aug. (Advt. Section) 21/2 This 3 bedroom, 1 bath home will make a super starter for a young family. **1980** *Times* 6 Feb. 6/6 Local authorities and builders should provide more 'starter' homes to meet the demand for lower priced small homes for sale, Mr John Stanley, Minister for Housing and Construction, said yesterday. **1928** *Correct Lubrication* 39 Starter motor spins without turning engine. **1971** R. DENTRY *Encounter at Kharmel* vi. 100 Pepper..leaned hard on the starter button. The starter motor set up a pulsating, piercing shriek. **1946** *Time* 29 July 64/2 It was inexpensive—a 20-piece 'starter set' sold for about $6. **1970** *Guardian* 17 Dec. 9/5 A starter set consisting of four soup bowls, four 10½-inch plates, four eight-inch plates, [etc.]. **1977** *Montgomery Ward Catal.* Spring–Summer 510/3 Men's starter set [of golf clubs]. **1925** *Morris Owner's Man.* 9 The starter switch should immediately be released. **1965** PRIESTLEY & WISDOM *Good Driving* ii. 19 The starter switch usually takes the form of a knob or button which is either pressed or pulled out.

starting, *vbl. sb.* Add: **1. a.** Also with *off* and *up* in some senses. Freq. *attrib.*

1821 M. EDGEWORTH *Let.* 29 Jan. (1971) 235, I hope this can be arranged as I found it a starting off point and I could not conclude the agreement without it. **1895** KIPLING in *Century Mag.* LI. 265/2 There was the same 'starting-off place'—a pile of brushwood. **1912** *Motor Man.* (ed. 14) iii. 108 Cars having compressed air starting-up devices are always equipped for rapid tyre inflation from the air pressure cylinder. **1927** [see *ACTIVATION]. **1946** *Happy Landings* July 1/1 The engine was not turned by hand through one cycle before the starting-up operation. **1959** *Times* 12 June 17/5 Extraordinary starting-up costs at the Company's new borate refinery. **1967** E. SHORT *Embroidery & Fabric Collage* i. 28 There is a definite starting-off point, namely the subject, which then has to be translated into a suitable flat pattern.

2. a. *starting cord.*

1977 D. MACKENZIE *Raven & Ratcatcher* viii. 114 He whipped the starting cord on the small outboard motor. It caught at the second attempt.

b. starting block, (usu. *pl.*) a shaped rigid block for bracing the feet of a runner at the start of a race; also *fig.*; **starting gate** *Sport,* (*a*) a barrier device used at the beginning of a race (esp. of horses) to ensure a simultaneous start for all competitors; (*b*) a point from which individual runs are timed, as in skiing etc.; also *transf.* and *fig.*; **starting grid** = *GRID 6 c; **starting handle,** a handle used to start a machine; *spec.* a detachable one that is turned to start the engine of a motor vehicle; **starting line,** a real or imaginary line used to mark the place from which a race starts; also *fig.*; **starting pistol,** a pistol used to give the signal at the start of a race; **starting salary,** the salary (on a pay-scale) earned at first by an employee taking up a new post.

1937 BRESNAHAN & TUTTLE *Track & Field Athletics* iii. 54 There are two opinions on the matter of support for the feet at the start of the sprints. One is that holes in the track be used as a means of foot support, while the other is that starting blocks on top of the track be used. *Ibid.* xvi. 455 Those who prefer to employ starting blocks rather than holes in the track claim that blocks have the advantage in that they protect the track and make adjustments..easier. **1961** F. C. AVIS *Sportsman's Gloss.* 63 *Starting blocks,* triangular pieces of wood fixed to the track and against which the sprinter's heels are pushed at the start of a race. **1977** J. WAINWRIGHT *Pool of Tears* 205 He crouched, like a sprinter on starting-blocks. **1983** *Listener* 29 Sept. 4/2 All the Opposition parties are poised nervously on the starting-blocks of the new political year. **1898** Starting-gate [in Dict., sense 2 a]. **1930** *Times* 24 Mar. 4/2 Numbered saddle cloths, the starting-gate, and the totalisator are among the reforms which came from them. **1940** C. DAY LEWIS tr. *Virgil's Georgics* I. 31 When racing chariots have rushed from the starting-gate. **1950** *Sun* (Baltimore) 18 Feb. 12/1 The competitors fear for life and limb when they are encased in the gate, which resembles the starting gate used for horses, and is designed to eliminate false starts. **1968** *Globe & Mail* (Toronto) 5 Feb. 19/3 The 18-year-old student was assessed a one-second penalty by the jury panel, which reviewed a claim by two officials that Debbie was too quick out of the starting gate. **1971** *Language* XLVII. 5 Acceptance of this very general position, however, does little more than put one in the proper starting gate. **1976** *New Yorker* 8 Mar. 105/1 Mount Sterling stumbled coming out of the starting gate, unseating his rider, Maple. **1957** Starting grid [see *GRID 6 c]. **1978** 'D. RUTHERFORD' *Collision Course* 100 Positions on the starting grid are allocated on practice times. **1876** Starting handle [in Dict., sense 2 a]. **1886** D. CLERK *Gas Engine* ix. 242 The starting handle is then let go, and the motor piston runs over its ports. **1932** D. L. SAYERS *Have his Carcase* xii. 145 After..exercise on the starting-handle, they had diagnosed trouble with the ignition. **1973** P. AUDEMARS *Delicate Dust of Death* x. 136 They left the bus... Perhaps they could not start it... I tried the starting handle myself. It was jammed. **1906** Starting-line [see *repair station* s.v. *REPAIR *sb.*[2]]. **1920** [see *BATON *sb.* 2 b]. **1962** A. NISBETT *Technique Sound Studio* x. 173 Anything but sheer surrealism was doomed to remain stickily on the starting-line. **1974** *Howard Jrnl.* XIV. 84 In a meritocratic society those whose powers of oral and written expression are extremely limited are left at the starting line in the race for social status. **1982** J. JARVER *Athletics Fundamentals* 20/1 The aim of the sprint start is to get the athlete away from the starting line as fast as possible. **1935** 'N. BLAKE' *Question of Proof* ii. 30 Get set! Go!! That was the starting-pistol you heard. **1962** A. NISBETT *Technique Sound Studio* x. 178 A modified revolver is better than a starting pistol. **1969** H. PERKIN *Key Profession* iv. 138 New assistant lecturers and junior lecturers..came in..at starting salaries much lower than those in schoolteaching. **1973** *Nature* 7 Dec. p. i, Starting salary would be in the vicinity of £3,000.

startle, *v.* **3. a.** Delete † *Obs.* and add later example.

1972 R. ADAMS *Watership Down* v. 18 To rabbits, everything unknown is dangerous. The first reaction is to startle, the second to bolt. Again and again they startled, until they were close to exhaustion.

b. (Later example.)

1961 R. GRAVES *More Poems* 42 In the course of travel, you must have startled at Some coign of true felicity.

Hence **sta·rtlement,** the state or condition of being startled, alarm; hence, something that gives rise to this.

1927 *Chambers's Jrnl.* Feb. 92/2 No startlement was in her face by now. **1960** 'S. Harvester' *Chinese Hammer* i. 10 A strange expression of startlement came into her cool dark eyes. **1975** *Islander* (Victoria, B.C.) 4 May 3/3 Even so he [*sc.* a mouse] was dreadfully nervous and would leap like a miniature kangaroo at the least startlement.

start-up, *sb.*[2] Also **startup.** [f. vbl. phr. *to start up*: see *start *v.* 23 c, e.] The action or process of starting up a series of operations, a piece of machinery, a business, etc. Also *attrib.*

1945 H. D. Smyth *Gen. Acct. Devel. Atomic Energy Mil. Purposes* ix. 94 In estimating time schedules this 'start-up' or 'equilibrium' time must be added to the time of construction of the plant. **1954** *Trans. IRE on Nuclear Sci.* I. 3/1 During startup the behavior of the reactor is similar to that of an amplifier with positive feedback. **1959** *Wall St. Jrnl.* (Eastern ed.) 18 Dec. 9/1 Start-up expenses connected with new store openings have been heavy. **1968** *Globe & Mail* (Toronto) 13 Jan. B 5/4 Production target is late 1969 with startup to have cost more than $90-million. **1975** P. R. F. Mathijsen *Guide to European Community Law* II. iv. 87 It is proposed that modern agricultural enterprises be set up with special aids such as start-up grants, investment aid and guaranteed credits. **1976** B. Jackson *Flameout* (1977) iv. 63 The flight data recorder..tape-recorded engine start-up, takeoff, climbout, [etc.]. **1980** *Daily Tel.* 20 Mar. 28 (Advt.), They will assume responsibility for the start-up, management, organisation, and profitability of large work sites. **1983** *Sunday Times* 23 Jan. 56/1 The fund is designed to take advantage of the tax relief introduced in 1981 for investors putting up to £20,000 a year into start-ups. **1983** *Times* 19 Feb. 15 (*heading*) Business start-up funds worth the risk for top taxpayers.

starty, *a.* (Earlier example.)

1861 Mrs. Stowe *Pearl of Orr's Island* I. ix. 70 The little feller was very starty and fretful in his sleep last night.

starvation. Add: **2. b.** *starvation diet, line, point, rations.*

1848 Mill *Pol. Econ.* I. ii. xii. 433 Wages may fall below starvation point. **1869** J. Greenwood *Seven Curses of London* iii. 46 The child is welcome to live on starvation diet just as long as it may. **1915** Mrs Belloc Lowndes *Diary* 3 Mar. (1971) 56 British prisoners..have one cup of coffee with no milk or sugar..a 2 lb. loaf of bread for two days..Practically starvation rations. **1925** Joyce *Let.* 25 Mar. (1966) III. 117, I have now been put on a starvation diet by way of adding to my present pleasures. **1937** 'G. Orwell' *Road to Wigan Pier* v. 80 A man and wife on twenty-three shillings a week are not far from the starvation line. **1957** P. Worsley *Trumpets shall Sound* 15 This does not mean that Melanesians always live near the starvation-line. **1977** D. Williams *Treasure by Degrees* i. 16 The production of pure food.. unadulterated by mechanical or chemical intervention ..would have put the nation on a starvation diet. **1977** D. Francis *Risk* v. 56 If he caught me..he'd..leave me in the dark on starvation rations.

3. Also *colloq. ellipt.* for *starvation cold.*

1967 E. Grierson *Crime of One's Own* xi. 89 Queer day to leave it open. It's starvation. **1977** *Lancashire Life* Mar. 68/3 They mostly had open top decks and open staircases, and it was starvation in the winter.

starve, *v.* Add: **II. 7. e.** Phr. *starve the crows* and varr. = *stone the crows* s.v. *crow *sb.*[1] 3 d. *Austral. slang.*

1918 H. Matthews *Saints & Soldiers* 116 'Starve the crows,' howled Bluey in that agonised screech of his. **1936** A. Russell *Gone Nomad* vi. 46 Starve the crows! I laugh ev'ry time I think of it. **1966** G. W. Turner *Eng. Lang. Austral. & N.Z.* vi. 118 The well-known *stone the crows*.. occurs in such forms as *starve the wombats*..*starve the ninnies* and several more. **1966** 'J. Hackston' *Father clears Out* 156 Trooper Newbigun turned his horse's head and rode off with such dignity that Albert Horne said, just like an Australian, 'Gawd starve the crows!' **1968** *Courier-Mail* (Brisbane) 18 Nov. 10/7 Though the Dad and Dave expression 'Starve the lizards' is well enough known it has taken the spring of 1968 to bring about a similar but far from fanciful phrase for the flying foxes.

starved, *ppl. a.* Add: **d.** *Pottery.* Of a glaze: lacking the expected brilliance after firing.

1964 H. Hodges *Artifacts* ii. 52 Under-firing may result in starved glazes which have a dull appearance. **1968** H. Powell *Pottery Handbk. Clay, Glaze & Colour* ii. 56 A starved glaze is lacking in shine. *a* **1977** *Harrison Mayer Ltd. Catal.* 18/2 Starved glaze. The glaze surface is dull in areas which have been adjacent to porous refractories during firing. As the term implies glaze volatiles are sucked away from the surface of the glaze by the porous refractory.

starver. Add: **2.** *Austral. slang.* A saveloy.

1941 Baker *Dict. Austral. Slang* 71 *Starver*, a saveloy. **1959** D. Niland *Big Smoke* 211, I know what the things I eat cost me. Starvers, crumpets, stale cakes, speckled fruit, pies.

stash, *v.* Add: Also **stach. 1.** (Earlier example.) Also *absol.*

1794 *Sessions Papers* 17 Sept. 1200/2 He says, Miller, it is, *stash*, I am satisfied.

2. To conceal, to hide; to put aside for safe keeping; to stow or store. Freq. with *away.* Formerly *Criminals' slang*; orig. *U.S.* in revived mod. use.

1797 *Humphry Potter's Dict. Cant & Flash Lang.* (ed. 3) 55 *Stach*, to conceal a robbery. **1821** *Sessions Papers* 14 Dec. 66/1 He begged of me to *stash* it, which means say nothing about it. **1914** Jackson & Hellyer *Vocab. Criminal Slang* 80 *Stash*,..to hide;..to cease talking; to 'plant'. **1927** *Dialect Notes* V. 477 Billy he done stashed the jug in th' brush, an' now the damned ol' fool caint find hit! **1937** C. R. Cooper *Here's to Crime* v. 102 A friend of mine had it stached in his cellar, in a fruit jar. **1937** D. Runyon in *Collier's* 16 Jan. 9/4 She must have some scratch of her own stashed away somewhere. **1944** *Daily Progress* (Charlottesville, Va.) 25 May 6/6 A customer at least has a sporting chance to pick up a bottle of brandy, gin, or rum if the dealer doesn't have a bottle of old Kentucky corn julep stashed away under the counter for him. **1952** *Manch. Guardian Weekly* 20 Mar. 4/3 The big gift already stashed away in the farmers' bank accounts. **1962** J. Heller *Catch-22* vi. 51 Just when I was all set to really start stashing it away they had to manufacture fascism and start a war. **1970** R. Price *Howling Arctic* i. 15 Travel proved too difficult after a while so they stashed the sledges and walked on. **1974** F. Forsyth *Dogs of War* (1975) I. i. 39 With all fees paid, he netted a cool £500,000, which was still stashed in the Zwingli Bank. **1978** J. A. Michener *Chesapeake* 670 The watermen ferried dead birds to the ice shelf, stashed them and returned to fetch others.

stash (stæʃ), *sb. slang* (orig. and chiefly *U.S.*). Also **stach.** [f. the vb.] **1. a.** Something, or a collection of things, stashed away; a hoard, stock; a cache.

1914 Jackson & Hellyer *Vocab. Criminal Slang* 80 *Stash*,..used as a noun in the sense of something cached. **1942** Berrey & Van den Bark *Amer. Thes. Slang* § 207/5 *Cache*..stach, stash, stash-away. **1954** Webster, *Stash*,.. something stashed away or the place where it is stashed. **1969** *New Yorker* 31 May 90/1, I liked..the stash of Pucci shifts. **1970** G. Jackson *Let.* 26 Mar. in *Soledad Brother* (1971) 199, I *want* my food and drink from the people's stash. **1975** B. Garfield *Hopscotch* xxv. 257 If he told Oakly the truth about going to ground then he'll want to clean out his stash..he's..got to have money. **1979** *Daily Tel.* 10 Apr. 3/2 Chief Insp. Newark said he was satisfied Barnes had no stashes of money hidden away. **1980** *Encounter* May 37 Even crane-crews angle For a share of the stash, Their lines urging up A grey, enormous catch.

b. A cache of an (illegal) drug; a quantity (of a drug); the drug itself. (See also quot. 1942.)

1942 Berrey & Van den Bark *Amer. Thes. Slang* § 509/12 *Stash*, concealed equipment for taking narcotics. **1953** W. Burroughs *Junkie* iii. 36 Taking junk hidden by another junkie is known as 'making him for his stash'. It is difficult to guard against this form of theft because junkies know where to look for a stash. **1959** [see *bust *sb.*[3] f]. **1967** *Trans-Action* Apr. 11/1 Someone cruises by in a car and brings a nice 'stash' of 'weed'. **1968** T. Wolfe *Electric Kool-Aid Acid Test* xi. 133 The Hermit ...was..keeper of the communal acid stash down there in the cave. **1975** *High Times* Dec. 11/1 Anyone who turns stash knows that most people will pay any price to get high. **1978** *N.Y. Times* 30 Mar. B1/2 A number of dubious substances, such as 'African Yohimbe Smokestuff'. This, the label said, should be added 'to your regular stash to turn your domestic green into African Red'. **1982** *Guardian* 14 Dec. 11/6 The hairy young man in Lee Cooper jeans..asking 'Anyone seen my stash?'

2. *slang* (orig. *Criminals'*). A hiding-place, a hide-out; a rendezvous; a dwelling, 'pad'.

1927 *Amer. Speech* II. 390/2 A *stash* is a hiding-place. **1930** R. Chadwick in *Liberty* 23 Aug. 33/2 If we were on a bank job in a strange city the stash would be in a room we had rented several weeks in advance. In a small town, though, you don't have any stash, because an hour after you moved in everybody in the burg would be checking in. **1946** Mezzrow & Wolfe *Really Blues* viii. 132 No Hotel Ritz for us this time; our stash was over some kind of feed store. **1963** L. Deighton *Horse under Water* xviii. 77 We set up 'Art for the Average Guy, Inc.', just a little stash on East 12th. **1965** *Listener* 7 Jan. 31/2 Susan Sontag went to see Philip Johnson, the New York architect, or rather she 'moseyed along to his stash on Park'.

stasiology (stæsiǫ·lŏdʒi). *rare.* [tr. F. *stasiologie* (see quot. 1954), f. Gr. στάσι-ς party, faction (see Stasis in Dict. and Suppl.): see -ology.] The science or study of political parties.

1954 B. & R. North tr. *M. Duverger's Pol. Parties* 422 The development of the science of political parties (it could perhaps be called *stasiology*). **1966** K. West *Power in Liberal Party* p. vii, There is now a field of academic enterprise known as analytical stasiology whose practitioners believe that by constructing a series of conceptual frameworks one may arrive at a 'science' of political parties.

stasipatric (stæsipæ·trik), *a. Biol.* [f. Gr. στάσις Stasis + πάτρα fatherland (f. πατήρ father) + -ic.] Applied to a form of speciation in which new taxa are considered to arise within the geographical range of the parent species, each part of which comes to be occupied by one of the new taxa. Hence **stasipa·trically** *adv.*

1967 M. J. D. White et al. in *Austral. Jrnl. Zool.* XV. 298 If a term, equivalent to allopatric and sympatric, is needed to describe the process of direct conversion of an essentially continuous population into a number of contiguous taxa (races, semispecies, or species) by the spread of chromosomal rearrangements around which isolating mechanisms develop, one might perhaps choose the adjective *stasipatric*, which is intended to indicate the essentially unchanging geographic range of the superspecies. **1968** *Science* 8 Mar. 1069/1 In the case of a chromosomal rearrangement which first establishes itself near the edge of a species distribution, one can imagine it spreading both inwards through the range of the species (stasipatrically) and outwards into previously unoccupied territory (allopatrically). **1973** L. S. Dillon *Evolution* x. 138/2 The stasipatric model is not designed to displace the established ones but to supplement them.

stasis. Restrict *Path.* to sense in Dict. and add: Also pronounced (stæ·sis). **1. b.** *gen.* Inactivity; stagnation; a state of motionless or unchanging equilibrium.

1920 *Glasgow Herald* 30 Nov. 9 The prevailing mood of Labour is indefinite; a condition of stasis has been caused by the coal strike and the dread of unemployment. **1930** W. Empson *Seven Types of Ambiguity* vii. 245 He is drawn taut between the two similar impulses into the stasis of appreciation. **1933** T. S. Eliot *Use of Poetry & Use of Criticism* vi. 103 Arnold represents a period of stasis; of relative and precarious stability, it is true, a brief halt in the endless march of humanity in some, or in any direction. **1940** E. Muir *Story & Fable* v. 186 This could be done by so controlling the chemical processes of the body as to produce a self-subsistent balance, an everlasting, living stasis. **1943** *Sewanee Review* LI. ii. 337 Art, according to Dedalus-Joyce, tends toward the achievement of *stasis*, which implies a state of contemplation, of detachment from the *kinesis* of life. **1972** *Times Lit. Suppl.* 1 Sept. 1020/3 We see him in the moment of stasis before action. **1978** J. Updike *Coup* (1979) iii. 91 A religion whose antipodes are motion and stasis.

c. In the psychoanalytical theory of Wilhelm Reich (see *Reichian *sb.* and *a.*), a hypothetical accumulation of unused or repressed sexual energy.

1942 T. P. Wolfe tr. *Reich's Function of Orgasm* iii. 58 The role of sexual stasis in increasing antisocial and perverse sexual impulses. *Ibid.* 361 *Stasis*, the damming-up of sexual energy in the organism, thus the source of energy for the neuroses. **1953** in *Wilhelm Reich: Sel. Writings* (1961) 12 *Stasis neurosis*, all somatic disturbances which are the immediate result of the stasis of sexual energy, with stasis anxiety at its core. **1973** D. Boadella *W. Reich* vii. 194 There are two fundamental biological responses to sexual stasis, or any other blockage to emotional functioning.

2. [Gr. στάσις in sense 'faction, discord'.] Party faction, civil strife.

1933 R. J. Bonner *Aspects of Athenian Democracy* v. 91 Solon tried to strengthen the government against sedition, or *stasis*, as the Greeks called it, by requiring every citizen to take one side or another in case of serious party strife. **1956** A. W. Gomme *Commentary on Thucydides* II. 374 From *stasis* in Kerkyra to *stasis* in the Greek world generally..to universal conditions of *stasis* and war as its stimulus. **1963** M. I. Finley *Anc. Greeks* 51 The dividing-line between politics and sedition (*stasis* the Greeks called it) was a thin one in classical Greece, and often enough *stasis* grew into ruthless war. **1975** N. G. L. Hammond *Classical Age of Greece* 166 The weakening of traditional obligations and the revolution in the economy which arose from the war were among the factors which led to the outbreak of *stasis*, civil war, in 411 and 410 at Athens.

stat[1] (stæt). Colloq. abbrev. of *Photostat b.

1960 'E. McBain' *Give Boys Great Big Hand* v. 40 Here are the stats, kid. **1971** C. Fick *Danziger Transcript* (1973) 81 Make stats of all the graduation and group pictures. **1977** J. Aiken *Last Movement* i. 33 Wonderful reviews... I'll send you stats of all the notices.

stat[2] (stæt). Colloq. abbrev. of Statistic *sb.*, Statistics. Cf. *math[3]. orig. and chiefly *U.S.*

1961 Webster, *Stat*,..statistics. **1973** *Amer. Speech* 1970 XLV. 86 *Stat*, Elementary Statistics. **1976** *Springfield* (Mass.) *Daily News* 22 Apr. 39/1 A key stat: Marcel Dionne had only two shots Tuesday night. He scored on one, had another in the second period. **1977** *Rolling Stone* 5 May 46/3 Certainly, his stats in spring training were not impressive; his earned run average was over 4.00.

stat. (stæt), *adv. Pharm.* [Abbrev. of L. *statim.*] On a prescription: immediately.

1875 W. H. Griffiths *Lessons on Prescriptions* iv. 18 *Stat.*, immediately. **1971** *Lancet* 25 Sept. 700/2 *Stat.*, to be given at once.

stat- (stæt), *prefix.* [f. Stat(ic *a.* and *sb.*] Used in combination with the names of the practical electrical units to form the C.G.S. electrostatic system of units, as *statampere, statcoulomb, statfarad, statgauss, statohm, statvolt.*

[**1903** A. E. Kennelly in *Trans. Amer. Inst. Electr. Engin.* XXII. 534 In a comprehensive system of electromagnetic terminology, the electric C.G.S. units should also be christened... They might be denoted by the prefix *abstat*. Thus the C.G.S. electric unit of e.m.f. would be the abstatvolt.] **1920** *Proc. Amer. Philos. Soc.* LIX. 365 B_e is the electric flux density in 'statgausses'. **1925** W. H. Timbie *Elements of Electricity* xvi. 584 A statcoulomb is a small unit of charge, one coulomb being equal to 3×10^9 statcoulombs. **1932** S. S. Attwood *Electric & Magnetic Fields* i. 19 The unit of potential is an erg per statcoulomb and is called the statvolt in the electrostatic C.G.S. system. **1937** H. L. Curtis *Electr. Measurements* ii. 11 The prefixes *ab* and *abstat* were proposed by Kennelly ... The latter has generally been shortened to *stat*. No one of the proposed names has been adopted by any international organization. **1939** J. B. Whitehead *Electricity & Magnetism* vi. 62 The name of the electrostatic unit of capacitance is the statfarad. One farad is equal to 9×10^{11} statfarads. **1958** Condon & Odishaw *Handbk. Physics* A-9/2 The cgs unit of charge is called the esu or the statcoulomb. It is the unit defined by using dynes of force and cm of distance and adopting $4\pi\epsilon_0 = 1$. The corresponding unit of current is called the statampere, defined as the flow of one statcoulomb per second. *Ibid.* A-11/1, 1 statohm = $c^2/10^9$ ohms..with $c = 2{\cdot}997930 \times 10^{10}$ cm/sec. **1963** Jerrard & McNeill *Dict. Sci. Units* 12 In recent years the prefix stat has sometimes been used to denote electrostatic units, thus 1 stat volt = 300 practical volts, 1 stat ampere = $(1/3) \times 10^{-9}$ ampere. This prefix is an abbreviation for abstat which was proposed for electrostatic units at the same time as ab was suggested for electromagnetic units.

statal, *a.* Restrict *rare* to sense in Dict. For *a* **1864** Edw. Bates (W.) read **1862** E. Bates in *Official Opinions Attorneys Gen.* X. 388, and add later examples. Also of a state in other federations.

1880 A. Tourgée *Fool's Errand & Invisible Empire* II. xi. 489 Public education flourished as a part of the statal economy. **1949** *Times* 7 Feb. 5/3 All the states outside this special category have already been merged with provinces or have joined one or another of the six great statal groups.

2. *Linguistics.* Of a passive verbal form: expressing a state or condition rather than an action (opp. *actional *a.*).

1935 [see *actional *a.*]. **1961** R. B. Long *Sentence & its Parts* v. 119 Thus *have* has no passive when it is statal. **1968** *Language* XLIV. 236 The 'statal passives' are quite different in their internal representations from the true passives, and actually are not passives at all. **1975** *Ibid.* LI. 362 The ambiguity is between the 'statal' and 'dynamic passive' meaning.

statalon, var. *statolon.

statary, *a.* Restrict † *Obs.* to senses in Dict. and add: **3.** *Ent.* (stē^i·tări). Pertaining to or designating army ants during that phase of their life cycle when they return to a fixed colony each night.

1933 *Jrnl. Compar. & Physiol. Psychol.* XV. 297 When in the 'statary' condition, [ant] colonies do not appear as susceptible to the atmospheric changes that apparently furnish the stimuli for the bivouac-change movements of nomad colonies. **1940** *Jrnl. Compar. Psychol.* XXIX. 434 Swarm division is exceptional in a statary colony, but is a regular morning event in a nomadic colony. *Ibid.* 435 Smaller swarms..characterize the statary period. **1972** *Sci. Amer.* Nov. 73/3 The actual regulator of the ants' nomadic and statary behavior, as Schneirla eventually demonstrated, was not some external influence but the breeding cycle within the colony.

state, *sb.* Add: **I. 4. a.** (Further examples.) Also in generalized or abstract sense: each of the possible modes of existence of a system; the condition of a device that determines what output it produces for a given input.

1937 A. M. Turing in *Proc. London Math. Soc.* XLII. 250 We know the state of the system if we know the sequence of symbols on the tape, which of these are observed by the computer.., and the state of mind of the computer. **1942**, etc. [see *Markov]. **1954** *Jrnl. Franklin Inst.* CCLVII. 170 Once a stable state has been reached for all secondary relays, then further circuit changes can occur only if modification is made in the input state. **1961** F. M. Reza *Introd. Information Theory* ii. 54 Let an experiment have a finite number of *n* possible outcomes, $a_1, a_2, \ldots,$ and a_n, called states. We assume the process to be of the finite Markov type and initially in the state *k*. **1962** A. Gill *Introd. Theory of Finite-State Machines* i. 6 Roughly, the state of a finite-state machine at any given sampling time is that variable which, together with the input symbol, enables one to predict the output symbol. *Ibid.* iv. 130 Let *M* be an *n*-state machine with the input alphabet $X = \{\xi_1, \xi_2, \ldots, \xi_p\}$. **1964** F. L. Westwater *Electronic Computers* ii. 21 The reliable and stable electronic devices are so far two-state devices... If we had a three-state device we could..develop a ternary system of arithmetic. **1979** J. R. Gibson *Electronic Logic Circuits* i. 5 Logic elements may be combined to form multiple-state systems and the states of such systems may be used to represent numbers in systems other than the binary one.

b. *spec.* in *Physics*, a condition of an atom or other quantized system described by a particular set of quantum numbers; *esp.* one characterized by the quantum numbers *n, L, S, J,* and *m.* Cf. *level *sb.* 3 e.

1913 N. Bohr in *Phil. Mag.* XXVI. 5 If in these expressions we give *τ*, different values, we get a series of values for W, *ω*, and *a* corresponding to a series of configurations of the system. According to the above considerations, we are led to assume that these configurations will correspond to states of the system in which there is no radiation of energy; states which consequently will be stationary as long as the system is not disturbed from outside. **1925** *Astrophysical Jrnl.* LXI. 39 Every spectral line is now believed to be emitted (or absorbed) in connection with the transition of an atom (or molecule) between two definite (quantized) states, of different energy-content—the frequency of the radiation being exactly proportional to the change of energy. **1929** N. V. Sidgwick *Electronic Theory of Valency* ii. 18 These states are distinguished by the fact that in them the electron possesses an integral number..of quanta of energy. **1935** P. A. M. Dirac *Princ. Quantum Mech.* (ed. 2) i. 11 A state of a system may be defined as an undisturbed motion that is restricted by as many conditions or data as are theoretically possible without mutual interference or contradiction. **1935** Condon & Shortley *Theory Atomic Spectra* iv. 122 The terms are designated as ^2S (doublet *S*), ^2P, ^2D, ... according to the *P* value of the configuration from which they arise. The separate levels are designated by adding the value of *j* as a superscript, thus $^2S_{\frac{1}{2}}$ ... To specify an individual state the value of *m* is given as a superscript. **1955** E. B. Wilson et al. *Molecular Vibrations* x. 246 The selection rules for overtone frequencies will next be considered. These are transitions between the ground vibrational state and an excited state in which one quantum number is greater than one and all other quantum numbers are zero. **1970** [see *level *sb.* 3 e]. **1972** DePuy & Chapman *Molec. Reactions & Photochem.* iii. 43 Formaldehyde, which is planar in its ground state, distorts slightly toward a pyramidal structure in the S_1 state. **1978** P. W. Atkins *Physical Chem.* xix. 631 The isotope ^{57}Co decays slowly..and forms an excited nuclear state of ^{57}Fe.

5. a. (Examples of *the* (or *a*) *state of affairs.*) *spec.* in the philosophy of L. Wittgenstein (1889–1951): see quots. 1922, 1962.

1776 *St. James's Chron.* 23–25 May 4/1 Administration had, to the Scandal of all good Government, suppressed every Thing relative to the true State of Affairs in America. **1909** G. B. Shaw *Press Cuttings* 31 We [women] should lose our influence completely under such a state of affairs. **1911** E. L. Thorndike *Animal Intelligence* vi. 245 By a satisfying state of affairs is meant one which the animal does nothing to avoid. **1922** tr. *Wittgenstein's Tractatus* 31 It would..appear as an accident, when to a thing that could exist alone on its own account, subsequently a state of affairs could be made to fit. *Ibid.* 35 Objects contain the possibility of all states of affairs. *Ibid.* 43 The picture contains the possibility of the state of affairs which it represents. **1958** R. L. Green *Land of Lord High Tiger* ii. 33 Sad affairs of State! Sad state of affairs! Affairs in a sad state! **1962** M. Cranston tr. *Hartnack's Wittgenstein & Mod. Philos.* ii. 13 A 'state of affairs' is a fact that in itself does not consist of facts... A state of affairs is a combination of possible facts. *Ibid.* 14 If an elementary sentence, or, better, an elementary proposition is true, then the state of affairs which is spoken of exists. **1973** A. Kenny *Wittgenstein* v. 73 States of affairs, we are told, are independent of one another.

e. *state of the art*: the current stage of development of a practical or technological subject; freq. (esp. in *attrib.* use) implying the use of the latest techniques in a product or activity.

[**1889**: see Status 4.] **1910** H. H. Suplee *Gas Turbine* 6 It has therefore been thought desirable to gather under one cover the most important papers... In the present state of the art this is all that can be done. **1955** *Jrnl. R. Aeronaut. Soc.* LIX. 471/1 Flight instruments and flight techniques of human pilots had to be brought up to a state where automatic flying could be fitted into a consistent state-of-the-art picture. **1957** R. A. Heinlein *Door into Summer* (1960) v. 69 Engineering is the art of the practical and depends more on the total state of the art than it does on the individual engineer. **1967** *Technology Week* 23 Jan. 18/1 (Advt.), Poseidon's requirements range from weapon effects on electronics to the design and use of state-of-the-art test checkout equipment. **1970** J. Earl *Tuners & Amplifiers* iv. 79 An average magnetic cartridge at the current state of the art produces an output of 1 mV per channel for each velocity unit of 1 cm/S. **1970** *Daily Tel.* (Colour Suppl.) 9 Oct. 7 Our highly sophisticated, technological defence establishment is advancing the state-of-the-art weaponry into new and therefore secret areas. **1975** *Language* LI. 1009 What emerges about the state of the art in linguistics is incidental to the presentation of L[abov]'s analysis of language use in various speech communities. **1976** *National Observer* (U.S.) 27 Mar. 15/2 State-of-the-art solar research is well advanced in New Mexico. **1976** *Offshore Platforms & Pipelining* 16/3 Except for an innovation or two, the platform is state-of-the-art and no more than an extension of existing capabilities. **1978** *Sci. Amer.* Apr. 64/3 In the 1950's C. Miller Fisher.. proposed that anastomosis, or joining, of cerebral arteries beyond the point of occlusion might be appropriate in some stroke cases, but such manipulations were then still beyond the state of the art. **1978** *SLR Camera* Aug. 54/1 It is still not so easy to produce decent pictures at such a venue, even when one is replete with 'state of the art' cameras, long lenses and fast film.

f. *State of the Union message*: a yearly address delivered by the President of the U.S. to Congress, giving the Administration's view of the state of the nation and its plans for legislation.

[**1787** *Constitution as formed for U.S.* II. iii. 10 He shall from time to time give to the Congress information of the state of the union.] **1945** *Newsweek* 15 Jan. 30 (*caption*) Three days before the President's State of the Union message, the 79th Congress takes its oath of office. **1959** *Ann. Reg. 1958* 182 The President appeared in person before both Houses of Congress on 9 January to deliver his State of the Union Message. **1968** W. Safire *New Lang. Politics* 427 State of the Union *messages* (preferred over speeches, addresses, or reports..) have inclined to be lengthy statements of legislative intent. **1974** *Guardian* 31 Jan. 2/7 President Nixon's sixth—and very possibly his last—State of the Union message.

g. *the state of play*: the position in which a matter or business stands at a particular time.

1966 *Rep. Comm. Inquiry Univ. Oxf.* II. 56 Receiving applications..and keeping colleges informed on the 'state of play' on each candidate. **1971** A. Garve *Late Bill Smith* i. 38 You know the state of play, you can handle everything. **1979** R. Mutch *Gemstone* v. 56 Write me a short report... I want the state of play. I want it accurate and I want it now.

14. b. *Bibliography.* (See quots. 1931.)

1931 P. H. Muir *Points* 12 A word is still needed to describe changes made before any publication takes place. These changes may be made while the entire edition is still in the publisher's hands, they may take place at the printer's, at the binder's, or even at a stage intermediate between the issue of some of the review copies and the actual date of publication. Any differences that may arise before that time will be referred to as 'states'. *Ibid.* 13 It is probable that copies of the book in all three states will be issued on the same day. They will all be 'first issues'; but some will be first, some second, and others again third 'states' of the first edition. **1931** G. Worthington *Bibliogr. Waverley Novels* p. viii, I have.. decided to use the word 'State' whenever between two copies of a first edition there are differences of sufficient importance to be noticed; and my 'First State' is the variety which I believe to be preferable..to any other. *Ibid.* 37 Guy Mannering... There are four States of the first edition. **1949**, etc. [see *issue *sb.* 14 b (ii)]. **1972** *Scholarly Publishing* III. 123 The text was published almost simultaneously in English, French, and German, all with the same title. To distinguish between the various states and issues is nearly hopeless.

IV. 31. c. (Earlier Amer. example.)

1634 *Mass. Bay Rec.* (1853) I. 117 When I shalbe called to give my voice touching any such matter of this state, wherein ffreemen are to deale, [etc.].

33. b. Short for *State Department* (sense 41 a below). *U.S.*

1955 W. Tucker *Wild Talent* xi. 151 Somebody down at State had to soothe his ruffled feelings. **1971** R. Ludlum *Scarlatti Inheritance* I. ii. 18 It took an executive order from the President to get it out of State. **1979** H. Kissinger *White House Years* ii. 29 The new President wanted to change the negotiating instructions on Vietnam drafted at State that reflected the approach of the previous Administration.

c. Preceded by the name of a State: short for *state university* (sense 38 e below).

1928 *Time* 29 Oct. 28/3 Penn mauled Penn State, 14–0. **1975** J. Wyllie *Butterfly Flood* (1977) xxiv. 177, I can outswim you any time at all. I used to swim for Penn State. **1980** 'R. B. Dominic' *Attending Physician* ii. 11 Two students in Ohio State sweatshirts.

VII. 38. a. (Further examples.)

1881 E. W. Hamilton *Diary* 5 June (1972) I. 144 It is certainly a great misfortune that the three foremost men on the front Opposition bench should be dependent on State aid. **1885** State school [see Real *a.*[2] 10]. **1917** A. S. Neill *Dominie Dismissed* ii. 27 Our rulers..send the rest of the sons of the community to State schools where they are trained to be disciplined and content with their lot. **1937** *Discovery* Oct. 305/2 State aid..might ultimately be the only hope of British agriculture. **1943** Koestler *Arrival & Departure* IV. 165 State-bureaucracies and managers establish themselves in vital hedgehog positions. **1944** Wyndham Lewis *Let.* 20 Aug. (1963) 378 But Stalin has a working state-system, with the air purged of humbug. **1948** J. Towster *Political Theory in U.S.S.R.* iii. 42 The Party..was not yet equipped to substitute collective-farm and state-farm production for kulak production. **1972** *Listener* 23 Nov. 690/2 With the inevitable rise in food prices..the Government..[should] introduce state subsidies to stabilise prices. *a* **1974** R. Crossman *Diaries* (1975) I. 351 If he stays in the state system—in the village school and then in Banbury. **1977** B. Freemantle *Charlie Muffin* iv. 43 Had she been born in a council house..and attended a state school..Janet would have been a slag.

e. (Further examples.)

For numerous other *attrib.* uses see *D.A.E.* and *D.A.*

1831 J. M. Peck *Guide for Emigrants* 256 One sixth part is to be..bestowed on a state college or university. *a* **1857** *Michigan Gen. Statutes* (1882) I. 171 The board of state auditors are hereby authorized..to procure plans, drawings and estimates for a state capitol. **1885** State park [see *land-jobbing* s.v. *land *sb.*[1] 12]. **1925** L. S. Dunaway *What Preacher Saw* 81 Jeff Davis declared that the ground on which the new state capitol was constructed was 'too poor for two Irishmen to raise a row on!' **1941** *N.Y. Times Mag.* 26 Jan. 19/3 Police work forms only part of the State trooper's duties. **1952** *Mind* LXI. 471 Suppose we then see him in earnest conversation with a scout from the state university. **1964** M. Banton *Policeman in Community* iv. 94 Many of the State police forces again are very different. The men wear big hats like the Canadian mounties and concentrate upon highway patrol. **1969** C. Burke *God is Beautiful, Man* (1970) 30 They took a trip to a place that looked like a state park. **1976** *National Observer* (U.S.) 1 May B5/4 The bulk of the newly admitted enjoyed a style of training, in junior and state colleges, little superior to that of the high school. **1976** A. Price *War Game* I. ix. 173 He's a New Englander... He left his state university nine years ago.

40. b. (Further examples.)

1833 J. S. Mill in *Jurist* IV. 14 Let the State endowments be once withdrawn from the church of England. **1842** —— in *Morning Chron.* 13 Jan. 3/6 If an established church is not to be independent of state control, no established church ought to exist. **1848** in A. Prentice *Tour in U.S.* viii. 76 A real, state-paid bishop, whilome a minister of the Scotch Relief Kirk. **1856** Geo. Eliot in *Westm. Rev.* X. 64 Its patent machinery of state-appointed functionaries. **1876** *Fortn. Rev.* 1 Apr. 630 Proof that, as the *Katheder-Socialisten* maintain in Germany, the part of state-intervention will go on steadily increasing. **1887** G. B. Shaw *Let.* 8 June (1965) I. 173 The sweeping away of our..wicked workhouse prisons in favour of State-owned farms and factories. **1891** H. Spencer *Justice* 270 Under the existing system of ownership, those who manage the land, experience a direct connexion between effort and benefit; while, were it under State-ownership, those who managed it would experience no such direct connexion. **1899** W. S. Churchill in *Morning Post* 6 Dec. 5/7 There will be those who will dream another dream of a brave system of State-aided—almost State-compelled—emigration. **1901** *Edin. Rev.* Apr. 453 In Germany we have seen a State-paid clergy help to create and keep on foot the great parliamentary party of the Centre. **1926** H. Sheehy-Skeffington *Let.* 15 Feb. in *Lett. of Sean O'Casey* (1975) I. 168 In no country save in Ireland could a State-subsidized theatre presume on popular patience. **1927** Carr-Saunders & Jones *Social Structure Eng. & Wales* 148 To complete the tale of State-provided benefits that school children may receive. **1927** A. Huxley *Proper Studies* 220 In most modern countries the only state-supported orthodoxy is a sexual orthodoxy. **1942** *Contemp. Jewish Rec.* V. 274 The state-controlled *Kolkhoz* or *Sovkhos* systems in Soviet Russia. **1946** J. W. Day *Harvest Adventure* xviii. 301 No National Park or State-planned 'lung' could offer lovelier scenery so near a manufacturing area. **1946** State-run [see *private *a.* 4 d]. **1952** C. P. Blacker *Eugenics: Galton & After* 185 France has a Minister for Population and a state-sponsored National Institute of Demographic Studies. **1958** A. Quinton in *Victorian Stud.* I. 254 [T. H.] Green's defence of state intervention is now generally recognised as an important intellectual preparation for the British Labour Party. **1973** *Listener* 17 May 635/1 That section of the Left which wants greater equality without a massive increase in state ownership. **1977** *N.Y. Rev. Bks.* 31 Mar. 22/3 On state control of industry, the pivotal socialist issue, he had no consistent views. **1978** S. Sheldon *Bloodline* iv. 69 He borrowed money on the real jewelry from the Crédit Municipal, the state-owned pawnshop. **1979** *Jrnl. R. Soc. Arts* CXXVII. 125/2 There was now state-aided scientific research.

41. a. state capitalism, a system of socialism whereby the State exerts exclusive control over a substantial proportion of the means of production, and over the deployment of capital created by this; hence **state-capitalist, -capitalistic** *adjs.*; **state-centred** *a.*, that centres on the State; **State Council,** the highest administrative and executive body of the People's Republic of China; **State Department** *U.S.*, the federal department for foreign affairs, presided over by the Secretary of State, = *Department of State* s.v. Department *sb.* 3 b; **State Enrolled Nurse,** a nurse enrolled on a State register and having a qualification lower than that of a State Registered Nurse; **state line** *U.S.*, the boundary line of a State; **state-oriented** *a.*, directed towards the State; **State Registered Nurse,** a nurse enrolled on a State register, and better qualified than a State Enrolled Nurse, **State rights:** also of States composing other federal nations; **State Scholarship,** a scholarship awarded by the State for study at a university; **state socialism,** socialism achieved by State ownership of public utilities and industry; hence **state socialist** *a.* and *sb.*; **state-socialistic** *a.*; **state vector** *Physics*, a vector in a space whose dimensions correspond to all the independent wave-functions of a system, the instantaneous value of the vector conveying all possible information about the state of the system at that instant; **state visit,** a visit by a head of state to a foreign country for ceremonial rather than official purposes; also *fig.*; **state-wide** *a.*, of, pertaining to, or extending over a whole state (usu. in sense 31 c; occas. sense 30); also as *adv.*

1903 D. Modell tr. *P. Kropotkin's Mod. Science & Anarchism* x. 94 Anarchism cannot see in the next coming revolution a mere exchange of monetary symbols for labor-checks, or an exchange of present Capitalism for State-capitalism. **1928** E. & C. Paul tr. *Stalin's Leninism* 436 The left-wing communists were of opinion that State capitalism is incompatible with the system of the proletarian dictatorship. **1978** Ld. Hailsham *Dilemma o Democracy* xvii. 110 Modern capitalism is the state capitalism of the Coal Board, British Rail or the Post Office. **1965** B. Pearce tr. *Preobrazhensky's New Economics* 153 In the Entente countries the economic system of the war period was state-capitalist to a considerably smaller extent. **1945** Koestler *Yogi & Commissar* iii. iii. 201 Soviet Russia is a State-Capitalistic totalitarian autocracy. **1957** K. A. Wittfogel *Oriental Despotism* 33 The state-centered system of land grants as it prevailed in early China. **1977** *Dædalus* Summer 53 Is the state-centered concept of international politics..still relevant to the age of interdependence? **1969** Plano & Olton *Internat. Relations Dict.* 179 *State Council*, the highest executive decision-making body of the state apparatus, comparable to the Council of Ministers in the Soviet Union. **1978** tr. *Documents 1st Sess. 5th National Congr. People's Republic of China* 153 The State Council is the Central People's Government and the executive organ of the highest organ of state power. **1790** *Deb. Congress U.S.* 1 Apr. (1834) 1505 The resolution laid on the table yesterday, respecting the State Department. **1836** in *Ann. Rep. Amer. Hist. Assoc. 1907* (1908) II. 117 This morning..I went to the State Department, to have a conference with the present Acting Secretary of State. **1930** *Times* (Weekly ed.) 9 Jan. 35/1 On the eve of its meeting the State Department published the New Year greetings exchanged between King George and President Hoover. **1970** E. Snow *Red China Today* (new ed.) 26 Under pressure he had himself made a State Department-accredited 'correspondent'. **1978** R. Ludlum *Holcroft Covenant* iii. 41 'It's the State Department. For you.' 'State? This is Lieutenant Miles, NYPA police.' **1961** *Nursing Mirror & Midwives' Jrnl.* 23 June 1143/2 The lettering on badges and certificates of existing State Enrolled Assistant Nurses will not be altered when the title is changed to State Enrolled Nurse as from June 28 this year. **1974** *Encycl. Brit. Macropædia* XIII. 399/1 Legislation in 1960 changed the title of a less qualified grade from state-enrolled assistant nurse to state-enrolled nurse. **1783** *Virginia Gaz.* 20 Dec. 2/3 George R. Clark, Surveyor State Line. **1868** *Harper's Mag.* June 123/2 He pronounced 'good-by' to the Prairie State, at the State line. **1973** R. L. Simon *Big Fix* (1974) xviii. 132, I was..driving into a desert dawn. I had already crossed the state line. **1961** *Encounter* Sept. 24/1 The political self-consciousness of the individual citizen is State-oriented. **1920** *Nursing Mirror & Midwives' Jrnl.* 17 July 270/1 A Bill for the State Registration of Nurses was drafted by the College in which it was provided that ..all the nurses on the College Register would automatically become State-registered nurses without further fee. **1965** D. Edwards-Rees *Story of Nursing* vi. 66 From 1925 onwards the only way for a new-comer to become a state-registered nurse was to take a three-year course and to pass the state examination at the end of it. **1977** P. Hill *Liars* ix. 117 On the mantelshelf were pictures.. one..of Rose in the full uniform of a State Registered Nurse. **1907** W. S. Churchill in R. S. Churchill *Winston S. Churchill* (1969) II. Compan. 1. 627 A more practical explanation of any inconsistency in the attitude of the States is to be found in the growing cleavage upon the question of State rights *versus* Federal authority. **1930** W. K. Hancock *Australia* vi. 121 In truth, Australian public opinion (even that section of it which is disposed to favour 'State rights') has only a fitful, ineffective interest in maintaining the Federal balance. **1944** *Ann. Reg. 1943* 63 State Scholarships to universities should be of such a value as to enable the holder to take full part in the life of the university. **1966** *Rep. Comm. Inquiry Univ. Oxf.* II. 27 Source of financial assistance... A college scholarship or exhibition and a State Scholarship or LEA award. **1879** G. J. Holyoake in *19th Cent.* June 1114 State socialism is one of the diseases of despotism. *Ibid.*, State Socialism, so far as any taste for it exists in England, is a growth of Toryism. *Ibid.* 1115 The only persons in this country likely to be suspected of the State Socialistic craze are the working class co-operators. *Ibid.* 1116 True co-operators are no State Socialists. **1912** State socialist [see *radical *sb.* 5 a]. **1930** W. K. Hancock *Australia* vii. 137 Mr. Eggleston says that the Victorians are destroying their State socialism by political sabotage. **1968** H. W. Laidler *Hist. Socialism* xliii. 739 The social legislation of Bismarck has often been referred to as state socialism. *Ibid.* 742 Mr. Hillquit's distinction between government ownership and collective ownership..was.. the distinction made between the state socialist and the democratic socialist approach. **1929** Condon & Morse *Quantum Mechanics* vi. 205 The components of the state vector along the different principal axes multiplied by their complex conjugates give the probabilities of each value for the state in question. **1951** *Physical Rev.* LXXXII. 914/1 Quantum mechanics involves two distinct sets of hypotheses—the general mathematical scheme of linear operators and state vectors with its associated probability interpretation and the commutation relations and equations of motion for specific dynamical systems. **1970** D. T. Gillespie *Quantum Mechanics Primer* iv. 41 The state of the system is completely described by the state vector in the sense that anything which is in principle knowable about the system at time t can be learned from the function $\Psi_t(x)$. **1794** H. Wilson *Let.* 12 Apr. in *Fingall Papers* (Nat. Libr. Ireland MS. 8023(5)), I think your resolution as to a certain complimentary State Visit is perfectly correct, both as to yourself and your Lady. **1857** C. M. Yonge *Dynevor Terrace* I. xiv. 218 On Monday we go to Leffingham... After that, more state visits, unless I can escape to Oxford. **1914** W. Owen *Let.* 1 Jan. (1967) 225, I had to buy a waistcoat today, to complete the black suit: for the State Visit to Mr. Aumont which French Politeness imposes. **1966** *Listener* 23 June 900/2 President de Gaulle arrives in Moscow for twelve-day state visit. **1979** G. St. Aubyn *Edward VII* vii. 320 He [*sc.* the King]..decided that he wished to pay a State Visit abroad. **1911** C. E. Persons et al. *Labor Laws* 62 A state-wide organization was sufficient to bring the necessary pressure to bear. **1927** [see *rodeo 3 b]. **1948** J. Towster *Political Power in U.S.S.R.* iv. 86 Maximum unification of all economic activity by one state-wide plan. **1954** W. Faulkner *Fable* 189 A horde of Federal agents and sheriffs and special officers like the converging packs of a state- or nation-wide foxhunt. **1974** *Hartsville* (S. Carolina) *Messenger* 22 Apr. 2-A/5 The American Patriot Reading Club will offer youngsters statewide the opportunity to become better acquainted with the men, women, places and events, which have been prominent in the history of our state and the nation. **1980** *News & Observer* (Raleigh, N. Carolina) 28 Oct. 22/3 That immunization of cats against rabies be required statewide, and that the N.C. Wildlife Resources Commission be permitted to hunt and trap foxes for rabies control.

b. state's evidence: see Evidence *sb.* 7 c; **States-rights:** hence **States-righter,** an advocate of States-rights; also in other federal nations.

1948 *States' Rights* (Birmingham, Alabama) 26 July 1/1 States' Righters is all right, but the term, 'Dixiecrats', leaves the wrong impression. **1959** *Times Lit. Suppl.* 28 Aug. 491/3 It undoubtedly rallied every states-righter and virtually every Southerner, however progressive, behind Governor Faubus. **1972** *Accountant* 30 Mar. 405/2 Mr Macaw is regarded as a devout 'States-righter', who is firmly opposed to the creation of any Federal body to control the securities industry [in Australia].

stated, *ppl. a.* **2. b.** *stated meeting* (earlier example).

1866 *Harper's Mag.* Apr. 676/2 At one of their stated weekly meetings recently there was a large attendance.

statehood. For 'Chiefly with reference to the U.S.' read 'Orig. with reference to the U.S.' and add later examples.

1952 *Times* 9 Dec. 9 (*heading*) Solid achievements [by Israel] after four years of Statehood. **1971** I. Deutscher *Marxism in Our Time* (1972) v. 99 In a vast part of the continent a struggle was indeed going on for the achievement of independent statehood and nationhood. **1976** *Time* 27 Dec. 14/3 What the Palestinians want most of all is the sense of national identity that would arise from statehood.

State house. Add: **4.** *N.Z.* A house owned and let by the government.

1941 W. B. Sutch *Poverty & Progress in N.Z.* vii. 153 In the building of State houses of high quality a suggestion as to necessary standards has been made. **1964** B. Crump in *N.Z. Listener* 11 Dec. 5/3 It was a state house with shrubs and flowers in a street full of state houses with flowers and shrubs. **1978** B. Mason in *Islands* Aug. 15 After years of waiting, they got a State house last summer.

stateless, *a.* Add: **c.** Not being a citizen of any state; having no nationality.

1930 E. F. W. Gey van Pittius *Nationality within Brit. Commonw.* xiii. 133 A person of dual nationality can at least enter more than one country and seek protection from both while abroad. Not so the stateless person. **1957** C. Day Lewis *Pegasus* 36 He travels on, not only blind But a stateless person. **1968** J. Lock *Lady Policeman* xv. 132 The alien—a forty-seven year old Jugoslav-born stateless person—looked at her blankly. **1981** G. Markstein *Ultimate Issue* 153 In the absence of valid documents, we must grade a suspect stateless.

Hence **sta·telessness,** the condition of having no nationality.

1930 E. F. W. Gey van Pittius *Nationality within Brit. Commonw.* xiii. 132 In case of statelessness, which is the reverse of dual nationality or multiple nationality, an unfortunate individual is placed in the unenviable position of being without any country at all. **1959** *Times* 24 Mar. 9/5 The fundamental theory that statelessness should be overcome or reduced by the application of the principle of *jus soli* (the law of the soil) under which the nationality of a State is acquired by birth on its territory. **1963** H. Arendt *Eichmann in Jerusalem* x. 155 This was one of the few cases in which statelessness turned out to be an asset.

stately, *a.* Add: **4. a.** *stately home*: originally in allusion to quot. 1827; now a fixed phrase designating a great country-house. Also *attrib.* and *Comb.*

1827 F. Hemans in *Blackw. Mag.* Apr. 392 The stately Homes of England, How beautiful they stand! **1831** J. Brown *Let.* 26 Oct. (1912) 26 There is certainly something unapproachable in the 'stately homes of England'. **1848** A. Brontë *Tenant of Wildfell Hall* III. xv. 311, I.. looked back, for one last view of her stately home. **1874** Jewitt & Hall (*title*) The stately homes of England.. illustrated with 210 engravings on wood. **1920** D. H. Lawrence *Touch & Go* iii. i. 68 This is what happens to the stately homes of England—they buzz with inky clerks, or their equivalent. **1934** Wodehouse *Right Ho, Jeeves* xiv. 167 Some stately-home owners of the name of Stretchley-Budd, hanging out in a joint called Kingham Manor. **1938** N. Coward *Operette* i. vii. 54 The Stately Homes of England How beautiful they stand, To prove the upper classes Have still the upper hand. **1945** B. Goolden *Ichabod* ix. 50 A group of persons restricted to the Services, the stately homes of England, and a line running roughly from Stanhope Gate to Eaton Square. **1959** Duke of Bedford *Silver-Plated Spoon* xi. 215 We had jumped straight into the front rank of the stately homes business. **1977** B. Pym *Quartet in Autumn* v. 45 There would be visits to a safari park and to the stately homes that offered the best attractions.

statement. Add: **2. a.** Also *transf.* and *fig.*

1953 W. M. Ivins *Prints & Visual Communication* i. 3 Since the invention of writing there has been no more important invention than that of the exactly repeatable pictorial statement. **1958** *Listener* 18 Sept. 437/3 Apart from some inherent nastiness in the story there is a fundamental weakness in its theatrical statement. **1970** *New Yorker* 26 Sept. 29/3 We had in mind thirty or forty people making a quiet statement by riding together. **1977** C. McFadden *Serial* (1978) xl. 86/2, I wish you'd stop shaving your goddamn legs. You might not know it, but you're making a *statement*.

b. *Computers.* An expression in a program language that specifies some operation or task, corresponding to one or more instructions according to the context and the level of the language.

1957 *Proc. Western Joint Computer Conf.* 188/2 He.. programmed the job in four hours, using 47 FORTRAN statements. **1957** D. D. McCracken *Digital Computer Programming* xviii. 215 The automatic coding systems directed toward scientific calculations accept problem statements in a form similar to ordinary mathematical language. **1959** M. H. Wrubel *Primer of Programming for Digital Computers* vi. 126 There are statements for performing arithmetic; statements for branching and looping; and input and output statements. **1967** W. F. Sharpe *Introd. Computer Programming using BASIC Lang.* i. 6 Every statement must begin with a legal command (after the line number, if any). **1973** J. K. Hughes *Pl/I Programming* i. 8 The statement to input the data.. should be specified. This could be accomplished with the statement get list (A, B, C, D, E); Notice how all PL/I statements are ended with a semicolon. **1981** Monds & McLaughlin *Introd. Mini & Micro Computers* vii. 99/1 An assembler translates a machine oriented language, ie, a language where, in general, one statement gives rise to one machine instruction... A compiler translates a problem-oriented language..into machine code. Each statement in the language usually gives rise to more than one, and sometimes many, machine instructions.

3. b. (Earlier example.)

1885 W. Whitman *Daybks. & Notebks.* (1978) II. 375 Half-annual 'Statement' from D Mckay $20.71 'ts for 6 mo's preceding Dec 1, '85.

c. statement of affairs *Accounting*, a list of assets and liabilities not expressed as a formal balance sheet.

1895 *Reports Tax Cases* (1907) III. 456 Every man and every company having foreign or colonial investments, of course, knows of the interest arising from them, takes note of it and enters it in any statement of affairs which may require to be made up. **1928** R. G. Williams *Elem. Bk.-Keeping* xiv. 240 The preparation of the statement of affairs may possibly depend upon information which is not supplied by the books of account, and often undue reliance must be placed upon the trader's memory. **1978** J. Kellock *Elem. Accounting* xi. 184 The term 'statement of affairs' is one commonly used in the subject of incomplete records and may be defined as a list of assets and liabilities. **1981** *Daily Tel.* 19 Dec. 17/6 In the statement of affairs presented at the creditors' meeting £31,000 of client account balances appeared as part of the net assets of the company. **1983** *Ibid.* 12 Mar. 19/1 Not only was there a complete absence of a statement of affairs—the receiver said that he had been unable to lay his hands on any of the company's books—but it was apparent from the scant information he was able to provide that the liabilities are far in excess of known assets.

5. Special Comb. (in sense 2): **statement-form** *Logic* = *propositional function* s.v. *PROPOSITIONAL *a.* b.

1942 J. Findlay in *Mind* LI. 261 A statement-form is an expression containing variables such as x, y, etc., which gives rise to statements when expressions with a constant meaning are substituted for those variables. Thus 'x is long' is a statement-form. **1950** M. G. White in M. Farber *Philosophic Thought in France & U.S.* 711 How shall we define or make clear the meaning of the statement-form '*x* is a history of *y*'? **1961** E. Nagel *Structure of Sci.* v. 95 Instead of being statement-forms the postulates of the theory appear to be statements.

statemental (stēⁱtme·ntăl), *a.* [f. Statement + -al.] That makes, consists of, or is characterized by a statement or statements.

1939 C. W. Morris in *Kenyon Rev.* I. 413 Scientific discourse is, in summary, statemental or predictive in character. **1955** J. L. Austin *How to do Things with Words* (1962) vi. 72 The primary or primitive use of sentences must be..statemental or constative. **1976** [see *sentential *a.* 2 b].

state-monger, states-monger. For *Obs.* exc. *arch.* read Now *rare* or *arch.*

1891 F. W. Bain *Antichrist* I. 53 The Revolutionary statesmongers were far too much in a hurry. **1965** C. Campos *View of France* x. 241 Perhaps..France is the source of light, as a certain tall statemonger would have it. Or perhaps Arnold was right after all and the English are a more earnest nation.

Stater[3] (stēⁱ·təɹ). *Irish Hist.* [f. State *sb.* + -er[1].] A member of the Irish Free State army.

1925 S. O'Casey *Juno & Paycock* III. 111 Ah, why didn't I remember that then he wasn't a Die-hard or a Stater, but only a poor dead son! **1936** 'N. Blake' *Thou Shell of Death* xiii. 239 During the Civil War..the Staters and the Republicans had a battle in the garden. **1965** L. Fleming *Head or Harp* x. 83 The streets themselves were full of 'Staters'.

state-room. Add: **3. a.** (Earlier examples.)

1774 J. Schaw *Jrnl. Lady of Quality* (1921) i. 22 Our Bed chamber which is dignified with the title of State Room, is about five foot wide and six long. **1832** F. Trollope *Domestic Manners of Americans* (ed. 2) I. xvii. 259 They occupied a state-room which Captain Hall had secured for his party.

b. (Earlier example.)

1853 *Southern Standard* (Charleston, S. Carolina) 31 Aug. 2/5 Messrs. Eaton & Gilbert..have built a beautiful car for the Hudson River Railroad which is divided into state rooms of eight feet square.

stateship (stēⁱ·tʃip). *Irish Hist.* [f. State *sb.* + -ship.] = Tuath.

1917 D. Figgis *Gaelic State Past & Future* 11 To make more easy the general administration of the country, he [*sc.* Cormac] regrouped the administrative units of the country. Until then the nation had consisted of a number of separate stateships. **1918** —— in *Studies* VII. 259 For the unit of the Irish polity—sometimes spoken of as the Gaelic State—was the Tuath. It was at once a political and an economic unit; a stateship of a state. **1918** A. de Blacam *Towards Republic* iii. 24 Along the western counties, where the Irish language still predominates, traces of the life of the stateships linger to this day.

Sta·teside, stateside, *a.* and *adv. colloq.* (orig. and chiefly *U.S.*). Also **states side** and hyphened. [f. *State-s* (State *sb.* 31 d) + Side *sb.*[1] 15 b.] **A.** *adj.* Of, in, or pertaining to the continental United States of America.

1944 Karig & Kelley *Battle Report* I. vii. 151 Hearing that several United States news correspondents were in Soerabaja it occurred to him that Stateside newspapers might carry stories of the air attack. **1952** *Chambers's Jrnl.* Aug. 486/1 After the biennial yacht-race to Honolulu is over..the problem of how to return the yachts to their stateside ports can no longer be postponed. **1960** *Encounter* Feb. 31/2 The kids keep up with the latest Stateside fad. **1967** A. Diment *Dolly Dolly Spy* vi. 80 She was tall and slim, as most of those Stateside career women are. **1975** tr. *Melchoir's Sleeper Agent* II. 148 Larry numbly examined his mangled, disfigured hands. 'I.. guess I bought myself a Stateside ticket.' **1979** *Sci. Amer.* Feb. 27/2 Agent Orange and its stateside analogues, much used defoliants for weeds and forest cover.

B. *adv.* Towards or in the continental United States of America.

1945 *Sun* (Baltimore) 12 Mar. 9-0/6 'Stateside' is a mighty popular word out here [*sc.* in Guam] because a service man going 'stateside' is going home. **1950** 'D. Divine' *King of Fassarai* xvii. 137 You're just fresh from States-side. You'll see what I mean when you've been on the island for a week. **1963** L. Deighton *Horse under Water* xliv. 176 Fernie fixed the consignment to a ship heading stateside. I notified my contacts in New York. **1966** E. McGirr *Funeral was in Spain* 74 I'm going back states side in a few days. **1969** *Oz* Apr. 27/2 This guy knew some of the Angels State-side, or at least he thinks he knows. **1976** M. Machlin *Pipeline* xxxix. 426 I'm willing to cash in my chips, drag up stateside, and get going on something else.

statesman[1]**.** Add: **1.** *elder statesman*: see *elder *a.* 1 c.

stateswoman. Add: Hence **sta·teswomanship; sta·teswomanlike, -ly** *adjs.*

1850 Thackeray *Pendennis* II. vi. 62 She..discharges I don't know what more duties of British stateswomanship. **1959** C. Pankhurst *Unshackled* xii. 205 The signatories of this stateswomanly letter included Viscountess Acheson, the Hon. Mrs. Guy Baring. **1966** *Punch* 30 Mar. 442/1 Mrs. Indira Gandhi..will 'meet and talk with the Prime Minister', either at the airport or a nearby hotel. With stateswomanlike caution, of course, she'll be rehearsing her formal greeting with a blank after the Mister.

stathmokinesis (stæ:þmokinī·sis). *Biol.* and *Med.* [ad. F. *stathmocinèse* (A.-P. Dustin 1938, in *Compt. Rend. de l'Assoc. des Anatomistes* XXXIII. 209), f. Gr. σταθμό-ς station, stage + κίνησις motion.] The type of cell division produced by substances such as colchicine, characterized by a halt or long delay at metaphase. Hence **sta:thmokine·tic** *a.*, (of a drug) that produces stathmokinesis; applied also to the method of measuring rates of cell division by means of such a drug.

1945 *Bot. Rev.* XI. 148 While some cells showed complete pycnosis, normal telophase stages and cytoses occurred. Some cells assumed normal telophase stages and formed giant or polyploid nuclei. Dustin proposed the name of 'stathmocinesis' for this type of indirect division and applied the name of 'stathmocinetic poison' to colchicine. He contended that the arrest of the nuclear division in the metaphase was preceded by a phase of excitation which distinguished this poison from those which merely inhibited division. **1971** *Brit. Jrnl. Cancer* XXV. 692 Since the stathmokinetic method we used cannot provide information about the proportion of cells actually in the proliferative cycle, the proportion or index of arrested metaphases..can only be used to find the potential doubling time..of the tumour cell population. **1977** W. A. Aherne et al. *Introd. Cell Population Kinetics* iii. 18 (*heading*) Metaphase arrest (stathmokinesis). *Ibid.*, The stathmokinetic agents in use today are colchicine, its derivative Colcemid, and the increasingly popular vinca alkaloids vinblastine and vincristine.

static, *a.* and *sb.* Add: **A.** *adj.* **3. b.** *static friction* (see quot. 1878).

1878 *Phil. Trans. R. Soc.* CLXVII. 509 Coulomb pointed out the necessity of distinguishing between the friction which resists the relative movement of surfaces already in motion, or what is now called kinetic friction, and the friction which tends to prevent surfaces at rest from being set in motion, or what is now called static friction. **1922** Glazebrook *Dict. Appl. Physics* I. 389/2 The subject of static friction is of considerable importance in the theory of the stability of engineering structures. **1980** J. W. Hill *Intermediate Physics* iv. 29 The block should, in absolutely frictionless conditions, begin to move however small the applied force but in practice static friction opposes the movement.

c. *Econ.* Of or pertaining to an economic system in a state of equilibrium. Cf. *statics 1 d.

1899 J. B. Clark *Distrib. of Wealth* iii. 31 What a static theory openly and intentionally puts out of sight—namely, changes that alter the mode of production. *Ibid.* v. 60 The study of the unreal static state is a heroic..use of the isolating method of study. **1904** J. N. Keynes *Scope & Method Pol. Econ.* (ed. 3) iv. 147 An economic theory is termed *static* if it is based on the assumption of ..a state in which there occurs no essential modification of the general conditions under which production and consumption, distribution and exchange, are carried on. **1947** P. A. Samuelson *Foundations Econ. Analysis* xi. 312 Gustav Cassel..considers Economic Dynamics to be a third stage of analysis, following a pure Static Economy and a 'quasi-static' Uniformly Progressive Economy. **1974** A. S. Campagna *Macroeconomics* iii. 50 Static analysis is concerned with states of equilibrium, and static models inquire into the forces leading to, maintaining, and reestablishing, if necessary, the equilibrium condition.

4. c. *Phonetics.* Of consonants, = Continuant *a.* 2; of tones, not changing pitch during utterance.

1931 [see *kinetic *a.* 5]. **1939** L. H. Gray *Foundations Lang.* 53 All consonants can be uttered by themselves whether they are *static* (or *continuant*), i.e., can be held continuously without changing quality (notably nasal, lateral, rolled, fricative, and sibilant sounds..); or are *kinetic*, i.e., cannot be so held. **1958** R. Kingdon *Groundwork Eng. Intonation* p. xxii, *Static tone*, a tone in which the voice remains steady on a given pitch throughout its duration. *Ibid.* 4 The Static Tones are the level tones, accompanied by stress, which are used on the words to which it is desired to give prominence in the sentence, but to which no particular feeling is attached. **1961** [see *kinetic *a.* 5]. **1968** B. M. H. Strang *Mod. Eng. Structure* (ed. 2) vi. 92 Kingdon divides the notes and tunes of English speech into two kinds, the level or Static Tones, and the moving or Kinetic Tones. **1969** D. Crystal *Prosodic Systems & Intonation in English* iv. 158 *Stress.* Perceivable increase in loudness accompanied by unmarked pitch movement (the norm in the pitch-range system, static tone).

6. c. *Computers.* Applied to a store in which the data are held at fixed positions in the device, and any location can be accessed at any moment.

1947 A. W. Burks et al. in *Coll. Wks. J. von Neumann* V. 44 We distinguish two broad types of such devices: static, and dynamic or pulse-type accumulators. **1970** O. Dopping *Computers & Data Processing* x. 134 A ferrite core memory..is an example of a static memory, while a drum memory..is a dynamic memory in which a particular memory can be read or written only when the continuously rotating drum is at a certain angular position. **1977** J. C. Boyce *Digital Computer Fund.* viii. 212 The basic building block of the static memory discussed in this section is a 16-pin integrated circuit.

7. Special collocations (mostly in sense 3): *static characteristic* (*curve*) (Electronics), a graph showing the relationship between two parameters of a valve, transistor, etc., measured under steady conditions (strictly at zero frequency and with no load impedance); *static line*, a line connecting a parachute to the body of an aircraft and serving to open and release it automatically when tensioned by the movement of the parachutist away from the aircraft; *static pressure*, the pressure of a fluid on a body when the latter is at rest relative to it; *static-pressure tube* = *static tube* below; *static test*, a test of a device or object in a stationary position, or under conditions that are constant or change only gradually; so *static-test* vb. trans.; *static testing* vbl. sb.; *static thrust*, thrust generated by a stationary aero-engine or rocket engine; *static tube* (Aeronaut.), the part of the pitot-static head that registers static pressure, consisting of a tube aligned parallel to the airflow, closed at the forward end, and having holes along its length; *static water*: during the war of 1939–45, a store of water with no pressure of its own intended for use as an emergency supply, esp. in fighting fires.; freq. *attrib.*, as *static-water tank*.

1919 *Wireless World* May 77/2 From the static characteristic of a valve..it is clear that if the grid voltage varies between sufficiently small limits, the law of variation will be exactly reproduced in the anode circuit. **1939** H. J. Reich *Theory & Applications Electron Tubes* iii. 43 Strictly a static characteristic is one obtained with steady voltages, whereas a dynamic characteristic is one obtained with alternating voltages. **1975** D. G. Fink *Electronics Engineers' Handbk.* vii. 39 The performance of a transistor over wide ranges of current and voltage is determined from static characteristic curves. **1930** C. Dixon *Parachutes for Airmen* ii. 20 The 'Guardian Angel' was a typical example of the 'automatic' design. It was fitted into a tube fixed at the side of the aeroplane, with a static line attached to the harness on the airman. **1966** M. R. D. Foot *SOE in France* iv. 78 All a parachutist has to do is to jump through the hole; his parachute is opened automatically by a thin wire called a 'static line' which his own weight breaks. **1977** *R.A.F. News* 30 Mar.–12 Apr. 3/3 If new members decide they want to move on to free-fall parachuting, they must first make six static line jumps. **1915** W. E. Dommett *Aeroplanes & Airships* 103 *Pressure head*, a combination of pitot tube and static pressure or suction tube. **1923** Glazebrook *Dict. Appl. Physics* V. 66/2 The air thus blows tangentially past these holes, and the pressure within the tube is equal to the static pressure of the surrounding air. **1948** C. E. Chapel *Aircraft Basic Sci.* i. 21/1 The center of pressure can be located for each angle of attack by installing parallel rows of static pressure tubes at right angles to the leading edge of a wing flush with the upper and lower surfaces. **1978** J. D. Anderson *Introd. Flight* iv. 95 Static pressure is a consequence of just the purely random motion of the molecules. **1905** *Jrnl. Iron & Steel Inst.* LXVII. 486 Overheating..will produce brittleness under shock or vibratory stress, although static tests may have given fairly satisfactory results. **1918** Cowley & Levy *Aeronautics* ix. 176 Fig. 97 gives thrust and torque required to drive the propeller for a 'static test', i.e. when the forward speed is zero. **1961** *Time* (Atlantic ed.) 24 Feb. 12/2 The Saturn has been static-tested, but will not be operational until 1965. **1962** *B.S.I. News* July 9/1 The 'static' test used..in approving well over a million Kite-marked safety belts is extremely effective in finding out any weakness. **1966** *McGraw-Hill Encycl. Sci. & Technol.* XI. 610a/2 The static test facilities must be capable of handling and disposing of the hot gases..that are expelled from the rocket. **1968** A. E. Roy tr. *T. de Galiana's Conc. Encycl. Astronautics* 259/1 The complete rocket, held in a test-stand, is then static tested. **1950** G. G. Smith *Gas Turbines & Jet Propulsion* (ed. 5) xii. 205 (*heading*) Static testing. **1958** F. A. Warren *Rocket Propellants* x. 173 Because of the dangers involved in static testing, special precautions must be taken to protect personnel. **1962** F. I. Ordway et al. *Basic Astronautics* vii. 319 Static testing may be divided into two categories: powerplant static testing and vehicle capture firing. **1916** M. A. S. Riach *Air-Screws* viii. 89 The 'Static' thrust of an air-screw on an aeroplane is usually measured by attaching a spring balance to the rear portion of the machine and attaching a rope from the spring balance to some fixed support. **1952** A. Y. Bramble *Air-Plane Flight* x. 153 The problem of providing the essential static thrust for take-off found its solution in the variable-pitch propeller. **1962** F. I. Ordway et al. *Basic Astronautics* vii. 319 Some of the common measurements made..are given below.

(i) Thrust (static thrust developed by the engine) [etc.]. **1923** GLAZEBROOK *Dict. Appl. Physics* V. 66/1 A 'head', consisting of two parts—the 'pressure' or 'Pitot' tube and the 'static' tube—is fixed on some exposed part of the aircraft. **1940** A. C. KERMODE *Mechanics of Flight* (ed. 4) ii. 29 In modern types the Pitot tube is connected to the inside of a capsule..while the Static tube is connected to the casing of the instrument. **1965** V. H. BRIX tr. *Martynov's Pract. Aerodynamics* vi. 141 The most widely used instrument for measuring static pressure is the static tube or sonde. **1944** *Ourselves in Wartime* 108/2 Thousands of static water tanks were established in parks, squares and in the basements of bombed buildings, so that never again would there be a shortage of water through the destruction of the mains by the enemy. **1958** L. W. TANCOCK in *Aspects of Translation* 31 You may remember those tanks of water stored in our towns against fires caused by enemy action. We had none in North Wales, but..near where we lived a torrent came tumbling down the valley and a large notice stood by indicating that this was *static water*. **1976** 'J. CHARLTON' *Remington Set* xxiii. 119 This place used to be an airfield in the war... Under here there's a big static water tank.

B. *sb.* **4. a.** Atmospherics; radio noise.

1913 *Wireless World* Nov. 508/2 Communication will also be had with New Orleans, which the static formerly prevented. **1938** D. CANFIELD *Fables for Parents* II. 124 That woman who talks about cooking is coming on splendidly. Not a speck of static. Wouldn't you like to bring your sewing over and listen? **1950** 'N. SHUTE' *Town like Alice* v. 156 He wanted to see a live broadcast of 'Much-Binding-in-the-Marsh' which he listened to on short wave from Brisbane when the static permitted. **1960** *Practical Wireless* XXXVI. 413/1 The background noise caused by external static can be troublesome. **1978** R. LUDLUM *Holcroft Covenant* xvii. 196 There was a sudden burst of static from a radio speaker beneath the dashboard.

b. In *fig.* use, aggravation or interference; confusion, fuss, trouble, criticism. *slang* (orig. *U.S.*).

1926 MAINES & GRANT *Wise-Crack Dict.* 8/1 *Full of static*, not worth listening to. **1953** W. BURROUGHS *Junkie* (1972) viii. 77 An Sol said, 'Hell, I love junk... But if I can't use it without I get static all the time from the law, I'll get off junk and stay off.' **1969** C. YOUNG *Todd Dossier* 154 If I notified Security it would just mean a lot of fuss, ..where was the requisition, all that static. **1974** L. DEIGHTON *Spy Story* xvii. 186 Spare me the static... Why didn't you lay it on for me, about working for the goddam Brits? **1979** D. ANTHONY *Long Hard Cure* v. 42 The words are full of static, a reaction to that attack.

5. Static electricity. Freq. *attrib.*

1916 'B. M. BOWER' *Phantom Herd* xiv. 233 All that negative I took to-day is chock full of 'static'. **1951** KOESTLER *Age of Longing* 195 The umbrellas..had a tendency to charge the people who carried them with static, which sometimes discharged itself in crackling sparks at a handshake, kiss or other bodily contact. **1956** *Planning* XXII. 128 Static elimination is the removal of the harmful electric charges which accumulate on fibres and thin sheets during manufacturing processes. **1978** *Hi-Fi News* Sept. 130/1 (Advt.), Not unlike a common magnet attracting iron particles, static scavenges and draws dust particles onto the record surface. **1979** *Globe & Mail* (Toronto) 5 May 8/1 The winter smell of the settlement has become that of laundry aids—fluffers and static eradicators—whose smells are wafted into the icy air.

-static, formative element (f. Gr. στατικός causing to stand, stopping: see STATIC *a.* and *sb.*) used in the senses (*a*) 'inhibiting flow', as in HÆMOSTATIC *a.* and *sb.*; (*b*) 'inhibiting growth', as in *BACTERIOSTATIC *a.*, *FUNGISTATIC *a.*

staticisor (stæ·tisəizəɹ). *Computers.* [f. STATIC *a.* + -ISE[1] + -OR.] A device which converts a succession of bits into an array of simultaneous states, thereby storing them.

1949 WILLIAMS & KILBURN in *Proc. Inst. Electr. Engineers* XCVI. III. 82 Information may be represented 'dynamically' by pulses, which only exist transiently, or 'statically' by d.c. coupled flip-flop circuits, which retain the information until purposely reset to a standard condition... The set of flip-flop circuits is called a 'staticisor'. **1956** *Electronic Engin.* XXVIII. 154/2 The diodes in one horizontal row store the binary digits of the same significance in each of the words, and all have access to the trigger V_2 in the input-output staticizor. **1960** HALEY & SCOTT *Analogue & Digital Computers* vii. 191 The digits are transient and must therefore be stored or converted into a static form by setting a row of five staticisors.

So **sta·ticize** *v. trans.*, to store by means of a staticisor.

1952 *Electronic Engin.* XXIV. 30/1 In almost every design, a modest number of electronic triggers is retained since they allow words to be set up ('staticized') or discharged ('dynamicized') at different rates. **1960** HALEY & SCOTT *Analogue & Digital Computers* vii. 193 Once the function digits have been 'staticised' there comes the problem of decoding.

statics. Add: **1. d.** *Econ.* That part of economic theory which examines the forces and conditions obtaining at a state of equilibrium in an economic system, without consideration of changes through time; esp. as *comparative statics* (see quot. 1974).

1871 W. S. JEVONS *Theory Pol. Econ.* p. viii, The nature of Wealth and Value is explained by the consideration of indefinitely small amounts of pleasure and pain, just as the theory of Statics is made to rest upon the equality of indefinitely small amounts of energy. **1891** J. N. KEYNES *Scope & Method in Pol. Econ.* iv. 141 In so-called economic statics we are frequently engaged in examining the effects of particular changes. **1920** A. MARSHALL *Princ. Econ.* (ed. 8) v. v. 366 The problem of normal value belongs to economic Dynamics: partly because Statics is really but a branch of Dynamics. **1947** P. A. SAMUELSON *Foundations Econ. Analysis* ii. 8 This method of comparative statics is but one special application of the more general practice of scientific deduction in which the behavior of a system (possibly through time) is defined in terms of a given set of functional equations and initial conditions. **1954** W. JAFFÉ tr. *Walras's Elem. Pure Economics* viii. 117 Had I supposed utility to be a *variable* functionally related to time, then time would have had to figure explicitly in the problem. And we should then have passed from economic *statics* to economic *dynamics*. **1963** R. E. KUENNE *Theory of Gen. Econ. Equilibrium* i. 15 Comparative statics is a *method* of employing static models analytically by imposing changes upon the data of the model. **1974** A. S. CAMPAGNA *Macroeconomics* iii. 50 With a model in equilibrium any change in the variables will cause the model to react until a new equilibrium is reached. The comparison of these two equilibrium states is called comparative statics.

† **2.** = *STATIC *sb.* 4 a. *Obs.*

1918 in WEBSTER Add. **1921** *Sci. Abstr.* B. XXIV. 156 On the North Atlantic coast the statics come in large proportion from the S.W. **1926** *Glasgow Herald* 15 May 4 A wall of 'statics' may be responsible for the fact that no wireless messages have been received from the airship for some time.

station, *sb.* Add: **II. 7. b.** *to keep station, on station.*

1923 *Man. Seamanship* (Admiralty) (ed. 2) II. x. 176 The leading ship should therefore at once reduce speed, even though the other is keeping station on her. **1939** *War Illustr.* 2 Dec. 372/3 The absolute necessity of maintaining the order in which their ships are placed in the convoy, i.e. to keep station, and not to alter course except at the order of the commodore of the convoy. **1972** *Lebende Sprachen* XVII. 149/1 *On station*, the status of an ocean station vessel when within the limits of the assigned ocean station. **1979** *Courier-Mail* (Brisbane) 1 Jan. 15/4 Quentin Fogarty managed to get film on the return flight of a large glowing orange object keeping station with the aircraft about 8 km away. **1982** *Times* 31 Mar. 4/4 HMS Endurance will remain on station as long as is necessary.

11. b. (Earlier example.)

1848 *Alfred in India* 12 There are also numbers in the civil service, and they reside at what are called *stations*.

c. *Air Force.* An aerodrome where personnel are employed or garrisoned.

1911, etc. [see *air-station* s.v. AIR *sb.*[1] B. III. 7]. **1922** *Encycl. Brit.* XXXI. 85/1 At the outbreak of the World War the stations on the organized east coast system of aerial patrol were as follows:—Eastchurch, [etc.]. **1942** T. RATTIGAN *Flare Path* I. 5, I suppose you came to see someone up at the station. **1977** *Daily Tel.* 7 Nov. 2 The Service's Ground Branch is most seriously affected, with one in three group captains nominated for command making it known at pre-selection stage that they are not interested in taking over their own station.

13. d. A mission station; a mission (MISSION *sb.* 6).

1834 J. A. WILSON *Jrnl.* 2 Jan. in *Missionary Life & Work in N.Z.* (1889) I. 7 We are..satisfied with the central position of the station. The large tribes are within a circle of twenty miles. **1851** H. R. RICHMOND *Jrnl.* in *Richmond-Atkinson Papers* (1960) I. ii. 85 On Monday evening we arrived at Mr Ashwell's station at Tukapoto. **1883** C. F. WILDER *Sister Ridnour's Sacrifice* 229 The converts..have been for many weeks at the station. **1923** O. SCHREINER *Thoughts on S. Afr.* 16 A minister of the Dutch Reformed Church..came to spend a night at our station. The accommodation of an up-country mission house is limited.

e. *U.S.* A branch post office.

1896 *Ann. Rep. U.S. Postmaster General* 14 All detail matters relating to the establishment and discontinuance of post offices, the establishment of stations,..would be superintended personally by the district supervisors. **1939** J. L. FLOHERTY *Make Way for Mail* x. 158 Twenty-four sub-postal stations are connected by tube system with the general post office. **1960** E. K. MEADOR *Billion Dollar Pork Barrel* i. 20, I..was appointed a regular clerk..at the same station where I had been working as a sub-carrier. **1977** *Times Lit. Suppl.* 18 Feb. 187/4 (Advt.), P.O. Box 307, Times Square Station, New York.

f. A broadcasting station; an establishment or organization transmitting radio or television signals. Cf. *radio station* s.v. *RADIO sb. 7; *television station* s.v. *TELEVISION 3 c.

1912: see *radio station* s.v. *RADIO *sb.* 7. [**1913** *Wireless World* Apr. 8 (*caption*) Aden Wireless Station.] **1922** *Science & Invention* Feb. 937/2 We amateurs and experimenters sit by our cozy fireside..and enjoy wireless telephone music sent out by the now famous Westinghouse broadcasting station at Newark, or from one of the dozen other stations. **1923** *Daily Mail* 13 May 8/2 You turn the handle a quarter of an inch, 'tuning'-in to the Cardiff station. **1944** S. S. MCKAY *W. Lee O'Daniel & Texas Politics, 1938–1942* i. 22 In addition to the WBAP programs the Doughboys were taken to Dublin every Wednesday night for a program over a small station there. **1959** A. WEBSTER *Roots* II. i. 37 She turns the radio on, turning the dial knob through all manner of stations and back again until she finds some very loud dance music. **1969** *Listener* 6 Feb. 177/2 The daily output of all these stations is remarkable considering their limited resources in money, staff and equipment. **1978** J. IRVING *World according to Garp* xix. 432 The Vermont station carried the game..from Philadelphia.

g. A location in an automated system (e.g. for data processing or a manufacturing process) where a particular operation takes place.

1948 *Math. Tables & Other Aids to Computation* III. 150 The card reading unit is similar to a standard IBM Reproducing Punch, except that a full reading station has been inserted ahead of the punching station. **1949** B. L. DAVIES *Technol. Plastics* xvii. 317 Each one of a number of moulds is placed at a station round the table and a cam device is provided for opening it and ejecting the moulding automatically as the table rotates. **1976** *Sci. Amer.* Feb. 77 (*caption*) The three components..are mounted on an underbody shuttle and carried rear end first past five welding stations in sequence.

h. *colloq.* The headquarters of an intelligence service.

1973 A. MANN *Tiara* vii. 57 Would you ask the station to let me know each day what they hear? **1975** N. LUARD *Robespierre Serial* iv. 18 A member of the Paris station, a young cypher clerk. **1978** R. CASSILIS *Winding Sheet* I. xiv. 44 He was a good man... A good Head of Station.. who hadn't forgotten his tradecraft.

14. (Earlier example.) Also *N.Z.*

1822 J. DIXON *Voyage to N.S.W.* 47 There have, however, been instances of stock-keepers, at distant stations, having been murdered. **1845** W. DEANS *Let.* 25 Nov. in J. Deans *Pioneers of Canterbury* (1937) 100 There will be no stations so far inland here as there are in Australia. **1851** E. SHORTLAND *Southern Districts N.Z.* xiii. 245 We arrived early in the afternoon at the native station near Lake Wairewa. **1930** [see *HOMESTEAD *sb.* 2 b]. **1950** *N.Z. Jrnl. Agric.* May 463/1 Years previously, when the present farm was part of a large station.

V. 28. (sense *11 c, 13 b) *station commander*; (sense *13 f) *station director, manager, operation*; (sense *13 h) *station chief*; (sense 14) *station holder, horse, man, manager, owner*; (sense 20) *station announcer, buffet, manager, platform* (earlier example).

1964 'J. H. ROBERTS' *'Q' Document* (1965) ii. 54 The blaring voice of the station announcer calling the trains. **1939** N. COWARD *To step Aside* 61, I had some tea with her in the station buffet at Dieppe. **1941** J. D. CARR *Case of Constant Suicides* i. 15 Drinking slopped tea..in a steamy station-buffet. **1978** D. KYLE *Black Camelot* viii. 119 He went into the station buffet and bought a cup of tea and a Banbury cake. **1974** W. GARNER *Big Enough Wreath* iv. 41, I have a station chief in London. **1943** C. H. WARD-JACKSON *It's a Piece of Cake* 8 We've a new Station Commander who is keen on physical training, and life is one long parade from six in the morning till ten at night. **1972** *Police Rev.* 1 Dec. 1569/2 Why should not the station commander himself take action? **1978** R. V. JONES *Most Secret War* xliv. 419 The Station Commander told Hartley that he had been watching all three squadrons. **1923** J. REITH *Diary* 25 Oct. (1975) ii. 132 Very busy on new regulations for SB... I am leaving it more to the station directors. **1878** E. S. ELWELL *Boy Colonists* 27 When the men..wanted any of these articles for *personal use*..the station-holder sold them to them. **1911** C. E. W. BEAN *'Dreadnought' of Darling* vii. 75 Leagues away even from the homestead cows or the station horses. **1966** 'J. HACKSTON' *Father clears Out* 14 No station horse of any standing would have approved of our little farm. *Ibid.* 174 Fearfully I looked round as if at that moment one of the station men would come riding up and find me with the dead sheep. **1911** C. E. W. BEAN *'Dreadnought' of Darling* xvii. 167 One station manager told us that he had found scores of them [*sc.* rabbits.] dead around their burrows. **1962** *B.B.C. Handbk.* 30 The station managers must aim to build a partnership between the broadcaster and the community. **1965** *Guardian* 11 Feb. 16/4 Stationmasters in the London-Midland region of British Rail..would be replaced by station managers, who would have wider powers. **1977** D. L. ALTHEIDE in Douglas & Johnson *Existential Sociol.* iv. 142 Secondly, there is the relation of the news to the overall station operation, including sales, production, and programming. **1911** E. M. CLOWES *On Wallaby* iii. 69 A station-owner's life, even in these days, is not all beer and skittles. **1968** K. WEATHERLY *Roo Shooter* 42 Three weeks later it rained... The station owners smiled. **1886** KIPLING *Plain Tales from Hills* (1888) 117 Nobody ever dreamed of seeing him handcuffed on a station platform.

29. station agent, (*a*) chiefly *U.S.*, a person in charge of a stage-coach or railway station; (*b*) a person working for an intelligence service; **station break** *U.S.*, a break (*BREAK *sb.*[1] 8 k) between radio or television items or programmes, during which the station identifies or advertises itself; **station hand:** also *N.Z.*; **station head,** the chief of an intelligence service headquarters; **station-keeping:** also *transf.* and as *ppl. a.*; **stationman,** a person employed on the (underground) railways, as a platform attendant, porter, etc.

1857 *Trans. Illinois Agric. Soc.* II. 25 The active co-operation of this company, through its station agents. ..in bringing forward an interesting show. **1879** E. J. SIMMONS *Mem. Station Master* (1974) ix. 131 The Long and Narrow Railway paid their station-agent better than the Great Smash Company. **1910** J. HART *Vigilante Girl* xv. 203 He stopped at the stage station... When the station agent looked to see what the man had written [etc.]. **1948** *Westerners Brand Bk.* (Denver Posse) 21 Louis J. F. Jaeger..was the Butterfield station agent at Fort Yuma. **1974** J. GRADY *Six Days of Condor* 109 Who do you suppose was station agent out of Taiwan? **1949** *Consumer Rep.* May 236/2 A 'station-break' can..be inserted between the close of one commercial program and the opening of the next. **1971** D. E. WESTLAKE *I gave at Office* (1972) 133 I've been in this business long enough to know a lead-in for a station break when I see one, and that finish was a natural, so I took a station break. **1930** L. G. D. ACLAND *Early Canterbury Runs* 1st Ser. i. 8 When an old fashioned squatter or station hand used the word 'homestead' he used it to signify the owner's residence. **1974** J. GRADY *Six Days of Condor* 108 He worked his way..from special field agent to station head. **1962**

Punch 18 Apr. 597/3 A British scheme 'envisages'.. 'twelve station-keeping active-relay satellites'. **1971** *Daily Tel.* 14 Sept. 2/6 The 'station-keeping' device would be useful in fog..to indicate the correct distance behind the vehicle in front. **1952** *Britannica Bk. of Year* 667/1 *Stationman*,..a platform attendant of the London Transport (Underground) railways. **1963** *Times* 24 May (London Underground Centenary Suppl.) p. vii/4 Passengers refused to leave trains at the haughty ordering of stationmen who refused to give any explanation of why the journey could not continue. **1968** *Daily Tel.* (Colour Suppl.) 13 Dec. 14/1 The wild adventures of train controllers and station men, or signalmen and porters as they used to be called in the dull old days. **1974** P. Wright *Lang. Brit. Industry* i. 19 Notice that on the London tubes, the 'degrading' rank of *porter* has been engulfed in *stationman*.

stationarity. Add: More widely, the state of being stationary or unvarying; stationariness; constancy.

1955 M. Loève *Probability Theory* ix. 418 In the integral stationarity case, the basic ergodic inequality takes very simple forms. **1972** *Nature* 8 Dec. 338/1 Hot spots have been hypothetically identified as mantle plumes and their stationarity with respect to the Earth's spin axis demonstrated. **1973** *Sci. Amer.* July 8/2 The demographic behavior of these nations is pointing in the direction of a rough equilibrium of deaths and births, that is, stationarity. **1973** *Animal Behaviour* XXI. 181/1 The assumption of stationarity of the processes in equation (7) seems justified if one bears in mind that the animals observed lived under constant conditions.

stationary, *a.* Add: **1. d.** *stationary bicycle, bike* (N. Amer.), a fixed machine, resembling a bicycle, used in fitness exercises.

1962 E. Lucia *Klondike Kate* ii. 53 And pedalled for hours on the stationary bicycle to keep her figure. **1969** *Sears Catal.* Spring/Summer 400/2 Stationary Bike... Pedal for miles without leaving the comfort of your own home. Chain-driven pedal action gives you the same exercise as regular bicycle. **1976** *Woman's Day* (U.S.) Nov. 154/2 If you don't want to be on public display, try a stationary bicycle or running in place in your bedroom.

e. Physics. *stationary wave* = *standing wave* s.v. *standing *ppl. a.* 11 e.

1856 D. Lardner *Hand-bk. Nat. Philos.* IV. iv. i. 350 (*heading*) Stationary waves. **1867** J. Tyndall *Sound* 101 The step of a water-carrier is sometimes so timed as to throw the surface of the water in his vessel into stationary waves, which may augment in height until the water splashes over the brim. **1905** *Brit. Pat. 8200* In consequence of the interference of the impressed and reflected oscillations, the phenomenon of 'stationary waves' ..is produced. **1962** Walshaw & Jobson *Mechanics of Fluids* xii. 387 By passing light through the divergent part of a supersonic nozzle, the existence of stationary waves inclined to the stream at the appropriate Mach angle may be confirmed on a shadowgraph.

f. Of an artificial satellite: geostationary.

1970 *Gloss. Aeronaut. & Astronaut. Terms* (*B.S.I.*) xviii. 3 *Stationary satellite*, a synchronous satellite in a circular, equatorial orbit, moving in the direction of rotation of the primary body. **1979** *Sci. Amer.* Feb. 58/1 Data on the expanses not accounted for by the World Weather Watch are provided by five geosynchronous ('stationary') weather satellites, [etc.].

2. b. *stationary state* (Physics), a steady state; *spec.* any of the stable orbits of the electrons in the Bohr model of the atom.

1900 *Rep. Brit. Assoc. Adv. Sci.* 634 If we are given the probability that the coordinates of the system may be between given limits, then a condition for the stationary state is that the mean values of the accelerations of $\frac{1}{2}mv^2$, $\frac{1}{2}nw^2$, $\frac{1}{2}mw^2$ are zero. **1913** N. Bohr in *Phil. Mag.* XXVI. 7 The dynamical equilibrium of the systems in the stationary states can be discussed by help of the ordinary mechanics, while the passing of the systems between different stationary states cannot be treated on that basis. **1932** *Jrnl. Chem. Soc.* 359 Each spectral term, multiplied by Planck's constant, may be taken to represent, for the corresponding stationary state of the atom, the work necessary to remove the electron to an infinite distance from the proton. **1974** G. Reece tr. *Hund's Hist. Quantum Theory* v. 67 Bohr now sums up his results as follows: in the 'stationary states' classical mechanics is used. **1977** I. M. Campbell *Energy & Atmosphere* iv. 65 Under normal conditions, E:C* will be the type of reactive intermediate to which the Stationary State Approximation can be applied, i.e. $d[E{:}C^*]/dt = 0$.

c. *Math.* That is not instantaneously changing; associated with a derivative whose value is zero.

1901 G. A. Gibson *Elem. Treat. Calculus* vi. 105 Since $f'(x)$ measures the rate of change of the function it is usual to class those values of the function for which $f'(x)$ is zero as stationary values. **1902** Snyder & Hutchinson *Differential & Integral Calculus* xiii. 153 A point at which the direction of bending changes from positive to negative, or *vice versa*..is called a point of inflexion, and the tangent at such a point is called a stationary tangent. **1954** H. R. Cooley *First Course Calculus* v. 89 Points at which the derivative is equal to 0 are sometimes called stationary points. They are points at which, if a particle were progressing along a curve from left to right, its vertical motion would be momentarily stopped. **1978** K. Ahmad *Trad. & Mod. Math.* 83 A stationary point is a point at which $dy/dx = 0$. Maxima, minima and points of inflection are stationary points.

d. *Statistics.* Applied to a series of observations that has attained equilibrium, so that the expected value of any function of a section of it is independent of the time for which it has been running.

1938 H. Wold *Stud. in Analysis of Stationary Time Series* 1 Observational series which describe phenomena changing with time may be roughly classified in two broad categories, viz. evolutive and stationary. *Ibid.*, Stationary time series are unchanging in respect to their general structure. The fluctuations up and down in such a series may seem random or show tendencies to regularity—in any case, the character of the series is, on the whole, the same in different sections. **1968** P. A. P. Moran *Introd. Probability Theory* iii. 151 A set of numbers, p_i, $i = 6, 1, \ldots$, such that $p_i \geq 0$, $\sum_i p_i = 1$, $p_i = \sum_j p_{ij} p_j$, will be called a 'stationary distribution' of the process. **1975** *Nature* 11 Dec. 490/1 Two assumptions are commonly made about earthquakes: first, that their occurrence has a stationary random Poisson distribution.

station-house. Add: **2.** Also *U.S.*, the police-station itself.

1870 *Galaxy* Feb. 272 An headquarters of police..is called in New York a station-house, though in many other places this word is more correctly used to indicate a stopping house on railroads. **1931** H. F. Pringle *Theodore Roosevelt* i. xi. 138 He arrived..at a station house in the lower part of the city, and interrupted the meditations of the sergeant. **1963** *Listener* 4 Apr. 585/1, I began my police career in June, 1951. After three months' training I was assigned to the W.54th Street station house. **1979** *Honolulu Advertiser* 8 Jan. D-1/4 2,000 Hasidic Jews stormed a Brooklyn police station-house.

5. Also *N.Z.*

1888 A. McKay in *Bull. N.Z. Geol. Survey* No. 1. 4 The station-house was so far wrecked. **1933** L. G. D. Acland in *Press* (Christchurch) 4 Nov. 15/7 *Men's hut*, house where the station hands live. On some stations it is called the *station house*.

stationnaire (stēiʃənēə·ɹ). *Obs.* exc. *Hist.* [Fr.] A naval guard-ship, stationed at a foreign port for the use of an ambassador.

1895 *F.O. 64/1351* (Public Record Office) No. 284 He feared the arrival of the second stationnaires would inevitably excite ill-feeling amongst the Mahomedans. **1914** R. Rankin *Inner Hist. Balkan War* xii. 364 As yet no warships were at hand except the weakly-armed 'stationnaires' or European guard-ships which at all times lie in the Bosphorus for the use of the Ambassadors. **1922** *Glasgow Herald* 21 Dec. 9/3 As regards the Foreign Embassy stationnaires, Lord Curzon said that he had never thought they could be detrimental to Turkey's sovreignty. **1958** M. Buchanan *Ambassador's Daughter* vi. 68 Ambassadors accredited to the Sublime Porte before the Turkish Revolution..were given a summer residence on the shores of the Bosphorus,..with an armed sloop or *stationnaire* always anchored in the vicinity in case of a rising of the Turks.

station-wagon. Also **station wagon, (-)waggon.** † **1.** *U.S.* **a.** A type of horse-drawn covered carriage, used for conveying passengers. *Obs.*

1894 *Hub News* 23 May 77/1 Business has been fairly good this spring... Traps are in most demand, next come buggies, cutunders, and business rockaways or station wagons. **1901** *Varnish* 15 July 253/1 Then we would all know the difference between a cabriolet and an extension-top phaeton; a station wagon and a rockaway.

b. A similar type of motorized carriage.

1904 *Motor World* 21 Jan. 680/2 The station wagon is a new model exhibited the first time this year. **1904** *Sci. Amer.* 30 Jan. 99/1 Manufacturers of Electric Broughams, Landaus,..Station Wagons, Surreys.

2. orig. *U.S.* An estate car; a saloon motor car with a rear door or doors, and capable of carrying goods as well as passengers.

1929 *N.Y. Times* 6 Jan. xi. 1/5 The Ford Motor Company is having its own exhibition... The three new models added to the line are on display there. These are the town sedan, the convertible cabriolet, and the station wagon. **1930** *Amer. Speech* V. 276 The other commercial bodies have usually retained old names—*delivery wagon, station wagon*. **1942** *E. African Ann. 1941–2* 11/1 *Safari* cars..have box-bodies, of the station-wagon model. **1949** F. Maclean *Eastern Approaches* ii. iii. 200 This was a new cut-down Ford station waggon, with room in it for six people and a certain amount of kit. **1951** 'J. Wyndham' *Day of Triffids* v. 88 We kept on foot for a while, looking out for a suitable car. After a mile or so we found it—a station-waggon. **1969** *Sydney Morning Herald* 24 May 55/4 (Advt.), Datsun station waggon. **1976** *Encounter* June 9/2 They advanced, the distinguished party,..down the steps, into Halpert's Dodge station wagon, where, along with two sacks of lawn fertiliser, they fitted comfortably.

statism. Restrict *rare* to senses in Dict. and add: **3. b.** = *étatisme.

1919 *Sociol. Rev.* XI. 62 Traditional phrases such as 'The Appeal to Democracy', 'Freedom for Little Nations', etc.,..have been used so often, with so poor a result during the past century, in which all the time 'individualism' and 'statism' have been struggling together for supremacy and power under their cover. **1940** *Sun* (Baltimore) 5 Nov. 5/7 Republican Senator Charles L. McNary concluded his Vice-Presidential campaign tonight with the charge the New Deal is 'taking deeper and deeper refuge in paternalism and statism'. **1945** A. Huxley *Let.* 8 Aug. (1969) 531 Men and women..brought up under Statism..have been taught to believe that the State is more important than the individual. **1962** *Times Lit. Suppl.* 23 Nov. 919/1 Anarchic egocentricity thus tugs against a Mum-providing statism. This has caused schizophrenia in British Labour. **1970** *Daily Tel.* 1 Dec. 9/4 In South America today..various forms of Marxist-inspired Statism are establishing themselves. **1979** *Time* 2 Apr. 52/2 The shortfall itself is rooted in policies that have led to too much statism and not enough private initiative.

statist, *sb.*[1] Add: **3.** (With capital initial.) A member of a conservative Belgian nationalist party which sought to maintain the power of the provincial assemblies or States in the late eighteenth century.

1909 *Cambr. Mod. Hist.* VI. xviii. 653 Only a short time was, however, to elapse before they [*sc.* States General] split asunder into two irreconcilable parties—the Statists of van der Noot..and the Democrats of Vonck. **1921** E. Cammaerts *Belgium* 11 'Statists' and 'Vonckists'. **1966** V. R. Lorwin in R. A. Dahl *Pol. Oppositions in Western Democracies* v. 149 The Statists, or Van der Nootists, opposed the reforms of Joseph II; they sought to maintain the customs and privileges of the established Catholic Church and the narrowly based oligarchy of landowners, masters of urban crafts, and nobles who dominated the sclerosed provincial assemblies or Estates. **1974** *Encycl. Brit. Macropædia* XI. 157/1 Van Der Noot made a triumphant entry into Brussels, where he and his 'Statists' were supported by the Estates of Brabant.

4. A supporter of statism.

1976 *National Observer* (U.S.) 24 Apr. 17/2 So much for rent control, just one of many well-meant disasters visited upon us by the statists. **1979** *N.Y. Rev. Bks.* 25 Oct. 49/1 McCagg sees Stalin as a 'statist', more interested, that is, in building the Soviet state than in the Communist Party.

statist (stēi·tist), *a.* [f. Statism: see -ist.] Of, pertaining to, advocating, or based on statism.

1960 *New Statesman* 9 Jan. 26/2 Tory propagandists and Labour re-thinkers share in the admiration of the new 'statist' economic system we have in Britain. **1960** *New Left Rev.* May–June 6/2 Communist and Labour fundamentalists of the 'statist' variety. **1973** *Advocate-News* (Barbados) 8 May 3/2 In other systems, the co-operatives has been the peripheral to the main sector, whether capitalist or statist. **1976** K. Joseph *Monetarism is not Enough* 17 But the whole economy is not private. Nearly two-thirds is statist, and insensitive in itself to contraction of the money supply. **1977** *N.Y. Rev. Bks.* 27 Oct. 26/3 They include not only members of the intelligentsia but also working people who have experienced statist authoritarianism, rigidity, narrowness, and felt impelled to speak up, however discreetly. **1979** *New Society* 9 Aug. 295/2 The commitment to democracy was real in the later Marcuse—including a commitment to defend existing democratic liberties against statist and fascist incursions.

statistic, *sb.* **1. b.** Delete ¶ and substitute for entry: A quantitative fact or statement. (Examples.)

1880 'Mark Twain' *Tramp Abroad* xvi. 148 There is not a statistic wanting. It is as succinct as an invoice. This is what a translation ought to be. **1928** H. Belloc *Hist. England* III. iii. 244 Before the siege-piece had been developed as a fairly reliable arm, a city or a castle wall was attacked in one of five ways... There was direct attack... There was a starving out of the garrison... Probably, if a statistic could be made, the latter would be found the most commonly successful method of the true Middle Ages. **1934** *Punch* 14 Mar. 292/2 Few citizens realise that there *is* any river traffic other than the boat race. Let me give them a statistic:—At least 3,000 craft of all sizes pass under Waterloo Bridge every week. **1949** E. Hyams *Not in our Stars* xvi. 198 Although the first dead was a horror and a tragedy, the ten thousandth was a statistic. **1973** *Times* 24 Apr. 12/2 The statistic of 22·2 unemployed to every notified vacancy in Scotland. **1975** *Nature* 11 Sept. 81/1 A more pertinent statistic is that about 98% of all trips taken with second family cars, lie within the 50-mile range of present battery technology.

c. *Statistics.* Any of the numerical characteristics of a sample (as opposed to one of the population from which it is drawn). Cf. *parameter 2 f.

1922, etc. [see *parameter 2 f]. **1925** R. A. Fisher *Statistical Methods for Research Workers* iii. 43 The utility of any particular statistic, and the nature of its distribution, both depend on the original distribution. **1976** *Biometrika* LXIII. 438 The sample sizes are enormous, the smallest being 23517, so that under the null hypothesis this statistic should be distributed as a χ^2 variate with $x_0 - 3$ degrees of freedom.

statistical, *a.* Add: **2. c.** *statistical significance* = *significance 3.

1938 *Jrnl. Parapsychol.* II. 210 The primary requirement of statistical significance is met by the results of this investigation. **1971** *Jrnl. Gen. Psychol.* LXXXV. 68 None of the..interactions reached statistical significance. **1974** *Jrnl. Dental Res.* LIII. 763/2 Whether to use the standard test for statistical significance or the Bechhofer test depends on the problem that is studied.

d. Of a branch of science, or a physical process or condition: not absolutely precise but dependent on the probable outcome of a large number of small events, and so predictable; *statistical mechanics*, the description of physical phenomena in terms of a statistical treatment of the behaviour of large numbers of atoms, molecules, etc., esp. as regards the distribution of energy among them; hence *statistical-mechanical* adj.

1885 J. W. Gibbs in *Proc. Amer. Assoc. Adv. Sci.* XXXIII. 57 (*heading*) On the fundamental formula of statistical mechanics, with applications to astronomy and thermodynamics. **1900** *Rep. Brit. Assoc. Adv. Sci.* 617

The statistical dynamics of the distribution of the molecules. **1902** J. W. GIBBS (*title*) Elementary principles in statistical mechanics. **1917** *Proc. K. Akad. van Wetensch. te Amsterdam* XIX. 578 The statistical mechanical explanation Boltzmann gave of it [*sc.* the second law of thermodynamics] rests on statistical foundations which are destroyed by the introduction of the quanta. **1927** [see *FERMI-DIRAC]. **1945** H. D. SMYTH *Gen. Acct. Devel. Atomic Energy Mil. Purposes* ix. 102 Such effects are used in six 'statistical' separation methods: (1) gaseous diffusion (2) distillation... In all these 'statistical' methods the separation factor is small so that many stages are required. **1955** H. B. G. CASIMIR in W. Pauli *Niels Bohr* 132 As long as this phenomenon [*sc.* superconductivity] is not understood an essential element is lacking in our comprehension of statistical mechanics and of the nature of the solid state. **1955** FRIEDMAN & WEISSKOPF in *Ibid.* 138 The statistical method of determining the yield of nuclear reactions gives a reasonable account of their most important features. **1956** E. H. HUTTEN *Lang. Mod. Physics* iv. 149 This H-function may be taken as the statistical-mechanical analogue of entropy, since it exhibits a one-sided change in time. **1962** J. RIORDAN *Stochastic Service Systems* iii. 28 The system is said to be in statistical equilibrium... It is not without changes, for probabilities are still in question, but the probabilistic description of its behavior in time is invariant with time. **1964** J. D. BERNAL in *Proc. R. Soc.* A. CCLXXX. 302, I found..that we did not know much about heaps and that to understand heaps we had to open a new subject, that of statistical geometry. *Ibid.* 307 It would be very well worth while to examine the purely geometrical properties of random close-packed aggregates without holes, particularly in relation to kinds of lines that can be drawn through neighbouring points. This should be one of the first tasks of the proposed statistical geometry. **1971** *Nature* 13 Aug. 450/1, I believe that the most widespread opinion is that quantum mechanics can be 'grafted' onto the classical statistical mechanics of Boltzmann and Gibbs and that therefore quantum mechanics does not require anything essentially new. **1974** G. REECE tr. *Hund's Hist. Quantum Theory* i. 14 The great achievement of statistical physics was that of deriving thermodynamics from mechanical principles. *Ibid.* iii. 46 In the years 1902–7 Einstein completed a basis for statistical thermodynamics.

statistically, *adv.* Add: *statistically significant*: see *SIGNIFICANT *a.* 5.

statisticize, *v.* Add: Also *intr.*, to collect or employ statistics. Hence **stati·sticizing** *vbl. sb.*

1927 *Sunday Express* 17 July 11 Miss Inderrieden has reduced desertions to a percentage basis. She says that the wife is to blame in fifty percent. of desertions... This is a dreadful specimen of statisticising. It means absolutely nothing. **1971** *Nature* 30 Apr. 602/3 The objective ..is not to help budding statisticians to statisticize but to help experimental scientists to experiment properly.

statistics. Add: **1. a.** (Earlier example.)

1770 W. HOOPER tr. *Bielfeld's Elem. Universal Educ.* III. xiii. 269 The science, that is called statistics, teaches us what is the political arrangement of all the modern states of the known world.

2. a*. = *vital statistics* s.v. *VITAL *a.* Also *transf. colloq.*

1958 *Times* 24 Feb. 11/3 It is a pretty thought to contemplate all those statistics hipping and swaying and shimmering. *Ibid.* 13 Nov. 9/4 To-day, except for the slightly high waist-lines and one or two modified trapezes, feminine statistics were where nature intended them to be. **1960** *Punch* 3 Aug. 148/2 An enticing girl with yellow hair and sound statistics. **1978** O. WHITE *Silent Reach* vi. 61 Next time you get into position, try squeezing her statistics.

3. *Physics.* The statistical description appropriate to the behaviour and properties of an ensemble of many atoms, molecules, etc., esp. as regards the distribution of energy among them; *spec.* = *quantum statistics* s.v. *QUANTUM 7 a.

[**1873** J. C. MAXWELL in *Nature* 25 Sept. 440/1 The modern atomists have therefore adopted a method which is I believe new in the department of mathematical physics, though it has long been in use in the Section of Statistics.] **1900** *Phil. Mag.* XLIX. 114 In the case of a gas, of which the statistics are assumed to be regular, the potential energy remains approximately constant. **1903** [in Dict., sense 2 a]. **1909** *Proc. R. Soc.* A. LXXXIII. 86 The general thesis of which a development is here attempted is thus the molecular statistics of distributions of energy. **1927** [see *FERMI]. **1928** [see *BOSE-EINSTEIN]. **1950** W. J. MOORE *Physical Chem.* xii. 356 In deriving the Boltzmann statistics, we assumed that the individual particles were distinguishable and that any number of particles could be assigned to one energy level. **1979** *Sci. Amer.* Feb. 89/1 Two fundamental categories of particles, the fermions and the bosons. These categories are distinguished by the intrinsic angular momentum, or spin, of the particles, and by their statistics, or behavior in groups.

stative, *a.* and *sb.* Add: **A.** *adj.* **3.** Now also applied to languages other than Hebrew, to sentences, and to words other than verbs.

1930 F. R. BLAKE in J. T. Hatfield et al. *Curme Vol. Linguistic Stud.* 38 All temporal and locative relations have theoretically three aspects, a stative indicating existence or rest at a time or place (time when, place where), an ablative indicating continuance or motion from a time or place.., and a terminal indicating continuance or motion to a time or place. **1939** L. H. GRAY *Foundations of Lang.* vii. 202 The stative verb expresses 'the state of being in a certain condition'. **1964** *Language* XL. 78 Stative verbs occur with the nasal simulfix and typically with stative prefixes. **1967** FENN & TEWKSBURY *Speak Mandarin* 3 The stative sentence consists of a subject and a stative verb. **1970** *Language* XLVI. 830 English adjectives, much like English verbs, seem to divide into *stative* and *active* ones. **1979** *Trans. Philol. Soc.* 230 A fundamental distinction exists in Abkhaz between stative and non-stative (or dynamic) verbs.

B. *sb.* Now also applied to languages other than Hebrew, and to words other than verbs.

1966 J. E. BUSE in C. E. Bazell *In Memory of J. R. Firth* 54 These constraints may be used to divide full-words into the four sub-classes of verb, stative, noun and negative. **1973** *Canad. Jrnl. Linguistics* XVIII. 103 In order to explain the possessive function of statives and the limitations of this function in Sechelt, it is necessary to consider a cross-section of occurrences of this verbal aspect and to define its semantic range.

stato-. Add: **sta:to-acou·stic** *a. Anat.*, pertaining to the senses or faculties of both equilibration and hearing; *spec.* the epithet of the eighth cranial nerve (the vestibulo-cochlear nerve); **sta·tocone** [Gr. κονία dust], each of the large number of granules in the statocyst of some animals, similar to a statolith, but smaller; also, an otolith in a vertebrate; also **statoco·nia** *sb. pl.*; **statolith** (later examples); also, an otolith in a vertebrate.

1958 *Gray's Anat.* (ed. 32) 144 The ganglia of the vagus, glossopharyngeal, stato-acoustic (in part), facial and trigeminal nerves are derived from the ganglion-crest, but they migrate ventrally and soon come to lie on the ventrilateral aspect of the hind-brain. **1964** J. Z. YOUNG *Model of Brain* vii. 122 There is thus the possibility of correct interaction of visual and stato-acoustic information, these being the two chief systems that project to the mid-brain roof. **1974** D. & M. WEBSTER *Compar. Vertebr. Morphol.* xi. 255 (*caption*) Cross section through a mammalian upper myelencephalon, just behind the cerebellum, showing the relationships of the abducens, facial, and statoacoustic cranial nerves. **1910** PARKER & HASWELL *Text-bk. Zool.* I. XII. 707 Each statocyst [in molluscs] may contain a number of minute statocones or, more usually, a single, larger statolith. **1963** *Biol. Bull.* CXXV. 441 In the labyrinth of teleosts there are generally three large statoliths... Most other vertebrates, however, have otolith masses consisting of a very great number of small statoconia held more or less firmly together by an organic gel. **1979** *Nature* 30 Aug. 832/1 Inner ear sensory surfaces from the Pacific herring..were prepared... After removal of the statoconia (otoliths) the tissues were dehydrated. **1980** *Gray's Anat.* (ed. 36) 1205/1 The gelatinous mass into which the cilia project is flatter and is termed an otolithic membrane.., because it contains numerous minute crystalline bodies called otoliths, otoconia, or statoconia. **1955** *Sci. News* XXXVI. 92 Even plants which have no statoliths respond to gravitational stimuli. **1962** D. NICHOLS *Echinoderms* vi. 83 These are tiny fluid-filled spheres containing calcareous statoliths, the differential movement of which is registered in special nerves. **1969** *Nature* 28 June 1229/1 Starch statoliths are mobile starch grains found in almost all plant organs that respond to gravity. **1975** *Ibid.* 2 Oct. 380/2 Statoliths of at least one species of cephalopod are composed of aragonite, a stable form of calcium carbonate.

statolon (stæ·tǒlǫn). *Biochem.* Also *erron.* **statalon.** [Prob. a blend of mod.L. *stoloniferum* (see below and STOLONIFEROUS *a.*) and *-STATIC.] A complex polysaccharide obtained from the mould *Penicillium stoloniferum,* now known to contain a fungal virus which is an antiviral agent, stimulating the release of interferon.

1961 PROBST & KLEINSCHMIDT in *Federation Proc.* XX. 441/2 A fermentation broth of *Pen. stoloniferium* [sic] prophylactically inhibits a number of viruses both in animals and in tissue culture... The active principle, designated as statolon, has been subjected to a variety of purification procedures. **1964** *Proc. Nat. Acad. Sci.* LII. 741 Statolon is a complex anionic polysaccharide with a relatively high content of galacturonic acid. **1967** *New Scientist* 10 Aug. 300/2 W. J. Kleinschmidt and L. F. Ellis have now refined the technique of fractionating statalon, and have discovered, to their surprise, that one of the active fractions contained numerous virus-like hexagonal particles... They have confirmed that..it is these particles that are responsible for stimulating interferon activity in mice. **1971** *Sci. Amer.* July 28/2 Eli Lilly and Company demonstrated the presence of a fungal virus in statalon, an extract of another penicillium species. **1976** P. COLLARD *Devel. Microbiol.* v. 64 There are a number of compounds that either stimulate the production of interferon in the host cells, as does Statolon, originally believed to be a fungal product but now shown to be a virus, or release interferon which is already pre-formed in the cells. **1978** *Nature* 29 June 760/1 Tilorone, statolon and Newcastle disease virus (NDV), all potent inducers of interferon in mice, induced a marked increase in spleen cell cytotoxicity.

stator[2]. Add: **1.** (Earlier example.)

1895 S. P. THOMPSON *Polyphase Electr. Currents* v. 113 In describing the parts of polyphase motors..[we] shall call the rotating part the rotor, and the stationary part the stator.

2. More widely, an immovable part of any turbine; *spec.* a stator blade (see sense 3 below), or a row of such blades.

1916 J. W. M. SOTHERN *Marine Steam Turbine* (ed. 4) VIII. 424 The turbine consists of two principal parts, the rotor or moving part, and the cylinder (sometimes called the 'stator') or stationary part. **1951** COHEN & ROGERS *Gas Turbine Theory* vi. 133 Each stage will consist of one rotating row followed by a stator but it is usual to provide an additional stator row at entry to guide the air correctly into the first rotor. **1962** F. I. ORDWAY et al. *Basic Astronautics* x. 404 The rotor turns within the stator, which is a series of blades arranged in a circle around the inside wall of the compressor housing. **1967** N. E. BORDEN *Jet-Engine Fundamentals* 80 The first four stages of the high-pressure compressor are provided with variable stators, automatically positioned by hydraulic actuators. **1971** P. J. MCMAHON *Aircraft Propulsion* iv. 124 Figure 4.2 shows a view in the radial direction of the blading of a compressor stage—rotor plus stator—with the stators of the previous stage included for completeness.

3. *attrib.* and *Comb.*, as *stator coil, winding*; **stator blade**, a small stationary aerofoil fixed to the casing of an axial-flow turbine, rows of which are positioned between the rows of rotor blades.

1946 G. G. SMITH *Gas Turbine & Jet Propulsion* (ed. 4) iv. 58 Stator blades to direct the air flow between stages will also be of either steel or light alloy. **1977** J. L. KERREBROCK *Aircraft Engines & Gas Turbines* v. 120 There are normally three types of blade row in an axial compressor: the inlet guide vanes, the rotor blades, and the stator blades. **1904** W. R. BOWKER *Dynamo, Motor & Switchboard Circuits* 102 The 'stator' coils are arranged in a six-pole grouping. **1895** S. P. THOMPSON *Polyphase Electr. Currents* v. 113 The stator winding is usually the primary, the rotor winding secondary.

stats (stæts). Colloq. abbrev. of STATISTICS.

1. (With capital initial.) A department responsible for collecting or recording numerical facts or data.

1942 N. BALCHIN *Darkness falls from Air* vi. 102 Why not give Stats. a new man and leave Giles where he is? **1953** D. PARRY *Going up—going Down* iv. 130 He visited the Stats. Branch. **1966** M. WOODHOUSE *Tree Frog* i. 2 Do you know what we pay those girls in Stats?

2. = STATISTICS 2 a.

1962 L. DEIGHTON *Ipcress File* x. 64, I am not a statistician... I was getting pretty fed up with his house-breaking stats. **1974** Cleveland (Ohio) *Plain Dealer* 26 Oct. 4-D/1 The positon statistics have been impressive even though individual stats for many have not shocked anyone. **1975** *New Yorker* 14 Apr. 90/1 Drove to Fort Lauderdale.., found the ballpark, parked, climbed to the press box, said hello, picked up stats and a scorecard, took the last empty seat, filled out my card. **1981** J. WAINWRIGHT *Tainted Man* 169 The bumpf... This never-ending paper crap. Stolen cars, crime stats.

3. = STATISTICS 1 a.

1970 *Guardian* 15 Jan. 13/3, I..went on to stress the importance of what..I have decided to dub stats education... It's..vital that people should know more about statistics.

statue, *sb.* Add: **1. c.** *pl.* The name of various children's games which involve the players standing still in different postures.

1906 *Dialect Notes* III. 158 *Statues, n.*, the name of a game in which children pose. **1916** N. DOUGLAS *London Street Games* 41 Catch-in-the-Rope is also for boys and girls, and so is..Statues... When you play this game you have to line yourselves up against a wall or a house; then the judge comes along and pulls one of you forwards and in that moment you have to make a posture and a face.. and pretend to be a statue. **1935** E. FARJEON *Nursery in Nineties* v. 240 She quickly suggests a game, Magical Music, or Forfeits, or Statues. She..thumps the only tune to which Statues can be played. **1950** B. PYM *Some Tame Gazelle* xxi. 236 When they realized that a prayer was being said, they stood stiffly with the urn, like children playing a game of 'statues'. **1981** L. DEIGHTON *XPD* xliv. 356 'You're moving,' called Stein loudly. It was a good-natured complaint of the sort that children might use when playing the game of 'statues'.

2. *statues game.*

1975 'D. JORDAN' *Black Account* II. xxxv. 175 Guy stood by the door like a child playing the statues game.

statued, *ppl. a.* Add: **2.** (Earlier example.)

1731 L. THEOBALD *Orestes* IV. iii. 57 The Statued Goddess born in solemn Pomp, Guarded, as 'twere the Spoils of hostile Bands?

status. Add: Now usu. with pl. **statuses** (stē̆ⁱ·tǒsėz). **1. b.** *status asthmaticus,* the condition of a patient during a prolonged severe asthmatic attack; also *ellipt.*, = status epilepticus.

1947 DORLAND & MILLER *Med. Dict.* (ed. 21) 1392/1 Status asthmaticus. **1962** J. H. BURN *Drugs, Med. & Man* xviii. 179 Sometimes the attacks (asthma) follow one another so steadily that the patient's life is in danger. He is then said to be in 'status asthmaticus' and in the past patients have often died. **1971** *Where* Dec. 360/1 There was no sign of epilepsy until she was two and a half, when she went into status (a condition where the fits follow one another without pause).

3. a. (Examples of pl. use.) Also *social status.*

1852 MILL *Pol. Econ.* (ed. 3) II. IV. vii. 331 As to civil and social *status*, in framing a new reform bill..the opportunity was not taken. **1873** [in Dict.]. **1901** G. B. SHAW *Socialism for Millionaires* in *Fabian Tract* No. 107. 15 A millionaire does not really care whether his money does good or not, provided he finds his conscience eased and his social status improved by giving it away. **1936** R. LINTON *Study of Man* viii. 114 There are no rôles without statuses or statuses without rôles. **1946** D. L. SAYERS *Unpopular Opinions* 120 The commercial middle classes acquired the plutocratic and aristocratic notion that the keeping of an idle woman was a badge of superior social status. **1955** T. H. PEAR *English Social Differences* i. 25 Each individual..can have many statuses. **1960** D. POTTER *Glittering Coffin* iv. 54 The links between job and social status..are too often taken for granted. **1970** C. T. RESTREPO in I. L. Horowitz *Masses in Lat. Amer.* xiv. 517 Cultural ascent in society refers to the acquisition of those cultural forms corresponding to a higher class or social status. **1977** R. HOLLAND *Self & Social Context* v. 89 Occupants of similar statuses may support each other against threats from members of a role-set, as when teachers support each other against parents of their students.

5. a. *attrib.* or as *adj.* That confers prestige on its possessor; having a high social status; superior.

1950 M. MEAD *Male & Female* xiii. 266 A caustic critic has labelled the one child of middle-class families as a 'status child', a child that merely gives the parents the status of *having had* a child. **1956** C. W. MILLS *Power Elite* iv. 79 As a status model the debutante declined. **1960** S. KAUFFMANN *If it be Love* I. viii. 113 A status-car, matched to your income, and a station wagon. **1961** A. SMITH *East-Enders* vii. 122 One of the status cafés on the edge of the East End, beautifully kept. **1964** A. HUNTER *Gently Sahib* iv. 33 The locals had taken him a room at the Angel Inn, the status hotel in Abbotsham. **1977** D. MORRIS *Manwatching* 125 What the rapist wants is..the total, abject subjection of his victim... This is Status Sex, and it is not by any means an exclusively human pattern of activity.

b. *Comb.*, as (sense 3) *status-conscious, -dissenting, -ridden* adjs.; **status anxiety**, anxiety about one's social status, esp. the fear of losing it; **status group(ing)**, any group of people who have similar social standing (see quot. 1978); **status-seeker**, one who is concerned with improving or demonstrating his social status; hence **status-seeking** *vbl. sb.* and *ppl. a.*; **status symbol**, a possession or asset sought or acquired as a symbol of social prestige; hence **status-symbolism**; **status system**, a social structure or organization in which status derives from one's position or achievement in some aspect of the group's activity; **status-trophy** *rare* = *status symbol* above.

1959 *Encounter* Sept. 58/1 The political conflicts of the 'fifties..were..explained by sociological concepts such as 'status anxiety'. **1971** HALSEY & TROW *Brit. Academics* xiii. 329 This may be due to the status anxiety associated with marked social mobility. **1959** V. PACKARD *Status Seekers* (1960) i. 6 Wives..tend to be more status conscious than their husbands. **1974** tr. *Wertheim's Evolution & Revolution* 234 Asian peasants are generally status conscious and..the more prosperous ones often recognize mutual social obligations only towards those whom they consider to be their peers. **1956** J. M. MOGEY *Family & Neighbourhood* viii. 140 The remainder of St. Ebbe's people we may call, by contrast, status-dissenting. **1965** *New Society* 4 Feb. 26/3 On the newer suburban housing estates..a new species has developed, the *status dissenting* working class person. **1910** Status group [in Dict., sense 2 a]. **1978** *Listener* 19 Jan. 77/3 Status groups—for example, peers of the realm or vagrants—are social networks of those who share similar social prestige. **1964** *Punch* 29 July 172/2 We hear a lot about status-groupings in the US. **1953** *Observer* 16 Aug. 7/5 Miss Thurburn can move us to admiring recognition when she deals with..the status-ridden society. **1962** *Guardian* 14 Aug. 5/3 The prestige notions of a Pakistani civil servant are almost as inflexible as those found in our own status-ridden society. **1959** V. PACKARD *Status Seekers* (1960) i. 7 The status seekers..are people who are continually straining to surround themselves with visible evidence of the superior rank they are claiming. **1979** *United States 1980/81* (Penguin Travel Guides) 214 There are no phone calls to take, except for those status-seekers foolish enough to have telephones in their cars. **1951** R. R. SEARS in Parsons & Shils *Toward General Theory of Action* 477 Secondary motivational systems..between mother and child...include aggression, dependency, self-reliance..and status-seeking. **1960** *Guardian* 23 Dec. 6/6 The status-seeking educational system. **1962** *Punch* 31 Jan. 227/3 Status-seeking, broken marriages, intrigue among research staff of Midland firm. **1962** E. SNOW *Red China Today* (1963) xl. 300 It should not be supposed that they are any less outer-directed than the status-seeking sons of Madison Avenue. **1976** J. WAINWRIGHT *Who goes Next?* 52 This over-expensive, status-seeking building. **1955** Status symbol [see *sign-vehicle* s.v. *SIGN *sb.* 12 b]. **1957** *Wall St. Jrnl.* 29 Oct. 1/1 The most common sources of interoffice rivalry over status symbols involve such obvious executive trappings as the size of the desk, the quality of drapes and carpets in private offices, [etc.]. **1965** G. MAXWELL *House of Elrig* v. 77, I was singled out as a target for jealousy by those whose parents would have liked 'a handle to their names' and whose status-symbol cars compared spectacularly with the modest and practical conveyances my mother chose. **1981** *Church Times* 23 Oct. 10/2 A fragment of the true Cross—a status symbol if ever there was one. **1957** *Wall St. Jrnl.* 29 Oct. 9/2 In their place he introduced a highly formalized system of status symbolism. **1968** *Punch* 7 Aug. 183/2 The main design criteria [*sic*] of motor-manufacture is now neither comfort nor status-symbolism, but simple safety. **1942** WARNER & LUNT *Status System Mod. Community* ii. 16 We shall hereafter refer to the eighty-nine behavioral situations (or statuses) as social positions or statuses, and the total social system of Yankee City as the positional or status system. **1978** *Listener* 12 Jan. 35/2 Our Martian would quickly conceptualise pair-bonding in what we call marriage, scientific organisations in the social relations of discovery, status systems in the relations of dominance and submission, and so on. **1964** AUDEN in *Listener* 1 Oct. 525/2 This unpopular art which cannot be..hung as a status-trophy by rising executives.

statusful (stēɪ·tǝsfŭl), *a.* [f. STATUS + -FUL.] Having or conferring (high) social status or distinction.

1969 *Daily Tel.* (Colour Suppl.) 17 Oct. 57/1 Ordering a 22-carat Dunebuggy with ocelot seats and rhinestone headlamps in a bid for statusful individuality. **1975** *Times* 22 Aug. 10/1 'Statusful speakers', like BBC newsreaders. **1977** J. A. FISHMAN in H. Glass *Lang., Ethnicity & Intergroup Relations* i. 37 It is not ethnicity *per se* that is of concern to it but the recrudescence of less statusful, narrower, 'peripheral' identities. **1978** *Amer. Speech* LIII. 14 Its use implies the user's special familiarity.. with that less statusful or less responsible class of people who have such special familiarity and use the term.

status quo. Add: (Later *attrib.* examples.) *status quo ante*: the state of affairs previously existing (also *absol.*).

1877 [in Dict.]. **1951** W. STEVENS *Let.* 9 Mar. (1967) 709 Everything is now proceeding in status quo ante. **1965** H. KAHN *On Escalation* xiii. 244 It is normal that *status quo* nations will tend to be crisis-avoiding nations. **1967** *Listener* 27 July 103/1 Supposing that Israel withdrew, and that the Arabs were re-supplied with arms, we should be back at a sort of status quo ante. **1971** *Guardian* 6 Dec. 13/8 The TUC puts its money firmly on the need for a 'status quo' declaration by the employer. In other words, the unions insist that the employer must..abandon his authority to change a work practice or agreement without the blessing of his employees... Workers can be expected to observe procedures only if they contain a 'status quo' clause and the employer observes it. **1976** *New Yorker* 24 May 115/2 There is a great move to the status quo ante. **1978** R. LEWIS *Inevitable Fatality* vi. 163 The attempts by Sir Henry Monroe to return QWARTA [*sc.* a company] to a *status quo* position.

statusy (stēɪ·tǝsi), *a. colloq.* [f. STATUS + -Y[1].] Possessing, indicating, or imparting a high status.

1962 *Guardian* 29 Nov. 7/1 No matter how many irrelevant if statusy pieces the 'New Yorker' publishes. **1964** *Punch* 22 Jan. 112/2 As statusy a combination as you can get. **1969** *Time* 26 Sept. 72/2 Pretty soon about 85% of the kids smoked. It got to be a really statusy thing. **1971** *Daily Colonist* (Victoria, B.C.) 3 Sept. 21/6 Katherine Gibbs, who in 1911 founded the statusy secretarial school that bears her name.

statute, *sb.* Add: **9. statute labour** (further Canad. examples).

1831 M. O'BRIEN *Jrnl.* 16 Feb. (1968) xvi. 155 We shall have a share as the statute labour employed on the Street will then come upon the side lines. **1895** W. ELKINGTON *Five Years in Canada* vi. 52 Every person owning property is required to put in a certain amount of work every year on Government roads or fireguards; it is called Statute Labour. **1968** E. RUSSENHOLT *Heart of Continent* IV. xii. 223 The Council of Assiniboia for 1901.. abolishes statute labor, that time-honored method of doing road-work.

statute-book. **2.** *on the statute-book* (later examples).

1934 G. B. SHAW *On Rocks* II. 253 You will have to wait two years and go through the whole job again before you can get your Bill on the statute book as an Act of Parliament. **1972** *Times* 2 Feb. 16/6 His Lordship thought as the Act was already on the statute book the judge was fully entitled to have regard to it.

statutory, *a.* Add: **2. b.** *statutory company*, a company created by statute, as distinguished from a chartered company or a joint-stock company; also, any company other than one incorporated by royal charter; *statutory holiday*, a holiday established by statue; *statutory instrument*, a common type of subordinate legislation (see quot. 1946); *statutory meeting*, a general meeting of the members of a company, held in accordance with a statute; *spec.* the first such meeting, held between one and three months after the company is entitled to commence business; *statutory rape* (*U.S.*), sexual intercourse with a female who is below the age of consent (whether it occurs against her will or not); *statutory tenant*, a person who is legally entitled to remain in possession of premises although his tenancy of them has expired; so *statutory tenancy*.

1915 *Act* 5 & 6 *Geo. V* c. 44 § 2 The expression 'statutory company' means any railway company, canal company, dock company, water company, or other company incorporated by special Act, who are for the time being authorised under such an Act to construct, work, own, or carry on any railway, canal, dock, water, or other public undertaking, and includes any person or body of persons so authorised. **1970** M. GREENER *Penguin Dict. Commerce* 108 Certain contracts are not binding unless made by deed. These are: (1) gratuitous promises, (2) transfers of *shares* in statutory *companies* [etc.]. **1911** *Daily Colonist* (Victoria, B.C.) 18 Apr. (Mag. section) 7/3 Yesterday [*sc.* Easter Monday] was a statutory holiday and many Victorians took advantage of the fact to drop their daily business cares. **1975** *Globe & Mail* (Toronto) 2 June 5/7 He also increased to double time-and-a-half, the pay for policemen working on statutory holidays. **1976** *Alyn & Deeside Observer* 10 Dec. 28/4 (Advt.), Refuse Collection... Due to the incidence of Christmas and New Year statutory holidays it has been necessary to re-arrange certain collection days. **1946** *Act* 9 & 10 *Geo. VI* c. 36 § 1(1) Where by this Act or any Act passed after the commencement of this Act power to make, confirm or approve orders, rules, regulations or other subordinate legislation is conferred on His Majesty in Council or on any Minister of the Crown then, if the power is expressed —(a) in the case of a power conferred on His Majesty, to be exercisable by Order in Council; (b) in the case of a power conferred on a Minister of the Crown, to be exercisable by statutory instrument, any document by which that power is exercised shall be known as a 'statutory instrument'. *a* **1974** R. CROSSMAN *Diaries* (1976) II. 549 The issue the journalists were raising concerned a statutory instrument. **1851** *Bradshaw's Railway Directory, Shareholder's Guide, Manual, & Almanack* 164 The statutory meetings held in March and September. **1900** *Act* 63 & 64 *Vict.* c. 48 § 12 Every company limited by shares and registered after the commencement of this Act shall, within a period of not less than one month nor more than three months from the date at which the company is entitled to commence business, hold a general meeting of the members of the company, which shall be called the statutory meeting. **1970** M. GREENER *Penguin Dict. Commerce* 313 The report should be certified by the auditors, if any, and must be delivered to the Registrar of Companies. It must also be sent to each member fourteen days before the statutory meeting. **1898** *Northwestern Reporter* LXXV. 439 The respondent was convicted of statutory rape. **1959** *Time* 26 Oct. (Canadian ed.) 99/2 His taste for young flesh led to three statutory rape scandals..but the older he got, the more he [*sc.* Errol Flynn] seemed a cardboard sinner. **1977** I. SHAW *Beggarman, Thief* I. iv. 54 They jailed him on the charge of statutory rape. **1920** *Act* 10 & 11 *Geo. V* c. 17 § 15 Conditions of statutory tenancy. **1928** *Daily Mail* 25 July 7/3 Mr. Hunt's case was that he owned the freehold of 294, Upper Richmond-road and occupied two rooms. Mr. Sullivan was the statutory tenant. **1972** *N.Y. Law Jrnl.* 10 Oct. 19/2 The parties concede that the defendants' occupancy of the apartment after the expiration of the lease was that of 'statutory tenants', since the premises were rent controlled under the City Rent and Rehabilitation Law. **1973** *Country Life* 3 May (Suppl.) 17 (Advt.), 3-bedroomed flat let unfurnished to statutory tenant.

3. b. Required for the sake of appearances; having only token significance. Used esp. with reference to the formal inclusion of women in male-dominated areas of activity.

1968 *Guardian* 31 July 1/6 Lord Conesford..was protesting against the cold and abstract 'statutory woman'. **1970** *Listener* 19 Nov. 707/2 Mary Stocks..was in great demand as a Statutory Woman, serving on one government committee and commission after another. **1977** *Observer* 1 May (Colour Suppl.) 12/4 I've noticed that most committees nowadays have a statutory woman on them.

Staunton (stǭ·ntǝn). The name of Howard *Staunton* (1810–74), English chess-player and writer, used *attrib.* and *absol.* to designate chess-men of a design now accepted as standard.

[**1891** R. B. SWINTON *Chess for Beginners* ii. 5 A chess-board and a set of men are necessary. The latter alone are to be purchased at all prices, from sets in 'African ivory', after Staunton's pattern, down to flimsy wooden pieces. *Ibid.* 7 Your wooden men..will..be easily identified with the drawings of Staunton's men which form headpieces to the..chapters.] **1898** *Dict. Nat. Biogr.* LIV. 117/1 Staunton's name was conferred on the set of chess-men which are recognised as the standard type among English-speaking peoples. His 'Chess Player's Text-book' was issed in 1849, without date, to be sold with the Staunton chessmen. **1913** H. J. MURRAY *Hist. Chess* II. x. 773 Chessmen of fanciful shapes and forms are often made as curiosities. For actual play, most players would prefer to use the 'Staunton chessmen', the pattern of which Howard Staunton designed in 1849. **1951** G. FRANKAU *Oliver Trenton* ix. 77 The set of ivory Stauntons I won from him. **1959** L. BARDEN *Chess* ii. 14 The pieces of a 'Staunton design' are..the most popular nowadays... The photograph shows what they look like in your Staunton-type set. **1977** M. KELLY in D. Marcus *Best Irish Short Stories* II. 66 The Staunton with its austere lack of pretension. **1979** P. ALEXANDER *Show me Hero* iv. 55 A chess-board and one of the earliest Staunton sets.

stave, *sb.*[1] Add: **I. 2. i.** [Cf. Norw. *stav.*] A vertical wooden post forming part of the framework of a building, usu. a stave church (see sense 8 c below); also, a plank used in the walls of such a construction.

1915 H. G. LEACH *Scandinavia of Scandinavians* II. xiii. 162 In architecture, the most distinctive survivals from the Middle Ages in Norway are the so-called 'stave' churches, tepee-like structures, built of wooden staves, rising roof above roof. *Ibid.*, Stave churches often contain elaborate wooden carvings which have served as models for modern Norwegian decoration... This is especially true of the church of Urnaes.., one of the earliest existing stave structures, with its intricate animal and vegetable motives. **1974** *Encycl. Brit. Micropædia* IX. 539/1 The stone foundation of the stave church supports four horizontal wooden beams, from which rise four corner posts, or staves.

7. b. An alliterating letter in a line of Old English verse. Also *head-stave.* Cf. G. *stab, hauptstab.*

1894 H. SWEET *Anglo-Saxon Reader* (ed. 7) p. lxxxv, In our texts..the letters or staves are in italics. *Ibid.*, We denote the first and second verse of each line by I and II respectively. II..has only one stave called the head-stave, while I has either one or two called under-staves.

1959 R. B. Le Page in *Jrnl. Eng. & Gmc. Philol.* LVIII. 434 The two alliterating staves, one in each half-line, have a definite structural function. **1962** K. Malone *Widsith* 67 Grammatically *fela ic monna* makes a unit but because of the m-stave that binds the two halves of the line together the on-verse must be classified as D in spite of the f-stave.

IV. 8. c. stave church [tr. Norw. (Bokmål) *stavkirke*], a church built with walls of upright planks or staves, of a type mainly built in Norway from the eleventh to the thirteenth century; **stave mill** *N. Amer.*, a mill making cask-staves.

1915, etc. [see sense 2 i above.] **1933** F. Lingstrom *This is Norway* facing p. 12 (*caption*) Borgund Stave Church in Laerdal. **1936** A. W. Clapham *Romanesque Archit.* viii. 189 A highly remarkable class of building in timber, which includes the celebrated mast or stave-churches of Norway. **1968** G. Jones *Hist. Vikings* II. iii. 116 An oak-built stave church at some time destroyed by fire. **1937** R. Flannagan *County Court* 188 Widowed five years before by an automobile accident, she had held on to her late husband's chain of stave-mills and had prospered. **1957** *Daily Progress* (Charlottesville, Va.) 7 May 15/8 Blake and other stave mill operators say they will remain in business as long as it is profitable. **1968** E. R. Buckler *Ox Bells & Fireflies* vi. 102 If there was urgent need of ready money..you worked off and on in the stave mill.

stavies, var. *stovies *sb. pl.*

Stavka (sta·fkă, sta·vkă). [Russ., f. *stavit'* to put, place.] The general headquarters of the Russian army.

1928 *Daily Express* 16 July 8 The actual relations between the Stavka (G.H.Q.) and the Duma are revealed clearly for the first time. **1931** W. S. Churchill *World Crisis* VI. ix. 142 By August 6 the Russian General Headquarters—in future called the Stavka—learned definitely that the German main forces..were entraining for the French front. **1949** I. Deutscher *Stalin* 466 The *Stavka*, the Red Army's G.H.Q., was in his offices in the Kremlin. **1963** P. Fleming *Kolchak* xiv. 158 The swollen Stavka, besides embodying all the worst technical vices of Russian military bureaucracy, was rotten to the core with dishonesty, nepotism and intrigue.

stay, *sb.*[1] Add: **1. b.** Also, a supporting wire or cable on an aircraft.

1894 O. Chanute *Progress in Flying Machines* 237 This main aeroplane..is trussed and stiffened in every direction by wire stays. **1908** H. G. Wells *War in Air* x. 317 It had taken only an hour or so to substitute wing stays from the second flying machine and to replace the nuts he had himself removed. **1919** S. Camm *Aeroplane Construction* xiii. 108 The various wires used in construction may be classified into four distinct types: the solid wire stay, the straining cord or cable used for stay wires, the extra flexible cable used for controls, and the swaged tie rods in plane or streamline form.

3. stay-wire, (*b*) a supporting wire on an aircraft.

1919 [see sense 1 b above]. **1969** K. Munson *Pioneer Aircraft 1903–14* 9 The superposed horizontal surfaces, A, formed by stretching cloth upon frames of wood and wire, constitute the 'wings' or supporting part of the apparatus. They are connected to each other through hinge-joints by upright standards and lateral stay-wires.

stay, *sb.*[2] Add: **5. a.** *stay-making* (earlier example).

1843 Dickens *Let.* 2 Nov. (1974) III. 589 Trades... I think of..stay-making [etc.].

b. stay braid (example).

1759 *Newport* (Rhode I.) *Mercury* 26 June 4/3 To be sold by Jacob Richardson,..Stay Braid and Cord.

stay, *v.*[1] Add: **4. e.** (Earlier example with *down.*) Also *to stay over* (orig. *U.S.*): to stop overnight; *to stay with*: to remain in the mind or memory.

1884, etc. [see *over *adv.* 9 b]. **1895** Kipling *Day's Work* (1898) 175 She had 'stayed down three hot weathers', as the saying is, because her brother..could not afford the expense of her keep at even a cheap hill-station. **1942** A. Woollcott *Let.* 26 May (1946) 260, I want to tell you that seldom has anything I have heard stayed with me like your reading of that first poem in the *Spoon River Anthology.* **1973** *Christian Science Monitor* 12 July 19/4 On the way home that stayed with me, 'The whole world needs mothering'. **1981** E. A. Taylor *Cable Car Murder* (1983) xviii. 130 We had a satisfying visit. I stayed over, and she took me to the train the next morning.

6. b. (Earlier example.) Also used outside U.S.

1843 *New Mirror* 23 Sept. 385/2 And now we have put her in black and white, where she will 'stay put'. **1891** 'L. Malet' *Wages of Sin* IV. v. 217 It takes a lot of latent strength to sit, either mentally or physically, really still. Not to fidget. To 'stay put', in short. **1924** J. Buchan *Three Hostages* vii. 102 He's able enough; but he won't stay put, and that makes him pretty well useless. **1936** F. Clune *Roaming round Darling* xv. 139 Here, for the time being, Sturt must 'stay put', while the Poet and I begin rolling down the Darling. **1959** *Globe & Mail* (Toronto) 17 Aug. 3/8 Fire Chief Dawson told him to stay put until the car could be pulled away safely. **1978** R. Busby *Garvey's Code* xii. 159, I keep the gun. And you stay put.

8. b. (Later examples.) Also *U.S.*

1951 *Amer. Speech* XXVI. 75/1 'Do you stay here?' In common Negro parlance *stay* is used for 'live' but is heard otherwise. **1959** A. Fullerton *Yellow Ford* v. 45 'Would you care to stay round here, man?' I had not caught on, at first, to her meaning: the verb 'stay' is used in South Africa when in England we'd say 'live'. **1962** W. Faulkner *Reivers* i. 13 Mr Wimbush stays a solid eight miles from town. **1980** D. Moraes *Mrs Gandhi* p. xiii, In March 1977..my wife..and I went to see her in New Delhi, at 1 Safdarjang Road, the house where she had stayed since she first became Prime Minister in 1966.

c. Similarly, *to be here to stay.*

1936 M. Mitchell *Gone with Wind* xli. 739 Everyone knew hard times were here to stay. **1947** [see *post-industrial* s.v. *post- B. 1 b]. **1966** *Listener* 5 May 661/3 It's a small question, though, when viewed against the more important fact that Mahler is indubitably here, and here to stay. **1969** *Ibid.* 31 July 135/1 In all the present uncertainties about the future of radio, one thing seems certain: local radio is here to stay, and we shall have more of it. **1971** J. Wainwright *Dig Grave* 85 'I don't go for them [*sc.* automatic gears]. They'll kill real driving.'..'They're here to stay, mate, whether you go for 'em, or not.' **1976** *Guardian* 17 Apr. 13/8 Multinationals are here to stay.

12. b. For *U.S. colloq.* read *colloq.* (orig. *U.S.*) and add: Also *fig.*, to concentrate on, to apply oneself to, to continue with.

1956 H. Kurnitz *Invasion of Privacy* i. 12 I gave you an order. Stay with it. **1961** 'A. A. Fair' *Stop at Red Light* (1962) vii. 108 That adds up, Donald. Stay with it. You're doing fine. **1969** *Guardian* 15 July 7/1 These astronauts..have an amazing capability to stay with their tasks. **1976** 'J. Ross' *I know what it's like to Die* xxv. 158 I've got to stay with it [*sc.* a police inquiry]. I can't just drop it. **1982** *Times* 6 Feb. 15 (*heading*) Fed stays with its tight money policy.

II. 17. b. *to stay the course*: to hold out to the end of a race. Freq. *fig.*

1885 *Daily Tel.* 11 Nov. 3/7 Doubts are also entertained..concerning her [*sc.* a horse's] ability to stay the course. **1916** *Times* 8 May 9/1 If we are to 'stay the course' set before us, other sections must be prepared for greater sacrifices. **1939** A. Huxley *After Many a Summer* I. viii. 103 'Do you suppose you'd still be a scholar and a gentleman?'..'One will certainly have stopped being a gentleman,' he answered. 'One's begun to stop even now, thank heaven.' 'But the scholar will stay the course?' **1966** *Listener* 10 Mar. 365/3 There was much to be learnt from this programme—about metal fatigue, for instance—for those who could stay the course. **1983** *Verbatim* IX. iv. 16/2 When President Reagan exhorted Senators and Congressmen to stay the course, the actual meaning of his words was the opposite of his intended meaning.

31. stay-away, (*b*) an act or process of staying away, esp. from work; also as *adj.*; **stay-down** *a.*, of, pertaining to, or designating a strike staged by miners staying down a mine; **stay-in** *a.*, of, pertaining to, or designating a strike in which the strikers remain in their place of work; also *absol.* as *sb.*, (one who participates in) a strike of this kind; **stay-up** *a.*, of stockings: remaining in place without garters or suspenders; also *absol.* as *sb.*

1940 *Sun* (Baltimore) 10 Sept. 7/2 A 'stay-away' strike by hundreds of Allegany county school children continued into its second week today, with parents' support. Students said the 'stay away' was a protest against the consolidation program of the Allegany County Board of Education. **1963** *Listener* 28 Feb. 363/1 The calls for general work-stoppages during recent years have been 'stay-aways' directed against political and urban restrictions rather than against employers. **1976** *Times* 24 Aug. 1/4 Thousands of people in Soweto heeded a call not to go to work... Whether the mass stay-away..reflected widespread support for the strike call is unclear. **1948** *Sun* (Baltimore) 11 Feb. 3/1 (*heading*) 'Stay-down' strikers occupy British mine. *Ibid.*, Three hundred miners are staging a 'stay-down' strike in the Waleswood mine. **1948** *Times* 23 Feb. 3/1 More than 400 delegates from all parts of the South Wales coalfield at Cardiff on Saturday discussed measures to stop the wave of stay-down strikes. **1980** *Listener* 29 May 686/2 Miners in Hungary were winning themselves better conditions with a new tactic, the stay-down hunger strike. **1915** *Political Q.* May 95 The Withdrawal of Labour Committee..advised the men ..to adopt the 'stay-in' strike. **1926** *Times* 29 Apr. 5/7 (*heading*) Lock-out of 'stay-in' strikers. **1937** *Amer. Speech* XII. 32 When this type of action takes place during working hours..it is a *sit-down, folded arms* or *crossed arms* strike. When it is prolonged beyond that period, it becomes, in addition, a *stay-in.* **1944** *Time* 12 June 14/1 Some of the stay-ins crowded out on to the balconies. **1950** Millis & Brown *Wagner Act to Taft-Hartley* viii. 278 In the 'stay-in' strike..management was locked out and kept off the job. **1968** *Amer. Speech* XLIII. 63 Drop-outs and stay-ins have been noted. **1949** *Sun* (Baltimore) 20 July 4 No roll—stay up tops. **1953** *Ibid.* 20 July (E ed.) 3 No supporters are necessary for they have their own stay-up tops! **1969** J. Gardner *Complete State of Death* ix. 174 Her woollen kaftan riding up to display the dark elasticized top of her stay-up stockings. **1973** *Nation* (Barbados) 25 Nov. 3 (Advt.), Nylon Stay-ups 99 c.

stay-at-home, *a.* and *sb.* Add: **A.** *adj.* Also *spec.* avoiding going abroad on military service.

1946 W. S. Churchill *Victory* 78 You hear all this talk by the stay-at-home Left Wing *intelligentsia* that the soldiers will hold us guilty if we do not have a new world waiting for them on their return.

B. *sb.* **a.** (Earlier example.) Also *spec.* one who avoids going abroad on military service. Also *transf.*

1836 Dickens *Let.* ? 27 Nov. (1965) I. 200 Mrs. Dickens is a great stay-at-home just now. **1883** A. Pinkerton *Spy of Rebellion* xxv. 499 Extravagant ideas of a struggle which should be 'short, sharp and decisive', were the only ones entertained by the great army of 'stay at homes'. **1918** *Nation* (N.Y.) 7 Feb. 131/1 Students.. accused as stay-at-homes, unwilling to fight and suffer for the Fatherland. **1949** E. Hyams *Grape Vine in England* 143 Not by any means all the root-dwelling insects change into winged insects. The stay-at-homes winter among the roots of the vines. **1981** A. Cooke in *N.Y. Times Mag.* 19 July 6/4 We..sent in 'technicians' and followed them up with a blood sacrifice, but burdened the stay-at-homes with no extra taxes.

b. A staying at home, *spec.* a strike.

1959 [see *neon world* s.v. *neon 3 a]. **1960** *Guardian* 20 Apr. 18/1 They disagreed on whether the stay-at-home should be for a day or a week. **1976** *Times* 24 Aug. 1/4 If today's stay-at-home is maintained..the organizers will have demonstrated that they are capable of arranging mass protests among urban blacks.

Staybrite (stēi·brəit). [f. Stay *v.*[1] + an arbitrary respelling of Bright *a.*] A proprietary name for a make of stainless steel.

1925 *Metallurgist* I. 153/2 Dr. Westgren..prepared photograms of this chromium-nickel steel—known as 'Staybrite'—in both the fully quenched and softened condition. **1930** *Engineering* 11 Apr. 486/1 Some trouble had been experienced with Staybrite jackets. **1937** G. Frankau *More of Us* ii. 26 In hall of nearest-marble, gay With Staybrite, stood old Dorkins, butler hoary. **1937** *Trade Marks Jrnl.* 7 July 820 *Staybrite*...Stainless steels. Firth-Vickers Stainless Steels Ltd.,..Sheffield. **1964** Bird & Hallows *Rolls-Royce Motor-Car* II. 244 Staybrite radiator shell, single-point suspension and pressure radiator cap.

Stayman (stēi·mæ̃n). The name of Samuel M. *Stayman* (b. 1909), an American authority on contract bridge, used *attrib.* and *absol.* to designate a convention used in bidding at contract bridge.

1952 S. M. Stayman *Expert Bidding at Contract Bridge* vi. 53 The bidding method that has become known as the 'Stayman' Convention was not named by me. I was the first to describe it in print (in..1945), and bridge players ..called it by my name. **1955** —— *Compl. Stayman System of Contract Bidding* viii. 83 The Stayman System takes a position in the centre of the two popular standards. **1962** *Times* 4 Apr. 6/7 The use of artificial 'asking' bids such as the Neapolitan One Club, the Stayman Two Clubs and the Blackwood conventions. **1972** *Guardian* 26 June 12/4 When asked if I play Stayman, I find it difficult to answer. There are many versions of this convention. **1976** *National Observer* (U.S.) 10 July 15/1 The partnership also was playing 'double barrel' Stayman in which two clubs shows a weak hand and two diamonds forces to game.

stay-put (stēi·put), *sb.* and *a.* *colloq.* Also **stay put, stayput.** [f. vbl. phr. *to stay put*: see Stay *v.*[1] 6 b.] **A.** *sb.* **a.** A refraining from movement or travel. (Stress variable.)

1941 Koestler *Scum of Earth* 194 It is a sort of general stay put. *Ibid.* 204 Crowd of smart civilians queuing up to get petrol for their cars—and actually getting it in spite of stay-put order.

b. One who refuses to move, one who stays at home. Chiefly *Austral.*

1967 Partridge *Dict. Slang* Suppl. 1388/2 *Stay-put*, one who holds his ground ('stays put'): coll., esp. Australian: since ca. 1950. **1977** C. McCullough *Thorn Birds* vi. 120 Things were more amicable between vagabonds and stay-puts.

B. *adj.* Remaining where or as placed; during which one remains in one place. Also, refusing to move, refraining from travel.

1962 *N.Y. Times Mag.* 9 Sept. 77/1 (Advt.), Other important details you'll like: the grow-feature for extra long wear, our new stay-put moccasin foot. **1963** *Guardian* 13 July 4/5 A stay-put holiday at one resort. **1968** *Daily Tel.* (Colour Suppl.) 13 Dec. 31/1 In the United States, a mobile home can have two bedrooms... Some cost almost as much as a stay-put house of comparable size. **1969** *Sears Catal.* Spring/Summer 22 Fashion-back jeans and shorts with soil release... Bar tacked. Stay-put zipper. Band waist, belt loops. **1973** *Times* 13 Jan. 12/8 A centre for touring as well as for stayput holidaymakers. **1977** *Borneo Bull.* 7 May 2/1 Thirty four of Miri's stay-put squatter families who have been defying eviction deadlines for two years have won their battle for land.

stay-pu·tter. *colloq.* [f. as prec. + -er[1].] One who refrains from moving.

1927 J. Adams *Errors in School* ii. 41 Leaving this suggestion of a restricted meaning of the term *idea* to the tender mercies of the stay-putters. **1971** 'E. Fenwick' *Impeccable People* xix. 105, I don't understand you stay-putters, but you're probably wise people.

stchi. Add: Also **shchi** (now the usual form), **shtchee, shtchi, shtshi,** etc. (Earlier and further examples.)

1824 J. D. Cochrane *Narr. Pedestrian Journey through Russia* iv. 105, I never entered a cottage, but shtshee (a cabbage soup), with meat, milk and bread, were.. placed before me unasked. **1901** *Daily Chron.* 14 June 3/4 The delicious and universal cabbage soup is not in English letters *Stchie*,..but—as nearly as maybe—*Shtchi.* **1904** *Westm. Gaz.* 21 Apr. 7/1 The dish of shtchee—fermented cabbage and meat—with vodka, he greatly enjoyed. **1905** *Ibid.* 21 Jan. 16/1 That extraordinary mixture of pickled cabbage, meat broth, and about a hundred other ingredients which goes by the name of *shtshi*. **1941** A. L. Simon *Conc. Encycl. Gastron.* III. 18/2 The most popular form of cabbage soup in France is called *Garbure*; the Russian edition of it is known as *Stschi.* **1958** W. Bickel tr. *Hering's Dict. Classical & Mod. Cookery* 113 *Schtschi*, Russian Cabbage Soup. **1971** *Times* 9 Aug. 5/8 [Soup made from wild sorrel] is a welcome change in the summer and is called *green schchi* (*schchi* being the traditional cabbage soup). **1973** R. Martin *Internat. Dict. Food & Cooking* 259/2 *Shchi*, (*Russian*), green vegetable soup of meat *bouillon* and cabbage. **1977** *N.Y. Rev. Bks.* 14 Apr. 10/4 In exchange for a few dissident intellectuals the Ibanskians import from America tons of *shchi*, the Russian national dish of cabbage soup.

stead, *sb.* **III. 12. f.** For *dial.* read *dial.* and *colloq.* and add later examples. Now usu. considered (also as *'stead*) to represent Instead *phrasal comb.*

1903 K. D. Wiggin *Rebecca of Sunnybrook Farm* xxvi. 279 Rebecca's fifty dollars had to be swallowed up in a mortgage, 'stead of goin' towards school expenses. **1916** G. B. Shaw *Pygmalion* II. 121, I want to be a lady in a flower shop stead of selling at the corner of Tottenham Court Road. **1939** Joyce *Finnegans Wake* 283 They ought to told you every last word first stead of trying every which way to kinder smear it out poison long. **1971** *Black World* Oct. 62/1 The sweet-potato bread was a dollar quarter this time stead of dollar regular. **1978** J. Thomson *Question of Identity* x. 100 He'd've been all right with me... 'Stead of which..he marries her.

steadite (ste·dəit). [f. the name of J. E. Stead (1851–1923), English metallurgist + -ite[1].] **1.** *Metallurgy.* A constituent of phosphorus-rich irons and steels which is a eutectic of austenite and iron phosphide (and sometimes also cementite) and contains dissolved phosphorus.

1902 *Jrnl. Iron & Steel Inst.* LXI. 118 Mr. A. Sauveur (Boston)..suggested [in correspondence]..'Steadite', to designate the eutectic alloy of iron and the phosphide Fe_3P formed in iron rich in phosphorus. **1925** *Machinery* XXVI. 501/1 Steadite is distributed throughout the metal and gives the abrasive action previously mentioned. **1964** S. H. Avner *Introd. Physical Metall.* xi. 327 Steadite is relatively brittle, and with high phosphorus content, the steadite areas tend to form a continuous network outlining the primary austenite dendrites. **1975** *Brit. Foundryman* LXVIII. 106/1 Phosphorus..segregates in the last portion to solidify, known as steadite, which is composed of iron, iron carbide and iron phosphide.

2. *Min.* A siliceous variety of apatite, usu. containing iron, found as yellowish needles in basic slag.

1911 V. A. Kroll in *Jrnl. Iron & Steel Inst.* LXXXIV. 130 In the new mineral, which..he [*sc.* the author] distinguishes by the name of Steadite, measurement of the angles reveals the occurrence of the hexagonal system. **1950** *Mineral. Mag.* XXIX. 184 Steadite is frequently a late constituent to crystallize; its crystals are the commonest in the vugs of basic slags. **1951** *Science* 29 June 755/2 Metallographic studies..prove the presence of cohenite, steadite, and schreibersite, as well as troilite. The percentage of nickel is about double that of the meteorite fragments found in the same area.

steady, *sb.* Add: **1. a.** *spec.* in Newfoundland, a part of a river which has little or no perceptible current. (Later examples.)

1842 J. B. Jukes *Excursions in & about Newfoundland* II. 241, I understood from a salmon-fisher, the only person inhabiting the neighbourhood, that a succession of 'steadies', with occasional rapids, may be met with for twelve miles farther. **1907** J. G. Millais *Newfoundland* xi. 206 At noon we entered a beautiful 'steady'. **1969** H. Horwood *Newfoundland* i. 4 The canoe..bounced joyously past the white water into the still and foam-flecked steady below.

b. A regular boyfriend or girlfriend. *colloq.* (orig. *U.S.*).

1897 F. Moss *Amer. Metropolis* III. ix. 172 Her 'steady' is Jim Clarke. **1927** *Vanity Fair* Nov. 132/3 His steady has quit him for another or he is lonesome for her. **1950** 'N. Shute' *Town like Alice* 313, I suppose he's turning into Rose's steady. **1960** Auden *Homage to Clio* 56 You won't find a steady in *that* museum Unless you prefer Tea with a shapeless angel to bedtime With a lovely monster. **1978** *Daily Mirror* 12 Jan. 3/4 Meanwhile Rod was flying off to Rio—with a farewell kiss for his latest 'steady', 23-year-old model Bebe Bluell.

steady, *a.* (and *adv.*) Add: **A.** *adj.* **4. e.** (Earlier example.)

1857 A. Mathews *Tea-Table Talk* II. 343 Ceylon coffee, heretofore steady and pressing for immediate sale, is now inactive.

f. *Cricket.* Of a batsman or his play: consistent, safe, cautious.

1826 S. Maunder in R. Dagley *Death's Doings* 54 A steady Player, careful of his fame, May have a *good long Innings*. **1833** *New Sporting Mag.* V. (Cricketers' Reg.) 13 This style [of bowling] Pilch met by steady play. **1857** T. Hughes *Tom Brown's School Days* II. viii. 398 To the suggestions that Winter is the best bat left, Tom only replies, 'Arthur is the steadiest, and Johnson will make the runs if the wicket is only kept up.' **1890** J. Lillywhite *Cricketers' Annual* 143 W. G. Turnbull: A steady bat, but lacking power; should hit more at loose balls. **1924** H. De Sélincourt *Cricket Match* iv. 104 As a matter of sad fact there was no steady and reliable batsman upon the side. *Ibid.* v. 159 He felt a batsman, pure and simple; and decided that he was..in for a good, steady display of batting.

6. c. Of a boyfriend or girlfriend: regular or constant. *colloq.* (orig. *U.S.*).

1887 *Lantern* (New Orleans) 23 July 2/2, I expect my steady company at the house this evening. **1922** S. Benson *Poor Man* v. 127 She had just mislaid her last steady beau, so she was at the moment a little susceptible. **1932** J. Dos Passos *1919* 43 Della let Joe kiss her when they said good night and he began kinder planning that she'd be his steady girl. **1975** D. Lodge *Changing Places* iii. 126 She's become Charles Boon's steady girl friend. **1977** *Rolling Stone* 5 May 47/4 He has no steady girl.

B. *adv.* **a.** Also *to go steady*, to keep regular company (*with* someone) as a boyfriend or girlfriend. *colloq.* (orig. *U.S.*).

1905 E. Wharton *House of Mirth* II. xiii. 493, I thought we were to be married: he'd gone steady with me six months and given me his mother's wedding ring. **1923** *Saucy Stories* 1 Mar. 78/1 Puzzled, she asked him, Well, wasn't we... Didn't you go with me steady? **1946** *Coast to Coast 1945* 136 Are you going steady with anyone, Billy? **1962** M. Urquhart *Frail on North Circular* xii. 70 Noticing a huge, cheap ring on Joan's finger. 'Where'd you get that?' 'It's a going steady ring.' **1978** F. Weldon *Praxis* xx. 163 I'm going steady with one of the young doctors.

b. Also in other contexts or *transf.* Freq. in colloq. phrases expressing caution, as *steady as she goes, steady on* (*with* something), *steady there*, etc.; *steady the Buffs* (Buff *sb.*[2] 6), hold on! keep calm! be careful!

1825 H. Wilson *Mem.* II. 162 Here the men, forgetful of the caution..began to draw [their swords]. Steady there!! Never a finger or a high to move. **1853** C. Brontë *Villette* I. ix. 168 She was going to bestow on me a kiss.. but I said, 'Steady! Let us be steady, and know what we are about.' **1888** Kipling *Story of Gadsbys* 6 I'd like to see Mr Khan being rude to that girl! Hullo! Steady the Buffs! **1893** *Illustr. London News* 18 Feb. 222/2 (Advt.), Steady there, Spencer with the milk, Rosebery here has not had a drop yet. **1903** G. B. Shaw *Man & Superman* II. 70 Here! Mister! arf a mo! steady on! **1936** A. Ransome *Pigeon Post* xiii. 140 'Sorry,' sobbed Titty. 'Awfully sorry. I didn't mean to.'..'All right, Titty... All right... Steady on.' **1953** N. Jacob *Morning will Come* xiii. 241 He was growing nervous, and kept saying, 'Steady, Charles, steady the Buffs!' **1959** J. Verney *Friday's Tunnel* i. 12 Here, steady on with the sugar, greedy guts. **1971** *Time* 30 Aug. 4/2 No changes were contemplated in the Administration's approach. 'Steady as she goes was the watchword,' said Shultz. **1972** J. Wainwright *Night is Time to Die* 155 Steady the Buffs! (thought Ripley). He's goading you. **1976** in R. Crossman *Diaries* II. 307 The 'steady as she goes' budget was welcomed by foreign bankers. **1976** *Shooting Times & Country Mag.* 18 Nov. 28/2 Opening gates, and holding them open without a hound rushing into the field, at the words 'steady there!' **1979** A. Williamson *Funeral March for Siegfried* xxxiii. 167 'She had last year been Andersson's mistress—' 'Here, steady on!' cried Von Wolstenholm..purple with indignation.

steady, *v.* Add: **1. c.** (Further example.)

1876 G. M. Hopkins *Wreck of Deutschland* iv, in *Poems* (1967) 52, I steady as a water in a well, to a poise, to a pane.

5. Also with *up*.

1932 E. Waugh *Black Mischief* iii. 104 When you're convinced he's steadied up a bit, let him have chambers of his own in one of the Inns of Court. **1963** *Times* 2 Feb. 5/1 The port's Trawler Officers' Guild asked the owners to co-operate in steadying up the men who go on board from the public houses and take bottles with them on late-night sailing.

steadyish, *a.* (Later example.)

1924 H. De Sélincourt *Cricket Match* iv. 104 Gauvinier tried to arrange for a steadyish man to go in at No. 7.

steady state. [f. Steady *a.* + State *sb.*]

1. An unvarying condition; a state of equilibrium.

1885 *Electrician* 10 Jan. 180/1 With special arrangements (solenoidal) of impressed force, there is no transmission of energy in the steady state. **1905** *Nature* 27 July 293/2 His [*sc.* Planck's] ensemble of systems has not yet reached a statistical 'steady state'. **1930** Ruark & Urey *Atoms, Molecules & Quanta* ix. 272 These five quantum numbers may be taken as those required to fix the steady states of an atom in a strong magnetic field. **1963** *Wall St. Jrnl.* 19 Aug., It long had been held by many scientists that the universe is in a steady state, that, in its general features, it is the same now as it always has been. **1971** *Nature* 8 Jan. 75/1 If present patterns..continue, the annual death rate from lung cancer will increase from about 15,000 to more than 45,000 in the steady state that will be attained in the 1980s. **1977** *Lancet* 3 Sept. 509/2 Plasma-carbamazepine concentrations were in steady state in all patients.

2. *attrib.* (freq. with hyphen). **a.** *gen.*

1909 *Phil. Mag.* XVII. 251 There is no *a priori* reason why there should not be different 'steady state' formulæ corresponding to different kinds of matter. **1942** *Jrnl. Appl. Physics* XIII. 710/2 The steady state current is then the difference of the expressions for the total current and for the transient current. **1965** H. I. Ansoff *Corporate Strategy* iii. 32 The microeconomic theory of the firm..is basically a steady-state theory concerned with successive equilibrium conditions. **1970** J. Earl *Tuners & Amplifiers* iii. 66 For good quality listening we should not go in for anything less than..8W steady-state power per channel. **1976** *Conservation News* Nov./Dec. 22/1 The author is sceptical that steady-state economics will ever find practical application, since people's desires for consumption show no evidence of having a reasonable upper limit. **1977** A. Hallam *Planet Earth* 296 Hutton and Lyell were postulating a steadystate Earth—ceaseless piecemeal local change was occurring. But the consequence of such change was to maintain from the indefinite past to the indefinite future an overall, constant equilibrium in the terrestrial economy. **1978** P. Marsh et al. *Rules of Disorder* iv. 112 Evidence for the existence of a 'steady-state' system of rules and a sense of social propriety.

b. *Astr.* Used with reference to any cosmological theory which embraces the principle that on a large scale the universe is essentially unchanging in time and space; *spec.* the theory propounded by Bondi, Gold, and Hoyle of an isotropic universe expanding at a constant rate, with matter being continuously created so that the mean density of the universe remains constant.

1948 Bondi & Gold in *Monthly Notices R. Astron. Soc.* CVIII. 252 (*heading*) The steady-state theory of the expanding universe. **1955** *Sci. News* XXXVII. 22 The steady-state theory was designed to overcome a difficulty in the world-models of general relativity which no longer exists. Until a few years ago it was thought that these gave a value for the age of the universe..which was too small to satisfy other astrophysical evidence. **1969** *Times* 23 June 6/7 The steady state theory..says that the universe looks roughly the same from any position and at any time in the past, present or future. **1971** J. Z. Young *Introd. Study Man* xxvi. 363 There are other versions of steady-state cosmologies according to which new galaxies are continuously being formed from newly created matter. **1973** [see *radio astronomy]. **1977** J. Narlikar *Struct. Universe* iv. 132 With the help of the PCP [Perfect Cosmological Principle], Bondi and Gold were able to deduce a number of important properties of the steady-state Universe. As we shall see.., they were able to deduce that such a Universe must continually expand. **1978** Pasachoff & Kutner *University Astron.* xxix. 732 If we have indeed discovered radiation from the big bang itself then clearly the steady state theory is discredited.

Hence **steady-stater,** an advocate of a steady-state theory of the universe.

1966 *Time* 11 Mar. 51 As the galaxies move farther away from each other, steady-staters believe, new galaxies are constantly being formed. **1973** 'D. Halliday' *Dolly & Starry Bird* xiii. 188 Black holes..according to theory are nonluminous stars..concealing whole galaxies..to the satisfaction of all the Steady Staters.

steak. 1. a. Add to def.: or specifying how it should be cooked, as *stewing steak* (meat from a less tender cut: see *stewing *vbl. sb.* b).

2. c. (Earlier and later examples.) Cf. *Hamburger 2.

1884 *Boston Jrnl.* 16 Feb. 2/2 We take a chicken and boil it. When it is cold we cut it up as they do meat to make Hamburg steak. **1951** *Good Housek. Home Encycl.* 502/2 *Hamburg steak*, a fried or baked flat cake of freshly minced seasoned steak, very popular in the United States.

3. *steak dinner, pie* (examples), *sandwich*; *steak hammer, tongs* (earlier example); in names of restaurants or other eating-places serving mainly beefsteak, as *steak bar, house, restaurant*; **steak and kidney**, used *attrib.* to designate a pie or pudding containing a mixture of beefsteak and kidney; also *ellipt.*; **steak au poivre** (*o* pwāvrə), beefsteak flavoured with coarsely crushed peppercorns before cooking; = *pepper steak* s.v. *pepper *sb.* 5; **steak Diane** (‖ di͵a·n), a dish consisting of thin slices of beefsteak fried with seasonings, esp. Worcestershire sauce; **steak knife,** (*a*) a butcher's knife; (*b*) a serrated table knife; **steak tartare**, a dish consisting of raw minced beefsteak mixed with egg and seasonings.

1910 Steak and kidney [see *say *v.*[1] B. 1 a]. **1930** H. Burke *Cookery Bk.* 103 Steak and kidney pudding... Put in the beef and kidney (see Steak and Kidney Pie recipe). **1960** I. Jefferies *Dignity & Purity* iv. 59 Cobb..spirited us off to a nearby pub for steak and kidney pud. **1965** L. Sands *Something to Hide* ix. 154 The sight of the steak-and-kidney glistening succulently between them. **1977** C. McCullough *Thorn Birds* ix. 206 The seven of them sat in the small dining room eating steak-and-kidney pie. **1953** Beard & Watt *Paris Cuisine* 132 Steak au poivre. **1976** 'F. Clifford' *Drummer in Dark* iv. 17 Avocado vinaigrette and steak au poivre... Choosing didn't take long. **1971** *Guardian* 10 June 7/8 Fire damaged a kitchen, restaurant, and steak bar in..Hull yesterday. **1957** *Gourmet Cookbk.* II. 270 (*heading*) Steak Diane. **1974** W. Garner *Big Enough Wreath* viii. 103 The waiter [was] serving his steak Diane. *a* **1964** C. Whitney in D. Macarthur *Reminiscences* viii. 271 We were seated and served a steak dinner. **1979** *Tucson* (Arizona) *Citizen* 20 Sept. 8 c/1 About 2,000 steak dinners will be served. **1934** Webster, Steak hammer. **1974** *Habitat Catal.* 81/3 Wooden steak hammer with a square toothed head knocks coarser cuts of steak into succulent shape. **1762** J. Boswell *Jrnl.* 15 Dec. (1950) 86, I went into the City to Dolly's Steak-house in Paternoster Row and swallowed my dinner by myself. **1954** I. Levin *Kiss before Dying* III. v. 178 They went to a steak house on Fifty-second street. **1977** B. Roueché *Fago* (1978) II. iii. 101 There was a steakhouse restaurant across the street. **1895** *Montgomery Ward Catal.* Spring & Summer 447/2 Steak knives,..12 inch blade... No butcher shop would be without them after a trial. **1951** *Catal. of Exhibits, South Bank Exhib., Festival of Britain* 59/2 Steak knife, hollow-ground blade. **1959** L. Smith *One Hour* xxv. 321 Even now, I see those steak knives cutting through the meat. **1979** N. Hynd *False Flags* v. 43 The barman gave

Mason a steak knife. The sandwich arrived. 1723 J. NOTT *Cook's & Confectioner's Dict.* sig. Kk2, To make a Stake-Pye. 1791 J. WOODFORDE *Diary* 8 Aug. (1927) III. 291 We did our best and gave them some Beans and Bacon..Stake Pye and a Codlin Pudding. 1930 H. BURKE *Cookery Bk.* 103 Steak Pie. Follow the Steak and Kidney Pie recipe, omitting the kidney. 1981 'M. YORKE' *Hand of Death* xiv. 121 He went home to the steak pie Nancy had prepared. 1970 J. UPDIKE *Bech: a Book* 199 We..made all those steak restaurants in the East Fifties light up like seraglios under bombardment. 1941 B. SCHULBERG *What makes Sammy Run?* v. 85 Sammy had his mouth full of..steak sandwich. 1979 J. VAN DE WETERING *Maine Massacre* ix. 123 Would you like a sandwich? A steak sandwich? 1911 A. FILIPPINI *Internat. Cook Bk.* 676 (*heading*) Steaks, Tartare. 1958 *Observer* 26 Jan. 5/6 A steak tartare. 1969 'M. UNDERWOOD' *Shadow Game* ii. 22 Peacock was having Steak Tartare...rather appropriate food for one who dwelt in a ruthless world of sophisticated gangsterism. Raw meat! 1845 E. ACTON *Mod. Cookery* (ed. 3) vii. 161 If..it should be necessary, for want of steak-tongs, to use a fork, it should be passed through the outer skin..of the steak.

steal, *sb.*[2] Add: **1. b.** (Earlier example.)

1872 *Daily Gaz.* (Little Rock, Arkansas) 1 Apr., Of all the swindles and steals that have ever been proposed or carried out in our State, this is the largest and boldest.

c. *colloq.* (orig. *U.S.*). A bargain.

1942 BERREY & VAN DEN BARK *Amer. Thes. Slang.* § 546/2 Advantageous purchase; a bargain,..*steal.* 1951 *N.Y. Herald-Tribune* 14 Dec. 6 The asking price is $45,000, but I'm pretty sure you could get it for 43,000, and at that price it's a *steal.* 1960 *News Chron.* 2 May 3/1 At £30,000 it was a steal. I think it's worth £75,000. 1969 C. DRUMMOND *Odds on Death* vi. 142 A car like this..is a steal at three thousand quid. 1979 *Fortune* 15 Jan. 67 A sentimental gesture, but it was a steal—a quarter of a million acres for less than $10 an acre!

3. b. (Earlier and later examples.)

1867 *Chicago Times* 26 July 5/2 Norton made first base, but, on essaying Berthrong's steal, he was similarly ousted. 1908 [see *RUN DOWN *sb.* 1]. 1949 *Oregonian* (Portland) 10 Aug. III. 4/1 Davis overthrew second in an attempt to nail Hale on a steal. 1976 *National Observer* (U.S.) 12 June 14/3 Don't worry. I give the steal sign, and if you're thrown out, I'll take the blame. 1976 *Washington Post* 19 Apr. D 4/4 Washington's glamour boy also struck out when he labeled the Yanks' Roy White 'an excellent steal man, 15 for 16 last year' only to correct himself a minute later by giving White 16 steals in 31 attempts last season.

c. *Basketball.* An act of obtaining possession of the ball from an opponent.

1974 *State* (Columbia S. Carolina) 15 Feb. 3-B/4 Then, on a steal, Iona tied it up 62–62.

steal, *v.*[1] Add: **I. 1. g.** With a person as quasi-obj., in phr. *to steal* (someone) *blind*, to rob or cheat (someone) totally or mercilessly. *colloq.* (orig. *N. Amer.*).

1974 *Times* 28 Feb. 9/5 Mr. Howard Hughes, the eccentric multimillionaire..replied: 'Because he's a no-good, dishonest son of a bitch, and he stole me blind.' 1975 *Citizen* (Ottawa) 29 Oct. 21/2 Trustee Dalton McGuinty..said there was no other way to keep students from 'stealing us blind'. 1977 I. SHAW *Beggarman, Thief* I. ii. 21 We'd've been stolen blind without him. 1978 D. BAGLEY *Flyaway* xxi. 182 These people are Fulani... We're not staying here—they'd steal us blind.

4. h. *to steal (the) picture, scene, show*: (*colloq.* (orig. *U.S.*)) in theatrical contexts, to outshine unexpectedly the rest of the cast; also *transf.*, to become or make oneself the centre of attention; *to steal* (one's) *thunder*: see *THUNDER *sb.* 3 c.

1928 *Amer. Speech* III. 368 If a 'part' actor leaves a better impression on the audience and critics than the 'star',..the 'part' actor or actress 'steals' the picture. 1934 *Everyman* 24 Aug. 201/2 (*caption*) It seems we've stolen the show, Aussie. 1937 H. G. WELLS *Brynhild* ix. 143 He appeared in bright new flannels,..the best-looking author in the bunch. He stole the picture. 1941 F. SCOTT FITZGERALD *Last Tycoon* iii. 37 'Somebody been catching flies on him?' she asked—a phrase for stealing scenes. 1942 E. WAUGH *Put out More Flags* iii. 189 They came to the little party.., and stole the scene. 1963 AUDEN *Dyer's Hand* 185 Short of cutting him [*sc.* Falstaff] out of the play altogether, no producer can prevent him from stealing the show. 1979 *Tucson Mag.* Jan. 55/3 Kate Gardiner could well steal the show in the delectable role of Dorine.

5. g. (Earlier examples.) Also in Basketball and Ice Hockey, and *fig.*

1836 *New Sporting Mag.* Oct. 361 [The batsmen's scores] added to the byes they stole, and the wide balls bowled, sufficed to make a hands of eighty-six runs. 1851 J. PYCROFT *Cricket Field* x. 196 A sharp runner..will often try a long-stop's temper by stealing runs. 1862 *Sunday Mercury* (N.Y.) 13 July 6/2 Creighton..made his base by a missed fly-catch of Sawyer's; Brainard and Young getting their runs by stealing in on the pitcher and catcher. 1936 *Philadelphia Rec.* 31 July 15/1 No Landon speech is likely to startle anybody. You know in advance that he will never take a full cut at the ball, try to steal a base or catch a line drive with one hand. 1938 M. DUTTON *Hockey* vi. 110 It is hard enough to steal the puck in your own end zone, without trying to regain a lost puck in the other fellow's. 1942 C. BEE *Basketball Library* IV. ii. 7 An attempt to 'steal' the ball from a good dribbler often leaves the defensive player out of position. 1968 *Globe & Mail* (Toronto) 5 Feb. 18/3 Ballantyne was ahead 5–3 going into the sixth end, but Lawrie tied it up in the seventh and stole one in each of eighth and ninth for the victory. 1978 *Boston Globe* 4 Jan. 42/2 Hollins stole the ball with seven seconds to play and scored.

6. c. (Earlier example.)

1743 W. ELLIS *Mod. Husbandman* July xvi. 77 One of my Hen Pheasants..got Abroad, and stole her Nest.

stealage, *a.* **a.** (Earlier example.)

1769 J. WEDGWOOD *Let.* 7 Apr. (1965) 72 On calculating the expence, breakage, and stealage by Sea, and comparing it with Land Carriage, I find there is about half saved.

steam, *sb.* Add: **I. 6. c.** Cheap wine laced with methylated spirits; methylated spirits as an intoxicant. *Austral.* and *N.Z. slang.*

1941 BAKER *Dict. Austral. Slang* 71 *Steam*, cheap wine, esp. laced with methylated spirits. 1963 A. LUBBOCK *Austral. Roundabout* 59 To my regret, I never got a chance to sample either 'plonk', or 'steam'! 1966 J. K. BAXTER *Pig Island Lett.* 36 I'd give old Rose the go-by For a bottle of steam tonight.

7. d. Also, *under one's own steam*; *like steam* (Austral.), furiously; *to let off steam*: also *fig.*, to relieve one's pent-up energy by vigorous activity; to give vent to one's feelings, esp. harmlessly; *to run out of steam*: see *RUN *v.* 66 c.

1863 *Blackw. Mag.* Feb. 249/1 This is a free country, and a few eloquent or blustering Radicals serve to 'let off the steam' of their class. 1869 H. JAMES *Let.* 16 Apr. in J. Strouse *Alice James* (1980) viii. 138, I feel an irresistible need to let off steam periodically & to confide to a sympathetic ear the impressions which the week has generated in my soul. 1905 H. LAWSON *Coll. Verse* (1968) II. 4 We was draftin' 'em out for the homeward track and sharin' 'em round like steam. 1912 CONRAD in *English Rev.* XI. 311 We are not allowed to bring them in under their own steam. 1916 H. J. LASKI in *Holmes–Laski Lett.* (1953) I. 25, I intend to write you a weekly letter to Washington—for I must let off steam somewhere. 1949 J. SYMONS *Bland Beginnings* 142 'Would you be kind enough to..see Miss Cleverly home.' 'That's not necessary... I can move under my own steam.' 1976 J. I. M. STEWART *Young Pattullo* iii. 72 It's just a dining club letting off steam. 1979 B. HARDY *World owes Me Nothing* 102, I hammered at the door like steam and over he came and opened it.

8. b. Short for *steam radio*, sense 17 below.

1959 C. MACINNES *Absolute Beginners* 112, I heard one of your arias on the steam, last evening. 1960 *Spectator* 15 July 103 John Arlott over on steam is still the best of the commentators. 1973 G. TALBOT *Ten Seconds from Now* (1974) v. 83 Frank Gillard..crowned his Corporation career by becoming Managing Director of Radio, our 'Head of Steam'.

12. *steam-bakery, bath* (earlier and later examples), *heater, radiator.*

1794 J. B. S. MORRITT *Let.* 24 June (1914) ii. 47 After a violent steam bath, they would run out and roll in the snow. 1879 *Bradstreet's* 22 Nov. 2/1 In close rooms close stoves are better than steam radiators. *a* 1884 KNIGHT *Dict. Mech.* Suppl. 861/1 *Steam Heater*,..a low pressure steam-heating apparatus. 1903 ADE *In Babel* 29 For ten years it had braced itself against the onsweeping rush of big machine-shops and steam-bakeries. 1962 A. LURIE *Love & Friendship* xii. 228 That..asthma kind of like a steam radiator. 1967 G. F. FIENNES *I tried to run Railway* ii. 7 The second [mistake was] to report myself for pulling off the steam-heater pipe. 1977 C. MCCULLOUGH *Thorn Birds* xi. 251 Hot nights in Gilly were bearable compared to this steam bath.

13. *steam-stack, trap.*

1877 Steam trap [see TRAP *sb.*[1] 8 b]. 1935 JOYCE *Let.* 28 Aug. (1957) 381, I would also like a pleasure yacht with a steamstack. 1955 *Times* 12 July 1/6 Before ordering any steam trap ask for its expectation of life. It is no use saving on steam equipment to pay it out later servicing traps.

14. *steam dredge, dredger, drill, -dryer, elevator, -mill* (examples), *press* (later examples), *shovel* (hence *-shovelful*), *trowel, -trumpet.*

1815 D. DRAKE *Nat. & Statist. View Cincinnati* iii. 137 The most capacious..building in this place is the Steam Mill. 1861 *Mitchell's Maritime Reg.* 1651/3 The launch of the Ancona, a very fine steam dredger, of 300 tons, recently took place at Southampton. 1873 H. JAMES *Let.* 25 Apr. (1974) I. v. 373 It was once a goodly old palace and though pitifully inconvenient as a hotel, is charminger to stay in than if it had a steam elevator. 1877 *Encycl. Brit.* VII. 464/1 The construction of large river steam dredges is now carried on by many engineering firms. 1879 R. J. BURDETTE *Hawk-Eyes* 25 The depot policeman looked in to say to him that if he was tired out, he would send in a section hand or the steam shovel to give him a spell. 1880 *Harper's Mag.* Aug. 344/2 The grist from it [*sc.* the tide mill] is said to be of a better quality than from the steam-mills, as being less heated in the process. 1904 *Jrnl. Inst. Electr. Engin.* XXXIII. 965 Steam-dryers are fitted in the flues of two of the boilers. 1906 T. ROOSEVELT *Let.* 20 Nov. (1919) 182 There the huge steam-shovels are hard at it; scooping huge masses of rock and gravel and dirt. 1906 W. DE MORGAN *Joseph Vance* xli. 367 He told how she and he were awakened by the sudden stoppage of the screw, followed by the roar of the steam-trumpet. 1925 L. R. HARRIS in *Messenger* VII. 387/1 A so-called 'steam-drill'..guaranteed to drill a hole faster than any ten men could drill one in the old way with sledge hammer and steel. 1928 *Observer* 15 Apr. 5/4 The people in the restaurants shovel food into their mouths as the steam-trowel takes up its load of earth. 1937 *Discovery* Dec. 362/2 All advances in technique such as the steam press and the linotype, had been developed by the news-printer and later used by the book-printer. 1966 T. PYNCHON *Crying of Lot 49* iii. 65 A wildcat transistor outfit that..was underselling even the Japanese and hauling in loot by the steamshovelful. 1972 J. MOSEDALE *Football* vii. 95 After a trip through the steam presses, caps and uniforms were either too large or too small. 1978 J. IRVING *World according to Garp* iv. 79 His mouth still reminded Garp of a steam shovel's power.

15. *steam barge, bus, ferry* (examples), *ferry-boat, hopper* (HOPPER[1] 6), *launch* (earlier example), *lawn-mower, locomotion, locomotive, lorry, omnibus, railway, schooner, yacht* (later examples).

1819 *N.Y. Even. Post* 4 Jan. 2/5 Steam sch[oone]r Ramapo, Reid, New Orleans. 1834 J. B. PURCELL *Jrnl.* 21 Mar. in *Catholic Hist. Rev.* (1919) V. 253 Mr. Mtgomery an hour & ½ in crossing the River in Steam-ferry boat. 1842 J. MCDONOGH *Papers* (1898) 65 The steam ferry which runs from one side of the river to the other lands a short distance below my house. 1866 *Mitchell's Maritime Reg.* 18 Aug. 1033/3 Messrs. C. and W. Earle launched from their yard a steam barge [named *Lion*] the first of its class built in Hull. 1869 *Bradshaw's Railway Man.* XXI. 34 A steam ferry across the river Severn. 1872 F. TREVITHICK *Life Richard Trevithick* II. xxi. 207 Cast-iron wheels were ordered with a view to steam locomotion in the Cordilleras. *Ibid.* xvii. 26 The high-pressure steam-puffer ..moved..towards the broken mass..and..changing its powers from steam-crane to steam-locomotive, conveyed it to the port. 1877 *Encycl. Brit.* VII. 464/2 The steam hoppers employed to receive and remove the dredgings carry about 500 tons of excavations. 1878 C. SCHREIBER *Jrnl.* 30 June (1911) II. 155 The Embassy steam launch met us. 1890 G. MEREDITH *Let.* 14 Apr. (1970) II. 997, I am promised a steam-yacht to take me up at Oban. 1902 H. C. MOORE *Omnibuses & Cabs* I. iv. 38 The first real steam omnibuses, the 'Era' and 'Autopsy', were invented by Walter Hancock, of Stratford, and placed on the London roads in 1833. 1915 *Naut. Gaz.* 31 Mar. 4/1 The Panama Canal has brought us the steam schooner and other Pacific curiosities. 1916 *Law Rep. I King's Bench* 148 The defendants, who were brewers, used a Steam lorry weighing five tons, for the purpose of delivering beer from their premises to various public-houses served by them. 1923 *Blackw. Mag.* Nov. 681/1 In the harbour.. there were lying odd craft... The one romance of life for these steam-hoppers..had been quenched. 1928 J. MASON *Before Mast in Sailing Ships* 174 He was picked up by a steam barge which happened to be passing. 1933 V. SOMMERFIELD *London's Buses* 5 (*caption*) Three of Hancock's Steam Buses, 1832 to 1836. 1946 G. FOREMAN *Last Trek of Indians* 116 A steam ferryboat was in service. 1946 NOBLE & JUNNER *Vital to Life of Nation* vi. 88 Sumner..began experimenting in the design of a steam wagon in 1889, a year or two later producing a steam lawn mower. *Ibid.* 96 (*caption*) A London steam omnibus of 1902. 1958 *Listener* 11 Sept. 379/2 He was knocked down and killed by a steam lorry. 1965 D. ARUNDELL *Sadler's Wells* xi. 144 Mrs. Warner and Phelps were shown arriving..in a first-class steam-railway carriage. 1970 F. MCKENNA *Gloss. Railwaymen's Talk* 1 Most steam locomotive depots in England are embedded in the older parts of our towns and cities. 1971 *Sat. Rev.* (U.S.) 6 Nov. 86/3 The purpose of the California steam-bus project is to demonstrate how effectively city buses can operate at low levels of exhaust emission. 1977 D. JACK *Leyland Bus* i. 11 The back-bone of the business was production of steam lawn-mowers selling with 30-inch roller at £85 each. 1977 H. FAST *Immigrants* I. 72, I got two steam schooners, wooden ships, six hundred tons each. 1980 *Times* 25 June 4/2 The inaugural voyage of the National Trust's restored 1859 steam yacht the Gondola took place on Coniston Water yesterday.

16. a. *steam-bent, -hauled, -heated, -operated, -set.* Also with vbl. sbs., as *steam-bending, cleaning, -heating*; and vbs., as *steam-bend, -clean* (trans.).

a 1884 KNIGHT *Dict. Mech.* Suppl. 861/1 In Campbell & Pryor's method of steam heating for dwellings, the steam boiler and radiators are inclosed in a heating room in the cellar. 1890 *Harper's Mag.* Sept. 576/1 The Kents lived in a steam-heated flat. 1917 S. GRAHAM *Priest of Ideal* iv. 53 This mansion, with its good roof and closed windows and doors, and probably steam-heating to keep out the damp. 1934 *Discovery* Nov. 314/1 In 1934 the German railways made some striking accelerations in the schedules of their steam-hauled expresses. 1936 *Ibid.* Nov. 357/1 Acceleration of steam-operated trains in Great Britain continues. 1946 *Nature* 5 Oct. 474/1 This at once prompted Rudall to examine the effect of 50 per cent urea on steam-set β-keratin. 1949 *Sun* (Baltimore) 14 Dec. 5/2 Already, automobile 'laundries' and firms that steam-clean buildings have been told to cease operation. 1956 *Handbk. Hardwoods* (Forest Prod. Res. Lab.) 2 Classification of timbers according to their steam-bending properties is..based mainly on the minimum bending radius of sound, clear specimens 1 in. thick at a moisture content of about 25 per cent. 1956 *Amer. Speech* XXXI. 86 Advertisement of Adelaide Steam Cleaning Service. 1962 J. T. MARSH *Self-Smoothing Fabrics* ix. 122 It is not necessary to employ a special chamber for curing, but only the usual steam-heated cylinders or a stenter. *Ibid.* ii. 9 The steam-set fabric has a pleasant handle, and good crease recovery. 1966 A. W. LEWIS *Gloss. Woodworking Terms* 106 *Oak, Japanese*..easier to work than European oak. Steam-bends excellently. 1973 *Times* 4 Oct. 24/5 The chair is demountable and consists of eight wooden staves..steam-bent into a soft, flowing outline. 1977 *Modern Railways* Dec. 493/3 Steam-hauled excursions would be operated over this short length. 1978 *Detroit Free Press* 2 Apr. 2F/4 The natives claim 'the diggers', which is even more impolite than calling them Aussies, come to this spectacular thermal display to get their suits steam-cleaned for free.

b. Objective, as *steam-raising.*

1923 *Engineering* 26 Jan. 101/2 The boilers, furnaces ..economisers, coal bunkers and other details of the steam-raising equipment are carried by the steel framework of the building. 1979 *Improved Energy Efficiency* (Shell Internat. Petroleum Co.) 5 Substantial savings are possible in steam-raising.

17. steam age, the era when trains were drawn by steam locomotives; also *attrib.* or as *adj.*, belonging to this era; *fig.* out-of-date; **steam beer,** a Californian effervescent beer; **steam calliope** *U.S.* = *steam-organ*; **steam car** (earlier U.S. and later examples); **steam-carriage** (earlier example); **steam cracking,** the thermal cracking of petroleum using steam as an inert diluent which reduces polymerization and increases the yield of olefins; hence **steam-cracked** *a.*; **steam cracker,** an installation for this process; **steam curing,** the curing or hardening of a material by treatment with steam; hence **steam-cure** *v. trans.*; **steam-cured** *ppl. a.*; **steam distillation** *Physical Chem.*, distillation of a liquid in a current of steam, used esp. to purify at temperatures below their normal boiling points liquids that are not very volatile and are immiscible with water; hence (as a back-formation) **steam-distil** *v. trans.* and *intr.*; **steam-doctor** (earlier example); **steamfitter,** one who installs the pipes of a steam-heating system; a steam-heating engineer; **steam fly,** the small brown cockroach, *Blattella germanica,* commonly found in kitchens and bathrooms; **steam heat:** see sense 12 in Dict.; now *spec.* (the heat produced by) a steam-generating central heating system, used in passenger trains and buildings; **steam iron,** an electric iron containing water which is heated and emitted as steam from its flat surface to assist in the pressing of clothes; † **steam-kettle,** a kettle used in sick-rooms to create a moist warm atmosphere (*obs.*); **steam line,** a line in a phase diagram representing the conditions of temperature and pressure at which water and water vapour are in equilibrium in the absence of ice; **steam organ** (later examples); **steam point,** (*a*) a temperature at which liquid water and water vapour are in equilibrium; *spec.* the boiling point of water under standard atmospheric pressure; (*b*) *N. Amer.*, a metal pipe which is driven into frozen earth and down which steam can be passed in order to thaw the ground for mining; **steam radio,** colloq. name for sound radio, considered outmoded by television; hence, a radio receiver; **steam-raiser,** a person employed in an engine shed to light the fires of locomotives and raise steam; **steam room,** (*b*) *U.S.*, a vapour bath; **steam table** *U.S.*, a table in a cafetaria, etc., slotted to hold containers of cooked food kept hot by steam circulating beneath them; **steam turbine:** see TURBINE 1 b.

1941 AUDEN *New Year Letter* III. 66 The genius of the loud Steam Age. **1961** *Spectator* 4 Aug. 181 The jet-age author gets the same sort of romance out of beaten-up old Dakotas..as steam-age Robert Louis Stevenson did from a schooner. **1978** W. GARNER *Möbius Trip* (1979) I. i. 34 Suppose you're..a bullion dealer. You're not happy with your present security. It's a little bit steam age. **1898** *Western Brewer* XXVIII. 278/1 Steam beer.. is bottom fermenting... The steam beer mash is made according to the English downward mashing method. **1941** *American Neptune* Oct. 402 Claus Spreckels is the reputed inventor of the great San Francisco speciality, steam beer. **1959** *San Francisco Chron.* 28 June 1 There won't be a drop of steam beer in Northern California after a few more days. **1974** W. R. HUNT *North of 53°* xv. 102 Many saloons served the 'choicest goods' and steam beer at two bits a glass. **1868** *Daily Territorial Enterprise* (Virginia City, Nevada) 29 Aug. 3/1 Even a steam calliope would not cause our firm nerves to tremble as vigorously as this worst of all combinations of unsweet tones. **1936** J. DOS PASSOS *Big Money* 164 The clanking roar of the rollercoaster and the steam-calliope. **1976** *St. Louis Post-Dispatch* 16 Sept. 1/2 A steam calliope is the ransom for the return of Nipper. **1833** *Amer. Rail Road Jrnl.* II. 225/2 The Steam Car accomplished the distance. **1903** J. FOX *Little Shepherd of Kingdom Come* v. 65 'Steam cars!' they cried. **1962** E. LUCIA *Klondike Kate* 7 They clambered aboard..the steam cars. **1969** *Listener* 3 July 31/3 Mr Donald Healey, developer of Austin-Healey sports cars, is rumoured to be building..a 140 m.p.h. steam car... The current spate of steam-car development projects. **1788** in *Rep. U.S. Comm. Patents 1849* (1850) 581 If any person..shall make..any elevator, hopper-boy, or any steam-carriage..without the consent of the said Oliver Evans. **1962** MURPHREE & CIPRIOS in *Mod. Petroleum Technol.* (ed. 3) ix. 318 The octane number of this steam-cracked naphtha ranges from about 80 to 100 research method (unleaded). **1968** *Economist* 2 Nov. 73/1 When finished, the plant will include a new steam cracker, with a production capacity of 340,000 tons a year of ethylene, 200,000 tons of propylene, [etc.]. **1959** *Petroleum Times* 25 Sept. 602/1 No. 3 olefine plant is..based on the steam cracking process. **1962** MURPHREE & CIPRIOS in *Mod. Petroleum Technol.* (ed. 3) ix. 318 Although the primary purpose of steam cracking is the production of light hydrocarbons, the process also produces material in the gasoline boiling range. **1977** *Shell in Base Chemicals* (Shell Internat. Petroleum Co.) 4 Benzene, toluene and mixed xylenes coming from oil are extracted in special plants from reformate and pyrolysis gasoline, formed when lower olefins are manufactured by the steam-cracking of liquid feedstocks. **1910** *Cement Era* VIII. 169/1 Blocks of 1 part cement to 8 parts sand and [*sic*] steam cured at 80 pounds pressure showed a crusting strength of 2,100 pounds per square inch. **1962** J. T. MARSH *Self-Smoothing Fabrics* xi. 177 It sometimes happens that, with cotton goods which have been steam-cured, the crease recovery is very slightly below that obtained in an atmosphere free from steam. **1909** *Chem. Abstr.* III. 1210 Steam-cured blocks may be made all winter. **1962** J. T. MARSH *Self-Smoothing Fabrics* xi. 176 It was possible to show a linear relation between the improvement in resistance to abrasion of steam-cured fabrics over dry-cured fabrics and the amount of steam present. **1907** *Engin. News* 5 Sept. 249/1 (*heading*) Effect of steam curing on the crushing strength of concrete. **1921** HATT & VOSS *Concrete Work* I. viii. 181 Steam curing is accomplished in curing tunnels with a roof of such a shape that it will drain the condensed moisture to the sides of the tunnel. **1967** M. CHANDLER *Ceramics in Mod. World* iv. 128 The whole assembly is..put into a steam-curing cabinet. **1923** W. M. CUMMING et al. *Systematic Org. Chem.* ii. 24 When the liquid to be steam-distilled is lighter than water, the small glass tube E is extended to the bottom of the receiver. **1964** *Oceanogr. & Marine Biol.* II. 152 The compound is reduced to trimethylamine with $TiCl_3$, which is then steam-distilled into an excess of standardized acid. **1974** ROSSER & WILLIAMS *Mod. Org. Chem. for 'A' Level* xiii. 253 If care is not taken to dry organic liquids thoroughly, the water/liquid mixture will often steam-distil over at a temperature lower than the actual boiling point of the pure liquid. **1904** *Analyst* XXIX. 385 (*heading*) Laboratory apparatus for steam distillation. **1954** *Thorpe's Dict. Appl. Chem.* (ed. 4) XI. 85/2 The chief advantage offered by steam distillation is that a substance of fairly low volatility can be separated from non-volatile impurities at a temperature much below its normal boiling-point. **1972** P. R. S. MURRAY *Princ. Org. Chem.* ix. 58 Steam distillation is most effective when one of the components to be separated..has a high molecular weight. **1830** *Cincinnati Chron.* 6 Feb. 2/3 The Mayor was induced..to issue his warrant for the apprehension of a black man calling himself Caesar Gimsoun, and practising in this city as a *steam doctor*. **1906** *Daily Colonist* (Victoria, B.C.) 12 Jan. 7/7 (Advt.), To plumbers, steam fitters etc. We have just received two carloads of iron pipes in all sizes. **1977** J. CROSBY *Company of Friends* xvii. 114 They both laughed...talking about the problems of the trade like steamfitters discussing occupational hazards. **1933** M. LOWRY *Ultramarine* iv. 184 'You shuffle them—' '—King of the steam-flies, eh—'. **1944** *Jrnl. R. Army Med. Corps* LXXXIII. 188 The steam fly or German cockroach. **1962** *New Scientist* 11 Oct. 75/1 The German cockroach, commonly referred to as 'the steam fly', is dark brown to tan in colour and is also very widely distributed. **1904** *Railway Mag.* XIV. 169/2 Since the general introduction of steam-heat..it appears to be an easy matter for the guard to simply turn a valve to supply sufficient steam to heat the cars comfortably. **1941** J. MASEFIELD *In Mill* 36 The winter steam-heat made it impossible to wear a coat while at work. **1974** *Times* 1 Apr. 14/5 Hugh Lawson, deputy city engineer of Nottingham, gave a speedy talk on his city's steam-heat system. **1951** *Good Housek. Home Encycl.* 154/2 Electronic steam irons are now available, but..are not always so effective as they might appear. **1962** *Which?* Sept. 270/1 If you want to avoid using a damp cloth or damping the clothes, then your choice may well be a steam iron. **1972** *Guardian* 30 Aug. 9/5 The opening for filling steam irons with distilled water is usually mingy, and the thing overflows. **1890** F. TAYLOR *Man. Pract. Med.* (1891) 356 In the intervals, the largyngitis is to be treated by a moist warm atmosphere (steam-kettle) and mild opiates as in other cases. **1879** Steam line [see *HOAR-FROST b]. **1937** M. W. ZEMANSKY *Heat & Thermodynamics* xi. 175 In the particular case of water..the vaporization curve is called the steam line. **1910** 'I. HAY' in *Granta* 11 June 12 Even the steam organs seemed to have stopped of their own accord. **1962** L. DAVIDSON *Rose of Tibet* vi. 106 It was as though he had been pushed into a steam organ at a fair. The stupefying blare of sound. **1895** *Jrnl. Chem. Soc.* LXVII. 196 It is absolutely necessary that the surface of the pyrometer should be free from all soluble salts when the steam point is being taken. **1909** *Yukon Territory* (Canada Dept. Interior) iv. 38 A steam point is an iron pipe of about 5½ feet in length,..connected to a boiler supplying the steam... The miner drives the steam point into the ground, where it is left..until a hole is thawed. **1965** *Jrnl. Chem. Physics* XLII. 274/2 In 1954 the size of the Kelvin degree was fixed by assigning the value 273·16°K to the triple point of water, so that the value of the steam point is now subject to experimental determination. **1974** W. R. HUNT *North of 53°* iv. 15 Steam points replaced wood fires for thawing and this greatly speeded the mining work. **1957** V. GIELGUD *Brit. Radio Drama 1922–1956* The flight from 'steam-radio' to television has become an admitted rout. **1961** *Radio Times* 6 Apr. 41/4, I am the proud possessor of 'square eyeballs', but still feel that the good old 'steam' radio has a winner in the *Scrapbook* series. **1976** J. SNOW *Cricket Rebel* 7 Overseas tours were followed equally avidly on the old 'steam' radio in the lounge. **1925** PATERSON & WEBSTER *Man. Locomotive Running Shed Management* viii. 114 The usual method is for the steam raiser to 'line' the grate along the firebox sides and well into the corners with coal, leaving the centre of the grate bare. **1947** H. WEBSTER *Locomotive Running Shed Pract.* 177 Following an interval of 30 minutes or so the fire is inspected by the steam-raiser who breaks it up and adds fresh fuel. **1972** *Village Voice* (N.Y.) 1 June 73/1 A steamroom in which vapors rise and good men fall. **1861** Steam table [see *hot plate* s.v. *HOT *a.* 12 c]. **1944** S. BELLOW *Dangling Man* 32, I looked around at the steam tables and the posters of foundering ships. **1976** M. MACHLIN *Pipeline* xiii. 154 Next to the sandwiches was a steam table with several containers of soggy-looking breaded veal cutlets.

steam, *v.* Add: **I. 7. c.** (Earlier examples.)

1842 C. FOX *Jrnl.* 29 May (1882) viii. 156 Steamed away to London Bridge and saw the Maurices. **1849** *Ibid.* 13 June xv. 244 Steamed to Chelsea, and paid Mrs. Carlyle a humane little visit.

9. d. *to steam open* (later examples). Similarly, *to steam* (a postage stamp, label, etc.) *off.*

1920 M. WEBB *House in Dormer Forest* xvi. 214 The kettle having complied, she began to steam the letter open. **1944** R. LEHMANN *Ballad & Source* I. vi. 49 She used to send us postcards... We steamed the stamps off. **1979** 'J. LE CARRÉ' *Smiley's People* (1980) xix. 242, I can still tap your phone, steam open your mail.

II. 11. Colloq. with *up.* **a.** To stir up or rouse (ardour, etc.). *rare.*

1919 F. HURST *Humoresque* 97 Ed says he'd never get him to steam up his nerve enough to call at a girl's house after her. **1931** *Daily Express* 21 Sept. 19/2 He was trying to steam up interest in the contest.

b. To rouse or excite (a person), esp. to anger; to agitate, upset.

1922 H. C. WITWER in *Collier's* 17 June 22/4 Are you asking me to go with you so's to steam Rags Dempster up? **1964** WODEHOUSE *Frozen Assets* iii. 61 She's one of those calm, quiet girls you'd think nothing would steam up. *a* **1974** R. CROSSMAN *Diaries* (1977) III. 366 The Department have steamed me up into the idea that I have got a terrible series of difficulties here.

12. With *up*: Agric., to subject (an animal) to steaming up (see *STEAMING *vbl. sb.* 5).

1947 V. C. FISHWICK *Dairy Farming* II. 164 We steam-up our heifers and cows, and feed a balanced milk-production ration during the lactation period. **1959** *Observer* 15 Nov. 3/1 There are no special hazards in artificial twinning provided that the cow is generously fed—steamed up as it is called in farming language—before calving. **1969** N. W. PIRIE *Food Resources* iii. 104 The extreme case is the process known as 'steaming up' or 'flushing' ewes before mating. The extra food given.. increases the probability of conception.

steamboat. Add: **a.** (Earlier *attrib.* examples.)

1821 *Deb. Congress U.S.* 28 Dec. (1855) 44 The jurisdiction had only embraced steamboat navigation. **1847** [see *raft-man* s.v. *RAFT *sb.*[1] 5].

c. *Comb.*, as **steamboat Gothic** *adj. phr.* (*U.S.*), used to designate an ornamented style of architecture typical of houses built by retired steamboat captains in the mid-nineteenth century.

1962 W. FAULKNER *Reivers* viii. 166 The big rambling multigalleried multistoried steamboat-gothic hotel where the overalled aficionados..gathered..each February. **1970** K. PLATT *Pushbutton Butterfly* (1971) iv. 43 The beautiful old mansions with their bay windows, ornate Steamboat Gothic cornices and mouldings.

steamboating *vbl. sb.*, (*a*) (earlier examples); also **steamboatman** *U.S.*, one who works on a steamboat, esp. a steamboat owner or captain.

1826 MALTHUS *Diary* 7 July (1966) 263 Dr Brown said that the introduction of Steam boating had quite altered the habits of the people of Glasgow. **1828** MRS. B. HALL *Let.* 7 June in *Aristocratic Journey* (1931) xxii. 288 Two nights more and we shall have done with it and have no more steamboating in this country. **1875** 'MARK TWAIN' in *Atlantic Monthly* Jan. 69/1 When I was a boy, there was but one permanent ambition among my comrades... That was, to be a steamboatman. **1910** D. W. BONE *Brassbounder* 251 Sailormen walk fore and aft; steamboat men, athwart. **1929** G. L. ESKEW *Pageant of Packets* ii. 101 All the steamboatmen when in New Orleans did their banking at the Banque des Citoyens.

steamed, *ppl. a.* (In Dict., s.v. STEAM *v.*) Add: **1.** In the simple senses of the vb. (Examples of *steamed pudding.*)

1884 N. LAKE *Menus made Easy* viii. 149 *Pouding soufflé*—a very light steamed pudding. *Ibid.* viii. 150 *Pouding à la Snowdon*—a steamed pudding of suet, breadcrumbs, brown sugar and marmalade. **1945** *ABC of Cookery* (Ministry of Food) xvii. 61 Most modern steamed puddings are made by one or other of the cake-mixing methods already described. **1978** K. WEBBER *Bk. Winter Cooking* 93 Boiled or steamed puddings can be stodgy.

2. With *up.* **a.** Excited or roused, esp. to anger; agitated, upset. Freq. in phr. *all steamed up.* Rarely without *up. colloq.*

1923 H. C. WITWER in *Cosmopolitan* Sept. 72/2, I was a bit steamed up about her making my popular sex ridiculous by going boy-crazy at fifty. **1935** J. HARGAN *Gloss. Prison Lang.* 8 *Steamed*, envious, angry. **1936** M. H. BRADLEY *Five-Minute Girl* v. 79 If she was all steamed up like this over embroidery silks, he thought, what would she be when he told his news? **1943** P. CHEYNEY *You can always Duck* vi. 101, I reckon he's a bit steamed up over my allure. **1953** K. AMIS *Lucky Jim* xiv. 148 People get themselves all steamed up about whether they're in love or not. **1965** M. BRADBURY *Stepping Westward* vii. 330 People live naked in this country [*sc.* the USA]. If you get steamed up you let everyone know. **1979** G. F. NEWMAN *List* ii. 22 They sounded pretty steamed with him. **1980** D. BOGARDE *Gentle Occupation* ii. 44 The General insists it is sent to all the Brigades. He's getting very steamed up about the bloody little thing.

b. Drunk, intoxicated. Rarely without *up. slang.*

1929 M. A. GILL *Underworld Slang* 10/2 *Steamed up*, drunk. **1950** *Landfall* June 126 Little Spike is six foot two and has a reputation for being a hard case when he is steamed-up. **1971** J. TERRELL *Bunkhouse Papers* xii. 156 A cowman sat next to the houseman, and he was steamed with liquor so that he slumped a little to one side.

3. With *up*. Of a glass surface, etc.: covered or bedewed with condensed vapour.
1972 G. Lyall *Blame the Dead* xv. 106, I went along to the buffet car..and stared at the steamed-up window.

steam-engine. b. (Later examples.)
1934 *Railway Wonders of World* I. 309/1 There is one factor, however, where the steam engine will probably always score, and that is in its greater length of useful life and lower maintenance costs. **1970** F. McKenna *Gloss. Railwaymen's Talk* p. iii, The crash of the coal hopper.. and the noise of steam engines preparing for their journeys no longer disturb the peaceful inhabitants of Mortimer Terrace and Highgate Road.

steamer. Add: **5. b.** *steamer rug, trunk* (earlier example).
1886 in *New Canaan Hist. Soc. Ann.* (1959) 19/1 A steamer trunk I believe they call them; something to hold necessary articles on their voyage. **1890** S. Hale *Let.* 22 Dec. (1919) 253 It is..so cold..that we are sitting close up to the grate..and all wound about with the heaviest steamer rug! **1977** H. Fast *Immigrants* vi. 365 They were covered by a big steamer rug.

6. c. A steam locomotive engine or train.
1837 W. Tayler *Diary* 22 Sept. (1962) 51 We passed the Southampton rail road and was just in time to see the steamer go past, with about forty cars fastened to it full of gravel.
1961 *Times* 16 Aug. 9/4 This strong feeling, stimulated in this decade by the departure of the 'steamer', has served to produce something of a golden age in railway literature. **1972** *Times Lit. Suppl.* 10 Nov. 1377/3 All over Britain people are banding together to buy, restore and, they hope, run a steamer. **1975** 'J. Lymington' *Spider in Bath* ix. 156, I meant a real locomotive. A steamer. **1981** *Railway Mag.* Mar. 115/3 No. 765 is the first main-line steamer of the decade to be returned to active duty.

7. a. (Earlier example.)
1870 *Daily News* 15 Oct. 7/4 Alarming Fire at the Gaiety Restaurant... The 'call' for engines was rapidly responded to, no fewer than eight steamers being soon present.

8. b. = *long-neck clam* s.v. *long-neck 2 b, freq. eaten as a delicacy. Also *steamer clam*.
1909 *Rep. Mollusk Fisheries Mass.* (Mass. Comm. Fisheries) 179 Small clams, or 'steamers', are shipped in the shell. **1947** P. A. Morris *Field Guide Shells of our Atlantic Coast* 89 *Mya arenaria*... Known by such names as 'long clam', 'soft-shelled clam', 'steamer clam', and 'long-necked clam', it lives in the muds and gravels between the tides. **1960** J. J. Rowlands *Spindrift* 84 The delicious steamer clam of the North Atlantic is becoming scarce. **1977** [see *quahaug, quahog].

† **10.** The name of a back-stroke in swimming (see quots.). *Obs.*
1861 'R. Harrington' *Swimming* 10 The 'steamer'.. consists in striking the water violently with the foot, raising each leg alternately out of the water to do so. **1879** *Boy's Own Ann.* I. 415/3 The Steamer... Lie on the back, point your feet as much as possible, and then strike them alternately into the water, the knees being kept quite stiff.

11. *Rhyming slang.* [Abbrev. of *steam tug* = 'mug'.] = Mug *sb.*[5] 1; also *spec.* a male homosexual, esp. one who seeks passive partners.
1932 G. S. Moncrieff *Café Bar* vii. 63 The mug became pleasanter... 'I'm a porter, at some service flats in Victoria..What's your friend do?' the steamer asked genially. **1936** J. Curtis *Gilt Kid* xxxvi 258 If you think I'm going to make a steamer of myself and let you hang about half a dozen more charges on me, you're mistaken. **1958** *Times Lit. Suppl.* 2 May 237/4 Terry..spending his time..among the young homosexuals and their 'steamers' **1968** G. J. Barrett *Guilty, be Damned!* viii. 95 You might get yourself caught. The Police are a lot sharper than steamers give them credit for being. **1978** M. Puzo *Fools Die* iv. 48 The third player at the table was a 'steamer', a bad gambler who chased losing bets.

steamie (stī·mi). *Sc.* Also **steamy.** [f. Steam *sb.* + -ie.] A public wash-house.
1926 *Glasgow Herald* 19 Oct. 8 The perambulator holds much besides..the baby... In the poorer parts of the city the washing is conveyed to and from the 'steamy' thereon. **1935** *Scottish Educ. Jrnl.* 8 Mar. Suppl. p. vi/2 Modern sanitation has..caused the coining of 'steamie' (the public wash-house). **1958** *3rd Statistical Acct. Scotl.* V. iii. xvii. 560 Attendances at the 'steamies' in the year were just short of 1,800,000. **1969** *Dumfries & Galloway Standard* 29 Oct. 1 There was still a need for the 'steamie' as launderettes were not as cheap as the council maintained. **1978** *Times* 18 May 24/1 It was the talk of the steamie, so to speak. It was a topic of conversation at the company.

steaming, *vbl. sb.* Add: **4. a.** (Earlier example.)
1836 *Southern Lit. Messenger* II. 696 Steaming from Washington to Baltimore is an improvement upon that route at least.

b. *Comb.*, as **steaming light**, a white light carried on the masthead of a steamship under way at sea by night.
1909 *Man. Seamanship* (Admiralty) II. i. 29 *Navigation lights*,..oil ones..consist of steaming light, in charge of 2nd captain of forecastle, who is responsible for placing it; after steaming light..; starboard bow light..; and port bow light. **1947** *Sea Breezes* iv. 139/2 A steamer appeared, also carrying steaming lights.

5. With *up*. In *Agric.*, the provision of extra food to farm animals as preparation for reproduction.
1943 R. Boutflour in *Agriculture* L. 306 It is now over twenty years since I coined the expression 'steaming up'; the reason for its choice was to imply that a definite preparation was required. **1947** V. C. Fishwick *Dairy Farming* ii. 156, I believe in steaming-up and preparation for calving. This is how you get the milk. **1953** K. Russell *Princ. Dairy Farming* xiii. 153 The amount of steaming-up ration to be fed as concentrates is then decided by two factors—the condition of the cow or heifer and her probable milking capacity. **1960** *Farmer & Stockbreeder* 19 Jan. 122/3 Cows require 'steaming up' prior to calving.

steaming, *ppl. a.* Add: **3.** Used as a substitute for a strong expletive: consummate, 'blithering'. *slang.*
1962 *Listener* 13 Dec. 1024/3 A cautionary tale concerning a real steaming nit of a British civilian. **1965** A. Garner *Elidor* xix. 147 Roland! You great steaming chudd! Come back!

steamless (stī·mlės), *a.* [f. Steam *sb.* + -less.] Without steam; that has run out of steam or is not propelled by steam. Also of a railway: not carrying steam-engines.
1920 *Blackw. Mag.* Apr. 573/2 The N.T.O. insisted on placing the skipper of the steamless tug under arrest. **1967** *Gloss. Sanitation Terms* (*B.S.I.*) 49 *Steamless inlet*, a device to reduce the amount of steam produced in filling a bath with hot water. **1970** *Railway Mag.* Oct. 544/2 My old room facing the now steamless railway.

steam-roller. Add: **b.** (Later examples, esp. of such a force used to a political end.)
Russian steam-roller: with reference to Russian military capacity in the war of 1914–18.
1896 Lloyd George *Let.* 6 Aug. (1973) 106 One of them [*sc.* M.P.s] threatened to pass a steamroller over me yesterday... Killed the Military Lands Bill. Just heard from Balfour. That's their steamroller. **1912** *Chicago Tribune* 3 June 2/2 The Roosevelt adherents..expect through publicity to prevent the operation of the steamroller. **1916** G. B. Shaw in *N.Y. Times* 9 Apr. vi. 1/3 A combination of the British fleet, the French Army, and the Russian steam roller. **1934** J. Hilton *Goodbye, Mr. Chips* xiii. 89 The Battle of the Marne, the Russian steam-roller, Kitchener. **1952** *Sun* (Baltimore) 7 July 2/4 Meanwhile Taft's men proceed on the lines slammed down by Elihu Root's steamroller. **1976** *Listener* 5 Feb. 132/3 The Soviet military doctrine of the so-called 'steamroller approach'—huge numbers of well-disciplined, fit and adequately trained privates, as distinguished from the élitist concept of an all-volunteer army, like Britain's.

steam-roll *v.*: also **stea·mroll;** (*b*) *fig.*; also, to force or drive in a given direction (cf. *steam-roller *v.* 2); **steam-rolling** *vbl. sb.* (*fig.* examples).
1914 *Times* 29 Aug. 6/2 Our task is stonewalling, and that of the Russians is steamrolling. **1915** F. M. Hueffer *Good Soldier* iv. v. 274 So Edward and Nancy found themselves steam-rolled out and Leonora survives. **1955** *Times* 15 Aug. 5/4 The big screen, Vistavision, the Hollywood technique, and all the rest of it will steamroll the lightness and gaiety of the original idea out of all recognition. **1975** *Times* 21 July 1/8 The ruling party..will steamroll the endorsement through. **1976** *Conservation News* Sept./Oct. 22/1 The main TV companies have made *some* attempt to cover the most excessive speculation and steamrolling of community rights.

stea·m-roller, *v.* [f. the sb.] Also as one word. **1.** *trans.* To crush or level with a steam-roller; to force with a steam-roller.
1913 *New Statesman* 26 July 497/2 To attempt to get through his poems in Classical Prosody is like trying to ride a bicycle over miles of newly-stoned road not yet steam-rollered. **1940** V. Brittain *Testament of Friendship* xix. 361 What had happened..to the mortal remnants of those slaughtered thousands?..Had they been ploughed, exploded and steam-rollered into the soil?

2. *fig.* **a.** To crush or break down, as with a steam-roller; to ride roughshod over; to overwhelm or squash. Freq. in *Pol.* contexts.
1912 *Chicago Daily Tribune* 7 June 1/4 They [*sc.* the Taft men] assent..that they will 'steam roller' the Roosevelt contests with a vengeance. **1918** G. B. Shaw in *Daily Chron.* 12 Jan. 5/2 He hammered poor Mr Walsh with trenchant repetitions of his chivalrous Christian phrase, and steamrollered him amid thunderous plaudits. **1921** *Round Table* June 651 His block majority, with which, if necessary, he could steam-roller opposition. **1930** G. B. Shaw *What I really wrote about War* xi. 283 An Ally [*sc.* Russia] on whom we had depended to steamroller our enemies on their eastern front. **1953** *Manch. Guardian Weekly* 3 Dec. 4/1 It would be a tragedy if the personal intimate side of British elections was steam-rollered into a flat monotony. **1982** *N. & Q.* Apr. 174/2 The book seems..to be an example of that kind of academic system-building where the subtleties of a text are 'steamrollered' in the interests of interpretative 'schemes'.

b. To push (a measure or bill) *through* (a legislative assembly, committee, etc.) by forcibly overriding opposition.
1947 A. W. Grantham in *Hong Kong Hansard* 31 July 257 It is too readily assumed that because there is a majority of Officials the slightest wish of Government is 'steam-rollered' through this Council. **1960** *Times* 1 Mar. 12/3 Certainly, each measure is steam-rollered through. **1964** *Daily Tel.* 27 Feb. 1/1 They accused him..of having 'steam-rollered the Bill through the Cabinet'.

c. To force (someone) *into* (a course of action, situation, etc.).
1959 *Economist* 18 Apr. 212/2 If the Government is steamrollered into granting a flat rate increase for all these pensioners right across the board, this will be the third successive general election which has been immediately preceded by such a step. **1959** P. Bull *I know Face* ii. 42 Luckily Robert and I..were not steamrollered into a phoney romance to appease the fans and newshawks.

3. *intr.* With *adv.* or *prep.* To proceed (esp. to continue speaking), regardless of opposition or interruption.
1969 D. Francis *Enquiry* i. iii. 38 Gowery steamrollered on. 'You found certain objects.' **1970** J. Porter *Rather a Common Sort of Crime* iii. 31 The Hon. Con steamrollered happily through the interruption. **1977** *Evening Gaz.* (Middlesbrough) 11 Jan. 13/8 Walker steam-rollered in with a 4–3 finish to win 16–15!

steamship. (Earlier attrib. examples.)
1866 'Mark Twain' *Lett. from Hawaii* (1967) 24 The permanent establishment of a San Francisco and Honolulu steamship line. **1884** *List of Subscribers* (London & Globe Telephone Co.) 11 Culliford & Clark Steam Ship Brokers.

steamy, *a.* Add: **3.** *fig.* Salacious; lustful, sexy, 'torrid'. Cf. Hot *a.* 6 c in Dict. and Suppl.
1970 *Daily Tel.* 19 June 7/4 Making Marilyn Roberts semi-nude curiously lessens the eroticism of one originally steamy scene. **1976** M. Machlin *Pipeline* xii. 139 Once he remembered a steamy necking session out in the middle of a field of oats. **1980** R. McInerny *Second Vespers* (1981) xv. 108 It was a moral outlook, one that had never..been disturbed by the steamy fiction that was her steady diet.

steamy, var. *steamie.

stearate. Add: Also, an ester of stearic acid (later examples).
1899 *Jrnl. Chem. Soc.* LXXV. 358 (*table*) [Amylic] *n*-stearate. **1904** *Ibid.* LXXXVI. i. 284 *iso*Amyl stearate is a neutral, white solid melting at 21°. **1950** Kirk & Othmer *Encycl. Chem. Technol.* V. 845 *n*-Butyl stearate.. is a colorless liquid... It is of value in compounding lubricating oils and as a lubricant for the textile and molding trade, in special lacquers, and as a waterproofing agent. **1976** [see *sorbitan].

steato-. Add: **steatoge·nic** *a.* [*-genic], tending to produce steatosis; **steatorrhœa:** delete and see as main entry below.
1956 *Nature* 14 Jan. 75/1 Experiments on phosphorus poisoning and steathogenic [*sic*] (Handler) diets in which thioctic acid normalizes the fat content of the liver. **1980** *European Jrnl. Cell Biol.* XXII. 567 After 7 days, steatosis developed in all animals on steatogenic diet alone.

steatopyga. Add: **steatopygia,** etc.: also *transf.* in *Archæol.* with reference to figurines that display steatopyga; also **steatopy·gial** *a.*, **steatopy·gism** (both *rare*).
1900 *Jrnl. Anthropol. Inst.* XXX. 253 In..the figure from Adalia..the steatopygia is by no means so pronounced, and is further concealed by the rudeness of the workmanship,..and the abbreviated treatment of the lower limbs. **1901** W. Ridgeway *Early Age of Greece* I. 66 In the graves female figurines have been found, some steatopygous, one of slighter type and tattooed. **1910** M. C. Harrison tr. *Mosso's Dawn of Mediterranean Civilization* ix. 150 (*caption*) Neolithic steatopygic figure, Knossos. **1912** Wace & Thompson *Prehist. Thessaly* xii. 225 The..statuettes reported to have been found at Sparta..are clearly of the mainland..type. The legs are short and stumpy, the heads are round, and the steatopygy is most marked. **1923** A. Huxley *Antic Hay* ii. 24 Gumbril's Patent Small-Clothes... A comfort to all travellers, civilization's substitute for steatopygism, indispensable to first-nighters. **1932** J. G. D. Clark *Mesolithic Age in Brit.* iii. 48 Resting on the living rock was found a curious object of shale, thought by the Abbé Breuil to partake of the nature of a phallus or a degenerate steatopygic figurine. **1966** J. Mellaart *Chalcolithic & Early Bronze Ages in Near East & Anatolia* ii. 28 The figurines, both male and female.., show naked or near-naked persons with hands at the waist... The women are slender with small breasts, and exaggerated stomach, enormous navel and a strongly marked pubic triangle, but no steatopygy. **1971** *Ann. Brit. School at Athens* LXI. 66 This figurine..is almost flat, and it is significant that.. about half of those from Crete are steatopygous only when viewed from front or rear; from the side they are seen to be almost flat. **1973** F. Garvie tr. *Buchholz's Prehistoric Greece & Cyprus* 99/2 Thera. Crudely formed, ill-proportioned female clay statuette, with steatopygia, moulded breasts and disc eyes. **1978** J. Updike *Coup* (1979) v. 182 The steatopygial silhouettes of naked mortals.

† **stearrhœa** (stī,ărī·ă). *Med. Obs.* [a. G. *stearrhœa* (J. H. L. Kunzmaun (or C. W. Hufeland) 1824, in *Jrnl. d. pract. Heilkunde* LIX. 45), f. Gr. στέαρ (see Steato-) + ῥοία flux.] = next.
1842 W. J. E. Wilson *Pract. & Theoret. Treat. Dis. Skin* xiv. 290 (*heading*) Augmentation of secretion. Stearrhoea. **1913** *Q. Jrnl. Med.* VI. 242 The term stearrhoea, or steatorrhoea, has had an unfortunate history. It was originally employed..to designate passage of liquid fat with the stools, but was applied later, by Erasmus Wilson, to the disease of the skin commonly known as seborrhoea.

steatorrhœa (stī,ătorī·ă). *Med.* Also **-rrhea.**

[Alteration of prec.: see Steato-.] **1.** The excretion of fat with the stools.

1859 R. G. Mayne *Expos. Lex. Med. Sci.* (1860) 1202/2 *Steatorrhœa*, term for a fatty dejection. **1903** E. L. Opie *Dis. Pancreas* xiii. 315 In some cases of pancreatic disease ..fat is discharged with the fæces as an oily, yellow fluid, and the condition may be designated a true steatorrhœa. **1923** A. E. Garrod *Inborn Errors of Metabolism* (ed. 2) ix. 167 Apart from the steatorrhœa there was nothing to suggest disease of the pancreas in either case. **1956** *Nature* 4 Feb. 237/1 These organisms were obtained from a patient with steatorrhœa.., it would appear that fat synthesis of this type [of bacterium] might make a significant contribution to fæcal fat. **1974** R. M. Kirk et al. *Surgery* vi. 100 The stones may occlude the orifice of the pancreatic duct, preventing exocrine..secretions from reaching the bowel, resulting in steatorrhoea.

2. = Seborrhœa. Now *rare* or *Obs.*

1878 W. J. E. Wilson *Lect. Dermatol. 1876–8* 259 Steatorrhœa in its commonest form, namely, steatorrhœa simplex or steatorrhœa oleosa..is illustrated by the model No. 571, which affords a striking example of this affection. **1899** *Allbutt's Syst. Med.* VIII. 759 The name seborrhœa (more correctly steatorrhœa) is not a satisfactory one.

Stechkin (ste·tʃkin). [The name of Igor Yakovlevich *Stechkin*, Soviet engineer, its designer.] A Soviet 9mm automatic or semi-automatic machine pistol. Also *attrib.*

1962 *Guns Rev.* May 23/2 The Soviets..in 1961 produce[d] an article ostensibly similar in function if not in cyclic rate, to the egregious Star of 1934. It is known as the Stechkin Machine Pistol or 'APS' in Russian notation. **1974** 'J. Graham' *Bloody Passage* v. 82 A Stechkin..A true machine pistol. Best I've seen since the Mauser. **1979** K. Bonfiglioli *After You with Pistol* xv. 109 The owner of the tan-coloured hand was grasping a large, crude Stechkin automatic pistol... The Stechkin is by no means a lady's handbag-gun. **1981** J. Trenhaile *Kyril* i. 4 'You have the gun?' In answer Yevchenko pressed a Stechkin into Stanov's hand.

Stedman (ste·dmæ̆n). The name of Fabian *Stedman* (*fl.* 1670), used *attrib.* and in the possessive to designate a method of change-ringing devised by him. Also *absol.*

1731 *Norwich Gaz.* 11 Sept. 4/1 That most noted and harmonious Peal on 7 Bells called Stedman's Triples. **1813** W. Shipway *Campanologia* I. 98 Let a ringer choose what method he will, it must still be on Stedman's principle. **1814** *Ibid.* II. 187 Doubles, or, as commonly called, a Stedman Grandsire, is completed by two singles. **1903** C. D. P. Davies *Stedman* 1 Throughout the whole province of Change Ringing, there is no more delightful method than Stedman. **1931** E. Morris *Hist. & Art Change Ringing* 78 The Norwich ringers performed a 'touch' of Stedman Cinques. **1957** *Encycl. Brit.* III. 375/2 Stedman's principle, which is *sui generis*, consists in the three front bells ringing their six possible changes, while the remaining pair or pairs of bells dodge. **1975** *Islander* (Victoria, B.C.) 16 Mar. 13/1 They rang a quarter peal of Stedman's triples for Canada's Centennial year.

‖ **steekgras** (stiə·kχras). *S. Afr.* Also † **stick-grass; steek-grass.** [Afrikaans, f. *steek* to prick + *gras* Grass *sb.*[1]] Any of several grasses of the genus *Aristida* or *Andropogon*, having spiky awns which damage the fleeces of sheep.

1838 J. Alexander *Exped. Discovery Interior Africa* I. ix. 237 The Boschmans have a peculiar mode of fishing in the 'Oup river; they make conical baskets of stick grass, which is as thick and hard as quills. **1893** W. Spilhaus in J. Noble *Illustr. Official Handbk. Cape & S. Afr.* (rev. ed.) xiv. 314 A year or two ago the Colony was troubled with a particularly obnoxious seed, that of the 'steekgrass' (*Andropogon contortus*, Ness, and *Aristida congesta*, R. and T.). **1896** R. Wallace *Farming Industries Cape Colony* v. 99 'Steekgrass' is the colonial name applied to a number of species..having long sharp awns attached to their seeds. **1913** C. Pettman *Africanderisms* 474 *Andropogon contortus*..is also a steekgras, but it is not the common one. **1954** D. D'Ewes *Mydorp* vii. 57 The seeds of the *steekgras* stuck in our stockings and bored relentlessly through to prick the skin. **1975** *Stand. Encycl. S. Afr.* XI. 382/1 Stick-grass or steekgras (*Aristida congesta*) is a biennial pioneer grass.

steel, *sb.*[1] Add: **I. 1. a.** (Later examples.)

With a few exceptions the term is now usu. restricted to iron alloys containing not more than 1·7% carbon.

1866 G. Ede *Managem. Steel* (ed. 4) ii. 15 Steel is a compound of iron and carbon... The carbon rarely exceeds two per cent. **1895** E. L. Rhead *Metallurgy* xi. 137 Steel proper contains from 0·5 to 1·5 or 1·7 per cent. of carbon. **1946** *Thorpe's Dict. Appl. Chem.* (ed. 4) VII. 47/1 Steel may be roughly defined as an alloy of iron and carbon containing up to 1·7% carbon, all of the carbon being in the combined condition. A second definition, distinguishing it from cast or wrought iron, is that it has been produced in the molten condition, and a third states that steel can be hardened by quenching from a suitably high temperature. There are..certain exceptions to all these definitions. **1967** A. H. Cottrell *Introd. Metall.* xi. 135 At present, about 80 per cent of steel in Britain is made by the open hearth process. **1976** *Sci. Amer.* July 68/2 For the iron to be made into steel (defined as iron with a carefully controlled carbon content of 1·7 percent or less) the sulfur, the silicon and the excess carbon must be removed. **1983** *Steel Times* Aug. 424/1 Even in the mildest of mild steels, with a carbon content of not more than 0·2% carbon, some other elements are present.

e. The name of a cold shade of grey resembling the colour of steel; steel-grey. Also as *adj.*

1851 E. Ruskin *Let.* 28 Dec. in M. Lutyens *Effie in Venice* (1965) II. 236 Falkenhayn gave..to Jane a steel glacé silk dress. **1881** [see *Burgundy 2 d]. **1895** *Montgomery Ward Catal.* Spring & Summer 9/2 Chambray mixtures in steel or blue with narrow white stripes. **1914** [see *beaver[1] 2 c]. **1925** in M. & N. Ward *Home in Twenties & Thirties* (1978) 39 Maids' morning dresses of strong washing gingham..in blue, grey, butcher, or steel.

II. 11. a. *steel-mesh.*

1944 M. Laski *Love on Supertax* xi. 103 A tall steel-mesh gate. **1976** J. Wheeler-Bennett *Friends, Enemies & Sovereigns* v. 156 King Peter attributed his father's, King Alexander's, death to the fact that..he had not worn his steel-mesh bullet-proof shirt.

13. *steel man, plant, town.*

1921 *Daily Colonist* (Victoria, B.C.) 1 Oct. 9/3 Mr. Fraser outlined the benefits that would come..from the erection of a steel plant here. **1922** L. Mumford in H. E. Stearns *Civilization in U.S.* 10 The steel towns of the Ohio [River]. **1961** *Universe* 27 Jan. 2/4 Steelmen There. Pope John on Monday received members of the council of the European coal and steel authority. **1976** *National Observer* (U.S.) 24 Jan. 1/1 East Chicago, Ind., a smoky Lake Michigan steel town that isn't exactly famous for its esthetic splendor even when the sun shines. **1977** *Times* 19 Dec. 13/3 Sound arguments have been put forward by many respected steelmen for moving away from the large integrated coastal works. **1979** *Steel Times Internat.* Sept. 91/2 The building of a new steelplant.

14. (Earlier example.)

1880 'Mark Twain' in *Mark Twain Let. Writer* (1932) iii. 48 The best picture I have had yet is the steel frontispiece to my new book.

15. a. *steel-bright* (later example), *-hard, -sharp, -straight, -strong, -thin*; *steel-blue* (later examples), *-grey* (later examples).

1916 A. Huxley *Burning Wheel* 8 The adamant core and the steel-hard chain. **1920** E. Sitwell *Wooden Pegasus* 32 Dusty voice that throbs with heat, Hoping with its steel-thin beat To put stitches in my mind. **1921** J. Buchan *Path of King* i. 9 The world put on a new dress, all steel-blue and misty green... Spring had fairly come. **1923** D. H. Lawrence *Birds, Beasts & Flowers* 29 Sit beside the steel-straight arms of your fair women. *Ibid.* 177 Steered and propelled by that steel-strong snake of a tail. **1944** Blunden *Shells by Stream* 4 Steel-sharp might Which blows the babe and nurse to atoms in the night. **1944** A. L. Rowse *English Spirit* xiii. 105 Narrow temples and steel-grey eyes. **1954** L. MacNeice *Autumn Sequel* 95 She ascends where steelbright rays impinge. **1976** 'Z. Stone' *Modigliani Scandal* II. i. 69 A steel-blue Mercedes coupé. **1977** A. Giddens *Stud. in Social & Polit. Theory* 23 His sombre characterization of the 'steel-hard cage' of the modern social order. **1978** 'M. M. Kaye' *Far Pavilions* iv. 73 The steel-grey curtain of the rain.

16. *steel-erector*; *steel-piercing, -rolling, -using* (examples).

1932 Auden *Orators* III. 102 Our steel-piercing bullet, our burglar-proof safe. **1959** *Daily Tel.* 12 Dec. 1/2 Loss of work because of steel shortages in car and other steel-using industries. **1960** *Times* 22 Mar. 12/1 The site of many industries and the country's largest steel-rolling mill. **1974** 'J. Ross' *Burning of Billy Toober* xi. 100 Almost permanently unemployed but registered as a steel-erector. **1977** *Whitaker's Almanack 1978* 757/1 Some of the country's [*sc.* Nigeria's] more important industrial installations include a steel-rolling mill. **1977** *Time* 19 Sept. 48/3 The relatively brisk pace of the economy is boosting demand in many steel-using industries.

17. *steel-born, -clad* (later example); *steel-barred, -bosomed, -grated, -lined, -nerved, -rimmed, -shafted, -studded, -tipped.*

1909 *Westm. Gaz.* 11 Nov. 5/2 A new steel-studded tyre. **1924** W. J. Locke *Coming of Amos* xvi. 211 What kind of steel-nerved wisp of a woman are you? **1926** 'C. Barry' *Detective's Holiday* vii. 66 A pair of steel-rimmed spectacles. **1929** L. MacNeice *Blind Fireworks* 8 The steel-bosomed siren calling bitterly. **1930** Blunden *Poems* 139 But steel-born bees, birds, beams invade. **1935** Kipling in *Times* 17 July 19/4 In the steel-grated prisons where I cast him. **1947** Dylan Thomas *Let.* 12 Apr. (1966) 302 In steel-barred rooms, where Mussolini personally had.. interrogated. **1950** *Times* 22 May 4/3 Four golfers and a caddy..were carrying steel-shafted clubs. **1954** L. MacNeice *Autumn Sequel* 94 The steel-clad troops begin arriving from the rear to rally or harry their humble fellows. **1972** P. Buckland *Irish Unionism* I. viii. 215 Armed raiders who had removed the steel-lined shutters from the windows. **1973** M. Russell *Double Hit* xx. 149, I just don't believe that an accidental swipe with a squash racket, even a steel-shafted one, would have killed a man. **1974** J. Aiken *Midnight is a Place* x. 290 The duels..which the men..fought, using no weapons but the steel-tipped clogs on their feet. **1978** R. Ludlum *Holcroft Covenant* xv. 174 The face was strong, the eyes behind the steel-rimmed spectacles alert.

18. steel band, (*a*) *Mus.*, a band composed of musicians who play (chiefly calypso-style) music on steel drums; so **steel bandsman,** a musician in a steel band; (*b*) *Austral.* [Band *sb.*[2] 12], 'hard thin stratum of ferruginous and siliceous material lying below the sandstone roof and above the opal dirt' (J. S. Gunn *Opal Terminol.* (1971)); **steel bender** (see quot. 1921); **steel-bow(ed)** *a. U.S.*, (of spectacles) having steel frames; **steel driver** *U.S.*, one who makes holes for explosive charges, using a steel stake and a sledgehammer; **steel drum** *Mus.*, a percussion instrument originating in the West Indies, made out of an oil drum with one end beaten down and divided into grooved sections to give different notes; hence **steel drummer; steel-facing,** the process of covering an engraved metal plate with a film of steel to increase its durability; hence **steel-faced** *a.*; (as back-formation) **steel-face** *v. trans.*; **steel fixer,** a skilled steel worker in the construction industries; **steel frame,** a framework, esp. of a building, made of steel; also *fig.*; freq. *attrib.*; hence **steel-framed** *a.*; also **steel framework; steel guitar** = *Hawaiian guitar* s.v. *Hawaiian *a.* and *sb.* II.; **steel-hardened** (later example); **steel orchestra** = *steel band* above; **steel pan** = *pan *sb.*[1] 1 f; **steel tape,** (*a*) a measuring tape made of steel; † (*b*) tape made of steel for use as a recording medium (*obs.*); **steel trap:** also *fig.* (chiefly in *attrib.* use) and in U.S. phr. *smart as a steel trap* and varr.; **steel wool,** fine strands of steel matted together, used as an abrasive, esp. for scouring.

1949 *Caribbean Quarterly* I. I. 30 The audience was introduced to..Trinidad's own steel band. **1950** *Bull. Austral. Bur. Mineral Resources* No. 17. 27 The first or upper level is indicated by the presence of a very thin and hard band of siliceous sandstone known as the 'Steel Band'. **1960** *Times* 17 Sept. 7/6 The steelband competition of the Trinidad music festival. **1967** *Sunday Mail Mag.* (Brisbane) 8 Jan. 6/7 Then comes eight to twelve feet of quartzite..and often after that, a layer of hard siliceous sandstone known as the 'steelband'. **1974** E. Ambler *Dr. Frigo* I. 15 He had collapsed while listening to the steel band. **1948** *Trinidad Guardian* 16 June 5/6 (*heading*) Judge advises steel bandsman to mend ways. **1967** *Listener* 31 Aug. 277/2 The steel bandsmen can play anything well: without a conductor and from memory. **1921** *Dict. Occupational Terms* (1927) § 279 *Steel bender*,.. bends steel rods and girders in hand operated or power press, into required shape, to form framework for concrete. **1939** M. Spring Rice *Working-Class Wives* iii. 53 An unemployed steel-bender in Newcastle. **1963** *Times* 10 June 8/1 The accent on industrialized building and the increasing development over recent years in concreting have created a great new demand for new skilled labour such as scaffolders, concreters, steelbenders and fixers. **1834** in *Proc. Mass. Hist. Soc.* (1924) LVII. 258 Appears to be a pleasant fellow, with frightful whiskers and steel bow spectacles. **1932** Steel-bowed [see *notion-peddler* s.v. *notion 9 c]. **1950** W. Faulkner *Lo* in *Coll. Stories* III. 390 From the pocket of his dressing gown he took a pair of steel-bowed spectacles. **1916** in *Jrnl. Amer. Folk-Lore* (1919) XXXII. 505 He [John Henry] was a steel driver and was famous in the beginning of the building of the C & O Railroad. **1973** A. Dundes *Mother Wit* 586 The story of John Henry is powerful whether there was an actual steel-driver named John Henry or..not. **1952** *Holiday* Feb. 94/2 Rainbow-uniformed dandies parade and compete in making music on tuned steel drums from oilcans. **1971** *West Indian World* 12 Nov. 7/1 Trinidad.. known..for its calypso singers and steel-drum bands. **1978** *New York* 3 Apr. 31 (Advt.), A cool drink slakes your thirst, steel drums stir your blood. **1960** *Times* 17 Sept. 7/6 This influenced the steeldrummers to discard their tubes and bars and to use tops of oil-drums hung from the neck. **1975** R. L. Simon *Wild Turkey* (1976) x. 60 The reggae band..had a steel drummer who could go day and night and enough dope to turn on a rock festival. **1884** J. S. Hodson *Guide to Art Illustration* II. iii. 213 The proper thickness of copper having been deposited in the mould, the shell is filed or ground flat on the back, and the face coated with a deposit of iron,—a process commonly called steel facing. **1897** Singer & Strang *Etching, Engraving* iii. 61 Steel-faced it may be printed over and over again.., for as soon as the steel face should wear off, the plate can be again immersed in the electrotyper's bath [etc.]. **1937** *Discovery* Mar. 76/2 The burr [in drypoint] being raised, will quickly wear, owing to the rubbing and the pressure it receives in printing. To overcome this a fine film of iron is deposited by an electric process on the plate. This is called steel-facing. An unfaced drypoint will yield only four or five first-class impressions before the burr starts to wear. A steel-faced plate will give as many as fifty. **1961** Webster, Steel-face, v. **1965** Zigrosser & Gaehde *Guide Coll. Orig. Prints* iii. 26 An invention of the mid-nineteenth century..steel-facing... The reason steel-faced prints have acquired a bad name is that they have often been printed in a slipshod manner. *Ibid.* v. 86 It used to be standard practice among professional etchers to steel-face the copperplate. **1936** *Record* Apr. 219/3 There is an awakening of interest amongst another section of building trade workers, namely, the steel benders and fixers. **1949** *Transport & General Workers' Record* June 26/3 (*heading*) Steel fixers and tubular scaffolders. **1974** Steel fixer [see *precasting *vbl. sb.*]. **1898** *Engineering* 8 July 39/3 An architect is made responsible for the general arrangement of the building..while the steel frame or skeleton is the work of a skilful engineer experienced in such matters. **1906** G. A. T. Middleton *Mod. Buildings* IV. xiv. 134/2 Probably the most thorough example of steel-frame construction yet erected in England is that of the Ritz Hotel, Piccadilly. **1922** Lloyd George in *Hansard Commons* 2 Aug. 1513, I can see no period when they can dispense with the guidance and the assistance of this small nucleus of the British Civil Service, of British officials in India—this 1,200 in a population of 315,000,000... They are the steel frame of the whole structure. **1928** M. Muggeridge in *Young Men of India* XL. 624 There is that amount of truth in the contention of the Die-hard as against that of the sentimental liberal—it must be a steel frame or nothing. **1948** O. Bondy in E. de Maré *New Ways of Building* 70 It was not until the 1890's that the first complete steel-frame buildings were erected in the U.S.A. **1980** J. Boyd-Carpenter *Way of Life* v. 59 To this day they [*sc.* the *Carabinieri*] are, I believe, the steel frame of the distracted Italian Republic. **1906** G. A. T. Middleton *Mod. Buildings* IV. xiv. 134/2 A steel framework may often be used with considerable economy, as is evidenced by the number of steel-framed structures that are now springing up. **1974** D. Seaman *Bomb that could*

Lip-Read iii. 23 His steel-framed grey suitcase. **1906** Steel framework [see *steel-framed* adj. above]. **1940** *Engineering* 1 Nov. 343/3 The steel framework..embedded in the concrete. **1925** *Glasgow Herald* 19 Mar. 8/7 Those two seductive Hawaiian instruments, the ukulele and the steel guitar. **1974** V. GIELGUD *In such a Night* ix. 90 The nerve-battering provided by invisible steel guitars. **1980** *Guardian Weekly* 13 July 1/2 It has all the grisly mod military cons: an isolated water supply, a purified air system, steel-hardened concrete. **1952** S. SELVON *Brighter Sun* xii. 233 Crowds jumped up to the music of steel orchestras. **1971** *News-Advocate* (Barbados) 20 Mar. 7/1 (Advt.), Dancing to the rhythmic beats of the..Elk Owls steel orchestra. **1973** *Nation* (Barbados) 23 Dec. 8 Trinidad's famed steel pans [will] be produced in masse in England. **1983** *Times* 7 Jan. 2/1 [He] was employed for several years by the local education authority to teach steel pan playing in schools. **1900** Steel tape [see TAPE *sb.*[1] 2 a]. **1901** *Electrician* 26 Apr. 7/2 The next [electromagnet] is connected to a microphone circuit to convey the record to the steel tape. **1949** S. J. BEGUN *Magnetic Recording* i. 10 A recording made on steel tape..has been played more than 100,000 times with no measureable deterioration after a slight initial falling off in output level. **1977** J. F. FIXX *Compl. Bk. Running* vii. 90 Measure off a half-mile with a steel tape. **1872** MRS. STOWE *Oldtown Fireside Stories* 57 She was a little thin woman, but tough as Inger rubber, and smart as a steel trap. **1899** A. M. BINSTEAD *Gal's Gossip* 127 He posted sentinel, bright and ready as a new steel-trap. **1921** D. H. LAWRENCE *Tortoises* 32 Little old man, Scuffling beside her..Parting his steel-trap face, so suddenly and seizing her scaly ankle. **1937** E. S. GARDNER *Case of Dangerous Dowager* i. 8 You're going up against a crook who is smart as a steel trap. **1972** *Publishers' Weekly* 17 Apr. 19/1 He's rather amused by what he calls his steeltrap memory. 'I have a tight grip on things in inverse proportion to their importance.' **1896** *Iron Age* 9 Apr. 871/2 The interesting product 'steel wool' is intended for use in all cases where sandpaper, emery paper, pumice stone and materials of a kindred nature are employed. **1947** J. C. RICH *Materials & Methods of Sculpture* vi. 169 'Fire-skin' may be removed by rubbing the work with steel wool, which is available in several grades, varying from very coarse to very fine. **1958** *Listener* 16 Oct. 627/1 Scour round the inside with a steel wool soap-pad. **1977** C. MCCULLOUGH *Thorn Birds* xvii. 444 His thick mane of hair was exactly the color of steel wool.

steel, *v.* **5.** (Later examples.)

1977 *Sci. Amer.* May 61/3 Iron that has been 'steeled' with that much carbon will not deform under stresses of less than 140,000 p.s.i. *Ibid.* Oct. 127/1 It seems evident that by the beginning of the 10th century B.C. blacksmiths were intentionally steeling iron.

steel-head, *sb.* Add: Also **steelhead 1.** (Later example.) Also *attrib.*, as *steelhead trout.*

1911 *Rep. U.S. Comm. Fisheries 1908* 317/2 *Salmo* is represented by..the steelhead trout. **1946** [see *CUT-THROAT 5 b]. **1968** *Times* 22 Oct. 3/3 Another species of trout, the steelhead, has been found to suffer from a vascular disease. **1976** *Vernon* (B.C.) *Daily News* 21 June 20A/5 Sea-going Rainbow are known as *steelhead* trout.

2. (Examples.)

1888 G. TRUMBULL *Names & Portraits of Birds* 112 William Wagner, a well known Washington gunner, tells of hearing it called Water-Partridge and Steel-head. **1917** T. G. PEARSON *Birds Amer.* I. 153/1 They are extremely tough, hardy little birds and gunners know them by such names as Tough-head, Hard-head, Steel-head, etc.

steelheader (stī·hedəɹ). *N. Amer.* [f. STEEL-HEAD *sb.* + -ER[1].] One who fishes for steelhead trout. Hence **stee·lheading** *vbl. sb.*

1948 *Game Trails in Canada* Feb. 25 The average steelheader that lands one in three seems quite content. **1954** *Daily Progress* (Charlottesville, Va.) 5 Nov. 13/1 They had gone out steelheading that morning. **1964** *Vancouver Province* 14 Feb. 18/1 The Gold River has blanked many a good steelheader. **1971** *Islander* (Victoria, B.C.) 24 Jan. 3/1 She had learned to avoid the cardinal sins of steelheading. **1972** *Daily Colonist* (Victoria, B.C.) 1 Jan. 21/3 April is the awakening month, when..steelheaders shift to trout fishing.

steel he·lmet. [f. STEEL *sb.*[1] + HELMET *sb.*]

1. A helmet made of steel (or other metal), worn as a form of protection in conditions of war.

1916 R. ASQUITH *Let.* 23 May (1980) IV. 263 One fearful addition to the honours of War since I have been away is the steel helmet which we all have to wear now, when in the shell area. **1940** *War Illustr.* 5 Jan. 563/1 It was not until February 1916 that the first steel helmets were issued to the British troops in the last war, but in this war they are an essential part not only of the soldiers' equipment but of that of the police, the A.F.S. and A.R.P. workers. **1978** A. PRICE *'44 Vintage* v. 52 Knitted cap-comforters instead of berets or steel helmets.

2. (With capital initials.) [tr. G. *STAHLHELM.] An organization, founded in 1918 by F. Seldte, of German ex-service men (and others, from 1924) drawn mainly from the Nationalist Party and having a strong conservative bias; a member of this.

The organization was dissolved in 1935, and refounded under the Federal Republic in 1951.

1925 *Spectator* 28 Mar. 487/1 How could he really fail to stand for monarchy when he is championed by such societies as the 'Steel Helmet League' and the 'Front Fighters'? **1926** *Times* 25 May 14/3 The Nationalist 'Steel Helmet' organization. *Ibid.*, Most of the 'Steel Helmets' wore iron crosses. **1932** H. R. KNICKERBOCKER *Germany —Fascist or Soviet?* 137 The four militant organizations are the Republican Reichsbanner, the National Socialist Storm Troops, the Conservative Steel Helmets, and the Communist Red Front. **1933** E. A. MOWRER *Germany puts Clock Back* 94 The Steel Helmet, or Confederation of Front-line Soldiers, the most respectable of the private armies, was founded on Christmas Day, 1918. **1983** C. MCCARRY *Last Supper* 32 A Steel Helmet, wearing two Iron Crosses on his civilian jacket..seized the weedy young man.

Hence **steel-he·lmeted** *a.*, wearing a steel helmet.

1926 *British Worker* 10 May 1/3 Thus all the display of steel-helmeted troops, all the tearing about of motor-cars filled with special constables..have failed of their object. **1977** N. SAHGAL *Situation in New Delhi* xvi. 159 One of the students informed him it was the police or perhaps the army—many were steel-helmeted and the boy could not tell.

steeling, *vbl. sb.* **3.** (Later example.)

1977 *Sci. Amer.* Oct. 125/1 If bloomery iron is treated in a certain way, it can be transformed into an alloy that is for most purposes far superior to bronze. That treatment is steeling, and its initial discovery was probably accidental.

steel pen. 1. (Later examples.)

1892 'Mark Twain' *Amer. Claimant* vii. 71 Steel pens on his table with the ink-bottle. **1922** JOYCE *Ulysses* 8 He fears the lancet of my art as I fear that of his. The cold steelpen. **1975** *Islander* (Victoria, B.C.) 16 Feb. 10/3 By 1803 producers could no longer keep pace with the consumption of quills and the first steel pen came into use. **1983** *Daily Tel.* 10 Mar. 14/4 The steel-pen writing is brisk and persuasive.

steely, *a.* Add: **5. b.** *steely-eyed.*

1964 D. F. DOWD in I. L. Horowitz *New Sociology* 60 Steely-eyed, if amiable, technicians. **1976** *Saturday Night* Mar. 82/3 A haughty Trudeau is seated at a press conference giving some questioner that familiar steely-eyed look of his.

6. Also in *Comb.*

1922 JOYCE *Ulysses* 252 Bronze By Gold Heard The Hoofirons, Steelyringing.

steenbrass. Now usu. **steenbras.** Substitute for def.: Any of several marine fishes of the family Sparidæ, esp. the red steenbras, *Petrus rupestris*, the silver steenbras, *Sparodon durbanensis*, or the white steenbras, *Lithognathus lithognathus.* (Further examples.)

1893 [see *KINGKLIP]. **1931** *Times Lit. Suppl.* 16 Apr. 301/2 Many of the Cape fish, such as the geelbek,..the steenbras. **1958** *Cape Times* 20 May 2/2 Fishermen have been bringing in some fine, big red-steenbras... Anglers on the rocks have..had good hauls of smaller fish including white stumpnose, galjoen and white steenbras. **1973** [see *KABELJOU].

steening, *vbl. sb.* Add: Also **steyning. 1.** (Later examples.)

1926 T. E. LAWRENCE *Seven Pillars* (1935) I. x. 80 The well was old, and broad, with a good stone steyning, and a strong coping round the top. **1939** *Oxoniensia* IV. 94 They might have been stones used to edge or pave the mouth of the well, as similar fragments of stone occurred in most wells, but they could not be taken as steyning.

steenstrupine (stī·nstrupīn). *Min.* [f. the name of Knud J. V. *Steenstrup* (1842–1913), Danish geologist + -INE[5].] A silicate and phosphate of rare-earth and other elements (chiefly cerium, sodium, calcium, iron, and manganese), found as dark brown or black rhombohedral crystals. Also (*rare*) **stee·nstrupite.**

1882 J. LORENZEN in *Mineral. Mag.* V. 67 The analysis of this mineral has shown it to be a new species, and, as suggested by Prof. Johnstrup, I have therefore given it the name of *Steenstrupine*, after Mr. *Steenstrup*, who.. first found the mineral. **1901** *Meddelelser om Grønland* XXIV. 204 The steenstrupite is found partly in pegmatitic veins and partly embedded in grained albite. **1943** *Mineral. Abstr.* VIII. 369 The unit-cell dimensions of steenstrupine..show a similarity to those of apatite. **1977** *Jrnl. R. Soc. Arts* CXXV. 406/2 The peralkaline nepheline syenites of Ilímaussaq in south Greenland, where the main mineral is steenstrupine (silicate and phosphate of rare earths, sodium, niobium, tantalum, thorium and uranium).

steentjie (stīᵊ·nkʸi). *S. Afr.* Also **steen(t)je.** [Afrikaans, dim. of Du. *steen* stone.] Either of two small marine fishes of the family Sparidæ, *Spondyliosoma emarginatum* or *Sarpa salpa* (= *STREPIE).

1893 H. A. BRYDEN *Gun & Camera S. Afr.* xx. 448 We caught also..steenje, another small fish, which we cut up principally for bait. **1913** W. W. THOMPSON *Sea Fisheries Cape Col.* 154 *Cantharus emarginatus*..Steentje. **1930** C. L. BIDEN *Sea-Angling Fishes of Cape* ix. 166 The men.. caught many steentjies which were scaled and pulped with a baton and baited whole on the big lines. **1957** S. SCHOEMAN *Strike!* iii. 88 There are two species of fish commonly referred to as steentjies, namely the common steentjie..alias strepie,..and the blue or bank steentjie.

steep, *a.*, *sb.*[2], and *adv.* Add: **A.** *adj.* **3. g.** *steepest descent(s)* (Math.), used with reference to a method of finding a minimum of a function of two or more variables by repeatedly evaluating it at a point displaced from the previous point in the direction that locally involved the greatest drop in its value.

1939 *Proc. R. Soc.* A. CLXIX. 484 In the method of steepest descents the displacement affects all co-ordinates and affects them in the ratio of their residual forces. **1943** *Bull. Amer. Math. Soc.* XLIX. 18 We now choose the line along which the motion proceeds so that the descent is as steep as possible (lines of steepest descent). **1974** ADBY & DEMPSTER *Introd. Optimization Methods* iii. 57 The steepest descent method uses the Jacobian gradient **g** to determine a suitable direction of movement.

6. *steep-fronted.*

1936 *Nature* 21 Mar. 491/2 The test piece is flashed over with a steep-fronted impulse in about a microsecond or less.

C. *adv.* **4.** *steep-cut* (earlier example).

1888 KIPLING *Lett. Marque* (1891) xv. 115 Up rough banks..down steep-cut dips.

stee·phead. *U.S.* (orig. *local*). *Physical Geogr.* [f. STEEP *a.* + HEAD *sb.*] A nearly vertical slope, from the base of which springs emerge, at the head of a pocket valley (see *POCKET *sb.* 13).

1918 *10th & 11th Ann. Rep. Florida Geol. Survey* 27 A characteristic feature of this topography is the development of what is [*sic*] known locally as 'steepheads'. *Ibid.*, The depth of the steephead from the plateau is usually from 50 to 60 or more feet. **1942** O. D. VON ENGELN *Geomorphol.* xxii. 569 Pocket valleys of similar origin are also of widespread occurrence in northwestern Florida where they are known as steep-heads. **1971** [see *pocket valley* s.v. *POCKET *sb.* 13].

steeple, *sb.*[1] Add: **I. 4*.** *transf.* A steeple-shaped formation of the two hands, with the palms facing and the extended fingers rising to meet at the tips.

1940 *Detective Fiction Weekly* 26 Oct. 9/1, I..waited for him to begin. He made a steeple of his hands. 'Now it is a very simple matter.' **1972** T. P. MCMAHON *Issue of Bishop's Blood* (1973) iii. 35 He was sighting at me carefully along the top of the steeple made by his manicured fingers. **1978** G. VIDAL *Kalki* ii. 33 When I put out my hand, she made a steeple with her hands, and bowed. This was my first experience with the Hindu pranam, or greeting.

II. 6. steeple clock, (*a*) a clock fixed to a steeple; (*b*) *U.S.*, an antique mantel or shelf clock (see quot. 1959).

1830 [in Dict., sense 5 a]. **1923** W. I. MILHAM *Time & Timekeepers* xx. 368 There are two kinds of clocks, however, which came into vogue shortly after 1850 and are usually classed among 'antiques' and not among the endless varieties of modern clocks. These are the small, spring-driven, brass shelf clock often in a rose-wood veneer case and the steeple clock, sometimes called the 'Sharp Gothic'. **1959** L. GROSS *Housewives' Guide to Antiques* viii. 114 The steeple clock of the mid-nineteenth century was another popular mantel clock. It takes its name from the steeple-like appearance of its case. **1976** R. B. PARKER *Promised Land* (1977) xvi. 97 There was an old steeple clock with brass works on the mantle.

steeple, *v.* Add: **3.** (Later *poet.* example.)

1922 BLUNDEN *Shepherd* 81 The cornel steepling up in white shall know The two friends passing by.

4. *trans.* To place (the fingers or hands) together in the shape of a steeple.

1968 A. MACLEAN *Force 10 from Navarone* iv. 59 The German captain leaned back in his chair and steepled his fingers. **1975** W. SAFIRE *Before Fall* VI. vi. 446 Nixon.. was relaxed when seated, steepling or folding his hands. **1977** G. SCOTT *Hot Pursuit* ii. 18 He steepled his fingers and looked wisely at me across the desk-top.

steepling *ppl. a.*: also *fig.*

1955 *Times* 28 June 3/2 He struck a steepling blow, but he fell into Kenyon's hands standing just inside the ropes beneath the Nursery Clock Tower. **1977** *Guardian Weekly* 17 July 24/4 McCosker hooked at it and sent a steepling catch to Underwood at mid-on. **1982** *Daily Tel.* 20 Aug. 9/4 The steepling rises in standing charges.

steeplechase, *sb.* Add: **1.** (Earlier examples.)

Quot. 1805 in Dict. is in error for 'Steeple-race'.

1793 *Sporting Mag.* Apr. 57/2 The Hon. Mr. O'Hea and Captain Magrath ran a Steeple-chace, near Galloway. **1803** W. TAPLIN *Sporting Dict. & Repository* II. 486 This kind of chase [*sc.* Wild-Goose chase]..was long since changed to a *train scent*, (that is, a drag across the country;) better known by the denomination of a *steeple chase.*

3. (Earlier example.)

1892–3 *T. Eaton & Co. Catal.* Fall & Winter 67/1 Games..errand boy, steeplechase, yacht race [etc.].

steepled, *ppl. a.* Add: **5.** Of the fingers or hands: brought together in the form of a steeple.

1971 P. O'DONNELL *Impossible Virgin* x. 212 Tapping the tips of his steepled fingers together. **1981** 'L. EGAN' *Miser* (1982) ii. 26 'Not much criminal practice,' said Jesse, brooding over his steepled hands.

steepler (stī·pləɹ). *Cricket.* [f. STEEPLE *v.* + -ER[1].] = SKYER, esp. one from which the batsman is caught out.

1959 *Times* 7 Aug. 4/2 He was caught and bowled off a steepler. **1963** *Times* 5 Feb. 3/6 Parfitt at long-on judged a steepler well to end the innings. **1976** *Cricketer Internat.* Sept. 35/2 Crockham Hill caught everything, including two stupendous steeplers in the last over.

steer, *sb.*[1] Add: **2. a.** *Comb.* Designating events or participants in a rodeo, as *steer roper, wrestler; steer bulldogging, roping, wrestling.*

1910 *Oregon Daily Jrnl.* 30 Sept. 18/5 Steer roping contest for championship of the northwest. **1912** *Oregon Sunday Jrnl.* 18 Sept. 2/1 Among the many events to be featured at the Round-Up this year is the world's championship wild steer bull-dogging contest. **1914** *World's Work* (N.Y.) Feb. 445/2 It by no means follows that a good steer roper is a good calf roper. **1922** *N.Y. Times* 12 Nov. I. 5/2 One of the conditions of the steer-wrestling contests is that the contestants will suffer a 'ten-second fine' for 'loosening or knocking off horns'. **1923** *Ibid.* 11 Aug. 16/4 Steer Wrestlers Here. Twenty-three contestants in the 'steer-wrestling' or 'bull-dogging' competitions..arrived in New York yesterday. **1924** *Glasgow Herald* 17 June 9 The 'steer-roping', which at Saturday's display met with some public disapproval, was withdrawn. **1968** R. F. Adams *Western Words* (rev. ed.) 305/1 *Steer wrestling*, one of the five standard rodeo events; also called *bulldogging*. The contestant rides alongside a running steer, jumps from his saddle to the steer's head, stops it, and twists it to the ground with its head and all four feet pointing in the same direction. **1976** *Billings* (Montana) *Gaz.* 16 June 1-c/3 University of Wyoming steer wrestler Shawn Madden took an early lead in the second go-round of steer wrestling, throwing his animal in 3·67 seconds. **1979** *Sunset* Apr. 6/3 Horses will compete in 36 classes, including calf and steer-roping events.

b. Special combination. **steerhide** *N. Amer.*, the hide of a steer; *spec.* leather made from this or from the hide of a similar beast.

1921 *Jrnl. Amer. Leather Chemists Assoc.* May 295 (*heading*) On certain characteristics of fresh steer hide. **1925** J. R. Arnold *Hides & Skins* ii. 32 The thickest part of a steer hide is over the rump. **1948** H. G. Kates *Luggage & Leather Cards Manual* 184 Steerhide leather is extensively used because of its adaptability to tooling. **1979** *PN Rev.* IX. 39/1 All winter your brute shoulders strained against collars, padding and steerhide over the ash hames.

steer (stīᵊɹ), *sb.*[5] *slang* (orig. *U.S.*). [f. Steer *v.*[1]] A piece of advice or information; a tip, a lead. (See also quot. 1970.)

1899 C. H. Hoyt *Texas Steer* (typescript) iv. 21 You're going back to Texas to give the voters of my district a steer. What's that steer to be? **1924**, etc. [see *bum *a.*]. **1926** *Flynn's* 16 Jan. 638/2 An' divvy with th' crooked barkeep for a steer or some kind of a tip if th' stunt panned out ok. **1935** L. E. Lawes *Cell 202, Sing Sing* iv. 553 You're both on the wrong steer..thinkin' about the devil when all the while it's the man himself deserves your attention. **1959** 'M. M. Kaye' *House of Shade* x. 127 All I've done is to give you a wrong steer, and make bad worse. **1970** D. Francis *Rat Race* vi. 79 I'd have to go round the Luton complex...could probably get a steer home from there, from the twenty-four hour radar. **1982** *Times* 21 Apr. 16/1 Steers from Smiths Industries on its financial performance are obviously worth listening to.

steerer. 3. (Earlier example.)

1873 'J. Morris' *Wanderings of Vagabond* xix. 210 Let us now take a peep into the brace room, while the steerer and his victim are on their way to it.

steering, *vbl. sb.* Add: **1. b.** *Meteorol.* The process by which pressure systems, precipitation belts, etc., are moved by temperature gradients or winds.

1919, etc. [see *steering line*, sense 3 b below]. **1944** Hewson & Longley *Meteorol. Theoret. & Appl.* xxiv. 428 The changes in pressure at the earth's surface are controlled by atmospheric movements at levels of 4 km and higher, the process whereby this occurs being known as 'steering'. **1956** S. Petterssen *Weather Analysis & Forecasting* (ed. 2) I. xiii. 277 From the point of view of theory it is difficult to make any distinction between the steering and the blocking of the movement of sea-level cyclones. **1959** R. E. Huschke *Gloss. Meteorol.* (Amer. Meteorol. Soc.) 541 *Steering*, in meteorology, loosely used for any influence upon the direction of movement of an atmospheric disturbance exerted by another aspect of the state of the atmosphere.

c. *Electronics.* The switching of pulses from one part of a circuit to another.

1956, etc. [see *steering circuit, diode*, sense 3 a below]. **1962** Simpson & Richards *Physical Princ. Junction Transistors* xvi. 410 In many bistable circuits,..trigger pulses of opposite polarity must be used alternately..or pulses of one polarity must alternately be switched from one collector or base to another. The latter process, which is usually performed by diodes or auxiliary transistors, is called steering. **1969** J. J. Sparkes *Transistor Switching* v. 122 Two quite distinct methods of controlling the penetration of pulses to the transistor are available, namely pulse steering by applying logic voltages to *SA* or *RA*, or pulse gating via additional diodes at the pulse inputs.

2. (Later examples.)

1970 K. Ball *Fiat 600, 600D Autobook* ix. 103/2 The first step in dismantling the steering is to remove the steering wheel. **1977** *Western Morning News* 30 Aug. 8/2 (Advt.), Austin 2200. Blue. Power-assisted steering.

3. a. (sense 1 a) *steering-bridge*; (sense *1 b) *steering principle*; (sense *1 c) *steering circuit, diode*; (sense 2) *steering angle, arm, axle, circle, knuckle, lever, linkage, rod.*

1936 *Proc. Inst. Automobile Engineers* XXX. 757 The angle of the front wheels or 'steering angle' is particularly important. **1902** A. C. Harmsworth et al. *Motors & Motor-Driving* 216 With a broken steering arm..a car.. may be hurled into a ditch. **1978** D. Clarke *Car* 84/1 All but the last type of box require a system of linkages to take the movement created by the drop arm..to the steering arms on the wheels. **1912** *Motor Man.* 87 Details of steering axle with steering arms and connecting bar. **1902** *Chambers's Jrnl.* Oct. 739/1 He left the bridge, roused all hands, and arraigned them on the steering-bridge. **1912** *Motor Man.* 88 Whichever wheel is on the inside of the steering circle turns through a wider angle than the outer wheel does. **1970** K. Ball *Fiat 600, 600D Autobook* ix. 108/2 The steering circle diameter on the Multipla is 28 feet 10 inches. **1956** L. P. Hunter *Handbk. Semiconductor Electronics* xv. 23 In order to operate the trigger in a binary fashion, it is necessary to provide steering circuits. **1971** J. H. Smith *Digital Logic* iv. 58 Steering circuits..control the operation of the gates. **1957** R. F. Shea *Circuit Engin.* x. 337 (*caption*) Bistable multivibrator with steering diodes for high-speed triggering. **1962** Simpson & Richards *Physical Princ. Junction Transistors* xvi. 410 Steering diodes may be used in a similar way at other electrodes and for other circuits than the simple bistable one. **1904** *Sci. Amer. Suppl.* 27 Aug. 23953/2 The front axle is provided with ball-bearing steering knuckles. **1970** K. Ball *Fiat 600, 600D Autobook* viii. 98/2 Remove the upper end shaft retaining nut from the steering knuckle and the two washers. **1866** *Eng. Mech.* 6 Apr. 33/1 Velocipede. SL is the steering lever. **1915** *Autocar Handbk.* (ed. 6) xv. 219 This steering lever is mounted upon a short spindle or shaft which is carried in bearings in the steering gear box. **1970** K. Ball *Fiat 600, 600D Autobook* viii. 97/2 The steering linkage also differs from that on the Sedan. **1945** F. A. Berry et al. *Handbk. Meteorol.* x. 818 Guiding of surface systems by the upper-level flow has been referred to as the steering principle. **1963** *Meteorol. Gloss.* (Met. Office) (ed. 4) 254 Application of the steering principle is most successful in the type of situation..in which almost straight thickness lines intersect a well marked pattern of surface vorticity. **1909** R. W. A. Brewer *Motor Car* xv. 148 The transverse arm on the off side is connected to the steering rod, generally by means of a knuckle joint. **1977** 'J. Gash' *Judas Pair* ix. 106 She twisted something near the steering-rod. The engine muted instantly into a deep, steady thrum.

b. steering box, a housing attached to the body of a motor vehicle that encloses the end of the steering column and the gearing that transmits its motion to the next members; **steering column,** a columnar assembly in a motor vehicle or motor bicycle carrying at its top the steering wheel or handle-bars and transmitting their motion to the rest of the steering gear; **steering line** *Meteorol.* (see quot. 1959); **steering lock,** (*a*) (example); (*b*) also, a similar mechanism fitted to the steering assembly of a motor vehicle, as an anti-theft device; **steering-oar** (earlier and later examples); † **steering pillar** = *steering column* above (*obs.*); **steering post** = prec.; on early motor vehicles (see also quot. 1904); **steering wheel,** (*b*) (examples); (*c*) also, a road wheel of a motor vehicle by which steerage is effected.

1913 W. E. Dommett *Motor Car Mechanism* xiii. 118 The method of mounting the steering box and column is clearly shown. **1970** K. Ball *Fiat 600, 600D Autobook* ix. 103/1 The linkage between the steering box and wheels is via a pair of symmetrical track rods and a central link rod connecting the pitman arm to a relay level. **1903** *Motor* 27 May 348/1 The steering column of the motor-bicycle is..a vitally important part. **1931** D. L. Sayers *Five Red Herrings* xxiii. 262, I was jammed up behind the steering-column. **1976** *Derbyshire Times* (Peak ed.) 3 Sept. 20/5 The single steering column stalk that operates lights, wipers, washers and flasher has too much to do. **1919** J. Bjerknes in *Geofysiske Publ.* I. ii. 1 As the line thus gives the momentaneous direction of the cyclone, it may, for practical purposes, be called the steering line. **1923** N. Shaw *Forecasting Weather* v. 155 The dividing line of the cyclone from the centre towards the eastern or advancing side is called the steering line or more recently, warm front. **1959** R. E. Huschke *Gloss. Meteorol.* (Amer. Meteorol. Soc.) 541 *Steering line*, according to Bjerknes' cyclone model, the line of convergence (corresponding to the warm front of a wave cyclone) which tends to be parallel to the direction of motion of the cyclone at the line's point of juncture with the cyclone center. **1955** *Times* 10 May 7/6 The greatest asset in this connexion.. is the admirable steering lock, with which the car can be turned in 37ft. and can be driven into small parking spaces. **1960** O. Gregory tr. *Spoerl's Living with Car* 212 Various devices.., some of which lock ignition and steering simultaneously... These locks are by no means impossible for a thief to cope with. However, if he has to choose between a car with one of these steering locks and one without he is likely to choose the one without. **1971** A. Price *Alamut Ambush* ix. 104 The new Triumph has a steering lock—it would be a verra difficult car to move. **1816** H. Ker *Travels* 30 In endeavouring to run the outside of a sawyer, I ran with my stem athwart it, and unshipped my steering oar, which I lost. **1938** B. L. Burman *Blow for Landing* 298 The black lifted the steering oar... The rafts began to speed down the water. **1904** A. C. Harmsworth et al. *Motors & Motor-Driving* 218 Looseness between steering wheel and end of steering pillar can be found at any time. **1921** W. H. Berry *Mod. Motor Car Practice* xvi. 324 A long chassis with a large engine involves a steering pillar of considerable length. **1904** A. B. F. Young *Compl. Motorist* iv. 118 The steering post, being situated in the middle of the car, and the steering tiller available on either side, it is possible for the driver to sit either on the right-hand or left-hand side of the car. **1969** J. Gores in *Ellery Queen's Mystery Mag.* Dec. 145/2 He was impaled on the steering post. **1902** A. C. Harmsworth et al. *Motors & Motor-Driving* 217 The free or direct gear moves with the impulse or pressure brought against the steering wheels or one of them by any ruts or obstructions on the road. **1907** R. W. Whitman *Motor-Car Princ.* x. 159 The irreversible type is used for all but the lightest cars, and..it prevents any movement from being transmitted from the wheels to the steering wheel or lever. **1912** *Motor Man.* 231 A weakened [tyre] cover will, as a general rule, give a considerable period of further service mounted on a steering wheel. **1915** *Autocar Handbk.* (ed. 6) xv. 220 It is very important..that the steering road wheels should be easily movable by means of the hand steering wheel... If a car is travelling on a much-rutted road the steering wheels tend to fall into the ruts. **1970** K. Ball *Fiat 600, 600D Autobook* ix. 103/2 Pry off the horn button from the steering wheel with a screwdriver.

steering (stīᵊ·riŋ), *ppl. a.* [f. Steer *v.*[1] + -ing[2].] *steering committee* (orig. *U.S.*): a committee set up to determine the order of business for another body, or to manage the general course of an operation. Also *steering group, sub-committee.*

1887 *Courier-Jrnl.* (Louisville, Kentucky) 6 Feb. 2/2 A steering committee upon the order of business for the remainder of the session was appointed. **1918** H. W. Dodds *Procedure in State Legislatures* iv. 56 Just as the power of standing committees developed when the number of bills introduced had become too large for consideration by the whole house, so the steering committee emerged when measures approved by the standing committees increased until a further selective agency became an irresistible temptation. **1955** *Times* 19 July 6/4 The steering committee making arrangements for the conference of Ministers on further European integration met to-day in Brussels. **1966** N. Johnson *Parliament & Administration* i. 22 The Chairman of the Estimates Committees presides over sub-committee A (now called the Steering sub-committee). **1974** 'E. Lathen' *Sweet & Low* ii. 20 Only three people are really important..the members of the steering committee. **1977** *Wandsworth Borough News* 7 Oct. 14/5 The Steering Group officially recognised by the Council's Recreation Committee at that meeting has met regularly and has discussed such matters as management, development, and use of the building. **1979** 'D. Meiring' *Foreign Body* v. 57 We have all read the Steering Committee's exhaustive report.

steersman. Add: **1. a.** Also, one who sits at the stern of a canoe and steers. *N. Amer.*

1774 Hearne & Turnor *Jrnls.* (1934) 122 The Pataroon or Steersman of each Cannoe has 50£ pr annom. **1791** [in Dict.] **1801** [see *middleman 5 c]. **1897** E. Coues *New Light Early Hist. Greater Northwest* I. 29 The steersman, finding himself within reach of the shore, jumped upon the rock with one of the midmen. **1968** [see *bowsman].

Stefan (ste·fæn). *Physics.* The name of Josef *Stefan* (1835–93), Austrian physicist, used *attrib.* and in the possessive with reference to a law discovered by him (see J. Stefan 1879, in *Sitzungsber. der Österreich. Akad. der Wissensch. in Wien* LXXIX. 391), as **Stefan('s) constant, law** = *Stefan–Boltzmann constant, law* (see next).

1898 *Sci. Abstr.* I. 391 The author's attempt to realise Kirchhoff's conception of an equivalent to an absolutely black body in the shape of a uniformly heated hollow space with a small opening, and test Stefan's law, which maintains that the radiation of such a body is proportional to the 4th power of its absolute temperature. **1923** Glazebrook *Dict. Appl. Physics* III. 711/1 By the Stefan-Boltzmann law.., and a knowledge of Stefan's constant, the whole radiation from the blackened surface is known. *Ibid.* IV. 569/1 Apart from this constant Stefan's law leads straight to Maxwell's law of radiation pressure. **1962** *Newnes Conc. Encycl. Electr. Engin.* 718/1 Here ϵ is the Stefan or total-radiation constant. **1966** [see *Planck('s) equation* s.v. *Planck]. **1979** T. B. Akrill et al. *Physics* xxviii. 377/2 For a non-black or 'grey' body we can apply Stefan's law in the form $P_{tot} = \epsilon\sigma AT^4$, where ϵ is called the total emissivity of the body and is a number always less than 1.

Stefan–Boltzmann (ste·fæn bōᵘ·ltsmæn). *Physics.* The names of Josef *Stefan* (see prec.) and Ludwig Eduard *Boltzmann* (1844–1906), Austrian physicists, used *attrib.* with reference to a law independently discovered by them (L. E. Boltzmann 1884, in *Ann. der Physik u. Chemie* XXII. 291; see also prec.), as **Stefan–Boltzmann constant,** the constant in the Stefan–Boltzmann law, equal to $5{\cdot}67 \times 10^{-8}$ J m^{-2} s^{-1} K^{-4}.; **Stefan–Boltzmann law,** the law which states that the total radiation emitted by a black body is proportional to the fourth power of its absolute temperature.

1898 *Sci. Abstr.* I. 391 The Stefan–Boltzmann law is confirmed to within 3 to 8%. **1915** R. A. Houstoun *Treat. Light* xxv. 448 By considering such a cycle Boltzmann proved that the total radiation from a black body was proportional to the fourth power of its absolute temperature. This law had been stated previously but erroneously by Stefan as holding good for all bodies, and as the amended version was due to Boltzmann, it is very often referred to as the Stefan–Boltzmann law. **1954** [see *langley]. **1958** Condon & Odishaw *Handbk. Physics* vi. i. 15/1 The total radiation crossing unit area in unit time in all directions in one hemisphere is usually written σT^4, where σ is called the Stefan–Boltzmann constant. **1977** I. M. Campbell *Energy & Atmosphere* i. 13 This is related to T through the Stefan–Boltzmann law: $E(T) = \sigma T^4$ where σ is known as the Stefan–Boltzmann constant and has value $5{\cdot}672 \times 10^{-8}$ for T in Kelvin and $E(T)$ in Wm^{-2}.

stegomyia (stegomǝi·ă). [mod. L. (F. V. Theobald 1901, in *Jrnl. Trop. Med. & Hygiene* IV. 235/1), f. STEGO- + Gr. μυῖα fly.] A mosquito of the genus formerly so called, now usually regarded as a sub-division of the genus *Aedes*, which includes tropical and sub-tropical species responsible for the transmission of yellow fever.

1911 A. ALCOCK *Entomol. for Med. Officers* v. 96 (*heading*) Genera of the Stegomyia type. **1915** G. B. SHAW in *New Statesman* 10 July 326/2 The same result could have been obtained by inoculation with anopheles vaccine and stegomyia emulsion. **1920** *Glasgow Herald* 6 July 6/4 The success of General Gorgas's methods can be gauged..after a campaign extending over eight years against the stegomyia. **1932** *Discovery* Oct. 326/2, I [*sc.* Robert Ross] then examined a small *Stegomyia*. **1971** J. D. GILLETT *Mosquitos* iii. 46 Other *Stegomyia* also at times glide through the water head-first.

steigerite (stǝi·gĕrǝit). *Min.* [f. the name of George *Steiger* (1869–1944), U.S. chemist + -ITE[1].] A monoclinic hydrated aluminium vanadate, $AlVO_4.3H_2O$, found as a canary-yellow powdery coating on vanadium-containing concretions.

1935 E. P. HENDERSON in *Amer. Mineralogist* XX. 769 A new yellow, hydrous aluminum vanadate, $Al_2O_3{\cdot}V_2O_5{\cdot}6{\cdot}5H_2O$, which has been named steigerite, is here described. **1959** *Amer. Mineralogist* XLIV. 336 Electron micrographs of steigerite from Gypsum Valley, Colorado ..show that the material is composed of thin, poorly developed laths and angular flakes.

stein. (Earlier and later examples.)

1855 *Trans. Hist. Soc. Lancs. & Cheshire* VII. 190 The 'Moss Pottery'..was..confined to the making of common red-clay ware, for domestic use, as jowls, steins, flower-pots, &c. **1897** [see PRETZEL, BRETZEL]. **1915** *Sat. Even. Post* 13 Feb. 52/3 So I sat down and et with 'em and had a few steins of beer. **1976** *Billings* (Montana) *Gaz.* 27 June 1-c/6 Beer was flowing at 50 cents a stein—three for $1. **1981** *West Lancs. Even. Gaz.* 18 July 8/4 A night on the town turned sour when a 22 year-old man hit a glass collector in the face with a beer stein.

Steinberger (ʃtǝi·nbǝ̄ɪgǝɪ). [Ger., f. the name *Steinberg* (also used) of the vineyard where the wine is produced.] A white wine produced near Hattenheim in the Rheingau.

1833 C. REDDING *Hist. & Descr. Mod. Wines* vii. 205 The Steinberger..takes rank after the Schloss-Johannesberger among these wines. It has the greatest strength, and yet is one of the most delicate, and even sweetly flavoured. **1894** J. L. W. THUDICHUM *Treat. Wines* 201 The *Johannisberg* is the only rival of the Steinberg. **1907** *Hatch, Mansfield Price List* Jan. 18 (Advt.), *Steinberg*, magnificent wine, with great body. **1926** M. SHAND *Bk. Wine* vi. 187 The number of classified districts in the Rheingau, from one or other of which all but three of its wines (Steinberger, Markobrunnen, and Schloss Vollrads) take their first name. **1951** *Good Housek. Home Encycl.* 508/2 The best Hock, which is sold under a number of well-known names, e.g. Johannisberger, Steinberger. **1965** O. A. MENDELSOHN *Dict. Drink & Drinking* 322 Starting at simple Steinberger and ending at the almost hallowed Steinberg Kabinett.

Steiner (ʃtǝi·nǝɪ). *Math.* The name of Jakob *Steiner* (1796–1863), Swiss geometer, used *attrib.* and in the possessive to designate various mathematical concepts suggested by him: **a.** *Steiner triple* or *triplet system* (see quot. 1939); so *Steiner triplet*; also *Steiner system*, a generalization of the triple system to other numbers (see quot. 1974). [Steiner first described such systems in *Jrnl. f. d. reine u. angewandte Math.* (1853) XLV. 181.]

1939 R. C. BOSE in *Annals Eugenics* IX. 354 Steiner (1853) proposed the problem of arranging *N* things in triplets, such that every pair occurs in just one and only one triplet. Such an arrangement may be called a simple triple system or a Steiner's triplet system. **1963** H. J. RYSER *Combinatorial Math.* viii. 100 The Steiner triple system of order 7 is the same as the projective plane of order 2 in the preceding chapter. **1966** *Annali di Matematica* LXXI. 199 The *Steiner* system *S*(5, 8, 24) is an arrangement of 24 elements in sets of 8, such that any 5 of the elements belong to exactly one set. **1974** I. ANDERSON *First Course Combinatorial Math.* vii. 102 A Steiner system *S*(*l*, *m*, *n*) is a collection of *m*-element subsets of an *n* element set *B* such that every *l*-element subset of *B* lies in exactly one of the *m*-element sets. *Ibid.*, A Steiner triple system is an *S*(2, 3, *n*) for some *n*. **1980** *Sci. Amer.* May 14/2 Since Steiner triplets are not ordered, the solution is of course unique.

b. Used with reference to the problem of finding the set of line segments of minimum total length needed to connect a given set of points in a metric space.

1941 COURANT & ROBBINS *What is Math.?* vii. 359 In Steiner's problem three fixed points *A*, *B*, *C* are given. It is natural to generalize this problem to the case of *n* given points. *Ibid.* 360 To find the really significant extension of Steiner's problem we must abandon the search for a single point *P*... Given *n* points..to find a connected system of straight line segments of shortest total length such that any two of the given points can be joined by a polygon consisting of segments of the system. **1961** *Canad. Math. Bull.* IV. 143 Given a triangle T with the vertices a_1, a_2, a_3, to find in the plane of T the point p which minimizes the sum of the distances $|pa_1| + |pa_2| + |pa_3|$. p, called the Steiner point of T, is unique. **1968** *SIAM Jrnl. Appl. Math.* XVI. 1 A Steiner minimal tree for given points $A_1, .., A_n$ in the plane is a tree which interconnects these points using lines of shortest possible total length. In order to achieve minimum length the Steiner minimal tree may contain other vertices (Steiner points) beside $A_1, .. A_n$. **1979** *Sci. Amer.* Apr. 37/1 First is the Steiner problem of the shortest roads linking many cities.

Steinert (ʃtǝi·nĕɹt). *Path.* [The name of H. G. W. *Steinert* (b. 1875), German physician, who described the disease in 1909 (*Deutsche Zeitschr. f. Nervenheilkunde* XXXVII. 58).] *Steinert's disease* = *myotonia atrophica* s.v. *MYOTONIA 2 b.

1932 *Index Medicus* XII. 429/1 (*heading*) Cachetic form of myotonia atrophica (Steinert's disease). **1948** F. B. CARLSEN tr. *Thomasen's Myotonia* vii. 94 Steinert's disease invariably set in in later life, generally between the ages of twenty and thirty. **1963** [see *MYOTONIA 2 b].

Steinhäger (ʃtǝi·nhēgǝɹ). Also **-haeger**, (*erron.*) **-hager.** [Ger., f. the name *Steinhagen* of the town, in Westphalia, where it is produced.] A spirit made from juniper-berries; a measure or glassful of this.

1959 M. CROSLAND tr. *Rovan's Germany* 180 Many fine spirits are made in Germany..a white *eau-de-vie* in Westphalia called *Steinhäger*. **1964** L. DEIGHTON *Funeral in Berlin* xl. 239 Coffee, doughnuts and tiny glasses of Steinhager. **1966** R. THOMAS *Cold War Swap* i. 9 Steinhaeger is best when drunk ice cold and washed down with a liter or so of beer. **1968** 'J. LE CARRÉ' *Small Town in Germany* xvii. 273 He drank a Steinhager from the tray. The mat stuck to the stem of the glass. **1976** R. PERRY *One Good Death* xi. 172, I handed him the flask of Steinhager... Muller took a generous swig.

Steinheim (ʃtǝi·nhǝim). The name of a village twelve miles north of Stuttgart, West Germany, used *absol.* or *attrib.* in **Steinheim skull** to designate a Middle Pleistocene fossil hominid known from a skull found there in 1933 by Karl Sigrist and described as *Homo steinheimensis* by F. Berckhemer in 1936 (*Forschungen & Fortschritte* XII. 349/2).

1946 F. E. ZEUNER *Dating Past* ix. 296 If the geological age of the Steinheim Skull were settled..we should at least know whether he, or his ancestor, lived in the middle Pleistocene. **1973** B. J. WILLIAMS *Evolution & Human Origins* x. 170/1 The Steinheim skull also comes from a gravel pit. *Ibid.* 170/2 In facial features Steinheim could indeed be a good ancestor for the later Neandertals.

Stein–Leventhal (ʃtǝin le·vĕntāl). *Path.* [The names of I. F. *Stein* (1887–1976) and M. L. *Leventhal* (1901–71), U.S. gynæcologists, who described the condition in 1935 (*Amer. Jrnl. Obstetrics & Gynecol.* XXIX. 181–91).] *Stein–Leventhal syndrome*: a hormonal abnormality in women characterized by enlarged polycystic ovaries, infertility, and oligomenorrhœa, often with hirsutism.

1950 F. A. SIMMONS in Meigs & Sturgis *Progr. in Gynecol.* II. 334 These curves are common in the 'Stein–Leventhal syndrome', a condition wherein poor or non-ovulatory cycles are thought to be caused by polycystic ovaries. **1972** *Brit. Med. Jrnl.* 20 May 457/2 A second ovarian cause of amenorrhoea is the Stein–Leventhal Syndrome.

Steinmann (ʃtǝi·nmæ̆n). *Surg.* The name of Fritz *Steinmann* (1872–1932), Swiss surgeon, who described the device in 1907 (*Zentralbl. Chir.* XXXIV. 939), used in the possessive and *attrib.* to designate a surgical pin that may be passed through one end of a major bone for traction or setting.

1916 ROBERTS & KELLY *Treatm. Fractures* i. 77 (*heading*) Technic of application of Steinmann's nails. **1925** WILSON & COCHRANE *Fractures & Dislocations* xv. 546 Steinmann's pin has now been largely superseded in general use by the calipers, or ice-tongs, which grasp, but do not penetrate the bone. **1933** P. B. MAGNUSON *Fractures* iii. 25 The use of the Steinmann pin is not advisable except in skilled hands. **1974** A. HENRY in R. M. Kirk et al. *Surgery* xvi. 370 A Thomas's splint is fitted, and skeletal traction set up through a Steinmann's pin.. in the proximal tibia.

Steinway (stǝi·nwē[i]). The name of Henry Engelhard *Steinway* (1797–1871), celebrated German piano-builder, used *attrib.* or *absol.* to designate a piano manufactured by him or by the firm which he founded in New York in 1853.

1875 T. YELVERTON *Teresina in Amer.* ii. 181 In the latter there was one of the best pianos (a Steinway) that I touched in America, where good pianos are by no means rare. **1889** G. B. SHAW in *Star* 13 July 4/4 She was presented with a Steinway Grand. **1905** A. BENNETT *Sacred & Profane Love* III. v. 260 The piano, a Steinway in a hundred Steinways. **1933** E. WHARTON *Human Nature* 172, I always knew fashionable people could barely distinguish a barrel-organ from a Steinway. **1965** J. M. CAIN *Magician's Wife* (1966) ii. 18 At one end of the room was a Steinway baby grand. **1977** *New Yorker* 19 Sept. 64/2, I pictured a sea of Steinways to choose from in Juillard's basement. **1981** J. JOHNSTON *Christmas Tree* 130 There was a piano, a beautiful Steinway concert grand... The only reality was the room with the Steinway.

Steinwein (ʃtǝi·nvǝin). [Ger.] The name of a dry white wine produced in the Steinmantel vineyards, near Würzburg, Bavaria, and sold in special bottles called Bocksbeutel.

1833 C. REDDING *Hist. & Descr. Mod. Wines* vii. 206 The Steinwein of 1748, brought in 1832 seventy pounds the ahm. This may serve to show how much these wines gain by age. **1843** *Penny Cycl.* XXVII. 456/2 The Steinwein must not be confounded with the Steinberger wine of the Rhine. **1920** G. SAINTSBURY *Notes on Cellar-Bk.* xii. 177 The popular form seems to have been..the *bocksbeutel* flasks of Steinwein. **1966** H. YOXALL *Fashion of Life* xxiii. 212 At Würzburg..a dinner with salmon and *Steinwein*. **1980** *Times* 9 Aug. 8/7 The Steinburg vineyard, whose fame caused Franconian wines to be referred to as 'Steinwein'.

Stelazine (ste·lăzīn). *Pharm.* Also **stelazine.** [f. *Stel-*, of unkn. origin + *AZINE.] A proprietary name for trifluoperazine.

1958 *Brit. Med. Jrnl.* 12 July 91/1 A short pilot trial of the drug stelazine was undertaken with 25 chronic psychotic patients. **1958** *Trade Marks Jrnl.* 23 July 738/1 *Stelazine* 772,994. Azine chemical compounds for use in medicine and pharmacy. Smith, Kline & French Laboratories Ltd., London. Manufacturing Chemists.—9th January, 1958. **1965** *Nursing Times* 5 Feb. 187/2 In hospital the phenothiazine tranquilizers seem most useful for relieving the fear and tension prominent at this stage. Stelazine (trifluoperazine) seems particularly useful. **1976** H. FERGUSON *Confessions of Long Distance Acid Head* 45 This hospital did not even stock the drug Stelazine which had, apparently, cured me when I had my first nervous breakdown.

stele. Add: **2.** [ad. F. *stèle* (Van Tieghem & Douliot 1886, in *Bull. de la Soc. bot. de France* XXXIII. 216).]

stelk (stelk). *Anglo-Ir.* [Prob. ad. Ir. *stailc* stubbornness, sulkiness, (in Co. Donegal) starch: cf. STALK *sb.*[1]] A cooked vegetable dish made with onions, mashed potatoes, and butter, or other ingredients.

1844 W. CARLETON *Traits & Stories Ir. Peasantry* (new ed.) II. 167 Norah..sent you a crock of her own lard. When you're makin'..*sthilk*.., if you slip in a lump of this, it'll save you the price of butther. *Ibid.*, *Sthilk* is made by bruising a quantity of boiled potatoes and beans together. The potatoes, having first been reduced to a pulpy state, the beans are but partially broken. It is then put into a dish, and a pound of butter or rendered lard thrust into the middle of it. **1890** D. A. SIMMONS *List Words & Phr. S. Donegal* 16 *Stelk*, champ, food made of pounded potatoes. **1949** 'M. INNES' *Journeying Boy* xiii. 162, I greatly fear that for dinner now we shall have to fall back upon stelk. **1971** *Guardian* 10 July 9/6 Stelk.. is alternatively known as champ and consists of spring onions simmered in milk.

stell, *sb.*[5] (Earlier example.)

1801 J. BARROW *Trav. Interior S. Afr.* I. vi. 360 The animal had been shot through the body by a *stell-roar* or trap-gun, set by a Hottentot.

stellacyanin (stelăsǝi·ănin). *Biochem.* [f. the name *Estelle* (see quot. 1967) after *PLASTOCYANIN.] An intensely blue copper-containing protein found in the latex of the Japanese lac tree, *Rhus vernicifera*.

1966 W. G. LEVINE in J. Peisach et al. *Biochem. of Copper* 377 Omura,..in the course of purifying *Rhus* laccase.., separated a second, blue, copper protein which Peisach later named stellacyanin. **1967** J. PEISACH et al. in *Biochem. Jrnl.* CCXLII. 2857/2 The authors would like to thank..Dr. Tsuneo Omura, whose permission was kindly given to name stellacyanin after Mrs. Estelle Peisach. **1976** *Nature* 27 May 346/1 Stellacyanin..and umecyanin have about 110 and 130 amino acids with a single cysteine residue plus one disulphide bridge.

‖ **Stella Maris** (ste·lă mæ·ris). [L., lit. 'star of the sea'.] A title given to the Virgin Mary (see SEA-STAR 1), used allusively of a protectress or a guiding spirit.

1876 GEO. ELIOT *Dan. Der.* III. v. xxxvii. 113 If a man could paint the woman he loves..as the *Stella Maris* to put courage into the sailors..so much the more honour to her. **1897** O. WILDE *Let.* 31 May (1962) 583 Even for the sheep who has no shepherd there is a Stella Maris to guide it home. **1913** W. J. LOCKE *Stella Maris* i. 1 Stella Maris—Star of the Sea! That was not her real name. No one could have christened an innocent babe so absurdly. *Ibid.* 2 Walter Herold.., one night of storm and dashing spray, seeing the light, burning steadily like a star.., cried: 'Stella Maris! What a name for her!'

stellar, *a.* Add: **1.** (Later example.)

1975 *Physics Bull.* Nov. 484/3 Astrophysicists use the term white dwarfs to describe objects which are stellar, that is to say luminous by themselves, but with a low luminosity and a small radius.

3. Having the quality of a star (STAR *sb.*[1] 5 in Dict. and Suppl.); leading, outstanding. So **ste·llardom**, stardom. orig. and chiefly *U.S.*

1883 *N.Y. Mercury* 3 Nov. 2/2 Effie Ellsler's dramatic stellardom is at an end and the supporting cast will be disbanded. **1883** *Sunday Mercury* (N.Y.) 4 Nov. 7/3 A fine specialty performance will be given by selected stellar artists. **1912** M. B. Leavitt *Fifty Years Theatr. Managem.* xxx. 464 In those days a theatrical star was obliged to work his way up to the rungs of the legitimate ladder until he was found worthy of ranking in stellardom. .. It made good actors,..who have since taken their places as leaders in the stellar ranks. **1932** Kaufman & Ryskud *Of Thee I Sing* I. iv. 75 The two centre chairs are conspicuously empty, obviously waiting for the stellar pair. **1950** J. Dempsey *Championship Fighting* 26 It is only in..'partial' punches that the body-weight does not play a stellar role. **1958** Wodehouse *Cocktail Time* xviii. 156 A man of regular habits, he would normally have shrunk from playing a stellar role in an E. Phillips Oppenheim story. **1964** W. C. Putnam *Geol.* ix. 215/1 Second of the factors is the nature of the ground. San Francisco, 1906, and Long Beach, 1933, both [earthquakes] in California, are stellar examples of the importance of this control. **1976** *Times Lit. Suppl.* 25 June 804/5 The most spectacular book sale held this spring... The stellar attraction was the whole Book of Daniel, twelve leaves, from the Trier copy of the 42-line or Gutenberg Bible, 1455. **1977** *Amer. N. & Q.* XV. 94/1 He has eschewed the glitter of Hollywood which has lured and made stellar personalities out of so many of his fellow novelists.

stellarator (ste·lăreɪtǫɪ). *Physics.* [f. Stellar *a.* (see quot. 1951) + L. *-ātor* (see -or 2 and cf. Eng. *generator*).] One kind of toroidal apparatus for producing controlled fusion reactions in a hot plasma, distinguished by the fact that all the controlling magnetic fields inside it are produced by external windings.

1951 L. Spitzer *Proposed Stellarator* (U.S. Atomic Energy Commission NYO-993) 4 Since the proposed system generates power and neutrons by reactions similar to those occurring in the stars, the device analyzed below is called a 'Stellarator'. **1967** Condon & Odishaw *Handbk. Physics* (ed. 2) IV. xi. 209/2 The feature that distinguishes a stellarator from a torus with solenoidal windings alone is the presence of helical windings around the channel which cause the magnetic-field lines to be twisted in such a way that as the particles drift they are constantly turned back toward the channel center. **1980** *Ann. Rep. U.K. Atomic Energy Authority 1979–80* 32/1 Another type of toroidal magnetic trap studied at Culham is the stellarator. **1981** *Nature* 19 Feb. 625/1 The tokamak must create the longitudinal current in the plasma by a transformer effect, and so must be pulsed. The stellarator, on the other hand, can in principle be run statically.

stellate, *a.* Add: **3. b.** *Esp.* in *Anat.*, as *stellate cell*, any of various types of cell with long processes, as a Langerhans cell, a Kupffer cell, or an astrocyte (sense *a); *stellate ganglion*, the lowest of the three cervical ganglia of the sympathetic trunk; *stellate reticulum*, a layer of cells with long processes within the enamel organ of a developing tooth.

1890, etc. [see *Langerhans]. **1895** A. H. Smith *Dental Microsc.* p. xvii, Stellate reticulum of enamel organ. **1899** [in Dict., sense 3 a]. **1901,** etc. [see *Kupffer]. **1918** *Gray's Anat.* (ed. 20) 935 The accelerator fibres of the heart leave mainly through the second and third thoracic nerves and pass to the stellate ganglion. **1921** Tilney & Riley *Form & Function Central Nervous Syst.* xli. 749 Immediately beneath the layers of large and medium-sized pyramidal cells is a stratum containing a number of small monopolar stellate cells belonging exclusively to the Golgi type II. **1945** [see *astrocyte]. **1969** W. A. Beresford *Lect. Notes Histol.* xxiv. 169 'Mesectoderm' cells..induce overlying ectodermal lamina to separate into tooth germs and provide for each an enamel organ with its pulp/stellate reticulum and inner and outer epithelia. **1980** *Gray's Anat.* (ed. 36) 1129/1 The cervicothoracic (stellate) ganglion is..much larger than the middle cervical ganglion, being probably formed by the coalescence of the lower two cervical segmented ganglia with the first thoracic.

stellate, *v.* (Later example.)

1948 [see *stellation 7].

stellated, *a.* Add: **1. b.** *Geom.* Of a polygon, polyhedron, or polytope: capable of being generated from a convex polygon, etc., by extending the edges, etc., until they once more meet at a new set of vertices, etc. [The sense is due to L. Poinsot, who used F. *étoilé* in *Jrnl. de l'École Polytechn.* (1810) IV. 41).]

1859 A. Cayley in *Phil. Mag.* XVII. 123 It is shown by Poinsot..that, besides the regular polyhedrons of ordinary geometry, there are (of course in an extended signification of the term) four new regular polyhedrons, viz. an icosahedron, which I will call the great icosahedron.., and three dodecahedrons, which I will call the great dodecahedron.., the great stellated dodecahedron.., and the small stellated dodecahedron. **1931** *Proc. Cambr. Philos. Soc.* XXVII. 206 Consider..the 'small stellated dodecahedron' { , 5}, bounded by pentagrams. **1952** Cundy & Rollett *Math. Models* iii. 83 These four beautiful solids were unknown to the ancient world and were not discovered until modern times. The two with star faces—the two stellated dodecahedra—were found by Kepler (1571–1630); the others with regular faces and star vertices—the great icosahedron and dodecahedron—by Poinsot (1777–1859). **1976** I. Lakatos *Proofs & Refutations* i. 62 Take for instance the 'great stellated dodecahedron' (fig. 15). It consists, like the 'small stellated dodecahedron' of pentagrams, but differently arranged. It has 12 faces, 30 edges and 20 vertices, so that $V-E+F=2$.

stellation. 7. (Later examples.)

1938 H. S. M. Coxeter et al. *Fifty-Nine Icosahedra* i. 1 We enumerate and describe the polyhedra that can be five Platonic solids by stellation, *i.e.*, by extending or 'producing' the faces until they meet again, always preserving the rotational symmetry of the original solid. **1948** —— *Regular Polytopes* xiv. 264 The first stellation of {5, 3, 3} is constructed by stellating the 720 pentagons into $\{\frac{5}{2}\}$'s, and the 120 dodecahedra into $\{\frac{5}{2}, 5\}$'s. The result is $\{\frac{5}{2}, 5, 3\}$. **1971** *Sci. Amer.* Dec. 114/2 The five Platonic solids are complete of their symmetrical kind. By mixing regular polygon faces, however, Archimedes made 13 more solids. These can be variously extended by putting cells on faces, called stellation, or by cutting away cells whenever that process can reveal new regular polygon faces within.

stelled, *a.* For † *Obs.* read '*Obs.* exc. *poet.*' and add: **b.** (Later example.)

1949 Blunden *After Bombing* 41 Thence the eye soon travelled over much green plain, Swathed with plats blush-dyed, with blue meres stelled.

Steller (ste·ləɪ). The name of Georg Wilhelm *Steller* (see next), used *attrib.* or in the possessive to designate certain animals associated with his explorations, as *Steller's* (*eider*) (*duck*), a black and white duck with reddish underparts, *Polysticta stelleri*, found in Siberia, Alaska, and Canada; *Steller('s) jay*, a blue jay with a dark crest, *Cyanocitta stelleri*, found in western North America; *Steller's sea-cow*, an extinct sirenian, *Hydrodamalis stelleri*, once found in the Bering Sea; *Steller('s) sea-lion*, a large sea-lion, *Eumetopias jubata*, found in the northern Pacific. Cf. Stellerine.

1814 tr. *G. H. von Langsdorff's Voyages & Travels* II. i. 23 My curiosity was particularly directed to..Steller's sea-cow. **1828** C. L. Bonaparte *Amer. Ornithol.* II. 44 The Steller's Jay is one of those obsolete species alluded to in the preface to this volume. **1884** *Bull. U.S. Nat. Mus.* No. 27. 162 Steller's Duck..Arctic and subarctic coasts. **1902** *Bull. Amer. Mus. Nat. Hist.* XVI. 111 The northern and southern Sea Lions, often known respectively as Steller's Sea Lion and Forster's Sea Lion. **1917** Steller's jay [see *mountain jay* s.v. *mountain 9 c]. **1938** P. A. Taverner *Birds of Canada* 104 Steller's Eider... The smallest and the least eider-like of any of the birds known under that name. **1947** L. G. Ingles *Mammals California* 88 Steller Sea Lion bulls weigh up to 1,800 pounds. **1948** *Pacific Discovery* Jan. 14/2 Steller jays, bald eagles, mountains of wild geraniums,..these are the Teton country. **1957** P. J. Darlington *Zoogeography* vi. 400 Steller's Sea Cow..was hunted to extinction. **1963** *Times* 11 Feb. 14/4 One of these was an account of Steller's Eider Duck. **1968** G. Maxwell *Raven seek thy Brother* viii. 103 No one had ever proved whether or not the..beautiful little duck called Steller's Eider..actually bred in Varanger Fjord. **1972** *Village Voice* (N.Y.) 1 June 75/2 In the dense fir forests you can hear..the scream of the steller's jay. **1972** L. Hancock *There's a Seal in my Sleeping Bag* vii. 145 The rocky shores..are used by the Steller sea-lions as hauling-out grounds. **1975** *Islander* (Victoria, B.C.) 27 Apr. 3/1 He has been studying California and Steller's sea lions in Barkley Sound. **1976** *Ibid.* 27 June 2/2 When the potatoes were small, many Steller jays came to rob the patch.

stellerite (ste·lĕrəit). *Min.* [ad. G. *stellerit* (J. Morozewicz 1909, in *Bull. internat. de l'Acad. des Sci. de Cracovie* (Math.-Nat. Classe) II. 350). f. the name of Georg Wilhelm *Steller* (1709–46), German naturalist and explorer of the Komandorski Islands in the Bering Sea where the first samples were found: see -ite¹.] A zeolite, $CaAl_2Si_7O_{18}.7H_2O$, found as tabular orthorhombic crystals.

1909 *Jrnl. Chem. Soc.* XCVI. II. 1028 A new zeolite, stellerite, has been found at the N.W. Cape of Copper Island, one of the Komandorski islands in the Aleutian Group. **1968** *Amer. Mineralogist* LIII. 511 *Stellerite*, a valid orthorhombic end member of a continuous series with monoclinic stilbite. **1973** *Lithos* VI. 85 The walls of large cavities and fractures are lined with polycrystal aggregates of stellerite.

stelleroid (ste·leroid). *Zool.* [f. mod.L. *Stelleroidea* (J. W. Gregory in E. R. Lankester *Treat. Zool.* (1900) III. xiv. 237), f. F. *stelléride* (J. B. P. A. de Lamarck *Hist. Nat. Animaux sans Vertèbres* (1816) II. 527): see Stellerid and -oid.] A star-fish or a similar invertebrate belonging to the class Stelleroidea.

1900 J. W. Gregory in E. R. Lankester *Treat. Zool.* III. xiv. 237 This list of characters is quite sufficient to mark off the Stelleroids from all other Echinoderms. **1935** Twenhofel & Shrock *Invertebr. Paleontol.* vi. 190 Stelleroidea—..referring to the starlike appearance of the stelleroid. **1962** D. Nichols *Echinoderms* iv. 62 They were burrowers, and, like some recent stelleroids, sat in the substratum with only the arm-tips exposed above the surface. **1970** R. M. Black *Elements Palaeontol.* ix. 105 The stelleroids, too, are vagrant.

Stellite (ste·ləit), *sb.* Also **stellite.** [? f. L. *stell-a* star + -ite¹.] Any of various cobalt-based alloys that usu. contain chromium and small amounts of tungsten and molybdenum and are used for their great hardness and their resistance to heat.

A proprietary name in the U.S.

1913 *Engin. Mag.* XLV. 840/2 It is an alloy of cobalt, chromium, and tungsten and has been called 'Stellite' by its inventor, Mr. Elwood Haynes. **1916** *Official Gaz.* (U.S. Patent Office) 3 Oct. 267/2 The Haynes Stellite Co.... *Stellite*... Metal alloys. **1937** *Jrnl. R. Aeronaut. Soc.* XLI. 330 The mean thermal expansion coefficients of the stellites were obtained between 20°C and a higher temperature ranging from 100°C to 850°C. **1975** Bram & Downs *Manuf. Technol.* iii. 79 Stellite can be purchased in bars of round or square section for manufacturing cutting tools. **1980** *Daily Tel.* 11 Sept. 7 (Advt.), The new 1300cc 'A' Plus unit with stellite faced valves.

Hence **ste·llite** *v. trans.*, to coat with Stellite; **ste·llited** *ppl. a.*, **ste·lliting** *vbl. sb.*

1934 *Jrnl. R. Aeronaut. Soc.* XXXVIII. 329 If only one part is to be 'stellited' it is better to treat the valve. *Ibid.*, The 'stelliting' of the valve stem and neck..would also be beneficial. **1937** *Ibid.* XLI. 330 The cracking of stellited steels is attributed to this difference in expansion. **1959** *Engineering* 9 Jan. 49/2 The journal portions of extension shafts on the vanes are Stellited and ground to provide a wear resistant bearing surface.

Stellwag (ste·lvag). *Med.* [The name of Carl *Stellwag* von Carion (1823–1904), Austrian ophthalmologist.] *Stellwag's sign*: orig., retraction of the upper eyelid in thyrotoxicosis (called also Dalrymple's sign); now often applied to the diminished blinking that normally accompanies it.

1887 *Brit. Med. Jrnl.* 26 Mar. 680/1 A married woman, aged 32, with marked retraction of the left upper eyelid (Stellwag's sign), no proptosis, and no goître. **1907** *Practitioner* Nov. 733 [In exophthalmic goitre] the margins of the eyelids are unduly separated (Dalrymple's sign); the upper lid tardily follows the eyeball in its downward movements (von Graef[e]'s sign); there is diminished frequency of winking (Stellwag's sign). **1950** R. I. Pritikin *Essent. Ophthalm.* vii. 321 Stellwag's sign—infrequent winking. **1973** R. S. Dillon *Handbk. Endocrinol.* vi. 248/1 'Stellwag's sign' is retraction of the upper eyelids producing apparent widening of the palpebral opening associated with infrequent and incomplete blinking.

stem, *sb.*¹ Add: **4. i.** *pl.* The legs. *slang.*

1860 Hotten *Dict. Slang* (ed. 2) 227 *Stems*, the legs. **1927** *Vanity Fair* XXIX. 67/2 Among some of Conway's more famous expressions are:..'Stems' and 'Gambs' (legs). **1970** C. Major *Dict. Afro-Amer. Slang* 109 *Stems*, the legs.

j. More fully *drill stem*: (*a*) (also *auger stem*) in percussion drilling, a heavy metal rod above the bit in a string of tools, used to provide added weight; (*b*) in rotary drilling, = *grief stem* below; also, the entire drilling column; *grief stem*: in rotary drilling, the rod at the top of the drilling column, having a square cross-section so that it fits in and is turned by the rotary table; = *kelly *sb.*² 4.

drill-stem test: a test of the potential of a well in which a sample of the oil or gas is allowed to run into the drill pipe for a short time before the hole is completed, the flow being measured and the fluid recovered; so *drill-stem testing* vbl. sb.

1880 J. F. Carll *Geol. Oil Regions Warren, Venango, Clarion & Butler Counties* III. xxviii. 300 On the down stroke the auger-stem falls 20 inches, while the sinker-bar goes down 24 inches. **1907** *Internat. Libr. Technol.: Rock Boring* 13 The tools consist of a rope socket, sinker bar, jars, stem, and bit. *Ibid.* 15 Auger or Drill Stem.—This part of the string of tools..is made about 30 feet long in some cases. **1922** B. Redwood *Petroleum* (ed. 4) II. 402 The lower end of the drilling-rod or casing with the bit is passed through the rotary table provided with grip rings or square 'grief' stem and clamped tight enough to cause it to revolve. **1938** D. Hager *Practical Oil Geol.* (ed. 5) viii. 252 After drilling into an oil stratum, some idea of productivity may be gained by making a drill-stem test. **1939** —— *Fund. Petroleum Industry* ix. 210 When the kelly is deep enough for a joint of drill stem, the kelly and bit are pulled out. **1951** K. K. Landes *Petroleum Geol.* ii. 51 The string of tools consists of the bit..; the stem, into which the bit fits; the jars; and the socket. **1962** E. J. Lynch *Formation Evaluation* viii. 291 Drill stem testing is the most hazardous of all drilling operations. **1965** E. Lehner et al. in G. J. Williams *Econ. Geol. N.Z.* xix. 350/2 Both the Taramakau and Arahura wells.. encountered faint traces of oil in the Brunner Sandstone at 5,700 ft and 5,030 ft respectively, but drill-stem tests of these zones yielded only salt water. **1973** J. W. Jenner in Hobson & Pohl *Mod. Petroleum Technol.* (ed. 4) iv. 108 A drilling bit..is attached to a heavy drill stem suspended by a cable from a cantilever arm, the Walking Beam, at the surface. **1976** L. St. Clair *Fortune in Death* i. 8 The drill stem had snapped... 'Stem crystalize?' 'Yep. Damned basalt is hard as the drill.'

k. Similarly, a drill used by a burglar or safe-breaker. *U.S. Criminals' slang.*

1914 Jackson & Hellyer *Vocab. Criminal Slang* 81 *Stem, noun.* Current among yeggs. A steel drill. **1926** J. Black *You can't Win* x. 133 Get the 'dan' and 'stems' (drills), and put them safely away. **1935** *Flynn's* 16 Mar. 102/1, I was inserting a 'stem' (drill) in a brace when I heard a most peculiar noise.

5*. a. A principal railway line, from which other tracks may branch; = *main stem.

1832 [see *main stem]. **1869** *Bradshaw's Railway Man.* XXI. 426 *Assets.* Main Stem..Lebanon Branch extension ..Richmond Branch. **1934** in *Amer. Ballads & Folk*

Songs i. 24 The manifest freight Pulled out on the stem behind the mail.

b. A street, esp. one frequented by beggars and tramps (see also quot. 1923); also, = *MAIN STREET a; *transf.*, an act of begging. *U.S. slang.*

1914 [see *MOOCH *v.* 6]. **1923** N. ANDERSON *Hobo* i. 4 Every large city has its district into which these homeless types gravitate. In the parlance of the 'road' such a section is known as the 'stem' or the 'main drag'. **1929** *Amer. Speech* IV. 345 *Stem*, act of begging; also a street where one begs. **1931** 'D. STIFF' *Milk & Honey Route* v. 59 The hobo also damns the hash houses along the stem. **1936** *New Republic* 15 July 289/1 The appearance of the applicant is perhaps not so important as in the case of private residences or on the 'stem'. **1955** D. W. MAURER in *Publ. Amer. Dialect Soc.* XXIV. 133 This is all done on the *stem* or street.

7. (sense 5 b) *stem-form, -formant; stem-final, -formative, -initial* adjs. (all also *absol.* as sb.); *stem-forming* adj.

1949 E. A. NIDA *Morphology* (ed. 2) ii. 34 All stem-final vowels before vowel suffixes are lost. **1965** *Canad. Jrnl. Linguistics* X. 130 It seems that Chipewyan and Navaho treat it as a stem final, while Mattole treats it as a stem initial. **1973** A. H. SOMMERSTEIN *Sound Pattern Anc. Greek* ii. 17 There is a large class of nouns ending, in the nominative singular, in -εύς [-éws]..which have a stem-final [w] when a consonant follows. **1928** O. JESPERSEN *Internat. Lang.* II. 97 The bare stem-form of many adjectives would not be euphonious enough. **1966** *English Studies* XLVII. 53 These genetive [*sic*] 'causative' objects disappear in early ME and give place to objects in stem-form or prepositional types. **1935** G. K. ZIPF *Psycho-Biol. of Lang.* iv. 144 A stem-formative (or stem-formant) is a morpheme added to the root either at the beginning (prefix) or at the end (suffix) or tucked inside (infix) to make the stem (root plus formant) to which endings are added. **1964** K. L. PIKE in D. Abercombie et al. *Daniel Jones* 428 The stem is made up of three monosyllabic roots plus three following stem-formative syllables. **1968** CHOMSKY & HALLE *Sound Pattern Eng.* 130 In short, there are 'stem-forming' vowels / i / and / u / which are deleted in final position..but which remain before certain affixes. **1978** *Language* LIV. 220 Most stem-forming suffixes consist of a single segment, and a certain amount of homophony results. **1949** E. A. NIDA *Morphology* (ed. 2) ii. 15 When stem-initial consonants are aspirated, the reduplicated consonant has the same point of articulation, except that it is unaspirated. **1965** [see *stem-final* above]. **1977** *Word* 1972 XXVIII. 223 The inappropriate stem-initial consonants.

8. stem analysis *Forestry*, (an) investigation of the past growth of a tree by study of a series of cross-sections of its trunk taken at different heights; **stem borer,** an insect larva that bores into plant stems; **stem cell** *Biol.*, (*a*) a cell in the stem of an organism (*nonce-use*); (*b*) a cell of a multicellular organism which is capable of giving rise to indefinitely more cells of the same type and from which certain other kinds of cell arise by differentiation; **stem-cup,** a Chinese porcelain goblet of a type with a wide shallow bowl mounted on a short base, first made in the Ming dynasty; **stem family** *Sociol.* [tr. F. *famille-souche* (F. le Play *La Réforme Sociale en France* (1866) I. iii. 249)], a family unit in which property descends to a married son who remains within the household, other (esp. married) children achieving independence on receipt of an inheritance; **stemflow** *Forestry*, precipitation which reaches the ground after running down the branches and trunks of trees; **stem ginger,** a superior grade of crystallized or preserved ginger; **stem-glass,** (*a*) a tall narrow glass vase for the display of a single flower or flowers; (*b*) a drinking-glass mounted on a stem; **stemline** *Med.*, the group of cells having a chromosome number that is (one of) the most frequent in a mixed population, esp. of tumour cells; **stem mother** *Ent.* = *FUNDATRIX 2; **stem root,** a root that develops from the stem of a plant, esp. on a lily from just above the top of the bulb; so **stem-rooting** *a.*, producing roots of this kind; **stem rust,** any of various fungus diseases of plants that produce spots on the stems; *esp.* that caused by *Puccinia graminis* on wheat and other cereals, marked by rows of black telia on the stems; **stem stitch:** also used more widely in *Embroidery* (earlier example); **stem succulent,** a plant chiefly native to dry regions, distinguished by a fleshy stem and often very small leaves or spines; **stemware,** stemmed glass drinking-vessels; **stem-winder,** (*c*) also, an enterprising or energetic person; an impassioned talker or public speaker; (*d*) *slang*, a rousing speech; **stem-winding** *a.* (earlier example); also *transf.*

1895 W. SCHLICH *Man. Forestry* III. I. vi. 83 The investigation of the progress of increment throughout the life of a tree is called a stem analysis. **1974** *Forest Sci.* XX. 75/2 In the comparisons to be discussed, three sets of stem analysis data were used, one for noble fir, one for Douglas-fir, and one for red alder. **1921** H. T. FERNALD *Appl. Entom.* xxxiii. 340 Superfamily Tenthredinoidea (The Saw-flies and Stem Borers). **1939** *Geogr. Jrnl.* XCIII. 140 The crop [of rice] would be destroyed by rats and stem-borers. **1972** J. MINIFIE *Homesteader* xv. 121 The Manitoba maple was subject to a stem-borer which destroyed its growing tips. **1885** Stem cell [in Dict., sense 7]. **1896** E. B. WILSON *Cell* iii. 111 In *Ascaris megalocephala univalens*..each of the first two cells receives two elongated chromosomes... In one of them, which is destined to produce only somatic cells, the thickened ends of each chromosome..degenerate... In the other cell, which may be called the stem-cell.., all the chromatin is preserved and the chromosomes do not segment into smaller pieces. **1959** W. ANDREW *Textbk. Compar. Histol.* vi. 234 The cells of this organ, while they include many lymphocytes, apparently serve as stem cells for all of the types of white corpuscles. **1970** *Sci. Jrnl.* June 32/3 The production of a continuous supply of spermatozoa from the testis is ensured by the continued existence of germ cells which form a reservoir of stem cells from which future spermatozoa are derived. **1915** R. L. HOBSON *Chinese Pottery & Porcelain* II. xii. 208 In the Bushell collection there are some beautiful reproductions of the Ch'êng Hua 'stem-cups'. **1942** *Burlington Mag.* June 151/2 The part of the base immediately below the stem-cup is a rather squat form of the Venetian bell base. **1980** *Catal. Fine Chinese Ceramics* (Sotheby, Hong Kong) 36 A *Longquan* (Lung Ch'üan) *Celadon stemcup* with plain circular bowl raised on a ribbed columnar foot. **1936** ZIMMERMAN & FRAMPTON *Family & Society* vii. 125 The stem-family..unites one married child to the paternal household, and supplies all the other offspring in a 'state of independence [with a dowry] which the patriarchal family does not give them'. **1947** P. H. LANDIS *Your Marriage & Family Living* i. 5 The stem family is about halfway between the great family of historic rural societies and the small, individualistic family of urban industrial societies. **1977** P. LASLETT *Family Life & Illicit Love in Earlier Generations* v. 211 In certain eighteenth-century areas of Austria and Germany, where a stem family arrangement prevailed..the old were allotted a familial situation which gave to retirement an institutional form. **1941** *Jrnl. Forestry* XXXIX. 521/1 Stemflow, although apparently not related to crown-length density, tree height, basal area, or crown area, does tend to increase with excess or deficit of height of tree as compared with adjacent trees. **1967** M. E. HALE *Biol. Lichens* vii. 96 Stemflow on trees..has been shown to be enriched, relative to throughflow, with potassium and calcium. **1980** SPURR & BARNES *Forest Ecol.* (ed. 3) ix. 230 Airborne dust, ash, and gaseous aerosols may also become attached to or impacted on tree surfaces and carried to the soil as throughfall and stem flow. **1922** A. WARD *Encycl. Food* 224 Crystallized ginger is also made from the young roots. The best grades, selected for uniform size and appearance, are called 'stem ginger'. **1977** *Times* 2 Sept. 10/5 The menu offers..bananas with stem ginger. **1922** JOYCE *Ulysses* 224 He took a red carnation from the tall stem-glass. **1974** L. DEIGHTON *Spy Story* xvii. 187 A stem glass from the ice-box, really cold Beefeater and..seven per cent dry vermouth. **1979** B. HINES *Price of Coal* I. 14 He..took down a tinted stem-glass..[and] selected his favourite bloom. **1953** LEVAN & HAUSCHKA in *Jrnl. Nat. Cancer Inst.* XIV. 5 Chromosome numbers and the concept of 'stemline'... The chromosome class with the highest number of cells, and the adjacent classes, represent the types mainly responsible for growth and characterize the principal stemline of each tumour. **1962** *Lancet* 27 Jan. 218/2 Several cases of mosaicism in mongolism have been reported... Two of these cases were mosaics with three stemlines, 46, 47, and 48 chromosomes; and two with two stemlines, 46 and 47 chromosomes. **1972** *Science* 23 June 1340/3 The establishment of this pattern was based on the analysis of stemlines, sidelines, and single deviating cells in 80 primary and 20 metastatic tumors. **1878** *Entomologist's Monthly Mag.* XIV. 224 An enormous single egg, from which, undoubtedly, will come the stem-mother. **1907, 1923** [see *FUNDATRIX 2]. **1979** *Vole* Dec. 40/2 Here the mated females [*sc.* grain aphides] hide the eggs that will come through the winter. These hatch in the late spring.., becoming 'stem mothers' that grow up to fly in quest of grain fields. **1901** G. JEKYLL *Lilies for Eng. Gardens* iii. 8 It should be planted six to seven inches deep, as it forms stem roots. **1978** B. MATHEW *Larger Bulbs* 85 Some species [of *Lilium*] produce a tuft of roots from the stem just as it emerges from the bulb, these stem-roots partly acting as extra support. **1896** T. W. SANDERS *Encycl. Gardening* (ed. 2) 19 *Artocarpus*... Propagation: By stem-rooting firm shoots in Feb., March; suckers at any time. **1974** H. G. W. FOGG *Compl. Handbk. Bulbs* vii. 91/1 This stem-rooting lily should be planted at least 4 ins deep. **1899** M. A. CARLETON *Cereal Rusts U.S.* 57 The stem rust..is not constant in occurrence, but will occasionally miss one or two years. **1923** *Jrnl. Agric. Res.* XXIV. 979 There are several biologic forms of stem rust of wheat. **1946** K. S. CHESTER *Nature & Prevention of Cereal Rusts* xiv. 199 Disproportionate emphasis..has been laid on stem rust..in wheat. **1979** TANOUS & RUBINSTEIN *Wheat Killing* (1980) ix. 57 There's some stem rust around... The black spores of the rust were clearly visible. **1873** *Young Englishwoman* June 299/1 The embroidery is worked..in satin and stem-stitch, and point-russe. **1897** J. C. WILLIS *Man. & Dict. Flowering Plants & Ferns* I. iii. 182 In the stem-succulents the leaves are reduced to scales or thorns. **1966** E. PALMER *Plains of Camdeboo* xvi. 258 It is the stem succulents..that are the most typical of Cranemere —Euphorbias, Stapeliads, and other such..most of them leafless, the work of the leaves being done by the stems and so protected from excessive transpiration; or bearing leaves for a short time only. **1929** *Sears Catal.* Fall 898/1 One of the newest creations in stemware. **1966** H. NIELSEN *After Midnight* (1967) xv. 194 A small, circular dinner table..had been meticulously set with china, silver and stemware. **1926** in J. F. Dobie *Rainbow in Morning* 85 He's a stemwinder and go-getter. **1942** BERREY & VAN DEN BARK *Amer. Thes. Slang* § 422/5 *Speech-maker*,.. stemwinder, vitalics, *a forceful talker.* **1973** T. H. WHITE *Making of President 1972* (1974) viii. 210 After all the calls to unity,..a stemwinder in the old tradition from Hubert Humphrey,..appearances by Muskie and Kennedy, Sargent Shriver was formally nominated for Vice-President. **1977** *Time* 3 Jan. 55/2 The 1,008 cadres and 24 fraternal foreign delegations..endured no fewer than 55 speeches, including an eight-hour stem-winder by Le Duan. **1867** *Rep. Comm. Patents 1866* (U.S.) 1115 Either side of the case of the stem-winding watch is opened by pressure upon the head of the winding arbor. **1966** *Atlantic Monthly* Sept. 90 A stem-winding sermon by Reverend Cecil Todd..can be obtained by sending one dollar to *Revival Fires* in Joplin, Missouri.

stem, *v.*² Add: **6. a.** *Skiing.* [ad. G. *stemmen.*] To decelerate (esp. before a turn) on a traverse descent by weighting the upper ski and angling its outer edge into the snow, causing the ski to turn downhill.

1904 E. C. RICHARDSON *Ski-Running* 41 (*caption*) *The proper way to stem...* A good stemming-spoor is at once known by the broad track of the braker. **1935** *Punch* 6 Feb. 164/3 *Stemming.*—Your ordinary straight running will lack the easy confidence..it should have unless I first show you how to stem, which is the only legitimate way of applying the brake other than using complicated turns like the christiania or the telemark. **1948** H. INNES *Blue Ice* x. 249 Jill stopped then and I stemmed. We were standing at the end of the snowshed. **1970** N. FLEMING *Czech Point* i. 22, I sideslipped at first, grew tired of it, stemmed for a while and then had just started to take the slope straight when the shot was fired.

b. The vb. in Comb., as **stem-Christiania,** a turn made by stemming and lifting the lower ski parallel as the manœuvre is completed (less advanced than the full *CHRISTIANIA); hence as colloq. abbrev. **stem-Christie** (also *v. intr.*, to turn in this manner); **stem turn,** an elementary turn made by stemming and then bringing the unweighted ski parallel in the new line; also *transf.* and as *v. intr.*, to make a stem turn or turns.

1922 V. CAULFEILD *Ski-ing Turns* xii. 228 The Stem-Christiania, like the Stem turn, is mainly used for down-hill turning on hard snow... A downhill turn can..be made more sharply by the Stem-Christiania than by any other means except a jump. **1961** *Times* 7 Jan. 7/6 The tried and basic essentials of the snowplough and the stem-christiania in particular. **1936** *Sierra Club Bull.* Feb. 57, I soon began very short linked stem-christies with the aid of the inner pole. **1942** 'N. SHUTE' *Pied Piper* ii. 20 At each new slope of snow he thought to see John come hurtling over the brow, stem-christie to a traverse, and vanish in a white flurry that sped down into the valley. **1972** 'M. YORKE' *Silent Witness* vi. iv. 141 They stem-christied inexpertly over the wide plateau. **1922** V. CAULFEILD *Ski-ing Turns* vii. 123 The Stem turn is impossible in heavy soft snow or breaking crust... There are two forms of the Stem turn... The Pure Stem turn is only possible on gentle slopes... The Lifted Stem Turn can be employed for down-hill turning on moderately steep slopes. **1938** [see *CHRISTIE]. **1959** M. GILBERT *Blood & Judgement* ix. 98 Petrella..started straight off down the pavement, did a stem turn at the corner... 'At least he can still walk,' said Borden. **1973** J. GOODFIELD *Courier to Peking* xiii. 171 They were moving downhill with the competence of an Olympic skier in a slalom race, stem-turning neatly at every snake-like twist of the road.

stem, *v.*⁴ Add: **3. a.** (Earlier examples.)

In quot. 1724 the senses of *stem* and *strip* are confused (*D.A.E.*).

1724 H. JONES *Present State of Virginia* 40 It lies till they have Leisure or Occasion to *stem* it (that is pull the leaves from the Stalk) or *strip* it (that is to take out the great Fibres). **1797** G. IMLAY *Topogr. Descr. Western Terr. N. Amer.* (ed. 3) 248 This done, you stem the tobacco, or pull out the middle rib of the leaf.

b. (Earlier example.)

1873 *Trans. Illinois Dept. Agric.* X. 61 The grapes were pressed without stemming.

4. To beg or 'panhandle' on the streets. Cf. *STEM *sb.*¹ 5* b. *U.S. slang.*

1924 'DIGIT' *Confessions 20th Century Hobo* 12 *Stemming*, begging, cadging. **1931** 'D. STIFF' *Milk & Honey Route* viii. 84 Panhandling falls into two classes: the domestic type..and a kind carried on in the streets and known as 'stemming'. **1937** *Lit. Digest* 10 Apr. 12/2 *Stemming*, panhandling in cities.

5. a. *fig.* To derive or take origin *from*; to spring from. (The principal modern sense.) orig. *U.S.*

1932 A. H. QUINN *Soul of Amer.* 131 The policy of vigorous intervention in the affairs of the nations bordering on the Caribbean Sea stems from Roosevelt's administration. **1937** R. S. MORTON *Woman Surgeon* i. 15, I realize now that my apparent indifference to suitors for marriage stemmed from my determination to study medicine. **1942** W. FAULKNER *Go down, Moses* 86 He knew what he had seen in his father's face..something.. not stemming from any difference of race nor because one blood strain ran in them both. **1949** *Here & Now* (N.Z.) Nov. 27/1 From this stemmed a whole line of high-grade thrillers. **1952** B. SMALLEY *Study of Bible in Middle Ages* 358 Both literal and spiritual exposition stemmed from Origen. **1958** *Times* 11 Feb. 11/7 The whole of this trouble has stemmed entirely from your own behaviour. **1961** I. FLEMING *Thunderball* xviii. 194 The source of his wealth was unknown but did not stem from funds held in Italy. **1976** H. WILSON *Governance of Britain* x. 183 Bills normally stem from the legislative arm. **1979** J. GRIMOND *Memoirs* vi. 98, I believe that much that is wrong with attitudes and organisation in Britain stems from the war.

b. To extend *back to* in origin. Also, to arise *out of*.

1937 *Sun* (Baltimore) 24 Nov. 2/7 Wall Streeters said the controversy stemmed back to the annual report issued by Mr. Gay as president of the exchange last August. **1959** N. Lofts *Heaven in your Hand* 99 The whole thing stemmed back to the beliefs in the African witch-doctors. **1965** *Listener* 11 Nov. 740/1 It is sometimes claimed that race antipathy stems out of the same order of cultural differences. **1974** *Times Lit. Suppl.* 26 Apr. 430/3 There is still doubt and conflict here, stemming back to the ancient world.

stemma. Add: **1. c.** A diagram which represents a reconstruction on stemmatic principles of the position of the surviving witnesses in the tradition of the transmission of a text, esp. in manuscript form. Cf. *STEMMATOLOGY.

1930 W. P. Shepard in *Mod. Philol.* XXVIII. 130 The claim that the Lachmannian method can deduce..the *ipsissima verba* of the author, takes no account of the fact that an author may change his mind...and the final and most telling objection to this method..is the fact that in practice it..leads to the establishment of a dichotomous 'stemma', a family tree. **1942** J. B. Severs in *English Institute Ann.* 1941 79 And so we deal with each of our families in turn, until the manuscripts in each family have been completely outlined... Thus we build up a complete stemma, or genealogical chart, for our whole body of manuscript. **1949** *Oxf. Classical Dict.* 889/1 Where one witness depends on two or more other witnesses, i.e. where the transmission is 'contaminated' and the stemma 'convergent', it is seldom possible to ascertain the type of interrelationship by stemmatics. **1962** E. J. Dobson in Davis and Wrenn *English & Medieval Studies* 136 We thus arrive at the stemma shown by the unbroken lines in the diagram. **1982** *N. & Q.* Feb. 77/2 The meticulous detail of information is made clear by stemma diagrams. for those with the courage to penetrate the complexity.

stemmaˑtic, *sb.* and *a.* [a. G. *stemmatik* (P. Maas in *Byzantinische Zeitschrift* (1937) XXXVII. 289), f. L. *stemma(t-)* Stemma + -ic.] **A.** *sb. pl.* **stemmatics** = *stemmatology.

1949 [see *stemma 1 c]. **1958** B. Flower tr. *P. Maas' Text. Criticism* 42 Errors arising in the course of transcription are of decisive significance in the study of the interrelationships of manuscripts—I may be allowed to use the term 'stemmatics'. **1968** Reynolds & Wilson *Scribes & Scholars* v. 140 The classic statement of the theory of stemmatics is that of Paul Maas. **1975** *Times Lit. Suppl.* 15 Aug. 928/4 There has been a tendency to see stemmatics as something born in an instant. **1980** *Early Music Gaz.* Jan. 13/3 Source studies and stemmatics play an increasingly important role in musicology.

B. *adj.* Of or pertaining to a textual stemma or stemmata; concerning the reconstruction of the interrelationships between the readings of manuscripts of a text, esp. as *stemmatic theory*.

1958 B. Flower tr. *P. Maas' Text. Criticism* 44 Such errors are so rare..that we cannot rely on being able to find one to establish every stemmatic relationship. **1968** Reynolds & Wilson *Scribes & Scholars* 140 In practice the stemmatic theory has serious limitations. **1980** *Early Music Gaz.* Jan. 13/3 Alejandro Planchart concluded that traditional stemmatic theory (after Paul Maas) best fits the text transmission of plainsong.

stemmatology (stemătǫˑlŏdʒi). [f. L. *stemma(t-)* Stemma: see -ology.] The study which attempts to reconstruct the tradition of the transmission of a text or texts (esp. in manuscript form) on the basis of the relationships between the readings of the various surviving witnesses; this sphere of scholarship.

1942 *Essays & Studies* XXVII. 43 In what may be called stemmatology, the veterans..have done brilliant work. **1981** *N. & Q.* Feb. 1/2 Mr. Hamer..attempts a 'provisional' stemma. The darkness of conflicting and 'contaminated' evidence might have made a less brave man shrink from stemmatology.

stemming, *vbl. sb.*[2] Add: **2.** *Skiing.* The action of *stem *v.*[2] 6 a.

1904, etc. [see *snow-ploughing *vbl. sb.*] **1935** P. Frankau *I find Four People* v. 311 We circled on our awkward attempts at stemming, frozen and undecided.

Sten (sten). Also **sten.** [Acronym f. the initial letters of the surnames of the designers, R. V. *S*hepherd and H. J. *T*urpin + *En*field, Greater London (see quot. 1942[1]), after *Bren.] More fully, *Sten gun.* A type of light, rapid-fire, sub-machine-gun. Also *fig.* and *attrib.*

1942 *Times* 16 July 8/3 It [*sc.* the gun] was known as the Schmeisser gun, and the Sten was merely a slight modification of it... The Ministry of Supply was not justified in taking to itself high praise for the speed of production of the Sten, and in giving the country the false impression that 'Colonel S' and 'Major T' invented and designed the gun. **1942** 'G. Orwell' *Diary* 7 Aug. in *Coll. Ess.* (1968) II. 442 Last night for the first time took a Sten gun to pieces. **1959** 'N. Blake' *Widow's Cruise* 99 He went off into a sten-gun burst of Greek. **1971** B. W. Aldiss *Soldier Erect* 255 It was bloody murder. I had shed the set, and went in firing the sten from the hip. *Ibid.* 261 In my ammo pouch, against the sten magazines, I had stuffed the picture of Hanuman. **1974** S. Gulliver *Vulcan Bulletins* 18 Automatic weapons like Stens and Sterlings.

Hence **Steˑn-gun** *v. trans.*, to shoot at or kill with a Sten gun; **Steˑn-gunner,** one who operates a Sten gun.

1949 Koestler *Promise & Fulfilment* ii. v. 280 There is..no conceivable justification..for Sten-gunning the representative of an international body. **1961** *Times* 8 Mar. 13/6 The Tunisian stengunners outside the luxury hotel: the Hiberno-Scandinavian-Afro-Asian chatter in the café below United Nations headquarters.

Stender (steˑndəɹ, ʃt-). *Biol.* and *Med.* Also **stender.** [The name of Wilhelm P. *Stender*, a manufacturer of Leipzig.] *Stender dish*: a shallow glass dish.

1900 Dorland *Med. Dict.* 637/1 Stender-dish. **1904** *Bot. Gaz.* XXXVII. 12 A simpler..method is to float a quantity of these spores on the surface of water half filling a stender dish. **1978** G. C. Brown *Introd. Histotechnol.* xi. 174 Other items that should be stored at the staining bench in adequate quantities are:..Stender dishes for frozen sections.., in three sizes.

Stendhalian (stan̆dā·liăn), *a.* and *sb.* [f. *Stendhal*, the nom-de-plume of the French writer Henri Beyle (1783–1842) + -ian.] **A.** *adj.* Characteristic or suggestive of the writings of Stendhal. **B.** *sb.* A follower or devotee of Stendhal or his works.

1907 G. B. Shaw *Mahor Barbara* Pref. 150 The sensation first came to me from Lever and may have come to him from Beyle, or at least out of the Stendhalian atmosphere. **1928** *Sunday Express* 8 Apr. 7/4 The Stendhalians are invariably cynics who delight in heartlessness and selfishness. **1937** Wyndham Lewis *Blasting & Bombardiering* 53, I was not surprised, luckily, when I became a lion, to find this gilded tamer a tough customer. I began studying her ways with curiosity, this spoilt and cocksure goddess of the ocean wave. I filled a notebook with Stendhalian observations. **1950** *Essays & Studies* III. 86 In this sense the Stendhalian analogy of crystallization may be applied equally to the reasons of the intellect as to the reasons of the heart, of which reason itself comprehends nothing. **1968** E. Hyams *Mischief Makers* vi. 99, I had gone flabby; no Stendhalian hero. **1980** A. Alpers *Life Katherine Mansfield* ix. 163 Murry [was] ..starting a huge Stendhalian novel.

stengah (steˑŋă). Also **stingah.** [ad. Mal. *setengah* half.] A half measure of whisky with soda (sometimes water), popular amongst the British in Malaysia.

1899 *Munsey's Mag.* XXI. 697/1 The majority of young Englishmen and Germans fared equally well when they limited the numbers of whiskies and sodas (or 'stengahs') which they drank. **1903** W. Del Mar *Around World through Japan* vii. 64 A 'peg' of whiskey and tonic-water, followed by a *stengah* (the Malay word for half, usually pronounced *stinger*) or split drink. **1927** *Blackw. Mag.* June 726/1 At this establishment we learn all about gin-slings and 'Stingahs'. **1948** M. Laski *Tory Heaven* i. 14 Stewards..to bring him..stengahs and pahits whenever he wanted them. **1966** D. Forbes *Heart of Malaya* xiii. 156 Malays could not be seen publicly knocking back *stengahs.* **1975** 'G. Black' *Big Wind* i. 18 When I was a boy in Malaysia a whisky-soda was called a *stengah.* It hasn't been for twenty-five years.

steno (steˑno). Colloq. abbrev. of: **a.** Stenographer (also *attrib.*), or abbrev. Stenographic *a.* orig. and chiefly *U.S.*

1906 J. F. Kelly *Man with Grip* 36 This bright young lady was on the waiting list of a steno. agency. **1928** 'L. North' *Parasites* ii. 34 (*heading*) 'Stalls' and stenos. *Ibid.* vii. 89 That Whispering Slim guy seems to be falling for that steno' of his. **1935** *Motion Picture* Nov. 40/2 Frances Dee..skyrockets to new importance with an amazingly fine performance as a small town steno who wins a five-thousand-dollar lottery. **1958** E. Birney *Turvey* v. 49 There was a good-lookin steno all alone. **1971** D. E. Westlake *I gave at Office* (1972) 19 He led the unsuccessful attempt to ban miniskirts in the steno pool. **1978** P. Boardman *Worlds of Patrick Geddes* ix. 342 A social workers' weekly..sent a stenotypist to take them [*sc.* lectures] down and a department editor to check up on the steno.

b. Stenography. *U.S.*

1946 *N.Y. Times* 1 Apr. 42/3 (Advt.), Girl, genl office work, typ, some steno. **1954** *Los Angeles Times* 21 Mar. 3/2 (Advt.), Clerk—lite steno..$200 start. **1973** *N.Y. Law Jrnl.* 20 July 16/2 (Advt.), *Law secretary*...legal experience and excellent skills required, dictaphone and light steno.

steno-. Add: **stenobaˑthic** *a. Biol.* [Gr. βάθ-ος depth], (of aquatic life) limited to or found at only a narrow range of depths; **stenohaline** (-hēⁱ·ləin) *a. Biol.* [Gr. ἅλιν-ος of salt], (of aquatic life) adapted to only a narrow range of salinity; **stenohyˑdric** *a. Biol.* [Hydro-], adapted to only a narrow range of humidities; **stenoˑphagous** *a. Zool.* [-phagous] (see quot. 1926); **stenopoˑdium** *Zool.* [Podium], a narrow, two-branched crustacean limb the flexibility of which is provided by joints; **stenothermal** *a.* (further examples); [ad. G. *stenotherm* (K. Möbius 1871, in *Jahresber. d. Commission z. wissensch. Untersuchung d. deutschen Meere in Kiel* (1873) I. 139)]; hence **steˑnotherm, stenotheˑrmic** *adjs.*; **stenotoˑpic** *a. Biol.* Gr. τόπ-ος place] (see quot. 1949).

1902 Stenobathic [see *eurybathic *a.*]. **1975** B. Fell *Introd. Marine Biol.* xi. 92 A deep-water stenobathic species, when brought too rapidly to the surface in a net, suffers disruption of the internal organs. **1930** *Biol. Rev.* V. 350 Most stenohaline marine invertebrates are poikilosmotic: their body fluids have an osmotic pressure which is the same as that of the external medium. **1973** P. A. Colinvaux *Introd. Ecol.* xx. 278 When temperature or salinity may fluctuate widely without seriously affecting individuals, the species are called eurythermal or euryhaline; when slight changes of temperature or salinity are fatal to animals or plants, they are called stenothermal or stenohaline. **1953** E. P. Odum *Fund. Ecol.* iii. 27 Stenohydric—Euryhydric refers to water. **1974** *Ciba Foundation Symp.* XX. 56 In general, relative humidities below 60% (temperatures of 21–28°C) are deleterious for these stenohydric species. **1926** A. S. Pearse *Animal Ecol.* iii. 72 Animals that have a narrow range of foods are called stenophagous and those that eat a wide variety are euryphagous. **1976** *Environmental Entomol.* V. 46/2, 21 (46%) of 46 identified species of phytophagous insects found associated with *A*[*mbrosia*] *dumosa* in southern California were stenophagous. **1932** Borradaile & Potts *Invertebrata* xii. 298 Since..the phyllopodium possesses the same two rami, and bears them, though not as a distal fork, yet in the same way as a great number of limbs of the first type, it is well not to use a name which might imply that there is a constant difference in respect of the rami between the limbs of the two types. We shall therefore call the first type the stenopodium, referring to its usually slender form. **1967** P. A. Meglitsch *Invertebrate Zool.* xviii. 755/1 A good case can be made for thinking of stenopodia as the more primitive form of crustacean appendage. **1888** Stenotherm [see *eurytherm *a.*]. **1964** *Oceanogr. & Marine Biol.* II. 284 Most stenosaline organisms live either in the ocean (polystenosaline forms) or in fresh water (oligostenosaline forms). These terms are analogous to steno- or eurytherm and just as relative in their meaning. **1937** *Brit. Birds* XXX. 247 It should be borne in mind that whereas the adult bird is stenothermal (warm-blooded), in the young the thermotaxic arrangements are undeveloped. **1973** P. A. Colinvaux *Introd. Ecol.* xx. 279 Between about 55°C and 40°C the algal mats are largely made up of filamentous blue-green algae, but these plants are rather stenothermal and will not actively grow at temperatures below 40°C. **1926** A. S. Pearce *Animal Ecol.* ii. 34 Animals are often classified into two groups: stenothermic and eurythermic, the former being restricted to a narrow range of temperature changes and the latter having ability to live through a wide range. **1965** B. E. Freeman tr. *Vandel's Biospeleology* xxiii. 384 Summer cysts containing the adults of stenothermic species [of copepods] are formed during the warm season. **1949** J. H. Kenneth *Henderson's Dict. Sci. Terms* (ed. 4) *Stenotopic*, having a restricted range of geographical distribution. **1967** *Oceanogr. & Marine Biol.* V. 546 This species is also stenotopic; it needs exposed rocky shores, but where the wave-action is not too strong. **1976** *Nature* 24 June 695/1 A major terminal extinction event..will tend selectively to eliminate the larger, more specialised, more stenotopic species.

stenog (stenǫˑg). Also with full point. Colloq. abbrev. of Stenographer. So as *v. intr.*, to write in shorthand or type. orig. and chiefly *U.S.* Cf. *steno.

1905 'O. Henry' in *N.Y. World Mag.* 2 Apr. 3/1 Not being able to stenog, she could not enter that bright galaxy of office talent. **1909** *Fra* (East Aurora, N.Y.) Mar. 82/1 The Stenog wanted a new set of curtains. **1912** Wodehouse *Prince & Betty* ix. 132 If I was good enough for him to marry when I was a stenog., he's good enough for me to marry when I'm a plute. **1941** B. Schulberg *What makes Sammy Run?* vi. 103 'Start typing up that last scene, Ellen,' Kit told the stenog. **1967** *Spectator* 20 Oct. 468/3 Julie Andrews, as tireless Millie the faithful stenog.

stenographer. Add: Now also *spec.* a shorthand typist.

1921 *Dict. Occup. Terms* (1927) § 939 *Stenographer*,.. shorthand typist; wholly engaged in taking down letters, ..etc., in shorthand from dictation of another, and in transcribing them on typewriter. **1978** A. Maling *Lucky Devil* xxx. 159 Taught herself stenotyping, and now she's a legal stenographer.

stenographist. (Examples.)

1839 *Spirit of Times* 20 Apr. 74/2 Paris swarms with scribblers of indifferent merit, authors of well founded pretensions, editors, stenographists, vaudevillists, translators, compilers, and correctors of work. **1845** *Times* 19 Aug. 4/5 England alone has despatched 30 stenographists (short-hand writers). **1905** J. Joyce *Let.* 28 Feb. (1966) II. 83 If I had..a clever stenographist I could *certainly* write any of the novels I have read lately in seven or eight hours.

stenol (stīˑnǫl). *Chem.* [f. *st(er)ol, blended with inserted *en* (see -ene); cf. *stanol.] Any sterol having one carbon–carbon double bond in its skeleton.

1949, 1958 [see *stanol]. **1968** *Lipids* III. 397/2 Derivatives of many Δ[24]-stenols undergo loss of two nuclear hydrogen atoms together with the side chain. **1979** *Nature* 25 Jan. 287/2 Core 16..was analysed for its sterol (stenol + stanol), stanone, and sterene contents.

stenosing (stĭnōᵘ·siŋ), *a. Med.* [f. Stenos(is + -ing[2].] Causing or characterized by stenosis.

1903 A. Stengel tr. *Riegel's Dis. Stomach* ii. 392 This condition..closely resembles the stenosing gastritis described by Boas. **1971** *Brit. Med. Bull.* XXVII. 26/2 A stenosing ulcer of the small bowel.

stenosis. Delete ‖. For '**1866**...(1880)' read '**1880**...(ed. 4)', and add earlier example.

1872 [see *mitral *a.*].

stenotype. Add: **2.** = STENOTYPER. Also *stenotype machine.*

1913 *Chambers's Jrnl.* Feb. 189/2 An English device of this kind appeared upon the market—the stenotype. **1942** *Amer. Cinematographer* Apr. 190/1 A secretary sits over in one corner with a stenotype, faithfully recording, ad verbatim, everything that's said. **1946** A. HUXLEY *Let.* 27 Oct. (1969) 555 We have just sent her stenotype machine over. **1970** J. HANSEN *Fadeout* xix. 161 He left them with a fat young sergeant and a..woman who ran a stenotype machine. **1976** *New Yorker* 5 Apr. 82/2 The stenotype machine, above which Gnusse could see the court reporter's fingers poised.

stenotypy. Add: **stenotyper** (later examples); **stenotypist** (later examples); also **steno·typic** *a.*, of, pertaining to, or printed by stenotypy (*rare*); **stenoty·ping.**

1889 *Cent. Dict.*, Stenotypic. **1908** *Chambers's Jrnl.* Oct. 765/1 A simple machine, the 'stenotyper', has been devised. *Ibid.* Oct. 766/1 One stenotypist can be retained.. solely for dictation purposes. **1946** *Nature* 17 Aug. 217/2 A judicious combination of this privilege [*sc.* emendation] with verbatim reporting by the new stenotypic method has resulted in a lively and informal record. **1951** *Catal. Exhibits, South Bank Exhib., Festival of Britain* p. liii, The only British system of stenotyping (machine shorthand). **1978** Stenotyping [see *STENOGRAPHER]. **1979** 'A. HAILEY' *Overload* II. viii. 148 A male stenotypist, who was keeping the official commission record, flipped back through the folded tape of his notes. **1980** 'E. ANTHONY' *Defector* ix. 223 There was a stenotyper who recorded every word spoken.

Stensen (sti·nsən, ste·nsən). *Anat.* Also (*erron.*) **Stenson.** The name of Niels *Stensen* (1638–86), Danish anatomist, used in the possessive and with *of* to designate structures investigated by him, as: **a.** *Stensen's duct*, the duct of the parotid gland. Cf. STENONIAN *a.*

[**1803** C. BELL *Anat. Human Body* III. II. ii. 463 The duct of this gland [*sc.* the parotid] was discovered by Needham, and afterwards by Steno: it is very often called Steno's duct.] **1867** W. SHARPEY et al. *Quain's Elem. Anat.* (ed. 7) II. 816 The parotid duct, named also Stenson's duct (d. Stenonianus), appears at the anterior border of the gland. **1977** G. D. ZUIDEMA *Johns Hopkins Atlas Human Functional Anat.* xiii. 56/2 Surrounding the [oral] cavity and exiting into it are the major salivary glands: the parotid (Stensen's duct), the submaxillary (Wharton's duct), and the sublingual glands.

b. Each of two (sometimes four) canals through the bony palate, running from just behind the incisor teeth to each half of the nasal cavity; also the orifices of these canals in the bony palate.

1867 W. SHARPEY et al. *Quain's Elem. Anat.* (ed. 7) I. 45 This aperture may be seen to be divided into four smaller foramina, two of which placed laterally are the incisor foramina, called also foramina of Stenson. **1871** Canals of Stenson [see *JACOBSON]. **1893** Stenson's canal [see *JACOBSONIAN *a.*]. **1936** L. B. AREY *Developmental Anat.* (ed. 3) vii. 182 Fusion between the median palatine processes and the palate is incomplete, so that in the midplane there is a gap, the incisive foramen, flanked by the incisive canals (of Stenson). These become covered with mucous membrane. **1969** G. N. C. CRAWFORD tr. *Donath's Anat. Dict.* 480 *Stenon's (Stensen's) foramen*, foramen incisivum: one of the inferior openings of the incisive canals.

stent (stent), *sb.*[5] *Med.* Also **Stent, stint.** The name of Charles R. *Stent* (d. 1901), English dentist. **a.** Used *attrib.*, *absol.*, and in the possessive to designate a substance invented by him for taking dental impressions; also, an impression or cast of a part or body cavity made of this or a similar substance, and used to maintain pressure on it so as to promote healing, esp. of a skin graft.

The form *Stents* is a proprietary name.

1878 [see *impression material* s.v. *IMPRESSION *sb.* 9]. **1899** *Trade Marks Jrnl.* 15 Feb. 155 *Stents*... A composition, sold in tablet form, specially intended for taking impressions of the gums and for like dental purposes. Caroline Stent, 5, Coventry Street, London, W.C.; dentist and manufacturer of dental composition. **1920** H. D. GILLIES *Plastic Surgery of Face* i. 10 An impression of the Sulcus is taken with warm Stent. *Ibid.*, The dental composition used for this purpose is that put forward by Stent, and a mould composed of it is known as a 'Stent'. **1939** S. FOMON *Surgery of Injury & Plastic Repair* ii. 128 Over irregular areas and where the base lacks resistance, such as on the eyelids and neck, and in inaccessible areas, like the nose and mouth..the use of dental modeling compound, commonly referred to as stent, is invaluable, as it acts in the dual capacity of pressure dressing and splint. *Ibid.* xvii. 1268 All cicatricial tissue beneath the surface is removed to form a pocket into which a stent mold covered with a razor graft, raw side out, is buried and sutured in place. **1961** WEBSTER, *Stent*, also *stint*. **1961** *Brit. Med. Dict.* 1350/1 *Stent's composition*, a proprietary form of composition used in dentistry, and in skin grafting. **1964** R. BATTLE *Plastic Surgery* x. 234 An impression of the raw surface [of the eyelid] must be taken in Stent's wax.

b. A tube implanted temporarily in a vessel or part.

1964 *Jrnl. Prosthetic Dentistry* XIV. 1168 All stents must be removed daily and cleaned. A pipestem cleaner is effective in cleaning the tube. **1975** *Year Bk. Ear, Nose & Throat* 114 Packing consists of a rayon basket with cellulose sponges in the meatus. Sutures and packing are removed after 7 days. Stents are not used. **1978** *Sci. Amer.* Apr. 67/1 A soft Teflon tube called a stent is placed in the vessel to keep the lumen open and facilitate the suturing. **1980** D. M. MAHONEY in R. C. A. Weatherley-White *Plastic Surg. Female Breast* vii. 203/2 At the time of the surgery, the physician lacerates the common bile duct and the liver. Both are successfully repaired but the common bile duct, of course, requires a stint.

stenter, *sb.* Add: **2.** (Later examples.) In mod. use, a machine through which fabric is carried mechanically while under sideways tension.

1911 C. SALTER tr. *Poileyn's Dressings & Finishings for Textile Fabrics* xxii. 244 The stenter and drying machine has been greatly improved by the addition of the longitudinal stretching device. **1939** A. J. HALL tr. *Hünlich's Textile Fibres & Materials* iv. 152 The fabric may be dried and stretched simultaneously on a hot air stenter. **1962** J. T. MARSH *Self-Smoothing Fabrics* ii. 9 The alternative use of radiant heat units mounted over the stenter is also quite common. **1973** *Materials & Technol.* VI. vii. 458 By the time the fabric has travelled the 50 or 60 ft.. which represents the length of the stenter, it is practically free from alkali and shows no further inclination to contract.

stenter, *v.* Add: Also, to pass (fabric) through a stenter. (Later examples of the vbl. sb.)

1946 A. J. HALL *Stand. Handbk. Textiles* iv. 228 The modern machine undertakes both the drying and the stentering. **1962** J. T. MARSH *Self-Smoothing Fabrics* xi. 171 The water content of the fabric may be reduced to a figure which prevents any migration during stentering. **1973** *Materials & Technol.* VI. vii. 458 Cotton fabrics are treated with the caustic soda solution while they are in open width on a powerful 'stentering' machine in which the fabric is anchored by its edges as it travels through.

stentorophonic, *a.* **2.** (Later example.)

1914 C. MACKENZIE *Sinister St.* II. IV. i. 834 The whirr of the ventilating fans, the stentorophonic orchestra, the red-faced raucous atom on the stage combined to irritate him beyond farther endurance.

† **stentorphone** (ste·ntǫɹfōᵘn). *Obs.* [f. STENTOR[2] + *-PHONE.] An electrical device for reproducing sounds, esp. the human voice, with increased intensity.

1921 *Punch* 2 Feb. 86/1 At Oxford Circus I have known What townmen call the 'stentorphone'. **1927** *Dancing Times* June 357/1 *Al fresco* dancing under cover is provided, with stentorphone music.

step, *sb.* Add: **I. 1. f.** Chiefly *pl.* Any of various children's games (see quots.). Cf. *Grandmother's* (*Foot*)*steps* s.v. *GRANDMOTHER *sb.* 1 d.

1909 J. H. BANCROFT *Games for Playground* 188 Step... The object of the game is for the players who are lined up in the rear to advance forward until they cross the line where the counter is stationed [etc.]. **1940** N. MARSH *Surfeit of Lampreys* (1941) ix. 127 The childish game of Steps in which, whenever the 'he' has his back turned, the players creep nearer. **1969** I. & P. OPIE *Children's Games* vi. 189 'May I?' is the usual name, but sometimes the game is known as 'Steps', 'All Sorts', 'Walk to London', 'Variety', or 'Mother, May I?'.

3. a. Also in phr. *a step in the right direction; a step up*, a rise in social status; a higher position on a ladder of success.

1877 C. READE *Woman-Hater* I. i. 190 A little money was given her for a bad purpose. She has used it for a frivolous one. That is 'a step in the right direction'—jargon of the day. **1919** H. S. WALPOLE *Jeremy* xii. 294 Going to school..was a mixed business; but the balance was now greatly to the good. It was a step in the right direction towards liberty and freedom. **1926** N. COWARD *Easy Virtue* II. 86, I don't consider my position in this house a step up... It's been..the most demoralising experience. **1939** L. M. MONTGOMERY *Anne of Ingleside* xxi. 137 'It'll be a step up for a Plummer if you marry a Mitchell,' Ma said. **1954** *Encounter* May 52/1 Eventually she became a model—a further step-up—and she received her first film-part in that capacity. **1974** J. POPE-HENNESSY *R. L. Stevenson* i. 32 The Thomas Stevensons ..made..a final move to..Heriot Row. This was in all senses a step up, for Heriot Row..was considered one of the most delectable residential streets in Edinburgh. **1976** *Glasgow Herald* 26 Nov. 6/1 Extensions of the fishing limits around our coasts to 200 miles..are a step in the right direction.

c. *Astronautics.* = *STAGE *sb.* 11* b.

1932 D. LASSER *Conquest of Space* vi. 103 Each step, as it is called, is a complete rocket motor, containing fuel, combustion chambers, exhausts, etc. **1956** *Spaceflight* I. 5/2 Each extra step multiplies the total weight by a factor of up to ten, so that..rockets of more than five stages are not often contemplated. **1966** H. O. RUPPE *Introd. Astronautics* I. ii. 35 There are cases when a two-step design can do the mission but a one-step rocket cannot.

4. b. Similarly *out of step.*

1961 *Listener* 9 Nov. 768/2 There is also the problem, with direct current lines, of providing what is called the reactive power—power where the current is out of step with the voltage—for the operation of converter equipment.

5. step by step. a. Also, with pauses at regular intervals. (Later examples.)

1893 [in Dict., sense 5 c]. **1966** *McGraw-Hill Encycl. Sci. & Technol.* XIII. 355/1 A shaft which can be driven step-by-step in a vertical direction and subsequently can be moved step-by-step in a rotary direction.

c. (Further examples.) *Esp.* (of mechanisms and the like) moving with pauses at regular intervals; *spec.* in *Teleph.*, with reference to one type of automatic switching, in which successive switches establish contact by a step-by-step movement first in a vertical and then horizontally in a rotary direction.

1845 *Brit. Pat. 10,838* 15 The Invention of causing the two elementary actions..to produce a step by step motion of an indicator in two contrary directions, for the purpose of giving signals. **1879** *Specifications of Patents* (U.S.) 9 Dec. 392/2 An electro-automatic central [station] for telephone exchanges provided with a step-by-step action. **1911** A. B. SMITH *Mod. Amer. Telephony* xxvi. 700 Their devices were usually based on some step-by-step ratchet action. **1933** [see *STROWGER]. **1938** G. H. SEWELL *Amateur Film-Making* iv. 46 The apparatus available to the amateur printer is all of the step-by-step type. Here the films remain stationary for a fraction of time opposite the printing aperture while the exposure is made. **1973** [see *STROWGER].

d. *fig.* Involving or comprising a series of distinct stages or operations, often devised to facilitate the accomplishment of something.

1918 C. I. LEWIS *Survey of Symbolic Logic* ii. 134 This is a 'step by step' definition. **1937** MICHELL & BELZ *Elem. Math. Analysis* II. x. 608 The elementary fractions are of the first type.., as we shall now demonstrate by the use of a step-by-step process. **1957** K. A. WITTFOGEL *Oriental Despotism* 284 The step-by-step rise of a new system of landed property. **1968** *Daily Tel.* 8 Nov. 17 Very clear instructions and step-by-step diagrams for making a glove puppet. **1980** 'R. B. DOMINIC' *Attending Physician* xx. 182 [He] had been subjecting Fournier's narrative to step-by-step dissection.

7. e. The movement through a fixed linear or angular distance made by a stepping device (see *STEPPING *ppl. a.*) in response to an applied voltage pulse.

1957 *Control Engin.* Jan. 74/1 The simple rugged construction of this new unit leads to high reliability, speeds to 100,000 steps per minute. **1964** *IEEE Trans. Automatic Control* IX. 102/2 Several companies..offer step motors with maximum stepping rates in excess of 3000 steps per second. **1974** T. E. BELINY in B. C. Kuo *Theory & Applications of Step Motors* x. 209 Load torque may actually vary somewhat from step to step.

8. b. A melodic interval of a single degree of the scale (i.e. a tone or semitone) (later examples). Cf. LEAP *sb.*[1] 7.

1907 C. E. KITSON *Art of Counterpoint* iv. 50 If the.. third and fourth crotchets are discordant with the C.F. the part must proceed in the same direction by step to the next concord. If the next step will not produce a concord, the passage must be rearranged. **1930** A. M. RICHARDSON *Helps to Fugue Writing* v. 27 If the two missing beats were supplied thus..the result would be impossible cacophony. The only thing to do is to transpose this last group a step lower. **1952** A. O. WARBURTON *Melody Writing & Analysis* I. 7 When a melodic part moves by step it is said to be 'conjunct'. When it moves by leap it is 'disjunct'. **1971** A. HOPKINS *Talking about Sonatas* iv. 58 The Exposition of the Hammerklavier ends with three giant steps.

10. b. *to watch* (or *mind*) *one's step*, to be careful about one's actions, to tread warily. (Chiefly admonitory.) *colloq.*

1934 'G. ORWELL' *Burmese Days* viii. 139 You watch your step. Tom Lackersteen may be a drunken sot, but he's not such a bloody fool that he wants a niece hanging round his neck for the rest of his life. **1935** D. L. SAYERS *Gaudy Night* vii. 154, I can have a word with her and tell her to mind her step. **1955** M. GILBERT *Sky High* xii. 168 The Inspector... Bit of an awkward mood... I'd mind my step, if I were you. **1977** P. D. JAMES *Death of Expert Witness* I. 23 He seems to be taking quite an interest in you... You'd better watch your step.

II. 12. d. (Earlier example.)

1816 JANE AUSTEN *Emma* I. xiii. 240 They arrived, the carriage turned, the step was let down.

f. *Eton Fives.* The shallow step which divides the court into an inner and outer part.

1890 A. C. AINGER *Fives* 463 The vertical face of the 'step' does not reckon as part of the floor of the court. **1897** [see *HOLE *sb.* 4 e]. **1975** *Oxf. Compan. Sports & Games* 290/2 Running across the court is a shallow step 10 ft. (3·05 m.) from the front wall, dividing the court into an inner or upper court and an outer or lower court.

g. *to go up the steps*: to be committed or appear for trial at a higher court, esp. the Old Bailey. Also in related phrs. *slang.*

1931 [see *BOTTLE *sb.*[2] 1 g (*a*)]. **1938** F. D. SHARPE *Sharpe of Flying Squad* 334 *Up the Steps*, being committed to the Sessions or Assizes. **1952** 'J. HENRY' *Who lie in Gaol* iv. 62 They think it's wonderful 'to go up the steps'—to be sent for trial at the Old Bailey. **1962** *John o' London's* 25 Jan. 82/1 You'll go up the steps.

III. 15. c. *Aeronaut.* An edge built across the float or hull of a seaplane or hydroplane, giving its outline the form of an inverted step and designed to facilitate its separation from the water; *on the step*, with the part of the hull forward of the step out of the water.

1911 *Flight* 25 Nov. 1026/1 Each hydroplane has two steps, the middle step being halfway back from the bow. **1913** *Aeroplane* 24 Apr. 482/1 The [flying] boat got up on its step in a few yards. **1934** W. NELSON *Seaplane Design* vi. 54 Floats without steps tend to cling to the water with a tenacity that requires abnormal power for the take-off. **1935** *Sun* (Baltimore) 10 Oct. 24/4 As the clipper reached Middle River its speed increased until it was flying over the water on the hydroplane step. **1936** J. GRIERSON *High Failure* v. 91 After about half a mile of almost imperceptible acceleration, [the seaplane] Robert Bruce 'got on to the step' and began to hydroplane. **1952** A. Y. BRAMBLE *Air-Plane Flight* xi. 167 The floats are curiously shaped on their under sides, having a sudden discontinuity of surface known as a 'step'. **1983** D. STINTON *Design of Aeroplane* ix. 359 It is necessary to break down the suction by ventilation..and this is done by making a step about half-way along the planing bottom, slightly aft of the aircraft CG.

17*. A change in the value of some quantity, esp. voltage, occurring over a negligibly short interval of time. Freq. *attrib.*

1940 in *Chambers's Techn. Dict.* 806/1. **1958** W. G. HOLZBOCK *Autom. Control* iii. 20 Assume that Figure 3–3c represents the change in level seen in Figure 3–5 after a step change in valve position..closes the valve slightly. **1959** W. I. CALDWELL et al. *Frequency Response or Process Control* ii. 15 If the input to the controller undergoes a step change of 1 psi, then the controller output will be a step equal in magnitude to the setting of proportional gain. **1962** SIMPSON & RICHARDS *Physical fPrinc. Junction Transistors* xv. 372 i_0i s the change of output current resulting from the application of a sudden step of input current. **1973** *Nature* 23 Nov. 220/1 Where *C* is membrane capacitance, *i* is membrane current and *V* is the magnitude of the applied voltage step. **1975** G. J. KING *Audio Handbk.* ii. 41 Although a perfect step-wave (i.e. one of zero rise time) cannot, of course, be produced, a good evaluation of amplifier rise time is possible.

18. step-collar, a collar with a V-shaped opening at the junction of the collar and lapel (cf. *step-roll* (*collar*) below); **step-dance** (examples); also as *v. intr.*; **step-dancer** (examples); **step flaking** *Archæol.*, secondary flaking of a flint tool to produce a strong, ridged cutting edge; **step function** *Math.* and *Electronics*, a function that increases or decreases abruptly from one constant value to another; **step-gable** = *corbie-gable* s.v. CORBIE 3 (cf. STEPPED (*ppl.*) *a.*, quot. 1833); hence **step-gabled** *a.*; **step iron,** an iron projection fixed into a wall or the like to serve as a support for the foot when ascending; **step motor,** a stepping motor (see *STEPPING *ppl. a.*); **step pattern** *Art Hist.*, a simple geometric pattern progressing in steps; **step printer** *Cinemat.* (see quots.); hence (as back-formations) **step print** *v. trans.*, **step printing; step print** *sb.* (see quot.); **step response,** the output of a device in response to a step input (*STEP *sb.* 17*); **step rocket,** a rocket of two or more stages; **step-roll (collar),** a rolled step-collar (cf. ROLL-COLLAR); **step saver** *U.S.*, a kitchen designed to reduce the necessity of walking between units, etc.; also *attrib.*, as *step-saver kitchen*; hence **step-saving** *a.*; **step-stool,** a stool which can convert into a short step-ladder; **step wedge** *Photogr.*, a line of contiguous rectangles each of a uniform neutral shade but getting progressively darker from white (or light grey) at one end to black (or dark grey) at the other; also *transf.*; **step-wise** *adv.* (see as main entry below).

1895 J. P. THORNTON *Sectional Syst. Cutting* 104 Step collar vest. **1977** *Summit* (Austin Reed Mag.) Autumn 41 Step collar dress suit..with satin facings £69. **1887** KIPLING *Plain Tales from Hills* (1888) 103 Orth'ris began rowlin' his eyes an' crackin' his fingers an' dancin' a step-dance for to impress the Headman. **1946** D. HAMSON *We fell among Greeks* xix. 204 The Bishop of Kozáni, who was in full regalia on the speaker's platform, executed a step-dance. **1950** A. CLARKE *Coll. Plays* (1963) 297 It was younger than the mayflies That step-danced above it. **1969** in Halpert & Story *Christmas Mumming in Newfoundland* 67 Sometimes janneys 'step-dance'. **1896** STUART & PARK *Variety Stage* iii. 42 The sentimental vocalist, the male impersonator..and the step-dancer were familiar performers. **1969** in Halpert & Story *Christmas Mumming in Newfoundland* 214 True step-dancers in 'Coughlin Cove' have learned their art from their fathers or grandfathers. **1931** R. A. SMITH *Sturge Coll. Flints from Britain* 30 Implement of triangular section... There is some undercutting along both sides, sometimes called resolved flaking or step flaking. **1959** J. D. CLARK *Prehist. Southern Afr.* vi. 146 The Fauresmith tools were made by using what is known as *step flaking*. **1971** *World Archaeol.* III. 161 Macroscopic inspection also revealed woodworking wear in the form of distinctive step-flaking (the result of progressive wear and resharpening of the working edge). **1946** H. CRAMÉR *Math. Methods Statistics* vi. 53 Any non-decreasing function..may be represented..as the sum of a step-function and an everywhere continuous function, both non-decreasing and uniquely determined. **1947** R. LEE *Electronic Transformers & Circuits* iv. 99 It is obtained by applying a step function voltage to the series R_sL_sC circuit. **1967** *Oceanogr. & Marine Biol.* V. 32 Assuming the sea to be at rest at $t=0$, elevations were found due to northerly stress fields, the stress magnitude varying in time either exponentially, or as a step-function, or as a single half sine wave. **1971** J. H. SMITH *Digital Logic* iv. 74 In the circuit described here the input signal is a step function. **1921** *Glasgow Herald* 8 Jan. 6 It is a whitewashed house, with step-gables. **1937** *Times Lit. Suppl.* 18 Dec. 954/3 The step-gabled houses at Llanedwen. **1978** R. FEDDEN et al. *Hughenden Manor* (1980) 8 Its delightful step-gabled entrance, wood-strutted to the yard. **1912** F. N. TAYLOR *Main Drainage of Towns* vii. 139 Step irons are let into the walls of the shaft.., but sometimes a small wrought-iron ladder is substituted. **1973** R. D. SYMONS *Where Wagon Led* xvi. 260 The wagon was swept down at right angles to the team. My neighbour yelled for the rope, which I threw. He caught the loop and fastened it to the step-iron. **1961** E. M. GRABBE et al. *Handbk. Automation, Computation, & Control* III. xxii. 55 Small step motors have three to six times as much stall torque as the same size a-c servo motor. **1974** B. C. KUO *Theory & Applications of Step Motors* i. 3 High-speed printers of up to 3000 lines per minute can be driven satisfactorily with step motors. **1908** *Encycl. Relig. & Ethics* I. 842/1 'Step' patterns occur in the *cloisonné* settings of Teutonic jewels. **1959** E. A. FISHER *Anglo-Saxon Archit. & Sculpt.* 74 The simple *step pattern* also was common in Celtic art of the pagan period, though it was rare in Celtic Christian art and may have been an independent invention of the Celtic people. **1953** K. REISZ *Technique Film Editing* xiii. 207 Shot 32..was too short for the present film and had to be step-printed to the needed length. **1960** O. SKILBECK *ABC of Film & TV* 125 *Step Print.* Most Positives are made on a continuous process machine in which they run in contact with the Negative; but for some purposes, step printing, Frame by frame, is used. **1930** *Sel. Gloss. Motion Pict. Techn.* (Acad. Techn. Bureau Hollywood), *Step printer,* machine which prints a positive, a frame at a time. **1959** W. S. SHARPS *Dict. Cinematogr.* 120/1 *Step printer,* a printer in which the film to be printed and the raw stock are moved intermittently, and are stationary whilst being exposed one frame at a time. **1959** ZIMMERMAN & MASON *Electronic Circuit Theory* viii. 368 (*caption*) Approximating the step response of a linear *RC* coupling circuit including stray capacitances. **1967** *Electronics* 6 Mar. 9/1 (Advt.), Step response over the full 4½-inch span..is 40 milliseconds. **1932** D. LASSER *Conquest of Space* vi. 104 The step-rocket will ascend to a far greater height than a unit rocket of the same weight. **1946** *Sun* (Baltimore) 23 Dec. 2/4 The 'Tiamat' is a 'step' rocket—that is, it has a rocket booster mounted on its tail. **1966** H. O. RUPPE *Introd. Astronautics* I. ii. 26 Optimization of step rockets poses some very interesting problems. **1881** *Record of Fashion* 27 July 178/2 Step roll is the most suitable style for most of the goods now fashionable. **1901** P. N. HASLUCK *Tailoring* 99 Step-roll collar vest. **1967** *Boston Sunday Globe* 23 Apr. B59/3 The large kitchen..is a stepsaver when the dining room is being used. **1974** *State* (Columbia, S. Carolina) 1 Apr. 9-B/8 (Advt.), Spanish style home includes 3 bedrooms, 2 full baths, cozy den, patio, step saver kitchen with built-ins, enclosed garage and central air. **1978** *Detroit Free Press* 16 Apr. F9/5 (Advt.), 4 bedroom Quad..featuring..step-saving kitchen with all built-ins. **1966** J. POTTS *Footsteps on Stairs* (1967) iii. 38 Hazel had to laugh, just at the sight of him up there on the step-stool. **1931** *Phil. Trans. R. Soc.* A. CCXXX. 91 The intensities were estimated by covering part of the lines with a step-wedge of aluminium foil..and making use of the known absorption-coefficient of aluminium for CuKα rays. **1936** F. R. NEWNES *Technique Colour Photogr.* (ed. 2) iii. 39 The print from the blue filter negative will show less contrast than the others... If the white end of the step wedge is white, then the black end will only be a dark grey. **1962** *Which?* May 135/1 A black and white film's characteristic curve can be obtained by photographing a grey step wedge..and measuring the densities of the grey steps in the picture in relation to their known real densities. **1971** *Jrnl. Oil & Colour Chemists' Assoc.* LIV. 881 A method of achieving this was evolved using a step-wedge produced by gradually increasing the exposure in strips across the film.

step, *sb.*[2] Colloq. abbrev. of *stepfather, -mother, -son,* etc. Cf. STEP- and the associated main entries.

1895 C. M. YONGE *Long Vacation* ii. 15 Anyone would have thought those poor boys were her steps, not good old Lamb's. **1913** ROWNTREE & KENDALL *How Labourer Lives* iii. 227 There are three 'steps', Mr. Hopwood's children by a former marriage. **1933** G. HEYER *Why shoot Butler?* ii. 23 'You should not encourage your friend to talk disloyally about her brother.'..'He's only a "step".' **1939** A. THIRKELL *Before Lunch* ii. 43 She's an angel. Not a bit like a step. I really think she married father so that she could look after Denis and take me about a bit. **1954** E. EAGER *Half Magic* 155 *Step,*..short for *step-father.* **1971** O. NORTON *Corpse-Bird Cries* iv. 68 They're not her natural parents. They're both steps.

step, *v.* Add: **I. 2. c.** Of an electromechanical device: to move a small, fixed distance in response to an input pulse.

1957 GOODE & MACHOL *System Engin.* iv. 48 The switch steps up through the various banks, taking 0·1 sec to arrive at the first and 0·1 sec to go to each succeeding one. **1958** [see *STEPPING *ppl. a.*]. **1964** *IEEE Trans. Automatic Control* IX. 98/1 The idea of mechanically stepping in angle goes as far back as the clock escapement. **1974** B. C. KUO *Theory & Applications of Step Motors* i. 4 Many solenoid type motors can step only in one direction. **1978** [see *STEPPER 4].

3. e. *step-and-repeat* adj. phr. In photographic printing, etc., involving or pertaining to a procedure in which performance of an operation and progressive movement of something involved in it occur alternately. Also *absol.*

1933 N. MONTAGUE in W. Atkins *Art & Pract. Printing* III. xii. 91 The second method consists of exposing a negative on to a coated plate, moving it a definite distance, exposing again and repeating the process... Thus by means of this 'step and repeat' method..one negative may be used for printing a large number of copies. **1954** J. SOUTHWARD *Mod. Printing* (ed. 7) II. xxxv. 388 The key forme is now made up..for step and repeat. **1967** E. CHAMBERS *Photolitho-Offset* vi. 65 Where multiple repeats are required with great precision step-and-repeat machines are necessary. These are most versatile, and can be used for multi-negative work for postage stamps, labels, cheque backgrounds and the like. **1977** J. HEDGECOE *Photographer's Handbk.* 256 (*heading*) Step-and-repeat images.

II. 12*. To cause to move or progress intermittently; to cause to assume successively larger or smaller values.

1960 *McGraw-Hill Encycl. Sci. & Technol.* XIII. 356/1 Magnets are provided to step the shaft by means of a pawl mechanism. **1971** *Sci. Amer.* June 85/1 If a series of adjacent loops is energized in sequence, a bubble will be stepped along from one loop to the next. **1977** *New Scientist* 7 Apr. 9/2 You can 'step' the laser from one frequency to another in this way, but cannot tune it continuously. **1977** *Offshore Engineer* Aug. 7/1 In the case of the larger Bass Strait fields..price rises are likely to be stepped.

III. 15. step on or **upon —. b.** *to step on the gas*: see *GAS *sb.*[2] Also, *to step on it* († *her*). *colloq.* (orig. *U.S.*).

1923 R. CROTHERS *Mary the Third* II. i. 53 This is life! Go on, Lynn! *Step on her*! (Lynn bends lower over the wheel.) **1926** MAINES & GRANT *Wise-Crack Dict.* 13/1 *Step on it,* hurry. **1930** F. L. PACKARD *Jimmie Dale & Blue Envelope Murder* xxii. 316 Then for heaven's sake step on it, old man! **1939** G. GREENE *Confidential Agent* IV. ii. 283 'Step on it, Joe.' They ricocheted down the rough path. **1957** 'N. SHUTE' *On Beach* i. 27 Get up into it, and I'll step on it and show you how she goes. **1974** K. CLARK *Another Part of Wood* vi. 234 His aim was to complain to M. Jean Zay that he was not getting enough drink. 'Tell him to step on it' he repeated. **1981** C. LEOPOLD *Night Fishers of Antibes* lxxv. 201 All he had to do was to put the Citroën into second and step on it.

IV. 21. step down. a. Also *fig.*, to withdraw or retire from office. orig. *U.S.*

1890 *Stock Grower & Farmer* 3 May 3/2 If the bureau cannot do this, let the members of it, the lunkheads, step down and resign. **1945** *Sun* (Baltimore) 22 Sept. 5-0/1 (*heading*) Henry Ford steps down: Grandson becomes president of motor company. **1983** *Times* 30 Aug. 1/2 Mr Menachim Begin has pledged to make a final announcement..about..his intention to step down as Israel's sixth prime minister.

c. Substitute for def.: to reduce (the voltage of a supply); to reduce the voltage of (a supply). (Later examples.)

1938 [see *scanning coil* s.v. *SCANNING *vbl. sb.* 5]. **1978** *Gramophone* Jan. 1340/3 It is also very safe, since it uses only a 12-volt supply, stepped down by a small isolating mains transformer.

25. step off d. *intr.* To die. Cf. *step out,* sense 26 e below. *slang. rare.*

1926 E. WALLACE *Man from Morocco* iii. 21 There will only be the bit of money I have when I—er—step off.

26. step out. c. (Earlier example.)

1806 J. DAVIS *Post-Captain* xii. 74 The sailors were making a run of the tackle-falls, and Mr. Hurricane..was heard to exclaim,..'Step out, men! step out! Walk away with him, cheerly!'

e. To die; to disappear. *U.S. slang.* ? *Obs.*

1844 *Yale Lit. Mag.* IX. 381 Of the other pieces..some will be found in the present number..and the remainder have '*stept out*'. **1851** T. A. BURKE *Polly Peablossom's Wedding* 177 Ay, dead!—stepped out!—d—d—dead as Tecumseh! **1903** A. D. MCFAUL *Ike Glidden* xxx. 277 He is the cause of my ruin. Yes, that is why he stepped out when he did.

f. To appear in company or society; *spec.* to accompany or walk out (*with* a person of the opposite sex); to consort (*with* a lover). *N. Amer. dial.* and *colloq.*

1907 'MARK TWAIN' in *Harper's Mag.* Dec. 44/2, I thought what a figure I should cut stepping out amongst the redeemed in such a rig. **1918** *Dialect Notes* V. 28 *To step* [*out*], vb. i. To go out with a jane. Usually with an unvirtuous intention. General, but especially college communities. **1934** T. E. SULLINGER *Children of Divorce* 9 It affords the father an opportunity to find out how his former wife is spending his alimony, who she is 'stepping out with'. **1936** L. LEFKO *Public Relations* 27 She must be cultured—none of those speak-easy belles you step out with will do. **1940** *Chatelaine* June 59/3 Sally's stepping out again! **1955** D. W. MAURER in *Publ. Amer. Dial. Soc.* XXIV. 190 [Support] will continue as long as she does not have anything to do with men; as soon as she 'steps out' and the fact becomes known, her support stops. **1977** *Detroit Free Press* 11 Dec. 11-B/1 Woodard believes Rae is stepping out with Frank.

g. To parachute *out* of a (disabled) aircraft. *R.A.F. slang.*

1942 B. J. ELLAN *Spitfire* p. x, If you are unlucky enough to get shot down yourself, you..step out. **1953** R. CHISHOLM *Cover of Darkness* I. ii. 24 He climbed to ten thousand and he and his observer stepped out as we used to say.

h. *to step out of line*: see *LINE *sb.*[2] 28 b.

28. step up. g. (Later examples.) Also (more commonly), to increase (the voltage of a supply).

1909 *Electrician* 2 July 463/1 By means of the three resonance relays..the telephone current was stepped up to 10^{-2} amperes and audible working obtained. **1956** A. H. COMPTON *Atomic Quest* i. 14 Step up the voltages used in our experiments with nuclei, and we should expect to produce interesting nuclear reactions. **1980** J. W. HILL *Intermediate Physics* xxi. 205 The transformer can step up or step down voltages.

h. *fig.* To raise to a higher level or standard, by a stage or stages. More widely, to advance gradually; to increase, intensify.

1920 *Glasgow Herald* 8 July 7 They would suggest that this increase..should be 'stepped up' over a period of years. **1931** *Amer. Speech* VII. verso rear cover (Advt.),

Can you 'step-up' education to meet the new requirements of society? **1938** *Sun* (Baltimore) 5 Sept. 8/8 Soon after they had cleared the Hanover street bridge they stepped up their stroke. **1941** *Punch* 19 Feb. 173/2 People have.. stepped their ideas up..about the telephone; I mean, nowadays very few of them actually brush their hair before answering. **1958** *Spectator* 18 July 117/1 The output..could be quickly stepped up. **1967** *Listener* 23 Mar. 390/2 An Aden nationalist leader says terrorist activity will be stepped up when U.N. mission arrives. **1978** K. HUDSON *Jargon of Professions* ii. 50 The war in Vietnam was being stepped up. **1982** *Times* 25 Oct. 6/1 The Solidarity underground..stepped up its pressure this weekend on..the beleaguered Polish leader.

V. 29. The vb.-stem in combination with advbs. and preps. **step-on** *a. U.S.*, that may be operated by pressure of the foot. See also STEP-DOWN, -IN, -OUT, -UP below.

1945 *Richmond* (Va.) *Times-Dispatch* 9 Nov. 24 (Advt.), Step-on pail. **1978** *Detroit Free Press* 5 Mar. A 20 (Advt.), Powerful cleaner has..Convenient step-on switch, easy-change bag holder.

step-. Add: (Later examples of derived and associated forms in somewhat limited currency.) *step-papa* (earlier example).

The concept of orphanage is no longer relevant to the meaning of the *step-* combinations. Consequently, the relationships of *step-brother, -sister*, etc., may be considered to refer reciprocally to children of a later as well as a former marriage: i.e. step-brother = half-brother, etc. A step-parent may be created by marriage to a divorced or a bereaved person.

1893 'MARK TWAIN' in *Century Mag.* Jan. 346/2 Yes; he's my steppapa, and the dearest one that ever was. **1924** G. B. STERN *Tents of Israel* vii. 105 Val,..the eldest step-grandchild..had returned from Vienna especially not to miss the occasion. **1936** M. MITCHELL *Gone with Wind* xlvii. 844 Ah ain' gwine leave Miss Ellen's gran' chillun fer no trashy step-pa ter bring up. **1959** 'E. H. CLEMENTS' *High Tension* v. 83 His step-cousin's [neck] rose..from an open-necked shirt. **1960** M. SPARK *Ballad Peckham Rye* vii. 130 Your step-dad's on about young Leslie. **1962** *Listener* 10 May 828/1 A comic private detective, besides step-mum and callous dad. **1974** D. FRANCIS *Knock Down* xii. 146 My new step-mama will be able to maintain us in the style to which we are accustomed. **1980** M. MCMULLEN *My Cousin Death* (1981) vii. 82 He's some kind of step-relative, and he's on his uppers. **1982** *Listener* 23—30 Dec. 12/1 Christmas for many will either be as desolate as an Oxford Street Santa's heart or so extended—what with the myriads of stepfathers, stepmothers, step-siblings, step-uncles and step-aunts—as to conjure up images of those family groupings which American family therapists love to gather for what they call 'working together'.

ste·p-down, *a.* and *sb.* [f. vbl. phr. *to step down*: see STEP *v.* 21.] **A.** *attrib.* or as *adj.*

1. In sense 21 c of the vb.: causing or pertaining to a reduction in voltage or some other quantity.

1893 [in Dict., s.v. STEP *v.* 21 c]. **1929** *Exper. Wireless* VI. 307/2 This reduces the step down ratio required in the potentiometer. **1947** R. LEE *Electronic Transformers & Circuits* vi. 172 Driver transformers are usually step-down because the grid potentials are relatively low. **1959** *Motor Man.* (ed. 36) 95 It has a stepdown gear which reduces the speed of the propeller shaft in a ratio which is usually between 5 to 1 and 4 to 1. **1961** *Wall St. Jrnl.* (Eastern ed.) 14 Nov. 10 (Advt.), With Con Edison's step-down rates, the more electricity you use, the less it costs per kilowatt-hour. **1981** *Daily Tel.* 22 July 12/6 For really rough going there is a 1·96:1 step-down ratio for four-wheel-drive.

2. In sense 21 a of the vb. Esp. from or in which one steps to a lower level. Chiefly *U.S.*

1949 *Newsweek* 28 Nov. 56 (*caption*) Hudson enters lower-priced field with smaller version of step-down car. **1954** *Sun* (Baltimore) 8 Mar. 20/1 Dr. Clifford M. Witcher ..calls his device a 'step-down detector'. When the user approaches a curb, a flight of steps or the edge of a subway platform, the detector buzzes a warning. **1966** A. R. BELLAMY in *Biochim. & Biophys. Acta* CXXIII. 102 (*title*) RNA synthesis in exponentially growing tobacco cells subjected to a step-down nutritional shift. **1976** *Billings* (Montana) *Gaz.* 27 June 5-D/4 (Advt.), Three bedrooms, step-down living room, and main floor family room with fireplace.

B. *sb.* **1.** A reduction or decrease.

1922 [see *REGENERATIVE *a.* (and *sb.*) 2 b]. **1962** A. NISBETT *Technique Sound Studio* ix. 165 The result is a sudden step-down in volume and quality just before the second signal appears on the tape.

2. The act of stepping down or withdrawing from a position.

1973 *Guardian* 7 June 2/4 In a cleverly disguised step-down from the position that these controversial logs would never be released, Mr Nixon's spokesman said today that..the documents would now be turned over.

Stephanian (stĭfēⁱ·niăn), *a. Geol.* [ad. F. *stéphanien* (A. de Lapparent *Traité de Géol.* (ed. 3, 1893) 819), f. *Stephan-us*, latinized form of Saint-*Etienne*, name of a city in central France where it is represented: see -IAN.] Of, pertaining to, or designating the uppermost division of the Carboniferous in Europe, especially where represented by coal-bearing formations. Also *absol.*

1901 *Jrnl. Geol.* IX. 196 The flora of the Caradons stage contains a mingling of uppermost Westphalian species with Stephanian types. **1903** A. GEIKIE *Text-bk. Geol.* (ed. 4) II. 1051 Stephanian. **1912** A. J. JUKES-BROWN *Student's Handbk. Stratigr. Geol.* (ed. 2) x. 317 A few small tracts of Stephanian measures occur in Brittany and Normandy... The most northern of these is at Littry.., the Coal-measures here..being conformably overlain by Permian Beds, and they belong, therefore, to the latest phase of the Stephanian. **1931** GREGORY & BARRETT *Gen. Stratigr.* vii. 118 The Stephanian is absent from the N. of France and Westphalia, and is present in numerous coalfields preserved in basins in the pre-Palaeozoic rocks of the Central Plateau of France. **1959** [see *DINANTIAN *a.*]. **1963** [see *SAKMARIAN *a.*].

stephanotis. For mod.L. read 'mod.L. (L. M. A. A. Dupetit-Thouars *Genera Nova Madagascariensia* (1806) 11' and add: **1.** (Earlier examples.)

1843 *Curtis's Bot. Mag.* LXX. 4058 (*heading*) Copious-flowering Stephanotis. **1869** S. R. HOLE *Bk. about Roses* iii. 41 The stove, truly, is a gladness and refreshment—gay..with the golden Allamandas,..the bridal Stephanotis.

2. (Earlier and later examples.)

1895 *Army & Navy Co-op. Soc. Price List* 716/1 A new fragrant Toilet Water in Jockey Club, White Rose, Stephanotis, [etc.]. **1980** M. FORSTER *Bride of Lowther Fell* xvi. 244 The perfume was..stephanotis, faint and unbelievably fragrant.

Stephen: see *even Stephen* s.v. *EVEN *a.* 14 d.

ste·p-in, *sb.* and *a.* [f. vbl. phr. *to step in*: see STEP *v.* 24.] **A.** *sb.* A garment or shoe put on by stepping into it; *spec.* in *pl.*, loose drawers (more recently, brief panties) for women (chiefly *U.S.*).

1922 *Woman's Home Compan.* June 70 (*caption*) The children like to wear step-ins. **1928** *Sunday Dispatch* 15 July 16 The same *couturière* is all for 'step ins' for swimmers. **1934** [see *SCANTY *sb.*]. **1939** M. B. PICKEN *Lang. Fashion* 131/1 *Step-in*, shoe with no obvious method of fastening, usually held on snugly by an elastic gore. **1946** WODEHOUSE *Money in Bank* xxvii. 234 A bottle of brandy which she..kept stowed away..in a drawer underneath her step-ins. **1958** S. ELLIN *Eighth Circle* (1959) II. xx. 208 Her brassière and step-ins plastered wetly to her body. **1964** P. WHITE *Burnt Ones* 86 Eileen began to pull. Her step-ins had eaten into her. **1975** J. GORES *Hammett* (1976) xxii. 153 The upended torcher wore no step-ins under her tight red sequins.

B. *attrib.* or as *adj.* Designating a garment or shoe of this type.

1923 *Weekly Dispatch* 18 Feb. 12 Step-in cami-knickers. **1960** *Amer. Speech* XXXV. 79 These dresses were listed variously as..'a step-in sundress of acetate', and 'a step-in charmer'. **1975** *Times* 3 May 8/2 The 'step-in' dress with buttons down the front, which permitted a woman to step into a dress instead of pulling it over her head.

Stepin Fetchit (ste·p'n fe·tʃit). *U.S.* Also **Steppin Fetchit.** [*Stepin Fetchit*, the stage-name of Lincoln Theodore Perry (b. 1902), a popular Black vaudeville actor noted for playing a series of fawning characters in Hollywood films of the 1920s and 1930s. For earlier uses of the sb. phr. *step and fetch it* applied to persons, see *Eng. Dial. Dict.*, *Dialect Notes* (1903) II. 301, (1914) IV. 113.] A type of a shuffling, obsequious, Black servant. Hence, any servile Black man; an Uncle Tom. Also *attrib.*

1940 F. SCOTT FITZGERALD *Let.* 1 Feb. (1964) 597 This way of looking at war gives great scope for comedy without bringing in Stepin Fetchit and Hattie McDaniel as faithful negro slaves. **1951** MCWHINEY & SIMKINS in A. Dundes *Mother Wit* (1973) 588/1 The mere mention of a ghost makes him shake as actively as Step'in Fetch'it under the influence of an Arctic breeze. **1967** P. WELLES *Babyhip* xvii. 121 He shrugged his shoulders in his phoney Steppin Fetchit pose and went home leaving a perfectly groovy [chess] strategy unfinished. **1968** *N.Y. Times* 21 Feb. 56/3 He talks disparagingly of comics and other artists who don't fill the role of rebel. Among these he lists Danny Thomas, Jack Benny, Woody Allen and 'Stepin Fetchit Negroes doing the same thing under a new veneer'.

stepless, *a.* Add: **2.** Continuously variable; capable of being given any value within a certain range.

1969 *Jane's Freight Containers 1968–69* 23 adv., Speed control is through the Wessex Carbon Pile, providing smooth, stepless acceleration. **1971** *Engineering* Apr. 111/2 (Advt.), This equipment provides stepless current adjustment over the full range of the..generator. **1973** *Physics Bull.* Feb. 110/1 The instruments in this range produce stepless DC voltage outputs. **1978** *Amateur Photographer* 2 Aug. 6/2 Stepless shutter speed range of 1/1000th to 4 seconds + B.

Hence **ste·plessly** *adv.*

1958 *Times Rev. Industry* Oct. 67/3 The rate of travel.. can be varied steplessly by a knob on the body. **1977** *Design Engin.* July 73/2 Frequency and amplitude can be steplessly varied during operation.

Stepney (ste·pni). Also **stepney.** [f. the name of *Stepney* Street, Llanelli, the place of manufacture.] **1.** A spare wheel for a motor vehicle, comprising a ready-inflated tyre on a spokeless metal rim, which could be clamped temporarily over a punctured wheel. Also *stepney wheel*. Now *Hist.* exc. in Bangladesh, India, and Malta, where = any spare wheel.

1907 *Westm. Gaz.* 3 Dec. 4/3 The popularity of the Stepney Wheel has never been more clearly demonstrated than at the Olympia Show. **1910** G. K. CHESTERTON *Alarms & Discussions* 179 Then he said, 'And I left the Stepney behind.' **1911** *Daily Chron.* 5 Jan. 4/7 Wales claims the origin of the 'stepney', the spare wheel and tyre. **1928** *Evening News* 7 Aug. 9/2 None of your detachable wheels, rims, or Stepneys! **1929** H. NICOLSON *Let.* 22 July in J. Lees-Milne *Harold Nicolson* (1980) xvi. 376 [In Berlin he was like] a stepney wheel of a car that is seldom taken out of the garage. **1937** *Autocar Handbk.* (ed. 13) xi. 196 With the introduction of pneumatic tyres came the puncture, and soon the 'Stepney' appeared: a spare rim and tyre fitted with clamps. **1971** *Listener* 11 Nov. 653/1 After jacking up the car, one of them turned to me and said: 'Have you a Stepney?' 'Yes, in the boot,' I answered... It takes an old Edwardian like me to know that a Stepney was an attachable wheel-rim, which came in about 1907 and went out about ten years later. You wouldn't hear the term in England now, but in Malta it is the *ordinary* word for a spare wheel. **1973** *Opinion* (Bombay) July 31 It helps to have a few holes in the roof of the car and to go about without a Stepney. **1975** J. DAY *Bosch Bk. Motor Car* 178 An early attempt to make puncture mending less troublesome was the Stepney spare wheel of T. M. and W. Davies in 1904. **1977** *Navbharat Times* (Bombay) 2 June (Advt.), Yezdi stepney wheel complete with tyre, tube, hub and bearings. **1980** L. LEWIS *Private Life of Country House* iii. 35 About 1920 we bought a secondhand T model Ford... In case of punctures there was a Stepney wheel to be clamped on to the rim to get you home.

2. *fig.*

1928 E. SUTTON tr. *A. Londres's Road to Buenos Ayres* ii. 18, I told her I had a woman already in Buenos Ayres, that she could only be my little sweetheart, as we say, or my 'stepney', if you like that better. **1929** E. LINKLATER *Poet's Pub* xxvi. 282 Redemption being carried as a kind of stepney on the best of all possible worlds. **1979** P. NIHALANI et al. *Indian & Brit. Eng.* 1. 167 Dr X may not be able to give his talk—we'd better arrange for a stepney.

ste·p-out. *Oil Industry.* [f. vbl. phr. *to step out*: see STEP *v.* 26.] In full *step-out well*. A well drilled beyond the established area of an oil or gas field to find out if it extends further.

1948 *Bull. Amer. Assoc. Petroleum Geologists* XXXIII. 1082 Step-out well No. 55, 1 kilometer east of No. 26, is now drilling. **1955** *N.Y. Times* 28 Aug. I. 72 Common practice is to drill 'step outs' at specified distances in all four directions from a discovery well. **1962** F. E. WELLINGS in M. J. Wells *Oil Industry Tomorrow* 32 Step-out wells make [*sic*] the usual division between exploratory wells and development wells. In development wells, if they are intelligently done, the percentage of success is very high,..but less so for the step-out wells. **1977** *Offshore Engineer* Aug. 19/3 Well 3/8-3, south of Ninian, found a hydrocarbon accumulation which has been extended into block 3/7 to the west with a step-out. **1979** *Jrnl. R. Soc. Arts* CXXVII. 407/1 The Gas Council..have indicated a wish to sink step-out wells on the Goathorn Peninsula and on the Studland Peninsula.

stepped, (*ppl.*) *a.* Add: **1.** Also *spec.* of the float or hull of a seaplane or hydroplane. Cf. *STEP *sb.* 15 c.

1911 *Flight* 9 Dec. 1074/2 The float consists of a three-stepped hydroplane. **1951** [see *hard chine* s.v. *HARD *a.* (*sb.*) 22].

2. Carried out or occurring in stages or with pauses, rather than continuously.

1935 *Proc. R. Soc.* A. CLII. 597 The prolific branching of the main part of the first stroke of a series arises solely from downward branching in the stepped leader which precedes it. **1944** *Jrnl. Iron & Steel Inst.* CL. 128A, The causes of the distortion of steel parts during heat treatment are analysed and methods of preventing it, including austempering and other forms of stepped quenching, are discussed. **1977** J. HEDGECOE *Photographer's Handbk.* 125 If you project a transparency using a zoom lens, you get a similar effect to stepped zoom. **1981** *Sci. Amer.* Mar. 28/1 Subsequent leaders..move an order of magnitude faster than the first stepped leader in the freshly ionized gas.

3. With *up*. Raised by degree to a higher standard or level; increased, intensified.

1933 *Sun* (Baltimore) 22 Nov. 20/2 Demands were being made on brewers for a 'stepped-up' beverage, whereas the normally brewed beer runs about four per cent. **1941** *Battle of Britain Aug.–Oct. 1940* (Ministry of Information) 26 Twenty Dornier 215's were encountered over the London Docks flying in a diamond formation escorted by Me 109's 'stepped up' to 22,000 feet. **1955** *Times* 22 Aug. 9/6 Mr. Sinclair Weeks, Secretary of Commerce, to-day announced 'a stepped up programme' to make public as quickly as possible non-classified research reports of industrial significance by the Atomic Energy Commission. **1963** P. FLEMING *Kolchak* xx. 212 They themselves were frightened men, and this combined with the necessarily stepped-up tempo of the interrogation to make them hectoring and exigent. **1976** *National Observer* (U.S.) 23 Oct. 4/4 But he concedes that post officials are 'a little concerned' about handling the stepped-up volume of business over the Christmas season if the strike continues.

stepper. Add: **2. a.** (Earlier and later examples.) Now *Obs.*

1846 *Swell's Night Guide* 59, I does the safe, if they cops me it's nix; six veeks, a fly at the stepper and turn up. **1891** 'F. W. Carew' *No. 747* xvi. 188 Toiling under our heavy burdens up that everlasting staircase—as Tony Klism said, it was ever so much worse than 'the stepper'.

4. In full *stepper motor.* A stepping motor (see *stepping *ppl. a.*).

1961 *Control Engin.* May 116/1 Applications employing interlocked steppers are ballistic missile prelaunching exercises, reconnaissance drone control, and precise positioning of radioactive fuel elements. *Ibid.* Nov. 103/1a, Stepper motor resembles the conventional ac servomotor except that its winding is excited by a stream of pulses from a multivibrator. **1976** Nasar & Boldea *Linear Motion Electric Machines* ix. 255 Some of the advantages of linear stepper motors are ease of control.. and locking force. **1978** R. P. Hunter *Automated Process Control Systems* xiv. 328 The VR stepper requires its windings to be energized in the proper sequence for predictable operation. Also, it can be made to step bidirectionally.

stepping, *vbl. sb.* Add: **1. e.** With *up.* The action of *step *v.* 28 h.

1958 *Listener* 24 July 112/1 This would involve a stepping-up of supplies from Persia and from Venezuela. **1965** D. Francis *For Kicks* i. 8 There were trials and prison sentences..and a stepping-up of regular saliva and urine tests.

f. The step-by-step movement of a stepping device (see *stepping *ppl. a.*).

1960 *McGraw-Hill Encycl. Sci. & Technol.* XIII. 356/2 These selectors may be arranged for..absorbing the digit pulsed without any stepping of the switch. **1964** [see *step *sb.* 7 e]. **1974** B. C. Kuo *Theory & Applications of Step Motors* i. 4 There are many different versions of switches and actuators which give stepping motion through the principle of solenoid action. **1977** *Engin. Materials & Design* Aug. 41/1 Medium power switching types provide operating voltage ranges from 6 to 110V dc and 6 to 220V ac, with latching and stepping facilities in selected items.

stepping (ste·piŋ), *ppl. a.* [f. Step *v.* + -ing[2].] Of an electric motor or other electro-mechanical device: designed to make a rapid succession of small, equal movements in response to a pulsed input, each pulse causing one movement.

1957 Goode & Machol *System Engin.* iv. 48 Consider a stepping switch acting as a line finder in a telephone system. **1958** J. G. Truxal *Control Engineers' Handbk.* v. 69 Besides stepping relays and the Ledex rotary solenoid, few digital devices are available that can step from one point to another rapidly enough to be useful as a control-system output actuator. **1975** *Physics Bull.* July 319/3 The precision divided tables may be fitted with calibrated hand wheels or driven by either stepping motors or dc gear motors. **1979** *Nature* 12 July 121/1 The electrodes were advanced through the brain with a stepping microdrive..until a cell or process was penetrated.

ste·p-up, *a.* and *sb.* [f. vbl. phr. *to step up*: see Step *v.* 28.] **A.** *attrib.* or as *adj.* **1.** Causing or pertaining to an increase in voltage.

1893 [in Dict., s.v. Step *v.* 28 g]. **1903** C. H. Sewall *Wireless Telegr.* iv. 149 The transmitter of the DeForest system uses..a step-up transformer to increase the voltage. **1947** R. Lee *Electronic Transformers & Circuits* v. 142 Input Transformer,.. Step-up ratio 1:20. *Ibid.* 188 If the transformer is step-up, C_1=[etc.]. **1977** *Gramophone* Oct. 744/2 A particular criticism levelled towards moving-coil cartridges is that their output is so low as to require a step-up transformer.

2. Furnished with a step to a higher level. Also, of a room with such a feature.

1958 J. Myerscough *Procession of Lancs. Martyrs & Confessors* xix. 260 A typical example of the 'step-up' chapel provided for Catholics in the days of persecution may be seen..in Alston Lane, Grimsargh. **1979** *Arizona Daily Star* 5 Aug. (Advt. Section) 13/1, 2 bdrms., 2 full baths, step-up dining area.

B. *sb.* **1.** An increase in rate or quantity; an intensification.

1922 Glazebrook *Dict. Appl. Physics* II. 889/1 The amplifying action of a valve is usually more a question of potential step-up than of ratio of power output to power input. **1944** *Times* 26 May 2/1 We should probably finish the war with very nearly the same step-up in engine power over the present war period as occurred between 1914–18. **1972** *Newsweek* 10 Jan. 14/3 Coupled with the increasingly hard line adopted by both negotiating teams in recent weeks, the step-up in the air war might even jeopardize the continuation of the talks themselves.

2. Chiefly *pl.* A step taken on to a platform (such as a bench, etc.) and back again, repeated as a fitness exercise.

1973 *Observer* 7 Oct. 28/1 A middle-aged actor keeping his paunch at bay with weights and interminable step-ups. **1978** *Kingston* (Ontario) *Whig-Standard* 15 July 15/2 Stations 5–9 include such exercises as..chin-ups and step-ups.

stepwise (ste·pwəiz), *adv.* and *a.* Also with hyphen. [f. Step *sb.* + Wise *sb.*[1] II.] **A.** *adv.* **1.** Like or in a series of steps.

1888 [in Dict., s.v. Step *sb.* 18]. **1902** *Jrnl. R. Inst. Brit. Architects* 20 Dec. 101 The balustrade of its upper flight rising step-wise, and showing at intervals the sockets of its colonnade. **1950** *Jrnl. Neurophysiol.* XIII. 193 The response builds either step-wise or abruptly to a complex series of peaks at 5–8 msec.

2. *Mus.* = *by step* s.v. Step *sb.* 8 b.

1955 G. Abraham in H. Van Thal *Fanfare for E. Newman* ii. 12 A purely harmonic cadence, the separate parts moving stepwise, even chromatically, with a much less decisive cadential effect rhythmically.

3. In a series of distinct or separate stages; with intermittent pauses, not continuously.

1971 J. Z. Young *Introd. Study Man* iii. 55 It may be that the new mRNA is synthesized stepwise in the nucleus. **1972** *Science* 2 June 1014/2 The details of.. whether the velocities increase smoothly or stepwise.. cannot be resolved without additional data.

B. *adj.* **1.** *Mus.* Of musical progression, etc.: occurring or arranged regularly in steps (Step *sb.* 8 b in Dict. and Suppl.).

1920 S. Macpherson *Melody & Harmony* i. 4 In the above extracts there is a considerable amount of 'conjunct' (i.e. step-wise) movement. **1930** A. M. Richardson *Helps to Fugue Writing* vii. 37 A progression like the following does not look interesting..but by supplying embellishments it can be made much more effective... The thirds need not be stepwise. **1949** W. Piston *Counterpoint* (rev. ed.) i. 20 In the Corelli example the upward octave skip is both preceded and followed by a downward stepwise movement. **1952** A. O. Warburton *Melody Writing & Analysis* I. 7 After stepwise movement it is usually wise to leap in the opposite direction. **1979** *Early Music* Jan. 138/2 The manuscripts..specify 'clarinet' on the title-page, and include stepwise movement in their lower register.

2. = *step-by-step* attrib. or quasi-adj. s.v. Step *sb.* 5 c.

1934 *Jrnl. Amer. Chem. Soc.* LVI. 913/1 The development of a complex polymer must require a series of consecutive reactions... It is necessary to assume that the first-formed polymers possess an ordinary double bond and are capable of being isolated. This scheme will be called 'stepwise'. **1954** [see *degradation[1] 4 c]. **1960** Koestler *Lotus & Robot* I. i. 43 The result of this stepwise dismantling of reality is that consciousness alone remains. **1975** N. Chomsky *Logical Struct. Linguistic Theory* x. 469 Transformational analysis permits the stepwise formation of complex phrases from already constructed simple phrases. **1980** *Jrnl. R. Soc. Arts* May 348/2 Step-wise mutations in the bacterium..are shown to produce corresponding changes in the synthesized amidase.

sterane (stiᵊ·rēⁱn, ste·rēⁱn). *Min.* and *Chem.* [f. *ster(oid + -ane.] Any of a class of saturated hydrocarbons with a steroid structure which are found in crude oils and derived from the sterols of ancient organisms; orig., † the compound whose molecule consists of the saturated nucleus only.

1951 *Jrnl. Chem. Soc.* 3527 The substance (II) shall be named gonane (preferred) or sterane (alternative). **1969** *Geochim. & Cosmochim. Acta* XXXIII. 1307 The C_{27}, C_{28} and C_{29} steranes are present in the bitumen from the Green River oil shale and..they were derived from cholesterol, ergosterol, stigmasterol or related sterols. **1973** *Nature* 27 Apr. 603/1 These steranes and terpanes represent the complete reduction of naturally occurring steroids or terpenoids to relatively stable fossil molecules which preserve intact the complete molecular skeleton and stereochemistry of their precursors. Steranes..provided convincing proof for the biological origins of petroleums.

stercolith (stə̄·ɪkoliþ). *Med.* [f. L. *sterc-us* dung + -o + -lith.] = Stercorolith.

1910 *Practitioner* July 106 We came upon another abscess cavity, from which a typical appendicular stercolith was dislodged. **1973** Earnest & Sleisenger in Sleisenger & Fordtran *Gastrointestinal Dis.* cxii. 1531/1 A smaller, rounded, smooth hard mass of stool which cannot be expelled is called a stercolith or enterolith.

stercorarian. Restrict † *Obs. rare* to senses in Dict. and add: **B.** *adj. Biol.* [f. mod.L. *Stercoraria,* name of a section of the genus *Trypanosoma* (C. A. Hoare 1964, in *Jrnl. Protozool.* XI. 203/1).] Used to designate those species of *Trypanosoma* which occur in the digestive tract of the secondary host, and are transmitted in its fæces. Cf. *salivarian *a.*

1964 C. A. Hoare in *Jrnl. Protozool.* XI. 203/2 It must be admitted that not all Stercorarian trypanosomes can be fitted with certainty into the above subgenera,..since the life cycle of many of them is still unknown. **1971, 1977** [see *salivarian *a.*].

stercorite (stə̄·ɪkŏrəit). *Min.* [f. L. *stercor-āre* to manure with dung, f. *stercus* dung + -ite[1].] A hydrated acid phosphate of sodium and ammonium, $Na(NH_4)HPO_4.4H_2O$, occurring as colourless triclinic crystals; microcosmic salt.

1850 T. J. Herapath in *Q. Jrnl. Chem. Soc.* II. 73 This being the first instance in which the ammonio-phosphate of soda has been met with as a natural production, I propose to class it amongst our minerals under the name of 'Stercorite'. **1975** *Mineral. Abstr.* XXVI. 125/2 The X-ray powder data of stercorite from Chincha Islands, Peru, prove that the mineral corresponds with [*sic*] the synthetic $Na(NH_4)HPO_4.4H_2O$.

stercorolith. Add: Now superseded by *stercolith.

stereo[2]**.** Add: **stereo card,** a card on which are mounted a pair of stereoscopic photographs; **stereo pair,** a pair of photographs showing the same scene from slightly different points of view, so that when viewed appropriately a single stereoscopic image is seen.

1975 *New Yorker* 26 May 11/3 (Advt.), Also on view are such items as a glass-plate camera from the period and stereo cards mounted in hand-operated viewers. **1976** *Church Times* 3 Dec. 6/5 Two handsome books contain, respectively, a stereoscopic viewer with facsimiles of old stereocards, and a lively illustrated history of stereographic photography. **1943** H. T. U. Smith *Aerial Photographs* iii. 79 Ink marks..detract seriously from the effectiveness of depth perception, particularly when on only one photo of a stereo pair. **1966** [see *photo-interpretation* s.v. *photo- 2]. **1977** J. Hedgecoe *Photographer's Handbk.* 299 One reason why stereo cameras have gone out of favour is that you can easily make stereo-pairs with an ordinary camera.

stereo (ste·rio, stiᵊ·rio), *a.* and *sb.*[3] *colloq.* [Abbrev. of *stereophonic *a.*, *stereophony.] **A.** *adj.* = *stereophonic *a.*

1954 *Wireless World* Jan. 7/1 The first full-length stereophonic film to be released was Walt Disney's 'Fantasia', ..with stereo sound photographically recorded on four tracks on a separate sound film. **1958** *Times* 20 Jan. 10/4 What stereo discs have achieved is to combine these two channels in one groove traced by one stylus. *Ibid.*, When the B.B.C. establishes stereo broadcasts..it may give a new lease of life to radio manufacturers. **1960** *Practical Wireless* XXXVI. 299/2 A variety of instrumental, choral and solo recordings, both monaural and binaural (stereo). **1963** *Which?* Jan. 3/1 Equipment for reproducing stereo records is more elaborate than for mono, and relatively few stereo record players are sold. **1976** 'A. York' *Dark Passage* xii. 144 The stereo cassette recorder was switched on. **1977** G. Scott *Hot Pursuit* xv. 147 My heartbeat began to pound as though stereo headphones had been clamped to my head.

B. *sb.* **1.** = *stereophony.

1956 *Radio & Television News* Aug. 35/1 (*heading*) What should stereo do? **1957** *Audio* Jan. 12/2 Tape is the only logical medium for stereo. **1958** *Observer* 20 Apr. 10/5 In adding another dimension to our listening, stereo represents a most significant advance in the quest for concert-hall realism. **1961** *John o' London's* 5 Oct. 396/4 The new Decca issue..presents both works in first-class stereo. **1970** *Jrnl. Audio Engin. Soc.* XVIII. 624 The transmission of four-channel stereo by means of FM-multipler techniques. **1972** *Daily Tel.* 9 Aug. 13/1 The BBC is to start programmes in stereo on Radios 1 and 2 from the end of September.

2. Any stereophonic apparatus for playing records or tapes. Cf. *stereogram[2].

1964 *House & Garden* Nov. 62/2 (*caption*) The wall unit houses the stereo. **1971** *Daily Tel.* 24 Sept. 12, I am unable to understand pop words seated 3ft away from a high quality stereo. **1976** P. Cave *High Flying Birds* iv. 52 Lorna showed us into the villa and put some low, slow background music on the stereo. **1980** J. Gardner *Garden of Weapons* I. iii. 37 You got full sound in the Charlton house? And a stereo? I can't live without music.

stereo-. Add: **ste:reo-acu·ity,** the sharpness of the eyes in discerning separation along the line of sight; **ste·reo-camera,** a camera for simultaneously taking two photographs of the same thing from adjacent viewpoints, so that they will form a stereoscopic pair; **stereo-ci·lium** *Anat.*, an immotile cell process of certain epithelial cells of the male reproductive tract and the labyrinth of the ear, similar to a cilium at low magnifications only; hence **stereo-ci·liary** *a.*; **stereo-comparator,** substitute for both defs.: an instrument enabling two different photographs of the same region to be seen simultaneously, one by each eye, either to detect any change (in the case of photographs of the night sky taken at different times) or to make measurements of the area depicted in stereoscopic photographs; (further examples); **ste:reocontro·l** *sb. Chem.*, the control of a synthesis by the choice of reagents and reaction conditions so as to produce a product with a desired stereochemical conformation; also as *v. trans.*, to control thus; **ste:reocontro·lled** *ppl. a.*; **ste·reo-diagram,** a diagram intended to show the three-dimensional structure of something; **ste:reoelectro·nic** *a. Chem.*, pertaining to the relative positions of the electron orbitals in reacting molecules; hence **ste:reoelectro·nically** *adv.*; **ste:reofluoro·scopy** *Med.*, the production of X-ray images which can be interpreted in three dimensions; = *stereoradiography* below; hence **stereoflu·oroscope,** an instrument for producing such images; **ste:reofluorosco·pic** *a.*; **stereogno·sis.** [Gr. γνῶσις means of knowing], the stereognostic sense or faculty; **stereo-isomer** (earlier example); **stereo-isomeride** (later example); now *obs.*; **ste:reoisomeriza·tion** *Chem.*, the conversion of one stereoisomer into another; hence (as back-formations) **ste:reoiso·merize** *v. intr.*, to undergo stereoisomerization; *trans.*, to cause the stereoisomerization of (a compound); **ste:reoiso·merized** *ppl. a.*, **-iso-merizing** *vbl. sb.*; **stereomi·crograph,** a micrograph that conveys a vivid impression of depth, such as one obtained with a scanning electron microscope; **stereomi·croscope,** a binocular microscope that gives a stereoscopic view of the subject; **ste:reomuta·tion** *Chem.*, the conversion of a *cis-* to a *trans-*isomer or vice versa; **stereo-photo** *a.* : see *stereo-photographic* adj. in Dict.; also as *sb.*, a stereophotograph; **ste:reophotogra·mmetry,** photogrammetry by means of stereophotography; hence **ste:reophotogramme·tric** *a.*; **stereo-photograph** (examples); **stereopla·ni-graph** *Cartography* [a. G. *stereo-planigraph*], a machine which plots a map of an area semi-automatically under the guidance of the operator as he views a stereoscopic pair of aerial photographs of it; **ste·reoplotter,** an instrument used for plotting maps of an area from stereoscopic aerial photographs that are projected on to the plotting table; **ste:reo-plo·tting** *a.* that is a stereo-plotter; **stereora·diograph,** a stereoscopic radiograph; so **ste:reoradiogra·phic** *a.*, **-gra·phically** *adv.*; **ste:reoradio·graphy** = *stereofluoroscopy* above; **Ste·reoscan, ste·reoscan,** a proprietary name for a scanning electron microscope; hence (as *stereoscan*), a picture obtained with a scanning electron microscope; **ste·reoviewing** *vbl. sb.*, stereoscopic viewing.

1942 *Summary Progress Rep. Tests of Stereoscopic Vision* (Harvard Univ. Psycho-Educational Clinic, Publ. Bd. No. 55797) 1 The objects of this investigation were: (1) to appraise tests of stereo-acuity in current use. **1974** *Nature* 13 Sept. 141/1 Stereoacuity falls in the region of the resolution of the Calcomp plotter, so it could not be measured. **1959** *Observer* 7 June 3/4, I have had a stereo-camera for five years now and the range of new experiences it can offer is constantly widening. You can photograph people and they are three-dimensional people, frozen in a moment of time. **1961** *New Scientist* 19 Oct. 173/2 The Japanese workers used a stereocamera to record the contours of waves generated by the model. **1977** Stereo-camera [see *stereo pair* s.v. *STEREO[2]]. **1933** Stereocilium [see *kinocilium* s.v. *KINO-]. **1950** A. W. HAM *Histol.* xxviii. 659/2 The epithelium [of the epididymis] is tall and regular, and tufts of large nonmotile stereocilia..project toward the lumen from the free margins of the cells. **1970** J. BABEL et al. *Ultrastructure Peripheral Nerv. System* 270 Every vestibular sensory cell carries 80–100 stereocilia..and one kinocilium... The stereocilia of the hair cells of the cristae are exceedingly long. **1979** *Nature* 30 Aug. 832/2 The stereociliary array [in the herring utricle] consists of rows of stereocilia which decrease in height the further away they are from the kinocilium. **1908** Stereocomparator [see *stereoplotter* below]. **1939** *Geogr. Jrnl.* XCIII. 240 An improved stereocomparator for air triangulation. **1950** *Jrnl. R. Aeronaut. Soc.* LIV. 619/2 In cases where co-ordinate measurements are made in a precise stereocomparator, the prints are made on a non-distorting surface such as sensitised aluminium foil. **1975** J. B. HARLEY *O.S. Maps* i. 11 By means of self-recording stereocomparators precise pairs of measurements of co-ordinates are made on pairs of overlapping aerial photographs. **1970** *Jrnl. Macromol. Sci.: Chem.* A. IV. 1014 A very useful technique for the exploration of the stereocontrol of ionic polymerizations. **1979** *Tetrahedron Lett.* Oct. 3805 Unique stereocontrol in aldolization at C6 of penicillanates through modification of solvent and cation has been observed. **1959** Stereocontrol *v.* [see *STEREOREGULATE *v.*]. **1969** *Jrnl. Amer. Chem. Soc.* XCI. 5675 (*heading*) Stereo-controlled synthesis of prostaglandins $F_{2\alpha}$ and E_2 (*dl*). **1975** *Ibid.* XCVII. 5873 Formylation followed by acidic treatment effects cyclobutyl ring cleavage to an enol lactone which constitutes a net stereocontrolled geminal alkylation with introduction of a one-carbon and a three-carbon chain differentially functionalized. **1945** M. F. GLAESSNER *Princ. Micropalaeont.* v. 96 (*caption*) Stereo-diagram of a segment of *Loftusia persica* Brady. **1979** *Nature* 13 Dec. 681/2 (*caption*) Stereodiagram of three molecules in the crystal lattice as they are stacked along the *c* axis in what looks like a continuous double helix. **1956** *Jrnl. Amer. Chem. Soc.* LXXVIII. 6273/1 The tendency of bromine to adopt the axial orientation in the bromination of an enol would seem to indicate that stereoelectronic control is unusually large in this case since the opposing steric effect is certainly quite large. **1972** *Ibid.* XCIV. 3657/1 It is expected that σ-π conjugation would have similar stereoelectronic requirements to p-π conjugation. **1956** *Ibid.* LXXVIII. 6272/2 Addition reactions to the Δ^6-double bond..take place predominantly from the α- rather than the β-direction despite the fact that these are stereoelectronically controlled. **1978** *Further Perspectives Org. Chem.* (CIBA Found. Symp. New Ser. No. 53) 94 The cyclization step is likely to be stereoelectronically impeded. **1932** *Lancet* 2 Jan. 47/2 The perfection of a stereofluoroscope for use in hospitals is reported. **1942** *Radiology* XXXVIII. 392/1 Stereofluoroscopes continue to gather dust, or go to the junk heap. **1928** *Lancet* 3 Mar. 442/2 The latest development in stereofluoroscopic work. *Ibid.*, The law governing stereofluoroscopy has not been fully recognised. The law stated simply is that angles of vision which the X rays make with the body should be identical with those made by the vision of the observer of the body... Early in the days of X rays the tubes were of a size which rendered stereofluoroscopy impossible. **1964** *Radiology* LXXXII. 125 A test of depth perception in 62 subjects strongly suggested that binocular stereofluoroscopy provided an advantage in the perception of depth over the clues available from motion parallax alone. **1900** DORLAND *Med. Dict.* 637/2 Stereognosis. **1905** A. W. CAMPBELL *Histol. Stud. Localisation Cerebral Function* viii. 205 Damage to this part of the brain is attended by disorder of high and combined forms of sensation, such as the muscle sense and that of stereognosis. **1980** D. JENSEN *Human Nerv. System* xiv. 212/2 Faulty stereognosis provides an early indication of cortical damage. **1894** Stereo-isomer [see *HEXONIC *a.*]. **1938** *Biochem. Jrnl.* XXXII. 1627 The pentose phosphoric acid most readily attacked..is not the *d*-arabinose-5-phosphoric acid..but is the stereoisomeride *d*-ribose-5-phosphoric acid. **1943** *Jrnl. Amer. Chem. Soc.* LXV. 1524/2 Oxidation ..was the only reasonable interpretation six years ago when the stereoisomerization of carotenoids was still unexplored. **1977** *Jrnl. Organometallic Chem.* CXXV. 185 This approach has enabled us to determine the lowest energy (threshold) rearrangement mode occurring in the stereoisomerization of these [β-diketonate] complexes. **1952** *Jrnl. Gen. Physiol.* XXXVI. 306 Some of them [*sc.* carotenoids] stereoisomerize even at room temperature. *Ibid.*, A general procedure for stereoisomerizing carotenoids is to heat them in solution. **1962** L. ZECHMEISTER *Cis-Trans Isomeric Carotenoids* v. 56 An attempt to stereoisomerize β-carotene epoxides..did not afford *cis* compounds but furanoid oxides. *Ibid.* 51 The following ratios of unchanged to stereoisomerized starting material were found in the recovered pigment. **1952** *Jrnl. Gen. Physiol.* XXXVI. 306 The possibility that there exists a stereoisomerizing enzyme—a vitamin A or retinene isomerase. **1956** *Nature* 17 Mar. 516/2 Electron micrographs and stereomicrographs showing the surface characteristics and microfibrillar texture of keratin fibres were exhibited. **1975** J. G. EVANS *Environment Early Man Brit. Isles* i. 10 (*caption*) Stereomicrograph of pollen grains of *Fraxinus excelsior*, ash, × 2570. **1962** *Radiology* LXXIX. 31/1 The image on the output phosphor was viewed through a low-power stereomicroscope. **1978** FRIEDMAN & SANDERS *Princ. Sedimentol.* xiii. 417/2 Cuttings from cable-tool drilling are..examined with a stereomicroscope. **1955** *Jrnl. Chem. Soc.* 3446 The *cis*-nitro-acid..on reduction gives about equal quantities of *cis-* and *trans*-amino acid, thus indicating that some stereomutation occurs during reduction. **1975** *Jrnl. Amer. Chem. Soc.* XCVII. 238/2 Pyrolysis of cyclopropane or its substituted derivatives causes..stereomutation (e.g., *trans* → *cis-cyclopropane*-$1,2\text{-}d_2$). **1972** *Science* 9 June 1116/2 Turnbull's contribution consists chiefly of figuring the Field Museum's Trinity (Albian Cretaceous) mammal teeth by means of stereophotos. **1930** *Geogr. Jrnl.* LXXV. 159 Stereo-photogrammetric methods. **1936** *Ibid.* LXXXVII. 99 To carry out a stereo-photogrammetric examination of the northern aspect and valleys of Mount Everest. **1913** *Engin. News* 27 Mar. 604/2 A method by which the troubles arising in photogrammetric surveys are eliminated is based on the principle of making the necessary measurements on stereoscopic pictures, and is called stereophotogrammetry. **1950** *Engineering* 14 July 28/3 The application of aerial photography and stereo-photogrammetry to large-scale railway surveys. **1980** I. NEWTON in K. B. Atkinson *Devel. Close Range Photogrammetry* I. vi. 129 Stereophotogrammetry has made it possible to analyse the size and shape of the palate in far greater detail than hitherto. **1865** H. SIDGWICK *Let.* Apr. in A. & E. M. Sidgwick *Henry Sidgwick* (1906) iii. 129, I got your stereo-photograph (what is the short for it?) at 113 Rue de Sebastopol. **1902** *Year Bk. Photogr.* 1902 162 The effect described will be at once apparent in the stereo-photograph. **1959** *Observer* 7 June 3/4 To look at your first stereo-photograph can be an experience as climactic as seeing the Mediterranean for the first time. **1980** I. NEWTON in K. B. Atkinson *Devel. Close Range Photogrammetry* I. vi. 127 An analysis of surgically corrected abnormal faces has been undertaken in the USA from stereophotographs taken pre- and post-operatively. **1906** J. A. FLEMER *Elem. Treat. Phototopographic Methods* x. 309 Dr. Pulfrich has devised a stereoplanigraph which is being made by the Carl Zeiss firm in Jena. **1974** P. R. WOLF *Elements of Photogrammetry* xiv. 320 Each projector of the C-8 stereoplanigraph has the customary three angular rotations, but translations are introduced as movements of the reference mirrors. **1908** *Geogr. Jrnl.* XXXI. 544 An instrument.. which makes the plotting of points and the reading of heights nearly automatic. To distinguish it from the stereo-comparator it has been called a stereo-plotter, as it combines the offices of the stereo-comparator and plotting board. **1979** *Photogrammetric Engin. & Remote Sensing* XLV. 802/1 Systemhouse has developed a universal analytical stereoplotter system with the primary theory of operation of an analytical stereoplotter being applied to its fullest extent. **1927** *Geogr. Jrnl.* LXX. 358 (*heading*) An attempt to describe Mr. Wild's stereo-plotting machine—the Autograph. **1975** J. B. HARLEY *O.S. Maps* i. 11 With the 1:10 000 series control points are plotted on a stable plastic sheet... A stereo-plotting machine is then used to derive map and contours, with the operator plotting the detail..in relation to the control points. **1945** *Light Metals* VIII. 269/2 The stereo radiograph, corresponding to a multiplicity of shots from different angles, is produced on a single film, an important economic advantage. **1965** D. N. & M. O. CHESNEY *Radiographic Photogr.* xiii. 319 In order to have perception of depth, various methods are available for viewing stereoradiographs. **1975** *Radiology* CXV. 455/1 Stereo radiographs usually eliminate the problem of matching sources, since the two views are more similar, but they do not always permit accurate 3-D reconstruction. **1936** *Amer. Rev. Tuberculosis* XXXIV. 517 Stereoradiographic examination of the chest on the same day revealed a widely disseminated infiltrative process throughout the right lung field. **1965** D. N. & M. O. CHESNEY *Radiographic Photogr.* xiii. 319 The anteroposterior projection of the sacro-iliac joints made stereoradiographically. *Ibid.* 317 In stereoradiography a pair of radiographs is taken. **1968** *Official Gaz.* (U.S. Patent Office) 12 Mar. TM 69/2 Cambridge Instrument Company Limited, London... *Stereoscan* for electron microscopes and parts and fittings therefor... First use on or about Mar. 31, 1966. **1970** AMBROSE & EASTY *Cell Biol.* xi. 377 The form of the ruffles is clearly seen in the Stereoscan picture. *Ibid.*, The Stereoscan allows us to see these contacts directly. **1970** *New Scientist* 27 Aug. 419/2 We were able to confirm using the stereoscan microscope that, as skin ages, the amount of extension possible in the fibre network is progressively limited. **1973** *Trade Marks Jrnl.* 11 Apr. 701/2 *Stereoscan*... Stereoscopic scanning electron microscopes and parts and fittings therefore included in Class 9. Cambridge Instrument Company Limited..; manufacturers. **1974** *Physics Bull.* Mar. 103/1 Many types of instrument are discussed, from the earliest use of a single lens to the present day field-ion and stereoscan electron microscopes. **1979** *Nature* 1 Mar. 102/2 Plates, including stereoscans, of pollen grains and spores. **1968** *Times* 1 Nov. 6/8 The idea is to carry automated photographic mapping to the full extent possible and to use stereo-viewing for interpretation. **1973** *Nature* 17 Aug. 413/1 Recently, direct stereoviewing has been developed for use in the scanning microscope.

ste·reoblock. *Chem.* [ad. It. *stereoblocchi* (G. Natta et al. 1957, in *Chim. e Industr.* XXXIX. 276/2): see STEREO- and BLOCK *sb.*] A segment of a polymer chain possessing stereoregularity. Also *attrib.*, as *stereoblock polymer*, a polymer the chains of which contain such segments.

1957 *Chem. Abstr.* LI. 12536 New linear high polymers of α-olefins are described which are distinguished by the presence within the macromol. of chain portions of different steric configurations. Designated 'stereoblock' polymers.., these differ from the block copolymers in that the former are obtained by polymerization of a single type of monomer. **1959** GAYLORD & MARK *Linear & Stereoregular Addition Polymers* 483 As originally defined by Natta, stereoblock polymers of α-olefins are polymers consisting of macromolecules containing crystallizable segments having isotactic structure and noncrystallizable segments. Actually, these macromolecules may consist either of both isotactic and atactic segments or of adjacent isotactic segments having different steric configuration... In practice, amorphous polymers, considered as atactic, may contain very short stereoblocks. **1979** C. H. BAMFORD in R. N. Haward *Developments in Polymerisation* II. 253 The 'hopping' of a propagating chain from an isotactic to a syndiotactic matrix (or vice versa) could give rise to a stereoblock daughter polymer. **1980** *Jrnl. Polymer Sci.: Polymer Physics Ed.* XVIII. 630 The length and the type of junctions between isotactic stereoblocks affects the crystallization of polypropylene.

stereochemistry. Add: Also, the stereochemical properties *of* something; a stereochemical configuration or arrangement. [After G. *stereochemie* (V. Meyer 1890, in *Ber. d. Deut. Chem. Ges.* XXIII. 568), *stereochemisch* adj. (Auwers & Meyer 1888, in *Ibid.* XXI. 789).]

1905 *Rep. Brit. Assoc. Adv. Sci. 1904* 169 The stereochemistry of nitrogen has..attracted considerable attention. **1969** *Jrnl. Leeds Univ. Union Chem. Soc.* XI. 43 The important stereochemistries are octahedral.., tetrahedral.., and square planar. **1972** *Nature* 21 Jan. 180/3 Nyholm's researches in transition metal chemistry..were particularly concerned with metal carbonyl, metal–metal bonded systems, unusual stereochemistries and..the reactivity of coordinated organic groups. **1972** DEPUY & CHAPMAN *Molec. Reactions & Photochem.* vi. 84 It is often observed that related thermal and photochemical processes, while both stereospecific, give products with differing stereochemistry.

Hence **stereoche·mically** *adv.*, as regards the relative spatial positions of atoms; **stereo-che·mist,** an expert or specialist in stereochemistry.

1890 *Jrnl. Chem. Soc.* LVIII. II. 970 The authors regard the existence of stereochemically isomeric azo-compounds as doubtful. **1935** TIPSON & STILLER in Harrow & Sherwin *Textbk. Biochem.* ii. 84 Where the two monoses are not identical, four stereochemically different disaccharides are theoretically capable of existence. **1937** *Nature* 10 July 49/2 The stereochemist is catered for in the precise directions given for the synthesis and complete optical resolution of that useful stereochemical agent, α-phenylethylamine. **1963** *Times* 23 Jan. 15/1 From there he went in 1905 to the University of Zurich to work with Alfred Werner, the distinguished stereochemist. **1974** GILL & WILLIS *Pericyclic Reactions* iii. 75 The stereochemically distinguishable modes of addition on a single olefin component.

stereogram[2] (ste·rio-, stiə·riogræm). [f. *STEREO *a.* + *RADIO)GRAM[2].] An instrument for stereophonic reproduction of sound combining a radio and gramophone in a single cabinet; a stereo radiogram. Cf. *STEREO *sb.*[3] 2.

1958 *Daily Mail* 27 Aug. 3/5 Some stereograms have both amplifiers and speakers inside one cabinet. **1976** *Gramophone* Nov. 914/1 Continuing their tradition of manufacturing single-unit stereograms, Thorn Consumer Electronics have just announced the latest in the line. **1977** M. JANCATH *Seatag* II. xi. 122 The stereogram in the corner stopped.

stereology (steri-, stiəri,ǫ·lŏdʒi). [f. STEREO- + -LOGY.] The science of the reconstruction of three-dimensional structures from two-dimensional sections of them.

1963 *1st Internat. Congr. Stereology* ii. 2 With the aid of a Greek pocket dictionary we [*sc.* Hennig & Elias] coined the word Stereology. **1967** *Proc. 2nd Internat. Congr. Stereology* 1 Stereology is three-dimensional interpretation of flat images or extrapolation from two to three-dimensional space. *Ibid.* 2 An announcement in a few journals brought 11 scientists together on the Feldberg Mountain in the Black Forest 11–12 May, 1961. The word stereology was then coined and the International Society for Stereology was founded. **1974** *Nature* 29 Nov. 412/1 Stereology has revealed that there is a continuous increase in mitochondrial volume during the cycle. **1977** N. T. James in Meek & Elder *Analytical & Quantitative Methods Microsc.* 20 An absolute requirement of stereology s that the test samples should be representative of the test tissue.

Hence **stereolo·gical** *a.*, of, pertaining to, or by stereology; **stereolo·gically** *adv.*; **stereo·-logist,** one skilled in stereology.

1963 *1st Internat. Congr. Stereology* v. 3 The..arithmetical and geometrical principles which I now assume to be those generally employed by nature and therefore of common interest to stereologists. *Ibid.* vi. 21 The stereological field includes all the investigations in respect to the three-dimensional structures. **1972** *Science* 12 May 655/1 Like all stereology..stereological shape determination is a matter of geometrical probability. *Ibid.*, Simple shapes can be identified stereologically by measuring the length and width of each profile of a feature in section, classifying the quotients length/width of many profiles, and applying mathematical rules elaborated by the reviewer. **1975** *Nature* 10 July 151/2 Articles on high resolution, dark-field microscopy, in-focus phase contrast and stereological techniques. **1981** *McGraw-Hill Yearbk. Sci. & Technol.* 376/2 This relationship has been defined stereologically by Eq. (5).

stereometer[1]. Add: **3.** *Cartography.* Any of various instruments for measuring the parallax of a feature depicted in a stereoscopic pair of aerial photographs.

1911 *Encycl. Brit.* XXV. 900/1 The stereometer may be regarded as a modification of the stereocomparator. **1940** C. A. Hart *Air Photogr.* vi. 178 In order that the stereometer may be moved easily while maintaining a direction parallel to the base-line of the pair of photographs, a parallel-guidance mechanism is often fitted. **1974** P. R. Wolf *Elem. Photogrammetry* viii. 150 Parallaxes of points may be measured stereoscopically. This method employs a stereoscope in conjunction with an instrument called a parallax bar and also..a stereometer.

stereometric, *a.* Add: Hence **stereome·trically** *adv.*

1890 in Webster. **1928** B. J. Leggett *Theory & Practice Radiol.* III. ix. 430 If..we radiograph this pelvis stereometrically and then reconstruct the pelvis in space by the method above, we are in a position to directly and accurately measure this diameter by means of suitable orthographic apparatus. **1972** *Science* 9 June 1136/1 The relative volume of extracellular space was estimated stereometrically.

stereophonic (ster*i*o-, stɪ̆ᵊr*i*ofǫ·nik), *a.* [f. Stereo- + Phonic *a.* (*sb.*).] Giving the impression of a spatial distribution in reproduced sound; *spec.* employing two or more channels of transmission and reproduction so that the sound may seem to reach the listener from any of a range of directions.

1927 *Wireless World* 26 Jan. 117/2 A marked improvement in quality of reproduction will be noticed, due to the phase-difference introduced by the distance between loud-speaker and phones. This phase-difference also varies with the frequency of the sounds reproduced, and thus a constantly varying difference in phase produces the stereophonic effect so superior to ordinary reproduction. **1940** *Nature* 3 Aug. 174/1 Demonstrations of the stereophonic reproduction of music and speech were given at the Carnegie Hall. **1953** *Sun* (Baltimore) 3 Aug. 16/7 Many picture men believe in the long-range possibilities of theater TV, but they also think that standardization of stereoscopic, stereophonic, wide screen equipment will have to come first. **1957** *Observer* 8 Sept. 10/2 An incredibly lush stereophonic music score exploits all the Hollywood clichés and adds some of its own. **1958** *Times* 14 Jan. 8/3 The B.B.C. last night carried out an experiment in the London area in stereophonic sound transmission. **1958** *Listener* 16 Oct. 605/1 Recently stereophonic disks have been introduced which have brought 'stereo' within reach of a much wider public. **1969** *Islander* (Victoria, B.C.) 6 July 5/2 Travellers enjoy a movie and stereophonic music through individual ear phones. **1977** *Rep. Comm. Future of Broadcasting* 13 in *Parl. Papers 1967–77* (Cmnd. 6753) VI. 1 The BBC.. introduced stereophonic broadcasting in 1966. Stereo was also provided by the IBA's local radio VHF transmissions.

Hence **stereopho·nically** *adv.*, in a stereophonic manner; as regards, or by means of, stereophony.

1940 *Nature* 3 Aug. 174/1 A symphony concert produced in Philadelphia was transmitted over telephone wires to Washington and there reproduced stereophonically. **1958** *Times* 4 Aug. 10/2 After a fly has been buzzing stereophonically round her..a flash-back considerately takes over the task of explanation. **1969** *Amateur Photographer* 16 July 75/1 Testing for stereo should be done with recordings which have been proved to be satisfactory themselves stereophonically. **1972** K. Bonfiglioli *Don't point that Thing at Me* ii. 16 Martland..busied himself coaxing a few more decibels out of the stereo equipment... The Flying Scotsman whooped stereophonically for a level-crossing. **1977** *Gramophone* Sept. 504/2 You cannot distinguish the players stereophonically but quality and playing are excellent.

stereopho·nics, *sb. pl.* [f. prec.: see -ic 2.] Stereophonic techniques; stereophonic sound.

1958 *Punch* 22 Jan. 153/1 As yet there has been no talk of marrying these clever stereophonics with the echo-chamber, but it is bound to come. **1973** D. Francis *Slay-Ride* v. 65 Arne..switched Beethoven on again fortissimo... I sat resignedly..while the stereophonics shook the foundations. **1975** *Listener* 2 Oct. 448/1 Getting your ears in phase with different sound sources, otherwise called stereophonics.

stereophony (ster*i*-, stɪ̆ᵊr*i*,ǫ·fŏni). [f. as prec.: see -y[3].] Stereophonic reproduction; stereophonic sound.

1950 *Wireless World* Sept. 327/1 The first broadcast of stereophony, the system in which sources of sound are restored to their relative positions in space, took place in France on June 19th, 1950. **1958** *Manch. Guardian* 30 June 5/3 Even on monaural discs the equipment..gives a remarkable impression of stereophony. **1972** *Daily Tel.* 31 Jan. 7/5 The BBC started experiments with stereophony in 1926.

stereopsis (ster*i*-, stɪ̆ᵊr*i*,ǫ·psis). [f. Gr. στερε-ός solid (see Stereo-) + ὄψις power of sight.] The ability to perceive depth and relief by stereoscopic vision.

1911 Stedman *Med. Dict.* 826/1 *Stereopsis,* stereoscopic vision. **1920** *Arch. Opthalmol.* XLIX. 64 When the facts are known it is quite possible that visual tests will not stop with measuring the acuity of each eye and the color sense, but that a certain standard of stereopsis will be required. **1961** *Lancet* 22 July 168/2 No stereopsis has been demonstrated in any of these patients. **1972** *Sci. Amer.* Aug. 86/3 By providing very precise localization of objects in visual space, stereopsis can be regarded as the *raison d'être* of binocular vision.

Hence **stereo·ptic** *a.*; **stereo·ptically** *adv.*, with an appearance of depth; stereoscopically.

1931 *Arch. Ophthalmol.* VI. 139 Stereoptic reactions of a grade above the lowest are observable in ordinary fishes, but the lowest grade is probably not represented in any surviving species. **1972** *Sci. Amer.* Apr. 65/3 One can also feed the three-dimensional coordinates into a computer and obtain simple ball-and-stick drawings that can be viewed stereoptically, enabling one to visualize the folded chain of the protein in three dimensions. *Ibid.* Aug. 120/2 No one believes that the anatomical retina could possibly be given information on any large scale from the mind; there are few, if any, outgoing pathways. Therefore, Julesz conjectures, the eidetic image is formed later than the image on the retina but earlier than the stereoptic image, perhaps much earlier. **1976** *Billings* (Montana) *Gaz.* 24 June 16-A/1 More pictures were taken Wednesday on Viking's fourth pass over the site, Chryse, by Viking's twin cameras. They were lined up to photograph overlapping strips which can be viewed stereoptically for a three-dimensional effect.

stereoregular (ster*i*o-, stɪ̆ᵊr*i*ore·gi*ŭ*lăɹ), *a.* *Chem.* Also **stereo-regular.** [f. Stereo- + Regular *a.*] Of a polymer: having each substituent atom or group on the main polymer chain oriented in the same manner on the chain with respect to the neighbouring atoms or groups. Of a reaction: giving rise to such a polymer.

1959 Gaylord & Mark *Linear & Stereoregular Addition Polymers* 473 The most significant new developments have involved the successful preparation of stereoregular polymers from monomers..which previously had only yielded atactic polymers. **1961** *Industr. Chemist* Feb. 74/2 Although stereoregular polymers prepared with Ziegler-type catalysts are now of considerable commercial interest, research is continuing in attempts to obtain stereo-specific polymers by other, and perhaps less complex, catalysts. **1962** *Engineering* 12 Jan. 57/1 The increasing commercial availability of the 'stereo-regular' synthetic rubbers. **1971** *Sci. Amer.* Dec. 50/3 One striking example of the ability of catalysts to perform highly selective molecular alterations is the stereoregular polymerization of olefins pioneered by Karl Ziegler and Giulio Natta. **1979** C. H. Bamford in R. N. Haward *Developments in Polymerisation* II. 251 Stereoregular poly(methyl methacrylate) can function, under suitable conditions, as a template for the polymerisation of the monomer.

Hence **ste:reoregula·rity.**

1959 *Jrnl. Polymer Sci.* XLI. 80 A decrease in polymerization temperature could result in increased regularity as a result of a simultaneous improvement in stereoregularity, linearity, and head-to-tail structure. **1964** *Ibid.* II. A. 4642 Stereoregularity was noticed in acetaldehyde polymerization only when solid boron-trifluoride-etherate was used as the initiator. **1976** *Makromol. Chemie* CLXXVII. 1475 The four catalyst systems employed for the *cis* polymerization..give polymers with a different degree of stereoregularity. This could depend on a different stereoregulating power of the catalysts. **1979** *Jrnl. Polymer Sci.: Polymer Chem. Ed.* XVII. 2022 There was no significant difference between the stereoregularities of the polymers obtained with cesium naphthalene and fluorenylcesium as catalyst. This result indicates that the difference in initiator anions ..did not affect stereoregulation.

stereoregulate (ster*i*o-, stɪ̆ᵊr*i*ore·gi*ŭ*lēⁱt), *v.* *Chem.* [f. Stereo- + Regulate *v.*] *trans.* To cause (a polymerization or its product) to be stereoregular. So **ste:reore·gulated** *ppl. a.*, **-re·gulating** *vbl. sb.* and *ppl. a.*; **ste:reoregula·tion.**

1959 Gaylord & Mark *Linear & Stereoregular Addition Polymers* 476 Even the application of free radicals as initiators does not rule out the formation of stereoregulated addition polymers. *Ibid.* 478 The propagation reaction will be stereoregulated or stereocontrolled and the polymer will be tactic, which means that the individual monomers in the chain will overwhelmingly be added in one of the different possible ways and the resulting macromolecule will display stereospecificity, i.e., a high degree of internal orderliness. *Ibid.*, Experience..has shown that stereoregulating effects are strongest in the case of Ziegler-type catalysts. *Ibid.* 479 It appears that a methyl group at the alpha carbon atom is favorable for stereoregulation. **1961** *Industr. Chemist* Feb. 73/1 (*heading*) Nature of the stereoregulating catalysts. **1962** E. L. Eliel *Stereochem. Carbon Compounds* xv. 448 The 'stereoregulated' (i.e. isotactic or syndiotactic) polymers have higher densities, higher melting points, and lower solubility than the atactic polymers. **1976, 1979** Stereo-regulating, -regulation [see *stereoregularity]. **1979** C. H. Bamford in R. N. Haward *Developments in Polymerisation* II. 249 The stereoregulating influence of added prepolymers has been shown to be more pronounced at lower temperatures.

stereoselective (ste:r*i*o-, stɪ̆ᵊ:r*i*osīle·ktiv), *a.* *Chem.* [f. Stereo- + Selective *a.*] Of a reaction: producing a particular stereoisomeric form of the product preferentially, irrespective of the configuration of the reactant; = *stereospecific *a.* 1 a.

Orig. (quot. 1957) = *stereospecific *a.* 2.

1957 *Jrnl. Amer. Chem. Soc.* LXXIX. 1595/2 Comparable *trans* eliminations in open-chain systems are stereoselective. **1959** *Ibid.* LXXXI. 110/1 A stereospecific process is one in which the configuration of the product is related to that of the reactant... A stereoselective process is one in which there is no relationship between the configuration of the reactant and that of product but one in which there is a definite driving force for forming one of the possible stereoisomeric products. **1962** E. L. Eliel *Stereochem. Carbon Compounds* xv. 436 All stereospecific processes are stereoselective, but not all stereoselective processes are stereospecific. For example, the low-temperature free-radical addition of hydrogen bromide to the 2-bromo-2-butenes..is both stereospecific and stereoselective in that the cis olefin gives *meso*-2,3-dibromobutane whereas the trans olefin gives the *dl*-dibromide. At higher temperature the reaction is still stereoselective (formation of 75% *dl* isomer to 25% meso isomer) but no longer stereospecific; both olefins now give the same product mixture. **1968** [see *stereospecific *a.* 2]. **1979** *Canad. Jrnl. Chem.* LVII. 646/1 Our synthesis [of sucrose] was predicated upon the stereoselective methoxybromination of the diene 8.

Hence **ste:reosele·ctively** *adv.*; **ste:reosele·ction, ste:reoselecti·vity,** the property or fact of being stereoselective.

1956 *Jrnl. Amer. Chem. Soc.* LXXVIII. 1171/1 The decreased stereoselectivity of ketonization..in the 2-methyl-3-phenylindanone system as compared with the 1-phenyl-2-benzoylcyclohexane situation. **1957** *Ibid.* LXXIX. 1594/2 The fact that eliminations from I and II ..occur stereoselectively rules out the possibility of an intermediate carbanion of any but very short half-life. **1968** S. I. Miller in V. Gold *Adv. in Physical Org. Chem.* VI. 186 We shall then describe a number of causes of stereoselection associated with bonding, steric, thermodynamic [etc.] factors. **1974** Gill & Willis *Pericyclic Reactions* vi. 191 Likewise the *trans*-alkene is formed in the other processes with fairly high stereoselectivity. **1979** *Tetrahedron Lett.* 4867 (*heading*) Stereoselection in the $AlCl_3$-catalysed ene additions of chloral to 1,2-dialkyl ethylenes. **1979** *Canad. Jrnl. Chem.* LVII. 646/1 A new synthesis of sucrose in which all of the steps involved proceeded with complete stereoselectivity. **1980** *Chem. in Brit.* XVI. 518/1 He was able to put one of the carbon-carbon bonds in place stereoselectively creating two of the six contiguous chiral centres on the left hand side of the molecule.

stereospecific (ste:r*i*o-, stɪ̆ᵊ:r*i*ospĕsi·fik), *a.* *Chem.* Also **stereo-specific.** [f. Stereo- + Specific *a.*] **1. a.** Of a reaction: = *stereoselective *a.* Also of a catalyst: causing a reaction to be (more) stereoselective.

1949 *Jrnl. Amer. Chem. Soc.* LXXI. 3866/2 The reaction giving rise to the acetates was at least 90% stereospecific since the ratio of the yield of the acid phthalate of racemate I to the yield of the acid phthalates of other alcohols was ten to one. Stereospecificity of even a higher degree was found in the II series. **1957** [see *atactic *a.* 3]. **1958** *Chem. Abstr.* LII. 1106 (*heading*) Isotactic and other stereospecific polymers. **1959** *Times Rev. Industry* Feb. 57/1 Using the stereospecific catalysts developed in Germany by K. Ziegler, Professor Natta in Milan had succeeded in producing, from propylene gas, useful polymers which he characterized as isotactic. **1960** *Times* 19 July (Royal Soc. Tercentenary Suppl.) p. xiv/3 The past decade has seen the emergence of various stereospecific syntheses. **1966** *Petroleum Handbk.* (ed. 5) 215/2 There are two possibilities in building up the polymer chain [of propylene]; the methyl groups can be situated either at random on both sides of the chain or on one side of the chain only (stereospecific polymerization). **1968** [see sense 2 below]. **1978** J. A. Brydson *Rubber Chem.* i. 8 Stereospecific catalyst systems..led to the availability of..rubbers with a much more controlled molecular architecture than had been obtained before. **1979** *Jrnl. Org. Chem.* XLIV. 3374 The determination of the configuration at C-24 of the revised structure of oogoniol..was accomplished by the stereospecific synthesis of the model compounds..which contain the oogoniol side chain.

b. Of a polymer, esp. rubber: = *stereoregular *a.*

1959 *Times* 27 Apr. (Rubber Industry Suppl.) p. ii/7 Polymer chemists have long yearned to synthetize such stereo-specific polymers found to occur so prevalently in Nature. **1961** [see *stereoregular *a.*]. **1966** *Petroleum Handbk.* (ed. 5) 224/1 In the last few years..a new family of synthetic rubbers—the stereospecific rubbers—have been developed. **1974** J. Ford-Smith tr. *Heinisch's Dict. Rubber* 447/1 Examples of stereospecific polymers are cis-1:4-polyisoprene and cis-1:4-polybutadiene.

2. Of a reaction or process: yielding a product, or having a rate, that depends on the particular stereoisomeric form of the starting material.

1959, 1962 [see *STEREOSELECTIVE *a.*]. **1968** I. L. FINAR *Org. Chem.* (ed. 4). II iv. 126 The term stereospecific reaction has been used in the same sense as stereoselective reaction, but now the tendency is to restrict the use of stereospecific to a reaction in which different stereoisomers produce different products or act at different rates. **1970** J. H. QUASTEL in Ehrenpreis & Solnitsky *Neurosci. Res.* III. 15 Stereospecific effects are also observed in cerebral amino acid exchange reactions; for example, elevated cerebral L-lysine is more effective than elevated cerebral D-lysine in increasing L-lysine exchange. **1978** *Biochem. Pharmacol.* XXVII. 653/1 The finding that the R-enantiomer of gliflumide binds less strongly [than the S-enantiomer] indicates that antidiabetic drugs are bound to plasma by a stereospecific process.

Hence **ste:reospeci·fically** *adv.*, in a stereospecific manner: **ste:resopecifi·city**, the property or state of being stereospecific.

1949 Stereospecificity [see sense 1 a above]. **1955** *Jrnl. Amer. Chem. Soc.* LXXVII. 4567/1 *cis*-Propenyllithium prepared from *cis*-2-bromopropene with lithium in ether.. reacts stereospecifically with benzaldehyde..to give..the alcohol with the same configuration as that of the starting bromide. **1965** PHILLIPS & WILLIAMS *Inorg. Chem.* I. x. 383 Other monomers can be stereo-specifically polymerized. **1970** *Jrnl. Polymer Sci.* A. VIII. 988 The stereospecificity of these catalysts is remarkable since they yield polybutadienes with a very high 1,4 content. **1970** J. H. QUASTEL in Ehrenpreis & Solnitsky *Neurosci. Res.* III. 15 Studies of the stereospecificity of amino acid uptake in vivo have shown..that the L-amino acid usually penetrates the brain to a greater extent than the corresponding D-isomer. **1979** *Jrnl. Chem. Soc.: Chem. Comm.* 918/2 Oxidation of labelled hexa-1,5-dienes with permanganate generates four new chiral centres with complete stereospecificity. *Ibid.* 920/2 The oxidative cycloaddition constitutes a method for the formation, stereospecifically, and in a single step, of four chiral centres from an achiral, acyclic reactant.

stereotactic (steri*o*-, stiᵊri*o*tæ·ktik), *a.* [f. STEREO- + TACTIC *a.*² (*sb.*²).] †**1.** *Biol.* = THIGMOTACTIC *a.* *Obs. rare.*

1902 *Q. Jrnl. Microsc. Sci.* XLVI. 171 There appear to me to be yet two possible explanations of the penetration [of sperm into the egg]: (1) it is due to reaction to a stereotactic stimulus; (2) it is purely mechanical.

2. *Biol.* and *Med.* = *STEREOTAXIC *a.*

1954 *Amer. Jrnl. Roentgenol.* LXXI. 441/2 A new type of stereotactic instrument for use in man. **1961** *Lancet* 2 Sept. 552/1 Stereotactic operations for parkinsonism. **1976** *New Scientist* 26 Feb. 427/2 Some of the patients will undergo stereotactic brain surgery, which enables lesions to be placed very precisely in the required parts of the brain.

Hence **stereota·ctically** *adv.*

1934 in WEBSTER. **1949** *Jrnl. Neurophysiol.* XII. 371 Electrolytic lesions were made..at a site determined stereotactically. **1966** *Arch. Neurol.* XIV. 334/2 Cross and Green, utilizing microelectrodes placed stereotactically in the hypothalamus of rabbits, studied the activity of single units, presumably single cells.

stereotaxic (steri*o*-, stiᵊri*o*tæ·ksik), *a.* *Biol.* and *Med.* [f. STEREO- + TAX(IS + -IC.] Involving or designed for the accurate three-dimensional positioning and movement of objects inside the brain.

1908 HORSLEY & CLARKE in *Brain* XXXI. 63 The foundation of the stereotaxic instrument is a rigid quadrilateral rectangular frame..the ends of which..can be approximated by joints which slide on the lateral bars. **1919** S. PAGET *Sir V. Horsley* 189 R. H. Clarke..also devised a stereotaxic apparatus, probably the most complex of all the mathematical instruments of physiology. **1935** *Arch. Neurol. & Psychiatry* XXXIV. 162 With the aid of the Horsley-Clarke stereotaxic instrument, lesions were placed in..the hypothalamus in forty adult cats. **1969** *New Scientist* 30 Jan. 230/1 The stereotaxic.. procedure reaches deep areas of the brain. **1971** *Nature* 8 Jan. 131/1 The brain was exposed from above and a fine knife lowered between the two hemispheres until the blade was at the correct stereotaxic setting for the supraoptic commissure. **1971** 'D. HALLIDAY' *Dolly & Doctor Bird* xvi. 247 Nothing short of stereotaxic surgery will ever obliterate the events of..that night.

Hence **stereota·xically** *adv.*

1964 *Jrnl. Neurophysiol.* XXVII. 754 Electrolytic lesions produced by passing 3-mA anodal d.c. for 10 sec. through a stereotaxically guided stainless steel electrode with 1 mm. bared at the tip. **1979** *Nature* 4 Jan. 52/1 I.c. cannulae (o.d. 0·6 mm) were implanted stereotaxically in male Wistar rats.

stereotaxis (steri*o*-, stiᵊri*o*tæ·ksis). *Biol.* [f. STEREO- + TAXIS.] †**1.** *Biol.* = THIGMOTAXIS. *Obs. rare.*

1897 C. B. DAVENPORT *Exper. Morphol.* I. iv. 105 (*heading*) Effect of molar agents in determining the direction of locomotion—thigmotaxis (stereotaxis) and rheotaxis. **1902** *Q. Jrnl. Microsc. Sci.* XLVI. 175 The passage of the spermatozoa through the gelatinous coat..is more or less in a radial direction as regards the egg... The phenomenon is possibly due to stereotaxis, but a purely mechanical explanation seems to the author more probable.

2. *Biol.* and *Med.* Also **ste·reotaxy.** Stereotaxic surgery.

1959 SCHALTENBRAND & BAILEY (*title*) Einführung in die stereotaktischen Operationen. Introduction to stereotaxis. **1959** L. V. AMADOR et al. in *Ibid.* I. 5/2 Most of the childrens [*sic*] brains were discarded because at the present stage stereotaxy will most likely be applied to adults only. **1974** C. B. T. ADAMS in R. M. Kirk et al. *Surgery* xiv. 284 This may be done by 'bimedial leucotomy' cutting the white matter under direct vision from above or by undercutting the orbital part of the frontal cortex from below (by open operation or by stereotaxis). **1974** *Lancet* 13 July 106/1 (*heading*) Stereotaxy for obesity.

stereotype, *sb.* Add: **3. b.** A preconceived and oversimplified idea of the characteristics which typify a person, situation, etc.; an attitude based on such a preconception. Also, a person who appears to conform closely to the idea of a type.

1922 W. LIPPMAN *Public Opinion* vi. 93 A stereotype may be so consistently and authoritatively transmitted in each generation from parent to child that it seems almost like a biological fact. **1935** G. W. ALLPORT in C. Murchison *Handbk. Social Psychol.* xvii. 809 Attitudes which result in gross oversimplifications of experience and in prejudgements...are commonly called biases, prejudices, or stereotypes. **1948** KRECH & CRUTCHFIELD *Theory & Probl. Social Psychol.* II. v. 171 The concept of stereotype ..refers to two different things. (1)..a tendency for a given belief to be widespread in a society... (2)..a tendency for a belief to be oversimplified in content and unresponsive to the objective facts. **1960** T. HUGHES *Lupercal* 42 Who lived at the top end of our street Was a Mafeking stereotype, ageing. **1968** W. E. LAMBERT et al. in J. A. Fishman *Readings Sociol. of Lang.* 487 American students of English-speaking backgrounds who are in the process of studying the French language have a generally negative set of stereotypes about the basic personality characteristics of French-speaking people. **1974** *Howard Jrnl.* XIV. 102 The stereotypes which society has of the offender, are quickly matched by stereotypes which many offenders create of society. **1981** *Church Times* 23 Oct. 9/1 The neatly dressed unmarried lady (never without handbag)..is definitely not the narrow stereotype our media would have us think she is.

c. *Zool.* A stereotyped action or series of actions performed by an animal (see *STEREOTYPED *ppl. a.* c).

1966 R. A. HINDE *Animal Behaviour* xxiii. 389 In captivity animals often develop behaviour stereotypes or tics which are repeated monotonously. **1971** *Sci. Amer.* June 117/1 Although subordinate males had no chance to mate with hens at the display grounds, they did perform mock matings... Mounting a pile of dry cow manure or a log or simply squatting on the ground, they would go through the stereotype of mating actions: treading the object, fluttering their wings, lowering their tail and even in some cases ejaculating.

stereotyped, *ppl. a.* Add: **b.** Also *spec.* in *Psychol.* (see quot. 1934).

1934 H. C. WARREN *Dict. Psychol.* 262/2 *Stereotyped* (*responses*), characterizing certain responses which are always performed in substantially the same manner. **1950** T. WIESENGRUND-ADORNO et al. *Authoritarian Personality* IV. xvi. 627 He..personalizes his own stereotyped hostility. **1957** [see *CONSUMMATORY *a.* 2]. **1968** A. STORR *Human Aggression* ii. 11 This mechanism is easily set off, and, like other emotional responses, it is stereotyped and, in this sense, 'instinctive'.

c. *Zool.* Of an animal's action or behaviour: repeated though serving no obvious purpose.

1934 E. S. RUSSELL *Behaviour of Animals* i. 8 Their [*sc.* chaffinches'] behaviour is mainly instinctive, independent of previous experience, and to a considerable extent stereotyped and invariable. **1950** G. SIRCOM tr. *Hediger's Wild Animals in Captivity* viii. 88 M. Holtzapfel ..was able..to remove a long standing stereotyped movement in an armadillo..kept on a slippery and therefore unbiological floor, by providing a layer of earth ten inches deep. **1970** R. A. & B. M. MAIER *Compar. Animal Behavior* xvii. 356 Stereotyped movements displayed during courtship can evolve out of general movement patterns.

Hence **ste·reotypedness,** the quality or state of being stereotyped.

1977 *Spare Rib* June 37/1 The visual equivalents tend to have a journalistic stereotypedness about them. **1979** *Trans. Philol. Soc.* 140 We also learn a good deal about.. live Old Persian speech, many features of which, owing to the wretchedly small number of OP inscriptions and the stereotypedness of most of them, have remained hitherto well beyond our reach.

stereotypical (steri*o*-, stiᵊri*o*ti·pikăl), *a.* [f. STEREOTYPE *sb.* + -ICAL.] Of, pertaining to, or resembling a stereotype (sense *3 b). Also *spec.* in *Psychol.*, designating behaviour which is repeated without variation irrespective of the particular circumstances. Cf. STEREOTYPIC *a.*

1949 *Commentary* July 41/2 The stereotypical Negro, the unstinting giver. **1950** T. WIESENGRUND-ADORNO et al. *Authoritarian Personality* IV. xix. 747 Only by identifying stereotypical traits in modern humans..can the pernicious tendency towards all-pervasive classification.. be challenged. **1957** P. LAFITTE *Person in Psychol.* v. 50 Co-operation on a ground of stereotypical distrust is not the same as co-operation on a ground of confidence. **1968** S. STUCKEY in A. Chapman *New Black Voices* (1972) 439 Small wonder we have been saddled with so many stereotypical treatments of slave thought and behavior. **1975** *Nature* 25 Dec. 750/1 Furthermore, a similar class of stereotypical behaviour is elicited by the DA agonist apomorphine. **1981** *Times Lit. Suppl.* 29 May 602/1 It boasts some fine performances and some stereotypical Allen dialogue.

stereotypically, *adv.* Add: (*c*) so as to constitute a stereotype (sense 3 b); in a stereotypical manner; (*d*) *Zool.*, as a stereotyped action.

1950 T. WIESENGRUND-ADORNO et al. *Authoritarian Personality* I. iii. 98 The inner conflict is replaced by a new conflict between groups: the stereotypically moral 'we' and the stereotypically immoral 'they'. **1950** G. SIRCOM tr. *Hediger's Wild Animals in Captivity* viii. 76 The path stereotypically followed by a dingo. **1975** *Daily Tel.* 19 Nov. 14/3 Do all minority faces look stereotypically alike or are they depicted as genuine individuals? **1977** *Time* 26 Dec. 40/1 A throughly Episcopal church in Darien, Conn., an almost stereotypically proper and affluent Northeastern suburb. **1980** *Times* 3 June 11/6 The Nordic countries, which we might stereotypically expect to be sober and/or tormented, are just that.

stereotyping, *vbl. sb.* Add: **3.** *Zool.* = *STEREOTYPY 3.

1950 G. SIRCOM tr. *Hediger's Wild Animals in Captivity* viii. 76 This stereotyping is not serious, yet it shows clearly enough that the animals's surroundings need enrichment. **1967** *Animal Behaviour* XV. 64 There were no significant differences between any of the groups in spot-picking, route-tracing, or total stereotyping.

stereotypy. Add: **2.** (Further examples.)

1934 H. C. WARREN *Dict. Psychol.* 262/2 *Stereotypy*, a pathological phenomenon consisting in the endless repetition of fragmentary or apparently senseless words, apparently useless movements, or of certain postures. **1948** [see *CATATONIC *a.*]. **1976** M. HAMILTON *Fish's Schizophrenia* (ed. 2) iii. 58 A stereotypy is a movement which is not goal-directed and which is carried out in a uniform way, but some mannerisms which are abnormal exaggerations of expressive movements may be confused with stereotypies; however they are not executed in such a rigid way.

3. *Zool.* The frequent repetition by an animal of an action that serves no obvious purpose.

1934 E. S. RUSSELL *Behaviour of Animals* v. 98 Examples of this stereotypy or rigidity of instinctive behaviour. **1967** *Animal Behaviour* XV. 63/2 In this stereotypy, a bird would repeatedly touch the tip or side of the bill to a particular spot. **1981** *Ibid.* XXIX. 4/1 Inappropriate and often perseverant stereotypy can be elicited in many animals by raising them in abnormal and restricted environments.

4. *gen.* The state or quality of being stereotyped (sense b).

1950 T. WIESENGRUND-ADORNO et al. *Authoritarian Personality* I. iii. 94 One striking characteristic of the imagery in anti-Semitic ideology is its *stereotypy*. **1973** O. SACKS *Awakenings* i. 36 Witty and precise in her speech without significant stereotypy or stickiness of thought. **1976** *Word 1971* XXVII. 128 This stereotypy of semantic relations of nouns reported by Bowerman decreases as mean sentence length increases.

steric, *a.* Add: Hence **ste·rically** *adv.*, by, or as regards, the three-dimensional arrangement of atoms.

1918 *Jrnl. Chem. Soc.* CXIV. I. 127 If only one group is sterically hindered, then reactions can take place at both tertiary amino-groups. **1959** *New Scientist* 19 Feb. 399/1 Propylene,..using a Natta catalyst, can be turned into straight chains of polypropylene molecules, with all the arms or side groups projecting in the same direction: that is to say, they are sterically oriented. **1974** GILL & WILLIS *Pericyclic Reactions* v. 130 The face to face interaction of the two π-systems is the only mode that is geometrically and sterically feasible.

stericks. (Later example.)

1859 C. BRAY *Let.* 26 June in *Geo. Eliot Lett.* (1954) III. 94 We had Sara in strong stericks all the way home, because she had missed her final chance of explanation and advice from you.

sterilant (ste·rilănt). [f. STERIL(IZE *v.* + -ANT¹.] A sterilizing agent. **a.** An agent used to make something free of plant life or micro-organisms; a herbicide or disinfectant.

1955 *Proc. 12th Ann. North Central Weed Control Conf.* 45/1 The estimated erodibility of the soil treated with various sterilants..is shown in Table 3. **1960** *Farmer & Stockbreeder* 12 Jan. 71/1 In the dairy, a mobile washing-up trough on castors is filled with 30 gallons of hot water with added detergent and sterilant. **1960** *Agronomy Jrnl.* LII. 707/2 The best way to relieve the erosion hazard is to eliminate the weeds with soil sterilants so that crops can be produced that will leave a protective cover. **1973** *Nature* 20 Oct. 455/2 Leaflets were..surface sterilized in 1·5% sodium hypochlorite solution (10 min). The sterilant was removed by 8 successive washes with sterile water. **1979** *Arizona Daily Star* 8 Apr. A1/2 The formula containing 2,4,5-T is used as a sterilant on driveways and brick walks to prevent plant growth.

b. An agent used to render an organism incapable of producing offspring.

1961 *Jrnl. Economic Entomol.* LIV. 688/1 Tests were made to determine the effect of the sterilant on copulation by treated males and on zygote formation in females inseminated by them. **1973** J. J. MCKELVEY *Man against Tsetse* iii. 197 When the flies are released, they can transmit this sterilant venereally to their mates and again shatter the potential of the fly to increase in numbers. **1978** *Times* 4 Sept. 13/4 There is no problem in producing sterilization substances; the difficulty lies in finding a sterilant that does not have side effects and in persuading wild animals to take it regularly.

sterile, *a.* Add: **8. sterile-male** *Biol.*, used *attrib.* to designate the technique of controlling a natural population by releasing large numbers of sterile males into it, so that females that mate only with these do not reproduce.

[**1955** E. F. KNIPLING in *Jrnl. Econ. Entomol.* XLVIII. 459/1 The purpose of this paper is to consider the possibility of controlling insects by releasing sexually sterile males among the existing population.] **1959** *Science* 9 Oct. 903/1 The possibility of controlling animal populations by the sterile-male method is not necessarily limited to insects. **1975** *Nigerian Jrnl. Entomol.* I. 181 Because of the ease of preparation, good-keeping quality and re-useability of the [bat's wing] membrane, it..may have a very important role in the control of tsetse flies in Africa by the use of the sterile male technique. **1980** *Adv. Vet. Sci. & Compar. Med.* XXIV. 166 Screwworm populations subjected to autocidal control by the sterile-male technique.

sterilization. Add: Also *fig.*, esp. in *Econ.* Cf. sense 6 of the *vb.*

1938 *Times* 15 Feb. 14/2 'Sterilization' is the word used to describe the Treasury's policy of limiting the expansion of credit which would follow if the imports of gold were used as a basis for the expansion of the note issue or bank credits. **1942** *Sun* (Baltimore) 20 Jan. 10/2 The fall or 'sterilization' of Singapore could contribute to a clearing of the way for Japanese naval debouchment into the Indian Ocean. **1955** *Times* 3 Aug. 12/2 The Swiss authorities would be the first to admit that the sterilization of deposits..cannot be held to promise a solution of the problem posed by the existence of too much money and lack of sufficient opportunities for investing it. **1968** R. A. MUNDELL *International Econ.* xviii. 256 Sterilization (or neutralization) policy is a specific combination of monetary and exchange policy. When the central bank buys or sells foreign exchange the money supply increases or decreases. The purpose of sterilization policy is to offset this effect. **1974** A. K. SWOBODA in Johnson & Nobay *Issues in Monetary Econ.* 66 Keeping the money supply at its initial level involves a lower rate of sterilization operations when non-trade goods are present.

sterilize, *v.* Add: **4.** Also, to render harmless.

1939 *Economist* 8 July 64/2 The Reich Government..is evidently thinking a good deal more of its own commercial ambitions in East Europe and..of ways and means of breaking up the embryonic 'Peace Front' by sterilising Poland as an anti-German military power.

6. *Econ.* To inhibit the use of resources in order to exercise control over the economy, esp. to control the balance of payments by taking offsetting action to hold down the money supply.

1930 *Economist* 3 May 1007/2 The directors conclude a somewhat discursive report with remarks upon the wastefulness of sterilised gold, which they regard as one of the principal causes of the fall in commodity prices. **1935** A. D. GAYER *Monetary Policy & Econ. Stabilization* ii. 32 By the consistent utilization of the devices of 'offsetting' and 'sterilising'..the total media of payments were regulated independently of her [*sc.* America's] resources. **1936** *Sun* (Baltimore) 6 June 16/1 Such action would be aimed primarily at sterilizing the mobile gold received from abroad. **1938** *Times* 15 Feb. 14/2 No more gold will be 'sterilized' by the Treasury. **1942** *Sun* (Baltimore) 11 Feb. 1/3 Such a technique would 'sterilize' the money..; that is, keep it from building up the nation's purchasing power. **1944** *Ibid.* 3 Apr. 9/3 WPB suggested..that legislation be proposed to 'sterilize' such reserves to keep them from affecting the economy. **1968** R. A. MUNDELL *International Econ.* x. 149 The practice of 'sterilizing' the monetary effects of foreign exchange (or gold) purchases and sales has become widespread as countries look for means of adjusting the balance of payments other than that implicit in price level (or interest rate) adjustments. **1977** C. & D. S. AMMER *Dict. Business & Econ.* 180 Even though the United States is no longer on the gold standard, the term [*sc.* sterilization] continues to be used with the understanding that not gold but other reserves ..are being sterilized.

7. *Town Planning.* To preserve (a piece of land) from building or other development.

1935 A. P. HERBERT *What a Word!* i. 18 The Town-planners and Green-Belters, when they propose to 'sterilize' a given area, mean that it shall *not* be sterile, that it shall produce *nothing* but vegetation and natural life, as opposed to buildings. **1937** *Times* 27 July 11/2 The council have also accepted offers to sterilize, free of compensation, the attractive Duncombe Farm estate at Ivinghoe, comprising 64 acres, on the understanding that there will be no building on the adjoining land. **1942** *Rep. Comm. Land Utilisation in Rural Areas* 71 in *Parl. Papers* (Cmd. 6378) IV. 497 The term 'green belt'..has come..to mean a belt of open land..to be 'preserved' from building (or, as is often said, 'sterilised'). **1973** *Town & Country Planning* Nov. 495 Any urban growth entailing the phased development of land would become impossible under site-value rating, except given some action to sterilize the land concerned, which would be precisely contrary to the aim of stimulating development.

sterks, sturks (stɜ·ɹks). *Austral. slang. rare.* [? abbrev. f. STERCORACEOUS *a.*] A fit of depression, irritation, annoyance. Also **ste·rky** *a.*, having loose bowels from fear.

1941 BAKER *Dict. Austral. Slang* 71 *Sterks, give one the*, to infuriate, annoy, depress. **1944** J. DEVANNY *By Tropic, Sea & Jungle* 162 The croc disappears, and there's Ernest, standing up to his waist in the water..scared as hell, but too game to come out... So my dad goes in. He's a bit sterky too. **1959** D. FORREST *Last Blue Sea* 24 He just gives me the sturks.

sterling, *sb.* and *a.* Add: **A.** *sb.* **4. c. sterling area**, the group of countries (chiefly of the British Commonwealth, from 1947 officially known as *scheduled territories*: see *SCHEDULED *ppl. a.* b) that from 1931 to 1972 pegged their exchange rates to sterling, or kept their reserves in sterling and not in gold or dollars, and transferred money freely amongst themselves; also *sterling bloc(k)*, *group*; **sterling balances**, deposits in sterling which are held in British banks by overseas creditors (see also quot. 1948).

1932 B. BLACKETT in *Times* 23 Jan. 12/4 What I have called the sterling area is sufficiently large and diversified to enable it to be to a very large extent self-contained. **1935** *Economist* 5 Jan. 1/2 The devaluation of the dollar and of the currencies of the sterling group..means that the currency value of the world's existing gold supply has immensely increased. *Ibid.* 26 Jan. 216/2 They might reasonably hope for a moderate increase in trade during the coming year, particularly, between countries within the 'sterling *bloc*'. **1937** A. HUXLEY *Ends & Means* v. 41 This has already been done in the case of the Sterling Bloc, which is composed of countries whose rulers have decided that it is worth while to co-ordinate their separate national plans so that they shall not interfere with one another. **1948** G. CROWTHER *Outline of Money* (ed. 2) v. 170 Overseas countries, especially those of the Commonwealth, were content during the war to sell more to Britain than they bought from her, and to take bank deposits in London..in payment of the difference. These were the famous 'sterling balances'. **1949** KOESTLER *Promise & Fulfilment* xv. 166 On February 22, 1948, Palestine was at short notice expulsed from the Sterling Block. **1956** R. S. SAYERS *Financial Policy* viii. 235 The Sterling Area became a legal entity, an area inside which payment in sterling was unrestricted. **1977** *Time* 24 Jan. 14/1 In the past three decades, few remnants of that empire have bedeviled the British more than the 'sterling balances'—deposits from governments and private parties abroad that are kept in British banks and government bonds. **1979** H. WILSON *Final Term* 3 The Sterling Area was dismantled at a stroke.

B. *adj.* **3. c.** *absol.* Sterling silver tableware.

1974 *State* (Columbia, S. Carolina) 3 & 4 Mar. G2/1 Sterling promises to grow both more valuable, and more beautiful, with time. Its luminous beauty..is destined to take on the soft, lustrous patina..prized by so many collectors of antique silver. **1977** 'E. MCBAIN' *Long Time no See* iv. 48 The women cleaned house for other women, soaping fine china and polishing heavy sterling.

Sterling (stɜ·ɹlɪŋ), *sb.*² The proprietary name of a sub-machine gun made by the Sterling Armament Company Limited.

1958 J. BOLAND *League of Gentlemen* v. 100 Orderly piles of automatic weapons of all types—Stens, Brens, and Sterlings—were on the racks. **1969** M. PUGH *Last Place Left* vii. 46 One of them ran his torch up and down me, while a second man held the tip of his Sterling into the light. **1971** J. WAINWRIGHT *Last Buccaneer* II. 237 He hefted the Sterling sub-machine gun. **1974** S. GULLIVER *Vulcan Bulletins* 18 Automatic weapons like Stens and Sterlings. **1975** *Trade Marks Jrnl.* 21 May 1034/2 Sterling 976,708. Sub-machine guns; and parts and fittings included in Class 13, sold in kits for modifying the calibre of rifles. Sterling Armament Company Limited, 9 Berkeley St., London. Manufacturers and Merchants.—22nd June 1971.

stern, *sb.*³ Add: **2. a.** Also, the rear part of an aircraft.

1931, etc. [see *STERN-POST]. **1942** *R.A.F. Jrnl.* 16 May 17 There is..a turret in the extreme stern.

8. sterndrive [*DRIVE *sb.* 6] *Naut.* (chiefly *N. Amer.*), an inboard engine connected to an outboard drive unit at the rear of a power-boat; **stern-line** (earlier example); **stern-trawler**, a trawler whose nets are operated from the stern of the vessel.

1968 *N.Y. Times* 9 Feb. 31 When they appeared on the water about eight years ago, they looked like outboards with the power head sawed off... Variously called stern drives, inboard-outwards, [etc.].., they are one of the hottest items in recreational boating. **1976–7** *Sea Spray* (N.Z.) Dec./Jan. 94/1 'Best way to beat the opposition is to join 'em' would seem to be the philosophy behind a decision by C. W. F. Hamilton Marine Ltd to offer OMC, MerCruiser and Volvo sterndrives through its dealers. **1880** 'MARK TWAIN' *Tramp Abroad* xvii. 157 Lay her in shore and stand by to jump with the stern-line the moment she touches. **1961** *Times* 9 Aug. 5/2 A large stern-trawler..has been ordered by J. Marr and Son, of Hull. **1977** *Grimsby Even. Tel.* 5 May 8/3 A new French stern trawler landed over 1,700 kits of blue ling on Grimsby Fish Docks this week. **1982** *Daily Tel.* 29 July 2/4 The last modern stern trawler fleet in Britain was being forced into an increasingly nomadic existence.

Stern (stɜɹn), *sb.*⁴ The name of Avraham *Stern* (1907–42), used *attrib.* in *Stern gang* or *group* to designate a militant Zionist organization (officially *Loḥame Ḥerut Yisra'el* Fighters for the Freedom of Israel) founded by him in 1940.

1944 *Nation* 2 Dec. 685/1 The so-called Stern gang, with 150 active members. **1947**, etc. [see *IRGUN]. **1959** I. JEFFERIES *Thirteen Days* iv. 51 One of the two terrorist groups was called the Stern Gang. **1963** D. LEITCH in Sissons & French *Age of Austerity* iii. 64 The Stern Gang was responsible for the murder of Lord Moyne, Minister resident in Cairo, in November 1944. **1978** L. HEREN *Growing up on The Times* iii. 86 The Stern Gang was a savage organisation which even Koestler could not defend despite his theory that ruthlessness was essential for human progress.

Hence **Ste·rnist** *a.* and *sb.*

1944 *Nation* 2 Dec. 685/2 Nathan Friedman-Yellin, the thirty-one-year-old Sternist chief. *Ibid.* 686/1 The Sternists' chief weapon is murder. **1949** KOESTLER *Promise & Fulfilment* I. viii. 92 The Sternists were believers in unrestricted and indiscriminate terror. *Ibid.* II. v. 279 Then a Sternist girl came in who once made international news. **1978** L. HEREN *Growing up on The Times* iii. 83 Goldschmidt..assumed that the Sternist philosophy, which was never made clear to me, would prevail.

Sterno (stɜ·ɹno). *U.S.* A proprietary name for solidified alcohol supplied in containers for use as fuel for cooking stoves, etc.

1915 *Official Gaz.* (U.S. Patent Office) 11 May 672/1 *Sterno.* S. Sternau & Co., New York, N.Y. Filed Mar. 24, 1915... Solid fuel composed mainly of alcohol. Claims use since Jan. 12, 1915. **1935** Z. N. HURSTON *Mules & Men* I. ix. 186 Somebody had squeezed the alcohol out of several cans of Sterno and added sugar, water and boiled-off spirits of nitre and called it wine. **1958** *Washington Post* 1 Nov. 1/3 They drink stuff like..Sterno (liquefied and strained 'canned heat'). **1969** *Trade Marks Jrnl.* 30 July 1237/2 *Sterno...* Solid fuels consisting mainly of alcohol. Colgate-Palmolive Company,..New York, State of New York 10022, United States of America; Manufacturers. **1978** R. DOLINER *On Edge* (1979) xvii. 223 There was no electricity... He cooked his meals over a can of Sterno. **1979** P. THEROUX *Old Patagonian Express* i. 16 Survival techniques at home.. cooking on Sterno stoves and the like.

sterno-. Add: **sternopleu·ron** (also **-pleurum**, † **-pleura**; pl. **-pleura**) *Ent.*, in flies, each of the two hard plates of the body wall to which the middle two legs are attached, protecting parts of the sides and parts of the underside; so **sternopleu·ral** *a.*, of or pertaining to the sternopleuron, or to the sternum and the pleura.

1884 C. R. OSTEN-SACKEN in *Trans. Entomol. Soc. London* 503 *Sternopleura*; it is that portion of the mesosternum which, from its position, forms a part of the pleura... It is convenient to have a separate name for it. *Ibid.*, *Sternopleural suture*, horizontal suture below the dorsopleural and parallel to it; separates the mesopleura from the mesosternum. *Ibid.* 510 Sternopleural bristles. **1925** A. D. IMMS *Gen. Textbk. Entomol.* III. 600 The sternopleuron is situated below suture 2 and above the anterior coxa [of the thorax of Diptera]. *Ibid.*, The mesopleuron is the area in front of the root of the wing between the noto- and sterno-pleural sutures. **1961** J. E. COLLIN *Brit. Flies* VI. 108 Sternopleura with a bare polished patch. **1975** *Nature* 25 Dec. 666/2 Studies of polygenes affecting sternopleural bristle number in *Drosophila melanogaster. Ibid.* 668/1 The distribution of small bristles on the ventral part of the sternopleurum.

stern-post. Also in an aircraft (see quot. 1969).

1931 *Flight* 10 Apr. 324/2 Cases have occurred of the raised flange on plate NA 507, which secures the stern-post to the top longeron, bending and cracking in way of the taper pin. **1939** C. H. L. NEEDHAM *Aircraft Design* II. ix. 157 Where tail-plane supporting members attach to the fin stern post, the resultant compressive load should be taken into account. **1969** *Gloss. Aeronaut. & Astronaut. Terms* (*B.S.I.*) III. 5 *Stern post*, a single member terminating a fuselage, hull or float. **1979** D. B. THURSTON *Design for Flying* xv. 233 The afterbody sternpost and deadrise angles required for a stable hull are set forth... These data are based upon actual water handling characteristics of many seaplanes.

sternutator (stɜ·ɹniutēⁱtǫɹ). [f. *sternutat-* (in STERNUTATORY *a.* and *sb.*, etc.) + -OR.] A substance that causes nasal irritation; *esp.* a poison gas that causes irritation of the nose and eyes, pain in the chest, and nausea.

1922 *Encycl. Brit.* XXXII. 111/2 The sternutators were originally considered from the point of view of putting a man temporarily out of action by a violent fit of sneezing. **1951** KIRK & OTHMER *Encycl. Chem. Technol.* VII. 136 The introduction of sternutators in the form of aerosols as a gas warfare agent was a deliberate attempt by the Germans in World War I to penetrate the gas-mask canister and thus force demasking. **1971** [see *JUGLONE].

stern-wheel, *v.* (Earlier example.)

1807 in *Tennessee Hist. Mag.* (1919) V. 62 Struck a large and stubborn sawyer, two or three feet below the surface of the water in a rapid current—stern wheeled with rapidity.

steroid (stiᵊ·roid, ste·roid). *Biochem.* [f. *STER(OL + -OID.] Any of a large class of naturally occurring or synthetic organic compounds characterized by a nucleus of 17 carbon atoms in the form of four fused rings (three containing six carbon atoms and one containing five) and with varying substituents and degrees of unsaturation, the members of which include sterols, many sex and adrenocortical hormones, insect hormones, bile acids and alcohols, cardiac-active glycones, and some sapogenins and alkaloids, and many of which have important pharmacological uses. Freq. *attrib.* or as *adj.*, as *steroid chemistry, hormone.*

anabolic steroid, a steroid whose anabolic effects predominate over the masculinizing ones.

1936 CALLOW & YOUNG in *Proc. R. Soc.* A. CLVII. 194 The term 'steroids' is proposed as generic name for the group of compounds comprising the sterols, bile acids, heart poisons, saponins and sex hormones. **1956** *Nature* 28 Jan. 188/2 We have observed the effects on wool growth of treating sheep with adrenocorticotrophic hormone and with cortical steroids. **1959** S. DUKE-ELDER *Parsons' Dis. Eye* (ed. 13) xiv. 151 In ophthalmology, these steroids may be administered locally or systemically. **1960** [see *PROGESTATIONAL *a.*]. **1961** *Nature* 30 Sept. 1368/1 New anabolic steroids with low androgenic activity. **1969** *Times* 16 Jan. 4/8 Steroid hormones, which are excreted in the urine, are one of the many body chemicals that follow a daily fluctuation. **1969** J. A. VIDA *Androgens & Anabolic Agents* i. 2 Since anabolic steroids promote protein synthesis in the muscular system, these drugs find important application in clinical medicine to speed up healing of wounds. **1971** *Brit. Med. Bull.* XXVII. 26/1 The amount of oestrogen in steroid contraceptives influences the hazard of thrombo-embolism. **1972** *Nature* 21 Jan. 125/1 Steroids are small and rather simple molecules which nevertheless elicit a complex array of biochemical responses in their target tissues, often leading to profound changes in growth and differentiation. **1974** M. C. GERALD *Pharmacol.* xix. 355 Anabolic steroids..have been used by football players, weight lifters, and athletes. *Ibid.* xxi. 384 Digitalis glycosides consist of an aglycone fraction that has a steroid nucleus. **1977** *Daily News* (Perth, Austral.) 19 Jan. 49 The British National Racehorse Trainers' Federation has officially admitted that anabolic steroids have been in common use throughout the training profession for several years.

Hence **steroi·dal** *a.*, possessing the structure of, or pertaining to, a steroid.

1938 *Jrnl. Amer. Chem. Soc.* LX. 1736/2 Arguments are advanced to indicate that the steroidal hormones and bile acids do not originate from cholesterol. **1957** *Ibid.* LXXIX. 3222/1 Bromination of the steroidal sapogenin side chain. **1963** KATZMAN & ELLIOTT in Florkin & Stotz *Comprehensive Biochem.* X. iii. 72 A number of methods have been developed for the quantitative estimation of the steroidal estrogens. **1972** *Lancet* 22 Sept. 611/1 Little is known about the growth and steroidal activity of the human ovarian follicle. **1977** *Listener* 18 Aug. 208/2 The wild yam, the source of steroidal compounds used as the starting material for oral contraceptives.

steroidogenesis (stɪroi:d-, steroi:do-dʒe·nĕsis). *Biochem.* [f. *STEROID + -O + -GENESIS.] The biosynthesis of steroids.

1951 *Recent Progress Hormone Res.* VI. 220 We have investigated the effects of several variables on the ACTH-controlled steroidogenesis of the isolated adrenal. **1970** *Nature* 28 Nov. 885/1 This second monograph.. deals with the pathways of steroidogenesis of the ovary and testis. **1979** *Experientia* XXXV. 159/2 The cyclic AMP-dependent protein kinase may be involved in the processes of spermatogenesis and steroidogenesis as animals reach sexual maturity.

Hence **steroi:doge·nic** *a.*, pertaining to or having the property of steroidogenesis.

1951 *Recent Progress Hormone Res.* VI. 240 Our data suggest the possibility that steroidogenic organs should be visualized as assembly-line processing plants, where specific groups are introduced in a highly specialized way. **1959** *Endocrinology* LXV. 29 Saline extracts of beef diencephalon were assayed in the decerebrate dog for steroidogenic activity. **1974** D. & M. WEBSTER *Compar. Vertebr. Morphol.* xiii. 313 In amphibians the chromaffin tissue is embedded in the ventral portion of the kidney along with steroidogenic tissue.

sterol (stɪᵊ·rǫl, ste·rǫl). *Biochem.* [The ending of *CHOLESTEROL, *ERGOSTEROL, etc., used substantively.] Any of a class of solid, unsaturated steroid alcohols that occur naturally both free and in combination as esters or glycosides and are classified according to their origin as mycosterols, phytosterols, zoosterols, and marine sterols.

1913 *Biochem. Jrnl.* VII. 617 It is now proposed to limit the terms zoo- and phyto-sterol to sterols which are found as tissue constituents of animals and plants respectively. **1939** A. HUXLEY *After Many a Summer* I. v. 65 Those sterols!..Always linked up with senility. The most obvious case, of course, was cholesterol. **1959** L. F. & M. FIESER *Steroids* xi. 358 The characteristic sterol fraction from freshwater green algae (*Chlorophyceae*) is the common sitosterol mixture of higher plants. **1975** *Lipids* X. 542/1 Sterols have been isolated from both adult and juvenile ivy in free and esterified form. Stigmasterol..is the main component. **1979** *Jrnl. Org. Chem.* XLIV. 3378/1 Algae and fungi produce sterols with 24β configurations, while most higher plants produce sterols with 24α configurations.

-sterol (stĕrǫl), *suffix. Biochem.* [f. *CHOLE)-STEROL.] A formative element in the names of many sterols, as in *ERGOSTEROL, *PHYTOSTEROL.

-sterone, formative element in the names of some steroids, as in *ANDROSTERONE, *PROGESTERONE. [ad. G. *-steron*, f. *ster*(*ol* *STEROL + *ket*)*on* KETONE. App. first used in G. *androsteron* (*Zeitschr. f. phys. Chem.* (1934) CCXXIX. 167) and *luteosteron* (*Ber. d. Deut. Chem. Ges.* (1934) LXVII. 1271).]

sterrettite (ste·rĕtəit). *Min.* [See quot. 1940 and -ITE¹.] A hydrous basic phosphate of scandium occurring as transparent, usually colourless, orthorhombic crystals, and now identified with kolbeckite (eggonite).

1940 LARSEN & MONTGOMERY in *Amer. Mineralogist* XXV. 513 A few specimens contain orthorhombic crystals distinct from any previously described mineral... The mineral is named sterrettite in honor of Dr. Douglas B. Sterrett who was one of the first investigators of the Utah and Nevada variscite deposits. **1959** *Bull. Geol. Soc. Amer.* LXX. 1648 Powder patterns of sterrettite and kolbeckite showed that their cell sizes are identical with that of synthetic $Sc(PO_4).2H_2O$.., indicating that the major cation might be scandium rather than aluminum. **1968** *Amer. Mineralogist* LIII. 1227 In the course of this work, the supposed Al phosphate sterrettite..was identified..to be scandium phosphate, $Sc(PO_4).2H_2O$, identical with kolbeckite.

stertorousness. (Example.)

1845 POE *Facts of Mr. Valdemar's Case* in *Amer. Rev.* Dec. 563/1 The stertorous breathing ceased—that is to say, its stertorousness was no longer apparent.

stet. Add: (Earlier and later examples.) The direction occasionally signifies that a non-standard or irregular form should be retained. Cf. SIC *adv.*

1755 J. SMITH *Printer's Gram.* xi. 277 Where words are struck out that are afterwards again approved of, they mark dots under such words, and write in the Margin, *Stet.* *a* **1966** 'M. NA GOPALEEN' *Best of Myles* (1968) 295 A colossal imposition who will..cause your heart to beat like a sludge-hammer (*stet*).

Also as *v. trans.*, to write 'stet' against (an accidental deletion, miscorrection, etc.).

1895 G. B. SHAW *Let.* 16 Dec. (1965) I. 581 If you disagree with my deletions, you can dot them under and 'stet' them. **1968** K. MARTIN *Editor* i. 19 On the same line I had 'stetted' another word which had been accidentally crossed out. **1975** J. BUTCHER *Copy-Editing* iii. 26 Stet American and all unusual spellings that are to be retained.

Stetson (ste·tsǫ̆n). Also **stetson.** The name of John Batterson *Stetson* (1830–1906), American hat manufacturer, used *attrib.* and *absol.* to designate hats made by the company founded by him, esp. one with a broad brim and high crown associated with cowboys of the western U.S. Also applied *loosely* to other hats in this style.

A proprietary term in the U.S.

[**1895** *Montgomery Ward Catal.* Spring & Summer 274/1 Cow Boys' sombrero hats... J. B. Stetson's 'Boss of the Plains'. **1897** *Sears, Roebuck Catal.* 234/1 The world famous J. B. Stetson sombrero hat..crown 4½ inch; brim 4 inch.] *c* **1900** in *Amer. Mail Order Fashions* (1961) 27 Every railroad man knows that the Stetson hat is just the right style and shape for his business. **1903** *Everybody's Mag.* Dec. 739/2 'Send for me if you want me again,' says Redruth, and hoists his Stetson and walks off. **1906** *Official Gaz.* (U.S. Patent Office) 6 Mar. 290/1 *Stetson.* Hats and caps. John B. Stetson Company, Philadelphia, Pa. Filed Apr. 14, 1905. Used ten years. The name 'Stetson'. **1924** *Westm. Gaz.* 26 Aug. 5/5 The modern coster wants to wear a Stetson hat. **1940** W. FAULKNER *Hamlet* I. ii. 38 Pat Stamper..standing there at the gate to his rope stock pen, with that Stetson cocked and his thumbs still hooked in the top of his pants. **1953** D. CUSHMAN *Stay away, Joe* 19 He had donned for the occasion a new flame-red shirt and a thirty-dollar Stetson hat. **1967** *Telegraph* (Brisbane) 17 Apr. 4/1 He was amused at the surprise that greeted his announcement that the hat he was wearing—a snappy, small-brimmed business model—was also a Stetson... 'Stetson is a brand name. We make all kinds of men's hats.' **1970** *Guardian* 31 Dec. 2/7 His [*sc.* J. B. Stetson's] first hat was a 10-gallon Western, an ancestor of the stetsons worn by President Lyndon Johnson. **1978** D. BLOODWORTH *Crosstalk* II. xxi. 164 Idi Amin..went around twice talking to the hijacked passengers..wearing..a big stetson hat.

Hence **Ste·tsoned** *a.*, wearing a Stetson.

1935 A. G. MACDONELL *Visit to America* xiii. 235 Fort Worth, overgrown village of spurred and Stetsoned cow-punchers. **1969** *Time* 8 Aug. 55/1 John Wayne as a pistoled and Stetsoned Captain Bligh. **1972** D. A. PAILIN in Cox & Dyson *20th-Cent. Mind* III. iv. 120, I remember a Stetsoned rancher arriving at a Texas seminary. **1976** *National Observer* (U.S.) 1 May 7/3 They're often joined by Russian trawlermen or Stetsoned Oklahomans.

Steuben (st(i)ūbe·n, st(i)ū·bĕn). The name of the *Steuben* Glass Works at Corning, N.Y., founded in 1903, used *attrib.* to designate fine glassware made there, esp. the decorative engraved crystal produced since 1933. Also *absol.*

1920 *Official Gaz.* (U.S. Patent Office) 16 Mar. 529/2 *Steuben.* Corning Glass Works, Corning, N.Y. Filed Nov. 19, 1919. No claim being made to the exclusive use of the word 'Steuben' apart from the mark as shown in the drawing. *Particular description of goods.*—Cut Glass and Artistic Glassware. *Claims use* since about Jan. 1, 1904. **1941** G. S. & H. MCKEARIN *American Glass* ix. 422 A small, well formed vase blown from gold-ruby glass..is an opaque pink. It may also be a Steuben piece. **1948** J. S. PLAUT *Steuben Glass* ii. 9 Steuben glass is made by the so-called 'off-hand' process. **1958** 'S. MARLOWE' *Second Longest Night* I. iii. 19 He was carrying a cocktail glass, expensive Steuben, in his right hand. **1967** 'R. FOLEY' *Fear of Stranger* (1968) viii. 89 Her Steuben bud vase held an assortment of brushes. **1968** L. J. BRAUN *Cat who turned on & Off* ii. 23 Oh, what a lovely shop... She's got some old Steuben... Look at this decanter! **1979** *United States 1980/81* (Penguin Travel Guides) 556 Corning Glass Center, Corning, New York: An area has been set aside for visitors where the fine Steuben glass is hand-formed and engraved.

Stevengraph (stī·vĕngrɑf). [Proprietary term, f. the name of the inventor Thomas *Stevens* (1828–88), a ribbon weaver of Coventry + -GRAPH.] A type of coloured woven silk picture produced during the late 19th century by the firm founded by Stevens.

1879 *Bookseller* 2 June 510/1 Mr. Stevens, of Coventry, has produced two interesting 'Stevengraphs'—one the four-horse Mail Coach..the other the Railway Locomotive. **1928** *Trade Marks Jrnl.* 4 July 1075 Stevengraph ... Woven labels of cotton, or in which cotton predominates. Thomas Stevens (Coventry) Limited, Stevengraph Works,..Coventry. **1957** W. S. LE VAN BAKER *Silk Pictures of Thomas Stevens* I. i. 15 An amazing third-dimensional effect is achieved in the tiny woven silk pictures known as 'Stevengraphs'. **1964** A. ADBURGHAM *Shops & Shopping* xix. 226 The weaving of dress labels was a development from the Stevengraphs... Many other ribbon firms copied the idea of Stevengraphs to see them through the depression. **1967** *Daily Tel.* 21 Oct. 13/1 A pair of Stevengraphs, illustrating Columbus leaving Spain and arriving in the New World made £105 (Hicks). **1971** G. A. GODDEN *Stevengraphs* i. 13 The..decorative silk-work pictures known as Stevengraphs were first introduced ..as a gimmick at the York Exhibition which was opened on 7 May 1879. **1980** *Daily Tel.* 8 Dec. 7/1 (Advt.), Wednesday 10 December 12 noon Baxter Prints & Stevengraphs. Viewing: Day Prior and Morning of Sale until 11 am.

stevensite (stī·vĕnzəit). *Min.* [f. the name of Edwin A. *Stevens* (1795–1868), U.S. inventor and businessman and founder of the Stevens Institute of Technology in Hoboken, New Jersey: see -ITE¹.] A brown, pink, or white magnesium-containing mineral of the montmorillonite group.

1889 A. E. FOOTE in *Naturalist's Leisure Hour* XIII. 31/1 Stevensite 5c to 1·50. **1896** A. H. CHESTER *Dict. Names Minerals* 257 Stevensite... This name was suggested in 1873, at a meeting of the N. Y. Lyceum of Natural History, but not published, though soon after used on labels. **1916** *Amer. Mineralogist* I. 44 In the old Hartshorn quarry, in Springfield Township, Essex County, New Jersey, Mr. Louis Reamer..discovered a single vein of a peculiar mineral, called by the quarrymen 'magnesium' (= talc?)... It proved to be essentially identical with the hitherto imperfectly known stevensite. **1962** W. A. DEER et al. *Rock-Forming Minerals* III. 231 Brindley (1955) described stevensite as a talc-saponite interlayered mineral, whereas Faust and Murata (1953) and Faust *et al.* (1959) regard it as a smectite with a defect structure in which a small proportion of layers with the 'attributes of talc' play only a minor role. **1979** *Sci. Amer.* Apr. 81/2 A good example is the alkaline chemical sedimentation that deposits limestones, cherts, phosphates and magnesium-based clay minerals, including attapulgites, sepiolites and stevensites.

Stevenson (stī·vĕnsən). *Meteorol.* [The name of Thomas *Stevenson* (1818–87), Scottish engineer and meteorologist (and father of R. L. Stevenson), who devised it (*Jrnl. Scottish Meteorol. Soc.* (1864) I. 122).] *Stevenson* (formerly *Stevenson's*) *screen*: a wooden box supported on a stand above the ground and made with doubly louvred sides and a double top with ventilation holes, so that thermometers or other instruments mounted inside it are sheltered from sunlight and precipitation and effectively register properties of the outside air.

1881 W. MARRIOTT *Hints Meteorol. Observers* 10 The thermometers must be mounted in the Stevenson's screen. **1884** *Bull. Philos. Soc. Washington* VI. 24 The Stevenson screen and the double louvre screens in general. **1923** GLAZEBROOK *Dict. Appl. Physics* III. 491/1 Owing to the intense solar radiation experienced in the tropics, it has been held..that the ordinary Stevenson screen is unsuitable for use in low latitudes. **1970** J. P. GLASGOW in H. W. Mulligan *African Trypanosomiases* xv. 355 Meanwhile maximum temperatures (in a Stevenson screen four feet above the ground) rose to 41°.

Stevensonian (stīvĕnsōᵘ·niăn), *a.* (and *sb.*). [f. the name of the writer Robert Louis *Stevenson* (1850–94) + -IAN.] Of, pertaining to, or characteristic of R. L. Stevenson or his writings. Also as *sb.*, an admirer of R. L. Stevenson or of his writings.

1897 T. DAVIDSON *Let.* 29 Mar. in R. B. Perry *Thought & Char. of W. James* (1935) I. 756 Nothing but a happy-go-lucky Stevensonian adventuresomeness. **1900** *Fortn. Rev.* Jan. 97 He did not underrate *Kidnapped* as a whole. 'By far the most human of my labours hitherto,' is his verdict, anticipating that of all the true Stevensonians. **1913** *Smart Set* No. 3. 45/1 That polished peanut style that passes for Stevensonian English in the 'culture' clubs. **1923** G. K. CHESTERTON in *Illustr. London News* 22 Sept. 512/2 It was..the essence of the Stevensonian spirit that the melancholy was not incurable even if the misfortune was incurable. **1928** *Observer* 22 Jan. 15/1 Bouvet Island is a Stevensonian treasure island, bare, uninhabited, bleak. **1939** *John o' London's Weekly* 9 June 363/2 A new detective novelist..whose equipment includes..a good homespun prose with Stevensonian echoes. **1974** J. Pope-Hennessy *R. L. Stevenson* vi. 118 Meredith did.. start off on a portrait of Louis Stevenson, in the guise of 'Gower Woodseer' [in]..*The Amazing Marriage* [but] the Woodseer of the later part..is not consistent with the Stevensonian youth we encounter at the beginning.

stevioside (stī·viosəid). *Chem.* [ad. F. *stévioside* (Bridel & Lavieille 1931, in *Jrnl. de Pharm. et de Chim.* XIV. 105), f. mod.L. *Stevi-a*, f. the name of P. J. Esteve (d. 1566), Spanish botanist + -ia[1]: see *-oside.] A glycoside, $C_{38}H_{60}O_{18}$, present in the leaves of a Paraguayan herb (*Stevia rebaudiana*) and comparable in sweetness to saccharin.

1931 *Chem. Abstr.* XXV. 4553 Dieterich named the principle eupatirin, which B[ridel] and R. [Lavieille] changed to stevioside. **1968** *Times* 3 Dec. 10/8 The weed, known to botanists as Stevia rebaudiana.., grows up to 1½ ft. high. Its leaves have a surprisingly sweet taste, the active principle being known as stevioside. **1978** *Nature* 9 Feb. 495/1 Stevioside, a triterpene glycoside, which is readily extracted from the leaves of *S. rebaudiana*, is being produced on a commercial scale in Japan... Stevioside, which is approximately 300 times sweeter than sucrose, is not a permitted food additive elsewhere.

stew, *sb.*[2] Add: **III. 8.** (sense 5) *stewgravy*, *-jar*; **stew-bum** *U.S. slang*, a tramp, *spec.* one who is habitually drunk (cf. *bum *sb.*[4] 1).

1902 *Bookman* (N.Y.) Aug. 541/2 The dictum of the ordinary tramp (the 'gay-cat' and stew-bum). **1918** [see *dingbat 1]. **1952** B. Harwin *Home is Upriver* xiii. 127 How come you to be a drunk damn' stew-bum when I found you? **1922** Joyce *Ulysses* 167 Scoffing up stew-gravy with sopping sippets of bread. **1913** D. H. Lawrence *Sons & Lovers* 79 The stew-jar was in the oven.

stew (stū, stiū), *sb.*[4] *U.S.* colloq. abbrev. of *stewardess c.

1970 D. Harper *Hijacked* (1971) 23 If a stew flies five years, she'll keep on as long as the company lets her. **1975** B. Meggs *Matter of Paradise* (1976) v. iii. 122 She had been with Pan Am herself as a 'stew'. **1979** S. Barlay *Crash Course* I. 6 I'm Mara. I used to be a stew myself.

stew, *v.*[2] Add: **2. b.** Also (of an infusion of tea, etc.), to 'stand' on the leaves, etc. Also *transf.*, of the pot containing it.

1906 *Rep. Brit. Assoc. Adv. Sci.* 783 There is found in tea and coffee an astringent substance which gives the well-known bitter taste to the infusions when they are allowed to 'stew'. **1942** *R.A.F. Jrnl.* 3 Oct. 25 An imposing enamel teapot stands on top, quietly stewing. **1979** W. H. Canaway *Solid Gold Buddha* xxiv. 158 The tea stewed for fifteen minutes or so.

c. (Later examples of *to leave to* (or *let*) *stew in one's own juice*.) Also in the senses: To be left to one's own devices, to be kept in a state of uneasy suspense, and *ellipt.*, as *to leave* (one) *to stew*, *to let* (one) *stew*.

1921 Galsworthy *To Let* ii. vii. 184 'Please don't let me bother you if you've got people.' 'Not at all... I want to let them stew in their own juice for a bit.' **1928** W. S. Maugham *Ashenden* vii. 116, I left her to stew in her own juice for a week before I went to see her. She was in a very pretty state of nerves by then. **1934** 'G. Orwell' *Burmese Days* ii. 38 Office babus are the real rulers of this country now... Best thing we can do is to shut up shop and let 'em stew in their own juice. **1961** B. Fergusson *Watery Maze* xv. 378 The Japanese in Tenasserim could safely be left to stew in their own juice once we had Rangoon. **1976** W. Greatorex *Crossover* 182 'It was me,' Calder said. 'I made up the story.' Calder let them stew in the silence. **1980** *Church Times* 3 Oct. 9/2 After letting us stew for three months, the Lord served up a miracle in the form of a perfect house for us in Berkeley.

3. e. To fret; to suffer anxiety or suspense; to be in an agitated state.

1917 S. Lewis *Innocents* xviii. 208, I was suspicious of these fellows that are always petting and stewing over their wives in public. **1930** E. B. White *Lett.* (1976) 91 White has been stewing around for two days now, a little bit worried. **1932** 'A. Bridge' *Peking Picnic* iii. 31 He seemed to be stewing, so I told him to come over and have a cocktail later on. **1949** E. Pound *Pisan Cantos* lxxx. 92 Stewing with rage Concerning the landlady's *doings* with a lodger unnamed. **1956** W. H. Whyte *Organization Man* x. 129 They don't want a man to fret and stew about his work. **1974** R. Harris *Double Snare* xviii. 133, I wouldn't let them go to life imprisonment... Why shouldn't they stew a little? **1979** *Tucson Mag.* Mar. 23/1 City planners don't just sit around and stew over traffic congestion.

steward, *sb.* Add: **1. e.** One employed on a train to serve meals, drinks, etc., to passengers and to attend to other needs. Also one with similar duties on a motor coach or aeroplane.

1906 *Railway Epicurean* July 9 Harvey's chefs and stewards have the food products of a continent at their command. **1915** *Proc. Amer. Assoc. Dining Car Superintendents* xv. 44 Instead of the steward asking, 'All on one check?' we instruct our stewards to, in a quiet way, get around to one of the party and ascertain whether one or more checks are desired. **1928** *Lit. Digest* 13 Oct. 70/3 The 'Nitecoach' carries a crew of three, driver, steward, and porter. **1931** *Sci. Amer.* Oct. 236/3 The steward, who now becomes the [airline] passenger's guide on land, is trained to supply any desired information. **1939** [see *air hostess* s.v. *air *sb.*[1] B. III. 4]. **1955** F. O'Connor *Wise Blood* i. 15 There was a steward beckoning people to places and handing out menus. **1975** *Economist* 11 Jan. 20/2 The £100,000 placed in the plane at Heathrow was recovered and the only damage, to a luckless steward, was one police dog-bite. **1979** P. Theroux *Old Patagonian Express* iii. 59 It was the steward from the dining car... 'Lunch!' he yelled. 'First call for lunch!'

11. Also occas. = *shop steward* s.v. *shop *sb.* 9 c.

1943 *Sun* (Baltimore) 13 Oct. 8/4 Union local stewards ..voted to end their stoppage. **1977** *Times* 6 May 1/6 The stewards are also pointing out that they are at one with management.

13. steward boy, for (sense 1 d) read: = *house-boy* s.v. House *sb.*[1] 23 (later examples).

1962 *Sat. Even. Post* 5 May 80/3 Her evening spent in helping Fossey's old stewardboy to beat carpets. **1977** *Daily Times* (Lagos) 25 Feb. 22/4 (Advt.), Driver, Steward boy, Houseboy, wanted.

stewardess. Add: **c.** A female attendant on a passenger aircraft who attends to the needs and comfort of the passengers; = *air hostess* s.v. *air *sb.*[1] B. II. 4. Also, a similar attendant on other kinds of passenger transport.

1931 *United Airlines News* Aug. 5/2 (*caption*) Uniformed stewardesses employed on the Chicago–San Diego divisions of United. The picture shows the original group of stewardesses employed. **1937** *Sun* (Baltimore) 22 Apr. 6/1 (Advt.), America's *first* railroad adds another to its long list of *firsts*... A uniformed Stewardess who is also a graduate nurse! She looks after your comfort en route [etc.]. **1958** 'Castle' & 'Hailey' *Flight into Danger* i. 12 He ducked into the aircraft..joined shortly by a stewardess..who smiled at him and made fast the door. **1968** M. Woodhouse *Rock Baby* x. 104 The stewardess announced our landing. **1978** R. Ludlum *Holcroft Covenant* iii. 40 In two chairs against the wall sat the captain of the 747 and the stewardess assigned to its first-class lounge. **1981** *Christian Sci. Monitor* 28 July 6/1 Rooms at the St. James's club, a luxury bus with two stewardesses, and a special room overlooking the Strand.

stewardship. Add: **2. b.** *Eccl.* The responsible use of resources, esp. money, time, and talents, in the service of God; *spec.* the organized pledging of specific amounts of money etc. to be given regularly to the Church. Also *attrib.*

1899 C. M. Sheldon (*title*) His brother's keeper; or, Christian stewardship. **1931** D. W. P. Strang *Studies in Christian Stewardship* i. 4 The philosophy of Stewardship can claim no less an authorship than that of our Lord Himself. **1938** H. Gerlinger *Money Raising* vi. 98 This lack of development of a social consciousness on the part of students is clearly due to the fact that practically no systematic effort is made to implant the idea of stewardship in undergraduates. **1950** *Christian Cent.* 22 Nov. 1392/2 There is only one legitimate answer to the financial problem..to..teach our people to practice Christian stewardship. **1951** *National Council Outlook* May 12/1 The delegates asked for consolidation of stewardship and fund-raising efforts in the Council. **1959** *Christian Stewardship of Money* i. 5 The movement..has broadened out into an attempt to recover and to teach the principles of the right Christian attitude towards the use of money. For want of a less archaic word this attitude is called 'Stewardship'. **1980** *Oxf. Diocesan Mag.* May 15/3 The book deals with man's attitude to the natural world in general and his Christian stewardship in relation to its resources.

attrib. **1931** D. W. P. Strang *Studies in Christian Stewardship* i. 5 The Stewardship movement has..developed momentum mainly in the New World. **1942** *Christian Cent.* 1 July 829/1 (*heading*) United stewardship campaign might go even further. **1962** P. Ferris *Church of England* ix. 175 Stewardship advisers..were soon appointed in most dioceses. **1979** *Oxf. Diocesan Mag.* Dec. 9/2 Stewardship campaigns are essentially teaching missions. *Ibid.* 10/1 Pastoral reorganisation and the stewardship movement have worked together to foster a sense of responsibility in parishes.

stewartite (stiu·ərtəit). *Min.* [f. the name of the *Stewart* mine, Pala, San Diego County, California, where it was found + -ite[1].] A hydrous basic phosphate of manganese and ferric iron, $MnFe_2(PO_4)_2(OH)_2.8H_2O$, found as pleochroic orange-yellow to colourless triclinic crystals.

1912 W. T. Schaller in *Jrnl. Washington Acad. Sci.* II. 143 Stewartite. Probably triclinic. A hydrous manganese phosphate from the Stewart Mine, after which it is named. **1975** *Neues Jahrb. für Mineralogie: Abhandl.* CXXIII. 148 Laueite, pseudolaueite, and stewartite occur in a similar paragenesis which is confined to the late stage hydrothermal leaching and oxidation of primary triphylite-lithiophilite, $Li(Fe,Mn)[PO_4]$, in granitic pegmatites.

stewed, *ppl. a.*[1] Add: **a.** (Examples with reference to tea.)

1908 A. Bennett *Old Wives' Tale* iv. iii. 509 The lounge tea, which in any case would have been undrinkably stewed. **1924** Kipling *Debits & Credits* (1926) 309 Drinking stewed tea with your meat four times a day. **1977** M. Hinxman *One-Way Cemetery* i. 7 The old man poured some stewed tea into a couple of mugs.

d. *slang* (orig. *U.S.*). Drunk. Also in phr. *stewed to the ears* (*eyebrows*, *gills*, etc.). Cf. *pickled *ppl. a.*[1] 2.

1737 *Pennsylvania Gaz.* 6 Jan. 2 The Drinkers Dictionary... Stew'd. **1871** A. A. Wright *Diary* in J. Wright *Generations of Men* (1959) v. 63 A very jolly party..we kept it up till daylight. I got pretty well stewed. **1912** *Pedagogical Seminary* Mar. 97 [expressions denoting] *Intoxication*..'half stewed'. **1922** S. Lewis *Babbitt* xxix. 347 He saw you out the other night with a gang of totties, all stewed to the gills. **1925** Wodehouse *Sam the Sudden* iii. 29 'My opinion is that he was as tight as an owl'. 'Stewed to the eyebrows'. **1930** J. Dos Passos *42nd Parallel* 9 They're a bunch o bums and hypocrytes, stewed to the ears most of em already. **1945** B. Macdonald *Egg & I* (1946) iv. xvi. 176 Yewgene got stewed and run into a tree. **1958** P. de Vries *Mackerel Plaza* vi. 82 A casual observer not familiar with him would have thought he was stewed to the gills as he rose and wobbled over to join me. **1978** J. Carroll *Mortal Friends* v. ii. 522 He wondered if Cushing had collected himself. He wondered if Cushing was stewed.

stewing, *vbl. sb.* **b.** (Earlier and later examples.)

1726 J. Gay *Let.* in *Corresp. J. Swift* (1963) III. 168 Take a knuckle of Veal... In a Stewing pan put it. **1921** *Daily Colonist* (Victoria, B.C.) 25 Oct. 6/1 (Advt.), Boneless Stewing Beef, per lb. 12½c. **1948** *Good Housek. Cookery Bk.* ii. 159 Stewing steak is commonly used, but other meats (kidney and liver) may be made into a brown stew. **1969** M. Kelly *Write on Both Sides* xxiii. 102 He took out the shopping list... Stewing steak, mushrooms, onions. **1978** E. Malpass *Wind brings up Rain* xiv. 149 She'd got stewing beef in the oven.

stewy, *a.* Add: Also, resembling stew.

1967 [see *gas-stove* s.v. *gas *sb.*[1] 7].

Steyr (ʃtəiɹ). The name of a town in Upper Austria used *attrib.* and *absol.* to designate a kind of automatic pistol made there.

1920 H. B. C. Pollard *Automatic Pistols* iii. 24 The latest product of the Steyr factory, the celebrated armoury of the Mannlicher firm, is the 1916 *Steyr Mannlicher* pistol. *Ibid.* 26 Taking the Steyr in comparison with the Parabellum, it is less complicated than the latter, but not so well designed or easy to shoot with. **1934** G. Burrard *Identification of Firearms & Forensic Ballistics* vii. 144 The rifling used in revolvers and self-loading pistols may be divided conveniently into the following..types: *Steyr type*, four grooves; right-hand twist; grooves and lands of equal width. Used in all earlier self-loading pistols, such as the Borchardt. **1972** R. Gadney *Seduction of Tall Man* ii. v. 154 This is a Steyr pistol, made in Austria. .. Fixed barrel, detachable seven shot magazine. **1974** A. Price *Other Paths to Glory* ii. viii. 211 The battered remains of an Austrian Steyr which he had bought.

sthreal, sthreel, varr. *streel *sb.*

‖ **stiacciato** (stiatʃ[i]ā·to). *Sculpture.* Also schiacciato. [It. *schiacciato*, (Tuscan) *stiacciato*, pa. ppl. of *schiacciare* (*stiacciare*) to flatten.] Very low relief. In full *stiacciato-relievo* or *relievo stiacciato*. Also *attrib.*

1862 J. C. Robinson *Ital. Sculpture of Middle Ages* 26 To him [*sc.* Donatello] is..due the invention of that.. method of low relief, which is often..called the 'Donatello style'... The ancient Florentine writers on art designated this style 'relievo stiacciato', (flattened relief)..but..it has become obsolete even in Italy. **1899** R. Glazier *Man. Historic Ornament* 51 Donatello also carried the art of low flat relief called '*Stiacciato*' to the greatest perfection. **1940** *Burlington Mag.* Mar. 76/1 The design of the buildings in lowest relief in the background is hardly imaginable without the precedent of Donatello's *stiacciato* reliefs. **1947** J. C. Rich *Materials & Methods of Sculpture* i. 8 Flat relief, *stiacciato-relievo*, is the lowest possible true relief. In this form, the effects are achieved by means of contour outlines and finely incised lines. The projection is very slight and there are no undercuts in this type of relief. **1957** H. W. Janson *Sculpture of Donatello* II. 31/1 A *schiacciato* panel 'reads' more like a picture than like a conventional relief.

stibadium (stibē[i]·diəm). *rare*[−1]. [a. L. *stibadium* a. Gr. στιβάδιον, dim. of στιβάς bed of straw.] A semicircular couch.

1840 Browning *Sordello* v. 174 He that sprawls On aught but a stibadium suffers... goose, Puttest our lustral vase to such an use?

stibio-. Add: **stibiopa·lladinite** *Min.*, a palladium antimonide, approximately Pd_5Sb_2, occurring as white or grey hexagonal crystals; **stibiota·ntalite** *Min.*, an oxide of antimony and tantalum, $SbTaO_4$, occurring as transparent brown or yellowish orthorhombic crystals in which niobium replaces some of the tantalum.

1929 P. A. Wagner *Platinum Deposits & Mines S. Afr.* i. 12 The other [mineral], a palladium antimonide, described by H. R. Adam.., from the pegmatitic ore of Tweefontein,..it is proposed..to name stibiopalladinite. **1976** *Amer. Mineralogist* LXI. 1249 Stibiopalladinite from the type locality, Farm Tweefontein, near Potgietersrust, Transvaal, South Africa, is considered to have a composition between Pd_5Sb_2 and Pd_8Sb_3. **1893** G. A. Goyder in *Proc. Chem. Soc.* IX. 184 (*heading*) Stibiotantalite: a new mineral. **1973** *Canad. Mineralogist* XII. 77/2 Sb, Bi, and As are characteristic trace elements in many well-differentiated Li-rich pegmatites... Stibiotantalite is presently known from about 10 localities in the world, all of them of this type.

stibocaptate (stibokæ·ptē[i]t). *Pharm.* [f. Stib- + -o + *-capt-* in 'antimony dimer*capto*-succinate', a chemical name for the substance (see Mercaptan) + -ate[4].] An antimony-containing drug used in the treatment of schistosomiasis and administered by intramuscular injection.

1962 *Trop. Dis. Bull.* LIX. 1281/1 (Index), Stibocaptate. **1967** *Lancet* 21 Jan. 130/2 Monthly intramuscular injections of stibocaptate 10 mg. per kg. body-weight proved to be the best treatment for Zanzibari schoolboys infected with *Schistosoma hæmatobium.* **1977** *Proc. R. Soc. Med.* LXX. 762/2 Stibocaptate (Astiban)..is the only antimonial used for schistosomiasis in the United Kingdom. **1978** *Nature* 22 June 628/1 Stibocaptate (antimony dimercaptosuccinate, Astiban), one of the more than 10,000 antimonials that have been synthesised, is still on the WHO list as a complementary drug.

stibophen (sti·bǒfen). *Pharm.* [f. STIB- + -O + PHEN(-.] The compound pentasodium antimonybis(catechol-3,5-disulphonate) heptahydrate, which is used principally in the treatment of schistosomiasis, and is administered by intramuscular or intravenous injection.

1941 *Brit. Pharmacopœia 1932* Add. III. 22 (*heading*) Stibophen. **1941** *Q. Jrnl. Pharmacy & Pharmacol.* XIV. 43 A further study of the effect of pH on the stability of stibophen solutions is being made. **1950** *Amer. Jrnl. Trop. Med.* XXX. 266 Fuadin, also known as 'stibophen', another trivalent [antimony] compound, which contains 13·6 per cent antimony, was introduced in 1929 for the treatment of Egyptian schistosomiasis. **1977** *Brit. Jrnl. Dermatol.* XCVII. 308 The patient was treated with 25 injections of stibophen..2 ml intramuscularly on alternate days.

stichtite (sti·tʃtəit). *Min.* [f. the name of R. C. *Sticht* (1856–1922), of Australia + -ITE[1].] A hydrated carbonate of magnesium and chromium, $Mg_6Cr_2(OH)_{16}CO_3.4H_2O$, occurring as trigonal crystals of a pink, lilac, or purple colour.

1910 W. F. PETTERD in *Papers & Proc. R. Soc. Tasmania* 167 *Stichtite*... This is beyond doubt an unrecorded mineral species which has hitherto been known under the name of kammererite... The writer has great pleasure in dedicating this new mineral species to Mr. Robert Sticht, the..general manager of the Mt. Lyell Mining and Railway Company. **1977** *Austral. Gemmologist* XIII. 103/1 Stichtite..occurs as a deep purple to rose pink soft waxy mineral as knots and veins in serpentine.

stick, *sb.*[1] Add: **I. 4. b.** Proverbial phr. *a stick to beat* (someone or something) *with* (perh. with ref. to the proverb: see quot. 1782). Also contrasted with *carrot* (= reward): see *CARROT *sb.* 2 a.

1653 D. OSBORNE *Let.* 24 July (1903) 125 What reason had I to furnish you with a stick to beat myself withal? [**1782** F. HOPKINSON *Misc. Essays* I. 266 A proverb.. naturally occurs on this occasion: It is easy to find a stick to beat a dog.] **1889** G. B. SHAW in *English Illustr. Mag.* Oct. 49 A few of us go to Bayreuth because it is a capital stick to beat a dog with. **1928** D. H. LAWRENCE in *Evening News* 8 May 8/4 The last stupid stick with which the old can beat the young. **1962** *Listener* 5 Apr. 597/2 Israel has sometimes been just another stick with which the Arabs beat each other. **1966** *Ibid.* 9 June 824/2 The Liberals had been glad to use the horror [at Turkish atrocities] felt by people in Britain as a stick with which to beat the Conservatives.

c. Hence (without article) *transf.*, severe physical handling, 'punishment'; *fig.* unfavourable criticism, censure, reproof. Usu. in phrases *to come in for, get, give,* or *take stick.*

1942 *E. African Ann.* 1941–2 115/1 The Italians nipped across from Diredawa, and, as the troops say, 'gave us stick'. **1956** *People* 13 May 14/8 As usual the Australians are getting plenty of stick from the armchair critics. **1967** J. BURKE *Till Death us do Part* vii. 116 He went out on the booze... She didn't half give him some stick when she found out. **1977** J. WAINWRIGHT *Nest of Rats* III. v. 205 We took some stick, and we gave some stick... I belted that face. **1980** *Daily Tel.* 11 Apr. 19/2, I told him that he could expect trouble from the branches... He will come in for some stick over this.

i. A conductor's baton.

1849 *Hamilton's Celebrated Dict.* s.v. *Battre la mesure,* To mark the time by beating with the hand or with a stick etc. **1884** F. NIECKS *Dict. Mus. Terms* s.v. *Bâton,* A stick used for beating time. *Ibid.* s.v. *Taktstock,* a conducting stick. **1920** A. BOULT *Handbk. Technique Conducting* 7 The conductor has, therefore, had to learn to show his ideas on the interpretation of a work by means of his stick and hand. **1931** *Times Lit. Suppl.* 14 May 394/2 Stickless conducting..may suffice in ordinary class-room teaching; but in the interests of festival work ..it is better to accustom all singers to watch a stick and to train up a generation of conductors who know the technique of using it. **1955** *Times* 2 Feb. 6/3 There were moments when a loose movement of the stick gave away a little concentration in the quiet entries of the strings. **1978** *Gramophone* Feb. 1390/1 His mentor was band leader Joe Loss. 'When Loss used a stick the bounce and freedom within a beat was masterly.'

5. c. (Earlier example.)

in front of the sticks: at the wicket, batting.

1840 J. C. W. in *Sporting Mag.* Aug. 333 (Cricketing Extraordinary) New *stumps* are wanted to the number of six, So, good Mr. Charon, pray lend us the *sticks*! **1924** LAWRENCE & SKINNER *Boy in Bush* ii. 22, I was captain of the first football eleven... And not bad in front of the sticks.

e. *Assoc. Football.* Phr. *between the sticks*: between the goal-posts, keeping goal.

1950 *Sport* 7–11 Apr. 14/3 Good news for Reading fans is that goalkeeper George Marks is expected to be back between the Elm Park sticks at the start of season 1950–1951. **1976** *Wymondham & Attleborough Express* 19 Nov. 23/4 Wortwell could not produce the form of recent weeks and crashed heavily to their hosts. David Loome took over between the 'sticks'.

7. *to up stick(s.* For (*lit.* and *fig.*) read: also *fig.* (usu. in form *up sticks*), to prepare to move, pack up, get going; to pack up and go, remove oneself. (Earlier and further examples.)

1839 *Knickerbocker* XIV. 141 Why, in the name of common sense, do you not up sticks and off? **1854** [see UP *adv.*[1] 29]. **1859** D. BUNCE *Trav. with Dr. Leichhardt* ix. 141 The place was so muddy as to render it necessary to 'up sticks!' and start for another..camping ground. **1877** *Harper's Mag.* Jan. 213/2 If any man tries hard words with me, I knocks him down, up sticks, and makes tracks. **1920** C. A. W. MONCKTON *Some Experiences of New Guinea Resident Magistrate* xxii. 262 Up sticks and away for Port Moresby and Sir Francis Winter. **1958** P. SCOTT *Mark of Warrior* II. 168, 0700 we up sticks here and get well under cover a mile into the jungle. **1967** *Economist* 21 Oct. 306/1 If businesses can up-sticks from Quebec.., they are being tempted to do so. **1972** G. GREEN *Great Moments in Sport: Soccer* i. 28 Neil Franklin ..upped sticks..and departed to Bogotá. **1978** *Guardian Weekly* 26 Mar. 21/2 What on earth impels a man..suddenly to up sticks at 84 and come back to this distressful country?

II. 8. f. Of bread, esp. as *French stick.* Cf. *BATON *sb.* 1 c, *bread-stick* s.v. *BREAD *sb.* 10, *GRISSINO.

1909 [see *bread-stick* s.v. *BREAD *sb.* 10]. **1943** A. SIMON *Conc. Encycl. Gastron.* IV. 59/2 (*heading*) Grissini or salt sticks. **1959** *Times* 9 Mar. (Britain's Food Suppl.) p. xii/5 Her French sister who shops three times a day for her French sticks in order to get them really fresh. **1962** *Woman* 8 Dec. 51/3 A stick of French bread. **1972** *House & Garden* Feb. 98/2 Swiss fondue... Sesame seed sticks.. make a happy accompaniment. **1980** *Sunday Times* (Colour Suppl.) 20 Jan. 57/3 *French stick,* long thin loaf with thick golden crust.

10. d. Also, in *Journalism,* a measure of copy, corresponding to about two column-inches.

1898 *Scribner's Mag.* May 579/1 He talked amiably enough; he said nothing he ought not to have said, but Linton [*sc.* a reporter] got five sticks out of it (a half column). **1932** G. GREENE *Stamboul Train* II. i. 44 They've asked me for a quarter of a column, but they'll cut it down to a couple of sticks. **1966** —— in *New Statesman* 25 Feb. 254/1 The ceremony could not possibly rate more than a couple of sticks in tomorrow's paper.

e. (Later examples in jazz and rock music.) Hence *pl.*, a nickname for a drummer. *Naval slang.*

1926 *Melody Maker* Sept. 56 The tambourine is..played with the sticks. **1933** *Metronome* Oct. 51/2 Playing with the sticks widely separated on the head of the snare drum is a common fault. **1977** *Gay News* 24 Mar. 32/3 Drummer Rat Scabies (also 19) is very fast with the sticks.

1909 J. R. WARE *Passing Eng.* 234/1 *Sticks,*..drummer. **1916** 'TAFFRAIL' *Carry On* 27 A drummer goes by the name of *sticks,* from the implements with which he beats his drum. **1950** KERR & JAMES *Wavy Navy* 263 *Sticks,* the ship's drummer.

i. = *joy-stick* s.v. *JOY *sb.* 10. Also occas., a gear lever in a motor vehicle.

1914 H. ROSHER *Let.* 11 Aug. in *In R.N.A.S.* (1916) 13 Mr. Strutt, our instructor.., controls the engine switch and covers your hand on the stick. **1927** C. A. LINDBERGH *We* v. 76 Pulling the stick back to go up. **1929** *Daily Express* 7 Nov. 1/1 On two occasions the pilot had to pull his stick back sharply, and once we only just cleared the tree tops. **1948** W. FORTESCUE *Beauty for Ashes* xxvii. 210 From their demeanour and that of the pilot, who handed 'the stick' over to a friend while he came to see that I was comfortable, one might almost have thought that this was my own private bomber. **1971** R. DENTRY *Encounter at Kharmel* iii. 42 Pepper threw the gear stick into neutral, applied the handbrake firmly, switched off... She..moved the stick back to first. **1977** *R.A.F. Yearbk.* 31/1 The Hawk is very docile in the stall and..control is immediately regained once the stick is moved forward.

j. The propeller of an aircraft (*rare*). *dead stick*: see *DEAD *a.* D. 2.

1917 *Editor* 21 Apr. 358 The propeller itself is generally known as the 'prop' or 'stick'.

k. = *ski stick* s.v. *SKI *sb.* 2 b.

1961 WEBSTER, *Stick rider,* a skier who makes excessive use of ski poles. **1963** *Amer. Speech* XXXVIII. 207 *Sticks,*... Slang for skis, and also for ski poles. **1972** 'M. YORKE' *Silent Witness* ii. 14 He stacked his skis and sticks in..the rack. **1977** C. WOOD *James Bond, Spy who loved Me* ii. 15 He stamped hard into his skis.. and stabbed at the snow with his sticks.

l. *Surfing.* A surfboard.

1967 J. SEVERSON *Great Surfing* Gloss., *Stick,* a surfboard. **1967** *Internat. Surfing* III. III. 29 Because of the lack of length when changing to a shorter board, different techniques from surfing a longer board are required. Margo Godfrey and Mike Purpus offer some helpful advice on adjusting to the short stick.

11. c. (Earlier and later examples.)

1879 *Macmillan's Mag.* Oct. 503/1 'What tools will you want?'..He said, 'We shall want some twirls and the stick (crowbar)'. **1934** P. SAVAGE *Savage of Scotland Yard* xxiii. 252 It's a fair cop. I'll go quiet, and here's my stick (jemmy). **1960** [see *LOID].

g. *the sticks*: a remote, thinly populated, rural area; the backwoods; hence, in extended (freq. depreciatory) use, any area that is off the beaten track or thought to be provincial or unsophisticated; esp. in phr. *in the sticks.* orig. *U.S.*

1905 N. DAVIS *Northerner* 78 Billy is a cane-brake nigger; he'll take to the sticks like a duck to water when he's scared. **1914** R. LARDNER in *Sat. Even. Post* 7 Mar. 8/1, I will have to slip you back to the sticks [i.e. the minor baseball leagues]. **1921** *Daily Colonist* (Victoria, B.C.) 22 Oct. 11/3 Judge Landis..has not yet consigned Babe Ruth to oblivion for..playing in the sticks for exhibition money. **1926** WHITEMAN & MCBRIDE *Jazz* xiii. 254 They had..all the real New Yorker's prejudice against 'the sticks'. **1936** J. DOS PASSOS *Big Money* 61 Mighty nice of you to ask me. I been out in the sticks... It makes you feel good to see folks from the other side... This is the nearest thing to Paree I've seen for some time. **1941** W. C. HANDY *Father of Blues* (1957) ix. 126, I continued ..playing for dances, touring on the road and through the sticks and giving concerts. **1958** C. KOCH *Boys in Island* 101 What can y' expect, way out here in the sticks? **1968** J. LOCK *Lady Policeman* ix. 79 Where's that? I know, it's somewhere in the sticks. **1971** *N.Z. Listener* 27 Sept. 3/2 The 'real' New Zealand..is out there in the sticks, under the open sky, where men have dirt on their elbows. **1974** *New Society* 7 Feb. 309/1 The idea of 'provincial' journalists working 'out in the sticks' has strong pejorative overtones. **1977** *Daily Express* 29 Jan. 39/2 More fighting talk came from Swindon striker Dave Syrett. 'Most people regard us as a bunch of farmers from out in the sticks,' he said.

h. A cigarette or cigar; *spec.*, a cigarette made with marijuana; also *stick of tea, weed* (cf. *TEA *sb.* 7 c, *WEED *sb.*[1] 3 c). See also *cancer stick* s.v. *CANCER *sb.* 5, *Thai stick* s.v. *THAI *a.*

1919 W. H. DOWNING *Digger Dialects* 17 *Consumption stick,* a cigarette. **1935** E. FARJEON *Nursery in Nineties* 348 Papa..smokes all day long, but only affords himself the cheapest..sticks, except when Aunt Mary Albery sends him a hundred Coronas for Christmas. **1938** [see *MARY 1 d]. **1940** R. CHANDLER *Farewell, my Lovely* xiv. 68 Evidence of what? That a man occasionally smoked a stick of tea, a man who looked as if any touch of the exotic would appeal to him. **1957** C. MACINNES *City of Spades* I. v. 28 'I'll roll you a stick.'..I lit up... 'Good stuff. And what do they make you pay for a stick here?' **1959** L. LIPTON *Holy Barbarians* iii. 78 Rolling their sticks of 'tea', they looked like a ring of kindergarteners. **1965** W. SOYINKA *Road* 24 Say Tokyo reaches out a stick of weed to him which he accepts behind his back. **1978** T. WILLIAMSON *Technicians of Death* xiv. 121 He got his first 'buzz' with a blend of Thai stick and opium.

12. c. *U.S. slang.* = *SHILL *sb.*

1926 MAINES & GRANT *Wise-Crack Dict.* 14/1 *Stick,* a confederate who wins or loses at dealer's will. **1931** G. IRWIN *Amer. Tramp & Underworld Slang* 182 The cash the 'stick' wins is handed back to the operator of the game ..and the stick never has enough of his employer's money to make it worth his while to decamp. **1966** E. V. CUNNINGHAM *Helen* (1967) ix. 129 A shill is also called a stick, and the role of the shill or stick is to make the customer relax and feel at ease.

13*. *Mil.* **a.** A number (usu. five or six) of bombs dropped in quick succession from an aircraft.

1940 *Illustr. London News* 18 May 669 (*caption*) A 'stick' of five bombs has just burst across her bows. **1940** *Times* 6 Dec. 4/1 Seeing a convoy in the road, we dropped a stick plumb in the centre of it. **1942** *Tee Emm* (Air Ministry) II. 100 If you, as bomb aimer..watch a stick of bombs on a town you'll notice that they appear to move outwards... When they hit they form a *curved* stick. **1956** W. SLIM *Defeat into Victory* VI. xxi. 500 British officers, watching from the ground the fall of each stick of bombs. **1975** T. ALLBEURY *Special Collection* iv. 18 There were dull thuds as another stick of bombs was dropped.

b. A group of parachutists jumping in quick succession.

1943 *Combined Operations* (Min. of Information) ii. 19 They [*sc.* airborne troops] practise dropping from an aircraft, first in 'slow' then in 'quick' pairs, until they are proficient enough to drop in 'sticks'. **1949** F. MACLEAN *Eastern Approaches* III. ix. 414, I had decided to jump first with the others following in a 'stick'. **1955** J. THOMAS *No Banners* xiv. 127 The despatcher yelled hysterically: 'Now, a nice stick of three!' **1974** C. RYAN *Bridge Too Far* III. iii. 156 As the pilot held it steady on course, Mitchell saw the entire stick of paratroopers jump right through the fire. **1982** *Times* 5 June 4/6 The 15 marines in our 'stick' jumped through the [helicopter] door..with weapons ready.

III. 14. e. (Further examples.) Also with other adjectives.

1846 *Swell's Night Guide* 49 Which of us had hold of the crappy..end of the stick? **1930** E. WAUGH *Vile Bodies* viii. 143 My private schoolmaster used to say, 'If a thing's worth doing at all, it's worth doing well.'..But these young people have got hold of another end of the stick, and for all we know it may be the right one. They say, 'If a thing's not worth doing well, it's not worth doing at all.' **1934** C. DAY LEWIS *Hope for Poetry* vii. 42 Although Lewis's analysis convinces us..as being correct in detail, we are compelled to feel that Lawrence rather than Lewis had got hold of the right end of the stick. **1939** 'G. ORWELL' *Coming up for Air* IV. vii. 283 Listen, Hilda. You've got hold of the wrong end of the stick about this business. **1959** 'M. CRONIN' *Dead & done With* iv. 61 I've had the rough end of the stick ever since I got here. **1977** P. SCOTT *Staying On* (1978) i. 14 Always..I have the mucky end of the stick. But then I am only part of the fixtures and fittings.

i. *up the stick*: pregnant. *slang.* Cf. *up the pole* s.v. *POLE *sb.*[1] 1 b.

1941 BAKER *Dict. Austral. Slang* 71 *Stick, up the:*

(of a girl or woman) to be pregnant. **1958** [see *BUN *sb.*[2] 1]. **1968** R. LAIT *Chance to Kill* i. 10 Mary up the stick; funny how everyone counts the months. **1976** J. I. M. STEWART *Memorial Service* ix. 160 Do you know what it's like, Cyril, to be a decent and penniless young man who isn't sure he hasn't got his girl up the stick?

j. *to cut one's stick*: see CUT *v.* 43; *more than you can shake a stick at*: see *SHAKE *v.* 5 b.

IV. 15. a. *stick microphone, mike.*

1961 C. WILLOCK *Death in Covert* xii. 212 The interviewer from ITN..was holding a stick microphone. **1961** *Listener* 19 Oct. 622/3 Uncle Dimbleby is seated (with stick mike) among a 'representative cross-section' of the British public. **1976** B. JACKSON *Flameout* (1977) IV. xii. 204 He saw him [*sc.* the pilot] speak into the stick microphone attached to his headset.

16. stick-and-carrot *adj. phr.* [see *CARROT *sb.* 2 a], characterized by both the threat of punishment and the offer of reward; **stick-back** *a.*, designating a kind of wooden chair having a back formed by upright rods or sticks; **stickball** *U.S.*, a game played with stick and ball; *spec.* (*a*) improvised baseball played with a stick and soft ball; (*b*) an American Indian ball game resembling lacrosse, played by the Indians of the South-eastern U.S.; **stick bean,** a runner bean; **stick-bomb,** a bomb or grenade with a protruding rod or stick for firing or throwing (cf. also *STICK *v.*[1] 35); **stick dance,** any of various kinds of folk-dance in which the dancer holds a stick and (in some dances) beats it against the sticks of other dancers; **stick-dressing,** the art of making shepherd's crooks (cf. *stick-dresser,* sense 15 b); **stick-fighting** *W. Indies*, a kind of martial art; hence **stick-fighter; stick-figure,** a matchstick figure (see *match-stick* (*c*) s.v. *MATCH *sb.*[2] 5), a pin-man; **stick fixed** *Aeronaut.*, the control column of an aircraft held in one position; freq. *attrib.*; **stick force** *Aeronaut.*, the force or effort needed to move the control column of an aircraft or hold it in position; **stick free** *Aeronaut.*, the control column of an aircraft allowed to move freely, unguided by the pilot; freq. *attrib.*; **stick (hand-)grenade,** a grenade with a handle; **stick-handling** *vbl. sb.* orig. and chiefly *N. Amer.*, the handling of one's stick in ice hockey (or occas. in other sports) (cf. *stick-work* (a)); also fig.; hence (as back-formation) **stick-handle** *v. intr.*, to control the puck (in ice hockey) with one's stick; also **stick-handler; Stick Indian** *Canad. colloq.*, a member of the North American Indian peoples inhabiting the forests of British Columbia and the Yukon [properly a loan transl. of Chinook Jargon *stick siwash* forest Indian, a term used by the Coast Indians for those of the interior in this area.]; **stick loaf:** occas. used = *French stick*, sense 8 f above; **stick-man,** (*a*) *slang*, a pick-pocket's accomplice (cf. *stick slinger*); (*b*) *U.S. colloq.*, a croupier; (*c*) *W. Indies* = *stick-fighter* above; (*d*) *rare* = *stick-figure* above; **stick-shaker** *Aeronaut. colloq.*, a device which causes the control column to vibrate when the aircraft is close to stalling; **stick shift** *N. Amer.*, a manually operated mechanism for changing gear; a gear lever; **stickwork,** (*b*) something made from, or fashioned by the use of, sticks.

1963 *Times* 4 Mar. 11/7 President Ayub has..given himself stick-and-carrot powers to deal with the 'Ebdonians'. **1977** 'J. LE CARRÉ' *Hon. Schoolboy* vi. 136 It's a stick and carrot job. If you don't play, the comic will blow the whistle on you... That's the *bad* news... The good news is five hundred US into your hot little hand. **1783** *Narragansett Hist. Reg.* (1884) II. 314 Three good large Windsor or Stickback Chairs. **1923** *Heal & Son Catal.: Kitchen Furniture* 2 Unpolished Stickback Windsor Small Chair..12/6. **1963** *Guardian* 21 Aug. 6/6 A pale oak gate-leg table is set off by six flame stick-back chairs. **1978** *Cornish Guardian* 27 Apr. 10/4 (Advt.), Swivel chairs, ..wheel back and stick back chairs, easy chairs [, etc.]. **1824** *Nantucket Inquirer* 12 Jan. 3/5 No person shall play Foot-ball or Poke, Stick-ball or Swinger, within the compact part of the Town of Nantucket. **1934** E. NEWHOUSE *You can't sleep Here* xii. 154 Two contending stickball teams left the gutter to see what was up. **1946** *Life* 11 Nov. 91/1 On the Cherokees' Qualla Indian Reservation in North Carolina..the Wolftown Wolves met the Wolftown Bears in a crucial game of stickball... The game of stickball, which is a primitive version of modern lacrosse, was centuries old when De Soto led a Spanish expedition through Cherokee territory in 1540. **1947** *Commentary* May 464/1 Sometimes we became so engrossed by a punchball or stickball game that night would fall without anyone's being aware of it. **1953** *Sun* (Baltimore) 1 Apr. (B. ed.) 12/1 Governor McKeldin can remember romping barefooted in the neighborhood, playing stickball. **1979** *United States 1980/81* (Penguin Travel Guides) 533 A recreation of an early-18th-century Cherokee Village, where Cherokees in costume dance, play at stickball, work at crafting baskets, [etc.]. **1981** *TV Picture Life* Mar. 32/1 A group of young black children playing stickball on the streets of New York. **1906** *Dialect Notes* III. 158 *Stick bean*,..pole bean. **1980** J. GARDAM *Sidmouth Lett.* 134 D'you want some beans?.. Stick beans? **1916** in C. F. S. Gamble *Story N. Sea Air Station* (1928) xiii. 222 The silent firing of projectiles varying in size from the Mills grenade to the 250-lb. stick bomb. **1925** FRASER & GIBBONS *Soldier & Sailor Words* 270 *Stick-bomb*, a type of trench-mortar bomb attached to a hollow steel rod which passed down the bore of the projectile. **1940** *Illustr. London News* 10 Feb. 167/1 A charge with 'stick-bombs' —a form of hand grenade. *Ibid.* 167/2 (*caption*) The patrol reaches the enemy lines, overwhelming them with the threat of 'stick-bombs'. **1899** KIPLING *From Sea to Sea* II. xxv. 12 A Zanzibar stick-dance, such as you see at Aden on the coal boats. **1907** SHARP & MACILWAINE *Morris Bk.* I. 39 In the Stick and Handkerchief dances, pairs..stand near enough to clap hands or tap sticks with each other. **1950** BLESH & JANIS *They All played Ragtime* (1958) 13 The banjo-ragtime rhythms of dances like the buck and wing, the Virginia Essence, the stick and the sand dances, and the soft-shoe routines. **1982** N. PAINTING *Reluctant Archer* vii. 113, I was also roped in..to play the piano for rehearsals of the stick dance which David Raeburn had introduced into his production of *The Shoemaker's Holiday*. **1968** P. JENNINGS *Living Village* 187 Stick-dressing..is the making of shepherds' crooks. A stick is dressed down, a ram's horn is put on top of it and the whole thing is polished. **1956** *Caribbean Q.* IV. III & IV. 194 Later this aristocrat's masque was adopted by batonyé or stick fighters. **1968** E. LOVELACE *Schoolmaster* i. 12 'Who say that?' Miguel asked hotly, growing angry, and moving up and down like a stickfighter in a rage. **1956** *Caribbean Q.* IV. III. & IV. 192 Antagonisms are relaxed from time to time by fêtes, when the traditional pastimes of dancing, singing and stick-fighting are enjoyed, with liquor and food. **1974** *Trinidad Guardian* 2 Nov. 5/2 (Advt.), African culture in all forms. Dance, Stick-fighting, Drumming, Calypso, [etc.]. **1965** I. A. RICHARDS in *Times Lit. Suppl.* 27 May 439/2 A stick-figure man is very different from any man but *is* a little like his silhouette or his shadow on a screen. **1976** *New Yorker* 9 Feb. 94/3 Weiss projects no character, he remains a stick figure. **1978** S. SHELDON *Bloodline* xxiv. 259 He was like a stick figure drawn by a child, with angular arms and legs, and a dry, unfinished face sketched on top of his body. **1945** *Jrnl. R. Aeronaut. Soc.* XLIX. 617/2 The stick movements the pilot has to make to control the aircraft are related to the stick fixed stability, while the stick forces he has to exert are related to the stick free stability. **1961** A. W. BABISTER *Aircraft Stability & Control* iii. 63 The stick fixed static margin is related to the elevator movement (or stick movement) to trim the aircraft. **1937** *Jrnl. R. Aeronaut. Soc.* XLI. 960 The stick forces required to operate them [*sc.* flaps] increased too rapidly with speed. **1942** *Tee Emm* (Air Ministry) II. 85 The stick force needed, say, to take violent avoiding action may be much too great. **1961** A. W. BABISTER *Aircraft Stability & Control* iii. 63 We shall now derive the relation between the stick force the pilot has to apply to hold the aircraft in a glide and the stick free static margin. **1983** E. BROWN *Wings of Weird & Wonderful* xvi. 100 The latter aircraft was the less pleasant to fly as the stick continually hunted either side of neutral, and there was no build up in stick force with increase in speed. **1945** Stick free [see *stick fixed* above]. **1961** Stick free [see *stick force* above]. **1918** E. S. FARROW *Dict. Mil. Terms* 586 *Stick grenade*, a grenade attached to a stick and thrown over short distances like a dart. **1979** O. SELA *Petrograd Consignment* 53 Boris..took out two stick grenades and a Mills bomb. **1923** Stick hand-grenade [see *HAIRBRUSH 2]. **1929** *N.Y. Times* 10 Mar. XII. 8/1 Trottier staged a prize play when he stickhandled his way through the entire American team. **1969** M. BRAITHWAITE *Never sleep Three in Bed* (1970) xv. 182 Back in 1926, he really couldn't skate very well, but he could stick-handle like a fiend. **1915** *Official Ice Hockey Guide* 17 Hill of Cornell.. is very fast, a good stick handler. **1958** *Rosetown* (Saskatchewan) *Eagle* 29 May 10/1 Dick..Elliot, plugger type, stick handler, back-bone of the team. **1904** *Ice Hockey & Ice Polo Guide* 35 Stick-handling, like confidence, coolness, strength and speed, is acquired by practice... The better you can handle your stick the more effective player you will be, because stick-handling is one of the essentials of the game. **1962** *Times* 28 Feb. 4/4 Cool lacrosse at Cambridge... Cambridge..played calmly, showing glimpses of..skilful stick-handling. **1976** *Ottawa Citizen* 24 Dec. 2/3 They did some nifty stickhandling through government red tape. [**1869** L. SMITH *Let.* 30 Oct. in *Rep. Indian Affairs 1969* (U.S.) (1870) 567 Twice a year most of the Indians make a trip up the Stikine River to Talyan, at which place the Stick tribe reside.] **1885** F. SCHWATKA *Rep. Mil. Reconn. Alaska 1883* 76 The so-called 'Stick' Indians of the interior are seen in the villages near the trading stores. **1887** G. M. DAWSON *Notes on Indian Tribes of Yukon* 14 They are classed with the 'Stick Indians', by the coast tribes. **1963** R. SYMONS *Many Trails* vii. 72 Snowshoes are known only as a strange accoutrement of the 'Stick Indians'. **1980** *Times* 15 Dec. 1/8 Britons returned home with..wines, stick loaves and under-ripe Camemberts. **1861** J. BINNY in H. Mayhew *London Labour* Extra Vol. (1862) 282/2 While drinking at the bar, one of the women tries to rob him... A man who is called a 'stickman', an accomplice..of hers, comes to the bar... If they have by this time secured the booty, it is passed to the latter, who thereupon slips away. **1931** *Amer. Speech* VII. 116 *Stick-man*,..a croupier in a gambling joint. **1952** *Evening News* (Port of Spain, Trinidad) 28 Jan. 8/2 A Trinidad stickman held his stick at both ends when going into action. **1958** *Newark* (New Jersey) *Star-Ledger* 23 Mar. 102/4 Then the stickman rakes in the dice, picks them up, and tosses them back to the shooter. **1966** J. DOS PASSOS *Best Times* ii. 47, I sent Arthur a cartoon..of warmongers..hanging from the arc lights on Fifth Avenue, while two stickmen..danced the carmagnole in the foreground. **1975** [see *POGUE]. **1980** J. SCOTT *Hunted* i. 8 He shoved the counters forward and the stickman flicked them into place. **1962** *Flight Internat.* LXXXI. 330/1 At 70 kt the stick shaker rattled again, but there was still plenty of aileron control. **1979** *Daily Tel.* 9 Aug. 7/2 The F.A.A. has proposed that an additional 'stick-shaker' be installed to warn the pilot when the plane loses enough speed and lift to approach a stall. **1960** *Wall St. Jrnl.* 13 Oct. 26 (Advt.), 'Welcome back, standard transmission.'.. A great majority of those who buy sports cars specify the 'stick shift' for the fun of it. **1976** 'E. MCBAIN' *Guns* (1977) vii. 200 Bucket seats in beige leather, stick shift on the floor. **1923** KIPLING *Irish Guards in Great War* I. 164 They [*sc.* the trenches] had been French..and [were] riveted with strange French stickwork. **1929** B. OLIVER *Cottages of England* iii. 44 The pricked treatment.., as also the scratched patterns, were equally the common finish to cottage exteriors all over Suffolk and Essex. Nothing looks better than this delightful Essex 'stickwork'. **1933** B. RACKHAM *Guide to Ital. Maiolica* i. 5 Lead-glazed earthenware with decoration done..by scratching with a pointed instrument.. through a surface layer of..'slip'... Wares of this kind are..called..*sgraffito*... The phrase *a stecco* ('stickwork') is generally used..in referring to this process. **1977** *Penguin Dict. Decorative Arts* 759/1 *Stickwork.* Small objects such as chess-men, egg-cups, snuff-boxes, etc. made from sticks of various types of wood assembled by the same technique as in Tunbridge ware and then turned on a lathe.

Stick, *sb.*[5]: see *STICKIE, STICKY.

stick, *v.*[1] Add: **I. 1. f.** To inoculate, to give a hypodermic injection to; to introduce a hypodermic needle into (a person). *U.S. colloq.*

1946 *Sun* (Baltimore) 19 June 10/1 Though he [*sc.* the traveler] surely has been 'stuck' for every known disease, no telling how often he will be halted by health officers and cast into quarantine. **1963** *New Yorker* 25 May 42/2 'Fraid I've got to stick you once more. **1969** E. WELTY in *New Yorker* 15 Mar. 43/1 The floor nurse came in to feed Mr. Dalzell, then stick him with a needle.

II. 6. e. *Vingt-et-un.* To decline the opportunity of adding to one's hand.

1931 W. V. TILSLEY *Other Ranks* 147 A little group in the centre of the room sprawled on their blankets, playing pontoon. 'I'll stick!' 'Twist one!' 'Busted!' **1950** [see *BUST *v.*[2] f]. **1956** R. FULLER *Image of Society* vii. 188 'In other words the bank is sticking at sixteen,' said Cawsey, amused at his own turn of phrase. **1976** G. SIMS *End of Web* iii. 22 Hello, young Clive. Still sticking on seventeens? .. I'm coming round for another pontoon lesson shortly.

7. b. (Further example.)

1977 J. F. FIXX *Compl. Bk. Running* iv. 49 One must stick at one's sport if it is to continue doing any good.

c. Also with a thing as object.

1907 J. M. SYNGE *Lett. to Molly* (1971) 172, I cannot 'stick' these plays any more. **1922** A. S. M. HUTCHINSON *This Freedom* IV. iii. 279, I couldn't stick the place. **1928** *Daily Tel.* 27 Mar. 9/1, I resigned..because I could stick the chief's bullying no longer. **1960** D. STOREY *This Sporting Life* I. ii. 29, I couldn't stick the sight of him standing up there against the Batley skyline.

8. c. Also, of a criminal charge: to be substantiated, take effect. Of an order or decision made by a court of justice, legislature, or other authority: to be implemented or complied with. Hence with wider application, esp. in phr. *to make* (something) *stick*, to make (that thing) effective; to clinch; to substantiate.

1932 [see *RAP *sb.*[1] 4 e]. **1942** *Sun* (Baltimore) 12 June 1/7 A..program of cooperation designed (1) to hasten the defeat of Germany and (2) to make that defeat stick. **1944** *Ibid.* 7 Feb. 1/1 The Department of Labor..would be empowered to hand down decisions 'which will stick and not be vetoed by any other Federal agency'. **1951** E. PAUL *Springtime in Paris* xvi. 324 Every officer at the Commissariat of the 5th had been itching to get Oudin, on any charge at all that could be made to stick. **1963** 'S. WOODS' *Taste of Fears* xiv. 148 'They couldn't make it stick,' said his uncle, positively... 'No evidence.' **1971** A. PRICE *Alamut Ambush* xii. 147 God knows whether the Americans and the Russians can make the cease-fire stick. **1981** *Times Lit. Suppl.* 9 Jan. 25/1 Picasso now taught himself how to use a poetic, half-theatrical imagination to make his art 'stick', while at the same time..taking pains to avoid the illustrational.

12. c. *to stick in one's throat*, (*b*) of a statement, proposal, notion, belief, etc.: to be difficult to swallow, to be unacceptable.

1843 DICKENS *Let.* 1 Feb. (1973) III. 434 Your dedication to Peel stuck in my throat. **1885** E. W. HAMILTON *Diary* 3 May (1972) II. 855 To luncheon..with F. Rothschild to talk over politics... What sticks in his throat is Chamberlain's programme—his quack remedies for the agricultural labourer, of whose real wants he has no experience. **1924** G. B. SHAW *St. Joan* Pref. p. li, The truth sticks in our throats with all the sauces it is served with. **1938** W. S. MAUGHAM *Summing Up* lxxvi. 310 This notion has long stuck in my gizzard. **1953** A. J. TOYNBEE *World & West* vi. 98 The new religions which were now being offered..would have stuck in a philosopher's throat if the missionary had not sugared the strange pill for him. **1958** C. P. SNOW *Conscience of Rich* xxxi. 232, I didn't like refusing, but it stuck in my gullet to help that blasted group of reds. **1976** A. PRICE *War Game* II. i. 193 Weston would find the accident..sticking in his throat, a question much too sharp to be swallowed.

18. d. *imp.* (or in constructions with equivalent force) and followed by *up* as a coarse expression of contemptuous rejection. Also *ellipt.* Similarly euphem. phr. *stick it in your ear* (U.S.). Cf. *SHOVE *v.* 10 e, *STUFF *v.*[1] 14* a.

1922 S. LEWIS *Babbitt* xix. 240 Bad luck, old dear, and you can stick your job up the sewer! **1939** R. STOUT *Some Buried Caesar* xi. 153 All right. Take your name and stick it up your chimney and go to hell. **1941** BAKER

Dict. Austral. Slang 71 *Stick it!*, a contemptuous ejaculation. **1948** D. Ballantyne *Cunninghams* xx. 105 He had a good mind to tell Basil Fisher to stick his run. **1960** Wentworth & Flexner *Dict. Amer. Slang* 520/1 *Stick it* (*something*) *up your* (*one's*) *ass* (taboo),..the strongest reply to the question, 'What shall I do with this?' **1971** P. Driscoll *White Lie Assignment* ii. 20 If you do earn your thousand pounds you can stick it, d'you hear? Stick it right up where it belongs. I don't want a penny of it. **1973** *Houston Chron.* 21 Oct. 12/7 Members of the House are suggesting to members of the Senate that they take this idea and stick it in their ears. **1977** *Daily Tel.* 22 June 17/8 After the hearing Mr Jeeves said: 'They can stick their cottage. I shall not move into it.'

21. b. (Earlier example.)

1876 [see *cold *a.* 12 b].

c. *to be stuck for*: to be at a loss how to obtain; to be unable to think of. *colloq.*

1937 in Partridge *Dict. Slang.* **1963** 'J. le Carré' *Spy who came in from Cold* iv. 32 'Who's Mr. Ironside?'..'I don't think he exists... He's her big gun when she's stuck for an answer.' **1965** A. J. P. Taylor *Eng. Hist. 1914–45* viii. 267 The Conservatives were strong in resistance. They were stuck for a positive programme. **1969** *Guardian* 31 July 6/1 Any time you're stuck for a meal.. come around. **1977** D. Beatty *Excellency* iv. 53 He might have discovered a snag..got stuck for some spare.

23. a. *to be stuck with*: to be saddled with, unable to get rid of (an unwanted person or thing). orig. *U.S.*

1848 [in Dict.]. *a* **1860** *Providence Jrnl.* in J. R. Bartlett *Dict. Americanisms* (ed. 3) 458 We got stuck with a bad lot of paper, and were obliged to stick it on to our readers. **1943** F. J. Bell *Condition Red* iv. 47 So it was our coal, and we were stuck with it. **1959** W. Kennedy in M. Ross *Arts in Canada* 136/1 We architects of the mid-twentieth century seem to be stuck with the gods who made us—Gropius, Corbusier. **1962** E. O'Brien *Lonely Girl* iv. 36 He bought me a grey astrakhan with a red velvet collar, and a flared skirt. 'I'm stuck with you now,' he said.. while he surveyed the coat from behind. **1972** *Guardian* 22 Mar. 16/2 Westminster..cannot apply a totally British solution to an Irish problem. But being stuck with it, the British Government has to try to muddle through. **1979** R. Jaffe *Class Reunion* (1980) 14 Emily hated being 'petite', which was a euphemism for getting stuck with all the short boys on blind dates.

d. For (U.S. slang) read (slang, orig. *U.S.*) and add: also *esp.*, to be fond of, enamoured of, in love with.

1886 *Lantern* (New Orleans) 20 Oct. 3/2 Poor Charles Ernest is so stuck on a fairy named Emma Brown, that she can make him do anything she wishes. **1897** Kipling *Captains Courageous* x. 221 I'm not stuck on myself any just now—that's all. **1909** J. Masefield *Tragedy of Nan* i. 9 'Er father, as she's so stuck on—'E was 'ung. **1938** G. Greene *Brighton Rock* vii. ii. 295 I'd stake you a fiver she's straight. Why—you told me yourself—she's stuck on you. **1939** A. Huxley *After Many a Summer* ii. iii. 207 You'd say she was kind of stuck on the fellow. **1967** P. Shaffer *Black Comedy* 55, I don't mean that's why he popped the question... He's always been stuck on you. **1974** A. Lurie *War between Tates* (1977) vi. 128 Sandy, who was rather pathetically stuck on her for a while, took her to hear *The Magic Flute*.

e. *to get stuck into*: to lay into, make a physical attack on (someone); to make a serious start on, get down to (a task, a meal, etc.). Hence *to get stuck in*, to pitch in, get down to it. *colloq.* (orig. *Austral.*).

1941 Baker *Dict. Austral. Slang* 31 *Get stuck into*, to engage a person in a bout of fisticuffs. To tackle a job with a will. **1942** G. Casey *It's harder for Girls* 228 A bit o' peace..after you an' Winch nearly getting stuck into each other at the pub. **1948** C. Fry *Thor with Angels* 3 You get stuck Into some work, you whitebellied weasel. **1958** I. Cross *God Boy* xix. 160 Though arithmetic wasn't my best subject, I was quite glad at the idea of getting stuck into some figures. **1962** *Observer* 18 Feb. 23/4, I heard a terrific clanging downstairs and went down to see Pancho getting stuck into the gas meter with an iron bar. **1974** A. Morice *Killing with Kindness* iii. 31 He reached out a hand and promptly got stuck into his beloved evening paper.

1948 S. Matthews *Feet First* x. 57, I have no time for that 'get stuck in' policy that is sometimes advised in cup-ties or local derbys. Once one side starts tackling with too much vigour there is inevitable retaliation and loss of tempers. **1959** G. Slatter *Gun in my Hand* v. 51 Gives us a hand sometimes on the mixer..Gets into his old mocker and gets stuck in. **1961** B. Crump *Hang on a Minute, Mate* 158 Mrs Wagner brought in two plates of food..and told them to get stuck in. **1971** *Where* Sept. 260/2 He flung out his arms like a Petticoat Lane trader, and got stuck in. In five minutes he had an audience.

IV. 26. stick to —. **f.** Also *to stick to one's last* (with allusion to the proverb: see Last *sb.*[1] 2 c).

1927 Galsworthy *Castles in Spain* 92 Conrad had always a great regard for..workmen who stuck to their last and did their own jobs well. **1939** A. Powell *What's become of Waring?* viii. 227, I don't know why he wanted to meddle with writing at all. It wasn't his avocation. He should stick to his last. **1956** A. Wilson *Anglo-Saxon Attitudes* i. i. 19 You're not a member of the University Press Syndic... Stick to your last.

27. stick with —. **e.** To adhere to (an account, plan, etc.); to be faithful to, support.

1915 J. London *Jacket* iv. 28 Stick with it. Don't ever let'm know. **1958** M. L. King *Stride toward Freedom* vii. 127 We would stick with them through their difficulties. 'We must remain together,' we kept repeating. **1976** M. Machlin *Pipeline* xlviii. 505 'I've known all along it was a Goddamn fool plan.'.. 'Then why have you stuck with it so long?'

V. 27*. stick around. *intr.* To wait, remain in the vicinity, not to go away. *colloq.* (orig. *N. Amer.*).

1912 J. Sandilands *Western Canad. Dict. & Phrase-bk.*, *Stick around*, wait about, hang around, or loaf around. The Canadian sport will stick around in the expectation of meeting the boys and having a good time. **1915** S. Lewis *Trail of Hawk* iii. 28 Stick around, son, and sit in any time, and I'll learn you some pool. **1919** E. Jordan *Girl in Mirror* iv. 79 I'm going to 'stick around', and guide them for a few days. **1943** P. Cheyney *You can always Duck* vi. 99 'I'm givin' no guarantees,' I tell her. 'But maybe I'll stick around. We'll see. So long, honey.' **1959** 'S. Ransome' *I'll die for You* ix. 109 You stick around, Mr. Fisher, where I can find you when I want you? **1979** A. Fox *Threat Warning Red* xvi. 248 You'll be asked to come over here next week..and you'll have to stick around for a day or two.

32. stick out. b. Also in various colloq. phrases, esp. *to stick out a mile*. *to stick out like a sore thumb*: see *sore *a.* 9 f.

1933 E. Waugh *Scoop* ii. i. 119 'Have you noticed it?' 'Yes..it sticks out a mile.' **1949** [see *road-sign* s.v. *road *sb.* 9 b]. **1952** M. Allingham *Tiger in Smoke* i. 16 You couldn't miss him. He stuck out like a lighthouse. **1977** 'H. Carmichael' *Grave for Two* iv. 48 'You're saying she's left him.'..'Sticks out a mile.'

c. (Earlier and later examples of *to stick it out*.)

1882 'Mark Twain' *Let.* 17 May (1917) I. 419, I have promised Osgood, and must stick it out. **1889** —— *Conn. Yank.* xxvi. 334 The proprieties required me to stick it out. **1914** G. B. Shaw *Misalliance* 17, I really couldnt stick it out with Jerry, mother. **1929** J. B. Priestley *Good Companions* iii. ii. 509 If you went, I'm durned sure I couldn't stick it out another week. **1981** P. P. Read *Villa Golitsyn* i. vi. 41 He stuck it out for a week and then shinnied down a drainpipe.

e. (Later example.) *to stick one out* (examples).

1910 A. Bennett *Clayhanger* i. vii. 49 She would not hear a word about the toast being a little hard... Maggie ..'stuck her out' that the toast was in fact hard. **1915** F. M. Hueffer *Good Soldier* iv. i. 224 That checked Florence a bit; but she fell back upon her 'heart' and stuck out that she had merely been conversing with Edward. **1916** A. Bennett *Lion's Share* vii. 53, I knew he was going to be ill when I left him in the cabin, but he stuck me out he wasn't.

i. *to stick one's neck out*: see *neck *sb.*[1] 3 e.

34. stick up. k. For *Austral.* read orig. *Austral.* and add *U.S.* examples. Also, (*Criminals' slang*) of the police: to hold up (a suspect).

1904 'O. Henry' *Cabbages & Kings* xvii. 302, I couldn't take it with me, not knowing but what the monkeys might stick me up. **1926** J. Black *You can't Win* vii. 81 Anyway we'll sure be stuck up and frisked at Evanston. **1971** *Black Scholar* Sept. 32/2 It was the night he, Shotgun and Big Daddy stuck up the policy clearing house. **1978** S. Brill *Teamsters* iii. 76 They had served time for sticking up a variety store in Akron, Ohio.

† **n.** *Cricket.* To put a batsman on the defensive. *Obs.*

1864 *Baily's Mag.* Sept. 297 Grundy and Wootton.. put every batsman on the defensive, stuck them up, man after man, over after over,..and then sent each back to the Pavilion. **1891** W. G. Grace *Cricket* ix. 243 There are some bowlers who, by their wonderful accuracy of length, stick up the batsmen and get wickets on the most perfect grounds. **1904** P. F. Warner *How we recovered Ashes* v. 70 Rhodes stuck up all the batsmen, with the exception of Trumper.

o. In phr. *stick 'em up*: an (armed) robber's order to his victim to raise his hands above his head; = *hands up!* s.v. Hand *sb.* 54. Usu. imp. *slang* (orig. *U.S.*). (Cf. *put them* (or *'em*) *up* (ii) s.v. *put *v.*[1] 53 a (e).)

1931 [see *reach *v.*[1] 12 c]. **1938** G. Greene *Brighton Rock* v. iii. 203 The children were scouting among the rubble with pistols from Woolworth's... Someone said in a high treble: 'Stick 'em up.' **1972** Wodehouse *Pearls, Girls, & Monty Bodkin* vi. 76 Sequences of spine-chilling drama, with people telling other people to stick 'em up and prodding them in the stomach with pistols.

VI. 35. stick-bomb = *sticky bomb* s.v. *sticky *a.*[2] 5; **stick-jaw:** also *spec.*, toffee; also *transf.*; **stick-pin** *U.S.*, any (ornamental) pin that is merely stuck in (as distinguished from a safety pin), esp. a tie-pin; also *attrib.*; hence **stick-pinned** *ppl. a.*; **stick-slip,** alternate movement and cessation of movement of one surface over another as a result of frictional forces; freq. *attrib.*; **sticktight,** (*b*) in full, *sticktight flea*; a small flea, *Echidnophaga gallinicea*, which infests poultry; **stickwater,** the liquid that is squeezed out when cooked fish are compressed during the manufacture of fish meal and fish oil.

1943 J. H. Fullarton *Troop Target* xxiv. 175 Along comes a Jerry tank. Kiwi goes in with stick bombs. Jerry hops out with his shirt-tail alight. Kiwi shoots him. **1971** 'A. Hall' *Warsaw Document* viii. 89 The main doors breached with five stick-bombs. **1894** R. Wells *Toffy & Sweets* 14 Stick-jaw. **1932** L. Golding *Magnolia Street* ii. v. 352 Hush, Annie, hush! Here's some stick-jaw! **1938** Auden & Isherwood *On Frontier* iii. ii. 108 Gone to a demonstration, I suppose, to shout stickjaw slogans with the rest. **1950** 'R. Crompton' *William—the Bold* i. 13 'Look! There's some real stick-jaw toffee,' said Henry. **1895** *Montgomery Ward Catal.* Spring & Summer 172 Fine solid gold scarf and stick pins. **1906** 'O. Henry' in *N.Y. World Mag.* 18 Dec. 2/2 He wore his tie drawn through a topaz ring instead of fastened with a stick pin. **1928** 'S. S. Van Dine' *Greene Murder Case* v. 64, I was only looking for that old emerald stick-pin you borrowed and never returned. **1973** M. Crowell *Greener Pastures* 132 A dapper tree sparrow, dark stickpin spot on his soft gray breast. **1939** *Proc. R. Soc.* A. CLXIX. 378 The friction is fluctuating violently, and the measurement again shows that the motion is proceeding by a process of 'stick-slip'. **1940** *Phil. Trans. R. Soc.* CCXXXIX. 1 Certain substances..are able to prevent this 'stick-slip' motion and allow continuous sliding to take place. **1958** *Engineering* 14 Mar. 339/2 The movement of the ram is completely free from 'stick-slip' phenomena because of the small but significant clearance between piston and cylinder. **1959** *Times* 13 Oct. 4/4 This 'stick-slip' as it is called can make the steering stiff to move initially. **1975** *McGraw-Hill Yearbk. Sci. & Technol.* 21/2 The jerky motion happens because—under the pressure and temperature conditions of the shallow part of the Earth's lithosphere—rock exhibits a property known as stick-slip. **1915** F. C. Bishopp *Fleas as Pests* (U.S.D.A. Farmers Bull. 683) 7 The sticktight flea, or southern chicken flea,..the most important of our live-stock infesting species. **1955** W. W. Denlinger *Compl. Boston* ii. 77 These sticktights abound in neglected..chicken houses. **1962** Gordon & Lavoipierre *Entomol. for Students of Med.* xxxv. 218 Another species of burrowing flea,..the so-called 'sticktight flea', on rare occasions attacks man. **1915** *Rep. U.S. Comm. Fisheries 1914* App. III. 25 An apparatus for evaporating the water which is separated from the oil and known as 'stick water' has recently been installed... The residue or 'stick' will average about 9 per cent ammonia. **1945** *Poultry Sci.* XXIV. 379/1 The stickwater from fish-meal manufacture added materially to the riboflavin potency of a feed. **1965** G. H. O. Burgess et al. *Fish Handling & Processing* x. 237 Acidification of the dilute stickwater coagulates some of the fine suspended solids and these are sometimes recovered by further centrifuging.

b. stick-at-it *colloq.*, a plodding conscientious person; **stick-to-it-iveness** *colloq.* (orig. *U.S.*), dogged perseverance.

1909 H. G. Wells *Tono-Bungay* ii. ii. 162 I'm a boiler-over, not a simmering stick-at-it. **1867** in E. B. Custer *Tenting on Plains* (1889) xvi. 520 With the stick-to-it-iveness of a fox-hound when once on a trail. **1908** *Daily Express* 15 May 1/4 Success..is mostly hard work. It's work and it's stick-to-it-iveness. You've got to keep at it all the time. **1934** J. A. Lee *Children of Poor* i. 19 With the irresponsibility of my..father and my mother's stick-to-itiveness, I can..fashion an edifice and then.. set the whole show toppling. **1979** *N.Y. Rev. Bks.* 8 Feb. 10/3 This man who made his million apparently more by stick-to-itiveness than brilliance.

c. stick-on *a.*, that sticks on or can be stuck on; adhesive.

1925 J. W. Bigger *Handbk. Bacteriol.* 60 Stick-on labels may be used, but these must never be licked in a bacteriological laboratory. **1941** *Sun* (Baltimore) 13 Aug. 16/6 There also will be speakers on the stick-on spray.. and other matters of interest to apple growers. **1962** L. Deighton *Ipcress File* i. 13 In crude stick-on letters the film title said *Jay. Leeds.* **1967** *Punch* 22 Nov. 780/1 False eyelashes, interchangeable wigs, adhesive eyebrows, stick-on fingernails. **1972** *Guardian* 11 Aug. 9/6 Another story book you make yourself with stick-on shapes.

stick, *v.*[2] Add: **7.** To strike (a person) with a stick.

1937 Partridge *Dict. Slang* 830/1 *Sticked* (, *be*), (to be) caned. **1962** M. Duffy *That's how it Was* iv. 44 The whole of 3A was sticked..Miss Wilkinson..smacking the outstretched palms. **1982** *Sunday Sun-Times* (Chicago) 17 Oct. 138/1 Edmonton's Ken 'The Rat' Linseman was suspended..for sticking Toronto's Russ Adam during an exhibition game [of hockey].

stickability (stikăbi·lĭti). *colloq.* [f. Stick *v.*[1] + Ability.] Capacity for endurance, persistence, perseverance, staying power.

1888 *Voice* (N.Y.) 10 May 7/3 Stickability..is the most important ability a farmer can possess. **1905** *British Weekly* 28 May 193/2 To be able to take rebuffs happily and still go on requires, to use a coined word, 'stickability'. **1922** *Chambers's Jrnl.* Sept. 634/2 The foreigner has supplanted the middle and lower class Chilian in nearly every branch of industry in which the quality best described as 'stickability' is required. **1962** *Daily Tel.* 17 Aug. 18/1 All too many lack any degree of 'stickability' and flit from job to job like butterflies. **1976** P. Donovan *Relig. Lang.* iv. 45 Those engaged in such activities get their stickability..from the quite reasonable assumption that unless someone persists.., there is little chance of any discovery being made.

stickage. (Earlier and later examples.)

1734 J. T. Desaguliers *Course of Experimental Philos.* I. iii. 89 We are to have regard to..the Quantity of *Stickage* or Friction; which differ according to the..Nature of the Materials. **1961** *New Scientist* 27 July 216 Most metals tend to stick to other metals they touch in a deep vacuum. Bearings must be found to prevent such stickage. **1968** *Encycl. Polymer Sci. & Technol.* IX. 33 Too much waxing can lead to further stickage.

sticker[1]**.** Add: **3. a.** (Later examples in sense 'one who persists in a task'.)

1916 *Anzac Bk.* 130 He was no 'sticker', and in the third year of his medical course he had side-tracked himself. **1967** C. Fremlin *Prisoner's Base* xii. 84 Daphne did not believe in dropping things; she was, as she would have told you, a Sticker. **1979** N. Hynd *False Flags* viii. 71 Bobby wasn't any quitter. He was a sticker.

d. (Earlier and later examples.)

1832 P. Egan *Bk. Sports* xxii. 344/2 At the *bat* and the *bottle* they find him a *sticker*. **1855** F. Lillywhite *Guide* to Cricketers 56 A 'sticker' with 'confidence' was all that was required, to have turned the 'tide' in their favour. **1977** *Times* 12 July 10/1 When Chappell was adding 55 with O'Keeffe, who is well known as a sticker, there were visions of England having to make 175, perhaps 200, today.

f. *U.S. colloq.* A thorn or bur.

1889 H. H. McConnell *Five Years a Cavalryman* iv. 35 The leaves when submitted to the action of fire in order to burn off the sharp stickers, are used as food for cattle. **1898** G. F. Atherton *Californians* 231 Trennahan.. plucked the 'stickers' from his trousers. **1899** M. Going *Field, Forest, & Wayside Flowers* 350 When the 'stickers' are at last picked or rubbed off, they fall to the ground. **1945** B. Macdonald *Egg & I* (1946) iii. viii. 94 My hair and shoulders were full of twigs and stickers.

5. a. For *U.S.* read orig. *U.S.* and add later examples. Also *spec.* a small adhesive notice designed to be stuck in a conspicuous place and used to publicize a cause, commodity, or place. Also *attrib.* in **sticker price** *N. Amer.*, the advertised price (of a commodity).

1919 *Nation* (N.Y.) 117/2 Defendants..had printed millions of seditious 'stickers'. **1934** J. M. Cain *Postman always rings Twice* ii. 13 About three o'clock a guy came along that was all burned up because somebody had pasted a sticker on his wind wing. I had to go in the kitchen to steam it off for him. **1943** K. Tennant *Ride on Stranger* xvii. 185 Plastering it [*sc.* a vessel] with stickers demanding the guest's release. **1955** W. Gaddis *Recognitions* i. v. 192, I left all my luggage there covered with the most adorable stickers from everywhere, my dears, every chic hotel you ever heard of. **1959** *Listener* 21 May 884/1 An English 'sticker' about Nuclear Disarmament on the door of..the students' canteen. **1962** E. Godfrey *Retail Selling & Organ.* ix. 91 Special delivery instructions.. should be written clearly..on a special sticker attached to the despatch docket. **1967** [see *bumper *sb.*[1] 5 c]. **1970** *Globe & Mail* (Toronto) 25 Sept. B4/7 The company said the sticker or suggested retail prices, which include federal excise taxes..are up an average of $136. **1976** J. I. M. Stewart *Memorial Service* xvi. 273 His magazine's supposed to be coming out tomorrow. Have you seen the stickers for it?

b. A postage stamp. *Criminals' slang.*

1904 'No. 1500' *Life in Sing Sing* 253/1 *Stickers*, postage stamps. **1926** J. Black *You can't Win* ix. 107 You're a cinch to get some coin and a bundle of stickers out of every 'P.O.' You can peddle the stamps anywhere.

Hence **sti·cker** *v. trans.*, to affix a sticker (sense 5 a) to; **sti·ckered** *ppl. a.*; **sti·ckering** *vbl. sb.*

1972 *Daily Colonist* (Victoria, B.C.) 3 Feb. 48/8 The system started in 1963 in Monterey Park, Calif., where 5,000 stickered homes had been broken into only 19 times and about 6,000 non-marked homes suffered more than 2,000 burglaries. **1976** *Publishers Weekly* 29 Mar. 41/1 The titles are produced by Dent in London. Dutton warehouses its inventory in this country and the titles are stickered for the U.S. market here. **1977** *Periodical* XL. 196 Nothing vexes me more than to go into a bookshop and find not just one price sticker on the book jacket, increasing the price, but sometimes two or more... The stickering is a burdensome business.

Stickie, Sticky (sti·ki). *Ir. slang.* [f. Stick *v.*[1]: see -y[6], -ie.] A member of the official I.R.A. or Sinn Fein. Usu. in *pl.* Also **Stick** *sb.*[5]

1972 *Times* 21 Aug. 10/3 Who'll stop the boys fighting with the stickies (official IRA)? **1978** F. Burton *Politics of Legitimacy* 188 'Stickies' is the widespread term used to designate the Official IRA/Sinn Féin. I heard two accounts of the origin of the term and both were somewhat apocryphal. One referred to the fact that the Official IRA 'stuck' to the existing organization whereas the Provisionals broke away. The other explained the name by referring to the fact that the Provisional IRA Easter Lilies were pinned to their supporters' clothes whereas the Officials had theirs stuck on. **1978** D. Murphy *Place Apart* ii. 37 The Officials are also known as the Stickies (or Sticks). *Ibid.* vi. 110 Her son..was 'executed' last year as a punishment for deserting from the Stickies. **1979** *An Phoblacht* 29 Sept. 3/5 In a typical pro-British statement..the Sticks' chairman in South Antrim, Kevin Smyth, accused the IRA of 'gross sectarianism' in bombing the Lisburn premises. **1979** J. B. Bell *Secret Army* 446 The term Stickies or Sticks came from the Official Republican innovation of putting gum on the back of the Easter Lily commemoration badge while the Provos stuck to the conventional pin.

stickily (sti·kili), *adv.* [f. Sticky *a.*[2] + -ly[2].] In a sticky manner.

1908 Kipling *Actions & Reactions* (1909) 102 The Hive was half hidden by smoke... They heard a frame crack stickily. **1937** *Times* 12 July 5/1 The game started rather stickily. **1942** 'A. Bridge' *Frontier Passage* iii. 39 'Is he dead?'..'Supposed to be—very stickily finished off by the Reds, when they caught him.' **1973** *Times Lit. Suppl.* 9 Mar. 257/2 The book manages, in fact, to make something stickily implausible out of several familiar conventions.

stickiness[1]. Add: Also, hesitancy, stubbornness; awkwardness, unpleasantness.

1933 C. Mackenzie *Water on Brain* viii. 115 Major Hunter-Hunt let his emotion over the stickiness of the Treasury evaporate in a deep sigh. **1947** 'N. Blake' *Minute for Murder* viii. 167 He had not imagined..that there was anything more in Billson's recalcitrance..than his usual official stickiness. **1948** Wodehouse *Spring Fever* xiii. 126 The intense stickiness of the situation. **1962** J. D. MacDonald *Girl* xii. 186 You do seem to have involved her in some sort of stickiness.

sticking, *ppl. a.* Add: **3.** (Earlier examples of *sticking-out.*) Also † *sticking-off.*

1834 C. M. Yonge *Let.* 4 July in C. Coleridge *Charlotte Mary Yonge* (1903) iv. 123 There were two great sticking-out boxes like pulpits. **1843** C. Ridley *Let.* Feb. in U. Ridley *Cecilia* (1958) x. 118 Really it will be tiresome if he grows up with large, sticking-off ears. **1892** C. M. Yonge *That Stick* I. ii. 32 She had such horrid sticking-out ears.

sticking-point. Add: **2.** A point at which one sticks and beyond which one refuses to go; a subject upon which one will not yield or compromise; an obstacle.

1965 *Listener* 23 Sept. 441/1 As a politician he has been mild to the point of compromise. But one sticking point for him has been India's unity. **1970** *Globe & Mail* (Toronto) 25 Sept. 3/2 An early sticking point is expected to come when the Russians raise the question of reopening the Port of Vancouver to the supply ships. **1981** *Church Times* 27 Mar. 12/5 It is not the matter of women priests that is the main sticking point.

stick-in-the-mud. Add: Hence **stick-in-the-muddish** *a.*

1936 M. Mitchell *Gone with Wind* xxviii. 481 It wasn't hidebound and stick-in-the-muddish like the older towns and it had a brash exuberance that matched her own. **1959** A. Salkey *Quality of Violence* x. 158 He's slow and easy and a little 'stick-in-the-muddish'.

stick-out, *a.* and *sb.* Add: Also **stickout.** **A.** *adj.* **2.** *U.S. slang.* Outstanding.

1948 *Daily Progress* (Charlottesville, Va.) 27 Jan. 9/1 After that, you have to scratch your head to think of another stickout box office attraction. **1958** *Washington Post* 19 June C1/6 Kramer's only hope for a stickout newcomer would be Australia's Mal Anderson against Gonzales.

B. *sb.* **2.** *U.S. slang.* **a.** A horse that seems a certain winner. **b.** An outstanding sportsman.

1937 D. Runyon in *Collier's* 11 Sept. 70/3 This mare Cara Mia is a stick-out. **1942** Berrey & Van den Bark *Amer. Thes. Slang* § 636/4 Good player,..*stickout.* **1949** *Sun* (Baltimore) 2 July 9/1 A 'stickout' on paper, Nokomis was in front most of the way along the six-furlong route. **1951** *Daily Progress* (Charlottesville, Va.) 26 Sept. 13/8 His former players now coaching send stickouts in his direction. **1958** *Washington Post* 26 June C1/1 As for third base, ball players and fans alike have no range of choice. Frank Malzone of the Red Sox is a stickout.

stickum (sti·kəm). *N. Amer. colloq.* [f. Stick *v.*[1] + Um, 'um.] A sticky or adhesive substance; gum, paste; pomade. Also *transf.* and *fig.*

1909 *Dialect Notes* III. 376 *Stickum*,..mucilage, paste. **1936** *Christian Sci. Monitor* 14 Aug. 1/3 See that he is keeping the quality of his postage stamp stickum up to standard. **1963** C. D. Simak *They walked like Men* ix. 48 We used to shave them and give them facials and all of them wanted stickum on their hair. **1969** R. Williams in D. Knight *100 Yrs. Sci. Fiction* 303 The fact still remains, this machine makes every man self-sufficient, it takes the stickum right out of society. **1978** J. Irving *World according to Garp* viii. 157 Wet with sweat and sweet with the lush stickum of sex. **1980** *Globe & Mail* (Toronto) 23 Aug. 1/1 (*heading*) Gaudaur strikes at stickum. Football commissioner Jake Gaudaur has instructed referees to rule ineligible players who use excessive amounts of adhesive on their hands.

stick-up, *a.* and *sb.* Add: **A.** *adj.* (Earlier example.)

1854 'C. Bede' *Further Adventures of Mr. Verdant Green* ii. 5 A modest-looking young gentleman, who appeared to be..ill at ease in his frock-coat and 'stick-up' collars.

B. *sb.* **2.** *slang* (orig. *Austral.*, now chiefly *U.S.*). **a.** = Hold-up b.

[**1887** W. H. Suttor *Austral. Stories Retold* 41 A body of men, mostly armed, met us. We at first thought it was a case of 'stick up'.] **1904** 'O. Henry' in *McClure's Mag.* Apr. 611/1 The first 'stick-up' I was ever in happened in 1890... It will explain how most train robbers start. **1910** H. Lawson *Skyline Riders & Other Verses* 62 Scott that fired at Brummy Hughson, when the 'stick-ups' used to be. **1930** *Punch* 26 Feb. 236/1 He was reminded..that he had worked on the Babylon stick-up, and consented to come clean. **1944** *Sun* (Baltimore) 18 Mar. 12/1 The bank manager told police that the bandit..drew a gun and said: 'This is a stickup.' **1955** H. Kurnitz *Invasion of Privacy* (1956) vii. 53 Morley..told him they wanted to fake a stick-up. Then he shoots..the holdup man. **1972** [see *pull *v.* 19 f].

b. One who robs by 'sticking up' his victims; = Hold-up a. ? *Obs.*

1905 *N.Y. Times* 2 Jan. 4/1 The 'stick-up' is always a powerful man, whose duties are to intimidate intruders and kill them if necessary, while the others are at work on a safe. **1936** [see *bimbo[2]].

c. *attrib.* = *hold-up 2; *esp.* in *stick-up man.*

1905 *N.Y. Times* 2 Jan. 4/1 The man..is declared to be a typical 'yeggman of the stick-up' class. **1909** G. R. Chester *Making of Bobby Burnit* xiv. 169 Our local Hicks would rather be robbed by a lot of friendly stick-up artists. **1924** G. C. Henderson *Keys to Crookdom* 396 *Assaulter*, rough guy, hard bird..stick-up man, thug. **1930** [see *cool *v.* 3 e]. **1935** D. Runyon in *Cosmopolitan* Jan. 63/3 A fast stick-up job without any foolishness about it, maybe leaving any parties we come across tied up good and tight. **1950** *Times* 7 Feb. 8/4 It was the story of a 'stick-up' plot being hatched. **1973** 'H. Howard' *Highway to Murder* vii. 80 The old man got knocked off by a stick-up guy at the filling station where he worked. **1979** G. F. Newman *List* i. 3 Any moron could get a gun and become a stickup man.

sticky, *a.*[2] Add: **1. a.** (Later examples.) Also *fig.*

1909 G. Stein *Three Lives* 27 The horses dragged the carriage slowly over the long road, sticky with brown clay. **1939** *Amer. Speech* XIV. 262 The listener often hears,..if the subject is a thief, 'He has sticky fingers.' **1940** N. Mitford *Pigeon Pie* v. 95 'I have just labelled a few little things of my own..' she said, putting a sticky one firmly on to the giant radiogram. **1956** H. Gold *Man who was not with It* (1965) i. 3 They were caught..like the flies caught wriggling in sticky-paper. **1976** A. Miller *Inside Outside* i. 16 To safeguard the money from the sticky fingers of some of the boys.

c. *sticky wicket* (earlier example). Also *fig.*, esp. in phr. *to bat* (or *be*) *on a sticky wicket*: to contend with great difficulties (*colloq.*).

1882 *Bell's Life in London* 29 July 4/6 The ground.. was suffering from the effects of recent rain, and once more the Australians found themselves on a sticky wicket. **1952** *National News-Let.* 24 Jan. 244 It must be clearly understood that Mr. Churchill was batting on a very sticky wicket in Washington. **1957** P. Kemp *Mine were of Trouble* ix. 177 Until substantial reinforcements could arrive we should be batting, in the language of Mr. Naunton Wayne, on a very sticky wicket. **1964** *Language* XL. 239 Enmeshed in these remarks, however, is a sticky wicket. **1971** *Cabinet Maker & Retail Furnisher* 24 Sept. 517 When it comes..to moulded plastics of various kinds, then the timber producer is on a stickier wicket.

d. *fig.* Sickly, mawkish, sentimental, 'soppy'.

1864 [implied at Stickiness[1]]. **1915** R. Frost *Let.* 11 Nov. (1964) 17 He needn't go calling himself sticky names like Gayheart in public. **1925** N. Coward *Fallen Angels* i. 16, I hope you're not..hurt at our refusing to call you Jasmin?..It's a sticky name, isn't it—for the house? *a* **1961** O. Sitwell in Webster s.v., Invest childhood with a sticky but romantic gloss.

e. *colloq.* (orig. *U.S.*). Of the weather: humid, muggy.

1895 in *Funk's Stand. Dict.* *a* **1961** in Webster, A hot and sticky hour or two on shore. **1977** *Washington Post* 30 June F2/4 Hot, sticky summer weather—the kind of weather that seems to attack the mind as well as the body with its oppressiveness. **1983** *National Trust* Spring 16/1 On one of those stifling, sticky days of this curious summer.., at rehearsal, the Philharmonia Orchestra and Norman del Mar were all in shirt sleeves.

3. a. (Later U.S. examples.)

1937 *Sun* (Baltimore) 28 June 12/1 Several recent offerings have been described as 'sticky' by dealers—meaning only partially sold. **1960** *Wall St. Jrnl.* (Eastern ed.) 5 Dec. 7/2 Underwriters released two sticky' corporate debt issues to the free market.

b. *Econ.* Of prices, interest rates, wages, etc.: resistant to change, slow to respond to altered conditions.

1930 *Economist* 6 Sept. 453/1 In many cases the amount of available stock has been limited, and when a fair supply has been in sight prices have proved surprisingly 'sticky'. **1936** J. M. Keynes *Gen. Theory Employment, Interest & Money* iv. xvii. 232 Wages tend to be sticky in terms of money, the money-wage being more stable than the real wage. **1939** G. Myrdal *Monetary Equilibrium* vi. 136 When we talk about sticky and flexible prices we are already thinking in terms of indices of different price levels. **1971** D. C. Hague *Managerial Economics* iv. 94 The idea that the kinked demand curve is likely to be found where there is oligopoly has led to the widespread feeling that in oligopoly prices will be 'sticky'. **1978** *Daily Tel.* 18 Dec. 14/7 Building society rates tend to follow movements in market rates only rather erratically and usually with a time-lag. As economists say they tend to be 'sticky'.

4. *colloq.* **a.** Of a person: difficult to cope with, awkward, uncooperative; strait-laced, punctilious, particular, tending to make difficulties (*about* or *over* something).

1882 L. Troubridge *Life amongst Troubridges* (1966) 162 Rather a sticky audience who evidently thought it vulgar to laugh, and only sniggered into their pocket handkerchiefs. **1925** T. E. Lawrence *Let.* 3 Nov. (1938) 486 I've got too many subscribers, so am very sticky over these last copies. **1933** C. Mackenzie *Water on Brain* viii. 115 Personally I've always advocated the spending of money. The only snag is the Treasury. They've been sticky lately. **1935** Wodehouse *Luck of the Bodkins* iii. 34 He didn't actually call me a waster..but his manner was sticky. **1937** E. Bowen in *New Statesman* 6 Nov. 727/2 Be a shade too punctilious and you are sticky; make a little too free and you are a pariah. **1940** Graves & Hodge *Long Week-End* ix. 135 Even the stickiest British families seemed ready to abandon their mistrust of the cinema, if the vulgar American scene could only be replaced by a wholesome British one. **1953** J. Bingham *Five Roundabouts to Heaven* iii. 26 Sometimes aunt Emily was a bit sticky about paying up. **1960** *Times* 15 Oct. 8/7 We had to be immaculately turned out... Father was very 'sticky' about this. **1972** J. Philips *Vanishing Senator* (1973) iii. ii. 127 Bernstein will tell you. If he acts sticky have him call me.

b. Of a situation, issue, period of time, etc.: awkward, presenting great difficulty, disagreeable owing to hardship or danger; of a social function: slow to start, stiff, uncomfortable.

1915 D. O. Barnett *Lett.* 86 We had a rather sticky time in the trenches..as the enemy's artillery and snipers showed 'a certain liveliness'. **1930** 'Sapper' *Finger of*

Fate 17 You have the alternative of a sticky five minutes with three savage Alsatians. **1930** V. SACKVILLE-WEST *Edwardians* i. 17 What was Miriam's party like, Lucy? Sticky, as usual? **1946** WODEHOUSE *Money in Bank* xix. 155 It is a human trait to keep on hoping, however sticky the outlook. **1955** *Times* 22 Aug. 2/7 The play became rather sticky and it looked like one or two fouls before the umpires blew on a B.A.O.R. player. **1958** *Listener* 16 Oct. 621/3 This medley of the fine arts and show business may be accommodated to a pleasant pattern later on: it made a sticky start. **1958** [see *PATCH *sb.*^{1} 5 b]. **1960** L. COOPER *Accomplices* I. ii. 17 It was the stickiest do I've ever been in and I thanked God I'd been taught to fight. **1976** *Lancs. Evening Post* 7 Dec. 1/5 Preston South Labour MP Mr Stan Thorne..faced the prospect of a sticky interview with Government whips. **1977** B. PYM *Quartet in Autumn* xv. 127 He was so used to sticky church occasions that a lunch with two former colleagues should have been well within his powers. **1979** *Nature* 7 June 461/2 The sticky issues, however, will be over the appropriate forms of accountability and responsibility.

c. Phr. *to come to a sticky end* (or occas. *finish*): to die or come to grief in violent or exceptionally unpleasant circumstances.

1915 H. ROSHER *In R.N.A.S.* (1916) 40, I wish we could get out to the front... I would much rather come to a sticky end out there than here. **1930** J. COLLIER *His Monkey Wife* xviii. 255 Even if our love affair did come to a horrible sticky end, yet there's so much between us. **1930** J. B. PRIESTLEY *Angel Pavement* xi. 566 Never mind, he'll come to a sticky finish before he's done. **1959** F. MACLEAN *Back to Bokhara* iii. 152 The reformers..have usually come to a sticky end. **1970** 'D. HALLIDAY' *Dolly & Cookie Bird* ix. 142 The heroines I've seen come to a sticky end because while the murderer's still running around no one calls in the police. **1980** *Church Times* 19 Dec. 12/3 Some cast away all chances of redemption till they come to a sticky end.

5. a. Special collocations: **sticky-back**, a small photograph or poster with a gummed back; also *attrib.* or as *adj.*; **sticky bomb**, an anti-tank grenade covered with an adhesive substance to make it stick to its target; **sticky dog** *Cricket colloq.*, a sticky wicket; **sticky end** *Genetics*, an end of a DNA double helix at which one strand extends a few nucleotides beyond the other, unpaired; **sticky-fingered** *a.*, apt to steal, light-fingered; **sticky tape** = *adhesive tape* s.v. *ADHESIVE *a.* 1.

1913 A. H. DAWSON *Dict. Slang* 184 *Sticky-backs*, photographs about the size of a postage-stamp with gummed backs. **1922** JOYCE *Ulysses* 56 Stamps: stickyback pictures. **1939** 'G. ORWELL' *Let.* 4 Jan. in *Coll. Essays* (1968) I. 378 The commonsense thing to do would be to accumulate the things we should need for the production of pamphlets, stickybacks etc. **1940** W. S. CHURCHILL *Let.* 6 June in *Second World War* (1949) II. I. viii. 149 It is of the utmost importance to find some projectile which can be fired from a rifle at a tank... The 'sticky' bomb seems to be useful for..this. **1962** L. DEIGHTON *Ipcress File* vi. 38 It was a sticky bomb about as big as two cans of soup end to end; on impact its very small explosive charge spread a sort of napalm through tank visors. **1925** D. J. KNIGHT in *Country Life* 18 July 95/1 If you..get a chance of bowling on one of these 'sticky dogs', as we call them. **1928** *Daily Express* 9 July 17/1 Should he bat first or should he put Somerset in and hope for a 'sticky-dog' wicket? **1982** P. TINNISWOOD *More Tales from Long Room* vii. 86 That great Groundsman in the sky has secured his covers... And when the sun appears again, as appear it always will, there will be no 'sticky dog' and play will be resumed on time. **1968** *New Scientist* 18 July 142/1 This [enzyme] can be used for linking up small nucleotide sequences by what Professor Khorana calls the 'sticky end' technique. **1976** *Sci. Amer.* Dec. 108 (*caption*) The circle of viral DNA replicates, producing multiple copies that are then cleaved by a specific viral enzyme to give rise to the linear form with 'sticky' ends. **1980** AYALA & KIGER *Mod. Genetics* ix. 327 The purified p184 DNA is mixed with purified DNA from another plasmid..also possessing *Eco* RI sites. The mixture is cleaved with pure *Eco* RI enzyme at a temperature that permits the sticky ends to come apart and reanneal..to form larger hybrid plasmids. **1890** BARRÈRE & LELAND *Dict. Slang* II. 305/2 *Sticky-fingered*.., thievish or covetous. **1932** D. ACLAND *Sticky Fingers* xxv. 314 What a crew we are—sticky-fingered, every one of us. **1982** *Daily Tel.* 23 July 30/3 Mr Steel announced menacingly that a list of sticky fingered policemen had been made available. **1958** *Times* 4 Aug. 9/1 What is the sense of combining the most obdurate kind of fastening (sticky tape, for instance) with the flimsiest of paper bags? **1973** R. PARKES *Guardians* ix. 162 The naked body had been strapped into the armchair with yards of sticky tape.

b. *Comb.* **sticky-out** *a. colloq.*, that protrudes or sticks out.

1928 D. L. SAYERS *Unpleasantness at Bellona Club* x. 118 She has a bad skin and rather sticky-out teeth. **1957** *Woman's Jrnl.* May 51/1 People who had bright red hair and sticky-out teeth and glasses weren't the sort..that any parents wanted to adopt.

sticky (sti·ki), *sb.* [Ellipt. use of STICKY *a.*^{2}]

1. *slang.* Something that is sticky, *spec.* (*a*) an adhesive material; (*b*) a sticky wicket.

1859 HOTTEN *Dict. Slang* 102 *Sticky*, wax. **1937** PARTRIDGE *Dict. Slang* 831/1 *Sticky*,..sticking-plaster: lower and lower-middle class coll. **1954** A. G. MOYES *Australian Batsmen* 184 Again, the 'sticky' provides plenty of excitement. **1966** I. JEFFERIES *House-Surgeon* viii. 154 Bring me some more sticky and that pint of blood in the fridge. **1967** PARTRIDGE *Dict. Slang* Suppl. 1390/2 *Sticky*, ..since late 1940's, usu. cellulose tape (Sellotape, Scotch tape, etc.). **1975** *Daily Mail* 3 June 11/2 As well as cash, the thieves took 'stickies'—the slang term for postage, national insurance and TV licence stamps. **1982** *Private Eye* 13 Aug. 13/2 All you ever get in the Alps is some ghastly sticky made out of rotting Edelweiss.

2. A film of which the action is slow-moving. *nonce-wd.* (*humorously* after *movies*).

1936 E. M. FORSTER *Abinger Harvest* 51 British ladies and gentlemen turn the movies into the stickies for old Elstree's sake.

stickybeak (sti·kibīk). *Austral.* and *N.Z. colloq.* Also **sticky-beak.** [f. STICKY *a.*^{2} + BEAK *sb.*^{1}] An inquisitive person; one who sticks his nose into others' affairs, a Nosey Parker. Also *attrib.*

1920 B. CRONIN *Timber Wolves* ix. 159 I've told the girls to give out that we've gone fishing, if any stickybeaks get to asking why we ain't visible no more. **1934** *Bulletin* (Sydney) 7 Feb. 10/1 One objection to 'party' telephone lines is the stickybeak subscriber. **1936** M. FRANKLIN *All that Swagger* xlix. 442 Fortunately such 'sticky-beaks' were few. **1948** D. W. BALLANTYNE *Cunninghams* I. v. 24 He wasn't like those other stickybeak kids, he reckoned. **1965** R. MCKIE *Company of Animals* i. 30 Fire is a strange thing to a jungle elephant. It's foreign. And because it's foreign and he's a stickybeak, he investigates. **1970** K. BENTON *Sole Agent* vi. 69 She rang me up, she did, the sticky-beak, the prying old cow!

Hence **sti·ckybeak, sticky-beak** *v. intr.*, to pry, to snoop; **sti·ckybeaking** *vbl. sb.*

1934 *Bulletin* (Sydney) 12 Sept. 20/2 Special traps were set outside for any crocs. that might stickybeak. **1945** L. GLASSOP *We were Rats* II. xi. 65 You deny me the right to think as I like... You must prod, and pry, and stickybeak. **1966** P. CARLON *Running Woman* xv. 144, I paused on my way back, looking at those houses. Such a temptation..to sticky-beak. **1969** *Coast to Coast 1967–68* 9 Mind your own business... I don't have to put up with you and your sticky-beaking into my affairs.

stictane (sti·ktē^{i}n). *Biochem.* [f. mod.L. *Stict-a* (f. Gr. στικτός spotted), name of a genus of lichens + -ANE.] Any of a class of pentacyclic triterpanes, unsaturated derivatives of which occur in some lichens.

1973 W. J. CHIN et al. in *Jrnl. Chem. Soc.: Perkin Trans.* I. 1437 Ten new triterpenes, derived from a new triterpane system for which the name stictane is proposed, have been isolated from the hexane extractives of the lichens named in the title [sc. *Sticta coronata*, etc.]. **1976** *Ibid.* 857/1 Stictane..and the related flavicane..have an 8α-methyl group and a boat structure for ring B rather than the usual 8β-methyl group and chair ring B, hitherto found in pentacyclic triterpenoids. **1979** *Org. Mass Spectrometry* XIV. 160/1 We present detailed analysis of the mass spectral fragmentations of ten stictane triterpenoids.

stictic (sti·ktik), *a.*^{2} *Chem.* [tr. G. *stictinsäure* stictic acid (Knop & Schnedermann 1846, in *Jrnl. f. prakt. Chemie* XXXIX. 367), f. as prec.: see -IC.] *stictic acid*: a depsidone, $C_{19}H_{14}O_9$, found in many lichens.

1868 WATTS *Dict. Chem.* V. 431 According to Knop and Schneedermann [*sic*]..the acid of *Sticta pulmonacea*, which they call stictic acid, is distinct from cetraric acid, though very much like it in composition and properties. **1935** *Jrnl. Chem. Soc.* 1380 We have now made a detailed comparison of the two acids..and found them to be identical in every way. Accordingly, since stictic acid was discovered and named first.., we propose that the name scopuloric acid should be abandoned. **1963** *New Scientist* 14 Mar. 588/1 The lichen synthesises appreciable amounts of the extra-cellular, water-soluble constituents of lichen acids, atranorin and stictic acid. **1979** *Lichenologist* XI. 321 Chemical examination of two similar specimens..showed stictic acid to be present in the squamulose specimens and absent from the others.

stiction (sti·kʃən). [f. *st*(*atic fr*)*iction*.] = *static friction* s.v. *STATIC *a.* 3 b.

1946 *Jrnl. R. Aeronaut. Soc.* L. 365/1 'Stiction' might be caused by foreign bodies silting up round these pistons. **1953** *Electronic Engin.* XXV. 11/2 Armature stiction due to residual magnetism in the iron circuit..is normally overcome by facing the pole piece or armature, or both, with some non-magnetic coating. **1976** *Gramophone* Nov. 905/2 The bearings use tiny ball-races and the 'stiction' is of a very low order, some five-thousandths of a gram in both planes.

stiddy (sti·di), *adv. E. Anglian dial.* [f. STEAD *sb.*] Instead (*of*).

1946 J. W. DAY *Harvest Adventure* iv. 57 If they'd left the rabbits to the workin' men we'd ha' had 'em in our bellies stiddy of the poor things suffocatin' in their burrows. **1971** *Country Life* 11 Mar. 533/1 Owd Bob, he cut a slice or tew out of it [a stranded sturgeon] with a hatchet an' all the roe runned away. That's where he done wrong. If we'd a-kept that roe in we'd a-got four bob a pound for it... Stiddy o'that we only got fi'pun from the fishmonger in Ely.

stiebel, var. *SHTIBL.

Stiegel (stī·gĕl). The name of Henry William *Stiegel* (1729–85), German-born American manufacturer of iron and glass, used *attrib.* and *absol.* to designate glassware made by him or resembling his work.

[**1773** *Pennsylvania Packet* 8 Mar. 3/2 An Elegant Assortment of Henry William Stiegle's Glass is to be Sold.] **1906** *Bull. Pennsylvania Museum* 5 Jan., The Stiegel glassware was of better quality than any produced elsewhere in the United States. **1922** *Country Life* May 49/2 I'd rather have it than any other piece of Stiegel I ever saw. **1949** *Hobbies* June 104/1 Until quite recently the majority of our collectors were in the habit of calling all old blown glass either Stiegel or Wistar. *Ibid.* 104/2 All can not be the proud possessors of Stiegel sugar bowls in sparkling cobalt, creamers in lovely shades of amethyst. **1961** E. M. ELVILLE *Collector's Dict. Glass* 18/2 Other factories followed the Stiegel fashion, especially in Ohio and Pittsburgh districts. **1974** J. GARDNER *Corner Men* viii. 64 Peter was..about to pour vodka into a Stiegel-type glass. **1977** FLEMING & HONOUR *Penguin Dict. Decorative Arts* 759/1 The term 'Stiegel glass' is commonly applied to most c18 American pattern-moulded wares.

Stieltjes integral (stī·ltʃəz). *Math.* [Named after Thomas-Jan *Stieltjes* (1856–94), Dutch-born French mathematician, who first considered such integrals in 1894 (*Ann. de la Faculté des Sci. de Toulouse* VIII. J.2).] A definite integral in which the value of a function is summed, not uniformly over an interval, but in accordance with some other function which assigns weightings continuously or discontinuously within the interval.

[**1910** H. LEBESGUE in *Compt. Rend.* CL. 86 On désigne sous le nom d'*integrale de Stieltjes*..l'opération fonctionnelle faisant correspondre à $f(x)$ un nombre défini de la façon suivante.] **1914** *Proc. London Math. Soc.* XIII. 131 The definition of the integral of a continuous function with respect to a monotone increasing function given by Stieltjes..is defined to be the Stieltjes integral. **1952** J. C. C. MCKINSEY *Introd. Theory Games* ix. 169 Since the Stieltjes integral is defined by means of a complicated limiting process, it should not be an occasion for surprise that it does not always exist. **1980** A. J. JONES *Game Theory* 276 Technically we are using Stieltjes integrals here.

stifado (stifā·do). Also **stifato, stiffado, stiphado, stuffado.** [a. mod.Gr. στιφάδο, presumably f. It. *stufato* stew; cf. STUFATA.] A Greek dish of meat stewed with onions and other vegetables, esp. tomatoes.

1950 E. DAVID *Bk. Mediterranean Food* 76 Stuffado (a Greek ragoût). Cut 2 lbs. of steak into large pieces. Brown them in oil with 3 lb of small onions and several cloves of garlic. Into the same pan put ½ pint of thick and highly seasoned tomato purée and a glass of red wine. Simmer slowly for 4 or 5 hours. **1952** M. LO PINTO *New York Cookbk.* ix. 145 (*heading*) Stifato (beef stew). **1962** M. SOPER *Encycl. European Cooking* 329 (*heading*) Greek beef stew. *Stiphado.* **1975** I. MURDOCH *Word Child* 210 'What's for din-dins at your place?' 'Smoked salmon. Stifados. Lime soufflé.' **1977** T. HEALD *Just Desserts* i. 16 I'd like the Fritto misto and then the Stiffado.

stiff, *a.*, *sb.*, and *adv.* Add: **A.** *adj.* **I. 2. b.** *stiff one, stiff 'un*, (*a*) earlier example; (*b*) *slang*, a racehorse certain to lose or not to run at all (cf. sense 2 f below and *STIFF *sb.* 3 b); (*c*) *slang*, a forged note or cheque (properly sense 1: cf. STIFF *sb.* 2).

1823 P. EGAN *Grose's Dict. Vulgar Tongue* (rev. ed.), *Stiff ones*, of no use, dead men. **1871** 'HAWK'S-EYE' *Turf Notes* 11 Most assuredly it is the bookmakers that profit by the 'safe uns', or 'stiff uns', as..horses that have no chance of winning are called. **1890** BARRÈRE & LELAND *Dict. Slang* II. 306/2 There are two bookmakers in Melbourne nicknamed 'the Undertakers', because of their fondness for laying against *stiff 'uns*, which, in this case, means horses that are certain not to run. **1895** A. GRIFFITHS *Criminals I have Known* 228 He had been 'took' with the 'stiff uns' on him, and was sent to the 'boat' (penal servitude). **1897** in Farmer & Henley *Slang & its Analogues* (1903) VI. 365/2 Do not invest money Until you read The Rialto. Never on stiff 'uns, wrong 'uns, or dead 'uns. **1953** *Sat. Even. Post* 4 Apr. 18/3 'I put over a couple of stiff ones,' is the way a paperhanger describes an operation.

e. Intoxicated, drunk. Cf. *STIFF *sb.* 4 c. *U.S. slang. rare.*

1737 *Pennsylvania Gaz.* 6 Jan. 2/2 He's Stiff. **1900** *Dialect Notes* II. 65 *Stiff, adj.*,..very drunk. **1957** N. ALGREN *Walk on Wild Side* I. 6 Getting stiff on the courthouse steps while denouncing the Roman Catholic clergy was a feat which regularly attracted scoffers and true believers alike. **1975** G. V. HIGGINS *City on Hill* i. 9, I always got stiff on the Fourth because it was the only way I could listen to all that crap.

f. *Sport.* Of a horse or athlete: certain (to win). Also of an event: certainly won, 'in one's pocket'. Cf. sense 2 b above. *slang.* ? *Obs.*

1890 BARRÈRE & LELAND *Dict. Slang* II. 306/2 *Stiff for*, (sporting Australian), certain for. The metaphor here is something that cannot be diverted (or averted). After the Melbourne Derby and Cup of 1880, Grand Flaneur was considered *stiff for* every race for which he was entered. **1912** *Punch* 21 Aug. 168/3 He ought to have this event absolutely stiff at the next Olympic Games.

g. Unlucky. *Austral.* and *N.Z. slang.*

1919 W. H. DOWNING *Digger Dialects* 47 *Stiff* (adj.), unlucky. **1922** A. WRIGHT *Colt from Country* 124 'On'y just got cut out of second place,' declared Knocker. 'Ain't a man stiff?' **1930** *Bulletin* (Sydney) 3 Dec. 22/3 ''Struth!' gasped Chips. 'If we're not stiff! Nothing doing for two days, Tommy.' **1958** *N.Z. Listener* 27 June 6/3 Then came the third Test... Maybe they were a bit stiff to lose that, but once again I think it was just that lack of solidity in the middle of the pack.

6. Also *fig.*

1939 F. THOMPSON *Lark Rise* ii. 42 Their talk was stiff with simile. **1977** B. PYM *Quartet in Autumn* iv. 34 That season of the year was stiff with festivals.

8. e. Severe, stern; angry.

1856 THACKERAY *Miscellanies* II. 272 The old gent cut up uncommon stiff. **1930** W. S. MAUGHAM *Cakes & Ale* viii. 104, I wrote a pretty stiff letter to the librarian.

f. *Cricket.* Of a batsman: tending to play stubbornly in a defensive manner.

1869 *Field* 28 Aug. 176/3 This lucky escape seemed to endow the 'stiff batsman' with more than ordinary vigour. **1877** C. BOX *English Game of Cricket* xxvi. 461 *Stiff bat*, usually applied to a batsman who stubbornly defends his wicket. **1885** R. H. LYTTELTON in *J. Lillywhite's Cricketers' Compan.* 16 Midwinter..[was] a stiff and careful bat.

11. a. *stiff as a poker* (earlier and further examples); *to keep a stiff upper lip* (earlier example); hence *stiff-upper-lip* adj.; also as *v. intr.* and *adv.*; also *stiff-upper-lipped* adj., *stiff-upper-lippery*, *stiff-upper-lippish* adj., *stiffupperlippishness*.

1798 G. COLMAN *Heir at Law* (1800) III. ii. 34 The last lord Duberly's father..with a wig as wide as a wash-tub and stuck up as stiff as a poker. **1815** *Massachusetts Spy* 14 June 4/4, I kept a stiff upper lip, and bought [a] license to sell my goods. **1876** E. W. HEAP *Diary* 22 Mar. in *Publ. Amer. Dial. Soc.* (1969) LII. 55 Frozen as stiff as a poker last night. **1934** J. BUCHAN *Free Fishers* xviii. 297 Old Utterson is as stiff as a poker, and would keep us arguing till midnight. **1958** *Listener* 16 Oct. 621/3 She criticizes herself for being too stiff-upper-lipped about the tragedy that she faces. **1961** A. O. J. COCKSHUT *Imagination of Charles Dickens* viii. 116 He oscillated between indignation, self-pity, and reticence of the stiff-upper-lip English school. **1961** *John o' London's* 19 Oct. 447/2 The second film contains a firmly disciplined..undercurrent of Miniverish stiff-upper-lippery. **1963** *Listener* 3 Jan. 42/1 It was all very improbable and too stiff-upper-lippish to have been written by anybody but an anglophile Frenchman. **1973** *New Society* 31 May 483/2 MPs, in praising stiffupperlippishness, used sex as a stalking horse. **1977** *Broadcast* 14 Nov. 10/3 The British are stiff upper-lipping through power cuts. **1978** W. F. BUCKLEY *Stained Glass* xv. 153 As you say, we must be stiff-upper-lip formal. **1979** *Verbatim* Autumn 14/2 Two of the men, an upper-class Indian and an English Colonel, share a British university education, and they have a private joke of using *pip-pip!, I say,* and *stiff upper lip* expressions to each other. **1979** *Evening News* 6 Feb. 7/4 With rakish Parker, Prince Philip found that he could relax from the strains of state business and stiff-upper-lippery. **1983** *Listener* 20 Jan. 33/1 Nigel Anthony is the stiff-upper-lipped adventurer.

b. In predicative use (cf. *RIGID *a.* 1 d): to an extreme degree, as *to bore* (*scare*, etc.) *stiff*.

1905 *McClure's Mag.* May 100/1 He was scared stiff to hear that Morrow was in town. **1918** W. J. LOCKE *Rough Road* ix. 107, I think I ought to tell you that you're boring Durdlebury stiff. **1923** R. D. PAINE *Comr. Rolling Ocean* ix. 150 When that crazy fireman broke loose just now, I was scared perfectly stiff. **1928** F. B. YOUNG *My Brother Jonathan* II. v. 284 She bores everybody she meets stiff with talking about him. **1933** [see *FEED *v.* 6 h]. **1952** [see *FRONT *sb.* (and *a.*) 3 b]. **1956** *English* Summer 46 Billy Temple, who announced in Westminster School Hall that 'the longer poems of Milton bored him stiff'. **1964** I. MURDOCH *Italian Girl* xii. 137, I was scared absolutely stiff of Otto finding out.

11*. *Math.* Of a differential equation: having a solution that shows completely different behaviour over widely different scales of time (or other independent variable).

1952 CURTISS & HIRSCHFELDER in *Proc. Nat. Acad. Sci.* XXXVIII. 235 In the study of chemical kinetics, electrical circuit theory, and problems of missile guidance a type of differential equation arises which is exceedingly difficult to solve by ordinary numerical procedures. A very satisfactory method of solution of these equations is obtained by making use of a forward interpolation process... The differential equations to which this method applies are called 'stiff'. **1973** *Physics Bull.* June 340/2 'Stiff' differential equation problems also have been the principal reason for combined analogue-digital (hybrid computer) simulation. **1979** *Nature* 18 Jan. 201/2 It would be interesting to extend the present work to the case of Bianchi-type models filled with a perfect fluid of equation of state: $p = (\gamma - 1)\rho$, which covers Zel'dovich's stiff equation of state.

II. 16. Delete 'Now only of spirits-and-water.' (Later examples.) Also of tea and *loosely*, denoting a generous measure.

1904 H. JAMES *Golden Bowl* I. xviii. 212 You must awfully want your tea..so let me give you a good stiff cup. **1919** WODEHOUSE *Coming of Bill* (1920) II. xi. 213 Mr. Penway's eyes..fell upon the bottle of Bourbon... He sprang at it and poured himself a stiff dose. **1929** T. WOLFE *Look Homeward, Angel* xxxv. 522 A stiff drink of gin. **1951** 'J. WYNDHAM' *Day of Triffids* i. 21, I was shaky again, and..could have done with a stiff drink. **1970** G. F. NEWMAN *Sir, You Bastard* vii. 192, I think you've earned a very stiff scotch. **1975** D. LODGE *Changing Places* ii. 67 'Wow,' said the woman. 'You mix a stiff drink.' **1977** K. O'HARA *Ghost of Thomas Penry* xv. 149 They went off and poured themselves a stiff one each.

19. b. *Finance.* = TIGHT *a.* 10 c. Now *rare* or *Obs.*

1845 *Punch* 11 Oct. 164/2 Money's stiff they say. **1912** *Q. Rev.* July 103 Money is in such keen demand all the world over that the rates tend to become high, whereupon it is called 'stiff' or 'tight'.

20. b. *stiff-brim, -leg.*

1896 'MARK TWAIN' in *Harper's Mag.* Aug. 356/1 It was the first season anybody wore that kind—a black stiff-brim stove-pipe. **1930** *Engineering* 10 Oct. 449/2 The material—sand and gravel—was..unloaded by means of a stiff-leg derrick. **1932** W. FAULKNER *Light in August* ii. 27 He wore a tie and a stiffbrim straw hat that was quite new. **1943** *Sun* (Baltimore) 26 Nov. 6/3 The tower was first welded together on the ground. It was then lifted into its foundation by heavy lines attached to two high especially built 'stiff-leg' cranes.

c. stiff-arm *v. trans.* (occas. *absol.*), to fend off or push with a stiff arm; hence *fig.*, to rebuff or reject; also as *sb.* (usu. *attrib.*) in Rugby and U.S. Football, the act of tackling or fending off a tackle with a stiff arm; **stiff-neck**, an obstinate, haughty or self-righteous person; cf. STIFF-NECKED *a.*

1927 G. S. LOWMAN *Pract. Football* vii. 85 In all stiff arm and shifting have the body slightly inclined toward the tackler. *Ibid.* xii. 218 When playing in the line, the defensive center should stiff-arm his opponent back into the play. **1934** CRISLER & WIEMAN *Pract. Football* vii. 86 The ball carrier is more easily stopped in the hole than anywhere else, since he cannot dodge, sidestep, reverse or stiff-arm at that point. **1945** *Tee Emm* (Air Ministry) V. 50 Ward off attack by kicking or stiff-arming the shark... Kick or stiff-arm a shark to push him away. **1950** *Sport* 24–30 Mar. 9/1 Vindictive hacking and 'stiff arm' jabs were the rule rather than the exception. **1968** *Listener* 8 Aug. 189/2 There had been the fury of the British backs meeting persistent stiff-arm and late tackling, although these almost automatic fouls were only occasionally penalised. **1973** [see *PLACE *sb.*[1] 9 d]. **1974** A. A. THOMPSON *Swiss Legacy* xviii. 185 She tried to slam the door, but McAllister stiff-armed it violently against the wall. **1921** *Blackw. Mag.* Feb. 251/1 The stiff-necks of Victoria's entourage would have been painfully shocked. **1962** E. SNOW *Red China Today* (1963) i. 18 The young stiff-neck dismissed them angrily and told me I could do as I pleased about disposing of my excess but if I carried it I'd have to pay. **1975** *New Yorker* 28 Apr. 124/2 A repatriated American stiffneck who has been imprisoned by the North Vietnamese finds his particular solace in not budging an inch from the mindless chauvinism he set out with.

d. *stiff-bosomed, -elbowed, -jointed, -legged, -limbed, -shirted, -winged*; **stiff-arsed** *slang* (see quot. 1937).

1937 PARTRIDGE *Dict. Slang* 831/2 *Stiff-arsed*, haughty; supercilious. **1971** B. MALAMUD *Tenants* 70 If you think you..are going to be stiffassed and uptight by what I say, maybe we ought to call it off before we start? **1925** WODEHOUSE *Carry On, Jeeves* ix. 238 Then lay out one of the gents' stiff-bosomed [shirts]. **1942** W. FAULKNER *Go Down, Moses* 74 A white stiff-bosomed collarless shirt beneath a pique vest. **1956** H. GOLD *Man who was not with It* (1965) vi. 50, I..walked imperfectly awake, stiff-elbowed, thick-tongued, and dim-sighted. **1973** M. AMIS *Rachel Papers* 190 In this fashion, with twelve stiff-elbowed tugs, he has wanked into her head. **1743** W. ELLIS *Mod. Husbandman* Oct. i. 126 Its stiff-jointed, high-coloured, long Straw. **1876** 'MARK TWAIN' *Tom Sawyer* xvi. 142 They felt rusty, and stiff-jointed, and a little homesick. **1854** DICKENS *Hard Times* III. i. 263 In staggering over the universe with his rusty stiff-legged compasses, he had meant to do great things. **1922** JOYCE *Ulysses* 428 Bloom..blunders stifflegged, out of the track. **1914** 'SAKI' *Beasts & Super-Beasts* 65 Old Shep, the white-nozzled, stiff-limbed collie. **1973** M. AMIS *Rachel Papers* 23 In normal circumstances, with her embarrassment in any kind of pre-coital conversation, her unassumingly pretty face, the stiff-limbed movements: you were a plaything of her unease. **1918** G. FRANKAU *One of Them* iv. 34 The patient lights of brougham or rarer car shine, Waiting stiff-shirted squires and ladies fair. **1933** DYLAN THOMAS *Let.* Nov. (1966) 51 Please don't go all stiff-shirted on me. **1901** *Practitioner* Mar. 241 Why not an 'Epic of Malaria'?..But such a theme would surely spur the stiffest-winged Pegasus to empyrean flights. **1977** *Devon Wetlands* (Devon County Council) vii. 26 Fulmars ..have a characteristic stiff-winged, gliding flight.

B. *sb.* **2. b.** Money. *slang.*

1897 'OUIDA' *Massarenes* i. 6 They are astonishing—biggest income in the United States... Made their 'stiff' there, and come home to spend it. **1930** BELLOC *New Cautionary Tales* 58 He wrang his hands, exclaiming, 'If I only had a bit of Stiff How different would be my life!'

3. b. A racehorse which is unlikely to win; *spec.* one which is not intended to win. Cf. *STIFF *a.* 2 b. *U.S. slang.*

a **1890** in Barrère & Leland *Dict. Slang.* (1890) II. 306/1 'What do they mean by a *stiff* in the race?' 'That means generally a horse that on public form should win the race, and that either the jockey, trainer, or horse has been 'fixed' so that he will not win.' **1935** D. RUNYON *Money from Home* 197 There is also a rumor that Follow You is a stiff in the race. **1944** *Sun* (Baltimore) 21 Sept. 17/5 We either get shut out or find we are on a stiff which won't run.

4. a. Also a tramp; a migratory or unskilled worker.

1901, etc. [see *BINDLE[2] a]. **1915** *Truth* 20 Jan. 90/2 A hopeless shortage of the best labour on the one hand, and an unusual proportion of 'stiffs' on the other. **1927** W. EDGE *Main Stem* iii. 16 No stiff ever got information about a job through a telephone directory. **1963** H. GARNER in R. Weaver *Canad. Short Stories* (1968) 2nd Ser. 41 Who would listen to a harvest stiff in the middle of the tobacco country? **1976** E. WARD *Hanged Man* iii. 13 The driver.. reached out to pull Burnett into the dusty cab. Construction stiff. A wandering freemasonry.

b. A mean, disagreeable, or contemptible person (freq. *big stiff*). Also joc. and *loosely*, a man, a fellow; *working stiff*, an ordinary working man. *slang* (orig. *U.S.*).

1882 in *Colorado Quarterly* (1956) Winter 271 Cap. Cline, that lonely old stiff..is now demonotized. **1896** G. ADE *Artie* ii. 17 There I set like a big stiff for five hours. *Ibid.* iv. 36, I do n't come in here to give coin to no such stiffs as you. **1914** [see *NANNY-GOAT 3]. **1925** C. CONNOLLY *Let.* 28 Feb. in *Romantic Friendship* (1975) 61 He was described..as 'rather a stiff' which is true at present. **1930** *Punch* 26 Feb. 228/2 He said 'You big stiff!' in a very loud voice and went. **1930** J. DOS PASSOS *42nd Parallel* v. 403 Charley said that working stiffs ought to stick together for decent living conditions. **1936** WODEHOUSE *Laughing Gas* viii. 82 He had told me this man was a pretty good sort of old stiff. **1949** *Daily Ardmoreite* (Ardmore, Oklahoma) 23 Feb. 18/6 A select group of working stiffs in high government circles have run into 20 assorted kinds of complications. **1951** E. PAUL *Springtime in Paris* vii. 139 Hold your trap, you old stiff. **1967** *Sun* 23 Apr. 5/8 A bad customer..a stiff who orders the table d'hôte and nothing to drink. **1975** *N.Y. Times* 8 Jan. 35/1 And if a black man did buy a house, hey, we knocked on his door and said hello. If he was a nice guy, great. If he was a stiff, well, I know lots of white stiffs, too. **1977** *Guardian Weekly* 10 July 15/2 The idea of two young working stiffs [*sc.* Woodward and Bernstein] carrying off the prize is irresistible to youngsters with their careers before them.

c. A drunkard (see also quot. 1969). Cf. *STIFF *a.* 2 e.

1907 J. LONDON *Road* 170 Robbing a drunken man they call 'rolling a stiff'. **1969** *Telegraph* (Brisbane) 3 Oct. 42/1 We get all types of no-hopers here—hoboes, bums, 'alcos', homosexuals and 'stiffs' (methylated spirits drinkers). **1976** N. THORNBURG *Cutter & Bone* vi. 135 It had taken a good part of the day just to locate the poor stiff.

d. *Football.* A member of a reserve team. Freq. in *pl. slang.*

1950 *Sport* 22–28 Sept. 4/1 On Saturday the Forest 'stiffs' romped home to a 5–1 victory over Halifax. **1967** M. PROCTER *Rogue Running* xxv. 164 He became one of the 'stiffs', a second-team man who only played for the first team when a better man was ill, or injured. **1970** *Sun* 5 Sept. 28/6 (*heading*) Gunners sign Metchick for stiffs.

stiff, *v.* Restrict † *Obs.* to senses in Dict. and add: **3.** To cheat; to refuse to pay or tip (a person). *slang* (orig. and chiefly *U.S.*).

1950 *Sat. Even. Post* 15 July 124/3 It was a signal for the waiter to hustle over and put the arm on the customer who was trying to stiff him. **1968** J. M. ULLMAN *Lady on Fire* (1969) vi. 85 He's still haggling over the bill..trying to stiff me for a thousand less than agreed on. **1978** *Detroit Free Press* 5 Mar. B 3/1 Some New York waiters will tell you that the wealthiest men stiff you on a tip. **1979** *Globe & Mail* (Toronto) 31 May 2/5 Agents are still going bankrupt, but now it means they are leaving debts with the wholesalers and airlines. They aren't stiffing the consumer. **1982** *Washington Post* 9 Jan. 21/2 What is McCarthy doing when he refuses to tip a waiter who has given good service?.. He may be cursed by the waiter he stiffs. *Ibid.* 21/3 Instead of stiffing his servers, McCarthy should be stiffing their employers.

4. To kill; to murder. Cf. STIFF *sb.* 3 a. *slang.*

1974 R. L. SIMON *Wild Turkey* (1976) xiv. 104 'The Japanese girl..was found stiffed in an air-conditioning duct.'..'Stiffed?' '*Asesinato.*' **1978** C. EGLETON *Mills Bomb* vii. 73 Did she blow their cover too? Is that how they got stiffed in Prague?

stiffener. Add: **2. a.** Also *spec.* a card, such as a cigarette card, used to stiffen a packet, envelope, etc.

1926 *Chambers's Jrnl.* 10 July 497/2 'Stiffener', the name by which the cigarette-card has always been, and still is, known in the trade. **1967** A. DAVIS *Package & Print* 55 Cigarette cards..were originally intended as stiffeners (and always known in the trade by this name). The first printed stiffeners were produced in America in 1879. **1971** D. POTTER *Brit. Eliz. Stamps* x. 114 As an added attraction they include a stiffener—a card which reduces damage to the envelope in transit—with informative technical and background data.

3. A fortifying or reviving drink, *spec.* an alcoholic one. *slang.*

1928 D. L. SAYERS *Unpleasantness at Bellona Club* ii. 12 Dick Challoner..took the gasping Fentiman away into the deserted library for a stiffener. **1973** G. MITCHELL *Murder of Busy Lizzie* xiv. 161 I'll buy you a stiffener in the bar. **1978** J. PUDNEY *Thank Goodness for Cake* 128 Another visit to the loo for a stiffener... There are always drinks on the way home.

stiffening, *vbl. sb.* Add: **2. c.** *Naut.* Heavy goods taken on board a ship as ballast (see quot. 1894). Cf. *stiffening order*, sense 3 in Dict.

1894 H. PAASCH *From Keel to Truck* (ed. 2) 463/1 *Stiffening*, is the term given to any weighty substances taken on board a vessel for the purpose of making her 'Stiff', i.e. less crank. Stiffening (whether consisting of ballast or a portion of the outward cargo) is put in vessels which do not remain upright without having sufficient weight in the bottom. **1902** B. LUBBOCK *Round the Horn* 29 We are waiting now for our 'stiffening', as we dare not take our last 400 tons of coals out until we get a like weight of grain. **1924** R. CLEMENTS *Gipsy of Horn* vi. 115 We heard one morning that we were chartered, and proceeded to shift ship down to the coal-tips to take in our 'stiffening'—just sufficient coal, that is, to ballast the ship. **1975** *Islander* (Victoria, B.C.) 23 Feb. 6/3 The *Pamir* was taken in tow with a small amount of coal ballast aboard for stiffening.

stiff-necked, *a.* Add: Also *transf.*

1963 *Times* 23 Apr. 13/2 Fortunately the recent exchanges promise slightly less stiff-necked attitudes on both sides.

stiffness. Add: **1. b.** *spec.* (*a*) the force required to produce unit deflection or displacement of an object; (*b*) the maximum deflection of a beam divided by its span or length. (Later examples.)

1893 H. T. Bovey *Theory of Structures* iii. 190, $dP_1/dl = EA/L$, and EA/L is consequently a measure of the longitudinal stiffness of a bar. *Ibid.* vi. 389 If *D* is the maximum deflection of a girder of span *l* under a load *W*, then *W*/*D*, or more usually *D*/*l*, is a measure of the stiffness of the girder. **1922** Glazebrook *Dict. Appl. Physics* I. 808/2 The stiffness of a beam is usually measured by the maximum deflection, when loaded, divided by the span. **1925** J. Case *Strength of Materials* xxiv. 386 The 'stiffness' of a spring is the load required to produce unit deflection. **1969** C. O. Raspor in W. R. R. Park *Plastics Film Technol.* iv. 88 The tensile modulus is often used as a measure of film stiffness. This quantity is obtained by calculating the ratio of a stress to strain at a certain point on a tensile stress–strain curve. **1978** *Sci. Amer.* Dec. 116 (*caption*) Stiffness of an isolated muscle (the change in the force developed by the muscle when it is stretched, divided by its change in length) increases as the muscle is stretched.

stiffy (sti·fi). *U.S. slang.* [f. Stiff *a.* or *sb.* + -y[6].] **1.** A beggar who pretends to be paralysed.

1917 'A.-no. 1' *Coast to Coast with Jack London* ii. 22 The fellow..was a hobo. He introduced himself as 'Stiffy Brandon'. His moniker indicated that for a beggar craft he had chosen the one which imposed upon the credulous..the awful affliction of the paralytic. **1956** S. Harris *Skid Row, U.S.A.* ii. 38 Red Bill was the best stiffy in New York.

2. A naïve or stupid person.

1965 *Liberator* (N.Y.) Aug. 23/1 'You a trick, Dan—a stiffy,' Herman said. 'You so square Little Orphan Annie could put game on you.' *Ibid.*, Stacked broads rushed in on the arms of stiffies straight from the cornfields; you know—them cats with the cowboy hats and ice-cream suits. Some stiffs. **1966** C. Keil *Urban Blues* v. 118 Negro artists who find their way into white concert halls still find it necessary to 'hip' those 'stiffies' in the audience who insist on clapping their hands in a martial manner.

Stiggins (sti·ginz). The surname of a character in Dickens's *Pickwick Papers* (1836–7), used as the type of the pious humbug.

1916 [see *holy *a.* 4 c]. **1931** A. Huxley *Let.* 25 Sept. (1969) 355 That horribly snuffling Stiggins tone! **1935** *Times* 5 Jan. 6/3, I do protest strongly at any attempt to revive the activities of the Prudes on the Prowl, the spying of the Stigginses, and the chortling of the Chadbands.

stigmal, *a.* Delete *rare*[−0] and add examples.

1957 *Imms's Gen. Textbk. Entomol.* (ed. 9) 683 It runs along the front margin as the marginal vein and gives off a short stigmal vein. **1962** Gordon & Lavoipierre *Entomol. for Students of Med.* xli. 246 The hard and the soft ticks..possess a pair of stigmata, surrounded by a rounded chitinised plate (known as the stigmal plate) on each side of the body.

stigmasterol (stigmæ·stĕrǫl). *Biochem.* [ad. G. *stigmasterin* (Windhaus & Hauth 1906, in *Ber. d. Deut. Chem. Ges.* XXXIX. 4380) f. Physo)stigma: see *-sterol.] A phytosterol, $C_{29}H_{48}O$, present in Calabar beans (*Physostigma venenosum*) and soya beans.

1907 *Chem. Abstr.* I. 1002 The compound..from the tetrabromide is termed stigmasterol. **1940** *Industr. & Engin. Chem.* Aug. 1138/1 Because of its chemical structure, stigmasterol is an excellent material for the synthesis of the hormone progesterone. **1975** *Lipids* X. 544/2 Sterol patterns of adult and juvenile ivy leaf were essentially identical, with quantities of sterol per 100 g fresh leaf being:..stigmasterol, 9 mg.

stigmergy (sti·gmɜ̄ɹdʒi). *Ent.* [ad. F. *stigmergie* (P.-P. Grassé 1959, in *Insectes Sociaux* VI. 62), f. Gr. στιγμ-ός pricking + ἔργ-ον work: see -y[3].] The process by which the results of an insect's activity act as a stimulus to further activity.

1959 tr. P.-P. Grassé in *Insectes Sociaux* VI. 79 The stimulation of the workers by the very performances they have achieved is a significant one inducing accurate and adaptable response, and has been named stigmergy. **1965** *Symp. Zool. Soc. Lond.* XIV. 128 Experimental evidence would seem to be desirable before accepting stigmergy as the explanation of all co-ordinated constructional behaviour. **1981** *Atlantic Monthly* July 49 There is a similar phenomenon in entomology known as stigmergy.

Hence **stigme·rgic** *a.*

1970 G. Ordish tr. *R. Chauvin's World of Ants* i. 41 At some point there seems to be a brake on the stigmergic process when the stimulation has gone beyond a certain stage. **1971** E. O. Wilson *Insect Societies* xi. 229/2 Stigmergic responses are evidently major elements in nest construction by social insects.

‖ **Stijl** (stəil). [Du., = style.] The name of a movement in art and architecture associated with the Dutch periodical *De Stijl* (1917–32), founded by Theo van Doesburg and Piet Mondrian, and devoted to the principles of neo-plasticism. Freq. with article *de.* Also *attrib.* and as *adj.*

1934 [see *neo-plasticism]. **1936** A. H. Barr *Cubism & Abstract Art* 142 In his *Volume construction* of 1918..the sculptor Vantongerloo applied the *Stijl* love of rectangles to sculpture. *Ibid.* 158 Other of Gropius' buildings at Dessau were even more *Stijl* in character. **1945** R. Motherwell tr. *Mondrian's Plastic Art* 14 In 1915, Theo van Doesburg..was making analogous researches. Together we formed a small group of artists and architects: the De Stijl Group. **1962** H. Myers tr. *Pingaud's Holland* 168 The *De Stijl* ('The Style') group, founded in 1917, is dedicated to the fight for a geometric art. **1974** *Encycl. Brit. Macropædia* IX. 516/1 Whereas the Bauhaus offered freedom of expression.., de Stijl offered dogmatic straitjackets of verticals, horizontals, and primary colours.

stilb (stilb). *Physics.* [a. F. *stilb* (A. Blondel in *Recueil des Trav. & Compt. Rend. des Séances* (Internat. Commission on Illumination, 1923) V. 88), f. Gr. στίλβ-ειν to glitter.] A unit of luminance equal to one candela per square centimetre.

1940 in *Chambers's Techn. Dict.* **1942** *Jrnl. Optical Soc. Amer.* XXXII. 355/2 The names, *phot* and *stilb* were ..coined by Blondel (1921) and are in general use on the Continent. **1953** [see *nit *sb.*[4]]. **1963** van Wijk & Ubing in W. R. van Wijk *Physics of Plant Environment* iii. 90 In photometry a black body at the temperature of melting platinum (2042·16 °K) is used as a standard light source. It has by definition a surface brightness of 60 candelas per cm² or 60 stilb, when viewed in a direction perpendicular to the surface.

stilbamidine (stilbæ·midīn). *Pharm.* [f. Stilb(ene + *amidine* (f. Amid(e + -ine[5]).] A diamidine derivative, $(H_2N)(HN)C{\cdot}C_6H_4{\cdot}CH{:}CH{\cdot}C_6H_4{\cdot}C(NH)(NH_2)$, of stilbene which has antiprotozoal properties and has been used, usu. in the form of its isethionate, in the treatment of trypanosomiasis and leishmaniasis.

1941 [see *pentamidine]. **1958** J. H. Burn *Lect. Notes Pharmacol.* (ed. 5) 110 Stilbamidine is no longer used [in the treatment of leishmaniasis] because it is toxic to the 5th nerve. **1977** *Jrnl. Pharmacol. & Exper. Therapeutics* CCI. 555/1 Pentamidine, stilbamidine and their close analogs are known to interfere with nucleic acid and protein synthesis.

stilbœstrol (stilbī·strǫl, -be·strǫl). *Pharm.* Also (*U.S.*) **stilbestrol.** [f. Stilb(ene + Œstr(us + -ol.] † **a.** A synthetic derivative, $HOC_6H_4{\cdot}CH{:}CH{\cdot}C_6H_4OH$, of stilbene having slight œstrogenic properties; also, any derivative of this. *Obs.*

1938 E. C. Dodds et al. in *Nature* 5 Feb. 248/1 In view of the fact that 4:4′-dihydroxystilbene is the mother substance of a series of œstrogenic agents, we suggest that it may be termed stillbœstrol. **1938** *Nature* 2 July 34/1 (*heading*) Oestrogenic activity of alkylated stilbœstrols. **1943** *Vitamins & Hormones* III. 233 This substance..is known as diethylstilbestrol, the term stilbestrol being used for the parent substance.

b. A powerful synthetic nonsteroidal œstrogen, $HOC_6H_4{\cdot}C(C_2H_5){:}C(C_2H_5){\cdot}C_6H_4OH$, used, often in the form of its dipropionate, in hormone therapy, as a postcoital contraceptive, and as a growth-promoting agent esp. in cattle and sheep; = *diethylstilbœstrol* s.v. *diethyl 2.

1939 *Lancet* 7 Oct. 788/1 Oral administration of the synthetic œstrogen, stilbœstrol, will inhibit implantation of the ovum in the rat and rabbit. **1943** *Vitamins & Hormones* III. 233 In Great Britain the substance is commonly known as stilbestrol, although it should, of course, be referred to as diethylstilbestrol. **1957** [*œstrogenic *a.*]. **1959** *Times* 29 Apr. 12/6 Farmers were warned yesterday that breeding stock should not be implanted with stilbœstrol. **1976** Smythies & Corbett *Psychiatry* xi. 209 Stilboestrol given to men reduces libido.

‖ **stile antico** (stī·le antī·ko). *Mus.* [It., lit. 'old style'.] The strict contrapuntal style of the sixteenth century, esp. as exemplified in the works of Palestrina.

1944 W. Apel *Harvard Dict. Mus.* 550/2 *Palestrina style*... As early as the 17th century this style, under names such as *stile antico, stile osservato*..had become 'classical' in the Roman school. **1959** *Collins Mus. Encycl.* 624/2 *Stile antico*, the contrapuntal style of the 16th cent. as practised by Italian composers and formulated by Italian theorists in the 17th and early 18th cent. **1968** *New Oxf. Hist. Music* iv. x. 521 This consciously conservative tendency among Catholic composers..resulted in the ultimate petrifaction of the Palestrinian *stile antico*, which artificially survived well into the eighteenth century. **1974** *Early Music* July 197/1 A dull *stile antico* section for 'Domine fili unigenite'. **1976** *Ibid.* July 274 Cavalli's final work, the Requiem, looks backwards also, but its use of the *stile antico* is not quite so remote as that in the psalms.

‖ **stile concitato** (stī·le kǫntʃitā·to). *Mus.* [It., lit. 'excited style'.] A baroque style developed by Monteverdi, emphasizing dramatic expression and excitement.

1926 H. Prunières *Monteverdi* iii. v. 180 The semiquavers of the *stile concitato* express their terror at the menace of the god. **1940** *Music & Letters* Apr. 244 Monteverdi..claimed, in the preface to the volume in which the 'Combattimento' is printed, to have originated a new *stile concitato*. **1947** M. F. Bukofzer *Mus. Baroque Era* (1948) ii. 38 Monteverdi enriched the *concertato* style by an important innovation: the *stile concitato* (style of agitation) in which he turned the measured tremolo of the *gorgia* to dramatic effect. **1959** *Listener* 16 Apr. 692/3 He admired the *stile concitato* of Monteverdi. **1967** *Ibid.* 18 May 665/2 These were part of Monteverdi's *stile concitato*, a style he cultivated..to express wrath, anger, indignation.

‖ **stile rappresentativo** (stī·le ra:prezentatī·vo). *Mus.* [It., lit. 'representative style'.] The vocal style of recitative used by Italian musicians of the early seventeenth century (see quot. 1938).

1886 F. Praeger tr. *E. Naumann's Hist. Mus.* I. xv. 525 At first the opera was variously styled according to the individuality of the composer... The style itself was generally called *Stile rappresentativo*. **1915** *Strad* Jan. 299/1 The so-called *stile rappresentativo* of Florence was claiming more and more adherents and ministers; Monteverde, likewise, was moved by the ever-expanding ripple. **1938** *Oxf. Compan. Mus.* 896/2 *Stile rappresentativo*... The term was used by the early Roman composer of oratorio, Cavalieri, and the contemporary Florentine composers of opera..to indicate the use of their invention of recitative..which aimed rather at *representing* the sense and the natural inflection of the speaking voice than at providing the enjoyment of pure musical beauty. **1947** M. F. Bukofzer *Mus. Baroque Era* (1948) ii. 25 The emergence of the *stile rappresentativo* or recitative about the year 1600 has often been regarded as the most important turning point in the entire history of music. **1959** N. C. Carpenter *Mus. in Medieval & Renaissance Universities* iv. 357 University learning..led such people as Vincenzo Galilei..to experiment in a new musical style based upon his concept of Greek music, the *stile rappresentativo*, with its close affinity between words and music. **1980** *Early Music* July 298/1 But we should not let the polemics of the day in favour of monody obscure the very close, though perhaps not immediately apparent, bond between the expressiveness of the *stile rappresentativo* and the concept of melody that pervades the fabric of many polyphonic works from the second half of the 16th century.

stiletto, *sb.* Add: **2.** Restrict † *Obs. rare*[−1] to sense in Dict. and add: **b.** Short for *stiletto heel* (see sense *5).

1959 *New Statesman* 10 Oct. 464/3 She came..smooching forward, her walk made lopsided by the absence of one heel of the stilettos. **1960** *Guardian* 18 Mar. 10/6 Wearing stilettos, you are, of course, tiptoeing. **1967** O. Wynd *Walk Softly, Men Praying* ii. 13 She wobbled slightly on worn-over stilettos.

5. stiletto heel, a very narrow, high heel on women's shoes, fashionable esp. in the 1950s; a shoe with such a heel; hence **stiletto-heeled** *a.*

1953 *Daily Tel.* 10 Sept. 8/4 One of the models..in the ..winter collection..has the new stiletto heel, 3½ in high and just large enough at the base to cover a sixpence. **1981** M. Hardwick *Chinese Detective* ix. 73 She was in black slip and stockings and four-inch stiletto heels. **1959** *Times* 13 May 10/7 The iniquitous effect of stiletto-heeled shoes on the modern woman's feet. **1973** M. Amis *Rachel Papers* 124 At this kind of speed it was advisable to place the stiletto-heeled shoe, kept in a side-pocket for this purpose, over the gear-stick to prevent it jiggering like a pump-drill.

still, *a.* and *sb.*[2] Add: **A.** *adj.* **1. d.** (Earlier example.) Used also of soft drinks, to distinguish them from the carbonated variety.

1777 P. Thicknesse *Year's Journey* I. v. 31 The difference between still Champaigne, and that which is *mousser*, is owing to..the time of year in which it is bottled. **1949** *Acct. Soft Drinks Industry in Brit.* 1942–48 iii. 37 A number of beverages essential for some purpose, such as health..were excluded from the general restrictions... The list of these drinks included..sugar-free drinks for diabetics..and still spa waters. **1981** *Soft Drinks Rep.* 1. 2 *Mineral and Bottled Water.* This includes natural spring water products which are either still or naturally or artificially sparkling. *Ibid.* 11. 9, 2·5 billion litres of diluted still drink was consumed in 1980.

3. a. (Allusive examples of *still small voice*: I *Kings* xix. 12.)

1769 T. Gray *Ode for Music* 6 Sweeter yet The still small voice of Gratitude. **1847** C. Brontë *Jane Eyre* II. iv. 101 Strong wind, earthquake, shock, and fire may pass by: I shall follow the guiding..of that still small voice which interprets the dictates of conscience. **1874** J. G. Whittier *Poet. Wks.* 458/1 Speak through the earthquake, wind and fire, O still, small voice of calm! **1918** L. Strachey *Eminent Victorians* 64 In such a situation the voice of self-abnegation must needs grow still and small indeed. **1953** P. C. Berg *Dict. New Words in English* 14 The still small voice of Professor Bryant..has a few good words to say in favour of these 'abominations'. **1983** *Daily Tel.* 25 Mar. 20/5 If it is not too late, may a still small voice be allowed to publicise a fact not yet revealed by either the protagonists or critics of the Budget?

8. still-air *a.*, (*a*) *Aeronaut.*, applicable or calculated for a state of no wind; (*b*) not employing forced draught.

1913 *Captain* Sept. 1072/2 A machine with still-air speed of 57 miles per hour was sent up to fight a gale for 400 yds. **1948** *Jrnl. R. Aeronaut. Soc.* LII. 600/2 We often read..of two aircraft of widely varying characteristics being compared over similar still-air ranges. **1951** 'N. Shute' *Round Bend* vi. 177 She had tankage for twelve hundred gallons, giving her a still-air range of about two thousand miles. **1960** *Farmer & Stockbreeder* 19 Jan. 108/1 Game birds are not..easy to hatch..in the big cabinet.. machines... Reasonably good results, on a small scale,..

can be got from the more old-fashioned still-air machines. **1961** P. W. BROOKS *Mod. Airliner* iv. 100 A payload of 6,000 lb. was required for a still-air range of 3,500 miles. **1977** *Shooting Times & Country Mag.* 13–19 Jan. 26/2 Small incubators—those that take 100–200 pheasant eggs—are nearly always the 'still air' type and depend on convection currents for ensuring air movement.

B. *sb.*[2] †**5.** *slang.* A still-born child; a still-birth. *Obs.*

1864 HOTTEN *Slang Dict.* 247 *Stills*, the undertaker's Slang term for still-born children. **1897** [see *MISS *sb.*[4]].

6. a. An ordinary photograph, as distinguished from a motion picture; *spec.* a single shot from a film (or a specially posed photograph of a scene from it) for use in advertising. Freq. with defining word, as *cinema still, film still*, etc.

1916 *Independent* 5 June 86 (*caption*) A striking 'still' from the film 'The Fall of a Nation'. **1922** *Glasgow Herald* 12 Oct. 6 Mr Johnson succeeded in exposing 25,000 feet of film and in taking some 1000 'stills'. **1938** *Archit. Rev.* LXXXIII. *caption facing* p. 72 Two aspects of a turbulent age are seen in 'The Temple of Janus',..wherein the figures of the Furies are arrested as in a cinema 'still'. **1945** H. READ *Coat of Many Colours* xxix. 142 We may select 'stills' for their closed form—for their pictorial composition—but the film itself is essentially open form. **1957** *Times* 25 Nov. 11/3 The story of that enchanting film *The Red Balloon* illustrated with film stills and with a photographic cover in colour. **1962** E. SNOW *Red China Today* (1963) xv. 109 McDermott and I used our Canons taking stills. **1972** C. WESTON *Poor, Poor Ophelia* (1973) xxvi. 164 The photo was a standard publicity still. **1976** *Oxf. Compan. Film* 66/1 *Frame stills* are reproductions of single frames from the film itself... They convey the true feeling of a film more exactly than can a posed production still. **1978** 'A. GARVE' *Counterstroke* I. 88 George had brought along a full-face 'still' of Lacy.

b. *attrib.* (as *sing.* or *pl.*).

1922 *Opportunities in Motion Picture Industry* (Photoplay Research Society) 47 Ask the first director you meet where you can find the still man. *Ibid.* 48 Still pictures are made for the publicity department. *Ibid.* 50 Seldom are the many lights placed for the movie camera exactly suited to the still camera. *Ibid.*, The still cameraman is of necessity a versatile flea. **1925** R. BEETHAM in E. F. Norton *Fight for Everest 1924* 324 His time was so fully taken up with cinema work that most of the still photography had to be done by other members of the party. **1928** [see *news-reel* s.v. *NEWS *sb.* (*pl.*) 6 c]. **1963** *Movie* July/Aug. 27/4 The still pictures have greater effect than the newsreel shots. **1964** C. WILLOCK *Enormous Zoo* ix. 165 Roger spent one whole afternoon trying to get the moment of entry and exit from the sandstone burrow with a stills camera. **1964** M. MCLUHAN *Understanding Media* II. xx. 193 The physical and psychic *gestalts*, or 'still' shots, with which they [*sc.* Freud and Jung] worked were much owing to the posture world revealed by the photograph. **1974** *Times* 16 Nov. 10/6 It was through stills photographs that the public were first introduced..to the stars. *Ibid.* 10/7 The stills men would retouch the negative. **1974** M. TAYLOR tr. *Metz's Film Lang.* i. 12 Rudolf Arnheim recognises that..still photography produces an impression of reality much weaker than that of the cinema. **1981** *Gossip* (Holiday Special) 54/3, I met her on a film I did a while back. She was the still photographer.

7. *Naut.* An instruction to cease work and stand to attention conveyed to a ship's crew by the boatswain's pipe.

1933 'L. LUARD' *All Hands* 140 Pipe the still, Cox'un. **1963** [see *PIPE-DOWN].

still, *adv.* Add: **6. c.** **still and all**: nevertheless, even so; after all. *colloq.*

1829 G. GRIFFIN *Collegians* I. vii. 140 Lord K..gave him a lease o' that farm... Still an' all, Myles do be poor, for he never knew how to keep a hoult o' the money. **1928** F. N. HART *Bellamy Trial* iv. 104 Still and all, I believe that he was there precisely when he said he was. **1942** G. MARX *Let.* 16 Dec. (1967) 32 Still and all, as Lardner would say, it's a very cozy little place. **1963** A. LUBBOCK *Austral. Roundabout* 77 'Still-and-all,' they said, 'it's no use worrying over things y' can't help, is it?' **1969** *Guardian* 18 Aug. 9/5 Still and all, it is surely time to desist in good grace. **1978** R. MOORE *Big Paddle* (1979) i. 4 Still and all, if you see something I haven't, let me know.

stillage, *sb.*[1] Add: **2.** Now *spec.* a pallet, frame, or similar structure used for storage of goods. Also *collect.*

1963 K. HUDSON *Industrial Archaeol.* vii. 111 Old fittings and furnishings which might well remain *in situ* at old factories..include..wooden stillages. **1970** *Cabinet Maker & Retail Furnisher* 25 Sept. 629/1 Each stillage is 36 in × 24 in × 6 ft high, and provides storage for 150 headboards... Customers who take regular bulk deliveries are offered these stillages on loan. **1976** *Listener* 22 July, Stacking of components in wooden stillage instead of metal bins.

stillage (sti·lėdʒ), *sb.*[2] Chiefly *U.S.* [f. STILL *sb.*[1] + -AGE.] The residue remaining in a still after a fermentation, usu. of grain or molasses, and removal of the alcohol by distillation.

1940 *Sun* (Baltimore) 5 Apr. 11/7 The experiments.. were designed to determine the value of distillers' dry rye grains and stillage as substitutes for other grains in feeding cattle for the market. **1945** *Industr. & Engin. Chem.* June 534/1 Distilleries processing molasses are frequently confronted with the problem of disposing of stillage. **1963** *Agric. & Biol. Chem.* XXVII. A19/2 (*heading*) Nutritional studies on the utilization of distiller's stillage. **1979** *Nature* 6 Dec. 551/1 The total output of stillage in Brazil is equivalent in biological oxygen demand to the untreated sewage produced by a city of 200 million inhabitants.

still-birth. Add: Also **stillbirth. 1.** (Further examples.) Also, formerly, birth of a child alive or with a beating heart, but not breathing.

1880 *Brit. Med. Jrnl.* 9 Oct. 596/2 Stillbirth—Resuscitation after two hours and five minutes. **1913** R. W. JOHNSTONE *Text-bk. Midwifery* xxxvii. 397 The infant is born in a state of suspended animation—its heart continues to beat, but it makes no effort to breathe or to move. 'Still birth' is therefore not the same thing as the child's being born dead, although death may supervene if prompt treatment is not applied. **1920** O. ST. J. MOSES *Man. Obstetr.* xviii. 269 In the pale or white form of still-birth the chances of recovery are much less. **1940** BROWN & GILBERT *Midwifery* l. 468 In certain circumstances, the fœtus continues to live as a fœtus external to the mother for some time—10 to 20 minutes—and it may die as a fœtus and be counted as a still-birth. **1947** G. I. STRACHAN *Textbk. Obstetr.* VIII. 699 The term 'stillborn' is therefore applied when the fœtus fails to maintain an independent existence, although some authorities..have attempted to make a division into (*a*) dead birth in which the fœtus is obviously dead and exhibits neither heart beat nor respiration, and (*b*) stillbirth in which the heart is beating but respiration is never established. It is simpler, however, to employ the term 'stillbirth' to cover both these states. **1971** *Reader's Digest Family Guide to Law* 197/2 Even a still-birth—where a child is born dead after at least 28 weeks of pregnancy—must be registered as a birth. **1972** S. G. CLAYTON et al. *Obstetrics by Ten Teachers* (ed. 12) liii. 642 If the heart is beating after delivery, even though there is no sign of respiration, the death of a child born after 28 weeks should not be included as a stillbirth but as a neonatal death.

2. A still-born child.

1963 BUTLER & BONHAM *Perinatal Mortality* 210 Only six of the 'stillbirths' weighed 1,000 grams or less and were born before 28 weeks gestation. **1969** M. M. GARREY et al. *Obstetrics Illustrated* 469/1 A stillbirth is a baby that does not breathe or show any other sign of life after being completely separated from its mother.

still-born, *a.* Add: Also **stillborn. 1.** (Further examples.) Also, formerly, born alive but not breathing.

1896 W. A. N. DORLAND *Man. Obstetr.* II. vi. 706 It is a very common occurrence for a child to be born with the respiratory functions in abeyance: such a child is said to be asphyxiated. If efforts at resuscitation prove ineffectual, it is said to have been stillborn. **1899** H. D. CHAPIN in C. Jewett *Practice of Obstetrics* xxviii. 617 Fœtal death must be distinguished from asphyxia... In the latter the heart is pulsating, reflexes are present, and there may be feeble attempts at respiration... The distinction between a dead born and a still born infant can usually be made by the rapid fall of rectal temperature in the former. **1936** O'D. BROWNE *Man. Pract. Obstetr.* xix. 170 Technically, if an infant is born alive but never breathes, it is said to be stillborn; if the heart has ceased to beat after birth, deadborn. **1953** *Act 1 & 2 Eliz. II* c. 20 § 41 'Still-born child' means a child which has issued forth from its mother after the twenty-eighth week of pregnancy and which did not at any time after being completely expelled from its mother breathe or show any other signs of life, and the expression 'still-birth' shall be construed accordingly. **1955** W. P. D. LOGAN in Holland & Bourne *Brit. Obstetr. & Gynæcol. Practice: Obstetrics* xxxix. 1140 In certain countries children born alive but dying within a stipulated number of days are registered as stillborn.

B. as *sb.*, a still-born child. Also *fig.*

1913 J. LONDON *Let.* 30 Jan. (1966) 369 For goodness sake, don't let's have a still-born of it. **1977** *Lancet* 30 July 257/1 She gave birth to a pair of male twins, one of which was a stillborn with no malformations. The other boy is normal and healthy.

stilleite (ʃti·ləˌəit). *Min.* [ad. G. *stilleit* (P. Ramdohr in *Geotektonisches Symp. zu Ehren von H. Stille* (1956) 482), f. the name of Hans W. *Stille* (1876–1966), Ger. geologist: see -ITE[1].] Native zinc selenide, ZnSe, found as grey or black cubic crystals.

1957 *Amer. Mineralogist* XLII. 584 (*heading*) Stilleite. **1970** *Mineral. Abstr.* XXI. 316/1 Mix crystals of ZnSe.., known as the mineral stilleite, and CdSe..were synthesized at 800° to 1200°C.

still-fishing, *vbl. sb. N. Amer.* [f. STILL *a.* + FISHING *vbl. sb.*[1]] The practice of fishing from one spot, esp. with a baited line.

1883 *Century Mag.* July 383/1 The Floridians..use a long rod or pole for still-fishing. **1902** J. TURNER-TURNER *Giant Fish Florida* iii. 49 Still-fishing, the old-fashioned method of angling, is practised under the lea of some islands only on days that do not permit of your getting out into the Pass. **1963** P. A. PARSONS *Compl. Bk. Freshwater Fishing* xxiii. 250 Crappies may be caught by drifting, trolling, still-fishing, and casting. **1971** *Islander* (Victoria, B.C.) 7 Nov. 13/2 Which method calls for the most skill—bait fishing (sometimes called still fishing) or artificial lure angling?

Hence (as back-formation) **still-fish** *v. intr.*

1903 *Outing* XLII. 716/1 We could..troll or cast or still-fish with light tackle. **1953** *Sunday Sun Mag.* (Baltimore) 25 Oct. 28/4 Whether you fish on a comfortable party boat..or simply sit on a piling and still-fish,.. it's the best kind of relaxation there is. **1974** M. HOYT *Thirty Miles for Ice Cream* i. 4 We still-fished for perch.

still-house. (Later U.S. examples.)

1834 A. PIKE *Prose Sk. & Poems* 24 Our party reached the still house in the valley. **1884** 'C. E. CRADDOCK' *In Tennessee Mountains* II. 118 Josiah Tait had put his troubles in to soak at the still-house. **1927** *Greensboro* (N.C.) *Daily News* 24 Apr. II. 7/5 One time I was sent fur to bury a feller who had been found dead by a still house over yon side the Roan. **1976** *Lancet* 18 Dec. 1358/2 Mountaineers' distrust of government for the past half-century has had vastly more to do with the antisocial environmental, economic, and developmental policies of half a dozen Federal agencies..than with overturning mash barrels and knocking down stillhouses.

still-hunt, *sb.* Add: **2.** (Earlier and later examples.) Also *transf.* and *fig.*

1828 M. S. BIDWELL *Let.* in *Toronto Publ. Libr. MSS* B104. 69 Under the guidance of Mackenzie, who did not conduct himself with the caution and reserve of a new member, the House went on a still hunt for grievances. **1876** *N.Y. Tribune* 28 Aug. 4/4 It will be well for the Republican managers to bear in mind that a 'still hunt' is Gov. Tilden's favorite campaign method. **1916** 'B. M. BOWER' *Phantom Herd* ii. 32 I'm out on a still hunt for some real boys. **1936** H. HAGEDORN *Brookings* ix. 131 He took to riding afternoons in Forest Park along the western edge of the city, on a persistent, still-hunt for a site. **1948** E. N. DICK *Dixie Frontier* 241 Sometimes a candidate..slipped off and went on a 'still hunt'; that is, he visited the people house-to-house and attended small gatherings unheralded.

still-hunt, *v.* **2.** (Earlier and later examples.)

1858 *Harper's Mag.* Oct. 615/2 An old woodsman..had been, without success, still-hunting. **1863** E. H. WALSHE *Cedar Creek* 107 You see I'm often away trapping or still-hunting. **1942** W. FAULKNER *Go down, Moses* 149 Once, still-hunting with Walter Ewell's rifle, he saw it [*sc.* a bear] cross a long corridor of down timber where a tornado had passed.

Stilling (ʃti·liŋ), *sb.*[3] *Ophthalm.* The name of Jakob *Stilling* (1842–1915), German ophthalmologist, used *attrib.* and in the possessive with reference to a test for colour-blindness based on the use of pseudo-isochromatic plates which he devised (*Arch. Ophthalmol.* (1879) VIII. 164).

1896 J. E. JENNINGS *Color-Vision & Color-Blindness* vii. 75 Stilling's plates are of practical value, and should be used in conjunction with the worsted test. **1925** M. COLLINS *Colour-Blindness* iii. 59 These students were examined [for colour blindness] in the course of the ordinary laboratory period by means of Stilling's Tables, and some of them failed completely to pass the tests. **1935** *Discovery* Jan. 15/2 Colour blindness tests (such as the Edridge Green or Stilling tests) are not much use in choosing men for this work. **1954** S. DUKE-ELDER *Parsons' Dis. Eye* (ed. 12) xx. 345 Stilling's original tests have now been largely replaced by Ishihara's.

still life. Add: **a.** (Earlier *attrib.* examples.) Also *fig.*

a **1784** G. A. STEVENS *Let.* in T. Wilkinson *Mem.* (1790) IV. 196 My existence now cannot properly be called living, but what painters term *still life*; having since February 13, been confined in this town gaol for a London debt. **1821** P. EGAN *Life in London* II. i. 156 It was not the still-life Beauty of the Sculptor and the Artist. **1831** F. REYNOLDS *Playwright's Adventures* vii. 112 This still-life personage, devoting the whole of her mind and time to her pianoforte.

b. A painting of such objects. Pl. *still lifes.*

1957 *Encycl. Brit.* XXI. 408/1 The first signed and dated pure still life..was painted in 1504. **1961** R. B. LONG *Sentence & its Parts* ix. 206 Sometimes regular plurals replace even firmly established native irregular plurals: for example, in *she does still lifes.* **1970** *Oxf. Compan. Art* 1097/1 The development of the typical still life took place mainly in the Netherlands. **1981** *Daily Tel.* 30 Dec. 10/3 After the war, the artist returned to his delicate, vague, surrealist landscapes and little still-lifes.

Still's disease (stilz). *Path.* [Named after Sir George Frederic *Still* (1868–1941), English physician, who first described the disease in 1896 (*Med.-Chir. Trans.* (1897) LXXX. 47).] A condition affecting children, characterized by arthritis and ankylosis and now believed to be a form of rheumatoid arthritis.

1905 *Lancet* 27 May 1424/2 Though Still's disease was of the nature of a multiple joint affection no changes in the bones or the cartilages were observed. **1936** W. SHELDON *Dis. Infancy & Childhood* xxiii. 596 In some children the changes in and around the joints make up almost the entire clinical picture, but more often there is an accompanying lymphatic reaction, as shown by enlargement of the superficial lymphatic glands and enlargement of the spleen (Still's disease). **1974** A. HENRY in R. M. Kirk et al. *Surgery* xv. 303 Rheumatoid arthritis occurring in childhood (Still's disease..) is probably not a separate entity.

Stillson (sti·lsən). Also **Stilson, stilson.** The name of Daniel Chapman *Stillson* (1830–99), used *attrib.* and *absol.* to designate an adjustable pipe wrench invented by him in 1869 and originally manufactured by his employers, the Walworth Company of New York.

1902 *Sears Catal.* 563/3 The Stillson Pipe wrench is too well known to require a lengthy description of same. **1903** *Sci. Amer.* 10 Oct. 266/1 Your kit is not complete unless it includes the famous Stillson wrench which is particularly adapted for turning out the best work without crushing the pipe in the least. **1945** *Walworth 1842–1942* (Walworth Company Inc.) 42 The sales of the Stillsons are highly sensitive to changes in economic conditions. **1960** E. L. DELMAR-MORGAN *Cruising Yacht Equipment & Navigation* xiv. 162 It used to be said by the old-time mechanics that refractory pipe joints suddenly made themselves loose when they saw you pick up a Stillson. **1961** J. SEYMOUR *Fat of Land* v. 67, I spend half the night

..working in the blizzard or the deep frost with 'stilsons' ..and other esoteric devices. **1971** F. HAMILTON *World Encycl. Dogs* 119 The undershot lower jaw [of a boxer].. gives a leverage similar to that of the plumber's Stilson wrench; once contact is made it cannot be broken; a pull just makes it tighter. **1978** J. GORES *Gone, no Forwarding* (1979) x. 62 Balland was out of his car, eight-inch Stillson wrench..in hand.

still-stand. Add: Also **stillstand. 1. b.** *Physical Geogr.* A condition in which there is no crustal movement in a region or no change in sea-level.

1896 *Bull. Geol. Soc. Amer.* VII. 393 The English School denies..the probability or even the possibility of a period of still-stand long enough for essentially complete subaerial denudation close to sea level, but assumes the possibility of a period of still-stand or of slight depression continuous and long enough to allow the sea waves to plane off the sinking lands. **1937** WOOLDRIDGE & MORGAN *Physical Basis Geogr.* xv. 218 The cycle [of erosion] can only move uninterruptedly to its close if it coincides with a period of still-stand, *i.e.* of unvarying base-level, unaffected by major climatic changes. **1966** J. WYCKOFF *Rock, Time, & Landforms* iv. 103 All believe that the reduction of vast. lofty highlands by erosion demands time spans of the order of 25 million years, during which there is virtual stillstand—that is lack of uplift. **1972** R. A. DAVIS *Princ. Oceanogr.* xx. 322 One of the most prevalent and significant types of evidence is the presence of terraces which were formed during still-stands of sea level.

still water. 2. (Earlier example.)

1832 W. D. WILLIAMSON *Hist. Maine* I. 66 The Metawamkeag..has frequent falls and intervening still-waters.

stillwellite (sti·lwelait). *Min.* [f. the name of F. L. *Stillwell* (1888–1963), Austral. geologist + -ITE[1].] A borosilicate of lanthanons and calcium, (Ln,Ca)$BOSiO_4$, found as brown rhombohedral crystals.

1955 MCANDREW & SCOTT in *Nature* 10 Sept. 509/2 The presence of stillwellite was discovered in 1954 during a mineralogical investigation of radioactive ore..34 miles east of Mt. Isa in north-western Queensland. **1971** *Doklady Acad. Sci. U.S.S.R.: Earth Sci. Sections* CCI. 182/1 The above data on our synthesis of the lanthanum analogs of stillwellite indicate that this borosilicate may be more widespread in nature than was previously thought.

stilt, *sb.* Add: **1.** Delete ? *Obs.* exc. *dial.* Occas. also with reference to other farm implements. (Later examples.)

1957 E. E. EVANS *Irish Folk Ways* x. 129 The Irish were amazed when they first saw a ploughman with a Scots plough both driving the horses and holding the stilts. **1971** *Country Life* 20 May 1203/1, I take the 'stilts' of the big grass cutter and struggle behind it. **1973** *Ibid.* 22 Feb. 474/1 My going to the plough that morning wasn't the first occasion upon which I had set my hands to the stilts.

6. stilt heel, (a shoe with) a high heel; **stilt-heeled** *a.* (later examples); **stilt-root,** an aerial root, arising from the trunk or lower branches of a tree, and acting to provide support; hence **stilt-rooted** *a.*; **stilt-walker** (*a*) (earlier example).

1973 R. RENDELL *Some lie & some Die* vi. 49 She was.. dressed..in..full, longish skirt, stilt heels. **1948** 'P. WENTWORTH' *Traveller Returns* xi. 64 The sheer black stockings, and the stilt-heeled shoes. **1980** 'L. EGAN' *Motive in Shadow* iii. 39 She was wearing..stilt-heeled black patent leather pumps. **1894** F. W. OLIVER tr. *Kerner's Nat. Hist. Plants* I. 756 Trees whose erect trunks are supported by tabular roots and those which are provided with stilt-roots may at the same time develop columnar roots from their branches. **1930** *Discovery* Nov. 381/1 No account of jungle vegetation..is complete without some mention of the trees with the curious stilt roots and those with the even stranger buttress roots. **1974** H. MACINNES *Climb to Lost World* xii. 221, I pointed..at a stilt-rooted tree which had grown up with stilts at least fifteen feet clear of the ground... Young stilt roots were growing into the swamp from its base. **1863** A. J. MUNBY *Diary* 20 May in D. Hudson *Munby* (1972) 162, I saw.. two young female acrobats or stiltwalkers..forlorn and pitiable in their satin shoes & spangles.

Stilton. Add: **a.** *Stilton cheese*: orig. also applied to similar cheeses made elsewhere, but since 1969 restricted to that made in the counties of Leicester, Derby, and Nottingham by members of the Stilton Cheese Makers Association. (Further examples.)

a **1864** J. CLARE in *Sel. Poems & Prose* (1967) 25 He.. seldom got astride of a saddle save when he gave old Dobbin a holiday from the plough to carry his Dame to the Fair to sell her Stilton cheese. **1930** L. G. D. ACLAND *Early Canterbury Runs* 1st Ser. ii. 30 In the 'fifties and early 'sixties [in New Zealand] they got two shillings a pound for their butter, tenpence for cheese, and eighteenpence for stilton cheese. **1969** *Trade Marks Jrnl.* 5 Feb. 234/1 Stilton 831,407 Class 29. Cheese. The Chairman, The Stilton Cheese Makers Association, Melton Mowbray, Leicestershire.—28th Feb. 1962. **1973** *Leicester Mercury* 24 Dec. 8/1 The public in the States is being..misled into purchasing the Purity brand of Stilton cheese in mistaken belief that it is the genuine product produced in England.

b. (Earlier example.)

1826 E. CRAVEN *Mem. Margravine of Anspach* I. v. 190 The Margrave had at his table good cream, and Stilton, or Berkeley hundred, made under my direction.

c. *attrib.*

1966 *Daily Tel.* 15 Nov. 15/2 The Stilton recipe..goes back to the 18th century... In seeking the trade mark, Stilton makers expressed fears that the same fate would befall the Stilton..as happened to the Cheddar. **1969** *Ibid.* 11 Apr. 19/5 Yesterday,..the Stilton Cheesemakers Association..obtained their trademark. **1971** *Sunday Times* (Colour Suppl.) 28 Mar. 36/1 Much the best way of tackling the half cheese on the table is with a knife with a long sharp pointed blade—not a Stilton spoon. **1973** *Leicester Mercury* 24 Dec. 8/1 (*heading*) Stilton men up in arms over 'spurious cheese'.

stilty, *a.* **2.** (Earlier example.)

1845 W. B. S. TAYLOR *Hist. Univ. Dublin* 339 The *stilty dignity* which is to be found in some other places.

‖**stilyaga** (stilya·gă). Also **stilyag.** Pl. **-gi.** [*Russ.* (*colloq.*), lit. 'stylish person'.] In the U.S.S.R.: a young person who affects stylish dress as an expression of rebellion, non-conformity, etc.

1955 H. HODGKINSON *Doubletalk* 55 The *stilyag* who goes in for 'style' in his clothes. **1959** *Listener* 5 Feb. 236/2 Soviet Russia has her..'teddy-boys', who are there called *stilyagi. Ibid.*, The introspective, thoughtful, humble type has taken the place of the *stilyaga.* **1960** *Guardian* 25 Feb. 4/1 Young people in Russia..wear the 'stilyagi' clothes that mark them as non-conformists. **1965** 'A. BURGESS' in *Times Lit. Suppl.* 22 Apr. 317/2 A trip to Russia showed me that *stilyagi* behaved much like our own (as they were then) teddy-boys. **1973** T. ALLBEURY *Choice of Enemies* xxiv. 129, I had difficulty in changing the money because one of the 'stilyagi' recognised me.

‖**Stimmung** (ʃti·muŋ). Also **stimmung.** [Ger.] Mood, spirit, atmosphere, feeling.

1909 W. M. URBAN *Valuation* v. 123 We may cite certain impressionistic or symbolic styles where the general mood or *Stimmung* is almost palpable. **1923** R. FRY *Let.* 13 May (1972) II. 534 Words as you use them..give me more of what the Germans call *stimmung*..than painting can ever do. **1939** E. H. W. MEYERSTEIN *Let.* 4 Apr. (1959) 222 He [*sc.* Eliot] cannot keep the poetic *stimmung* up as long as Bridges can. **1948** WYNDHAM LEWIS *Let.* 18 Oct. 463, I could not help imbibing from my very American father much Stimmung, a certain sentiment, and a lot about the Civil War. **1961** *Times* 23 Mar. 16/6 The Riffelalp had its own *stimmung.* **1972** *Guardian* 12 Aug. 8 The 'Kaiserwalzer'..is..[an] emanation of the Viennese spirit, Stimmung. **1980** R. ADAMS *Girl in Swing* iv. 59 In memory the whole *Stimmung* changes and our recollections become like a story we have read before.

stimoceiver (sti·mosīvəɹ). [f. STIM(ULATE *v.* + -O + RE)CEIVER[1].] A radio transmitter and receiver implanted in the head which transmits information about the brain and receives signals which electrically stimulate the brain.

1967 *N.Y. Times* 22 Mar. 49/1 Dr. Delgado's laboratory is developing an instrument, called a 'stimoceiver', that takes advantage of the increasing sophistication of circuit technology and microminiaturization. **1968** J. M. R. DELGADO et al. in *Jrnl. Nerv. & Mental Dis.* CXLVII. 331/1 The integration of the three-channel units for radio stimulation and EEG telemetry constitutes the stimoceiver. *Ibid.* 338/2 A new instrument called 'stimoceiver' has been developed for the stimultaneous multichannel recording and stimulation of the brain by FM radio waves in completely unrestrained subjects. **1979** *Amer. Jrnl. Orthopsychiatry* XLIX. 367/2 The grim prospects of a burgeoning psychosurgical technology for widespread telemetric surveillance of behavior via transponders, stimoceivers, and brain pacemakers *à la* Schwitzgebel, Meyer, and Delgado are adumbrated.

stimulable, *a.* Add: (Later example.) Hence **stimulabi·lity.**

1944 *Mind* LIII. 90 Most of the essayists, having a good deal of vitality themselves, are eminently stimulable. **1975** *Year Bk. Ear, Nose & Throat* 36 If nerve stimulability is lost.

stimulant, *sb.* **2. b.** Delete parenthetical comment and add earlier examples.

1848 MILL *Pol. Econ.* II. v. vi. 425 Among luxuries of general consumption, taxation should by preference attach itself to stimulants. **1859** —— *Liberty* v. 180 To tax stimulants for the sole purpose of making them more difficult to be obtained, is a measure differing only in degree from their entire prohibition.

stimulatory, *a.* and *sb.* Restrict *rare* to sense b in Dict. and add: **a.** (Later examples.)

1968 *Times* 21 Oct. 7/1 The buds exert a differential influence during the season, being inhibitory in winter and stimulatory in spring. **1975** *Nature* 7 Aug. 487/2 Either germinating seeds or soil may provide the substrates for growth of the stimulatory micro-organisms. **1981** *Times* 27 Aug. 9/2 Even with the stimulatory measures, however, the deficit does not seem likely to be excessive in the years to come.

stimulus. Add: **2. a.** (Earlier example.)

1791 W. ENFIELD *Hist. Philos.* II. i. 18 Among the philosophical works of Cicero, we do not now find his *Hortentius*,..which Augustine confesses operated upon his mind, as a powerful *stimulus* to the pursuit of wisdom.

3. c. *Psychol.* Any specific change in physical energy or an event (whether internal or external to the organism) which excites a nerve impulse and gives rise to a reaction.

1894 CREIGHTON & TITCHENER tr. *Wundt's Human & Animal Psychol.* 16 The processes of motion which, by their operation upon our senses, give rise to sensations, we commonly denominate *stimuli*, or more particularly *sense-stimuli*... Thus we regard the sound-waves of the air or the light-waves set up in surrounding space as stimuli corresponding to our sensations of sound and light. **1919** J. B. WATSON *Psychol.* i. 9 The goal of psychological study is the ascertaining of such data and laws that, given the stimulus, psychology can predict what the response will be; or..given the response, it can specify the nature of the effective stimulus. **1957** E. R. HILGARD *Introd. Psychol.* (ed. 2) 596/1 *Stimulus*, some specific physical energy impinging on a receptor sensitive to that kind of energy... Any objectively describable situation or event..that is the occasion for an organism's response. **1980** E. L. DECI in E. Staub *Personality* ii. 43 People do not respond to objective external stimuli; they respond to stimuli *as they perceive them.*

5. *attrib.* and *Comb.*, as (sense *3 c) *stimulus-complex, control, -error, intensity, -object, -pattern, -situation, -threshold, -value, -word*; **stimulus diffusion** (see quot. 1940); **stimulus generalization,** the fact that the response elicited by one stimulus can also be elicited by other stimuli associated with but not identical to the original; **stimulus-response,** abbrev. form of *stimulus-and-response*, used *attrib.* or as *adj.* to denote this process, esp. when considered as the basic element in the study of sense perception, learning or behaviour modification; = S-R s.v. *S 4 a.

1924 R. M. OGDEN tr. *Koffka's Growth of Mind* 87 Fine differences in the stimulus-complex may lead to opposite reactions. **1954** W. H. MELCHING in E. L. Wikes *Secondary Reinforcement* (1966) II. ii. 143 The presence (or absence) of the buzzer during conditioning and extinction was assumed to be an important component of the stimulus complexes. **1956** *Psychol. Monogr.* LXX. v. 2/2 A method which involved a greater degree of stimulus control than has usually been achieved in research on discrimination. **1979** H. K. RODEWALD (*title*) Stimulus control of behavior. **1940** A. L. KROEBER in *Amer. Anthrop.* XLII. 1 (*title*) Stimulus diffusion. *Ibid.*, It is the idea of the complex or system which is accepted, but it remains for the receiving culture to develop a new content. This somewhat special process might therefore be called 'idea-diffusion' or 'stimulus diffusion'. **1978** *Language* LIV. 207 If diffusion is to be thought of as operating between the sub-areas, it can only be 'stimulus diffusion'. **1909** E. B. TITCHENER *Text-bk. Psychol.* I. § 66.218 The observer tends to judge, not in terms of sensation, but in terms of stimulus... This error,..is known technically as the stimulus error. **1949** *Mind* LVIII. 452 The Stimulus-error and the Constancy Hypothesis are particular forms of this fallacy. **1943** C. L. HULL *Princ. Behavior* xii. 183 The reaction involved in the original conditioning becomes connected with a considerable zone of stimuli other than, but adjacent to, the stimulus conventionally involved in the original conditioning; this is called *stimulus generalization.* **1977** in Honig & Staddon *Handbk. Operant Behavior* xi. 316/2 Another possibility is that the mechanism underlying conditioned reinforcement is stimulus generalization. **1909** *Amer. Jrnl. Psychol.* XX. 4 A progression of stimulus intensities such that the differences of corresponding sensation between any consecutive pairs are equal to one another. **1933** *Psychol. Abstr.* VII. 538/1 The relationship between stimulus intensity and duration in the motor nerve of the frog. **1921** *Psychol. Rev.* XXVIII. 398 The dependence of a stimulus-object upon its setting is especially familiar in the case of contrasting colors or objects. **1970** *Jrnl. Gen. Psychol.* Apr. 151 The strength with which an unfamiliar stimulus-object elicits a particular mediational process. **1924** R. M. OGDEN tr. *Koffka's Growth of Mind* iii. 137 The phenomenon corresponding to a given stimulus-pattern. **1950** *Mind* LIX. 187 A red shape presents a stimulus pattern that I react to immediately. **1921** *Psychol. Rev.* XXVIII. 390 The response member of a stimulus-response couple may consist of a group of reactions. **1927** L. L. BERNARD *Introd. Social Psychol.* viii. 109 Tropism is not a stimulus–response process in the same sense that reflexes and instincts are. It makes use of stimulus-response mechanisms. **1957** E. R. HILGARD *Introd. Psychol.* (ed. 2) i. 21/1 Stimulus-response theory (or S-R theory, as it is commonly called) asserts that all behavior is in response to stimuli. **1964** E. A. NIDA *Toward Sci. Transl.* iii. 40 In most actual instances of communication, verbal symbols enter into a chain of stimulus-response situations. **1980** *Dædalus* Spring 23 This evidence of central control over receptors ..affected the picture of the stimulus-response relationship that had dominated psychology for decades. **1923** OGDEN & RICHARDS *Meaning of Meaning* iii. 139 The excitation of part of an engram complex, which is called up by a stimulus..similar to a part only of the original stimulus-situation. **1977** A. GIDDENS *Stud. in Social & Polit. Theory* i. 76 All descriptive predicates, however 'theoretical', are learned in conjunction with definite stimulus-situations. **1897** C. H. JUDD tr. *Wundt's Outl. Psychol.* 254 The stimulus from which the resulting psychical process, for example, a sensation, can be just apperceived, is called the *stimulus-threshold.* **1935** L. BLOOMFIELD in C. Hockett *Bloomfield Anthol.* (1970) 310 His audience will respond only to the exact stimulus-value of his words. **1962** *Science Survey* XV. 251 Now the 'stimulus value' of a moving object depends not only on the actual capacity of the eye to detect and evaluate movement, but [etc.]. **1905** *Psychol. Bull.* II. 249 The influence of the grammatical form of the stimulus-word on the reaction is rather striking. **1971** *Jrnl. Gen. Psychol.* Apr. 281 Stimulus words were carefully selected in order to control for associative response frequencies.

sting, *sb.*[1] Add: **7*.** *Aeronaut.* A rod-like support used in wind-tunnel testing (see quot. 1933).

1933 *Gloss. Aeronaut. Terms (B.S.I.)* III. 20 *Sting*, a light rod attached to and extending backwards from a body for convenience of mounting for test in a wind tunnel. **1948** *Jrnl. R. Aeronaut. Soc.* LII. 240/1 In this work the model was supported from the rear by means of a sting. **1959** *Engineering* 6 Feb. 188/1 The model support consists of a quadrant and sting.

sting, *sb.*[2] Add: **5. a.** Also in phr. *a sting in the tail* and varr.

1657 [in Dict.]. *c* **1820** BLAKE *On Homer's Poetry* in *Compl. Writings* (1972) 778 Those who will have Unity exclusively in Homer come out with a Moral like a sting in the tail. **1926** *Times* 7 Sept. 17/5 The sting of this book is in its tail. **1952** A. CHRISTIE *They do it with Mirrors* 192 Don't say it. I'm suspicious of these village parallels. They've always got a sting in the tail. **1979** A. WILLIAMSON *Funeral March for Siegfried* xxxii. 165 He..added a sting in the tail. 'Of course, if the murderer were one of you, an interloper would not be necessary.'

b. Freq. in phr. *to take the sting out of* (something). (Earlier and later examples.)

1860 *Bailey's Mag.* Oct. 42 Hayward's..rare defence completely took the sting out of the Surrey bowling. **1942** *R.A.F. Jrnl.* 3 Oct. 24 It has taken the sting out of the Adjutant. **1956** B. HOLIDAY *Lady sings Blues* (1973) xix. 157, I was so happy I cried. People like Lena took the sting out of other little people. **1977** *Jrnl. R. Soc. Arts* CXXV. 464/1 This defence consists in establishing..that the derogatory words—or at least their sting—were true.

c. *Austral. slang.* (*a*) Strong drink, 'stingo'; (*b*) a drug, *spec.* one administered to a racehorse in the form of an injection.

1929 K. S. PRICHARD *Coonardoo* 60 'Misses his three square meals a day and sting,' Bob explained. **1949** L. GLASSOP *Lucky Palmer* 36 They're going to give it the sting. They'll hit it with enough dope to win a Melbourne Cup. **1958** F. HARDY *Four-Legged Lottery* 173 The 'smarties' soon found stings that didn't show on a swab. **1972** J. DE HOOG *Skid Row Dossier* 4 You can share a bottle of sting (methylated spirits) down a lane.

d. *slang* (chiefly *U.S.*, orig. *Criminals'*). (*a*) A burglary or other act of theft, fraud, etc., esp. one that is carefully planned in advance and swiftly executed; (*b*) a police undercover operation designed to ensnare criminals.

1930 *Liberty* 20 Sept. 77/1 The hustlers would sit around planning their stings and I guess about half of the jobs pulled in southern Ohio that year started in my parlor. **1955** *Publ. Amer. Dial. Soc.* XXIV. 76 The *sting* we described involved a wallet obviously *on its feet.* **1975** *Courier-Mail* (Brisbane) 11 Mar. 6/8 A transaction between a jewellery salesman and a professed buyer with $230,000 in his pocket was intercepted yesterday by a cab driver who made off with the cash. Investigators believe the theft was a set-up 'sting'. **1976** *National Observer* (U.S.) 13 Mar. 6/3 The Sting also produced leads to three murders and several other unsolved major crimes. **1977** *Tel.* (Brisbane) 24 Aug. 25/2 'Sting' officers operated in old warehouses and run-down storefronts, developed close contacts with loose-lipped thugs who believe they dealt with fellow criminals. **1982** *Sunday Times* 14 Nov. 15/2 The Miami 'sting' was so well set up that it survived a remarkable breach of security. **1983** *Observer* 30 Jan. 10/2 His second reaction was to inform the American authorities and get their approval for an elaborate and costly 'sting'.

sting, *v.*[1] Add: **2. e.** *to sting* (someone) *for* (something): to induce (someone) to give (money, etc.) by begging or borrowing in an exploitative manner. *slang* (orig. *U.S.*).

1903 *Kansas City Daily Star* 21 Apr. 6/7 An undergraduate is no longer 'stuck' for a dinner, a seat at a play, a railroad ticket; he is 'stung'. **1940** N. MARSH *Surfeit of Lampreys* (1941) ii. 34 We hope to sting Uncle G. for two thousand [pounds]. **1973** WODEHOUSE *Bachelors Anonymous* iii. 26 He wants to make a touch... He even stung me for a bit the other day. **1976** P. CAVE *High Flying Birds* iv. 46 You still letting that bum sting you for drinks?

f. To swindle or overcharge (someone); to involve (someone) in financial loss. Freq. in *pass.* Cf. sense 2 d in Dict. *slang* (orig. *U.S.*).

1905 [see *BUNDLE *sb.* 2 h]. **1922** S. LEWIS *Babbitt* iii. 27 Guess I'll have to get down to the office now and sting a few clients. **1923** *Daily Mail* 22 Jan. 8 [He] told me.. he stood to lose some enormous number of millions of marks if Germany went *phut*... He seemed hurt when I said I was very glad if he got stung for trading with the enemy. **1927** WODEHOUSE *Small Bachelor* vii. 121 'How much did you pay?' 'Three hundred dollars.' 'You were stung... The stock is so much waste paper.' **1943** K. TENNANT *Ride on Stranger* vii. 62 In this world you've got to sting or get stung. **1955** M. ALLINGHAM *Beckoning Lady* v. 82 You sting 'em when the time comes. **1974** 'E. LATHEN' *Sweet & Low* xi. 108 Big names do not like getting stung. **1981** *London Mag.* July 15 I've no idea how much her son pays her... I like to think she's really stinging her son.

stingaree. (Earlier example.)

1838 *Papers Mirabeau Buonaparte Lamar* (1922) II. 87 To crown the whole Sergeant Bryant was cut on the foot with an oyster shell, and Mr. Edington was stung by a Stingaree.

stinge (sti·ndʒ). [Back-formation from STINGY *a.*] A stingy person. Hence as *v. intr.* (*rare*), to behave in a stingy manner.

1914 'BARTIMEUS' *Naval Occasions* xxi. 185 Accustomed to tribute tendered with a lavish hand, Arabella decided that this must be a 'proper stinge'. **1937** *Boy's Own Paper* 3 Dec. 143/1 The barber can't stand stinges. **1937** V. SACKVILLE-WEST *Pepita* II. iii. 205, I couldn't see why a person ready to spend hundreds of pounds should be equally ready to stinge over a stamp or a ball of string. **1977** C. BOYLAN in D. Marcus *Best Irish Short Stories* II. 113 Elizabeth had got herself a job. 'Well, I had to... My, Morgan has become a stinge.'

stinger[1]. Add: **3.** Also *Austral.*, an exceptionally hot or cold period of time.

1899 'S. RUDD' in Murdoch & Drake-Brockman *Austral. Short Stories* (1951) 103 My! it'll be a stinger to-night. **1942** E. LANGLEY *Pea Pickers* (1958) II. vii. 167 The next day was a stinger... It dawned sultry red.

4. A long structure attached to the stern of a pipe-laying barge which supports the pipe as it enters the water and prevents it from buckling.

1958 *Offshore Drilling* Oct. 11/2 The 'stinger' is final cradle [*sic*], submerged 85 feet off the stern of the lay barge, which holds the pipe to a 2500 ft. radius to prevent any undue strain during the process of lowering it into the underwater trench. **1966** M. J. LAMB in *Exploiting the Ocean* (Marine Technol. Soc.) 296 A 'stinger' is used in deep water to limit the sag in the pipe. **1969** [see *OVERBEND *sb.*]. **1976** *Offshore Platforms & Pipelining* 6/3 Key changes include..the addition of 160-ft truss-type stinger in place of the usual pontoon stinger.

stinger[3] (sti·ŋəɪ). Corruption of *STENGAH. Also used as the name of various other mixed drinks or cocktails (see quots. 1973, 1976).

1901 *Scribner's Mag.* Jan. 106 Two 'stingers' were brought... A 'stinger'..is a noggin of Scotch whiskey, enlivened by much or little, according to individual taste, of the local buzz-water. **1903** [see *STENGAH]. **1916** H. L. WILSON *Somewhere in Red Gap* ix. 376, I found 'em in the palm grill, or whatever it's called, drinking stingers. **1928** [see *ROUND *sb.*[1] 20 a]. **1942** D. POWELL *Time to be Born* (1943) x. 242 Have another daiquiri... Or change to a stinger. **1961** I. FLEMING *Thunderball* xv. 156 After they had had coffee and a stinger at the bar they separated and went to the [gaming] tables. **1973** *Sat. Rev. Society* (U.S.) May 45/1 B & B Stinger. 3 parts B & B Liqueur, 1 part White Creme de Menthe. **1976** *Scotsman* 24 Dec. (Weekend Suppl.) 3/7 A Stinger..is a better drink, being creme de menthe well laced with brandy, and stronger.

stinging, *ppl. a.* Add: **1. a.** *stinging lizard,* one of several North American lizards, esp. a spiny lizard of the genus *Sceloporus,* also called a scorpion.

1870 J. C. DUVAL *Adventures Big-Foot Wallace* xlv. 294 They chaw tobacco and drink whiskey even in the wintertime, when the 'cow-killers' and stinging-lizards are all frozen up. **1889** H. H. MCCONNELL *Five Years a Cavalryman* 77 The 'scorpion' or 'stinging lizard' abounds. **1926** J. K. STRECKER in J. F. Dobie *Rainbow in Morning* (1965) 61 The true scorpion is popularly called a 'stinging lizard', this misnomer being in common use throughout the state of Texas.

stingo. Add: **b.** *fig.* Vigour, energy, vim; *to give* (a person) *hot stingo* = *to give it hot* s.v. HOT *a.* 11 d. ? *Obs.*

1885 *Punch* 22 Aug. 86/3 It's rare fun, by Jingo! I give 'em hot stingo. **1927** *Daily Tel.* 19 July 15 To keep in good trim and add stingo to your efforts in sport. **1927** GALSWORTHY in A. A. Horn *Ivory Coast* Foreword 5 A gorgeous book..full of sheer stingo. **1928** *Observer* 18 Mar. 23/3 Some shanties, sung by Raymond Newell and a chorus, are full of stingo.

stingy, *a.* Add: **2.** (Earlier example.)

1781 J. WOODFORDE *Diary* 22 Feb. (1924) I. 302, I was very stingy this morning alias in a bad humour and made Nancy uneasy by my talking.

4. d. Meagre, spare, circumscribed.

1927 E. M. FORSTER *Aspects of Novel* viii. 205 [James's] characters..are constructed on very stingy lines. They are incapable of fun, of rapid motion, of carnality.

6. Of the brim of a hat: narrow. Also as *sb.*, a narrow-brimmed hat. *U.S.* (*Black English*).

1965 *Liberator* Aug. 23/2 He was neat from toe to stingy. **1969** N. COHN *AWopBopaLooBop* (1970) ix. 86 He wore Stingy Brim straw hats, tight pants, lurid shirts.

stink, *sb.* Add: **1. c.** A contemptible person, a stinkard. *slang.*

1916 JOYCE *Portrait of Artist as a Young Man* 8 Rody Kickham was a decent fellow but Nasty Roche was a stink. **1918** E. POUND *Let.* 4 June (1971) 137 Meredith is, to me, chiefly a stink. I should never write on him as I detest him too much ever to trust myself as critic of him. **1950** R. MOORE *Candlemas Bay* v. 281 And the rest of you little stinks, shut up, too! **1972** D. DEVINE *Three Green Bottles* 102 That stink, Celia Armitage, had somehow found out.

3. a. Also, a row or fuss; a furore (later examples). Now chiefly in phrs. *to raise* (*kick up, make*) *a stink.*

1907 [see *JIM-HICKEY]. **1913** KIPLING *Diversity of Creatures* (1917) 293 We *mustn't* be tried! It'll make an infernal international stink. **1942** *Tee Emm* (Air Ministry) II. 81 Do you do it merely because there's a stink if you don't? **1948** 'N. SHUTE' *No Highway* ii. 31, I remember the Russians kicking up a stink. **1959** 'M. CRONIN' *Dead & done With* iv. 56 The first thing he'd do when he got back was see his M.P. and kick up a stink. **1976** L. SANDERS *Hamlet Warning* (1977) iii. 31 [She] commanded a world press. She could raise a tremendous stink if she chose to do so.

b. *like stink,* furiously, intensely. Cf. LIKE *adv.* 1 b. *colloq.*

1929 R. C. SHERRIFF *Journey's End* I. 40 If you see a Minnie coming..you have to judge it and run like stink sometimes. **1938** M. ALLINGHAM *Fashion in Shrouds* xv. 240 It's raining like stink. **1945** 'P. WOODRUFF' *Call Next Witness* II. v. 114 He clapped in his heels and rode like stink. **1955** M. ALLINGHAM *Beckoning Lady* iii. 40 The telephone's here..and when it rings you have to run like stink before the caller gives up. **1972** D. DEVINE *Three Green Bottles* 11 She wasn't really clever, she just worked like stink.

c. In other colloq. phrases (parallel to the use of *hell* and similar words).

1942 *R.A.F. Jrnl.* 16 May 26, I bet they've been giving old Jerry stink this afternoon. **1977** I. SHAW *Beggarman, Thief* I. ii. 21 We'd've been in a stink of a mess without him.

4. Now used principally of Chemistry.

1914 'I. HAY' *Lighter Side School Life* iv. 116 Master Nixon..had pointed out that it would be a good thing to enrol as a member some one who understood 'Chemistry and Stinks generally'. **1928** R. CULLUM *Myst. Barren Lands* xi. 107 You can't afford to use up the source that gives you a living so you can carry on with your stinks. **1945** 'R. CROMPTON' *William & Brains Trust* vii. 129 'English isn't bad, 'cause ole Sarky can't see what you're doin' at the back, an' Stinks isn't bad, 'cause you can get some jolly good bangs if you mix the wrong things together.' **1955** [see *LAB *sb.*[2]]. **1961** A. WILSON *Old Men at Zoo* i. 37 Eventually..the laboratory work will be on a scale that will make this place look like a school stinks room.

5. stink beetle = *stink bug*; **stink bomb,** a small hand-missile which emits a nauseating smell when broken, typically thrown by schoolboys; also *transf.*; **stink-bug,** substitute for def.: a shield bug of the family Pentatomidæ, which includes many species that feed on plants and eject a strong-smelling liquid if attacked; (earlier example); **stink-finger:** in coarse slang phr. *to play* (*at*) *stink-finger* (see quot. 1903) (now *rare* or *obs.*); **stink-fish,** (*a*) *S. Afr.* = *bamboo-fish* s.v. *BAMBOO *sb.* 3; (*b*) *Ghana* = *stinking fish* (*b*) s.v. *STINKING *ppl. a.* 2 a.

1889 H. VAUGHAN-WILLIAMS *Visit to Lobengula* (1947) xxv. 162, I must mention the stink beetles, as they are called. They all emit the most horrible stench when killed or even touched. You get them all over South Africa. **1979** *Jrnl. Arid Environments* II. 101 When stink-beetles of the genus *Eleodes* are placed in a bottle.., their fumes will kill other insects placed inside the bottle. **1915** D. O. BARNETT *Let.* 26 June 192 It seems that the tobacco stores had amalgamated with a stink-bomb dépôt. **1922** A. HADDON *Green Room Gossip* iv. 117 At this juncture there was a good deal of sneezing and coughing in the auditorium... Both stink bombs and 'electric snuff' were thrown from the gallery. **1958** 'J. BYROM' *Or be he Dead* xiii. 167 He lobbed this [conversational] grenade..as innocently as a child with a stinkbomb. **1974** D. RAMSAY *No Cause to Kill* I. 38, I used to sit in the library wishing I had a stink bomb to set off under her nose. **1877** BARTLETT *Dict. Americanisms* (ed. 4) 647 Squash-bug... A small yellow bug, injurious to the vines of squashes, melons, and cucumbers... In Connecticut, called a stink-bug. **1903** FARMER & HENLEY *Slang* VI. III. 369/1 *To play at stinkfinger,*..to grope a woman. **1934** H. MILLER *Tropic of Cancer* 282, I had no Odette Champsdivers with whom to play stinkfinger. [**1902** *Marine Investigation in S. Afr.* I. 116 Bamboesvisch. Stinkvisch. Scarce in Cape Town market, but common in Saldanha Bay.] **1913** Stink-fish [see *bamboo-fish* s.v. *BAMBOO *sb.* 2]. **1962** C. BAETA *Prophetism in Ghana* ii. 17 Adherents of the Twelve Apostles Church..are not allowed to eat pork, stink-fish, shark's meat or snails.

stink, *v.* Add: **2. b.** Also *to stink of* (or *with*) *money*: to be 'offensively' rich. *slang.*

1877 E. PEACOCK *N.W. Lincs. Gloss.* 239/2 A very proud man is said to '*stink wi'* pride', a very rich one to '*stink o'* brass'. **1922** JOYCE *Ulysses* 9 Touch him for a guinea. He's stinking with money. **1932** I. BROWN *Marine Parade* xii. 152 We must do our best. He stinks of money. Will you fix up about rooms and for God's sake let's have a decent dinner.

e. To exhibit or savour of moral (artistic, etc.) decay. Of persons: also, to be despicable or completely incompetent. Of actions, phenomena, etc.: also *spec.* in phr. *to stink to* (*high*) *heaven. colloq.*

1934 J. T. FARRELL *Young Manhood of Studs Lonigan* viii. 121, I watched you guys go through signal practice. You stunk! **1956** H. KURNITZ *Invasion of Privacy* xv. 99 She regarded Zorn bleakly. 'You stink, Michael Zorn,' she said. **1963** 'D. CORY' *Hammerhead* iv. 61 Sofia was the actress of the family. I stink.

1936 *Metronome* Feb. 61/2 *Stinks,* what one pub thinks of another's tunes. **1940** 'N. BLAKE' *Malice in Wonderland* I. v. 61 Big Business does rather stink, doesn't it? **1959** H. HOBSON *Mission House Murder* iii. 21 Rock an' Roll came in..now that's out—that stinks too. **1963** C. D. SIMAK *They walked like Men* ix. 53 'How did you know that?' 'Just a guess,' I said. 'This whole thing stinks to heaven.' **1973** *Times* 23 May 16/4 The affairs of Lonrho stunk to high heaven. **1979** R. JAFFE *Class Reunion* (1980) II. ii. 196 Chris would make it be like the old days. But the old days had stunk too.

5. b. With *up.* To cause (a place) to stink. Also *fig. colloq.* (orig. and chiefly *U.S.*).

1956 B. HOLIDAY *Lady sings Blues* (1973) vii. 65 The manager got panicky and began to holler at me that I was stinking up his Grand Terrace. **1967** C. DRUMMOND *Death at Furlong Post* xi. 140 Harassed fat women cooking *sauerbraten* and stinking up the place with the smell of vinegar. **1977** D. MACKENZIE *Raven & Ratcatcher* iii. 44

A rumour..that..I was allowed to resign rather than stink-up the fair name of the Serious Crimes Squad. **1979** R. JAFFE *Class Reunion* (1980) III. iii. 319 He was sweet even though he did stink up her bedroom because he always forgot to open the window.

stinkaroo, var. *STINKEROO.

stinker. Add: **1.** (Later examples as a term of abuse.) Also in weakened uses, esp. banteringly and in mock-contempt. Now *slang.*

1922 [see *HOUSE *sb.*[1] 4 c]. **1936** M. ALLINGHAM *Death of Ghost* xx. 237, I will show that stinker! **1949** A. HUXLEY *Let.* 6 Mar. (1969) 593 Saying what a stinker he is, both in bed and out. *c* **1951** T. ROETHKE *Selected Lett.* (1968) 170 After your generous words, I feel a terrible stinker questioning everything. **1962** WODEHOUSE *Service with Smile* viii. 120 Is that you, Stinker? **1975** *Daily Mail* 30 May 3/6 A gang of 'real stinkers' have raided a top wartime air ace and stolen his most prized souvenir—a 6ft. German propellor.

3. Also formerly, a rank cigar or cigarette. (Earlier and later examples.)

1834 *Proc. Geol. Soc.* II. 21 The greater part of the workings are only shallow pits, touching merely the sulphureous beds, locally called 'stinkers'. **1924** N. COWARD *Rat Trap* I. 11 There are cigarettes in that silver box, Keld; stinkers on one side, and opulent Turkish on the other. **1935** WODEHOUSE *Luck of Bodkins* iv. 42 Have you such a thing as a stinker?..And a match? **1961** J. W. ANDERSON *Fur Trader's Story* iii. 23 At Moose Factory, I saw the last of the sulphur matches ('stinkers' we used to call them) which were in their day considered a great advance on the striking of flint on steel to make fire. **1970** B. CARTLAND *We danced All Night* vii. 198 Virginian cigarettes were first called 'stinkers', then 'gaspers', and were considered a little vulgar.

6. *fig.* **a.** A strongly-worded letter; a disagreeable review or other communication. *slang.*

1912 *World's Work* Apr. 509/1 The principal content of this mail proved to be, as usual, a very long and wordy 'stinker'. **1936** WODEHOUSE *Young Men in Spats* vi. 157 For weeks..Stiffy had been yearning to write an absolute stinker to old Wivelscombe, telling him exactly what he thought of him. **1945** L. DURRELL *Spirit of Place* (1969) 81, I was afraid..that you would write me a stinker calling me a peach fed sod. **1953** E. M. FORSTER *Hill of Devi* 228, I composed a stinker... H. H. supervised it and decried any attempt at moderation.

b. More widely, something repugnant because of its difficulty or unendurable nature. *colloq.*

1917 KIPLING *Diversity of Creatures* 241 The second stanza..of that Ode is what is technically called a 'stinker'. **1941** S. J. BAKER *Dict. Austral. Slang* 72 *Stinker*, a disagreeable, highly unpleasant and often humid day. **1947** *Penguin New Writing* XXIX. 100 During the war the standard [of films] was undeniably high, with the exception of a few frank stinkers such as *Half-Way House.* **1959** D. HEWETT *Bobbin Up* 170 Already the sky was pale and smoky with the promise of 'another stinker'. **1967** *Listener* 9 Feb. 196/2 Stylistically, the Royal Victoria Hospital is indeed a stinker. **1979** H. R. F. KEATING *Inspector Ghote draws Line* xv. 149 The headache..has become a real stinker now.

c. In phr. *to come a stinker* = *to come a cropper* s.v. CROPPER[3] (chiefly in the work of P. G. Wodehouse). *slang.*

1923 J. MANCHON *Le Slang* 293 *To come a stinker*, ramasser une pelle. **1936** WODEHOUSE *Laughing Gas* iv. 41 And then..the engagement went and busted itself up. One moment, it was buzzing along like a two-year-old... The next, it had come a stinker. *a* **1975** —— *Sunset at Blandings* (1977) iii. 26 Lack of the stuff [*sc.* wealth] is always the rock on which the frail craft of love comes a stinker where Blandings is concerned.

stinkeroo (stiŋkĕrū·). *slang* (orig. *U.S.*). Also **stinkaroo.** [f. STINK *sb.* or *v.*: see *-EROO.] Something of a very low standard; a very bad performance. Also, a furore or 'stink'.

1934 D. RUNYON in *Collier's* 24 Nov. 8/3 The contest.. turns out to be something of a disappointment, and, in fact, it is a stinkeroo, because there is little skill and no science whatever in it. **1946** *Sun* (Baltimore) 21 June 16/4 The fight last night was a 'stinkeroo' and should be investigated. **1951** J. B. PRIESTLEY *Festival at Farbridge* ii. 54 They've sunk two-and-a-half million dollars in this new stinkaroo that opens tonight. **1958** B. NICHOLS *Sweet & Twenties* ix. 120 It caused an absolute stinkaroo in the women's colleges. **1973** *Daily Tel.* 24 Nov. 11/7 Many of the critics' notices [of the play] were unfavourable, referring to it as 'an antique', 'a puerile affair' and 'a stinkaroo'.

stinking, *ppl. a.* Add: **1. e.** As an intensifier: 'offensively', in *stinking drunk, rich* (somewhat *derog.*); also *absol.* and const. *with,* having too much (money, etc.). Cf. sense *2 b of the vb. *colloq.*

1887 *Lantern* (New Orleans) 12 Feb. 3/1 Dey had four bottles er booze and got stinkin' 'fore two o'clock. **1926** L. H. NASON *Chevrons* iii. 96 He went off and got stinking drunk. **1934** E. WAUGH *Handful of Dust* iii. 115 'Tight that night.' 'Stinking.' **1940** E. POUND *Cantos* lvi. 62 Sangko stinking with graft. **1945** E. S. GARDNER *Case of Golddigger's Purse* ii. 9 Not only is he rich but he's *stinking* rich. **1956** A. CHRISTIE *Dead Man's Folly* ii. 27 Stinking with money—absolutely stinking! **1965** *New Statesman* 19 Mar. 462/2 The father meets old cronies and gets stinking drunk. **1978** N. MARSH *Grave Mistake* iv. 111 She was in affluent circumstances, stinking rich in fact. **1980** D. BOGARDE *Gentle Occupation* i. 22 The only thing to do is to get absolutely stinking... It was the best thing in the world for despair: a good skin-full.

2. a. stinking fish, (*a*) in allusion to the phr. *to cry stinking fish* (sense 1 a): something worthless or rotten; (*b*) *Ghana* (see quot. 1973).

1935 E. R. EDDISON *Mistress* vi. 98 Have I not proof of 's loyal mind within reason: his refusing on't when Lessingham did offer it? Nay, 'twas but stinking fish then: 'twas under suzerainty. **1968** J. ABRUQUAH *Torrent* ii. 29 You are treated nice when you are a stranger instead of having little bits of dried stinking fish and kenkey thrown at you. **1973** K. A. SEY *Ghanaian Eng.* vii. 90 *Stinking fish,* fish preserved with salt and used for seasoning 'soups' and 'stews'. **1981** N. J. CRISP *Festival* xi. 260 Vincent Consel said to his editor, 'I detect the faint aroma of stinking fish.'

stinkingly, *adv.* Add: **2.** Excessively, extraordinarily. Cf. sense *1 e of the ppl. a. *colloq.*

1906 R. FRY *Let.* 14 Jan. (1972) I. 248 The Raphael.. [is] stinkingly pretty and gives me no aesthetic pleasure. **1951** M. KENNEDY *Lucy Carmichael* II. i. 65 He is.. frightfully good-looking..and stinkingly rich. **1957** J. BRAINE *Room at Top* xxvi. 207 We got really stinkingly sozzled... I don't believe that I've ever drunk so much before. **1979** N. FREELING *Widow* xxvi. 158 A bungalow, very large and super and stinkingly rich.

stinko (sti·ŋko), *predic. a. slang* (orig. *U.S.*). [f. STINK *v.* + *-O[2].] **a.** Of a very low standard; very bad. Cf. *STINKEROO. *rare.*

1924 F. SCOTT FITZGERALD *Let.* 20 Dec. (1964) 174, I thought *The White Monkey* was stinko.

b. Intoxicated; blind drunk. Also as quasi-advb., *stinko drunk,* (joc.) *paralytico.*

1927 *New Republic* 9 Mar. 72/1 The following is a partial list of words denoting drunkenness now in common use in the United States..stinko. **1936** P. G. WODEHOUSE *Laughing Gas* ix. 92 Are you really such a poor judge of form as to imagine that I am stinko? **1942** E. WAUGH *Put out More Flags* iii. 182 'Darling, she was plastered.' 'Are you sure?' 'My dear, stinko paralytico.' **1954** G. SMITH *Flaw in Crystal* 55 They generally come every night for a week and get stinko every night. **1960** S. H. COURTIER *Gently dust Corpse* ii. 21 We ought to be getting stinko together today. An anniversary, see. **1974** D. RAMSAY *No Cause to Kill* II. 132 Jessie's a lush. Stinko most of her waking time. **1976** *National Observer* (U.S.) 6 Nov. 12/6 Poor unfortunates who get stinko drunk every day on skid row.

c. Over-supplied (*with* money, etc.). *rare.*

1960 *Sunday Express* 28 Feb. 3/3, I should be a stockbroker or someone stinko with money.

† **Stinkomalee** (sti:ŋkǒmălī·). *Obs.* Also **Stinkomiles.** [Fanciful combination f. STINK *sb.* or *v.* + TRINCOMALEE.] A disrespectful sobriquet of London University. Hence **Sti:ncomale·an** *a.*

1825 T. HOOK in *John Bull* 25 Dec. 413/1 In consequence of the nature of the property [beside a stagnant pond] the first act of the Council has been to give a new and distinguishing name to the Institution—instead of the London College, or Carmarthen-street University, as heretofore, it is in future to be called—*Stinkomalee!* **1827** T. CREEVEY *Let.* 14 Apr. in J. Gore *Creevey Papers* (1963) xiii. 223 The enlightened moderns who are now founding Stinkomiles College at the end of Gower Street. **1844** A. H. CLOUGH *Let.* 24 Nov. (1957) I. 141 It would be far better to be at Stinkomalee (the London University acknowledges that agnomen,..does it not?). **1849** —— *Let.* 15 Feb. in *Ibid.* I. 242, I have accepted the Stincomalean position. **1851** T. ARNOLD *Let.* 14 Sept. (1966) 205, I saw..that you had been made Professor of English at University College, London. Do you still call that institution by the irreverent name of Stinkomalee?

stink-pot. Add: **5. a.** A term of abuse for a person or (*rarely*) a thing. *slang.*

1854 T. WOOLNER *Let.* 4 Oct. in *Geo. Eliot Lett.* (1954) II. 176, I will not..display the filthy contaminations of these hideous satyrs and smirking moralists—..stink pots of humanity. **1916** JOYCE *Portrait of Artist* v. 230 Go away from here, he said rudely. Go away, you stinkpot. **1928** D. H. LAWRENCE *Let.* Aug. (1932) 744 Whether I shall have the strength to put my nose into that stinkpot of an island [*sc.* England], I don't know. **1948** D. BALLANTYNE *Cunninghams* xx. 267 They can call me miserable old stinkpot. **1959** I. & P. OPIE *Lore & Lang. Schoolch.* ix. 155 These syllables are used..to turn a verb or adjective into a descriptive noun, as:..fuss-pot, stinkpot, [etc.]. **1973** R. LUDLUM *Matlock Paper* xii. 112 *Nowhere* does your signing this little stinkpot say you *agree* to retire from the scene.

b. A machine which emits foul exhaust fumes: esp. a truck or motor-boat. *slang.*

1972 B. GARFIELD *Line of Succession* (1974) II. 155 Mario had..a hatred of stinkpot powerboats. **1977** H. FAST *Immigrants* I. 55 They're gone now, all of them [*sc.* fishing-boats with sails]. Nothing but stinkpots—I'm sorry—oil burners. **1978** D. BAGLEY *Flyaway* xxi. 179 The truck broke through..and it killed them... Lousy stinkpots! Never have liked them except when I'm in a hurry.

stinkweed. Add: **c.** Any of several other plants with an unpleasant smell.

1932 [see *khaki bos, bush* s.v. *KHAKI D.]. **1954** *Sun* (Baltimore) 4 June 21/1 Due to the fact that its leaves, when crushed, are very disagreeable to get next to, the *ailanthus* is also known as 'stinkweed'. **1970** J. H. GRAY *Boy from Winnipeg* 153 My job was to graze the cattle slowly..keeping them out of the stinkweed which, I was warned, spoiled the butter.

stinky (sti·ŋki), *a.* (*sb.*). [f. STINK *sb.* + -Y[1].] = STINKING *ppl. a.* Also as *sb.*

1888 KIPLING *Plain Tales* 238 Now we've got the [joss-]sticks mixed with a lot of glue, and they..smell stinky. **1949** N. R. NASH *Young & Fair* I. ii. 17 What if you had a stinky summer? **1958** S. A. GRAU *Hard Blue Sky* v. 317 'And he does smell,' she said, 'phew'.. 'Go on, stinky,' Annie told him. **1966** L. KIRSTEIN *Rhymes & More Rhymes of PFC* 163 Stinky shorts, dead shoes, sodden shirt. **1972** D. RAMSAY *Little Murder Music* 190, I think human nature is pretty stinky. **1982** *Observer* 25 Apr. 7/6 To get where he is and stay there he must have had to do some pretty stinky things. His is a pretty stinky country, after all.

stint, *sb.*[1] Add: **II. 6. a.** Also, a portion of land allotted for pasturing a limited number of sheep or cattle.

1849 *Gloss. Provincial Words Teesdale, Co. Durham* 125 *Stint,* a limited number of cattle gaits. **1904** in *Eng. Dial. Dict.* V. 768/1 The marshes of Skinburness, &c.,..were not enclosed in 1811 as were the commons, but were divided into stints, 400 being made out of 1,008 acres. **1954** M. BERESFORD *Lost Villages* vi. 204 Abandoned cornfields tumble first to grass and weed... The flocks which had been stinted could now have their stint enlarged. **1975** *Country Life* 11 Dec. 1676/2 As winter sets in, the salt marshes on the English side of the Solway will be grazed by..hill sheep from the Lake District. The 'stints' (pasturage for sheep and cattle) are owned by the Solway-side farmers.

7. a. Also, a period of time spent on a particular job; a turn (at doing something).

1955 S. WILSON *Man in Gray Flannel Suit* (1956) xxii. 170 After college had come a brief stint in the Army. **1957** *Economist* 21 Dec. 1073/1 No really outstanding executives for private business have ever been ready to take on a stint in the hardest jobs that industry in this country has to offer. **1965** *Listener* 24 June 933/2 This is the end of my stint for *The Listener.* **1976** H. WILSON *Governance of Britain* vii. 130 His three or four weeks' compulsory stint as 'Minister in Attendance' at Balmoral. **1978** S. BRILL *Teamsters* viii. 307 He..then served a stint as a railroad brakeman.

stint, var. *STENT *sb.*[5]

stipe[2] (stəip). *slang.* Also *rarely* **stip.** [Abbrev. of STIPENDIARY *a.* and *sb.*] **1.** A stipendiary magistrate.

1860 HOTTEN *Dict. Slang* (ed. 2), *Stipe,* a stipendiary magistrate. **1956** S. HOPE *Diggers' Paradise* xvi. 141 The 'stipe'..had failed to find a permanent job to his liking in Britain. **1966** F. SHAW et al. *Lern Yerself Scouse* 65 *De Stipe,* the Liverpool Stipendiary Magistrate. **1978** *New Society* 28 Sept. 710/1 Roberts devoted the remainder of his..speech to remembering odd little incidents in the early career of the senior 'stip'.

2. A stipendiary racing steward. Chiefly *Austral.*

1922 *Daily Mail* 13 Nov. 11 The *Daily Mail* scheme for invigorating turf supervision... The plea for 'stipes' is a newspaper stunt. **1930** *Bulletin* (Sydney) 8 Jan. 35/1 And all the stipes and vets. and docs. galore..Wouldn't change that. **1963** *Truth* (Wellington, N.Z.) 9 July, Stipe should have acted [at Trentham races]. **1969** D. FRANCIS *Enquiry* i. 13 Stipendiary Stewards, officials paid by the Jockey Club... The Stipe who had been acting at Oxford was notoriously the most difficult. **1977** *Australian* 15 Jan. 20 The racing page screamed Stipes Probe Jockey.

stiphado, var. *STIFADO.

stipple, *sb.* Add: **3.** *stipple-engraved* adj.

1936 [see *line-engraved* s.v. *LINE *sb.*[2] 32]. **1961** E. M. ELVILLE *Collector's Dict. Glass* 77/1 A stipple engraved wineglass with the standing figure of a small boy with a bird on his wrist. **1973** *Country Life* 6 Dec. 1931 (Advt.), Stipple engraved goblet..circa 1785.

stipple, *v.* **1. c.** (Earlier example.)

1765 T. H. CROKER et al. *Compl. Dict. Arts & Sciences* II. s.v. *Miniature,* The whole appears as if strippled [*sic*] or wrought with points.

stipulation. Add: **2. c.** *U.S. Law.* An agreement between opposing parties (or their counsels) relative to the course of a judicial proceeding; a requirement or condition of such an agreement.

1802 *South Carolina Rep.* (1817) II. 162 The Court opened a stipulation entered into between the insurers and the insured, by which it was agreed that one case should decide all others. **1828** *U.S. Supreme Court Rep.* XXVI. 448 The want of possession, if consistent with the stipulations of the parties,..has never been held to be, *per se,* a badge of fraud. **1876** *Ibid.* (1877) XCIV. 278 Stipulations between counsel relative to the course of proceeding in a cause pending in this court cannot be withdrawn by one party without the consent of the other. **1909** *Northeastern Reporter* LXXXVIII. 786/1 By that stipulation the defendants had the right of inspection before final acceptance of the goods. **1948** *Pacific Reporter* (1949) XCIX. 956/1 The contents of the proposed stipulation with reference to the repairs of the damage as to sidewalks, are merely instructions to workmen. **1977** *National Observer* (U.S.) 8 Jan. 18/1 Agreements to something he [*sc.* your counsel] calls 'stipulations' pour from his eager lips so thick and fast that soon a miasma of confusion covers you. Eventually you learn that a stipulation is a point or condition agreed upon between the litigants.

stipulative (sti·piulătiv), *a.* [f. STIPULATE *v.* + -IVE.] That stipulates or specifies as an essential condition. *spec.* in *stipulative definition* (Logic), the act of stipulating what a word, phrase, etc. shall be used to mean; a definition so stipulated.

1950 R. Robinson *Definition* ii. 19 By 'stipulative definition' I mean establishing or announcing or choosing one's own meaning for a word. **1956** J. Hospers *Introd. Philos. Anal.* i. 51 We are stating what *we* are going to mean by it... We are stipulating a meaning, and we have a stipulative definition. **1965** E. J. Lemmon *Beginning Logic* 33 A definition such as *Df* ↔ may be called a *stipulative* definition. **1976** A. R. Lacey *Dict. Philos.* 48 Stipulative definitions are *prescriptive* in that they prescribe how a word is to be used. **1981** P. A. Angeles *Dict. Philos.* 59 When Norbert Wiener coined the word 'cybernetics' he gave it the stipulative definition: 'the science of communication and control systems'.

stir, *sb.*³ Add: **1.** Also without article, esp. in phr. *in stir.* (Later examples.)

1926 [see *jolt *sb.* 4 b]. **1939** J. Steinbeck *Grapes of Wrath* ii. 19 When you been in stir a little while, you can smell a question comin' from hell to breakfast. **1970** G. F. Newman *Sir, You Bastard* ii. 79 Tasting stir, Goldby suddenly realized he was the wrong side of thirty for acquiring the habit. **1977** 'E. Crispin' *Glimpses of Moon* xii. 250 You get better conditions than that in stir.

2. *Comb.* (Designating) a person deranged, etc., by long imprisonment, esp. as *stir-crazy.* Also *fig.* *Criminals' slang* (chiefly *U.S.*).

1908 J. M. Sullivan *Criminal Slang* 24 *Stir crazy, prison crazy,* a man whose mind has become affected by serving long sentences. **1924** G. C. Henderson *Keys to Crookdom* 419 *Stir bugs,* prison crazy. **1925** *Flynn's* 18 Apr. 116/2 *Stir-bug,* one whose mentality has been broken by confinement in prison. **1926** *Clues* Nov. 162/2 *Stir-simple,* been in so long they are losing their mind. **1929** M. A. Gill *Underworld Slang* 10/2 *Stir nut,* convict effected [*sic*] by long confinement. *Ibid.*, *Stir simple,* convict effected by long confinement. **1932** 'Spindrift' *Yankee Slang* 60 *Stir crazy,* nervous dread of free convicts who have served a long term and fear to return to prison. **1935** N. Ersine *Underworld & Prison Slang* 72 *Stirnuts,* mentally hazy because of long imprisonment. **1939** J. Steinbeck *Grapes of Wrath* iv. 36, I wonder what the stir-bug I got for a cell-mate is doin'. *Ibid.* xvi. 241 Maybe I'm kinda stir-nuts. *Ibid.* xx. 342 If say a fella's goin' stir-bugs..why, you know it 'fore it happens. **1950** H. E. Goldin *Dict. Amer. Underworld Lingo* 212/2, I must be gettin' stir-bugs or blowing my top (going insane) altogether. **1950** Patterson & Conrad *Scottsboro Boy* ii. vii. 133 Howard was stir-crazy. He would go around the prison saying to anybody about anybody, 'I kill the sonofabitch, I sure kill the sonofabitch.' **1956** P. I. Wellman *Death on Prairie* xxiv. 225 The latter came back after two years in prison with his mind gone—'stir simple' to use a modern slang phrase. **1960** *Washington Post* 29 Jan. A14 A Democratic President would go 'stir crazy' without a depression or war to occupy his time. **1972** J. Wambaugh *Blue Knight* v. 74 She's..an ex-con and stir crazy as hell... She's got a phobia about jails.

sti·r-fry, *v.* orig. *U.S.* [Stir *v.*] **a.** *trans.* Chiefly in Chinese cookery: to fry (meat, vegetables, etc.) rapidly on a high heat, while stirring and tossing them in the pan. Also *absol.*

1959 C. B. T. Lee *Chinese Cooking for Amer. Kitchens* 82 Add all ingredients except egg roll skin and beaten egg. Stir-fry for 3 minutes. *Ibid.* 102 Stir-fry onions for 2 minutes. **1969** *Guardian* 16 July 16/4 Stir-fry the vegetables. **1972** K. Lo *Chinese Food* i. 11 After the vegetables have been stir-fried for a minute or two the meat is returned to the pan and stir-fried together with the vegetables. **1976** 'M. Delving' *China Expert* viii. 93 'You were in trouble with police,' she said, stir-frying thin strips of beef and vegetables. **1982** *Daily Tel.* 14 Jan. 15/4 Draw in prepared beef and stir/fry for 10 mins.

b. The vbl. phr. used *attrib.*

1959 *House Beautiful* June 146/1 The nub of stir-fry cooking is the chopping, so that all ingredients are in uniformly small pieces. **1976** *Publishers Weekly* 19 Apr. 76/1 Soufflés, stir fry cookery, casseroles. **1981** J. Mann *Funeral Sites* xii. 77 Ian..had spent some time making a Chinese stir-fry dinner.

Also **sti·r-fried** *ppl. a.*; **stir-fry·ing** *vbl. sb.*

1959 C. B. T. Lee *Chinese Cooking for Amer. Kitchens* 64 *Chow* (stir-frying). This is the most popular method of Chinese cooking and is called either stir-frying or sautéing at high heat. *Ibid.* 65 Do not try to attempt more than two stir-fried dishes at one meal. **1972** K. Lo *Chinese Food* i. 45 All that quick-fried dishes require is a very short period of stir-frying over high heat with a couple of tablespoons of oil. **1980** *Redbook* Oct. 136/2 To save time and money in the kitchen, Denise does a lot of stir-frying and uses a slow cooker. **1981** *Sunday Tel.* 6 Dec. 13/5 Stir-fried shredded beef with bean sprouts and celery.

stirk. 1. (Later examples.)

1880 W. H. Patterson *Gloss. Antrim & Down* 100 *Stirk, sb.* a cow one or two years old. 'A bull *stirk*,' a young bull. **1909** D. Houston *'E Silkie Man* 4 Fan Kirsty tethered 'e stirk. **1949** *Scotsman* 17 May 8/7 130 Store cattle including 60 choice West of Ireland black polled bullocks and stirks,..and 30 North of Ireland stirks. **1973** *Stirling Observer* 25 July 7/2 They had on offer 51 dairy cattle,..64 accredited calves, 49 non-accredited calves and 81 store cattle and stirks... Charolais heifer stirks sold to £148,..Hereford heifer stirks sold to £107. **1978** *Morecambe Guardian* 14 Mar. 22 (Advt.), Rearing Calves and Stirks, Fat Cattle and Slaughter Cows. **1979** L. Derwent *Border Bairn* i. 15 Her brother, the shepherd.. accepted me more or less as one of his flock. A yowe or a gimmer, a stirk or a stot.

Stirling¹ (stə̄·ɹliŋ). [The name of the Revd. Robert *Stirling* (1790–1878), Scottish minister and engineer.] *Stirling* (or † *Stirling's*) *cycle,* the thermodynamic cycle on which an ideal Stirling engine would operate, consisting of an isothermal expansion, a drop in temperature at constant volume by giving up heat to a regenerator, an isothermal compression, and an increase in temperature at constant volume by gaining heat from the regenerator; *Stirling* (or † *Stirling's*) *engine,* orig., an external-combustion air engine invented by Stirling (*Brit. Pat. 4081* (1816)); more widely, a mechanical device used to provide either power or refrigeration and operating on a closed regenerative cycle, the working fluid being cyclically compressed and expanded at different temperatures; also *ellipt.* as *Stirling.*

1845 *Minutes Proc. Inst. Civil Engineers* IV. 348 (*heading*) Description of Stirling's improved air engine. *Ibid.* 359 In Mr. Stirling's engine the intense heat of the fire did not come into actual contact with the pistons. **1887** *Encycl. Brit.* XXII. 523/1 Stirling's cycle is theoretically perfect whatever the density of the working air. **1889** C. H. Peabody *Thermodynamics of Steam-Engine* xi. 174 A recent hot-air engine made on the same principle as Stirling's hot-air engine. **1943** E. H. Lewitt *Thermodynamics Applied to Heat Engines* (ed. 3) iii. 57 The Stirling cycle is thermodynamically reversible owing to the action of the regenerator. **1963** *Engineer* CCXIV. 1063/1 A Stirling cycle machine operates on a closed regenerative thermodynamic cycle. **1973** *Sci. Amer.* Aug. 81/2 In practice Stirling engines do not work on the Stirling cycle. It is not possible to have isothermal (constant temperature) compression and expansion processes. **1980** *Times* 16 Oct. (Internat. Motor Show Suppl.) p. xiv/8 Most of the technology of the Stirling has been established since the Second World War,..but mainly for vehicle and industrial duties rather than aircraft.

Stirling². The name of Allan *Stirling* (1844–1927), Scottish-born American engineer, used *attrib.* to designate a water-tube boiler invented and patented by him (*U.S. Pat. 381,595* (1888)), usu. consisting of three interconnected upper steam and water drums and one or two lower water drums, connected by banks of inclined water-tubes which are heated by combustion gases and bent to enter the drums radially.

1889 *Amer. Machinist* 23 May 12/1 (Advt.), The Stirling Water Tube Boilers have unusually large steam and water spaces and well-defined circulation. **1924** F. J. Drover *Coal & Oil Fired Boilers* ii. v. 143 For from 1,000 to 10,000 sq. ft. of heating surface the standard Stirling boiler consists of three steam drums and two mud drums. **1940** H. M. Spring *Boiler Operator's Guide* iv. 117 The Stirling boiler..is one of the first types of bent-tube boiler to come into common use.

Stirling³. *Math.* The name of James *Stirling* (1692–1770), Scottish mathematician, used *attrib.* and in the possessive to designate concepts in the theory of numbers, as **Stirling('s) approximation** or **formula,** either of two functions of an integer n which are approximations for factorial n when n is large, viz. $n! \sim n^n/e^n$ and (more accurately) $n! \sim \sqrt{(2\pi n)}n^n/e^n$; **Stirling('s) number,** a member of either of two arrays used in combinatorics, first described by him (*Methodus Differentialis* (1730)), *spec.* (*a*) the number of ways of arranging the integers 1 to m in n disjoint non-empty ordered sets, the first element of each ordered set being the least; (a Stirling number of the first kind); (*b*) the number of ways of partitioning the integers 1 to m into n disjoint non-empty sets; (a Stirling number of the second kind).

1938 *Biometrika* XXX. 220 The first order term in Stirling's approximation to $m!$ **1948** Glasstone *Textbk. Physical Chem.* (ed. 2) xi. 874 Since N is a large number, viz., the Avogadro number, it is possible to use the Stirling approximation and to replace $\ln N!$ by $N \ln N - N$. **1970** Ashby & Miller *Princ. Mod. Physics* ii. 35 We can obtain an approximate analytical expression..by using Stirling's approximation for the factorials: For large n, $\ln (n!) \propto \frac{1}{2}\ln (2\pi) + (n+\frac{1}{2}) \ln (n) - n$. **1978** P. W. Atkins *Physical Chem.* xx. 650 Stirling's approximation is that x large: $\ln x! \quad x \ln x - x$. **1908** T. J. I'A. Bromwich *Introd. Theory Infinite Series* 461 (*heading*) Stirling's asymptotic formula for the gamma-function when x is real, large and positive. **1934** I. S. & E. S. Sokolnikoff *Higher Math. for Engineers & Physicists* xiii. 383 The first term of this series bears the name of Stirling's formula and gives satisfactory results even for small values of n. **1940** Glasstone *Text-bk. Physical Chem.* x. 861 By Stirling's formula $1/N!$ is approximately equal to $(e/N)^N$ if N is large. **1962** W. J. Moore *Physical Chem.* (ed. 4) vii. 233 This expression is evaluated by means of the Stirling formula, $\log N! = (N+\frac{1}{2}) \log N - N + \frac{1}{2} \log 2\pi$. **1928** *Amer. Math. Monthly* XXXV. 77 The Stirling Numbers are characterized by many very beautiful properties. **1933** *Tôhoku Math. Jrnl.* XXXVII. 255 (*caption*) Table of Stirling's numbers of the first kind. *Ibid.* 277 The Stirling number of the second kind can be obtained by aid of a problem of probability. **1966** F. N. David et al. *Symmetric Functions & Allied Tables* v. 226 Stirling's Numbers of the first kind...1 1 2 6 24 120 720...1 3 11 50 274 1764...1 6 35 225 1624...1 10 85 735...1 15 175... 1 21...[etc.]. *Ibid.* 223 Stirling's Numbers of the second kind...1 1 1 1 1 1 1...1 3 7 15 31 63...1 6 25 90 301... 1 10 65 350...1 15 140...1 21...[etc.].

stirrer. Add: **1. d.** One who stirs up trouble or discontent; an agitator, a trouble-maker. *colloq.* (chiefly *Austral.*).

1963 T. & P. Morris *Pentonville* xi. 247 Other prisoners described him as a *stirrer* rather than a leader in that he got others to do the dirty work for him. **1970** *Sunday Truth* (Brisbane) 28 June 4/3 He was no stirrer. He came quietly to Brisbane made the scene for six months or so then quietly drifted back a few weeks ago to his favorite haunts around Kings Cross. **1973** C. Mason *Hostage* vii. 104 'You're a born boat-rocker.' 'D'you think so? A stirrer, they'd call it at home.' **1977** *Sounds* 9 July 15/2 He's an absolute stirrer with very little concept of what our job is. **1982** *Observer* 13 June 16/1 Jessica Mitford is what Australians call a stirrer, meaning a person with a talent for causing trouble.

stirrup, *sb.* Add: **1. c.** *up in the stirrups* (earlier example).

1812 J. H. Vaux *Vocab. Flash Lang.* in *Mem.* (1964) 277 A man who is in swell street, that is, having plenty of money, is said to be up in the stirrups.

2. c. Delete † *Obs.* and add: Now *spec.* the strap itself. Also, a similar strap attached to women's stretch trousers or slacks. orig. *U.S.* in recent use.

1955 *Sun* (Baltimore) 7 Jan. (B ed.) 15/1 [Baseball] The stockings, modeled after those of the Boston Red Sox. The stirrup—that cutaway portion which extends down into the shoe—will be orange. **1963** *Women's Wear Daily* 23 Sept. 15/1 Rayon/nylon twill stretch pants. ..hi rise, back zip, no stirrups. **1967** *Boston Sunday Herald* 26 Mar. (Advt. Section), Comfy elastic waist, neat stitched pleat, self-fabric stirrups. **1980** *Times* 19 Feb. 8/4 The major buyers have bought..denims, dungarees, stirrup trousers (they used to be called ski pants) in the now obligatory stretch fabrics.

e. Also, each of a pair of supports for holding the legs of a female patient raised and apart, as during childbirth.

1936 H. J. Stander *Williams' Obstetrics* (ed. 7) xv. 406 In the hospital she is..placed on a suitable delivery table,..the legs held in position by adjustable stirrups. **1977** M. French *Women's Room* (1978) i. 69 The humiliation of being in stirrups and having people peer at her exposed genitals whenever they chose.

8. stirrup pump, a portable hand pump held steady by a stirrup-like foot-plate and used, esp. in the war of 1939–45, for extinguishing small fires and incendiary bombs with water drawn from a bucket and directed by a hose.

[**1902** *Shand, Mason & Co.'s Portable Fire Appliances* 3b, This is another adaptation of the 'London Brigade' Hand Pump. The pump is..provided with a stirrup, by means of which it can be used with an ordinary house pail.] **1939** C. C. Ramsay *Fire-Fighting in Peace & War* vi. 41 The Home Office specification insists on a stirrup pump with a 30-ft. length of ½-in. rubber tubing (hose). **1939** *Punch* 27 Sept. 342/1 The long day, with its stream of gas-masks, sandbags, stirrup-pumps, dugouts,..had drawn to a close. **1974** M. Gilbert *Flash Point* xx. 165 He..had a stirrup pump, a relic of the last war, ready primed in the hall.

stishovite (sti·ʃŏvəit). *Min.* [f. the name of S. M. *Stishov*, Russian geochemist, who first synthesized it in 1961: see -ite¹.] A dense, tetragonal polymorph of silica, formed at very high pressure and found in meteorite craters. Cf. *coesite.

1962 E. C. T. Chao et al. in *Jrnl. Geophysical Res.* LXVII. 419/1 Stishov and Popova (1961) recently synthesized a high-density polymorph of SiO_2 at 1200°–1400°C and at a pressure reported to be above 160,000 atmospheres... In honor of the senior author of the paper announcing the synthesis of this new polymorph, we propose to name the new mineral stishovite. **1971** I. G. Gass et al. *Understanding Earth* i. 35/1 The diamonds occasionally contain minute inclusions of coesite..but do not contain stishovite, another polymorph forming at even higher pressures. **1978** *Nature* 20 Apr. 714/2 Stishovite is the highest pressure polymorph of silica. It possesses the rutile structure with a density of 4·28 g cm^{-3} and is characterised by sixfold coordination of silicon by oxygen.

stitch, *sb.*¹ Add: **I. 2. d.** *pl.* Fits of laughter; esp. in phr. (*to have,* etc., someone) *in stitches.* Occas. *sing.* = *laugh *sb.* 4 b. (See also sense 2 a, quot. 1601.)

1935 *Motion Picture* Nov. 41/1 A laugh festival that will have you in stitches from its opening scene to its ridiculous but uproarious climax. **1952** E. O'Neill *Moon for Misbegotten* i. 65 Listen to Jim still in stitches. It's good to hear him laugh as if he meant it. **1968** A. Diment *Great Spy Race* ii. 18 The party's in a house right opposite. It'll be a stitch, Phil. You must come. **1969** O. Blakeston *For crying out Shroud* vi. 56 I've got some new gear that will give you stitches. **1981** D. M. Thomas *White Hotel* iv. i. 139 She had them in stitches with her absurd—but true—anecdotes. **1983** *Listener* 20 Jan. 38/4 The sardonic puppets, C4s, had my anglophone family in stitches.

II. 7. (Earlier *fig.* example.)

1837 F. D. Maurice *Let.* Feb. in F. Maurice *F. D. Maurice* (1884) I. xiv. 224, I consider..whether we ought to take up our stitches (not intentionally dropped) at the age of twenty-four [*i.e.* go to a university].

III. 13. stitch welding, a form of spot welding in which a series of overlapping spot welds is produced by a machine which makes each weld and advances the work automatically; hence (as back-formation) **stitch weld** *sb.* and *v. trans.*; **stitch-welded** *ppl. a.*; **stitch welder,** a machine that performs stitch welding.

1934 *Welding Industry* Aug. 223/1 A continuous spot welding machine is shown... This is often called stitch welding. *Ibid.* Dec. 348/1 A development which is the logical consequence of the attempt to speed up the spot welding process is the so-called continuous spot or stitch welder. **1946** *Philips Resistance Welding Handbk.* i. 18 Stitch welders, which have been described as the sewing machines of the resistance welding industry, are either pneumatically or mechanically driven to produce a very large number of spots in rapid succession. **1951** *Trans. Inst. Welding* June 90/1 A seam weld is considered better than a stitch weld, because of its more regular formation. **1958** *Times Rev. Industry* July 26/2 The components [of the gas turbine] are stitch-welded around the circumference. **1961** J. A. OAKES *Welding Engineer's Handbk.* xxiii. 243 (*caption*) Set-up for stitch welding a steel door. **1972** *Automobile Engineer* Jan. 12/1 The fuel tanks are stitch-welded to the sides of the chassis. **1978** D. R. ANDREWS *Soldering, Brazing, Welding & Adhesives* iii. 65 For stitch welding the electrodes are automatically opened and closed between the making of consecutive welds and the work is moved while the electrodes are parted.

stitch, *v.*[1] Add: **II. 3.** (Later *fig.* examples.)

c **1862** E. DICKINSON in *Poems* (1955) I. 300, I saw no Way—The Heavens were stitched—I felt the Columns close. **1936** L. MACNEICE tr. *Aeschylus' Agamemnon* 68, *I* stitched this murder together; it was my title. **1961** *Daily Tel.* 16 Nov. 21/3 The precast concrete sections are 'stitched' together with 33 miles of 1⅛ in diameter high tensile steel strand. **1973** M. AMIS *Rachel Papers* 220 My father..crossed his little legs and stitched his fingers.

9. stitch up. f. Of a criminal, etc.: to cause (a person) to be convicted, esp. by informing or manufacturing evidence. Also *gen.*, to swindle, to overcharge exorbitantly.

1970 G. F. NEWMAN *Sir, You Bastard* v. 142 Your confederate has just about stitched you up. **1977** *New Society* 7 July 6/2 Both Sheila and Gary have many stories of being 'stitched up' by the police or fleeced. Gary says the Dip Squad—the special police patrol looking for pickpockets—are 'a bunch of wankers'. **1977** *Woman* 3 Sept. 30/3 After shelling out £1.50 for a fold-up version [of an umbrella] she found that she'd been stitched up... Two spokes were broken. **1978** F. BRANSTON *Sergeant Ritchie's Conscience* I. v. 69 Those [rivals] who wouldn't be frightened he stitched up, his favourite method being to sell an opponent some drugs, then inform on him to the police.

sti·tchdown. [f. STITCH *v.*[1] + DOWN *adv.*] A shoe or boot on which the lower edge of the upper is turned outward and stitched on to the sole; a veldt-shoe. Also *stitchdown shoe.*

1840 E. STIFF *Texan Emigrant* vii. 95 During the intolerable hot weather in the summer of 1838, the same Kentucky jeans pants, the same pair of stitchdowns,.. adorned the tall and disproportioned outward man. **1916** F. PLUCKNETT *Introd. Boot & Shoe Manuf.* xxx. 258 The 'veldtschoen', or 'stitchdown', has passed through so many stages that no description of it would correctly describe its production in all factories. The principal idea is that the edge of the upper (except just around the heel) shall be turned outward instead of being folded over the edge of an insole, and that this projecting flap shall be attached to the sole with a vertical thread seam. **1940** *Chambers's Techn. Dict.* 888/2 *Veldtschoen*,..a sandal-like form of shoe in which the upper is attached directly to the sole by a row of stitches near the edge. Also called *stitchdown shoes.* **1969** T. C. THORSTENSEN *Pract. Leather Technol.* xv. 248 The stitchdown shoe differs from the Littleway in that the insole is fastened to the upper by flairing the upper outward rather than inward.

sti·tchless, *a.* [f. STITCH *sb.*[1] + -LESS.] Without stitches; *spec.* (formerly) of a tennis ball, put together without stitches or a stitched seam. Also, 'without a stitch', unclothed.

1927 *Daily Tel.* 22 Mar. 15/6 W. H. Powell..was beaten... It was due..to the fact that Powell is not yet used to the stitchless ball. **1939** JOYCE *Finnegans Wake* 451 I'd plant you..on the electric ottoman in the lap of lechery, simpringly stitchless with admiracion. **1953** M. PEAKE *Mr. Pye* xvi. 128 She had left her clothes on a high rock... 'My child..' said Mr. Pye '..my stitchless child.'

stiver, *v.* Add: **2.** *trans.* To ruffle (the hair); to make it bristle or stand on end. Also with *up*.

1886, etc. in *Eng. Dial. Dict.* **1924** GALSWORTHY *White Monkey* I. viii. 61 Michael stivered his hair. **1926** —— *Silver Spoon* I. v. 34 Michael stivered up his hair.

stivered *ppl. a.* (later examples); **stivery** *a.* (examples).

1892 S. HEWETT *Peasant Speech* (E.D.D.), Didee iver zee sich a stivery head as 'er 'th agot? 'Er lüketh 's-of 'er'd been drawed drii a brimbly 'ädge back'ards. **1918** GALSWORTHY *Five Tales* 127 He looked like a stuffed man..sitting there, with..his stivered hair. **1928** —— *Swan Song* I. iii. 19 Dabbing at his hair, bright and stivery, he straightened his tie and ran down. **1939** N. MARSH *Overture to Death* v. 58 The stivered grass was washed with colour, and before him his own attenuated shadow appeared.

stoat, *sb.* Add: *fig.* Also, a treacherous fellow; a sexually aggressive man, a lecher.

a **1960** E. M. FORSTER *Maurice* (1971) xxx. 138 His feeling for Dickie required a very primitive name... What a stoat he had been! **1978** C. EGLETON *Mills Bomb* xxii. 208 'Would it surprise you to learn that he was a fag?' 'You've got it wrong; everyone knew he was a stoat.'

stochastic, *a.* Restrict Now *rare* or *Obs.* to sense in Dict. and add: **2. a.** Randomly determined; that follows some random probability distribution or pattern, so that its behaviour may be analysed statistically but not predicted precisely; *stochastic process* = *random process* s.v. *RANDOM *a.* 1 b.

[**1917** L. VON BORTKIEWICZ *Die Iterationen* 3 Die an der Wahrscheinlichkeitstheorie orientierte, somit auf 'das Gesetz der Grossen Zahlen' sich gründende Betrachtung empirischer Vielheiten möge als Stochastik..bezeichnet werden. **1923** A. A. TSCHUPROW in *Metron* II. 461 Every stochastical (1) theory of statistics sees in the empirical statistical numbers images of certain really significant quantities—reflected confuse[d] images blurred ..by the Chance. [*Note*] (1) I use the word 'stochastical' as synonymous to 'based on the theory of probability'—cf. J. Bernoulli, *Ars Conjectandi*, Basileae, 1713, p. 213 'Ars Conjectandi sive Stochastice nobis definitur ars metiendi quam fieri potest exactissimi probabilitates rerum' and L. v. Bortkiewicz, *Die Iterationen*.] **1934** *Proc. Nat. Acad. Sci.* XX. 376 A stochastic process is defined by Khintchine to be a one parameter set of chance variables: $\mathbf{x}(t)$, $-\infty < t < \infty$. **1943** *Rev. Mod. Physics* XV. 32 That we should be able to idealize Brownian motion as a Markoff process appears very reasonable. But we should be careful not to conclude too hastily that every stochastic process is necessarily of the Markoff type. **1957** *New Scientist* 20 June 17/3 A new approach to population dynamics was needed, and quite recently this has been provided by J. G. Skellam in the form of a stochastic model which allows the experimentalist to regard his population as a random variable at each instant in time, and is much more flexible than the earlier deterministic equations. **1968** P. A. P. MORAN *Introd. Probability Theory* iii. 108 We have already dealt with some simple cases of successive trials in which the probabilities at each stage depend on what has happened before... As the successive stages can be regarded as successive instants of time the sequence of events may be regarded as a 'random' or 'stochastic'..process. **1971** KIMURA & OHTA *Theoret. Aspects Population Genetics* iii. 33 In any finite population, gene frequencies are subject to stochastic change due to random sampling of gametes. **1979** *Sci. Amer.* Mar. 64/2 (Advt.), The key was recognizing that the star formation process was 'stochastic'. That is, new massive stars are not necessarily created adjacent to a supernova; rather, a probability exists for their formation.

b. *Mus.* Applied (orig. by Iannis Xenakis (b. 1922), Romanian-born Greek composer) to music in which the overall sound structure is determined, but internal details are left to chance or are established mathematically by composer or computer (by the laws of probability or otherwise).

1958 Y. XENAKIS in *Gravesaner Blätter* IV. 112 (*title*) In search of a Stochastic music. *Ibid.* 121 This *glissando* passage has been taken as an example, for it comprises every problem of this Stochastic music controlled by arithmetic. **1963** T. PYNCHON *V.* x. 292 He got around to talking stochastic music and digital computers with one technician. **1969** *Sat. Rev.* (U.S.) 28 June 56/2 Though much has been written, especially by Xenakis himself, on the technique of 'stochastic' music, most of it is utterly unintelligible to the layman. **1975** *New Yorker* 19 May 90/1, I heard a Balinese gamelan one night and the Strasbourg Battery in Yannis Xenakis's latest 'stochastic' composition the next. **1978** P. GRIFFITHS *Conc. Hist. Mod. Music* xi. 169 Iannis Xenakis..has also used computers as calculating aids in the composition of his 'stochastic' music, where the musical form is made analogous to a stochastic process (i.e. one ruled by laws of probability, such as a sequence of dice throws).

stochastically *adv.*, delete † and add later examples; **stochasti·city,** the property of being stochastic.

1947 *Biometrika* XXXIV. 228 The efficiency of any two tests would be identical, in the conditions stated, if the coefficient of correlation between them was ± 1 because then, of course, they would be functionally, and not stochastically, related. **1968** P. A. P. MORAN *Introd. Probability Theory* v. 247 X is said to be 'stochastically larger' than Y if $F(x) \leqslant G(x)$ for all x. **1971** *Jrnl. Statistical Computation & Simulation* I. 42 Refinement in modelling eventuates a requirement for stochasticity. **1979** *Nature* 9 Aug. 459/2 The explanation..is to the contrary of the conventional explanation of these non-seasonal cycles in terms of demographic stochasticity.

stocious (stōᵘ·ʃəs). *slang* (chiefly *Anglo-Ir.*). Also **stotious.** [Of uncertain origin.] Drunk, intoxicated.

1937 *News Chron.* 20 Feb. 8/6 Slang also appeals to our elementary sense of humour, as when we say of a man who is drunk that he is..stotious. **1949** C. GRAVES *Ireland Revisited* i. 20 Words to discriminate the various degrees of intoxication... You have..spifflu, langers, and stocious. The last word rhymes with atrocious and means thickly speaking drunk... We were unable to find anybody who had ever seen it in print. **1952** *Caribbean Quarterly* II. IV. 27 Since when you become so damn stocious? *a* **1966** 'M. NA GOPALEEN' *Best of Myles* (1968) 119 A young man charged with delivering them was found stotious in a doorway. **1970** M. KENYON *100,000 Welcomes* xx. 174 'She's stotious,' Rafferty said. **1980** J. O'FAOLAIN *No Country for Young Men* v. 115 'Coming home stocious five nights a week,' said Doris.

stock, *sb.*[1] Add: **I. 3. d.** (Earlier example in sense of a language group.)

1730 W. WOTTON *Discourse Confusion Babel* 15 So that though this will invincibly prove the Gradation and Derivation of different Dialects from a common Stock, yet it will not prove the actual Formation of some essentially different Tongues which I here contend for.

IV. 28. b. (Earlier example.)

1817 W. SCOTT *Let.* 29 Oct. (1933) V. 4 Like the Highlandman's gun, she wants stock, lock, and barrel, to put her into repair.

V. 41. (Later examples.)

1877 A. I. ROOT *ABC Bee Culture* 158/1 Our pure Italian stocks could have been opened, and their queens removed, scarcely disturbing the cluster. **1930** W. HERROD-HEMPSALL *Bee-Keeping* I. vi. 315 A 'Swarm' is a cluster of bees and their queen only; a 'Colony' consists of the bees and queen living on combs containing brood.. and food; a 'Stock' includes the latter together with the home in which the bees are residing. **1980** R. J. & W. E. HOWE *Practical Beekeeping* vi. 49 When a stock of ten frames is broken up into a number of nuclei, the flying bees from these nuclei will return to their old stand.

VI. 52. b. (Earlier example.)

1870 'MARK TWAIN' in *Galaxy* Oct. 575/1 The 'chance' theory..is..calculated to inflict..pecuniary loss upon any community that takes stock in it.

c. *fig.* Reputation, esteem, credit.

1930 *Times Lit. Suppl.* 17 Apr. 334/4 He found British stock very high in North Germany. **1942** *R.A.F. Jrnl.* 27 June (recto rear cover), The stock of the R.A.F. is high in the Soviet. **1955** *Times* 24 June 10/2 General Perón's stock still seemed to be rising to-day as the country gradually returned to normal conditions. **1979** A. BOYLE *Climate of Treason* viii. 237 This minor triumph sent up the personal stock of Philby.

53. c. = *STOCK-CAR 2. *U.S.*

1951 *Sun* (Baltimore) 11 Oct. B24/1 The Philadelphia district will be well represented when the 100-mile National Championship, for sportsman stocks, gets the green flag at the Langhorne Speedway, Sunday. **1979** *Arizona Daily Star* 1 Apr. C 12/5 Tucson Dragway will run its weekly racing program today, with the junior pro stocks..topping the racing.

56. d. *Theatr.* A stock company; repertory. Chiefly *U.S.*

1916 *Variety* 27 Oct. 12/1 The Alcazar stock is enjoying satisfactory business. **1933** M. LINCOLN *Oh! Definitely* vii. 73 'He had been getting three pounds a week in stock' but would 'take two-ten for town'. **1937** *Daily Tel.* 14 Aug. 9/1 No money will induce them [*sc.* good actors] to bury themselves in Stratford..under 'stock' conditions. **1962** *Listener* 16 Aug. 242/2 Between her junior and senior years in college..she played summer stock.

57. a. (Earlier examples.)

1730 C. CARTER *Compl. Pract. Cook* 1 A good Stock of strong Broth Well made, and good Gravies well drawn off, are very principal Ingredients in the Composing of all Made-Dishes of boil'd Meats. **1747** H. GLASSE *Art of Cookery* ix. 78 An Oyster Soop. Your stock must be made of any Sort of Fish the Place affords.

b. (Later examples without prefix in Paper-making.)

1924 S. LEICESTER *Pract. Stud. for Paper Manufacturers* v. 116 The mistakes in sizing are some of the most difficult to elucidate... The stock used may be the cause. **1963** R. R. A. HIGHAM *Handbk. Papermaking* ii. 45 Distinct variations occur between one batch of stock and another with regard to treatment, colour, temperature, consistency, retention of additives, etc.

c. Cinematographic film.

1897 C. F. JENKINS *Picture Ribbons* 27 The film is of transparent celluloid, one side of which is coated with a sensitive emulsion, that for the negative being much more rapid than the positive stock. **1909** *Moving Picture World* 3 July 11/2 The non-inflammable film stock is now being issued by so many manufacturers. **1938** *Times* 15 Mar. 12/3 A twelve-minute film on 16 mm. stock, shown privately in Liverpool. *Ibid.*, The technical quality of the film is excellent, super-panchromatic stock giving rich quality to shots which are themselves carefully composed. **1974** C. PRIEST *Your Bk. of Film-Making* i. 23 The film is twice as wide as 8 mm film stock.

VIII. 62. stock split *U.S.*, the division of a stock into an increased number of shares; hence **stock splitting**; cf. *split-up* s.v. *SPLIT-.

1955 *Times* 6 July 9/3 According to the Associated Press, the directors of General Motors Corporation have to-day recommended a three-for-one stock split to be voted on by stockholders at a special meeting on September 23. **1959** *Economist* 28 Feb. 788/1 Stock splitting (the American equivalent of the British scrip or bonus issue). **1967** *N.Y. Times* (Internat. ed.) 11–12 Feb. 9/6 Your first bonus report will be our list of 30 stock split candidates. **1977** *Dædalus* Fall 85 Tests indicate that stock prices quickly adjust to changes in public information (announcements of stock splits, dividend increases, etc.).

63. a. *stock-agent, -auction, -breeding, -carrying, -driver, -driving, -farm* (later examples), *-farmer* (later example), *-feed* (later examples), *-inspector, -rearing, -sale, -station* (earlier examples), *-theft, -thief, -trader, -train* (examples), *-yard* (later examples); *stock-proof* adj.; **stock and station** *Austral.* and *N.Z.*, used *attrib.* to designate firms or their employees dealing with farm products and supplies; **stock horse** (earlier example); **stock-rider** (later examples); **stock-route** (later examples); **stock-whip** (earlier and later examples); also as *v. trans.*, to beat with a stock-whip.

1933 *Press* (Christchurch, N.Z.) 9 Sept. 15/7 Dealers and stock-agents use various terms..to make failing mouthed sheep sound younger. **1977** *Weekly Times* (Melbourne) 19 Jan. 11/3 Barney, the stock agent, was looking him straight in the eye when he said: 'If I were you, Clarence, I'd sell the lot and run some sheep.' **1881** *Adelaide Observer* 22 Oct. 44/1 He was suspicious of all stock and station salesmen. **1908** in D. J. Gordon *Handbk. S. Austral.* 327 (Advt.), Bagot, Shakes, & Lewis, Limited. Stock and station agents. **1930** L. G. D. ACLAND *Early Canterbury Runs* 1st Ser. ii. 13 Ford and Newton, who were the leading Christchurch Stock and Station Agents. **1965** G. MCINNES *Road to Gundagai* vii. 113 Here were the big mortgage and stock-and-station houses where wool was finally baled and cleaned for export. **1948** W. FAULKNER *Intruder in Dust* (1949) vi. 134 Monday was stock-auction day at the sales barns behind the Square. **1937** R. H. LOWIE *Hist. Ethnological Theory* viii. 114 This yields..the sequence of (a) hunting-gathering; (b) hoe-culture; (c) hoe-culture with stock-breeding; (d) 'agriculture'. **1957** *Times Lit. Suppl.* 8 Nov. 678/3 Professor Nichols makes a comprehensive review of the genetic basis of modern stockbreeding. **1866** J. MURRAY *Descr. Province Southland* 9 The stock-carrying capacity of the natural herbage is of course variable. **1960** *Farmer & Stockbreeder* 12 Jan. 78/1 He brought back the idea of loose-housing..and introduced it at Langhill to cater for the additional stock-carrying capacity of the next-door, buildingless farm then being acquired. **1851** *Lyttelton* (N.Z.) *Times* 19 Apr., A settlement of whale-fishers and stock-drivers. **1871** *Republican Rev.* (Albuquerque, New Mexico) 27 May 1/3 M. Maloney..arrived here on Thursday, being sent ahead to employ stock drivers. **1867** H. PHILLIPS *Jrnl. Rockwood* 29 Sept. 88 (typescript), T.A.P. & I.I. stock driving. **1874** J. C. MCCOY *Hist. Sk. Cattle Trade* 92 [The farm] is allowed to lay awaste, whilst its owner has turned to stock-driving. **1848** *Senate Rep. 30th U.S. Congr. 1 Sess.* No. 75. 29 Some five hundred head of beef cattle were taken from the government stock farm. **1912** M. NICHOLSON *Hoosier Chron.* 27, I own a stock farm near Lexington. **1894** *Harper's Mag.* Apr. 676/2 'Crit' Marston, the young blue-grass stock-farmer, is a favorite throughout all that section. **1960** *Farmer & Stockbreeder* 15 Mar. 113/1, I am growing ten acres each of stockfeed peas and beans. **1970** *Oxford Times* 30 Oct. 14 Demand for stockfeed potatoes would be far greater than usual. **1846** H. WEEKES in Rutherford & Skinner *New Plymouth Settlement* (1940) 1. vi. 124 'Peter' was an excellent stock-horse, would follow cattle like a dog. **1888** *Century Mag.* Feb. 507/1 At every shipping point..stock inspectors..jealously examine all the brands on the live animals or on the hides of the slaughtered ones. **1930** L. G. D. ACLAND *Early Canterbury Runs* 1st Ser. iii. 47 He then became Stock Inspector in the North Island, but quarrelled with his superiors. **1948** V. PALMER *Golconda* ii. 15 He might have been a country teacher or a stock-inspector. **1915** *N.Z. Jrnl. Agric.* 20 Feb. 190 If the long shoots of this plant [sc. *Eleagnus*] are interlaced while the hedge is growing it makes a close and excellent stock-proof fence. **1960** *Farmer & Stockbreeder* 15 Mar. 123/2 The Monmouthshire style of hedging..gives a real stock-proof fence. **1915** *Chambers's Jrnl.* Jan. 47/2 A son of his anticipated this kind of stock-rearing many years ago in Manitoba. **1960** *Farmer & Stockbreeder* 29 Mar. 12/3 An 81-acre Northants stock-rearing and feeding farm has been sold for £9,800. **1908** E. J. BANFIELD *Confessions of Beachcomber* II. iii. 314 A stockrider..in..flash riding-boots. **1973** *Parade* (Melbourne) Sept. 30/2 The authorities were able to choose exactly the sort of men they wanted from the hundreds of adventurers, prospectors, settlers and stock-riders who offered their services. **1901** M. FRANKLIN *My Brilliant Career* xxxiv. 286 An overgrown old orchard, skirting one of the great stock-routes. **1977** *Meanjin* (Austral.) XXXVI. 1. 69 Cattle cross on the stockroutes. **1948** W. FAULKNER *Intruder in Dust* (1949) vi. 134 Stock-sale day unlike Sunday was a man's time. **1843** J. BACKHOUSE *Narr. Visit Austral. Colonies* xxiii. 264 Accompanied by the Agricultural Superintendent, we walked to a stock-station..where three men are placed in charge of some cattle. **1847** A. HARRIS *Settlers & Convicts* xiii. 252 It was ..not till noon..that we succeeded in finding the nearest stock-station. **1904** *Transvaal Agric. Jrnl.* July 573 Stock theft has always been a great source of worry and trouble to the farming community of this country. **1955** L. G. GREEN *Karoo* xvii. 199 Crime in the karoo usually means stock-theft. *Ibid.* ix. 112 The hunt for a stock-thief who fled into the poort. **1958** *Johannesburg Sunday Times* 28 Sept. 14/9 A quiet-spoken, slightly-built man has become the terror of stock-thieves in the Evaton and Losberg areas. **1942** W. FAULKNER *Go Down, Moses* 248 A back-street stock-trader's boarding house. **1948** —— *Intruder in Dust* (1949) vi. 134 The men with their stock-trader walking-sticks not even stopping. ? **1906** in J. V. Allen *Cowboy Lore* (1971) I. 19 Another train run in to my stock train. **1961** R. P. HOBSON *Rancher takes Wife* xiv. 171 By the time the stock train pulled in..we had a count on the herd. **1852** *Harper's New Monthly Mag.* Dec. 25/1 The Australian 'stockman' is a sort of Europeanized Tartar... His food is beef and 'damper'... In his 'run' the stockman is king: his cattle are his subjects; his saddle is his throne; his sceptre is the stock-whip. **1853** J. ROCHFORT *Adventures of Surveyor in N.Z.* iv. 42 If the natives had not lent her [*sc.* the mare] to me he would have gone over and stock-whipped them. **1901** M. FRANKLIN *My Brilliant Career* i. 4 Father came to my rescue, despatching the reptile with his stock-whip. **1936** *shaw's Railway Man* XXI. 428 *Expended...* Union stock whip and blanket, And bury me deep. **1955** J. CLEARY *Justin Bayard* viii. 111 He tried to hit me, and old Thaddeus stockwhipped him. **1958** R. STOW *To Islands* i. 17 What's the use of holding it against Mr. Heriot that he used to be a handy man with a stockwhip? **1869** *Bradshaw's Railway Man* XXI. 428 *Expended...* Union stock yards Chicago.. §100,000. **1911** C. E. W. BEAN *'Dreadnought' of Darling* xv. 145 The wind..piled it uselessly over every fence and stockyard. **1929** K. S. PRICHARD *Coonardoo* iv. 51 They wandered from the stock-yards to the shade-miah. **1958** L. DURRELL *Mountolive* viii. 162 The mauve-veiled evening voices of Alexandrians uttering stockyard quotations. **1963** *Times* 16 Jan. 6/6 Born in the stockyards district (where he still lives) and where as a 'stockyards cowboy' he once herded cattle from pen to pen. **1978** D. GREIG *Daisy* v. 54 In Chicago we stayed at the Hotel on Lake Michigan, near the famous Stockyards where, as they used to say, the unfortunate animals went in whole at one end and came out the other processed into fifty different products.

b. *stock carp.*

1785 J. WOODFORDE *Diary* 20 Oct. (1926) II. 211 Mr. Townshend..sent me 20 brace and ½ of stock Carp.

65. stock book (earlier examples); also *spec.* a book in which a record is kept of the animals which make up the stock of a farm; **stock-boy,** (*a*) *Austral.*, an Aboriginal employed to look after cattle or other stock; (*b*) *U.S.*, a boy employed by a business firm to look after stock; **stock-building** = *STOCK PILING *vbl. sb.*; **stock control** (see quot. 1943); **stock cube,** a cube of concentrated, dehydrated meat stock sold for use in making soups, stews, etc.; **stock culture,** an uncontaminated culture of a micro-organism maintained continuously and available as a source of experimental material; **stock knife,** (*a*) delete †, add later examples, and substitute for def.: a knife for cutting wood, *esp.* one used by a clogger for shaping the soles of clogs; (*c*) a stockman's knife; **stock-pot** (earlier and later examples); **stock rail** *Railways*, each of the outer fixed rails at a set of points.

1835 J. F. COOPER *Monikins* I. ii. 32 Love was a sentiment much too pure and elevated for one whose imagination dwelt habitually on the beauties of the stock-books. **1847** A. HARRIS *Settlers & Convicts* xiii. 260 Outside the yard..is..set a table with the stock book, pens, and ink, and in that the cattle are registered. **1882** W. D. HAY *Brighter Britain!* I. viii. 202 We keep a stock-book, in which every beast is entered. **1937** E. HILL *Great Austral. Loneliness* xli. 305 In Kimberley and the Territory lubras are even to-day recognised as the best 'stock-boys'. **1955** J. CLEARY *Justin Bayard* iv. 58 The stockboys had roped the piebald now and thrown a saddle on him. **1972** R. MILNER in W. King *Black Short Story Anthol.* 376 This receptionist thought I had come about a stock-boy job, you dig. **1979** D. ANTHONY *Long Hard Cure* x. 86 He owns a chain of department stores..one of those self-made men, who went to work at fourteen as a stockboy. **1967** A. BATTERSBY *Network Analysis* (ed. 2) xiii. 221 They will be high during the first few months because of retail stock-building. **1977** *Financial Results of Oil Majors 1976* (Shell Internat. Petroleum Co.) 8 The increase in demand, combined with some stock-building at the end of the year in anticipation of a significant rise in oil prices, raised oil production outside the USSR, Eastern Europe and China to 47 million barrels daily in 1976. **1943** *Princ. Production Control* (*B.S.I.*) 7 *Stock control*, the means by which the correct quantity and quality of material and components are made available according to the production plan, and excessive stocks avoided. **1962** A. BATTERSBY *Guide to Stock Control* v. 48 The calculations can conveniently be summarized on the Stock Control Form..and a specimen set of figures is shown. **1976** J. LUND *Ultimate* iii. 29 They talked..on the economics of warehousing and stock control. **1965** *Listener* 26 Aug. 317/2 Add enough water to almost cover the meat, and the stock cubes. **1979** *Times* 29 Sept. 15/5 Do you keep a stockpot..and boil it daily?..Cookery books..have a sneaky way of implying that stock cubes will never do. **1903** *Jrnl. Hygiene* III. 2 Gelatin plates were then made from the broth culture; if only a single species developed, agar tube-cultures were prepared and used as the stock-cultures of the organism. **1979** *Jrnl. Appl. Bacteriol.* XLVII. 381 The maintenance of stock cultures of lactic acid bacteria in small microbiological laboratories may present a technical problem. **1955** R. P. HOBSON *Nothing too Good for Cowboy* i. 16 He cut the moosehide wrapping with his stock knife. **1968** J. ARNOLD *Shell Bk. Country Crafts* 105 The shaping of clogs from these clefts is done with a stock knife... It consists of a stout blade with a long projecting handle. **1978** *Lancashire Life* Apr. 49/2 The tools a sole-cutter used were three in number—stock-knife, hollower and gripper. **1845** E. ACTON *Mod. Cookery* i. 3 Never..set the soup by in it, but strain it off..and fill the stock-pot immediately with water. **1917** *Harrods Gen. Catal.* 964/1 Extra heavy bellied Stockpot, enamelled Pearl Grey outside and in. **1928** 'O. DOUGLAS' *Eliza for Common* x. 128 Some quite dull books read like that—as if the author had simply thrown everything in, a sort of stock-pot of a book. **1931** R. CAMPBELL *Georgiad* i. 18 His melancholy recipes for 'happiness'.. How to 'rechauffe' the stock-pot of desire. **1960** E. DAVID *French Provincial Cooking* 158 The pot.. is usually a tall straight-sided or slightly bulbous stock-pot made of earthenware, copper, enamelled iron, or heavy aluminium. **1982** *Daily Tel.* 14 Jan. 15/5 Put.. chine bone into stockpot, cover with water,..and simmer. **1850** *Civil Engin. & Archit. Jrnl.* XIII. 270/1 The top of the switch not being mitred into the underside of the bearing surface of the stock rail, it is not liable to be locked by the barbing over of the stock from the pressure of the wheels. **1890** W. H. COLE *Notes on Permanent-Way Material* i. 20 The points or switches are..so adjusted to their respective stock-rails that when one switch is pressed against its stock-rail the other is drawn away, and thus one line of metals or the other is made continuous. **1935** E. BEAL *Railway Modelling in Miniature* ii. 36 Then solder the stock-rail for the other track.

B. *adj.* For '(in attributive use only)' read '(usu. in attributive use)'.

1. a. *stock model*; *stock-type* adj.; **stock shot** *Cinemat.* = *library shot* s.v. *LIBRARY[1] 3; **stock size** (later examples).

1926 *Daily Colonist* (Victoria, B.C.) 4 July 3/1 (Advt.), The car was a stock model in every respect except for a 48-gallon gasoline tank and changes in the top, back seat and tire carrier. **1941** B. SCHULBERG *What makes Sammy Run?* vi. 93 A shoe-string producer told him he had bought the stock shots from *Hell's Angels*. **1974** *Radio Times* 14 Mar. 11/4 Processed chases up and down stock-shot ski slopes. **1952** M. LASKI *Village* xix. 262 Margaret was lucky, she was stock-size, not like Wendy herself who had always had to have everything made for her. **1980** *Country Life* 3 July 78/2 Our model girl was stock size and everything was too big for her. **1958** *Spectator* 1 Aug. 170/1 A stock-type Vauxhall Velox.

2. *stock author, burlesque, comedy* (earlier example), *star*; **stock actor** (earlier example); also *stock actress*; **stock character,** a dramatic character representing a type in a conventional manner and recurring in many works; (cf. sense 3 a below); **stock piece** (earlier and later examples); **stock play** (earlier example).

1839 MARRYAT *Diary Amer.* 2nd Ser. II. xiii. 121 The American *stock* actors, as they term those who are not considered as *stars*. **1921** E. O'NEILL *Diff'rent* II. 243 She resembles some passé stock actress of fifty made up for a heroine of twenty. **1824** J. DECASTRO *Mem.* 154 T. Dibdin, esq., succeeded him..as the stock author of that theatre. **1864** 'P. PATERSON' *Glimpses of Real Life* xxv. 240 Jones keeps a stock author, and does not rely on outsiders. **1916** *Variety* 27 Oct. 12/1 Stock burlesque at the Lyric is moderately successful. **1864** H. MORLEY *Jrnl.* 16 Jan. (1866) 325 The *gracioso* was a popular addition made by Lope de Vega to the stock characters of a Spanish play. **1893** [see *CLOAK *sb.* 6]. **1976** *Country Life* 12 Feb. 346/1 In *Albert Herring*, Britten took stock characters—pompous mayor, stolid policeman,..overbearing lady of the manor. **1812** *Dramatic Censor 1811* 27/1 Among all the stock comedies which the Theatres are in the habit of representing, this is, in our idea, one of the very best. **1804** W. COOKE *Mem. C. Macklin* 408 It was always one of the stock pieces which he engaged himself to perform. **1843** *Ainsworth Mag.* IV. 135 His.. acting contributed greatly to the success of the drama, though it had not sufficient stamina to become 'a stock piece'. **1708** L. DOWNES *Roscius Anglicanus* 8 Note, That these being their Principal Old Stock Plays. **1856** A. C. RITCHIE *Mimic Life* I. ii. 44 As the 'stock star' of a popular theatre, in Boston, she had shone several years in the dramatic firmament.

3. a. Also with reference to fictional characters of a standardized or conventional type (cf. *stock character*, sense 2 above); also *transf.*

1940 W. S. MAUGHAM *Books & You* p. xii, The characters..are not very interesting, and most of them are the stock figures of Victorian fiction. **1951** M. MCLUHAN *Mech. Bride* (1967) 118/2 The 'good girl' is the nineteenth-century stock model which has long been merged with the mother image. **1960** [see *EXURBANITE *a.*]. **1963** [see *CLICHÉ 3]. *a* **1963** L. MACNEICE *Astrol.* (1964) vi. 200 Catering for stock-type 'individuals' (all humanity being divided into 12 groups). **1980** J. GARDNER *Garden of Weapons* II. vii. 185 A man full of bounce, like the stock uncle known to all large families.

b. Special collocations: **stock bowler** *Cricket*, a reliable but unspectacular bowler; hence **stock bowling**; **stock response,** an automatic and superficial reaction to a literary device (see quot. 1939); also *transf.* and *fig.*

1968 *Listener* 11 July 61/2 Connolly, in 1964 a strenuous but pedestrian fast bowler, has reduced his pace, developed swing and cut, and become an admirably steady stock-bowler. **1976** J. SNOW *Cricket Rebel* 37, I could no more be regarded as a stock bowler relying on line and length to keep the scoring in check. *Ibid.* 77 Only occasionally did he call upon me to do a stock bowling job with the intention of closing the game up. **1925** I. A. RICHARDS *Princ. Lit. Crit.* xxv. 203 Against these stock responses the artist's internal and external conflicts are fought, and with them the popular writer's triumphs are made. **1939** BROOKS & WARREN *Understanding Poetry* 639 *Stock response*, the general uncritical response made on conventional or habitual grounds to a situation, subject, phrase, or word in literature. Advertisers frequently attempt to appeal to stock responses. **1957** A. THWAITE *Home Truths* 40 Or will it seem Merely the self-duped mind's harangue at Death, The stock-response still raging in the shroud? **1961** K. TYNAN *Curtains* I. 8 The stock response of terror in the face of matricide has vanished. **1966** 'K. A. SADDLER' *Gilt Edge* ix. 128 'Well,' he said continuing, and just in time as I was running out of stock responses. **1975** *Times* 20 Sept. 6/3 If Agatha Christie works almost entirely with what the critics call 'stock responses', she knows..how to take advantage of our responding in a stock way to..stock situations.

4. In non-*attrib.* use.

1966 *Listener* 25 Aug. 288/3 The authors gave us sharply observed characters—stock, but none the worse for it. **1977** *Hot Car* Oct. 88/2 The diesel comes stock with a servo. **1979** *Jrnl. R. Soc. Arts* Nov. 776/2 The stereotypes are used in a relatively straightforward way, as stock as the London brick.

stock, *sb.*[4] Add: **b.** A discordant intrusion of igneous rock which has a roughly oval cross-section and steep sides, and is smaller than a batholith.

1898 *Jrnl. Geol.* VI. 706 It will be found advantageous to discriminate between bysmalith and stock by limiting the term stock to such bodies as occupy nearly vertical tubes or funnels of indefinite depth in rocks of any and all kinds..and which maintain such a relation to them as to appear to belong to the category of dikes. **1916** *Yukon Territory* (Canada Dept. Interior) iii. 35 Occasional pebbles derived from the various dikes and stocks outcropping along the valleys. **1944** [see *LACCOLITH]. **1955, 1957** [see *INTRUDE *v.* 5]. **1977** A. HALLAM *Planet Earth* 69/1 The upper surface [of a batholith] is generally irregular, with upwardly projecting stocks and dikes that may be the only surface clue to the much larger body at depth.

stockade, *sb.* Add: **2. c.** A prison, esp. a military one.

1865 *Atlantic Monthly* Mar. 286/2 'Is it a pen?'..'Yes, yours,' retorted one of the guard, with a grin,—'the Stockade Prison.' **1882** W. D. HAY *Brighter Britain!* I. 23 A man..on a subsequent conviction, might be sent to the Stockade (prison) without the option of a fine. **1905** [in Dict., sense 2 a]. **1906** *Daily Colonist* (Victoria, B.C.) 16 Jan. 2/5 [Two men] will be sent to the convict stockade on the islands in the tropics off the coast. **1945** *Richmond* (Va.) *News-Leader* 10 Oct. 8/1 'Stockade' in army language is synonymous with jail. **1979** P. GOSLING *Zero Trap* xix. 191 'What's a glasshouse?'..'A prison,' Skinner explained... 'The stockade,' Laura amplified. 'That's what they call it in the [U.S.] Army.'

stock-broker, stockbroker. Add: **b. stockbroker belt,** any prosperous residential area in the Home Counties favoured by stockbrokers or other affluent businessmen; also *transf.* of similar areas elsewhere; usu. with *the*; similarly **Stockbroker('s Tudor,** a facetious term for a style of mock-Tudor architecture supposed to be favoured by such people.

1960 [see *BELT *sb.*[1] 5 a]. **1961** *Spectator* 14 Apr. 523 They live in the Sussex stockbroker-belt. **1968** *Listener* 22 Aug. 248/2 A moderately successful novelist..bored with his stockbroker-belt home. **1976** J. I. M. STEWART *Young Pattullo* ii. 24 She had been brought up in a stockbroker belt in the Home Counties. **1981** M. JON *Wallington Case* iv. 24 It's a large house in..the stockbroker-belt, not far from Wilmslow. **1939** O. LANCASTER *Homes Sweet Homes* 70 (*heading*) Stockbrokers Tudor. **1940** GRAVES & HODGE *Long Week-End* xi. 180 In 'Stockbroker's Tudor' houses..ingenuity was displayed in olde-worlde disguise. **1958** J. CANNAN *And be a Villain* i. 6 Next best were these Stockbrokers' Tudor jobs built immediately before the first world war. **1959** *Good Food Guide* 98 Unlike Victorian Gothic, Stockbroker Tudor and suchlike varieties, this medieval mansion is perfect in every detail, except date. **1980** D. CLARK *Poacher's Bag* iv. 81 It had been an old inn. Now it had sprouted wings in stockbroker Tudor.

stockbrokerage (later examples).

1952 S. KAUFFMANN *Philanderer* (1953) ii. 26 It reminded her of her father (a minor officer of a stockbrokerage firm). **1972** *Publishers Weekly* 6 Mar. 24/1 Her husband..has his own stockbrokerage firm on Wall Street.

sto·ck-car. [f. STOCK *sb.*[1] + CAR *sb.*[1]] **1.** A truck or wagon for transporting cattle or other livestock by rail. *U.S.*

1858 *Pennsylvania Rail Road Ann. Rep.* 14 The rolling stock [included]..188 Eight-wheeled Stock Cars. **1875, 1898** [in Dict. s.v. STOCK *sb.*[1] 63 a]. **1920** *Proc. 3rd Nat. Country Life Conf.* 12 They shot me across the country in a stock car. **1949** *Exciting Western* May 55/1 Another group was bringing the cattle up the Texas trail to ship east in the stock cars.

2. A racing car which has the basic chassis of an ordinary commercially produced vehicle but is extensively modified for use in racing. orig. *U.S.*

1914 *Automobile* 9 Apr. 792/2 It was a more strenuous test than ever staged in America in the days of stock cars. **1927** *Sat. Even. Post* 21 May 71 America's fastest stock car. **1935** EYSTON & LYNDON *Motor Racing & Record Breaking* viii. 73 They have been rivalled by reconstructed 'stock' cars. **1960** *Daily Tel.* 26 Sept. 1/8 (*heading*) Stock car ploughs into 10-deep crowd. **1982** *Times* 16 June 10/3 Andretti raced cars, stock cars, midgets, whatever presented itself.

3. *attrib.*, as *stock-car driver, racer, racing,* etc.

1914 *Automobile* 9 Apr. 800/1 Chairman Richard Kennerdell and his Contest Board are at work on the stock car rules. **1955** *Times* 17 May 10/1 A woman stock car driver..died in a Coventry hospital to-night from injuries received in an accident while she was competing in a stock car meeting. **1960** *News Chron.* 26 Sept. 1/5 He organises stock-car and jalopy racing. **1969** A. LURIE *Real People* 114 Nick Donato proposed that we should all go and watch what he called 'my kind of racing'—at the stock-car track over in Dryden. **1973** 'D. JORDAN' *Nile Green* vi. 29 Ramshackle, blaring taxis, weaving round the squares with the recklessness of stock-car drivers. **1976** B. BOVA *Multiple Man* (1977) viii. 87 Become a stock car racer. It's a helluva lot safer. **1976** A. DAVIS *Television* 67 The programmes close with classified results..including American and Gaelic football, stock car racing, canoe slalom and hurling.

stocker. Add: **6.** A warehouseman or stockkeeper. Also (*U.S.*), an assistant engaged to look after stock held for sale by a business firm.

1921 *Dict. Occup. Terms* (1927) § 940 *Stock keeper, stocker*, a warehouseman..who keeps stock book showing amount of stock (as distinguished from stores). **1976** *Billings* (Montana) *Gaz.* 27 June 5-E/4 At age 14 or 15, cashiers, salesmen, stockers, baggers, gas pumpers, car washers,..can work. **1979** *Arizona Daily Star* 5 Aug. (Advt. Section) 5/10 Full time person to work in our yard as salesperson and stocker.

7. *U.S. colloq.* A stock-car; a stock-car racer.

1976 *Harper's Mag.* Jan. 20 You simply can't believe the noise of these engines. Stockers, motorcycles, needle-nosed dragsters..tear the night apart for hours. **1976** *Time* 27 Sept. 82/3 Stock cars... Richard Petty, king of the stockers, won $378,865 last year. **1978** *Time* 25 Sept. 88 Members of the National Association for Stock Car Auto Racing..rolled up to the 'diplomatic entrance' in their Day-Glo colored 'stockers'.

stock exchange. Add: **b.** *attrib.*

1849 J. FRANCIS *Chronicles & Characters Stock Exchange* xv. 288 It was proved that one million had been wasted in commissions and military preparations; in Stock Exchange transactions and Stock Exchange jobbing. **1877** R. GIFFEN (*title*) Stock Exchange securities. **1922** JOYCE *Ulysses* 521, I shall..suck my thumping good Stock Exchange cigar. **1940** T. S. ELIOT *East Coker* III. 11 The Stock Exchange Gazette, the Directory of Directors. **1957** *Encycl. Brit.* XXI. 420/1 After 1954 all members of the council (from 30 to 36 in number) were to be elected by stock exchange members generally.

stock-fish, stockfish. Add: **2.** [ad. Afrikaans, f. Du. *stokvis* stockfish, hake.] Also † **stok-fish.** The South African hake, *Merluccius capensis*, of the family Gadidæ, a large marine food fish. *S. Afr.*

1823 W. W. BIRD *State of Cape of Good Hope in 1822* viii. 159 The hottentot, jacob evert, elft, hake or stockfish, the king klipfish, the steen brazen, and the stompneus are all of excellent quality. **1853** L. PAPPE *Edible Fishes Cape of Good Hope* 31 The cured or dried Cape Stok-fish is an excellent dish. **1913** W. W. THOMPSON *Sea Fisheries Cape Colony* ii. 48 The larger fish, such as..steenbras, stockfish,..are caught with fish bait. **1930** [see *KINGKLIP]. **1947** K. H. BARNARD *Pict. Guide S. Afr. Fishes* iii. 83 The stockfish has become one of the mainstays of the South African fishing industry.

stockholding, *vbl. sb.* or *ppl. a.* Add: (Further examples.) Also, (of or pertaining to) the practice of holding material in stock.

1961 *Wall St. Jrnl.* 26 Apr. 3 Ralph Gish, manager of the funds' investment departments, said common stock holdings have been increased in these industries. **1962** A. BATTERSBY *Guide to Stock Control* ii. 18 If the cost of the material goes up, the amount of capital invested in stock also increases, and so does the stockholding cost. **1965** *Mod. Law Rev.* XXVIII. v. 555 Loss to other outlets of fast-selling titles..can have a devastating effect on stockholding booksellers. **1971** *Engineering* Apr. 123 (Advt.), This van is just one of many which provide a service from stock-holding depot to the customer... With 29 stock-holding depots strategically placed throughout the British Isles, you are assured personal service. **1981** *Times* 26 Jan. 15/2 A group of smaller stockholding concerns is said to have formed a consortium through which it can buy and distribute cheaper foreign produced steel. **1981** J. SUTHERLAND *Bestsellers* i. 18 The stockholding bookshop would be sacrificed to the bookstand in the supermarket.

Stockholm (stǫ·khōᵘm). The name of the capital city of Sweden, used *attrib.* in **Stockholm syndrome** (see quots.); **Stockholm tar,** a kind of tar prepared from resinous pinewood and used in shipbuilding, skin ointments, etc.

1978 *Practitioner* Feb. 297/1 Mr Vaders had a mild case of 'Stockholm syndrome'... Named after the dramatic and unexpected realignment of affections in the Sveriges Kreditbank robbery, this syndrome consists of a positive bond between hostage and captor, and feelings of distrust or hostility on the part of the victim towards the authorities. **1980** C. MOOREHEAD *Fortune's Hostages* ix. 183 The phrase 'Stockholm syndrome' was coined, probably in America, to explain this strange affection the victims of kidnappings and sieges come to feel for the men who hold them prisoner. **1867** *Chambers's Encycl.* IX. 296/1 The Stockholm tar, which is so widely used in shipbuilding. **1929** R. HUGHES *High Wind in Jamaica* ii. 50 He did envy the chap whose job it was to dip his hand in a great pot of aromatic Stockholm tar, and work it into the dead-eyes. **1976** *Country Life* 5 Feb. 298/3 Sailmaking..was very hard on the hand, and..open cracks in the skin, were a frequent source of trouble... For this 'Stockholm' tar was provided by the ship owners.

Stockholmer (stǫ·khōᵘməɹ). [f. prec. + -ER[1].] A native or inhabitant of Stockholm.

1938 *Daily Tel.* 22 Jan. 12/3 Modern Stockholmers..are accustomed to fairly substantial midday meals in restaurants. **1968** P. B. AUSTIN *On Being Swedish* iii. 21 To be *jäktad* (literally 'chased'), to be the victim of a mad whirl of engagements such as can only lead to stomach ulcers, is the contemporary Stockholmer's life-style. **1983** *Times* 30 June 13/4, I live in Stockholm and, like the vast majority of Stockholmers, buy a monthly card that gives me unlimited access to the underground and buses.

stocking, *sb.* Add: **7. a.** *stocking-heel* (earlier example).

1888 KIPLING *Story of Gadsbys* 1 (*stage direction*), Spreads stocking-heel on open hand for inspection.

c. *stocking knitter* (later example), *-maker* (later examples).

1921 *Dict. Occup. Terms* (1927) § 374 *Stocking knitter*,.. a frame hand..who attends a power-driven frame adjusted to knit elastic hosiery. **1779** in J. R. Anderson *Burgesses of Glasgow* (1935) 117 Wilson, Gabriel, stocking-maker. **1812** J. MELISH *Trav. in U.S.A.* II. 55 Professions exercised in Pittsburg:..stocking-makers, taylors, printers, book-binders.

d. stocking bar, a counter or bar in a shop at which stockings are sold; **stocking cap,** a knitted woollen hat with a long tapered end which hangs down from the crown; **stocking filler,** a small present suitable for putting in a Christmas stocking; also *fig.*; **stocking mask,** a thin nylon stocking pulled over the face to disguise the features, used esp. by criminals; hence **stocking-masked** *a.*; **stocking stuffer** *N. Amer.* = *stocking filler* above; **stocking tights** = *TIGHTS *sb. pl.* c; **stocking top** (later examples).

1962 *Guardian* 23 Feb. 8/3 The idea of a stocking bar came from America eight years ago. **1965** Stocking bar [see *BAR *sb.*[1] 28 b]. **1902** Stocking cap [in Dict., sense 7 b]. **1978** *Times* 4 Mar. 22/5 The fishermen still wear their shirts and trousers of Portuguese tartan and long black stocking caps. **1959** *Listener* 10 Dec. 1054/1 A useful stocking-filler at 2s. is a gardener's measuring beaker, graduated for almost all fertilizers, insecticides, etc. **1973** *Radio Times* 20–27 Dec. 3 How's this for a stocking-filler? *Radio Times* has a complete Christmas package for you. **1979** M. BABSON *Twelve Deaths of Christmas* xx. 109 Just tiny bits and pieces. Stocking fillers, small tokens. **1966** *Times* 16 May 10 Three men in stocking masks raided Martins Bank in South Audley Street. **1978** G. GREENE *Human Factor* I. ii. 25 He might object to a stocking mask all the same. **1971** *Daily Tel.* 24 Sept. 2/8 Six stocking-masked bandits..ambushed a lorry at Bethnal Green yesterday. **1977** N. ADAM *Triplehip Cracksman* xviii. 186 Corny stocking-masked villains. **1976** *Globe & Mail* (Toronto) 7 Dec. 24/7 Rockefellers don't stress paperbacks this time of year—the market for stocking stuffers is apparently limited. **1977** *Time* 17 Jan. 28/2 Around holiday season, stocking-stuffer items like *The Slipper and the Rose* usually show up, all covered in glitter and good will. **1967** *Economist* 5 Aug. 517/1 Manufacturers report orders..up by 23 per cent, mainly thanks to the invention of stocking tights..to go under mini skirts. **1977** J. WAINWRIGHT *Nest of Rats* I. i. 9 One leg of her stocking-tights badly torn. **1859** GEO. ELIOT *Adam Bede* III. vi. liii. 305, I can count a stocking-top [in knitting] while a man's getting 's tongue ready. **1935** N. MITCHISON *We have been Warned* I. ii. 19 To wear the sgian dhu in his stocking top, as he was allowed to with the kilt. **1978** R. H. LEWIS *Antiquarian Bks.* ii. 47 Nina Hamnet..remembered..for her disconcerting habit of keeping her money in her stocking tops.

stocking-foot. Add: **d.** The loose or pendent part of a stocking-cap. *rare*[−1].

1921 D. H. LAWRENCE *Sea & Sardinia* v. 161 The old boy brings his stocking-foot over the left ear.

Hence **stocking-footed, (-feeted)** *a.*, having stocking-feet; in stocking-feet.

1926 J. F. DOBIE *Rainbow in Morning* (1965) 99, I had a bay, white-faced, and stocking-footed horse called Buck. **1973** Stocking-feeted [see *leather-jacketed* s.v. *LEATHER *sb.* 5 d].

stock-in-trade. Add: **b.** Also *attrib.*

1931 L. H. MYERS *Prince Jali* ii. 26 The point was that his parents and the world each presented the other with something intelligible, they presented stock-in-trade figures between whom a stock-in-trade intercourse was possible. **1970** P. OLIVER *Savannah Syncopators* 100 These repertoires of traditional songs, stock-in-trade lines and phrases and sudden original words and verses. **1977** *Word 1972* XXVIII. 190 Bloomfield discussed such stock-in-trade instances as *adder* (for *nadder*), *newt* (for *eft*), and *apron* (for *napron*), to illustrate one type.

stockist (stǫ·kist). [f. STOCK *sb.*[1] + -IST.] One who stocks (certain) goods for sale.

1922 *Autocar* 10 Nov. 52 We are Stockists of High grade Cars. **1941** *Picture Post* 3 May 32/1 Write for style folder and name of nearest stockist to Swallow Raincoats Ltd. **1956** *People* 13 May 14/1 (Advt.), See the many other advantages at your local stockist. **1977** D. J. ELLIOTT in D. Marcus *Best Irish Short Stories* II. 150 Our range of Sheer Elegance shampoos and lipsticks. Ask for samples at our nearest stockists.

stock-jobber. b. (Examples.)

1833 *Niles' Reg.* XLIV. 570/1 The 'black-leg' in the gambling houses..more fairly takes the chances of the play, than the stock-jobber on 'change. **1911** H. S. HARRISON *Queed* 107 If a man became the greatest stock-jobber in the world, who would remember him after he was gone.

stock-keeping, *vbl. sb.* (Earlier example.)

1844 W. WAKEFIELD in *N.Z. Company Rep.* (1845) XVII. 139 The sport of hunting them [*sc.* deer]..would afford a manly amusement to the young Colonists, fitting them for the more serious occupations of stock keeping and wool growing.

stockman. Add: **1.** (Further Austral. examples.)

1862 R. HENNING *Let.* 2 Nov. (1966) 113 Mr Palmer was not at home, but we were received by an amiable stockman. **1911** C. E. W. BEAN *'Dreadnought' of Darling* xi. 100 The subordinate hands on the station—..the groom, stockman, rouseabouts—live in the men's huts, close behind the homestead. **1929** K. S. PRICHARD *Coonardoo* 5 Nowadays..aboriginal stockmen usually receive a small wage as well as payment in kind by rations. **1944** *Living off Land* iv. 94 Before the sun rises..the stockman's 'boys' are back with the horses. **1962** A. UPFIELD *Will of Tribe* iii. 27 'You have two white stockmen.'..'Just the two,' replied the cattleman. **1978** O.

White *Silent Reach* xviii. 191 'Where are the stockmen?' ..'Out looking for the Dalziel girl.'

Hence **sto·ckmanship,** the art of raising or looking after livestock.

1959 *Farmer & Stockbreeder* 22 Dec. (Suppl.) 7/2 As science develops...the art of good farming will remain—the art of knowing when and how to work the soil, the art of stockmanship. **1969** J. G. S. & F. Donaldson *Farming in Britain Today* II. xviii. 170 Efficient planning of the battery can almost eliminate the need for skilled stockmanship. **1979** *Daily Tel.* 1 May 11/2 Stockmanship, record-keeping, observation, simple disease control..will be the necessary tools of his [*sc.* the pigman's] trade.

stock-market. Add: **1. c.** *attrib.*

1930 W. C. Brooks *How Stock Market Really Works* viii. 121 There followed closely upon the Hatry crash the break of the stock market boom in New York. **1951** M. McLuhan *Mech. Bride* (1967) 7 Speed of communication and movement makes possible at the same time such diverse facts as stock-market operations, international armies, [etc.]. **1964** —— *Understanding Media* xxi. 207 The classified ads (and stock-market quotations) are the bedrock of the press. **1977** *Listener* 17 Apr. 204/1 The great stock market crash of 1929.

stock out. *Business.* [f. Stock *sb.*[1] + Out *adv.*] An occurrence of being out of stock of an item wanted by customers.

1957 Clark & Gottfried *Dict. Business & Finance* 339/1 Stock-out. **1967** E. Duckworth in Wills & Yearsley *Handbk. Management Technol.* 107 Because delivery from the wholesaler was so short the consequences of any 'stock out' would not be serious. **1969** J. Argenti *Managem. Techniques* v. 26 Symptoms: frequent stock-outs or frequent disposals of surpluses. **1979** *Washington Post* 22 June A 12/3 Its allocation rules 'do not prevent long lines, stockouts, and early closings at retail outlets'.

stockpile (stǫ·kpəil), *sb.* orig. *U.S.* Also **stock-pile, stock pile.** [f. Stock *sb.*[1] + Pile *sb.*[3]] **1.** A pile of coal or ore accumulated at the surface after having been mined.

1872 *Trans. Amer. Soc. Civil Engineers* II. 30 This covers the cost from miners' hands to cars or stock pile. **1912** C. E. van Barneveld *Iron Mining in Minnesota* 140 For lighter stripping work and stock-pile loading, the 70-C Bucyrus is quite largely used. **1958** *Engineering* 7 Feb. 188/1 Limestone is fed into a swing hammer-mill either direct from tipping lorries or by bulldozing from a stock pile.

2. a. A reserve or store of goods or commodities, esp. one accumulated in anticipation of shortage or market fluctuation.

1942 *Sun* (Baltimore) 15 Jan. 1/2 The facilities of new car dealers will be used to store for a year or more an estimated 130,000 new passenger automobiles under a 'stock pile' plan. **1943** *Times* 15 Dec. 5/6 The complete success achieved was due to..the statesmanship of all nations represented, especially those with resources outside their occupied lands and therefore able to make stockpiles of supplies at the expense of other nations less fortunate. **1957** *Economist* 30 Nov. 791/1 In the postwar years the cartel has not been restrictive. Helped by stockpile buying of industrial diamonds and by a demand for gems as a hedge against inflation, its policy has been to hold prices down rather than force them up. **1958** *Manch. Guardian* 25 Feb. 16/6 No wool from the British stockpile is included in this week's catalogue. **1962** *Economist* 20 Jan. 249/3 The United States will not now authorise sales of stockpile tin below £965 a ton. **1970** *Listener* 23 July 107/3 Most European countries keep a 2 months' stockpile of oil by government command. **1972** D. Haston *In High Places* xii. 150 The supplies were flowing well through the icefall;..there was a great stockpile at Camp I.

b. *spec.* An accumulation of nuclear weapons.

1946 *Rep. Internat. Control Atomic Energy* (Dept. of State, Washington) III. i. 31 How can a strategic balance be maintained between nations so that stockpiles of fissionable materials will not become unduly large in one nation and small in another? **1947** *Nature* 11 Jan. 48/1 A.D.A. should take over..the right of ensuring that any dangerous products were consumed in [atomic] power plants and that no excessive stockpile be produced. **1955** [see *atomic *a.* 2 e]. **1957** *Times* 6 Nov. 9/6 Mr. Dulles said to-night that the United States was considering the problem of establishing stockpiles of nuclear weapons in Europe for N.A.T.O. forces' use in case of emergency. **1969** *Daily Tel.* 16 Sept. 22/7 The threat of nuclear war was increasing every day with the mounting nuclear stockpiles. **1976** *Survey* Summer–Autumn 193 The total explosive energy that could be released by the strategic stockpile is a measure frequently used to compare US and Soviet forces.

c. *fig.*

1945 J. Steinbeck *Cannery Row* xvii. 104 The sea rocks and the beaches were his stock pile. **1957** *Listener* 21 Nov. 826/1 Imperialist behaviour built stockpiles of national resentment. **1966** *Electronics* 31 Oct. 23 Stockpiles of good technical men in some of the aerospace companies. **1982** R. Ludlum *Parsifal Mosaic* viii. 111 What he learned—what he *thinks* he learned—has turned him into a stockpile of nitro.

sto·ckpile, *v.* orig. *U.S.* [f. the sb.] **1.** *trans. Mining.* To heap up (ore, coal, etc.) in piles at the surface.

1921 E. W. Davis *Magnetic Concentration of Iron* 136 It may be necessary to mine, crush, and roast perhaps three tons of ore, cob, fine grind, and concentrate two tons of ore, dewater and agglomerate one ton of ore, stockpile one-half ton of ore, and dispose of two tons of tailings. **1937** —— *Magnetic Roasting of Iron Ore* 3 The ore being treated is a coarse tailing product rejected from existing concentration plants. It is in ideal physical condition for this process and is of no value at the present time, altho it has been mined, crushed, and stock-piled.

2. a. To accumulate a stock of (something); *spec.* to build up a stock of (nuclear weapons). Also *absol.*

1943 *Sun* (Baltimore) 28 Apr. 7/4 The Government at last began to 'stockpile' 100 octane gasoline. **1947** *Ibid.* 1 Jan. 6/3 It can be assumed that similar weapons..are now being perfected and stock-piled for future use. **1957** *Times* 18 Nov. p. xxxii/1 Decisions to buy and stockpile or to hold off and release stocks are, no doubt, dictated by consumer demand. **1959** *Listener* 16 July 88/2 President De Gaulle's refusal to allow American nuclear warheads to be stockpiled on French territory. **1974** G. Markstein *Cooler* lxxvii. 254 She..had stock-piled the pills the medical officer gave her until she had collected a fatal dose. **1976** *Country Life* 11 Mar. 638/2 It looked as if inflation would mean ever-advancing prices so wine merchants..started to stockpile.

b. *fig.*

1959 *News Chron.* 9 July 4/5 To stockpile acting talent of splendid calibre. **1959** *Daily Tel.* 2 Sept. 16/1 Employers urged to 'stockpile' labour. **1966** [see *sack *v.*[1] 8 a]. **1975** *Language for Life* (Dept. Educ. & Sci.) xxiv. 347 Pre-service education is not a phase in which the intending teacher must stockpile resources for a lifetime.

Hence **sto·ckpiled** *ppl. a.*; **sto·ckpiler.**

1951 *Business Week* 24 Nov. 26 (*heading*) Stockpilers are dipping in now and then to keep both civilian and military industry going. **1972** *Sci. Amer.* Jan. 22/1 There could be uncertainties about the performance of stockpiled weapons. **1979** *Guardian* 23 May 15/1 Agonised consumers deciding whether to take the stock-piled bread out of the freezer and fill it up with petrol.

sto·ckpiling, *vbl. sb.* orig. *U.S.* [f. *stockpile *v.* + -ing[1].] **1.** The action of making a stockpile of goods, raw materials, or nuclear weapons.

1943 *Sun* (Baltimore) 20 July 9/4 Suspension of purchases of Australian wool for stockpiling. **1946** *Rep. Internat. Control Atomic Energy* (Dept. of State, Washington) II. v. 25 It is, furthermore, clear that the stockpiling of appreciable quantities of fissionable material suitably denatured, must precede the development of these safe power reactors. **1953** E. Hyams *Prophecy of Famine* 41 But to do so would upset our stock-piling and other contingency supplies. **1959** *Listener* 18 June 1066/2 France's refusal to allow stockpiling of American atomic weapons on French soil for the Nato fighter-bomber force.

2. *attrib.* and *Comb.*, as *stockpiling act, policy, programme, purchase, purpose.*

1946 *Times* 26 July 7/1 This week President Truman has signed the Strategic and Critical Materials Stockpiling Act. **1945** *Sun* (Baltimore) 30 Mar. 7-0/5 The committee will review the food procurement and stockpiling policies of war agencies. **1943** *Ibid.* 20 July 9/4 Officials of agencies concerned with the stockpiling program. **1944** *Times* 14 Feb. 7/1 Certainly it would hardly be wise to start a 'stockpiling' programme. **1949** *Times* 10 Sept. 5/7 The article provides safeguards against..injuring British interests in their commercial export as a result of stockpiling purchases. **1947** *Sun* (Baltimore) 20 Dec. 2/4 To facilitate the procurement of such raw materials by the United States for stockpiling purposes.

sto·ck-take, stocktake, *sb.* [f. the vb.] An instance of stock-taking.

1972 J. Brown *Chancer* (1974) xii. 139 Three bad stock-takes and you're out. First stock-take I had it wasn't bad... The next big stock-take, the area manager, he came down. **1973** *Daily Tel.* 13 Apr. 18 The introductory work of stocktaking and separating VAT stock took two hours above that required by an efficient business for a normal necessary periodical stocktake. **1979** *Ibid.* 29 June 3/1 The committee decided to lock the door to ensure the 'privacy' of the club bars and stock after a stock-take before handing over to a new steward.

stock-work. (Earlier and later examples.)

1808 R. Jameson *Syst. Mineral.* III. xi. 255 A Stockwerk, is a mountain-mass of greater or less extent, traversed in all directions by a very great number of small veins. **1957** *Mineral. Mag.* XXXI. 588 In these the tin ores occur as stockworks of topaz-bearing greisen.

stød (stǭd). *Linguistics.* [Da., lit. 'push, jolt'.] A glottal stop or catch (see quot. 1973).

1954 Pei & Gaynor *Dict. Linguistics* 204 *Stød*, the Danish term for *glottal stop*.., often used by phoneticians for other languages, too. **1964** J. C. Catford in D. Abercrombie et al. *Daniel Jones* 36 *Voiced creak* may be one form of the 'stød' in Danish. **1973** J. D. O'Connor *Phonetics* vii. 237 Danish has the same stress system as English with the addition that each stressed syllable may or may not have the 'stød' or glottal stop added to it (in fact, it is rarely a complete stop but rather a short period of creaky voice). **1977** C. F. & F. M. Voegelin *Classification & Index World's Lang.* 140 Subdialectal division into Northern and Southern on the basis of the so-called 'stød' feature, usually a 'glottal creak' in Southern corresponding to pitch-stress phenomena in Northern Danish. **1980** *Amer. Speech* LV. 61 The Danish words that have the glottal catch or stød are generally those with accent 1 elsewhere in Scandinavia.

stodge, *sb.* Add: **1. b.** Also *spec.* heavy and usu. fattening food (often with little nutritional value). *colloq.*

1963 R. I. McDavid *Mencken's Amer. Lang.* 296 *Pudding* implies what we normally call *stodge.* **1963** *Times* 13 Feb. 5/2 If the prisoner could not tolerate all the 'stodge' he became undernourished. **1976** *Milton Keynes Express* 25 June 4/5 Remember that no exercise programme will work if not backed by sensible eating patterns and cut out stodge from today. **1980** *Times* 28 Nov. 3/2 The writers complain of surviving on stodge like potatoes and rice.

2. b. (Earlier example.)

1903 Farmer & Henley *Slang* VI. 373/2 *Stodge*,..a heavy meal.

c. Food of any kind. *slang.*

1890 Barrère & Leland *Dict. Slang* II. 307/2 *Stodge*,.. (popular and thieves), food. **1917** 'Taffrail' *Sub* ii. 72 Cream, jam, mineral waters and all other sorts of 'stodge'. **1929** F. C. Bowen *Sea Slang* 133 *Stodge*, food, generally used in the gunroom only. **1940** M. Marples *Public School Slang* 167 *Stodge* (Rugby),.. = food—e.g. 'I've got a box of stodge.'

4. A hard effort; an unfulfilling occupation.

1846 J. C. Patteson *Let.* in C. M. Yonge *Life J. C. Patteson* (1874) I. iii. 58 Reading books for the second or third time is light work compared to the first stodge at them. **1873** C. M. Yonge *Pillars of House* II. xxiv. 34 To let him go on here in the stodge is a bit of short-sightedness I can't understand.

5. = *stodger.

1922 E. V. Lucas *Genevra's Money* xxiii. 152 How silly of us to think he was going to be a stodge.

stodge, *v.* Add: **4.** (Examples.)

1912 F. M. Hueffer *Panel* I. iii. 93, I tell you, I'm tired! Used up! I must have comfort, quiet! I can't stodge away any more. *Ibid.* 98, I plodded and stodged for just that, and nothing else. **1928** —— *Last Post* II. iii. 259 They ought no longer to go stodging along in penury. **1939** D. Jones *Let.* 17 Jan. in R. Hague *Dai Greatcoat* (1980) ii. 89 Writing is odder than painting... One seems to stodge on and scratch out for hours and days and then sometimes..something breaks through. **1959** *Listener* 29 Oct. 748/2 Poor Dr. Bronowski seems fated to the *pas seul*... His fellows stodge around, looking severe and sagacious and sound and sensible.

5. To walk or trudge through mud or slush; to walk with short heavy steps. Occas. *trans.*, to trudge through (mud). *dial.* or *colloq.*

1854 A. E. Baker *Northampt. Gloss.* II. 306 *Studging*, walking with short heavy steps; always used with the adjunct along. 'He goes *studging* along.' **1902** *Aberdeen Weekly Free Press* 7 June 3/6 A polissman wha was comin' stodgin' doon the street. **1920** W. Deeping *Second Youth* xxiii. 195 The 'Old Man' and his orderly stodged back again up a waterlogged communication trench. **1929** —— *Roper's Row* viii. 83 She had seen the feet of cattle stodging the mire in Melfont. *Ibid.* xiii. 138 A very stout woman..stodged round the grave after the service was over.

stodger (stǫ·dʒəɪ). *colloq.* [f. Stodg(y *a.* + -er[1].] A stodgy person; one who is lacking in spirit or liveliness. Hence **sto·dgery,** behaviour characteristic of such a person.

1905 *Punch* 25 Jan. 62/1 The other regular old stodgers who go to all the parties within a radius of six miles. **1907** *Punch* 9 Jan. 20/2 Well, father's quite right, they are the most awful stodgers. You know they are. **1920** W. Deeping *Second Youth* iv. 31 If you were starving, Miles, I suppose you would walk down Oxford Street and say nothing. What stodgery! We middle-class people are hopeless!

stodgy, *a.* Add: **2. a, b.** (Earlier and later examples.) Also applied to other objects, activities, etc.

1874 L. Troubridge *Life amongst Troubridges* (1966) 89 We had meant to play Rats and Ferrets, but we had to begin a stodgy game of Old Maid. **1885** C. M. Yonge *Nuttie's Father* I. x. 111 One of the stodgey [*sic*] old clergymen in books. **1976** J. I. M. Stewart *Memorial Service* ii. 24 The stodgy lime-streaked effigy of Provost Harbage..is really more congruous with the spirit of the place. **1977** *National Observer* (U.S.) 1 Jan. 5/4 It was a stodgy old company when he came to it as president of the international division. **1977** *Time* 31 Jan. 13/2 Leidigkeit, 38, has brought scandal and notoriety to Bonn's Ermekeil Strasse, formerly a quiet, slightly stodgy row of shops, middle-class town houses and student flats.

d. Applied *loosely* to music, its performance, interpretation, etc.

1934 C. Lambert *Music Ho!* v. 294 The stodgy and academic imagination of *Verklarte Nacht.* **1959** *Times* 12 Jan. 12/3 It was surprising that Miss Puppulo was so stodgy in some early miniatures at the start of the programme. **1974** *Early Music* Apr. 81 It is so easy..for four viols to be too stodgy. **1978** R. Donington in J. M. Thomson *Future of Early Music in Britain* 14 The dodge.. is to get that massive resonance without sounding in the least thick and opaque and stodgy and Straussian.

stoep. Delete || and add: Also † **stoop** (cf. Stoop *sb.*[3]). **a.** (Earlier and later examples.)

1797 A. Barnard *Let.* 10 July in *S.Afr. a Century Ago* (1901) 57 As for the young Dutchmen, I saw hardly any; the young ones prefer smoking their pipes on the *stoep.* **1798** —— *Jrnl.* 21 May in *Lives of Lindsays* (1849) III. 457 Their *stoop* was covered with a set of large idle boors in their blue jackets, sons of the family—men who do hardly anything beside eating and smoking. **1804** J. Barrow *Trav. Interior S. Afr.* II. ii. 104 He..parades the *stoop*, or raised platform before the door. **1805** *Gleanings in Afr.* ii. 17 A stone terrace, extending the whole length of the house, and elevated a few feet above the level of the street, is the grand promenade of the family; this is called the *Stoop.* **1939** tr. *E. N. Marais's My Friends the Baboons* ix. 101 We could follow the whole tragedy step by step from the stoep of Mr. van Heerden's house. **1966** E. Palmer *Plains of Camdeboo* ii. 26 A wide stoep running round three sides in the manner of Karoo houses. **1980** *Listener* 17 July 66/3 A farmer's wife in Natal..sitting..on the stoep.

b. *stoep lantern, plant*; **stoepsitter,** one who habitually sits idly on the stoep of his house.

1971 *Het Suid Western* 14 May 9 Wrought iron porch or stoep lanterns, wired in new condition—R5 each. **1961** *Argosy* Mar. 20 She attended to her stoep plants. **1934** C. R. Swart *Africanderisms* (typescript), *Stoepsitters*,..a sluggard or lazy person; sometimes humorously applied by townsmen to farmers, who used to spend much of their time on the stoep, drinking their favourite beverage, coffee. **1948** O. Walker *Kaffirs are Lively* 92 They don't work. They're stoep-sitters, coffee-tipplers and pipe-spitters. **1972** *Sunday Times* 24 Sept. 19 Topical remarks, especially by the three 'stoepsitters', are made through the play.

stog, *v.*[2] Add: **1.** Also *fig.*

1928 J. Y. T. Greig *Breaking Priscian's Head* 60 Old pedantic grammarians stogged to the neck in Latin, have done their work too well.

stogy, *a.* and *sb.* Add: Now freq. *stogie.* **A.** *adj.* **b.** (Examples.)

1903 Farmer & Henley *Slang* VI. 373/2 *Stogy-cigar*, a rough coarse cigar. **1930** J. Omwake *Conestoga Six-Horse Bell Teams* 118 The Conestoga wagon gives its name to the Stogie cigar, a great thin coarse one, supposed to have been originally a foot long and made for the delectation of the wagoner.

B. *sb.* **b.** (Earlier and later examples.)

1873 J. O'Connor *Wanderings of Vagabond* 52 After the lunch liquors and cigars (red-eye and stogies), the best the place afforded, were introduced by the host. **1916** C. Sandburg *Chicago Poems* 47 He lighted a three-for-a-nickel stogie. **1930** J. Dos Passos *42nd Parallel* 19 He was smoking a thin black stogy of a sort Fainy had never seen before. **1957** V. Packard *Hidden Persuaders* ix. 103 The man who puffs on his cigar is sucking his thumb while the man who chews vigorously on his stogie is a nail biter.

Stoic, *a.* Add: **3.** *Comb.*, as *Stoic-Christian, -Epicurean, -Megaric* adjs.

1933 A. N. Whitehead *Adventures of Ideas* iii. 43 These doctrines have all weakened the Stoic-Christian ideal of democratic brotherhood. **1948** L. Spitzer *Linguistics & Lit. Hist.* 15 *Pantagruélisme*, the name given by Rabelais to his stoic-epicurean philosophy. **1966** *Philos. Rev.* LXXV. 246 Rescher takes these..as evidence that Arabic logic was directly influenced by the Stoic-Megaric tradition.

stoicheiometry. Add: Now usu. thus (in the U.K.) or as **stoichio-**. In mod. use, the quantitative relationship between the substances in a reaction or compound. (Further examples.)

1971 W. F. Pickering *Mod. Analytical Chem.* iv. 153 It can also be used to determine the stoichiometry of reactions occurring in solution. **1975** R. F. Brown *Organic Chem.* viii. 192 Stoichiometry, the weight relations in chemical reactions, must be kept in mind in the study of rates of reaction.

stoichiometric *a.* (further examples).

1921 *Jrnl. Geol.* XXIX. 533 The stoechiometric relation between MgO and FeO in olivine and bronzite. **1962** J. H. White *Inorganic Chem.* ix. 108 The formation of solid solution does not appear to be very different [from that of metallic compounds] except that..no stoichiometric relationship between the constituent metals exists. **1965** Phillips & Williams *Inorganic Chem.* I. viii. 296 Metal fluorides but not hydrides are stoicheiometric.

stoicize, *v.* (Earlier example.)

1718 C. Hayes tr. *Addison's Dissertation upon Roman Poets* 42 Pompey..ought to have been very much stoiciz'd indeed, who, despoil'd of all the Goods of Fortune, could place the Sum of his Felicity in meer naked Virtue.

Stoico- (stōᵘ·iko), combining form of L. *stōicus* or Gr. *στωϊκός* Stoic, as in *Stoico-Platonic, -sybaritical* adjs.

1979 M. A. Screech *Rabelais* iii. 38 The inerrant Stoico-Platonic Christian sage. **1822** M. Edgeworth *Let.* 12 June (1971) 406 He and Harriet and Fanny too declare it is too much trouble to hold a parasol. I believe you too are of the same *Stoico-sybaritical* sect so I will waive the subject.

Štokavian (ʃtǫkā·viǎn), *sb.* (and *a.*). Also **Shtokavian, Stokavian, stokavian.** [f. Serbo-Croat *štokavščina* (*štokavski* adj.): see -ian.] A widely spoken dialect of Serbo-Croat on which the literary language is based. Also *attrib.* or as *adj.*

[**1911** *Encycl. Brit.* XXIV. 695/2 Servian is sometimes called *shtokavski* because the Servian word for 'what' is *shto*, whereas the Croats say *cha* for *shto*, and therefore their language is called *chakavski*.] **1925** P. Radin tr. *Vendryès's Lang.* 291 In Italy, in the province of Campobasso, there is a Serbo-Croatian colony..which..speaks a dialect of the Stokavian type. **1939** L. H. Gray *Foundation of Lang.* 355 *Serbo-Croatian*, with three dialects conventionally named according to the way in which they form the word for 'what': *Štokavian* (the basis of the literary language), *Čakavian*, and *Kaykavian*. **1949** R. Jakobson *Slavic Languages* 4 Serbocroatian from East to West presents three basic groups: Štokavian, Čakavian and Kajkavian. **1964** M. Partridge *Serbo-Croatian* 13 Three distinct basic dialects exist in spoken Serbo-Croatian. They are referred to as *čakavian, kajkavian* and *štokavian* according to whether the word 'ča?', 'kaj?' or 'što?' is used respectively as the interrogative pronoun meaning *what*? **1974** *Encycl. Brit. Macropædia* XVI. 867/1 The literary Serbo-Croatian language was formed in the first half of the 19th century on the basis of the Shtokavian dialects that extend over the greater part of the Serbo-Croatian territory in Yugoslavia. **1976** *Language* LII. 375 The dat. sg. + *i* here..represents a morphological change rather than a phonological difference between kajkavian and štokavian. **1977** *Archivum Linguisticum* VIII. 91 In štokavian Serbo-Croat (on which the standard language is based), the rising accent is a disyllabic one.

stoke(s (stōᵘk(s)), *sb.*[4] *Physics.* [f. *Stokes[1]. Proposed in Ger. by M. Jakob 1928, in *Zeitschr. f. techn. Physik* IX. 22/1.] The unit of kinematic viscosity in the C.G.S. system, equal to 1 cm.^{2} sec.$^{-1}$

1931 G. Barr *Monogr. Viscometry* i. 4 Jacob [*sic*] has proposed that the C.G.S. unit be called the 'stokes', but the suggestion has not yet had time to bear fruit. **1934** [see *centistoke(s)]. **1961** V. L. Streeter *Handbk. Fluid Dynamics* 1. 14 The unit of one square centimeter per second is called a stoke. The centistoke (= 0·01 stoke) is often a more convenient unit. **1964** Sabersky & Acosta *Fluid Flow* i. 10 In the c.g.s. system,..the unit of absolute viscosity..is called a poise, and the unit of kinematic viscosity, 1 cm.^{2}/sec., is called a stoke.

stoke, *v.*[2] Add: **1. a.** Also, to feed or build up (a fire).

1942 E. Langley *Pea-Pickers* x. 148 The hut was warmed by a little red fire which the fair-haired comrade stoked. **1971** G. Jones in Jones & Elis *Twenty-Five Welsh Short Stories* 106 That night, when he went into the house, he saw that the big iron double bed had been moved down into the middle of the kitchen and a great furnace of a fire stoked up in the chimney.

c. To excite, thrill, elate. *slang* (chiefly *Surfing*).

1963 *Pix* 28 Sept. 63 A good stomping movement that 'stokes' the tourists is worth two extra points. **1965** *S. Afr. Surfer* I. 3/3 Your magazine stoked me out of my mind. *Ibid.* 7/1 We will let him stoke you on some of the modern variations of body riding.

2. Also *absol.* with *up.*

1901 'R. Andom' *Troddles & Us & Others* iv. 47 Troddles stoked-up on bread-and-butter pudding to such an extent that I wondered how on earth he could..drag himself about. **1946** R. Lehmann *Gipsy's Baby* 29, I have often noticed how much less greedy children of the proletariat are than others. One would imagine that they would be more absorbed in the problem of stoking up. **1975** J. Symons *Three Pipe Problem* xvi. 155 They sat in one of the high-backed compartments where the punters came to stoke up after their losses.

3. stoke-up *slang*, a large or sustaining meal.

1955 J. Thomas *No Banners* xv. 133 Later..it would be possible to go to the black-market eating-houses for an occasional 'stoke-up'.

stoked *ppl. a.* (later examples in sense *1 c of the vb.); also, keen or 'hooked' *on. slang.*

1963 [see *board *sb.* 1 b]. **1968** *Surfer Mag.* Jan. 47/3, I realized they're really stoked. **1969** *Sunday Mail* (Brisbane) 2 Feb. 20/3 I'm stoked on Chinese food. **1970** *Studies in English* (Univ. Cape Town) I. 33 People bitten by the *surf bug*..are really *stoked* on surfing. **1976** *N.Y. Times Mag.* 12 Sept. 40/1 Something like 10 million Americans..are stoked on floating about three inches over the paved surfaces of planet earth. Their flotation device is the new, Nasworthy-improved skateboard. **1977** *Skateboard Special* Sept. 2/1 The guy was really stoked but he fell off a nose wheelie and ended up taking a trip to McDonalds.

Stokes[1] (stōᵘks). *Physics.* The name of Sir George *Stokes* (1819–1903), Irish-born physicist and mathematician, used in the possessive and *attrib.* to designate concepts and phenomena discovered by him or arising out of his work: **a.** *Stokes' theorem*: the theorem that the line integral of a vector function round a closed path is equal to the surface integral of the curl of the function over any surface bounded by the path.

1893 J. J. Thomson *Notes Recent Res. Electr. & Magnetism* i. 10 Now by Stokes' theorem $\int (Xdx + Ydy + Zdz)$ taken round a closed circuit is equal to [etc.]. **1940** E. T. Bell *Development Math.* xviii. 364 Stokes' theorem, its proof, and its generalizations have developed into a thriving industry of modern analysis. **1975** R. L. Ferrari *Introd. Electromagnetic Fields* vi. 109 We have postulated Maxwell's equations in their integral form... Using the vector calculus rule, Stokes' theorem, these can be transformed into differential relationships required to hold everywhere in space.

b. *Stokes' law*: the statement (not always true) that in fluorescence the wavelength of the emitted radiation is longer than that of the radiation causing it. Also *Stokes' line, shift*, etc., with reference to spectral emission lines at a lower frequency than the stimulating or incident radiation.

[**1902** *Encycl. Brit.* XXXII. 124/1 According to the experimental law of Stokes, the wave-lengths of the fluorescent radiation are longer than those of the radiation which excites it.] **1926** R. W. Lawson tr. *Hevsey & Paneth's Man. Radioactivity* v. 57 It is the same condition as that with which we meet in optics in connection with the occurrence of fluorescence according to Stokes' law. **1949** P. Pringsheim *Fluorescence & Phosphorescence* ii. 163 The fourth row of the same table shows..the distances of the first Stokes line from the exciting line. *Ibid.* vii. 556 Even if the absorption and emission correspond to the same electronic transition,..relatively large Stokes shifts have a great probability [in crystal phosphors]. **1973** *McGraw-Hill Yearbk. Sci. & Technol.* 307/1 Other consequences of the transient nature of the scattering are that the Raman-shifted (Stokes) pulse is both narrowed in time and delayed with respect to the exciting pulse. **1975** D. H. Burrin in Williams & Wilson *Biologist's Guide to Princ. & Techniques Pract. Biochem.* v. 146 The energy emitted from these molecules in regaining the ground state within a period of less than 10^{-8} s gives rise to a fluorescent peak, showing the Stokes' shift. **1978** P. W. Atkins *Physical Chem.* xvii. 562 (*caption*) Stokes and anti-Stokes rotational Raman lines.

c. *Stokes' law* (or *formula*): the statement that the resisting force on a spherical particle moving through a fluid is $6\pi\eta Vr$ (where η is the viscosity of the fluid, V the speed of the particle, and r its radius), so that its limiting rate of fall is $2gr^2\rho/9\eta$ (where g is the acceleration due to gravity and ρ the difference in density between the particle and the fluid).

1910 *Rep. Brit. Assoc. Adv. Sci. 1909* 407 To test Stokes's formula for air, the size, density, and terminal velocity of fall of some spherical spores were determined. **1936** *Discovery* Nov. 349/2 This period [of settlement of dust particles] is dependent on the application of Stokes' law, and hangs on particle size, density, etc. **1968** P. A. P. Moran *Introd. Probability Theory* ix. 431 Assume that the particle, besides being spherical, is large enough for Stokes law to give a good estimate of the resisting force. **1974** G. S. Ormsby in P. L. Moore et al. *Drilling Practices Manual* vi. 158 Since Stokes Law applies in a sand trap, large quantities of barites..may be settled from weighted drilling fluids. **1983** *Sci. Amer.* Apr. 128/2 Many of the grains in Middle Eastern coffee are too large to fall according to Stokes's law.

Stokes[2] (stōᵘks). The name of Sir Wilfrid *Stokes* (1860–1927), English engineer, used *attrib.* and *absol.* to designate a type of trench mortar invented by him.

1915 W. S. Churchill *Let.* 7 Sept. in M. Gilbert *Winston S. Churchill* (1972) III. Compan. ii. 1167 In the early part of June, Lloyd George and I were shown the Stokes gun in action. **1919** [see *Lewis[3]]. **1919** *Athenæum* 25 July 664/1 'Stokes', the name of the inventor of the T.M., has, by metonymy, come to mean the trench mortar gun itself (so 'Nissen' = hut; 'Armstrong' = hut). **1923** Kipling *Irish Guards in Great War* II. 146 Our own two-inch Stokes in the front line strove to cover the noise by separate rapid fire. **1930** G. B. Shaw *What I really wrote about War* (1931) 241 The thermit shower was produced by firing from Stokes guns a cloud of shells packed with it. **1974** A. Price *Other Paths to Glory* i. i. 16 Their dead hanging on the unbroken barbed wire among the dud shells and unexploded Stokes mortar bombs.

Stokes–Adams (stōᵘks,æ·dămz). *Med.* The names of William *Stokes* (1804–78) and Robert *Adams* (1791–1875), Irish physicians, who described the condition in 1846 (*Dublin Q. Jrnl. Med. Sci.* II. 73) and 1827 (*Dublin Hosp. Rep.* IV. 414) respectively, used *attrib.* to designate occasional transient cessation or extreme slowness of the pulse, esp. when caused by heart-block.

1903 R. H. Babcock *Dis. Heart* xxiv. 634 The diagnosis of Stokes-Adams disease presents difficulty when the paroxysms are characterized only by vertigo and increase of an already existing bradycardia. **1922** *Lancet* 13 May 933/2 In a woman of 49 with complete heart-block, who was under observation for seven days and nights, severe Stokes-Adams attacks were recurring almost every minute. **1947** Scherf & Boyd *Cardiovascular Dis.* xxii. 318/1 In this book the term Stokes-Adams attacks will embrace all types [of circulatory standstill] resulting from a change of cardiac activity irrespective of whether they are due to cardiac standstill or tachycardia... We deal with a syndrome and not a disease entity. **1974** *Ciba Symposium* New Ser. XX. 133 AV blocks of all kinds, from first-degree block to complete block, including the Stokes-Adams syndrome.

stokesite (stōᵘ·ksəit). *Min.* [f. *Stokes[1] + -ite[1].] A hydrated silicate of calcium and tin, $CaSnSi_3O_9.2H_2O$, found as colourless, transparent orthorhombic crystals.

1899 A. Hutchinson in *Phil. Mag.* XLVIII. 480 Among the specimens..recently acquired for the Cambridge Mineralogical Museum, has been found a crystal whose characters prove it to belong to a new mineral species. This mineral I propose to call Stokesite in honour of Sir George Gabriel Stokes, Bart., whose jubilee as Lucasian Professor was this year celebrated by the University. **1977** *Mineral. Mag.* XLI. 413 Stokesite in very small amounts has been reported at two localities in Czechoslovakia..while at Corrégo do Urucum, Brazil, it has been found..as spherical clusters of crystals up to 3 cm diameter.

Stokowskian (stǫkǫ·vskiǎn), *a.* and *sb.* [f. the name of Leopold *Stokowski* (1882–1977), English-born American conductor + -an.] **A.** *adj.* Of, pertaining to, or characteristic of Stokowski.

1961 *Times* 19 June 9/2 Inappropriate infusions of Stokowskian sensuousness marred..his interpretation of Orff's *Carmina Burana.* **1977** *Gramophone* Apr. 1556/2 The Stokowskian concentration and persuasiveness will be hard for anyone to resist. **1978** *Ibid.* Jan. 1263/3 The Schubert is by Stokowskian standards given an unmagical performance.

B. *sb.* An admirer of Stokowski.

1975 *Gramophone* Aug. 322/2 It is very much a performance for Elgarians as well as for the Stokowskians. **1978** *Ibid.* Jan. 1308/2 Still, Stokowskians will want this, although I am sure they will lament with me that CBS scheduled this record before the *Pastoral* Symphony, which Stokowski was due to record when he died.

stole, *ppl. a.* Add: (Later examples.) Now *colloq.*

1923 [see *HISN, HIS'N]. **1976** *Billings* (Montana) *Gaz.* 20 June 5-D/1 (Advt.), *Found* in Missoula: Male Great Dane Cross. Approx. 1½ yrs. old. Stole in Blgs. last Fall or Winter.

stolewise (stōᵘ·lwəiz), *adv.* [f. STOLE *sb.*[1] + WISE *sb.*[1]] Draped like a stole.

1922 JOYCE *Ulysses* 19 Buck Mulligan slung his towel stolewise round his neck.

Stolichnaya (stalī·tʃnaiă). [Russ., lit. 'of the capital, metropolitan'.] The proprietary name of a variety of Russian vodka.

1966 L. DEIGHTON *Billion-Dollar Brain* xi. 98 Stolichnaya..the only vodka I will drink. **1969** *Official Gaz.* (U.S. Patent Office) 25 Feb. TM 145 Stolichnaya. V/O Sojuzplodoimport. **1973** *Radio Times* 20 Dec. 110/4, 1 bottle Russian vodka (Nureyev recommends Stolichnaya). **1975** *Trade Marks Jrnl.* 4 June 1163 Stolichnaya Vodka. ..998,200. Vodka. Vsesojuznoje Objedinenie Sojuzplodoimport..32/34 Smolenskaja Square, Moscow, U.S.S.R.; Manufacturers and Merchants. —11th Sept. 1972. **1977** J. WAMBAUGH *Black Marble* (1978) i. 3 He.. stealthily withdrew the bottle of Stolichnaya from the pocket of his raincoat.

‖ **stolkjærre** (stu·lkyerə). Also **stolkjaerre.** [Norw. (Bokmål), f. *stol* seat, STOOL *sb.* + *kjærre* cart.] A two-wheeled cart with seats for two persons. Hence as *v. intr.*, to ride in such a cart.

1885 *One & a Half in Norway* 125 The court-yard of the station was quite busy with carrioles and stolkjærres. **1924** *Public Opinion* 9 May 454/2 The traveller in stolkjærre or automobile ascends to snow-mantled plateaux. **1932** *New Yorker* 9 Apr. 59/2 Yachting on the Trollfjord, stolkjærreing through the Naeroedal, automobiling in the Baltic Capitals.

‖ **Stollen** (ʃtǫ·lən). Also **stollen, Stolle.** [Ger.] A rich fruit loaf, often made with nuts added.

1906 E. OSWALD *German Cookery for English Kitchen* 200 Stolle... Prepare the yeast as in recipe 'Napfkuchen'. **1927** *Daily Express* 20 Dec. 5/3 Germany has a cake similar to the Polish Strutzel, called Stollen. The dough should be made in the same way with quarter pound each chopped mixed peel, melon, angelica, prunes, and raisins, ..for a filling, and the icing made with lemon juice. **1959** H. SLESAR *Grey Flannel Shroud* (1960) i. 15 Fine European baked goods, the stollen and strudel and delicate little kuchen. **1975** *Woman* 17 May 15/3 There are more than 200 types of bread made in Germany, like..Stollen, a famous dryish bread filled with glacé fruit, almonds, raisins and currants. **1977** [see *PFEFFERKUCHEN]. **1977** *Sunday Tel.* (Colour Suppl.) 5 June 13/2 Church remains an integral part of the day, the marzipan in the stollen bread.

stolon. Add: Hence **stolo·nial** *a.*, of or pertaining to stolons.

1911 [see *EPICARDIAC *a.*]. **1964** *Oceanogr. & Marine Biol.* II. 317 High salinities..caused..reduction of stolonial material and fusion of hydranths.

‖ **stolovaya** (stalōᵊ·vaiă). [Russ.] A canteen, a cafeteria.

1943 E. M. ALMEDINGEN *Frossia* ix. 329 It is dinner time. Come on, let us eat at the station *stolovaya.* **1976** 'S. HARVESTER' *Siberian Road* vii. 75 The swingdoors of the *stolovaya* shut behind the Russian. **1982** *Spectator* 27 Mar. 21/3 The food in a Russian *stolovaya* (or 'diner').

STOLport (stǫ·lpǭɪt). orig. *U.S.* Also **STOL-port, stolport,** etc. [f. *STOL* (see *S 4 a), after *AIRPORT.] An airport for aircraft which need only a short runway for take-off and landing.

1968 *N.Y. Times* 14 Jan. 1/1 A stolport would serve planes that make a 'short take-off and landing'. They use runways much shorter than those required by commercial jets. **1968** *Science News* 7 Sept. 230 (*caption*) Frenetic ground travel to and from New York's main airports may be replaced by STOL-ports along the Hudson river. **1975** *Sunday Sun* (Toronto) 12 Oct. 17/1 As the plan suggests, the airport and the STOLport would take over all of Toronto's air travel eventually. **1976** *Globe & Mail* (Toronto) 16 Feb. 5/5 Nordair [is] getting permanent access to the Toronto island Airport and the Victoria STOLport in Montreal. **1980** *Times* 3 June 19/5 The company has drawn up plans for a 2,000ft 'stolport' (short takeoff and landing airport) in the east Shetlands basin. **1982** *Times* 24 June 3/4 A group of companies is proposing to build a small airport, to bring a different kind of transport interchange to the docklands known as a Stolport (Stol stands for short-take-off-and-landing).

Stolypin (stalī·pin). [The name of Pyotr Arkadyevich *Stolypin* (1862–1911), Russian conservative statesman.] **1.** *Stolypin's necktie,* the noose. *colloq.*

1909 J. R. WARE *Passing Eng.* 234/2 *Stolypin's necktie* (*Europ. Politics, 1897*), the final halter. This term was brought into fashion in 1907 (Nov.–Dec.), at a Duma then recently assembled in St Petersburg. One Rodicheff, an extreme Radical, brought in the term on 30th November 1907. **1974** *Encycl. Brit. Micropædia* IX. 583/1 Stolypin ..instituted a network of courts-martial... Within the few months of their existence they used 'Stolypin's necktie' (the noose) to execute more than 1,000 defendants.

2. Used *attrib.* and *absol.* to designate a type of railway carriage made for the transport of prisoners.

1970 HARARI & HAYWARD tr. *Amalrik's Involuntary Journey to Siberia* xi. 127 This was a so-called 'Stolypin' car, specially constructed for the transport of prisoners... They are named after the Tsarist Prime Minister and Minister of the Interior who introduced them after the first Russian Revolution of 1905. **1974** T. P. WHITNEY tr. *Solzhenitsyn's Gulag Archipelago* I. II. i. 491 The prisoners got used to calling this kind of railroad car a *Stolypin* car, or, more simply, just a *Stolypin.*

stoma. Add: **3.** *Surg.* A permanent opening made into a hollow organ; *spec.* one made from outside the body. Freq. *attrib.*, as *stoma patient, therapy.*

1937 R. SCHINDLER *Gastroscopy* xiv. 269 In cases of gastric resection the stoma of resection is generally easily seen if the 85° instrument is used. **1943** H. L. BOCKUS *Gastro-Enterol.* I. xxxi. 633 The stoma which is too large allows food to enter the jejunum immediately after eating. **1952** *Jrnl. Amer. Med. Assoc.* 25 Oct. 812/2 A special clinic devoted to intestinal stomas of all types has been established recently at the hospital. **1977** *Lancet* 15 Oct. 806/1 How often in a lifetime does a patient with an ileostomy have to return to hospital or seek advice from the Ileostomy Association or a stoma therapist? **1978** *Jrnl. R. Soc. Med.* LXXI. 519 All of these patients have become well rehabilitated, helped particularly by the excellent stoma-therapy services at these two hospitals. **1978** K. P. KRETSCHMER *Intestinal Stoma* 115 A stoma patient is well advised when entering an unfamiliar locality to inform himself first of bathroom facilities. **1980** *Recent Adv. Surg.* X. 281 Courses for the training of stomatherapists. **1981** *West Lancs. Evening Gaz.* 14 Jan. 14 (Advt.), Victoria Hospital Gastro Enterology Services Unit Stoma Therapy Nursing Service..are looking for a person who has the ability to communicate and assess the patient's psychological and social needs.

Hence **sto·mal** *a.*

1952 W. M. CRAPPER in F. A. Jones *Mod. Trends Gastro-Enterol.* xviii. 464 A stomal ulcer may appear, as we have seen recently, where a woman aged 73 developed ulceration 9 months after gastro-jejunostomy for a duodenal ulcer. **1979** J. P. DELANEY et al. in Najarian & Delaney *Gastrointestinal Surg.* 191 The only way symptoms of stomal gastritis can be relieved is by diversion of the upper gastrointestinal juices away from the stomach.

stomach, *sb.* **6. a.** For † *Obs.* read Now *rare* and add later examples.

1859 EARL GRANVILLE *Let.* in E. Fitzmaurice *Life Granville* (1905) I. xii. 344, I ought to..tell you of..the enormous weight off my stomach when I failed [to form a government]. **1965** E. B. WHITE *Let.* July (1976) 533 The city is very strange this summer—alternately deserted and packed, and the nearness of Harlem always in everybody's stomach.

10. a. *stomach muscle, ulcer, upset*; good for the stomach, *stomach powder.*

1965 P. O'DONNELL *Modesty Blaise* xviii. 199 Instinct tensed her stomach-muscles an instant before the woman dropped on her with both knees. **1911** E. WHARTON *Ethan Frome* vii. 135 I've a good mind to go and hunt up those stomach powders I got last year... Maybe they'll help the heart-burn. **1972** V. CANNING *Rainbird Pattern* vi. 115 He was restless himself from a substantial dinner and lay awake for hours wishing he had brought some stomach powder. **1945** A. HUXLEY *Let.* 27 May (1969) 527 He interferes with the normal functioning of his own body and worries or strains himself into stomach ulcers. **1961** L. MUMFORD *City in History* xv. 473 Definite ailments, like stomach ulcers and high blood pressure, seem to be aggravated by the strain of living, say, within sound of a busy motorway or airport. **1960** L. COOPER *Certain Compass* 23 Adrian said that he had a stomach upset, and went back. **1976** D. CLARK *Dread & Water* v. 102 Mugs..if used communally..can serve to pass germs among the party, causing stomach upsets.

stomachy, *a.* Restrict *dial.* to senses in Dict. and add: **4.** Of the voice or vocal sounds: deeply resonant, as if produced in the stomach. *colloq.*

1936 E. M. FORSTER *Abinger Harvest* II. 101 The soloist ..invites his 'friends' in a stomachy voice to rise in their shirt-fronts and shout. **1975** 'D. RUTHERFORD' *Mystery Tour* iv. 71 His rich stomachy laugh.

stomatal, stomatitis, stomato-. Add: Also with pronunc. (stōᵘ·-).

stomiatoid (stōᵘ·-, stǫ·miătoid), *sb.* and *a.* *Zool.* [f. mod.L. name of suborder *Stomiatoidei,* f. generic name *Stomias* (H. R. Schinz in G. L. C. F. D. Cuvier *Thierreich* (1822) II. 310), f. Gr. στόμ-α mouth + -IA[2]: see -OID.] **A.** *sb.* A deep-sea fish of the suborder Stomiatoidei, distinguished by a large mouth and rows of photophores on its sides. **B.** *adj.* Of or pertaining to a fish of this kind or the suborder as a whole.

1957 E. LE DANOIS *Fishes of World* vi. 178 The smaller stomiatoids with formidable teeth prey on other midwater, deep-sea fishes. **1974** *Nature* 8 Nov. 98/1 They [*sc.* hatchetfishes] form one of the major groups of the stomiatoid fishes. **1976** *Jrnl. R. Soc. Arts* Apr. 251/2 Stomiatoid and lantern fishes..have large, highly sensitive eyes and marvellous arrays of light organs.

stomion (stǫ·miǫn). *Gr. Archæol.* Pl. **stomia.** [a. Gr. στόμιον, dim. of στόμα mouth.] The entrance to an ancient tomb.

1934 E. GJERSTAD et al. *Swedish Cyprus Expedition* I. 35 Three chambers..roughly circular, or oval in shape with horizontal floors, and steeply sloping tunnel-shaped stomia. *Ibid.* 47 The proper dromos of Chamber B was never excavated. The stomion is very long and slightly curved eastwards. **1946** *Ann. Brit. School at Athens* XLI. 79 The tombs were entered by a narrow passage (*dromos*), sometimes wider below than above, with a rectangular doorway (*stomion* in *SEC* descriptions) closed by a limestone slab. **1969** V. KARAGEORGHIS *Cyprus* iii. 152 Towards the middle of the 7th century the same tomb was re-used by cutting a passage through the filling of the dromos of the first burial to provide access to the *stomion* of the chamber. **1970** *Mariner's Mirror* LVI. 390 Anchors ..were broken in antiquity before being used as fill in the stomion of a tomb last closed in the 11th century B.C.

stomium (stōᵘ·miəm). *Bot.* [mod.L., coined in Ger. (K. Goebel 1901, in *Organogr. d. Pflanzen* II. 753), f. Gr. στόμιον (see prec.).] In ferns, a part of the wall of the sporangium which ruptures to release the spores.

1905 I. B. BALFOUR tr. *Goebel's Organogr. of Plants* II. 575 A point of opening which we may designate the stomium occurs in all sporangia which discharge their spores into the air. **1936** A. J. EAMES *Morphol. Vascular Plants* xii. 263 The annulus [of the Cyatheaceæ] is complete and oblique (nearly vertical) with a poorly defined stomium. **1969** F. E. ROUND *Introd. Lower Plants* xiii. 156 The sporangial head has a cluster or ring of thickened cells (annulus) which acts as the dehiscence mechanism working on a weaker region of unthickened cells (stomium).

stomp (stǫmp), *v.*[2] Chiefly *U.S.* (orig. *dial.*). [Var. STAMP *v.* in senses of branch II.] **1. a.** *intr.* = STAMP *v.* 2 a. Also *fig.*

1803 J. DAVIS *Trav. U.S.A.* x. 382 He began to *stomp* upon me, and ax if I had yet got enough. **1936** C. CARMER *Listen for Lonesome Drum* 74, I stomped on his hand. **1961** C. MCCULLERS *Clock without Hands* vii. 148 He took down his records of German lieder..and stomped on them, stomping with such despair and fury that not a groove of the records remained unshattered. **1971** B. MALAMUD *Tenants* 65 In the last piece Harry..is painted white by three brothers after they had considered stomping on him..for what he did. **1973** *Observer* 25 Nov. 28/4 They stomped all over Newport County.., winning 3–1.

b. = STAMP *v.* 2 b.

1914 *Dialect Notes* IV. 156 *Stomp, v.i.*, var. of *stamp*, to strike the foot forcibly and noisily downward. **1917** *Ibid.* 400 *Stomp*.., tread heavily or noisily with one or more feet.. 'He *stomped* on the floor as hard as he could.' **1928** J. PETERKIN *Scarlet Sister Mary* 147 Tell Doll not to stomp so hard. **1940** *Time* 29 July 40 They banged, rattled, beat, blew, stomped. **1969** *New Scientist* 17 July 119/2 The astronaut will be asked to stomp on the surface several times to produce observable seismic signals. **1982** B. CHATWIN *On Black Hill* xvi. 77 The bull bellowed; horses stomped in their stalls.

c. = STAMP *v.* 2 e.

1919 E. POUND *Quia Pauper Amavi* 18 He stomped into my bedroom. **1941** *Time* 13 Oct. 15/3 Mr. Ford stomped out, grinding his teeth. **1953** W. BURROUGHS *Junkie* (1972) ii. 23 Whitey was stomping up and down the length of the bar trying to promote some free drinks. **1956** J. MASTERS *Bugles & Tiger* 87 Biniram unpacked my suitcase, threw my pyjamas on the bed, and stomped out. **1967** G. STEINER *Lang. & Silence* 138 He stomps like a boisterous giant through a literature often marked by slim volumes of whispered lyricism. **1971** B. W. ALDISS *Soldier Erect* 89 He came stomping along the edge—for a moment I thought he was going to dive in after me, boots and all! **1981** 'J. GASH' *Vatican Rip* vii. 61 I'd never seen people move so fast... Everybody simply stomped hurriedly past.

2. a. *trans.* = STAMP *v.* 3 a. Also *fig.*

1916 in H. Wentworth *Amer. Dial. Dict.* (1944) 593/1 Before you stomp all that snow off. **1941** H. SKIDMORE *Hawk's Nest* 2 [She] stomped the red clay from her feet. **1954** *Ladies' Home Jrnl.* Oct. 116/3 Any passerby could look through the glass and see if the teacher inside were perhaps being pinned to the wall or stomped into the floor. **1971** B. PATTEN *Irrelevant Song* 40, I will make all that is possible step out of time To a land of giant hurrays! where the happy monsters dance And stomp darkness down. **1981** M. C. SMITH *Gorky Park* I. iii. 45 The host's carload entered, stomping snow off their boots.

b. *to stomp one's feet.* Cf. STAMP *v.* 3 c.

c **1927–34** J. TOOMER in *Black Scholar* (1971) Jan. 8, I teased the girls. I sent notes. I stomped my feet and made strange noises. **1941** *Sat. Even. Post* 10 May 113/2 Fern stomped feet against the floor. **1955** *Birmingham* (Alabama) *News* 14 July 55/2 She stomped her feet in the manner in which she testified she saw Colin walking toward the car to take the battery. **1972** *Jazz & Blues* Nov. 5/1 They jitterbugged to 'One O'Clock Jump' and stomped their feet to 'Maple Leaf Rag'.

c. To stamp or trample on (a person, etc.). Also *transf.*

1934 C. CARMER *Stars fell on Alabama* 165, I fixes to stomp him to death... There I was stompin' jest like I'd stomped a thousand coons. **1942** *R.A.F. Jrnl.* 16 May 28 The Indians then began a victory dance. Before the dance was over..the..British fliers were stomping the ground in customary style. **1959** N. MAILER *Advts. for Myself* (1961) 201, I never could stomach the relish with which soldiers would describe how they had stomped some faggot in a bar. **1967** *Daily Progress* (Charlottesville, Va.) 1 May C2/6 Jerry got into an argument with his mother and his father shouted: 'I'm gonna stomp you!' **1975** D. LODGE *Changing Places* ii. 86 He saw Carol jumping up and down on the mountainous figure of the black wrestler, 'Stomp me baby, stomp me,' he moaned.

d. With *out*. = STAMP *v.* 3 d. Chiefly *transf.*

1936 *Sun* (Baltimore) 4 Dec. 12/3 We are against crime. Crime should be 'stomped' out. **1940** W. FAULKNER *Hamlet* I. iii. 82 That first Snopes will turn around and stomp the fire out. **1941** *Time* 29 Dec. 22/1 Castillo would use his new powers..to stomp out Nazi propaganda agents. **1976** *Science* 10 Sept. 982/1 Despite government efforts to stomp it out..the banned anticancer drug Laetrile has a steady..market..in the United States.

e. To beat *out* (a rhythm) with one's foot.

1973 *Black World* Mar. 61/2 Arms open wide, he stomped out a savage drum beat: 'Kill! kill! kill! kill!'

f. To tramp or trudge between (a series of places).

1977 'J. LE CARRÉ' *Hon. Schoolboy* xv. 331 He was reduced to stomping the air-freight agencies, asking about a firm called Indocharter.

3. Chiefly *Jazz.* **a.** *trans.* To perform (a dance) to a lively, stamping rhythm.

1926 B. KRENZ (*song-title*) Stomp your stuff. **1926** in R. S. Gold *Jazz Lexicon* (1964) 297 When they start dancin'—Stompin and prancin'—the dance called the sugar foot stomp. **1978** *Amer. Poetry Rev.* July/Aug. 45/2 'Stomping the blues' is also dancing with the get down style of dance-beat-oriented people.

b. With *off*. To beat (a tempo) with one's foot as a signal to a jazz band to start to play; also, to signal to (a band) in this way. Also *absol.* or *intr.*

1925 in R. S. Gold *Jazz Lexicon* (1964) 298 (*tune-title*) Stomp off, let's go. **1960** H. O. BRUNN *Story Orig. Dixieland Jazz Band* vi. 68 For this reason LaRocca was not allowed to 'stomp off' his band in the usual fashion. **1961** *Artesian* Winter 33 They stomped off the solid beat. **1970** W. APEL *Harvard Dict. Mus.* (ed. 2) 441/2 In the earliest forms of jazz the leader 'stomped off' the tempo (gave it by tapping his foot).

c. *intr.* To dance or play a stomp. Cf. *STOMP *sb.* 1.

1925 (*tune-title*) Everybody stomp. **1929** (*tune-title*) I'm gonna stomp, Mr. Henry Lee. **1937** C. CONNOLLY in L. Russell *Press Gang!* 80 And then dancing, while.. David stomps on the piano. **1957** D. HAGUE in S. Traill *Concerning Jazz* 112 A resurgence of swing in evidence.. and Dixieland still stomping here and there. **1968** *Daily Mail* 16 Mar. 6/1 'Ullo, darlin', can you stomp?' my rocker friend Jonny asked gaily. I looked puzzled. 'It's the new Rocker dance,' he explained. **1974** *Ibid.* 16 Oct. 6/4 He does not stomp quite so energetically these days.

Hence **stomped** (stǫmpt) *ppl. a.*

1946 R. BLESH *Shining Trumpets* iv. 95 A stomped and hand-clapped rhythmic base. **1950** —— & JANIS *They all played Ragtime* ix. 176 Nor is erudite musical analysis needed to differentiate ragtime from jazz when one has heard him play the *Maple Leaf* in the authentic St. Louis manner and then follow with his own complex stomped version 'along the lines of jazz creation'.

stomp (stǫmp), *sb.* orig. and chiefly *U.S.* [f. prec.] **1. a.** Chiefly *Jazz.* A lively dance, usu. involving heavy stamping; also, a tune or song suitable for such a dance; stomping rhythm. Also *attrib.*

1912 (*tune-title*) Stomp dance. **1923** (*tune-title*) House rent stomp. **1926** *Amer. Mercury* Apr. 388/1 Hot jazz (which the Charleston and the Stomp—ye gods, what a name!—are bringing back, worse luck!). **1929** WODEHOUSE *Summer Lightning* iv. 108 Leopold's justly famous band, its cheeks puffed out and its eyeballs rolling, was playing a popular melody with lots of stomp in it. **1933** *Fortune* Aug. 90/3 Gene Gifford has composed and arranged some of the neatest exercises in *stomp* (very fast) time. **1940** *Swing* June 24/2 Fundamentally, there are two types of jazz—blues and stomps... Stomp tunes are gay; blues are mournful. **1952** *Mademoiselle* Dec. 120/3 The great era of the stomp was the twenties. **1956** H. KURNITZ *Invasion of Privacy* xiii. 85 She opened..with '*Vissi d'arte*' from Tosca..and to close, a hot and authentic stomp. **1968** *Daily Mail* 16 Mar. 6/5 Others did the stomp, an accelerated calypso, one of the most energetic and difficult dances I have ever tried to learn. **1977** J. WAINWRIGHT *Do Nothin' till you hear from Me* vii. 116 An outfit, straight from a 'viper session' could take a stomp, play it at..a nice, bouncy pace, and it came out faster than seemed mortally possible.

b. A heavy stamping step to the beat of such a dance.

1927 *Observer* 6 Feb. 15/7 Once you get the stomp—the peculiar beat of the foot—and you both hit the floor and not a neighbour's ankle, it is quite suitable as a ballroom dance. **1940** *Time* 25 Nov. 41/1 Dancer Massine [pieces out] simple footwork with deft body movements, well-timed claps and stomps. **1942** *Sat. Even. Post* 14 Feb. 20/2 A fast double shuffle that should have climaxed in a stomp. **1971** B. MALAMUD *Tenants* 217 Some of the youths try to imitate the newly married couples shaking their hips and shoulders but give it up and break into a stomp, shake, and whirl.

2. A party characterized by lively dancing to popular music; *spec.* a rent party.

1926 WHITEMAN & MCBRIDE *Jazz* viii. 177 The 'stomp' consisted of a barbecue with music afterwards, during and before. The guests raised a purse to save their host's home and also composed a new blues for the occasion. **1940** [see *G.I. 2 a]. **1967** E. A. GOLLSCHEWSKY in *Coast to Coast 1965–66* 86 The stomp crowd breaking up down at the Junior Citizens' Hall. **1977** P. DICKINSON *Walking Dead* III. iii. 230 The villagers met..for dances—those noisy nights half-way between revivalist meetings and beer-hall stomp.

3. A heavy, tramping gait or walk; *on the stomp*: tramping or trudging from place to place.

1971 B. W. ALDISS *Soldier Erect* 205 The parade-ground stomp was out in Dimapur, where it raised too much dust; the fashion was for a sort of brisk stroll, a gun-fighter's walk. **1977** 'J. LE CARRÉ' *Hon. Schoolboy* xvi. 392 He went on the stomp for refugee and orphan stories. **1982** *Times* 6 Sept. 7/1 A stomp along the cliff path, talking all the way.

stomper (stǫ·mpəɹ), *sb.* [f. *STOMP *v.*^{2} + -ER^1.] **1.** *pl.* Shoes or boots; *spec.* large, heavy shoes. Cf. STAMPER *sb.* 4; *waffle stomper* s.v. *WAFFLE *sb.*^{1} *U.S. slang.*

1899 B. W. GREEN *Word-Bk. Virginia Folk-Speech* 366 *Stompers*, large heavy shoes. **1945** L. SHELLY *Jive Talk Dict.* 19/1 *Stompers*, pair of shoes. **1974** K. MILLETT *Flying* (1975) II. 233 The Left wears its jeans and stompers. **1979** B. MALAMUD *Dubin's Lives* vii. 257 Dubin wore two scarves..waffle stompers, earmuffs.

2. *Jazz.* A person who performs a stomp.

1925 in B. Rust *Jazz Records 1897–1942* (1972) I. 758 (*recording artists*) The Dixie Stompers. **1927** *Music* 5 Jan. 50/2 (*heading*) Red and Miff's Stompers. **1944** *Amer. Speech* XIX. 268 In sharp contrast to the power-aggressiveness group [of names of boys' clubs] is a small but well defined group that might be called the rakish: Top Hats..Ramblers, Stompers, Hepcats. **1959** *Encounter* Sept. 51/1 Richard Waring..turns Oberon into a vocal, melodramatic, and *bravura* stomper. **1968** *Blues Unlimited* Nov. 17 A host of harpists, guitarists and stompers.

stompie (stǫ·mpi). *S. Afr. slang.* [a. Afrikaans, dim. of *stomp* STUMP *sb.*^{1}] A cigarette butt; also, a partially-smoked cigarette, esp. one stubbed out and kept for relighting later.

1947 L. ABRAHAMS in B. Sachs *H. C. Bosman: S. Afr. Opinion—Trek Anthol.* (1971) 235 He stubbed out the stompie on the kerb. Pushing it into his pocket, he came over. **1959** J. MEIRING *Candle in Wind* ii. 32 She pulled a stompie out of her pocket and lighted it. **1969** A. FUGARD *Boesman & Lena* 37 The whiteman stopped the bulldozer and smoked a cigarette... He threw me the stompie. **1981** A. PATON *Towards Mountain* v. 34 The smell [of tobacco smoke] was made worse by his habit of keeping stompies in his pockets, a stompie being a cigarette not fully smoked, then stubbed out, and stored away for future use.

stomping (stǫ·mpiŋ), *vbl. sb.* Chiefly *U.S.* [f. *STOMP *v.*^{2} + -ING^1.] **1.** The action of stamping or treading heavily.

1819 M. EDGEWORTH *Let.* 28 Jan. (1971) 164 Made such a stomping about the room that Mr. Sneyd could not think what was the matter. **1950** BLESH & JANIS *They all played Ragtime* ix. 166 The term 'stomp', used to designate a hot number of dynamic rhythm, was derived in New Orleans from the stomping of bare feet in the Bamboula and the Congo. **1976** *National Observer* (U.S.) 27 Mar. 2/5 The debate..was marked by howls, foot-stomping, angry exchanges.

2. *Jazz.* The action of dancing or playing a stomp.

1930 R. WRASKOFF (*song-title*) Stomping! Hot stomp. **1936** in R. S. Gold *Jazz Lexicon* (1964) 297 (*song-title*) Stomping at the Savoy. **1941** W. C. HANDY *Father of Blues* i. 6 That was real stomping. **1963** *Pix* 28 Sept. 62 Rubber soled sneakers are fine for stomping but you can get an extra two points for owning a pair of huaraches.

3. *transf.* An attack in which the victim is trampled upon. More generally, a beating. Cf. *STOMP *v.*^{2} 2 c. *U.S. colloq.*

1958 *Washington Post* 13 Sept. D3/5 A coroner's jury yesterday found Robert C. Gerald..responsible for the death by stomping of Hazel R. White. **1967** *Daily Progress* (Charlottesville, Va.) 1 May C2 (*heading*) Threatened with 'stomping' boy kills parents, granddad. **1971** J. MANDELKAU *Buttons* xiv. 155, I grabbed him by the hair when he didn't answer and started to swing him around and punch him in the face... You know what he cried? 'I know where it's at. I can take a stomping!' **1977** L. O'DONNELL *Aftershock* xv. 217 The beating and the stomping weren't necessary.

4. *Comb.*, as **stomping ground** = *stamping ground* s.v. STAMPING *vbl. sb.* 3.

1854 in *Amer. Speech* (1940) XV. 397/1 Crossing the top of said ridge to a white oak & 2 chesnut saplings by the edge of a stomping-ground. **1937** *Dialect Notes* VI. 617 This is the stomping ground of Pecos Bill. **1950** A. LOMAX *Mister Jelly Roll* 42 New Orleans was the stomping grounds for all the greatest pianists in the country. **1977** 'J. LE CARRÉ' *Hon. Schoolboy* xiii. 307 The East was his natural stomping ground.

stomping (stǫ·mpiŋ), *ppl. a.* Chiefly *U.S.* [f. *STOMP *v.*^{2} + -ING^2.] **1.** *Jazz.* That plays, or is played, in the manner of a stomp; exciting with a heavy, 'swinging' rhythm; also, that dances the stomp.

1927 H. FORD et al. (*song-title*) Stompin' fool. **1950** BLESH & JANIS *They all played Ragtime* viii. 160 New Orleans, not St. Louis, made the real impact on Chicago music,..as it developed into stomping jazz with much ragtime retained. **1956** M. STEARNS *Story of Jazz* (1957) xvi. 187 A series of stomping bands swung along this circuit. **1968** P. OLIVER *Screening Blues* v. 151 Joe Pullum, a Houston singer who was accompanied on *Joe Louis Is the Man* by Andy Boy's stomping piano. **1972** *Jazz & Blues* Sept. 12/2 The number seems to be based on 'Way Down Upon The Swanee River' but is played by Fats as a fast boogie-woogie piece with a stomping left hand.

2. = STAMPING *ppl. a. U.S.*

1942 *Time* 9 Feb. 28/2 Brazil's Aranha..announced to stomping, cheering crowds that Brazil..had..'broken her diplomatic and commercial relations with Germany'.

stompneus. Substitute for def.: Either of two edible fishes found off the coast of southern Africa, the red and silver *Chrysoblephus gibbiceps* or the silvery *Rhabdosargus globiceps*, both of the family Sparidæ. (Later examples.)

1945 *Cape Argus Mag.* 20 Oct. 1 Often we hooked two together—silverfish, panga, stompneus, elft. **1953** *Cape Times* 4 Mar. 2/4 Kabeljou, yellowtail, white stompneus and stockfish were all caught in Hermanus.

-stomy (stŏmi), f. Gr. στόμ-α mouth, opening + -Y^3, used in *Surg.* to form the names of operations in which (*a*) an opening is made into the internal organ denoted by the preceding element, as in *COLOSTOMY, GASTROSTOMY; or (*b*) a permanent connection is made between the internal organs indicated, as in *gastro-duodenostomy* and *gastro-gastrostomy* s.v. *GASTRO-.

stone, *sb.* Add: **1. c.** A meteorite; now *esp.* one containing a high proportion of silicates or other non-metals.

1628 J. HOSKINS *Let.* in N. Wallington *Hist. Notices* (1869) I. i. 14 As it is reported, there fell divers stones, but two is certain, in our knowledge. **1796** *Gentleman's Mag.* LXVI. 845/1 Various instances are alleged of such falling stones, or, as they may be denominated, extinguished meteors. **1802** *Phil. Trans. R. Soc.* XCII. 212 Have not all fallen stones, and what are called native irons, the same origin?..Are all, or any, the produce or the bodies of meteors? **1809** *Jrnl. Nat. Philos.* XXIII. 233 Account of a meteoric stone..that fell in the circle of Ichnow. *Ibid.*, Several persons..got out the stone, which was above two feet beneath the surface of the snow... A professor of natural philosophy..considered it..as ferruginous. **1826**, etc. [see *IRON *sb.*^{1} 1 d]. **1977** A. HALLAM *Planet Earth* 24 Freshly fallen stones are usually quite cool to the touch.

d. A fashion shade of yellowish or brownish grey; stone-colour. Also *attrib.* or as *adj.* Cf. sense 19 in Dict.

1848 E. RUSKIN *Let.* 10 May in W. James *Order of Release* (1947) v. 107 A stone silk dress with two broad flounces. **1865** M. EYRE *Lady's Walks in South of France* i. 10 The colours most in vogue are some shade of grey, stone, or buff. **1890** [see *box-cloth* s.v. *BOX *sb.*^{2} 24]. **1907** *Yesterday's Shopping* (1969) 157/2 Paints mixed ready for use... White, light stone, dark stone, middle stone, black. **1923** *Daily Mail* 2 June 1 In delightful shades of Fawn,.. Dove Grey, Stone, Beaver. **1977** *Times* 18 Aug. 23/6 *Rover* 3·5 *litre*..blue with stone leather interior.

2. g. *artificial stone* (see quot. 1967).

1722 *Brit. Pat.* 447 Thomas Ripley..and Richard Holt..have been at much labour..for the finding out and inventing 'A certain compound liquid metall never before known and used by the Antients or Moderns, by which artificiall stone and marble is made.' *c* **1778** [see *LITHODIPYRA]. **1868** *Building News* 10 Apr. 248/2 (*heading*) Ransome's artificial stone. *Ibid.* 3 July 448/2 A method of manufacturing artificial granite..has just been patented by Mr. P. M. Parsons. **1935** *Economist* 9 Feb. 321/1 The two trades..which represent the largest consumers of cement are 'public works contracting, etc.', and 'artificial stone and concrete manufacturing'. **1935** [see *RECONSTRUCTED *ppl. a.* a]. **1967** *Gloss. Highway Engin. Terms (B.S.I.)* 37 *Artificial stone*, a form of precast concrete in which the finished surface resembles that of natural stone.

j. (Earlier example in *Curling*.)

1824 [see *HOG *sb.*^{1} 10].

7. a. (Earlier and later S. Afr. examples in sense 'diamond'.)

1884 MRS. CAREY-HOBSON *At Home in Transvaal* 184 He had placed no stones in the bank since Graham had been on the Fields. **1891** E. GLANVILLE *Fossicker* xxix. 292 The cooling mud has closed around the 'stones', taking the impress of every angle and facet. **1946** S. CLOETE *Afr. Portraits* 109 His favourite stone was his blink klippie—his shining stone—the first diamond to be found in Africa. **1972** *Panorama* Dec. 27 'Stones' are usually over one carat (a carat being 200 milligrams). Anything smaller falls in the 'melee' category.

b. *spec.* in *Criminals' slang*, a diamond (see also quot. 1955).

1904 'No. 1500' *Life in Sing Sing* 252/2 *Stone*, diamond. **1936** J. CURTIS *Gilt Kid* xxiv. 240 Ten nicker for a little stone like that. **1955** D. W. MAURER in *Publ. Amer. Dial. Soc.* xxiv. 122 A man's tie-pin, seldom worn nowadays, was a prop. If it had a diamond setting, it was referred to as a stone.

c. *Austral.* Opal or opal-bearing material; an opal. Also *to be on stone*, to have struck opal stone. Also *N.Z.* (see quot. 1965).

1895 *Rep. N.S.W. Dept. Mines* 68 A patch of stone was taken about the end of the year which brought £1,200. **1921** K. S. PRICHARD *Black Opal* iv. 33 You don't suppose Jun'd try to take the stones off of him, do you? **1924**

T. C. Wollaston *Opal* iv. 61 The men were not 'on stone', it seemed, but perhaps I could change the luck? **1965** G. J. Williams *Econ. Geol. N.Z.* iii. 20/2 *Stone*, a miner's term for payable [*sc.* auriferous] quartz. **1967** A. Kalokerinos *In Search of Opal* 18 Stones that are worth $2,000 or more on the field are found at a rate that would not exceed one per week.

14. c. In phr. *to give a stone and a beating to* (Racing slang): to outrun easily, despite carrying a heavier weight. Also *transf.*, to surpass. Now *rare*.

1885 *Daily News* 4 Feb. 5/2 *Canis vulpis* is, as a rule, able to give, intellectually speaking, and in language germane to the matter, 'a stone and a beating' to the majority of his pursuers. **1906** *Punch* 18 Apr. 286/3 Their Smokeroom is deliciously comfy, and can give a stone and a beating to ours at the Camellia.

18. a. attrib. *stone-cliff, -heap* (later examples). **b.** Objective, etc. *stone-haunting* adj. **c.** Instrumental, etc. *stone-bearded, -faced* (later examples), *-flagged, -headed* (earlier example), *-horned, -ribbed, -strewn* adjs.

1922 Joyce *Ulysses* 141 A man supple in combat: stonehorned, stonebearded, heart of stone. **1912** E. Pound *Ripostes* 26 Storms, on the stone-cliffs beaten. **1932** W. Faulkner *Light in August* xvi. 355 This time he indicates the stonefaced woman; she may or may not be listening to what he is saying. **1973** M. Woodhouse *Blue Bone* ix. 82 The Eisenwald Volksklinik was..a huge stonefaced structure. **1904** E. Wharton *Italian Villas* i. 53 The house is built about three sides of a raised stone-flagged terrace. **1978** J. Wainwright *Jury People* v. 16 The room had a stone-flagged floor. **1933** Auden *Poems* (ed. 2) 43 By pot-holed becks A bird stone-haunting, an unquiet bird. **1829** G. Griffin *Collegians* I. viii. 170 The difference which existed between..an English halberd and a stone-headed gai-bulg. **1868** *N. & Q.* 15 Aug. 165/2 The game Set-a-Foot is still played by the rising generation who frequent Park Square, Regent's Park, under the name of Stone Heaps. **1941** F. Thompson *Over to Candleford* 356 They ran..and wrestled the whole way, or pushed each other over stone-heaps or into ditches. **1977** *New Yorker* 17 Oct. 37/3 Her stone heap... My mother spreads out soapy white laundry on these stones, so that the hot sun will bleach them even whiter. **1922** Stone-horned [see *stone-bearded* above]. **1936** L. B. Lyon *Bright Feather Fading* 19 The bone-Bare garden steep, the stone-ribbed land. **1853** M. Arnold *Poems* 179 The climbing gourd-plant's leaves Muffled its walls, and on the stone-strewn roof Lay the warm golden gourds. **1974** R. Adams *Shardik* x. 71 The bear's trail led on through the bushes to emerge in open, stone-strewn woodland.

19. a. *stone-bright, -cold* (examples in quasi-advb. attrib. use, esp. in phr. *stone cold sober* = utterly sober), *-comfortless* adjs.

1916 E. Pound *Lustra* 26, I have known the stone-bright place, The hall of clear colours. **1913** F. H. Burnett *T. Tembarom* xxxiv. 435 It'd be stone-cold safe to rush things. **1937** T. Rattigan *French without Tears* iii. i. 65 Are you stone-cold sober? **1958** A. Sillitoe *Saturday Night & Sunday Morning* vii. 111 We've been stone-cold sober since Canning Circus. **1969** C. Armstrong *Seven Seats to Moon* v. 59, I could have been stone-cold-dead in Chicago! **1979** O. Sela *Petrograd Consignment* 144 Unlike the other revolutionaries, the Bolsheviks..were resolutely stone-cold sober. **1924** D. H. Lawrence in M. Magnus *Mem. Foreign Legion* 13 There I had a big and lonely, stone-comfortless room. **1769** J. Wedgwood *Let.* 1 Dec. (1965) 85 We have nobody making white ware here, only stone white ware. **1949** E. Pound *Pisan Cantos* lxxxiv. 129 Carrara Snow on the marble Snow-white against stone-white.

b. Intensively with adjs. in non-similative use (after *stone-broke* adj., sense 20 a below): completely, utterly, 'plumb', as *stone crazy, drunk, mad*, etc. Also in adj. relation to sb., complete, utter, 'dead'; excellent. Cf. *stone ginger* (b), sense 20 a below. *slang.*

1928 *Lawn Tennis & Badminton* 23 June 255/2 Few could have foreseen that the two doubles would have been the 'stone certainties' for Britain that they proved to be. **1933** Partridge *Words, Words, Words!* 214 India gives us..*piache*, mad... On the analogy of *stone mad, stone piache* was employed for a change. **1935** Z. N. Hurston *Mules & Men* (1970) i. iii. 66 You must be stone crazy! Why, dis hide is worth five thousand dollars. **1947** K. Tennant *Lost Haven* ix. 126 Oh, don't let him think of the punt again—that was the stone finish! **1959** *Esquire* Nov. 70 *Stone*, adjective meaning complete. Example: He's a stone musician. **1960** *Observer* 25 Dec. 7/7 If..he were stone rich and lived in a big drum in the country. **1968** *Blues Unlimited* Dec. 12 First things developed was the set of four reissue albums labelled 'Legendary Masters'; three being stone blues albums. **1970** D. M. Davin *Not here, not Now* iii. vi. 202 This was the finish, the stone end of it. **1978** *N.Y. Times* 30 Mar. A21/1 A little later another patrol..declared him stone drunk, and confiscated his documents and his car keys.

c. As *adj.*, excited; intoxicated with drink or drugs, 'stoned'. *U.S. slang. rare.*

1945 L. Shelly *Jive Talk Dict.* 19/1 *Stone* (adj), excited or intoxicated. **1960** R. G. Reisner *Jazz Titans* 165 *Stone*, drunk or high.

20. a. stone-breaker (earlier U.S. example); **stone-broke** *a.* (earlier and later examples); **stone bruise** chiefly *N. Amer.*, an injury to the feet caused by walking on stony ground; hence **stone-bruised** *a.*; **stone cell** (earlier example); **stone cist** *Archæol.*: see Cist 1 a; **stone-craft,** the art or skill of working in stone; sculpture; **stone cream,** a traditional blancmange-like sweet served cold on a base of jam; **stone-dust,** dust or powder made of particles of broken stone; hence **stone-dusting,** the introduction of stone-dust to the air in a mine to render the coal-dust less combustible; **stone-dust** *v. trans.*, with place as obj.; **stone face** *U.S. colloq.*, a person whose features reveal no emotions; a poker-faced person; esp. in phr. *great stone face* in playful allusion to Hawthorne's tale (see bracketed quot. 1850); **stone-field,** an expanse of ground covered with large stones; *spec.* = *Felsenmeer; **stone frigate** *Naut. slang*, a Naval shore establishment or barracks (see quot. 1948); formerly *spec.* a naval prison; also *transf.*; **stone garland** *Geomorphol.*, a low bank or terrace of large stones occurring on a steep slope and curved downwards so as to resemble a garland or necklace; **stone ginger,** (*a*) see sense 17 b in Dict.); (*b*) *slang*, a certainty, a 'sure thing' (cf. sense 19 b above); also as adj., certain; **stone guard,** an attachment serving to prevent stones entering the air-intake system of a motor vehicle or aeroplane; a similar device protecting another part of a vehicle; **stone-hand** (later examples); **stone kist,** var. *stone cist* above; **stone line** *Geomorphol.*, a layer of isolated stones between subsoil and underlying rock; also, the line of stones that this appears as in a section through the soil; **stone net** *Geomorphol.*, a network of stone rings or polygons; **stone pavement** *Geomorphol.*, an area of ground covered with large flattish stones; **stone polygon** *Geomorphol.*, a naturally occurring arrangement of stones in the approximate form of a polygon; **stone ring,** (*a*) *Geomorphol.*, a natural circle of stones on the ground, similar to a stone polygon; (*b*) *Archæol.* = *stone circle*; **stone river,** a dense, stream-like accumulation of rocks and large stones occurring along a valley bottom or down a slope; *esp.* one of those in the Falkland Islands; **stone run** = *stone river* above; **stone stripe** *Geomorphol.*, one of the evenly spaced bands of coarse rock debris separated by finer material that occur on slopes in cold environments.

1827 S. Rodman in B. Swan *New Bedford in 1827* (1935) 8 Occupied most of the day at my house lot. Made a further trial of my stone breaker, the weight raised by a horse. **1886** H. Baumann *Londinismen* 196/2 Stone-broke. **1933** *Bulletin* (Sydney) 20 Dec. 10/3 There was a hardy war-time story of a stonebroke Digger. **1981** O. Bernier *Pleasure & Privilege* xii. 197 Naples wasn't exactly short of mobility... Some were stone broke. **1805** Lewis & Clark *Orig. Jrnls. Lewis & Clark Expedition* (1904) II. 290 We have a lame crew just now,..one with a bad stone bruise. **1885** *Cent. Mag.* Nov. 29/1 Angy, who was complaining of a stone-bruise, got up. **1976** T. Walker *Spatsizi* xi. 122 The continuous descent over rough ground lamed one saddle horse with a stone bruise. **1909** 'O. Henry' *Roads of Destiny* xxi. 354 Five of my best staff-officers fell, suffering extremely with stone-bruised heels. **1875** Bennett & Dyer tr. *Sachs's Textbk. Bot.* ii. 106 The polyhedral stone-cells (sclerenchyma) in the flesh of pears are arranged in groups. **1888, 1934** Stone cist [see *passage grave* s.v. *Passage *sb.* 16 b]. **1903** J. R. Harris *Dioscuri in Christian Legends* 37 We recognized stonecraft amongst the arts of the Dioscuri. **1931** *Catholic Bull.* (Dublin) June 578 Metal-work, stone-craft, and architecture. **1861** Mrs. Beeton *Bk. Househ. Managem.* 747 Stone cream of tous les mois...½ lb. of preserve, 1 pint of milk, 2 oz. of lump sugar, 1 heaped tablespoonful of tous les mois, 3 drops of essence of cloves, 3 drops of almond-flavouring... When rather cool, but before turning solid, pour the cream over the jam. **1973** E. Sprigge *Life of Ivy Compton-Burnett* v. 78 They liked fish, too, and junket, and that old favourite among puddings, stone cream. **1896** M. E. Wilkins *Madelon* xxix. 330 Damned foolishness, that does more harm to the world than the shattering of all the commandments into stone-dust. **1920** *Chambers's Jrnl.* Mar. 266/2 This fact is taken advantage of to localise explosions in some American mines by mixing the first rush of air with stone-dust. **1930** *Engineering* 28 Feb. 295/3 Stone-dusting in coal mines was not considered to be injurious in Poland. **1975** *Telegraph* (Brisbane) 13 Nov. 16/2 No agreement was reached between union and management on stone dusting Kianga No. 1. [**1850** Hawthorne *Great Stone Face* in *Nat. Era* 16 Jan. 16/1 The Great Stone Face, then, was a work of Nature..formed on the perpendicular side of a mountain by some immense rocks, which had been thrown together in such a position, as, when viewed at a proper distance, precisely to resemble the features of a human countenance.] **1949** *Life* 5 Sept. 82/2 (*heading*) The great stone face [of Buster Keaton]. **1960** *Newsweek* 25 Jan. 90/2 Here is the Great Stone Face on the most famous element of this vanishing art, his dead pan. **1972** J. Mosedale *Football* iv. 47 Even in high school his classmates called him the 'Great Stone Face'. **1977** *Rolling Stone* 21 Apr. 88/3 Only a stoneface could resist smiling. **1906** *Jrnl. Geol.* XIV. 103, I feel sure that these immense block-fields of Bear Island are formed in quite the same manner as the Falkland stone-runs... The only differences between the two occurrences are differences of topography and age: in Bear Island a great plain forming a stone-field, in the Falkland Islands valleys filled at the bottom by stone-rivers. **1959** A. H. McLintock *Descr. Atlas N.Z.* p. xv, At the timber line there is a locally heavy scrub belt..passing into snow-tussock grasslands, stone-fields, and herb moor. **1978** O. White *Silent Reach* viii. 87 It gets harder when you hit the..stonefields. **1917** M. T. Hainsselin *Grand Fleet Days* iv. 15 Where I met her was in a Stone Frigate—that is to say, a Naval Shore Establishment. **1929** F. C. Bowen *Sea Slang* 134 *Stone frigate*, a naval gaol or, more recently, any shore establishment. **1948** Partridge *Dict. Forces' Slang* 182 *Stone frigates*, Royal Naval Barracks or Shore Establishments; they are usually named after the old frigates. **1955** 'N. Shute' *Requiem for Wren* iii. 81 She found that *H.M.S. Mastodon* was a stone frigate. It was Exbury Hall, about three miles up the Beaulieu River from the Solent. **1979** *Mariner's Mirror* LXV. 51 H.M.S. *Thunderer* (our title as a 'stone frigate') has since prospered... It is planned amongst other things to produce a book on the history of the college. **1932** E. Antevs *Alpine Zone Mt. Washington Range* iv. 62 A balsam fir forest..grows normally up to the stone garland. **1977** R. J. Small *Study of Landforms* x. 326 If the slope becomes a little steeper, the polygons give way to 'stone garlands'. **1936** J. Curtis *Gilt Kid* iv. 41 It was stone-ginger, you thought, that you'd get a smashing job up here. **1943** J. A. W. Bennett in *Amer. Speech* XVIII. 90 'That's a stone ginger' (a dead certainty) conceals the name of a famous and unbeatable horse, Stone Ginger [in New Zealand]. **1972** G. F. Newman *You Nice Bastard* 348 *Stone ginger*, a million; certainty. **1936** *Times* 19 Oct. 8/4 The chromium-plated radiator has an integral stoneguard. **1947** *Jrnl. R. Aeronaut. Soc.* LI. 287/2 The best solution of the problem of the stone guard would be to abolish the guard, and eliminate stones and other refuse by momentum-separation. **1958** *Times* 22 Sept. 12/6 Superficially it [*sc.* a motor car] had many attractive qualities..a detachable silver stone-guard before the radiator. **1981** *Buses* Dec. 535/1 This ex-Liverpool Atlantean..has acquired a stone guard in front of the windscreens. **1921** Stone hand [see *Imposer b]. **1978** L. Davidson *Chelsea Murders* xxv. 156 He.. was rapidly rewriting lines for the stone-hand. **1926** Stone kist [see *round barrow* s.v. *Round *a.* 15 a]. **1980** D. K. Cameron *Willie Gavin* vi. 54 There was hardly a year when the winter ploughs did not turn up an old hunter..crouched still in his cold stone-kist. **1938** C. F. S. Sharpe *Landslides & Related Phenomena* iii. 24 This layer [of rock fragments] outcrops in natural and artificial cuts and marks the approximate boundary between the base of..the 'B' horizon of the soil and the 'C' horizon or parent rock material. Where well developed it appears as a broken line of stones suggesting the name *stone-line* here used. **1969** C. Ollier *Weathering* iv. 46 The profiles in many tropical countries have rock..overlain by a stone line, overlain in turn by fairly uniform, fine grained 'soil'. **1975** R. V. Ruhe *Geomorphology* vii. 127/3 A stone-line surface usually differs topographically from the present land surface. **1949** *Jrnl. Geol.* LVII. 143 Stone nets, stone stripes, and soil stripes have formed on high, flat erosion surfaces..in the Wind River Mountains, Wyoming. **1977** D. & V. Weyman *Landscape Processes* iv. 69/2 Stripes are found on slopes above 4° and seem to be stone nets elongated by downslope movements of slope debris. **1969** E. Watson tr. *Tricart's Geomorphol. of Cold Environments* ii. ii. 109 Moist Climates with Severe Winters: Mountain Type... Stone polygons and stone stripes (as well as stone pavements, which are typical), are fairly frequent. **1977** D. & V. Weyman *Landscape Processes* iii. 52/1 In general, desert surfaces show only a shallow weathering layer. Bare rock outcrops are common and many other areas have a stone pavement of coarse material. **1924** Huxley & Odell in *Geogr. Jrnl.* LXIII. 208 We propose here to style the two forms 'stone-polygons' and 'fissure-polygons' respectively. The stone-polygons are represented at one extreme by isolated stone-circles, while at the other they may become drawn out into a series of elongated mud-strips separated by strips of stone. **1950** [see *Patterned *ppl. a.* b]. **1970** R. J. Small *Study of Landforms* x. 327 The reason why stone polygons as a whole vary so much in size (their diameters range from 0·5 to 15 metres) is not understood. **1924** *Geol. Mag.* LXI. 509 (*heading*) Formation of 'stone rings' in rocks which are being shattered by frost action. **1954** J. R. R. Tolkien *Fellowship of Ring* i. vii. 141 The stone-rings upon the hills. **1957** J. K. Charlesworth *Quaternary Era* I. xxvii. 572 The severer frost in the lower, sodden layers produces the finer material and brings it to the surface, pushing the coarser to the sides. The stone-rings so produced grow outwards from their centres to build a polygonal network. **1980** *Sci. Amer.* July 67/1 As a result the term now coming into favour as a description of these megalithic enclosures is stone ring. **1877** C. W. Thomson *Atlantic* II. iv. 246 At the mouth of the valley the section of the 'stone river' exposed by the sea is like that of a stone drain on a huge scale. **1894** J. Geikie *Gt. Ice Age* (ed. 3) xl. 723, I do not think there can be much doubt that the 'stone-rivers' of the Falkland Islands are of the same nature and origin as the rubble-drifts already described in connection with the glacial phenomena of Europe. **1956** W. Edwards in D. L. Linton *Sheffield* 20 Newer Drift... This is well developed on the hillsides in the Millstone Grit country—for example, on Burbage Moor..—its content of large gritstone blocks betraying its presence, especially where these are concentrated in 'stone-rivers'. **1969** C. Ollier *Weathering* xii. 214 Block-streams (stone rivers) also have sharp edged and angular blocks, and occur in the same areas as blockfields. **1906** *Jrnl. Geol.* XIV. 101 The large old stone-runs of the Falkland Islands evidently were formed in a period of the past with a climate more severe than the present. **1950** *Geol. Mag.* LXXXVII. 106 The The stone runs of the Falklands extend over a greater area than is at present exposed, since they are masked by vegetation. **1934** *Proc. Geologists' Assoc.* XLV. 174 Fig. 24 ..shows the stone-stripes in cross section one to two inches thick lying in shallow depressions in the clay-loam. **1978** A. L. Bloom *Geomorphology* xv. 363 Like sorted polygons, stone stripes require active freeze-thaw processes but are not restricted to regions of permafrost.

b. stone-fish: esp. the highly venomous *Synanceja verrucosa*, of the family Scorpænidæ, a bottom-dwelling fish resembling a small rock, found in tropical seas and bearing venom glands at the base of the dorsal fin spines; (later examples); **stone roller** (earlier example).

1908 E. J. BANFIELD *Confessions of Beachcomber* I. iv. 143 Beware of the stone fish.., the death adder of the sea. **1947** I. L. IDRIESS *Isles of Despair* xxxv. 234 The lancet of the hideous little stone fish in his salamander coat. **1971** *Islander* (Victoria, B.C.) 20 June 5/2 The ugliest fish in the sea (and one of the most dangerous) is the stonefish. **1878** C. HALLOCK *Sportsman's Gaz.* 386 The 'stone toter', or 'stone roller', is a far better variety.

stone, *v.* Add: **1. b.** In colloq. phr. *stone the crows*: see *CROW sb.[1] 3 d. Similarly *stone me*: an exclamation of astonishment.

1961 SIMPSON & GALTON *Hancock* 38 *Tony*: Any room for a littl'un? (*Laughs*). *They stare at him frostily. Tony* (*laugh dries*): Cor, stone me. **1967** *Listener* 21 Dec. 815/2 Mrs Dale speaks. 'Why hello, Jim—Cor, stone me, what a booze up we had last night up the BMA.' **1979** J. WAINWRIGHT *Tension* 183 Stone me!—next thing I know I have a..hand-grenade here in my pocket.

3. a. Also, to cover or shut *up* with stones. Also *fig.*

1889 V. MCNABB *Let.* 24 Apr. in F. Valentine *Father Vincent McNabb* (1955) I. ii. 62 Every little fountain of grief seems stoned up. **1953** A. BRYANT *Story of England* iii. 68 His [*sc.* Jesus'] body had vanished from the tomb in which it had been stoned up.

9. a. To become intoxicated with drink or drugs (with *out*, to the point of unconsciousness). **b.** *trans.* To render intoxicated or (*fig.*) ecstatic. Also *refl.* Chiefly as (*ppl.*) *a.*: see *STONED *ppl. a.* and *a.* 7. *slang* (orig. *U.S.*).

1952 G. MANDEL *Flee Angry Strangers* 139 I'd rather stay with the tea. It's great pod. I don't want to stone out. **1959** *Jazz* Fall 290, I heard Phineas Newborn play 'I'll Remember April' two Mondays ago at The Five Spot and he completely stoned me. *a* **1961** T. CAPOTE in WEBSTER (1961) s.v., Planned to stone himself with vodka. **1972** J. BROWN *Chancer* iii. 38 You smoke Egyptian Black, that will stone you out of your head.

stone age. Add: **b.** *fig.*, esp. as the type of an outmoded or unsophisticated era. Also *attrib.* and as *adj.*

1927 KIPLING in *Maclean's Mag.* 15 Sept. 52/4 The old lady..was primitive Stone-Age—bless her! She looked on us as a couple of magicians. **1937** F. SCOTT FITZGERALD *Let.* 5 July (1964) 15 The girls who were what we called 'speeds' (in our stone-age slang) at sixteen were reduced to anything they could get at the marrying time. **1959** M. LASKI *Offshore Island* III. 84 I've enjoyed civilization too much to be happy in a new stone age. **1973** R. THOMAS *If you can't be Good* (1974) xvi. 147 Back in the mid-fifties was back in the stone age. It was way before the Pill. **1981** *Quarto* May 4/2 In the age of computerised type-setting, the technology of the book trade seems more and more stone age.

stone-blue. Add: **2.** (Earlier and later examples.)

1860 C. BRONTË *Emma* in *Cornh. Mag.* Apr. 494 Bright stone-blue is a colour they like in dress. **1962** *L. L. Bean Catal.* Spring 11 Ladies Knee Sox..Colors: Stone Blue, Stone Green.

stone-boat. **2.** For *U.S.* read *U.S.* (chiefly *North.*) and *Canad.* (Earlier and further examples.)

1859 N. P. WILLIS *Convalescent* 75 A *stone-boat* would run glibly over such a shallow snow! **1901** 'R. CONNOR' *Man from Glengarry* 189 In the afternoon the colt was put through her morning experience, with the variation that the stone-boat was piled up with a fairly heavy load of earth and stone. **1962** J. ONSLOW *Bowler-hatted Cowboy* viii. 79 A stone-boat is best described as a heavy wooden sled, on which can be hauled rocks and stones..dead cows, sick cows, or other heavy objects.

stoned, *ppl. a.* and *a.* Add: **7.** *slang.* **a.** Drunk, extremely intoxicated (see also quot. 1952). Freq. const. *on.* Chiefly *predic.*, esp. in phr. *to get stoned.* Cf. *STONE *sb.* 19 c. orig. *U.S.*

1952 *Life* 29 Sept. 67/2 Like boiled snails, bop jokes certainly are not everybody's dish, but those who acquire the taste for them feel cool, gone, crazy and stoned. *Ibid.* 67/3 *Stoned*, drunk, captivated, ecstatic, sent out of this world. **1955** *Amer. Speech* XXX. 305 *Stoned out of his skull*, intoxicated to an intense degree. **1957** J. KEROUAC *On Road* (1958) I. xiii. 90, I had finished the wine..and I was proper stoned. **1968** *Listener* 28 Nov. 735/2 He would only be taken in charge if he was drunk: were he to spend his ten shillings on getting stoned out of his mind the police would happily accommodate him. **1972** R. REID *Canadian Style* (1973) iv. 144 Then they all laugh and get stoned. **1976** P. CAVE *High Flying Birds* ii. 18 We drive off the ferry at Roscoff late in the afternoon, both well and truly stoned on cut-price booze.

b. In a state of drug-induced euphoria, 'high'; also, incapacitated or stimulated by drugs, drugged. orig. *U.S.*

1953 ANSLINGER & TOMPKINS *Traffic in Narcotics* 315 *Stoned*, under the influence of drugs. **1956** 'E. MCBAIN' *Cop Hater* (1958) ix. 85 You're an H-man..and we know you copped three decks a little while back. Are you stoned now, or can you read me? **1967** M. M. GLATT et al. *Drug Scene* viii. 97 Addicts know these dangers, one for example describing graphically how in a 'stoned' state he had stepped out in front of a car. **1971** 'D. HALLIDAY' *Dolly & Doctor Bird* x. 129 They're all lying around in there wearing beads and stoned out of their skulls on French Blues. **1981** M. LEITCH *Silver's City* viii. 65 If he'd been pissed, he reflected, instead of stoned, he might still be in khaki, but, as it was, the old man had a down on drugs, and so it was a dishonourable discharge or nothing.

c. *fig.*

1952 [see sense 7 a above]. **1963** R. I. MCDAVID *Mencken's Amer. Lang.* 742 A cool cat..is..much of the time stoned on wine, pot.., heroin or an overdose of Zen Buddhism. **1969** *Listener* 17 July 88/3 We are, by any definition, stoned on liberty, smashed by self-fulfilment; the real need now is for silence and what used to be called classical restraint—and irony. **1980** *Times Lit. Suppl.* 31 Oct. 1220/5 He [*sc.* Tom Robbins] is also a moralist, and although superficially he belongs to the 'stoned' school of American fiction, along with Brautigan, Kotzwinkle et al, there is a more interesting comparison to be made with the work of Aldous Huxley.

d. With *out.*

1968 A. DIMENT *Great Spy Race* iii. 39 He..[was] chortling in his stoned out way. Tim was really blocked. **1972** R. K. SMITH *Ransom* I. 23 Joyboy had been a stoned-out junkie. **1977** *Rolling Stone* 13 Jan. 51/1 We even have a comedy collection—the Firesign Theatre's *Forward into the Past*, a double album's worth of puns, alliterations, slapstick and stoned-out mayhem.

stone jug. Add: **3.** *Rhyming slang.* = MUG *sb.*[5] Cf. *STEAMER 11.

1923 J. MANCHON *Le Slang* 296. **1974** P. WRIGHT *Lang. Brit. Industry* xiv. 128 When the Duke of Edinburgh visited one of the Astley collieries in the 1950s, he so satisfied the miners..that one of them was moved to say to the local press, 'He's no stone jug, yon mon.' This was the highest possible praise from a South Lancashire miner.

stonemason. (Earlier Amer. example.)

1758 C. SMITH *Let.* 23 Feb. in *Lett. to Washington* (1899) II. 269 Our Stone Masons has been Sick, Ever Since you have been Away, and our Stone Work is much Behind hand.

stone-wall, *sb.* Add: **2. b.** As an epithet for one who seeks to confound by dogged resistance. Chiefly applied to Thomas Jonathan ('*Stonewall*') Jackson (1824–63), Confederate general during the American Civil War. (The earlier *fig.* use.)

1862 *Texas Almanac Extra* 18 Sept. 1/1 Stonewall Jackson was marching on Baltimore with 40,000 men. **1863** G. MEREDITH *Let.* 7 Jan. (1970) I. 185 Busy my good sir, so as to drive the pen as fast as Stonewall Jackson is driving the federals. **1867** *John Lillywhite's Cricketers' Compan.* 46 'Young Stonewall'—as he [*sc.* H. Jupp] has been called—was in immense form. **1902** E. B. V. CHRISTIAN in Alverstone & Alcock *Surrey Cricket* iii. 82 The eleven..received very valuable additions in Tom Humphrey and Jupp, or 'young Stonewall', the 'old Stonewall' being Mortlock, who still played. **1970** R. LOWELL *Notebook* 120 Above your fire the blood-crossed flag of the States, A Stonewall Jackson, a Twenty-two at half-cock.

3. (Examples in *Cricket* and *Lawn Tennis.*)

1885 F. GALE *Hon. Robert Grimston* iii. 25 The well-known stone-wall cricketer, Mr. A. Haygarth. **1895** J. N. PENTELOW *England v. Australia* 37 Lucas played the stonewall game. **1932** E. BOWEN *To North* vi. 57 He played..a stonewall game and beat Emmeline.

stonewaller (later examples).

1895 J. N. PENTELOW *England v. Australia* 20 Boyle gave the young stonewaller still better assistance. **1958** *Economist* 2 Aug. 361 He indicated to the Austrians that he thought Mr Dulles the chief western no-man and habitual stonewaller. **1971** *Jamaican Weekly Gleaner* 17 Nov. 27/1 Mrs. A. D. Scott, regarded as one of the toughest stonewallers ever to play locally, was not very happy on the very fast surface.

stonewall, *v.* Add: **b.** For 'orig. and chiefly *Australian*' read orig. *Austral.* and add later examples; *trans.* (later examples); also, to block (an enquiry, request, etc.); to obstruct (a person or organization). Now chiefly *N. Amer.*

1964 M. GOWING *Britain & Atomic Energy 1939–1945* xiii. 344 The Combined Policy Committee discussed the matter but the Americans stonewalled. **1972** *Accountant* 23 Mar. 373/2 Often in the past, the Budget speech has been preceded by the unreality of questions to the Chancellor which his junior Ministers have had to stonewall with the traditional: 'I cannot anticipate my right hon. Friend's Budget statement.' **1974** *Newsweek* 11 May 23/2 The President himself..served notice that he would stonewall any further demands for tapes in the Watergate scandal. **1974** *Globe & Mail* (Toronto) 10 Dec. 6/2 What the Government does not seem to realize is that in the process of stonewalling the Opposition, it has, itself, compromised the independence of Mr. Munro. **1976** D. HIRO *Inside India Today* 260 The Congress administration stonewalled again, when Mishra died..and the opposition demanded a 'high power' inquiry. **1982** *Daily Tel.* 25 Jan. 12/7 The Nixon administration..also gave the world 'stonewall' as a verb and then got out in the attempted practice thereof.

stoney (stōᵘ·ni). *dial.* Also *Sc.* **staney, stanie; stonie.** [Var. STONY *a.*] A child's coloured marble made of stone or a stone-like material.

1856 *N. & Q.* 2nd Ser. I. 283/2 Stone marbles are called *stoneys*, and clay ones *commoneys*, though *Dutch alleys* are only *stoneys* enamelled. **1868** *Little Corporal* May 67/3 Chinies, Stonies, and Agates, some large and some small. **1885** 'J. STRATHESK' *More Bits from Blinkbonny* (ed. 2) ii. 33 Those played with were called 'taas', and consisted of 'marbles, stanies, frenchies, moral-leggers', etc. **1919** W. WINGATE *Poems* 74 Reddies and stanies for 'moshie' or 'ring'. **1956** G. E. EVANS *Ask Fellows who cut Hay* xxiv. 215 Single marbles were placed in a long line, as many marbles as there were players... The player stood at the end of the line, an agreed distance from the first marble, or *stoney* as it was called. **1965** *Press & Jrnl.* (Aberdeen) 13 Apr. 6/4 A good 'staney', a hard stone boolie which could be hurled against the school wall without breaking.

stonk (stɒŋk). [?Echoic.] **1.** *dial.* Also **stunk.** (See quot. 1841). Also, a game of marbles; a coloured marble.

1841 JAMIESON *Dict. Sc. Lang.* II. 503/1 *Stunk*, the stake put in by boys in a game, especially in that of marbles. **1896** *Manch. City News* 10 Oct., The game is called 'stonks' oftener than marbles. *Ibid.*, A brown or other coloured marble is a 'stonk' and counts one.

2. *Mil. slang.* A concentrated artillery bombardment. Also *fig.*

1944 W. ROBSON *Let.* 8 May (1960) 94 Our gunners were in readiness for the great stonk we requested at nightfall. **1947** D. M. DAVIN *Gorse blooms Pale* 197, I wasn't so crackers I wasn't still listening for that bloody stonk to come screaming down on us. **1961** *Times* 27 Nov. 6/5 The 'stonks' that Mr. Brown and his regional organizers are now going to bring down. **1975** D. CLARK *Premedicated Murder* iv. 65 'We were AGRA.' 'Army Group Royal Artillery..thickening up on other people's stonks and barrages.' **1981** LD. HAREWOOD *Tongs & Bones* ii. 45 You could never tell..if your arrival would bring down an artillery 'stonk' on your head.

Hence as *v. trans. Mil. slang*, to bombard with concentrated artillery fire.

1944 *Daily Tel.* 15 May 6 Here was one more message before we left—that British troops on a captured ridge were being 'stonked' heavily. **1946** R. ALLEN *Home made Banners* xi. 136 Moaning Minnie..was the name they gave to the German multiple mortars that stonked their positions, wherever they were, a minimum of twice and a maximum of several dozen times in each twenty-four hours.

stonker (stɒ·ŋkəɪ), *v. slang* (chiefly *Austral.* and *N.Z.*). [f. *STONK + -ER[5].] *trans.* To render useless; to put out of action, thwart. Also, to kill, destroy; to defeat or outwit. Now chiefly as *pa. pple.*

1919 W. H. DOWNING *Digger Dial.* 48 *Stonker*, exterminate; kill; strike out. **1928** *Bulletin* (Sydney) 15 Feb. 26/4 Then one [shell from a gun] comes in and stonkers 'Iggins and the Company Sergeant-Major. **1941** BAKER *Dict. Austral. Slang* 72 *Stonker*, to defeat, outwit, put out of action. **1945** R. L. SEDDON *Whims of W.A.A.F.* 4 Benzine restrictions have stonkered my car. **1959** G. SLATTER *Gun in my Hand* xiv. 201 He went and stepped on a bloody mine. Stonkered the poor bastard properly.

Hence **sto·nkered** *ppl. a.* (also *spec.* drunk; excessively intoxicated; extremely tired).

1924 *Truth* (Sydney) 27 Apr. 6 *Stonkered*, to be very drunk. **1925** FRASER & GIBBONS *Soldier & Sailor Words* 271 *Stonkered*, put out of action. **1932** A. W. UPFIELD *Royal Abduction* 250 'Why don't they shut off the confounded thing?' 'Too stonkered with surprise, I'll bet.' **1940** F. SARGESON *Man & Wife* (1944) 76 Once they were a bit stonkered the boys would want to have a bo-peep at the bird while he was asleep. **1948** V. PALMER *Golconda* xix. 161 There were one or two old chaps on the executive who were glad enough to see me stonkered. **1963** A. LUBBOCK *Austral. Roundabout* 44 Two on 'em there was, lyin' stonkered in the road. **1967** K. GILES *Death & Mr. Prettyman* ii. 59 It won't help. I know when I'm stonkered. **1970** *Private Eye* 22 May 16 I'm pretty stonkered. Where can we get a snooze round here?

stony, *a.* For '7–9 stoney' read '7– stoney' and add: **2. d.** Of a meteorite or meteoritic material consisting mostly of silicates and other non-metals.

1802 *Phil. Mag.* XIII. 23 (*heading*) Experiments and observations on certain stony and metalline substances which at different times are said to have fallen upon the earth. **1866** *Catal. of Meteorites* (Geol. Survey of India) 8 Two classes of meteorites or solid bodies which have been known to fall to the earth's surface, namely, 1st, stony masses, or aërolites, (often with particles of iron)—and 2nd, masses chiefly iron, or aërosiderites. **1898** *Amer. Jrnl. Sci.* CLV. 63 It seems probable that certain of the stony meteorites that have been found are really the matrices in which some of the iron nodules, formed perhaps many miles distant, were embedded at the moment they entered our atmosphere. **1926** E. A. FATH *Elem. Astron.* xiv. 196 The three classes have the following general composition:..Iron Meteorites... Stony-iron Meteorites... Stony Meteorites.—These consist essentially of silicate minerals with minor amounts of metallic alloys and sulphides. **1981** *Times* 23 Jan. 14/5 The fossil falls into the class known as 'H-chondrite', stony meteorites containing a large amount of iron.

5. c. (Examples of phr. *stony silence.*)

1911 M. BEERBOHM *Zuleika Dobson* vii. 90 The Duke did not try to break the stony silence in which Zuleika walked. **1979** A. BRINK *Dry White Season* IV. iv. 301 They were still staring at me in stony silence, their young dark faces expressionless.

d. (Earlier example.)

1886 [see *BROKE *ppl. a.* 3].

6. b. *stony-faced*; **c. stony-broke** *a.* (earlier example); **stony-iron** *sb.* and *a.*, used to designate meteorites which contain appreciable quantities of both stony material and iron.

1890 Stony-broke [see *pebble-beached* adj. s.v. *PEBBLE *sb.* 5 b]. 1933 M. ARLEN *Man's Mortality* xv. 315 Manteuffel, staring stony-faced towards the darkness..appeared not to have heard his question. 1975 F. BRESLER *You & Law* 81 Even in this stony-faced sector of the law, fairness prevails. 1918, 1962 Stony-iron [see *MESOSIDERITE]. 1969 *Times* 9 Apr. 7/3 Stony-iron meteorites have been found in several Hopewell burial mounds. 1978 D. W. SEARS *Nature & Origin of Meteorites* iii. 73 Stony-iron meteorites are traditionally defined as having approximately equal proportions of stony material and iron. At various times, four groups of stony-iron meteorites have been defined, but since two of these contain only one meteorite each we need here consider only two in any detail: the pallasites and the mesosiderites.

stooge (stūdʒ), *sb. slang* (orig. *U.S.*). [Origin unknown; the possibility that it represents an altered form of *student* has been suggested (students having frequently been employed as stage assistants).] **1. a.** A stage hand. **b.** A stage assistant, esp. one who acts as the butt or foil for a leading character; a feed, straight man. **c.** The assistant of a conjuror or similar performer. **d.** *transf.*

1913 *Sat. Even. Post* 1 Nov. 64/4 Ben, I want you to plant one of your stooges in that coop with a couple of smoke-pots, so that we'll get the effect of Jack coming through the thickest of it. 1929 *Variety* 24 July 1/1 Stuges perform on the floor with dead-pan faces and unconscious feet beating out the time-step. 1936 R. E. SHERWOOD *Idiot's Delight* II. iii. 129, I was a stooge for Zuleika, the Mind Reader. 1936 WODEHOUSE *Laughing Gas* xxii. 238 You expect me, do you, not only to act as a stooge for you in front of the camera, but to sit smiling in the background while you horn in and swipe my interview? 1940 —— *Eggs, Beans & Crumpets* 166 She's a conjuror's stooge... A conjuror's assistant, don't you know. 1941 *Punch* 14 May 468/1 A lament for the absence of that long-suffering, superbly resilient feminine stooge, *Margaret Dumont* [as partner of the Marx brothers]. 1955 W. R. MATTHEWS *Brit. Philosopher as Writer* 12 In it [*sc.* one kind of philosophical dialogue] the author sets up one or more 'stooges', who..can be made to ask just the questions which he, in the person of another character, can answer. 1967 M. ARGYLE *Psychol. Interpersonal Behaviour* vi. 112 Subjects took part in three three-minute discussions with stooges trained to stare, at distances of two, six and ten feet. 1977 *Spare Rib* June 28/2 Our humour is inter-reactive, there's no stooge. 1979 *Sci. Amer.* May 22/1 A common method of cheating is to rely on what magicians call a 'stooge': someone who is watching behind a screen and sending secret signals to the psychic by any one of scores of little-known techniques. 1982 *Jewish Chron.* 9 July 10/3 Their roles—ventriloquist and dummy, reciter and interrupter, smart alec and stooge.

2. A newcomer, a novice (in certain *spec.* contexts: see quots.).

1930 J. LAIT *Big House* i. 6 A first-timer [in prison] is a 'stooge'. 1935 J. HARGAN *Gloss. Prison Lang.* 8 *Stooge*, first offender. 1942 FORBES & ALLEN *Ten Fighter Boys* 55 As the squadron was on readiness most of the day, training was difficult to do, but we did some. However, within a fortnight the squadron moved south to 'K': we stooges were left behind with one pilot to finish off training.

3. A person whose function is merely to carry out another's directions; an unquestioningly loyal or obsequious subordinate, a lackey; a person used as an instrument by someone behind the scenes, a cat's paw. Also *fig.*

1937 H. G. WELLS *Brynhild* vi. 85, I have to..proclaim you. Be your Aaron. Your John the Baptist. Your—Stooge! 1937 —— *Star Begotten* vii. 128 He assembled by wire and telephone all his most trusted henchmen, tools, stooges, subordinates, intimates. 1944 *Times* 6 Jan. 8/3 'If the Beveridge plan is adopted, does it mean that we shall all become State stooges?'.. 'No... I have been a Civil servant myself, and I rather resent the suggestion that a Civil servant is a stooge.' 1948 *Observer* 7 Mar. 4/2 Communists have no use for democratic Socialists except as stooges, and the end they are working for is not Socialism but the totalitarian police-State. 1951 *Negro Hist. Bull.* (U.S.) Feb. 111/1 Black stooges mouthing the sentiments of the white politicians. 1952 R. A. KNOX *Hidden Stream* xvii. 157 If I see a rather nice picture in a shop and..buy it, is that because..I can't resist buying it? But if so, surely my will is not really free: it is just a sort of stooge. 1957 M. SPARK *Comforters* iii. 69 At first I thought she was running a gang, but now, all things considered, I think she may be their stooge. 1960 *Washington Post* 28 Apr. A 22/1 But..his habit of surrounding himself with stooges and sycophants, inevitably led to the debacle after an egregiously fraudulent election. 1978 *Detroit Free Press* 5 Mar. A 11/1 Joshua Nkomo and Robert Mugabe..branded the moderate African leaders as 'sworn stooges of Premier (Ian) Smith'.

4. *R.A.F.* In war-time: a flight during which one does not expect to encounter the enemy. Also *attrib.* and in *stooge-around*.

1942 T. RATTIGAN *Flare Path* I. 37 It's a raid, I suppose. *Teddy.* It's not exactly a practice stooge-around. 1945 C. H. WARD-JACKSON *It's a Piece of Cake* 57 *Stooge patrol*, a patrol on which the pilot does not see, or expect to see, the enemy. 1952 M. TRIPP *Faith is Windsock* v. 86 At one stage we saw a Fortress orbiting slowly, presumably on a stooge with a team of W/Ops jamming enemy frequencies.

5. *attrib.* and *Comb.*

1940 *Punch* 1 May 482/3 His Lordship..was taken on as a stooge fiance in order to camouflage Felicity's unprincipled intentions. 1948 PARTRIDGE *Dict. Forces' Slang* 183 *Stooge pilot*, a pilot employed in flying-training aircraft carrying untrained navigators or gunners. 1957 R. N. CAREW HUNT *Guide to Communist Jargon* xxxiii. 115 The Communists..introduced one-party government, and the various stooge-parties the existence of which they permitted had no influence in determining policy. 1958 *Observer* 16 Mar. 17/6 The sententious, almost stooge-like, quality associated with the chorus in Greek tragedy.

stooge (stūdʒ), *v.* [f. the sb.] **1.** *intr.* To act as a stooge (senses 1 and 3) (*for* someone). *slang.*

1939 R. CHANDLER *Big Sleep* xviii. 135 We're glad to stooge for a shamus of his standing. 1955 J. THOMAS *No Banners* xxii. 214 One of the *Milice* degenerates who stooged for the Gestapo. 1973 'G. BLACK' *Bitter Tea* viii. 122 For a time Jeremy stooged in espionage, but that must have hurt his feet. 1979 *Sci. Amer.* May 22/3 That Strang often stooged for Geller is well established.

2. *slang* (orig. *R.A.F.*). Of an aircraft: to cruise (*about, around*, etc.). Hence *gen.*, to drift, wander, move randomly.

1941 *Illustr. London News* 9 Aug. 165/2 (*caption*) We just stooged about watching the bombers drop their loads. 1942 T. RATTIGAN *Flare Path* I. 19 We were stooging along over the Dutch coast. 1942 [see *BEAT *v.*[1] 40 i]. 1953 G. HEYER *Detection Unlimited* xiii. 208 Stooging round with me, and thinking how much better you could do the job yourself. 1956 'J. WYNDHAM' *Seeds of Time* 136 The streets became..full of crowds stooging around. 1958 M. K. JOSEPH *I'll soldier no More* xiii. 238 Been in 691 Squadron, stooging around the Channel ports all winter. 1973 'N. GRAHAM' *Murder in Dark Room* xviii. 128, I noticed the Austin in the mirror... That made me think I'd seen another black Austin stooging around fairly recently.

Hence **stoo·ging** *vbl. sb.*

1944 *Times* 26 Jan. 4/2 Anti-submarine patrols form another vitally important part of the Coastal Air Force's work; it is often dull, monotonous 'stooging', but is also often well rewarded. 1960 D. STOREY *This Sporting Life* I. ii. 62, I don't want the thought of your stooging always lying over me. 1978 J. GARDNER *Dancing Dodo* xviii. 134, I did some stooging—keeping cave, you know.

† **stook** (stuk), *sb.*[2] *Obs. slang.* Also **stoock.** [Possibly ad. G. *stück* piece.] A pocket-handkerchief. Also *Comb.*, as **stook-buzzer, -hauler**, one who steals pocket-handkerchiefs.

1859 HOTTEN *Dict. Slang* 103 *Stook*, a pocket-handkerchief. *Stook hauler*, or *buzzer*, a thief who takes pocket-handkerchiefs. 1862 H. MAYHEW *London Labour* Extra vol. 25 *Stook-buzzers*, those who steal handerchiefs. 1889 E. SAMPSON *Tales of Fancy* 18 A dirty face, and a still more dirty 'stook'. 1893 P. H. EMERSON *Signor Lippo* xiv. 48 All I get is my kip and a clean mill tog, a pair of pollies and a stoock.

stookie (stu·ki), *Sc.* and *north. dial.* Also **steuke, stoukie.** [dial. var. STUCCO *sb.*] **1.** Plaster of Paris; any plaster-like substance.

1796 *Edin. Mag.* May 385 The carved wood an' polish'd stoukie. 1948 *Proc. Sc. Anthrop. & Folklore Soc.* III. iii. 83 When the doorstep had been washed, the careful housewife could draw designs and patterns with white 'stookie'. 1968 in *Sc. Nat. Dict.* (1974) IX. 60/3 My stooky halfed in two and I had to go back into hospital.

2. A plaster statue, a wax figure or dummy. Also *transf.*, a slow-witted person, a block-head.

a 1828 T. BEWICK *Howdy & Upgetting* (1850) 13 Dinna sit there leyke steuke, and sit and say nowse. 1895 W. C. FRASER *Whaups of Durley* xv. 219 Jamie sat like a stookey wi' a face as red as a partan's tae. 1903 J. LUMSDEN *Toorle* 193 Because, ye stupid stookie, I step aside for none. 1931 A. J. CRONIN *Hatter's Castle* II. iii. 256 Did ye notice the stookies in the window? 1934 J. BUCHAN *Free Fishers* xix. 314 Give her your arm..and don't stand glowering like a stookie. 1948 *Aberdeen Press & Jrnl.* 27 May 4/1 The civic representatives all standing like 'stookies' as they had not got the words of the Psalm they were singing.

stool, *sb.* Add: **2. b.** (Earlier example.)

1836 DICKENS *Let.* ?27 July (1965) I. 157 If you write me word that you will give him a stool, he shall sit himself upon it forthwith.

18. a. (Earlier example.) Also *transf.*, a person employed as a decoy by criminals.

1825 *Huntington* (N.Y.) *Town Rec.* (1889) III. 322 No person [shall] be permitted to gun with macheanes or stools in sd. Town. 1847 J. ROACH *Let.* 20 May in T. Coleman *Passage to America* (1972) xi. 183 There is three hundred emigrants in the Rochester tonight... The head man is a 'Stool'—make him jump.

b. A police informer. Cf. *stool-pigeon*, sense 19 b in Dict. and Suppl.

1906 G. E. STEVENS *Wicked City* 233 Under others were inscribed: 'He is a "stool".'..'He was croaked by the cops.' 1915 J. LONDON *Jacket* ii. 10 They laughed at him and turned him away..for the stool that he was. 1932 E. WALLACE *When Gangs came to London* xv. 129 I'm not so sure that I want to tell you anything—I never was a stool. 1939 J. STEINBECK *Grapes of Wrath* xx. 338 I'll come for ya tonight. Maybe I'm wrong. There's stools aroun' all a time. 1962 B. COBB *Murder: Men Only* I. 12 He said he wasn't a stool, he wasn't giving anybody away.

19. b. stool-pigeon (*a*) (earlier examples); (*b*) a police informer.

1830 *Workingman's Gaz.* (Woodstock, Vermont) 1 Dec. 79/2 A wag who keeps an oyster cellar in Newark advertises, among other things, 'wildbirds domesticated and stool pigeons trained to catch votes for the next Presidency—warranted to suit either party.' 1836 W. IRVING *Astoria* I. 137 One man..was used like a 'stool pigeon', to decoy the others. 1844 [see *ROPER 5]. 1845 *Yankee* (Boston) 9 Aug. 2/6 If this business is so profitable to thieves, how much do those [*sc.* police officers] make out of it who encourage the stool pigeon business? 1849 *Bankers' Mag.* Aug. 89 The senior high constable of Philadelphia..recollected that Harry White..who he had been lately using as a 'stool pigeon', or secret informer, had informed him..that 'a big thing' was coming off shortly. 1850 *Congress. Globe* 18 July 1403/1 Sheltering this aggression, on the part of the United States, behind 'poor New Mexico', who is only a stool-pigeon. 1910 E. A. WALCOTT *Open Door* 134 Rafferty..assured the chief that he would pass word to certain stool-pigeons to keep their eyes and ears open for trace of the missing canvas. 1930 *Times Lit. Suppl.* 4 Dec. 1047/3 Occasionally a masterful rogue arose who shot a few people as 'stool-pigeons', even though they had never imparted any information to the police. 1974 J. THOMSON *Long Revenge* ii. 23 A stool pigeon planted in a local Gestapo prison to eavesdrop on the detainees.

stool, *v.* Add: **4. a.** (Earlier example.)

1842 W. P. HAWES *Sporting Scenes* I. 55 I'll tell you all about that..the next time we're stooling snipe together.

b. *intr.* To act as a stool or stool-pigeon; to inform *on* (someone). Chiefly *U.S. slang.*

1911 [see *BOOB *sb.* 1]. 1938 *Amer. Speech* XIII. 191/2 *To stool*, to act as a stool-pigeon. 1950 PATTERSON & CONRAD *Scottsboro Boy* III. v. 224 There were little mice in Kilby. They ran in the cells. They weren't the trouble that the big rats were, though, them that stooled on you. 1960 'E. MCBAIN' *See them Die* v. 48 You'd stool on Pepe for that rotten cop?..A stoolie is a stoolie. 1973 'B. MATHER' *Snowline* xi. 133 'I stand in a sort of special relationship with these bums. If they thought I was stooling on them—well, you see what I mean?' 'No,..I don't see that putting me in touch..could possibly be construed as stooling. I'm not a policeman.'

stoolie (stū·li). *U.S. slang.* [f.*STOOL *sb.* 18 b or *stool(-pigeon)* (s.v. STOOL *sb.* 19 b) + -IE.] A police informer, a stool-pigeon.

1924 G. C. HENDERSON *Keys to Crookdom* 419 *Stool pigeon*, a spy, stoolie, squealer. One who betrays his fellow crooks. 1930 'E. QUEEN' *French Powder Mystery* p. xiv, Without the stool-pigeon a huge percentage of felonies would remain unsolved... Our problem is to find a 'stoolie' who will part with the tip. 1947 *Sun* (Baltimore) 13 Sept. 8/1 Victor Mature..succeeds in winning sympathy for Nick against odds, overcoming even the stigma which attaches to the stoolie. 1958 'E. MCBAIN' *Killer's Payoff* (1960) viii. 79 The policeman trusted the stoolie's information... The stoolie trusted the policeman... Cops were averse to working with pigeons they did not know and trust. 1960 [see *STOOL *v.* 4 b]. 1974 T. P. WHITNEY tr. *Solzhenitsyn's Gulag Archipelago* I. iii. 128 'There is no way out! You have to confess to everything!' whisper the stoolies who have been planted in the cell. 1978 LAROSA & TANENBAUM *Random Factor* (1979) 60 When Parker put the pressure on, some stoolie somewhere would turn the man he was looking for.

stoop, *sb.*[3] Add: **b. stoop ball** *N. Amer.*, a ball game resembling baseball, but in which the ball is thrown against a stoop or building rather than to a batter.

1941 B. SCHULBERG *What makes Sammy Run?* ix. 166 Kids yelling at each other in a stoop-ball game. 1947 *Commentary* May 463/2 As one of a large family of games such as stoopball..it demands an ability to maneuver freely. 1959 J. D. SALINGER in *New Yorker* 6 June 102/2 Stoopball, for the information of rural readers, is a ball game played with the support of a flight of brownstone steps or the front of a apartment building. 1978 G. A. SHEEHAN *Running & Being* vii. 90 We knew our block... Knew which steps to get pointers in stoop ball.

stoop, *v.*[1] Add: **III. 14. stoop crop** *N. Amer.*, a crop whose cultivation demands stoop labour; **stoop labour** *N. Amer.*, agricultural labour performed in a stooping (or squatting) position; **stoop tag** *N. Amer.* = *SQUAT TAG.

1928 *Sat. Even. Post* 10 Mar. 170/2 He does heavy field work—particularly in the so-called 'stoop crops' and 'knee crops' of vegetable and cantaloupe production. 1939 J. STEINBECK *Grapes of Wrath* xix. 316 Lettuce, cauliflower, artichokes, potatoes—stoop crops. 1967 *PTA Mag.* (U.S.) June 5 He was one of the migrant workers who follow the course of stoop crops through California fields and valleys. 1943 *Sun* (Baltimore) 3 Aug. 11/1 Asparagus cutting ordinarily is a specialized stoop-labor job. 1959 *Economist* 7 Mar. 876/1 Some harvesting can be done mechanically, but most crops still require back-breaking 'stoop' labour. 1972 *Islander* (Victoria, B.C.) 23 Apr. 13/2 Most moved down to southern Ontario to do back-breaking stoop labor in its sugar-beet fields. 1979 G. SWARTHOUT *Skeletons* 89 There are eight million illegals in the country... It would be one thing if they were all agricultural—stoop labor, fruit- and produce-pickers, so on. 1898 F. P. DUNNE *Mr. Dooley in Peace & War* (1899) 179 Little Flora an' little Fauna playin' stoop-tag aroun' a whale..or engagin' in some other sport iv childhood! 1955 W. GADDIS *Recognitions* I. iii. 146 The critics!..They're like a bunch of old maids playing stoop-tag in an asparagus patch.

stoopid (stū·pid), *a.* and *sb.* Non-standard (often joc. or playful) repr. of STUPID *a.* and *sb.*

1848 THACKERAY *Vanity Fair* xl. 362 Hold your tongue, you stoopid old fool. *Ibid.* lv. 499 Shut your mouth, you old stoopid. 1854 MRS. GASKELL *Let.* 2 Sept. (1966) 303 Many happy returns of your birthday..I hope it won't be a 'stoopid' day. 1902 F. G. ELLERTON *Let.* 11 Aug. in

S. Bailey *John Bailey* (1935) 83 Glad you had a little slap at that stoopid old Swinburne. **1913** R. BROOKE *Let.* 24? Nov. (1968) 537 I'm going to spend 5 days a week there, and three in London (that's 8, stoopid). **1956** N. MARSH *Off with his Head* (1957) x. 211 Lor', Dulcie, what a stoopid gel you are. **1978** C. STORR *Winter's End* xi. 131 'I didn't like your being angry with me.' He began with a denial..then checked himself. 'I was stoopid.'

stop, *sb.*[2] Add: **I. 1. g.** An act of stopping and questioning a suspected person.

1968 J. LOCK *Lady Policeman* iii. 21 These stops winkled out the juveniles who had absconded. **1970** P. LAURIE *Scotland Yard* ii. 47 He appreciates encouragement, and has been advised..about stops on the street.

II. 12. Also in *Photogr.*, a diaphragm or (orig.) a perforated plate for reducing the effective diameter of the lens of a camera or enlarger (now usu. built into the apparatus); hence used as a unit of change of relative aperture (or exposure or film speed), a reduction of one stop being equivalent to a halving of any of these.

1858 SUTTON & WORDEN *Dict. Photogr.* 255 The principle of this form of lens will be best understood by discussing, in the first place, the case of a single plano-convex lens, with a stop in front. **1883** *Photogr. Simplified* 23 Always focus with the largest stop, so as to get as much light as possible, and afterwards insert a stop which gives the necessary sharpness. **1902** G. B. SHAW *Let.* 11 Aug. (1972) II. 282 A slow plate and a suitably small stop will prolong the exposure sufficiently to make it manageable by hand with a cap. **1955** MORGAN & LESTER *Leica Man.* (ed. 13) ii. 75 With lenses of short focal length, the addition of 62·5mm extension results in the true aperture being nearly 2 stops smaller than the marked f-numbers. **1961** G. MILLERSON *Telev. Production* iii. 36 Lens diaphragms are graduated in units called stops or f-numbers. **1977** H. INNES *Big Footprints* II. iii. 179 The light's going to be tricky... It'll soon be dusk. If I were you I'd open up a stop. **1979** *Amat. Photographer* 10 Jan. 90/1 The extra two stops of film speed obtained by raising 400ASA to 1600 are invaluable under such conditions.

III. 16. (Later examples.) Now freq. in phrase *to pull out all the stops,* to make every possible effort.

1927 *Oxford Mag.* 20 Oct. 3/2 He may be said to have 'pulled out all his stops'. He gave the University a speech which for ease, eloquence and felicity could not readily be surpassed or indeed equalled. **1955** A. L. ROWSE *Expansion of Elizabethan England* 123 As his rebellion progressed Tyrone had to pull out the Catholic stop. **1957** *Economist* 5 Oct. 20/2 A Russian admiral on a good will naval visit to the Syrian port of Lattakia was serenading nationalism with all the right stops out. **1965** MRS. L. B. JOHNSON *White House Diary* 20 Dec. (1970) 341 This evening we gave a State Dinner... We opened up all the stops and the Christmas carols rang forth. **1974** A. PRICE *Other Paths to Glory* I. vi. 77 'But they have no idea who did it?' 'Not from what I heard... I know they're pulling out all the stops, though.' **1978** P. MCCUTCHAN *Blackmail North* ii. 20 We'll be doing our best, all stops out.

IV. 17. d. *Cryptography.* A character representing a punctuation mark.

1915 [see *NULL *sb.*[1] b]. **1939** F. PRATT *Secret & Urgent* 18 *Stops* are punctuation marks, usually sentence endings, for which special characters are provided, sometimes placed after each word.

e. Short for *full stop*: (*a*) as used, spelt out, in a telegram; (*b*) = *PERIOD *sb.* 11 b.

1936 [see *LITERARY *a.* 3 b]. **1964** F. CHICHESTER *Lonely Sea & Sky* xxxii. 333 Another exciting telegram.. which read, 'Delighted to see that you have achieved your ambition to beat your own record Stop.' **1977** *Times* 7 Oct. 15/5 Sir, Almost all who write you on this subject assume that high productivity is desirable, stop.

18. b. (Later examples.) Also = *PERIOD *sb.* 11 b.

1861 GEO. ELIOT *Let.* 6 Oct. (1954) III. 456 There is a point of disgust..which one feels must make a full stop, and call for a *Finis* in friendship. **1923** P. SELVER tr. *Čapek's R.U.R.* I. 10 It was in the year 1920 that old Rossum the great physiologist, who was then quite a young scientist, betook himself to this distant island for the purpose of studying the ocean fauna, full stop. **1962** *Observer* 1 July 8/5 The controversy has been between those who say yes, full stop, and those who say yes, but... **1971** R. AMBERLEY *Ordinary Accident* x. 92 Once he sends for a lawyer then that will be full stop.

V. 28. a. (Earlier example in sense 'the game of Newmarket'.)

1886 W. B. DICK *Mod. Pocket Hoyle* (ed. 11) 343 Newmarket, or Stops. This game is played in a similar manner to the game of 'Boodle'.

† **28*.** *Cricket.* A fielder standing three or four yards behind the wicket, a little on the off side. *Obs.* Cf. *BACK-STOP b, *long-stop* s.v. LONG *a.*[1] 18 d.

1773 in H. T. Waghorn *Cricket Scores, Notes, &c.* (1899) 90 All England. May, Lumpey, bowlers; Minshul, Miller, Parmore (stop). Hampshire. Bret, Nyren, bowlers; Small, Sutton, Lear (stop). **1851** W. CLARKE in W. Bolland *Cricket Notes* 129 In laying out your field, you should be careful in selecting good men for your principal places, such as wicket keeper, point, stop, short slip.

V. 29. stop band *Electronics*, a band of frequencies which are highly attenuated by a filter; **stop bath** *Photogr.*, a bath for arresting the process of the preceding bath, esp. development, by neutralizing any of its chemical that may still be present; **stop bead** [BEAD *sb.* 6 b] (see quot. 1964); **stop-butt,** a slope or bank constructed behind the targets at a rifle-range to stop bullets; **stop button,** a button or switch which is pressed or pulled to stop the action of a machine; **stop chords** *Jazz,* chords played on the first beat of every bar or every other bar, as the only accompaniment to a solo; **stop chorus** *Jazz,* a solo accompanied by stop chords; **stop consonant** = sense 19 b; **stop-cylinder,** a printing press in which the cylinder is stopped to permit the return of the reciprocating carriage; **stop lamp,** a light on the rear of a motor vehicle, which is automatically illuminated when the brakes are applied; **stop light,** (*a*) = *stop lamp* above; (*b*) *N. Amer.* = *stop sign* below, also *fig.*; **stop list,** (*a*) a list of persons, etc., deprived of particular rights, privileges, or services; *spec.* a list of persons with whom members of an association are forbidden to do business; (*b*) a list of prohibited books; (*c*) a list of words to be omitted from a concordance or index; hence **stop-list** *v. trans.*, to include in a stop list; **stop log,** a log or plank, or a beam or plate of concrete or steel, fitting between vertical grooves in walls or piers to close a water channel; **stop-netting** = *stop-net* (*b*); **stop sign,** a sign indicating that traffic should stop; *N. Amer.* spec., a red traffic-light; **stop signal,** a signal indicating whether a train should stop; **stop time** *Jazz,* a stop chorus or a series of stop chords; **stop volley** *Lawn Tennis* (see quot. 1928); **stopway,** an area at the end of an airfield runway in which an aircraft can be stopped after an interrupted take-off; **stop word,** a word (usu. one of a set of the words most frequently occurring in a language or text) that is automatically omitted from or treated less fully in a computer-generated concordance or index.

1922 Stop band [see *passband* s.v. *PASS *sb.*[2] 17 b]. **1959** KUH & PEDERSON *Princ. Circuit Synthesis* xiii. 200 The frequency where the pass- and stopbands coalesce is called the cutoff frequency. **1978** *Internat. Jrnl. Electronics* XLV. 247 Filters are designed with various frequency characteristics for the pass band and the stop band and also with predefined zeros in the stop band. **1898** H. MACLEAN *Pop. Photographic Printing Processes* iv. 42 To counteract some more or less over-toning..what is termed a 'stop' bath is used. **1967** E. CHAMBERS *Photo-litho-Offset* v. 58 The required number of contacts are made on lith type plates, developed, passed into the stop-bath and etch-bleached in the usual manner. **1980** D. FRANCIS *Reflex* xiii. 151, I set out the trays of developer and stop bath and fixer. **1876** *Encycl. Brit.* IV. 496/1 An inner or stop bead is mitred round on the inside to complete the groove or channel for the lower sash. **1964** J. S. SCOTT *Dict. Building* 155 *Stop bead,* a bead mitred round the inner edge of a sash window to prevent the inner sash from swinging into the room. **1976** R. DAY *All about House Repair & Maintenance* 62 Broken sash cords are easily removed... First remove the stop bead on the inside. **1864** A. WALKER *Rifle* (ed. 2) 114 If at a smaller angle it would, instead of acting as a stop-butt [etc.]. **1923** KIPLING *Land & Sea Tales* 177 The long shed of the Village Rifle Club reeked with the oniony smell of smokeless powder, machine-oil, and creosote from the stop-butt. **1963** W. H. FULLER *Small-Bore Target Shooting* i. 25 Stop butt or bullet catchers. **1940** N. MARSH *Surfeit of Lampreys* (1941) xiv. 209 When we'd got about half-way d-down she started screaming... I shoved down the stop button. So we stopped... Just below the first floor. **1977** J. WAINWRIGHT *Day of Peppercorn Kill* 120 He glanced at the tape-recorder, pressed the 'stop' button and said, 'We need a new reel.' **1941** *Musical Q.* Jan. 52 The second chorus is played with great feeling by the clarinet to a background of 'stop chords', a very effective device of the New Orleans style. **1958** R. HARRIS in P. Gammond *Decca Bk. of Jazz* iii. 45 *Dipper Mouth* with a hot theme stated by the ensemble; a superb Dodds solo against stop chords; [etc.]. **1942** BERREY & VAN DEN BARK *Amer. Thes. Slang* § 578/10 *Stop chorus,* a chorus in which the orchestra plays only one note in every one or two measures as a background for a tap dancer or other soloist. **1968** P. OLIVER *Screening Blues* ii. 67 The singer 'reading on down' to each new chapter [in sermon-like recitations] against the stop chorus of the pianist or a full jazz band. **1975** Stop consonant [see *PRESSURIZATION]. **1978** *Maledicta* II. 111 Rising tones in Thai do not co-occur in syllables ending in a stop consonant. *a* **1877** KNIGHT *Dict. Mech.* I. 671/2 The stop-cylinder press, designed for woodcut printing. **1980** B. CRUTCHLEY *To be Printer* ii. 21 'And what do you know about printing?' I was about to reply..: 'Well, I can tell the difference between a two-rev and stop-cylinder,' (those were basic types of printing machine). **1959** *Motor Man.* (ed. 36) viii. 217 Sidelamps, headlamps, rear lamps and stop lamps should also be examined for bulb failure. **1979** *Southern Star* (Eire) 29 Sept. 2/6 Defendant was fined £3 for having no stop lamp, £3 for having no rear lamp and £3 for having no number plate lighting. **1930** D. MACKAIL *How Amusing!* 190 His stop-light flickered almost ceaselessly as he crawled round the square. **1931** O. NASH *Hard Lines* 45 But there is no stoplight For a talkative cosmoplite. **1950** *How to drive Car* (ed. 18) xi. 88 Most cars are now fitted with direction indicators and 'stop' lights. The latter are automatic if properly maintained and come on when the brakes are applied. **1978** *Verbatim* Sept. 7/2 The tremendous role that traffic signals play in our national consciousness (it can be argued that the entire Interstate system was built in order to get around —and under and over—stoplights). **1920** *Daily Tel.* 18 May 16/5 The association published his name on their stop list, the object of which was to prevent all members of the association having any trade relations with the offending agent. **1949** *Rep. Committee on Resale Price Maintenance* 54 in *Parl. Papers 1948–49* (Cmd. 7696) XX. 383 Only the 'open price-cutter' who advertised that he was committing a breach of the conditions of sale was immediately stop-listed. **1958** *Times* 13 Mar. 11/3 A nation with what is reported to be over 1,000 books on the stop-list had got enough censorship. **1963** *Times* 28 Jan. 9/2 Merseyside was on the original list but within a few months, because of the motor industry's plans and other new projects, was put on the stop-list. Last week it was restored to the active list. **1963** [see *re-list* vb. s.v. *RE-5 a]. **1970** *Computers & Humanities* IV. 167 This program segment provides for two stoplists. **1974** *Times* 5 Feb. (Europa Suppl.) p. xiv/5 With credit cards the vendor has to check against the stop list (to check on people who have had their accounts stopped, or cards that have been reported missing). **1975** O. SELA *Bengali Inheritance* xxi. 185, I intend to hold your passport... I'm also putting you on a stop list at Kai Tak [airport]... I don't want you disappearing. **1979** J. E. ROWLEY *Mechanised In-House Information Syst.* I. 74 Words in a title are compared with a stop-list, to suppress the generation of useless index entries. **1930** *Engineering* 6 June 725/3 Each weir is divided into six bays by piers, between which stop logs can be placed, while for emergency regulation..low level Stoney sluices are provided. **1973** *Detroit Legal News* 30 Aug. 13/2 Two feet of the south stop-log chamber wall at the Fairview Pumping Station was removed and had to be replaced with new reinforced concrete. **1927** Stop-netting [see *RUN-BACK 2]. **1981** *Sunday Tel.* 4 Oct. 16/3 A badly-flighted lob cleared the stop-netting. **1934** *Amer. Speech* IX. 114/2 Those who drive have to make allowances for *stop streets* and *stop signs.* **1951, 1972** [see *RUN *v.* 40 d]. **1976** *S. Wales Echo* 27 Nov. 9/3 Pleaded guilty by letter to failing to conform to a stop sign while on his motor-cycle. **1923, 1963** Stop signal [see *HOME B. 2 d]. **1929** *Musical Q.* XV. 611 As to what possibilities such free-will tricks as the jazz 'break', stop-time, the harmony chorus, an exaggerated syncopation, etc., hold for the development of musical form beyond jazz itself, he would be bold who would predict. **1966** *New Yorker* 11 June 135 The Onward was playing 'Victory Walk', an engaging stop-time number. **1978** *N.Y. Times* 30 Mar. c16/2 Even in strongly swinging situations, jumping brightly through crisply muted breaks and stop time, the singing flow of Mr. Vaché's playing is never lost. **1915** M. E. MCLOUGHLIN *Tennis as I play It* 56 That is when a 'stop-volley' is employed to drop a ball just over the net. **1928** B. NUTHALL *Learning Lawn Tennis* 106 One of the most useful strokes in the game..is what is called the 'stop volley'... It is necessary to be quite close to the net to play it. The racket is just put in the way of the ball, which drops dead on the other side of the net. **1978** *Times* 4 July 19/2 Ground strokes were spiced with many a delicate angled cross-court chip, the stop volley, the lob and smash. **1960** in *Guide to Civil Land Aerodrome Lighting* (*B.S.I.*) 7 *Stopway,* a defined rectangular area at the end of a runway which has been selected or prepared as a suitable area in which aircraft can be stopped after an interrupted take off but which is not suitable for use as part of the runway. **1980** *Observer* 2 Nov. 6/8 A.. DC-10 from Delhi ran from the runway on to the stopway, the hard section on either side, which is meant to be firm enough to take the weight of aircraft. **1969** *Computers & Humanities* III. 135 If stop words are desired, the user can either specify his own or request a standard list which is encoded within BIBCON. **1979** J. E. ROWLEY *Mechanised In-House Information Syst.* I. 74 The stop-list or stopword list contains words under which entries are not required, such as the, he, is, a and in some circumstances, machine, processing, plant, etc. **1982** *N. & Q.* Oct. 385/1, I understand that a microfiche concordance of the stop words will soon be available.

stop, *v.* Add: **II. 15. c.** (Earlier example.) Also, to hit (game).

1845 *Punch* 25 Jan. 46/2 Out they [*sc.* the hares] rushed from every quarter—so many—that it was often impossible to 'stop' more than one out of half-a-dozen.

e. *colloq.* (orig. *Mil.*). To be hit by (a bullet). Phrases *to stop one*: to be hit or killed; *to stop a packet*: see *PACKET *sb.* 1 f.

1901 *Boy's Own Paper* 5 Oct. 14/2 After the battle of Spion Kop, one man, who was hit in seven places, said that he had stopped a whole volley himself. **1915** *Sphere* 6 Nov. 144/1 A man's troubles begin rather than end when he 'stops' a German or Turkish bullet. **1916** E. V. LUCAS *Vermilion Box* clxxxiv. 213 Poor boy, I do so hope he manages not to 'stop one'—which is what being hit is called here. **1929** J. BUCHAN *Courts of Morning* I. xiii. 152 If I hadn't thought of that head-crashing dodge, I think I might have stopped a bullet. **1933** H. S. WALPOLE *Vanessa* IV. i. 682 Maurice stood there wishing that he might 'stop one' before he had to go over the top. *a* **1976** A. CHRISTIE *Autobiogr.* (1977) v. ii. 234 You stop one, you've had it, and you've left behind a young widow.

f. To drink; usu. in phr. *to stop one,* to take a drink. *Austral. slang.*

1924 *Truth* (Sydney) 27 Apr. 6 *Stop one,* to take a drink. **1929** K. S. PRICHARD *Coonardoo* xxix. 279 Geary poured himself a drink. 'Hi, Dick,' he called, 'could you stop one?' **1936** A. RUSSELL *Gone Nomad* x. 78 Then, jerking his finger knowingly, 'I s'pose yer could stop one?' I could. I needed that rum. **1937** PARTRIDGE *Dict. Slang* 835/2 *Stop a pot,* 'to quaff ale,' C. J. Dennis.

21. a. (Later examples in conventional phrases indicating that there is no obstacle to an action.)

1951 M. KENNEDY *Lucy Carmichael* II. iii. 94 You.. make an entrance if you like. I'm not stopping you. **1970** *Globe & Mail* (Toronto) 28 Sept. 23/2 (Advt.), Make the break with Tradition. What's to stop you? Certainly not the price. **1973** R. Thomas *If you can't be Good* (1974) xx. 180 'I wanta see Connie Mizelle,' he said. 'What's stopping you?' 'Not a damn thing,' he said. 'Let's go.'

c. *to stop the show* (orig. *U.S.*); to cause an interruption of a performance by provoking prolonged applause or laughter, or requests for encores. Cf. *show-stopper, -stopping* adj. s.v. *show *sb.*[1] 22.

1926 *Amer. Speech* I. 437/1 When an act proves to be such a wow that it is forced to respond to encore after encore and the remainder of the acts on the program must wait until the audience will allow them to go on, it is said to 'stop the show cold'. **1933** *Fortune* Aug. 92/1 Jim Europe had stopped the show with *St. Louis Blues.* **1957** R. Hart-Davis *Let.* 19 May in *Lyttelton–Hart-Davis Lett.* (1979) II. 103 The Gibbon quotation stopped the show long enough for me to consult my scrappy notes. **1966** 'M. Renault' *Mask of Apollo* vi. 107 This line, as I had feared it might, stopped the show. **1977** *Times* 13 June 15/4 *The Merchant of Venice* [was] performed by the Ibadan Boys' Grammar School... A British widower['s].. son..was cast as the Prince of Morocco. His opening line stopped the show: 'Mislike me not for my complexion—.'

d. To give a still picture of (a moving object).

1937 *Star* (Kansas City) 8 Aug. 3 The camera 'stops' the action of a chorus in training. **1937** *Discovery* Nov. 353/1 Anyone can find a gannet, and any shutter working to 1/500 sec. will 'stop' it. **1950** A. Huxley *Themes & Variations* 161 On Alexander's [tomb] the monster has been 'stopped', as the photographers say, in the act of shooting up from the doorway leading into the vault.

33. a. stop down. Also *absol.* and *intr.* for *pass.*

1971 P. Purser *Holy Father's Navy* xiv. 75 Can you stop down to make it look like dusk? **1978** *SLR Camera* Aug. 46/1 As the lens is focused through these various degrees of magnification the lens automatically stops down.

b*. stop off = senses 21 a, 23 b, and 24 a. Now *rare* or *obs.*

1891 W. B. Yeats *Let.* 21 Jan. (1954) I. 162 Ellis..may do some of my chapters himself... Providence has stopped off his terrible activity for the present with twelve lectures for the University Extension. **1892** —— *Lett.* (1954) II. 201, I helped to stop off another man of learning the other day who came trying to get a book from Unwin to do. **1902** H. James *Wings of Dove* VII. xxv. 382 Having suffered him to insist almost convicted her of indelicacy. Why hadn't she stopped him off? **1904** G. B. Lancaster *Sons o' Men* 47 Stop that row, Tommy... Stop it off. **1929** T. E. Lawrence *Let.* 22 July (1938) 666 Dirty Dogs, they *have* stopped off poor Trotsky.

III. 35. b. For *U.S.* read orig. *U.S. to stop over* (earlier and later examples); *to stop off* (earlier and later examples).

1855 *Knickerbocker* XLVI. 604 He had 'stopped off', he said, to see a friend. **1857** M. J. Holmes *Meadow-Brook* xvi. 182 Wishing to see a friend of his who lives here, we have stopped over one train. **1873** 'Mark Twain' & Warner *Gilded Age* xxiv. 218 Once when you renewed your ticket after stopping over in Baltimore. **1892** *Harper's Mag.* Feb. 437/2, I stopped off overnight to see about something for a friend. **1925** D. H. Lawrence *Let.* ?7 Nov. (1962) 864 It is great fun stopping off in Switzerland to see you. **1952** M. Laski *Village* xii. 173 'Shall we stop off soon and eat our lunch?' asked Roy and at the next field-gate they dismounted. **1970** G. F. Newman *Sir, You Bastard* viii. 244 Stopping off after court for an early liquid lunch. **1971** *Daily Tel.* 29 Dec. 10 Many people suffer from jet fatigue and on long-distance routes often go to the additional expense of stopping over somewhere on the way to recuperate.

c. *to stop in*: to pay a brief visit, 'drop in'. *U.S.*

1904 *Dialect Notes* II. 421 *Stop in, vb. i.*, to call. 'I *stopped in* at his house one day.' **1925** T. Dreiser *Amer. Tragedy* (1926) I. II. xxxvi. 402 He stopped in, not at all sure that on this first occasion he would be able to broach the dangerous subject. **1953** J. Cheever in *New Yorker* 22 Aug. 23/2 He was rude to his friends when they stopped in for a drink. **1963** *Jrnl. Amer. Med. Assoc.* 26 Oct. 459/1 He was found dead in his crib by a family friend who had stopped in at the home. **1979** *Yale Alumni Mag.* Apr. (Suppl.) cn17/3 Classmates are eagerly invited to stop in!

d. With *by*: (*a*) as *adv.*, = sense 35 c above; (*b*) as *prep.*, to call at, visit (a place). orig. *U.S.*

1905 *Dialect Notes* III. 96 *Stop by, v. phr.*, to call, to visit. 'I believe I'll *stop by* and see Bud.' **1923** *Ibid.* V. 244 *Stop by*, v. phr., to visit. '*Stop by* my house.' **1928** F. N. Hart *Bellamy Trail* v. 172 They were going to stop by for her. **1943** T. Pratt *Barefoot Mailman* i. 11, I picked him up when I stopped by at St. Augustine. **1953** N. Gordimer *Lying Days* II. v. 48 It was Ludi, he would stop by at the old Plaskett's on the way to say hullo—. **1957** *New Yorker* 2 Nov. 89/3 Don't wait..stop by your favorite shop and try one today. **1964** Mrs. L. B. Johnson *White House Diary* 8 Apr. (1970) 103, I had asked Mrs. MacArthur and her son..to stop by the White House to warm up and have a cup of tea. **1973** M. Amis *Rachel Papers* 20, I mentioned that Gloria would probably be stopping by later on.

36. b. *to stop out* (examples); *spec. N. Amer.*, to interrupt one's higher education for a time in order to pursue some other activity.

1926 I. S. Cobb *Some United States* xi. 257 I'm a Virginian—at present stopping out in Kentucky. **1942** Berrey & Van den Bark *Amer. Thes. Slang* § 214/7 *Stop out*, to stay away from home all night. **1971** *Less Time, More Options* (Rep. Carnegie Commission on Higher Educ.) vii. 28 Colleges and universities can assist by.. encouraging students to have work or service experience before entering college, to stop out while in college to obtain it, or both. **1977** *N.Y. Times* 16 Jan. IV. 9/1 Paul Marantz is stopping out. He's one of the estimated two million college undergraduates..who last year left school to spend some time in the outside world, or to try out some other form of education, but who do plan to return eventually and earn their degrees.

37. e. *Bridge.* To refrain from increasing one's bid beyond a specified level. Const. *in.*

1959 *Listener* 5 Feb. 265/1 The British pair stopped in Five Hearts. **1964** Frey & Truscott *Official Encycl. Bridge* 533/1 *Stopping below game*, the decision to 'stop on a dime' in two no trump or three of a major may be influenced by a variety of factors.

IV. 43. a. stop-tap, the time at which drinks cease to be served in a public house.

1938 F. D. Sharpe *Sharpe of Flying Squad* xxiii. 240 Bob said that they hadn't *passed by* any public houses and that it was after 'stop tap' that they were passing the shop. **1940** Dylan Thomas *Portr. Artist as Young Dog* 228 If you go for a constitutional after stop-tap along the sands you might as well be in Sodom and Gomorrah. **1960** V. Jenkins *Lions down Under* 103 The 'five o'clock, to six o'clock swill' in the bars of New Zealand cities—for 'stop-tap' is at six—is also a phenomenon to be avoided. **1975** R. Lewis *Part of Virtue* vi. 147 Next evening, after stop tap, he was putting some crates out behind the pub.

b. *Cinematogr.* Combinations of the verb with a sb., with reference to the technique of stopping the camera between frames in order to produce special effects, esp. animation; as *stop-action, -frame, -motion, -shot*, etc.

1912 F. A. Talbot *Moving Pictures* 201 When the 'stop' call was given the witch disappeared from the stage... The strange effects produced in the witch's cave were obtained both by double printing and the 'stop-motion'. **1915** J. B. Rathbun *Motion Picture Making* 73 Trick street scenes, commonly known as 'stop' pictures. **1933** G. H. Sewell *Commercial Cinematography* x. 155 Stop-motion is..the method of cine-photography in which one, two, or three frames..are taken at one time, the camera being stopped and the subject re-arranged after each shot or group of shots. **1959** Halas & Manvell *Technique Film Animation* xxii. 274 The technique for stop-action puppet work must be worked out in terms of single motion-picture frames. **1966** *Listener* 14 July 67/1 The stop-shots neatly made each point. **1968** *Guardian* 22 Mar. 10/4 The stop-frame technique in which the puppets are photographed separately for each movement. **1976** R. B. Parker *Promised Land* (1977) xx. 122 Powers was quiet. We all were. It was like a stop frame in instant replay. **1980** *Sci. Amer.* Apr. 84/1 A glass is a solid that can be regarded as a stop-action photograph of a liquid.

44. stop and frisk *a.*, of or pertaining to the stopping and searching of suspects by the police; so **stop-and-search, stop-search-question**; **stop-and-start** *a.*, alternately stopping and starting; **stop-me-and-buy-one,** a travelling vendor of refreshments, usu. ice-creams [from the slogan on the refrigerated box at the front of Wall's Ice-Cream tricycles]; also *attrib.*; **stop-off,** (*b*) the act of stopping off (see 35 b); a place where one stops off; also *attrib.*; **stop-out,** (*a*) *colloq.*, one who stays out late; (*b*) *N. Amer.*, a student who interrupts his or her studies for a time in order to pursue some other activity; an interruption of studies for this purpose; also *attrib.*; **stop-over,** (also **stopover**), (*a*) (earlier and later examples); (*b*) permission given to a passenger to break his journey (now *rare* or *obs.*); (*c*) a place where a journey is broken; also *fig.*

1967 *Economist* 21 Oct. 286/1 The cases to be heard this year are a mixed bag. Those involving the criminal law and the police—particularly 'stop and frisk' laws—may be the most controversial. **1975** *New Yorker* 2 June 101/1 A Terry stop is what civil libertarians sometimes refer to as stop-and-frisk. **1974** *Spartanburg* (S. Carolina) *Herald* 25 Apr. A 10/1 A federal court judge began hearing arguments Wednesday on whether to halt the hotly debated police 'Operation Zebra' stop-and-search dragnet for the black killer or killers of 12 whites. **1950** J. G. Davis *Dict. Dairying* 62 The feed to the dies is done with a variable stop-and-start motion, allowing the strip time to stop while the die punches out the shape. **1961** *Times* 4 May 13/6 The stop-and-start tendencies of our economy. **1976** *Woman's Day* (U.S.) Nov. 50/2 If you do a lot of stop-and-start driving,..change every three months or 3,000 miles. [**1935** *Automobile & Carriage Builders' Jrnl.* LXXV. 4/1 'Stop me and buy one.' The latest type of cycle carrier for ice-cream vending.] **1935** *Food* Oct. 3/1 A holiday spent in a number of South Coast towns suggests that England is..becoming as ice-cream-minded as North America. The last three hot summers have provided a golden harvest for the familiar tricycle. But even more recent..has been the appearance..of the 'ice-cream parlour'... 'Come in and have one' is evidently proving as alluring a slogan as the more familiar 'Stop me and buy one'. **1936** N. Coward *To-Night at 8.30* 49 Asked if I'd got an ice-cream wafer... What did she think I was, a 'Stop me and buy one'? **1939** N. Monsarrat *This is Schoolroom* xi. 228 To..buy an ice from the stop-me-and-buy-one man. **1947** Dylan Thomas *Let.* 11 Apr. (1966) 300 There were stop-me-&-buy-one bicycle boys selling, not ice-cream, but bottles of Chianti. **1979** D. Robinson *Eldorado Network* III. xliii. 288 Ice-cream. Stop-me-and-buy-one, the Eldorado man on a tricycle. **1912** J. Sandilands *Western Canad. Dict. & Phrase-bk.*, *Stop-off* or *stop-over privileges*, an arrangement made with the ticket agent to break a railway journey at some place where the passenger wishes to make a short halt. **1931** C. Beaton *Jrnl.* Feb. in *Wandering Years* (1961) x. 226 En route for home there was a three-week stop-off in Paris. **1947** *Sun* (Baltimore) 18 Jan. 4/2 Is the police court merely a stop-off between one back room and the next? **1958** *Times Lit. Suppl.* 7 Mar. 125/3 London, New York, Paris, Rome come to life not as tourist centres, holiday stop-offs, but as places of work. **1977** *Horse & Hound* 14 Jan. 25/2 Cost of the trip is £530 return (excursion, 21 days–6 months, no stop-offs). **1906** E. Dyson *Fact'ry 'Ands* ii. 24 'See,' cried Annie—'See, you dirty stop-out!' She placed the hat on the floor and danced wildly amongst the feathers. **1941** Baker *Dict. Austral. Slang* 72 *Stop-out*, an inveterate gadabout, esp. a woman. **1966** F. Shaw et al. *Lern Yerself Scouse* 27 *Yer a derty stopout*, you are a nocturnal reveller. **1971** *Less Time, More Options* (Rep. Carnegie Commission on Higher Educ.) vi. 13 That service and other employment opportunities be created for students between high school and at stop-out points in college. *Ibid.* 21 Those who plan to continue with academic study either directly or after a stop out. **1971** *Time* 27 Sept. 79/3 Still, many stop-outs do better academically than their less-seasoned classmates, if only because they are a year older. **1974** *Globe & Mail* (Toronto) 31 Oct. 1/5 The so-called stopout students, those who postponed entering university immediately after high school graduation, now are starting to go back to school. **1881** *Harper's Mag.* Apr. 767/2 They are allowed stop-over tickets which give them the privilege of turning their stock out at any place for the winter, and then sending them on in the spring to market. **1885** *Outing* (U.S.) Nov. 150/2 There I took advantage of what, in railroad parlance, is called a 'stop-over'. **1905** *Chambers's Jrnl.* Jan. 87/1 At Vancouver I stepped on board a Canadian Pacific Railway steamer bound for Hong-kong, with a stop-over on my second-class ticket. **1928** *Blue Peter* July p. iv (Advt.), A Convenient Stopover. Honolulu is a regular port of call for passenger steamers crossing to or from the Orient. **1953** I. Levin *Kiss before Dying* I. ii. 11 College would only be an unnecessary stopover on the road to..success. **1959** *Economist* 20 June 1106/1 Mr Khrushchev will round off his Scandinavian tour in August by a two or three day stop-over in Helsinki. **1976** *National Observer* (U.S.) 22 May 18/6 From New York the round-trip economy fare is about $1,600, with stopover privileges in London and Nairobi. Because it's a very long flight, you can use the stopovers. **1973** *Time Out* 2–8 Mar. 10/3 More recently they have been performing stop-search-question late night patrols in Hornsey which have resulted in such serious crime detection as arresting people with a quid's worth of dope.

stop-and-go (stǫp ənd gōᵘ), *a.* Also **stop and go.** [f. Stop *v.* + And *conj.* + Go *v.*] **1.** = *stop-go *adj.* 1.

1926 G. Frankau *My Unsentimental Journey* xi. 145 St. Louis; where the men..have the most elaborate 'stop and go' signs for their traffic. **1935** D. L. Sayers *Gaudy Night* viii. 177 Its modern bustle of cars and complication of stop-and-go lights. **1942** *Policy on Rotary Intersections* (Amer. Assoc. State Highway Officials) 1 There is discussion of design speeds, interweaving lengths, curves, geometric shapes, sight distance, roadway widths, cross slope, curbs, islands, lighting, stop-and-go control and special adaptations of rotary intersections. **1962** N. Freeling *Love in Amsterdam* I. 61 Don't use your brain. Be a farmer holding a stop-and-go sign.

2. = *stop-go *adj.* 2.

1943 F. L. Wright *Autobiogr.* (rev. ed.) IV. 329 No need to get tangled up in spasmodic stop-and-go traffic. **1972** *Jazz & Blues* Nov. 32/1 He also evinces real invention over the stop-and-go rhythms of *Departure.* **1977** 'E. McBain' *Long Time no See* vii. 94 His stop-and-go typing irritated Carella.

3. = *stop-go *adj.* 3.

1961 *Times* 5 Jan. 11/5 The short-term 'stop-and-go' remedies of recent years..deal with the symptoms rather than the disease. **1961** *Hansard Commons* 7 Nov. 850 Before the right hon. Member for Monmouth we had the present Prime Minister as Chancellor. He was a 'stop and go' man. **1962** *Listener* 10 May 817/2 The new-found interest in planning in Tothill Street was a direct reaction to the stop-and-go policies of 1959 and 1960.

stopbank (stǫ·pbæŋk). *Austral.* and *N.Z.* Also **stop-bank.** [f. Stop *sb.*[2] + Bank *sb.*[1]] A levee, an embankment.

1950 G. Wilson *Brave Company* xiii. 196 The clean lines of the river and the stopbank. **1958** S. Ashton-Warner *Spinster* 54 All them kids on the stopbank. **1965** S. T. Ollivier *Petticoat Farm* xv. 198 Stop-banks were raised against rivers. **1977** *N.Z. Herald* 5 Jan. 1-6/4 The Auckland Harbour Board controls to the tidal boundary at Bonds Rd, Matatoki, a vast acreage that has built up outside the stopbanks.

stope, *v.* Add: **2.** *Geol.* Of magma or a magmatic body: to make *its way* by stoping; also, to subject to stoping.

1908 *Amer. Jrnl. Sci.* CLXXVI. 19 The latter are regarded as then stoping their way up into the overlying shell. **1932** F. F. Grout *Petrogr. & Petrol.* III. 202 No batholith is known to have stoped its way to the actual surface. *Ibid.* 203 Some rocks are stoped and assimilated more readily than others. **1962** W. T. Huang *Petrology* iv. 104 If the specific gravity is lower than the corresponding solid rock, a magma could stope its way into rocks of similar chemical composition.

Hence **stoped** *ppl. a.*

1932 F. F. Grout *Petrogr. & Petrol.* III. 203 The stoped blocks may dissolve before moving far. **1970** K. C. Jackson *Textbk. Lithol.* ii. 38 The margin of the magma body becomes cluttered with scattered stoped blocks of wall rock.

stop-go (stǫp gōᵘ), *a.* and *sb.* [f. Stop *v.* + Go *v.*] **A.** *adj.* **1.** Of signs or lights: indicating alternately to traffic that it should stop or that it should go.

1918 *Wells Fargo Messenger* Feb. 94/3 The copper flashed us a smile as he gave his stop-go apparatus another twist. **1952** M. Steen *Phoenix Rising* ii. 50 They were.. held up..by 'Stop'-'Go' signs. **1965** *Motor* 17 July 1/2 The long queues of cars waiting at the wrongly timed stop-go lights.

2. Alternately stopping and going, or acting and not acting.

1960 *Times* 10 Oct. 16/1 In their new 'stop-go' style they were infinitely the more dangerous. **1973** 'M. Innes' *Appleby's Answer* iii. 32 Their taxi made only a tedious stop-go progress. **1980** *Times Lit. Suppl.* 2 May 503/4 Would that English historical journals discussed, for example, the implications for future research of the stop-go policy of recruitment of graduates to history departments.

3. *Econ.* Of, pertaining to, or designating a policy of alternately restricting demand, in order to contain inflation, and expanding credit, in order to reduce unemployment.

The earlier designation of the policy was *stop-and-go* (see *stop-and-go *a.* 3).

1962 *Daily Tel.* 21 Feb. 10 It is precisely these 'stop-go' policies of successive Chancellors which have been a major cause of our export troubles. **1965** *Listener* 3 June 817/2 The British Government then in office found its negotiating position undermined by gossip and arguments at home about the imminence of devaluation of the pound sterling as the only way out of the old stop-go circle. **1971** *Business Week* 13 Nov. 146/3 Yet Ulman and Flanagan conclude that governments have a strong tendency to choose stop-go policies. **1975** J. De Bres tr. *Mandel's Late Capitalism* xiv. 455 The 'Stop-Go' pattern of the British economy in the first post-war Tory era is the classical example of such a relatively autonomous credit cycle. **1979** *Dædalus* Spring 47 In Sweden, special factors reduced the country's vulnerability to uncontrollable money wage increases, hence to disruptive policies of the stop-go variety.

B. *sb.* *Econ.* A stop-go policy; the economic cycle resulting from this.

1964 S. Brittan *Treasury under Tories* vii. 208 This was the event which turned the business community violently against 'stop-go' and made it look with a less jaundiced eye on national planning. **1966** *Listener* 2 June 808/2 Does more inflation mean more difficulties with the balance of payments and more 'stop-go'? **1972** *Accountant* 23 Mar. 365 What evidence is there to convince management and industry that the new phase of expansion which the Chancellor's proposals should generate will not, as on so many previous occasions, culminate within some 18–24 months in a revival of 'stop-go' and balance of payments difficulties? **1976** K. Joseph *Monetarism is not Enough* 10 We refused to believe that it was the drug which had caused the need for a stop, hence we still say 'stop-go', but it is the go which causes the stop, not vice-versa.

stoping, *vbl. sb.* Add: **b.** *Geol.* The process by which intruding magma detaches blocks of the surrounding rock.

1903 R. A. Daly in *Amer. Jrnl. Sci.* CLXV. 272 (*heading*) The hypothesis of overhead stoping† by deep-seated magmas. [*Note*] †A technical mining term meaning to excavate upwards or sideways to remove ore. **1903** —— in *Bull. U.S. Geol. Surv.* No. 209. 102 Magmatic stoping would tend to weaken the earth's crust immediately above the intruding body. **1939** Bailey & Weir *Introd. Geol.* xlii. 237 On the whole, stoping is probably the most important method of emplacement. **1977** A. Hallam *Planet Earth* 69/1 Intrusions are emplaced in various ways: for example,..by stoping, a process of gradual movement involving the dislodging of the blocks of country rock and their incorporation—perhaps even assimilation—into the magma.

stoppable (stǫ·păb'l), *a.* [f. Stop *v.* + -able; cf. Stoppability.] That can be stopped.

1934 in Webster. **1977** *Time* 3 Jan. 20/1 Stop most anyone you see—they're generally stoppable—and he or she will soon be spinning you a web of recollection to entertain you both. **1982** *Economist* 16 Oct. 18/1 The dangers threatening Lebanon's Palestinians are not academic; they are both foreseeable and stoppable.

stoppage. Add: **7. b.** A cessation of work owing to disagreement between employer and employees; a strike or a lock-out.

1902 *Encycl. Brit.* XXV. 554/1 The adjustment of differences that might otherwise lead to stoppage. *Ibid.* XXXIII. 14/1 To distinguish stoppages as strikes or lock-outs according to the source of the original demand for a change of conditions would lead to a very arbitrary and misleading classification. **1926** *Publishers' Circular* 29 Dec. 895/3, 1926... The year of the General Stoppage. **1966** *Listener* 1 Sept. 302/2 An American-owned engineering works in north-west London is to close down because of stoppages and the economic squeeze. **1976** *West Lancs. Evening Gaz.* 8 Dec. 1/2 More than 350 Blackpool Corporation busmen agreed unanimously to give authority to the TGWU's North Lancashire District Committee to call them out on a one-day stoppage in support of their Fylde colleagues.

stopped, *ppl. a.* Add: **2. d.** *Bridge.* (See quots.) Cf. *stopper *sb.* 7 e.

1901 R. F. Foster *Foster's Bridge* 35 A Suit is Stopped when you can make one trick in it, or can compel the adversary to quit it and lead something else. **1929** M. C. Work *Compl. Contract Bridge* iv. 20 A suit is stopped when the bidder holds such cards in it that he can be sure of taking at least one trick in that suit.

9. *Carpentry.* Of a chamfer, housing, etc.: closed, not running the whole length of a member. Cf. Stop *v.* 30.

1918 *Woodwork Joints* 167 The sketch to the right shows 'stopped housing', the groove coming to within ½in. of the front edge of the shelf. **1934** P. A. Wells *Design in Woodwork* ii. 15 The number of joints can be trebled by variations such as 'through', 'stopped' or 'secret' dovetails. **1949** W. J. West *Woodwork* ix. 78 To cut stopped housings start by using a mallet and chisel to chop out a slot of the required depth. **1979** A. B. Emary *Woodworking* iii. 18 At (a) is seen the stopped housing joint where the recess has been terminated a short distance from one edge and the piece which fits into the recess has been cut to fit round the stopped end.

stopper, *sb.* Add: **1. g.** *Assoc. Football.* A player whose function is to block attacks on goal from the middle of the field. Also *attrib.* as *stopper centre-half.*

1934 D. Jack *Soccer* 124 The defensive pivot..is essentially a 'stopper', a destructive player if you like. **1941** *Daily Mail* 10 Feb. 4/2 Though occasionally outwitted by Lawton, Dykes made himself a nuisance as a stopper. **1951** *Sport* 16–22 Mar. 9/1 He was an admirable foil for two clever attacking halves, for he was a stopper pure and simple. **1961** *Times* 10 Feb. 19/6 A fundamental change in tactics with the arrival of the 'stopper' centre-half. **1978** *Time* 3 July 53/2 He spent the first half, at his own behest, in the unlikely role of a stopper on Paolo Rossi—and very nearly gave away a goal.

7. d. *Rowing.* The after part of a rowlock.

1897 J. Jeffery *Rowing* 8 That part against which the oar is pressed in rowing is called the 'thowl', and the opposite, or after-thowl, is called the 'stop', or 'stopper'. **1904** G. Rixon *Rowing & Sculling* 2 In some stock gigs it will be found that there is not sufficient room between the thowl and stopper, causing the oar to stick or 'lock' on a full reach forward.

e. *Bridge.* A card of such value that it can reasonably be counted on, in conjunction with other cards in the same suit, to take a trick in that suit. Cf. *stopped *ppl. a.* 2 d.

1901 R. F. Foster *Foster's Bridge* 112 When the make is original, a guarded king is very likely a stopper in the dealer's suit. **1913** F. Irwin *Auction High-Lights* 101 To bid 'a no-trump' declares nothing actually, except general help. The bid is often made on three stoppers. *Ibid.* 105 Four diamonds to the jack might not prove a stopper if the card next to the jack did not happen to be the ten-spot, but it is, and a sequence-stopper is always safe. **1933** *Times* 24 Jan. 13/4 This is a conventional and artificial response. It does not guarantee a 'stopper' in Spades. **1959** T. Reese *Bridge Player's Dict.* 222 Some players bid 1 NT on a fair balanced hand even when they have no stopper. **1978** *Detroit Free Press* 2 Apr. 19c/2 If North has a diamond stopper, he bids no trump.

f. Something which attracts and holds attention; something striking or impressive. *colloq.* Cf. *show-stopper* s.v. *show *sb.*[1] 22.

1968 *Punch* 21 Feb. 269/1 'What's your snap reaction, Jack?' broke in Gringeworth. 'It's um, well, certainly a stopper,' said Tubstraw. 'My God! It's the stopper of the century!' exclaimed Gringeworth. **1973** *Times* 21 Feb. 13/8 'A memorable image.' 'It's a stopper.'

stopping, *vbl. sb.* Add: **I. 1. b.** *stopping off*: also *attrib.*; *stopping out*; *stopping-over.*

1942 Berrey & Van den Bark *Amer. Thes. Slang* § 45/2 Small town,..*stopping-off place.* **1966** 'A. Hall' *9th Directive* iv. 41 I'll need up-to-the minute information ..final itinerary..stopping-off points, so forth.

1971 *Time* 27 Sept. 79/1 The trend of stopping out is growing..partly because the draft law now gives young men with high lottery numbers a new freedom. **1977** *N.Y. Times* 16 Jan. IV. 9/1 Stopping out..has become so popular on some campuses that the notion of graduating in four years seems almost quaint.

1932 *New Yorker* 4 June 38 You leave Seattle July 9, and do a bit of stopping-over at Yokohama, Tokio, and other Japanese ports.

III. 7. *stopping distance*; **stopping-house** *Canad.*, a house offering accommodation to travellers; a boarding-house or rooming-house; **stopping-place,** (*a*) (earlier and later examples); (*b*) *Canad. Hist.*, a stopping house, or a settlement where groups of travellers customarily stop for food and lodging; **stopping rule** *Statistics*, any rule in sequential testing or sampling for deciding when an investigation should be terminated, dependent on the cumulative trends in the results obtained.

1947 *Highway Code* 10 The good driver knows how stopping distances increase with speed, and drives accordingly. **1883** *Prince Albert* (Saskatchewan) *Times* 18 Apr. 1/5 The road from Carrot River crosses the South Saskatchewan at this point where there is now a first class ferry and stopping house. **1912** H. Footner *New Rivers of North* 235 None of the stopping-houses along this trail have progressed beyond the most primitive stage. They provide a floor for you to sleep on and a fire-place, in some cases a stove for you to cook your food on; that is all. **1970** R. & J. Paterson *Cranberry Portage* i. 4, I got a stoppinghouse here... My rooms is all full up. **1827** A. Sherwood *Gazetteer Georgia* 37 *Camp c.* in the N.W. part of the Warren..and well known as a stopping place. **1836** C. Fox *Jrnl.* 31 Aug. in *Memories of Old Friends* (1882) ii. 5 Dr. Buckland was an outside *compagnon de voyage*, but often came at stopping places for a little chat. **1878** J. M. LeMoine *Chronicles of St. Lawrence* 21 When being jolted in a two-wheeled post stage, without springs, over these villainous roads, the traveller will do well to fix beforehand the stopping places (for meals), as hostelries are few and far between. **1909** A. D. Cameron *New North* 28 We 'make tea' at Sturgeon Creek (the Namao Sepee of the Indians), the first of the 'stopping-places' or Waldorf-Astorias of the wilderness. **1950** Stopping place [see *lay-by *sb.* 1 c]. **1953** *Jrnl. R. Statistical Soc.* B. XV. 9 Thus if a history of the population is available over some period of time, $\lambda + \mu$ can be estimated from the observed number of incidents and the Ui, and $\lambda/(\lambda + \mu)$ from the proportion of the incidents that are births; the details will depend on the stopping rule. **1960** P. Armitage *Sequential Med. Trials* ii. 17 The design of the trial is determined entirely by the stopping-rule. **1978** *Brit. Jrnl. Cancer* XXXVIII. 760/1 Investigators were also asked whether they used any formal or informal stopping rules for the early termination of trial if treatment differences should develop.

stopple, *sb.*[1] Add: **1. d.** = *ear-plug* (*b*) s.v. *ear *sb.*[1] 16. *U.S.*

a **1961** in Webster, s.v., A stopple must be fitted into the ear canal so that noise does not leak around the edges. **1965** J. M. Cain *Magician's Wife* (1966) xvi. 121 He must put stopples in his ears to account for his failure to answer, in case his phone had rung. **1977** *New Yorker* 12 Sept. 161/3 (Advt.), Noise? No problem. Flents Ear Stopples seal it out.

stoppo (stǫ·pōᵘ). [f. Stop *sb.*[2] or *v.* + -o[2].]

1. *slang.* A rest from work.

1938 J. Phelan *Lifer* xii. 120 What's the chances for a 'stoppo', Reg?

2. *Criminals' slang.* An escape, a get-away, esp. in phrase *to take stoppo*, to make a rapid escape in order to avoid detection. Freq. *attrib.*, with reference to rapid escape by car, in *stoppo car, driver, man.*

1935 G. Ingram *Cockney Cavalcade* v. 78 'I took stop-o.' In other words, ran away from the police. **1949** Partridge *Dict. Underworld* 712/1 *Take stoppo*, to be obliged to run away... To take heed when the look-out cries 'Stop!' **1974** *Listener* 7 Nov. 595/3 Boys who are going to be stoppo drivers—driving stolen escape cars. **1975** M. Kenyon *Mr Big* xx. 192 Walk, then, to the stoppo car... And wait... Till Slicker comes. **1978** J. Gardner *Dancing Dodo* xxxv. 279 Dobson..held the clutch down, took off the hand brake and let his toe press gently on the accelerator... 'It's a stoppo man's take-off,' the instructor said.

stop-watch (stǫ·pwǫtʃ), *v.* [f. the sb.] *trans.* To time with a stop-watch.

1973 J. Wainwright *Devil you Don't* 19 We being timed?..Stop-watched? **1977** B. Freemantle *Charlie Muffin* xvii. 166 Cuthbertson..had insisted on final rehearsals..stop-watching the journey and testing the surveillance.

stop-work (stǫ·pwɒ̈ɪk), *a.* Also as one word. [f. Stop *v.* + Work *sb.*] **1.** *Austral.* and *N.Z.* Designating a meeting that requires employees to stop working in order to attend. Also *ellipt.* as *sb.*

c **1926** 'Mixer' *Transport Workers' Song Bk.* 25 With their silly bluff and twaddle, And their stop-work meetings, too, By which I'm not allowed to work Till their business is through. **1941** *Argus* (Melbourne) 15 Nov. 3/6 A stopwork meeting of builders' workers. *Ibid.*, Mr. Howitt said congress regretted the stopwork meeting. **1946** K. Tennant *Lost Haven* (1947) x. 138 Jack Starbrace called a little stop-work meeting and addressed it. **1957** *Landfall* 11 Apr. 278 But it was a good day for a stop-work. **1977** *N.Z. Listener* 15 Jan. 6/4 A great many immigrants, probably the majority, were never involved in any kind of trade unionism in Britain and would not have recognised a 'stop-work' meeting if they had actually fallen over one!

2. *N. Amer.* Designating an order requiring work to stop.

1972 *Even. Telegram* (St. John's, Newfoundland) 28 June 1/1 The federal cabinet has authorized a stop-work order. **1973** *N.Y. Law Jrnl.* 26 July 2/1 This is an article 78 proceeding to rescind a 'stop work' order issued by the New York City Department of Buildings.

storage. Add: **1.** (Examples relating to *Computers.*)

1946 Goldstine & von Neumann in J. von Neumann *Coll. Wks.* (1961) V. 24 It may be seen from the fact that each binary digit requires essentially one relay or one pair of vacuum tubes..that this form of storage rapidly becomes quite expensive. **1964** T. W. McRae *Impact of Computers on Accounting* ii. 38 These early machines.. were fitted with magnetic tape storage. **1973** C. W. Gear *Introd. Computer Sci.* vii. 309 We must develop a scheme for allocating storage as it is needed and 'recovering' it when structures using it are deleted.

2. b. *cold storage* (earlier and later examples).

1877 *Illustr. London News* 3 Mar. 203/1 A..company called Cold Storage Wharf..undertakes to provide cold storage accommodation for fresh meat..and all produce of a perishable nature, from all parts of the world. **1926** *Daily Express* 11 May 1/3 No difficulty was experienced at any of the cold storage centres. **1933** *Discovery* Apr. 126/1 Canning and freezing both eliminate the risk of spoilage by moulds and bacteria which are a constant danger in cold storage. **1946** *Nature* 21 Dec. 920/2 Fruit cold-storage research has continued.

fig. **1897** *Outing* XXX. 367/1 Still that stony stare and his reiterated, impertinent queries... A cold-storage air arose between us. **1920** W. Perrett *Peetickay* 3 It seemed ..that the thing to do would be to apply the stenographic principle to the consonants... That plan is now in cold storage. **1951** A. Huxley *Let.* 22 July (1969) 637 It seems to be rather a shame that this anthology-with-comments, which cost me a lot of work..should remain indefinitely in cold storage. **1979** A. Boyle *Climate of Treason* xi. 420 If he did idly question why the Soviet Union had kept their guests in cold storage for so long, Philby soon found a ready answer.

d. *Computers.* The placing or keeping of data and instructions in a device from which they can be retrieved as needed.

1909 *Sci. Proc. R. Dublin Soc.* XII. 80 The present design of the machine provides for the storage of 192 Variables of twenty figures each. **1945** J. VON NEUMANN in B. Randell *Origins Digital Computers* (1973) 358 R has also the properties of a memory. Indeed, it is the natural medium for long time storage of all the information obtained by the automatic device on various problems. **1958** *Listener* 11 Dec. 983/2 For high-speed storage, the magnetic cores of the present machines will give way to films of special iron alloys deposited *in vacuo* upon ceramic plates. **1978** J. P. HAYES *Computer Archit. & Organization* v. 325 The physical processes involved in storage are sometimes inherently unstable, so that stored information may be lost over a period of time.

5. *storage device, medium, register, space.*

1946 *Electr. Engin.* LXV. 389 Each is a complete adding and subtracting machine, and functions as a storage or memory device. **1955** *IRE Trans. Electronic Computers* IV. 16/1 This report deals with a storage device utilizing magnetic cores to achieve fairly large amounts of information storage with a relatively moderate amount of circuitry. **1972** D. LEWIN *Theory & Design Digital Computers* vi. 185 Storage devices may have either destructive or non-destructive read-out of the stored data. **1947** A. W. BURKS et al. in J. von Neumann *Coll. Wks.* (1963) V. 40 There still remains the problem of automatic integration of this storage medium with the machine. **1966** *Sci. Amer.* Sept. 80/1 Magnetic materials ..supply the principal storage medium in computers. **1946** *Ann. Computation Lab. Harvard Univ.* I. 14 Each storage register consists of twenty-four electro-magnetic counter wheels. **1965** HOLLINGDALE & TOOTILL *Electronic Computers* 114 In most computers an individual storage register is not a separate entity, either physically or conceptually, and the term *storage location* is more appropriate. **1936** *Discovery* May 158/1 It may well revolutionise library methods and solve the eternal question of storage-space. **1979** D. MALLETT *Greatest Collector* ix. 84 Richard Wallace..bought no furniture, not wishing, perhaps, to add to the already acute problems of storage space.

6. storage heater, (*b*) = *night storage heater* s.v. *NIGHT *sb.* 14; hence **storage heating,** heating by means of storage heaters; **storage life** (see quot. 1971[1]); **storage location** *Computers,* a place in a store capable of storing one unit of data and usu. specifiable by an address; **storage protection** *Computers,* the protection of storage locations against unauthorized or accidental reading or writing; **storage ring** *Physics,* an approximately circular accelerator in which particles can be effectively stored by being made to circulate continuously at a high energy; **storage tube** *Electronics,* any of various kinds of electron tube which store the information or image applied to them so that it can be retrieved at a later time; **storage unit,** (*a*) one of a set of domestic cupboards; (*b*) a unit that serves as storage for a computer; **storage wall,** a partition wall consisting of cupboards, often designed to be opened from either side.

1961 *Listener* 19 Oct. 629/1 For an existing house the storage-heater system works out very favourably. A good-looking storage-heater with thermostatic control.. costs £22 10s. 6d. **1977** B. PYM *Quartet in Autumn* x. 88 Mrs Pope's sister apparently being too mean to switch on the storage heaters before January. **1961** *Listener* 19 Oct. 629/1 A storage-heating installation. *Ibid.* 629/2 The chief disadvantage of storage-heating is the comparatively slow reaction to sudden big outside-temperature changes. **1971** *Gloss. Terms Quality Assurance (B.S.I.)* 8 *Storage life,* the specified length of time prior to use for which items which are inherently subject to deterioration are deemed to remain fit for use under prescribed conditions. **1971** *Country Life* 9 Sept. 643/1 How can the storage life of vacuum-packed bacon be extended? **1949** D. R. HARTREE *Calculating Instruments & Machines* 96 Different means have to be used for identification of a storage location on a wire. **1964** T. W. MCRAE *Impact of Computers on Accounting* i. 10 If we have 100 storage locations, each one of which can store one character, we will divide this up into ten words, each word containing ten storage locations. **1965** G. B. DAVIS *Introd. Electronic Computers* 223 A storage protection feature is an optional feature not usually found on small computers. **1970** O. DOPPING *Computers & Data Processing* ix. 128 In a computer with storage protection, a program can modify the contents of storage only within a prescribed area assigned to the program. **1956** G. K. O'NEILL in *Physical Rev.* CII. 1418/2 (*heading*) Storage-ring synchrotron: device for high-energy physics research. *Ibid.*, Two 'storage rings', focusing magnets containing straight sections one of which is common to both rings, are built near the accelerator. **1965** *New Scientist* 18 Mar. 692/2 They accelerated two comparatively low energy beams of electrons to 300 MeV in a linear accelerator; they steered these beams into two 'storage rings' built adjacent to one another in the form of a figure of eight, and finally made them collide head-on at the point where the two rings touch. **1978** *Nature* 20 July 202/1 PETRA, Europe's 19 GeV on 19 GeV electron-positron storage ring under construction..near Hamburg, has circulated its first beam around the ring and stored it 'for several minutes'. **1946** *Radar: Summary Rep. & Harp Project* (U.S. Nat. Defense Res. Comm., Div. 14) 144/1 Storage tube. **1947** *Electronics* Sept. 80/1 Specific applications of this storage tube include use in simultaneous multicolor and three-dimensional presentation of radar or sonar data. **1975** D. G. FINK *Electronics Engineers' Handbk.* VII. 30 The correlation is a storage tube that receives a visual input to a photoemissive film..and later compares the original image with a similar image. **1951** *Catal. of Exhibits, South Bank Exhib., Festival of Britain* 125/2 Storage unit. **1964** T. W. MCRAE *Impact of Computers on Accounting* vii. 199 A magnetic tape reel is a remarkably compact storage unit. **1978** J. MCNEIL *Consultant* xi. 117 Two lines of storage units ran at right angles to the wall. **1978** J. KELLOCK *Elements of Accounting* xii. 215 Hardware includes the storage unit, arithmetic unit, control unit, and all the input and output devices used with the computer. **1945** NELSON & WRIGHT *Tomorrow's House* xi. 132 (*caption*) It is only a step to the use of such equipment [*sc.* storage cabinets] to form the walls themselves—a device which we have named the 'storagewall'. **1959** *House & Garden* July 43/2 The dining-room, linked to the kitchen by a storage wall. **1970** *Observer* 18 Oct. 35/1 Ideally, every room in every house needs a storage wall.

store, *sb.* Add: **11. b.** *Computers.* = *MEMORY *sb.* 2 d.

1837 C. BABBAGE in B. Randell *Origins of Digital Computers* (1973) 21 The Store may be considered as the place of deposit in which the numbers and quantities given by the conditions of the problem are originally placed, in which all the intermediate results are provisionally preserved, and in which at the termination all the required results are found. **1919** A. MACFARLANE *Lect. on Ten Brit. Physicists* 80 Directive cards to transfer numbers from the store to the mill and from the mill to the store. **1948** *Nature* 8 May 712/1 The general ideas for a large automatic calculating machine are to be found in the designs of Charles Babbage for an 'analytical engine'... It was to work by means of plungers passing through punched cards, and was to contain a 'store' for numbers... The main components of any digital computing machine were then described... There must be a store to hold numbers and instructions. **1948** *Proc. R. Soc.* A. CXCV. 283 Stores have been operated with thirty-two lines and with sixty-four lines, each line containing thirty-two digits; 12 in. diameter cathode-ray tubes were used. **1964** F. L. WESTWATER *Electronic Computers* iv. 59 To read a word out of the store we have to open a gate at the end, and this permits pulses to escape. **1968** *Brit. Med. Bull.* XXIV. 191/1 The basic configuration of any computer consists of a store, a suitable input and output device, and a control mechanism. **1977** *Sci. Amer.* Sept. 130/1 In the context of electronics 'memory' (or, in British usage, 'store') usually refers to a device for storing digital information.

12. a. (Further examples.)

The use of the word in this sense has not become common in the U.K. except in *Comb.*, as *chain store, department store* (see under the first elements), *store detective* (see sense 13 d below), in which it still refers to a large shop.

1839 W. WAKEFIELD in *N.Z. Jrnl.* (1840) No. 9. 112 It partly belongs to Captain Mayhew, an American, who has a store on it. **1862** *Times* 1 Sept. 5/1 At one corner of the street was a little provision and drapery store kept by an old woman. **1956** H. G. DE LISSER *Cup & Lip* ii. 22 The shops—or stores, as they are invariably called in the West Indies—were open. **1975** *Encounter* Jan. 41/2 But for chrissake—that's 'Christ's sake' in American, chaps—has anybody ever gone away from a shop—meaning 'store', youse guys—empty-handed through ignorance of some one of these local variants?

13. b. *store barn, cupboard* (earlier example), *-shop; store-boat* (earlier and later examples).

1926 D. H. LAWRENCE *David* xii. 87 And she shall have her handmaidens about her, and her store-barns of wool. **1797** *State Papers & Publick Documents U.S.* (1815) II. 436 On the 21st of January, the ice began to give way, and their store-boat arriving on the 28th, they proceeded on the 31st for the Natchez. **1944** T. D. CLARK *Pills, Petticoats, & Plows* 25 In the Louisiana sugar belt, barge store boats eased along the back ways of sugar plantations receiving stolen goods. **1841** C. FOX *Jrnl.* 5 May in *Mem. Old Friends* (1882) vii. 123 We went all over his comfortable house..choosing papers, positions of store cupboards, and other important arrangements. **1888** C. M. YONGE *Our New Mistress* xii. 109, I went into one of those great store shops where they sell all sorts of things. **1972** E. WHITE in W. King *Black Short Story Anthol.* 366 Jill.. passes the store-shops of the Jews.

d. For *U.S.* and *colonial* read chiefly *N. Amer. store buyer, detective, porch; store cheese, clothes* (examples), *pants, tea* (earlier example), *teeth* (examples); **store church:** see quot. 1948; = **storefront church;* **store pay** (examples).

1965 *Harper's Bazaar* Feb. 21/3 The entirely new role of the store buyer. **1980** *Times* 12 Aug. 8/4 Store buyers.. still come to Paris, but..to see the ready-to-wear. **1982** *Times* 3 Aug. 6/1 This week, there weren't any store buyers. **1863** P. S. DAVIS *Young Parson* 61 One plate of 'store cheese', and half a bread-basket of ginger crackers. **1894** *Rep. Vermont Board Agric.* XIV. 25 A full cream store cheese is run through a grinder. **1948** H. L. MENCKEN *Amer. Lang.* Suppl. II x. 591 A *store-church* is one set up in a vacant store or in the front room of a dwelling house. **1961** C. HIMES *Black on Black* (1973) 60 She hid in Rev'end Sinner's store church when she run away. **1840** *Knickerbocker* XVI. 262, I felt an awe of young ladies in 'store clothes'. **1872** [see *boiled shirt* s.v. *BOILED *ppl. a.* 2]. **1944** B. JOHNSON *As much as I Dare* 294 These young men did not want to give up their store clothes. **1907** *St. Nicholas* Oct. 1106/2 He wondered how the store detectives worked to find a man who might be picking pockets in a great crowd. **1968** J. LOCK *Lady Policeman* xix. 157 They had been detained by the store detective. **1979** R. RENDELL *Make Death love Me* vi. 59 A woman had grabbed him and he'd only just escaped the store detective. **1891** 'O. THANET' *Otto the Knight* 4 Thar, store pants an' gallowses! Make haste an' putt 'em on! **1932** *Atlantic Monthly* Apr. 475/1 Steve-john..was..a bronze perfection—Celini's 'Perseus' in store pants. **1942** W. STEGNER *Mormon Country* 126 Smart alecs had money to jingle in their store pants. **1842** R. H. BONNYCASTLE *Canada & Canadians* II. 180 A quintal of fish..is worth 12*s.* 6*d.* in hard cash, or 14*s.* 6*d.* store pay. **1891** S. M. WELCH *Recoll. Buffalo 1830–40* 353 The workmen were to receive..only half cash, the remainder in trade—store pay, *i.e.*: in orders on the employers or other stores for such goods as they needed. **1905** J. S. CARTER *Story of Dundas* 51 The store-keeper bought the settlers' produce but would give them only trade in return, or what was known as 'store pay'. **1934** C. M. WILSON *Backwoods Amer.* ii. 16 Hired boys are among the most cherished perpetrators of store-porch mirth. **1949** B. A. BOTKIN *Treas. S. Folklore* p. xix, The rural south is a land of the out-of-doors come up to the door and even indoors, where the 'gallery', the store-porch, the kitchen..are made for story-telling. **1843** 'R. CARLTON' *New Purchase* I. ix. 64 'Tisn't nun of your spice-wood or yarb stuff, but the rale, gineine *store* tea. **1878** *Brooklyn Monthly* June 185/1 It occurred to me that a brief description of the sensations experienced might be of interest to any of my readers who are contemplating a new set of 'store teeth'. **1951** C. LYNCH-ROBINSON *Last of Irish R.M.s* vi. 113 When I first got my new 'store teeth' in, they worried me. **1975** *Budget* (Sugarcreek, Ohio) 20 Mar. 8/6 Mrs. Gintz is a sister to O.K. Brown, the dentist that pulled my last teeth, and made me some store teeth.

14. In *Comb.* with adjs. or ppl. adjs., as **store-bought,** bought (often ready-made) from a store; also *fig.*; also **store-boughten** *U.S.*; **store-wide,** operating or applying throughout the whole of a store.

1952 J. STEINBECK *East of Eden* xvi. 181 Would you say they were made clothes or store bought? **1953** *Manch. Guardian Weekly* 1 Oct. 2 She swayed like a riven oak over her failure to compete with 'powder and store-bought hair'. **1962** *Times* 4 May 9/6 It has become 'common sense' to substitute a store-bought, ready-made universe for the disquieting uniqueness of actuality. **1970** *Islander* (Victoria, B.C.) 22 Nov. 5/1 Those home-garden farmers aimed for near total independence from store-bought produce. **1981** *Farmstead Mag.* Winter 63/2 Pickled mushrooms..bring an outrageous price, in delicatessen shops, if you can find them and the storebought ones don't taste nearly as good as those pickled at home. **1883** ZEIGLER & GROSSCUP *Alleghanies* 91 Two good-natured-looking young men dressed in..'store-boughten' coats, and homespun pantaloons. **1933** L. I. WILDER *Farmer Boy* viii. 54 Clothes..made of store-boughten cloth, woven by machines. **1974** M. LAURENCE *Diviners* ii. 29 Storeboughten cookies are looked down on. **1938** *Sun* (Baltimore) 8 Sept. 3/1 A union demand for..a store-wide seniority plan. **1979** *Tucson* (Arizona) *Citizen* 3 Oct. 10/A (Advt.), Tremendous storewide savings.

store, *v.* Add: **4. d.** *Computers.* To retain a physical representation of (data or instructions) that enables them to be subsequently retrieved.

1909 *Sci. Proc. R. Dublin Soc.* XII. 78 An Analytical Machine must have some means of storing the numerical data of the problem to be solved. **1937** H. H. AIKEN in *IEEE Spectrum* (1964) Aug. 69 It is necessary that numbers may be removed from the calculating units and temporarily stored in storage positions. **1945** J. VON NEUMANN in B. Randell *Origins Digital Computers* (1973) 356 A distinction must be made between the specific instructions given for and defining a particular problem, and the general control organs which see to it that these instructions..are carried out. The former must be stored in some way. **1948** *Nature* 8 May 712/2 In all these machines there is provision for storing numbers, say in the scale of 2, in certain places. **1964** F. L. WESTWATER *Electronic Computers* ix. 144 Inside a computer, alphabetical characters and numerals are both stored as numbers. **1972** D. LEWIN *Theory & Design Digital Computers* vi. 184 The speed of computers is limited by the time required to store and retrieve information.

e. *Computers.* To transfer *into* a store or storage location.

1964 *Ann. N.Y. Acad. Sci.* CXV. 654 The speed of the computer is fixed by the length of time required to read information from or store information into one of the 1,024..12-bit memory locations. **1973** C. W. GEAR *Introd. Computer Sci.* ii. 37 The CPU can be told to load a number into its accumulator from a specific cell in the memory..or to store a number from the accumulator into memory.

6. *Comb.*: **store-and-forward** *Telecommunications,* used *attrib.* with reference to a data network in which messages are routed to one or more intermediate stations where they may be stored before being forwarded to their destinations.

1963 *On Line Data Processing* (Inst. Electr. & Electronics Engineers) 63 The store and forward switching system must interconnect with line switching facilities. **1980** R. L. FREEMAN *Telecommunication Syst. Engin.* ix. 429 The ARPANet connects dispersed computers of various manufacture and varying design. The subnet providing that connection is a form of store and forward system and must deal with such problems as routing, buffering, synchronization, [etc.].

stored, *ppl. a.* Add: **1. c.** *stored program,* a program that is stored in a computer in the same way as data, *esp.* one that can be automatically manipulated like data; freq. *attrib.*

1957 D. D. MCCRACKEN *Digital Computer Programming* i. 4 We speak of modern computers as being stored program machines. **1964** *Ann. N.Y. Acad. Sci.* CXV. 654 The LINC is a small stored-program digital computer which uses transistor circuitry and a random-access ferrite-core memory. **1970** O. DOPPING *Computers & Data Processing* vi. 93 The use of a stored program, which can be modified by the machine itself, is one of the basic ideas in the design of a computer. **1983** *Sci. Amer.* Jan. 92/3 The stops and combination pistons [of the organ]..

are under the control of microprocessors having stored-program capabilities.

storefront, *sb.* (and *a.*). orig. and chiefly *U.S.* Also **store-front, store front.** [f. STORE *sb.* + FRONT *sb.*] **1. a.** The side of a shop facing the street; (a building with) a shop window.

1880 G. W. CABLE *Grandissimes* 376 A large porte-cochère..[opened] upon the banquette immediately beside and abreast of the store-front. **1922** F. FARRINGTON *Meeting Chain Store Competition* iii. 37 You can make your store front as conspicuous as a red front Atlantic and Pacific Tea Co. store front and still make it infinitely more attractive. **1945** *Planning Store of Tomorrow* (National Retail Merchants Assoc.) 6/1 Some are specialists on store fronts, but can do or supervise an intelligent job on interior layout. **1962** E. SNOW *Red China Today* (1963) lxx. 538 Some of the old foreign store fronts (such as Whiteaways) now exhibited shining lathes and other machines. **1974** R. L. SIMON *Wild Turkey* iii. 19 [A] shocking pink storefront temporarily labeled 'The Institute of Oral Love'. **1977** *Guardian Weekly* 4 Dec. 12/5 This indifference..turns storefronts not into show-cases for the articles sold by the shops but into museums of all the goods that were once sold there or will be sold at some future date. **1979** *United States 1980/81* (Penguin Travel Guides) 73 This little deli is just a storefront on a shopping-center strip, so look carefully.

b. A room or rooms at the front of shop premises, esp. as used for some other purpose.

1972 *N.Y. Times* 3 Nov. 22/2 The two fully staffed and fully equipped Nixon storefronts in the area contain busy volunteers. **1973** *Houston Chron.* (Texas Mag.) 14 Oct. 2/1 The Hare Krishna sect..is big business. It began in an East Village store front in New York. **1976** *National Observer* (U.S.) 7 Feb. 20/3 Performances first held in storefronts and lofts and later in streets, parks, and other public places. **1982** S. PARETSKY *Indemnity Only* vii. 83 She ran a clinic in a shabby storefront down the street.

2. *attrib.* and *Comb.*, as *storefront cinema, headquarters, industry, location, restaurant, theatre, window*; **storefront church**, a shop building used as a church or meeting place, esp. by small evangelical groups; also *store-front mission, synagogue, temple.*

1938 C. HIMES *Black on Black* (1973) 167 For one hundred and fifty dollars he leased a storefront church in the heart of the slums and poverty. **1957** *Economist* 28 Sept. 1031/2 The Negro newcomer from the South..may attend a 'storefront church', of uncertain denomination, in a rented shop with the display window painted over. **1968** P. OLIVER *Screening Blues* ii. 62 Infinitely smaller, but important because of their numbers and their devout followings of tiny congregations, are the multitude of store-front churches which line the streets in the Negro areas of the main urban centres. **1973** A. DUNDES *Mother Wit* 175 Professor Dillard..examines the names of store-front churches... The individual words in store-front church names may be SE (Standard English). **1967** *Daily Tel.* 16 Feb. 19/6 The Storefront Cinema..is a rented shop that has been converted into a miniature cinema. **1976** *National Observer* (U.S.) 3 Apr. 5/1 He has more than 25 store-front headquarters in every one of the state's nine congressional districts. **1967** *Economist* 6 May 563/2 Everywhere in Bangkok there are store-front industries where people are beating metal, mending things by hand, getting used to machines. **1970** *Globe & Mail* (Toronto) 25 Sept. 11/4 Government information centres in 'store-front locations'. **1978** *Sunday Mail TV Suppl.* (Brisbane) 23 July 2/2 The pair operate a store-front mission in a lower class area. **1978** *Chicago* June 208/1 We've always liked to brag about Chicago's Mom-and-Pop storefront restaurants. **1975** A. BERGMAN *Hollywood & Le Vine* (1976) vii. 80 A store-front synagogue in Brooklyn. **1965** D. HENDERSON in S. Henderson *Understanding New Black Poetry* (1973) III. 269 The ritual is black The ritual is in the storefront temple On the corner. **1973** E. BULLINS *Theme is Blackness* 7 Sweating out long, hot summers in store-front theaters. **1976** *National Observer* (U.S.) 2 Oct. 15/1 A Teletype machine, set in the store-front window of the bureau.

3. *attrib.* passing into *adj.* **a.** Of, pertaining to, or designating legal aid or citizen's advice organizations which operate from shop premises in order to be easily accessible.

1971 *Sunday Sun* (Brisbane) 31 Oct. 20/2 Why..can't we have legal offices in poor areas offering cheap legal aid along the lines of America's 'store-front' lawyers. **1973** *Courier-Mail* (Brisbane) 9 June 1/3 A 'store front' legal and general advice system will be available cheaply to Brisbane people in a few weeks. **1973** *Globe & Mail* (Toronto) 2 Aug. 8/7 (Advt.), Store-front Citizenship Office now open..to answer your questions about how you can become a Canadian citizen. **1974** *Index-Jrnl.* (Greenwood, S. Carolina) 18 Apr. 6/1 A group called Resource One operates a storefront 'people's computer', a cross between a hip encyclopedia and a community bulletin board. **1974** *Courier-Mail* (Brisbane) 25 Apr. 2/4 Australia's first 'store front' legal aid office will open in Ipswich tomorrow. **1975** *Weekend Mag.* (Montreal) 1 Nov. 8/2 Robert Cooper..is a lawyer with an extraordinary string of..achievements in his chosen field, including the opening of Canada's first storefront law office. **1979** N. HARTLEY *Quicksilver* i. 19 Storefront law offices, giving free legal advice to minority groups.

b. Of, pertaining to, or characteristic of a storefront church.

1972 J. L. DILLARD *Black English* v. 217 We see evidence of formal styles of Negro Non-Standard in the speech of the storefront preachers. **1973** *Black World* Sept. 31 'Tambourines' has the impelling, fervent, and nervous rhythms of the 'store-front' spiritual or gospel hymn. **1976** *National Observer* (U.S.) 1 May B 2/3 Store-front religion offered solace and precious respectability to mothers whose families were collapsing around them. **1978** J. UPDIKE *Coup* (1979) v. 173, I hope that stuff hasn't taken you in; it's just our usual native storefront I'm-comin'-home-Jesus routine.

stork (stǭɹk), *v. U.S. slang.* [f. the sb., with reference to the nursery fiction that babies are brought by the stork: see sense 1 c.] *trans.* To make pregnant.

1936 A. HUXLEY *Eyeless in Gaza* xxv. 353 What would you do if the fever frau had the misfortune to be storked? **1968** R. STOUT *Father Hunt* (1969) xiii. 157 'Didn't she stop because she was pregnant?'.. 'Yes,' he said. 'She was storked.' **1977** *Amer. Speech 1975* L. 67 *Stork vt*, make pregnant. 'Jim storked her; that's why she's not back up here this year.'

sto·rkbird. *nonce-wd.* [f. STORK *sb.* + BIRD *sb.*] = STORK *sb.*

1922 JOYCE *Ulysses* 416 Madam, when comes the storkbird for thee?

storm, *sb.* Add: **I. 1. f.** *any port in a storm*: see *PORT *sb.*[1] 1 c.

g. In pl. *ellipt.* for storm windows. *N. Amer.*

1952 *Home Building in Canada* Oct.–Nov. 22/2 If you are wondering which windows and when to protect with storms, the answer is simple—all of them, from October to April. **1968** *Globe & Mail* (Toronto) 17 Feb. 45 (Advt.), Complete with drapes, aluminum, storms and screens. **1973** *N.Y. Law Jrnl.* 1 Aug. 3/2 Alwin J. Dovale, installer of storms and screens. **1977** *Chicago Tribune* 2 Oct. II. 7/1 Maybe next year I can afford real storms with the money I'll save on utility bills.

3. a. Freq. in phr. *to weather the storm.*

1671 [see WEATHER *v.* 4 b]. **1802** [in Dict.]. **1849, 1853** [see WEATHER *v.* 4 b]. **1868** [in Dict.]. **1924** *Nation & Athenæum* 26 Jan. 603/1 His plight was serious; but he weathered the storm. **1934** F. W. CROFTS *12.30 from Croydon* viii. 95 He had come to an arrangement with his uncle whereby he hoped to weather the storm.

e. *up a storm* adv. phr., vehemently, violently, with enthusiasm or energy. *U.S. colloq.*

1953 J. STREET *Civil War* iv. 55 The editors just r'ared back in the omnipotence of Jove and pontificated up a storm. **1956** B. HOLIDAY *Lady sings Blues* (1973) xviii. 149 After Marietta taught me, I knitted up a storm and got real fancy. I made cable-knit sweaters for Bobby Tucker and his little boy. **1965** *Charlottesville* (Va.) *Daily Progress* 29 Apr. 6/1 When I ask him to go to the store for me he starts to wheeze up a storm and tells me he is a sick man. **1967** *Boston Sunday Herald Mag.* 30 Apr. 19/3 Right now she's cooking up a storm in preparation for the rash of friends who will be stopping by on their way to Expo. **1972** *TV Guide* (U.S.) 15 Jan. A54/1 Aretha Franklin sings up a storm and impersonates top female vocalists. **1974** K. MILLETT *Flying* (1975) v. 518, I will console myself with material goods. I will shop up a storm. **1983** *Oxford Times* 29 Apr. 3/7 Youngsters from the First Yarnton Brownies have been knitting up a storm to make a blanket for Mother Theresa in India.

III. 6. a. *storm flake, -month, -rack, -song, -spirit.*

1876 Storm flake [see *scroll-leaved* adj. s.v. *SCROLL *sb.* 6 a]. **1894** *Stonyhurst Mag.* Feb. 233 And like the storm-months smote the earth. **1878** O. WILDE *Ravenna* 14 As from the storm-rack comes a perfect star! **1926** J. N. CAMERON in *Oxford Poetry* 14 The haggard storm-rack of disastrous days. **1925** BLUNDEN *English Poems* 40 While on her soul the stormsong bursts, and groanings Knell through roof and flue. **1929** —— *Near & Far* 41 Storm-spirit, coil your lightnings round mad towers.

b. *storm-bitten, -damaged, -driven, -rent* (later example), *-threatened, -tormented, -torn, -troubled* adjs.

1939 W. B. YEATS *Last Poems* 6 A small forgotten house that's set On a storm-bitten green. **1980** *New Age* (U.S.) Oct. 26/1 Eight acres of storm-damaged apricots. **1841** J. G. WHITTIER *Poet. Wks.* (1898) 190/2 Loose rock and frozen slide, Hung on the mountain-side, Waiting their hour to glide Downward, storm-driven! **1900** W. S. CHURCHILL in *Morning Post* 1 Jan. 6/2 These tall figures, full of animated movement, clad in dark flapping clothes, with slouch, storm-driven hats. **1850** E. B. BROWNING *Poet. Wks.* (1904) 141/1, I lack your daring, up this storm-rent chasm To fix with violent hands a kindred god. **1977** Storm-threatened [see *QUANTUM 5 d]. **1844** POE in *Columbian Mag.* Dec. 275/2 Storm-tormented ocean of his thoughts. **1876** J. G. WHITTIER *Poet. Wks.* (1898) 247/2 The storm-torn plumes Of old pine-forest kings. *c* **1958** E. M. FORSTER *Life to Come* (1975) 199 They flew round and round the basilica.., they shot through its roof into the storm-torn night. **1850** E. BRONTË *Wuthering Heights* 489 No coward soul is mine, No trembler in the world's storm-troubled sphere.

d. storm apron *U.S.*, a waterproof sheet used to cover the front of an open carriage in wet weather; **storm boat** *Mil.*, a light but powerful boat used for conveying attacking troops across rivers; **storm cellar** orig. and chiefly *U.S.*, a cellar or dugout made to be a place of refuge from a storm; also *transf.* and *fig.*; **storm centre** (later *fig.* examples); **storm choke,** a safety valve installed in an oil-well pipe below the ocean surface, designed to stop the oil flow should it exceed a predetermined rate as a result of damage at the wellhead; **storm coat** orig. and chiefly *U.S.* (earlier and later examples); **storm collar,** a coat-collar which may be turned up and fastened close round the neck; **storm door:** for *U.S.* read orig. *U.S.* and add later examples; **storm drain,** a drain built to carry away excess water in times of heavy rain; **storm flag,** (*a*) (example); **storm-flap,** a piece of material designed to protect an opening or fastening from the effects of rain, as on a tent, coat, etc.; **storm-house** (example); also, a shelter from the weather on a boat; **storm-jib** (earlier example); **storm lantern** orig. *U.S.* = *hurricane-lamp* s.v. HURRICANE 3 a; **storm-proof** *a.*, (*a*) (later example); also, protected from or affording protection from stormy weather; **storm rubber** *N. Amer.*, a rubber overshoe; **storm sewer** *U.S.* = *storm drain* above; **storm shutter** (earlier example); **storm surge** *Oceanogr.*, an abnormal raising of the sea level in a region as a result of the wind and atmospheric pressure changes associated with a storm; **storm-trysail** (earlier and later examples); **storm wind**: *spec.* a wind having a speed within certain limits (see quots. and cf. STORM *sb.* 1 b); **storm window,** (*c*) *N. Amer.*, a detachable window put up in winter to form an insulating double window.

1895 *Montgomery Ward Catal.* Spring & Summer 591/2 *Storm Aprons.* These aprons are held firmly in position on the dash..forming an unbroken water-shed over front of dash. No mud, snow, or rain can settle inside of carriage. **1943** L. I. WILDER *These Happy Golden Years* xxix. 260 Back in his [buggy] seat, he unrolled the rubber storm apron. **1945** *Sun* (Baltimore) 27 Feb. 3/1 The sergeant..took them back to the road to carry the stormboat down to the river and launch it. **1945** *Finito! Po Valley Campaign* (15th Army Group) 12 Each 20-foot, powered, plywood storm boat. **1920** G. ADE *Hand-Made Fables* 30 The Money-lender beat it to a Storm-Cellar. **1929** J. F. DOBIE *Vaquero of Brush Country* 151 Storm cellars in north Texas, Oklahoma, and Kansas still preserve its architecture. **1962** F. I. ORDWAY et al. *Basic Astronautics* xii. 503 One..suggestion is that a special 'storm cellar' be constructed within the spacecraft, a well-shielded area into which the crew could retreat. **1971** J. H. GRAY *Red Lights on Prairies* ii. 36 When the first oratorical thunder clapped, the chief, the mayor..took to the storm cellars to wait for the storm to blow over. **1977** J. CLEARY *Vortex* i. 8 People build storm cellars to retreat to. **1965** *Listener* 30 Sept. 481/2 Europe is no longer the storm centre in world affairs. The clouds have shifted to Asia. **1978** M. PUZO *Fools Die* xxix. 335 She was having a good time standing outside the party storm center. **1966** P. HINDE *Fortune in North Sea* viii. 154 The first safety valve is installed and left at the bottom of each production well at sea, and is known as the Storm Choke. **1975** *North Sea Background Notes* (Brit. Petroleum Co.) 40 Precautions are taken to shut down production automatically on any failure of the wellhead or flow-line by installing suitable safety valves. These are the 'storm choke' in the well bore,..and the surface safety valve. **1830** J. F. WATSON *Annals of Philadelphia* 179 In the year 1749, I met with the incidental mention of a singular over-coat, worn by captain James as a storm coat, made entirely of beaver fur. **1849** THOREAU *Week Concord Riv.* 250 He ran along over the wet stones like a wrecker in his storm coat. **1953** 'S. RANSOME' *Drag Dark* (1954) i. 16 The corpse..wore..a tan gabardine storm-coat, and big galoshes. **1974** 'J. Ross' *Burning of Billy Toober* i. 7 His stiff-fabric stormcoat. **1981** *Daily Tel.* 30 Mar. 18/5 Snug, high-collared storm coats are ready to roam Tibetan mountains. **1898** *T. Eaton & Co. Catal.* Spring & Summer 124/1 Men's Klondike mining coats,.. with 6-inch storm collar and capot to pull over the head. **1899** [see *EMPIECEMENT]. **1931** *Daily Mail* 26 May 1/4 (Advt.), West Riding suiting coats... Smart Storm Collar and pull-in Belt. **1939** H. M. MINER *St. Denis* ii. 25 Storm doors or built-on entries are put on the houses in winter. **1977** *Grimsby Even. Tel.* 27 May 17/7 (Advt.), Freehold semi-detached house... Porch with storm door. Entrance Hall. **1960** C. ACHEBE *No Longer at Ease* ii. 16 His car was parked close to a wide-open storm drain from which came a very strong smell of rotting flesh. **1974** N. GORDIMER *Conservationist* 218 The English-language evening paper published a picture of a pet dog being rescued from a flooded storm-drain by the fire brigade. **1896** *Weather Bureau Bull.* (U.S.) No. 80. 7 Two storm flags (red with black centers), displayed one above the other,..announce the expected approach of tropical hurricanes. **1929** *T. Eaton & Co. Catal.* Spring & Summer 373/1 Palmetto Tent... Insect-proof mosquito door and rear window with storm flap operated from inside. **1968** J. IRONSIDE *Fashion Alphabet* 41 *Trench-coat*... This short-cape effect is often called a 'storm cape' or 'storm flaps'. **1972** *Village Voice* (N.Y.) 1 June 13/2 (Advt.), Nylon Mountain Tent... Rear screen window with storm flap. **1973** *Shooting Times & Country Mag.* 7 July 37/2 (Advt.), Zip full length from neck to hem, covered by storm flap. **1836** T. POWER *Impressions Amer.* I. 31 She..had stump-royal masts, and a storm-house abaft. **1839** *Southern Lit. Messenger* V. 8/2 The James Cropper..was fitted with..a storm house over the wheel. **1887** *Harper's Mag.* Dec. 119/1 Two men..were bending down at the storm-house in front of her parlor-door. *c* **1810** W. HICKEY *Mem.* (1960) xiii. 207 It blew so hard we could scarcely carry a close-reefed mainsail and storm-jib. **1895** *Montgomery Ward Catal.* Spring & Summer 553/2 Cold Blast or Storm Lantern: is made on the same principle as street lamps, with wind break. **1923** W. DEEPING *Secret Sanctuary* xx. 207 He..lit the storm-lantern he used at night, and extinguished the lamp. **1964** D. VARADAY *Gara-Yaka* vi. 51, I hurried to the hut with a storm lantern. **1976** *Norwich Mercury* 17 Dec. 6/7 If the light fails, you use a storm lantern. **1901** Storm-proof [see *COVER-ALL, COVERALL *sb.*]. **1909** *Chambers's Jrnl.* May 335/2 The lamp is stormproof, and is unaffected by cold weather, while it constitutes the safest form of street-lighting that has yet been devised. **1968** R. M. Patterson *Finlay's River* 224 So I set up a good storm-proof camp on a level point between two streams. **1895** *Montgomery Ward Catal.* Spring & Summer 522/3 Woman's Storm Rubber: nothing better for wet weather. **1924–25** *T. Eaton & Co. Catal.* Fall & Winter 146/2 Women's first quality Black Storm Rubbers with round toes and low heels. **1887** W. E. S. Fales *Brooklyn's Guardians* iii. 43 The improvements contemplated the repairing of the great thoroughfares..; the construction of storm sewers. **1941** *Sun* (Baltimore) 16 Sept. 9/3 Silting-up of the channel, due, it is said, to discharge from storm sewers. **1978** J. Irving *World according to Garp* iv. 77 The storm sewers bogged. **1834** E. W. Brayley *Graphic & Historical Illustrator* 395/1 All the windows..are protected by storm-shutters. **1929** A. T. Doodson *Rep. Thames Floods* 5 If there are no tidal predictions available the problem of separating the storm surge from the tidal oscillation is by no means easy. **1956** *Proc. R. Soc.* A. CCXXXVII. 325 The problem [of the mathematical solution of tides in a closed channel] is increased in difficulty when a storm surge of a non-periodic character is superposed upon the periodic tide. **1970** D. A. Ross *Introd. Oceanogr.* vii. 229 In the Gulf Coast area of the United States, storm surges have been known to raise the water level as much as 7m. **1851** H. Melville *Moby Dick* III. xxxvii. 213 A storm-trysail was set further aft. **1967** L. S. Tawes *Coasting Captain* 259, I slacked off my storm trysail sheet. **1923** Storm wind [see *gale *sb.*[3] 1 a]. **1959** *Gloss. Meteorol.* (Amer. Meteorol. Soc.) 545 *Storm wind*, in the Beaufort wind scale, a wind whose speed is from 56 to 63 knots (64 to 72 mph). **1933** L. I. Wilder *Farmer Boy* xxii. 174 They fitted storm doors and storm windows on the house. **1956** W. R. Bird *Off-Trail in Nova Scotia* ii. 51 She's always nagging Sam to take off the storm windows, whitewash the fence. **1978** *Detroit Free Press* 5 Mar. c21/1 (Advt.), 3 Track Storm Window $20.95 each.

e. storm cock (further examples).

1819 M. Edgeworth *Let.* 26 Jan. (1971) 160 When a dark black cloud threatens a heavy shower..then the storm-cock cries or screams. **1896** A. E. Housman *Shropshire Lad* 17 So braver notes the storm-cock sings To start the rusted wheel of things. **1978** *Country Life* 7 Sept. 630/1 The mistle thrush..will sing in the wildest weather and fully justify its vernacular name of storm-cock.

Stormont (stǭ·ɹmǫnt). The name of a suburb of Belfast, used to denote: (*a*) the administration presided over by the Secretary of State for Northern Ireland (the Northern Ireland Office), housed at Stormont Castle; (*b*) the Northern Ireland parliament which met at the Parliament House in the grounds of Stormont Castle from 1920 until its suspension in 1972.

1934 H. Maxwell *Ulster was Right* 9 The Act which created Stormont provided also for a similar Parliament in Dublin. **1935** *Frontier Sentinel* 22 June 4/4 The strongest supporter of Stormont rule. **1938** *Irish News* 3 Feb. 2/3 Stormont is not a de jure Government. **1949** St. J. Ervine *Craigavon Ulsterman* iii. x. 418 Some very queer fish have been elected to Stormont,..but Stormont, at its worst, has never declined to the depths of Leinster House. **1957** *Times* 9 Dec. p. ii/3 The Government of Northern Ireland Act by which Stormont was established in 1920 was not a response to local demands. **1971** H. Wilson *Labour Govt.* xxxv. 719 Our own back-benchers expressing their criticisms of Stormont and the Unionists in speeches designed to strengthen the arm of the Home Secretary. **1972** *Guardian* 25 Mar. 1/2 Mr Brian Faulkner, who has been Northern Ireland's sixth Prime Minister..will tender his resignation on Tuesday... He will end the existence of that..provincial assembly which has become known.. by the name of the building where the Parliament sits—Stormont. **1975** *Times* 10 Sept. 1/3 Stormont officials attempted to put a brave face on the situation.

sto·rm-trooper. Also **storm trooper, stormtrooper.** [f. as next + -er[1].] **1.** A member of the storm-troops, esp. the Nazi S.A.

1933 *Palestine Post* 2 Apr. 4/1 The Nazi storm-troopers at noon on Friday, cleared the Berlin law courts of Jewish judges. **1941** B. Schulberg *What makes Sammy Run?* vi. 101 'Jews,' he said bitterly..like a storm-trooper. **1958** *Listener* 14 Aug. 238/2 The Nazi storm-trooper. **1973** R. Lacey *Sir Walter Raleigh* xvii. 129 The ordinary English levies..were no match for the Spanish stormtroopers. **1976** J. McClure *Rogue Eagle* iii. 57 Formidable fellow like Vorster, ex-stormtrooper general. **1977** A. Ecclestone *Staircase for Silence* v. 89 He did not foresee a time when..stormtroopers and commandos would appear.

2. *transf.* and *fig.*

1943 C. Himes *Black on Black* (1973) 220, I suppose you have been reading about the birth of the storm troopers in Los Angeles, the reincarnation, or rather I should say, the *continuation* of the vigilantes, the uniformed Klansmen. **1956** R. Macaulay *Towers of Trebizond* ii. 23 Some of the leaflets had 'Catholic Commandos' printed on them, and others 'Protestant Storm Troopers', and Father Chantry-Pigg did not know which of these two bands of warriors he disliked most. **1958** *Spectator* 1 Aug. 163/2 The toughest Nationalists, Plaid Cymru's Storm Troopers. **1976** *Birmingham Post* 16 Dec. 4/1 The Gay movement in the city is concerned about a kind of creeping apathy coming over some of its former storm-troopers. **1978** M. Page *Pilate Plot* (1979) x. 160 A place within..easy reach in which Von Hassen's storm-troopers would find their activities heavily restricted.

sto·rm-troops, *sb. pl.* Also **storm troops.** [tr. G. *sturmtruppen.*] **1. a.** = *shock troops* s.v. *shock *sb.*[3] 7 b. Also *fig.*

1917 *Punch* 27 June 409/3 Special 'storm troops'—men picked for their youth, vigour and daring, to carry out counter-attacks—are now a feature of the German Armies. **1922** C. E. Montague *Disenchantment* ix. 125 Canadians and Australians..were the 'storm troops', the men who had to be sent for to do the tough jobs. **1924** J. Ross *Years of My Pilgrimage* xxx. 283, I had heard from my friend, Sir Henry Wilson, F.M., that the use of storm troops was an extravagant way of utilizing men. **1933** J. Buchan *Prince of Captivity* iii. i. 274 They were violent German nationalists..true storm-troops, ready for any forlorn hope and prepared to use any means however devilish. **1943** C. Day Lewis *Word over All* 42 Spent as storm-troops after defeat or triumph, Deeply indifferent. **1973** *Black Panther* 11 Aug. 8/3 Tommassi said he was offered $5,000 to use his storm troops as registrars.

b. *spec.* The troops of the Nazi *Sturmabteilung.

1923 *Times* 15 Jan. 10/4 Bands of 'storm troops' paraded the streets, singing the Fascist war songs. **1933** *Granta* 26 Apr. 370/1 We believe that only now has come the time to see these issues in themselves, out of the context of cruelty and outrage which Herr Hitler's storm-troops created for them. **1954** B. & R. North tr. *M. Duverger's Pol. Parties* i. i. 36 In the case of the National Socialist Storm Troops the initial element was the squad (*schar*). **1982** T. Keneally *Schindler's Ark* xxxiii. 344 An influential officer in the S.A. (the Sturmabteilung, or Storm Troops).

2. *sing.* **a.** A branch or detachment of storm troops.

1935 [see *Nazi *a.*]. **1938** J. Cary *Castle Corner* 483 A soldier picked by lot for the storm troop.

b. *attrib.*

1939 S. Spender tr. *E. Toller's Pastor Hall* i. 14 Go and ask the Stormtroop Leader to come in. **1958** *Times* 3 Sept. 11/3 The outbreaks will have served a useful purpose if they oblige the public to understand that the Storm Troop mentality exists in England, too. **1981** *Listener* 2 July 7/1 Röhm..was jailed on 29 June [1934] by a worried Heines, and other storm-troop leaders.. were due to arrive the next day.

Hence **sto·rm-troop** *v. intr.*, to behave in an aggressive manner like storm-troops; so **sto·rm-trooping** *ppl. a.*

1960 *News Chron.* 5 Jan. 4/5 The storm-trooping birdbrains of Notting Hill. **1974** *Times* 10 May 22/6 The National Union of Students goes storm-trooping about the country's universities suppressing..freedom of speech. **1977** *Sounds* 9 July 31/3 This is the nucleus of the band, who charge in with a stormtroopin' instrumental romp through the Byrds 'Eight Miles High'.

Storthing. (Later examples with spelling *Storting.*)

1955 *Times* 23 June 11/6 King Haakon VII..was formally elected by the Storting, the Norwegian Parliament, on November 18, 1905. **1964** *Ann. Reg. 1963* 267 The Storting on 28 March passed a Bill concerning Norway's participation in a common defence system for the European section of NATO. **1977** *Time* 26 Sept. 17/3 From the beginning, the race for control of the Storting (Parliament) had been regarded by most Norwegians as a 'destiny election' for the Labor Party's brand of socialism.

story, *sb.*[1] Add: **I. 4. e.** Also in catch-phrase *that's the story of my life*, etc., used of something that supposedly epitomizes one's life or experience.

1964 *Punch* 11 Mar. 385/3 It's the story of my life—looking for small watch-straps. **1969** *Time* 30 May 22/3 In 13 years, he's been a hard-liner in criminal cases. That's the story of his life.

6. d. (*that is*) *another story* (earlier and later examples); (*to be*) *the same story*: a repetition of some occurrence; similarly *a different story*; *the old story*: see *old *a.* 7 e.

1818 Scott *Heart Midl.* II. xiii. 308 But if she's gaun to look after the kye at St. Leonard's, that's another story. **1905** *American Mag.* May 107/1 It has been the same story in every strike the man has undertaken, though it has been a longer job in most cases. **1940** A. Christie *Sad Cypress* ii. iii. 128 As a matter of fact, it was Nurse O'Brien who set me on the track; but that's another story. **1958** 'Castle' & 'Hailey' *Flight into Danger* i. 20 The met report was reasonable... In a month or so's time it'll be a very different story. **1966** 'H. Calvin' *Italian Gadget* v. 64 'Brains?..I haven't shown much evidence of them here... But that's another story,' he added hastily. **1979** J. Crosby *Party of Year* xxiii. 146 Let's look at the back stairs.—Same story there... The door was of steel.

e. For *U.S.* read orig. *U.S.* and add later examples. Now chiefly = *news story* s.v. *news *sb.* (*pl.*) 6 b.

1905 E. Wallace *Four Just Men* v. 86 'A very good story,' said the chief complacently, reading the proofs. **1942** *Sphere* 27 June 409/1 Each regional editor acquires stories from his own Embassy or exiled Government as well as sending out his own reporters for stories of special interest to his country. **1961** C. Willock *Death in Covert* xii. 203 One headline said: *Regency Bucks Ride Again*, and the sub-head to the same story complained: *Last time a man was blown up.* **1976** *Task of Broadcasting News* (B.B.C.) ii. 17/1 'Story' is only a journalist's professional jargon for an item of news. The proper place for it is a news bulletin.

III. 9. *story-ballet, -film*; **storyboard,** a large surface on which is displayed a series of rough drawings representing a shot-by-shot breakdown of a planned film (*spec.* used of advertising commercials); **story-book:** also *attrib.*; freq. *fig.* with allusion to the conventionally happy ending of children's stories or popular romances (cf. *fairy-tale); **story conference,** a meeting of editorial and production staff to discuss a film script; **story editor,** one who advises on the content and form of film or television scripts; **story-line,** an outline of the principal stages by which a story (esp. a film script) unfolds; also *transf.*; **story-paper** (earlier example).

1951 *Ann. Reg. 1950* 396 'Story ballets' with music that had been specially composed to fit a ballet scenario. **1964** *Listener* 23 Apr. 668/2 Story-ballets on special scenarios. **1942** *Amer. Cinematographer* Apr. 188/3 A story board is a large 4 × 8 foot piece of wallboard or celotex, on which the story sketches are pinned in rows with aluminum push-pins. **1952** *Jrnl. Soc. Mot. Pict. & Television Engineers* LIX. 298/1 The storyboard will then show how much time is to be consumed between these majors. **1962** *Rep. Comm. Broadcasting 1960* in *Parl. Papers* 1961–2 (Cmnd. 1753) IX. 259 70 The storyboards or scripts of all advertisements are scrutinised by the Advertising Copy Committee. **1975** R. Hill *April Shroud* xii. 154 A huge sheet of card pinned to the wall. On it were pasted a series of drawings... 'Yeah, that's my story board.' **1844** C. M. Yonge *Abbeychurch* xiv. 298 It is only a failure in story-book justice. Lucy is too noble a creature to be rewarded in story-book fashion. **1913** E. C. Bentley *Trent's Last Case* xv. 309 The national fondness for doing things in a story-book style. *a* **1944** K. Douglas *Alamein to Zem Zem* (1946) xix. 124 She looked like a story-book nurse, clean, slim, pretty, and smiling. **1973** P. Moyes *Curious Affair of Third Dog* iii. 32, I call that a real story-book happy ending. **1926** G. Frankau *My Unsentimental Journey* xvi. 217 Casey Williams explained a story-conference, which appears to be something like a board meeting. **1975** R. L. Simon *Wild Turkey* (1976) xi. 71, I found the producer's office... Graskow was in the middle of a story conference. **1940** I. Crump *Our Movie Makers* ii. 21 In every studio there is a story editor, with numerous assistants who are always on the watch for stories. **1950** C. Beranger *Writing for Screen* xx. 165 The story then goes to the head of the department, the story editor. If the story editor approves of it, he in turn gives it to an associate producer or to the studio head who can order its purchase. **1966** *Writing for BBC* v. 24 A post peculiar to [television] Drama Group is that of the Story Editor... He is concerned with the content of the script, rather than its technical requirements... His role..is that of adviser, not 'rewrite man'. **1981** N. Tucker *Child & Book* v. 142 Story editors may be pushed fairly hard to think of new material for plots. **1937** A. Calder-Marshall in C. Day Lewis *Mind in Chains* 64 Proceeding from the lot of the film-worker to the nature of capitalist story-films, we find that they have a uniform basis. **1961** K. Reisz *Technique Film Editing* i. 36 This contempt for the simplest requirement of a story-film—the ability to create the illusion of events unfolding in logical sequence. **1941** B. Schulberg *What makes Sammy Run?* vi. 103 I've been after them to make a Jefferson picture..if I can only hammer out the goddam story line. **1956** *B.B.C. Handbk. 1957* 82 The most noticeable trend in variety production has been recent efforts to develop the situation comedy-type show with the continuing story-line. **1967** M. McLuhan *Medium is Massage* 92 Older societies..demanded story lines. Today's humor, on the contrary, has no story line—no sequence. **1972** G. Jones *Kings, Beasts, & Heroes* i. i. 8 'The Three Stolen Princesses' is an elaborate and complicated type of folktale..tolerating a considerable choice of alternatives by the story-teller without losing its story line. **1886** F. H. Burnett *Little Lord Fauntleroy* xi. 218 Then he looked at the story papers.

stoss (stǫs, ‖ʃtǫs), *a. Geol.* [G. *stoss-*, f. *stossen* to push, thrust.] Designating the side of any object that faces a flow of ice or water; also *transf.* Freq. in *stoss-side* [partial tr. G. *stoßseite*, † also used]; *stoss-and-lee* attrib. phr. (see quot. 1947).

[**1848** J. G. Cumming *Isle of Man* xv. 249 The general appearance of its eastern, as compared with its western side, described by Swedish naturalists under the term *stoss seite* or weathered side, indicates in some measure that fact.] **1878** C. H. Hitchcock *Geol. New Hampshire* III. iii. ii. 180 The sides most worn are those which have been struck. We often speak of the struck or *stoss* and the lee sides of these rounded edges. **1891** R. D. Salisbury *Geol. Surv. New Jersey* 47 There was also more rapid erosion upon the north or stoss side of hills than upon the southern or lee side. **1905** J. Geikie *Structural & Field Geol.* xx. 310 The smoothed face is termed the Stoss-seite, and the non-glaciated face, the Lee-seite. **1920** [see *lee side b]. **1928** T. C. Chamberlin *Two Solar Families* 180 Let us picture the accretions..as running in convergently at one end of the axis of the core (the stoss end) and as running out divergently at the other (the lee end). **1947** R. F. Flint *Glacial Geol. & Pleistocene Epoch* v. 72 The persistently asymmetric arrangement of bosses and small hills in a strongly glaciated district, each hill having a comparatively gentle abraded slope on the stoss side and rougher quarried slope on the lee side, is termed stoss-and-lee topography. **1968** R. W. Fairbridge *Encycl. Geomorphol.* 435/1 These small glaciated knobs generally display a gently sloping, striated and polished upstream (stoss) slope and an oversteepened lee slope. **1971** I. G. Gass et al. *Understanding Earth* xiii. 171/1 The abundant ripples of beaches are..about 1 cm high... They move forward under the current by stoss-side erosion and lee-side avalanching.

‖ **stotinka** (stǫ·tinka). Usu. in *pl.* **-ki.** [Bulg.] A Bulgarian unit of currency, one-hundredth of a *lev*; a coin of this value.

1892 F. C. Higgins *Introd. Copper Coins Mod. Europe* 91 *Bulgaria*, 1881.—2, 5, and 10 'Stotinki'. **1902** *Encycl. Brit.* XXVI. 451 The monetary unit is the *lev*, or 'lion'..

nominally equal to the franc, with its submultiple the *stotinka* (pl. *-ki*), or centime. **1933** *Whitaker's Almanack* 546/1 Bulgaria—*Lev* of 100 *Stotinki*. **1976** A. GREY *Bulgarian Exclusive* vii. 48 I'll bet you fifty *stotinki* that he'll start telling us anti-communist jokes.

stotious, var. *STOCIOUS.

stotty (stǫ·ti). *north. dial.* [Origin unknown.] In full, *stotty cake*. A soft roll split and filled with meat or cheese.

1971 *Guardian* 5 July 4/6 The traditional local [Tyneside] foods such as leek and suet puddings, stotty cake. **1975** *Times* 20 Sept. 11/5 The bar snacks..include.. stotties, which are a local version of a bap, split and filled with meat or cheese. **1982** *Times* 12 Aug. 3/4 Most of the gunners come from north-east England, and Councillor Joseph Hall, Mayor of Sunderland, welcomed them as they left their aircraft. They were given..large portions of locally made pease pudding and stotty cake.

stoush (staʊʃ), *v. Austral.* and *N.Z. slang*. Also † **stouch.** [Orig. uncertain: perh. rel. to *stashie* uproar, quarrel (*E.D.D.*, *S.N.D.*).] To thrash or beat (a person); to punch or strike; to fight.

1893 J. A. BARRY *Steve Brown's Bunyip* 66 I'll get stoushed over this job yet. Brombee's got it in for me. **1894** *Bulletin* (Sydney) 5 May 13/3 'Then 'e biffed me.' 'And did yer stouch him back?' **1900** H. LAWSON *On Track* 148 'If you don't,' said Steelman, 'I'll stoush you.' **1924** KIPLING *Debits & Credits* (1926) 309 'What *your* crowd down under are suffering from is growing pains. You'll get over em in three hundred years or so—if you're allowed to last so long.' 'Who's going to stoush us?' Orton asked fiercely. **1941** K. TENNANT *Battlers* xxvi. 281 What with not being allowed to stouch any of the coves in charge of this turnout. **1945** [see *QUILT *v.*[3] a]. **1965** E. LAMBERT *Long White Night* 79 Get out of that bloody car while I stoush yer!

stoush (staʊʃ), *sb. Austral.* and *N.Z. slang*. Also † **stouch.** [f. the vb.] Fighting; also, *to take stoush*, to receive a beating. A brawl or fight; a scrap, 'punch-up'.

1908 H. FLETCHER *Dads & Dan between Smokes* 32 He looked as though he liked bein' hit an' took stoush fer breakfast every mornin'. **1914** C. J. DENNIS in *Bulletin* (Sydney) 16 July 47/1 Wot's jist plain stoush wif us..is 'valler' [*sc.* valour] if yer far enough away. **1924** *Truth* (Sydney) 27 Apr. 6 *Stouch*, a fight; to assault. **1945** R. S. CLOSE *Love me Sailor* 149 It was like the old days when I got Ernie into some stoush ashore just for the hell of fighting him out of it. **1952** J. CLEARY *Sundowners* (1960) iii. 129 The warmonger. You start any more stoushes.. and..it'll be the finish of you. **1966** *Weekly News* (N.Z.) 22 June 59/4 The final folly was that it was the Lions and not Otago who were principally responsible for the 'stoush' of the first half of Saturday's game. **1970** D. M. DAVIN *Not here, not Now* iv. i. 229 I've played football against him. He's a good man in the stoush, no doubt about that.

stout, *a.* Add: **I. 3. a.** Also, *stout fellow*: see *FELLOW *sb.* 9 a.

II. 6. a. For ?*Obs.* read 'Now only *U.S. dial.*' and add later examples.

1882 'MARK TWAIN' *Stolen White Elephant* 269 Your word 'stout' means 'fleshy'; our word 'stout' usually means 'strong'. **1913** *Dialect Notes* IV. 54 That calf's terrible stout; he pretty near pulled me all over the field. **1962** W. FAULKNER *Reivers* iv. 82 Let Lucius get out... He's younger than me and stouter too for his size.

12. c. *stout party*, a fat person (*humorously*). Esp. in catch-phrase *collapse of stout party* (see quot. 1975).

1855 *Punch* 25 Aug. 80/1 (*caption*) *Stout Party*: Well, I'm sure! What can possess those skinny creatures to wear round hats, I can't think,—making themselves so conspicuous! **1949** M. ALLINGHAM *More Work for Undertaker* vii. 102 'Do you will the stout party to give you the sixpences?' he ventured. **1957** R. G. C. PRICE *Hist. Punch* iii. 96 The florescence of the 'collapse of stout party' type of caption comes later [than the 1860s]. **1959** [see *PEARLY *sb.* b]. **1975** R. PEARSALL *Collapse of Stout Party* 4 To many people Victorian wit and humour is summed up by *Punch*, when every joke is supposed to end with 'Collapse of Stout Party', though this phrase tends to be as elusive as 'Elementary, my dear Watson' in the Sherlock Holmes sagas.

stouter. Add: (Later example.) Cf. *STROUTER.

1819 L. A. ANSPACH *Hist. Island Newfoundland* 430 The place where the operation of curing the cod-fish is performed, is a *stage* or covered platform erected on the shore, with one end projecting over the water, which is called the *stage-head*, and which is fortified with stouters.

stove, *sb.*[1] Add: **6.** (sense 3) *stove-plant* (earlier example); (sense 5) *stove-lid* (U.S.), *-oven*, *-tile*, *-wood* (U.S.); **stove enamel,** a vitreous enamel that is sufficiently heat-resistant to be used on stoves; hence **stove-enamelled** *a.*, **stove-enamelling; stove lifter** *N. Amer.*: see LIFTER 2 a.

1907 *Yesterday's Shopping* (1969) 11/1 Stove enamel polishing paste..tin, 0/2. **1949** KIRK & OTHMER *Encycl. Chem. Technol.* IV. 165 White baking finishes may be classified in four general types: (1) kitchen-cabinet enamels, (2) refrigerator finishes, (3) washing-machine finishes, and (4) stove enamels... Stove enamels are intended for use on the trimmings for stoves... A maximum temperature of 200°F is encountered. **1958** *Observer* 13 Apr. 10/2 A durable finish chromium rather than aluminium, and vitreous enamel..rather than stove enamel. **1912** C. H. B. QUENNELL in L. Weaver *House & its Equipment* 103 A few years ago, and in the case of the cheaper ones to-day, baths were 'stove-enamelled'. **1977** *Custom Car* Nov. 85/1 (Advt.), 100E Jaguar IRS complete with crossmember, stove enamelled, all new parts. **1939** *Jrnl. R. Aeronaut. Soc.* XLIII. 607 It is desirable therefore, that in cases where stove-enamelling treatments or other processes involving re-heating at elevated temperature have to be applied to duralium, [etc.]. **1876** 'MARK TWAIN' *Tom Sawyer* i. 17 She could have seen through a pair of stove lids just as well. **1929** W. FAULKNER *Sound & Fury* 318 'I came in here to burn them up' ..I says, looking at him and opening the stove lid. **1886** *Harper's Mag.* Nov. 835/1 We'll have a real egg and cinder flip with the hot stove-lifter in it when we get back. **1927** M. DE LA ROCHE *Jalna* xxv. 306 She up and shied the stove lifter at my 'ead. **1855** E. ACTON *Mod. Cookery* (rev. ed.) ii. 70 Set the dish into a gentle oven... A stove-oven, if the heat be properly moderated, will answer for the baking. **1968** *Globe & Mail* (Toronto) 13 Feb. 30/4 (Advt.), 4 Bedrooms, large family room. Fireplace! Walkout! Stove Oven! **1778** W. COWPER *Let.* 3 Dec. (1904) I. 151, I made Mr. Wrighte's gardener a present of fifty sorts of stove plant seeds. **1860** *Inventory Objects Mus. Ornamental Art, S. Kensington* 51/1 German enamelled stove tile; allegorical figure under an arcade.—Dated 1567. **1936** *Burlington Mag.* Sept. 111/1 The occurrence..on the jug of a relief corresponding to one on a green-glazed stove-tile. **1960** R. G. HAGGAR *Conc. Encycl. Cont. Pott. & Porc.* 269/2 Stoves and stove-tiles were made from the sixteenth until the eighteenth centuries, the earlier stove-tiles having flat surfaces with relief decorations and concave cylindrical backs. **1867** D. R. LOCKE *Swingin' round Cirkle* 159, I held a stick of stove wood suspended over his head. **1929** W. FAULKNER *Sound & Fury* 332 Then she..stacked stovewood into her crooked arm. **1972** *News & Observer* (Raleigh, N.C.) 30 Dec. 4/2 We don't hear much about stove wood [nowadays].

stove, *v.*[1] Add: **5. b.** To heat so as to fuse a coating to the object being coated. Also *absol.*, and *intr.* (of the coating) for *pass*.

1951 *Industrial Finishing* IV. 184/1 Unless the article is suspended approximately equidistant from the emitting surfaces there will be a risk of it being unevenly stoved. **1954** *Archit. Rev.* CXVI. 132 The undersides of most metal deckings are ribbed, and the steel ones are usually finished with red oxide, 'stoved' on. **1962** D. W. HISLOP in H. W. Chatfield *Sci. Surface Coatings* xviii. 531 A finish which stoves in half an hour at 150° C on sheet metal may require three times as long..at the same temperature when applied to a heavy casting. *Ibid.* 532 To be sure that a finish has been stoved adequately, a recording instrument is used with a thermocouple in contact with the painted metal. *Ibid.* 537 These lamps may be arranged in banks to give a high heating intensity. They enable paint films on suitable objects..to be stoved in times of a few seconds. **1977** *Hot Car* Oct. 73/1 It first etches and then stoves so that the finished coating (they say) is a really corrosion resistant lacquer around five times the thickness of factory wheel lacquer. **1979** J. D. SANDARS et al. *Man. Colour Matching* 129 Apply 25–30 micron dry films to burnished degreased mild steel. Stove for appropriate times.

stove, *ppl. a.* Add: **1.** (Earlier example.) Also **stove-in.**

1850 H. MELVILLE *White Jacket* I. iv. 20 Eternally talking of line-tubs, Nantucket, spermoil, stove boats, and Japan. **1897** KIPLING *Captains Courageous* iv. 98 They found..a gin-bottle, and a stove-in dory, but nothing more. **1979** 'A. HALL' *Scorpion Signal* xix. 223 A stove-in radiator with rusty water blowing out of it.

2. stove-up. Run-down, exhausted; worn out. Chiefly *predic.* of persons. *N. Amer. slang*.

1901 A. C. HEGAN *Mrs Wiggs of Cabbage Patch* ix. 127 If I was n't so stove up, an' nobody was n't lookin', I'd jes' skitter 'round this here yard like a colt! **1942** BERREY & VAN DEN BARK *Amer. Thes. Slang* § 129/12 *Physically run-down*,..stove-up. **1955** R. HOBSON *Nothing too Good for Cowboy* xvi. 175 You look stove-up, boy, what's the trouble with that hind leg of yours? **1960** H. LEE *To kill Mockingbird* viii. 81 Mr. Avery'll be in bed for a week—he's right stove up. He's too old to do things like that. **1974** D. SEARS *Lark in Clear Air* i. 18 An elderly man in levis and stove-up range-boots was..in the lower bunk.

stoved, *ppl. a.*[1] Add: **5.** *stoved enamel* = *stove enamel* s.v. *STOVE *sb.*[1] 6.

1926–7 *Army & Navy Stores Catal.* 311 The patent 'Peveril' grate..in best bright black stoved enamel, which does not require blackleading. **1967** *Times Rev. Industry* May 53/3 A good deal of paint is exported as the cellulose finish of a car, the stoved enamel surface of a washing machine or the paintwork of a jet airliner.

stoven, *ppl. a.* (Earlier example.)

1851 H. MELVILLE *Moby Dick* II. xiv. 122 The terrific wreck of the stoven planks.

stove-pipe. Add: **3. b.** More recently, = *drain-pipe* (fig.) s.v. *DRAIN *sb.* 5. Also *attrib.*, as *stove-pipe trousers*.

1955 T. H. PEAR *Eng. Social Differences* vii. 176 Narrow stove-pipe trousers. **1970** *Globe Mag.* (Toronto) 26 Sept. 5/2 The greasers..wear stove pipes, grey with pin stripes. **1978** *Sunday Times Mag.* 18 June 43/2 The names are Mazurca and Maier, cheap pink shirts against blond hair, stovepipe trousers above bare ankles and feet.

c. A portable trench mortar. *U.S. Mil.*

1920 H. H. BISSELL *Hist. Sixty-Third U.S. Infantry* 37 It didn't prevent their finding ranges, or getting the maximum of performance out of the old 'Stove-pipes'. **1957** R. LECKIE *Helmet for my Pillow* vi. 236, I remained.. spared the ordeal of carrying mortar shells to the 'stove-pipe' crews.

stovies (stō·viz), *sb. pl. Sc.* and *north. dial.* [f. STOVE *v.*[1] 6.] A dish of potatoes stewed in a pot; a potato stew. Also *attrib.*

1893–4 R. O. HESLOP *Northumb. Words* II. 687 Hey! lass, is the stavies [*sic*] no ready yit? **1894** J. INGLIS *Oor Ain Folk* iv. 40 One day there was a fine dish of 'stoved taties' for dinner... The lads would..have 'the stovies' finished before he had a chance to start. **1907** in *Ochtertyre Ho. Bk. Accomps* 258 *Stovies*, potatoes stewed fine with dripping or fat bacon, onions and spice, and served hot. **1939** M. SPRING RICE *Working-Class Wives* vi. 144 Her main dish is 'stovies' made with onions, potatoes and water; she never puts either dripping or meat into them. **1971** S. WALKER *Highland Cookbk.* 77 Plain stovies are excellent with beef stew or mince..Put as many peeled and sliced potatoes as you need in a pot [etc.]. **1973** *Courier & Advertiser* (Dundee) 26 Feb. 7/1 A liquid gas portable stove..would have barely supported our stovie pot!

stoving, *vbl. sb.* **b.** (Later examples.)

1952 *Industrial Finishing* V. 201/2 How efficiency of drying..can be increased with existing stoving equipment. **1962** D. W. HISLOP in H. W. Chatfield *Sci. Surface Coatings* xviii. 531 All paint stoving ovens can be a hazard as the solvent vapour/air mixture is a potential fire risk. **1972** *Materials & Technol.* V. viii. 215 The use of these oils in water-thinnable stoving paints has been more successful. *Ibid.* xi. 363 Anti-corrosive stoving primers for cars. **1982** W. M. MORGANS *Outl. Paint Technol.* (ed. 2) I. xiii. 221 The combination of urea resin with non-drying alkyd is used very widely for stoving finishes of almost all types.

stow, *v.*[1] Add: **6. stow away. a.** (Earlier example of jocular use.)

1858 M. TUCKETT *Diary* 24 Nov. (*c* 1975) 21 We stowed away a good breakfast.

b. (Later example.) Also, to conceal oneself on board a train or aeroplane.

1929 R. HUGHES *High Wind in Jamaica* vii. 168 Otto was a Viennese by birth, but had stowed away in a Danube barge when he was ten years old, had taken to the sea, and thereafter generally served in English ships. **1973** *Times* 8 Aug. 7/3 A Brazilian youth was sent home ..after stowing away on board a South African Airways aircraft by mistake.

stowaway. Add: **1.** (Earlier and later examples.) Also, one who steals a passage by aeroplane.

1850 *Morning Chron.* 22 July 6/1 All the passengers were summoned on deck that their names might be read over, their tickets produced, and a search made in the steerage, and in every hole and corner of the ship, for 'stow-aways'. **1922** [see *SCRATCH *sb.*[1] 5 b]. **1973** *Times* 8 Aug. 7/3 (*heading*) Stowaway takes wrong flight.

2. *gen.* Something stowed away. Also, a place where things may be stowed.

1913 E. F. BENSON *Thorley Weir* iii, For all these weeks Charles had never touched the cupboard except to insert some further stowaway. **1915** W. J. LOCKE *Jaffery* xx, Of all the stowaway places under my control..only one is locked. **1928** *Daily Express* 21 Mar. 5/3 The window-seat top lifts up, and this makes another good stowaway for toys.

STP (es tī pī). orig. *U.S.* Also **S.T.P.** [Prob. f. the initial letters of *S*cientifically *T*reated *P*etroleum, the commercial name of a motor-oil additive which was being extensively advertised when the drug first appeared.] A synthetic hallucinogenic drug chemically related to amphetamine but having effects similar to those of LSD; 2,5-dimethoxy-4-methylamphetamine.

1967 *Village Voice* (N.Y.) 13 Apr. 7/2 STP is a new psychedelic drug which..has become the most sought-after high on the psychedelic scene. **1967** *Guardian* 4 July 7/1 A new drug being used by the 'hippies' who inhabit San Francisco... For want of a name the hippies call it STP—a trade mark for an oil additive. **1969** *Oz* May 21/2 Alexander 'Sashe' Shulgin, the brilliant chemist who is best known to the public for his synthesis of STP (which was later illegally distributed in a dose form twice that 'recommended'). **1971** *It* 2–16 June 8/5 Those 80,000 doses of S.T.P. in the peanut butter jar that we were saving for an emergency. **1974** M. C. GERALD *Pharmacol.* xvii. 328 DOM is 2,5-dimethoxy-4-methylamphetamine to the chemist and STP (serenity, tranquillity, and peace) to the drug user.

strabismic, *a.* Add: (Earlier and later examples.) Also *fig.*

1855 *Lancet* 12 May 479/1 If the strabismic eye be brought into play, it assumes a normal condition, and moves in obedience to the will. **1915** H. DE SÉLINCOURT *Realms of Day* ii. 8 The weak and dim-eyed, who blame life for their own strabismic will-lessness. **1955** W. GADDIS *Recognitions* II. viii. 695 A small figure clutching a filthy dollar bill fixed him with a strabismic stare. **1975** *Nature* 20 Nov. 199/1 If a kitten is made strabismic by sectioning an eye muscle..their neurones are found to receive input from one eye or the other, but very few receive input from both.

‖ **stracciatella** (stratʃiate·lă). [It.] A soup made with stock, eggs, and cheese.

1954 E. David *Italian Food* 66 *Stracciatelle*, a Roman soup but common all over Italy, and extremely good. **1963** R. Carrier *Great Dishes of World* 54 Stracciatella alla Romana... Bring chicken stock to a fast boil and add egg mixture. **1978** *Chicago* June 221/1 A sumptuous selection of delectables: stracciatella fiorentina, soup made with whipped egg and spinach and topped with cheese. **1981** M. Nabb *Death of Englishman* i. iii. 95 *Stracciatella!* Good fresh broth, eggs laid ten minutes ago.

Stracheyan (strēi·tʃiăn), *a.* [f. the name of the English biographer and critic Giles Lytton *Strachey* (1880–1932) + -an.] Of, pertaining to, or characteristic of Strachey or his style of writing.

1927 *Observer* 9 Oct. 6/2 Mr. Burdett's 'Gladstone'.. owes to Mr. Strachey nothing but its size; it is a Victorian revaluation on a Stracheian scale. **1958** *Sunday Times* 22 June 6/4 A profusion of fancy adjectives and Stracheyan present participles. **1967** *Punch* 25 Oct. 639/2 The tone of it, if not derisive and iconoclastic in quite the Stracheyan manner, is none the less far from hushed and reverential. **1974** K. Clark *Another Part of Wood* v. 174, I had escaped from the infection of Stracheyan irony that influenced my chapter on the Ecclesiologists.

straddle, *sb.* Add: **I. 1. a.** Also *fig.*

1914 Lloyd George in *Times* 20 Sept. 4/4, I do not believe he [*sc.* the German Emperor] meant all these speeches; it was simply the martial straddle he had acquired.

b. (Examples.)

c **1842** G. D. Prentice *Prenticeana* (1860) 110 A writer in the 'True Whig' justly represents Mr. Tyler as standing with 'a foot on one boat and a foot on the other'... Although his Accidency's legs are not of the shortest, his straddle is becoming inconveniently wide. He will soon be as badly split as his party. **1934** H. Vines *This Green Thicket World* 21 The two springs that were little more than a man's straddle apart boiled up.

3. (Earlier examples.)

[*c* **1842**: see sense 1 b above.] **1843** *Knickerbocker* XXII. 233 These are..subjects for the straddle. The fence..is our only..safety on these p'ints.

4. (Earlier example.)

1864 W. B. Dick *Amer. Hoyle* 177 If the dealer choose, he may, in turn, double the *straddle*.

4*. A positioning of discharged shots, bombs, etc., such that some fall short of and some beyond the target (see also quot. 1973), esp. used as a deliberate form of attack or for range-finding. Freq. with reference to naval warfare. Cf. *straddle *v.* 5 c; *straddling *vbl. sb.*

1915 in M. Gilbert *Winston S. Churchill* (1972) III. Compan. i. 486 Four rounds will be wasted for every hit made in addition to the rounds used before the straddle is obtained. **1918** [see *straddle *v.* 5 c]. **1926** *Sci. Amer.* Aug. 104/1 They were liable to be wrecked by the first 'straddle' of an enemy's salvo. **1944** *Times* 27 Apr. 4/7 Depth charges were dropped from a low height in a perfect straddle. **1973** J. Quick *Dict. Weapons & Military Terms* 423/1 In range, or in deflection, when projectiles from a salvo fall both over and short of, or to both the left and right of, the target, a straddle is obtained.

III. 7. straddle carrier, a vehicle for manœuvring large containers, bulk loads of timber, etc., by straddling and lifting them beneath its chassis; **straddle harvester, machine,** an agricultural device which straddles rows of bushes or plants, etc., to facilitate the picking of the fruit; **straddle mill** (examples); so **straddle milling** *vbl. sb.*, the milling of two parallel faces of a workpiece simultaneously by means of a pair of cutters on a single shaft; **straddle-mill** *v. trans.*; **straddle truck** = *straddle carrier* above; **straddleways** *adv.* = *straddle-wise* adv. in Dict.

1950 *Dock & Harbour Authority* XXXI. 157/2 Another method of conveying baulks of timber, iron pipes and other similar goods is by petrol or diesel driven 'straddle' carrier. **1969** *Jane's Freight Containers 1968–69* 9/1 Provisions for straddle carrier handling. **1977** D. Grossman *Samsom Management Lexicon* vi. 36 At the extreme, straddle carriers may have a span wide enough to straddle several railway tracks or roadways and are used for the *intermodal* transfer of containers between road and rail. [**1967** *Amer. Fruit Grower* May 20/1 (*caption*) Also a straddle-type, the Krebs harvester..has hand shakers on both sides.] **1976** 'D. Halliday' *Dolly & Nanny Bird* vii. 85, I lurched creaking up the stairs like a blackcurrant straddle harvester. **1975** *N.Z. Jrnl. Agric.* Sept. 39/2 The larger British 'straddle' machines..are used to harvest some berry fruits. **1898** Straddle mill [see *side mill* s.v. *side *sb.*¹ 27]. **1905** W. S. Leonard *Machine-Shop Tools* (ed. 3) xxvi. 436 The straddle-mill..is of course the quickest for shapes having an even number of sides. **1919** H. D. Burghardt *Machine Tool Operation* ii. xii. 255 When any considerable number of pieces are to be milled it will be advisable to straddle-mill them. **1922** P. Gates *Jigs, Tools & Fixtures* v. 53 In the case of the component at b calling for 'straddle' milling, the fixture can be made adaptable, so that in the case of horizontal machines.. the fixture could be arranged on angle plate..and vertically 'straddle' milled. **1954** Straddle milling [see *side milling* vbl. sb. s.v. *side *sb.*¹ 27]. **1958** *Listener* 25 Sept. 458/1 The [timber] yards, where the fork-lift and straddle trucks scurry about loading and stacking. **1968** *N.Z. News* 25 Dec. 5/5 Straddle trucks are by no means new to the timber industry, but this vehicle..offers features never before incorporated in these utility vehicles. **1919** H. S. Walpole *Secret City* i. iii. 10, I can imagine Lawrence standing straddleways on the deck of the *Jupiter*, his short thick legs wide apart.

straddle, *v.* Add: **1. d.** Also *fig.*

1969 B. Rubens *Elected Member* ii. 18 Now, it was Norman, on the same bed, with a different illusion, but an illusion all the same, while between his father and Dr Levy in the kitchen, straddled the same uneasy truth.

2. (Earlier example.)

1802 D. Wordsworth *Jrnl.* 8 Feb. (1941) I. iii. 108 We met our patient bow-bent Friend... He straddled and pushed us with all his might; but we soon outstripped him.

5. a. Also *fig.*

1970 A. Toffler *Future Shock* xx. 424 Advanced telecommunications mean that participants in a social future assembly need not literally meet in a single room, but might simply be hooked into a communications net that straddles the globe. **1981** *Economist* 24 Jan. 28/2 Bank holding companies can straddle state lines (including foreign banks that were lucky enough to establish branches before the 1980 deadline).

c. For *Naut.* read *Gunnery* and substitute for def.: To fire at (a target) with shots, bombs, etc., so that they fall in a straddle (sense 4*). (See also quot. 1941.) (Later examples.)

1918 'B. Copplestone' *Silent Watchers* viii. 165 When, say, the shots of one salvo fall beyond the mark and the shots of the next come down on the near side, the mark is said to be 'bracketed'. When the individual shots of a salvo fall some too far and others too short, the mark has been 'straddled'. A *straddle* is a closed-in bracket. **1941** *Christian Sci. Monitor* 6 Mar. 4/7 'To straddle a target'.. no longer means..range-finding shots placed each side of the target. To the bombardier, the phrase describes the split-second triggering of a stick of bombs upon an objective. **1943** *Sun* (Baltimore) 28 Aug. 2/4 The crew of a plane..sprayed the deck of one submarine with machine-gun bullets, straddled it with depth charges and caused the U-boat to explode internally.

6. (Earlier example.) Also *absol.*

1838 J. C. Neal *Charcoal Sk.* 133 Sometimes I was a-one side, sometimes a-t'other, and sometimes I straddled till the election was over, and came up jist in time to jine the hurrah. **1878** *N.Y. Tribune* 29 Mar. 4/5 Whenever Mr. Randall doesn't straddle a question, he gets on the wrong side of it. **1880** *Daily Union* (San Diego, Calif.) 5 Sept. 1/3 For once in his life, therefore, Hendricks didn't straddle. He put both feet down on the wrong side, and tipped the whole party up. **1906** *N.Y. Even. Post* 6 Dec. 8 Eleven Senators answered yes, four no, and four straddled.

7. (Earlier examples.)

1864 W. B. Dick *Amer. Hoyle* 177 The 'blind' may be doubled by the player to the left of the eldest hand, and the next player to the left may at his option *straddle* this bet. **1872** [see *blind *sb.* 9].

8. *to straddle the market* (see quots.). *U.S. Exchange slang.*

1870 W. W. Fowler *Ten Years in Wall St.* 128 Going long and short of stocks, at the same time, is what is technically called 'Straddling' the market. **1900** S. A. Nelson *ABC Wall St.* 161 A speculator who has bought and is long of one stock, and sold and is short of another, has straddled the market. **1907** M. Rollins *Money & Investments* 383 *Straddle the market*, an understanding of 'Selling Short' is first necessary. One has 'straddled the market' when he is 'short' of one stock and 'long' of another.

straddling *vbl. sb.* (later examples).

1919 *Athenæum* 23 May 360/1 For a well-known method of range-finding..the Navy [has] the term 'straddling'. **1949** *San Francisco News* 14 Mar. 14/2 Despite the local board's straddling, the Legislature, fortunately, voted to continue the centers for another year. **1957** O. Parkes *British Battleships* lxxviii. 458 He proposed that the armoured cruiser..should be placed at his disposal for.. 'straddling' tests.

straddle, *adv.* Add: (Later example.) Also const. *of.*

1857 *Quinland* I. 24 He found a crazy fellow sitting straddle of a grave, holding on to the tombstone. **1919** J. Masefield *Reynard the Fox* 12 Molly Wolvesey riding straddle. **1930** W. Faulkner *As I lay Dying* 79 They had already dragged the backboard back from where Quick found it upside down straddle of the ditch about a mile from the spring. **1935** Z. N. Hurston *Mules & Men* i. vii. 163 It's a story 'bout a man sittin' straddle of a cow.

straddle-bug. Add: Also **straddlebug. 2.** *colloq.* A politician who is non-committal or who equivocates; one who 'straddles' (sense 6).

1872 *Kansan* (Newton, Kansas) 5 Sept. 2/1 We think it well that the people..not see quite so much of the straddle-bug business carried on by a few. **1896** *N.Y. Sun* 13 May 1/3 McKinley isn't a gold-bug, McKinley isn't a silver bug, McKinley's a straddle-bug. **1939** *Newsweek* 21 Aug. 14/2 If we nominate conservative candidates, or lip-service candidates, on a straddlebug platform, I personally..will find it impossible to have any active part in such an unfortunate suicide of the old Democratic party. **1948** *Sat. Even. Post* 10 July 33/3, I will not support either a conservative or a straddlebug.

straddly (stræ·dli), *a. rare*⁻¹. [f. Straddl(e *v.* + -y¹.] That straddles; long-legged.

1921 E. M. Forster *Let.* 21 July in *Hill of Devi* (1953) 98 Returned on foot, buying some toys—straddly black horses, but they will be difficult to pack.

strafe, *v.* Add: Also with pronunc. (strēif). Also **straff.** (Earlier and further examples.) In later Mil. usage, to attack from low-flying aircraft with bombs or machine-gun fire, etc.; also *transf.* and *fig.*

1915 A. D. Gillespie *Lett. from Flanders* (1916) 240, I never saw a billet like this for flies... We are trying poison too, but however we may 'strafe' there are just as many left. *Ibid.* 251 They only sent a few shells, and the first seemed to burst in their own trench..and I expect someone will be 'strafed' for it. **1916** 'Boyd Cable' *Action Front* 45 Straff the Germans and all their works, particularly their mine works! **1917** J. M. Grider *War Birds* (1927) 33 A regular army West Point major came over from Paris to look us over Sunday and straffed hell out of us in front of the British colonel and his staff. **1918** Galsworthy *Five Tales* 273 If I did my duty as a special, I should 'strafe' her for that. **1925** *Atlantic Monthly* Nov. 657 They're going to strafe us when we start out. **1942** *R.A.F. Jrnl.* 3 Oct. 36 Within ten minutes, enemy aircraft were straffing the ship. **1944** *Sun* (Baltimore) 12 Dec. 20/1 Most of the fighter escort of the 1,600 bombers..dropped to telephone-pole level to strafe trucks and trains heading from Frankfurt to the Saarbrucken battle zone. **1959** N. Mailer *Advts. for Myself* (1961) 42 They started to strafe the beach and the trenches. **1965** *Listener* 16 Dec. 1012/1 At least the latter straffed right and left with an energetic disregard for anything but her own sense of superiority. **1979** B. Parvin *Deadly Dyke* xv. 81 The Stone Cottages were..in need of repair, their paintwork peeling and strafed by the Fenland winds. **1982** *Daily Tel.* 18 Jan. 4/8 Filipino officials have denied a claim by Tokyo that their air force strafed the Japanese oil tanker.

Hence **stra·fer; stra·fing** *ppl. a.*

1916 O. Seaman *Made in England* 31 Is it the absent strafer's kiss On whose account this plaint they utter? **1930** C. R. Samson *Fights & Flights* 98 We left a car to attend to the Zeppelin strafers and take their mechanics away. **1979** M. Page *Pilate Plot* iv. 50 Some illusory protection from any Turkish Air Force strafer that appeared overhead. **1979** R. Cox *Auction* ii. 41 Strafing fighters passed so low that they were often below the level of the hill.

strafe (strāf, strēif), *sb. slang.* Also **straff.** [f. the vb.] A fierce assault; an attack from low-flying aircraft. Also *fig.*, a reprimand.

1915 in *Naval Rev.* (1916) IV. 267 The usual daily straff. **1916** [in Dict. s.v. Strafe *v.*] **1918** J. M. Grider *War Birds* (1927) 73 The C.O. and Capt. Horn, our new flight commander, were all set for a big straff because we were supposed to be back at nine. **1935** D. L. Sayers *Gaudy Night* xvii. 372 We was expectin' a bit of a strafe. **1939** *War Illustr.* 11 Nov. 288/1 (*heading*) German officer called Polish campaign a 'strafe' expedition, not a war. **1944** *R.A.F. Jrnl.* Aug. 262 Jerry is up to his nightly strafe. **1979** *Guardian* 24 July 19/1 The people who organize dinners..for foreign panjandrums have..received a rocket... The subject of the strafe was the standard of food. **1980** J. L. Carr *Month in Country* 69 I'd prayed eloquently enough in my signal-pit during big strafes.

strafing (strā·fiŋ, strēi·fiŋ), *vbl. sb. slang.* Also **straffing.** [f. Straf(e *v.* + -ing¹.] Fierce attacking; bombarding; bombing or machine-gunning from low-flying aircraft. Also *fig.*, a dressing-down.

1915 in *Naval Rev.* (1919) IV. 267 Not much straffing on either side. **1919** E. H. Jones *Road to En-Dor* vii. 70 The escape..was followed by a very severe 'strafing' of the whole camp. **1923** *Contemp. Rev.* Jan. 16 Mr. Bonar Law endured this moral strafing with dogged heroism. **1927** E. W. Springs *Nocturne Militaire* 75 I'm going to get a strafing when I get in. **1945** *Finito! Po Valley Campaign* (15th Army Group) 27 Spitfires and Mustangs weaved in strafing sorties over the enemy's positions. **1969** I. Kemp *Brit. G.I. in Vietnam* iii. 60 Diving aircraft ..swept close past us on their strafing runs. **1971** S. Hill *Strange Meeting* iii. 169 But when the strafing finally stopped, everything just went quiet. **1979** T. Barling *Olympic Sleeper* iv. 51 Let us hope the Zionists don't make a strafing run on the ship.

straggle, *sb.* Add: **2.** Also, a thin, lank, or untidy growth (of hair). Also *Comb.*

1978 H. Wouk *War & Remembrance* i. 7 His once-thick brown hair was a gray straggle. **1979** C. MacLeod *Family Vault* xviii. 117 Edith, puffy-faced and straggle-haired, stumped upstairs.

straggle, *v.*¹ Add: **1. e.** Also, of hair: to spread in lank or untidy strands.

1940 R. Chandler *Farewell, my Lovely* xvii. 106 Her dirty hair straggled on the pillow. **1958** A. Sillitoe *Saturday Night & Sunday Morning* i. 17 Her hair straggled untidily over the pillow.

straggler. Add: **4.** Also *spec.* in Austral. and N.Z., a stray unbranded animal or one that falls behind or is overlooked in a round-up. Also *fig.*

1848 H. W. Haygarth *Recoll. Bush Life Austral.* vi. 56 Innumerable animals of every kind of brand, and others with no brand at all, and known as 'stragglers', are mixed with the herds in the interior. **1860** G. Duppa in S. S. Crawford *Sheep & Sheepmen Canterbury* (1949) v. 46 Complete dipping flock..deliver stragglers. **1928** 'Brent of Bin Bin' *Up Country* xvii. 296 Then I'm going to have a good fling and settle down with a straggler if I can't get the bell ewe. **1933** L. G. D. Acland in *Press* (Christchurch, N.Z.) 16 Dec. 21/8 *Straggler*, sheep that has been left on the country at a muster. It is usual to go over the country again to pick them up. **1953** O. E. Middleton in C. K. Stead *N.Z. Short Stories* (1966) 186 Shepherding the stragglers would be Charlie's strong-eyes, Beau and Belle. **1972** P. Newton *Sheep Thief* 188 Sheep that have been missed in a main muster are 'stragglers'. To get them in may necessitate a special muster.

straggling, *vbl. sb.*[1] Add: **a.** *spec.* in *Nucl. Physics*, a spread of the energies, ranges, etc., of charged particles about a mean value as a result of collisions undergone in their passage through matter.

1912 *Phil. Mag.* XXIII. 902 After going a given time the α particles will have straggled out, and some will be moving faster than others. I have not succeeded in finding the amount of this straggling. **1930** E. RUTHERFORD et al. *Radiations from Radioactive Substances* iv. 112 The first experiments to estimate the straggling of the α particles were made by the scintillation method. **1950** D. HALLIDAY *Introd. Nucl. Physics* iv. 121 We can have straggling effects caused by varying energy losses in the source (source straggling), by departure of the beam from parallelism (angular straggling), and by characteristics of the detecting and recording equipment (instrument straggling). **1971** *Canad. Jrnl. Physics* XLIX. 1015 (*caption*) Comparison of experimental and theoretical range and range straggling values of ^{224}Ra ions in gases. **1979** *Physical Rev.* A. XIX. 111/1 Measurements of the energy straggling of ^{16}O ions with energies from 5 to 50 MeV passing through Al foils of thickness 100–500μg/cm² were described.

straggly, *a.* (Earlier example.)

1862 J. A. SYMONDS *Let.* 2 Feb. (1967) I. 327 The evergreens..are growing very straggly in parts.

straight, *a.*, *sb.* and *adv.* Add: **A.** *adj.* **2. d.** (Later examples.)

1940 W. FAULKNER *Hamlet* III. ii. 200 Lying flat on his back in the darkness with his eyes open and his arms straight beside him, thinking of nothing. **1955** *Simple Gymnastics* ('Know the Game' Ser.) 6/1 When your knees are as high as this, squeeze your legs together and lay back with straight arms.

3. a. Also in collocation with *narrow*, esp. in phr. *straight and narrow path*, a course of conventionally moral and law-abiding behaviour; freq. *ellipt.* in colloq. usage as *straight and narrow.* Cf. *strait and narrow* s.v. *STRAIT a. 3 b.

A misinterpretation of Matt. vii. 14 'Because strait is the gate, and narrow is the way which leadeth vnto life, and few there be that finde it.'

1842 J. E. LEESON *Hymns & Scenes of Childhood* 25 Loving Shepherd, ever near, Teach Thy lamb Thy voice to hear; Suffer not my steps to stray From the straight and narrow way. **1912** T. DREISER *Financier* xxiii. 253 In his younger gallivantings about places of ill repute, and his subsequent occasional variations from the straight and narrow path, he had learned much of the curious resources of immorality. **1930** J. DOS PASSOS *42nd Parallel* IV. 275 Robbins..said that he..would have to follow the straight and narrow. **1959** D. BUCKINGHAM *Wind Tunnel* xx. 161 He had unwittingly caused Madelaine to take a far more serious step off the straight and narrow. **1970** *Times* 13 Feb. 10/4 It may be counted for consistency..that the White Paper should not have flinched..once again to sign-post the straight and narrow path. **1978** F. WELDON *Praxis* x. 73 It's only the fear of pregnancy which keeps girls on the straight and narrow.

b. Delete † *Obs.* (Later examples.)

1898 G. B. SHAW *You never can Tell* II. 241 She takes his hand and presses it, with a frank, straight look into his eyes. **1922** T. S. ELIOT *Waste Land* (1923) ii. 12 He wants a good time. And if you don't give it him, there's others will, I said... Then I'll know who to thank, she said, and give me a straight look.

e. Also, straightforward, not evasive.

1959 A. SILLITOE *Loneliness of Long-Distance Runner* ii. 178 'You'll get five years in Borstal if you don't give me a straight answer,' he said. **1973** J. PORTER *It's Murder with Dover* vii. 70 Dover generously gave him a straight answer to a straight question. 'No,' he said. **1979** 'A. HAILEY' *Overload* IV. viii. 333 Nim, give me the straight dope behind this Yale thing. What went wrong?

g. *Lawn Tennis.* Applied to the sets in a match where the winner has not conceded a set. Also *fig.*

1895 *Official Lawn Tennis Bull.* 4 July 103 Stevens's persistent and accurate ground-strokes from the baseline, and his ability to reach and return everything safely proved too much for Fischer, who was beaten rather badly in straight sets. **1911** *Wright & Ditson's Official Lawn Tennis Guide* 12 Except in the second set of this match, the two Doyles..were completely outclassed and Waidner and Gardner made rather easy work, winning in straight sets. **1936** E. C. POTTER *Kings of Court* vi. 99 If Brookes had been able to hold his service..it might have gone for a straight-set win. **1949** D. C. COOMBE *Hist. Davis Cup* 222 Petra won both his singles in straight sets. **1961** *Times* 4 Jan. 11/3 Miss McAlpine should have won in straight sets. **1971** LAVER & COLLINS *Educ. Tennis Player* xxiii. 273, I picked up a little Spanish in that stretch of straight-set victories. **1980** *Guardian* 20 Sept. 10/3 (*heading*) Straight set winners.

h. Consecutive, in unbroken sequence. *colloq.* (orig. *U.S.*).

1899 J. LONDON *Let.* 30 Apr. (1966) 35 He spent 48 straight hours with me a couple of days before he went. **1963** *Wall St. Jrnl.* 25 Jan. 31/3 American Photocopy Equipment stock was the most active stock for the second straight day. **1971** LAVER & COLLINS *Educ. Tennis Player* xxv. 291 I had won 30 straight matches since losing to Newcombe in June, the week before Wimbledon. **1976** *Morecambe Guardian* 7 Dec. 8/9 Vale got off to a good start through their No. 1 Mike Ashby who won in fine style in three straight games. **1977** *Listener* 10 Mar. 295/1 Company earnings..had reflected their 16th straight annual gain.

i. *Racing.* Designating a bet which backs (a horse, etc.) to win. Cf. PARI MUTUEL.

1928 *Daily Sketch* 10 Aug. 20/4 It..can be used either for straight or place betting. **1974** P. ARNOLD *Bk. Gambling* viii. 88/1 If there are three to six runners, a straight forecast pool is also run. Bettors are required to name the first two horses to finish, in the correct order. **1976** *Webster's Sports Dict.* 427/2 *Straight*,..[in] pari-mutuel betting. First place at the finish. When a straight wager is made, the bettor collects only if the competitor wins.

j. Straightforward, simple, uncomplicated. *colloq.*

1936 *Discovery* Aug. 254/1 It is possible to perceive a sharp demarcation between what may be called 'straight dowsing' and 'divination proper'. **1957** *Times Lit. Suppl.* 18 Oct. 625/3 Any editor worth his salt is grateful to have slips, oversights, straight mistakes and insensitivities pointed out. **1962** *Times* 5 July 15/5 The tapes all emerged as inferior in straight comparisons. **1972** WODEHOUSE *Pearls, Girls, & Monty Bodkin* x. 143 Would he be cut in on the gross receipts, do you think, or is he on a straight salary?

6. a. Also in colloq. use, law-abiding as opp. criminal. Cf. *to go straight* (*b*), sense 5 of the adv. below.

1977 J. WAINWRIGHT *Day of Peppercorn Kill* 37 Inky was straight... Ten years ago, Inky had walked away from prison..and, since that day, he hadn't put a foot wrong.

c. (Earlier example.)

1853 C. M. YONGE *Heir of Redcliffe* II. v. 70 If the right motives did not suffice to keep one straight..why then I should be..utterly good for nothing.

d. *slang* (orig. *U.S.*). Conventional, respectable, socially acceptable. Also *spec.* (*a*) heterosexual; not practising sexual perversions; (*b*) not using or under the influence of drugs; sober, abstinent.

1941 G. W. HENRY *Sex Variants* II. 1176 *Straight*... Also employed as meaning not homosexual. *To go straight* is to cease homosexual practices and to indulge—usually to re-indulge—in heterosexuality. **1959** M. ZANE *Easy Living* vii. 90 'You don't want a slug [of brandy], huh?' 'No thanks. I'm straight.' **1960** WENTWORTH & FLEXNER *Dict. Amer. Slang* 524/1 *Straight*,..honest; normal. Depending on the context, denotes that the person referred to is not dishonest, not a drug addict, not a homosexual, and so forth. **1965** *San Francisco Examiner* 5 Sept. 5/1 A lot of us have 'straight' friends. **1966** A. YOUNG in A. Chapman *New Black Voices* (1972) 147 Why dont you buy this joint off me so I can be straight for lunch. **1967**, etc. [see *FREAK *sb.*[1] 4 c]. **1968** *Globe & Mail Mag.* (Toronto) 13 Jan. 6/1 Some straight (heterosexual) people also go there to watch the drag show (a floor show put on by men dressed and acting like women). **1971** *Psychol. Today* May 43/1, I can see patterns, form, figures, meaningful designs in visual material that does not have any particular form when I'm straight. **1971** 'M. UNDERWOOD' *Trout in Milk* xx. 167 'Every perversion catered for.'..'And what's yours, Mr Slatter?'..'I'm straight.' **1975** *N.Y. Times Bk. Rev.* 30 Nov. 42/3 A fastidiously distant man without the hint of a sex life, straight or otherwise. **1976** J. CROSBY *Snake* (1977) ix. 43 Few of the revolutionary youth..threw it all up and came back to the straight world. **1978** V. MARTIN *Set in Motion* v. 96, I wish I had some dope. I haven't been straight this long in years. **1981** Q. CRISP *How to become a Virgin* vi. 88 All his spare attention was given to pointing out which bars were gay or had been gay, which restaurants were straight though run by homosexuals and so on.

7. b. Freq. in phr. *to play a straight bat* and varr. Also *fig.*

1944 BLUNDEN *Cricket Country* vii. 79 He simply played the straight-bat game. **1973** *Times* 11 June 13/7 The British too..owed much of their greatness to their own self-esteem, and to the legend of straight bat, stiff upper lip, probity and detachment. **1975** *Times* 1 Dec. 5/1 Mr Wilson and Mr Callaghan intend to play a straight bat at the EEC conference. **1979** 'J. LE CARRÉ' *Smiley's People* (1980) xiv. 164 When it came to the big stuff he always played a straight bat.

8. a. Also attributively, esp. in phr. *to keep a straight face.*

1953 H. MILLER *Plexus* (1963) iv. 137 All I felt called upon to do was to keep a straight face and pretend that everything was kosher. **1972** J. PORTER *Meddler & her Murder* x. 128 Miss Jones..managed to keep a straight face... The margarine represented a small secret triumph. **1974** *Scotsman* 22 Apr. p. ix, Only in oil can you break off kelly and set down on rams while keeping a straight face.

c. Also, free from debt.

1914 F. M. FORD *Let.* 22 Dec. (1965) 60 Of course if Conrad is not yet straight I don't want to exact this. **1960** *Jazz Rev.* Sept.–Oct. 14 He was straight at this time—saved his money and everything. **1966** *Listener* 8 Sept. 335/2 In the ten years after the war we made a huge effort to get straight by austerity and stringent controls.

d. In colloq. phrases, as *to get* (*something*) *straight*, to make (something) clear, to reach an understanding; *to keep* (*someone*) *straight*, to keep (someone) informed.

1862 J. BLACKWOOD *Let.* 17 Mar. in *Geo. Eliot Lett.* (1956) IV. 22, I suppose there is nothing in your remarks about language to clash with my paper last month. Keep me straight about this. **1920** S. LEWIS *Main St.* xiv. 167 Will,..I must get this straight. Some one said..all the doctors hate each other. **1946** MEZZROW & WOLFE *Really the Blues* viii. 124 Get this straight, we pure-and-simple jazzmen didn't scoff the 'serious' composers. *Ibid.* xi. 194 When he got straight on my version of *My Blue Heaven* I played the second harmony sax part along with him. **1946** J. B. PRIESTLEY *Bright Day* x. 320 I'm going to risk telling you something... It's all ancient history, but..we might as well get it straight.

e. *U.S. slang.* Of a drug-user: drugged, 'high' (*HIGH *a.* 16 c). Cf. sense 6 d above.

1946 MEZZROW & WOLFE *Really Blues* xii. 217, I know I'm gonna get straight now, I know you gonna put me on. **1951** *Life* 11 June 120/1 While the cops were in the apartment they seized five teen-agers who came up to be put straight. **1965** *Life* 26 Feb. 86/4 Once the addict has had his shot and is 'straight' he may become admirably, though briefly, industrious. **1971** E. E. LANDY *Underground Dict.* 178 *Straight*,..1...off drugs; clean. 2. A drug addict will use the word 'straight' to mean to use a drug—eg. *I've got to get straight.*

9. For *U.S.* read 'orig. *U.S.*' **a.** (Later examples.) *to vote the straight ticket*: also *fig.*

1934 J. O'HARA *Appointment in Samarra* (1935) vi. 171 You want ginger ale with yours, or straight? **1940** H. G. WELLS *Babes in Darkling Wood* II. iii. 194 She'll give up the ice, I expect, and settle down to straight Martini and gin. **1950** 'D. DIVINE' *King of Fassarai* xv. 119 'I'd like a coke.'..'Little rum in it?'..'Straight coke.' **1977** M. HINXMAN *One-Way Cemetery* xx. 146 She handed him his glass. 'Soda?' 'Straight.' **1979** *Guardian* 30 Oct. 10/4 People who vote the straight green ticket—rucksacks, sperm whales, recycling, and free-range hens.

b. (Earlier example.)

1864 W. B. DICK *Amer. Hoyle* 167 It [*sc.* Twenty-Deck Poker] is controlled by the same rules as Common or Straight Poker.

d. *Mus.* Applied to a kind of jazz characterized by adherence to a score or set orchestration and a lack of improvisation, or to a player of this kind of jazz. Also, of music or a musician: 'serious' or dance-band as opposed to jazz; = *LEGITIMATE *a.* 2 e.

1926 *Melody Maker* Feb. 15/2 His father was..one of the finest 'straight' saxophonists in the world. **1927** *Ibid.* Apr. 329/3 The band is well drilled..but relies on stereotyped orchestration and 'straight' rendering. Moreover, there is nothing like enough solo work. **1928** [see *HOT *a.* 8 g]. **1934** S. R. NELSON *All about Jazz* ii. 40 This training is very useful where an orchestra has played for the cabaret, or any diversion where 'straight' music is employed. **1936** *Swing Music* Apr. 37/1 Red Nichols was ..a great 'straight' jazz trumpet. **1938** *Oxf. Compan. Music* 777/2 It appears that the terms *Straight Jazz* (or *Sweet Jazz*) and *Hot Jazz* apply respectively to jazz played as written and jazz in which the extempore element is prominent. **1947** *Penguin Music Mag.* May 28 Antony Hopkins has been much more affected by the jazz element in other 'straight' composers' works than by the original thing. **1961** *Guardian* 16 Mar. 11/1 [He] is a 'straight' musician with some experience of jazz. **1971** *Daily Tel.* 20 Jan. 10/6 A programme which covered fields as diverse as Renaissance polyphony, newly-commissioned music, both straight and jazzy, and swinging close-harmony arrangements.

e. Of animals: pure-bred. Cf. *straight-bred*, sense 7 a of the adv. below.

1972 P. NEWTON *Sheep Thief* x. 80 They were straight merinos and pretty touchy to handle.

9*. a. *Theatr.* 'Serious' as opposed to popular or comic. Cf. LEGITIMATE *a.* 2 b in Dict. and Suppl.

1895 *N.Y. Dramatic News* 6 July 2/1 Trilby is the only 'straight' theatrical entertainment now left in New York. **1908** *Variety* 16 May 15/1 A steady succession of comedy numbers..gave the two 'straight' acts closing the bill an almost impossible task to accomplish. **1928** *Observer* 1 Jan. 11/4 Miss Gertrude Lawrence will then make her first appearance in 'straight' drama. **1928** *Punch* 23 May 582/3 The character-actors have no doubt an easier task than the 'straight' actors. **1932** *Daily Express* 27 June 3/3 Being determined to go into straight plays, she learned some poetry. **1937** *Sunday Express* 21 Feb. 21/5 Luckily he has Naunton Wayne handling his best lines, revealing in his first straight part an easy sense of situation and character to back up his known comedy brilliance. **1959** H. PINTER *Birthday Party* I. 4 This is a straight show... No dancing or singing... They just talk. **1970** *Guardian* 19 Aug. 6/4 Feldman..has since appeared as a straight man..in a couple of Johnny Speight TV plays. **1981** V. GLENDINNING *Edith Sitwell* xi. 151 Edith...loved music halls, which she preferred to the straight theatre.

b. *Vaudeville.* Applied to a performer who assumes a passive role as a feeder (FEEDER 11) or butt for a comedian; also *transf.*

1923 *N.Y. Times* 15 July VI. 1/6 The method of the comedy team remains more or less unvaried. The team is composed, in the first place, of a comedian and a 'straight' man. **1933** P. GODFREY *Back-Stage* iii. 37 The music-hall cross-talk act, where one of the characters is 'straight' and the other the comedian. **1957** [see *FEEDER 11]. **1961** *Sunday Express* 18 June 19/1 For eight years he had been 'straight man' to Sid Field, one of the great comics. **1973** R. HILL *Ruling Passion* II. ii. 101 Pascoe looked doubtful. He was used to playing Dalziel's straight man. **1979** J. BARNETT *Backfire is Hostile!* i. 26 Smith knew he was being used as a straight man but played along with it.

c. Applied to a 'serious' novel, film, etc. which employs the conventional techniques of its art form.

1936 'J. TEY' *Shilling for Candles* vi. 59 She was at that time shooting her first straight film. **1942** H. HAYCRAFT *Murder for Pleasure* ix. 203 Mr. Carr-Dickson..has been an incomparable boon to the English 'straight' detective story. **1953** A. UPFIELD *Murder must Wait* x. 90, I write..straight novels, not these beastly thrillers. **1977** *Listener* 30 June 866/4 Most crime reviewers have..been arraigned by novelists who think they would have got better treatment in straight novel columns. **1981** F. MCSHANE *Sel. Lett. R. Chandler* p. xv, He..rendered the actualities of American life as vividly and independently as any 'straight' novelist.

10. c. straight A('s) *U.S.*, uniform top grades; **straight-armed** *a. Cricket*, with the arm unflexed; *spec.* † designating a style of round-arm bowling with a straight arm, or an exponent of this style (*obs.*); **straight arrow** *N. Amer. slang*, an honest or genuine person; also as *adj.* and *adv.*; **straight-backed** *a.*, (*a*) (earlier example of a person); **straight chain** *Chem.*, a chain of atoms that is neither branched nor closed in on itself to form a ring; usu. *attrib.* (with hyphen); **straight cut** *Cinemat.*, a complete cut between sequences (as opposed to a fade or a dissolve); **straight drive** *Cricket*, a drive in which the ball is struck back down the pitch towards or past the bowler; also as *v. trans.*; hence **straight driver, straight driving** *vbl. sb.*; **straight-edge(d) razor** = *straight razor* below; also *ellipt.*; **straight eight** *Mech.*, (a motor vehicle having) an internal combustion engine with eight cylinders arranged in a straight line; freq. *attrib.*; similarly *straight four*, *straight six*; (cf. *IN-LINE *a.* 1 a); **straight-faced** *a.*, solemn, serious (cf. sense 8 a in Dict. and Suppl.); hence **straightfacedly** *adv.*, **straightfacedness; straight fight,** an election in which there are only two candidates; **straight goods** *U.S. slang*, the truth; an honest person; **straight-grain(ed)** *a.* (see quot. 1929); **straight job** *U.S. slang*, a single-unit truck, one with its body built directly on to its chassis; **straight leg** *U.S. Mil. slang*, a member of the ground staff as opposed to one of the flying personnel (see also quot. 1967); **straight mute,** a simple cone-shaped mute for a trumpet or trombone; **straight pein** *a.*, designating a type of hammer which has the pein in line with the handle; freq. *absol.* as *sb.*; **straight razor,** a razor with a long blade that folds into its handle for storage, a cut-throat razor (see *CUT-THROAT 1 d); **straight-run** *a. Chem.*, (of a petroleum fraction) produced by distillation without cracking or other chemical alteration of the original hydrocarbons; **straight stitch,** in *Embroidery*, a single, short, detached stitch; also as *adj.*, designating a simple type of sewing-machine; hence **straight-stitching** *a.*; **straight time** *a.* orig. and chiefly *U.S.*, of or relating to remuneration received for work performed within normal or regular hours; also *absol.* (cf. OVERTIME *sb.* a in Dict. and Suppl.).

1926 *Amer. Oxonian* July 98 It isn't merely four years of football, four years of straight A, and ten thousand activities that make a winner [of a Rhodes Scholarship]. **1948** *Chicago Daily News* 20 Sept. 18/2 In pre-medical college Jim S. was a brilliant student—straight A's. **1960** *Encounter* Nov. 29/1 The straight-A students..sometimes slipped away without anyone's noticing. **1980** *TWA Ambassador* Oct. 77/2, I have a daughter who is the movie-star type, brighter than hell and has straight A's in college. **1827** *Sporting Mag.* Nov. 11/1 If necessary, admit the straight-armed bowling, allowing it to go as high as the shoulder, so that the back of the hand be kept under when the ball is delivered. **1828** *Ibid.* Feb. 244/2 Straight-armed bowlers are invariably slow bowlers. **1934** W. J. LEWIS *Lang. Cricket* 31 Various obsolete names applied to round-arm bowling when it was first introduced:..*straight-arm* (or *-armed*) *bowling*, i.e. with the arm extended horizontally. **1961** *Times* 12 July 4/5 Suttle gathering runs with that curiously rigid, straight-armed hook of his. **1969** *Time* 22 Aug. 43 The new eco-activists include groups as straight-arrow as the Girl Scouts. **1969** *New Yorker* 11 Oct. 194 Smith, a wonderfully old-fashioned straight arrow. **1977** C. MCFADDEN *Serial* (1978) xliv. 95/1, I keep trying to tell you, I'm really a straight arrow. **1978** *Daily Colonist* (Victoria, B.C.) 6 Sept. 31/3 Tell the truth no matter what. And be straight-arrow about it. **1978** J. L. HENSLEY *Killing in Gold* iv. 52, I hated not playing it straight-arrow with Ed. **1819** M. EDGEWORTH *Let.* ?10 Mar. (1971) 181 Lady Elizabeth's mother a fine straight-backed thin dried benevolent smiling eyed looking woman whom I like much. **1890** J. B. TINGLE tr. *E. Hjelt's Princ Gen. Org. Chem.* I. ii. 18 If the carbon atoms of a nucleus are joined together in a single straight chain, they are said to form a simple or normal chain. **1934** *Jrnl. Franklin Inst.* CCXVIII. 145 Among organic chemical compounds the straight-chain hydrocarbons are of particular interest because of the simplicity of their properties. **1965** PHILLIPS & WILLIAMS *Inorg. Chem.* I. iv. 138 A relatively simple example is provided by the difference between the branched and straight-chain hydrocarbons. **1971** Straight chain [see *ladder polymer* s.v. *LADDER *sb.* 6]. **1953** K. REISZ *Technique Film Editing* iii. 245 While the spectator is still laughing, he is already plunged—through a straight cut—into the next sequence. **1959** Straight cut [see *CUT *sb.*² 14*]. [**1877** C. BOX *Eng. Game Cricket* xxvi. 449 *Drive*, a hard forward hit; it is designated on, off, or straight according to the course taken by the ball.] **1898** K. S. RANJITSINHJI *With Stoddart's Team* (ed. 4) iv. 72 McKenzie plays with a very straight bat,..most of his runs being obtained by straight drives on either side of the bowler. **1927** G. A. TERRILL *Out in Glare* v. 95 Clement played his first ball defensively;..off-drove the next for three. Fosbery straight-drove the next for two. **1959** J. FINGLETON *Four Chukkas to Australia* xvi. 135 He straight-drove Davidson. **1971** *Times* 15 Feb. 8/2 Jenner..made some punishing straight drives off Lever. **1925** *Country Life* 8 Aug. 214/1 Of all the glorious straight drivers I have ever seen, commend me to J. N. Crawford. **1904** P. F. WARNER *How we recovered the Ashes* vii. 119 There was a Lyons-like power about his straight driving. **1972** *Sat. Rev.* (U.S.) 27 May 4/2 When I was a small boy, my father used a straight-edged razor... I tried using a straightedge, but I was a generation too late... I went over to the safety razor. **1973** J. ROSSITER *Manipulators* i. 8 He shaved his flat cheeks..with a straight-edge razor. **1926** A. HUXLEY *Jesting Pilate* II. 197 Heroes invariably have the time to drive in Straight-Eights from Salt Lake City to New York. **1928** *Punch* 17 Oct. 439/3 Several new 'straight eight' cars have recently been announced. The advantages of the eight-in-line unit are obvious. **1954** *Motor Man.* (ed. 35) ii. 25 (*caption*) Daimler Straight-eight 36 h.p. petrol engine. **1963** BIRD & HUTTON-STOTT *Veteran Motor Car* 53 This formed the basis for the small, fast revving straight-eights so particularly associated with the name of Bugatti. **1982** *Times Lit. Suppl.* 5 Mar. 249/5 The engine of the Type-41 Bugatti illustrated..is a straight-eight with all its cylinders in line. **1975** *Business Week* 30 June 14/2 Pierce was, Crichton tells us with the straight-faced assurance that makes his readers wonder what is fiction and what is fact, 'a man destined to be so notorious that Queen Victoria herself expressed a desire to meet him'. **1983** *Washington Post* 6 Mar. H 6/3 O'Down just turned 21. With the innocence of the newly famous, he's straight-faced when he says, 'I want to grow old gracefully.' **1977** *Guardian Weekly* 17 July 11/3 They were told straight-facedly [that] the new Israeli premier was going all out to convince the Arabs that in their own interests Israel should keep the West Bank. **1982** *N. & Q.* Apr. 142/1 One cannot help feeling that the straight-facedness of the glossing..detracts from the complete understanding of the passage. [**1900** *Times* 3 Oct. 8/2 Dundee, where there will this time be a straight party fight, without the interposition of a labour candidate.] **1910** *Times* 12 Jan. 9/1 Another very noticeable feature of the London elections is that there will be a straight fight between the Government candidate and the Opposition nominee in all but three constituencies. **1957** *Ann. Reg. 1956* 26 Comparisons had been complicated by the appearance or disappearance of Liberal candidates. Here..the comparison was between two straight fights. **1959** *Motor Man.* (ed. 36) ii. 38 The crankshaft is arranged so that the pistons operate in exactly the same manner as they do in a straight-four engine. **1892** *Harper's Mag.* Dec. 138 I'm givin' yu' straight goods, yu' see. **1903** B. KENNEDY *Sailor Tramp* I. xix. 156 What do I know.. about him? Why that he's all right. That he's straight goods. **1922** E. O'NEILL *Anna Christie* III. 181 You'd die laughing sure if I said that meeting you that funny way that night in the fog, and afterwards seeing that you was straight goods stuck on me, had got me to thinking for the first time. **1922** —— *Hairy Ape* iv. 40 Is all dat straight goods? **1880** J. W. ZAEHNSDORF *Art Bookbinding* xx. 88 Should the leather be 'straight grain', it must only be creased in the one direction of the grain. **1929** C. J. H. DAVENPORT *Roger Payne* ii. 44 He [*sc.* Roger Payne] found that if a piece of morocco was slightly damped, and then vigorously rolled on itself by hand, that all its original markings became much more apparent. This leather when dry was found to have acquired a permanent surface configuration like a series of small, more or less parallel, wavy lines, which is now known as 'straight grain', largely found, for the first time, on many of Payne's finest bindings. **1963** Straight-grain [see *paste grain* s.v. *PASTE *sb.* 8]. **1892** W. L. ANDREWS *Roger Payne* 16 The materials used by Roger Payne as coverings for his bindings were almost without exception either straight-grained morocco or russian leather. **1956** H. M. NIXON *Broxbourne Library Styles & Designs Bookbindings* 193/1 Material: Red straight-grained morocco, over pasteboards. **1955** *Amer. Speech* XXX. 92 *Straight job*, a single-unit truck, usually equipped with dual wheels. **1978** S. BRILL *Teamsters* v. 170 About thirty trucks, all 'straight jobs' (that is, one-unit vehicles rather than tractors pulling trailers) were backed against a ramshackle warehouse. **1951** *Sun* (Baltimore) 24 July 17/3 Witnessing the maneuver from the sidelines were a number of anxious ground officers or 'straight legs'. **1967** *Everybody's Mag.* (Austral.) 18 Jan. 36/2 Today, in Vietnam, Australians are again catching up on American Army slang... An airborne soldier is called a Trooper, and he knows his counter-part on the ground as a Straight-leg. **1926** *Melody Maker* Feb. 23/1 The modern player must be prepared to use every kind of mute, and novelties are constantly being produced. Most of the latter provide 'stunt'..effects as against the 'straight' mute, which merely softens the tone of the instrument. **1961** A. BERKMAN *Singers' Gloss. Show Business Jargon* 61 The most popular mutes for trumpet and trombone are the Straight Mute, which softens the volume about fifty per cent, retaining a certain amount of 'attack' quality; the Cup Mute, [etc.] **1904** J. L. BACON *Forge-Practice* i. 11 Several other types..are illustrated... *A* is a straight-pene,..and *C*, a riveting-hammer. **1957** R. LISTER *Decorative Wrought Ironwork* ii. 11 Hammers.. used by blacksmiths vary considerably in size and shape. One type is called a *straight pane*; its head has a slightly convex face at one end and a wedge-shaped termination or pane (sometimes formerly called a *pen*) at the other. **1964** [see *PEEN *sb.*]. **1975** R. A. SALAMAN *Dict. Tools* 223/1 The Scotch pattern [of hammers used in coopering] has a round face with chamfered neck... The straight pane is used for flaring hoops..to follow the bulge of the cask. **1959** E. FENWICK *Long Way Down* v. 41 If you can use plain soap and don't mind a straight razor. **1976** 'TREVANIAN' *Main* (1977) iv. 73, I use a straight razor. **1921** *Nat. Petroleum News* (U.S.) 15 July 76/2 Such a product as 68–70 straight-run gasoline is made principally from fresh crude. **1934** *Industr. & Engin. Chem.* May 501/1 Similar studies were made of a 'reformed' gasoline produced by cracking a West Texas straight-run gasoline. **1973** HADLEY & TURNER in G. D. Hobson *Mod. Petroleum Technol.* (ed. 4) xii. 441 The petroleum chemicals industry can call upon a variety of feedstocks, including natural gas and straight-run oil fractions. **1973** *Guardian* 11 June 7/4 The Datsun 240K GT Skyline..[has] an ordinary straight-six cylinder engine. **1918** E. A. ARCHER *Needlecraft* ix. 99, I will start with chain-stitching... Start by taking a straight stitch on the line. **1934** M. THOMAS *Dict. Embroidery Stitches* 194 Straight or Stroke Stitch consists of single isolated satin stitches of any desired length and worked in any required direction over short traced lines which have to be covered. **1961** *Observer* 28 May 33/1 The cost of a sewing-machine can vary... Simple straight-stitch machines can be had for £25 to £30 hand operated. **1967** E. SHORT *Embroidery & Fabric Collage* ii. 51 Even on a simple straight-stitching domestic machine a wide variety of effects may be obtained. **1944** *Sun* (Baltimore) 13 Oct. 7/7 Straight-time earnings (which include incentive payments and merit increases). **1958** *Listener* 10 July 43/2 The widely recognised problem of maintaining reasonable balance of earnings between semi-skilled workpeople paid by results and others—possibly highly skilled—who are traditionally paid on a straight-time basis. **1971** *Daily Colonist* (Victoria, B.C.) 7 Oct. 1/3 The construction workers..were working 60-hour weeks at straight time for an hourly rate of $2.27.

B. quasi-*sb.* and *sb.* **1. e.** *the straight*: the truth. Esp. in phr. *to get* (*at*) or *hear the straight*. *U.S.*

1866 C. H. SMITH *Bill Arp* 35 You should git the straight of it from one who seen it with his eyes. **1900** E. A. DIX *Deacon Bradbury* 266 *You*'ve heared th' straight of it, Mr. Leavitt. **1902** G. H. LORIMER *Lett. Self-Made Merchant* xviii. 271 No one except the widow ever really got at the straight of Bud's conduct. **1951** H. GILES *Harbin's Ridge* xviii. 161, I wanted to get the straight about this piece of land Faleecy John wanted. **1977** 'L. EGAN' *Blind Search* iii. 38 Tell you something, I never heard the straight of that anyway. **1982** 'W. R. DUNCAN' *Queen's Messenger* xxv. 372 It will be recorded properly in the archives... The straight of it will exist.

3. a. Also, a straight portion of a road; also *fig. back straight*: see *BACK- B.; *home straight* = *HOME-STRETCH. Cf. STRETCH *sb.* 8 in Dict. and Suppl.

1903 *T.P.'s Weekly* 2 Jan. 248/1 Good, I'm in the straight now!..Thank Heaven that's done. **1953** K. AMIS *Lucky Jim* i. 15 The car darted forward on to the straight. **1958** *Times* 20 Aug. 2/7 Miss Itkina, of Russia, used the inside lane intelligently and was well ahead of the opposition entering the long home straight. **1968** P. DICKINSON *Weathermonger* iv. 59 You'll have to do the map-reading. ..I'll teach you as soon as we come to a safe bit of straight where we can't get surprised. **1976** *West Lancs. Even. Gaz.* 13 Dec. 9/1 (Advt.), Scalextric, including pits, chicane, straights, 90 degree. **1977** *Arab Times* 14 Dec. 10/2 In the longer sprint, the 400 m, Ayad Mooshari and Ali Sulaiman were easily the strongest runners in the home straight.

b. *Aeronaut.* A run or flight in a straight line (without turning).

1911 *Aeroplane* 19 Oct. 471/2 In evening Sabelli rolling and Richey doing straights on brevet machine, the latter damaging chassis slightly in landing. **1914** H. ROSHER *In Royal Naval Air Service* (1916) i. 20 Yesterday I did five straights (straight flights) alone.

5. a. (Earlier and later examples.) *inside straight*, four cards which will form a straight if a fifth card of a particular value is added.

1841 *Spirit of Times* 1 May 102/1 This last name [*sc.* Falseful] is taken from the players of *twenty-deck poker*, and is used by them to represent a '*straight*', or ace, king, queen, jack, and ten. **1866** C. H. SMITH *Bill Arp* 39 The Yankees had a strait, which would have taken Forrest and raked down the pile. **1903** 'O. HENRY' *Roads of Destiny* 210 He always would play jack, queen, king, ace, deuce for a straight. **1934** M. ELLINGER *Poker* 163 The odds against filling an inside straight flush are 3 to 1. **1951** *Amer. Speech* XXVI. 99/2 *Inside straight*, a possible straight which is open in the middle, for example: 4-5--7-8. It takes a gut shot to hit it. **1968** V. NABOKOV *King, Queen, Knave* p. ix, I can only hope that my good old partners, replete with full houses and straights, will think I am bluffing. **1977** G. V. HIGGINS *Dreamland* i. 11 Never draw to an inside straight.

b. *Shooting.* A perfect score, with every shot fired making a hit.

1903 *Forest & Stream* 21 Feb. 160/1 In the 10-bird event Wade..and Curran each made a straight. **1931** L. B. SMITH *Better Trapsmanship* vii. 101 In the Atlantic Indian shoot in September, 1927, there were two 100 straights turned in for the championship. **1976** *Shooting Mag.* Dec. 36/2 Three more straights [in skeet shooting] were shot by Minards, P. Spear and J. Cording.

6. *slang.* **a.** orig. *U.S.* Unadulterated or very strong whisky. Cf. sense 9 a of the adj.

1862 *Harper's Mag.* Aug. 312/1 [The] primer was simply a gill of Bourbon straight. **1905** 'O. HENRY' in *N.Y. World Mag.* 12 Nov. 8/1, I managed to soak in a little straight. **1928** *Collier's* 29 Dec. 42/2 There is Juarez whisky, for instance. It is sometimes called 'American Straight'.

b. A cigarette, esp. one containing ordinary tobacco as opposed to marijuana.

[**1923** J. MANCHON *Le Slang* 296 *A straight = a straighter = a straight cut*, une cigarette en tabac de Virginie.] **1959** *Esquire* Nov. 70 J *Straight*,.. an ordinary cigarette. **1973** W. TUTE *Resident* iii. 53 'I..never will be a dope head. I don't drop and I don't smoke—except straights.' 'You mean ordinary cigarettes?' 'Yes.' **1977** *Radio Times* 1–7 Apr. 41/4 *Straights*, cigarettes.

7. a. *Vaudeville.* A stooge; a 'straight' performer (see sense 9*b of the adj. above).

1933 P. GODFREY *Back-Stage* xviii. 228 They had teamed up together, with Dora doing the 'straight' and Fred the red-nosed comedy stuff. **1941** J. P. MARQUAND *H. M. Pulham, Esquire* xxix. 312 'A straight,' Bill said.

'Don't you know what a straight is? A straight's someone in a skit who has all the jokes thrown at him.'

b. In absol. use of the adj. (sense *6 d): one who conforms to the conventions of society; one who does not take drugs; a heterosexual. *slang* (orig. *U.S.*).

1967 *Observer* (Colour Suppl.) 4 Dec. 28 *Straight*, conventional person, one who does not use cannabis. **1967** W. & J. Breedlove *Swinging Set* xii. 146 The easy atmosphere..the abundant evidence of abundant wealth attract not only 'straights', but a variety of sexual thrill-seekers. **1968** J. D. Macdonald *Pale Grey for Guilt* (1969) xii. 152 We don't bug the straights and why shouldn't they leave us alone? **1969** *Gandalf's Garden* iv. 25/2 George King..has spent his life in a service that causes Straights to back away muttering 'crack-pot'. *c* **1971** *Come Together* iii. 7/1, I have danced with a boy at a straight party where we were the only two gay people and the straights were looking at us. **1974** 'K. Royce' *Trap Spider* vii. 111 'I'm not having the stink of pot in this place.'..'You straights are all the same.' **1974** K. Millett *Flying* (1975) iii. 279 Unctuous homosexual eager to prove its human worth to these archetypical straights. **1977** *Gay News* 24 Mar. 10/4 It was a campaign shared and supported by a number of gays—even straights. **1980** *Daily Mirror* 10 Apr. 13/4 Straights prefer 'mums and dads' type pop music made by bands like Boomtown Rats, Blondie and, more recently, Police.

8. A shoe designed to be worn on either foot.

1934 *Times* 5 Feb. 13/5 In the seventeenth century men's and women's shoes and slippers seem without exception to be straights. **1968** J. Ironside *Fashion Alphabet* 125 During the Dark Ages, shoes were cut as 'straights', both shoes having the identical shape. **1976** *Sunday Post* (Glasgow) 26 Dec. 6/5 My late father used to tell of bootmaking in his young day. People ordering footwear had to say they wanted a right and left. Otherwise they were supplied with 'straights', which fitted either foot.

C. *adv.* **1. g.** *to think straight*: to think clearly or logically. *colloq.*

a **1916** H. James *Sense of Past* (1917) ii. 60 He had already..asked himself when he should be able so to detach himself as to think at all straight about his book. **1973** 'C. Aird' *His Burial Too* xiii. 115, I can't begin to think straight as it is. **1980** P. G. Winslow *Counsellor Heart* x. 137 He rubbed his forehead. 'I haven't been thinking straight. Excuse me.'

2. c. *straight away*: now usu. written as one word: cf. Straightaway *a.*, *sb.* and *adv.* in Dict. and Suppl. (Later examples.)

1910 *Sphere* 20 Aug. p. vi/1 Radley flies a mile straight-away at a speed of 75 miles an hour. **1923** *Daily Mail* 26 May 9 It was so evident that Evander had been badly hurt that he was straightaway withdrawn. **1948** M. Laski *Tory Heaven* v. 65, I said straightaway..that I'd like to be a land-agent. **1978** *Church Times* 23 June 14/1, I would confess straightaway that I have often envied my Anglican brethren when I was in the pastoral ministry.

5. Phr. *to go straight*: (*a*) *colloq.*, to behave honourably; (*b*) *colloq.*, to reform, to desist from criminal activities (cf. sense *6 a of the adj.); (*c*) *slang*, to conform to social conventions, *spec.* by renouncing drugs or homosexuality (cf. sense *6 d of the adj.).

1845 [in Dict.] **1888** [see Go v. B. 4 a]. **1940** Blunden *Poems 1930–40* 76 Fixing his pinchers on the snake, Thus spake The crab: 'It's Time for you, mate, To go straight; No more crooked habits.' **1968** [see *do *v.* B. 11 m]. **1973** *To our Returned Prisoners of War* (U.S. Secretary of Defense, Public Affairs) 5 *Go straight*, (1) Give up the use of drugs. (2) Return to an approved life style. **1977** D. E. Westlake *Enough!* ii. 59 'He's a fag.'..'Well, maybe he's trying to go straight.'

6. (Earlier example.) Also used *colloq.* as *int.* or intensively: really, certainly, definitely.

1874 A. J. Munby *Diary* 22 Apr. in D. Hudson *Munby* (1972) 366 'Mrs Skeats,' I said to her, quite straight, 'Do you really think I could wish to be a lady?' **1894** A. Chevalier *in Humorous Songs*, 'Straight,' says I, 'I'm on the job, for better or for wuss.' **1898** J. D. Brayshaw *Slum Silhouettes* 3, I could kill yer wiv my little finger. I could, straight. **1914** D. H. Lawrence *Prussian Officer & Other Stories* 211 I'm awfully sorry, I am, straight, Lois. **1949** J. R. Cole *It was so Late* 61 She was a smasher—straight she was! **1969** D. Francis *Enquiry* xi. 141 'You've never seen nothing like it,' he said. 'You wouldn't know it was a car, you wouldn't straight.'

6*. orig. *U.S.* **a.** *slang.* Without adornment, admixture, or dilution. Cf. sense 9 a of the adj.

1869 S. Bowles *Our New West* 135 We had to take our victual and drink 'straight',—plain ham and bread and butter and black coffee,—or go without. **1873** J. H. Beadle *Undeveloped West* 528 We lived on Navajo bread, coffee, and 'commissary butter', straight. **1902** L. McKee *Land of Nome* 234 It was a rude shock..when I saw 'Little Casino' standing by the bar and drinking her whisky straight. **1947** *This Week Mag.* 10 May 13/2 She was a bold..camp in days gone by and still drinks her liquor straight.

b. Jazz. *to play (it) straight*: to play without improvisation, but according to a score or set orchestration. Cf. sense 9 d of the adj. above.

1933 *Fortune* Aug. 90/3 It seems to be congenitally impossible for Negro dance musicians to play *straight*. **1934** S. R. Nelson *All about Jazz* iii. 66 Listen to the tune played 'straight', or as written. **1948** Manone & Vandervoort *Trumpet on Wing* 26 Then we would play it straight. **1960** M. T. Williams *Art of Jazz* iii. 18 The average listener is disappointed in anything played 'straight'.

c. *colloq.* In a straightforward or simple manner; without embellishment or affectation; seriously, without 'hamming'. Cf. senses 9*a, c of the adj. above.

1961 A. Berkman *Singers' Gloss. Show Business Jargon* 84 *Straight*, (Mus.) As written, with no variations. (Thea[tr.]) without comedy (e.g. 'play it straight'). **1975** *Country Life* 25 Dec. 1799/1 He was able to render these [folk] songs 'straight', not in the cultured, genteel manner usually affected on the concert platform. **1976** *S. Wales Echo* 23 Nov. 1/4 Eric and Ernie played it straight but still had their 'audience' laughing. **1978** *N.Y. Times* 30 Mar. c16/1 One can strike for authenticity: collect old scripts and have them read, straight, by good actors.

6.** *U.S. colloq.* Consecutively, in a row. Cf. sense 3 g of the adj. above.

1949 H. Robbins *Dream Merchants* (1950) 45 Haven't you got any other films? People are getting tired of the same show for three weeks straight. **1951** R. Bradbury *Silver Locusts* 106 He had been working in one of the new colonies for ten days straight, and now he had two days off and was on his way to a party. **1973** [see *series 17 a]. **1976** *National Observer* (U.S.) 7 Feb. 9/4 It [*sc.* a stove] has an automatic thermostat that adjusts the damper, and can be loaded to burn for 12 hours straight.

7. a. *straight-flying*, *-hanging*, *-standing*; **straight-bred** *a.*, pure-bred, descended from one breed only (cf. sense *9 e of the adj.); **straight-cut** *a.*, (*a*) cut on straight lines; (*b*) *slang*, honest, respectable; (*c*) applied to cigarettes made from tobacco with the leaves cut lengthwise into long strands; freq. *absol.* as *sb.*; **straight shooter** *slang* (chiefly U.S.), an honest person (cf. *square shooter* s.v. *square *a.* 14 a).

1898 *Breeder's Gaz.* XXXIV. 199/3 The Gazette is asked for information in reference to certain so-called 'pure' or 'straight-bred' strains of pedigreed cattle. **1840** Straight-cut [in Dict.]. **1868** G. M. Hopkins *Jrnl.* 14 Aug. (1959) 185 Fine. There were the travelling stack clouds with straight-cut under-sides. **1884** *Illustr. London News* 18 Oct. 383/1 Cigarette smokers..will find the Richmond Straight Cut No. 1 superior to all others. **1895** *Irish Times* 16 July 3 (Advt.), Kinney's straight-cut cigarettes. **1927** G. W. Deeping *Kitty* ii. 21, I want some cigarettes,—straight-cuts—. **1936** J. Curtis *Gilt Kid* xiv. 139 He could..pick up a girl, even a straight-cut, and have her walk arm-in-arm with him. **1939** Joyce *Finnegans Wake* 156 As british as bondstrict and as straightcut as when that broken-arched traveller from Nuzuland. **1925** J. Gregory *Bab of Backwoods* ii. 17 Whatever Dick Gale had done pointed the straight-flying arrow for Bab's following. **1935** *Amer. Speech* X. 192/1 [In writing on fashion] adjectives [*sic*] in combination with present participles are common, as in *much-looking* and *straight-hanging*. **1960** *Times* 18 Jan. 15/2 Straight-hanging coats with flat backs are a speciality. **1928** S. Lewis *Man who knew Coolidge* ii. 155 'I'll make the law and you furnish my fee,' he used to say—but laughingly, of course, because he was a real square straight-shooter. **1969** G. M. Brown *Time to Keep* 176 'He's the decentest skipper ever I sailed with... Strict, but very fair in his dealings.' 'A straight shooter.' **1978** M. Puzo *Fools Die* xxxiii. 376 She came from a place where the people were straight shooters. **1913** D. H. Lawrence *Sons & Lovers* xii. 334 The big, straight-standing woman was trying to estimate the situation.

b. **straight-ahead**, simple, straightforward; *spec.* (orig. *U.S.*) with reference to popular music, pure, unadorned; **straight-up**, (*b*) *colloq.*, exact, complete; true, trustworthy; also as quasi-*adv.* (*i*) truthfully, honestly; = Straight *adv.* 6 in Dict. and Suppl.; (*ii*) *U.S.*, unmixed, undiluted (cf. sense 9 a of the adj.).

1836, etc. Straight-ahead [in Dict.]. **1964** *Down Beat* 17 Dec. 30 'McSplivens' is a straight-ahead blues. **1977** *It* May 27/2 Just high energy, straight ahead rock 'n roll of the seventies. **1910** A. Bennett *Clayhanger* i. ix. 71 This new Licensing Act will close every public-house..at eleven o'clock, and a straight-up eleven at that! **1936** J. Curtis *Gilt Kid* v. 52 But Maisie was the only girl he had ever loved! That was straight-up. **1963** L. Deighton *Horse under Water* xlix. 211 'What's the trouble?' I asked. 'I'm being followed,' he said. 'Really,' I said. 'Straight up,' he said. 'I wasn't sure until today.' **1973** W. J. Burley *Death in Salubrious Place* vii. 150, I don't know where he is, Mr Gill, straight up, I don't. **1975** B. Garfield *Death Sentence* (1976) v. 30 He..beckoned the barmaid. 'Dewar's straight up, darlin'.' **1976** *Listener* 8 Jan. 23/1 It proved to be a completely wasted sacrifice, for the programme it gave space to..was a straight-up disaster. **1979** D. Sanders *Queen sends for Mrs Chadwick* 137 You might have something going there. That's if this is straight up. **1982** R. Hill *Who guards a Prince* ii. vii. 149 You looked honest to me..and you sounded like a straight-up guy.

straight-arm, *a.* and *sb.* [Straight *a.* 1 d.] **A.** *adj.* Performed with the arm stiff or unflexed; *spec.* in Cricket = *straight-armed* adj. s.v. *straight *a.* 10 c.

1807 *Sporting Mag.* July 192/1 The straight-arm bowling, introduced by John Willes, Esq. **1946** E. O'Neill *Iceman Cometh* iii. 177 [Rocky] Leans over the bar and stops Lewis with a straight-arm swipe on the chest. **1977** *Time* 21 Nov. 28/2 New Jersey's Democratic Governor Brendan Byrne, whose self-effacing campaign style consists of a strained smile and straight-arm salute.

B. *sb. N. Amer. Football.* An act of warding off an opponent or making room for oneself with the arm held straight. Also *fig.* Cf. *stiff-arm* s.v. *stiff *a.* 20 c.

1903 W. T. Reid in W. Camp *How to play Football* (ed. 2) 85 Under no circumstances can a back use his 'straight-arm' more effectually than in the broken field running that forms such a big part of back-field work. **1927** G. S. Lowman *Pract. Football* xii. 225 He must have good use of the straight-arm and must be able to hit and pivot. **1951** M. McLuhan *Mech. Bride* (1967) 141/2 The numerous variants on straight-arm tactics, from lynch law to the third degree, all reduce to inner panic as their origin. **1969** *Maclean's Mag.* Aug. 3/1 He had to get his kicks, like many of us, by watching the Good Guys belt the Bad Guys and imagining that it was him down there, handing out straight-arms.

Hence as *v. trans.* and *intr.* (also *transf.*); **straight-arming** *vbl. sb.*

1934 Webster, Straight-arm *v. trans.* **1934** Crisler & Wieman *Pract. Football* vii. 81 (*heading*) Straight-arming. **1966** R. H. Rimmer *Harrad Experiment* (1967) 95 They stamped on feet, straight-armed, jammed people in the middle, and cursed them. **1980** 'R. B. Dominic' *Attending Physician* xix. 174 Ben..did not pause, but straight-armed his way through the human barrier.

straightaway, *a.*, *sb.*, and *adv.* Add: **A.** *adj.* Also, of other courses or paths: direct, without bending or turning.

1903 G. V. Hobart *Out for Coin* 89 Out of the chute in to the straightaway course they foamed, that heaving, seething mass of horseflesh. **1913** *Captain* Sept. 1072/2 In straight-away flights even higher speeds have been established. **1977** *New Yorker* 16 May 115/1 The fifteenth, a straightaway 490-yard par 5, can be reached with two big blows.

B. *sb.* (Earlier and later examples.) Also, a straight section of a road or racecourse, etc. Cf. Straight *sb.* 3 in Dict. and Suppl. Chiefly *U.S.*

1878 C. Hallock *Hallock's Amer. Club List & Sportsman's Gloss.* p. xi, *Straight-away*, a straight course without a turn, for racing boats. **1926** E. Hemingway *In our Time* xiii. 188 Finally they made the last turn and came into the straightaway. **1935** *Sun* (Baltimore) 31 Jan. 11/6 On straightaways, Lieutenant Klein said, these pursuit planes made still higher speeds with the '100-octane'. **1954** [see *prop *v.*[1] 4]. **1957** J. Kerouac *On Road* (1958) iii. ix. 234 A long Nebraskan straightaway. **1966** J. Pearl *Crucifixion of Pete McCabe* (1967) iii. 30 Once they were on the wide main highway, McCabe relaxed... Donovan could not get in too much trouble on the straightaway. **1978** L. Pryor *Viper* ii. 31, I backed off the throttle for the U-turn at the end of the straightaway.

C. *adv.*: see Straight *adv.* 2 c in Dict. and Suppl.

straighten, *v.* Add: **1. a.** Also with *up*, to bring on to a straight or level course.

1911 Grahame-White & Harper *Aeroplane* 136 Instead of performing the evolution which is known as 'straightening up' a machine, just before coming into contact with the ground, M. Chavez continued on his downward course, at a steep angle, and struck the ground with great violence.

2. Also *transf.* of persons: to put (someone) right, esp. by explanation.

1956 B. Holiday *Lady sings Blues* (1973) iv. 42 Excuse me, Mom, I'm sorry, but I got to straighten this whore out. **1979** W. Styron *Sophie's Choice* xii. 355 Look, Sophie, you're confusing me. Straighten me out. Please.

3. Also in slang use (see quot. 1970).

1944 C. Hines *Black on Black* (1973) 198, I had to get them people straight and get 'em straightened fast. **1946** Mezzrow & Wolfe *Really Blues* xii. 216 I'm short a deuce of blips but I'll straighten you later. **1970** C. Major *Dict. Afro-Amer. Slang* 110 *Straighten*, to straighten someone is to tell her or him the truth or to pay back money borrowed.

4. a. *to straighten up*: for (U.S.) read (orig. U.S.). (Later example.) Also in *gen.* use, to adopt a straight or level course. Also *to straighten out* (also *fig.*).

1914 [see *flatten *v.* 2 b]. **1917** *Times* 5 July 6/5 Two machines..swerved and one started to fall for some hundreds of feet before it straightened out and regained flying speed. **1921** *Rev. of Reviews* Aug. 99/2 The..expectations ..that the Silesian tangle was straightening out have proved quite illusory. **1939** G. B. Shaw *In Good King Charles's Golden Days* i. 31 Newton straightens up and stares. **1940** W. Faulkner *Hamlet* i. ii. 36 All of a sudden they [*sc.* mules] straightened out and I mind how I was thinking what a good thing it was they was pointed away from the wagon when they straightened out.

b. *colloq.* To settle *up* an account or debt (with someone).

1915 D. H. Lawrence *Let.* Dec. (1948) 66 But I haven't had the bill yet: I will straighten up with you when it comes. **1966** *Amer. Speech* XLI. 297 *Straighten up*, pay a bill.

5. *trans.* To bribe or corrupt. Also with *out*. *slang* (orig. *U.S.*).

1923 E. Wallace *Missing Million* xxiii. 182 They said they'd tried to straighten you. **1960** [see *knock *v.* 10 i]. **1976** J. O'Connor *Eleventh Commandment* v. 67, I didn't fancy being in the hands of the Wiltshire police. I couldn't straighten them, but I had one in London straightened. **1982** *Observer* 15 Aug. 22/4 Somebody who has been successfully bribed to do something has been 'straightened out'.

straightening, *vbl. sb.* Add: **a.** Also with *out*.

1900 'MARK TWAIN' in *McClure's Mag.* XIV. 287/1 With this straightening-out and classification of the dreamer's position to help us, perhaps we can put ourselves in his place. 1978 S. BRILL *Teamsters* vi. 226 She went to a friend of Arnie's who she thought was straight.. and asked him to talk to Arnie for her about straightening out.

straight forward, straightforward, *a.* **5.** (Earlier example.)

1829 P. EGAN *Boxiana* 2nd Ser. II. 601 The *Streatham Youth* is a *straight-forward* fellow—*honest* upon all occasions.

straight-out, *a.* Add: (Earlier example.) Also straightforward, unqualified, genuine.

1848 W. ARMSTRONG *Stocks* 9 The Stock is to be delivered and paid for upon a certain day—these are sometimes termed straight out contracts. 1873 'MARK TWAIN' *Gilded Age* xxv. 228 Buying committees for straight-out cash on delivery. 1912 T. DREISER *Financier* 57, I don't like it as well as I do the straight-out brokerage business. 1947 A. P. GASKELL *Big Game* 118 It's not just a straight-out romance? 1973 E. S. GARDNER *Case Postponed Murder* (1977) viii. 106 It isn't any trap. It's a straight-out business proposition.

strain, *sb.*[1] Add: **II. 7. c.** *strain 19, Strain 19*: a strain of the bacterium *Brucella abortus* which is used as a live vaccine against brucellosis in cattle and as a killed vaccine in horses.

1930 *Jrnl. Agric. Res.* XLI. 669 Strain 19 that had been isolated one and one-half years previously was used in the preparation of the vaccine administered to calves. 1959 *Vet. Ann.* I. 88 There have been several reports of infection of human beings with strain 19 vaccine. 1970 T. G. HUNGERFORD *Dis. Livestock* (ed. 7) 718/2 Injection of Strain 19 into the horse is followed by severe systemic reaction... As a result, killed Brucella abortus vaccine was originally used, but it is thought that the living Strain 19 giving a violent reaction offers a better hope of success.

10. *Comb. strain-specific* adj.; *strain-specificity*.

1964 M. HYNES *Med. Bacteriol.* (ed. 8) xxiv. 350 Many examples are now known of viruses which cause malignant tumours in animals. Most are species-specific or even strain-specific. 1947 *Ann. Rev. Microbiol.* I. 362 There was a sharp strain specificity with sedimented antigen and less with the residual.

strain, *sb.*[2] Add: **II. 9. c.** *to take the strain*, in a tug of war: see quots.; *fig.*, to assume a burden, take a responsibility.

1912 *Games & Nav. Milit. Tournament* 3 The pulls will be started by the Referee by word of mouth:—'Take the strain', on which both teams will put a strain on the rope without pulling. 1927 W. E. COLLINSON *Contemporary English* 38 Among the other field sports I might single out.. the tug of war with its expressions to take the strain (i.e. when each side pulls the rope taut before the signal for the tug is given by the dropping of a handkerchief), and to pull one's weight.., both of which lend themselves to figurative use.

10. d. *Life Insurance.* An expense or financial liability incurred by an insurance office which is not covered by reserves accumulated from the relevant policies.

1910 *Encycl. Brit.* XIV. 670/2 It is obvious that office B, which has a margin of income 50% greater than that of office A, is so much better able to bear any unusual strain in addition to the ordinary expenditure. 1929 F. L. COLLINS in R. C. Simmonds *Life Assurance Text-bk.* 128 The true risk which the office runs consists not in the whole sum assured, but in the difference required in the case of death to supplement the reserve value which it already has in hand...technically termed the 'strain'. 1941 *Economist* 15 Mar. 344/1 When a premature death occurs, the loss to the office, known technically as the 'strain', is the difference between the policy moneys payable and the reserve carried, and it follows that this 'strain' will be much greater in the case of a young life than an old one. 1965 FISHER & YOUNG *Actuarial Practice of Life Assurance* I. ii. 29 The net premium method of valuation failed to take account of this uneven incidence of expenses and caused what is termed a new business strain. It required the setting up of initial reserves which could not have been derived from the first premium since that had been largely or even entirely expended in the cost of the first year's risk and expenses.

10*. Phr. *strain and stress* (with reference to senses 9 and 10; cf. *stress(es) and strains* s.v. *STRESS *sb.* 5*).

[1842 *Penny Cycl.* XXIII. 101/2 *Strain* and *Stress*. ([See] *Materials, Strength of.*)] 1856 *Phil. Trans. R. Soc.* CXLVI. 488 (*heading*) On the measurement of strains and stresses. 1857 E. B. BROWNING *Aurora Leigh* v. 385 We, staggering 'neath our burden as mere men, Being called to stand up straight as demi-gods, Support the intolerable strain and stress Of the universal. 1872 J. G. WHITTIER in *Pennsylvania Pilgrim* 94 Take from our souls the strain and stress, And let our ordered lives confess The beauty of thy peace. 1935 *Discovery* Sept. 270/1 Many [stelae] have successfully resisted the strains and stresses of the passing centuries. 1941 H. G. WELLS *You can't be too Careful* v. i. 240 After a tremendous constructive effort after the war, and after a phase of experimental strain and stress. 1962 J. DILL in *Into Orbit* p. xix, Space flight..would expose the Astronauts to greater strains and stresses, both physically and mentally, than most pilots had ever had to face.

V. 15. *strain-free, -veined* adjs.; **strain ageing** *vbl. sb. Metallurgy*, the cold working of iron and steel followed by ageing, either at room temperature or at temperatures up to the recrystallization temperature; also, the resultant increase in hardness and decrease in ductility; so **strain-aged** *ppl. a.*; **strain energy**, (*a*) *Mech.*, energy stored in a body as a result of work performed on it; (*b*) *Chem.*, the excess heat of formation of a cyclic molecule over the value calculated from similar bonds in unstrained molecules; **strain gauge** *Engin.*, a device for indicating the strain of a material or structure at the point of attachment; **strain hardening** *vbl. sb. Metallurgy*, increase in strength and hardness and decrease in ductility of a metal as a result of strain ageing; so **strain-harden** *v. intr.*, to undergo strain hardening; **strain-hardened** *ppl. a.*; **strainmeter** *Engin.* = *strain gauge* above; **strain rosette** *Engin.* = *ROSETTE *sb.* 5 f; **strain-slip cleavage** *Geol.*, a rock structure in which there are parallel, closely-spaced shear planes with transverse microscopic folds between adjacent ones.

1966 *Trans. Metall. Soc. A.I.M.E.* CCXXXVI. 1198/1 (*heading*) The yield-point phenomenon in strain-aged martensite. 1979 *Jrnl. Materials Sci.* XIV. 386 A strain-aged low carbon (~0·1% C) temper-rolled 16-gauge sheet steel which has been subjected to..ageing temperatures of 80 and 100°C. 1934 *Proc. Amer. Soc. Testing Materials* XXXIV. II. 48 The authors have applied the principle that strain ageing and blue brittleness of ferrous materials are but different manifestations of the same phenomenon. 1967 A. H. COTTRELL *Introd. Metall.* xxi. 394 In mild steel strain ageing usually takes a few days at room temperature, or about 30 minutes at 100°C, the rate being controlled by the diffusion of nitrogen and carbon atoms. 1926 PIPPARD & BARROW *Building Res. Board Techn. Paper* No. 1. 2 The total strain energy of the beam is made up of three components due to bending, torque and shear. 1939 *Jrnl. Amer. Chem. Soc.* LXI. 1871/2 The relative heats of hydration may be employed to evaluate the strain energy in cyclopentene only after correction has been made for these steric effects. 1976 A. L. TERNAY *Contemp. Org. Chem.* vii. 197 The cyclopentane ring is puckered and..the cyclohexane ring exists largely in the chair form. If these compounds did not adopt these geometries, their strain energy would increase. 1977 WILLEMS & LUCAS *Struct. Analysis for Engineers* (1978) iii. 34 For the purposes of this text..all work done by external actions A_i acting through corresponding displacements D_i will be converted into kinetic and strain energy, and no energy losses will occur. 1946 *Nature* 26 Oct. 583/1 Well-annealed glass is strain-free when uniformly heated. 1978 *Solid State Communications* XXVII. 713 (*heading*) Ferromagnetic resonance in strained and strain-free single crystal nickel films. 1910 *Engin. Rec.* LXI. 767/2 (*caption*) Strain gauge or extensometer for deformation of webs or beams. 1948 'N. SHUTE' *No Highway* i. 9 He had a few strain gauges mounted on various parts of the structure. 1972 L. M. HARRIS *Introd. Deepwater Floating Drilling Operations* xv. 160 Strain gauges on marine-riser joints have been used to evaluate fatigue damage and to locate stress concentrations. 1977 *Proc. R. Soc. Med.* LXX. 172/2 Mouth pressure and œsophageal pressure are monitored using strain-gauge transducers. 1959 C. E. BIRCHENALL *Physical Metall.* vi. 124 Alloys always strain-harden more effectively than pure metals. 1968 B. AVITZUR *Metal Forming* viii. 201 When a material is deformed at a temperature above its crystallization temperature, it does not strain-harden. 1914 W. ROSENHAIN *Introd. Stud. Physical Metall.* xiii. 300 All ordinary wrought metals show signs of 'cold work' and are more or less strain-hardened. 1960 *Jrnl. Appl. Physics* XXXI. 687/1 It is usually difficult to study the behavior of individual dislocations in strain-hardened crystals because so many dislocations are present. 1914 W. ROSENHAIN *Introd. Stud. Physical Metall.* xiii. 300 It is generally desirable to continue the working operations until a moderately low temperature is reached. This will result in slight strain-hardening of the metal. 1973 J. G. TWEEDDALE *Materials Technol.* II. iv. 75 In metallic materials particularly, and in some other crystalline materials, mechanical deformation in certain circumstances gives rise to strain hardening. 1916 *Metallurgical & Chem. Engin.* XIV. 551/1 The strainmeter is not affected by vibration, and it can be used under difficult conditions. 1939 *Jrnl. R. Aeronaut. Soc.* XLIII. 544 The strain meter..first made it possible to investigate the behaviour of the fast-moving and more inaccessible parts, such as crankshaft, airscrew, etc., during flight. 1979 *Bull. Seismol. Soc. Amer.* LXIX. 1983 Four invar-wire strainmeters have been operated in shallow trench sites.. beside the San Andreas fault. 1938 *Engin. News-Record* 10 Mar. 370/3 The strains and stresses computed on the above form are pictured, in relation to the strain rosette on the plating, in Fig. 6. 1950 J. H. MEIER in M. Hetényi *Handbk. Exper. Stress Analysis* 400 The equi-angular strain rosette..is best suited in cases where the direction of the principal strains cannot be established approximately before test. 1886 T. G. BONNEY in *Q. Jrnl. Geol. Soc.* XLII. I. 95 Subsequent work..has thrown additional light upon the..kind of cleavage..in which the cleavage-planes cut across the undulating bands of the constituent minerals. Of this structure I possess one or two excellent examples..which makes it clear that the structure is an example of the strain-slip cleavage (Ausweichungs-Clivage) of Dr. Heim. 1954 J. F. KIRKALDY *Gen. Princ. Geol.* x. 127 Less perfectly graded rocks..may develop not the true slaty cleavage, due to re-orientation of the minerals, but a strain-slip cleavage, produced by closely spaced planes of movement. 1969 BENNISON & WRIGHT *Geol. Hist. Brit. Isles* vii. 137 The first thrusts have been folded by N–S fairly open folds and associated asymmetric small folds have a strain-slip cleavage. 1922 JOYCE *Ulysses* 714 The cause of a brief sharp unforeseen heard loud lone crack emitted by the insentient material of a strainveined timber table.

strain, *v.*[1] Add: **II. 12. b.** Also of the ears.

1943 J. WEDGE in K. Rhys *More Poems from Forces* 313 Ears are straining for a distant 'boom'.

strainedness. (Later example.)

1901 [see *over-elaboration* s.v. *OVER- 29 d].

strainer. Add: **2. b.** *N.Z. ellipt.* for *strainer post* below.

1933 E. JONES *Autobiogr. Early Settler* xviii. 77, I know of a wire fence which was erected with wire strainers 70 years ago. 1950 *N.Z. Jrnl. Agric.* Apr. 347/3 Reinforced concrete strainers and intermediate posts are preferable to wood. 1961 B. CRUMP *Hang on a Minute, Mate* 43 They'd been splitting the short ends of logs into posts and strainers.

4. strainer post chiefly *N.Z.* = *straining post* s.v. STRAINING *vbl. sb.* 6 a.

1921 H. GUTHRIE-SMITH *Tutira* xviii. 148 A kerosene case nailed to the top of a strainer-post. 1950 *N.Z. Jrnl. Agric.* Apr. 347/3 At the ends of each fence should be a good strainer post stayed in position in the normal way. 1965 S. T. OLLIVIER *Petticoat Farm* ix. 132 If she walked round the drain she could climb on the corner strainer post and get a view of the house. 1968 J. ARNOLD *Shell Bk. Country Crafts* 101 End or corner strainer posts are supported by diagonal struts.

strainful (strē^i·nfŭl) *a.* [f. STRAIN *sb.*[2] + -FUL.] Causing or filled with strain; stressful.

1935 G. FRANKAU *Three Englishmen* lxix. 607 It came to Andrew—not for the first time in these strainful days—how great, whatever the outcome of this ordeal, would be the relief of its end. 1957 *Psychol. Rev.* LXIV. 142/2 There is no built-in incentive for the foreigner to maintain a cognitively strainful regimen of attending further to speech sounds.

straining, *vbl. sb.* Add: **6. b.** *straining-cloth* (later example), *-spoon*.

1915 J. LONDON *Let.* 26 Jan. (1966) 445 Note his.. pasteurization of utensils and of straining-cloths over the milk-pails. 1912 C. MACKENZIE *Carnival* xxxvi. 342 Here were also brass ladles and straining spoons and a pair of bellows. 1960 H. HAYWARD *Antique Coll.* 269/2 *Straining spoon*, spoon with pierced bowl, found either in large sizes for gravy or similar use or in teaspoon size with thin, tapering stem and pricket top, used for skimming leaves from teacups.

strainless (strē^i·nlės), *a.* [f. STRAIN *sb.*[2] + -LESS.] Produced without strain; free from strain. Hence **strai·nlessly** *adv.*

1907 G. B. SHAW *John Bull's Other Island* II. 39 Aunt Judy comes down the hill,..a contented product of a narrow, strainless life. 1927 *Daily Tel.* 10 Feb. 16/4 Eluding the volleying vigilance of the Australian by drives as supremely accurate as they were strainlessly produced. 1927 N. V. SIDGWICK *Electronic Theory of Valency* xiv. 237 We are..not justified in assuming..that the resulting angles are 'strainless'. 1975 R. F. BROWN *Org. Chem* xii. 322 It was not until 1890 that Sachse proposed strainless ring puckering for cyclohexane and larger rings.

strainometer (strē^iṉǫ·mĭtəɹ). [f. STRAIN *sb.*[2] + -OMETER.] = *strain gauge, strainmeter* s.v. *STRAIN *sb.*[2] 15.

1915 *Jrnl. Iron & Steel Inst.* XCI. 605 The strainometer, besides measuring the axial deformation, enables the amount of bending to be accurately calculated. 1978 *Invest. Urology* XVI. 208/2 The strainometer constantly monitored changes in vas deferens diameter which occurred with spontaneous contractions.

strait, *a.*, *sb.*, and *adv.* Add: **A.** *adj.* **I. 3. b.** *strait and narrow* (*ellipt.*), a conventional, limited procedure or way of life. Cf. *straight and narrow* s.v. *STRAIGHT 3 a.

1952 S. KAUFFMANN *Philanderer* (1953) xv. 247 Not that I wandered from the respectable bourgeois strait-and-narrow. 1979 *Listener* 1 Mar. 322/2 She seems to feel it is rather daring of her to be the great defender of Arnold Bennett's reputation—and I felt she might have risked one or two dashes off the strait and narrow.

5. strait-jacketed *ppl. a.*, confined in a strait jacket (chiefly *fig.*); **strait-jacketing** *vbl. sb.* and *ppl. a.*

1894 G. B. SHAW *Let.* 2 Dec. (1965) I. 462 The dramatist is so strait-jacketed in theories of conduct that he cannot even state his conventional solution clearly. 1937 *Times Lit. Suppl.* 16 Oct. 743/3 It is a great story, a little strait-jacketed by the official style of the *communiqués*. 1955 Straitjacketed [see *lock-step* s.v. *LOCK *sb.*[2] 20]. 1950 *Times* 20 Mar. 3/3 Tendencies towards reducing Socialist democracy to a minimum, including the strait-jacketing of opinion and the suppression of the initiative of the people. 1965 K. H. CONNELL in Glass & Eversley *Population in Hist.* xvii. 433 The Malthusian theory, freed of its mathematical strait-jacketing, had a precise relevance to Irish conditions. 1977 *N.Y. Rev. Bks.* 26 May 17/1 Paradoxically, he finds liberation in a succession of instrumental works, the Trio, Symphony, Concerto, and two Quartets, all written according to certain principles of Schoenberg's new, reputedly strait-jacketing twelve-tone system. 1979 *Time Out* 5–11 Oct. 20/3 The possible straitjacketing effect of producing another revue.

B. *sb.* **3. d.** *pl.* *up the Straits* (see quot. 1962); in the Mediterranean. *Naut. slang.*

1916 'Taffrail' *Pincher Martin* i. 2 'Er commander's a werry nice gentleman; 'e was shipmates along o' me in th' *Duncan* up the Straits six year ago. 1962 W. Granville *Dict. Sailors' Slang* 115/1 *Straits, up the*, serving on the Mediterranean Station in the Straits of Gibraltar.

11. Straits Chinese, (a) Chinese born in one of the former Straits Settlements; also *attrib.* or as *adj.*; **straits oil**, a type of fish-oil (see quot. 1902), formerly made from fish caught in the straits between Newfoundland and Labrador; also *ellipt.*

1897 *Straits Chinese Mag.* Mar. 1/2 A Straits Chinese Magazine has been started; and although its name indicates that it will mainly be controlled and carried on by Straits Chinese, nevertheless within its columns will be discussed all matters of interest to Straits people generally. 1968 *Radio Times* 28 Nov. 20/2 Straits Chinese: Joyce Galbraith recalls..the Chinese she knew in Singapore. 1969 J. M. Gullick *Malaysia* i. 28 The modern descendants of the earliest wave of Chinese immigration several centuries ago are the 'Straits Chinese' whose forebears intermarried with local women. 1970 M. Pereira *Pigeon's Blood* xiv. 156 The manager..was a Straits Chinese by the name of Yee-Shen, originally a native of Malacca. 1850 *Rep. U.S. Comm. Patents 1849* 165, I..claim..the combination of the straits oil with the magnesia. 1897 C. T. Davis *Manuf. Leather* (ed. 2) 229 The oil is clarified and bleached by boiling and filtering. Thus refined it is called 'straits'. 1902 *Rep. U.S. Comm. Fish & Fisheries* 226 'Straits oil' and 'bank oil' were formerly well-known grades of cod oil, but these are now made entirely from menhaden.

straked, *ppl. a.* For † *Obs.* read Now *rare* and add later example.

1939 A. Ransome *Secret Water* xxix. 343 He could not help smiling..at the memory of the savages ringed, straked and spotted in the war-paint of mud.

stram. *v. intr.* For *U.S. colloq.* read *U.S. colloq.* and *dial.* (now *Obs.* or *rare*) and substitute for def.: To stretch out the limbs; to walk in a flourishing manner. (Earlier and later examples.)

1792 F. Burney *Jrnl.* 27 June in *Jrnls. & Lett.* (1972) I. 209 He bowed without looking at her, & she strammed away, still, however, keeping in sight. *a* 1852 F. M. Whitcher *Widow Bedott Papers* (1856) xxv. 306 She..strammed right across the room and sot down. 1866 W. Gregor *Dial. Banffshire* 184 *Stram, v.n.* to walk with a rude, noisy step. 1890 *Dialect Notes* I. 19 *Stram*, flourish the limbs. It is used in two ways: (1) 'to go stramming along the street', 'to stram about the room', that is, stride with ado and bustle; and (2) 'to stram about in bed' = flounder, kick about. 1927 *Amer. Speech* III. 138 A young child crying and displaying temper was said to 'kick and stram'. This word *stram* means in older English 'to recoil with violence and noise', which gives a vivid picture of a child in a tantrum.

‖ **strambotto** (stræmbǫ·to). Pl. **strambotti**. [It.] An Italian verse form of eight lines, common esp. in the 15th and 16th centuries and freq. set to music.

1914 G. Warrack *Folk Songs of Tuscan Hills* p.v., Of the verse-form which belongs to the Sicilian equivalent of the *Rispetto*, the *Canzona* or *Strambotto*, an octave of lines alternately rhyming, there is said to be only one example amongst the Tuscan poems. *Ibid.*, Tigri notes that the octave poems amongst the *Rispetti* are sometimes also in the Pistoian mountains called *Strambotti* (a word derived..from *strani motti* = 'strange words, quaint conceits'); some writers give this name to the Sentention Rispetti. 1931 J. Torbarina *Italian Influence on Poets of Ragusan Republic* II. iii. 143 Their origin..is the ottava of the Italian *strambotto*. Though it had its prime towards the end of the preceding century, the *strambotto* continued to flourish far into the Italian Cinquecento. 1960 *New Oxf. Hist. Music* III. xi. 395 The collection [*sc.* the fourth book of Petrucci's frottole] contains 47 *strambotti*, 19 *frottole*, 14 *ode*, and 9 *sonetti*. The appearance of *strambotti* in such great number is noteworthy, for although their artistic value is low indeed, from this form developed the later *ottava rima*. 1980 *Early Music* Jan. 104/2 Among the other compositions there is a *barzelletta* setting and a *strambotto* both by Cara, a number of *ballate mezzane*, and a sonnet.

stramin (stræ·min). [ad. Da. *stramin*, maker's name for the material.] A kind of coarse sacking formerly used for making nets for sea fishing.

1914 *Jrnl. Marine Biol. Assoc. U.K.* X. 328 The nets used were constructed on the system of the Petersen young-fish trawl, and three qualities of material were used. These were coarse sacking ('Stramin'), with mesh $\frac{1}{16}''$ square; cheesecloth,..and mosquito netting. 1925 *Ibid.* XIII. 769 The material known as 'stramin',..on account of its cheapness and durability compared with silk makes large nets for everyday use a possibility. 1936 *Nature* 30 May 915/1 The larger tunicates were abundant in the stramin net. 1959 H. Barnes *Oceanogr. and Marine Biol.* ii. 25 (*caption*) Large stramin net coming to the surface. This is made from fairly coarse material and is used to catch the larger zooplankton organisms. 1970 *Jrnl. Marine Biol. Assoc. U.K.* L. 709 The previous stramin mesh has been replaced with a knitted Terylene material, which has a higher porosity than stramin, and is less expensive than either stramin or nylon.

strand, *sb.*[1] Add: **3. a. strandflat** [partial tr. Da. *strandflade*, lit. 'beach expanse' (H. Reusch 1894, in *Norges Geol. Undersøgelse* No. 14. 1)], a very wide rocky platform, close to sea level, that extends along much of the Norwegian coastline between cliffs and the sea; (with *a* and *pl.*) any particular part of this.

[1906 *Q. Jrnl. Geol. Soc.* LXII. 87 Raised rock-platforms of marine origin..were found along the Norwegian coast, and had been termed strandflade or 'coast-plane [*read* -plain]' by Dr. Reusch.] 1922 *Skrifter utgit av Videnskabsselskabet i Kristiania 1921: Mat.-Nat. Kl.* No. 11. 60 At Tangen, on the south side of Sogne Fjord,..there is a well-marked strandflat..on which the houses are situated. 1934 R. A. Daly *Changing World Ice Age* v. 166 Along the coast of southern Norway the strandflat is a composite of three benches, with inner edges respectively 30 to 40 meters and 15 to 18 meters above sea and a few metres..below sea-level. 1940 *Geogr. Jrnl.* XCVI. 96 The origin of strandflats has interested many writers. 1954 W. D. Thornbury *Princ. Geomorphol.* xvii. 436 The Strandflat along the west coast of Norway, which is thought by some to be of marine origin, has a maximum width of 40 miles. 1972 J. L. Davies *Geogr. Variation Coastal Devel.* vi. 87 The enormous width of strandflats in some places makes it difficult to conceive of them as extraordinarily extensive shore platforms and their origin remains obscure.

b. strand-wolf: for *Hyæna striata* substitute *Hyæna brunnea*; (earlier example).

1786 G. Forster tr. *Sparrman's Voy. Cape of Good Hope* I. 165 Two other voracious animals of this kind are found in Africa, which are distinguished by the names of mountain-wolf and strand-wolf.

strand, *v.*[2] **3.** (Earlier example.)

1894 J. E. Davis *Elem. Mod. Dressmaking* 116 Very careful workers strand their button-holes—*i.e.* carry a thread of silk across each edge over which to work the stitch.

‖ **Strandbad** (ʃtræ·ntbād). Also **Strand-Bad**. [Ger.] In Germany and in German-speaking countries: a bathing-place by natural waters, an open-air swimming-pool.

1939 N. Monsarrat *This is Schoolroom* III. xvii. 391 We had..our first bathe in a little Strand-Bad sheltered by trees. 1959 P. Townend *Died o' Wednesday* ix. 149 From a multi-coloured knot of bathers at the river *Strandbad* occasional faint cries drifted up to the terrace.

stranded, *ppl. a.*[2] Add: **4.** Of a fur garment: made of skins which have been cut into diagonal strips and resewn.

1935 O. Hacking *Home Furriery* iii. 16 Work the next cut in the same way, breaking through the little joins in the centre and sides piece by piece... This way of dealing with the skin gives lovely stranded effects. 1977 *Lancashire Life* Dec. 109/2 (Advt.), A gorgeously rich coat in warm-coloured pastel mink has big revers, beautifully stranded sleeves and a full skirt for perfect winter warmth and elegance. 1978 *Times* 26 Aug. 22/7 Fully stranded new mink coats from £950.

stranding *vbl. sb.*[2] (In Dict. s.v. Strand *v.*[2]) Add: **b.** In the working of furs: (see quots. 1950, 1968).

1935 O. Hacking *Home Furriery* iii. 15 (*caption*) Dropping and stranding. 1950 *N.Z. Jrnl. Agric.* June 597/1 Some technical terms in [fur] workmanship..should be understood... Stranding or letting out means cutting and sewing a pelt in such a way that it becomes longer and narrower than it was originally; it is done with mink and fitch. 1968 J. Ironside *Fashion Alphabet* 153 *Stranding*. This is the process of lengthening and narrowing a skin by cutting and resewing in a series of diagonal strips.

Strandlooper. Substitute for entry: **Strandlooper, Strandloper** (stra·ntlupəɹ). Also with small initial. Rarely as two words or with hyphen. [a. Afrikaans *strandloper*, f. Du. *strand* Strand *sb.*[1] + *looper* walker: cf. Land-loper.] **1.** *S. Afr.* Any of several sand-plovers of the genus *Charadrius*, found in coastal regions.

1731 G. Medley tr. *Kolb's Descr. Cape of Good Hope* II. 157 The Dutch call this Bird *Strand Loper*, i.e. Shore-Courser. 1875–84 [in Dict., sense 2]. [1972 *Evening Post* (Port Elizabeth) 9 Sept. 2 They [*sc.* ostriches] find the little sandplovers (strandlopertjies) on the farm a nuisance. These little birds dart at them frequently.]

2. *S. Afr.* **a.** A member of a people, related to the Bushmen and Hottentots, living on the southern shores of S. Africa from prehistoric times until the present millennium. **b.** A member of a people, perh. to be identified with the above, found on the Namibian coast.

1838 [see *Saldanier]. 1846, etc. [in Dict., sense 1]. 1900 *Jrnl. Anthropol. Inst.* XXX. 47, I have not much to say about the remains of the 'strand loopers' or 'shore walkers', as they have been called, from their habit of life. 1919 H. H. Johnston *Compar. Study Bantu & Semi-Bantu Lang.* I. ii. 23 This Strandlooper either co-existed alongside the Bushman or preceded and was followed by this specialized desert negro. 1928 C. Dawson *Age of Gods* i. 11 There is reason to think that this race [*sc.* Boskop Man] was the ancestor of the modern South African Hottentot and Bushman, for the remains of an intermediate type—the vanished race of Strandloopers—has been discovered and all three types agree in certain cranial characteristics. In size of brain, however, there is a steady diminution from the 1,700 c.c. or more of Boskop through the Strandlooper skulls. 1948 L. G. Green *So Few are Free* xvi. 216 Some authorities believe that the 'Strandlopers', extinct in South Africa, may survive on the Kaokoveld coast. 1951 [see *river-debris* s.v. *River *sb.*[1] 4 d]. 1956 *Cape Times* 27 July 3/5 Three Hottentots of the *strandloper* race, said to be the last of their kind, attended a gathering of Kaokoveld Natives addressed by..Dr. Verwoerd..in the north-west of South West Africa. 1975 *Eastern Province Herald* (Port Elizabeth) 4 Aug. 4 A skeleton believed to be that of a Strandloper Hottentot, who was buried in the traditional position with legs drawn up and hands placed across the knees, has been unearthed near Sedgefield, the coastal resort. 1981 *Sci. Amer.* Aug. 92/1 They appeared to fill a niche at the edge of western Europe similar to that of the aboriginal Tasmanians in the Pacific, the Patagonians in sub-polar South America and the Hottentot 'strandloopers' of South Africa.

3. *Archæol.* Usu. *pl.* Any prehistoric people who were nomadic about coastal areas or inland shores.

1935 *Proc. Prehistoric Soc.* I. 12 The strandloopers who have left the kitchen-middens in Denmark. 1939 V. G. Childe *Dawn Europ. Civilization* (ed. 3) i. 8 *Asturian* is the term applied to the culture of strandloopers who succeeded the Azilians on the coasts of North Spain. 1956 *Antiquity* XXX. 48 A peripheral culture, which has lost its vitality, a 'strand-loper' type of existence. 1974 G. Jenkins *Bridge of Magpies* ii. 37 The investigation of sea-shore middens belonging to *Strandlopers*—'Seashore Walkers'—who were a vanished Stone Age race of Sperrgebeit nomads. 1975 J. G. Evans *Environment Early Man Brit. Isles* v. 103 In the north of Britain, and especially along the coasts of the North Channel, groups of people known as 'Strandloopers', who subsisted to a considerable extent on shellfish, are represented by the Larnian and Obanian industries.

4. A beachcomber or vagrant.

1939 Joyce *Finnegans Wake* 110 What child of a strandlooper but keepy little Kevin..would ever have trouved up on a strate that was called strete a motive for future saintity by euchring the finding of the Ardagh chalice by another heily innocent and beachwalker. 1952 *Chambers's Jrnl.* Feb. 87/2 The man turned out to be a strandlooper—a coloured beachcomber, one who shared the food of the gulls.

Hence **stra·ndlooping** *ppl. a. Archæol.*, nomadic about coastal areas or lake shores; also as *vbl. sb.*

1959 *New Scientist* 12 Mar. 562/1 The Kennet of about 7,000 years ago was a series of connected lakes surrounded by forest, a site which must have been ideal for a strandlooping people. 1975 J. G. Evans *Environment Early Man Brit. Isles* v. 105 For part of the year, the inhabitants probably forsook their industrial and strandlooping activities and moved inland to obtain their living by other means. 1976 J. Hawkes *Atlas of Early Man* 44/2 Strand looping as well as fresh water and sea fishing intensified. 1978 R. Bradley *Prehist. Settlement of Britain* 94/1 Early fishing, fowling and strandlooping are all compatible with one another.

‖ **Strandveld** (stræ·ndvelt, ‖ stra·ntfelt). *S. Afr.* Also † **strand veld, Strandveldt**, etc.; **strandveld.** [Afrikaans, f. Du. *strand* Strand *sb.*[1] + *veld* Veldt, veld.] The southernmost coastal strip of Africa, in the district of Bredasdorp.

1875–84 R. B. Sharpe *Layard's Birds S. Afr.* (rev. ed.) 47 Mr. John Van Byl's farm, Nacht-wacht in the Strand-Veldt. 1880 *Trans. S. Afr. Philos. Soc.* I. III. 196 The variety is usually termed the 'Strandveldt' (sea-coast) locust. 1912 *S. Afr. Agric. Jrnl.* July 35 In the Bredasdorp district it [*sc.* lamziekte] occurs on the flats of the strand veld and is prevalent along the mountain ranges in the strand veld. 1953 *Cape Times* 3 Apr. 2/6 *Bredasdorp*... Mr. Hennie Geldenhuys has..killed two lynx which marauded farms in the strandveld area of the district in the summer. 1974 *Standard Encycl. S. Afr.* X. 319/2 The Strandveld is..a marine terrace, some 30 to 45 metres above sea-level... The main portion is the Western Strandveld, round Elim, which is level or undulating and where agriculture is practised... To the south of the town of Bredasdorp lies the Eastern Strandveld, a drier terrain of chalky dune-sand.

strange, *a.* Add: **I. 10. e.** *Particle Physics.* Epithet of those sub-atomic particles that have a non-zero value of the strangeness quantum number.

So called orig. because they had lifetimes much longer than was expected from their being produced by the strong interaction.

1956 M. Gell-Mann in *Nuovo Cimento* IV. Suppl. 850 We shall refer to the nucleon.., the antinucleon.., and the pion..as 'ordinary particles' to distinguish them from the 'strange particles', K-particles and hyperons. 1965 H. Muirhead *Physics Elem. Particles* i. 20 The discoveries of new particles have occurred sometimes as a result of a theoretical impetus and sometimes by accident. The strange particles fall into the latter category. 1973 L. J. Tassie *Physics Elem. Particles* vi. 51 A typical strange particle is the Λ^0, an uncharged particle which decays with a mean lifetime of $2{\cdot}5 \times 10^{-10}$ s. 1974 Frauenfelder & Henley *Subatomic Physics* xiii. 358 To construct strange mesons and strange baryons, at least one strange quark is needed. 1975 *Physics Bull.* Apr. 177/1 There are two nonstrange quarks, u and d, a doublet under SU(2), and a strange quark which is a singlet under SU(2). 1977 *Sci. Amer.* Oct. 58/3 There must be a set of lightest strange particles, which have no states of lower mass to which they can give the *s* quark. These are the *K* mesons and the lambda baryon (Λ).

13. b. Now *dial.* and *N. Amer.* (Later examples.)

1904 *Eng. Dial. Dict.* V. 804/2 *Strange*... 1. *adj.*.. *W*[est]*m*[oreland]. Also said of one who professes to be in ignorance of some matters it is well known he understands. 'Thoo's neea casion to makt seea strange, thoo knows o' t'time.' **1937** P. K. DEVINE *Devine's Folk Lore of Newfoundland* 33 *To make strange*, to be afraid or timid. 'Don't make strange,' said to a guest sitting down to eat. **1966** *Amer. Speech* XLI. 295 [Newfoundland] *Don't make strange*. Said to make a guest feel at home. **1974** P. GZOWSKI *Bk. about this Country* 173/1 The luxury of a babysitter is rare—besides, the baby makes strange, and no babysitter with knowledge aforehand would come near!

III. 16. c. For † *Obs.* read Now *rare* and add *strange-moulded*.

1917 D. H. LAWRENCE *Look! We have come Through!* 135 Also she who is the other has strange-moulded breasts.

Stra·ngelove. Also **strangelove.** The name of the character Dr. *Strangelove* from the film of that title (1963) directed by Stanley Kubrick, used *transf.* to designate one who ruthlessly considers or plans nuclear warfare. Freq. *attrib.* and with *Dr.*

1968 *Listener* 16 May 638/1 Dr Strangelove is still at it... He has realised that the hydrogen bomb may yet prove to be a limited..means of annihilating the human race. His current concern is with finding ways of doing it more cheaply..and with greater gusto. **1972** *Village Voice* (N.Y.) 1 June 10/4 In the strangelove language of the AEC, the accident exceeded the 'maximum credible accident' established as a possibility for the installation in the AEC's Hazards Summary. **1973** *Guardian* 22 Feb. 11/3 The Strangelove school, of which Dr Kissinger is a charter member, sees the world as a series of problems that can be manipulated by US money, technology, and bombs. *Ibid.* 28 Feb. 10/6 Professor William Shockley the exponent of sterilisation for low IQ subjects..went into a Dr Strangelove act. **1975** *University* (Princeton Univ.) Winter 5/1 *The Physicists* makes a Strangelove even out of Einstein. **1976** 'R. B. DOMINIC' *Murder out of Commission* xv. 137 Dean Kennison was no Dr Strangelove, yearning to set off bigger and better bangs. **1980** *Times* 12 Aug. 10/7 Nervousness about a latterday Dr Strangelove getting his itchy finger on the button.

Hence (**Dr.**) **Stra·ngelovean, -ian** *a.*; **Stra·ngelovism,** a word or expression characteristic of one who toys with the concept of nuclear war.

1967 *Newsweek* 27 Mar. 47 Words like deterrent, credibility, overkill and doomsday machine became familiar, and were even kidded in such movies as 'Dr. Strangelove'. Now development of anti-ballistic missiles has produced a second generation of Strangelovisms. **1969** *Washington Post* 23 Apr. A16/4 Mendel Rivers..suggested that nuclear weapons be used if necessary to 'bring this crowd to its knees'... Such 'strangelovisms' from that source are of course not new. **1971** P. DICKSON *Think Tanks* 4 Outside Washington, D.C.,..a group of analysts is fighting the wars of the 1990's in a $50,000 Strangelovean game room to see who wins, why, and with what weapons. **1977** *Time* 11 Apr. 13/1 The concepts are often Strangelovean. **1978** *Chatelaine* (Canada) Dec. 41/3 There was something Dr. Strangelovian about these top-level intellectuals who discussed top-secret scenarios.

strangeness. Add: **3.** *Particle Physics.* A quantized property of hadrons, now attributed to the *s* quark, that is conserved in strong and electromagnetic interactions but not in weak ones and is represented by a quantum number *S* equal to the hypercharge of a particle minus its baryon numbers.

1956 M. GELL-MANN in *Nuovo Cimento* IV. Suppl. 852 Since we have $S=0$ for ordinary particles and $S \neq 0$ for 'strange' ones we refer to *S* as 'strangeness'. **1960** *New Scientist* 5 May 1126/2 Like electric charge, the total magnitude of strangeness remains constant in a nuclear process. Not so, however, for the decay phenomena... Decay forces violate strangeness-conservation. **1963** S. TOLANSKY *Introd. Atomic Physics* (ed. 5) xxiii. 397 Whilst the strangeness number seems to play a basic part in the baryon reactions it does *not* operate in the case of the leptons... The concept of isospin is hardly appropriate to the leptons and with this falls away the significance of strangeness too. **1965** H. MUIRHEAD *Physics of Elementary Particles* ix. 396 The classification of particles using the hypercharge quantum number is more economical in numbers than one involving strangeness. **1972** [see *HYPERCHARGE]. **1981** *Sci. Amer.* June 57/1 Strangeness conservation is now understood to be not a fundamental principle like energy conservation.. but a consequence of the detailed theory of the strong interactions.

stranger, *sb.* (and *a.*). Add: **3. b.** (Earlier example.)

1798 COLERIDGE *Frost at Midnight* 20 Only that film, which flutter'd on the grate, Still flutters there... Ah me!..How often in my early school-boy days, With most believing superstitious wish Presageful have I gaz'd upon the bars, To watch the *stranger* there!

4. b. (Earlier examples.)

a **1674** T. TRAHERNE *Centuries of Meditations* (1927) III. ii. 151, I was a little stranger, which at my entrance into the world was saluted and surrounded with innumerable joys. **1787** J. WOODFORDE *Diary* 6 May (1926) II. 320 Mrs. Custance was brought to bed of a Boy about 11 o'clock this Morn'. She with the little stranger as well as can be expected.

c. Now in gen. colloq. use, to address one who has not been seen for some time.

1934 E. O'NEILL *Days without End* II. 59 Hello, Stranger. **1969** *New Yorker* 3 May 34/3 'Well, stranger, where've you been?' she greeted me. 'Why didn't you come back like you said?' **1973** *Weekly News* (Glasgow) 11 Aug. 5/1 (*caption*) Hello, there, stranger! **1977** F. PARRISH *Fire in Barley* iii. 31 'Mornin', stranger,' said.. the landlord. 'How's the old lady keepin'?' 'Fairish,' said Dan.

d. Esp. in phr. *to be* (*quite*) *a stranger* and varr., said of an infrequent visitor.

c **1807** JANE AUSTEN *Watsons* in J. Leigh *Mem. Jane Austen* (1871) 349 'So Emma,' said he, 'you are quite a stranger at home.' **1860** C. M. YONGE *Friarswood Post-Office* vii. 115 Ha! Harold King! Well, to be sure, you are a stranger! **1910** A. BENNETT *Clayhanger* III. vii. 378 'Well, Mr. Clayhanger,' said the steward... 'You're quite a stranger.' **1916** JOYCE *Portrait of Artist* (1969) 219 You are a great stranger now. **1937** A. UPFIELD *Mr. Jelly's Business* xx. 211 Hello, Mr. Muir! You're quite a stranger. **1962** G. AVERY *Greatest Gresham* ix. 162 Well, if it isn't the kiddies from next door. Why, you are strangers these days.

e. *Austral.* and *N.Z.* An animal which has strayed from a neighbouring flock or herd.

1852 J. R. CLOUGH *Jrnl.* 11 Feb. in *Deans Lett. 1840–54* (1937) 290 Branded 57 calves..counted all the other cattle; 201 of them strangers. **1933** L. G. D. ACLAND in *Press* (Christchurch, N.Z.) 16 Dec. 21/8 *Stranger*, a sheep of a neighbour's on your own run. **1965** J. S. GUNN *Terminol. Shearing Industry* II. 28 *Stranger*, a strange sheep, probably from an adjoining property, which has joined the flock being shorn. **1972** P. NEWTON *Sheep Thief* xvi. 137 There was nothing unusual in..having a few 'strangers' (neighbour's sheep) on the place.

5. b. (Earlier examples.)

1705 *House of Commons Jrnl.* 31 Oct. 6/2 *Ordered*, That the Serjeant at Arms, attending this House, do, from time to time, take into his Custody any Stranger or Strangers, that he shall see, or be informed of to be, in the House, or Gallery, while the House, or any Committee of the Whole House, is sitting. **1795** tr. *C. P. Moritz's Trav.* 58 The members call aloud to the gallery, *withdraw! withdraw!* On this the strangers withdraw.

strangle, *sb.* Add: **4. strangle-hold** (non-*attrib.* examples of *fig.* use).

1930 G. B. SHAW *Apple Cart* p. x, This purely inhibitive check on tyranny has become a stranglehold on genuine democracy. **1939** *Daily Tel.* 18 Dec. 6/4 Hitler knows and fears the stranglehold of the British and Allied blockade. **1980** I. COLEGATE *Shooting Party* (1982) 7 The stranglehold of the rich on the life-blood of the working man.

strangle, *v.* Add: **3. b.** Also with *off.*

1918 D. H. LAWRENCE *New Poems* 38 The frost has.. ruthlessly strangled off the fantasies Of leaves.

strangler. Add: **1. a.** *spec.* in *Bot.*, an epiphytic plant which eventually sends its roots to the ground and smothers its host.

1895 J. RODWAY *In Guiana Forest* 91 The strangler is now ready for its deadly work. The forest giant..is bound by cords which are stronger than iron bands. **1952** P. W. RICHARDS *Tropical Rain Forest* ii. 21 The third section of dependent plants, here termed stranglers.. begin life as epiphytes and later send roots to the ground. **1960** N. POLUNIN *Introd. Plant Geogr.* xiv. 435 Stranglers ..begin life as epiphytes but later send down roots to the soil. **1976** *Hortus Third* (L. H. Bailey Hortorium) 288/1 *Clusia*..dioecious trees and shrubs, occasionally more or less epiphytic or stranglers.

b. *strangler fig, vine.*

1955 *Sci. Amer.* Apr. 74/2 The strangler fig in the tropical jungle, which kills other trees to reach the light, is a rare type. **1962** *Times* 6 Apr. 7/2 Strangler figs..envelope and kill other trees. **1976** *Publishers Weekly* 12 Jan. 50/3 'Nanny' grows upon the family like a strangler vine upon a tree.

2. = *CHOKE *sb.*[1] 7.

1925 E. W. KNOTT *Carburettor Handbk.* i. 29 Easy starting devices... First, stranglers or air chokes which reduce the main air supply by means of a suitable shutter or similar device, the use of which increases the suction on the main fuel orifice or jet far beyond the normal state of affairs. **1976** J. WATSON *Understanding your Car* v. 27 A second butterfly valve, mounted above the spray tube..is known as a strangler, and by cutting off most of the air it greatly increases the suction on the jet to give a very rich mixture for starting.

stranskiite (stræ·nski,əit). *Min.* [ad. G. *stranskiit* (H. Strunz 1960, in *Naturwissenschaften* XLVII. 376/1), f. the name of I. N. *Stranski* (b. 1897), Bulgarian-born physical chemist: see -ITE[1].] An arsenate of zinc and copper, $Zn_2Cu(AsO_4)_2$, found as blue triclinic crystals.

1960 *Amer. Mineralogist* XLV. 1315 (*heading*) Stranskiite. **1978** *Ibid.* LXIII. 213 Inclusions of intergrown stranskiite, $Zn_2Cu(AsO_4)_2$, and schultenite, $PbHAsO_4$, in massive tennantite from Tsumeb, Southwest Africa, have been investigated by X-ray diffraction and X-ray fluorescence.

strap, *sb.* Add: **15*.** *Typogr.* Short for *strap-line*, sense 17 below.

1960 A. HUTT *Newspaper Design* vii. 128 Essentially the strap is a single-line affair. **1981** A. GRAHAM-YOOLL *Forgotten Colony* xviii. 238 A photograph of the man.. was splashed over the front page of the Buenos Aires evening newspaper..with a strap that read: 'This is how our English friends see us.'

16. a. With the meaning 'that has a strap', as (sense 3) *strap watch.*

1926 *Daily Colonist* (Victoria, B.C.) 11 July 9/4 (Advt.), Strap Watch. Guaranteed accurate and dependable. Handsome case. Leather strap. **1962** K. ORVIS *Damned & Destroyed* xxiv. 181, I dropped my eyes to my strap-watch.

17. strap-end *Archæol.*, the metal fastening on a strap (sense 3); **strap-game** (examples); **strap handle** *Ceramics*, a handle on a vessel such as a jug or ewer which is in the form of a loop and flattened like a narrow strap; hence **strap-handled** *a.*; **straphanger,** (later examples); also *fig.*, one who commutes to work by public transport; **strap-line** *Typogr.*, a subsidiary heading printed above a headline; **strap-rail** (examples).

1973 *Oxf. Univ. Gaz.* CIII. Suppl. v. 18 *Mr A. R. Lake*: Presented a 12th-century bronze strap-end from near Bicester, Oxon. **1977** *Antiquaries Jrnl.* LXII. 420 Belt-buckles and strap-ends of the later Roman Empire. **1847** *Knickerbocker* XXIX. 281 He was accused of having 'come the strap-game' over a native. **1873** J. H. BEADLE *Undevel. West* vii. 140 A score of 'smart Alecks' relieved of their surplus cash by betting on the 'strap game'. **1939** J. D. S. PENDLEBURY *Archaeol. Crete* iii. 134 The small size of the strap handles is also an indication of date. **1972** *Trans. Oriental Ceramics Soc.* XXXVIII. 65 A stoneware ewer, ovoid with a short spreading neck and double strap-handle. **1957** V. G. CHILDE *Dawn Europ. Civilization* (ed. 6) vii. 131 Strap-handled jugs. **1915** W. CATHER *Song of Lark* II. v. 195 In the street-car..she sat staring at the waistcoat buttons of a fat strap-hanger. **1950** A. J. DEUTSCH in D. Knight *100 Yrs. Sci. Fiction* (1969) 169 The other seats were filled, and there were a dozen or so strap-hangers. **1981** *Times* 5 Aug. 10/4 Washington.. commuters..are not strap-hangers like New Yorkers, Londoners and Parisians. **1960** A. HUTT *Newspaper Design* vii. 128 The use of subsidiary lines—*strap-lines* over headings, *tag-lines* following them—has become a feature of headline practice. *Ibid.*, *Strap-lines* are most suitable over double-column headlines. **1979** *Guardian* 9 Oct. 10/7 Lord Beaverbrook..sometimes put a strap-line over the story saying that the piece didn't represent editorial policy. **1874** B. F. TAYLOR *World on Wheels* I. xiii. 105 Years ago, he rode on a train of the old Toledo & Adrian Railway—strap-rail at that. **1948** *Exhibit Finder* (Museum of Sci. & Industry, Chicago) 3 The story of the early days of railroading is further traced by samples showing the progress of rail manufacture from strap rail, flat as a pancake, to the heavy crowned rail of today.

strap, *v.*[1] Add: **1. e.** *to strap* (oneself) *in*: in an aircraft, to fasten one's safety belt. Also *absol.* (occas. with *up* or without *adv.*).

1913 *Flight* 20 Sept. 1040/2 Neither the pilot nor passenger was strapped in. **1919** J. BUCHAN *Mr. Standfast* I. ix. 173 He signalled to me to strap myself in..and he proceeded to practise 'stunts'—the loop, the spinning nose-dive, and others. **1958** 'CASTLE' & 'HAILEY' *Flight into Danger* v. 72 Better strap yourself in... You must have watched the pilot quite a lot. **1962** L. DEIGHTON *Ipcress File* v. 31 The steward helped him strap in. **1970** 'R. LLEWELLYN' *But we didn't get Fox* vii. 69 She waited for me to strap, started a jet..and taxied down the loop. **1977** *R. Air Force Yearbk.* 29 The excellent leverage of the straps is a noteworthy point and enables the pilots to strap in tightly and securely. **1977** 'O. JACKS' *Autumn Heroes* v. 69 Gerry Steinberg was strapping up beside his pilot.

f. *intr.* for *pass.* To admit of being fastened by means of a strap.

1924 A. D. SEDGWICK *Little French Girl* I. v. 37 Grey shoes strapping across the instep with a buckle.

7. Comb.: **strap-down** *a. Astronautics*, applied to an inertial guidance system in which the gyroscopes are fixed to the vehicle rather than mounted in gimbals; **strap-on** *a.*, that can be attached by a strap or straps; in *Astronautics*, applied to a booster rocket mounted on the outside of the main rocket so as to be jettisonable; also as *sb.*, such a booster.

[**1962** FERNANDEZ & MACOMBER *Inertial Guidance Engin.* viii. 308 The strapped-down gyro reference package..has become widely used as a guidance aid in ballistic missiles where high accuracy is not required.] **1963** SLATER & AUSMAN in C. T. Leondes *Guidance & Control Aerospace Vehicles* iii. 82 A system of this sort..is sometimes inelegantly called 'strapdown'. **1983** *Times* 8 June 2/8 The IMU system uses specially designed and positioned gyros attached to the body of the missile, called strapdown gyros. **1966** *Sci. News* 13 Aug. 107 Solid propellant strap-ons could be used to raise the Saturn V's orbital payload..to as much as 427,000 pounds. **1968** *New Scientist* 31 Oct. 231 The vehicle..appeared to have a two-stage core with four strap-on boosters. **1975** *Aviation Week* 12 May 21/1 Viewed from below a climbing booster, the procedure would appear like the petals of a flower opening if all four strap-ons separated at the same moment. **1981** J. SUTHERLAND *Bestsellers* x. 111 Such 'novelties' as strap-on shark fins. **1982** *Aviation Week* 14 June 18 the U.S. vehicle..uses strap-on solid boosters and integral liquid propulsion to launch itself.

S-trap: see *S I. 2 c.

stra·p-hang, *v. colloq.* Also **straphang.** [Back-formation from *straphanger* s.v. STRAP *sb.* 17.] *intr.* To be a straphanger in a railway carriage, etc. Also *fig.*

1908 O. JESPERSEN in *Englische Studien* LXX. 119 You strap-hang on the Subterranean. **1917** *Daily Mail* 28 Aug. 2/5, I think those weary girls look like tired little flowers as they strap-hang for half an hour or more. **1931** GALSWORTHY *Maid in Waiting* vii. 55 The only..difference..between Parties is that one Party sits in the National 'Bus, and the other Party strap-hangs. **1937** W. H. AUDEN in Auden & MacNeice *Lett. from Iceland*

v. 55 The bowler hat who straphangs in the tube. **1959** *Times Lit. Suppl.* 24 Apr. 237/4 Miss Charles straphangs from fashion on a journey whose destination does not interest her. **1974** K. Royce *Trap Spider* viii. 141, I still wonder what happened to her; it's not usually a happy ending with girls who strap-hang with rats like Laurie Yates. **1982** Barr & York *Official Sloane Ranger Handbk.* 100/1 In the Europe Supermarket in Old Brompton Road, or strap-hanging in the tube from Gloucester Road, astonishingly you meet *more* people you know.

Hence **stra·p-hanging** *vbl. sb.* and *ppl. a.*

1919 *Electrician* LXXXII. 497/2 The somewhat elaborate provision made for 'strap hanging'. **1920** *Cycling* 5 Feb. p. i (Advt.), The strap-hanging problem is easily solved by the satisfied owner of a Rudge-Whitworth. **1928** *Daily Express* 22 Dec. 7/2 (*heading*) Straphanging rule dispute. **1945** [see *keynote *v.*]. **1957** L. Durrell *Justine* I. 53 Here, where the general impression of British culture suggested parsimony, indigence, intellectual straphanging—here I would pass the evening alone. **1972** C. Fremlin *Appointment with Yesterday* i. 8 Every straphanging commuter in London.

strapless, *a.* Add: *spec.* of women's dress: without shoulder straps. Also *absol.*

1935 *Mademoiselle* Feb. 91/3 Strapless and backless brassiere. **1946** *Vogue* Aug. 90/2 In another seventy-five years he'll probably be all for Picasso and your strapless frock. **1955** N. Fitzgerald *House is Falling* i. 13 Her strapless, white swim-suit. **1969** A. Lurie *Real People* 92 Anna May came out, in a cerise strapless satin evening gown. **1973** *Country Life* 8 Mar. 633/2 Slinky dresses that have the finest of straps or are completely strapless. **1980** *Daily Tel.* 13 Oct. 19/3 Strongest revival of all—the straight-across strapless.

‖ **strapontin** (strapoǹtæ̃n). [Fr.] A tip-up seat, usu. additional to the ordinary seating in a theatre, taxi, etc., esp. in France.

1926 W. J. Locke *Old Bridge* v. xviii. 270 Perella insisted on sitting on the little seat, so that Silvester should be at the back with Beatrice. 'He loves it—hates *strapontins*.' **1927** *Observer* 29 May 12/3 As for the strapontins, which, at every performance of a successful play, block up all the gangways, actors and managers agree that they are dangerous. **1934** H. Miller *Tropic of Cancer* 179 Carl was sitting opposite us, on the *strapontin*. **1965** P. H. Newby *One of Founders* iv. 113 Hedges.. climbed in behind Prudence, seated himself on a well-upholstered strapontin, and allowed himself to be driven off.

strapped, *ppl. a.* **2.** For *U.S. slang* read *slang* (orig. *U.S.*) and add: (Further examples.) Now freq. const. *for*. Also in extended use. Also *cash-strapped* adj.

1935 *Sun* (Baltimore) 13 Mar. 2/6 PWA is not yet 'strapped' for funds. **1936** L. C. Douglas *White Banners* ix. 193 If he had been strapped, the chances were he would have bought a hat to-day. **1936** M. Franklin *All that Swagger* xlviii. 437 Also she was strapped for ready money. **1952** Wodehouse *Pigs Have Wings* i. 23 A bit strapped for the ready, eh? **1958** L. Wolff *Low Level Mission* iii. 76 The Axis powers had always been strapped for oil; the specter of a shortage..haunted the two dictators. **1960** J. Lodwick *Asparagus Trench* 7 Fortunately, neither was strapped for children. **1968** *Sunday Mail Mag.* (Brisbane) 8 Dec. 13/3 Strapped for cash he and the dancers tossed their luggage by night from fire escape. **1973** *Times* 7 Dec. 18/7 (*caption*) If only we could be sure the Stringalongs are as strapped for petrol as we are, we could risk asking them to dinner. **1976** *Time* 5 Apr. 37/1 Cash-strapped Chrysler is stepping up preparations to bring out its first domestic subcompact late next year. **1977** *Time* 25 July 48/3 By the spring of 1974, the whipsaw effect of recession and rising costs—particularly for oil which fuels 80% of Con Ed's generating capacity—left the company strapped. **1979** *Church Times* 2 Nov. 10 The Roman Church is almost everywhere strapped for ready cash. **1982** *Times* 18 Dec. 9/1 Cash-strapped countries like Iran and Libya are producing flat out.

strapper[1]. Add: **2.** (Later Austral. examples.)

1963 M. L. West *Gallows on Sand* i. 3 The strappers who stood round the tracks in the misty mornings trying to pick Saturday's winners. **1970** *Sunday Truth* (Brisbane) 19 July 30/6 He checked to see if he was registered as a strapper with any turf club in the country.

5. A worker who furnishes or secures a thing with straps.

1881 *Instructions to Census Clerks* (1885) 79 Leather Goods..Maker. Strapper. **1921** *Dict. Occup. Terms* (1927) § 047 *Strapper*, puts up straps of wood or steel in support of roof in machine cut coal face. *Ibid.* § 345 *Strapper*, attaches straps to bags, trunks, etc.

strappy (stræ·pi), *a.* [f. Strap *sb.* + -y[1].] Of footwear or clothes: having straps.

1977 *Observer* (Colour Suppl.) 31 July 18/3 Bags, handluggage, strappy evening sandals. **1978** *Detroit Free Press* 16 Apr. (Detroit Suppl.) 20 (Advt.), Strippy, strappy stripes of canvas, wedged high, to put spring snap in your steps. **1980** *Daily Tel.* 21 July 13/1 There are strappy Fifties-style sundresses.

Strasburg. Add: Now usu. with spelling Strasbourg. **a.** *Strasbourg goose*, a goose fattened in such a way as to enlarge the liver for use in pâté de foie gras (see Pâté 1 a in Dict. and Suppl.); *S. pâté*, formerly = *S. pie* in Dict. but now usu. a goose pâté not enclosed in pastry.

1857 C. M. Yonge *Dynevor Terrace* I. xv. 240 A Strasburg goose nailed down and crammed before a fire becomes a Strasburg pie. **1877** E. S. Dallas *Kettner's Bk. of Table* 277 The liver of the Toulouse duck..is by most good judges preferred even to that of the Strasbourg goose. **1969** J. Fraser *Clap Hands* v. 76 Byron's passion for Liquorice Allsorts was rapidly diminishing... Every week..he was fed a large box of them, like a Strasbourg goose. **1860** Dickens *Uncommercial Traveller* (1861) xiv. 204 An unopened Strasbourg pâté fresh from Fortnum and Mason's. **1980** D. Bloodworth *Trapdoor* x. 56 They sat perched on high stools..with a pot of taramasalata,.. an opened tin of Strasbourg pâté, a loaf of brown bread.

b. Used to designate the European Parliament, established in 1958, which has its seat in the premises of the Council of Europe at Strasbourg.

1972 *Guardian* 14 July 10/2 There is now some recognition at Strasbourg that with the coming of new members it must change its ways. *Ibid.* 23 Oct. 12/2 No doubt progress towards an effective European Parliament must take time. There are nevertheless measures which can be taken at once to lift Strasbourg out of its futile and legalistic rut. **1976** *Times* 8 Mar. 13/1 (*heading*) Who governs, Strasbourg or Westminster?

strass[2]. Delete *rare*$^{-0}$ and add: **2.** A kind of waxed straw with a silky appearance, used for dress trimmings, etc.

1926 *Westm. Gaz.* 10 Mar. 7/3 Raspberry red strasse (a sort of waxed straw) was made into rosettes for a trimming on one black frock. **1927** *Daily News* 8 Apr. 2/2 Beneath the large strass-trimmed finish to the belt in front fell a full panel of white georgette trimmed with strass.

stratal, *a.* (Later examples.)

1966 S. M. Lamb *Outl. Stratif. Gram.* 1 These several systems may be called stratal systems, and each may be said to be associated with a stratum of linguistic structure. **1967** D. G. Hays *Introd. Computational Linguistics* viii. 162 A stratal conversion is a mapping or transduction of the representation of an utterance on one stratum into the representation of the same utterance on an adjacent stratum.

strategic, *a.* Add: **2.** Of, pertaining to, or designating nuclear weapons intended to destroy an enemy's capacity to make war. Cf. *tactical *a.* 1 c.

1957 *Listener* 26 Dec. 1056/1 Nobody has managed..to draw an effective distinction between 'strategic' and 'tactical' atomic weapons. **1957** *Times* 18 Nov. p. x/2 Between 1946..and 1950, strategic stockpiling had hardly begun. **1958** *Spectator* 21 Feb. 219/1 If Russia were to launch a major attack on the West, even with conventional forces only, the West would have to hit back with strategic nuclear weapons. **1961** *Listener* 14 Dec. 1012/1 The idea was not to create a complete system of strategic deterrence under Nato, but one large enough to meet certain specific problems. **1965** H. Kahn *On Escalation* v. 92 A high degree of escalation could easily be involved ..if it were a strategic-weapons submarine. **1969** *Times* 27 Oct. 9/1 The discussions which will open between the United States and Russia in Helsinki next month are... the long awaited Salt discussions—the strategic arms limitation talks. **1978** *Orbis* XXII. 319 A desire to strengthen the linkage between theater- and strategic-nuclear forces. **1979** *Financial Rev.* 28 Sept. 10/5 It is not that the doctrine of strategic deterrence is being discarded, but that it is being constantly adapted to new technologies as each side seeks to prevent the other from gaining a decisive advantage.

3. Of, pertaining to, or designating materials essential to a country for fighting a war.

1958 *Economist* 26 July 283 A relaxation of the embargo on strategic exports to communist countries has been in the wind for some time. **1959** *Listener* 10 Dec. 1023/1 On the British side there is the question of the so-called strategic controls. This is the agreement between Great Britain and certain other Western countries not to export to the U.S.S.R. certain goods which might be used for military purposes. **1969** Plano & Olton *Internat. Relations Dict.* iii. 76 Some of the most critical strategic materials include foodstuffs, aluminum, cadmium, copper, magnesium, [etc.]. **1981** *Financial Rev.* (Sydney) 24 Apr. 54/2 Germanium is one of about two dozen metals called 'strategic' because they are vital to defence and industry, but available in large supplies only from foreign sources.

4. Special collocations: *strategic bombing*, the bombing of an enemy's territory with the aim of disrupting its economy and destroying morale; hence *strategic bomber*, an aircraft used for this purpose; cf. *tactical *a.* 1 b; *strategic hamlet*, a settlement or reservation for accommodating potential terrorists or their supporters under surveillance (esp. with reference to the Vietnam war); *strategic studies*, the analysis of conflict in international relations in all its aspects.

1961 *Listener* 14 Dec. 1012/1 If it becomes unwise.. to consider basing MRBMs or strategic bombers in Europe. **1977** *Sci. Amer.* Aug. 26/3 The Backfire's capability as a strategic bomber—defined as a bomber that can reach the other country's territory—is certainly less significant than that of U.S. bombers based in Europe or on aircraft carriers. **1941** *Nineteenth Cent.* Sept. 163 Bombing of cities..is a true example of strategic bombing. **1966** *Listener* 27 Oct. 616/2 The very foundation stone of the independent service—strategic bombing—becomes a stumbling block. **1963** *Times* 21 Jan. 9/7 A vast campaign to build 'strategic hamlets' has been launched in every province... President Ngo Dinh Diem has described 1962 as the 'year of the strategic hamlets'. **1973** *Black Panther* 30 June 11/3 Smith's program involves the concepts of the 'strategic hamlet' and 'pacification'; to round up peasants from areas where guerilla forces show signs of gathering support (they will then be relocated to centers where they are surrounded by police barricades). **1975** *New Yorker* 5 May 131/1 What were *we* doing to the South Vietnamese, with our 'strategic hamlets' and 'free-fire zones'? **1959** *Times* 18 Feb. 12/1 The chairman and council of the Institute for Strategic Studies held a reception yesterday evening. **1981** *Listener* 5 Nov. 530/1, I.. started a postgraduate seminar in strategic studies.

strategize (stræ·tĭdʒəiz), *v. U.S.* [f. Strategy + -ize.] *intr.* To formulate a strategy or strategies; to plan a course of action. Hence **stra·tegizing** *vbl. sb.*

1943 *Sun* (Baltimore) 8 Nov. 6/3 The delay in bringing the bill to the House floor for action developed because both sides were 'strategizing'. **1977** *Dædalus* Fall 134 Four competing hypotheses can be posed for the explanation of kinship rules: detailed genetic control, rational strategizing, complete cultural determinism, and coupled cultural and genetic control. **1978** *New Scientist* 21 Sept. 873 Men in dark suits and homburg hats will be commissioning think tanks to strategize. **1983** *Washington Post* 3 June A 3 Back in those days [*sc.* the 1960s]..you didn't have to strategize and study and do the kind of homework on your cases that you have to do now.

strategy. Add: **2. d.** In (theoretical) circumstances of competition or conflict, as in the theory of games, decision theory, business administration, etc., a plan for successful action based on the rationality and interdependence of the moves of the opposing participants; also *transf.* (see quot. 1979).

1944 von Neumann & Morgenstern *Theory of Games* i. 44 The same arguments which forced us to consider sets of imputations instead of single imputations necessitate the abandonment of that narrow concept of 'standard of behavior'. Actually we shall call these sets of rules the 'strategies' of the game. **1954** *Psychol. Bull.* LI. 406/2 A *strategy* is a set of personal rules for playing the game. For each possible first move.., your opponent will have a possible set of responses. **1965** H. I. Ansoff *Corporate Strategy* vi. 118 A *grand* or *mixed* strategy is a statistical decision rule for deciding which particular pure strategy the firm should select in a particular situation. **1969** R. Farquharson *Theory of Voting* iv. 20 Any procedure can be represented as a game by assuming that each voter makes a plan in advance regarding the course of action he will take in every division which can arise. Any such plan may be called a 'strategy'—the voter's set of strategies constitutes the complete range of such possible plans. **1979** *Science* 25 May 795/2 Gideon Louw..laments the widespread biological use of the word 'strategy' because of the implication of rational choice..but..there is no simpler way to label possible evolutionary designs.

Stratfordian (strætfoə·ɹdiăn), *sb.* (*a.*). [f. the name of the town *Stratford*-upon-Avon, War., birthplace of William Shakespeare + -ian.] **1.** One who lives in or was born in Stratford-upon-Avon.

1821 J. Saunders *Let.* 8 June in A. Mathews *Mem. Charles Mathews* (1839) III. ix. 204 Intreating a line when you have anything desirable to impart to the Stratfordians. **1909** 'Mark Twain' *Is Shakespeare Dead?* 58 Stratfordians who were not Stratfordians of Shakespeare's day, but later comers. **1963** *Times* 12 Feb. 11/4 It is likely that the Stratfordians thus deprived of some edification from the pulpit were less put out than those who now find the harmonies of a concert-platform sadly broken.

2. A supporter of the view that Shakespeare was the author of the plays generally attributed to him. Also as *adj.* Cf. *Shakespearian *a.* (and *sb.*) b.

1908 G. Greenwood *Shakesp. Probl. Restated* 172 Really, really, there must be some limits even to Stratfordian demands on our credulity! *Ibid.* 226 The futilities which are gravely trotted out by enthusiastic Stratfordians as valuable evidence to illustrate the life of Shakespere. **1912** [see *over-prove* s.v. *over- 27 a]. **1930** P. Allen *Case for E. de Vere as Shakespeare* 6, I remained an orthodox Stratfordian until 1923. *Ibid.* 26 All these discoveries and inferences..were fast and firmly establishing the case for Oxford, at the same time that they were destroying utterly the Stratfordian arguments. **1962** *Economist* 28 July 364/2 His work..made him a 'convinced Stratfordian'.

stratification. Add: **1. b.** The placing of seeds close together in layers between layers of moist sand, peat, or the like in order to preserve them or promote germination; also extended to the placing of seeds in such a medium other than in layers.

1914 Moon & Brown *Elem. of Forestry* vi. 103 Commercial houses rarely practice stratification, because they have storehouses where moisture conditions are kept uniform. **1928** *Jrnl. Forestry* XXVI. 775/2 Stratification of these seeds for one to four months previous to planting has been found to hasten greatly their germination. **1976** H. L. Edlin *Nat. Hist. Trees* xiv. 181 The seeds of ash trees..and many other common genera..require stratification for sixteen months.

2. e. *spec.* in Sociology, the formation and establishment of social or cultural levels resulting from differences in occupation and political, ethnic, or economic influence.

1927 P. Sorokin *Soc. Mobility* ii. 13 Unstratified society ..is a myth which has never been realized in the history of mankind... The forms and proportions of stratification vary, but its essence is permanent. **1944** S. PUTNAM tr. *da Cunha's Rebellion in Backlands* ii. 117 It was natural that the deep-lying layers of our ethnic stratification should have cast up so extraordinary an anticlinal as Antonio Conselheiro. **1962** *Guardian* 22 June 20/2 The so-called gulf between science and literature..led to no social stratification. **1981** R. FLETCHER *Sociol.* vii. 200 Specific interest groups and a changing ethnic composition are the elements most likely to be troublesome in..problems of social stratification.

f. The existence in a lake or other body of water of two or more distinct layers differing in temperature, density, or the like.

1898 *Amer. Naturalist* XXXII. 26 It is in a condition of 'inverse stratification', as Forel calls it, when the colder water is above the warmer. **1935** P. S. WELCH *Limnology* iv. 51 Exceptional meteorological conditions may..prevent stratification completely. **1952** *Phil. Trans. R. Soc.* B. CCXXXVI. 355 (*heading*) Water movements in lakes during summer stratification. **1972** M. G. GROSS *Oceanography* vii. 191 Well-developed density stratification of the open ocean inhibits strong vertical currents. **1973** P. A. COLINVAUX *Introd. Ecol.* xviii. 249 If a lake is highly productive, thermal stratification has some interesting consequences for the bottom water.

g. Variation in the richness of the fuel-air mixture during the period of its introduction into the cylinder of an internal-combustion engine.

1922 H. R. RICARDO *Internal-Combustion Engine* I. v. 75 In order to increase the range of power as far as possible, every effort is made to encourage stratification. **1981** *Sci. Amer.* May 45/1 The stratification also makes it possible to burn fuel-air mixtures so lean in fuel that they would not burn if the fuel were uniformly mixed with the air.

2*. *Statistics.* The (usu. notional) division of a population into distinct groups from each of which a proportion of an overall sample may be taken.

1920 A. L. BOWLEY *Elements of Statistics* (ed. 4) II. iv. 336 The stratification of a universe of measurable objects is also treated by Mr. Yule. **1934** *Jrnl. R. Statistical Soc.* XCVII. 608 This method of stratification..gives an improvement in precision. **1957** KENDALL & BUCKLAND *Dict. Statistical Terms* 282 The process of stratification may be undertaken on a geographical basis, *e.g.* by dividing up the sampled area into sub-areas on a map. **1966** *Rep. Comm. Inquiry Univ. Oxf.* II. 420 In drawing the sample stratification by college and subject was used to the greatest possible extent. **1967** G. WILLS in Wills & Yearsley *Handbk. Management Technol.* 187 This process of stratification..can only be carried out if you have details of the relevant population of shops by region, type, etc. **1977** *Lancet* 28 May 1142/2 With stratification for hospital, age, and year of admission, the maximum-likelihood estimate of uniform risk ratio was 3·3.

stratificational (strætifikeɪ·ʃənăl), *a.* [f. STRATIFICATION + -AL.] **1.** *Linguistics.* Of or pertaining to the concept of language as a series of strata or structural layers, esp. *stratificational grammar, linguistics,* whereby language is envisaged and analysed in terms of a number of different strata, each with its own rules of formation and related to each other.

1962 S. M. LAMB (*title*) Outline of stratificational grammar. *Ibid.* 3 The code relating each pair of neighboring strata is a set of *stratificational rules. Ibid.* 6 Stratificational analysis may be described as a process of *emicization* followed by the description of the results. **1966** *Georgetown Univ. Monogr. Ser. Lang. & Linguistics* XVII. 87 The picture of the organization of language in terms of four strata can conveniently be called stratificational. **1968** P. M. POSTAL *Aspects Phonol. Theory* iv. 89 By abandoning any vestige of a natural relation between phonetic and phonemic representations, stratificational phonemics has completely lost contact with these early motivations. **1970** *Canad. Jrnl. Linguistics* XV. 97 Since this hypothesis is independent of the concept of strata, it seems sensible to call the grammar to be developed here a *relational network grammar*, rather than a stratificational grammar. **1972** D. G. LOCKWOOD *Introd. Stratificational Linguistics* i. 5 Stratificational theory may eventually be able to provide evidence on the relation of the neural networks to the storage of knowledge. **1977** P. STREVENS *New Orientations Teaching of English* vi. 79 Very little..stratificational theory..could be thoroughly taught and learned during, say, a two-year training college course.

2. Of or pertaining to social or cultural strata.

1963 *New Society* 3 Oct. 30/3 The evolution of American jazz has been correctly recognised..as a musically expressed protest movement against the existing stratificational order. **1968** *Canad. Jrnl. Linguistics* XIII. 126 The variables studied..showed stratificational patterns clearly identifiable with different social levels of the community.

Hence **stratifica·tionalism**, adherence to the theory that language comprises several structural layers; **stratifica·tionalist**, one who holds this theory.

1968 *South Atlantic Bull.* Mar. 1/3 Dashing across the empty plains from a distant Danish horizon comes a new band, the troop of Stratificationalism. **1969** R. I. McDAVID in *2nd & 3rd Lincolnland Conf. on Dialectology* (1972) 1 There seems to be diffidence on the part of Lamb's stratificationalists. **1973** *Amer. Speech 1969* XLIV. 287 Pike or Lamb might charge that James D. McCawley's 'Prelexical Syntax' is arcane from the point of view of a tagmemicist or stratificationalist. **1978** *Language* LIV. 170 If it can be said to have a dominant philosophy, it would be stratificationalism.

stratified, *ppl. a.* Add: **1. a.** (Earlier example).

1799 [see POLYGENOUS *a.* 1].

e. Of a lake or other body of water: exhibiting stratification. [tr. F. *stratifié* (F. A. Forel 1880, in *Bibliothèque Univ.: Arch. des Sci. physiques et nat.* IV. 94).]

1881 *Proc. Boston Soc. Nat. Hist.* XXI. 66 In summer the return current takes place at no great depth, because then the water is stratified according to its temperature. **1910** E. M. WEDDERBURN in Murray & Pullar *Bathymetrical Surv. Sc. Fresh-Water Lochs* I. 104 As winter draws on the lake becomes thermally stratified. **1957** G. E. HUTCHINSON *Treat. Limnol.* I. v. 334 Not only can a lake oscillate as a whole, but if it is stratified, the various layers of different density can oscillate relative to one another. **1972** M. G. GROSS *Oceanography* xi. 301 Tidal currents [in an estuary] cause mixing between layers, so that the waters become only moderately stratified. **1980** G. E. FOGG in Barnes & Mann *Fund. Aquatic Ecosystem* ii. 37 Sometimes lakes are permanently stratified, as for example in tropical regions.

f. *Sociol.* (Cf. *STRATIFICATION 2 e.)

1927 P. SOROKIN *Social Mobility* ii. 11 If the economic status of the members of a society is unequal, if among them there are both wealthy and poor, the society is *economically stratified.* **1960** V. PACKARD *Status Seekers* xxii. 325 Life is said to be more stable and serene in clearly stratified societies. **1969** C. D. DARLINGTON *Evol. of Man & Soc.* xviii. 422 The urban society was still stratified and even more highly stratified, but the strata and their boundaries had changed.

g. *stratified charge*: in an internal-combustion engine, a rich mixture for ignition in each cycle followed by a lean one for combustion, usu. achieved by having a side chamber in each cylinder into which the mixture for ignition is introduced; freq. *attrib.*

1931 D. R. PYE *Internal Combustion Engine* vi. 148 (*caption*) Thermal efficiencies obtainable at weak petrol-air mixtures with 'stratified charge' operation. **1953** H. R. RICARDO *High-Speed Internal Combustion Engine* (ed. 4) xviii. 366 Two alternative schemes were tried:..(2) The use of a stratified charge in which the mixture immediately in the zone of the sparking-plug is very much richer than that in the main body of the combustion space. **1976** *National Observer* (U.S.) 22 May 9/4 The Japanese car is..powered with a larger version of the stratified-charge engine. **1981** *Sci. Amer.* May 45/1 Direct-injection stratified-charge engines have efficiency advantages comparable to those of the diesel.

2. *Statistics.* Employing, or obtained by means of, the technique of stratification.

1920 A. L. BOWLEY *Elements of Statistics* (ed. 4) II. iv. 333 In a non-stratified selection we should have had σ = ·0141. **1934** *Jrnl. R. Statistical Soc.* XCVII. 567 This method has been called by Professor Bowley the method of stratified sampling. **1956** *B.B.C. Handbk. 1957* 104 This Survey employs part-time interviewers..who each day question some four thousand people—a sample or cross-section of the adult public... (Technically speaking, the sample used is a stratified quota sample.) **1980** *Nature* 1 May 5/3 One [technique] is stratified sampling, in which the site was first divided into 20 metre by 20 metre squares, and then four randomly selected one metre by one metre trenches excavated within each of the larger squares.

stratiform, *a.*² Delete *rare*⁻¹ and add later examples.

1885 [see CUMULIFORM *a.*]. **1944** H. C. WILLETT *Descriptive Meteorol.* iv. 92 These high stratiform clouds are spread over large areas where convection is extensive in the lower atmosphere. **1978** *Bull. Amer. Meteorol. Soc.* LIX. 518 (*heading*) An analytical model of snowflake growth in stratiform clouds.

stratify, *v.* Add: **1. c.** To preserve or promote the germination of (seeds) by stratification.

1905 *Terms Forestry & Logging* (U.S. Dept. Agric., Bureau of Forestry) 23 *Stratify*, to preserve tree seeds by spreading them in layers alternating with layers of earth or sand. **1916** J. W. TOUMEY *Seeding & Planting* vii. 104 Some of the pines and junipers germinate so slowly that the seed is usually stratified for a year before sowing. **1949** *Q. Jrnl. Forestry* XLIII. 169 The seed is stratified in wet sand for six weeks before sowing at a temperature of 34° F. **1960** *New Scientist* 12 May 1210/3 When seeds of certain shrubs or trees are stratified—stored in moist sand at 41° F. to break their dormancy—the amount of moisture in the sand may markedly influence the percentage germination subsequently achieved.

2. c. *Statistics.* To subdivide (a population) into groups in order to take a stratified sample. Also *absol.*

1949 F. YATES *Sampling Methods for Censuses & Surveys* iii. 25 A population may be stratified for two or more different characteristics... Thus we may stratify farms according to size and according to geographical regions. **1966** *Rep. Comm. Inquiry Univ. Oxf.* II. 420 It was possible to stratify by college and proposed subject. *Ibid.* 424 The names under Social Studies were further stratified according to college thus: Nuffield, St. Antony's, and others. **1967** G. WILLS in Wills & Yearsley *Handbk. Management Technol.* 187 In most cases..the statistician can..stratify the list of 27,000 names [of shops] in terms of the region of the country they are in, [etc.]. **1970** J. E. FREUND *Statistics* xi. 285 Stratified sampling..can be very effective provided one stratifies with respect to truly relevant characteristics of the population.

3. Also, to become stratified.

1935 P. S. WELCH *Limnology* iii. 15 Criteria which would make a lake include only those bodies of standing water which are of considerable expanse and which are deep enough to stratify thermally. **1980** R. S. K. BARNES in Barnes & Mann *Fund. Aquatic Ecosystems* i. 14 Water bodies stratify when stable density differences are generated, often as a result of surface heating.

stratigraphic, *a.* Add: (Later *transf.* example.) Also *fig.*

1972 *Computers & Humanities* VII. 39 One of the most characteristically archaeological of these uses is the generation and printing of stratigraphic backplots of artifacts and other items in a site. **1976** *Jrnl. Asian Studies* XXXV. 636 Another stratigraphic approach to Indian society.

strato-. Add: **1.** Also used in forming other terms, as **stra·totype** *Geol.*, a particular group of strata chosen as defining a named stratigraphic unit or boundary; freq. *attrib.*; **stra·tovolca:no** Geol. [ad. G. *strato-vulkan* (K. von Seebach 1866, in *Zeitschr. d. deutsch. geol. Ges.* XVIII. 644)], a volcano built up of alternate layers of lava and ash.

1965 *Bull. Amer. Assoc. Petroleum Geologists* XLIX. 1701/1 The most effective means of providing a chronostratigraphic unit with fixed and uniform limits..appears to be by the designation of a specifically bounded section of rock strata as the stratotype of this unit. **1969** *Proc. Geol. Soc. Lond.* Aug. 142 A standard stratigraphical scale expresses the relative ages of rock in agreed terms defined by boundary points in stratotype sections. **1972** J. A. COUVERING in Bishop & Miller *Calibration of Hominoid Evolution* 247 Stage-age names..are put in quotation marks when used in a sense which differs from the strict definition of the stratotype. **1978** *Nature* 16 Nov. 258/2 The rich foraminiferal and molluscan faunas at these localities establish the correlation of the beds..with the Jemmys Point Formation in Gippsland, the stratotype of the Kalimnan Stage (early Pliocene). [**1885** A. GEIKIE *Text-bk. Geol.* (ed. 2) 227 Von Seebach..distinguished two volcanic types. 1st, Bedded Volcanoes (Strato-Vulkane), composed of successive sheets of lava and tuffs, and embracing the great majority of volcanoes.] **1957** G. E. HUTCHINSON *Treat. Limnol.* I. i. 25 The typical large volcano with a well-developed crater is an intermediate or composite structure, usually built of alternating layers of lava and cinders, and therefore called a stratovolcano. **1973** *Sci. Amer.* Aug. 67/1 These later lavas form the great stratovolcanoes, some still active, that dominate the Andean chain. **1977** *Whitaker's Almanack 1978* 1037/2 Merapi, a strato-volcano on the island of Java, has been active for several centuries.

2. [f. *STRATO(SPHERE.] **a.** Used to form the names of various kinds of high-altitude aircraft, as *stratocruiser, -fortress, -freighter, -jet, -liner, -plane, -tanker.*

All but *stratoplane* are the names of aircraft built by the Boeing Airplane Company, but only *Stratoliner* (formerly also *Stratocruiser*) is a proprietary name (in the U.S.).

1944 *Sun* (Baltimore) 15 Nov. 8/2 An announcement by the Boeing Aircraft Company of a 'Stratocruiser' for post-war production... A military prototype of the Stratocruiser..is undergoing tests. **1966** D. FRANCIS *Flying Finish* iv. 48 The pressurized stratocruiser which took us [to New York]. **1953** *Britannica Bk. of Year* 28/1 The Boeing YB-52, an eight-engine jet swept-wing Stratofortress designed gradually to replace the intercontinental B-36, made its first flight. **1981** *Nature* 17 Dec. 606/2 The massive wide-area saturation bombing from B-52 stratofortresses alone ultimately added up to 800,000 tonnes of bombs. **1947** *Sun* (Baltimore) 10 July 2 (*caption*) The Boeing Aircraft Company's 'Stratocruiser', passenger-carrying counterpart of the 'Stratofreighter', is shown as it takes off on its initial test flight at Seattle. **1947** *Daily Progress* (Charlottesville, Va.) 18 Dec. 10/1 The XB4 Stratojet, described as potentially the world's most powerful plane, made its initial test hop yesterday. **1955** *Times* 20 June 3/5 One 'Stratojet' bomber succeeds another as the latest weapon of defence. **1938** *Sun* (Baltimore) 8 June 3/2 Two other new transports, the Boeing 'Stratoliner' and the Douglas DC-4. **1939** *Official Gaz.* (U.S. Patent Office) 26 Dec. 805/1 Boeing Aircraft Company... Stratoliner. For airplanes and structural parts thereof. **1955** M. MCCARTHY *Sights & Spectacles* (1959) 162 Stratoliners from Kansas City ferry-in patrons for *Guys and Dolls.* **1933** *Daily Progress* (Charlottesville, Va.) 16 Nov. 6/4 Clues to the tail-winds that may push future strato-planes on high-speed flights through the stratosphere were sought..here today by astronomers watching the Leonid meteor shower. **1936** *Discovery* Apr. 125/2 The efficiency of the reaction-motor beginning where that of the propeller leaves off, at approximately the 10-mile level,..raises the question as to whether certain makers of hush-hush 'stratoplanes' are not working along the wrong lines. **1955** *Ann. Rep. 1954* (Boeing Airplane Co.) 15/2 The new military airplane, to be known as the KC-135 Jet Stratotanker, will be an advanced version of the prototype. **1980** *Times* 1 Feb. 3/3 (*caption*) A woman stratotanker pilot in the United States Air Force at RAF Fairford, Gloucestershire, yesterday, after a refuelling mission.

b. Used in the sense 'travelling in, suitable for travel in, the stratosphere', in *stratonaut* [f. *-naut* after AERONAUT, *ASTRONAUT], *stratosuit.*

1934 *Amer. Speech* IX. 236/2 According to C. E. Mason, the New York *Times* coined the word *stratonaut* to describe venturers in the stratosphere. **1936** *Nature* 27 June 1053/1 A general introduction which is packed with references to Magellan and Copernicus on one hand, and the stratosphere explorers (*stratonauts*) and theoretical investigators of the expanding universe on the other. **1937** C. G. PHILP *Conquest of Stratosphere* 6 Seventy-four years ago..those gallant pioneers, Glaisher and Coxwell,..claimed to have reached a height of 7 miles, into the lower stratosphere..without a single essential of the modern stratonaut, for they had no oxygen apparatus. **1945** *Sun* (Baltimore) 23 June 3/2 (*caption*) An airman wears a new flexible pressurized 'Strato-suit' of rubberized fabric.. for use in high-altitude flying. **1949** *Jrnl. Brit. Interplanetary Soc.* VIII. 40 Doubtless considerable improvements have been effected in stratosuits since the Haldane-Davis original.

stratopause (stræ·topǭz). *Meteorol.* [f. *STRATO(SPHERE + PAUSE *sb.*] The upper limit of the stratosphere, separating it from the mesosphere. (In current use at a greater height than formerly: cf. *STRATOSPHERE 2.)

1950 S. CHAPMAN in *Jrnl. Atmospheric & Terrestrial Physics* I. 121 Taking stratosphere to denote the nearly isothermal region above the troposphere, its upper boundary, where the temperature first begins to increase upwards more rapidly than is common in the lower stratosphere, would be the stratopause. **1963** *Q. Jrnl. R. Meteorol. Soc.* LXXXIX. 156 At its meeting in June 1962, the executive committee of the World Meteorological Organization passed a resolution on the terminology.. for the high atmosphere. It is as follows:..(a) Stratosphere: Region (situated between the tropopause and stratopause) in which the temperature generally increases with height. (b) Stratopause: The top of the inversion layer in the upper stratosphere (usually around 50 to 55 km). **1979** *Jrnl. Atmospheric Sci.* XXXVI. 1616/1 Large [meridional wind] oscillations are seen near the stratopause (~50 km) with a period of about 2 days and an amplitude as large as 30 m s^{-1}.

stratosphere (stræ·tǒsfiᵊɹ). [f. STRATUM + -O + SPHERE *sb.*] †**1.** *Geol.* [ad. G. *stratosphäre* (E. Suess *Das Antlitz der Erde* (1901) III. I. i. 4).] (See quots.) *Obs.*

1908 H. B. C. SOLLAS tr. *Suess's Face of Earth* III. i. 2 So great is the part played by stratified deposits in the structure of the earth's crust that we might be tempted to speak of the *stratosphere* of the earth in contradistinction to the *scoriosphere* of the moon. **1909** *Ibid.* IV. xv. 546 The stratosphere, or younger sedimentary envelope has been formed almost entirely at the expense of the Sal envelope.

2. *Meteorol.* The region of the atmosphere extending from the top of the troposphere up to a height of about 50 km. (the stratopause), in the lower part of which there is little temperature variation with height in temperate latitudes and in the higher part the temperature increases with height; formerly, the lower part of this region only (up to a height of about 20 km.).

1909 *Sci. Abstr.* A. XII. 208 (*heading*) Variation in height of the stratosphere (isothermal layer). **1909** W. N. SHAW *Free Atmosphere in Region of Brit. Isles* 47 M. Teisserenc de Bort has introduced the words 'troposphere' and 'stratosphere' to denote these two layers. *Ibid.* 48 Such evidence as we have goes to show that the stratosphere is a region of comparative calm. **1923** *Daily Mail* 26 Feb. 5/4 In this stratosphere it has been ascertained from balloon soundings that the temperature ceases to fall with an increase in height,..up to a level of 13½ miles, the highest attained so far by any instrument of man. **1934** *Discovery* Mar. 57/2 Professor Piccard, the Belgian physicist, was the first to make a successful flight [by balloon] into the stratosphere. **1937** *Jrnl. R. Aeronaut. Soc.* XLI. 414 It is likely to be many years before stratosphere flight, flights at heights of 40,000 feet and over, will become the commercially paying proposition which its enthusiasts believe it ultimately will be. **1951** 'J. WYNDHAM' *Day of Triffids* ii. 39 Somewhere high up in the stratosphere, he and Comrade Baltinoff found themselves attacked by the planes. **1951** [see *exosphere* s.v. *EXO-]. **1960** M. NICOLET in J. A. Ratcliffe *Physics of Upper Atmosphere* ii. 19 The stratosphere is essentially that region where the temperature increases, or at least does not decrease, with altitude. **1963** [see *STRATOPAUSE]. **1980** *Nature* 27 Nov. 347/1 Air samples, collected cryogenically at different heights of the stratosphere, were analysed for carbon dioxide.

3. *Oceanogr.* The bottom layer of the ocean, in which (by analogy with the original meaning of sense *2) there is little temperature variation with depth.

1937 *Nature* 26 June 1085/1 The oceanic troposphere, like the corresponding section of the atmosphere, is a relatively shallow layer marked by steep temperature gradients which contrast strongly with the more even conditions of the stratosphere. **1942** H. U. SVERDRUP et al. *Oceans* iv. 141 From analogy with the atmosphere, Defant (1928) has applied the terms troposphere and stratosphere to two different parts of the ocean. Troposphere is applied to the upper layer of relatively high temperature that is found in middle and lower latitudes and within which strong currents are present, and stratosphere to the nearly uniform masses of cold deep and bottom water. *Ibid.*, Within the oceanic stratosphere the salinity is very uniform. **1966** R. W. FAIRBRIDGE *Encycl. Oceanogr.* 940/2 The oceanic stratosphere refers to the nearly uniform masses of cold deep water and bottom water.

4. *transf.* and *fig.* An upper region, esp. in a hierarchy; a high, or the highest, plane, level, or rank.

1951 M. MCLUHAN *Mech. Bride* (1967) 62/1 The bathroom has been elevated to the very stratosphere of industrial folklore. **1952** *Observer* 3 Feb. 5/8 Their father was a big Paris dealer who moved in the stratosphere with Anatole France and de Goncourt. **1958** *Listener* 9 Oct. 578/2 To come down from the stratosphere of critical intentions to the rough terrain of poetry itself. **1965** B. SWEET-ESCOTT *Baker Street Irregular* vii. 188 Since August 1943 the stratosphere had begun to take our work in the Balkans seriously. *a* **1974** R. CROSSMAN *Diaries* (1975) I. 609 They were astonished that Harold had upped me into the stratosphere. **1975** *Country Life* 16 Jan. 138 With the fall-front secretaire..we are well-up in the stratosphere in terms of furniture... It was sold for 45,000 gn. **1980** *Daily Tel.* 3 Nov. 16 At various times she has advanced three different reasons for keeping the [minimum lending] rate in the stratosphere.

stratospheric (strætǒsfe·rik), *a.* [f. prec. + -IC.] **1.** Of or pertaining to the stratosphere; occurring or performed in the stratosphere.

1920 W. J. HUMPHREYS *Physics of Air* x. 191 Let a stratospheric column be dropped bodily a distance *dh*, and let the surrounding air come in until equilibrium is again established. **1935** *Jrnl. R. Aeronaut. Soc.* XXXIX. 194 This plea is often put forward by the protagonists of so-called stratospheric aviation. **1945** *Washington Post* 10 Oct. 1/3 Development of even greater bombers capable of operating at stratospheric altitudes..is a certainty. **1959** *Daily Tel.* 30 Nov. 1/6 A balloon descending from a stratospheric study of the planet Venus landed safely in a meadow 20 miles north of Manhattan, Kansas, to-day. **1980** *Nature* 27 Nov. 347/2 The stratospheric CO_2 mixing ratio is not constant with height but rather decreases with increasing height.

2. *fig.* On a scale, from a point of view, or of a pitch, so high as to be suggestive of the stratosphere; *esp.* of a cost: = *ASTRONOMICAL *a.* 1 b.

1935 *Sun* (Baltimore) 16 Feb. 2/1 This bill..requires Congress to abdicate. It requires the country to lean on a dubious dream... Changes made by the Senate committee ..in no sense change the stratospheric realities of the bill itself. **1958** K. GOODWIN in P. Gammond *Decca Bk. of Jazz* xiii. 149 His ability to produce stratospheric screamers with apparent ease was utilized to add bite and drive to the brass sections. **1966** *Economist* 19 Nov. 778/1 It might at least consider supporting stratospheric French suggestions for so-called 'solving of the key currency problem' by the admitted archaism of raising the world price of gold. **1973** *Daily Tel.* 17 Nov. 29/3 To prevent gilt-edged prices from falling even further and yields from escalating to even more stratospheric heights. **1980** *Jewish Chron.* 29 Feb. 17/3 Stratospheric admission prices for a suburban commercial venture.

stratosphe·rically, *adv. colloq.* [f. prec. + -AL[1] + -LY[2].] To a stratospheric degree, 'astronomically'.

1946 J. W. DAY *Harvest Adventure* xx. 331 This type of oratory was something very rich and rare, obviously from an intellect stratospherically above the plain, blunt, and fairly honest opinions held by the rank and file of Newark Labour. **1961** B. FERGUSON *Watery Maze* x. 237 The stratospherically high priority afforded him for the journey did not really do him much good.

Stratovision (stræ·tovi3ən). *U.S. Television.* Also **stratovision.** [f. *STRATO(SPHERE + *TELE)VISION.] A proprietary name for a system whereby television programmes are broadcast to a wide area by retransmission from a circling aircraft.

1945 *Cleveland* (Ohio) *Plain Dealer* 10 Aug. 1/5 The stratovision system simply puts the antenna and transmitter in an airplane flying in lazy circles 30,000 feet above the earth. **1946** *Official Gaz.* (U.S. Patent Office) 14 May 197/1 *Stratovision* for radio receiving and/or transmitting sets, television receiving and sending apparatus, [etc.]. **1948** *Sun* (Baltimore) 6 Oct. 19/4 If the World Series goes beyond five games, the East Coast and mid-West can see the remaining contests. A linking of the two networks by stratovision plane would provide the largest audience in television broadcast history. **1959** *Washington Post* 24 Dec. A1/7 Four transmitters on the Purdue campus will send two simultaneous programs to the plane, which will travel in a 10-mile circle 23,000 feet above Montpelier... The system, known as 'stratovision', is designed to explore the value of the plane in reaching hundreds of thousands of students at one time. **1964** B. GROB *Basic Television* (ed. 3) v. 85 The UHF channels 66 to 83 are available for experimentation with this airborne television system called stratovision.

stratum. Add: Now usu. with pronunc. (strā·tǒm, *pl.* strā·tă). **6. a.** (Earlier and later examples of *social stratum.*)

1886 T. H. S. ESCOTT in P. Bailey *Leisure & Class in Victorian England* (1978) iii. 58 A social movement..is now steadily progressing on a lower social stratum. **1927** P. SOROKIN *Social Mobility* 141 There has never existed a society in which vertical social mobility has been absolutely free and the transition from one social stratum to another has had no resistance. **1973** E. BERCKMAN *Victorian Album* 50 This murder..must have been in too drab a social stratum..to attract even contemporary attention.

b. Earlier and later examples of *social strata*: cf. sense 6 a in Dict. and Suppl.

1890 W. JAMES *Princ. Psychol.* I. iv. 121 Habit..keeps different social strata from mixing. **1937** R. H. LOWIE *Hist. Ethnological Theory* vi. 57 It is hard to understand how Morgan could have missed the social strata of the caste-ridden Oceanians. **1968** G. P. MITCHELL *Dict. Sociol.* 182 In theory social strata are made up of individuals and families.

c. *Statistics.* Each of the groups into which a population is divided in the technique of stratified sampling.

1920 A. L. BOWLEY *Elements of Statistics* (ed. 4) II. iv. 332 It may happen..that the universe consists of different regions or strata in which the chances are different, and the question arises whether we should proceed at random .., or..partially arrange the choice so as to take the same proportion out of each region or stratum. **1952** A. HALD *Statistical Theory with Engin. Applications* xvii. 495 In sampling investigations of industrial products stratified sampling is often useful. For example, when a lot is being loaded a random sample of items may be taken from every truckload, the truckloads being the strata. **1960** *Jrnl. Amer. Statistical Assoc.* LV. 105 If the sample is allocated to the strata in proportion to the number of elements in the strata, it is virtually certain that the stratified sample estimate will have a smaller variance than a random sample of the same size. **1980** HAWKINS & WEBER *Statistical Analysis* xi. 295 Stratified sampling is appropriate only if the variable of interest is relatively homogeneous within strata and heterogeneous among strata.

¶ **d.** The form *strata* used as sing., with pl. *stratas*.

1937 *Times Lit. Suppl.* 27 Nov. 910/2 He marries a penniless girl of a lower social strata than himself. **1946** M. PEAKE *Titus Groan* 159 The mixture of cunning and honesty which he did not yet perceive to be a still deeper strata of Steerpike's cleverness. *Ibid.* 177 The abstract language with which they communicated their dizzy stratas of conjecture. **1971** *Timber Trades Jrnl.* 14 Aug. 20/2 The era of the family business is now a complex structure of top, middle and lower stratas. **1980** *Good Housekeeping* Nov. 181/4 After this comes a strata of accessories.

7. Delete ? *Obs.* **a.** (Later examples.)

1955 T. H. PEAR *Eng. Social Differences* i. 23 Within the wholesale trade there are interesting strata-differences. **1962** *Conveyancing (Strata Titles) Act* in *Statutes of New S. Wales 1961* 129 'Strata plan' means a plan which.. shows the whole or any part of the land comprised therein as being divided into two or more strata, whether or not any such stratum is divided into two or more lots. **1977** [see b below]. **1982** *Polit. Sci. Q.* XCVII. 482 The manipulation of ethnicity or of strata-local forces.

b. (in sing. form.)

1955 T. H. PEAR *Eng. Social Differences* vi. 144 Neighbouring families for whom class-consciousness..was usually submerged below stratum-consciousness. **1977** *Dædalus* Fall 73 Country-wide strata consciousness and a less pronounced stratum formation of ethnic, religious, or regional elements.

c. Special Combs.: **strata-bound** *a.*, confined to a single stratum or group of strata; **strata title** *Austral.* and *N.Z.*, the freehold or leasehold of or title to a stratum or storey (or more than one) of a building.

1962 *Econ. Geol.* LVII. 272 It is..reasonable to expect that a majority of strata-bound ore fields will be readily explainable on explicit grounds of tectonic history. **1979** *Nature* 15 Nov. 247/1 Uranium mineralisation, for the most part, is strata-bound and occurs in breccia matrix and vugs. **1962** *Statutes of New S. Wales 1961* 128 (*title*) Conveyancing (strata titles) act. **1977** *Courier-Mail* (Brisbane) 7 Apr. 17/2 Many strata title (home units) property owners risk serious financial loss because of inadequate legal insurance on their units. **1977** *N.Z. Herald* 5 Jan. 2–16/2 (Advt.), Home unit, Avondale, as new, strata title, 2 brms, internal garage.

Straussian (strau·siăn), *a.* and *sb.* [f. the name of (1) the German composer Richard *Strauss* (1864–1949), or (2) the Viennese family of composers of whom Johann *Strauss* II (1825–99) was the foremost member + -IAN.] **A.** *adj.* **1.** Of, pertaining to, or characteristic of the music of Richard Strauss.

1910 G. B. SHAW in *Nation* 19 Mar. 969/2 To those of us who are neither deaf nor blind nor anti-Straussian critics (which is the same thing), she was a superb Elektra. **1949** A. HUXLEY *Ape & Essence* ii. 24 Flawlessly pure of all Wagnerian lubricity and bumptiousness, all Straussian vulgarity! **1954** *Grove's Dict. Mus.* (ed. 5) VIII. 129/1 He wrote..some fine songs for voice and orchestra,..of which 'Hymnus' and 'Gesang der Apollopriesterin' (Op. 33) are the most characteristic of Straussian rapture. **1963** *Times* 8 Mar. 15/3 Earlier in the work he had not shown the same ability to sustain a true Straussian intensity of feeling. **1979** *Guardian* 26 Mar. 14/5 It was no disappointment to find Italian verismo rather than Straussian opulence.

2. Of, pertaining to, or characteristic of the music of the Strauss family.

1935 *Punch* 8 May 561/2 The scheme and time of the play..has prevented him from suggesting or—except in a brief snatch of the *Blue Danube*—borrowing from the glories of the Straussian epoch. **1958** *Listener* 21 Aug. 285/1 The commonplace of a Straussian waltz.

B. *sb.* An admirer of Richard Strauss; an exponent of his music.

1959 *Times* 17 Nov. 16/4 With that renowned Straussian, Mr. Rudolf Kempe, now..available to take charge, the London Symphony Orchestra assembled all its forces on Sunday..so that the second half of the programme could be devoted to *Also sprach Zarathustra.* **1967** *Guardian* 13 June 7/3 Straussians all think it [sc. *Die Frau ohne Schatten*] *the* masterpiece. **1977** *Gramophone* June 64/1 A lack of sensuousness and ardour in the first half of the work is something which many Straussians won't readily forgive.

stravaig, *v.* For *Sc.* and *north.* read *Sc.*, *north,* and *Ir.* and add further examples. Also in general literary use, and occas. *trans.* with *road* as obj.

1831 S. LOVER *Legends & Stories of Ireland* p. xxiv, *Stravaig*, to ramble. **1876** C. M. YONGE *Three Brides* I. xvi. 279 Her own children, which it is a shame to see stravaging about the place! **1929** E. BOWEN *Last September* I. viii. 93 They do be stravaging about always and not contented at all. **1934** T. E. LAWRENCE *Let.* 23 Nov.

38) 830 Visit it, sometime, if you still stravage the ls of England in a great car. **1958** S. BECKETT *From ndoned Work* 14, I might be sprawling in the sun sucking my pipe..wondering what there was for ier, instead of stravaging the same old road in all thers.

ravinskian (strävi·nskiăn), *a.* (and *sb.*). o **Stravinskyan.** [f. the name of *Stravinsky* e below) + -AN.] Of, pertaining to, or racteristic of the Russian-born composer or Fyodorovich Stravinsky (1882–1971) or music. Also as *sb.* = *STRAVINSKYITE.

925 F. TOYE *Well-Tempered Musician* iii. 74 vinsky himself was put up to defend Tchaikowsky, whom all the Stravinskians..had been constantly ring for years. **1947** D. MILHAUD in *Stravinsky's tics of Music* p. xi, The *Poetics of Music* brings to t the indissoluble relationship between the two ects of the Stravinskyan temperament: that is, his ic and his philosophy. **1958** *Times* 22 Feb. 3/7 hart had absorbed his Stravinskian predilection. 2 *Times* 29 Mar. 8/5 Sir William, whose attitude to cs is Stravinskyan..is ready to forecast critical tions to his work. **1968** *Listener* 1 Aug. 153/2 Britten's berant cantata..is informed by a Stravinskian nomy of gesture and dramatic style. **1978** *Gramophone* 174/1 The second [movement is] a sonata—very avinskian yet it could not be by Stravinsky but only Malcolm Williamson.

o **Stravi·nskyite**, a devotee of Stravinsky's sic.

924 C. GRAY *Survey Contemp. Music* 132 The devotees he Russian ballet, the Stravinskyites, seek the satis-ion of normal human activities in art. **1949** G. F. GHT in *Penguin Music Mag.* IX. 82 The majority of musical world divided into two irreconcilable camps: Stravinskyites and the Anti-Stravinskyites. **1961** *es* 12 Apr. 6/5 Elsewhere all praise—and a rap on the ckles for all those Stravinskyites who stayed at ne.

aw, *sb.*[1] Add: **I. 1. d.** The colour of straw, ale brownish-yellow.

799 in M. Edgeworth *Parent's Assistant* (1800) (ed. 3) 119 Mr. Davis, slate-color and straw. **1897** *Sears, buck Catal.* 231/2 Silk Mitts..in the following colors: cy blue, lemon, straw, cardinal. **1923** *Daily Mail* 19 . 5 A full range of new colourings, including Peach, non, Straw, Rose. **1942** *R.A.F. Jrnl.* 3 Oct. 15 A vy, oily liquid, from straw to black in colour. **1978** S. BYATT *Virgin in Garden* xi. 111 Red was defiance, l avarice, straw plenty. Green was hope, but sea-green inconstancy.

. *poppy straw*: see *POPPY *sb.* 8.

I. 5. g. (Earlier and later examples.) Now a. made from paper or plastic.

851 *London at Table* III. 52 *Mississippi Punch.* Let u use a glass tube or straw to sip the nectar through.) BARTLETT *Dict. Americanisms* (ed. 3) 90 *Cobbler*,..a k made of wine, sugar, lemon, and pounded ice, and ibed through a straw or other tube. **1888** RUSKIN *terita* III. ii. 57, I..saw the Bishop of Oxford taught Sir Robert Inglis to drink sherry-cobbler through a w. **1926** 'O. DOUGLAS' *Proper Place* xxxi. 286 She.. 1 had Alistair supremely happy drinking lemonade ugh a straw. **1926** [see *soda straw* s.v. *SODA[1] 7]. **1953** AN THOMAS in *Listener* 17 Sept. 459/2 They gave him ttle with a straw. **1967** R. A. WALDRON *Sense & Sense el.* vi. 116 A drinking-*straw* is nowadays usually made plastic. **1982** H. ENGEL *Ransom Game* viii. 45, I led for a vanilla shake... The straw stood up un-d in..the froth.

. Used as a means of deciding something by ance (lit. by choosing the shortest (or gest) from among several straws held so as conceal one end); phr. *to draw a straw* or *aws*, to draw a lot or lots.

832 [see DRAW *v.* 34]. **1939** WODEHOUSE *Uncle Fred Springtime* i. 13 It was the person on whom life had ast the..task who must be considered to have drawn short straw. **1959** R. BRADBURY *Day it rained Forever* Sundays we draw straws for who wears the suit the a night.

. c. (Earlier and later examples.) Now esp. *traw in the wind* (usu. in *pl.*).

1654 J. SELDEN *Table-Talk* (1689) 31 Take a straw throw it up into the Air, you shall see by that which the wind is. **1799** W. COBBETT *Porcupine's Works* 01) X. 161 'Straws' (to make use of Callender's old kneyed proverb) 'Straws serve to show which way the d blows.' **1823** BYRON *Don Juan* XIV. viii, You know don't know that great Bacon saith 'Fling up a straw, ll show the way the wind blows.' **1927** A. ADAMS *ach on Beaver* vii. 99 'As straws tell which way the d blows,' remarked Sargent, 'this day's work gives us lean line on these company cattle.' **1939** MADGE & RRISSON *Britain, by Mass-Observation* ii. 107 Yet ough agents in the constituencies, and straws in the d like West Leicester, came a slightly better indication popular sentiment. **1960** C. P. SNOW *Affair* xxv. 334 ere have been other things, straws in the wind, maybe, ch give reason to think that contemporary standards ong a new scientific generation are in a process of line. **1975** *Language for Life* (Dept. Educ. & Sci.) xii. These are straws in the wind. What they indicate is degree to which learning and the acquisition of lan-ge are interlocked. **1983** *Listener* 27 Jan. 3/1 As MPs e already pointed out in the debate, Captain Nick ker of HMS *Endurance* had detected straws in the d.

. *to have straws in one's hair* (and varr.): be insane, eccentric, or distracted.

1890 'L. CARROLL' *Nursery 'Alice'* x. 39 That's the March Hare, with the long ears, and straws mixed up with his hair. The straws showed he was mad—I don't know why. Never twist up straws among *your* hair, for fear people should think you're mad!] **1923** WODEHOUSE *Inimitable Jeeves* vii. 72 When your uncle the Duke begins to feel the strain a bit and you find him in the blue drawing-room sticking straws in his hair, old Glossop is the first person you send for. **1925** —— *Carry On, Jeeves!* vi. 142 His [*sc.* a psychiatrist's] outlook on life has become so jaundiced through constant association with coves who are picking straws out of their hair. **1937** D. L. SAYERS *Busman's Honeymoon* xviii. 346 (*heading*) Straws in the hair. **1962** 'S. WOODS' *Bloody Instructions* ix. 100 Dennis Dowling..brought with him an atmosphere of mingled drama and insanity. Antony thought: 'definitely straws in the hair' as soon as he opened the door.

10. e. *potato straw*: see *POTATO *sb.* 7.

f. A plastic phial in which bull semen is stored for artificial insemination.

1966 *Canad. Jrnl. Compar. Med. & Vet. Sci.* XXX. 109 The use of plastic straws would..encourage volume storage of high quality semen from young sires. *Ibid.* 111/1 Better fertility results can be anticipated with straw packaged semen as compared with that packaged in glass ampoules. **1982** *Sunday Times* 12 Sept. 45/2 The firm..specialises in artificial insemination..in cattle, and expects Pickles [*sc.* a bull] eventually to produce 40,000 'straws', or phials, of semen a year. These straws will be frozen, and sold to cattle breeders all over the world at about £50 a time.

III. 11. (Earlier examples.)

1829 P. EGAN *Boxiana* 2nd Ser. II. 681 *Hall*..went briskly into the ring, and tossed up his Dunstable straw. **1849** *Theatr. Programme* No. 5. 45/2 (Advt.), Charles Vyse, manufacturer of Leghorns and Straws to the British and Foreign Courts.—30 Ludgate-street.

IV. 13. a. *straw pulp.*

1888 CROSS & BEVAN *Text-bk. Paper-Making* vi. 101 The presse-pâte system is largely adopted for straw pulp. **1937** E. J. LABARRE *Dict. Paper & Paper-Making Terms* 238/2 Straw pulp is prepared by cooking straw with soda.

b. *straw-clutching.*

1962 L. DAVIDSON *Rose of Tibet* iii. 65 Every bit of straw-clutching, every bit of hope..was followed instantly by a reaction of dismay.

c. *straw-bottomed* ppl. adj.

1749 SMOLLETT tr. *Le Sage's Gil Blas* (1750) II. IV. xi. 137 We quitted the hermitage, leaving..two old straw-bottomed chairs.

14. straw ballot = *straw vote*; **straw basher** *slang*, a straw hat or boater; **straw-blond(e** *a.*, applied to hair of a pale, yellowish blond colour; also *absol.*, this colour; **straw-board** (earlier and later examples); also, a piece of this material; **straw boss** orig. *U.S.*, a subordinate or assistant foreman; **strawboy** *Ir.* (see quots.); **straw braid** (earlier example); **straw-bug** *slang*, a strawberry; **straw-dry** *a.*, as dry as straw, very dry; **straw-foot**: see *HAY-FOOT; **straw-gold**, the colour of straw; = sense 1 d above; **strawline**, a light rope used to pull a heavier one into position, esp. in Logging; **straw-man**, (*b*): delete *U.S.* and add examples; **straw-pale** *a. rare*[−1], as pale as straw; **straw poll** orig. *U.S.* = *straw vote*; **straw potatoes**, very thinly cut potato chips; **straw tick** *U.S.* [TICK *sb.*[2]], a straw-filled mattress; **straw vote**: for *U.S.* read orig. *U.S.* (earlier and later examples).

1932 Straw ballot [see *straw poll* below]. **1967** *Canad. Ann. Rev. 1966* 63 RIN..polled 27·7 per cent of the vote in a Université de Montréal straw ballot. **1901** Straw basher [see *BASHER[2]]. **1931** A. J. CRONIN *Hatter's Castle* II. xii. 421 A stiff, board-like straw-basher. **1928** E. O'NEILL *Strange Interlude* I. 25 Her straw-blond hair, framing her sunburned face, is bobbed. **1973** A. HUNTER *Gently French* v. 47 Her hair was a warm straw blonde. **1850** *Rep. Commissioner Patents 1849* (U.S. Patent Office) 305 [The] said process is peculiar to the use of strawboard. **1862** *Harper's Mag.* June 135/1 He was making a personal examination of straw-board shoes provided for those who have gone to be soldiers. **1885** G. F. GREEN in Rattray & Mill *Forestry & Forest Products* xviii. 474 Wood-pulp boards, straw-boards, and mill-boards are sometimes referred to as 'paste-boards'. **1956** H. WILLIAMSON *Methods Bk. Design* xix. 321 Millboards are harder and more solid than strawboards. **1894** W. H. CARWARDINE *Pullman Strike* ix. 117 These employees..had been so ground between the upper millstone of 'low wages' and the nether millstone of 'high rents', the continued oppression of the 'straw bosses', [etc.]. **1915** S. LEWIS *Trail of Hawk* II. xiii. 132 He had laughed away the straw boss who tried to make him go ask for a left-handed monkey-wrench. **1945** 'N. SHUTE' *Most Secret* viii. 172 Them Frenchies won't work right without they have a straw-boss. **1976** L. ST. CLAIR *Fortune in Death* x. 98 Dime-stores, cafeterias, moving to a new job..every time some greasy straw boss ran his hand up my skirt. **1894** C. R. BROWNE in *Proc. R. Irish Acad.* 3rd Ser. III. 352 Mr. Michael Lavelle..informs me that he has heard that sometimes, on the occasion of a wedding, 'straw-boys' go round with long straw masks on, and if they do not get either money or liquor will threaten to break the windows and furniture of the house. **1937** C. M. ARENSBERG *Irish Countryman* iii. 106 The 'strawboys'—privileged masqueraded figures whose mock-dangerous invasion of the wedding feast has been dignified to represent a last remnant of a primeval bride-capture. **1968** A. GAILEY in *Folk Life* VI. 90 In parts of Fermanagh there survive even to the present day traces of an old ceremony performed by groups of..young men, disguised latterly in..straw masks.., but in former times..wearing complete suits of straw. They interrupted the festivities following the solemnisation of marriages in the country districts, and were known simply as the Strawboys. **1864** *Harper's Mag.* Oct. 578/2 He laid all kinds of evil results at the door of straw braid. **1908** A. HUXLEY *Let.* 29 June (1969) 28 Latest News Stop Press Strawbugs for tea. **1959** I. & P. OPIE *Lore & Lang. Schoolch.* ix. 155 These syllables [*sc.* -*bug*, -*gog*, etc.] are used..to replace the second half of a word, as: newbug, rasbug, strawbug, goosegog, and wellygogs. **1951** W. DE LA MARE *Winged Chariot* 47 Unlike the plant called 'everlasting', this [*sc.* poetry] Never straw-dry, sapless, or sterile is. **1963** *Glamour* Nov. 23 Even hair that's straw-dry turns silky. **1963** A. LUBBOCK *Austral. Roundabout* 3 Here are fine expenses of pasture, turning to straw-gold in summer. **1977** J. AIKEN *Last Movement* i. 20 Her hair had been..a pale Scottish straw-gold. **1956** *Amer. Speech* XXXI. 152 *Strawline*,..a small-size wire rope which hauls the heavy logging cables into position. **1975** *Islander* (Victoria, B.C.) 22 June 7/4 A strawline was taken across the river by boat, then each cable was pulled to the other side by the horses. **1896** L. T. HOBHOUSE *Theory of Knowl.* 59 The straw man was easily enough knocked over by the critic who set him up. **1934** A. WOOLLCOTT *While Rome Burns* 76, I have often challenged one of these straw-man authorities. **1946** KOESTLER *Thieves in Night* 328 The authorities..only got the Rumanian captain and his crew, who couldn't give away much as all their dealings had been with straw men under assumed names. **1981** 'M. HEBDEN' *Pel is Puzzled* xviii. 180 He seemed active enough, but there seemed an awful lot lacking in him... Was he really just a straw man? **1922** W. B. YEATS *Seven Poems* 13 Under the shadow of stupid straw-pale locks. **1932** C. E. ROBINSON *Straw Votes* iv. 52 The newspaper or magazine conducting a straw poll by the ballot-in-the-paper method prints a straw ballot in the publication for a certain period of time before an election. **1944** *Chicago Tribune* 26 Oct. 12/2 (*heading*). New deal area lifts F.D.R. in N.Y. straw poll. **1958** *Spectator* 6 June 722/1 In my own straw poll I found two electors who were going to vote Liberal for the first time. **1978** *Nature* 6 Apr. 484/3 A straw poll taken three weeks ago at a meeting of faculty professors..voted 23 to 3 against approving the proposal. **1904** C. H. SENN *New Cent. Cookery Bk.* (rev. ed.) 596 Pommes Pailles (Straw Potatoes). **1959** *Times* 6 Apr. 13/5 Serve with sweet corn and straw potatoes. **1931** *Amer. Speech* VII. 169 Most of these [mattresses and ticks] were filled with corn husks, straw or hay, and were called 'husk ticks', 'hay mattresses', and 'straw ticks'. **1949** L. I. WILDER *Long Winter* viii. 68 They must fill the straw ticks with hay, because there was no straw in this new country. **1954** W. FAULKNER *Fable* 195 He was sleeping on a straw tick in the lodge room over the store. **1866** *Cleveland* (Ohio) *Leader* 6 Oct. 4/2 A straw vote taken on a Toledo train yesterday resulted as follows; A. Johnson 12; Congress, 47. **1887** *San Francisco Thunderbolt* 4 Nov. 1 The straw vote taken at the 'Report' office is unreliable. **1977** R. HOLLAND *Self & Social Context* v. 175 A special session on legal registration produced a straw vote which revealed an even balance of viewpoint.

strawberry. Add: **I. 1. b.** A sea anemone, probably a variety of *Actinia equina*, the body of which resembles a strawberry.

1856 G. TUGWELL *Man. Sea-Anemones* ii. 33 Here is 'the strawberry', whose body is mottled with red and green, after the fashion of that pleasant fruit. **1856** GEO. ELIOT *Jrnl.* 8 May–26 June in *Lett.* (1954) II. 243 It was a crescendo of delight when we found a 'Strawberry'..in a low tide pool. **1971** *Oxf. Bk. Invertebrates* 14/1 Particularly common is the 'strawberry' variant [of the beadlet anemone] in which the body is crimson with green spots.

c. The fruit of certain seaweeds resembling a strawberry. (Perhaps a misunderstanding by Kipling.)

1897 KIPLING *Capt. Cour.* iii. 53 The hook had fouled among a bunch of strawberries, red on one side and white on the other.

4. (Later examples.)

1897 *Sears, Roebuck Catal.* 222/1 They [*sc.* scarves] consist mostly of combination colors, just a few of which are blue, lavender, light green, cherry, strawberry, [etc.]. **1922** JOYCE *Ulysses* 492 A blond feeble goosefat whore in a tatterdemalion gown of mildewed strawberry lolls spread-eagle in the sofacorner. **1954** [see *ALIZARIN]. **1974** *Harrod's Xmas Catal.* 19 Luggage..in colourful Vinyl: light tan, orange, blue, or strawberry.

5*. Applied to things resembling a strawberry in shape or colour. **a.** An emery bag in the shape of a strawberry.

1903 K. D. WIGGIN *Rebecca of Sunnybrook Farm* vi. 66 She polished her needles to nothing, pushing them in and out of the emery strawberry. **1937** [see *emery cushion* s.v. *EMERY *sb.* 3]. **1976** P. CLABBURN *Needleworker's Dict.* 99/1 *Emery cushion* (emery bag, emery ball, strawberry), small pincushion, often in the shape of a strawberry, which is filled with emery powder... If needles become damp and rusty they are run through the cushion to make them shiny and smooth again.

b. A sore or bruise, esp. one caused by friction with the ground. *N. Amer. colloq.*

1921 *Daily Colonist* (Victoria, B.C.) 13 Oct. 11/4 'Strawberry', or open sore, on his hip, caused by sliding bases and constantly reopened. **1937** *Pittsburgh Press* 11 Jan. 27/5 Here are some expressions commonly used..; *Strawberry*, a bruise from sliding [etc.]. **1981** *Washington Star* 19 Mar. D 1 'Look at that,' he said, hitching up his knickerbockers to reveal matching strawberries just above both knees, red and angry-looking. At least, they used to call them 'strawberries'. He still does.

c. A nose having the colour of a strawberry, esp. as the result of heavy drinking.

1949 PARTRIDGE *Dict. Slang.* (ed. 3) Addenda 1188/1 *Strawberry*,..a red nose: Cockney's. **1980** C. SMITH *Cut-Out* ix. 62 His nose..had turned..to the characteristic boozer's strawberry.

II. 6. Also *strawberry pink, red.*
1939 JOYCE *Finnegans Wake* 207 The lellipos cream to her lippeleens and the pick of the paintbox for her pommettes, from strawbirry reds to extra violates. **1952** A. G. L. HELLYER *Sanders' Encycl. Gardening* (ed. 22) 113 [*Cirrhopetalum*] *Amesianum*, old gold, single haired, lower sepals strawberry-red. **1956** G. DURRELL *My Family & Other Animals* ii. 28 (*heading*) The strawberry-pink villa.

7. a. *strawberry bed* (later examples), *box* (also *fig.*).
1787 J. WOODFORDE *Diary* 15 Oct. (1926) II. 352, I was very busy this morning in my Garden making some new Strawberry Beds. **1892** W. B. YEATS *Countless Kathleen* ii. 34 My asparagus and strawberry beds Are trampled into clauber. **1936** 'R. HYDE' *Passport to Hell* vi. 93 Life just one strawberry-box after another. **1951** *Dict. Gardening* (R. Hort. Soc.) IV. 2042/1 An infected Strawberry bed should be cleared by burning all the plants. **1965** G. MCINNES *Road to Gundagai* iii. 35 All about us they [*sc.* passengers] were vomiting into 'strawberry boxes'.

b. *strawberry cream* (earlier example), *shortcake.*
1792 J. WOODFORDE *Diary* 26 June (1927) III. 359 Dinner..a very fine Leveret rosted, Strawberry Cream, Jelly. **1841** L. B. SWAN *Jrnl.* 20 June (1904) 28 We had a new dish, 'Strawberry Short Cake' very fine indeed. **1953** G. W. BRACE *Spire* xi. 93, I had strawberry shortcake... Hot biscuits, yellow cream, and quite often wild berries.

c. *strawberry-breasted.*
1878 G. M. HOPKINS *Poems* (1967) 77 Star-eyed strawberry-breasted Throstle.

8. strawberry bass (earlier and later examples); **strawberry blite,** substitute for def.: a herb, *Chenopodium capitatum*, with triangular leaves and heads of small flowers followed by fruit resembling a strawberry; (later examples); **strawberry blond(e)** *a.*, applied to hair of a light reddish blond colour; as *sb.*, the colour itself; a person with hair of this colour; **strawberry dish** *Silver-work* (see quot. 1977); **Strawberry Fields** *slang* [prob. f. *Strawberry Fields Forever*, title of a song (1967) by John Lennon and Paul McCartney] = *LSD^2; **strawberry guava,** a shrub or small tree, *Psidium cattleianum*, of the family Myrtaceæ, native to tropical America and bearing white flowers and large edible berries; also, the red or yellow fruit of this tree; **Strawberry Hill** *Archit.*, the name of the house in Twickenham bought in 1747 and rebuilt by Horace Walpole after the Gothic style, used *attrib.* to designate the style of early Gothic Revivalist architecture inspired and epitomized by this house; **strawberry perch** (earlier example); **strawberry pot,** a large garden pot with pockets in its sides, designed to contain growing strawberry plants; **strawberry tomato,** substitute for def.: *U.S.*, a ground-cherry of the genus *Physalis* or its edible fruit; (earlier and later examples); **strawberry tree,** (*b*) add: also = MADROÑO; (later examples); (*c*) (earlier and later examples); **strawberry weevil,** a small black and white beetle, *Anthonomus signatus*, found in eastern North America, where it lays its eggs in strawberry buds, so that no fruit is formed.
1867 T. F. DE VOE *Market Assistant* 294 Calico bass, speckled bass, or partridge-tailed bass.—This fish is also known among our fishermen as the 'strawberry bass'. **1947** B. W. DALRYMPLE *Panfish* 81 You'd think there be Strawberry Bass..in there. **1900** L. H. BAILEY *Cycl. Amer. Hort.* I. 290/2 The common Strawberry Blite..has been introduced to the trade as a pot-herb. **1943** FERNALD & KINSEY *Edible Wild Plants* iii. 180 The Strawberry-Blite, one of the most striking plants of Canadian clearings, on account of its masses of brilliant red pulpy fruits, may be used as a potherb like spinach. **1970** *Beaver* Winter 23 Strawberry spinach, also known as ..strawberry blite, is similar to its close cousin, lamb's quarters. **1884** E. W. NYE *Baled Hay* 98 That is what is ..sprinkling my strawberry blonde hair with gray. **1887** *Courier-Jrnl.* (Louisville, Kentucky) 6 Feb. 12/2 Seventeen young women, with hair ranging from strawberry blonde to deep crimson, are seated..on a long platform. **1895** PALMER & WARD *Band played On* (song) 4 Casey would waltz with a strawberry blonde, And the Band played on. **1958** *Daily Express* 17 Mar. 1/4 An unassuming strawberry blonde. **1977** B. BAINBRIDGE *Injury Time* ii. 19 Alma's hair, rinsed to an unusual shade of strawberry blonde. **1941** *Burlington Mag.* Aug. 68/1 A set of four strawberry dishes—also silver-gilt, by Paul Crispin, 1734. **1977** FLEMING & HONOUR *Penguin Dict. Decorative Arts* 766/1 *Strawberry dish*, a type of late C17–C18 English silver dish, deeper but no larger than a plate, rather thin with punched decorations in the C17, more substantial and usually with a scalloped rim in the C18. It is improbable that such dishes were used originally only for strawberries. **1971** *Tel.* (Brisbane) 27 Oct. 3/1 A youth had seven tablets of LSD, known as 'Strawberry Fields', when picked up in a city hotel by detectives. **1976** H. FERGUSON *Confessions Long Distance Acid Head* 22 Then came the fatal trip which led..to my fleeing to India to forget. I was on Blue Cheer, I think, though it could have been Strawberry Fields. **1901** L. H. BAILEY *Cycl. Amer. Hort.* III. 1460/2 Strawberry Guava. Shrub or small tree, 10–20 ft. high... Pulp fleshy, soft and juicy, purplish red next the skin,..sweet and acid, with a strawberry-like fragrance and flavor. **1976** *Monitor* (McAllen, Texas) 7 Nov. 1C/1 (*caption*) The strawberry guava, a shrublike tree, produces a fig-like fruit almost cherry-sized that can be eaten raw and can also be made into jellies. **1836** R. GRIFFIN *Hist. Audley End* v. 127 The chapel..was newly fitted up..according to the fashion of the day, with..clustered pilasters, and a groined ceiling, in the style called after its patron, *Strawberry Hill Gothic.* **1891** T. G. BONNEY in *Hist. Houses of United Kingdom* 90 A room..now serves as a chapel... It is..a specimen of Strawberry Hill Gothic. **1928** A. HUXLEY *Point Counter Point* xix. 344 The fantastic towers and pinnacles of Gattenden Castle, built..in the most extravagant style of Strawberry Hill Gothic. **1977** *Times* 6 Aug. 3/3 The eleventh duke [of Norfolk] rebuilt it [*sc.* Arundel Castle] in the Strawberry Hill baronial fantasy style. **1877** C. HALLOCK *Sportsman's Gazetteer* 378 Strawberry Perch. ..*Pomoxys hexacanthus.* **1946** M. FREE *All about House Plants* ix. 67 'Strawberry pots' made of earthenware.. are much used, suitably planted, for patio decoration in California. **1977** JELLICOE & ALLEN *Town Gardens to live In* xi. 125/2 (*heading*) A handmade strawberry pot. It will take twenty-eight plants. **1862** M. D. COLT *Went to Kansas* ix. 133 The strawberry tomatoes..are indigenous to the soil. **1919** E. L. STURTEVANT *Notes on Edible Plants* 432 *P. lanceolata*..was among the strawberry tomatoes grown at the New York Agricultural Experiment Station in 1886. **1969** *Oxf. Bk. Food Plants* 126/2 The ground cherry, which is also called 'Strawberry Tomato'.., is an annual, native in parts of eastern and central North America. **1792** A. MENZIES *Jrnl.* 2 May in *Menzies' Jrnl. of Vancouver's Voy.* (1923) 20 The Oriental Strawberry Tree..at this time a peculiar ornament to the Forest by its large clusters of whitish flowers & ever green leaves, but its peculiar smooth bark of a reddish brown colour will at all times attract the Notice of the most superficial observer. **1813** H. MUHLENBERG *Catalogus Plantarum Americæ Septentrionalis* 25 Euonymus *Americanus*, (burning bush, strawberry tree). **1838** J. C. LOUDON *Arboretum & Fruticetum Britannicum* II. 1117 The Arbutus, or Strawberry Tree...Robust evergreen shrubs, or low trees. **1866** *Trans. Illinois Agric. Soc.* VI. 391 The Strawberry Tree, with its delicate foliage, green wood and beautiful berries. **1975** D. MCCLINTOCK *Wild Flowers of Guernsey* 155 The Strawberry Tree..has established itself in Jersey. **1884** *Ann. Rep. Michigan State Hort. Soc. 1883* 155 This strawberry weevil..was described by Thomas Say. **1929** AUCHTER & KNAPP *Orchard & Small Fruit Culture* xiv. 486 Strawberry Weevil..lays its eggs in the flower buds and then girdles the stem so as to prevent further development. **1976** *Islander* (Victoria, B.C.) 30 May 10/2 Another expense was combating the strawberry weevil.

strawflower (strǭ·flau^ə^ɹ). *N. Amer.* [f. STRAW *sb.*^{1} + FLOWER *sb.*] = EVERLASTING *sb.* 4; esp. *Helichrysum bracteatum*, a perennial herb of the family Compositæ, native to Australia, whose variously coloured flowers are often dried and preserved.
1924 L. H. BAILEY *Man. Cultivated Plants* 786 Strawflower..frequently grown as an 'everlasting'. **1933** L. BLOOMFIELD *Language* x. 160 The *straw-* in *strawberry* is phonetically the same as the *straw-* in *strawflower.* **1972** F. MASON *Roads to Liberty* 10 She had tucked a pair of blue-dyed strawflowers into the dark hair above her ear.

straw hat. Add: Also **strawhat. 2.** *U.S. Theatr.* A summer theatre; a theatre operating during the summer only and presenting various productions or companies. Freq. *attrib.*
1935 *Variety* 12 June 62/4 (*heading*) Nearly 100 straw hat troupes will dot eastern landscape. **1936** A. GREEN in *Esquire* Sept. 160/3 A summer stock (legit) is a 'straw hat'. **1946** *Life* 5 Aug. 81/1 More than 125 straw-hat theaters now adorn the eastern sea-coast. **1948** *Sun* (Baltimore) 24 June 16/1 They appeared in the same roles last year on the strawhat circuit. **1952** *Ibid.* 10 June (B* ed.) 10/1 The play is not the thing this week at the Maryland strawhat. **1968** *N.Y. Times Bk. Rev.* 23 June VII. 5/4 They finagle their way into the strawhat dramatic workshop of a famous theater guru.

Hence **straw-hatter,** a straw-hat theatre, or play presented in one; **straw-hatting** *vbl. sb.*, work in straw-hat theatres.
1949 *N.Y. Times Mag.* 21 Aug. 24/4 The trick of operating a successful straw-hatter is to build up a steady clientele—a sizable number of people who get the habit of regular attendance because they have learned that the general average of production is good. **1950** *Wall St. Jrnl.* 4 Aug. 9 The Howard Lindsay-Russell Crouse straw hatter ('Life with Father') subsequently made Broadway. **1950** *Richmond* (Va.) *Times-Dispatch* 9 Dec. 5/1 Straw-hatting is arduous.

strawish, *a.* For †*Obs.* read *rare* and add later examples.
1598 J. FLORIO *Worlde of Wordes* 253/1 *Pagliaresco*, made of strawe, strawish. **1978** B. FREEMANTLE *Clap Hands* viii. 50 Thinning strawish hair... A very ordinary sort of man.

strawy, *a.* **4.** (Later example.)
1957 T. HUGHES *Hawk in Rain* 20 With love so like fire they dared not Let it out into strawy small talk.

straying, *vbl. sb.* **b.** For †*Obs. rare*$^{-1}$ read Now only *arch.* and add later examples.
1884 *Eng. Illustr. Mag.* Dec. 152/2 Thoughts that had gone astraying half across the globe. **1936** AUDEN *Look, Stranger!* 56 And Garbo's and Cleopatra's wits to go astraying.

stray-running, *ppl. a. rare*$^{-1}$. [f. STRAY *a.* or *v.*^{2} + RUNNING *ppl. a.*] That runs astray.
1914 D. H. LAWRENCE *Prussian Officer & Other Stories* 251 What am I frightened of him for? Why, for you, you stray-running little bitch.

streak, *sb.*^{1} Add: **2. g.** (Examples.)
1892 G. M. STERNBERG *Man. Bacteriol.* I. viii. 75 We commonly make a streak upon the surface of cooked potato or solidified blood serum in studying the development of various bacteria on these culture media. **1939** A. J. SALLE *Fund. Princ. Bacteriol.* ix. 133 The last streaks should thin out the culture sufficiently to give isolated colonies. **1969** SIROCKIN & CULLIMORE *Practical Microbiol.* ii. 17 It will be observed that away from the initial streak, the growth is less dense and discrete colonies are present.

h. *Hairdressing.* A strand or strands of hair fashionably tinted, esp. in a light colour. Cf. *HIGH LIGHT 1 b.
1949 *Queen* 21 Dec. 39 Light streaks are again fashionable. These can be tinted to match an evening dress—the colour can be washed out next day. **1956** ASHLEY & STEVENSON *Hair Design & Control* xi. 127 When introducing blonde streaks, or tipping, it assists to segregate the streak or section of hair concerned by means of a piece of cloth or Cellophane. **1966** J. S. COX *Illustr. Dict. Hairdressing* 144/1 *Streaks*, light strands of hair deliberately contrived to enhance the appearance. **1979** R. RENDELL *Make Death love Me* v. 40 She and Pam argued as to whether it was possible to put blonde streaks in one's hair at home.

3. c. *like a streak* (earlier examples). Also *quick as a streak* and *transf.*
1839 *Knickerbocker* XIII. 298, I see him yesterday afternoon..starting off like a streak, to go to Norridgewock. **1849** C. LANMAN *Lett. from Alleghany Mts.* xi. 89 The water wheeled my head round to the hole, and in I went quick as a streak. **1887** M. E. WILKINS *Humble Romance* 376 He went past me like a streak when I was coming up the road. **1920** C. SANDBURG *Smoke & Steel* 138 Maybe I will light out like a streak of wind.

d. *slang* (orig. *U.S.*). A rapid move; (a journey undertaken at) a fast rate. Also *fig.*
a **1861** T. WINTHROP *John Brent* (1862) xxii. 243 She's got the old man to take care of and follow off on his next streak. **1865** A. D. WHITNEY *Gayworthys* 141 She's going a good streak, ain't she? **1875** J. G. HOLLAND *Sevenoaks* iv. 60 We'll wopse 'im up in some blankits, an' make a clean streak for the woods. **1909** R. A. WASON *Happy Hawkins* 280 She was in the habit of estimatin' just how little nourishment it would take to run her to the next feed, gettin' it into her in the shortest possible time, an' then makin' a streak for it. **1960** *Twentieth Cent.* Dec. 556 His streak to stardom.

e. *to talk a streak*, to talk fast or constantly; *to talk a blue streak*: see *blue streak* (*b*) s.v. *BLUE *a.* 13.
1915 J. LONDON *Jacket* v. 37 He sleeps most of the watch, and we can talk a streak. **1968** T. WOLFE *Electric Kool-Aid Acid Test* xxvii. 373 Robertson's talking a streak. It's a grand speech.

4. b. *colloq.* (orig. *Austral.*). A tall, thin person.
1941 BAKER *Dict. Austral. Slang* 73 *Streak*, a tall, lean person. **1947** K. TENNANT *Lost Haven* iii. 57 Thank goodness he hadn't told that long, gabbling streak about Cherry. **1959** I. & P. OPIE *Lore & Lang. Schoolch.* ix. 169 There is a fusion of terms between those for the thin and lanky lad and those for the overgrown... Epithets include:..streak or streaker, Tower of London, walking barge pole, [etc.]. **1966** *Listener* 3 Mar. 317/1 That long streak of misery in a blue shirt.

6. b. (Earlier examples.) Also in phr. (*on*) *a losing* (or *winning*) *streak*, (experiencing) a series of losses (or wins). Hence, a series (of games, etc.) of a specified kind.
1843 *Knickerbocker* XXI. 303, I had 'struck a streak of bad luck'. **1865** 'MARK TWAIN' in Harte & 'Twain' *Sk. Sixties* (1926) 205 There never was a bad James in the Sunday-school books that had such a streak of luck as this sinful Jim. **1871** B. HARTE *Luck of Roaring Camp* 34 We've had a streak of bad luck since we left Poker Flat. **1912** C. MATHEWSON *Pitching in a Pinch* xi. 233 But what's a new hat against a losing streak or a batting slump? **1950** *Daily Ardmoreite* (Ardmore, Okla.) 30 Apr. D. 6/2 Last year's edition of the Indians set one of the hottest paces in the league before folding with a long losing streak. **1963** A. BARON *Lowlife* xi. 107 The old song inside my head, *don't be mad, don't walk out of a winning streak.* **1967** *Boston Globe* 5 Apr. 51/5 It is also fair enough to figure the 76ers will end the Celtics' streak of eight straight National Basketball Assn. titles. **1968** *Globe & Mail* (Toronto) 3 Feb. 35/6 Toronto Marlboros snapped Montreal Junior Canadiens' unbeaten streak at 10 games. **1972** 'H. CARMICHAEL' *Naked to Grave* xvi. 183 Mrs Davey won quite a lot of money... She said something to him about Mrs Davey's winning streak. **1973** G. MOFFAT *Deviant Death* ix. 125 The police were on a losing streak and they knew it. The questions were just form. **1980** *Times* 19 Feb. 11/5 Their winning streak includes the Boat Race record.

6*. Any of various virus diseases of plants which cause discoloured stripes to appear on their leaves; = *streak disease*, sense *7 below.
1930 *Discovery* June 196/1 Other important virus diseases of plants include..streak of maize,..and many others. **1936** J. JOHNSON in *Phytopathology* XXVI. 285 The writer has repeatedly observed a disease of tobacco in the field that is characterized by a necrosis of, or along, the veins of the leaf... The term 'tobacco streak' is.. proposed as perhaps the simplest and most suggestive for this malady. **1939** *N.Z. Jrnl. Sci. & Technol.* A. XX. 365 In New Zealand, pea-streak has not been observed other than at Palmerston North. **1952** GRAM & WEBER *Plant Dis.* iii. 387/2 Heavy dressings of stable manure make the symptoms of tomato streak worse. **1963** L.

Bos *Symptoms Virus Dis. in Plants* 39 The term 'streak', such as in 'cocksfoot streak' or 'pea streak', is confusive and insufficient. The name does not indicate whether the streak is chlorotic or yellow, such as in 'cocksfoot streak', or is necrotic, such as in 'pea streak'. **1977** J. KRANZ et al. *Diseases, Pests & Weeds in Tropical Crops* 21 Maize streak has not been reported from Europe or the Americas.

7. streak camera, a camera which uses the principles of streak photography; also, an electron-optical analogue of this allowing the resolution of events of the order of a picosecond duration and used esp. in high-speed spectroscopy (see quots. 1973, 1977); **streak culture,** substitute for def.: a bacterial culture made by drawing the point of an infected needle or the like over the surface of a solid culture medium; (earlier and later examples); **streak disease** = sense 6* above; **streak photography,** a form of photography in which film is automatically and rapidly moved past the open shutter of a camera, allowing a one-dimensional record of high-speed events to be made which can be reconstituted optically; so **streak photograph; streak plate,** (*a*) *Bacteriology,* (a vessel containing) a streak culture; (*b*) *Min.,* a small tablet of unglazed porcelain on which minerals may be rubbed to ascertain the colour of the streak (sense 2 d); **streak virus,** a virus causing a streak disease in plants.

1962 *Sci. Amer.* May 102/2 For this purpose we use a streak camera. **1973** *Ibid.* June 60/2 In the streak camera, which has an electronic circuit fast enough to measure picosecond events, light from a slit is focused onto a cathode where electrons are released and accelerated towards a phosphorus substance, which emits light. A voltage increasing with time..streaks the electrons across the phosphor so that electrons released at earlier times appear at a different position on the phosphor than electrons released later. **1977** *Jrnl. R. Soc. Arts* CXXV. 772/2 Direct linear measurement of pulse durations by electron-optical streak-cameras, in which the time-into-space transformation is brought about by deflecting an electron-optical slit image across the output phosphor of an image-tube. **1892** G. M. STERNBERG *Man. Bacteriol.* I. viii. 75 Koch made 'streak cultures' by drawing the point of a platinum needle, charged with bacteria, over the surface of a gelatin or agar plate. **1926** A. BULLEID *Text-bk. Bacteriol.* vii. 62 An examination of the culture tube with the naked eye will reveal the presence of 'colonies' on or in the medium, according to whether the culture was made on the surface (streak culture) or into the medium (stab or shake culture). **1923** W. F. BEWLEY *Dis. Glasshouse Plants* vi. 132 The organism from the tomato can cause a number of 'stripe' or 'streak' diseases of other plants. **1925** *Rep. Proc. Imperial Bot. Conf.* 132 (*heading*) Streak disease, an infectious chlorosis of sugar-cane. *Ibid.* 133 Streak disease in maize has been known in Natal for many years. **1938** *Jrnl. Agric. Res.* LVI. 747 A virus disease of peas.., manifested by a streaking of the stems and leaves and a spotting of the pods, was observed under greenhouse conditions..in the fall and winter of 1934. The disease.. resembles the streak disease described by Linford, in 1929, as occurring in pea fields throughout the United States. **1970** LIEBSCHER & KOEHLER tr. *Fröhlich & Rodewald's Pests & Dis. Tropical Crops* 240 Leaves [of sugar cane] infected with streak disease exhibit light-coloured, short and long streaks along the veins. **1950** *Jrnl. Appl. Physics* XXI. 448/2 (*caption*) Streak photograph illustrating the motion of the platform of the instrument shock testing machine. *Ibid.* 445/1 Methods of streak photography are easy to perform and can often be done with ordinary laboratory equipment. **1952** G. A. JONES *High Speed Photogr.* ix. 181 Streak photography is mainly of value in the case of luminous objects. **1980** *Sci. Amer.* May 102/2 The course of growth over time also appears to be continuous, as can be seen in time-lapse motion pictures, multiple-exposure photographs and streak photographs. (A streak photograph is made with a camera in which the lens is left open and the film moves at a constant speed.) **1895** *Buck's Handbk. Med. Sci.* Suppl. 83/1 'Streak-plates' are made on gelatine and agar, after the medium has been poured in the plates and become solidified, by drawing an infected needle across them in four or five parallel courses. **1898** BRUSH & PENFIELD *Man. Determ. Mineral.* (ed. 15) v. 228 The streak of a mineral..may be quickly determined by rubbing it on a piece of white, unglazed porcelain... Pieces of unglazed porcelain, called streak-plates, are made especially for this purpose. **1964** J. SINKANKAS *Mineral. for Amateurs* viii. 202 Hematite crystals appear quite black, but when rubbed across a porcelain streak plate, the characteristic deep red trace shows the true color. **1966** *McGraw-Hill Encycl. Sci. & Technol.* III. 616/2 Streak plates are incubated in a closed vessel in which the air is replaced by an inert oxygen-free gas. **1930** *Ann. Appl. Biol.* XVII. 623 Our maize streak virus was taken from a naturally streaked maize plant. **1948** *Phytopathology* XXXVIII. 421 To determine the incidence of the streak virus in wild and crop plants, collections were made in areas near infected tobacco fields.

streak (strīk), *sb.*^{2} *slang* (orig. *U.S.*). [f. *STREAK *v.*^{2} 6 c.] An act of running naked in a public place; = *STREAKING *vbl. sb.* 4. Also *attrib.* Cf. STREEK, STREAK *v.* 5 in Dict. and Suppl.

1974 *Newsweek* 4 Feb. 63/3 A student who participated with 125 others in a co-educational streak has been suspended from school. **1974** *Daily Tel.* 11 Mar. 16 High spirits may account for some streaks, and sheer frustration or a desire to insult society for others. **1974** *Newsweek* 18 Mar. 42/3 Any number of other streak-watchers didn't react at all. **1980** *Times* 5 Jan. 3/5 [He] ran down Dean Street, Soho, on New Year's Eve, wearing only shoes while taking part in a 'streak' for charity.

streak, *v.*^{2} Add: **2. b.** *Bacteriology.* To draw an infected needle or the like lightly over the surface of a solid culture medium in order to initiate a culture in which there is a varied density of growth: used with either the needle or the medium as obj. Also, to transfer (a bacterial specimen) in this way.

1910 [implied at *STREAKING *vbl. sb.* 1]. **1927** R. A. KELSER *Man. Veter. Bacteriol.* vi. 70 By going to the end of the streak with a sterile needle and streaking that portion down, the end of such down streak will contain but very few bacteria. **1934** A. T. HENRICI *Biol. of Bacteria* xii. 203 It is often advisable to streak a second or even a third plate without recharging the wire loop. **1949** KELLY & HITE *Microbiology* xi. 147 The specimen is streaked out with a sterile inoculating needle. **1969** SIROCKIN & CULLIMORE *Practical Microbiol.* ii. 17 Streak out a loopful of the broth culture using the aseptic techniques described. **1976** WILLIAMS & SHAW *Micro-Organisms* x. 124 (*caption*) Streaking a plate with pure cultures. **1977** *Lancet* 29 Oct. 906/1 A bacteriological loop is used to sweep across the surface of a young culture of the isolate and is then streaked across one end of the strip. **1980** *Nature* 21 Feb. 793/1 Faecal specimens were collected on sterile 'Cultures'..and streaked onto MacConkey plates.

c. *Hairdressing.* To tint (the hair) with streaks (*STREAK *sb.*^{1} 2 h). Cf. *STREAKING *vbl. sb.*^{1} 3.

1965 R. CORSON *Fashions in Hair* xiv. 625 Women developed an experimental urge and began streaking their hair.

6. a. (See STREEK, STREAK *v.* 5. The spelling *streak* is now standard, probably through assoc. of the vb. with STREAK *sb.* 3 c.) (Further examples in gen. use.)

1768 A. ROSS *Fortunate Shepherdess* 51 O'er hill an' dale she forcefully did dreel; A' road to her was bad an' gueed alike, Nane o't she wyl'd, but forret still did streak. **1834** *New Monthly Mag.* XLI. 465 Away we 'streaked' at the rate of twelve miles an hour against the current. **1888** P. GILLMORE *Days & Nights by Desert* xx. 170 True, it was wounded; but as it 'streaked' across the plain, from the pace it was going, no one would have thought so. **1915** H. ROSHER *In Royal Naval Air Service* (1916) 50, I climbed to 2,000 feet and streaked off over the Channel. **1931** *Punch* 28 Oct. 456/1 The village kids..used to spend most of their leisure in pushing the door ajar in order to set it [*sc.* an electric bell] going and then streak for home. **1955** 'A. GILBERT' *Is she Dead Too?* vii. 128 'So you opened the door—' 'And Tom [*sc.* a cat] streaked out.' **1973** E. LEMARCHAND *Let or Hindrance* viii. 94, I got out at last, and streaked up to the bungalow.

b. *trans.* To cause to move fast or like lightning.

1912 W. DEEPING *Sincerity* xviii. 137 She shot well, very few of her arrows streaking their way through the sunlight to stand slantingly in the grass. **1928** *Daily Express* 19 June 17/2 He hit only three 4's, and..streaked one from Staples dangerously through the slips when 28. *Ibid.* 25 June 17 Chapman..'streaked' several shots through the slips. **1970** J. HOWARD *Please Touch* 2 When supersonic transports streak 330 passengers to their destinations.

c. *intr.* To run naked in a public place as a stunt. Cf. *STREAK *sb.*^{2} *slang* (orig. *U.S.*).

1973 [implied at *STREAKING *vbl. sb.*^{1} 4]. **1974** *Runner's World Mag.* Feb. 9/1 During the winter of 1958–9 a group of us 'streaked' all over Berkeley. **1974** *Daily Tel.* 5 Mar. 3/6 At Memphis State University, the dean issued a warning that students caught 'streaking' would be suspended. **1974** *Globe & Mail* (Toronto) 18 Mar. S1/1 Phil Esposito, stripped as though to streak, held court in the cluttered quarters, tall, dark, unquiet. **1979** *Daily Tel.* 12 Jan. 9/3 The girls..had danced on the lawns in the nightdresses, 'streaked' to chapel and enjoyed midnight parties.

Hence **strea·ker**^{2}, one who runs naked in a public place; also *attrib.*; **streak-in** [*-IN^3], a communal act of running naked in a public place.

1973 *Time* 10 Dec. 14/2 Streakers generally race nude between two unpredictable points. **1974** *Newsweek* 4 Feb. 63/3 One Los Angeles radio station broadcast 'streaker alerts' to warn the populace that naked youths were on the loose. **1978** D. BLOODWORTH *Crosstalk* xiii. 104 The streaker had invaded the Brasserie Lipp in Paris at lunch-time. **1978** J. IRVING *World according to Garp* xi. 210 A young woman had reported that she was approached by an exhibitionist—at least, by a streaker. **1974** *Kingston* (Ontario) *Whig-Standard* 8 Mar. 3/2 The mass streak-in started near Victoria and Leonard Halls. **1974** *Times* 9 Mar. 4/8 Some of the students were arrested when a 'streak-in' turned into a riot.

streaking, *vbl. sb.* (In Dict. s.v. STREAK *v.*^{2}). Add:

1. (Examples in *Bacteriology*: cf. *STREAK *v.*^{2} 2 b.)

1910 HISS & ZINSSER *Text-bk. Bacteriol.* viii. 148 (*heading*) Separation of bacteria by surface streaking. **1949** KELLY & HITE *Microbiology* xi. 147 Though the streaking must be done carefully and according to some plan, it must be performed speedily. **1973** R. G. KRUEGER et al. *Introd. Microbiol.* iv. 169/1 Aerobic organisms..are inoculated onto the surface of the solidified medium by a procedure called streaking.

2. *Television.* A picture condition in which the trailing edges of areas of a particular colour are extended by streaks of the complementary colour.

1956 AMOS & BIRKINSHAW *Television Engin.* II. (*caption facing* p. 27) An image of test card C as reproduced by a video-frequency amplifier giving short-term streaking. **1975** B. GROB *Basic Television* (ed. 4) xix. 411 The streaking is especially evident trailing to the right after the edges of numbers or letters in the picture... The cause is phase distortion with time delay for low video frequencies up to about 200 kHz.

3. *Hairdressing.* (See quot. 1966.)

1966 J. S. COX *Illustr. Dict. Hairdressing & Wigmaking* 144/1 *Streaking,* the bleaching of a few strands of hair in the coiffure. **1975** *Time Out* 30 May 63/4 (Advt.), Streaking including cut & blow £5.50. **1976** *Southern Even. Echo* (Southampton) 3 Nov. 2/3 (Advt.), Fashion cutting, blow drying, shampoo and set and streaking.

4. The act of running naked in a public place. Cf. *STREAK *v.*^{2} 6 c, *STREAK *sb.*^{2}

1973 *Time* 10 Dec. 14/2 Another statistic in a growing Los Angeles-area fad: streaking. **1974** *Washington Post* 6 Mar. B3 Lady Godiva established the political importance of streaking. **1977** D. MORRIS *Manwatching* 210 The phenomenon of 'streaking'..is a strange example of an act that *only* has value as a deliberate Overexposed Signal.

streaky, *a.* Add: **2. b.** Also *absol.* as *sb.*

1969 *Listener* 17 Apr. 535/3 An angst-ridden fly on the ceiling: 'What is my life? Hanging about dustbins, crawling up drains, promiscuous sex on a rasher of *streaky.* There must be more to life than just pleasure.' **1973** *Tel.* (Brisbane) 5 Apr. 29/3 If she [*sc.* a housewife] wants half-a-pound of streaky she is likely to be called 'dear' by Britain's grocers. **1979** A. PARKER *Country Recipe Notebk.* vi. 82 Pot-roasted pork streaky (belly of pork) is better cold than hot.

stream, *sb.* Add: **2. f.** (*a*) (Later example.)

1937 W. R. INGE *Rustic Moralist* IV. i. 234 What ought the helpless *intelligentsia* to do? Not to float with the stream, a feat which any dead dog can accomplish.

4. f. See *ON STREAM *adv. phr.* and *a.*

6. a. Examples of time considered as a continuous flow.

1597 SHAKS. 2 *Hen. IV* IV. i. 70 Wee see which way the streame of Time doth runne. **1739** HUME *Treat. Hum. Nature* II. III. 276 When we turn our thought to a future object, our fancy flows along the stream of time. **1846** J. S. MILL in *Edin. Rev.* Oct. 356 Authentic history, as we ascend the stream of time, grows thinner and scantier. **1896** L. T. HOBHOUSE *Theory of Knowl.* II. xix. 465 Think of the whole page as the stream of time advancing from the top downwards. **1914** B. RUSSELL *Our Knowl. External World* vi. 167 A truer image of the world..is obtained by picturing things as entering into the stream of time from an eternal world outside.

d. *stream of thought* = *STREAM OF CONSCIOUSNESS.

1890 W. JAMES *Princ. Psychol.* II. xix. 79 This consciousness must have the unity which every 'section' of our stream of thought retains so long as its objective content does not sensibly change. **1921** J. VARENDONCK *Psychol. of Day-Dreams* iv. 293 Only such terminations of fore-conscious streams of thought as are in relation with acknowledged desires..of our conscious life can come to the surface. **1938** W. S. MAUGHAM *Summing Up* 223 Of the other experiments that have been made [by the novelist] the most important is the use of the stream of thought... It was tempting to explore greater depths of character by an imaginative picture of the subconscious of the persons of his invention. **1961** *John o' London's* 2 Feb. 109/3 The author includes many.. remarks..on the Ulysses characters, providing fascinating insights into what Joyce was getting at with his stream-of-thought vignettes.

e. *Educ.* A division in a school according to ability or to subjects studied; a group of pupils selected in this way.

1938 [see *MULTILATERAL *a.* 4]. **1946** M. L. JACKS *Total Education* iv. 59 The Headmaster of a Senior School tells me that his main difficulty lies not with the A stream nor with the C stream,..but with that solid mass in the middle. **1953** *Manch. Guardian* 11 May 6/10 On entry at eleven, each child is given intelligence tests and group tests in arithmetic and English, and on the result is placed in the appropriate stream (both the Douglas schools have a six-stream, Ramsey a four, and Castle Rushen a three-stream entry). **1959** *Observer* 20 Dec. 22/2 Perhaps we can totter along somehow, and for a time, by prolonging the 'stream' system into university education. **1966** J. PARTRIDGE *Middle School* iii. 41 It is clearly recognized that the 'A' stream contains the most intelligent boys and the 'D' stream the least. **1977** J. AIKEN *Last Movement* i. 31, I never actually taught her..because she was in the science stream and I was tutoring in business methods.

9. a. *stream-name.*

1922 E. EKWALL *Place-Names of Lancashire* 25 It *might* be an old stream-name..and might have given name to the forest. **1960** P. H. REANEY *Orig. Eng. Place-Names* v. 81 It is also possible that this (and other names) may contain a stream-name *ec(c)les*, as in Ecchinswell.

b. *stream-cut* adj., *-cutting* vbl. sb.

1970 R. J. SMALL *Study of Landforms* ix. 314 Pediments form not at the bases of fault-scarps but beneath the retreating walls of stream-cut valleys. **1973** *Nature* 2 Mar. 40/1 In a streamcut channel, the Ganurgarh shales intercalated with limestone have been exposed. **1957** G. E. HUTCHINSON *Treat. Limnol.* I. i. 47 Since there is little or no stream-cutting below such lakelets, they may persist longer than do the lakes dammed by the main mass of the slide.

c. stream-flow orig. *U.S.*, flow of water in streams and rivers; the rate or amount of this in any one stream or from any particular area; **stream function** *Physics,* a mathematical function of position defined so that lines along which it has a constant value are the streamlines of a flow or the lines of force of a field.

1902 W. P. MASON *Water-Supply* (ed. 3) vi. 269 The forest acts as a 'governor' of stream flow, rather than as a means of increasing precipitation. **1922** GLAZEBROOK *Dict. Appl. Physics* I. 498/2 It has been possible..to deduce the total run-off or stream flow from a drainage area from the difference of rainfall and the computed evaporation over that area. **1971** *Sci. Amer.* Sept. 142/3 The cooling water required by power plants already constitutes 10 percent of the total U.S. streamflow. **1979** *Bull. Amer. Meteorol. Soc.* LX. 560 (*heading*) A method for assessment of effects on streamflow by orographic cloud seeding in the Colorado Rocky Mountains. **1879** H. LAMB *Treat. Math. Theory Motion of Fluids* iv. 67 If *P* move about in such a manner that the value of ψ does not alter, it will trace out a curve such that no fluid anywhere crosses it, *i.e.* a stream-line. Hence the curves ψ = const. are the stream-lines, and ψ is called the 'stream-function'. **1937** S. L. GREEN *Hydro- & Aero-Dynamics* ii. 19 When $w = \phi + i\psi$ is a function of $z = x + iy$ the conditions $\phi_x = \psi_y$, $\phi_y = -\psi_x$ are satisfied, and these conditions are exactly the same as those satisfied by the velocity potential and the stream function for an irrotational motion in two dimensions. **1979** BERTIN & SMITH *Aerodynamics for Engineers* ii. 44 The existence of a stream function is a necessary condition for a physically possible flow.

stream, *v.* Add: **II. 14.** *Educ.* In a school, to divide (pupils) into streams (sense *6 e); to place (a pupil) in a stream.

1957 *Listener* 12 Dec. 997/1 The Russians..neither stream nor select their children... All are expected to reach a common standard. **1966** J. PARTRIDGE *Middle School* iii. 41 The boys are thus streamed according to recognized ability. **1973** *People's Jrnl.* (Inverness & Northern Counties ed.) 4 Aug. 9/2, I suppose they had their problems trying to get me 'streamed'. **1980** *Times* 7 May 15/3, I got myself streamed at Manchester Grammar towards the sciences.

streamed, *a.* Restrict † *Obs.* to sense in Dict. and add: **2.** *Educ.* Of a school, esp. a comprehensive school: organized in classes of pupils of like rather than mixed ability. Also of pupils: grouped according to ability.

1962 *Guardian* 30 Mar. 10/5 There are some very good streamed schools. **1968** *Listener* 4 July 8/3 In streamed comprehensive schools..all advantages lie with the children of middle-class parents. *a* **1974** R. CROSSMAN *Diaries* (1977) III. 391 She has got four different streamed groups and a fifth group of backward children. **1978** *Times* 28 July 4/8 The bottom classes of streamed schools..often.. get the worst teachers.

streamer, *sb.* Add: **2. f.** A long narrow strip of coloured paper used as a festive decoration or rolled up to unwind when thrown (at a celebration, etc.).

1857 C. M. YONGE *Dynevor Terrace* I. xvi. 262 The [Christmas] tree became more laden, and the streamers and glass balls produced a more brilliant effect. **1918** A. BENNETT *Jrnl.* 14 Nov. (1932) II. 242 The feature of last night was girls with bunches of streamers which they flicked in your face as you passed. **1930** E. RICE *Voyage to Purilia* xii. 155 The room was gay, with streamers of coloured paper and with large gas balloons. **1959** M. SHADBOLT *New Zealanders* 239 She..found herself waving farewell to her tearful parents from the deck of a ship. Only then, as the tangling streamers snapped across the widening water, did she remember to be surprised at herself. **1980** *Daily Tel.* 25 Nov. 15/6 This useful company also supplies carnival and party novelties including balloons.., dance streamers,..lucky dip prizes and stocking fillers.

g. = *BANNER *sb.*[1] 2 c. Also *transf.*

1909 G. R. CHESTER *Making of Bobby Burnet* xix. 230 Use two-inch streamers clear across the page. **1922** U. SINCLAIR *They call me Carpenter* 88 The headlines flamed before my mind's eye—streamer heads, all the way across the sheet. **1938** F. D. SHARPE *Sharpe of Flying Squad* xxv. 254 Then a very good crime reporter called a portico thief a cat-burglar and the story got a streamer headline. **1957** [see *BANNER *sb.*[1] 2 c]. **1963** *Times* 19 Apr. 8/5 Invitations to browse in these places, moreover, occasionally decorate the discreet vans of the Stationery Office. But this form of streamer on the van is technically known as a 'filler', which means that it is used only when the space is not required for boosting some new publication.

h. *Angling.* A fly with feathers attached, which simulates a small fish; also, the feathers so employed. Freq. *attrib.*, chiefly as *streamer fly.* orig. and chiefly *U.S.*

1919 D. CARROLL *Fishing, Tackle & Kits* 265 The white bucktail with the red feather streamers in the shape of a tail made the trout strike. **1929** *Field & Stream* June 65/3 (Advt.), Dixie Wiggler..different colored streamers. **1930** *Forest & Stream* Mar. 202/2 A lure which is justly famous in a few restricted localities..is the Streamer Fly... This fly is tied in more or less conventional hackle style with a two- or three-inch streamer feather as a tail. **1952** J. VENIARD *Fly Dressers' Guide* xiii. 140 *Streamer Flies.* This type of fly is immensely popular in America, but its possibilities in the United Kingdom have never been seriously considered. The nearest approach we have to it is the 'lure', which consists usually of two or three hooks in tandem with a long wing. The idea is very much the same..the main difference being that many of the 'streamers' are tied to represent the small fish on which game fish feed, whereas most of the lures are just brightly coloured 'attractors'. **1971** K. DRAPER *Trout Flies in N.Z.* ii. 41 One of the most popular types of tie is the Parson's Glory style of streamer. This fly is closely allied to the American streamer fly which is tied in much the same manner except that the long neck or saddle hackles 'stream' free. **1975** D. J. COLLYER *Fly-Dressing* xi. 167 Seven years ago I received..two very interesting flies, both streamers..designed by Lew Oatman, an American, to imitate small fish.

3. b. Restrict † *Obs.* to sense in Dict. and add: In mod. use, a long, thin component or appendage of the tail of some comets.

1909 G. F. CHAMBERS *Story of Comets* iii. 23 Although comets usually have but one tail, 2 are not uncommon, whilst even that number is often increased by the presence of slender streamers, which are virtually independent tails. **1931** [see *JET *sb.*[2] 4 c (i)]. **1972** D. C. KNIGHT *Comets* 13 The tail of Donati's comet of 1858 was some 50 million miles long..and was split into two or three streamers.

f. A filamentary luminosity sometimes seen to extend from an electrode in a gas when the potential difference is not great enough to produce a spark or arc; a similar feature that extends from a cloud or something on the ground prior to a stroke of lightning along the same path.

1910 *Encycl. Brit.* V. 883/1 Bright curved streamers starting from the negative terminal. **1934** *Physical Rev.* XLVI. 101/2 The breakdown in argon is similar to that in helium except that no glow discharge is observed and no anode streamer forms. **1935** *Proc. R. Soc.* A. CLII. 597 The leader to the first stroke consists of a series of streamers moving downwards in a step-by-step manner. **1953** MEEK & CRAGGS *Electr. Breakdown of Gases* iii. 159 In a 6-cm. gap with a 0·05-mm. point, the streamers gradually lengthen, as the voltage is raised, to 1·1 cm. and then breakdown occurs. **1972** *Jrnl. Physics D* V. 2179 Photomultiplier investigations..have shown that the streamers are weakly luminous channels, and that almost all the ionization phenomena are concentrated at their tip. **1979** J. G. NAVARRA *Atmosphere, Weather & Climate* ix. 298 When the leader stroke approaches the ground, a discharge streamer is extended from the ground up to the leader and completes the channel.

6*. [f. the sb.] *Educ.* With a categorizing letter prefixed: a child belonging to that stream in a school, or one whose abilities are adapted to such a stream; esp. *C-streamer,* a child of little academic ability.

1966 *Guardian* 4 Apr. 6/1 C-stream children in a competitive society have the makings of failure before they start... Let us take it that eventually the C-streamer has been taught to read. **1967** *Punch* 20 Dec. 952/3 These.. riddles will hold ten-year-olds enthralled until *next* Christmas—or even, in the case of certain C-streamers, the one after. **1970** *Sunday Times* (Colour Suppl.) 18 Jan. 8/1 They are C-streamers, from poor homes.

7. b. *Physical Chem.* Applied to a type of molecular orbital possessing a single nodal plane and formed out of identical atomic orbitals of the same phase from each of the atoms in the ring or chain backbone of the molecule.

1966 PHILLIPS & WILLIAMS *Inorg. Chem.* II. xxvii. 348 The lowest benzene π (aromatic) orbitals of the 'streamer' kind, one from each benzene, have nodes only in the planes of the benzene rings, and taken in combination are therefore either of the A_{1g} or A_{2u} type symmetry. **1974** GILL & WILLIS *Pericyclic Reactions* iv. 117 The lowest hexatriene level (ψ_1) is the typical 'streamer' orbital (i.e. $\pm\pm\pm\ \pm\pm\pm$) which is of *A* symmetry with respect to C_{2y} and of *S* symmetry with respect to the mirror plane σ_{yz}.

streaming, *vbl. sb.* Add: **f.** *Educ.* The practice of dividing pupils in a school into streams (sense *6 e). Also, the allocation of pupils to different schools according to ability.

1954 *Brit. Jrnl. Psychol* XLV. 147 Present methods of streaming in primary and secondary schools do not give the more backward as good a chance to make up. **1961** *New Left Rev.* Jan.–Feb. 6/2 A streaming system..with secondary modern, technical and grammar-type schools. **1966** D. JENKINS *Educated Society* v. 200 An argument for turning all Secondary schools into Comprehensive schools with a strong streaming system. **1971** *Where* Sept. 262/2 The practice of streaming—classifying children according to their abilities in reading, writing and arithmetic—is gradually becoming suspect. **1980** *Daily Tel.* 10 Dec. 16/6 The proposals include phasing out of church schools, single sex schools, and streaming.

streaming, *ppl. a.* Add: **1. b.** Of a cold: accompanied by copious running of the eyes and nose.

1923 W. R. INGE *Lay Thoughts* (1926) III. vii. 229 Persons..suffering from streaming colds, which are quite as infectious as..mumps or chicken-pox. **1982** *Guardian Weekly* 26 Dec. 22/1 One is sorry for foreigners, both as a Christian duty and because they tend to have streaming colds.

stream-line, *sb.* Add: Now usu. **streamline. 1. a.** Also *Aerodynamics.* In mod. use, a line such that, at any instant, the direction of the tangent at any point is the direction of the flow of fluid at that point. (This definition is equivalent to that in Dict. for the special case of steady flow.) (Earlier and later examples.)

1868 W. J. RANKINE in *Engineer* 16 Oct. 285/1 A stream-line is the line, whether straight or curved, that is traced by a particle in a current of fluid. **1945** R. VON MISES *Theory of Flight* ii. 23 In the case of an unsteady flow the streamlines, *i.e.*, the curves whose tangents have the velocity direction are, in general, not the pathways of the particles. **1971** G. M. HIDY *Waves* iv. 47 Streamlines generally bear no relation to particle paths because different fluid elements form different streamlines at given times. **1980** BOBER & KENYON *Fluid Mech.* iv. 124 If the flow is steady then a fluid particle will move along a streamline.

b. *attrib.* (*a*) Designating motion of a fluid that is free from turbulence, so that it can be represented by a pattern of streamlines that either is constant or changes steadily with time.

1898 [in Dict.]. **1916** H. BARBER *Aeroplane Speaks* 62 To secure a stream-line motion of the air free from eddies. **1957** G. E. HUTCHINSON *Treat. Limnol.* I. v. 251 The only simple way of observing regular streamline or laminar flow is adjacent to some smooth surface over which a slow current is passing. **1979** A. L. LYDERSEN *Fluid Flow & Heat Transfer* i. 2 This type of motion, where the velocity at a certain point is constant and independent of time, is termed laminar flow. It is sometimes called streamline flow or viscous flow.

(*b*) Having or being a shape such that the flow of a fluid round it is smooth, and there is no separation of streamlines from the surface; more widely, shaped so as to reduce air or water resistance; *streamline wire,* a wire of elongated cross-section.

1907 F. W. LANCHESTER *Aerodynamics* i. 20 In an actual fluid, bodies of other than streamline form experience resistance apart from that directly due to viscosity. *Ibid.* iii. 102 In the hydrodynamic theory of an inviscid fluid, every conceivable body is of stream-line form. **1909** [in Dict.]. **1914** *Automobile Topics* 30 May (Advt., back cover), That beautiful stream-line Car. **1918** W. L. COWLEY *Aeronautics* iv. 93 The following table gives the resistance coefficients of aeroplane stream line wires, of fineness ratio 3:1. **1919** G. WHALE *Brit. Airships* 160 The remaining two engines are carried in a small streamline car situated amidships. **1928** E. CADBURY in C. F. S. Gamble *Story North Sea Air Station* xxii. 408, I..seized a scarf, goggles and helmet, tore off my streamline coat, and, semi-clothed..took a running jump into the pilot's seat. **1929** *Jrnl. R. Aeronaut. Soc.* XXXIII. 360 In aeronautical nomenclature a 'streamline body' is one about which the flow of a real fluid..approximates very closely to a steady flow of the hypothetical inviscid fluid, except in a very thin layer called the 'boundary layer', surrounding the exposed surfaces. *Ibid.* 361 The ideally streamline aeroplane cannot exist. **1936** J. C. CORLETT *Rigging & Airframes* v. 108 On the final inspection of streamline wires they must be checked for 'safety'. **1953** M. RAUSCHER *Introd. Aeronaut. Dynamics* vi. 259 The theory of the ideal fluid comes very close to representing the actual flow conditions about a streamline body in a fluid of low viscosity.

(*c*) *fig.*

1933 S. SPENDER *Poems* 44 Where only a low streamline brightness Of phosphorus on the tossing hills is white. **1942** *R.A.F. Jrnl.* 2 May 21 The camp is the last word in streamline modernity. **1967** B. J. BANFILL *Pioneer Nurse* xi. 129 Snow, in long streamline drifts, covered the now familiar objects.

c. Used predicatively as *adj.* in preceding senses.

1907 F. W. LANCHESTER *Aerodynamics* i. 27 If..we assume continuity as hypothesis, then all bodies must be streamline. **1922** *Daily Mail* 3 Nov. 2 The body of the car is streamline according to British practice. **1929** *Jrnl. R. Aeronaut. Soc.* XXXIII. 366 The b.h.p. required.. should not be seriously influenced by interference, provided that the interference does not cause the flow to cease being streamline. **1936** B. JONES *Elem. Pract. Aerodynamics* vii. 115 Wherever possible the airplane parts that would cause parasite drag are made streamline in shape. **1971** J. W. IRELAND *Mech. of Fluids* viii. 234 Oil of specific gravity 0·9 and viscosity 1 poise is pumped through a 5 cm diameter pipe at the rate of 280 litres/min. Show that the flow is streamline.

d. A contour of a body that is coincident with a streamline of flow round it; *loosely,* a smooth, flowing outline.

1917 D'A. W. THOMPSON *Growth & Form* xvi. 673 The naval architect learns a great part of his lesson from the investigation of the stream-lines of a fish; and the mathematical study of the stream-lines of a bird..has helped to lay the very foundations of the modern science of aeronautics. **1936** B. JONES *Elem. Pract. Aerodynamics* vii. 117 Any non-streamlined body can have its resistance or drag greatly reduced merely by the addition of a blunt nose and a tapered tail. If the contour is also a continuous curve the shape approaches the ideal streamline. **1943** KOESTLER *Arrival & Departure* ii. 41 He was able to re-draw in his mind the curve of Odette's knees.., the streamlines of her jumper. **1944** W. FORTESCUE *Mountain Madness* xxiv. 162 If my curls were grey, at least I had kept my stream-line.

strea·mline, *v.* Also stream-line. [f. the sb.] **1.** *trans.* To give a streamline form to. Chiefly as *STREAMLINED *ppl. a.*, *STREAMLINING *vbl. sb.*

1918 H. BARBER *Aeroplane Speaks* (ed. 6) 61 From the designer's point of view it always pays to stream-line detrimental surface. **1927** HALDANE & HUXLEY *Anim. Biol.* xiii. 316 The air-sacs..are used to stream-line the body. **1927** *Daily Tel.* 27 Sept. 9/5 It appears that Flight-Lieut. Kinkead came down because the spinner, a metal fitting streamlining the propeller boss, came off.

2. *fig.* **a.** To slim; to remodel on smooth, uncluttered lines. Also *absol.*

1935 P. B. HAWK (*title*) Streamline for health. **1937** *Denver Post* 27 Jan. (Mag. Section) 9 (*heading*) Streamline your dance frock.

b. To simplify, esp. in order to make more efficient or better organized.

1936 *Sun* (Baltimore) 2 Nov. 13/5 Those who watch financial fashion observe a tendency to streamline capital set-ups for tax purposes. **1947** *Hansard Commons* Written Answers 2 Dec. 46, I am anxious to do all I can to streamline controls. **1950** A. Huxley *Let.* 16 Mar. (1969) 620 Chapters might be 'streamlined'. **1957** *New Yorker* 26 Oct. 60/2 The producers got panicky and decided to 'streamline' the production, stressing professional finish. **1958** *Post Office Mag.* Apr. 117/2 The Ministry are co-operating with us all..on streamlining general building methods. **1974** *Whitaker's Almanack 1975* 812/1 Through its advisory services, it helps its member governments to ..streamline health services.

streamlined (strī·mləind), *ppl. a.* Also **stream-lined.** [f. prec. + -ED[1] (early uses derived from the sb.).] **1.** Having a streamline form; designed so as to reduce air or water resistance.

1913 *Aeroplane* 30 Oct. 480/1 Its [*sc.* an aeroplane's] small span and carefully streamlined body. **1916** [see *CLEAN *a.* 13 c]. **1928** C. F. S. Gamble *Story North Sea Air Station* 10 Her two stream-lined gondolas..were designed to be capable of sustaining severe impact loads when alighting on water. **1930** *Observer* 16 Feb. 17/5 She has oval, instead of stream-lined funnels. **1948** M. Laski *Tory Heaven* iv. 58 I'd thought of..one of the old Lagondas..but I believe everything's streamlined these days. **1968** O. S. Nock *Railway Enthusiast's Encycl.* 279 From 1923 onwards, the 'Cheltenham Flyer' of the G.W.R. claimed the honours until the advent of the L.N.E.R. streamlined trains. **1977** C. McCullough *Thorn Birds* xvii. 439 Nowadays even the ocean liners were streamlined, hulls shaped like destroyers to get there faster.

2. *fig.* **a.** Having smooth, flowing, or elongated lines; slender.

1934 H. Read *Art & Industry* 3 'Streamlined' is popularly, if inaccurately, used as a term of approval for the design of any object in daily use. **1935** *Amer. Speech* X. 194/1 Terminology from other fields aids the fashion editors... The *streamlined* silhouette came in with the new automobile. **1937** *Nation* 15 May 559/2 The cows came from their stables down a runway into a streamlined building. **1944** A. Holmes *Princ. Physical Geol.* v. 63 The effects of shearing or flowage give the rocks a new structure, due to the stream-lined arrangement of the platy and elongated minerals. **1951** M. McLuhan *Mech. Bride* (1967) 96/1 Streamlined, synthetic blondes—these are at once abstract and exciting. **1966** Wodehouse *Plum Pie* 75 Dieting continues to be all the go..and the number of those who hope to become streamlined by pushing their plates away untasted increases daily. **1976** *Country Life* 1 Apr. 805/2 The two aspects of the ubiquitous Deco that have caused such confusion in recent terminology, the one still curved and flowing (Streamlined Moderne), the other angular and machine-style (Zig-Zag Moderne).

b. Efficient; simplified, having inessentials removed.

1937 *Words* May 100/1 Our streamlined professors. **1942** E. Paul *Narrow St.* xvii. 128 Clever women..manipulated high statesmen, financiers and stream-lined executives as if the men were marionettes. **1947** A. Huxley *Let.* 9 Mar. (1969) 568 We might think in greater detail about..a stream-lined construction for the revised Goldsmith. **1957** L. F. R. Williams *State of Israel* ix. 156 This..end is secured by an ingenious, stream-lined, procedure which makes the guillotine unnecessary. **1971** *Daily Tel.* 15 Jan. 15/5 A streamlined, yet cosy, kitchen overlooks a tiny paved garden. **1979** *Tucson* (Arizona) *Citizen* 20 Sept. 3 c/2 The majority's reasons for dissolving the former trustees included a desire..to make 'more streamlined' decisions regarding control of health care costs and treatment of indigents.

strea·mliner. [f. as prec. + -ER[1].]

a. A stream-lined train.

1938 *Times* 14 Oct. 15/6 One of the latest streamliners to be put into operation is that of the Reading Line between New York and Philadelphia. **1946** D. C. Peattie *Road of Naturalist* v. 55 To read the country while you run is possible even from a streamliner. **1958** J. Kerouac *On Road* ix. 229 A hundred and ten miles an hour straight through, an arrow road, sleeping towns, no traffic, and the Union Pacific streamliner falling behind us in the moonlight. **1967** O. Wynd *Walk Softly* v. 72 The Fuji is a great train, a streamliner, everything shiny and new. **1982** Whitehouse & Allen *E. Treacy—Railway Photographer* 85 A streamliner takes the 5.25 to Euston past Wavertree.

b. One who streamlines.

1943 F. L. Wright *Autobiogr.* iv. 321 Invention.. looking for salvation to the engineer, the streamliner, and the elevator, has been trying to..hold the profits of superconcentration.

c. *gen.* Something streamlined.

1968 *Church Times* 13 Sept. 18/3, I hear you have sold your old house and are looking for a streamliner.

strea·mlining, *vbl. sb.* [f. as prec. + -ING[1].]

1. a. Streamlined shape or design. **b.** The action of giving something a streamlined shape.

1918 H. Barber *Aeroplane Speaks* (ed. 6) 61 The weight of the stream-lining is always paid for many times over by the greater velocity and consequent increase of lift due to the decreased drift. **1921** *Discovery* Apr. 98/1 This probably is partly due..to the careful streamlining of the machine [*sc.* an aircraft] and the sensible distribution and installation of the engines. **1932** D. L. Sayers *Have his Carcase* vi. 76 The car glided away amid the reverent murmurings..of persons gathered..to admire its streamlining. **1936** *Discovery* Feb. 40/1 To diminish air-resistance by the streamlining of both engine and train. **1950** *Times* 5 May 5/6 A large engine does not necessarily mean a large wash. Bad streamlining and excessive speed create the wash. **1955** *Sci. Amer.* Mar. 90/3 The streamlining of birds of course is the envy of all aircraft designers. **1965** H. Hood in R. Weaver *Canad. Short Stories* (1968) 2nd Ser. 219 'That's quite a car, Mister.' 'Yes, that's what they call streamlining.' **1980** *Daily Tel.* 24 Sept 12/2 The drag factor of a car is becoming an increasingly significant item... It is, loosely, what used to be referred to as the streamlining effect.

2. *transf.* and *fig.* **a.** The action or result of giving smooth, flowing lines to something.

1934 *Punch* 19 Dec. 691/1 This 'streamlining' bunkum is spreading from the sordid realms of mere mechanics to those of everyday life, even to human physiognomy. **1937** G. Frankau *More of Us* vi. 70 '*I* find these modern figures far too arty,' Continued Sophie, obviously not repining Tho' hers had long since faltered from streamlining. **1940** Graves & Hodge *Long Week-End* xi. 181 The use of streamlining as a modern style in domestic objects.

b. Simplification of procedures, an organization, or the like to improve efficiency.

1959 *Daily Tel.* 24 July 5/7 (*heading*) Railway streamlining to be speeded. **1965** *Listener* 3 June 822/2 The streamlining of the administrative and financial planning structure was as urgent as was the physical planning in 1961. **1970** *Daily Tel.* 18 Mar. 2/5 As a result of a streamlining operation the weekly expenses had been cut from £1,200 to £700. **1978** R. Lewis *Inevitable Fatality* ii. 42 If there's to be a *streamlining*..some heads will have to roll.

stream of consciousness. [f. Stream *sb.*] **1.** *Psychol.* An individual's thoughts and conscious reaction to external events experienced subjectively as a continuous flow. Also *loosely* (influenced by sense *2), an uncontrolled train of thought or association.

1855 A. Bain *Senses & Intellect* 359 The concurrence of Sensations in one common stream of consciousness,—in the same cerebral highway. **1890** W. James *Princ. Psychol.* I. ix. 239 Consciousness..does not appear to itself chopped up in bits... A 'river' or a 'stream' are the metaphors by which it is most naturally described. In talking of it hereafter, let us call it the stream of thought, of consciousness, or of subjective life. **1908** W. McDougall *Introd. Social Psychol.* i. 15 Psychology must not regard the introspective description of the stream of consciousness as its whole task. **1928** D. H. Lawrence *Lady Chatterley's Lover* xiv. 253 The quiver was going through the man's body, as the stream of consciousness again changed its direction, turning down-wards. **1942** M. McCarthy *Company She Keeps* vi. 251 Damn my stream of consciousness, her mind said. **1959** Penfield & Roberts *Speech & Brain Mechanisms* iii. 47 Ganglionic patterns that preserve the record of the stream of consciousness. **1975** C. Fremlin *Long Shadow* xx. 142 Cynthia's stream-of-consciousness soon meandered obediently back to the matter in hand. **1979** K. R. Popper in Popper & Eccles *Self & its Brain* iii. 157 When we—actively—try to be passive, there may be something like a stream of consciousness; but normally we are active, and then there is.., rather, organized procedures of problem-solving.

2. *Lit. Criticism.* A method of narration which depicts events through this flow in the mind of a character; an instance of this.

[**1918** M. Sinclair in *Little Rev.* Apr. 6 In identifying herself with this life which is Miriam's stream of consciousness Miss Richardson produces her effect of..getting closer to reality than any of our novelists.] **1939** S. S. O'Casey *Let.* Apr. (1975) I. 792, I differ from you.. in your contention that my 'dream fantasies & streams of consciousness' are 'foreign to my best style'. **1961** W. C. Booth *Rhetoric of Fiction* iii. xi. 324 The deep plunges of modern inside views, the various streams-of-consciousness that attempt to give the reader an effect of living thought and sensation, are capable of blinding us to the possibility of our making judgments not shared by the narrator or reflector himself. **1964** M. McLuhan *Understanding Media* xxix. 296 Here [*sc.* in *David Copperfield*] was the stream of consciousness, perhaps, in its original form before it was adopted by Proust and Joyce and Eliot. **1971** B. Malamud *Tenants* 162 Bill took on a sort of stream-of-consciousness and heavily overworked association. **1978** I. B. Singer *Shosha* xiii. 233, I had also read in a literary magazine about the kind of literature called the 'stream of consciousness'.

3. *attrib.* (freq. with hyphens).

1931 *N. & Q.* 1 Aug. 74/1 This is in part a development from the 'stream of consciousness' method. **1942** *Q. Jrnl. Speech* Feb. 4/2 *This Lonely Heart*, a stream-of-consciousness play. **1955** L. P. Hartley *Perfect Woman* iii. 24 Do you think the stream-of-consciousness method has come to stay, or have Joyce and Virginia Woolf exhausted it? **1958** *Listener* 16 Oct. 603/2 The late Dorothy M. Richardson was one of the earliest exponents of the 'stream-of-consciousness' novel. **1975** B. Garfield *Death Sentence* (1976) iii. 22 He darted from topic to topic... He wasn't a stream-of-consciousness talker. **1982** *Times* 7 Apr. 9/8 A stream-of-consciousness chess match.

streek, streak, *v.* **5.** This sense is now usu. spelt *streak* and regarded as part of Streak *v.*[2] in Dict. and Suppl. (q.v., sense 6).

streel, *v.* Add: (Earlier and later examples.) Hence as *sb.*[1], a straggling, untidy procession of persons; **stree·ler,** a disreputable, idle person; **stree·ling** *vbl. sb.*

1805 E. Cavanagh *Let.* 20 Aug. in Londonderry & Hyde *Russian Jrnls.* (1934) ii. 182 In walk'd a Grenadier of a Man..& after him streal'd in at his heels a Girl. *c* **1874** D. Boucicault in M. R. Booth *Eng. Plays of 19th Cent.* (1969) II. 202, I was thrying to get away from him..but he was at my heels all the way, and Tatthers at his heels. A nice sthreel we made along the road. **1907** J. M. Synge *Playboy* ii. 48 An ugly young streeler with a murderous gob on him. **1927** E. Bowen *Hotel* xvi. 184 Miss Fitzgerald's party going forward in the leisurely and spread-out manner called in Ireland 'strealing'. **1937** G. Frankau *More of Us* ii. 30 Remembered she her own pre-ducal streelings: Some boy she had filched from her own mother dear; When all the other world that either knew was Ealing's? **1943** J. Stuart *Taps for Private Tussie* iv. 57 It was after four o'clock when Aunt Vittie and Grandma came strealin up the Turnpike from town. **1971** T. Kilroy *Big Chapel* ix. 177 She never went anywhere without a streel of children.

streel (strīl), *sb.*[2] Chiefly *Anglo-Ir.* Also **sthreal, sthreel.** [ad. Ir. *s*(*t*)*raoill*(*e*) untidy or awkward person; cf. *straille* wench or untidy girl and prec.] A disreputable, untidy woman; a slut.

1842 S. Lover *Handy Andy* xliii. 322 To marry a thrampin' sthreel like that—a great red-headed Jack. **1909** G. B. Shaw *Press Cuttings* 36 Not out o bed yet! Go and pull her out be the heels, the lazy sthreel. **1919** —— *O'Flaherty V.C.* in *Heartbreak House* 185, I thought that covetious sthreal in there was a walking angel; and now if ever I marry at all I'll marry a Frenchwoman. **1922** Joyce *Ulysses* 354 She did look a streel tugging the two kids along with the flimsy blouse..like a rag on her back and a bit of her petticoat hanging like a caricature. **1936** M. Franklin *All that Swagger* xx. 188 That streel must have gone off with James Fullwood. **1961** 'F. O'Brien' *Hard Life* i. 11 A streel of a girl with long lank fair hair arrived to look after myself and the brother. **1970** D. M. Davin *Not Here, not Now* i. i. 8 She certainly kept the house in trim, even if she always looked a bit of a streel. **1978** D. Murphy *Place Apart* iv. 78 Jimmy wouldn't like a streel.

Hence **stree·lish** *a.*; **stree·lishness.**

1936 M. Franklin *All that Swagger* xxii. 218 Belike she has picked up some of me brogue as well as some civilised habits, if she doesn't fall back into her streelishness. **1974** E. O'Brien in *New Review* Apr. 35/2 We saw this wild creature coming... Her costume was streelish.

streepje, var. *STREPIE.

street, *sb.* Add: **2. f.** *the street*: also = *Fleet Street* s.v. *FLEET *sb.*[2] 2 b.

1932 *News Chron.* 11 Feb. 6/3 A year ago he was coming back as Editor to the Street. **1963** L. Meynell *Virgin Luck* v. 101 The Street isn't the best place to come looking for a job at the moment. **1976** 'J. Welcome' *Grand National* viii. 123 Things were bad on the street... Two dailies were..expected to be unable to survive.

g. *Physics.* More fully *vortex street* [tr. G. *wirbelstrasse*]. An arrangement of vortices in which they form two parallel lines with clockwise rotation in one and anticlockwise rotation in the other; similarly *cloud street.*

1927 *Proc. R. Soc.* A. CXVI. 170 These vortex bands.. roll up and form what is commonly known as a vortex street. **1929** *Aircraft Engin.* I. 124/3 Vortices in a 'street' of two rows. **1936** *Proc. R. Soc.* A. CLIV. 68 For any given street the distance between consecutive vortices remains remarkably constant. **1954** [see *cloud street* s.v. *CLOUD *sb.* 12]. **1956** A. A. Townsend *Struct. Turbulent Shear Flow* vii. 144 For higher Reynolds numbers, either the vortex street forms very close to the cylinder or the circulation is itself unstable. **1973** *Times* 29 Jan. 14/4 As a fish swims it produces a turbulent 'vortex street' of whirling water behind it. **1978** R. S. Scorer *Environmental Aerodynamics* ix. 340 Cloud streets occur over land temporarily in the morning, and occasionally in the evening. *Ibid.* 341 Streets are common over the sea, particularly where the air stream is being slowly warmed.

h. *the street*: the streets regarded *loosely* as the realm of the common people, and esp. as the source of popular political support.

1931 [see *NAZI *sb.*]. **1954** B. & R. North tr. *M. Duverger's Pol. Parties* i. i. 38 The Storm troops wrested from the Communist and Socialist crowds their dominance of the street. **1969** *Listener* 24 Apr. 555/3 This was the street taking over a modern state in a way which hasn't happened, I think, at any other time in our history. It was as if this country had been taken over by the Black and Tans.

i. *the street* (U.S. slang): the world outside prison or other confinement, freedom.

[**1931** G. Irwin *Amer. Tramp & Underworld Slang* 185 *Streets*, freedom, and so called by prisoners in confinement.] **1935** J. Hargan *Gloss. Prison Lang.* 8 *Street, hit the*, to be released. **1956** B. Holiday *Lady sings Blues* (1973) xviii. 144, I was too busy thinking about 'the street' all the time and the life I'd left. **1966** J. Mills *Panic in Needle Park* xix. 184 It is no accident that our patients refer to the world outside [the hospital] as 'the street'; they cherish their mobility, the opportunity to escape difficult relationships, very highly. **1977** E. Leonard *Unknown Man No. 89* iv. 35 The jury believed Robert Leary and he was allowed to return to the street.

3. a*. *on the street*: (*a*) *U.S. slang*, outside prison, at liberty; (*b*) *slang*, by illicit trafficking (with reference to the acquisition of drugs); (*c*) *colloq.*, out of work, unemployed.

1935 N. Ersine *Underworld & Prison Slang* 73 *Street, n.*, figuratively, freedom. 'Another year will see him on the street.' **1951** W. Faulkner *Requiem for Nun* iii. 251 They worked their fines out on the street. **1977** *New Yorker* 24 Oct. 64/3 A number of men who are heterosexual on the street practice homosexuality in prison. **1979** *Guardian* 30 Oct. 8/5 We have either an extremely successful therapeutic service, or people are obtaining the drugs which they want 'on the street'. **1980** J. Wainwright *Venus Fly-Trap* 12 It's *my* living, too... If I upset that crowd, I could be on the street.

g. Also (with hyphens) *attrib.* Also (*U.S.*) *the man on the-street.* Similarly *the woman in the street.*

1926 GALSWORTHY *Silver Spoon* III. xi. 305 She had the political cynicism of the woman in the street. **1928** *Amer. Speech* IV. 134 The American newspaper man.. speaks a patois bewildering to the man on the street. **1942** G. GREENE *British Dramatists* 20 We notice the quality which reached its height in the great comedies ..a kind of man-in-the-street poetry. **1962** A. NISBETT *Technique Sound Studio* vii. 130 A sort of convention has arisen whereby 'man-in-the-street' interviews are cut together by simple editing. **1964** R. K. GOLDSEN in I. L. Horowitz *New Sociol.* 89 We must endeavor to make sociological knowledge as inescapable for men-on-the-street as are..the virtues of the latest detergent. **1973** *Observer* (Colour Suppl.) 4 Feb. 15/4 He really wanted to please the man on the street and the man on the street knew it. **1977** E. W. HILDICK *Vandals* I. ii. 17 Tape-recorded man- and woman-in-the-street interviews.

h. *by a street*: by a wide margin (esp. of a sporting victory).

1962 *Times* 5 Nov. 4/1 Oxford..could have won by a street before half time. **1971** *Daily Tel.* 28 Sept. 30/1 He already knew what most of us had already calculated—that Bodell had won by a street. **1977** *Time Out* 17–23 June 65/5 The Scots should win the drinking by a street. **1982** *Age Monthly Rev.* (Melbourne) Mar. 11/3 Any label embracing such a wide range of usage is too wide by a street.

i. *to be up* (*down*, † *in*) *one's street*: to be suited to someone's taste or ability.

1903 FARMER & HENLEY *Slang* VII. 10/1 *Street*.., a capacity, a method; a line: *e.g.* 'That's not in my street' = 'I am not concerned' or 'That's not my way of doing,' etc. **1929** *Publishers' Weekly* 21 Dec. 2813/2 A great many of the books published today are, as the saying is, right up her street. **1937** *Forward* 13 Nov. 1/2 We Labour people can the more easily say these things because some of his activities were 'up our street'. **1945** E. WAUGH *Brideshead Revisited* II. iv. 259 She is a jolly attractive girl, the sort of girl any chap would be glad to have—artistic, too, just down your street. **1955** KNIGHT & GEORGE *Advice to Student of French* 67 The historical line of enquiry is outside your scope, but the analysis of the book or books is right down your street. **1960** L. COOPER *Accomplices* I. vi. 55 John Pollard got me the job and..I loved it... It was right up my street. **1977** *It* May 28/1 If you like Miles Davis's 'In a Silent Way' then Don Cherry has a new release which is just up your street.

j. *to play* or *work both sides of the street* (orig. and chiefly *U.S.*): to ally oneself with both sides, to behave inconsistently and opportunistically.

1938 *Sun* (Baltimore) 8 Sept. 1/2 Our friends of the New Deal have the devil's own nerve when it comes to working both sides of the street... Mr. James A. Farley..can reel off a speech as pious as the heart could wish and he can play the part of Jobmaster General with all the ruthlessness of the Tammany school of politics. **1951** E. KEFAUVER *Crime in Amer.* xvii. 202 He played both sides of the street and made contributions to candidates of both major parties. **1969** *Listener* 13 Feb. 196/3 Amnesty International has to play both sides of the political street in seeking to obtain the release of political prisoners... Information usually comes either from the press or through prisoners' friends, but known domestic or foreign opponents of a regime are not..necessarily the best channel for bringing influence to bear.

4. a. *street accident, band, battle, beggar* (later example), *bookie, -bookmaker, -bookmaking, clothes, cry* (earlier example), *decoration, fair, -fight* (further examples), *-fighter, game, gang, market, meeting, music* (earlier example), *organ, party, patrol, photographer, piano, preacher, riot, -rioter, -singer* (earlier example), *-singing* (later example), *song, theatre, -trader, -trading, vendor, violence, warfare.*

1892 KIPLING *Many Inventions* (1893) 164, I heard Keller saying, as though he were watching a street accident, 'Give him air. For God's sake, give him air.' **1980** J. HONE *Flowers of Forest* I. i. 14 An essential witness in a street accident. **1838** DICKENS *Nicholas Nickleby* (1839) ii. 6 Street bands are on their mettle in Golden Square. **1977** *New Statesman* 2 Sept. 292/1 The traditional Trinidadian street bands and dancers. **1936** *New Yorker* 7 Mar. 29/1 In 1923..the Commissioner..in a street battle routed the brownshirts. **1978** 'A. STUART' *Vicious Circles* 21 Last night's riots in Milan where fascists had fought communists in a running street battle. **1976** *Birmingham Post* 16 Dec. 5/5 Patrick Haplin, a street beggar, will celebrate Christmas in prison—for the tenth consecutive year. **1939** *John o' London's Weekly* 2 June 320/2 He gets himself..into minor social difficulties, finding himself one day..in the police cells in Kennington, accused of being a street-bookie. **1980** G. M. FRASER *Mr. American* xxiv. 479 Unless ultimately he could break them, he might as well go back to catching street bookies. **1939** H. HODGE *Cab, Sir?* xvi. 238 We [*sc.* cabmen] have come to look on the police-court dock as a normal trade risk—just as street-bookmakers and prostitutes do. **1981** R. SAMUEL *East End Underworld* xiv. 179 They kept a big cat's meat shop, but his real money came from street bookmaking. **1908** M. MORGAN *How to dress Doll* vii. 63 (*heading*) *Dolly's street clothes.* Here is Dolly dressed for a walk. **1981** M. C. SMITH *Gorky Park* i. 10 In his street clothes Arkady was slovenly. **1858** *Punch* XXIV. 103 The value of the houses ..is daily diminishing by reason of the Street Cries, which render the place uninhabitable. **1911** *Encycl. Brit.* XXIX. 759/2 Street decoration. **1969** *Guardian* 18 Dec. 9/1 There are fewer street decorations..store displays are less lavish. **1872** B. JERROLD *London* xix. 158 These street-fairs are held chiefly on Saturday nights and Sunday mornings. **1982** 'E. MCBAIN' *Beauty & Beast* viii. 130 Calusa's street fairs during..March and April, when the tourists were thickest. **1930** E. POUND *XXX Cantos* ix. 35 And he fought in Fano, in a street fight. **1976** *Sunday Mail* (Glasgow) 26 Dec. 1/2 Late-night revellers were terrified when several running street fights broke out. **1970** K. PLATT *Pushbutton Butterfly* (1971) ix. 102, I promised my mother I would only marry a street fighter. **1890** *Public Ledger* (Philadelphia) 9 Dec. 6/5 Mr. Stewart Culin..recently delivered a lecture in Brooklyn, on children's street games. **1969** I. & P. OPIE *Children's Games* p. vi, There is no town or city known to us where street games do not flourish. **1942** E. WAUGH *Put out More Flags* i. 32 A Glasgow millionaire..who had started life in a street gang. **1979** *Amer. Speech* 1976 LI. 61 Their speech is closer to standard than is that of the adolescent street-gang members. **1870** D. J. KIRWAN *Palace & Hovel* xxxiv. 507 The roughest audience..wandered right and left..to..choke the thoroughfare to buy in the street market, which was now—eleven o'clock—at the height of commercial prosperity. **1922** V. WOOLF *Jacob's Room* viii. 157 The street market in Soho is fierce with light. **1982** *Listener* 16 Dec. 34/3 Beware street-market tapes at silly prices, even if they have well-known brand names. [**1923** R. MACAULAY *Told by Idiot* I. xii. 46 She attended street labour meetings in the east [end].] **1933** 'G. ORWELL' *Down & out in Paris & London* xxv. 183 There were street meetings... In the East India Dock Road the Salvation Army were holding a service. **1982** R. MANHEIM tr. *Grasse's Headbirths* vi. 85 Street meeting in the pedestrian zone. **1829** *Harlequin* 20 June 48 Street music is on the march... At Ascot, some glee-singers received two sovereigns for singing before the Royal Stand. **1849** E. RUSKIN *Let.* 28 Oct. in M. Lutyens *Effie in Venice* (1965) I. 54 This Milan is a most wonderful place for street organs. **1964** G. MITCHELL *Death of Delft Blue* i. 15 If you go there [*sc.* Amsterdam], be sure to look out for the street organs, the barrel-organs, you know. **1953** *Times* 3 June 8/1 The most popular events were the street parties. In some 30 or 40 streets the inhabitants had clubbed together to hold parties, starting, as a rule, with tea for the children. **1977** *New Yorker* 27 June 52/1 London's celebrations of the Queen's Silver Jubilee seemed like one mammoth street party. **1976** *Guardian* 12 Apr. 20/7 All good police officers know that the street patrol on foot..is the classic champion over the scourge of street crime. **1945** E. WAUGH *Brideshead Revisited* I. vi. 132 Here..is a group taken by a street photographer. **1981** 'S. CAUDWELL' *Thus was Adonis Murdered* xviii. 230 The street photographers and sellers of souvenirs continued about their business. **1857** *Punch* XXXII. 40 All music sounds alike to him, whether it be the Handel of the organ-loft or the handle of the street piano. **1903** [see *PLUNK *v.* 1 b]. **1978** L. DEIGHTON *SS-GB* xix. 166 Douglas stopped to give a penny to an old man at the handle of a street piano. **1878** *Golden Hours* X. 85/2 Moxy looked up quickly into the face of an old black 'mammy' who..had paused for a moment to listen to the words of the street preacher. **1916** G. B. SHAW *Androcles & Lion* p. xii, The horror of the High Priest was perfectly natural: he was a Primate confronted with a heterodox street preacher uttering what seemed to him an appalling and impudent blasphemy. **1977** J. GILLIS *Killers of Starfish* (1979) v. 35 He pretended he was a street preacher once and people put pennies and dimes in his hat to save the sinners. **1980** L. ST. CLAIR *Obsessions* i.16 Perhaps there would be no more street riots and shooting. **1900** KIPLING *Let.* 24 July in C. Carrington *Rudyard Kipling* (1955) xiii. 314 We advanced against 'em [*sc.* the Boers] as if they were street-rioters that we didn't want to hurt. **1789** C. BURNEY *Hist. Mus.* III. 64 It seems to have been the wish of illiterate and furious reformers, that all religious offices should be performed by field-preachers and street-singers. **1958** E. ROUTLEY *Eng. Carol* 228 Television probably accounts in part for the decline of street-singing. **1891** R. FRY *Let.* 4 Mar. (1972) I. 129 There is a good deal of spontaneous music in the Italians... Their street songs are perfect of their kind. **1959** W. R. BIRD *These are Maritimes* x. 274 There were street songs brought out over the years from the old country. **1959** G. WICKHAM *Early Eng. Stages* I. iii. 51 Specially erected platforms..in market squares or other open spaces..are usually known by such names as 'booth theatres', *théâtres de la foire*, or simply 'street theatres'. **1977** *Spare Rib* May 16/1 I'd like to do street theatre, but it's not that easy in a place like Sheffield. **1870** D. J. KIRWAN *Palace & Hovel* xxvi. 395 These dog-sellers are the keenest street-traders to be found in London. **1979** S. BRETT *Comedian Dies* i. 17 [He] spoke with the brash confidence of an East End street-trader. **1903** *Act* 3 *Edw. VII* c. 45 § 2 Any local authority may make bye-laws with respect to street trading by persons under the age of sixteen. **1977** J. THOMSON *Case Closed* viii. 99 They'd kept their street-trading licence and..they'd go round the local markets selling clothing. **1872** B. JERROLD *London* ii. 23 Stopped by street vendors of all descriptions. **1978** N. LONGMATE *Hungry Mills* vii. 100 His heart went out to the inexperienced street-vendors he encountered. **1977** *Times* 22 Jan. 4/4 The two days of street violence [in Cairo] which took more than 60 lives. **1830** in *Times* (1982) 7 June 14/7 Locomotive Carriages might be used with great advantage in cases of Riot and Street Warfare. **1938** 'G. ORWELL' *Homage to Catalonia* x. 174 Few experiences could be..more nerve-racking than those evil days of street warfare.

b. *street architecture, -corner* (earlier and further examples), *-crossing, -end* (earlier example), *island, lamp* (earlier example), *map, -name* (later example), *plan, -side* (later examples).

1933 J. BETJEMAN *Ghastly Good Taste* vi. 99 The true eighteenth century tradition, which lavished adornment on the interior and did not worry as much about street architecture. **1978** *Architectural Design* 5 June 314/2 Shaw's Albert Hall Mansions of 1879–81..are excellent as street architecture. **1836** DICKENS *Sk. Boz* 2nd Ser. ii. 22 The policeman at the street corner. **1944** [see *FEEL *v.* 9 e]. **1978** J. WAINWRIGHT *Jury People* xxxvi. 118 Yobbo types, tearaways, bully-boys, street-corner louts. **1875** 'MARK TWAIN' in *Atlantic Monthly* May 571/1 Go on until you know every street-crossing, the character, size, and position of the crossing stones, [etc.]. **1956** D. GASCOYNE *Night Thoughts* 26 Street-crossing islands stand becalmed. **1977** R. L. WOLFF *Gains & Losses* II. iii. 243 The virtuous street urchin who has never heard of Christ..raises himself..to the proprietorship of a muddy street-crossing as a sweeper. **1890** KIPLING *Life's Handicap* (1891) 79 A lamp at a street-end. **1919** J. BUCHAN *Mr. Standfast* x. 187 A hundred yards away a bomb fell on a street island. **1934** *Sun* (Baltimore) 31 May 5/3 A hard-driving taxi driver ignored a red signal, threatened the traffic policeman's knees, missed the street island by a hair [etc.]. **1799** C. B. BROWN *Arthur Mervyn* I. iv. 33 [The room's] height and spaciousness were imperfectly discernible..by gleams from a street lamp. **1964** L. DEIGHTON *Funeral in Berlin* vii. 52 Spectacles produced a street map and..began marking circles here and there. **1978** T. ALLBEURY *Lantern Network* x. 141 The street map showed it as a small road off the Brighton Road. **1970** J. MCN. DODGSON *Place-Names Cheshire* I. p. xliv, As a rule, street-names not recorded before 1700 are excluded. **1929** *Woolley's Ludlow Guide* (ed. 18) 44 (*caption*) Street plan of Ludlow. **1978** W. J. BURLEY *Wycliffe & Scapegoat* iii. 55 Wycliffe studied the street plan. 'Here we are. Albert Terrace.' **1974** *New Yorker* 29 Apr. 47/1 The odd oarsman..looks forlorn seen from the bridges or the streetsides. **1977** *Antiquaries Jrnl.* LVII. 251 The building extended only for the width of the streetside room..from the street frontage.

c. *street lighting* (examples).

1916 G. B. SHAW *Androcles & Lion* p. lxxii, The sportsmen, the musicians, the physicists, the biologists will get their apparatus for the asking as easily as their bread or, as at present, their paving, street lighting, and bridges. **1979** *Time* 8 Jan. 23/2 In 1975 Gacy became a trustee of the Norwood Park Township Street Lighting District.

d. *attrib.* passing into *adj.*, with reference to the streets as the focus of modern urban life, esp. among the poor and contrasted with polite society. Often with the implication of illegal dealings (esp. drug-trafficking), or the sharp-wittedness needed to survive 'on the streets'. orig. *U.S.*

1967 'T. WELLS' *Dead by Light of Moon* xiii. 126 A street merchant is a con artist who pretends to sell stolen goods. **1967** *Trans-Action* Apr. 5/1 Street culture exists in every low income ghetto. It is shared by the hustling elements of the poor, whatever their nationality or color. **1972** *N. Y. Times* 24 Dec. IV. 6 Murphy called a news conference to announce that 57 pounds of heroin with an estimated street value of more than $10-million had been stolen. **1973** D. BARNES *See the Woman* (1974) 73 His name is Frederick L. Pepper... He's got a street name of 'Red Pepper'. **1976** R. CONDON *Whisper of Axe* I. xv. 87 The street price for one kilogram of heroin is one million two hundred thousand dollars. **1979** W. J. FISHMAN *Streets of East London* 74/1 A street culture based on the pub. **1980** *Brit. Med. Jrnl.* 6 Dec. 1511/1 Phencyclidine is now a class 2 controlled substance in the United States—and after marijuana has become the most widely abused 'street drug' in North America. **1982** R. LEIGH *Girl with Bright Head* ii. 12 She wasn't street tough but neither was she a runaway kid up from the provinces.

e. street-Arab (earlier and later examples); **street-boy** (earlier example); **street-child,** a homeless or neglected child who lives chiefly in the streets; **street crime** *U.S.*, a crime such as robbery, assault, etc., committed on the streets; **street fighting,** fighting conducted in the streets, esp. on a large scale for political or revolutionary ends; **street floor** *U.S.* = GROUND-FLOOR; **street furniture,** objects such as post-boxes, road-signs, litter bins, etc., placed in the street for public use or assistance (orig. a planners' term); **street girl,** a homeless or neglected girl who lives chiefly in the streets; a prostitute; **street-grid,** an arrangement of streets crossing at right angles to each other; **street hockey** *N. Amer.*, a variety of ice hockey played on the street; **street jewellery,** painted enamel advertising plates considered as collectors' items; **street kid** = *street child* above; **street-legal** *a.*, applied to a motor vehicle which satisfies the legal requirements for roadworthiness; **street level,** (*a*) ground-floor level; (*b*) *fig.*, the level of direct contact with the public or of operation on the streets; **street-light,** (*b*) (later examples); **Street name** *U.S.* [after *WALL STREET], the name of a stock-brokerage firm, bank, or dealer in which stock is held on behalf of the purchaser; **street people** orig. and chiefly *U.S.*, (*a*) homeless or vagrant people who live on the streets, esp. as a protest against the conventional values of society; (*b*) people involved in petty crime in the urban underworld; (*c*) *spec.* people dealing in the illicit supply of drugs 'on the street'; **street rod** orig. *U.S.* (see quot. 1954); hence **street rodding** *vbl. sb.*; **street-scape,** a view or prospect provided by the design of a (city) street or streets; **street scene,** the spectacle of life in the streets; **street-smart** *a. U.S. slang* = *street-wise* adj. (*b*) below; also **street-smarts,** the ability to live by one's wits in an urban environment;

street-to-street *a.*, of fighting: taking place in the streets; **street tree**, a tree planted at the side of a street to enhance the view; **street urchin** (later examples); **street village**, a long, narrow village formed of buildings along either side of a main street; **street warden**, (*a*) an air-raid warden assigned to a particular street or streets; (*b*) a warden selected to look out for certain social problems in a particular street or streets; **street-wise** *a. slang* (orig. and chiefly *U.S.*), (*a*) familiar with the outlook of ordinary people in an urban environment; (*b*) cunning in the ways of modern urban life; **street worker** orig. *N. Amer.*, a social worker whose concern is with juvenile delinquents.

1859 G. A. SALA *Twice round Clock* 388 Street Arabs, threw 'cart-wheels' into the midst of the throng. **1924** LAWRENCE & SKINNER *Boy in Bush* 49 The children.. were singing..with a sort of street-arab abandon. **1854** DICKENS *Hard Times* I. xvi. 127, I was a ragged street-boy. **1863** —— *Mrs Lirriper's Lodgings* i, in *All Year Round* Extra Christmas No. 3 Dec. 8/2 You must allow me to inform you..that my grandson is *not* a street-child. **1959** I. & P. OPIE *Lore & Lang. Schoolch.* xii. 232 The street-child today with his soot-blackened face and red-daubed nose, rattling a tin, is a much more demure creature than his predecessors. **1982** G. WAGNER *Children of Empire* vii. 123 Three-quarters of his young life had been spent in the workhouse, yet technically he was a 'street child'. **1973** *Listener* 20 Sept. 364/1 You'd expect.. New York to take a highly sophisticated view of the drug problem, for it is more subtle in its operations here,..and responsible for more street crimes—robberies and rapes—than in any other State. **1978** *Chicago* June 162/2 The state's attorney's office..must prosecute virtually all local street crime, leaving meager resources for long, complex investigations. **1832** F. MACERONI (*title*) Defensive instructions..on..street and house fighting. **1900** W. S. CHURCHILL in *Morning Post* 12 July 7/7 The cavalry halted on the hills for a while, the general being desirous of obtaining the formal surrender of Heilbron, and so preventing street-fighting or bombardment. **1981** *Times* 6 July 13/1 Within a few months there have been three major eruptions of street fighting, all of which have included an ethnic element. **1927** DOUBMAN & WHITAKER *Organization & Operation of Department Stores* vii. 162 The first or street floor of a store is the most desirable for selling. **1972** H. KEMELMAN *Monday the Rabbi took Off* xxvi. 170 Why would he take an apartment on a street floor here? **1944** J. C. RIDDELL *Rep. Post War Housing* 11 In all future planning there should..be the closest co-operation between all departments and services responsible for the erection of street furniture and small buildings. **1976** *Cumberland & Westmorland Herald* 27 Nov., We don't want to waste officers' time..on more street furniture which costs a fortune today. **1907** G. B. SHAW *Major Barbara* I. 206 You have had the education of a lady... Don't talk like a street girl. *a* **1911** [see *MOST *adv.* 4]. **1979** *Maledicta* III. 11 For a budding sexologist I must have been uncommonly naive, but I swear that I didn't catch on that these were street girls' joints till it dawned on me, while sorting out my notes, that I seemed to have a disproportionate number of sexual idioms. **1948** *Antiquity* XXII. 173 The wide road leading to its main entrance from the east is plainly out of alignment with the street grid on the west side of the Forum block. **1964** *Listener* 27 Aug. 300/2 The avenue slices diagonally across the basic street-grid. **1964** *Globe & Mail* (Toronto) 15 Dec. 41/8 He brought a fresh approach to street hockey when he began trying to teach Frank how to shoot a puck. **1976** *New Yorker* 26 Apr. 90/3 Meynell and I played marbles, mumblety-peg, running games, street hockey, primitive baseball, stoop ball, games of imagination. **1978** BAGLEE & MORLEY *Street Jewellery* 9 Street jewellery, flashing in the winter sunlight, gleaming in gaslight..—the enamel sign. **1982** *Arts North* June 9 (*caption*) Street jewellery—one of the saucier enamel signs from the fascinating exhibition at the Dorman Museum. **1929** E. WILSON in *New Republic* 17 Apr. 256/2 The money with which the street-kids have been playing craps. **1977** *Rolling Stone* 5 May 55/1 You could go to New Delhi or Calcutta, there are thousands of street kids there. **1976** *Casper* (Wyoming) *Star-Tribune* 29 June 19/1 (Advt.), Yamaha 125. Street legal. Good condition. **1980** *Dirt Bike* Oct. 58/3 The rear fender is plastic, which is a rarity on street legal bikes. **1934** *Archit. Rev.* LXXV. 214/3 The storey built above the street-level floor was called a solar. **1963** 'J. LE CARRÉ' *Spy who came in from Cold* xv. 140 Branch Secretaries with..a good record of stimulating mass action at street level. **1974** 'E. LATHEN' *Sweet & Low* xi. 114 He reached street level. **1976** *Times* 6 Sept. 2/3 Plans are advanced to open..an office in Belfast..accessible to both communities. An effort will be made to concentrate organization at street level. **1982** G. F. NEWMAN *Men with Guns* ix. 69 Kohn avoided contact with street-level hoods... Now he was a respectable businessman. **1955** E. BLISHEN *Roaring Boys* iii. 128 The street lights..were on early. **1969** L. MICHAELS *Going Places* 27 Streetlights glowed in a receding sweep. **1930** C. F. HODGES *Wall Street* 383 When a security is registered in the name of a recognized brokerage firm, usually members of the Exchange, it is said to be in a 'Street Name'. **1933** *North Western Reporter* CCXLVI. 660/1 The court properly instructed as to the 'street name' custom of the exchange..submitted to the jury the question of fact [etc.]. *Ibid.* 664/2 Evidence sustained finding that customer's repudiation of broker's purchase of stock in 'street name', instead of customer's name, was made within reasonable time. **1976** E. STEWART *Launch!* (1977) 35 'And I want to know how much the brokerage houses are holding in street names.' All the brokerage houses had street-name accounts, stock bought and traded for clients in the broker's name. **1967** *Trans-Action* Apr. 5/1 In Los Angeles, members of.. street groups sometimes call themselves 'street people', 'cool people', or simply 'regulars'. **1969** *Guardian* 24 May 1/3 The precincts inhabited by Berkeley's hippies and 'street people'. **1972** *National Observer* (U.S.) 27 May 7/2 There's evidence that methadone has become almost as popular as heroin among addicts. Street people say so. **1976** *Billings* (Montana) *Gaz.* 4 July 2-B/3 'At first, we got mostly street people,' said Nyberg. 'Lately our patients have begun to be from the higher social levels.' **1954** *Amer. Speech* XXIX. 103 *Street rod* (*job, roadster, etc.*), *n.* A hot rod suitable for street use, one of the competition types. The 'street rod' is distinguished from the 'track car', which is intended primarily for drag-strip or lakes racing. **1972** *World of Wild Wheels* (Custom Car) 58/1 Street rods don't have to be American based—just tinged with American thought. **1977** *New Society* 3 Mar. 436/2 Custom-car cruisers, in their glistening, overpowered improvisations... The monthly influx of around 250 'street rods' causes a solid traffic jam. **1976** *Panorama* (Austral.) Dec. 4 One of Australia's fastest-growing sports is street rodding—turning pre-1948 cars into sparkling, high-performance vehicles which belie their age. **1924** *Glasgow Herald* 8 Mar. 9 Where aerial invaders left ugly.. scars in the streetscape noble new buildings have already appeared. **1979** *Jrnl. R. Soc. Arts* Nov. 770/2 Giorgio Grassi and others have designed housing blocks as long arcaded streetscapes. **1870** D. J. KIRWAN *Palace & Hovel* xxvi. 407 The great..attraction among the multifarious street scenes of London, is the Punch and Judy show. **1979** *N.Y. Times Mag.* 30 Sept. 37/2 The girls' mother, Ada, is down on the stoop, watching the street scene as if it were television. **1976** *National Observer* (U.S.) 1 May 5/1 Rizzo is tough, street-smart, charming in his own special way. **1976** *N.Y. Times* 9 Aug. 30 To be free, however, requires street-smarts, the cunning of the survivor. **1978** *Time* 3 Apr. 61 Norris also sought out local black leaders and followed their street-smart advice. **1978** *New Yorker* 20 Nov. 113 They thought always about winning, and, one way or another, they almost always did win. Like the A's, these Yankees have street-smarts. **1983** *Underground Grammarian* VII. III. 7/2 Frank will be demoted to the lowliest rank in education, teacher, so that those adaptable street-smart kids can go and apply their skills in *her* classroom. **1945** *Finito! Po Valley Campaign* (15th Army Group) 33 Street-to-street battles. **1976** *Southern Even. Echo* (Southampton) 12 Nov. 10/3 She recalls the street-to-street fighting that became an everyday feature. **1911** W. SOLOTAROFF *Shade-Trees in Towns & Cities* p. ix, This book treats particularly of the planting and care of street-trees. **1981** *Garden* CVI. 443/2 They [*sc.* local authorities] might be persuaded to plant street trees. **1977** Street urchin [see *street-crossing*, sense *4 b]. **1978** J. KRANTZ *Scruples* vi. 168 Jake..had a droll and artful street-urchin look to him and typically Black Irish coloring. **1949** *Ann. Assoc. Amer. Geographers* XXXIX. 261 *Street Villages* (*Strassendörfer*), the name being used only for those villages which were founded on an existing route. **1974** C. TAYLOR *Fieldwork in Medieval Archaeol.* vi. 142 Caxton..is now a long street village on either side of the Old North Road. **1940** N. LAST *Diary* Oct. *Nella Last's War* (1983) 78 Our street warden called tonight... He wanted to know if we had buckets, stirrup-pumps, blankets, bandages, [etc.]. **1973** *Daily Tel.* 8 Jan. 2/2 Mrs Green said her organisation wanted street wardens whose job 'for perhaps £1 a week' would be to call on old people each morning. **1980** *Church Times* 11 Apr. 6/4 Much is said about almost every activity that laypeople can undertake—forming a 'Jesus gang', personal witness, acting as street wardens, helping the bereaved, befriending the elderly. **1965** *New Yorker* 27 Mar. 78 A [social] worker therefore had to be wary as well as trustful, be security minded as well as loving, and be 'street-wise' as well as compassionate. **1971** *N.T. Times* 18 June 37 Take a dirt-poor Sicilian peasant kid fresh out of steerage. Make him scrappy and street-wise. **1977** H. FAST *Immigrants* v. 321 Al Smith, street-wise Catholic from New York. **1980** *Times Lit. Suppl.* 1 Aug. 867/5 The learned men on the council of the SPR were not, as we would say now, 'street-wise'. **1981** *Daily Tel.* 27 Nov. 16/2 Their [*sc.* young blacks'] values place a premium on being 'street-wise',..that is, being able to survive in the rough and tough world of the streets. **1964** *Maclean's Mag.* 25 Jan. 23 Almost all of them have quit school. The street-worker has become so friendly with them that he can sometimes return stolen goods before the police are even aware of the theft. **1973** 'J. PATRICK' *Glasgow Gang Observed* xxi. 219 Adolescents..did not know how to react to the non-evaluative, non-judgmental approach of the street worker.

street-car. 1. For *U.S.* read *N. Amer.* and add further examples.

1887 *Grip* (Toronto) 5 Feb. 6/2 Toronto law is plain and hard—no streetcars out on Sunday. **1915** D. R. CAMPBELL *Proving of Virginia* 108 So I shall bid you good-by and take a street car home. **1929** M. DE LA ROCHE *Whiteoaks* iv. 58 They boarded a street car and stood together, swaying, hanging by the straps,..oblivious of the other passengers. **1931** W. G. MCADOO *Crowded Years* iv. 44 The street cars went like sleepy tortoises; they were pulled by mules. **1947** *Partisan Rev.* XIV. 366 They returned in a streetcar, although Jasper wanted to take a taxi. **1947** T. WILLIAMS (*title*) A streetcar named Desire. **1968** *Globe & Mail* (Toronto) 15 Jan. 17/1 Bus companies reported delays and power failure contributed to the problems of city street cars. **1974** *Plain Dealer* (Cleveland, Ohio) 26 Oct. 5-D/1 The people who came to the Barons-Rangers game that night long ago came by streetcar and bus and by shank's mare as well as by auto. **1978** *Detroit Free Press* 16 Apr. (Record) 9/4 The Warsaw street cars stop sixty or seventy meters from the gates of the ghetto.

2. A shell. *Mil. slang.*

1920 C. R. HERR *Company F Hist.: 319th Infantry* 22 The air was filled with the sounds of the shells as they lazily went on their way towards the back lines of both sides 'Street cars'..the boys called them. **1950** R. CHANDLER *Let.* 18 May (1966) 78 Doesn't he [*sc.* Partridge] overlook some of the most commonly used words of soldier-slang? E.g...'street cars' or 'tram cars' for heavy long range shells.

streetman. Add: **2. b.** A petty criminal who works 'on the street', esp. as a pickpocket or drug pedlar. *U.S. slang.*

1908 'O. HENRY' *Gentle Grafter* 161 I'd like to shake hands with Parley-voo Pickens, the greatest street man in the West. **1974** *Publishers Weekly* 21 Jan. 80/3 He is playing partner to the pusher whose street man is keeping the girl hooked. **1981** W. H. HALLAHAN *Trade* ii. 41 They were the perfect team, the tough street man and the elegant boardroom manipulator.

Strega (strē·gă). The proprietary name of a kind of Italian liqueur flavoured with orange; a drink or glassful of this.

1910 *Trade Marks Jrnl.* 19 Jan. 104 Liquore Strega. Liqueurs. The firm trading as Ditta Giuseppe Alberti. **1920** D. H. LAWRENCE *Lost Girl* xvi. 358 Pancrazio took her to the place where she could drink coffee and a strega. **1922** —— *Aaron's Rod* xiv. 203 The waiter rattled off a list, beginning with Strega and ending with cherry brandy. **1938** E. AMBLER *Cause for Alarm* iv. 63, I found..an empty Strega bottle. **1948** W. S. MAUGHAM *Here & There* 25, I ordered coffee and strega, which is the best liqueur they make in Italy. **1974** K. CLARK *Another Part of Wood* v. 179 The only penalty was that the meal traditionally ended with quantities of Strega, which gave one a sore head the next day.

strength, *sb.* Add: **1. d.** Freq. in phr. *strength of character.*

1836 J. H. NEWMAN *Parochial Sermons* III. i. 3 Of course men who make such sacrifices, often evidence much strength of character in making them. **1863** N. HAWTHORNE *Our Old Home* I. 74, I have not found reason to suppose that the English dowager of fifty has actually greater courage, fortitude, and strength of character than our woman of similar age. **1919** G. B. SHAW *Heartbreak House* II. 52 You know, Ellie has remarkable strength of character. I think it is because I taught her to like Shakespear when she was very young. **1957** *Oxf. Dict. Chr. Ch.* 583/2 It was owing to Gregory, in whom firmness and strength of character were tempered by gentleness and charity, that many of these evils were conquered. **1975** *Economist* 15 Mar. 38/3 Mike Denness had the job sewn up after his batting performances against India last summer... His batting efforts..show his strength of character.

j. (Later examples.) In *Telecommunications* also with following numeral, indicating signal strength as shown on a meter.

1914 *Rep. Brit. Assoc. Adv. Sci. 1913* 132 These instructions would include directions for simultaneous observations of..the strength of the time-signals..and the average strength and frequency of strays. **1923** *Radio Times* 28 Sept. 2/1 We can take the following as useful ranges from one of the main broadcasting stations for good strength on the head telephones. **1968** J. SANGSTER *Touchfeather* xvi. 188 He finally got the message, strength five. 'What do you want?' **1979** P. NIESEWAND *Member of Club* i. 6 'I've got them, but they're only hearing me strength two.'..'How do you hear them?' 'Strength five.'

2. e. *the strength of*: the point or meaning of, the essential facts about (*ellipt.* in quot. 1958). Esp. in phr. *that's about the strength of it*: that is what it amounts to (cf. *that's, (about) the size of it* s.v. *SIZE *sb.*[1] 10 f); *to get the strength of*: to understand. *colloq.* (orig. and chiefly *Austral.* and *N.Z.*).

1908 H. FLETCHER *Dads & Dan: between Smokes* 112 'So yous thinks I'se wore out,..an' past patchin' an' mendin'?' 'That's about ther strength of it.' **1916** C. J. DENNIS *Moods of Ginger Mick* 63 Then, bit be bit, Mick gits the strength uv it. **1926** K. S. PRICHARD *Working Bullocks* xv. 136 Now..I'll just give you the strength of Red Burke... They say there never was a good Burke. **1943** N. MARSH *Colour Scheme* v. 93, I don't get the strength of it myself. He wouldn't say much. **1946** K. TENNANT *Lost Haven* (1947) ix. 129 If it hadn't been for her engine..you might just as well have left her on the sand-bar to go to pieces... That's about the strength of it. **1958** F. NORMAN *Bang to Rights* I. 10 The strength was that he'd got nicked for ponceing off his old woman. **1965** A. PRIOR *Interrogators* x. 188 'Just passing and you saw the door was open?' He laughed. 'Well, yes, that's just about the strength of it.' **1969** *Advertiser* (Adelaide) 12 May 5/4 Get the strength of this: You [*sc.* Australians] talk about bankos and trunks—is that English? **1974** J. CLEARY *Peter's Pence* vi. 178 'What's the strength of all this?' 'Strength?' Kessler's English didn't run to Australian colloquialisms. 'What's the point, the meaning?'

f. *give me strength*: used as an expression of exasperation.

1967 'S. WOODS' *And shame Devil* 251 'Give me strength,' said O'Brien helplessly. 'I'll try to explain.' **1970** K. BENTON *Sole Agent* xviii. 194 'You make all my plans sound so drab and sordid.' 'Oh give me strength!'

16*. *strength through joy* [tr. G. *kraft durch freude*]: a movement founded in Germany by the National Socialist Party in 1933 to promote physical and cultural recreational activities among working people. Also *transf.* and *fig.* (Freq. with capitals and hyphens.)

1935 G. DIMITROV *Working Class against Fascism* in *Rep. 7th World Congress* (1936) 43 In the Hitler Youth Leagues, in the sports organizations, in the *Kraft durch Freude* organisations (*Strength Through Joy*). **1939** *Ann. Reg. 1938* iii. 201 During the first days after the 'Anschluss', 10,000 [Austrian] workers..inclined to Communism and Socialism, had been invited for a fourteen-day trip to Germany where they found a hearty welcome and were shown the institutions of the *Kraft durch Freude* (strength through joy) movement. **1943** *Tribune* 4 June 19/1 The strength-through-joy brigades you will have met Whose mouths are baggy and whose hair is scented. **1962** L. R. BANKS *End to Running* II. iv. 177 Full of an awful sort of phoney strength-through-joy. **1967** T. STOLPER tr. *G. Stolper's German Economy* v. 152 Annual paid vacations, inexpensive theaters and concerts, and all the other activities of the party's leisure time organization—'Strength through Joy' (*Kraft durch Freude*). **1973** 'G. BLACK' *Bitter Tea* x. 156 The girl..looked as if she had graduated from one of Lee Kuan Yew's strength-through-joy courses. **1975** *Listener* 16 Jan. 71/3 Physical fitness was a Nazi fetish..bronzed young Germans cultivating 'strength through joy'. **1979** J. GARDNER *Nostradamus Traitor* xv. 86 'They sent me up to Scotland.' It was a toughening-up course at a Strength Through Joy Camp... Survival. Living off the land.

17. *strength-(to-)weight ratio*; *strength-giving* (earlier example), *-sapping*, *-showing* adjs.

1845 J. R. LOWELL in *Amer. Rev.* Aug. 137, I saw them in all higher moods, and durst Face their strength-giving eyes. **1961** *Times* 6 Dec. 3/4 Both boxers kept up a strength-sapping pace. **1939** N. DE V. HART *Bridge Players' Bedside Bk.* 133 North's Two Spades is a true strength-showing reverse, because South has to raise the bidding level to three in order to put North back to clubs. **1967** *Bridge Players' Encycl.* 490/1 *Strength-Showing Bids*, in some special situations a suit bid can be used to show strength rather than length or control. **1978** *Jrnl. R. Soc. Arts* CXXVI. 682/2 The primary incentive for the development of titanium was without doubt its strength-to-weight ratio and the potential of this property in aircraft construction. **1945** F. S. STEWART *Airframe Materials* i. 2 The strength-weight ratio of materials used in airframes is of such great importance.

strep (strep), colloq. abbrev. of (*a*) STREPTOCOCCUS (freq. *attrib.*); (*b*) *STREPTOMYCIN.

(*a*) **1927** *Amer. Speech* II. 313/2 A streptococcus infection of the throat becomes a 'strep throat'. **1941** R. CHANDLER *Let.* 1 Feb. (1981) 19 Awfully sorry to hear you had been sick. I know what the streps can do to a person. **1956** [see *STAPH]. **1962** A. LURIE *Love & Friendship* iv. 68 There's germs flying round in the air.., pneumonia and bronchitis and strep. **1966** H. KEMELMAN *Saturday the Rabbi went Hungry* iv. 25 It's a strep infection, the doctor says. **1974** [see *SHET, SHED]. **1980** *Daily Tel.* 6 Oct. 14/6 Strep infections can cause breathing disorders, shock, bleeding and meningitis in newborn babies.

(*b*) **1959** J. BRAINE *Vodi* vi. 85 They'd tried strep. and P.A.S. **1961** C. COCKBURN *View from West* i. 6 Hallucinated myself by the effects of streptomycin—we soon all got very matey with this potent drug and called it strep.

strephosymbolia (stre:fosimbōᵘ·liă). *Psychol.* [mod.L., f. Gr. στρέφειν to turn, twist + σύμβολ-ον (see SYMBOL *sb.*[1]) + -IA[1].] (See quot. 1937.)

1925 S. T. ORTON in *Arch. Neurol. & Psychiatry* (Chicago) XIV. 610 The term 'congenital word-blindness' because of its association with the acquired condition and the implications therefrom, does not seem to be properly descriptive of this disability, and I would therefore like to offer the term 'strephosymbolia'..as a descriptive name for the whole group of children who show unusual difficulty in learning to read. **1937** —— *Reading, Writing & Speech Problems in Children* 214 *Strephosymbolia*, a delay or difficulty in learning to read..characterized by confusion between similarly formed but oppositely oriented letters, and a tendency to a changing order of direction in reading. **1968** E. J. KAHN *Harvard* xiv. 223 There are students who should be exempt from language requirements because they suffer from strephosymbolia—an affliction that makes it difficult..to see the ends of written words in unfamiliar languages.

strepie (strī·pi). *S. Afr.* Also **streepie, streepje.** [Afrikaans, f. *streep* STRIPE *sb.*[3] + -IE.] A small fish, the striped karanteen, *Sarpa salpa*. Cf. *KARANTEEN.

1913 [see *bamboo-fish* s.v. *BAMBOO *sb.* 2]. **1945** *Cape Argus* 27 Jan. 4/8 Half an inch of her wool..tied to a 'streepie' hook, caught about a dozen small fish. **1957** S. SCHOEMAN *Strike!* iii. 89 The strepie, with its beautiful gold and silver colouring, is the favourite prey of the elf. **1974** *Stand. Encycl. S. Afr.* X. 320/1 Strepie..is one of the most beautiful and best-known bait fishes in southern Africa.

‖ **strepitoso** (strepitō·so), *a.* (*adv.*) *Mus.* [It., lit. 'noisy, loud'.] A direction indicating that a composition be played in a spirited or boisterous manner. Also as *sb.*, a piece designed to be played in this manner.

1801 T. BUSBY *Compl. Dict. Mus.*, *Strepitoso*.., a word signifying that the movement to which it is prefixed is to be performed in an impetuous, boisterous style. **1876** STAINER & BARRETT *Dict. Mus. Terms* 410/1 *Strepitoso* (*It.*), noisy, impetuous. **1946** E. BLOM *Everyman's Dict. Mus.* 596/2 *Strepitoso* (It.=noisy), a direction suggesting a forceful and spirited perf., but more often used in the sense of a climax growing in force and speed. **1966** *Listener* 17 Feb. 256/3 The first act finale of both operas ends with a canonic *andantino* in A flat leading to a prolonged *strepitoso* in C major.

† **strepsinema.** *Cytology. Obs.* [f. Gr. στρεψι-, comb. form of στρέφειν to twist + νῆμα yarn.] A condition of the nucleus during cell division, characterized by pairs of chromosomes twisted around one another or in the form of twisted rings; in most cases applied to diplotene nuclei.

1900 H. H. DIXON in *Proc. R. Irish Acad.* VI. 2 In the next stage (fig. 2) the nucleus is in what I would suggest to call the 'strepsinema' condition. The chromatin appears in much the same condition as in the preceding stage, except that in many places it may be seen that the two portions of the thread are more or less loosely twisted together. **1911** *Q. Jrnl. Microsc. Sci.* LVII. 15 The onset of synizesis coincides with the entrance of the nucleus into strepsinema. **1925** E. B. WILSON *Cell* (ed. 3) ii. 126 A noteworthy peculiarity of the spireme sometimes seen is a twisting of the longitudinal halves about each other to form a strepsinema; but this is much less common in the somatic mitoses than in meiosis.

† **strepsitene.** *Cytology. Obs.* [ad. F. *strepsitène* (V. Grégoire 1907, in *La Cellule* XXIV. 372), f. prec.: see *-TENE.] = prec.

1911 *Q. Jrnl. Microsc. Sci.* LVII. 14 Following immediately after the bouquet is the strepsitene or diplotene stage, in which the conjugants which were temporarily united in the pachytene loops separate again. **1925** E. B. WILSON *Cell* (ed. 3) vi. 544 Sooner..or later.., the threads are plainly longitudinally double (diplonema); and the two threads, especially in the later stages, are often spirally twisted about each other to form the strepsinema or strepsitene. These various conditions cannot as yet be very logically separated as distinct stages.

strepto-. Add: **streptostylic** *a.*, (further examples); now used with reference to the free articulation of the quadrate bone with the squamosal rather than to any taxonomic group; [ad. G. *Streptostylica*, name of a group (H. Stannius 1856, in von Siebold & Stannius *Handb. der Zootomie* (ed. 2) II. 45)]; so **stre·ptostyly**, streptostylic condition. Also used as comb. form of STREPTOCOCCUS, STREPTOCOCCAL *a.*, as in *STREPTODORNASE, and of *Streptomyces* (see *STREPTOMYCETE), as in *STREPTOVARICIN.

1933 *Univ. Calif. Publ. Zool.* XXXVII. 524 A comparison of the streptostylic condition in these salamanders with that in certain reptiles..shows great differences in both skeleton and muscles, such that no homology is possible. **1980** *Nature* 21 Feb. 779/1 Streptostylic quadrates are found in fossil lizards before the appearance of mesokinesis and occur in animals with limited mesokinetic potential such as *Uromastix* and *Ctenosaura*. **1925** J. S. KINGSLEY *Vertebrate Skeleton* (ed. 2) 335/2 (Index), Streptostyly. **1933** *Univ. Calif. Publ. Zool.* XXXVII. 521 In a study of some Pacific coast salamanders, it was found that at least three species..possess a pivoting squamosal... Streptostyly, so far as the writer has been able to learn, is otherwise unknown in Amphibia. **1973** *Nature* 11 May 72/2 The articulation of the maxillae with the nasals and premaxillae reveals how streptostyly was associated with an akinetic skull in *Hesperornis*.

streptocarpus. (Earlier example.)

1828 J. LINDLEY in *Bot. Reg.* XIV. 1173 (*heading*) Cape Streptocarpus.

streptodornase (streptodǭ·ɹnēⁱz). *Pharm.* and *Biochem.* [f. STREPTO(COCCAL *a.* + *D(E)O(XY)R(IBO)N(UCLE)ASE.] A deoxyribonuclease, or a group of such enzymes, produced by some streptococci and used in conjunction with streptokinase to bring about the dissolution of purulent and fibrinous exudates.

1949 S. SHERRY et al. in *Jrnl. Clinical Investigation* XXVIII. 1094/1 The word 'Streptodornase' has been employed in this article as an abbreviation of streptococcal desoxyribose nuclease. **1977** *Proc. R. Soc. Med.* LXX. 571/1 Skin testing to streptokinase-streptodornase, candida and phytohaemagglutinin proved negative.

streptokinase (streptokəi·nēⁱz). *Pharm.* [f. as prec. + *KINASE.] An enzyme produced by hæmolytic streptococci which activates plasminogen to form plasmin and is given intravenously to dissolve intravascular blood clots.

1944 CHRISTENSEN & MACLEOD in *Jrnl. Gen. Physiol.* XXVIII. 581 Streptococcal fibrinolysin, also a misnomer in the light of present knowledge, may be termed 'streptokinase', analogous to 'enterokinase' or 'mold kinase'. **1969** *Brit. Med. Jrnl.* 29 Mar. 812/1 Nine patients with arteriographically proved pulmonary embolism have been treated by a 36-hour infusion of streptokinase. **1978** F. X. HASSELBERGER *Uses of Enzymes* x. 122 A controlled experiment..confirmed the superiority of streptokinase over heparin (a chemical anticoagulant) in reducing deaths due to acute myocardial infarction.

streptomycete (streptoməi·sīt). *Bacteriology.* [f. mod.L. *Streptomycetes*, pl. of *Streptomyces*, generic name (Waksman & Henrici 1943, in *Jrnl. Bacteriol.* XLVI. 339), f. STREPTO- + Gr. μύκης fungus.] A bacterium of the genus *Streptomyces*, which belongs in the family Streptomycetaceæ of spore-forming, mould-like bacteria and comprises aerobic forms that grow as branching filaments, form spores in chains, and occur chiefly as saprophytes in soil.

1956 CARTER & SMITH *Microbiol. & Pathol.* (ed. 6) xxxii. 494 The streptomycetes are of medical importance because they are the source of the antibiotics, streptomycin, [etc.]. **1961** *Lancet* 12 Aug. 377/2 A large variety of mould products have been reported effective in cancer in man, from myxomycetes to streptomycetes. **1977** R. W. THOMA *Industr. Microbiol.* 51 Rigorous proof for genetic recombination via transduction or transformation among streptomycetes is still lacking. **1978** *Nature* 31 Aug. 844/2 C. Stuttard..reported the isolation of virulent transducing phage in a chloramphenicol-producing streptomycete.

streptomycin (streptoməi·sin). *Pharm.* [f. prec.: see *-MYCIN.] An antibiotic, $C_{21}H_{39}N_7O_{12}$, produced by the soil bacterium *Streptomyces griseus*, which was the first drug to be successful against tuberculosis but is now used chiefly in conjunction with other drugs because of its toxic effects. Also *Comb.*

1944 A. SCHATZ et al. in *Proc. Soc. Exper. Biol. & Med.* LV. 67/1 Because of its similarity to streptothricin, this substance may be designated as streptomycin, derived from the generic name that has recently been given to the aerial-mycelium producing and sporulating group of actinomycetes, namely *Streptomyces*. **1948** 'G. ORWELL' *Let.* 4 Feb. in *Coll. Ess.* (1968) IV. 404 We are now sending for some new American drug called streptomycin which they say will speed up the cure. **1961** *Lancet* 29 July 247/2 Streptomycin-resistant strains [of gonococci] remained.. susceptible to penicillin. **1973** *Sci. Amer.* Sept. 130/2 Streptomycin and isoniazid have diminished the need for state tuberculosis sanatoriums. **1974** M. C. GERALD *Pharmacol.* xxvi. 457 Streptomycin binds to the ribosome in such a manner that incorrect amino acids are laid down, thus resulting in the formation of a nonfunctional protein. **1978** *Antimicrobial Agents & Chemotherapy* XIII. 430 Combinations of penicillin and gentamycin have been shown to be synergistic against all strains of enterococci, including those resistant to penicillin and streptomycin.

streptosolen (streptosōᵘ·lĕn). [mod.L. (J. Miers 1850, in *Ann. Mag. Nat. Hist.* 2nd Ser. V. 208), f. STREPTO- + Gr. σωλήν pipe.] A climbing evergreen shrub, *Streptosolen jamesonii*, of the family Solanaceæ, which is native to Colombia and Ecuador and bears clusters of orange flowers.

1938 J. S. DAKERS *Mod. Greenhouse* vii. 105 Streptosolen..has orange scarlet flowers produced in bunches. **1952** R. GENDERS *Greenhouse* xv. 150 Streptosolen..is a grand evergreen plant for covering a wall of a lean-to house. **1976** *Homes & Gardens* Aug. 75/2 At the minimum heat mentioned, little more than that needed to keep out winter frost, climbers one can grow include..blue plumbago, orange streptosolen, [etc.].

streptothricin (streptoþri·sin, -þrəi·sin). *Biochem.* [f. mod.L. *streptothric-*, STREPTOTHRIX + -IN[1].] Each of a group of related antibiotic but toxic compounds, $C_{13}H_{21}N_6O_7$-$(C_6H_{12}N_2O)_n$, produced by the soil bacterium *Actinomyces lavendulæ*.

1942 WAKSMAN & WOODRUFF in *Proc. Soc. Exper. Biol. & Med.* XLIX. 207 A new substance can now be added to this list of antibiotic agents. This substance has been obtained from a soil *Actinomyces*, and is designated as *streptothricin*, derived from the early generic designation *Streptothrix*, given to this group of organisms. **1955** *Sci. News Let.* 21 May 326/3 Two other antibiotics, streptothricin and noformicin, ..are effective against Newcastle disease virus in the test tube. **1963** BARBER & GARROD *Antibiotic & Chemotherapy* vi. 89 This first antibiotic of any value resulting from this investigation was streptothricin, which..was subsequently found to be too toxic for clinical use. **1972** *Jrnl. Antibiotics* XXV. 501 All the available preparations of antibiotics of this type were mixtures of six streptothricins differing in the number of L-β-lysine residues (1 in streptothricin F, 2 in streptothricin E and so on to 6 in streptothricin A). **1978** *Res. in Vet. Sci.* XXV. 110 The number of worms remaining in the infected dogs after one or more treatments with this streptothricin complex.

streptothricosis (stre:ptoþrikōᵘ·sis). *Vet. Sci.* Also **-trichosis.** [f. as prec. + -OSIS.] A usu. chronic, sometimes fatal disease caused by actinomycetes and producing scabs on the skin of cows and other farm animals, esp. in the wet season in tropical regions.

1927 *Ann. Rep. Veter. Dept., Northern Provinces, 1926* (Nigeria) 10 Contagious Impetigo or Streptothricosis... This disease made its appearance in the Government herd [of cattle] at Vom. **1971** D. L. DOXEY *Veter. Clinical Path.* xiv. 267 Although formerly classed as of differing aetiology, cutaneous streptothricosis in cattle, mycotic dermatitis in cattle, sheep, goats and horses, and strawberry foot rot of sheep, are all caused by the same organism, *Dermatophilus congolensis*. **1973** AINSWORTH & AUSTWICK *Fungal Dis. Animals* (ed. 2) 135 Dermatophilosis, especially in cattle (streptotrichosis) and sheep (mycotic dermatitis, strawberry foot-rot), occurs in many tropical and temperate countries as acute local infections of the skin following damage by prolonged soaking, insolation, tick bites or other agencies.

streptovaricin (streptovæ·rĭsin). *Pharm.* [f. mod.L. *Strepto-myces* (see *STREPTOMYCETE) + VARI(OUS *a.* + *-MY)CIN.] Each of a group of related antibiotics produced by the bacterium *Streptomyces spectabilis*.

1957 P. SIMINOFF et al. in *Amer. Rev. Tuberculosis* LXXV. 582 A new antimicrobial complex, streptovaricin, is produced by *Streptomyces spectabilis*, n. sp. The complex consists of at least five microbiologically active, closely related components which have been named streptovaricins *A*, *B*, *C*, *D*, and *E*, respectively. **1972** *Accounts Chem. Res.* V. 60/1 The streptovaricins all contain an identical carbon skeleton and..they differ from one another in the degree of oxygenation and degree of acetylation.

streptozotocin (streptozǫ·tǝ̄ʊsin). *Pharm.* [f. as prec. + *-zoto-*, of unkn. origin + *-MY)-CIN.] An antibiotic substance obtained from *Streptomyces achromogenes* that damages insulin-producing cells and is used to induce diabetes in laboratory animals.

1960 J. J. VAURA et al. in *Antibiotics Ann. 1959–60* 234 Streptozotocin is a new antibiotic produced by a streptomycete isolated from the soil. **1972** *Jrnl. Pharm. Sci.* LXI. 491/1 Chemically streptozotocin is a *N*-methyl-*N*-nitrosourea derivative..of D-glucosamine. **1976** A. MARBLE et al. in G. S. Avery *Drug Treatment* xv. 421/1 Streptozotocin, another hyperglycaemic drug, has been similarly used in cases of malignant insulin-secreting tumour. **1980** *Nature* 3 Jan. 100/1 Proinsulin mRNA was purified from rat B-cell tumours induced with streptozotocin and nicotinamide.

Strepyan (stre·piăn), *a.* *Archæol.* Also **Strepyian.** [ad. F. *Strépyien*, f. *Strépy*, name of a town (the type site) in Belgium: see -AN.] Of or belonging to a palæolithic culture of Europe supposed to have existed before the Chellean. Freq. *absol.*

[**1904** A. RUTOT in *Bulletin Société d'Anthropologie de Bruxelles* XXIII. Mém. 1. 15 Les industries éolithiques quaternaires et des pièces qui se rapportent absolument à notre transition de l'Éolithique au Paléolithique ou du Mesvinien au Chelléen, c'est-à-dire au Strépyien.] **1910** J. McCABE *Prehistoric Man* i. 12 It is usual to admit three stages in the earlier Paleolithic, the names of which are taken from the French sites where we find them best exhibited... Advanced students, like M. Rutot, add an earlier stage (the Strepyian). **1911** W. J. SOLLAS *Ancient Hunters* v. 112 The distinctive character of the Strepyan industry, according to M. Rutot, is that all the implements retain a considerable part of the original crust of the flint nodule. **1914** J. GEIKIE *Antiquity of Man in Europe* ii. 43 The 'Strepyan', on the other hand, is marked by the presence not only of simple flakes but of primitive forms of the Chellean *coup de poing*. **1927** PEAKE & FLEURE *Apes & Man* vi. 90 The Strépyan, more often termed by others pre-Chellean, are accepted under the latter name by most archaeologists as being merely a very early type of Chellean. **1948** A. L. KROEBER *Anthropology* xvi. 631 Rutot's Mesvinian stage of the Eolithic is recognized as probably a Belgian facies of the oldest Levalloisian or Pre-Mousterian, his Strepyan as being Chellean—all of them Palaeolithic and Pleistocene. **1961** L. D. STAMP *Gloss. Geogr. Terms* 532 *Acheulian*,..a cultural stage.. characterized by a certain type of chipped stone implements. The more usually accepted stages are:..Eolithic, Strepyan, pre-Chellean.

stress, *sb.* Add: **I. 3. g.** *Psychol.* and *Biol.* An adverse circumstance that disturbs, or is likely to disturb, the normal physiological or psychological functioning of an individual; such circumstances collectively. Also, the disturbed state that results.

1942 *Endocrinology* XXXI. 420 When the normal animal is subjected to stress the adrenal cortices show hypertrophy. **1953** FRUTON & SIMMONDS *Gen. Biochem.* xxxvii. 843 Similar reduction in the adrenal ascorbic acid and cholesterol is observed when normal animals are subjected to a variety of stress [*sic*] (injury, cold, heat, drugs, toxins, lack of oxygen, etc.). **1955** H. BASOWITZ et al. *Anxiety & Stress* i. 7 Anxiety has been defined in terms of an affective response; stress is the stimulus condition likely to arouse such response. **1959** *New Scientist* 12 Nov. 927/1 Some examples of the diseases thought to result from stress are high blood pressure, peptic ulceration and coronary thrombosis. **1968** PASSMORE & ROBSON *Compan. Med. Stud.* II. xxxvi. 8/1 Parenthood itself can be a stress for the immature adult. **1973** R. M. MAY *Model Ecosystems* iii. 60 Equation (3.21) tends to require that each species encounters greater competitive stress from its own, rather than from the other, species. **1976** *Sci. Amer.* July 55/1 The familiar human experience described as stress (caused by many factors, including fear, physical trauma, severe heat or cold or even extreme joy) has as a common denominator an increased secretion of adrenal steroids. **1978** S. LEVINE et al. in H. Ursin et al. *Psychobiol. of Stress* i. 4 When the psychologically threatening or arousing aspects of a situation were altered, classical stresses such as fasting and heat no longer activated the pituitary-adrenal system. **1979** *McGraw-Hill Yearbk. Sci. & Technol.* 374/1 Cacti suffering from water stress become fully rehydrated within 24 hr following a heavy rain.

5. c. Substitute for def.: A force acting on or within a body or structure and tending to deform it; now usu. the intensity of this, the force per unit area. (Further examples.)

As orig. defined by Rankine the stress was the equal and opposite reaction of the body to the force, rather than the force itself (see quots. 1855, 1856 in Dict.).

1876 *Encycl. Brit.* IV. 285/2 There are three kinds of stress, due to tension, compression, and shearing. *Ibid.* The ultimate strength of the material is measured by the maximum intensity of stress which it can bear, or in other words, by the stress which the unit area of cross section can bear. **1925** J. CASE *Strength of Materials* i. 2 When we wish to give the stress a numerical value it is desirable.. to refer to the stress in relation to the area of the cross section... The total force acting on a section, divided by the area of that section, is called the stress intensity or, more often, simply the stress. [*Note*] In future when we use the word 'stress' without qualification it must be understood to mean 'intensity of stress'. **1938** LAURSON & COX *Mech. of Materials* i. 2 Total stress is a force... Intensity of stress, however, is expressed in units of force divided by units of area. **1960** H. K. PRESTON *Practical Prestressed Concrete* i. 3 The same beam..is prestressed by a force of 54,000 lb... This force creates a uniform compressive stress of +1,000 psi over the entire cross section of the beam. **1979** *Nature* 23 Aug. 670/1 Arctic sea-ice breaks under wind stress throughout the year, exposing leads of open water.

5*. Phr. *stress(es) and strain(s)* (with reference to senses 3 and 5; cf. *strain and stress* s.v. *STRAIN *sb.*² 10*).

1854 C. PATMORE *Angel in House* I. VIII. viii. 118 Puzzled and fagg'd by stress and strain. **1856** *Phil. Trans. R. Soc.* CXLVI. 481 (*heading*) Elements of a mathematical theory of elasticity... Part I. On stresses and strains. **1935** *Discovery* Sept. 259/1 The interdependent mechanical stresses and strains. **1952** *Sat. Rev.* (U.S.) 20 Sept. 38/2 There never are stresses in government, but *stresses* and *strains*. **1959** M. STEEN *Tower* I. vi. 85, I realised what the last few years, with their stresses and strains, had done to us both. **1960** *Times* 13 Jan. 15/2 Wrestling once again with unknown aeronautical quantities and resolving new propositions in stress and strain. **1979** *Jrnl. R. Soc. Arts* CXXVII. 363/2 New stresses and strains in the relationships between..Britain and the remaining territories.

III. 10. (sense 3 d) *stress area*; (sense 3 g) *stress reaction*, *situation*, *symptom*; (senses 5 c, 8) *stress-pattern*; (sense 8) *stress-difference*, *-point*, *-shift*; **stress analysis** *Engin.*, the theoretical or experimental study of the stresses within a mechanical structure in relation to its function; hence **stress analyst; stress-breaker** *Dentistry*, a device attached to or incorporated in a partial denture to reduce the occlusive forces that have to be borne by the underlying tissue and the teeth to which the denture is attached; so **stress-breaking** *vbl. sb.* and *ppl. a.*; **stress-broken** *ppl. a.*; **stress concentration** *Engin.*, a local increase in the stress inside an object; also, a stress raiser; **stress contour** *Phonetics*, a sequence of varying levels of stress within an utterance; **stress corrosion** *Metallurgy*, the development of cracks as a result of the combined effects of stress and corrosion; freq. *attrib.*; **stress diagram** *Mech.*, a diagram that represents graphically the stresses within a framed structure; **stress-dilatancy** *Physics*, dilatancy that occurs as a result of applied stress; **stress disease,** a disease that occurs as a result of continual exposure to stress; **stress fracture** *Med.*, a fracture of a bone caused by the repeated application of a high load; **stress-free** *a.*, pertaining to or possessing freedom from mechanical or biological stress; **stress grading** *vbl. sb.*, the grading of timber according to its strength, as estimated from the number and distribution of knots and other visible defects; so **stress grade** *sb.* and (with hyphen) *v. trans.*; **stress-graded** *ppl. a.*; **stress-group** *Phonetics*, a group of syllables forming a rhythmic unit with one primary stress; **stress incontinence** *Med.*, a condition found chiefly in women in which a (usu. small) escape of urine occurs when the intra-abdominal pressure increases suddenly, as in coughing or lifting; **stress interview,** an interview in which there is a deliberate attempt to subject a candidate to stress by the nature of the questioning; **stress mark,** (*a*) *Phonetics*, a symbol or a diacritical mark indicating that a syllable carries stress; (*b*) *Photogr.*, a mark on a photographic print caused by friction or pressure on the film surface; hence **stress-marked** *a.*; **stress maximum** *Phonetics*, the tonic accent; **stress mineral** *Petrol.*, a mineral whose formation in metamorphic rocks is believed to be dependent on shearing stress; **stress-neutral** *a.* *Linguistics*, designating a derivational or inflectional suffix which plays no part in the placing of stress within a word; hence **stress-neutrality; stress phoneme** *Linguistics*, a phoneme whose contrastiveness consists in a distinctive degree of stress; **stress raiser** *Engin.*, a feature in the shape or composition of an object that gives rise to a local increase in stress; **stress relaxation** *Engin.*, a decrease of stress occurring in a material when the associated deformation remains constant; **stress relief** *Metallurgy*, the reduction of residual stress in a material by thermal treatment; also **stress-relieve** *v. trans.*, **-relieved** *ppl. a.*, **-relieving** *vbl. sb.* (freq. *attrib.*); **stress-strain** *adj. phr. Engin.*, pertaining to or depicting the relation between mechanical stress and the strain it produces; **stress-timed** *a. Phonetics*, designating or pertaining to a language in which primary stresses occur at approximately equal intervals, irrespective of the number of unstressed syllables in between; hence **stress-timing.**

1926 PIPPARD & BARROW in *Building Res. Board Techn. Paper* No. 1. 1 The bow girder..presents an interesting problem in stress analysis. **1980** *Strain* XVI. 132/2 The stress analysis of turbine components for the new hydro-electric pumped storage system. **1950** M. HETÉNYI *Handbk. Exper. Stress Analysis* p. v, Several principal methods and literally hundreds of individual tools and artifices constitute the 'arsenal' of the experimental stress analyst. **1976** B. JACKSON *Flameout* (1977) ii. 32 His career as stress analyst with Lockheed Aircraft. **1973** *Times* 17 Apr. 1/2 His brief will be to review the functions and relationship of the two bodies to enable them to make the most effective contribution in strengthening the voluntary housing movement in stress areas. **1930** H. P. Boos in I. G. Nichols *Prosthetic Dentistry* xxxvii. 600 Stress-breakers can be used in conjunction with the tube successfully. **1955** J. OSBORNE *Dental Mech.* (ed. 4) x. 215 (*caption*) Split casting type of stress breaker. **1930** L. M. FARNUM in I. G. Nichols *Prosthetic Dentistry* xxxvi. 593 Stress-breaking construction is indicated where there are no posterior abutments on one or both sides of the mouth. **1963** C. R. COWELL et al. *Inlays, Crowns, & Bridges* xi. 118 This form of bridge incorporates a stress-breaking device, which allows limited movement at one of the joints between pontic and retainer. **1973** D. H. ROBERTS *Fixed Bridge Prostheses* ix. 152 The dovetail and slot introduces a certain degree of 'stress-breaking' between the two parts of the bridge, and because of this the retainers..are far less likely to fail. **1955** J. OSBORNE *Dental Mech.* (ed. 4) ix. 150 In cases when the teeth are periodontally affected, stress-broken designs may be employed. **1925** TIMOSHENKO & LESSELLS *Appl. Elasticity* i. 10 A semi-circular groove in a strip subjected to tension..also produces very high stress-concentration. **1936** [see *stress raiser* below]. **1977** E. J. HEARN *Mech. of Materials* xviii. 477 If..stress concentrations such as notches, keyways, holes, etc., are present in the bar, these will result in local stress increases. **1958** A. A. HILL *Introd. Linguistic Struct.* 28 Stress contours differ from pitch contours in that two phrases are never united into a single stress contour. **1971** *Language* XLVII. 269 It appears that the stress contours of English sentences are determined in a simple and regular way by their underlying syntactic structures. **1931** *Jrnl. Iron & Steel Inst.* CXXIV. 723 Stress corrosion of metals. **1967** A. H. COTTRELL *Introd. Metallurgy* xxiii. 467 In stress-corrosion cracking there is usually very little overall corrosion. **1973** A. PARRISH *Mech. Engineers' Ref. Bk.* (ed. 11) v. 77 The higher Mo bearing steels offer more resistance to stress corrosion cracking than 18/8; stress relief treatment (two hours at 870°C) after fabrication considerably reduces the risk of cracking. **1873** J. G. MEDLEY *Roorkee Treat. Civil Engin. in India* (ed. 3) I. xxv. 550 Loads on Roofs naturally divide themselves into two sets... Hence two distinct Stress-diagrams must be drawn, one for each system of load. **1919** PIPPARD & PRITCHARD *Aeroplane Structures* viii. 72 Probably the most satisfactory method of determining the forces in the individual members of a structure is by means of the stress diagram. **1965** G. M. MILLS *Theory of Structures* ix. 168 The variation of stress along a given axis may be shown graphically by means of a stress diagram. **1924** O. JESPERSEN *Philos. Gram.* xvii. 231 The old compound *mankind* (now stressed on the second syllable) comprises all human beings, but the younger *mankind* (stressed on the first syllable) is opposed to *womankind*. (The stress-difference, as made in N.E.D., is not, however, recognized by everybody.) **1971** *Language* XLVII. 261 The analysis given..correctly predicts the existence of a stress difference associated with the two readings of sentences like *The parable shows what suffering men can create.* **1944** G. W. S. BLAIR *Survey Gen. & Appl. Rheol.* iii. 31 The exceptions [to this rule] are..(*c*) Materials whose consistency is increased by increasing the stress (as distinct from the strain) applied to them. This phenomenon has been little studied, but may be referred to as 'stress-dilatancy'. **1962** *Proc. R. Soc.* A. CCLXIX. 500 (*heading*) The stress-dilatancy relation for static equilibrium of an assembly of particles in contact. **1979** *Geotechnique* XXIX. 341 Rowe's (1962) stress-dilatancy relation..allows indirect measurement of this angle [*sc.* of interparticle friction] based on triaxial compression tests on dense..samples. **1948** *Observer* 13 June 5/5 Absenteeism which arises..from those once..despised causes which passed under names such as neurasthenia and described to-day as stress diseases. **1966** G. E. EVANS *Pattern under Plough* viii. 96 It is more enlightened and scientific in psychosomatic and stress diseases for medicine to address itself as much to the man as to the actual disease. **1952** R. WATSON-JONES *Fractures* (ed. 4) I. xv. 343 (*heading*) Fatigue or stress fractures. **1983** *Brit. Med. Jrnl.* 12 Nov. 1449/1 Stress fractures are widely recognised in running. **1946** *Nature* 5 Oct. 475/1 After discussing the effect of swelling on the sorption isotherm he proceeded to derive a stress-free isotherm. **1961** *Economist* 21 Oct. 249/1 A stress-free cruising speed of 70-75 mph. **1978** D. BLOODWORTH *Crosstalk* xxiv. 188 Stress-free mice are far better performers. **1941** *Grading Rules for Structural Timber* (*B.S.I.*) 2 A further standard for the compressive stress grading of these species for use in compression and tension members..is being prepared. **1944** (*title*) Grading rules for stress-graded timber. (B.S.I.) *Ibid.* 4 The present revision has been undertaken..to provide for stress grades higher than 800 lb. f. **1971** *Timber Trades Jrnl.* 21 Aug. 26/2 Typical yields of sawn timber have been..graded by the stress-grading machine installed by Timber-lab at Princes Risborough. *Ibid.* 23/3 The timber for all the main structural components was visually stress-graded to a minimum of 50 grade before use. **1973** *Materials & Technol.* VI. i. 27 In Britain, four basic stress grades are specified for sawn softwood, and three for laminated timber. *Ibid.*, Visual stress grading is not a difficult operation, but requires considerable experience. **1876** H. Sweet in *Trans. Philol. Soc.* **1875–6** 473 We find..that every sentence can be analyzed into smaller groups characterized by one predominant stress-syllable, round which the others group themselves... In our first sentence there are two such stress groups... A word is, phonetically speaking, a stress-group. **1959** J. T. Pring *Colloq. Eng. Pronunc.* 56 A stress-group is formed by a strongly stressed, pro-minent syllable, together with any unstressed, non-prominent syllables which cluster about it. **1935** A. W. Bourne *Midwifery for Nurses* ii. 24 Stress incontinence is due to a weakening of the supports of the bladder. **1972** Law & Friedman *Midwifery* xiv. 334 The patient is then asked to strain down and any tendency to prolapse of the vaginal walls is noted. She is then asked to cough to determine whether any stress incontinence is present. **1955** *Explorations* Feb. 7, I examined stress interviews as well as non-directive ones. **1978** *Jrnl. R. Soc. Arts* CXXVI. 270/1 Whilst stress interviews in which the interviewer sets out to be provocative or rude may have been appropriate for the selection of American Special Services personnel during the war, I would not recommend them for civilian use. **1888** H. Sweet *Hist. Eng. Sounds* 8 The stress marks are put before the element on which the stress begins. **1918** *Photo Miniature* Mar. 41 *Stress marks*, scummy appearance or black lines on a bromide or D.O.P. print, caused by..the sensitive paper being rubbed against the negative or other sheets of paper, or any sharp pressure. **1919** *Brit. Jrnl. Photogr. Alm.* 251 Free from tendency to give rise to stress or abrasion marks. **1961** *Amer. Speech* XXXVI. 221 Tone patterns illustrated by Kingdon's tonetic stress marks in ascending order of complexity. Indicates the force of each pattern on basic grammatical constructions. **1968** L. A. Mannheim tr. *Fritsche's Faults in Photography* III. 331 Most enlarging papers are largely protected against stress marks by an emulsion supercoating. **1964** R. H. Robins *Gen. Linguistics* iv. 138 In a word stressed on a non-initial syllable, in stress-marked languages, the stressed articulation usually begins on the consonant. **1969** *Computers & Humanities* III. 136 The next step in this project is to replace orthographic entries with phonetic entries... Then, stress maxima will be determined and various features of meter tabulated and analyzed. **1971** *Language* XLVII. 588 Thus in *the mangy dog*, the stress on the first syllable of *mangy* is a stress maximum. **1918** A. Harker in *Q. Jrnl. Geol. Soc.* LXXIV. p. lxxvii, Shearing stress manifestly favours the production of sericite and the chlorites, of albite [etc.]... These may conveniently be styled stress-minerals. **1952** H. Ramberg *Origin Metamorphic & Metasomatic Rocks* 119 It has yet to be proved..that any of the suggested stress minerals really are such. **1965** G. J. Williams *Econ. Geol. N.Z.* x. 158/1 The chief constituent of all specimens he examined is a variety optically identical with the stress-mineral antigorite. **1971** *Language* XLVIII. 269 If word stress is assigned prior to syntactic transformations, then it follows automatically that transformationally attached affixes are stress-neutral. **1972** *Ibid.* XLVIII. 336 He [*sc.* Lakoff] suggests that the NSR [*sc.* Nuclear Stress Rule] might precede the assignment of word-stress; this destroys the principle of the phonological cycle, and again fails to explain the stress-neutrality of transformationally placed affixes. **1954** S. Robertson *Devel. Mod. Eng.* (rev. ed.) iv 77 In English, any word of two or more syllables has its own stress-pattern **1968** R. A. Lyttleton *Myst. Solar Syst.* vi. 193 Tektites reveal series of dark and light bands associated with the internal stress-pattern. **1980** *Early Music* July 403/2 Freed from the obligations of setting a poetic text, from the need to conform to text stress-patterns and changes of poetic mood, a composer might indulge in the exploration of thematic material to the full. **1933** L. Bloomfield *Language* xvii. 295 In modern English verse..the author shapes his wording so that stress-phonemes at certain intervals. **1968** Chomsky & Halle *Sound Pattern Eng.* 26 He [*sc.* the speaker] need not make a choice among various 'stress phonemes'. **1932** D. Jones *Outl. Eng. Phonetics* (ed. 3) xxviii. 223 The lengths separating the 'stress-points' or 'peaks of prominence' of the syllables. **1956** *Kenyon Rev.* XVIII. 466 Mr. Chatman has shown the metrical stress-points in each line, but in my judgment he has misplaced them in lines 2, 12 and 14. **1936** *Trans. Amer. Inst. Mining & Metall. Engineers* CXX. 32 Yet another field in which correlation of metallographic and mechanical methods is needed is the study of the relative seriousness of 'inherent' and 'imposed' sources of stress concentration —'stress raisers', as Gillett has aptly called them. **1978** R. J. Gray in McCall & French *Metallogr. in Failure Analysis* 240 The surfaces must be free of machining marks that could serve as stress raisers where a fissure and subsequent fracture could occur. **1966** Lazarus & Opton in C. D. Spielberger *Anxiety & Behavior* x. 227 The second phase involved the plan to manipulate 'ego-defense' processes so as to reduce stress reactions while subjects watched a stressful film. **1979** D. A. Bakal *Psychol. & Med.* iii. 86 The capacity of any situation to produce stress reactions depends on the characteristics of individuals. **1943** *Jrnl. Chem. Physics* XI. 127/1 As a result of their studies of stress relaxation..of polyvinyl acetate held at constant elongation these authors conclude that the polymer is composed of a netted system of chains through which interpenetrates a system of relatively free chains. **1959** *Jrnl. Iron & Steel Inst.* CXCII. 198/3 Stress relaxation tests at a constant total strain of 0·15% for times exceeding 20 000 h on three low-alloy steels. **1979** R. P. Brown *Physical Testing of Rubbers* xi. 200 Stress relaxation is the measurement of change of stress with time under constant strain. **1935** *Symp. Welding Iron & Steel* (Iron & Steel Inst.) II. 42 Stress relief by heat treatment reduced the stresses to approximately 10 per cents of those existing in the plates as welded. **1973** [see *stress corrosion* above]. **1980** *Metallography* XIII. 69 A stress-relief treatment at 600–650°C results in the transformation of ferrite primarily to $M_{23}C_6$ carbide. **1935** *Symp. Welding Iron & Steel* (Iron & Steel Inst.) II. 47 The whole member was now stress-relieved in the furnace and delivered to the machine shop for completion of the work. **1980** *Metallography* XIII. 59 Large components are invariably stress relieved to reduce the residual stresses generated in welding. **1935** *Symp. Welding Iron & Steel* (Iron & Steel Inst.) II. 46 The stress-relieved grid was next planed on a planer and planed top and bottom. **1980** *Metallography* XIII. 59 (*heading*) Microstructural transformations in stress relieved type 316 stainless steel weld metal. **1938** D. K. Bullens et al. *Steel & its Heat Treatment* (ed. 4) I. v. 140 Finish machining is then done and a final stress-relieving draw given..at 1050°, holding 48 hr. at temperature and furnace cooling. **1956** *Jrnl. Iron & Steel Inst.* CLXXXIII. 99/2 Stress relieving of 11-ft. dia. electrically welded steel duct. **1980** *Jrnl. Nucl. Materials* XCI. 189 The stress-relieving treatments [of Zircalloy-4] were made at..773,'793 and 813 K, during 1 and 2 hr. **1888** H. Sweet *Hist. Eng. Sounds* 124 This law of stress-shift in weak diphthongs explains the INorth. *am = eom*: weak *eom* became first *eam*.., then *eám*, and finally, by dropping the almost inaudible *e*, *am*. **1930** T. Sasaki *On Lang. R. Bridges' Poetry* 91 It has been the rule in the English blank verse since Chaucer not to tolerate stress-shift (or inversion of accent) in the fifth foot. **1972** M. L. Samuels *Linguistic Evol.* iii. 36 Later in Germanic stressing on the root-syllable was generalised, and because of this stress-shift the voiced allophones..were no longer in complementary distribution, [etc.]. **1959** *New Scientist* 12 Nov. 927/2 Much was still to be understood of the intermediate steps between the stress situation and the decrease in circulating eosinophils. **1972** 'T. Coe' *Don't lie to Me* xviii. 149 That premonition of something being wrong that sometimes strikes people in stress situations. **1886** K. Pearson in I. Todhunter *Hist. Theory Elasticity* I. 503 There exist certain materials for which even in a state of ease the stress-strain relation is not linear; that is to say the stress-strain curve..is not a straight line even for very small elastic strains. **1923** Glazebrook *Dict. Appl. Physics* V. 56/2 This will be the most convenient place in which to treat of the stress-strain relations of a doped fabric. **1956** *Nature* 24 Mar. 561/1 Papers..dealt with the measurement of residual stresses in cold-drawn tubes;..and stress-strain characteristics of metal at high rates of strain. **1973** J. G. Tweeddale *Materials Technol.* I. iv. 79 Having derived the respective stress and strain values it is possible to study the tensile characteristics of a material from a graph comparing these values—a stress–strain diagram. **1958** *Times Lit. Suppl.* 17 Oct. 596/4 A cold in the head is more often than not a stress-symptom with which one must learn to live. **1977** P. Dickinson *Walking Dead* 1. i. 24 At a certain point of over-crowding..[rats] manifest stress symptoms. **1946** K. L. Pike *Intonation Amer. Eng.* III. 35 Many non-English languages..tend to use a rhythm which is more closely related to the syllable than the regular stress-timed type of English. **1956** [see *isochronic *a.* 3]. **1980** *English World-Wide* I. 1. 108 RP is stress-timed, with primary stress recurring at roughly even intervals through a sentence. **1964** M. A. K. Halliday et al. *Linguistic Science* iii. 72 The English type of rhythm is known as 'stress-timing'.

stress, *v.*[1] Add: **3. d.** In contexts of *Biol.* and *Psychol.*: cf. *stress *sb.* 3 g.

1973 *Country Life* 7 June 1859/2 The transfer to a new environment stresses the calves, and it is now that latent infection will show itself. **1975** *Verbatim* Sept. 5/2 An analysis of the tapes will show exactly how stressed he was, stated the author of a book on certain intelligence methods. **1979** *Sci. Amer.* Nov. 65/1 When the reovirus-infected mice were stressed by injection with a large dose of glucose, however, it became quite clear that their ability to metabolize glucose had become impaired.

stressable (stre·săb'l) *a.* *Linguistics.* [f. Stress *v.*[1] + -able.] Capable of being stressed. Also **stressabi·lity.**

1964 W. S. Allen in D. Abercrombie et al. *Daniel Jones* 6 In verse, as in the language, not every heavy syllable is stressed; it is only *stressable*. **1964** *English Studies* XLV. 495 He investigates its relation to Latin phonology, which in the realm of accent is characterized by the category of stressability. **1972** *Language* XLVIII. 295 The statement 'B is stressable' is to rule out cases like anaphoric noun phrases, which are not stressable. **1977** *Ibid.* LIII. 28 We agree that the stressability of prepositions is to be handled by the rules of the grammar rather than poetry, but we differ substantially on the specific analysis.

stressed, *ppl. a.* Add: **3.** *Engin.* Subjected to mechanical stress; *spec.* = *prestressed *ppl. a.*; *stressed skin*, an outer covering of an aircraft or other structure that bears a significant part of the stresses and contributes to the overall strength and stiffness; usu. *attrib.*

1930 *Flight* 11 Apr. 411/2 Recently a monoplane of orthodox aerodynamic design was completed by the company, employing the stressed-skin type of wing construction. **1951** *Archit. Rev.* CX. 342/1 The roof is of stressed-skin plywood construction formed by two skins of exterior ply panel grade on an internal timber framework. **1954** [see *diagrid]. **1966** *Daily Tel.* 10 Aug. 18/2 American steel was being bought for the 'highly stressed' parts of future British-built nuclear submarines. **1968** *Punch* 13 Nov. 688/3 British Railways 'revolutionary gas-turbine advanced passenger train with stressed-skin, aircraft-type construction'. **1979** *Jrnl. Magnetism & Magn. Materials* XI. 76 Uniaxially stressed semiconductors.

stressful, *a.* Add: Also, causing or inclined to cause stress.

1952 *Psychosomatic Med.* XIV. 311/2 Characteristically in the patient with chronic fatigue, the stressful activity is implicit rather than explicit. **1966** O. Norton *School of Liars* vi. 104 'How do you protect a man like him from stress?'..'By not being stressful yourself.' **1972** C. M. Parkes *Bereavement* iii. 32 Situations that tend to produce alarm are regarded as *stressful*. **1978** *Detroit Free Press* 5 Mar. D4/4 Are you always changing things in your life, changing jobs, changing residences?..If so, subtract two years. Too much change is stressful.

stressman (stre·smæn). *Engin.* Pl. **stressmen.** [f. Stress *sb.* + Man *sb.*[1]] = *stress analyst* s.v. *stress *sb.* 10.

1935 C. G. Burge *Compl. Bk. Aviation* 260/2 The 'stressman' may be able to suggest practical methods of lightening the weight. **1954** Veale & Radford *Aircraft for All* iv. 62 Stressmen..check the strength of every major part. **1960** *Times* 1 Apr. 2/3 (Advt.), Hunting Aircraft Limited have vacancies for..aerodynamicists, stressmen, design draughtsmen. The work programme embraces both high and low speed military and civil aircraft. **1975** *Offshore Engineer* Sept. 134/1 There is provision for override so that when needed the system can operate continuously—say during a period of bad weather or, as Desmond Thurgood, Seatek's chief stressman, points out, during installation.

stressor (stre·səɹ). *Psychol.* and *Biol.* [f. Stress *sb.*, *v.*[1] + -or.] A single condition or agent that constitutes a stress for an organism (see *stress *sb.* 3 g).

1950 H. Selye *Physiol. & Path. of Exposure to Stress* 9 The expression systemic stress is used here to denote a condition in which..extensive regions of the body deviate from their normal resting state. In accordance with the common usage of the word 'stress', the term 'systemic stress' is sometimes loosely employed also to denote the stimuli which cause systemic stress. In this sense, it is preferable however, to speak of alarming stimuli or 'stressors'. **1958** *Proc. 10th Internat. Congr. Entomol.* IV. 727 (*heading*) Crowding as a stressor [in insects]. **1962** *Lancet* 27 Jan. 200/2 It has long been known that the response of schizophrenic patients to stressor agents is dulled. **1969** *Nature* 4 Oct. 18/2 Stress results from a threat, real or apparent, to the biological integrity of the animal. More simply—a 'stressor' can be defined as any stimulus or situation which causes maladaptive behaviour. **1972** C. M. Parkes *Bereavement* i. 4 Loss of a close relative is normally a major stressor.

stressy (stre·si), *a. rare.* [f. Stress *sb.* or *v.*[1] + -y[1].] Characterized by stress, *spec.* in the prosody of G. M. Hopkins; in which stress is conspicuous.

1880 G. M. Hopkins *Lett. to R. Bridges* (1955) 107, I think you have missed the clue. You take the rhythm for three triple time, iambs and anapaests say, and four feet to a line (except the refrain). But to get this you have to skip..a whole foot as marked and stressy as any other foot. **1961** *Times Lit. Suppl.* 18 Aug. 549/4 Neither of these versions reveals the bold, thoroughgoing 'stressy' flexibility of genuine sprung rhythm.

stretch, *sb.* Add: **1. i.** *Baseball.* An action used in pitching (see quots.).

1939 E. J. Nichols *Hist. Dict. Baseball Terminol.* 75 *Stretch*,..a pitcher's straightening of his arms above his head preliminary to delivering the ball. **1951** H. Turkin *Official Encycl. Baseball* 572 The pitching delivery can be broken down and analyzed to reveal six distinct actions: windup, stretch, leg lift, stride, body pivot and follow through... The stretch brings the pitching arm behind the head. **1976** *Webster's Sports Dict.* 428/2 *Stretch*,..a movement a pitcher uses instead of a windup when there are runners on base. *Ibid.* 429/1 The stretch, with its integral pause, allows the pitcher to throw to the base to try to pick off the runner or to keep him close to prevent his stealing without interrupting the pitching motion and making a balk.

j. *Aeronaut.* Modification of an existing aircraft design to increase its capabilities, esp. by lengthening the fuselage; capacity for this allowed for in a design.

1954 *Economist* 11 Sept. 2/2 However much 'stretch' may have been designed into the two machines—and the evidence suggests it was not too great—these changes in elements outside the designer's control mean modifications..delays. **1960** *New Scientist* 30 June 1640/1 The modifications involved in stretch are chiefly concerned with stress and control parameters. **1976** *Farnborough Internat. Exhibition* (Official Programme) 46/2 The Lynx design is capable of considerable 'stretch', says Westland.

2. d. Freq. in phr. *by any* (or *no*) *stretch of the imagination.*

1942 T. Bailey *Pink Camellia* xv. 122 Peter could not, by any stretch of the imagination, be compared to that Satan of the Scriptures who came so inopportunely to the Garden. **1957** *Pract. Wireless* XXXIII. 573/2 Most neutral leads..have registered between 5 and 25 volts R.M.S., voltages which cannot, by any stretch of the imagination, be called lethal. **1977** A. Ecclestone *Staircase for Silence* iv. 77 The church they belong to seems hopelessly stuck fast in a way of life that by no stretch of the imagination can be described in terms of leaven or salt or light.

4. c. Now chiefly *at full stretch*: to capacity; working fully or as hard as possible.

1934 G. B. Shaw *On Rocks* I. 221, I am an overworked.. man,..having to keep my mind at full stretch all the time struggling with problems. **1955** *Times* 1 June 10/1 United States tire manufacturers are still working at full stretch. **1977** *Evening Post* (Nottingham) 27 Jan. 4/5 Wilford power station, Nottingham, has been at full stretch to meet heavy demand.

6. g. *Linguistics.* A definable extent (of text or speech).

1961 M. A. K. Halliday in *Word* XVII. 250 Language is patterned activity. At the formal level, the patterns are patterns of meaningful organization: certain regularities are exhibited over certain stretches of language activity. **1964** *English Studies* XLV (Suppl.). 56 It certainly seems worth while trying to bring more system into stretch-of-speech analysis in general by studying the potentialities and realities of absence of sound, sound zero. **1967** D. G. Hays *Introd. Computational Linguistics* x. 171 As the text is being prepared, each stretch between unit boundaries is compared with the contents of the exclusion list. **1972** J. McH. Sinclair *Course in Spoken Eng.: Grammar* 3 Strict grammatical relationships need only be made across stretches of language a few words long. **1973** A. H. Sommerstein *Sound Pattern Anc. Greek* i. 1 The final chapter..contains a summary..of the rules of the part of Greek phonology that I have investigated, a stretch of text written in the form it would have before the application of these rules, [etc.].

7. b. Also *loosely*, a prison sentence (freq. with preceding numeral signifying the number of years). Also *transf.*

1949 'M. Innes' *Journeying Boy* ix. 109 If we were getting him a stretch, we could go to bed feeling we had done something useful. **1951** P. Branch *Lion in Cellar* xx. 222 He's in Joe Gurr again. He got nicked in Cardiff on a snout gaff... It's only a two stretch and a lot of the Boys had their collars felt. **1957** G. Thomas *Gazooka* 42, I owed it to him now to see that he would not be saddled with another stretch under the probation officer or in a reform school for an offence which was not..immoral. **1960** S. Claydon *Lesson in Murder* v. 75, I was going to serve my stretch, come out, and get a job. **1967** J. Morgan *Involved* 40 What do you think he'll get for this lot, guv'nor, ten? I suppose a ten stretch is the least he can expect. **1976** K. Bonfiglioli *Something Nasty in Woodshed* ix. 106 'Porridge'..means penal servitude. There is a legend..that if..on the last morning of your 'stretch', you do not eat up all your nice porridge, you will be back in durance vile within the year.

8. Chiefly *U.S.* **a.** Also *attrib.* (esp. = 'home-stretch') as *stretch run, turn.*

1934 D. Runyon in *Collier's* 3 Mar. 42/3 Gallant Godfrey comes to the conclusion that Westrope is working on him in a stretch run. **1944** *Sun* (Baltimore) 14 Apr. 14/1 Backers of Sollure had no worries all through the stretch run. **1949** *Time* 10 Oct. 42/2 They had less reason to thank their own bats than the batty stretch-run performance of the Cardinals. **1972** *N.Y. Times* 4 June v. 1/4 Shortly after the field hit the stretch turn, Run the Gantlet moved into the lead position. **1978** *Detroit Free Press* 2 Apr. 2E/1 Craig's Corner, a 7-year-old gelding, won the Carolina Cup steeplechase at Camden, S.C., with a strong stretch run before a race record crowd of 30,000-plus. **1979** *Internat. Herald Tribune* 31 Oct. 23/3 It would be the clubhouse turn in the United States, but this was the Vaal Racing Club in the Orange Free State of South Africa, where the horses run clockwise, so it was really the stretch turn.

b. *home-stretch*: see *home-stretch. *back stretch* = *back-straight* s.v. *back- B.

1839 *Picayune* (New Orleans) 2 Apr. 2/2 He went to work himself, soon passed the old black, made all sorts of a brush while rounding the last turn and commencing the back stretch. **1868** H. W. Woodruff *Trotting Horse Amer.* xii. 122 On the back-stretch..Mr. Duffy asked me if I could ride it out without tiring. **1903** A. Adams *Log of Cowboy* xv. 237 He was speeding her on the back stretch. **1931** *Daily Express* 21 Sept. 11/5 Box stalls were built around the walls, while in other parts of the ballroom were reproduced in miniature the back stretch and the home stretch of the track. **1933** *Boys' Mag.* XLVII. 119/2 He shot by a little group of runners, and in the back-stretch was hard upon the heels of the four leaders. **1948** *Life* 21 June 32 (*caption*) Dewey, Taft and Stassen will get away fast, but watch out for Dark Horse Vandenberg on the backstretch. **1970** *Toronto Daily Star* 24 Sept. 21/4 The jock had to check her twice on the backstretch.

c. *transf.* and *fig.*

1949 *Sun* (Baltimore) 9 Aug. 14/3 Baseball's 1949 stretch is now only a few furlongs away. Oddly enough, conditions in the two leagues have been somewhat reversed since last April. **1957** *Baseball Digest* Jan.–Feb. 15 Despite Joss' great work in the stretch, the season ended with the Indians in second place. **1972** *Publishers' Weekly* 12 June 9 (Advt.), Put your money on *Miss Elizabeth Arden* to win in the stretch. **1976** *Billings* (Montana) *Gaz.* 20 June 1E/3 Friday when he led the second round by one shot, Mahaffey expressed disappointment that shoddy putting down the stretch prevented him from running away from the field. **1976** *National Observer* (U.S.) 6 Nov. 5/1 Ford, at the very last, was doing something right. Most of the polls showed he was closing fast on Jimmy Carter, who was limping badly down the stretch.

stretch, *v.* Add: **I. 1. b.** Also (*slang*), to kill (a person). Cf. Lay *v.*[1] 56 b in Dict. and Suppl.

1902 Kipling *Traffics & Discoveries* (1904) 11 He said if you stretched a man at his prayers you'd have to hump his bad luck before the Throne as well as your own. **1953** M. Gilbert *Fear to Tread* viii. 107 Once..Annie had a husband. She got tired of him, so she 'stretched him with a bottle'.

V. 16. a. Also, to straighten, to remove the curl from (hair).

1963 W. Soyinka *Lion & Jewel* 9 Her hair is stretched Like a magazine photo. **1971** C. Achebe *Girls at War* (1972) 58 Now Abigail was a lady; she could sew and bake ..put on powder and perfumes and stretch her hair.

VI. 21. c. *colloq.* To eke out (food), esp. to serve a greater number of people than originally intended.

1923 *Chambers's Jrnl.* Christmas 858/2 The problem of how to stretch a supper made for two to fit three. **1951** H. MacInnes *Neither Five nor Three* xiii. 184 She began worrying how far she could stretch the beef stew now simmering on the stove. **1974** N. Freeling *Dressing of Diamond* 80 She had made stuffing for the trout, to stretch them a bit. **1977** C. McCarry *Secret Lovers* viii. 98 She wondered if I was free to have dinner at her house... They were having something that the cook could stretch for three.

d. *Cinemat.* To adapt (a silent film) for projection on sound equipment by duplicating alternate frames so that the speed of action is not distorted.

1953 L. J. Wheeler *Princ. Cinematogr.* v. 145 Many occasions arrive when it is desirable to 'stretch' an original negative, that is, assuming an old, silent negative, is required to be printed into a sound film. **1965** *Listener* 11 Feb. 231/3 If a silent film (sixteen frames/sec.) is projected on a sound projector (twenty-four frames/sec.), the action appears too fast. To rectify this, silent films are sometimes 'stretched' by making a special print in which every other frame is printed twice. **1969** *Observer* 26 Jan. 7/4 The technique of stretching them [*sc.* silent films] to run at 24 or 25 frames a second..has been known and used for very many years. **1976** *Oxf. Compan. Film* 664/2 Makers of compilation films often incorporate old footage without stretching it, with the result that modern audiences have come to regard all silent film as comic.

e. *Engin.* To increase the capability or power of (an aircraft, power plant, etc.).

1960 *New Scientist* 30 June 1640/1 Engine power again was an essential factor in stretching the Viscount. **1967** *Economist* 8 July p. xxvi/3 The newest Gardener engine now runs at 1,800 rpm to give 180 bhp—still with remarkable fuel economy. This is near the far limit to which this engine can be stretched without supercharging. **1979** *Nature* 19 July 187/3 Why is it necessary to scale up to 1,300 MW? Doesn't the ability to replicate and perhaps stretch the 250 MW Dounreay prototype fast reactor give sufficient insurance against the risk of long-term uranium scarcity?

22. d. Also in colloq. phr. *to stretch it* (or *things*): to go too far, to go beyond the limits of credibility; to exaggerate.

1965 M. Allingham *Mind Readers* xx. 212 Rightie ho. If you say so. Any friend of yours is a friend of mine but that's stretching it. **1974** M. Hastings *Dragon Island* xi. 96 'I can't believe that by some chance Jones found himself with *two* people in whom he had special interest.' 'That would be stretching it.' **1975** R. Stout *Family Affair* ix. 83 Everyone in Washington is connected..with Watergate. That's stretching it, but not much. **1980** R. Hill *Killing Kindness* v. 46 It's stretching things a bit... Still, it's worth checking.

e. *colloq.* To cause (someone) to exert himself to the utmost of his talents or abilities, esp. with regard to learning or employment.

1951 C. Morgan *Breeze of Morning* i. v. 25, I had found that he always 'stretched' me in the way I liked, and gave me confidence by having such unswerving confidence in himself. **1960** C. Day Lewis *Buried Day* i. 23 Under such conditions, an only child may become precocious, stretching himself unnaturally to meet the adult world on its own terms. **1968** *Guardian* 21 Nov. 10/5 He is satisfied by being a bishop; he says he felt a need to be stretched by some equally big job. **1978** D. Devine *Sunk without Trace* iv. 36, I hear good reports of your work... I fear, however, we're not stretching you enough. **1983** *Times* 8 Jan. 3/8 Local education authorities..could ensure..that the curriculum suited and stretched all children.

23. b. *Jazz.* To play without restraint, esp. in a solo. Const. *out.*

1961 *N.Y. Times Mag.* 25 June 39/3 When a cat stretches out, he can make the moon on his own thrust or horn. **1962** *Down Beat* 5 July 35/3, I heard this group in person, at the Village Gate, and they stretched out. **1968** *Crescendo* June 12/2 Everybody really had a chance to stretch out and play what and how they wanted to.

VII. 24. a. stretch forming *vbl. sb. Mech.*, a process in which sheet metal under tension is shaped by the pressure of a punch to the required contour; hence **stretch-form** *v. trans.*; **stretch mark**, a linear mark on the skin (esp. of the stomach or thighs) when it has been distended by pregnancy or obesity; = *stria 2 e; **stretch receptor** *Physiol.*, a sensory receptor that responds to the stretching of tissue; **stretch reflex** *Physiol.*, a reflex contraction of a muscle resulting from the stretching of the same muscle; **stretch spinning** (see quot. 1957).

1951 G. Sachs *Princ. & Methods Sheet-Metal Fabricating* v. iii. 470 In most instances a part is stretch-formed from a rectangular blank. **1973** J. G. Tweeddale *Materials Technol.* II. iv. 85 (*caption*) Stretch forming a curved shape. **1942** *Iron Age* 4 June 49 (*heading*) Stretch-forming contoured sheet metal aircraft parts. **1951** *Archit. Rev.* CIX. 166/1 It can be spun into a bell-like shape, or it can be shaped on a stretch-forming machine, which pulls it into shape over a former. **1973** J. G. Tweeddale *Materials Technol.* II. iv. 85 Stretch forming uses a principle that involves applying a uniaxial tension to a thin plate,..and then pushing a controlled shape progressively into the surface of the tensioned sheet. **1960** F. W. Goodrich *Maternity* iii. 59 The development of 'stretch marks' in the skin of the abdomen and thighs is not unusual. **1970** D. Marlowe *Echoes of Celandine* viii. 143 'The marks you see..are not stretch-marks even though I have had three children.'..She then turned around..revealing scars..across her thighs. **1972** G. Bourne *Pregnancy* vi. 110 Stretch marks may occur at puberty on the buttocks and also on the breasts, especially if a girl is overweight. **1980** *Family Med. Guide* (R. Soc. Medicine) ix. 210/1 Cushing's syndrome is characterized by..thinning of the skin which may lead to large stretch marks, and a tendency to bruise easily. **1936** C. L. Evans *Starling's Princ. Human Physiol.* (ed. 7) xxxvii. 906 The lung evidently possesses stretch receptors similar in their responses to those of muscle. **1961** *Listener* 23 Nov. 858/1 If the animal [*sc.* an octopus] cannot use information from internal stretch receptors in its muscles, it will not be able to define the relative positions of the sense organs on the suckers that it uses to pick up an object. **1969** J. H. Green *Basic Clin. Physiol.* ix. 52/2 As one breathes in, the lungs expand, and stretch receptors in the lungs send sensory information up the vagus nerve to the respiratory centre cutting short inspiration. **1916** C. Asayama in *Q. Jrnl. Exper. Physiol.* IX. 278 Quick stretching of tibialis anticus by a sharp pull on its tendon ..elicits a reflex contraction of the muscle... It may be termed a stretch-reflex. **1978** B. W. Payton in G. Ross *Essentials Human Physiol.* ix. 478 Stretch reflexes occur in all muscles but are particularly obvious in those involved in maintaining posture. **1925** *U.S. Patent 1,528,219* This extract..prevents adhesion of the filaments in multiple spinning, and thereby greatly promotes 'stretch spinning'. **1957** *Textile Terms & Definitions* (Textile Inst.) (ed. 3) 96 *Stretch spinning*, a process of spinning whereby the filaments are substantially stretched at some stage between extrusion and collection.

b. Used *attrib.* or as *adj.* to designate various (usu. synthetic) fibres or fabrics which are elastic or capable of stretching, and garments, etc. (which may stretch to provide close fitting) made from them. Occas. *absol.* as *sb.*

1956 *Jrnl. Textile Inst.* XL. 280 A stretch yarn in which the deformation is produced by suitable combinations of heat-setting and twisting. **1957** *Times* 18 Nov. 11/4 Ties..by Jacques Fath with matching nylon stretch socks. **1959** *Times* 12 Jan. 11/3 Courtauld's process to obtain resilient stretch-nylon yarn. **1961** *Listener* 16 Nov. 825/2 My favourite example comes from a very modish American magazine... 'As contemporary..as C. P. Snow and stretch-pants.' **1962** *Guardian* 23 Feb. 8/5 Until recently I had never found a fine stretch which did not ladder quickly. **1963** *Harper's Bazaar* Jan. 50 Stretch slacks and cardigan in gold and silver. **1963** *Daily Mail* 24 Aug. 5/1 (Advt.), 100% Nylon Stretch Tights. **1963** *Economist* 7 Sept. 840/2 The most promising..growth area ..is..in 'stretch' fabrics. **1964** *Woman* 18 Jan. 13 Keep your stretch pants slender. **1968** *Vogue* 15 Apr. 60 Snug-topped bubble dress..of sun red stretch. **1972** *Times* 22 May 10/2 Too-tight stretch nylon socks cause many foot troubles. **1977** 'J. Fraser' *Hearts Ease in Death* xiv. 166 The chair..was fitted with one of those cheap stretch covers with a large floral pattern. **1978** J. Gores *Gone, no Forwarding* xiii. 76 A wide-hipped woman in red stretch slacks. **1980** *Times* 19 Feb. 8 The now obligatory stretch fabrics.

stretchabi·lity. [f. Stretchable *a.*: see *-bility.] Capability of being stretched.

1940 H. R. Mauersberger *Matthews's Textile Fibers* (ed. 5) xx. 863 On cold-drawing, nylon becomes exceedingly strong and elastic. But elasticity means more than 'stretchability'. The degree to which a stretched material recovers its original length is a measure of true elasticity. **1959** Potter & Corbman *Fiber to Fabric* (ed. 3) iv. 60 Stretch yarns..when subjected to certain methods that use heat to set crimp in thermoplastic filament yarns.. increase their stretchability. **1962** *Listener* 22 Mar. 510/2 What he does..is to measure the 'strength' of a flour.. by measuring the 'stretchability' of the dough it makes. **1967** E. Chambers *Photolitho-Offset* i. 9 It [*sc.* zinc] also stretches more before breaking—this stretchability being sometimes useful to correct mis-register. **1978** *Detroit Free Press* 5 Mar. 30 (Advt.), We tested it for launderability, durability, stretchability and shape retention.

stretchable, *a.* (Later examples.)

1889 A. James *Diary* 16 Nov. (1965) 56 She seems as large a joke as ever, an embodiment of the stretchable, a purely transatlantic and modern possibility. **1975** L. Blue *To Heaven with Scribes & Pharisees* iv. 39 Jewish cooking..inclines to casseroles and stews, which are infinitely stretchable.

stretched, *ppl. a.* Add: **5.** Of an aircraft, engine, etc.: increased in size or operating capacity; based on a smaller or less powerful design. Cf. *stretch *v.* 21 e.

1960 *New Scientist* 30 June 1639/2 The Super-VC 10, which BOAC has just ordered off the drawing-board, is an example of a 'stretched' aeroplane. **1966** *Wall St. Jrnl.* 13 Jan. 1 Their orders of 'stretched' jets—conventional models expanded to carry more passengers—will also have to be carefully considered. **1967** *Economist* 8 July p. xxvi/3 Operators are suspicious of 'stretched' engines. **1972** *Daily Tel.* 26 Sept. 6/7 The car is a stretched version of the latest Daimler Double-Six, itself developed from the Jaguar XJ12. **1978** *Ibid.* 23 Feb. 6/8 Improvements in technology mean that the British Hovercraft Corporation's 'stretched' SRN-4 is likely to be used on some of the established 100–150 mile European routes.

stretcher, *sb.* Add: **II. 6. a.** (Earlier example.)

1833 *Reg. Deb. Congr. U.S.* 22nd Congr. 1 Sess. App. p. xli, [Duty] on square wire used for the manufacture of stretchers for umbrellas..twelve per centum ad valorem.

9. a. Also, a camp-bed used as a spare bed in a house, etc. Chiefly *Austral.* and *N.Z.*

1943 *Amer. Speech* XVIII. 86 A common article of furniture [in New Zealand] is a *stretcher*—a folding camp bed or cot, often used to provide temporary sleeping accommodation in a house. **1974** *Weekend Mag.* (Montreal) 18 May 21/1 All summer cottages in those days had two or three camp cots or 'stretchers', with flat wire springs and small mattresses, which could be folded up and stuffed under beds for use when unexpected or surplus guests arrived. **1980** B. Mason *Solo* 30 Tim, I got the stretcher out. It's quite sound. Needs a dust, that's all. I'm giving you three blankets. That should be enough.

11. (Later examples.)

1885 *Outing* (U.S.) Oct. 77/1 The trout..were lusty, vigorous fellows, and with a 'Silver Doctor' as a stretcher, I managed to forget myself..completely. **1938** W. C. Platts *Mod. Trout Fishing* vii. 59 Two flies—a stretcher, or tail fly, and one dropper—is rather risky. **1963** A. N. Marston *Newnes Encycl. Angling* 249/1 *Stretcher*, the bottom fly on a wet-fly cast made up of two or more flies. Usually called a tail fly.

III. 12. **stretcher case**, an injured or sick person needing conveyance on a stretcher; **stretcher strain** *Metallurgy*, a furrowed marking on the surface of a metal produced by local deformation.

1917 'CONTACT' *Airman's Outings* v. 118 On this occasion there was good reason for the delay, as we ceded the right of way to a hospital ship and waited while a procession of ambulance cars drove along the quay and unloaded their stretcher cases. **1978** R. V. JONES *Most Secret War* xxxvi. 310 The Navy would not take him because as a stretcher case he would occupy as much space on board ship as four men standing up. **1931** *Metal Progress* Sept. 90/1 Stretcher strains (or more appropriately 'worms') are the shop names for the phenomenon known as the 'Lines of Lüder', after Lüder of Magdeburg, who first described them in 1860. **1971** *Steel in U.S.S.R.* I. 899 (*heading*) Causes of the formation of strain lines (stretcher strains) when drawing stainless-steel tubes.

stretcher (stre·tʃəɹ), *v.* [f. the sb.] *trans.* To carry *off* or convey (an injured or sick person) on a stretcher.

1976 *Daily Mirror* 15 Mar. 30/6 The sickening blow of seeing Gary Locke stretchered off in only the seventh minute. **1978** J. UPDIKE *Coup* (1979) i. 7 The beer-crazed mob of American boobs cheers..the crunched leg of the unhome-team left tackle as he is stretchered off the field. **1980** K. ROYCE *Third Arm* v. 52 He did not himself feel shock until after Adams had been stretchered from the car. **1982** *Times* 11 June 6/4 Casualties..were stretchered to a field hospital.

stre·tchiness. [f. STRETCHY *a.* + -NESS.] The quality of being stretchy; elasticity.

1963 *Economist* 7 Sept. 840/2 A slight stretchiness can be woven into two directions. **1976** A. FARRER *Interpretation & Belief* 208 In this way I stretch my terms and I do not know how much they ought to be stretched. At this point the stretchiness of terms in my descriptions to myself of my own experience comes into play.

stretching, *vbl. sb.* Add: **c.** **stretching-board,** (*c*) *Leather-manuf.* = *stretch-bench* s.v. STRETCH *v.* 24; **stretching-course** (later example).

1976 T. WALKER *Spatsizi* v. 47 He taught me how to skin, showing me how to turn the hides fur side out before they were quite dry and then pull them back on the stretching board. **1973** L. RUSSELL *Everyday Life Colonial Canada* v. 60 Each layer of bricks was called a course; the parallel arrangement was a stretching course and the transverse a heading course.

stre·tch-out. Chiefly *N. Amer.* Also unhyphened. [f. STRETCH *v.* + OUT *adv.*] **1.** A practice of requiring workers, esp. in textile industries, to do extra work or operate extra machines for little or no additional pay.

1933 *Sun* (Baltimore) 30 June 12/1 The 'stretch-out' is a scheme for getting more work done in the textile mills with less labor. **1933** E. CALDWELL *God's Little Acre* v. 84 The mill can't get us back unless they shorten the hours, or cut out the stretchout, or go back to the old pay. **1934** *Sun* (Baltimore) 17 Aug. 1/3 Wage increases, shorter hours, differentials in the higher wage brackets, and an end to the 'stretch-out' are objectives to be sought in the strike. **1943** *Ibid.* 14 June 10/7 A managerial stretch-out which prostrates war workers is intolerable.

2. A practice of slackening production schedules as an economy, so that a set quantity will be produced over a longer period; a postponement of the date of fulfilment of orders or contracts, etc.

1946 [see sense 3 below]. **1952** *N.Y. Times* 16 Aug. (Late city ed.) 14/1 The North Atlantic defense program, already handicapped by a 'stretch-out'. **1959** *Wall St. Jrnl.* 14 Jan. (Eastern ed.) 2/4 The stretchout is understood to apply to the date at which the two aircraft were to go into flight and become 'operational'. **1960** *Times* 21 Nov. (Canada Suppl.) p. xiii/3 Stretch-out of deliveries has been broadly accepted by the industry. **1969** *Look* 29 Apr. 57/3 Support on the part of so many in the diocese made this patient waiting over weeks of time much easier. But the long stretch-out freed us. **1979** *Aviation Week & Space Technol.* 13 Aug. 9 Neither the abandonment of the B-1 by the current Administration nor its stretchout of the MX missile..speeded up SALT.

3. *attrib.*

1934 *Sun* (Baltimore) 1 Sept. 2/4 It has failed to do anything about solving the 'stretch-out' problem. **1946** *Ibid.* 10 May 15/3 A 'stretch-out' plan, under which those employed will work less hours weekly, will be adopted soon. **1960** *Times* 21 Nov. (Canada Suppl.) p. xiii/2 The viability of a satisfactory stretch-out arrangement depends on the transfer of contracts from the weaker to the stronger mining operations. **1967** *Canad. Ann. Rev.* *1966* 75 The Prime Minister announced a major increase in the amounts allocated to vocational and technical training in the stretch-out period.

stretto, *adv.* and *sb.* Add: **A.** *adv.* (Earlier example.)

1740 J. GRASSINEAU *Mus. Dict.* 240 *Stretto*, shortened, is often used to signify that the measure is to be short and concise, therefore quick.

B. *sb.* **a.** Also *transf.*

1962–3 *Sight & Sound* Winter 19/1 Finally, there are the flashbacks and then the stretto of flashbacks, as if, at the end, Colin Smith were still attempting to make up his mind. **1963** J. WIESENFARTH *H. James* v. 104 The *coda* begins in Chapter XII and ends with Chapter XIV in a *stretto*. **1979** *UCT Studies in English* (Univ. Cape Town) Sept. 38 Pope mimics the convention: *The Rape of the Lock* is threaded with premonitory phrases which he gathers into a *stretto* as the climax draws near.

b. *stretto maestrale* [cf. *MAESTRALE] (see quot. 1946).

1876 STAINER & BARRETT *Dict. Mus. Terms* s.v. *Maestrale, Stretto maestrale*, a term sometimes applied to the stretto of a fugue when in canon. **1910** E. PROUT *Anal. J. S. Bach's Forty-Eight Fugues* 13 As the subject appears in a complete form in all the groups of the entries now under notice,..we have here an example of a stretto maestrale. **1946** E. BLOM *Everyman's Dict. Mus.* 672/1 *Stretto maestrale*,..a S[tretto] in which the fugal subject not only appears in close, overlapping entries, but is carried through from beginning to end at each entry. **1948** G. OLDROYD *Technique & Spirit of Fugue* ix. 143 It is a specimen of '*stretto maestrale*' in which a phrase in its full length is repeated in canon throughout all the strands. **1959** J. V. COCKSHOOT *Fugue in Beethoven's Piano Mus.* v. 68 This four-fold entry foreshadows the final section, with an effect of *stretto maestrale*.

streusel (stroi·zĕl, strū·zĕl, ‖ʃtroi·zĕl). Chiefly *U.S.* [Ger., f. *streuen* to sprinkle.] A crumb-like topping for cakes and pastries made from fat, flour, cinnamon, and sugar; a confection with such a topping. Freq. *attrib.*, esp. as *streusel cake, kuchen.*

1909 L. MEIER *Art of German Cooking & Baking* xvii. 335/2 (*heading*) Streusel Coffee Cake. Preparation of the Streusel. **1910** M. MALZBENDER *Pract. Man. for Confectioners, Pastrycooks & Bakers* (rev. ed.) iii. 66/2 Streusel Kuchen. Proceed same as No. 6 only put streusel on top before baking. **1952** L. J. MITCHELL *Lüchow's German Cookbk.* xi. 183 (*heading*) Apple crumb cake (Apfel Streuselkuchen). *Ibid.*, For the Streusel, coarsely mix ⅜ cup butter, the flour, sugar and cinnamon with a pastry blender. **1957** M. E. SHOWALTER *Mennonite Community Cookbk.* i. 27 (*heading*) 'Streusel Kuchen' *Raised Coffee Cake*... Let rise 1½ hours. Sprinkle with streusel crumbs. **1960** 'A. KNOX' *Cooking Austrian Way* (rev. ed.) 202 (*heading*) Streusel Cake *Streuselkuchen*... This is a cake with a yeast dough and a streusel mixture on top. **1966** W. S. RAMSON *Austral. Eng.* viii. 161 Some unrecorded borrowings from German may be in local use in parts of South Australia. Price noted..*streuselkuchen*, 'cake', [etc.]. **1976** *Woman's Day* (U.S.) Nov. 104, no. 14 Mashed Potatoes/Peach Streusel/Gingerbread. **1977** C. MCFADDEN *Serial* (1978) xx. 46/1 Sam wanted to buy a Sara Lee streusel cake.

streuth, var. 'STREWTH in Dict. and Suppl.

strewage (strū·ėdʒ). [f. STREW *v.* + -AGE.] = STREWING *vbl. sb.* b.

1902 J. H. SKEINE *Pastor Agnorum* 266 The waking of that Syrian refugee..after his sleep among the great strewage of rocks on a down of Canaan. **1929** R. BRIDGES *Test. Beauty* III. 894 Vestiges of his stony asceticism imbue all time, thick as the strewage of his flinty tools, disseminate wheresoe'er he hath dwelt. **1940** C. F. C. HAWKES *Prehist. Found. Europe* ii. 13 The basement-beds below it, formed of the strewage of older land-surfaces.

strewn field. *Geol.* Also **strewnfield.** [f. STREWN *ppl. a.* + FIELD *sb.*] A part of the earth's surface over which tektites of a similar age are found.

1937 *Proc. R. Soc. Victoria* XLIX. 167 There are no records of the discovery of australites in towns within the australite 'strewn field'. **1961** *Sci. Amer.* Nov. 63 (*caption*) Estimates of ages of tektites in strewn fields are based on ages of rocks with which they are found. **1973** *Nature* 16 Feb. 431/1 Tektites..are apparently limited to four large areas (strewnfields) and four corresponding ages.

'strewth. Add: Also **streuth, strewth, 'strooth, 'struth, struth.**

1913 A. J. REES *Merry Marauders* ix. 149 'Strooth! he's looked up all our lines. **1915** [see *KING-PIN 2]. **1925** [see *GARN *int.*]. **1933** M. LOWRY *Ultramarine* ii. 75 Gawd strewth, you're some fellow, you are! **1938** P. LAWLOR *House of Templemore* xvii. 186, I have made a string bookshelf just like you had. Streuth! So you have. **1954** A. SETON *Katherine* xiv. 235 "Struth," said Edmund. ..'High time I got me *some* wife.' **1975** P. G. WINSLOW *Death of Angel* iv. 86 Strewth, they've made a mess of this office. **1977** *Sunday Sun* (Brisbane) 30 Jan. 29/1 Struth! What next? says Sam.

stria. Add: **2. d.** (Earlier and further examples.) Also in *sing.*

1859 *Phil. Trans. R. Soc.* CXLVIII. 3 The discharge did not exhibit the uniform white light of the Torricellian vacuum, but striæ in confused or irregular forms. **1883** [see *STRIATED *ppl. a.* 1 e].

e. *Med.* Also *stria atrophica* [mod. L. *atrophica* (see ATROPHIC *a.*)]. A stretch mark; *stria gravidarum* [L., gen. pl. of *gravida* pregnant woman], one on a pregnant woman, usu. darker than the surrounding skin; *stria albicans* (pl. *albicantes*) [L., pres. pple. of *albicāre* to make or be white], a former stria gravidarum that has become light-coloured following delivery.

1867 *Jrnl. Cutaneous Med.* I. 142 None of the early writers have alluded to any other cause of the striae atrophicae than over-distension. **1880** *Trans. Amer. Gynecol. Soc.* IV. 141 These cicatrices are usually described as red or white shining striæ, marking the skin..of pregnant and multiparous women. **1884** R. & F. BARNES *Syst. Obstetric Med. & Surg.* I. viii. 294 Striæ gravidarum. **1906** T. W. EDEN *Man. Midwifery* i. 51 *Striæ gravidarum* appear on the abdominal wall... They are pearly..when recent, but afterwards they become pale and silvery (*striæ albicantes*). **1968** D. C. BETHEA *Introd. Maternity Nursing* iii. 25 Thin, red streaks, called striae gravidarum, occur on the breasts of some pregnant women. **1970** C. LERCH *Maternity Nursing* v. 61/2 In subsequent pregnancies new striae appear in addition to the silvery white markings of the previous pregnancy.

striatal: see *STRIATUM.

striate, *a.* Add: **2.** *Anat.* Epithet of the striatum (esp. in sense *a) and the blood vessels supplying it.

1890 BILLINGS *Med. Dict.* 599/2 *Striate arteries*, small twigs from anterior and middle cerebral arteries that.. supply corpus striatum. **1902** D. J. CUNNINGHAM *Text-bk. Anat.* 837 An inferior striate vein descends on each side from the substance of the corpus striatum. **1907** *Arch. Neurol.* III. 42 Homonymous visual defects are due to disease and destruction of the striate cortex. **1921** TILNEY & BASSETT *Form & Functions Central Nerv. Syst.* xliv. 805 In its process of evolution from the lower vertebrates to mammals, the primordial portion of the striate body corresponds to the globus pallidus. **1948** A. BRODAL *Neurol. Anat.* iv. 73 The striate body, the corpus striatum, consists of large grey nuclear masses.. subdivided by fibre strands into different portions. **1968** PASSMORE & ROBSON *Compan. Med. Stud.* I. xxiv. 52/2 The striate area..contains extra fibres which widen the outer lines of Baillarger into a broad white band. *Ibid.* 72/1 The striate artery..supplies the medial part of the head of the caudate nucleus and putamen and the anterior part of the internal capsule. **1978** *Nature* 3 Aug. 423/1 Posteriorly, the striate cortex is so distinct and uniform that its borders are visible, in histological sections, even to the naked eye.

striate, *v.* Add: Also *fig.*

1979 D. HOFFMANN in *Harvard Guide Contemp. Amer. Writing* xii. 579 Clarity and strength striate the poems of Charles Edward Eaton.

striated, *ppl. a.* Add: **1. a.** Also *fig.*

1923 H. CRANE *Let.* 2 Mar. (1965) 129 Striated with nuances, nervosities, that we are heir to.

d. Of muscle: = STRIPED *ppl. a.* 1 c.

1846 W. B. CARPENTER *Man. Physiol.* iii. 199 When the striated Muscular Fibre is examined still more closely, it is found to contain an assemblage of very minute elements. **1851, 1866** [in Dict., sense 1 a]. **1959** W. ANDREW *Textbk. Compar. Histol.* ii. 48 The muscular tissue in man and other vertebrates is of three chief types: (1) smooth, (2) cardiac, and (3) skeletal. The last two types frequently are referred to as striated because of the cross-striations on the fibers. **1982** [see *SKELETAL *a.* b].

e. Of an electric discharge: exhibiting striæ (sense 2 d).

1852 *Phil. Trans. R. Soc.* CXLII. 100 In a well-exhausted receiver containing a small piece of phosphorus, the discharge is throughout its course striated by transverse non-luminous bands. **1883** *Rep. Brit. Assoc. Adv. Sci.* *1882* 31 A stria, with its attendant dark space, forms a physical unit of a striated discharge. **1942** J. D. STRANATHAN *'Particles' Mod. Physics* iii. 71 Small amounts of impurity in the gas affect the striated positive column greatly. **1973** J. YARWOOD *Electricity & Magnetism* xiv. 503 For a striated positive column, the number of ions per unit volume is least at the bright edge of the striation.

striation. Add: **2. b.** *Electr.* = STRIA 2 d (in *sing.*).

1902 *Encycl. Brit.* XXVIII. 47/2 The bright parts of the striations are slightly concave to the positive electrode. **1942** J. D. STRANATHAN *'Particles' Mod. Physics* iii. 67 As the pressure is still further reduced..the striations become more coarse and indistinct, and the Crookes dark space lengthens. **1973** [see *STRIATED *ppl. a.* 1 e].

striatum (strəi,ēⁱ·tŏm). *Anat.* Pl. **striata.** [mod.L., neut. of *striātus* STRIATE *a.*]. **a.** The corpus striatum, a body of grey matter within each cerebral hemisphere comprising the lentiform nucleus (i.e. the globus pallidus and the putamen) and the caudate nucleus; some writers also include the claustrum. **b.** (Now the more usual use.) = *NEOSTRIATUM, i.e. the putamen and the caudate nucleus only.

[**1803** C. BELL *Anat. Human Body* III. I. iii. 87 The corpora striata are smooth, cineritious convexities... These bodies are called striata, from the intermixture of the medullary matter, which gives the appearance of striæ when they are cut.] **1889** J. LEIDY *Elem. Treat. Human Anat.* (ed. 2) xv. 751 The striatum, or corpus striatum, appears in the body of the lateral ventricle as a smooth, convex gray eminence projecting from its outer wall. **1948** A. BRODAL *Neurol. Anat.* iv. 73 The putamen and the caudate nucleus together constitute the neostriatum (often collectively called on account of their similarities the striatum). **1971** N. G. SUTTON *Anat. Brain & Spinal Medulla* vii. 102 The claustrum is often considered part of the striatum, that is a detached part of the putamen, but it has also been thought to be an included portion of the cortex of the insula. **1978** *Nature* 23 Feb. 767/1 The rats were decapitated and the corpus striatum ipsilateral to the lesion, the contralateral unlesioned striatum and striata from unlesioned animals were assayed.

Hence **stria·tal** *a.*, of or pertaining to the striatum.

1926 *Jrnl. Nerv. & Mental Dis.* LXIV. 9 All kinds of striatal tremors..are action-tremors. **1937** *Arch. Neurol. & Psychiatry* (Chicago) XXXVIII. 737 One can infer that hippocampal activity..through the striatal connections regulates attitudes of emotional expression. **1974** D. & M. WEBSTER *Compar. Vertebr. Morphol.* xi. 268 It is not definitely established whether some or all of the bird's striatal structures are related to the mammalian striatum.

striature. Add: Also *fig.*
1918 F. HACKETT *Ireland* xiii. 362 This striature of Catholics and Protestants, nationalists and anti-nationalists, Irish and Scotch-Ulstermen, is by no means so insufferable as the tenor of argument may indicate.

strich, var. *STRITCH.

strickle, *v.* (Later examples.)
1927 *Jrnl. Inst. Metals* XXXVII. 25 Red-hot sand was used to fill this space and strickled off level with the top of the mould. **1934** *Proc. Inst. Brit. Foundrymen 1932–1933* XXVI. 548 It [*sc.* stucco] is a splendid material and can be swept or strickled to very fine limits.

strict, *a.* Add: **I. 3. a.** (Later example.)
1897 F. THOMPSON *New Poems* 68, I, the boundless strict savannah Which God's leaping feet go through.

8. e. Logic. *strict implication*: a relationship holding between propositions in which it is impossible for the antecedent to be true and the consequent false. Cf. *material implication* s.v. *MATERIAL *a.* 2 b.
1912 C. I. LEWIS in *Mind* XXI. 526 Intensional disjunction bears the same relation to inferential or 'strict' implication that extensional disjunction bears to the algebraic or 'material' implication. **1933** C. A. MACE *Princ. Logic* iv. 68 This is clearly a different sense of implies, and is sometimes called strict implication. **1947** H. REICHENBACH *Elem. Symbolic Logic* viii. 379 The calculus of strict implication..constitutes a system of this kind. **1977** *Fontana Dict. Mod. Thought* 206/1 The systems of strict implication are the basis of contemporary modal logic.

II. 11. d. *strict liability*: a liability which does not depend upon intent to commit an offence.
1896 *Rep. Cases N.Y. Court of Appeals* CLI. 142 The weight of the argument..is in favor of the rule of strict liability which requires a public official to assume all risks of loss. **1926** *Law Q. Rev.* XLII. 51 The description of the rule in *Rylands* v. *Fletcher* as an example of absolute liability in tort is unhappy in view of some half dozen exceptions which are admitted as qualifications of it. 'Strict liability' seems to be a better term. **1935** *California Law Rev.* May 431 Liability on the ground of nuisance should not be confused with the doctrine of absolute or strict liability for certain classes of lawful acts. **1945** W. T. S. STALLYBRASS *Salmond's Law of Torts* (ed. 10) ii. 20 A period of strict liability, an 'unmoral period, is succeeded by a period of fault liability, a moral' period. **1953** *N.Y. Univ. Law Rev.* XXVIII. 1076 The courts have made no inroads upon strict liability for damage done by animals ferae naturae, nor upon scienter liability. **1979** *Internat. Jrnl. Sociol. of Law* Feb. 54 In short, by substantially removing the issue of intention from the crimes of employers, the 1844 Act took a substantial step towards the doctrine of strict liability.

12. b. *strict tempo*: in Music, a strict and regular rhythm; freq. used *attrib.* with reference to a kind of ballroom dancing to music with such a rhythm.
1936 F. G. HAWKES *Studies in Time & Tempo* vi. 35 If the proper rhythmical effect..is to be secured, the observance of accurate and strict *tempo* becomes an absolute necessity. **1958** P. GAMMOND *Decca Bk. Jazz* xxv. 320 The vacuities of 'strict tempo' and the morbid sex neurosis of the modern 'sob' song. **1959** F. NEWTON *Jazz Scene* xiii. 230 'Strict tempo' dancing, the foundation of the mass ballroom vogue among the British working class,..grew in a direction diametrically opposed to jazz. **1961** *Listener* 23 Nov. 887/2 A champion strict-tempo dancer. **1978** F. MULLALLY *Deadly Payoff* vi. 81 Strict-tempo ballroom dancing: the slow foxtrot, the quickstep, the waltz. **1982** WARNER & SANDILANDS *Women beyond Wire* ii. 19 The strict-tempo orchestra which reeled off foxtrots and quicksteps.

strictarian (striktē°·riăn), *sb.* and *a.* *rare.* [f. STRICT *a.*: see *-ARIAN.] **A.** *sb.* One holding rigidly conformist views. **B.** *adj.* Characteristic of a strictarian.
1867 [see *-ARIAN]. **1926** *Chambers's Jrnl.* Mar. 153/1, I was not churlish enough or strictarian enough to decry that acceptance. **1931** A. L. ROWSE *Politics & Younger Generation* ix. 251 These are points in Marxism, particularly in the orthodox, strictarian interpretation of it, that are open to criticism.

‖ **stricti juris** (stri·ktəi dʒū°·ris, stri·kti yu°·ris), *adv. phr. Law.* Also **stricti iuris.** [L., lit. 'of strict law'.] Strictly according to the law; according to law as opposed to equity. Also as quasi-*sb.*, the practice of strict interpretation of the law.
1684 G. MACKENZIE *Institutions Law of Scotland* IV. i. 342 Some actions are stricti juris; in which the Judge is to follow the strict prescript of the Contract upon which the Action is raised. **1704** T. WOOD *New Inst. Imperial or Civil Law* IV. iii. 327 Some *stricti juris*, where the Judge cannot depart from the strict terms of the Contract. **1845** H. BROOM *Sel. Legal Maxims* v. 242 Defences which were not admissible or valid *stricti iuris*. **1971** R. D. BAKER *Judicial Rev. in Mexico* vii. 185 The rule of *stricti iuris* (*estricto derecho*) requires the courts to confine their attention to and base their decisions exclusively on those conclusions of law. **1977** A. WATSON *Society & Legal Change* ii. 12 *Stipulatio*..was a unilateral formal contract of strict law (*stricti iuris*) but the formalities were far from complicated.

strictly, *adv.* Add: **9.** *colloq.* (chiefly *U.S.*). Definitely; exclusively. Phr. *strictly for the birds*: see *BIRD *sb.* 5 d.
1938, 1945 [see *MICKEY MOUSE 2]. **1947** [see *MODEL *sb.* 7 e]. **1951** [see *man-hungry* s.v. *MAN *sb.*[1] 20]. **1977** *Amer. Speech 1975* L. 67 *Strictly*.., absolutely, honestly, sincerely, definitely. 'My teacher is handsome, strictly!'

‖ **stricto sensu** (stri·kto se·nsu). Also *erron.* **strictu sensu.** = *SENSU STRICTO.
1931 [see *FOLSOM]. **1972** *Mod. Law Rev.* XXXV. I. 55 In the case of custom *stricto sensu* lack of consensus enhances the importance of the consolidating effect of time. **1976** *Times Lit. Suppl.* 17 Sept. 1176/3 'A philosophical analysis of the feasibility' of the structuralist enterprise *stricto sensu*. **1979** *Nature* 22 Feb. 599/1 Thus 'mosaic' RNAs produced by splicing are *strictu sensu* recombinant molecules in that they contain data drawn from different parts of the genome.

stricture, *sb.*[1] Add: **I. 1. b.** *Phonetics.* Partial or complete closure of the air-passage in the articulation of speech sounds.
1943 K. L. PIKE *Phonetics* vii. 120 At the time in the production of some sound when any moveable part of the vocal apparatus causes any *stricture* (the partial or complete closure of an air passage) it becomes an *articulator*. **1962** B. M. H. STRANG *Mod. Eng. Structure* 31 Articulated sounds may further be differentiated by the variable shape of the articulators and strictures involved in their production. **1964** J. C. CATFORD in D. Abercrombie et al. *Daniel Jones* 26 The articulatory stricture *generates* turbulent airflow. *Ibid.* 32 These five major phonatory stricture types.

strictu sensu, ¶ var. *STRICTO SENSU.

stride, *sb.* Add: **1. b.** Esp. in phr. *to take* or *make strides*: to make progress.
1926 J. S. HUXLEY *Essays in Pop. Sci.* 21 Great strides have been taken in this field too during the last twenty years. **1934** *Discovery* Dec. 362/2 Photography for all purposes has made immense strides latterly. **1956** J. B. WILSON *Lang. & Pursuit of Truth* i. 14 The development of a good system of notation made it possible to take great strides in our mathematical knowledge. **1976** *Field* 18 Nov. 979/1 Great strides have been made in short term forecasting in the last five years.

c. Phr. *to lengthen* (or *shorten*) *one's stride*. Also (U.S.) *to lengthen* (or *shorten*) *stride*.
1925 E. F. NORTON *Fight for Everest: 1924* 32 On April 8 we lengthened our stride and covered 12 miles. **1978** *Washington Post* 24 Mar. B6/2 Her many backers had some anxious moments as she shortened stride after a clear lead at the head of the stretch. **1980** H. D. WESTACOTT *Walker's Handbk.* (ed. 2) iv. 60 On level ground use your natural stride and resist any temptation to lengthen it. On a gradient the stride should be shortened.

3. c. (Earlier and later *fig.* examples.) Freq. in phrases, as *to get into one's stride*, *to hit one's stride*, *to put* or *throw* (someone) *out of* (or *off*) *his stride*.
1890 S. WEBB *Let.* in J. MacKenzie *Victorian Courtship* (1979) viii. 104, I had a bad week... But I have 'got into my stride again' now. **1919** *Punch* 12 Mar. 210/1 The operator won the first game before I could get into my stride. **1933** A. POWELL *From View to Death* i. 19 Conversationally, Zouch was getting back into his stride and he knew that by the evening he would be in good form. **1941** E. S. GARDNER *Case of Haunted Husband* viii. 53 He threw me out of my stride for a whole half day. **1946** K. TENNANT *Lost Haven* (1947) xiv. 226 'Why, I had a talk with him only the other night.' 'Did you?' Dipper asked, put out of his stride. **1955** H. KURNITZ *Invasion of Privacy* (1956) xii. 77 It was late in the working day..but ..Louis Stradling was just hitting his full stride. **1967** N. FREELING *Strike out where not Applicable* 85 'Who told you that?'..The young man was thrown out of his stride. **1978** D. DEVINE *Sunk without Trace* xxii. 202 He was disappointed. He didn't think I'd let a man like Max Sapiro put me off my stride. **1983** *Listener* 27 Jan. 21/1 But when Mr. Maccoby gets into his stride of explaining the mechanisms of what has so often been the loathsome behaviour of so-called Christians to Jews, his book becomes of potent interest.

d. Also (chiefly *U.S.*) without possessive adj. (Later examples.)
1941 B. SCHULBERG *What makes Sammy Run?* iii. 48 It was funny to see him taking the Vendome [*sc.* an expensive restaurant] in stride too. **1974** *Publishers Weekly* 7 Jan. 49/2 Coach John Wooden..has taken it all in stride. **1976** *New Society* 3 June 521/1 Everyone understood what it meant to be photographed and took the request in stride.

4. c. Delete ? *Obs.* and add later examples.
1922 JOYCE *Ulysses* 344 A navy threequarter skirt cut to the stride showed off her slim graceful figure to perfection. **1939** *Country Life* 11 Feb. p. xxxiii/2 (Advt.), There is plenty of stride; the knees are well formed; the lines and run of seams are perfectly executed.

d. *pl.* Trousers. Also occas. breeches; jeans. *slang.*
1889 A. G. MURDOCH *Scotch Readings* (Ser. 3) 26 His two legs, which were encased in a pair of all but skin-tight 'strides'. **1889** CLARKSON & RICHARDSON *Police!* xxv. 346 If the 'Peter' (cash-box) can be found, that is at once appropriated, as also are a man's 'strides' (trousers). **1914** JACKSON & HELLYER *Vocab. Criminal Slang* 81 *Strides*,..a pair of trousers. **1924** *Truth* (Sydney) 27 Apr. 6 *Strides*, trousers. **1932** L. MANN *Flesh in Armour* 291 His tunic and light coat were of the ultra fashionable style, and his strides would not have disgraced an officer of the Guards. **1947** D. M. DAVIN *For Rest of our Lives* xxxviii. 196 Trying to get his strides up. **1950** 'N. SHUTE' *Town like Alice* ix. 261 Could you get into a pair of my strides? **1960** 'A. BURGESS' *Doctor is Sick* xxvi. 211 He handed a crumpled bundle to Edwin, saying: 'You'll 'ave to take my strides.'..The trousers, Edwin found, were too short. **1973** M. AMIS *Rachel Papers* 186 The Oxford University candidate was to be seen in T-shirt and khaki strides. **1980** B. MASON *Solo* 91, I wiped damp hands on my serge strides.

6*. Ellipt. for *stride piano* (see sense 7 b below).
1956 PANASSIÉ & GAUTIER *Guide to Jazz* 260/2 *Stride*, a piano style much in use by soloists about 1930. **1969** *Listener* 6 Feb. 186/3 Peterson stands at the end of a long and honourable tradition of jazz piano playing originally known as 'Harlem stride'. The stride refers to a left-hand vamping method using alternating tenths and note clusters at least an octave apart. **1975** *New Yorker* 19 May 6/2 Jaki Byard, who displays a confident feel for ragtime, stride, and more modern piano styles, has fun with bassist Major Holley.

7. b. *Jazz.* Used *attrib.* to designate a style of piano-playing in which the left hand alternately plays a single note and a chord that is an octave (or more) higher; *esp.* in **stride piano** (hence **stride pianist**); also *stride accent, bass, tempo*, etc.
c **1938** N. E. WILLIAMS *His Hi de Highness of Ho de Ho* 35/2 'Gut tempo' and 'stride tempo' usually are intelligible only to our own musicians. **1950** BLESH & JANIS *They all played Ragtime* x. 192 He could play the ragtime stride bass, but it bothered him because his stomach got in the way of his arm, so he used a walking bass instead. **1952** B. ULANOV *Hist. Jazz in Amer.* iv. 29 'Stride piano', the particular pride and joy of Fats Waller and, before him, of innumerable ragtime pianists, comes from the blues. *Ibid.* 30 The blues is usually played in unaccented four/four time or with stride accents. **1955** L. FEATHER *Encycl. Jazz* 289 His lacy, charming melodies sometimes contrast with 'stride' passages of great intensity. **1959** *Jazz Rev.* June 14/1 He [*sc.* James P. Johnson]..developed the New York style of 'stride' piano from the rags of Scott Joplin and the southern Negro cotillion and set dances. **1978** *Listener* 29 June 841/2 An exhilarating two hours of Fats Waller numbers..accompanied on stage by the celebrated stride pianist, Luther Henderson. **1983** *Listener* 20 Jan. 10/2 Its earliest landmark was James P. Johnson's stride-piano showpiece 'Carolina Shout'.

stride, *v.* Add: Pa. pple. also **strode** (*colloq.*).
1936 'R. WEST' *Thinking Reed* iii. 89 From youth he had strode through the twenty-four hours at the pace of a Marathon race. **1951** R. LYND *Essays on Life & Lit.* I. 27 But a *gauche* big farmer's son in a white coat..had strode past her roughly. **1972** *Observer* (Colour Suppl.) 24 Sept. 23/2 The clear mental picture of the battlefront with which he had so boldly strode into Samsonov's headquarters. **1980** *New Yorker* 24 Mar. 127/1 (Advt.), No consumer advocate has yet strode forth to defend and protect the interests of those who can afford a $30,000 sport coupe.

7. *Jazz.* To play stride piano (see *STRIDE *sb.* 7 b).
Found only in the gerund or participial form *striding*.
1944 *Metronome* Nov. 17/3 Alberta Simmons, from down in the Jungles, could beat the average man 'striding'. **1958** P. GAMMOND *Decca Bk. of Jazz* xv. 187 Nobody else has compounded so many pianistic devices—the delayed note, the tremolo, the dazzling run, the striding bass—into such a homogeneous quiddity.

stridency. Add: (Examples in sense 1 b of *STRIDENT *a.*)
1968 CHOMSKY & HALLE *Sound Pattern Eng.* 329 Stridency is a feature restricted to obstruent continuants and affricates. **1976** *Word 1971* XXVII. 220 This appearance of the Stridency distinction among Stops and Continuants evidently does not generalise immediately to the affricates. **1979** *Canad. Jrnl. Linguistics* XXIV. I. 20 It incorporates both articulatory (anteriority-coronality) and acoustic (stridency) features.

strident, *a.* Add: **1. b.** *Phonetics.* Of the articulation of a consonantal sound: characterized by friction that is comparatively turbulent. Also as *sb.*, a consonant articulated in this way.
1956 JAKOBSON & HALLE *Fundamentals of Lang.* 31 Strident/mellow: acoustically—higher intensity noise *vs.* lower intensity noise; genetically—rough-edged *vs.* smooth-edged. *Ibid.* 42 Mellow constrictives, opposed to strident constrictives, or strident plosives (affricates) opposed to mellow plosives (stops proper) do not appear in child language before the emergence of the first liquid. **1965** *Amer. Speech* XL. 9 *T* cannot follow a dental stop or *S* follow a strident (sibilant). **1968** CHOMSKY & HALLE *Sound Pattern Eng.* 329 Strident sounds are marked acoustically by greater noisiness than their nonstrident counterparts. **1976** *Word 1971* XXVII. 220, /s/..[and] /f/..also embody the Strident vs. Mellow distinction and are both + Strident.

strider. Add: **2.** *U.S.* = *pond-skater* s.v. *POND *sb.* 4.
1974 A. DILLARD *Pilgrim at Tinker Creek* xi. 189, I read that striders are attracted to any light. **1978** *Sci. Amer.* Apr. 134/1 When the strider stands on the surface film, it is supported by its long, slender middle and hind legs.

strife. Add: **1. f.** *Austral. colloq.* Trouble, disgrace, difficulties. Freq. in phr. *in strife.*

1963 A. LUBBOCK *Austral. Roundabout* 45 'By cripes!' said the landlord, 'I bet you was in strife after that.' **1966** *Sunday Mail Mag.* (Brisbane) 9 Jan. 2/2 He's having trouble with his irrigation. His sudax is coming along all right but he's often in strife priming his pump. **1966** P. MATHERS *Trap* 15, I reckon she needs..a bloody flogging... She'll get us all in strife, he finished. **1969** 'A. GARVE' *Boomerang* iv. 147 'Keep close on my tail,' he called. 'If you get in any strife, bang on your horn.'

5. *strife-weary* adj.; *strife-torn* ppl. adj.

1972 R. D. WALSHE in G. W. Turner *Good Austral. Eng.* xi. 227 The ego ceases to be a shifting strife-torn no-man's-land between the armies of the id and the superego. **1983** *Times* 30 Mar. 7/2 She flies there today on her third tour of the strife-torn Brahmaputra valley state in the past 10 weeks. **1949** KOESTLER *Promise & Fulfilment* III. i. 302 Millions of war-worn, strife-weary people longing to find peace.

striggle (stri·g'l), *colloq.* [perh. f. STR(AGGLE *v.*[1] + W)IGGLE *sb.*] A wavy line.

1906 W. DE MORGAN *Joseph Vance* xxx. 286 I've got him [*sc.* a fly out of the milk]! But he's brought a long striggle of cream out with him. **1963** V. NABOKOV *Gift* iv. 220 This old diary, which was written in an even hand with little striggles and was in a home-made code.

strikable (strəi·kab'l), *a.* [f. STRIKE *v.* + -ABLE.] **a.** That may be struck. **b.** Of an issue: that may provoke an industrial strike.

1904 J. P. MANNOCK *Billiards Expounded* I. i. 23 The various 'strikable faces' of a ball. **1977** *Washington Post* 18 May C2 The idea of 5-day mail service is a 'strikeable issue'.

strike, *sb.* Add: **6. d.** Infestation of a sheep or cow with flies whose larvæ burrow into the skin; an occurrence of this. Freq. with preceding sb.

1933, etc. [see *blow-fly strike* s.v. *BLOW-FLY b]. **1933,** etc. [see *MULES]. **1934** *Bulletin* (Sydney) 26 Sept. 22/1 The C.S.I.R. regards dipping in the light of only 'perhaps rendering the sheep less favorable for strike, but a measure not to be relied upon'. **1937,** etc. [see *fly-strike* s.v. *FLY *sb.*[1] 11]. **1952** I. E. NEWSOM *Sheep Dis.* vi. 140 In South Africa..*L[ucilia] cuprina* is thought to be responsible for 90 per cent of the strikes either alone or in combination with other flies. **1972** *TV Vet Sheep Bk.* xlviii. 143/1 In Britain strike usually starts when the lambs start scouring. **1975** *N.Z. Jrnl. Agric.* Sept. 65/1 One measure for blowflies' resistance to insecticides is the time that it takes, after a spray or dip, for implanted larvae to establish a strike. **1977** *Bulletin* (Sydney) 22 Jan. 16/3 The blowfly costs rural industry $70 million a year in sheep and cattle strike.

e. A sudden military attack concentrated on selected targets; also occas. *concr.*, the force used in such an attack. Also (chiefly with reference to the use of nuclear weapons) preceded by a qualifying word, as *first-strike, pre-emptive strike, second strike*: see under the first elements.

1942 [see *strike patrol*, sense 20 below]. **1943** T. DUDLEY-GORDON *Coastal Command at War* ii. 16 When the Admiralty desires a special reconnaissance or strike to be 'laid on'. **1943** *Yank* 19 Nov. 3 But, when the last strike returned, there were no bullet holes, no torn fabric and the pilots climbed out unhurt. **1945** [see *air strike* s.v. *AIR B. III. 2]. **1963** *Ann. Reg. 1962* 520 The purpose of these bases can be none other than to provide a nuclear strike capability against the Western hemisphere. **1972** *Newsweek* 10 Jan. 1/1 Described by the Pentagon as 'protective-reaction' strikes, the bombings in fact signaled to the world the continuing U.S. interest in Southeast Asia. **1979** H. KISSINGER *White House Years* xxiii. 983 The Son Tay raid was accompanied by a two-day strike by 200 airplanes against North Vietnamese supply installations.

f. *bird-strike*: see *BIRD *sb.* 9.

9. a. Freq. with preceding qualifying word, as *general, outlaw, selective, sit-down, stay-away (-down, -in), sympathetic, wild-cat strike*: see under the first elements. Also *fig.*

1907 R. DUNN *Shameless Diary of Explorer* xv. 201 Miller's stomach went on strike after we washed in the glacier stream.

b. *transf.* A concerted abstention from a particular economic, physical, or social activity on the part of persons who are attempting to obtain a concession from an authority or to register a protest; esp. in *hunger strike, rent strike* (see *HUNGER *sb.* 4, *RENT *sb.*[1] 4 c).

1889, etc. [see *hunger strike* s.v. *HUNGER *sb.* 4]. **1911** G. B. SHAW *Getting Married* 220 Ive told our last four Prime Ministers that if they didnt make our marriage laws reasonable there would be a strike against marriage. **1934** *Sun* (Baltimore) 8 Nov. 10/4 People with fixed incomes necessarily buy less. There are indignation meetings and 'buyers' strikes'. **1937** *Ibid.* 30 Aug. 8/1 The falling birth rate indicates that 'mankind cannot be forced or bribed to produce children'... The present 'birth strike' will continue until necessary social readjustments are effected. **1938** *Ibid.* 28 Jan. 22/1 Forty-eight tenants of an apartment building..started a 'strike' January 1, demanding rent reductions. **1965** B. PEARCE tr. *Preobrazhensky's New Economics* 167 A consumers' strike is the limit which arises to state planning whenever the state's prices exceed the level acceptable to the private market. **1970,** etc. [see *rent strike* s.v. *RENT *sb.*[1] 4 c].

1976 *Gramophone* Dec. 1052/1 The Lysistrata plot about the women stopping a war by going on sexual strike.

11. (Earlier examples.) Also, the sudden discovery of an accumulation of natural gas. orig. *U.S.* (For 67 d read 68 d.)

1852 L. CLAPPE *Shirley Lett. Calif. Mines* (1922) 131 They are always longing for big strikes [of gold]. **1855** H. HELPER *Land of Gold* 296, I may make a 'strike', but that is mere speculation. **1864** [see *oil strike* s.v. *OIL *sb.*[1] 6 e].

12. Restrict *U.S.* to senses in Dict. and add: **a.** Also *Ninepins.* (Earlier and later examples.) Also *fig.*

1859 *Atlantic Monthly* Nov. 641 Strike: terms of the game of nine-pins. **1939** H. MILLER *Cosmological Eye* 219 *Of Human Bondage* was a great book, he thought. I thought so too and I scored another strike for the constable on my mental blackboard. **1958** [see *FRAME *sb.* 11 g]. **1974** *Cleveland* (Ohio) *Plain Dealer* 13 Oct. C. 8/3 Marge opened her third game with nine strikes in a row, but left the 5-9 pins on her first ball in the 10th frame on the way to her 275 game and 614 series.

b. (*a*) Earlier examples.) (*b*) Also, a pitched ball recorded against the batter. (Earlier and later examples.) Esp. as one of three counts against the batter.

1841 *Picayune* (New Orleans) 25 May 2/2 If 'Edith' wishes to see 'a great strike'.., let her walk down Water street..and see *the* 'bachelors' make the ball fly. **1845** in *Appletons' Ann. Cycl. 1885* (1886) X. 77/2 Players must take their strike in regular turn. **1856** *Spirit of Times* 22 Nov. 197/2 The striker should also be compelled to run on such occasions, strike or no strike. **1867** *Ball Players' Chron.* 4 July 6/2 Their batting was of a superior character, two of their players..each making some powerful strikes. **1868** H. CHADWICK *Base Ball Player's Bk. Reference* 75 Mills called 'one strike' on him. **1912** C. MATHEWSON *Pitching* 12 It put me in the hole with the count two balls and one strike. **1942** *Sun* (Baltimore) 3 Apr. 18/7 The machine will throw 75 per cent more strikes in a given number of pitches than a human. **1974** *Anderson* (S. Carolina) *Independent* 19 Apr. 4B/7 The Citadel scored on a missed third strike and two errors.

(*c*) *fig.* Usu. preceded by a numeral or enumerative adj. and const. *against* or † *on.* Something to one's discredit, a black mark.

1938 *New Republic* 26 Jan. 336/1 All movements for social good will..have two strikes on them before they start. *a* **1939** in E. J. Nichols *Hist. Dict. Baseball Terminol.* (Unpublished Ph.D. thesis, Pennsylvania State College) Appendix I, p. iv, You therefore are starting with two strikes against him. It's up to you to hit one into the bleachers and send yourself home. **1943** *Official Rep. Deb. House of Commons Canada* 31 May 3196/2, I am a little afraid that a man who approaches that board claiming exemption as a conscientious objector goes to bat with three strikes against him. **1956** B. HOLIDAY *Lady sings Blues* (1973) xxi. 169 The only evidence they've got is on me. I've got one strike against me. **1962** J. GLENN in *Into Orbit* 16, I knew that I might have a couple of small strikes against me... I was not a college graduate. ..Also..I was probably a little older than most of the men NASA was considering. **1968** *Globe & Mail Mag.* (Toronto) 13 Jan. 3/2 The student council also did nothing. Strike one for student power. **1975** *Listener* 13 Feb. 204/1 One of the main strikes against Ted Heath was that he did not 'come over' on the box. **1979** 'S. WOODS' *This Fatal Writ* 129 The discovery of your man, injured, would have been an additional strike against him.

c. *Cricket.* The right of the batsman to receive the next ball. Also without article.

1886 *Cricket* 20 May 137/1 Seeing over sixty runs scored, he, strange to relate, did not succeed in getting a strike. **1955** [see *FARM *v.*[2] 6]. **1963** A. ROSS *Australia 63* iii. 83 He played McKenzie fine of Harvey at cover, called euphorically, in an effort to keep the strike, for a second, and was run out. **1976** J. SNOW *Cricket Rebel* 57 Geoff Boycott took first strike leaving 'Ollie' [Milburn] at the non-striker's end.

d. *U.S. Football.* A forward pass, straight into the hands of the receiver.

1947 *Richmond* (Va.) *Times-Dispatch* 9 Nov. B7/7 Brown threw a perfect 'strike' to Elliott on the 10-yard ribbon, but the lanky freshman end dropped the ball. **1972** J. MOSEDALE *Football* v. 72 To this strike-tossing forward passer..went the plaudits of the nation.

20. (sense 3 c) *strike bushel* (earlier example); (sense 6 e) *strike aeroplane, aircraft, carrier, Command, patrol, power, trainer, wing*; also *strike-attack, -reconnaissance* attrib. phrases; (sense 8) *strike-faulting* vbl. sb.; (sense 9) *strike action, benefit, call, committee, leader* (example), *meeting, money, movement, notice, record, wave, weapon*; *strike-free, -happy, -prone, -ridden, -torn* adjs.; **strike-bound** *a.*, immobilized by a strike; **strike-breaker** (earlier example); **strike-breaking** *vbl. sb.*, the action of a strike-breaker; also as *ppl. a.*; hence (as back formation) **strike-break** *v. intr.*; **strike force,** (*a*) a military force equipped to deliver a (nuclear) strike; (*b*) a police unit organized for rapid and effective action against crime; **strike-slip** *Geol.* (orig. *U.S.*), the component of the slip of a fault in a horizontal direction, parallel to the strike; also as *adv.*; freq. *attrib.*, esp. in *strike-slip fault*, a fault in which motion was predominantly parallel to the strike; **strike zone** *Baseball*, an imaginary rectangle 17 inches wide, stretching from the height of the batter's armpits to that of his knees, within which the pitcher must throw the ball for the pitch to be called a strike.

1949 *Britannica Bk. of Year* 606/2 Minority groups.. threatening and, from time to time, taking strike action by way of protest. **1977** M. EDELMAN *Polit. Lang.* vii. 131 Wage demands their fellow workers would otherwise be free to back with strike action if necessary. **1965** *New Scientist* 22 Apr. 217/1 The Hawker Siddeley Buccaneer naval strike aeroplane might be modified to suit the RAF. **1957** *Times* 22 Aug. 6/6 The supersonic strike aircraft which Hawker Aircraft are developing as a private venture. *Ibid.*, The fact that it is described as a strike aircraft indicates that it can be used as a bomber as well as a fighter. **1980** *Daily Tel.* 24 Sept. 4/8 Iraqi transport aircraft have been withdrawn to the safety of bases in Jordan, beyond the reach of Iran's strike aircraft. **1977** *R.A.F. News* 11–24 May 1/5 The two squadrons operate in the same maritime strike attack role. **1896** *Rep. Proc. Internat. Typogr. Union N. Amer.* 22/1, $48,087.18.. [were] paid during the two years in strike and lockout benefits. **1949** *Britannica Bk. of Year* 687/1 *Strike-bound*, prevented from moving, travelling, sailing etc. by a strike or strikes. **1956** *B.B.C. Handbk. 1957* 121 The editors of strike-bound national dailies and periodicals. **1982** *Daily Tel.* 3 Aug. 22/4 Strike-bound Sealink ships have.. moored at the two Holyhead berths. **1961** *Economist* 6 May 525/1 Individual exporters and importers should be allowed to send their own staff in to get their own goods on and off the ships, if their staff will agree to strike-break in this way. **1904** *N.Y. Even. Post* 4 Aug. 2 [Half of] the strike breakers are men who, having been idle for a time, simply wanted a chance to make a little ready money. **1905** *Amer. Mag.* May 107/2 It is quite a new profession, this strike breaking, a curious evolution of modern industrial methods. **1920** *Manch. Guardian News Bull.* 10 Sept. 2/1 A direct incitement to strike-breaking. **1978** S. BRILL *Teamsters* x. 362 The police sent an armed convoy to escort a strikebreaking truck. **1858** TROLLOPE *Three Clerks* I. i. 12 Young Tudor had produced a very smart paper on the merits—or demerits—of the strike bushel. **1976** Strike call [see *stay-away* s.v. *STAY *v.*[1] 31]. **1966** *Daily Tel.* 18 Aug. 1/4 'Straight Laced' is the first multi-national strike-carrier exercise for some years. **1968** *Ann. Reg. 1967* 27 The White Paper envisaged..the merging of the RAF's Fighter and Bomber Command into a new Strike Command. **1949** *Britannica Bk. of Year* 210/2 The men's allegiance to the strike committee outweighed their loyalty to the union. **1925** N. E. ODELL in E. F. Norton *Fight for Everest: 1924* 299 There is considerable evidence of strike-faulting which would explain this. **1965** G. J. WILLIAMS *Econ. Geol. N.Z.* iii. 30/2 Some ore was won from a 390 ft shaft, but both strike- and cross-faulting seem to have disrupted the lode. **1961** *Listener* 14 Dec. 1011/2 The development of nuclear strike forces by Britain and France. **1973** *Black Panther* 1 Sept. 11/2 Federal and local strike forces smashed into homes and offices in a series of pre-dawn raids. **1947** *Sun* (Baltimore) 2 Jan. 17/1 If operations are strike-free, enough steel can be turned out to restore within a few months a balance between supply and demand. **1982** *Times* 23 Mar. 8/7 The reductions in strike-free days. **1955** *Times* 26 May 11/5 We are being placed on a par with other 'strike-happy' industries. **1913** W. OWEN *Let.* 19 Oct. (1967) 201 You should set up as Suffragette, Dublin-Strike-Leader, or Schoolmistress, so that you would be *obliged* to speak for seven hours a day. **1978** P. BOARDMAN *Worlds of Patrick Geddes* vii. 246 The strike leader had the reputation of being a dangerous man. **1926** *Brit. Gaz.* 12 May 1/7 Large crowds of them congregated in the streets, while some abortive strike meetings were held in the squares. **1913** D. H. LAWRENCE in *Westm. Gaz.* 13 Sept. 2/2 Strike-money is paid in the Primitive Methodist Chapel. **1932** *Sun* (Baltimore) 13 Sept. 8/3 The certain futility of the 'strike' movement. **1926** *Brit. Gaz.* 12 May 2/2 The *Weston Mercury*, Weston-super-Mare, reports that after strike notices had been received the local branch of the Typographical Association decided to return to work. **1942** Strike patrol [see *ROVER[1] 3 e]. **1959** *Time* 23 Feb. 22/3 U.S. strike power is still supreme now. **1961** *Daily Tel.* 22 Apr. 9/2 The strike-prone motor industry. **1963** *Times* 2 Feb. 9/2 Adopting American nuclear warheads for its strike-reconnaissance aircraft missiles defending the North American continent. **1938** *Encycl. Brit. Bk. of Year* 614/1 In 1936 there were but 156 strikes..; a rather typical strike record for Canada. **1967** *Spectator* 8 Dec. 706/2 Two of our favourite illusions are that we are among the most strike-ridden nations on earth, and that every strike brings chaos in its wake. **1913** W. LINDGREN *Mineral Deposits* ix. 121 The strike-slip is the component of the slip parallel with the fault slip. *Ibid.* 126 The expressions 'normal' and 'reverse' may be used in connection with oblique and dip faults, even when these are strike-slip or oblique slip faults. **1932** C. R. LONGWELL et al. *Textbk. Geol.* I. xii. 315 (*caption*) Broken lines show the displacement (slip), and its three components—throw, heave, and strike-slip—measured along axes at right angles to each other. **1964** W. C. PUTNAM *Geology* vi. 146/2 Ordinarily, in order to establish whether or not movement has been strike-slip or dip-slip, it is necessary to have layered rocks with strongly differing dips cut by the fault. *Ibid.* 147/1 The actual movement as demonstrated by the outcrop was strike-slip. **1971** I. G. GASS et al. *Understanding Earth* xxiii. 327/2 The San Andreas is called a strike-slip fault. **1977** *Sci. Amer.* Apr. 36/2 In Mongolia most earthquakes are associated with strike-slip faulting. **1977** *Belfast Tel.* 28 Feb. 7/9 The crisis at strike-torn Leyland deepened. **1967** *Observer* 26 Nov. 2/6 The Jaguar strike-trainer which was born.. in the Anglo-French agreement of 1965. **1957** *Encycl. Brit.* XXI. 469/1 The strike waves that accompanied the Russian revolutions of 1905 and 1917. **1955** *Times* 26 May 11/5 The apparently indiscriminate use of the strike weapon. **1944** *Hansard Commons* 7 Mar. 1910 In conjunction with the strike wings of Coastal Command and R.A.F. fighters our Light Forces have constantly attacked enemy convoys in the Channel. **1948** *Sporting News Dope Bk.* 119 The umpire shall rule it a ball even though it passed over the heart of the plate within the strike zone. **1950**

Official Baseball Rules ii. 17 The strike zone is that space over home plate which is between the batter's armpits and the top of his knees when he assumes his natural stance.

strike, *v.* Add: The pa. pple. *stricken* remains common in U.S. (esp. legal) use. (Examples in various senses.)

See also sense 13 a below.

1906 *Federal Reporter* (1907) CXLVII. 451 All of the testimony given by the witness..is withdrawn and stricken out of this case. **1938** *Congress Rec.* 24 May 7405/2 That the Committee do..report the bill back to the House with the recommendation that the enacting clause be stricken out. **1976** *National Observer* (U.S.) 9 Oct. 7/4 A new trend in comics has stricken down many of the old taboos.

III. 13. a. Also (*U.S.*) const. *from*. The *absol.* use has now been revived in the U.S., esp. in legal contexts and *colloq.*, in the *imp.*, annulling or reversing what the speaker has just said.

The pa. pple. form *stricken* is common in the legal examples of this sense.

1829 *Rep. Supreme Court Tennessee* (1832) IX. 229 That an attorney may be stricken from the roll for good cause, none can doubt. **1915** *Southwestern Reporter* CLXXV. 661/1 No further steps..were taken in the case until the February term, 1904, of the Magoffin circuit court, when it was stricken from the docket. **1973** *N.Y. Law Jrnl.* 19 July 4/2 The Convention..voted 132 to 49, to strike that section from the Constitution.

1957 *Reports Supreme Court Kansas* (1958) CLXXXI. 623 In our opinion the reply was erroneously stricken. **1965** *Pacific Reporter* CCCCIV. 230/2 Where..a second clause appears which expresses a different intent and declares a life estate plus a remainder which is void under the rule, the qualifying clause will be stricken. **1973** *N.Y. Law Jrnl.* 31 Aug. 19/2 Motion to strike the statement of readiness is granted. **1978** *N.Y. Times* 29 Mar. B3/4 Over strong objections from the prosecutor, Sybil R. Moses, Judge William J. Arnold ordered the question stricken.

1963 R. I. McDavid *Mencken's Amer. Lang.* xi. 754 In television we might note *mark it* and *strike it*, directions to stage hands to chalk out the position for scenery and then rub out the mark for the next set. **1976** R. M. Stern *Will* I. ii. 17 Do you..believe that the crash was not an accident? Strike that. We will look into it with an open mind. **1977** H. Greene *FSO-1* ii. 16, I don't give a damn what the congressman says. Strike that: I *do* give a damn.

b. Phr. *to strike* (a medical practitioner, etc.) *off the register*: to remove (that person's name) from the register of qualified practitioners and thereby forbid him or her to practise. Usu. *pass.*

1911 G. B. Shaw *Doctor's Dilemma* p. xciii, Execute the doctor, if necessary, *as* a doctor, by striking him off the register. **1936** A. Christie *Cards on Table* xvi. 157, I heard him say he'd get Dr. Roberts struck off the—Medical Register, would it be? **1951** 'E. Crispin' *Long Divorce* xvi. 199 We can and shall get him struck off the register.

IV. 24. b. Also with particular kind of work as obj.

1878 Trollope *Is he Popenjoy?* III. xix. 251 She had on one occasion threatened to strike lecturing.

c. (Later examples.) Now only *N. Amer.* Also in wider but analogous contexts.

1930 J. Dos Passos *42nd Parallel* I. 117 She'd worry Mac about striking his boss for more pay. **1941** *Sun* (Baltimore) 23 Sept. 12/2 Now the affected union, the Seafarers' International Union of the AFL, serves formal notice that it will strike every ship on which it has contracts. **1946** *Ibid.* 16 Jan. 4–0/1 They [*sc.* students] held a mass meeting, staged a snake dance, struck their classes, and otherwise asserted themselves, in protest over the resignation of..a football coach at the university. **1950** Patterson & Conrad *Scottsboro Boy* II. vii. 137 Right here we struck the whole squad. No one would do any work till the question of slowing down the work was settled. **1968** *Globe & Mail* (Toronto) 1 Feb. B10/3 The union will strike company plants in five U.S. cities. **1978** *N.Y. Times* 29 Mar. A20/4 Photoengravers voted 177 to 0 yesterday to strike The New York Times and The Daily News.

V. 28. f. *Cinemat.* To make (another print) *from* a motion picture film.

1970 A. Fowles *Dupe Negative* xiv. 192 I've got four hundred feet of 35 mm. ECO original here... How long will it take to strike a master positive? *Ibid.* 196 The piece of film that actually runs through the camera is called the original..from which all subsequent prints are struck.

30. a. (*b*) (Later examples with a match as subject.)

1957 'R. West' *Fountain Overflows* i. 14 And I think the matches are wet, they won't strike. **1962** J. Braine *Life at Top* ii. 31, I heard a match strike and smelled cigar smoke.

(*c*) Also *imp.* as a mild imprecation (cf. sense 46 c in Dict. and Suppl.). Chiefly *Austral.* and *N.Z.*

1936 A. Russell *Gone Nomad* vi. 44 'Strike a light!' he broke in suddenly. 'See them?' **1960** I. Cross *Backward Sex* ii. 39 'Strike a light,' he hissed... 'Get over here, quick,' he said. 'Have a bloody look, man.'

44. b. (Later examples.)

1904 *Sun* (N.Y.) 23 Aug. 1 The storm twister struck Willow Lakes about 9 o'clock. **1976** *Daily Mirror* 16 July 13/3 Earthquakes killed 275 people and injured 2,000 early yesterday as they struck Indonesia's tropical holiday island of Bali.

46. c. *strike me pink*: see *pink *a.* 8. Also (*Austral.* and *N.Z.*) *ellipt.* as *strike!*

1915 C. J. Dennis *Songs of Sentimental Bloke* (1916) 43 'Ah, strike!' she sez. 'I wish that I could die!' **1960** B. Crump *Good Keen Man* 116 Strike, he went crook! Who the hell was responsible? Had we been blasting fish?

VII. 66. e. Also, in pass. constr., to be favourably impressed by (an idea, suggestion, etc.). Now *colloq.*

1899 J. K. Jerome *Three Men in Boat* i. 17 The only one who was not struck with the suggestion was Montmorency. **1938** C. P. Conigrave *Walk-About* ix. 50, I don't think he's too struck on my going back to Rosewood. **1940** 'N. Shute' *Old Captivity* iv. 110, I don't know that I'm so struck on this, sir.

68. d. (Earlier examples.) *to strike it rich* (earlier examples). Also in similar *fig.* phrases.

1835 C. F. Hoffman *Winter in West* II. 47, I hear that he has lately struck a lead. **1852** L. Clappe *Shirley Lett. Calif. Mines* 216 When a company wish to reach the bedrock as quickly as possible, they sink a shaft..until they 'strike it'. **1854** *California Daily Chron.* 19 May 3/7 Messrs. Emory & Bacon, just above the claim of Messrs. Meredith & Co., have also struck it rich. **1862** 'Mark Twain' *Let.* (1917) I. iii. 76 Well, if you haven't 'struck it rich—' that is, if the piece of rock you sent me came from a *bona fide ledge*—and it looks as if it did. *c* **1863** T. Taylor *Ticket-of-Leave Man* III. 47 He..had to bolt to Australia—struck an awfully full pocket at the diggings, and is paying off his old ticks like an emperor. *fig.* **1884** 'Mark Twain' *Huck. Finn* xxi. 208 We struck it mighty lucky. **1953** [see *pay-dirt* s.v. *pay- 2]. **1975** *Sydney Morning Herald* 15 Nov. 55 West Indies batsmen struck pay dirt aplenty in the SCG yesterday. **1977** A. C. H. Smith *Jericho Gun* vi. 85 He didn't mind a penny. It was what he had always thought he would do when he struck it.

e. *intr.* Colloq. phr. *to strike lucky*, to hit a vein of good fortune.

1951 *Sport* 6–12 Apr. 17/1 Birmingham struck lucky because several London clubs refused to give Graham Warren a trial. **1984** *Financial Times* 31 Jan. 17/7 The Bush strikes lucky more often than any fringe theatre has a right to.

VIII. 71. Also, to reach (a figure, loss, or profit) by balancing an account.

1880 *Tax Cases* I. 500 In striking their annual profits so as to fix the sum divisible as dividend, the Railway Company have gone upon actual expenditure, and not upon a mere estimate of probable wear and tear. **1932** *Economist* 16 Jan. 127/2 For years past the banks have been building up contingency reserves by appropriations made before and after striking their net profits. **1955** [see *clearing-bank* s.v. *clearing *vbl. sb.* 8]. **1980** *Daily Tel.* 30 July 1/4 Last year's loss..was struck after allowing for depreciation of £87 million and interest payments of £188 million.

75. e. For (See quot.) read: 'To induce (a person) to pay money on the promise of getting him votes, legislative favors, etc.' (*D.A.E.*), and add earlier examples.

1859 G. W. Matsell *Vocabulum* 87 *Strike*, to get money from candidates before an election, under the pretense of getting votes for them. **1883** M. de L. Landon *Wit & Humor of Age* 345 He had a way of striking the politicians who wanted a favor out of the Governor.

76. a. (Earlier and later examples.) Also, † of an electric charge, to pass as a spark (cf. sense 43 a); of an electric discharge, to come into being; also *transf.* of the tube containing it.

1777 T. Cavallo *Compl. Treat. Electr.* III. iii. 163 When the jar is charging, and the charge is become so high as to strike through half an inch of air. **1827** *Phil. Mag.* I. 344 If the distance be greater than that over which the charge can *strike* in the form of a spark, or with explosion. **1929** *Ibid.* VIII. 1100 The uncertain delay which occurs between the instant at which the requisite voltage is applied to the lamp and that at which the discharge strikes. **1962** J. H. & P. J. Reyner *Radio Communication* v. 237 Once the tube has struck, however, the current can be maintained with a somewhat lower anode potential.

c. *trans.* To bring (an arc) into being. Cf. sense 30 a.

1891 [in Dict., sense 76 a]. **1930** *Engineering* 7 Feb. 173/2 Oil..played an important part in quenching the arc which was struck when those contacts were separated. **1950** Gill & Simons *Mod. Welding Technique* xi. 129 On occasion it may be found difficult to strike an arc. **1976** C. Bradshaw *Metall. for Schools* xi. 143/1 An arc is struck between the electrode and the workpiece.

77. b. *U.S. Naut.* (See quot. 1952[1].)

1952 J. V. Noel *Naval Terms Dict.* 212 *Strike*..to work for, as in..'he is striking for chief'. *Strike for*..to learn the trade of. **1952** *MSTS Bull.* May 9/1 Few and far between are those who don't 'strike' for a rating during their short or long Navy career.

IX. 79. strike down. e. *trans.* To hold invalid (chiefly in legal contexts). *U.S.*

1894 *Congress. Rec.* 12 Dec. 267/1, I do not care who strikes down class legislation in this country. **1951** *Federal Reporter* (1952) CXCIII. 250/2 The court's opinions make abundantly clear its intention to strike down the entire arrangement. **1964** *Mod. Law Rev.* XXVIII. III. 343 Their main agreement had been struck down by the Restrictive Practices Court. **1979** *Tucson* (Arizona) *Citizen* 3 Oct. 4c/2 The decision..struck down a..Superior Court ruling.

82. strike off. a. *spec.* in *pass.*, of a medical practitioner, solicitor, etc.: to be struck off the register (see sense 13 b above).

1937 A. J. Cronin *Citadel* IV. xxi. 424 You remember the case of Jarvis, the manipulator, several years ago, when he got some cad of a doctor to anaesthetise for him. He was struck off, instanter. **1958** J. Cannan *And be Villain* i. 20 He'd be struck off if he was the least bit naughty. **1965** A. Christie *At Bertram's Hotel* xvi. 153 We still call him Dr. Stokes although he's been struck off. **1983** *Times* 12 Oct. 3/4 Mr Parsons is asking Mr Justice Vinelott to order that Mr Davies be struck off.

83. strike out. i. (Earlier and later examples in Baseball.) Also *fig.*

1853 *Oregonian* (Portland) 2 July 1/5 No doubt they will find that strikers have struck out. **1866** *N.Y. Herald* 28 Aug. 8/2 Pennington was third man at the bat, and struck out. **1937** *New Yorker* 19 June 30 The senator had his hopes, but he struck out on three wide 'ha's'. **1974** *Los Angeles Times* 13 Oct. III. 10/2 Garvey grounded to short. Ferguson struck out.

k. *trans.* Of a pitcher in Baseball, to put (a batter) out by pitching three strikes to a batter. *U.S.*

1939 E. J. Nicholls *Hist. Dict. Baseball Terminol.* (Unpublished Ph.D. thesis, Pennsylvania College) 75 *Strike-out king*, a pitcher who is noted for the large number of times he strikes out opposing batters. **1968** *Washington Post* 4 July C1/8 It was the third time in the game that he struck out the side. **1975** *New Yorker* 14 Apr. 92/2 He struck out two of the first three Yankee batters, without really trying his fastball.

X. 88. strike-back, used *attrib.* to designate the capacity of making a retaliatory nuclear strike; **strike me blind** *slang* (see quots.); **strike-out,** an out in baseball, called when a batter has made three strikes; also *attrib.* and *fig.*; **strike-over** *U.S.*, the typing of a character on a spot occupied by a character typed previously; **strike through** *Printing* (see quots.).

1962 *Listener* 29 Mar. 539/2 It was clear that we would soon..have a sufficiently invulnerable strike-back nuclear capacity. **1966** Schwarz & Hadik *Strategic Terminology* 44 *Strike-back capability*, nuclear forces which could survive an enemy first strike and then be used against him in a second strike. **1901** S. H. King *Dog-Watches at Sea* 146 Rice was known as 'strike me blind'. **1936** B. M. Adams *Ships & Women* viii. 180 The dish..called 'strike-me-blind'. Boiled rice, with black-strap molasses. **1911** J. B. Foster *How to Pitch* 72 It happens to be a pitcher..of the strike-out kind. **1922** E. J. Lanigan *Baseball Cycl.* II. 39/1 Another top-notcher joined them in the person of Thomas Ramsey, eminent strike-out king. **1937** *Philadelphia Rec.* 23 Mar. 15/1 Mr. Roosevelt has..grown into the stature of a strike-out king. **1967** *Boston Sunday Herald* 14 May II. 3/3 Six of his strikeouts came in those innings. **1978** M. Puzo *Fools Die* xvi. 170 After Pfc. Hiller was recalled, his case would be evaluated by a Regular Army board. Another strikeout. **1950** *Richmond* (Virginia) *Times-Dispatch* 3 Oct. 1/8 A patent on typewriter type designed to permit strikeovers on letters in about 11 per cent of common typing errors. **1978** W. White *W. Whitman's Daybooks & Notebooks* I. p. xxii, Corrections, strike-overs, inserted words..I have transcribed exactly the way Whitman has left them. **1958** T. Landau *Encycl. Librarianship* 290/2 *Strike through*, penetration of the type impression from the verso to the recto of a page due to improper pressure or faulty make-ready. **1979** G. A. Glaister *Gloss. Bk.* (ed. 2) 464/1 *Strike through*, a fault caused when the oily medium in printing ink soaks into and through the paper, making it translucent.

striker. Add: **I. 2. e.** For † *Obs.*$^{-0}$ read *rare*$^{-1}$ and add example.

1970 J. H. Gray *Boy from Winnipeg* 69, I also first got to know horses that were strikers.

3. f. *Tanning.* One who smooths and stretches skins either by hand or by means of a machine. Also *striker-out*.

1921 *Dict. Occup. Terms* (1927) §338 *Striker, striker-out*, (i) lays wet hide or skin on a slate or marble slab or table, and rubs it with a hard 'slicker' tool, of stone or steel, to stretch it, drive out excess of moisture, smooth it, and to close grain; (ii) sets rollers of a machine..in motion..and passes skin or hide between revolving rollers. **1972** *Classification of Occupations* (Dept. Employment) III. 24/2 *Finishing machine operator*... Other titles include.. Striker.

4. (Earlier example in Baseball and later examples in Cricket.) In Assoc. Football and Hockey, a forward whose main function is to seek to score goals. In *Rugby Football* = *hooker[1] 6.

1816 [see *play *v.* 17 f]. **1862** *Sunday Mercury* (N.Y.) 13 July 6/2 The Excelsiors led off, Young being their first striker, and he sent the ball flying to left field. **1891** W. G. Grace *Cricket* viii. 235 It is the striker's duty to call [for a run] if the ball is hit in front of the wicket. **1963** J. Greaves *Soccer* vii. 73 If John White or another Spurs' player is bringing the ball up..I move into a position ready to race through and be first to the ball when he pushes it forward. It is the ball goal-strikers dream of. *Ibid.* 74 Remember, the striker never takes it for granted ..he goes after the ball on every occasion. **1973** *Daily Mail* 24 July 27/1 John White, Bristol's 30-year-old reserve hooker,..replaces ex-Coventry striker John Gray. **1974** M. Weir *Women's Hockey for Seventies* 96 Before the ball is hit the right striker is sprinting out to the right wing and the right wing is cutting into the space she has made. *Ibid.* 8 It is confusing for a defence to have to cater for elusive strikers. **1974** *Encycl. Brit. Macropædia* 257/2 The striker does not have to run after he has hit the ball. **1980** *Daily Tel.* 20 Mar. 34/3 Wales, without Chester striker Ian Rush, could not break down the Irish defence.

6. b. (Later examples.)

1898 *Harper's Mag.* Apr. 700/2 My 'striker' had just left me, with instructions to have my horse fed. **1929** B. Davis *Truth about Geronimo* 107 Geronimo's son demanded the post of striker (servant) to me. **1948** *Time* 14 June 9/3 He takes the same attitude toward Congress as he would to a striker who fails to put the proper polish on his boots.

c. (Earlier and later examples.)

1836 *Spirit of Times* 9 July 162/2 An awkward looking *striker* of old Thompson's holding her by the cheek of the bridle. **1853** 'P. Paxton' *Stray Yankee in Texas* 335 To a few he [*sc.* John Murel] confided the extent of his design, and to each of these gave the authority to enlist all the minor villains of their acquaintance. The latter were termed Strikers and used but as tools. **1873** J. H. Beadle *Undevel. West* xi. 184, I had published a severe criticism of this Judge Smith. His 'strikers' now had me at Court as defendant. **1883** 'Mark Twain' *Life Mississippi* xxix. 315 [Murel's gang of robbers] was composed of two classes: the Heads or Council..[and] the active agents..termed strikers.

d. An engineer's apprentice on a steamboat. Also in extended use: see quots. 1944, etc.

Cf. also quot. 1891 at sense 3 b in Dict.

1872 [see *mud-clerk* s.v. *mud *sb.*[1] 5]. **1875** 'Mark Twain' in *Atlantic Monthly* XXXV. 70/2 He turned up as apprentice engineer or 'striker' on a steamboat. **1944** K. D. McCracken *Baby Flat-Top* 53 In the Navy a striker is a seaman or fireman who is working particularly hard in order to convince his superiors that he ought to become a petty officer of some kind. **1955** C. S. Forester *Good Shepherd* 104 An electrician's mate and his striker stood behind him. **1963** *Amer. Speech* XXXVIII. 45 *Striker*, a [truck] driver's helper. **1970** *National Fisherman* Aug. 21-A/1 Emery Brown as rigman or 'striker' [on a shrimp boat]..testified in person during this trial.

III. 18. striker-boat (examples); hence *striker boatsman*.

1891 Striker boat [in Dict., sense 3 b]. **1950** *Richmond* (Va.) *Times-Dispatch* 23 July (Mag. Section) 5/1 When a bunch [of fish] is spotted, a striker boat, manned by a striker boatsman, is sent out to indicate the direction in which the fish are moving.

striking, *vbl. sb.* Add: **1. e.** *Tanning.* The process of smoothing and stretching skins. Also *striking-out*. Freq. *attrib.*

a **1877** Knight *Dict. Mech.* III. 2429/1 Striking-machine. **1882** *Encycl. Brit.* XIV. 385/2 For striking or pinning by hand the hide is dampened with water, thrown over a beam, and worked all over the grain side with a striking pin. *Ibid.*, Striking machines are now very generally used for the operation. **1897** C. T. Davis *Manuf. Leather* (ed. 2) 378 The 'striking out' was performed on mahogany tables. **1920** *Conquest* Nov. 38/3 Stretching and smoothing [hides] with a striking-pin (a two-handled tool triangular in sections). **1942, 1953** [see *setting *vbl. sb.*[1] 13 a].

3. striking-circle *Hockey* (see quots.); **striking distance** (earlier example); **striking force,** (*a*) the force with which a projectile strikes; (*b*) a military force held in readiness for sudden attack; **striking-plate** (*b*) (see quot. *a* 1877); **striking platform** *Archæol.*, a flat area on a core of flint or stone on which a blow is struck to detach a flake; **striking price** *Stock Exch.* (see quots. 1973, 1982).

1890 F. S. Creswell *Hockey* 11 No goal can be scored unless the ball be hit by one of the attacking side from within the striking circle. **1906** *Official Handbk. Hockey Assoc.* 120 In front of each goal shall be drawn a white line 4 yds. long, parallel to, and 15 yds. from, the goal line. This line shall be continued each way to meet the goal line by quarter-circles having the goal posts as centres. The space enclosed by these lines and the goal lines, including the lines themselves, shall be called the striking circle. **1961** F. C. Avis *Sportsman's Gloss.* 219/1 *Striking circle*, in Hockey the space immediately in front of goal, really a rough *semi*-circle, 15 yards from the goal line. **1751** B. Franklin *Exper. & Observations Electricity* 62 A needle..will draw the fire from the scale silently at a much greater than the striking distance. **1881** Striking force [in Dict.]. **1917** T. E. Lawrence *Lett.* (1938) 230 Force 3 is our striking force (of perhaps 6,000 not bad men) and may be able to rush Deraat, or at least should cut off the garrison there. **1944** [see *air strike* s.v. *air *sb.*[1] B. III 2)]. **1965** J. A. Michener *Source* (1966) 793 The well-trained Jews of the Palmach—an abbreviation for the Plugat Machatz, 'striking force', organized in 1941 to resist the threatened German invasion. *a* **1877** Knight *Dict. Mech.* III. 2429/2 *Striking-plate*, the device by which the wooden centering of an arch is lowered when the arch is completed. **1876** *Encycl. Brit.* IV. 311/2 Figure 55 shows the *striking plates* and *wedges* by which the centre is lowered after the completion of the arch. **1913** *Proc. Prehistoric Soc. E. Anglia* I. III. 311 The flaking..is of a very high order, dexterous vertical blows, with well-masked cones of percussion, and striking platforms being supplemented by the most regular and fine edge-work. **1949** K. P. Oakley *Man Tool-Maker* 25 Each blow is delivered obliquely downwards near the edge of some conveniently placed flattish area (the striking platform), usually the scar of a flake previously struck off. **1977** L. L. Johnson in Hill & Gunn *Individual in Prehistory* x. 218 Collapsed platforms were noted only where there was no retouch on the striking platform. **1961** K. S. Most *How to make Money on Stock Exch.* iii. 35 Suppose I have a..well-founded belief that Woolworths' shares are going to rise in price..I shall have to pay out £335 plus purchase costs for every 100 shares. I may not have this money available..so I arrange to give the price of a call option, say, 5s. per share, for the right to buy 100 Woolworths' shares at any time during the next twelve weeks at a price of, say, 66s., being the 'striking price' at the end of the previous Account. **1973** N. Searle *Successful Investments* 85 *Striking price*, the price at which the holder of an option has the right to effect a purchase or sale. **1982** *Times* 9 Nov. 19 With a tender offer for sale, investors tender at the price they are prepared to pay. The issuing house works down the list to the lowest price at which the issue is totally subscribed. This becomes the 'striking price'.

Strindbergian (strindbɜ̄·ɹgiăn), *a.* [f. the name of the Swedish dramatist Johan August *Strindberg* (1849–1912) + -ian.] Of, pertaining to, or characteristic of Strindberg or his writings.

1913 G. B. Shaw *Quintessence of Ibsenism* (Completed ed.) Pref. p. xiii, An eminent bacteriologist filled three columns of The Times with a wild Strindbergian letter. **1934** C. Lambert *Music Ho!* iv. 265 It [*sc.* Soupault's *Death of Nick Carter*] reads..like an elaborate stage direction from some super-Strindbergian play. **1954** *Encounter* May 51/1 [The Swedes] are inclined to examine themselves with a touch of Strindbergian introspection. **1966** J. Fowles *Magus* xliv. 281 Brought up, like bacilli in a test-tube, on a culture of such pure Strindbergian melancholia. **1974** R. Rendell *Face of Trespass* viii. 70 An old Swedish film full of pale Strindbergian people.

Strine (strəin), *a.* and *sb. joc.* (orig. *Austral.*). Also **'strine.** [imit. of alleged Austral. pronunc. of *Australian*, coined by Alistair Morrison in 1964 under the pseudonym 'Afferbeck Lauder' (Strine pronunc. of 'alphabetical order').] **A.** *adj.* Australian. **B.** *sb.* **a.** An Australian. **b.** The English language as (allegedly) spoken by Australians.

1964 A. Morrison in *Sydney Morning Herald* (Sat. Mag.) 19 Dec., (*heading*) New light on the Strine language, by Afferbeck Lauder, Professor of Strine Studies, University of Sinny. *Ibid.*, Selected translations of everyday words will be of interest..also to overseas vistas and to the many New Strines in our mist. **1965** 'A. Lauder' (*title*) Let stalk Strine. **1965** *Listener* 2 Sept. 340/1 While I was there they discovered a new dialect or speech pattern called Strine. Strine is simply the way the word 'Australian' sounds if you slur and twist it enough. **1967** *Daily Express* 6 May 13/6 He said in a broad Strine accent: [etc.]. **1973** E. McGirr *Bardel's Murder* iv. 93 Iced beer stops up the nose which is why you Yanks and also the Strines talk so funny. **1974** *Times* 21 Dec. 10/6 'The *legs*, Ealing, go for the *legs*!' she exhorted in a strong 'strine accent. **1980** [see *roomette].

string, *sb.* Add: **I. 1. f.** Also *fig.*, a limitation, condition, or restriction attached to something. Freq. in phr. *no strings attached* (cf. *no strings* s.v. *no *a.* 5 d). Also (with hyphen) as adj. phr. Hence *strings-attached a.* (*rare*). orig. *U.S.*

1888 in *Dict. Amer.* (1951) II. 1665/1 Bob Ingersoll says there is a string to it. **1930** *Randolph Enterprise* (Elkins, W. Va.) 19 Dec. 4/2 All the propositions with a string to them remind us of the..First of April joke. **1948** G. E. Kirk *Short Hist. Middle East* viii. 242 The masses are accustomed to poverty and will listen to their own political leaders rather than to foreigners who offer them opulence with a political 'string' attached. **1951** in M. McLuhan *Mech. Bride* (1967) 90/1 It has for its elements ..imagination with no strings attached. **1953** S. Plath *Johnny Panic & Bible of Dreams* (1977) II. 151 Would he ask her out..just for herself, no strings attached? **1960** *Washington Post* 16 Nov. A16/2 Much has been said about the desirability of aid without strings, and a strong case can be made for this in some areas where the need is economic. Certainly any strings ought to be obvious. **1969** *Daily Tel.* 12 Dec. 1/1 The Government is to give a new £7 million loan to Upper Clyde Shipbuilders...The new loan would not carry any 'strings'. **1971** *Nature* 16 Apr. 420/2 A 'substantial' effort will be made in the category called *l'aide au développement*, a strings-attached arrangement whereby state loans proffered for industrial development must be repaid if the project proves successful and profitable. **1976** *Women's Rep.* Sept./Oct. 2/1 The feminist-run clinics in Australia..who persuaded the government to fund them (no strings attached). **1980** *Forest Products News* (Wellington, N.Z.) XVII. 1. 2/2 As a gesture of goodwill, NZFP has given 'no-strings-attached' aid to an experimental forestry venture in Northland. **1981** J. B. Hilton *Playground of Death* v. 58, I could aspire to be his assistant editor... He was very proud of the *Examiner's* freedom from strings.

i. Also *fig.* in *to pull strings*, to exert influence privately. Cf. *string-pulling* vbl. sb., sense 32 below.

1924 M. Kennedy *Constant Nymph* III. xvi. 213 With half a dozen strings within her reach, she had not made up her mind which to pull. **1938** M. Allingham *Fashion in Shrouds* xxii. 404 I've been trying to pull a few strings myself..but there's an ominous frigidity on all sides. **1955** G. Greene *Loser takes All* I. v. 26 Rice is still short, but I'm certain Aunt Marion can pull strings with the grocer. **1960** *News Chron.* 30 Jan. 3/8 She admits she will pull any strings to get things done. **1979** R. Jaffe *Class Reunion* (1980) II. viii. 265 He couldn't be dumb or they wouldn't have accepted him at Le Rosay. On the other hand, his father had strings to pull everywhere.

m. Also in phrases (freq. *attrib.*) with *sealing-wax*, used to denote the unpretentious apparatus with which great discoveries may be made.

1962 *Daily Tel.* 5 Mar. 20/5 The traditional British method of scientific research with 'string and sealing wax' will pay rich dividends. **1969** *New Scientist* 28 Aug. 422/2 Systems which are..still in the string and sealing-wax stage of development. **1972** *Physics Bull.* July 393/1 The individual with his sealing wax and string has been replaced by the battalion with a multimillion pound particle accelerator. **1975** *Nature* 2 Oct. 349/1, I have been told that it is impossible to 'put the clock back'. The assumption is that the age of string, sealing wax and enthusiasm has gone for ever. **1976** *Sci. Amer.* Oct. 138/2 Blackett's world was no longer Rutherford's string-and-sealing-wax one.

n. A hoax or trick. Cf. String *v.* 15 in Dict. and Suppl., *stringer 9. *U.S. slang.*

1851 T. A. Burke *Polly Peablossom's Wedding* 92 Of course Mabe was innocent of the 'string'. **1937** E. H. Sutherland *Professional Thief* iii. 69 Many other short-con games have been played, including the gold-brick,.. the strap, the string (a variation of the string). [*sic:? read* strap].

o. A fashion shade of the natural colour of string, a light greyish-brown. Also *attrib.* or as *adj.* Cf. *string-colour, -coloured,* sense 31 b in Dict.

1914 *Queen* 24 Oct. 2 (Advt.), Colours—champagne, silver, Wedgwood, sky, string. **1923** *Daily Mail* 7 June 6 In Ivory, String, Beige, Light Grey. **1949** *Dict. Colours Interior Decoration* (Brit. Colour Council) III. 26/1 *String*, a colour standardised by B.C.C. in 1934. A similar colour is here shown under the name of String Beige. **1963** *Harper's Bazaar* May 17 (Advt.), In navy, string, cedar, nut brown or black calf... In cardinal, white or string calf. **1972** *Vogue* June 13/1 A kind of warm biscuit shade that some paint-makers bluntly term 'string'.

p. (See quot. 1964.) Usu. *attrib.* (see *string underwear, vest,* sense 32 below) or as *adj.*

1964 *Which?* Apr. 123/1 There are four main types of knit for men's underwear—*plain*; *interlock*; *cellular*, *mesh* or *eyelet*; and *string*... String fabrics are mesh fabrics, but of a very open structure—the holes may be nearly one inch across, and the fabric is usually in the form of thick strands joined together. This type originated in Norway, where the fishermen used to cut up their old fishing nets and wrap them round their bodies to keep warm when fishing in icy weather. **1966** 'A. York' *Eliminator* viii. 156 His underwear was Norwegian string. His coat was a Burberry.

4. c. (Later examples.) Freq. (with hyphen) *attrib.*

1943 J. B. Priestley *Daylight on Saturday* xxxi. 245 He was one of that select..group of second-string personages for whom the party..had always to provide. **1958** *People* 4 May 19/1 The man who may take over as second string to Tony Lock is Mike Allen, of Northampton. **1965** *Times Lit. Suppl.* 25 Nov. 1058/3 Moore was a kind of second-string Clarence Darrow. **1977** C. McCullough *Thorn Birds* iv. 80 The big Queensland blue brute that led the dog pack took a slavish fancy to the priest and followed him without question, meaning Frank was very definitely the second-string man.

d. (Later *attrib.* examples.) Also, of a team.

1934 *Times* 14 Feb. 6/3 In the first string match P. Q. Reiss (R.A.F. Club) just beat S. N. Capel-Cure by three games to two. *Ibid.* 3 Mar. 6/4 The match was decided on the last fight, that between the first-string welter-weights. **1951** *Sport* 27 Jan.–2 Feb. 3/1 On Saturday, 'Archie' kept goal for the Rochdale second string. **1972** J. Mosedale *Football* iii. 32 Walter Camp named him a second-string All-American. **1976** *Norwich Mercury* 19 Nov. 10 Terry Medwin's finest moment so far as Norwich City Reserves' coach was in defeat. The second string went down 3–2 in September at Tottenham.

6. c. A very scanty bikini (see quot. 1974[1]).

1974 *W* 14 June 17/2 The latest—The String—looks like a winner on the beaches of other countries too... Held by thin strings, it's just two tiny triangles—front and back—worn with a mini-bra. **1974** *Times* 13 Aug. 5/6 The String, a sort of cache-sexe sized bathing suit from Brazil which is now sweeping America. **1977** *Courier-Mail* (Brisbane) 5 Nov. 1/4 They were what we call 'strings'—just a string holding them up.

II. 12. c. (Examples.)

1848 B. A. Baker *Glance at New York* 11, I have beat Miss Wilson one string. **1855** J. Holbrook *Ten Years among Mail Bags* 60 Just allow me twenty on a 'string'. **1871** G. W. Peck *Adventures of Terence McGrant* iii. 22 I'd do it to him half a string. **1924** *Billiards Mag.* June 46/1 Kreshel beat the coast's amateur three-cushion titlist, 80–44. The score of the first block was 40–14, with the string completed in 110 innings.

14. d. *transf.* = *stable *sb.*[1] 2 b. *U.S. slang.*

1913 G. J. Kneeland *Commercialized Prostitution in N.Y. City* iv. 77 A single girl, at times a 'string' of girls, 'working' for them [*sc.* pimps] on the street or in houses. **1946** *Amer. Mercury* Sept. 272/2 Promoters of commercialized prostitution look to two main sources for replenishing their 'stables' or 'strings' of girls. **1982** L. Block *Eight Million Ways to Die* (1983) x. 87 She wants out of my string of girls.

15. b. Orig. (more fully *string of tools*), the drilling bit and weights that occupy the hole in drilling for oil, etc.; in mod. use, the entire drilling assembly in the hole (so *drilling string*); also, the coupled lengths of drill pipe or of casing in the hole.

1895 W. T. Brannt *Petroleum* vii. 182 The string of tools—the bit, the auger-stem and jars, with the sinker-bar—are [*sic*] more than sixty feet long. **1929** Babbitt & Doland *Water Supply Engin.* vii. 160 The only tools on the string in spudding are usually the auger stem and the spudding drill. **1939** D. Hager *Fund. Petroleum Industry* viii. 181 A string of cable tools consists of the bit, stem, jars, sinker bar or sub, and rope socket. The parts of the string are all joined by tool joints and fastened to the drilling cable or line by means of the rope socket. **1947** *Richmond* (Va.) *Times-Dispatch* 12 Mar. 11/2 Pacific Western's well contains the longest 'string' of casing ever run into a well—16,406 feet. **1963** G. Sell *Petroleum Industry* iii. 53 The swivel is so designed as to allow the drilling string to rotate freely on roller bearings. **1976**

M. Machlin *Pipeline* xxvii. 318 Can you imagine old Wilbur all touted out in greasy coveralls, working the string on some well up in the slope? **1979** R. Piper *Story of Oil* vi. 23 When boring for oil, a separate engine, apart from the one that raises and lowers the drill string, is needed to turn the drill stem.

c. *Math.*, etc. A sequence of symbols or linguistic elements in a definite order.

1932 Lewis & Langford *Symbolic Logic* iii. 49 Propositions are not strings of marks, or series of sounds, except incidentally. **1940** W. V. O. Quine *Math. Logic* vii. 284 Now *x* is a string of accents, symbolically Ac *x*, if every initial segment of *x* ends in an accent. **1954** *Jrnl. Assoc. Computing Machinery* I. 120/2 A finite, possibly null, sequence of members of the alphabet is called a string. **1955** N. Chomsky *Logical Struct. Linguistic Theory* (microfilm, Mass. Inst. Technol.) viii. 356 There are cases where similar strings have intuitively quite different interpretations, but where we can discover no grounds.. for assigning different markers to them. **1958** [see *identifier 2 c]. **1970** J. Lyons *Chomsky* 58 The ambiguity of such strings as *old men and women*. **1977** *Word* 1972 XXVIII. 91 The surface string of such sentences indeed looks perfectly straightforward—an adjective with comparative inflection and a comparative marker. **1979** *Sci. Amer.* Oct. 138/3 It was hoped that by transforming the statements of mathematics into strings of meaningless symbols to be combined according to the rules of logic, whatever unavowed principles of reasoning had given rise to the paradoxes would be revealed.

d. *Computers.* A linear sequence of records or data.

1956 *Jrnl. Assoc. Computing Machinery* III. 147 Areas are set aside for shuttling strings of control fields back and forth until a completely sorted sequence is obtained. **1964** C. Dent *Quantity Surveying by Computer* iii. 34 After the second pass tapes *A* and *B* contain the data in strings of four items. **1979** Page & Wilson *Introd. Computational Combinatorics* iii. 49 Two strings of r, s items respectively are each in ascending order in the main store of a computer.

16. e. A continuous series of successes or of failures. orig. and chiefly *U.S.*

1890 Barrère & Leland *Dict. Slang* II. 313/2 A common expression in America is 'to get in a *string*', applied to any kind of fortunate series. **1898** H. M. Blossom *Checkers* 170 Well, I've had my hard luck, and 'played out the string'. **1967** *Boston Herald* 8 May 16/5 Womack preserved the victory that ended a four-game losing string for New York. **1968** *Globe & Mail* (Toronto) 15 Jan. 19/1 The victory stretched the Canadiens' unbeaten string to nine games. **1973** *Times* 17 Apr. 14/6, I try to take it in my stride and relax, and not get too nervous about continuing a string. **1976** *Billings* (Montana) *Gaz.* 27 June 1-F/2 The Mustangs stretched their scoreless string to 12 innings before finally connecting in the fourth inning.

f. *Sport.* (See quot. 1961.) Also *spec.* in Bowling, a succession of strikes. *N. Amer.*

1961 Webster, *String*, a fixed or standard number of turns at play in a game or competition. **1970** *Globe & Mail* (Toronto) 28 Sept. 21/4 Fred Harrison failed to win any..prize money in the Ace Bowling Centre's men's open five pin tournament but he..included a perfect 450 game in his 10-game string. **1979** Ritger & Allen *Compl. Guide Bowling Spares* 228/1 *String*, a number of continuous strikes. Also, in some areas, one game of bowling.

17. a. (Earlier examples.)

1875 *Chicago Tribune* 23 Nov. 7/3 [She] always had a full string at measuring-time. **1889** *Current Lit.* Apr. 314/1 Presently his week's 'string' averaged twelve thousand a day.

b. (See quots.)

1892 *Dialect Notes* I. 207 When he [*sc.* a correspondent] comes to make up his bill, he takes all the articles he has written for a given period and pastes them together, end to end. This he calls his *string*. **1913** W. G. Bleyer *Newspaper Writing & Editing* iii. 55 On some papers the correspondents clip out all of their news stories and paste them together in a 'string' which they send in once a month, so that the telegraph editor may pay them according to the length of the 'string'.

III. 25. (Later examples.)

1854 *Trans. Mich. Agric. Soc.* VI. 177 The strings of fence will average eight and three-quarter rails high. **1903** A. Adams *Log of Cowboy* 17 On the Mexican side there was a single string of high brush fence.

28. (Earlier example.)

1809 T. D. W. Dearn *Bricklayer's Guide* 101 This projection frequently occurs, and in many instances serves as an agreeable relief to the eye, if of no other use; it is sometimes called a *string*.

30*. *Billiards.* A string-line, a baulk-line. *U.S.*

1857 *Spirit of Times* 30 May 200/1 The player in hand can play at any ball, the largest half of which lies outside the string. **1872** 'Mark Twain' *Roughing It* 336 Cheese it, pard; you've banked your ball clean outside the string. **1964** Sullivan & Crane *Young Sportsman's Guide to Pocket Billiards* viii. 77 Through the head spot is drawn the 'head string'. This is a line that passes through the head spot and the two center diamonds on the opposing side rails (near the head end of the table). There are comparable designations—'foot spot' and 'foot string'—at the opposite end of the table. **1974** *Rules of Game* 80/1 Each player takes a cue ball, and plays it against the foot cushion from behind the head string.

31. a. *string box* (earlier and later examples); *string man* (later *Hist.* example), *player*; **c.** instrumental, as *string-soled*, *-tied* adjs.

1839 Dickens *Nicholas Nickleby* xxxvii. 354 Paper, pens, ink, ruler, sealing-wax, wafers, pounce-box, string-box, fire-box..all had their accustomed inches of space. **1926–7** *Army & Navy Stores Catal.* 120/2 Household string box..containing a ball of fine, medium, and coarse brown string. **1980** R. Adams *Girl in Swing* xix. 255 She came back with the other two saucepans, the lemon-squeezer, the string-box and two brown-paper parcels. **1971** *Country Life* 23 Dec. 1776/3 The peacock for the most distinguished person at the high table was carried into the dining-hall with pompous ceremony on a gold or silver-gilt charger by the most elegant lady of the assembled company, attended by trumpeters, pipers and stringmen. **1923** *Daily Mail* 6 Feb. 7 All the string-players pulled their weight. **1979** *Jrnl. R. Soc. Arts* CXXVII. 385/2 The Council has approved this year's awards of scholarships to enable young string players and singers to undertake advanced studies. **1924** *Blackw. Mag.* Oct. 556/2 We steal softly on our string-soled shoes down the stairs. **1925** J. Gregory *Bab of Backwoods* xxiii. 285 There was a string-tied canvas bag, as long as her open palm. **1960** *Farmer & Stockbreeder* 2 Feb. 5/3 Hay from £9 10s to £10, loose in stack; in bales, string-tied, £10 to £10 10s.

32. string analysis *Linguistics*, a method of analysing sentences as linear strings; **string art** *U.S.*, the art of making decorative pictures by winding yarn round nails driven into a flat surface; **string bass** *Jazz*, a double-bass; also *transf.*, the player of a double-bass; **string-bean,** (*a*) (earlier examples); (*b*) *U.S. colloq.*, a tall thin person; also *transf.*; **string bikini** = sense 6 c above; **string bog** *Physical Geogr.*, a boggy area containing long, high banks of silty material; **string correspondent** = *stringer 11; **string cot** = *string bed* (cf. Cot *sb.*^{4} 1); **string drum,** a musical instrument, consisting of a rectangular box over which strings are stretched, and played by striking the strings with a stick; **string figure,** a figure made by passing a length of string round the fingers of both hands (cf. Cat's-cradle); so **string game; string glove,** a glove knitted or crocheted of coarse mercerized cotton yarn; **string man** = *stringer 11 (see also sense 31 a in Dict. and Suppl.); **string point, proof:** in sugar manufacture, a degree of concentration at which the boiled sugar may be drawn out in the form of a thread; **string-pulling** *vbl. sb.*, the act of exerting influence, esp. behind the scenes; cf. Wire-pulling *vbl. sb.*; hence **string-puller; string puppet,** a puppet actuated by means of strings, a marionette; also *fig.*; **string slum** *U.S.*, a row of unsightly buildings along the side of a road (see quot. 1939^2); **string tie** orig. *U.S.*, a very narrow necktie worn as a bow; **string-tone** *Mus.*, the sound of bowed stringed instruments; hence **string-toned** *a.*; **string vest,** a man's vest or singlet made from an open-knit fabric (cf. sense 1 p above); also *string underwear*.

[**1960** *Language* XXXVI. 63 Positively, it leads to the development of a string constituent analysis in which grammatical strings are discovered and described.] **1962** Z. S. Harris (*title*) String analysis of sentence structure. **1972** Hartmann & Stork *Dict. Lang. & Linguistics* 221/2 A string analysis of the sentence *Today we heard three shots in the park* would be as follows: *We heard shots* is the elementary sentence; *today* is an adjunct to the left of the elementary sentence; *in the park* is an adjunct to the right of the elementary sentence; *three* is an adjunct to the left of the word *shots*. **1972** *Creative Crafts* Aug. 21/1 Our ship bounding over gleaming silver waves is an excellent example of fascinating string art, the fool-the-eye craft which makes curves from straight lines. **1975** *String Art Encycl.* 41 (*caption*) A traditional fruit display looks different..when you stitch it using the string-art technique. **1927** *Melody Maker* Aug. 771/2 Their instrumentation..which, when playing on Sundays, is a combination of piano, flute, 'cello, violin, string bass and tymps. **1930** *Ibid.* Jan. 27/1 The pianist and string bass must be particularly complimented on the steadiness of their playing. **1956** M. Stearns *Story of Jazz* (1957) xvii. 205 The string-bass began to 'walk', or play melodic figures instead of pounding away at one or two notes. **1977** J. Wainwright *Do Nothin'* iii. 39 'Occupation?' 'Musician... String bass.' *Ibid.* xi. 197, I turn to the string-bass man. **1759** E. Holyoke *Diary* 11 July in G. F. Dow *Holyoke Diaries* (1911) 20 First Str[ing] Beans y^s. year. **1801** *Spirit of Farmers' Museum* 244 Her neck-beef sausage, and her tough string beans. **1936** Wodehouse *Laughing Gas* xi. 114 'Gee!' he said. 'Are you one of those English Oils?' 'I am. Or, rather, I was.' 'I always thought they were string-bean sort of guys without any chins.' **1975** R. H. Rimmer *Premar Experiments* (1976) i. 70 Ellen, I know you can't help it, but you remind me of a starving, stringbean kitten that wandered into our house when I was a kid. **1977** *New Yorker* 3 Oct. 80/2 'Did Germany need living space?' Hellmann asked, translating the stringbean's German word. **1974** *McCall's* Nov. 10/1 Winter vacation time is coming and the string bikini is still with us—better, if not bigger, than ever. **1976** 'E. McBain' *Guns* (1977) vii. 194 The tall sleek blonde in the white string bikini. [**1956** *Contrib. Gray Herbarium Harvard Univ.* CLXXVIII. 62 These bog ridges are the strings of the *Strangmoor* of European authors.] **1959** *Geogr. Jrnl.* CXXV. 145 A particularly well defined form [of patterned ground feature] are the string bogs, or *strängmoore*, which occur particularly in eastern Canada. **1973** A. L. Washburn *Periglacial Processes & Environment* iv. 151 Although string bogs or closely similar features have also been observed far north of tree line and well within the zone of continuous permafrost.., most investigators agree they are not necessarily indicative of permafrost. **1960** *Spectator* 24 June 920 Later he became a 'string correspondent' sending items to all the local papers, and he also sold jokes at a dollar apiece. **1969** B. Moore *Workers in World News* i. 6 To return to our Paris correspondent, as well as the news coming to him through the newspaper in whose office he worked, he would probably have his own 'stringers'—or string correspondents—in the different provincial centres. **1895** Kipling *Day's Work* (1898) 178 Scott..laid himself down to rest on a string cot in a bare room. **1960** R. P. Jhabvala *Householder* ii. 83 A string-cot had been put up for her in the living-room. **1940** *Amer. Speech* XV. 125 'Ionisation', written for percussion instruments and piano, requires the use of *bongos*, *sirens*.., *guiro*, *claves*, *maracas*, *tarole*, and *string-drum*. **1976** D. Munrow *Instruments Middle Ages & Renaissance* v. 33/4 Various names have been used for the string drum... The thick gut strings are stretched over an oblong sound box and tuned to the key-note and fifth of the pipe so as to provide a drone accompaniment. All the strings are struck at the same time with a small stick held in the right hand. **1902** *Man* II. 146 Many travellers have stated that various peoples, more or less primitive, amuse themselves by making string figures to which the general term of 'cat's cradle' is usually applied. **1963** K. Vonnegut *Cat's Cradle* v. 20 His fingers made the string figure called a 'cat's cradle'. **1879** *Jrnl. Anthropol. Inst.* IX. 26 Now as to the origin of the string games among these Malays (Dayaks) and Polynesians, it is evident that they did not learn them from Europeans. **1910** *Encycl. Brit.* X. 601/2 In particular it is found that the string game called 'cat's cradle' in various forms is of very wide diffusion, being found even in Australia. **1949** 'J. Tey' *Brat Farrar* xxiv. 217 Did I put my string gloves in the locker? **1978** A. Morice *Murder by Proxy* iii. 32 His coat, cap and string gloves..were neatly arranged on a chair. **1943** C. Hollingworth *German just behind Me* ix. 150 By means of bribing his assistant I got a telephone call to my own 'string man' in Belgrade in order that my paper should know I was alive. **1968** M. Allingham *Cargo of Eagles* viii. 98 I'm the string man in these parts... I..write for the *Gazette* at Nine Ash and keep a watching brief for the *Globe* in town. It's called stringing. **1909** Jones & Scard *Manuf. Cane Sugar* vii. 198 The highly concentrated juice is boiled to 'string' or crystallising point... The admission and subsequent discharge of the juice are so regulated, that by the time the latter has reached the point of withdrawal, it has been concentrated to 'string' point. **1909** H. C. P. Geerligs *Cane Sugar* 214 The consistency of the liquid being such that a sample can be drawn out in the form of a thread, the liquid is said to be boiled to 'string proof'. **1915** —— *Pract. White Sugar Manuf.* 80 String-proof boiling should entirely be discarded. **1961** *Guardian* 27 Sept. 10/4 International string-pullers still try to make the Congo dance to their tunes. **1977** D. Ramsay *You can't call it Murder* i. 51 Judith contrived, with the aid of a venerable string puller..to gain admittance. **1949** *Ann. Reg. 1948* 330 The same political manœuvres, corruption, and string-pulling by moneyed interests..were discernible. **1970** E. R. Johnson *God Keepers* (1971) xiv. 146 The choice between public-opinion pressure and Lucchese string-pulling pressure. **1982** W. Buchan *John Buchan* x. 192 At Londonderry House..many believed, important political strings were pulled. The importance of that string-pulling was probably exaggerated. **1937** W. S. Lanchester (*title*) Hand puppets and string puppets. **1970** G. F. Newman *Sir, You Bastard* iv. 126 The visit was nothing more than a test to see just how much the firm's man he was, to see how he would interpret the string-puppet role. **1980** S. Brett *Dead Side of Mike* iv. 39 Two Italian string-puppets in silver armour. **1939** *Sun* (Baltimore) 25 Mar. 8/2 A bill designed to halt the growth of string slums along the public highways by conservative zoning has been pending before the Judiciary Committee of the State Senate for weeks. *Ibid.* 24 Oct. 12/1 The string slums walling in sections of the highways are composed of hot-dog stands, ramshackle overnight cabins, automobile graveyards, cheap dance halls, gaudy taverns and a host of other hideous business places. **1950** *Ibid.* 28 Apr. 18/3 Once string slums come into being, they stay. **1895** *Montgomery Ward Catal.* Spring & Summer 95/2 Men's folding string ties. **1916** *Daily Colonist* (Victoria, B.C.) 22 July 12/6 (Advt.), Red, white and blue string ties. Made of a nice quality silk crepe de Chine. **1942** J. D. Carr *Seat of Scornful* xi. 152 He welcomed them..wearing a shiny black alpaca suit and a string tie. **1976** L. Henderson *Major Enquiry* xvi. 108 He was dressed in a dark blue suit..pale blue shirt and string tie. **1928** J. P. Dunn *Student's Guide to Orchestration* xii. 54 String tone permeates every orchestral movement of any length. **1968** A. Niland *Introd. Organ* ii. 30 Undulating stops..are usually of string tone. **1938** *Oxf. Compan. Mus.* 669/1 *Geigen Principal*.., a sort of slightly string-toned diapason of 8- or 4-foot length and pitch. **1967** D. Pinner *Ritual* vii. 70 He shoved his nylon socks and string underwear in the first drawer he found. **1951** *Catal. of Exhibits, South Bank Exhib., Festival of Britain* 96/1 Khaki trousers..String vests.. Long cashmere pants. **1983** *Listener* 3 Feb. 19/3 You can always..don your string vest and boxer shorts and bang hell out of a rowing machine.

string, *v.* Add: **1. e.** To fit (a thing) with the necessary strings or ties to keep it firm or in place.

[**1805** *Edin. Bk. Prices* 61 Stringing or banding.] **1931** *Henley's ABC Gliding & Sailflying* 232 Having sewn up all the edges neatly, the next operation is 'stringing' the wing to keep the fabric tight to the ribs.

3. c. *to string on*: for *vulgar* read *Austral.* and *N.Z. slang*. (Earlier example.)

1881 A. Bathgate *Waitaruna* 142 A barmaid in one of its hotels..is popularly known as 'Goodall's stringer'... She makes herself agreeable to those who frequent the house, and so she 'strings them on' and induces them to spend their money there.

10. a. Also *spec.* to place (pipes) end to end along the line of a trench, in preparation for welding them together.

1949 *Our Industry* (Anglo-Iranian Oil Co. Ltd.) (ed. 2) v. 163 The pipes are strung out along the line of the trench and placed into position alongside or over it on temporary supports, and the lengths are then connected by electric welding. **1957** *Oil & Gas Reporter* VI. 1141 The service of 'stringing pipe' for oil and gas pipe lines does not, within and of itself, constitute a transportation of property. **1966** *Petroleum Handbk.* (Shell Internat. Petroleum Co.) (ed. 5) 266/2 The construction phases consist of: clearing and grading the right of way, hauling and 'stringing' the pipe, [etc.]. **1968** *Sunday Mail* (Brisbane) 29 Sept. 12/2 The first pipes will be 'strung out' this week.

11. b. *fig.* To stretch (something) *out* in order to make it last.

1867 'MARK TWAIN' *Sk. New & Old* (1875) 73 What is the use of stringing out your lives to a lean and withered old age? **1894** —— in *North Amer. Rev.* Apr. 447 It [*sc.* the story] is not strung out as I have strung it out, but it is all there. **1977** P. HILL *Fanatics* 125 They're just stringing it out, putting off the evil hour.

12. d. To extend or continue. Const. *along, out.*

1869 'MARK TWAIN' *Lett. to Publishers* (1967) 21 So much of the 400 or 500 pages still left are reprint, and so will string out a heap. **1877** —— in *Atlantic Monthly* Nov. 591/1 Isaac knelt down and began to pray: he strung along, and strung along..till everybody had got tired. **1896** —— in *Harper's Mag.* Aug. 351/2 Well, the time strung along and along, and that fellow never come!

d. *to string along with*: to accompany, to agree with, to support or go along with (usu. without undue enthusiasm). Occas. without const. *colloq.* (orig. *U.S.*).

1927 *Vanity Fair* (N.Y.) Nov. 67/2 To this day the B. F. Keith chain call the small-time 'The Family Time' but the players still string along with the theatrical paper [sc. *Variety*]. **1937** J. STEINBECK *Of Mice & Men* 59 Funny how you an' him string along together. **1946** *Sun* (Baltimore) 31 May 15/1 The majority of the bettors decided to string along with Blind Path, a well bred youngster making his seasonal debut. **1950** 'S. RANSOME' *Deadly Miss Ashley* ix. 103 String along, won't you? Don't let me down. **1955** M. ALLINGHAM *Beckoning Lady* iii. 39 She had been..much younger than the crowd which had grown up with Minnie, but she had strung along with them. **1960** WODEHOUSE *Jeeves in Offing* vii. 75, I string along with that school of thought. **1972** L. P. DAVIES *What did I do Tomorrow?* ix. 114, I wasn't going to be taken in. I'll string along, I thought. **1978** A. GILCHRIST *Cod Wars* xi. 109 If at some particular moment, they were stringing along with those other departments and accepting..a continued tough line of policy, then my warning telegrams might seem tactless, tiresome, inept.

e. *to string out*: to be under the influence of a drug. Cf. *STRUNG *ppl. a.* 4 c. *U.S. slang.*

1967 WENTWORTH & FLEXNER *Dict. Amer. Slang* Suppl. 706/1 *String out,* to use or be addicted to narcotics; to be 'high' on a drug. **1970** *Sunday Tel.* 20 Dec. 6/6 How long did you string out?

15. a. For *U.S. slang* read *slang* (now chiefly *U.S.*). (Earlier and later examples.)

1812 J. H. VAUX *Vocab. Flash Lang.* in *Mem.* (1964) 251 To banter or jest with a man by amusing him with false assurances or professions, is also termed *stringing* him, or *getting* him *in tow.* **1846** *Swell's Night Guide* 133/1 *String, to,* to impose on a person's belief by some joke or lie. **1898** A. M. BINSTEAD *Pink 'Un & Pelican* v. 115 She strung him for fifty bob on an old tea-chest an' a jar o' pickled inyuns! **1931** P. MACDONALD *Crime Conductor* I. i. 3 'It isn't!' said the Assistant Editor incredulously. 'You're stringing me!' **1959** 'R. MACDONALD' *Galton Case* xviii. 147 They were stringing you. They just don't want a woman in the way. **1982** H. ENGEL *Ransom Game* i. 5, I guess I don't have any reason to believe they'd string me.

b. *to string* (someone) *along*: to fool or deceive (someone); *spec.* to encourage (someone) to remain in a state of misplaced confidence. Cf. sense 3 c in Dict. *colloq.* (orig. *U.S.*).

1902 G. H. LORIMER *Lett. Merchant* xviii. 270 Clytie had been stringing the old lady along, intending to produce Bud's spook as a sort of..climax. **1924** P. MARKS *Plastic Age* xviii. 206 I'm afraid that he's just stringing me along, trying to encourage me. **1933** D. L. SAYERS *Murder must Advertise* ix. 158 He told me to string him along. And afterwards, quite suddenly, he told me to give him the push. **1943** K. TENNANT *Ride on Stranger* viii. 84 'If he was taking you to lunch..you might work us in somewhere.' 'String him along, kid,' Douglas encouraged... 'We're with you.' **1959** H. HOBSON *Mission House Murder* xviii. 123 How do I know you're not stringing me along, just to get Sharon to go back? **1962** A. LURIE *Love & Friendship* xi. 208 Why not string Dr. Flory along? **1978** H. C. RAE *Sullivan* I. iii. 39, I don't appreciate being strung along by a contract employee.

16. *intr.* To work as a stringer (sense *11).

1960 G. EDINGER *Twain shall Meet* xv. 187 European journalists, stringing for papers in America or Britain. **1966** E. WEST *Night is Time for Listening* ii. 49 'It's not an assignment,' Darsoss said. 'I've been stringing.' **1972** *Maclean's Mag.* June 82/1 Fred Cleverly is a CBC news reporter in Winnipeg. He also strings for the Toronto *Star.* **1977** I. SHAW *Beggarman, Thief* III. ii. 202 An old newspaperman in Elysium, Ohio, who occasionally strings for us when there's anything of interest happening in that part of the world.

‖ **stringendo** (strindʒe·ndo), *adv.* (*a.*) and *sb. Mus.* [It., gerund of *stringere,* to press, squeeze, bind together.] **A.** *adv.* (*a.*). A direction indicating that a composition be played with increasing speed and excitement. Also *transf.* and *fig.*

1853 GEO. ELIOT *Let.* 2 Dec. (1954) II. 129 Mrs. Pitt scolds the servants, *stringendo & fortissimo,* while I am dressing. **1894** G. B. SHAW in *World* 25 Apr. 24/2 Wagner thought it sufficient to indicate the necessary changes of tempo by such hints as 'ritenuto', 'stringendo', and the like. **1922** JOYCE *Ulysses* 207 *Stephen* (*Stringendo.*) He has hidden his own name, a fair name, William, in the plays, a super here, a clown there, as a painter of old Italy set his face in a dark corner of his canvas. **1959** *Times* 30 Oct. 4/7 A tendency to exaggerate the stringendo passages. **1977** *Gramophone* Nov. 837/1 His tempo for the funeral march is barely faster than Boult's, but it seems much more so thanks in part to his *stringendo* manner.

B. *sb.* (Pl. **stringendi.**) A passage played in this manner.

1937 R. JAQUES tr. *A. Cortot's Stud. Mus. Interpretation* 154 From the bars before the *stringendo* the upper C sharps of the left-hand part may be played by the right hand. **1978** *Gramophone* Feb. 1405/2 One finds the latter [*sc.* Karajan]..readier to indulge in *stringendi,* urging things on, where Giulini's combination of concentration and steadiness is compelling in quite a different way.

stringent, *a.* **5.** (Example.)

1870 J. K. MEDBERY *Men & Mysteries Wall St.* v. 69 Money is 'very active', and the loan market 'stringent'.

stringer. Add: **5. a.** Also, a long horizontal member serving to support or tie together a bridge.

1940 *Sun* (Baltimore) 24 May 19/5 The last span between piers 36 and 37 was closed today, engineers said, and work is being rushed on floor beams, stringers and decking. **1960** [see *cream-truck* s.v. *CREAM *sb.*[2] 7]. **1976** *Columbus* (Montana) *News* 24 June 6/6 The best method to improve the bridges is to install more stringers.

d. (Earlier example.)

1848 *Rep. Comm. Patents 1847* (U.S.) 72 One patent has been granted for improvements in the rail, and the manner of fastening it to the stringers.

f. *Aeronaut.* A spanwise member of a wing, parallel to the spars, used to give lateral stiffness to the ribs; also, a longitudinal member of a fuselage, serving to reinforce and stiffen the skin and assisting it to carry direct load.

1918 *Flight* 4 July 740/2 The main [wing] ribs consist of ply wood webs socketted into grooved spruce flanges, which are tapered off..except where they are met by a longitudinal stringer. **1920** *Ibid.* 12 Aug. 879/2 To this main [fuselage] structure is added stringers which bring the outside form up to a streamline shape. **1928** CHATFIELD & TAYLOR *Airplane & its Engine* xii. 212 As even the main ribs are very light, they must often be supported against tipping over sidewise. This is done by means of light wood stringers, which run parallel to the spars. **1932** M. LANGLEY *Metal Aircraft Construction* v. 113 The slightly curved contours of stringers may be achieved by rolling them to template immediately they come off the draw bench. **1945** *Aeroplane* 17 Aug. 185/2 The multiplicity of stringers forms an impressive skeleton upon which a preformed skin is laid in large panels of over 30 ft. in length. **1961** B. FERGUSSON *Watery Maze* vii. 160 This was *Bachequero's* first venture in anger since her conversion, and she was no doubt straining every plate and stringer to do herself credit. **1973** 'A. HALL' *Tango Briefing* ix. 111 The whole of the airframe began shivering as the stringers took the strain.

g. *Surfing.* (See quot. 1962.)

1962 T. MASTERS *Surfing made Easy* 65 *Stringers,* pieces of wood laminated into the surfboard foam for decoration and rigidity. **1965** J. POLLARD *Surfrider* ii. 21 Those strips of wood used in foam boards to add lateral strength are called 'stringers'. **1968** W. WARWICK *Surfriding in N.Z.* 16/3 Today about 50% of all surfboards are built with a centre stringer of either wood or fibreglass, whereas up to about 1966 nearly all boards had some kind of stringer.

9. = *STRING *sb.* 1 n. *U.S. slang. rare.*

1851 T. A. BURKE *Polly Peablossom's Wedding* 89 He never lacked assistance from his acquaintances whenever he had concocted a 'stringer'.

10. *Metallurgy.* A microstructural feature consisting of a narrow vein of inclusion or alloy constituent oriented parallel to the direction of metal working.

1942 C. G. JOHNSON *Metallurgy* (ed. 2) x. 187 Fig. 103 illustrates a slag stringer in steel that caused failure in the hardening operation. **1959** *Jrnl. Iron & Steel Inst.* CXCI. 353/1 Forging draws out the carbides into long stringers running in the direction of hot working. **1976** *Sci. Amer.* Nov. 106/3 The most significant difference between bending and stretching is the role of microscopic impurities or inclusions that are not metallic... During hot-rolling they become elongated into 'stringers'.

11. A newspaper correspondent paid in proportion to the quantity of his published work (cf. *STRING *sb.* 17 b). Hence, a correspondent employed part-time; *spec.* one employed to report on events in a particular place. Also *transf.* Freq. *attrib.* orig. *U.S.*

1952 *Time* 21 Jan. 7/1 Saporiti was in Portugal when he first started as a stringer (part-time correspondent) for *Time* in the spring of 1946. **1952** *Iowa Quest* 31 Jan. 3 (*heading*) 11 students hold 'stringer' jobs. **1956** *Sun* (Baltimore) 28 Aug. 4/6 Even the wire services used mainly stringer correspondents to cover trial. **1958** *Spectator* 31 Oct. 570/2 A free-lance reporter (formerly a stringer for *Confidential*). **1962** *Rep. Comm. Broadcasting 1960* 315/2 in *Parl. Papers 1961–2* (Cmnd. 1753) IX. 259 Organisation of independent television news: camera crews and 'stringer' cameramen. **1970** *Radio Times* 30 Apr. 10/4 Every weekday BBC radio puts out 5½ hours of news and current affairs programmes to Britain. It employs 17 full-time foreign correspondents and nearly 100 stringers, mostly newspapermen. **1973** H. TREVELYAN *Diplomatic Channels* vii. 116 They [*sc.* intelligence services] employ stringers to get caught and occasionally exchanged; but these are regarded by proper spies as an inferior form of life and are not admitted to the international spy confraternity. **1979** E. KOCH *Good Night Little Spy* viii. 65 He was a so-called 'stringer'; he was not attached to any one newspaper and freelanced for several of them.

stringily (stri·ŋili), *adv.* [f. STRINGY *a.* + -LY[2].] So as to be stringy, so as to resemble string.

1940 G. FRANKAU *Self-Portrait* i. 19 My childhood acquired..a horror of macaroni, with which—cooked stringily à l'Anglais—we were compulsorily fed when we stayed for 'afternoon class'. **1976** SCOTT & KOSKI *Walk-In* (1977) ii. 17 One lonely and sullen girl in cut-offs and sweat shirt, hair hanging stringily to her waist.

stringing, *vbl. sb.* **1. b.** (Later examples.)

1952 *Iowa Quest* 31 Jan. 3/5 'Stringing' is interesting and has provided many aspiring journalists with valuable on-the-job training. **1970** A. FOWLES *Dupe Negative* iii. 23 I'd shot an interview with him..on a stringing job for the BBC. **1973** *Times* 3 July 18/7 Lyall then did more years in the editor's chair..before devoting himself to stringing.

† **stringlet** (stri·ŋlet). *U.S. Obs.* [f. STRING *sb.* + -LET, after *ringlet.*] A long wisp of hair.

a **1852** F. M. WHITCHER *Widow Bedott Papers* (1856) xv. 154 Them great long stringlets a danglin' down her cheeks. **1874** *Rep. Vermont Board Agric.* II. 600 Faded-out hair upon either side, with stringlets hanging half-way to the ground from hip and shoulder.

stringy, *a.* Add: **1. c.** Designating defective cotton or wool, esp. cotton which has been imperfectly scutched.

1902 W. I. HANNAN *Textile Fibres Commerce* 115 The cotton which is struck off by the beater blades of the scutcher should be removed away from the beater's course immediately; any delay at this stage may cause the fibres to become contorted into very curious shapes, and such cotton is then termed *stringy.* **1932** E. MIDGELEY *Technical Terms Textile Trade* II. 215 *Stringy,* wool partially matted in fibre and drawn into a slightly ropy form. The stringing of wool is usually due to inefficient scouring. **1950** *Mercury Dict. Textile Terms* 481/1 *Stringy cotton.* This is a defective cotton produced by ginning wet or unripe seed cotton, or sometimes by a wrong adjustment of the brushes that take the lint from the ginsaws.

2. Also of hair: thin, tending to hang in strands. Also *Comb.*

1956 J. CHEEVER in *New Yorker* 14 Jan. 26/1 Her light hair was long and stringy. **1981** P. THEROUX *Mosquito Coast* xviii. 234 The stringy-haired man.

stringy-bark. Add: **a.** (Earlier example.)

1801 [see *BLACKBUTT].

b. (Earlier example.) Also, the wood of one of these trees.

1848 W. WESTGARTH *Australia Felix* vi. 73 These natives appear to like also the fruit of the pandanus, of which large quantities were found in their camps, soaking in water contained in vessels formed of stringy-bark. **1901** M. FRANKLIN *My Brilliant Career* i. 3 The stringy bark roof of the salt-shed..protected the troughs from rain. **1928** 'BRENT OF BIN BIN' *Up Country* vi. 94 On that early journey when it rained they hove to under the drays, well-covered by tarpaulins supplemented by stringy-bark lean-tos. **1977** *Weekly Times* (Melbourne) 19 Jan. 39/2 The basic materials used are local gum and stringy bark.

c. Also as *sb.*, an inhabitant of the outback, an uncouth person.

1836 J. F. O'CONNELL *Residence Eleven Yrs. New Holland* 49 Let us suppose the suitor an old 'stringy-bark', such being the soubriquet in which inland settlers rejoice. **1861** H. EARLE *Ups & Downs* 59 She would never have had the bad taste to prefer a stringy bark like me to such a fine-looking, first-class fellow as yourself. **1892** H. NISBET *Bushranger's Sweetheart* iv. 30 He was a larikin of the larikins, this tiny Stringy Bark, who haunted my thoughts.

strio-. For 'striæ' read 'striatum' and add: **strioni·gral** *a.*, epithet of nerve fibres running from the corpus striatum to the substantia nigra; **striopa·llidal** *a.*, epithet of nerve fibres running from the neostriatum to the globus pallidus (the palæostriatum).

1920 S. W. RANSON *Anat. Nerv. Syst.* xi. 164 The function of the substantia nigra is equally obscure... There terminates within it a bundle, consisting of both direct and crossed fibers from the corpus striatum, the strionigral tract. **1970** *Brain Res.* XVII. 125 As part of an analysis of the intrinsic and extrinsic connections of the caudate nucleus some information has been obtained on the termination of the strio-pallidal and strio-nigral fibres. **1937** J. H. GLOBUS *Pract. Neuroanat.* I. 156 Through the red nucleus, the rubrospinal tract is brought in continuity with part of the striopallidal system. **1970** Strio-pallidal [see *strio-nigral* adj. above].

strioscopy (strəi,ǫ·skǒpi). *Physics.* [f. STRIO- (here of unkn. significance) + -SCOPY.] A form of electron microscopy in which the beam is focused on to the specimen as a hollow cone of particles, giving a bright image on a dark field.

1967 *Jrnl. Electron Microsc.* XVI. 11 The contrasts obtained by the contrast-stop method are better than those of strioscopy. **1974** *Physics Bull.* Sept. 397/2 Castaing contributes a chapter on the prism-mirror analyser, Fert on strioscopy. **1979** J. R. Fryer *Chem. Applications Transmission Electron Microsc.* ii. 62 Normal dark field technique either tilts the incident beam, or displaces an objective aperture, so that the primary beam does not contribute to the final image, whilst strioscopy physically stops the axial primary beam passing.

So **striosco·pic** *a.*

1972 P. W. Hawkes *Electron Optics* iii. 89 In a commercial instrument..that makes provision for strioscopic illumination, as this type of illumination is called, a third condenser..is provided below the annular aperture to match the latter exactly to the objective aperture. **1973** *Nature* 17 Aug. 412/1 Strioscopic methods are also of potential value for high resolution work.

strip, *sb.*[2] Add: **1. f.** A sequence of small drawings telling a comic or serial story in a newspaper, etc. Freq. as *comic strip*. Also *transf.* orig. *U.S.*

1920 L. N. Flint *Editorial* x. 229 In the paper..the week-day issues contain a preponderance of syndicate features—'comics', 'strips'..and continued stories. **1920** C. Sandburg *Smoke & Steel* 47 The comic strips in the papers. **1928** *Daily Sketch* 7 Aug. 4/2, I keenly appreciate the qualities that make Pop the greatest comic strip in the world. No comic strip artist..has the same facile and generic lines the creator of Pop possesses. **1939** Joyce *Finnegans Wake* 537 Such wear a frillick for my comic strip, Mons Meg's Monthly, comes out aich Fanagan's Weck. **1943** D. Powell *Time to be Born* iv. 95 She had a curious impression of being in a Buck Rogers strip..and gazing into another planet. **1955** Auden *Shield of Achilles* ii. 38 Mild-looking middle class boys Who read the comic strips. **1967** *Listener* 21 Dec. 821/3 This feedback from strip to pop and back into strip again is very noticeable. **1979** *Tucson* (Arizona) *Citizen* 20 Sept. 7B/6 Why, you might wonder, would Universal and NBC risk an expensive space comic strip like 'Buck Rogers'?

g. = *air-strip* s.v. *Air *sb.*[1] B. III. 7. Also *fig.* See also *fighter strip* s.v. *Fighter 4, *landing-strip* s.v. *Landing *vbl. sb.* 8.

1936 W. H. McCormick *Mod. Bk. Aeroplanes* xi. 106 The strip extends across the landing-ground. **1944** *Yank* 14 Jan. 10 As a draftsman working for the Australian government, he helped plan both strips. **1958** 'N. Shute' *Rainbow & Rose* i. 9 This is the only strip in the vicinity? **1962** M. McLuhan *Gutenberg Galaxy* 64 Greek celature as a take-off strip for the medieval manuscript culture. **1977** *Whitaker's Almanack 1978* 756/2 Several flying strips are also in use by light aircraft [in Nigeria].

h. A street noted for its night-clubs, bars, gambling houses, etc. Freq. with def. article and capital initial (orig. with reference to *Sunset Strip* in Hollywood: see quot. 1974). *slang* (chiefly *N. Amer.*).

1939 *California* (Federal Writers' Project, Calif.) 193 Further west on Sunset Boulevard..is a section popularly known as 'the Strip'. **1941** B. Schulberg *What makes Sammy Run?* vii. 124 The wind sweeping down the Strip from the sea. **1957** *MacLean's Mag.* 6 July 33/1 The many-tongued enclave known as the Strip is cut off..by a near-Gothic stone pile that straddles the Avenue [*sc.* Spadina Avenue in Toronto] just north of College Street. **1967** W. Murray *Sweet Ride* vi. 89 The Place is located in the heart of the Strip. It..had once catered to a touristy clientele. **1968** *Globe & Mail* (Toronto) 3 Feb. 23/1 Visit the main floor bar of the Brown Derby at Dundas and Yonge, the crossroads of the Yonge Street 'strip' which includes seven bars within a block-and-a-half. **1971** *Guardian* 8 July 3/1 Bangkok has its own strip, the new Petchburi Road extension: miles of girlie bars, short time hotels, and soul food snack bars. **1974** *Encycl. Brit. Macropædia* XI. 109/2 Sunset Boulevard meanders 21 miles west from the state park..to the sea. A one-mile section of the boulevard becomes the 'Sunset Strip', or simply the 'Strip'. **1976** *Publishers Weekly* 21 June 62/2 Rush Street was a nightlife strip, virtually deserted during the day. **1978** S. Brill *Teamsters* iv. 124 Just over to the right is the strip—a row of flickering neons wrapped around bold signs that advertise 'go-go girls' and 'live dancers'.

i. *to tear* (someone) *off a strip, to tear a strip off* (someone) and varr.: to upbraid or reprimand (someone); *to lose a strip, to have a strip torn off*, to be reprimanded or receive a dressing-down. *colloq.* (orig. *R.A.F. slang*).

1940 N. Monks *Squadrons Up* ii. 56 For any breaches of discipline..he would 'tear a strip' off the luckless pilots. **1940** 'N. Shute' *Landfall* i. 25 Dickens tore me off a strip just now. **1942** T. Rattigan *Flare Path* i. 30, I didn't particularly like doing it, and I had the hell of a strip torn off about it afterwards. **1952** E. F. Davies *Illyrian Venture* iv. 71 Nicholls used to tear tremendous strips off Trayhorn. **1957** L. P. Hartley *Hireling* 42 If my wife saw me wearing one, she would tear me off a strip. *a* **1963** J. Lusby in B. James *Austral. Short Stories* (1963) 225 It's all right... I've just lost a strip, too. **1967** *Listener* 31 Aug. 264/1 Mr Kosygin..tore great strips off almost every major industry for inefficiency, or shoddy work, or both. **1979** 'M. Hebden' *Death set to Music* ix. 99 He'd clearly suspected it might have been Nosjean's [idea] and had been hoping to be able to tear a strip off him.

j. A track used for motor-racing. See also *drag strip* s.v. *Drag *sb.* 1 f. *U.S.*

1941 *Sun* (Baltimore) 30 Aug. 13/1 Dick Pending has the racing strip in good condition and unless more rain comes tomorrow, the track will not be too bad. **1946** *Ibid.* 2 Oct. 16/5 The racing strip has been brought around slowly to peak form. **1977** *Custom Car* Nov. 5/4 The drivers of these American cars are also quite happy with the racing. They enjoy chasing the slower cars down the strip.

k. = *strip light* (*b*), sense 6 a below.

1970 R. Crawford *Kiss Boss Goodbye* ii. iii. 68 The basement was..warmed by wall-heaters and lit by soft-pearl strips. **1981** I. McEwan *Comfort of Strangers* x. 133 The room was small, windowless and heavily perfumed. It was lit by a fluorescent strip.

l. *Cricket.* The narrow band of ground lying between the wickets.

1976 J. Snow *Cricket Rebel* 30 None of England's fast bowlers had been particularly menacing during the first Test on a typically sluggish Edgbaston strip. **1977** *Sunday Times* 9 Jan. 28/6 MCC's other team in Bengal found a better wicket for batting at Dacca than the mutilated strip at Calcutta.

5*. *colloq.* The clothing worn by and distinguishing a football team.

If the original sense is 'clothing to which a player strips down', this sense should properly be placed under Strip *sb.*[3]

1974 *Evening News* (Edinburgh) 8 Oct. 16/3 Postal United, the East of Scotland League club, had their strip stolen from a car in the Hailesland Park area. **1977** *Shoot* 18 June 4/4 The national strip of Zambia is green jerseys, orange shorts, and black stockings. **1981** 'G. Gaunt' *Incomer* xiv. 87 The [football] team were..passing flagon bottles around. Frank & Bob were..in a corner, having changed into strip early, and managed to grab a bottle between them.

6. (sense *1 f), *strip advertisement, form, heroine*; (sense *1 g) *strip landing ground*; **strip architecture** *U.S.*, the types of building or other features characteristic of strip development; **strip-built** *a. rare*$^{-1}$, that has been subjected to strip or ribbon development; **strip cartoon,** a sequence of cartoons (sense *2) telling a (comic) story; freq. *attrib.*; hence **strip cartoonist; strip chart, stripchart,** a long roll of (usu. graduated) paper on which the pen of an automatic recording device can trace changes of a measured quantity with time by moving the paper past the pen at a constant rate; usu. *attrib.*, designating recorders using such rolls; **strip-cropping,** (*a*) *U.S.*, a system of land cultivation in which crops of different types and habits of growth are sown alternatively in strips along the contours of a hill, etc., to prevent soil erosion (cf. *contour cropping* s.v. *Contour *sb.* 4); (*b*) the practice of growing crops in strips (cf. *strip farming* below); **strip-cultivation,** (*a*) = *strip farming* below; (*b*) *Archæol.*, the practice of using strip lynchets in farming; **strip development** *U.S.* = *ribbon development* s.v. *Ribbon *sb.* 10 a; **strip-farm** *v. trans. U.S.*, to cultivate (land) in strips along the contours of a hill, etc., to prevent soil erosion (cf. *strip-cropping* (*a*) above); **strip farming** *Hist.*, a system of land cultivation in which the land was divided up into long narrow strips and allocated to different peasant-farmers; **strip-grazing** *Agric.*, a system of farm management in which strips of land are alternately grazed and kept empty; rotational grazing; hence **strip-graze** *v. trans.*, to graze (land or livestock) in this way; **strip-grazed** *ppl. a.*; **strip light,** (*a*) *Theatr.*, any device to provide diffused stage lighting by mounting several lamps in a row, as on a batten, in a trough, etc.; (*b*) a lighting device, now usu. in the form of a tubular fluorescent lamp, for providing a continuous line of light; also as *v. trans.*; hence **strip-lighted** *ppl. a.*; **strip-lighting** *vbl. sb.*; **strip line, stripline** *Electr.*, a *Microstrip; **strip-lit** *a.* = *strip-lighted* ppl. adj. above; **strip-lynchet** *Archæol.*, a horizontal terrace used for cultivation; a long, narrow lynchet (sense *2 b); **strip mill** *Metallurgy*, a rolling mill specially designed for the production of metal strip; **strip mine** *U.S.*, a mine worked by strip-mining; also as *v. trans.*, to obtain or exploit by strip-mining; **strip-mined** *ppl. a.*, **strip-miner; strip mining** *vbl. sb. U.S.*, a method of mining in which surface material is removed in successive parallel strips to expose the mineral, the spoil from each new strip being placed in the previously excavated one; **strip packaging,** a method of packaging small items, liquids, etc., in which individual sachets are formed (from plastic or metal foil), filled and heat-sealed in a single process; **strip park** orig. *U.S.*, a long, narrow park developed alongside a road, canal, etc. (cf. *strip development* above); **strip printer,** a photocomposing device which prints characters on a strip of paper or film; also, any device which prints on a narrow roll of paper; **strip steak** *U.S.* (see quot. 1962) (cf. *strip-loin*); **strip system** = *strip farming* above; **strip-wound** *a.*, wound with strips, esp. of metal.

1938 Strip advertisement [see *Before A. 5 c]. **1976** *New Yorker* 15 Mar. 27/3 'Strip' architecture—the endless miles of trailer parks, gas stations, used-car lots, Taco Bells, etc.,..that fan out from every American metropolis—has its own validity. **1936** C. Day Lewis *Noah & Waters* 15 Strip-built roads that stray Out like suckers to drain the country. **1936** *Discovery* Dec. 384/1 Shopkeeper's bill of the early 18th century. Note the smokers conversing about their tobacco, quite in the modern 'strip-cartoon' style. **1950** *Times* 2 Mar. 6/5 Separate or detachable sections or supplements comprised wholly or mainly of strip cartoons. **1967** E. Short *Embroidery & Fabric Collage* iii. 60 The coverlet tells the story of Tristan, in a series of scenes showing different incidents, in the manner of a strip cartoon. **1974** *Listener* 24 Jan. 118/1 Under the strip-cartoon image lies a message that is often puritanical. **1953** *New Internat. Yearbk. 1952* 47/1 J. C. Bancks, Australia's most popular strip-cartoonist, was creator of Ginger Meggs. **1950** *Instruments* XXIII. 260/3 (Advt.), New 'Pneumatic Capacilog' air-operated strip-chart recorder is completely self-contained. **1966** *N.Y. Times* 3 Feb. 33 The computer recorded wave variations that often are undetectable to the eye of a physician using the traditional strip chart. **1978** *Nature* 12 Oct. 520/2 The outputs are recorded on stripchart recorders, allowing a maximum resolution of 100 ms. **1936** *Sun* (Baltimore) 18 Aug. 3/5 This would be effected through..a blending of 'soil depleting' crops with grasses by a system of 'strip-cropping'—a strip of crops and a strip of grass. **1949** Martin & Leonard *Princ. Field Crop Production* v. 125 Strip cropping, now widely advocated, has been practiced for generations in sections of Pennsylvania. **1976** *S. Wales Echo* 26 Nov. 8/6 If you have plenty of cloches you could accomplish what is called strip cropping. This means that sowings are arranged in alternate strips so that cloches can be moved sideways from one strip to the next and back as required. **1932** Kendrick & Hawkes *Archaeol. in England & Wales 1914–31* x. 173 The Celtic system..lasted to reach its height in Roman times, and makes a striking contrast to the strip cultivation of the Saxon and medieval open fields. **1974** C. Taylor *Fieldwork in Medieval Archaeol.* iii. 28 These terrace-like features [*sc.* strip lynchets] on hillsides are the remains of medieval strip cultivation. **1955** *Sun* (Baltimore) 7 Jan. 19/5 Shops in long-established business districts are predominantly in 'strip' developments; that is, strung out along principal highways that bisect the neighborhood. **1980** *Blair & Ketchum's Country Jrnl.* Oct. 68/1 The arrival of new kinds of people or a new industry or housing developments and strip developments loomed all the larger in many small towns. **1943** *Sun* (Baltimore) 8 Sept. 18/1 The corn rows follow the lay of the land on the contour and the land is strip-farmed.. with the corn rows acting as dams to check losses of soil and moisture. **1913** A. D. Hall *Pilgrimage Brit. Farming* xiv. 103 The strip farming..prevails over all the land [of the Isle of Axholme] which we may suppose to have been dry in medieval times. **1962** H. R. Loyn *Anglo-Saxon England* i. 20 Pre-Saxon strip farming has been recognized at sites in Wessex..and in Cumberland, Northumberland and South Scotland. **1949** *Radio Times* 15 July 17/2 Those inter-planetary adventures we find, in strip form, in almost every comic. **1960** *Farmer & Stockbreeder* 12 Jan. 78/1 One part [of a herd] is housed and milked in a modern and double row cowshed and is strip-grazed in summer. *Ibid.* 79/1 The kale is no longer strip-grazed. **1971** *Power Farming* Mar. 29/1 It was particularly useful for direct-drilling kale, which could then be strip grazed. **1976** *Burnham-on-Sea Gaz.* 20 Apr. 22/3 Although being ..strip grazed on a paddock system..the herd has shown that it can milk well. **1960** *Farmer & Stockbreeder* 15 Mar. 133/1, I shall be going in for milk production. Please suggest a ration based on strip-grazed beet tops, swedes, kale, hay, oats, barley and beet pulp. **1955** *Times* 6 June 4/5 Some farmers are such convinced believers in strip grazing that in the larger fields they use two electric fences, one at the feeding face and one as a back fence to keep the animals off the grass that should be starting to grow again. **1975** *Country Life* 26 June 1702/3 Strip-grazing..involves using two swards, one solely for grazing..and used for a succession of years..and the other sward used more often as a shorter ley for conservation. **1967** *Listener* 21 Dec. 822/1 The idea of a strip-heroine for middle-aged onanists is surely a gloomy one. **1938** *Flight* 21 July 60/1 It is in fact a strip landing ground with natural wind buffers. **1920** S. Lewis *Main Street* xviii. 221 Sending to Minneapolis for..a strip light. **1927** *Proc. Inst. Civil Engin.* CCXXIV. 160 The manometer is illuminated by a 'strip light'. **1934** S. Gold *Neon* xxii. 61 The question of strip-lighting the building over the entire front is usually entertained only by cinemas. **1963** Parker & Smith *Scene Design & Stage Lighting* xvi. 292 One form of stage-lighting instrument that predates the invention of the incandescent lamp is the striplight, which produces the effect of a line of light by means of a number of sources. **1972** P. Lively *Driftway* i. 1 Big strip lights on the ceiling reached away almost as far as you could see. **1981** 'J. Ross' *Dark Blue & Dangerous* xx. 109 A corridor flanked with strip-lighted offices. **1926** *Gloss. Terms Electr. Engin.* (Brit. Engin. Stand. Assoc.) 146 *Strip lighting*, a system of lighting in which a number of lamps, usually of tubular form, and installed in line with one another, so as to give the impression of a more or less continuous strip of light. **1934** S. Gold *Neon* xxii. 61 A combination of colours in strip-lighting gives a charming effect to an otherwise straightforward display. **1976** L. Deighton *Twinkle, twinkle Little Spy* iv. 39 The entrance hall..was brightly lit by indirect strip-lighting set into the ceiling. **1952** *Proc. IRE* XL. 1658/2 In the case of strip lines, the line conductor is a thin narrow ribbon of metal either cut from sheet or deposited. **1967** *Electronics* 6 Mar. 58/2 The military believes recent advances in stripline versions of Butler matrixes..can produce faster memory units. **1974** *Physics Bull.* Apr. 153/3 The copper conductors..are suitable for high resolution stripline and ground plane applications. **1960** *Guardian* 14 Apr. 9/3 Illuminated..by ..strip-lit shelves. **1973** M. Amis *Rachel Papers* 131 Cat's crap on the strip-lit kitchen floor, musty wine-shop smells from the dining-room, objects tingled to flayed senses. **1928** *Antiquity* II. 172 Their..observations..of the ..long-strip lynchets of Saxon and medieval times. **1929** *Ibid.* III. 174 The strip lynchets..on sloping ground, are made stable..by the facing of masonry. **1975** J. G. Evans *Environment Early Man Brit. Isles* vii. 168 Today, where ridge and furrow and strip lynchets are preserved they are generally under permanent pasture. **1983** *Out of Town* June 26/2 Bands of quite difficult ground are often stepped and striped by patterns of 'strip lynchets'... The strip lynchets..were gradually bitten into the hillslopes by ploughs that were hauled (approximately) along the contours. **1910** H. P. Tiemann *Iron & Steel* 286 Bar mills, also called merchant mills or, on account of the special product which they make..rod mill, hoop mill or strip mill. **1945** *Times* 26 Feb. 5/7 The strip mill for light sheet and tin plate, the continuous billet mill..[etc.] all belong to this type. **1980** *Times* 19 Feb. 2/5 Wide sheet steel from the BSC's strip mills..is widely used in the manufacture of domestic 'white goods'. **1934** *Coal Age* Oct. 376/3 The spread of trailer operation at Southwestern strip mines reflects a number of advantages. **1970** *New Scientist* 21 May 364/2 Nuclear explosions are also planned for strip-mining large deposits of non-ferrous metals in the northern territories. **1976** *Billings* (Montana) *Gaz.* 1 July 2-A/4 The high court has dramatized the need for a national strip mine law so that everybody plays according to the same rules in extractable resource development. **1978** *Peace News* 6 Oct. 7/2 Stewart Udall, Secretary of the Interior, gave approval to WEST to strip-mine vast areas of Indian land for coal. **1936** *Coal Age* Oct. 415/1 Strip-mined coal, under early production conditions,.. generally sold at prices substantially under those for deep-mined coal. **1980** *Sci. Amer.* Oct. 160/3 The reclamation of strip-mined land involves the relatively simple processes of flattening the piles of overburden, replacing the top-soil and replanting it. **1946** *Sun* (Baltimore) 19 Nov. 4/5 Mark McCauley, Davis (W. Va.) strip miner convicted of first degree murder..was sentenced to be hanged. **1977** *Economist* 23 Apr. 52/3 Despite the small proportion of stripminers in the United Mineworkers Union, the union as a whole has withdrawn its support for federal legislation. **1935** *Coal Age* Feb. 91/1 This first-and-second method of strip mining cannot be employed economically with shovel equipment which must operate down in the cut. **1949** *Hansard Commons* 19 May 706 Strip-mining, as it is known in America, and opencast work in regard to gypsum..or any..base metal is essentially a mining problem. *Ibid.* There were..technicians in the country.. familiar with American strip-mining methods. **1977** *Economist* 23 Apr. 52/2 The technique of stripmining—clearing the topsoil above a coal seam to scoop out the coal with bulldozers—once seemed an answer to low productivity. **1969** L. S. Mounts in W. R. R. Park *Plastics Film Technol.* v. 140 Many products can be packaged in water soluble films with advantage. These include..industrial and agricultural products like sprays, chemical additives and strip packaging of seeds. **1975** C. F. Ross *Packaging of Pharmaceuticals* i. 4 Sachets, filled automatically on suitable strip-packaging machines. **1938** *Sun* (Baltimore) 24 June 12/3 The financial operations..seem likely to leave the Eastern United States with their third 'strip park', the others being the Shenandoah Skyway and the park at Natchez, Miss. **1972** *Times* 7 June 4/3 A number of smaller strip-parks, which people could walk to..would be..useful. **1962** *Amer. Lithographer* Apr. 90/3 An automatically-timed exposure light has been added to the Strip Printer Photo Composing Machine Model 299. **1965** R. R. Karch *Graphic Arts Procedures* (ed. 3) xiii. 331 The Strip Printer is used to produce lines of type in various sizes on paper or 35 mm. film. **1976** *Times* 8 June 10/5 By adding a simple keyboard and strip printer to a standard telephone, the telephone terminal could..interact with a computer. **1962** J. N. Winburne *Dict. Agric. & Allied Terminol.* 769/2 *Strip steak*, the steak cut from the loin strip of a beef carcass. **1977** *Rolling Stone* 30 June 111/3 His guitar style is taut and as lean as a strip steak. **1954** J. Keith *Fifty Yrs. Farming* xi. 125 Over a great part of Britain there developed the common-field and strip system. **1965** R. Whitlock *Short Hist. Farming in Britain* i. 20 In conjunction with the pattern determined by the type of plough, arose the Saxon strip system of fields. **1907** Hobart & Ellis *Armature Construction* xi. 265 Windings for a strip-wound barrel type of armature. **1962** *Times* 26 Feb. (Canada Suppl.) p. vii/2 (Advt.), Hydraulic pressure cylinders in steel, stripwound, etc.

strip, *sb.*[3] Add: **2.** *colloq.* (orig. *U.S.*). An act or the practice of removing one's clothes or of striptease. See also *strip *v.*[1] 24 b.

1928 *Variety* 12 Dec. 46/3 Why do women principals try to do strip numbers against the competition of experienced runway specialists?..Columbia, by the way, seems to be leery of the limit in strip at this telling. **1956** B. Holiday *Lady sings Blues* (1973) v. 54 He kept on doing this slow elaborate strip. **1966** *Guardian* 9 July 8/3 Perhaps ten [clubs] provide regular striptease. Up to ten provide strip occasionally. **1971** R. Petrie *Thorne in Flesh* vi. 86 Dahlia does a strip... I auction the things she takes off.

strip, *v.*[1] Add: **I. 1. a.** Also const. *down, off,* in *intr.* for *refl.* use.

1947 'A. P. Gaskell' *Big Game* 22 You're not supposed to strip off but I had. **1962** D. Francis *Dead Cert* xi. 124 I'm glad it's you that's got to strip off and get soaked, and not me. **1976** D. Barnes *Yesterday is Dead* ii. 272 After taking a leak he'd strip down and jack off.

e. *to strip* (*well*, etc.): to have a good body, to have a pleasing appearance when stripped.

1815 T. Belcher *Art of Boxing* ix. 33 James Belcher.. stripped remarkably well, and displayed much muscle. **1932** D. L. Sayers *Have his Carcase* ix. 106 He strips better than I should have expected... Better shoulders than I realised, and, thank Heaven, calves to his legs. **1955** T. H. Pear *English Social Differences* ix. 201 Such boys, to use the drill-instructor's expression, 'strip better'.

h. (Later *intr.* examples.)

1897 *National Police Gaz.* 26 May 14/2 It is fully expected that he will not only strip in much better fettle at Epsom than he did for the Guineas, but run a remarkably different horse altogether. **1973** *Times* 26 Feb. 12/8 Skymas runs in the Wills Premier Chase at Haydock this week, and will certainly strip fit.

i. *intr.* To perform a strip-tease act. *colloq.* (orig. *U.S.*).

1929 *Variety* 25 Sept. 53/3 She has the unadornment stuff to herself, since the other gals never strip beyond regulation soub garb. **1939** Joyce *Finnegans Wake* 68 She stripped teasily for binocular man. **1962** J. D. MacDonald *Girl, Gold Watch & Everything* vii. 86 I'm working a place, Rio's, up North Miami, singing and sort of stripping some, but not down to raw. **1976** 'E. McBain' *Guns* (1977) ii. 49 'Jocko said you used to be a stripper.' 'Yeah, but..I haven't been stripping for seven, eight years now.'

3. b. Delete 'now *rare*'. (Later examples.)

1881 'Mark Twain' *Prince & Pauper* xxiii. 385 The pickpockets had stripped him of his last farthing. **1919** G. B. Shaw *Heartbreak House* ii. 81 Are you one of those who are so sufficient to themselves that they are only happy when they are stripped of everything, even of hope? **1936** J. Buchan *Island of Sheep* i. vii. 130 They had only to get hold of Haraldsen..to strip him bit by bit of his possessions. **1950** C. S. Forester *Midshipman Hornblower* 262 The last visit of Spanish ships of war had stripped the place of almost all its stores, and many of the dockyard hands had been pressed as seamen at the same time.

4. b. To pull off the winter growth of hair from (a dog); to pluck. Cf. *stripping *vbl. sb.*[1] 1 a.

1930 E. C. Ash *Pract. Dog Bk.* xi. 197 Stripping a coat is in the varieties of Terriers most important. Powdered chalk is well rubbed into it. The long hair is then plucked out. **1931** *Daily Tel.* 21 May 1/3 Dogs stripped.

7. e. *slang* (orig. *U.S.*). To unpack or unload (a load, container, lorry, etc.).

[**1950** *Western Folklore* IX. 119 *Pulled, stripped,* or *gutted a load,* lost a load of logs.] **1963** *Amer. Speech* XXXVIII. 45 *Strip a load, v. phr.*, to unload a truck. **1968** *Wall St. Jrnl.* 27 Sept. 34/2 Management agreed to allow the dockworkers to strip and stuff containers in which mixed types of cargo had been packed. **1970** *Times* 16 Sept. (Road Haulage Suppl.) p. vii/9 The [overladen] container..should be devanned (or stripped, to use container parlance) and delivered on two vehicles. **1972** *Guardian* 8 May 20/2 According to the dockers' leader..those terms..are for..the same guarantees over 'stuffing' (packing) and 'stripping' (unpacking) the containers. **1973** *Amer. Speech* 1969 XLIV. 208 *Strip her*, unload a trailer.

8. (Later examples.) Now freq. in contexts of the inspection or repair of motor vehicles, engines, etc. Also with *down*. Cf. *stripped *ppl. a.* c.

1937 *Discovery* May 164/1 Part of the necessary machinery could not be stripped down to parts small enough to be carried by mules over the narrow and difficult trails. **1958** *Listener* 13 Nov. 778/1 He drives the thing [*sc.* a car] straight into the repair shop at the back and has it stripped down. **1972** *Daily Tel.* (Colour Suppl.) 20 Oct. 10/4 At the end of 36,000 miles the engines were stripped and every component measured and meticulously examined. **1981** B. Hines *Looks & Smiles* 26 His bike..had also been stripped down to the frame.

II. 11. a. Also *spec.*, to remove paint or varnish from woodwork, etc. Cf. *stripped *ppl. a.* b.

1908 P. N. Hasluck *Cassell's House Decoration* 171/2 All the washing and stripping should be done first. The wallpaper must be removed, and the paint stripped. **1956** *Pract. Householder* July 596/1 A number of preparations.. are intended to strip off only one coat at a time... I prefer the type which strips several coats. **1981** *New Homemaker* Apr. 90/1 (Advt.), Stripping isn't the soul-destroying job it used to be... Powerful Ronseal strips without scraping.

14. Also, to harvest (a crop).

1891 R. Wallace *Rural Econ. & Agric. Austral. & N.Z.* i. 6 Twenty acres of grain can be stripped per day. **1938** *Sun* (Baltimore) 6 Sept. 2/7 The corn almost ready to strip. **1979** *Verbatim* Summer 8/1 In Queensland a wheat crop is *headed*, in Victoria *stripped*.

III. 17. c. (Later example.)

1978 D. Bagley *Flyaway* xxv. 230 I've got a spare differential... The bastards are always stripping so I've made it a habit to keep a spare.

23*. *Physics.* **a.** To deprive (an atom or ion) *of* an electron, or (a molecule) *of* an atom. Also *absol.*

1933 O. H. Blackwood et al. *Outl. Atomic Physics* xiv. 305 Throughout the interior of a star, atoms do not exist in what we consider their ordinary conditions... Near the center of the star they are assumed to be stripped of nearly all their planetary electrons. **1936** *Trans. Faraday Soc.* XXXII. 350 One empirical molar weight of $C_2H_4S_4$ in suspension in water is first 'stripped' of two sulphur atoms with sodium hydroxide. **1954** H. E. Huntley *Nuclear Species* i. 4 By stripping the atoms which lay in its path of one or more of its orbital electrons the swiftly moving particle produced large numbers of positively charged ions and free electrons. **1969** *Times* 22 Apr. 6/3 Large amounts of energy are needed to strip the calcium atoms of their electrons before accelerating them into the target of plutonium atoms. **1970** *Sci. Amer.* Aug. 32/3 The ions are stripped not only in the terminal but also halfway down the positive acceleration column. **1978** L. Válvi *Atom & Ion Sources* i. 35 At low impact energies only the outer shell can be stripped of its electron.

b. To remove (an electron or other particle) *from* an atom, ion, nucleus, etc. Also const. *off.*

1935 B. Jaffe *Outposts of Science* ix. 349 This recoiling nucleus spends its energy of motion in stripping electrons from other atoms near it. **1947** *Physical Rev.* LXXII. 1003 A simple theory of neutron production, according to which the proton is 'stripped' from the deuteron by striking a target nucleus. **1958** *Ann. Physics* III. 275 In a deuteron stripping reaction, the rôle of the incident deuteron is to present at the target nucleus surface a neutron or proton ready to be captured (or 'stripped' off). **1979** *Sci. Amer.* Aug. 122/2 The star..becomes a white dwarf: a star with a core consisting of a highly compressed gas of atomic nuclei (mostly helium nuclei) and the electrons stripped from them.

23. a.** *Oil Industry.* To separate (crude oil or gas) into fractions, to fractionate; to extract or recover (a light fraction) *from* a mixture.

1922 D. T. Day *Handbk. Petroleum Industry* II. 324 The great bulk of crude handled was still stripped in batch stills. **1931** Hoffert & Claxton *Motor Benzole* viii. 226 It is essential that the benzole should be stripped from the wash oil as completely as possible. **1938** A. E. Dunstan et al. *Sci. of Petroleum* II. ii. xxv. 1559/2 The latent heat of vaporization of the components stripped from the oil is supplied by the sensible heat of the oil. **1979** *Liquefied Petroleum Gas* (Shell Internat. Petroleum Co.) 3 The aim of this scheme is to 'strip' the large amounts of associated gas which were previously flared and then separate LPG and other heavier gas liquids for export.

b. *Chem.* To extract or recover (a solute) *from* a solvent previously used in its extraction.

1962 Cotton & Wilkinson *Adv. Inorg. Chem.* xxxii. 906 The protactinium can be stripped from the solvent by aqueous acid fluoride solutions. **1980** *Sci. Amer.* Jan. 59/3 Both are recovered by using a complexing agent to dissolve the metal selectively into a dilute solution and then stripping the metal from the solution.

23*.** *Printing.* To mount (copy) in the correct position on a sheet for use in making a printing plate; freq. const. *in*. Also, to make (a flat) thus.

1937 R. W. Polk *Pract. of Printing* (ed. 2) xli. 291 If a number of pictures are to be used together, and the sizes of the originals are not in proper proportion to each other, separate exposures are made for each size, the necessary reductions made, and the resulting negatives are 'stripped' together in proper position on the composite negative plate... If the sizes are not in proper proportion, separate negatives must be made and stripped in on the plate. **1948** R. R. Karch *Graphic Arts Procedures* viii. 232 After the negatives or positives of illustrations and type matter have been prepared.., the job must be stripped on a layout so that press plates may be made. *Ibid.* 233 Positives used for stripping flats for the deep-etch process are stripped on a piece of transparent acetate. **1964** R. W. & E. W. Polk *Pract. of Printing* (ed. 6) xl. 304 (*caption*) A masking sheet with negatives stripped in. *Ibid.* 306 Positioning and attaching films on a masking sheet is called stripping a flat. **1967** Karch & Buber *Offset Processes* v. 142 After the film is developed, the negative is washed and dried. It is then 'stripped' or placed in a predetermined position on a special type of paper for the plate maker who will expose the image onto the offset plate. **1975** J. Butcher *Copy-Editing* iv. 39 Combined line and half-tone may be used for a photograph that needs some lettering or a scale; this is usually done by stripping a line negative into a half-tone negative.

IV. 24. a. strip cell, a cell in which a prisoner is subjected to sensory or physical deprivation; **strip-down**, (*a*) *U.S. colloq.*, a car which has been stripped down and reassembled so as to improve performance; (*b*) the dismantling or disassembly of an engine, etc. (cf. sense 8 above); **strip-poker** orig. *U.S.*, a game of poker in which a losing player sheds a garment as a penalty or forfeit; **strip-search,** a search of a prisoner during the course of which he is stripped naked; also as *v. trans.*; = *skin-search* s.v. *skin *sb.* 13; **strip the willow**, a Scottish country dance performed by couples in longways sets.

1971 *New Society* 1 July 15/1 A strip-cell. This contains only a mattress on a bare floor. **1973** *Black Panther* 7 July 9/2 If the guards wanted to they could turn on a light in the ceiling, but I was always kept in the dark, and nude. That is part of the deprivation, why the soul breaker is called a strip cell. **1950** *Sun* (Baltimore) 6 Oct. (B ed.) 7/4 Juveniles who have been racing the highways in stepped-up strip-downs. **1963** *Times* 24 May (London Underground Suppl.) p. xii/5 The trains were withdrawn from service and sent to Acton, where they undergo a comprehensive strip-down. **1969** *Daily Tel.* 18 Feb. 5/5 Repair is in progress. A strip-down survey of the refinery is being undertaken. **1929** M. Lief *Hangover* i. 9 'How about a fast game of strip-poker?' she suggested. **1935** G. Greene *England made Me* ii. 86 Two girls playing strip poker. **1961** *Times* 14 June 16/3 There had been a 'strip-poker' party that night. **1978** D. Williams *Treasure up in Smoke* xix. 169 'He..suggested some kind of poker.'..'Strip poker?' **1947** Strip-search [see *run-over 1]. **1970** G. F. Newman *Sir, You Bastard* vii. 189 The arrested men were strip-searched and made to await the DI's pleasure. **1979** *Tucson* (Arizona) *Citizen* 3 Oct. 10c/5 A woman sentenced for drunken driving should not be strip-searched. *Ibid.*, Subjected to extreme trauma by a strip-search. **1924** *Scottish Country Dance Bk.* I. 16 Strip the Willow or Drops of Brandy... Running step is used all through this dance. **1980** L. Lewis *Private Life of Country House* xii. 166 'Strip the Willow', a country dance in which couples in turns came from the ends of two rows to perform some steps in the middle.

b. [Sometimes, f. *strip *sb.*[3] 2.] In various

slang or *colloq*. Combs. in sense *1 i, as *strip act, bar, dancer, girl, party, show, song*; **strip club**, an establishment providing entertainment in the form of strip-tease; **strip joint** [JOINT *sb.* 14 a in Dict. and Suppl.] *slang* = prec.

1950 A. COOKE in *Manch. Guardian Weekly* 13 July 13/2 The all-American cult of the 'strip act'. **1963** R. I. McDAVID *Mencken's Amer. Lang.* 728 Today the higher-priced girls are often connected with burlesque or work in strip-bars. **1975** D. LODGE *Changing Places* ii. 96 One of the South Strand strip bars. **1960** *Spectator* 12 Aug. 236 That strip clubs have been multiplying in London recently is generally known. **1962** *Ibid.* 7 Dec. 883 The strip-club owner who intends to fight..on a campaign against entertainments tax. **1973** J. M. WHITE *Garden Game* 36 The neon lights of the strip-clubs and restaurants. **1946** D. RUNYON *Short Takes* 236 There were cut-outs of guys with their arms around hula dancers and around strip dancers. **1961** *Times* 21 Sept. 15/2 The strip-girl loved by a foolish, tiresome but engaging missionary. **1951** *Sun* (Baltimore) 27 June 30/3 Prince Georges County Sheriff Carlton Beall began a crackdown on what he called 'strip joints'. **1959** *Times Lit. Suppl.* 13 Mar. 148/4 Gambling rooms, saloons and strip joints. **1975** D. LODGE *Changing Places* ii. 95 He now stands gawping incredulously at the strip-joints that jostle each other all along Cortez Avenue. **1959** *Times* 19 June (Queen in Canada Suppl.) p. iv/5 Police are always cracking down on private strip parties. **1972** J. BROWN *Chancer* viii. 110 These strip parties—young business blokes—you know. **1967** *Listener* 5 Oct. 437/3 One of the old Windmill strip shows. **1971** *New Scientist* 10 June 641/2 Their dirty raincoats..have been snapped up by strip-show patrons. **1937** HART & KAUFMAN *You can't take it with You* III. 171 She kept singing a strip song while Mrs. Kirby undressed.

strip, *v.*³ Add: **1. b.** *strip cup* (see quot. 1962).

1941 ROADHOUSE & HENDERSON *Market-Milk Industry* iv. 67 (*caption*) Strip cup used for detecting abnormal milk. The first stream of milk from each teat is milked into the strip cup through the fine mesh screen. **1950** *N.Z. Jrnl. Agric.* Mar. 265/1 Every cow should be tried, using a strip cup, before putting on the machines. **1955** J. G. DAVIS *Dict. Dairying* (ed. 2) 37 The routine use of strip-cups in the cowsheds will assist in the prevention of mastitis spreading. **1962** J. N. WINBURNE *Dict. Agric. & Allied Terminol.* 769/1 *Strip cup*, a small metal cup or vessel with a fine wire strainer or inner liner into which the first streams of milk from each teat are milked from the cow for examination to detect any indication of mastitis infection or any other abnormal condition of the milk or udder. **1975** CAMPBELL & MARSHALL *Sci. providing Milk for Man* xiv. 337 The California Mastitis Test (CMT) is much more sensitive in detecting inflamed quarters than is the strip cup.

stripe, *sb.*³ Add: **1. d.** *pl.* A prison uniform (with reference to the stripes with which it is patterned). *U.S. slang.*

1887 *Courier-Jrnl.* (Louisville, Kentucky) 29 Jan. 3/2 He changed his stripes for a suit of citizens' clothes. **1905** B. TARKINGTON *In Arena* 22 I'm going to clear this town of fraud, and if Gorgett don't wear the stripes for this my name's not Farwell Knowles! **1940** W. FAULKNER *Hamlet* III. ii. 212 He had never seen convicts' stripes before either. **1943** P. STURGES in Gassner & Nichols *Best Film Plays 1943–44* 279/1 He's going to be in jail, Trudy, for a long time. He can't do you any good in stripes, honey.

e. A narrow strip of magnetic material along the edge of a cine film on which the sound may be recorded.

1954 R. H. CRICKS tr. *Bau's How to make 8 mm. Films as Amateur* 169 The magnetic stripe is coated between the perforations and the edge of the film. **1972** *Amateur Photographer* 12 Jan. 65/3 Fujicascope SH1... Sound unit: Magnetic sound stripe, 6w amplifier. **1973** *Sci. Amer.* Dec. 49/1 Sights and sounds the camera records stay together on the super 8 film in synch during processing. Spoken comment can be added to the magnetic stripe during projection.

f. *U.S.* A line which forms part of the marking on a sports pitch or court. Cf. LINE *sb.*² 7 f.

1967 *Boston Herald* 1 Apr. 17/1 Kennedy led the visitors with 17 points, 11 from the foul stripe. **1974** *State* (Columbia, S. Carolina) 3 Mar. 1-D/7 We wanted to keep him off the foul line (Stewart made one of two from the stripe).

2. *to pull stripes*: see *PULL *v.* 19 h.

8. a. For *U.S.* read orig. *U.S.* and add later examples.

1943 L. ADAMIC *My Native Land* 137 Trubar scored a great cultural victory and set a national-linguistic precedent for men of his stripe. **1968** *Guardian* 9 Apr. 9/3 Negro organisers of all stripes, urging their footloose young 'to keep your cool'. **1979** *Daily Tel.* 6 Sept. 4/2 Guyana, led by a Socialist of another stripe.

stripe, *v.*² Add: **2. d.** To apply a magnetic stripe to (a cine film). Cf. *STRIPE *sb.*³ 1 e.

1954 R. H. CRICKS tr. *Bau's How to make 8 mm. Films as Amateur* 169 You then send your film to a suitable firm which 'stripes' it—i.e., coats a narrow strip of magnetic material along its whole length. Two methods of striping have been proposed. **1960** R. BATEMAN *Movie-Making as Pastime* ix. 58 A 'magnetic stripe' system is becoming more widely used... Experiments in 'striping' 8 mm film have been made.

striped, *ppl. a.* Add: **1. b.** *striped bass*, a large North American fresh-water or marine bass of the genus *Roccus*, esp. *R. saxatilis* (earlier and later examples); *striped gopher*, a ground squirrel, *Citellus decemlineatus*, found in North America; *striped mouse*, a mouse with one or more stripes along its back, found in Africa and belonging to the genus *Rhabdomys* or *Lemniscomys*; *striped squirrel*, one of several small rodents with striped markings, esp. the North American chipmunk; (earlier examples); *striped tuna* = *skipjack tuna* s.v. *SKIPJACK 4.

1796 J. MORSE *Amer. Universal Geogr.* I. 203 The Striped Squirrel is still less than the [red squirrel]. **1818** *Amer. Monthly Mag.* II. 295 The striped bass..is another excellent salt-water fish. **1854** THOREAU *Walden* 323, I am on the alert for the first signs of spring, to hear..the striped squirrel's chirp. [**1900** H. A. BRYDEN *Animals Afr.* v. 48 The pretty little Striped Barbary Mouse..is a very different kind of animal.] **1922** *Pacific Fisherman* Feb. 12/2 Striped tuna..is required to be designated with the qualifying adjective 'striped'. **1932** *Discovery* Nov. 364/2 Pythons are so sluggish that they have been nibbled to death by striped mice. **1941** E. T. SETON *Trail of Artist-Naturalist* 299 Gone..also the striped gopher, whose labyrinths are only four inches down. **1951** TRESSLER & LEMON *Marine Products of Commerce* (ed. 2) xx. 445 Skipjack..is also known as the striped tuna from the markings on the body. **1956** W. R. BIRD *Off-Trail in Nova Scotia* ii. 48 I've been after striped bass in many places up and down the coast of America but this is the best of them all. **1963** G. H. THOMSON *Crocus Country* xx. 133 At this time [*sc.* 1905] there were quite a few striped gophers left, though later they entirely disappeared, driven out, it was said, by their bigger grey cousins. **1973** *Stand. Encycl. S. Afr.* IX. 248/1 Some, like the striped mouse.., are diurnal. **1974** *Calhoun Times* (St. Matthews, S. Carolina) 18 Apr. 3/3 Some 200 striped bass are swimming through Lakes Marion and Moultrie with special tags attached.

c. (Earlier example.)

1850 *Phil. Trans. R. Soc.* CXL. 515 Muscles are now named according to their function, voluntary and unvoluntary; or according to their structure, striped and unstriped.

f. *striped trousers*, (typically worn by civil servants, businessmen, etc.), used allusively to indicate the wearer's status, and, by extension, bureaucracy, formality, etc.; by metonymy, a civil servant, etc.; so *striped-trouser(ed)* adj.; similarly (chiefly *U.S.*) *striped pants*. Cf. *PIN-STRIPE, *PIN-STRIPED *a.*

1933 DYLAN THOMAS *Let.* Oct. (1966) 37 Oh to look.. different from the striped trouser lads. **1945** 'G. ORWELL' in *New Saxon Pamphlets* III. 38 The striped-trousered ones will rule, but so long as they are forced to maintain an intelligentsia, the intelligentsia will have a certain amount of autonomy. **1946** KOESTLER *Thieves in Night* 220 At the end emerged the striped-trousered finished product. **1958** S. HYLAND *Who goes Hang?* xxxiii. 140 He was almost in tears. Black tears with striped trousers. **1968** W. SAFIRE *New Lang. Politics* 398/2 The diplomatic niceties of 'striped-pants' diplomacy. **1972** M. GILBERT *Body of Girl* xxiv. 206 A crook in striped trousers turns my stomach. **1974** 'D. KYLE' *Raft of Swords* x. 97 They may be useful. So may the striped-trousers in the Foreign Secretary's entourage. **1976** G. MARKSTEIN *Man from Yesterday* xi. 59 'Who's had to apologize?' 'The gentlemen in striped pants.' **1977** *Time* 9 May 22/3 His youthful diplomatic appointee's aversion to striped-pants airs. **1977** 'J. LE CARRÉ' *Honourable Schoolboy* i. 24 Ring every damned striped-pants in the Colony! **1981** *New Standard* 1 Sept. 14/6 An old-fashioned striped-trouser diplomat.

g. Of cine film: having a magnetic stripe (*STRIPE *sb.*³ 1 e).

[**1956** J. J. ROSE *Amer. Cinematographer Hand Bk. & Ref. Guide* (ed. 9) 7 (Advt.), Your pre-striped film with magnetic sound lip-synchronized to your picture.] **1972** E. & D. SCHULTZ *How to make Exciting Home Movies* xi. 131 Your splicer can get magnetized when it's used on a film already striped.

2. (Earlier example.)

1839 *Morning Post* (Boston) 4 July 2/2 She made a remark, which, if reported in full, would make one of O.F.M. [*sc.* Our First Men] feel decidedly striped.

striper (strəi·pəɹ). *colloq.* [f. STRIPE *sb.*³ + -ER¹.]

1. Usu. as *two* (*two and a half, three, four*)-*striper*: an officer in the Royal Navy or U.S. Navy (from the stripes worn to denote rank). In later use, in the army, a lance-corporal (*one-striper*), corporal (*two-striper*), sergeant (*three-striper*).

1917 M. T. HAINSSELIN *Grand Fleet Days* xv. 118 But nowadays you find them lolling and sprawling in all the most comfortable armchairs, while the three-striper has to take a high chair or else go to his cabin! **1918** L. E. RUGGLES *Navy Explained* 146 *Two striper.* Instead of saying 'he was a lieutenant', many men say 'he was a two-striper', meaning that he wore two stripes on his cuff. If the officer was a lieutenant commander he would wear two-and-a-half stripes, hence 'he was a two-and-a-half striper'. **1920** *Blackw. Mag.* Mar. 320/2 A dapper two-and-a-half-striper, R.N., dashed alongside in an obviously Navy gig, and scrambled aboard. **1936** *Nat. Geogr. Mag.* LXIX. 799/2 The three-striper looked me up and down. **1950** G. HACKFORTH-JONES *Worst Enemy* i. 20 It made me remember how I felt when some pompous four-striper came slumming or snooping on board my submarine. **1954** *Sun* (Baltimore) 11 Dec. 13/4 Some 250 other 'stripers' were named brigade officers for the period ending March 17. **1977** [see *SPEC *sb.*⁴]. **1978** A. PRICE *'44 Vintage* iii. 41 A two-striper like himself. **1978** H. WOUK *War & Remembrance* i. 10 Bill, isn't that a three-striper slot?

2. = *striped bass* s.v. *STRIPED *ppl. a.* 1 b.

1945 *Richmond* (Va.) *Times-Dispatch* 29 Aug. 22/1 It may be stated that in the West as in the North, the fish is called the striped bass or simply the striper. **1955** *Field & Stream* June 51/1 So far as is known, this is the first fresh-water lake in the entire country to be stocked with adult stripers. **1961** J. STEINBECK *Winter of our Discontent* xv. 292 Stripers come in sometimes. **1974** *Spartanburg* (S. Carolina) *Herald-Jrnl.* 21 Apr. B6/5 A hybrid is a cross between a striper and a white bass.

stripey (strəi·pi). [f. STRIPE *sb.*³ + -Y⁶ (in sense 2, ad. Afrikaans *strepie*): cf. STRIPY *a.*]

1. *Navy slang.* A long-service able seaman; one with good-conduct stripes.

1942 *Gen* 1 May 42/1 'What's the buzz, Stripey?'.. 'Dunno,' curtly responded the Bosun's Mate. **1945** 'TACKLINE' *Holiday Sailor* i. 8 Stripey was a small, middle-aged A.B. **1977** [see *RATE *sb.*¹ 9 c].

2. *Afr.* Also **stripie.** = *STREPIE.

1964 A. TREW *Smoke Island* viii. 133 Ezekiel was fishing in a deep pool; at his side were four or five mullet and as many 'stripeys'. **1969** *Guardian* 8 Mar. 7/6, I glimpsed his outstretched pectoral fins for a moment and saw the flash of purple. He was a stripie.

stripiness (strəi·pinės). [f. STRIPY *a.* + -NESS.] The condition of being stripy.

1958 tr. *Herberts' Artists' Techniques* III. 273 The tendency to stripiness can be avoided by stippling the paint on with a sponge. **1960** *Textile Terms & Definitions* (Textile Inst.) (ed. 4) 144 *Stripiness* (warp knitting), longitudinal defects caused by yarn variation or structural distortion in warp-knitted fabric.

strippable (stri·păb'l), *a.* [f. STRIP *v.*¹ + -ABLE.] **1.** Of a coating: capable of being stripped off or removed.

1950 *Effects Atomic Weapons* (U.S. Sci. Lab., Los Alamos) x. 333 Another possibility in connection with protection against radioactive contamination..is to use strippable coatings. **1980** *Daily Tel.* 16 Dec. 11/4 The wallpapers are trimmed, washable and strippable.

2. *U.S.* Of a mineral deposit: capable of being strip-mined.

1975 *N.Y. Times* 24 Mar. 20/2 Their entrepreneurial thrust to exploit what industry spokesmen call the West's 'Persian Gulf' of strippable coal. **1978** *Time* 17 Apr. 74/3 When they do [legislate], Western strip-mine owners fear up to 80% of the region's strippable tonnage will be ruled off limits.

stripped, *ppl. a.* Add: **a.** (Further examples. Cf. *STRIP *v.*¹ 23*, 23**.)

1931 HOFFERT & CLAXTON *Motor Benzole* iv. 61 After the removal of the benzole in the scrubbers, the gas is usually referred to as stripped gas. **1933** O. H. BLACKWOOD et al. *Outl. Atomic Physics* xiv. 305 The electrons and the more or less stripped nuclei together are assumed to form a gas, which acts like a perfect gas even at huge densities. **1947** *Physical Rev.* LXXII. 1008/2 It is just the narrowness of the cone which distinguishes the stripped neutrons from those produced by direct nuclear encounters. **1978** *Nature* 7 Sept. 41/2 Stripped iron nuclei in a hydrogen plasma under central solar conditions, according to the classical Debye—Hückel model, would undergo phase separation for concentrations well below the cosmic abundance value.

b. *spec.* Of wood (esp. pine) used for furniture or domestic woodwork, etc.: that has had the accretions of paint or varnish removed, so as to reveal the natural grain and colour.

1934 M. ALLINGHAM *Death of Ghost* ix. 105 The high narrow room with its top lights and stripped pine panelling. **1966** A. CHRISTIE *Third Girl* iv. 31 Long Basing.. had two antique shops, one mostly consisting of stripped pine chimney pieces. **1976** *Listener* 15 July 49/2 He likes corner cabinets and stripped pine. **1976** *Lancs. Even. Post* 7 Dec. 14/5 (Advt.), Chairs include set eight stripped beech. **1981** 'M. YORKE' *Hand of Death* xx. 189 A customer called. Lynn sold her a stripped-pine chair.

c. *stripped-down* adj., that has had all superfluous or extraneous parts removed; also *fig.* Esp. (orig. *U.S.*) applied to a motor vehicle so adapted in order to improve engine performance. Also of a machine: disassembled, dismantled. Cf. STRIP *v.*¹ 8 in Dict. and Suppl.

1946 [see *HOPPED *a.* 3]. **1958** *Times* 24 Nov. (Canada Suppl.) p. iv/4 In 1959, General Motors will introduce a small, stripped-down Chevrolet, which will be billed as a 'new' small car. **1961** R. B. LONG *Sentence & its Parts* 494 'Kernels.' This term is applied to stripped-down nucleuses [of sentences]. **1973** A. MACVICAR *Painted Doll Affair* vi. 66 A pimpled hairy youth in overalls wriggled out from underneath a stripped-down car. **1975** *New Yorker* 7 July 78/3 'Blue Lou' is short, stripped-down, and full of business. **1978** *Archit. Design* 5 June 310/2 The stripped-down classicism promoted by men [*sc.* architects] like Burnet and Richardson. **1979** J. GARDNER *Nostradamus Traitor* xlix. 237 They travelled in a stripped-down Heinkel 111. **1980** J. CARTWRIGHT *Horse of Darius* v. 66 He laid out the stripped-down Kalashnikov, the plasticine, the detonators.

stripper¹. Add: **1. b.** *colloq.* (orig. *U.S.*). A performer of strip-tease.

1930 *Variety* 3 Dec. 54/5 (*heading*) Detroit censor pinches four stock strippers. **1945** P. CHEYNEY *I'll say she*

Does! ii. 42, I was a stripper one time... I had a feature spot in the programme. **1950** *Manch. Guardian Weekly* 13 July 13/2 A couple of famous strippers and a beloved Broadway comedian appeared in something called 'Wine, Women, and Song'. **1960** *New Left Rev.* Mar.–Apr. 45/2 The calculated obscenity of the stripper's act. **1972** C. WESTON *Poor, Poor Ophelia* v. 27 She unzipped her.. mini-dress, and with the grace of a professional stripper, stepped out of it. **1980** *Times* 21 Oct. 12/6 (*caption*) Why should it only be male strippers who are subsidized?

2. b. *Oil Industry.* A still for the fractionation of oil or oil products.

1930 H. S. BELL *Amer. Petroleum Refining* (ed. 2) xii. 222 Reboiling coils are sometimes used as strippers. **1938** A. E. DUNSTAN et al. *Sci. of Petroleum* II. II. xxv. 1559/2 Reheaters, when used, usually have been placed on the oil stream flowing from one of the lower plates of the stripper. **1961** D. PETRIE *Petroleum* xi. 64 In order to make the fractionation process even more exact, each fraction when it leaves the tower is led into another smaller fractionating tower called a 'side stripper'. **1975** W. G. ROBERTS *Quest for Oil* (rev. ed.) viii. 85 The purpose of the stripper is to remove small amounts of vapour from the liquid entering it.

c. *Physics.* In a particle accelerator, a section containing metal foil or gas at a high positive potential, which removes electrons from the ions passing through it. Also *attrib.*

1959 *Nuclear Instruments & Methods* IV. 123/2 The image size and beam divergence required at the object point for the accelerator are limited by the dimensions of the stripper tube. **1974** J. B. A. ENGLAND *Techniques in Nuclear Structure Physics* I. iii. 268 There is usually little to choose in final beam intensity between foil strippers and gas strippers for hydrogen and helium ions. **1979** *Sci. Amer.* Apr. 47/2 The aiming mechanism would first direct the negative-hydrogen beam at the target and then pass it through a gas 'stripper' for neutralization.

3. (Earlier example.)

1843 J. H. GREENE *Exposure Arts & Miseries Gambling* (1845) 121 When cards are prepared as I have above described, they are called *strippers*.

4. a. A bleaching agent or solvent used to remove colour from fabrics before re-dyeing. Cf. STRIP *v.*[1] 21.

1909 A. MORRIS in Rothery & Edmunds *Mod. Laundry* II. xl. 150 Permanganic acid in the form of its potash or soda salt is a powerful oxidizing stripper. **1957** *Woman* 16 Nov. 25/4 Light over dark won't go, but if you want to try it you'll need a colour 'stripper'.

b. A chemical preparation used to remove paint, varnish, etc., from a surface; *paint stripper*: see *PAINT *sb.* 6.

1937 A. JONES *Cellulose Lacquers, Finishes & Cements* xii. 241 Wax has been objected to as a thickening agent as it settles out and the paint remover or stripper requires frequent and repeated shaking. **1949** C. H. HAYWARD *Woodworker's Pocket Bk.* 4 Many proprietary strippers are now available. **1979** C. CURZON *Leaven of Malice* ii. 22, I had bought..cleaning agents, strippers, filler for the cracks..in the plaster.

stripper². (Later example.)

1917 L. A. KLEIN *Princ. & Practice Milk Hygiene* i. 5 Cows in which lactation is about to cease are called 'strippers'.

stripper³ (stri·pəɹ). *Oil Industry.* [? f. STRIPPER², by analogy with a low-yielding milk cow.] More fully, *stripper well.* An oil well in which production has dwindled to only a few barrels a day.

1930 *Oil & Gas Jrnl.* 18 Dec. 48/2 The proration committee is working out a plan safeguarding the interest of operators owning small and shallow producing wells... Nothing will be done that might cause the abandonment of the stripper wells. **1931** *Ibid.* 8 Jan. 26/1 There would apparently be nothing to do but to abandon these old strippers as having exceeded their useful life. **1976** *Watertown* (S. Dakota) *Public Opinion* 6 July 7/5 Throughout the United States marginally productive oil wells known as 'strippers' account for more than 13 percent of domestic production. **1980** *Fortune* 24 Mar. 64/1 Independents will also get a break on oil from 'stripper' wells, which produce ten or fewer barrels a day.

strippeuse (stripǭ·z). *joc.* [An alteration of *STRIPPER¹ 1 b, perh. after *danseuse.*] A (female) performer of strip-tease.

1939 *Life* 2 Jan. 15/2 Last year blonde Della Carroll was première strippeuse at New York's Paradise restaurant. **1960** [see *IN *a.* 2 a]. **1962** *Times Lit. Suppl.* 26 Oct. 827/5 An eminent 'strippeuse' at Las Vegas.

stripping, *vbl. sb.*[1] Add: **1. a.** (Later examples.)

1952 W. H. KIRK *Sewell's Dogs & their Management* (rev. ed.) iv. 76 Proper trimming or stripping is a long, tedious, and continuous work. **1974** R. RENDELL *Face of Trespass* xiv. 134 Mr Greenberg doesn't have a surgery on Saturday afternoons... We're only open for clipping and stripping.

b. (Further examples. Cf. *STRIP *v.*[1] 23*, 23**, 23***.)

1922 D. T. DAY *Handbk. Petroleum Industry* II. 324 Stripping may be held to mean a complete removal of all light fractions down to those of lubricating value, and represents the initial refining process. **1943** *Ann. Reg. 1942* 364 Saha..suggested that both the stripping of the atoms and their high velocities are due to a nuclear reaction analogous to fission. **1949** MELCHER & LARRICK *Printing & Promotion Handbk.* 283/2 When two or more photographic negatives are used together to make one printing plate, the process of combining them is known as 'stripping'. **1955** [see *DESORPTION]. **1972** *Physics Bull.* Mar. 145/1 After stripping the nitrogen ions..will behave like deuterons or alpha particles in the injection channel into the synchrotron. **1977** L. VÁLYI *Atom & Ion Sources* iv. 251 An alternative method for the production of multiply charged ions is the stripping of electrons in the interaction of singly charged positive ions. **1980** J. R. WALKER *Graphic Arts Fund.* vi. 116/1 (*caption*) Light table makes good work surface for stripping.

3. *stripping agent, bench, cement, column, desk, foil, operation, still*; **stripping-bill(e)**, a bladed implement or bill used in besom-making; **stripping-knife,** (*b*) a knife used in the stripping of wallpaper or paint from surfaces.

1958 M. G. LARIAN *Fund. Chem. Engin. Operations* xiii. 495 In desorption dissolved gases are removed from a liquid by contacting the liquid with a suitable gas (the desorbing or stripping agent), or a volatile liquid is separated from a relatively nonvolatile solvent. **1967** E. CHAMBERS *Photolitho-Offset* v. 51 A stripping bench, layout and lining tables are essential... The former provides the illuminated working surface on which the various images can be positioned. **1968** J. ARNOLD *Shell Bk. Country Crafts* v. 97 The cuttings are prepared for use with chopping and stripping-billes for the coarse and finer work. **1974** P. W. BLANDFORD *Country Craft Tools* ii. 38 The besom broom maker called his general-purpose tool a 'chopping bill' and had a lighter one with more curve to the point called a 'stripping bill'. **1967** E. CHAMBERS *Photolitho-Offset* v. 50 With face-up stripping a stripping cement is first applied to the base support. **1930** H. S. BELL *Amer. Petroleum Refining* (ed. 2) xii. 222 If withdrawn as a finished product, the light ends must be removed and this is usually accomplished in a separate small stripping column. **1967** E. CHAMBERS *Photolitho-Offset* v. 55 (*caption*) Bench-type illuminated stripping desk. **1972** *Physics Bull.* Mar. 144/3 An aluminium stripping foil of density 40 μg cm⁻² was therefore used at the high energy end of the Linac to convert the particles to $^{14}N^{7+}$. **1927** W. DEEPING *Kitty* xx. 254, I could lend you a plank and a couple of step-ladders, and a stripping-knife. **1951** *Good Housek. Home Encycl.* 210/1 A paper-hanger's stripping knife, which is a flat, fairly flexible, steel-bladed knife. **1948** R. R. KARCH *Graphic Arts Procedures* viii. 232 (*heading*) The stripping operation. **1980** J. R. WALKER *Graphic Arts Fund.* vi. 116/2 (*caption*) Stripping operations require sharp knives, scissors and brushes for opaquing pinholes. **1931** HOFFERT & CLAXTON *Motor Benzole* viii. 225 The function of a modern stripping still is to remove the remaining benzole from the hot oil leaving the preheater.

strippy, *a.* Delete *rare* and add later examples.

1963 *Times* 20 Apr. 11/6 Veneered with carefully matched figured or burr walnut,..with drawer fronts, fall flaps and door framing straight or herringbone cross-banded with strippy walnut. **1978** *Detroit Free Press* 16 Apr. (Detroit Suppl.) 20 (Advt.), Strippy, strappy stripes of canvas [sandals], wedged high, to put spring snap in your steps.

strip-tease. *colloq.* (orig. *U.S.*). Also **strip tease, striptease.** [Back-formation from next.]

1. A kind of entertainment in which a female (occas. a male) performer undresses gradually in a tantalizingly erotic fashion before an audience, usu. to music; an instance of this.

[**1930** *Variety* 1 Oct. 49/4 Girls have the strip and tease down to a science.] **1936** *Variety* 2 Dec. 70/5 An undersea ballet, veil waving number and a mild strip tease by the entire chorus, which required little feeling, were nicely executed. **1937** *Daily Tel.* 29 Apr. 22/2 Can anything be said in defence of the present public interest in 'strip-tease' and nudist or semi-nudist displays on stage? **1943** *Scrutiny* XI. 286 The business-cum-Riviera set of which he is the representative in fiction (on the stage—strip-tease) were very pally with Goering and Co. **1960** *News Chron.* 23 Sept. 10/2 Strip-tease..can be banal. **1978** G. GREENE *Human Factor* II. iii. 75, I thought dinner in the Café Grill and afterwards a spot of strip-tease.

2. In *transf.* and *fig.* use.

1937 *Hansard Commons* 20 Apr. 1623 We had a display of what I believe is now known as 'strip-tease', in which we were kept in tantalising expectation of what was to come. **1956** E. LINKLATER *Dark of Summer* iv. 62 The whole female art of novel-writing—is an exquisitely prolonged strip-tease. **1969** I. & P. OPIE *Children's Games* 13 They snatch the girls' ties or hair ribbons and call it 'Strip Tease'. **1982** J. O'FAOLAIN *Obedient Wife* i. 26 'Do you feel I owe you a confidence?' 'No..if I come here to do a strip-tease, it doesn't mean *you* have to.'

3. In *attrib.* use. **strip-tease artist,** a performer of strip-tease.

1936 *N.Y. Post* 15 Sept. 13/1 Gypsy Rose Lee is at once the Bernhardt, the Duse and the Joan Crawford of Strip-Tease girls. **1939** A. HUXLEY *After Many a Summer* I. vi. 71, A strip-tease dancer in a Western mining-camp. **1944** 'G. ORWELL' in *Horizon* X. 237 A strip-tease act. **1947** H. A. SMITH *Low Man on Totem Pole* viii. 68 Miss Lee turned to a paragraph in the magazine in which Henry L. Mencken was represented as having coined a word to describe a strip-tease artist. **1953** C. DAY LEWIS *Italian Visit* i. 25 Whoever would master the truth by which your provocative, charming Strip-tease universe lives. **1958** N. MARSH *Singing in Shrouds* v. 101 That damn' spiritual striptease session. **1968** P. OLIVER *Screening Blues* vi. 251 As the strip-tease artist compares with the artist's model, so the seductive effects of slow unveiling are more stimulating erotically than the starkly naked. **1979** C. MACLEOD *Family Vault* xi. 71 Does it disgust you..that your..husband once made a fool of himself over a striptease dancer?

Hence as *v. intr.*, to perform a strip-tease act; **strip-teaseuse,** joc. alteration of *STRIP-TEASER (cf. *CHANTEUSE, *STRIPPEUSE, etc.); **strip-teasing** *vbl. sb.* and *ppl. a.*; **stripteuse** = *strip-teaseuse* above.

1937 G. FRANKAU *More of Us* 185 Dalliest thou, strip-teasing and beachcombing, On some far southern beach of Gallic joy. **1937** *Variety* 31 Mar. 69/1 Kraus is accused by John S. Sumner, head of the vice society, of permitting strip-teasing in his show. **1941** *Sun* (Baltimore) 8 Mar. 20/2 (*caption*) Strip-teaseuses Betty Coette..and Winnie Garrett. **1942** *Time* 28 Sept. 40/3 Gipsy Rose Lee, stripteuse turned woman of letters. **1951** *Sun* (Baltimore) 27 June 30/3 A blond stripteuse was arrested at a Silver Hill night spot. **1957** *Times Lit. Suppl.* 11 Oct. 611/1 Little Rose Louise was..new to burlesque, and able to gasp at strip-teasing Flossie. **1958** *Listener* 18 Sept. 418/2, I..drove to a night club, where a girl stripteased while lashing a whip. **1960** *News Chron.* 22 Sept. 3/1, I have given up strip-teasing to be with my husband. **1962** *Guardian* 23 Feb. 9/4 A strip-teasing woman. **1977** J. MITFORD *Fine Old Conflict* vii. 118, I was temporarily in despair, hoping against hope that something would turn up. It did, in the shape of a former stripteaseuse whom I had met at a PW party.

strip-teaser. orig. *U.S.* [f. STRIP *v.*[1] + *TEASER[1] 2 g.] A performer of strip-tease; an ecdysiast or stripper.

1930 *Variety* 26 Nov. 40/2 The main b[ox] o[ffice] lure is the girls, those known as 'strip teasers'. **1935** E. E. CUMMINGS *Let.* 29 Jan. (1969) 135, I recommend the Irving Place Burlesk (stripteasers in excelsis). **1952** *Chambers's Jrnl.* Feb. 71/1 There was not a pinpoint of light anywhere, not a glimmer from the long line of caravans parked round the square, where the Parisian Strip-teasers slept beside their watchful mothers. **1960** *News Chron.* 25 Feb. 5/8 They got Trixie Kent, our strip-teaser, to autograph one or two scraps of clothing. **1982** *Washington Post* 22 Jan. (Weekend section) 47/1 Despite its new soigné image, the essential pulse of Baltimore remains the rhythmic tic-toc of a stripteaser's tassels.

stritch (stritʃ). Also **strich.** [Origin uncertain.] A musical instrument resembling a straightened alto saxophone. (Chiefly associated with the American jazz musician Roland Kirk, b. 1936.)

1960 *Downbeat* 4 Aug. 13/1 Kirk haunted music stores, examined all kinds of antique instruments, many of them remnants of the 19th century... When he found what he was looking for..they weren't saxophones at all... One was a stritch, the other a manzello. **1962,** etc. [see *MANZELLO]. **1969** *Punch* 12 Mar. 393/2 The manzello and strich..sound fine as solo instruments or as sudden quasi-orchestral interludes in a tenor solo. **1977** *Time* 19 Dec. 53/1 Kirk played the manzello (a quasi-saxophone), the stritch (a horn resembling a dented blunderbuss) and the tenor sax together.

strivingly, *adv.* (Later example.)

1890 W. JAMES *Princ. Psychol.* II. xxi. 315 The impulse to take life strivingly is indestructible in the race.

strobe (strōᵘb), *a.* and *sb.* [f. first syllable of STROBOSCOPIC *a.* and related words.] **A.** *adj.*

1. = STROBOSCOPIC *a.*

1942 *Amer. Cinematographer* Sept. 422/3 Adjust the speed of the projector until the bars on the 'strobe' band corresponding to the number of blades in the projector shutter appear to stand still. **1949** H. LURAY *Strobe* viii. 110 (*caption*) A classic strobe shot. Drop of milk splashing on a plate covered by a thin layer of milk. **1962** *Amer. Jrnl. Physics* XXX. 925/2 Strobe photography is an area that has not been saturated at science fairs. **1966** *McGraw-Hill Encycl. Sci & Technol.* XIII. 187/1 Stroboscopic or 'strobe' photography is generally understood to refer to pictures of both single and multiple exposure taken by flashes of light from electrical discharges. **1978** *Oceans* May–June 39/1 Flash bulbs or strobe (electronic flash) lighting is often used to restore lost colors and provide light for an exposure.

2. Special collocations: *strobe disc,* a disc with alternate light and dark sectors of equal size for checking the speed of rotation of something, its appearance being steady only when this speed is related in a definite way to the periodicity of the illumination; *strobe lamp, light,* an electric light that can be made to flash on and off rapidly and automatically; also (*U.S.*), an electronic flash for a camera; so *strobe-lighted, -lit* adjs.; *strobe pulse* (Electronics) (see quot. 1971).

1942 *Amer. Cinematographer* Sept. 423/1 Check the strobe disc for synchronization. **1967** *Nature* 23 Dec. 1173/1 The correct speed of a gramophone turn-table may be checked by viewing a strobe disk illuminated by electric light supplied by the a.c. mains. **1974** *Sci. Amer.* Aug. 108/3 The solution of the problem of stopping fast action lies in an electronic flash lamp. The duration of most 'strobe' lamps owned by amateurs is about 5×10^{-4} second, which is sufficiently brief for many events of interest. **1975** *Gramophone* Jan. 1297 (Advt.), Dots on the outer rim of the SR717 are illuminated by the built-in strobe lamp. **1962** N. MAXWELL *Witch-Doctor's Apprentice* vi. 68 Augusto helped a lot, lugging the Strobe light and holding his flashlight so that I could check my camera settings. **1971** R. BUSBY *Deadlock* vii. 98 Pulsating strobe lights left Leric with a fragmented picture of girls. **1978** *Sci. Amer.* June 128/1 My best clue came from examining the floating drops under a strobe light set near the frequency of oscillation, so that the flashing light effectively slowed the vibration of the drops. **1979** *Listener* 18 Oct.

517/3 A strobe-lighted production number that sends images flashing around the vast auditorium. **1967** P. Welles *Babyhip* ii. 36 It's not everyone who can have a strob-lit [*sic*] dream of love. **1972** *Listener* 23 June 845/1 Weird strobe-lit collages. **1946** *Jrnl. Inst. Electr. Engineers* XCIII. IIIA. 318/2 The operator had under his control a variable-range strobe pulse which he could bring into coincidence with the target echo. **1967** *Electronics* 6 Mar. 117/1 (*caption*) The level detector senses the moment when C_{int} reaches zero volts and generates a strobe pulse. **1971** *Gloss. Electrotechnical, Power Terms* (*B.S.I.*) III. vi. 18 *Strobe pulse*, a pulse, of duration less than the period of a recurrent phenomenon, used for scrutinizing a particular epoch of that phenomenon... In radar, a strobe pulse is sometimes made to follow automatically the echo from a moving object.

B. *sb.* **1.** = *strobe disc*, sense *A. 2 above.

1942 *Amer. Cinematographer* Sept. 423/1 Watch the strobe for any changes in projector speed.

2. *Electronics.* = *strobe pulse*, sense *A. 2 above.

1946 *Jrnl. Inst. Electr. Engineers* XCIII. IIIA. 319/1 In the A.I. Mark IV [radar] equipment, the search was a progressive outward movement of the strobe from zero to maximum range, followed by a rapid fly-back to zero. **1953** *Electronic Engin.* XXV. 191/1 Photographing a C.R.O. trace using a reference waveform as a strobe. **1959** *Ibid.* XXXI. 136/2 The *X* displacement may be dissociated from the phase of the strobe (time scale). **1980** D. G. Green *Digital Techniques & Systems* iv. 49 The strobe determines the times at which the *S* and *R* input signals should be effective.

3. a. = *strobe light*, sense *A. 2 above. **b.** Stroboscopic photography.

1949 H. Luray *Strobe* v. 73 You will know which size flash bulb your strobe approximates. *Ibid.* vii. 101 Strobe is used outdoors very much like flash. **1962** *Amer. Jrnl. Physics* XXX. 925/1 The strobe was flashing at three times the frequency of the wave. **1968** J. D. MacDonald *Pale Grey for Guilt* (1969) xii. 153 Maybe the music got too loud... Maybe it was the strobes. **1975** J. Rathbone *Kill Cure* II. vi. 48 For one brief moment she saw the man full face, caught in the jerky light of the strobe.

strobe (strōᵘb), *v.* [f. prec.] **1.** *trans. Electronics.* To gate (*gate *v.*[1] 2 a) by means of a strobe pulse.

1947 *Wireless World* Aug. 290/1 Work was also carried out on 'strobing' a portion of the time base. **1950** [see *gate *v.*[1] 2]. **1981** Nashelsky & Boylestad *Devices* xi. 391 The output remains high unless strobed.

2. *intr. Cinemat.* and *Television.* To exhibit or give rise to strobing.

1959 Halas & Manvell *Technique Film Animation* xix. 232 Fairly light colours do not strobe so much as white. **1965** *Punch* 12 May 684/1 Before my very first TV appearance the studio manager tried to get me to change clothes with him... He then explained that the black and white check I was wearing would 'strobe'—an optical illusion whereby the wearer of any pattern containing vertical or horizontal stripes appears to vibrate. **1982** *Observer* 12 Dec. 26/3 Don't blink, don't sniff, don't stick your chin up, don't slouch, don't wave your hands about, don't wear stripes (they 'strobe'), look at the person you're talking to, *smile*.

3. *fig.* (*intr.* and *trans.*) To flash.

1977 R. E. Harrington *Quintain* vi. 53 Possible explanations flashed through his mind..thoughts strobing across his mind. **1980** J. McNeil *Spy Game* ix. 103 The fire strobed rosy light onto the burnished yew furniture.

Hence **strobed** *ppl. a.*

1980 D. C. Green *Digital Techniques & Systems* iv. 49 A clocked or strobed flip-flop will change only when a clock pulse is received.

strobilanthes (strobilæ·nþīz). [mod.L. (K. L. Blume *Bijdragen tot de Flora van Nederlandsch Indië* (1826) 781), f. Strobilus + Gr. ἄνθος flower, in reference to the shape of the young inflorescence.] A herb or subshrub of the genus *Strobilanthes*, belonging to the family Acanthaceæ, native to tropical Asia, and bearing clusters of blue or white tubular flowers.

1836 *Curtis's Bot. Mag.* LXIII. 3517 (*heading*) Mr. Sabine's strobilanthes. **1918** R. N. Parker *Forest Flora Punjab* 386 In most floras all the Strobilanthes are described as shrubs but I have not found the Punjab species shrubby. **1944** J. Corbett *Man-Eaters of Kumaon* (1946) 17 A bed of strobilanthes, the bent stalks of which were slowly regaining their upright position, showed where.. the tigress had passed. **1979** A. J. Huxley *Success with House Plants* 375/1 A strobilanthes cannot tolerate temperatures below about 55°F.

strobing (strōᵘ·biŋ), *vbl. sb.* [f. *strobe *v.* + -ing[1].] **1.** The action of *strobe *v.* 1.

1959 *Electronic Engin.* XXXI. 130/2 Strobing consists of sampling a repetitive waveform at what to all intents and purposes is an instant in the repetition period. **1981** Nashelsky & Boylestad *Devices* xi. 390 Figure 11.5 shows how a 311 comparator can be used with strobing.

2. a. *Cinemat.* Jerkiness in what should be a smooth movement on the screen. **b.** *Television.* An irregular movement and loss of continuity sometimes seen in lines and stripes in a television picture.

1959 Halas & Manvell *Technique Film Animation* xix. 231 When objects are panned through the screen area, strobing always appears to be worst (on standard 5 inch field) when the distance of movement is between ·125 and ·500 inch per frame. **1961** G. Millerson *Technique Television Production* iii. 52 Where..tiling, venetian blinds, etc., are seen at such a distance that their surface appears as close horizontal lines, line-beating or strobing will occur. **1973** R. Dougall *In & Out of Box* xxiii. 280 Ties..could be noisy or even loud, so long as they had no horizontal or diagonal patterns which caused 'strobing'. **1980** *Radio Times* 25 Nov.–5 Dec. 102/2 There are a few rules about television clothes... Some patterns can make the picture go all funny—what's known as strobing.

strobo- (strōᵘ·bo), formative element f. the first syllable of Stroboscope, etc., as in **stro·botorch**, a light source designed to give very brief flashes of light at a known rate; **stro·botron** [*-tron], a gas-filled cold-cathode discharge tube used as a strobotorch, the flashing rate being determined by the frequency of the voltage applied to a control grid.

1951 *Electronic Engin.* XXIII. 187/3 It is..possible to link the flashing rate of the strobotorch to an electrical contractor..fitted on the mechanism. **1970** *Nature* 15 Aug. 731/1 A sheet of white translucent plastic was placed between the geometrical figure and the strobotorch. **1937** Germeshausen & Edgerton in *Electronics* Feb. 12/1 In this paper a tube, named the Strobotron, is described which has been developed primarily for producing stroboscopic light. **1949** *Jrnl. R. Aeronaut. Soc.* LIII. 460/1 The cathode ray tubes, amplifiers, and strobotron lamps, together with their power supplies, are built into one case. **1966** *McGraw-Hill Encycl. Sci & Technol.* XIII. 190/1 A thyratron or a strobotron can be used as a trigger tube in place of the switch *S*.

stroboscope. Add: Also with pronunc. (strōᵘ·bŏ-).

stroboscopic, *a.* Add: Also with pronunc. (strōᵘbŏ-). Also, involving or pertaining to rapid flashes of light. (Further examples.)

1949 H. Luray *Strobe* i. 22 Real stroboscopic lighting equipment with ample light output can do wonderful things. **1959** L. A. Mannheim *Successful Flash Photogr.* 130 (*heading*) Stroboscopic shots. *Ibid.*, A stroboscopic flash outfit. **1971** *Nature* 11 June 397/2 Lately there has been a fad in this area for dances to be held under stroboscopic lighting. **1980** J. W. Hill *Intermediate Physics* iv. 35 Stroboscopic photography (where photographs are taken by a camera at intervals of fractions of seconds on the same film) shows this.

Hence **strobosco·pically** *adv.*, by means of a stroboscope or stroboscopic illumination.

1919 *Proc. Nat. Acad. Sci.* V. 174 All measurements were made by the Michelson interferometer viewed stroboscopically. **1932** *Phil. Mag.* XIII. 163 The nature of the instability induced by sound in smoke jets has been examined stroboscopically and by means of photography. **1951** *Electronic Engin.* XXIII. 430/1 The valve structure may be observed stroboscopically while subjected to vibration and the offending portion detected visually. **1977** D. Goldstein et al. *Test System for Evaluations of Armors using Duplicate Fragments* (U.S. Patent 4,044,599), By using stroboscopically-controlled illumination, the high-speed flight of the fragments can be captured on one photograph.

stroboscopy (strob-, strǫ̆bǫ·skŏpi). [f. Stroboscope + -y[3].] **a.** The use of stroboscopic techniques or apparatus. **b.** Stroboscopic effects.

1932 *Sun* (Baltimore) 17 Sept. 16/4 Such effects are produced through the principle of stroboscopy, applications of which already make possible the photography of rapidly whirling objects. **1971** Chin-Wu Kim in W. O. Dingwall *Survey of Linguistic Sci.* 22 A slowed-down or stationary appearance in stroboscopy is due to an electromechanical apparatus of the stroboscope. **1980** S. L. Lyons *Exterior Lighting* ii. 31 A special effect of flicker is that termed stroboscopy in which rotating or rhythmically moving objects may give the illusion of being stationary.

stroganoff (strǫ·gănǫf). Also **stroganov, strogonoff** and with capital initial. [a. Fr., f. the name of the 19th-cent. Russian diplomat Count Paul *Stroganov.*] A dish of strips of beef cooked in a sauce containing sour cream. In full, *beef stroganoff, bœuf stroganoff.*

1932 A. Heath *Good Food* 30 Beef *Strogonoff*..slices from a fillet of beef..cut..into shortish, thin strips.. onions and mushrooms..cook..in butter..add..thick sour cream. **1937** 'Countess Morphy' *Kitchen Library* IV. 50 (*heading*) Bœuf Strogonov (Russian). **1944** E. M. Almedingen *Dasha* vi. 235 All of it sounds as tidy as pieces of beef in the Strogonov dish. **1955** *Good Food Guide 1955–56* 341 Steak maison, tournedos Rossini and bœuf Stroganoff. **1961** *Listener* 28 Dec. 1107/2 In Leningrad's smartest restaurant I ordered beef strogonoff. **1964** 'D. Shannon' *Death-Bringers* (1966) vi. 72 It's Beef Stroganov, and it's hot. **1969** D. Lambert *Angels in Snow* ii. 48 'What's for dinner?' Harry asked. 'Strogonoff,' said his wife. **1980** A. N. Wilson *Healing Art* xiv. 157 Did you get Gale to fix you..her strogonoff, followed by bilberry strudel?

Stroh (strōᵘ). The name of the inventor Charles *Stroh* (fl. 1901) used *attrib.* to designate stringed instruments (chiefly of the violin class) having an aluminium plate and horn attachment in place of a wooden body, formerly used for recording purposes.

1902 *Encycl. Brit.* XXXI. 766/1 The recent invention of the Stroh violin. **1923** [see *phonofiddle]. **1934** C. Lambert *Music Ho!* iv. 257 The old pre-electric horn recording, with its euphoniums instead of 'cellos, and its handful of Stroh violins. **1947** F. W. Gaisberg *Music on Record* vi. 79 Stringed instruments we recorded by a subterfuge. We substituted the Stroh violin for violins and violas. **1979** *Oxf. Jun. Compan. Mus.* (ed. 2) 314/1 *Stroh violin*, a violin that has an aluminium plate and a trumpet bell instead of the normal wooden body. Invented in 1901 by Charles Stroh for use in the early recording studios, where primitive microphones could only pick up sound aimed directly at them (which..the trumpet bell could do). There are also Stroh violas, cellos, mandolins, and guitars.

stroke, *sb.*[1] Add: **13. f.** *to put* (someone) *off* (his) *stroke*, to distract (someone) from his course of activity; to disconcert or disturb. *colloq.*

a **1914** Joyce *Stephen Hero* (1944) xx. 103 Besides girls praying put me off my stroke. **1922** —— *Ulysses* 285 Put you off your stroke. **1965** J. Gale *Clean Young Englishman* iv. 167 The note put me right off my stroke. I was trying to tell the audience what the war in Algeria was really like... But somehow I never finished what I wanted to say. **1977** R. Perry *Dead End* iii. 41 She must have..seen the bodies..but it didn't put her off her stroke at all.

14. d. *to pull a stroke*, to play a dirty trick. Cf. *pull *v.* 19 e. *slang.*

1970 P. Laurie *Scotland Yard* 293 *Pull a stroke, to*, to play a dirty trick. **1974** J. McVicar *McVicar* i. ii. i. 109 It would be wrong to let Charlie go... He's pulled too many strokes.

17. b. For ? *nonce-use* read *colloq. rare* and add later example.

1914 Joyce *Dubliners* 153, I don't say Hynes.—No, damn it, I think he's a stroke above that.

d. In *Telegraphy*, the name of the signal for an oblique stroke. Now usu. *colloq.*, a spoken representation of a solidus. Freq. used as *conj.* to indicate or stress alternatives: or else, alternatively.

1884 W. Lynd *Pract. Telegraphist* i. 27 The oblique stroke is to be signalled 'stroke', thus—'FI three stroke five FF', meaning 3/5 (three shillings and fivepence). **1965** M. Allingham *Mind Readers* xv. 153, I have my own feel, of course, which would be 'glad stroke laughing-at' in his case. **1971** J. Yardley *Kiss a Day keeps Corpses Away* ii. 39 The Truman stroke Eisenhower regime. **1974** G. Markstein *Cooler* xlvii. 171 ABPQ stroke 113 stroke 1. Ah yes. Is that your national registration number? **1977** N. J. Crisp *Odd Job Man* iii. 28 One dozen cardigans, stroke thirty-three, blue, for knitwear.

e. *spec.* in *Logic* = *Sheffer('s) stroke* s.v. *Sheffer.

1925 Whitehead & Russell *Principia Math.* (ed. 2) I. p. xvi, The symbol '*p*/*q*' is pronounced: '*p* stroke *q*'... All the usual truth-functions can be constructed by means of the stroke. **1952** R. L. Wilder *Introd. Found. Math.* ix. 220 Since P[rincipia] M[athematica] was first published, with its two undefined symbols (or 'logical constants')..it has been shown that *one* undefined symbol..[is] sufficient. The symbol referred to is / and is called 'stroke'. **1975** P. K. Bastable *Logic* 189 Later he [*sc.* Russell] preferred to become acquainted with implication through defining it as 'Either not *p* or *q*' or, like Sheffer and Nicod, in terms of the stroke functor.

24*. *Basket-making.* A single movement analogous to a stitch in sewing or knitting; the result of this.

1912 T. Okey *Art of Basket-Making* vii. 59 Where an even number of pairs of leagues or sticks is used, the centre strokes lie alternate, and not side by side. *Ibid.* 154 *Stroke*, any complete movement in basket-work: analogous to a stitch in needlework. **1960** E. Legg *Country Baskets* iii. 29 And now for the strokes, which are comparable with 'stitches' in knitting... The strokes are indeed simple and few.

25. c. stroke-maker *Cricket*, a batsman who plays attractive, attacking strokes; hence **stroke-making; stroke-ornamented** *a. Archæol.* (see quot. 1970); **strokeplay** *Cricket*, the playing of attractive, attacking strokes; hence **stroke-player.**

1927 *Observer* 5 June 21/5 A beautiful stroke-maker, he [*sc.* H. W. Austin] is pleasant to watch. **1976** J. Snow *Cricket Rebel* 84 Nurse could be a brilliant and savage stroke-maker on his day, but could graft when necessary. **1956** R. Alston *Test Commentary* iii. 23 One of the features of the morning's play was the stroke-making of.. Van Geloven. **1977** *World of Cricket Monthly* June 87/1 He impressed the Lord's gathering with his crisp stroke-making. **1925** V. G. Childe *Dawn Europ. Civilization* xii. 172 The second ware may..be called stroke-ornamented pottery. Its forms are rather more angular than those of spiral-meander pottery. *Ibid.* xviii. 272 Hut foundations..yielded sherds with curvilinear decoration and others recalling the Danubian stroke-ornamented ware. **1970** Bray & Trump *Dict. Archaeol.* 222/1 *Stroke-ornamented ware*, pottery with zigzag patterns made by a series of distinct jabs rather than continuous lines. It was current during the centuries after 4000 BC in Bohemia, west Poland, Bavaria and central Germany. **1930** C. G. Macartney *My Cricketing Days* ii. 14 Perhaps this sort of cricket was an aid to stroke play, perhaps not, but as far as I can see, it never did me any harm. **1979** *Daily Tel.* 19 May 29/1 Any doubts about his form or fitness were violently dismissed in a morning of rich strokeplay. **1935** *Times* 20 July 13/5 Some of the English cricketers now getting past their prime are still stroke-players. **1963** A. Ross *Australia 63* x. 183 There were, on the

England side, three stroke-players capable of enhancing any Test, on the Australian side two.

stroke, *sb.*^{2} Delete † *Obs.* and add: Also, an act of stroking, esp. by way of caress.

1953 H. E. BATES *Nature of Love* iv. 36 She gave her hair a long deep casual stroke with the brush.

2. An act of copulation. *slang. rare.*

1785 GROSE *Classical Dict. Vulgar Tongue* s.v., *Stroke. To take a stroke,* to take a bout with a woman. **1976** P. CAVE *High Flying Birds* ii. 19, I happened to be engaged upon a variation of the sexual act known as the 'Birmingham Stroke' at the time our little love-nest started rolling.

3. A comforting gesture of approval or congratulation (see also quot. 1964). Hence, a flattering or friendly remark, etc., esp. one made in order to help or manipulate another. Cf. *STROKE *v.*^{1} 1 e. Now chiefly *U.S. colloq.*

1964 E. BERNE *Games People Play* 15 By an extension of meaning, 'stroking' may be employed colloquially to denote any act implying recognition of another's presence. Hence a *stroke* may be used as the fundamental unit of social action. An exchange of strokes constitutes a *transaction,* which is the unit of social intercourse. **1969** T. A. HARRIS *I'm OK, You're OK* iii. 45 The Adult has something to work on: what must I do to gain their strokes, or their approval? **1973** *Houston* (Texas) *Chron. Texas Mag.* 14 Oct. 4/1 The popular saying around PDAP [*sc.* The Palmer Drug Abuse Program] is 'different strokes for different folks', and that's the basis of the program. **1978** M. PUZO *Fools Die* xi. 122 He started off dishing out some nice strokes. With an admiring smile he told me how smart I was, how honest, so absolutely reliable. **1981** *TV Picture Life* Mar. 12/3 Let's face it, everybody needs their strokes and that would be very ego-satisfying.

4. Special combinations: **stroke book,** a pornographic book; **stroke house** *U.S.,* a cinema where pornographic films are shown.

1972 *Pussycat* XXIII. LIX. 10/1 For a stroke book, the quality of writing is astonishingly good. **1978** T. GIFFORD *Glendower Legacy* (1979) 73 I'm just going to pig out at home, look at a stroke book... As a matter of fact, I've taken to writing for stroke books. **1971** *Atlantic Monthly* July 52 He would camp in the 42nd Street stroke houses and come back with tales of what they were getting away with now.

stroke, *v.*^{1} Add: **1. e.** In recent use, to reassure (a child, etc.) by approval or congratulation (see also quot. 1964). Hence, to manipulate (another) by means of flattery, persuasion, etc.; to compliment. Cf. *STROKE *sb.*^{2} 3. Chiefly *U.S. colloq.,* esp. in political contexts.

1964 [see *STROKE *sb.*^{2} 3]. **1969** T. A. HARRIS *I'm OK, You're OK* iii. 48 If a two-year-old concludes *I'm OK,* does this mean his *OK* is the product of 'self-stroking' and, if so, how does a small child stroke himself? **1973** T. C. HUSTON in L. Chester et al. *Watergate* iv. 43 Mr. Hoover should be called in privately for a stroking session at which the President [*sc.* Nixon] explains the decision he had made. **1975** *Atlantic Monthly* Mar. 44 It's Show Biz, man—a bunch a' egomaniacal people using a captive audience to stroke themselves. **1977** *Time* 17 Oct. 20/1 Carter also stroked the Jerusalem government by promising that the U.S. would never attempt to impose a Middle East settlement. **1978** *New Yorker* 9 Jan. 41 He tells his client, 'It's looking pretty good. We'll stay on top of it.' This is what is known as 'stroking' the client. **1981** *Observer* 11 Jan. 6/5, I think he's still a little kid from Hoboken, who likes to be stroked by Presidents.

stroke, *v.*^{2} Add: **I. 4*.** Of a bell: to chime the strokes of (the hour, etc.). *poet. rare*$^{-1}$.

1902 HARDY *Poems of Past & Present* 132 As the hope-hour stroked its sum, You did not come.

III. 6. b. Of an oarsman or crew: to row at (a certain number of strokes per minute).

1928 *Times* 11 Aug. 5 The winner stroked an average of 28 to Gunther's 30. **1976** C. FREUD in *Webster's Sports Dict.* 431/1 With 500 yards to go, the Cairo Police, stroking 38, edged past Oxford.

7. *Sport.* To hit or kick (the ball) smoothly and elegantly; to score in this manner.

1960 J. FINGLETON *Four Chukkas to Australia* xvi. 136 He..raved of the manner in which Cowdrey stroked the ball. **1962** [see *CROSS *sb.* 22 e]. **1972** *Even. Telegram* (St. John's, Newfoundland) 24 June 1/1 Bernie Allen stroked his first home run of the season. **1976** *Wymondham & Attleborough Express* 3 Dec. 27/4 Wortwell fought back and were awarded a spot kick only for Webb to stroke the ball straight to the keeper.

stroll, *v.* **3.** Delete † *Obs.* and add later examples. Chiefly *U.S.* in recent use.

1956 H. GOLD *Man who was not with It* (1965) vi. 50 Her laughter rang out as we strolled a business street of the suburb. **1974** *New Yorker* 3 June 76/3 (Advt.), Hike forest trails, stroll lovely gardens. **1977** *Gay News* 24 Mar. 23/1 They taxi to the Toilet and stroll the dock strip at 3 am.

stroller. Add: **6.** A child's push-chair, esp. a collapsible buggy.

1920 *Sears, Roebuck & Co. Catal.* Fall 1049/2 Stroller Style Carriage... Body made of selected reeds finished in the natural shellac color. **1922** *Ibid.* Spring 590/2 Select your stroller or collapsible sulky from this page and you will be satisfied with service given. **1932** *Babies, just Babies* Dec. 63/3 (Advt.), Baby walker, stroller and go-cart combined. **1954** W. MCCULLOUGH *Illustr. Handbk. Child Care* vii. 144 We saw the Smithsonian Institute and art galleries today. So glad we brought along his stroller. We just fold it up and pack it in the car. **1962** J. R. BERNARD in *Southerly* XXII. II. 97 We keep stroller as meaning saunterer but we add the meaning of baby's push-cart. **1977** N. SAHGAL *Situation in New Delhi* i. 5 Young women in bright coats briskly pushing strollers carrying rosy bundled babies.

7. A casual shoe. Normally in *pl.*

1948 *Woman & Beauty* Oct. 118/2 For shoes I picked a pair of black suède strollers. **1953** R. CHANDLER *Long Good-Bye* xi. 64 On his feet were black moccasin type ties, the kind..that are almost as comfortable as strollers. **1958** J. CANNAN *And be Villain* viii. 177 She stepped into her 'strollers'. **1970** *Washington Post* 30 Sept. B5/3 (Advt.), Softy suede stroller... Soft-walk into fall.

strom, strum. For *dial.* read *dial.* and *Naut.* and add: **2.** Chiefly in form **strum. b.** *Naut.* (See quots.) Also *strum-box, -plate.*

1894 H. PAASCH *From Keel to Truck* (ed. 2) 172/1 *Strainer; strum; strum-box,* terms applied to perforated plates, wire-clothes or any other objects fitted to allow the entry or exit of water or other fluids, but preventing the passing of any refuse matter. **1948** R. DE KERCHOVE *Internat. Maritime Dict.* 739/2 *Strum plate,* a plate fitted in pump suctions, deck scuppers, sea cocks, having a number of small holes in it to allow water to pass, but designed to stop foreign matter that would clog the piping. **1962** A. G. COURSE *Dict. Naut. Terms* 192 *Strum box,* a square metal box with perforated sides fitted round the bottom of a suction pipe in a ship's bilges. **1975** *B.S.I. News* July 21/2 Strum boxes for ships.

stroma. Add: **2. c.** *Bot.* The colourless fluid surrounding the grana inside a chloroplast.

1914 M. DRUMMOND tr. *Haberlandt's Physiol. Plant Anat.* i. 37 In some cases the characteristic pigment [of chromoplasts] is suspended in a colourless protoplasmic matrix (or stroma)..in the shape of minute globules or vesicles (grana). **1979** KRAMER & SCOTT *Cell Concept* iv. 80 The chemical changes in photosynthesis go on in the chlorophyll in the granules on the lamellae and are completed in the stroma.

stromatolite (strōu·mătolǝit). *Geol.* [ad. G. *stromatolith* (see next): see -LITE.] A laminated calcareous sedimentary structure built up by algae or bacteria. Cf. *oncolite* s.v. *ONCO-.

1930 PEACH & HOME *Chapters on Geol. Scotl.* vi. 214 The structures referred to above as resembling the *Stromatolites* of Kallowsky [*sic*] are considered to be of the nature of a chemical deposit brought about by the action of organisms such as algae. **1957** *Prof. Papers U.S. Geol. Surv.* No. 294-D. 129/1 The present study discriminates between fossil algae and stromatolites. **1969** DUNBAR & WAAGE *Hist. Geol.* (ed. 3) viii. 182/2 Since these deposits preserve only the gross form of the colony, the algae cannot be identified biologically and the deposits are simply called stromatolites. **1979** D. ATTENBOROUGH *Life on Earth* i. 22 The blue-green pillars of Hamelin Pool are living stromatolites.

Hence **stromatoli·tic** *a.,* of the nature of or pertaining to stromatolites.

1933 *Trans. Geol. Soc. S. Afr.* XXXV. 35 The main interest of the rocks is centred in the abundance amongst them of stromatolitic limestones. **1955** *Jrnl. Paleont.* XXIX. 723/2 (*heading*) Recent stromatolitic sediments from south Florida. **1978** *Sci. Amer.* Sept. 86/3 Microfossils have been identified in some 45 stromatolitic deposits.

stromatolith (strōu·mătoliþ). *Geol.* [f. mod.L. *stromat-* STROMA + -LITH.] **† a.** A laminated rock structure with a complex interleaving of igneous and sedimentary components. *Obs.* **b.** [a. G. *stromatolith* (E. Kalkowsky 1908, in *Zeitschr. der Deutsch. geol. Ges.* LX. 68).] = *STROMATOLITE.

1916 W. G. FOYE in *Jrnl. Geol.* XXIV. 791 The noun 'Stromatolith' may be defined as a rock mass consisting of many alternating layers of igneous and sedimentary rocks in sill relationship. **1918** *Jrnl. Geol.* XXVI. 608 The stromatoliths are the sedimentary equivalent of the calcareous and siliceous 'sinter' of the hot springs. **1933** *Q. Jrnl. Geol. Soc.* LXXXIX. 415 These bodies—stromatoliths—are composed of chlorite or chlorite with zones of a brown or green-brown isotropic mineral. **1963** D. W. & E. E. HUMPHRIES tr. *Termier's Erosion & Sedimentation* xi. 223 The Cyanophyceae can give rise to carbonaceous substances (bogheads) in the form of 'water-blooms' and can also precipitate calcareous 'biscuits', stromatoliths and calcareous muds.

Hence **stromatoli·thic** *a.,* of the nature of or pertaining to a stromatolith.

1916 W. G. FOYE in *Jrnl. Geol.* XXIV. 791 The term batholithic' does not describe the true character of these areas and the term 'stromatolithic' is suggested in its place. **1936** *Geogr. Jrnl.* LXXXVII. 534, I recognized..a palaeozoic series which extends from the stromatolithic Cambrian to a lower carboniferous formation. **1963** D. W. & E. E. HUMPHRIES tr. *Termier's Erosion & Sedimentation* xvii. 343 The stromatolithic limestones of the Precambrian.

Strombolian, *a.* Add: Also **strombolian.** Applied to (the stage of) a volcanic eruption in which there are repeated or continuous explosions of moderate force with the ejection of gases and bombs of lava. (Earlier and later examples.)

1897 I. C. RUSSELL *Volcanoes N. Amer.* i. 9 These two volcanoes belong to the explosive type,..but illustrate two quite well marked phases of that type, which..are termed the Strombolian stage and the Vesuvian stage,—the former characterized by long-continued but mild activity, the second by periods of rest broken by explosions of extreme violence. **1974** *Nature* 2 Aug. 385/1 Between these eruptions, activity on the volcano had been restricted to strombolian explosions and the extrusion of lava at the bottom of..the summit crater. **1976** P. FRANCIS *Volcanoes* iii. 108 Strombolian activity..is a bit noisier than Hawaiian, but it's still not particularly dangerous.

strong, *a.* **1. a.** Delete note and add: *strong man*: see as main entry below. Also *strong woman,* a designation for a woman who publicly exhibits feats of strength, as in a circus.

[**1936** J. S. CLARKE *Circus Parade* v. 46 Sandwina..was, until recently, the strongest woman in the world.] **1952** R. MANNING-SANDERS *Eng. Circus* xx. 284 Coming now to the *strong man* act, let us say at once that 'strong' men and 'strong' women, *are* strong men and women. **1953** K. TENNANT *Joyful Condemned* xx. 193 Stretched on the sofa lay Rene McGarty..looking like something between a lady wrestler and a circus strong woman. **1975** *Listener* 28 Aug. 275/3 Mildly humiliating experiences, such as being..manhandled by a circus strongwoman.

f. *strong silent* (*type,* etc.): see *SILENT *a.* 1 a.

6. b. (Earlier examples.)

1840 J. S. MILL in *Westm. Rev.* XXXIII. 260 The strong points of each [*sc.* Bentham and Coleridge] correspond to the weak points of the other. *c* **1869** TAYLOR & DUBOURG *New Men & Old Acres* I. 22 Perhaps you didn't know Bunter was such a way... Humour is his strong point.

9. d. Also *fig.* in phr. *strong meat* (alluding to Heb. v. 12: see quot. 1526 in Dict.), applied to something acceptable only to strong or instructed minds.

1837 [see MEAT *sb.* 1 b]. **1909** H. G. WELLS *Tono-Bungay* I. i. 26 Gulliver was there unexpurgated, strong meat for a boy perhaps. **1965** *Listener* 21 Oct. 640/2 *Nineteen Eighty-Four* was prefaced by a warning that it was not for nervous listeners. There was no such warning before Shirley Jenkins's *The Child*... Yet this too was.. strong meat, dealing..with the thought stream of a woman on the point of giving birth.

10. d. Of a field of force.

1903 J. J. THOMSON *Conduction of Electricity through Gases* ii. 21 If we..apply a strong electric field between the plates. **1930** PAULING & GOUDSMIT *Structure of Line Spectra* ix. 159 The resultant magnetic moment of the atom in a very strong field, such that the spins and orbital moments of the individual electrons are quantized relative to the field. **1978** PASACHOFF & KUTNER *University Astron.* xxvii. 699 A related prediction of general relativity is that 'clocks' run slower in a stronger gravity field than they do in a weaker.

e. *Physics.* Applied to the strongest of the four known kinds of force between particles, which acts between nucleons and other hadrons when closer than about 10^{-13} cm. (so that protons in an atomic nucleus remain bound together despite the repulsive force due to their electric charge), and which conserves strangeness, parity, and isospin.

1947 *Nature* 4 Oct. 453/2 We refer to any particle with a mass intermediate between that of a proton and an electron as a meson... In using this term, we do not imply that the corresponding particle necessarily has a strong interaction with nucleons. **1953** *Physical Rev.* XCII. 833/2 Let us suppose that both..have interactions of three kinds: (i) Interactions that rigorously conserve isotopic spin. (We assume these to be strong.) (ii) Electromagnetic interactions...(iii) Other charge-dependent reactions, which we take to be very weak. **1954** *Progress Theoret. Physics* XII. 107/2 Contrary to the case of electric charge, *v*-charge is defined only for such particles that have strong nuclear interactions and its conservation is violated by the weak interactions responsible for decays. **1973** *Sci. Amer.* Aug. 34/2 All the particles discovered to date participate in strong interactions except the photon and the four weakly interacting leptons. **1975** *Nature* 5 June 453/1 The electromagnetic interaction is responsible for the force between charged particles, its strength is 1/137 that of the strong force. **1978** PASACHOFF & KUTNER *University Astron.* ix. 261 For nuclear fusion to begin, atomic nuclei must get close enough to each other so that the nuclear force, technically called the strong force, can play its part.

12. b. Restrict † Obs. to sense in Dict. and add: Also in more recent Canad. use, *strong wood(s)* [tr. Canad. Fr. *bois fort(s)*], a region of thick afforestation. Freq. *attrib.* (see also quot. 1921).

1794 D. M'GILLIVRAY 12 Oct. *Jrnl.* (1929) 34 Soon after their departure 2 tribes of Assinoboines arrived..called Strong Wood & ..Grand River Assiniboine [*sic*]. **1800** A. HENRY *Jrnl.* 5 Sept. in E. Coues *New Light Early Hist. Greater Northwest* (1897) I. iii. 83 We had a quarter of a mile of strong wood to pass through. **1861** *Canad. Naturalist* Dec. 438 The Strong-wood Reindeer inhabit the thickly wooded parts of the District. **1921** A. HEMING *Drama of Forests* 15 The several zones of the Canadian wilderness are locally known as the Coast Country—the shores of the Arctic Ocean and Hudson Bay; the Barren Grounds—the treeless country between Hudson Bay and the Mackenzie River; the Strong Woods Country—the whole of that enormous belt of heavy timber that spans Canada from east to west; the Border Lands—the tracts of small, scattered timber that lie between the prairies and the northern forests; the Prairie Country; the Mountains; and the Big Lakes. **1969** E. W. MORSE *Fur Trade Canoe Routes* II. iv. 45 The North Saskatchewan formed roughly the boundary of the 'strong woods' region where the furs were harvested.

14. d. (Earlier *fig.* example.)
1745 YOUNG *Night-Thoughts* VIII. 15 Men, who think nought so strong of the romance, So rank Knight-errant, as a Real Friend.

19. c. *Math.* Of a mathematical entity or concept: implying more than others of its kind; defined by more conditions.
1950 W. FELLER *Introd. Probability Theory* I. viii. 156 We shall prove a much stronger statement. **1955** M. LOÈVE *Probability Theory* 18 Now we can..use the supplementary requirement that the additive property of P remains valid for denumerable sums... This is the celebrated Borel strong law of large numbers. **1964** A. P. & W. ROBERTSON *Topological Vector Spaces* iii. 47 This topology is denoted by $\beta(E',E)$ and is sometimes called the strong topology on E'. **1971** G. GLAUBERMAN in Powell & Higman *Finite Simple Groups* i. 44 Here the condition of p-stability is too strong to be useful. **1979** *Proc. London Math. Soc.* XXXVIII. 338 We say that a linear operator L on $\mathcal{A}$ is a strong Feller operator if $Lf \in \mathcal{C}$ whenever $f \in \mathcal{M}_k$.

22. b. (Earlier example.) Occas. *transf.* with reference to non-Teutonic languages.
1833 *Philol. Museum* II. 385 No *weak* verb ever in process of time became *strong*, while strong verbs do become weak. **1946** BINCHY & BERGIN tr. *Thurneysen's Gram. Old Irish* 335 According to the way in which these stems are formed, two main classes of verbs can be distinguished, for which the terms 'strong' and 'weak' verbs are borrowed from the grammar of the Germanic languages. Strong verbs are without exception primary... Weak verbs are for the most part denominative. **1962** C. WATKINS *Indo-European Origins of Celtic Verb* II. 116 In the strong (non-derivative) verb..the present still exhibits numerous divergent formations.

24. b. Hence *fig.*, as (one's) *strong suit*: something at which one excels. Also *strong card*, a particular advantage or forte. *colloq.*
1865 'MARK TWAIN' *Sketches New & Old* (1875) 33 Jumping on a dead level was his strong suit. **1884, 1898** [see SUIT *sb.* 20 a]. **1899** ADE *Fables in Slang* 138 Marie was a Strong Card. The Male Patrons of the Establishment hovered around the Desk long after paying their Checks. Within a Month the Receipts of the Place had doubled. **1936** E. M. FORSTER *Abinger Harvest* I. 16 As my husband points out, that is one of our strong cards. **1940** G. FRANKAU *Self-Portrait* lxiii. 388 Adaptability has always been one of my strong suits. **1970** R. LOWELL *Notebook* 140 Dating children with trash was your strong suit.

25. *strong-armed* (example), *-blooded, -bodied* (later examples), *-charactered, -elbowed* (later example), *-gutted, -jawed, -membered, -muscled, -thewed.*
1785 Strong-bodied [see *BAAS]. **1850** J. G. WHITTIER *Elliott* in *National Era* 10 Jan. 6/4 Strong-armed as Thor! **1907** *Munsey's Mag.* Dec. 309/1 The *piccola* looked up at the dark..strong-jawed face. **1922** JOYCE *Ulysses* 525 He wrote pencilled messages offering his nuptial partner to all strongmembered males. **1922** D. H. LAWRENCE *England, my England* (1924) 82 He looked so strong-blooded and healthy. **1926** —— *Plumed Serpent* vii. 130 White men sitting there would have been strong-muscled and frank. *a* **1930** —— *Etruscan Places* (1932) iii. 74 This sense of vigorous, strong-bodied liveliness is characteristic of the Etruscans. **1930** S. SPENDER *Twenty Poems* 3 Weapons men use, stone, sling, and strong-thewed bow He will not know. **1931** R. GRAVES *To Whom Else?* 11 With their strong-gutted and capacious bellies Digested stones and glass like ostriches. **1944** BLUNDEN *Shells by Stream* 31 Strong-elbowed and with wondrous beard, Whose statue's this? **1960** C. DAY LEWIS *Buried Day* ii. 44 My father..[had] the expression of an actor playing the part of a strong-charactered, resolute, if moody, man. **1978** W. F. BUCKLEY *Stained Glass* xvii. 169 He was strong-jawed, with a splotchy face that showed the ravages of frostbite.

26. strong-back, (*a*) substitute for def.: any of several plants used in the West Indies to make medicinal infusions; (later examples); (*b*) (later examples); also in extended uses, esp. a beam placed across an access cover to secure it in position; **strong-eyed** *a.* chiefly *N.Z.*, of a sheep-dog: possessed of good powers of controlling sheep; hence **strong eye,** (*N.Z.*, a sheep-dog with) this ability; **strong joint** *U.S. slang* (see quots. 1935, 1938); **strong stress** *Prosody*, accentuation which falls on syllables separated by a varying number of unstressed syllables, characteristic of certain poetic traditions, as Old English alliterative verse.
1927 M. W. BECKWITH *Notes Jamaican Ethnobotany* 28 Strong-back..For a weak back drink a little as tea each day. **1927** G. BRADFORD *Gloss. Sea Terms* 176/2 *Strongback*, a steel (or wood) beam placed across a hatch to support the sections of the hatch covers... A spar lashed to and running between the old style davits to steady them and to aid in controlling and securing the boat. **1953** C. S. FORESTER *Hornblower & Atropos* xvi. 253 The next morning Hornblower watched launch and longboat start off with strongbacks erected in their sterns, and blocks and tackles rigged on them. **1953** *Caribbean Q.* III. 1. 10 There are two or three kinds of strong-back (to make strengthening tea). **1970** M. SLATER *Caribbean Cooking for Pleasure* 21/2 In Jamaica, fish soup is 'Fish Tea' and sometimes called 'Strong Back', but this term is applied to anything nourishing 'make strong back'. **1977** *Austral. Sailing* Jan. 38/3 The strongback on which the mast is stepped is made as a complete trussed girder beam which is placed as a unit inside the shell. **1934** J. LILICO *Sheep Dog Mem.* 4 My father..taught me how to prevent the several faults that the strong-eyed young dog will assuredly acquire if not taken in time. **1949** G. W. C. HARTLEY *Shepherd's Dogs* ii. 3 Excessively strong-eyed dogs. *Ibid.* 5 The pup is from a 'strong-eye' strain. **1952** *Arena* (N.Z.) XXXI. 2 Shepherding the stragglers would be Charlie's strong-eyes, Beau and Belle. **1977** *Field* 13 Jan. 55/2 A dog which can 'will' his sheep into submission requires what shepherds term a strong (or dominant) eye. **1926** MAINES & GRANT *Wise-Crack Dict.* 14/1 *Strong joint*, unfair or cheater's game. **1935** N. ERSINE *Underworld & Prison Slang* 73 *Strong joint*, a crooked gambling house. **1938** F. CHESTER *Shot Full* xi. 98 A 'pick-out'. This is another form of 'strong-joint', or never-win game. **1963** Strong-joint [see *flat joint* s.v. *FLAT *a.* 15]. **1959** *PMLA* LXXIV. 1. 588 The two main alternative principles of English meter..are actually two kinds of stress—strong stress (the Old English, the *Piers Plowman* tradition) and syllable stress (the Chaucer-Tennyson tradition). **1973** *Studies in Eng. Lit.: Eng. Number* (Tokyo) 22 There was no mention of Anglo-Saxon verse as a forerunner of sprung rhythm... There is..little reason to suppose that Hopkins derived his sprung rhythm from strong-stress verse.

strong, *adv.* Add: **1. c.** *to come out strong* (earlier example); *to come on strong* (orig. U.S.), to adopt or exhibit aggressive behaviour; to perform or contest successfully.
1860 *Players* I. 147 Many a fair lady must have lost her heart when she saw Mr. J. M. on his twentieth birthday, when he came out 'strong' at a fancy dress ball. **1970** H. E. ROBERTS *Third Ear* 5/2 *Come on strong*, to do something to a superlative degree, to an extreme; to 'pour it on'. **1976** *Honolulu Star-Bull.* 21 Dec. E-1/5 Young guys who've never had experience come on too strong and that's how a fight with a host starts. **1979** *Tucson* (Arizona) *Citizen* 28 Apr. B. 1/1 The Kings came on strong at the onset of the third period, outscoring the Suns, 15–6.

strong, *v.* Restrict † *Obs.* to sense a and add: **b.** (Later examples.) Also, to cause (one) to smell strong. Now only *U.S. local.*
1913 H. KEPHART *Our Southern Highlanders* xiii. 283 A verb will be coined from an adverb... Or from an adjective... Baby, that onion 'll strong ye! **1941** E. P. O'DONNELL *Great Big Doorstep* xviii. 250 The coffee gunna strong you soon, darling.
c. *to strong it*, to behave excessively, to exaggerate. *slang.*
1964 *New Statesman* 10 Apr. 555/2 'To strong it' means to overdo something, like taking more than 30 purple hearts in one night. **1970** G. F. NEWMAN *Sir, You Bastard* iii. 108 Don't you think that's stronging it?

strong, *sb. Austral. slang.* [f. the adj.] In phr. *the strong of* (a person or thing) = *the strength of* s.v. *STRENGTH *sb.* 2 e.
1916 A. WRIGHT *Under Cloud* 31 Don't yer want to own up? Some reason for wantin' to preserve yer incog, I suppose. What's th' strong of it? **1938** X. HERBERT *Capricornia* 566 What's the strong of you? What's the questioning for? I've done nuthin'. **1959** E. LAMBERT *Glory thrown In* 161 'What's the strong of this joint?' demanded Doc brusquely. 'Not an undertaker's is it?'

strong arm, *sb.* (and *a.*) orig. *U.S.* **A.** *sb.* Used *transf.* and *fig.* with reference to power: see sense 1 b of the adj. Cf. LONG *a.* 1 c.
2. With *the*: physical force or violence considered as a means of action, *spec.* in the course of robbery. Cf. STRONG HAND.
1836 M. HOLLEY *Texas* xiv. 322 This military council.. distributed lots to the inhabitants, contrary to all law, but that of the *strong arm.* **1903** A. H. LEWIS *Boss* 316 He was all for th' strong-arm, an' th' knock-about! It's a bad system. Nothin's lost by bein' smooth, Gov'nor. **1907** J. LONDON *Road* 169 Into the man's back goes his knee; around the man's neck..passes his right hand, the bone of the wrist pressing against the jugular vein. Barber Kid throws his whole weight backward... It is the strong arm. **1948** *Daily Express* 2 Oct. 1/5 Modern youngsters..get panicky and use the strong arm.
3. A criminal who resorts to violence; one who is employed or hired to use force against persons.
1907 J. LONDON *Road* 159 A world of rods and gunnels, blind baggages and 'side-door Pullmans'.. 'strong arms' and 'bindle-stiffs'. **1932** 'SPINDRIFT' *Yankee Slang* 60 *Strong arm*, bouncer or 'chucker out' for speakeasies and Honkytonks. **1978** N. J. CRISP *London Deal* ii. 21 He was a strong arm for an ambitious East End team which.. incurred the displeasure of the incumbent mob.
B. *attrib.* or as *adj.* (stress on first syllable). **1.** Of a person: having or showing strength of arm; physically powerful; *spec.* of a criminal: resorting to violence, esp. for hire or in the case of robbery. Freq. in phr. *strong-arm man.*
1897 ELDRIDGE & WATTS *Our Rival, the Rascal* ix. 281 The ordinary robber of to-day is frequently and familiarly styled by his 'pals', a 'strong arm man'. **1904** 'No. 1500' *Life in Sing Sing* 257/2 *Strongarm guy*, highway robber. **1931** *Times* 24 Sept. 11/2 A large force of gunmen and 'strongarm men'..was soon effective in breaking down the resistance of the strikers. **1947** J. MULGAN *Report on Experience* x. 125 It comes down to cases with two strong-arm men who call round and offer a beating-up. **1953** J. PHELAN *Underworld* i. 21 A strong-arm chap is, roughly speaking, a bruiser, one who, for a pound or two, will punch some one on the nose, or start a fight in a pub, or even sometimes assault the police. **1973** D. WESTHEIMER *Going Public* ii. 27 Your strongarm boy won't always be around to save your skin.
2. Of an action: involving the use of physical violence. Also of policies, etc.: characterized by a display of (excessive) force; heavy-handed, oppressive, bullying.
1901 'J. FLYNT' *World of Graft* II. 18, I had been inclined to believe that the 'strong-arm' crimes were committed by men who were transients in the city. **1930** P. MACDONALD *Link* vii. 109 The law was in a pair, and with..a little strong-arm stuff of their own, got the two apart. **1951** E. PAUL *Springtime in Paris* xi. 202 The Communists began strong-arm tactics to discourage the timid from seeing things at night. **1973** WODEHOUSE *Bachelors Anonymous* xii. 160 The strong-arm methods favoured by both counsellors might, of course, be resented, for he had no official knowledge that his love was returned. **1978** S. BRILL *Teamsters* vii. 288 The Vice-President has a record of strong-arm robbery.
Hence **stro·ng-arm** *v. trans.*, to treat roughly or manhandle (a person); to rob with violence, to coerce; to seize (something) by force; also *intr.*, to proceed in an aggressive, bullying manner; **stro·ng-arming** *vbl. sb.*
1903 *Monthly Maroon* (Chicago) June 444 If he refused, Phil..was to strong-arm him while Tommy took away the badge. **1937** E. HEMINGWAY *To have & have Not* III. vii. 130 Don't try to strong arm it away from me. **1941** BAKER *Dict. Austral. Slang* 73 *Strongarm, to*, to act in a bullying fashion. **1948** LAIT & MORTIMER *New York* xi. 114 Mugging..in old Chicago days called 'strong-arming'. **1954** D. DODGE *Lights of Skaro* vi. 215, I strong-armed my way out like a hero. **1965** D. FRANCIS *Odds Against* xiii. 179 He was strong-arming Brinton. **1969** *Daily Colonist* (Victoria, B.C.) 27 Feb. 35/1 A new trial was ordered by the B.C. Court of Appeals for a man jailed..in connection with a Prince George strongarming. **1977** *Observer* (Colour Suppl.) 5 June 42/3 The OAS had financed themselves initially by strong-arming contributions from rich settlers, who usually shared their sympathies.

strongers (strǫ·ŋəɹz). *slang.* [f. STRONG *a.* + *-ER[6].] **1.** = *SOOGEE-MOOGEE a. *Naut.*
1929 F. BOWEN *Sea Slang* 135 *Strongers*, any strong cleaning preparation such as spirits of salt. **1961** F. H. BURGESS *Dict. Sailing* 202 *Strongers*, a compound cleaning mixture, caustic, etc., made up for use; also spirits of salts, acids, etc., undiluted.
2. = STRONG DRINK. *slang. rare.*
1939 JOYCE *Finnegans Wake* 58 Swiping rums and beaunes and sherries and ciders and negus and citronnades too. The strongers.

stro·ng-ha·nded, *a. rare.* [f. STRONG HAND + -ED[2].] † **1.** = STRONG *a.* 5 e. *Obs.*
1818 H. B. FEARON *Sk. Amer.* 224 The wealthy or 'strong-handed' farmer..owns five to twelve hundred acres.
2. Of a ship: well-manned. Also by synecdoche, of a ship's captain: in charge of a well-manned ship.
1827 J. F. COOPER *Red Rover* I. ii. 45 It is plain enough, by the manner in which his [a captain's] sails are furled, that he is strong-handed. **1844** —— *Afloat & Ashore* I. v. 129 He took us on board purely out of a national feeling, for his ship was strong-handed without us.
3. Forceful, imperious.
1949 I. DEUTSCHER *Stalin* vi. 178 Stalin..secured a more impressive abode for his Commissariat through a strong-handed intervention in a somewhat comic scramble between the commissars for accommodation.

strongly, *adv.* Add: **1. i.** *Physics.* By means of the strong interaction (see *STRONG *a.* 10 e).
1960 P. ROMAN *Theory Elementary Particles* v. 460 The K^-, but not the K^+, can react strongly with nuclear matter. **1977** *Sci. Amer.* Oct. 58/2 A strongly decaying hadron exists for only 10^{-23} second before it breaks up into less massive hadrons.
2. b. (Examples in *Math.*: cf. *STRONG *a.* 19 e.)
1955 M. LOÈVE *Probability Theory* ix. 442 Since..T is bounded and linear, every B_λ is..a strongly closed linear subspace of B. **1966** E. H. SPANIER *Algebraic Topology* ix. 510 Let X be a strongly simple space. **1979** *Proc. London Math. Soc.* XXXVIII. 507, K is said to be a spectral compact convex set if A and V are in spectral duality, and K is said to be strongly spectral if in addition [etc.].

strong man. **1.** A man of great physical strength; *spec.*, one who displays his strength professionally, as in a circus.
1699, etc. [see STRONG *a.* 1]. **1841** THACKERAY *Loose Sk.* ii, in *Britannia* 15 May 315/3 A vast number of booths and exhibitions..no less than four companies of strongmen..'the Indian strong men'; 'the strong men with the fairy pony', &c. **1872** BROWNING *Fifine at Fair* 23 The Strong Man, whom..by-and-by You shall behold do feats. **1908** *Variety* 16 May 15 Blocksom and Burns, the 'strong' men,..have bookings at hand which, if accepted, will keep them busily playing in the west all summer. **1954** [see *beefcake* s.v. *BEEF *sb.* 5]. **1977** C. WOOD *James Bond* xii. 99 He was..the product of a union between the strong man of a travelling circus and the Chief Wardress at the Women's Prison.
2. A dominating man; the man who exercises effective control of an organization; *spec.*, one who exercises absolute political power.
1859 MILL *Liberty* iii. 119, I am not countenancing the sort of 'hero-worship' which applauds the strong man of genius for forcibly seizing on the government of the world

and making it do his bidding in spite of itself. **1879** [see STRONG *a.* 3 d]. **1886** KIPLING *Plain Tales from Hills* (1888) 89 He called on the biggest and strongest man that the Government owned, and explained that he wanted an appointment at Simla on a good salary. The compound insolence of this amused the Strong Man. **1924** A. D. SEDGWICK *Little French Girl* II. ix. 165 They were both agreed on the necessity of a strong man for France and on many lopped heads. **1943** E. A. PEERS *Spain in Eclipse* I. ii. 39 The erstwhile 'strong man', President Azaña, emerged out of his silence. **1961** P. KEMP *Alms for Oblivion* ii. 29 Pluto had been nominated Minister Without Portfolio; Marshal Phibul, the 'Strong Man' of the country,..was under arrest. **1969** D. ACHESON *Present at Creation* (1970) xxi. 187 Colonel Juan Perón, the President and 'strong man' of Argentina. **1977** *Westindian World* 3–9 June 12/1 The other is Major General Ziaur Rahman, who became President of Bangladesh only a few weeks ago (though he had been the country's strongman for some time).

3. *attrib.*

1962 C. WALSH *From Utopia to Nightmare* ix. 122 A strong-man government. **1977** *Times* 12 July 14/3 Strongman rule has provided the region with comparative stability..and, in the case of South Korea and Singapore, phenomenal economic growth.

strong-minded, *a.* Add: **b.** (Earlier example.)

1843 DICKENS *Mart. Chuz.* (1844) iv. 42 Then there was the widow of a deceased brother.., who being almost supernaturally disagreeable, and having a dreary face and a bony figure and a masculine voice, was..what is commonly called a strong-minded woman.

strong-mindedness (earlier example.)

1849 C. BRONTË *Shirley* II. xii. 294 With all her strictness, with all her 'strongmindedness', she could gain no command over them.

strong point. **1.** *one's strong point*: see STRONG *a.* 6 b.

2. *Mil.* [tr. G. *feste stellung*: see STRONG *a.* 8 and POINT *sb.*[1] A. 19.] A specially fortified position in a defence system. Also *transf.* and *fig.*

1915 E. DANE *Battles in Flanders* x. 183 An orchard, triangular in shape and bounded along each face by a road, which the Germans had fortified. This, one of the strong points of the German second line, the Devons carried by storm. **1931** *Times Lit. Suppl.* 30 Apr. 350/3 Billets, water-supply, roads, wiring, strongpoints, fighting. **1946** D. L. SAYERS *Unpopular Opinions* 100 Nobody was quite ready to coerce Britain into giving away her colonies, dependencies, and scattered strong-points. **1957** *Times* 16 Feb. 7/5 Its simple existence is a strong-point in the struggle to maintain our standards against the spread of the 'new illiteracy'. **1978** L. HEREN *Growing up on The Times* iii. 66 The Jewish Agency..had been determined to establish as many Jewish strongpoints as possible in an effort to extend its territorial claims. **1980** *Sci. Amer.* Mar. 56/1 Preserved under the city is a record of its development since the year of its founding in A.D. 71 as a strongpoint for the Roman Ninth Legion.

3. *R.A.F.* (See quots.)

1946 D. HAMSON *We fell among Greeks* i. 18 The strong-point is normally a powerful bolt and shackle fitted into the framework of the aircraft at the point of exit of the parachutist. To it are attached the static-lines from each man's parachute. **1951** *Gloss. Aeronaut. Terms* (*B.S.I.*) III. 15 *Strong point*, a fitting in an aircraft which is capable of transmitting a shock load and to which the static line or strop is attached. **1958** P. KEMP *No Colours or Crest* iii. 40 The sergeant clipped the static lines of our parachutes to the 'strong-point', a stout wire running along the fuselage beneath the roof.

Strongyloides (strǫndʒiloi·dīz). *Med.* and *Vet. Sci.* Also **strongyl-**. [mod.L. (B. Grassi 1879, in *Rendiconti R. Ist. Lombardo di Sci. e Lett.* XII. 233), f. *Strongyl-us* (see STRONGYLE[1]) + *-oides* (see -OID).] Nematode worms of the genus of the same name; also, = *STRONGYLOIDIASIS.

1911 *Jrnl. Exper. Med.* XIV. 6 Most of the patients were admitted for malaria, so that the strongyloides were incidentally found as a result of the routine stool examinations. **1929** A. S. CHANDLER *Hookworm Dis.* vii. 287 Sandground himself, as the result of a light and brief *Strongyloides* infestation, apparently remained immune for at least 14 months. **1958** *Jrnl. Amer. Med. Assoc.* 22 Nov. 1651/2 Careful examination of serial sections of large intestine..failed to reveal any Strongyloides in this tissue. **1974** PASSMORE & ROBSON *Compan. Med. Stud.* III. xii. 56/1 In many British soldiers who acquired the infection when prisoners of war in the Far East, strongyloides has persisted for more than 25 years.

strongyloidiasis (strǫːndʒiloidəi·ăsis). *Med.* and *Vet. Sci.* [f. *STRONGYLOID(ES + *-IASIS.] Infection with or a disease caused by nematode worms of the genus *Strongyloides* (family Rhabditidæ), esp. *S. stercoralis*, a threadworm infesting the human and the canine gut in tropical and subtropical regions, causing diarrhœa.

1930 E. C. FAUST *Human Helminthol.* xxxiii. 538 (*heading*) Strongyloidiasis. **1935** *Arch Path.* XIX. 782 In certain cases in which strongyloidiasis had been active for several months the presence of filariform, postfilariform and preadolescent worms in the respiratory passages suggested hyperinfection. **1977** *Lancet* 28 May 1121/2, 1 patient with strongyloidiasis had an increased total number of IgG-labelled cells in the lamina propria.

strongyloidosis (strǫːndʒiloidōᵘ·sis). *Med.* and *Vet. Sci.* [f. as prec. + -OSIS.] = prec.

1911 *Jrnl. Exper. Med.* XIV. 7 Of 54 cases of strongyloidosis..none had been subject to diarrhea. **1957** SMITH & JONES *Vet. Path.* xiii. 494 It is generally believed that severe and fatal strongyloidosis is likely to occur only in man or animals debilitated from faulty nutrition or other factors. **1969** J. R. GEORGI *Parasitol. for Veterinarians* viii. 134 Canine strongyloidosis has been much feared in the past and demands respect in the future as a menace to human health. **1980** *Acta Parasitol. Polonica* XXVII. 89 Anatomical and pathological changes in animals that have died of the strongyloidosis consist mostly of changes in the respiratory and alimentary systems.

strongylosis (strǫndʒilōᵘ·sis). *Vet. Sci.* and *Med.* [f. mod.L. *Strongyl-us* (see STRONGYLE[1]) + -OSIS.] Infection with or a disease caused by nematode worms (strongyles) of the genus *Strongylus* or the family Strongylidae containing it, which are parasites of many domestic animals.

1892 O. FLEMING tr. *Neumann's Treat. Parasites* IV. ii. 580 (*heading*) Bronchial and pulmonary strongyloses. **1928** *Daily Tel.* 7 Aug. 9/4 Strongylosis, or grouse disease, is an infection produced by parasitic worms in the intestines, which are found to be present in almost all grouse. **1969** J. R. GEORGI *Parasitol. for Veterinarians* ix. 164 Although *Nematodirus* spp. infections are ordinarily not associated with clinical disease, serious outbreaks have been attributed to *N. battus*. This strongylosis is characterized by..very severe and debilitating diarrhea. **1981** *Equine Vet. Jrnl.* XIII. 35 (*heading*) Ischaemic myocardial fibrosis and aortic strongylosis in the horse.

strontian (strǫ·ntiăn), *a.* *Min.* [f. STRONT(IUM + *-IAN 2.] Of a mineral: having a (small) proportion of a constituent element replaced by strontium.

1930 W. T. SCHALLER in *Amer. Mineralogist* XV. 573 Strontium—strontian. **1959** [see *ELLESTADITE].

strontium. Add: Now usu. with pronunc. (strǫ·ntiəm). *strontium* 90, a radioactive isotope of strontium which is one of the chief products of the fission of uranium 235, can pass from fall-out into plants and animals and hence into human tissue (where it is concentrated in bones and teeth), and has been used in radiotherapy.

1955 *Sci. News Let.* 28 May 345/1 Strontium 90 is of particular interest because, being chemically similar to calcium, it may be deposited in human bone. **1961** *Lancet* 12 Aug. 366/1 Measurements of strontium 90 in human bone in the United Kingdom. **1978** *Jrnl. R. Soc. Arts* CXXVI. 257/1 Two fission products, Strontium 90 and Caesium 137 have particularly awkward half-lives of about 30 years.

strool (strul). *Sc.* Also **strule**. [? ad. Sc. Gaelic **sruil* stream (*srùlach* abounding in streams).] A stream (of water or other liquid). Also *fig.*

1867 G. W. DONALD *Poems* 17 The water comes doon in perfect strools upon's. **1920** D. H. EDWARDS *Men & Manners* 236 There's juist a dreeble o' a strule at the burn spoot. **1922** JOYCE *Ulysses* 756 Sending me that long strool of a song out of the Huguenots to sing in French.

'strooth, var. 'STREWTH in Dict. and Suppl.

strop, *v.*[1] Add: **1.** Also *transf.* and *fig.*

1841 [in Dict.]. **1944** 'PALINURUS' *Unquiet Grave* III. 72 The parrot stropping its beak on the bars of the cage. **1957** C. DAY LEWIS *Pegasus* 25 The river endlessly stropping its tides against the embankment. **1974** 'J. HERRIOT' *Vet in Harness* vii. 51 'I think a beef sandwich would go down rather nicely, Jim,' he murmured, as he stropped his carving knife on a steel.

strophanthidin (strofæ·nþidin). *Pharm.* [f. next + *-IDIN.] A poisonous steroidal aglycone, $C_{23}H_{32}O_6$, which is prepared by hydrolysis of strophanthin-K and is a stimulant of heart muscle.

1888 T. R. FRASER in *Proc. R. Soc. Edin.* XIV. 373 All mineral acids..resolve strophanthin, even in the cold, into glucose and a substance which I have named strophanthidin. **1962** H. L. KERN et al. in A. Pirie *Lens Metabolism Rel. Cataract* 394 The aglycone, strophanthidin, abolished the active transport of sugars..by intestine of hamsters. **1978** *Nature* 1 June 389/1 The aglycone strophanthidin was preferred to cardiac glycosides such as ouabain because its effects are more readily reversible.

strophanthin (strofæ·nþin). *Pharm.* [f. STROPHANTH(US + -IN[1].] Any or all of several polycyclic glucosides obtained from certain varieties of plants of the genera *Strophanthus* and *Acokanthera* and used as cardioactive drugs; *G-* or *g-strophanthin* (also *strophanthin-G, -g*) [L. *g(rātus* agreeable], the primary active component, $C_{29}H_{44}O_{12}$, of the mixture obtained from *S. gratus*, *A. schimperi*, or *A. ouabaio*; also called *ouabane*; *H-*, *h-strophanthin*, etc., [L. *h(ispidus* hairy], a mixture of the glucosides obtained from the seeds of *S. hispidus*; *K-*, *k-strophanthin*, etc., [*K(OMBÉ], $C_{36}H_{54}O_{14}$, the principle extract from *S. kombe*, also called *KOMBÉ.

1873 *Pharm. Jrnl.* III. 524/2 From this extract [of seeds of *Strophanthus Hispidus*, D.C.] Dr. Fraser succeeded in separating a very powerful active principle, which he proposes should be named strophanthin. **1927** *Blackw. Mag.* May 582/1 Strophanthin, its [*sc.* strophanthus'] laboratory derivative is a drug commonly used by the medical profession. **1940** *Elsevier's Encycl. Org. Chem.* Ser. III. XIV. 270, h-Strophanthin is a mixt. of glycosides from the seeds of Strophanthus hispidus. **1960** J. J. LEWIS *Introd. Pharmacol.* xii. 356 Ouabain (G-strophanthin) is a crystalline glycoside obtained from *S. gratus*. **1962** H. L. KERN et al. in A. Pirie *Lens Metabolism Rel. Cataract* 389 The cardiac glycosides, gitalin and strophanthin K, produced effects [on the transport of potassium and anaerobic glycolysis in calf lens] comparable to ouabain. **1978** *Acta Physiol. Acad. Sci. Hungaricae* LI. 166 The therapeutic and toxic effects of strophanthin and digoxin on the heart were studied in the 6–7-week old human embryo.

stroppy (strǫ·pi), *a.* *colloq.* [? abbrev. of OBSTREPEROUS *a.* with altered stem-vowel.] Bad-tempered, rebellious, awkward, obstreperous, unruly. Hence **stro·ppiness.**

1951 H. HASTINGS *Seagulls over Sorrento* II. i, in *Plays of Year 1950* IV. 76 There ain't nothing clever about answering him back and being stroppy. **1964** J. BURKE *Hard Day's Night* iv. 80 'Have you got a licence for it?' 'Oh, don't be so stroppy.' **1968** [see *SHIT *sb.* 1 g]. **1969** *New Statesman* 31 Oct. 633/3 It anyhow seems to me (perhaps out of stroppiness) that the good toys aren't all necessarily the ones that teach how to count or measure. **1973** J. WAINWRIGHT *Devil you Don't* 116 All that balls about 'with respect'...Honesty. Stroppiness. **1977** *Guardian Weekly* 27 Feb. 5/4 Those who didn't know him well..missed the stroppy radicalism of his spirit. **1983** *Listener* 14 Apr. 37/1 Susan, on the other hand, is street-wise and stroppy.

stroud. Add: **1.** (Later U.S. examples.)

1846 T. L. MCKENNEY *Mem.* I. i. 21 It was not so much a competition in blankets, and strouds, and calicoes..as in whiskey. **1872** *Rep. Indian Affairs 1871* (U.S.) 459 Blankets, leggings, strouds, paints.

3. (Later examples.)

1751 G. CROGHAN in *Pennyslvania Colonial Rec.* (1851) V. 531, I gave him a Strowd Shirt, Match Coat [etc.]. **1934** P. H. GODSELL *Arctic Trader* 39 A dozen other drivers, all clad in..blue stroud leggings and fur caps.

Strouhal (strau·ăl, strū̆·ăl, ‖ strōᵘ·hal) *Mech.* [The name of Čeněk (or Vincent) *Strouhal* (1850–1922), Czech scientist.] *Strouhal number*: a dimensionless number used in the study of the vibrations produced in a body by a fluid flowing past it, defined as $\nu d/v$ (or $v/\nu d$) where v is the fluid velocity, ν the frequency of the vibration, and d the effective diameter of the body.

1949 *Proc. R. Soc.* A. CXCVIII. 175 The results are expressed in the form of Strouhal number: $S(R)=fd/U_0$, where $R=U_0d/\nu$. **1975** *Offshore Engineer* Dec. 42/3 For an isolated stationary cylinder the Strouhal number is fairly constant for a wide range of Reynolds numbers.

strouter (strau·təɹ). *Newfoundland.* [Perh. f. dial. form of STRUT *sb.*[2]: cf. also STOUTER.] A heavy post used to support and strengthen the end of a fishing stage or wharf; = STOUTER.

1895 *Jrnl. Amer. Folklore* VIII. 31 *Strouters*, the outside piles of a wharf, which are larger and stronger than the inner ones. **1937** P. K. DEVINE *Folk Lore Newfoundland* 50 *Strouters*, the perpendicular posts at the front end of a fishing stage, jammed firmly into the sea bottom, and having rails nailed across to make the ladder for getting into and out of boats. **1973** *Even. Telegram* (St. John's, Newfoundland) 25 Oct. 3 You could hear a tin can bonking against the strouters or the rocks down there in the landwash. **1975** V. BUTLER *Little Nord Easter* 61 For the shores [of a wharf] there'd be strouters. They'd be called strouters and they'd be a little larger, probably seven or eight inches in diameter. **1975** *Canad. Antiques Collector* Mar.–Apr. 23/1 In the fishery we have such terms as:.. strouters (perpendicular posts which support the front of a fishing-stage).

Strowger (strau·gəɹ). *Teleph.* The name of Almon B. *Strowger*, U.S. telephone engineer, used *attrib.* with reference to an exchange switching system proposed by him in 1891 (U.S. Patent 447,918), involving successive step-by-step switches.

1900 K. B. MILLER *Amer. Telephone Pract.* (ed. 3) xxxiv. 459 The most important idea..in all of the Strowger automatic work, was that of simplifying the contacts for the different line wires. **1901** J. E. HOMANS *ABC of Telephone* xx. 268 A Strowger exchange in Atlanta, Ga., has as many as 500 subscribers. **1933** K. B. MILLER *Telephone Theory & Pract.: Automatic Switching* iii. 22 Of the three general types of automatic or machine-switching systems, 'step-by-step', 'power-driven', and 'all-relay', the former, also called the 'Strowger system', will be treated in this chapter. **1967** *Times Rev. Industry* July 19/1 There are three types of telephone exchange in use; one is the Strowger which has been the standard British equipment ever since we introduced the automatic exchange. **1973** *Nature* 16 Feb. 416/1 The antiquated Strowger step-by-step switching on which Britain's telephones deplorably now depend.

struck, *ppl. a.* Add: **4. b.** *struck-off*: of persons in certain professions, debarred from practising by having one's name deleted from the register of those qualified. Cf. *STRIKE *v.* 13 b, 82.

1963 *Sunday Express* 27 Jan. 23/3 A struck-off doctor—now a dope addict. **1972** E. ROUTLEY *Puritan Pleasures of Detective Story* II. vii. 74 An unexpected meeting with a struck-off solicitor turned private detective. **1976** E. WARD *Hanged Man* xxix. 189 Are *you* really a doctor?.. You sound like a struck-off vet.

7. e. *struck joint* (Building): a joint in which the mortar between two courses of bricks is sloped inwards so as to be flush with the surface of one but below that of the other.

1876 *Notes Building Construction* II. xiii 219 Struck Joints should be formed by pressing back the upper portion of the joint while the mortar is moist, so as to form a sloping surface which throws off the wet. **1948** *Archit. Rev.* CIV. 20 (*caption*) Brick external walls are finished in buff face brick with struck joints. **1978** S. MARTIN *Build your own House* (ed. 7) v. 75 The flush joint and the struck weathered joint are formed with a trowel.

7*. Of, pertaining to, or affected by an industrial strike. Chiefly *U.S.*

1894 S. & B. WEBB *Hist. Trade Unionism* ii. 80 Finding that the yarn was for a 'struck shop'. **1937** *N.Y. Times* 16 June 1/6 The Republic Steel Corporation..asked for a mandamus writ to compel Postmaster General Farley.. to deliver to people in its struck plants 'all matter properly mailable'. **1939** *Sun* (Baltimore) 21 July 2/6, 60,000 butchers in retail shops would refuse to handle 'struck products'. **1947** *Ibid.* 14 Oct. 24/1 The league said it would withdraw its charges.., provided the union would delete its 'closed shop' and 'struck work' clauses. **1962** *Aeroplane* 12 Apr. 16/1 Since 1958 the same eight airlines ..have had a mutual aid agreement whereby a 'struck' company receives from the others any excess revenues attributable to the strike, less additional expenses. **1968** *Globe & Mail* (Toronto) 3 Feb. B5/3 Men and women who make a living by working on struck newspapers. **1977** *Time* 27 June 35/2 Not since World War II, when President Roosevelt threatened to call out the armed forces to reopen struck mines, has the union played such an important role in the nation's well-being.

struck (strʌk), *sb.* [Subst. use of STRUCK *pa. pple.* and *ppl. a.*] A bacterial disease of sheep causing sudden convulsive death after few symptoms; orig. more loosely in *dial.* use.

[**1784**: see STRIKE *v.* 45 d]. **1903** *Jrnl. S.-E. Agric. College* XII. 86 First and most prominent is the disease commonly known as 'struck', or 'struck in the blood'. These terms appear to be somewhat loosely applied to any cases of sudden death in sheep... There is, however, especially in the marsh lands of Kent,..a disease in which few symptoms of a definite character are ever seen, owing to the rapid approach of death, and to which the term 'struck' is intended to be applied. [**1904** *Eng. Dial. Dict.* V. 827/1 Ken[t]. A sheep which dies suddenly of a disease akin to apoplexy is said to die 'struck'.] **1929** *Jrnl. Compar. Path. & Therapeutics* XLIII. 1 The term 'struck' is applied by the farming community [of Romney Marsh] to a rapid and fatal disease where post-mortem examination reveals an acute inflammatory condition in one or more of the following parts of the body: areas of muscular tissue, organs in the abdominal cavity, and organs in the thoracic cavity. **1966** T. DALLING *Internat. Encycl. Vet. Med.* I. 640 The classical type [of *Clostridium perfringens* Type C] was shown to be the cause of 'Struck' (Romney Marsh disease). **1972** *TV Vet Sheep Bk.* lxii. 169/1 All the clostridial diseases—enterotoxaemia, pulpy kidney, lamb dysentery, struck (blackleg),..can and should be prevented by vaccinating the ewe flock.

structural, *a.* Add: **2.** *structural engineering*, the branch of civil engineering concerned with large modern buildings and other structures; so *structural engineer*.

1896 *Engineering Index 1892–5* II. 412 Structural engineering. Courses in —. See Engineering Education. **1912** *Register of Former Students* (Mass. Inst. Technol.) 65 Burleigh, Cha(rle)s R(andall)..structural engineer and chief draughtsman. **1924** *Times Trade & Engin. Suppl.* 29 Nov. 248/2 Structural engineers are irregularly employed. *Ibid.*, Some of the finest structural engineering in the world was done in the Black Country. **1943** A. RAND *Fountainhead* I. i. 15 Of course, no one denies the importance of structural engineering to a future architect. **1977** *Modern Railways* Dec. 488/1 The APT project placed a complex set of inter-related demands on the structural engineer.

4. d. *Chem.* Of or pertaining to the arrangement of atoms in a molecule; *structural formula*, a plane schematic method of representing the structure of a molecule by using punctuation (as $CH_3\cdot CH:CH_2$) or lines (as $CH_3—CH=CH_2$) to indicate the position and nature of the bonds between constituent atoms; *structural isomerism*, a form of isomerism in which molecules having the same constituent atoms may have different structures, the atoms being joined in different sequences; so *structural isomer*.

1872 *Phil. Mag.* XLIII. 241 (*heading*) On the relations between the atomic hypothesis and the condensed symbolic expressions of chemical facts and changes known as dissected (structural) formulæ. **1876** *Ibid.* II. 162 To so-called normal butylic alcohol is generally assigned the structural formula $CH_2(C_3H_7)OH$. **1926** J. READ *Textbk. Org. Chem.* xii. 215 The various kinds of isomerism encountered up to the present point are all included under the general title of structural isomerism. Structural isomers are substances possessing the same molecular formula but different structural formulæ. **1951** I. L. FINAR *Org. Chem.* I. i. 6 It is always desirable to show the arrangement (if known) of the atoms in the molecule, and this is done by means of structural formulæ or bond-diagrams. **1980** C. W. SPANGLER *Org. Chem.* I. i. 17 Such branching produces structural isomers, compounds having identical molecular formulas, but whose carbon backbones are arranged differently in three-dimensional space. *Ibid.* 18 If another atom (or group) is bonded to the carbon system (say, chlorine), positional isomerism as well as structural isomerism becomes possible. *Ibid.* 19 There are many different methods of writing structural formulas for organic molecules.

e. *Biol.* Of a gene: that specifies the amino-acid sequence of a polypeptide.

1959 PARDEE, JACOB, & MONOD in *Jrnl. Molecular Biol.* I. 177 The situation revealed with the present system, namely a genetic 'complex' comprising, besides the 'structural' genes (*z, y*) a repressor-making gene (*i*) whose function is to block or regulate the expression of the neighbouring genes is, so far, unique for enzyme systems. **1966** E. A. CARLSON *Gene* xxiv. 229 The repressor was assumed to be incomplete. Thus the structural genes would be transcribed and their enzymes would synthesize a metabolite. **1976** F. J. AYALA *Molecular Evolution* ii. 12 Substitutions in the DNA nucleotide sequence of a structural gene may result in changes in the amino acid sequence of the polypeptide encoded by the gene, although this is not always the case because of the degeneracy of the genetic code.

5. In the Social Sciences, Psychology, and other disciplines, such as Linguistics, connected with the analysis of social, mental, or linguistic organization. **a.** Of, pertaining to, involving, or resulting from those aspects of a system concerned with the formal laws and relations of its structure, as distinguished from function or phenomenon; also, relating to or connected with the 'deep' structures that are considered to generate 'surface' structures. Cf. *deep structure* s.v. *DEEP *a.* IV. c; *FUNCTIONAL *a.* 2 c.

1884 W. JAMES in *Mind* IX. 19 The contrast is really between two *aspects*, in which all mental facts without exception may be taken; their structural aspect, as being subjective, and their functional aspect, as being cognitions. **1890** O. T. MASON in *Ann. Rep. Smithsonian Inst.* (1891) 527 A complete syllabus of anthropology would include—first, what man is, and second, what man does. What man is may be denominated *structural anthropology*; what man does, *functional anthropology*. **1908** *Philos. Rev.* XVII. 651 The book is a very pronounced example of the structural type of psychology. **1917** *Internat. Jrnl. Amer. Linguistics* I. 177 The existence of phonetic shifts, and the presence of structural similarities are too numerous. **1932** M. FORTES tr. *Petermann's Gestalt Theory* ii. 33 The concept leads to a theory of reactions..which is characterized by Köhler's key-word 'structural reaction'. **1940** C. C. FRIES in *Language* XVI. 199 (*heading*) On the development of the structural use of word-order in modern English. **1944** *Social Res.* XI. 99 A Beethoven symphony where from a part of the whole we could grasp something of the inner structure of the whole itself. The fundamental laws, then, would not be piece-meal laws but structural characteristics of the whole. **1952** C. C. FRIES *Structure of English* iv. 58 One of the basic assumptions of our approach here to the grammatical analysis of sentences is that all the structural signals in English are strictly formal matters that can be described in physical terms of forms, correlations of these forms, and arrangements of order. **1952** A. R. RADCLIFFE-BROWN *Structure & Function in Primitive Society* 11 When we are dealing with a structural system we are concerned with a system of social positions. **1958** *Eng. Jrnl.* XLVII. 479 Structural ambiguity, on the other hand, results from the arrangement of the words, that is, from the structure of the utterance. It is sometimes known as syntactic ambiguity and, in older logic books, as amphiboly. **1962** R. JAKOBSON *Sel. Writings* I. 654 An analysis of the structural laws which underlie language and its evolution necessarily leads us to ascertain a limited set of actually given structural types. **1963** JACOBSON & SCHOEPF tr. *Lévi-Strauss's Structural Anthropology* p. viii, Two papers..are published here for the first time in conjunction with fifteen others that seem to me to elucidate the structural method in anthropology. **1964** H. HARTMANN *Ego Psychol.* xiv. 289 The genetic viewpoint had to be supplemented by a structural approach, though Freud never quite explicitly stated this. **1974** *Howard Jrnl.* XIV. 37 Worsening structural inequalities... (We shall use the term 'structural' to refer to housing, education, employment, income and race.) **1974** I. ROSSI *Unconscious in Culture* 70 The same structural code is at work in mind, society, and physical reality. **1975** G. STEINER *After Babel* ii. 77 Hamann's opening statement..and his..dictum that theories of language and of economics will prove mutually explanatory..set out *in nuce* much of Lévi-Strauss's structural anthropology. **1976** G. S. KLEIN *Psychoanal. Theory* 10 Basic tendencies that are often implied in the 'structural point of view' of contemporary psychoanalysis.

b. Special collocations: *structural analysis*, analysis of a system in terms of its general characteristics or structure; hence *structural analyst*; *structural change* (see quot. 1972); *structural description* = *structural analysis* above; *structural-functional* adj., that takes account of both structure and function; so *structural-functionalism*; *-functionalist* adj. and *sb.*; *structural grammar* (see quot. 1975); *structural integration*, a technique of deep massage developed by Ida P. Rolf (see *ROLF); *structural linguistics*, the study of a language viewed as a system made up of interrelated elements without regard to their historical development (cf. *descriptive linguistics* s.v. *DESCRIPTIVE *a.* 3 b); hence *structural linguist*; *structural linguistic* adj.; *structural psychology*, an approach to the study of consciousness which relies on the introspective analysis of simple experience into elements; *structural semantics*, the study of the sense relations that may be established between words or groups of words; hence *structural semanticist*; *structural-semantic* adj.; *structural unemployment*, unemployment resulting from reorganization in the structure of industry due to technological change, etc., rather than from fluctuations in supply and demand; *structural word* = *empty word* s.v. *EMPTY *a.* and *sb.* C (cf. *grammatical word* s.v. *GRAMMATICAL *a.* 2; *structure word* s.v. *STRUCTURE *sb.* 8).

1898 E. B. TITCHENER in *Philos. Rev.* VII. 465, I believe..that the best hope for psychology lies today in a continuance of structural analysis. **1901** H. OERTEL *Lectures on Study of Lang.* i. 45 We are here concerned with the method only of Humboldt's structural analysis. **1940** *Language* XVI. 216 This is the neglect of the method of structural analysis, i.e. of organized synchronic description. **1974** tr. *Wertheim's Evol. & Revol.* i. 91 Weber's views are more than once mentioned as having paved the way for structural analysis. **1979** F. KERMODE *Genesis of Secrecy* iv. 80 When the structural analysts have done their work, interpretation may take over. **1964** Structural change [see SC s.v. *S 4 a]. **1972** R. A. PALMATIER *Gloss. Eng. Transformational Gram.* 168 *Structural change*.., the generalization of the operation which a particular transformation performs..; the right-hand side of a transformational rule. **1964** Structural description [see SD s.v. *S 4 a]. **1977** *Language* LIII. 15 The *ö* of *hösli* was not affected because, after all, phonetically it didn't meet the structural description of Lowering. **1947** T. PARSONS in Parsons & Henderson tr. *Weber's Theory Social & Econ. Organization* 20 A second type [of conceptual scheme]..may be called a generalized structural-functional system. **1977** J. D. DOUGLAS in Douglas & Johnson *Existential Sociol.* i. 6 The classical structural-functional paradigm of social theory grew out of and progressively diverged from this mechanistic model. **1958** *Listener* 28 Aug. 308/1 The first great proponent of structural-functionalism, Radcliffe Brown, failed to get beyond metaphor and analogy when he sought to explain his method. **1977** *Scott. Jrnl. Sociol.* I. 186 A sense that differs both from American structural-functionalism, in which structure is merely descriptive, and from French structuralism, in which it is 'reductive'. **1976** E. LEACH *Culture & Communication* i. 3 Others..offer structural-functionalist explanations. **1977** *Dædalus* Summer 64 Like many structural-functionalists, he regards as unproblematical the processes by which corporations and other 'surface structures' come into existence. **1949** W. O. BIRK (*title*) Structural grammar for building sentences. **1975** *Language for Life* (Dept. Educ. & Sci.) 594 *Structural grammar*, a grammar intended to explain the working of language in terms of the functions of its components and their relationships to each other without reference to meaning. **1963** *Systematics* I. 66 (*heading*) Structural integration. **1975** *Sat. Rev.* (U.S.) 22 Feb. 15/3 The body reformation methods called structural integration (commonly known as rolfing, after its developer Ida Rolf). **1949** *Archivum Linguisticum* I. 1. 89 The functional interpretations of language given by structural linguists are justified. **1951** *Language* XXVII. 8 We must remember the particular attention which structural linguists in the United States have bestowed upon non-culture languages. **1958** *New Statesman* 6 Sept. 288/3 The new advance guard, the Structural Linguists, round on the New Critics as amiable old pipe-smoking fuddy-duddies. **1954** U. WEINREICH in *Word* X. 389 Structural linguistic theory now needs procedures for constructing systems of a higher level out of the discrete and homogeneous systems that are derived from description. **1962** *New Yorker* 10 Mar. 158/2 For the scientific study of language the Structural Linguistic approach is superior to that of the old grammarians. **1940** *Amer. Speech* XV. 438/2 Harris, Zellig S. Rev. of L. H. Gray, Foundations of Language... Some useful remarks on 'structural' linguistics. **1941** A. W. DE GROOT in *Archives Néerlandaises de Phonétique Expérimentale* XVII. 71 (*title*) Structural linguistics and phonetic law. **1945** *Word* I. 58 With structural linguistics as the chief interest of some workers, area may be expected to play a more central role,—to be, in effect, a specialized point of departure. **1948** *Lingua* I. i. 23 'Structural linguistics' is a method, it is not a science and 'structuralism' is nothing but a collective name for general linguistic and explanatory grammatical examination of certain phenomena. **1959** J. C. CATFORD in Quirk & Smith *Teaching of English* vi. 168 Professor Quirk..is talking about the approach to the scientific study of language which is known as 'structural linguistics'. **1972** D. LODGE *20th Cent. Lit. Crit.* 545 Structural linguistics goes beyond the description of any particular language to pursue the 'deep structures' that are common to all languages. **1898** E. B. TITCHENER in *Philos. Rev.* VII. 449 (*title*) The postulates of a structural psychology. **1933** J. C. FLUGEL *Hundred Yrs. Psychol.* IV. ii. 229 (*heading*) 'Structural' and 'functional' psychology. **1980** J. M. CARROLL (*title*) Toward a structural psychology of cinema. **1973** *Archivum Linguisticum* IV. 67 The structural-semantic category system of Soskin and John (1963). **1977** J. LYONS *Semantics* I. iv. 102 One of the points that Saussure and other structural semanticists have insisted upon is that each language has, not only its own stock of forms, but also its own system of meanings or concepts. **1962** D. H. HYMES in J. A. Fishman *Readings Sociol. of Lang.* (1968) 103 An ethnographic semantics..should be a structural analysis, achieving the economies of the rules of a grammar in relation to a series of analyses of texts. In the past generation Jakobson and his associates have done most to develop such a structural semantics. **1977** J. LYONS *Semantics* ix. 270 From its very beginnings structural semantics..has emphasized the importance of relations of paradigmatic opposition. **1932** A. H. HANSEN *Econ. Stabilization* ix. 148 By structural unemployment..we mean unemployment caused by changes in the structure of industry that are of a non-recurring type. **1966** *Economist* 29 Jan. 407/2 The boom of the past years has brought jobs for Negroes and for the unskilled, in the teeth of cries that 'automation' and 'structural unemployment' meant that such people had no hope of finding work. **1979** *Guardian* 31 May 735/3 The spectre of 'structural unemployment'—the likelihood that some of today's young people will never have a job. **1940** BRYANT & AIKEN *Psychol. Eng.* iv. 38 A distinction is made between 'full' and 'empty' words, the latter being what are known as 'structural' words. **1966** J. DERRICK *Teaching Eng. to Immigrants* i. 8 If we take our first example again, 'The man is hitting the horse' we find we can substitute any one of a hundred or more different items for the words *man, hit* and *horse*... But if we try to do the same thing at one of the other places in the sentence, we find we can only substitute a limited set of words... The words in these places, where the choice is limited, are what writers have called the structural or grammatical words of the language, while the other words have been called content words or lexical items.

c. = *STRUCTURALIST 2.

1953 *College Composition & Communication* IV. iv. 124 The structural objection to the traditional use of *language* is that the account of the mechanisms becomes distorted beyond reason. **1959** *Word* XV. 176 The newly established chair of General Linguistics and Phonetics (which was, incidentally, the first structural academic position to be established anywhere).

structuralism (strɒ·ktiŭrăliz'm). [f. STRUCTURAL *a.* + -ISM.] **1.** *Psychol.* A method, connected esp. with the American psychologist E. B. Titchener (1867–1927), of investigating the structure of consciousness through the introspective analysis of simple forms of sensation, thought, images, etc.

1907 J. R. ANGELL in *Psychol. Rev.* XIV. 64 If you adopt as your material for psychological analysis the isolated 'moment of consciousness', it is very easy to become so absorbed in determining its constitution as to be rendered..oblivious to its artificial character. The most essential quarrel which the functionalist has with structuralism..arises from this fact. **1927** M. BENTLEY in C. Murchison *Psychologies of 1925* 390 However important or trivial we shall find the accomplishments of structuralism to be, we must recognize the gain in clear thinking which accrued to Titchener's sharply drawn distinction between the analytical psychology of structure and the descriptive psychology of mental operation and functional performance. **1930** *Times Lit. Suppl.* 19 Jan. 508/3 Modern schools of psychology, Structuralism, and Functionalism. **1968** *Internat. Encycl. Social Sci.* XV. 610 The movement called 'structuralism' which was founded in Germany by Wilhelm Wundt and transplanted to the United States by Edward B. Titchener of Cornell University.

2. Any theory or method in which a discipline or field of study is envisaged as comprising elements interrelated in systems and structures at various levels, the structures and the interrelations of their elements being regarded as more significant than the elements considered in isolation; also, more recently, theories concerned with analysing the surface structures of a system in terms of its underlying structure. **a.** *gen.*

1951 *Mind* L. 270 Braithwaite evidently believes that the whole philosophy of structuralism breaks down over the question of a combining relation. **1968** *Sunday Times* 10 Mar. 52 Structuralism is a technique for analysing any kind of symbolic system. Its break with the past consists in refusing to take note of the appropriateness of symbols for the things they symbolise. **1969** P. ANDERSON in Cockburn & Blackburn *Student Power* 246 Namier's legacy to English historiography was thus inevitably equivocal. His structuralism was rapidly suppressed from memory. **1970** M. LANE *Structuralism* 31 Structuralism, then, is a method whose primary intention is to permit the investigator to go beyond a pure description of what he perceives or experiences..in the direction of the quality of rationality which underlies the social phenomena in which he is concerned. **1971** C. MASCHLER tr. *Piaget's Structuralism* i. 4 We come upon at least two aspects that are common to all varieties of structuralism: first, an ideal..of intrinsic intelligibility supported by the postulate that structures are self-sufficient. **1972** *Sci. Amer.* Sept. 50/3 Structuralism recognizes that information about the world enters the mind not as raw data but as highly abstract structures that are the result of a preconscious set of step-by-step transformations of the sensory input. **1973** *Film Comment* May/June 52/1 In recent years, structuralism and semiology have received much attention as methods for analyzing and interpreting film... Structuralism..attempts to analyze comparatively the deep structures, thus locating those distinctive features common to all of man's cultural and social expressions. **1975** *New Rev.* II. xiv. 55/1 (*title*) Is your structuralism really necessary? *Ibid.* 57/2 Is not the case for temporalism overwhelmingly stronger than the case for structuralism? **1978** *History Workshop* Autumn 3 British Marxist structuralism exalts theoretical practice to the point where it seems to become an end in itself. **1980** *London Rev. Bks.* 15 May 3/2 Structuralism is the philosophy of those in the universities and thereabouts who are not philosophers.

b. *Linguistics.* Applied to theories in which language is considered as a system or structure comprising elements at various phonological, grammatical, and semantic levels, esp. after the work of F. de Saussure (1857–1913).

1945 E. A. CASSIRER in *Word* I. 99 (*title*) Structuralism in modern linguistics. *Ibid.* 104 If the adherents and defenders of the program of linguistic structuralism are right, then we must say that in the realm of language there is no opposition between what is 'formal' and what is merely 'factual'. **1953** A. MARTINET in A. L. Kroeber *Anthropol. Today* 577/1 It would seem that the teaching of Ferdinand de Saussure has, directly or indirectly, influenced most of linguistic structuralism. **1964** *English Studies* XLV (Suppl.). 33 They intend..to stress the importance of semantic studies..(as a necessary counterpart to formal structuralism). **1968** J. LYONS *Introd. Theoret. Linguistics* x. 443 It is one of the cardinal principles of 'structuralism', as developed by de Saussure and his followers, that every linguistic item has its 'place' in a system and its function, or value, derives from the relations which it contracts with other units in the system. **1972** *Language* XLVIII. 419 Structuralism proper in linguistics began with phonology. **1976** *Archivum Linguisticum* VII. 152 With the rise of structuralism, linguistics turned back upon itself, so to say, and tended to abstract away from the social matrix of language.

c. *Anthrop.* and *Sociol.* The theories or methods of analysis concerned with the structure or form of human society or social life; also, following the work of the French anthropologist Claude Lévi-Strauss (b. 1908), theories concerned with the deeper structures of communication from which the surface structures or 'models' evolve.

1955 R. FIRTH in *Jrnl. R. Anthropol. Inst.* LXXXV. 1 All British social anthropologists are structuralists in their use of the analytical principles developed by this method. But the rigidity and limitations of a simple structuralism alone have come to be more widely perceived. **1969** A. G. FRANK *Latin Amer.* (1970) ii. 68 The pioneering service..of those latter students of economic development and cultural change is precisely that they drop all pretense and practice of social scientific structuralism. **1973** J. REX *Discovering Sociol.* ix. 118 French structuralism has to be sharply distinguished from the structuralism of Radcliffe-Brown with which it compares itself, and the structuralism of Simmel and Weber, of which it remains largely ignorant. **1978** J. Z. YOUNG *Programs of Brain* 299/1 *Structuralism*, a movement in social science originated by Claude Lévi-Strauss, which supposes that social structures depend upon certain basic characteristics of human brain programs.

structuralist (strɒ·ktiŭrălist), *sb.* (and *a.*). *Social Sci.* and *Humanities.* [f. STRUCTURAL *a.* + -IST.] **1.** An advocate or adherent of a structural approach (see *STRUCTURAL *a.* 5 a) or of a theory of structuralism.

1907 J. R. ANGELL in *Psychol. Rev.* XIV. 67 Dwelling as the structuralist is supposed to do upon the problem of determining the irreducible elements of consciousness and their characteristic modes of combination. **1922** W. McDOUGAL in *Amer. Jrnl. Psychiatry* Jan. 347 Mott and the other structuralists..would..dismiss the second alternative with contempt. **1949** *Archivum Linguisticum* I. 184 A survey of post-neogrammarian views on language, viz. those of Saussure..and the Danish 'structuralists'. **1965** *Economist* 25 Sept. p. xxvi/2 Some extreme structuralists argue that demand deflation is actually likely to increase cost inflation. **1975** G. STEINER *After Babel* ii. 83 More than a century before the modern structuralists, Humboldt notes the distinctive binary character of the linguistic process. **1982** *Listener* 18 Nov. 17/2 Structuralists and post-Structuralists maintain that the notion of the author as the creator of his works is merely a modern consolation prize.

2. *attrib.* or as *adj.*

1907 J. R. ANGELL in *Psychol. Rev.* XIV. 62 The most lucid exposition of the structuralist position still remains, so far as I know, Titchener's paper, 'The Postulates of a Structural Psychology'. **1929** W. B. PILLSBURY *Hist. Psychol.* xvi. 271 The structuralist school..holds that consciousness is directly observable and is composed of simple, definitely describable elements. **1955** *Jrnl. R. Anthropol. Inst.* LXXXV. 1 The air of enchantment which for the last two decades has surrounded the 'structuralist' point of view. **1955** *Times* 11 June 5/5 In contrast to much of to-day's painting..which is considered finished when it has reached the stage which, in any other epochs, would have been called the sketch, Structuralist painting is carried to completion in strict obedience to the scientific laws of colour-form structure **1963** *Indian Econ. Rev.* Feb. 67 The monetarist-structuralist controversy is an argument over the remedy for inflation, the monetarist taking supply as given and recommending a contraction of demand, the structuralist..taking demand as given [etc.]. **1965** N. CHOMSKY *Aspects of Theory of Syntax* ii. 67 Such a system is apparently what is implicit in modern taxonomic ('structuralist') grammars. **1970** J. LYONS *Chomsky* 29 The 'structuralist' approach was by no means confined to Boas and his successors in America. **1970** *Sunday Times* 15 Nov. 32/2 Today when we go to Paris, we can read structuralist novels, look at structuralist paintings and hear structuralist music. Even newspaper cartoons and gourmet meals are subjected to structuralist interpretations. **1976** *Archivum Linguisticum* VII. 152 Even present-day transformational grammar, though quite remote from classical structuralist thought, singles out a 'fluent speaker' set apart from the disturbing influences of social variation. **1979** A. R. PEACOCKE *Creation & World of Science* i. 29 This more narrowly functionalist account of myth has given way, following the lead of Lévi-Strauss, to a 'structuralist' account.

structuralistic (strɒ:ktiŭrăli·stik), *a.* [f. *STRUCTURALIST *sb.* + -IC]. Characteristic of a structuralist or of structuralism; structuralist.

1957 H. WHITEHALL in N. Frye *Sound & Poetry* 134 Both criticism and linguistics, in their modern phases, are structuralistic in attitude. **1972** *Jrnl. Social Psychol.* LXXXVII. 37 Mental imagery and image formation have recently become a topic of concern again, after avoidance of such structuralistic phenomena for 50 years or more. **1978** *Studies in Eng. Lit.: Eng. Number* (Tokyo) 134 Her idea of 'structure' is structuralistic, and this is no coincidence.

structuralize (strɒ·ktiŭrălaiz), *v.* [f. STRUCTURAL *a.* + -IZE.] *trans.* = STRUCTURE *v.*; also, to apply structural theories or analysis to (something). So **stru:cturaliza·tion**; **stru·cturalized** *ppl. a.*; **stru·cturalizing** *vbl. sb.*

1936 K. MANNHEIM *Ideology & Utopia* iii. 128 All that has become intelligible, understandable, rationalized, organized, structuralized, artistically, and otherwise formed, and consequently everything historical seems in fact to lie between these two extreme poles. **1953** C. E. BAZELL *Linguistic Form* iii. 29 Distributional criteria seldom provide grounds here for a narrower structuralisation. **1964** H. HARTMANN *Ego Psychol.* iii. 64 Once structuralization has taken place, they [*sc.* ego interests of the id] become partly independent in the service of the ego. **1965** *Canad. Jrnl. Linguistics* Spring 142 Once Kiowa was structuralized, however, it turned out that it made the same distinctions in vowel type that the Tanoan languages made. **1975** *Times Lit. Suppl.* 21 Nov. 1394 (*heading*) Structuralizing in Sumatra. **1977** *Dædalus* Fall 70 Far-reaching changes in the political regimes could affect the functioning of economic institutions and the structuralization of social hierarchies.

structurate (strɒ·ktiŭreɪt), *v. rare.* [f. STRUCTURE *sb.* + -ATE[3].] *trans.* = prec. So **stru·cturated** *ppl. a.*

1937 *Mind* XLVI. 512 The physical sciences are in a happy position, because their numerical world is mathematically structurated. **1978** *Eng. Jrnl.* Dec. 20/1 You say you've been grammaticized, transformalized, and structurated.

structuration (strɒktiŭrē̆ɪ·ʃən). [f. STRUCTURE *v.* + -ATION.] The condition or process of organization in a structural form.

1927 *Brit. Jrnl. Psychol.* XVIII. 6 After many such changes an image may represent a vast structure of meanings, and so 'structuration' may be attributed to it. **1934** *Mind* XLIII. 110 In man the main feature, because the *dynamic* feature, of his development consists in the structuration of his propensities into sentiments. **1952** W. SPROTT *Social Psychol.* iii. 52 All groups..tend towards structuration which is evidenced by..a role system, an ethos, a certain formalization of action-patterns. **1973** A. GIDDENS *Class Struct. Advanced Societies* xi. 201 The influence of paratechnical relations upon working-class structuration. **1973** *Screen* Spring/Summer 11 Semiology opens out that process in its disengagement of the heterogeneity of codes at work in the structuration of film. **1980** *Times Lit. Suppl.* 26 Sept. 1072/1 It might be more appropriate to speak of the differential structuration of life chances as constituting classes.

structure, *sb.* Add: **3. d.** Also *spec.* in *Linguistics. deep structure*: see *DEEP *a.* IV. c; *surface structure*: see *SURFACE *sb.* 6 d.

1961 Y. OLSSON *On Syntax Eng. Verb* ii. 27 Both collocation and colligation operate syntagmatically... They are examples of *structures* constituted by *elements*. **1965** *Language* XLI. 73 The nested structures are phrase types which are in clear structural contrast in the language.

8. *structure-dependence, dependency, sensitivity; structure-borne, -dependent, -independent, -sensitive* adjs.; **structure-function** *attrib. phr.*, pertaining to both structure and function; **structure plan** *Local Government*, a plan drawn up by a local planning authority for the development, use, conservation, etc., of a prescribed area of land; hence **structure planning**, the preparation of such a plan; **structure word** = *structural word* s.v. *STRUCTURAL *a.* 5 b.

1962 A. NISBETT *Technique Sound Studio* ii. 38 Structure-borne noises are almost impossible to eliminate and rebuilding work is complicated by the need to avoid all noisy work when nearby studios are recording. **1972** *Lebende Sprachen* XVII. 37/2 *Structure-borne noise*, a condition when the sound waves are being carried by a solid material. **1976** N. CHOMSKY *Reflections on Lang.* I. i. 33 The principle of structure-dependence is not learned, but forms part of the conditions for language learning. **1976** *Times Lit. Suppl.* 17 Dec. 1590/4 By structure dependency he [*sc.* Chomsky] means, and I mean, that the significance of any feature is determined by its position in a structure. **1965** Structure-dependent [see *ANALYSABILITY]. **1978** *Logophile* VIII. 5/2 All syntactic operations in language are structure-dependent. **1963** *Canad. Jrnl. Linguistics* VIII. 59 (*heading*) A structure-function description of Terena phrases. **1977** *Dædalus* Fall 115 For the moment I want to draw the kind of structure-function distinction we might adopt, say, in discussing walking: what it is versus where it might take you. **1964** E. A. POWER *Introd. Quantum Electrodynamics* i. 5 Also even the structure-independent radiation damping term depends on the arrow sign of time—unlike the fundamental equations themselves—because in calculating the radiation field boundary conditions at infinite time are involved. **1976** N. CHOMSKY *Reflections on Lang.* I. i. 33 Construct a structure-dependent rule, ignoring all structure-independent rules. **1971** *Act* 19 & 20 *Eliz. II* c. 78 §7 The local planning authority shall..prepare and send the Secretary of State..a structure plan for their area. **1980** *Oxford Times* 12 Dec. 10/4 Policy E1 of the Structure Plan says that the Council will restrain growth of employment in the county as a whole. **1973** *Times* 8 Sept. 14/6 He made it plain that he did not expect an end to the structure planning process, the framework for regulating development which every local planning authority is expected to prepare. **1976** *Alyn & Deeside Observer* 10 Dec. 16/1 The strange spectacle of two Conservative councils locked in a fierce exchange over structure planning. **1936** *Jrnl. R. Aeronaut. Soc.* XL. 593 The strength of a crystal across a crystal plane is a structure-sensitive property. **1970** *Language* XLVI. 261 We demonstrate the use of transformational rules applied to the output of structure-free grammars as a means of generating symmetrical strings which are not only structure-sensitive but context-sensitive as well. **1976** *Times Lit. Suppl.* 17 Dec. 1590/4 My emphasis on structure sensitivity in 'natural' situations leads me to look for leads in linguistics. **1956** *Publ. Amer. Dial. Soc.* XXVI. 59 A listing by parts of speech brings out the numerical superiority of nouns, and the relatively small number of structure words borrowed. **1965** Structure-word [see *FUNCTOR 2].

structure, *v.* Delete *rare* and add: **a.** (Later examples.) Also, to establish a hierarchy of relationships or a pattern in (something). Also *absol.* and *loosely*, to construct, form, or organize. So **stru·cturing** *ppl. a.*

1933 *Mind* XLII. 176 It is the architectonic (supreme and structuring) principle or spirit regulating in their mutual relations all other structuring activities. **1949** M. MEAD *Male & Female* xv. 296 This has been an accurate picture of the way in which we have structured our society, with women as keepers of the house.., and men as keepers of women in the house. **1955** AUDEN *Shield of Achilles* i. 16 When, on some windless day Of dejection, unable To name or to structure. **1960** L. PINCUS *Marriage* III. 221 An inhibited response structured by..these unconscious dilemmas. **1962** *Amer. Speech* XXXVII. 107 Bloomfield..calls /r/ a 'vocaloid' and says it may be syllabic..but he has it function as a consonant when structuring the final consonant clusters of English. **1971** *Sci. Amer.* Aug. 91/1 Input/Output tables provide management..with a powerful new tool for forecasting and measuring the indirect as well as the direct inter-industry relationships that structure our industrial economy. **1974** R. HELMS *Tolkien's World* v. 98 The parallel plot-lines of Book III..are both structured by the laws of providential control and of the cause-and-effect morality. **1978** *Guardian Weekly* 10 Sept. 17/4 A secret study memorandum..which helped structure Carter's decision last month to use trade restrictions. **1979** *Nature* 23 Aug. 652/1 The chemical exchanges among uplands, marshes and coastal waters are important in structuring these ecosystems.

b. To give (someone or something) a place in a structure; to absorb or integrate into a pattern or system.

1954 J. A. C. BROWN *Social Psychol. Industry* vi. 174 Aggressiveness as a response to this has become structured into his basic personality. **1955** C. CHERRY in B. I. Evans *Stud. in Communication* iii. 60 The individuals were to be structured into social coherence. **1959** M. DOLINSKY *There is no Silence* iii. 44 You don't easily structure the unusual or the exotic. **1977** A. GIDDENS *Stud. in Social & Polit. Theory* i. 70 Criticism thus cannot be terminated within the sphere of science itself, but must concern itself with the standards or values which structure science as one mode of activity among others.

c. To present or manipulate (a situation, etc.) in such a way as to elicit desired responses or effects.

1966 *Listener* 10 Mar. 342/2 Parents who are trying to train their children make use of verbal explanations to structure the situation. **1971** J. B. CARROLL et al. *Word Freq. Bk.* p. ix, His assistance was also essential in.. structuring the survey to reflect curriculum divisions and publications diversity. **1973** *Howard Jrnl.* XIII. 282 Treatment..is a matter of so structuring the environment..that aversive consequences..follow unwanted or undesirable behaviour. **1975** *Language for Life* (Dept. Educ. & Sci.) x. 145 He must structure the learning so that the child becomes positively aware of the need for a complicated utterance.

structured, *ppl. a.* Add: **1.** (Later examples.)

1929 A. N. WHITEHEAD *Process & Reality* 138 The enduring object..may be conceived as independent of the structured society. **1940** C. S. SHERRINGTON *Man & his Nature* xi. 353 There is the difficulty that the outward process on analysis proves always to be 'granular', quantal, 'structured'; the inner process to be structureless, non-quantal. **1962** H. A. GLEASON in Householder & Saporta *Problems in Lexicography* 91 Occasionally sets of language phenomena are observed which, though apparently structured, seem not to be so rigorously structured as this. **1968** *Guardian* 12 June 8/4 The taking of hallucinogenic drugs, where the objective is..to erase the influence of structured experience and organisation of perceptual material in order to explore some kind of world beyond the structures. **1980** P. HILL *Savages* iii. 46 The boys are not criminals... They need a structured group, a sense of belonging.

2. a. Organized or arranged so as to produce a desired result. Also *loosely*, formal, organized, not haphazard.

1959 *Listener* 17 Dec. 1079/1 The use of measured or structured arguments to get at the causes of such interesting phenomena as millionaires or strikes. **1968** *Brit. Med. Bull.* XXIV. 189/2 The computer can accept data only in a highly structured (digital) form. **1975** *Language for Life* (Dept. Educ. & Sci.) v. 59 In certain cases the object was to equip the mother with the ability to work through a structured programme with her child. **1976** *Ann. Rep. Manpower Services Comm. 1975–76* iv. 30/1 The review is intended to provide a framework within which choices can be made and resources allocated in a more structured way. **1977** *Cornish Times* 19 Aug. 8/7 It will provide all learning opportunities through the medium of formal teaching processes, planned excursions, structured and unstructured play and recreational experiences.

b. Of a computer program: organized in a logical way to facilitate debugging and modification; *spec.* composed of linked but distinct modules each having one entry point and one exit point, so that the program may be read straight through; so *structured programming* vbl. sb.

1966 *Information Processing 1965* II. 448/1 (*heading*) On solving large structured programs. **1972** *Bit* XII. I. 38 (*heading*) An experiment in structured programming. **1974** D. D. MCCRACKEN *Simplified Guide to Fortran Programming* vi. 110 This makes it possible to write the program without a GO TO . . . This..is one aspect of structured programming, which holds great promise of converting programming from a hit-or-miss craft into an engineering science. **1978** L. A. LEVENTHAL *Introd. Microprocessors* vi. 250 In structured programming only single logic structures are used. Bohm and Jacopini showed that any program could be written by using only three structures. 1. A sequential structure . . . 2. A conditional structure of the IF-THEN-ELSE type . . . 3. A loop structure of the DO-WHILE type . . . The computer executes P repeatedly as long as A is true. **1983** *Personal Computer World* Sept. 216/2 If a program is badly structured..altering one part of the program may have unforeseen effects in a completely different part.

structuredness (strʌ·ktiŭɹdnės). [f. STRUCTURED *ppl. a.* + -NESS.] The quality of being structured.

1966 S. BEER *Decision & Control* xiv. 350 He refers to the gain in structured-ness that accompanies the entropy change in a biological system as a gain in the *maturity* of that system. **1970** *Jrnl. Gen. Psychol.* July 69 The tasks of the Wechsler..are not composed of stimuli all of the same degree of structuredness. **1974** *Lang. Sciences* Aug. 27/2, I am personally convinced that the focus on structuredness has been and will be as heuristic..in semantics as it has been in phonology and grammar. **1977** *Lancet* 22 Jan. 172/1 The data are too few at present to indicate whether the use of H.C.G. in addition to myelin or cancer basic protein will significantly improve the specificity of the M.E.M. test and the related test for the 'structuredness of cytoplasmic matrix' as means for detecting the presence of malignant disease.

stru·cturing, *vbl. sb.* [f. STRUCTURE *v.* + -ING[1].] The action of the verb.

1951 M. MCLUHAN *Mech. Bride* (1967) 77/1 The emotional structuring which results..from affection that is tendered or withdrawn. **1958** *New Scientist* 25 Sept. 887/2 While apes and infants struggle towards some sort of structure-formation, the human artist of today struggles to free himself from all structuring or imagery. **1962** H. A. GLEASON in Householder & Saporta *Problems in Lexicography* 92 Crossing grammatical structure in various ways are..other types of structurings, some of them, at least, so different in form as to be unrecognizable as structure by the methods of descriptive linguistics. **1965** H. I. ANSOFF *Corporate Strategy* (1968) i. 19 One part of the administrative problem is concerned with organization: structuring of authority and responsibility relationships, work flows, information flows, [etc.]. **1970** T. LUPTON *Managem. & Social Sci.* (ed. 2) ii. 35 The factors which influence the structuring of social relationships. **1977** M. EDELMAN *Polit. Lang.* v. 92 This kind of cognitive structuring exemplifies the selective perception of information to reinforce established beliefs. **1980** *Amer. Speech* LV. 42 A toponymic dialect would be shaped.. also by other important factors:..by the structuring of onomastic fields.., by the sequence of naming, [etc.].

structurism (strʌ·ktiŭriz'm). [f. STRUCTURE *sb.* + -ISM.] The artistic theory or practice of a structurist (sense *2).

1963 *New Republic* 16 Feb. 26/3 Biederman..has written several books expounding Structurism as a future imperative. **1965** *Minneapolis Tribune* 21 Mar. (Arts Sect.) 1/4 His work evolved into the painted aluminium reliefs that represent his latest effort. These carried him through an attitude called constructionism to structurism. **1970** *Time* 26 Jan. 37 Biederman himself, having grandly declared that both painting and sculpture were obsolete, arrived at what he has come to call 'structurism'—reliefs that have the dimension of sculpture and the color of painting. **1973** *Phaidon Dict. Twentieth Cent. Art* 35/1 Biederman rejected Constructivism and termed his 'new art' Structurism—three-dimensional constructions in which small single-coloured rectangles are placed on a solid-coloured background, at right angles to the background and to each other.

structurist. Restrict *rare* to sense in Dict. and add: **2.** An artist whose work emphasizes underlying structural forms and processes in nature; applied esp. to the U.S. artist Charles Biederman (b. 1906) and by him to earlier artists in whose work he perceived this tendency. Also *attrib.* or as *adj.*

1958 C. BIEDERMAN *New Cézanne* viii. 61 Monet alone is the great Structurist innovator for the 19th century. It is Cézanne who is the great Structurist innovator for the 20th century! *Ibid.* 77 The genuine Structurist is indifferent to the slick materials of industry. **1959** —— in *Structure* 2nd Ser. I. 16/1 Artists no longer found their art but only their method of art, not in the creations but only in the creative method of nature's structural process. I call this the Structurist direction of art. **1960** *Guardian* 2 Feb. 7/5 The post-cubist collage-makers and other pioneer abstract 'structurists'. **1967** *Times* 17 Mar. 12/5 The trustees [of the Tate Gallery] have also recently acquired 'Structurist Relief. Red Wing No. 20' 1954–65, by Charles Biederman. *Ibid.* Biederman's 'structurist' work developed from a study of Mondrian. **1970** *Sat. Rev.* (U.S.) 17 Oct. 54 He and others 'in curriculum development and teacher training have been guilty for years of structuring canvases and of choosing the brushes and paints'. And yet how many structurists are willing to abandon that on which they depend? **1976** J. VAN DER MARCK in *Charles Biederman* (Minneapolis Inst. Arts) 64 That gradual development, from the simple to the complex, which is a tenet of the Structurist philosophy.

structurization (strʌ:ktiŭrəizēi·ʃən). [f. STRUCTURE *sb.* + -IZATION.] The process of giving a structure to something or of arranging material into an organized pattern.

1950 *Brit. Jrnl. Psychol.* Dec. 129 Do [rumours]..take their origin almost wholly from 'within' the mind... Or do they arise as 'constructions' or structurizations of the stimulus situation, produced by the peculiar attitude, which itself was formed under the influence of the special situation of a crisis? **1955** H. READ *Icon & Idea* iii. 60 Then, on the basis of this symbolic activity and of intuitive thought generally, a representational structurization of space becomes possible. **1958** C. BIEDERMAN *New Cézanne* viii. 62 Having failed, out of fear of the consequences of Cézanne's geometrical structurizations, they [*sc.* the Cubists] now switched their attention to the surface aspects of Cézanne. **1969** *New Scientist* 6 Nov. 304/3 For him [*sc.* Grèco],..the concept of structure and the process of structurization..are essential for the understanding of human intelligence.

structurize (strʌ·ktiŭrəiz), *v.* [f. STRUCTURE *sb.* + -IZE.] *trans.* To give a structure to (something), to organize structurally.

1958 C. BIEDERMAN *New Cézanne* iv. 37 The brush stroke structurizes color. *Ibid.* 48 Art is now directed towards a 'constant reality', structurized by 'constant relationships'. **1968** *Times* 18 Dec. 9 Research capacities are being structurized to the optimum in every single economic branch in order to meet the country's requirements of the scientific and technological revolution.

strudel (strū·d'l, ‖ ʃtrū·d'l). [a. Ger., lit. 'eddy, whirlpool'.] A baked sweet of Austrian origin, made of very thin layers of pastry with a filling, usu. of fruit. Also used *attrib.* to denote the kind of dough or pastry used in such confections. *apfelstrudel, apple strudel*: see *APPLE *sb.* B. II.

1893 *Encycl. Pract. Cookery* II. 525/2 *Strudels*, a kind of pancake or fritter made in Germany. **1903** *Jewish Encycl.* IV. 257/2 The *strudel*, or single-layered jelly or fruit cake, takes the place of the pie for dessert. **1915** L. KANDER *'Settlement' Cook Book* (ed. 7) xxi. 251 Prepare Strudel dough,..fill with kraut and other above ingredients. **1923,** etc. [see *apple strudel* s.v. *APPLE *sb.* B. II]. **1932** [see *LEKACH]. **1941** B. SCHULBERG *What Makes Sammy Run?* ix. 225 *Strudel*,..still hot... Sammele used to say I made the best *strudel* in the whole world. **1950** *Here & Now* (N.Z.) Dec. 26/1 Whether visitors to Vienna went to the big expensive hotels..or ordered a quick meal in a coffee-house..they always kept haunting memories of *schnitzels, strudels* and cakes. **1960** [see *SCHNITZEL]. **1972** F. B. MAYNARD *Raisins & Almonds* 31 She was baking while I watched..the miracle of the strudel. **1981** *Times* 19 Mar. 8/6 Feta cheese and phyllo or strudel pastry are.. sold in shops specializing in Greek or Cypriot foods.

'strue (strū), schoolboy's abbrev. of CONSTRUE *v.* and *sb.*

1903 FARMER & HENLEY *Slang* VII. 14/2 *Strue*, verb, (schools'), 'construe'. **1906** D. COKE *Bending of Twig* viii. 122 But mind, you've promised to sap out the 'strues, and 'strue them to me. *Ibid.* 125 Russell..made Lycidas extend his 'struing services to six more mornings' work.

struggle, *sb.* Add: **3.** *Comb.*, as **struggle-buggy** *U.S. slang*, a motor vehicle; *spec.* an old and battered one; **struggle meeting**, [tr. Chinese *dòuzhēng huì*], in Communist China: a meeting at which those who have aroused official or public disfavour are criticized or denounced.

1925 *College Humor* Sept. 20/2 I'll say you can park in my struggle buggy. **1946** Struggle-buggy [see *RINKY-DINK *a.*]. **1966** F. SCHURMANN *Ideology & Organization in Communist China* v. 318 'Struggle meetings' were held throughout China in which offending cadres were attacked, and by mass demand removed from office. **1973** *Times* 21 Mar. (China Trade Suppl.) p. viii/5 Officials who have been through 'struggle meetings', because they were considered to be bureaucratic..are likely to be sufficiently shaken by the experience to avoid arousing such resentments in the future.

struma. Add: **1. c.** *struma lymphomatosa* [mod.L., coined in Ger. (H. Hashimoto 1912, in *Arch. f. klin. Chir.* XCVII. 219)], = *Hashimoto's disease* s.v. *HASHIMOTO; *Riedel's struma* [*RIEDEL], a rare condition of uncertain status in which the thyroid becomes hard, nodular, and fibrotic.

1931 *Arch. Surg.* XXII. 548 Recent writers have stated that struma lymphomatosa is the early stage of Riedel's struma, despite the fact that Hashimoto..definitely rejected such a relationship. **1947** H. Selye *Textbk. Endocrinol.* 714/2 The etiology of struma lymphomatosa is unknown but its histologic characteristics are not typical of inflammatory lesions. **1966** [see *Riedel]. **1974** S. L. Robbins *Path. Basis Dis.* xxix. 1328/1 In years past, Riedel's struma was thought to be the fibrotic end-stage of struma lymphomatosa.

strumble (strʌ·mb'l), *sb. rare*⁻¹. [f. Strumble *v.*[1]] A rumble.

1938 Belloc *Sonnets & Verse* 180 Beneath His feet are implacable fate, and panic or night, and the strumble of the hungry river of death.

strumitis (strumai·tis). *Path.* [f. Strum(a + -itis.] Inflammation of a goitrous thyroid gland.

1889 *Buck's Handbk. Med. Sci.* VII. 96/1 Inflammation of the thyroid gland (thyroiditis, strumitis) is most commonly seen as the accidental or intentional result of remedial measures employed in the treatment of goitre. **1955** S. C. Werner *Thyroid* v. 745 Thyroiditis appears in acute, subacute, and chronic forms... If the acute disorders have their onset in pre-existing goiter, the disease is often termed strumitis.

strumming (strʌ·miŋ), *ppl. a. rare.* [f. Strum *v.* + -ing[2].] Sounding like a strummed instrument.

1887 Hardy *Woodlanders* III. vii. 140 She fancied that she could hear, above the sound of her strumming pulse, the vehicle. *a* **1911** D. G. Phillips *Susan Lenox* (1917) II. xxv. 553 As a menace, as a prophecy, the old women and the hunchback and the strumming piano had gone forever.

strung, *ppl. a.* Add: **3.** Also, extended, continuing in a long series.

1978 *Language* LIV. 91 This falls short of accounting for strung-out MI correspondences where relative orderings remain the same.

4. For 'String *v.* 4' read 'String *v.* 3'. **a.** *strung-up* (later examples). Also (*N. Amer. slang*) *strung out* (overlaps with sense c below).

1933 M. de la Roche *Master of Jalna* xv. 198 She worries greatly over the child and that keeps her in a strung-up state. **1967** *N.Y. Times* 18 Aug. 22 'These are very strung-out kids with individual hang-ups,' said Jim Fouratt..describing the modern runaway. **1974** M. Haskell *From Reverence to Rape* 208 Martha Vickers' spoiled, strung-out younger sister. **1979** K. M. Peyton *Marion's Angels* ix. 137 You don't think she might have —? Oh, Christ! She was strung up when she left me. We both were. **1980** *Globe & Mail* (Toronto) 20 Mar. T1/5 She takes to the streets daily in response to calls from tenants to investigate nuisance neighbours who might be strung out emotionally.

c. *strung out*: weak or ill, esp. as a result of drug addiction; hence, addicted to, using, or 'high' *on* drugs. *slang* (orig. and chiefly *U.S.*).

1959 *Esquire* Nov. 70 *Strung Out*, in bad physical condition. **1960** *Jazz Rev.* Nov. 8/2 Unfortunately it was at this period he acquired the 'monkey' and frequently was strung out. **1965** *N.Y. Post* 3 Dec. 45/1 If one spends time talking to marijuana users, one can only conclude that the entire college population is 'strung out' thrice weekly. **1966** *San Francisco Chron.* 29 June 3 Acid does nothing for me... I love to get strung out on pot. **1973** *Black World* Aug. 59/1 The horns..lef' by some strungout junky musician. **1977** *Guardian Weekly* 30 Oct. 15/4 Young people get strung out on heroin.

strunt, *sb.*[1] Add: Also, the whole tail.

a **1930** D. H. Lawrence *Phoenix* (1936) 16 Wag thy [*sc.* a puppy's] strunt, then!

strunzite (strʌ·nzait). *Min.* [ad. G. *strunzite* (C. Frondel 1957, in *Neues Jahrb. f. Min.: Monatshefte* 222), f. the name of K. Hugo *Strunz* (b. 1910), German mineralogist: see -ite[1].] A hydrated basic phosphate of manganese and iron, $MnFe_2(PO_4)_2(OH)_2.8H_2O$, found as tiny yellow hair- or lath-like monoclinic crystals and produced by the weathering of manganese and iron phosphates.

1958 C. Frondel in *Naturwissenschaften* XLV. 38/1 Among the outstanding problems in the mineralogy of the hydrated phosphates of iron and manganese has been the identity of a straw yellow mineral first recognized in 1947... The writer takes pleasure in naming this mineral after Dr. Hugo Strunz, Professor of Mineralogy at Berlin. **1975** *Mineral. Record* VI. 71/2 Stewartite, strunzite, and cacoxenite, which in our specimens are confined to oxidized assemblage[s], are the products of weathering.

strut, *sb.*[3] Add: **c.** A type of slow and complicated dance or dance-step.

[**1917**: see *shimmy *sb.*[2] 1]. **1937** [see *Big Apple* s.v. *big *a.* B. 2]. **1970** C. Major *Dict. Afro-Amer. Slang* 111 *Strut*.., a fancy-step slow dance. **1979** R. B. Gillespie *Crossword Mystery* i. 17 He..executed a few soft-shoe steps which merged into a strut.

strut, *v.*[1] Add: **7. f.** *to strut one's stuff*: to display one's ability. *U.S. slang.*

1926 C. Van Vechten *Nigger Heaven* ii. vi. 242 Some one cried, Strut your stuff, Lasca! **1935** [see *roller *sb.*[1] 18 d]. **1941** *Sun* (Baltimore) 30 Aug. 13/1 Rain today made the prospect for off-going for the first card, thus giving the 'mudders' an opportunity to strut their stuff. **1972** *N.Y. Times* 3 Nov. 28/1 The company is going to strut its stuff, with nothing more in mind than to entertain, in Washington Square, near the Arch. There will be singing and dancing and acting and acrobatics. **1977** *Rolling Stone* 30 June 121/2 (Advt.), Each run is equipped with a super, custom-designed sound system, so you can 'strut your stuff' or 'space walk' to your favorite tunes.

g. *intr.* To dance the strut. Cf. *strut *sb.*[2] c.

1975 *Time Out* 8 Aug. 67/1 D'you wanna shake, strut, shimmy, jive, twist, waltz, mash potato, tango, tap or conga?

'struth, var. 'Strewth in Dict. and Suppl.

struthonian (strūþōᵘ·nian), *a.*, (*sb.*) *joc.* [Irreg. f. L. *struth-io*: see -ian and Struthious *a.*] Tending to 'hide one's head in the sand', like the ostrich (see *sand *sb.*[2] 2 d), and so to ignore unwelcome facts (Koestler's word). Also as *sb.*, one who does this. Hence **strutho·nianism.**

1963 A. Koestler in *Encounter* July 7/1 One need not be an economist to find these figures disconcerting. But there is a struthonian answer to them (from struthio the Latin for ostrich). Your Old Struthonian will start with some disparaging remarks about statistics in general, and ..then explain that Britain started the Industrial Revolution, and that accordingly it is only natural..that other nations, which started later, should grow at a faster rate. **1966** *Listener* 18 Aug. 223/2 Housing, with doubtful justification, lags behind needs, and continues to take a lion-hearted and struthonian view of the climate. *Ibid.* 224/1 A fine piece of struthonianism is the failure to accept the fact that teenagers are now in practice sexually active. *Ibid.* 25 Aug. 279/1 It is unfortunate that Professor Wisdom should perpetuate Arthur Koestler's barbaric derivative struthonian... If *leonine*, then *struthionine*, or nothing.

strüverite. Add: **2.** *Min.* An oxide of titanium containing tantalum and ferric iron, found as black tetragonal crystals having a metallic lustre. [a. It. *strüverite* (F. Zambonini 1907, in *Rend. dell'Accad. d. Sci. fis. e matem.* (Napoli) XIII. 46).]

1907 *Mineral. Mag.* XIV. 411 Strüverite. **1908** *Ibid.* XV. 78 The mineral strüverite occurs as a rare accessory constituent of the pegmatite which is found in large detrital masses in the neighbourhood of Craveggia (Val Vigezzo, northern Piedmont). **1917** [see *mossite]. **1974** *Mineral. Abstr.* XXV. 236/1 Strüverite, tanteuxenite and tantalanatase from the pegmatites near the town of Chepelare, Central Rhodopes [Bulgaria].

Struwwelpeter (strū·əlpītəɹ, ‖ʃtru·vəlpē:tər). Also *erron.* **Struwelpeter.** The name of a character in a children's book of the same name by Heinrich Hoffmann (1809–94), used *attrib.* to designate (a person with) long, thick, and unkempt hair. Also *transf.* Also *Comb.*, as *Struwwelpeter-haired.* Hence **Struwwelpeterdom,** (of hair) the condition of being thick and untidy. Cf. *shockheaded Peter* s.v. *shock-headed *a.*

1909 W. J. Locke *Septimus* iii. 37 He passed his hand through his Struwelpeter hair. *Ibid.* xxii. 351 His hair.. reached the climax of Struwelpeterdom. **1920** E. Sitwell *Wooden Pegasus* 78 As he rides on his rocking-horse All Struwwelpeter-haired. **1927** 'G. Daviot' *Man in Queue* vii. 82 The artist's eyebrows disappeared in the Struwwelpeter hair. **1958** P. Kemp *No Colours or Crest* x. 228 The Commissar was a small, squat man with very bright eyes and a *Struwwelpeter* shock of black hair. **1959** C. Spry *Favourite Flowers* xxv. 188 The flowers [of *Anemone alpina*] were over and I saw for the first time what Mr. Drake calls the 'Struwwelpeter' seed heads. **1973** R. W. Clark *Einstein* xi. 269 William Rothenstein, making notes for his remarkable portrait of Einstein who is presented as a Struwelpeter character, smiling from an aureole of almost electrified hair.

strychninization (stri:kninəizē̍ⁱ·ʃən). [f. as next + -ization.] The act of applying strychnine.

1898 in *Syd. Soc. Lex.* **1933** *Ann. Rep. London Co. Council* IV. iii. 143 After strychninisation of the gyrus uncinatus and lobus pyriformis, fits could be induced by olfactory stimulation. **1951** J. F. Fulton *Frontal Lobotomy* ii. 47 Strychninization of the posterior hypothalamus activates the dorsomedial nuclei. **1974** *Proc. Soc. Exper. Biol. & Med.* CXLV. 979 (*heading*) Subcortical multiple unit activity..during strychninization of the cerebral cortex in the female rat.

strychninize (stri·kninəiz), *v.* [f. Strychnine + -ize.] *trans.* To apply strychnine to.

1934 in Webster. **1938** *Jrnl. Neurophysiol.* I. 69 The distribution of the spikes within the cytoarchitectonic area, of which a part has been strychninized. **1951** P. D. MacLean in J. F. Fulton *Frontal Lobotomy* ii. 57 Then we strychninized the nucleus. **1980** *Pavlovian Jrnl. Biol. Sci.* XV. 58/1 The response was made single by strychninizing a larger area of cortex.

Hence **stry·chninized** *ppl. a.*

1938 *Jrnl. Neurophysiol.* I. 72 Farther away from the strychninized locus spikes are absent. **1978** H. Takeuchi in Chalazonitis & Boisson *Abnormal Neuronal Discharges* 161 The strychninized somatic abnormal biopotential was similarly subjected to temperature changes.

strychnization (striknəizē̍ⁱ·ʃən). [f. Strychn(ia + -ization.] = *strychninization.

1916 *Q. Jrnl. Exper. Physiol.* IX. 356 Slight strychnisation of the dorsal mechanisms..gives rise to a typical complex of symptoms. **1924** *Proc. R. Soc.* B. XCVI. 272 Local strychnization of the central nervous system.. yields good results in investigations on the sensory mechanisms of the spinal cord.

stryddag (strē̍ⁱ·tdaχ). *S. Afr.* Pl. **stryddae.** [Afrikaans, lit. 'struggle day, day of battle'.] An Afrikaner political party rally. Also *transf.*

1950 *Cape Times* 26 July 1/3 Mr. C. R. Swart, Minister of Justice, told a Nationalist Party stryddag here yesterday that he was not prepared to reintroduce public hangings. **1961** *Ibid.* 11 Jan. 1/6 In Britain he will be able to give the moderately-phrased versions of *apartheid* far more expertly and convincingly than in heated debates in Parliament or during *stryddae* in the platteland. **1972** *Daily Dispatch* 14 Apr. 10 The day of the big stryddag is over. Those large crowds will never again drive across the veld to hear emotional appeals to the blood. **1978** *Pace* Dec. 51 On Sunday, Chief Buthelezi is going to.. address an all-black *stryddag* in Soweto.

stschi, var. Stchi in Dict. and Suppl.

Stuart (stiū·ăɹt). Also formerly **Stewart.** The name of the British royal family from 1603 to 1688, used *attrib.* to designate that period of history and applied esp. to artefacts, buildings, etc., of that date or style.

1873 C. M. Yonge *Pillars of House* IV. xxxvi. 50 Here's the dining-room—This is the middle period, the Stewart style part. **1880** E. Glaister *Needlework* viii. 87 Some oak chairs, probably of early Stuart date. **1922** S. Weyman *Ovington's Bank* ix. 104 Long-backed Stuart chairs. **1937** *Discovery* Aug. 231/1 The penny of Tudor and Stuart times. **1973** *Country Life* 5 Apr. 909/2 He has treated the wainscot of the Stuart bedroom..in a similar manner to the Stuart staircase. **1981** V. Glendinning *Edith Sitwell* i. 12 Renishaw Hall..retained within its walls..most of its Stuart and Regency past.

stub, *sb.* Add: **7. e.** A short length of wire used in flower-arranging. Cf. *stub wire*, sense 11 below.

1951 R. A. Birch et al. *Mod. Florist* ix. 83 On the bench is fixed the wire tidy..a set of upright metal cylinders or holders into which the wires, or 'stubs', are placed. *Ibid.* 88 Next we come to 'invisible wiring' with ordinary stubs. **1960** V. Stevenson in T. A. Price et al. *Retail Florist's Handbk.* iii. 66 Stem wires, often called stub wires (one assumes because they are stubbed into the design), vary from 3½ to 18 inches in length... Twenty gauge..is the most widely used wreath stub. **1963** M. Smith *Arranging Flowers* viii. 83 With a very fragile stem it is best to lay a stub-wire against it..and to twist fuse-wire round both the stub and the stem to bind them together.

9. a. Also *spec.* the butt or stump of a cigar or cigarette.

1855 'Q. K. P. Doesticks' *Doesticks, what he Says* xvi. 133 Perhaps they expect us to smoke 'stubs', like the newsboys. **1869** [in Dict.]. **1873** J. H. Beadle *Undevel. West* 787 Even little darkeys watch for the 'old stubs' as they are thrown away. **1914** B. M. Bower *Flying U Ranch* 187 He spat upon the burnt end of his cigarette stub from force of the habit that fear of range fires had built. **1973** T. Pynchon *Gravity's Rainbow* (1975) iii. 309 The two of them sit there, passing a cigarette back and forth, till it's smoked down to a very small stub.

11. stub-end, (*b*) *U.S.*, the unconnected end of a stub track; (*c*) a cigarette stub (in quot. *fig.*); **stub station** *U.S.*, a railway station at which the tracks terminate; **stub-switch** (examples); **stub-tail,** (*b*) also used of maize (later example); (*c*) a short and thick or broad tail; also *fig.*; **stub-toed** *a.*, of a shoe: having a broad toe; **stub track** *U.S.*, a railway track, usu. at a terminus, connected to another at one end only; also *stub-end track* (cf. *stub-end* (*b*) above); **stub wing** *Aeronaut.* (see quot. 1956); hence **stub-winged** *a.*; **stub wire** = sense 7 e above.

1896 *Engineering News* XXXVI. 27/1 When a long stub-end track gets full of empties, the cars at the stub end are likely to remain for weeks and months. **1900** *Ibid.* XLIV. 377/2 Stub-end tracks should generally be in pairs, with crossovers near the ends, so that the engine of one incoming train can be got out without waiting for its train. **1903** W. M. Camp *Notes Track Constr.* I. vi. 466 An arrangement that is sometimes provided where inbound, outbound and transfer houses are consolidated at one point is to have parallel stub tracks, with the inbound house on one side, the outbound house on the opposite side and the office between them, at the stub ends of the tracks. **1932** Auden *Orators* iii. 85 Stub-end of year that smoulders to ash of winter. **1916** J. A. Droege *Passenger Terminals* v. 104 The head or stub station is an end-of-the-line station. *Ibid.*, Practically all the terminals in New York City are built on the stub station plan. **1929** *Amer. Railway Engineering Assoc. Man.* xiv. 960 The through and loop types of station are superior to the stub station from the standpoint of train operation. **1885** G. Mordecai *Rep. Terminal Facilities* 6 The tracks are of good material, laid with stub switches and railfrogs. **1903** W. M. Camp *Notes Track Constr.* I. 292 The stub switch, with its open joint in winter and tight joint in summer, with a loose head block to be tampered with every few days. **1873** *Spider & Fly* iv. i. 19 This corn is the Illinois growth of 1857, and is called 'stub-tail' because about one-third of it is rotten. **1938** L. MacNeice *Zoo* 234 They [*sc.* bears] showed their stub-tails. **1973** *Times* 17 May 35/1 Compared with the 1100 it has a more streamlined bonnet curving down to a low radiator grille, and a stub tail somewhat reminiscent of the Hillman Avenger. **1930** J. Dos Passos *42nd Parallel* 134 He'd..clatter up and down stairs making a tremendous racket with his stubtoed ironplated shoes. **1896** *Engineering News* XXXVI. 27/1 The empty car storage tracks on Mr. Derr's diagram are very long stub tracks, which are objectionable. **1921** *Railway Engin. & Maintenance of Way Cycl.* 348/1 A freight terminal is commonly considered an important freight station served by stub tracks. **1956** *Railway Track & Structures Cycl.* (ed. 8) 425/2 Bumping posts are obstructions placed at the end of stub tracks. **1931** *Flight* 2 Jan. 16/2 The lower stub wings form part of the landing gear structure. **1956** W. A. Heflin *U.S. Air Force Dict.* 496/2 *Stub wing*,..1. A short wing, esp. as used on certain autogiros. 2. That part of a wing on certain airplanes that lies next to the fuselage, to which the rest of the wing, separately built, is attached... 3. Short for 'stubwing stabilizer.'..*Stubwing stabilizer*, a hydro-stabilizer on a flying boat. **1958** *Times Rev. Industry* Aug. 39/2 The [Rotodyne] fixed stubwing..takes over the task of supporting the aircraft. **1957** *Times Survey Brit. Aviation* Sept. 2/6 Bristol are sending the stub-winged twin-rotor Type 173. **1960, 1963** Stub wire [see sense 7 e above]. **1976** *Eastern Even. News* (Norwich) 22 Dec. 4/8 (Advt.), Oasis (dry and wet). Dried flowers. Stub wires and a large selection of containers.

stub, *v.*[1] Add: **9. a.** Also *fig.*

1957 *Economist* 19 Oct. 194/1 At a time when the Middle East has become more of a happy hunting ground for Russians seeking friends and influence than ever before, it is on Turkey that they are always stubbing their toe. **1967** [see *goods *sb. pl.* 2 b]. **1976** 'J. Ross' *I know what it's like to Die* xix. 126 It was a reputable organisation. At least, insofar as it hadn't stubbed its corporate toes on, or interfered with, anything under the supervision of the superintendent's own bailiwick.

b. Also *transf.* and *fig.*

1875 C. B. Lewis *Quad's Odds* 480 The writer will stub along through life with a heart full of joyfulness. **1878** B. F. Taylor *Between Gates* 241 An old whaler stubbing about estimated him [*sc.* a whale] at sixty barrels.

12. *trans.* To extinguish (a cigarette) by pressing the lighted end of the stub against a hard object. Freq. with *out.* Also *fig.*

1927 *Daily Express* 28 Oct. 5 A new glass ash tray with cigarette rests has a glass stopper fitting in at the back which is used for stubbing one's smokes... On the stubber a Greek girl dancing, scarf in hand [is represented]. **1930** J. Cannan *No Walls of Jasper* 116 He stubbed out his cigarette and smiled at her. **1955** P. Larkin in *Listener* 8 Sept. 373/1, I lie Where Mr. Bleaney lay, and stub my fags On the same saucer-souvenir. **1962** J. Braine *Life at Top* xxvi. 277, I looked round for an ashtray and for the fifth time since nine o'clock stubbed out my cigarette on the floor. **1970** R. Lowell *Notebk.* 214 A hand prepared to stub out liberty. **1974** 'E. Ferrars' *Hanged Man's House* xv. 149 There was always something that you could do with a cigarette, light it, draw on it, tip ash off it, stub it out. **1978** S. Radley *Death & Maiden* xi. 109 She stubbed out her cigarette with sudden vigour.

stubbed, *ppl. a.* Add: **6.** Chiefly, of a toe: injured by being struck against something. Cf. Stub *v.*[1] 9 a in Dict. and Suppl. orig. *U.S.*

1890 *Brighton* (Colorado) *Reg.* 11 Jan. 4/1 Montana is the 'stubbed-toe State'. **1958** J. G. MacGregor *North-West of 16* viii. 111, I don't suppose a city boy, or even a modern farm boy, knows what a stubbed toe is. Maybe that's just as well, because they were most painful. **1977** *Evening Gaz.* (Middlesbrough) 11 Jan. 4/5 None of the hair-raising stunts he performs for his TV series Some Mothers Do 'Ave 'Em led to any injury greater than a stubbed finger. **1978** B. Bainbridge *Young Adolf* xviii. 101 Testily he kicked at the..wood... Recoiling, he curled his stubbed toes within his boot.

7. *stubbed-out*: of a cigarette, extinguished by being pressed against a hard object.

1975 O. Sela *Bengali Inheritance* xxv. 218 A single stubbed out Stuyvesant in the ashtray. **1979** *N.Y. Rev. Bks.* 8 Feb. 13/4 No other writer since Noël Coward can have so constantly punctuated dialogue and action with a ritual pattern of lighting-up, inhalation, smoke-rings, and stubbed-out butts.

stubber. Add: **2.** A contrivance against which a cigarette is stubbed out.

1927 [see *stub *v.*[1] 12].

stubble, *sb.* Add: **5.** objective, *stubble-burner, -burning*; instrumental, as *stubble-covered* adj.; **stubble-fed** *a.*, of poultry: fed on the stubble left in a reaped field; hence **stubble-feeding; stubble-grown** *a.* = *stubble-covered* adj. above; **stubble-jumper** *slang* (chiefly *Canad.*), a prairie farmer (see also quot. 1946); **stubble-quail,** a brown, black, and white quail, *Coturnix pectoralis*, native to southern Australia.

1980 *Sunday Times* 24 Aug. 1/7 Can stubble-burners be controlled? **1973** *Times* 24 Aug. 2/5 The National Union of Agricultural and Allied Workers yesterday called for regulations to control stubble burning. **1976** A. Price *War Game* 1. ii. 48 There hadn't been so much stubble-burning this year, he noted approvingly. **1916** Joyce *Portrait of Artist* (1969) ii. 61 Stephen often glanced with mistrust at his trainer's flabby stubblecovered face. **1882** W. D. Hay *Brighter Britain!* I. 224 Cricket-fed turkey would shame any stubble-fed bird altogether. **1928** *Daily Express* 6 Oct. 4/6 These stubble-fed geese are the best of all for eating. **1960** G. E. Evans *Horse in Furrow* xii. 172 There were two kinds of shacking; *Lammas shack*..and *Michaelmas shack*, stubble-feeding after the corn harvest. **1916** Joyce *Portrait of Artist* (1969) v. 227 Good evening, gentlemen, said the stubblegrown monkeyish face. **1946** *California Folklore Q.* Apr. 164 'Top hands', 'sodbusters', 'hay stopers', 'stubble jumpers',..denote farmers who have turned to mining, and these terms are always opprobrious. **1961** *Sun* (Vancouver) 4 July 1/1 The prairie farmer, to those of us who don't know him well, is a stock comic character. Clod-hopper, we call him, and stubble-jumper. **1973** *Islander* (Victoria, B.C.) 19 Aug. 12/1 An authentic stubble-jumper from the prairies was looked upon as being at the very bottom rung of the social and employment ladder. **1848** J. Gould *Birds Austral.* V. plate 88 The name of Stubble Quail has been given to it by the colonists of Van Diemen's Land, from the great numbers that visit the fields after the harvest is over. **1921** Matthews & Iredale *Man. Birds Austral.* I. 224 Stubble-quail... Head, neck, entire back and scapulars rufous-brown and black streaked with white. **1965** *Austral. Encycl.* VII. 316/1 The stubble-quail, which is closely allied to the quail of Europe, is confined to southern Australia and Tasmania.

stubborn, *a.* Add: **4.** *stubborn-hearted* (later example).

1906 W. B. Yeats *Poems, 1899–1905* 55 Women are hard and proud and stubborn-hearted.

Stubbsian (stɒ·bziăn), *a.* [f. the surname *Stubbs* (see below) + -ian.] **1.** Of, pertaining to, or characteristic of the English painter George *Stubbs* (1724–1806), or his work.

1960 *Times* 4 Nov. 16/7 Ferneley's brand of aristocratic elegance is splendidly represented, especially in the 'Five Hunters in the Park at Deene' (a Stubbsian subject with a better understanding of space than Stubbs). **1963** *Times* 1 May 5/7 Stubbs, of course, ranges over the whole field of conversation pieces, portraiture, wild life and landscape as well as horse painting;..and there is a picture of almost Stubbsian quality by George Garrard.

2. Of or pertaining to William *Stubbs* (1825–1901), historian and Bishop of Oxford, or his historical opinions.

1979 *English Hist. Rev.* XCIV. 487 By 1934 Kenneth Pickthorn's study of *Early Tudor Government*..still framed its argument in Stubbsian terms by denying that the period had much of a constitution at all aside from the medieval idea of the supremacy of law.

stubby (stɒ·bi), *sb. Austral. slang.* Also **stubbie.** [f. Stubby *a.*] **1.** A short, squat beer-bottle with a capacity of 375 ml. Also *Comb.*, as *stubby beer bottle.*

1957 *Encycl. Brit.* IV. 106/2 A variety of standardized forms and sizes of bottles are in use, including the so-called Stubby, Steinie, Packie, Export and Single Trip bottles. **1966** *Sunday Truth* (Brisbane) 8 May 33/7 Well-known transport man generally likes to have a 'stubbie' of beer at home each evening. **1968** F. Hardy *Unlucky Australians* 49 He threw an empty stubby into the box and went to the refrigerator for a full one. **1969** *Sunday Truth* (Brisbane) 23 Nov. 37/7 Both as a safety measure and a fight against litter, I advocate the absolute banning of the stubby beer bottle. **1972** G. Morley *Jockey rides Honest Race* 165 Phil opened the freezer and pulled out four stubbies. **1977** *Mod. Boating* (Austral.) Jan. 88/1 Buy another stubby at the bar to gather strength to try again in half an hour.

2. Usu. *pl.* Shorts (see Short *sb.* 6 d in Dict. and Suppl.).

1977 *Australian* 7 Apr. 3 Stubbies—the football shorts with pockets—have become an international fashion... Although the Stubby is a very Australian name—thought of in the context of short shorts to go with short bottles of beer—Mr Phillips is confident they will become as American as apple pie. **1982** *Guardian* 18 Dec. 11 'Stubbies', slang for both the shorts they wear..and the bottles from which they drink. *Ibid.* 11/4 (*caption*) 'Stubbies' (shorts) and pot bellies predominate on Australia's popular side.

‖**Stube** (ʃtū·bə). Also **stube.** [Ger., lit. 'room, parlour'.] = *Bierstube.

1946 S. Spender *European Witness* 138 He invited me to join the other officers in going to a drinking Stube. **1956** E. Berckman *Strange Bedfellow* vii. 66 The dimness and coolness of the village *Stube.* **1967** J. Eastwood *Little Dragon from Peking* xvii. 153 Hilde, the maid of all work, had already mopped the wooden floor of the *Stube.* **1969** A. Glyn *Dragon Variation* viii. 232 In a gasthof in the Maria-Josephastrasse, Jeff Falkner sat at a window, staring out at the snow. The others were downstairs playing chess in the stube. **1980** J. Cartwright *Horse of Darius* x. 149 A *stube* full of hearty people drinking beer.

stuc, stuck. Restrict † *Obs.* to sense in Dict. and add: **2.** = Stucco *sb.* 1 b.

1932 T. Corkhill *Conc. Building Encycl.* 207 *Stuc*, plasterwork to imitate stone. **1971** *Country Life* 14 Oct. 969/1 Its walls are of *stuc*, by M. Germain, an imitation of dressed Caen stone.

stuccador(e (stɒ·kădōᵊɪ). Also **stuccodore.** [irreg. ad. It. *stuccatore*; cf. Sp. *estucador.*] A worker in stucco. Cf. Stuccoer.

1952 *Archit. Rev.* CXI. 201/3 Its Tapestry Room with Floral Zephyrs by James 'Athenian' Stuart and a Saloon with walls marvellously decorated by Italian stuccadores. **1956** *Essays in Crit.* VI. 324 The iconography of other eighteenth-century arts (Tiepolo's painting, the interior plasterwork of Dublin stuccodores), is still that of the High Renaissance. **1972** *Canad. Antiques Collector* Mar.–Apr. 15/1 The interiors..are as exuberant and varied as the stuccodores through seventy years of changing taste (1730–1800) could make them. **1973** *Country Life* 10 May 1306/2 The Schmuzer family..whose activity as mason-stuccadors persisted right into the Rococo period. **1978** A. Laing in A. Blunt et al. *Baroque & Rococo* iv. 241/1 In Bavaria it was a Wessobrunner stuccador, Joseph Schmuzer (1683–1752), who was most successful in creating a local practice as the architect of parish churches, extending his competence from stucco to masonry.

stucco, *sb.* Add: **2. b.** A house plastered with stucco.

1976 C. Weston *Rouse Demon* (1977) xi. 50 The Simmons house turned out to be a two-story Monterey-style stucco. **1981** P. Mallory *Killing Matter* xvi. 167 A blue stucco at the corner of Delgado and Harding.

stuccoist (stɒ·kouˌist). = Stuccoer. Cf. *Stuccador(e.

1945 J. Lees-Milne *Jrnl.* 26 Sept. in *Prophesying Peace* (1977) 238 Lord Leigh assured me..that the plasterwork was by Cipriani, which I find hard to believe unless there was an earlier stuccoist of the same name as the well-known painter. **1969** M. Whinney *Home House* 19 In November 1775 Joseph Rose, Adam's principal stuccoist, was paid £603.10.0.

stuck, *ppl. a.* Add: **5.** With advs. forming adjs. with reference to attachment or sealing by adhesive, etc., as *stuck-down, -on.*

1908 Kipling *Actions & Reactions* (1909) 101 The Hive shook beneath the shattering thunder of a stuck-down quilt being torn back. **1940** *Chambers's Techn. Dict.* 815/2 *Stuck-on soles* (*Shoes*), shoe soles in which the upper inner sole and the outer sole are attached together by means of strong cement; used for women's and children's shoes. **1960** *Farmer & Stockbreeder* 15 Mar. Suppl. 7 A whitewood bedside cabinet is given a stuck-on veneer finish. **1978** D. Francis *Trial Run* xviii. 228 One of them handed me a stuck-down envelope.

stuckness (stɒ·knės). [f. Stuck *ppl. a.* + -ness.] The condition of being stuck or unable to move or progress.

1969 J. S. Bruner in Elkind & Flavell *Stud. Cognitive Devel.* 225 Let me characterize that growth briefly as moving from a diffuse distractibility in the weeks immediately following birth to a stage of stuckness where attention has an 'obligatory character', to use Stechler's phrase. **1974** R. M. Pirsig *Zen & Art of Motorcycle Maintenance* xxiv. 278 The first [problem] is stuckness, a mental stuckness that accompanies the physical stuckness of whatever it is you're working on.

stud, *sb.*[1] Add: **II. 5. d.** One of a series of small devices protruding slightly above the surface of a road and used to demarcate traffic lanes; *spec.* = *cat's eye 5.

1935, etc. [see *road stud* s.v. *road *sb.* 9 b]. **1939** L. MacNeice *Autumn Jrnl.* viii. 33 The metal studs in the sleek macadam. **1943** *Ann. Reg. 1942* 386 A traffic stud insecurely fixed..flew up and injured a cyclist. **1958** *Spectator* 8 Aug. 190/2 The road studs known as cat's eyes. **1975** R. Hoban *Turtle Diary* xxxii. 151 There were reflecting studs in the road. **1978** *Highway Code* 18 Coloured reflecting road studs may be used with white lines—white studs mark the lanes or centre of the road, while the edge of the carriageway may have red studs on the left-hand side and amber by the central reservation of dual carriageways. Green studs may be used across lay-bys and side roads.

e. = *ear-stud* s.v. *ear *sb.*[1] 16.

[**1873**: see *ear-stud* s.v. *ear *sb.*[1] 16.] **1968** J. Ironside *Fashion Alphabet* 172 *Stud*, a plain 'knob' on the ear. **1979** N. Freeling *Widow* xxiii. 143 Garnet studs in the pale fleshy lobes of the ears.

6. See also *press-stud.

7. g. One of a number of metal pieces set into the tyre of a motor vehicle to improve roadholding in slippery conditions. *N. Amer.*

[**1909** *Westm. Gaz.* 11 Nov. 5/2 Messrs. B. F. Goodrich will exhibit their all-rubber non-skids, in which the rubber studs form an integral part of the tread, as well as a new steel-studded tyre.] **1963** *Pop. Mechanics* Sept. 24 *PM* tried one version of Season Safety Stud tires on a glassy smooth skating rink and found performance impressive. **1976** *National Observer* (U.S.) 13 Nov. 10/4 In Illinois, Minnesota, and Wisconsin studded tires have been barred this year for the first time. In Michigan a new law permits studs only if they meet certain rigid—and some say impossible—specifications.

IV. 9. stud-ear-ring = *ear-stud* s.v. *ear *sb.*[1] 16; cf. sense 5 e above; **stud welding,** a method of welding in which an arc is struck between a stud and the base metal, producing a pool of molten metal into which the stud is driven to form a weld.

1919–20 *T. Eaton & Co. Catal.* Fall & Winter 394/3, 14k stud earrings, set with diamond. **1966** [see *ear-stud* s.v. *ear *sb.*[1] 16]. **1973** E. Linington *Crime by Chance* i. 10 Sue..put on makeup and small stud earrings. **1941** A. C. Davies *Sci. & Pract. Welding* iv. 298 (*heading*) Stud welding or studding. **1962** *Engineering* 20 Apr. 527/1 Stud welding has the advantage that there is no distortion of the flanges of the steel beams. **1975** Bram & Downs *Manuf. Technol.* ii. 57 Stud welding is a form of electric-arc welding.

stud, *sb.*[2] Add: **4. c.** = Stud-horse 2. Chiefly *U.S.*

[**1890** J. P. Quinn *Fools of Fortune* 188 Next to the banking games in the estimation of the betters comes poker, both 'draw' and 'stud'.] **1933** D. Runyon in *Collier's* 28 Jan. 8/1 A proposition may be only a problem in cards, such as..how often a pair of deuces will win a hand in stud. **1942** W. FAULKNER *Go down, Moses* 26 'Stud,' Mr Hubert said. 'One hand. You to shuffle, me to cut, this boy to deal.' **1979** REESE & FLINT *Trick 13* 64 In seven-card stud a player who stays in the pot till the finish receives two cards face down, four face up, and one face down.

d. A man of (reputedly) great sexual potency or accomplishments; a womanizer, a habitual seducer of women. In weakened uses: as a familiar term of address among men; a boy-friend or escort.

Particularly common since *c* 1960.

1895 W. RYE *Gloss. E. Anglia* 217 *Stud*, a nickname given to a man from his love of venery (Wilton, 1877). **1909** *Dialect Notes* III. 377 *Stud (-horse)*, *n.*, a stallion. Also used as a term of familiar address among men. 'Hello, old stud, how are you?' **1955** *Amer. Speech* XXX. 305 [Wayne University slang] *Stud*, a ladies' man. **1959** C. MACINNES *Absolute Beginners* 165 The chick sits on cushions in the front part, with a brolly, and her stud heaves the thing along with a hop pole, just like gondolas. **1970** B. MOORE *Luck of Ginger Coffey* iv. 88 Throwing her across this bed yesterday, pleased with yourself for being the great stud. **1964** S. BELLOW *Herzog* 154 Still in fleeting moments the young and glossy stud—such as he really had never been. **1974** M. HASKELL *From Reverence to Rape* 250 In the sixties we came to realize that the figure of the stud (the gamekeeper, the 'macho' Latin, the gigolo) is, like the sex-starved woman, largely a figment of male homosexual fantasy. **1981** S. RUSHDIE *Midnight's Children* III. 395 A notorious seducer; a ladies'-man; a cuckolder of the rich; in short, a stud.

e. Hence (without explicit sexual significance): a man, a fellow, esp one who is well-informed; a youth. *U.S. slang* (chiefly *Blacks'*).

1929 M. A. GILL *Underworld Slang* 10/2 *Stud*, man. **1944** D. BURLEY *Orig. Handbk. Harlem Jive* 70 If you're a hipped stud, you'll latch on. **1946** MEZZROW & WOLFE *Really Blues* (1957) 379 *Stud*, guy, man. **1963** E. J. GAINES in *Sewanee Rev.* Autumn 550, I mean a stud's going to drink eggnog, and he isn't going to put whiskey in it. **1967** W. MURRAY *Sweet Ride* x. 169 We're looking for a couple of studs..Jimmy the Head and Jawbone. **1970** R. D. ABRAHAMS *Positively Black* ii. 46 But who's this stud they call Billy?

5. (sense 1) *stud-fee*, *-master*; **stud-book:** also *transf.* and *fig.*, a catalogue of aristocratic pedigree, esp. = *BURKE *sb.*, *DEBRETT *sb.*; **stud-poker** (now the commonest form): (earlier and later examples).

1888 KIPLING *Story of Gadsbys* (1891) viii. 122 'Fraid you won't be entered in the Stud Book correctly unless you go Home? **1933** D. L. SAYERS *Murder must Advertise* xi. 198, I think I know the stud-book pretty well. I was not aware that you had a cousin Bredon. **1982** R. BARNARD *Death & Princess* xii. 122 Lady Dorothy..can drone on endlessly about her family tree... She's a sort of walking stud-book. **1922** JOYCE *Ulysses* 540 What's our studfee?..You fee men dancers on the Riviera, I read. **1953** X. FIELDING *Stronghold* 48 My stud-fee's as low as you like—I'd do it for nothing. **1937** E. RICKMAN *On & Off Racecourse* i. 3 Their best horses are placed at stud.. or are sold to other stud-masters. **1975** *N.Z. Jrnl. Agric.* Sept. 60/3 New Zealand studmasters have proved their ability through the years. **1864** W. B. DICK *Amer. Hoyle* 167 *Stud poker*.., in all essential particulars, is like the other Poker games. **1922** S. LEWIS *Babbitt* xxv. 295 All the way north he pictured the Maine guides: simple and strong and daring, jolly as they played stud-poker in their unceiled shack. **1959** 'B. MATHER' *Achilles Affair* I. i. 13 He and Finnessy were playing murderous stud poker. **1978** E. TIDYMAN *Table Stakes* II. iii. 191 The best stud poker player who ever sat down among them.

6. *attrib.* or *adj.* use of sense 4 d above: manly, displaying a masculine sexual character. Hence *loosely* in commendation: fine, excellent. Chiefly *U.S. slang.*

1944 AUDEN *Sea & Mirror* in *For Time Being* iii. 56 The stud contralto gargling through her maternal grief. **1969** *Sat. Rev.* (U.S.) 5 July 28 There's nothing like a head-shrinker..for putting you where you're at. That's stud. **1971** *Black Scholar* Sept. 45/1 He had learned the stories about stud broads..but he knew Christine 'used' to be a stud broad. **1977** *Amer. Speech* **1975** L. 67 *Stud.* 1: *adj*, outstanding, having all the attributes approved of by the group.

studded, *ppl. a.* Add: **1. c.** Of a tyre: provided with studs (*STUD *sb.*[1] 7 g).

1966 *Better Homes & Gardens* Jan. 14/2 Studded snow tires made their debut in many of the snow belt states last winter. **1970** *Toronto Daily Star* 24 Sept. 39/1 Studded tires were causing costly damage to city streets.

student[1]. Add: **2. b.** A scholar at an institute of primary or secondary education. orig. *U.S.*

1900 E. E. BROWN in N. M. Butler *Monographs on Educ. in U.S.* 183 In these laboratories [high school] students perform representative experiments in the science they are pursuing. **1924** *Junior High School Clearing House* Mar. 6/1 It was felt..that to single out the student who excelled in scholarship was usually to recognize native abilities but not necessarily serious effort. **1936** *Evening Citizen* (Glasgow) 29 Aug. 4/6 [In the United States] even schoolboys and schoolgirls are students. **1962** *Dict. Canad. English: Beginning Dict.* 644/2 *Student*... 2. a person who is studying in a school, college, or university: *That high school has 3,000 students.* **1976** *Times* 5 Aug. 14/7 We have primary school students, presumably working for BAs in Plasticine; the National Union of School Students; and graduation day for high school students... Formerly people were schoolboys or schoolgirls until they became undergraduates.

c. An inexperienced user of illegal drugs; *spec.* one who takes small or occasional doses. *U.S. drug-users' slang.*

1936 [see *joy-popper* s.v. *JOY *sb.* 10]. **1949** [see *JUNKIE]. **1951** [see *SATURDAY NIGHT 1].

5. a. *student activism, activist, body, counselling, demonstrator, duel, exchange, grant, hostel, leader, politics, protest, revolt, revolution, riot, unrest, violence*; appositive, as *student nurse*.

1977 *Hongkong Standard* 14 Apr. 4/4 The University of the Philippines, a hotbed of student activism before Mr Marcos declared martial law in September 1972. **1969** 'E. LATHEN' *When in Greece* x. 114 He had almost forgotten his role as a student activist. **1906** W. JAMES *Mem. & Stud.* (1911) xiv. 362 Above all things, offer the opportunity of higher personal contacts. A university provides these anyhow within the student body. **1979** A. PRICE *Tomorrow's Ghost* ii. 26 We're not infiltrating the delectable student body. **1959** *Listener* 19 Mar. 515/1 This sort of thing must surely have been studied by university psychology departments before now—particularly in America, where 'student counselling' is respectable. **1968** 'J. LE CARRÉ' *Small Town in Germany* ii. 13 Student demonstrators..overturned the American Ambassador's car. **1911** Student-duel [see *MENSUR]. **1979** J. LEASOR *Love & Land Beyond* iii. 48 Men..take pride in bearing scars of student duals on their cheeks. **1971** K. DICK *Ivy & Stevie* 42 I've been to Potsdam, Amsterdam, Königsberg. .. Sort of student exchange holidays. **1965** *Students' Handbk.* 1965 (Univ. Coll. London Union) 43 For years the Councils of the N.U.S...have reiterated a call for the abolition of the Means Test on parental incomes used in the assessment of student grants. **1974** Student grant [see *inflation-proofing* s.v. *INFLATION 8]. **1960** *N.U.S. Year Bk.* 35 This year marks the eleventh in which the Union has maintained a student hostel in the Bloomsbury area. **1977** R. BARNARD *Blood Brotherhood* xvi. 182 It was the address of a student hostel. **1962** E. SNOW *Red China Today* (1963) i. 20 Huang Hua, whom I knew as a student leader when I taught briefly at the American-supported Yenching University. **1932** *Lancet Commission on Nursing* v. 46 Each 'student nurse', as they are called, is attached to a nursery class with part-time practical work with little children. **1956** K. HULME *Nun's Story* xvii. 287 She listened deliberately now to the talk of her student nurses. **1954** P. TOYNBEE *Friends Apart* ii. 35, I used my freedom to become..violently caught up in the excitement of student politics. **1965** *Granta* Summer 9/1 The worst tactical mistake the SRC could make is not to dissociate itself from the old idea of 'student protest'. **1976** D. CLARK *Dread & Water* vi. 133 We'd had a student protest at the gate. **1969** *Listener* 8 May 630/2, I said that western civilisation today was being challenged from within... The most obvious symptom is the outbreak of what is commonly called 'student unrest', or 'student revolt'. **1978** P. BOARDMAN *Worlds of Patrick Geddes* xi. 403 In 1930, an event occurred which took the old and hardy critic of universities himself by surprise: a student revolt. **1968** *Punch* 31 July 168/1 When the student revolution intervened the group moved to England. **1968** *Listener* 4 July 1/1 'Student riots', 'student violence', 'the movement for student power'—these are phrases that have been used to cover a wide variety of actions and attitudes and opinions. **1966** J. MITFORD in *Vogue* (U.S.) 15 Mar. 93/1 Campuses throughout the country, undergoing the 'wave of student unrest', are producing their share of women individualists. **1968** Student violence [see *student riot* above].

b. student card, a card or ticket issued to members of a student body, and usu. entitling the holder to certain privileges; **student power,** the exercise of authority within a school, college, or larger sphere by students (cf. *POWER *sb.*[1] 4 f); **student(s') union** = UNION *sb.*[1] 10 c; also applied to a similar association or building at other centres of higher education, and *loosely*, to a national association of students, formed to promote the welfare and views of its members (cf. *N.U.S.* s.v. *N II. 1); **student teacher,** a student of a university or training college who teaches in a school for a certain period, as part of the qualification for a teaching certificate (cf. PUPIL TEACHER); hence **student-teachership; student-teaching; student-teacher** *a.*, designating the relation between students at a school or college and their teacher or teachers (cf. *pupil-teacher* adj. s.v. *PUPIL *sb.*[1] 3 b).

1973 *Sat. Rev. Society* (U.S.) May 53/2 Cost of the 16-hour program: $50 ($30 for anyone with a student card). **1975** P. THEROUX *Gt. Railway Bazaar* iii. 51 She was a student and..had a student card... A card got each one a 50 percent reduction on the ticket. **1968** *Listener* 21 Mar. 365/3 He will go to any lengths to placate and excuse the brutally vocal ginger group of Student Power. **1973** *Times* 15 Oct. 17/1 Student power alone would not have toppled the government unless circumstances were very much in their favour. **1891** Students' Union [see UNION *sb.*[1] 10 c]. **1916** J. BUCHAN *Power-House* v. 134 It had something to do with the Slav States of Austria and an Italian Students' Union, and it threatened..to be dangerous. **1967** M. KENYON *Whole Hog* i. 12 The student union cafeteria always had..fried, boiled or scrambled eggs. **1977** P. JOHNSON *Enemies of Society* xii. 171 It was Margaret Thatcher..who, in the winter of 1970–1, changed the wording of the official regulations to allow public money to be handed over to the Student Unions. **1982** A. TAYLOR *Caroline Minuscule* iii. 30 The forthcoming motion the Students' Union were planning..deploring violence. **1909** *Rep. Board Educ. 1907–8* 57 During 1907 the new method of providing for the preliminary education of Elementary School Teachers, which is known as the 'Bursar System', has been brought into operation... The prospective Teacher either goes direct into a Training College..or..obtains an appointment as a Student-Teacher. **1953** W. MOORE *Bring Jubilee* (1955) xiii. 122 That personal, face-to-face, student-teacher relationship. **1973** E. MCGIRR *Bardel's Murder* ii. 47 When I started.. there was no difficulty in getting student teachers because they could use the rod. **1910** *Rep. Board Educ. 1908–9* 56 Upon..the passing of the necessary leaving examination, two alternative courses are immediately open to him—to proceed to a Training College or to proceed to Student-Teachership. **1970** *Daily Tel.* 23 Oct. 13/8 In the 'bad old days' of student-teachership, despite our huge classes we knew how to deal with 'emotional and learning disorders' without the aid of drugs! **1929** MYERS & HARSHMAN *Training Secondary Sch. Teachers* 17 Regulations relative to prerequisites for student-teaching.

studentess (earlier U.S. example); **stu·denting** *nonce-wd.* [-ING[1]], studying; an object of study.

1834 *Knickerbocker* IV. 120 The Collegiate Institute.. was originally designed to afford its fair studentesses all the advantages usually obtained by the best educated of the other sex. **1922** JOYCE *Ulysses* 739 That delicate looking student..nearly caught me washing through the window only for snapped up the towel to my face that was his studenting.

Student[2] (stiū·dĕnt). *Statistics.* The pseudonym of William Sealy Gossett (1876–1937), English brewery employee, used *attrib.* and in the possessive to designate statistical concepts devised by him, as *Student('s) (t-)distribution*, a statistical distribution which is that of a fraction whose numerator is drawn from a normal distribution with a mean of zero and whose denominator is the root mean square of k terms drawn from the same normal distribution (where k is the number of degrees of freedom); *Student's (t) test*, a test for statistical significance that uses tables of this distribution.

1929 *Nature* 17 Aug. 267/1 This is not to say that the deviation from 'Student's' t-distribution..may not have a real application. **1935** R. A. FISHER *Design of Experiments* iii. 38 (*heading*) Student's t test. **1937** YULE & KENDALL *Introd. Theory Statistics* (ed. 11) xxiii. 440 We proceed to give one or two examples of the way in which the 'Student' distribution is generally used to test the significance of various results obtained from small samples. **1938** *Biometrika* XXX. 223 As the theory of mathematical statistics has developed, the significance of 'Student's' test has been elaborated from many angles and deeper meanings associated with it than its author had ever dreamed of. **1968** P. A. P. MORAN *Introd. Probability Theory* vii. 326 Since t is scale-invariant its distribution is independent of σ, and is known as 'Student's t-distribution with $n-1$ degrees of freedom'. **1980** *Brit. Med. Jrnl.* 29 Mar. 890/2 The serial changes in mean daily volume, time taken, and flow were pooled and assessed with student's two-tailed t test.

stu·dentish, *a.* [f. STUDENT + -ISH[1].] Pertaining to, characteristic of, or resembling an (undergraduate) student; student-like, esp. in dress or opinion.

1934 *Times Lit. Suppl.* 9 Aug. 552/3 Her spectacles, her studentish clothes, her pride in her degrees..combine to make her an almost lovable character. **1979** *Church Times* 7 Dec. 7/3 Their very appearance was not studentish: 'puritans predominated, all with clean short hair, inexpensive shoes, mass-produced clothes well cared for'.

studentize (stiū·dĕntəiz), *v. Statistics.* Also **Studentize.** [f. *STUDENT[2] + -IZE.] *trans.* To subject (data) to studentization; chiefly as **stu·dentized** *ppl. a.*, applied esp. to data that have been standardized by division throughout by their estimated standard deviation, and to quantities derived therefrom; **stu:dentiza·tion** (see quot. 1957).

1938 *Suppl. Jrnl. R. Statistical Soc.* V. 80 This theory has been developed further, and quite a number of large-sample results have been 'studentized'. By this we mean that a statistic whose sampling distribution involves the unknown standard deviation of the population is modified so that its distribution involves only quantities calculated from the sample. **1939** *Biometrika* XXXI. 21 In a recent paper H. O. Hartley..has suggested a systematic method of obtaining probability levels for 'studentized' functions. **1957** KENDALL & BUCKLAND *Dict. Statistical Terms* 284 *Studentisation*, the process of removing complications due to the existence of an unknown parent scale-parameter by constructing a statistic whose sampling distribution is independent of it; especially by dividing a statistic which is of a certain degree in the observations by another statistic of the same degree. **1959** H. SCHEFFE *Analysis of Variance* ii. 28 In the next chapter we will apply the distribution of the Studentized range. **1972** *Biometrika* LIX. 165 Duncan's modification also starts with the studentized range test.

stud-horse. Add: **2.** (Earlier and *absol.* examples.) (The usual form is now *STUD *sb.*[2] 4 c or *stud-poker* s.v. STUD *sb.*[2] 5.)

1879 *Rep. Cases at Law Supreme Court of State of Arkansas* (1881) XXXIV. 442 The proof..showed that he did bet chips, or checks, at a game played with cards, called 'stud', or 'stud-horse', poker; being somewhat different from other games called 'straight poker' and 'draw poker'. **1882** in *Colorado Q.* (1956) IV. III. 271 Brownie Lea is leading stud horse at Del Norte. **1920** C. E. MULFORD *Johnny Nelson* ii. 19 He's a travelin' eddicator in th' innercent game of draw—or was it studhoss, Nelson?

studiable, *a.* Delete *nonce-wd.* and add: Also, capable of being studied or observed.

1971 *Jrnl. Gen. Psychol.* Jan. 172 The activities of single cells studiable by microelectrode techniques. **1982** *Times Lit. Suppl.* 23 Apr. 465/3 He does give a studiable picture of how Los Angeles may have sleep-walked into this unassimilable truth.

studio. Add: **2. c.** *Cinematogr.* A room in which a cinematographic film is shot. Hence, a film-making complex including film studios and attendant offices and premises (also in *pl.*); the company which runs this. Cf. *film studio* s.v. *FILM *sb.* 7 c.

1911 C. N. BENNETT et al. *Handbk. Kinematogr.* xiii. 102 Covered-in studios provided with expansive glass roofs for daylight work..are hardly among the first flights of commercial Kinematographic enterprise. **1923** *Variety* 15 Nov. 18 (*heading*) Hollywood studios moving to less costly locations. **1928** *Morning Post* 20 Oct. 4/3 The 'dedication' of Fox's new 8,000,000-dollar Movietone Studio at Los Angeles. **1937** A. HUXLEY *Let.* 12 July (1969) 423 With regard to the handling of my work, I am prepared to authorize you to take up the matter with film studios. **1956** H. KURNITZ *Invasion of Privacy* iii. 26 The actor was undoubtedly a handsome youngster... Five studios were squabbling over him now. **1971** *Guardian* 2 Dec. 11/2 The studio, Paramount, was 'not happy with it' [*sc.* a film] and failed to promote it.

d. *Radio* and *Television.* In a broadcasting station, etc.: a room from which items are broadcast live or in which they are recorded for subsequent transmission; the premises housing such a studio or studios. Also *pl.*

1922 J. REITH *Diary* 29 Dec. (1975) ii. 129 Newcastle... Here I really began my BBC responsibility. Saw transmitting station and studio place. **1923** *Radio Times* 5 Oct. 38/3 'Romeo and Juliet' is being..broadcast from our own studio. **1938** *Encycl. Brit. Bk. of Year* 633/2 The apparatus will operate satisfactorily either in natural or artificial light, the technique used in the television studio being somewhat similar to that in a film studio. **1968** M. BRAGG *Without City Wall* xxviii. 255 The television studios..were on the edge of town. **1972** *Daily Tel.* 6 Jan. 1/2 Mr Wilson, Leader of the Opposition, visited a television studio yesterday morning to pre-record his contribution to the programme.

e. A room used for recording and editing music, etc. to be reproduced on a gramophone record or similar medium.

1928 [see *recording studio* s.v. *RECORDING *vbl. sb.* 5]. **1932** *Daily Mirror* 21 Oct. 10/3 It is good watching a record being made in a gramophone studio. **1955** L. FEATHER *Encycl. Jazz* 341 The bands of Hundy Kirk, Count Basie, Hot Lips Page and Eddie Durham, the last two being studio-assembled combinations. **1977** *Rolling Stone* 24 Mar. 55/4 Ten months devoted to Fleetwood Mac's album has left Buckingham spindly and studio wan.

f. = *studio flat*, sense 3 b below. orig. *U.S.*

1942 D. POWELL *Time to be Born* (1943) v. 100 Amanda's furnished 'studio'..was..a one-room apartment. **1962** P. MOYES *Death on Agenda* vi. 94 [The flat] was what is known on the Continent as a studio—that is to say, a one-room bachelor apartment with its own tiny hallway, off which led a box-sized kitchen and a dwarf bathroom. **1977** I. SHAW *Beggarman, Thief* IV. i. 365 Home was a nasty little one-room studio near the university.

3. a. (Later examples in broadcasting and recording: cf. sense 2 above.)

1922 [see sense 2 d above]. **1944** L. MACNEICE *Christopher Columbus* 16 The radio dramatist must..be studio-conscious, remembering what results can..be obtained. **1956** B. HOLIDAY *Lady sings Blues* (1973) iii. 35 Benny [Goodman] was a radio-studio musician who talked a lot then about having his own band one day. **1972** P. BLACK *Biggest Aspidistra* I. iii. 28 The studio announcer introduced the band and the place, and wished the nation good night.

b. Special Combs. (senses *2 c, d) *studio audience, manager*; **studio apartment** *U.S.* = *studio flat* below; **studio bed, couch,** a couch which converts into a bed; **studio flat,** a flat containing a spacious room with large windows, which is or resembles an artist's studio; more recently, a small one-roomed flat, **studio party,** an informal party held in an artist's studio; also, a social gathering at a film studio: **studio portrait,** a posed photograph, as taken in a photographer's studio; **studio potter,** a potter (freq. one of a small group) who works in a studio producing hand-thrown pottery; hence **studio pottery**; **studio theatre,** (an) experimental theatre.

1903 *Archit. Rec.* July 240 The most economical way of combining a good high studio with an economical disposition of space would be to make the studio apartment two-storied in the service and living portions, and only one-storied in the space devoted to the studio. **1929** *Washington Post* 1 Sept. 6/5 Studio Apartment $100. **1949** *Archit. Rec.* Nov. 125 At the foot of the San Jacinto mountains, this small group of studio apartments is keyed to the needs..of a specific class of tenant—artists who spend part of the year in Palm Springs. **1978** J. IRVING *World according to Garp* xix. 428 Roberta went to ..Duncan's live-in studio... Duncan's studio-apartment. **1932** *B.B.C. Year Bk. 1933* 20 Comedians probably most need the stimulus of the crowded hall, for which the 'studio audience' is a poor substitute. **1977** B. PYM *Quartet in Autumn* x. 90 The radio offered a choice of comedy, with a braying studio audience. **1963** M. MCCARTHY *Group* vi. 118 Across the room, a big lumpy studio bed was covered with a black velveteen spread. **1931** *Sears, Roebuck Catal.* Spring 662 New 'Sun Bed' Latest Style Couch... This new type davenport-bed or studio couch. **1977** A. SCHOLEFIELD *Venom* I. 3 His bedroom..had been designed..as a bed-sitter..and the bed itself was a studio couch. **1934** A. HUXLEY *Let.* 13 Oct. (1969) 385 We are in London for the winter—having found a studio flat, miraculously large. **1970** K. GILES *Death in Church* ii. 31 He had what they call a studio flat —bed, gas fire and tiny kitchenette. **1937** R. CHANDLER in *Blask Mask* Jan. 19/1 The call letters of the station revolved in neon letters... I..got to see a Mr. Dave Marineau, studio manager... 'We get one in the radio column about every second month. We're a small station still.' **1980** S. BRETT *Dead Side of Mike* i. 13 'I'm sorry, I don't speak BBC. What's an SM?' 'Studio Manager. Knob-twiddler..tape-machine starter and what you will.' **1909** E. NESBIT *Daphne in Fitzroy St.* xvii. 275 'Meals in studios are always rather like picnics.'..'Oh, yes,' she said. 'I've been to lots of studio parties. They're great fun, aren't they?' **1931** R. H. HEATON *Perfect Hostess* 110 (*heading*) Miss Eighteen borrows the Attic for her first Studio Party for her young friends from the Slade. **1974** A. MORICE *Killing with Kindness* viii. 59, I had met her..at a studio party. **1938** M. ALLINGHAM *Fashion in Shrouds* xviii. 329 The story had made..headlines on the front pages, most of which also carried studio portraits of Miss Adamson. **1978** F. OLBRICH *Desouza pays Price* xv. 93 A signed studio portrait of herself taken with a soft-focus lens. **1940** B. LEACH *Potter's Bk.* iii. 43 A potter's prime need is good clay. Whether he be industrial, peasant or studio potter the raw material of which pots are made is of fundamental importance. **1979** *China Now* Mar./Apr. 9/1 We saw the sort of simple country pots that we as studio potters (people actively engaged in making pots ourselves—by hand in a machine age) so much admire. **1959** J. & D. V. BAKER *Pottery Bk.* III. x. 59 At a studio pottery (generally a small pottery with perhaps half a dozen partners or employees..) machinery plays the least possible part. **1980** *Times* 11 Dec. 16/6 At Sotheby's Belgravia studio pottery was also making high prices. **1933** P. GODFREY *Back-Stage* xiii. 160 The studio or art theatre exists..to prevent dramatic art from being wiped out by the commercially minded. **1965** *Listener* 20 May 738/1 What we most lack today..is the type of experimental studio-theatre that flourished in Stanislavsky's lifetime. **1971** J. ELSOM *Theatre outside London* x. 172 There will be a high fly-tower, a studio theatre, fine foyers, a restaurant and good backstage facilities.

‖ **studiolo** (stūdiōu·lo). [It., lit. 'small study'.] A private study hung with paintings.

1926 J. E. JEFFERY tr. *R. de la Sizeranne's Celebrities Ital. Renaissance* 180 She [*sc.* Isabella d'Este] heard that the decorations ordered for her *studiolo* at Mantua were not progressing, for Luca Liombeni, the painter, was a dawdler. **1958** *Times* 14 Nov. 16/4 Later developments, such as the '*Studiolo*' group, Pietro Candido, Salviati, and Tibaldi, are not represented. **1968** *N.Y. City* (Michelin Tire Corp.) 57 The major attraction of the Italian section is the 'studiolo', or private study, from the Ducal Palace at Gubbio (Umbria). **1978** M. GIROUARD *Life in Eng. Country House* vi. 166 The books..in the *trompe l'œil* paintings in the *studiolo* of Federigo Montefeltro at Urbino.

‖ **studium** (stiū·diŏm). *Hist.* [late L. (4th.-cent.) use of L. *studium* STUDY *sb.*] = STUDY *sb.* 9. Also, = next.

1610 [see STUDY *sb.* 9]. **1673** J. RAY *Observations Journey Low-Countries* 342 The *Studium*, called the *Sapienza*, where are the public Schools [in Siena]. **1834** [see next]. **1902** *Encycl. Brit.* XXXIII. 602/1 Immediately after 1168 allusions to Oxford as a *studium* and a *studium generale* begin to multiply. **1936** *Times Lit. Suppl.* 2 May 361/2 Out of such enterprises developed the medieval university. It grew and was not made. Later, of course, there was deliberate creation: there was the *studium* at Naples, brought into being by Frederick II. **1961** P. KIBRE *Scholarly Privileges Middle Ages* ii. 19 The measure requiring the rectors..to take the oath that they would not seek the removal of the studium from the city [of Bologna] was retained.

‖ **studium generale** (stiū·diŏm dʒenerēi·lĭ, -ā·lĭ). *Hist.* Pl. **studia generalia** (-ēi·liă, -ā·liă). [med.L.: f. as prec. + *generāle*, neut. sing. of *generālis* GENERAL *a.*] A medieval university which did not only receive scholars from its own locality (an earlier equivalent of the *universitas* UNIVERSITY); = *general study* s.v. STUDY *sb.* 9.

1834 *Edin. Rev.* Oct. 215 The oldest word for an unexclusive institution of higher education, was *studium*, and *studium generale*—terms employed in the twelfth and thirteenth centuries, and retained in those which followed. **1895** H. RASHDALL *Univ. Europe Middle Ages* I. 9 A Studium Generale meant a School of general resort, but in its origin the expression was a wholly popular and extra-legal one. *Ibid.* 10 In the latter half of the Thirteenth Century this unrestricted liberty of founding Studia Generalia gradually ceased. **1928** *Daily Tel.* 10 July 12/4 Where the liberal Arts and Sciences of a complete Studium Generale may be cultivated and practised. **1966** H. WIERUSZOWSKI *Medieval Univ.* I. i. 16 The term *studium generale* was used for schools of higher learning until late in the fifteenth century... Gradually..the term 'university' replaced the word *studium*.

study, *sb.* Add: **6. b.** *a quick study* (also *transf.* in general contexts).

1900 J. K. JEROME *Three Men on Bummel* i. 13 Muriel is master of six pieces already, as perhaps you know; and all the other children are quick studies. **1954** M. EWER *Heart Untouched* ix. 164 She had learnt something in these last few days. She was a quick study. **1974** P. DE VRIES *Glory of Hummingbird* xiii. 197 We'll brush him up. He's a quick study. He's not a Neanderthal.

7. b. Hence applied to the face registering an expression of incredulity, etc. (*colloq.*).

1886 C. M. YONGE *Chantry House* II. xiv. 136 Emily's countenance was a study. **1964** C. CHAPLIN *My Autobiogr.* x. 156 You should have seen his face watching you, it was a study! **1973** *Press & Jrnl.* (Aberdeen) 3 Aug. 7/3 We stopped for lunch at a little rustic inn. Specialite de la maison—chicken and chips with frozen peas on the side. Archie's face was a study.

12. (sense 5) *study-leave, tour*; (sense 8) *study-bedroom*; **study circle,** a group that meets regularly to discuss a particular topic of study; **study group** = prec.; freq. an investigative committee formed by a political, industrial, or other body for this purpose.

1930 *Times Educ. Suppl.* 26 July 332/2 Study-bedrooms for 108 inmates. **1978** J. I. M. STEWART *Full Term* i. 15 Schools that are a bit lavish with study-bedrooms for senior boys. **1938** L. MACNEICE *I crossed Minch* vi. 84 They've no team spirit, they won't take part In our study circles and community art. **1979** B. G. SKINNER *Robert Exon* iv. 31 Study circles, Chapter meetings. **1926** *Scribner's Mag.* Sept. 8/2 The Foundation is accumulating a body of literature on Positive Health, for the use of individuals and organized study groups. **1948** *Ann. Reg. 1947* 223 Before the conference came to an end thirteen of the participating countries decided to create a 'study group' to examine the possibility of creating a general European Customs union. *a* **1974** R. CROSSMAN *Diaries* (1975) I. 75 The only thing I need really mention is the dinner held at Arnold Goodman's house for my Rent Bill study group. **1961** *Times* 12 Oct. 13/7 The huge expansion of universities has..made it more difficult for them [*sc.* members of staff] to take study-leave. **1982** M. DUKE *Flashpoint* vi. 44 A spell of study-leave before you take on the new job. **1937** *John o' London's Weekly* 7 May 209/2 A tin to keep my damp cake of soap from coming into contact with the bristles of my toothbrush during studytours. **1977** *Jrnl. R. Soc. Arts* CXXV. 519/2 Approximately 90 former Bursary winners made study tours abroad.

study, *v.* Add: **I. 1. a.** Now only *U.S. colloq.*, to make a close study of (a subject), to 'bone' *up* (*on, in*), esp. in preparation for some display of knowledge (*intr.* use of sense 7 b).

1946 *Chicago Daily News* 25 June 31/3 Ah'll git a li'l closer, an' study up on him! **1956** R. ROBINSON *Landscape with Dead Dons* xiii. 114, I am sure that if you once studied up a little in psychology you would be as struck as I was. **1970** N. ARMSTRONG et al. *First on Moon* vi. 131 He had studied up on vineyards so he could tell wonderful stories about them. **1980** J. BALL *Then came Violence* ii. 10 'We know quite a lot about Pasadena,' he said. 'Have you been studying up?' the chief asked.

2. a. (Later examples with *about*).

1844 *Yorks. Comet* No. 1. 1 Moare Ah studied aboot it an' war it pottered me. **1895** *Dialect Notes* I. 374 *Study*, talk, discuss, consider... 'I studied about her to my man when I got home.' **1940** W. FAULKNER *Hamlet* IV. i. 244, I was absent-minded one night when I was staking them out. Studying about something else and forgot how long the wire was. **1965** 'MALCOLM X' *Autobiogr.* (1966) xiii. 306, I studied about if I just *should* happen to say something to her—what would her position be?

II. 7. b. (Examples.)

1880 'MARK TWAIN' *Tramp Abroad* 412 Studying up the subject of Alpine climbing. **1922** JOYCE *Ulysses* 728 He knows a lot..about the body and the insides..often wanted to study up that myself.

stuff, *sb.*[1] Add: **II. 3. c** Esp. in phr. *bit of stuff.* Now chiefly in slang use, with or without epithet, of a woman or girl. Cf. *BIT *sb.*[2] 4 f, h.

1828 *Subaltern's Log Bk.* II. 164, I entered the house in great spirits, fancying myself, to make use of a slang phrase, a very good bit of stuff. **1858**, etc. [in Dict.]. **1909** in J. R. Ware *Passing Eng.* 31/1 He waited for a bit of stuff near the stage door of the Comedy Theatre. He was an elderly cove and he had great patience. **1971** B. W. ALDISS *Soldier Erect* 10 The infantry myth that one spent one's whole leave yanking it up some willing bit of stuff in a pub yard.

4. d. (Earlier example.)

1851 S. RUTTER *Hints to Gold Hunters* 12 The principal use of the washpan is in rewashing the partially washed stuff taken from the rocker.

III. 6. g. Narcotics, 'dope'. Phr. *on the stuff*, addicted to drugs, on drugs. *slang* (orig. *U.S.*).

1929 *Amer. Speech* IV. 345 *Stuff*, dope. **1934** [see *MAIN-LINE *v.*]. **1935** A. J. POLLOCK *Underworld Speaks* 84/1 *On the stuff*, addicted to dope. **1952** *Sunday Times* 3 Feb. 5/4 There has lately been a lot of research into the sale of narcotics (or 'junk' or 'stuff') and their effects on addicts. **1959** 'F. NEWTON' *Jazz Scene* 292 Jive talk.. contains all the fancy-dress devices of private languages.. the never-ending substitution of new passwords into the group for new codes..the use of neutral and general words for highly specific things (e.g. *on the stuff*, or simply *on* for drug addiction). **1965** *New Statesman* 20 Aug. 248/3 Addicts have a secret language, which changes like a code. The commonest current name for heroin is 'stuff'. **1973** L. HELLMAN *Pentimento* 290 'His room-mate's on the stuff.' This then new way of saying dope..was no surprise. Years before she had told me her son was on the stuff. **1976** H. FERGUSON *Confessions Long Distance Acid Head* 65 'Yes. You were the bloke who got done for someone else's stuff..weren't you?' It was a junkie whom I had met in Ashford.

7. c. See also *HOT STUFF a.

e. *to do one's stuff*: to do what is required or expected of one; to perform one's role. *colloq.*

Quot. 1663 may belong to another sense.

1663 G. Fox *Jrnl.* (1694) I. 266 A while after, when the priest had done his stuff, they came to the friends again. **1922** *Radio News* (U.S.) IV. 854/1 (*caption*) Take a look at S. M. Brown, Chief on the Mauretania, 'doing his stuff' in the saloon. **1930** T. E. Lawrence *Lett.* (1938) 677 That portable was good at Miranshah. I hope yours is doing its stuff. **1933** *Bulletin* (Sydney) 19 Apr. 29/4 Australia will be represented in this event by Alan Bruce, who has been doing his stuff in London. **1946** F. Sargeson *That Summer* 144 If you knew how to do your stuff you never could tell but what it mightn't end up in a date. **1959** [see *anti-aircraft *a.*]. **1967** G. F. Fiennes *I tried to run a Railway* vi. 70, I go when I can for the fun of hearing Richard doing his stuff. **1972** Wodehouse *Pearls, Girls, & Monty Bodkin* ii. 27 The Bishop and assistant clergy and the bridesmaids shall be encouraged to line up and do their stuff. **1976** *Daily Times* (Lagos) 27 Aug. 30/2 Ghana's Johnny Francois and a few others did their stuff abroad and, gradually, the panel took root.

f. *that's the stuff* (*to give them* or *to give the troops*): that is what is particularly appropriate to the situation, that is what is required.

1923 'Bartimeus' *Seaways* vii. 98 George Grayson and his Flock of Fascinating Flappers presents a screaming farce: The Giddy Governess! That's the stuff to give the troops! **1927** *Daily Express* 13 Oct. 12 That, if one may be pardoned the colloquialism, was the stuff to give them. **1942** H. C. Bailey *Dead Man's Shoes* xiv. 63 'A new married man with a lovely wife spends half the night with a police inspector he meets by chance! That's not the stuff to give the troops.'..'No, it don't sound natural.' **1943** J. B. Priestley *Daylight on Saturday* vii. 46 'We're always glad to have suggestions from anybody.' 'That's the stuff,' said Mr. Ogmore. **1977** P. D. James *Death of Expert Witness* ii. i. 53 Inspector Blakelock.. was always ready for his tea... 'That's the stuff to give the troops,' he would invariably say.

g. *to know one's stuff*: to be experienced or knowledgeable in one's subject, profession, etc. *colloq.*

1927 *Amer. Speech* II. 277 *Know your onions* or *know your stuff*, have grasp of your subjects. **1935** *Swing Music* June 111/1 The Little Man of the Rhythm Clubs did himself proud in this test paper. He knows his stuff. **1938** G. Greene *Brighton Rock* iii. i. 108 'This doctor,' she says, 'he knows his stuff?' **1945** R. A. Knox *God & Atom* x. 132 All I have written could have been written very much better by someone who, in an expressive modern phrase, knew his stuff. **1952** J. Steinbeck *East of Eden* xxxiii. 46 It's a lulu. Kate sure knows her stuff. **1967** M. Argyle *Psychol. Interpersonal Behaviour* ix. 166 His [*sc.* the supervisor's] influence will be accepted more readily if it is believed that he really knows his stuff. **1973** A. Christie *Postern of Fate* iii. vii. 174 'He gave me a lot of knowledge about planting things.' 'Yes, he knew his stuff, as you might say.'

8. e. *gen.* Used *loosely* to denote any collection of things about which one is not able or willing to particularize (a weakened application of senses 6, 7); material, matter, business. *colloq.*

1922 [see sense 7 e above]. **1949** 'G. Orwell' *1984* ii. ii. 123 You thought I was a good Party member. Pure in word and deed. Banners, processions, slogans, games, community hikes—all that stuff. **1967** R. Brautigan *Trout Fishing in America* (1970) 83 One spring day she had me ascend to the attic and clean up some boxes of stuff and throw out some stuff and put some stuff back into its imaginary proper place. **1977** J. D. MacDonald *Condominium* xxxvii. 370 Once they left we were going to move his stuff out and change the locks.

f. Hence, with preceding epithet.

1929, etc [see *kid *sb.*[1] 6]. **1932** S. Gibbons *Cold Comfort Farm* xiii. 191 She had best not pull any Cinderella stuff on me. **1939** *Punch* 5 July 9/1 'Sam,' they said to him, 'what's wrong? You can bowl much better stuff than that.' **1948** *Sporting Mirror* 21 May 7/3 Jack Martin may also be available for fast stuff on occasions. **1974** *Times Lit. Suppl.* 26 Apr. 440/3 The principal message [of Hochhuth's comedy *Lysistrate und die NATO*] is largely straightforward feminist stuff. **1976** *National Observer* (U.S.) 9 Oct. 2/4 The threat of another oil embargo is always serious stuff here. **1978** D. Williams *Treasure up in Smoke* xiii. 120 What he said was pretty strong stuff... He fairly laid into Mr O'Hara.

9. b. *N. Amer.* In various sports, the spin or 'work' imparted to a ball in order to make it vary its course; the type of control which effects this. Also *fig.*

1905 *Sporting Life* (U.S.) 9 Sept. 1/1 If I tried some of the stuff that certain pitchers use and escape bumping, I have an idea that the fielders would never stop..hitting. **1913** *Harper's Weekly* 13 Sept. 21/2 Weilman, the giant Brown, is another [pitcher] who has the 'stuff'. **1927** *Daily Tel.* 21 Feb. 13/6 T. A. Workman, their captain, was in wonderfully good form against Commander S. W. Beadle, finding an almost perfect length for an American service which had plenty of 'stuff' on it. Beadle could not do anything with it, and was kept on the defensive throughout. **1936** J. T. Farrell *World I Never Made* v. 68 The O'Neills are proud of their name, and they got as much stuff on the ball in the game of life as old Three-fingered Brown has when he toes the mound. **1947** *Sun* (Baltimore) 3 Apr. 20/1 He is only 20 years old, has a good arm and has much of the well known stuff on the ball. **1967** Varner & Harrison *Table Tennis* v. 51 These spinners are often one-ball hitters; they vary their 'stuff' until you yield a loose return, which they efficiently kill. **1970** J. H. Gray *Boy from Winnipeg* 152 That got us seats behind home plate where we could watch the stuff, mainly curves, that the pitchers were putting on the ball. **1981** *Washington Star* 30 Apr. c 4/1 'I really had good stuff tonight,' the lefthander said in a post-game radio interview. 'My slider wasn't great at the beginning, but my fastball really was good.'

10*. Phr. *not to give a stuff*, etc. = *not to give a fuck* s.v. *fuck *sb.* 2. Cf. *stuff *v.* 14* a. Chiefly *Austral.* and *N.Z. slang.*

1976–7 *Sea Spray* (N.Z.) Dec./Jan. 62/1 Well, deep down inside I don't really give a stuff. **1974** *Bookseller* 19 Jan. 117/3 A word or two of criticism: I don't give a stuff for your great managing director. **1977** *Bulletin* (Sydney) 22 Jan. 100/3 The list goes on and on and on and as it grows so does the feeling amongst the blokes in the bush that no one gives a stuff. **1979** N. Gordimer *Burger's Daughter* i. 42 In the end no one cares a stuff who's in jail or what war's on, so long as it's far away. **1980** B. Mason *Solo* 207, I don't give a stuff if it was or not. That spoke to me. Opened up my life, things I'd forgotten.

11. c. stuff-over *a.*, applied to chairs, etc., which are upholstered by having the material drawn over the frame of a fixed seat and secured beneath; also *absol.* as *sb.*, a stuff-over seat.

1915 R. S. Bowers et al. *Furniture Making* xxxi. 353 Stuffover chair and settee. **1963** *Times* 2 Feb. 11 The slip-in seat is almost universal and the stuffover almost unknown in Portuguese Chippendale chairs. **1972** *Country Life* 1 June 1414/1 Regency mahogany dining chairs..with stuffover seats. **1976** *Liverpool Daily Post* 11 Dec. (Advt.), For sale, stuff-over roll back (Chesterfield Settee in silk damask.

stuff, *v.*[1] Add: **8. e.** To pack or load (a freight container). *slang.*

1965 R. B. Oram *Cargo Handling* vi. 115 Containers can come into..a Consolidation Depot where they are stuffed with miscellaneous general cargo. **1968** [see *strip *v.*[1] 7 e]. **1972** *Timber Trades Jrnl.* 13 May 44/1 The dockers threaten to continue the ban until their demands are met which include the exclusive right to stuff (pack) and unstuff (unpack) containers. **1972** *Nature* 11 Aug. 301/2 British dockers are..asking that members of their union should have a right to employment at the centres at which containers are stuffed with goods.

14*. a. Used in coarse expressions of contempt or defiance. Cf. *fuck *v.* 2; *stuffed *ppl. a.* 6.

1955 P. Larkin *Less Deceived* 30 Ah, were I courageous enough To shout *stuff your pension!* **1958** F. Norman *Bang to Rights* 168 The geezer just got up and told him to stuff his job. **1962** J. Wain *Strike Father Dead* iv. 205 Very well, they could keep the whole outfit. And stuff it. I wasn't even going to stay in the same miserable country. **1965** 'T. Hinde' *Games of Chance* i. iii. 99 'Stuff you,' I said. **1973** J. Porter *It's Murder with Dover* i. 2 He should have taken a stronger line... Told old Crouch to stuff it. **1976** W. Trevor *Children of Dynmouth* xi. 204 She goes up to him and tells him to stuff himself and in a flat half-minute he's belting the old lorry up the London road. **1977** *Time* 28 Mar. 11/1 Stuff the criticism. He said what he was going to do. He won the election and now he's doing it.

b. *vulg. slang.* (With male subject) to copulate with (someone). Occas. *intr.*

1960 B. Moore *Luck of Ginger Coffey* iv. 85 Trying to stuff another man's wife, is that your idea of being a friend? **1977** F. Raphael *Cracks in Ice* (1979) 333 *Satura*..can also be applied, since it was originally adjectival, to a pregnant woman and to a sausage, both of which, in vulgar parlance, can clearly claim to have been stuffed. **1982** J. Scott *Uprush of Mayhem* vi. 63 You come all the way from the city..to stuff—to have intercourse with her. **1983** *Sunday Times* 16 Jan. 35/3 He was sacked from Eton for stuffing the boys' maids.

stuffado, var. *stifado.

stuffage. Delete † *Obs.* and add: **1.** (Later examples.)

1943 *Aeronautics* Jan. 34/1 An aeroplane should be stripped for action and not a stuffage of gadgets. **1963** C. Roberts *Buried Books* 13 The discarded papyrus MS used as stuffage for the binding cannot conceivably be later.

stuffed, *ppl. a.* Add: **6.** Phr. *get stuffed*: used as a coarse imprecation. Cf. *stuff *v.*[1] 14* a, b.

1952 M. Tripp *Faith is Windsock* x. 155 'Get stuffed,' he said savagely. **1968** M. Richler in R. Weaver *Canad. Short Stories* 2nd Ser. 188 'Why don't you tell Leopold to go get stuffed?' 'Because we need the foreign currency.' **1975** *Weekend Mag.* 1 Nov. 16/2 [He] told the Tories in so many words to get stuffed; he had no intention of telling them anything important, he proposed to deal only with the government. **1979** R. Rendell *Make Death love Me* vii. 69 Who're you giving orders to? You can get stuffed.

7. Special collocations: **stuffed monkey**, a type of biscuit or cake made with almonds; **stuffed olive**, a stoned (usu. green) olive filled with pimento; **stuffed owl** [from the title of an anthology, ult. derived from Wordsworth's *Misc. Sonnets* iii. xiii], used *attrib.* with reference to poetry which treats trivial or inconsequential subjects in a grandiose manner; hence **stuffed-owlish** *a.*; **stuffed pepper**, a cooked dish of green or red pepper (capsicum) de-seeded and filled with tomatoes, rice, meat, etc.; **stuffed shirt** *colloq.* (orig. *U.S.*), one who is pompous and conservative, but usu. ineffectual; hence **stuffed-shirted** *a.*; **stuffed-shirtedness**; **stuffed vine leaves**, an eastern (esp. Greek or Turkish) dish consisting of vine leaves wrapped round a savoury mixture of rice, onion, etc.

1892 I. Zangwill *Children of Ghetto* I. 14 The confectioners' shops, crammed with 'stuffed monkeys' and 'bolas'. **1943** A. L. Simon *Conc. Encycl. Gastron.* IV. 127/2 *Stuffed Monkey* (S. Africa... Place the one half on a flat baking-sheet, cover with the filling or stuffing... Put the other half of the pastry over the filling; press the edges firmly together. **1962** *Listener* 11 Jan. 107/3 'Stuffed monkey' is a rich cake popular on the Continent. **1967** K. Giles *Death in Diamonds* iv. 78 Another cupper and a plate of stuffed monkeys. **1897** Kipling *Captains Courageous* ix. 198 Try a stuffed olive. **1920** [see *angel('s)-food(-cake)* s.v. *angel *sb.* B. 2]. **1967** P. Jones *Fifth Defector* i. 4 He took a smallish savoury, a stuffed olive, and popped it into his mouth. [**1930** Wyndham Lewis & Lee (*title*) The stuffed owl: an anthology of bad verse.] **1941** Blunden *Thomas Hardy* xii. 264 Hardy's poems.. have their share of stuffed-owl simplicities. **1957** R. A. Knox *On Eng. Translation* 12, I will not entertain you.. with choice specimens of really stuffed-owl renderings in this field; such as that famous translation from the Italian, about the medieval story of a woman who was turned into a horse. **1960** *Guardian* 13 May 6/7 Of the longer pieces, 'The Cruel Place' is the most stuffed-owlish. **1864** V. Davis *Let.* 8 Oct. in C. V. Woodward *Mary Chesnut's Civil War* (1981) xxvii. 663 Colonel Lubbock was funny about your breakfast—and your stuffed peppers. **1960** 'E. McBain' *Killer's Payoff* ix. 89, I was going to call you for that stuffed-pepper recipe.. you used for the last buffet. **1978** H. Kaplan *Damascus Cover* vii. 69 Boys..carried trays laden with soup and stuffed peppers. **1913** W. S. Cather *O, Pioneers!* 144 He characterized Frank Shabata by a Bohemian expression which is the equivalent of stuffed shirt. **1939** C. Day Lewis *Child of Misfortune* iii. iii. 287 These women and their stuffed-shirt escorts. **1969** *Islander* (Victoria, B.C.) 23 Feb. 7/1 He had no time at all for the 'stuffed-shirt' types which were beginning to show in the north [of Canada]. **1976** *Country Life* 26 Feb. 496/3 The American President (a stuffed shirt) and two visiting Arab oil sheiks are held to ransom. **1977** A. J. Ayer *Part of my Life* viii. 197 The head of the section, who disliked Cummings for his indifference to spit and polish and his preference for the company of the French cook and mechanics to that of the more stuffed-shirted Americans. **1981** 'J. Ross' *Dark Blue & Dangerous* xxii. 127 You sounded so awfully priggish..stuff-shirted..I do like you ..in spite of your stuffed-shirtedness. **1939** A. Heath *Open Sesame* 120 Vine Leaves, Stuffed. **1978** H. Kaplan *Damascus Cover* xv. 148 A man sitting on a straw stool eating stuffed vine leaves sunk in goat's milk.

stuffer. Add: **3.** An advertising leaflet or similar material enclosed with other literature, esp. when sent by post.

1942 [see *filler[1] 2]. **1971** *Oxf. Univ. Gaz.* (Ann. Rep. Delegates Univ. Press) 5 The Promotion Department had to prepare, produce, and distribute 875,000 stuffers, 550,000 prospectuses. **1972** *Publishers Weekly* 31 Jan. 94/3 The prices they wish printed on the mailing piece, circular, stuffer, etc. **1976** *New Yorker* 12 Apr. 120/3 There was a program stuffer with a word-and-picture collage printed on one side and a full chronology of Tharp choreographies on the other.

stuffiness. Add: **4.** A formal or strait-laced attitude.

1926 Galsworthy *Silver Spoon* iii. vi. 262 The book breaks through the British 'stuffiness' which condemns any frank work of art. **1933** *Times Lit. Suppl.* 9 Nov. 776/4 We see Angrove's clerical stuffiness gradually dispelled by the Greek sun and sea. **1975** J. R. L. Anderson *Death in North Sea* vi. 112 Mr Wilson more than made up for his initial stuffiness... I took him into a small bar.

stuffing, *vbl. sb.* Add: **1. a.** The putting of fraudulent votes into a ballot-box. Also *ballot stuffing.* Cf. Stuff *v.*[1] 8 d.

1976 *Birmingham Post* 16 Dec. 2/9 Special see-through ballot boxes were used to show that no pre-vote 'stuffing' had taken place. **1977** *Time* 3 Jan. 10/2 Apparently defeated in his first try for the state senate in 1962, he fought to prove ballot stuffing by the boss of Quitman County. **1979** *Internat. Jrnl. Sociol. of Law* Feb. 71 In actual fact, during the civilian rule, they occasionally employed illegal means..and the stuffing or disappearance of ballot-boxes to help ruling party candidates.

2. e. *to put stuffing into*: to add strength or substance to. *colloq.*

1938 [see *page *v.*[1] c]. **1977** P. Harcourt *At High Risk* iii. v. 179 The whisky and wine I had drunk weren't making me rash..but they were putting some needed stuffing into me. **1979** J. Sherwood *Hour of Hyenas* iv. 44 She really puts the stuffing back into these women. Some of them even learn to cope with their dreadful husbands.

stuffless, *a.* Delete *nonce-wd.* and add earlier and later examples.

1896 Belloc *Verses & Sonnets* 23 The tiny stuffless voices of the dark. **1932** W. De La Mare *Early Novels of Wilkie Collins* in J. Drinkwater *Eighteen-Sixties* 90 The best of them [*sc.* Collins' characters] are triumphantly in the round;..those in the background are somewhat stuffless in effect.

stuffy, *a.* Add: **2. b.** (Earlier example.)

1813 Jane Austen *Pride & Prejudice* I. xvi. 173 They were superior to the broad-faced stuffy uncle Philips, breathing port wine, who followed them into the room.

5. Prim, formal, strait-laced, pompous; boring, conventional.

1895 Kipling *Day's Work* (1898) 181 'You might have

come to me to begin with,' said Scott stiffly... 'Well, you need't be stuffy about it.' **1904** E. NESBIT *Phoenix & Carpet* i. 11 It's awfully stuffy for a chap not to be allowed out in the evenings. **1922** J. CANNAN *Misty Valley* xv. 245 Cousin Innes was very stuffy about it when you got engaged. But all we wanted was for you to be happy, Claire. **1948** E. WAUGH *Let.* 24 Nov. (1980) 293, I went to one stuffy upper class dinner party on my first night & I go to another tonight. **1965** *Listener* 16 Sept. 418/2 Some of them have grasped the BBC's main dilemma, which is that it ought..to be in the widest, not in any 'stuffy' sense, an instrument of culture and education. **1979** R. JAFFE *Class Reunion* (1980) I. ii. 34 Every man I meet wants to go into business. They're all so stuffy.

stuggy, *a.* Add: Also *transf.*

1945 P. WOODRUFF *Call Next Witness* II. 59 Quite as heavy a weight as his stuggy little brown mare was meant to carry. **1960** L. FIELDEN *Natural Bent* ix. 250 Ships with high noses and short noses, ships with long lines and stuggy lines.

Stuka (stū·ka, ʃ-). Also **stuka.** [Abbrev. of G. *sturzkampfflugzeug* dive-bomber.] A dive-bomber of the German air force, esp. as used in the war of 1939–45.

1940 *Sun* (Baltimore) 23 May 1/5 The awful destruction which German *Stukas* (dive bombers) wreak. **1942** *Ann. Reg. 1941* 12 On January 10 German Stuka dive-bombers ..made an attack..on a British convoy. **1942** *Daily Tel.* 23 Mar. 1/5 Fighters and stukas operate from the more forward flying ground at Tmimi. **1946** A. LEE *German Air Force* iii. 37 The Stuka pilot went straight to a specialist dive-bomber school. **1956** D. M. DAVIN *Sullen Bell* vii. 151 Sounds worse than a lot of screaming stukas. **1962** *Times* 7 June 16/5 After the drone of Stukas has died away. **1969** G. MACBETH *War Quartet* 21 So we would die..Picked into pulp by stukas. **1973** S. B. JACKMAN *Guns covered with Flowers* viii. 127 This was how the Stuka pilots must have seen it [*sc.* Warsaw], open and defenceless in the bomb-sights. **1980** *Daily Tel.* 16 Oct. 16/5 Sunset and sand. Stukas and sand. Food, flies, hospital, home—and sand.

Hence **stu·ka** *v. trans.*, (*pass.*) to be attacked by Stukas.

1946 *Amer. Speech* XXI. 208, I served with the British Eighth Army in the desert.., but I never heard *sand happy. Bomb happy*, yes, when a bloke had been Stuka'd too often. **1977** N. FAULKS *No Mitigating Circumstances* vii. 80 On one lovely afternoon, I was sitting there with the G3 when we were Stuka'ed. **1980** *Daily Tel.* 16 Oct. 16/6 One moves from page to page, one moment 'brewing up', another being 'stuka-ed', to the cameo of a desert sunset.

stultificatory (stɒːltifikēi·tŏri), *a.* [f. STULTIFICATION: see -ORY².] = STULTIFYING *ppl. a.*

1931 *Times Lit. Suppl.* 21 May 400/2 Further penetration into the processes of the universe is self-stultificatory. **1972** D. BELL in Cox & Dyson *20th-Cent. Mind* I. vi. 180 A transcendental and intuitionist philosophy which Mill saw as internally inconsistent, obscurantist, and stultificatory of the progress of both science and philosophy.

stuma: see *STUMER 3.

stumblebum (stɒ·mb'lbɒm). Also **stumble bum, stumble-bum.** *slang* (orig. and chiefly *U.S.*). [f. STUMBLE *v.* + *BUM *sb.*⁴] **a.** A worthless, clumsy, or inept person; a 'down and out', a drunkard.

1932 E. HEMINGWAY *Death in Afternoon* 297 American word would be awkward bum, stumble-bum, flat-footed tramp. **1935** *Punch* 11 Dec. 652/3 An American gangster is stated to have begun his career by starting as a stumble-bum. **1936** [see *PALOOKA]. **1940** G. FRANKAU *Self-Portrait* xxxi. 178 The good old English word for a posterior, which possesses a different meaning (cf. 'stumblebum'—a guy who comes home drunk) in America. **1954** *Sun* (Baltimore) 11 Feb. 1/4 He became a ragged stumble-bum, raging drunkenly through the village and selling mediocre poetry. **1955** D. KEENE *Who has Wilma Lathrop?* x. 93 He had a stubble of beard that made him look like a stumblebum. **1966** A. LA BERN *Goodbye Piccadilly* xii. 113 These stumble-bums may have stumbled across the real culprit. **1970** *Guardian* 25 Sept. 10/5 Iago is a red-necked farm boy... He's a stumblebum. **1981** *Times Lit. Suppl.* 11 Sept. 1042/1 The Eisenhower of the war years has lost much of his lustre, and the successful organizer of Montgomery, Bradley and Patton has been reduced by some writers to the level of a strategic stumble-bum.

b. *attrib.* or as *adj.* Also *fig.*

1940 *Topeka* (Kansas) *Daily Capital* 16 Jan. 4/4 Russia's stumblebum campaign in Finland. **1952** B. WOLFE *Limbo '90* (1953) VI. xxii. 372 It made its slapstick stumblebum way back and forth. **1975** N. FREELING *What are Bugles blowing For?* xii. 75 Airs and graces with plain stumblebum cops. **1981** *Washington Post* 23 July C9/4 Joe Benjamin has a nihilistic, stumblebum-drunk son (splendidly played by Michael Rothhaar).

stumer. Add: **1. a.** Also *attrib.*, as *stumer cheque.*

1926 F. M. FORD *Man could stand Up* II. iii. 140 Two [were] awaiting court-martial for giving stumer cheques. **1944** P. CHEYNEY *They never say When* i. 18 Tell him to get in touch with Effie and get that stumer cheque from her and issue a writ against Swayle. **1962** *Listener* 11 Jan. 98/1 People who cash stumer cheques. **1972** L. LAMB *Picture Frame* xvii. 149 Nice old Mr Murgatroyd got your picture back from the man who gave you a stumer cheque.

b. *Austral.* Also **stoomer** (-ū-). (See quots.)

1898 *Bulletin* (Sydney) 17 Dec. (Red Page), A *stoomer* or *stumer* is a man without money. **1900–10** O'BRIEN & STEPHENS *Materials Dict. Austral. Slang* (MS.), *Come a stoomer*, stake a bet and lose everything. **1941** S. J. BAKER *Dict. Austral. Slang* 73 *Stumer*, (in gambling or racing) a bankrupt, a defaulter... *Come a stumer*, to crash financially, esp. in a racing bet.

2. *gen.* Something which is worthless; a failure, a 'flop', a 'dud'. Also used of persons.

1886–96 A. R. MARSHALL in Farmer & Henley *Slang* (1903) VII. 18/1 The merry stumer. **1902** *Sporting Times* 1 Feb. 3/1 He..had given her as security a 'stumer' in the shape of an unfinished history of Corsica. **1923** WODEHOUSE *Inimitable Jeeves* xii. 132 The agony of having put his little all on a stumer that hadn't finished in the first six. **1925** FRASER & GIBBONS *Soldier & Sailor Words* 273 *Stumer*, an expression used commonly to denote a shell that had failed to explode. **1928** GALSWORTHY *Swan Song* II. iv. 140 There is no good in me... You've pitched on a stumer. **1934** *Punch* 10 Jan. 50/1 *Myself*... No, drama. Young couple sight-seeing in mine. Old Miner guide. Roof falls, water rises. *Daphne.* Sounds like a stumer. Are you going to give it a run? **1970** *Daily Tel.* 9 Feb. 15/1 While in the course of a year countless shares will establish new lows only half a dozen will turn out to be real stumers and eventually worthless. **1976** *Times* 21 Feb. 15/3 Eclecticism guarantees that in a period like this the [Tate] collection will come to include a fair proportion of stumers. **1980** R. HILL *Spy's Wife* iv. 25 Don't be such a stumer!.. Fetch them.

3. Also **stuma.** A state of agitation; a sweat or 'stew'.

1932 AUDEN in *Rev. Eng. Studies* (1978) Aug. 284 Poor old Ma in a perfect stuma. **1936** —— *Look, Stranger!* 36 Behind your simple sense of humour You hide the boss's simple stuma. **1941** S. J. BAKER *Dict. Austral. Slang* 73 *Stumer, in a*, in a 'stew', worried, angry.

stumm, var. *SHTOOM *a.*

1974 L. DEIGHTON *Spy Story* iv. 41 So far, both sides have kept stumm about these operations. **1981** G. MARKSTEIN *Ultimate Issue* 209 Keep stumm about how you heard... You can always say you picked up a rumour.

stummick, repr. dial. and pop. pronunc. of STOMACH *sb.*

1888 KIPLING *Soldiers Three* (1890) 38 He was pegged out..on his stummick, a peg to each arm an' leg. **1936** M. MITCHELL *Gone with Wind* xxii. 372 De Yankees is comin'!.. Dey'll run dey baynits in our stummicks! **1947** K. TENNANT *Lost Haven* x. 157 If I was ever *you*, Mollie, or if I ever developed scales on me stummick, which amounts to the same thing..I'd be able to wriggle under rocks. **1977** J. AIKEN *Five-Minute Marriage* v. 88 You didn't ought to go out giving lessons on an empty stummick.

stump, *sb.*¹ Add: **2. c.** *up a stump*: perplexed, in difficulties (see also quot. 1834). Cf. *up a tree* s.v. TREE *sb.* 7. *slang* (orig. and chiefly *U.S.*).

1829 S. KIRKHAM *Eng. Gram.* 206 Hele [= he will] soon be up a stump. **1834** W. G. SIMMS *Guy Rivers* II. 241 Brooks..in backwood parlance, was 'considerably up a stump'—that is to say, half drunk. **1880** 'MARK TWAIN' *Tramp Abroad* xxxvi. 402 The public reciter..would find himself 'up a stump' when he got to the church bell. **1924** GALSWORTHY *White Monkey* I. xii. 100 Look here, Uncle Soames, I'm up a stump. **1944** DUNCAN & NICKOLS *Mentor Graham* 147 For once in his life, work had him so up a stump that he could not snatch a moment for study or reading.

8. Restrict † *Obs.* to sense in Dict. and add: **b.** To leave one's home, job, or settled way of life, to move. Also without possessive pronoun. Cf. *to pull up stakes* s.v. STAKE *sb.*¹ 1 e.

1955 'A. GILBERT' *Is she Dead Too?* xiii. 227 Seems to have pulled up his stumps now he's married again. Wonder if they left an address. **1974** M. BUTTERWORTH *Man in Sopwith Camel* I. i. 19 I've been trying to bully him into pulling up stumps and doing something with the rest of his life.

9. c. An act of stumping a batsman out. Also *stump-out*. Cf. STUMP *v.*¹ 8.

1859 *All Year Round* 23 July 305/2 All clever catches, and clever stumps too. **1871** 'THOMSONBY' *Cricketers in Council* 38 A stump-out may send the batsman back to his friends. **1912** A. A. LILLEY *Twenty-Four Years in Cricket* v. 61 Stover's wicket-keeping was remarkable... He..was always able to gather the ball with ease, and thus create for himself the maximum of certainty in.. effecting a possible stump.

d. *pl.* Close of play, when stumps are drawn. Chiefly *Austral.*

1954 J. H. FINGLETON *Ashes crown Year* xxv. 268 England carried on to stumps. **1962** *Times* 3 Dec. 3/2 He looked to be coasting through to 'stumps' when Benaud bowled him. **1977** *World of Cricket Monthly* June 30/2 Bold tactics by Intikhab..carried the Pakistani score to 6-249 at stumps.

† **16*.** A stringed instrument of the lute family (see quots.). *Obs.* exc. *Hist.*

a **1623** in *R. Johnson's Compl. Works for Solo Lute* (1972) 22 (*music title*) Alman To the Stumpe. **1947** E. BLOM *Everyman's Dict. Mus.* 674/1 *Stump*, an obs. string instrument of the Cittern type invented *c.* 1600 by Daniel Farrant. **1961** A. BIRCH in A. Baines *Mus. Instr. through Ages* vii. 166 There were other instruments too, for accompanying the voice or for solo playing, 'stump', 'poliphant', 'penorcon', but little more than their names has survived. **1976** D. MUNROW *Instr. Middle Ages & Renaissance* ix. 83/4 Of the stump there are no surviving examples or descriptions though the name does suggest a small instrument. One piece of stump music is extant, however, entitled *Alman R. Johnson to the stump by F.P.*..giving the impression that the stump was a wire-strung equivalent of the theorbo.

17. (sense 2) *stumpwood*; (sense 14) *stump oration, oratory* (earlier example), *speech* (earlier example).

1831 *Constellation* (N.Y.) 12 Feb. 98/2 You see, sir, I want an office, for, as I told 'em in my stump horation twict, the man..is the very one that ought to be awarded. **1811** E. FLETCHER *Let.* 11 Jan. (1965) 26 For you must know that the people in these parts get into office by 'Stump oratory' or praising and electioneering for themselves. **1820** J. FLINT *Lett. from Amer.* (1822) 251 The harangues are called stump-speeches. **1953** *Forestry Abstr.* XIV. 296/2 Miscellaneous notes are appended on: splitting stumpwood with explosives.., and Spruce and Pine stumpwood for the manufacture of fibreboards. **1977** *Ibid.* XXXVIII. 44/2 (*heading*) Determining the volume of stumpwood and rootwood in *Picea abies*.

18. stump-grubber, a machine designed to excavate the stumps of trees after the trees have been felled (cf. *stump-machine*); **stump-grubbing,** the excavation of tree-stumps by manual or mechanical means; **stump-jump** *a.*: also *absol.* as *sb.*; **stump jumper** *U.S.*, a countryman or hillbilly (cf. *stubble-jumper* s.v. *STUBBLE *sb.* 5); **stump plant,** a cutting consisting of a short cut-back stem and roots which may or may not be pruned; **stump topgallant mast** (earlier example); **stump water** *U.S.*, the rain-water which collects in the stumps of hollow-trees, associated esp. with folk remedies and charms; **stump word,** a word formed by abbreviating a single longer one, esp. by reducing it to a single syllable (freq. the first) or the minimum necessary for understanding; cf. *CLIPPING *vbl. sb.*² 2 c; **stump-work** (later *attrib.* examples).

1971 *Sylwan* CXV. x. 19 Investigation of the technical and economic efficiency of the Odyniec stump-grubber. **1977** *Forestry Abstr.* XXXVIII. 580/1 The specifications of the stump-grubbers are tabulated, and data are given on stump-grubbing performance. **1938** M. RICHARDSON in B. A. Botkin *Treas. S. Folklore* (1949) III. i. 442 He went on the stump-grubbing gang, soon as he got to the Farm. **1961** *Forestry Abstr.* XXII. 582/1 (*heading*) Using a vibratory shock method in stump-grubbing. **1977** Stump-grubbing [see *stump-grubber* above]. **1911** E. M. CLOWES *On Wallaby* xi. 297 Those people who..were once in undisputed possession of these mountains and forests—before the days of the axe and saw, the 'stump-jump', and the 'mallee roller'. **1936** J. H. STREET *Look Away* xiii. 87 That's the home of the hillbillies. Some folks call 'em 'stump-jumpers'. **1944** in H. Wentworth *Amer. Dial. Dict.* 606/2 She musta been one o' these West Virginia stump-jumpers. **1953** *Brit. Commonw. Forest Terminol.* I. 36 *Cutting, root and shoot*, one consisting of a pruned tap-root and cut-back stem. Syn...stump plant. **1960** *Forestry Abstr.* XXI. I. 31/1 Stump plants made from 1-year seedlings were planted in pots. **1804** in *Naval Docs. U.S. Wars with Barbary Powers* (U.S. Office Naval Rec.) (1942) IV. 346 You will know my ship by her having stump top Gl Masts. **1892** J. C. HARRIS *Uncle Remus & Friends* 290 De way ter git rid er ha'nts wuz ter git some prickly-pear root en bile it in stump-water en sprinkle it 'roun' de yard. **1972** J. S. HALL *Sayings from Old Smoky* 133 'His head is full of stump water.' That is, 'He don't use his brain.'..Possibly 'stump water in the head' meant originally that the person had been affected by magic, that is, was 'teched in the head', or dazed. **1922** O. JESPERSEN *Language* II. ix. 169 We come to those changes which result in what one may call 'stump-words'. ..Words may undergo violent shortenings both by children and adults. **1963** *Amer. Speech* XXXVIII. 156 Other stump words or clipped forms such as *info, auto.* **1971** Stump word [see *MELO]. **1938** *Burlington Mag.* Oct. 172/2 Stuart 'stump-work' embroidery. **1958** *Times* 25 Nov. 18/6 A highly important Venetian glass mirror with stumpwork panels. **1971** *Country Life* 10 June 1426/2 A mirror framed in stumpwork embroidery made in England three centuries ago.

stump, *a.* **4. stump-nose,** substitute for def.: = STOMPNEUS in Dict. and Suppl.; (earlier example).

1838 [see *KLIPFISH 1].

stump, *v.*¹ Add: **2. b.** (Earlier example.)

1803 G. COLMAN *John Bull* IV. i. 41 Now, Sir, you and I'll stump it.

13. (Examples.)

1857 A. LINCOLN in H. Binns *Life A. Lincoln* (1927) 181 Like the boy that stumped his toe..it hurt too bad to laugh. **1891** *Harper's Mag.* Feb. 364/2 Mus' be powerful sorrowful ter set at home an' shed tears lest he mought her stumped his toe on the road.

17. b. (*c*) In extended use, const. *with.*

1956 'C. BLACKSTOCK' *Dewey Death* ii. 35, I hope the department will stump up with a decent wreath. **1958** *Listener* 9 Oct. 569/2 The Americans stumped up with *The Old Man and the Sea.*

c. (Earlier example, with person as obj.)

1853 J. PALLISER *Solitary Rambles* v. 126, I..reminded him how completely he had stumped me up that afternoon.

stumpage. 1. (Earlier example.)

1835 *Knickerbocker* V. 423 Such rough words as tariff jobbing, cuts, stumpage.

stumper. 3. (Further example.)

1833 in P. Norman *Scores & Annals W. Kent Cricket Club* (1897) 73 Herbert..is such a wonderous stumper.

stumping, *vbl. sb.*¹ Add: **1. b.** (Earlier example.)

1844 W. LILLYWHITE *Hand-bk. Cricket* 15 No byes, overthrows, stumping, or catching out behind wicket allowed.

3. *Comb.*, as **stumping machine** *N. Amer.* = *stump-machine* s.v. STUMP *sb.*¹ 18; **stumping powder,** an explosive used for clearing land of tree stumps.

1871 G. EASTON *Trav. Amer.* xiii. 129 Until time has so destroyed the roots that, with the aid of a pair of oxen and a 'stumping machine', the stumps can be removed with comparative ease. **1906** *Daily Colonist* (Victoria, B.C.) 30 Jan. 5/5 An experiment in clearing Island lands by the aid of a steam stumping machine is shortly to be made in the vicinity of Duncan. **1973** L. RUSSELL *Everyday Life Colonial Canada* ii. 31 Later a 'stumping machine' was used. It consisted of a very heavy wooden tripod, with a stout, vertical iron screw mounted at the apex. **1921** *Daily Colonist* (Victoria, B.C.) 6 Apr. 5/4 The regulations under which the Provincial Department of Agriculture will issue funds for the purchasing of cheap stumping powder to farmers have been approved. **1955** R. P. HOBSON *Nothing too Good for Cowboy* i. 11 The cattle company..has exploded like a can of stumping powder.

stun, *v.* Add: **6.** *Comb.* **stun gas,** a gas that incapacitates by causing temporary confusion and disorientation; **stun grenade,** a grenade that only stuns through its sound and flash; **stun gun,** a gun that fires shot which stuns without causing serious injury.

1968 *Punch* 21 Feb. 253 Here is a run-down of anti-crowd devices which other nations, notably America, are developing:..stun gas; gas which temporarily blinds. **1977** *Times* 19 Oct. 1/4 The 'stun' grenades which played such a vital part in enabling the West German commando unit to overcome the terrorists..were supplied by Britain. **1981** A. WINCH *Blood Money* xxi. 236 The stun grenades..looked like unmarked beer cans and provided a deafening explosion, a blinding flash. **1971** *Sunday Times* 30 May 5 The stun gun has already been used effectively by the Alameda County Sheriff's Department who are called in whenever student riots at Berkeley become too much for the local police. **1975** *Nature* 13 Feb. 495/3 One hopes that the [polar bear tagging] expedition will be equipped with a supply of stun-guns.

stung, *ppl. a.* Add: **2.** *Austral. slang.* Drunk. Cf. *STUNNED *ppl. a.* 2.

1919 W. H. DOWNING *Digger Dialects* 48 *Stung*,.. drunk. **1952** T. A. G. HUNGERFORD *Ridge & River* 62 The old bloke's stung already, and the pubs aren't even opened yet! **1965** W. DICK *Bunch of Ratbags* 219 We had arrived at Doreen's sister's wedding-reception about an hour ago and by now we were all half stung. **1970** K. SLESSOR *Bread & Wine* 154 To a total abstainer, the line 'I am stung, stung to the heart of me' would convey, I suppose, nothing so coarse as the associations which I find in it.

stunned, *ppl. a.* (In Dict. s.v. STUN *v.*) Add: **2.** *Austral.* and *N.Z. slang.* Drunk. Cf. prec.

1919 W. H. DOWNING *Digger Dialects* 48 *Stunned* (adj.), drunk. **1933** 'P. CADEY' *Broken Pattern* xii. 129 I'm afraid I got a bit stunned... I had one over the odd.

3. Phr. *like a stunned mullet* [MULLET¹]: dull, stupefied. *Austral. slang.*

1953 BAKER *Australia Speaks* 267 [Similes] Dullness: (looking) like a stunned mullet. **1963** J. O'GRADY *Things they do to You* 147, I returned and lay on the bed like a stunned mullet. **1977** *Australian* 16 May 1 Mr Hawke said yesterday the Federal Government had responded like a stunned mullet to his acceptance of the proposed Industrial Relations Bureau.

stunner. 1. (Earlier example.)

1829 P. EGAN *Boxiana* 2nd Ser. II. 417 The blow was a *stunner*, and visible on his forehead.

stunt, *sb.*² Add: **1. a.** (Earlier example.) Also *spec.* in aerobatics.

1892 R. H. DAVIS *West from Car Window* 13 They went about it as gleefully as schoolboys at recess doing 'stunts'. **1909** *Flight* 11 Sept. 552/2 He made the machine dart down as though it were going to pitch to earth head foremost, but when within about 20 feet of the ground, without effort he brought it horizontal again. These are what Americans style 'stunts'. **1915** W. E. DOMMETT *Submarine Vessels* viii. 88 Of course, nothing in the nature of 'stunts', such as are performed by airmen, are tried. **1927** C. A. LINDBERGH *We* i. 13 We did a few stunts over the fair-grounds to get everyone's attention.

b. (Earlier and later examples.) Also *spec.* in Advertising, Journalism, etc., a 'gimmick' or device for attracting attention.

1878 S. BUTLER *Let.* 7 Feb. (1955) 174 It was a stunt for advertising the books, so I sent them. **1919** 'R. N. ETIENNE' *Strange Tales from Fleet* 27 The 'stunt' was over, and two brief hours had prevented the twelfth Cruiser Squadron from cutting off the enemy light forces. **1922** *Daily Mail* 13 Nov. 11 The plea for 'stipes' is a newspaper stunt. **1930** *Lancet* 7 June 1264/1 It has even been whispered, Sir, that there are too many 'stunts' (if this word may appear in your columns), too little science, but this is just malicious gossip. **1942** *Sun* (Baltimore) 29 Dec. 13/2 It would be a good stunt for us fellows to learn all the tricks of the Coast Guard and then we could turn rum runners! **1968** J. R. ACKERLEY *My Father & Myself* vii. 61 My brother's assignment was what we called a 'stunt', a common affair, in this case important if only because the Brigadier had set his heart on it. **1975** *Sunday Times* (Colour Suppl.) 20 July 12/2 His bi-sexuality..was attracting sensational publicity. How much of this was simply a stunt?

c. A stint, a task, an exercise. orig. *U.S.*

1880 *Hermean* (N.Y.) 256 Ye have heard it said by those of old time, 'A rolling stone gathers no moss,' but by reason perhaps of its having been used as a 'stunt' for our childhood in the copy books, we seldom realize how beautiful and full of wisdom is the adage. **1904** G. H. LORIMER *Old Gorgon Graham* 85 And you set the other at a twelve-hour stunt of making all the beds you've mussed. **1921** G. B. SHAW in G. C. Williamson *John Keats Memorial Vol.* 176 Milton can do a stunt of geniality, as in *L'Allegro*.

d. In wider use, a piece of business, an act, enterprise, or exploit.

1904 *Sun* (N.Y.) 8 Aug. 5 He took lessons in holding the life net..and the other stunts firemen are taught. **1913** R. BROOKE *Coll. Poems* (1918) p. lxxxiv, Then I do my pet boyish-modesty stunt and go pink all over. **1920** C. BAX *Square Pegs* 21 *Hilda.* You'll drive me frantic If you're not just the teeniest bit romantic. *Gioconda.* It isn't done. You're absolutely wrong In asking me to do that stunt. So long! **1928** [see *PEEP *sb.*¹ 2 b]. **1964** C. HASSALL *Rupert Brooke* vii. 277 'So of course you were frank and boyish?' asked Mrs. Cornford, on hearing he [*sc.* Rupert Brooke] had just met Henry James. 'Oh yes,' he said, 'Of course I did the fresh, boyish stunt, and it was a great success.'

2. a. *attrib.*, as *stunt artist, flying, pilot*, etc.

1904 W. H. SMITH *Promoters* iii. 75 He might have made a successful actor, of the modern 'stunt' sort. **1916** C. WINCHESTER *Flying Men* 112 Trick flying, or 'stunt' flying as it is colloquially called, can only be attempted with impunity by those aviators who have had some experience. **1922** H. L. WILSON *Merton of Movies* 174 Ain't I a good stunt actress? **1931** *Morning Post* 18 Feb. 6/4 (*heading*) 'Stunt' pilot's escape. **1931** *Everyman* 23 Apr. 388/2 We are on the eve of a reaction from the 'stunt Press', he believes—the Press of competitions and coupons and catchpenny sensations. **1938** M. MCCARTHY in *Partisan Rev.* Feb. 35 In the actual production of Gielgud's *Hamlet* and Welles's *Caesar*, the exploiter, that is, the stunt artist, wears a more successful disguise. **1971** *Flying* Apr. 46/3 He is in the stunt-flying business. **1976** M. MAGUIRE *Scratchproof* iv. 53 'Remember to stretch the line tight,' the stunt arranger emphasized. **1977** D. ANTHONY *Stud Game* vi. 37 After the war Dusty became a stunt pilot for the movies. **1981** *Times Lit. Suppl.* 13 Feb. 177/5 The black-and-white plates which illustrate the book..reveal completely new aspects of the works of art reproduced, without ever verging on the stunt photography which so often distorts Baroque sculpture in books written by less scrupulous authors.

b. Special Comb.: **stunt-drive** *v. intr.*, to drive a car for stunts (sense 1 a), esp. for making dangerous film sequences; hence **stunt-driving** *vbl. sb.*; **stunt man,** one who performs dangerous feats, esp. as a stand-in for a film actor.

1966 J. CLEARY *High Commissioner* v. 96, I used to stunt-drive in the old Ealing comedies. **1975** *New Yorker* 21 Apr. 92/3 One can disregard obvious high-risk occupations, such as stunt-driving. **1930** *Aberdeen Press & Jrnl.* 23 Jan. 2/6 To those who wish to get plenty of excitement out of life our advice is—Be a movie stunt man. **1953** C. A. LINDBERGH *Spirit of St. Louis* II. vi. 275 We walked over to a group of pilots, mechanics, and stunt men. **1953** DYLAN THOMAS *Let.* (1966) 416, I cry to myself as I kick clear of the cling of my stuntman's sacking. **1968** P. GEDDES *High Game* viii. 101 He'd worked, off and on, as a stunt-man in movies. **1977** *New Yorker* 27 June 84/3 The successful stunt man explained that his plan had been to scale the tower a day earlier.

stunt (stʊnt), *v.*³ [f. STUNT *sb.*²] **a.** *intr.* To perform stunts (in quots. with reference to aerobatics). **b.** *trans.* To use (an aeroplane) for the performance of stunts.

1917 'CONTACT' *Airman's Outings* p. xxiii, They could turn, climb, and stunt quicker than any two-seater. **1928** *Daily Mail* 9 Aug. 7/1 The aeroplane was apparently 'stunting' at a height of between 2,000 and 3,000 feet. **1928** *Daily Tel.* 18 Sept. 11/4 There is no reason why the autogiro should not be stunted. **1953** C. A. LINDBERGH *Spirit of St. Louis* II. vi. 421 DHs aren't built like Jennies. .. And you can't stunt 'em like a Jenny either—no rolls or loops. **1970** L. DEIGHTON *Bomber* iv. 64 When the Luftwaffe was officially born in 1935 Peter Redenbacher was stunting a Bücker Jungmann biplane above the heads of Hitler, Göring, the foreign Press and a deliriously happy German crowd.

Hence **stu·nter, stu·ntist,** one who performs or organizes stu·nts; **stu·nting** *vbl. sb.* and *ppl. a.*

1914 G. HAMEL *Flying* 212 It [*sc.* the Royal Flying Corps] talks shop..and indulges in rude health and proper pride, discouraging 'stunting' and heroics. **1922** *Daily Mail* 2 Nov. 5 Some of the members of the Committee.. went on the Council as economy 'stunters'. **1923** *Glasgow Herald* 14 July 7 Close on five o' clock the 'stunting' planes came to earth. **1925** *Public Opinion* 31 July 107/3 When the political stuntists saw fit to mobilise. **1927** C. A. LINDBERGH *We* vi. 94 The De Havilands were not considered safe for hard stunting. **1928** *Observer* 18 Mar. 17/2 Two officers..who are considered to be the best 'stunters' in the force. **1940** G. FRANKAU *Self-Portrait* xlvi. 285 The stunt merchant, for all his stunting, had a creed. **1970** R. BLAKE *Conservative Party* viii. 253 The Conservatives, in spite of having a real point, incurred the charge of 'stunting' when they used such expressions as 'Gauleiter Laski'. **1978** *Detroit Free Press* 16 Apr. (Cartoon Suppl.) 1/2 (Advt.). Boys' deluxe MX motocross style bike... Not for stunting or off-road use.

stunty, *a.* Add: **3.** Having the character of a stunt, extravagant, 'gimmicky'.

1981 *Daily Tel.* 27 Jan. 13/4 Cardin's minis do not look stunty or contrived.

stupe, *sb.*² Add: (Later U.S. examples.) Also as *adj.*

1967 'T. WELLS' *Dead by Light of Moon* (1968) i. 15 His assistant, a big stupe called Jersey Eng. **1967** E. MCGIRR *Here lies my Wife* v. 151 He carries on..all the time. He's stupe. **1977** *Time* 25 Apr. 46/3 She tells him that true love has washed away her sins and the pure and simple stupe embraces her.

stupend (stiūpe·nd), *v. rare.* [Back-formation from STUPENDOUS *a.*] *trans.* To amaze, dumbfound. (G. B. Shaw's word.)

1904 G. B. SHAW *Let.* 6 Dec. (1972) II. 470 You will be stupended at my meanness in this obvious & cheap retort. **1927** —— *Let.* 2 Feb. in *To a Young Actress* (1960) 113 The discovery that you actually wanted me to shew that daub to Charlotte has perfectly stupended me.

stupendous, *a.* Add: Now freq. in trivial use.

1892 E. DOWSON *Let.* in *N. & Q.* (1962) Mar. 102/1, I have become the victim of the most stupendous cold which has ever occurred to me, & fear that I shall spend tomorrow in bed. **1939** *Airman's Gazette* Dec., All aircraft off duty being allowed to..view the stupendous, side-splitting entertainment. **1942** E. PAUL *Narrow St.* ii. 15 The *marc* was undiluted—stupendous, in fact. **1959** C. L. WRENN *Word & Symbol* (1967) 35 That stupendous scholar, Max Förster.

‖ **stupor mundi** (stiū·pǫɹ mu·ndī, stiū·pǫɹ mɒ·ndəi). L. phr.: the marvel of the world; an object of admiring bewilderment and wonder. Cf. STUPOR 2 b.

The phrase was originally used by the thirteenth-century historian Matthew Paris to describe the Emperor Frederick II of Germany.

1879 *Encycl. Brit.* IX. 732/2 The general contemporary opinion regarding Frederick II. is expressed in the words *stupor mundi*:..wonder and perplexity are the predominant sentiments which..[the contemplation of his career] even yet awakens. **1946** R. LOWELL *Lord Weary's Castle* 5 Over the drum-beat of St. Stephen's choir I hear him, *Stupor Mundi.* **1980** J. A. T. ROBINSON *Roots of Radical* ii. 22 What is easier is to preen ourselves on our 'comprehensiveness' without realising that it is in every sense a *stupor mundi*, an object of incredulous disbelief to the world and even our fellow Christians.

Sturge–Weber (stɒ̄ɹdʒ we·bəɹ). *Path.* [The names of W. A. *Sturge* (1850–1919) and F. P. *Weber* (1863–1962), English physicians, who described the syndrome in 1879 and 1922 respectively.] *Sturge-Weber syndrome* or *disease*: a congenital syndrome in which a diffuse malformation of blood-vessels on one side of the head produces port-wine nævus on the face and lesions of the brain, usually resulting in fits and mental retardation.

1935 H. BERGSTRAND in *Abstr. 2nd Internat. Neurol. Congr., London* 124 Sturge-Weber's disease is a syndrome comparable with von Recklinghausen's..and Bourneville's diseases. **1974** J. H. MENKES *Textbk. Child Neurol.* x. 412/2 The coincidence of a facial vascular disease and seizures suggests Sturge-Weber disease.

sturine (stiūᵊ·rīn, -in). *Biochem.* Also **-in.** [a. G. *sturin* (A. Kossel 1896, in *Zeitschr. f. physiol. Chem.* XXII. 180) f. pop.L. *sturiōn-em* STURGEON: see -INE⁵.] A protamine extracted from the testicles of fish of the genus *Accipenser*, esp. *A. sturio* and *A. guldenstadtii*, sturgeons of the Baltic and Caspian Seas.

1896 [see *SALMINE]. **1960** *Adv. Protein Chem.* XV. 34 In the case of sturine, both procedures..yield two NH_2-terminal amino acids, alanine and glutamic acid. **1977** *Bull. Exper. Biol. & Med.* LXXXIII. 710 The proportion of added DNA to be bound with spheroblasts untreated with sturine was 18%.

‖ **Sturmabteilung** (ʃtu·ɹmaptai:luŋ). [Ger., lit. 'storm detachment'.] A paramilitary force forming part of the German National Socialist Party, founded in 1921 and deprived of power in 1934. Abbrev. S.A. (s.v. *S 4 a).

1923 *Times* 22 May 11/1 At the headquarters of the [Nazi] organization near the Gärtnerplatz Theatre, the visitor is confronted in the main hall by the notice 'Sturm-Abteilung' (Storm-troop section). Newspaper correspondents..are not very welcome. **1932** E. LENGYEL *Hitler* x. 145 Germany is divided into five Sturm Abteilung inspections. **1977** M. WALKER *National Front* i. 19 They [*sc.* Mosley's army] had neither the numbers nor the organization of Hitler's *Sturmabteilung* or Mussolini's *Squadristi.* **1977** [see *S.A.* s.v. *S 4 a].

‖ **Sturmbannführer** (ʃtu·ɹmbanfū:rəɹ). Ger., = 'battalion leader'.] An officer in the *Schutzstaffel* (formerly part of the *Sturmabteilung*).

1955 J. THOMAS *No Banners* xxv. 246 The *sturmbannführer* literally foamed at the mouth. **1965** M. SPARK *Mandelbaum Gate* i. 13 Freddy..felt an urge to explain that he was not a mass-butcher and that he had never desired to become a *sturmbannführer.* **1978** T. ALLBEURY *Lantern Network* viii. 99 A fresh-faced blond German with the insignia of a Sturmbannführer.

Sturmer (stɒ̄·ɹməɹ). Also **sturmer.** The name of a village near Haverhill, on the Suffolk–Essex border, used *attrib.* or *absol.* in

Sturmer apple, Pippin to designate a late-ripening dessert apple belonging to a variety developed there in the 1830s by S. and J. Dillistone (fl. 1827–50) and distinguished by yellowish-green skin, sometimes slightly russetted, and crisp, creamy-white flesh.

1831 *Catal. Fruits cult. in Garden* (Hort. Soc.) (ed. 2) 37 Apples... Sturmer Pippin. **1847** *Gardeners' Chron.* 27 Feb. 135/2 When the Nonpareil is getting over, the Sturmer Pippin. then in perfection, comes in to supply its place. **1851** R. Hogg *Brit. Pomology* 190 The Sturmer Pippin was raised by Mr. Dillistone, a nurseryman at Sturmer, near Haverhill, in Suffolk, and was obtained by impregnating the Ribston Pippin with the pollen of the Nonpareil. **1877** E. S. Dallas *Kettner's Bk. of Table* 35 Dessert Apples... February—Sturmer Pippin. **1950** *N.Z. Jrnl. Agric.* Aug. 191/1 Good sources of vitamin C include..sturmer apples. **1959** [see *delicious *a.* 2 b]. **1971** R. Petrie *Thorne in Flesh* x. 133 A flow of customers beyond the carefully stacked pyramids of Sturmers and Jonathans swelled and dwindled.

‖ **Sturm und Drang** (ʃtuɹm unt draŋ): see *storm and stress* s.v. Storm *sb.* 3 d.

[**1844** F. L. J. Thimm *Lit. of Germany* 85 This period, so styled by Goethe, after the title of one of the dramas of Klinger, 'Sturm und Drang'.] **1857** C. Kingsley *Two Yrs. Ago* III. i. 29 One of the Sturm-und-drang party, of course; the express locomotive school, scream-and-go-ahead. **1873** Gostwick & Harrison *Outl. German Lit.* xvi. 228 That time of 'Sturm und Drang', when writing wild poetry was regarded as the object of life. **1925** L. P. Smith *Words & Idioms* iii. 105 In that wild period, which was called at the time *Genieperiode*, but has since acquired the name of *Sturm und Drang*, the great watchwords *Genius*, *Originality*, and *Creative* acquired a resonance.. which they had certainly never possessed in England. **1950** M. J. C. Hodgart *Ballads* ix. 152 The philosophical and political obsessions which attracted the *Sturm und Drang* writers to folksong. **1973** *Listener* 28 June 862/3 The Romantic poets..loved the word 'storm' as a synonym for energy, in phrases like *Sturm und Drang*, 'storm and thrust'.

transf. **1885** H. Conway *Family Affair* III. v. 85 His *sturm und drang*, his emotional days, were well over... He had not bowed his knee to the intense, nor sacrificed on the altar of the incomprehensible. **1909** A. Nicolson *Let.* 24 Mar. in H. Nicolson *Sir Arthur Nicolson* (1930) xi. 305 When we have passed through the present 'Sturm und Drang' period, I should not be surprised if we were to find both France and Russia gravitating rapidly towards and Central Powers. **1938** E. Bowen *Death of Heart* I. v. 86 Eddie..wrote some pamphlets, which were printed by a girl who had a press in a loft. Arts and crafts had succeeded *Sturm und Drang*. **1962** J. Heller *Catch-22* iii. 29 Only when all the *Sturm und Drang* had been left far behind would he tip his flak helmet back wearily on his sweating head and stop barking directions to McWatt at the controls. **1978** H. Frank *Single* vi. 137 She wanted..mortification, punishment, Sturm und Drang.

S-turn: see *S 2 c.

Sturt (stɜ̄ɹt), *sb.*[4] The name of Charles *Sturt* (1795–1869), Australian explorer, used *attrib.* or in the possessive in **Sturt('s) (desert) pea** to designate a plant collected by him in 1844, *Clianthus formosus*, a trailing perennial herb of the family Leguminosæ, native to desert regions of Western Australia and bearing racemes of red or white flowers blotched with black at the base.

1865 J. E. Tenison-Woods *Hist. Discovery & Exploration Austral.* I. i. 29 Some of the species are engraved in one account of his [*sc.* Dampier's] voyage, amongst which appears the beautiful clianthus, known to the colonists as Sturt's Desert Pea. **1911** W. R. Guilfoyle *Austral. Plants* 114 'Sturt's Desert Pea'..or 'Australian Glory Pea' (biennial), flowers scarlet. **1933** [see *clianthus]. **1936** I. L. Idriess *Cattle King* iv. 27 The bluebush a sombre carpet splotched by scarlet patches of Sturt's desert pea. **1949** D. Walker *We went to Australia* xix. 183 The sturt pea is the most sensational [wild flower of West Australia]. **1966** *Times* 11 Nov. (W. Australia Suppl.) p. iv/2 There is the spectacular Sturt pea, sprawling crimson and black-hearted, on the red earth. **1977** *Caravan World* (Austral.) Jan. 37/3 The scarlet splash of Sturt's Desert Pea..mellowing the stark red earth. **1979** D. Bellamy in *Radio Times* 1–7 Dec. 5/1 Many Australian plants..have adapted to withstand bush fires... Sturt's Pea, the first plant to bloom after the ravages of fire.

stushie (stʊ̄·ʃi, sti·ʃi).). *Sc.* Also **stashie, stishie.** [Origin unknown.] A disturbance, uproar, row, fracas.

1824 G. Smith *Douglas Travestie* 12 Mony an aukward stashie was he in. **1840** G. Webster *Ingliston* xxviii. 289 The haill toun's been in a stushie about it. **1926** 'H. MacDiarmid' *Penny Wheep* 8, I lo'e the stishie o' Earth in space. **1959** M. Pugh *Chancer* 68 Big trouble from the film company... They're in a stushy. Some of the survivors started creating hell about the film. **1973** *People's Jrnl.* (Inverness & Northern Counties ed.) 24 Nov. 17/4 (*heading*) Army 'Samaritans' caused a stushie on the road to Durness. **1980** G. Hammond *Reward Game* vii. 96 Do you still want Briesland House, or did this morning's stishie put you off it for life?

stuss (stʊs, stʊʃ). *U.S.* [ad. Yiddish *shtos*, perh. a. G. *stoss* push, stack.] A form of faro.

1912 A. H. Lewis *Apaches of N.Y.* 35 Jigger owned a stuss-house in Forsyth Street. *Ibid.*, Between them they would divide the harvest of the stuss. **1913** [see *pipe-fiend* s.v. *pipe *sb.*[1] 11 b]. **1930** D. Runyon in *Sat. Even. Post* 5 Apr. 48/3, I do not wish to play stuss. *Ibid.* 72/1 It is what is called a stuss house, and many prominent citizens of the neighbourhood are present playing stuss. **1975** *Way to Play* 207/3 Stuss is also known as Jewish faro. It is a simplified form of faro, with a larger percentage in the house's favor.

stutter, *sb.*[2] Add: Also *transf.*

1974 C. Ryan *Bridge Too Far* iv. vi. 263 As he neared the ground the stutter of machine guns and the dull thud of mortar bursts seemed to engulf him. **1981** M. E. Atkins *Palimpsest* ii. 12 The car engine—with..the merest apology of stutter—cut out completely.

stutter, *v.* Add: **1. b.** (Later examples.) Also *fig.*

1931 Nordhoff & Hall *Falcons in France* 236 Guns were stuttering faintly on every side. **1935** J. Steinbeck *Tortilla Flat* ii. 26 The lawyer..climbed into his Ford and stuttered down the hill. **1963** *Times* 11 Feb. 4/1 Meanwhile, the F.A. Cup stutters forward, step by step. **1976** *Scottish Rev.* Summer 8 Tractors stutter in and out of fields.

2. Also *fig.*

1929 *Oxford Poetry* 12 And the map stutters inarticulate lines.

stuttering, *ppl. a.* (Later *transf.* and *fig.* examples.)

a **1918** W. Owen *Poems* (1963) 44 Only the stuttering rifles' rapid rattle Can patter out their hasty orisons. **1946** D. C. Peattie *Road of Naturalist* iv. 44 Turning out editorials of a rare charm and delicate fancy while the stuttering telegraph battered on his eardrums. **1980** L. Cody *Dupe* iii. 23 Even Selwyn's stuttering typewriter was silent.

S-twist: see *S 8.

style, *sb.* Add: **II. 13. c.** Proverbial phr. *the style is the man.*

[**1624** R. Burton *Anat. Melancholy* (ed. 2) 7 It is most true, *stylus virum arguit*, our stile bewrayes vs. **1753** G. Buffon *Histoire Naturelle* VII. p. xvii, Le style est l'homme même.] **1901** G. B. Shaw *Caesar & Cleopatra* 208 Going to Caesar's books, and concluding that the style is the man. **1901** A. Whyte *Bible Characters: Stephen to Timothy* civ. 72 If the style is the man in Holy Scripture also,..we feel a very great liking for Luke. **1942** H. F. Heard *Reply Paid* (1943) ix. 141 Usually I don't like to have my style modified. 'The style is the man.' **1978** *Language* LIV. 284 In describing Achilles' speech, we have also been describing his character, since 'style is the man'.

III. 23. (Later examples.) Also *gen.*, one's characteristic manner of acting or reacting. Phr. *to cramp one's style*: see *cramp *v.* 5 c.

1937 C. Odets *Golden Boy* I. iii. 47 Joe knows his own needs, as he says. Don't ask him to change his style. **1970** G. F. Newman *Sir, You Bastard* viii. 247 It hadn't been his original intention to make her suffer, but he couldn't alter his style. **1978** S. Brill *Teamsters* vi. 260 Lying low just isn't his style.

24. b. Also, more generally, attractive or impressive quality; originality.

1967 *Trans-Action* Apr. 11/1 Style is difficult to define as it has so many referents. It means to carry one's self well, dress well, to show class... A person with style must also show respect..for another's superior power. **1968** *Listener* 13 June 761/3 Jack, the prime Kennedy,.. had a quality which practically everybody recognised as 'style'. **1979** R. Jaffe *Class Reunion* (1980) II. xi. 288 How much more dignified it would have been if Rusty could have trusted her... But Rusty had never had style.

V. 28. (in sense 21 d) *style manual, sheet*; **style analysis,** analysis of the characteristic style of an artist, writer, composer, etc., or of a school or period, on the basis of which attribution of a particular work can be made; **style-book** (*b*): for *U.S.* read orig. *U.S.* and add examples; **style critic,** an expert in style analysis; **style-setter,** someone who or something which sets the fashion; so **style-setting** *ppl. a.*

1927 E. Rickert *New Methods for Study of Lit.* 274/2 (Index), Subjectivity in style analysis. **1953** M. Schapiro in A. Kroeber *Anthropol. Today* 290/1 The refinement of style analysis has come about..through problems in which small differences had to be..described precisely. **1955** H. Read *Icon & Idea* vi. 112 Then are many other factors which can be used in style analysis..but though all these stylistic traits build up to an index of the painter's personality, they do not..indicate the painter's awareness of a self. **1969–70** *Computers & Humanities* IV. 41 These results, minor as they are, are of a nature that has not been achieved in any other use of the computer for style analysis in music. **1973** *Black World* Nov. 5/1 Conventional histories of music and style-analysis texts generally ignored the subject of the Black man's contribution to music. **1898** (*title*) Stylebook of the Chicago Society of Proofreaders. **1930** [see *Negro 1 d]. **1981** K. Waterhouse *Daily Mirror Style* 5 In most newspaper offices there is to be found a manual known as the style-book which lays down..the paper's rules on the usage of words and punctuation. **1959** *Times* 26 May 13/5 On that hypothesis David stays as the author of the 75 pictures,..finally reinstated by modern style-critics. **1978** *Jrnl. R. Soc. Arts* CXXVI. 718/2 He may be the less inclined to indulge in wild or subjective speculation than the style critic. **1922** (*title*) Style manual of the Government printing office (U.S. Govt. Printing Office). **1964** E. D. Seeber (*title*) A style manual for students. **1959** *News Chron.* 1 July 3/1, I have a feeling it is going to be a style-setter. **1960** *Ibid.* 29 Feb. 6/7 Princess Margaret has always been a style-setter. **1955** Keepnews & Grauer *Pictorial Hist. Jazz* iii. 44 Earl Hines..quickly developed into an outstanding and style-setting pianist. **1960** *Farmer & Stockbreeder* 1 Mar. 44/2 The Fordson Dexta with its proved style-setting three cylinder Diesel engine. **1924** H. L. Mencken *Let.* 7 Dec. (1961) 272 Have you such a thing as a Style Sheet for The Atlantic? **1982** R. Quirk *Style & Communication in Eng. Lang.* i. 16 This is not, of course, to say that the existence of the 'style sheet' mentality is always advantageous.

style, *v.* Add: **7.** To design, arrange, make, etc., in a particular (esp. fashionable) style.

1934 J. Rorty *Our Master's Voice Advertising* 11 'Styling' clothes, kitchens, automobiles—everything, in the interest of more rapid obsolescence and replacement. **1936** H. L. Mencken *Amer. Lang.* (ed. 4) 194 The American liking for short cuts in speech, *e.g.*..*to style* for *to cut in accord with the style.* **1958** J. Cannan *And be a Villain* i. 25 The fashions of the day, styled to suit *gamines.* **1958** *Observer* 25 May 17/2 Mgr. Knox seems to have styled his translation to fit in with the least sufferable conceptions of this, really, stout-hearted young girl. **1976** 'Z. Stone' *Modigliani Scandal* III. iv. 137 Her hair had been styled by Sassoon.

-style, *suffix*, forming adjs. and advbs. **1.** Appended to adjs. **a.** Forming adjs. having the sense 'resembling or characteristic of something that is—'.

1934 *Discovery* June 174/1 He will have to put up at a Japanese style hotel. **1958** *Listener* 11 Sept. 368/1 He was dressed in European-style clothes. **1960** W. Thorp *Amer. Writing in 20th Cent.* 296 A series of events.. convinced [them] that revolution, Russian-style, would never take place in America. **1966** [see *sedan 1 c]. **1975** *Country Life* 20 Mar. 747/2 Elegant regency-style restaurant.

b. Forming advbs. with the sense 'in a manner that is—'. *colloq.*

1967 G. Kelly in *Coast to Coast 1965–6* 95 Bill Beatty leant across the table, his cigarette dangling casual style from his fingers. **1976** T. Sharpe *Wilt* (1978) vi. 61 We're here idyllicstyle, cruising down the river in the good old summertime.

2. Appended to sbs., forming advbs. and adjs. with the general sense '(in a manner) characteristic of or befitting—'.

The advb. use is highly colloq.

1944 W. Saroyan *Human Comedy* xxiv. 166 He whistled, newsboy style. **1949** *Amer.-German Rev.* Apr. 10 Meals were served family-style. **1973** *Guardian* 31 Jan. 5/2 An election-style budget.

styled, *ppl. a.* Restrict † *Obs. rare* to sense in Dict. and add: **2.** Of a person's hair: professionally arranged, cut, or set.

1958 *Spectator* 27 June 833/2 Another of the old gang in hacking jacket and styled hair mincing over to a seat. **1977** E. Leonard *Unknown Man No. 89* ii. 13 His styled hair..glistened.

3. With prefixed sb., adj., etc., forming combs. indicating the origin or provenance of the style.

1958 *Spectator* 11 July 56/2 Manhattan-styled clerical tuxedos. **1966** *Melody Maker* 15 Oct. 19 After an Alpert-styled 'Taste of Honey'.., he introduced a couple of new numbers. **1976** B. Bova *Multiple Man* (1977) v. 64 Their Bavarian-styled paneled dining room.

styler (stəi·ləɹ). [f. Style *v.* + -er[1].] **1.** = *stylist 2 a, b. *rare.*

1960 *Lebende Sprachen* V. 35/2 [Clothing industry vocabulary] *Designer, styler, stylist,* Modellmacher, Modelleur (Bekleidung). **1972** *Classification of Occupations* (Dept. Employment) III. 257/2 Dolls' hair styler.

2. A device for styling hair.

1971 *Wall St. Jrnl.* (Eastern ed.) 1 Apr. 1/5 Bercy Industries..has doubled its own forecast of men's hair styler sales... The response to stylers cheers retailers. **1976** *Honolulu Star-Bull.* 21 Dec. B-3/1 (Advt.), Save $5! women's 1200-watt styler-dryer.

styling. Add: **2.** The action, process, or result of *style *v.* 7.

1928 *Publishers' Weekly* 9 June 2370 Recourse to art for investing conventional merchandise with fresh or added appeal has been the chief reliance of post-war sales strategy. It has been termed 'Styling' in some quarters. **1939** *Archit. Rev.* LXXXVI. 62/1 It is scarcely conceivable that any but an American designer would have designed such a building: it is 'styling' applied to architecture. One can only hope that this same 'styling' will not later be applied to Town Halls. **1958** *Observer* 25 May 11/3 The styling of clothes for small children has now passed out of the hands of British makers. **1959** *Daily Tel.* 27 Aug. 11/3 This same firm which now also makes Pilot [television] models with slightly different styling. **1966** *Listener* 17 Nov. 712/2 A new automobile... Engineering and 'styling' costs were $9,000,000. **1975** G. Howell *In Vogue* 206/2 Teddy Boys would go to a barber for 'styling'. **1980** *Times* 29 Feb. 23/4 Smooth, wedge-shaped styling makes for a distinctive appearance.

stylism (stəi·liz'm). [f. Style *sb.* + -ism.] A stylistic device or effect; emphasis on style.

1928 H. Crane *Let.* 5 Feb. (1965) 317, I am not as original in some of my stylisms as I had thought I was. **1942** [see *abstractional]. **1958** *Times* 30 Sept. 3/1 The German company..proves to be a finely cast body of actors with an inevitably stronger feeling for classical stylism. **1971** R. apRoberts *Trollope* i. 15 Both symbolic explanation and *stylism*, then, are overworked for fiction.

stylist. Add: **1. b.** *transf.* In sport or music, one who plays with style.

1897 K. S. RANJITSINHJI *Jubilee Bk. Cricket* iii. 118 A young player of much promise—essentially a stylist, with brilliant strokes all round the wicket when set. **1898** —— *With Stoddart's Team* (ed. 3) i. 34 Hayward is essentially a stylist. **1969** *Listener* 3 Apr. 470/3 He's also perhaps the most original clarinet stylist in the British Isles. **1981** *Best of Karate '81* Spring 35/2 (*caption*) A Japanese stylist from Indiana, he has won virtually every major title available.

2. orig. *N. Amer.* **a.** In industry, esp. the retail clothing and car industries, one whose job is to create, co-ordinate, or promote the latest fashions or designs for a firm's commodities.

1928 *Daily Express* 18 July 12 The post of 'stylist' has been created during the last year in some of the better Canadian and American stores. The duties consist of linking departments,..informing the bag department of the trend of fashion in the shoe section, and the glove department what is happening in the costume department. *Ibid.* 24 Sept. 7 Harrods Fashion Buyers and Stylists. **1956** *Stanford Law Rev.* July 628 The General Motors stylist Harley Earl cannot be split into five pieces. **1958** *Spectator* 20 June 817/3 The quality and style of 'St. Michael' garments are the product of close collaboration between the Buying Executives, Stylists and Technologists. **1978** *Jrnl. R. Soc. Arts* CXXVI. 538/1 Mr. Nader caused a greater fundamental change to the appearance of cars than did a hundred stylists or engineers.

b. One who styles hair; = *hair-stylist* s.v. *HAIR *sb.* 10.

1937 R. STOUT *Crime on her Hands* (1939) ii. 23, I could have got a job as a stylist, or..started a hat shop. **1962** *Times* 3 Feb. 9/4 Where are the barbers or even the hairdressers now? They have become stylists to a man or woman. **1968** [see *CRIMPER[1] 1 b]. **1979** *West Lancs. Evening Gaz.* 10 Nov. 11 (Advt.), Wanted—all-round Stylist—male/female.

stylistician (stəilisti·ʃən). [f. STYLISTIC *a.* and *sb.* + -IAN.] One who studies stylistics.

1939 *Language* XV. 257 One misses the subtler approach of the 'stylisticians' of today. **1948** L. SPITZER *Linguistics & Lit. Hist.* iv. 136 In general, stylisticians have rather shied away from Diderot. **1957** *Archivum Linguisticum* IX. 148 He shares the weakness of other stylisticians, in claiming to have found the Philosopher's Stone. **1969** CRYSTAL & DAVY *Investigating English Style* 12 The stylistician is on precisely the same footing as anyone else. **1980** *Times Lit. Suppl.* 11 Jan. 28/1 He makes extensive use of the rhetorical device known to stylisticians as 'free indirect speech'.

stylometric (stəilome·trik), *a.* [f. STYLE *sb.* + -O + *-METRIC.] Of or pertaining to stylometry.

1935 H. W. B. JOSEPH *Essays in Anc. & Mod. Philos.* i. 1 The first book of Plato's *Republic*..may be earlier in date than those which follow. This view about it has strong support from 'stylometric' investigations. **1964** *Guardian* 17 June 9/3 Mr Thomson..determined..to use stylometric methods to investigate the Baconian controversy. **1971** *Computers & Humanities* V. 302 The goals are:..to establish stylometric criteria based on preferred sounds, to see if significant differences in phonemic and phonetic frequencies exist between prose and verse. **1982** *Times Lit. Suppl.* 26 Nov. 1322/2 Most unsettling is his claim, on stylometric grounds long invaluable in the study of Plato, that the so-called 'common books'..are Eudemian, not Nicomachean.

stylometry (stəilǫ·mėtri). [f. as prec. + -METRY.] The technique of making statistical analyses of the features of a literary style, esp. by means of a computer. Hence **stylo·metrist**, one who practises this technique.

1945 R. G. COLLINGWOOD *Idea of Nature* 58 Scholars.. have analysed the language of the Platonic dialogues statistically... Whatever view is taken of Platonic 'stylometry' in its more detailed development. **1953** *Classical Q.* XLVII. 80 This admission that only equal amounts of text should have been compared..had the effect of largely invalidating his own and most earlier attempts to order the dialogues by relative affinities of style. Stylometrists ignored the warning... The effect was..to discredit mechanical stylometry. **1972** *Ibid.* May 89 (*heading*) The new stylometry. *Ibid.*, Stylometry can be defined as the use of numerical methods for the solution of literary problems. **1979** *Sci. Amer.* Nov. 34/2 The 50,000 words of the 14 epistles attributed to St. Paul are a challenge to the stylometrist. *Ibid.* 34/3 Forensic stylometry is at least an inhibition to the temptation on the part of police officers to adjust the admissions they present in court.

stylopization (stəi:lǫpəizē[i]·ʃən). *Ent.* [f. as STYLOPIZED *pa. pple.* and *ppl. a.* + -IZATION.] The state of being or becoming stylopized.

1882 *Trans. Entomol. Soc. London* 228 The effects of stylopisation vary very much in different specimens. **1956** G. LAPAGE *Veterinary Parasitol.* xiv. 416 The Strepsitera are commonly known as 'stylops'. The bees and wasps in which they are parasitic undergo, as a result of their effects, changes known as 'stylopisation'. **1980** *Ann. Entomol. Soc. Amer.* LXXIII. 448/1 Morphological characters often modified as a result of stylopization include clypeal pigmentation, pollen-carrying hairs, and wing venation.

stylostatistics (stəi:lǫstăti·stiks). [f. STYLE *sb.* + -O + STATISTICS.] The application of statistical methods to the analysis of features of literary style.

1956 G. HERDAN *Language as Choice & Chance* i. 8 The main division [of the book] is according to the four main branches of quantitative linguistics: Stylostastics, Statistical Linguistics, Information Theory, and Linguistic Duality. *Ibid.* ii. 14 That the 'mood' of a text of considerable length should be reflected in the relative frequency of a linguistic form..,—this is precisely what stylostatistics claims to achieve. **1962** A. ELLEGÅRD *Who was Junius?* vi. 97 (*heading*) Identification by stylostatistics. **1964** G. HERDAN in H. G. Lunt *Proc. 9th Internat. Congr. Linguists* 323 Stylostatistics leads to establishing the general laws for the use of language as a necessary preliminary of the determination of divergencies from these laws in individual style.

stylus. Add: Pl. **styluses, styli. 2. a.** Substitute for def.: A tracing-point used to produce the written record in a chart recorder, telegraph receiver, or the like. (Further examples.)

Quot. 1892 in Dict. belongs to the next sense.

1966 *McGraw-Hill Encycl. Sci. & Technol.* XI. 382/1 By the use of a coated chart or an inked ribbon between the stylus and the chart, an intermittent record is made. **1971** MAGRAB & BLOMQUIST *Measurement Time-Varying Phenomena* v. 182 A voltage will be applied to the coils of the writing system which will cause the slider and writing stylus to move in proportion to the voltage, thus obtaining a recording.

b. = *NEEDLE *sb.* 3 e.

1879 *Year-Bk. of Facts* 88/2 In that patent he [*sc.* Edison] describes a means of recording ordinary telegraph signals by a chisel-shaped stylus indenting a sheet of paper. **1892** W. GILLETT *Phonograph* 12 Instead of one stylus serving for the two purposes, there are now two; one, the recorder, having a very keen edge,..and the other, the reproducer, having a tiny knob highly polished. **1904** S. R. BOTTONE *Talking Machines & Records* 48 The recording stylus is now seldom made of steel, except only in the very commonest forms of recorders; but is usually made of..sapphire. **1943** *Gramophone* July 29/3 The stylus is a small sapphire carried on the toe of an L-shaped holder. **1960** *Practical Wireless* XXXVI. 370 (Advt.), Turnover sapphire styli. **1962** A. NISBETT *Technique Sound Studio* iv. 87 The hot-stylus method.. helps to smooth the wall as the cutter moves on. **1975** *Times* 17 Sept. 16/3 Nowadays, you have a 'cartridge' with a 'stylus' in it, and the [gramophone] arm is called a 'pick-up'.

fig. **1936** DYLAN THOMAS *Coll. Poems* (1952) 37 The grooved land rotating, that the stylus of lightning Dazzle this face of voices on the moon-turned table.

stymie, *sb.*[2] (Earlier example.)

1834 *Rules of Musselburgh Golf Club* in C. B. Clapcott *Rules of Golf of 10 Oldest Golf Clubs* (1935) 66 With regard to Stimies the ball nearest the hole if within six inches shall be lifted.

stymie, *v.* Add: **2.** *fig.* To impede, obstruct, frustrate, thwart (a person, an activity, or a project).

1902 G. ADE *Girl Proposition* 70 In about 8 minutes he had the Regular Fellow stymied and Hazel was leaning against him. **1922** A. HADDON *Green Room Gossip* vii. 154, I looked like being stymied because I couldn't sing in tune. **1933** WODEHOUSE *Mulliner Nights* v. 183 There came the shrill cry of a Hunting Bishop stymied by a hat-stand. **1938** *East Liberty* (Pittsburgh) *Tribune* 26 Aug. 1/5 (*heading*) New recreation center at Mellon Field 'stymied'. **1946** J. W. DAY *Harvest Adventure* xvi. 274 Mr John Loverseed..raised this whole question..in spite of repeated attempts by the Ministry of Agriculture to stymie him. **1957** *Economist* 2 Nov. 389/1 It is hard to visualise Afghans and Albanians, Salvadoreans and Sudanese quickly triumphing over the very real difficulties that have stymied the five-power group. **1966** L. DURRELL in *Sat. Even. Post* 4 June 68/3 Coco was for selling her to a local clinic, but once more we were stymied by this public holiday. The clinic was shut. **1980** *Daily Tel.* 28 July 24/3 France's participation in the military force had merely been to stymie an intended intervention by troops from Pacific area countries.

stymied, *ppl. a.* Add: Also *fig.*

1937 PARTRIDGE *Dict. Slang* 844/1 *Stymied*,..awkwardly placed; nonplussed. **1974** P. DE VRIES *Glory of Hummingbird* vii. 97, I was worried about a stymied affair with a girl with whose parents I was getting on swimmingly.

styptic, *a.* Add: **1. b.** *styptic pencil*, a stick of styptic substance used to stem the bleeding of small cuts.

1908 *Sears, Roebuck Catal.* 799/2 Styptic Pencils. Used when shaving. Will instantly stop bleeding. **1936** G. GREENE *Gun for Sale* vii. 211 Plying his styptic pencil, sticking the cotton-wool on the longer wounds. **1961** I. FLEMING *Thunderball* i. 9 Bond dabbed with the blood-stained styptic pencil at the cut on his chin. **1978** *Observer* 26 Mar. 29/7 He had dropped his styptic pencil down the washbasin.

Stypven (sti·pvĕn). *Med.* Also **stypven.** [f. STYP(TIC *a.* and *sb.* + VEN(OM *sb.*] The dried and purified venom of Russell's viper for use in solution as a local hæmostatic and a blood coagulant; **Stypven time**, coagulation time measured when Stypven is added as a coagulant.

Stypven is a proprietary name in the U.S.

1940 *Lancet* 17 Aug. 195/1 This venom..is very efficient in bringing about the rapid formation of a strong clot when applied to a bleeding surface. It is supplied under the name of Stypven by Messrs. Burroughs Wellcome and Co. **1948** *Official Gaz.* (U.S. Patent office) 20 Jan. 409/2 Burroughs Wellcome & Co. (U.S.A.) Inc., New York... *Stypven.* For dry viper venom... Claims use since 1937. **1955** *Lancet* 1 Oct. 692/1 'Stypven' times were estimated on all the samples as follows: To 0·1 ml. of warmed plasma was added 0·1 ml. of stypven... Immediately after, 0·1 ml. of calcium chloride was added, and the clotting-time was recorded. **1961** *Ibid.* 2 Sept. 503/1 In these men, the whole-blood clotting-time, silicone clotting-time, calcium clotting-time.., prothrombin-time, and 'Stypven' time were estimated in duplicate weekly for eight weeks. **1976** *Ibid.* 6 Nov. 995/2 The stypven time (Russell viper venom) of P.P.P. reflects the amount of available active phospholipids which may be dietary in origin.

styrene (stəi[ə]·rīn). *Chem.* [f. STYR(AX + -ENE.] **1.** A colourless, toxic, aromatic liquid, $C_6H_5 \cdot CH{:}CH_2$, orig. obtained from the storax tree (hence called STYROL or STYROLENE) and now recovered as a by-product of petroleum. Also called *vinylbenzene* and *phenylethylene*.

1885 I. REMSEN *Introd. Study Compounds of Carbon* 343 Styrene... This hydrocarbon is contained in liquid storax... It is formed by distilling cinnamic acid with lime. **1926** H. G. RULE tr. *J. Schmidt's Text-bk. Org. Chem.* II. iii. 331 Styrene, phenyl-ethylene, vinyl-benzene, $C_6H_5 \cdot CH{:}CH_2$, is the simplest representative of the olefine derivatives [of benzene]. **1947** *Sun* (Baltimore) 17 Apr. 2/5 Styrene was not explosive, Thomas said, but would burn as rapidly as gasoline. **1956** *Sci. News* XLII. 41 Hydrocarbons and low boiling organic compounds..are becoming increasingly important industrially owing to the development of petrochemicals,..which include polythene, styrene and synthetic rubber. **1978** J. R. HOLUM *Org. & Biol. Chem.* viii. 163 Polystyrene, made from styrene, has phenyl groups on alternate carbons of the main chain.

2. = *POLYSTYRENE. Also *attrib.*

1938 *Encycl. Brit. Bk. of Year* 147/1 To the growing family of synthetic resins and plastics, 1937 saw added Styrene, characterized by clarity, low initial colour, and thermoplastic properties. **1969** *Islander* (Victoria, B.C.) 6 July 8/2 Keeping food hot or cold en route is important —a styrene foam chest has exceptional insulating ability. **1972** J. POTTER *Going West* 45 Every can was found to have a double bottom. Nuggets of gold lay embedded in white styrene between the two sheets of tin.

3. Special Combs.: **styrene-acrylonitrile**, the combination of styrene and acrylonitrile, esp. as copolymers in a rubber; usu. *attrib.*; **styrene-butadiene**, the combination of styrene and butadiene, esp. as copolymers in a rubber; usu. *attrib.*; **styrene monomer**, the monomeric form of styrene; = sense *1; **styrene oxide**, the toxic epoxide, $C_6H_5 \cdot \underbrace{CH{-}CH_2}_{O}$; **styrene plastic**, any or all of the plastic materials that may be made using styrene; **styrene resin**, any compound formed by the polymerization of styrene.

1957 H. R. SIMONDS *Conc. Guide to Plastics* ii. 71 A styrene-acrylonitrile copolymer is available from Bakelite Co. **1977** R. A. DICKIE in M. O. W. Richardson *Polymer Engin. Composites* iii. 177 Results are presented..on several rubber-modified polystyrene and styrene-acrylonitrile copolymers. **1958** *Times Rev. Industry* Apr. 51/1 The synthetic S.B.R. (styrene-butadiene rubber) being tough and hard wearing, is good for tire treads. **1978** D. R. PAUL in Paul & Newman *Polymer Blends* II. xii. 59 A patent..describes bonding an ethylene-propylene-diene terpolymer rubber..to styrene-butadiene rubber.. by a graft. **1947** I. THOMAS *Injection Moulding Plastics* iii. 168 The base material for polystyrene is styrene monomer. **1971** R. D. DEANIN in Tobolsky & Mark *Polymer Sci. & Materials* xiv. 335 These [polyesters] are mixed with about one-half their weight of styrene monomer. **1939** *Jrnl. Amer. Chem. Soc.* LXI. 997/2 The reaction of styrene oxide and hydriodic acid results in a primary alcohol. **1979** *Experientia* XXXV. 241/2 The observed differences in the metabolism of styrene oxide can be assigned theoretically to 2 possible factors. **1943** D. W. BROWN *Handbk. Engin. Plastics* ii. 27 (*heading*) Styrene plastics. **1947** *Brit. Catal. Plastics* 51/2 (*heading*) Methyl methacrylate and styrene plastics. **1937** R. S. MORRELL *Synthetic Resins* i. 16 The vinyl and styrene resins are used as lacquers and in nitro-cellulose finishes. **1959** E. C. BERNHARDT *Processing of Thermoplastic Materials* III. 628 (*heading*) Styrene resins.

Hence **sty·renated** *ppl. a.*, containing styrene in chemical combination; **styrena·tion**, the process of chemically adding styrene.

1954 KIRK & OTHMER *Encycl. Chem. Technol.* XIII. 146 Styrenated drying oils, and styrenated alkyds as a base for many protective coatings..illustrate still further uses for styrene. *Ibid.* 177 The rate of the styrenation reaction and the clarity of the product are influenced by the kind and amount of unsaturation present in the oil. **1972** H. WARSON *Applic. Synthetic Resin Emulsions* v. 252 It is not readily possible to form a styrenated oil or alkyd in emulsion form directly. *Ibid.* 253 A maleinized oil is used as the basis for styrenation in the ammoniacal form.

styria, styriate(d, varr. STIRIA, STIRIATE(D.

Styrofoam (stəi[ə]·rŏfōᵘm). Chiefly *U.S.* Also **styro-.** [f. *POLY)STYR(ENE + -O + FOAM *sb.*] A proprietary name for a variety of foam plastic.

1950 *Official Gaz.* (U.S. Patent Office) 11 July 403/1 Dow Chemical Co...*Styrofoam*... For irregular solid masses of multicellular expanded synthetic resinous material and granular masses of the same material comminuted. **1962** *Punch* 19 Dec. 881/1 How to make.. lambs from glass fibre, angels from styrofoam. **1969** *Jane's Freight Containers 1968–69* 438/3 Insulated container. Rectangular, with styrofoam insulation between aluminium panels. **1971** *Islander* (Victoria, B.C.) 11 July 2/1 The styrofoam in the deckhead was wonderful in keeping it relatively cool below. **1973** R. HAYES *Hungarian Game* ii. 20 Each item was cradled in plush-lined styrofoam... Nothing could rattle. **1978** G. VIDAL *Kalki* vi. 135 Geraldine was referring to the top part of a huge Styrofoam statue of Vishnu. **1981** *Times Lit. Suppl.* 6 Mar. 254/2 A styrofoam beaker of instant coffee.

suabe (swā·bə, swē^i^b). *Mus.* [It., ad. G. *Schwabe* SWABIAN.] *suabe flute*: an organ flute-stop.

1855 E. J. HOPKINS *Organ* 119 *Suabe-flute*,..a tenor c Manual Stop of 4 feet, formed of wood pipes, with inverted mouths. It's tone is liquid and clear, and not so loud as the Wald-flute. **1907** *Musical Times* 1 Aug. 514/2 Swell Organ..Voix celestes..Suabe flute 4 ft. **1954** *Grove's Dict. Mus.* (ed. 5) VI. 358/2 *Suabe flute*, a 4-ft open flute stop of medium scale, said to have been invented by William Hill. The tone is a soft variety of that of the Clarabella.

suave, *a.* Add: The pronunc. (swāv) is now standard. **3.** (Earlier example.)

1831 F. REYNOLDS *Playwright's Adventures* iv. 63 St Alm was anything but *suave*.

suavify, *v.* For *rare*$^{-0}$ read *rare*$^{-1}$ and add example.

1825 *Spirit of Public Jrnls. for 1823* (ed. 2) 444 Eating much tends to suavify the mood.

sub, *sb.* Add: **4.** (Earlier examples in Sporting and Printing contexts.)

1864 *Field* 9 July 22/1 Lillywhite was caught by Yescombe, a 'sub'. **1876** *Scribner's Monthly* Apr. 838/1 He consented finally to allow another printer to take his place in the 'Clarion' office—temporarily, and as his 'sub' only. **1887** *Irish Times* 24 May 7/7 D. Carbery c. sub. b. W. G. Downey 1.

6. (Earlier examples of sense 'subscription'.)

1805 M. L. WEEMS *Let.* 9 Jan. (1929) II. 310 In 18 hours subscriptioneering I obtaind from the Legislature 100 subs. to Sydney. **1833** J. ROMILLY *Diary* 12 Mar. (1967) 30 Fairly bullied Waud & Jones into subscribing to my Blencowe cause:—got 4 others subs today. **1898** W. S. CHIRCHILL *Let.* 5 Aug. in R. S. Churchill *Winston S. Churchill* (1967) I. Compan. II. 956, I have to pay £40 for one charger, £35 for the other & £20 subs to the mess.

8. a. = SUBMARINE *sb.* 3. Also Comb., as *subchaser* = *submarine chaser* s.v. *SUBMARINE *sb.* 3 b.

1917 J. M. GRIDER *Diary* 29 Sept. in *War Birds* (1927) 21 We were supposed to look out for gulls which they say usually follow in the wake of a sub. **1918** L. E. RUGGLES *Navy Explained* 124 *Sub-chaser*, a small, swift, light draft boat used to hunt submarines. **1931** 'TAFFRAIL' *Endless Story* xxi. 333 'Sub-chaser' 28, manned by the French, broke down in the Atlantic 700 miles from the Azores and was given up for lost. **1936** *Nat. Geogr. Mag.* LXIX. 799/1 Seamanship..includes instruction on how to.. maneuver..such craft as subchasers and motor launches. **1968** A. DIMENT *Bang Bang Birds* ii. 16 Boris snooping round Holy Loch and the nuclear subs. **1977** *New Yorker* 29 Aug. 20/1 A subchaser lurches forward on the calm water and comes to a stop as a black sub surfaces at its side.

b. = *SUBMARINE *sb.* 4 b. *U.S. colloq.*

1955 *Sat. Even. Post* 1 Jan. 16 'I tell you,' a sandwich-shop operator said, 'Subs are taking over.' **1976** R. B. PARKER *Promised Land* ii. 5, I was ready to settle for Ugi's steak and onion subs.

sub, *v.* Add: **2.** (Earlier examples.) In *gen.* use, to act as a substitute. Also *trans.*, to substitute (something). Chiefly *U.S.*

1853 'MARK TWAIN' *Let.* 26 Oct. (1917) I. i. 26, I am subbing at the Inquirer office. *Ibid.*, If I want it, I can get subbing *every night* of the week. **1926** *Amer. Mercury* Dec. 465/2 When a new act was placed last on a programme, *Variety* put it: 'Fred and Daisy Rial subbed in the walk-out assignment.' **1943** *Sun* (Baltimore) 17 Sept. 8/2 (*heading*) Subbing camera for gun, corporal 'shoots' zeros. **1950** A. LOMAX *Mister Jelly Roll* (1952) 218 The lord of New Orleans piano was scratching hard for a living.., subbing for other piano players who showed up drunk on their jobs. **1974** *Globe & Mail* (Toronto) 24 July 10/2 Toronto Executive Alderman Arthur C. Eggleton subbing for Mayor David Crombie. **1981** B. GRANGER *Schism* (1982) x. 88 Father Malachy is subbing for the pastor at St. Mary's... The pastor broke his leg, jogging.

3. (Earlier examples.) Also *to sub up*: to pay up or subscribe.

1874 C. HOLLOWAY *Jrnl. Visit to N.Z.* 22 Apr. (*typescript*) I. 57 In some instances the dissipated individual had to sub a few shillings of the Landlord to help him on the road. **1874** HOTTEN *Slang Dict.* 314 *Sub*, to draw money in advance. **1942** O. JESPERSEN *Mod. Eng. Gram.* VI. 546 *Sub* = subsidy or subsistence.., also subscription ..and as a vb., esp. *sub up* 'subscribe'. **1958** G. MITCHELL *Spotted Hemlock* vii. 75 'Wasn't that rather expensive?'.. 'I believe Tony Biancini subbed up.'

4. Also, *to sub the purple*: see *PURPLE *sb.* 7 b.

5. [SUBSTRATUM 4.] In the manufacture of photographic film: to coat with a substratum (see quot. 1965). Chiefly as *vbl. sb.*, the process of applying a substratum; the substratum itself.

1941 T. T. BAKER *Photographic Emulsion Technique* x. 179 The film base may be wiped or cleaned prior to subbing... The cleaned and substratumed film base is coated at a fairly rapid rate. **1958** H. BAINES *Sci. Photogr.* vi. 83 The rear side of roll film and sheet film is subbed (substratum coated). **1965** M. J. LANGFORD *Basic Photogr.* ix. 161 The manufacturer first 'keys' both sides of the film base or coats them with a foundation layer of gelatin and cellulose ester known as the 'subbing' layer. Next, the emulsion is coated over the subbing on the face of the film. **1977** J. HEDGECOE *Photographer's Handbk.* 263/1 Other non-porous surfaces should be pre-coated with the subbing which is normally supplied with the emulsion.

sub, *Latin prep.* Add: **14*.** **sub specie æternitatis,** 'under the aspect of eternity', i.e. viewed in relation to the eternal; in a universal perspective. [Cf. Spinoza *Ethices* (*a* 1677), in *Opera Posthuma*, 1677, V. xxix. 254.] Hence **sub specie temporis,** viewed in relation to time rather than eternity.

1896 W. CALDWELL *Schopenhauer's System* v. 268 Art enables us somehow to see things *sub specie aeternitatis*. **1911** *Encycl. Brit.* XXI. 441/2 The nature of any fact is not fully known unless we know it in all its relations to the system of the universe, or, in Spinoza's phrase, *sub specie aeternitatis*. **1925** A. HUXLEY *Let.* 21 Apr. (1969) 247 There, on the other side of the water, are one hundred and five million beings whose sole function—if you look at their lives sub specie aeternitatis—is to provide people like us with money. **1935** E. R. EDDISON *Mistress* 20 This man, as I have long observed him, looked on all things *sub specie æternitatis*; his actions all moved..to slow perfection. **1952** V. A. DEMANT *Relig. & Decline of Capitalism* iii. 70 Hence what was true *sub specie aeternitatis* in the liberal aim is being lost. **1973** G. M. BROWN *Magnus* vii. 139 If..we could look with the eye of an angel on the whole history of men, *sub specie aeternitatis*, it would have the brevity and beauty of this dance at the altar.

1928 L. HODGSON in A. E. J. Rawlinson *Essays on Trinity & Incarnation* viii. 378 Perhaps the best one can do is to speak of God as ἀπαθής *sub specie aeternitatis* but παθητικός *sub specie temporis*. **1944** W. TEMPLE *Let.* 12 Jan. (1963) 142, I have treated the Son and the Spirit as God *sub specie temporis* and the Father as God *sub specie eternitatis*. **1960** *Encounter* XV. 77 *Sub specie temporis* his Combination Rooms say more to us than Beckett's wet and windy plains.

14.** **sub specie mortis,** in the face of death.

1955 *Times* 26 May 3/4 The ninth symphony, we are told, is poignant in that it was his last and written *sub specie mortis*. **1964** *Listener* 21 May 849/3 Written *sub specie mortis*, they are his [*sc.* Mahler's] most 'existentialist' works.

14*.** **sub verbo** = *sub voce*, sense 15 in Dict.; abbreviated *s.v.* (see *S 4 a).

1902 J. M. BALDWIN *Dict. Philos. & Psychol.* II. 358/2 Many citations in Eisler, Wörterb. d. philos. Begriffe, sub verbo.

15. sub voce (examples). Cf. VOCE.

1859 *N. & Q.* 23 Apr. 341/1 Skinner, *Gloss.*, *sub voce*, evidently understands the word in this sense. **1871** *Ibid.* 9 Dec. 487/1 See Halliwell's *Dict.*, sub voce 'Braid'.

sub-, *prefix.* Add: **I. 1. a. subti·dal** *Ecol.*, situated or occurring below the low tide mark.

1939 CLEMENTS & SHELFORD *Bio-Ecol.* x. 313 The subtidal community reaches up into the tidal area. **1979** R. BREWER *Princ. Ecol.* v. 231 It is usual to recognize three zones on both sandy and rocky shores. These are the intertidal zone itself, a supratidal zone above it.., and the subtidal zone.

(*b*) In derived advbs., as **subgla·cially** *adv.*, under an ice sheet or glacier.

1909 WEBSTER, Subglacially. **1978** *Nature* 8 June 456/2 Lava flows which were erupted subglacially in southwestern Iceland.

b. subglo·ttal, -lary·ngeal, -te·ctal (the tectum of the skull); **sub-ge·nual** *a.*, situated below the knee; **sub-gingi·val** *a.*, situated or occurring beneath the gums, esp. between the gum-margins and the teeth.

1934 WEBSTER, Subgenual. **1935** R. E. SNODGRASS *Princ. Insect Morphol.* xvii. 527 Proximally, below the 'knee', is a large fan-shaped subgenual organ. **1978** H. V. DALY *Introd. Insect Biol. & Diversity* vi. 109/1 Subgenual organs are found in many insects but are lacking in Archeognatha, Coleoptera, and Diptera. **1898** H. H. BURCHARD *Text-bk. Dental Path. & Therapeutics* xxiv. 456 By subgingival deposits are meant calculi which are first deposited in the annular depression between the gum-margin and a tooth. **1979** WILLIAMS & ELLIOTT *Basic & Appl. Dental Biochem.* xii. 224 Dental plaque covers the tooth (supragingival plaque) and extends over the tooth surface of the gingival pocket (subgingival plaque). **1932** W. L. GRAFF *Language & Languages* i. 33 Even if we assume that the subglottal force of expiration is the same.., on leaving the larynx its strength is.. weakened. **1970** *Language* XLVI. 313 It would seem difficult to ascertain whether a change in fundamental frequency is due to a change in the tension of the laryngeal muscles or to a change in the subglottal air pressure. **1901** *Proc. Zool. Soc. London* I. 281 The sub-laryngeal pouch is essentially a cæcal diverticulum of the ventral wall of the larynx, between the thyroid and cricoid cartilages. **1949** KOESTLER *Insight & Outlook* 391 A continuous flow of physiological processes, involving.. sublaryngeal movements (inner speech). **1940** *Chambers's Techn. Dict.* 818/2 *Subtectal*, lying beneath the roof, as the roof of the skull. **1975** *Nature* 30 Oct. 738/1 In the vertebrates below mammals, the tectal and subtectal areas are the main centres of termination of sensory pathways.

(*b*) *subconjuncti·vally, -glo·ttically, -pi·ally.*

1907 *Ophthalmoscope* V. 383 The conjunctival cicatrice had been divided subconjunctivally. **1974** *Nature* 11 Oct. 553/2 Grafts..placed on Fischer hosts that had been inoculated subconjunctivally..were rejected abruptly. **1975** *Year Bk. Ear, Nose & Throat* 317 Direct laryngoscopy showed adducted cords with an absent lumen subglottically. **1950** *Jrnl. Neurophysiol.* XIII. 192 A fine steel needle electrode thrust subpially into the substance of the acoustic tubercle.

e. *su·b-ice*; **subso·lidus** *Geol.*, existing or occurring in conditions corresponding to a point in a phase diagram below a solidus, i.e. when the system is wholly solid.

1959 *Times* 9 Jan. 11/6 Apart from the exposed mountains near the coast, sub-ice hill and dale occur. **1973** *Nature* 20 Apr. 539/3 New chapters in the history of the continent will be based on the results of continued palaeomagnetic studies, much deep sea drilling and to a lesser extent sub-ice drilling. **1952** B. MASON *Princ. Geochem.* x. 232 We must..consider the phase changes that may take place in solid solutions in the subsolidus region. **1979** *Nature* 15 Mar. 220/1 This mineral assemblage could be produced by hot-pressing the above composition in subsolidus conditions.

2. a. *subadjacent* (later example); *subirrigate*: see also *SUB-IRRIGATION.

1922 JOYCE *Ulysses* 653 He..gained retarded access to the kitchen through the subadjacent scullery.

3. a. su·b-floor, a floor serving as a base for another floor; **su·b-frame,** a secondary frame; *spec.* (*a*) in carpentry and building, the frame for the attachment or support of a window or door-frame, or of panelling; (*b*) in a vehicle, the frame on which the coachwork is built, as distinct from the chassis; **substra·tosphere,** the upper part of the troposphere, immediately below the stratosphere.

1893 J. P. ALLEN *Pract. Building Construction* viii. 122 Double floors may sometimes mean that the flooring or floor-boards are laid on the joists in two thicknesses.. the bottom thickness being straight-jointed..; while the other..is laid in the ordinary way above the sub-floor, as the bottom one is called. **1929** W. C. HUNTINGTON *Building Construction* vi. 264 This type of construction is greatly superior to that which rests the studs on a sole plate placed on top of the sub-floor. **1973** *Building Materials* (MTP Construction) 186 Any sub-floor can be levelled and smoothed. **1929** *Motor* 1 Oct. 33 (Advt.), A sub-frame, on which the body is built, isolates the coachwork from the chassis and prevents distortion; the sub-frame being mounted on the chassis by supports having a certain degree of flexibility. **1944** N. W. KAY *Pract. Carpenter & Joiner* vi. 138 Care must be taken to prevent any damage by shrinkage. One method..is to form a sub-frame within the main frame. D shows a sub-frame, to carry the glazing, tongued into the frame of the door. **1968** D. BRAITHWAITE *Fairground Archit.* v. 88 At least two further wagons were required for 'loose stuff'—— sub-frames, gates and shutters, roundings and so on. **1979** *Daily Tel.* 1 Dec. 18 (Advt.), For Sale. Mini 850, 1969, 47,000 miles... New sub-frame, reconditioned gear-box. **1937** *Popular Sci. Monthly* Nov. 68/2 Aerial Battles miles above the earth..are foreshadowed by a substratosphere plane placed under test by the U.S. Army Air Corps. **1952** *Chambers's Jrnl.* Feb. 84/2 Another day Byrd flew over a never-ending succession of mountain-ranges, which looked as if they were suspended in the substratosphere.

II. 5. b. *sub-leader* [LEADER[1] 12], *-network*; **submuni·tion** chiefly *U.S.*, (usu. *pl.*) small, short-range guided missiles; also *sing.*; **su·bstorm** *Meteorol.*, a disturbance of the earth's magnetic field restricted to certain, usu. polar, latitudes and typically manifested as an aurora and other upper atmospheric phenomena.

1913 S. O'CASEY *Let.* 8 Mar. (1975) I. 23 The Editor recently, in a sub-leader, advised all his readers to go and see pictures exhibited in the Central Branch of the Gaelic League. **1975** *Aviation Week & Space Technol.* 6 Oct. 15/2 Improvement of the BLU-63 submunition bomblet with two basic sizes of fragments. **1983** *Financial Times* 2 Dec. 2/3 Clusters of anti-armour submunitions which would be fired from stand-off positions. **1956** J. KLEIN *Study of Groups* iv. 50 This will be useful when we wish to analyse sub-networks. **1978** *Sci. Amer.* June 95/1 Clos's design is based on the idea of building a large network out of smaller networks called subnetworks. **1961** AKASOFU & CHAPMAN in *Jrnl. Geophysical Res.* LXVI. 1339/2 Each such event, which Birkeland.. called a polar elementary storm, is here called a *DP* substorm. **1969** *New Scientist* 25 Sept. 669/3 These are the 'substorms' which manifest themselves as aurorae and associated magnetic disturbances. **1979** *Nature* 22 Feb. 649/1 Measurements were made during a magnetic substorm which appeared together with the polar light on 25–26 February, 1978.

c. (*a*) *sub-code* [*CODE *sb.*[1] 3 d], *-cycle, -entry, -function, -genre, -hierarchy, -item, -literature, -part* (later examples), *-plot* [PLOT *sb.* 6], *-problem, -sense, -society, -substantiality, -system* (later examples), *-theme, -theory, -topic, -war, -world*; **sub-goal** *Psychol.*, something that must be achieved on the path to the main objective.

1960 R. JAKOBSON in T. A. Sebeok *Style in Lang.* 352 For any speech community..there exists a unity of language, but this over-all code represents a system of interconnected subcodes. **1967** *Language* XLIII. 752 Variants of one and the same code, realized by means of different information channels, are called 'subcodes'. **1973** S. HEATH in *Screen* Spring/Summer 215 The distinction between cinematic codes and sub-codes is initially made in *Langage et Cinéma* as that between general and particular cinematic codes. **1953** A. K. C. OTTAWAY *Educ. & Society* 45 A sub-cycle was here set up within the whole economic setting. **1974** *Sci. Amer.* June 78/2, I have omitted the important subcycles of nitrogen and phosphorus, two elements that are strongly related to the origin of life and to biological processes in general. **1876** C. A. CUTTER *Rules for Dictionary Catalog* 13 Class entry with specific or class subentry. **1979** G. N. KNIGHT *Indexing* vi. 106 If it is a sub-entry itself that errs with excessive references, then the remedy is to turn it into a cross-reference to a separate heading having its own sub-entries. **1949** KOESTLER *Insight & Outlook* x. 153 Like all means towards an end (or subfunctions in non-teleological language) [etc.]. **1969** H. R. F. KEATING *Inspector Ghote plays Joker* iii. 35, I regard it as a sub-function of my post to make person-to-person contact with as many people in your department as possible. **1976** *N.Y. Times* 13 Jan. 40/5 This was because she belonged to, if in fact she hadn't pretty much created a subgenre of the mystery novel. **1980** *Times Lit. Suppl.* 7 Nov. 1262/2 One of the major subgenres of science fiction (works dealing with robots and computers). **1932** E. C. TOLMAN *Purposive Behav.* 459/1 (*Index*) Sign-objects.. become sub-goal-objects. **1967** M. ARGYLE *Psychol. Interpersonal Behaviour* v. 91 Driving a car from A to B involves the sub-goals of getting the engine started, getting the car moving in top gear, and getting to the intermediate points X, Y and Z. **1977** *Dædalus* Fall 121 The theory includes the representation of the task environment, the definition of goals and subgoals,..and the order in which alternative courses of action will be explored. **1962** H. C. CONKLIN in Householder & Saporta *Probl. Lexicogr.* 128 Subhierarchies of varying 'depths' are often discernible within larger hierarchic structures. **1928** in W. K. Hancock *Australia* (1930) v. 90 In the existing Customs tariff there are 259 items or sub-items which provide *ad valorem* duties of 40 per cent. or over. **1961** WEBSTER, *Subliterature*,..inferior literature that does not survive the test of time. **1974** *Times Lit. Suppl.* 1 Feb. 105/1 Though it is important to acquaint oneself with best-sellers and sub-literature.., the chief stress should be on literature of enduring aesthetic worth. **1949** KOESTLER *Insight & Outlook* x. 135 A sub-whole composed of sub-parts, which in themselves are sub-wholes, and so on. **1976** LIEBERMAN & RHODES *Compl. CB Handbk.* xi. 233 Each applicant..must follow the procedure prescribed by Subpart 1 of Part 1 of this chapter. **1916** C. HUGON tr. *Creizenach's Eng. Drama in Age of Shakespeare* v. 255 In those cases where a comic sub-plot runs side by side with the main plot. **1962** G. K. HUNTER *John Lyly* iv. 237 The sub-plot episode of the pages and Grim the Collier of Croydon in Edwardes' Damon and Pithias. **1907** W. JAMES *Mem. & Stud.* (1911) x. 236 So the great problem splits into two sub-problems. **1980** *Sci. Amer.* Feb. 30/3, I shall treat such issues as special subproblems of allocation. **1947** E. PARTRIDGE *Usage & Abusage* 134/2 *Titanic*..is frequently employed with the sub-sense of 'extraordinarily powerful'. **1981** *Dictionaries* II.–III. 168 Brockhaus lists it as an example illustrating a sub-sense of *Blut*. **1951** E. E. EVANS-PRITCHARD *Soc. Anthropol.* i. 13 Its boundaries include..peoples of near and further Asia, north Africa, and parts of Europe—an almost limitless number of..societies and sub-societies. **1922** JOYCE *Ulysses* 385 *Entweder* transsubstantiality *oder* consubstantiality but in no case subsubstantiality. **1957** V. W. TURNER *Schism & Continuity in African Society* i. 1 This book is..an attempt to analyse..the form and functioning of a sub-system, the village, within a wider system, the totality of Ndembu society. **1972** W. LABOV *Language in Inner City* ii. 64 BEV..is best seen as a distinct subsystem within the larger grammar of English. **1949** M. MEAD *Male & Female* xvii. 345 In this story there is a sub-theme of the girl's mother's flirtation with a younger man. **1981** A. PATON *Towards Mountain* xxxiv. 307 The birth and rise of Afrikaner nationalism is one of the most powerful subthemes of my life story. **1951** PARSONS & SHILS *Toward Gen. Theory of Action* i. 28 Economic theory..only becomes a distinctive subtheory of the general theory. **1897** O. J. NAVE *Topical Bible* 4 Under the subtopic, *Instances of*, are grouped all the illustrative facts that occur in the Scriptures relating to each subject. **1923** *Notes from Ireland* Nov. 120/2 All this time a sub-war rages. **1949** KOESTLER *Promise & Fulfilment* I. x. 114 The year..ended with the first encounters in the sub-war between the British Foreign Office and the future State of Israel. **1890** W. JAMES *Princ. Psychol.* II. xxi. 291 The popular mind conceives of all these sub-worlds more or less disconnectedly. **1983** *Times* 10 Jan. 22/7 A sort of sub-world of smacked bottoms and scrawny mothers-in-law.

(*b*) With derived adjs., as *sub-intentional*, *-intentioned*, *-systemic*.

1957 P. LAFITTE *Person in Psychol.* ix. 121 A projective test..is designed to elicit what might be called sub-intentional behaviour, including the whole range of covert behaviour that the person cannot report directly. **1968** *Internat. Encycl. Soc. Sci.* XV. 387/2 Subintentioned deaths are those in which the deceased played an important indirect, covert,..or unconscious role in his own demise. **1961** WEBSTER, Subsystemic. **1966** S. BEER *Decision & Control* xvi. 428 The prefrontal lobe of the cortex..has no specific sub-systemic control responsibilities. **1977** *Dædalus* Summer 81 The functionings of their subsystemic parts..and of the whole are to be understood with the aid of general systems theory.

d. *sub-smile* (earlier example); **sub-optimiza·tion** (see quot. 1967).

1964 T. W. MCRAE *Impact Computers on Accounting* iii. 93 Cyberneticists are for ever emphasizing the dangers of sub-optimization. **1967** E. DUCKWORTH in Wills & Yearsley *Handbk. Management Technol.* 119 *Sub-optimization*—the achievement of optimum working of, say, one department of a company without regard to the effect this may have on the rest of the organization. **1852** C. M. YONGE *Two Guardians* viii. 140 A certain sub-smile about the corners of his mouth.

6. a. *sub-conductor*.

1947 H. G. FARMER *Royal Artillery Concerts* v. 15 For many years Zavertal would rehearse the orchestra for months without giving the slightest heed to the military band, which was left to the sub-conductor (the Serjeant Major) and his subordinates. **1976** D. STEELE in H. Procter-Gregg *Beecham Remembered* I. 109 He came across the orchestra bridge to start untangling the confusion caused by Weingartner's being quite out of touch..with his sub-conductors.

7. a. Also of immaterial or abstract entities. *substring* (*STRING *sb.* 15 c), *-tree* (TREE *sb.* 6 b (*e*)), *-unit*; **su·b-channel** *Radio*, a distinct division of a channel or frequency band; **su·bgrain**, a small grain contained within another grain in a metal; **sub-hori·zon**, a layer within an existing archæological or soil horizon; **su·blattice** *Physics*, a coextensive part of a fuller lattice, obtained by considering all the members having some property not possessed by the other members; **su·b-shell** *Physics*, in an electron shell, the complete set of orbitals capable of being occupied by electrons of identical azimuthal quantum number *l*.

1959 *Wall St. Jrnl.* 30 June 1/4 Multiplexing...is a technique by which a radio station can divide its regular channels into subchannels and transmit two or more sound signals at the same time. **1970** J. EARL *Tuners & Amplifiers* i. 24 Other features found in tuner-amplifiers.. are automatic mono/stereo switching.., a low-pass filter for reducing the stereo sub-channel noise when the aerial signal is not quite strong enough for noise-free stereo reception, [etc.]. **1955** *Phil. Mag.* XLVI. 1343 Recent work..has shown that many of the dislocations left inside a metal after deformation are arranged along surfaces forming low angle boundaries between neighbouring regions of crystal, these latter being called subgrains, cells, or particles. **1975** *Nature* 10 Apr. 489/1 Granular xenoliths..show various strain effects, including undulose extinction.., slip-planes, and subgrain development. **1928** *Bull. Amer. Soil Survey Assoc.* IX. 36 Other sub-horizons are designated as A_1, A_2, etc. **1973** P. A. COLINVAUX *Introd. Ecol.* iii. 45 (*caption*) There may be several subhorizons in each of the main horizons and roots may penetrate them all. **1959** W. F. DE JONG *Gen. Crystallogr.* II. 101 Either the direct lattice..is congruent (similar) with the elementary Bravais lattice, or one is a sub-lattice of the other. **1973** H. D. MEGAW *Crystal Structures* viii. 174 Physicists who are less used to describing any but very simple periodic structures,..use the very misleading term 'sublattice' for a Bravais array. **1976** *Physics Bull.* July 294/2 In a crystal the atomic lattice can divide into two interpenetrating sublattices so that most, if not all, of the neighbours of an atom on one sublattice belong to the other. **1930** RUARK & UREY *Atoms, Molecules & Quanta* ix. 272 The *n*, *l*, and *s* quantum numbers can still be assigned to individual electrons, and, therefore, the shells and subshells can be designated in terms of these numbers. **1959** G. TROUP *Masers* 161 We take as an example Cr^{+++} which has 3 electrons in the unfilled outermost sub-shell. **1980** H. H. SISLER et al. *Chem.* viii. 209 For electrons in *s* subshells, we find that the probability distribution..is independent of direction in space and varies only with distance from the nucleus. **1955** N. CHOMSKY *Logical Struct. Linguistic Theory* (microfilm, Mass. Inst. Technol.) vi. 202b *Z′* differs from *Z* only in that it contains a substring *Y* replacing the substring *X* of *Z*. **1966** D. G. HASS in *Automatic Transl. of Lang.* (NATO Summer School, Venice, 1962) 145 In natural languages, texts can be segmented into recurrent substrings. **1972** *Computer Jrnl.* XV. 232/2 Each co-ordinate of *T* specifies a set to which a substring of *A* belongs. **1947** *Proc. Cambr. Philos. Soc.* XLIII. 26 We call *S* a subtree of *L* if $p_0(S) = 1$ and $p_1(S) = 0$. **1972** R. J. WILSON *Introd. to Graph Theory* iv. 51 Let $T_1, \ldots, T_k$ be the subtrees obtained from *B* by removing the vertex *v* and every edge incident to *v*. **1976** J. S. GRUBER *Lexical Structures in Syntax & Semantics* II. i. 219 Instead of writing the lexical attachment rules as transformations, we will write them as terminal subtrees. **1936** *Economist* 7 Mar. 530/1 The promoters buy specified blocks of securities and deposit them with named trustees, who issue an agreed number of 'sub-unit certificates' against them. **1950** *Cold Spring Harbor Symp. Quantitative Biol.* XIV. 69/1 The phenomenon that the asymmetric unit in the crystal is a submultiple..of the molecular weights found in the ultracentrifuge, and..that excelsin..splits into 3n subunits. **1980** *Times* 15 Jan. 14 DNA is a long chain-like molecule composed of four different chemical subunits.

b. *sub-caste*, *-clan*, *-clone* (also as vb. trans.), *-flight* [*FLIGHT *sb.*[1] 1 h], *-nation* (also *-nationalism*), *-unit* (later example).

1892 H. H. RISLEY *Tribes & Castes Bengal* I. 78 The Bauris are divided into the following nine sub-castes. **1974** tr. *Wertheim's Evolution & Revolution* iii. 240 Even if a sub-group within a caste..has constituted itself as a separate sub-caste, such a collective step will generally imply a disruption of recognized family ties. **1954** Subclan [see *PARAMOUNT *a.* 1 c]. **1961** *Virology* XIII. 160/2 Subclones showing the morphology characteristic of the superinfecting virus were plated for virus release. *Ibid.*, Clones showing the morphology characteristic of the original virus were subcloned. **1977** *Jrnl. Protozool.* XXIV. 28/1 The plausible inference can be drawn that doublet and singlet subclones from a single source do not differ in the kinds of genes or of other molecules they contain. **1978** *Nature* 7 Dec. 579/2 We subcloned the mixed progeny of the cross. **1941** *Hutchinson's Pictorial Hist. War* 14 May–8 July 216/2 Dive-bombers usually approach at about eight thousand feet or so, and on arriving over the target break up into sub-flights of three. **1935** A. M. CARR-SAUNDERS in Huxley & Haddon *We Europeans* viii. 256 We might..contrast America with Europe, regarding the European nations as sub-nations, that is as communities with a lower degree of distinction. **1967** M. AYUB KHAN *Friends not Masters* x. 183 We will remain 'sub-nations' if we do not join together to offer united resistance to power pressures. **1957** *Economist* 7 Sept. 739/2 This theoretically sensible policy ran up against the sub-nationalism of the local peoples. **1974** G. W. CHOUDHURY *Last Days United Pakistan* i. 1 Emerging Bengali regionalism or sub-nationalism. *a* **1944** K. DOUGLAS *Alamein to Zem Zem* (1946) 13 He allotted me two tanks, as a troop, there not being enough on the squadron strength to make sub-units of more than two tanks.

(*b*) *subnational*.

1977 *Jrnl. Commonwealth & Compar. Pol.* XV. 236 In 1968 the 81 successful UNIP candidates included 24 politicians at subnational levels.

c. *sub-area*, *-centre*, *-epoch*, *-interval* (later examples), *-phase*, *-zone*.

1926 *British Gaz.* 12 May 2/3 A service of corporation 'buses has been started in the sub-area of Keighley. **1980** *Amer. Speech 1976* LI. 235 The second map..shows the boundaries of twelve dialect areas and subareas of Scottish English. **1953** L. KUPER *Living in Towns* 304 Library books had been issued from sub-centres in local schools. **1977** *Lancet* 5 Nov. 946/1 The health centre and subcentres provided additional support. **1910** *Geol. Fören. i Stockholm Förhandl.* XXXII. 1146 (*heading*) Gothi- and Finiglacial sub-epochs. **1940** A. H. SUTTON in *Bull. Geol. Soc. Amer.* LI. 1402 Subepoch—subseries. These terms as herein proposed are applicable to the first subdivisions of epochs and series respectively. **1962** D. R. Cox *Renewal Theory* ii. 30 To obtain (1) from first principles, divide the time interval (O, *t*) into a large number *k* of small subintervals of length Δt, where $k\Delta t = t$. **1980** A. J. JONES *Game Theory* ii. 109 Then divide the interval [0, 1] into three equal subintervals. **1936** *Discovery* Oct. 329/1 Measles and certain skin affections..are the result of these sub-phase mutations. **1977** *Antiquaries Jrnl.* LVII. 392 It is simply a sub-phase of one phase..of a conservative..coinage. **1903** Subzone [see *SECULE]. **1969** BENNISON & WRIGHT *Geol. Hist. Brit. Isles* ix. 213 The 6 goniatite stages called after goniatite genera..were formally called zones but they are stages further divided into 16 zones (and many subzones).

d. *sub-depot*; *subdiscipline*, *-field*, *-speciality*, *-specialty*, *-task*.

1938 *Times* 13 Sept. 17/6 The opening of a further sub-depôt for recruits at the air station at Dishforth, Yorks. **1976** *Daily Mail* (Hull) 30 Sept. 5/1 Councillors at Selby, concerned at the possibility of an Army Ordnance sub-depot being purchased by the Central Electricity Generating Board. **1958** W. STARK *Sociol. Knowl.* i. 31 The relation of the two sub-disciplines to each other. **1982** *Sci. Amer.* Nov. 52/1 Answers to these questions call for close collaboration among earth scientists from many subdisciplines. **1902** W. JAMES *Var. Relig. Exper.* ix. 195 For them the soul is only a succession of fields of consciousness: yet there is found in each field a part, or sub-field, which figures as focal and..from which..the aim seems to be taken. **1964** GOULD & KOLB *Dict. Soc. Sci.* 510/2 Political behaviour has come to be regarded as a sub-field, within the social sciences. **1968** N. CHOMSKY *Lang. & Mind* ii. 24 Linguistics..is simply the subfield of psychology that deals with these aspects of mind. **1977** *Dædalus* Fall 59 These subfields have been codified and systematized in an attempt to bring them into closer relation with theoretical frameworks. **1971** *Optometry Today* 15 Vision care needs of the aging patient have virtually produced a subspeciality within the opto-metric profession: vision care of the aging. **1980** *Jrnl. R. Soc. Med.* LXXIII. 758/1 Between four and seven reviews within six subspecialities of medicine. **1963** *Lancet* 5 Jan. 42/2 Some of the subspecialties such as skins and eyes. **1961** *Communications Assoc. Computing Machinery* IV. 438/2 A request, by a task, to call in and execute a sub-task causes..a new task (the subtask called) to be added to the task list, with the appropriate precedence and priority. **1971** *New Society* 26 Aug. 373/1 My first subtask is..to move the ramp... This sets up the subsubtask of computing the coordinates. **1982** *Sci. Amer.* Jan. 123/2 The several concurrent processes can be different subtasks of a single program.

e. *Math.* Prefixed to sbs. to denote an entity which is contained in some similar entity, in that each of its elements is also an element of the latter and that it shares the characterizing properties of the latter, as *subalgebra*, *-field*, *-formation*, *-graph*, *-manifold*, *-matrix*, *-module*, *-object*, *-ring*. Also SUBGROUP b, *SUBSEQUENCE[2], SUBSET *sb.*[2]

1933 Subalgebra [see *LATTICE *sb.* 3**]. **1979** *Proc. London Math. Soc.* XXXVIII. 315 Let A_N be the closed subalgebra of $L(H_N)$ generated by the operators $T_1, \ldots, T_N$ and set *H*. **1940** E. T. BELL *Devel. Math.* xi. 239 The final outcome may be roughly described as an analysis of the structure of fields with respect to their possible subfields and superfields. **1971** G. HIGMAN in Powell & Higman *Finite Simple Groups* vi. 209 $Q(\alpha)$ is the real subfield of the field of the 5-th roots of unity. **1966** tr. *Gericke's Lattice Theory* iv. 71 We shall show that the set of sub-formations of a formation..relative to a given axiom system..that satisfies a condition yet to be formulated forms a complete lattice. **1931** *Proc. Nat. Acad. Sci.* XVII. 125 A subgraph *H* of a graph *G* is a graph formed by dropping out arcs from *G*. **1979** PAGE & WILSON *Introd. Computational Combinatorics* iv. 76 Given a graph G = (P, L) then G′ = (P′, L′) is a subgraph if P′ is a subset of P and L′ is a subset of L. **1963** H. FLANDERS *Differential Forms* v. 52 A manifold **M** is called a submanifold of a manifold **N** provided there is a one-to-one smooth mapping $j: \mathbf{M} \to \mathbf{N}$ which has this..property. **1970** G. K. WOODGATE *Elem. Atomic Struct.* viii. 152 The matrix of *H′* which has to be diagonalized breaks up into submatrices of given *M*. **1980** A. J. JONES *Game Theory* iii. 149 There are nine 2 × 2 submatrices obtained by deleting the *i*th row and *j*th column from *A*. **1965** J. J. ROTMAN *Theory of Groups* iv. 68 A subset *W* of the *R*-module *V* is a submodule of *V* in case it is a subgroup of

V which is closed under scalar multiplication. **1981** *Amer. Math. Monthly* LXXXVIII. 53 Submodules of finitely generated free modules over a principal ideal domain are free and need no more generators. **1965** Subobject [see *PROPER *a.* 5 c (i)]. **1979** *Proc. London Math. Soc.* XXXVIII. 245 The subobjects of N^+ in *E* which contain the point ∞ are in 1–1 correspondence with closed ideals of subsets of **N**. **1937, 1969** Subring [see *IDEAL *sb.* 3].

8. *sub-entitle* vb. (earlier U.S. example), *-functional* adj.

1845 POE in *Amer. Whig Rev.* II. 127/1 It is to be regretted that 'The Spanish Student' was not sub-entitled 'A Dramatic Poem', rather than 'A Play'. **1904** *Amer. Naturalist* Jan. 6 Hypohippus of the middle Miocene with subfunctional lateral digits..is an instance of arrested evolution.

9. *sub-classify* vb. (earlier example); *sub-classification* (earlier example), *-component, -kind*; **su·b-carrier** *Telecommunication*, a carrier wave used to modulate another carrier; **sub-fraction**: see also as main entry in Suppl.; **su·blevel** *Physics*, each of a group of energy levels of an atom or nucleus which coincide under a coarse approximation or when some factor (as a magnetic field) is removed; **su·bline** *Genetics*, a variant arising in an inbred line and distinguished by a trait usu. inherited from a genetically impure ancestor; **su·bpassage** *sb. Biol.* and *Med.*, the passage of a strain of micro-organisms cultivated in one animal through another, esp. to increase the virulence; also as *v. trans.*; hence **su·bpassaging** *vbl. sb.*; **subsa·tellite** *Astronautics*, a satellite of a satellite; *spec.* a small artificial satellite released from another satellite or spacecraft; **sub-u·nderwriter** *Econ.*, one who underwrites part of a liability (esp. a share issue) underwritten by another; so **sub-u·nderwrite** *v. trans.*, **sub-u·nderwriting** *vbl. sb.*

1953 REED & RUSSELL *Ultra High Frequency Propagation* xi. 411 Subcarrier modulation, wherein a subcarrier spaced in the order of 10 kc from the highest modulating frequency is modulated with the desired intelligence, would provide all desired carrier amplitude variations at frequencies much in excess of any presently conceivable lobe modulation frequency. **1976** *Which?* Sept. 204/1 We measured how well the sets filtered from the audio output ..the 38Hz sub-carrier frequencies—parts of the complex signal that tell the tuner that a stereo programme is being broadcast. **1873** M. DEWEY in G. Dawe *Melvil Dewey* (1932) 320 Sub-classify each, or any, of these eighty-one (hundred) classes... A Dictionary of Science would receive no sub-classification but remain simply with main class number. **1965** N. CHOMSKY *Aspects Theory Syntax* i. 17 The syntactic component of a generative grammar contains a *transformational* subcomponent. **1973** L. L. & J. M. CONSTANTINE *Group Marriage* xviii. 199 In the interpersonal dimension, we identified two subcomponents. **1843** MILL *Logic* II. III. xxii. 135 Examining every known sub-kind included in the larger kind. **1968** *Listener* 4 July 6/1 The campus novel, a literary sub-kind that has languished these last years, is surely in for a revival now that dons have had the heady experience of being news. **1963** G. TROUP *Masers & Lasers* (ed. 2) 183 Paramagnetic resonance is usually observed between sub-levels of the term having lowest energy. **1971** *Sci. Amer.* Oct. 91/2 In a nonuniform [electrostatic] field such nuclei will exhibit energy levels that are split into a number of sublevels corresponding to the number of allowed orientations of the nucleus. **1948** *Jrnl. Genetics* XLIX. 92 A tumour arising in one subline would be foreign, to some degree at least, to another subline. **1981** *Nature* 19 Feb. 626/1 Many of the major sublines of common inbred strains [of mice]..have arisen as a result of genetic contamination in the past. **1934** WEBSTER, Subpassage, *sb.* **1947** *Ann. Rev. Microbiol.* I. 19 Pneumococci..maintained by rapid subpassage through mice. **1969** *Parasitology* LIX. 352 Parasites isolated from the parasitaemia..were subpassaged at 4-day intervals. **1970** B. G. F. WEITZ in H. W. Mulligan *African Trypanosomiases* vi. 114 Variants sometimes reverted to a 'parent' antigenic strain type when rodent subpassage was prolonged. **1978** *Nature* 14 Sept. 132/2 Tumours have been serially subpassaged 3× to date. **1970** *Ibid.* 12 Dec. 1061/1 Lincicome has shown that in calorically restricted mice the number of hosts that developed maximal infections and the intensity of the parasitaemia are increased by subpassaging. **1894** J. J. ASTOR *Journey in Other Worlds* II. i. 126 There will be no danger from meteors or sub-satellites here..for anything revolving about the moon at this distance would be caught by the earth. **1956** *Time* (Canadian ed.) 24 Dec. 53/1 The inflated sub-satellite is a balloon of Mylar plastic ·0025 in. thick covered with an aluminium film ·0006 in. thick. **1978** *Nature* 5 Oct. 430/1 We have attempted..to interpret lunar palaeomagnetism as observed ..in widespread crustal magnetic anomalies mapped by magnetometers on Explorer 35 and the Apollo 15 and 16 subsatellites. **1935** *Economist* 13 July 65/1 He did, however, sub-underwrite the issue, which was discussed with him previous to the date of the prospectus. **1959** *Ibid.* 18 Apr. 256/1 The sub-underwriters get 1 per cent of the amount they have underwritten. **1982** *Daily Tel.* 6 Mar. 1/7 A large proportion..is paid out to other financial institutions, called sub-underwriters. **1955** *Times* 11 July 14/1 Firm applications..have already been received ..for 300,000 shares on sub-underwriting terms. **1981** *Times* 8 Jan. 11/3 Brokers to the issue..completed the subunderwriting of the issue yesterday afternoon.

III. 12. a. *sub-Himalayan* (earlier example).
1847 [see *SHERPA 1].

b. *sub-equatorial* (also *fig.*).

1909 WEBSTER, Subequatorial. **1935** H. H. BASHFORD *Lodgings for Twelve* 108 Apart from the excitements incident to the relief of Ladysmith and Mafeking, the Boer War—at any rate to the average undergraduate—was a sub-equatorial and not very important affair. **1977** *Sci. Amer.* Apr. 106/2 This is the earliest-known evidence of metallurgy in the entire subequatorial region.

14. a. Also with the sense 'numerically less than', and in derived advbs. *sub-literary, -molecular, -morphemic, -optimal* (hence *-optimally*), *-optimum, -phonemic* (hence *-phonemically*); **sub-bitu·minous** *a. Geol.*, (of coal) of inferior quality to bituminous; intermediate in rank between bituminous coal and lignite; **subce·llular** *a. Biol.*, smaller than a cell; occurring inside a cell; **sub-compa·ct** *a. U.S.*, designating a car which is smaller than a compact one (see *COMPACT *ppl. a.*[1] II. 1 b); also *absol.* as *sb.*; **subfree·zing** *a.*, designating or characterized by a temperature lower than the freezing-point of water; **sublu·minal** *a.* [L. *lūmen, lūmin-* light], having or being a speed less than that of light.

1908 *Econ. Geol.* III. 136 The term 'sub-bituminous' was recommended and formally adopted by the [U.S. Geological] survey for all official publications. **1949** F. J. PETTIJOHN *Sedimentary Rocks* xii. 366 Subbituminous, semibituminous, and semianthracite coals are transitional coal types. **1979** B. L. C. JOHNSON *Pakistan* xi. 161/1 The estimates of reserves of Lower Tertiary lignitic to sub-bituminous coal range between 449 and 478 million tonnes. **1953** *New Biol.* XV. 120 There are too many examples in which patterns arise..within single cells (and thus demand a theory dealing in sub-cellular units). **1964** G. H. HAGGIS et al. *Introd. Molecular Biol.* ii. 20 Some enzymes are localized in certain sub-cellular structures. **1978** *Sci. Amer.* Dec. 68/2 Myoglobin combines with the oxygen released by red cells, stores it and transports it to the subcellular organelles called mitochondria. **1967** *Wall St. Jrnl.* 24 Feb. 1/1 AMC [*sc.* the American Motors Corporation] also is thinking of building a 'subcompact' car that would compete directly in size and price with Volkswagen. **1971** *Flying* Apr. 68/2 (Advt.), A different-looking subcompact with the spirit of a sporty car. **1980** *Times* 12 Dec. 24/3 Chrysler extended the close-down of its Belvidere, Illinois, assembly plant, which makes sub-compact cars. **1958** *N.Y. Times* 15 Dec. 2/6 The Weather Bureau warned that subfreezing temperatures would continue today. **1979** P. THEROUX *Old Patagonian Express* iii. 51 Two feet of snow in Boston. Chaos and death. Power cuts in sub-freezing weather. **1952** *New World Writing* Apr. 234 Even *aficionados* of murder fiction will concede..that except in the hands of a few writers it has been a sub-literary product—characters unreal, dialogue artificial, plots highly improbable. **1980** *Jrnl. R. Soc. Arts* Apr. 302/1 He illuminates..this curious sub-literary genre in such a way that even serious students gain a profitable exposure to materials not often considered in length. **1969** *Physics Today* May 45/3 Particles traveling at sub-luminal and those traveling at luminal velocities are two entirely distinct kinds of objects. **1980** *Sci. Amer.* Aug. 76/2 The expansion that appears from the earth to be superluminal would be relativistic but still subluminal when measured by the slower clocks of the source itself. **1935** *Discovery* Dec. 353/1 Raindrops may form on sub-molecular electrically-charged units, or ions. **1964** G. H. HAGGIS et al. *Introd. Molecular Biol.* 338 Study of the mechanism of enzyme action is in a sense submolecular biology. **1947** C. F. HOCKETT in *Language* XXIII. 321 A scholar deciphering a dead language written in a non-phonetic or semi-phonetic orthography, may achieve good control of the tactics and semantics of the language, but remain in almost total ignorance of anything sub-morphemic. **1964** E. A. NIDA *Toward Sci. Transl.* iii. 41 Certain submorphemic elements can also be recognized, e.g. the sound symbolism of *ush* in *gush, flush, blush, slush* and *mush*. **1901** *Amer. Jrnl. Physiol.* IV. 477 If the stimulation is sub-optimal, the animal will seek the source of light. **1980** *Sci. Amer.* Sept. 134/1 On the whole, however, India remains a case of stunted, suboptimal growth, burdened as it is with the world's largest single national mass of poverty and unemployment. **1901** *Amer. Jrnl. Physiol.* IV. 478 The supra-optimally stimulated organism moves from the source, the sub-optimally stimulated one moves towards the source, of light. **1958** *Times Rev. Industry* Sept. (London & Cambridge Economic Bull.) p. iii/1 A larger labour force..had to be..deployed sub-optimally. **1937** *Ann. Reg. 1936* 59 Attention was given to the social importance of nutrition due to the realisation that sub-optimum nutrition is common and widespread. **1950** Suboptimum [see *LINOLENATE]. **1935** *Language* XI. 102 A sub-phonemic variation which the observer himself uses will generally escape his notice. **1969** *Archivum Linguisticum 1965* XVII. 109 By no means all subphonemic changes eventually become phonemic. **1981** *Amer. Speech 1977* LII. 171 Along the Atlantic seaboard, subphonemic vowel differences are common. **1955** C. F. HOCKETT *Man. Phonol.* 160 The worker who sets up fewer 'phonemes' must cover less 'subphonemically' but correspondingly more 'superphonemically'.

b. Similarly combined with sbs. (forming words used chiefly *attrib.*), as *sub-cabinet* (chiefly *U.S.*), *-microgram, -proletariat, -threshold, -zero*; **submi·llimetre** *a.*, less than a millimetre in size or length; pertaining to or employing electromagnetic waves of such a length; also **su:bmillime·tric** *a.*

1956 R. J. DONOVAN *Eisenhower* v. 66 Almost as soon as the Cabinet rises each week, Rabb meets with a group of sub-Cabinet officers. **1974** P. GORE-BOOTH *With Great Truth & Respect* 389 The process of an important and difficult decision is remarkable... It passes through a hierarchy or a sort of sub-cabinet or both. **1981** *Economist* 24 Jan. 24/3 Lower appointments to sub-cabinet jobs are still being made and will be for some weeks. **1965** PHILLIPS & WILLIAMS *Inorg. Chem.* I. xvi. 576 Work on natural polonium has been limited to the sub-microgram scale. **1976** *Nature* 10 June 454/1 Gibberellins are amongst the most potent of the naturally occurring plant growth regulators and exert maximal activity in most tissues when present in sub-microgram quantities. **1955** *Jrnl. Appl. Physics* XXVI. 1384/1 Submillimeter radiation was produced when a pulsed, bunched high-energy electron beam was passed through a simple rectangular wave guide. **1973** *Physics Bull.* May 305/3 Submillimetre spectroscopy, or far infrared spectroscopy as it is more frequently termed, is a field in which there has been much activity during the last 15 years. **1976** *Sci. Amer.* June 127/1 All one had to do was to drop his view to the submillimeter level, where little creatures abound that are still new to science. **1975** *Nature* 6 Mar. 39/2 The mystery of the submillimetric limb brightening [of the sun]. **1958** *Listener* 30 Jan. 186/1 Today the population of the delta belongs to the class which, I believe, sociologists call the rural sub-proletariat. They are landless or almost landless peasants who seek casual employment in agriculture or anything that comes along. **1974** M. B. BROWN *Economics of Imperialism* iv. 87 Nor can we overlook..the role of migrant labour as a 'sub-proletariat' in Europe today. **1979** *Dædalus* Spring 105 The institutionalization of a subproletariat, and the creation of ethnic ghettos in the large urban areas are..examples of the changes taking place. **1937** BEST & TAYLOR *Physiol. Basis Med. Practice* lxiii. 1225 If a second stimulus also of subthreshold strength..be sent into the nerve an impulse is set up. **1976** *Ann. Rev. Microbiol.* XXX. 234 Negative chemotaxis appears to be largely an all-or-none response to a threshold concentration, but weaker effects caused by prolonged exposure to subthreshold concentrations probably also occur. **1942** O. NASH *Face is Familiar* 137 And nobody is prompter In the face of hell, high water, and sub-zero thermomter. **1980** R. MCCRUM *In Secret Place* xii. 113 He's having a sub-zero feud with Hayter.

c. Compounded with a further prefix, as **sub-mi·cro-** *Chem.*, involving amounts less than those typical of microanalysis; also used as an independent word.

1945 *Jrnl. Biol. Chem.* CLXI. 589 In order to estimate the P content of these solutions, a submicroprocedure.. having a range of 0·2 to 3 γ of P was employed. **1964** N. G. CLARK *Mod. Org. Chem.* xxiv. 496 The isolation of minute quantities of material from biological sources has necessitated even greater refinements, so that sub-micro techniques (requiring 30–50 μg) have been developed during recent years. **1974** [see *MICRO- 8 b].

18. *sub-neolithic* (also *fig.*), *-Roman* adjs.

1905 A. J. EVANS in *Ann. Brit. School at Athens* X. 22 This stratum, to which the name 'Early Minoan I.' may be conveniently applied, shows naturally a greater survival of Neolithic elements... In its general complexion indeed it may be described as 'Sub-Neolithic'. **1956** E. E. CUMMINGS *Let.* 11 Mar. (1969) 248 Good Freudians were quick to suggest that my superego suffers from sub-neolithic trends. **1962** H. R. LOYN *Anglo-Saxon England* i. 39 Wheel-made pottery of sub-Roman character. **1977** *History* LXII. 175 We cannot, however, expect that these works will ever provide information about the sub-Roman centuries.

IV. 19. *sub-historical, -literate, -mature, -moral, -solid* adjs.; **sub-econo·mic** *a.*, not justifiable on purely economic grounds; **subinhi·bitory** *a.*, (of a dose of a drug, chemical, etc.) enough to hinder but not prevent microbial growth; **sublu·minous** *a.*, dim; *spec.* in *Astr.*, of less luminosity than the normal; **subse·xual** *a. Genetics*, characterized by or being a form of parthenogenetic reproduction in which the first division of meiosis occurs, with crossing-over, but not the second (reduction) division; **subso·cial** *a. Biol.*, applied to species of spiders or insects that live gregariously but without a fixed social organization; **subvo·cal** *a.*, designating an unarticulated level of speech comparable to thought; hence **subvo·cally** *adv.*

1948 *Rep. Native Laws Commission 1946–48* (Dept. Native Affairs, S. Afr.) 4/2 Government assistance..in respect of sub-economic schemes has all along been linked with the condition that the municipality should bear a share of the loss. **1971** *Leader* (Durban) 7 May 1/5 The Verulam Town Board has announced its intention to erect..100 sub-economic houses. **1980** *Sci. Amer.* Jan. 50/2 He created a two-way grid of categories based on the degree of geological knowledge (known deposits, inferred deposits and probable deposits) and on current economics (economic, subeconomic and uneconomic). **1940** K. MANNHEIM *Ideology & Utopia* 128 Besides this sub-historical biological element a spiritual, transcendental element is also to be found in this sphere. **1973** R. J. W. EVANS *Rudolf II* ii. 45 Such a view..has survived in sub-historical writing and belles-lettres. **1956** M. HYNES *Med. Bacteriol.* (ed. 6) ix. 123 Serial culture of susceptible organisms in the presence of sub-inhibitory concentrations of an antibiotic results in the emergence of bacteria that can flourish in the presence of enormous concentrations of the antibiotic. **1976** *Ann. Rev. Microbiol.* XXX. 64 Some strains of *M. osloensis* produce such a preponderance of coccal cells that their true nature can only be ascertained in films from media with subinhibitory concentrations of penicillin. **1958** J. BERRY in J. A. Fishman *Readings Sociol. of Lang.* (1968) 743 In subliterate societies (in most of Tropical Africa for example) where book-production is at the best financially hazardous, the need for exotic type can have a deterrent effect on book production. **1973** R. A. CRAMPSEY *Puerto Rico* 13 In 1940 the bulk of the people were subliterate or illiterate. **1864** Subluminous [in Dict.]. **1959** *Encounter* July 53/2 The photography is that chocolate-marshmallow kind of subluminous chiaroscuro. **1969** O. J. Eggen in S. S. Kumar *Low-Luminosity Stars* I. i. 22 Photometric parallaxes have been derived for the 27 stars in Table III which are very probably subluminous. **1976** *Progress in Sci. Culture* (E. Majorana Centre) Spring 52 Extragalactic sources can be classified in order of luminosity as follows (1) subluminous galaxies, such as M 31, (2) normal galaxies, [etc.]. **1899** Submature [see *peneplanation]. **1922** C. A. Cotton *Geomorphol. N.Z.* I. xxviii. 415 The coast has passed through the stage of youth and has become sub-mature. **1951** *Jrnl. Sedimentary Petrol.* XXI. 128 Definition of the four stages of textural maturity... I. Immature stage... II. Submature stage. Sediment contains very little or no clay, but the non-clay portion.. is still itself poorly sorted... III. Mature stage... IV. Supermature stage. **1965** G. J. Williams *Econ. Geol. N.Z.* xiii. 192/1 A submature valley formed on this surface, later to be dammed by a basalt flow. **1946** *Mind* LV. 115 A will-less saint would be a sub-moral being, a fine creature perhaps, but not a responsible moral agent. **1937** C. D. Darlington in *Nature* 30 Oct. 761/2 Other mechanisms occur in the dog roses and with certain kinds of parthenogenesis whereby, as in *Œnothera*, a large part of the genes are prevented from recombining. With such systems stability has been achieved at the expense of variability, and we have arrived at what we may call a sub-sexual method of reproduction. **1947** —— & Mather *Elements of Genetics* xii. 266 As compared with sexual species variation is much reduced but it still occurs. The new apomictic species is thus often subsexual. **1928** W. M. Wheeler *Social Insects* i. 13 The insects included in categories (1) to (5) may be designated as 'infrasocial'; those of (6), which are more interesting for our purposes may be called 'quasisocial' or 'subsocial'. **1958** *Science* 2 May 1046/1 Social organization in the main groups of social bees..did not arise..through subsocial family groups. **1976** *Sci. Amer.* Mar. 101/3 Michener's second evolutionary route he calls subsocial. On this route only one level of behavior precedes eusociality; it is characterized by solitary rather than communal nest building. The solitary female [spider] remains at the nest, however, and cares for her young. **1922** Joyce *Ulysses* 674 The decocted beverages, allowing for subsolid residual sediment of a mechanical mixture, water plus sugar plus cream plus cocoa, having been consumed. **1934** M. Ten Hoor in *Jrnl. Philos.* XXXI. 534 The responsibility for descriptive analysis and psychological definition..has been accepted..by..the behaviorists... This theory..in its extreme form..contends that thought is nothing but subvocal speech. **1980** A. Kenny *Aquinas* iii. 78 Aquinas has a clear grasp of the relationship between the intellect and the imagination when thought takes place in mental images or in subvocal speech. **1961** E. J. Furlong *Imagination* vii. 77 The words 'the Chapel' are subvocally present to me along with the visual object.

b. In derived advbs., as *submaturely*.

1900 *Proc. Boston Soc. Nat. Hist.* XXIX. 309 In central France..the initial form was an uplifted and submaturely dissected peneplain, in which valleys with incised meanders have been..developed. **1913** *Bull. Geol. Soc. Amer.* XXIV. 201 The submaturely dissected scarp.

19*. a. With adjs. derived from the names of persons, used to designate something in the manner of but inferior to their work, characteristic style, etc. (Chiefly in nonce-formations.)

1934 E. Sitwell *Aspects Mod. Poetry* i. 18 Mr. Housman was followed by a school of poets, rather loosely held together by their sub-Wordsworthian ideals. **1959** *Listener* 5 Feb. 258/2 A laboured sub-Wodehousian straining after slapstick instead of farce. **1962** *John o' London's* 10 May 459/2 The opening has a sub-Chaplinesque quality. **1967** J. Philip et al. *Best of Granta* I. 16 Following the editorial come five sub-Miltonic stanzas. **1977** P. Johnson *Enemies of Society* xi. 154 One prominent sub-Marxist 'scientist' who constantly uses the crisis-mechanism, to justify, among other things, the use of positive censorship, when possible, is Herbert Marcuse.

b. Hence, prefixed simply to the names of persons.

1963 *Times Lit. Suppl.* 5 Apr. 235/2 Here is the eternal sex-life of the American college girl told in the eternal sub-Salinger..style. **1968** J. Bingham *I love, I Kill* xi. 132 It was called *Deeper in the South*..kind of sub-Tennessee Williams. **1977** *Listener* 28 July 122/3 A pregnant older lady who paints sub-Ernst surrealities.

20. b. *subtranslucent* adj.

1868 J. D. Dana *Syst. Mineral.* (ed. 5) v. 194 Plasma... Rather bright-green to leek-green, also sometimes nearly emerald-green, and subtranslucent or feebly translucent. **1955** Brown & Dey *India's Mineral Wealth* (ed. 3) 623 The bloodstones are subtranslucent, dark green chalcedony speckled with red; the moss agates..perfectly translucent stones.

c. su:bacroce·ntric *a. Cytology* = *subtelocentric* adj. below; **subhe·dral** *a.*, applied to crystals having partially developed faces, or incompletely bounded planes; **su:bmeta-ce·ntric** *a. Cytology*, applied to a chromosome with the centromere almost in the middle, so that the two chromosome arms differ slightly in length; also *ellipt.* as *sb.*; **su:bteloce·ntric** *a. Cytology*, applied to a chromosome with a centromere near one end, but not as near as in an acrocentric chromosome; also *ellipt.* as *sb.*

1906 W. Cross et al. in *Jrnl. Geol.* XIV. 698 *Subhedral*, partly bounded by crystal faces, hypantomorphic, hypidiomorphic. **1961** M. J. D. White *Chromosomes* (ed. 5) ii. 23 Intermediate types exist..so that we may describe particular chromosomes 'subacrocentric' or 'metacentric'. **1963** *Austral. Jrnl. Zool.* XI. 8 Four pairs of subacrocentrics, whose short arms are in most cases large enough to be distinctly visible in the preparations. **1963** *Jrnl. Nat. Cancer Inst.* XXXI. 642 The diploid complement of 22 pairs of chromosomes consists of 5 median metacentrics, 3 subtelocentrics, [etc.]. **1964** *Ibid.* XXXII. 858 This system was arrived at by the arrangement of metacentric chromosomes in descending size order followed by submetacentric and subtelocentric chromosomes arranged in a similar manner. **1964** *Hereditas* LII. 211 Chromosomes..with arm ratios of 3·0 or higher are classed as ST ('subtelocentric'). **1973** *Nature* 5 Oct. 262/1 The diploid karyotype of *U. limi* consisted of twenty-two chromosomes, eighteen metacentrics and four submetacentrics. **1975** G. Anderson *Coring* ii. 35 (*caption*) Porous network of medium-grained euhedral to subhedral dolomite rhombs. **1976** *Jrnl. Cellular Physiol.* LXXXVII. 104 The four groups (I, metacentric; II, submetacentric; III, subacrocentric; and IV, acrocentric) were defined for this purpose by the ratio, short/long arm length. **1980** *Canad. Jrnl. Genetics & Cytol.* XXII. 421 There are three SAT-chromosomes (arm ratio (r) = 1·74–1·92), four metacentric chromosomes (r = 1·07–1·14), seven submetacentric chromosomes (r = 1·22–1·68) and seven subtelocentric chromosomes (r = 1·75–2·42).

e. *subcircular* (later examples), *-rectangular* adjs.

1940 *Antiquity* XIV. 16 The hopelessly decayed traces of a large wooden object, apparently subrectangular in plan. **1957** G. E. Hutchinson *Treat. Limnol.* I. ii. 171 Subcircular, a less perfect approach to circular form. **1970** R. J. Small *Study of Landforms* iv. 121 King..has postulated that in many parts of Africa stream incision along joints has given rise to a subrectangular drainage pattern. **1979** *Geogr. Mag.* July 668/3 Sub-circular pans on the Essex marshes.

g. *subcurative, -fertile*; **subcli·nical** *a.*, not giving rise to any observable symptoms; **subpa·tent** *a.*, (of a parasite or parasitic infection) present but not detectable; of or pertaining to such an infection; **subte·rtian** *a. Med.*, applied to a severe form of malaria caused by the sporozoan *Plasmodium falciparum* and to the sporozoan itself; also *ellipt.* as *sb.*, subtertian malaria.

1919 R. Ross *Suggestions for Care of Malaria Patients* 7 A severe type in which the paroxysms..are often found to recur every day and at irregular times..is caused by the malignant tertian parasite, sometimes called the 'subtertian' parasite (*Plasmodium falciparum*). **1926** *Q. Rev. Biol.* I. 399/2 In many infections the patent period is followed by a Subpatent Period of indefinite length. **1930** M. F. Boyd *Introd. Malariol.* ii. 32 It would appear that resistance may be established earliest to subtertian, and more slowly in tertian and quartan. **1946** *Nature* 17 Aug. 243/2 With the addition of subcurative doses of 'Mapharsen', the amount of penicillin required to cure rabbit syphilis is reduced to a fraction of that required when penicillin is used alone. *Ibid.* 5 Oct. 487/2 L.V. is responsible for a certain number of cases of epididymal inflammations, many of them of a subclinical type. **1947** *Ann. Rev. Microbiol.* I. 49 Subpatent infections persisted in some individual ducks for as long as eight months after they had been inoculated with sporozoites. **1954** Martin & Hynes *Clin. Endocrinol.* (ed. 2) viii. 187 It is difficult to assess the efficiency of therapy in a subfertile male. **1954** *Brit. Med. Jrnl.* 6 Feb. 293/2 It has been found that in indigenous East Africans the sickle-cell trait affords a considerable degree of protection against subtertian malaria. **1971** *Observer* (Colour Suppl.) 31 Oct. 10/1 Like many men her husband seemed to be subfertile but was by no means infertile. **1974** J. R. Baker in *Trypanosomiasis & Leishmaniasis* (Ciba Foundation Symposium No. 20) 32 Parasites may often be subpatent, that is, too scanty to be detected by microscopic examination. **1978** *Jrnl. R. Soc. Med.* LXXI. 507 The spectrum of illness is wide, from severe and prostrating to mild and, probably, subclinical. **1979** *Tropenmedizin u. Parasitologie* XXX. 239/1 Infected cows treated with subcurative doses of trypanocidal drugs. **1979** E. Nnochiri *Textbk. Imported Diseases* iv. 59 *P*[*lasmodium*] *falciparum* infections, in contrast, are insidious in onset with irregular fever which subsequently becomes subtertian (i.e. between 36 and 48 hours) in periodicity.

h. *subclinically, -terminally*.

1954 *Amer. Jrnl. Public Health* XLIV. 575/2 It was ascertained that previous infection of a child with Type 2 or Type 3 virus failed to prevent his becoming infected subclinically with Type 1 virus. **1963** R. P. Dales *Annelids* ix. 182 The rectum opening subterminally at a dorsal anus.

22. *subfertility*; **sub-song**, the part of a bird's song that is softer and less well defined than its characteristic series of notes and is believed to have no territorial significance.

1948 Martin & Hynes *Clin. Endocrinol.* viii. 157 Several examinations are advised before diagnosing subfertility and they should be performed as soon as possible after ejaculation. **1962** H. Lourie *Question of Abortion* xxiii. 201 The sub-fertility clinics, the clinics dealing with sterile marriages. **1971** *Daily Colonist* (Victoria, B.C.) 21 Aug. 22/2 Male subfertility is the main factor in 45 per cent of childless marriages. **1925** E. M. Nicholson in *Field* Dec. 31/3 Even the chaffinch..has a very low rambling, warbling sub-song with no fire or decision about it. **1948** *Brit. Birds* XLI. 51 The sub-song was occasionally replaced by the typical loud burst of song characteristic of this species [*sc.* the redstart]. **1979** *New Scientist* 17 May 537/1 Subsong is a rather soft and rambling type of singing..in which the bird seems to try out various sounds for itself.

23. *subsulphide*.

1868 Subsulphide [see *plumbous *a.* 2]. **1976** *Nature* 15 Jan. 109/3 Vanadium subsulphide β–V_3S is known to have a tetragonal unit cell.

‖ **suba** (ʃʊ·bă). [Hungarian.] A type of long sheepskin cloak worn by Hungarian shepherds.

1925 G. A. Birmingham *Wayfarer in Hungary* xiv. 130 The *suba* is a long cloak of sheepskin reaching to the ankles. It has no sleeves... Only when the weather is bad is the *suba* fastened in front. **1939** *Times Lit. Suppl.* 4 Nov. 636/4 The Hungarian shepherd's 'suba', a magnificently voluminous sheepskin cloak. **1971** *Nat. Geogr. Mag.* Apr. 481 (*caption*) Shepherds wear huge suba to escape autumn's chill. **1979** J. Snowden *Folk Dress of Europe* 25 In the last century, the *suba*, a sheepskin cloak, was developed from primitive peasant wear to a garment of considerable elaboration and costliness... Circular, or nearly so,..the *suba* was cut with radial sections joined to a shoulder yoke. The long seams..were decorated.. on the skin side.

subacid, *sb.* **1.** (Earlier example.)

1785 A. Seward *Let.* 7 June (1811) I. 75 That tetchy unprovoked spleen..clouding and staining the lustre of fine talents, and many excellent qualities... Let us all take warning, and correct our acids and sub-acids of every sort.

subacute. Add: **c.** *subacute sclerosing panencephalitis*, a frequently fatal degenerative disease of the central nervous system, caused by reactivation of a measles virus some years after the original infection.

1950 J. G. Greenfield in *Brain* LXXIII. 150 The name *subacute sclerosing encephalitis* therefore appears fully justified. Dr. van Bogaert's term 'leuco-encephalitis' emphasizes the characteristic damage to the white matter, but leaves out of account the cortical changes which are also important. Perhaps the term 'Panencephalitis' already adopted by Pette (1942) for forms which attack both grey and white matter could be usefully employed here, i.e. 'Subacute sclerosing panencephalitis'. **1967** *Brit. Med. Jrnl.* 5 Aug. 352/2 Measles complement-fixing and haemagglutination-inhibiting antibodies have been found in the serum of 22 patients with subacute sclerosing panencephalitis in significantly higher titre than in controls.

subadole·scent, *sb.* and *a.* [Sub- 19.] **A.** *sb.* = *preadolescent *sb.* **B.** *adj.* = *preadolescent *a.* a.

1957 R. A. Heinlein *Door into Summer* ii. 32 Did you ever try to discuss with a subadolescent something the child does not want to talk about? **1977** W. M. Spackman *Armful of Warm Girl* 33 An enlarged snapshot of two baby boys and two sub-adolescent girls.

subadult (sʊbæ·dʊlt, sʊbădʊ·lt), *a.* and *sb.* [Sub- 19.] **A.** *adj.* Not fully adult. **B.** *sb.* A subadult individual.

Applied chiefly to animals (cf. *preadult* s.v. *pre- B. 1).

1903 *Nature* 3 Dec. 112/1 A subadult Australian barn-owl in which large bunches of the nestling down are retained on the legs. **1934** Webster, Subadult *n.* **1946** *Nature* 28 Dec. 927/1 The author distinguishes between juvenile, young, sub-adult and adult, in that order of ascending age [of mammals]. **1962** B. Harrisson *Orang-Utan* iii. 108 Sub-adults, who have left their mothers, cuddle in pairs to get additional warmth. **1975** *Sci. Amer.* May 56/3 Lions are termed cubs until they are two years old and subadults between the ages of two and four. **1976** *Ibid.* Apr. 118/3 Subadult crocodiles often form a semicircle where a channel enters a pan, facing the inrushing water and snapping up the fish that emerge from the river.

‖ **subak** (sū·băk). Also **soebak.** [Balinese.] A Balinese rice-growers' co-operative, organized to ensure equitable distribution of water for irrigation.

1921 *Man. Netherlands India* (Admiralty) xi. 373 In the..construction of aqueducts..the Balinese excels. Moreover, the natives have their own irrigation associations or *subaks*. **1926** H. Norden *Byways of Tropic Seas* ix. 159 Balinese economic life is governed by *Soebak*, a communistic organization which came into being for the joint irrigation of rice fields. **1937** M. Covarrubias *Island of Bali* (1972) iii. 67 Disputes concerning ricefields or irrigation water are settled by the council of a special agricultural society, the *subak*. **1957** K. G. Wittfogel *Oriental Despotism* 25 In Bali the peasants are obliged to render labor service for the hydraulic regional unit, the *subak*, to which they belong. **1972** *Times* 11 Nov. 13/4 The brilliant green *sawahs*..are tended by village co-operatives, the *subaks*.

subaltern, *sb.* **3.** (Earlier examples.)

1685 tr. *Arnauld & Nicole's Logic* II. ii. 169 If they differ in Quantity only, and agree in Quality, as A.I. and E.O. they are call'd Subalterns. **1816** *Elements of Logic* II. iii. 47 Propositions which differ only in quantity are called subalterns.

sub-aqua (sʊ:bæ·kwă), *a.* [Adj. use of L. phr. *sub aqua* under water: cf. Sub- I.] Of or pertaining to underwater swimming or diving performed (esp. as a sport) with the assistance of an aqualung. Also *ellipt.* as *sb.*, sub-aqua swimming.

1955 *Neptune* Aug. 31/1, I was..surprised to learn that..few members of the British Sub-Aqua Club were interested in..spearfishing. **1959** *Listener* 8 Jan. 67/3 The 'sub-aqua-jet' which provides motive power for an under-water swimmer. **1962** *Underwater Swimming* ('Know the Game' Ser.) 3/1 The formation of sub-aqua clubs throughout the country. **1976** *Milton Keynes Express* 1 June 11/2 Saturday's attractions include demonstrations of..swimming, life-saving, sub aqua and weight-lifting. **1978** *Times* 14 July 26/3 Sub-aqua diving is one of the country's leading growth sports.

subaqueous, *a.* Add: **4.** In *fig.* use, lacking real substance or strength; wishy-washy.

1960 C. DAY LEWIS *Buried Day* i. 15 The whole picture, clear yet elusive, is bathed in a brooding, sub-aqueous light. **1970** H. BRAUN *Parish Churches* xix. 228 During the last fifty years an inevitable reaction has introduced pallid sub-aqueous treatments [of stained-glass windows], less obstructive to light but lacking all the ancient warmth and liveliness. **1977** *Listener* 28 July 122/3 A sort of subaqueous, loopy, transcendental speculation about female identity.

subarctic, *a.* Add: **2.** [SUB- 18.] Also **Subarctic.** Applied to a European climatic period that followed the Arctic and preceded the Preboreal.

1876 [see *ARCTIC *a.* 3]. **1935** *Discovery* July 198/2 Relics from Arctic and Subarctic times during and soon after the last glaciation are still to be found in Scotland. **1973** P. A. COLINVAUX *Introd. Ecol.* vii. 93 There is peat between the Dryas-bearing bottom mud and the first line of stumps, a gradation probably, but one that could be used as a stratigraphic unit. It represented the sub-arctic period.

Subarian (siŭbāri·ăn), *a.* and *sb.* Also **Subaraean.** [f. Akkadian *Subar(tu* 'Assyria' + -IAN.] **A.** *adj.* Of or pertaining to the Subarian people (see below) or their language. **B.** *sb.* **a.** (A member of) an ancient people of northern Mesopotamia in the 3rd and 2nd millennia B.C., sometimes identified with the Hurrians. **b.** The language (written in cuneiform) of this people. Cf. *HURRIAN *sb.* and *a.*, *MITANNI.

1923 C. J. GADD *Fall of Nineveh* 20 In his own building records Nabopolassar says, 'I slew the Subaraean, and turned the enemy's land into mounds and ruins.' *Ibid.*, Throughout these references, it is most probable that the enemy is the same, though described indifferently as Subaraean and Assyrian. **1926** —— in *Revue d'Assyriologie* XXIII. 63 The suffix *-ia* which is in constant use to form shortened names has long been established as a characteristic of Subaraean. **1939** [see *PAPUAN *sb.* 2]. **1964** G. ROUX *Anc. Iraq* xi. 166 Babylon was attacked by a coalition of Elamites, Guti, 'Subarians' (Assyrians) and people from Eshnunna. **1974** *Encycl. Brit. Micropædia* V. 222/3 The Hurrian language, once improperly called Mitannian or Subarian, exists chiefly in four varieties of cuneiform.

sub-asse·mbly. [SUB- 7 a.] A unit assembled separately but designed to be incorporated, with other such units, into a larger manufactured product; also, the production of sub-assemblies. Cf. *ASSEMBLY 1 c.

1919 *Brit. Manufacturer* Nov. 29/1 Parallel with the Finished Part Stores is the sub-assembly stores. **1924** W. J. HISCOX *Factory Lay-Out, Planning & Progress* ii. 29 The term 'sub-assembling' is used when two or more component parts are assembled together to form one part... Sometimes the 'sub-assembly' merely covers the fitting of a pin to a certain part. **1941** *Sun* (Baltimore) 21 Feb. 30/5 The Omaha plant will be used to assemble bombers from sub-assemblies and parts supplied by the automotive and other non-aeronautical enterprises. **1952** F. ALLEN *Big Change* II. vii. 111 The Ford assembly line, with its subassemblies, was unique. **1967** *Electronics* 6 Mar. 171/1 (*caption*) Three subassemblies constitute IBM's new mass production computer for varied aerospace applications. **1973** J. G. TWEEDDALE *Materials Technol.* II. iv. 73 Such mechanically-wrought products can form the primary material for further mechanical manipulation..into fairly complex sub-assembly components.

Hence (as a back-formation) **sub-asse·mble** *v. trans.*; **sub-asse·mbling** *vbl. sb.*

1924 Sub-assembling [see *sub-assembly* above]. **1940** *Sun* (Baltimore) 28 Nov. 1/2 Parts are manufactured and sometimes 'sub-assembled' at plants where idle machinery and man power are available.

subatla·ntic, *a.* Also **Subatlantic, sub-Atlantic. 1.** (In Dict. s.v. SUB- 1 e.)

2. [SUB- 18.] Pertaining to or designating a European climatic period that followed the Sub-boreal and which is still current. Also *absol.*

1876 [see *ARCTIC *a.* 3]. **1935** *Discovery* July 198/2 A fair number of these species has even survived the last climatic phase, the humid Subatlantic time (after 500 B.C.). **1957** E. E. EVANS *Irish Folk Ways* xiv. 186 The onset of the sub-Atlantic climatic deterioration in the last millennium B.C. seems to have accelerated the peat-forming processes. **1975** J. G. EVANS *Environment Early Man Brit. Isles* vi. 149 The growing of cereals [in Yorkshire]..would have been difficult..at any time since the onset of the Sub-atlantic.

subau·dible, *a.* [SUB- 14, 19.] **1.** Not loud enough to be audible. Also *fig.*

1839 [in Dict. s.v. SUB- 19]. **1928** E. BLUNDEN *Undertones of War* vii. 109 A good joke: but with this sub-audible meaning.

2. Of a frequency: lower than the lowest audible frequency. Of a sound: too low-pitched to be audible.

1922 *Proc. IRE* X. 253 It may be at sub-audible, or super-audible frequencies. **1978** *Gramophone* June 128/2 Superimposed on this are subaudible tones successively at 4, 5, 6, 8, 10 and 12 Hertz.

Sub-bo·real, *a.* Also **sub-Boreal.** [SUB- 18.] Pertaining to or designating a European climatic period that followed the Atlantic and preceded the Subatlantic. Also *absol.*

1876 [see *ARCTIC *a.* 3]. **1935** *Discovery* July 198/2 The Atlantic period was followed by another drier, continental phase, the Subboreal, lasting from 2500 till 500 B.C. **1963** H. N. SAVORY in Foster & Alcock *Culture & Environment* iii. 27 Primitive man, at least under sub-Boreal climatic conditions, had a choice of two main routes which gave him relatively easy access to the Glamorgan uplands from the coastal area of settlement. **1975** J. G. EVANS *Environment Early Man Brit. Isles* iv. 84 The sequence is overlain by peat of Atlantic and Sub-boreal age.

‖ **subbotnik** (su·bǫtnik). Pl. **-niki,** (anglicized) **-niks.** [a. Russ. *subbótnik,* f. *subbóta* Saturday: cf. SABBATH.] In the Soviet Union, the practice or an act of working voluntarily on a Saturday, for the benefit of the collective; = *SATURDAYING *vbl. sb.*

The practice originated with workers on the Moscow–Kazan railway in Moscow on 10 May 1919. The meaning given in quot. 1920 is imprecise.

1920 *19th Cent.* Sept. 399 This mutilation was due to an accident which had happened to him while he was a *subbotnik*. *Subbotniki*..are workmen who work on Saturday (*Subbota*) for the benefit of the Government: there is quite a large *subbotnik* movement in Russia. **1921** L. TROTSKY *Defence of Terrorism* viii. 136 The flourishing, unprecedented in the history of humanity, of labor voluntarism in the form of *subbotniks* (Communist Saturdays). **1959** C. LANDAUER *Europ. Socialism* I. xxvii. 772 The response to the call for *subbotnik* work left much to be desired. **1975** T. P. WHITNEY tr. *Solzhenitsyn's Gulag Archipelago* II. III. i. 14 Soon after that there began the Communist 'subbotniki'—'voluntary Saturdays'. **1979** *Nature* 16 Aug. 532/3 The Vietnamese economy is in such an urgent state that 75% of the proceeds of this year's *Subbotnik*, the Saturday in April when Soviet citizens contribute a day's work for the good of the economy, are to be devoted to Vietnam.

sub-bo·ttom, *a.* [SUB- 1 e.] Of or pertaining to what is underneath the sea-bed.

1949 *Trans. Amer. Geophysical Union* XXX. 7 The most clear-cut sub-bottom echoes are found in the region which shows least topographic relief. **1968** [see *PROFILING *vbl. sb.* 3]. **1975** *Petroleum Rev.* XXIX. 103/1 Sub-bottom profiler.

sub-ca·libre, *a.* Also (*U.S.*) **sub-caliber.** [SUB- 5 c.] Of a projectile: smaller in calibre than the gun from which it is fired, and discharged from a secondary tube set inside the main barrel. Also, of, pertaining to, or employed in the firing of sub-calibre projectiles.

1876 E. H. KNIGHT *Amer. Mech. Dict.* III. 2434/1 *Subcaliber projectile*,..a projectile for cannon or small-arms, of smaller diameter than the bore of the gun from which it is fired. **1909** *Teachers' Assembly Herald* 13 Apr. 19/1 Arms. Double-barreled shot-gun, pocket rifles, sub-calibre or auxiliary barrels. **1917** W. S. CHURCHILL in M. Gilbert *Winston S. Churchill* (1977) IV. Compan. I. 131 This after all is only applying the sub-calibre principle to actual service. **1946** T. C. OHART *Elements Ammunition* vii. 179 The subcaliber gun is mounted on a large gun tube for practical purposes. **1967** F. W. HACKLEY et al. *Hist. Mod. U.S. Mil. Small Arms Ammunition* I. II. vii. 93 *Subcaliber cartridges*. These..were at first called 'ball cartridges for artillery drill cartridges'. They were designed to be fired from subcaliber barrels mounted within..the main artillery gun tube. **1973** J. QUICK *Dict. Weapons & Mil. Terms* 426 Subcaliber ammunition is adapted for firing in weapons of larger caliber by sub-caliber tubes.

sub-ca·tegory. [SUB- *7 e, 9.] A subsidiary category; a subsection of a category; *spec.* in *Maths.* and *Linguistics.*

1909 WEBSTER, Sub-category *sb.* **1931** A. POPE *Introd. Lang. Drawing & Painting* II. iv. 63 It is well to stop in the joyous enthusiasm of thinking out new categories and subcategories. **1949** KOESTLER *Insight & Outlook* iv. 37 First, bisociation is not the same thing as ambiguity; ambiguity is merely a subcategory of it. **1956** R. REDFIELD *Peasant Soc. & Culture* 24 Typologies of Latin-American cultures or of the peasant subcategory of such cultures. **1972** A. G. HOWSON *Handbk. Terms Algebra & Anal.* xix. 98 Hence, *Ab* is a *functor* from G to the *subcategory* of Abelian groups and homomorphisms. **1982** *Sci. Amer.* Mar. 91/1 He divided the galaxies into two main classes, ellipticals and spirals, with several subcategories.

Hence **sub-ca·tegorize** *v. trans.*, to place in or divide into sub-categories; **su:b-categoriza·tion.**

1965 N. CHOMSKY *Aspects of Theory of Syntax* ii. 95 Rules..which analyze a symbol in terms of its categorial context, I shall henceforth call *strict subcategorization rules.* **1965** Subcategorize [see *pre-adjectival* s.v. *PRE- B. 1 d]. **1971** J. ANDERSON in A. J. Aitken et al. *Edin. Stud. Eng. & Scots* 69, I would like to consider some of the set of phenomena that we could reasonably require a subcategorisation of the modal verb in English to provide an explanation for. **1979** *Dictionaries* I. 14 The initial capitals are subcategorized and provided with lower-case letters and figures.

subce·ption. *Psychol.* A blend of *subliminal perception* (see quot. 1949).

1949 MCLEARY & LAZARUS in *Jrnl. Personality* XVIII. 171 An experiment which confirms the notion that subjects give discriminatory galvanic skin responses to visual stimuli presented at tachistoscopic speeds too brief for correct verbal report. The implied perceptual process is termed by the authors *subception* (verb form—to *subceive*). *Ibid.* 179 It is suggested that the level of perceptual activity indicated by this finding be called *subception.* **1958** *New Biol.* XXVII. 29 The subject remains unaware not only of the stimulus but also of the fact that his 'guesses' are being biased. For this effect the word 'subception' has been coined. **1959** *Manch. Guardian* 2 July 4/6 The techniques of 'subception' would be of no value to advertising agents... Subception effects which could be obtained under laboratory conditions would be masked..in real life. **1977** R. O. VIITAMÄKI in von Fieandt & Moustgaard *Perceptual World* xxi. 557 The subception effect has implications not only for perceptual theory but..also..in the fields of personality and clinical psychology.

sub-cheese (su·btʃī·z). *Mil. slang* (orig. *Anglo-Indian*). Also **sub-cheeze, -chiz,** [ad. Hind. *sab* all + *chiz* thing (see CHEESE sb.[2]).] The lot; everything; all that there is. Also in phr. *the whole sub-cheese.*

[**1864** HOTTEN *Slang Dict.* 98 The expression *cheese* may be found in the Gipsy vocabulary, and in the Hindostanee and Persian languages. In the last *chiz* means a thing. *Ibid.* 250 *Sub*, all. *Anglo-Indian.*] **1874** E. LEAR *Jrnl.* 4 May (1953) vii. 132 Then came the long and stumbling descent until the last village, where were all the coolies, and sub-cheese (everything). **1895** KIPLING *Day's Work* (1898) 181 She's as clever as a man... Settled the whole *subchiz* (outfit) in three hours. **1919** W. H. DOWNING *Digger Dialects* 60 Subcheese, the lot. **1962** M. MALGONKAR *Combat of Shadows* xxiv. 184 And the cricket pavilion, and the game cottage, the whole subcheeze. **1971** B. W. ALDISS *Soldier Erect* 251 Of course we were lugging our ammo, machine-guns, mortars, and the whole *subcheeze* with us.

su·b-clause. [SUB- 5 c, 9.] **1.** *Law.* A subsidiary section of a clause. Also *transf.*

1927 *Tax Cases* (1928) XI. x. 801 Notwithstanding anything in sub-clause (7) of Clause 20A contained the amounts credited to members under this clause shall not be deemed to be amounts withdrawn from Reserve Fund for the purposes of that sub-clause. **1946** *All England Law Reports* II. 577 In that sub-clause it is provided that the wife is to support, maintain and educate the child. **1959** I. & P. OPIE *Lore & Lang. Schoolch.* viii. 136 There are also some sub-clauses in the code [of oral legislation concerning possession]. **1974** *Williams' Law Wills* (ed. 4) v. 1067 My trustees shall hold such dwelling..upon trust to sell the same with full power (subject to the provisions of sub-clause (e) of this clause) to postpone the sale.

2. *Gram.* A clause that is subordinate to a main clause.

1934 PRIEBSCH & COLLINSON *German Lang.* vi. 311 *So dass* (with *so* drawn out of the main clause into the sub-clause). **1957** R. W. ZANDVOORT *Handbk. Eng. Gram.* I. vi. 86 The subjunctive may be used in nominal sub-clauses depending on a main clause expressing will or wish. **1966** *English Studies* XLVII. 261 The independent use of subclauses in expressive speech is not restricted to *that*-clauses. **1983** *Times* 5 Oct. 32/7 He would launch into the last paragraph only to find that he had put in one sub clause too many.

subcli·max. *Ecol.* [f. SUB- 22 + *CLIMAX 4 b.] A point in an ecological succession at which a plant community is prevented by climatic or other factors from reaching its natural climax.

1916 F. E. CLEMENTS *Plant Succession* vi. 107 Such apparent climaxes are always subordinate to the normal developmental or climatic climax, and may accordingly be distinguished as subclimaxes. **1926** TANSLEY & CHIPP *Aims & Methods in Study of Vegetation* ii. 9 Such an edaphic climax may be a climatic sub-climax. **1941** J. S. HUXLEY *Uniqueness of Man* iii. 104 If grassland is not the natural climax of plant life, but is only a 'sub-climax',..then it will stand very heavy grazing. **1952** *Jrnl. Ecol.* XL. 105 It appears..that this is in reality a grazing sub-climax vegetation. **1979** *Nature* 11 Oct. 425/2 Weedy herbs support fewer fungal parasites than do climax and subclimax herbs in the US.

subconscious, *a.* Add: **1. a, b.** *absol.* (Later examples.)

1890 J. M. BALDWIN *Handbk. Psychol.* (ed. 2) iv. 57 This whole field in its relation to consciousness has been well called the sub-conscious, from the fact that images formerly in consciousness have now fallen below the threshold, but may rise again..when the stimulation of the centres is sufficient. **1914** [see *CO-CONSCIOUS *a.* and *sb.*]. **1928** H. G. & C. F. BAYNES tr. *Jung's Two Essays Anal. Psychol.* v. 67 The personal unconscious, of which I also speak as the 'subconscious', in contrast to the absolute or collective unconscious, contains forgotten memories, suppressed..painful ideas..apperceptions sometimes described as below the threshold (subliminal). **1934** J. M. CAIN *Postman always rings Twice* xvi. 187 There's a guy in No. 7 that murdered his brother, and says he didn't really do it, his subconscious did it. **1957** V. PACKARD *Hidden Persuaders* iii. 27 With all this interest in manipulating the customer's subconscious, the old slogan 'let the buyer beware' began taking on a new and more profound meaning. **1977** B. PYM *Quartet in Autumn* i. 6 Something of this may have been in Norman's subconscious as he turned the pages of his newspaper.

subconsciousness. 1. (Earlier example.)

1874 G. H. LEWES *Probl. Life & Mind* (Ser. 1) I. 141

Neural processes which formerly were accompanied by Consciousness sink into Sub-Consciousness.

subcontinent. Add: Now also with main stress on second syllable. (Later examples.) More recently applied commonly to India, Pakistan, Bangladesh, and Sri Lanka.

1947 J. STEVENSON-HAMILTON *Wild Life S. Afr.* xiii. 94 The springbuck..is the only representative of the gazelle group, which is found in the sub-continent. **1954** B. & R. NORTH tr. *M. Duverger's Pol. Parties* II. i. 210 In Latin America, a general tendency towards the two-party system is perceptible, though it is generally.. deformed by the revolutions, *coups d'état*, gerrymandering..characteristic of..that sub-continent. **1971** R. RUSSELL in *Aziz Ahmad's Shore & Wave* 7 The novel in Urdu, as in all the modern languages of the South Asian sub-continent, is of very recent growth. **1972** *Times of India* 28 Nov. 11/4 Mr. Azad outlined his Government's views on the political problems of the sub-continent. **1978** L. HEREN *Growing up on The Times* v. 175 Many Indians refused to accept the partition of the sub-continent.

subcontinental, *a.* Add: **3.** [SUB- 5 b.] Of or pertaining to a subcontinent, *spec.* the Indian subcontinent (see prec.).

1973 *Guardian* 5 Mar. 5/2 'I've been a Pakistani for 24 years,' she says, though her accent remains softly Irish and not at all subcontinental. **1975** R. JACKSON *S. Asian Crisis* iii. 66 The situation in East Pakistan had been represented..as yet another round in the perennial quarrel between the two sub-continental states.

subcontract, *v.* Add: **3.** (Later examples.) Formerly, of the sub-contractor; now often with contractor or work as subj. Also with *out.*

1939 *Daily Tel.* 18 Dec. 12/8 Outworkers required to sub-contract large and regular orders of light clothing. **1955** *Times* 19 Aug. 10/1 Hall Telephone will..be able to employ its factories to greater advantage by undertaking the manufacture of the James Gordon products, which hitherto have been sub-contracted by that company. **1972** *Daily Tel.* 20 Mar. 18/3 Most of the engineering parts are sub-contracted out. **1981** *Brit. Med. Jrnl.* 4 July 51/2 He worked on a commission of 15% on surgery sales, the middleman (the general practitioner) had nothing to do with it, and the surgical operation was subcontracted out.

sub-crea·tion. [SUB- 5.] J. R. R. Tolkien's word for the process of inventing an imaginary or secondary world, different from the primary world but internally consistent.

1947 J. R. R. TOLKIEN in *Essays presented to Charles Williams* 51 This aspect of 'mythology'—sub-creation, rather than either representation or symbolic interpretation of the beauties and terrors of the world—is, I think, too little considered. **1974** R. HELMS *Tolkien's World* vi. 123 He needed to tell himself..that the cosmos is friendly to sub-creation, because it echoes its own chief and most joyous activity.

Also **sub-crea·tor,** one who engages in sub-creation.

1947 J. R. R. TOLKIEN in *Essays presented to Charles Williams* 51 In such 'fantasy', as it is called, new form is made; Faërie begins; Man becomes a sub-creator. **1972** P. H. KOCHER *Master of Middle-Earth* (1973) vii. 201 He..is lifted up to live above himself, as is the sub-creator of secondary worlds of fantasy at the height of his inspiration.

sub-crea·tive, *a.* [SUB- *5 c (*b*), 8.] Of or pertaining to sub-creation or secondary creation. Hence **sub-crea·tively** *adv.*

Quot. 1860 shows a nonce-use of this word.

1860 [in Dict. s.v. SUB- 8]. **1947** J. R. R. TOLKIEN in *Essays presented to Charles Williams* 71 To many, Fantasy, this sub-creative art which plays strange tricks with the world and all that is in it, combining nouns and redistributing adjectives, has seemed suspect, if not illegitimate. **1958** —— *Lett.* (1981) 286 In this Myth the rebellion of created free-will precedes creation of the World (Eä); and Eä has in it, subcreatively introduced, evil, rebellious, discordant elements of its own nature. **1974** R. HELMS *Tolkien's World* vi. 122 As artist, he is incomplete, impotent, without the presence of the other element in sub-creative activity—his community.

subcri·tical, *a.* Also **sub-critical.** [SUB- 14.] **1.** *Metallurgy.* Less than the critical temperature above which ferrite changes into austenite; *subcritical annealing*, annealing in which the temperature is not raised above this.

1930 *Trans. Amer. Inst. Mining & Metall. Engineers, Techn. Publ.* No. 348. 5 The quenching to this subcritical temperature must be rapid enough to preserve the austenite essentially unchanged. **1935** M. A. GROSSMANN *Princ. Heat Treatment* viii. 113 Subcritical annealing will not induce as much softness as a full anneal. **1980** G. KRAUSS *Princ. Heat Treatment Steel* v. 115 Process and recrystallization annealing are similar subcritical annealing treatments usually applied to restore ductility to cold worked steel products.

2. Of a flow of fluid: slower than the speed at which waves travel in the fluid.

1941 *Civil Engin.* Mar. 171/1 The terms 'tranquil' and 'rapid' have been used..in connection with the Froude criterion... The frequently used terms 'low-velocity' and 'high-velocity' are..just as inept as the ambiguous 'subcritical' and 'supercritical'. **1943** R. C. BINDER *Fluid Mech.* xiv. 215 The hydraulic jump is an abrupt transition between what might be called supercritical and subcritical flow. **1981** *Sci. Amer.* Apr. 138/2 A ridge across a streambed provides an example of how a barrier can create supercritical flow, a standing wave and a hydraulic jump in an initially subcritical flow.

3. *Nucl. Physics.* Containing or being less than the critical mass (*CRITICAL *a.* 7 b).

1945 D. DIETZ *Atomic Energy in Coming Era* xii. 146 It was seen..that the mechanism of the bomb would have to bring sub-critical masses of the material together quickly. **1961** *Engineering* 7 Apr. 487/1 Two new light-water moderated and natural-uranium fuelled subcritical assemblies are appearing on the nuclear market in this country. **1978** *Nature* 9 Feb. 497/3 Chain reaction is unlikely, since the mass of uranium used in such satellites is normally subcritical.

subcu·ltural, *a.* Also **sub-cultural.** [SUB- 5, 7.] Of or pertaining to a subculture. Also, that is inferior to or below the general cultural level.

1933 *Brit. Jrnl. Psychol.* July 2 The residual group of patients..may be termed the subcultural type. This type is..a collection of persons who are healthy, apparently sound neurologically.., but who lack intelligence. **1937** *Discovery* July 223/2 The sub-cultural social defective must be recognised as such..and the able child made an economic asset. **1958** B. BERNSTEIN in J. A. Fishman *Readings Sociol. of Lang.* (1968) 223 Within the last thirty years in both the fields of sociology and psychology there has been an increasing awareness of sub-cultural and social class influences upon behaviour and in particular learning. **1968** D. L. CLARKE *Anal. Archaeol.* vi. 234 Ethnologists..have drawn attention to the material equipment of the lower-level sub-cultural segments outlined by sociology. **1979** *Internat. Jrnl. Sociol. of Law* VII. 242 This order is not instilled by sanctions, at least not primarily so, but partly guaranteed by extra-legal normative structures (ethical norms, group norms, subcultural norms etc.).

su·bculture, *sb.* Also **sub-culture.** **1.** *Biol.* and *Med.* [SUB- 9.] A culture (of bacteria or the like) started from another culture; the process of starting a culture in this way.

1886 E. KLEIN *Micro-Organisms & Dis.* (ed. 3) v. 43 From the individual and separate colonies, it is then easy by re-inoculation of gelatine tubes..to start pure subcultures of the different species. **1899** [in Dict. s.v. SUB- 9]. **1911** *Jrnl. Path. & Bacteriol.* XV. 94 In subculture it grew on plain agar. **1962** *Lancet* 5 May 933/1 Amongst the 240 staphylococcal strains tested..64 showed discrete colonies of this kind and they were tested by subculture on to the same concentration of drug. **1971** *Nature* 16 July 174/1 Subcultures of the bacterial cultures were carried out at 7 day intervals to maintain vigorous stocks.

2. [SUB- 7.] A group or class of lesser importance or size sharing specific beliefs, interests, or values which may be at variance with those of the general culture of which it forms part.

1936 R. LINTON *Study of Man* xvi. 275 While ethnologists have been accustomed to speak of tribes and nationalities as though they were the primary culture-bearing units, the total culture of a society of this type is really an aggregate of sub-cultures. **1937** *Brit. Jrnl. Psychol.* Apr. 358 We may regard the adjusted group.. as a small culture pocket or subculture within the larger culture. **1948** T. S. ELIOT *Notes towards Definition of Culture* iv. 75 We may find ourselves led to the conclusion, that every sub-culture is dependent upon that from which it is an offshoot. **1955** T. H. PEAR *Eng. Soc. Differences* iii. 111 The extravert's and the introvert's idea of good manners and goodwill, even in the same sub-culture-pattern, are very different. **1963** T. PYNCHON *V.* xii. 361 Anyone who continues to live in a subculture so demonstrably sick has no right to call himself well. **1970** G. JACKSON *Let.* 4 Apr. in *Soledad Brother* (1971) 214 We are a subsidiary subculture, a depressed area. **1976** DEAKIN & WILLIS *Johnny go Home* v. 82 The [social] workers dress like their clients... Only their accents betray them as not being part of the sub-culture they are ministering to.

su·bculture, *v.* *Biol.* and *Med.* [f. prec., sense 1.] *trans.* To produce a subculture of. Hence (with variable stressing) **subcultured** *ppl. a.*, **subculturing** *vbl. sb.*

1899 G. NEWMAN *Bacteria* 339 The contained bacteria will reveal themselves in characteristic colonies, which may be..sub-cultured. **1919** *Lancet* 2 Aug. 189/2 After eight subculturings in broth..all the strains had become agglutinable to para. B serum. **1930** *Forestry* IV. 66 Sub-culturing was done with small pieces of rhizomorph, and all cultures so made continued to produce rhizomorphs in great abundance. **1949** H. W. FLOREY in H. W. Florey et al. *Antibiotics* I. i. 18 This contaminating organism..was subcultured. **1967** M. E. HALE *Biol. Lichens* i. 8 Ideally the algae should be isolated and subcultured. **1970** *Nature* 25 July 383/1 Subcultured gonococci were exposed to antiserum alone. **1974** *Ibid.* 2 Aug. 383/2 Diploid fibroblast cultures can be propagated..only for a finite number of subculturings.

sub-deb. *slang* (chiefly *U.S.*). Now *rare.* [*SUB- 14 b.] A girl who will soon 'come out' as a social débutante. Hence, less specifically, a girl in her mid-teens. Also *fig.* and *attrib.*

1917 M. R. RINEHART (*title*) Bab: a sub-deb. *Ibid.* i. 14 Is it fair also, I ask, that in the best society a girl is a Sub-Deb the year before she comes out? **1930** *New Statesman* 1 Nov. 114/1 *The Little Review*, born in Chicago, a 'sub-deb' in California, debutante in New York, defunct in Paris. **1936** M. H. BRADLEY *Five-Minute Girl* 116 Margaret, two years older than Alva..and there was Joyce, the subdeb. **1939** [see *DATING *vbl. sb.* c]. **1944** W. S. MAUGHAM *Razor's Edge* vii. 278 The living-room would do very well for the sub-deb dances which it would be her pleasant duty to give. **1947** *Time* 6 Jan. 20/3 The season's debutantes danced their way into society while eager sub-debs looked on.

Also **sub-de·butante** *U.S.*

1934 in WEBSTER. **1959** V. PACKARD *Status Seekers* xiii. 186 The girl..must be invited to the right sub-debutante parties.

subdialect. Add: Hence **su:bdiale·ctal** *a.*, of or pertaining to a subdialect.

1960 *Amer. Speech* XXXV. 218 Least likely to be widely accepted is Hoenigswald's general theory as to the origin of sound change... He revives the old substratum theory in a subdialectal setting. **1978** *Language* LIV. 10 The pattern of free variation (presumably representing subdialectal variation).

subdivision. Add: **2. c.** *N. Amer.* An area of land subdivided into plots for the erection of houses; a housing estate.

1911 *Daily Colonist* (Victoria, B.C.) 29 Apr. 13/2 Willows Beach Subdivision... The subdivision adjoins the well known Uplands Subdivision. **1926** G. FRANKAU *My Unsentimental Journey* xv. 209 The straight road through your new 'sub-divisions' (Anglicé—building lots). **1947** *Publ. Amer. Dial. Soc.* VII. 22 'Village' has always been the common term for a small settlement, but does not appear in the name itself unless this is a subdivision name: *Sunset Village, Pilgrim Village.* **1960** V. PACKARD *Waste Makers* (1961) xxiv. 299 The 'country' place in the suburbs loses its 'semirural' character as soon as a subdivision goes up beyond it..(even though a subdivision house..in the suburbs may be preferable to an old row house in the city). **1979** *Tucson* (Arizona) *Citizen* 20 Sept. 1A/1, 1,700 displaced residents..left flooded parts of 25 subdivisions in Harris and Galveston counties.

subdominant, *a.* Add: **2.** *Ecol.* Designating a species which is prevalent in a community, but below the dominant in precedence. Also as *sb.* Cf. *DOMINANT *a.* 8.

1909 GROOM & BALFOUR tr. *Warming's Oecol. Plants* xxxv. 139 Every community consists of dominant and sub-dominant species, as well as of others that are more or less dependent upon these and occur only here and there. **1923** *Ecology* IV. 13 Species belonging to life-forms of subordinate rank (i.e. subdominant species) have also to be considered. **1933** [see *CO-DOMINANT *sb.*]. **1969** *Gloss. for Landscape Work* (*B.S.I.*) v. 39 *Sub-dominant*.. Of a species, that species in a mixed crop which is selected to come next in precedence to the dominant.

subduct, *v.* Restrict 'Now *rare*' to senses in Dict. and add: **5.** *trans.* and *intr.* *Geol.* To move sideways and downwards underneath a neighbouring lithospheric plate.

1971 *Nature* 29 Jan. 309/2 A Mesozoic foldbelt..makes up the periphery of West Antarctica, suggesting that seafloor was once subducted along this margin. **1974** *Ibid.* 13 Sept. 102/3 Since the Lower Miocene eastern Sicily has been the border zone between colliding continental blocks and the oceanic lithosphere subducting beneath the Calabrian arc. **1975** *Sci. Amer.* Nov. 98/2 It is puzzling..that the Pacific plate can move laterally for 6,000 kilometers before it subducts. **1977** A. HALLAM *Planet Earth* 100 (*caption*) The dense oceanic plate..is being subducted beneath the lighter continental plate.

Hence **subdu·cted, subdu·cting** *ppl. adjs.*

1975 *Sci. Amer.* Nov. 93/1 If the subduction ceases altogether, the subducted segment of the lithosphere will lose its identity and become part of the surrounding mantle in roughly 60 million years. *Ibid.*, At a velocity of one centimetre per year the subducting plate will be assimilated at a depth of about 400 kilometres. **1980** J. G. NAVARRA *Earth, Space, & Time* i. 17/1 The subducted plate is believed to be more dense than the mantle into which it plunges because it is colder. **1980** *Economist* 16 Aug. 64 Where two plates collide, one plate plunges beneath the other... The world's deep ocean trenches mark the graves of such 'subducting' plate edges.

subduction. Restrict 'Now *rare*' to senses in Dict. and add: **5.** *Geol.* [a. F. *subduction* (A. Amstutz 1951, in *Arch. des Sci.* IV. 326).] The sideways and downward movement of the edge of a lithospheric plate into the mantle beneath a neighbouring plate; **subduction zone,** a strip along which this is occurring.

1970 *Nature* 14 Nov. 659/1 The lateral displacement of continents involves at least partial destruction in subduction zones of either the plate on which they are borne or of another plate. **1972** *Sci. Amer.* Mar. 33/2 Along one edge of a crustal plate there is a subduction zone, usually marked by a trench. **1972, 1975** [see *OBDUCTION 2]. **1975** *Sci. Amer.* Nov. 89/2 The deepest trenches of the world's oceans, including the Java and Tonga trenches and all others associated with island arcs, mark the seaward boundary of subduction zones. **1980** J. G. NAVARRA *Earth, Space, & Time* i. 17/2 Subduction along the Java Trench where the Indo-Australian Plate is moving under the Indonesian island chain..fueled the 1883 eruption of Krakatoa.

subdue, *v.* Add: **2. f.** In phr. *to be subdued to what one works in*: to become reduced in capacity to the standard of one's material (in allusion to SHAKES. *Sonnets* cxi.).

1907 W. RALEIGH *Shakespeare* iv. 107 Shakespeare accepted the facts, and subdued his hand to what it worked in. **1912** L. STRACHEY *Landmarks in French Lit.*

iv. 92 Their [*sc.* the Elizabethans'] work has vanished from the stage, and is today familiar to but a few of the lovers of English literature. Shakespeare alone was not subdued to what he worked in. **1926** G. M. TREVELYAN *Hist. Eng.* v. iii. 559 When a man, in defending his country from foreign conquest, has to rely on certain forces, he ceases to be capable of criticizing them. He becomes subdued to the material in which he works.

su·bdwarf, *sb.* and *a.* *Astr.* [SUB- 22.] **A.** *sb.* A star which when plotted on the Hertzsprung–Russell diagram lies just below the main sequence, being less luminous than dwarf stars of the same temperature. Cf. *SUBGIANT.

1939 G. P. KUIPER in *Astrophysical Jrnl.* LXXXIX. 548 Three classes of objects of special interest are expected to be found..: (1) white dwarfs; (2) intermediate white dwarfs or, more generally, stars not over 2 or 3 mag. below the main sequence... The second group extends almost along the whole main sequence. Since these stars merge into the main sequence and are much more similar to main-sequence stars than to white dwarfs.., the name 'subdwarfs' is suggested for this class of stars, in analogy with 'subgiants'. **1962** *New Scientist* 3 May 218/2 Some hot subdwarfs are found from their spectra to have helium but virtually no hydrogen. **1979** *Nature* 24 May 305/1 The observations of CH Cygni reported here were made to determine whether a symbiotic star is a binary system composed of an M6 giant and a hot subdwarf, or whether it is a cool star surrounded by a thick corona.

B. *adj.* Designating such a star.

1981 *Nature* 8 Oct. 432/2 The most likely explanation.. is that the atmospheres are untypical of the subdwarf stars as a whole.

sub-edit, *v.* Add: (Earlier example.) Also *absol.*

1855 D. G. ROSSETTI *Let.* 23 Jan. (1965) I. 241 He sub-edits the *Leader.* **1915** WODEHOUSE *Psmith, Journalist* xx. 145, I am Psmith. I sub-edit.

sub-editor. (Earlier example.)

1834 [see *city-editor* s.v. *CITY 9].

subfamily. Add: **1. b.** A subdivision of a human family, *spec.* one living within a primary family group (see quot. 1964).

1964 *Census of Population* 1960 (U.S. Dept. Commerce) I. I. p. lviii/2, A subfamily is a married couple with or without own children, or one parent with one or more own children under 18 years old, living in a housing unit and related to the head of the household or his wife. **1970** S. L. BARRACLOUGH in I. L. Horowitz *Masses in Lat. Amer.* iv. 129 Some such units have incomes close to those of sub-family producers.

2. *transf.*, esp. in *Linguistics.*

1856 W. D. WHITNEY in *Jrnl. Amer. Oriental Soc.* V. 195 The various sub-families and even closer kindred dialects had deviated too widely from their original and from one another. **1972** R. J. WILSON *Introd. Graph Theory* viii. 119 We call a transversal of a subfamily of *S* a partial transversal of *S.* **1978** *Language* LIV. 181 The Southern sub-family merged *i* with *ī* and *u* with *ū.*

sub-fra·ction. [SUB- 9.] **1.** *Math.* (In Dict. s.v. SUB- 9.)

2. *Biochem.* Any one of the portions into which a fraction may be further divided. Cf. *FRACTION *sb.* 7.

1946 *Nature* 5 Oct. 474/1 The division of the combined cystine in wool into four sub-fractions of different chemical reactivity. **1962** V. N. OREKHOVICH et al. in A. Pirie *Lens Metabolism Rel. Cataract* 324 We succeeded in dividing β-crystallin of cattle lens into β_1- and β_2-crystallin..and γ-crystallin was divided into three sub-fractions. **1978** *Jrnl. Neurochem.* XXX. 563 A subfraction, derived from the microsomal fraction of rat cerebral cortex,.. appears to be enriched in receptor sites for a number of potential neurotransmitters.

Hence **su:bfractiona·tion** *Biochem.*, the process of separating a fraction into further components.

1955 *Biochem. Jrnl.* LX. 615/1 This subfractionation has not brought to light any enzymic heterogeneity in the granules. **1978** *Jrnl. Neurochem.* XXX. 783 The possibility that these findings might reflect merely contamination of myelin with other membranes was tested by subfractionation.

subfusc, -fusk, *a.* and *sb.* Add: Now usu. in form **subfusc. a.** Also *spec.* of clothing: dark, as prescribed by the regulations of the Universities of Oxford and Cambridge for examinations and other formal occasions; (later examples).

1930 W. J. LOCKE *Town of Tombarel* v. 163 Cousin Hortense in some sort of unremarkable subfusc raiment. **1973** *New Society* 1 Nov. 259/3 His clothes very subfusc—grey suit, polished black shoes, the only brightness a purple and red bowtie. **1978** G. GREENE *Human Factor* v. i. 232 Two women who might have been sisters in their similar subfusc clothing waited by what he guessed was a confessional box.

fig. (Later examples.)

1927 C. PARSONS in *Oxford Poetry* 24 Lost in what corner of this maze, With mind already dyed subfusc. **1949** C. P. SNOW *Time of Hope* v. xxxiii. 280 Allen..made subfusc, malicious, aunt-like jokes at Getliffe's expense. **1958** L. DURRELL *Balthazar* x. 210 The frail subfusc moonlight glancing along the waves. **1970** N. MARSH *When in Rome* iv. 106 Mailer seemed to me to be, in a subfusc sort of way, cocksure.

b. (*b*). (Later examples with reference to university examination dress.)

1944 A. L. ROWSE *Eng. Spirit* xxxvii. 260 Black-gowned young men and women, all dutifully clad in *sub fusc.* **1961** E. WILLIAMS *George* xx. 320, I was able to keep up the illusion of study by twice donning sub-fusc and walking down to the Examination Schools in white tie and mortar-board.

su·bgiant. *Astr.* [SUB- 22.] A star which when plotted on the Hertzsprung–Russell diagram lies between the main sequence and the giants; a star similar to a giant of the same spectral type but less luminous. Cf. *SUBDWARF *sb.* and *a.*

1937 *Astrophysical Jrnl.* LXXXV. 383 Three bright 'subgiants' having well-determined trigonometric parallaxes. **1943** W. W. MORGAN et al. *Atlas Stellar Structure* 6 For the stars of types F–K, class IV represents the subgiants and class III the normal giants. **1978** H. L. SHIPMAN *Introd. Astron.* xi. 296 Star *A* becomes a rather unusual type of star, a subgiant—a low-mass, very dim, small red giant.

su·bgrade. 1. *Road* and *Railway Engineering* [SUB- 3 a.] The layer, either natural or constructed, lying immediately beneath the foundations of a road or railway line. Cf. SUBSTRATUM 4 b.

1893 G. A. PERKINS et al. in *Rep. Mass. State Highway Comm.* v. 78 The subgrade, or the ground on which the large stones rest, should be thoroughly compacted by rolling. **1906** *Engin. Rec.* 14 Apr. 478/3 The reduced quantity of broken stone required, when it is laid on a firm sub-grade. **1930** *Engineering* 1 Aug. 139/3 Maintenance of a mile of gravel road, including the sub-grade. **1962** *Ibid.* 30 Mar. 439 The stresses transmitted to the subgrade by a high quality structural are so small. **1979** *Railway Gaz. Internat.* Jan. 52/2 Protection of the subgrade against frost.

2. [SUB- 9 (*a*).] A subsidiary grade; one within a grade.

1919 *Sociol. Rev.* XI. 90 We might perhaps recognise.. an intermediate group, concerned chiefly with relations between sub-grades. **1931** J. S. HUXLEY *What dare I Think?* vi. 218 In this stage of thought there are, of course, many sub-grades.

subgroup. Add: **a.** No longer 'Chiefly *Nat. Hist.*'. (Later *gen.* examples.)

1935 *Planning* II. XLI. 6 Utility Services..has been working in three or four sub-groups, one of which dealing with transport has produced the survey contained in broadsheet No. 21. **1961** Y. OLSSON *Syntax Eng. Verb.* ii. 30 One sub-group is independent, for its extra-lingual correlation, of the speech-situation in which its terms are employed. **1978** K. HUDSON *Jargon of Professions* 10 Changes in the technology of communication have made it far easier for one cultural sub-group to hear the members of another group talking.

b. More widely, any group all of whose elements are elements of a larger group. (Earlier and later examples.)

1887 *Amer. Jrnl. Math.* IX. 51, I use 'self-conjugate sub-group' in translating Klein's 'ausgezeichnete Untergruppe' and Jordan's 'groupe permutable.' **1937**, etc. [see *PROPER *a.* 5 c]. **1975** I. STEWART *Concepts Mod. Math.* vii. 104 If I gave you a group of order 615 you would know, without any information about the multiplication table, that its subgroups cannot have any orders other than 1, 3, 5, 15, 41, 123, 205, and 615.

Hence **su·bgroup** *v. trans.*, to divide or classify into subgroups; **sub-grouping,** a subsidiary grouping or subgroup; the action of dividing or classifying into these.

1922 E. WALLACE *Flying Fifty-Five* xi. 67 They also were grouped and sub-grouped and indexed. **1956** J. KLEIN *Study of Groups* 168 It must be established that these sub-groupings are not thrown up by chance. **1960** *Amer. Speech* XXXV. 216 The two final chapters [of H. M. Hoenigswald, Language Change & Linguistic Reconstruction] deal with..the procedures for the subgrouping of language families. **1977** *Lancet* 1 Jan. 9/1 The I.Q. data from this study have been subgrouped according to whether the immersion accident occurred in the hot or the cold months of the year. **1978** *Language* LIV. 468 Dyen concerns himself with three topics: the AN homeland, the subgrouping and external relationships of the AN language, and reconstruction.

subharmo·nic, *sb.* and *a.* Also **sub-harmonic.** [SUB- 9.] **A.** *sb.* An oscillation with a frequency equal to an integral submultiple of another frequency. Freq. *attrib.*

1924 W. N. BOND in *Nature* 8 Mar. 355/2 The production of the half frequency easily, of the third frequency with care, and of the fourth frequency faintly..leaves little doubt that the frequencies obtainable are all submultiples of the fundamental applied frequency... These forced vibrations might be described as sub-harmonics. **1940** H. F. OLSON *Elem. Acoustical Engin.* vii. 137 It has been analytically shown..that subharmonics are possible in certain vibrating systems. **1952** [see *frequency divider* s.v. *FREQUENCY 5]. **1961** M. L. GAYFORD *Acoustical Techniques & Transducers* III. 67 A curvature of the sides of the [loudspeaker] cone assists the suppression of subharmonics. **1976** *Gloss. Terms Mech. Vibration & Shock* (*B.S.I.*) 12 *Subharmonic response*, a response of a mechanical system exhibiting some of the characteristics of resonance at a frequency having a period that is an integral multiple of the period of the periodic excitation. **1978** A. B. PIPPARD *Physics of Vibration* I. ix. 253 Each subharmonic is stable over a limited range of excitation.

B. *adj.* Involving or being a subharmonic.

1940 H. F. OLSON *Elem. Acoustical Engin.* vii. 137 Another feature of subharmonic phenomena is the relatively long time required for 'build up'. **1962** A. NISBETT *Technique Sound Studio* 245 Paper cones are often corrugated to reduce any tendency to 'break up' radially and produce sub-harmonic oscillations. **1978** A. B. PIPPARD *Physics of Vibration* I. ix. 253 The pin is shown making contact with the cone every other cycle of the latter, and therefore responding in the octave subharmonic mode.

sub-head. Add: **3.** (Examples from newspaper journalism.)

1889 T. CAMPBELL-COPELAND *Ladder of Journalism* vi. 42 The first line..should consist of from twelve to fifteen letters, presenting in the briefest form..the subject of the article; beneath which, the sub-head of twelve words or thereabouts, making a line and a half, should be placed. **1927** *Amer. Speech* II. 239/2 For a very long story, 'subheads' are usually provided, brief crosslines in bold face type the same size as the body type. **1961** C. WILLOCK *Death in Covert* xii. 203 One headline said: *Regency rakes ride again,* and the sub-head to the same story complained: *Last time a man was blown up.* **1979** D. ANTHONY *Long Hard Cure* vii. 64 The news story..was on the front page, under the subhead: *Maniac claims fourth victim.*

Hence **su·bhead** *v. trans.*, to furnish with a sub-heading; also *fig.*

1877 *Harper's Mag.* Dec. 45/2 One of them was heading and sub-heading cable dispatches from the seat of war. **1949** *Scrutiny* XVI. 52 He [*sc.* C. E. M. Joad] contrasts the present period, which he subheads as 'foreheads defiantly low', with the happy time of his youth. **1978** W. WHITE in W. Whitman *Daybks. & Notebks.* II. 415 The account, which totals more than 26 column inches in the *Times,* ends with a section subheaded 'The Poet Greets His Friends'.

subheading. (Earlier example.)

1874 *Catal. Apprentices' Libr.* (N.Y.) p. v, Headings containing a large number of titles are subdivided into sub-headings to facilitate reference.

sub-human, *a.* Add: **1. b.** as *sb.* One who is less than human; a person of sub-human instincts.

1957 R. CAMPBELL *Portugal* iv. 62 This..moray..was fed chiefly on recalcitrant slaves..devoured before the gloating eyes of the subhuman who was its owner. **1970** G. JACKSON *Let.* in *Soledad Brother* (1971) 247 Would you like to know a subhuman... I'm not a very nice person...more kin to the cat than anything else, the big black one.

Hence **sub-huma·nity,** the quality of being sub-human, less than human existence; (*rarely*) a level of creation below the human race; **sub-hu·manly** *adv.*, in a sub-human manner, bestially.

1909 G. B. SHAW in *Nation* 28 Aug. 787/2 Mr. Chesterton..finally excogitates, as a proof of my superhumanity or sub-humanity, exactly the reason that would have been given by one of Wellington's private soldiers. **1929** A. HUXLEY *Do what You Will* 75 They live..subhumanly..they sink..towards a repulsive subhumanity. **1939** J. CARY *Mister Johnson* 157 They have become a new kind of creature, a sort of subhumanity which can smile and eat and live at a level of corruption and misery which would kill a real human being. **1966** 'H. MACDIARMID' *Company I've Kept* ii. 50 As soon as you make allowances..then you are opening the floodgate for mediocrity and..you are submerged under a tide of subhumanity. **1970** G. GREER *Female Eunuch* 262 Is it too much to ask that women be spared the daily struggle for superhuman beauty in order to offer it to the caresses of a subhumanly ugly mate?

su:b-irriga·tion. [SUB- 2 a.] The irrigation of land from beneath the surface, esp. by means of underground channels or pipes.

1880 *News & Press* (Cimarron, New Mexico) 19 Aug. 1/6 Sub irrigation for wheat would be too expensive. **1904** *Bull. Bur. Census, U.S. Dept. Comm. & Labor* No. 16. 25/1 In one of the systems of subirrigation the water is carried through pipes 14 inches below the surface. **1930** *Amer. Speech* VI. 11 Subirrigation is accomplished by allowing water to stand in deep ditches from which it soaks laterally. **1979** R. ADAMS et al. *Dry Lands* viii. 116/1 Sub-irrigation..is normally achieved either by creating an artificial water-table just below the ground surface or by burying a drip irrigation system or a network of perforated pipes.

Hence **subi·rrigate** *v. trans.* (also *absol.*), **subi·rrigated** *ppl. a.*

1903 [in Dict. s.v. SUB- 2 a]. **1933** *Nat. Geogr. Mag.* Feb. 189 (*caption*) The soil is remarkably fertile and is subirrigated by springs in the surrounding hills. **1950** H. B. ROE *Moisture Requirements in Agric.* viii. 229 On Elgin Bench..the subirrigated district includes an area of about 60,000 acres. **1976** D. GOLDBERG et al. *Drip Irrigation* i. 10 Drainage systems were utilized to function as a double action system, draining surplus water yet sub-irrigating through the same medium in a reverse operation.

subitaneous, *a.* Add: **b.** *Biol.* Of the egg of a small aquatic invertebrate: hatching soon after it is laid. Cf. *resting egg* s.v. *RESTING *ppl. a.* 1 b.

1950 *Adv. Genetics* III. 240 From the fertilized eggs (the ephippial eggs) there emerge, after a shorter or longer resting period, exclusively females, the eggs of which (the subitaneous eggs) develop parthenogenetically in the brood chamber of the female. **1979** *Nature* 30 Aug. 722/1 Both quick-hatching (subitaneous) and resting eggs are produced but neither kind was believed to be fertilised, though in *Chaetonotus* two types of subitaneous egg have been reported.

subitize (sɒ·bitəiz), *v. Psychol.* [f. L. *subitus* SUBITE *a.* + -IZE.] *intr.* and *trans.* To apprehend immediately (the number contained in a small sample). Hence **su·bitizing** *vbl. sb.*

1949 E. L. KAUFMAN et al. in *Amer. Jrnl. Psychol.* LXII. 520 A new term is needed for the discrimination of stimulus-numbers of 6 and below... The term proposed is *subitize*... We are indebted to Dr. Cornelia C. Coulter, the Department of Classical Languages and Literatures, Mount Holyoke College, for suggesting this term. *Ibid.*, If no discontinuities had appeared in the results, no distinction between subitizing and estimating could have been drawn. **1971** *Jrnl. Gen. Psychol.* Jan. 121 The number of items in an array capable of being subitized. **1981** *Nature* 15 Oct. 569/2 Judgements of 'small' numerosities..are ordinarily attributed to subitizing.

subject, *sb.* Add: **III. 16.** (Earlier example.) Also, *first* (*second*) *subject*, the primary (or subsidiary) theme of a composition, esp. in sonata-form; (earlier and later examples).

1752 C. AVISON *Ess. Mus. Expression* I. ii. 28 In the greater Kinds of musical Composition, there is a principal or leading *Subject* or Succession of Notes, which ought to prevail, and be heard throughout the whole Composition. **1771** C. BURNEY *Present State Mus. in France & Italy* 49 The first subject is judiciously returned to while it still vibrates on the ear. **1876** STAINER & BARRETT *Dict. Mus. Terms* 411/1 In sonata form there should be two chief subjects, called first and second. **1883** GROVE *Dict. Mus.* III. 752/1 The Father of the Symphony [*sc.* Haydn] enriched his new Art-form with a Second Subject, so constructed as to enhance the beauty of the Primary Theme by the introduction of some form of expression distinctly opposed to it. **1955** J. F. RUSSELL in H. Van Thal *Fanfare for Ernest Newman* 148 It is difficult to remember a Mozart first subject, for example, in which the common chord is not melodically employed. **1977** *Gramophone* June 90/2 Walton brilliantly exploits every conceivable kind of antiphony..the Worcester Cathedral choristers angelically distanced in the gentle second-subject at 'The glorious company of the Apostles'.

IV. 18. a. (sense 8) *subject clause, complement,* (also 13) *-oriented* adj.; (sense 13) *subject-changer*; (sense 14) *subject card, catalogue* (earlier example), *cataloguing, entry* (earlier example), *heading, index* (earlier example), *list* (earlier example), *reference* (earlier example); **subject-term** *Logic* = sense 7 b.

1869 C. A. CUTTER in F. L. Miksa *Charles Ammi Cutter* (1977) II. xxiv. 168 The subject-cards would..be copied from these author-cards. **1982** D. L. FOSTER *Managing Catalog Department* (ed. 2) iii. 72 The best way to divide the catalog..is to divide the subject cards from the others within each drawer. **1873** M. DEWEY in G. Dawe *Melvil Dewey* (1932) 323 By this plan any books may be found without a catalogue since the library is in itself a full classed subject catalogue. **1900** E. W. HULME in *Libr. Assoc. Rec.* 5 Nov. 571 (*heading*) Principles of dictionary subject-cataloguing in scientific and technical libraries. **1748** RICHARDSON *Clarissa* (1785) II. 160 But I asked him, If he had any news by his last letters from London: A question which he always understands to be a *subject-changer*; for otherwise I never put it. **1978** I. MURDOCH *Sea* 164 'Been to Ireland lately?' This always set Perry off and was a guaranteed subject-changer. **1957** R. W. ZANDVOORT *Handbk. Eng. Gram.* III. vi. 165 *What*..may introduce a subject clause, an object clause,..a predicative clause, or a clause preceded by a preposition. **1939** H. E. PALMER *Gram. Spoken Eng.* (ed. 2) II. 80 A certain number of adverbs may be used as subject-complements, i.e. as complements to..verbs of incomplete predication. **1869** C. A. CUTTER in *N. Amer. Rev.* CVIII. 115 In the New Catalogue, on the contrary, the subject entry is the fullest. **1874** *Catal. Libr. Mercantile Libr. Assoc. San Francisco* p. vi, Subject-headings, when there are two or more titles, are denoted by a separate line in the same [fount]. **1973** M. AMIS *Rachel Papers* 60, I indent subject-headings, co-ordinate footnotes, mark cross-references in red and blue biros. **1861** *Catal. N.-Y. State Libr.: Gen. Libr., 1st Suppl.* p. xii, *Subject-Index.*—In the Index following the catalogue, the subjects of the books are arranged alphabetically. **1875** C. A. CUTTER in *Nation* 14 Oct. 252/1 'Analysis'—that is, reference under subjects to topics discussed in certain books incidentally but not at sufficient length to justify the insertion of the book in the subject-list. **1964** *Language* XL. 77 Middle voice embraces at least five subtypes: (1) subject-oriented action, [etc.]. **1975** *Language for Life* (Dept. Educ. & Sci.) xii. 189 The primary school teacher is likely to conceive of his task in terms of integrated rather than subject-oriented work. **1876** *Public Libr. in U.S.A.* (U.S. Bureau Educ.) I. xxvii. 542 A dictionary catalogue (author- and anonymous-title entries with imprints,.. subject-references to the classed part). **1880** W. H. S. MONCK *Introd. Logic* v. 39 A particular proposition is not limited to some *only* of the objects denoted by the subject-term. **1980** A. KENNY *Aquinas* ii. 34 The word 'substance' can be used to refer to the thing that sentences such as the above are about: the object for which the subject-term of the sentences stands.

b. Used appositively in senses 7–9, as *subject-object, -predicate, -verb* adjs.

1933 *Jrnl. Philos.* XXX. 65 We have described those features of subject-object situations whereby the narrowness of a point of view is escaped. **1936** J. R. KANTOR *Objective Psychol. Gram.* xvi. 222 The logical essense of these cases can be clearly discerned in the fact that the nominative and accusative are subject-object cases. **1977** DOUGLAS & JOHNSON *Existential Sociol.* p. xi, Experimental or other methodological protocol can produce the so-called subject-object dualism. **1900** B. RUSSELL *Leibnitz* ii. 12 The question whether all propositions are reducible to the subject-predicate form is one of fundamental importance to all philosophy. **1980** A. KENNY *Aquinas* ii. 51 Sentences which are of subject-predicate form. **1935** G. K. ZIPF *Psycho-Biol. of Lang.* v. 234 One cannot determine *a priori* what actual proportion of spoken English consists of simple subject-verb sentences. **1979** *Amer. Speech 1976* LI. 134 Of the nine problems covered, subject-verb agreement receives a thorough treatment.

su·bjecthood. [-HOOD.] **1.** [SUBJECT *sb.* I.] The state or condition of being a subject; = SUBJECTION 2.

1927 C. C. MARTINDALE *Christ is King* v. 93 The vast duty of our subjecthood almost narrows itself to this. **1968** *Economist* 17 Feb. 16/1 In the Kenya independence settlement devised by Mr Duncan Sandys in 1963,..they were offered the chance either to acquire Kenyan citizenship, or to have full rights of British subjecthood, including passports.

2. *Gram.* [SUBJECT *sb.* II.] The state of being a subject (of a sentence, etc.).

1976 *Classical Q.* XXVI. 38 The 'with' idiom expresses not the idea of means, but rather that of subjecthood or even agency. **1979** *Trans. Philol. Soc.* 223 The insertion of this reciprocal marker is shown to be sensitive to the transitive subjecthood, either actual or at some initial stage of derivation, of the affix it replaces.

subjective, *a.* **4. d.** (Earlier example.)

1853 J. S. LE FANU in *Dublin Univ. Mag.* Dec. 723/1 Was this singular apparition..the invention of my poor stomach? Was it, in short, *subjective* (to borrow the technical slang of the day) and not the palpable aggression and intrusion of an external agent?

subjectivistic, *a.* (Earlier example.)

1884 W. JAMES in *Unitarian Rev.* Sept. 210, I will.. speak rather of *subjectivism*, and the *subjectivistic* point of view.

subjectivity. 4. (Earlier example.)

1854 A. G. HENDERSON tr. *V. Cousin's Philos. Kant* viii. 177 The subjectivity of human reason; this it is that troubles Kant.

subjee. Add: Also **sabji, sabzi, subzee.** (Earlier and later examples.)

1826 W. AINSLIE *Materia Indica* II. II. i. 39 Banghie.. (Tam[ool])... Subjah..(Duk[hanie] and Hind[oostanie]). **1883** W. DYMOCK *Vegetable Materia Medica of Western India* 603 Cannabis sativa, Linn., Var. Indica... Leaves, Bháng, Siddhi, Sabzi (Hind. Beng. and Bomb.). **1893** —— et al. *Pharmacographia Indica* III. 320 *Sabzi* or *Sabji*, an infusion of Bhang with black pepper, anise and sugar. In Bengal milk, and cucumber and melon seeds are added. **1938** R. P. WALTON *Marihuana* xi. 190 Bhang. Also known as Subjee—is the larger leaves and capsules of the cannabis compressed in balls and sticky layers with here and there some flowers between. *Ibid.* 195 *Subzee*, an infusion of bang.

subjunct (sɒ·bdʒɒŋkt). *Gram.* [f. L. *subjunctus*, pa. pple. of *subjungĕre* SUBJOIN *v.*: cf. ADJUNCT *ppl. a.* and *sb.*] In Jespersen's terminology, a word or group of words of the third rank of importance in a phrase or sentence. Cf. *PRIMARY *sb.* 9, *ADJUNCT *sb.* 5 b.

1914 O. JESPERSEN *Mod. Eng. Gram.* II. xii. 283 The adjunct in *perfect simplicity* is a shifted subjunct of the adjective contained in the substantive *simplicity*, cf. *perfectly simple.* We may call these *shifted subjunct-adjuncts.* **1924** —— *Philos. Gram.* vii. 97 For tertiary we may use the term *subjunct*, and quaternary words.. may be termed *sub-subjuncts.* **1935** [see *ADJUNCT *sb.* 5 b].

subjunctive, *sb.* Add: **1. b.** *Comb.*, as **subjunctive-equivalent,** an expression which conveys the subjunctive mood by a construction involving an auxiliary verb and an infinitive.

1927 E. A. SONNENSCHEIN *Soul of Grammar* ii. 87 Modern English makes a large use of 'subjunctive-equivalents,' e.g. expressions formed by combining a tense..of the verbs 'shall', 'will', 'may', 'let', with an infinitive. **1965** F. BEHRE in *English Studies* Apr. 89 But now is perhaps the right moment to question the fitness of using the term 'subjunctive-equivalent' in contemporary English.

su·blanguage. [SUB- 5 c.] A specialized language or system of notation that occurs only in certain contexts or is used only by certain people among those who speak the same ordinary language.

1934 WEBSTER, *Sublanguage*, a subordinate language; a dialect. **1951** J. HOLLOWAY *Lang. & Intell.* x. 182 These sub-languages include arithmetic and geometry..; chess notation; musical notation [etc.]. **1966** M. GROSS in *Automatic Transl. of Lang.* (NATO Summer School, Venice, 1962) 134 Of course a translation from L_1 to L_2 need not be an exact mapping between L_1 and L_2, but there may be a large sublanguage of L_2. **1972** *Science* 23 June 1304/3 In a sub-language..such as the jargon of surgeons, the information is carried mainly by the kernels. **1973** G. W. TURNER *Stylistics* i. 26 Such sub-languages as the language of telegrams, newspaper headlines, advertisements or knitting patterns.

sub-le·thal, *a.* [SUB- 19, 20.] **a.** *Med.* Of a drug, treatment, etc.: having an effect (only just) less than lethal.

1896 [in Dict. s.v. SUB- 20 g]. **1910** HANSON & ZINSSER *Textbk. Bacteriol.* xii. 195 (*heading*) Active immunization with sublethal doses of fully virulent bacteria. **1937** *Ann. Reg. 1936* 59 Experimental epidemiologists showed the importance of latent and sub-lethal infection. **1947** *Radiology* XLIX. 303/1 At sublethal doses, the minimum granulocyte count occurs at about the same time as in non-survivors. **1977** J. L. HARPER *Population Biol. Plants* xvi. 493 These are the pathogens that kill young seedlings,..that convert sub-lethal damage done by other causes into lethal damage.

b. *Genetics.* Of an allele or a chromosomal abnormality: = *SEMI-LETHAL *a.*

1935 *Jrnl. Heredity* XXVI. 357/2 Hadley reported the inheritance of a sub-lethal, hairless defect in Holsteins [*sc.* a breed of cattle]. **1946** *Nature* 16 Nov. 722/2 When a gene is sublethal, as are those for hæmophilia and achondroplasic dwarfism, its elimination by natural selection is in approximate equilibrium with its appearance by mutation. **1961** R. D. BAKER *Essent. Path.* xi. 274 'Sublethal genes' are those which produce malformations compatible with life in the uterus but responsible for death soon after birth.

Hence **suble·thally** *adv.*

1958 *Science* 4 July 32 (*heading*) Delayed deaths in sublethally X-rayed F_1 hybrid mice injected with parental strain spleen cells. **1978** *Nature* 13 Apr. 625/2 Sublethally irradiated adult BALB/c mice.

sublimate, *v.* Add: **5. c.** *trans.* in *Psychoanal.* To refine or direct (instinctual energy), esp. that of the sexual impulse, so that it is manifested in more socially acceptable ways. Also *absol.* and *intr.*

1910 J. J. PUTNAM in A. A. Brill tr. *Freud's Three Contrib. Sexual Theory* p. vii, The instincts with which every child is born..may be refined ('sublimated')..into energies of other sorts. **1916** C. E. LONG tr. *Jung's Coll. Papers Anal. Psychol.* 141 Here we are confronted by an energetic effort to sublimate the fear into an eager desire for knowledge. **1921** R. MACAULAY *Dangerous Ages* vi. 112 You have some bad complexes, which must be sublimated. **1953** J. STRACHEY et al. tr. *Freud's Compl. Psychol. Wks.* VII. 50 The perversions..—by being 'sublimated'—are destined to provide the energy for a great number of our cultural achievements. **1967** M. L. KING *Trumpet of Conscience* iv. 69 This rare opportunity for bloodletting was sublimated into arson. **1974** 'S. WOODS' *Done to Death* 195 If she had guilt feelings..she might have sublimated them this way.

absol. and *intr.* **1933** J. JASTROW *House that Freud Built* vi. 136 We sublimate as we grow in psychic stature. **1955** H. HARTMANN in A. Freud *Psychoanal. Study of Child* X. 12 Melanie Klein..equates the capacity to cathect ego activities with libido with the capacity to sublimate. **1973** H. MCLEAVE *Question of Negligence* xxiii. 183 Some boy jilted her..thirty years ago. Now she sublimates like mad and expends all her pent-up emotion on her patients.

sublimating *vbl. sb.* (examples in *Psychoanal.*).

1913 E. JONES *Papers on Psycho-Anal.* xx. 416 (*heading*) The value of sublimating processes for education and re-education. **1923** J. S. HUXLEY *Ess. Biologist* vii. 276 Dominant ideas at work in the sublimating process.

sublimated, *ppl. a.* Add: **4.** *Psychoanal.* Of a (sexual) instinct, feeling, etc.: that has been refined and made more socially acceptable.

1911 *Amer. Jrnl. Psychol.* XXII. 436 If the transference is successful, be it a purely erotic feeling, or a sublimated one of respect.., there springs up the feeling of sympathy. **1923** J. S. HUXLEY *Ess. Biologist* vii. 271 A sublimated instinct has more and higher values attached to its satisfaction than one unsublimated. **1951** E. JONES *Ess. in Applied Psychol.* II. xiii. 320 A given sublimated interest ..may represent one of the described stages. **1966** G. ONN tr. *Wyss's Depth Psychol.* I. ii. 194 Sublimated ideas may also temporarily sink back into the unconscious, regress and become symbols of complexes.

sublimation. Add: **5. c.** *Psychoanal.* The refining of instinctual energy, esp. that of the sexual impulse, and its manifestation in ways that are socially more acceptable.

1910 A. A. BRILL tr. *Freud's Three Contrib. Sexual Theory* 58 It must be through these roads that the attraction of the sexual motive powers to other than sexual aims, the sublimation of sexuality, is accomplished. **1920** B. LOW *Outl. Psycho-Anal.* (ed. 2) iii. 81 If the sublimation-process can afford an adequate outlet for the psychic energy accompanying the primitive desires, we achieve a fairly satisfactory adjustment. **1925** I. A. RICHARDS *Princ. Lit. Crit.* xxxi. 232 If we do not extend the 'sublimation' theory too far..it may be granted that in some cases the explanation is in place. **1943** H. READ *Educ. through Art* vi. 177 Sublimation is thus the transformation of instinctive egoistic drives, wishes and desires onto socially useful or socially approved thoughts, ideals and activities. **1957** G. FABER *Jowett* v. 84 [His] extraordinary energy..may, perhaps, have been derived..from a perpetual 'sublimation' of the energy which most men release in acts of sex. **1977** R. L. WOLFF *Gains & Losses* vii. 404 *Zoe*..is the first novel to sound the notes which novelists were so often to repeat. Scepticism of Christian evidences, sublimation of doubt in sex, [etc.].

6. b. *Psychoanal.* The result of the refinement or transmutation of sexual or instinctual energy.

1926 *Internat. Jrnl. Psycho-Anal.* VII. 44 Thus Leonardo's genital activity..was wholly merged in his sublimations. **1955** H. HARTMANN in A. Freud *Psychoanal. Study of Child* X. 13 We know much more about the origin of specific contents of sublimations. **1973** *Jrnl. Genetic Psychol.* Mar. 153 It is out of the basic societal repression/inhibition of drives that sublimations are born.

Hence **sublima·tional** *a.*

1934 in WEBSTER. **1935** *Mind* XLIV. 348 Sublimational, substitutional or Changeling psychology may be Freudian, but it surely is not the only 'scientific' psychology. **1943** A. HUXLEY *Let.* 4 Mar. (1969) 487 A revival of cerebrotonic philosophy in some..form, with a practical system of sublimational outlets, seems to be the only hope.

sublimatory, *a.* Restrict † *Obs.* to senses in Dict. and add: **3.** *Psychoanal.* Pertaining to sublimation of instinctual energy or of the sexual drive.

1943 A. STRACHEY *New Ger.-Eng. Psycho-Anal. Vocab.* 66 Relating to sublimation; sublimatory. E.g...sublimatory processes. **1955** H. HARTMANN in A. Freud *Psychoanal. Study of Child* X. 16 We will tend to see in sublimation..a continuous process which..does not exclude temporary increases or decreases in sublimatory activities. **1968** *Psychoanal. Rev.* LV. 10 This concrete orientation occurred along with a reduced capacity for fantasy release or other sublimatory behavior. **1981** *Internat. Jrnl. Psychoanalytic Psychotherapy* VIII. 461 The newly liberated creative capacity permitted an important sublimatory release.

subliminal, *a.* Add: **c.** In collocations which denote exploitation of the idea that people can be unconsciously influenced by messages or other stimuli projected just below the threshold of awareness, as *subliminal advertising, propaganda,* etc.

1957 *Times* 18 Sept. 9/5 The report in your columns to-day from your New York Correspondent on subliminal advertising must be taken as a timely warning of an encroachment, if not upon the physical freedom, certainly upon the free will of the cinema and television audiences of the near future. **1957** *Technology* Nov. 328/4 The process—christened 'subliminal projection' because the message is transmitted at sub-threshold intensities—is ready for commercial exploitation. *Ibid.* 334/4 'Subliminal' propaganda—briefly flashing a suggestion on a cinema or television screen for subconscious observation. **1958** *Times* 5 July 7/2 A committee of the Institute of Practitioners in Advertising has reported on the subject of 'subliminal communication'. **1968** *Punch* 23 Oct. 563/1 Won't it [*sc.* the Government] use every trick in the book —including subliminal TV appeals and pressures—to make us buy more and more? **1975** *Perceptual & Motor Skills* XLI. 847 (*title*) Effect of subliminal stimuli on consumer behavior: negative evidence. **1981** J. E. ALCOCK *Parapsychol.* iv. 72 It is even unclear from the reports whether the increase in popcorn and cola sales occurred only after the exposure to subliminal advertising.

Hence **subli·minally** *adv.*, in a manner which is subliminal or below the threshold of sensation or consciousness.

1892 F. W. H. MYERS in *Proc. Soc. Psychical Res.* VIII. 438 Similar subliminal activity is going on also along the *red to violet* spectrum of which we are supraliminally as well as subliminally cognisant. **1902** W. JAMES *Var. Relig. Exper.* x. 237 Subjects who are in possession of a large region in which mental work can go on subliminally. **1963** *Observer* 7 Apr. 22/2 The way it [*sc.* a book] is presented, with a cover more than subliminally reminiscent of the Leopard. **1977** J. GARDNER *Werewolf Trace* xxiv. 195 They also had a tape on the video link..which Harvester wanted to play through subliminally while Joseph watched the news.

sublingual, *a.* (*sb.*) **A.** *adj.* **1.** Delete † *Obs.* and add later examples.

1958 *Martindale's Extra Pharmacopœia* (ed. 24) I. 67 *Aleudrin*... Isoprenaline sulphate, available as Solution containing 1% for inhalation, and as Sublingual Tablets of 20 mg. **1980** *Amer. Speech* LV. 52 Nitroglycerine sublingual tablets given to heart patients for angina.

Hence **subli·ngually** *adv.*, under the tongue.

1945 *Proc. Soc. Exper. Biol. & Med.* LVIII. 185/1, 4000 units of penicillin in 0·05 gm of zephiran was administered sublingually to a man. **1961** *Lancet* 9 Sept. 587/2 Testosterone was given sublingually. **1980** *Monthly Index Med. Specialities* Feb. 76/3 Lingraine... Ergotamine tartrate 2mg; green tab. Migraine [etc.]... 1 sublingually at onset of attack.

su:b-lingui·stic, *a.* **1.** [SUB- 19.] Not fully linguistic; expressed in a level below that of language.

1933 L. BLOOMFIELD *Language* ix. 148 These shortened forms occur in various languages; their relation to normal speech is obscure, but evidently they represent a kind of *sub-linguistic* communication, in which the ordinary meaning of the forms plays no part. **1956** J. WHATMOUGH *Language* I. 7 May 'thought' be not merely sub-linguistic, but also non-linguistic, or both? **1977** 'A. BURGESS' *Beard's Roman Women* v. 108 I'm American, so there won't be any language problem. Not that there'll be any need for language. Sublinguistic activity, let's call it.

2. [*SUB- 5 c (*b*).] Of or pertaining to a sub-language.

1976 *Amer. Speech 1974* XLIX. 266 The changes involved in these expressions are not sublinguistic.

sublittoral, *a.* Add: (Further examples.) *spec.* in *Ecol.*, applied to the inshore biogeographic zone normally taken as extending from mean low tide to the edge of the continental shelf.

1909 E. WARMING *Œcol. Plants* IV. xli. 172 Sub-littoral 'region':—Ranges from below low-tide mark down to a depth of twenty fathoms (40 metres); here algae of all colours are represented. **1931** [see *PROFUNDAL *a.* and *sb.*]. **1937** T. A. & A. STEPHENSON in *Trans. R. Soc. S. Afr.* XXIV. 360 It [*sc.* a particular zone of a beach] is occasionally exposed to a considerable extent, when maximal spring tides coincide with calm weather. This region we propose to call the Sublittoral Fringe. **1971** *Nature* 9 Apr. 402/2 In the Mediterranean, *Dardanus* inhabits sandy bottoms with some exposed rocks..from sublittoral to moderate depths down to 100 m.

B. *sb.* The sublittoral zone.

1961 in WEBSTER. **1964** V. J. CHAPMAN *Coastal Vegetation* i. 1 So far as algae are concerned, the sublittoral will extend downwards to the point where algae cease to grow. **1980** HISCOCK & MITCHELL in J. H. Price et al. *Shore Environment* II. i. 333 The real downward extent of the sublittoral..is often ignored by field workers.

Hence **subli·ttorally** *adv.*, in sublittoral regions.

1964 *Oceanogr. & Marine Biol.* II. 260 Sublittorally, the distribution of the radioactivity on the sea bottom is not uniform. **1971** *Nature* 9 Apr. 402/2 All are essentially warm temperate to tropical species occurring sublittorally in the Mediterranean, the Eastern and South Atlantic.

sublunar, *a.* and *sb.* Add: **A.** *adj.* **2.** *Navigation* and *Astr.* Applied to a point on the surface of the earth which lies on a line joining the centre of the moon and the centre of the earth, i.e. a point at which the moon is vertically overhead.

1938 P. V. H. WEEMS *Air Navigation* (ed. 2) xvi. 263 The geographical position of a heavenly body is the point on the earth's surface that has the body in its zenith; in other words the substellar, subsolar, or sublunar point. **1971** *Nature* 31 Dec. 537/2 Most large earthquakes occur after the epicentral region has passed the sublunar or subsolar point.

su:b-machi·ne-gun. [SUB- 5 b.] A light portable machine-gun firing ammunition of the same type and calibre as a pistol. Cf. *THOMPSON.

1926 [see *THOMPSON]. **1934** *Sun* (Baltimore) 4 Dec. 3/5 None of these companies manufacture the deadly submachine gun in popular use by criminals. **1942** J. STEINBECK *Moon is Down* 2 Grey-helmeted men who carried sub-machine-guns in their arms. **1951** 'J. WYNDHAM' *Day of Triffids* vi. 112, I dropped down, pulling Jocella with me as the clatter of a sub-machine gun began. **1965** J. A. MICHENER *Source* (1966) 816 Little Vered in her boxlike hat came darting in with her submachine gun spurting. **1973** G. GREENE *Honorary Consul* III. iii. 132 A stranger stood there waving a sub-machine gun at him.

su·b-man. [*SUB- 14 b.] A man of markedly inferior development or capacities.

1921 R. A. FREEMAN *Social Decay & Regeneration* 248 As we are accustomed to speak of a man whose bodily and mental qualities are such as to lift him far above the common level, as a super-man, so we may conveniently refer to one who is to a like degree below the average as a sub-man. **1939** DYLAN THOMAS *Let.* 14 Sept. (1966) 237 Submen from the islands of crabs. **1951** N. M. GUNN *Well at World's End* xxix. 277 The Cromagnons, those sub-men who painted their bisons on the walls of far interior caves. **1964** *Punch* 28 Oct. 655/2 Peter Cook with his sub-man monologues. **1981** P. AUDEMARS *Gone to her Death* vii. 123 What do they do now? Send these apes—these sub-men—to a reform school.

submarginal, *a.* (*sb.*) Add: **2.** [SUB- 19.] Of land: not capable of being farmed profitably.

1930 *Economist* 9 Aug. 272/1 It permits the survival of sub-marginal farms which plainly ought to be driven out of cultivation by the operation of economic forces. **1938** *Encycl. Brit. Bk. of Year* 24/2 In the autumn of 1937 a long-term programme for agriculture was announced [in the U.S.]. It included:..crop insurance, retirement of submarginal land, and price adjustment payments. **1970** E. FLORES in I. L. Horowitz *Masses in Lat. Amer.* ix. 336 Public lands could not be given to anybody simply because they were submarginal.

submarine, *a.* and *sb.* Add: The noun may also be stressed on the final syllable. **A.** *adj.* **1.** Also *fig.*

1917 T. S. ELIOT *Prufrock & Other Observations* 35 His laughter was submarine and profound Like the old man of the sea's. **1925** A. HUXLEY *Those Barren Leaves* v. i. 348 He found himself adding, with a kind of submarine laughter below the surface of his voice: 'Do you think you *can* make an end?'

2. (Further examples.) *submarine boat* (earlier examples.)

Later examples tend to merge with the recent *attrib.* use of the *sb.* (sense 3 b below).

1807 T. JEFFERSON *Let.* 16 Aug. in *Writings* (1853) V. 165, I have ever looked to the submarine boat as most to be depended on for attaching them [*sc.* torpedoes to the cable of a ship]. **1818** *Monthly Mag.* Feb. 46/2 His boat at this time he called the submarine boat, or the plunging boat. **1897** *Knowledge* 1 Jan. 20/1 All the great naval Powers are busily engaged in bringing submarine warfare to a perfect system of attack. **1919** *Daily Mail Year Bk.* 76/2 One and a half year's unrestricted submarine war. **1940** *Times* 11 June 7/4 Someone has blundered—Dr. Goebbels, or the German submarine command, or both. **1979** O. SELA *Petrograd Consignment* 17 The chiefs of the [German] civil, military and naval cabinets..had decided to end the blockade by declaring unrestricted submarine warfare.

B. *sb.* **3. b.** *attrib.* and *Comb.* in many obvious uses. **submarine chaser,** a small patrol boat equipped for military operations against submarines; **submarine pen:** see *PEN *sb.*[1] 2 e; **submarine scout** = *BLIMP 1.

1908 C. FIELD *Story of Submarine* 183 The rise of the Russian submarine flotilla. **1914** C. M. DOMVILLE-FIFE *Submarines* 9 The submarine fleets of England, France, Russia, [etc.]. **1915** W. E. DOMMETT *Aeroplanes & Airships* vi. 75 In place of an enemy camp or railway junction, we get the submarine base or dockyard. **1917** *Daily Mail* 5 Mar. 5/4 Expert officials of the [U.S.] Navy department devised a scheme for placing on board merchant ships.. two or three small boats as submarine-chasers. **1917** *Jane's All the World's Aircraft* 78c The 'Blimp' or Submarine Scout, evolved by the British Naval Air Service. **1931** W. G. CARR *By Guess & by God* 261 Lieutenant Johnson was 'submarine-minded'. He loved them. **1941** *Hutchinson's Pict. Hist. of War* 14 May–8 July 193 Fast revenue cutters of the U.S. coastguard service..are now in service with the Royal Navy as submarine chasers. **1942** *Sun* (Baltimore) 17 Mar. 1/5 That the submarine-killer is not instantly available is due to the same old cause—we did not start early enough. **1954** P. K. KEMP *Fleet Air Arm* 35 The first of the famous S.S., or Submarine Scout, airships. **1959** *Encounter* Jan. 13/1 The Polaris submarine-launched missile. **1975** B. MEYRICK *Behind Light* xiv. 190 They had to raise and lower the submarine nets. **1979** J. SHERWOOD *Hour of Hyenas* xiv. 163, I know Georgiades' boat..former Nazi navy submarine chaser.

4. *slang.* † **a.** A doughnut. *U.S. Obs.*

1916 *Independent* 9 Oct. 77 'Two submarines and a mug of murk—no cow!' orders the waiter. **1942** BERREY & VAN DEN BARK *Amer. Thes. Slang* § 91/25 *Doughnuts,*.. sinkers, submarines.

b. A type of sandwich; = *HOAGIE; *poor boy* (*sandwich*) s.v. *POOR *a.* (*sb.*) 8. Freq. *attrib.* as *submarine roll, sandwich.* Cf. *SUB *sb.* 8 b. Chiefly *U.S.*

1955 *Sat. Even. Post* 1 Jan. 16/2 The submarine is a noble edifice built of meats, cheeses, fish—preserved and pickled—and fresh vegetables and greens, all stuffed into a whole long loaf of bread and laved generously with oil, herb-flecked vinegar and other delicious lubricants. **1961** WEBSTER, Submarine sandwich. **1967** *Amer. Speech* XLII. 279 (*title*) The submarine sandwich: lexical variations in a cultural context. **1973** Submarine roll [see *HOAGIE]. **1973** *Kingston* (Ontario) *Whig-Standard* 11 July 7/2 Who are the biggest fans of the Jaycee beer garden where beer and submarine sandwiches are sold? **1979** *Tucson* (Ariz.) *Mag.* Sept. 68/2 Real bargains in pizzas, submarines and dinner platters.

submarine *v.*: (*b*) *intr.*, to act or move like a submarine (*fig.*); **submariner** (-mæ·rĭnəɹ), a member of the crew of a submarine; **su·b-marining** (also -ī·niŋ) *vbl. sb.*, the use of or activity with submarines; also *attrib.* and as *ppl. a.*; **submarinism** *disused* = *submarining* vbl. sb. above.

1911 *Chambers's Jrnl.* Feb. 170/1 'Ought to prove a tidy job for us, though,' he muttered with some anxiety, 's'long as she don't take to submarinin' first.' **1915** *Times* 1 Feb. 9/3 All is fish which comes into the net of the submariner. **1915** *Glasgow Herald* 30 Mar. 8 The commander of the U16, which sank the British steamer Dulwich and the French vessels Ville de Lille and Dinorah, discussed 'submarinism' from the standpoint of one who had experience. **1915** *Spectator* 13 Nov. 645/2 America's last word as to submarining in the North Sea. **1917** R. LORD *Captain Boyd's Battery, A.E.F.* (1919) 24 *Submarine,*.. let's submarine, etc.—to submerge, to make onself scarce in the presence of impending duty. **1918** G. FRANKAU *One of Them* xxii. 170 That Hand before whose Thumb the Cave-men bow, Whose oiled Palm guides the submarining mermans. **1927** *Westm. Gaz.* 23 May 6/2 The war advanced the study of submarinism and aviation. **1946** G. MILLAR *Horned Pigeon* viii. 96 A submariner named Mike Caplatt produced an original musical comedy. **1966** M. R. D. FOOT *SOE in France* iv. 62 The most active submarining spell. **1971** *Wall St. Jrnl.* 12 Mar. 1/4 Occupants [of a crashing car] could 'submarine' under an inflating bag and thus not be protected by it. **1972** J. BROOME *Convoy is to Scatter* I. 24 Submarining then was a human rather than a technological way of life, full of individuals who stamped one's memory with their character. **1976** J. LEE *Ninth Man* I. 5 If they stumbled into trouble on the beach, they could claim they were submariners. **1981** *Sunday Times* 26 Apr. 3/5 The 10-year-old dummy [in a test of safety belts] 'submarined'—that is, he slid forward under the belt, which tightened across his stomach and around his neck.

submerge, *v.* **3.** Delete 'Now *rare*' and add later examples.

1903 A. H. BURGOYNE *Submarine Navigation* II. 162 Having reached the 'limit of visibility' it becomes necessary to submerge. **1915** *Glasgow Herald* 30 Mar. 8 In the vicinity of the enemy or when weather conditions make it necessary we submerge. **1930** W. FAULKNER *As I lay Dying* 146 We submerge in turn, holding to the rope, being clutched by one another. **1958** J. LEWIS in C. S. Lewis *Lett. to Amer. Lady* (1969) 72 He comes up for air now and then, blows a few pathetic bubbles, then submerges again. **1974** P. LOVESEY *Invitation to Dynamite Party* xiv. 172 Put the boat in diving trim... To submerge, push down the ballast-levers.

submerged, *ppl. a.* Add: **a.** Also *Naut.*, operating or being under water (esp. of or relating to a submarine).

1902 H. C. FYFE et al. *Submarine Warfare* 258 When running submerged the submarine is lighter than her displacement. **1914** C. W. DOMVILLE-FIFE *Submarines* 10 Each of the 1,500 surface warships..carries the means for delivering submarine attacks in its torpedoes and surface and submerged discharging tubes. **1928** C. F. S. GAMBLE *N. Sea Air Station* 311 Their maximum submerged speed was, for a limited period, as much as 9 knots.

c. Engin. *submerged-arc welding*, a method of arc welding with a bare metal electrode in which both arc and electrode tip are entirely covered by a loose flux powder fed to the welding area.

1945 *Industry & Welding* Apr. 78 (*heading*) Submerged arc welding steps up production of invasion boat assemblies. **1952** [see *BURDEN *sb.* 6]. **1975** BRAM & DOWNS *Manuf. Technol.* ii. 57 The submerged-arc welding process must be automatic.

submergence. b. (Earlier example.)

1871 GEO. ELIOT *Middlemarch* (1872) I. I. iii. 33 The secondary importance of ecclesiastical forms and articles of belief compared with that spiritual religion, that submergence of self in communion with Divine perfection.

submergible, *a.* Delete *rare* and add later examples.

1936 *World Petroleum* VII. 246 (*heading*) Submergible barges for Gulf Coast drilling. **1977** *Offshore Engineer* May 98/3 A submergible, electrically driven tide recorder is available from Benthos.

submersible, *a.* and *sb.* Add: **B.** *sb. spec.*, a small submersible vessel designed for use in underwater exploration or drilling or recovery operations, etc.

1959 *Time* (Atlantic ed.) 23 Mar. 56/2 The *Skipjack* is the consummation of a long program to give the U.S. its first true submersible designed primarily for underwater work. **1967** *Listener* 18 May 657/2 Three of the bombs were soon recovered. The fourth—in the sea—nearly eluded an armada of warships, 'submersibles', and 'submarines'. **1973** D. KYLE *Raft of Swords* (1974) vi. 50 An oil company..had..been considering the purchase of a German submersible..small submarines for underwater industrial and defence use. **1980** *Daily Tel.* 14 Nov. 17 The film never gets round to it, being so preoccupied with salvage vessels, submersibles and diving bells, trying to locate, miles down, the dear old Titanic.

su:b-microsco·pic, *a.* [SUB- 14.] Too small to be seen even with the aid of a microscope; also *absol.*

1912 *Chem. Abstr.* VI. 1014 (*heading*) Methods for the recognition of submicroscopic structures. **1938** S. CHASE *Tyranny of Words* iii. 20 The submicroscopic, which we do not consciously see or feel. **1954** *Sat. Rev.* (U.S.) 19 June 48/1 'Reality' is apperceived on three levels: macroscopic, microscopic, sub-microscopic. **1978** H. MCLEAVE *Borderline Case* (1979) xiii. 133 A submicroscopic particle that struck and then went to earth.

Also **su:b-microsco·pical** *a.*; **su:b-microsco·pically** *adv.*

1934 *Amer. Jrnl. Sci.* CCXXVII. 284 A regularly repeated twinning of submicroscopically small units can give rise to an apparently homogeneous crystal. **1949** *Jrnl. Iron & Steel Inst.* CLXIII. 270/2 This heat might melt a sub-microscopically thin layer of metal. **1953** C. WAKELEY *Med. Dict.*, Sub-microscopical. **1954** *Ann. Reg. 1953* 373 The determination of the structure of molecules in the sub-microscopical genes that regulate heredity. **1961** *Lancet* 2 Sept. 546/1 We have to continue the search for the basis of this specificity at the submicroscopical level. **1976** *Dermatologica* CLIII. 209 No submicroscopical alterations of the cytoplasm were found in the interacting cells. **1981** *Acta Crystallogr.* A. XXXVII. 754/1 The diffraction of such submicroscopically intergrown twins is calculated for lamellae and blocks.

submi·niature, *a.* [SUB- 14.] Even smaller than what is described as 'miniature'; very much reduced in size. Chiefly used in *Electronics* and *Photogr.*

1947 *Electronics* June 160/2 (caption) Oscillator circuits of the two units..are printed on the outer surface of a steatite cylinder housing the subminiature tube. **1956** *Spaceflight* I. 28/1 There are two alternative designs, one using subminiature valves and the other transistors. **1968** *Amateur Photographer* 1 May 13/2 Sizes [of camera] below 35mm are usually called sub-miniature. **1977** 'J. LE CARRÉ' *Hon. Schoolboy* vi. 123 Four lozenges of subminiature film..and a battered subminiature camera.

Hence **submi:niaturiza·tion**, the development or use of subminiature devices, esp. in electronics.

1949 *Aviation Week* 11 Apr. 18/1 Not content with 'miniaturization' of electronic equipment for airborne installations, engineers are now utilizing 'subminiaturization' of this material to reduce its size and weight. **1957** *Circulation* XVI. 764/1 The transition from antisubmarine warfare to phonocardiography involved mainly subminiaturization of the transducer and adaptation of the amplifiers to the recording instruments used in routine clinical phonocardiography. **1960** *Analog Science Fact/Fiction* Nov. 108/2, I don't know what genius indulged his yen for subminiaturization,..but he carried it too far.

submission. Add: **1. c.** In legal use, a theory of a case put forward by an advocate. Cf. SUBMIT *v.* 7.

1922 *Westm. Gaz.* 20 Dec. 7/1 In my submission..this woman was called by the police as the only corroboration which they produced. **1923** *Ibid.* 4 Jan. 3/7 It was put to the Court that there should be no difference in the rates of wages for similar work in different localities,..but the Court could not uphold this submission. **1976** *Daily Tel.* 20 July 3/2 In my submission it is nonsense.

submucosal, *a.* Add: (Examples.) Also, = SUBMUCOUS *a.* 2 b.

1951 WHITBY & HYNES *Med. Bacteriol.* (ed. 5) v. 55 The sub-mucosal lymphatic plexus is much nearer to the surface than that of the skin. **1975** *New Yorker* 22 Dec. 75/1 There was no evidence of any intradermal, submucosal, or subcutaneous hemorrhaging. **1978** *Jrnl. R. Soc. Med.* LXXI. 359 The ileal spout was excised and showed a significant submucosal haematoma.

Hence **submuco·sally** *adv.*

1977 *Lancet* 8 Oct. 771/2, 0·5–1·0 ml was injected submucosally.

subna·sal, *a.* **1.** [SUB- 1 b.] *Anat.* (See quots.)

1882 A. THOMSON et al. *Quain's Elem. Anat.* (ed. 9) I. 80 Subnasal or spinal point, the middle of the inferior border of the anterior nasal aperture at the base of the nasal spine. **1951** B. Z. SELIGMAN *N. & Q. Anthrop.* (R. Anthrop. Inst.) (ed. 6) I. 11 *Nasal height*,..the distance between the nasion, which is the point of junction of the nasal and frontal bones in the midline, and the subnasal point, which is the point at which the lower end of the nasal septum meets the upper lip.

2. [SUB- 19.] Not quite or somewhat nasal in tone. *rare*$^{-1}$.

1936 R. LEHMANN *Weather in Streets* I. ii. 39 Cool voice, with an edge of sub-nasal gentility.

subnormal, *sb.* Add: **2.** [SUB- 14: see sense b of the adj., below.] *Educ.* and *Psychol.* One who is below normal in academic or general ability.

1916 L. M. TERMAN *Measurement of Intelligence* vi. 78 Conversely, we may say regarding the subnormals that:—the child testing at (about) 90 is equaled or excelled by 80 out of 100. **1956** J. F. HORNER *Summary of Scientology* 15 The children who get extra attention are the subnormals. **1975** N. O'CONNOR in Kirman & Bicknell *Mental Handicap* iv. 102 The generally slowed reaction time to both visual and auditory, simple and complex stimulus-response situations which characterizes all subnormals.

subnormal, *a.* Add: **b.** *Educ.* and *Psychol.* Of a level of intelligence and general ability which is below a predetermined standard of normality. See also *educationally subnormal* adj. phr. s.v. *EDUCATIONALLY *adv.*

1919 H. WOODROW *Brightness & Dullness in Children* ii. 22 In 1904, the French Minister of Public Instruction made him [*sc.* Binet] a member of a commission appointed for the purpose of organizing classes for subnormal children... How were subnormal children to be positively distinguished? **1935** C. L. BURT (*title*) The subnormal mind. *Ibid.* ii. 77 In another 12 per cent. the parent, though not intellectually subnormal, was more or less unstable. **1940** A. O. HECK *Educ. Exceptional Children* xxiii. 342 Frequently, children are referred to as bright, average and subnormal. **1958** K. LOVELL *Educ. Psychol.* xii. 149 Those whose IQ's are within the range from about 80–55 will usually be classified as educationally subnormal. **1975** N. O'CONNOR in Kirman & Bicknell *Mental Handicap* iv. 102 Within the subnormal group, abnormal EEG was a poor indicator for prognosis.

subnormality. Add: **b.** *spec.* The condition of being mentally subnormal; *severe subnormality* (see quot. 1959). Also *Comb.*, as **subnormality hospital**, a hospital for patients who are severely subnormal.

1935 C. L. BURT *Subnormal Mind* i. 8, I shall restrict myself to those forms of subnormality which seem to be chiefly mental in their origin. **1959** *Mental Health Act* 7 & 8 *Eliz. II* lxxii § 4 (2) In this Act 'severe subnormality' means a state of arrested or incomplete development of mind which includes subnormality of intelligence and is of such a nature or degree that the patient is incapable of living an independent life. **1965** *Mod. Law Rev.* XXVIII. v. 580 Persons who..receive local authority services for sub-normality. **1968** *Economist* 21 Dec. 37/2 Had she been of below average intelligence she could have been sent to a subnormality hospital. *a* **1974** R. CROSSMAN *Diaries* (1977) III. 664 No, out on tour studying the sub-normality hospitals, but I thought I would come down and put in an appearance.

subnu·clear, *a.* *Physics.* [SUB- 14.] Smaller than or occurring in an atomic nucleus; relating to such particles or to phenomena involving them.

1964 *New Scientist* 20 Feb. 458/1 The frontier of physics has lain, since the war, in the field of sub-nuclear particles. **1964** M. GOWING *Britain & Atomic Energy 1939–45* 16 These two theories [of Schroedinger and Bohr]..form the basis of all modern atomic, nuclear, and sub-nuclear physics. **1969** *Times* 5 Feb. 13/7 The classification is part of the conceptual order which physicists are trying to impose on the sub-nuclear particles. **1981** C. H. L. SMITH in J. H. Mulvey *Nature of Matter* iii. 61 In the 1930s..protons and neutrons were the only sub-nuclear particles known.

suborbital, *a.* and *sb.* Add: **A.** *adj.* **2.** [SUB- 19.] Being or having a trajectory that does not make a complete orbit of a planet.

1959 *N.Y. Times Mag.* 11 Oct. 18/1 The moment has come, after months of training, testing and short, suborbital flights, when one of seven carefully chosen men climbs into a space capsule perched high on the nose of an Atlas rocket. **1967** *New Scientist* 16 Nov. 424/1 The Soviet Union seems to have developed a sub-orbital missile, and the implications of the new weapon have been quickly realized. **1977** A. HALLAM *Planet Earth* 28/2 This hypothesis demands that the impact is sufficiently catastrophic to vaporize large amounts of surface and subsurface rock, the gases being ejected into suborbital trajectories.

subordinate, *a.* Add: **2. b.** *subordinate legislation* Law (see quots.).

[**1841** G. C. LEWIS *On Govt. of Dependencies* 52 Legislation is subordinate when the sovereign person or body delegates the legislative power to an inferior authority, which issues or makes the law.] *Ibid.*, A power of subordinate legislation is sometimes *direct*;..the laws made in virtue of it are issued avowedly..by the subordinate legislature. **1901** C. ILBERT *Legislative Methods & Forms* p. v, Chapter III deals with what I have called subordinate legislation, that is to say, that part of the law which is enacted, not directly by the supreme legislature, but under delegated powers. **1917** *Erskine May's Treat. Laws Parl.* (ed. 12) xxiii. 567 Something must be said here of those administrative orders, rules and regulations which constitute what is sometimes called delegated or subordinate legislation. **1975** J. P. MORGAN *House of Lords & Labour Government* ii. 63 An equally important function is their work on subordinate legislation, a subject that requires a section to itself. **1980** *Oxf. Compan. Law* 758/1 Subordinate or delegated legislation takes many forms, rules, regulations, and orders made by Ministers of the Crown, frequently in the form of statutory instruments; [etc.].

subo·rdinator. [f. SUBORDINATE *v.* + -OR.] Something which subordinates; *spec.* in *Gram.*, a subordinating conjunction.

1962 C. L. BARBER in F. Behre *Contrib. Eng. Syntax* 25 Clauses of time.., most of them introduced by *when*..; the next commonest subordinators in these clauses are *until*..and *while*. **1965** *Language* XLI. 242 Connectors are divided into subordinators (subordinating conjunctions)..and coordinators. *Ibid.*, Subordinators link the sentence they introduce with either a preceding or a following superordinate structure. **1978** *Ibid.* LIV. 140 In only one case in our data did we observe Level I possibly in use as a status subordinator between adults.

subpœna, *sb.* Add: **2. c.** In Lat. phrases: *subpœna ad testificandum* [L., in order to testify], *subpœna duces tecum* [DUCES TECUM] (see quot. 1980).

1768 BLACKSTONE *Comm.* III. xxiii. 382 In the hands of third persons they [*sc.* books and papers belonging to the parties] can generally be obtained by rule of court, or by adding a clause of requisition to the writ of *subpoena*, which is then called a *subpoena duces tecum*. **1808** E. H. EAST *Rep.* IX. 476 The precedents of the common subpœna ad testificandum are scarcely more ancient than that of the subpœna duces tecum. **1891** *Weekly Notes* 12 Dec. 195/1 This was a motion..to set aside a writ of *subpœna duces tecum*. **1909** *Law Jrnl. Rep. King's Bench Div.* LXXVIII. 120/2 This case must not be taken as a precedent for any supposed rule that a person summoned on *subpœna ad testificandum* may get it set aside by swearing that he can give no relevant evidence. **1944** *All England Law Reports* (1945) I. 274 The party on whose behalf the motion is made has been required by a *subpœna ad testificandum* and *duces tecum* to appear before the district auditor. **1965** *Annual Practice* I. 881 Any party in any cause or matter may by *subpœna ad testificandum* or *duces tecum* require the attendance of any witness before an officer of the Court. **1980** *Oxf. Compan. Law* 1195/1 It [*sc.* a subpœna] takes two forms, *subpoena ad testificandum*, when the recipient is called to give evidence, and *subpoena duces tecum*, when he is required to bring documents or papers relevant to the controversy for examination by the court.

su·bpopulation. 1. (In Dict. s.v. SUB- 3.)

2. a. [SUB- 7 a.] A population forming part of a larger population. **b.** [SUB- 9.] One derived or originating from some other population.

1959 *Heredity* XIII. 217 This gene flow..prevented the divergence of the two sub-populations. **1961** *Lancet* 9 Sept. 586/2 Serious outbreaks have occurred mainly because substantial poorly vaccinated subpopulation groups have remained—for example, lower socioeconomic groups in the U.S.A. **1964** S. LIEBERSON in J. A. Fishman *Readings Sociol. of Lang.* (1968) 553 Such subpopulations as social classes, juvenile delinquents, racial, ethnic, and tribal populations, age groups, regions, and occupational groups. **1971** J. Z. YOUNG *Introd. Study Man* xxvii. 385 Like all populations, ours is composed of many subpopulations, differing from each other not only outwardly but in their gene structure. **1974** J. W. DRAKE in Carlile & Skehel *Evolution in Microbial World* 53 Microbial subpopulations frequently become extinct. **1979** *Sci. Amer.* Mar. 53/1 Could it be that they represent a subpopulation of tumor cells endowed with the particular characteristics making for successful metastasis?

su·bprogram. *Computers.* [SUB- 5 c.] = *SUBROUTINE.

1947 *Math. Tables & Other Aids to Computation* II. 358 Nor can it [*sc.* a computer] be directed to repeat automatically sub-programs within the same total program. **1965** *Math. in Biol. & Med.* (Med. Res. Council) IV. 205 All the sub-programs that enter into the FIDAC system are listed in a manual, which specifies for each what user-input parameters are required and what values they may take on. **1979** *Sci. Amer.* Dec. 87/1 The most important technique for limiting the complexity of computer programs is the use of subprograms: self-contained pieces of programming that are named, stored in a library and called on to perform their particular computation as part of the execution of other programs.

su·b-range. 1. [SUB- 5 b.] A subsidiary range (of mountains).

1859 [in Dict. s.v. SUB- 5 b].

2. [SUB- 7 c.] A range of values or conditions within a larger range.

1956 A. A. Townsend *Struct. Turbulent Shear Flow* iii. 45 In this subrange [of Reynolds numbers], the motion is independent of the viscosity. **1968** Fox & Mayers *Computing Methods for Scientists & Engineers* iii. 50 The computed value at r_e, and the given $y_0 = \alpha$, . . provide boundary values for solution by linear equations in this first sub-range.

subregion. Add: (Later examples, chiefly in non-geographical use.)

1898 A. N. Whitehead *Treat. Universal Algebra* I. i. 125 A region defined by any ρ independent letters lying in a region of $\nu - 1$ dimensions, where ρ is less than ν, is called a subregion of the original region. **1959** G. & R. C. James *Math. Dict.* 374/1 *Subregion*, a region within a region. **1974** *Nature* 11 Oct. 531/1 The periventricular areas of the hypothalamus were further dissected into four subregions and assayed for adrenaline. **1977** *Verbatim* Dec. 7/2 Cultural maps, such as those provided by Odum and Vance, would have been more useful than his reprinted essay from PMLA in identifying the subregions of the South.

sub-regional *a.* (later examples).

1946 *Richmond* (Va.) *News Leader* 7 Feb. 3/3 The Richmond sub-regional office of the Veterans Administration will be open . . until 5 P.M. **1966** [see *leisure *sb.* 6 a and c]. **1977** *Lancet* 14 May 1054/1 We were surprised to read . . that the treatment of leukæmia should no longer be regarded as regional or subregional.

su·broutine. *Computers.* [Sub- 5 c.] A routine designed to be stored in a computer's memory so that longer, self-contained programs can make use of it any number of times without its being written into the program each time.

c **1946** Goldstine & von Neumann in J. von Neumann *Coll. Wks.* (1961) V. 25 Both . . machines are controlled by instructions punched into several tapes and they can be ordered to switch from one to the other as desired. They are usually referred to as 'master routine' and 'subroutine' tapes. **1948, 1951** [see *routine *sb.* (*a.*) 1 d]. **1956** G. A. Montgomerie *Digital Calculating Machines* xii. 248 We then transfer control to this subroutine whenever it is required, and arrange for its last action to be the transfer of control back to the main programme. **1959** M. H. Wrubel *Primer of Programming for Digital Computers* iv. 100 Use the subroutine for sinh *x* and cosh *x* to construct a program for calculating $f = \sinh (x+y)/\cosh x \cosh y$. **1973** C. W. Gear *Introd. Computer Sci.* iv. 156 Any built-in subroutines and functions required by the program are loaded with it. **1980** R. L. Duncan *Brimstone* xi. 272 'We . . can't handle the master program . . . So we'll attack the subroutines.' . . The computer responded.

sub-Saha·ran, *a.* [Sub- 1.] Situated or originating in regions bordering on the Sahara desert.

1955 *Ann. Amer. Acad. Political & Social Sci.* Mar. 13/1 The fact that sub-Saharan Africa has so large a number of distinguishable languages makes impressive documentation. **1969** *Times* 22 Oct. (Ghana Suppl.) p. i/2 Ghana was the pacesetter for modern Africa when it became the first sub-Saharan black country to move from colonial status to independence. **1978** J. Updike *Coup* (1979) iii. 121 This French villa spun of sub-Saharan materials.

su·bsample. [Sub- 9(*b*).] A sample drawn from a sample.

1909 Webster, Sub-sample, *n.* & *v.t.* **1913** *Econ. Geol.* VIII. 134 Each sample has thus been divided into 10 subsamples which may be used to estimate roughly the probable error. **1939** *Brit. Jrnl. Psychol.* XXX. 76 Burt chose his subsample of persons to be not only equal in average to one another, but equal to the average of all. **1959** H. Barnes *Oceanogr. & Marine Biol.* i. 32 (*caption*) Stempel (Suction) pipette. Used for taking an aliquot from a plankton sample. The sub-sample is contained between the curved part of the plunger and the barrel of the pipette. **1972** H. J. Eysenck *Psychology is about People* ii. 92 The actual mean scores for P, E and N in the general population, and in various sub-samples graded by sex, age and class are known.

Hence **su·bsample** *v. trans.*, **su·bsampling** *vbl. sb.*

1909 Subsample *v.* [see the sb. above]. **1959** H. Barnes *Oceanogr. & Marine Biol.* i. 32 If larger nets are employed then it [*sc.* the catch] may have to be sub-sampled and only a fraction counted . . . There are various ways of such sub-sampling. **1969** R. Lange *Chem. Oceanogr.* v. 79 It is . . useful to organize the numbers of the bottles for subsampling in such an order that [etc.]. **1971** *Nature* 4 June 290/2 They were subsampled for metal analysis and placed 0·8 m above ground in three locations downwind of Swansea.

subscriber. Add: **2. d.** One who pays a regular sum for the hire of a telephone line.

1878 (*title*) List of subscribers (Bell Telephone Co. of N.Y.). **1922** [see *dialling tone* s.v. *dialling *vbl. sb.* 4]. **1934** Haldane & Huxley *Animal Biol.* xii. 272 The telephone bells of all the subscribers would start ringing. **1978** *Broadcast* 6 Mar. 10/2 Viewdata is transmitted along normal telephone lines . . . Identifying the caller, the computer responds with a personalized greeting to the subscriber.

3. Special Comb.: **subscriber trunk dialling,** a telephone service by which subscribers can make trunk calls without the assistance of an operator, by dialling the exchange code and the number required; abbrev. *STD* (see *S 4 a).

[**1950** *Post Office Electr. Engineers' Jrnl.* XLIII. 170/2 If, at some future date, subscriber-to-subscriber trunk dialling is introduced, a national numbering scheme and a translator trunk dialling system may be introduced.] **1952** *Prof. Papers Inst. P.O. Electr. Engineers* No. 203. 1 Subscriber Trunk Dialling in the United Kingdom . . . The possibility of extending the range over which subscribers can dial their own calls has received increasing attention by many telephone administrations. **1979** M. Underwood *Victim of Circumstance* iii. iii. 183 With subscriber trunk dialling and unitemised telephone accounts, it's very difficult to trace calls.

subscript, *sb.* Add: **2. b.** *Computers.* A symbol (notionally written as a subscript but in practice usually not) used in a program, alone or with others, to specify one of the elements of an array.

1957 *Proc. Western Joint Computer Conf.* Feb. 190/1 The programmer may also employ subscripted variables having three independent subscripts. **1966** R. V. Jamison *FORTRAN Programming* vi. 83 We cannot write these subscripts in the usual lowercase manner with an actual lowering of the subscript. Instead we write, for example, X(4), X(7) for x_4, x_7. **1973** C. W. Gear *Introd. Computer Sci.* iii. 145 A three-dimensional array . . is an array of two-dimensional arrays. It is accessed by specifying three subscripts. Thus, if the array is B, we can refer to B[I, J, K]. **1982** R. S. Forsyth *Pascal at Work & Play* xii. 172 Execution errors occur when a program attempts something illogical or impossible . . . Typical examples are division by zero and trying to use a subscript outside the bounds set for the array. **1983** [see *subscripted *a.*].

So **su·bscripting** *vbl. sb.*, the action of providing with a subscript or subscripts; the use of subscripts.

1959 *Communications Assoc. Computing Machinery* Feb. 4/1 Unfortunately, many algebraic languages now in use . . do not allow subscripting of subscripts. **1972** Bergmann & Bruckner *Introd. Computers & Computer Sci.* x. 342 In FORTRAN the subscripting is different; the subscripts run from 1 through *n*. **1981** A. R. Miller *BASIC Programs* iii. 39 A matrix is referenced by its name, which can be a single alphabetic character, or a string of characters. The indices are given as subscripts except in computer programs, where subscripting is not possible.

subscripted (sɒ·bskripted), *a.* [f. Subscript *sb.* + -ed[2].] Having a subscript, provided *with* a subscript; *spec.* in *Computing*, specified out of an array by means of a subscript or subscripts.

1957 [see *subscript *sb.* 2 b]. **1972** W. Labov *Language in Inner City* iv. 153 The subscripted parentheses indicate optional elements that co-occur. **1983** *Daily Tel.* 19 Sept. 12/6 Subscripted variables take the form A(x), x being the value (or address) of the subscript . . . Subscripted string variables, needed to store strings of text, include a dollar sign, thus: 40 LET A$(6) = 'BUG'.

subscription. Add: **10. a. subscription book,** (*b*) (earlier example); **subscription television** (also **T.V.**) *N. Amer.*, a television service which provides programmes for subscribers.

1870 'Mark Twain' *Lett. to Publishers* (1967) 31 You will make the finest success of it that has ever been made with a subscription book. **1955** *How to unscramble Subscription T.V.* (Zenith Radio Corporation, U.S.), Subscription T.V. can provide you and your family with the best of entertainment . . major sports events . . education . . carefully prepared programs for your children . . at a *nominal* price . . when *you* want it . . *if* you want it . . and without ever having to leave the family room of your home. **1962** *Rep. Comm. Broadcasting 1960* 271 in *Parl. Papers 1961–2* (Cmnd. 1753) IX. 259 We now recommend that no service of subscription television be authorised. **1973** C. Sagan *Cosmic Connection* viii. 62 An unmanned roving vehicle on Mars could probably be supported by subscription television.

subsea·, *a.* and *adv.* Chiefly *Oil Industry.* [Sub- 1 e.] **A.** *adj.* Situated or occurring beneath the surface of the sea.

1909 [see *air-borne *a.*]. **1962** *Offshore* July 19 Equipment manufacturers have accelerated their research and development of sub-sea wellheads and auxiliary equipment. **1977** *Financial Times* 1 Apr. 11/1 Figures . . suggest that over the life of North Sea oil development at least $20bn (at current prices) will be spent to make sure that platforms, pipelines, and sub-sea well systems are safe and in good working order. **1980** F. C. F. Earney *Petroleum & Hard Minerals from Sea* iv. 129 The oil companies' interest in subsea completion systems.

B. *adv.* Below the surface of the sea.

1971 *Bull. Amer. Assoc. Petroleum Geologists* LV. 1694/2 The gas-oil contact is at 6,636 ft subsea. **1977** *Offshore Engineer* May 49/1 The top of the reservoir formation is 1,800m subsea.

sub-sequence[2] (sɒ·bsīkwĕns). [Sub- 7 a, *e.] A sequence contained in or forming part of another sequence; *spec.* in *Math.*

1908 [see *oscillatory *a.* 3]. **1958** R. C. Moore *Introd. Hist. Geol.* (ed. 2) iv. 80 The second division of the Huronian Sequence, named the Cobalt Sub-sequence, has an aggregate thickness of more than 12,000 feet. **1972** A. G. Howson *Handbk. Terms Algebra & Anal.* xxii. 109 This definition formalises the notion of a subsequence as a sequence derived from the original sequence by the omission of a number (not necessarily finite) of terms. **1975** N. Chomsky *Logical Struct. Linguistic Theory* ix. 329 The term arrangement of *t** may not be the same as the term arrangement of the transformation *T* defined in terms of *t*, although the latter term arrangement must be a subsequence of the former.

subsequent, *a.* and *sb.* Add: **A.** *adj.* **2. d.** Applied to a stream or valley that has developed its course so as to follow rock that is more easily eroded, and consequently in most cases following the strike of the rock. (Further examples.)

1954 W. D. Thornbury *Princ. Geomorphol.* v. 113 Because of the coincidence of subsequent valleys with belts of weak rock it is usually concluded that any valley which follows such a course is a subsequent valley. This may not be true, for the valley may have been on the weak rock from the beginning. **1970** R. J. Small *Study of Landforms* vii. 233 The most significant feature . . will be the appearance and growth of 'subsequent' streams, which by the process of headward erosion will extend along lines of geological weakness.

B. *sb.* **2.** *Physical Geogr.* A subsequent stream (see sense A. 2 d in Dict. and Suppl.).

1895 W. M. Davis in *Geogr. Jrnl.* V. 144 The Welland, Gwash, Chater, and Eye being parts of consequent streams that have been captured by subsequents. **1956** D. L. Linton *Sheffield* 42 Its headstream the Doe Lea has the aspect of a true subsequent, but from Staveley northwards though it maintains the direction of the Doe Lea this is no longer that of the strike of the rocks. **1970** R. J. Small *Study of Landforms* vii. 234 In an area where the structure comprises a series of anticlines and synclines, one is tempted . . to regard all synclinal streams as longitudinal consequents and all anticlinal streams as subsequents.

su·bsere. *Ecol.* [Sub- 5.] A secondary sere (see quot. 1926). Cf. *prisere.

1916 [see *prisere]. **1926** Tansley & Chipp *Aims & Methods in Study of Vegetation* ii. 19 A new sere beginning after the succession has been stopped by the destruction of some later phase . . we distinguish as a secondary sere or subsere. **1938** Weaver & Clements *Plant Ecol.* (ed. 2) iii. 78 Seres . . on secondary areas, such as lumbered, burned, flooded, or otherwise denuded ones, are termed subseres. **1964** V. J. Chapman *Coastal Veg.* i. 3 Should an area of dune that has developed to forest become destroyed by burning a new succession would arise, but this would be known as a subsere.

subserve, *v.* **3. a.** Delete † *Obs.* and add later *poet.* examples.

1840 Browning *Sordello* iii. 533 Old engagements out he blots For aye: Taurello shall no more subserve. **1968** T. Kinsella *Nightwalkers* 60 We dwell together in urgency; Dominate, entering middle age; subserve, Aborting vague tendencies with buttery smiles.

subset, *sb.*[2] Add: A set all the elements of which are contained in another set. (Further examples.)

1911 *Trans. Amer. Math. Soc.* XII. 285 Among such [compact] assemblages one very important class are those which have the property that the first derived set (*E'*) of every subset (*E*) of (*D*) is closed. **1928** *Amer. Jrnl. Math.* L. 521 In studying these difficulties we are led to the introduction of a new notion of a subset of a point set being connected through the complement of the point set. **1961** M. A. K. Halliday in *Word* XVII. 276 Subsets progressively differentiated as the degree of collocational likeness set as defining criterion increases. **1968** E. T. Copson *Metric Spaces* v. 67 Let *a* and *b* be two points of a subset *A* of a metric space *M*. **1977** J. L. Harper *Population Biol. Plants* xiii. 416 There are 45 species of *Heliconius*, each specializing on its own sub-set of *Passiflora* species. **1980** *Amer. Speech 1976* LI. 165 We cannot always extrapolate from a corpus to the language in general or even to some subset of the language.

subshrub. (Later examples.)

1886 G. Nicholson *Illustr. Dict. Gardening* II. 168/1 Hypericum . . . An extensive genus . . of greenhouse or hardy, evergreen or deciduous, herbs, shrubs, or subshrubs. **1957** R E. Woodson et al. *Rauwolfia* i. 11 The smallest species appears to be . . a truly rhizomatous subshrub only six inches tall. **1980** *Country Life* 13 Mar. 790/1 Among sub-shrubs profitably treated as herbaceous and cut back to the ground now is mint-scented, sunbasking *Elsholtzia stauntonii*.

subsidiarity (sɒbsidiæ·riti). [tr. G. *subsidiarität* (1931, paraphrasing Pope Pius XI in *Rundschreiben über die gesellschaftliche Ordnung* (*Quadragesimo Anno* § 80); cf. F. *subsidiarité* and Subsidiary *a.*] The quality of being subsidiary; *spec.* the principle that a central authority should have a subsidiary function, performing only those tasks which cannot be performed effectively at a more immediate or local level.

1936 B. W. Dempsey tr. *O. von Nell-Breuning's Reorganization of Social Econ.* x. 206 The Pope repeats the same statement . . : 'Of its very nature, the true aim of all social activity should be to help individual members of the social body, but never to destroy or absorb them.' This is the frequently mentioned and famous principle of *Subsidiarity of Social Activities*, also called the principle of *Subsidiarity of Associations*, a fundamental principle of Christian social doctrine. **1964** S. Attanasio tr. H. Küng's *Structures of Church* vii. 215 Is there a *criterion* with respect to the exercise of the papal pastoral office in the individual dioceses? . . Post-Vatican theology developed a criterion: This is the *principle of subsidiarity* which, according to Pius XII, 'is valid for social life in all its organizations, and also for the life of the *Church* without prejudice to her hierarchical structure'. **1967** *New Catholic Encycl.* XIII. 762/1 The principle of subsidiarity is broadly concerned with the limits of the right and duty of the public authority to intervene in social and economic affairs. **1976** J. P. WOGAMAN *Christian Method of Moral Judgment* v. 142 According to the doctrine of subsidiarity, as developed in various papal encyclicals, social problems should be dealt with at the most immediate (or local) level consistent with their solution. **1980** J. H. WHYTE *Church & State in Mod. Ireland* (ed. 2) vi. 163 Concepts such as vocationalism, the principle of subsidiarity, and the danger of excessive State control. **1982** *Times* 18 Sept. 7/5 The 'principle of subsidiarity'—a meaningless or even misleading phrase in English—is being discussed in the European Parliament in connection with eventual revision of the Treaty of Rome. It is defined to mean that the European Community's activities should be limited to those which are better performed in common than by member states individually.

subsidiary, *a.* Add: **1. c.** *subsidiary company*, a company controlled by a holding company. Cf. SUBSIDIARY *sb.* 2 c(*b*).

1916 F. G. UNDERHAY *Income Tax* 272 (*Index*), Subsidiary company. **1928** *Daily Mail* 25 July 18/6 The net dividends received from the Subsidiary Companies amounted to £24,808 1s. 11d. **1970** M. GREENER *Penguin Dict. Commerce* 170 A subsidiary company must state in its accounts the name of its ultimate holding company and the country where this is incorporated.

subsistence. Add: **11.** Also, with reference to the process of farming, esp. on poor agricultural land or with simple technology, merely to maintain a bare living, and without producing a significant surplus for trade, as *subsistence agriculture, crop, economy, farming; subsistence farm, farmer*; (sense 10) **subsistence level,** the economic level at which only the bare necessities of life can be provided; **subsistence wage,** the amount of money a person must earn in order to achieve a minimal standard of living.

1937 Subsistence agriculture [see *cash-crop* s.v. *CASH *sb.*[1] 3]. **1940** Subsistence crop [see *subsistence farm* below]. **1940** E. HUNTINGDON *Princ. Econ. Geogr.* 711 (Index), Subsistence economy. **1962** R. S. THOMAN *Geogr.* III. viii. 150/1 The crudest of subsistence economies need not involve markets. **1971** *World Archaeol.* III. 171 Hunting.. is considerably less important in the overall subsistence economy than foraging. **1940** WHITBECK & WILLIAMS *Econ. Geogr. S. Amer.* (ed. 3) ii. 57 Subsistence crops are found both on tiny subsistence farms and on the commercial plantations. **1951** A. L. ROWSE *England of Elizabeth* vi. 231 He was no mere subsistence farmer. **1980** *Jrnl. R. Soc. Arts* Mar. 175/2 Let us take as an example..a subsistence farmer debating whether to produce a surplus for sale. **1949** W. SMITH *Econ. Geogr. Gt. Brit.* I. i. 44 As long as subsistence farming was practised..price fluctuations had only a limited significance. **1962** *Listener* 22 Mar. 496/1 They are undergoing the transition from subsistence farming to being a landless proletariat. **1978** A. J. HUXLEY *Illustr. Hist. Gardening* i. 13 The final stage of collapse back into subsistence farming after conquest and pillage is..all too frequent. **1923** H. W. B. JOSEPH *Labour Theory of Value in Karl Marx* ii. 44 Marx believed in the so-called 'iron law of wages', in accordance with which there is a constant tendency under capitalism for wages to sink to the bare subsistence-level. **1978** A. J. HUXLEY *Illustr. Hist. Gardening* i. 11 Communities have to raise themselves above subsistence level before they can really afford to grow..plants not strictly utilitarian. **1926** *British Worker* 10 May 3 Mr. Herbert Smith told to running bursts of sympathy the story of the miners' patient struggle to retain a subsistence wage. **1982** *Washington Post* 17 July A4/4 Many..have also, it is alleged, worked long hours for subsistence wages.

subsolar, *a.* Add: **2.** Also *Astr.* (Further examples.)

1910 G. L. HOSMER *Textbk. Pract. Astron.* xiv. 175 If an observer measures an altitude of the sun he locates himself on the circumference of a circle whose centre is the sub-solar point. **1938** [see *SUBLUNAR *a.* 2]. **1970** N. ARMSTRONG et al. *First on Moon* ix. 195 As you get closer to the subsolar point you can definitely see browns and tans on the ground. **1978** PASACHOFF & KUTNER *University Astron.* xv. 409 Because of Mercury's slow rotation, the subsolar point is not always at the same place on the surface and so is not eternally heated.

subso·nic, *a.* (and *sb.*). [SUB- 14.] **A.** *adj.* **1. a.** Pertaining to, involving, capable of, or designating speeds less than the speed of sound. Cf. *SUPERSONIC *a.* (and *sb.*) 2 a.

1937 *Jrnl. R. Aeronaut. Soc.* XLI. 1099 The drag coefficient rises..as the velocity of sound is reached, and.. remains very much higher than the sub-sonic figure. **1946** *Ibid.* L. 907/2 The National Physical Laboratory has examined the possibility of using flexible walls in high-speed subsonic tunnels. **1958** *Times* 9 Jan. 5/5 It is..to carry 95–100 passengers, cruising at high subsonic speeds of around 600 m.p.h. **1973** *Times* 5 Feb. 13/5 Capacity now exceeds demand for subsonic flight in the mass market. **1978** *Jrnl. R. Soc. Arts* CXXVI. 685/1 The breakdown of the direct operating costs (DOC) per passenger mile for a typical subsonic aircraft is indicated in Table III.

b. *ellipt.* as *sb.* An aircraft not made to travel faster than sound. Cf. *SUPERSONIC *a.* (and *sb.*) 2 b.

1970 *New Scientist* 10 Dec. 445/2 This aircraft will cruise at a higher altitude than the subsonics. **1975** *Nature* 31 Jan. 299/1 Ozone reduction could then be kept near the current reduction due to aircraft alone..for fleets up to 4,000 747-class subsonics at 11 km..or 1,000 at 13 km. **1977** *Jrnl. R. Soc. Arts* CXXV. 361/1, I originally planned to cover supersonics as well as subsonics.

2. = *INFRASONIC *a.* 1. Cf. *SUPERSONIC *a.* 1. *rare.*

1961 in WEBSTER. **1976** *Gramophone* Sept. 513/2 Arm mass problems are reduced on record warps, causing less intermodulation and unwanted sub-sonic cone movement of the loudspeakers.

Hence **subso·nically** *adv.*

1962 *Economist* 8 Sept. 944/1 The aircraft have to fly mainly supersonically but in part subsonically. **1977** *Daily Tel.* 12 Dec. 2/7 The Indonesian decision to allow Concorde to fly subsonically through its air space.

su·bspace. [*SUB- 7 e.] **1.** *Math.* A space (*SPACE *sb.*[1] 16*) that is wholly contained in another space, or whose points or elements are all in another space.

1931 H. P. ROBERTSON tr. *Weyl's Theory of Groups & Quantum Mech.* i. 20 $\mathfrak{R}$ is decomposed into mutually perpendicular sub-spaces. **1946** *Nature* 12 Oct. 513/1 He has studied problems of deformation of sub-spaces, of 'imbedding', of automorphism, and of the variation of multiple integrals. **1968** P. A. P. MORAN *Introd. Probability Theory* v. 226 Particular subspaces of the space of all distributions. **1979** *Proc. London Math. Soc.* XXXVIII. 221 Let X and Y both be subspaces of the Hilbert space of all square summable sequences.

2. *Sci. Fiction.* A physical space in which motion and communication are supposed to occur free of their usual limitations, or subject to different laws.

1955 *Mag. Fantasy & Sci. Fiction* Aug. 106/1 The subspace radio had announced his coming, and preparations consonant with his exalted rank had been made. **1976** L. NIVEN in R. Bretnor *Craft Sci. Fiction* 180 *FTL, hyperdrive, hyperspace, subspace*, all refer to means of traveling faster than light in an otherwise relativistic universe.

subspecies. Hence **su:bspecia·tion** [cf. *SPECIATION], the evolutionary development of a subspecies or subspecies.

1942 E. MAYR *Systematics & Origin of Species* vii. 169 Subspeciation, that is geographic variation, has actually brought about the formation of unquestionably new species of birds. **1952** E. O. DODSON *Textbk. Evolution* xvi. 314 Subspeciation is the ordinary prerequisite to speciation in the neo-Darwinian scheme. **1956** PETERSON & FISHER *Wild America* iii. 43 Roger nearly always starts a difficult subject, like..subspeciation, when I'm threading my way through the stickiest London traffic. **1978** *Nature* 22 June 603/1 Four species [of *Plasmodium*]..are stipulated, three of which exhibit subspeciation.

substance. Add: **8. b.** *substance P* (Biochem.): an undecapeptide thought to be involved in the synaptic transmission of nerve impulses, esp. pain impulses.

[**1931** EULER & GADDUM in *Jrnl. Physiol.* LXXII. 80 This standard preparation, which we call *P*, dissolved easily in water to form a practically clear solution.] **1934** GADDUM & SCHILD in *Ibid.* LXXXIII. 1 This unidentified substance has been known in the laboratory for some time as substance P, and will be referred to under this name. **1964** W. G. SMITH *Allergy & Tissue Metabolism* vi. 71 Substance P, which is a pharmacologically active polypeptide.., stimulates guinea pig ileum. **1979** *Sci. Amer.* July 69/3 Enkephalin and another peptide, substance P, have been implicated in pain perception, substance P with the transmission of pain-related impulses and enkephalin with their suppression.

sub-sta·ndard, *a.* [SUB- 14.] **1.** Of a quality or size less than that which is normally or officially regarded as standard.

1909 in *Cent. Dict.* Suppl. **1930** *Daily Express* 6 Oct. 13/1 The famous 'Marshella'..sub-standard [stockings]... Special lot..slightly sub-standard. **1947** *Mind* LVI. 313 A race of philosophers from whom it is the fashion to expect somewhat sub-standard ratiocination. **1952** C. P. BLACKER *Eugenics: Galton & After* 312 The mother is frequently sub-standard mentally. **1964** D. MACARTHUR *Reminiscences* VI. 157 He took a substandard force and welded it into a weapon so deadly as to take command of the air whenever it engaged the enemy. **1975** M. SULLIVAN *Watch how you Go* i. 22 They lived all their long lives under sub-standard conditions, and accepted them.

2. Of speech: not conforming to standard usage; *spec.* employing forms which are widely used but are considered incorrect.

1933 L. BLOOMFIELD *Language* iii. 50 In such communities the non-standard language can be divided, roughly, to be sure, and without a sharp demarcation, into *sub-standard* speech, intelligible at least, though not uniform, throughout the country, and *local dialect*. **1951** TRAGER & SMITH *Outl. Eng. Struct.* 84, *I have knowed* can be called substandard or 'incorrect'. **1964** *English Studies* XLV. (Suppl.). 149 St. Mary's Lane, Lewes, is called 'Simmery Lane' in local sub-standard speech. **1977** *Word* 1972 XXVIII. 264 It is much more prevalent in the north, especially in substandard and rural speech.

3. *Cinemat.* Of film: less than 35 mm. wide; *spec.* 16 mm. wide.

1934 *Discovery* Feb. 47/2 [Films] shot on standard 35 mm film-stock before being reduced to the sub-standard non-flam 16 mm normally required for class-room use. **1940** *Chambers's Techn. Dict.* 818/1 Sub-standard sizes in use are 17·5, 16, 9·5 and 8 mm., as contrasted with the standard 35 mm. **1953, 1959** [see *NARROW GAUGE 2].

substantial, *a.* Add: **9.** (Later examples.) More recently also in a somewhat weakened sense, esp. 'fairly large'.

1957 W. S. CHURCHILL *Hist. Eng.-Speaking Peoples* III. 218 A substantial section of the population, which included the most prominent if not always the most powerful of French citizens, were largely exempt from taxation. **1976** *Sunday Times* 30 May 24/4 (Advt.), It is mandatory that candidates have experience of..the control and motivation of a substantial work force.

substantia nigra (sɒbstæ·nʃiă nəi·gră). *Anat.* [mod.L., = black substance.] A curved layer of grey matter in the brain that extends from the pons to the subthalamic region on each side, separating the tegmentum of the midbrain from the crus cerebri, and forming part of the extra-pyramidal system.

1882 *Quain's Elements Anat.* (ed. 9) II. 315 A section into the crus cerebri shows the two parts of which it is composed to be separated from one another by a tract of dark coloured grey substance known as the substantia nigra. **1923** [see *PARKINSONISM]. **1961** *Lancet* 26 Aug. 446/1 A tiny old hæmorrhage in one substantia nigra, and a small periaqueductal glial scar, were the only focal lesions found. **1976** SMYTHIES & CORBETT *Psychiatry* iv. 41 The dopamine system is divided into several portions. The main one has its cell bodies in the substantia nigra.

substantive, *a.* **1. e.** (Earlier example.)

1854 T. TROUBRIDGE *Let.* 30 Dec. (MS.), I daresay they will make my Brevet rank *substantive* which is the new word they have coined for a *real* Lt. Colonelcy.

su·bstation. [SUB- 7 d.] **1.** A building or establishment subordinate to a principal station or office.

1881 *Rep. Indian Affairs* (U.S.) 45 The temporary establishing of two substations for the police..resulted in the locking up of the offenders. **1891** [see SUB- 7 d]. **1933** *Jrnl. R. Hort. Soc.* LVIII. 162 Only two varieties have been recommended for extended trial at the sub-stations. **1982** 'M. HEBDEN' *Pel & Bombers* ii. 12 The sous-brigadier who ran the substation at St. Blaize.

2. A station at which electrical current is switched, transformed, or converted, intermediate in rank between a generating station and a low-tension distribution network.

1901 [see SUB- 7 d]. **1933** *Archit. Rev.* LXXIII. 2 The scheme of building included..a university sub-station for electric power which supplies the laboratories. **1968** [see *FEEDER 10 a]. **1976** P. R. WHITE *Planning for Public Transport* viii. 162 Substation costs were greatly reduced, and more powerful locomotives permitted.

3. *Telephony.* (See quots.)

1922 W. AITKEN *Automatic Telephone Systems* I. 3 We have, therefore, a *sub-station* at the subscriber's office, which may consist of one, or a plurality of direct lines, or a small switchboard. **1940** *Chambers's Techn. Dict.* 818/1 *Sub-station* or *subscriber's station* (*Teleph.*), a subscriber's telephone located on his premises.

subste·llar, *a.* **1.** *Navigation* and *Astr.* [SUB- 1 a.] Applied to a point on the surface of the earth which lies on a line joining some particular star and the centre of the earth, i.e. a point at which the star is vertically overhead.

1910 C. L. POOR *Nautical Sci.* vii. 154 To find the substellar point..it is necessary for the observer to know the sidereal time at which the observation is made. **1938** [see *SUBLUNAR *a.* 2]. **1967** P. VAN DE KAMP *Princ. Astrometry* ii. 19 The terrestrial longitude and latitude of a substellar point equal the Greenwich Hour Angle (GHA) and declination of the star.

2. *Astr.* [SUB- 14.] Much smaller than a typical star.

1973 *Physics Bull.* Nov. 648/1 The shock wave preceding a black hole of substellar mass could explain both the scale of damage caused and the visual effects observed. **1978** *Nature* 24 Aug. 781/1 The resolution and sensitivity of the spinning infrared interferometer suggest other applications, for example, to cool features other than planets (such as dust rings or substellar companions).

substituend (sɒbsti·tiuĕnd). [ad. L. *substituend-us*, gerundive of *substituĕre* SUBSTITUTE *v.*] A thing that can be put in the place of another, *spec.* in *Linguistics* or *Logic.*

1955 N. CHOMSKY *Logical Struct. Linguistic Theory* (microfilm, Mass. Inst. Technol.) viii. 432 We would naturally expect the substituend Y_1 to play the same role in the overall structure of the sentence as did the term Y_2 for which it is substituted. **1965** *Philos. Rev.* LXXIV. 473 We must have..an appropriate nominal *substituend* of *x*. **1976** *Analysis* XXXVI. 81 The anaphoric substituend of a proform, if there is one, is (possibly a grammatical variant of) its antecedent.

substitutable, *a.* Delete *rare* and add later examples.

1905 W. JAMES *Meaning of Truth* (1909) v. 132 Reality ..is always defined as a terminus within the general possibilities of experience; and what knows it is defined as an experience *that 'represents' it, in the sense of being substitutable* for it in our thinking. **1941** *Mind* L. 167 Both the original word and all signs substitutable for it stand independently for universals. **1961** R. BRAIN *Speech Disorders* v. 57 Even a phoneme is abstract, since it stands for and represents an indefinite variety of mutally substitutable phones. **1980** A. KENNY *Aquinas* ii. 58 It is tantamount to a predicate variable for which no predicate is substitutable.

Hence **substitutabi·lity.**

1907 W. JAMES *Meaning of Truth* (1909) vii. 175 The relations..which we epistemologists study, relations of adaptation, of substitutability, of instrumentality, of reference and of truth. **1922** tr. *Wittgenstein's Tractatus Logico-Philosophicus* 171 Equations express the substitutability of two expressions. **1957** A. C. L. DAY *Outl. Monetary Econ.* xxxi. 395 There may also be a high or low degree of substitutability in consumption in each country. **1979** *Nat. Westminster Bank Q. Rev.* Nov. 33 Each occupation should be compared with a group of workers where there is some close, short-run substitutability i.e. where there is a fair degree of movement between the two labour markets.

substitute, *sb.* Add: **I. 3.** (Earlier examples.)
1777 *Jrnls. Continental Congress U.S.* (1907) IX. 1002 The laws which have been enacted in the State of Pennsylvania, permitting the furnishing of substitutes to perform militia duty. **1779** J. WOODFORDE *Diary* 30 Sept. (1924) I. 266, I let my man Ben have my little Mare to go to Norwich this morning to try to get a Substitute to serve for him in the Militia.

4. b. *spec.* in *Sport,* a player who replaces another after a match has begun. Abbrev. *sub* (see SUB *sb.* 4 in Dict. and Suppl.).
1849 [in Dict., sense 4 a]. **1916** [see *BENCH *sb.* 1 c]. **1951** *Sport* 30 Mar.–5 Apr. 6/1 Of course, the idea of substitutes in both Association and Rugby football is not new. **1976** *Southern Even. Echo* (Southampton) 17 Nov. 23/4 When Saints beat Wolves 6–2 in the Second Division last month, the appearance..of Martin Patching as substitute was lost into obscurity because of the emphatic margin of victory.

II. 5. b. A person or thing that becomes the object of love (or another emotion) deprived of its natural outlet. Formerly only with qualifying noun, as *father, mother substitute*: see the first elements in Suppl. Cf. *SURROGATE *sb.* (*a.*) 2.
1956 L. DURRELL *Justine* I. 78 For her we, her lovers, had become only mental substitutes for this first childish act—so that love, as a sort of masturbation, took on all the colours of neurasthenia. **1964** C. ISHERWOOD *Single Man* 23 Jim is the substitute I found for a real son. **1973** E. CALDWELL *Annette* (1974) II. iv. 50 I'd say that enormous teddy bear is a substitute till some boy comes along with the real thing she's after.

6. e. *Philol.* A word that can stand in the place of another, e.g. a pronoun.
1807 WEBSTER *Philos. & Pract. Gram. Eng. Lang.* 15 *Substitutes,* words which are used in the place of other words or of sentences. **1933** L. BLOOMFIELD *Language* ix. 146 In every language we find certain forms, *substitutes*... In English, the pronouns are the largest group of substitutes. **1958** C. F. HOCKETT *Course in Mod. Linguistics* xxx. 253 The substitutes in this sentence are the morpheme *he* (in the word *his*) and the morpheme *do* (in the word *did*). *He* refers to *John*: it is John's hat which John puts on.

substitute, *v.* Add: **4.** (*c*) More recently, used incorrectly for REPLACE *v.* 3 a.
1974 *Daily Tel.* 25 July 6/7 The tribunal concludes that British Rail's proposal to compensate..at rates of four, five and six per cent. are inadequate and substitutes them with levels of five, $7\frac{1}{2}$ and 10 per cent. **1978** *Maledicta* II. 176 Most commonly they are typically formed by substituting *diavolo* with other terms. **1980** *Coal: Energy for Future* (Shell Internat. Petroleum Co.) 3 OECD coal demand is likely to..grow much more rapidly as national actions to substitute oil by coal begin to take effect.

5. Freq. with *for.* (Later examples.)
1953 [see *FURAN]. **1962** *Listener* 17 May 883/1 But how could it satisfactorily substitute for the complexity and psychological depth abandoned in hacking the novel down to size? **1965** *Language* XLI. 239 A construction.. which may substitute for a word..is a phrase. **1975** *Sci. Amer.* Feb. 36/1 An ion of ferrous iron..can easily substitute for a magnesium ion.

substitution. Add: **7.** Also, the replacement of one atom or group of atoms in a molecule by another. (Further example.)
1964 N. G. CLARK *Mod. Org. Chem.* xix. 381 The typical reactions of aromatic hydrocarbons are those of nuclear substitution, whereby one or more of the available hydrogen atoms attached to the nucleus are replaced by substituents derived from the reagent.

11. *gen.* Replacement (*of* one thing) *by* another. See sense 4 of the vb. in Dict. and Suppl.
1888 [see GRAVITATION 1]. **1938** R. D. CHARQUES *Footnotes to Theatre* II. 89 Some of the advocates of the.. pictorial theatre went even so far as to recommend the substitution of the living actors by two-dimensional puppets. **1969** G. STEDMAN JONES in Cockburn & Blackburn *Student Power* 28 The political upheavals within the university in the last years are not the product of an imaginary substitution of workers by students. **1978** *Financial Results Oil Majors, 1977* (Shell Internat. Petroleum Co.) 7 In Europe, oil products demand declined by 1 per cent due to warmer weather, a generally weak economic performance and substitution by other energy sources, particularly hydro-electricity.

12. Special Comb. **substitution group** *Math.,* a group all the elements of which are substitutions (SUBSTITUTION 5 b); now usu. called *permutation group.*
1889 [see *INTRANSITIVE *a.* 4]. **1916** G. A. MILLER et al. *Theory & Applications Finite Groups* i. 10 It will be proved..that every finite group can be represented as a substitution group.

substitutional, *a.* Add: **2. c.** *Metallurgy.* Of an alloy: involving the substitution at certain lattice sites of atoms of the minor component for those of the major component; *substitutional site,* a lattice site in an alloy at which atomic substitution occurs.
1940 [see *INTERSTICE 1 b]. **1966** C. R. TOTTLE *Sci. Engin. Materials* viii. 186 Where complete or partial solid solubility exists and the solute atoms are too large to occupy interstitial positions, they replace solvent atoms at random in the lattice, and are accordingly referred to as substitutional. **1969** *Physics Bull.* May 167/2 To have the desired effects the implanted impurity atoms must eventually occupy isolated substitutional sites within the lattice. **1980** CHOMEL & COTTU in P. Haasen *Strength of Metals & Alloys* II. 1017 Substitutional alloy softening only results from a thermal component reduction of the flow stress.

substituti·vity. *Logic.* [f. SUBSTITUTIVE *a.* 2 b + -ITY.] The capacity of terms to function as logically equivalent substitutes for one another (see quot. 1965).
1940 W. V. QUINE *Math. Logic* 96 This restriction gives rise..to the following..substitutivity principle. **1943** [see *IDENTICAL *sb.* 1]. **1945** *Mind* LIV. 358 Subject to certain important restrictions pointed out recently by Prof. W. V. Quine, we may accept what he calls the principle of substitutivity as applied to class-identity. **1959** K. R. POPPER *Logic of Sci. Discovery* 343 One of our axioms would become redundant, *i.e.* our axiom of substitutivity. **1965** *Jrnl. Philos.* LXII. 139 Quine, Frege, and Russell approach problems connected with *oratio obliqua* constructions determined to defend Leibniz's Law, the principle of substitutivity, sometimes referred to as 'the indiscernibility of identicals'. **1976** *Language* LII. 3 The sense of 'referential' represented by a pair of heavy parentheses is different from the standard one in terms of substitutivity of identicals.

substrate, *sb.* Add: **2.** *Biochem.* The substance upon which an enzyme acts, i.e. whose reaction it brings about.
1907 *Bio-chem. Jrnl.* II. 143 When the relative amount of substrate is large, catalase is rapidly changed into an inactive form. **1938** [see *ADENOSINE b]. **1962** VAN HEYNINGEN & WALEY in A. Pirie *Lens Metabolism Rel. Cataract* 336 Proteolytic enzymes are often characterized by their action on substrates which are not known to be the natural substrates of the enzyme *in vivo.* **1978** J. R. HOLUM *Org. & Biol. Chem.* xiii. 270 Many enzymes are named by attaching the suffix -ase to the name of the compound, called the substrate, whose reaction the enzyme catalyzes.

3. *Biol.* The surface or material on which any particular organism occurs or grows.
1908 W. M. BAYLISS *Nature of Enzyme Action* ii. 7 A name is frequently needed for the substances on which enzymes exert their activity... On the whole, 'substrate,' already used by many writers, seems to answer the purpose best. **1949** W. C. ALLEE et al. *Princ. Animal Ecol.* x. 158 The surface of water is an important substrate for life, though not nearly so important as the surface of land. **1967** M. E. HALE *Biol. Lichens* iv. 61 A large group of lichens..have high fidelity for limestone and other basic substrates. **1976** *Nature* 15 July p. xiii (Advt.), An order of Crustacea common on sandy or muddy substrates all round the European coasts. **1977** J. L. HARPER *Population Biol. Plants* xxiv. 765 The variations in substrate that undoubtedly occurred..in the field were eliminated by using a standard potting compost throughout the experiment.

4. Any underlying bulk phase, layer, etc., on which something is deposited. Cf. SUBSTRATUM 4.
1937 *Nature* 24 July 158/1 In recent years, the practice has grown up among workers in surface chemistry of using the word 'substrate' to denote the bulk phase underlying a surface film, regardless of the fact that this word has been in general use for a much longer time to denote the substance upon which an enzyme acts. **1954** *Electronic Engin.* XXVI. 296 The applied metal film..adheres well to the substrate. **1960** [see *EPITAXIALLY *adv.*]. **1967** *Times Rev. Industry* May 76/1 The use of polythene in coating paper and other substrates for packaging a variety of goods. **1974** *Physics Bull.* June 225/3 Spiller and Segmuller's x ray waveguide consists of a 30–50 nm thick layer of boron nitride between a substrate and cover layer of sapphire.

substratum. Delete ‖ and add: **5. a.** *Linguistics.* Elements or features of a language which are identified by linguists as being relics of, or due to the influence of, an earlier extinct language, usually of the same region. Cf. *SUPERSTRATUM 2 a.
1922 O. JESPERSEN *Language* xi. 192 Many scholars have recently attached great importance to the..influence exerted by one language on another in those cases in which a population abandons its original language and adopts that of another race... There is thus created what is now generally termed a *substratum* underlying the new language. **1933** L. BLOOMFIELD *Language* xxi. 386 There is no sense in the mystical version of the substratum theory, which attributes changes, say, in modern Germanic languages, to a 'Celtic substratum'. **1956** J. WHATMOUGH *Language* IV. 51 We have superimposed or adjacent languages (superstratum, substratum, and adstratum). **1972** H. KURATH *Studies in Area Linguistics* 120 The phonemic system of Gullah shows some clear influence of the African substratum.

b. *attrib.* and *Comb.,* as *substratum influence, language,* etc.; **substratum theory,** a theory that attributes linguistic change to the influence of a substratum language.
1933 L. BLOOMFIELD *Language* xxi. 386 The substratum theory attributes sound-change to transference of language: a community which adopts a new language will speak it..with the phonetics of its mother-tongue. **1937** J. ORR tr. *Iordan's Introd. to Romance Linguistics* i. 12 An historical summary of the substratum problem. **1952** R. HALL in *Lingua* III. 144 The basic prerequisite for the possibility of substratum influence is a language transfer which takes place through a stage of bilingualism. **1954** *Word* X. 395 Diachronic dialectology deals ..with convergence, i.e. it studies partial similarities increasing at the expense of differences (traditionally, substratum and adstratum studies..and the like). **1962** BURRILL & BONSACK in Householder & Saporta *Probl. Lexicogr.* 189 Words which had the force of generic terms in substratum languages may not be understood as generic terms by the present-day populace. **1973** *Archivum Linguisticum* IV. 110 In regard to the so-called Black English, William A. Stewart was the first to advocate a creole substratum theory. **1980** *English World-Wide* I. 1. 150 It is not legitimate to compare a static description of creole with a static description of a substratum language.

substructure. Add: **su·bstructured** *a.* [-ED^2], having a substructure.
1952 GERTH & MARTINDALE tr. *M. Weber's Anc. Judaism* III. x. 254 Babylonia and Egypt knew no unified, religiously substructured ethic. **1971** *Black Scholar* June 52/2 The substructured prison movements are gaining momentum.

subsumptive, *a.* (Earlier example.)
1807 R. KIRWAN *Logick* II. ix. 521 Those *subsumptive* and illative words, *but, now, therefore.*

subta·bulate, *v. Math.* [SUB- 9.] *trans.* To expand (a mathematical table) by systematic interpolation; to evaluate (a tabulated function) for a set of values of the argument in between the tabulated ones. Hence **subta·bulated** *ppl. a.*; also **su:btabula·tion.**
1924 WHITTAKER & ROBINSON *Calculus of Observations* iv. 57 We may obtain without difficulty formulae for subtabulation based on central-difference formulae. **1936** *Suppl. Jrnl. R. Statistical Soc.* III. 87 The differences of subtabulated values. *Ibid.* 93 Then..the original table is subtabulated over the range required to tenths, hundredths or thousandths. **1947** *Math. Tables & Other Aids Computation* II. 286 He had made independent subtabulations in each interval. **1952** D. R. HARTREE *Numerical Analysis* v. 78 A set of subtabulated values. **1956** F. B. HILDEBRAND *Introd. Numerical Analysis* v. 146 This problem would occur..if a function were initially tabulated for increments of 0·1 in *x* and it were required to subtabulate the function for increments of 0·01. **1975** *Nature* 16 Oct. 541/1 The principle adopted in this project was to compute accurate values at rather widely spaced values of the argument, and to produce values at the required tabular interval by systematic interpolation or subtabulation.

subtee·n, *sb.* (and *a.*) orig. *U.S.* [*SUB- 14 b.] **a.** A child belonging to the age-group next below teenage. Freq. *pl.*
1952 *Amer. Speech* XXVII. 73 Bonds department store, 16 Feb.: Adv. announcing opening of 'Infants to *Subteens* Shop'. **1960** *Twentieth Cent.* Nov. 389 The sub-teens, the pocket-money market,..have never been considered anything but children. **1964** *Discovery* Oct. 31/2 Even the sub-teens of the 1960's interpret all too readily the Freudian symbolism of Peter Pan. **1976** *Publishers Weekly* 7 June 75/1 Subteens and teens with an ambition to get into journalism.

b. *attrib.* passing into *adj.,* esp. with reference to clothing designed for the older preteenage girl.
1953 *Sun* (Baltimore) 22 July 5/5 (Advt.), Very special purchase! Regular 5.98 and 7.98 sub-teen cottons. **1962** *Sunday Express* 4 Feb. 14/6 Dating is now an accepted thing in the age group known as 'subteen'. **1968** P. WELLES *Babyhip* xxii. 151 Armed with enormous shopping bags, they descended on the subteen department. **1978** M. FARREN *Feelies* 146 The sub-teen girls in the crowd went even wilder.

Also **subtee·nage** *a.*; **subtee·nager.**
1959 *New Statesman* 7 Nov. 631/3 He is a pervert.. interested emotionally only in pubescent girls, subteenagers as they are known in American advertising. **1960** P. GOODMAN *Growing up Absurd* v. 117 This is the meaning, surely, of the publicity that has been trumped up for the Little League, the baseball teams of subteenagers sponsored and underwritten by various business firms. **1963** *Times Lit. Suppl.* 8 Feb. 91/4 (Advt.), He lives in Switzerland and is married with two sub-teenage daughters. **1968** *Punch* 3 July 3/2 A friend is worried at Wimbledon's chauvinistic effect on his sub-teenage kids. **1977** *Washington Post* 20 Feb. D4/2 He keeps horses and a pony for two subteenage daughters. **1980** *Ibid.* 5 Oct. A22/3 There are a 'tremendous' number of subteenagers who abuse a variety of drugs and alcohol.

subtense, *sb.* Add: **a.** Also, the angle subtended by a line at a point. (Further examples.)
1958 *Engineering* 21 Feb. 231/3 Fig. 4 shows the composite picture for the Horseshoe Falls, the angles signifying the angular subtense of any part of the Falls at the floodlights. **1974** *Nature* 3 May 86/2 The test strips.. had a subtense of between 1° and 2°. *Ibid.* 13 Dec. 535/2 Stereo blending does not work well when the angular subtense of the line joining the speakers exceeds about 60°.

su·btest. [SUB- 5 c, 7 a.] A test which is subsidiary to or forms part of a main test, esp. (*Psychol.*) in aptitude assessment.

1939 *Brit. Jrnl. Psychol.* July 21 In normal mental test theory there is a test variable (consisting, if need be, of several sub-tests which are used additively). **1961** *Lancet* 26 Aug. 487/1, I also heartily endorse his call for a refinement in the constituent subtests of psychological batteries, so that intellectual functions may be more precisely identified. **1968** W. E. LAMBERT in J. A. Fishman *Readings Sociol. of Lang.* (1968) 480 It is clear from these analyses that the subtests of the Modern Language Aptitude Test..are generally highly correlated with intelligence. **1976** *Word 1971* XXVII. 320 It includes subtests of vocabulary, oral comprehension, sentence completion, spelling, and grammar.

su·btext. † **1.** (See SUB- 3 a in Dict.)

2. [SUB- 5 c.] An underlying theme in a piece of writing (esp. in a novel or play). Also *transf.*

1950 E. R. HAPGOOD tr. *C. Stanislavski's Building Character* viii. 113 What do we mean by subtext? What is it that lies behind and beneath the actual words of a part?..It is the manifest, the inwardly felt expression of a human being in a part, which flows uninterruptedly beneath the words of the text, giving them life and a basis for existing. **1960** S. MOORE *Actor's Training: Stanislavski Method* iii. 27 An artistic, rich imagination will also contribute a great deal when an actor interprets the lines and fills them with the meaning that lies behind, the 'subtext'. **1964** *Evergreen Rev.* Dec. 78/1 The modern style of interpretation..digs 'behind' the text, to find a sub-text which is the true one. **1973** *Times* 2 Jan. 7/8 Also admirable was the manner in which Prince underlined the subtext of naturalism that lies beneath the very obvious symbolic superstructure. **1978** G. VIDAL *Kalki* i. 16 Whenever I got the chance I gave my pitch, which, basically, is the subtext of *Beyond Motherhood*.

subtha·lamic, *a. Anat.* [SUB- 1 b.] Situated below the thalamus.

1882 *Quain's Elements Anat.* (ed. 9) II. 326 The fibres [of the crura]..are seen diverging at the side of the subthalamic tegmental region into the inner capsule. **1962** *Gray's Anat.* (ed. 33) 1025 The floor of the diencephalon..forms the subthalamic tegmental region. This, together with the anterior part of the floor and the immediately adjacent parts of the side wall, comprise the hypothalamus. From the functional point of view, however, the subthalamic tegmental region is usually excluded from the hypothalamus. **1973** *Brit. Med. Jrnl.* 15 Dec. 666/1 A vascular lesion of the subthalamic nucleus results in sudden onset of violent choreic movements in the contralateral half of the body.

subtha·lamus. *Anat.* [SUB- 1 f.] A region of grey and white matter in the brain at the base of the diencephalon, below the thalamus and adjacent to the substantia nigra and the red nucleus.

1920 S. W. RANSON *Anat. Nervous Syst.* xiv. 222 The hypothalamus consists of three parts: (1) the pars optica hypothalami,..(2) the pars mamillaris hypothalami, and (3) the subthalamus. **1946** F. W. JONES *Buchanan's Man. Anat.* (ed. 7) 1378 The inferior surface of the thalamus is related to..the subthalamus, which intervenes between the thalamus and the tegmental part of the mid-brain. **1974** D. & M. WEBSTER *Compar. Vertebr. Morphol.* xi. 261 Just ventral to the dorsal thalamus is the ventral thalamus (sometimes called the subthalamus), which is primarily concerned with somatic motor functions.

Subtiaba (*s*ubtiā·bă). [The name of a village, (San Juan Bautista de) *Subtiaba*, earlier *Sutiaba*, (see quot. 1891): perh. of Nahuatl origin.] **a.** (A member of) an Indian people of western Nicaragua. **b.** The Tlapanec language of this people (no longer spoken), formerly considered to have Hokan affinities but now regarded as Otomanguean. Formerly also **Subtia·ban.** Also *Comb.*, as **Subtiaba-Tlapanec,** a group of related central American Indian languages, including Subtiaba.

[**1878** S. HABEL in *Smithsonian Contrib. Knowl.* No. 269. 24, I proceeded to Leon. Here I collected as many words and sentences as I could of the *Raburochi* language, spoken in the neighboring village of Sutiaba.] **1891** D. G. BRINTON *Amer. Race* 159 The Subtiabas are inhabitants of the valley of that name near the modern city of Leon in Nicaragua. **1911** THOMAS & SWANTON *Indian Languages of Mexico & Central Amer.* 77 Mangue..was the most northwesterly tribe of the series, the area occupied extending..northwards from the territory of the Subtiaba (Squier's Nagrandans) 'along the Gulf of Fonseca'... *Subtiaban* (*Synonyms*: Nagrandan, Maribi). This language..forms a dictinct family. **1925** E. SAPIR in *Amer. Anthropol.* XXVII. 402 Subtiaba, a language now spoken by only a small number of Indians in a village near Léon, on the Pacific slope of Nicaragua... For a long time the language was believed to be an isolated one.. But it appeared later that it is very closely related to Tlappanec or Yopi, a language spoken in the state of Guerrero in Southern Mexico. **1935** P. RADIN in *Internat. Jrnl. Amer. Linguistics* VIII. 45/1 Lehmann succeeded in demonstrating quite clearly that Tlappanec was closely related to the Subtiaba language of Nicaragua. **1965** *Canad. Jrnl. Linguistics* Spring 100 The third constituent of Hokan-Coahuiltecan, Subtiaba-Tlappanec. **1978** *Language* LIV. 507 Both papers are crucially concerned with a particular language known in two dialectal forms, Subtiaba (extinct, of Nicaragua) and Tlapanec (still spoken in Guerrero, Mexico).

subtilin (sɒ·btilin). *Pharm.* [f. L. *subtil-is* slender + -IN[1].] Any of a group of polypeptides of differing antibiotic activity (*subtilin A, B, C*) derived by culture from *Bacillus amyloliquefaciens* (orig. identified as *B. subtilis*), the most potent of which are used against Gram-positive bacteria and certain pathogenic fungi.

1944 JANSEN & HIRSCHMANN in *Arch. Biochem.* IV. 298 The substance thus differing from tyrothricin has been named *subtilin* by the authors. **1948** *Sun* (Baltimore) 9 Jan. 5/1 Recently publicized 'wonder drugs' include.. subtilin. **1948** C. H. HASSAL in *Nature* 28 Feb. 318/1 By use of the latter procedure, followed by dilution of the alcoholic extract with adjustment of the *p*H to 2·3, an active concentrate, which we will term subtilin *C*, was obtained. **1966** *McGraw-Hill Encycl. Sci. & Technol.* XIII. 230/2 Subtilin A, the major component of the subtilin family, is separated by partition chromatography. **1976** J. S. GLASBY *Encycl. Antibiotics* 334/1 A further antibiotic isolated from cultures of *Bacillus subtilis*, subtilin may be produced by both surface and submerged growth on various media. The associated antibiotic subtilin C..appears to be identical..in all respects except that it gives no colour reaction with $FeCl_3$ solution.

subtilisin (sɒbti·lisin). *Biochem.* [f. L. *subtīlis* slender + -IN[1].] Any of a group extracellular proteinases derived from strains of *Bacillus amyloliquefaciens* (orig. identified as *B. subtilis*).

1953 GÜNTELBERG & OTTESEN in *Compt. Rend. des Travaux du Laboratoire Carlsberg: Ser. Chim.*•XXIX. 47 Since..the *B. subtilis* proteinase appears to be a rather well defined enzyme..we feel that it will be appropriate to give it a name, and we propose to call it 'subtilisin'. **1968** A. WHITE et al. *Princ. Biochem.* (ed. 4) xii. 255 This is indicated by the finding that the subtilisins, proteolytic enzymes of *Bacillus subtilis* of different genetic origin, possess entirely different amino acid sequences. **1980** *Developmental Biol.* LXXVIII. 383/2 Protease activity of subtilisin and trypsin was confirmed with Azocoll..as substrate at pH 7·0.

sub-title, *sb.* Add: **1.** (Earlier examples.)

1825 T. H. HORNE *Outlines for Classification of Library* 86 To each Volume should be prefixed..an Alphabetical Table of the several Titles and sub-titles. **1865** GEO. ELIOT *Let.* 16 Sept. (1956) IV. 203 Mr. Lewes..thinks my suggestion as to the sub-title acceptable.

3. *Cinemat.* and *Television.* A caption which appears on a cinema or television screen, esp. to translate the dialogue or to explain the action. Freq. in *pl.*

1909 *Moving Picture World* 27 Feb. 235/1 If the audience is not given time to read the sub-titles or if they are indistinct..the spectators lose the thread. **1924** WODEHOUSE *Leave it to Psmith* i. 30 What he did not know about erring wives and licentious clubmen could have been written in a sub-title. **1931** B. BROWN *Talking Pictures* xi. 287 Another [camera]..photographs a sub-title tablet about a foot across and illuminated by a couple of arc lamps. **1944** [see *DUB *v.*[5]]. **1957** M. SUMMERTON *Sunset Hour* x. 140 The French film was mediocre. I ignored the sub-titles, testing my ear on the dialogue. **1975** G. HOWELL *In Vogue* 5/1 The subtitles to films brought American slang to Britain... 'Beatrix Esmond goes nix on the love-stuff.'

sub-title, *v.* Add: **b.** *Cinemat.* and *Television.* To furnish (a film or programme) with subtitles. Also **su·btitled** *ppl. a.*; **su·btitler; su·btitling** *vbl. sb.*

1930 E. V. KNOX in *Living Age* 1 Apr. 188 It is a *lingua franca*, or a *lingua californica*... The subtitlers have created a wilderness and called it prose. **1948** *Brit. Film Rev.* Apr. 10 The Cinemas of Great Britain are now showing the sub-titled films so well known to readers in other parts of the world. *Ibid.*, It cannot be said that subtitling in England is uniformly good. **1950** *Jrnl. Soc. Motion Picture & Television Engin.* Nov. 536 Several operations are necessary in order to subtitle pictures. **1968** *Punch* 31 Jan. 154/3 The sub-titler..can sum up a passage of flashy philosophy in one profound-seeming sentence. **1979** K. CONLON *Move in Game* vi. 71 'Tell me some more about academic life.'.. 'Well... There were subtitled foreign films.' **1982** *English World-Wide* III. 1. 53 Films are virtually all subtitled.

subtopia (sɒbtōᵘ·piă). Also **Subtopia.** [Blend of SUBURB and UTOPIA: cf. SUBURBIA.] A disparaging term for: Suburbia regarded as an ideal place. Applied more generally to areas of undifferentiated, ill-planned, and ugly suburban development; unsightly suburbs which encroach on the countryside,

1955 I. NAIRN in *Archit. Rev.* CXVII. 365 There will be no real distinction between town and country. Both will consist of a limbo of shacks, bogus rusticities, wire and aerodromes, set in some fir-poled fields... Upon this new Britain the *Review* bestows a name in the hope that it will stick—*Subtopia*. **1960** KOESTLER *Lotus & Robot* II. 277, I loathe crooners and swooners,..neon and subtopia. **1963** A. ROSS *Australia 63* iv. 102 The descent from Utopia to Sub-topia is steep and short. **1971** *Country Life* 2 Sept. 566/1 Will there still be English villages as we know them, or will they have merged into an unending subtopia in which town and country have become indistinguishable? **1976** W. J. BURLEY *Wycliffe & Schoolgirls* vii. 123 The killer was a man of the suburbs..at home in a neatly patterned subtopia.

subtopian, *a.* and *sb.* Also **Subtopian.** [f. prec. + -AN.] **A.** *adj.* Of, pertaining to, or characteristic of subtopia.

1955 I. NAIRN in *Archit. Rev.* CXVII. 372 The other is the panic reflex to the spread of Subtopia, which attempts improvements using standards which are themselves Subtopian. **1963** *Times Lit. Suppl.* 3 May 321/2 For a man with such a harrowing tale to tell Mr. Camp ought not to be so reassuringly readable..He will be avidly read by the subtopian commuters and their desperate wives. **1973** J. LEASOR *Host of Extras* i. 24 This subtopian hinterland of back-to-back houses and outside privies.

B. *sb.* A resident of subtopia.

1958 N. MACKENZIE *Conviction* 11 Those parts of it [*sc.* Britain] that remain unspoiled are falling into the hands of the subtopians. **1972** I. BROAT (*title*) The Subtopians.

Hence **subto·pianism,** the characteristics or ideals of subtopia; **subto·pianize** *v. trans.*, to render subtopian.

1959 *Cambr. Rev.* 25 Apr. 447/2 One can imagine some of them..trying to show that this eclipse was a bad thing, for which broadcasting, subtopianism, Trade Unions and the Welfare State were jointly to blame. *a* **1963** C. S. LEWIS *Poems* (1964) 62 One huge celestial charabanc, will stink and roll Through patient heaven, subtopianized from pole to pole. **1970** *New Scientist* 13 Aug. 342/2 It needed the motor-car to..subtopianize suburbia.

subtotal, *sb.*, *a.* (and *v.*) [f. SUB- + TOTAL *a.* and *sb.*, *v.*] **A.** *sb.* (stressed *su·btotal*) [SUB- 9.] An intermediate total; a total of part of a group of numbers to be added.

1906 *U.S. Patent 823,474*, Fig. 4, showing means for printing marks or characters indicating both totals and subtotals. **1921** J. A. V. TURCK *Origin Mod. Calculating Machines* 168 A feature common to recording of added columns of numerical items is the distinguishing characters for clear, sub-totals and totals by the use of letters, stars and other marks. **1952** D. R. HARTREE *Numerical Analysis* ii. 20 After each contribution is added, a subtotal is taken, then the next contribution is set and added. **1977** *New Yorker* 29 Aug. 54/2, I kept the new totals in conformity with their figures but changed the supporting details and some subtotals.

B. *adj.* (stressed *subto·tal*) *Surg.* [SUB- 20 g.] Involving the removal of only part of an organ or tissue.

1908 *Practitioner* Dec. 788 Surgeons adopted what has been called hysterectomy with intraperitoneal treatment of the stump, or subtotal hysterectomy. **1977** *Lancet* 29 Oct. 899/2 The natural history of the disease may be interrupted by ablative therapy (subtotal thyroidectomy or the use of radioiodine).

Hence **su·btotal** *v. trans.*, (*a*) to add (numbers) so as to obtain a subtotal; (*b*) to obtain a subtotal from the contents of (a register, etc.).

1936 *Suppl. Jrnl. R. Statistical Soc.* III. 95 The contents of any register may be totalled,..or sub-totalled, i.e. printed without clearing the register. *Ibid.* 99 Several prints of the function may be obtained by inserting more non-add steps after position 8, and sub-totalling register 5 on each of these. **1956** G. A. MONTGOMERIE *Digital Calculating Machines* xii. 250 This causes the accumulator to be sub-totalled into register 117.

subtracter. Add: **3.** *Electronics.* = *SUBTRACTOR.

1950 W. W. STIFLER *High-Speed Computing Devices* xiii. 284 The subtracter which is subtracting a large number from a smaller generates an extra carry pulse at the end of the arithmetic operation. **1970** *IEEE Trans. Computers* XIX. 720/1 A cascade of these subtracters, controlled by a multiplier recorder, provides multiplication.

subtracting, *vbl. sb.* Add: Also as *ppl. a.*

1956 J. L. STEWART *Circuit Theory & Design* ix. 289 (*caption*) A two-tube subtracting circuit.

subtractive, *a.* Add: **a.** Also in *Linguistics*, of a morph or morpheme. Cf. *REPLACIVE *a.*

1948, etc. [see *REPLACIVE *a.*]. **1953** [see *PORTMANTEAU *sb.* 4 d]. **1968** *Amer. Speech* XLIII. 203 Primary graphemic shortenings..may be divided into the subtractive and the replacive.

c. *Photogr.* Of or pertaining to the production of a coloured photographic image by passing white light through a series of filters which absorb or subtract different parts of the spectrum. Cf. *ADDITIVE *a.* c.

1906 E. J. WALL tr *Konig's Natural-Color Photogr.* 1. 23 (*heading*) Three-color printing, or the subtractive method of three-color photography. **1916** G. L. JOHNSON *Photogr. in Colours* ix. 141 Processes..which depend on the 'three-colour' principle are daily growing in favour... There are two forms of this process, the 'subtractive' one..and the 'additive' method. **1935** [see *ADDITIVE *a.* c]. **1957** V. J. KEHOE *Technique Film & Television Make-Up* 219 The dye images form the composite color pictures by subtractive synthesis. **1978** *SLR Camera* Dec. 61/1 This subtractive method is the most commonly used in modern colour printing.

B. *sb.* Something that is subtracted or deducted from another quantity; *spec.* in *Linguistics*, a subtractive morph or morpheme.

1949 E. A. NIDA *Morphology* (ed. 2) iv. 103 Such bound forms are either (1) nonclitics—additives, replacives, subtractives. **1954** *Word* X. 224 The same comment applies to 'subtractives'. **1979** *Daily Tel.* 21 Nov. 18 Apart from the purchase of a stamp..the ½p is no more than an additive to or subtractive from some other price.

subtractor (sɒbtræ·ktəɹ). *Electronics.* [f. SUBTRACT *v.* + -OR.] A circuit or device that produces an output dependent on the difference of two inputs or of multiples of them. Cf. *SUBTRACTER.

1950 W. W. STIFLER *High-Speed Computing Devices* 450/1 (Index), Subtractor [*in text as* subtracter]. **1953** A. D. & K. H. V. BOOTH *Automatic Digital Calculators* vi. 36 An adder or subtractor requires the provision of some form of register in which the sum is to be stored. **1970** J. EARL *Tuners & Amplifiers* v. 118 The signals from these [microphones] are fed into an 'adder/subtractor' network, giving two outputs, one L+R and the other L−R. **1977** J. G. GRAEME *Designing with Operational Amplifiers* vii. 177 To combine addition and subtraction with integration, the summing and differencing techniques of adders and subtractors are applied to integrators.

subtribe. (Later examples of peoples.)

1857, etc. [see *HAPU]. **1958** G. LIENHARDT in Middleton & Tait *Tribes without Rulers* 103 A tribe is divided into subtribes, its largest political segments. **1977** *Time* 19 Dec. 21/3 Its population of 2·5 million citizens includes members of 76 ethnic groups, mostly subtribes of the Tswana.

subtype. Add: *spec.* a subdivision of a type of micro-organism.

1951 WHITBY & HYNES *Med. Bacteriol.* (ed. 5) xii. 203 By preparing specific Vi phages more than 20 types and sub-types of the typhoid bacillus have been recognized. **1963** *Lancet* 12 Jan. 92/2 Three serotypes are known, but subtypes of type 2 have recently been demonstrated in some animal species. **1979** *Sci. Amer.* Jan. 66/1 That particular subtype of the influenza virus had been the agent of the pandemic of 1918, which killed 20 million people worldwide.

Hence as *v. trans.*, to assign to a subtype; to classify in terms of subtypes; **su·btyping** *vbl. sb.*

1973 *Lancet* 20 Oct. 867/1 Relatives of 9 blood-donors were also subtyped; all had the same subtype as the index case to which they were related. *Ibid.* 869/1 The value of subtyping as an epidemiological tool. **1977** *Ibid.* 15 Oct. 803/2 A multiply resistant strain of type-19 (not yet subtyped) *Streptococcus pneumoniæ* was isolated. **1980** *Brit. Jrnl. Psychiatry* CXXXVII. 502/1 Subtyping of schizophrenia into paranoid and non-paranoid subtypes.

Subud (subu·d). [Contraction of Skr. *suśīla* good disposition, *budh* to awake, learn, *dharma* custom (see quot. 1968).] A system of exercises by which the individual seeks to approach a state of perfection through the agency of the divine power; hence, a movement (founded in 1947 and led by the Javanese mystic Pak Muhammad Subuh, b. 1901) based on this system.

1958 J. G. BENNETT *Concerning Subud* vi. 111 Subud.. the perfect harmony of the inner life (Budhi) and outer life (Suśila) that is attained when our entire being is submitted to the Will of God. **1959** A. HUXLEY *Let.* 12 Aug. (1969) 874 Subud is simply a technique for reproducing the quaking of the early Quakers—a release via the muscles. **1962** *Lancet* 26 May 1125/2 As Subud has taken some hard knocks in your columns, I feel that someone ought to speak up for the 5000–6000 members of the Subud movement in this country. **1968** E. VAN HIEN *What is Subud?* ii. 25 Subud is a contraction of three Sanskrit words: Susila Budhi Dharmi. In Subud terminology, these have been interpreted as follows: Susila means 'right living'. Budhi refers to 'the higher powers and capacities latent in man himself'. Dharma means 'submission to the Will of God'. Taken together, they mean 'Right living according to the highest that is possible for man in submission to God's Will'. **1969** M. SUBUH *Basis & Aim of Subud* 5 It is also necessary to explain that Subud is neither a kind of religion nor a teaching, but it is a spiritual experience awakened by the Power of God. **1972** N. SAUNDERS *Alternative London* xviii. 176 Subud forms a link between psychotherapy and mysticism as roads to self-realisation.

suburban, *a.* and *sb.* Add: **A.** *adj.* **4.** Special collocations: *suburban line*, a railway line which runs between the centre of a city and its suburbs; *suburban neurosis*, a form of neurosis said to occur esp. among suburban housewives which is associated with feelings of boredom, loneliness, and lack of personal fulfilment; *suburban sprawl*, the straggling and often ill-planned expansion of the suburbs of a city over a large area of adjacent countryside; an instance of this.

1869 *Bradshaw's Railway Man.* XXI. 379 The Suburban line, from the Salt River station to Wynberg, is now open. **1926** *Times* 6 May 3/1 Skeleton services were run on main and suburban lines, and more trains are promised to-day. **1972** C. FREMLIN *Appointment with Yesterday* i. 10 South Coast, this [ticket] office... Suburban line, opposite Platform Six. **1938** S. J. L. TAYLOR in *Lancet* 26 Mar. 759/1, I hope to show that environment plays no less a part in the production of what I venture to call 'the suburban neurosis' than it does in the production of physical disease. **1962** *Listener* 6 Dec. 948/2 The so-called 'suburban neurosis' is due to society's having failed to provide a constructive role for these mothers. **1983** *Jrnl. Amer. Acad. Child Psychiatry* XXII. 172 (*heading*) The nuclear family, suburban neurosis, and iatrogenesis in Auckland mothers of young children. **1949** H. BLUMENFELD in *Social Forces* Oct. 59/1 The Association poses the alternative of 'self-contained towns' versus 'suburban sprawl'. **1958** *Listener* 19 June 1022/3 The transformation of most of the country into a gigantic suburban sprawl. **1972** *Country Life* 6 Jan. 18/1 The suburban sprawl that characterises much of the eastern seaboard of the northern United States.

B. *sb.* **2. b.** (Earlier and later examples.)

1841 S. BAMFORD *Passages in Life of Radical* (ed. 2) I. xxxiv. 203 He passed on, leaving those warm-hearted suburbans capering and whooping like mad. **1926** R. MACAULAY *Crewe Train* II. vi. 129 Don't waste time arguing about the accepted premises of life, of which one is that suburbans are dull. **1977** *Transatlantic Rev.* LX. 197 She laughed..being confused by Mr and Mrs Superb the Semi-Detached Suburbans strolling their Sealyhams, for woodpeckers.

Also **suburbaniza·tion**, the act of suburbanizing or the condition of being suburbanized; an instance of this; **subu·rbanized** *ppl. a.*, rendered suburban; **surbu·rbanly** *adv.*

1921 *Edin. Rev.* Jan. 111 The local feeling of the less suburbanised Home Counties continues to object. **1926** *Daily Tel.* 3 Aug., In the urbanisation or suburbanisation of the country motor transport is destined to be even more effective than railways. **1938** *Archit. Rev.* LXXXIII. 216/3 It is gratifying to find *Country Life* adding its own opposition to a tendency which, if not soon halted, will result in literally nation-wide suburbanization. **1951** N. PEVSNER *Middlesex* 55 Finchley Parish had only 1,500 inhabitants in 1801 and still only 7,000 in 1871. Thereafter suburbanization set in. **1963** S. S. IKRAMULLAH *Purdah to Parliament* ii. 17 The mentality and attitude of those who lived in these parts were also suburbanly correct. **1977** *Time* 25 Apr. 35/2 We are going to go on with suburbanized homes. **1978** H. CARPENTER *Inklings* iv. 64 They still went on walking tours, until the increasing suburbanisation of the countryside and the outbreak of war brought that annual event finally to a halt.

Suburbia. Add: Now often **suburbia.** (Earlier and later examples.) Freq. rather disparagingly. Also in N. Amer. and general contexts, and (*poet. nonce-use*) as quasi-*adj.*

1895 E. PUGH (*title*) A street in Suburbia. **1922** L. MUMFORD in H. E. Stearns *Civilization in U.S.* 13 'Suburbia' is used here in both the accepted and in a more literal sense. On one hand I refer to the fact that the growth of the metropolis throws vast numbers of people into distant dormitories where..life is carried on without the discipline of rural occupations and without the cultural resources that the Central District of the city still retains. **1925** WODEHOUSE *Sam the Sudden* xiv. 99 The early morning patois of Suburbia, which is the English language filtered through toast and marmalade. **1936** T. SHARP *Eng. Panorama* vi. 94 H. G. Wells..anticipated with extraordinary accuracy (and, as it seems to-day, with a maddening optimism) the universal suburbia which is already upon us. **1947** AUDEN *Age of Anxiety* III. 76 A married tribe commutes, mild from suburbia. **1967** MCLUHAN & FIORE *Medium is Massage* 72 It gave us darkest suburbia and its lasting symbol: the lawnmower. **1970** G. F. NEWMAN *Sir, You Bastard* iii. 92 The deposit on their admission to suburbia was managed jointly.

subvent, *v.* Restrict † *Obs.* rare^{-1} to sense in Dict. and add: **2.** = SUBVENTION *v.*

1921 *Discovery* Nov. 293/1 The excavations authorised and subvented by the French Government began in 1880 and have been continued to the present time. **1965** *New Statesman* 23 Apr. 646/1 The only question is, should the taxpayer continue to subvent [the Catholic education system]? **1976** *Times Lit. Suppl.* 25 June 793/2 A..fear of subventing the profits of commercial firms.

subve·rsive, *sb.* [f. the adj.] A subversive person; one who wishes to overthrow a political regime. Also *transf.* and *fig.*

1887 G. MEREDITH *Let.* Feb. (1970) II. 853 Londoners, ..ladies, dandies, mild revolutionists, total subversives, would mob together. **1927** *Weekly Dispatch* 23 Oct. 1/2 The fight against subversive anti-Fascism ceased. The subversives were crushed. **1951** *Manch. Guardian* 30 June 5/5 They [*sc.* the Chinese] have had quite a lesson in Korea and would hesitate before moving into Burma, except as subversives. **1954** I. DEUTSCHER *Age of Permanent Revolution* 14 He [*sc.* Trotsky] stakes everything on the change and upheaval that Time, the great subversive, must bring about. **1977** F. ORMSBY *Store of Candles* 49 At high tide the sea is under the city, A natural subversive. **1978** 'J. HIGGINS' *Day of Judgment* v. 75 You specialized in handling subversives, revolutionary movements generally and so on.

subvi·tal, *a.* (*sb.*) [SUB- 19 a.] **a.** *Genetics.* Of a gene: causing the death of a significant proportion of the individuals carrying it, but not as many as a semi-lethal gene. Also as *sb.* Cf. *LETHAL *a.* 1 d, *SEMI-LETHAL *a.* and *sb.*

1948 E. HADORN in *Symp. Soc. Exper. Biol.* II. 181 We may even come across mutants, or organ systems of lethals, that behave during a first sensitive period as subvital factors, during a second period as semi-lethals, and during a third period as true lethals. **1951** T. DOBZHANSKY *Genetics & Origin of Species* (ed. 3) iii. 67 About 57 percent of the second and 49 percent of the third chromosomes which were free of lethals or semilethals were 'subvital' in homozygotes. A subvital is a deleterious gene or gene complex which causes..the death of less than half of the homozygotes. **1962** [see *LETHAL *a.* 1 d]. **1978** *Acta Embryol. Exper.* I. 101, 80·9% of them survive the ill effects of the mutation; it is, therefore, considered a subvital mutation.

b. *Biol.* Not fully alive; having only some of the characteristics of living systems.

1954 *New Biol.* XVI. 10 Amongst the energy-providing materials are needed also 'sub-vital' systems which, using the energy provided, can grow and split and thus reproduce themselves.

su:bvocaliza·tion. [SUB- 22; cf. *subvocal* s.v. *SUB- 19.] The act or process of articulation with the lips or other speech organs silently or with barely audible sound, esp. while reading.

1947 G. T. BUSWELL in *Scientific Monthly* June 542/2 Completely silent reading, or 'nonoral' reading..is carried on without subvocalization. **1960** A. W. EDFELD *Silent Speech* II. vi. 88 The quotient between the rate of oral reading and the rate of silent reading was used as the measure of subvocalization. **1966** *New Scientist* 29 Dec. 738/1 'Subvocalization' in its most familiar form..consists of audible whispering while reading to oneself. **1974** *Nature* 8 Nov. 121/1 They were instructed to hold their tongues firmly between their teeth and lips while listening and were told to minimise subvocalisation.

Hence [as a back-formation] **subvo·calize** *v. trans.* and *intr.*, to utter or form (words) by subvocalization; **subvo·calizer**; **subvo·calizing** *ppl. a.*

1947 G. T. BUSWELL in *Scientific Monthly* June 542/2 Few persons listening to a lecture follow the speaker by subvocalizing after him the words he speaks. **1947** —— in *Elem. School Jrnl.* Dec. 193/2 Persons who subvocalize in silent reading have a much slower rate than those who suppress all tendencies to deal with words separately. *Ibid.* 194/2 They were subvocalizers, the victims of a method of teaching reading that fixed oral-reading habits first. **1964** *Jrnl. Educ. Psychol.* LV. 339 Subvocalizers exhibited a higher mean lip movement and a slower mean breathing rate than did nonsubvocalizers. **1966** *Science* 16 Dec. 1467/2 An individual who subvocalizes to any great extent is limited to a top reading speed of approximately 150 words per minute—a maximum attainable while reading aloud. **1966** *New Scientist* 29 Dec. 738/3 Of 17 subvocalizing college students out of 50..nearly all managed to reduce their involuntary vocal activity to nil within five minutes. **1978** K. AMIS *Jake's Thing* xv. 153 Jake had subvocalized an oath.

subway, *sb.* Add: **a.** (Earlier and further examples.) Also, for the passage of vehicles.

1825 HOOD & REYNOLDS *Odes & Addresses* 7 Speak up —or hath he hid his name To crawl thro' 'subways' unto fame Like Williams of Cornhill? **1869** *Bradshaw's Railway Man.* XXI. 454 Thames Subway. Incorporated..for making and maintaining a subway, under the river Thames, from Deptford to the Isle of Dogs. Length, 582 yards, with various roads and approaches. **1954** *Gloss. Highway Engin. Terms* (*B.S.I.*) 25 *Subway*, an underground passageway or tunnel to permit traffic movement or to accommodate pipes and cables underneath a structure, road or railway.

b. For *U.S.* read 'Chiefly *N. Amer.* (orig. *U.S.*)' and add earlier and further examples. Freq. *attrib.*

1893 *Massachusetts Acts & Resolves* 1420 The mayor of the city of Boston shall appoint..three commissioners.. to be known as the board of subway commissioners. **1906** *Daily Colonist* (Victoria, B.C.) 27 Jan. 2/5 An aged woman was killed by a subway train today while trying to go into a car in which the door had been closed. **1919**, etc. [see *METRO[2]]. **1941** B. SCHULBERG *What makes Sammy Run?* i. 22 They were walking down the steps to the subway arm in arm. **1951** E. PAUL *Springtime in Paris* v. 106 They stood there staring at the subway map. **1968** *Globe & Mail* (Toronto) 17 Feb. 48/3 (Advt.), An apartment.. minutes from the Davisville subway station. **1971** *New Society* 18 Aug. 322/2 The [Glasgow] underground (never called the tube)... Glaswegians persist in calling it the subway. **1979** R. JAFFE *Class Reunion* (1980) I. viii. 117 The subway kiosk in Harvard Square.

2. Special Comb.: **subway alumni** *sb. pl.* (U.S. slang), city-dwelling supporters of a college football team who, though not graduates of the college, attend games or follow the results through the news media (also *transf.*).

1947 *Sun* (Baltimore) 3 Nov. 15/8 Many letters have come in attacking Army for dropping Notre Dame... These letters came from Notre Dame's subway alumni, not from Notre Dame. **1960** *Washington Post* 7 Apr. D7 Silky Sullivan, the hero of the 'subway alumni', went into the 1958 Derby as the sentimental favorite. **1982** *Chicago Sun-Times* 26 Oct. 91 Faust would be having a devil of a time staying in the good graces of Notre Dame alumni (real and subway).

Hence as *v. intr.* (N. Amer. colloq.), to travel by subway or underground railway.

1929 M. LIEF *Hangover* 307 He subwayed up to Times Square. **1945** *PM* (N.Y.) 15 Apr. M4/2 We subwayed to Brooklyn. **1968** *Globe & Mail* (Toronto) 17 Feb. 46 (Advt.), You drive a Mercedes, but want to subway to the office.

subzee, var. SUBJEE in Dict. and Suppl.

‖ **succah** (su·kă, suka·). Also **sukkah,** [Heb. *sukkāh*, lit. 'hut'.] One of the booths in which a practising Jew spends part of the Feast of the Tabernacles. Cf. *SUCCOTH.

[**1819** *Christian Spectator* I. 126/2 They made booths, in Hebrew *succoth*, that is, sheds or hovels of thorn bushes.] **1875** J. PICCIOTTO *Sk. Anglo-Jewish Hist.* xvi. 140 The Succoths [*sic*] or tabernacles were then, as at present, decorated with fruits and flowers. **1905** *Jewish Encycl.* XI. 660/2 The sukkah or booth was to be a structure especially built for the festival. **1925** *Public Opinion* 4 Sept. 220/3 A sukkah for use during the Feast of Tabernacles. **1970** *New Yorker* 20 June 32/2 The Rabbi's disciples escorted her personally into the *sukkah.* **1979** *Jewish Chron.* 7 Dec. 39/1 Tradition has it that the minute Yom Kippur ends, you dash out and erect the first plank of the Succah. Tradition in our house has it that as soon as Succot is over, you dash out looking for the first Chanucah presents. **1981** C. POTOK *Bk. of Lights* (1982) vi. 191 'What do you want built, chaplain?' 'It's called a succah. It's a kind of booth or hut with wooden sides and an open roof covered with leaves and branches.'

succeed, *v.* Add: **13.** Also in proverbial phr. (see quots.).

1840 T. H. PALMER *Teacher's Man.* 223 'T is a lesson you should heed, Try, try again; If at first you do n't succeed, Try, try again. **1857** W. E. HICKSON *Try Again* in *Moral Songs* 8 'Tis a lesson you should heed, Try, try, try again. If at first you don't succeed, Try, try, try again. **1915** E. B. HOLT *Freudian Wish & its Place in Ethics* iii. 103 The child is frustrated, but not instructed; and it is in the situation where, later on in life, we say to ourselves, 'If at first you don't succeed, try, try again!' **1960** I. JEFFERIES *Dignity & Purity* v. 91 Not to worry... If at first you don't succeed, try, try, try again. *a* **1976** A. CHRISTIE *Miss Marple's Final Cases* (1979) 39 You musn't give up, Mr. Rossiter. 'If at first you don't succeed, try, try, try again.'

‖ **succès** (sükse). [Fr., = SUCCESS *sb.*] Used in phrases with reference to types of artistic success or acclaim, as *succès de scandale* (də skandal), success due to notoriety or scandalous character; *succès d'estime* (destim), a critical rather than a popular or commercial success; *succès fou* (fu), a success marked by wild enthusiasm. Also *transf.* and *fig.*

[**1826** *New Monthly Mag.* Dec. 578 Merely that lukewarm approbation, which in Paris is termed *un succès d'estime.*] **1859** *Once a Week* 13 Aug. 136/1 My second attempt..will be something more substantial than a mere *succès d'estime.* **1878** J. A. C. MORISON *Gibbon* vi. 86 The book was..a *succès fou.* **1887** R. CHURCHILL *Let.* 2 Mar. in W. S. Churchill *Lord Randolph Churchill* (1906) II. xvii. 291, I think the Government are earning a rather second-rate kind of *succès d'estime.* **1896** G. B. SHAW *Our Theatres in Nineties* (1932) II. 35 Mr Cartwright..enjoyed ..a sort of *succès de scandale.* **1908** MRS. H. WARD *Diana Mallory* III. xvi. 331 She would find herself a *succès fou*—people tumbling over each other to invite her, and make a show of her. **1919** 'C. DANE' *Legend* 56 The first two books were a *succès d'estime.* **1928** *Observer* 1 Jan. 8 The success which Victor Margueritte's novel 'La Garçonne' made all over Europe..was chiefly a succès de scandale. **1948** W. FORTESCUE *Beauty for Ashes* xix. 142 It was hard work creating something from nothing, but very great fun, and had the usual *succès fou* of all dramatic performances coached by the founder. **1965** A. J. AYER in *Listener* 4 Nov. 700/2 The result was *Language, Truth and Logic...* Though it had an almost immediate *succès de scandale,* its tenets..had a respectable philosophical ancestry. **1977** *Daily Tel.* 17 Mar. 14/3 It has already won a *succès d'estime* in the United States, and seems likely also to become a cult work here. **1978** *Christian* V. 86 What caught on with a succès fou and drew in the spiritual élite of the generation in tens of thousands was a Benedictine reform movement. **1979** M. HILEY *Victorian Working Women* I. iv. 48 *The Pictorial World*..was obviously hoping for some *succès de scandale* by splashing women in trousers across its front page.

success, *sb.* Add: **3. b.** *success of esteem, success of scandal,* tr. *succès d'estime, succès de scandale* s.v. *SUCCÈS.

1880 Success of esteem [in Dict.]. **1916** G. SAINTSBURY *Peace of Augustans* iii. 144 The extraordinary power of the close of *Vathek* has secured it..a success of esteem. **1926** C. E. MONTAGUE *Rough Justice* III. vii. 99 Notorious novels, successes of scandal, that lived as hard and about as long as super-impudent ball-dresses. **1939** D. CECIL *Young Melbourne* vii. 191 *Glenarvon* had a success of scandal; three editions were called for within a few weeks. But it dealt the death blow to..Caroline's social position. **1958** W. PLOMER *At Home* xii. 175 They [*sc.* publishers' readers] are liable to advise the rejection of typescripts that might have popular success and be moneymakers, or success of esteem followed perhaps by durability and influence.

6. a. *attrib.,* as *success ethic, hunter, rate, value,* etc.

1923 W. STEVENS *Let.* 11 Feb. (1967) 236 Aside from this absurd hero-worship, or success-worship, the town is purely a business place. **1946** *Nature* 17 Aug. 242/2 A success-rate of syphilis prevention of more than 97 per cent was claimed to be unequalled by any other mode of treatment. **1949** *Success-goal* [see *open-class* s.v. *OPEN *a.* 22 a]. **1951** M. McLUHAN *Mech. Bride* (1967) 35/2 They remain avid customers for the success manuals and beauty treatments which by themselves constitute a large line of merchandise. **1955** KOESTLER *Trail of Dinosaur* 93 The same is true of obsessional success-hunters in every field. **1957** R. K. MERTON *Social Theory* (rev. ed.) v. 170 The distribution of success-values among economic and social strata. **1965** H. HENDIN in A. Giddens *Stud. in Social & Polit. Theory* ix. 311 His legal ambitions were excessive and he found it impossible to compromise with his grandiose success fantasies. **1977** *Time* 13 June 44/2 They are an uncommonly interesting lot, whose lives and habits illuminate what achievement means today in the society that invented the success ethic.

b. *Comb.,* as **success story** *colloq.* (orig. *U.S.*), (*a*) an account of a success; (*b*) an instance of a successful venture, an achievement, etc.

1925 *Ladies' Home Jrnl.* Feb. 28/2 (*heading*) A great success story. **1938** *Time* 14 Nov. 84/2 Last year, when the U.S. Circuit Court of Appeals ruled that physicians might send contraceptives by mail, her career became a 'success story'. **1954** W. K. HANCOCK *Country & Calling* vii. 203 Departments would naturally prefer to get 'a good press', whereas we were bound by our instructions to write critical history, not 'a success story'. **1973** *Nature* 9 Nov. 58/1 The study of X-ray sources is one of the great success stories of present-day astrophysics. **1978** *Jrnl. R. Soc. Arts* CXXVI. 755/2 A comparative success story is the inundation of the ancient city of Nagarjunakonda to make way for a great hydro-electric project.

succession. Add: **IV. 14. f.** *Ecol.* The sequence of ecological changes in which one group of plant or animal species is replaced by another.

1860 H. D. THOREAU in *N.Y. Weekly Tribune* 6 Oct. 6/6 (*heading*) The succession of forest trees. **1899** *Bot. Gaz.* XXVII. 95 The ecologist..must study the order of succession of the plant societies in the development of a region. **1904** *Univ. Nebraska Stud.* IV. 332 Such succession herbaria are the natural outgrowth of formational ones. **1926** TANSLEY & CHIPP *Aims & Methods in Study of Vegetation* ii. 7 Vegetation, when left to itself, tends to change in a definite direction..and this change we call succession. **1957** G. E. HUTCHINSON *Treat. Limnol.* I. xv. 834 It is not impossible that the element plays some part in regulating phytoplankton succession. **1975** *Sci. Amer.* May 90/1 Forest succession proceeds too slowly for it to be observed directly.

g. *Geol.* A group of strata whose order represents a single chronological sequence.

1940 *Bull. Amer. Assoc. Petroleum Geologists* XXIV. 309 Near Las Vegas an apparently conformable succession of marine beds, mostly limestone, is designated as the Bird Spring formation. **1976** *Jrnl. Geol. Soc.* CXXXII. 121 The study area covers..the eastern half of the flysch succession. **1979** D. ATTENBOROUGH *Life on Earth* ii. 36 The limestones at the top of the Moroccan succession are about 560 million years old.

V. 15. succession powder (earlier example); **succession state,** a state which comes into existence after the overthrow or division of a previous state (used orig. of those states which succeeded the dismembered Austro-Hungarian Empire in 1919).

a **1821** MRS. PIOZZI in A. Hayward *Autobiogr., Lett. & Lit. Remains Mrs. Piozzi* (1861) I. 356 In Italy it was supposed to have been the succession powder mingled with chocolate whilst in the cake, not in the liquid we drink. Acqua Toffana, and succession powder (polvere per successione) were administered, as I have heard, with certain although ill-understood effects. **1924** Succession state [see *NATIONALISTICALLY *adv.*]. **1943** C. HOLLINGWORTH *German just behind Me* ii. 14 Like Romania it [*sc.* Yugoslavia] is a 'Succession State'. **1973** *Times Lit. Suppl.* 23 Mar. 318/2 Now that the breakaway of Bangladesh has effected a second partition of the Indo-Pakistani subcontinent, there has been renewed interest in all three succession states in the long-standing controversy over whether the first partition was either inevitable or necessary.

successional, *a.* Add: **2. c.** *Ecol.* Of or pertaining to ecological succession. Cf. *SUCCESSION 14 f.

1922 R. H. YAPP in *Jrnl. Ecol.* X. 13 The Successional Habitat practically agrees with Clements' developmental concept of habitat. **1967** M. E. HALE *Biol. Lichens* vii. 99 Successional stages leading to forested stands. **1979** *Sci. Amer.* Feb. 73/2 The Swiss have come increasingly to rely on natural tree types and natural successional trends as a basis for their silviculture.

successor. Add: **c.** *attrib.,* as *successor-designate*; **successor state** = *succession state* s.v. *SUCCESSION 15.

1958 D. TAIT in Middleton & Tait *Tribes without Rulers* 197 His companion is generally his successor-designate in the office. **1974** P. GORE-BOOTH *With Great Truth & Respect* 388, I set up a committee of three, consisting of Colin Crowe, Dennis Greenhill, my successor-designate, representing the Foreign Office and Jack Johnston representing the Commonwealth Office, to meet daily. **1930** *Economist* 9 Aug. 274/1 A century ago the present 'successor States' of the Hapsburg and Ottoman Empires might have been economically self-sufficient. **1971** H. MACMILLAN *Riding Storm* xvi. 537 The complicated intrigues and rivalries among the successor states of the old Turkish Empire.

succinct, *a.* **2.** (Later example.)

1958 S. J. PERELMAN *Most of S. J. Perelman* 491 Now, Messieurs, exposition is wearisome, so I will be succinct.

succinylcholine (sɒːksinəilkōᵘ·līn). *Pharm.* Also **succinyl choline.** [f. SUCCINYL + *CHOLINE.] The ion $[\text{—}CH_2COO{\cdot}(CH_2)_2\overset{+}{N}(CH_3)_3]_2$ formed by esterification of succinic acid with choline; also, a halogen salt of this, given intravenously as a short-acting muscle relaxant and local anæsthetic; = *SUXAMETHONIUM.

1950 *Chem. Abstr.* XLIV. 2124 It is shown that succinyl choline produces strong curarizing effects. **1952** [see *SCOLINE]. **1965** J. POLLITT *Depression & its Treatment* vi. 80 Occasionally recovery from succinyl choline is delayed and artificial respiration required for an extended period. **1974** M. C. GERALD *Pharmacol.* iii. 52 Alcohol.. and the skeletal muscle relaxant succinylcholine are broken down by the enzymes alcohol dehydrogenase and pseudocholinesterase, respectively.

succinylsulphathiazole (sɒːksinəilsɒlfaþəi·ăzōᵘl). *Pharm.* Also **-sulf-.** [f. SUCCINYL + *SULPHATHIAZOLE.] A poorly absorbed sulphonamide derivative which is used in the treatment of gastrointestinal infections and is inactive until hydrolysed to sulphathiazole in the body; 4′-(thiazol-2-ylsulphamoyl)-succinanilic acid, $C_3H_2NS{\cdot}NH{\cdot}SO_2{\cdot}C_6H_4{\cdot}NH{\cdot}CO{\cdot}(CH_2)_2COOH$.

1941 *Proc. Soc. Exper. Biol. & Med.* XLVIII. 129 (*heading*) Succinyl sulfathiazole, a new bacteriostatic agent locally active in the gastrointestinal tract. **1981** H. J. ROGERS et al. *Textbk. Clinical Pharmacol.* xix. 647 Only 5–10% of these drugs are absorbed... Examples are phthalylsulphathiazole and succinylsulphathiazole, both of which hydrolyse to sulphathiazole.

succorance (sɒ·kərəns). *Psychol.* Also **succourance.** [f. SUCCOUR *v.* + -ANCE.] A term used in some forms of personality assessment to describe the need for help, sympathy, and affection as a psychogenic force. Hence **su·ccorant** *a.*

1938 H. A. MURRAY *Explorations in Personality* ii. 83 *Succorance* (Succorant attitude), to seek aid, protection or sympathy. *Ibid.* iii. 181 The Succorance drive seeks a nurturant O. *Ibid.* 182 The Succorant need is always a sub-need. **1944** L. MUMFORD *Condition of Man* ii. 75 He builds his life around the themes of rejection and succorance. **1953** *Brit. Jrnl. Psychol.* Nov. 333 *Succourance*: some heroes show their great need of support, encouragement, care and protection. **1973** *Jrnl. Genetic Psychol.* June 185 Femininity involved being more..succorant. **1977** H. G. BURGER in B. Bernardi *Concept & Dynamics of Culture* 421 The nine behavioral systems of man were stated on unclear empirical grounds by Beatrice Whiting (1963:7): succorance, or asking help from others, [etc.].

succotash. (Earlier example.)

1751 J. MACSPARRAN *Diary* 4 Aug. (1899) 47 Mʳdined with us upon Suckatash and Ham.

‖ **Succoth** (suko·t). Also † **Souccoth; Succot, Sukkot(h.** [a. Heb. *sukkôṯ,* pl. of *sukkah*: cf. *SUCCAH.] = *Feast of Tabernacles* s.v. TABERNACLE *sb.* 1 b.

1882 tr. *L. Kompert's Scenes from Ghetto* 102, I hope you will be back in time for the *Souccoth.* **1888** H. POLANO *Talmud* III. 244 Making a tabernacle for thyself during Succoth. **1905** *Jewish Encycl.* IX. 583/1 Number of days on which the several ceremonies of Sukkot are observed. **1907** I. ZANGWILL *Model of Sorrows* ii, in *Ghetto Comedies* 20 When *Succoth* (Tabernacles) came, again no money, no bread. **1921** *Daily Colonist* (Victoria, B.C.) 16 Oct. 15/7 The Jewish folk of Victoria will observe Succoth, the original Thanksgiving Day of ancient Israel, better known as the Feast of the Tabernacle—on October 16. **1944** M. SAMUEL in M. W. Weisgal *Chaim Weizmann* I. 88 The Jews were more transfigured by *their* celebration of Shavuoth and Sukkoth than the Russian peasants by *their* thanksgiving celebrations. **1973** *Synagogue Light* Sept., Passover and Succoth are of seven days duration. **1974** *Times* 8 Oct. 10/1 The Soviet authorities allowed.. about 90 Jews to hold a picnic..to mark the *Sukkot,* a religious festival. **1979** [see *SUCCAH].

succubus. 1. (Later examples.)

1950 A. CLARKE *Coll. Plays* (1963) 315 Branduv is sleeping with a succubus. **1958** L. DURRELL *Balthazar* vii. 167 Thirst *can* be quenched like this, by inviting a succubus to one's bed. **1969** J. UPTON tr. *R. Diaz Sánchez's Cumboto* 261 The dream reoccurred many times, it was the work of a clever succubus who came to my cot regularly to conduct her oneiric concert. **1977** A. CARTER *Passion of New Eve* ii. 27, I would..remember the myth of the succubus, the devils in female form who come by night to seduce the saints.

succuss, *v.* Add: **b.** *Homœopathy.* To shake (a preparation of a drug) vigorously.

1910 *Encycl. Brit.* XIII. 646/1 To make the 2× potency, 10 drops or 10 grains of this first dilution or trituration are mixed with 90 drops of pure alcohol..and are succussed or triturated. **1938** D. SHEPHERD *Magic of Minimum Dose* 264 The 12th potency..is prepared..by diluting one drop in a hundred and shaking or succussing violently. **1974** *Homoeopathy* June/July 86 Between each dilution he [*sc.* Hahnemann] succussed (shook vigorously) the medicine.

succussion. Add: **c.** *Homœopathy.* The vigorous shaking of a preparation of a drug.

1848 HEMPEL & QUIN tr. *Jahr's New Manual* II. 1059 *Succussion,* shaking. **1910** *Encycl. Brit.* XIII. 646/1 The continuation of the dynamization of trituration or succussion develops a spiritual acurative agency. **1938** D. SHEPHERD *Magic of Minimum Dose* 21 This trituration or succussion is a most important part of the preparation of the drug. **1974** *Homoeopathy* June/July 86 This process of dilution and succussion seemed to give the remedy more energy and a greater healing effect.

such, *dem. adj.* and *pron.* Add: **A. 4. β.** sich (further examples).

1846 DICKENS *O. Twist* (rev. ed.) xv. 81 Oh, you naughty boy, to make me suffer sich distress. **1863** *Southern Confederacy* (Atlanta) 13 May 2/1 The buryal squad organized *fust* and foremost, and begun to inter their money and spoons and 4 pronged forks and sich like. **1890** KIPLING in *Scots Observer* 28 June 149 Don't call your Martini a cross-eyed old bitch; She's human as you are—you treat her as sich. **1938** M. K. RAWLINGS *Yearling* xvi. 185 'Is that true, Buck?' Buck whittled busily. 'Now if you was to tell me a tale,' he said, 'I'd not ask you no sich of a question.' **1953** E. SIMON *Past Masters* III. 191 'But I did it in my own time,' said Monro... 'There ain't no sich thing, old son.' **1981** P. MACDONALD *One Way Street* i. 9 These bloody English..have put their imprint on this place in sich a way as to make yew want to heave.

B. V. 24. Also in phr. *or some such* (also *somesuch*): or some such thing.

1967 D. FRANCIS *Blood Sport* iii. 35 He was in France on business wasn't he, or somesuch. **1972** *Daily Tel.* 11 Apr. 22/5 Plan will be to approach them with proposals for short and sharp bursts of selling with stamps—stamp weeks or somesuch. **1973** R. PARKES *Guardians* vii. 122 The doctor believed it might aid expiation or abreaction or some such.

suck, *sb.*[1] Add: **1. c.** An act of fellatio. *coarse slang.*

1941 G. W. HENRY *Sex Variants* II. 1177 A real suck seems to be one in which orgasm and ejaculation are induced. **1972** *Screw* 12 June 21/2 They start their separate ways through a variety of fucks and sucks and lesbian encounters.

† **9.** A breast-pocket. *Criminals' slang. Obs.*

1821 D. HAGGART *Life* 26 He returned the screaves to his lil, and placed it in his suck. **1923** *Chambers's Jrnl.* 6 Oct. 716/1, I..pulled the dub of the outer jigger from his suck.

10. *slang.* A sycophant; esp. a schoolboy who curries favour with teachers. Cf. SUCK *v.* 25 e in Dict. and Suppl.; *sucker-up* s.v. *SUCKER *sb.* 14.

1900 FARMER *Public School Word-Bk.* 197 *Suck, subs.* (University), a parasite, a toady. **1907** B. M. CROKER *Company's Servant* xx. 213 He was just a suck—that's all. **1916** JOYCE *Portrait of Artist* (1969) i. 11 We all know why you speak. You are McGlade's suck. **1955** W. GADDIS *Recognitions* II. ii. 373 The shade of the boy whom he had not seen since they were boys together (Martin was Father Joseph's 'suck') lived on the air as though they had parted only minutes before.

11. *pl.* as *int.* Used as an expression of contempt, chiefly by children. Also in phr. *sucks to you* and varr. *slang.*

1913 C. MACKENZIE *Sinister Street* I. I. vii. 98 This kid's in our army, so sucks! **1922** F. HAMILTON *P.J.: Secret Service Boy* iv. 178 'S', he announced, '*u,c,k,s,t,o,y,o,u.*' **1935** N. MITCHISON *We have been Warned* I. 28 Brian is a baby. Oh sucks, oh sucks on Brian. **1945** E. WAUGH *Brideshead Revisited* II. v. 287 It's great sucks to Bridey. **1952** 'C. BRAND' *London Particular* xv. 191 A most regretable air of sucks to you. **1968** *Melody Maker* 30 Nov. 24/5 This is a rotten record—yah boo and sucks. **1974** *Times* 4 Mar. 9/5 Sucks boo, then, with acting like this, to that new National Theatre down the road. **1978** 'J. LYMINGTON' *Waking of Stone* ii. 45 'Sucks to you!' she said..tossing her head so her pigtails swung. **1983** *Listener* 19 May 11/1 The council treated the urbane Mr Cook to the politician's equivalent of 'Yah, boo, sucks'.

12. *Canad. slang.* A worthless or contemptible person. Cf. *SUCK *v.* 15 f; *suck-hole* s.v. *SUCK-.

1974 *Globe & Mail* (Toronto) 8 Mar. 1/6 The teachers are copping out. They're now saying, if we can't have our way, then we're going to be sucks and refuse to work. **1975** *Citizen* (Ottawa) 28 Oct. 1/1 A neighbor described Rob as 'a quiet guy who was always getting put down a lot. Lots of people used to call him a suck... He didn't do much socially or in the way of sports.'

suck, *v.* Add: **I. 1. f.** (See quot. 1960.) With person or part as obj. Cf. sense 23* below. *coarse slang.*

1928 in A. W. Read *Lexical Evidence from Folk Epigraphy Western N. Amer.* (1935) 78, I suck cocks for fun. **1960** WENTWORTH & FLEXNER *Dict. Amer. Slang* 527/2 *Suck v.i., v.t.* 1 [taboo] to perform cunnilingus or, esp., fellatio. **1972** *Screw* 12 June 21/2 Characters fuck and suck each other like *real* people do. **1973** E. BULLINS *Theme is Blackness* 79 You heard what I said, bitch.. take me to dinner and suck mah dick and et cetera fa dessert.

II. 9. c. *to suck the hind tit* or *teat*: to be inferior or have no priority. Also *intr.* with *on. slang* (orig. *U.S.*).

1940 W. V. T. CLARK *Ox-Bow Incident* iv. 244 'Well,' he said, 'if you like to suck the hind tit.' **1951** N. MONSARRAT *Cruel Sea* III. vi. 179 You have n't a hope... As far as radar is concerned, corvettes are sucking on the hind tit. **1963** *Time* 8 Nov. 47, I don't want these kids around here to suck on a hind tit when it comes to getting a good education. **1975** *Weekend Mag.* (Montreal) 31 May 20/2 Radio, no matter what you've read about the Radio Revolution, still sucks the hind teat at the CBC.

10. a. *suck it and see* (see quot. 1951). Now used *attrib.* and *absol.* (also with hyphens) to denote experimental methods.

1951 PARTRIDGE *Dict. Slang* (ed. 4) Add. 1189/2 *Suck it and see!* A derisive c[atch-]p[hrase] retort current in the 1890's. **1968** *New Scientist* 3 Oct. 10/1 Biologists..prefer to employ the 'suck it and see' approach adopted by Harold Wilson to politics rather than the impractical (?) idealism of Michael Foot. **1973** *Nature* 2 Mar. 16/2 In the best tradition of 'suck it and see' Fowlis has attempted to use such a velocimeter to measure the flow of both mercury and the liquid alloy NaK. **1976** *New Scientist* 16 Dec. 636/1 Types of experiment that could be usefully or uniquely performed in space:..'suck-it-and-see' experiments to explore a new environment (such as the plant growth and spider-web-spinning variety). **1979** *SLR Camera* June 42/3 It's difficult to lay down any hard and fast recommendations for using fill-in lighting; it's really a suck-it-and-see situation.

III. 15. e. To practise fellatio (or cunnilingus). *coarse slang.*

1928 in A. W. Read *Lexical Evidence from Folk Epigraphy Western N. Amer.* (1935) 78 My cock is only 10 ins long so if any one would like to suck meet me here 9 pm. **1960** [see sense 1 f above]. **1975** E. HANNON *Doors* 123 White chicks dig suckin, that's a fact. That's cause suckin's sophisticated. **1977** M. T. BLOOM *13th Man* (1978) viii. 148 The pimp said: 'She wouldn't suck so she couldn't make a living. I had to send her back.'

f. To be contemptible or disgusting. *slang.* Cf. *SUCK *sb.*[1] 12.

1971 *It* 2–16 June 3/2 Polaroid sucks! For some time the Polaroid Corporation has been supplying the South African government with large photo systems..to use for photographing blacks for the passbooks..every black must carry. **1976** G. V. HIGGINS *Judgment of Deke Hunter* vi. 59, I had a lousy summer... I thought it sucked, and I bet next summer'll suck too. **1978** M. GORDON *Final Payments* xi. 193 All the hotels have the same pictures. The last one, the food sucked.

VI. 22. b. suck (a)round. *intr.* To go about behaving sycophantically. Occas. *ellipt.* Cf. sense 25 e in Dict. and Suppl. *slang* (orig. and chiefly *U.S.*).

1931 *Princeton Alumni Weekly* 22 May 798/1 If 'drag' or 'hot dope' is necessary one usually 'sucks around' for it. **1934** G. ADE *Let.* 27 June (1973) 186 As for the Landis party on July 10th I have had no invitation but maybe I could suck around and get one. **1940** M. MARPLES *Public School Slang* 169 Thus a boy is said to *suck round*, if he tries to ingratiate himself. **1941** B. SCHULBERG *What makes Sammy Run?* xi. 209 The tycoon who spends the first part of his life sucking and crushing, and the last part giving away dimes. **1979** 'A. HAILEY' *Overload* III. xiv. 273 Logically, she should go to the city editor. She might have done it, too, if the son-of-a-bitch hadn't handed her that coach-and-team crap earlier today. Now it would look as if she was sucking around him because of it.

23*. suck off. *trans.* To cause (someone) to experience an orgasm by fellatio or cunnilingus. *coarse slang.* Cf. sense 1 f above.

1928 in A. W. Read *Lexical Evidence from Folk Epigraphy Western N. Amer.* (1935) 79 When will you meet me to suck me off? **1941** G. W. HENRY *Sex Variants* II. 1176 The object of *suck* can be either the organ or the person; but the object of *suck off* is usually the person, who is mentioned within the idiom, e.g. 'to suck him off'. **1959** W. BURROUGHS *Naked Lunch* 76 Equilibrists suck each other off deftly. **1969** FABIAN & BYRNE *Groupie* (1970) vii. 50 He listened superciliously..and, spreading his legs, asked me to 'suck him off' to make him less uptight. **1971** *Guardian* 27 Sept. 14/5 One American GI is forcing a Vietnamese woman to suck him off. **1976** J. CROSBY *Snake* (1977) xxxv. 222 Elf has had a busy night... Sucking me off till all hours.

25. e. For *'Schoolboy slang'* read *'slang* (orig. *Schoolboys*'). (Later examples.) Cf. *sucker-up* s.v. *SUCKER *sb.* 14.

1936 M. MITCHELL *Gone with Wind* xl. 719 We hear how you suck up to the Yankees..to get money out of them. **1945** E. WAUGH *Brideshead Revisited* II. iv. 261, I imagine she's been used to bossing things rather in naval circles, with flag-lieutenants trotting round and young officers on-the-make sucking up to her. **1957** R. K. MERTON *Social Theory* (rev. ed.) viii. 270 Data in *The American Soldier* on what was variously called brown-nosing, bucking for promotion, and sucking up. **1963** D. OGILVY *Confess. Advert. Man* (1964) i. 15, I despise toadies who suck up to their bosses; they are generally the same people who bully their subordinates. **1966** [see *CRAWL *v.*[1] 3 c]. **1979** J. COOPER *Class* (1980) vi. 131 Harry Stow-Crat also has to suck up to neighbouring farmers in case he should want to hunt over their land.

suck-. suck-hole: restrict † to sense in Dict. and add: (*b*) *U.S.*, a whirlpool, a pond; (*c*) *Canad.* and *Austral. slang*, a term of abuse (cf. *SUCK *sb.*[1] 12); hence as *v. intr. slang* (orig. and chiefly *Canad.*), to curry favour.

1909 *Dialect Notes* III. 377 *Suck-hole, n.*, a whirlpool. Common [in East Alabama]. **1961** PARTRIDGE *Dict. Slang* Suppl. 1302/2 *Suck-hole, v.*, to toady, as in 'He won't suck-hole to anyone'; hence, to cringe; low Canadian; C. 20. **1964** F. O'ROURKE *Mule for Marquesa* 200 They rode on toward the small water hole... Dolworth led them off a plateau down the rocky trail to the suckhole under the rock ledge. **1966** P. MATHERS *Trap* 12 Our progressive mayor..and his pack of scabby suckhole mates. **1968** J. WAINWRIGHT *Edge of Extinction* 48 He can roast to hell—then go suckholing to Old Nick. **1970** *Globe Mag.* (Toronto) 31 Oct. 4/2 No matter how strong I could become there was still someone in this city of 470,000 who thought I was a suckhole. **1972** J. METCALF *Going down Slow* vii. 128 Can't even fix yourself a sandwich without suckholing round that man.

suck-egg. Add: **c.** Used *attrib.* to designate a dog regarded as the type of viciousness or worthlessness. Also *transf. U.S. dial* (chiefly *South* and *Midland*).

1892 *Dialect Notes* I. 232 He is as mean as a suck-egg dog. **1927** P. GREEN *Unto Such Glory* in *One-Act Plays for Stage & Study* 3rd Ser. 104 He's a dirty low-down suck-egg dog. **1931** *Virginia Q. Rev.* Jan. 102 Hayes got up and slunk off like a suck-egg dog caught in the hen-house. **1958** 'W. HENRY' *Seven Men at Mimbres Springs* ix. 107 But I will be a suck-egg son of a bitch if I can't tie my good arm behind me, stand on my bad leg only, and still whup me the living daylights out of any skinny little Alabama bast—.

sucker, *sb.* Add: **I. 1. b.** For *U.S.* read orig. *N. Amer.* (Earlier and later examples.)

1838 *Patriot* (Toronto) 29 May 1/2 It's true that pigs has their troubles like humans—constables catches 'em, dogs bites 'em, and pigs is sometimes as done-over suckers as men. **1927** A. CONAN DOYLE *Case-Bk. Sherlock Holmes* 92 I'll see this sucker and fill him up with a bogus confession. **1941** [see *PLAY *v.* 24 a]. **1957** *Essays in Crit.* VII. 47, I confess to being a sucker myself, if not for Malory, for Welsh legend. **1960** P. GOODMAN *Growing up Absurd* iii. 65 Our present poor are absolute sheep and suckers for the popular culture which they cannot afford, the movies, sharp clothes, and up to Cadillacs. **1973** L. MEYNELL *Thirteen Trumpeters* iv. 57 He got..a tiny percentage out of the total takings of the Casino. The more suckers who turned up and the more each sucker spent the better pleased he was. **1979** *Financial Rev. Survey* (Sydney) 22 Oct. 11/2 Look at the advertising man himself. He's the biggest sucker in town. From rotary engines to studded blue jeans—you'll find 'em at the agency. **1981** M. GEE *Dying, in Other Words* 58 Elsie laughed when she told about Pelham and called her a sucker, and said that she ought to ask him for money, men often liked giving you money, it was part of the game.

9. g. *Golf.* (See quot. 1931.) orig. *U.S.*

1931 *Daily Express* 2 Sept. 1/5 The United States Golf Association passed a special rule permitting 'suckers'—that is, balls embedded in the mud—to be lifted and cleaned without penalty. **1963** *Times* 9 Jan. 4/3 There do not seem to have been any 'suckers', although some of Ray's towering drives were repeatedly expected to produce them.

III. 13. For *local* read *colloq.* (orig. *local*) and add later examples. Also *spec.* (chiefly *N. Amer.*), a lollipop; *all-day sucker*: see *ALL *a.* IV. b.

1907 *Dialect Notes* III. 250 *Sucker, n.*, a kind of hard candy held by a small wooden stick and sucked. 'Let's buy suckers.' **1938** *Times* 13 Jan. 14/5 One of them said: 'I'll buy some suckers.' **1956** J. SYMONS *Paper Chase* xii. 91 A window in which gobstoppers, liquorice bootlaces and sherbet suckers nestle. **1962** J. LUDWIG in R. Weaver *Canad. Short Stories* (1968) 2nd Ser. 242 'I got no money for suckers,' the woman said nastily. **1971** *Islander* (Victoria, B.C.) 19 Sept. 4/3 The small children eagerly hunted suckers that had been hidden in a large hay wagon. **1977** E. JONG *Loveroot* 45 Little sugar suckers with sour centers.

IV. 14. (sense 1 b) *sucker bait, bet, list, punch, trap*; **sucker-bashing** *Austral. slang* (see quots. 1945, 1953); **sucker-disk** = SUCKER *sb.* 10; **sucker-rod** (earlier example); **sucker-up** = *SUCK *sb.*[1] 10 (cf. SUCK *v.*[1] 25 e in Dict. and Suppl.).

1939 *Amer. Speech* XIV. 80/2 *Mootch* is a derisive term applied to a careful customer... Retailers lose money on the 'mootch', because he buys only those things offered as 'sucker bait' or 'specials'. **1976** 'TREVANIAN' *Main* (1977) xiii. 249 'Have you any reason to think you might be in trouble?' he asks. But she is not taking sucker bait like that. She smiles. **1945** J. A. ALLAN *Men & Manners in Austral.* 89 Before that the settlers had cut the scrub a foot above ground, piled the refuse round the stumps, and fired it as the new shoots appeared. Even after that, 'sucker bashing'—which had raised the cost of clearing to 15/– an acre—had still been needed. **1953** BAKER *Australia Speaks* iii. 80 *Sucker bashing*, work at cutting down saplings. **1962** *Australasian Post* 25 Oct. 40 Whilst sucker-bashing at Mirambigo Station. **1920** *Collier's* 26 Mar. 22/3 You actually intend *makin'* a sucker bet like that? **1979** *Tucson* (Arizona) *Citizen* (Weekender Mag.) 28 Apr. 9/3 Don't buy much insurance. Cover your potential catastrophic losses with insurance, but not your minor setbacks. Remember that the way insurance companies make money is by taking as many sucker bets as possible. **1964** *Oceanogr. & Marine Biol.* II. 412 The functional histology of the sucker-disk of two British regular echinoids..has been described. **1977** *Playgirl* May 76/2 The sucker-disc mouth [of a lamprey] was stuck solidly to the smooth skin on J. T.'s right side. **1910** *Collier's* 17 Dec. 25/1 'Sucker lists', as the promoters call the roster of victims..are traded and passed on. **1966** T. PYNCHON *Crying of Lot 49* v. 114 After a week of anxiously watching the mailbox..getting nothing but sucker-list stuff through the regular deliveries. **1981** E. AMBLER *Care of Time* v. 65 If they're pulling names on the sucker list, they can forget mine. I'm not available. **1947** *Amer. Speech* XXII. 122/2 *Sucker punch*, a hit or punch delivered without warning. **1950** J. DEMPSEY *Championship Fighting* 50 The right lead is called a sucker punch. **1979** N. HYND *False Flags* xxii. 201 It was a sucker punch... The fist landed, breaking his nose. **1865** *Harper's Mag.* Apr. 571/1 Small engines are used in most cases, with hardly sufficient power ro raise the sucker-rod out of a deep well. **1953** POHL & KORNBLUTH *Space Merchants* xvi. 156 Warren Astron had never returned to his sucker-trap on Shopping One. **1973** *Sunday Advocate-News* (Barbados) 16 Dec. 3/5 So this Christmas, shop wisely, avoid the sucker traps. **1911** F. SWINNERTON *Casement* ii. 66 'Suckers-up' (those who sought by illegitimate means to ingratiate themselves with the manager). **1976** P. LIVELY *Stitch in Time* i. 10 Toady, said Maria to it [*sc.* a cat] silently, sucker-up.

sucker, *v.* Add: **4.** *trans.* To cheat, to trick. *slang* (orig. and chiefly *U.S.*).

1939 *Sat. Even. Post* 14 Oct. 78/1 It was a little deal I got suckered on. **1948** *Chicago Tribune* 27 Mar. I. 1/4 Apparently we are again going to be suckered into approval of a glorified world WPA. **1958** J. & W. HAWKINS *Death Watch* (1959) 87 We're going to sucker the killer out in the open. **1971** L. GRIBBLE *Alias the Victim* xii. 184 He had been suckered badly. What had to be done was to get away. **1978** J. GORES *Gone, no Forwarding* (1979) xv. 90 Delaney suckered us into making a payment which he now claims is an admission of guilt because we made it.

sucket. For † *Obs.* read 'Now rare exc. *arch.* and *Hist.*' and add: **a, b, d.** (Later examples.)

a. **1929** E. LINKLATER *Poet's Pub* xii. 144 The table already gleamed with..jumbals and marchpane and suckets of one kind and another. **1959** P. VANSITTART *Tournament* xiv. 115 Suckets shaped as unicorns, swans, frogs.
b. **1917** A. WAUGH *Loom of Youth* 10 'Those who can, do, while those who can't, teach.' This choice sucket.. comes consolingly to the ears of one whom the chances and caprices of life may have thrown casually on the preceptorial beach.
d. **1938** CURRIER & BUHLER *Marks Early Amer. Silversmiths* 165 Forks were apparently unknown except for serving—to which use were doubtless put the small sucket-forks..for sweetmeats. **1956** G. TAYLOR *Silver* v. 112 The three prongs were curved, unlike the two prongs of the sucket fork. **1977** FLEMING & HONOUR *Penguin Dict. Decorative Arts* 768/2 *Sucket fork*, an implement with a spoon at one end and a two-pronged fork at the other, intended for eating fruit, especially *succade*.

sucking, *vbl. sb.* Add: **3. a. sucking-pot** (later example); **sucking reflex** *Biol.*, the instinct to suck as possessed by the young of all mammals; **sucking response** *Biol.*, the action of sucking as a response to some stimulus or influence; **sucking-up** *slang*, sycophancy.
1843 C. A. F. PARKE *Let.* 19 Aug. in U. Ridley *Cecilia* (1958) xi. 125 She uses a sucking pot, but the Old Crab thinks that she sucks in wind. **1923** T. P. NUNN *Education* 167 An infant is born in vigorous possession of the sucking reflex. **1974** *Biol. Abstr.* LIX. 2593/2 An otherwise normally developed female rabbit without ears may have lost them when still in the nest due to a 'sucking-reflex' among its siblings, such as that which occurs among young mice. **1938** *Jrnl. Genetic Psychol.* LIII. 369, 49 per cent of sleeping infants gave sucking responses to stimulation of the lips. **1975** *Jrnl. Compar. Physiol. & Psychol.* LXXXVIII. 796 Monitoring sucking responses to a rubber teat revealed that..the vigorous oral activity continued largely unabated. **1946** B. MARSHALL *George Brown's Schooldays* ii. 7 'Thank heaven my people sent me here with a decent grub box.' 'But what has a grub box to do with being caned..?' Brown asked. 'The gentle art of sucking-up, of course... Not to the beaks.' **1978** 'M. INNES' *Ampersand Papers* I. v. 44 He wasn't doing any sucking-up act on Archie.

sucking, *ppl. a.* Add: **6. sucking louse,** a blood-sucking ectoparasite of mammals belonging to the order Siphunculata (or Anoplura); **sucking stomach** *Zool.*, a stomach in certain invertebrates that expands so as to provide a food reservoir (formerly interpreted as the means by which the animal imbibed fluid).
1910 R. DOANE *Insects & Disease* iv. 54 The sucking lice..are suspected of carrying some of these same diseases. **1950** *N.Z. Jrnl. Agric.* Jan. 68/1 Sucking louse: This parasite [of pigs] is very common in New Zealand. **1962** GORDON & LAVOIPIERRE *Entomol. for Students of Med.* xxxvi. 223 Members of the order Anoplura, all of which are known as 'sucking lice' possess 'sucking' mouthparts borne on an elongated head. **1886** F. R. CHESHIRE *Bees & Bee-Keeping* I. vii. 94 Cook calls the honey-sac the 'sucking stomach', using an old, but extremely misleading, title. **1925** A. D. IMMS *Gen. Textbk. Entomol.* 98 The organ is then known as the food-reservoir or 'sucking stomach', but the latter expression is misleading and incorrect.

suckle, *v.* **3.** *intr.* Delete *rare* and add later examples.
1966 P. SCOTT *Jewel in Crown* I. 28 Their children, three girls and two boys to date (apart from the one still suckling..) sat on the front benches. **1977** *Sci. Amer.* Aug. 80/3 Since the evicted joey may continue to suckle for another four months, the female red kangaroo may have three offspring in the 'pipeline' at any one time: a dormant blastocyst, a small joey nursing and developing in the pouch and a larger young-at-foot still suckling.

sucrase (s¹ū·krē¹z). *Biochem.* [f. F. *sucre* SUGAR *sb.* + *-ASE.] An enzyme that catalyses the hydrolysis of disaccharides to monosaccharides; *spec.* that which catalyses the hydrolysis of sucrose to glucose and fructose; = INVERTIN, *INVERTASE, *SACCHARASE.
1900 in B. D. JACKSON *Gloss. Bot. Terms.* **1901** *Jrnl. Chem. Soc.* LXXX. I. 180 The isolation of 'sucrase' the actual enzyme of cane sugar inversion from yeast in a pure form appears..to be hopeless. **1954** A. WHITE et al. *Princ. Biochem.* xvii. 397 Specific disaccharases for sucrose and lactose, named sucrase and lactase, respectively, are supposed to occur also in the intestinal juice. **1974** *Encycl. Brit. Micropædia* IX. 640/1 Sucrase is produced by the mucous membrane cells lining the walls of the small intestine. **1981** M. TOPOREK *Basic Chem. Life* xix. 271 Evidence at present indicates that..maltase, sucrase, and lactase are not actually secreted into the intestinal lumen.

‖ **sucrier** (sükrie). [Fr.] A sugar-bowl, usu. made of porcelain and with a cover.
1869 C. SCHREIBER *Jrnl.* 9 Oct. (1911) I. 50 A Bow (sprigged) sucrier with cover and acorn top. **1904** E. DILLON *Porcelain* p. xxi, Sèvres porcelain. Two small *sucriers..Gros bleu* and green ground, with birds on branches painted in white reserves. **1960** *Times* 18 June 11/2 But odd pieces—*sucriers*, cup and saucers, teapots—can be obtained at moderate cost. **1975** *Country Life* 4 Dec. (Suppl.) 43/1 Chelsea-Derby sucrier, c. 1770.

sucrose. Mark sense in Dict. † *Obs.* and add: **1. b.** *spec.* a white crystalline sugar, $C_{12}H_{22}O_{11}$, which can be derived from sugar-cane, sugar beet, and in lesser quantities from most other plants, and is used as a sweetener; = *SACCHAROSE.
In chemical terms, sucrose is an optically active disaccharide composed of D-fructose and D-glucose and having a structure described by the systematic name α-D-glucopyranosyl-(1,2)-β-D-fructofuranoside.
1857 W. A. MILLER *Elem. Chem.* III. ii. 54 Cane sugar or Sucrose ($C_{12}H_{11}O_{11}$).—This variety of sugar is chiefly otained from the sugar cane. **1888** BLOXAM *Chemistry* (ed. 6) 644 Sucrose fuses at 160°C. (320°F.), and does not crystallize on cooling. **1903** A. J. WALKER tr. *Holleman's Textbk. Org. Chem.* I. 274 On hydrolysis sucrose yields *d*-glucose and *d*-fructose in equal proportions. **1964** N. G. CLARK *Mod. Org. Chem.* viii. 138 Molasses is the dark syrup remaining after the removal of crystallized sugar from evaporated sugar-cane juice or the aqueous extract of sugar beet; it contains between 40 and 50 per cent of sucrose (table sugar). **1980** C. W. SPANGLER *Org. Chem.* I. xii. 248 Lactose and sucrose are two of the more common disaccharides.
2. *attrib.* and *Comb.*, as **sucrose (density) gradient** *Biochem.*, a gradient of sucrose concentration used in the centrifugation of biological media to prevent convection currents; freq. *attrib.*; **sucrose phosphate,** any of the esters that can be formed between sucrose and phosphoric acid; **sucrose phosphorylase,** a bacterial enzyme which catalyses the breakdown of sucrose, ultimately producing glucose-1-phosphate and fructose.
1944 *Jrnl. Exper. Med.* LXXIX. 304 Concurrent experiments..performed without the protective action of a sucrose gradient showed no indication of a sedimentation boundary. **1947** *Ann. Rev. Microbiol.* I. 362 Friedewald & Pickels.., by centrifugation in a sucrose density gradient so as to reduce convection, noted differences between PR8 and Lee strains. **1968** H. HARRIS *Nucleus & Cytoplasm* iii. 43 (*caption*) Sucrose-density-gradient sedimentation pattern of a crude extract of *Escherichia coli* cells exposed to [^{14}C] uracil for 20 seconds. **1979** *Biochim. & Biophysica Acta* DLXIV. 191 Sucrose density gradient analysis of the postribosomal fraction of muscle and liver revealed that the sedimentation profiles of the synthetases of the two tissues were similar. **1938** *Chem. Abstr.* XXXII. 5920 The rabbit paw was injected with 10 cc. of 2% aq. solns. of..Ca sucrosephosphate. **1960** *Plant Physiol.* XXXV. 269/2 Any sucrose-phosphate which is formed is ultimately dephosphorylated by enzymes in sugar beet tissue at some stage prior to storage in the root. **1979** *Infection & Immunity* XXIV. 868/1 Hydrolysis of sucrose phosphate would be expected to yield glucose 6-phosphate and fructose. **1943** *Jrnl. Biol. Chem.* CLI. 360 It is possible to obtain active preparations of sucrose phosphorylase relatively free of invertase and phosphatase. **1977** *Jrnl. Molecular Catalysis* II. 453 The interest in sucrose phosphorylase lies in the fact that a stable and re-usable insoluble preparation can be useful for both preparative and analytical purposes.

suction. Add: **4. b. suction dredge** *Engin.*, a type of dredge employing a suction pump, used in the dredging of soft material from sea-beds and river bottoms; hence **suction dredger,** a vessel which carries a suction dredge; **suction dredging** *vbl. sb.*; **suction gas,** the town gas produced by a suction plant; **suction lift** *Mech.*, the height to which a liquid can be drawn up a pipe by suction; **suction plant,** a form of gas producer (see PRODUCER 3) in which the blast is induced by suction; **suction pressure** *Bot.* [tr. G. *saugkraft* suction force (Ursprung & Blum 1916, in *Ber. d. Deutsch. bot. Ges.* XXXIV. 539)], the force with which a cell can imbibe water, being the difference between the pressure exerted by the cell walls on the cell contents and the osmotic pressure of the contents; **suction stroke,** in an internal-combustion engine, a piston stroke in which fresh mixture is drawn into the cylinder; also, *suction sweeper*.
1901 *Daily Colonist* (Victoria, B.C.) 27 Oct. 3/2 Next Monday..the first suction dredge ever operated in the western part of the Dominion will be given a trial. **1940** *Sun* (Baltimore) 4 Dec. 6/3 Excavations by huge dipper and suction dredges already are under way at both ends of the canal. **1977** *New Yorker* 20 June 68/2 Suction dredges are portable, cheap, irresistible to a certain class of lone, adventuring miner. **1911** *Daily Colonist* (Victoria, B.C.) 6 Apr. 14/5 Plans are being prepared for a new suction dredger of the type of the King Edward for use in British Columbia coast waters. **1930** *Engineering* 13 June 760/1 The sand backing was filled in over the bank by suction dredgers. **1974** H. R. COOPER *Pract. Dredging* (ed. 2) i. 10 (*caption*) A powerful pump, a floating platform, a pipe and disposal system...that is the simple anatomy of the Suction Dredger. **1965** G. V. WILLIAMS *Econ. Geol. N.Z.* vii. 69/2 These sands were washed beyond the narrow confines of the Ohinemuri River..where they were worked by suction-dredging some years ago. **1974** H. R. COOPER *Pract. Dredging* (ed. 2) p. x, During the 12 years since the first edition of *Practical Dredging* was published, trailing suction dredging methods have become increasingly important. **1907** *Daily Mail Year Bk.* 75/2 Suction-gas has been adapted to marine purposes. **1936** BONE & HIMUS *Coal* xxiv. 417 By the year 1901 'Suction-Gas Plants' were established on the market. *Ibid.* 418 A typical 'suction gas', generated from gas-coke, with air saturated with steam at 51·7°C, contains CO_2=5·15, CO=25·45, H_2=13·10, CH_4=0·30, and N_2=56·00 per cent. **1909** N. HAWKINS *Mech. Dict.* 559/2 Suction lift. **1940** KRISTAL & ANNETT *Pumps* ii. 103 It is a generally accepted rule that 15-ft. suction lift is a safe operating condition. **1976** C. P. KITTREDGE in I. J. Karassik et al. *Pump Handbk.* II. 148 A positive value of h_s is called a suction head while a negative value of h_s is called a suction lift. **1909** *Rep. Brit. Assoc. Adv. Sci. 1908* 826 A suction plant costs less and occupies less ground space, but the gas made in it is not so strong as in the older form of pressure plant. **1920** H. C. GREENWOOD *Industr. Gases* III. 344 Suction plants have an advantage in the reduction of risk of carbon monoxide poisoning owing to the prevailing negative pressure. **1922** W. STYLES in *Biochem. Jrnl.* XVI. 728, I propose for this quantity, already described as a force and a power, but which is in reality a pressure, the term 'suction pressure'. **1958** *New Biol.* XXV. 38 Water moves from the soil to the leaves along a gradient which most European workers call a gradient of suction pressure or suction force and most Americans, a gradient of diffusion pressure deficit. **1978** *Physiol. Plant Path.* XIII. 275 Infection of tomato plants by *Meloidogyne javanica* resulted in increased suction pressure in the root system. **1904** R. T. MECREDY *Dict. Motoring* 169 The Suction Stroke... The descent of the piston naturally causes a vacuum in the combustion chamber, which at first was air and gas tight. **1933** V. L. MALEEV *Internal-Combustion Engines* v. 59 Temperature *ta* of the gases in the cylinder at the end of the suction stroke is higher than the outside temperature *ta*. **1941** NEWTON & SEEDS *Motor Vehicle* (ed. 3) xi. 172 The displacement of the piston on the suction stroke represents potential ability for forming a vacuum in the cylinder. **1920** *Chambers's Jrnl.* Nov. 830/1 A suction-sweeper that we have examined recently runs the electric type very close indeed. **1926–7** *Army & Navy Stores Catal.* 114/1 Whirlwind Suction Sweeper. Its revolving Brush sweeps the carpet... Its powerful suction sucks the dust into the dustproof container.
c. *spec.* in *Aeronaut.*, used *attrib.* to designate various devices concerned with controlling flow conditions in the boundary layer, as *suction aerofoil, control, slot,* etc.
1933 *Gloss. Aeronaut. Terms* (*B.S.I.*) VII. 58 *Suction face*, the side of an airscrew blade formed by the upper surfaces of its aerofoil elements. **1946** *Jrnl. R. Aeronaut. Soc.* L. 431/1 The suction aerofoil exhibits a large discontinuous fall of velocity followed by a gentle rising velocity from the position of the suction slot to the trailing edge. **1950** *Ibid.* LIV. 159/2 The suction wing principle must be associated with the flying wing layout for it to be truly advantageous. **1960** *Aeroplane* XCIX. 268/2 In spite of official reluctance to admit the potentialities of suction control of the boundary layer, the enthusiasts persist in their efforts. **1977** *Jrnl. R. Soc. Arts* CXXV. 350/1 The US..flew a modified twin-jet reconnaissance aircraft..in 1966 with suction slots which also achieved a high degree of wing laminar flow.

suctorian. Add: In mod. use *spec.* a protozoan of the class or subclass Suctoria, the adult form of which is usually sessile, lacking cilia and feeding by the use of suctorial tentacles. Also as *adj.* = SUCTORIAL *a.*
1931 R. R. KUDO *Handbk. Protozool.* xxxiii. 399 The body of a suctorian may be spherical, elliptical, dendritic, etc. **1939** *Jrnl. Cellular & Compar. Physiol.* XIV. 410 The tentacles of the suctorian protozoan Ephelota coronata.. are very long and thin. **1975** *Nature* 7 Aug. 467/2 Microtubules have also independently evolved into many other organelles of motility, such as..suctorian tentacles and haptonemata. **1980** J. N. FARMER *Protozoa* xvii. 678/1 The tentacles of suctorians included in this family are of one type, the feeding tentacles.

sucupira (su:kŭpī·ră). [a. Pg., f. Tupi *sucupira*.] A dark brown hardwood obtained from trees of the genus *Bowdichia* or *Diplotropis*, both native to South America, esp. Brazil, and belonging to the family Leguminosæ; also, a tree of either of these genera.
1924 RECORD & MELL *Timbers Trop. Amer.* II. 270 The woods commonly known as 'sucupira' are of a deep chocolate-brown color. **1950** *Archit. Rev.* CVII. 124 The photograph..shows..an office partition in 'sucupira', a rich purple hardwood. **1977** *Transatlantic Rev.* LX. 86 The colossal Ceibas, para nuts and sucupiras with their blue flowers high in the sun.

sudak. (Later example.)
1973 *Nat. Geogr. Mag.* May 612/1 All the strange but delicious bounty of the Volga, handsome, fat fish with names like sazan, sudak.

Sudan. Add: **2.** *Chem.* Used *attrib.* to designate various azo and diazo dyes mostly derived from 2-hydroxynaphthalene and anthraquinone, used as industrial dyes and biological stains: as *Sudan I* (also *1*), the orange-yellow azo dye, C_6H_5ROH (where R= —N:N·$C_{10}H_6$—); *Sudan II* (also *2*), the brown azo dye, $(CH_3)_2·C_6H_3·N:N·C_{10}H_6OH$; *Sudan III* (also *3*), the red diazo dye, $C_6H_5·N:N·C_6H_4·ROH$; *Sudan IV* (also *4*), the scarlet diazo dye, $CH_3·C_6H_4·N:N·C_6H_4(CH_3)·ROH$; *Sudan black* (*B*), the black diazo dye,

$$C_6H_5·R·R \overset{NH}{\underset{NH}{\diamond}} C(CH_3)_2.$$

1894 A. G. Green tr. *Schultz' & Julius' Syst. Survey Org. Colouring Matters* 66 (*table*) Sudan I..Benzene-azo-β-naphthol. $C_{16}H_{12}N_2O$. *Ibid.* 70 (*table*) Sudan II..Xylene-azo-β-napthol. $C_{18}H_{16}N_2O$. *Ibid.* 86 (*table*) Sudan III..Benzene-azo-benzene-azo-β-naphthol. $C_{22}H_{16}N_4O$. **1907** *Practitioner* Nov. 635 Fresh sections stained with Sudan III. **1956** [see *polybase]. **1961** R. D. Baker *Essent. Path.* iv. 40 The lipid is bound in the organ and does not have the physicochemical form necessary to absorb Sudan dye. **1966** T. S. & C. R. Leeson *Histology* i. 16/1 Fat can be detected in sections which have not been exposed to fat solvents by stains such as Sudan III, Sudan IV, and Sudan black B. **1974** Passmore & Robson *Compan. Med. Stud.* III. i. xxi. 14/2 Sudan black B stains the cytoplasm of the myeloid series, the intensity of the staining increasing with maturation.

3. *Sudan grass* (*U.S.*), a tall annual grass, *Sorghum sudanense*, which is cultivated for hay in dry regions of the United States. Also *ellipt.*

1912 *Yearbk. U.S. Dept. Agric. 1911* 72 Sudan grass.. is another example of a new forage crop that has become popular almost in one season. **1929** C. C. Deam *Grasses of Indiana* 325 Sudan grass has only recently been introduced into Indiana and its use as a hay crop is on the increase. **1949** *Hoard's Dairyman* 25 Oct. 756/3 Frost-nipped cane, sudan, pig weeds, Johnson grass, and flax are poisonous to cattle. **1964** Mrs. L. B. Johnson *White House Diary* 6 July (1970) 176 You can look down on the church spire in the valley below and the fields in between, with Sudan grass waving in the wind. **1978** J. Updike *Coup* (1979) i. 28 In the wide belt of transition between withered sudan and stark desert, there were islands of what had been, before the drought, pasture land.

Hence **su:danophi·lia** *Med.* [*-philia], the condition in which cells containing particular fatty or lipid structures can be stained with a Sudan dye; hence **su:danophi·lic** *a.*, capable of taking up Sudan stains.

1911 Stedman *Med. Dict.* 840/2 *Sudanophilia*,..a condition in which the leucocytes contain minute fat droplets which take a brilliant red stain when treated with 0·2 per cent Sudan III. **1954** E. W. Dempsey in R. O. Greep *Histology* xxvii. 745 (*caption*) The two sections are from two phases of secretion and illustrate the increased sudanophilia of the rodlike mitochondria during the phase of extrusion of fat from the cells. **1956** *Nature* 7 Jan. 48/1, I observed certain sudanophilic corpuscles which do not appear to have been previously described. **1961** R. D. Baker *Essent. Path.* iv. 40 Fat occurring normally in adipose tissue, adrenal cortex and corpus luteum absorbs Sudan dyes and is called sudanophilic. **1979** *Atherosclerosis* XXXIII. 486 Sudanophilia is evident in the upper thoracic portion and in the area of the renal arteries. **1980** *Ibid.* XXXV. 103 Polar coordinate mapping was used to determine the rate of progression of spontaneous sudanophilic coeliac lesions on the aortic wall in White Carneau pigeons.

Sudanese, *sb.* Add: Also in *Comb.*, as **Sudanese-Guinean** (see quots.).

1954 Pei & Gaynor *Dict. Linguistics* 207 *Sudanese-Guinean*, a family of African Negro languages, spoken by an estimated total of 50,000,000 persons... Some linguists consider Sudanese and Guinean as two independent families. **1967** M. Schlauch *Language* ii. 39 In a wide belt stretching across Northern Africa, bounded on the South by a line extending Eastwards from the shores of the Gulf of Guinea and then dipping still farther to the South, we find a chain of languages grouped together and known as Sudanese-Guinean.

Sudanic (sudæ·nik), *a.* and *sb.* [f. Sudan + -ic.] **A.** *adj.* = Sudanese *a.*; *spec.* of or pertaining to the Sudan or an extensive group of African languages spoken there and elsewhere in central, northern, and eastern Africa. **B.** *sb.* (One of) the Sudanic group of languages.

1912 D. Westermann *Shilluk People* i. 32 Hamitic languages..differ from the Sudanic languages chiefly in the grammatical gender. *Ibid.*, Numerous Shilluk-words, which most probably are Sudanic, are found in languages generally counted as Hamitic. **1913** N. W. Thomas *Anthrop. Rep. Ibo-Speaking Peoples of Nigeria* i. 141 The languages of West Africa, commonly called Sudanic, and spoken by the true negro, have been classified into four main groups—Eastern Sudanic, Central Sudanic, Middle and Western Sudanic. **1931** C. K. Meek *Sudanese Kingdom* iv. 184 Mlle. Homburge has recently written a paper attempting to prove a close connection between Ancient Egyptian, Fulani, Sudanic, and Bantu. **1936** *Discovery* June 171/1 The Nilotes of the Nile Valley, speaking Negro (Sudanic) languages and extending from the Anglo-Egyptian Sudan some 200 miles south of Khartum into Uganda. **1956** E. E. Evans-Pritchard *Nuer Relig.* iii. 104 They think easily in terms of Spirit but not in terms of medicines, the idea of which as it obtains among their Sudanic neighbours they seem scarcely able to grasp. **1956** A. W. Southall *Alur Society* ii. 24 The Bendi are also Sudanic speakers. **1957** Ld. Hailey *African Survey 1956* iii. 84 Negro (including Sudanic, Bantu, and Nilotic), and Hamito-Semitic. **1972** J. Biggs-Davison *Africa—Hope Deferred* iii. 24 The Sudanic economy was mainly rural and pastoral. **1977** *Sci. Amer.* Apr. 110/3 Ehret suggests that the names applied to cattle and sheep by many modern Bantu-speakers were probably derived from the non-Bantu languages known collectively as Central Sudanic. **1980** *Cambr. Encycl. Archaeol.* 342/1 The formative processes of the Early Iron Age complex took place in the country to the north-west, in the 'sudanic' belt of open grassland savanna on the northern fringes of the equatorial forest.

Sudanization (sudǎnəizēi·ʃən). [f. as prec. + -ization.] The action or process of making Sudanese in character, *spec.* with reference to the independence of the Sudan from Great Britain in 1956.

1951 *Britannica Bk. of Year* 44/1 The year was one of progress towards the government's declared object—the Sudanization and independence of the Sudan. **1955** *Times* 2 Aug. 5/2 The first stage in the 'Sudanization' of important posts held by foreigners, had been completed. **1970** H. Trevelyan *Middle East in Revolution* 19 Commissions were to be established to guide the Governor-General, to supervise Sudanisation of the Civil Service,..and to supervise the formation and work of the Constituent Assembly. **1978** S. Lloyd *Suez 1956* i. 12 A Sudanisation Committee to deal with the administration and defence forces.

Sudano- (sudā·no), used as comb. form of Sudan and its derivatives, as in *Sudano-Sahelian* adj.; **Sudano-Guinean** = *Sudanese-Guinean* s.v. *Sudanese *sb.* Cf. *sudanophilia (s.v. *Sudan).

1939 [see *Nilo-]. **1954** Pei & Gaynor *Dict. Linguistics* 207 Some linguists consider Sudanese and Guinean as two independent families; others, notably Delafosse, consider Sudano-Guinean and Bantu to be members of a larger linguistic group. **1979** *Nature* 18 Jan. 167/3 UNCOD therefore proposed giant transnational projects like..a joint livestock management programme in the Sudano-Sahelian countries.

sudden, *a.* **3. b.** Delete 'see quots.' and add: (*a*) a single toss used to decide an issue; hence in *Lawn Tennis*, a game played to break a tie; also in general sporting use (usu. *attrib.*), designating an additional competition or period of extra time in which the first to concede a game or score is immediately eliminated; (further examples); (*b*) *U.S.*, a potent alcoholic drink; (*c*) (see quot. 1886 in Dict.).

1863 C. Reade *Hard Cash* I. vii. 205 America is fertile in mixtures: what do we not owe to her? Sherry-cobbler, gin-sling..sudden death. **1865** 'Mark Twain' in *Californian* 18 Mar. 8/3 Our reserve (whom we had..kept out of sight and full of chain-lightning, sudden death and scorpion-bile all day..) came filing down the street as drunk as loons. **1927** W. E. Collinson *Contemp. Eng.* 36 *Sudden death* [is used] for a game played to bring a set to a sudden, decisive conclusion without playing out the full number. **1939** *Sun* (Baltimore) 21 July 15/8 Skipper Bill Barrow, of the Rochester Yacht Club, sailed his Thisbe II to victory today in a sudden-death race against defending champion Aphrodite. **1945** *Ibid.* 3 Mar. 7/2 Tech meets the winner tonight, and got this break by having its name picked out of a hat when the 'sudden death' playoff plan was decided on. **1946** L. P. Hartley *Sixth Heaven* viii. 162 'Game-ball all,' was called... 'Shall we play it out?' said Dick, 'or shall we have sudden death?' **1961** *Times* 29 Aug. 3/4 Player and..J. Herbert tied for the lead.. and then had a sudden-death play-off. **1972** 'E. Lathen' *Murder without Icing* xxvi. 224 'I hear that it wasn't a bad game.'..'Not bad! When it went into sudden death overtime?' **1974** *Times* 22 Jan. 10/7 The WCT circuit as a whole contains a controversial innovation: a 13-point tie-break with a 'sudden death' finish. This means that the first player to score seven points wins the tie-break whether he leads by two points or not. **1977** *Evening Gaz.* (Middlesbrough) 11 Jan. 14/6 These matches are 'sudden death' affairs, a single match in each round either home or away depending on the luck of each draw.

Sudeten (sudēi·tən), *a.* and *sb.* [Ger., the name of the *Sudeten* mountains in north-eastern Czechoslovakia.] **A.** *adj.* Of, pertaining to or designating the predominantly German-speaking area of Czechoslovakia in the vicinity of the Sudeten mountains (the Sudetenland) which was annexed by Germany from 1938 to 1945. Freq. as *Sudeten German*.

1937 *Times* 20 Oct. 13/2 (*heading*) Czechoslovakia and the Sudeten Germans. *Ibid.* 6 Dec. 11/5 (*heading*) Sudeten German quarrels. *Ibid.*, Dissensions within the Sudetendeutsch Party. **1939** *Encycl. Brit. Bk. of Year* 526 At the time of the annexation by Germany of the Sudeten areas of Czechoslovakia there were in the country some 5,000 refugees from the old Reich and from Austria. **1946** W. S. Churchill *Victory* 131 Henlein, Sudeten-German leader, committed suicide. **1959** W. F. Leopold in J. A. Fishman *Readings Sociol. of Lang.* (1968) 355 Sudeten Germans with Bavarian dialect adapt themselves slowly to Swabian. **1966** S. Mann *Collecting Playing Cards* iv. 84 (*heading*) The Franconian or Sudeten pattern (Sudeten-deutsch). **1968** [see the *sb.* below]. **1974** *Listener* 25 Apr. 530/2 The Sudeten 'problem' was being manipulated both by appeasers here and..by Hitler. **1982** S. G. Duff *Parting of Ways* xv. 135 Gradually, up to 1933, the Sudeten Germans had become reconciled to the [Czechoslovak] Republic.

B. *sb.* An inhabitant of the Sudetenland; a Sudeten German.

1938 H. Nicolson *Diary* 13 May (1966) 341 The Sudetens could not approve of a pro-Russian and anti-German policy. **1943** *Amer. Speech* XVIII. 200 The term *Sudetens*, extremely frequent in the news columns of 1938, did not exist before that year. **1968** K. Martin *Editor* xii. 252 The Sudetens had some real grievances, even though they were the best-treated minority in Europe... The Czech government knew that their real problem had nothing to do with Sudeten grievances.

Sudetic (sudēi·tik), *a.* Now *rare.* [f. *Sudet(en *sb.* + -ic: cf. G. *sudetisch.*] Of or pertaining to the Sudeten region of Czechoslovakia.

1907 *Muret-Sanders Encyclopaedic Eng.-German & German-Eng. Dict.* II. 710/3 *Sudeten..Gebirge*,..Sudetic Mountains. **1928** C. Dawson *Age of Gods* xii. 270 A movement of population was certainly taking place at this period, for the skulls of the Lengyel people belong not to the old 'Sudetic' type of the Danube region, but are distinctively Nordic. **1928** P. Selver tr. *Benes' My War Memoirs* xix. 481 The Austrian Minister..sent..the.. Allied Governments a protest against the attempt to retain the Sudetic Germans within Czechoslovakia. **1934** Priebsch & Collinson *German Lang.* i. ii. 37 Of less moment..are..the fair broad-heads of East Baltic type on the eastern periphery and a very primitive strain, called by Günther Inner Asiatic or Sudetic (from the Sudetes). **1938** *Manch. Guardian* 12 May 6/3 It is not clear what is meant by the 'extreme limit' to which the Czecho-Slovak Government is asked to go in its 'concessions' to the Sudetic German minority.

sudoite (sū·do,əit). *Min.* [ad. G. *sudoit* (G. Müller 1962, in *Naturwissenschaften* XLIX. 205/2), f. the name of Toshio *Sudo* (b. 1911), Japanese mineralogist and crystallographer: see -ite[1].] (See quot. 1963.)

1963 *Amer. Mineralogist* XLVIII. 214 G. Müller (1962) proposes 'sudoite' as a name for this dioctahedral series of phyllosilicates, as chlorite is the name of the analogous trioctahedral series. **1977** *Mineral. Abstr.* XXVIII. 16/1 An essentially regular interstratification of mica (sericite) and chlorite (sudoite) was found in an alteration area of the Matsumine Kuroko deposit of the Hanaoka mine.

suds, *sb. pl.* Add: **4. c.** For *U.S. slang* read '*slang* (orig. and chiefly *U.S.*)' and substitute for def.: Beer. (Earlier and later examples.)

1904 G. V. Hobart *I'm from Missouri* iii. 52 Who.. hoists a few dippers of suds?.. Dad! **1924** *Truth* (Sydney) 27 Apr. 6 *Suds*, beer. **1925** Fraser & Gibbons *Soldier & Sailor Words* 273 *Suds*, ale. **1926** *Flynn's* 16 Jan. 638/2 The boozeclerk give us th' high sign he had doped th' suds or skat. **1931** 'D. Stiff' *Milk & Honey Route* 177 Fill up on 'suds' for a dime. **1943** C. L. Sonnichsen *Roy Bean* 171 The bear..was still consuming his free bottle of suds. **1962** *Radio Times* 17 May 43 Let's split to your pad for some suds. **1975** *Globe & Mail* (Toronto) 8 Feb. 1/2 Before then, Labatt had only a marginal share of the suds market in Quebec. **1977** *Mod. Boating* (Austral.) Jan. 30/1 The figure propped half-standing on a bar stool, with his face in a glass of suds. **1979** *Tucson* (Arizona) *Mag.* Sept. 60/3 Sip suds out of glass jars while you wait.

5. in the suds a. (Later U.S. examples.)

1816 U. Brown *Jrnl.* 28 Sept. in *Maryland Hist. Mag.* (1916) XI. 234 We both in the sudds pretty much. *Ibid.* 29 Sept. 235 Thinking that I was not out of the sudds yet. **1887** R. T. Cooke *Happy Dodd* xxvii. 295, I shan't leave Mis' Payson in the suds.

suds (sɒdz), *v.* [f. the sb.] **1.** *trans.* To lather; to cover with soap-suds, or wash in soapy water.

1834 'C. Packard' *Recoll. Housekeeper* 12 Ma'am Bridge was *sudsing* the clothes in a tub before her. **1939** N. S. Colby *Remembering* ii. 62 She dipped my hair in a basin of hot water, sudsed it, rinsed it, and dried it with a towel. **1976** *S. Wales Echo* 27 Nov. 6/3 (Advt.), Rub-a-Dub Doll. Soap her and suds her. See how much fun a bath can be. **1981** P. Theroux *Mosquito Coast* xv. 185 The..splash of our foot-operated wheel sounded like a washing machine sudsing clothes.

2. *intr.* To form suds. *U.S.*

1893 M. A. Owen *Voodoo Tales* 5 An impertinent housewife had dared to affirm that her soap wouldn't 'suds'. **1972** *Fortune* Jan. 73/1 Detergent foam first became a matter of national concern in the early 1960's, when Representative Henry S. Reuss of Wisconsin, among others, pointed out that detergents were persisting, and sometimes sudsing, in the environment.

So **su·dsing** *vbl. sb.* and *ppl. a.*

1844 'J. Slick' *High Life N.Y.* II. 20 I'd gin myself a good sudsing in the wash hand basin. **1879** *Scribner's Monthly* Oct. 940/2 As soon as they begin to boil, remove them to the 'sudsing'-water. **1881** S. P. McLean *Cape Cod Folks* 167 A good poundin', and boilin', and sudzin', you need. **1957** T. Sturgeon in D. Knight *100 Yrs. Sci. Fiction* (1969) 134 Slim heard more water running and sudsing noises, and, by ear, followed the operation through a soaping and two rinses. **1971** *New Yorker* 6 Nov. 5 (Advt.), This rich, sudsing, mentholated cleanser was developed by dermatologists. **1978** *Nature* 6 Apr. p. xxvii/2 The concentrated detergent powder dissolves quickly to provide fast action, minimal sudsing, and free rinsing.

sudsable (sɒ·dzăb'l), *a.* [f. *suds *v.* + -able.] Capable of forming soap-suds; also of garments: washable in soapy water. Hence **sudsabi·lity.**

1951 *Sun* (Baltimore) 15 Dec. 10 (Advt.), She never has too many blouses..so lovable..so wearable..so sudsable. **1959** *Wall St. Jrnl.* 16 Dec. 9/2 More folks are becoming more conscious of the sudsability of their tap water. **1970** *Globe & Mail* (Toronto) 25 Sept. 16/2 (Advt.), Tam-and-scarf set in thick suds-able hand-crocheted acrylic.

sudser (sɒ·dzəɹ). *U.S. slang.* [f. Suds *sb. pl.* + -er[1].] A soap opera.

1968 *New Yorker* 30 Mar. 114/2 It has the suggestions of sadness and 'depth' that make it a kind of high-class sudser for women. **1975** *Ibid.* 5 May 31/1 This NBC half-hour TV sudser expired after fifteen months. **1982** *Washington Post* 8 Dec. c10 Clooney's autobiography.. has been turned into another drably shabby TV sudser.

sudsy, *a.* Add: Also *transf.* and *fig.* (Earlier and later examples.)

1866 *Harper's Mag.* Sept. 544/2 He's gone! across the sudzy sea. **1980** *Times Lit. Suppl.* 17 Oct. 1160/1 Thanks to Arianna Stassinopoulos's votive ministrations, Maria Callas has graduated from opera to the sudsier, sublimer realm of soap opera.

suède. *Delete* ‖ and add: Now usu. **suede. 1.** Now applied to other kinds of leather finished to resemble undressed kid-skin. Also an article, usu. a shoe, made of suede.

1923 [see *SAND *sb.*[2] 1 i]. **1957** M. B. PICKEN *Fashion Dict.* 211/1 *Suede*.., leather, usually calf, finished by special process, with flesh side buffed on emery wheel to produce napped, velvety surface. **1968** V. CANNING *Melting Man* viii. 237 The only spare shoes were a pair of ginger suèdes. **1970** *Daily Tel.* 2 Mar. 14 Ankle-length, shiny, wet-look coats, suèdes and leathers were often trimmed with fur. **1975** C. CALASIBETTA *Fairchild's Dict. Fashion* 324/2 *Suede*, leather, usually lambskin, doeskin, or splits of cowhide..that has been buffed on the flesh side to raise a slight nap. **1982** T. HEALD *Masterstroke* v. 103 A heavy dew underfoot..soaked through Bognor's suedes, moistening his socks.

2. *attrib.* and *Comb.*, as *suede-coloured, -gloved, -like,* adjs.; **suede brush,** a brush with which to brush suede; **suede cloth** = *SUEDETTE; **suede-footed** *a.* = *suede-shoed* adj. below; **suedehead** *slang* (see quot. 1970); **suede shoe,** a shoe made with a suede upper; chiefly used *attrib.* to denote: (*a*) resemblance to the rough texture of suede; (*b*) *fig.*, something which displays a spurious smartness (*U.S. colloq.*); **suede-shoed** *a.*, wearing suede shoes.

1951 *Catal. of Exhibits, South Bank Exhib., Festival of Britain* 30/1 Suede brush; Federation of British Rubber Manufacturers Association. **1967** 'K. O'HARA' *Unknown Man* ix. 81 A rubber suede-brush she used to buff the key-case. **1930** *Daily Express* 30 July 5/4 Suede cloth, which made its real appearance in furnishing last year. **1979** *Arizona Daily Star* 5 Aug. J 5/2 (Advt.), Soft supple suedecloth is in several styles. **1897** Suède-coloured [in Dict.]. **1938** J. W. DAY *Dog in Sport* iv. 64 It will take many generations of stupid women in Bayswater and *suède*-footed young men in Kensington to ruin the character of this eminently sensible working dog. **1979** —— in *East Anglian Mag.* Aug. 531/2 None of your suede-footed, whey-faced, sniffling little intellectuals. **1981** J. JOHNSTON *Christmas Tree* 121 Her suede-gloved hands clasped on her knee. **1970** *Time* 8 June 37 The skinheads are lineal descendants of the rockers—with an added touch of mindless savagery. When their hair grows a trifle longer, they refer to themselves as suedeheads. Skins or suedes, they specialize in terrorising such menacing types as hippies and homosexuals, Pakistani immigrants and little old ladies. **1974** P. CAVE *Mama* (new ed.) iv. 25 The suedehead kids weren't expecting any 'bovver'. **1971** *Country Life* 28 Oct. 1107/1 When some browsing animal blunders against them bursting their [*sc.* the puffballs'] suede-like skin. **1952** *News* (San Francisco) 27 Feb. 10/1 (*heading*) 'Suede-shoe boys' renew racket here. Home-owners warned on repair work. **1973** M. AMIS *Rachel Papers* 29 *Chronic* bronco was reserved for nicotined oldsters with suede-shoe lungs. **1979** *Tucson* (Arizona) *Citizen* 20 Sept. 1B/6 There are also a lot more 'pseudo-high rollers' in Phoenix, too, which is Mano's polite description of a phony. 'Suede shoe types,' he calls them. **1980** D. MARLOWE *Rich Boy from Chicago* iv. 52 He edited the college magazine (pre-Beat poetry, suede-shoe satire). **1938** *New Statesman* 21 May 863/2 The abusive semi-illiterate or the sleek, shinily tailored, down-at-heel, suède-shoed play-boy, who hawks inferior goods on their doorstep.

sueded (swē^i·dėd), *a.* [f. SUÈDE + -ED[2].] Of leather: buffed on the flesh side to raise a slight nap. Also of fabrics, etc.: provided with a nap.

1956 *Gloss. Leather Terms* (*B.S.I.*) 5 A fine soft leather ..sueded on the flesh side. **1962** *L. L. Bean Catal.* Spring 12 Ladies' bush coat and pant..styled from sueded cotton poplin. **1971** *Leader* (Durban) 7 May 5/5 (Advt.), Men's bri-nylon sueded warm winter shirts. **1976** *National Observer* (U.S.) 30 Oct. 9/3 (Advt.), Made of strong and supple full grain steerhide with the rough side out. Rich, sueded finish. **1978** *Textiles* (Manchester) VII. 46/2 Patterned and sueded fabrics.

suedette (swe^ide·t). Also **suèdette.** [f. SUÈDE + -ETTE.] A material designed to imitate the texture of suede, esp. a type of cotton or rayon fabric with a suede-like nap.

1915 *Chambers's Jrnl.* May 413/1 A cover of waterproofed suedette. **1930** *Daily Express* 30 July 4/5 To make a smart..tea cosy, cut out four pieces of material.. in suede, velvet, or suedette. **1960** *Pract. Wireless* XXXVI. 350/2 The cabinet is finished in cream rexine with a royal blue suedette surround and a blue and gold scale. **1962** *Punch* 23 May 785/3 Massive Mums in tartan trews and suèdette jackets. **1963** *Punch* 10 July 54/2 Apple-green suedette wallpaper. **1971** *Sunday Times* 6 June 33 Swimming in suede is the new thing; swimming in cotton suedette the next best. **1977** *Cosmopolitan* Feb. 19/1 Wore brown suedette shoes with thin black suits and thick regional accents.

‖**suerte** (suē^ə·ɹte). [Sp., lit. 'chance, fate, luck': cf. SORT *sb.*[1]] An action or pass performed in bull-fighting; one of the three stages of a bull-fight; = *TERCIO, TERTIO 2 a.

1838 *Q. Rev.* LXI. 418 'Suertes' or manners of killing the bull. **1893** CHAPMAN & BUCK *Wild Spain* v. 58 It is in this phase of the fight that we trace the origin of several of the *suertes* which are practised in the modern Corrida de Toros. **1910** *Encycl. Brit.* IV. 790 The fight is divided into three divisions (*suertes*). *Ibid.*, Then begins the *suerte de picar*, or division of lancing. **1932** R. CAMPBELL *Taurine Provence* 61 The estocada is the climax, to hasten ..which, all the other suertes (actions, passes, and feats) must be devoted. **1957** A. MACNAB *Bulls of Iberia* v. 53 The *banderilla* act is a 'decorative' *suerte* rather than one of 'punishment'. **1967** McCORMICK & MASCAREÑAS *Compl. Aficionado* i. 24 'The suerte of the varas' means the picador's work.

Suess (sūs). The name of Hans E. *Suess* (b. 1909), Austrian-born U.S. chemist, used *attrib.* to designate certain phenomena in radio-carbon dating, as **Suess effect,** the reduction in the proportion of carbon 14 in the atmosphere and plant life during the twentieth century as a result of the increased burning of fossil fuels, which lack that isotope; **Suess wiggle,** each of a series of relatively short-term irregularities, of disputed existence and origin, in the calibration curve obtained by dendrochronology for radio-carbon dating.

1957 *Proc. R. Soc.* A. CCXLIII. 562 An accurate assessment of the Suess effect can yield valuable data on the carbon cycle. **1976** *Nature* 8 July 128/1 There have probably also been periods of irregular fluctuation spanning a few hundred years (the so-called Suess 'wiggles'). **1977** *Sci. Amer.* May 86/3 There is uncertainty in interpreting the present era of solar activity from carbon-14 evidence because of the Suess effect. **1979** *Nature* 5 July 48/1 (*heading*) Confirmation of the Suess wiggles: 3200–3700 BC.

suet. Add: **2. suet-brained** *a.*, stupid; **suet crust,** a form of heavy pastry made with suet, esp. used for meat or fruit puddings; **suet-faced** *a.*, having a face with an unhealthy or colourless complexion; **suet-headed** *a.*, stupid.

1921 *Public Opinion* 26 Aug. 199/2 Even among the most suet-brained readers of the Morning Post there are some [etc.]. **1845** E. ACTON *Mod. Cookery* xvi. 406 (*heading*) Common suet-crust for pies. **1906** *Mrs. Beeton's Bk. Househ. Managem.* xxxi. 889 Suet crust..flour..suet.. baking-powder..salt..water. **1951** *Good Housek. Home Encycl.* 671/1 Make 6–8 oz. suet-crust pastry. **1977** 'E. CRISPIN' *Glimpses of Moon* xii. 231 Mrs Clotworthy is making a steak-and-kidney pudding with a thick suet crust. **1922** JOYCE *Ulysses* 166 A pallid suetfaced young man polished his tumbler knife fork and spoon with his napkin. **1937** E. POUND *Let.* 10 Mar. (1971) 291 Make it clear..that 200 words per subject is all that wildcat editing can get over on the suet-headed Brits.

suevite (swē^i·vəit). *Petrogr.* [ad. G. *suevit*, f. L. *Suēvia, Suēbia*, name of a region in W. Germany (see SWABIAN *a.* 1 a): see -ITE[1].] A type of welded braccia found associated with impact craters, similar to a tuff but showing signs of impact metamorphism; orig. such a rock from the Ries crater near Nördlingen in W. Germany.

1938 *Mineral. Abstr.* VII. 74 The tuffs (suevite) of the Nördlinger Ries are supposed to be rocks fused by the impact of the meteorite. **1970** *New Scientist* 23 July 174/3 The so-called 'suevite' rocks of the Ries are almost identical to some of the surface samples from the fragmented lunar 'regolith'.

suey pow (sū·i pau). *U.S. slang.* Also **suey-pow, sui pow.** [Orig. unknown.] (See quot. 1914.)

1914 JACKSON & HELLYER *Vocab. Criminal Slang* 82 *Suey pow, noun*, current amongst opium smokers. A sponge or rag used to cool and cleanse the face of an opium bowl. **1926** *Variety* 29 Dec. 7/4 The dopes and hop heads, with their 'stem',..'sui pow', [etc.]. **1939** [see *joy-pop* s.v. *JOY *sb.* 10].

Suez (sū·iz, sū·ĕz). The name of an Egyptian port [Arab. *al-Suways*] at the head of the Red Sea, used *attrib.* and *absol.* to denote the military and political crisis which resulted from the nationalization of the Suez Canal in 1956; *Suez group* (now *Hist.*), a group of Conservative MPs who opposed the withdrawal of British troops from the Suez Canal Zone in 1954; hence applied to other groups advocating the presence of British troops in the Middle or Far East.

1955 *Ann. Reg. 1954* 34 Anglo-Egyptian talks have been recently renewed in Cairo..and the so-called 'Suez group' in the Conservative Party, about 40 in number and led by Captain Waterhouse, had consequently become restive. **1958** H. NICOLSON *Diary* 18 June (1968) 350, I am very worried about the Lebanon situation, fearing it may prove a repetition of Suez. **1961** *Guardian* 6 Dec. 18/1 Captain Charles Waterhouse, one of the original 'Suez rebels' in the winter of 1956–7. **1962** *Hansard Commons* 13 Nov. 281/1 The hon. Member for Leeds, East spoke of my hon. Friend the Member for Inverness as being a member of the Suez Group. **1966** *New Statesman* 3 June 804/1 The cabinet's Suez Group (Wilson, Healey, Stewart and Bottomley) are prepared to bring back a good many servicemen following the end of Confrontation but want to maintain the bases till the late 1970s. **1968** M. JONES *Survivor* iii. 55 She could not remember events like Suez and Hungary. **1972** R. R. JAMES *Ambitions & Realities* ii. 104 What became known as 'the Suez Group' constituted the first organized element in the Conservative Party that viewed Heath with hostility. **1981** A. PRICE *Soldier no More* ix. 122 Ever since Suez the Americans had been bad friends with the Israelis.

suffer, *v.* **3. b.** (Earlier example const. *under*.)

1836 DICKENS *Let.* 15 Nov. (1965) I. 195, I..am still suffering under..a head-ache.

suffering, *ppl. a.* Add: **3. d.** *suffering cat*(*s*)*!* an exclamation expressing surprise or annoyance. Also *the suffering Moses* (cf. MOSES 1 c), etc.

1869 'MARK TWAIN' *Innocents Abroad* v. 52 The suffering Moses!—there ain't money enough in the ship to pay that bill! **1897** KIPLING *Captains Courageous* vi. 134 'Sufferin' Christianity!' sez Counahan (he always said that whin..he was not feelin' good). **1907** S. E. WHITE *Arizona Nights* xv. 217 Suffering cats, think how that fellow sized us up for a lot of pattern-made fools. **1931** S. LEWIS *Sel. Short Stories* (1935) 162 Suffering cats! You might have been one of your uncles still puttering around with dirty pitchforks back on the farm! **1948** G. H. JOHNSTON *Death takes Small Bites* v. 122 She doesn't think I've got any guts.' 'Well, sufferin' cat! What does she want? Alexander the Great?' **1977** J. PORTER *Who the Heck is Sylvia?* vi. 54 Oh, suffering cats, with that bunch of lecherous thugs it could have been *anybody!*

sufficient, *a.* Add: **1. c.** For *rare* read '*rare* exc. in allusion to or imitation of Matt. vi. 34'.

1766 A. ADAMS *Let.* 13 Oct. in L. H. Butterfield et al. *Adams Family Corr.* (1963) I. 56 Sufficient to the Day is the Evil thereof. **1917** H. B. TWYFORD *Purchasing & Storing* 323 A 'sufficient unto the day' policy has brought some rude jolts to many manufacturing establishments. **1921** GALSWORTHY *To Let* I. xii. 114 He never looks happy—not really happy. I don't want to make him worse, but of course I shall have to, when Jon comes back. Oh! well, sufficient unto the night! **1928** D. H. LAWRENCE *Lady Chatterley's Lover* ii. 18 Sufficient unto the day is the evil thereof. Sufficient unto the moment is the *appearance* of reality. **1960** C. DAY LEWIS *Buried Day* ii. 34 They watch the spring rise inexhaustibly—a breathing thread out of the eddied sand, sufficient to their day. **1967** S. BECKETT *Stories & Texts for Nothing* v. 93, I haven't been damned for what seems an eternity, yes, but sufficient unto the day, this evening I'm the scribe. **1983** E. ROSSITER *Lemon Garden* v. 72 'What about this hospital business?' Sufficient, I thought, unto another day.

2. c. *sufficient condition* (see quot. 1930). Cf. *necessary condition* s.v. *NECESSARY *a.* 1 d.

1914 B. RUSSELL *Our Knowledge of External Wrld.* iv. 109 In the hypothetical sense, continuity may be allowed to be a *necessary* condition if two appearances are to be classed as appearances of the same thing. But it is not a *sufficient* condition, as appears from the instance of the drops in the sea. **1923** C. D. BROAD *Sci. Thought* xiii. 499 Certain brain-events are the necessary and sufficient conditions of the occurrence of all our different sensations. **1930** L. S. STEBBING *Mod. Introd. Logic* xv. 271 A condition X is a *sufficient condition* of an occurrence A provided that whenever X is present A occurs. But if A may occur when X is absent, then X, though a sufficient is not a *necessary* condition of A. **1948** AMBROSE & LAZEROWITZ *Fund. Symbolic Logic* v. 83 The sufficient condition for *q*'s truth is given by '$p \supset q$'. **1949** [see *NECESSARY *a.* 1 d]. **1965** E. J. LEMMON *Beginning Logic* i. 28 Hence we shall say that, whenever it is the case that if *P* then *Q*, *P* is sufficient condition for *Q*, and, whenever it is the case that only if *P* then *Q*, *P* is a *necessary condition* for *Q*.

d. *sufficient statistic*, a statistic that contains all the information in the observations it is based on that is relevant to the estimate being made.

[**1922** R. A. FISHER in *Phil. Trans. R. Soc.* A. CCXXII. 316 The statistic chosen should summarise the whole of the relevant information supplied by the sample. This may be called the Criterion of Sufficiency.] *Ibid.* 359 In the case of the normal curve of distribution it is evident that the second moment is a sufficient statistic for estimating the standard deviation. **1972** A. W. F. EDWARDS *Likelihood* ii. 18 If we were certain that no other model would ever be contemplated, then the sufficient statistic could replace the original data as raw material for inductive inference.

suffisance. Restrict † *Obs.* to senses 1–6 and add: **7.** Now only with Fr. pronunc. (sufizaṅs). (Later *Lit.* examples.)

1917 D. H. LAWRENCE *Phoenix II* (1968) 82 The police-officer turned, saluted politely, and said, with the polite, intolerable *suffisance* of officialdom: 'Good evening! Trouble here!' **1925** —— *St. Mawr* 25 At the same time he was free of the Englishman's water-tight *suffisance*. **1957** S. SMITH *Coll. Poems* (1975) 344 Ah me the *suffisance* I drew therefrom What strength, what glory from that fattening fluid.

suffix, *sb.* Add: **3. suffix ablaut,** variation in the vowel of a suffix; **suffix language** (earlier example).

1900 E. BJÖRKMAN *Scand. Loan-Words in M.E.* I. 112 Here *aȝ* might depend on suffix-ablaut as in O.E. *fazen, faȝ*(*e*)*nian*. **1977** *Archivum Linguisticum* VIII. 80 We must now examine cases where SF apparently fails, despite a following [l] rather than [ɫ]. Several cases, such as *falaed, alaer* may be explicable on grounds of 'suffix ablaut'. **1874** H. BENDALL tr. *Schleicher's Compar. Gram.* 3 The Indo-European is therefore a suffix-language, together with the neighbouring languages of the Finnish stem.

Hence **su·ffixual** *a.* = SUFFIXAL *a.*

1901 J. HUGUENIN *Secondary Stress in Anglo-Saxon* 13 The inflected cases in which the suffixual syllable is lengthened by position are, the genitive and dative singular feminine, the accusative singular masculine, and the genitive plural. **1964** [see *MORA[1] 3 b].

suffling (sɒ·f'liŋ), *vbl. sb.* [f. SUFFL(E *v.* + -ING[1].] A sound as of blowing or heavy breathing.

1904 H. F. DAY *Kin O'Ktaadn* I. 11 The..whummle of horses and..sufflings of..cattle hint that 'fodder-time' is at hand. **1933** W. DE LA MARE *Lord Fish* 37 It was so full of the suffling and sighing, the music and murmuration of water.

Suffolk. Add: **a.** *Suffolk ham*; **Suffolk latch** (see quot. 1972); **Suffolk sheep,** a black-faced hornless sheep of a breed first developed in East Anglia, distinguished by a short fleece, large size, and the production of lean meat.

1855 E. ACTON *Mod. Cookery* (rev. ed.) xiii. 256 The receipt for the Suffolk ham. **1966** *Times* 28 Dec. 9/6 A genuine Suffolk ham man is Mr. R. Stiff of Kersey. He uses his own pigs and douses the hams in black treacle, spices and stout. They are then floated in tubs of sweet pickle. **1940** *Chambers's Techn. Dict.* 819/2 *Suffolk Latch* (*Join.*), a variant of the *Norfolk Latch*. **1972** *Country Life* 13 Jan. 98/1 The great variety of country door-latches would reward a study in depth: the well-known type, the 'Suffolk latch', is usually operated by a pivoted blade, which passing through the door and depressed by thumb pressure, lifts the latch. **1981** 'G. GAUNT' *Incomer* xviii. 117 Les Taunton thumbed down the Suffolk latch of the Queen's Head taproom and entered. [**1794** A. YOUNG *Gen. View Agric. Suffolk* XIII. 33 The Norfolk breed of sheep spread over almost every part of the county; and as the most famous flocks are about Bury..it has been observed, that they ought rather to be called the Suffolk breed.] **1893** J. WRIGHTSON *Sheep* viii. 75 The original Suffolk sheep existed in famous flocks during Arthur Young's time.

c. Also, = Suffolk punch, sheep.

1831 W. YOUATT *Horse* 39 The immense power of the Suffolk is accounted for by the low position of the shoulder. **1902** *Encycl. Brit.* XXV. 193/2 The Suffolk..probably took its origin in the crossing of improved Southdown rams with the old horned Norfolk ewes. **1928** [see *ACTIONED *ppl. a.*]. **1960** G. E. EVANS *Horse in Furrow* xiii. 181 He knew the Suffolks so well..that he could pick out a horse's breed by studying him. **1979** C. MACLEOD *Luck runs Out* (1981) ii. 21 Those gorgeous Clydesdales and Percherons and Belgians and Suffolks..with their brasses polished like gold. **1980** 'D. SHANNON' *Felony File* vii. 173 He's found the sheep... They're sixty dollars each. They're Suffolks.

Suffolker (sɒ·fəkəɹ). [f. SUFFOLK + -ER[1].] A native or inhabitant of Suffolk.

1849 DICKENS *Dav. Copp.* (1850) xi. 117 The men generally spoke of me as..'the young Suffolker'. **1910** H. M. DOUGHTY *Chron. Theberton* iii. 40 We Suffolkers never misplace H's. **1952** M. ALLINGHAM *Tiger in Smoke* vi. 100 We come from the same part of the country, sir. We're all Suffolkers. **1978** *East Anglian Daily Times* 7 Dec. 8/6 First was depicted the hitherto unseen paintings of a dead Suffolker, the late Cecil Howard Lay.

suffrage, *sb.* Add: **11. b.** Also *adult suffrage*.

1906 W. R. CREMER in *Hansard Commons* 25 Apr. 1572 If they once opened the door and enfranchised ever so small a number of females..it ultimately meant adult suffrage... Hon. Members had not really thought out what adult suffrage must lead to. **1910** *Hansard Commons* 11 July 55 The Member for Clitheroe explained with great explicitness what his object is. The hon. Gentleman's object is adult suffrage. That adult suffrage, of course, includes the vote for all adult women... The result of this adult suffrage, when it does come, will be a total electorate of 23,000,000 instead of 7,000,000. In that total electorate there will be a considerable majority of women. **1939** G. B. SHAW *Geneva* I. 16 The president and parliament are elected by adult suffrage every two years.

suffragette. Add: Also as *v. intr.* (in quot. *fig.*). **suffragettish, -ism** (examples). Also **suffragetty** *a.*

1909 H. G. WELLS *Ann Veronica* vii. 134 And her straight hair was out demonstrating and suffragetting upon some independent notions of its own. **1912** C. S. CHURCHILL *Let.* 7 Feb. in M. Soames *Clementine Churchill* (1979) vi. 76 Amy is kind, but more Suffragetty, Christian Sciency and Yankee Doodle than ever. **1913** G. B. SHAW *Let.* 4 Feb. in *B. Shaw & Mrs. Campbell* (1952) 79 That is the sort of thing that you vaguely lump into a cloud of abomination as Suffragettism. **1957** E. HYAMS *Speaking Garden* 75 What, in their time, were more ludicrous than suffragettism or antisepsis or anti-slavery? **1970** G. GREER *Female Eunuch* 295 The history of suffragettism.. is beyond the scope of this book. **1974** V. NABOKOV *Look at Harlequins* (1975) IV. iv. 173 Mrs. Noteboke, a stout dark lady in suffragettish tweeds.

suffragi (sufrāgī). Also **suffraggi.** [a. *sufragī*, repr. Egyptian Arab. pronunc. Turk. *sofraji*, f. Arab. *sufra* food, dining-table + Turk. agent-suffix *-ji*.] A waiter, butler or steward.

1924 *Blackw. Mag.* Feb. 246/2 Our suffragi and cook led a sort of troglodyte life for days. **1959** W. THESIGER *Arabian Sands* xiii. 247 In the new 'hotel'..there was electric light, fans, and tinned food served by a Sudanese suffragi. **1972** R. MAUGHAM *Escape from Shadows* iii. 136 Suffragis sprang up from nowhere with drinks, and I was offered one. **1979** *Stand* XX. IV. 34/2 The suffraggi puts a whisky before me.

suffragist. Add: Hence **suffragi·stic** *a.*, **suffragi·stically** *adv.*

1907 M. BEERBOHM in *Sat. Rev.* 13 Apr. 457/2 The shrill suffragistic cheers which punctuated the first performance. **1909** *Daily Chron.* 13 Nov. 6/4 The pageant had been preceded by an excellent entertainment, including several 'suffragistic' and other playlets. **1923** K. D. WIGGIN *My Garden of Memory* (1924) xiii. 121 Ella intrusively and suffragistically fluttered into the nest,..sadly complicating the family arrangements.

suffusive, *a.* (Earlier example.)

1872 GEO. ELIOT *Middlem.* I. II. xvi. 295 That agreeable after-glow of excitement when thought lapses from examination of a specific object into a suffusive sense of its connections with all the rest of our existence.

sugar, *sb.* Add: **1. e.** *colloq.* A lump or teaspoonful of sugar.

1962 L. DEIGHTON *Ipcress File* xxiii. 150 He poured coffee into a black wedgwood cup and put four sugars in. 'Raise the sugar count,' he said. **1978** C. MACLEOD *Rest you Merry* (1979) ii. 18 'Why don't I make us a cup of coffee?' 'Great idea. Three sugars in mine.' **1982** *Sunday Tel.* 18 Apr. 8/6 How many sugars they were allowed in their tea.

2. d. *slang* (orig. *U.S.*). A narcotic drug: spec. (*a*) heroin; *brown sugar* (see quot. 1974); (*b*) LSD (taken on a lump of sugar).

1935 A. J. POLLOCK *Underworld Speaks* 116/2 *Sugar and salt*, poisonous habit forming drugs; any of the white narcotics. **1951** *Evening Sun* (Baltimore) 27 Mar. 4/1 Dope in general was 'cement'..'sugar', etc. **1956** H. GOLD *Man who was not with It* (1965) iii. 27 You'll dream about the sugar yet. You'll wake up hot for it. No joy-popping, hear? Stay off, kid. **1967** M. M. GLATT et al. *Drug Scene* Gloss. 116 *Sugar*, dose of LSD on sugar lump. **1973** K. ROYCE *Spider Underground* viii. 118 We sat in a corner of this dark, smoke-infested hole that smelled of.. third-rate pot... 'What a place to pick,' I complained. 'It's the sort of dump the fuzz raid three times a week.'.. 'Relax, man. They hit us last night... That makes it safe, man. I'm not carrying sugar or anything. I don't touch the stuff.' **1974** *Indonesian Observer* 26 July 3/2 French police said this year they have seized 50·6 pounds (23 kilograms) of 'brown sugar' in the suitcases of 13 Chinese arriving at Orly airport enroute to Amsterdam. The brown sugar is 33 per cent heroin diluted with 60 per cent caffein and strychnine. **1978** D. MACKENZIE *Raven settles Score* (1979) 32 No more Hong Kong brown sugar. We'll be out of business. **1979** *Observer* 25 Nov. 4/1 Detectives call them the 'sugar people' and they are young, rich and blue-blooded. They are also heroin addicts. It is in an ironic double reference to the 'sugar daddy' parents and to the expensive white powder they inject or sniff.

e. *colloq.* A term of endearment. Also in Comb., as *sugar-babe, -baby, -pie*, etc.

1930 *Dialect Notes* VI. 85 *Sugar-pie*,..common term of endearment. **1930** J. H. COMBS in B. A. Botkin *Folk-Say* v. 245 A-settin' on the ice till my feet got cold, sugar-babe. **1936** M. MITCHELL *Gone with Wind* xxvi. 455 Scarlett said gratefully: 'Thank you, Sugarbaby.' **1936** J. CURTIS *Gilt Kid* vi. 68 When am I going to see you again, sugar? **1944** L. A. G. STRONG *Director* xvii. 135 See here, sugar. I'll take care of you. **1951** S. SPENDER *World within World* i. 26 No, you don't, sugar, you don't go out with your cold. **1962** J. D. MACDONALD *Girl, Gold Watch & Everything* vii. 87 What you do for a living, sugar? **1976** P. FLOWER *Crisscross* i. 10 'What's funny, sugar?' Sibyl said... Would he ever get Sibyl to stop calling him sugar? **1980** D. BRIERLEY *Blood Group O* 76 Okay, sugar, what are you looking for?

3. a. *sugar of lead, sugar of milk* (later examples).

1847 C. J. HEMPEL tr. *Rau's Organon of Specific Healing Art* lxii. 128 If triturated with sugar of milk, it [*sc.* phosphorus] changes to phosphoric acid in a very few hours. **1864** P. SQUIRE *Compan. Brit. Pharmacopœia* 161 *Sugar of Milk*... Crystallized Sugar obtained from the Whey of Cow's Milk by evaporation. **1895** *Montgomery Ward Catal.* Spring & Summer 252/3 Artists Tube Oil Colors..Silver White, Sugar of Lead, Terre Verte. **1975** *Nature* 23 Oct. 632/2 Something needed to be done to stop the watering of milk..and even so flagrant a malpractice as the use of 'sugar of lead', as lead acetate was called, to sweeten beer.

4. a. (*a*) *sugar basin* (earlier examples), *basket, bin, cube, dish* (earlier examples), *factory, icing* (later *comb.* and *fig.* examples), *industry, kettle* (earlier example), *knife* (later example), *lump, mill* (later examples), *mule, ration, refinery* (earlier example; also *fig.*), *scoop, thermometer, trade* (later example), *worker*. (*b*) *sugar field, grove, island* (later examples), *land, plantation*.

1785 *Daily Universal Reg.* 1 Jan. 3/2 (Advt.), Oval pierced sugar and cream basons, 10 oz. to 15 oz. a pair. *a* **1828** D. WORDSWORTH *Jrnl.* (1941) II. 81 A sugar-basin made of cocoa-nut. **1917** F. H. BIGELOW *Historic Silver of Colonies* 472/1 (Index), Sugar baskets. **1981** *Sunday Tel.* 18 Jan. 13/2 Garrads have augmented the exhibition with antique castors.., as well as sugar baskets, boxes, tongs and nippers. **1922** JOYCE *Ulysses* 58 There he is,..leaning against the sugar-bin in his shirt-sleeves. **1897** Sugar cube [see *CUBE *sb.*[1] 1 b]. **1978** T. ALLBEURY *Lantern Network* xi. 169 She was screwing up the paper from the sugar cubes. **1742** W. ELLIS *Timber-Tree Improved* II. 151, I was told..that this Wood makes fine Sugar-dishes, and other Turners-ware. **1765** J. WEDGWOOD *Let.* 17 June (1965) 34 The articles are..a slop basin, sugar dish with cover, [etc.]. **1908** KIPLING *Actions & Reactions* (1909) 96 They [*sc.* bees] took to cadging round sugar-factories and breweries. **1958** O. CAROE *Pathans* xxvi. 429 Peshawar, always famous for its sugar-cane, has been enriched with finer varieties which have turned the old village industry of *gur* into the great sugar-factories which now sustain the life of Pakistan. **1930** W. K. HANCOCK *Australia* iv. 81 Polynesians in their wild state never clamoured for admission to the Queensland sugar-fields. **1792** G. IMLAY *Topogr. Descr. Western Terr. N. Amer.* 136 Luxuriant sugar groves. **1847** *Ex. Doc. 31st U.S. Congress 1 Sess. House* (1849) No. 5. III. 629 A ridge covered with sugar maples, formerly an Indian sugar grove. **1948** E. N. DICK *Dixie Frontier* 247 A clump numbering from one hundred to three hundred trees was chosen for the operation. Such a clump came to be called a sugar grove. **1930** E. WAUGH *Labels* vii. 180 Gaudi has again introduced his 'sugar-icing' motive, translating it from tile and mosaic into carved stone. **1979** 'M. HEBDEN' *Pel & Faceless Corpse* xii. 123 The pink shirt had suddenly become sugar icing-coloured and hideously wrong. **1887** *Encycl. Brit.* XXII. 628/1 There are numerous modified and subsidiary processes connected with refining, as well as with all branches of the sugar industry. **1779** Sugar island [see *SCUTTLE *v.*[2] 1 a]. **1980** *Jrnl. R. Soc. Arts* Apr. 271/1 The UK has traditionally bought 50 per cent of the sugar consumed here on the world market, principally from the Sugar Islands of the Caribbean. **1834** J. KEMPER in *Wisconsin Hist. Coll.* (1898) XIV. 444 If ardor leads some of the [Sioux] hunters beyond the boundary stake, they can be punished by the soldiers by having their sugar kettles broken or their lodges torn down. **1949** *Caribbean Q.* I. 8 It was..the stalwart, armed with hoes and..sugar knives.., whose work would 'make or break' the proprietor. **1692** *Calendar Virginia State Papers* (1875) I. 44 We marcht to the Suggar Land. **1883** SWEET & KNOX *On Mexican Mustang through Texas* vii. 82 A great deal of the finest sugar-lands in the world. **1974** *Guardian* 23 Jan. 12/6 As far as sugar lands are concerned,..the Government is now the largest landowner. Tate and Lyle sold their lands to the last government. **1901** KIPLING *Kim* xii. 307 She chuckled like a contented parrot above the sugar lump. **1964** D. FRANCIS *Nerve* ix. 122 The dope has been given to the horses on sugar lumps. **1882** W. D. HAY *Brighter Britain!* I. viii. 221 If all the farmers in the district were to combine to grow beet-root on every acre they could plough,..even then it would hardly pay the sugar-mills, or possibly the farmers either. **1971** *Advocate-News* (Barbados) 24 Apr. 10/1 (Advt.), ⅓ acre house plots and/or cottage with sugarmill and swimming pool. **1908** *U.S. Dept. Agric. Farmers' Bull.* No. 334. 24 Sugar mules are those shipped south to use on the sugar farms of Georgia, Louisiana, and other Southern States. **1960** V. WILLIAMS *Walk Egypt* 71 A sugar mule, now, was a big fellow. He ate big, but he pulled big, and he would look big before the wagon. **1883** 'MARK TWAIN' *Life on Miss.* xl. 419 The great sugar plantations border both sides of the [Mississippi] river. **1978** 'A. YORK' *Tallant for Disaster* ii. 28 The burnt earth roadway which led to the sugar plantation. **1917** Sugar ration [see *RATION 3 c]. **1978** L. DEIGHTON *SS-GB* xxv. 237 Drink up your tea, that's a good boy. It's the last of the sugar ration. **1794** A. YOUNG *Trav. France* (ed. 2) II. xix. 539 The sugar refinery is a considerable business, there are 10 large and 17 smaller houses engaged in it. **1896** G. MEREDITH *Let.* 17 June (1970) III. 1236, I..can own her sweet to the ear, wondering what it is in her that extracts her deadly bitter from a sugar-refinery. **1916** *Daily Colonist* (Victoria, B.C.) 1 July 8/2 Mothers had been remembered by most of the workers, for there were bread boards, and sleeve holders, sugar scoops and wooden spoons. **1960** R. A. PARKER *Family of Friends* 89 The old days of the Quaker garb and the sugar-scoop bonnet were gone forever. **1977** *Time* 14 Nov. 21/1 The Concordski whistled down the runway for 33 seconds, sucking in air through four 'sugar scoop' intakes slung beneath its body. **1913** M. H. NEIL *Candies & Bonbons & how to make Them* 24 A sugar thermometer is generally used for testing the boiling syrup. **1887** *Encycl. Brit.* XXII. 625/1 Within the first twenty years of the 16th century the sugar trade of San Domingo expanded with great rapidity. **1973** *Sunday Express* (Trinidad) 1 Apr. 12/5 A delegation of sugar workers is to ..protest what they call the 'abandonment of the cane-growing industry'.

b. *sugar-broker* (example), *-growing* (earlier example), *-maker* (later examples), *-making* (later examples), *-planter* (later examples), *-producer, -producing* (earlier example), *rationing, -refiner* (later examples).

1841 *Picayune* (New Orleans) 10 June 2/3 Several dealers in sugar and sugar brokers were yesterday summoned before Recorder Bertus. **1816** *Niles' Reg.* 6 Apr. 81/1 The representatives of the sugar-growing states insist on a certain duty upon that article. **1835** J. J. AUDUBON *Ornith. Biogr.* III. 439 With large ladles the sugar-makers stirred the thickening juice of the maple. **1899** W. A. MACKAY *Pioneer Life in Zorra* 171 Not infrequently would the sugar-makers remain in the woods most of the night boiling down the sap. **1828** M. O'BRIEN *Jrnls.* (1968) I. iii. 27 During sugar-making time it will contain a furnace and other vessels. **1953** R. F. V. HEUSTON *Salmond's Law of Torts* (ed. 11) xiv. 566 In *Indermaur* v. *Dames* itself the hole in the floor was a defect but a necessary incident of sugar-making. **1842** *Niles' Reg.* 14 May 176/3 (*caption*) Sugar planters of Louisiana. **1926** J. MASEFIELD *Odtaa* i. 4 In the seventies others, from all parts of England, settled as sugar-planters along the northern sea coast in the Pituba country. **1983** A. BROOKNER *Look at Me* iv. 56 The wealthy sugar planter's daughter. **1881** *Harper's Mag.* Apr. 646 We met one of the largest sugar producers. **1974** *Guardian* 23 Jan. 12/4 Jamaica is the biggest sugar producer in the Commonwealth Caribbean. **1866** 'MARK TWAIN' *Lett. from Hawaii* (1967) 135 Maui.. that deservedly famous sugar-producing region. **1918** *Times* 29 Jan. 3/1 When sugar rationing actually came into operation, the workers..had to face considerable pressure. **1976** J. LEE *Ninth Man* 77 Talking about sugar rationing. **1879** G. W. BAGBY *Canal Reminiscences* 10 What was their petty thieving compared to the enormous pillage of the modern sugar refiner and the crooked-whiskey distiller? **1979** *Dædalus* Summer 113 Sugar refiners, soap boilers, glass blowers, and brewers..depended on continuously fired furnaces.

c. *sugar-cured* (earlier U.S. examples), *-free*, *-pink*.

1848 A. PRENTICE *Let.* 20 June in *Tour in U.S.* vi. 56, I tasted some excellent sugar-cured ham. **1889** *Judge* (U.S.) 12 Jan. 222/2 Beautiful red, sugar-cured ham. **1924** *Amer. Jrnl. Physiol.* LXVII. 635 Three other totally depancreatized dogs had been used for studying the administration of insulin..for several weeks, during which time their urine was never sugar-free for a period of more than 6 or 7 hours at a time. **1978** *N.Y. Times Mag.* 23 July 22/3 The absence of what had formerly been desirable is now proudly advertised: not only lead-free gas, but salt-free diets and sugar-free soft drinks. **1961** *House & Garden* Feb. 48 A..sofa covered in sugar-pink tafetta. **1978** 'M. M. KAYE' *Far Pavilions* xxi. 299 Rajastham..where..men..painted their houses blinding white or sugar-pink.

5. a. sugar-almond (later examples); **sugar aquatint,** a method of etching in which the artist draws his dark areas on a copper plate with a solution of black water-colour and sugar; **sugar-bag,** (*a*) a bag or sack for containing sugar, *esp.* a bag made of coarse thick paper specially coloured or (*Austral.* and *N.Z.*) of fine sacking; also used as a measure of quantity; (*b*) (in Austral. Aborigines' speech) a wild bees' honeycomb; **sugar-cake** (later examples); **sugar-camp** (earlier and later examples); **sugar card,** a ration card entitling the holder to a ration of sugar; **sugar-coated** *ppl. a.* (earlier example); also *fig.*; **sugar-crusher,** (*a*) a machine for crushing sugar-cane; (*b*) an implement for crushing sugar for use at table; **sugar daddy** [cf. *DADDY 3] *slang* (orig. *U.S.*), an elderly man who lavishes gifts on a young woman; also *transf.*; **sugar-house molasses** (earlier examples); **sugar mouse,** a sweet made of sugar in the shape of a mouse; **sugar nippers,** (*a*) an implement for cutting loaf sugar into lumps; (*b*) a pair of sugar tongs; **sugar-on-snow** *U.S.*, a delicacy made by pouring hot maple syrup on snow (SNOW *sb.*[1] 4 a); **sugar-paper,** coarse paper such as that used for making sugar-bags; **sugar puff,** (*a*) a puff (see PUFF *sb.* 5) made with sugar; (*b*) *pl.*, the proprietary name of a breakfast cereal; **sugar rag** *U.S.* = *sugar-teat*; **sugar sack,** a bag made of fine sacking for containing sugar; the sacking itself; **sugar sand** *U.S.*, a fine sand raised by the sap of the maple tree which results in a gritty sediment in maple syrup unless removed; **sugar shell** *N. Amer.*, a spoon with a shell-shaped bowl for serving sugar; **sugar sifter,** (*a*) see quot. 1875; (*b*) = *sugar caster*; **sugar snow,** (*b*) *N. Amer.*, a snowfall in the maple sugar season (see quot. 1932); **sugar soap,** an alkaline abrasive used to remove paint, and in solution for cleaning paintwork; **sugar stick,** also *fig.*; **sugar-teat** (later example); also **sugar-tit; sugar trough** *U.S.*, a wooden trough used for collecting maple sap; **sugar vase,** a tall sugar-container for use at table; **sugar-weather** *Canad.*, spring weather, characterized by cold nights and warm days, that starts the sap running in maple trees.

1935 *Amer. Speech* X. 193/2 The '*bonbon* [fashion] shades' included *icing blue* and *sugar almond pink*. **1973** G. GREENE *Honorary Consul* III. ii. 124 It [*sc.* a missal] might have been a first Communion present, for it closely resembled the sugar almonds..distributed on such occasions. **1962** D. BLAND *Illustration of Bks.* (ed. 3) viii. 155 Picasso used sugar aquatints in his Buffon, making two plates, one to print grey and the other black. **1764** *New Hampsh. Hist. Soc. Coll.* (1889) IX. 156, [I sent] also lb 14¼ Sugar bag with it. **1830** R. DAWSON *Present State of Australia* 136 The strange native pointed with his tomahawk to the tree and..repeated the words, 'Choogar-bag, choogar-bag, choogar-bag!' (sugar-bag) their English expression for honey, or anything sweet. **1864** R. HENNING *Let.* 27 Nov. (1966) 185 The other [aboriginal] has been..climbing gum-trees after 'sugar-bags', or wild honeycombs. **1882** *Cassell's Family Mag.* Nov. 756/2 The crowns..have two square corners like the bottom of a sugar-bag. **1913** D. H. LAWRENCE *Sons & Lovers* vii. 164 There's something very blue; is it a bit of sugar-bag? **1927** M TERRY *Through Land of Promise* 104 We found the others clustered round a bauhinia tree... 'We've got a sugar bag.' **1928** V. PALMER *Passage* I. v. 44 It was Uncle Tony standing with a sugar-bag over his shoulders. **1948** F. A. IREMONGER *William Temple* v. 81 A nine-year-old boy in a Bethnal Green school, who handed to his teacher one morning an untidy piece of blue paper torn from a sugar-bag. **1963** *N.Z. Listener* 6 Sept. 9/2 Reference to the price of a 'sugar' bag full of oysters. It drew my attention to the frequency with which we in New Zealand refer to a 'sugar bag' as a basic unit of quality. **1967** A. & D. REID *Paddle Wheels on Wanganui* 71 On another trip the same cabin boy acquired a sugar-bag of apples. **1923** Sugar cake [see *SAUERBRATEN]. **1977** A. WILSON *Strange Ride of Rudyard Kipling* ii. 110 The Durbar Room at the Queen's beloved Osborne House—not a very happy sugar-cake Moghul decoration. **1779** M. PATTEN *Diary* (1903) 400, I went to our shugar Camp and covered some fire steads with brush where we had Cabbage and french Turnip seed sowed to preserve them from Cattle. **1805** R. SUTCLIFF *Trav. N. Amer.* (1811) 184, I saw several sugar camps..where the sap is collected in small wooden troughs. **1959** R. CAMPBELL *I would do it Again* ii. 7 The neighbours gathered at the sugar camps. **1966** *Publ. Amer. Dial. Soc.* XXXVIII. 66 *Sugar camp.* This characteristically Midland [Illinois] term appears only once in the field interviews but with much more frequency in the checklists. **1917** H. H. HENSON *Jrnl.* 11 Dec. in *Retrospect* (1942) I. vi. 217, I started the day by filling up the new sugar cards for the household. **1875** 'MARK TWAIN' in *Atlantic Monthly* Aug. 195/1 Stephen sweetened him up and put him off a week. He called then..and came away sugar-coated again. **1935** *Motion Picture* Nov. 81/1 That keen humor, barbed sometimes, pointed always, but never other than good-natured and sugar-coated, has passed beyond our ken. **1977** R. L. WOLFF *Gains & Losses* ii. 197 The earliest [High Church] novelists..whose fiction amounted to little more than sugar-coated tracts. **1870** A. S. STEPHENS *Married in Haste* 366 He held a sugar-crusher in one hand. **1901** KIPLING *Kim* xv. 403 He felt..that his soul was out of gear with its surroundings—a cog-wheel unconnected with any machinery, just like the idle cog-wheel of a cheap Beheea sugar-crusher laid by in a corner. **1962** J. B. PRIESTLEY *Margin Released* I. i. 11 In winter, toddy, for which we had those silver sugar-crushers. **1926** G. FRANKAU *My Unsentimental Journey* ii. 32 There came another woman to the sofa; and spoke to me of 'sugar-daddies'. **1935** WODEHOUSE *Luck of Bodkins* xxi. 266 The morning papers had come aboard, reassuring citizens ..that sugar daddies were still being surprised in love-nests. **1959** [see *DOOR-MAT b]. **1973** *Times* 13 July (Motor Racing Suppl.) p. iii/2 The oil and petrol companies, for a long time the sugar-daddies of top class motor racing. *Ibid.* 20 Sept. 3/7 Norma Levy, a prostitute, had a 'sugar daddy' called Bunny who paid her rent and gave her a Mercedes car. **1848** W. E. BURTON *Waggeries* 35 Encomiums on the sweets of married life were drowned in sugar-house molasses. **1886** B. P. POORE *Perley's Reminisc.* I. 39 Many of the passengers visited the bar to imbibe Holland gin and sugar-house molasses—a popular morning beverage. **1931** A. UTTLEY *Country Child* xii. 115 She pinched the stocking from the toe to the top... There was a tin ball..filled with comfits, and an orange, and a sugar mouse. **1965** 'M. A. GIBBS' *Sugar Mouse* xv. 155 A sugar mouse, its chocolate eyes run to smudges, its paper ears flattened,..and its sugar hardened into rock. **1790** *Pennsylvania Packet* 1 Mar. 1/1 This Day ..will commence the Sale of a Large and General Assortment of..screw drivers, iron holders, sugar nippers. **1840** BARHAM *Ingol. Leg.* 1st Ser. 240 With those great sugar nippers they nipp'd off his 'flippers'. **1858** P. L. SIMMONDS *Dict. Trade Products, Sugar-nippers*, tools for cutting loaf-sugar into lumps. **1921** *Glasgow Herald* 14 July 5 A pair of George II. silver sugar nippers. **1981** *Sugar nippers* [see *sugar basket*, sense 4 a above]. **1947** *Publ. Amer. Dial. Soc.* VIII. 9 *Sugar on snow*,..'waxed' maple sugar served on snow. **1948** *Richmond* (Va.) *Times-Dispatch* 9 Jan. 16/1 As serious a breach of etiquette as eating 'sugar-on-snow' with a knife or beating one's grandmother in public. **1973** M. CROWELL *Greener Pastures* 173 It never fails to remind me..of our introduction to sugar-on-snow. **1926** *Paper Terminol.* (Spalding & Hodge, Ltd.) 24 *Sugar paper*, a common quality of wrapping paper made principally from paper waste. Used.. for sugar bags. **1972** *Guardian* 5 Dec. 16/7 Drawing paper ..Grey or off-white, good quality sugar paper. **1711** Sugar puff [see *RATAFIA 1]. **1736** [In Dict., sense 4 a]. **1957** *Trade Marks Jrnl.* 1 May 460 Sugar Puffs... Cereal preparations coated with sugar and flavoured with honey... Quaker Oats Limited. **1959** *Elizabethan* Apr. 10/1 You've taken all the Sugar Puffs which are sweet already and left me with one mouldy old bit of Shredded Wheat. **1962** J. BRAINE *Life at Top* xiii. 173, I want Sugar Puffs, Daddy, I do. And yoggy. And cheese. **1855** J. E. COOKE *Ellie* 203 Are you going..to make a sugar-rag for that baby up there? **1895** 'MARK TWAIN' in *Harper's Mag.* Dec. 136/1 Somebody fetch this sick doll a sugar-rag. **1938** *Daily Progress* (Charlottesville, Va.) 15 Feb. 1/6 Mayor J. Fulmer Bright..dubbed the concessions offered by the State a 'sugar-rag dipped in paregoric'. **1891** KIPLING *Light that Failed* ii. 18 Has any man here a needle? I've got a piece of sugar-sack. **1929** B. L. BURMAN *Mississippi* 78 Two beds, one made of automobile cushions nailed together and covered with a few folded sugar-sacks. **1965** S. T. OLLIVIER *Petticoat Farm* x. 140 The thin tired figure with the..sugar-sack apron and dishevelled hair. **1882** *Vermont Agric. Rep.* VII. 64 In the process of sugar making there was a point where it would combine with the lime, making 'sugar sand' or the malate of lime. **1949** [see *NITRE *sb.* 1 d]. **1975** *Islander* (Victoria, B.C.) 25 May 5/3 The strained [maple] syrup should sit to allow sugar sand to settle to the bottom of the mixture. **1895** Sugar shell [see *flat-ware* s.v. *FLAT A. *adj.* 15]. **1916** *Daily Colonist* (Victoria, B.C.) 12 July 7/1 Sale Goes Merrily On!..Sugar Shells, fine silver plate, plain, for 50c. **1875** Sugar sifter [in Dict., sense 4 b]. **1906** GALSWORTHY *Man of Property* I. vi. 88 Now, what did you give for that sugar-sifter? **1976** *Deeside Advertiser* 9 Dec. 9/6 She presented a cut glass sugar sifter to Mrs. Brockley, past president. **1826** A. ANDERSON *Diary* 20 Mar. in G. Sellar *Narrative* (1916) viii. 124 Gordon awakened us by shouting 'A sugar snow.' There had been a light shower of it during the night, and the air was soft. Holes were rebored, and there was a fine run of sap. **1932** L. I. WILDER *Little House in Big Woods* 92 It's called sugar snow, because a snow this time of year means that men can make more sugar... The snow will hold back the leafing of the trees, and that makes a longer run of sap. **1973** M. CROWELL *Greener Pastures* 149 Sugar snow is falling in those distinctive great feathery flakes that foretell the beginning of a maple sap run. **1930** C. H. EATON *Painting & Decorating* IV. XIII. 843 Sugar soap has a softening action on the water, and is not so liable [as soda]..to cause undue softening of the paint film. **1958** *Woman* 22 Feb. 14/3 Walls must be washed, brushed... Paintwork washed with sugar-soap, rinsed and allowed to dry. **1963** W. TEE *Painting & Decorating* viii. 67 When you have removed all traces of the sugar soap, mop up surplus moisture. **1892** *Irish Daily Independent* 4 July 5/5 We are not sugarsticks. *Ibid*, Sugarsticks..men whose steadfastness would melt away before a passing cloud. **1936** W. B. YEATS *Let.* 21 Dec. (1940) 124 He [*sc.* Wilfred Owen] is all blood, dirt & sucked sugar stick. **1938** M. K. RAWLINGS *Yearling* v. 51 The 'coon nibbled at his flesh and cried again. 'He wants his sugar-teat,' Fodder-wing said maternally. **1892** *Dialect Notes* I. 232 Sugar-tit. **1936** M. MITCHELL *Gone with Wind* viii. 145 Prissy produced the sugar-tit..and the baby's wails subsided. **1958** S. A. GRAU *Hard Blue Sky* 118 So she went into the bedroom and picked up the sugar tit and tucked it into his mouth. **1779** in *Proc. Mass. Hist. Soc.* (1886) 2nd Ser. II. 453 Made Sugar Troughs and Katch.[d] some Sap. **1837** R. BIRD *Nick of Woods* II. iv. 90 What should I do but see the old sugar-trough floating in the bushes. **1946** C. RICHTER *Fields* 17 She lifted the long bundle from out of the sugar trough. **1848** H. R. FORSTER *Stowe Catal.* 144 A pierced sugar-vase—with goats' heads. **1956** G. TAYLOR *Silver* ix. 202 *Sugar Vases.* Among the many varieties of vases is one based on the Greek volute-krater. **1981** *Sunday Tel.* 18 Jan. 13/1 Tate and Lyle's own collection..includes silver gilt sugar vases with tops, and the pierced ladles used with them. **1826** A. ANDERSON *Diary* 18 Mar. in G. Sellar *Narrative* (1916) viii. 124 Have had no sugar-weather this week; frosty with strong winds, and some snow. **1942** G. CAMPBELL *Thorn-Apple Tree* 97 When the March sun began to honeycomb the snow, and the sun was warm on the south side of the house, then came sugar weather.

b. sugar glider, a flying phalanger, *Petaurus breviceps*, found in Australia and New Guinea; **sugar squirrel** (later example); = *sugar glider* above.

1937 *Discovery* Dec. 365/1 Only fifteen inches in total length, with a lovely ash-grey coat.., the Sugar Glider is usually a gregarious creature. **1941** E. TROUGHTON *Furred Animals of Australia* 95 'Sugar Glider' is now adopted as being brief and suitable for popular use. **1972** *Sci. Amer.* Sept. 56/1 Males of the sugar glider..go even further. **1932** *Victorian Naturalist* XLIX. 97 When one has kept the 'Sugar Squirrel' in captivity and suffered keen bites from its long piercing teeth, one is able to appreciate the spitfire temper concealed in these beautiful little creatures.

c. sugar-berry (earlier and later examples); also, one of several other North American species of *Celtis*; **sugar (snap) pea,** add: = *MANGE-TOUT; (later examples); **sugar-tree,** (*a*) (earlier and later examples).

1818 W. P. C. BARTON *Compendium Floræ Philadelphicæ* I. 151 Celts occidentalis... Sugar-berry Tree. American Nettle Tree. **1896** *Chicago Rec.* 17 Feb. 4/6 He laid the groundwork..by cutting a sugarberry sprout. **1948** *Florida Anthropologist* May 19 This vegetation includes sugarberry, banyan, mulberry, papaya, saw palmetto and small plants. **1969** T. H. EVERETT *Living Trees of World* xiv. 129/1 The closely related sugarberry (*C. laevigata*), native from Indiana and Illinois southward, ..has a maximum height of 90 feet. **1907** A. FRENCH *Bk. Veg.* 198 Pea, edible-podded or sugar, is a type of pea with tender pods, which are eaten. **1951, 1972** Sugar pea [see *MANGE-TOUT]. **1980** *Ecology Center* (Berkeley, Calif.) *Newslet.* Oct. 6/2 A great crop of Sugar Snap Peas. **1705** R. BEVERLEY *Hist. & Present State Virginia* II. 21 The Honey and Sugar-Trees are likewise spontaneous, near the Heads of Rivers. **1949** *Chicago Tribune* 13 Mar. I. 6/4 The Crane Naval depot encroached upon some fine old sugar trees in Martin county.

sugar, *v.* Add: **2. a.** (Later examples.) *to sugar the pill* = *to gild the pill* s.v. GILD *v.*[1] 1 b.

1794 LD. ST. HELENS *Let.* 14 Oct. in A. Paget *Paget Papers* (1896) I. 66 They [*sc.* the Prussian Cabinet] have no right to complain, as I observe that you continued to gild and sugar over the pill which you were directed to administer. **1936** V. W. BROOKS *Flowering of New England* xv. 287 He liked to administer doses of moral quinine, and he never thought of sugaring his pills. **1954** N. MITFORD *Madame de Pompadour* xviii. 237 To sugar the pill of what was, in fact, his dismissal, a Cardinal's hat was procured for Bernis by Stainville. **1955** E. POUND *Section: Rock-Drill* lxxxix. 55 Louis Philippe suggested that Jackson stand firm And not sugar his language. **1978** J. CARROLL *Mortal Friends* v. ii. 521 The bishop sugared the request with his smile. **1978** [see *PILL *sb.*[2] 1 b].

c. To flatter. Also const. *up*.

1923 J. MANCHON *Le Slang* 300 *To sugar a person up*, flatter quelqu'un. **1939** R. CHANDLER *Big Sleep* ii. 25 It won't get you anything. Sugaring them never does. **1958** R. STOUT *And four to Go* iii. 172 There was no point in trying to sugar him. The damage..had been done the second he saw me. **1962** W. FAULKNER *Reivers* x. 219 When I sugars up a woman, it aint just empty talk.

4. Also *transf.*

1906 G. B. SHAW *Let.* 4 Apr. in *Florence Farr, Shaw, Yeats* (1946) 26 Your standard of work [*sc.* in acting]..is far too low... You sugar disgracefully except where you see your way to an effect. **1882** 'F. ANSTEY' *Vice Versa* viii. 166 Although (to use a boating expression) he 'sugared' with some adroitness, he was promptly found out, for his son had been a dashing and plucky player.

5. Used in imprecations, esp. as pa. pple.: = BLOW *v.*[1] 29. *euphem.*

1886 MRS. H. WOOD in *Argosy* XLI. 270 'Stephenson says he had blue eyes. Now Dick's are brown.' 'Eyes be sugared,' retorted the lawyer. **1903** [see *AMATEUR 3 b]. **1903** KIPLING *Traffics & Discov.* (1904) 107 War's declared at midnight. *Pedantics* be sugared! **1942** *Tee Emm*

(Air Ministry) II. 78 Real pilot be sugared. Real little show-off, more like! **1962** B. GLANVILLE *Diamond* xxi. 339 'They wouldn't talk to me.'..'Sugar them; you're too good for them.'

6. *trans.* To 'cook' or 'doctor'; *spec.* to give a specious impression of the amount of trade done by (a place of business, etc.). *colloq.*

1892 STEVENSON & OSBOURNE *Wrecker* xv. 239 Out of six thousand mats [*sc.* bags of rice], only twenty were found to have been sugared; in each we found..about twelve pounds of drug. **1894** *Daily News* 26 Dec. 5/3 'Sugaring a house'..in Birmingham..denoting a system of creating a fictitious appearance of business by privately giving away money to be spent at its bars.

sugarallie (ʃugəra·li). *Sc. colloq.* Also **sugarellie** (-e·li), **-olly** (-ǫ·li), etc. [A shortened form of *sugar alicreesh*, 16th-cent. Sc. *sukker lagrace*, *succour alacreische*, f. SUGAR *sb.* + Du. *lakk(e)ris* LIQUORICE, LICORICE.] **a.** Liquorice.

1812 P. FORBES *Poems* 21 Sulphur, salt fish, sugar allie. **1842** *Children in Mines Rep.* App. 465 in *Parl. Papers 1842* XVI. 1 Mother gives me 3d., which I spend in sugar-alleys and sweeties. **1876** S. R. WHITEHEAD *Daft Davie* iii. 53 The stock of candy and liquorice (known in that countryside by the name of 'sugar-ally'). **1915** A. S. NEILL *Dominie's Log* xviii. 206 To-night I have a great craving for a stick of twisted sugarelly—the polite call it liquorice. **1921** —— *Carroty Broon* xvii. 229 Long tubes of sugarella. **1947** L. DERWENT *Clashmaclavers* 87 Whiles a lucky-bag I'd try, Or sticky sugar-alla buy.

b. *Comb.* **sugarallie button**, a round sweet made of liquorice; **sugarallie hat**, a tall cylindrical hat, esp. as formerly worn by policemen; **sugarallie water**, a drink made by vigorously shaking a container in which water and a stick of liquorice have been placed.

1887 A. D. WILLOCK *Rosetty Ends* xx. 148 Havin' discovered that Flossie had a weakness for sugarellie buttons, Simpson has made it a habit to hae ane or twa o' thae sweetmeats in his pouch on courtin' nichts. **1887** J. McBAIN *Arbroath* 104 Their bonnets were replaced by 'sugarellie hats'. **1904** 'H. FOULIS' *Erchie* 65 The sugar-aully hats the polis used to hae. **1953** J. J. LAVIN *Compass of Youth* I. vi. 54 Yelling derisively: 'Sugarawlly Hat,' to the might and majesty of the law. **1889** J. M. BARRIE *Window in Thrums* xxii. 207 Bairns..shook their bottles of sugarelly water into a froth. **1923** W. D. LYELL *Justice-Clerk* I. iv. 26 What say ye to a sma' bottle o' sugaralie water? **1947** J. F. HENDRY *Fernie Brae* 10 Shall we make some sugarolly water?

sugar-bird. Add: **3.** Also, an African honey-eater of the genus *Promerops*.

1798 LADY A. BARNARD *Jrnl.* Apr. in *Lives of Lindsays* (1849) III. 408 The sugar-bird's tail..is long and elegantly formed. **1913** D. FAIRBRIDGE *That which hath Been* 30 The emerald-throated sugar-birds..darted from one pink protea to another. **1973** S. CLOETE *Company with Heart of Gold* 155 A sugar bird returned to its infinitesimal nest in the grey bush.

sugar-bush. Add: **1.** (Later examples.)

1842 [see *EIGHTY 2 c]. **1896** *Vermont Agric. Rep.* XV. 38 Does the location of a sugar bush determine the quality of the sugar? **1950** *N.Y. Times Mag.* 23 Apr. 46/2 'Sugar bush' is rarely heard in New Jersey, but in Pennsylvania it is the normal term. **1973** L. RUSSELL *Everyday Life Colonial Canada* xi. 144 The settler who would exploit his grove of maple trees or 'sugar-bush' cleared narrow roads through the woods.

2. Also, one of several other species of *Protea* rich in nectar. Cf. PROTEA in Dict. and Suppl.

a **1823** J. EWART *Jrnl.* (1970) ii. 14 The Protea of Linn[æus] called by the colonists the sugar bush, from the quantity of sweet juices the large and beautiful flowers contain. **1931** V. SAMPSON *Kom Binne* 28 The wild arums, the sugar-bush goblets of pink or cream. **1970** M. MULLER *Cloud across Moon* 239 The masses of white and pink sugar bushes were covered with nearly opened sticky, stiff flowers.

3. *U.S.* An evergreen shrub, *Rhus ovata*, native to southwestern North America and bearing yellow flowers followed by dark red berries.

1900 *West Amer. Sci.* X. 61 The Sugar-bush is a handsome evergreen shrub. **1931** G. H. VANSELL *Nectar & Pollen Plants California* 49 Sugar bush..of coastal southern California blossoms in winter. **1949** *Nature Mag.* Nov. 424/1 There is the gray of some manzanitas, the silver of white sage, the dark green of sugar bush. **1982** M. MILLAR *Mermaid* vi. 57 Drought-resistant native plants like ceanothus and sugar-bush.

sugar-candy. Add: Hence **sugar-ca·ndyish** *a.*, resembling sugar-candy.

1874 DISRAELI *Let.* Aug. in *Lett. to Lady Bradford* (1929) I. vii. 135 Her manners not only sugary but sugar-candyish. **1927** J. MASEFIELD *Midnight Folk* 172 A bowl of raspberries and cream with blobs of sugar-candyish brown sugar.

sugarellie, var. *SUGARALLIE.

sugarer (ʃu·gərəɹ). *slang.* [f. SUGAR *v.* + -ER[1].] One who shirks, *spec.* at rowing. Cf. SUGAR *v.* 4.

1904 W. G. EAST *Rowing & Sculling* 20 A sugarer, a man who, whilst rowing correctly, avoids putting in a full share of work. **1925** W. DEEPING *Sorrel & Son* xviii. 171 It was necessary to be neither a funk nor a sugarer.

sugaring, *vbl. sb.* Add: **4.** Bribery.

1891 J. P. QUINN *Fools of Fortune* 285 This payment is what the 'fakirs' call 'sugaring', and I have never known one of these officials for whom the dose could be made too sweet. **1902** S. E. WHITE *Blazed Trail* xvi. 117 The old-time logger found these two individuals susceptible to the gentle art of 'sugaring'.

sugar-loaf. Add: **3.** *sugar-loaf hill* (earlier and later examples).

1799 MALTHUS *Diary* 9 July (1966) 131 We..saw Doverfield..with his sugar loaf hills covered with snow. **1859** D. BUNCE *Travels with Dr. Leichhardt* iv. 29 There are two lofty sugar-loaf hills..which may be seen from Hobart Town. **1969** [see *FAVELA].

sugar-maple. Add: (Earlier example.) Also, the light-coloured wood of this tree.

1731 P. MILLER *Gardeners Dict.* s.v. Acer, There is another Sort of Maple, which is very common in Virginia, and is known by the name of the Sugar Maple. **1936** *Wood Products* Mar. 11/1 During recent years the U.S. Forest Products Laboratory..has investigated the weight and hardness of sugar maple. **1980** *Family Handyman* Sept. 63/2 A cubic foot of poplar weighs 26 lbs. compared to 39 lbs. for a cubic foot of sugar maple.

sugarolly, var. *SUGARALLIE. **sugarro,** var. *SAGUARO.

suggan. a. Restrict *Anglo-Irish* to first two meanings and add later examples of both. Also *attrib.* in *suggan chair*.

1888 YEATS *Fairy & Folk Tales* 133 She lulls them to rest in the low *suggaun* chair. **1922** JOYCE *Ulysses* 489 Bloom..leading a black bogoak pig by a sugaun. **1957** E. E. EVANS *Irish Folk Ways* xv. 207 When..the load is placed directly on the ass a simple 'sugan' is sometimes made—a ring of straw some fifteen inches in diameter bound with a fine straw rope. **1977** C. ROCKS in *Winter's Tales 23* 128 My da goes to his own sugan chair inside the hearth.

b. For 'a coverlet' read: *N. Amer.* (Usu. in form *soogan*, *sugan* (sū·gǎn).) A thick blanket or padded quilt suitable for camping out. (Earlier and later examples.)

For evidence of earlier but limited currency of this sense in Scotland see *S.N.D.*

1907 S. E. WHITE *Arizona Nights* 72 Sitting cross-legged on his 'so-gun' in the middle of the floor. **1915** *Dialect Notes* IV. 245 *Soogan*,..sheep herder's blanket. 'When they move, they just roll up the soogan and are off.' **1926** *Amer. Speech* I. 653/1 [Hobo lingo.] *Sugan*, a bed comforter. **1955** R. HOBSON *Nothing too Good for Cowboy* vii. 66 [I] saw Jimmy John shove him back into the soogans. **1974** D. SEARS *Lark in Clear Air* ii. 32 No matter how quick I turned out of my soogans I would see him up prowling around.

suggest, *v.* **1. e.** (Earlier example.)

1751 FIELDING *Amelia* I. III. iii. 187 The thought of going back at first suggested itself.

suggestibility. Add: **1.** Also in contexts where hypnosis is not involved.

1890 W. JAMES *Princ. Psychol.* II. xix. 97 This suggestibility is greater in the lower senses than in the higher. **1908** W. McDOUGALL *Introd. Social Psychol.* iv. 97 The measure of the suggestibility of any subject is, then, the readiness with which he thus accepts propositions. Of course, the proposition is not necessarily communicated in formal language, it may be implied by a mere gesture or interjection. **1924** W. B. SELBIE *Psychol. Religion* iv. 87 Such cases are generally those of persons in a high condition of suggestibility, and it often happens that suggestions do not become active..until they have..incubated in the unconscious realm. **1962** L. DEIGHTON *Ipcress File* 224 Tricayandamino-propene..can change brain's nerve cells and cells of membrane that sheath the cells... From this change the suggestibility of the subject is increased. **1972** *Jrnl. Social Psychol.* LXXXVI. 11 He demonstrated the importance of motivational and experiential factors in determining suggestibility.

suggestible, *a.* Add: **1.** Also in contexts where hypnosis is not involved.

1903 W. JAMES in *Harvard Monthly* Mar. 6 There is no test..by which, if a title or decoration, a public badge or mark, were to be won by it, some weakly suggestible or hauntable persons would not feel challenged. **1908** W. McDOUGALL *Introd. Social Psychol.* iv. 100 Children are..inevitably suggestible..because of their lack of knowledge and lack of systematic organisation of such knowledge as they have. **1921** *Discovery* Nov. 294/1 Children are more suggestible than grown persons, and women are more suggestible than men. **1955** *Times* 17 May 3/3 Orchestras being suggestible by professional training cannot wholly eliminate from their playing the implications of a conductor's gestures. **1981** F. HOYLE *Ice* ii. 39 He is very suggestible; if he is told he is stupid, he thinks he is stupid and behaves accordingly.

suggestio falsi (sǒdʒe·stio fæ·lsəi). Pl. **suggestiones falsi.** [mod.L., = suggestion of what is false.] A misrepresentation of the truth whereby something incorrect is implied to be true; an indirect lie. Often in contexts with *SUPPRESSIO VERI.

1815 H. MADDOCK *Princ. & Pract. Chancery* I. 208 Whenever *Suppressio veri* or *Suggestio falsi* occur..they afford a sufficient ground for setting aside any Release or Conveyance. **1855** *Newspaper & Gen. Reader's Pocket Compan.* I. 4 He was bound to say that the *suppressio veri* on that occasion approached very nearly to a positive *suggestio falsi*. **1898** KIPLING *Stalky & Co.* (1899) 36 It seems..that they had held back material facts; that they were guilty both of *suppressio veri* and *suggestio falsi*. **1907** W. DE MORGAN *Alice-for-Short* xxxvi. 389 That's suppressio veri and suggestio falsi! Besides, it's fibs! **1962** J. WILSON *Public Schools & Private Practice* i. 19 It is rare to find a positively verifiable untruth in a school brochure: but it is equally rare not to find a great many *suggestiones falsi*, particularly as regards the material comfort and facilities available. **1980** D. NEWSOME *On Edge of Paradise* 7 There are undoubted cases of *suppressio veri*; on the other hand, he appears to eschew *suggestio falsi*.

suggestion. Add: **8. suggestion-book** (later examples).

1931 W. HOLTBY *Poor Caroline* iv. 113, I put it down in the suggestion-book six weeks ago. **1967** V. GIELGUD *Conduct of Member* i. 11 The Suggestion Book of the Font-hill Club was much like others of its kind. Its contents..dealt with the apparent shortcomings of the House Committee.

suggestive, *a.* Add: **2. c.** (Earlier example in sense 'likely to make suggestions'.)

1846 DICKENS *Let.* 5 Oct. (1977) IV. 629, I shall have the greatest satisfaction..in putting you in communication with two or three gentlemen who I am sure will be most valuable, willing, and suggestive advisers.

d. (Earlier and later examples.)

1888 [implied at *SUGGESTIVENESS]. **1895** C. D. WARNER *Golden House* iii. 24 Her judges were cosmopolitans who had seen the most suggestive dancing in all parts of the world. **1924** R. MACAULAY *Orphan Island* xiv. 182 There were complaints, too, of fashions in dress, which, on the part of the younger females, were becoming immodest and suggestive. **1926** T. DREISER *Amer. Tragedy* I. xviii. 132 They..lay there laughing and yet in a most suggestive position. **1978** L. MEYNELL *Papersnake* iii. 51 Mabel, archpriestess of the art of suggestive repartee.

suggestiveness. Add: (Later examples in sense 2 d of the adj.)

1888 M. S. VAN DE VELDE *Random Recollections of Courts & Society* x. 252 Some foreigners..wondered at the excessive licence she permitted herself on the English stage, and the marked suggestiveness of her looks and gestures. **1913** MRS. BELLOC LOWNDES *Diary* 7 Jan. (1971) 42 We talked of English prudery, and..of *The Rosary* and its wonderful success, and I said I felt sure this was owing to the suggestiveness of certain scenes. **1963** L. DEIGHTON *Horse under Water* xxiii. 100, I noticed Singleton's lip curl..at H.K.'s suggestiveness.

suggestology (sɒdʒestǫ·lŏdʒi). [f. SUGGEST *v.* + -OLOGY.] The study of suggestion, a branch of parapsychology originated by a Bulgarian, Dr. Georgi Lozanov. Similarly **suggestopae·dia, suggesto·pedy** [Gr. παιδεία education], the application of suggestology to education, teaching by suggestion.

1970 OSTRANDER & SCHROEDER *Psychic Discoveries behind Iron Curtain* xxii. 293 With suggestopaedia the Bulgarians have expanded time in a very real sense, teaching you in a minute what usually takes many weeks to learn. **1970** *New Society* 31 Dec. 1155/1 This conference is called an 'International Symposium on the Problems of Suggestology'... Among the listed attractions is a visit to the research centre of suggestology in Sofia. **1973** OSTRANDER & SCHROEDER *Psi* xxii. 293 Suggestology is *not* hypnosis. With suggestology you are always in the waking state and aware of everything around you. **1978** HALL-POZHARLIEVA & PASHMAKOVA tr. *Lozanov's Suggestology & Outl. of Suggestopedy* i. 1 Suggestology, the science of suggestion, and its concomitant penetration into pedagogy, suggestopedy, is a newly developing science. **1980** *San Francisco Bay Guardian* 16–23 Oct. 30 (Advt.), Hypnosis/Self-Hypnosis with Dr. Leonard Elkind. Weight. Smoking. Autogenics. Suggestology. Self-Improvement.

sugi (sū·gi). Also 8 **ssugi, suggi.** [Jap.] = *CRYPTOMERIA.

1727 [see *HINOKI]. **1795** tr. *C. P. Thunberg's Trav.* (ed. 2) III. 123 *Ssugi* signifies Cedar wood. **1876** *Trans. Asiatic Soc. Japan* IV. 53 One piece of *sugi* of 6 by 3 by 0·4 ft. **1916** E. H. WILSON *Conifers & Taxads of Japan* 69 The Cryptomeria, or Sugi as it is called in Japan, is the noblest of the Japanese conifers. **1954** [see *Japanese cedar* s.v. *JAPANESE *a.* b]. **1970** J. KIRKUP *Japan behind Fan* iv. 137 A bus took me on the long winding road, through groves of immense *sugi* or Japanese cedar.

suh (sɒ), chiefly *U.S. Southern* and *Black* pronunc. of SIR *sb.* Cf. *SAH.

1894 KIPLING *Day's Work* (1898) 50 Most of your prominent siahs, suh, are impo'ted from Kentucky. **1901** W. CHURCHILL *Crisis* I. iv. 38 'T'ank you, Mistah Cantah,' wailed the poor woman, 't'ank you, suh... De Lawd Jesus'll rewa'd you, suh.' **1911** [see *HIDE *v.*[1] 2 c]. **1929** W. FAULKNER *Sartoris* II. 117 'Come on here and get in,' he commanded. 'Naw, suh. I'll walk.' **1940** H. G. WELLS *Babes in Darkling Wood* III. ii. 252 Cutting facts dead unless they wear the old school tie! 'Don't know you, suh.' **1971** *Black Scholar* Sept. 38/2 'Yes suh, officer,' she replied.

Sui (swē[i]). Also **Suy, Swi.** [Chinese *suí*.] The name of a dynasty which ruled in China from 581 to 618 A.D. and re-unified the country after the divisions of the Northern and Southern Dynasties period. Freq. *attrib.*

1738 J. B. DU HALDE *Descript. China & Chinese Tartary* I. 194 Thus ended the Dynasty nam'd Swi, the last of five petty ones. **1797** *Encycl. Brit.* IV. 653/1 The whole of their [*sc.* China's] emperors..are comprehended in 22 dynasties, mentioned in the following table..Chin.. Swi..Twang [etc.]. **1845** *Encycl. Metrop.* XVI. 550/1 The tower of Kao-ming-chi, with its gardens, temple and pavilions, erected by Kao-tsu of the Swi dynasty. **1897** J. MacGowan *Hist. China* xix. 261 Yang-Kien was forty-eight years old when he became Emperor... He gave his dynasty the name of Sui. **1910** *Encycl. Brit.* VI. 195/2 This period of disorder was brought to a close by the establishment of the Suy dynasty. **1958** W. Willetts *Chinese Art* I. v. 310 We are concerned only with the Sui and the first four reigns of the T'ang... The Sui Emperors were great patrons of Buddhism. **1969** *Guardian* 2 July 3/2 A 15-inch terra cotta horse of the Sui period (seventh century AD), is offered for £6,000. **1972** *Trans. Oriental Ceramics Soc.* XXXVIII. 29 Much that is ascribed to Sui ..should be placed in the opening generations of T'ang. **1979** A. Henning tr. *Myrdal's Silk Road* (1980) i. 11 Tashkent was known during the Sui dynasty.

‖ **suiboku** (*su*·ibǫku). [Jap., lit. 'liquefied ink', f. *sui* water + *boku* ink stick.] A style of Japanese painting in black ink on a white surface characterized by bold brush-work and subtle gradations of tone (see quot. 1970).

1912 E. F. Fenollosa *Epochs Chinese & Jap. Art* II. xi. 43 Kakei..made a decided change in Chinese landscape style: the 'In' style..in that he introduced the utmost decorative splendour of *notan*, or dark and light beauty. He made the strong shapes of his touches of glowing ink 'look as if they were falling in drops'. This is 'suiboku', or wet ink. **1959** R. Saito *Jap. Ink Painting* 13 Because of the value of the light and dark color of the sumi, and the taste and interest which come from each variation of the brush, suiboku painting really reveals the true spirit of the Oriental people. **1959** *Times Lit. Suppl.* 17 Apr. 218/4 The distinction is most apparent, and most interesting, in the field of *suiboku*—the monochrome painting practised by the *bunjin-ga*. **1970** *Oxf. Compan. Art* 1114/1 The essentials of *suiboku* were bold composition in the Chinese style, strength of brush-work, and nuance in the tone of the ink.

suicide, *sb.*[2] Add: **c.** (Further examples, esp. as *suicide letter, note, pact.*) Also *spec.* in *Mil.* use, designating highly dangerous or deliberately suicidal operations and persons, etc., involved in them, as *suicide aircraft, mission, squad,* etc.

1897 'Mark Twain' *Following Equator* lvii. 546 In India, the annual man-killings by snakes are..as forecastable as are the tiger-average and the suicide-average. **1911** *Daily Colonist* (Victoria, B.C.) 19 Apr. 4/3 Before he shot himself..he shot Miss Bovee three times, they having previously entered into a suicide pact. **1916** 'Boyd Cable' *Doing their Bit* iii. 47 You bombers of the 'Suicide Clubs' might note this. **1923** Kipling *Irish Guards in Gt. War* I. 67 There seemed no meaning or reason in the affair, unless it was a suicide-party of Germans who had run from the attack of the day before and had been ordered thus to die. **1928** A. C. Havlin *Hist. Company A, 102nd Machine Gun Battalion* 3 We were to serve as 'suicide squads' in the..26th Division. **1929** D. Hammett *Dain Curse* vii. 65 Your husband's letter sounded enough like a suicide letter..so you murdered him. **1938** 'E. Queen' *Four of Hearts* xxii. 293 Park left a suicide note to efface his trail and vanished. **1942** *R.A.F. Jrnl.* 13 June 15 If a 'suicide squad' job came along..it would be assumed that every man was ready for that sort of thing. **1945** *News Chron.* 1 June 4/5 Conferences..are believed to have included plans to counter the..suicide plane. According to a Tokio statement, these suicide attacks..are being developed by the..Japanese Naval Command. **1946** *Jrnl. R. Aeronaut. Soc.* L. 293 As with the pages devoted to German aircraft, so with those given to Japanese. They are full and informative, and end with brief interesting notes on suicide aircraft and the Baka flying bomb. **1954, 1956** [see *kamikaze *a.* 1]. **1963** 'D. Cory' *Hammerhead* x. 123 Fedora brushed what was left of the suicide pill on to the palm of his hand. **1969** R. Rendell *Best Man to Die* xv. 147 It's the seat on the driver's left that's called the suicide seat. **1971** *New Scientist* 11 Mar. 531/2 No civil defence measure would improve this state of affairs except perhaps the issue of suicide pills. **1974** 'S. Woods' *Done to Death* 127, I haven't told him about the suicide note. *Ibid.* 129 Mr Maitland's theory about the suicide letter is right. **1976** A. White *Long Silence* xviii. 158 'And the third objective?'..'Obviously to flee..and eventually return to England. None of you strikes me as the kind of fool who would accept a suicide mission.' **1977** A. Giddens *Stud. in Social & Polit. Theory* ix. 308 Her husband left her seven months later, and this precipitated her suicide attempt. **1978** *Times* 21 Nov. 6/4 Mr Jones had forced his followers to make a suicide pact with him. He predicted..all 1,200 members of the sect would die. **1979** T. Sharpe *Wilt Alternative* xvi. 149 Could have left a suicide squad to cover their retreat.

d. *Comb.*, as **suicide blonde** *slang*, a woman with hair dyed blonde (esp. rather amateurishly), a peroxide blonde; **suicide clause,** a clause in a life insurance policy which releases the insurer from liability if the insured commits suicide within a specified period; **suicide squeeze** *Baseball*, the action of a runner on third base in running for home as the ball is pitched (cf. *squeeze play).

1942 Berrey & Van den Bark *Amer. Thes. Slang* § 430/4 Bottle baby,..peroxide, suicide blonde, an artificial blonde. **1959** J. Braine *Vodi* vii. 104 'You don't have to whitter on about one little suicide blonde.' 'She's a real blonde,' Tom said. **1973** A. Sillitoe *Men, Women & Children* 174 The snow-white hair of a suicide-blonde flashed around: 'Hey up, Margaret!' **1902** C. L. Greene *Medical Examination for Life Insurance* 357 There can be little doubt that in the case of persons insured under policies containing a suicide clause, such deaths are very generally reported as accidental. **1976** 'L. Black' *Healthy Way to Die* x. 112 Eddie asks her if there is a suicide clause in the life policy. **1955** P. Richards *Mod. Baseball Strategy* xi. 129 The 'suicide-squeeze', which has the runner going home on the pitch, is absolutely certain to work—*if* the batter bunts the ball on the ground. **1974** *Los Angeles Times* 13 Oct. III. 9/5 It is properly called a 'suicide squeeze' because it calls for the runner to arrive at home plate at the same time as the ball.

suicidology (s[i]ūisəidǫ·lŏdʒi). [f. Suicide *sb.*[2] + -ology.] The study of suicide and its prevention. Hence **suicido·logist.**

[**1929** W. A. Bonger in *Psychiatrisch-Juridisch Gezelschap* 9 Feb. 3 De wetenschap van de zelfmoord, the *suicidologie* (cursivering van mij) zou men haar kunnen noemen, is ruim een eeuw oud.] **1964** E. S. Shneidman in *Contemp. Psychol.* IX. 371/2, I thank Louis Dublin, the Grand Old Man of Suicidology, for this book because in it he..has given us all new clues to suicide. **1967** —— *Bull. Suicidology* July 7/2 The 10-point program for suicide prevention here outlined is a mutual enterprise whose successful development depends on the active interest, support, and activities of 'suicidologists'. **1969** *Nature* 4 Oct. 12/2 The Johns Hopkins University in collaboration with the National Institutes of Mental Health has established a course in 'suicidology'. **1970** L. Lasagna in O. G. Brim et al. *Dying Patient* 96 The 'suicidology' program concept. **1976** E. S. Shneidman *Suicidology* 7 Suicidology is defined as the scientific study of suicidal phenomena. **1976** R. K. McGee in *Ibid.* 482 The volunteer suicidologist has become a vital component of the suicide prevention scene.

suid (s[i]*u*·[i]d), *sb.* and *a.* *Zool.* [f. mod. L. *Suidæ*: see Suidian *a.* and *sb.*] = Suidian *a.* and *sb.*

1957 P. J. Darlington *Zoogeogr.* vi. 403 Fossil suids.. are known only from the main part of the Old World. **1969** [see *bunodont *a.* and *sb.*]. **1970** B. G. F. Weitz in H. W. Mulligan *African Trypanosomiases* xviii. 419 Table 18.1 shows the results obtained by the Haemagglutination-Inhibition Test on ten suid feeds. **1976** D. Pilbeam in C. J. Jolly *Early Hominids of Africa* 509 Most workers can..sort..bovids from suids. **1980** *E. Afr. Med. Jrnl.* LVII. 333 *G. brevipalpis* fed mostly on suids.

sui generis. Add: Also used *attrib.*

1944 S. Putnam tr. *E. da Cunha's Rebellion in Backlands* ii. 60 Such a climate tends to create a *sui generis* pathology throughout the whole of the northern coastal strip. **1963** J. Lyons *Structural Semantics* i. 2 In this theory meaning is defined as a *sui generis* 'reciprocal relation between name and sense, which enables them to call up one another'. **1977** *Time* 4 Apr. 41/3 The superlative interpretations by the *sui generis* Budapest Quartet come from tapes of live performances at the Library of Congress in 1959 and 1961.

suikerbos (sǿĭ·kəɹbǫs). *S. Afr.* Also **suikerbosch, -bossie, zuikerbosch.** [Afrikaans, f. *suiker* Sugar *sb.* + *bos* Bush *sb.*[1]] = Sugar-bush 2 in Dict. and Suppl.

[**1793** tr. *C. P. Thunberg's Trav. Europe, Africa, & Asia* I. 292 The *Protea mellifera* (*Tulp-boom* and *zuyker-boom*) contains in its calyx a sweet juice.] **1822** W. J. Burchell *Trav. S. Afr.* I. ii. 18 The delicate Humming birds..are, in Southern Africa,..called by the Dutch colonists *Suiker-vogels* (sugar birds), from having been observed.. to feed principally on the honey of the flowers of the *Suiker-bosch* (sugar-bush). **1852** C. Barter *Dorp & Veld* vii. 74 We came upon knolls covered with the evergreen *Suiker bos* a graceful shrub. **1887** A. A. Anderson *Twenty-Five Years in Waggon* I. 210 The fine flat-topped Kameel doorn is very common, palms, baobab,..zuikerbosch, acacia. **1937** S. Cloete *Turning Wheels* 104 As he rode past a clump of soikerbos [*sic*] a duiker sprang out. **1950** M. M. Kidd *Flowering Plants Cape Peninsula* Pl. 34 June–Aug. Sugar Bush, Suikerbossie. **1952** *Cape Times* 4 Sept. 5/4 The five dozen selected proteas include..two varieties of the furry suikerbos type. **1971** *Cape Argus* 10 July 5 Now is the time to see all those lovely Proteas and suikerbossies in full bloom.

sui-mate (s[i]ū-əi,mē[i]t, s[i]ū·i-). *Chess.* [f. L. *suī* of oneself + Mate *sb.*[1]] = Self-mate *sb.* Also *ellipt.* (**sui**) and as *v. intr.*

1870 *Dubuque Chess Jrnl.* 1 Nov. 7 White sui-mates in ten moves. **1890** [see *retractive *a.* 3]. **1907** S. S. Blackburne *Terms & Themes Chess Problems* 21 Sui-mate Problem. One in which one player..compels the other to mate him. **1965** *New Statesman* 16 Apr. 625 This one is a 'sui in 5', and..what matters is for White to commit suicide..by forcing Black to mate him in five moves. **1966** *Ibid.* 11 Nov. 718/3 Many readers have let me know their gradual addiction to sui-mates.

suine (s[i]ū·əin), *a.* *nonce-wd.* [f. L. *sūs*, *su*- pig + -ine[1]: cf. L. *suīnus* (see Swine).] Pig-like, porcine.

1922 Joyce *Ulysses* 554 The suine scions of the house of Lambert.

suing, *vbl. sb.* Add: **4. a.** (Later examples.)

1946 *Law Rep.* (King's Bench Division) 18 Sept. (1947) 93 The plaintiff was incapable of suing. **1983** *Weekly Law Rep.* 22 July 884 By the grant of a stay the plaintiffs would be deprived of the juridical advantage of suing as plaintiffs in the Admiralty Court.

suiseki (su,isē·ki). [Jap., *sui* water + *seki* stone(s).] The Japanese art of arranging stones on a tray, often one containing shallow water.

1929 *Encycl. Brit.* III. 855/2 Some stones are placed on a tray with low-growing grass or bamboo... Another way of enjoying them, which has been for centuries and is still popular among the Japanese, is known as *sui-seki*... A natural stone of desirable shape is placed in a porcelain or bronze tray or dish with sand and water. **1972** *Islander* (Victoria, B.C.) 2 Dec. 7/2 Very short sections [of a yew log], an inch or two in thickness, could be used as bases for viewing stones after the Japanese suiseki fashion... The art of suiseki is popular in Japan. **1976** *N.Y. Times* 8 Aug. 24 As with all suiseki, the stones must be as found in nature, though they may be cleaned with a soft cloth or brush. However, they are never polished or sculpted.

suisse. Add: **2.** A soft French white cheese resembling *Neufchâtel. Usu. in the form *petit suisse*: see *petit *a.* (*sb.*) 5.

1892 Stevenson & Osbourne *Wreckers* v. 70 When I called for a *suisse*..I was bluntly told there were no more.

suit, *sb.* Add: **V. 18. † h.** A gold watch, usu. with seals, case, etc. *Criminals' slang. Obs.*

1718 C. Hitching *Regulator* 13 They [*sc.* pickpockets] greatly benefit; either by a Suit, *alias* Gold-watch,..or by a Wedge Lobb, *alias* Gold or Silver Snuff-Box. **1839** H. Ainsworth *Jack Sheppard* II. xiv. 40 A fence, or receiver,..bargaining with a..pickpocket, for a *suit*,—or to speak in more intelligible language, a watch and seals.

19. b. Now usually, a jacket and trousers of the same material, sometimes with matching waistcoat, and esp. for formal or office use.

1932 G. Greene *Stamboul Train* I. i. 7 He..required no longer..his suit from Savile Row..to hearten him. *a* **1953** E. O'Neill *Hughie* (1959) 8 He wears an ill-fitting blue serge suit. **1960** C. Day Lewis *Buried Day* ii. 43, I am standing..in a white suit and holding my broad-brimmed round straw hat.

c. Cf. **trouser suit.*

e. *birthday suit*: see also s.v. *birthday 3.

g. = *bathing-suit* s.v. *bathing *vbl. sb.* 2, *swim-suit* s.v. *swim *sb.* 10 b.

1883 L. Troubridge *Life amongst Troubridges* (1966) 165 Walked along..meaning to bathe... Ran down in our suits. **1949** D. Smith *I capture Castle* x. 162 We didn't bathe because none of us had brought suits. **1977** *Times* 16 June 13/6 The suit in our picture..is the first suit for ages..to cover up the spare tyre.

20. a. *long suit*: see Long *a.*[1] 5 b, *5 c.

b. (Earlier *fig.* example.)

1851 H. Melville *Moby Dick* I. v. 47, I quickly followed suit, and descending into the bar-room accosted the grinning landlord.

VII. 24. a. (senses 19 b, c) *suit coat, -jacket*; **suit bag,** (*a*) a protective covering for a suit which is not being worn; (*b*) a travelling bag designed to contain a suit of clothes; **suit length,** a piece of material of the right size for making into a suit; also *fig.*; **suit-weight,** used *attrib.* of fabrics of an appropriate thickness for making up into suits.

1966 *Olney Amsden & Sons Ltd. Price List* 5 Suit bag zipped 51/9 doz. **1978** W. Stovall *Presidential Emergency* i. 1 He set down his suit bag, underseater and attaché case. **1971** D. E. Westlake *I gave at the Office* (1972) 15 A guy..whose suitcoat collar was turned up indoors. **1972** *National Observer* (U.S.) 27 May 1/4 Wallace removed his suit coat, handed it to an aide, and moved forward to greet well-wishers. **1965** M. Shadbolt *Among Cinders* x. 79 The crumpled..suit-jacket with sleeves too short. **1977** *Transatlantic Rev.* LX. 69 She had taken off her suitjacket. **1924** J. Joyce *Let.* 30 Sept. (1957) II. 221 There is now a special cheap edition..about 1/11¼ per normal novel suitlength real continental. **1971** D. Lees *Rainbow Conspiracy* ii. 24 The foreman weaver in most mills is allowed to take any end pieces as part of his perks. .. More often than not he finds himself with a suit length. **1955** *Archit. Rev.* CXVII. 351 (*caption*) Light suit-weight Cheviot tweed by Michal Illan. **1963** *Guardian* 10 May 8/4 Tweed, flannel or other suit-weight woollen.

b. In *Bridge*, freq. as opp. to *no trump(s) *phr.*, as *suit-bid, -break, call, contract, declaration, double, game, -jump*; **suit preference signal,** a play of a card of a certain rank to indicate which suit one wishes one's partner to return.

1917 E. Bergholt *Royal Auction Bridge* I. 90 In some circles, the practice of raising partner's suit-bid, when no other bid has intervened, is considerably overdone. **1962** *Times* 24 Oct. 3/7 Why be forced into a higher contract which may be in jeopardy through unlucky suit-breaks? **1907** Suit call [in Dict., sense 24 a]. **1977** *Homes & Gardens* Feb. 14 Presumably he also appreciates the point I made above about playing unbalanced hands in a suit contract. **1910** W. Dalton *Saturday Bridge* iv. 65 (*heading*) Defensive suit declarations by the dealer. **1927** *Observer* 13 Mar. 27 The suit double..has several interesting aspects. **1910** W. Dalton *Saturday Bridge* vii. 89 There are two distinct games at Bridge, the No Trump game and the suit game. **1929** M. C. Work *Compl. Contract Bridge* 52 When determining whether to make a suit-jump of two or three..do not be influenced..by Queens or Jacks of other suits. **1934** H. Lavinthal in *Bridge World* June 5/1, I am offering a new convention for the defense. I call this convention the High-Low Suit Preference Signal. **1981** *Times* 14 Nov. 17/6 Where there is any risk of confusion, suit preference signals should not be applied to the first trick.

suit, *v.* Add: **9. d.** To fit (someone) *up* with a specific type of clothing, as for sport, protection, etc. Cf. *kit *v.*[1] 2. *U.S.*

1945 M. H. ALLEE *Smoke Jumper* iii. 24 A man suited up for smoke jumping would almost as soon fall into the fire itself as into deep water. **1970** *New Yorker* 24 Oct. 140/3 Yale suited up sixty men, including four quarter-backs. **1976** *Daily Tel.* 1 Sept. 3/3 Only when everyone [*sc.* U.S. policemen] is suited up is the order given to tackle a disorderly crowd. **1979** *Tucson Mag.* Apr. 66 (Advt.), Dave Bloom & Sons will suit you up for all your active sport needs.

13. b. *suit yourself*: do (or think) as you please, please yourself.

1897 KIPLING *Captains Courageous* i. 21 'You stole it.' 'Suit yourself. We stole it ef it's any comfort to you.' **1932** W. FAULKNER *Light in August* xxi. 478 'I reckon I'll ride back here,' she says... 'Suit yourself,' I says. And we drove off. **1953** K. TENNANT *Joyful Condemned* xiii. 120 'Just suit yourself.' Miss Pilcher shrugged her broad shoulders. **1977** 'M. UNDERWOOD' *Murder with Malice* xiii. 118 'I'll probably call back later.' 'Suit yourself,' the woman said, indifferently.

16. (Earlier and later examples.) Also, to match or be in accord.

1816 JANE AUSTEN *Emma* III. ii. 20 Frank Churchill is a capital dancer, I understand—We shall see if our styles suit. *a* **1817** —— *Persuasion* (1818) IV. v. 91 Mr. Elliot is an exceedingly agreeable man..but we should not suit. **1971** 'D. HALLIDAY' *Dolly & Doctor Bird* xiii. 193 I've done an Eysenck personality inventory on you both... You wouldn't suit.

17. e. To dress oneself *up* in clothing designed for a specific task or purpose.

1959 J. BLISH *Clash of Cymbals* viii. 191 We should suit up at the half-hour. **1967** *Boston Sunday Herald* 30 Apr. 1. 22/2 Jim Lyle headed for the flight line to suit up for a routine mission aboard one of the giant radar picket planes. **1975** 'A. HALL' *Mandarin Cypher* xi. 170 'Time to suit up, isn't it?'..I got into the wet-suit. **1978** G. A. SHEEHAN *Running & Being* xv. 206 He will suit up and get out on the roads.

sui·tcase. (In Dict. s.v. SUIT *sb.* 24.) Add: **1.** Now more generally, a piece of luggage in the form of an oblong case, usu. with a hinged side and a handle, for carrying clothes and other belongings.

1902 [in Dict. s.v. *SUIT *sb.* 24]. **1942** W. FAULKNER *Go Down, Moses* 235 The boy waked him at last and got him and the suitcase off the train. **1981** D. M. THOMAS *White Hotel* IV. i. 133 She realized they were travellers, for they were weighed down by rucksacks and suitcases.

2. Phr. *to live out of* (or *from*) *a suitcase* (or *suitcases*): to move between temporary accommodation, esp. hotels and boarding houses; to be a wanderer, to have no fixed abode.

1946 L. DURRELL *Let.* 25 Sept. in Durrell & Miller *Private Corr.* (1963) 229, I can't tell you what wonderful peace and quiet it is, having a house of your own after so many years living from suitcases in hotels. **1960** J. WEIGHTMAN tr. *H. de Montherlant's Sel. Essays* 181 To live for years on end out of a small suitcase..seemed so much part and parcel of my everyday life. **1969** *Photoplay* Jan. 69/1 'It never occurred to me it would take ten years to settle down,' Audrey said recently, after ten years of living out of suitcases. **1975** C. EGLETON *Skirmish* xiii. 132 He had spent the greater part of his life living out of a suitcase.

3. a. *attrib.* Designating devices small or compact enough to be fitted into a suitcase, usu. in connection with secret or criminal activities, as *suitcase bomb, radio*, etc.

1954 *Richmond* (Va.) *Times-Dispatch* 25 Mar. 16 (*heading*) Now the 'suitcase A-bomb'. *Ibid.* 16/2 All of which means that a 'suitcase atom bomb' is no longer a figment of the imagination. **1972** T. ARDIES *This Suitcase is going to Explode* xiii. 134 Suitcase bombs have been discussed..in public. *Ibid.* xvii. 188 Very damning stuff—such as the plans for constructing a suitcase nuclear bomb. **1974** L. DEIGHTON *Spy Story* xix. 207 Our boy with the suitcase radio set came in five by five. A powerful signal.

b. *Comb.*, as **suitcase farmer** *N. Amer.*, a farmer who is resident on his farm for only a small part of the year (see quots.).

1941 R. DILLER *Farm Ownership, Tenancy, & Land Use* 2 'Suitcase farmer' is a term used of farmers on the Great Plains who put in a crop of wheat in the fall and come back to harvest it the next summer, after having spent the winter in their permanent homes elsewhere. **1956** *Saturday Night* (Toronto) 13 Oct. 15/1 The wheat-marketing problem means the end of the 'suitcase farmer', who has been accustomed to spend only a few weeks on his land each spring and summer for seeding and harvesting. **1970** DUCKHAM & MANSFIELD *Farming Syst. World* II. ii. 114 A 'suit-case' farmer moves seasonally between his several farms.

sui·tcaseful. [f. prec. + -FUL.] As much as a suitcase will hold.

1928 *Daily Express* 11 Aug. 5/1 Sand tray with which the little ones can play by an open window. If it is possible to persuade a friend to bring back a suitcaseful of shore sand.., so much the better. **1965** J. FLEMING *Nothing is Number* II. v. 83 He..brought back a suitcaseful of these books. **1979** J. SHERWOOD *Hour of Hyenas* xvi. 189 If you'll let me have that suitcaseful of guns that madam lent you.

suite. Add: **2. c.** (Earlier example.) Now freq. with reference to a three-piece suite of two armchairs and a sofa.

1805 *Times* 7 Nov. 4/2 An elegant drawing-room suite of 5 curtains, chairs, &c...suites of chairs, sofas. **1920** 'O. DOUGLAS' *Penny Plain* v. 47 Can you imagine it furnished with a 'suite'..and a grand piano? **1974** I. MURDOCH *Sacred & Profane Love Machine* 244 She had chosen..the maroon armchairs of corded velvet (they could not afford a 'suite').

d. (*a*) (Earlier example); (*b*) substitute for def.: a set of instrumental compositions (orig. of movements in dance style) to be played in succession; also, an assemblage of movements from opera or ballet scores; (later examples).

1760 J. MAINWARING *Mem. Life G. F. Handel* 68 The two first movements of Handel's seventh suite in the 1st Vol. of his Lessons formerly stood for the Overture in his famous opera of Agrippina. **1893** G. B. SHAW *Music in London 1890–94* (1932) III. 1 The usual two or three concertos..selection of overtures, suite from the latest 'incidental music' composed for the theatres. **1902** *Encycl. Brit.* XXXI. 42/1 Edward Alexander MacDowell..has written..symphonic poems, overtures, and suites for orchestra. **1928** *Grove's Dict. Mus.* (ed. 3) V. 184/2 The composer..accepts the term 'suite' as one which allows him a freer hand than symphony and one which indicates more definiteness of design than symphonic poem. **1977** *Zigzag* June 39/4 Only in the lengthy 'Rangers At Midnight' suite do the band really go over the top into arty cleverness.

e. *Geol.* A group of related minerals, rocks, or the like, esp. ones from the same place.

1845 [in Dict., sense 2 a]. **1882** A. GEIKIE *Text-bk. Geol.* 648 The earliest system or connected suite of deposits in the Palæozoic series has received the name of Cambrian. **1934** *Bull. Amer. Paleont.* XXI. No. 71. 18 It is sometimes..convenient to bracket several intimately related members together into what are here called formational suites or in common speech 'suites'. **1937** HATCH & WELLS *Petrol. Igneous Rocks* (ed. 9) v. ii. 273 As it is difficult to speak of a suite of associated rocks of one age and derived from a common magmatic source as a 'province', the term comagmatic assemblage is preferred. **1951** [see *NOVÁČEKITE]. **1963,** etc. [see *ophiolite suite* s.v. *OPHIOLITE b]. **1972** *Sci. Amer.* Mar. 34/2 Delta and river deposits sweep back across the continent, covering the miogeocline with a suite of continental shales and conglomerates. **1974** *Nature* 15 Nov. 219/2 X-ray diffraction analysis of residue in specimens from the eastern United States showed the mineral suite: chlorite, gibbsite, illite, kaolinite, [etc.]. **1978** *Sci. Amer.* Sept. 85/2 Boundaries between such layers, where one characteristic suite of fossils gives way to another, provide the basis for dividing geologic time into eras, periods and epochs. **1980** *Encounter* May 16/1 Those rocks (second sample though they might be from a suite already sampled by Shackleton) were..among the most precious data which could possibly have been obtained for geology.

f. A set of jewellery, esp. one containing matching pieces.

1869 S. R. HOLE *Bk. about Roses* viii. 109 Let him display..casket after casket of lustrous gems. Then invite her to select her *suite*. **1888** *J. Simmons Illustr. Trade Catal.* 25 (*heading*) Coloured bright gold brooches and earrings. Separately, or in suites to match. **1936** *Watchmaker & Jeweller* Feb. 187/2 (*caption*) A costume suite of gilt jewellery. **1981** M. BABSON *Bejewelled Death* i. 14 The Orpington Bequest..was the last of the monumental suites..to have survived.

g. The set of components which forms a lavatory; hence also, (matching) bathroom furniture or fittings.

1926–7 *Army & Navy Stores Catal.* 325 The 'Colonial' Closet Suite, comprising strong Vulcanware closet-pan and trap..polished mahogany seat..cistern, cover and brackets, brass chain pull and pottery handle. **1951** *Catal. of Exhibits, South Bank Exhibition, Festival of Britain* 125/1 W.C. suite. **1966** *Guardian* 5 July 8/5 A tiled bathroom, with or without a coloured 'suite'. **1973** J. THOMSON *Death Cap* i. 15 Pale green bathroom suite, fitted carpets, the lot.

h. *Computers.* A collection of related programs which can be run one after the other without interruption.

1967 *Oxford Computer Explained* 9 This Suite is run twice a day. **1980** R. MCCRUM *In Secret State* xi. 98 It was just a suite of programmes that wasn't in Lister's index.

suiting, *vbl. sb.* Add: **5.** Now in wider use, and freq. *sing.* Also applied to the finished garments.

1923 A. HUXLEY *Antic Hay* iii. 34 A very small man.. popped out from a canyon..between two stratified precipices of mid-season suitings. **1930** *Daily Express* 8 Sept. 11/5 This cardigan type of tailored suit is made of a soft suiting tweed. **1957** L. DURRELL *Bitter Lemons* 44 His rusty, moth-bedevilled business suiting and wrinkled dicky suggested extremes of dreadful indigence. **1980** J. B. HILTON *Anathema Stone* iii. 28 [He] left the farm with a sample of his suiting in the jaws of a bull-mastiff.

Suk (sūk), *sb.* and *a.* **A.** *sb.* **a.** An East African people who inhabit an area on the Uganda-Kenya border; a member of this people. **b.** The Nilotic language spoken by the Suk. **B.** *adj.* Of or pertaining to this people or their language.

1902 H. JOHNSTON *Uganda Protectorate* II. xix. 847 The Sūk, like the Turkana, pierce the lower lip... The Sūk women sometimes shave the head. **1902** *Encycl. Brit.* XXXIII. 541/2 The languages spoken in the Uganda Protectorate belong to the following stocks..*Masai* (Bari, Masai, Elgumi, Turkana, Sūk, &c.). **1930** [see *NANDI *sb.*[2] and *a.*]. **1936** *Discovery* June 171/2 The Nandi, Masai, Turkana, and Sūk are perhaps the best-known tribes of this group. **1947** [see *KIPSIGIS]. **1953,** etc. [see *SEBEI]. **1963** *Times* 6 May 19/6 Mr. Jomo Kenyatta, president of the Kenya African National Union, today reminded a crowd already nursed to a happy pitch of electoral enthusiasm by the chanting and dancing of Suk and Kalenjin tribesmen. **1974** *Encycl. Brit. Micropædia* VII. 347/2 Linguists often divide the Nilotic languages into a western group..and a southern group, including Nandi and Suk.

suk, var. *SOUK.

sukebind (s[i]ū·kbəind). [Arbitrary formation: cf. BIND *sb.* 2, 3.] Name given by Stella Gibbons (see quot. 1932) to an imaginary plant associated with superstition and fertility, hence used allusively with reference to intense rustic passions.

1932 S. GIBBONS *Cold Comfort Farm* v. 75 In the fulness of summer, when the sukebind hangs heavy from the wains..'tes the same. **1968** *Listener* 19 Sept. 379/3 The sukebind twines lushly over the grave of Mary Webb, another esteemed pre-war novelist, and since Stella Gibbons planted the fatal seed, nobody has bothered to hack away the undergrowth to discover what lies beneath. **1975** *Times* 15 July 14/3 A Country Sports Fair conjures images of..young couples competing among the sukebind. **1982** W. GOLDING *Moving Target* 106 Mr Trevelyan's fascinating book... He climbed one or two family trees where the Sukebind was a-blowing.

sukey (sū·ki). *dial* and *colloq.* Also with capital initial and **suckey, sukie, suky.** [Dim. of *Susan, Susanna*, fem. name.] A tea-kettle.

The nursery rhyme 'Polly put the kettle on' (see quot. 1981) is known from 1841: *Oxf. Dict. Nursery Rhymes.*

1823 'J. BEE' *Slang* 167 Sukey, a tea kettle. **1875** E. TWEDDELL *Rhymes Cleveland Dial.* 40 Suckey was bolin' a gud un when we gat there. An' Ah..helpt to fettle t'tea. **1877** E. PEACOCK *N.W. Lincs. Gloss.* 244/2 *Suky*, a child's name for a tea-kettle. **1898** J. D. BRAYSHAW *Slum Silhouettes* 182 Now, Sukey boils; fill the teapot, Dick. **1919** 'W. N. P. BARBELLION' *Diary* 13 Feb. (1920) 95 Our sukie is an old copper one, and sings sometimes in splendid imitation of an orchestra tuning up. **1952** M. LASKI *Village* i. 13 I'll just get the sukey going, and then we'll have a nice cup of tea. **1981** *Jrnl. Lancs. Dial. Soc.* Jan. 46 Many people remember *sukey* as a name for the kettle. 'Sukey's boiling,' they would say. This must originate in the nursery rhyme 'Polly put the kettle on'.

sukh, var. *SOUK.

sukiyaki (sukiya·ki, ‖skī·yaki). Also **suki-yaki.** [Jap.] A Japanese dish, consisting of very thin slices of beef fried with vegetables in sugar and soy sauce, and often served with rice.

1920 *Japan Advertiser* 22 Aug. 5/1 Another name by which this dish [*sc.* nabe] is usually known outside of Tokyo, is suki-yaki. This is derived from suki, which means a spade, and yaki, to cook. **1932** H. A. PHILLIPS *Meet Japanese* xvii. 185 Beef *sukiyaki* tasted good after a long day's jaunt. **1935** B. WOON *San Francisco & Golden Empire* v. 62 The best *suki-yaki* restaurant is not in the Japanese quarter but in a Japanese hotel near the corner of California Street and Grant Avenue. Here tasteful *suki-yaki* dishes are cooked in chafing-dishes, Japanese style. **1943** H. MEARS *Year of Wild Boar* iii. 51 The Japanese who patronized this place..did so only to sample American culture, as in New York the American might dine in a Japanese *sukiyaki* restaurant. **1952** R. CUTFORTH *Korean Reporter* xvi. 147 There are other famous meals—*Sukiyaki*—a fry of chicken or beef with vegetables and soya. **1964** I. FLEMING *You only live Twice* xxii. 253 A highly spiced dish of *sukiyaki*, the national dish of beef stew. **1970** P. & J. MARTIN *Jap. Cooking* 72 Put a sukiyaki pan or a large, heavy frying pan over a portable cooking stove. **1977** *Time* 19 Dec. 43/1 (*caption*) Drama Coach Lee Strasberg cooks sukiyaki in Manhattan.

sukkah, var. *SUCCAH. **Sukkot(h,** var. SUCCOTH.

sulfa-, altered and U.S. form of *SULPHA-, used to form the name of certain drugs (in British English *sulpha-* also occurs): **sulfame·razine** (also **-izine**)[*-MER + *AZINE], the readily absorbed sulphonamide $CH_3·C_4H_2N_2·NH·SO_2·C_6H_4·NH_2$, now rarely used except in Sulphatriad; N[1]-(4-methylpyrimidin-2-yl)sulphanilamide; **su:lfaquino·xaline** [*QUINOXALINE], the sulphonamide $C_8H_5N_2·NH·SO_2·C_6H_4·NH_2$, used as a coccidiostat in the treatment of cæcal coccidiosis in poultry; *N*[1]-quinoxalin-2-ylsulphanilamide.

1943 A. D. WELCH et al. in *Jrnl. Pharmacol. & Exper. Therapeutics* LXXVII. 357 The chemistry of this compound, which will be referred to as sulfamerizine, has been described in the publications of several groups. **1945** *Brit. Med. Jrnl.* 3 Feb. 155/1 One new compound—sulphamerazine (or sulphamerizine)—has been the subject of much work in America. **1961** A. GOTH *Med. Pharmacol.* xli. 444 Sulfamerazine and sulfamethazine resemble sulfadiazine in most respects, except for the fact that they are excreted more slowly by the kidney. **1962** H. BURN *Drugs, Med. & Man* xx. 200 Various new substances were prepared in this way, among them sulphathiazole, sulphadiazine and sulphamerazine. These compounds were not only different from sulphanilamide, but were much more potent. **1977** *Approved Names 1977* (Brit. Pharmacopœia Commission) 81 Sulfamerazine. **1944** *Jrnl. Biol. Chem.* CLVI. 343 Recently, a new sulfonamide, sulfaquinoxaline, was introduced. **1961** *New Scientist* 21 Dec.

742/1 Sulfaquinoxaline and sulfadimidine were administered to turkeys either in their food or by intramuscular injection. **1976** *Nature* 17 June 621/2 The number of antagonists is now large, some of the best-known being.., sulphaquinoxaline and actinomycin D. **1977** *Approved Names 1977* (Brit. Pharmacopoeia Commission) 81 Sulfaquinoxaline.

Sulfasuxidine (sɒlfăsɒ·ksidīn). *Pharm.* [f. *SULFA- + *SUX- + *-IDINE.] A proprietary name for the drug succinylsulphathiazole.

1942 *Official Gaz.* (U.S. Patent Office) 6 Jan. 9/2 Sharp & Dohme, Incorporated, Philadelphia... *Sulfasuxidine* for pharmaceutical preparations useful as bactericides and as antiseptics. **1943** *Trade Marks Jrnl.* 26 May 223/1 *Sulfasuxidine*...Pharmaceutical substances for human use and for veterinary use..consisting wholly of sulphur compounds...Sharp & Dohms Ltd...1st April, 1942. **1976** A. I. BRAUDE *Antimicrobial Drug Therapy* i. 11 Succinylsulfathiazole (Sulfasuxidine) is a good example of how the para-NH_2 group becomes free after slow hydrolysis from its inactive form to the active sulfathiazole.

sulham (su·lhām). Also † **silham, sulam; selham.** [a. Arab. *zulḥam*.] A large Arab hooded cloak (properly distinguished from the burnous).

1791 W. LEMPRIERE *Tour from Gibraltar to Morocco* ix. 229 They then were obliged to uncover their cap or turban..and to wear instead of the *haick* the *sulam*, which is a cloak made of white or blue woollen cloth. **1809** J. G. JACKSON *Acct. Empire of Marocco* 138 The Berebbers wear drawers, and a cloak of dark blue cloth, called a Silham. **1817** J. RILEY *Narr. Loss Amer. Brig 'Commerce'* 198 The cloak, or sulam, is made of coarse black cloth. **1891** HALL CAINE *Scapegoat* (ed. 2) viii. 172 He drew forth from the folds of his selham a long knife. **1903** *Westm. Gaz.* 15 Jan. 5/1 The ladies..all wearing Moorish sulhams. **1907** F. CAMPBELL *Shepherd of Stars* vi. 72 Strange faces look out from the jellab and sulham hoods. **1921** *Chambers's Jrnl.* Jan. 22/2 A 'warm man' of merchandise, with robes of a surpassing whiteness, rich cloth selham or burnous, and brilliant lemon-coloured slippers. **1951** W. BLUNT *Black Sunrise* xvii. 201 After two or three courses Ismail took off his *selham* and *haik*. **1975** C. CALASIBETTA *Fairchild's Dict. Fashion* 64/1 *Burnoose*.., travelling cape..worn by Moors and Arabs in northern Africa. Also called a *selham*.

Suliote (sⁱū·liōᵘt) *sb.* (and *a*). Also **Souliot(e), Suliot.** [ad. Gr. Σουλιώτης: see -OTE.] An inhabitant of the Suli mountains in Epirus, of mixed Greek and Albanian origin. Also *attrib.* or as *adj*.

1812 BYRON *Ch. Har.* II. lxxii, Oh! who is more brave than a dark Suliote? **1827** F. G. HALLECK *Alnwick Castle & Other Poems* 10 Bozzaris ranged his Suliote band. **1832** T. GORDON *Hist. Greek Revol.* I. I. i. 76 The Souliotes, the flower of Albanian warriors, were driven from Epirus. **1852** G. F. BOWEN *Mount Athos, Thesaly, & Epirus* viii. 214 The Suliote hamlet of Kiafa. **1897** W. A. PHILLIPS *War of Greek Independence* vii. 127 Marko Botzares, the Suliot hero. **1900** 'ODYSSEUS' *Turkey in Europe* ix. 404 The Suliots have somehow acquired in popular estimation the reputation of being Greeks. As a matter of fact they were a tribe of Christian Albanians. **1910** *Encycl. Brit.* XI. 494/2 On the night of the 21st of August [1823] occurred the celebrated exploit of Marko Botzaris and his Suliotes: a successful surprise attack on the camp of the Ottoman vanguard, in which the Suliote leader fell. **1914** D. J. CASSAVETTI *Hellas & Balkan Wars* xv. 188 Old people would shake their heads sadly and ask if these empty-headed dolls could possibly belong to the same country as the grand Souliot women. **1952** C. M. WOODHOUSE *Greek War of Independence* i. 13 Parts of Crete remained..independent of all foreign rule. So to some extent did Souli, a wild precipitous district above the River Akheron in Epirus (Southern Albania); but the Souliotes were not strictly Greeks. **1973** D. DAKIN *Greek Struggle for Independence* i. 31 The wily Souliots, hoping to find out what Ali was really up to, sent a token force only. *Ibid.*, Back in Souli, Tzavellas and the chief of Souliot chiefs, Georgios Botsaris, decided to defy Ali.

sulk, *sb.*² **1. b.** (Earlier examples.)

1792 W. B. STEVENS *Jrnl.* 8 Oct. (1965) I. 48 The strange Sulk of a Day and a half, during our Northern Tour. **1836** J. ROMILLY *Diary* 21 Oct. (1967) 104 Much discussion (in wch the V.Ch. never joined, he being in a grand sulk).

Sulka (su·lkă). The name of *Sulka* & Co., shirtmakers and hosiers (est. 1895), of London and New York, used *attrib.* to designate exclusive fabrics (esp. silk) and garments made, designed, or sold by them. Freq. as *Sulka tie*.

1925 *Trade Marks Jrnl.* 21 Oct. 2307 *Sulka*... Shirtings and handkerchiefs, being linen piece goods. A. Sulka & Company.., New York City, New York, United States of America; merchants and manufacturers. **1944** A. HUXLEY *Time must have Stop* (1945) vi. 69 The beautifully fitting pearl-grey suit, the Sulka tie. **1963** E. LININGTON *Death of Busybody* x. 126 Mendoza's custom-tailored gray Italian silk and Sulka tie. **1981** 'E. LATHEN' *Going for Gold* ix. 99 Brad, wrapped in yards of Sulka silk, was pacing the floor.

sulky, *sb.* Add. **4.** (*b*) *sulky cultivator, plow* (earlier examples).

1867 *Trans. Ill. Agric. Soc.* VI. 49 Driving a sulky plow, and plowing his one-fourth acre. **1868** *Rep. Iowa Agric. Soc. 1867* 154 It is then plowed with double-shovel, or sulky cultivators.

sull (sɒ̄l), *v. U.S.* [Back-formation from SULLEN *a.*, *adv.* and *sb.*] *intr.* Of an animal, to balk; of a person, to become sullen or to sulk.

1869 *Overland Monthly* III. 127 A mustang..will both 'sull', (have the sulks) and 'buck'. **1891** 'O. THANET' *Otto the Knight* 29 The ox, he sulled,..an' Jim jes' guv 'im one on the head. **1902** *Dialect Notes* II. 246 *Sull*,..to hold a position with imperturbable obstinacy and a total disregard of surroundings, as a possum, or a hog in a corner. **1903** *Ibid.* 332 *Sull*,..to sulk; to balk. 'My oxens sull whenever they get hot.' 'She is a quare child and sulls whenever she is contrairied.' **1929** W. FAULKNER *Sound & Fury* 87 'She sulling again, is she,' Roskus said. **1938** M. K. RAWLINGS *Yearling* xxv. 327 Do he ever come here drunk, remember he ain't human when he gits to sullin'. **1949** *10 Story Western* May 11/2 Tell them slow motion sons to keep them cattle comin' before this drive balks and sulls. **1959** W. FAULKNER *Mansion* 10 All Frenchman's Bend knew Houston: sulking and sulling in his house all alone by himself since the stallion killed his wife four years ago.

Hence (rarely) as *sb.*, a sulky fit, a 'sulk'.

1972 E. WELTY *Optimist's Daughter* II. iv. 97 He's been in a sull ever since you married Judge McKelva and didn't send him a special engraved invitation to the wedding.

Sullan (sɒ·lăn), *a.* (and *sb.*). [f. the name of Roman general and dictator Lucius Cornelius *Sulla* (*c* 138–78 B.C.) + -AN.] Of or pertaining to Sulla or his party, or the laws and political reforms instituted by him. Also as *sb.*, a supporter of Sulla.

1866 W. P. DICKSON tr. *Mommsen's Hist. Rome* IV. v. iii. 90 The young Gaius Caesar..brought to trial..another Sullan officer Gaius Antonius. *Ibid.* v. 167 Antonius, originally a Sullan like Catilina. **1892** W. W. FOWLER *Julius Caesar* ii. 29 Caesar..fled in disguise into the mountains of Samnium. Here he was pursued and captured by the Sullan bloodhounds, who were everywhere. **1905** G. S. GORDON *Let.* 15 Nov. (1943) 10, I *cannot* get out of my head even now the Ontological proofs of the existence of God, the Sullan Constitution, Pericles and Athenian finance, and why Pleasure cannot be an ultimate Ethical end. **1923** T. R. HOLMES *Roman Republic* I. i. 59 The Sullan reign of terror was never forgotten by the Romans. **1949** L. R. TAYLOR *Party Politics in Age of Caesar* i. 21 The *optimates*, who were determined to save what they could of their Sullan prerogatives. **1974** A. WATSON *Law Making in Later Roman Republic* vi. 95 It is not proved that all these *leges* are Sullan. **1976** *Classical Q.* XXVI. 105 The Sullan reforms tell us a little about this.

sullen, *a.* Add: **6.** *sullen-eyed, -faced; sullen-blooming, -looking, -smiling.*

1879 O. WILDE in *Time* July 402 No sullen-blooming poppies stain thy hair. **1961** R. S. THOMAS *Tares* 47 And given to watching, sullen-eyed, Love still-born, as it was then. **1914** JOYCE *Dubliners* 117 A very sullen-faced man. **1919** J. MASEFIELD *Reynard the Fox* I. 29 Surly, Tall, shifty, sullen-smiling.

sulph-, sulpha- (sɒ·lfă). *Pharm.* Also (chiefly *U.S.*) **sulfa-**. [f. *SULPHA(NILAMIDE.] Formative element in the names of drugs derived from sulphanilamide, as **sulphace·tamide** [ACETAMIDE], the sulphonamide $CH_3CO{\cdot}NH{\cdot}SO_2{\cdot}C_6H_4{\cdot}NH_2$, which is used in the form of the sodium salt in the treatment of eye infections; N^1-acetylsulphanilamide; **sulphadi·azine** [*AZINE b], the readily absorbed sulphonamide $C_4H_3N_2{\cdot}NH{\cdot}SO_2{\cdot}C_6H_4{\cdot}NH_2$, which is used in the treatment of meningococcal meningitis; N^1-pyrimidin-2-ylsulphanilamide; **sulphadi·midine** [DI- + *PYRI)MIDINE], the readily absorbed sulphonamide $(CH_3)_2C_4H_2N_2{\cdot}NH{\cdot}SO_2{\cdot}C_6H_4{\cdot}NH_2$, used in the treatment of a wide range of systemic and urinary tract infections; N^1-(4,6-dimethylpyrimidin-2-yl)-sulphanilamide; **sulphafu·razole** [*FUR(AN + *PYR)AZOLE], the readily absorbed sulphonamide $(CH_3)_2C_3NO{\cdot}NH{\cdot}SO_2{\cdot}C_6H_4{\cdot}NH_2$, which is used in the treatment of infections of the urinary tract; N^1-(3,4-dimethyliosoxazol-5-yl)sulphanilamide = *sulphisoxazole* below; **sulphagua·nidine** [GUANIDINE], the poorly absorbed sulphonamide $HN{:}C(NH_2){\cdot}NH{\cdot}SO_2{\cdot}C_6H_4{\cdot}NH_2$, formerly used in the treatment of intestinal infections; N^1-guanidinylsulphanilamide; **sulphame·thazine** [METH(YL + *AZINE] = *sulphadimidine* above; **sulphame·thizole** [ME(THYL + THI(O- + *dia*)*zole* (f. DIAZO- + *-OLE)], the readily absorbed sulphonamide $CH_3{\cdot}C_2N_2S_2{\cdot}NH{\cdot}SO_2{\cdot}C_6H_4{\cdot}NH_2$, which is used in treating coliform infections of the urinary tract; N^1-(5-methyl-1,3,4-thiadiazol-2-yl)sulphanilamide; **su:lphametho·xazole** [METH(YL + *is*)*oxazole* s.v. *ISO- b], the sulphonamide $CH_3{\cdot}C_3HNO{\cdot}NH{\cdot}SO_2{\cdot}C_6H_4{\cdot}NH_2$, used in the treatment of respiratory and urinary tract infections, and as a component of the preparation co-trimoxazole; N^1-(5-methylisoxazol-3-yl)sulphanilamide; **su:lphametho:xypyri·dazine** [*METHOXY- + *PYRIDAZINE], the long-acting sulphonamide $CH_3O{\cdot}C_4N_2H_2{\cdot}NH{\cdot}SO_2{\cdot}C_6H_4{\cdot}NH_2$, used in the treatment of systemic and urinary tract infections; N^1-(6-methoxypyridazin-3-yl)sulphanilamide; **Sulphame·zathine,** a proprietary name for sulphadimidine (sulphamethazine); **sulphapy·ridine** [PYRIDINE], the readily absorbed sulphonamide $C_5H_4N{\cdot}NH{\cdot}SO_2{\cdot}C_6H_4{\cdot}NH_2$, which is used chiefly in the treatment of dermatitis herpetiformis; N^1-pyridin-2-ylsulphanilamide; **sulpha·rsenite,** any compound containing the elements sulphur, arsenic, and oxygen; **sulphasa·lazine** [SAL(ICYL + *AZINE], the sulphonamide $C_5H_4N{\cdot}NH{\cdot}SO_2{\cdot}C_6H_4{\cdot}N{:}N{\cdot}C_6H(OH)COOH$, which is used in conjunction with corticosteroids in the treatment of ulcerative colitis; 4-hydroxy-4′-(2-pyridylsulphamoyl)azobenzene-3-carboxylic acid; **Sulphatri·ad,** a proprietary name for a mixed sulphonamide drug containing sulphadiazine, sulphamerazine, and sulphathiazole, used in the treatment of acute infections; **sulphiso·xazole** *Pharm.* [*isoxazole* s.v. *ISO- b] = *sulphafurazole* above.

1941 *Pharm. Jrnl.* 29 Nov. 188/3 Sulphacetamide is a name which it has been proposed should be adopted for the preparation now known under the trade mark 'Albucid'. **1975** *Prescribers' Jrnl.* XV. 139 Sulphacetamide in the form of eye drops and ointment can produce sensitivity reactions on the skin around the eyes. **1940** R. O. ROBLIN et al. in *Jrnl. Amer. Chem. Soc.* LXII. 2002/2 In order to avoid possible confusion between sulfapyridine and sulfapyrimidine, the term sulfadiazines is suggested for these [pyrimidine] compounds. **1943** [see *SULPHATHIAZOLE]. **1956** I. L. FINAR *Org. Chem.* II. xviii. 668 Sulphadiazine..is less toxic than Sulphathiazole; it is the most widely used of the 'sulpha' drugs, its main use being for mild infections. **1980** *Jrnl. Med. Microbiol.* XIII. 131 At therapeutic levels in blood, trimethoprim and sulphadiazine singly produced mainly a bactericidal action on pathogens responsible for urinary-tract infections. **1950** *Brit. Med. Jrnl.* 12 Aug. 409/1 Sulphadimidine ('sulphamezathine') and Sulphamerazine (U.S.P.) have almost identical qualities. **1961** [see *sulfaquinoxaline* s.v. *SULFA-]. **1977** *Martindale's Extra Pharmacopoeia* (ed. 27) 1479/2 Sulphadimidine penetrates into cerebrospinal fluid less readily than sulphadiazine and is usually less effective than sulphadiazine in meningeal infections. **1961** *Lancet* 22 July 178/1 Rebollo..claimed a cure [for meningitis due to *Pseudomonas pyocyanea*] with sulphafurazole, given orally. **1976** *Ibid.* 11 Dec. 1276/1, 91 men with nongonococcal urethritis (N.G.U.) were randomly treated with..sulphafurazole (sulfisoxazole). **1941** *Jrnl. Amer. Med. Assoc.* 3 May 2019/2 For 2-sulfanilamidopyrimidine it [*sc.* the Council on Pharmacy and Chemistry of the American Medical Association] adopted the term sulfadiazine and for sulfanilylguanidine the term sulfaguanidine. **1943** *Listener* 16 Sept. 321/2 A quite new drug, sulphaguanidine, shows promise for the treatment of bacillary dysentery; it succeeds here..because much of it is not absorbed, and it therefore remains to act in the intestine. **1958** E. NEWBY *Short Walk in Hindu Kush* xviii. 220 Everyone..was now suffering from dysentery. We all munched sulphaguanadine tablets but even these failed. **1977** *Martindale's Extra Pharmacopoeia* (ed. 27) 1483/1 Sulphaguanidine has been employed for the treatment of local intestinal infections..though it has now been largely superseded by the less toxic sulphonamides, phthalylsulphathiazole and succinylsulphathiazole. **1942** *Lancet* 30 May 639/1 In the summer of 1941 our attention was drawn by Drs. Martin and Rose of the research laboratories of Imperial Chemical (Pharmaceuticals) Ltd. to a near relation of sulphadiazine..to which the name sulphamethazine has been given. **1951** A. GROLLMAN *Pharmacol. & Therapeutics* xxi. 434 Sulfamethazine.., the methyl derivative of sulfamerazine resembles the latter in action and is used for the same purposes as sulfamerazine and sulfadiazine. **1965** *Pharmacopeia U.S.A.* (ed. 17) 785 U.S.P. XVII Title..Sulfamethazine. Other Designation(s)...Sulphadimidine (*BP*). **1978** SPINELLI & ENOS *Drugs in Vet. Pract.* x. 135/1 Foot rot... The following can be used: 1. Sulfamethazine, starting with one intravenous injection [etc.]. **1952** *Chem. Abstr.* XLVI. 686 Sulfathiazole, sulfadiazine, and sulfamethizole have been detd. by this method in various pharm. prepns. **1977** *Lancet* 16 Apr. 863/2 Sulphamethizole and alkali were prescribed pending a culture report. **1960** *Antibiotics & Chemotherapy* (N.Y.) X. 572 A new sulfonamide compound, sulfamethoxazole, is identified chemically as 5-methyl-3-sulfanilamidoisoxazole. **1977** *Lancet* 2 July 4/1 Much of the shigellosis could be successfully treated with ampicillin trihydrate and closely related antibiotics, or with co-trimoxazole (trimethoprim and sulphamethoxazole). **1981** H. J. ROGERS et al. *Textbk. Clin. Pharmacol.* xix. 653 Sulphamethoxazole is about 50% metabolised so that much reaches the urine in an inactive form. **1956** *Antibiotic Med. & Clin. Therapy* III. 386 A new antibacterial sulfonamide, sulfamethoxypyridazine, has been studied in 67 patients. **1980** *Biochem. Pharmacol.* XXIX. 984/1 Kidney weight/body weight ratio, DNA and protein concentrations of kidney cortex were determined in 55-day-old rats repeatedly pretreated with saline, PAH, sulfamethoxypyridazine, cyclopenthiazide and phenobarbital, respectively. **1943** *Trade Marks Jrnl.* 6 Oct. 421/2 *Sulphamezathine*... Pharmaceutical organic substances being sulphanilamido compounds for veterinary use. Imperial Chemical (Pharmaceuticals) Ltd. **1944** *Pharmaceutical Jrnl.* 8 Apr. 154A/3 Imperial Chemicals (Pharmaceuticals), Ltd., now offer their 'Sulphamezathine' brand of sulphadimethylpyrimidine in the form of a stable solution of the sodium salt. **1970** *Country Life* 26 Feb. 491/1 The drinking water should be dosed with sulphamezathine to prevent coccidiosis. **1939** *Jrnl. Amer. Med. Assoc.* 7 Jan. 49/2 Recent reports from investigators indicate that a pyridine derivative of sulfanilamide..is apparently more promising in the treatment of certain types of pneumonia than sulfanilamide itself... The Council has therefore adopted the term 'sulfapyridine'. **1942** *Times* 30 Nov. 2/3 In 1939, by skilled use of the new drug sulphapyridine, it [*sc.* the fatality rate in spotted fever] was brought down to 33 per cent. **1957** [see *M AND B]. **1967** [see *SULPHANILAMIDE]. **1981** H. J. ROGERS et al. *Textbk. Clin. Pharmacol.* xix. 649 Sulphapyridine in low doses over prolonged periods may control dermatitis herpetiformis. **1859** Sulpharsenite [in Dict.]. **1868** J. D. DANA *Syst. Min.* (ed. 5) ii. 84 (*heading*) Sulpharsenites, sulphantimonites, sulphobismuthites. **1905** *Nature* 6 Apr. 534/1 To these minerals a third must now be added in hutchinsonite, a new sulpharsenite from the Binnenthal, which also contains thallium as an important constituent. **1954** Sulpharsenite [see *HUTCHINSONITE]. **1961** *Brit. Med. Jrnl.* 21 Jan. 5220/2 Sulphasalazine ('salazopyrin', 'asulfidine') has been used extensively in Sweden and America since 1941 in the treatment of colitis. **1977** *Lancet* 29 Oct. 931/1 Inflammatory bowel disease was diagnosed and the patient was put on intramuscular corticotrophin, sulphasalazine, and codeine phosphate. **1948** *Trade Marks Jrnl.* 12 May 348/2 Sulphatriad... Pharmaceutical preparations of sulphonamides... May & Baker Limited... Manufacturing chemists. **1950** 'N. SHUTE' *Town like Alice* vi. 184 The flies would probably result in dysentery but she knew what to do about that; she had plenty of sulphatriad. **1968** J. H. BURN *Lect. Notes Pharmacol.* (ed. 9) 101 If three sulphonamides are used together, as in Sulphatriad, only one-third of the amount of each need be used. **1965** *Pharmacopeia U.S.A.* (ed. 17) 785 U.S.P. XVII Title... *Sulfisoxazole.* Other Designation(s)... Sulphafurazole (*BP*). **1976** [see *sulphafurazole* above]. **1977** *Lancet* 2 July 4/1 Most of the *S. flexneri* strains were resistant to tetracycline, streptomycin, and sulphafurazole diethanolamine (sulfisoxazole dialomine). **1952** H. BECKMAN *Pharmacol. in Clin. Pract.* 648 The principal ones [*sc.* sulphonamides] in current use are sulfadiazine, sulfamerazine, Sulfamethazine..and sulfisoxazole.

sulpha (sʌ·lfă). *Pharm.* Also (chiefly *U.S.*) **sulfa.** [f. *SULPHA(NILAMIDE.] Any of the drugs derived from sulphanilamide. Usu. *attrib.*, as *sulpha drug*.

1942 B. BLIVEN *Men who make Future* i. 11 Within the past year or two, the magical effects of sulfanilamide in curing a whole series of diseases have been supplemented by..the other 'sulfa' drugs. **1951** E. A. MCCOURT *Home is Stranger* xiv. 211 She had asked Weary to get a prescription of some kind from Dr Harrington—sulpha, perhaps. **1956** *Sci. News* XLI. 18 Modifications of sulphanilamide have led to the extensive sulphanamide or sulpha group of drugs. **1967** *New Scientist* 16 Feb. 384/2 A fatal type of malaria..is now being effectively controlled by a new sulpha drug. **1973** E. ARNOLD *Proving Ground* (1974) xiv. 169 The nurses..applied sulfa powder and repacked and rebandaged the wound. **1975** B. WOOD *Killing Gift* (1976) III. ii. 94 I've given her some sulfa and a shot of codeine so she'll sleep.

sulphæmoglobin (sʌ:lfhīmoˌglōᵘ·bin). *Biochem.* and *Med.* Also **sulph-hæmoglobin, -hemoglobin,** (*U.S.*) **sulfhemo-.** [f. SULP(H- + HÆMOGLOBIN.] A sulphur-containing derivative of hæmoglobin, produced by its reaction with soluble sulphides or sulphides absorbed from the alimentary tract, and giving rise to the greenish discoloration found in putrefying cadavers.

1896 A. BRUCE tr. *Thoma's Text-bk. Gen. Path.* I. iii. 43 In poisoning by charcoal fumes, carbonic-oxide-hæmoglobin is formed, and in poisoning by sulphuretted hydrogen, sulph-hæmoglobin or sulph-hæmatin. **1908** HALL & DEFREN tr. *Abderhalden's Text-bk. Physiol. Chem.* xxiv. 561 This green shade is due to the formation of sulphhemoglobin, which, however, has never been prepared in a pure state. **1947** K. SIMPSON *Forensic Med.* xxviii. 314 Sulphaemoglobin forms naturally as post-mortem decomposition sets in. **1980** *Amer. Jrnl. Physiol.* CCXXXVIII. H745/2 This report concerns a method for 'labeling' red blood cells..by the formation of sulfhemoglobin.

Hence **su:lphæmoglobinæ·mia** [Gr. αἷμα blood], the presence of sulphæmoglobin in the blood, caused by drug-potentiated absorption of hydrogen sulphide from the alimentary tract, or direct assimilation of the sulpha group from any sulphonamide.

1910 *Jrnl. Amer. Med. Assoc.* 17 Dec. 2181/2 The patient was observed for some weeks, and as the ordinary blood examination failed to reveal any polycythemia or other abnormality to account for the condition, a tentative diagnosis of sulphemoglobinemia was made. **1961** A. S. MACNALTY *Brit. Med. Dict.* 1373/2 It [*sc.* sulphæmoglobin] is produced under the influence of many substances such as nitrates, chlorates, nitrites..etc., causing enterogenous cyanosis or sulphaemoglobinaemia. **1980** *Amer. Jrnl. Clin. Path.* LXXIII. 245/1 In one specimen, marked methemoglobinemia and sulfhemoglobinemia were also demonstrated.

sulphane (sʌ·lfēⁱn). *Chem.* Also (*U.S.*) **sulf-.** [a. G. *sulfane* (Fehér & Laue 1953, in *Zeitschr. für Naturforschung* VIIIB. 687/1): see -ANE.] Any of the hydrides of sulphur, H_2S_x.

1955 *Chem. Abstr.* XLIX. 15590 The results reported in this series, on compds. of the form H_2S_n, M_2S_n, and X_2S_n (M = alkali metal, X = halogen), indicate that they have a paraffin-like chain structure. The generic name *sulfanes* is suggested. **1968** BURTON & MACHMER in G. Nickless *Inorg. Sulphur Chem.* x. 340 The sulphanes are extremely sensitive compounds and hence are very difficult to prepare in the pure state. **1979** *Geophysical Research Lett.* VI. 807/1 We discuss the possible importance of gaseous elemental sulfur (particularly S_2, S_3..and S_4) and sulfanes (H_2S_n) in the lower atmosphere of Venus.

sulphanilamide (sʌlfăni·lăməid). *Pharm.* Also (*U.S.*) **sulf-.** [f. *sulphanilic* s.v. SULPH- (f. ANIL(INE + -IC) + AMIDE.] **a.** The amide of sulphanilic acid, which has wide bacteriostatic activity, has been used, esp. topically, in the treatment of infections due to hæmolytic streptococci, and is the parent compound of the sulphonamides; *p*-aminobenzenesulphonamide, $H_2N{\cdot}C_6H_4{\cdot}SO_2{\cdot}NH_2$.

1937 *Jrnl. Amer. Med. Assoc.* 17 Apr. 1340/2 The Council [on Pharmacy and Chemistry] has therefore formally adopted the nonproprietary name 'Sulfanilamide' for para-aminobenzenesulfonamide. **1942** *Times* 9 Oct. 2/4 A further long list of requirements was sent back from Moscow... The articles dispatched..have included:—530,000 blankets,..10,000 kilos sulphanilamide. **1953** M. LOWRY *Let.* 31 Oct. (1967) 345 The chief engineer has an ulcerated throat, and the ship itself is running on sulfanilamide. **1962** J. HELLER *Catch-22* xli. 428 Snowden ..shifted the position of his hips a bit so that Yossarian could begin salting the wound with sulfanilamide. **1967** *Martindale's Extra Pharmacopoeia* (ed. 25) 1376/1 Sulphanilamide,..together with the earlier derivatives, sulphapyridine and sulphathiazole, has been largely superseded by more effective and less toxic compounds. **1974** R. M. KIRK et al. *Surgery* ii. 27 Sulphanilamide powder is sometimes used topically on raw surfaces, in abscess cavities and body spaces such as the peritoneal and pleural cavities.

b. Any substituted derivative of this compound.

1961 in WEBSTER. **1962** H. A. KREBS in A. Pirie *Lens Metabolism Rel. Cataract* 351 The effects ..of sulphanilamides on the metabolism of *p*-aminobenzoic acid.

sulphatase (sʌ·lfătēⁱz). *Biochem.* Also (*U.S.*) **sulf-.** [a. G. *sulfatase* (C. Neuberg 1924, in *Naturwissenschaften* XII. 799/2), f. *sulfat* SULPHATE *sb.*: see *-ASE.] Any of a group of enzymes found chiefly in mammalian tissues which catalyse the hydrolysis of sulphuric acid esters.

1924 *Chem. Abstr.* XVIII. 3600 The new enzyme sulfatase. **1952** *Biochem. Jrnl.* LI. 585/1 The sulphatases differ with respect to the type of sulphuric acid ester upon which they act. **1964** A. WHITE et al. *Princ. Biochem.* (ed. 3) xl. 775 No sulfatase capable of effecting hydrolysis of sulfate esters of carbohydrates is known to be present in animal tissues. **1980** *Jrnl. Path.* CXXX. 243 The giant lysosomes contained both acid phosphatase and aryl sulphatase.

sulphate, *sb.* Add: **3. sulphate ion,** the ion SO_4^{2-}; **sulphate process** *Paper-making*, a method of manufacturing a tough brown paper involving the digestion of wood chips by sodium hydroxide and sodium sulphate to form the pulp; so **sulphate pulp**; cf. *KRAFT; **sulphate-reducing** *a. Biol.*, (of a process or micro-organism) bringing about the reduction of sulphate ions to sulphur; *spec.* applied to bacteria of the genera *Desulphovibrio* and *Desulphatomaculum*, which do this as part of their respiratory metabolism.

1902 G. S. NEWTH *Text-bk. Inorg. Chem.* (ed. 9) xi. 105 SO''_4, in the same way, stands for the sulphate ion, with its two negative charges. **1978** J. R. HOLUM *Org. & Biol. Chem.* xix. 411 The sulfur dioxide is then oxidized to sulfate ion, which is excreted by the kidneys. **1894** G. CLAPPERTON *Pract. Paper-Making* iv. 32 The former [process]..employs a solution of sodium compounds containing a large percentage of sulphate of soda, and is known as the sulphate process. **1963** R. R. A. HIGHAM *Handbk. Papermaking* v. 98 There are three basic alkaline processes, which are: Soda process, Sulphate (Kraft) process, Pomilio process. **1974** *Sci. Amer.* Apr. 55/1 Most soda pulp mills changed over to the kraft process (which is also often called the sulfate process). **1907** G. CLAPPERTON *Pract. Paper-Making* (ed. 2) iv. 36 During recent years the demand for 'sulphate' pulp has increased largely, owing to the development of 'Kraft' brown paper. **1962** F. T. DAY *Introd. Paper* ii. 19 The wood chips are cooked in digesters in a solution of caustic soda to produce soda pulp, or with a mixture of caustic soda and sulphate of soda to produce sulphate pulp. **1966** F. E. DEAN *Paper* ii. 36 Unbleached sulphate or 'kraft'..pulp..is used mainly for tough wrapping paper. **1926** *Science* 1 Jan. 24/1 The oil-field waters in which the sulphate-reducing bacteria occur are similar in general composition to seawater. **1954** *New Biol.* XVII. 67 Vastly greater amounts of sulphide are formed in nature by a single group of micro-organisms called the sulphate-reducing bacteria... Their sulphate-reducing process corresponds to the respiration of more normal organisms. **1979** *Arch. Microbiol.* CXXI. 261/1 Some sulfate-reducing bacteria are able to utilize colloidal sulfur as respiratory substrate.

sulphate, *v.* (Earlier example.)

1888 D. SALOMONS *Managem. Accumulators* (ed. 3) v. 58 If the positives sulphate the surface becomes very hard.

sulphathiazole (sʌlfăþəi·ăzōᵘl). *Pharm.* Also (*U.S.*) **sulf-.** [f. *SULPHA- + *thiazole* s.v. THIO- 1.] The readily absorbed sulphonamide $C_3H_2NS{\cdot}NH{\cdot}SO_2{\cdot}C_6H_4{\cdot}NH_2$, now rarely used; thiazol-2-ylsulphanilamide.

1939 *Jrnl. Amer. Chem. Soc.* LXI. 3593/2 The potentiometric titration curves for the acidification of 2% solution of the sodium salts of 2(*p*-aminobenzenesulfonamido)thiazole (Sulfathiazole) and sulfapyridine are submitted in Fig. 1. **1943** *Endeavour* Apr. 42/1 Sulphathiazole and sulphadiazine are now among the physician's sheet anchors in the treatment of meningitis, gonorrhoea and pneumonia. **1967** [see *SULPHANILAMIDE]. **1978** J. IRVING *World according to Garp* i. 7 Sulfathiazole was for the clap—with lots of water recommended.

sulphatide (sʌ·lfătəid). *Biochem.* Also (*U.S.*) **sulf-.** [SULPHAT(E *sb.* + -IDE.] Any of the group of lipids consisting of the sulphuric acid ester of a cerebroside.

1884 J. L. W. THUDICHUM *Treat. Chem. Constitution of Brain* i. 22 The albuminous substances of the brain may be considered as nitrogenised sulphatides, inasmuch as sulphur is an essential constituent. **1954** A. WHITE et al. *Princ. Biochem.* xxxii. 801 A number of less clearly defined lipids have also been recognized [in the brain], such as sulfatides... Only one sulfatide has been isolated and studied, cerebron sulfuric acid. **1966** *Lancet* 24 Dec. 1421/2 The predominance of sulphatide in the white matter of the brain in this disease has been noted by Lees. **1978** *Nature* 7 Dec. 625/1 The negative charge imparted by the sulphate group of the sulphatide does not seem to be the direct cause of its strong adhesion capacity, as other negatively charged lipids, such as ganglioside or phosphatidyl inositol, did not adhere strongly.

sulphation. Add: Conversion into a sulphate; incorporation of a sulphate ion, SO_4^{2-}, into a molecule. (Further examples.)

1957 *New Biol.* XXIV. 52 There is an informed opinion which asserts that sulphation is not necessary for metachromasia and that mucopolysaccharides without sulphur are also metachromatic. **1971, 1972** [see *SOMATOMEDIN]. **1975** *Nature* 24 Jan. 269/2 Somatomedin, previously known as 'sulphation factor',..stimulates the incorporation of $^{35}SO_4$ into costal cartilage. **1977** *Lancet* 22 Jan. 168/1 The mammary gland itself may be the site of sulphation [of vitamin D].

sulphazin (sʌ·lfăzin). *Pharm.* Also (chiefly *U.S.*) **sulfazin.** [Russ.] A drug consisting of a suspension of one per cent purified sulphur in peach oil, given intramuscularly to induce fever.

1970 *Time* 29 June 30/3 A Soviet drug called Sulfazin, which induces fever and temperature, is administered as a punishment. **1977** *Lancet* 23 July 185/1 There are reports of the use of sulphazin to produce a painful fever. **1979** H. FIRESIDE *Soviet Psychoprisons* iv. 82 If a patient speaks out against such brutality, he is subjected to punishment by overdoses of drugs or injections of sulfazin that make it 'painful for him even to stir'. **1981** M. C. SMITH *Gorky Park* I. xii. 185 Sulfazin was one of the favorite narcotics of the KGB.

sulphetrone (sʌ·lfĕtrōᵘn). *Pharm.* [f. SULPHONE with insertion of *t)etr(asodium* (f. TETRA- + SODIUM).] A trade name for the drug *SOLAPSONE.

1947 *Lancet* 20 Dec. 897/2 Two studies were made—(1) to assess the efficacy of streptomycin; and (2) to evaluate the possible synergic action of streptomycin and sulphetrone. **1959, 1974** [see *SOLAPSONE].

sulph-hæmoglobin, var. *SULPHÆMOGLOBIN.

sulphide, *v.* Add: (Example.) Also **su·lphiding** *vbl. sb.*

1950 R. W. MONCRIEFF *Artificial Fibres* viii. 105 The yarn was wound into skeins, and these were washed, sulphided, bleached and washed. **1955** E. E. LOENING et al. in R. S. Schultze *Sci. & Applic. Photogr.* 62 In the case of sulphiding, the left part of the curves is..absent. **1982** *Photogr. Sci. & Engin.* XXVI. 223/1 Sulfiding of the cathode can be minimized by poising the potential of the cathode more positive than −0·55 v.

sulphidic (sʌlfi·dik), *a. Chem.* [f. SULPHID(E *sb.* + -IC.] Of or containing sulphides.

1929 H. SCHNEIDERHÖHN in P. A. Wagner *Platinum Deposits & Mines S. Afr.* xvii. 208 (*heading*) The sulphidic ore minerals of the felspathic Harzburgite and Merensky 'reef'. **1959** *Times* 23 Sept. 19/6 Sulphidic minerals, mainly pyrites. **1978** *Metals* (Shell Internat. Petroleum Co.) 4 Rich sulphidic ores, such as those in the massive copper belt of Zambia/Zaire.., have been recovered by underground mining for many years.

sulphinpyrazone (sʌlfinpi·răzōᵘn). *Pharm.* Also (*U.S.*) **sulf-.** [f. SULPHIN(IC *a.* + *PYRAZ(OLE + -ONE.] The uricosuric drug $C_6H_5{\cdot}SO{\cdot}(CH_2)CH{\cdot}C_3HN_2O_2(C_6H_5)_2$, which promotes excretion of urates by inhibiting their reabsorption by kidneys; 1,2-diphenyl-4-(2-phenylsulphinylethyl)pyrazolidine-3,5-dione.

1958 *Arthritis & Rheumatism* I. 532 The present communication is concerned with G-28315 (4-[phenylsulfoxyethyl]-1,2-diphenyl-3,5-pyrazolidinedione). [*Note*] The generic name of this compound is sulfinpyrazone. **1961** *Lancet* 30 Sept. 763/2 Aspirin..could within a few days overcome the effects for which probenecid, sulfinpyrazone, or zoxazolamine had been prescribed. **1978** *Times* 2 Mar. 16/6 The American research project was set up to test the theory that the risk of this further thrombosis might be reduced by treatment with a drug, sulfinpyrazone, which acts on the blood platelets, the small cells that start the process of thrombosis. **1981** H. J. ROGERS et al. *Textbk. Clin. Pharmacol.* xvii. 569 Sulphinpyrazone (Anturan)..is a uricosuric drug related to phenylbutazone which prolongs platelet survival..without prolonging the bleeding time.

sulpho-. Add: In mod. use often repr. *SULPHONYL, as in *sulphochlorination, -lipid* below. **su:lphobromophtha·lein** *Pharm.* [BROMO- + PHTHALEIN] = *bromosulphthalein* s.v. *BROMO-; **su:lphochlorina·tion** *Chem.*, the introduction of the chlorosulphonyl group, $ClSO_2$—, into a molecule; **su·lpholipid** *Biochem.*, any of a class of lipids whose structures terminate with the sulphonate group, —SO_3^-.

1945 *Jrnl. Amer. Med. Assoc.* 4 Aug. 1001/2 A positive Hanger test or a strong sulfobromophthalein dye retention also provides valuable evidence [of hepatitis]. **1974** M. C. GERALD *Pharmacol.* ii. 34 Frequently employed diagnostic agents include..sulfobromophthalein for liver function tests. **1931** *Jrnl. Amer. Chem. Soc.* LIII. 2648 Phenols can be converted in phenolpolysulfonylchlorides by the action of chlorosulfonic acid. It also was noticed that the reagent caused four distinct types of reaction: namely, sulfonation, sulfochlorination, chlorination, oxidation. **1980** *Chem. in Brit.* XVI. 466/1 The sulphochlorination of paraffins to alkane sulphonyl chlorides is conducted in the presence of uv light. **1930** M. BODANSKY *Introd. Physiol. Chem.* (ed. 2) iii. 70 Aminolipids, sulfolipids, etc. —groups which are at present not sufficiently well characterized for classification. **1977** D. E. METZLER *Biochem.* ii. 112/2 Chloroplasts contain a large amount of a special sulfolipid.

sulphonamide (sɒlfǫ·nāməid). *Chem.* and *Pharm.* Also (*U.S.*) **sulf-.** [f. SULPHONE + AMIDE.] **a.** Any organic compound that is an amide of a sulphonic acid, characterized by the group —SO_2N=; *spec.* any of the drugs derived from sulphanilamide (and so containing this group). Freq. *attrib.*

1881 *Jrnl. Chem. Soc.* XL. 602 The [1:4:3] acid..is converted by ammonia into a sulphonamide crystallising in needles. **1947** *Sci. News* IV. 60 When new drugs like the sulphonamides or D.D.T. are developed, their chemical properties have been reported for thirty years or so, and it is their biological effects which are the true modern discoveries. **1959** *Times* 7 Dec. (Agric. Suppl.) p. vii/4 To prevent coccidiosis in chickens, nitrophenol, a sulfonamide..is added to the feed. **1964** N. G. CLARK *Mod. Org. Chem.* xx. 414 In most cases, the sulphonamides have convenient melting-points, and are admirably suitable for characterizing both sulphonic acids and amines. **1974** [see *POTENTIATED *ppl. a.*]. **1977** *Martindale's Extra Pharmacopoeia* (ed. 27) 1468/1 Because they are similar in chemical structure to *p*-aminobenzoic acid, sulphonamides interfere with the synthesis by micro-organisms of folic acid from *p*-aminobenzoic acid... The sulphonamides have been largely replaced by antibiotics in the treatment of infections.

b. *attrib.* and *Comb.*, as *sulphonamide drug, group* (of atoms or of drugs); *sulphonamide-resistant* adj.

1943 *Times* 16 June 5/7 Recent American figures suggest that one death occurs from the Sulphonamide drugs in every 2,571 deaths from all causes. **1959** *Sci. News* LI. 96 Antithyroid activity was first observed in some of the sulphonamide drugs, but the first compound used clinically, in 1943 by Astwood in America, was thiourea. **1979** DAVIES & LITTLEWOOD *Elementary Biochem.* iv. 83 Sulfonamide drugs are not effective in open, suppurating wounds; such wounds contain pus and other materials that are a source of *p*-aminobenzoic acid, which antagonizes the action of the sulfonamide drugs. **1939** *Brit. Med. Jrnl.* 5 Aug. 269/2 Sulphanilamide consists of a benzene ring to opposite ends of which are attached an amino group and a sulphonamide group. **1942** *Times* 21 Sept. 5/7 Another most important factor in saving life has been the series of new drugs, of which the sulphonamide group is the most important. **1942** *Proc. Soc. Exper. Biol. & Med.* L. 336 The present report is concerned with the *in vitro* and *in vivo* production of sulfonamide resistant strains of staphylococci. **1968** *Times* 12 Oct. 18/8 One of the organisms sometimes responsible for travellers' diarrhoea is now sulphonamide-resistant. **1981** H. J. ROGERS et al. *Textbk. Clin. Pharmacol.* xix. 649 Sulphadiazine is now only rarely used (with benzylpenicillin) in the treatment of meningococcal meningitis since sulphonamide-resistant meningococci are common.

sulphonate, *v.* (Earlier example.) Hence **su·lphonated** *ppl. a.*, **su·lphonating** *vbl. sb.*

1882 *Jrnl. Chem. Soc.* XLII. 196 The author could not obtain the salt 'A'..by sulphonating pure cymene. **1902** Sulphonating [in Dict.]. **1936, 1966** [see *SOAPLESS *a.* b]. **1972** *Materials & Technol.* V. 302 By the use of energetic sulphonating agents such as sulphur trioxide.., fatty acids can be sulphonated at the alpha carbon atom. The sulphonated acids have useful surface-active properties.

sulphonium (sɒlfōᵘ·niɒm). *Chem.* Also (*U.S.*) **sulf-.** [f. SULPH(UR *sb.* + *-ONIUM.] A hypothetical monovalent complex cation having a central sulphur atom bonded to three hydrogen atoms; also, any derivative of this in which one or more of the hydrogen atoms is replaced by organic radicals. Usu. *attrib.*

1894 [see *IODONIUM]. **1942** *Jrnl. Amer. Chem. Soc.* LXIV. 1165/1 The ability of dialkyl sulfides to react with ω-halogenated ketones with the subsequent formation of sulfonium halides has been known for some time. **1975** R. F. BROWN *Org. Chem.* xxix. 945 The sulfonium ions (R_3S^+) are much more stable than are the analogous oxonium ions (R_3O^+).

sulphonyl (sɒ·lfŏnəil). *Chem.* Also (*U.S.*) **sulf-.** [f. SULPHONE + -YL.] The divalent radical —SO_2—, derived from a sulphonic acid group by removal of the —OH group. Usu. *attrib.*

1920 *Chem. Abstr.* XIV. 1947 Place 3 g. of pulverized sulfonyl chloride in a round-bottomed flask. **1953** *Chem. & Engin. News* 5 Jan. 91/3 The inorganic name of the radical SO_2 is sulfuryl, while its organic name is sulfonyl. **1975** R. F. BROWN *Org. Chem.* xxix. 956 Some of the sulfonyl chlorides and esters have been used so often that trivial names have been coined.

Hence **su:lphonyla·tion,** conversion into a sulphonyl compound; (as a back-formation) **sulpho·nylate** *v. trans.*

1956 *Chem. Abstr.* L. 10677/1 (*heading*) Friedel-Crafts acylation and sulfonylation reactions. **1979** *Tetrahedron Lett.* Sept. 3790 The mild conditions used in this sulphonylation provide some advantages over the more usual preparative methods for unsymmetrical sulphones. **1980** *Chem. Abstr.* XCIII. 843/2 Thiazole hydrobromide was sulfonylated with..arsenesulfonyl chlorides to give the corresponding 7-sulfonylthiazolium chlorides.

sulphonylurea (sɒ̄:lfŏnəil,yūᵊrī·ă). *Pharm.* Also (*U.S.*) **sulf-.** [f. *SULPHONYL + UREA.] Any of the group of hypoglycæmic drugs containing the active grouping —SO_2·NH·CO·NH—, which are used orally in the treatment of diabetes.

1956 *Science* 6 Apr. 583/2 A statistically highly significant hypoglycemic response occurred in 34 of the patients with diabetes who were given the sulfonylurea. **1966** *New Scientist* 24 Nov. 433/1 The longing of diabetics for a hypoglycaemic drug which could be taken orally..was realized ten years ago when the sulphonylureas and diguanides were introduced. **1974** M. C. GERALD *Pharmacol.* xxv. 442 The oral hypoglycemic agents, the sulfonylureas such as tolbutamide and the biguanide phenformin, are useful agents for the treatment of the stable maturity-onset diabetes.

sulphur, *sb.* Add: **1. f.** The colour of sulphur, a greenish-yellow.

1924 R. CAMPBELL *Flaming Terrapin* ii. 32 Panthers' eyes..Flashed their pale sulphur on the sunless air. **1963** *Listener* 10 Jan. 84/2, I don't like the colours, especially the Ribena, pillarbox, scrofula, and sulphur.

5. c. (Earlier example.)

1801 M. EDGEWORTH *Belinda* I. viii. 240 Helena and her young companions now came into the room, bringing with them the sulphurs at which they had been looking.

8. sulphur bacterium *Biol.*, any of the bacteria which derive their energy from the oxidation of sulphur or inorganic compounds of sulphur; **sulphur cycle** *Ecol.*, the cycle of changes whereby sulphur compounds are interconverted between sulphates and hydrogen sulphide in the air and sulphates, sulphides, and sulphur in organisms and the soil; **sulphur print** *Metallurgy*, a print on photographic bromide paper showing the distribution of sulphur as sulphides in a steel surface with which it has been placed in contact; **sulphur shower** (earlier example); **sulphur soap,** a medicinal soap containing elemental sulphur for use in treating skin complaints; **sulphur-spring** (earlier examples).

1891 A. B. GRIFFITHS *Res. on Micro-Organisms* viii. 179 All belong to the class of 'sulphur-bacteria'..—that is, bacteria which in the presence of free hydrogen-sulphide oxidize sulphur, forming sulphuric acid. **1939** CLEMENTS & SHELFORD *Bio-Ecol.* iii. 101 Hydrogen sulphide is also acted upon by a remarkable group of sulphur bacteria. **1962** W. W. UMBREIT *Mod. Microbiol.* xv. 276/2 There are three major types of photosynthetic bacteria. The first two of them, the thiorhodaceae and the chlorobacteriaceae, are sulfur bacteria. **1979** ARMS & CAMP *Biology* x. 165 Purple and green sulfur bacteria (Thiorhodaceae) use hydrogen gas and hydrogen sulfide (H_2S) as hydrogen donors. **1967** *New Scientist* 9 Nov. 333/1 The continuation and evolution of life depends upon a stable eco-system. A characteristic of such a system is that cyclical transformations of the major biological elements take place within it—the carbon cycle, the nitrogen cycle, the sulphur cycle and so on. **1973** R. G. KRUEGER et al. *Introd. Microbiol.* xxx. 745/2 Bacteria can carry out each of the processes in the sulfur cycle; bacteria and certain colorless blue-green algae are the only known living agents of the steps involving interconversions of inorganic forms of sulfur. **1977** I. M. CAMPBELL *Energy & Atmosphere* viii. 289 More efficient dispersal of sulphur dioxide at source cannot be regarded as an acceptable long term solution, since that merely transfers the problem to another region or country, the problem intensified by the fact that the anthropogenic term in the sulphur cycle is of the same order of magnitude as the natural terms. **1912** *Jrnl. Iron & Steel Inst.* LXXXV. 380, I have adopted a method which is virtually a modification of the well known method of obtaining a 'sulphur print'. **1977** R. B. ROSS *Handbk. Metal Treatments & Testing* 373 Chemical analysis and micro-examination..require laboratory equipment and skilled personnel, whereas the Sulphur print may be used in relatively unsophisticated conditions. **1854** THOREAU *Walden* 340 The sulphur-like pollen of the pitch pine soon covered the pond and the stones and rotten wood... This is the 'sulphur showers' we hear of. **1894** A. WATT *Art of Soap-Making* xxi. 172 Sir H. Marsh's Sulphur Soap... A few drops of otto of roses are added to give the soap an agreeable fragrance. **1925** G. MARTIN *Mod. Soap & Detergent Industr.* II. II. iv. 34 Sulphur soaps, when dissolved in water, slowly evolve sulphuretted hydrogen, which gives them an unpleasant smell. **1953** J. DAVIDSOHN et al. *Soap Manuf.* I. xxii. 505 Sulfur soaps are frequently prepared in combination with beta-naphthol, tar, glycerine and camphor. **1785** T. JEFFERSON *Notes on Virginia* vi. 59 We are told of a Sulphur-spring on Howard's creek of Greenbriar. **1811** W. J. HOOKER *Jrnl. Tour in Iceland in 1809* 195 We could not resist the present temptation of alighting from our horses, to visit one of the sulphur-springs that lay in our route.

9. sulphur-bottom (**whale**), substitute for def.: Sibbald's rorqual (see *SIBBALD); (further examples); **sulphur** (**-crested**) **cockatoo,** a white cockatoo, *Kakatoe galerita*, with a yellow crest, native to Australia; **sulphur tuft,** a toadstool, *Hypholoma fasciculare*, with a yellow cap tinged with brown; **sulphur whale** (earlier example).

1851 H. MELVILLE *Moby Dick* I. xxxi. 221 Adieu, Sulphur-Bottom! **1934** R. CAMPBELL *Broken Record* iv. 94 These blue whales are the great sulphur-bottoms. **1959** A. C. HARDY *Open Sea* II. xv. 280 It [*sc.* Sibbald's rorqual] has also been called the sulphur-bottom whale on account of a yellowish scum of diatoms which these whales usually carry when they first return to polar waters again after visiting warmer latitudes for breeding. **1811, 1893** Sulphur (-crested) cockatoo [in Dict.]. **1908** E. J. BANFIELD *Confessions of Beachcomber* I. i. 17 Sulphur-crested cockatoos sail down upon the red raiment of the tree. **1963** *Times* 8 June 14/3 Probably the most talkative..is one of the four sulphur-crested cockatoos. **1909** E. W. SWANTON *Fungi* 115 'Sulphur-tuft'... Taste intensely bitter. Poisonous. **1979** *Country Life* 25 Oct. 1423/1 The fruiting bodies of sulphur tuft..also grow on tree stumps. **1829** T. C. HALIBURTON *Hist. & Statistical Acct. Nova Scotia* II. ix. 404 Fish-Whale Species. Sulphur Whale.

sulphur-. In words in the Dict. beginning thus the second 'u' when unstressed is marked with the pronunc. (-iŭ-); this is now often pronounced (-ə-) or (-ŭ-).

sulphuretum (sɒlfərī·tɒm). *Ecol.* Also (*U.S.*) **sulf-.** Pl. **sulphureta, -tums.** [mod.L., f. SULPHUR *sb.* + *-ETUM.] An ecological community of organisms, mainly consisting of sulphur bacteria, which metabolizes sulphur compounds in a closed subcycle of the larger environmental sulphur cycle.

1925 L. G. M. BAAS-BECKING in *Ann. Bot.* XXXIX. 615 The natural ecological community of these [sulphur] bacteria is a miniature cycle in itself, and will be called a sulphuretum. **1967** *New Scientist* 9 Nov. 333/2 One such ecosystem is known as the sulfuretum, based primarily on the sulphur bacteria and essentially anaerobic. *Ibid.*, Palaeochemical evidence, based on fractionation of the sulphur isotopes, has shown that sulfureta were active at least 2 × 10⁹ years ago.

sulphydryl. Add: Also (*U.S.*) **sulfhydryl.** (Examples.) = *MERCAPTO(-) b, *THIOL b.

1924 *Biochem. Jrnl.* XVIII. 1020 The sulphydryl compounds are apparently incapable of combining directly with molecular oxygen. **1946** *Nature* 3 Aug. 155/2 Manganese dioxide is reduced with great ease to form divalent manganese ion by sulphydryl compounds, for example, thioglycollic acid. **1978** *Bull. Amer. Acad. Arts & Sci.* Feb. 10 Elwood Jensen had already made important contributions to..our understanding of the role of sulfhydryl groups in protein structure.

sulpiride (sʌ·lpirəid). *Pharm.* [a. F. *sulpiride*, prob. f. *sul(f-* SULPH- + *pir-*, alteration of *pyr-* PYR(O-: see -IDE.] An anti-emetic and neuroleptic drug used in the treatment of gastro-intestinal disorders, vertigo, and psychiatric conditions; *N*-(1-ethylpyrrolidin-2-ylmethyl)-2-methoxy-5-sulphamoylbenzamide, $(C_2H_5)C_4H_6N(CH_3){\cdot}NH{\cdot}SO_2{\cdot}C_6H_3(OCH_3){\cdot}CO{\cdot}NH_2$.

1970 *Jrnl. Amer. Med. Assoc.* 10 Aug. 1076/1 The new drug sulpiride was tested to determine its effectiveness in the treatment of ulcerative colitis. **1976** *Lancet* 18 Dec. 1358/1 We concluded that sulpiride should be prescribed with care in hypertensive patients. **1979** *Nature* 11 Jan. 94/2 The antipsychotic drugs, molindone and sulpiride, and the antiemetic drug, metoclopramide, are dopamine antagonists when tested in the anterior pituitary or the brain.

sul ponticello: see *PONTICELLO b.

sultana. Add: **5.** (Later *Hist.* example.)

1935 P. P. ARGENTI *Occupation of Chios by Venetians (1694)* p. xxxix, The enemy fleet..consisted of twenty great sultanas, and thirty galleys and galliots, all under the command of the *Capoudân Pasha.*

7. Also produced in other parts of Turkey, Greece, and Australia. (Further examples.)

1855 E. ACTON *Mod. Cookery* (rev. ed.) xxi. 442 Sultana raisins are well adapted to these puddings, as they contain no pips. **1920** C. L. T. BEECHING *Mod. Grocer & Provision Dealer* III. viii. 163 The sultana raisin may be said to share in the good qualities of both the currant and the Valencia. **1938** C. J. Elliott *Retail Grocery Trade* xii. 108 The Australian sultana is a little larger than the Turkey and Smyrna variety. **1966** A. Uttley *Recipes from Old Farmhouse* 58 Add one ounce of sugar and one ounce of sultanas.

9*. = *busy Lizzie* s.v. *busy *a.* 11; *patient Lucy* s.v. *patient *a.* 5.

1938 M. K. Rawlings *Yearling* xxvi. 360 The church was decorated with..donations of house plants; sultanas and geraniums, aspidistras and coleas [*sic*]. **1977** [see *patient *a.* 5].

10. sultana grape, the white seedless grape from which sultanas are made.

1861 Mrs. Beeton *Bk. Househ. Managem.* 666 Sultana Grape... The white or yellow grape..produces the Sultana raisin. **1931** C. L. T. Beeching *Law's Grocer's Man.* (ed. 3) 513/2 The vine which grows the sultana grape is vigorous and upright. **1979** *Illustr. London News* Jan. 66/3 The sultana grape vineyards start a few kilometres to the east of Ayios Nikolaos.

sultanate. **1.** (Earlier example.)

1822 tr. *Malte-Brun's Universal Geogr.* I. xxii. 590 It would be rather interesting to enumerate the various denominations which designate the different states. The use of the terms empire, kingdom, sultanat, khonet, and others, will be learnt in the descriptive part of this work.

sultanize, *v.* **2.** (Earlier examples.)

1804 J. Mackintosh *Let.* 14 Aug. in *Mem.* (1835) I. v. 212 The Governor..is..an..intelligent man; but every Englishman who resides here very long, has..his mind either emasculated by submission, or corrupted by despotic power. Mr. Duncan may represent one genus, the Braminised Englishman; Lord W— is indisputably at the head of the other, the Sultanised Englishman. **1876** *Hansard Commons* 16 Mar. 103 It was not a wise thing to endeavour even in India to Sultanize the Crown.

sul tasto: see *tasto b.

sultry, *a.* Add: **2. b.** (*c*) (Earlier example.)

1880 'Mark Twain' *Tramp Abroad* xxv. 250 It was getting pretty sultry for me. I said to myself, 'Is it possible she is going to stop there, and wait for me to speak? If she does, the conversation is blocked.'

(*d*) Of a woman: lascivious or sensual, arousing sexual desire; also *transf.* and in *Comb.* orig. *U.S.*

1940 *Time* 7 Oct. 63/2 He watches..another become a sultry, sirenic dancer. **1946** *Sun* (Baltimore) 25 Apr. 12/1 There is also a ballet touch to Miss Horne's sultry song number, 'Love'. **1949** R. Harvey *Curtain Time* xvi. 160 Miss Nethersole specialized in sultry rôles and her performance in Daudet's *Sapho* was considered scandalous. **1956** *People* 13 May 4/4 Certainly none of the sultry Continental sirens stood a chance when Diana strolled on to the beach. **1977** C. Storr *Tales Psychiatrist's Couch* i. 6 She exuded an air of unsatisfied sexuality... She was what I'd call sultry. **1978** *Times* 30 Nov. 16/8 A trip to Rio to see the real thing—*real* sultry-eyed temptresses.

Sulu[1] (sū·lu). [Prob. ad. Sama-Bajaw dial. f. Tau Sug *sulúg* current.] = *Tau Sug.

1816 [see *Macassar 2]. **1898** D. C. Worcester *Philippine Islands & their People* viii. 201, I had made numerous attempts in Mindanao, Basilan, and Sulu to get an explanation of the Moro aversion to pork. **1908** N. M. Saleeby *Hist. Sulu* i. 133 Jolo is the Spanish representation..of the word Sulu... The complete form of the word is Sulug... The Sulus pronounce it and write it Sūg. *Sūg* means a sea current. *Ibid.* iii. 155 The ancient Sulus..had many myths relating to the marriages and heroic deeds of their gods. **1923** S. Y. Orosa *Sulu Archipelago & its People* v. 67 The people of the Sulu Province number over 170,000, roughly grouped as Sulus and Samals. The dominating and most advanced people are the Sulus or *Tao-Sug*, 'people of the current'. *Ibid.* vi. 72 The Sulu is of the brown or Malay race. **1936** G. A. Malcolm *Commonwealth of Philippines* iii. 39 The Sulus of whom I would speak..are Moros living in the Sulu Archipelago in the Philippine Islands. **1977** C. F. & F. M. Voegelin *Classification & Index World's Lang.* 41 Taw Sug= Tausug=Sulu=Joloano Sulu. Palawan, Philippines, northeast coast of Borneo. Closely related to Maranao.

‖ **sulu**[2] (sū·lu). [Fijian.] In Fiji: a length of cotton cloth wrapped about the body to form a sarong; hence, a type of sarong worn by both sexes (typically from the waist to the knee by men, and to the ankle by women). Also, a similar fashion garment worn by women.

1850 D. Hazlewood *Feejeean & English Dict.* 129/1 *Sulu-ma*, v. to put on a sulu, or dress... The difference between malo and sulu seems to be in the way in which it is worn: malo is sulu when put round the body and not between the legs. **1897** 'Sundowner' *Rambles in Polynesia* 7 For many years yet..the Polynesian islander will continue to wear his *sulu* or lava-lava, as the case may be. **1921** W. A. Chapple *Fiji—its Problems & Resources* ii. 22 His [*sc.* the Fijian's] sulu is his only garment,..a rectangular piece of cotton cloth that he folds round his loins and tucks in upon itself. **1926** *Glasgow Herald* 25 Sept. 4/5 Clad only in their sulus (or kilts). **1944** W. E. Harney *Taboo* (ed. 2) 135, I had only a loincloth—a sulu, as it is called. **1970** *Honey* June 86 Vivid multi-coloured patchwork slit sulu 11 gns, and tie top, 84s. **1977** *Times* 20 July 1/7 The staff of the Fijian High Commission had turned out in pinstripe *sulu* skirts and morning jackets.

sulvanite (sɒ·lvănəit). *Min.* [f. Sul(phur *sb.* + Van(adium + -ite[1].] A bronze-coloured sulphide of copper and vanadium, Cu_3VS_4, that usu. occurs massive, rarely as crystals having cubic symmetry, and is often chemically altered.

1900 G. A. Goyder in *Jrnl. Chem. Soc.* LXXVII. 1094 (*heading*) Sulvanite, a new mineral. **1974** *Amer. Mineralogist* LIX. 307/2 In all occurrences, sulvanite is coated with alteration minerals consisting of malachite, volborthite, and azurite.

sum, *sb.*[1] Add: **5.** (Later examples.)

1946 *R.A.F. Jrnl.* May 152 The *Bulletin* slowly built up a sum of good will among contributors. **1967** G. Steiner *Lang. & Silence* 31 Literature, philosophy, theology, law, the arts of history, are endeavours to enclose within the bounds of rational discourse the sum of human experience.

6. d. = *logical sum* s.v. *logical *a.* 7.

1918 C. I. Lewis *Survey of Symbolic Logic* iii. 185 The 'sum', $a+b$, denotes the class of those things which are either members of a or members of b (or members of both). **1934** W. V. Quine *System of Logistic* xvii. 171, $\epsilon'\alpha$ may be called the sum of the class of classes α. **1968** P. A. P. Moran *Introd. Probability Theory* iv. 185 The advantage of using half-open intervals is that if two of them abut, their sum is again a half-open interval. **1981** W. Marciszewski *Dict. Logic* 53 The union (sum) of sets: $x\in X\cup Y \equiv (x\in X)\vee(x\in Y)$.

14. *Comb.*, as **sum check** *Computers*, a check on the accuracy of a group of digits in which they are added together and the result compared with a previously computed sum (which may accompany the group as a check digit); also applied to similar checks in which a quantity other than a sum is employed; = *summation check* s.v. *summation[2] 6; so **sum-checked** *a.*

1962 R. V. Oakford *Introd. Electronic Data Processing Equipment* ii. 31 If a single *R* check bit is changed, the sum check will fail..in that row, but not in the four columns. **1972** *Computer Jrnl.* XV. 196/2 A similar routine deals with sum-checked binary input.

sum, *v.*[1] **1. a.** Delete 'Now *rare*' and add further examples.

1935 *Lancet* 11 May 1123/1 For the pig,..the combination of virus plus hæmophilic organism is much more potent than was to be expected from summing the mild diseases caused by the two agents acting separately. **1947** *Electronic Engin.* June 179/1 Suppose..that it is desired to sum the voltages from *n* sources. **1962** F. I. Ordway et al. *Basic Astronautics* vii. 325 The average lifetime.. may be easily determined by summing all lifetimes and dividing by 100. **1971** *Nature* 24 Dec. 485/2 He summed data of six previous studies..and demonstrated in the total sample an over-representation of the last-but-one position. **1977** J. G. Graeme *Designing with Operational Amplifiers* vii. 177 The number of signals that can be summed is limited only by increasing circuit errors.

b. Restrict † to *pass.* and add later example of *intr.* use.

1966 G. C. Hemmens *Structure of Urban Activity Linkages* i. 6 The matrix of linkage coefficients is a stochastic matrix where each row sums to one.

Sumac, var. *Soumak.

sumach, sumac. 2. a. (Later examples.)

1936 W. Faulkner *Absalom, Absalom!* vi. 214 The old street of the slave quarters—a jungle of sumach and persimmon. **1965** A. Lurie *Nowhere City* (1966) xv. 162 The sumac held them back with its woolly, awkward stems. **1980** *Hunting Ann.* 1981 42/2 Here, the berries of black haw, sumac, bittersweet and greenbrier are important even in winter.

Sumatra. Add: **c.** A variety of tobacco yielding a light-coloured leaf.

1911 B. Miall tr. *Cabaton's Java, Sumatra, & other Islands of Dutch East Indies* xi. 229 The Manilla variety [of tobacco]..has been..less largely used than the Deli (Sumatra) tobacco. **1912** A. E. Tanner *Tobacco* xii. 85 Leaf used for making British cigars consists of Sumatra, Borneo, and Havana. **1969** *Times* 24 Nov. (Congo Suppl.) p. vi/6 The main varieties [of tobacco] grown are Kentucky, White Burley, Sumatra and heavy Dark Western. **1975** N. Freeling *What are Bugles blowing For?* xiv. 84 He sat..smoking a small Dutch cigar as a treat: rather heavy—they had mixed some dark Brazilian leaf in with the light Sumatra tobacco.

Sumatran, *a.* Add: **b. Sumatran tiger**, a small tiger belonging to the subspecies *Panthera tigris sumatræ*.

1908 *Proc. Zool. Soc.* 890 Mr. R. I. Pocock..exhibited photographs of a Sumatran Tiger, recently purchased by the Society. **1945** F. Harper *Extinct & Vanishing Mammals of Old World* 310 The Sumatran Tiger.., although less common than formerly, is still numerous in various districts. **1976** *Guardian* 19 Apr. 7/6 Six Sumatran tiger cubs were born at Whipsnade last year.

sumbitch (sɒ·mbitʃ). *U.S. slang.* Contraction of *son of a bitch.

1975 O. Sela *Bengali Inheritance* xiii. 108 That sumbitch Winston would go far in Russia. **1976** M. Machlin *Pipeline* liii. 533 Play that 'I'm Dreaming of a Fat Paycheck'. That's a sumbitch! **1977** *Time* 7 Mar. 34/2 Strauss, you are a rich sumbitch. **1981** P. Mallory *Killing Matter* iv. 53 The sumbitch has sure got him a way with the womenfolk.

Sumero-. Add: **Sume·rogram**, a character or group of characters representing a Sumerian word, used in written Hittite (Akkadian, etc.) as a substitute for the equivalent (longer) word in that language.

1952 O. R. Gurney *Hittites* vi. 121 Hittite texts are liberally interspersed with purely Akkadian and Sumerian words, the latter usually written by single signs, the use of which as 'ideograms' (or better, 'Sumerograms') can often be recognized only by means of the context, for they may be the same signs that are normally used for mere syllables. **1965** J. Puhvel in W. Winter *Evidence for Laryngeals* 83 The Sumerogram used for *Ḫattusa-* reveals its meaning of 'Silver City'. **1983** *Trans. Philol. Soc.* 102 The increasing tendency to make use of Sumerograms and Akkadograms in place of syllabically written Hittite words.

‖ **sumi** (sū·mi). [Jap., = ink, blacking.] (See quot. 1958); = Indian ink. Cf. next.

1911 [see *dry brush* s.v. *dry *a.* C. 3]. **1958** M. L. Wolf *Dict. Painting* 285 *Sumi*, Japanese ink or blacking, composed of a mixture of carbon and glue molded into sticks or cakes. When rubbed into water on an inkstone, it becomes the common medium of the painter and writer. **1970** *Globe & Mail* (Toronto) 26 Sept. 26/4 There's another show close to sellout in Kazuo Hamasaki's Japanese sumi paintings.

‖ **sumi-e** (sū·mie). Also **sumi-ee, sumiye, sumi-ye.** [Jap.] Japanese ink painting; also *collect.*, sumi pictures. Cf. prec.

1938 D. T. Suzuki *Zen Buddhism & its Influence on Jap. Culture* I. ii. 24 Calligraphy in the Far East is an art just as much as *sumiye* painting. **1960** H. Hayward *Antique Coll.* 271/1 *Sumi-ye*, Japanese ink-pictures, i.e. painted in black only. **1965** W. Swaan *Jap. Lantern* xiii. 146 Lessons in *sumi-e* (Japanese style, ink painting). **1977** *Time* 17 Jan. 34/3 Every cut of the chisel seems to possess the final, unlaboured rightness of a brush stroke by a master of *sumi-e* (ink painting). **1981** G. MacBeth *Kind of Treason* xx. 196 On the wall he'd hung the *kakemono*.., a thin scroll in *sumi-ee* with a house under a mountain.

summa. 5. b. (Later example.)

1941 Swenson & Lowrie tr. *Kierkegaard's Concluding Unscientific Postscript* II. ii. v. 528 If it is postulated and granted that it is easy to understand that God becomes a particular man, so that the difficulty first emerges in the next fact, that He becomes a lowly and despised man—then in *summa summarum* Christianity is humor.

summability (sɒmăbi·liti). [f. Summable *a.*: see *-bility.] The property of being summable.

1904 *Q. Jrnl. Pure & Appl. Math.* XXXV. 43 In the treatment of certain questions fundamental in the theory we gained nothing by the introduction of the idea of absolute summability. **1968** P. A. P. Moran *Introd. Probability Theory* viii. 351 The study of the relative strengths of various methods of summability of series.

‖ **summa cum laude** (sɒ·ma kɒm lǫ·di, su·ma kum lau·di, -e), *adv.* (*adj.*, *sb.*,) *phr.* Chiefly *U.S.* [L., 'with highest praise'.] With highest distinction: designating a degree, diploma, etc., of the highest standard. Also *transf.* and *fig.* Occas. *ellipt.* as *summa*. Cf. *magna cum laude.

1900 [see *magna cum laude]. **1951** S. F. Nadel *Found. Social Anthropol.* i. 18 You may be said to have accomplished assimilation *summa cum laude*. **1962** *Listener* 16 Aug. 242/1 He was psychoanalyzed..presumably by what Buddy calls one of those '*summa-cum-laude* thinkers and intellectual men's-room attendants'. **1970** G. Greer *Female Eunuch* 295 Mrs Friedan is a *summa cum laude* graduate of Smith College. **1976** *N.Y. Rev. Bks.* 24 June 4/2 When Commencement Day arrived, Mrs. Plath..[came] to watch her daughter being awarded her *summa cum laude* certificate. **1976** *Time* 20 Dec. 18/2 James R. Schlesinger..*summa cum laude* and Ph.D in economics at Harvard. **1977** *New Yorker* 19 Sept. 47/3 She had just graduated summa cum laude from the University of Washington, in Seattle. **1978** F. Maclean *Take Nine Spies* iv. 132 At Hamburg Sorge had taken his doctor's degree in political science *summa cum laude*. **1980** M. Babson *Dangerous to Know* vi. 40 An interview with one of the graduates, *summa cum laude*, of the Fat Farm. **1980** *Sci. Amer.* Aug. 35/1 He left Harvard three years later with a most irregular but steadily brilliant record, graduating in three years with an A.B. summa in chemistry.

summand. Delete *rare* and add further examples.

1943 *Mind* LII. 243 Even in logic, 'all' means something more... It means..completeness of the logical summands. **1964** E. A. Power *Introd. Quantum Electrodynamics* iv. 53 Suppose then $n_j \geqslant 1$, and then in each of the N summands on the right one gets a contribution of $\lambda_\alpha = j$ for that particular summand. **1979** *Proc. London Math. Soc.* XXXVIII. 213 If (G,H) is a countably generated pair with $cd_RG \leqslant 1$, and I_HG a direct summand of I_G, then $H_\gamma G$.

summarizable (sɒ·mărəizăb'l), *a.* [f. Summariz(e *v.* + -able.] Capable of being summarized.

1970 *Nature* 23 May 774/2 In the last 18 pages chairmen attempt to summarize their sessions, but this is disappointing; it is not summarizable material. **1977** M. Cohen *Sensible Words* 139 Conventional intellectual historians who read merely for summarizable ideas.

summary, *sb.* Add: **4.** Special Comb.:

summary punch, a card punch that automatically punches the results obtained by a tabulator from a number of other cards; hence as *v. intr.*; **summary-punched** *a.*, **summary punching** *vbl. sb.*

1935 *Astron. Jrnl.* XLIV. 180/1 The wiring for the tabulator and summary punch is changed very little during the cycle. **1949** E. C. BERKELEY *Giant Brains* iv. 50 The reproducer..can..summary punch, or copy totals or summaries obtained in the tabulator into blank cards in the reproducer. **1956** G. A. MONTGOMERIE *Digital Calculating Machines* viii. 154 Automatic punches can also be connected to the tabulator to act as summary punches. **1957** N. CHAPLIN *Introd. Automatic Computers* xv. 341 Summary punching produces, by machine, cards that may contain variable and modified information derived from other cards. *Ibid.* 342 A summary punch machine.. usually does not produce more than one hundred summary punched cards per minute. **1970** O. DOPPING *Computers & Data Processing* iv. 75 The summary punch can punch information coming from the registers of the tabulator.

summate, *v.* Delete *rare* and substitute for def.: To add together or combine; *spec.* in *Physiol.*, with reference to nerve impulses, etc. Also *intr.* and *fig.*

1922 *Jrnl. Optical Soc. Amer.* VI. 550 When quite differently weighted, in terms of the relative powers of the three elementary processes to generate brilliance, the three chromatic curves should summate to yield the visibility curve. **1932** P. BLOOMFIELD *Imaginary Worlds* xiv. 246 Happiness does not summate. The happiness of ten million individuals is not a millionfold the happiness of ten. **1935** *Discovery* May 140/1 In order to see more clearly in a bad light, we instinctively keep on blinking and peering so that the recurring slight pressures by the eyelids are, when summated, capable of evoking phosphenes. **1935** WINTON & BAYLISS *Human Physiol.* (ed. 2) ix. 349 Responses which are partially or completely super-imposed are said to summate. **1951** G. HUMPHREY *Thinking* i. 17 The implication that stimuli may be linearly summated is accepted by representative objective psychologists. **1957** *Encycl. Brit.* III. 866/1 Similar documents may be assembled and summated before they are journalized. **1962** W. NOWOTTNY *Lang. Poets Use* iv. 78 The particulars which inhabit these schemes, though extraordinarily difficult to summate, permit themselves to be assimilated to a common ideogram of decline. **1970** *Jrnl. Gen. Psychol.* LXXXIII. 144 According to the second principle, two responses having the same form summate. **1971** A. C. GUYTON *Basic Human Physiol.* vi. 63/2 Not only can discharges from separate presynaptic terminals summate with each other, but rapidly successive discharges from the same presynaptic terminal can also summate.

2. *trans.* To summarize.

1955 G. GORER *Exploring Eng. Character* xiv. 269 If the 25 per cent of the population who say that they are influenced either regularly or occasionally by the advice of horoscopes are summated, one finds that there are very few categories where there is a variation of more than 3 per cent from the national norm. **1976** J. BAYLEY *Uses of Division* I. i. 24 It remained for Proust to summate the retrospective social novel.

Hence **summa·ted** *ppl. a.*

1938 J. NEWTON *Introd. Metallurgy* xiii. 406 In slag calculations use is sometimes made of 'summated' percentages by means of which oxides of similar chemical properties are grouped together and treated as a single constituent.

summation^{2}. Add: **3. a.** (Further examples.) Now *esp.* such addition in an electronic device.

1962 M. G. HARTLEY *Introd. Electronic Analogue Computers* iii. 23 An arrangement for the summation of three voltages. **1977** J. G. GRAEME *Designing with Operational Amplifiers* vii. 175 This characteristic makes possible signal summation and subtraction through the simple connection of summing or differencing resistors to the amplifier inputs. **1981** F. W. HUGHES *Op Amp Handbk.* viii. 206 The output signal may be a direct mathematical summation of the input signals or may include a determined amount of gain.

b. Substitute for def.: The process or effect by which repeated or multiple nerve impulses can produce a response that each impulse alone would fail to produce. (Further examples.)

1956 A. C. GUYTON *Textbk. Med. Physiol.* v. 45/1 If impulses occur too far apart in time..temporal summation will not occur. **1979** SPENCE & MASON *Human Anat. & Physiol.* xi. 293 During spatial summation, nerve impulses in many different stimulatory presynaptic cells travelling to a single postsynaptic cell may all arrive at the postsynaptic cell very close together in time.

c. *Psychol.* Cumulative action or effect (see quots.).

1921 E. J. KEMPF *Psychopathol.* i. 62 The tendency to suppress our affections may accumulate; that is, a summation of the repressing or suppressing egoistic wishes may occur. **1924** J. RIVIERE et al. tr. *Freud's Coll. Papers* I. 95 An assumption which is not improbable in itself—namely, that a *noxia* such as coitus interruptus attains its effect by summation. According to the disposition of the person..a longer or shorter time will be required before the effect of this summation becomes evident. **1955** J. STRACHEY et al. tr. *Freud's Compl. Psychol. Wks.* II. ii. 174 Even a hysteric can retain a certain amount of affect that has not been dealt with; if, owing to the occurrence of similar provoking causes, that amount is increased by summation to a point beyond the subject's tolerance, the impetus to conversion is given.

6. *summation network*; **summation check** *Computers* = *sum check* s.v. *SUM *sb.*^{1} 14.

1954 *Computers & Automation* Dec. 22/1 Summation check. **1969** JORDAIN & BRESLAU *Condensed Computer Encycl.* 498 One weakness of the summation check is its inability to detect transposed digits. **1968** D. EADIE *Introd. Basic Computer* xv. 347 In most analog computers the summation network is combined with an operational amplifier.

summative, *a.* Delete *rare* and add: (Later examples.) Also, cumulative, pertaining to accumulation.

?**1930** W. C. WILLIAMS *Sel. Essays* (1954) 103 We've got to experiment with technique long before the final summative artist arrives. **1931** *Brit. Jrnl. Psychol.* July 25 All such views of perception may be distinguished from summative or integrative theories by being called 'response' theories of perception. **1936** *Jrnl. Psychol.* II. 80 (*caption*) The summative efficiency of the samples. **1938** W. BENARY in W. D. ELLIS *Sourcebk. Gestalt Psychol.* viii. 105 In these examples brightness differences are the *reverse* of what a summative theory would have demanded. **1968** W. A. SCOTT in Lindzey & Aronson *Handbk. Social Psychol.* (ed. 2) II. xi. 218 We shall use the term *summative* to designate a scale that is scored by adding the response scores on its component items.

summatively (sʌmēⁱ·tivli), *adv.* [f. SUMMATIVE *a.* + -LY^{2}.] Additively, cumulatively.

1936 *Mind* XLV. 270 Everything that can be described 'organically' can also be described 'summatively'. It is simply a question of convenience. **1951** G. HUMPHREY *Thinking* iii. 103 Watt professes to hold..a contributory theory of mental energetics, one which derives motive power in the kind of experiment which he performed,.. summatively from task and reproductive tendency. **1976** *Nature* 4 Mar. 59/1 Baylor *et al.* showed that the cones of the red-eared turtle, *Pseudemys scripta elegans*, are summatively and reciprocally coupled over distances up to 50 µm.

summator (sʌmēⁱ·tǝ̆ɹ). [f. SUMMATE *v.* + -OR.] **1.** *Electr. Engin.* That which sums; *spec.* a device which sums the analogue or digital information it receives. Cf. INTEGRATOR.

1930 *Engineering* 11 Apr. 482/1 The summator proper consists of two parts, a series of small dials giving the total kilowatt hours recorded by all the individual meters and larger dials, on which the maximum demand in kilowatts is aggregated. **1953** *Proc. Inst. Electr. Engineers* C. I. 44/1 The summator operates on the same principle of current balance as the telemeter and its error term is the same. **1974** *Jrnl. Appl. Physiol.* XXXVII. 748/1 A problem..is the inherently slow response time of the continuous discharge integrators (usually called analog summators, or merely integrators) used to supply this running average.

2. *Psychol.* In full, *verbal summator*: (see quots.).

1936 B. F. SKINNER in *Jrnl. Psychol.* II. 71 The verbal summator is a device for repeating arbitrary samples of speech obtained by permuting and combining certain elemental speech-sounds. *Ibid.*, Apart from its use as a test, the summator is valuable in the study of other aspects of verbal behavior. *Ibid.* 73 The verbal summator ..evokes latent verbal responses through summation with imitative responses to skeletal samples of speech. **1957** C. E. OSGOOD et al. in Saporta & Bastian *Psycholinguistics* (1961) 293/1 Skinner (1936) has devised a 'verbal summator' technique for studying language behavior... Samples of meaningless speech sounds are repeated until the subject perceives some meaningful form —a kind of verbal inkblot. **1970** *Jrnl. Gen. Psychol.* Oct. 143 Skinner hoped to measure the strength and relative importance of verbal responses and intended that the verbal summator, or Tautophone, as it was subsequently named, should become the instrument for doing so.

summer, *sb.*^{1} Add: **4. a.** (*e*) (Further examples.)

1798 J. WOODFORDE *Diary* 11 June (1931) V. 121 Master Neville Custance called on us..being very lately come home from School for the Summer Vacation. **1875** TROLLOPE *Prime Minister* (1876) I. xv. 237 The lawyer's regular summer vacation had not yet commenced. **1942** O. NASH *Good Intentions* 179 A summer cold Is to have and to hold. **1970** J. CREASEY *Part for Policeman* vi. 53 What's the matter with him? Summer 'flu? **1975** *Times* 19 Apr. 9/2 Kathy had been in bed with a so-called summer cold..sniffling and sneezing. **1980** P. HARCOURT *Tomorrow's Treason* I. i. 23 What with leave and summer flu, we're already short of staff. **1982** R. TIMPERLEY *Face in Leaves* i. 11 The long summer vacation was stretching out ahead of me.

(*g*) (Later examples.)

1873 H. JAMES *Let.* 24 Mar. (1974) I. 355, I walk abroad in my summerest clothes and am warm. **1979** *Times of India* 17 Aug. 3/4 A wag remarks that half the city's population migrates to cooler climes during the 'summerest' month of May.

c. *summer apple* (example), *pearmain* (example), *pippin* (earlier example).

1795 J. JAY *Let.* 12 Dec. in *Columbia Lit. Columns* (1970) XIX. III. 43 Ten are Summer Pippins, a very large fair Yellow apple. **1870** J. W. MCCLUNG *Minnesota* xi. 154 Among the varieties [of apples]..are..Summer Pairmain, [etc.]. **1930** J. DOS PASSOS *42nd Parallel* II. 145 They ate sweet summerapples.

f. *U.S.* Designating tourists or those who visit a place for a summer holiday. Cf. *summer boarder*, sense 6 a below.

1886 *Leslie's Monthly* Feb. 203/1 Old Sampson don't like the Summer gentry. **1889** W. D. HOWELLS *Hazard of New Fortunes* I. 135 She frankly gave up her house to the summer-folks (as they call them in the country). **1892** *Rep. Vermont Board Agric.* XII. 139 To these more prominent places may be added a multitude of..attractive homes to the summer guest. **1898** E. N. WESTCOTT *David Harum* 286 Our friend had met quite a number of the 'summer people'. **1938** *Sun* (Baltimore) 24 Mar. 10/2 New England has been declining. Her rural areas are given over to a sort of subsistence farming or to the entertainment of 'summer people'. **1971** H. T. WALDEN *Anchorage Northeast* 19 So few 'summer people' are here that the term has little or no usage. **1977** *New Yorker* 10 Oct. 112/3 He is the native by the side of the road who, having been called stupid by the summer person exasperated at his inability to provide directions to Portland, says, 'Mebbee, but at least I ain't lost.' **1980** J. COATES *Sentimental Education* 124 She belonged to the town—she was not one of the summer people.

5. Indirect objective, *summer-going* adj.; instrumental, *summer-painted*, *-soothed*, *-tranced* adjs.; similative, *summer-happy*, *-kind*, *-merry*, *-sweet* adjs.; 'in or during summer', *summer-basking*, *-born*, *-green*, *-idle*, *-opened*, *-running*, *-shaded*, *-still*, *white* adjs.

1931 R. GRAVES *Poems 1926–30* 69 You are no more than weather, The year's unsteadfastness To which, now summer-basking,.. The mind pays no honour. **1975** *Language for Life* (Dept. Educ. & Sci.) xviii. 267 Many children..are likely to continue to need special help in the junior school, particularly those summer-born children who may have had only two years of early schooling. **1954** J. BETJEMAN *Few Late Chrysanthemums* 43 Oh sun upon the summer-going by-pass Where ev'rything is speeding to the sea. **1930** J. DOS PASSOS *42nd Parallel* 137 There was a blue haze at the end of every street of brick houses and dark summergreen trees. **1917** D. H. LAWRENCE *Look! We have come Through!* 104 And we're going to be summer-happy And summer-kind. **1955** E. BOWEN *World of Love* iv. 67 The summer-idle water dawdled in shallows. **1917** Summer-kind [see *summer-happy* above]. **1957** E. BLUNDEN *Poems of Many Years* 279 By the arched grey bridge of summer-merry streams. **1887** J. R. LOWELL in *Atlantic Monthly* Feb. 250 And listen while Old Hundred pours Forth through summer-opened doors. **1937** E. MUIR *Coll. Poems* (1960) 80 The lint-white stubble plain From which the summer-painted birds have flown A year's life on. **1972** *Trout & Salmon* Feb. 10/2 Clearly the nets are taking an excessive proportion of summer-running salmon. **1850** J. G. WHITTIER *Poet. Wks.* (1898) 340/1 Down the summer-shaded street A wasted female figure..Came rushing. **1883** R. BRIDGES *Prometheus the Firegiver* 37 Piloting over the wind-dappled blue Of the summer-soothed Aegean. **1925** A. HUXLEY *Sel. Poems* 38, I am a pool of waters, summer-still. **1945** W. DE LA MARE *Burning-Glass* 42 Summer-sweet as that wild rose. **1881** O. WILDE *Poems* 66 We too might waste the summer-trancèd day. **1918** D. H. LAWRENCE *New Poems* 9 The flagged, clean pavement summer-white.

6. a. summer boarder *U.S.*, one who lives at a boarding-house in the country in summer; hence **summer-board** *v. trans.*, to take (someone) as a summer boarder; **summer-boarding; summer camp** orig. and chiefly *U.S.*, a camp providing recreational and sporting facilities during the summer holiday period, usu. for children; **summer cottage** *N. Amer.*, a cottage, usu. at a holiday resort or in the country, occupied during the summer; hence **summer cottager,** one who occupies a summer cottage; **summer country** *N.Z.* (see quot. 1898); **summer eggs** (examples); **summer kitchen** *N. Amer.*, an extra kitchen, adjoining a house or separate from it, used for cooking in hot weather; **summer-long** *adv.* and *adj.*, (lasting) throughout the summer; **summer master** *Canad. Hist.*, a person in charge of a trading post for the summer only; **summer mastitis,** a severe inflammation of the udder of cows usu. associated with the bacteria *Corynebacterium pyogenes* or *Peptococcus indolicus*; **summer pruning,** the selective cutting back of branches of trees or shrubs during the growing season; hence **summer prune** *v.*; **summer-pruned** *ppl. a.*; **summer pudding,** a pudding made of stewed fruit (freq. raspberries and red currants) and bread; **summer resort,** a popular place of resort in the summer, esp. a summer holiday resort; also, the act of visiting such a place; **summer resorter** *U.S.*, one who frequents summer resorts; **summer road** *Canad.*, a road suitable for use all year round, as opp. to one used in winter only by sleighs; **summer sale,** a sale of merchandise at reduced prices in the summer, esp. by shops wishing to clear their seasonal stock; **summer sausage** *U.S.*, a type of dried or smoked sausage which can be made in winter and kept until summer; **summer school,** a school or course of education conducted by a university, etc., in the summer, esp. during the long vacation; **summer stock** *U.S.*, theatrical productions by a repertory company organized for the summer season, esp. at holiday resorts, freq. *attrib.*; **summer term,** that term of an academic year or of legal sessions which occurs before the summer vacation; **summer theatre**, a theatre operating only in summer; **summer-tilth** *dial.*, fallow land; the cultivation of such land; **summer-weight** *a.*, of clothes: light, suitable for wear in summer; also *transf.*; **summer wood** = *late wood* s.v. *LATE *a.*[1] 4.

1903 K. D. WIGGIN *Rebecca* x. 107 Mother has summer-boarded a lot o' the school-marms. **1847** H. N. MOORE *Fitzgerald & Hopkins* 73 And stated also that there were several summer boarders from the city present. **1879** *Harper's Mag.* July 164 A few quiet summer boarders took shelter for a season's rest. **1897** [in Dict., sense 4 a (*f*)]. **1949** *Sat. Even. Post* 25 June 47/2 At the end of one unusually arduous summer he put an ad in a Portland paper for summer boarders. **1880** *Harper's Mag.* Sept. 536/1 Summer boarding here can be had for one dollar per week. **1893** *McClure's Mag.* I. 242/2 The camp was founded by Mr. Ernest Berkeley Balch as a summer camp for boys. **1948** *Sat. Even. Post* 23 Oct. 87/2 He wants to send every youngster in Lawrence to summer camp for at least two weeks. **1958** R. LIDDELL *Morea* III. ii. 238 There [Cerigo] monasteries are, regrettably, regarded merely as summer camps for visitors. **1979** *Country Life* 24 May 1640/1 At the age of 14..I was packed off to a summer camp in the Welsh hills. **1840** *Montreal Transcript* 22 Dec. 402/2 Some owners of lots also propose putting up summer cottages. **1902** W. D. HOWELLS *Literature & Life* 49 A few houses of the past remain, but the type of the summer cottage has impressed itself upon all the later building, and the native is passing architecturally, if not personally, into abeyance. **1958** *Edmonton Jrnl.* 28 June 25/1 Schools and universities are closing their doors for the next few months and many Canadian households will begin the annual exodus to summer cottage or camp. **1948** *Chicago Tribune* 20 June VII. 12/5 Many summer cottagers will be happy to know that the same house makes a similar type of cream that repels chiggers. **1971** *Islander* (Victoria, B.C.) 2 May 6/1 In this strange fantasyland live 300 permanent residents and another 3,200 summer cottagers. **1898** MORRIS *Austral Eng.* 444/2 *Summer country, n.*, in New Zealand (South Island), country which can be used in summer only; mountain land in Otago and Canterbury, above a certain level. **1922** W. PERRY et al. *Sheep Farming in N.Z.* vii. 88 The higher country..which is likely to hold snow to some depth in the winter months, is termed 'summer country'. **1947** P. NEWTON *Wayleggo* (1949) 14 A large proportion of the country [in the South Island]—the shady and hindermost areas—is suitable for summer grazing [of sheep] only... Such country is known as 'summer country'. **1884** A. SEDGWICK tr. *Claus's Elem. Text-bk. Zool.* x. 418 The so-called summer eggs..produce generations containing no males. **1952** J. CLEGG *Freshwater Life Brit. Isles* xii. 169 These so-called 'summer eggs' are laid, perhaps twenty or more at a time. **1874** *Southern Mag.* XIV. 124 There was Charley's wife..flitting about from house to summer-kitchen. **1939** H. M. MINER *St. Denis* ii. 25 Airy summer kitchens, which do not retain the heat of the stove, are built onto the sides of the houses. Too exposed to be warm, these annex kitchens are evacuated in winter. **1924** E. SITWELL *Sleeping Beauty* xxvi. 95 When the thickest gold will thrive Summer-long in the combs of the honey-hive. **1960** C. DAY LEWIS *Buried Day* ii. 31 On and on droned the voices, blending slumbrously with..the summer-long hum of insects. **1980** *Beautiful Brit. Columbia* Summer 39 In the summer, you may examine thousands of items at the summer-long Crafts Centre. **1913** I. COWIE *Company of Adventurers* 228 Many of these journals were kept by a 'summer master', who was quite often a very illiterate laborer, who could barely scrawl phonetics in the book during the real master's absence on the annual voyage to and from headquarters with the furs and for the outfit. **1967** A. M. JOHNSON in *Saskatchewan Jrnls.* (Hudson's Bay Rec. Soc.) p. xxviii, He sent Bird to Buckingham House with instructions to leave the summer master in charge there. **1934** R. G. LINTON *Vet. Hygiene* (ed. 2) VI. 446 The well-known suppurative form of mastitis..is especially prone to attack dry cows and virgin heifers during the summer months... This form is often referred to as epidemic mastitis or summer mastitis. **1970** W. H. PARKER *Health & Dis. Farm Animals* xv. 212 Infection of a dry cow or unbred heifer with..summer mastitis, is as common in beef as in dairy breeds. **1786** Summer prune *v.* [in Dict., sense 5 a]. **1980** V. CANNING *Fall from Grace* vii. 118 They summer pruned the wistaria. **1960** *News Chron.* 6 Aug. 6/4 The summer-pruned laterals are further shortened. **1707** J. MORTIMER *Whole Art of Husbandry* xvii. 396 To the Boughs that put out in Spring, give a Summer pruning a little after Midsummer. **1725** [in Dict., sense 4 a (*e*)]. **1806** W. PONTEY *Forest Pruner* 235 As a general rule, we think summer is preferable to winter-pruning. **1895** *Meehan's Monthly* May 87/1 Summer pruning is especially effective with coniferous trees... One who understands this business of summer pruning an evergreen can so manage that the tree forms an absolutely perfect specimen. **1972** G. E. BROWN *Pruning Trees, Shrubs & Conifers* iii. 50 Summer pruning..promotes spur formation. **1933** E. C. CARVER *Pract. Catering* vi. 114 Summer pudding. Thin slices of stale bread, stewed fruit... Serve with cream or custard. **1974** P. HAINES *Tea at Gunter's* xx. 206 Heaping my plate with summer pudding..I looked at the bread on my plate, oozing deep crimson juice. **1832** *Louisville* (Kentucky) *Public Advertiser* 12 July 3/5 He has prepared his House and Garden at the lower end of Jefferson Street, for the purpose of making it a general *Summer Resort*. **1846** *Chambers's Miscellany* XIV. CXXI. 32 Musselburgh,..another pleasing summer resort, is situated two miles eastward. **1853** E. T. TURNERELLI *Kazan* II. i. 4 This village is a favourite place of summer-resort for the inhabitants. **1873** J. H. BEADLE *Undevel. West* xv. 257 For a summer resort one can spend weeks very pleasantly here. **1882** G. W. PECK *Peck's Sunshine* (1883) 125 He said he should at once begin..by boarding at a summer resort hotel. **1974** *Times* 12 Nov. 14/1 Mr and Mrs Ronald Heywood own a 56-bedroom two star hotel in a summer resort on the east coast. **1889** *Advance* (Chicago) 19 Sept. 673/3 At Astoria the summer resorters distribute themselves to the various beaches. **1907** 'MARK TWAIN' in *N. Amer. Rev.* Nov. 327 They respected these elegant summer-resorters. **1820** S. H. WILCOCKE in L. F. R. Masson *Les Bourgeois de la Compagnie du Nord-Ouest* (1890) II. 224 With the summer road they were acquainted and that, therefore, they followed. **1909** *Gow Ganda* (Ontario) *Tribune* 17 Apr. 6/2 What will be the cry on the summer roads when we reach those points where the dense forest and rocks obstructs the view ahead? **1974** E. C. STACEY *Peace Country Heritage* i. 7 A few farmers used the..summer road. **1899** J. F. FRASER *Round World on Bicycle* xxvi. 324 All the millinery shops in Oxford Street begin their early summer sales or spring-clearance sales. **1923** A. HUXLEY *Antic Hay* xvi. 223 If I wait till the summer sale, the crêpe de Chine will be reduced by at least two shillings. **1976** *Times* 2 Aug. 16/3 The usual summer sales hiatus. **1893** F. E. RHORER *Meat Man's Friend* 33 By making summer sausage the same as above, but allowing the meat to be very coarse, it is called Salami. **1965** *House & Garden* Jan. 60 Summer sausage or Thüringer. These terms are interchangeable with dried cervelas. In fact, all dried sausages of this type are called summer sausage. **1976** T. GIFFORD *Cavanaugh Quest* (1977) x. 181 She sliced thick chunks of summer sausage. **1860** J. C. PATTESON *Jrnl.* Sept. in C. M. Yonge *Life J. C. Patteson* (1874) I. ix. 473 In taking away natives to the summer school, it must be understood that some..are taken..merely to teach us their languages. **1871** E. EGGLESTON *Hoosier Schoolmaster* 1 You might teach a summer school. **1919** M. BEER *Hist. Brit. Socialism* II. IV. xiv. 294 In 1906 a Fabian Summer School was established. **1967** B. JEFFERIS *One Black Summer* (1968) i. 1 The grounds and buildings would be full of summer school students: doctors who longed to pot; dressmakers who yearned to try their hands at sculpture. **1971** *Daily Tel.* (Colour Suppl.) 3 Dec. 9/2 The lecturer..led his summer school audience down the howling avenues of Joycean puns. **1981** V. GLENDINNING *Edith Sitwell* xvi. 205 In August Edith had lectured..at a summer school in Cambridge. **1942** BERREY & VAN DEN BARK *Amer. Thes. Slang* § 587/4 *Straw hat*, a summer stock theater, in which plays are tried out. **1955** J. P. DONLEAVY *Ginger Man* vii. 64, I was once approached by a talent scout in summer stock. **1965** *New Statesman* 2 July 20/1 There is a very funny story about Maury Stein, a Summer Stock actor at Indian Lake. **1977** I. SHAW *Beggarman, Thief* III. vi. 262 'Where've you acted before?'..'Well..noplace.'..'Not even summer stock?' **1853** ROOT & LOMBARD *Songs of Yale* 4 Presentation Day is the sixth Wednesday of the Summer Term, when the graduating Class..are presented to the President as qualified for the first degree, or the A.B. **1859** J. A. SYMONDS *Let.* Feb. (1967) I. 181, I always connect it in my mind with that interminable Harrow Summer Term. **1922** *Times* 11 Oct. 11/5 During the last weeks of the Summer Term, at the request of the Lord Chancellor, I undertook the trial of undefended suits for divorce, and heard about four hundred cases. **1980** C. FREMLIN *With no Crying* ii. 8 It looked like being the best summer term ever... O-levels were still a full year away. **1801** *Monthly Mirror* June 414 'Make hay while the sun shines,' has been found a most salutary maxim at the summer theatres. **1938** L. BEMELMANS *Life Class* II. vii. 189 They were.. Bavaria's greatest peasant actors... Their theater, part of the inn, was not the usual..summer theater, a converted old barn, but a real theater. **1981** N. CRISP *Festival* i. 15 Who in their right mind..would have dreamed of a summer theatre at..a somewhat shabby would-be genteel spa. **1818** in Thirsk & Imray *Suffolk Farming 19th Cent.* (1958) 104 To leave all the muck, dung and compost made the last year and all hay, clover hay and summertilths. **1903** in G. E. Evans *Farm & Village* (1969) 160 Beans and Peas to be twice clean hoed or a clean summertilth. **1970** in —— *Where Beards wag All* viii. 89 Ploughing a long fallow or summer-tilth was a very hard and slow job for the man and his horses. **1883** *Graphic* 14 Apr. (Advt., rear cover), Youth's overcoat, summer weight. **1931** *Daily Tel.* 22 May 9/6 Summer-weight weaves in hopsack, tweed, and knitted mixtures. **1968** A. DIMENT *Bang Bang Birds* v. 66 It's hell trying to keep a crease in bottle green, summer-weight cavalry twill. **1977** *Time* 27 June 46/2 The story also has some pretty serious problems, or perhaps more accurately, some puzzling aspects for what is intended as summer-weight entertainment. **1896** W. R. FISHER in W. Schlich *Man. Forestry* V. i. 6 It [*sc.* springwood] contains less woody substance than the summer- or autumn-wood of the same annual zone. **1930** *Forestry* IV. 10 The greater length of the summer wood tracheids of the Sitka spruce is in accordance with the observations of Lee and Smith. **1982** *Sci. Amer.* July 35/2 These make the directly visible springwood ring, followed once the tree is great with leaf by a wider, denser, darker ring of mixed fibrous growth and small summerwood vessels.

b. summer crookneck, a small yellow or orange summer squash with a curved neck; **summer grape** (later examples); **summer squash**, substitute for def.: any of several varieties of the gourd *Cucurbita pepo* whose fruits are eaten young; (examples).

1890 *Amer. Naturalist* XXIV. 731 Summer crooknecks appeared in our garden catalogues in 1828. **1969** *Oxf. Bk. Food Plants* 122/1 'Summer Crookneck'..has bright yellow or orange, warty fruits, shaped like a crooked club. **1834** J. J. AUDUBON *Ornith. Biogr.* II. 92 The Summer Grape..occurs in all the barren lands of the Western Country. **1949** *Amer. Photography* Apr. 244/3 The summer grape is somewhat similar to the blue grape. **1815** W. BENTLEY *Jrnl.* 14 Aug. (1914) IV. 346 A more free use has been made of the summer squash than ever before known. **1902** *Harper's Bazaar* Sept. 766 There was nothing in her larder except a summer-squash pie. **1981** *Farmstead Mag.* Winter 37/1 Winter squash, of course, shares space in seed catalogs with its sister vegetable—the summer squash.

summer, *sb.*[3] Add: **1.** (Later example of *summer-up*.)

1960 J. BAYLEY *Characters of Love* iii. 130 Here the confident summer-up of Othello might become a little uneasy.

2. *Electronics.* A circuit or device that produces an output dependent on the sum of two or more inputs or of multiples of them.

1958 W. J. KARPLUS *Analog Simulation* ix. 234 Since the output voltage is proportional to the sum of the input voltages, this circuit is termed 'summer'. **1968** PASSMORE & ROBSON *Compan. Med. Stud.* I. ii. 5 The summer would have many input voltages, each one representing the factors for heat gain..or the heat loss. **1981** R. G. IRVINE *Operational Amplifier Characteristics* vii. 176 The gain of this circuit may be changed from unity by modifying the value of the feedback resistor on the inverting summer.

summer-game. 2. (Earlier example.)

1859 G. W. MATSELL *Vocabulum* 117 *Summer game*, playing merely for amusement. *Summer game*, playing a game for the benefit of another person with his money.

summerize, *v.* Restrict *nonce-wd.* to sense in Dict. and add: **1.** (Later example.)

1891 H. JAMES *Let.* 7 June (1981) III. 342 The Curtises go to India—or believe they do—in the autumn; so I suppose they summerize at the Barbaro.

2. *trans.* To prepare (something) for summer. Also *intr.* for *refl.* *U.S. colloq.*

1935 *Evening Sun* (Baltimore) 3 Apr. 9 Let Hutzler's summerize your home. **1949** *Sun* (Baltimore) 2 June 4 Come to K. Katz and 'summerize'! **1962** *Harper Motors, Inc.* (Charlottesville, Va.) *Advertising Let.*, This time of year you're probably deluged with offers from service stations to 'summerize' your car—that is, drain the anti-freeze, check the motor, and get ready for summer driving.

Hence **summeriza·tion**, the act or process of preparing a thing for summer.

1974 *Old Times* (Upper Canada College) Autumn 8 With..the summerization of the Patrick Johnson rink.. the quality of extracurricular programs..is greatly enhanced.

summer-land, summerland, *sb.* **2.** (Earlier examples.)

1861 *Herald of Progress* (N.Y.) 13 July 3/4 (*heading*) Tidings from the summer land. A plea in behalf of little children. **1869** *Spiritualist* 17 Dec. 19/3 He found that he could pass through the upper air with ease, and at last they reached what the Spiritualists call the 'Summer Land', but in reality the compound essence of seventeen summers distilled into one, would not equal it in loveliness. **1890** W. JAMES *Princ. Psychol.* I. x. 394 The odd thing is that persons unexposed to spiritualist traditions will so often act in the same way when they become entranced, speak in the name of the departed,..send messages about their happy home in the summer-land, and describe the ailments of those present.

summers (sʊ·məɹz), *adv. U.S.* [f. SUMMER *sb.*[1] + -S.] During the summer; each summer (for a number of years).

1907 'MARK TWAIN' *Christian Sci.* II. viii. 235 It [*sc.* a local Christian Science church] can appoint its own fan-distributors, summers. **1936** H. W. HORWILL *S.P.E. Tract* XLV. 192 A peculiar use of the plural form is illustrated in..'A niece of theirs had earned her way through College by waiting on the Atkins-Smythes' table, summers'. This usage is said to be a relic of the old adverbial genitive. **1976** *National Observer* (U.S.) 1 May 8/2 The limits have riled Pevsner since college days, when he worked summers in Europe.

summer season. Restrict *rare* to sense in Dict. and add: **2.** A period in summer for which people are employed in connection with seasonal or holiday entertainment, trade, etc.

1952 W. GRANVILLE *Dict. Theatrical Terms* 159 *Seasonal shop*, an engagement for the summer season in, say, a concert party or in a touring company that visits theatres which open only in the summer months. **1973** *Melody Maker* 4 Aug. 50/6 The Teign Valley Stompers from Teignmouth, Devon, who are at present enjoying a summer season on Pontin's Holiday Camps' Devon circuit, have engaged a new trombonist.

summer-time. 2. Add: (Later examples.) Now adopted in the U.K. for daylight saving from March to October (see quot. 1982). Cf. *British Summer Time* s.v. *BRITISH *a.* 5; *double summer-time* s.v. *DOUBLE *a.* 6.

1916 *Times* 26 Aug. 7/2 Of the changes which have already proved themselves to be changes for the better, that which immediately affects the greatest number of people is the introduction of 'summer time'. **1937** D. L. SAYERS *Busman's Honeymoon* vii. 158 October 2nd—sun would be setting about half-past five. No, it was Summer Time. Say half-past six. **1967** [see *British Standard Time* s.v. *BRITISH *a.* 5]. **1982** *Whitaker's Almanack 1983* 142 In the United Kingdom, Summer Time, one hour in advance of G.M.T. will be kept between 01h G.M.T. on the last Sunday in March and 01h G.M.T. on the day following the fourth Saturday in October. Thus, in 1983, Summer Time will be in force between March 27 and October 23.

summing, *ppl. a.* Add: **2.** *Electronics.* That performs summation; producing an output dependent on the sum of the inputs.

1948 *Electronics* Apr. 124/3 The summing amplifier..is widely used in d-c and a-c servomechanisms. **1960** ROGERS & CONNOLLY *Analog Computation in Engin. Design* ii. 13 When used in this manner, the operational amplifier is known as a summing amplifier. **1963** B. FOZARD *Instrumentation Nucl. Reactors* ix. 107 The point *b* corresponds to the summing junction in a computing amplifier. **1967** *Electronics* 6 Mar. 120/2 A network between the output of a_1 and the summing junction of a_3 can be set to bring the total loop phase shift to 360°. **1981** F. W. Hughes *Op Amp Handbk.* viii. 208 The inverting AC summing amplifier is similar to the inverting DC summing amplifier, except for the input capacitors.

summit, *sb.* Add: **3. b.** The highest level, *spec.* with reference to politics and international relations; also *ellipt.* for *summit conference, meeting,* etc., sense 4 below.

1950 W. S. Churchill in *Times* 15 Feb. 4/2 It is not easy to see how things could be worsened by a parley at the summit, if such a thing were possible. **1955** *Newsweek* 11 Apr. 44/1 Only if the Big Four Foreign Ministers reached 'a substantial measure of agreement' would a further conference be convened—at the summit. **1957** P. Frank *Seven Days to Never* i. 33 We haven't knuckled under, not at the Summit or anywhere else, and..the alliance stands. **1958** *Listener* 14 Aug. 220/2 Then came the Czestochowa raid; the decision for this must have been taken at the summit. **1959** *Economist* 11 July 92/2 While an agreement not to mention time limits may be enough to get from the foreign ministers' level to the summit, to reach a settlement there will require something more. **1967** *Spectator* 30 June 757/1 The most certain result of the Glassboro summit, in fact, is no more than that Mr. Johnson's standing at home is now rather higher. **1978** R. Ludlum *Holcroft Covenant* xxxi. 365 Since I left Brazil, I've not owned a weapon... I should like to have one now. Only for the duration of the summit.

4. summit meeting, a meeting between heads of government, etc., to discuss matters of international significance (cf. sense 3 b above); also *transf.*; similarly *summit conference, talks.*

1955 *Times* 23 June 8/3 The senator's resolution demanding that the United States should refuse to attend the 'summit' conference. **1959** *Encounter* Aug. 33/2, I was running out of pennies, and had to have a summit conference with the [telephone] operator. **1977** *Whitaker's Almanack 1978* 590/1 A unified political command for Egypt, Syria, and the Sudan was agreed at the end of the two-day tripartite summit conference in Khartoum. **1955** *N.Y. Times* 5 May 2/5, I say at this moment I see no reason for that summit meeting. **1963** *Ann. Reg. 1962* 208 Krushchev suggested a Summit meeting. **1977** Summit meeting [see SSRC s.v. *S 4 a]. **1955** *Times* 7 May 8/7 There are certainly no indications that Washington has modified its resistance to 'summit talks' with Russia in advance of preparatory soundings.

summit, *v.*[2] [f. *summit *sb.* 3 b.] *intr.* To take part in summit meetings.

1972 *Time* 5 June 40 Prime Minister Indira Gandhi is willing to summit with the chap (probably at the end of the month). **1973** *New Scientist* 5 July 30 Nixon the President, summiting and clowning with the visiting Brezhnev, and Nixon, the suspect, seeking to elude the Watergate noose. **1979** *Daily Mail* 23 Jan. 5/2 When he is not summiting in the sunshine there is apparently nothing like All Creatures Great and Small..to help him forget crumbling pay norms and secondary picketing.

summitee·r. [f. *summit *sb.* 3 b + -eer.] One who takes part in summit meetings. Hence **summitee·ring.**

1957 *Time* 16 Dec. 21/2 The man who..must lead NATO along the course the summiteers lay down. **1958** *Daily Mail* 31 July 4/3 Macmillan has emerged as a worthy Summiteer. **1962** *Observer* 18 Feb. 11/7 No one knows either what the country thinks about the pay pause or Mr. Macmillan's summiteering. **1978** *Guardian Weekly* 23 July 6 Hot from their discussions on how to save the world from an energy crisis, the six summiteers repaired to the 14th century Gymnich Castle, near Bonn, for dinner. **1982** *Economist* 20 Mar. 12/1 This month's summiteers are likely to turn a blind eye to the subject.

su·mmitry. [f. *summit *sb.* 3 b + -ry.] The practice of convening or holding summit meetings, or of using them as a diplomatic device.

1958 *Economist* 8 Feb. 479/1 The Western dislike of time-wasting summitry is due..to a feeling that even an inconclusive get-together would fill the democracies with a false sense of security. **1967** *Spectator* 28 July 97/1 Mr. Macmillan likened the preliminaries to the summitry so dear to his heart to a stately minuet. **1972** Ld. Gladwyn *Mem.* xvi. 276 The so-called science of 'Summitry' was now being pursued with zeal and intelligence by the Foreign Office. **1979** *Time* 2 Apr. 26/1 Jimmy Carter initiated his most stimulating success as President six months ago: his summitry that broke 30 years of bloodshed and stalemate to make possible a peace treaty between Egypt and Israel.

summoned, *ppl. a.* Add: Also in comb. with adv., as *summoned-up.*

1977 *New Yorker* 19 Sept. 108/2 Calling beautiful coaches for the harshly summoned-up emergency.

Sumner[2] (sʊ·mnəɹ). The name of Thomas H. *Sumner* (1807–76), U.S. shipmaster, used *attrib.*, in the possessive, and *absol.*, with reference to a method devised by him in 1837 of finding one's position on the surface of the earth, employing an approximate value of latitude or longitude based on dead reckoning, in conjunction with an astronomical observation, to calculate a number of positions that define a line that must contain the true position; so *Sumner line* = *position line* s.v. *position *sb.* 7 b.

1849 H. Raper *Pract. of Navigation & Naut. Astron.* (ed. 3) 345 (*heading*) Position on a line of bearing. [*Note*] Or 'Sumner's Method'. **1881** S. T. S. Lecky *'Wrinkles' in Pract. Navig.* ii. viii. 201 Unless the error of the latitude is greater than that assumed, the ship must be somewhere on this 'Line of position', which, for convenience, will henceforth in these pages be termed a 'Sumner line', after the American seaman who first brought this useful problem prominently to the notice of the profession. **1901** J. R. Walker *Explanation of 'New Navigation'* 8 The straight line is called the Sumner Line, or Line of Position. **1919** [see *position *sb.* 7 b]. **1924** R. Clements *Gipsy of Horn* xii. 228, I worked a Sumner, or position by double altitude. **1976** *Oxf. Compan. Ships & Sea* 845 *Sumner's position line*, a systemized method of finding a ship's position by means of a sight.

sumo (sū·mo). [Jap.] In Japan, a form of wrestling in which a wrestler wins a bout by forcing his opponent outside a circle or making him touch the ground with any part of his body except the soles of his feet. Freq. *attrib.*, esp. as *sumo wrestler, wrestling*; also *absol.*, a sumo wrestler.

1880 W. E. L. Keeling *Tourists' Guide Yokohama* 23 The wrestlers (*sumô*)..will not fail to interest him. **1893** *Jap. Soc. Trans. & Proc.* I. 19, I have seen English wrestling, and found it similar to Japanese *wrestling* (*Sumō*, not *Ju-jitsu*). **1923** J. Street *Mysterious Japan* ix. 103 The kind of wrestling known as *sumo* still maintains its ancient prestige as the national sport. **1934** [see *all-in 2]. **1936** K. Nohara *True Face of Japan* v. 220 Our taste for prodigies..is gratified by the corpulence of the *Sumo*. **1938** Bush & Kagami *Japanalia* 156/1 *Sumō* wrestlers are huge fellows. **1958** *Times* 27 Dec. 7/6 Such are the advance preliminaries of a bout of *sumo*, the national sport of Japan. **1964** I. Fleming *You only live Twice* i. 17 It is only the *sumo* wrestlers who drink *saké* in these quantities without showing it. **1966** *New Scientist* 28 July 182/3 Sumo wrestling, in which two monstrous men charge one another, clinch briefly and separate, with one the winner, usually in the space of a few seconds. **1974** *Daily Tel.* (Colour Suppl.) 22 Feb. 39/3 If one is to understand Japan in any depth, a realisation of the significance and the enjoyment of Sumo is as important as it is to appreciate the influence of soccer if one is to understand Britain. **1977** *Time* 4 July 52/2 Surpassing even such traditional Japanese sports as sumo wrestling, *bēsubōru* has become Japan's favorite sport. **1978** M. Kenyon *Deep Pocket* x. 125 This character was a sumo-wrestler, hewn from a cliff-face.

sumotori (sumotō[ə]·ri). [Jap., f. prec. + *tori* active partner in the performance of techniques.] A sumo wrestler.

1973 *Newsweek* 13 Aug. 92 Anyone who [tries] socking a sumotori in the stomach will gladly go back to brick walls. **1974** *Daily Tel.* (Colour Suppl.) 22 Feb. 39/3 The mature *sumotori* (as Sumo wrestlers are called) is about six feet tall and will weigh anything from 16 to 24 stone.

sump, *sb.* Add: **2. a.** (Further examples.) Also *fig.*

1963 T. & P. Morris *Pentonville* iii. 69 Pentonville represents one of the sumps of the English prison system; a receptacle into which the sludge is continuously drained. **1969** *Gloss. Terms Water Cooling Towers* (*B.S.I.*) 6 *Sump*, a lowered portion of the cold water basin floor for draining down purposes. **1975** *Sci. Amer.* Oct. 23/3 As fast as the heavy water leaked out it was collected in a sump and pumped directly back into the reactor.

c. A depression in the bottom of the crankcase of an internal-combustion engine, which serves as a reservoir of lubricating oil.

1907 *Westm. Gaz.* 9 Nov. 14/3 The oil is forced by a gear-driven pump from a sump in the crank-chamber. **1929** [see *skew gear* s.v. *skew *a.* 2]. **1950** *Brit. Repair Man.: Cars* 38/2 The oil filling orifice is housed in the valve top cover, and the sump, which is a steel pressing, has a capacity of 7½ pints. **1980** J. McClure *Blood of Englishman* i. 9 Droopy was removing the sump... He..extended a hand for a No. 8 ring spanner.

5. sump guard, a cowling for protecting the sump of a motor vehicle from perforation on poor roads.

1968 *Guardian* 6 May 5/5 The 1800 I was driving was standard except for a sump guard, essential on East African roads. **1980** J. Barnett *Palmprint* vii. 62 A heavy stone clanged against the sumpguard.

sump'n (sʌm[p]'n). Also **somepin, sumpin,** etc. Repr. colloq. (chiefly U.S., esp. Blacks') pronunc. of Something *sb.*, (*adj.*,) and *adv.*

1880 [see *kin var. Can *v.*[1]]. **1882** *Indianapolis Jrnl.* 5 Aug. 4/6 They's somepin kindo' hearty-like about the atmosphere. **1929** *Amer. Mercury* Sept. 50/2 Done sumpin' to fine captain one time didn't aim to do. **1938** C. Himes *Black on Black* (1973) 167 Ef'n yo' is God, den gimme somp'n tuh eat. **1951** X. Herbert in Murdoch & Drake-Brockman *Austral. Short Stories* 298 Git to jiggery out of it, you stinkin' rottin' black sumpen. **1961** Wodehouse *Ice in Bedroom* v. 41 Why not Heels Incorporated or Doublecrossers Limited or sump'n? **1976** *National Observer* (U.S.) 17 Apr. 17/1, I just want to tell him sump'n!

sumpter, *sb.* **3.** For † *Obs.* read 'Now *rare*' and add later example.

1958 L. Durrell *Balthazar* ii. 32 A liquid-eyed camel.. humped down the narrow street threatening to knock us down with its bulging sumpters of *bercim.*

sun, *sb.* Add: **I. 1. e.** (*i*) *the sun is over the foreyard* (*Naut.*): it is noon (the time at which the first drink of the day is taken).

1844 [see Fore-yard[2] 1]. **1862** 'Vanderdecken' *Yacht Sailor* ix. 123 It will be a favourable time to 'make the sun over the foreyard', and serve out grog in moderation to all hands. **1903** H. Holmes *Life & Adventures* 11 The sun's over the fore yard; no doubt they have spliced the main brace. **1962** W. Granville *Dict. Sailors' Slang* 115/2 *Sun over the foreyard*, time for drinking in the wardroom. Eight bells in the forenoon watch: mid-day. It is a traditional Naval convention never to drink before the sun clears the foreyard.

2. a. *rising sun* (later examples). Also, (*a*) as a decorative motif; (*b*) as the emblem of Japan (with ref. to the literal meaning of the country's name in Japanese: see *Nippon).

1840 J. Madison *Papers* III. 1624 [At the Constitutional Convention, 1787] Doctor Franklin, looking towards the President's chair, at the back of which a rising sun happened to be painted, observed..that painters had found it difficult to distinguish in their art, a rising, from a setting, sun. **1841** J. F. Cooper *Deerslayer* II. xii. 206 You are a man whose fathers came from beyond the rising sun; we are children of the setting sun. **1863** *Chambers's Encycl.* V. 683/1 *Japan* (native name, *Nipon*.. i.e., the Land of the Rising Sun). **1895** 'C. E. Craddock' *Mystery Witch-Face Mountain* 185 Some [quilts] were of the 'log cabin' and 'rising sun' variety. **1897** *Far East* 20 Mar. 83/2 The children of the Rising Sun. **1935** J. C. Lincoln *Cape Cod Yesterdays* 109, I ducked my tousled head under the..'rising-sun comforter' and fell asleep in spite of the racket. **1942** *R.A.F. Jrnl.* 2 May 1 It is difficult to form an exact picture of the air strength of the land of the Rising Sun. **1983** *Jewish Chron.* 27 May 15/3 The cupped-hand emblem replaces the now familiar rising sun logo [of the Jewish Welfare Board].

4. b. (*d*) For quot. 1727 substitute:

1688 J. Walker tr. *Pascal's Thoughts* xxxi. 246 This Dog is mine, said those poor Children; That's my place in the Sun: This is the beginning and Image of the Usurpation of all the Earth.

(Further examples.)

Quot. 1897 comes from a speech by Bernhard von Bülow, Chancellor of Germany; quot. 1901 is an example from Emperor Wilhelm II earlier than that in Dict.

[**1897** *Times* 7 Dec. 5/5 We desire to throw no one into the shade, but we also demand our own place in the sunlight.] **1901** *Times* 20 June 5/4 We have..fought for our place in the sun and have won it. It will be my business to see that we retain this place in the sun unchallenged, so that the rays of that sun may exert a fructifying influence upon our foreign trade and traffic. **1926** Galsworthy *Silver Spoon* i. iii. 22 Five million pounds spent on the organised travel of a hundred thousand working men..would infect the working class with a feverish desire for a place in the sun. The world is their children's for the taking. **1928** C. R. Longwell in *Theory Continental Drift* (Amer. Assoc. Petroleum Geologists) 145 Perhaps the very completeness of this iconoclasm, this rebellion against the established order, has served to gain for the new hypothesis a place in the sun. **1939** L. MacNeice *Autumn Jrnl.* viii. 35 Sun shines easy, but I no longer Docket a place in the sun. **1951** 'J. Tey' *Daughter of Time* vii. 96, I sure would hate a brother who took my credit and my women and my place in the sun. **1967** V. Lincoln *Private Disgrace* (1968) iii. 37 Lizzie longed for a place in the sun. But..her longing for popularity was self-defeating.

8. b. (Earlier example.)

1749 [see *cascade *sb.* 2 b].

II. 11. a. *sun-flush, -glaze, -glint* (earlier example), *-glory, -mote; sun-hero, -man.*

1924 G. B. Shaw *St. Joan* ii. 27 Joan (rising, with a sunflush of reckless happiness irradiating her face). **1958** C. Tomlinson *Seeing is Believing* (1960) 1 A quick gold, dyeing the uncovering beach With sunglaze. **1880** J. E. Watt *Poet. Sk.* 85 Oor sun-glints o' glory are followed by gloom. **1929** D. H. Lawrence *Pansies* 117 Men should group themselves into a new order Of sun-men..walking each in his own sun-glory. **1911** F. H. Woods in *Encycl. Relig. & Ethics* IV. 355/1 Cúchulainn as a sun-hero..was directly connected with Lug, the sun-god. **1929** Sun-man [see *sun-glory* above]. **1933** W. de la Mare *Fleeting* 96 The sun-motes where the mosses drowse.

b. *sun-film, -scorch.* See also *suntan *sb.* (and *a.*).

1930 E. Pound *XXX Cantos* ii. 11 Snipe come for their bath, bend out their wing-joints, Spread wet wings to the sun-film. **1907** W. De Morgan *Alice-for-Short* xix. 208 With her hair shaken out and only the least little shade of sun-scorch from long exposure on the inexhaustible sands.

c. *sun-canopy* (later example), *-filter, -lotion, -shield, -umbrella* (earlier examples).

1923 *Heal & Son Catal.: Kitchen Furnit. & Garden Furnit.* 10 Hammock..with sun canopy and fittings complete. **1970** *Cape Times* 28 Oct. 18/4 You can select your material from our large range of fabrics in tweed, sunfilter, satin, taffeta, shantung and parchment. **1979** P. Niesewand *Member of Club* vi. 40 The sun filter curtains were..green, yellow and orange stripes. **1967** H. Pinter *Tea Party* 49 You're off to Spain... What sun lotion do you use, Lois? **1974** W. Garner *Big enough Wreath* ix. 118 One of the two guards stepped out of the gate-house, sun-shields hiding his eyes. **1977** G. Scott *Hot Pursuit* iii. 29 The driver had my wrist... His other hand had to stay on the wheel and his knife was behind the sunshield. **1831** *Boston* (Mass.) *Transcript* 31 May 3/2 Light Sun Umbrellas..are offered at low prices. **1867** A. D. Whitney *Summer in Leslie Goldthwaite's Life* viii. 173 Miss Craydocke appeared..under her great brown sun-umbrella.

d. = affording maximum access to the sun; used, worn, etc., for sun-bathing; as *sun balcony, loggia, parlour, porch, room*; *sun-dress, -suit, -top*; *sun-chair.*

1971 'D. HALLIDAY' *Dolly & Doctor Bird* vii. 90 A sun balcony..ran round the..side of the villa. 1976 'W. TREVOR' *Children of Dynmouth* i. 19 Mrs Dass was reclining on a sun-chair in the bow-window. 1942 R. GODDEN *Breakfast with Nikolides* vi. 138 Her spotted sun-dress, her sun hat and sandals. 1976 I. MURDOCH *Henry & Cato* II. 319 Gerda was wearing a sun dress with shoulder straps. 1965 Sun loggia [see *pram-park* s.v. *PRAM[2] 3]. 1911 Sun-parlour [see *SOLARIUM 2 a]. 1940 AUDEN *Another Time* 92 The poor old fat banker in the sun-parlour car. 1918 M. B. COOKE *Threshold* 53 Joan went in search of Mr. Farwell and found him reading in the sun porch. 1955 Sun-porch [see *MAKE *sb.*[2] 13]. 1977 *Stornoway Gaz.* 27 Aug. 7/5 (Advt.), For Sale. Detached stone-built house..containing living room, bedroom, kitchen, bathroom, sun porch. 1907 E. WHARTON *Fruit of Tree* III. xxiv. 349 A glazed 'sun-room', mosaic pavements, a marble fountain. 1935 *Archit. Rev.* LXXVIII. 167 It contains nine different types of flat, each with an open balcony and a glass-enclosed sun-room that can be thrown open in fine weather. 1977 *Age* (Melbourne) 18 Jan. 9/6 (Advt.), Comp. an imposing ent. hall, a large and charming sittingroom,..mod. kitchen opens to an excellent sunroom. 1929 *Punch* 17 July p. xxxv/2 (Advt.), If preparing for a sun-bath, a swim, or both, slip into the Jantzen Sun-suit! 1971 'D. HALLIDAY' *Dolly & Doctor Bird* xi. 147, I got out into the garden in my sunsuit. 1937 *Night & Day* 29 July 22/2 Deeply to be deplored are such things as..sun-top dresses. 1972 W. ELLIS *Knife Edge* vi. 114 Emma..innocently seductive in her shorts and sun-top.

12. a. *sun-worshipper* (*transf.* example); *sun-worship* (earlier example); *sun-clouding, -creating, -defying, -disdaining, -enticing, -screening* adjs.

1930 R. CAMPBELL *Adamastor* 91 Stripped are the great sun-clouding planes. 1847 EMERSON *Poems* 84 None so backward in the troop,..But knows the sun-creating sound. 1879 LONGFELLOW *Poet. Wks.* (1910) 137 There is a mountain in the distant West That, sun-defying, in its deep ravines Displays a cross of snow upon its side. 1904 W. DE LA MARE *Henry Brocken* xiii. 150 The sun-disdaining eagle. *Ibid.* vii. 79 His sun-enticing thatch of hair. 1958 *Which?* I. IV. 17/2 CR had a number of the preparations tested for their sunscreening quality. 1813 *Monthly Rev.* LXXI. 477 The sun-worship of the Persians, and the manicheism of the Zend-Avesta..are classed with the monotheism of the Jews. 1966 B. H. DEAL *Fancy's Knell* v. 77 Her red bathing suit [was] brilliant against her white skin. Evidently she wasn't the sun worshiper the others were.

b. *sun-alight, -ambered, -bedazzled, -begotten* (later example), *-bemused, -bitten, -black, -blazoned, -bleached, -brown* (earlier example), *-bruised, -caught, -charged, -coloured, -compelled, -dappled, -dark, -darkened, -dazed, -delighted, -desired, -detested, -dimmed, -dozed, -driven, -eaten, -faded, -fed, -flaked, -flecked* (also *fig.*), *-flooded, -flushed, -fondled, -forgotten, -freckled, -gilded, -glazed, -kissed* (later examples, *spec.* of fruit, freq. with commercial spelling *-kist*), *-lashed, -licked, -mellowed* (*fig.*), *-parched, -ripened, -scarred, -scrubbed, -sculptured, -shafted, -shot, -shy, -soaked* (also *fig.*), *-stained, -strewn, -struck, -swung, -whitened* adjs.

1904 HARDY *Dynasts* I. I. v. 32 Till we sight Famed Milan's aisles of marble, sun-alight. 1951 W. DE LA MARE *Winged Chariot* 23 Sun-ambered, weathered, sweet as new-mown hay. 1946 —— *Traveller* 18 A dwindling, sun-bedazzled moon. 1912 —— *Listeners* 24 A sea Of sun-begotten grain. 1957 L. DURRELL *Bitter Lemons* 118 We'll all subside into sun-bemused tranquillity. 1920 H. G. WELLS *Mr. Britling sees it Through* I. iii. 72 It was a tall, lean, sun-bitten youngish man of forty perhaps. 1923 D. H. LAWRENCE *Birds, Beasts & Flowers* 46 Columns dark and soft, Sunblack men, Soft shafts, sunbreathing mouths. 1947 DYLAN THOMAS *Let.* 3 Aug. (1966) 318 Sunblack webfooted waterboys..bleed from the heat. 1919 V. WOOLF *Night & Day* xx. 275 The sun-blazoned windows. 1835 J. E. ALEXANDER *Sketches in Portugal* xi. 267 Peasants with long and sun-bleached hair floating about their shoulders..stood behind fruit and vegetable baskets. 1979 *Arizona Daily Star* 5 Aug. A10/3 The approaching slick has not hurt business at the long strip of sun-bleached sand. 1861 A. J. MUNBY *Diary* 19 May in D. Hudson *Munby* (1972) 93 His frank intelligent face..has a pure rich sunbrown tint. 1957 L. DURRELL *Bitter Lemons* 138 How could such a sun-bruised world be transformed? 1932 D. GASCOYNE *Roman Balcony* 9 A rusty and serrated leaf, Alive with sun-caught moisture. 1942 E. BOWEN *Seven Winters* 32 A pinkish suncharged gauze. 1926 D. H. LAWRENCE *Sun* iv. 13 She stood a few steps, erect, in front of the sun-coloured woman. 1922 JOYCE *Ulysses* 712 He would hear and somehow reluctantly, sun-compelled, obey the summons of recall. 1924 R. CAMPBELL *Flaming Terrapin* v. 80 The sun-dappled herds a-skipping to the song. 1983 A. PRICE *Gunner Kelly* II. 77 The sun-dappled pools where the stream idled between the trees. 1924 GALSWORTHY *Forest* IV. i, (*stage direction*) Franks comes in. Very sun-dark and thin. 1926 D. H. LAWRENCE *Sun* iii. 11 The child too was another creature, with a peculiar quiet, sun-darkened absorption. *Ibid.* i. 6 She went home, only half-seeing, sun-blinded and sun-dazed. 1942 J. MASEFIELD *Generation Risen* 70 Sun-delighted earth. 1925 BLUNDEN *English Poems* 55 It glittered mist and fire amain, Sun-desired, desiring. 1931 R. CAMPBELL *Georgiad* i. 25 Shame to show your sun-detested sight Among the sons of valour and delight. 1917 D. H. LAWRENCE *Look! We have come Through!* 101 The stars, in their sun-dimmed closes. *a* 1918 W. OWEN *Poems* (1920) 18 So we drowse, sun-dozed. 1909 E. POUND *Personae* 48 The stars of heaven sheathe their glory And sun-driven forth-goeth Settentrion. 1926 D. H. LAWRENCE *Plumed Serpent* xx. 343 She stepped across the sun-eaten plaza. 1887 KIPLING *From Sea to Sea* (1899) I. 34 The maroon cloth..is..neither strained nor meagre nor sunfaded. 1926 D. H. LAWRENCE *Sun* iv. 13 Her sun-faded fair hair in a little cloud. 1917 E. POUND *Lustra* 184 The air is solid sunlight, *apricus*. Sun-fed we dwell there. 1934 S. SPENDER *Vienna* iii. 30 The once sun-flaked walls. 1844 J. R. LOWELL *Poems* 17 Dim vistas, sprinkled o'er with sun-flecked green, Wound through the thickset trunks. *a* 1950 J. CLEARY in Murdoch & Drake-Brockman *Austral. Short Stories* (1951) 438 Her laugh is a warm, tumbling sound, sun-flecked and musical. 1904 M. A. VON ARNIM *Adventures of Elizabeth in Rügen* 156 Up there in the sun-flooded space among the shimmering bracken. 1862 G. M. HOPKINS *Poems* (1967) 10 So those Mermaidens crowded to my rock, And thicken'd, like that drifted bloom, the flock Sun-flushed. *a* 1960 M. TRIST in 'B. James' *Austral. Short Stories* (1963) 258 He was a nice baby, blue-eyed, fair-haired and with sun-flushed skin. 1935 L. MACNEICE *Poems* 42 The light on the sun-fondled trees. 1881 O. WILDE *Poems* 219 Bare to sun-forgotten fields the fire of the sun! 1925 S. O'CASEY *Let.* 7 Feb. (1975) I. 131 One can hardly look for the blossoming of roses in these sun-forgotten places. 1916 W. B. YEATS *Eight Poems*, Imagining a man, And his sun-freckled face. 1892 STEVENSON & OSBOURNE *Wrecker* xii. 190 Day after day, in the sun-gilded cabin, the whiskey-dealer's thermometer stood at 84°. 1960 J. BETJEMAN *Summoned by Bells* iii. 26 Only one harbinger of future woe Came to me in those far, sun-gilded days. 1915 W. J. LOCKE *Jaffery* iii. 36 A fair-bearded..giant..ran up and laid a couple of great sun-glazed hands on my shoulders. 1920 Sunkist [see *Sunshine State* s.v. *SUNSHINE *sb.* 6]. 1979 N. & I. LYONS *Champagne Blues* 172 I'll have a nice glass of tomato juice with a quarter of a Sunkist lemon. 1891 O. WILDE *Picture of Dorian Gray* ix. 161 The green, flickering, sun-lashed garden. 1926 D. H. LAWRENCE *David* ii. 18 He beats himself against the sun-licked pebbles. 1849 C. BRONTË *Shirley* xxxvi. 625 My intention was then formed, but not mature for communication; now it is ripe, sun-mellowed, perfect. 1848 J. R. LOWELL *Poems* 2nd Ser. 65 The next heart-beat, the wind-hurled pile,..Bursts rattling over the sun-parched roof. 1915 G. FRANKAU *Tid'apa* i. 7 Do you know our churchyard at Aden; lone tombs on a sun-parched plain. 1935 *Discovery* June 162/2 The fruit is fully sun-ripened and canned immediately after gathering. 1897 J. L. ALLEN *Choir Invisible* xv. 159 Frenzied fightings and awful deaths had left but the sun-scarred dust. 1955 P. LARKIN *Less Deceived* 19 And how remote that bare and sunscrubbed room. 1955 S. SPENDER *Coll. Poems 1928–53* 159 Already you are beginning to become Fallen tree-trunk with sun-sculptured limbs. 1910 W. DE LA MARE *Three Mulla-Mulgars* xiv. 193 Nod lifted his face and saw..the vast sun-shafted precipices. 1890 R. BRIDGES *Shorter Poems* IV. xiv. 75 I'll sit with my love in the scented hay: And watch the sunshot palaces high. 1936 C. DAY LEWIS *Noah & Waters* 52 Then plunge out of heaven upon his prey, Slanting and swiftsure as a sun-shot ray. *a* 1973 J. R. R. TOLKIEN *Silmarillion* (1977) xvi. 135 What errand have you, Dark Elf, in my lands? An urgent matter, perhaps, that keeps one so sun-shy abroad by day. 1910 H. G. WELLS *Hist. Mr. Polly* vii. 212 He..dreamt..of the East and West Indies until his heart ached to see those sun-soaked lands before he died. 1960 *Times* 29 Feb. 15/1 Falla's four sun-soaked dances of Spain. 1916 D. H. LAWRENCE *Twilight in Italy* 36 Her hands and her face were all sun-bleached and sun-stained. 1916 BLUNDEN *Harbingers* 3, I still can watch the purple-slumbrous main Fretting the sun-strewn air. 1794 T. DWIGHT *Greenfield Hill* VII. 154 Idolatry fans off the vernal breeze, And sun-struck Labour, phrenzied, sinks to peace. 1896 A. E. HOUSMAN *Shropshire Lad* xlii. 62 By blowing realms of woodland With sunstruck vanes afield..Content at heart I followed With my delightful guide. 1963 A. LUBBOCK *Austral. Roundabout* 14 Grey salt-bush, tufts of coarse brownish grass, and stony soil merge into the sun-struck distance. 1874 J. R. LOWELL in *Atlantic Monthly* May 588 Indifferent as the figures on a slate Are to the planet's sun-swung curve Whose bright returns they calculate. 1957 T. HUGHES *Hawk in Rain* 39 He smiles in a mirror, shrinking the whole Sun-swung zodiac of light to a trinket shape On the rise of his eye. 1848 J. R. LOWELL *Poems* 2nd Ser. 64 A great cloud edged with sun-whitened spray.

c. *sun-clear* (later example), *sun-gloved, -gold, -haired, -heavy, -leaved, -round, -sweet* adjs.

1945 W. DE LA MARE *Burning-Glass* 36 The grass takes on a shade Of paradisal green, sun-clear. 1939 DYLAN THOMAS *Map of Love* 6 Comes love's anatomist with sun-gloved hand Who picks the live heart on a diamond. 1911 E. POUND *Canzoni* 5 Guerdoned by thy sun-gold traces. 1938 S. SPENDER *Trial of Judge* I. 18 Let the nordic Sunhaired head be matched against cloud drifts. 1918 D. H. LAWRENCE *New Poems* 9 The glimmer of the limes, sun-heavy sleeping, Goes trembling past me up the College wall. 1939 DYLAN THOMAS in *Poetry* Feb. 26 The sun-leaved holy candlewoods. 1918 E. SITWELL *Clown's Houses* 14 Like wooden bumpkins' sun-round stare. 1937 W. DE LA MARE *This Year, Next Year* 50 Came the woodman with his axe into the sun-sweet glade.

d. *sun-drunk, -fast, -flashed, -glittering, -glowing, -honeyed, -peering* adjs.; *sunbask* vb. intr.

1967 C. B. CHRISTESEN in *Coast to Coast 1965–6* 29 When..taxed on this subject while sun-basking by herself on the top deck. 1925 A. HUXLEY *Selected Poems* 16 The sun-drunk petals. 1962 *Economist* 21 Apr. 250/1 The French have produced a [plastic] geranium which is guaranteed to be sunfast. 1905 Sun-flashed [see *IRIDESCE *v.*]. 1916 BLUNDEN *Harbingers* 11 Odysseus came..And called without my strong sun-glittering gates. 1926 D. H. LAWRENCE *Sun* iv. 14 Like a blot of ink on the pale, sun-glowing slope. 1953 DYLAN THOMAS *Under Milk Wood* (1954) 44 There's the clip clop of horses on the sun-honeyed cobbles of the humming streets. 1923 D. H. LAWRENCE *Birds, Beasts & Flowers* 84 John, oh John, Thou honourable bird Sun-peering eagle.

13. a. sun arc *Cinematogr.*, an arc lamp used to simulate sunlight in film production; **sun-back,** a low-cut back of a garment; also *attrib.*; **sunbaking** *vbl. sb. Austral.*, sunbathing; **sun-bath** (earlier example); **sun-bather,** one who takes a sun-bath; hence (as back-formation) **sun-bathe** *v. intr.*; **sun bed,** (*a*) a lightweight bed or couch for sun-bathing; (*b*) a bed designed for artificial sun-bathing in ultraviolet light; **Sunbelt** *U.S.* (also as two words) [*BELT *sb.*[1] 5 a], a zone consisting of the most southerly states of the U.S., extending from California in the west to the Carolinas in the east; **sun-bonnet** (earlier and later examples); hence **sun-bonneted** *a.*; **sun-break,** (*c*) = *BRISE-SOLEIL; **sun club,** a club for sun-bathers or naturists (*NATURIST 2); **sun compass,** a navigational device for finding true north from the observed direction of the sun, allowing for the time of day; also *fig.* and *attrib.*; **sun-cream,** a creamy preparation rubbed on the skin to protect it from sunburn or to promote sun-tanning; **sun-cure** (earlier example); **sun-dance** (earlier example); **sun-deck,** (*a*) (earlier example); (*b*) *N. Amer.*, a terrace or balcony situated so as to catch the sun; **sun-drenched** *a.*, soaked with sunshine; having (typically) very sunny weather; **sun-dry** *a.* = SUN-DRIED *a.*; **sun-dust,** the motes in a sunbeam; hence **sun-dusted** *a.*; **sun-extinct** *a. poet. nonce-wd.*, inwardly dead; **sun-eye** *poet.*, the sun; **sun flash,** a flash of sunlight; a device or pattern resembling this (see quots.); **sun furnace,** an apparatus constructed of mirrors designed to concentrate solar energy for use in high-temperature experiments and research; **sun gear** *Mech.* = *sun wheel* (*a*); **sun-glade** (earlier example); **sun-glass,** (*a*) (earlier examples); (*c*) *pl.*, spectacles with tinted lenses for protecting the eyes from sunlight; = *dark glasses* (*b*) s.v. *DARK *a.* 13 c; hence **sun-glassed** *a.*, wearing sun-glasses; **sun-glow,** (*a*) also, the colour of this; **sun-grazer** *Astr.* (see quot. 1982); so **sun-grazing** *a.*; **Sun Gun** *Cinemat.*, a proprietary term for a portable incandescent lamp; **sun-helmet** (earlier example); **sun hot** (see quot. 1961); **Sun King** [see *ROI SOLEIL], a sobriquet of Louis XIV of France; also *transf.* and *attrib.*; **sun-lamp,** an electric lamp designed to emit radiation of a similar type to that of sunlight; now esp. one that produces ultraviolet light for therapeutic purposes or to produce an artificial sun-tan; hence **sun-lamped** *a.*; **sun lounge,** (*a*) a room built largely of glass to admit the maximum amount of sunlight; (*b*) *U.S.* = *sun-bed* (*a*) above; **sun-lounger** = *sun-bed* (*a*) above; **sun-motor,** a machine which converts solar energy to another form of energy, such as electrical or mechanical energy; **sun-oil,** (*a*) oil rubbed on the skin to prevent sunburn or promote tanning; (*b*) = *sunflower oil* s.v. SUNFLOWER 4; **sun-painting** = *sun-printing* below; **sun-print** *Photogr.*, a print made from a negative by means of sunlight; a daylight print; so **sun-print** *v.*, **-printing** *vbl. sb.*; **sun-roof,** (*a*) = *sunshine roof* s.v. *SUNSHINE *sb.* 6; (*b*) a part of the roof of a house which is suitable for sunbathing; **sun-scald,** (*a*) esp. damage to trees caused by the bark being dried by excessive heat and wind; (earlier and later examples); **sun-scorch,** the burning of leaves by sunlight when a plant lacks sufficient water; also = *sun-scald*; **sunscreen,** (*a*) (see sense 11 c in Dict.); (*b*) a preparation intended to screen the skin from ultraviolet rays and thereby prevent sunburn; **sun-seeker,** (*a*) *Astronautics*, a photoelectric device used in satellites and spacecraft which maintains its orientation with respect to the sun and can be used to direct instruments and provide navigational information; (*b*) one seeking a sunny place for a holiday or to live in; **sun-shaft:** for *U.S.* read orig. *U.S.* and add later and *fig.* examples; **sunship** [-SHIP], a mock title for the sun; **sunspecs** *colloq.* = **sun-glass* (*c*); **sun-thickened oil,** a polymerized oil of a honey-like consistency, produced from linseed oil by action of the sun and used as a base in oil-painting; **sun valve,** a mechanical device which used the heat of the sun as it appeared or disappeared to turn a lighthouse light off or on; **sun visor,** a projecting shield on a cap, or a hinged screen mounted inside (formerly also outside) a motor vehicle, to shade the eyes from bright sunshine; **sun-wheel,** (*a*) (examples); (*b*) (example).

1928 *Amer. Speech* III. 366 'Back-spot'.., 'baby-spots', 'sunarcs', 'twins', 'floods' and others. **1930** *Sel. Gloss. Motion Pict. Technician* (Acad. Motion Pict. Arts & Sci., Hollywood), *Sun lamps,* a large lamp (*Sun Arc* or *Sun Spot*) reflecting its light by means of a parabolic mirror. **1933** *Sun* (Baltimore) 11 Aug. 8/7 Her sunback suit she casts aside, She is a nudist—off go things. **1934** *Times* 22 June 17/6 Many swimming and bathing suits now have a 'sun-back' and a high throat line. **1955** J. Potts *Death of Stray Cat* ii. 18 Summer people..in..their sunback dresses. **1935** E. Dark *Return to Coolami* xxiv. 262 He had wondered..if Susan liked surfing, if she liked sun-baking. **1977** *Best of Austral. Angler* 63/1 The middle of the day is mostly for sunbaking and dreaming. **1866** *Galaxy* 15 July 544 What you want..is a sun-bath daily. **1941** A. Christie *Evil under Sun* vi. 107, I oiled myself and sunbathed. **1978** 'A. York' *Tallant for Disaster* i. 17 Supposing the *Gazette* did learn that Mistress Castanos does sunbathe in the altogether? **1929** *Daily Express* 14 Jan. 19/3 The groups of Lido sun-bathers. **1973** H. Nielsen *Severed Key* xviii. 189 Sunny walked on the beach... The sun-bathers and surfers were far behind her. **1967** *Punch* 11 Jan. p. viii/2 The optimistic can snap up adjustable folding sun beds. **1979** *Sunday Express* 28 Jan. 16/6 Ever sat down on a foreign beach for a bit of blissful solitude only to find your local pub bore a couple of sunbeds away? **1980** *West Lancs. Even. Gaz.* 9 July 14 (Advt.), 'Mermaid Sontegra' Canopy Sun Beds £2 per half-hour session or course of 6 £10. **1983** *Daily Tel.* 31 Jan. 15/8 Sunbed lamps are designed to cut down ultra-violet B light, which burns before it tans. **1969** K. P. Phillips *Emerging Republican Majority* v. 438 Chart 134 illustrates how the electoral votes of the Sun Belt will have almost tripled in the half-century between 1920 and 1970. **1976** *National Observer* (U.S.) 24 Apr. 12/1 The movement is away from the noise, dirt, crime, and congestion of the oldest urban centers and to the so-called Sunbelt. **1980** *Christian Sci. Monitor* (Midwestern ed.) 4 Dec. 2/2 In some of the wooded parts of this bustling Sunbelt city, white-tailed deer have been spotted. **1837** *Southern Lit. Messenger* III. 332 She had on a deep sun-bonnet. **1941** J. Masefield *In Mill* 130 All the horses were wearing sun-bonnets and ear-flappers. **1981** M. Byrd *California Thriller* (1984) x. 82 She wore a sun-bonnet..and carried a clipboard. **1839** *Southern Lit. Messenger* V. 113/2 The bevy of sun-bonnetted lasses, who gave us of their pies and apples. **1947** *Archit. Rev.* CII. 148/1 Covering one-third of it is a key pattern of loggia-like sun-breaks, the scale of which is exactly double that of the rest of the elevation. **1969** J. Elliot *Duel* iii. iv. 275 The other creatures on the beach..sat under sun-breaks, walked in and out of the water, tinkered with boats. **1936** *Sun Bathing Rev.* June–July 43/2 (*heading*) Non-nudist sun clubs. **1950** *Sun Bather* Spring 23/1 That's my ideal sun-club. In the National Trust Land, on reserved beaches. In our own gardens, where suitable. **1978** *Lancashire Life* July 31/3 Although Lancashire has four Sun Clubs (naturist terminology for nudist camps), none is on the coast. **1925** *Nat. Geogr. Mag.* Nov. 523/2 In clear weather the sun compass enabled us to do accurate navigation... Mr. Albert H. Bumstead..invented it for our trip and I consider it a great contribution to science. **1947** *New Biol.* III. 14 The sun may be either to the left or to the right of a marching hopper and it appears that the hopper while marching keeps its direction with reference to the sun. That such 'sun-compass orientation' exists was proved by ingenious experiments in the field. **1967** J. Grierson *Heroes of Polar Skies* iv. 65 Byrd..expected to maintain his heading by the sun compass. **1966** L. Cohen *Beautiful Losers* i. 91 There is a tube of sun cream in the glove compartment. **1863** L. M. Alcott *Hospital Sketches* v. 70 Very soon after leaving the care of my ward, I discovered that I had no appetite, and cut the bread and butter interests almost entirely, trying the exercise and sun cure instead. **1849** M. H. Eastman *Dahcotah* p. xxii, The Sioux worship the sun. The *sun dance* is performed by young warriors who dance, at intervals of five minutes, for several days. **1897** M. Kingsley *Trav. W. Afr.* 130 The captain is on top of the sun deck most of the time. **1950** J. D. MacDonald *Brass Cupcake* (1955) ii. 15 The apartment has a big bedroom, sun deck, living room. **1970** R. Lowell *Notebk.* 111 Thirty raspberry bushes stacked on my sundeck. **1924** A. J. Small *Frozen Gold* ii. 47 He was no longer in the sun-drenched Spring. He had flung himself back..into the winter. **1929** *Radio Times* 8 Nov. 421/3 Honey..from sun-drenched meadows. **1979** R. Gillespie *Crossword Mystery* i. 27 The sun-drenched sidewalk. **1885** W. B. Yeats in *Dublin Univ. Rev.* June 110/2 And with a sun-dry weed He wrote it on the sands. **1909** H. G Wells *Tono-Bungay* i. ii. 51 The seaports of the sun-dry Levant. **1849** Thoreau *Week Concord Riv.* 373 The particles of golden light, the sun-dust, have..fallen like seeds on the earth. **1964** W. Golding *Spire* i. 10 Those two men posed so centrally in the sundust. **1946** R. S. Thomas *Stones of Field* 42 The breeze could bring..songs to his ear from the sun-dusted moor. **1929** D. H. Lawrence *Pansies* 120 It is only immoral to be dead-alive, Sun-extinct And busy putting out the sun In other people. **1931** C. Day Lewis *From Feathers to Iron* 23 That golden seed extends Beneath the sun-eye, the father, To ear at the earth's ends. **1960** H. Hayward *Antique Coll.* 272/1 *Sun flash horse brass,* a face piece, extremely popular in Kent,..originally a disc of latten..with its centre hand-raised into a high dome or boss and encircled with a wide, flat rim. **1971** J. S. Gunn *Opal Terminol.* 46 *Sunflash,* pattern exhibiting flashes of colour, usually weak, in a dark potch background. **1949** *Sun* (Baltimore) 25 Feb. 17/3 A sun furnace which..can concentrate the temperature of the sun's surface on a space about three inches in diameter. **1955** *Sci. News Let.* 21 May 328/2 French scientists are using the sun furnace to produce and study some minerals which are made at temperatures too high for ordinary furnaces. **1935** R. Trautschold *Standard Gear Bk.* xi. 173 The relative speed of the driven internal gear in terms of the speed of the driving sun gears. **1975** *Sci. Amer.* Dec. 120/2 When the motor drives the cylinder, the idler gear and its companion rotate as a planetary system around the sun gear that is fixed to the base. **1849** H. Melville *Mardi* I. xxxix. 152 He would not be able to perceive us, owing to our being in what mariners denominate the sun-glade, or that part of the ocean upon which the sun's rays flash with peculiar intensity. **1804** M. Lewis *Jrnl.* 19 Aug. in *Orig. Jrnls. Lewis & Clark Expedition* (1904) I. ii. 112 The main chief Brack fast with us & beged for a Sun glass. **1806** W. Clark *Jrnl.* 2 Apr. in *Ibid.* (1905) IV. xxiv. 236 An Indian whome I hired for a Sun glass. **1927** A. Conan Doyle *Case-Bk. of Sherlock Holmes* xii. 306 He *had* grey-tinted sun-glasses. **1976** 'B. Shelby' *Great Pebble Affair* 119 My sunglasses fell from my hand, cracking one of the hand-ground lenses. **1961** *John o' London's* 6 July 25/1 The sun-glassed eyes of the vacation-bound. **1972** K. Bonfiglioli *Don't point that Thing at Me* x. 86 Hatted and sun-glassed to the point of anonymity. **1977** *Western Morning News* 30 Aug. 4 (Advt.), 1976 Vauxhall Chevette 4-door Saloon. Sunglow. Low mileage, family saloon. **1965** *Observer* 17 Oct. 13/4 The comet may herald the return of a family of 'sun-grazing' comets..which produced some spectacular effects in the last century. *Ibid.*, One theory has suggested that this group of 'sun-grazers' may have been formed in the wake of the sun after it passed through a cosmic dust cloud. **1982** *New Scientist* 21 Oct. 158/3 Comets that pass near the Sun are called 'sungrazers'. **1961** *Official Gaz.* (U.S. Patent Office) 14 Nov. tm 49/1 Sylvania Electrical Products, Inc... *Sun Gun,* for motion picture camera lamps and reflectors. **1969** J. Whale *Half-Shut Eye* iii. 30 The battery-powered hand-lights which cameramen call sun-guns. **1976** *Listener* 12 Feb. 171/2 By shooting a gun numerous times and flashing a sun-gun, we persuaded hordes of bats to fly round the cave. **1879** *Cornh. Mag.* XXXIX. 516 Saint-Luc wore a sun-helmet. **1873** C. I. G. Rampini *Lett. from Jamaica* 179 Rockatone (stone) at ribber-bottom (bottom of the river) no know sun hot. **1961** F. G. Cassidy *Jamaica Talk* vi. 109 The oldest, and still current expression [for *noon*] is *sun hot.* **1939** O. Lancaster *Homes Sweet Homes* 26 Few of his fellow-sovereigns enjoyed the robust health of the Sun King. **1976** N. Thornburg *Cutter & Bone* xi. 258 The women were heavy and overdressed, with elaborate Sun King coiffeurs [sic]. **1977** *Time* 8 Aug. 37/1 Yves Saint Laurent, the Sun King of fashion. **1885** *List of Subscribers, Classified* (United Telephone Co.) (ed. 6) 87 Electric Sun Lamp & Power Co., Limited. **1934** L. Mumford *Metropolitan Milieu in City Devel.* (1946) ii. 34 Finally the sun lamps.. overcame the lack of real sunlight in these misplanned domestic quarters. **1957** C. MacInnes *City of Spades* ii. v. 141 You're getting so pale... You must have some sun-lamp treatment. **1980** J. Hone *Flowers of Forest* i. 61 An unreal tan... Something assumed..with lotions or sun-lamps. **1976** 'Trevanian' *Main* (1977) xi. 219 There is a lighter tone to his sun-lamped bronze around the ears, indicating that his haircut is fresh. **1910** *Bradshaw's Railway Guide* Apr. 1020 Linden Hall Hydro... Splendid winter garden and sun-lounge. **1971** [see *double-glazing* s.v. *double *a.* A. 6]. **1979** M. Babson *So soon done For* xiv. 103 The sun lounges, the chairs, the cushions..all belonged to the Norrises... She was reclining in one of the sunlounges. **1972** D. Lees *Zodiac* 191 We found ourselves side by side on one of the sun loungers. **1980** *Daily Tel.* 10 Dec. 3/7 A morning on your sun-lounger on one of Tobago's deserted beaches. **1884** *Cassell's Family Mag.* Mar. 252/1 The Sun-Motor. Our illustration gives a general view of the machine constructed by Captain J. Ericsson of New York, for utilising the sun's heat in producing mechanical power. *Ibid.* 252/2 The sun-motor may be very useful in some hot parts of the globe. **1952** 'J. Wyndham' in 'E. Crispin' *Best SF* (1955) The main batteries charged by the sun-motor. **1945** 'L. Lewis' *Birthday Murder* (1951) x. 151 Her face bare of lipstick and shining with sun oil. **1981** *Sci. Amer.* Feb. 62/3 The production of 'sunoil' amounted to 5.6 million tons in 1979–80. **1876** C. M. Yonge *Three Brides* I. ix. 142 The likeness of a young man..where the hard verities of sun-painting had refused to veil the haggard trace of early dissipation. **1971** *Country Life* 8 July 104/1 In the 1840s, before artists reacted violently against the threat posed by the new so-called sun paintings. **1858** *Lake Price Man. Photogr. Manip.* 218 Such a negative would suffer considerably by being sun-printed. *Ibid.*, Injured by sun-printing. **1928** Blunden *Undertones of War* viii. 78 A large sunprint on view at headquarters suspected many enemy mine-shafts. **1966** T. Pynchon *Crying of Lot 49* ii. 38 A small automobile with a sun roof. **1972** *Country Life* 15 June (Suppl.) 22/2, 5 bedrooms, bathroom, 2 w.c.'s, flat sun-roof. **1980** *Daily Tel.* 23 Jan. 14/4 Electrically operated sunroof and windows and central locking system are included as standard. **1855** *Trans. Mich. Agric. Soc.* VI. 158 The tree has received a sun scald, and the sap soured in consequence. **1932** Felt & Rankin *Insects & Diseases of Ornamental Trees & Shrubs* iv. 116 Beech, spruce and pines are subject to sun-scald. **1967** *New Scientist* 30 Nov. 546/2 The temperature of the fruit [*sc.* tomatoes] directly exposed to the sun is at least 5 to 10 deg C higher than the surrounding air, and this high temperature frequently causes sunscald. **1928** B. D. Jackson *Gloss. Bot. Terms* (ed. 4) 469/1 Sun scorch. The burning of foliage when the soil is parched. **1932** Felt & Rankin *Insects & Diseases of Ornamental Trees & Shrubs* iv. 115 The leaves may transpire more water than the roots can take up in a given length of time. This condition will cause sun-scorch of the leaves. **1950** *N.Z. Jrnl. Agric.* Jan. 5/2 Do not place them [*sc.* unripe tomatoes] at a window exposed to strong sunlight, as this will induce sun scorch and render the skin tough. **1969** *Gloss. Landscape Work* (*B.S.I.*) v. 28 Sun scorch (sunscald), damage caused to bark by unaccustomed exposure to the sun, for example, following the sudden removal of shade. **1958** *Which?* I. iv. 17/2 Some sunscreens are lotions, some oils, some creams, others aerosols. **1980** *Daily Tel.* 22 Feb. 15/2 Any exposed area of skin should always be protected, either by a moisturiser or—in hot sun—by a sunscreen. **1956** *Nature* 7 Apr. 645/1 The Royal Aircraft Establishment..is also studying the design of a sun-seeker for carriage in the rocket. The sun-seeker would be used for measurements of solar radiations and for obtaining ultra-violet pictures of the sun at high altitude. **1963** M. Caidin *Man-in-Space Dict.* 198 As used in manned spacecraft or robot satellites, the sunseeker 'seeks out' the sun by its brightness. An automatic pilot notes the position and angle of the sunseeker, and fires reaction jets to keep the spacecraft oriented on the basis of the position of the sun. **1970** *Times* 31 Dec. (Rev. of Year) p. vii./5 Sunseekers are beginning to look farther afield than the popular Spanish mainland. **1975** D. Francis *High Stakes* ix. 141 Selling dream retirement homes to elderly sun-seekers. *a* **1918** W. Owen *Poems* (1963) 64 Who's prejudiced Against a grimed hand when his own's quite dust, Less live than specks that in the sun-shafts turn. **1941** Blunden *Thomas Hardy* iv. 67 The secret of that apparent indifference was his lifelong purpose..of striking for truth under the intense sunshafts of philosophic poetry. **1974** F. Warner *Meeting Ends* i. 1 A sunshaft strikes the steeple by my room. **1836** Poe *Four Beasts in One* II. 206 You need not look up at the heavens; his Sunship is not there—at least not the Sunship adored by the Syrians. *That* deity..is worshipped under the figure of a large stone pillar. **1975** *Observer* (Colour Suppl.) 20 June 13/4 The Reactolite 90/20 lenses..capable of withstanding the impact of a $1\frac{1}{8}$ oz. steel ball dropped from a height of 50 in., more than double the requirement of the United States' stringent sunspec regulations. **1976** *Punch* 11 Aug. 234/1 Choose a chair and pull up a glass, push up the sunspecs and just drink in this room. **1935** E. Neuhaus tr. *Doerner's Materials of Artist* iii. 105 Sun-thickened oil is to be preferred to boiled oils, as also to the resin-oil varnishes. **1975** U. Dix tr. *Wehlte's Materials & Techniques of Painting* 389 Sun-thickened oil darkens rapidly when stored in tin canisters. **1910** *Chambers's Jrnl.* Sept. 620/2 One great feature of this beacon is the sun-valve, whereby the light is ignited and extinguished automatically at varying periods, according to the time of year. **1936** W. H. McCormick *Mod. Bk. Lighthouses* xi. 92 The light is automatically turned on and off..by placing the light in charge of an 'AGA' Sunvalve. **1975** Hague & Christie *Lighthouses* v. 159 Early in the present century the.. operation of unattended lighthouses..was revolutionised by the invention of the sun- or light-valve. This..consists of an arrangement of reflective gold-plated bars supporting a suspended absorbent black rod; when lit by the sun this rod absorbs the direct heat and that reflected from the other bars and expands downwards thereby cutting off the supply of gas. The first sun-valve was put into operation..near Stockholm in 1907. **1926** *Daily Colonist* (Victoria, B.C.) 8 July 2/1 Bright Sunshine is fine—enjoy it all the more by wearing a sun visor... A necessity to campers, sportsmen, etc. **1936** *Times* 19 Oct. 8/2 The inside fittings include..sun visors, footrests, etc. **1978** L. Heren *Growing up on The Times* ii. 30, I..had a large American Ford V8 car fitted with a sun visor projecting over the windscreen. **1827** Sun-wheel [see *planet-wheel* s.v. *planet *sb.*[1] 4]. **1965** *Daily Mail* 28 Oct. 7/3 If we convert the reverse wheel into a sun wheel (stationary wheel) by introducing a brake band, we'll get an intermediate gear ratio and three speeds. **1973** T. Pynchon *Gravity's Rainbow* i. 100 The symbol used is a rude mandala, a red circle with a thick black cross inside, recognizable as the ancient sun-wheel from which tradition says the swastika was broken.

b. sun-bear (later examples); **sun gem,** for *cornutus* substitute *cornuta* and add: distinguished by tufts of feathers on either side of the head; (examples); **sun-perch** (earlier and later examples); **sun plant,** (*a*) a small, half-hardy, annual herb belonging to one of several varieties of *Portulaca grandiflora,* native to Brazil and bearing single or clustered terminal flowers which open in sun; (*b*) a plant that grows best in full sunlight; **sun-rose:** cf. *Helianthemum; (earlier example); **sun-spider** = Solpugid; **sun-trout** (earlier example).

1894 N. B. Denys in W. W. Skeat *Malay Magic* (1900) v. 183 The Malayan Sun-bear, the only animal of the bear species in the Peninsula... It is black in colour, with the exception of a semi-lunar-shaped patch of white on the breast, and a yellowish-white patch on the snout and upper jaw. **1931** *Times Educ. Suppl.* 19 Sept. (Home & Classroom Suppl.) p. iv/3 Mr. Charles Tonge has presented a young Malay sun-bear. **1965** R. McKie *Company of Animals* ix. 146 Sun bears can become dangerous as their power increases with age. **1861** J. Gould *Monogr. Trochilidæ* IV. 212 (*heading*) Sun Gem. **1912** Brabourne & Chubb *Birds S. Amer.* 144 *Heliactin..bilophum..* Sun-Gem. **1804** Lewis & Clark *Orig. Jrnls. Lewis & Clark Exped.* (1905) VI. 174 In this lake there is also.. Sunperch. **1876** 'Mark Twain' *Tom Sawyer* xiv. 123 They were back again with some handsome bass, a couple of sun-perch and a small catfish. **1902** W. S. Gordon *Recoll. Old Quarter* 177 How full were the holes of crawfish, turtles, sun-perch, grindles, and of daring, voracious pike. **1887** G. Nicholson *Illustr. Dict. Gardening* III. 202/2 Sun-plant. Fl[owers] yellow, purple,..terminal. **1900** B. D. Jackson *Gloss. Bot. Terms* 260/2 Sun-plants, plants which prefer full sun-light: their stems are often short, the leaves have the palisade cells well developed. **1963** *Oxf. Bk. Garden Flowers* 140/2 Sun Plant. The yellow, pink, scarlet or purple cup-shaped flowers of this little plant from Brazil open in direct sunshine and close in shadow. **1979** W. M. M. Baron *Organization in Plants* (ed. 3) iii. 42 Shade plants can utilize low light intensities more efficiently than sun plants. **1822** Sun-rose [see *helianthemum]. **1959** *Southwest Rev.* XLIV. 137/1 An arachnid frequently, and naturally, confused with the true vinegarone is the solpugid—or wind-scorpion, wind-spider, or sun-spider. **1974** *Stand. Encycl. S. Afr.* X. 217/1 The sun-spider can easily be distinguished from all other arachnids by the two immense jaws at the front of the head. **1884** G. B. Goode *Fisheries U.S.: Nat. Hist. Aquatic Animals* I. 362 In the Southern Atlantic States it [*sc.* the squeteague] is called 'Grey Trout', 'Sun Trout', and 'Shad Trout'.

‖ **sun** (sʊn), *sb.*[2] Pl. **sun.** [Jap.] A Japanese

unit of length, equivalent to approximately 1·19 inches (3·03 centimetres).

1727 [see *SHAKU 1]. **1888** *Encycl. Brit.* XXIV. 490/2 Japan... Sun, 10 = shaku (11·948 inches = 10/33 metre), 6 = ken, 60 = cho. **1956** K. TOMIKI *Judo* i. 22 Regulations require that the surrounding mats be all 5 *sun* (about 6 inches) lower than the contest area.

sun, *v.* Add: **2. b.** Now esp. = *sun-bathe* vb. s.v. *SUN *sb.* 13 a. (Later examples.)

1933 V. WOOLF *Jrnl.* 13 Apr. in *Writer's Diary* (1953) 197 But we go today and I shall sun, with only a few books. **1968** *Sat. Rev.* (U.S.) 23 Nov. 48/1 Three beaches where you can swim and sun stark naked. **1976** E. DEWHURST *After Bail* vii. 90 The sun never does anything to my lily-white skin... Alan doesn't let me sun for too long.

sunbeam. Add: **1. d.** Someone, esp. a woman or girl, who enlivens or cheers another. Cf. (*little*) *ray of sunshine* s.v. *RAY sb.[1] 1 a.

1886 C. M. YONGE *Chantry House* II. xxi. 190 She was always a sunbeam, with her ever ready attention. **1900** C. H. CHAMBERS *Tyranny of Tears* IV. 128 We're all very sorry you're going—particularly cook. Cook's very strong in her attachments... Cook's words was, 'This'll be a dull 'ouse when the little sunbeam's gone.' **1943** F. THOMPSON *Candleford Green* viii. 133 Girls..of the type then called 'sunbeams in the home': good, affectionate, home-loving girls. **1970** G. HEYER *Charity Girl* x. 150 She couldn't conceive how she had ever contrived to exist without 'our sweet little sunbeam'.

sunburn, *sb.* Add: **2.** The name of a fashion colour.

1923 *Daily Mail* 11 Sept. 11 Nude, Sunburn, Mulatto, and all shades. **1932** *Barker's Sales Catal.* 27 Poplin tennis shirts... Guaranteed fast self colours of blue, champagne, helio, ivory, sunburn, white and light grey.

sunburn, *v.* **2.** (Later examples.)

1873 J. H. BEADLE *Undevel. West* xxix. 640 An Indian will 'sunburn' as much or even more than a white man. **1928** *Daily Mail* 6 Aug. 12/6 One girl tells me she 'doesn't sunburn easily'. **1962** L. DEIGHTON *Ipcress File* i. 14 He had a clear complexion that sunburnt easily.

sunburst. Add: **2. b.** *attrib.* of things designed or arranged as conventional or stylized representations of the sun and its rays; esp. *sunburst clock*, a clock framed by radiating arms; *sunburst pleat* = *sun-ray pleat* s.v. *SUN-RAY 2 b.

1908 *Sears, Roebuck Catal.* 362/2 Salt and pepper shakers. In beautiful sunburst pattern. **1920** *Glasgow Herald* 29 Apr. 6 Her bouquet was of 'sunburst' roses. **1927** A. E. W. MASON *No Other Tiger* xxiii. 260 They sold the lot—the emerald ring, the diamond sunburst ear-rings and all. **1939** M. B. PICKEN *Lang. of Fashion* 113/2 *Sunburst p*[*laits*], accordion-like plaits that are narrow at top and wider at the bottom, thus producing a flare. Fabric plaited on bias so that plaits radiate from a center. **1949** M. STEEN *Twilight on Floods* III. iv. 426 The gilt sunburst clock over the fireplace. **1962** M. KELLY *Due to a Death* ix. 152 There was a sunburst window over the hairdresser's door. **1969** M. TRIPP *Malice & Maternal Instinct* i. 6 A sunburst clock on one of the blue walls in the main room. **1980** *News & Observer* (Raleigh, N. Carolina) 28 Oct. 17/7 The sun set Sunday on the familiar sunburst insignia.

sundae (sʌ·ndeⁱ). orig. *U.S.* Also (*rarely*) **sundi.** [Origin uncertain. There exist a number of differing accounts both of the invention of the dish and of the coinage of its name.

The name is generally explained as an alteration of *Sunday*, either because the dish originally included left-over ice-cream sold cheaply on Monday, or because it was at first sold only on Sunday, having, according to some accounts, been devised to circumvent Sunday legislation. The alteration of the spelling is sometimes said to be out of deference to religious people's feelings about the word *Sunday*. For several accounts see H. L. Mencken, *The American Language* Suppl. I. (1945), pp. 376–7.]

A confection of ice-cream topped or mixed with crushed fruit, nuts, syrup, whipped cream, etc. locally also called *college ice*.

1897 W. A. BONHAM *Mod. Guide for Soda Dispensers* 126 Peach Sundae. Ice cream, vanilla or peach..5 ounces. Crushed or sliced peaches..2 ounces. Serve with a spoon. Pear, orange, raspberry and other fruit sundaes are made by adding the syrup or fruit to the ice cream. **1904** *N.Y. Evening Post* 21 May (Sat. Suppl.) 4/7 The Sundi, so popular at the confectioner's, can be prepared at home. Make a rich vanilla ice cream and over it pour the juice of your preserved fruits. **1904** *Minneapolis Times* 15 June 6 In one of the Jersey City churches fans and lemonade are distributed. Some brands of 'sundae' might be added with propriety. **1910** *Chambers's Jrnl.* July 431/1 A sundae—a mixture of ice-cream, soda-water, and raspberry juice. **1927** A. P. HERBERT *Plain Jane* 88 I'm fizzy and fiery and fruity and tense, So let's have a sundae and hang the expense! **1951** T. STERLING *House without Door* ii. 22 Year after year..Schrafft's had been serving lamb and mint jelly and hot fudge sundaes to others. **1970** *Kay & Co.* (Worcester) *Catal.* 1970/71, 896 Six Bohemian sundae glasses in the Zorka design... Perfect for all sweets.

Sundanese, *sb.* (Earlier example.)

1878 [see *MADURESE *a.* and *sb.*].

‖ **sundang** (sūndā·ŋ). [Malay.] A heavy two-edged sword used in Malaysia.

1902 *Encycl. Brit.* XXX. 497/1 Malays use...short broad swords called *sûndang*. **1936** G. B. GARDNER *Keris* i. 39 The *sundang* is two edged and may be straight or sinuous. **1947** R. WINSTEDT *Malays* 165 The type..is closer to the Bugis *sundang* or short sword. **1972** M. SHEPPARD *Taman Indera* 133 The largest member of the kris family is the *Sundang*, the sword kris. It originated in the Celebes... The Sundang is a cutting and slashing weapon and is not intended for thrusting.

Sunday, *sb.* Add: **1. c.** *a month of Sundays* (earlier example); *Sunday out* (earlier example); hence *Sunday outer*; *Sunday-go-to-meeting clothes* (earlier examples); also *ellipt.* as *Sunday-go-to-meetings*.

1831 Sunday-go-to-meetings [see *GO-TO-MEETING *sb.*]. **1831** J. R. MOTTE *Diary* 28 Aug. in A. H. Cole *Charleston goes to Harvard* (1940) 100 Rose at 7, and having shaved and dressed myself,—in Sunday-go-to-meeting clothes, started for a walk to Boston. **1841** *Punch* 21 Aug. 65/1 A veritable footman,..upon the occasion of his 'Sunday out'. **1846** D. CORCORAN *Pickings from Picayune* 49 The hoosier asked him if he thought him 'darn'd fool enough to dirty his Sunday-go-to-meetin' clothes'? **1847** J. CODMAN *Sailor's Life & Sailor's Yarns* 25 He..dressed himself in his 'Sunday-go-to-meetings'..and bade adieu to home. **1849** G. E. JEWSBURY *Let.* 29 Mar. (1892) 286 If I don't get a better letter from you, or at least a letter with something in it, you may pass 'a month of Sundays' at breakfast without any letter from me. **1879** DICKENS *Life Charles James Mathews* I. i. 30 A couple advanced who evidently did not belong to the usual class of 'Sunday outers'.

d. *pl. ellipt.* for: (*a*) Sunday clothes or best; (*b*) Sunday newspapers.

(*a*) **1901** 'MARK TWAIN' in *Century Mag.* Nov. 26/2 Tommy was..not in his Sundays, but in his dreadful work-clothes. **1933** *Punch* 14 June 663/1 Tom was busy brushing up his Sundays to go a-calling at the station-master's house. **1944** E. CARR *House of All Sorts* 89 Neither of them noticed the dust on his 'Sundays' as they smiled off down the street.

(*b*) **1949** E. BENN *Happier Days* x. 116 The Sundays and Weeklies were outside the squabbles of the Dailies. **1963** *Listener* 24 Jan. 175/3 An English reviewer, writing in one of the 'posh Sundays'..recently claimed that only Dubliners are now writing outstanding prose. **1976** T. STOPPARD *Dirty Linen* 9 They each carry several newspapers, a whole crop of the day's papers and the Sundays. **1983** *Listener* 27 Jan. 18/3 There are the smart Sundays, the *Guardian's* Agenda page on Monday mornings, and pieces such as this in the literate weeklies.

3. *Sunday('s) suit* (earlier example not in the possessive); carrying out an activity only on Sundays or for pleasure (on the analogy of **Sunday driver*, **Sunday painter*), as *Sunday architect, artist, golfer, novelist, poet, sailor*; **Sunday best** (earlier examples); also **Sunday's best** and *transf.* and *attrib.*; **Sunday child** (earlier example); **Sunday closing,** the closing on Sundays of shops, except for the sale of certain commodities, or of public houses, etc.; **Sunday driver,** one who drives chiefly at week-ends, freq. an unpractised, slow, or unskilful driver; **Sunday face:** for (*Sc.*) read (orig. *Sc.*); (later example); also **Sunday's face;** hence **Sunday-faced** *a.*; **Sunday joint,** a roasted joint of meat traditionally served for Sunday lunch; **Sunday lunch,** the traditional large meal served at midday on Sunday; **Sunday observance,** the keeping of Sunday as a day of rest and worship; **Sunday painter,** an amateur painter, one who paints purely for pleasure; often applied to a naïve painter (*NAÏVE *a.* 1 c), esp. Henri Rousseau; **Sunday punch** *U.S. slang*, a knock-out blow (of the fist); also *transf.*; **Sunday supplement,** an illustrated section issued with a Sunday newspaper, sometimes characterized by the portrayal of voguish living.

1978 *Listener* 6 Apr. 439/1 A small temple of individualism..by a Sunday architect. **1978** *Times* 12 Apr. 16/5 Those who think the Berlin Wall was built..for Sunday artists to exhibit their wares on. **1794** Sunday's best [see BEST *a.* 8 d]. [**1844** G. E. JEWSBURY *Let.* 17 Sept. (1892) 143 So, on the whole, you may set it down as one of the best good deeds you ever did—quite a 'Sunday best.'] **1846** *Amulet* 12 Some urchins, dressed out 'in their Sunday's best', all neatly clean. **1846** *Godey's Mag.* July 8/2 Like most of the nobility he dresses with the utmost plainness, hardly above the substantial Yankee 'squire' in his Sunday best. **1849** N. P. WILLIS *Rural Lett.* iii. 325 It was that kind of Sabbath weather in which Nature seems dressed and resting—every tree looking its 'Sunday best'. **1859** [see BEST *a.* 8 d]. **1969** R. BLYTHE *Akenfield* ii. 59 Sunday-best suits. **1886** C. M. YONGE *Chantry House* I. i. 8 He was punished for 'telling fibs', though the housemaid used to speak..of his being a 'Sunday child'. **1850** *Punch* 31 Aug. 92/2 The Sunday closing of the country Post was considered no other than an unmeaning rant of a party. **1863** *Punch* 28 Mar. 130 (*caption*) Probable effect of Mr. Somes's Sunday Closing Bill. **1881** *Act* 44 & 45 *Vict.* c. 61 s. 5 This Act may be cited as the Sunday Closing (Wales) Act, 1881. **1932** U. SINCLAIR *Candid Remin.* II. ix. 60 He would join the church, sign pledges, vote for Sunday closing. **1971** *Reader's Digest Family Guide to Law* 660/2 Some areas—parts of Wales and Monmouthshire—have Sunday closing [of public houses] by law. **1925** *New Yorker* 11 July 11/1 The Sunday painter is to the art-artist what the Sunday driver is to the owner of the Hispano or Rolls-Royce. **1942** *Sun* (Baltimore) 26 Jan. 18/3 Sunday drivers and sightseers accounted for more than seventy per cent of the total number of cars passing along the Eastern avenue road. **1975** L. DEIGHTON *Yesterday's Spy* xx. 161 The Sunday drivers creeping along the promenade. *a* **1779** D. GRAHAM *Writings* (1883) II. 51 Put on a Sunday's face, and sigh as ye were a saint. **1786** BURNS *What ails ye Now* in *Poems ascribed to R. Burns* (1801) 29 Wi' pinch I put a Sunday's face on, An' snoov'd awa' before the Session. **1906** E. DYSON *Fact'ry 'Ands* xiii. 165 His Trowsis had er slitherin' chin, 'n' ther Sunday face iv er sick sheep. **1910** T. S. ELIOT in *Harvard Advocate* 26 Jan. 114 Sunday: this satisfied procession Of definite Sunday faces. **1934** DYLAN THOMAS 18 *Poems* 25 For, sunday faced, with dusters in my glove, Chaste and the chaser, man with the cockshut eye. **1928** J. BUCHAN *Runagates Club* xii. 319 His clothes ..were workman-like, and looked as if they belonged to him—no more the uneasy knickerbockers of the Sunday golfer. *c* **1921** D. H. LAWRENCE *Mr. Noon* in *Mod. Lover* (1934) 172 They were socialists and vegetarians... None of the horrors of Sunday joints. **1980** 'M. HEBDEN' *Pel under Pressure* v. 47 He was lying on the floor, trussed up like a Sunday joint. **1932** E. M. DELAFIELD *Thank Heaven Fasting* III. ii. 263 Mr. Pelham was sleeping, after Sunday lunch. **1973** 'M. UNDERWOOD' *Reward for Defector* viii. 63 They sat down to roast lamb, roast potatoes, cauliflower with a cheese sauce and brussel sprouts... 'Mrs Tidmarsh enjoys cooking a proper Sunday lunch.' **1960** *News Chron.* 9 Mar. 6 Mr. Bratby may be a professional painter, but he is a Sunday novelist. [**1785**: see OBSERVANCE 1 a.] **1857** *Punch* 4 July 4/2 Having put down the Sabbatarians and secured rational liberty to the millions in respect to Sunday observance. **1973** J. WAINWRIGHT *High-Class Kill* 209 Pornographic literature—and blue films—and illegal gambling—and anything else the Sunday Observance crowd can think up. **1925** Sunday painter [see *Sunday driver* above]. **1948** R. O. DUNLOP *Understanding Pictures* iv. 26 Chief of these 'Sunday' painters was the *Douanier* Rousseau—so-called because he was for long a customs official. **1961** M. LEAKE tr. *Bouret's Henri Rousseau* 170 After the publication of this text [*sc.* R. Grey's *Henri Rousseau*] in 1922, the label 'Sunday-painters' became attached to the naïf and primitive painters and to the popular realist masters, and still survives. **1980** B. BAINBRIDGE *Winter Garden* xii. 88 He gathered there were few actual artists in the room. A General was pointed out to him and an Admiral, both retired. He supposed they were Sunday painters, rather like Churchill and Roosevelt. **1979** M. MCCARTHY *Cannibals & Missionaries* iii. 73 The Senator..calls himself a 'Sunday poet', so he doesn't publish. **1929** D. RUNYON in *Cosmopolitan* Oct. 64/1 If you argue with Dave the Dude too much he is apt to reach over and lay his Sunday punch on your snoot. **1944** W. W. ELTON et al. *Guide Naval Aviation* iv. 71 The real 'Sunday punch' of naval aviation is the torpedo bomber. **1979** E. NEWMAN (*title*) Sunday punch. **1973** H. NIELSEN *Severed Key* iii. 27 As the day cleared, a few hardy Sunday sailors took out their boats. **1830** in M. R. Mitford *Stories Amer. Life* I. 280 Sampson stood, in his Sunday suit, showing with his teeth an air of joyous satisfaction. **1905** E. WHARTON *House of Mirth* II. ix. 429 The photographer whose portraits of her formed the recurring ornament of 'Sunday Supplements'. **1913** [see *RINKY-DINK a.]. **1958** J. BLISH *Case of Conscience* I. iii. 36 Stop sounding like a Sunday supplement. You underestimate your own intelligence. **1979** M. TABOR *Baker's Daughter* i. 13 A basement in a Sunday supplement conversion.

Sundayfied *a.* (earlier example).

1870 *Bazar Bk. Decorum* 164 We are apt to be, as the French say, *endimanchés*, which we may translate by the coined word *Sundayfied*.

Sunday-school. Add: **1. a.** (Earlier *attrib.* example).

1792 *Looker-On* 24 Mar. 36, I really once detected her knitting stockings, for prizes to the Sunday-school girls.

b. *transf.* A school in which instruction in Socialist principles is given on a Sunday.

1901 *Young Socialist* Apr. 2 We ought to..muster as large an army as possible of young soldiers of our cause... This is already being done in our Socialist Sunday Schools. **1922** J. BUCHAN *Huntingtower* x. 198 Wee Jaikie went to a Socialist Sunday School last winter. **1930** A. P. HERBERT *Water Gipsies* xv. 217 Ernest assumed that it would be a treat for Jane to spend her Sunday afternoon at a proletarian Sunday School. **1978** *Times* 5 May 15/5 As long ago as 1918 to 1925 I attended a William Morris Sunday School in an English industrial city.

2. Used *attrib.* or as *adj.* with allusion to the sanctimoniousness, sentimentality, or strict morals held to be inculcated by Sunday-schools: primly moral.

1843 DICKENS *Mart. Chuz.* (1844) xxvii. 333 'Not the truth?' cried Tigg... 'Don't use that Sunday-school expression, please!' **1894** G. B. SHAW *Let.* 4 July (1965) I. 448 Ober Ammergau was a miserable, genteelified, Sir Noel Patonesque Sunday School piece of illustrated Bibleism: Bayreuth is very different. **1931** *Amer. Mercury* Nov. 352/2 *Gone Sunday-School*, said of a circus that has abolished the grift. *Ibid.* 354/2 *Sunday-school show*, a show on which gambling games for the public have been prohibited. **1952** S. KAUFFMANN *Philanderer* (1953) iii. 54 No, it doesn't matter how good he *is*; how good he tries to be, human good, not Sunday-school good. That's what matters. **1973** *Time* 25 June 6/2 Like the circus before it, the carnival is today largely a 'Sunday school' operation.

Su·nderland. The name of a town in Tyne and Wear, England, used *attrib.* to designate (*a*) a type of coarse cream-coloured ware, usu. decorated with a pink lustre and transfers, made there in the late eighteenth and nineteenth centuries; also similar ware made elsewhere; (*b*) less frequently, a type of coarse brown earthenware made in Sunderland in the nineteenth century.

1870 W. CHAFFERS *Marks Pott. & Porc.* (ed. 3) 587 The ware made here was..decorated with the pink metallic lustre so usual on the Sunderland jugs. **1874** [see *Newcastle pottery* s.v. *NEWCASTLE[1] 2]. **1911** J. F. BLACKER *19th-Cent. Eng. Ceramic Art* xvi. 396 The purple and pink lustre..decorated the white ware, which must be distinguished from 'Sunderland ware', the brown earthenware, resembling what is known in the trade as 'rockingham'. **1920** [see *PRATT]. **1937** J. R. HODGDON *Collecting Old Eng. Lustre* v. 34 There are many large bowls, mostly of the late Sunderland ware... Mrs Harpur..is an authority on Sunderland lustre. **1951** JOHN & BAKER *Old Eng. Lustre Pott.* xvi. 97 *Sunderland Ware* has always been reserved for a robust glazed brown earthenware lined with a white glaze and suitable for cooking. **1975** P. D. JAMES *Black Tower* iii. 87 A splendid Sunderland lustreware jug commemorating Trafalgar. **1979** 'J. GASH' *Grail Tree* xvi. 165 Dull pink lustres, universally known as 'Sunderland' ware, don't always come from Sunderland.

sundown, sun-down. Add: **2.** (Earlier example.)

1873 *Kansas Mag.* Sept. 207/2 A flaring sun-down dangled by its strings.

3. *U.S. colloq.* Used *attrib.* to designate one who practises as a doctor or lawyer, etc., outside normal working hours or in addition to his principal occupation. Cf. *SUNDOWNER 3.

1897 *Boston Transcript* 5 Aug. 5/1 There are sundown doctors, sundown lawyers and sundown ministers. **1904** L. DERVILLE *Other Side of Story* 42 A sundown doctor.. [is] a doctor who practices his vocation after four o'clock, when he can leave his desk in some Government office. **1949** *Sun* (Baltimore) 29 June 8/3 Attorneys practising in the county without maintaining offices there have come to be known as 'sundown' lawyers.

sundowner. Add: **1.** (Earlier examples.)

[**1846** C. P. HODGSON *Reminisc. Austral.* 302 A 'Sundowner' (? a task requiring no great exertion which lasts until sundown).] **1868** *Sydney Punch* 14 Nov. 198 (*heading*) The song of the sundowner.

2. orig. *Colonial* (esp. *S. Afr.*). **a.** An alcoholic drink taken at sunset. Also *transf.* and *attrib.*

1909 *Daily Chron.* 20 Oct. 6/7 The 'sundowner' refreshment of the West African late afternoon. **1921** *Chambers's Jrnl.* Jan. 43/1 Surely you are not going to refuse a solitary sundowner. **1932** E. WAUGH *Black Mischief* viii. 298, I said we'd drop into the Brethertons for a sundowner. **1947** W. S. MAUGHAM *Creatures of Circumstance* 37 See you again at six for a sun-downer. **1966** D. VARADAY *Gara-Yaka's Domain* x. 113 We had a good notion the herd would return for a 'sundowner'. **1978** G. GREENE *Human Factor* II. iv. 86 He sits there on a hot evening swilling his sundowners without a care in the world.

b. An evening drinks party.

1962 *Pretoria News* 9 Nov. 9/3 The war raged on, much to the delight of our sundowner guests. **1971** D. CREED *Trial of Lobo Icheka* xv. 149 I'll throw a Sundowner at your place tonight... Invite anyone you feel I might like to meet. **1973** J. J. MCKELVEY *Man against Tsetse* ii. 73 At the 'sundowners', or cocktail hours, heavy white socks seem safer and more comfortable than black ones.

3. *U.S. colloq.* One who practises as a doctor, etc., outside normal working hours or in addition to his principal occupation. Cf. *SUNDOWN, SUN-DOWN 3 and *MOONLIGHTER 3.

1886 *Turf, Field & Farm* 10 May 399/3 The night doctors gather the 'stiffs' and the 'sundowners' flourish around them with scalping knives. **1904** *Sun* (N.Y.) 14 Aug. 17 The Washington sundowner is so called because he practises a profession, usually medicine or dentistry, after the close of Government office hours, or after sundown.

sundries, *sb. pl.* Add: **a.** (Earlier examples.) Also (chiefly *Austral.*), in Cricket: the extras, or runs scored otherwise than off the bat.

1755 FIELDING *Voy. to Lisbon* 182 The whole pitiful 30 l. came pure and neat into the captain's pocket,.. attended with the value of 10 l. more in sundries, into the bargain. **1794** A. YOUNG *Trav. France* II. xix. 421 Live Stock..Corn..Tobacco..Sundries. **1867** *Australasian* 16 Mar. 332/1 With sundries forty-five, the innings closed for the very long score of 211. **1976** *0–10 Cricket Scene* (Austral.) 13/1 That 104 was seven runs more than the 11 New Zealanders could muster between them..excluding the 15 sundries.

b. sundriesman (earlier example).

1885 *List of Subscribers, Classified* (United Telephone Co.) (ed. 6) 84 (*heading*) Druggists' sundriesmen.

sundriness. (Later example.)

1878 W. BARNES *Outl. Eng. Speech-Craft* 86 The goodness of a speech should be sought in..its fulness of words for all things and time-takings which come, with all their sundrinesses, under the minds of men of the speech, in their common life.

sunfish, *sb.* Add: **3.** *U.S. colloq.* A manner of bucking. Cf. SUNFISH *v.*

1903 *Wide World Mag.* Mar. 548 A broncho named 'E.A.'..used a combination of 'sunfish' and 'twister'. **1939** P. A. ROLLINS *Gone Haywire* 260 One prodigious forward jump, then a 'sunfish', and the beast raced into a 'circle buck'.

sunfish, *v.* Add: (Later example.) Also *transf.*

1923 *Century Mag.* CVI. 831/2 Down across Texas it went sunfishin', back-flippin', side-windin'... The Staked Plains used to be heavily timbered until that big wind swiped the trees off. **1971** A. P. MCINNES *Dunlevy* 86 Sometimes the mare sunfished, but the girl stuck solidly. **1979** D. ANTHONY *Long Hard Cure* xxv. 195 He'd ducked ..and gone to one knee, sunfishing a little. His right arm moved..and his pistol boomed loud.

Hence **su·nfisher,** a horse that sunfishes; **su·nfishing** *ppl. a.* and *vbl. sb.*

1913 in *Dialect Notes* IV. 28 Sunfisher. **1923** *N.Y. Times* 16 Aug. 10/1 As Yak went by the sun-fishing longhorn sort o' sheered. **1924** W. M. RAINE *Troubled Waters* v. 47 Rocking chair [an outlaw horse]..was a noted fence rower, weaver, and sunfisher. *Ibid.* 52 Neither side-bucking nor pitching, sunfishing nor weaving could shake the lean-loined, broad-shouldered figure from his seat. **1961** R. F. ADAMS *Old-time Cowhand* 298 A 'sunfisher' was a hoss that twisted his body into a crescent, or, in other words, when he seemed to try to touch the ground with first one shoulder and then the other, lettin' the sunlight hit his belly. **1967** *Sunday Mail Mag.* (Brisbane) 12 Feb. 3/1 In the flash of a second, he'd switched from 'sunfishing' to 'corkscrewing'.

sunflower. Add: **4. sunflower oil** (earlier example); **Sunflower State** *U.S.*, a nickname for Kansas.

1768 *Pennsylvania Gaz.* 6 Oct. 2/3 The sun-flower oil may prove equally valuable with the best Florence oil, for diet or medicine. **1888** *Harper's Mag.* June 39/1 Her citizens affectionately speak of Kansas as the 'Sunflower State'. **1904** *Minneapolis Times* 7 June 6 The floods in Kansas are subsiding. There was danger for a time that the Sunflower state would grow a crop of pond lilies. **1965** MRS. L. B. JOHNSON *White House Diary* 2 Sept. (1970) 315 It was a pleasant journey back to the Ranch, flying over the flat, rich lands of Kansas..sunflowers everywhere, as big as salad plates. You can see why it's called the Sunflower State.

Sung (suŋ), *sb.* Also 7 **Sunga,** 8 and Pinyin **Song.** [Chinese *sòng.*] **a.** The name of a dynasty which ruled in China from 960 to 1279; a member of this dynasty. Also *attrib.*

1673 J. OGILBY *Nieuhoff's Embassy from East-India Co.* I. 249 The Tartars, after a long and tedious destructive War with this Family Sunga for seventy three years, conquer'd the whole Empire, extirpating the whole Family, and set up a new one call'd Ivena. **1738** J. B. DU HALDE *Descr. Empire of China & Chinese Tartary* I. 206 (*heading*) The Nineteenth Dynasty, call'd Song. **1745** tr. J. F. Gemelli Careri in A. & J. Churchill *Coll. Voy. & Trav.* (ed. 3) IV. II. iv. 313/1 When China was rul'd by the family of Sung. **1831** *Canton Miscellany* I. 28 Hwuytsung, an Emperor of the Sung Dynasty. **1893** D. C. BOULGER *Short Hist. China* v. 57 The folly of the Sungs had completed the discomfiture of the Kins. **1925** B. RACKHAM in R. Fry et al. *Chinese Art* 16 A further wide expansion of craftsmanship is shown by the manifold variety of wares of the Sung period. **1958** W. WILLETTS *Chinese Art* I. iii. 133 The Sung Emperors wanted to surround themselves with examples of ancient high art. **1977** *N.Y. Rev. Bks.* 26 May 21/2 (Advt.), To the Sung, poetry was a part of everyday life. **1979** *China Now* Mar./Apr. 9/2 For many practising potters the heights of Chinese ceramics were achieved during the Song Dynasty.

b. Used *attrib.* and *absol.* of the arts, design, and porcelain of the Sung period.

1885 *Trans. Asiatic Soc. Japan* XII. 171 The angular forms..of the Sung dynasty, usually called the *Sung-pan* ..or '*Sung-block*' printing. **1906** R. FRY *Let.* 2 Dec. (1972) I. 275 He's got..some first-rate early Chinese Sung pieces. **1933** *Burlington Mag.* Nov. 204/1 It is obviously a copy of a Sung or Yüan celadon dish. **1937** E. LINKLATER *Juan in China* xii. 222 I've plenty of things to show you, Ming, Sung, pictures, anything you like. **1943** D. WELCH *Maiden Voyage* xviii. 149 This is another type of Sung porcelain called Ying-Ching or 'shadow blue'. **1961** *Guardian* 19 May 9/7 The European eye cannot fail to respond to what it would call the romanticism of Sung landscapes. **1976** M. DELVING *China Expert* ii. 36, I shall hope that whoever stole the Sung vase will make his little slip.

sungar, sangar, *sb.* Delete ‖ and add: Now chiefly *Mil.* Also **sanger.** The spelling *sangar*, with pronunc. (sæ·ŋəɹ), is now usual. (Later examples.) Also, a strong point or fortified look-out post.

1938 D. FORBES *My Life in S. Afr.* v. 68 Small sangers were put up at other commanding positions to hold the enemy back until the fort was finished. **1944** *N.Y. Times* 25 Apr. 5/5 It was about noon..when he climbed out of his own 'sanger',—a type of rocky foxhole characteristic of this section [of Italy]. **1951** G. WILSON *Brave Company* vii. 135 Our sangars are much more elaborate. We have erected roofs reinforced by sandbags and screw pickets. **1962** *Times* 2 May 14/7 The pickets settled down in their *sangars* [in a wadi, W. Aden]. **1974** *Sunday Times* 17 Feb. (Colour Suppl.) 27/3 High look-out platforms called *sangars* [in Northern Ireland]. **1979** *Observer* 4 Mar. 11/1 The man on sangar duty must look out through a narrow slit and observe movements for up to four hours at a time. **1982** *Times* 12 June 5/4 To the commando crouching in his damp 'sanger', a slit trench built up with rocks, there has seemed little reason for the wait.

sungar, *v.* (Earlier example.)

1900 W. S. CHURCHILL in *Morning Post* 25 July 5/7 Both infantry and guns are strongly sangared among the rocks and stones of the kopjes.

sungates, *adv.* For †*Obs.* read 'Now only *arch.*' and add: Also **singates, sungaets.** (Later examples.)

1879 *Shetland Times* 20 Sept. 3/5 They paired and proceeded to the house, walking once round it 'singates', *i.e.* sun ways, or from left to right; that was to secure luck to the pair. **1890** J. SERVICE *Notandums* 100 She was tell't to tak her withershins nine times through a heap o' unwatered yarn, to tak the cat through't sungates aboot as many times again. **1916** A. HUXLEY *Burning Wheel* 49 Though they turn sungates to its widdershins. **1931** [see *NOUST].

sunk, *ppl. a.* **2.** Restrict Now *rare* or *Obs.* to senses in Dict. and add: **d.** *colloq.* Of a person: in a hopeless position, in trouble, in a mess. Freq. *hyperbolical.*

1922 [see *SPURLOS VERSENKT]. **1934** A. P. HERBERT *Holy Deadlock* 103 'Hell!' thought Mr. Ransom, 'we're sunk!' **1941** M. ALLINGHAM *Traitor's Purse* xx. 231 You can't say you're afraid we're sunk... Everyone's relying on you. **1951** J. FRAME *Lagoon* 56 If visitors come tonight I am sunk. **1960** G. SANDERS *Mem. Professional Cad* II. v. 136 If you go to a party with the impedimenta of a date, an overcoat or a hat, you are sunk.

4. b. *sunk band, cord*, a strip of cloth or string on which a binding is constructed, fitted in to furrows across the spine of the book; *sunk-enamel*, champlevé; *sunk garden*, a (portion of a) garden created below the natural level of the surrounding land, a sunken garden (SUNKEN *ppl. a.* 4).

1889 W. MATTHEWS *Mod. Bookbinding* 27 [Raised-band sewing] is three or four times the cost of the ordinary, or sunk-band, sewing... Sunk-band is the ordinary style of the book sewing of our time. Here the sheets are sawed with three or five furrows to admit the bands of twine. **1959** L. M. HARROD *Librarians' Gloss.* (ed. 2) 268 Sunk Bands (Cords)... Cords or bands..placed in grooves sawn into the backs of sections of a book. **1965** L. S. DARLEY *Introd. Bookbinding* 61 (*caption*) Sawing for sunk cords. **1929** *Times* 2 Nov. 10/4 The coral inlay, and red sunk-enamel (champlevé) on the handle. **1922** J. BUCHAN *Huntingtower* v. 93 A path which wound down to the sunk garden. **1973** *Country Life* 15 Nov. 1591/1, I bask on a stone seat in the sunk garden.

sunken, *ppl. a.* Add: **2.** *Comb.*, as *sunken-eyed.*

1851 H. MELVILLE *Moby Dick* I. xxxiv. 253 Your whales must be seen before they are killed; and this sunken-eyed Platonist will tow you ten wakes round the world, and never make you one pint of sperm the richer. **1971** S. HILL *Strange Meeting* 191 The men glanced up apprehensively as they passed along, and their faces had the sunken-eyed look of suppressed fear.

4. *sunken bath, living-room.*

1925 F. SCOTT FITZGERALD *Great Gatsby* (1926) v. 110 Through dressing-rooms and poolrooms, and bathrooms with sunken baths. **1979** J. MELVILLE *Wages of Zen* xi. 110 The tiled sunken bath was drained and clean. **1970** *Globe & Mail* (Toronto) 26 Sept. 42/3 (Advt.), 3 Bedrooms, 3 Washrooms, Electric Light Fixtures, Sunken Living Rooms. **1976** M. MACHLIN *Pipeline* xxxvii. 408 The entrance hall, which gave onto a white-carpeted, sunken living-room, looked as though a regiment of cavalry had galloped through it.

sunker (sɒ·ŋkəɹ). *Newfoundland.* [f. SUNK *ppl. a.* + -ER[1].] A submerged rock. Also *fig.*

c **1880** in G. S. Doyle *Old Time Songs & Poetry of Newfoundland* (1927) 29 We'll rant and we'll roar on deck and below, Until we see bottom inside the two sunkers. **1896** *Jrnl. Amer. Folklore* IX. 33 Among the peculiar words connected with the fishing I note the following:..*sunker*, a breaker. **1951** *Newfoundland & Labrador Pilot* I. 134 Duck Road shoal, about 4 cables north-eastward of Eastern head and Anchor Cove Sunkers. **1966** A. R. SCAMMELL *My Newfoundland* 63 The words don't seem to have a clear channel from me brain to me lips. Too many sunkers for 'em to ground on, I spose. **1973** *Maclean's Mag.* Jan. 16/1 At dusk, the Nordfjeld slammed onto a 'sunker', a rock that's awash at high tide, one mile off Flowers Cove.

sunket (sɒ·ŋkėt), *sb.*[2] *dial.* [Origin obscure.] A simpleton, a silly fellow.

1823 E. MOOR *Suffolk Words & Phrases* 409 Sunket. A child sickly and unpromising is so called—'Ah! 'tis a poor sunketing thing.' **1895** W. RYE *Gloss. Words E. Anglia* 219 *Sunket*,..a contemptuous appellation of a silly fellow. **1940** C. P. SNOW *Strangers & Brothers* 21 'You can't take sides with those sunkets against me,' said George. His voice had risen. We were used to the odd Suffolk words as his temper got up.

sunlight, *sb.* Add: **1. c.** *artificial sunlight*: see *ARTIFICIAL *a.* 5.

sun-lighted, sunlighted, *ppl. a.* (Earlier U.S. example.)

1787 M. TILGHMAN *Let.* 6 Oct. in *Maryland Hist. Mag.* (1926) XXI. 220 The bright, Sun-lighted Wedding proceedings.

su·nlighting, *vbl. sb.* [f. SUNLIGHT *sb.* + -ING[1].] **1.** The process, degree, etc., of the illumination of buildings by sunlight.

1961 [see *DAYLIGHTING *vbl. sb.* 2]. **1977** *Washington Post* 10 Apr. B5/1 Maximum sunlighting and, therefore, heat capture are assured in the winter when the sun is low.

2. (See quot. 1977.)

1977 D. N. BARON in *Brit. Med. Jrnl.* 22 Oct. 1080/1 If taking on paid outside work during night-time hours is moonlighting then let us call doing outside work (though unpaid) during daytime hours sunlighting. **1978** *Lancet* 14 Jan. 89/2 Then follow 3–4 years of internship or residency training..with opportunities of moonlighting and sunlighting. **1983** *N.Y. Times* 7 Feb. A2/3 Bureaucrats [in Madrid] practiced moonlighting to such an extent it turned into sunlighting.

Sunnism (sʊ̄·niz'm). Also **Sunniism.** [f. SUNNA or SUNNI + -ISM.] The doctrines or principles of the Sunnites.

1892 *Chambers's Encycl.* IX. 398/2 The moderate Shiism that has been the national religion of Persia since the native royal line of Safiides ascended the throne in 1499 is more Koranic than Sunnism. **1911** D. S. MARGOLIOUTH *Mohammedanism* v. 174 Nadir Shah attempted to substitute Sunnism. **1953** O. CAROE *Soviet Empire* iv. 50 The Samanids came from Baltch and enforced a rigorous form of Hanafi Sunniism. **1962** G. E. VON GRUNEBAUM *Mod. Islam* 11 The catholicity of Sunnism. **1983** S. AKHAVI in N. R. Keddie *Relig. & Pol. in Iran* vii. 129 His [*sc.* Shariati's] thought has more affinities to Shi'ism than to Sunnism.

sunny, *a.* **2. b.** Restrict † *Obs.* to phrases in Dict. and add: *sunny South*: the southern states of the U.S.

1846 *Spirit of Times* (N.Y.) 18 Apr. 96/2 The wish of his heart should always be, peace and prosperity to the 'Sunny South'. **1950** *Chicago Tribune* 11 Mar. 8/3 Eric, the redbird..flew by, fat 'n' sassy from a sojourn in the sunny South.

5. b. *sunny side* (*fig.* or in fig. contexts), (*a*) in phrases expressive of cheerfulness or optimism, esp. *on the sunny side of the wall*; (*b*) *on the sunny side of* (an age): on the right side of, i.e. less than (cf. SHADY *a.* 2 b); (*c*) *sunny side up*: of an egg, fried on one side only; hence *sunnyside egg*.

(*a*) **1831** E. TRELAWNY *Adventures Younger Son* II. viii. 61 Then, only looking at the sunny side of things, all was bright. **1837** [in Dict., sense 5]. **1858** TROLLOPE *Doctor Thorne* I. vi. 141 Mary..was..of the same age as Frank; but, as I..have so often said before, 'Women grow on the sunny side of the wall.' **1890** W. S. GILBERT *Gondoliers* II. 119 Live to love and love to live—You will ripen at your ease, Growing on the sunny side—Fate has nothing more to give. **1970** C. MAJOR *Dict. Afro-Amer. Slang* 111 *Sunny side (of the street)*, the 'good life'; luxury, leisure and comfort.

(*b*) **1865** *Atlantic Monthly* XV. 711 How many of us,.. on the sunny side of thirty, have gone through the 'Paradise Lost'? **1967** *Boston Sunday Globe* 23 Apr. (TV Week) 2/1 That's mighty high flying for a young Negro actor still on the sunny side of 30.

(*c*) **1901** *Dialect Notes* II. 149 *Sunny side up*,..of eggs, to fry [sic] on only one side. **1948** *Royal Air Force Rev.* Jan. 20/2 It's whizzo when you get a fried egg sunny-side-up for tea. **1953** A. CHRISTIE *After Funeral* xii. 101 Worried, bad-tempered and irritable in the office. *But* since his uncle's death that's all changed. He's like the breakfast eggs (if we had 'em). Sunny side up! **1967** [see *ONCE *adv.* B. 8 e]. **1971** H. HOWARD *Murder One* vii. 92 If he's made a funeral in the family he'll fry like a sunny-side egg. **1979** R. FIENNES *Hell on Ice* iii. 32 Ginnie ladled her sunny-side-up eggs' with semolina.

c. *Sunny Jim*, the name of an energetic character employed as the proprietary name for a brand of breakfast cereal; also used allusively, as a term of address, and as a nickname. Also *Sonny Jim* (influenced by SONNY).

'Sunny Jim was the creation of an American schoolgirl called Ficken (not Fincken) and the various jingles which accompanied him were written by Miss Minnie Hanff. It is believed that Sunny Jim was the winning entry in a competition run by the Force Food Company to find a suitable advertising character to promote "Force".' —C. Fincken (A. C. Fincken & Co. Ltd., manufacturers of Force), private let. to ed., 24 June 1983.

1903 *Poster*, High o'er the fence leaps Sunny Jim 'Force' is the food that raises him. **1904** *Trade Marks Jrnl.* 30 Mar. 381 'Sunny Jim'... Cereal Food Products. The firm trading as The 'Force' Food Company, 6, Holborn Viaduct, London, E.C.; Manufacturers. *c* **1904** *Story of Sunny Jim* (Force Food Co.), Jim Dumps was a most unfriendly man, Who lived his life on a hermit plan. He'd never stop for a friendly smile, But trudged along in his moody style. Till 'Force' one day was served to him, Since then they call him Sunny Jim. **1911** CHESTERTON *Innocence of Father Brown* xii. 315 Sir Aaron Armstrong was..comic... It was like hearing that Sunny Jim had hanged himself. **1911** 'I. HAY' *Safety Match* xii. 187 Mr. Blunt..cleared the topmost rail... 'Now then, Sunny Jim!' remarked a reproving voice. **1916** *Punch* 5 Apr. 229/1 [He] says he's quite a Sunny Jim, That buoyant health and youthful vim Are sticking out all over him. **1943** *Current Biogr.* (1944) 779/2 Vandegrift—so cheerful that he has earned the nickname 'Sunny Jim'—is..the toughest Marine Corps leader who ever charged at the head of his troops. **1960** D. STOREY *This Sporting Life* I. v. 127 'All right, all right! Don't preach, sonny. Hey!' she calls to the M.P. 'Hey sonnyjim! What kinda car has Arthur Machin got?' **1962** S. L. GOLDBERG *Joyce* i. 3 What his [*sc.* James Joyce's] early works do not portray.. is the aspect of his character that earned him the family nickname, 'Sunny Jim'. **1967** A. WILSON *No Laughing Matter* II. 127 Does your Mother know you're out, Sonny Jim? **1976** *Times* 6 Apr. 16/1 The new Prime Minister [*sc.* James Callaghan]..enjoys life... He is not called Sunny Jim for nothing.

6. a. *sunny golden, -winking.*

1922 JOYCE *Ulysses* 406 She dare not bear the sunny-golden babe of day. *Ibid.* 216 He walked by the treeshade of sunnywinking leaves.

sunnyasee, sunnyasi. Add: Also **sannyasi** (now the most usual form), **sanyas(s)i, san(n)yas(s)in.**

1812 J. MALCOLM in *Asiatick Researches* XI. 267 That crowd of holy mendicants, Sanyásís and Fakírs, with whom India swarms. **1854** GEO. ELIOT tr. *Feuerbach's Essence Christianity* xvii. 167 No regenerate man could assume the rank of a Sanyassi,..if he had not previously paid three debts. **1876** Sannyasin [see *BHIKSHU]. **1891** MONIER WILLIAMS *Brahmanism & Hinduism* 55 He was a Sannyāsī and an unmarried Smārta Brāhman. **1938** W. S. MAUGHAM *Writer's Notebk.* (1949) 280 At his birth his horoscope was taken, and the astrologer said that he would either become a very rich, successful man, a king among men, or a sanyasin. **1957** *Contributions to Indian Sociol.* I. 17 Now, what one is in the habit of calling Indian Thought is for the very great part the thought of the sanyasi. **1960** E. R. LEACH *Aspects of Caste in S. India, Ceylon & N.W. Pakistan* 6 It is open to every man to become a *sannyasi* and receive the adulations of his society. **1978** *Times* 5 Aug. 7/8 Dom Bede Griffiths, a Benedictine monk who has spent the past 16 years of his life as a *sannyasi*—a kind of hermit—at a Hindu ashram at Kerala in India. **1980** *Daily Tel.* 13 Feb. 15/4 She joined a group of sanyassins, and became fascinated with the guru's writings.

sun-ray. Add: **2. b.** *sun-ray pleat, pleated* adj., *pleating.*

1903 *Young Woman* XI. 318/2 For evening dresses accordion pleated—or sun-ray pleated—point d'esprit net is an ideal material. **1922** JOYCE *Ulysses* 731 The orange petticoat I had on with sunray pleats. **1935** *Times* 4 Nov. 9/3 Sunray pleating gives fullness from the knee. **1959** *Spectator* 2 Jan. 10/2 Short office skirts and dropping Spanish skirts and brisk housewifely sun-ray pleats. **1972** *Country Life* 25 May 1354/2 Sunray pleating is again in fashion. **1978** *Lancashire Life* Apr. 79/2 A tailored jacket which can be teamed with a sunray pleated skirt.

3. An (artificial) ultraviolet ray used for medical or cosmetic treatment. Chiefly *attrib.*, esp. in *sun-ray lamp*; formerly also *ellipt.* for *sun-ray treatment.*

1928 *Daily Express* 27 June 3/6 The speedy development of sun-ray clinics all over the country. *Ibid.*, The treatment of disease by artificial sun-rays. **1930** M. KENNEDY *Fool of Family* x. 89, I wonder if sunray treatment would do her good... Sir Ivor knew nothing of sun-ray, and he had no faith in doctors. **1954** 'N. BLAKE' *Whisper in Gloom* II. xii. 164 Does this young lady..own a sun-ray lamp? **1977** C. FREMLIN *Spider Orchid* xxii. 149 He looked from the bedside table to the sunray lamp.

sunrise. Add: **b. sunrise industry,** a new and expanding industry; cf. *sunset industry* s.v. *SUNSET 3.

1980 L. C. THUROW *Zero-Sum Society* (1981) iv. 95 We do need the national equivalent of a corporate investment committee to redirect investment flows from our 'sunset' industries to our 'sunrise' industries. **1980** *Economist* 23 Aug. 16/2 Those who try to shelter dying jobs in sunset industries, and thereby blight the prospects of growth of good jobs in sunrise ones. **1983** *Times* 20 Apr. 21/7 The traditional 'sunset' industries are a pain in the neck for the Industry Secretary. However much he tries to brush them under the carpet in favour of the glamorous 'sunrise' sector of high technology, they persist in creeping back into the public consciousness.

sunset. Add: **1. b.** *to ride* (*go, sail,* etc.) *off into the sunset*, phr. derived from a conventional closing scene of many films used, freq. ironically, to denote a happy ending.

1967 H. HARRISON *Technicolor Time Machine* (1968) iii. 28 He takes the girl with him and together they sail into the sunset to a new life. **1976** W. GOLDMAN *Magic* III. xii. 207, I didn't even bother getting mad at your crack about me going off into the sunset. **1977** *Times* 17 Feb. 6/4 Our black hero..rides off to freedom in the sunset.

3. *sunset-red* (examples; also as *sb.*), *-tinted* adjs.; **sunset-gun** (earlier U.S. example); **sunset home,** a home (HOME *sb.* 8) for the elderly, a 'twilight' home; **sunset industry,** an old and declining industry.

1840 THOREAU *Jrnl.* 16 June in *Writings* (1906) VII. 141 To hear..the bittern begin to boom from his concealed fort like a sunset gun! **1978** *Dædalus* Spring 220 A society that increasingly emphasizes..singles bars for the young and..sunset homes for the elderly. **1980, 1983** Sunset industry [see *sunrise industry* s.v. *SUNRISE b]. **1837** E. B. BROWNING *Epistle to Canary* (1913) 11 A spark of light from highest dawn, Which glows and opens..till sunset reds are likest to them. **1934** WEBSTER, Sunset-red adj. **1964** *New Yorker* 5 Sept. 86 (Advt.), Slip into the run-about shift...mirage aqua, sunset-red, cactus-green, burnt-clay. **1979** *Arizona Daily Star* 5 Aug. (Parade Suppl.) 24/2 (Advt.), These are handsome..books, smartly bound in sunset red, desert tan and cavalry blue. **1876** J. G. WHITTIER *Mabel Martin* (new ed.) 40 And sad the uncompanioned eves, And sadder sunset-tinted leaves. **1954** L. MACNEICE *Autumn Sequel* 33 The sunset-tinted Balloons were down.

b. *N. Amer. Pol.* Applied to legislation whereby a government agency or programme is automatically terminated at the end of a fixed period unless formally renewed.

1976 *National Observer* (U.S.) 5 June 1/1 The hottest political idea of the year is something called the sunset bill. *Ibid.* 1/5 Colorado recently became the first state to adopt sunset legislation. **1976** *Wall St. Jrnl.* 25 June 1/1 Colorado's new 'Sunset Law'. The experimental measure would terminate in six years the state's regulatory agencies..unless they justify their existence. **1978** *Globe & Mail* (Toronto) 15 Feb. 1/3 The Ontario Government is on the verge of embracing sunset law. **1982** *Times* 25 Feb. 7/8 It is not a wilderness protection Bill.. but a wilderness sunset Bill, that would end wilderness protection.

Hence **su·nset** *v.*, (*a*) *intr.*, to decline, sink (*rare*); (*b*) *trans.*, to subject to, or terminate by means of, sunset legislation (see sense 3 b above). (*N. Amer.*)

1933 V. MCNABB *Nazareth or Social Chaos* 30 The prodigal's prosperity which sunsets in beggary. **1978** *Canadian Broadcasting Corporation News* 1 June (*oral quot.*), [The] act would be sunsetted out of existence. **1979** *National Jrnl.* 17 Mar. 438/1 In the debate on the sunset bill..when it was passed by the Senate, we tried to figure out what exactly they thought they were sunsetting. **1982** *N.Y. Times* 28 Sept. B.10/4 His impatience is also displayed in his plans to 'sunset' the aeronautics board well before it is scheduled to expire.

sunshade. Add: **2.** (Earlier U.S. example.)

1842 *N.Y. Times* 22 Mar. (Advt.), Umbrellas, parasols and sun-shades manufactured at Newark, N.J.

5. *pl.* = *sun-glass* (*c*) s.v. *SUN *sb.* 13 a. Cf. *SHADE *sb.* 11 e.

1965 'LAUCHMONEN' *Old Thom's Harvest* ii. 24 The minister took off his sunshades and his naked eyes followed the girl. **1967** *Sunday Times* 28 May 18, I give a lot of speeches with my sunshades on.

sunshine, *sb.* Add: **2. a.** (Later example.) Now freq. as a colloq. form of address to any person. Cf. also (*little*) *ray of sunshine* s.v. *RAY *sb.*[1] 1 a.

1942 BERREY & VAN DEN BARK *Amer. Thes. Slang* § 184/1 Hap, Happy, Sunshine, a cheerful person. **1972** M. GILBERT *Body of Girl* iv. 43 Hullo, Sunshine. What can we do for you? **1976** P. CAVE *High Flying Birds* ii. 17, I turned back to the ticket man. 'OK now, sunshine?' **1976** *Daily Mirror* 16 Mar. 12/1 Mike Reid's cheery Cockney greeting seems to switch on every girl in the place. 'Hello sunshine,' he says.

6. sunshine law *U.S.*, a law making the official meetings and records of certain government agencies accessible to the public; **sunshine roof,** on a motor vehicle, a roof that can be slid open; = *sun-roof* (*a*) s.v. *SUN *sb.* 13 a; **Sunshine State,** (*a*) *U.S.*, any of several states (see quots.); (*b*) *Austral.*, Queensland; **sunshine-yellow** *a.* and *sb.*, (of) a bright shade of yellow.

1972 *Atlantic Monthly* Sept. 22 The state of Florida has adopted a 'sunshine law' which requires that all official meetings in which public business is transacted be open to the public. **1977** *National Observer* (U.S.) 22 Jan. 16/5 We need an all-inclusive 'sunshine law' in Washington so that special interests will not retain their exclusive access behind closed doors. **1982** *Times Lit. Suppl.* 26 Feb. 225/5 'Sunshine laws' have opened committee hearings to public scrutiny. **1929** *Daily Express* 12 Jan. 4/7 The royal coupé, with a sunshine roof. **1954** J. TRENCH *Dishonoured Bones* II. v. 72 He got out the old Austin..unfastening the sunshine roof. **1977** *Horse & Hound* 14 Jan. 44/3 (Advt.), Land-Rover..sunshine roof. **1893** L. WAGNER *Significance of Names* 36 New Mexico is The Sunshine State. **1918** S. S. VISHER *Geogr. S. Dakota* 60 South Dakota is known as 'the Sunshine State', not because it surpasses in this respect..states..in the southwest, but because of the contrast between South Dakota and the Eastern States and northern European countries from whence most of the persons not born in South Dakota came. **1920** *Monthly Weather Rev.* (U.S. Weather Bureau) Mar. 154/2 In this 'Sunshine State' [*sc.* California] we have 'Sunkist Orange'. **1947** *Time* 17 Mar. 42/2 Employees..are happier in The Sunshine State [*sc.* Florida] where living is so pleasant and healthful. **1962** C. ROHAN *Delinquents* 128 'If you ask me, all Brisbane's full of coppers and all of them bastards,' she said, expressing in one concise sentence the full theory of central government of the sunshine state. **1976** *Daily Record* (Glasgow) 30 Nov. 28/6 And although the Sunshine State has seen a few fancy sights the citizens of Palm Springs are in for an extra special treat next week. **1971** 'A. GILBERT' *Tenant for Tomb* i. 22 The plumber..wanted to install a bright blue bath..and had to be coaxed into substituting a sunshine-yellow one. **1975** A. FRASER *Whistler's Lane* x. 161, I bought myself a blouse in sunshine yellow.

sun-spot. Add: Now usu. **sunspot. 2. b. sunspot cycle,** the recurring increase and decrease in the number of sunspots, with a period averaging just over 11 years.

1922 H. S. JONES *Gen. Astron.* v. 126 There is a remarkable connection between the Sun-spot cycle and the occurrence of magnetic storms on the Earth. **1977** *Jrnl. R. Soc. Arts* CXXV. 157/1 Since the solar output appears to change by a good deal less than 1 per cent, even during solar flares, it is not surprising that weather events show very little correlation with the sunspot cycle.

3. *Cinemat.* A powerful arc lamp used to imitate the light from the sun in colour cinematography; = *sun arc* s.v. *SUN *sb.* 13 a.

1930 [see *sun arc* s.v. *SUN *sb.* 13 a]. **1976** H. R. F. KEATING *Filmi, Filmi, Inspector Ghote* iii. 29 We are using a great number of different lights for different purposes in filming, Five-Ks, Two-Ks, Sunspots, Solars, Babies.

4. A place that affords plentiful sunshine.

1976 *U.S. News & World Rep.* 2 Feb. 26/1 Most travelers favor sun spots. St. Maarten, in the Netherlands Antilles, leads the parade. **1983** *Listener* 6 Jan. 36/3 (Advt.), First choose your holiday sun-spot, then choose where to stay.

sunstone, sun-stone. Add: **5.** [tr. ON. *sólarsteinn.*] A stone whose exact properties are uncertain, mentioned in several medieval Icelandic sources.

'A semi-precious stone capable of being used as a burning-glass': P. G. Foote in *ARV: Jrnl. Scandinavian Folklore* (1956), XII. 26–40.

1874 CLEASBY & VIGFUSSON *Icelandic–Eng. Dict.* 579/2 *Sólar-steinn*, m. a sun-stone or loadstone, = leiðarsteinn, used by sailors to find the place of the sun on a cloudy day. **1947** J. E. TURVILLE-PETRE tr. *Story of Rauð & his Sons* 24 The King..sent a man out to observe the weather, and there was not a patch of clear sky to be seen. The King then asked Sigurd to determine how far the sun had travelled. He gave a precise answer. So the King had the sun-stone held aloft, and observed where it cast out a beam; the altitude it showed was exactly as Sigurd had said. **1968** *Carnegie Mag.* May 152/1 In overcast weather, a 'sunstone' determined the position of the sun. **1970** B. E. GELSINGER in *Mariner's Mirror* LVI. 222 Thorkild Ramskou..suggested that the sunstone was a crystal such as Iceland spar which polarizes light... The sunstone could thus indicate the position of the sun even though the sky was completely overcast. This description..harmonizes with non-Icelandic references to the sunstone... Pliny the Elder..described the sunstone or *solis gemma* as a white stone which casts rays of the sun. **1980** M. MAGNUSSON *Vikings!* vii. 191 Unfortunately, today's scholars do not rate the so-called sun-stone as a Viking Age navigational aid..; nothing is sacrosanct in the severe world of scholarship.

sunt. Add: Also **sont.** For *Acacia arabica* substitute *Acacia nilotica*. (Later example.)

1901 *Knowledge* June 138/2 The timber forming a raft is generally of the 'sont' tree.

sun-tan, *sb.* (and *a.*). (In Dict. s.v. SUN *sb.* 11 b.) Add: **1. a.** (Later examples.)

1958 M. K. JOSEPH *I'll soldier no More* xiii. 237 They're just out for a bit of suntan. **1980** *West Lancs. Evening Gaz.* 11 Aug. 10 (Advt.), A guaranteed suntan without sunburn.

b. In *Comb.* designating cosmetics which provide protection against sunburn and promote suntanning, as *sun-tan lotion, oil,* etc.

1934 *Beautycraft* July 19/1 To acquire a brown, healthy skin..it must be anointed plentifully with one of the good Sun-tan oils now on the market. **1938** E. AMBLER *Cause for Alarm* vi. 90 The points of his dress collar..were..smeared with grease and sun-tan powder. **1951** KOESTLER *Age of Longing* ii. 36 She felt herself go slightly pale under the sun-tan make-up. **1962** 'E. MCBAIN' *Like Love* ix. 132 Contents medicine cabinet...one tube suntan lotion, one bottle Seconal, one toothbrush. **1976** P. PARISH *Medicines* II. xli. 242 The effectiveness of suntan applications is..related to their ability to cut out the burning effects of the sun's rays.

2. *pl.* **a.** Lightweight, tan-coloured summer uniform worn by military personnel. **b.** Trousers forming part of this uniform or similar slacks for casual wear. *U.S.*

1937 *Amer. Speech* XII. 75/1 *Suntans*, summer uniform, made of lightweight material with sheen. **1945** E. NEWHOME in *New Yorker* 10 Feb. 22/1 He had removed only his tie and was lying..in his suntans. **1947** J. BERTRAM *Shadow of War* VIII. v. 279 We stared at the Commodore's drab suntans. **1958** 'E. DUNDY' *Dud Avocado* I. i. 7 The Left Bank uniform of the day, dark wool shirt and a pair of old Army suntans. **1960** J. UPDIKE *Rabbit, Run* 98 He takes clean Jockey pants, T-shirts,..a pair of laundered suntans..and a sports shirt from the closet. **1966** *Times* 28 Mar. (Austral. Suppl.) p. viii/4 The streets are full of people in shorts and suntans. **1972** W. MCGIVERN *Caprifoil* (1973) xiii. 217 Admiral Burkholder..wore suntans, and the collar of his shirt was open.

3. A light-brown fashion colour. Also as *adj.*

1937 [see *MIST *sb.*[1] 1e]. **1976** *Horse & Hound* 3 Dec. 17 (Advt.), Deep pile Borg washable numnah, foam filled. Pony or F.S. general purpose. Cream or suntan.

Hence as *v. trans.* and *intr.*, to expose (oneself) to the sun in order to acquire a tan; **su·n-tanned** *ppl. a.*; **su·n-tanning** *vbl. sb.* and *ppl. a.*

1821 Sun-tanned [in Dict. s.v. SUN *sb.* 12 b]. **1876** 'MARK TWAIN' *Tom Sawyer* xviii. 185 That swarthy, suntanned skin of his. **1932** *Sun* (Baltimore) 5 Sept. 6/2 The millions busy today suntanning themselves, picnicking in the country. **1938** W. DE LA MARE *Memory* 16 The suntanned soldiers. **1959** *Chambers's Encycl.* III. 762/2 Genetically or environmentally induced melanization (sun-tanning) of the skin may serve a useful function in screening out injurious short-waved fractions of the sunlight from the sensitive underlying tissues. **1961** *Times* 29 Nov. 13/6 Just the right amount of suntanning. **1976** B. SHELBY *Great Pebble Affair* 117 Donnely and I were suntanning on the roof. **1977** N. FAULKS *No Mitigating Circumstances* vii. 99, I had a little lawn tennis at Monfalcone as well as at Trieste, and had an idle, suntanning time.

Suntory (sɒntōᵊ·ri). Also **Suntori.** The proprietary name of a Japanese whisky.

1959 R. KIRKBRIDE *Tamiko* ii. 11 Here he was..without even a drink in his hand. 'A double Suntory,' he said to the baaten. **1960** *Trade Marks Jrnl.* 21 Dec. 1659/2 Suntory 809,445. All goods included in Class 33 [sc. alcoholic beverages]. Kabushiki Kaisha Kotobukiya (a Corporation duly organised and existing under the laws of Japan)..Osaka, Japan; Manufacturers.—15th Aug. 1960. **1967** 'J. H. ROBERTS' *February Plan* I. i. 17 He..remembered enough of his long unused Japanese to order a bottle of Suntori. **1975** R. L. DUNCAN *Dragons at Gate* (1976) iii. 99, I have ordered Kobe steaks... I have also requested a bottle of Suntory.

sun-up, sunup. For *local*, chiefly *U.S.* read: *local U.S.* (chiefly *Midland*), *Caribbean*, and formerly (perh. rendering Afrikaans *sonop*) *S. Afr.* Add: freq. in phr. *from sun-up to sundown.* (Earlier and further examples.)

1712 T. BANISTER *Let.* 12 Nov. in *Coll. Connecticut Hist. Soc.* (1924) XXI. 377 Wee Set out by or before Sun up, for Wyndham. **1826** J. F. COOPER *Last of Mohicans* I. iv. 69 One would think such a horse as that might get over a good deal of ground atwixt sun-up and sun-down. **1887** RIDER HAGGARD *Jess* xxxii. 305 Will you consent to marry me to-morrow morning at sun up, or am I to be forced to carry the sentence on your old uncle into effect? **1903** K. D. WIGGIN *Rebecca of Sunnybrook Farm* x. 102, I could teach school from sun-up to sun-down if scholars was all like Rebecca Randall. **1920** [see *KLOMP]. **1949** *Caribbean Q.* I. III. 45 Your face turned to sun-up. *a* **1963** S. PLATH *Crossing Water* (1971) 47 The blue hour before sunup. **1965** 'LAUCHMONEN' *Old Thom's Harvest* viii. 99 Another hour and it was sun-up. **1976** A. HALEY *Roots* (1977) cxiii. 646 Twenty-eight wagons were packed and ready to roll on the following sunup.

sunwards, *adv.* **2.** (Earlier example.)

1851 H. MELVILLE *Moby Dick* III. xxx. 189 Here, too, life dies sunwards, full of faith.

sunyasi, var. SUNNYASEE, SUNNYASI in Dict. and Suppl.

‖**sunyata** (sūnya·tā, ʃ-). *Buddhism.* Also **çūnyatā.** [Skr. *śūnyátā* emptiness, non-existence, f. *śūnyá* empty, void.] The concept of the essential emptiness of all things and of ultimate reality as a void beyond worldly phenomena.

1907 D. T. SUZUKI *Outl. Mahâyâna Buddhism* vii. 173 The emptiness of things (*çûnyatâ*) does not mean nothingness..but..conditionality or transitoriness of all phenomenal existences. **1916** A. COOMARASWAMY *Buddha & Gospel of Buddhism* v. 318 The *Prajñāpāramitās* are filled with..texts upon the Emptiness (*Sunyata*) of things. **1938** B. L. SUZUKI *Mahayana Buddhism* i. 15 Sunyata is what is left behind after an endless series of negations, and is therefore the most positive and fundamental of ideas. **1951** E. CONZE *Buddhism* v. 130 We must now make an effort to understand this all-important idea of *Emptiness*... What we call *emptiness* in English is *sūnyatā* in sanskrit. **1978** C. HUMPHREYS *Both Sides Circle* v. 57 What I call the mystical metaphysics of the *Madhyamika* (Middle Way) School, founded by Nagarjuna and expanded through several centuries into the ultimate concept of *sunyata*, 'no-thing-ness'.

‖**Sun Yat-sen** (sɒn yæt sen). Also **Sun Yatsen.** The Cantonese form of the personal name Sun I-xian, adopted by Sun Wen (1866–1925), founder in 1911 of the Republic of China, used *attrib.* to designate a modern style of clothing in China.

1946 O. LANG *Chinese Family & Society* ix. 77 Those who wear long Chinese gowns are usually old-fashioned men... Modern-minded officials wear black coats with high collars, the so-called 'Sun Yat-sen jackets', and tight trousers tucked into black or khaki puttees—a Western garment common in China. **1965** 'HAN SUYIN' *Crippled Tree* I. xvi. 222 Most of us had come to wear the Japanese students' uniform, which later was termed the Sun Yatsen suit, and is now spoken of as the Communist garb. **1977** 'S. LEYS' *Chinese Shadows* (1978) ii. 75 Impeccably cut Sun Yat-sen jackets. (*Note*) Chung-shan chuang, which a silly vogue in the West persists in calling a 'Mao jacket'—as if the present regime had invented it.

Sun Yat-senism (sɒn yætse·niz'm). Also as one word. [f. prec. + -ISM.] The political principles of Sun Yat-sen, which included Chinese nationalism, democracy, and the people's livelihood (the 'three principles of the people').

1927 *Observer* 17 July 20/2 The understanding between Chiang Kai-shek and Feng Yu-hsiang is precariously maintained by intermediaries, not by Sun Yat-senism. **1931** tr. *P. M. D'Elia's Triple Demism of Sun Yat-Sen* 41 Some authors have not hesitated to believe that they could make a certain distinction between 'Sunyatsenism' and 'Sunwenism'. **1957** CHIANG KAI-SHEK *Soviet Russia in China* I. i. 36 Officers and cadets at the Academy..formed a rival group named Society for the Study of Sun Yat-senism. **1979** *World Today* June 244 During his long career, Ho Chi Minh made a point of reassuring both Chiang Kai-shek and Mao Tse-tung that he was dedicated, first, to Sun Yat-senism and, later, to Marxism-Leninism-Mao Tse-tung thought.

sup (sɒp), *sb.*[2] *Math.* [f. *SUP(REMUM.] Supremum (of).

1940, 1949 [see *INFIMUM]. **1968** E. T. COPSON *Metric Spaces* i. 14 The supremum or least upper bound of *A*..is denoted by sup *A*.

sup, *v.*[1] Add: **2.** (Later examples.) Also const. *up.*

1869 [in Dict., sense 1 b]. **1898** J. MACMANUS *Bend of Road* 94 There wasn't a man ever supped from a noggin in Corradooey he couldn't sweep the floor with! **1952** M. TRIPP *Faith is Windsock* v. 86 Now sup up, as Arthur [a north-countryman] says, and have one on me. **1971** D. LEES *Rainbow Conspiracy* ix. 152 Sup up first—tha's let the beer get cold. **1977** SCOLLINS & TITFORD *Ey up, mi Duck!* III. 30 Men were content just to gossip and 'sup'.

supe. Add: (Later examples.) Also as *v. intr.*, to act as a supernumerary in a theatre. Cf. *SUPER *v.* I.

1893 W. K. POST *Harvard Stories* 107 Do you remember the time..that we saw the old man suping in that spectacular play? **1915** J. B. RATHBUN *Motion Picture Making* 72 'Westerns' are invariably taken in their proper locale, the 'supes' usually being drawn from the ranches and towns surrounding the studio. **1977** [see *SCOFF *v.*[1] 2 c].

super, *sb.* Add: **II. 3. a.** (Earlier examples.) Also in the context of films. Cf. *EXTRA *sb.* b.

1838 *Actors by Daylight* I. 112/1 Many of the old supers of course remained. **1844** DICKENS *Let.* 3 Jan. (1977) IV. 9 That extraordinary compound of odd scents peculiar to a theatre..accompanies me, as I meet perspiring supers in the narrow passage. **1924** GALSWORTHY *White Monkey* II. ii. 125 The lurid professions—film-super, or mannequin. **1930** E. WAUGH *Vile Bodies* ix. 155 The Colonel's somewhere in that little crowd singing the hymn... He was crazy to be allowed to come on as a super.

5. (Earlier and later examples.)

1857 F. COOPER *Wild Adventures in Austral.* 59 'Scotchy'..introduced me as a particular friend to Wilder the owner of that run, under the impression that a 'super' was required. **1864** C. R. THATCHER *Songs of War* 12 The Super issued Quite a rabid Proclamation. **1916** A. BENNETT *These Twain* iii. 33 The sole lecture of his répertoire, but it had served to raise him ever so slightly out of the ruck of 'Supers'. **1939** 'F. O'BRIEN' *At-Swim-Two-Birds* 80 The policemen were rounded up and marched across the prairies to the Circle N, as fine a body of men as you'd hope to see, myself and the super as proud as be damned at the head of them. **1953** 'N. BLAKE' *Dreadful Hollow* xv. 197 My dear old Super, Pop was always threatening to cut us off with a shilling. **1977** T. BERGER *Who is Teddy Villanova?* i. 1 My apartment, on the door of which the churlish super had posted a notice that tended to humiliate.

8. *Bookbinding.* [Origin unknown.] = *MULL *sb.*[7] (see quots. 1914, 1970). *U.S.*

1914 J. J. PLEGER *Bookbinding* III. 15 *Super*, a thin, loosely-woven, starched cloth glued on the back of books. **1916** *Rebacking Bks.* (Worcester County, Mass., Law Library) 7 The back had been hand sewed.., a strip of super between the bands pasted on the boards. **1940** PERRY & BAAB *Binding of Bks.* iii. 48 Super cloth (a sized cheese cloth) is too light for reinforcing purposes. **1967** [see *MULL *sb.*[7]]. **1970** R. K. KENT *Lang. Journalism* 130 *Super*,..a loose, open-weave cotton material used as reinforcement for the binding of a book: also called *crash*, or in England, *mull.*

9. [Short for *SUPERDUPER *a.* or *SUPERBOMB.] A colloquial name for the fusion or hydrogen bomb. Now chiefly *Hist.*

1951 W. L. LAURENCE *Hell Bomb* i. 3, I first heard about the hydrogen bomb in the spring of 1945 in Los Alamos... They were already considering preliminary designs for a hydrogen-fusion bomb, which in their lighter moments they called the 'Super-duper' or just the 'Super'. **1958** J. CLEUGH tr. *Jungk's Brighter than Thousand Suns* xvi. 259 In the discussions among those 'in the know' that arose in consequence of the news of the explosion in the Soviet Union one word was continually repeated which outsiders, at that time, would scarcely have understood. It was 'Super'. **1982** *New Scientist* 2 Sept. 642/2 It seems that the realisation of the Super, with its implications of mega-deaths, is not technically out of reach of any power which can produce a fission bomb.

III. [Absol. use of the adj.] **10.** *colloq.* High-octane or top-grade petrol.

[**1965**: see *PREMIUM 7 b.] **1967** 'G. DOUGLAS' *Death went Hunting* vi. 47 He wanted petrol—four of super, it was. **1978** *Country Life* 25 May 1502/2 French petrol has always been expensive... A gallon of super..costs about £1.37.

super (sū·pəɹ), *v.* **I. 1.** [f. SUPER *sb.* 3 a.] *intr.* To appear in a play or film as an extra or supernumerary. *Theatr. slang.*

1889 [implied in *supering* s.v. SUPER *sb.*]. **1920** J. FERGUSON in *Northern Numbers* 98 In Town she 'supered' and would just 'walk on'. **1938** G. B. SHAW *Let.* 20 Sept. in *B. Shaw & Mrs. Campbell* (1952) 323 All the élite of the profession over forty rushed down to Pinewood to super in it [*sc.* a film]. **1976** *New Yorker* 16 Feb. 26/1 Chance for man to super in new Met production of Aida.

2. [f. *SUPER *sb.* 8.] *trans.* To back (a book) with super. *U.S.*

1914 J. J. PLEGER *Bookbinding* III. 125 After enough books have been head-banded and supered.., put the backs together.

II. 3. [Short for SUPERANNUATE *v.*] *trans.* To remove (a pupil) from a school or form on account of age. Chiefly *pass.* Cf. SUPERANNUATE *v.* 3 a. *School slang.*

1902 'C. TURLEY' *Godfrey Marten, Schoolboy* xi. 135 'I have been in the Lower Fourth exactly four terms,' he went on, 'and my people are getting sick, and Sandy says I shall be 'supered' in a term or two.' **1923** E. W. HORNUNG *Old Offenders & Few Old Scores* 239 He was in our house, and super'd, poor beast! **1937** R. A. KNOX *Double Cross Purposes* v. 84 He always was a scug, till the day he was super'd. **1945** T. RATTIGAN *Love in Idleness* I. 8 He was super'd from Eton... Removed for not being in a high enough form.

4. [Short for SUPERIMPOSE *v.*] *trans.* To superimpose (a caption, etc.) on a film. *Television slang.*

1964 [see *CUE *v.*[2] a]. **1964** [see *CAPTION *sb.* 4]. **1966** G. N. LEECH *Eng. in Advertising* vi. 60 In the transcription [of a television commercial], italicised portions are 'supered' and capitalised portions are in the spoken commentary. **1975** *Listener* 9 Jan. 38/2 Why not super the characters' names towards the end of a play?

super, *a.* Restrict *Trade colloq.* to senses in Dict. and add: **1.** Now also preceding the sb. as *super foot.* Cf. *superficial foot* s.v. SUPERFICIAL *a.* 2 b.

1949 *Gloss Terms Timber* (*B.S.I.*) 23 Super. foot, a square foot of timber of the thickness stated, e.g. 'per super. foot of 1½ in'. **1953** *Brit. Commonw. Forest Terminol.* I. 57 Foot, superficial... A unit of volume equal to 1/12th of a cubic foot. In Australia and New Zealand, applied to standing trees, logs and sawn timber of any thickness, usually under the synonym *Super foot.* **1971** *Sunday Australian* 8 Aug. 4/3 A brick veneer home of this size contains 11,000 superfeet of timber.

3. *slang.* Very good or pleasant, first-rate, excellent, 'smashing'. Also as *int.*

This sense has developed from and overlaps with sense 2 in Dict.

[**1837** DICKENS *Pickw.* xli. 445 I'll be upon the wery best extra-super behaviour!] **1895** *Army & Navy Co-op. Soc. Price List* 15 Sept. 1079 White or black super opera bodice. **1923** [see *CABARET[1] 2b]. **1932** *Daily Express* 25 June 7/4 We have race meetings here, and super bathing. **1946** J. B. PRIESTLEY *Bright Day* xi. 327 This is jolly good, though. Super. **1954** 'R. CROMPTON' *William & Moon Rocket* i. 27 'Wizard,' said William. 'Super,' said Ginger. **1968** *Sunday Times* 25 Aug. 4/6 Doesn't almost everyone describe something mildly nice as 'super'. **1976** *Evening Post* (Nottingham) 13 Dec. 7/2 His wife Lee, said: 'Isn't it super? We can't get over it.'

super-, *prefix.* Add :This prefix, particularly in senses of branches II and III, has continued to be an important formative element in English. The sections in this article together with the following main entries contain a selection of those formations found more frequently during the last hundred years or so.

I. 2. a. (*b*) **su:perexcha·nge** *Physics* [ad. F. *superéchange* (H. A. Kramers 1940, in *Magnétisme* (Centre Nat. de la Recherche Sci. de France) III. 49)], an exchange force that acts between the electrons of two cations through those of an intervening anion, as in some antiferromagnetic materials; **superinvest** *v.*: delete † and add later example; **superprona·tion** = SUPINATION.

1950 *Physical Rev.* LXXIX. 354/1 This indicates that the superexchange directly through the O ion may be more powerful than that between locations making angles of 90° with the O ions. **1967** J. S. KOUVEL in J. H. Westbrook *Intermetallic Compounds* xxvii. 529/2 A remarkable feature of these superexchange interactions in ionic materials is that they almost always give rise to an antiparallel rather than parallel (i.e., ferromagnetic) alignment of moments. **1980** A. S. CHAKRAVARTY *Introd. Magnetic Properties Matter* xiv. 458 The superexchange mechanism..becomes the dominant factor if the separations between the magnetic ions are too large for the direct exchange mechanism to be operative. **1922** *19th Cent.* Oct. 594 Even sordidness itself has put off all its vileness, and is seen superinvested in beauty. **1907** *Practitioner* Apr. 486 The arms are fixed in a position of rigid extension, and frequently superpronation, so that the palms looked outward.

II. 4. a. (*a*) *super-legal, -moral, -muscan* [L. *musca* fly], *-physical, -sensational* adjs.; **su:peradiaba·tic** *a. Meteorol.*, being or involving a lapse rate greater than that of dry air when it rises and expands adiabatically (viz. approximately one degree centigrade per 100 metres), or a temperature gradient in any other fluid greater than that of an adiabatic expansion of the fluid during upward motion; **superlu·minal** *a.* [L. *lūmen, lūmin-* light], having or being a speed greater than that of light; **superna·tional** *a.* = *SUPRANATIONAL *a.*; hence **superna·tionalist** *a.*; **super-re·al** *a.* = *SURREAL *a.*; also as quasi-*sb.*; **super-reali·stic** *a.* = *SURREALIST, *SURREALISTIC *adjs.*

1925 *Nature* 28 Feb. 301/2 The frequent superadiabatic lapse-rates which occur in the bottom layer of the atmosphere. **1975** *Ibid.* 30 Oct. 748/1 Within the continental tectosphere..the thermal gradients are superadiabatic, and the dominant mechanism of heat transport is conduction, not advection. **1978** *Ibid.* 26 Oct. 726/2 The theory of corona formation [on the sun] is not well developed, and the computation of acoustic fluxes is critically dependent on the theory of superadiabatic convection. **1920** H. G. WELLS *Outl. Hist.* 478/2 He was a real monarch, super-legal. **1959** K. R. POPPER *Logic Sci. Discovery* ix. 236 Saying that they are 'spread with super-luminal velocity' is about as helpful as saying that twice two turns with super-luminal velocity into four. **1975** *Physics Bull.* Jan 13/1 The prospect of discovering superluminal particles is so appealing that the search is started afresh whenever there is an improvement or extension of experimental technique. **1980** Superluminal [see *subluminal* adj. s.v. *SUB- 14 a]. **1922** W. R. INGE *Outspoken Ess.* II. 131 It would be too absurd to suppose that our own State is the only specimen of these superhuman and supermoral individualities. **1960** K. AMIS *New Maps of Hell* (1961) iii. 84 Religious or quasi-religious feelings.. attach themselves to the super-intelligent or super-moral alien power. *a* **1902** S. BUTLER *Way of All Flesh* (1903) lxxx. 370, I..saw a fly alight on..hot coffee on which the milk had formed a thin skin... I noted with what..almost supermuscan effort he..made for the edge of the cup. **1929** S. LESLIE *Anglo-Catholic* xv. 208 The Bees which buzzed..throughout the Papal City, resembling supermuscan flies perched on the walls. **1898** F. W. MAITLAND *Roman Canon Law in Church of England* i. 8 The cosmopolitan, the 'extra-national', or 'super-national' tone of the work of these two English canonists. **1928** G. B. SHAW *Intelligent Woman's Guide Socialism* lxxxiii. 450 Substitute supernational morality, law, and action, for the present international anarchism. **1977** *Irish Democrat* Mar. 3/1 The process of merging the national Governments of western Europe into one supernational administration. **1979** *Dædalus* Winter 190 Andreas Papandreou and his Panhellenic Socialist Movement (PASOK) have been able to capitalize on a supernationalist stand. **1889** *Cent. Dict.*, Superphysical. **1924** W. B. SELBIE *Psychol. Relig.* 277 Various forms of super-physical life. **1935** S. BECKETT *Echo's Bones*, The sphincter..Potwalloping now through the promenaders This trusty all-steel this superreal Bound for home like a good boy. **1942** *Horizon* July 41 The best Winchester pictures..possess the quality of super-real mystery. **1952** R. CAMPBELL *Lorca* iv. 63 There are also curious nonsensical excursions into the super-real. **1926** A. HUXLEY *Essays New & Old* 185 The adventures of Felix the Cat are super-realistic in the highest degree. **1955** S. SPENDER *Making of Poem* vi. 103 The golden Romanticism has..claims to set up a super-realistic reality. **1888** Supersensational [see *non-spatial* s.v. *NON- 3]. **1943** H. READ *Educ. through Art* ii. 28 As for the mental activity called intuition, by which we do not mean any super-sensational faculty of the mind, but the apprehension of abstract quantities and relations..it is the basis of a fourth type of art.

(*b*) *superluminally.*

1979 *Nature* 18 Jan. 182/1 (*heading*) Superluminally expanding radio sources and the radio-quiet QSOs.

(*c*) In related sbs., as *supernationalism, -nationalist, -nationality*; **super-re·alism** = *SURREALISM; **super-re·alist** = *SURREALIST *sb.*; **super-rea·lity** = *SURREALITY.

1917 G. B. SHAW *Platform & Pulpit* (1962) 106 Supernationalism will be limited by general psychological homogeneity. **1980** *Encounter* May 94/1 It thus seems natural to expect an author such as Fleming..to endow his heroes with patriotism and his villains with a super-nationalism of the nastier kind. **1941** L. B. NAMIER in *Time & Tide* 5 July 558/1 The outlook and ideas of the modern supernationalists..are very largely of German origin. **1916** E. HOLMES *Nemesis of Docility* i. 16 Those nations cling tenaciously to their respective nationalities, as against the supernationality of Germany. **1933** *Bull. Mus. Mod. Art* Oct. 2/1 Superrealism is the most conspicuous movement. **1952** R. CAMPBELL *Lorca* iv. 65 The dream region of 'super-realism'. **1931** 'WYNDHAM LEWIS' *Diabolical Principle* 64 The cultural message of *Transition* is still further defined by the incorporation of the *dream-aesthetic* of the Super-realists into a body already reeking with 'romance'—indeed putrid with the excessive decomposition of that condition. *Ibid.* 65 The *infantile* is the link between the Super-realists and Miss Stein, as it is between Miss Stein and Miss Loos. **1934** H. READ in *Cinema Q.* III. 1. 17 Some painters call it a super-reality (*surréalité*). **1935** D. GASCOYNE *Short Survey Surrealism* v. 109 The more recent ideas of surrealism, which conceive super-reality as existing in the material world, objectively, as well as subjectively in the automatic thought of the unconscious. **1945** H. READ *Coat of Many Colours* xxxix. 198, I believe that in general the plastic arts will tend towards rationality and the poetic arts towards superreality.

5. c. *superfamily* (later examples), *superspecies* (later examples); **su·pergalaxy** *Astr.*, a supercluster; *spec.* = *local supercluster* s.v. *LOCAL *a.* 2 d; hence **supergala·ctic** *a.*

1953 E. MAYR et al. *Methods & Princ. Syst. Zool.* iii. 52 The age of specialization has resulted in a general pushing upward of the categories, subfamilies becoming families, and families becoming superfamilies. **1978** *Nature* 16 Nov. 264/2 All three families of humans and apes are included in the superfamily Hominoidea. **1971** *New Scientist* 29 July 245/1 His final choice of supergalactic equator gave highly positive concentration indices for galaxies in the northern galactic hemisphere. **1982** *Nature* 2 Dec. 409/1 At high supergalactic *z* coordinates the galaxy density is much lower than near the supergalactic plane $z = 0$. **1946** G. GAMOW in *Nature* 19 Oct. 549/1 The realm of galaxies as seen through Mt. Wilson telescope represents only a small part of a much larger system (a 'supergalaxy' in the super-Shapley sense) rotating round a distant centre. **1955** *Sci. Amer.* Mar. 42/1 One source of radio emission, extending over a long path across the sky, coincides with the plane of the supergalaxy of which the Milky Way is a part. **1971** *New Scientist* 29 July 245/1 The Supergalaxy is, in turn, composed of smaller clusters of galaxies, including the local cluster of about a dozen members, our Galaxy being one of them. **1931** E. MAYR in *Amer. Mus. Novitates* No. 469. 2, I propose for *Artenkreis* the more convenient term, Superspecies. I define superspecies as a systematic unit containing geographically representative species that have developed characters too distinct to permit the birds to be regarded as subspecies of one species. **1976** E. DELSON in C. J. Jolly *Early Hominids of Africa* 535 This reliance on superspecies is perhaps..a recognition of our own uncertainties.

f. *Biol.* **superfe·male,** a female with a higher ratio of X chromosomes to autosomes than normal females; **su·permale,** a male in which this ratio is lower than in normal males, or the ratio of Y chromosomes to autosomes is higher.

1922 *Amer. Naturalist* LVI. 63 If the intersexes result from an intermediate ratio of X [chromosomes] to autosomes because the X has a net female tendency, then it might be expected that by increasing the ratio of X to autosomes a superfemale would be produced, and conversely, a supermale by increasing the relative number of autosomes. **1955** [see *INTERSEX]. **1959** *Lancet* 12 Dec. 1088/1 The inappropriateness of the term 'superfemale' is emphasised by the discovery of a human 3X 2A individual whose primary and secondary sex characters are underdeveloped. **1969** *Guardian* 8 Mar. 3/1 The theory that so-called supermales—men with an extra male chromosome—might be born criminals has lost its first test in a United States court.

6. a. *super-minister; super-ministry.*

1946 *Nature* 24 Aug. 247/2 What the Haldane Report recommended, however, was, not placing responsible ministers under a super-minister, but the consolidation or grouping of departments into a small number of super-ministries with one responsible minister for each. *a* **1974** R. CROSSMAN *Diaries* (1977) III. 666 Benn and Crosland are now super-Ministers of industry and planning, the same level as Barbara and me. **1937** L. HART *Europe in Arms* xv. 191 Ideas of possible organization range from a super-Ministry which should..absorb the..existing departments to a small Ministry, superimposed, which should guide the Government. **1975** *Globe & Mail* (Toronto) 25 Nov. 5/3 Liberal leader Robert Nixon also pledged to end the three super-ministries if his party were elected.

b. *super-organism* (later examples), *-priority, -quality, -system*; **supergra·vity** *Physics*, (a theory of) gravity as described or predicted by a supersymmetric quantum field theory; **supersy·mmetry** *Physics*, a very general type of mathematical symmetry which relates fermions and bosons; hence **su:persymme·tric** *a.*

1976 *Physics Lett.* B. LXII. 335/1 The first order formulation with torsion is closely related to the description of supergravity in superspace. **1980** *Nature* 21 Feb. 717/3 Known as supergravity, the new theory attempts to treat the familiar gravitational field as only a component part of a more elaborate network of forces and fields. **1971** E. O. WILSON *Insect Societies* (1972) i. 1/2 The giant of all such 'superorganisms' is a colony of the African driver ant *Anomma wilverthi.* **1973** P. A. COLINVAUX *Introd. Ecol.* xl. 551 The ideas of the superorganism and the social entity no doubt acquired much of their plausibility from the prevalence of the phenomenon of ecological dominance in plant communities of the temperate zones. **1917** W. S. CHURCHILL *Let.* 19 Aug. in M. Gilbert *W. S. Churchill* (1977) IV. Compan. I. 141 At present the Admiralty claim a super priority upon all supplies. **1952** *Times* 30 June 6/7 Lord De L'Isle and Dudley, V.C...announced on June 7 that the R.A.F. was to be equipped with the GA5 as an all-weather fighter and that it would have 'super-priority'. **1922** JOYCE *Ulysses* 312 His superb highclass vocalism, which by its superquality greatly enhanced his already international reputation. **1960** *Times* 3 Oct. (John Harvey Advt. Suppl.) p. ii/3 Super-quality surgical steel. **1974** *Proc. 17th Internat. Conf. High Energy Physics* I. 254/1 A supersymmetric theory. **1982** *Nature* 26 Aug. 801/1 During the past year there has also emerged a growing interest in particle physics theories that not only unify the description of the three basic interactions (strong, weak and electromagnetic) but which are also supersymmetric. **1974** B. ZUMINO in *Proc. 17th Internat. Conf. High Energy Physics* I. 254/1 Fermi-Bose supersymmetry was introduced by Wess and the author. It connects Bosons with Fermions. Its existence was suggested by dual models (when formulated as two-dimensional field theories) and the name supergauge symmetry in four dimensions seemed a natural choice. The supergauge algebra having only a finite number of generators in four dimensions, it seems now reasonable to avoid the word gauge and adopt the expression Fermi-Bose supersymmetry, or simply supersymmetry, suggested recently by Salam and Strathdee. **1977** *Physics Today* Apr. 49/3 As far as I know, the only natural way to keep a scalar boson massless is to have a 'supersymmetry',.. which puts scalar fields in the same multiplet as massless fermion fields. **1978** *McGraw-Hill Yearbk. Sci. & Technol.* 356/1 Gauge supersymmetry treats all fundamental particles..on the same basis, accomplishes a fusion of space-time symmetries and internal symmetries.., and promises new types of renormalizable field theories as possible models for unified interactions, perhaps even including gravitation. **1934** WEBSTER, Supersystem. **1940** BRYANT & AIKEN *Psychol. Eng.* ii. 8 'Universal grammar', a norm or super-system which will comprehend all the various local systems. **1975** *Bio Systems* VII. 15/2 Having pure chemical systems for each of the three subsystems, we connect them to form a chemical supersystem.

c. *super-being, block* [BLOCK *sb.* 14], *-boss* [BOSS *sb.*[6]], *-brain, -car, -carrier* [*CARRIER 1 m], *-cinema, -city, -computer, -crook* [CROOK *sb.* 13], *-grid* [*GRID 8 a], *-gun, -hero, -heroine, -journalist, -liner* [LINER[2] 8 a], *-magic, -male* (see also sense 5 f), *-nation, -patriot, -port* [PORT *sb.*[1] 1], *-profit, -race* (examples), *-rich* [RICH *sb.* 11], *-salesman, -salesmanship, -ship, -sleuth, -speed, -spy, -stud* [*STUD *sb.*[2] 4 d], *-tanker* [*TANKER[1] 1 a]; **su·peralloy** *Metallurgy*, an alloy capable of withstanding high temperatures, high stresses, and often highly oxidizing atmospheres; **su·perbike,** a motor cycle with a nominal engine capacity of 750 cc. or more; **Super Bowl** *U.S. Football* [after *ROSE BOWL 2], the final of the National Football League championship, contested annually since 1967 (from 1970, a play-off between the winners of the two sections of the League, the National and the American conferences); **su·perchurch,** (*a*) a church formed by the amalgamation of separate churches; (*b*) a very large church; **su·percrat** *N. Amer.*, a powerful bureaucrat; **Super Glue,** the proprietary name of a strong adhesive; also **superglue; su·pergrass** [*GRASS *sb.*[1] 11*] (see quot. 1979); **super-hi·ghway** *N. Amer.*, a road designed for high-speed traffic, a motorway; also *fig.*; **su·perjet** a very large or fast jet aeroplane; also *attrib.* and *fig.*; **su·perloo** *colloq.*, a public convenience on certain British railway stations which offers a range of washing facilities, including showers; **su·per-rat,** a rat that is resistant to the action of the usual rat poisons; **superset** *Math., Linguistics,* etc., a set (*SET *sb.*[2] 10 c) which includes another set or sets; **su·persound** sound which is too intense to be endured, or of too high a frequency to be perceived (cf. *ULTRASOUND); **su·perstate,** a dominant political community, esp. one formed from an alliance or union of several nations; *spec.* = *SUPERPOWER 3; **su·perstore,** a large store selling a variety of goods and typically situated away from a town's main shopping area; a small hypermarket; **su·perwoman** (later examples); in recent use, a woman who fills successfully concurrent roles as career-woman, wife, and mother.

Many of these formations are not 'chiefly nonce'.

1953 C. L. CLARK *High-Temperature Alloys* xvi. 269 Up to the time of the introduction of these superalloys it was generally agreed that any alloy intended for high-temperature service should be processed and heat treated. **1981** *McGraw-Hill Yearbk. Sci. & Technol.* 325/1 Superalloys can operate for extended periods of time at temperatures about 1200°F (650°C), and provide resistance to hot corrosion and erosion. **1930** *Daily Express* 8 Sept. 2/4 A patient imagines—quite seriously—that he is a kind of super-being. **1980** I. WATSON *Gardens of Delight* iv. 28 Who's this 'God' you were telling my people about? An alien superbeing—is that it? **1970** *Cycle World* Oct. 34 Suzuki's entry in the 'Superbike' field just happens to be an excellent touring bike. **1976** *Good Motoring* Nov. 5/2 A strong quota of 'superbikes' in the 750cc-plus category. **1928** *Survey* (N.Y.) 1 Mar. 696/1 It is necessary to examine more closely the structure and use of these superblocks. **1975** *New Society* 14 Aug. 375/3 A whole superblock in front of the museum, including many publishers offices and landmarks.., would have gone. **1916** *Blackw. Mag.* June 813/2 The German super-bosses. **1977** *Listener* 12 May 608/2 The man..he most admires in Italian public life today, the Fiat superboss. **1966** *Los Angeles Times* 22 Oct. III. 1/5 The capacity of the Coliseum for the Super Bowl will be 90,000. **1979** *Arizona Daily Star* 1 Apr. H 4/1 One would think the question of desirability of rising profits was of the same genre as who should win the Super Bowl. **1928** G. CAMPBELL *My Mystery Ships* xi. 208 To find out what its [*sc.* the name's] origin is or what it means, we shall have to wait till the person with the super-brain who thought of it appears before the Invention Board. **1975** *Pix* (Austral.) 13 Nov. 42/5 Futurologist and 'super brain' Dr. Kahn..on a recent visit said the world would be better off if Australians worked harder. **1920** *Motor* 3 Nov. 113 (Advt.), The Supreme development of the British super-car. **1977** *Belfast Tel.* 17 Jan. 9/4 There is everything from the family saloon to the specialised super-cars. **1969** D. ACHESON *Present at Creation* xxii. 195 We urged sending a powerful naval force, including the newly commissioned supercarrier *Franklin D. Roosevelt.* **1978** *Times* 28 Jan. 4/8 Mr Brown was seeking to make optimum use of the Navy's power in face of the strengthened Soviet Navy, which is making supercarriers increasingly vulnerable. **1970** *Time* 25 May 76 Episcopalians are potential participants in the proposed multichurch Protestant merger, the Church of Christ Uniting. Should the Episcopal Church join the new super-church, [etc.]. **1977** *Time* 26 Dec. 41/2 The faithful throng to gaudy superchurches with 5,000 to 10,000 seats, green shag wall-to-wall carpeting, pit orchestras and Jesus rock bands. **1923** *Gramophone* Apr. 7/1 A terrace opposite Holland House (now I believe about to be pulled down for a super-cinema). **1931** *Ann. Reg. 1930* 48 Of the existing cinemas 85 per cent are now wired, and there has been a great advance in the building of new super-cinemas. **1955** *Times* 9 May 3/1 One of Madrid's super-cinemas, the Coliseum. **1958** A. TOYNBEE *East to West* 103 You find yourself interned in one of the standardized super-cities of the modern world. **1971** *Americana Ann.* 103 Paolo Soleri..planned..gigantic supercities towering high in the air or floating on water. **1968** N. WALFORD tr. *O. Johannesson's Great Computer* IV. 108 The generating of controlling computers must be entirely computer-controlled. This task..was performed..by linking together about a hundred computers..and combining them..to form a unit known as the supercomputer. Such a unit had sufficient capacity to breed new computers of its own type. **1982** *Times* 30 Apr. 17/2 The market for supercomputers, as they are generally known, is also set for rapid growth. **1972** *Newsweek* 11 Dec. 25 A slimmed-down, tidied-up..Nixon Inc. with..four or so White House-level supercrats. **1978** *Globe & Mail* (Toronto) 17 July 2/4 [The Ottawa] system has fewer than a dozen super-powerful bureaucrats who dominate the policy-making process. They are the supercrats, and Mr. Gotlieb is one of the more successful ones. **1934** S. G. HEDGES *Plague Panic* xxvi. 211 The organized police systems of the world had failed so utterly to bring this super-crook to book. **1979** *Daily Mail* 29 Jan. 6/3 The wanted man was a super-crook. **1977** *Drive* May–June 91/3 One of the latest superglue products..is a two-part, metal-to-glass adhesive. **1978** R. MARK *Office of Constable* xiii. 163 The age of the supergrass had arrived. **1979** *Observer* 8 Apr. 1/3 Twomey and Carpenter claim they were framed by a 'supergrass'—a police informer hoping for lenient treatment in return for turning in other villains. **1983** *Listener* 19 May 7/1 Following information from a supergrass, dozens of people alleged to be members of it had been arrested. **1950** *Times Rev. Industry* May 32/1 The projected 275/300kV British super-grid transmission system. **1979** *Nature* 8 Nov. 123/2 The extension of the Union-wide 'supergrid' of 1500 V DC transmission lines should, theoretically, allow power stations to be sited anywhere. **1915** *Chambers's Jrnl.* Oct. 661/2 The journalistic words 'superguns' [etc.]. **1929** *Encycl. Brit.* III. 367/1 As fast as the Liége forts fell to the super-guns. **1972** *Village Voice* (N.Y.) 1 June 53/2 Lee and Harry are inclined to put him down for killing the hawk with his supergun. **1917** 'CONTACT' *Airman's Outings* 211 The super-heroes of the war. **1980** *Dædalus* Spring 119 The only people foolish enough to believe in fairy tales and superheroes (the last survivals in the mythology of atheism). **1970** *Times* 22 Dec. 8 Miss Comic Strip will be..selected for her..desirability as an imaginary superheroine. **1925** *Amer. City Mag.* Apr. 373/1 The Super-Highway is unique... It will furnish an express motor traffic highway. **1949** *Word Study* May 1/2 A super-highway toward..success. **1978** J. A. MICHENER *Chesapeake* xiii. 799 She found Route 2, which took her to Route 695, the superhighway circumnavigating Baltimore. **1958** *Daily Herald* 3 Mar. 1/1 They [*sc.* aircraft firms] are talking in terms of a super jet liner capable of crossing the Atlantic in four hours with 150 passengers. **1964** S. BELLOW *Herzog* (1965) 241 The superjet carried him to Chicago in ninety minutes. **1978** *Detroit Free Press* 16 Apr. (Parade Suppl.) 20/3 Except for her, however, not a single person arrested fits the image usually associated with the superjet, 'fast lane' set. **1916** L. CURTIS *Let.* 13 Nov. in *Let. People India* (1917) 27 As a sort of super-journalist much of my information has been derived from pumping people with first-hand knowledge. **1976** *Listener* 6 May 554/1 The superjournalists have evidently conquered the supermarket, for the rise of Mr Bob Woodward and Mr Carl Bernstein is now being presented as almost as spectacular a saga as the fall of President Nixon. **1928** *Manch. Guardian Weekly* 31 Aug. 180/3 To enlarge their docks for the building of a super-liner. **1963** *Economist* 27 July 322 Cunard is still chasing its ambition of a new super-liner. **1969** *Daily Tel.* 17 Dec. 1/4 The charge for using the 'superloo' at Euston and Victoria will go up from 6d to 1s. **1972** *Travelling* Autumn 43/3 Edinburgh's Waverley Station..will provide superloos, catering facilities. **1921** T. R. GLOVER *Jesus in Exper. Men* i. 8 The early Christian..really used the Gospel as a sort of super-magic. **1972** D. KENNEDY *Recoll. Assiniboine Chief* 156 The old witch saw that she was thwarted by super-magic. **1970** G. GREER *Female Eunuch* 194 Her sister, killed because of the maleficent supermale. **1914** E. BARKER *Nietzche & Treitschke* 25 Treitschke looks to war as the expression of an exclusively national supernation. **1977** P. JOHNSON *Enemies of Society* xix. 248 Is there to be a huge African super-nation, based only on colour, but with immense racial differences within it? **1917** *N.Y. World* 7 Mar. 10/1 At a Carnegie Hall meeting of..superpatriots, Irving T. Bush was hissed because he defended the President of the United States. **1945** [see *SALISBURY STEAK]. **1977** *Private Eye* 13 May 16/1 That super-patriot the late Lord Beaverbrook. **1969** *Sunday Times* 16 Feb. 30/4 In addition to the container ship, another ship of the future is the LASH vessel (lighter-aboard-ship) that will cruise at high speeds, pausing only briefly at super-port gathering points to pick up or discharge its fleet. **1970** *Daily Colonist* (Victoria, B.C.) 9 Aug. 5/3 A second superport, providing modern bulk handling facilities. **1946** *Sun* (Baltimore) 9 July 2/2 He declares that Mr. Norton is trying to..swell employers' 'super-profits'. **1974** B. PEARCE tr. *Amin's Accumulation on World Scale* II. ii. 392 The origin and dynamics of the superprofits of monopolies. **1912** C. SAROLEA *Anglo-German Problem* i. 59 The German is convinced that he belongs to a super-race. **1979** *Jrnl. R. Soc. Arts* CXXVII. 324/2 A single pathogen genotype able to attack all of the components, the so called 'super-race'. **1974** *N.Y. Times* 13 Nov. 47/8 Armed with a new toxic rodent killer, the City Health Department opened a campaign yesterday to destroy a strain of 'super rats' breeding in the South Bronx. **1977** *New Scientist* 28 Apr. 200 This company has developed an anti-coagulant which is particularly effective against super rats..which are already prevalent in the United States and are now being reported in Europe and Asia. **1981** *Oxford Jrnl.* 27 Feb. 6 Pest controllers are battling against a breed of 'super-rats' which are immune to normal poisons. **1969** *Times* 5 May (Wall St. Suppl.) p. xii/2 Many of the super-rich of the United States live in Texas. **1982** *Country Life* 11 Mar. 666/2 This brilliant..novel about the super-rich in France. **1934** WEBSTER, Supersalesman. **1936** O. NASH *Primrose Path* 127 And a bright super-salesman Has sold you a pup. **1978** M. PUZO *Fools Die* xvi. 172 A very soft-selling supersalesman. **1933** *Sat. Even. Post* 7 Jan. 21 Super-salesmanship—1932 model. **1968** Supersalesmanship [see *SELL *v.* 3 j]. **1970** *Psychonomic Sci.* XXI (4) 235/3 There is no predetermined hierarchy of supersets and subsets. **1976** J. S. GRUBER *Lexical Structures in Syntax & Semantics* II. ii. 278 In this case we cannot allow the derived tree to be a subset of that in the lexical environment. The only alternative is to require that the derived tree be a superset of that in the lexical environment. **1937** *Sun* (Baltimore) 16 Nov. 12/1 The reasons that prompted the commission to advise against construction by this country of superships to rival the Queen Mary. **1974** *National Rev.* (U.S.) 1 Mar. 261 New sources of competitive coal have opened up in Australia, Canada, and South Africa, and again the specter of superships rises to plague us. **1974** *Aiken* (S. Carolina) *Standard* 24 Apr. 4-A/5 It's doubtful if the FBI will long retain, or ever again seek, the super-sleuth. **1942** *Pop. Sci. Monthly* Feb. 49/2 Sound waves too powerful for the human system to bear, and others too high in pitch for the human ear to hear, are new miracle-working tools in science and industry. In dozens of laboratories, scientists are perfecting sound-generating devices, and discovering new uses for supersound and ultrasound. **1952** *Chambers's Jrnl.* 1 June 363 Scientists have been having the time of their lives exploring super sound. **1927** *Glasgow Herald* 1 June 15 If we cleaved our way above the ocean at the superspeeds now contemplated. **1961** *Times* 17 Nov. 17/5 (Advt.), Current Ferranti activities include..Atlas (most advanced super-speed computer in the world). **1937** KOESTLER *Spanish Testament* i. 24 If one had taken them seriously, one might have imagined that half Esturil consisted of super-spies. **1980** R. HILL *Spy's Wife* viii. 53 Is she another Kremlin super-spy? **1918** O. GREGORY *Meccania* iv. 91 The Super-State must borrow from the Socialists the conception of an all-embracing power and activity. **1929** B. RUSSELL *Marriage & Morals* xv. 173 The control of the super-State over education would be a positive safeguard against war. *Ibid.*, Loyalty to the international super-State should everywhere be fought. **1935** J. E. C. WELLDON *Forty Years On* ii. 76, I have felt that the Darwinian theory of the survival of the fittest. was responsible for the German doctrine of the super-state, which, as the Germans conceived it, could only be Germany. **1941** A. HUXLEY *Let.* 27 Nov. (1969) 471 The super-states based on the three centres of heavy industry and advanced technology—Europe, North America and East Asia. **1959** N. MAILER *Advts. for Myself* (1961) 272 The iron commisars of the Soviet superstate. **1974** M. B. BROWN *Econ. Imperialism* ix. 225 The nation states, apart from the super-states—USA, EEC, Japan and the USSR—are forced into a client relationship with the giant companies. **1978** *New York* 3 Apr. 45/3 Loyalty to the superstate as a substitute for the supernatural. **1965** *Punch* 7 July 1/2 Why bother with exports when the superstore will take anything you care to make? **1980** *Times* 13 Feb. 3/2 Comparing superstores with local supermarkets is like comparing apples with oranges. **1975** *Time Out* 19 Sept. 25/1 Petersen, the latest in the 'Alvin Purple' brigade of Australian superstuds. **1921** *Mex Fuel Oil* (Anglo-Mexican Petroleum Co.) 7 These losses are being made good by the building of several supertankers, commencing with the *San Florentino*..18,000 tons. **1953** *Wall St. Jrnl.* 1 July 4/2 The S.S. New Jersey Sun, second of four supertankers being built for Sun Oil Co. **1977** *Whitaker's Almanack 1978* 1035/2 A serious problem would be the shipping and supertankers passing round Cape Horn. **1958** *Listener* 18 Dec. 1040/1 A picture of a girl maybe, fantastically beautiful, a blonde superwoman. **1975** S. CONRAN (*title*) Superwoman. **1976** *National Observer* (U.S.) 11 Sept. 20/5 The superwoman image ignores the reality of the average working woman or housewife.

III. 9. a. (*a*) *superdense, -fast, -luminous, -sumptuous*; **su·percolo:ssal** *a. U.S. colloq.*, very large, very good, stupendous; **super-coo·l** *a. slang* (orig. and chiefly *U.S.*), very cool (*COOL *a.* 4 e), relaxed, fine, etc.; also *absol.* as *sb.*; **superfatted** *a.*, (*b*) *slang*, of persons: overweight, fat; **superio·nic** *a. Physics*, having a high ionic electrical conductivity; also as *sb.*, a superionic substance; **superma·ssive** *a. Astr.*, having a mass many (i.e. typically between 10^6 and 10^9) times that of the sun; **superwea·k** *a. Particle Physics*, pertaining to or being a proposed interaction several orders of magnitude weaker than the weak interaction which would not be invariant under charge conjugation and space inversion jointly.

1934 WEBSTER, Supercolossal. **1937** *Amer. Speech* XII. 241/1 Supercolossal is an adjective heard several times orally in Colorado. **1938** WODEHOUSE *Code of Woosters* v. 130 Big is right, though perhaps 'super-colossal' would be more the *mot juste*. **1947** —— *Full Moon* v. 92 'Her profile. Lovely, don't you think?' 'Yup.' 'And her eyes. Super-colossal.' **1976** *National Observer* (U.S.) 17 July 6/3 The brand-new National Air and Space Museum here is a supercolossal mixture of show biz and science. **1970** T. WOLFE *Radical Chic & Mau-Mauing Flak Catchers* 131 The pimp style was a supercool style that was much admired or envied. **1975** *Radio Times* 23–29 Aug. 11/4 James Coburn was the nicest of all those Bond-type supercools. **1978** *Hot Car* July 91/3 They were super-cool amongst the sixties surfing set in the USA. **1981** *Times* 22 July 11/2 That style had itself been borrowed from younger Jamaicans, and the super cool they affected. **1967** *Listener* 27 Apr. 545/1 These observations ..imply an origin [of the Universe] from a superdense state 10,000 million years ago. **1977** *Time* 19 Sept. 50/1 The whole principle of diesel ignition is to raise the temperature of the fuel mixture by compressing it into a superdense mass in the cylinder. **1980** *Lok Sabha Deb.* (Delhi) 5 Aug. 264 A superfast train like the K.K. Express runs late by 5 to 6 hours. **1982** *Economist* 3 Apr. 120/3 It is at the frontiers of R and D now being done into superfast computers. **1927** WODEHOUSE *Small Bachelor* iii. 48 'Important people!' Mr. Waddington snorted sternly, 'A bunch of super-fatted bits of bad news.' **1947** L. HASTINGS *Dragons are Extra* ix. 212 A bald, double-chinned type who looked very like a super-fatted edition of ex-President Hoover. **1972** W. L. ROTH in *Jrnl. Solid State Chem.* IV. 60/1 Such solids, which may be called super ionic conductors, exhibit ionic conductivities that can be as large as inverse ohm-centimeters at temperatures ranging from near room temperature to 1200°C. **1972** *New Scientist* 11 May 321 A small and hardly known group of compounds called 'superionics' reveal exceptional electrical conductivity in the solid state. **1980** *Jrnl. Physics & Chem. Solids* XLI. 1323/1 The superionic conductors are characterized by their high ionic but very low electronic conductivity at room temperature. **1968** D. MOORE tr. *Schatzman's Struct. Universe* i. 15 If our present interpretations are correct, quasars are very remote and super-luminous. **1977** *Jrnl. R. Soc. Arts* CXXV. 215/1 The enigmatical 'quasars'..are thought to be immensely remote and super-luminous. **1967** Supermassive [see *RELATIVISTIC *a.* 2b]. **1981** *Economist* 24 Jan. 97/1 Still higher output would result from the collision of super-massive black holes containing, say, a mass equivalent to a million of earth's suns. **1922** JOYCE *Ulysses* 497 It is immense, supersumptuous. **1970** *Physical Rev.* D. II. 257 (*heading*) Unitarity and the phase of the mixing parameter in superweak theories. **1979** CHENG & O'NEILL *Elem. Particle Physics* ix. 206 If the Wolfenstein model is correct, there exists a 'superweak' fifth force in nature.

(*b*) *supercolossally*.
1966 *New Yorker* 1 Oct. 184 Both supercolossally ambitious and energetic men.

b. *super-civilized* adj. (also *absol.* as *sb.*); **superallo·wed** *a. Nucl. Physics,* (of a beta decay) having an exceptionally high probability of occurrence as measured by the product of the half-life of the initial state and a function of the energy and momentum of the emitted electron.
1950 *Rev. Mod. Physics* XXII. 397/2 The very lowest $\log_{10} ft \sim 3$ to 4 are allowed transitions between nuclei having similar nuclear wave functions. These transitions are called the superallowed transitions, while allowed transitions between nuclei not having very similar wave functions have log *ft* ranging from 4 to 6. **1964** *Physical Rev. Lett.* XII. 301/1 The transition from the ground state of ^{37}Cl to the 5·1-MeV excited state of ^{37}Ar is superallowed and has a large matrix element for neutrino absorption. **1975** *Nature* 18 Sept. 179/2 They start..from basic input experimental data—the lifetimes and energy release of certain particularly simple nuclear β decays known as superallowed transitions. **1929** 'R. CROMPTON' *William* i. 12 The Outlaws never made the pretence affected by the super-civilised, of indifference to their neighbours' affairs.

10. b. su·pervoltage *Physics* and *Med.*, a higher than usual voltage; *spec.* a voltage in excess of 200 kilovolts; usu. *attrib.* with reference to the use of X-rays generated using such voltages.
1934 *Illinois Med. Jrnl.* LXVI. 286/2 Much of the improvement claimed for super-voltage is available at 200 kilovolts. **1956** A. H. COMPTON *Atomic Quest* i. 14 The new physics laboratory..would include space for super-voltage equipment. **1976** *Lancet* 6 Nov. 992/2 Patients who received T.N.I. were all treated with supervoltage or megacurie equipment.

12. b. superoxide: in mod. use distinguished from peroxide (q.v. in Suppl.) and restricted to the anion O_2^-; (further examples).
1950 *Chambers's Jrnl.* Apr. 255/2 It [*sc.* a new life-saving apparatus] has depended upon finding a method for fairly large-scale production of the chemical used, namely potassium superoxide. **1965** PHILLIPS & WILLIAMS *Inorg. Chem.* I. xiii. 491 The metal oxides so far discussed contain the anion O_2^- only. There are also two other series of oxides, the peroxides and superoxides which contain the anions O_2^- and O_2^-respectively. **1979** *Experientia* XXXV. 245/2 The explanation for such action is the hypothesis that vitamin C can act as an antoxidant as well as oxidant, by generating superoxide.

IV. 13. supercalender *sb.* (earlier example); **super-tax:** abolished as an official term in the U.K. in 1929, but still in common (esp. *attrib.*) use; cf. *SURTAX *sb.*
1894 Super-calender [see *SHEAVE *sb.*[2] 3]. **1931** *Times Lit. Suppl.* 16 July 556/4 The incidence of income-tax and supertax on business profits. **1972** *Daily Tel.* 14 Jan. 13 Our friends, on hearing that we own two houses, put us in the super-tax class. **1978** F. OLBRICH *Desouza pays Price* v. 21 The Taj Mahal Hotel['s]..clientele consisted exclusively of those in the super-tax bracket.

VI. With reduplication of the prefix.

17. Used as an intensifier Cf. branch III.
1871 Super-superabundance [in Dict., sense 10a]. **1871** Super-superabundant [in Dict., sense 9a(*a*)]. **1871** Super-superabundantly [in Dict., sense 9a(*b*)]. **1934** 'J. SPENSER' *Limey breaks In* ix. 158 This warder was another of the variety known amongst prison populations as super-super bastards. **1937** A. CALDER-MARSHALL in C. Day Lewis *Mind in Chains* 60 The second stage was reached, where super- and super-super-films were made. **1963** *Supermarket & Self Service* (Johannesburg) Aug. 16/1 A further 'super-supermarket' of American-style dimensions, is under contemplation. **1974** T. P. WHITNEY tr. *Solzhenitsyn's Gulag Archipelago* I. II. iv. 590 Things were neat and clean, they said, and it was always warm, and the only work was mental work—and all of it super-supersecret.

18. Used to denote a further increase in rank or degree. Cf. branch II.
1971 *Nature* 26 Nov. 182/1 The observations would therefore seem to exclude super-clusters or the still greater hierarchy of super-super-clusters as the source of X-ray background. **1979** *Ibid.* 12 Apr. 615/1 Since nuclear shell theory predicts a further island of stability at Z = 164–184 ..we must consider whether the three peaks originate from decay of super-superheavy elements. **1980** *Sci. Amer.* July 112/1 In this way super-supercoiled molecules can be created, molecules that have many more superhelical twists than are usually present.

super-acid, *a.* Add: Also **super acid. 3.** Of, pertaining to, or designating a non-aqueous solution having very great protonating power.
1927 CONANT & HALL in *Jrnl. Amer. Chem. Soc.* XLIX. 3047 We investigate certain of the properties of these solutions in which salt formation is exceptionally complete, and we propose to call such solutions 'superacid solutions'. **1940** GLASSTONE *Textbk. Physical Chem.* xii. 959 On account of the very marked tendency of the $CH_3{\cdot}CO_2H_2^+$ ions to lose the proton they have taken up from the acid, the solutions exhibit acidic properties, e.g., in catalysis, of an exceptionally strong nature and so they have been called super-acid. **1968** *Accts. Chem. Res.* I. 202/1 The acidity of fluorosulfuric acid can be considerably increased by the addition of SbF_5 and SbF_5—SO_3, and the resulting solutions are the most highly acidic media known... These systems may therefore be justifiably called superacid media. **1979** *Science* 5 Oct. 14/3 Two superacid systems used very frequently are HSO_3F-SbF_5 (Magic Acid)..and HF-SbF_5 (fluoroantimonic acid).

B. *sb.* A solution of a strong acid in a very acidic solution, which is an extremely effective protonating agent; any acid stronger than some standard acid in either Brönsted acid (i.e., proton-donor) or Lewis acid (electron-acceptor) systems.
1968 *Jrnl. Amer. Chem. Soc.* XC. 2726/1 (*caption*) Chemistry in super acids. **1979** *Science* 5 Oct. 13/3 All protic acids stronger than 100 percent sulfuric acid should be classified as superacids. *Ibid.* 14/2 It is suggested that those [Lewis acids] stronger than anhydrous aluminum chloride..should be categorized as superacids. *Ibid.* 16/3 The astonishing acidity of Magic Acid and related superacids allows protonation of exceedingly weak bases.

Hence **superaci·dic** *a.* = *SUPER-ACID *a.* 3.
1979 *Science* 5 Oct. 14/3 These superacidic systems can be 10^{16} times stronger than 100 per cent sulfuric acid.

su:peraci·dity. [f. SUPER-ACID *a.*, after ACIDITY.] **a.** *Med.* (See quot.)
1900 DORLAND *Med. Dict.* 653/2 *Superacidity*, increase of the normal acidity of the gastric secretion.

b. *Chem.* The quality or state of being a superacid.
1927 *Jrnl. Amer. Chem. Soc.* XLIX. 3061 Our work indicates that the proximate cause of superacidity in a solution is an abnormally high value of the hydrogen-ion activity. **1979** *Science* 5 Oct. 14/2 It should always be kept in mind that superacidity encompasses both Bronsted and Lewis acid systems.

superadiabatic: see *SUPER- 4 a (*a*).

su:peraerodyna·mics, *sb. pl.* [f. SUPER-, with reference to the *upper* atmosphere.] The study of motion of and in a gas so rarefied that it has to be treated as a collection of individual particles rather than a continuous fluid. Hence **su:peraerodyna·mic** *a.*
1934 A. F. ZAHM in *Jrnl. Franklin Inst.* CCXVII. 153 (*heading*) Superaerodynamics. **1952** W. F. HILTON *High-Speed Aerodynamics* xiii. 351 The Mach number should be greater than the Reynolds number for superaerodynamic conditions to prevail. *Ibid.* 353 There is no reason why *M* should not be less than unity; i.e., a subsonic superaerodynamic flow could exist. **1957** *Jrnl. Aeronaut. Sci.* XXIV. 527/1 The mechanics of the kinetic theory of gases is employed to describe the drag force on the nose of a missile moving in the superaerodynamic region of the atmosphere. **1960** *McGraw-Hill Encycl. Sci. & Technol.* XIII. 293/2 It is convenient to divide superaerodynamics into three flow regimes.

superallowed, -alloy: see *SUPER- 9 b, 6 c.

supera·nnuable, *a.* [f. SUPERANNU(ATE *v.* + -ABLE.] (Of a post or salary) that entitles the holder to superannuation (sense 2).
1950 *Times* 27 Apr. 1/4 (Advt.), The above appointments are superannuable under the British Electricity Authority and Area Boards Scheme. **1960** *Times Lit. Suppl.* 18 Nov. 748/2 The appointment is superannuable. **1971** *Daily Tel.* 13 Apr. 6/6 (Advt.), A permanent superannuable post paying up to £2,691 per annum. **1978** *Nature* 18 May p. xxvii/1 (Advt.), Annual salary (superannuable) will be within the professional range which has a minimum of HK$131,640.

superannuate, *sb.* (Earlier example.)
1816 *Hist. Colleges Winchester, Eton & Westminster* 46 Boys between eighteen and nineteen years old, called superannuates.

superau·dible, *a.* **1.** [SUPER- 9 a.] Very loud. *nonce-use.*
1921 D. H. LAWRENCE *Tortoises* 47 That fragile yell, that scream, Super-audible.

2. [SUPER- 4 a.] Of a frequency: greater than the highest audible frequency; ultrasonic. Of a sound: too high-pitched to be audible. Now *rare.*
1922 [see *SUBAUDIBLE *a.* 2]. **1926** R. W. HUTCHINSON *Wireless* 237 The resultant wave is anything from 2,000 metres to, say, 12,000 metres in length (super-audible frequency). **1944** *Proc. IRE* XXXII. 735/2 Superaudible noise impulses which may be present.

super-bike: see *SUPER- 6 c.

superbity. Delete *rare* and add later examples.
1924 G. B. SHAW *St. Joan* p. ix, She went to the stake without a stain on her character except the overweening presumption, the superbity as they called it, that led her thither. *a* **1945** E. R. EDDISON *Mezentian Gate* (1958) xxix. 141 In her nose, a critical outward-regarding superbity that judged without appeal. **1979** C. P. SNOW *Coat of Varnish* xxxviii. 297 In spite of his superbity, he might possess a kind of self-protective cunning.

su·perbomb. [SUPER- 6 c.] **a.** Also **super bomb.** A fission bomb. *Obs.* exc. *Hist.*
1940 O. R. FRISCH in *Ann. Rep. Progr. Chem.* XXXVI. 16 Since the energy release in this reaction would be about 10^8 times larger than in ordinary chemical reactions..it has been feared that it might form the basis for the construction of a super-bomb exceeding the action of ordinary bombs by a factor of 10^6 or more. **1941** in H. D. Smyth *Gen. Acct. Devel. Atomic Energy Mil. Purposes* (1945) iv. 38 In such a reaction the energy would be released at an explosive rate which might be described as a 'super bomb'. **1964** M. GOWING *Britain & Atomic Energy 1939–45* i. 34 A chain fission reaction was a possibility, the inevitable question had arisen. Could this energy be harnessed for making a super bomb?

b. A fusion or hydrogen bomb. Cf. *SUPER *sb.* 9.
1951 W. L. LAURENCE *Hell Bomb* i. 3 'Is it true about the superbomb?' I asked him. 'Will it really be as much as fifty times as powerful as the uranium or plutonium bomb?' **1961** *New Statesman* 15 Sept. 330/1 For this interpretation not least among the exhibits in evidence is Krushchev's grim emphasis on his 100-megaton superbomb, which American experts regard as militarily poor but incredibly dirty. **1975** *Sci. Amer.* Oct. 106/2 It called for the fastest possible development of the hydrogen bomb, which was widely referred to at the time as the superbomb (or simply the Super).

Super-Bowl: see *SUPER- 6 c. **super-calender:** see SUPER- 13.

su:percalifra:gilistice:xpialido·cious, *a.* Also **supercalifragilistic;** formerly also other varr. [Fanciful: cf. *SUPER a. 3.] A nonsense-word used esp. by children, now chiefly expressing excited approbation: fantastic, fabulous.
Made popular by the Walt Disney film 'Mary Poppins' in 1964. The song containing the word was the subject of a copyright infringement suit brought in 1965 against the makers of the film by Life Music Co. and two song-writers: cf. quots. 1949, 1951. In view of earlier oral uses of the word sworn to in affidavits and dissimilarity between the songs the judge ruled against the plaintiffs.
1949 PARKER & YOUNG (*unpublished song-title*) Supercalafajalistickespialadojus. **1951** —— (*song-title*) Supercalafajalistickespeealadojus; or, The super song. **1964** R. M. & R. B. SHERMAN (*song-title*) Supercalifragilisticexpialidocious! **1967** *Decisions U.S. Courts involving Copyright 1965–66* 488 The complaint alleges copyright infringement of plaintiff's song '*Supercalafajalistickespeealadojus*' by defendants' song '*Supercalifragilisticexpialidocious*'. (All variants of this tongue twister will hereinafter be referred to collectively as 'the word'.) **1971** *Daily Tel.* 6 Nov 13/5 If you can stand more than a day of Supercalifragilisticexpialidocious entertainment you can settle in at the concrete Contemporary Resort Hotel. **1972** *Atlanta Constitution* 9 Apr. 20A/1 Disney World, the new supercalifragilisticexpialidocious tourist attraction created by the folks who brought you Mickey Mouse, is packing them into Orlando. **1980** *Amer. Speech* LV. 266 Whatever the ancestry of *supercalifragilisticexpialidocious*, it entered the general public consciousness as a result of the wonderful world of Disney. **1982** *N.Y. Post* 29 July 64/3 His eyes are willing unspoken words to life as though they were part of one of those supercalafragilistic electronic scoreboards.

supercharge, *sb.* Restrict *rare* to senses in Dict. and add: **3.** *Engin.* An explosive charge of higher than usual pressure in the cylinders of an internal-combustion engine; increased pressure of the charge.
1912 E. BUTLER *Evol. Internal Combustion Engine* vi. 69 It has been proposed by Clerk and others to employ super-compression of the charge.., the combustion cylinder thereby receiving a super-charge of air. **1948** *Petroleum Handbk.* (Shell Petroleum Co. Ltd.) (ed. 3) xxv. 356 The extra fuel has a certain cooling effect, and this permits an increase in boost (degree of supercharge). **1971** L. J. K. SETRIGHT *Power to Fly* v. 120 The immediate effect of the new fuel was to allow a greater degree of supercharge.

su·percharge, *v. Engin.* [SUPER- 9 b.] *trans.* To increase the pressure of the fuel-air mixture in (an internal-combustion engine).
1919 W. J. WALKER tr. *Devillers's Automobile & Aero Engines* xxiv. 384 Each compressor, having two compression strokes per revolution, can supercharge two cylinders. **1924** *Glasgow Herald* 6 May 4 The proposition of super-charging engines for sea-going and for road as well as for air service. **1966** *McGraw-Hill Encycl. Sci. & Technol.* VII. 208/2 Supercharging a two-cycle diesel engine requires some means of restricting or throttling the exhaust in order to build up cylinder pressure.

supercharged, *pa. pple.* and *ppl. a.* Add: **2.** *Engin.* **a.** Of the fuel-air mixture in an internal-combustion engine: increased in pressure by mechanical means. **b.** Of a vehicle or its engine: equipped with a supercharger.
1919 W. J. WALKER tr. *Devillers's Automobile & Aero Engines* xxiv. 387 The volume of the supercharged mixture remains sensibly constant during injection. **1943** J. B. PRIESTLEY *Daylight on Saturday* vii. 41 Where did Germany get her first super-charged aero engines from? **1955** *Times* 5 May 16/5 The newest of our engines to be publicly announced is a supercharged turboprop of 4,000 h.p. **1980** *Daily Tel.* 21 May 14/3 The preview of supercharged prototype models in Turin.

su·percharger. *Engin.* [f. *SUPERCHARGE *v.* + -ER[1].] A compressor that increases the pressure of the fuel-air mixture supplied to the cylinders of an internal-combustion engine. Cf. *BLOWER[1] 3 d.
1921 A. W. JUDGE *Automobile & Aircraft Engines* x. 452 The power required to drive the supercharger is about 6 per cent. **1946** *Happy Landings* July 3/1 The supercharger control..should be operated smartly. **1960** G. MAXWELL *Ring of Bright Water* II. x. 144 The supercharger screamed, dial needles moved with incredible rapidity towards red zones; I had a glimpse of the speedometer hovering at 145 m.p.h. **1980** *Daily Tel.* 21 May 14/3 Manufacturers have been increasingly attracted to the turbocharger because it is driven by waste gases from the exhaust, while

the supercharger is driven by a power take-off from the engine.

su·percharging, *vbl. sb. Engin.* [f. *SUPERCHARGE *v.* + -ING[1].] The action or use of a supercharger.

1922 *Encycl. Brit.* XXX. 41/1 Supercharging for high flying. **1937** *Discovery* Dec. 386 (caption) The McClelland two-stroke petrol turbine engine. The unfinned cylinders are pumps providing a supercharging effect. **1980** *Daily Tel.* 21 May 14/3 Fiat officials indicated that the ultimate intention was to apply supercharging to its small and medium volume production models.

superchurch: see *SUPER- 6 c.

su·perclu:ster. *Astr.* [SUPER- 5 c.] A cluster of objects that are themselves clusters (in quot. 1930, of stars, but now only of galaxies).

1930 R. J. TRUMPLER in *Lick Observatory Bull.* XIV. 187/2 It seems worth while to examine the hypothesis that our Milky Way system..together with the two Magellanic Clouds and about a hundred globular clusters form a cluster of extra-galactic objects which we may call the 'supercluster'. **1958** *Astron. Jrnl.* LXIII. 260/2 The local super-cluster of galaxies is an irregular assembly of groups, clouds and clusters dominated by the Virgo cluster in its center. **1970** *Nature* 19 Dec. 1137/1 Wolfe and Burbidge argue from these observations that super-clusters of galaxies..must definitely be ruled out. **1978** PASACHOFF & KUTNER *University Astron.* i. 6 Before we could enlarge our field of view another 100 times we might see a supercluster—a cluster of clusters of galaxies. **1982** *Daily Tel.* 1 Dec. 1/6 The largest-known object in the universe, a supercluster of millions of galaxies, has been discovered.

Hence **su·perclu:stering** *vbl. sb.*

1960 *Soviet Astron.* III. 910 We conclude that not only clustering, but also superclustering, is a general characteristic of the distribution of galaxies. **1971** D. W. SCIAMA *Mod. Cosmol.* vii. 96 The suggested scale of their clustering would be much the same in relation to their separation as is the case for the clustering or super-clustering of galaxies.

su·percoil, *sb. Biochem.* [SUPER- 5 c.] A coiled coil; *spec.* a structure sometimes assumed by DNA in which the double helix itself is coiled or looped. Cf. *SUPERHELIX.

1965 PEACOCKE & DRYSDALE *Molecular Basis Heredity* IV. 168 In the fibre, these molecules take the form of 'super-coils' in which the axis of the DNA helix is itself coiled with a pitch of 120Å and a diameter of 100Å. **1976** *Nature* 10 June 516/1 Supercoils could be introduced into progeny molecules either before sealing of the closed circular form, or subsequent to an initial closing of the molecule. **1980** *Sci. Amer.* July 100/2 Because the forces that stabilize the double helix are strong the closed circular molecules resist such underwinding, and..they compensate by forming supercoils.

su·percoil, *v. Biochem.* [f. prec. sb.] **a.** *trans.* To make (a molecule) into a supercoil. **b.** *intr.* To become a supercoil.

1967 *Jrnl. Molecular Biol.* XXV. 28 Only molecules in which both strands are intact can be supercoiled in either sense. **1971** *Nature* 29 Oct. 591/2 Segrest and Cunningham start with the tropocollagen molecule, a three-strand rope formed by supercoiling two identical helices termed α_1 and α_2. **1982** *Sci. Amer.* July 87/1 When the ethidium is removed, the ring [of DNA] supercoils.

Hence **su·percoiled** *ppl. a.*, having the structure of a coiled helix; **su·percoiling** *vbl. sb.*, the action or result of forming a supercoil; also *attrib.*

1967 *Jrnl. Molecular Biol.* XXV. 23 It would be desirable to have independent evidence on the direction of supercoiling and to obtain an estimate of the number of supercoiling turns. *Ibid.* 27 The supercoiled form of polyoma DNA can be converted to the unsupercoiled form by one single-strand scission. **1980** *Sci. Amer.* July 100/1 Affecting DNA's in a wide range of sizes and shapes (including some that are not organized into a double helix), supercoiling takes a variety of forms. **1980** *Proc. Nat. Acad. Sciences* LXXVII. 2445/1 A massive tangle of catenated supercoiled molecules.

supercolossal: see *SUPER- 9 a (*a*).

supercondu·cting, *ppl. a. Physics.* [f. SUPER- 9 b, tr. Du. *suprageleidend* (H. K. Onnes 1913, in *Versl. van de gewone Vergad. d. Wis- en Natuurk. Afdeeling, K. Akad. v. Wetensch. te Amsterdam* XXI. 1390).] Possessing no electrical resistivity; employing a substance in this state.

1913 H. K. ONNES in *Proc. Sect. Sci. K. Akad. Wetenschap. Amsterdam* XV. 1429 A thread of super-conducting mercury, if an ordinary conducting particle were present anywhere in the current path, could show resistance at that spot. **1935** *Discovery* July 213/2 The fascinating transition of metals into the super-conducting state when near to absolute zero. **1958** *Listener* 11 Dec. 984/1 A current once established in a superconducting lead ring will continue to flow indefinitely. **1966** C. R. TOTTLE *Sci. Engin. Materials* vi. 127 The superconducting state can be destroyed by the application of an external magnetic field. **1978** *Jrnl. R. Soc. Arts* CXXVI. 608/2 The savings from introducing superconducting generators are relatively small.

Hence (as a back-formation) **supercondu·ct** *v. intr.*, to conduct electricity without any resistance.

1964 *New Scientist* 20 Aug. 441 (*heading*) USSR field windings that superconduct. **1976** G. K. HAINES *Supercold, Superhot* v. 30 More than twenty-five elements have now been found that will superconduct.

supercondu·ction. *Physics.* [SUPER- 10 a:] = *SUPERCONDUCTICITY; conduction of electricity without resistance.

1940 E. F. BURTON et al. *Phenomena Temperature Liquid Helium* x. 322 It might be possible to explain the discrepancy..in the apparent number of superconduction electrons. **1959** *Electronic Engin.* XXXI. 589/2 Domains of ferromagnetism alternating with domains of superconduction, the latter having a magnetization antiparallel to the applied field.

su:perconducti·vity. *Physics.* [SUPER- 10 a.] The property of having zero electrical resistivity exhibited by some substances at temperatures close to absolute zero.

1913 H. K. ONNES in *Proc. Sect. Sci. K. Akad. Wetensch. Amsterdam* XV. 1428 (*heading*) Experiments on the possible influence of contact with an ordinary conductor upon the superconductivity of mercury. **1934** *Times Lit. Suppl.* 26 July 531/3 A similar property of superconductivity, acquired at specific low temperatures, has since been found also in a number of other metals and in certain alloys. **1959** *Sci. News* LI. 21 The idea of loss-free electromagnetic devices was immediately suggested when superconductivity was first discovered, and a number of efforts have since been made to find metals or alloys that would exhibit superconductivity at higher than [liquid] helium temperatures. **1978** *Jrnl. R. Soc. Arts* CXXVI. 608/2 Superconductivity..offers the prospect of lower capital costs and higher efficiencies than conventional generators for large units.

So **supercondu·ctive** *a.* = *SUPERCONDUCTING *ppl. a.*

1913 H. K. ONNES in *Proc. Sect. Sci. K. Akad. Wetensch. Amsterdam* XVI. 116 The actual degree of conductivity of the superconductive mercury. **1955** H. B. G. CASIMIR in W. Pauli *Niels Bohr* 119 There exist many metals that do not become superconductive in the temperature range in which they have been investigated. **1966** K. MENDELSSOHN *Quest for Absolute Zero* ix. 199 In 1930 de Haas and Voogd had found that wires of lead–bismuth alloy remained superconductive in magnetic fields as high as 20,000 oersted. **1972** *Physics Bull.* Oct. 615/1 The highest transition temperature for superconductive materials reported so far is 21 K in a three element compound, niobium–aluminium–germanium.

supercondu·ctor. *Physics.* [f. SUPER- 6 c, tr. Du. *suprageleider* (H. K. Onnes 1913, in *Versl. van de gewone Vergad. d. Wis- en Natuurk. Afdeeling, K. Akad. v. Wetensch. te Amsterdam* XXI. 1390).] A substance that becomes superconducting at sufficiently low temperatures; also, such a substance in the superconducting state.

1913 H. K. ONNESS in *Proc. Sect. Sci. K. Akad. Wetensch. Amsterdam* XV. 1429 A pushing forward of the electrons in the galvanic current through a super-conductor without performance of work. **1931** *Ann. Reg. 1930* 61 Meissner discovered that copper sulphide is a superconductor. *Ibid.*, Niobium carbide becomes a superconductor at 10° A. **1955** H. B. G. CASIMIR in W. Pauli *Niels Bohr* 119 At temperatures above the transition point..superconductors behave in all respects like these normal metals. **1959** *Sci. News* LI. 21 The real difficulty in the use of superconductors in magnetic devices is the fact that superconductivity is destroyed by fields of only a few hundred oersted. **1969** ROSE-INNES & RHODERICK *Introd. Superconductivity* i. 5 About half the metallic elements are known to be superconductors and..a large number of alloys are superconductors. **1983** *New Scientist* 24 Mar. 802/1 Like most of the organic superconductors already known, the new material loses its resistance only under high pressure.

su·perconscious, *a. Psychol.* [SUPER- 4 a.] Transcending human or normal consciousness. Also *absol.*

1884 F. W. H. MYERS in *Proc. Soc. Psychical Res.* II. 219 We shall come, perhaps, to find *super-conscious* as necessary a term as *sub-conscious*. **1904** HARDY *Dynasts* I. v. iv. 166 In that immense unweeting Mind is shown One far above forethinking; purposive, Yet superconscious. **1921** *Public Opinion* 28 Jan. 90/2 What the world needs is a man whose genius will come from the superconscious, the divine. **1940** A. HUXLEY *Let.* 12 Jan. (1969) 449 It looks as though there were a kind of spiral development, from unconscious animal, through conscious human up to what for lack of better words may be called super-conscious spiritual. **1953** R. F. C. HULL tr. *Jung's Psychol. & Alchemy* in *Coll. Wks.* XII. ii. 268 There are people who can never understand the unconscious as anything but a *sub*-conscious, and who therefore feel impelled to put a superconscious alongside or possibly above it.

Hence **superco·nsciousness.**

1898 *Advance* (Chicago) 27 Jan. 107/2 [Jesus] had now reached the state of mind known to Hindus as samahdo or super-consciousness, and there was no pain for him on the cross. **1901** *Harper's Mag.* CII. 788/1 Since this unpleasant whirl of superconsciousness had swept over him. **1940** *Mind* XLIX. 130 The condition of 'super-consciousness' which most Indian philosophers and mystics agree to be attainable in this life. **1962** M. SADHU *Samadhi* i. 13 The question of the higher aspects of consciousness in man, often called simply the Superconsciousness, is becoming more and more urgent.

su·percontinent. *Geol.* [SUPER- 6 c.] One of the large land masses that are thought to have existed in the geological past and from which two or more of the present continents are thought to be derived; = *PROTOCONTINENT. Cf. *GONDWANALAND, *LAURASIA, *PANGÆA.

1963 *Sci. Amer.* Apr. 89/1 According to Wegener all the continents had been joined in a single supercontinent about 200 million years ago. **1969** *Times* 25 Apr. 13/8 Australia and Antarctica are also thought to have been joined together, the land mass they formed being part of the supercontinent of Gondwanaland. **1970** [see *PANTHALASSA]. **1977** A. HALLAM *Planet Earth* 210 In the late Permian we thus encounter a single sea-less supercontinent, a phenomenon probably unique in the history of the Earth.

su:percontra·ction. [SUPER- 13.] The contraction of a hair or fibre to less than its original length after treatment with heat or chemicals.

1933 ASTBURY & WOODS in *Phil. Trans. R. Soc.* A. CCXXXII. 337 The appearance of the phenomenon of 'super-contraction' just described is perhaps the most striking manifestation of this change. *Ibid.* 359 A general effect to which we have ventured to attach the term 'super-contraction', to distinguish it from the property of a normal stretched hair, when wetted, of returning exactly to its original unstretched length. **1954** ALEXANDER & HUDSON *Wool* iii. 75 Supercontraction of unstrained fibres was first observed by Speakman. **1977** F. KIDD in R. S. Asquith *Chem. Natural Protein Fibers* ix. 394 Woods..recorded 50% supercontraction of Cotswold wool.

So **su:percontra·ct** *v. intr.* and *trans.*, to (cause to) undergo supercontraction; **su:percontra·cted, -contra·cting** *ppl. adjs.*

1933 *Phil. Trans. R. Soc.* A. CCXXXII. 365 With respect to the *minimum* (super-contracted) length,..permanent set develops even in hot water. **1953** R. W. MONCRIEFF *Wool Shrinkage* xxv. 352 Fibres..which had not been treated with diepoxybutane in the phosphate buffer did not subsequently supercontract in metabisulphite. **1954** ALEXANDER & HUDSON *Wool* iii. 76 Phenol is a much more effective supercontracting agent than formamide. **1962** W. J. ONIONS *Wool* ii. 38 Steam set fibres are also resistant to boiling 5 per cent sodium bisulphite, which supercontracts untreated fibres. **1977** F. KIDD in R. S. Asquith *Chem. Natural Protein Fibers* ix. 394 White skunk hairs..supercontract more in sodium metabisulfite than do human hairs.

supercoo·l, *v.* [SUPER- 9 b.] **a.** *trans.* To subject to supercooling.

1932 F. F. GROUT *Petrogr. & Petrol.* III. 232 In the absence of seeding some magma intrusions may be greatly supercooled. **1959** B. CHALMERS *Physical Metallurgy* vi. 265 The liquid of composition *O* is supercooled until a nucleus in one of the phases forms. **1976** *Nature* 22 July 323/2 The cell contents are readily supercooled.

b. *intr.* To undergo supercooling.

1940 *Lancet* 17 Feb. 303/2 The capacity to supercool may be abolished by soaking the skin in water, and skin which does not supercool may be induced to do so by leaving it unwashed for a week. **1959** B. CHALMERS *Physical Metallurgy* vi. 244 When a metal sample is sufficiently subdivided into isolated drops, some supercool to the extent of about $0{\cdot}2T_E$ before nucleation occurs. **1975** *Rev. Mod. Physics* XLVII. 454/1 The $A \to B$ transition [in liquid ^{3}He] strongly supercooled the first time the transition was made from temperatures considerably above T_0.

super-cool, *a.*: see *SUPER- 9 a (*a*).

supercoo·led, *ppl. a.* [SUPER- 9 b.] **a.** Liquid though below the freezing point. **b.** Apparently solid, but formed from a liquid without a definite change of phase and having (on the atomic scale) the disorder of a liquid.

1898 *Chem. News* 29 July 59/1 (*heading*) The variation with the temperature of the number of nuclei which are formed in different supercooled liquids. **1937** *Times* 14 Oct. 11/4 Local conditions may cause the moisture in a cloud to become, in the meteorologist's phrase, 'supercooled'. **1947** J. C. RICH *Materials & Methods Sculpture* xi. 329 Glass is sometimes referred to as a supercooled liquid, because the material has no definite melting point. **1966** C. R. TOTTLE *Sci. Engin. Materials* iii. 81 Any material possessing the properties of a supercooled liquid, having failed to crystallize and therefore being amorphous in structure, can be called a glass. **1980** *Jrnl. R. Soc. Arts* May 369/2 Silver iodide smoke particles can also provide 'kernels' on which ice crystals can grow in supercooled cloud.

supercoo·ling, *vbl. sb.* [SUPER- 9 b.] The cooling of a liquid to below its freezing point without solidification or without crystallization occurring; more widely, cooling to below the temperature of a phase transition without the change of phase occurring; reduction in the temperature of a phase transition.

1898 *Chem. News* 29 July 59/1 The number of points increase with strong super-cooling. **1922** GLAZEBROOK *Dict. Appl. Physics* I. 947/2 The supercooling of a vapour without condensation is analogous to the supercooling of a liquid without crystallization. **1963** R. A. FLINN *Fund. Metal Casting* ii. 21 Some supercooling usually ensues before initial crystallization. **1975** *Rev. Mod. Physics* XLVII. 463/2 This would explain..experiments [on ^{3}He] at melting pressure..where *no* superheating of the $B \to A$ transition is observed while supercooling of the $A \to B$ transition is common. **1980** S. A. MORSE *Basalts &*

Phase Diagrams iii. 28 Supercooling results from the fact that the nucleation of a crystal is a random process, requiring the accidental arrangement..of atoms in the pattern of the crystal structure, after which a crystal nucleus may grow at a great rate.

supercrat: see *SUPER- 6 c.

supercri·tical, *a.* [SUPER- 9 a.] **1.** Highly critical.

1610, 1661 [in Dict. s.v. SUPER- 9a]. **1937** *Even. News* 12 Feb. 11/1 Only the super-critical, rather cosmopolitan-minded audience of the West End still look coolly on their simple robust brand of humour.

2. Of, pertaining to, or designating a fluid at a temperature and pressure greater than its critical temperature and pressure.

1934 *Econ. Geol.* XXIX. 457 The first work on critical and supercritical phenomena of solutions was done by Hannay and Hogarth in 1879. **1968** *New Scientist* 27 June 697/1 Supercritical boilers probably present more problems. **1972** *Physics Bull.* Apr. 236 The use of supercritical helium for cooling superconducting and other low temperature equipment. **1981** E. CORLETT *Revolution Merchant Shipping* 40/1 Natural gas..at normal temperatures ..is supercritical... It cannot be liquefied by pressure unless below −82° C.

3. Of a flow of fluid: faster than the speed at which waves travel in the fluid. Of an aerofoil: giving rise to such a flow over much of its surface when its speed relative to the bulk fluid is subcritical, but in such a way that flow separation is largely avoided.

1941, etc. [see *SUBCRITICAL *a.* 2]. **1967** *Aviation Week* 24 July 25/1 Whitcomb describes the shape as a 'supercritical airfoil' because it enables aircraft in subsonic flight to achieve these higher critical Mach numbers before the normal drag rise is experienced in transonic flight. The shape of the upper surface of the transonic wing permits predominantly supersonic air flow to be maintained across the wing. **1969** *Ibid.* 17 Feb. 22/1 Improved version of the National Aeronautics and Space Administration's 'supercritical wing'..will begin test flights in mid-1970. **1977** *McGraw-Hill Yearbk. Sci. & Technol.* 422/1 Supercritical compressor blades. **1979** *Time* 2 Apr. 21/2 With only two engines and a 'supercritical' wing that cuts aerodynamic drag, it is the most fuel-efficient commercial jet flying today.

4. *Nucl. Physics.* Containing or being more than the critical mass (see *CRITICAL *a.* 7 b).

1950 GLASSTONE *Sourcebk. Atomic Energy* xiv. 394/2 The presence of stray neutrons in the atmosphere makes it impossible to prevent a chain reaction in a supercritical mass. **1958** J. CLEUGH tr. *Jungk's Brighter than Thousand Suns* xii. 191 If he passed the point or was not quite quick enough in breaking contact, the mass might become 'super-critical' and produce a nuclear explosion. **1973** *Nature* 23 Mar. 251/1 Assuming a relative ^{235}U abundance throughout the [hypothetical] planet equal to the terrestrial crustal abundance, there is just enough energy to disperse the planet if the ^{235}U could be assembled into a super-critical mass.

Hence **su:percritica·lity,** supercritical state.

1959 *Times* 5 Mar. 2/4 (Advt.), Join a section concerned with the assessment of criticality hazards in the handling and processing of fissile materials and to carry out theoretical research into the factors governing criticality and supercriticality. **1976** L. SANDERS *Hamlet Warning* (1977) I. xi. 95 The blast..would be well into the kiloton range. The trick was..to bring the mass to supercriticality uniformly and at the same instant.

su·percurrent. *Physics.* [f. *super-* in *SUPERCONDUCTOR, etc.] An electric current flowing without dissipating energy, as in a superconductor.

[**1936** *Nature* 16 May 824/1 The assumption for the supra-conductor is, that $I = I_c + I_s$... That is to say, there is a third sort of current I_s, call it the supra-current.] **1940** E. F. BURTON et al. *Phenomena Temperature Liquid Helium* x. 302 We must now recognize three entirely different kinds of electric current..: (1) the displacement current in an insulator..; (2) the ordinary conduction current..; (3) the super-current. **1962** *New Scientist* 22 Nov. 454/3 Superconductivity can also be destroyed by increasing the supercurrent itself beyond a critical value. **1966** K. MENDELSSOHN *Quest for Absolute Zero* x. 242 Superfluid flow, just as a persistent supercurrent, is distinguished by zero entropy. **1980** *Sci. Amer.* May 43/1 In the absence of a magnetic field, and with a current below a critical value, a supercurrent flows through the Josephson junction just as if the superconductor were not interrupted by the insulating barrier.

su:per-du·per, *a. colloq.* (orig. *U.S.*). Also **sooper-dooper, super-dooper, super duper.** [A reduplicated extension of SUPER *a.*] Especially splendid, powerful, etc.; exceptional, particularly good.

1940 *N.Y. Times* 27 Sept. 27/7 (Advt.), After seeing this new M-G-M sooper dooper musical smash, our little voice went pattering all over the house. **1942** *Fortune* Feb. 104/3 Joining the Hearst organization he rapidly became what he calls a super-dooper circulator in Milwaukee, Detroit, Boston. **1942** *Sun* (Baltimore) 5 Mar. 8/8 A week ago officers knew before the curtain rose that something super-duper was about to be staged. **1949** *Hansard Commons* 26 May 1490 They are now subsidising the building of a 'super-duper' liner to compete with the Cunard flagships. **1951** *People* 3 June 2/2 British Railways put on a super-duper Pullman car special from Victoria to Epsom. **1958** D. WALLACE *Forty Years On* i. 15 Super-duper rockets with fancy-nancy warheads. **1971** *News-Advocate* (Barbados) 20 Mar. 8/1 Now this promises to be a super duper weekend. **1975** *New Yorker* 24 Mar. 33/1 The Colony range from the modest Villa Torino unit..to the superduper Viking Executive units. **1978** M. PUZO *Fools Die* xvi. 181 There was one super-duper bicycle that I was sorry she had bought.

super-e·go. *Psychoanal.* [SUPER- 5.] A Freudian term for that aspect of the psyche which has internalized parental and social prohibitions or ideals early in life and imposes them as a censor on the wishes of the ego; the agent of self-criticism or self-observation. Also *transf.*

1924, etc. [see *ID^2]. **1938** *Times Lit. Suppl.* 26 Feb. 132/4 When the moral superego takes charge and the ego is no longer coercive but submissive. **1945** AUDEN *Coll. Poetry* 242 The fatal ease with which Conscience, i.e., the voice of God, is replaced by 'my conscience', i.e., the Super-Ego. **1958** M. ARGYLE *Relig. Behaviour* xii. 157 If religious behaviour is derived from the super-ego in some way, religion should have an irrational 'super-ego' quality about it. **1958** W. J. H. SPROTT *Human Groups* x. 173 The importance of the primary group can be expressed by saying that the group acts as the 'super-ego' of its members. **1965** *Listener* 2 Sept. 337/2 Lord Reith—one of the few twentieth-century Britons who have been willing to cast themselves as the community's superego. **1972** *Jrnl. Social Psychol.* LXXXVI. 157 The less dramatic resolution of the Oedipal complex experienced by females causes them to have a weaker superego than males. **1981** W. EBERSOHN *Divide Night* xi. 153 Freud..had decreed that the human psyche had three parts, the Id, the Ego, and the Super-ego.

superelevation. Add: **2.** Also *transf.* (see quot.)

1930 *Engineering* 14 Feb. 193/3 The spillway channels [of the dam] are curved, requiring large superelevation of the floor toward the outside.

supere·ssive, *a.* (and *sb.*) *Gram.* [f. L. *superesse* to be higher than, survive, remain + -IVE.] Designating a case or grammatical relation which expresses position above or on top of. Also *absol.* as *sb.*

1903 [see *INTROESSIVE *a.*] **1951** W. K. MATTHEWS *Languages U.S.S.R.* vi. 99 Marr and M. Brière..recognise secondary cases—a locative, an inessive..a superessive, a disjunctive, [etc.]. **1954** PEI & GAYNOR *Dict. Linguistics* 207 *Superessive,* in certain languages (notably, languages of the Finno-Ugric family) a declensional case, having the same denotation as the English preposition *on* or *upon.* **1971** D. I. SLOBIN in W. O. Dingwall *Survey Linguistic Sci.* 310 A variety of Hungarian case endings on nouns indicating such locative relations as illative, elative,..and superessive—that is, in plain English,..the directional notions of *into, out of,*..and the positional notion of *on top of.*

supere·tte. orig. and chiefly *U.S.* [f. *SUPER-(MARKET + *-ETTE.] A small supermarket.

1938 *Sat. Even. Post* 17 Sept. 85/3 It also developed a store called the 'Super-ette', which is a compact, limited-stock, self-service store. **1956** *Sun* (Baltimore) 10 Feb. 23/1 There were an estimated 67,500 'superettes' in 1953. **1963** *Listener* 10 Jan. 75/1 Supermarkets and superettes (the latter still large by British standards) together took over four-fifths of all American retail food trade in 1958. **1976** *Daily Times* (Lagos) 3 Nov. 12/1 (Advt.), A spacious van for traders, commercial houses,..supermarkets and superettes.

super-exchange, -fatted: see *SUPER- 2 a (*b*), 9 a (*a*).

superfe·cta. *U.S.* [f. SUPER- 6 c, after *perfecta.*] A method of betting in horse-racing whereby the bettor must pick the first four finishers of a race in the correct order.

1972 *Compton Yearbk. 1971* 532/2 *Superfecta,* a system of betting on races in which the bettor must pick the first, second, third, and fourth horses in this sequence in a specified race in order to win. **1972** *N.Y. Post* 1 Mar. 63/5 Besides superfectas, seats, TV..the track also plans to improve the lighting. **1973** *Sunday Mirror* 9 Sept. 20/2 The gang went to work on trotting races in New York, fixing 'superfecta' races. **1977** *Time* 21 Nov. 46/3 The growth of exotic betting devices—superfectas and the like—with their huge pay-offs represents an additional impetus to crooked horsemen.

superfemale: see *SUPER- 5 f.

su·perfix. *Phonetics.* [f. SUPER- 2, after *prefix, suffix,* etc.] A sequence of stress or other suprasegmental phonemes which is treated as part of the grammatical structure of words and phrases.

1951 TRAGER & SMITH *Outl. Eng. Structure* II. 56 Suprasegmental morphemes consisting of patterns of stress, with the possibility of including plus junctures, are called superfixes. Those consisting of pitches and a terminal juncture are called intonation patterns. *Ibid.,* A morphemic phrase consists of two or more bases, with their suffixes, and a superfix. **1954** [see *SIMULFIX]. **1956** H. WHITEHALL in *Kenyon Rev.* XVIII. 415 In their *Outline,* Trager and Smith have..assembled some..linguistic tools. Their exposition of the superfix..throws..light on the distinction between the verse of Wyatt, Donne,.. Hopkins, and Eliot in which superfix patterns function freely..as part of the rhythm, and the verse of Surrey, Pope, Tennyson, in which the superfixes are frozen..in the rhythm. **1965** [see *high-tone* s.v. *HIGH *a.* 22a]. **1972** HARTMANN & STORK *Dict. Lang. & Linguistics* 226/1 *Superfix,* term used to describe the suprasegmental or prosodic features of a particular word or utterance, e.g. the stress pattern which distinguishes modifier + noun *green house* from the compound noun *greenhouse.*

su·perflow. *Physics.* [f. *super-* in next.] Flow of a superfluid.

1939 *Canad. Jrnl. Res.* XVII A. 163 An ordinary flow of the whole fluid is superposed on the super-flow. **1966** [see *LAMBDA 4]. **1975** *Nature* 10 Jan. 93/3 It is superflow in the film which is responsible for the well known and dramatic phenomenon of the beaker of helium which empties itself while remaining upright.

superfluid (stress variable), *sb.* and *a.* *Physics.* [SUPER- 6 c, 9 a.] **A.** *sb.* (*su·perfluid*) A fluid that exhibits superfluidity.

1938 P. KAPITZA in *Nature* 8 Jan. 74/2 The helium below the λ-point enters a special state which might be called a 'superfluid'. **1950** [see *quantum liquid* s.v. *QUANTUM 7 a]. **1965** *Economist* 22 May 935/2 Helium itself behaves oddly. If cooled below 2·2 degrees K it becomes a 'superfluid'. **1974** *Nature* 15 Mar. 195/2 With the discovery of the new phases of ^{3}He, the number of known superfluids in nature has been doubled. **1982** *McGraw-Hill Yearbk. Sci. & Technol.* 227/1 The neutrons in a neutron star..are expected to form a *p*-wave-paired superfluid whose properties should be related to those of ^{3}He-A and B.

B. *adj.* (*superflu·id*) Exhibiting or pertaining to superfluidity.

1941 *Physical Rev.* LX. 357/2 We might regard liquid helium as if it consisted of a 'mixture' of two liquids—one is 'superfluid' without viscosity..and the other is 'normal'. **1947,** etc. [see *NORMAL *a.* 2 k.] **1968** C. G. KUPER *Introd. Theory Superconductivity* ii. 20 At any temperature $T < T_c$ only a fraction..of the electrons are in the condensate ('superfluid' electrons) and the remainder are 'normal' electrons. **1974** *Nature* 6 Dec. 441/2 Liquid ^{3}He.. under its own saturated vapour pressure..was found to undergo a superfluid transition at 0·93 mK.

superflui·dity. *Physics.* [SUPER- 10.] The property of flowing without viscosity or friction which, with other exceptional properties, is exhibited by the isotopes of liquid helium below certain temperatures; an analogous property of other collections of particles (as the electrons in a superconductor) that exhibit quantum effects on a macroscopic scale.

1938 *Physical Rev.* LIV. 952/2 The transport properties ..of liquid helium, when passing the λ-point actually change in a very conspicuous manner; thus one speaks of a 'superfluidity' and of a 'super-heat-conductivity'. **1955** H. B. G. CASIMIR in W. Pauli *Niels Bohr* 131 The Bose-Einstein gas is the only model known at present that leads to macroscopic wave functions at finite temperatures and the super-fluidity of liquid helium has almost certainly something to do with this model. **1967** *New Scientist* 25 May 454/1 In superconductivity, as in its counterpart superfluidity, we are faced with phenomena that are quite outside our ordinary physical experience. **1975** *Rev. Mod. Physics* XLVII. 430/1 Observation of fourth sound [in ^{3}He] proves the existence of superfluidity. **1976** *Sci. Amer.* Dec. 56/1 Under the name of superconductivity, superfluidity is also displayed by the conduction electrons in a great many metals and alloys.

su:perfluore·scence. *Physics.* [SUPER- 6 c.] The co-operative emission of radiation by a system of atoms as a result of fluorescence and the spontaneous correlation of excited atomic states; also, superradiance.

1966 *Jrnl. Appl. Physics* XXXVII. 682 (*heading*) Studies of ruby superfluorescence and population inversion. **1974** *Sci. Amer.* June 31/1 Since short-pulse laser systems must store large amounts of energy prior to pulse amplification, high gain coefficients in large-aperture amplifiers present two difficult problems. The first is termed superfluorescence. This is simply the normal fluorescence emitted spontaneously by the excited laser material, amplified by the gain of the material itself. **1975** BONIFACIO & LUGIATO in *Physical Rev.* A. XI. 1507/2 The system spontaneously creates correlations, i.e., a macroscopic dipole which gives rise to a pulse whose maximum intensity is proportional to N^2 and whose time duration is proportional to N^{-1}. We call this phenomenon superfluorescence. **1980** *Nature* 8 May 70/1 Superfluorescence produces radiation pulses which have much larger amplitudes than those which one would obtain in normal incoherent atomic radiation processes.

Hence **su:perfluore·scent** *a.*

1973 *Appl. Physics Lett.* XXII. 79/2 Figure 1 illustrates the repetitive superfluorescent pulses observed at 3370 Å in N_2. **1977** R. L. BYER in Harper & Wherrett *Nonlinear Optics* ii. 89 For efficient superfluorescent operation the input noise field must be amplified by approximately 10^{16}.

superfluous, *a.* (*sb.*) Add: **5.** Special collocations: *superfluous hair,* bodily hair considered to be unattractive in women, esp. on the face; *superfluous woman,* a woman unlikely to marry, because of a surplus of women over men in the population; also *superfluous girl.*

1876 GEO. ELIOT *Dan. Der.* II. III. xxi. 49 The sad faces of the four superfluous girls, each, poor thing.. having her peculiar world which was of no importance to any one else. **1800** in C. W. Cunnington *Feminine Attitudes* (1935) ii. 44, I shall sell a compound to take off all superfluous hair. **1873** *Young Englishwoman* Aug. 414/1

Will you kindly tell us..whether you know of any depilatory that may be safely used for the removal of superfluous hair? **1933** D. L. SAYERS *Murder must Advertise* iv. 69 Do you suffer from superfluous hair? **1976** CADOGAN & CRAIG *You're a Brick, Angela!* v. 74 Superfluous hair, poor complexions and excessive perspiration preoccupied many readers. **1886** L. M. ALCOTT *Jo's Boys* i. 22 There is a plenty for the 'superfluous women' to do... I..am very glad..that my profession will make me a useful..spinster. **1911** G. B. SHAW *Getting Married* Pref. 140 In our population there are about a million monogamically superfluous women, yet it is quite impossible to say of any given unmarried woman that she is one of the superfluous. **1978** CADOGAN & CRAIG *Women & Children First* vii. 133 The 1921 census showed a 1,700,000 surplus of women over men as a result of the slaughter of the war years..the so-called superfluous woman.

su·perfly, *a.* and *sb. U.S. slang.* [SUPER- 9 a: cf. FLY *a.* 1.] **A.** *adj.* **a.** Very good, excellent, the best (esp. in the context of drugs). **b.** *spec.* Typical of the film character Super Fly (see quot. 1975[1]). Also with capital initial.

1971 R. WOODLEY in *Esquire* Apr. 79/1 'That,' he said in crisp, sure tones, 'is top-shelf coke. Super-fly.' **1971** —— in *New York* 30 Aug. 29/1 They figure if the cat O.D.'d, it must have been some superfly dope. **1974** *Florida FL Reporter* XIII. 50/2 A kind of Swahili-speaking Superfly image. **1975** *Wentworth & Flexner's Dict. Amer. Slang* Suppl. 747/2 *Superfly*,..very wonderful, desirable, or attractive... Became popular after the 1972 motion picture *Super Fly*, about a cocaine dealer in Harlem. **1975** *Los Angeles Times* 14 July II. 5/3 Last year a ninth-grader impressed the entire student body on several occasions by wearing flashy 'super fly' suits. **1976** *National Observer* (U.S.) 8 May 16/2 Ban outlandish and distracting clothes... No Superfly suits, no platform shoes. **1977** E. LEONARD *Unknown Man No. 89* vii. 67 The beauty parlor... Get his superfly hair fixed up.

B. *sb.* [From the title of the film: see sense b of the adj. above.] One who sells illegal drugs, a 'pusher'.

1973 *Black Panther* 7 July 7/3 The high level dope pushers, the 'Super Flys', were the target. **1974** *Black World* Sept. 25/2 *Long Black Song* tells us, here in the 1970's, that the days of darky entertainers, superflies, sweetbacks, and Melindas, if not over, are numbered.

superfœtation, var. SUPERFETATION.

superfusate (s(j)ūpəɹfiū·zeɪt). *Med.* [f. *SUPERFUSE *v.* + *-ate*, after *filtrate, precipitate*.] Any solution which has been used in the process of superfusion.

1970 *Proc. Soc. Exper. Biol. & Med.* CXXXIII. 1373/2 The presence of a constant concentration of LH in the superfusate in this system furnishes an appropriate control to evaluate the release obtained in response to hypothalamic extracts. **1979** *Experientia* XXXV. 225/2, 5-min fractions of superfusate were collected serially in glass vials.

superfuse, *v.* Add: **1. b.** *Med.* To subject (tissue) to, or employ (fluid) in, the technique of superfusion. Also, of a liquid, to flow over the surface of (tissue) in a thin layer. Cf. *PERIFUSE *v.*

1953 *Brit. Jrnl. Pharmacol. & Chemotherapy* VIII. 322/1 Two tissues were suspended one above the other and the same fluid was superfused over them both. **1964** *Ibid.* XXIII. 360 The blood superfused the second tissue and was then returned to the jugular vein by gravity. **1975** *Nature* 25 Dec. 754/2 The exposed suboesophageal ganglia were superfused with continuously flowing snail Ringer. **1978** *Ibid.* 29 June 765/2 Each stream of blood superfused a separate collagen strip which was excised from the Achilles tendon of a rabbit.

Hence **superfu·sed** *ppl. a.*, subjected to superfusion; **superfu·sing** *ppl. a.*, that superfuses.

1953 *Brit. Jrnl. Pharmacol. & Chemotherapy* VIII. 322/2 Stoppage of the flow may itself cause contraction of superfused muscle. **1977** *Nature* 6 Jan. 85/2 Test solutions were assayed..by their effects on isolated, superfused smooth-muscle organs. **1980** *Ibid.* 3 Jan. 93/1 (*caption*) Potassium chloride was added..to the superfusing fluid for 2-min periods at intervals of 16 min.

superfusion. Add: **1. b.** *Med.* The technique of causing a stream of liquid to run over the surface of a piece of suspended tissue, keeping it viable and allowing the interchange of substances between it and the fluid to be observed.

1953 *Brit. Jrnl. Pharmacol. & Chemotherapy* VIII. 321/1 A piece of intestine may be suspended in air and kept in good condition by a stream of a suitable solution running over its surface... This technique may be called superfusion, since the fluid runs over the tissue, by analogy with perfusion, in which the fluid runs through the tissue. **1970** *Proc. Soc. Exper. Biol. & Med.* CXXXIII. 1373/2 Continuous superfusion of a single pituitary gland might also permit new approaches to the study of mechanisms and dynamics of LH release. **1980** *Nature* 3 Jan. 92/2 Superfusion of these slices for 2 min with Krebs' solution containing added KCl..increased the tritium overflow.

supergalactic, -galaxy: see *SUPER- 5 c.

supergene (s(j)ū·pəɹdʒīn), *a. Min.* [f. SUPER- 1 a: see *-GEN 3.] Of an ore or mineral: enriched or deposited by a downward-moving solution; involving deposition by a downward-moving solution.

1914 F. L. RANSOME in *Bull. U.S. Geol. Survey* No. 540. 153 The suggestion is offered that minerals deposited by generally downward-moving and initially cold solutions may be termed supergene minerals. **1944** [see *paravauxite* s.v. *PARA-[1] 2c]. **1977** A. HALLAM *Planet Earth* 112 Where leaching of sulfide ore deposits occurs, residual red and brown iron hydroxyoxide cappings (gossans) are left, and other elements can be carried down and precipitated in a zone of 'supergene' enrichment near the water table.

su·pergene, *sb. Genetics.* [f. SUPER- 6 c + *GENE.] A group of closely linked genes, freq. having related functions.

1949 DARLINGTON & MATHER *Elem. Genetics* ii. 46 Thus the cross between male and female is a back-cross for the X–Y pair of chromosomes or, if you like, the X–Y super-gene, and half the offspring are of each sex. *Ibid.* v. 118 The differences could be interpreted as two gene differences so closely linked as never to recombine (two-gene system). Or one of them could be regarded as associated with an inversion inhibiting recombination (one super-gene system). **1978** *Nature* 13 July 164/1 The *t* complex seems to provide an example of a 'supergene'—a large chromosomal segment with multiple genes involved in similar, or closely related functions.

su·pergiant, *sb.* and *a.* [SUPER- 6 c.] **A.** *sb.* **a.** A very large star that is even brighter than a giant, in many cases despite being relatively cool. (The dominant sense.)

1927 H. N. RUSSELL et al. *Astronomy* II. xxi. 725 Certain very bright stars, much more brilliant than the ordinary giants, are sometimes called super-giants. **1959** *Listener* 26 Feb. 370/2 A very brilliant white super-giant such as Rigel. **1978** PASACHOFF & KUTNER *University Astron.* xi. 294 The sun..is only one-millionth as luminous as the most brilliant of the red supergiants.

b. A supergiant galaxy (see sense b of the adj. below).

1975 S. VAN DEN BERGH in A. Sandage et al. *Stars & Stellar Systems* IX. xii. 531 Assuming the brightest stars in the Sc giant galaxy M33 to be similar to those in the Sc supergiant M100.

B. *adj.* **1.** *Astr.* **a.** Designating a star that is a supergiant.

1930 R. H. BAKER *Astronomy* ix. 372 Super-giant stars are extraordinarily luminous giants. **1973** *Daily Tel.* 29 Sept. 13/1 Under the best conditions it might be possible with glasses to glimpse the red supergiant star Antares in Scorpius. **1981** *Nature* 15 Oct. 513/1 Red giant and supergiant stars have long been favourites of professional and amateur astronomers.

b. Of a galaxy: in the brightest of five luminosity classes.

1960 S. VAN DEN BERGH in *Astrophysical Jrnl.* CXXXI. 216 The nomenclature for the luminosity classes has been chosen to agree with that used in the Yerkes system of stellar luminosity classification: (I) supergiant galaxy, (II) bright giant galaxy, (III) normal giant galaxy, (IV) subgiant galaxy, and (V) dwarf galaxy. **1978** *Sci. Amer.* Nov. 103/1 It [*sc.* the Perseus cluster]..harbors a centrally located supergiant elliptical galaxy, which is a strong radio source and is surrounded by an X-ray-emitting cloud and a massive halo of stars.

2. *gen.* Extremely large.

1977 *Time* 1 Aug. 37/1 In June a high-pressure air mass began building up just east of the Rockies. It stayed there, with some up-and-down movement of air, and slowly turned into a supergiant oven. **1981** *Sci. Amer.* Nov. 66/2 Several supergiant natural-gas fields were found north of the Arctic Circle.

su:pergranula·tion. *Astr.* [SUPER- 6 b.] A pattern of large convective cells, each thousands of miles across, covering the surface of the sun. So **supergra·nular** *a.*, of or pertaining to supergranulation; **supergra·nule,** an individual cell of this kind.

1962 R. B. LEIGHTON et al. *Astrophysical Lett.* CXXXV. 494 Some of the properties of the large cells suggest that they may be a giant system of convective cells—a supergranulation—analogous to the ordinary granulation but originating in deeper layers where the scale height is relatively great. **1964** *Astrophysical Jrnl.* CXL. 1120 The velocity cells (called 'supergranules')..have an average diameter of 32000 km. **1967** K. O. KIEPENHEUER in J. N. Xanthakis *Solar Physics* xiii. 385 Even large spots, with their strong magnetic fields and complex structures, seem to be tied into the pattern of the supergranular network. **1973** *Nature* 14 Dec. 412/1 Spicules..cluster favourably in regions of enhanced magnetic fields along supergranular boundaries within the chromosphere. **1976** D. F. GRAY *Observation & Analysis Stellar Photospheres* xviii. 442 The gas flow in a supergranule mimics that of the granule, but the size of the convective cell is about 20 times as large.. and there is no brightness variation across a supergranule. **1977** *New Scientist* 13 Jan. 77/1 The supergranulation 'cells', unlike the small convective granulations visible on the Sun's surface, are of the order of 15 000 to 30 000 km across.

supergrass, -gravity: see *SUPER- 6 c, b.

su·pergroup. a. [SUPER- 5 c.] A group composed of a number of other groups.

1943 M. SCHLAUCH *Gift of Tongues* 63 Finno-Ugric and Nenets..together form a super-group. **1969** *Proc. Geol. Soc.* Aug. 145 The following formal lithostratigraphical divisions are recognized: *Supergroup, Group, Formation, Member, Bed. Ibid.*, A supergroup consists of two or more adjacent and naturally related or associated groups. **1972** *Sci. Amer.* Sept. 133/2 In the next step most of these groups are combined, five at a time, to form 'supergroups' of 80 conversations each.

b. [SUPER- 6 c.] In rock music: a group formed by star musicians from different bands. Also *loosely*, an exceptionally talented or successful group.

1970 *Times* 7 Jan. 7/1 What the pop world calls a supergroup is a group formed by star musicians from ordinary groups. **1976** *Sounds* 11 Dec., I can only hope and pray that..two supergroups will emerge, but they have one hell of a name to live up to. **1976** *New Musical Express* 17 Apr. 23/3 They're what's already been described as a pub-rock supergroup. **1980** *Washington Post* 4 Dec. D 9 Last night, The Police filled a packed Warner Theater with a lithe, sensual and utterly danceable brand of rock that is going to propel them to supergroup status in the next few years.

superheat, *v.* Delete 'in order to increase its pressure' and add: More widely, to heat (a substance) above the temperature of a phase transition without the change of phase occurring.

1869 *Amer. Jrnl. Sci.* XCVII. 12 To subject the oils to a temperature above their boiling points, or in other words, to super-heat their vapors. **1939** CARPENTER & ROBERTSON *Metals* II. xiv. 1194 Marked changes in the structure of cast iron could be produced by superheating the melt, i.e. heating to a temperature considerably higher than that required to melt the metal.

superheated, *ppl. a.* Add: **1. a.** More widely, heated above the temperature of a phase transition without the change of phase occurring.

1931 G. W. TYRRELL *Volcanoes* vi. 161 Some of the material was melted up by the ascent of a highly superheated lava.

superheating, *vbl. sb.* Add: (*a*) Also more widely (cf. *SUPERHEAT *v.*).

1980 S. A. MORSE *Basalts & Phase Diagrams* iii. 28 Superheating of crystals above their melting temperature is a rare phenomenon.

superhea·vy, *a.* (and *sb.*). [SUPER- 9 a.] **a.** *gen.* Extremely heavy, heavier than the normal. Occas. as *sb.*

1952 *Sci. Amer.* May 44/1 It is a job for accurate balancing and gyroscope controls..and therefore an ideal spot for Hevimet, super-heavy Carboloy created-metal. **1974** *Physics Bull.* Dec. 578/3 The quarks give way to..superheavy mesonic matter and, ultimately, neutrons, protons and the lighter mesons. **1976** *Daily Times* (Lagos) 22 Sept. 30/1 That's how wrestling 'superheavy' Ray Apallon begins the open challenge to 'any of your Nigerian heavyweight wrestlers'.

b. *Nucl. Physics.* Of, pertaining to, or designating an element with an atomic mass or atomic number greater than those of the naturally occurring elements; *spec.* having an atomic number of 110 or more and belonging to a group having a limited range of proton/neutron ratios which confer enhanced stability against radioactive decay. Also as *sb.*, such an element.

1955 J. A. WHEELER in W. Pauli *Niels Bohr* 183 The superheavy nuclei that are neutron stable. **1962** L. DEIGHTON *Ipcress File* xviii. 107 Tritium is also called super-heavy hydrogen. **1970** *Physics Bull.* Dec. 534/2 The success of this view..has led to the suggestion that there exists a further 'island' of stability around mass number 300: superheavy nuclei which may have lifetimes from a fraction of a second, up to many years. **1971** *New Scientist* 18 Feb. 344/3 The radioactive counts from the mercury source showed the most promise for a superheavy. **1979** *Nature* 16 Aug. 549/2 There is no convincing evidence that superheavy elements have been discovered. **1980** *Physical Rev.* C. XXI. 1664/2 The recent theoretical estimates of low barriers..are supported by the failure to detect superheavies in the ^{48}Ca + ^{248}Cm reaction.

superhe·lical, *a. Biochem.* [f. *SUPERHELIX, after HELICAL *a.*] Belonging to or consisting of a superhelix.

1966 *Jrnl. Gen. Physiol.* XXXXIX. 125, I wonder whether you would explain again how you calculated the number of superhelical turns. **1974** *Nature* 5 Apr. 476/3 The superhelical structure imposes upon the DNA molecule a topological restraint. **1980** *Sci. Amer.* July 108/1 It is possible to gain a general understanding of how a left-handed superhelical coil..is transformed into a right-handed interwound superhelix by considering the linking number.

Hence **superhe·lically** *adv.*; also **su:perheli·city,** the state of being superhelical.

1974 *Nature* 20 Sept. 248/2 The affinity of the repressor for the operator..increases with increasing negative superhelicity up to a factor of approximately 14 for the DNA with −160 superhelical turns. **1978** *Ibid.* 12 Jan. 118/2 Superhelically wound oligonucleosome fibres. **1980** A. KORNBERG *DNA Replication* i. 25 Supertwisting, supercoiling, and superhelicity are terms for the twisting upon itself of the duplex DNA strands.

su·perhelix. *Biochem.* Pl. **-helices.** [SUPER- 5 c.] A helix formed from a helix; *spec.* a three-dimensional structure sometimes assumed by polypeptides, in which double protein or DNA helices are themselves coiled into a higher-order helix. Cf. *SUPERCOIL *sb.*

1964 G. H. HAGGIS *Introd. Molecular Biol.* iv. 80, α-Helices probably twist together like the strands of a rope, in keratin and myosin, to form super-helices. **1971** *Nature* 5 Nov. 27 (*caption*) Since the normal DNA double helix is right handed, the superhelix is more likely to be left handed. **1980** *Sci. Amer.* July 100/1 In the chromatin ..of higher organisms the DNA is wound around a core of protein to form a left-handed solenoidal superhelix.

su·perhet, colloq. abbrev. of next. Also *fig.*

1926 *Glasgow Herald* 12 Jan. 10 The real heart of a superhet set is the first detector. **1926** R. W. HUTCHINSON *Wireless* 236 The multivalve..'Super-Het' is scarcely a receiving set..for a beginner. **1937** [see *direct vision* s.v. *DIRECT *a.* 1 b]. **1951** R. HOGGART *Auden* vi. 195 So the scene for a work such as this [sc. *The Age of Anxiety*] must be a time-ridden, newspaper-headline-obsessed, 'superhet' city. **1960** *Practical Wireless* XXXVI. 342/2 The output is fed by a jack into the L.F. portion of a six transistor superhet. **1976** *CB Mag.* June 1/2 (Advt.), This handsomely styled 23-channel solid-state CB two-way radio features a..dual-conversion superhet receiver with RF stage.

superhe·terodyne, *a.* and *sb.* *Radio.* [f. *SUPER(SONIC *a.* (and *sb.*) + *HETERODYNE *a.*] **A.** *adj.* Employing or involving a method of radio reception (also used in television) in which a signal from a tunable local oscillator is combined with the incoming carrier wave to produce an ultrasonic intermediate frequency whose value is fixed and predetermined, so that it is unnecessary to vary the tuning of the subsequent amplifier and detector and increased selectivity and amplification are possible.

1922 *Wireless World* 1 Apr. 11/1 The Armstrong superheterodyne principle, in which the incoming signals are heterodyned before the first detector valve. **1934** *Times Rev. Year 1933* 1 Jan p. ix/4 Superheterodyne receivers were especially popular. **1966** *McGraw-Hill Encycl. Sci. & Technol.* XI. 257/1 Frequency-modulation (FM) receivers are almost always superheterodyne. **1976** *Gramophone* July 232/2 The superheterodyne circuit made modern radio possible. **1977** W. TUTE *Cairo Sleeper* vii. 128 'Hafiz the barman has a wireless set.'.. It was a superheterodyne job with valves.

B. *sb.* A superheterodyne receiver.

[**1921** *Q.S.T.* May 16/1 If a good U.S. amateur with such a set and an Armstrong Super could be sent to England, reception of U.S. amateurs would straightway become commonplace.] **1922** *Ibid.* July 7/1 Super-regeneration is..the method that makes two tubes do all the work that ten used to do in the super-heterodyne. **1933** K. HENNEY *Radio Engin. Handbk.* xvii. 449 The h-f superheterodyne seldom has high sensitivity, unless the first or h-f tube is regenerative. **1940** [see *CHASSIS 5]. **1965** *Wireless World* July 336/2 The various oscillators in superheterodynes have all set their own problems.

super-highway: see *SUPER- 6 c.

superimpo·sable, *a.* [f. SUPERIMPOSE *v.* + -ABLE.] Capable of being superimposed.

1920 in WEBSTER. **1925** *Rep. Proc. Imperial Bot. Conf. 1924* 41 Repeated examination in the same and different years of families derived from the same matings or selfings..gave rise to curves so similar as to be in many cases superimposable. **1933** *Jrnl. Theol. Stud.* XXXIV. 97 Private objects, such, e.g., as the different elliptical shapes seen by individuals at different distances, &c., from a circular plate, are often not compatible, congruent, or superimposable. **1971** *Nature* 9 July 106/2 The system is symmetric, for it is superimposable on its mirror image. **1979** *Dædalus* Summer 90 They are both interchangeable and superimposable.

superimpose, *v.* Add: **4.** *intr.* Of two figures or the like: to be capable of being brought into coincidence; to occupy the same positions in relation to their contexts.

1971 *Nature* 2 July 12/2 Counts from the highest polysome fraction superimpose on the zones corresponding to the two major light chains. **1972** *Sci. Amer.* Aug. 95/1 The degree to which the fields do not superimpose can be measured, and in this case there was a range of six degrees of horizontal disparity and two degrees of vertical disparity. **1975** *Nature* 10 Jan. 127/1 The sheets could then superimpose, forming the observed structures. **1978** *Ibid.* 27 July 389/2 (*caption*) Note that the peaks do not superimpose.

superimposed, *ppl. a.* **1. b.** (Earlier and later examples.)

1875 J. W. POWELL *Explor. Colorado Valley* 166 The beds in which the streams had their origin.. have been swept away. I propose to call such superimposed valleys. **1977** A. HALLAM *Planet Earth* 76/2 Alternatively, in superimposed drainage, the river courses may have initially developed on a cover of rocks whose structure was different to that of the rocks beneath, the upper beds having since disappeared through erosion.

su:perindivi·dual, *a.* (and *sb.*). [SUPER- 4 a.] Of or pertaining to that which is above or greater than the individual. Also as *sb.*

1916 F. VON HÜGEL *German Soul* 92 The moral relation between the individual and the super-individual unity. **1924** W. B. SELBIE *Psychol. Relig.* 150 The crowd will then act and feel, and express itself together. In doing so it becomes an entity or super-individual. **1936** J. KANTOR *Objective Psychol. Gram.* iv. 49 Those who would reject psychology from linguistics because linguistic phenomena are superindividual. **1943** *Mind* LII. 342 His [*sc.* Kant's] phrase *Bewusstsein überhaupt*, 'consciousness in general', though sometimes supposed to stand for a super-individual consciousness, might equally well..be taken to mean a character which all individual consciousnesses have in common.

Hence **su:perindivi·dualist, -individuali·stic** = *SUPERINDIVIDUAL *a.*; also [SUPER- 9 a], that favours a high degree of individualism.

1934 WYNDHAM LEWIS *Let.* 2 Nov. (1963) 223 Handicapped as we are under a super-individualist legislation—which allows the utmost licence in criticism of the State, in contradistinction to the Individual. **1943** *Mind* LII. 342 The majority of Kant's followers have, I suppose, adopted what I may call the 'super-individualist' interpretation. **1958** W. STARK *Sociol. Knowledge* i. 19 American society was also super-individualistic.

superinfe·ct, *v.* *Med.* [Back-formation from next.] *trans.* **a.** To cause (an infected cell) to be further infected *with* an organism of a similar kind. **b.** Of a bacterium or virus: to infect (a cell that already contains organisms of a similar kind).

1954 *Jrnl. Bacteriol.* LXVII. 696/1 Lysogenic cells were superinfected with phages. **1971** *Nature* 23 Apr. 496/3 By superinfecting it with a mixture of cat leukaemia and sarcoma virus the defective human virus might be helped. **1980** *Internat. Jrnl. Radiation Biol.* XXXVII. 120 When cells of *E. coli* are superinfected by phage λ, the phage DNA can appear in three distinct forms.

Hence **superinfe·cted, superinfe·cting** *ppl. adjs.*

1954 *Jrnl. Bacteriol.* LXVII. 698/2 The superinfected culture produces both the carried type and the superinfecting type of phage. **1961** *Virology* XIV. 220 The genetic incorporation of the superinfecting P2 was studied by examining the progeny of the superinfected cells. **1976** *Path. Ann.* XI. 259 Bacterial and, to a lesser extent, viral infections were also encountered in patients with multiple superinfecting organisms. **1981** *Virology* CIX. 74/1 The same concentration of PAA was also applied to the superinfected Raji cells.

su:perinfe·ction. *Med.* [SUPER- 15.] **a.** An infection occurring after or on top of an earlier infection, *esp.* as a consequence of treatment of the latter by broad-spectrum antibiotic or other therapy. **b.** The further infection of cells that are already infected with a similar organism, *esp.* as a technique in virology and immunology.

1922 *Stedman's Med. Dict.* (ed. 7) 972/2 *Superinfection*, ..a fresh infection added to one of the same nature already present. **1954** *Jrnl. Bacteriol.* LXVII. 702/2 The type of phage produced after superinfection was studied both in mass culture and in single burst experiments. **1961** *Lancet* 12 Aug. 352/2 Bacteræmia developed as a superinfection during antibiotic therapy. **1974** M. C. GERALD *Pharmacol.* xxvi. 459 While the incidence of superinfection is low with narrow-spectrum antibiotics such as penicillin, it is a common occurrence with tetracycline and other broad-spectrum antibiotics. **1981** *Virology* CIX. 72/1 Superinfection of the nonproducer cells with EBV..is known to induce synthesis of EA and MA.

superinte·lligent, *a.* **1.** [SUPER- 4 a.] Above or beyond the range of intelligence.

1960 [see *super-moral* s.v. *SUPER- 4 a].

2. [SUPER- 9 a.] Very highly intelligent.

1971 B. DE FERRANTI *Living with Computer* ix. 80 Recent work..demonstrates that by transplanting brain tissues super-intelligent animals can be produced. **1977** *Time Out* 28 Jan.–3 Feb. 60/4 (Advt.), Our labour force.. is super-intelligent.

superintendent, *sb.* and *a.* Add: **A.** *sb.* **1. e.** A police officer next above the rank of inspector.

1832 *Observer* 24 June 4/4 Mr. Thomas, the Superintendent of Police, F Division, came before..the presiding Magistrate. **1836** [in Dict., sense 1 a]. **1885** *Encycl. Brit.* XIX. 337/1 All promotions in the [police] service up to the rank of superintendent are made from the next rank below. **1907** G. B. SHAW *Major Barbara* Pref. 171 Those who pester our police superintendents with confessions of murder might very wisely be taken at their word and executed. **1936** G. HEYER *Behold, here's Poison* iv. 71 Things are more serious than I had supposed. This is Superintendent Hannasyde, of Scotland Yard. **1977** 'E. CRISPIN' *Glimpses of Moon* viii. 150 Not at all, Superintendent. Partial deafness must be quite a handicap in your profession.

superionic: see *SUPER- 9 a (*a*).

superiority. Add: **5.** Special Comb.: **superiority complex,** (*a*) *Psychol.*, an attitude of superiority which conceals actual feelings of inferiority and failure; (*b*) *gen.*, an exaggerated sense of personal superiority; (cf. *inferiority complex* s.v. *INFERIORITY 2).

1929 A. ADLER *Probl. Neurosis* vi. 87 In his business we find the man with a 'superiority complex': but if he were to lose his position..he would promptly go back to the expression of inferiority and make capital out of it. **1936** H. PREECE in *Crisis* Dec. 364/2 Each expression of this interest in the Negro is the manifestation of a definite superiority complex. **1945** A. L. ROWSE *English Spirit* xxxiii. 232 The English have a singular faculty for depreciating their great men. (Is it perhaps a form of superiority-complex?) **1979** *Nature* 11 Oct. 424/2 The Egyptian scientific community does not like or agree with the Israeli superiority complex.

superius (s^{i}upī^{ə}·riŏs). *Mus.* [a. L. *superius*, neut. (used as *sb.*) of *superior* SUPERIOR *a.*]. (See quots. 1801, 1876.) Also *transf.*, a person who sings this part.

[**1519** O. PETRUCCI *Motetti de la Corona* (heading) Libro secundo. (Superius.)] **1776** J. HAWKINS *Gen. Hist. Sci. & Pract. Music* II. I. vii. 86 *Quinible*..may rather mean a high part.., which in general lies above the tenor..and at others between the contretenor and the superius or treble. **1801** T. BUSBY *Dict. Mus.*, *Superius*,..the name by which the contrapuntists of the fifteenth and sixteenth centuries distinguished the *upper part* of any composition. **1876** STAINER & BARRETT *Dict. Mus. Terms* 412/1 *Superius*,..a name given to the upper part in a composition by the writers of the sixteenth century. **1907** *Grove's Dict. Mus.* (ed. 2) III. 631/1 'Le Parangon des Chansons', printed by 'Jaques Moderne'..in nine volumes..and..so arranged that the Superius and Tenor sit facing each other, on opposite sides of the table—the Superius reading from the lower half of the left-hand page, and the Tenor from the upper half. **1954** G. REESE *Music in Renaissance* i. 16 The *texture* in which a vocal top line (or, as this part is interchangeably called, treble, superius, cantus, or discantus) is supported by a subordinate, instrumental tenor and contratenor was much in vogue. **1970** *Proc. R. Mus. Assoc. 1969–70* 95 The fourth and final line of the text..telescopes the beginning and end of Sandrin's superius. **1977** *Early Music* Apr. 243/3 Surely..the superius should cadence on C with the other voices. *Ibid.* July 419/2 The superius of his motet *Sufficiebat*..is closely related to the tenor of Hayne's chanson *Mon souvenir*.

superjet: see *SUPER- 6 c.

superlative, *a.* Add: **2. c.** *superlative surprise*, the name given to an especially complicated method of change-ringing. Cf. SURPRISE *sb.* 5 b.

1788 W. JONES et al. *Key to Art of Ringing* xi. 179 Superlative Surprise... The above is an original composition of our own on purpose for this work, and has never yet been rung: the principle upon which it is founded, will..give it credit among amateurs of the art, for..it will plainly appear the most even treble bob peal..discovered. **1845** *Cambr. Chron.* 6 Dec. 4/3 The company of change-ringers, of Saffron Walden, performing..upwards of 1,200 changes of Superlative Surprise. **1874** W. BANISTER *Art & Science Change Ringing* 33 (*heading*) Superlative Surprise. **1931** E. MORRIS *Hist. Change Ringing* 458 Harry Withers..once..conducted a peal of Superlative Surprise at Selly Oak, Birmingham. **1965** W. G. WILSON *Change Ringing* 237/2 Superlative Surprise Major, 114.

su·perlattice. [SUPER- 5.] **1.** *Metallurgy.* An ordered arrangement of some of the atoms in a solid solution extending through large parts of it and coexisting with the disorder of the remaining atoms; also, a solid solution possessing this; = *SUPERSTRUCTURE 3.

1932 *Proc. R. Soc.* A. CXXXVI. 211 A structure of this kind is usually termed a superlattice (überstruktur). **1951** N. F. M. HENRY et al. *Interpret. X-Ray Diffraction Photographs* xv. 211/1 The use of the word 'superlattice' is unfortunate. The original German word *Uberstruktur* conveyed perfectly the concept of a new type of ordered structure being imposed on the existing disordered phase. This has nothing to do with the type of lattice. **1966** C. R. TOTTLE *Sci. Engin. Materials* viii. 187 Domains form and grow during normal superlattice formation, according to composition, temperature, and time of annealing. **1967** A. H. COTTRELL *Introd. Metallurgy* xiv. 190 When formed from true metals the structure is often an ordered solid solution or superlattice, in which the two species are arranged in some regular alternating pattern. **1978** *Nature* 9 Nov. 168/2 Evidence..that an FeNi $L1_0$ superlattice exists in the taenite of the Cape York and Toluca meteorites. **1979** [see *SUPERSTRUCTURE 3].

2. *Physics.* A small-scale periodicity in the composition of a semiconductor.

1970 *IBM Jrnl. Res. & Development* XIV. 61 We consider a one-dimensional periodic potential, or 'superlattice', in monocrystalline semiconductors formed by a periodic variation of alloy composition or of impurity density during epitaxial growth. **1977** *McGraw-Hill Yearbk. Sci. & Technol.* 380/1 Photocurrent measurements in the superlattice structures have made it possible to observe simultaneously quantum states and associated anomalous conductance.

superloo, -luminal, -male: see *SUPER- 6 c, 4 a (*a*), 5 f (and 6 c).

superman. Add: **1.** Also *loosely*, a man of extraordinary power or ability; a superior being.

1925 H. V. MORTON *Heart of London* 110 Above the kneeling priests is the Pharaoh, that ancient superman. **1942** *R.A.F. Jrnl.* 13 June 15 They are neither freaks nor super-men. *Ibid.* 18 The stories told in the newspapers to emphasise the superman qualities which the Commandos deny possessing. **1959** KOESTLER *Sleepwalkers* v. ii. 471 Both considered themselves supermen and started on a basis of mutual adulation. **1969** G. JACKSON *Let.* 28 Dec. in *Soledad Brother* (1971) 179 How could there be a *benevolent* superman controlling a world like this.

2. (With capital initial.) The name of an invincible hero with superhuman powers, including that of flight, introduced in an American comic strip (1938). Also *transf.* and *allusively*.

1938 *Action Comics* June 1 So was created..Superman! champion of the oppressed, the physical marvel who had sworn to devote his existence to helping those in need! **1940** *Time* 26 Feb. 44/3 Last week Superman took to the air in earnest, as a three-a-week serial. **1942** H. Haycraft *Murder for Pleasure* ix. 191 Converting Strangeway's wife Georgia into what Miriam Allen de Ford calls 'a sort of female Superman'. **1958** *Times Lit. Suppl.* 1 Apr. p. xx/4 The impression remains of a sense of values associated with 'Superman' and American comics. **1968** S. Ellin *Valentine Estate* III. iv. 142 'How the hell did he come to miss me?'..'You're Superman,' the first man answered. 'Bullets bounce off you.' **1976** *Survey* Winter 1 The..*New York Times*..in the past presented Henry Kissinger as a species of diplomatic superman. **1977** *New Scientist* 14 Apr. 59/3 Schlesinger..is riding high at present—pictured in a superman suit on a recent *Time* magazine cover. **1980** F. Weldon *Puffball* 77 'Now it's our turn.' 'I don't want it to be,' she said, as if he, like Superman, could turn the world the other way.

Hence **su·permanhood.**

1910 *Dublin Rev.* Oct. 344 Human nature..is likely to remain still exactly the same. Those who believe it to be travelling towards moral supermanhood have obviously not studied it. **1924** W. J. Locke *Coming of Amos* xix. 254 My vanity was pricked by what seemed to be her lack of confidence in my supermanhood. **1964** *Punch* 1 Apr. 507/3 Convincingly exciting, despite hero's slight leaning towards supermanhood.

su·permarket. orig. *U.S.* Also **super market.** [Super- 6 c.] **1. a.** A large self-service shop, selling a wide range of groceries and household goods, and freq. one of a chain of stores.

1933 *N.Y. Times* 25 Feb. 28/1 In a move interpreted by the trade as an effort to help both corporate chains and independent wholesale grocers fight the competition of 'super-markets' which have sprung up in the last two years, the Associated Grocery Manufacturers of America, Inc., yesterday drew up a proposed model law for States which may seek to prevent the sale of standard grocery products at or below purchase price. *Ibid.* 5 Mar. 11/4 For three months now a large supermarket in New Jersey has been doing a business reputed to average $100,000 a week. **1933** *Chain Store Age* (Gen. Merchandise ed.) June 95/1 The 'One-stop-drive-in super market' provides free parking, and every kind of food under one roof. **1949** R. Graves *Seven Days in New Crete* 121 We buyers..drifted round with our baskets, silently helping ourselves to whatever we wanted... The procedure recalled that of an American super-market. **1959** *Spectator* 25 Sept. 409/1 This applies particularly to supermarkets, whose whole economy depends on people going in to buy a can of beans and coming out with a dazed expression and three pounds' worth of groceries. **1969** *Islander* (Victoria, B.C.) 6 July 8/2 Your supplies..come from a good delicatessen and..your super market. **1978** *Oxford Consumer* Mar. 4/1 The change from counter to self-service stores in Britain only started in the late 1950's/early 1960's, when a supermarket was defined as having a minimum sales area of 2,000 sq. ft. **1979** M. Boyce *I was There!* 70 The pithead baths is a supermarket now.

b. *transf.* and *fig.*

1962 *Listener* 26 July 127/2 The Marshall Plan and this vast new Supermarket have destroyed the roots of that sickness. **1973** J. W. Polier in A. E. Wilkerson *Rights of Children* p. xiv, The 1970 White House Conference on Children announced that prepared reports would offer 'a supermarket of proposals'.

2. a. *attrib.*, as *supermarket chain, company, shopping*, etc.

1933 *N.Y. Times* 26 Feb. 15/8 The independent and corporate chain stores are standing together against the alleged menace of the 'super-market' competition. **1934** *Archit. Rec.* LXXVI. 206 Markets are now built up to the street line and are of the 'super-market' type. **1951** C. W. Mills *White Collar* I. ii. 25 As supermarkets mushroomed..the chains began to imitate their supermarket competitors. **1963** *Times Rev. Industry* Aug. 65/2 Premier..is one of the few supermarket companies proper with a highly developed and well integrated scheme. **1967** G. Wills in Wills & Yearsley *Handbk. Management Technol.* 192 A product which cannot gain distribution in the major supermarket chains may have a very high direct percentage distribution yet a low percentage sterling distribution. **1975** D. Lodge *Changing Places* iii. 115 We seem to have fixed on the same day for supermarket shopping. **1977** F. Parrish *Fire in Barley* ii. 24 A lifetime of deep-frozen scampi, supermarket Riesling, [etc.].

b. supermarket trolley, a wire basket on wheels which a supermarket customer can push around the shop collecting goods for purchase; also (U.S.) *supermarket cart.*

1972 *Even. Telegram* (St. John's, Newfoundland) 28 June 29/6 (Advt.), 5 supermarket carts. **1970** *Cape Times* 28 Oct. 21/3 (Advt.), Lawn mowers, kitchenware, glassware, 22 supermarket trollies. **1977** *Irish Times* 8 June 8/8, I wandered in to sit with the farmers, and saw a heifer that would fit into a supermarket trolley sell for £60. **1982** Barr & York *Official Sloane Ranger Handbk.* 95/1 He and his chums stage a mixed doubles wheelbarrow/piggy-back/supermarket trolley race down the High/the Broad/the Cornmarket.

Hence **su:permarketee·r** [-eer], a person or company involved in a supermarket business.

1960 *Spectator* 13 May 712 Nor have many of the supermarketeers realised that self-service in itself gets you nowhere. **1964** *Punch* 29 Jan. 174/3 Other supermarketeers include London Grocers. **1973** *Guardian* 17 Feb. 13/6 To ask them to cut their profits still further would, in the view of the supermarketeer, be both unjust and ineffective.

su·permart. [Super- 6 c.] = prec.

1954 *Archit. Rev.* CXVI. 234 Beneath the two major blocks..the lower floors will house shops, a supermart, a highways terminal, an art museum, [etc.]. **1961** *Guardian* 17 Feb. 8/6 The baby sitting up in the supermart trolley. **1978** P. Van Greenaway *Man called Scavener* xiv. 193 Take any name familiar to our age: a supermart..a refrigerator.

supermassive: see *super- 9 a (*a*).

su·permind. 1. [Super- 6 c.] A mind of exceptional capacity or ability; a person possessing such a mind.

1918 *Daily News* (Chicago) 5 Jan. 10/6 (*heading*) Four super-minds ruling in Loop. **1962** 'S. Ransome' *Without Trace* v. 50 Loot that wasn't dropping soon enough because..that high-geared supermind of Lynch's kept hanging fire. **1975** J. Taylor *Superminds* (1976) ix. 161 The view of a group of defence workers..who advised their government to liquidate all superminds as being a menace to security.

2. [Super- 5 a or 6 b.] An extended or superior mind that is a composite of many individual minds.

1941 L. MacNeice *Poetry of W. B. Yeats* vi. 126 This mind, for Yeats, is not so much the mind of God as the super-mind of humanity. **1965** *Listener* 1 July 26/1. This civilization exists in a corporate form, the individual thinking units of which have long ago been synthesized into one super-mind.

su·permu:ltiplet. *Physics.* [Super- 6 b.] **a.** A group of transitions in an atom between spectral terms of different multiplicity, all the transitions involving the same change in the orbital quantum number *l* of an electron from the same initial value.

1927 Russell & Meggers in *Sci. Papers Bureau of Standards* (U.S.) XX. 331 The five terms first mentioned are evidently closely related, and their combinations with the triad ^3P, $^3D'$, ^3F can be arranged in the form of a 'supermultiplet'. **1935** Condon & Shortley *Theory Atomic Spectra* ix. 245 The set of all lines arising in transitions between two polyads..having the same parent configuration is known as a supermultiplet. **1972** I. I. Sobel'man *Introd. Theory Atomic Spectra* xxxi. 313 By summing eqn. (31.48) over all transitions $J \rightarrow J'$ within the given multiplet we obtain the line strength of this multiplet... Summing over LL'..gives the line strength of the supermultiplet.

b. In particle physics, a multiplet (sense *b) in the broader sense, comprising particles of different hypercharge as well those of different charge.

1952 *Ann. Rev. Nucl. Sci.* I. 44 The two states belong to the same supermultiplet (in this case a single charge multiplet with $S = \frac{1}{2}$ and $T = \frac{1}{2}$). **1964** *New Scientist* 27 Feb. 523/3 The discovery of the omega-minus confirms that other groupings of particles into families or 'supermultiplets' are valid. **1972** G. L. Wick *Elementary Particles* v. 82 They thought that all these particles might belong to a larger multiplet, or supermultiplet, which connects both different isotopic spin and different strangeness.

supernacular, *a.* Add: (Later examples.) Also *transf.*

1920 G. Saintsbury *Notes on Cellar-bk.* 18 Some of the finer kinds [of sherry] are really supernacular—the best 'Tio Pepe', for instance. **1958** [see *devadasi].

supernatant, *a.* Add: **B.** *sb. Biol.* and *Med.* A supernatant substance.

1922 *Brit. Med. Jrnl.* 19 Aug. 297/2 To this high refinement..Otto, Munter, and Winkler attribute the potency of their products as compared with supernatants obtained by the centrifuge only. **1955** *New Biol.* XIX. 91 The supernatant is decanted and again spun usually at about 10,000 to 20,000 *g* for twenty minutes. **1977** *Proc. R. Soc. Med.* LXX. 192/2 The supernatants were decanted into plastic counting vials and mixed with 10ml Instagel.

su·pernate, *sb. Biol.* and *Med.* [f. prec., after *filtrate, precipitate.*] = *supernatant *sb.*

1943 *Jrnl. Immunol.* XLVI. 326 After centrifuging these mixtures the supernates were tested for the presence of a sheep-cell hemolysin. **1979** *Experientia* XXXV. 193/2 After decantation of the supernate into counting vials.

supernation, etc.: see *super- 4 a (*a*) and (*c*), 6 c.

supernaturalize, *v.* Add: Hence **su:pernaturaliza·tion.**

1933 *Downside Rev.* LI. 729 St Thomas gives no support ..to the original views of Rousselot..as to the need of a kind of supernaturalization of the (natural) intellectual powers in order to accept and assent to revelation. **1961** E. L. Mascall *Grace & Glory* i. 15 The sanctification and the supernaturalization of our whole being, body and soul alike—this is the purpose for which the Catholic Church and its whole sacramental equipment exist.

su:pernorma·lity. [f. Supernormal *a.* + -ity.] **a.** The quality of exceeding what is normal; an instance of this.

1909 O. J. Lodge *Survival of Man* I. i. 2 Assertions concerning psychological supernormalities have not only excited attention, but have rather notably roused the interest of careful and responsible students. **1922** *19th Cent.* Oct. 600 One of the first indications of potential genius in school children is unusual precocity or mental supernormality. **1955** W. Naylor *Silver Birch Anthol.* 8 The faculty of being able to deliver, week after week, words of wisdom..in this spontaneous fashion, is in itself evidence of supernormality. **1977** D. Morris *Manwatching* 277 Having exhausted one line of supernormality, we switch to another, selecting a new element for improvement and dwelling on that until it too has become stale.

b. [Super- 9 a.] The quality of being exceedingly normal. *rare.*

1945 *New Yorker* 7 Apr. 74/2 Now that the end [of the war] is practically at hand, the supernormality of the English is surprising.

superno·va. *Astr.* Pl. **-novae, -novas.** [Super- 6 c.] **1.** A star that undergoes a sudden and temporary increase in brightness like a nova but to a very much greater degree, as a result of an explosion that disperses most of the stellar material.

1934 Baade & Zwicky in *Physical Rev.* XLV. 138/1 Supernovae flare up in every stellar system (nebula) once in several centuries. **1934** —— in *Proc. Nat. Acad. Sci.* 15 May 254 The extensive investigations of extragalactic systems..have brought to light the..fact that there exist two well-defined types of..novae which might be distinguished as common novae and super-novae. **1939** [see *nova 2]. **1965** *Listener* 20 May 741/1 Only three supernovae, the stars of 1054, 1572, and 1604, have appeared in our Galaxy since records began. **1976** *Sci. Amer.* Dec. 89/1 Some supernovas may leave behind cosmic ashes in the form of a neutron star or black hole. **1977** *Whitaker's Almanack 1978* 155/1 One important source of radio noise is the Crab Nebula, which is known to be the remains of the supernova of A.D. 1054. **1978** Pasachoff & Kutner *University Astron.* xi. 296 On the average, Type I supernovae reach an absolute magnitude of −19 at peak brightness, while that of Type II supernovae is about 2 magnitudes fainter.

2. *fig.*

1965 *Listener* 14 Jan. 84/3 Look at the soft gleam of D major near the start of the development (bar 170)—the distant glow of fiery *supernova*, into the heart of which we are at length to be flung. **1974** *State* (Columbia, S. Carolina) 1 Apr. 10A/1 As far as the networks were concerned, the satiric supernova had burned out. **1979** *Tucson* (Arizona) *Citizen* 20 Sept. 7B/6 (*heading*) 'Buck Rogers' no supernova, but it won't wink out, either.

3. *attrib.*, as *supernova explosion, remnant.*

1960 *McGraw-Hill Encycl. Sci. & Technol.* XIII. 303/2 The remains of an old supernova explosion. **1975** *Sci. Amer.* Mar. 29/2 The Crab Nebula is the remnant of a supernova explosion. **1960** *McGraw-Hill Encycl. Sci. & Technol.* XIII. 304/1 Unexplained radio sources also may be from supernova remnants. **1978** Pasachoff & Kutner *University Astron.* xi. 296 Optical astronomers have photographed two dozen of these stellar shreds, which are known as supernova remnants.

supernumerary, *a.* and *sb.* Add: **A.** *adj.* **1. d.** *Genetics.* Of a chromosome: additional to the normal complement of autosomes and sex chromosomes. Cf. sense f of the *sb.* below.

1907 E. B. Wilson in *Biol. Bull.* XII. 304 The unpaired chromosome may be either present or absent in either the male or female, and hence is without significance in sex-production. It is in fact a kind of supernumerary chromosome, which I shall designate as the '*s*-chromosome' in order to distinguish it from the odd sex-chromosome of the usual type. **1927** *Jrnl. Agric. Res.* XXXV. 782 The distribution of a supernumerary chromosome to the four daughter cells has been studied and found to be erratic. **1969** Brown & Bertke *Textbk. Cytol.* xviii. 380/1 Supernumerary chromosomes are usually much smaller than the autosomes and for that reason have often been termed 'fragment' chromosomes.

B. *sb.* **1. e.** (Earlier example.)

1755 C. Charke *Life* 115 A poor, beggarly Fellow, who had been sometimes Supernumerary in Drury-Lane Theatre.

f. *Genetics.* A chromosome which may be absent from normal individuals of either sex, having little or no effect on phenotype and occurring irregularly.

1909 E. B. Wilson in *Jrnl. Exper. Zool.* VI. 150 The chromosomes in question are the ones which in earlier papers I have called the 'supernumeraries'. **1917** E. E. Carothers in *Jrnl. Morphol.* XXVIII. 469 Another variation which has attracted attention in our collection of Acridian material..is the presence in certain individuals of one, or sometimes two, entities which I shall designate as supernumeraries. They possess the staining capacity of chromatin. **1969** Brown & Bertke *Textbk. Cytol.* xviii. 381/1 A..peculiarity of supernumeraries which seems to indicate that they have genes for their own survival is preferential fertilization in corn.

superordinate, *a.* (*sb.*) Add: **a.** Delete 'Now only in *Logic*'. (Later examples.) Also *spec.* in *Gram.*

1934 Priebsch & Collinson *German Lang.* vi. 318 The older construction is characterized by the precedence of the superordinate infinite, e.g. *lassen tragen.* **1949** C. E. Bazell in *Travaux du Cercle Linguistique de Copenhague* V. 77 If..the functions of one member (e.g. the substantive) alone are similar to the functions of the whole group, this member is said to be superordinate. **1954** *Theology* LVII. 326 It would not necessarily be apparent which was the subordinate and which the superordinate sex. **1970** T. Lupton *Managem. & Social Sci.* (ed. 2) iii. 80 The superordinate manager must work hard to create conditions for the subordinate such that the latter will feel that he is being supported and encouraged. **1974** W. Rees-Mogg *Reigning Error* i. 21 Only those who appreciate my superordinate quality are fit to live in our new world of Nazism/Fascism/Soviet Communism. **1979** *Trans. Philol. Soc.* 37 In Italian promotion of the subordinate *si* into the superordinate clause..results in the unacceptable sequence *si si*.

b. *sb.* Also, that which is of a superior order or category.

1934 Priebsch & Collinson *German Lang.* vi. 318 Extensions of the infinitives and participles..sometimes follow their superordinates. **1957** R. W. Brown in Saporta & Bastian *Psycholinguistics* (1961) 505/1 The concrete noun..is likely to be more picturable than its superordinate. **1969** Greenfield & Bruner in J. S. Bruner *Beyond Information Given* (1974) xxi. 388 An itemized superordinate in labeling form. **1972** *Jrnl. Social Psychol.* LXXXVI. 302 The use of a superordinate ..functionally eliminated one element from the set.

superordination. Add: **2. b.** The condition of belonging to a higher or more powerful category or class; opp. *subordination.*

1952 V. O. Key *Politics, Parties, & Pressure Groups* (ed. 3) i. 4 Politics deals with human relationships of superordination and subordination,..of the governors and the governed. **1959** G. D. Mitchell *Sociol.* iii. 41 The relationship between father and son is one of super- and sub-ordination. **1975** A. Ryle *Frames & Cages* xiii. 121 The concept of superordination recurs through the book.

su:perorga·nic, *a.* (and *sb.*). *Sociol.* [Super- 4 a.] Applied to the social and cultural aspects of life which evolve from and transcend the individuals in society. Also *absol.* as *sb.*; occas. *transf.*

1862, 1876 [In Dict. s.v. Super- 4 a]. **1917** A. L. Kroeber in *Amer. Anthropol.* XIX. 163 (*title*) The superorganic. **1932** A. Raven (*title*) Civilization as divine superman. A superorganic philosophy of history. **1962** E. E. Evans-Pritchard *Ess. Social Anthropol.* ii. 34 Spencer clearly formulated the theory of gradual modification of species or structure..and..extended his evolutionary ideas to include the social or super-organic. **1968** *Internat. Encycl. Social Sci.* XV. 124/2 It was Spencer who coined the term 'superorganic', which, following its use by Kroeber in 1917 in his article 'The Superorganic', has been accepted as designating the unique and distinct elements in human behavior, and therefore as synonymous with 'culture'. **1973** P. A. Colinvaux *Introd. Ecol.* xl. 550 A first grand generalization was the persuasive philosophy of Clements and his disciples..who likened the climax stage to some superorganic being.

supero·vulate, *v. Physiol.* [Back-formation from *superovulation.] **a.** *intr.* To produce abnormally large numbers of ova at a single ovulation. **b.** *trans.* To cause (an animal) to do this. So **supero·vulated** *ppl. a.*

1956 *Nature* 3 Mar. 429/1 Fallopian tubes from a superovulated female, killed approximately 12 hr. after mating to one of these males, were fixed in Bouin. **1961** M. C. Chang in C. A. Villee *Control of Ovulation* 185 It seems that ovulation can be easily induced in the pregnant rabbits and that about half of the pregnant animals superovulate; that is ovulate a larger number of eggs than expected. **1970** *Sci. Jrnl.* May 50/2 Hormonal treatment can be used to get the female to superovulate. **1971** *Nature* 10 Sept. 125/2 Random bred female albino mice.. were superovulated with gonadotrophins. **1979** *Ibid.* 25 Jan. 298/2 Two-celled embryos were collected from super-ovulated donor ewes early on day 2 of their oestrous cycle. **1979** *New Scientist* 26 Apr. 269/2 [They] superovulated 14 heifer cows up to 10 times in rapid succession —and the cows responded with crops of up to 19 eggs at a single ovulation.

So **su:perovula·tion** [Super- 10 b].

1927 *Amer. Jrnl. Anat.* XL. 213 Superovulation, or the liberation of an unusual number of ova invariably occurs. **1981** *Sci. Digest* Aug. 89/1 They were beginning to suspect that superovulation..might be disrupting the internal reproductive environment.

superpe·rsonal, *a.* [Super- 4 a.] Transcending the limits of what is personal. Also *absol.* Hence **su·perperson, superpe·rsonalism, su:perpersona·lity.**

1860, 1899 [in Dict. s.v. Super- 4 a]. **1924** G. B. Shaw *Saint Joan* p. xvii, An appetite for evolution..[is] a superpersonal need. **1926** W. D. Lighthall *Superpersonalism* 26 We can proceed a stage further, and call it the Person of Evolution. But its vast and complex personality requires a differentiating term. May we not apply to it the term 'Superperson'? and call its personality a 'superpersonality', its point of view the 'superpersonal', the system of its study, 'Superpersonalism'? **1927** J. S. Huxley *Relig. without Revelation* i. 52 Metamorphosed from a divine person into a super-person. **1939** Auden in *I Believe* (1940) 20 But this does not warrant ascribing to a culture a super-personality, conscious of its parts as I can be conscious of my hand or liver. **1963** *Observer* 31 Mar. 11/3 The God hypothesis asserts the existence of some kind of supernatural personal or superpersonal being. **1977** *Rolling Stone* 21 Apr. 68/2 A chair is made by a person, so the world has to be made by a superperson.

superpla·stic, *a.* and *sb. Metallurgy.* [Super- 9 a, 10: see *superplasticity.] **A.** *adj.* Of, pertaining to, or designating a metal capable of extreme plastic extension under load; involving or characteristic of such materials.

1947 *Chem. Abstr.* XLI. 2375 The superplastic alloy cannot be a mixt. of solid solns. of Al and Zn. **1970** *New Scientist* 12 Mar. 504/2 One of the most suitable titanium alloys—Ti-318—is superplastic at 930°C if correctly worked, and can be made to stretch and flow like plastic. **1978** *Jrnl. R. Soc. Arts* CXXVI. 689/1 It is possible that the single heat cycle combination of superplastic forming and diffusion bonding will revolutionize the fabrication of titanium sheet structures for aircraft applications. **1978** *Nature* 16 Nov. 209/2 The consolidated product can have very fine grain sizes which in turn leads to great ductility at ambient temperature—even to superplastic behaviour.

B. *sb.* A superplastic metal.

1969 *New Scientist* 2 Jan. 22/2 This metal, after treatment which reduces the grain size to about a micrometre, behaves like a superplastic at room temperature—it can be stretched by a factor of about 10 in one direction without breaking. **1971** *Britannica Yearbk. Sci. & Future 1972* 406 While the superplastics are only starting to shed their image as laboratory curiosities, the fiber composites have almost arrived.

Hence **superpla·stically** *adv.*; **su:perplasti·city** [tr. Russ. *sverkhplastichnost'* (Bochvar & Sviderskaya 1945, in *Izvestiya Akad. Nauk SSSR: Otdelenie tekhnicheskikh Nauk* IX. 824)], the state or quality of being superplastic.

1947 *Chem. Abstr.* XLI. 2375 (*heading*) Superplasticity in zinc-aluminum alloys. **1969** *Sci. Jrnl.* June 75/2 At one time, it was considered that superplastic metallic alloys were amorphous-like and for this reason behaved superplastically. **1977** *Jrnl. R. Soc. Arts* CXXV. 348/1 The exploitation of superplasticity in titanium sheet opens the way for shaped components of reduced cost. **1978** *Ibid.* CXXVI. 688/1 When the temperature of the blank reaches 950°C the argon pressure is increased at a programmed rate to expand the blank into the tool superplastically.

superposable, *a.* Add: Hence **su:perposabi·lity,** the property of being superposable.

1913 *Jrnl. Chem. Soc.* CIII. 839 There are evidently two vertical planes of symmetry cutting diagonally through the ring carbon atoms, and it might be objected that the presence of these two planes of symmetry are in reality the cause of the superposability. **1963** R. Ballabh *Hydrodynamic Superposability* i. 1 The idea of superposability as regards fluid motions does not seem to have engaged the attention of mathematicians in a formal way until the year 1940. **1973** *Engin. Fracture Mechanics* V. 555 The same is practically true for elastomers also but, in addition, their ultimate properties are well described by a failure envelope which approximates time–temperature superposability.

su·perpower. Also **super power.** [Super- 6.]

1. [Super- 6 c.] orig. and chiefly *U.S.* Electrical power produced by the co-ordination and interconnection of existing power plants for greater economy and efficiency. Freq. *attrib.* Now *Hist.*

1921 W. S. Murray in *Prof. Papers U.S. Geol. Survey* No. 123. 11 On first presenting the subject considered in this report to the late Secretary of the Interior..I used the word 'superpower' to describe a system that would furnish power to the railroads and the industries within the territory between Boston and Washington that has now become more familiarly known as the superpower zone. **1921** *Independent* CVII. 316/2 The problems certain to arise within the circuit of the super-power zone are like those connected with the interstate and intrastate services of the railroads. *Ibid.* 317/2 The probable issues of super-power seem to make such a body [*sc.* a Federal control agency] inevitable. **1926** *Encycl. Brit.* (ed. 13) 681/2 The basis for a super-power system lies in the economy effected by the interconnection of electric power systems whose peak loads are reached at different times. **1983** T. P. Hughes *Networks of Power* xi. 297 Only one month after World War I ended, William S. Murray, a consulting electrical engineer, urged the secretary of the interior to prepare the ground for this superpower system.

2. [Super- 6 b.] Power of a greater kind or degree than the ordinary.

1922 D. H. Lawrence *Aaron's Rod* xviii. 269 Newly flushed with his own male super-power, he was going to have his reward. **1928** G. B. Shaw *Intelligent Woman's Guide* lxxxiii. 454 The more power the people are given the more urgent becomes the need for some rational and well-informed superpower to dominate them. **1931** *Times Lit. Suppl.* 26 Sept. (Home & Classroom Suppl.) p. iv/2 A super-power amplifier with an undistorted output of 125 watts. **1970** *New Society* 5 Feb. 231/3 This is an entity which has recently escaped from the dominance of Europe: and is now shadowed by the dominance of American superpower. **1975** *Microwave Jrnl.* XVIII. 50/3 The power of conventional microwave generating devices can be increased appreciably only through a matched increase of the..electron beam intensity. It is therefore tempting to use intense Relativistic Electron Beams to generate 'super power' microwaves. **1977** *N.Y. Rev. Bks.* 23 June 39/2 We do not, and cannot hope to, have a monopoly of 'superpower' in our world, as Rome had in hers.

3. [Super- 6 c.] A nation or state having a dominant position in world politics; one which has the power to act decisively in pursuit of interests which embrace the whole world; *spec.* the United States of America and the Union of Soviet Socialist Republics.

[**1930** *Economist* 12 July 63/2 The most important contributions to the Conference..were descriptions of what has actually taken place in the..control of super-power zones.] **1944** W. T. R. Fox *Super-Powers* ii. 20 There will be 'world powers' and 'regional powers'. These world powers we shall call 'super-powers', in order to distinguish them from the other powers..whose interests are great in only a single theater of power conflict. **1957** *Foreign Affairs* XXXV. 177 Britain is no longer a Super-Power. **1967** *Spectator* 30 June 758/2 Almost by definition superpowers do not have to care about face... America will continue to be a superpower whatever it does about Vietnam. **1971** *Guardian* 9 Dec. 12/1 China has..been drawn into a Super Power type of defence of Pakistan. **1977** E. Heath *Travels* viii. 166 What I saw when I arrived was a laudable achievement, possible only to a military commander with the resources of a superpower. **1978** J. Updike *Coup* (1979) ii. 54 Capital investments cleverly pried from the rivalry between the two superpowers (and that shadowy third, China, that has the size but not as it were the mass, the substance, to be called super).

superpronation: see *super- 2 a (*b*).

superra·diant, *a. Physics.* [Super- 9 a.] Involving or exhibiting superradiance.

1954 R. H. Dicke in *Physical Rev.* XCIII. 102/2 For want of a better term, a gas which is radiating strongly because of coherence will be called 'super-radiant'. **1974** *Sci. Amer.* June 126/1 The optical gain of the rapid discharge is so large that emission becomes superradiant, which means that the unit will lase without an optical cavity. **1978** *Nature* 20 Apr. 742/2 The word superradiant has often been misused..but is now taken to mean either the coherent radiation generated by a system of atoms possessing an externally created macroscopic polarisation rather akin to a phased array of dipoles, or alternatively the incoherent fluctuating radiation produced by a system of excited atoms possessing no initial polarisation but instead developing a cooperative decay behaviour through quantum correlations.

Hence **superra·diantly** *adv.*; also **superra·diance,** the spontaneous emission of coherent radiation by a system of atoms, esp. when the coherence is due to the initial correlation of the atoms by an external macroscopic polarization.

1965 *Physical Rev. Lett.* XIV. 589 (*heading*) Nuclear superradiance in solids. **1974** *Sci. Amer.* June 126/2 If the ultraviolet pulses are focused by a cylindrical lens to a line on the surface of the dye.., the dye will often lase superradiantly in visible light along the direction of the line. **1979** *New Scientist* 8 Mar. 763/2 The wave analogue of this process was called 'super-radiance': incident waves in certain modes would be amplified (rather than absorbed) by a rotating black hole, and would carry away some of the black hole's rotational energy.

super-rat: see *super- 6 c. **super-real,** etc.: *super- 4 a (*a*) and (*c*).

su:perregenera·tion. *Electronics.* [Super- 6 b.] Regenerative amplification in which self-oscillation is prevented by repeated quenching of the signal at an ultrasonic frequency.

1922 *Q.S.T.* July 7/1 At a meeting of the Institute of Radio Engineers, Edwin Howard Armstrong on June 7th gave his new invention of super-regeneration to a tense and expectant audience. **1922** E. H. Armstrong in *Proc. IRE* X. 244 This new result is obtained by the extension of regeneration into a field which lies beyond that hitherto considered its theoretical limit, and the process of amplification is therefore termed super-regeneration. **1943** F. E. Terman *Radio Engineers' Handbk.* ix. 664 Receivers employing superregeneration find their chief usefulness in the wavelength range 0·5 to 10 meters. **1975** R. L. Shrader *Electronic Communication* (ed. 3) xviii. 435/2 This type of superregeneration is often produced in RF amplifiers and is characterized by a wide band of spurious signals that it generates.

Hence **superrege·nerative** *a.*, employing or characterized by superregeneration; **superrege·neratively** *adv.*; **superrege·nerator,** a superregenerative device.

1922 *Q.S.T.* July 9/2 The super-regenerative amplifier. *Ibid.* 11/1 In the super-regenerator there is periodically sufficient positive resistance to wipe out this oscillation and hence it is not heard. **1934** *Wireless Engineer* XI. 35/1 The receiver may be made to function superregeneratively by increasing the s.g. voltage to the point of 'squegging'. **1948** Slurzberg & Osterheld *Essent. Radio* v. 232 Superregenerative detector circuits are used in light, compact, portable code receivers. **1959** R. L. Shrader *Electronic Communication* xvii. 542 When coupled to an antenna, the superregenerator radiates a very broad signal. **1965** *Guardian* 18 Jan. 16/3 The popular super-regenerative receiver..is the simplest and cheapest on the market. **1975** R. L. Shrader *Electronic Communication* (ed. 3) xviii. 434/2 A demodulator used in the past in the VHF range is the superregenerative detector.

supersaturation. Add: Also, the state of being supersaturated.

1876 *Phil. Mag.* II. 216 This is a consequence..of the condition of supersaturation being maintained even in solutions from which crystals of sugar are being deposited. **1941** [see *kern *sb.*² 3]. **1983** *Sci. Amer.* June 108/3 The concentration of dissolved nitrogen in the dolphin's muscle tissue was indicative of a degree of supersaturation that in a human diver would have been dangerous.

superscript, *sb.* Add: **2.** A superscript character.

1901 [see Subscript *sb.* 2]. **1927** [see *Kronecker delta]. **1945** F. A. Ficken in F. A. Berry et al. *Handbk. Meteorol.* ii. 144 In work with tensors, indices occur as superscripts as well as subscripts. **1970** G. K. Woodgate *Elem. Atomic Struct.* iv. 67 The notation for a level specifies the value of j as a subscript to the letter code for l. The superscript gives the..multiplicity of the term.

supersensible, *a.* (*sb.*) **a.** (Earlier example.)
1798 A. F. M. WILLICH *Elem. Crit. Philos.* 180 The *supersensible substratum* of nature is that object, of which we can determine nothing in an affirmative sense.

supersensitive, *a.* Add: (Further examples in *Physiol.* Cf. *SUPERSENSITIVITY 2.)
1949 CANNON & ROSENBLUETH *Supersensitivity of Denervated Structures* ii. 11 They are often quite easily rendered supersensitive to some agent, e.g., adrenaline, by preliminary treatment with one or another chemical substance, e.g., cocaine or thyroxine. **1962** *Nature* 3 Feb. 487/1 The increased secretory activity seen in the supersensitive submaxillary glands. **1978** *Life Sciences* XXIII. 1283 Rats were supersensitive to norepinephrine as well as to dopamine.

su:persensiti·vity. [SUPER- 10.] **1.** Great or excessive sensitivity.
1934 [see *FRAYED *ppl.a.*²]
2. *Physiol.* The state or fact of a tissue or organ having an increased sensitivity to stimuli, as manifested by a longer or increased response, a reduced threshold, or increased susceptibility.
1949 CANNON & ROSENBLUETH *Supersentivity of Denervated Structures* ii. 11 The term supersensitivity covers several possibly different phenomena. **1959** *Jrnl. Physiol.* CXXXXVII. 178 Organs chronically deprived of their motor nerves develop an increased sensitivity to the neurohumoral transmitter and to other chemical agents. This phenomenon is observed in several types of tissue, e.g. striated muscle, smooth muscle, ganglia and glands, and is known as denervation supersensitivity. **1963** *Pharmacol. Rev.* XV. 226 The changes and modifications of dose-response curves of sympathomimetic amines by various drugs or procedures known to cause super- and subsensitivity to this group of substances. **1974** *Sci. Amer.* Jan. 48/3 This partial denervation could conceivably lead to chemical supersensitivity, accessory sprouting of collateral nerve fibers or the formation of new synaptic contacts.

superse·xual, *a.* **1.** [SUPER- 4 a.] Beyond or outside the sphere of sexuality.
1895 *World* 20 Mar. 15/2 She had resolved from the very outset to maintain her companionship with Lucas on a supersexual basis. **1976** *Encounter* June 51 A pop-star pseudo-Christ has to be at once sexy, bisexual and supersexual, so as to cater simultaneously for all possible needs.
2. [SUPER- 9 a.] Having strong sexual appetites, highly sexed.
1970 R. D. ABRAHAMS *Positively Black* v. 112 This is done commonly by picturing men as supersexual animals who cannot control themselves when they see another woman.

su·persign. **1.** [SUPER- 3 a.] A diacritical mark written or printed above a letter.
1947 H. JACOB *Planned Auxiliary Lang.* 40 Supersigns were introduced to make Esperanto fully phonetic. **1958** J. BERRY in J. A. Fishman *Readings Sociol. of Lang.* (1968) 745 The supersigns interfere with spacing and involve 'kerning'.
2. [SUPER- 6 b] A combination of letters, figures, etc., forming a unit.
1976 J. J. WHITE in *Visible Lang.* X. 81 It is possible to view them as iconic 'supersigns'; i.e., as *collections* or *configurations* of symbolic signs (viz. words). *Ibid.*, Whether iconicity occurs at the sign or supersign level would be something which semiotic analyses would have to consider.

superso·nic, *a.* (and *sb.*) [f. SUPER- 4 a + L. *son-us* sound + -IC, as tr. F. *ultra-sonore.*] **1.** Of, pertaining to, or designating sound waves or vibrations with frequencies greater than those audible to the human ear or greater than 20,000 Hz.
This use of *supersonic* is now deprecated in scientific contexts, *ultrasonic* being the preferred term.
1919 *Electrician* 25 Apr. 494/2 The French have experimented with a system in which a continuous wave signal in heterodyned to a supersonic frequency. **1930** *Daily Express* 22 May 6/5 The wireless enthusiast, whether.. crystal-set owner or disciple of the supersonic heterodyne, will still have his moments of doubt. **1957** I. MURDOCH *Sandcastle* xiv. 224 The next act was to blow a long blast upon the supersonic whistle. **1975** *Gramophone* Jan. 1412/3 CD-4 employs a carrier tone at supersonic frequency (30,000 Hz). **1980** *Daily Tel.* 5 Mar. 17/4 The Fisheries Agency team is using supersonic waves of 24 kilohertz which..have proved effective in repelling the dolphins without affecting ordinary fish.
2. a. Involving, pertaining to, capable of, or designating speeds greater than (*spec.* up to five times) the speed of sound. Cf. *HYPERSONIC *a.*, *SONIC *a.*
1934 *Jrnl. R. Aeronaut. Soc.* XXXVIII. 866 (*heading*) Supersonic wind channel for model tests. **1936** *Aircraft Engineering* Sept. 260/2 The wing shows what the Germans call a 'supersonic profile', because the aeroplane is supposed to fly the greater part of its route at supersonic speeds. **1948** 'N. SHUTE' *No Highway* xii. 313 It [*sc.* an aircraft] was at the speed of sound... He said he'd been through to the supersonic zone several times. **1953** *Hansard Commons* 11 May 881 As for the problem of the supersonic bang, I must tell the hon. Gentleman that there is absolutely no solution in sight. In fact, we are probably in for some rather noisy times. **1972** *Nature* 18 Aug. 379/2 A low density tunnel for simulating supersonic and hypersonic flight at altitudes of 20 to 70 miles. **1978** *Jrnl. R. Soc. Arts* Dec. 37/1 The Concorde is to-day the precursor of much larger supersonic transport aircraft in years to come.
b. *ellipt.* as *sb.* An aeroplane capable of flying at speeds greater than the speed of sound.
1947 *Times* 1 Jan. 3/3 It is generally assumed here that cooperation in research will cover tests now being carried out by both countries in the field of supersonics, guided missiles, and the development of jet aircraft engines. **1962** *Listener* 5 July 36/2 The demand for supersonics came from the aircraft manufacturers. **1968** *Economist* 11 May 71/1 With jumbo jets and the supersonics on the horizon, aviation insurers had enough to worry about already. **1973** *Times* 24 May (Aviation Suppl.) p. vi/5 When supersonics have, by public demand, taken over all long-haul air services..we may well wonder what all the argument was about.
3. *colloq.* **a.** Very fast. **b.** Excellent, wonderful, exciting, etc. Also as *int.*
1947 *Argus Week-End Mag.* 25 Oct., Isn't he simply supersonic! **1954** C. DAVIES *Let.* 24 Dec. in B. Russell *Autobiogr.* (1969) III. ii. 96 My thoughts were speeding along with yours at a super-sonic rate. **1955** G. DORMAN *Swooping Vengeance* iv. 31 Ginge's eyes gleamed and he said eagerly,..'Gee, Wing! This *is* supersonic! Can I be in it too?' *Ibid.* v. 44 'Absolutely supersonic!' was Ginge's enthusiastic comment. **1963** *Listener* 17 Jan. 109/2 The unique problems with which the continent [*sc.* Africa] is struggling in an age of supersonic speed of change. **1972** R. GODDEN *Diddakoi* iv. 83 Miss Brooke made girdle scones..'Supersonic!' said Clem. **1980** *Daily Mail* 23 July 33 (Advt.), Young men required for supersonic battle of wits.
Hence **superso·nically** *adv.*
1952 *Chambers's Jrnl.* June 363/2 They [*sc.* rats] are being lured forth by their mating-note, produced supersonically, and trapped as they emerge. **1970** *Daily Tel.* 2 Sept. 26/6 The St David's Civic Society..has launched a national campaign to stop the Concorde flying supersonically over land.

superso·nics, *sb. pl.* (const. as *sing.*). [f. prec.: see -IC 2.] The science of sound waves or vibrations with frequencies greater than those audible to the human ear or greater than 20,000 Hz.
1925 *Nature* 9 May 690/1 The method adopted to measure the vibrational energy in the water at the high frequencies used in supersonics is interesting. **1952** *Chambers's Jrnl.* June 363/1 The urge to explore supersonics afresh arose from the infestation of reservoirs by seagulls... Scientists have been..studying the artificial application of supersonics, and..have evolved a method of producing a high-intensity beam of sound of any desired frequency. **1977** *Jrnl. R. Soc. Arts* CXXV. 361/1 Supersonics has a place by the end of the century.

supersound: see *SUPER- 6 c.

su·perspace. *Physics.* [SUPER- 5 d.] A concept of space-time arising out of the attempt to quantize the gravitational field, in which points are defined by more than the usual four co-ordinates; also, a space of infinitely many dimensions postulated to contain actual space-time and all possible spaces.
1971 *Daily Tel.* (Colour Suppl.) 7 May 35 Inside superspace there is neither space nor time. **1972** *Nature* 15 Dec. 382/2 This point of view, which leads to the notions of 'superspace' and quantum fluctuation of three geometries, was described by Professors K. Kuchař and J. A. Wheeler. **1974** A. BERRY *Next 10,000 Yrs.* 111 All the stars and galaxies that we can see are on the curved, solid part of the doughnut, while the hole in the middle represents the mysterious region of Superspace. **1975** *Physics Lett.* B. LVI. 178/2 The usual supersymmetry transformation is then a linear transformation in the 8 dimensional 'superspace' of z^A. **1976** B. ZUMINO in Arnowitt & Nath *Gauge Theories & Mod. Field Theory* 262 We call superspace a space whose points are labeled by four commuting coordinates x^α and by a number of additional totally anticommuting coordinates θ^a, $\theta^a\theta^b + \theta^b\theta^a = 0$, which also commute with the x^α. **1978** *Sci. Amer.* Feb. 138/3 The superspace theories are elegant but technically complicated. **1980** P. DAVIES *Other Worlds* v. 104 We may construct a different world for each shape of space. Stitching them altogether [*sic*] gives us an infinite-dimensional superspace. Contained in superspace are all the possible spaces... Each space of superspace will contain its own superworld of all possible particle arrangements.

su·perstar. [SUPER- 6 c.]
1. An outstanding performer in the theatre, music, sport, etc.; something exceptionally successful, advanced, etc. Freq *attrib.*
1925 W. DEEPING *Sorrell & Son* 130 You wouldn't expect a couple of cinema super-stars to be running away from publicity. **1936** 'RIFF' & 'RAFF' *They're Off!* v. 40 A..relation of my own was running a horse with no less a person than our super-star jockey in the saddle. **1969** N. COHN *AWopBopaLooBop* (1970) xx. 188 He became a superstar but he wasn't happy. **1972** *Guardian* 24 Feb. 14/4 [David] Frost's importance is not the super-star status. **1976** *Nature* 8 Apr. 471/1 Superstar technology is the name given by a working party of the Council for Science and Society to highly innovatory, large scale technical projects. **1978** *Detroit Free Press* 5 Mar. C 14 (Advt.), Hertz, the superstar in the Rent-A-Car industry has an immediate vacancy. **1980** M. FONTEYN *Magic of Dance* 32 From the Charleston it was an easy step to the emergence of a male superstar dancer. **1982** *London Rev. Bks.* IV. XXIV. 20/2 Star quality, however, was not at all what was looked for in those who played opposite a superstar like Kean.
2. *Astron.* A very important or powerful heavenly body. *rare.*
1929 S. LESLIE *Anglo-Catholic* iv. 58 He..meditated.. upon sun and moon, whose counter-changes and performances in the sky he followed with deep amaze. These super-stars of heaven never ceased to vary in effects. **1964** [see QSO s.v. *Q II. 2 b].
Hence **su·perstardom.**
1973 *Harper's Mag.* Oct. 111 Apparently, in the eyes of one dazzled by his own celebrity,..superstardom puts a man above the law. **1977** *Times Lit. Suppl.* 22 Apr. 479/2 Hollywood exacts its price for superstardom.

super-state, -store: see *SUPER- 6 c.

superstratum. Add: **2. a.** *Linguistics.* A language responsible for linguistic change (esp. in vocabulary) in another upon which it is imposed and over which it is temporarily dominant. Cf. *SUBSTRATUM 5 a.
[**1932** E. TAPPOLET in *Archiv für das Studium der neueren Sprachen* CXI. 234 Von ähnlichen Erwägungen geleitet, sprach von Wartburg (Leipzig) über die Wirkung des *Superstratums*.] **1953** J. B. TREND *Lang. & Hist. Spain* xii. 167 Spanish-speaking America offers an exceptionally favourable field for examining the linguistic concepts of substratum and superstratum. **1976** W. F. H. NICOLAISEN *Scottish Place-Names* vi. 84 The place-names created by a certain language form an adstratum to English names in one place, a superstratum in another, and a substratum in most places.
b. *attrib.* and *Comb.*, as *superstratum influence, language.*
1957 *Publ. Amer. Dial. Soc. 1956* XXVI. 100 A substratum influence is one derived from a dominated language, a superstratum from a dominant language. **1960** *Amer. Speech* XXXV. 234 Substratum languages can affect all features of grammar, whereas superstratum languages tend to affect vocabulary only. **1978** *Canad. Jrnl. Ling. 1977* XXII. 206 After surveying the distribution, function, and status of each Romance language..it discusses the thorny problem of the influence exerted by the so-called substratum and superstratum languages.

superstructure. Add: **1. c.** *Geol.* [tr. G. *oberbau* (C. E. Wegmann 1935, in *Geol. Rundschau* XXVI. 332).] A relatively shallow overlying layer of an orogenic belt that is unaffected by plutonic activity or metamorphism.
1944 *Proc. Geologists' Assoc.* LV. 69 A distinction must be drawn, he [*sc.* Wegmann] maintains, between happenings in the non-migmatitic superstructure (Oberbau) and the migmatitic infrastructure (Unterbau) lying below. **1972** J. G. DENNIS *Structural Geol.* xvii. 394 In many orogenic belts, the superstructure has not been preserved in place: most of it has been eroded or transported to the external zone as allochthons.
d. *Biochem.* The higher-order structure of a protein or enzyme molecule which is superimposed upon the sequence of amino-acids or nucleotide bases.
1962 A. SPECTOR in A. Pirie *Lens Metabolism Rel. Cataract* 334 The *N*-terminal residues of native proteins are probably not readily accessible to the enzyme since such groups are masked or buried in the superstructure of the molecule. **1973** *Nature* 7 Sept. 23/1 The term superstructure will be used to include the secondary and higher order structures that might be super imposed upon the primary base sequence of a nucleic acid. **1981** *Sci. Amer.* Feb. 60/2 (*caption*) Helical superstructures might be formed with increasing salt concentration.
2. b. *Pol.* and *Econ.* In Marxist theory, the institutions and culture which are considered to result from or reflect the economic system on which a society is based.
[**1903** *Social Democrat* VII. 274 The Greeks attained to a high pitch of civilization, with a slave class as the basis of its economic superstructure.] **1904** N. I. STONE tr. *Marx's Contributions Critique Pol. Econ.* 11 The sum total of these relations..constitutes the economic structure of society—the real foundation, on which rise legal and political superstructures. **1926** M. EASTMAN *Marx, Lenin & Sci. of Revolution* iv. 50 It is obvious that if the material basis positively *determined* the superstructure, we should not have to *disregard* the superstructure and examine the basis, for the one could be directly inferred from the other. **1943** J. A. SCHUMPETER *Capitalism, Socialism, & Democracy* xi. 121 We now turn to the cultural complement of the capitalist economy—to its socio-psychological superstructure, if we wish to speak the Marxian language—and to the mentality that is characteristic of capitalist society. **1960** E. R. GOODMAN in J. A. Fishman *Readings Sociol. of Lang.* (1968) 729 Man considered language as an element in the Marxist superstructure dependent upon the economic base of society... Just as this base might be changed by force, so Man thought, the linguistic superstructure should be impelled to develop toward its ultimate goal. **1975** *Chinese Econ. Stud.* VIII. IV. 10 The superstructure refers to the national government, army, law, and other political systems and their corresponding ideological forms, such as philosophy, literature, and fine arts. **1977** R. WILLIAMS *Marxism & Lit.* II. vi. 111 Cultural work and activity are not now, in any ordinary sense, a superstructure.
3. *Metallurgy.* = *SUPERLATTICE 1.
1932 *Proc. R. Soc.* A. CXXXVI. 216 The type of superstructure represented by Fe_3Al gives other lines [in an X-ray diffraction photograph]. **1979** *Nature* 11 Oct. 469/2 Ordered solid solutions (superstructures or superlattices), in which atoms of one kind segregate into a particular set of lattice positions, are usually obtained by slow cooling at the critical ordering temperature.

super-super-: see *SUPER- 17, 18. **supersymmetric, -symmetry:** see *SUPER- 6 b.

su:pertechnolo·gical, *a.* **1.** [SUPER- 9 a.] Involving or employing highly advanced technology.

1968 *Economist* 14 Dec. p. xxv/3 Some sort of middle course will be found, between the super-technological and the purely sociological. **1977** P. JOHNSON *Enemies of Society* xii. 164 The galaxy of star universities which formed the vertebrae of the super-technological East Coast.

2. [SUPER- 4 a.] Beyond or superseding the technological.

1973 *Nature* 6 Apr. 382/1 A branch of this water-drawing and wood-hewing supertechnological fraternity would be preserving health.

supervision. Add: **1. b.** Special Comb.: **supervision order,** a court order placing a child or young person under the supervision of a local authority or a probation officer in cases of delinquency, petty crime, etc.

[**1933** *Act* 23 & 24 *Geo. V.* c. 12 § 62 An order placing him..under the supervision of a probation officer, or of some other person appointed for the purpose by the court.] **1938** *Act* 1 & 2 *Geo. VI* c. 40 Supervision order in place of order committing to care of fit person. **1968** J. LOCK *Lady Policeman* xv. 126 The juvenile court placed her under a Supervision Order and she returned home. **1980** *Times Lit. Suppl.* 28 Nov. 1347/3 The usual treatment [in dealing with schoolboy truancy] is to place the child under a supervision order: he is then seen by a social worker or probation officer from time to time.

supervoltage, -weak, -woman: see *SUPER- 10 b, 9 a (*a*), 6 c.

suphrosyne: see *SOPHROSYNE.

supje, var. SOPIE in Dict. and Suppl.

supp (sʌp). Colloq. abbrev. of SUPPLEMENT *sb.*[1] 1 b. Usu. *colour supp.*

1968 *Punch* 6 Nov. 646/2, I don't want to..get myself interviewed in a colour-supp series. **1974** *Listener* 17 Jan. 95/1 To decorate a Mini outrageously for a colour supp. **1975** J. SYMONS *Three Pipe Problem* xv. 136, I read this *Observer* colour supp. piece, you see.

supper, *sb.*[1] Add: **1. c.** (Earlier example.)

1818 H. B. FEARON *Sk. Amer.* 44 A mechanic..has 3 meals a-day, coffee with fish or meat for breakfast; a hot dinner; and tea (called supper) in the evening.

4. *supper-bell* (earlier and later examples), *-board* (example), *-hour* (earlier example), *-table* (earlier example), *-tray* (earlier example); *supper-eater* (earlier example); **supper club,** a restaurant serving suppers and usu. providing entertainment; **supper dance,** (*a*) a dance after which the man escorts his partner into supper; (*b*) a dancing party at which supper is served; **supper house** (earlier example); **supper-party** (earlier example).

1770 P. V. FITHIAN *Let.* 30 Nov. in *Jrnl. & Lett.* (1900) I. 9 About seven the supper Bell rings. **1940** W. FAULKNER *Hamlet* I. iii. 77 Walking on toward the brazen sound of Mrs. Littlejohn's supper-bell. **1918** G. FRANKAU *One of Them* xx. 154 Gay with a thousand supper-boards, whose drink Was poured to rag-time tunes by Herman Finck. **1927** H. CRANE *Let.* 19 Dec. (1965) 313, I don't think I'll dare attend that supper club again. **1977** *New Yorker* 8 Aug. 66/3 Only after a time of heading a hotel and supper-club trio did he turn his hand to composing and arranging. **1885** F. C. BAYLOR *On Both Sides* 64 'A supper-dance, then,' he stupidly insisted. **1928** 'BRENT OF BIN BIN' *Up Country* xvi. 284 Thank heaven, here was the supper dance for which he was committed to good old Mrs Mac. **1948** M. LASKI *Tory Heaven* viii. 110 'May I have the supper-dance?' he had said to Penelope. **1979** S. SMITH *Survivor* xxvii. 253 The Christmas Eve supper dance was one of the biggest nights of the year in [hospital] sp9. **1799** MALTHUS *Diary* 29 May (1966) 37 We told him that we were no supper eaters. **1814** JANE AUSTEN *Mansfield Park* II. x. 227 Previous inquiries.. about the supper-hour. **1855** TROLLOPE *Warden* xvi. 265 It was a London supper-house. **1808** *Monthly Pantheon* I. 684/2 The more gay and fashionable may go to balls or supper parties. **1781** R. F. GREVILLE *Diary* 6 Aug. (1930) 12 At this time the distribution of the Supper Tables was mentioned to Him. **1847** C. BRONTË *Jane Eyre* I. v. 74 Monitors, fetch the supper-trays!

supper, *v.* **1. b.** (Earlier U.S. example.)

1805 R. PARKINSON *Tour Amer.* 68 Going to look at the horses after what is called suppering them up at night.

supperward. Add: Also as *adv.* (*U.S. rare*) = SUPPERWARDS *adv.*

1932 W. FAULKNER *Light in August* xv. 330 The townspeople began to move supperward.

supplantal. (Example.)

1891 *Harper's Mag.* June 69/1 The excitements of the day had..withdrawn his mind from..his fear of supplantal.

supple, *a.* Add: **8.** *supple-faced, -tempered, -thewed.*

1931 V. WOOLF *Waves* 100 The little men at the next table... Supple-faced, with rippling skins. **1865** J. R. LOWELL *Ode Recited at Commemoration* vi. 27 They could not choose but trust In that sure-footed mind's unfaltering skill, And supple-tempered will. **1959** R. GRAVES *Coll. Poems* 317 Free from the cramps of yesterday, Clear-eyed and supple-thewed.

supple-jack. Add: **3.** *U.S.* A toy representing the human figure, the limbs of which are manipulated by a string. Also *fig.* Cf. SUPPLE *a.* 2 c. ?*Disused.*

1776 M. CUTLER *Jrnl.* 17 June in *Life & Correspondence* (1888) I. 55 They made us several presents of the small affairs in the cabins, such as sweetmeats, cayenne-pepper, supple-jacks, cassada or bread..trinkets etc. **1791** W. MACLAY *Jrnl.* 25 Feb. (1927) xiv. 390 Schuyler is the supple-jack of his son-in-law Hamilton. **1835** A. B. LONGSTREET *Georgia Scenes* 13 Bob Simons danced..like a 'Suple-Jack'..when the string is pulled with varied force, at intervals of seconds. **1853** P. KENNEDY *Blackwater Chron.* x. 147 His body spread out as usual in his favorite position of a supple-jack distorted to the utmost. **1871** W. WHITMAN *Democr. Vistas* 30 How the millions of sturdy farmers and mechanics are thus the helpless supple-jacks of comparatively few politicians. **1904** *N.Y. Times* 8 July 5 Those political supplejacks who go about with sanctimonious moan, saying: 'The President is wrong, but we must support the President.'

supplement, *v.* Add: Freq. const. *by* and (more recently) *with.* (Later examples.)

1890 G. GISSING *Emancipated* I. I. v. 151 Then he strolled away and supplemented his meal with a fine bunch of grapes. **1940** H. G. WELLS *Babes in Darkling Wood* III. iii. 270 She realised she had forgotten her lunch, and she supplemented her tea with two boiled eggs. **1946** BIBLE (Rev. Stand. Version) 2 Pet. i. 5 Make every effort to supplement your faith with virtue. **1952** S. KAUFFMANN *Philanderer* (1953) vi. 97 When everyone else was making money, Robert was forced to supplement his insufficient income with his savings. **1977** K. M. E. MURRAY *Caught in Web of Words* vi. 105 He had spare time in which to supplement his income by literary work.

supplemental, *a.* Add: **a.** (Later examples.) Now chiefly *U.S.*

1952 *Sun* (Baltimore) 28 Aug. 1/3 The supplemental defenses of anti-aircraft artillery and infantry posts. **1958** *Yearbk. Agric. 1957* (U.S. Dept. Agric.) 769/1 *Supplemental irrigation*,.. irrigation during dry periods in regions where normal precipitation supplies most of the moisture for crops. **1966** K. AMIS in *New Statesman* 14 Jan. 52/1, I have never before met *supplemental* for *supplementary* except as the term for the second-bite-at-the-cherry examination for pass students at the University College of Swansea. **1969** D. ACHESON *Present at Creation* (1970) xviii. 159 A supplemental budget estimate was prepared. **1976** *Amer. N. & Q.* XV. 2/1 Supplemental to this special number of *AN&Q.* **1980** *Amer. Speech 1976* LI. 202 All of those partial records will be included in the atlas as supplemental evidence.

supplementarity (sʌplĭmentæ·riti). *rare.* [f. SUPPLEMENTARY *a.* + -ITY, after F. *supplémentarité* (J. Derrida).] The condition or quality of being supplementary.

1976 G. C. SPIVAK tr. *Derrida's Of Grammatology* II. iv. 314 In as much as we designate the impossibility of formulating the movement of supplementarity within the classical logos. **1979** C. NORRIS in *PN Rev.* X. 38/1 Writing is the example *par excellence* of a supplementarity which enters into the heart of all intelligible discourse.

supplementary, *a.* Add: **b.** (Further examples.)

Esp. of welfare payments. *Supplementary Benefits* replaced National Assistance in 1966.

1841 *Hansard Commons* 5 Mar. 1361 He had..felt it his duty late in the year, to bring forward a supplementary estimate of 22,000*l*, to carry into effect the recommendation of the naval and military commission, which increased the estimates for the whole year to 6,185,000 *l.* **1920** W. S. CHURCHILL *Let.* 3 Mar. in R. S. Churchill *Winston S. Churchill* (1969) II. Compan. II. xiii. 985 The House is now discussing peacefully the supplementary Estimates of the Navy. **1940** *Economist* 27 Jan. 141/2 The direct cost involved in the change over to a new central organisation for the payment of supplementary pensions is..nil. **1966** *Hansard Commons* 7 Mar. 1730/2 Will the right hon. Lady confirm whether supplementary benefits will now be the subject of Parliamentary Questions to her? **1966** *Whitaker's Almanack 1967* 1109/1 The supplementary pension may be claimed by persons over pension age and the supplementary allowance by persons aged 16 or over but under pension age, who are not in full-time work. **1973** B. MATHER *Snowline* vii. 85 He was getting nothing—unemployment pay, supplementary allowance—not a sausage. **1977** in R. Crossman *Diaries* III. 124 The House of Commons must annually debate and pass three Consolidated Fund Bills, authorizing the issue of the supply of funds to cover the civil and defence estimates and supplementary estimates. **1977** *Proc. R. Soc. Med.* LXX. 602/1 That there are five million people in receipt of supplementary benefit is as much a sign of affluence as poverty for of households receiving benefit 96% have television, 68% washing machines, 62% a refrigerator and 23% a car.

suppletion. Restrict † *Obs. rare* to sense in Dict. and add: **2.** *Linguistics.* The replacement of a form which is missing from a grammatical paradigm by one derived from a different root. Also *attrib.*

1933 L. H. GRAY in *Language* IX. 84 Athematic verbs, as well as their semantic equivalents elsewhere, seem peculiarly liable to suppletion by other verbs to furnish their aorists. **1942** BLOCH & TRAGER *Outl. Linguistic Anal.* iv. 58 Suppletion may be regarded as an extreme kind of internal change, in which the entire base..is replaced by another form. **1951** [see *MORPHOLEXICAL *a.*]. **1959** F. W. HOUSEHOLDER in Saporta & Bastian *Psycholinguistics* (1961) 21/1 It is always possible (with due allowance for irregularity and suppletion) to derive a related expression of structure B. **1978** *Language* LIV. 21 Cases of feminine suppletion like *mon amie* are not included.

suppletive, *a.* Restrict *rare* to sense in Dict. and add: **2.** *Linguistics.* Displaying suppletion. Also as *sb.*, a suppletive form.

1926 L. BLOOMFIELD in *Language* II. 161 If in a construction all the component forms are irregular, the whole form is *suppletive.* If *go* be taken as the stem of the verb, then the past *went* is suppletive. **1933** *Language* IX. 83 'Buy'..appears only in the aorist, serving as suppletive to the present and imperfect of ὠνέομαι. **1934** PRIEBSCH & COLLINSON *German Language* II. ii. 140 For the suppletive comparatives and superlatives cf. the Germanic section. **1957** S. POTTER *Modern Linguistics* iv. 101 *Aller* is suppletive (*aller, vais, irai*). **1964** R. H. ROBINS *Gen. Linguistics* v. 207 Such roots involving total variation among their allomorphs are sometimes called suppletive. **1976** J. S. GRUBER *Lexical Structures in Syntax & Semantics* II. ii. 303 The past tense is not used in those cases in which we have a suppletive form.

supply, *sb.* Add: **I. 4. b.** *in short supply*: see *SHORT *a.* 15 a.

II. 6. b. Also, a supply teacher.

1957 A. WILSON *Bit off Map & Other Stories* 152 'Why can't they get a Supply in?' 'Supply teachers need notification.' **1974** M. HIGGINS *Changeling* i. 7 Your replacement is only a supply, and..the Head'd be only too happy to have you back.

11. (Earlier and later examples of phr. *supply and demand.*)

1843 CARLYLE *Past & Present* IV. v. 368 The sixpence a day and supply-and-demand principle. **1919** M. BEER *Hist. Brit. Socialism* I. II. iv. 152 We have been dealing with pure theory, leaving out of account such factors as supply and demand. **1936** J. M. KEYNES *Gen. Theory Employment, Interest & Money* v. xxi. 292 Prices are governed by the conditions of supply and demand. **1976** J. SNOW *Cricket Rebel* 19 Most boys wanted to bat and because I could do both I usually found myself caught up with a ball in my hand due to the law of supply and demand.

III. 12. a. *supply train* (earlier example), *wagon* (earlier example); *supply-boat* (earlier example); also (partly with ref. to the supplies of an army and partly *gen.*) *supply base, depot, line, ship, station, store*; **supply day,** a day on which the House of Commons debates an Opposition motion criticizing the Government's proposed expenditure (cf. sense 10 a in Dict.); **supply drop,** the dropping of supplies by parachute; **supply house,** (*a*) *U.S.*, a commercial establishment selling supplies; (*b*) *Canad.*, a hut, tent, lean-to, or other structure, used as a storehouse; **supply-side** *a. Econ.* (orig. *U.S.*), pertaining to the supply side of the economy; hence, designating a policy designed to increase the incentives to produce and invest, by means of tax cuts; hence **supply-sider,** an advocate of this policy; **supply teacher,** a teacher supplied by the education authority to fill a (temporary) vacancy; hence, one who is regularly employed to do this; hence (as a back-formation) **supply-teach** *v. intr.*, to work as a supply teacher; **supply teaching** *vbl. sb.*

1958 L. URIS *Exodus* I. xviii. 101 It was a fenced-in area containing several acres of trucks and other rolling stock and a dozen enormous warehouses. During the war the depot had been a major supply base for the Allies in the Middle East. **1840** J. F. COOPER *Pathfinder* II. ix. 73 We shall lie in wait..to intercept their supply-boats. **1946** *May's Treat. Parliament* (ed. 14) xxv. 686 The House had attempted to counter this tendency [*sc.* the government's postponement of the discussion of estimates] by making one day each week a compulsory supply day. **1959** *Listener* 12 Mar. 441/1 The time allotted to the opposition for the criticism of policy and administration in supply days and so forth would not need to be curtailed. **1976** H. WILSON *Governance of Britain* i. 19 Defeated on a snap vote on a Supply Day debate on the stocks of cordite in government depots, he threw in his hand. **1918** E. S. FARROW *Dict. Military Terms* 596 Main supply depots are established at advanced bases or at convenient positions on the railway. **1921** *Daily Colonist* (Victoria) 18 Mar. 3/2 Two all-metal monoplanes have made an initial flight..carrying 1,000 pounds of gasoline each for the supply depot at Hay River. **1947** 'N. SHUTE' *Chequer Board* iv. 86 Last job was a Dakota squadron in South-East Asia Command. Supply drops, I suppose. **1978** T. ALLBEURY *Lantern Network* iii. 33 You have been given details of..suitable areas for supply drops. **1897** *Sears, Roebuck Catal.* 1 Sears, Roebuck & Co., (Incorporated), Cheapest Supply House on Earth, Chicago. **1905** L. MOTT *Jules of Great Heart* 161 A voyageur showed him to the supply-house, and he got some pemmican, tea and bread, and a blanket. **1957** V. J. KEHOE *Technique Film & Television Make-Up* xiii. 194 Get a small sized balsa wood head form from a hat supply house. **1975** *New Yorker* 7 July 73/1 While discarded manufactured objects found in the street or in junk shops may be richly charged with poetic and psychological associations..this is not the case with new supply-house items. **1942** *R.A.F. Jrnl.* 3 Oct. 11 We were detailed to attack Jerry's supply lines. **1956** D. L. LINTON *Sheffield* p. xxiii, It can serve the other towns of the region with wholesale and retail goods, professional and social services only over 'supply lines' that are relatively costly in maintenance, operation, or time.

1915 J. M. de Robeck in M. Gilbert *Winston S. Churchill* (1972) III. Compan. I. 753 The passage of supply ships for the Fleet through the Dardanelles with the forts still intact is a problem to which I can see no practical solution. **1975** *BP Shield Internat.* May 6 To enable it to continue operations for several days when supply ships cannot come alongside. **1976** *Wall St. Jrnl.* 9 Apr. 8/1 (*heading*) Supply-side fiscalism. *Ibid.* 15 Nov. 26/4 Supply-side fiscalists..agree that tax changes do not affect total demand, but they emphasize the effects on supply. **1980** *N.Y. Times* 22 June IV. 20 They recommend capital formation and other supply-side policies that have recently become fashionable. **1980** *Wall St. Jrnl.* 28 Feb. 24/3 Reception to 'supply-siders' was still hostile..when they criticized the economic models being used by the congressional budget committees for assuming that higher government spending was better for the economy than lower tax rates. **1981** *Christian Sci. Monitor* (Weekly Internat. ed.) 7 Sept. 20/3 The supply-siders who persuaded President Reagan to seek a balanced budget by cutting taxes. **1909** F. Ash *Trip to Mars* xxxiv. 262 Airships are of no use without a supply-station. **1885** *List of Subscribers, Classified* (United Telephone Co.) (ed. 6) 204 Supply Stores... Army & Navy Auxiliary Co-operative Supply, Limited... Civil Service Supply Associations, Limited. **1946** W. Faulkner *Portable Faulkner* 752 A pair of offices up a flight of stairs above the supplystore. **1968** *New Statesman* 22 Mar. 376/1, I am now supply teaching in London. **1980** J. Barnes *Metroland* III. i. 138, I was supply teaching in Wandsworth at the time: twenty-five quid a week for the privilege of having your bicycle tyres let down each week by different kids at different schools. **1902** Supply teacher [in Dict.]. **1963** S. Marshall *Experiment in Education* iii. 115, I happened to be ill..and the only supply teacher the L.E.A. could find at short notice was an Indian teacher. **1969** R. Godden *In this House of Brede* xv. 341 Father Gervase has gone as supply teacher for a fortnight to Bishop Palin's Grammar School for Boys. **1976** *Rhyl Jrnl. & Advertiser* 9 Dec. 20/5 (Advt.), Applications are invited from Qualified Teachers..who wish to be included on the Authority's list of Supply Teachers for Primary and/or Secondary Schools. **1957** *Kingston* (Ontario) *Whig-Standard* 24 Jan. 17/6 She told the students something of the practice and supply teaching possible while at college. **1976** *Times Lit. Suppl.* 13 Aug. 1006/5 He was a student at the London School of Economics, wanted to be a writer and did supply teaching for a living. **1860** H. Greeley *Overland Journey* 55 Our route..was no longer encumbered with great army supply-trains. **1866** A. D. Richardson *Secret Service* xix. 241 Their retreat was a stampede, leaving behind great quantities of ammunition..supply-wagons and ambulances.

support, *sb.* Add: **II. 7. d.** The solid substance or material on which a painting is executed.

1892 J. G. Vibert *Sci. of Painting* viii. 96 A picture is composed of three altogether distinct elements:— 1. The support, or the material substance painted on, as wood, canvas, stone, paper, etc. **1926** A. P. Laurie *Painter's Methods & Materials* iv. 53 Well-seasoned panels of wood form an excellent support for pictures. **1958** M. L. Wolf *Dict. Painting* 286 The *support* is covered with the *ground*..for evenness, and is then ready to receive the actual painting.

8. *Math.* The smallest closed set of elements outside which a given function or mapping is zero.

1964 A. P. & W. Robertson *Topological Vector Spaces* i. 18 Let $K(S)$ be the set of real (or complex) valued functions continuous and of compact support on the separated locally compact space S. **1967** MacLane & Birkhoff *Algebra* iv. 143 Show that the set of all functions f with finite support constitute a ring..under pointwise sum and convolution product. **1980** D. L. Cohn *Measure Theory* vii. 200 Define functions g_1 and g_2 by $g_1 = h_1$ and $g_2 = h_2 - (h_1 \wedge h_2)$. Then g_1 and g_2 are nonnegative, their supports are included in U_1 and U_2 respectively.

III. 9. *attrib.* **a.** That provides support or acts as a support.

1953 F. P. Magoun in *Speculum* XXVIII. 460 At least some of the *Riddles* is traditional, since verses from these appear in the support-evidence. **1962** *Listener* 29 Mar. 549/1 The British..could be fairly allowed to bring back a division [from Germany] to this country and let that division act in a support role. **1964** *Language* XL. 26 Old French developed a 'support vowel'..only where there would have been an unwieldy cluster otherwise. **1967** *Times Rev. Industry* June 20/2 The ratio of 'support staff' to salesmen. **1972** *Guardian* 2 Feb. 1 The dollar sank close to its new 'support floor'. **1975** *Offshore* Sept. 9/1 Now converted into a support ship for the North Sea. **1976** M. Machlin *Pipeline* liii. 526 By one p.m. Simon Orloff had climbed the twelve foot support member. **1976** *Spare Rib* Dec. 8/2 Up till now I've always done support gigs. **1977** C. McFadden *Serial* (1978) ix. 24/1 He was uptight about the support money he gave her. **1980** *New Age* (U.S.) Oct. 21/1 How important it is to use your personal support network, and your head, when dealing with illness.

b. *spec.* Designating stockings or tights reinforced with elastic yarn to support the muscles and veins of the legs.

1970 *Vogue* May 64/2 Ours is the *original* support stocking. **1971** *Ibid.* Nov. 26/1 Support tights don't have to be thick and ugly. *a* **1975** R. Crossman *Diaries* (1977) III. 640 These surgeons come and go but they know nothing about support stockings. **1975** *Guardian* 25 Mar. 13/5 Support hose or support tights are supplied through the Hospital Supply Service. **1976** *Times* 26 Mar. 10/3 The support tights market in America has been booming.

10. Special Combs., as **support barge,** a barge providing assistance for offshore oil-drilling; **support buying,** the purchase of a commodity, a currency, or stocks and shares, in order to encourage a price rise; **support cost,** the cost of supporting something; *spec.* the cost of supporting the armed services; **support group,** (*a*) a group of musicians taking a subordinate part in a concert; (*b*) a group of people giving support to a charitable or political organization; **support line** *Mil.*, the second line of troops in a battle; a trench occupied by such troops; **support price,** a minimum price for agricultural produce, maintained by support buying or deficiency payments; **support trench** *Mil.*, a trench forming part of a line of strong points in the rear of the strong points of the firing line.

1976 *Offshore Engineer* Apr. 5/1 Field operator Occidental has given a letter of intent for a long-term charter of the *Bredford*, the first purpose-built semi-submersible support barge. **1932** *Economist* 9 Jan. 69/2 The time to support prices was opportune. Support buying of high-grade bonds, particularly in the railroad list, has resulted in improvement of prices and a stronger tone in all security markets. **1969** *Times* 13 Jan. 11/1 There will..be support buying to support the levies in some cases. **1958** *Spectator* 14 Feb. 192/2 To talk about the foreign policy of a small Power would be a little ridiculous if international affairs consisted purely of rocket sites and support costs. *a* **1974** R. Crossman *Diaries* (1976) II. 208, I went across to the Party meeting on German support costs. **1969** *Listener* 10 July 59/1 After all this and the excellent support groups, the Rolling Stones were a musical disappointment. **1976** *Spare Rib* Dec. 13/1 Our support group is small so we have very few problems with disagreements on tactics, etc., but have to work harder. **1977** *Lancashire Life* Dec. 75/1 CARE's Wigan support group invited the organisation to inspect the building. **1917** W. Owen *Let.* 4 Feb. (1967) 430 We worked back through the reserve, & support lines to the crazy village where the Battalion takes breath. **1918** *Aussie* Aug. 10/1 In that sector of the front..there was a small town... Subsequently, as our Support Line settled down in front of it, it became the object of minute attention on the part of Fritz. **1971** S. Hill *Strange Meeting* ii. 110 Garrett had asked Hilliard to write to the men's relatives, as soon as they got into the support line the following day. **1943** *Sun* (Baltimore) 30 Jan. 18/4 So-called support prices, the minimum which canners may pay this year to growers who participate in the subsidy program,..are as follows. *Ibid.* 2 Oct. 6/2 The food planners tell us solemnly that this is not a subsidy program; it is a support-price program. **1949** A. McLintock *Descr. Atlas N.Z.* 44 Since the war 'support schemes' have also been established for wool and export meat, based on the reserve funds built up during the war and post-war periods of stabilisation..[but] in the long run 'support prices' cannot diverge very far from market realisations. **1974** *Times* 15 Jan. 1/7 The Council..had rejected..an immediate 10 per cent rise in the support price for beef paid to farmers. **1915** Support trench [in Dict., sense 1 e]. **1923** Kipling *Irish Guards in Great War* I. 40 The line of support-trenches was held.

support, *v.* Add: **12. c.** *Sport.* To be a supporter or follower of (a team, etc.). Cf. *supporter 5 b.

1952 J. Arlott *Concerning Soccer* viii. 122 The spectator has the loudest word; for the good of football he should support good football. **1962** K. Wolstenholme *Book of World Soccer* 55/2 When you think of all that, what other football club is there worth supporting? **1979** E. John in K. Keegan *Against the World* x. 071 I've always supported England, I've stood on the terraces at Wembley, so what I relish now is the sheer luck of having the privilege to travel with the team.

supportative (sǒpōᵊ·ɹtǎtiv), *a. rare.* [f. support *v.* + -ative.] = Supportive *a.*

An unnecessary formation, since the shorter *supportive* is completely established.—Ed.

1972 *Nature* 24 Mar. 154/2 These two basically different types of control are complementary and supportative. **1976** *Times* 22 July 14/2 (Advt.), A perceptive, sensitive and intelligent individual capable of organising our president in a supportative manner. **1981** *Spectator* 7 Feb. 19/2 Then follow the supportative words, the substructuration of Belonging.

supporter. Add: **3. g.** A jock-strap.

1895 *Montgomery Ward Catal.* Spring & Summer 488/3 The best fitting, most comfortable and effective supporter yet devised. Used by ball players, athletes and the theatrical profession generally. **1978** R. Doliner *On the Edge* (1979) iv. 66 The Senator pulled on his supporter, made a cup of his hand and laid himself gently to rest in the elastic sling.

5. b. One who supports a particular form of sport or who makes a practice of following the fortunes of a particular team, by attending matches, etc.

1922 *Glasgow Herald* 30 June 8 An enthusiastic supporter of baseball. **1928** *Daily Mail Year-bk.* 84/2 The supporters of the Chelsea F.C. **1972** T. Stoppard *Jumpers* I. 40 That he [*sc.* God] should have been taken up by a glorified supporters' club is only a matter of psychological interest. **1973** *Times* 24 Apr. 8/4 You have been wonderful supporters. I think I am very fortunate to play my last match in front of such wonderful people. **1976** *Milton Keynes Express* 2 July 42/6 There was a unanimous vote that a supporters' club be formed to further promote the need for a track in the area as soon as possible. **1980** *Daily Tel.* 19 Sept. 3/3 More than 30 supporters were ejected during the match, eight were still in police custody.

supporting, *ppl. a.* Add: **5.** Of actors or their roles, or of items in a programme of entertainment, usu. at a cinema: subordinate, less important.

1933 P. Godfrey *Back-Stage* v. 62 The fake star can be made to twinkle brightly by absorbing the surrounding light of the 'supporting cast'. **1939** *Chatelaine* Nov. 24/4 Some will continue for a while in minor productions and supporting roles. **1947** M. Gilbert *Close Quarters* vii. 108, I reached the cinema in time for the beginning of the supporting picture. **1953** [see *big stuff* s.v. *big *a.* B 2]. **1966** *Listener* 23 June 918/1 The supporting performances..are enthusiastically full-blooded. **1977** *Rolling Stone* 21 Apr. 31/3 Blondie begins to seek out that untapped audience with a supporting slot on Iggy Pop's American tour.

supportive, *a.* Delete *rare* and add later examples.

1954 H. C. Shands in *Amer. Jrnl. Orthopsychiatry* XXIV. 84 It is necessary that the anxious individual have available a supportive pattern of relationship to depend upon through the learning period. **1962** Henderson & Gillespie *Text-bk. Psychiatry* xi. 286 This sort of supportive psychotherapy is relevant in every case. **1965** *Listener* 30 Sept. 501/3 Supportive material, notes by the editor, and letters by other hands are made to fill in the picture. **1972** *Science* 20 Oct. 229/3 She appears to interpret her findings as supportive of a smaller proportion of genetic variance among blacks than among whites. **1973** *Black Panther* 23 June 6/2 She has vein trouble in her legs for which she wears supportive stockings. **1978** G. Vidal *Kalki* vi. 149 'Senator White says that..he's going to call Mr. Kalki, as a witness... Will Mr. Kalki be supportive?' 'Hopefully, Kalki is supportive of all of us all of the time and for all time.' **1980** *Daily Tel.* 6 Dec. 12/4 Most American psychotherapists now advertise themselves as 'supportive'.

Hence **suppo·rtiveness.**

1968 A. J. Tannenbaum in H. L. Foster *Ribbin'* (1974) i. 4 They have worked with the children..in order to win their confidence and provide supportiveness. **1978** *Nature* 17 Aug. 698/1 We have also tried to determine whether there was a dorso-ventral pattern of host supportiveness of tumour growth.

supposably, *adv.* (Earlier example.)

a **1866** J. Grote *Exam. Util. Philos.* (1870) vi. 107 The happiness of any supposably actual being.

suppose, *v.* Add: **8. b.** Also *I suppose*, ellipt. for *I suppose so*, as a hesitant or reluctant affirmative.

1959 'E. McBain' *'Til Death* (1961) v. 67 'I think that's wise, don't you?' 'I suppose.' **1973** S. Cohen *Diane Game* (1974) xii. 103 'Look how much good information is published by..guys at universities.' 'Yes, I suppose.' **1976** 'Trevanian' *Main* (1977) x. 206 'Is she a viable?'..'I suppose. She had reason and opportunity.'

d. *pass.* Now esp., to be expected, intended, or meant; to have as a duty, to be obliged.

The pronunc. of the pa. t. is often colloquially modified from (sǒpōu·zd) to (sǒpōu·st). The negative is, idiomatically, freq. used to mean 'to have a duty or obligation not (to do something)'.

1859 Dickens *Tale of Two Cities* III. x. 223 We saw the man, who was supposed to be at the gate, standing silent behind him. **1863** *Proc. Linnean Soc.* VII. p. xxvii, Still less does it seem consistent with that impartiality which every reviewer is supposed to possess. **1894** J. Pope *Mem. Rt. Hon. Sir John A. Macdonald* I. ii. 24 It appears that Mr. Baldwin considered this notice as sufficient to relieve him of the ordinary obligations which are supposed to govern the actions of Cabinet Ministers. **1902** 'R. Connor' *Glengarry Days* ii. 43 Girls are not supposed to be soldiers, are they, Margaret? **1914** G. B. Shaw *Misalliance* 86 Look here, Mr Percival: youre not supposed to insult my sister. **1931** *Morning Post* 31 Jan. 6 Officers..were not 'supposed' to keep a scrap log. **1949** E. Caldwell *This Very Earth* xi. 112 What's a girl supposed to do on Tuesday nights..? Bring her diary up to date? **1953** *N.Y. Herald-Tribune* 29 Apr. 4 They were supposed to address the lecturer as comrade. **1963** E. Albee *Who's Afraid of Virginia Woolf?* (1964) 84 When Daddy retired, he'd take over the college... That's the way it was supposed to be. **1969** A. Christie *Hallowe'en Party* xiii. 141, I brought her in lots of things that she was not supposed to eat. **1976** M. Machlin *Pipeline* xi. 134 That's more than the whole job was supposed to cost in the first place. **1976** P. & W. Proctor *Women in Pulpit* vi. 106 If that outburst was supposed to shock me because I'm a woman—forget it, brother!

supposite, *sb.* For † *Obs.* read *rare* and add: **1, 2.** (Later examples in form *supposit.*)

c **1882** G. M. Hopkins *Sermons & Devotional Writings* (1959) II. iii. 146 A person is defined a rational (that is/intellectual) supposit. **1929** tr. *St. Thomas Aquinas's Summa contra Gentiles* IV. IV. xxxiv. 144 Relative terms, nouns or pronouns, relate to the same supposit.

‖ **suppositio materialis** (sʊpǒzi·ʃio mătīᵊri-ē·lis). *Logic.* [med. L.] Reference to a word or phrase used simply as an example within a statement, and devoid of its normal semantic function.

1843 Mill *Logic* I. II. ii. 29 This employment of a word to denote the mere letters and syllables of which it is composed, was termed by the schoolmen the *suppositio materialis* of the word. **1921** W. E. Johnson *Logic* I. x. 169 The scholastic logicians introduced the phrase 'suppositio materialis'..but modern logicians have interpreted this phrase as equivalent to what they call the 'universe of discourse'. **1935** H. Straumann *Newspaper Headlines* ii. 67 The two sentences: 1. The first line of Gray's *Elegy* states a proposition, and 2. 'The first line of Gray's *Elegy*' does not state a proposition. Both utterances are true, but in the second case the validity entirely depends on the inverted commas. This phenomenon used to be well known in mediaeval scholasticism under the name of *suppositio materialis*, and it still plays an essential part in semantics. **1961** [see *HYPOSTASIS 8].

suppositious, *a.* Restrict Now *rare* or *Obs.* to senses 1 and 2 and add: **3. a.** (Later examples.)

1905 JOYCE *Let.* 12 July (1966) II. 97 We might take a small cottage outside Dublin... Not that I imagine that the atmosphere of our suppositious cottage could.. become more unpleasant to you than the atmosphere you are at present breathing. **1957** G. E. HUTCHINSON *Treat. Limnol.* I. iv. 231 Most of the evidence is purely suppositious. **1978** P. W. J. RILEY *Union of England & Scotland* 4 Although the island comprised more than one kingdom the term 'Great Britain' was already respectable usage... James [VI/I] now contemplated for this suppositious entity not only one king but one kingdom. **1982** *Christian Sci. Monitor* 26 Aug. 9/2 Being at the center of population has some commercial advantage for local inhabitants. The last stop of the suppositious point was at Mascoutah, Ill., in 1970—a town now dethroned by the new centre.

supposititious, *a.* **1. b.** (Later *fig.* example.)

1934 H. G. WELLS *Exper. Autobiogr.* I. v. 265 Russia.. is now no longer a Communism nor a democratic Socialism... It is a novel experimental state capitalism... It is the supposititious child of necessity in the household of theory.

suppositous (sǝpǫ·zitǝs), *a. nonce-wd.* [f. L. *suppositus*, pa. ppl. of *suppōnĕre*: see SUPPOSITUM.] Supposed, assumed.

1922 JOYCE *Ulysses* 686 An infinity rendered equally finite by the suppositous probable apposition of one or more bodies equally of the same and of different magnitudes.

suppress, *v.* Add: **8. a.** To prevent or inhibit (an action or phenomenon); *esp.* to eliminate, partly or wholly (electrical interference or unwanted frequencies).

1929 T. E. SHEA *Transmission Networks & Wave Filters* I. i. 20 For demodulation and recognition of signals the carrier frequency and one sideband may be suppressed. **1933** *Popular Sci.* Jan. 57/2 Interference troubles are present in abundance... To suppress these oscillations, 25,000-ohm resistors are placed in each spark plug lead. **1964** R. F. FICCHI *Electr. Interference* iv. 29 Shielding is the only practical method of suppressing interference which is radiated directly from a source. **1969** J. H. GREEN *Basic Clin. Physiol.* xvi. 91/2 The hormones of the adrenal cortex have an action in suppressing allergic responses. **1977** *Lancet* 5 Nov. 954/2 A 6-day course of oral dexamethasone at a dosage which would completely suppress A.C.T.H. in a person with adrenal insufficiency. **1980** PIERCE & POSNER *Introd. Communication Sci. & Systems* x. 224 A data signal with dc suppressed is sent through..single-sideband telephone links.

b. To fit with a suppressor.

1948 *Electronic Engin.* XX. 95 Garages and service stations are asked to co-operate in 'suppressing' cars already on the road. **1955** *Times* 31 Aug. 5/1 Everyone, he said, should beware of people who told them that all appliances must now be suppressed, especially if they were trying to sell suppressors. **1970** *AA Bk. Car.* 332 (*heading*) Suppressing the coil and the dynamo.

suppressant (sǝ̆pre·sănt). [f. SUPPRESS *v.* + -ANT[1].] An agent that suppresses or restrains; *spec.* (more fully *appetite suppressant*) a drug which suppresses appetite.

1958 *Jrnl. Amer. Med. Assoc.* 24 May 437/1 We were particularly impressed with the marked reduction in side-effects with the new drug, as compared with our previous experience with other appetite suppressants. **1968** *McGraw-Hill Yearbk. Sci. & Technol.* 189/1 material that is applied directly to the burning fuel to reduce the intensity or rate of burning is termed a suppressant. **1974** M. C. GERALD *Pharmacol.* ii. 28 One group of appetite suppressants is composed of indigestible gums that swell when they come into contact with the stomach's fluids. **1977** P. THEROUX *Consul's File* 73 Ayer Hitam was malarial, and the tablets we took..were only suppressants.

suppressed, *ppl. a.* Add: **c.** *Forestry.* Of a tree: growing in the lower levels of a forest.

1893 [see *DOMINANT *a.* 6]. **1938** J. S. BOYCE *Forest Pathol.* xvi. 388 In Germany suppressed trees of artificially infected red beech were found to be more susceptible to decay. **1976** [see *OVERTOPPED *ppl. a.*].

d. Fitted with an interference suppressor.

1959 *Which?* Aug. 91/1 All [clothes driers]..were stable .., and suppressed for TV, though none was completely suppressed for radio. **1970** *AA Bk. Car.* 332/3 (*caption*) On cars not fitted with suppressed high-tension leads or caps, insert individual line suppressors in each HT lead.

e. suppressed-carrier *Telecommunications*, usu. *attrib.* (see quot. 1924).

1924 S. R. ROGET *Dict. Electr. Terms* 251/1 *Suppressed carrier wave telephony*, a system of Carrier Current Telephony in which the excess of unmodulated carrier wave is filtered out and not transmitted, but re-introduced in the receiving apparatus in sufficient quantity to prevent distortion. **1935** [see *PILOT *sb.* 5*]. **1959** [see *PHASING *vbl. sb.* 1]. **1974** HARVEY & BOHLMAN *Stereo F.M. Radio Handbk.* ii. 12 In the Zenith-G.E. system..a suppressed-carrier or balanced modulator is employed.

suppressible, *a.* Add: Hence **suppressibi·lity**, capacity for being suppressed.

1973 *Clin. Endocrinol.* II. 369 There was a good correlation between a normal TRH response and normal thyroid suppressibility by T_3. **1977** *Lancet* 5 Nov. 954/2 Inadequate A.C.T.H. suppressibility in patients with Addison's disease while on treatment may be due to the maintenance of a secondary pituitary hyperplasia by inadequate replacement therapy.

suppression. Add: **7. a.** *Psychol.* The restraint or repression of an idea, an activity, or a reaction by something more powerful.

1880 W. JAMES *Coll. Ess. & Rev.* (1920) 197 What is this volition?..the permanent suppression of an idea although it may be immediately and urgently pleasant. *Ibid.*, What do we mean by 'suppression'? Either complete oblivescence, or such presence as to evoke the steady sentiment of aversion or negation. **1894** CREIGHTON & TITCHENER tr. *Wundt's Human & Animal Psychol.* 206 It may sometimes be observed that these phenomena of suppression do not extend to the entire image. **1951** T. C. RUCH in S. S. Stevens *Handbk. Exper. Psychol.* v. 172/2 Suppression exists in two forms. The first is termed 'suppression of motor activity'..and the second form is 'suppression of electrical activity'. **1971** K. H. PRIBRAM *Languages of Brain* vii. 138 Thus some sort of suppression of responsiveness must occur when an imbalance in the ordinary mode of excitation is produced, and their suppression exceeds the malfunction produced solely by disuse. **1974** ATKINSON & BIRCH in Atkinson & Raynor *Motivation & Achievement* xv. 274 The impact of some feature of the immediate environment is not so much an instigation to activity as the opposite, suppression of an activity.

b. *Psychoanal.* The action or result of (consciously) inhibiting an unacceptable feeling, desire, or memory. Cf. *REPRESSION 2 c.

1913 A. A. BRILL tr. *Freud's Interpretation of Dreams* v. 199 The theory of repression..asserts that such repressed wishes still exist, contemporaneously with an inhibition weighing them down. Language has hit upon the truth when it speaks of the 'suppression' of such impulses. **1926** J. S. HUXLEY *Ess. Pop. Sci.* vii. 72 Repression, suppression, sublimation, and the rest are [psychological] realities; and we are finding out how our minds do work. **1955** E. MOSBACHER tr. *Ferenczi's Final Contrib. Psycho-anal.* iv. 265 With suppression one does not feel the pain, only the *effort* which is necessary to 'alienate over' the pain. With repression one does not even feel this any longer. **1969** H. NAGERA et al. *Basic Psychoanal. Concepts* II. ix. 43 The possibilities range from complete suppression..to an intensity which is greater than the ideational content would lead one to expect. **1977** A. SHERIDAN tr. *Lacan's Four Fundamental Concepts Psycho-anal.* ii. 27 Is it not possible to see emerging from the text itself..the reality of the disappearance, of the suppression, of the *Unterdrückung*, the passing underneath?

8. *Electr.* Prevention of electrical interference.

1933 *Jrnl. Inst. Electr. Engineers* LXXIII. 543/2 Devices for the suppression of interference from many items of electrical plant, particularly domestic appliances, could be incorporated in future designs. **1964** R. F. FICCHI *Electr. Interference* vii. 110 Capacitors are used when suppression is required on two commutator motors. **1970** *R.A.C. Guide & Handbk.* 56 Radio Interference Suppression. Regulations made by the Postmaster General.

9. *Phonetics.* The lowering of normal stress levels in verse; an instance of this.

1956, 1973 [see *PROMOTION 1 f].

‖ **suppressio veri** (sǝ̆pre·ʃio vīǝ·rəi). [mod. L., = suppression of what is true.] Misrepresentation of the truth by concealing facts which ought to be made known. Cf. *SUGGESTIO FALSI.

1755 CHESTERFIELD in *World* No. 105. 632 Here is not only the *suppressio veri*, which is highly penal, but the *crimen falsi* too. **1815, 1855** [see *SUGGESTIO FALSI]. **1889** *Athenæum* 20 Apr. 500/3 There is an unintentional *suppressio veri* in his assertion. **1905** *Spectator* 25 Feb. 286/2 The English Church Union could hardly subscribe *ex animo* to an interpretation containing an important *suppressio veri.* **1950** M. HAY *Foot of Pride* v. 135 It would not be easy to find a more flagrant case of *suppresio veri* than this omission..of any reference to the notorious Rohling scandal. **1979** J. MELVILLE *Wages of Zen* iii. 28, I told him exactly who I am and, with a touch of *suppressio veri*, what I'm about.

suppressor. Add: **1. b.** *spec.* A device for stopping a machine or part to which it is fitted from causing electrical interference.

1930 *Engineering* 14 Nov. 626/1 A diagram..is given in Fig. 16, the transmitting and receiving suppressors being marked TS_1 and TS_2. **1948** *Electronic Engin.* XX. 95 An ignition suppressor for fitting in the H.T. supply lead from the coil. **1955** [see *SUPPRESS *v.* 8 b]. **1970** [see *SUPPRESSED *ppl. a.* d].

2. *Genetics.* A gene in whose presence the effects of some other gene are not expressed. Also *suppressor gene.*

1928 *Zeitschr. f. Induktive Abstammungs- und Vererbungslehre* XLVI. 85 (*heading*) The genetics of 'black suppressor' in Drosophila melanogaster. **1932** *Amer. Naturalist* LXVI. 323 That the suppressor is a translocated wild-type allelomorph rather than a mutation in another gene has been proved in certain cases. **1960** *Heredity* XV. 91 The phenotypic manifestation of the suppressor gene is hidden by the mutation *en.* **1966** *Ann. Rev. Microbiol.* XX. 409 The best characterized and most intensively studied of the suppressor mutations which affect the translation process are the suppressors of the two classes of mutants, 'amber' and 'ochre'.

3. *Electronics.* = *suppressor grid*, sense 4 below.

1937 F. E. TERMAN *Radio Engin.* (ed. 2) iv. 128 The virtual cathode in conjunction with the plate and suppressor grid forms the equivalent of a triode tube in which the suppressor is the grid. **1959** [see *GRID 5 a]. **1968** ROMANOWITZ & PUCKETT *Introd. Electronics* vi. 237 The suppressor is usually connected to the cathode and is thus at full negative potential with respect to the plate.

4. Special Combs.: **suppressor (T) cell** *Immunol.*, a thymus-dependent lymphocyte which can suppress the stimulation of antibody production in lymphocytes in the presence of antigen; **suppressor grid** *Electronics*, in a thermionic valve, a coarse grid situated between electrodes (usu. the screen grid and the anode) so as to stop secondary electrons emitted by the latter from reaching the former.

1972 *Jrnl. Immunol.* CVIII. 590/1 It is possible that there are separate populations of activator (*x*) and suppressor (*y*) T cells. **1979** *Jrnl. Exper. Med.* CXLIX. 1018 The suppressor T cells regulated the DH [*sc.* delayed hypersensitivity] in the induction stage. **1981** *Nature* 23 July 357/2 Nonspecific suppressor cells may be one explanation for the severe immunodeficiency and the recurrent infectious complications characteristic of patients with chronic GvHD [*sc.* graft-versus-host disease]. **1931** *Electronics* Nov. 176/2 In order to avoid the effects of secondary emission from the plate..an auxiliary electrode was inserted to suppress this secondary current. The advantages of this same sort of suppressor grid are utilized in the..power pentode design. **1944** *Electronic Engin.* XVII. 163 The suppressor grids are generally operated at cathode potential. **1974** HARVEY & BOHLMANN *Stereo F.M. Radio Handbk.* ii. 13 If a modulating signal is now applied, the bias on the suppressor grid is alternately raised and lowered in sympathy with the modulating signal.

supra-. Add: **I. 1. a. supracru·stal** *a.* and *sb. Geol.*, (a stratum, formation, etc.) lying above the basement rocks of the crust; **suprafa·cial** *a. Chem.*, (of a concerted reaction undergone by a molecule) involving the formation of two new bonds on the same face of the molecule; **suprali·ttoral** *a. Ecol.*, applied to a biogeographic zone normally taken as extending from mean high tide to the limit of influential sea spray or land vegetation; also *ellipt.* as *sb.*

1946 *Amer. Jrnl. Sci.* CCXLIV. 851 The supracrustal formations are subjected to folding, plastic deformation, fractures and thrusts in which the blocks of the basement also take part. **1973** *Nature* 21 Sept. 138/1 The Isua supracrustals may represent a shallow-water shelf facies. **1965** WOODWARD & HOFFMANN in *Jrnl. Amer. Chem. Soc.* LXXXVII. 2512/1 In the first process, here designated suprafacial, the hydrogen atom is associated at all times with the same face of the π-system. **1980** E. N. MARVELL *Thermal Electrocyclic Reactions* i. 5 Thus for a π bond a suprafacial process forms new connections on the same side of the nodal plane. **1909** WARMING & VAHL *Œcol. Plants* IV. xli. 173 Thus arises a kind of supra-littoral 'region'. **1949** T. A. & A. STEPHENSON in *Jrnl. Ecol.* XXXVII. 298 We therefore formally propose that the three main zones of the shore be called: Supralittoral Fringe, Midlittoral Zone, Infralittoral Fringe. **1967** *Oceanogr. & Marine Biol.* V. 464 The plants and animals living in the supralittoral zone can either tolerate or need a permanent or almost permanent emersion, but with moistening by sprays and waves. **1974** *Nature* 22 Feb. 520/2 The environmental significance of each of these.. seems to reflect various aspects of turbulence, turbidity, and/or desiccation in the littoral or supralittoral.

b. *supranuclear*: delete 6 b (further examples); *suprapatellar, -umbilical, -ventricular* (examples referring to VENTRICLE 1); **suprameatal** (-mi,ē[i]·tăl) *a.*, situated above the acoustic meatus; **suprao·ptic** *a.* situated above the optic chiasma; **suprase·llar** *a.*, situated or occurring above the sella turcica.

1893 W. MACEWEN *Pyogenic Infective Dis. of Brain & Spinal Cord* i. 9 The apex of this triangular depressed area points forward. The author proposes to name this area the supra-meatal triangle. **1922** *Brit. Med. Jrnl.* 29 July 164/2 Later experience in using this suprameatal angle as a guide has been extensive. **1980** *Gray's Anat.* (ed. 36) iii. 302/2 Immediately above and behind the meatus there is frequently a small depression with a bony spicule (suprameatal spine) in its anterior margin. This lies within the area of the suprameatal triangle. **1977** *Lancet* 12 Nov. 1029/2 One [patient] had periodic vertigo due to a supranuclear vestibular lesion. **1979** *Jrnl. Compar. Path.* LXXXIX. 503 The supranuclear cytoplasm of the superficial epithelial cells. **1921** TILNEY & RILEY *Form & Function Central Nerv. Syst.* xxxi. 550 Situated above the optic chiasm and in communication with the chamber of the third ventricle is a small canal which projects outward over the optic nerve. This is the supra-optic canal. **1980** K. E. MOYER *Neuroanatomy* xxviii. 70/2 The supraoptic nucleus is located directly over the lateral portion of the optic chiasm. **1902** D. J. CUNNINGHAM *Text-bk. Anat.* 293 The joint-cavity may communicate with bursæ situated in relation to the inner head of the gastrocnemius muscle and the tendon of the semi-membranosus muscle, besides the large supra-patellar bursa already described. **1975** L. M. ELSON *It's your Body* v. 284 (*caption*) Suprapatellar bursa. **1934** J. H. GLOBUS *Neuroanatomy* (ed. 6) I. 15 The diamond shaped somewhat depressed space outlined at the base of the brain is called the interpeduncular space..; and because it overlies the sella turcica in the base of the skull, it is often termed the suprasellar space. **1977** *Lancet* 9 Apr. 780/1 Air encephalograms were performed on 7 of the 12 patients with prolactin levels between 15 and 30 μg/l and in all 7 suprasellar extension of the tumour was found. **1906** *Practitioner* Dec. 781 Rolleston thinks that, for practical purposes, it is advisable to adopt Oppenheim's division of the reflex into a supra-umbilical and infra-umbilical zone. **1978** *Acta Path. Japonica* XXVIII. 288 Just after birth.., this female patient showed deep cyanosis and supraumbilical abdominal hernia. **1974** *Ciba Symposium* XX. 133 Localization of the infiltrate in the AV node blocks the supraventricular impulses when the atrial rate increases. **1979** *Brit. Med. Jrnl.* 15 Dec. 1553/2 Disopyramide..has been used to treat supraventricular and ventricular arrhythmias.

d. Phonology. *supradental* (also as *sb.*), *supraglottal* (also as *sb.*), *supralaryngeal.*

1926 B. KARLGREN *Philology & Ancient China* iv. 80 No pronouncement is here made about whether these sounds were hard, supradental ('cerebrals'), *tʂ-*, *tʂ'-*, *ʂ-*, etc., somewhat resembling English heart*sh*aped. **1969** *Language* XLV. 125 To say that the supradentals are merely occurrence phenomena of [r] plus dental leads to undesirable results. **1935** *Amer. Speech* X. 311/2 The quality of vowels depends not only on supra-glottal resonances, but..on the complex and variable sound emitted by the larynx. **1964** CRYSTAL & QUIRK *Prosodic & Paralinguistic Features in Eng.* iii. 39 Supraglottals may be tense or lax. **1979** *Amer. Speech 1978* LIII. 290 The supraglottal articulatory motions and positions used in human language..are not used by other animals at all. **1964** J. C. CATFORD in D. Abercrombie et al. *Daniel Jones* 29 Phoneticians should be able to classify 'voice qualities' and other phonatory activities in as systematic a way as they classify supralaryngeal articulation. **1978** *Amer. Speech* LIII. 292 They carefully measured chimpanzee supralaryngeal cavities.

II. 4. a. *supraconscious* (later example), *-decent, -dialectal, -individual, -literal, -logical, -normal* (later examples), *-racial, -regional, -sentential*; **su:pramole·cular,** composed of many molecules; higher in organization than a molecule; **su:prarela·tional,** of a postulated being or power that transcends or includes all that is relational.

1953 J. STRACHEY tr. *Freud's Interpret. of Dreams* in *Compl. Wks* V. vii. 615 We must avoid, too, the distinction between 'supraconscious' and 'subconscious', which has become so popular in the more recent literature of the psychoneuroses, for such a distinction seems precisely calculated to stress the equivalence of what is psychical to what is conscious. **1938** S. BECKETT *Murphy* v. 90 As different..as a *voyeur's* from a *voyant's*, though Wylie was no more the one in the indecent sense than Murphy was the other in the supradecent sense. **1960** P. DORF tr. M. M. Guxman in J. A. Fishman *Readings Sociol. of Lang.* (1968) 768 Even in the formation process of the new written Bashkir national language, the problem of working out a unified, supradialectal literary norm,..was in the twentieth century just as real as it was in eighteenth- and nineteenth-century Germany or Italy. **1936** *Mind* XLV. 293, I would fain hold..that the highest values are, not only supra-individual, but supra-national. **1949** *Archivum Linguisticum* I. 164 A mark of palatalization in the shape of a supraliteral meniscus. **1896** W. CALDWELL *Schopenhauer's System* i. 42 This fondness of Schopenhauer for the supra-logical character of intuition and genius has its dangerous side. **1936** *Essays & Studies* XXI. 136 In the case of words like 'spell' and 'Host' the supra-logical connotation and accidental associations reinforce the literal meaning. **1909** in *Cent. Dict.* Suppl. **1961** *Nature* 8 July 145/1 A supramolecular organization of the enzyme systems. **1976** *Sci. Amer.* July 65/1 One of the major challenges in cell biology today is the mapping of supramolecular structures such as membranes and ribosomes. **1902** W. JAMES *Var. Relig. Exper.* 484 Our supra-normal cognitions, if such there be, and if we are telepathic subjects. **1959** B. WOOTTON *Social Science & Social Pathology* ii. 59 Exceptionally difficult problems, failure to cope adequately with which might well be a sign,..of their lack of the supra-normal qualities which the situation demands. **1977** J. L. HARPER *Population Biol. of Plants* x. 328 Partial closure of stomata..usually occurs when supra-normal concentrations of CO_2 are applied to leaves. **1922** JOYCE *Ulysses* 717 With what antagonistic sentiments were his subsequent reflections affected?.. Abnegation? In virtue of..extraracial attraction, intraracial inhibition, supraracial prerogative. **1973** R. C. VAN CAENEGEM *Birth of Eng. Common Law* i. 14 The justices in eyre or itinerant royal judges..were called *justitiarii totius Angliae*, to indicate that their commission was supraregional. **1910** W. JAMES *Coll. Ess. & Rev.* (1920) 497 Mr. Bradley tumbles to philosophy's call. Down he slides, to the dry valley of 'absolute' mare's nests and abstractions, the habitation of the fictitious suprarelational being which his will prefers. **1936** *Mind* XLV. 538 His initially hopeless attempt to make sense..of freedom and individuality in terms of his supra-relational whole. **1961** Y. OLSSON *Syntax Eng. Verb* ii. 34 This constitutes a new kind of intersectional concord, often exceeding the limits of the sentence (*supra-sentential concord*).

b. *supra-clan, -class, -Elder, -language, -party, -village.*

1979 *Social Sci. & Med.* XIII. D. 209/2 Within these dispersed people, there was no supraclan political system to organize for mutual defense. **1952** C. BARDSLEY *Bishop's Move* viii. 96 A supra-class Church founded on Life and Love. **1977** M. WALKER *National Front* iv. 84 The NF's supra-class, supra-party appeal. **1958** D. TAIT *Tribes without Rulers* 193 There is no supra-Elder authority to impose a solution on recalcitrants of a district. **1975** *Amer. Speech 1972* XLVII. 253 Such supralanguage phenomena as rhyme and assonance in verse. **1974** tr. *Wertheim's Evolution & Revolution* iii. 245 The creation of supra-village organizations.

6. *supra-body, -burgher, -consciousness* (earlier example), *-council, -language, -organism, -parliament, -system.*

1967 M. AYUB KHAN *Friends not Masters* xi. 199 There was obviously no place for a supra-body of religious experts exercising a power of veto over the Legislature and the Judiciary. **1905** JOYCE *Let.* 19 July (1966) II. 99 Also desirables are..a sizeable beefsteak.., and..an intelligent supra-burgher like yourself to share the meal. **1911** A. MITCHELL tr. *Bergson's Creative Evolution* 275 It is consciousness, or rather supra-consciousness, that is at the origin of life. **1974** *Physics Bull.* Mar. 86/1 A formalized supra-council of scientific institutions. **1980** *Encounter* July 50/1 *Finnegan's Wake*..the project of a supra-language distinct to the given text. **1949** KOESTLER *Insight & Outlook* II. xi. 167 We must expect the ultimate achievement of a proportionate superiority in the mature human supra-organism. **1971** Supra-parliament [see *MULTINATIONAL *a.* and *sb.*]. **1964** *Language* XL. 274 Modern Greek has two independent and partial phonological suprasystems.

7. suprale·thal *a.*, exceeding what is lethal; so **suprale·thally** *adv.*; **suprama·ximal** *a. Physiol.*, greater than what is required to produce the maximum response; hence **suprama·ximally** *adv.*; **suprathe·rmal** *a. Physics*, having greater energy than that associated with thermal excitations; **supra-thre·shold** *a. Physiol.*, exceeding the threshold value required for the perception of a stimulus.

1957 *Jrnl. Exper. Zool.* CXXXVII. 426 A total continuous dose of 24 kr, referred to as a supralethal dose, was given to interphase cells at each exposure. **1979** *Nature* 11 Oct. 490/2 Supralethal doses of chemoradiotherapy followed by allogeneic bone marrow transplantation are being used to treat patients with acute leukaemia. **1955** *Jrnl. Exper. Zool.* CXXX. 190 (*heading*) Survival and cell division in supralethally x-irradiated giant amoebae following injection of nonirradiated protoplasm. **1975** *Nature* 20 Nov. 233/2 (*caption*) Supralethally irradiated rats. **1925** LIDDELL & SHERRINGTON in *Proc. R. Soc.* B. XCVII. 497 The reflex mode of employing the motor units is to subject them to an incitement which is 'supramaximal' in the sense that it is in excess..of that which is necessary to evoke in them individually their 'maximal' response. **1977** *Lancet* 30 Apr. 942/1 Desmedt and Borenstein have modified this test..by first applying a train of supramaximal stimuli at 3 Hz for 4 minutes. **1973** *Nature* 26 Oct. 465/1 The sciatic nerve was stimulated supramaximally at a rate of 6.4 Hz with square waves of 0.5 ms duration. **1969** *New Yorker* 12 Apr. 104/3 The three pots are the passive seismic experiment, the solar-wind experiment, and the suprathermal-ion-detector. **1980** *Nature* 29 May 285/1 Of perhaps even greater interest was an image of the suprathermal X-rays, or bremsstrahlung, derived from interactions of the hot electrons with ions from the exploding pusher. **1946** *Ibid.* 27 July 131/2 The strength of the stimulating current was gradually increased to threshold and supra-threshold values. **1980** VAN BOMMEL & DE BOER *Road Lighting* ii. 35 The supra-threshold level of visibility can be expressed in terms of the visibility level attainable.

III. 9. supracondu·cting *ppl. a.* [tr. Du. *suprageleidend*: see *SUPERCONDUCTING *ppl. a.*] = *SUPERCONDUCTING *ppl. a.*; so **supra-condu·ction, -conductive** *a.*, **su:praconducti·vity, supraconductor**; all now *rare.*

1932 *Nature* 10 Dec. 880/2 The application of mechanical stresses..raises the transition temperature of a supra-conducting metal. **1937** M. & B. RUHEMANN *Low Temperature Physics* IV. ii. 269 It is by no means clear whether at sufficiently low temperatures all metals become supra-conducting. **1932** *Nature* 10 Dec. 879 (*heading*) Electric supra-conduction in metals. *Ibid.*, Currents of electricity started in a ring of metal in the supra-conductive state will continue apparently undiminished in intensity. **1941** *Ibid.* 13 Sept. 317/1 It..appears that, in sufficiently pure and homogeneous samples of tantalum, the changes of electrical resistance..and specific heat accompanying the establishment of the supra-conductive state occur at one and the same temperature. **1930** *Engineering* 16 May 640/3 Some of the discoveries made by the late Professor Kamerlingh Onnes,..as, for instance, supraconductivity. **1962** P. J. & B. DURRANT *Introd. Adv. Inorg. Chem.* xviii. 591 Graphite does not show supraconductivity. **1976** *Progress in Sci. Culture* (E. Majorana Centre) Spring 90 The most important theoretical items were probably the nuclear analogy of supraconductivity..and the accounting of wave functions for deformed nuclei. **1933** *Nature* 14 Oct. 602/1 The use of a supra-conductor (therefore completely free from Joule heating) has been more than once suggested for the production of magnetic fields at low temperatures.

suprachoroid (s^{i}ūprăkō^{ə}·roid), *sb.* and *a. Ophthalm.* Also **-chorioid**, and in L. form **-chor(i)oidea.** [ad. mod. L.: see SUPRA- 1 b and CHOROID *a.* (*sb.*).] **A.** *sb.* A layer of loose cellular tissue lying between the choroid and the sclera. **B.** *adj.* Epithet of this layer.

1892 A. DUANE tr. *Fuchs's Text-bk. Ophthalm.* iv. 245 The suprachorioid..consists of numerous fine non-vascular but richly pigmented lamellæ lying between the chorioid proper and the sclera. **1896** W. A. FROST *Fundus Oculi* i. 12 Between the sclerotic and the choroid is some loose cellular tissue—the suprachoroidea. **1959** S. DUKE-ELDER *Parsons' Dis. of Eye* (ed. 13) i. 6 The greater part of the muscle is composed of meridional fibres running antero-posteriorly on the inner aspect of the sclera to find a diffuse insertion into the suprachoroid. **1962** *Gray's Anat.* (ed. 33) 1258 It [*sc.* the sclera] is separated from the outer surface of the choroid by an extensive perichoroidal space, which is traversed by an exceedingly delicate cellular tissue, termed the suprachoroid lamina. **1971** M. J. HOGAN et al. *Histol. Human Eye* viii. 386 The suprachoroidea lies between the choroid and the sclera and appears to be derived partly from each tissue. **1978** F. W. NEWELL *Ophthalmology* (ed. 4) i. 15/1 The outermost layer, the suprachoroid (*lamina fusca*), is made up of delicate lamellae composed of elastic and collagenous fibers to form a syncytium.

So **su:prachoroi·dal** *a.*, situated above the choroid.

1887 F. FERGUS tr. *Meyer's Pract. Treat. Dis. Eye* iv. 148 (*caption*) Supra choroidal space. **1918** J. H. PARSONS *Dis. Eye* (ed. 3) xvii. 334 Fuchs..attributes it to slight separation of the ciliary body, so that the aqueous percolates from the anterior chamber into the suprachoroidal space. **1975** *Symposium on Glaucoma: Trans. New Orleans Acad. Ophthalm.* xix. 304 The surgeon should then confirm that the probe may be introduced with equal facility.. into the space between the ciliary body and sclera which anatomists call the suprachoroidal space.

supracleithrum (s^{i}ūprăklǝi·þrǒm). *Zool.* Pl. **-cleithra.** [SUPRA- 1 c.] A dermal bone dorsal to the cleithrum in the pectoral arch of some fishes and amphibians.

1905 A. SEDGWICK *Student's Text-bk. Zool.* II. vii. 162 These bones are now often called supracleithrum, cleithrum and clavicle respectively. **1949** A. S. ROMER *Vertebr. Body* vii. 179 Above each cleithrum there are usually additional elements—typically a supracleithrum and post-temporal, and sometimes other bones as well—which curve upward and forward above the gill chamber and anchor the dermal girdle to the skull. **1981** PEARSON & BALL *Lect. Notes Vertebr. Zool.* iv. 52/1 Large clavicles occur in paleoniscoids and Polypterus, with large cleithra and smaller postcleithra, supracleithra, and post-temporals above them.

supracoracoid (s^{i}ūprăkǫ·răkoid), *sb.* and *a. Zool.* Also in L. form **-coracoideus.** [f. SUPRA- 1 c + CORACOID *a.* and *sb.*] **A.** *sb.* A muscle in some birds, amphibians, and reptiles which passes over the coracoid bone and is attached to the head of the humerus and to part of the sternum. **B.** *adj.* Of, pertaining to, or designating the supracoracoid.

1933 L. A. ADAMS *Introd. Vertebrates* iv. 86 (*in figure*) Supracoracoideus. **1949** SAUNDERS & MANTON *Man. Pract. Vertebr. Morphol.* (ed. 2) ix. 88 The supracoracoideus muscle elevates the wing. **1956** A. S. ROMER *Osteol. of Reptiles* vii. 308 Beneath the anterior end of the glenoid is a supracoracoid foramen (or coracoid foramen), carrying..the supracoracoid nerve. **1974** ANDREW & HICKMAN *Histol. Vertebr.* vi. 107/2 The powerful muscles of flight (pectoral and supracoracoid) are centrally located on the sternum. **1979** *Nature* 15 Mar. 247/2 It has been argued that the structure of the coracoid of *Archaeopteryx* would not have permitted the supracoracoideus muscle to function as a wing elevator.

supraliminal, *a.* (Later examples.)

1903 F. W. H. MYERS *Human Personality* I. i. 14 Sensations, thoughts, emotions, which..by the original constitution of our being, seldom emerge into that *supraliminal* current of consciousness which we habitually identify with ourselves. **1918** [see *OVERLEARN *v.*]. **1931** *Brit. Jrnl. Psychol.* Jan. 305 Another series [of observations] was made in which a supraliminal admixture of spectral light was reduced until the field appeared pure white. **1971** *Jrnl. Gen. Psychol.* Jan. 122 Manipulating intensity..from subliminal to supraliminal luminance results in..emergence of linear detail.

supra·tional, *a.* [SUPRA- 4 a.] Having power, authority, or influence that overrides or transcends national boundaries, governments, or institutions.

1908 [in Dict. s.v. SUPRA- 4 a]. **1924** J. C. W. REITH in *Radio Times* 29 Feb. 361/2, I like to think that wireless, as with music, is supra-national, a word coined, I believe, by Lord Cecil to indicate that which is above not only nationality, but something more even than international. **1941** *Burlington Mag.* Feb. 38/1 Mediaeval artists shared the common task of glorifying God under the guidance of a supra-national church. **1950** W. S. CHURCHILL in *Hansard Commons* 27 June 2147, I would add, to make my answer quite clear to the right hon. and learned Gentleman, that if he asked me, 'Would you agree to a supra-national authority which has the power to tell Great Britain not to cut any more coal or make any more steel, but to grow tomatoes instead?' I should say, without hesitation, the answer is 'No'. **1958** A. J. ZURCHER *Struggle to unite Europe 1940–1958* vii. 80 This first European supranational community set up its administrative offices in Luxembourg on August 10, 1952. **1962** A. SAMPSON *Anat. of Britain* xxvii. 429 The very biggest firms in Britain..belong more to an international, than a national economy. And in the Common Market they are likely to become much more supra-national. **1973** *Observer* (Colour Suppl.) 12 Aug. 19/3 They were 'inter-governmental' rather than 'supranational'—that is to say based on negotiation between sovereign Governments, not on the principle that the institution itself, operating as a unit, could overrule member Governments. **1977** M. WALKER *National Front* ii. 25 His [*sc.* Mosley's] book *The Alternative*, which advocated a European nationalism, a new supra-national state of Europe.

Hence **suprana·tionalism, su:pranationa·lity.**

1921 *Glasgow Herald* 14 Oct. 10 It was only a developed sense of supra-nationalism that would in the future make war unthinkable. **1930** *Tablet* 16 Aug. 206/2 The Popes held out..against every threat..which aimed at lowering the supra-nationality of the Papacy. **1955** A. L. ROWSE *Expansion of Elizabethan England* vii. 241 One sees, as against the supra-nationalism of the Habsburgs.., the nationalist assumption..that the Low Countries should govern themselves. **1959** *Times Lit. Suppl.* 3 Apr. 187/3 The actual degree of supranationality in these Communities. **1971** *Mod. Law Rev.* XXXI. VI. 607 It is clear that with the elements of supranationality are commingled features of a more typical international organisation. **1980** *Times Lit. Suppl.* 10 Oct. 1134/1 Supranationalism has lost what appeal it had in the 1950s.

supraopticohypophysial (s¹ūprăˌǫːptikohəi-pofi·ziăl), *a. Anat.* Also **-eal.** [f. *supraoptic* adj. s.v. *SUPRA- 1 b + -O + *HYPOPHYSIAL *a.*] Applied to a tract of nerve fibres in the brain running from the supraoptic nucleus to the hypophysis.

[**1937** *Jrnl. Path. & Bacteriol.* XLIV. 310 The fact.. seems to indicate that at this time the lesion was confined to the supraoptic-hypophyseal system.] **1943** STRONG & ELWYN *Human Neuroanat.* xvii. 317/2 They [*sc.* the connections of the hypothalamus with the posterior lobe of the hypophysis] are unmyelinated fibers which arise principally from the supraoptic and paraventricular nuclei and form a well defined bundle, the supraopticohypophysial tract. **1961** *Lancet* 2 Sept. 525/1 A lesion in the tuberal nuclei, with or without damage to the supraopticohypophyseal system, resulted in diabetes insipidus. **1980** K. E. MOYER *Neuroanatomy* xxxiii. 80 The supraopticohypophysial tract..comes principally from the supraoptic nucleus.

supra-pe·rsonal, *a.* [SUPRA- 4 a.] = *SUPERPERSONAL *a.*

1918 J. H. LECKIE *World to Come* II. 322 The notion.. of attaining some supra-personal state of being is not an idea that can appear reasonable. **1934** M. BODKIN *Archetypal Patterns in Poetry* 276 The sense of..a supra-personal life present within the group, which is made explicit in the writings of St. Paul. **1949** H. READ *Conc. Hist. Mod. Painting* vii. 249 The 'vibrations of the spirit' that then take place are..perhaps supra-personal, in that they assume the archetypal patterns into which mankind projects an explanation of its destiny. **1955** J. BURNABY *Christian Words & Christian Meanings* iii. 48 It may sometimes be wholesome for us to tell ourselves that God is not 'a person', but 'supra-personal', or even 'Absolute Being'. **1958** *Times Lit. Suppl.* 23 May 278/3 Its [*sc.* The Warburg Institute's] character is also suprapersonal, and it is never likely to lose its identity and be submerged in some more general apparatus of historical research. **1972** M. KIRKHAM in *Focus on Robert Graves* No. 3 (1973) 40 The feeling might be called impersonal, in the sense that it reflects..everybody's response to a general condition; a better word would be 'suprapersonal', to signify a going-beyond personality.

suprasegmental (s¹ūːprăsegme·ntăl), *a.* and *sb. Linguistics.* [f. SUPRA- 4 a + *SEGMENTAL *a.* 2 c.] **A.** *adj.* Designating a feature or features of a sound or sequence of sound other than those constituting the consonantal and vocalic segments, as stress, pitch, and intonation in English.

1941 TRAGER & BLOCH in *Language* XVII. 224 These two kinds of phonemes [*sc.* juncture and prosodic phonemes] are usually recognizable only as modifications of other sound-types; they are suprasegmental. **1942** C. F. HOCKETT in *Language* XVIII. 8 Features..which clearly extend over a series of several segmental groupings are *suprasegmental.* **1942, 1952** [see *PROSODIC *a.* 2]. **1953** [see *intrasegmental* s.v. *INTRA- 1]. **1968** P. KRATOCHVÍL *Chinese Lang. Today* ii. 35 The most striking suprasegmental feature of MSC syllables is the characteristic contour known as the tone. **1971** [see *PROSODEME]. **1975** N. CHOMSKY *Logical Struct. Linguistic Theory* iii. 111 In this study, suprasegmental features (pitch, stress, juncture) have not been seriously considered.

B. *sb.* A suprasegmental feature.

1955 N. CHOMSKY *Logical Struct. Linguistic Theory* (microfilm, Mass. Inst. Technol.) vii. 278 It has often been suggested that constituent structure be determined by considerations involving suprasegmentals. **1965** *Word Study* Feb. 2/2 Structural and contextual meanings are signaled largely by intonational clues, by such suprasegmentals as pitch, stress, and juncture. **1975** *Language* LI. 737 How we perceive duration, pitch, and intensity is an area that seldom receives serious attention in the literature on suprasegmentals. **1981** *Amer. Speech* LVI. 306 A summary of paralanguage, including suprasegmentals, hesitation phenomena, and nonlinguistic sounds.

Hence **su:prasegme·ntally** *adv.*, in terms of suprasegmental features.

1957 S. POTTER *Modern Linguistics* v. 105 Sentences may be described *suprasegmentally* in respect of the prosodemes of *length, stress* and *pitch.* **1970** J. W. GAIR *Colloq. Sinhalese Clause Structures* vi. 133 The focus may be marked only suprasegmentally, even if the form of the predicator indicates that the focus is elsewhere in the clause.

suprasensuous, *a.* (In Dict. s.v. SUPRA-SENSUAL *a.*) Add: (Later examples.) Also *absol.* with *the.*

1902 *Pop. Sci. Monthly* Apr. 519 The scientist often has recourse to the suprasensuous. **1947** A. EINSTEIN *Music in Romantic Era* III. xviii. 340 An idea which then led to the assertion that true, ideal music is not heard at all, but is non-sensuous and suprasensuous. **1957** J. I. M. STEWART *Use of Riches* 41 He knew why this picture was neither better nor worse than the Maremma or the La Verna... Brilliantly sensuous, it was yet suprasensuous.

supraspecies (s¹ū·prăspīːʃīz, -sīz). [f. SUPRA- 6 + SPECIES *sb.*] (See quot. 1940.) So **supraspeci·fic** *a.*, above the rank of a species.

1940 J. S. HUXLEY *New Systematics* 10 We may substitute the term 'species-group', reserving the term 'supraspecies' for groups of an intermediate nature, in which it is dubious whether the constituent groups are best called subspecies or species. **1942** E. MAYR *Systematics & Origin of Species* vii. 169 The term supraspecies..seems to me to be an unfortunate combination. **1961** Supraspecific [see *NOMENCLATURAL *a.*]. **1975** *Nature* 9 Oct. 516/1 Because supraspecific taxa have different numbers of species, their observed linearity is evidence for the ecological reality of supraspecific taxa.

suprasterol (s¹ūprăste·rǫl). *Biochem.* [ad. G. *suprasterin* (A. Windaus et al. 1930, in *Ann. d. Chem.* CCCCLXXXIII. 20): see SUPRA- + *-STEROL.] Either of two optically active polycyclic isomers (*suprasterol I, II*) of $C_{28}H_{44}O$ produced by prolonged irradiation of vitamin D.

1931 *Chem. Abstr.* XXV. 301 Ergosterol in EtOH, subjected to the action of Hg light at about 75° for 50 hrs., gives a mixt. of suprasterol I..and II. **1943** *Endeavour* Apr. 73/2 Calciferol itself [vitamin D] was also liable to be broken down further to inactive substances—toxisterol and suprasterols I and II. **1976** H. CAMPION et al. in B. E. C. Nordin *Calcium, Phosphate & Mineral Metabolism* xii. 452 Ergocalciferol itself can, under prolonged irradiation, undergo irreversible photoisomerization to compounds known as suprasterol$_2$ I.

supravital (s¹ūprăvəi·tăl), *a. Histology.* [SUPRA-.] Of a stain or the process of staining: involving living tissue, esp. blood, outside the body. Hence **supravi·tally** *adv.*

1921 *Arch. Internal Med.* XXVIII. 513 Janus green B .., used as a supravital stain in dilute solutions..stains mitochondria an intense green. *Ibid.* 515 The reticulum present in certain erythrocytes is seen as a delicate network and is best demonstrated by staining supravitally with brilliant cresyl blue or azur II. **1930** *Edin. Med. Jrnl.* XXXVII. 429 Supravital staining.—The process consists of the application of basic dyes to portions of tissues removed during life or immediately after somatic death. **1972** C. GURNEY in C. E. Mengel et al. *Hematology* i. 6 When stained supravitally with a number of special stains, these young cells show small dark granules. **1974** *Nature* 22 Feb. 551/2 The supernatant was then shaken from the wells and supravital stain was added.

supremacist (s¹upre·măsist), *sb.* and *a.* [f. SUPREMACY + -IST, orig. in *white supremacist.*] **A.** *sb.* One who believes in the supremacy of one of the races or of either of the sexes or of any other social group. **B.** *adj.* That is a supremacist. Orig. and freq. preceded by defining word: see also *male supremacist* s.v. *MALE *sb.* 4, *white supremacist* s.v. *WHITE *a.* 11 e.

1959, etc. [see *white supremacist* s.v. *WHITE *a.* 11 e]. **1961** WEBSTER, *Supremacist*.., an advocate or adherent of some concept of group supremacy; *esp*: *white supremacist.* **1968** in B. & T. Roszak *Masculine/Feminine* (1970) 256 Men..maintain a dominant position for themselves, and as supremacists, try to perpetuate that position of dominance. **1969** *Manifesto for N.Y. Radical Feminists* in J. Hole & E. Levine *Rebirth of Feminism* (1971) 443 The purpose of the male power group is to fulfill a need. That need is psychological, and derives from the supremacist assumption of the male identity. **1975** *Economist* 1 Feb. 24/1 Weaning the more sensible loyalists away from their Protestant supremacist partners. **1976** P. DRISCOLL *Barboza Credentials* v. iii. 217 An ultra-white brotherhood of supremacist bitter-enders. **1982** *Washington Post* 4 Mar. D 1/1 None of this football nonsense of airy polls full of supremacist blather.

So **supre·macism**: see *white supremacism* s.v. *WHITE *a.* 11 e.

Suprematism (s¹upre·mătiz'm). Also **suprematism.** [ad. Russ. *suprematizm.*] An artistic movement initiated by the Russian painter Kazimir Malevich in 1913; the abstract, geometrical style of art produced by this movement. Hence **Supre·matist**¹ (*a*) *sb.*, an adherent of Suprematism; (*b*) *adj.*, of, pertaining to, or characteristic of Suprematism.

[**1915** K. MALEVICH (*title*) Ot Kubizma do Suprematizma.] **1933** *Times Lit. Suppl.* 2 Feb. 76/3 The various channels in which the Futurist movement has run.. orphism..suprematism. **1936** *Bull. Museum of Mod. Art* Nov.–Dec. 6 Malevich, the Suprematist, passed through a proto-Dada phase in 1914. **1948** H. READ *Art Now* (ed. 3) iv. 104 Malevich and Tatlin revolted against the naturalistic tradition and established a completely geometrical style which they called *Suprematism.* **1955** *Archit. Rev.* CXVII. 226/1 Malevitsch, in *Bauhausbuch* No. 11, hopefully says of his own filleted and rectilinear aesthetic 'thus one may also call Suprematism an aeronautical art'. **1958** *Spectator* 14 Feb. 203/1 His Suprematist work exploiting a simple vocabulary of colours and shapes and rhythms. **1958** *Listener* 31 July 168/3 Malevich and the Suprematists reflected it, in a form so extreme and absolute that it led to the painting of a picture consisting of a white square on a white ground. **1972** [see *RAYONISM, RAYONNISM]. **1972** *Times* 13 Apr. 4/8 A Suprematist construction of about 1916..by Ivan Puni made £3,200. **1980** I. MURDOCH *Nuns & Soldiers* i. 80 He became a cubist, then a surrealist, then a *fauve*: a futurist, a constructivist, a suprematist.

suprematist²: see *white suprematist* s.v. *WHITE *a.* 11 e.

supreme, *a.* and *sb.* Add: **A.** *adj.* **2. a.** *Supreme Soviet*: the national legislature of the U.S.S.R.; also, the national legislature of any of its constituent republics.

1936 *Times* 15 June 11/4 The legislative assemblies will consist of one All-Union Parliament called the 'Supreme Council (or Supreme Soviet) of the U.S.S.R.'. **1947** *Ann. Reg. 1946* 218 M. Kalinin, chairman of the Presidium of the Supreme Soviet, resigned for reasons of health. **1957** *Whitaker's Almanack 1958* 950/1 The Union Republics and Autonomous Republics have Supreme Soviets..of their own..although their jurisdiction is severely circumscribed in favour of the central Government. **1974** tr. *Sniečkus's Soviet Lithuania* 67 The Supreme Soviet of the Lithuanian SSR has approved the Five-Year Plan for the economic development of the Republic for 1971–5. **1978** *Ann. Reg. 1977* 490 Article 90 [of the Constitution of the USSR 1977]. The term of the Supreme Soviet of the USSR, the Supreme Soviets of Union Republics, and the Supreme Soviets of Autonomous Republics shall be five years.

3. a. *the supreme sacrifice*: the laying down of one's life for one's country in battle. Also *transf.*

1916 W. M. CLOW *Evangel of Strait Gate* xv. 173 These young men..have gone down not only to the horror of the battlefield but to the gates of death as they made the supreme sacrifice. **1935** J. E. C. WELLDON *Forty Years On* i. 46 Citizenship demands at times the supreme sacrifice—as it was called during the Great War of 1914–18. **1955** J. BURNABY *Christian Words & Christian Meanings* vi. 104 The 'supreme sacrifice', in the cliché of the wartime newspaper, does consist in the carrying of disregard of self to the limit. **1965** J. A. MICHENER *Source* (1966) 491 Because He [*sc.* Christ] offered Himself as the supreme sacrifice two things happened. We were saved and He ascended to Godhood. **1981** HINCHLIFF & YOUNG *Human Potential* v. 98 When one speaks of the dead of two world wars as having made the supreme sacrifice, one means that the sacrifice was made for..one's country.

B. *sb.* **5.** *supreme of chicken* = *suprême de volaille* s.v. *SUPRÊME *sb.* (*a.*) 2 a.

1939 *Vogue's Cookery Bk.* 81 Supreme of Chicken. 1 chicken 4 eggs 1½ cups cream. **1959** A. CHRISTIE *Cat among Pigeons* xiv. 154 Ann Shapland..was sitting at a table..eating Supreme of chicken. **1983** *Out of Town* Dec. 72/2 The pastry case on the Supreme of Chicken.. was a little too generous.

‖ **suprême** (süprẹm), *sb.* (*a.*) [F., f. L. *suprēmus*: see SUPREME *a.* and *sb.*] **1.** A kind of sauce (see quot. 1906). Also ‖ *sauce suprême, suprême sauce.*

1813 L. E. UDE *French Cook* viii. 191 (*heading*) Filets of fowls sautés au suprême. **1846** A. SOYER *Gastronomic Regenerator* 342 Fillet three fowls.., sauté the same,.. sauce over with a sauce suprême. **1906** *Mrs. Beeton's Bk. Househ. Managem.* lxii. 1671 *Suprême*, a rich, delicately flavoured cream sauce, made from chicken stock, etc. **1936** LUCAS & HUME *Au Petit Cordon Bleu* 73 Pour over the following *suprême* sauce. **1948** *Good Housek. Cookery Bk.* 303 Suprême Sauce. Make as for Velouté sauce, but add up to ¼ pint of cream. **1961** *Harper's Bazaar* Feb. 72/2 There are three kinds of *roux*... Pale—for making *veloutés*, *suprême* sauces and *allemande* sauce.

2. a. In full, *suprême de volaille*: a dish consisting of breast of chicken or other poultry usu. served with a white sauce. **b.** The part of the bird used in making *suprême de volaille.*

1850 THACKERAY *Pendennis* II. i. 6 The supreme de volaille was very good. **1864** M. B. CHESNUT *Diary* 31 Jan. in C. V. Woodward *Mary Chesnut's Civil War* (1981) xxii. 551 Gumbo, ducks and olives, suprême de volaille. **1907** [see *JARDINIÈRE 2]. **1944** A. SIMON *Conc. Encycl. Gastron.* VI. Birds 111/2 The suprêmes are constituted by the meat on each side of the breast, from the point where the wing originates to the extremity of the stomach. **1975** *Times* 22 Feb. 7/2 Chicken Neptune—a suprême stuffed with prawns and butter and served with a shellfish sauce (£2.20). **1979** J. TOVEY *Entertaining with Tovey* 61 For cream soups I use a chicken..stock. Use..the bones of a bird from which you have cut the suprêmes. **1983** *Sunday Tel.* 17 Apr. 18/5 While they ladle out the mulligatawny or dish out the *suprême de volaille.*

supremo (sŭprī·mo, sŭprẹ̄¹·mo), *sb.* [f. Sp. (*generalissimo*) *supremo* supreme general.] **a.** A supreme leader or ruler; one holding the highest military or political authority.

The reference in quot. 1944 is to Earl Mountbatten of Burma, whose nickname this was during his period as Supreme Allied Commander, South-East Asia (cf. quot. 1966).

1937 C. S. FORESTER *Happy Return* iv. 43 No expostulation on his part would override the orders given by el Supremo. *Ibid.* 46 'Supremo,' sighed Hernandez... 'The captain came instantly on hearing your summons.' **1944** *Daily Express* 6 July 2/7 Why the Supremo?.. A handsome, romantic figure. Hence the Latin-sounding nickname. **1958** *Ibid.* 11 July 1/1 Now their advice and complaints can reach the Cabinet or the Prime Minister only through their 'supremo'—the chairman of the staff chiefs. **1966** E. H. COOKRIDGE *From Battenberg to Mountbatten* ix. 188 In June 1946 Lord Mountbatten's post as Supremo in South-East Asia came to an end and he returned to England. **1979** A. FOX *Threat Warning Red* ii. 21 Pat Cleary, a two-star British admiral, was the representative in Brussels of the American NATO supremo in Norfolk, Virginia.

b. *transf.* One who has overall charge of some department of government or sphere of activity.

1963 *Daily Express* 21 Oct. 1/4 Some, particularly in the Research Department, may follow the supremos into resignation. **1972** *Observer* 10 Dec. 2/7 The appointment of a Land Release Supremo with regional teams to unclog the machinery which is holding up the release of land. **1976** H. WILSON *Governance of Britain* iv. 97 The successful attack by other ministers to prevent him [*sc.* Herbert

Morrison] from becoming an economic supremo. **1983** *Private Eye* 17 June 7/1 A short list of possible replacements..included..the ruthless supremo of the Royal Philharmonic Orchestra.

supremum (s(i)uprī·mŏm). *Math.* [L., = highest, neut. of *suprēmus* (see SUPREME *a.* and *sb.*).] The smallest number that is greater than or equal to each of a given set of real numbers; an analogous quantity for a subset of any other ordered set.

1940, 1949 [see *INFIMUM]. **1968** E. T. COPSON *Metric Spaces* i. 13 An ordered field *S* is said to have the supremum property if and only if every non-empty subset of *S*..has a supremum in *S*. **1971** HADLEY & KEMP *Variational Methods in Economics* ii. 53 We now define U* as the supremum of levels of utility which can be maintained indefinitely.

suq, var. *SOUK.

sur-, *prefix.* Add: **sura·nal** *a. Zool.* = *supra-anal* adj. s.v. SUPRA- 1 b; also as *sb.*, a suranal plate; **surhu·man** *a. Lit.* = SUPERHUMAN *a.* (cf. F. *surhumain*).

1906 J. B. SMITH *Explan. Terms Entomol.* 135 *Suranal*, supra-anal. **1925** A. D. IMMS *Gen. Textbk. Entomol.* 41 The tergum of the last segment, whatever its numerical designation may be, is frequently referred to as the suranal plate or pygidium. **1962** D. NICHOLS *Echinoderms* v. 66 In the urchin immediately after metamorphosis the whole of the aboral surface is covered by an apical disk of plates, consisting of a central suranal, through which the anus opens, a ring of five basals, [etc.]. **1933** T. E. LAWRENCE *Let.* 1 Aug. (1938) 773 He takes figures of to-day and projects their shadows on to clouds, till they grow surhuman and grotesque. **1952** E. POUND *Personae* 56 Beauty That seems to be some quivering splendour cast By the immortal nature on this quicksand And by surhuman fates.

surah. (Earlier example.)

1873 *Young Englishwoman* May 234/1 Surah is a kind of twilled Indian silk tissue, extremely soft and brilliant.

suramin (sū·rămin). *Pharm.* Also **Suramin.** [Etym. unknown: perh. f. SURRA.] A complex symmetric urea used in the treatment of trypanosomiasis and filariasis. Also *suramin sodium.*

1941 *Brit. Pharmacopœia 1932* Add. iv. 33 Suramin is the symmetrical urea of the sodium salt of *m*-benzoyl-*m*-amino-*p*-methylbenzoyl-1-aminonaphthalene-4:6:8-trisulphonic acid. **1951** A. GROLLMAN *Pharmacol. & Therapeutics* xx. 416 Atoxyl..was the first drug used successfully in trypanosomiasis. Tryparsamide..was an improvement and with Suramin..is effective in the treatment of the early stage of the disease before the organisms appear in the spinal fluid. **1974** *Encycl. Brit. Micropædia* IX. 687/3 Suramin sodium, a white or pinkish powder soluble in water, is administered in an aqueous or saline solution. **1978** *Nature* 22 June 627/1 Three anti-trypanosomal drugs are listed by the WHO as essential for the treatment of human sleeping sickness caused by African trypanosomiasis. They are melarsoprol (Mel B), pentamidine (Lomidine) and suramin (Antrypol, Germanin).

surbahar (sā·ɹbahāɹ). [Bengali *surbāhār.*] A mellow-toned Indian stringed instrument or esraj, larger than a sitar.

1896 S. M. TAGORE *Universal Hist. Mus.* 88 A distinguished musician Babu Kally Prosonno Banerji..plays skilfully on the *Víná*, *Sur-báhár* and *Setár*. **1914** A. H. F. STRANGWAYS *Music of Hindostan* iii. 88 Next to the expressive *vinā* comes the dignified *surbahar*. **1927** *Grove's Dict. Mus.* (ed. 3) II. 706/1 The *Surbahar* (Calcutta) has sympathetic strings, a mellow tone, is fatiguing to play and expensive to buy. **1969** R. SHANKAR *My Music* i. 37/1 A cousin of the sitar is the large, deep-toned *surbahar*. **1979** *Radio Times* 6–12 Jan. 54/6 (*heading*) Imrat Khan plays surbahar and sitar.

surcharge, *sb.*[2] Add: **7.** *Civil Engin.* **a.** The part of a load that is above the horizontal plane containing the top of a retaining wall. **b.** A load placed upon uncompacted material to compress it.

1881 *Van Nostrand's Mag.* XXV. 336/2 The author found a wall of slag blocks having a batter of ⅓ of the height, and an effective thickness of 1 foot sustained a bank of broken slag 10 feet high, with a surcharge of some 5 feet more. **1930** *Engineering* 30 May 689/3 The heavy 24-in. steel beam..was intended for applying a surcharge to the filling in the bin. **1967** C. A. O'FLAHERTY *Highways* xii. 597 A surcharge of uncompacted material is added on top [of the embankment] to accelerate the outflow of water and the compaction of the underlying compressible material.

† **surculus.** *Bot. Obs.* Pl. **surculi.** [L., = young twig, branch, shoot.] (See quots. 1775, 1849.)

1775 ASH, *Surculus*, a shoot, a sucker, a slip; a middle branch between the larger and smaller ribs of a leaf. **1826** KIRBY & SPENCE *Introd. Entomol.* III. 227 The cocoon..is fastened by one side to the roots or surculi of Typha latifolia. **1849** J. H. BALFOUR *Man. Bot.* 639 *Surculus*, a sucker proceeding from the neck of a plant, and afterwards rooting, as in the Rose.

surd, *sb.* Add: **1.** (See also quots.) (Further examples.)

1908 G. H. HARDY *Course Pure Math.* i. 7 If a is a rational number, the two numbers $\pm\sqrt{a}$ are either rational or irrational, and..*generally* the latter. Numbers of this kind, when irrational, are called pure quadratic surds. A number $a\pm\sqrt{b}$..is sometimes called a mixed quadratic surd. **1959** G. & R. C. JAMES *Math. Dict.* 379/2 *Surd*, a sum of one or more irrational indicated roots of numbers. Sometimes used for irrational number. **1962** H. COHN *Second Course in Number Theory* iii. 40 If a, b, c are integers..we define the conjugate surds $\lambda=(a+b\sqrt{D})/c$, $\lambda'=(a-b\sqrt{D})/c$.

sure, *a.* and *adv.* Add: **III. 8. f.** Colloq. phr. *don't (you) be too sure*, do not depend too confidently (upon something).

1866 MAYNE REID *Headless Horseman* iii. 16 'Don't be too sure, all of ye,' said the surly nephew. **1916** G. B. SHAW *Pygmalion* v. 189 But dont you be too sure that you have me under your feet to be trampled on and talked down. **1942** T. BAILEY *Pink Camellia* xviii. 98 Don't be too sure. You're the girl I want, and I'm going to have you.

IV. 9. c. Now often in phr. *that's for sure*, placed at the end of the sentence.

1971 C. BONINGTON *Annapurna South Face* xiii. 156 We can't do it in the next two days..—that's for sure. **1981** C. ROSS *Scaffold* 106 Well, who's telling? Not me, that's for sure.

d. *sure thing*, a certainty, a secure prospect; freq. as asseverative affirmation: Yes, indeed! Also as *attrib. phr. colloq.* (orig. *U.S.*).

1836 J. HILDRETH *Dragoon Campaigns Rocky Mts.* 24, I say, stranger, didn't I say that old 'Slow and Easy' was a sure thing, in the end? **1848** *Sporting Life* 22 Jan. 269/1 Teetotum had the call for the July in the betting, and it was booked a sure thing for her. **1896** ADE *Artie* ii. 9 You never see such a sure-thing crowd in your life. *Ibid.* xvi. 147 'Sure thing,' says he. **1908** J. M. SULLIVAN *Criminal Slang* 2 *Sure thing gambler*, character who bets with suckers at race tracks. **1933** D. L. SAYERS *Murder must Advertise* v. 91 'Should you care to make one in our next dope-raid?' 'Sure thing. When do you expect it?' **1943** *Sun* (Baltimore) 22 Apr. 18/1 Ralph Root apparently thought Overlin was a sure thing. Roberts drew his whip. **1953** W. BURROUGHS *Junkie* iii. 38, I had one of his sure-thing croakers reach for a telephone on me. **1962** P. GREGORY *Like Tigress at Bay* v. 63 'Sure thing, boss,' she said lightly. **1963** N. MARSH *Dead Water* (1964) vi. 158, I appreciate your reluctance to form a theory too soon... But..it looks a sure thing to me. **1979** C. MACLEOD *Family Vault* xxiii. 150 'Would you mind getting this box for us?' 'Sure thing, Mr Verplanck.'

10. c. *sure-fire* adj. phr., certain to succeed or attain the desired end (occas. in predicative use). *colloq.* (orig. *U.S.*). Less frequently, *sure-shot* (chiefly *U.S.*).

[**1901** 'H. MCHUGH' *Down Line* 93 Swift often told himself that he could give Marshall P. Wilder six sure-fires and beat him down to the wire.] **1909** P. G. WILLIAMS in *Sat. Even. Post* 5 June 17/2 *Sure fire*, certain of success. **1912** *Variety* 18 May 8/2 The Rev. William Sunday (Billy) the evangelist or sure-fire evangelist, has done one of the worst 'financial flops' in the history of his travels. **1914** [see *FIXER 1]. **1926** WHITEMAN & MCBRIDE *Jazz* viii. 171 In the old days, it took six months to spread even the most sure-fire song over the United States. **1933** D. L. SAYERS *Murder must Advertise* iii. 41 He thought it was a sure-fire mascot. **1941** B. SCHULBERG *What makes Sammy Run?* ii. 28 The most surefire story sale that's come to Hollywood in years. **1952** J. STEINBECK *East of Eden* 79 The preacher turned over his hole-card, the sure-fire card. **1960** G. E. EVANS *Horse in Furrow* vi. 82 You could get a *sure-shot* cigar for tuppence in those days. **1967** N. FREELING *Strike out if not Applicable* 14 He had certain surefire jokes that were repeated all over Holland. **1974** G. F. NEWMAN *Price* vii. 238 Buy into Nu-Schoenberg... They're sure-fire, I promise you. **1983** *Listener* 16 June 8/1 The search for a sure-fire hit in American network television engages thousands of minds and millions of dollars every year.

B. *adv.* **3. a.** Now also *N. Amer. colloq.* (freq. introduced between subj. and vb., as a mere intensive).

1861 *Trans. Illinois Agric. Soc.* IV. 460 Once successfully transplanted it will live sure. **1876** 'MARK TWAIN' *Tom Sawyer* iv. 83 They're coming, sure. **1908** 'YESLAH' *Tenderfoot S. Calif.* i. 14 It sure was a cold night. **1933** J. COZZENS *Cure of Flesh* i. 20 Sure, the truck came. Is anything wrong? **1953** *Manch. Guardian Weekly* 22 Jan. 7 You sure left an awful mess in Washington. **1969** A. LURIE *Real People* 106 Parts of it were pretty, sure. In a phony way, like this place. **1975** R. DAVIES *World of Wonders* (1977) i. vii. 83 You didn't need feet to fly a plane, but you sure needed brains.

c. For *dial.* read '*colloq.* and *dial.*' and add earlier example. Now chiefly *N. Amer.* in independent affirmative use.

1803 G. COLMAN *John Bull* i. 4 *Den.* Troth, and myself, Mr. Dennis Brulgruddery, was brought up to the church. *Dan.* Why, zure! **1914** WODEHOUSE *Man Upstairs* 133 'Is that a fact?' 'Sure,' murmured Archibald. **1963** MRS. L. B. JOHNSON *White House Diary* 26 Nov. (1970) 11 If it had been a request to chop off one's right hand one would have said, 'Sure'. **1975** R. STOUT *Family Affair* xi. 130 I'm under arrest. I asked if you could finish your lunch, and they said sure, no hurry.

4. a. (Further examples.) *sure as hell* (U.S. slang), most certainly; (*as*) *sure as God made little apples*, etc.: see *APPLE *sb.* 1 b.

1824 SCOTT in *Edin. Weekly Jrnl.* 9 June 181/3 As sure as ever ye sit there, She'll tell the Bailie. **1828** J. NEAL *Rachel Dyer* xix. 238 He will get away if you turn your head... That he will! if you don't look sharp, as sure as my name is Peter P. **1856** C. M. YONGE *Daisy Chain* i. ii. 13 Madam, said I, you'll have to answer for your mother's death, as sure as my name's Dick May. **1944** E. S. GARDNER *Case of Black-Eyed Blonde* xx. 194 I'm telling you just as sure as you're sitting there, that if you don't get men out to Jason Bartsler's place, a murder is going to be committed. **1976** *Listener* 6 May 562/3 Wayne ..introduces me to Commemorativo Tequilla. 'It doesn't hurt your head, but it may hurt your back, as you sure as hell fall over a lot.'

C. Comb. *sure-handed* adj.

1930 M. MEAD *Growing up in New Guinea* iii. 23 The decisive, angry gesture..has taught him to be alert and sure-handed. **1962** *Times* 26 Feb. 4/1 [The French rugby team] were able to start attacks..and, surehanded, to develop them.

surefootedly, *adv.* (Examples.)

1936 *Discovery* Aug. 242/1 Clambering sure-footedly about the larger..trunks. **1977** *Times Lit. Suppl.* 15 Apr. 449/2 Walks surefootedly through the minefield that separates fulsome idolatry from condescending anecdotal chit-chat.

surely, *adv.* **II. 4. a.** (*b*) (Later examples.)

1876 C. M. YONGE *Three Brides* II. viii. 152 'I must go. Can I?' 'Surely, as soon as there is a train.' **1922** E. RAYMOND *Tell England* ii. i. 166 'Surely,' answered my companion, which was a new way he had acquired of saying 'yes'. **1975** M. RUSSELL *Murder by Mile* iii. 19 'Like to follow me along?' 'Surely.'

‖**Sûreté** (sürte). [Fr., = SURETY *sb.*, security.] In full, *Sûreté nationale*, the French police department of criminal investigation, controlled by the Ministry of the Interior. Also *transf.* of similar forces elsewhere.

Since 1966 amalgamated with the Prefecture of Police of Paris in the *Police Nationale*. The department was previously known as the *Sûreté générale* and the *Service de la Sûreté*, and was latterly also responsible for policing the provincial towns of France.

1871 *Observer* 9 Apr. 6/4 M. Ranc..was the chief of the *Sûreté Generale* under Gambetta. **1885** *Encycl. Brit.* XIX. 343/2 The *service de sûreté*, or detective department (out of uniform)..comprises a commissary, principal inspectors, brigadiers, and 211 inspectors. **1917** J. F. MACDONALD *Two Towns—One City* iii. i. 192 This foreign gentleman..represents the *Sûreté* (or Criminal Investigation Department) of Paris. **1926** D. L. SAYERS *Clouds of Witness* iii. 94, I have written to the Sûreté and the Crédit Lyonnais to produce his papers. **1935** A. CHRISTIE *Death in Clouds* xi. 115 At the Sûreté Poirot renewed acquaintance with the Chief of the Detective Force. **1955** *Times* 9 May 8/3 The Binh Xuyen garrison which has been occupying the headquarters of the Sûreté in Saigon. **1963** A. ORLOV *Handbk. Intelligence & Guerrilla Warfare* xii. 143 An old Soviet informant who was an officer of the French Sûreté Générale (Secret Police). **1973** 'M. INNES' *Appleby's Answer* x. 97 The great Vidocq, who transformed the efficiency of the Paris Sûreté by..insisting that his detectives should never forget a face. **1980** R. GRAYSON *Monterant Affair* xi. 94 The hotel was..within easy walking distance of Sûreté headquarters.

surf, *sb.* Add: **3.** Simple attrib., as *surf-beach, -beat, line*; locative, as *surf-bathe* vb., *-fish* vb., *-fisherman, -fishing* (examples), *lifesaver, lifesaving, -rider, -riding* (earlier example), *-swimming* (example); **surfboard** (later examples); hence as *v. intr.*, to ride on a surfboard (also *fig.*); **surfboarder, surf-boarding** *vbl. sb.*; **surf-bum** *slang*, a surfing enthusiast who frequents beaches suitable for surf-riding; cf. *ski bum* s.v. *SKI *sb.* 2 b; **surf-casting** *vbl. sb.*, fishing by casting a line into the sea from the shore; so (as a back-formation) **surf-cast** *v. intr.*, **surf-caster; surf-clam** (examples); **surf day,** a day marked by rough surf along the shore (see quot. 1854); **surf-grass,** any of several species of marine grass of the genus *Phyllospadix* (family Zosteraceæ), having thickened rootstocks and slender stems and growing underwater on rocky shores in temperate regions; **surf music,** a variety of rock music which celebrates the sport of surf-riding; **surf-ride** *v. intr.* [back-formation from *surf-riding* above] = *surf-board* vb. above; also *fig.* and as *v. trans.* and *sb.*; **surf safari** = *SURFARI.

1940 V. BRITTAIN *Testament of Friendship* xii. 192 You'll look at the Rhodes Memorial and the Union Buildings..; you'll..surf-bathe at Durban.., and then you'll begin to think you know everything. **1932** N. PALMER *Talking it Over* 137 Surf-beaches of any size are rare in the world. **1966** *Weekly News* (N.Z.) 19 Jan. 11/1 Mt. Maunganui is probably one of New Zealand's best-known surf beaches. **1977** *Herald* (Melbourne) 17 Jan. 14/4 Within 16 km of Wollongong are 17 superb surf beaches. **1873** 'MARK TWAIN' *Gilded Age* lx. 543 A receding of tides, a quieting of the storm-wash to a murmurous surf-beat. **1974** *Encycl. Brit. Micropædia* IX. 689/2 Surf beat, ocean waves of uncertain origin, with the relatively long periods of 1 to 5 minutes. These low-frequency waves appear to be related to the interaction of normal wind waves and swell. Surf beat is believed responsible for the generation of seiches in bays. **1931** T. E. LAWRENCE *Let.* 14 July (1938) 729 Here is a final report..on the little surf-board target. **1934** WEBSTER, *Surfboard, v.i.*, to ride the surf on a surfboard.—*surfboarding, n.* **1938** E. HEMINGWAY *Fifth Column* (1939) iii. iv. 103 Or what about Malindi where you can surfboard on the beach. **1962** *Coast to Coast 1961–62* 63 He wished he could stand up and walk away from Pammie and go out with the surfboard riders. **1962** M. McLuhan *Gutenberg Galaxy* 248 (*heading*) Heidegger surf-boards along on the electronic wave as triumphantly as Descartes rode the mechanical wave. **1953** *Pop. Mechanics* July 157 Hitching a ride on a beach-bound ocean wave with a featherlight surf-board is rated tops in water sports by practiced surf-boarders. **1969** *Britannica Bk. of Year 1968* 801/1 *Surfari*, a group of surfboarders who travel together in search of good surfing areas. **1964** *Sunday Mail Mag.* (Brisbane) 17 May 1 Surfboarding was virtually forgotten until the late 1930's. **1958** Surf-bum [see *petite *a.* 2]. **1971** Surf-bum [see *pipe-line *sb.* c]. **1975** *Country Life* 16 Jan. 131/2 Surf-cast for corvina..on a California beach and you will probably have to show your California fishing licence. **1968** 'S. Jay' *Sleepers can Kill* xxiv. 248 When you've walked through to the beach, you'll see a surfcaster, fishing by himself. **1928** *N.Y. Times* 8 Oct. 21/4 Charles Vollum of Philadelphia became surf casting champion of the United States today at the annual tournament of the Dover Fishing Club of Philadelphia. **1963** *Weekly News* (Auckland, N.Z.) 8 May 56/6 Pukehina surfcasting beach. Near Te Puke, Bay of Plenty, one of the best surfcasting beaches in New Zealand. **1979** *Angling* July 45/3 As a contemporary guide to the basics of general shorefishing it gives excellent surfcasting instruction. **1884** *Bull. U.S. Nat. Museum* No. 27. 260 Hen Clam, Surf Clam, or Sea Clam. Florida and Gulf of Mexico to Labrador. **1949** [see *skimmer *sb.* 1c]. **1978** *Times* 29 July 3/6 More than two weeks after the wreck..we saw millions of dead molluscs, urchins, razor and surf clams. **1854** G. W. Peck *Melbourne & Chincha Islands* 187 Often when the mornings are still, and the surface of the sea undisturbed by a ripple, the surf will be rolling tremendously on the narrow beaches... These are called 'surf-days', and special allowance is made for them in the charter parties of vessels loading at the islands. **1950** J. S. Learmont *Master in Sail* 60 Surf days did not count as working days. These surf days are peculiar to the northern part of the coast of Chile. **1940** O. H. P. Rodman *Handbk. Salt-Water Fishing* iii. 99 We will make a definite statement in regard to wetting down your cutty hunk line before you really start surf fishing. **1979** 'A. Blaisdell' *No Villain need Be* vii. 120 They like to surf-fish, and they claim rain..drives 'em in toward the beach. **1920** Heilner & Stick *Call of Surf* i. 5 Those great and goodly fish which so frequently take into their capacious jaws the bait of the surf fisherman. **1967** O. E. Middleton in *Coast to Coast 1965–66* 123 The surf-fishermen leaned out over the shallows. **1920** Heilner & Stick *Call of Surf* i. 4 Surf fishing is by no means a new development of the angler's art..but only of late years has it begun to achieve real popularity. **1949** S. K. Farrington *Fishing the Atlantic* iv. 82 Surf fishing at Narragansett should be a revelation. **1923** L. Abrams *Illustr. Flora Pacific States* I. 94 *Phyllospadix torreyi* S. Wats. Torrey's Surf-grass. **1981** *Sci. Amer.* Mar. 92/1 The sea grasses number 12 genera and..about 50 species... Eelgrass and surfgrass are familiar examples in temperate regions. **1977** *N.Z. Herald* 8 Jan. 1–6/4, I have been talking to the wife of a surf lifesaver, and she spoke of the apparent indifference people show on being saved from drowning. **1968** W. Warwick *Surfriding in N.Z.* 1 It is difficult to imagine how closely it was once associated with the surf lifesaving movement. **1887** O. J. Humphrey *Wreck of Rainier* 33 When the surf line was hauled tight the boat would run on the line and be kept head to the sea. **1923** H. Belloc *Sonnets & Verse* 1. 28 Above the surf-line, into the night-breeze; Eastward above the ever-whispering trees. **1965** P. L. Dixon *Compl. Bk. Surfing* 142 If the dory broaches in the surf line and turns over, bail out and get clear of oars and falling boat. **1965** *N.Z. Listener* 17 Dec. 4/1 The million-dollar industry of surf music, surf movies and surf-wear. **1977** *Sounds* 9 July 28/2 The Turtles started out playing surf music at High School hops in LA. **1953** 'S. Rattray' *Bishop in Check* 101 One-half per cent of them play tennis—or swim, or surf-ride. **1958** *Listener* 2 Oct. 494/1 This motorization wave is not something on which the rich alone can surf-ride. **1973** *Times* 1 June (Australia Suppl.) p. i/3 The Whitlam Government has been in office just six months tomorrow. For the Prime Minister it has been 'a surf ride so far'. **1976** *National Observer* (U.S.) 19 June 1/3 Now, surf-riding his victory in the California Presidential primary last week, he's racing to a showdown with Gerald Ford. **1882** *Hawaiian Almanac* 52 At one time they sent their champion surf-rider to compete with chiefs in the sport at Hawaii. **1981** L. Leamer *Assignment* iii. 43 They take this drug. They have learned this from these hippie surf-riders. **1882** *Hawaiian Almanac* 52 Among the various sports and pastimes of the ancient Hawaiians..the principal one..is that of surf-bathing, or more properly speaking, surf-riding. **1962** *Austral. Women's Weekly* 24 Oct. (Suppl.) 3/4 *Surf safari*, a trip around different beaches to find a good surf. **1858** R. M. Ballantyne *Coral Island* xxv. 305 'What sort of amusement is this surf swimming?'.. 'Each man..has got a short board or plank, with which he swims a mile or more to Sea, and then, gettin' on the top o' yon thunderin' breaker, they come to shore on the top of it.'

surf, *v.* Restrict *rare* to sense in Dict. and add: **2.** *intr.* To go surf-riding; to surf-ride. Also *transf.* and *fig.*

1917 *Chambers's Jrnl.* Apr. 280/2 The depth of the lagoon is trifling.., and this it is which makes surfing there so safe and enjoyable. **1932** *Ibid.* Aug. 462/2, I had snaps, too, of the children, riding or surfing, and of the whole family in their ocean-going yacht. *a* **1957** R. Campbell *Coll. Poems* (1960) III. 83 Over its surge in red tornadoes rolling My heart goes surfing on the waves of fire. **1965** *N.Z. Listener* 17 Dec. 4/5 Once a person is bitten by this surfing bug he seems to become insatiable. He surfs every day he can, the whole year round. **1970** *Motor Boat & Yachting* 16 Oct. 29/1 *La Russhe* surfed handsomely down the backs of the heavy swell and buried herself into the short steep seas on the way. **1976** M. Birmingham *Heat of Sun* iv. 51 Biriwa has..a comparatively safe beach..where you can surf when the tide is right.

3. *trans.* **a.** To ride (a boat) on the surf. **b.** To surf-ride at (a specified place).

1965 P. L. Dixon *Compl. Bk. Surfing* 18 Dories, canoes, sailing catamarans, and a few special motorboats can be surfed by experts. Where waves break far from shore and spill gradually forward. **1967** W. Murray *Sweet Ride* vi. 85 Ten years ago..no one surfed this place but him. **1968** *Surfer Mag.* Jan. 56/1 Paulo surfed a beach break off the famous Rio Copacabana called Posto Six Pier.

Hence **su·rfing** *vbl. sb.*, surf-riding, surf-boarding.

1955 A. Ross *Australia 55* xv. 214 The essential art of surfing is timing. **1959** H. Hobson *Mission House Murder* xviii. 119 When they'd had enough surfing, they brought the boards back up the beach. **1963** *Wall St. Jrnl.* 22 July 1 Surfin' music is characterized by a heavy echo guitar sound, supposed to simulate the roar of the surf. **1971** 'D. Halliday' *Dolly & Doctor Bird* i. 2 Skin diving, rum punches, calypso night-clubs, surfing, dancing, gambling.

surface, *sb.* Add: **1. b.** Also, *to scratch the surface (of)*: see *scratch *v.* 3 a.

3. f. *Aeronautics.* An aerofoil, considered as something whose intended effects arise superficially.

1843 *Mechanics' Mag.* 8 Apr. 277/2 The main surfaces.. are here placed one above the other, and each pair are connected together by strong shafts. **1912** W. Wright in C. C. Turner *Romance of Aeronautics* xvii. 178 A smaller surface set at a negative angle in front of the main bearing surfaces or wings will largely counteract the effect of the fore-and-aft travel of the centre of pressure. **1930** P. H. Sumner *Marine Aircraft* ii. 104 The larger the aeroplane the larger the control surfaces become and the loads necessary to move elevators, rudder and ailerons may become too heavy for the pilot to operate their surfaces. **1974** *Encycl. Brit. Macropædia* I. 377/1 The essential components of an airplane are a wing system to sustain it in flight, tail surfaces to stabilize the wing, movable surfaces (ailerons, elevators, and rudders) to control the attitude of the machine in flight, [etc.].

g. *surface-to-air, surface-to-surface* adj. phrs., of, pertaining to, or designating a guided missile designed to be launched from the ground or at sea, and directed respectively at a target either in the air, or elsewhere on the earth's surface. Cf. *air-to-air* adj. s.v. *air *sb.*[1] B. III. 1; *ground-to-air, ground-to-ground* s.v. *ground *sb.* 17 d; SAM s.v. S. 4 a.

1950 *Sun* (Baltimore) 7 Feb. 1/2 Research continues on these surface-to-air missiles. **1951** D. C. Cooke *Jets, Rockets & Guided Missiles* 146 This is a Surface-to-Surface Missile, Air Force, Third Model, Second Modification. **1954** *Jrnl. Brit. Interplanetary Soc.* XIII. 164 One of the first G.E.C. missiles, the Hermes A-1 is a development of the German Wasserfall in a surface-to-surface rôle. **1959** *Listener* 4 June 984/3 A British Thunderbird surface-to-air guided missile. **1962** *Times* 11 Aug. 6/1 The Government yesterday made their expected announcement that Blue Water, the surface-to-surface guided missile..is to be cancelled. **1978** P. McCutchan *Blackmail North* vi. 69 Russia's been supplying Libya with a big range of surface-to-surface and surface-to-air missiles.

6. a. *attrib.* in lit. sense, as *surface film* (also *spec.* in sense (*b*)); (*a*) in reference to the surface of the ground, as *surface exploration, find* (both *Archæol.*), *worker.*

1949 W. F. Albright *Archaeol. of Palestine* iii. 49 The great increase of surface exploration in Palestine in the middle decades of the nineteenth century. **1903** *Proc. R. Soc.* LXXII. 222 The influence of the stroking is therefore limited to a very thin surface film. **1981** O. N. Bishop *Physics* xvii. 161/2 The liquid closest to the surface of the object may show adhesion with it; there is often a surface film of liquid which is carried along with the object. **1917** Surface find [see *Iroquoian *a.* and *sb.*]. **1977** *Antiquaries Jrnl.* LVII. 324 The seal-matrices..derive either from excavations or from surface-finds at known sites. **1963** *Times* 2 Mar. 8/5 The miners' demands include pensions at 50 for underground workers and at 55 for surface workers.

(*d*) *Naut.* Designating ships which move on the surface of the water as opp. to submarine vessels, as *surface craft, ship, vessel, warship,* etc.; also *Comb.*, as *surface-borne, -sailing* adjs.

1905 *Trans. Inst. Naval Archit.* XLVII. 407 Misconceptions exist..as to the relative chances of accidents happening to boats compared with surface craft. **1910** C. W. Domville-Fife *Submarines of World's Navies* ii. 101 This is if the surface warship was steaming in an erratic course. **1915** W. E. Dommett *Submarine Vessels* 5 The term 'submersible vessels' should..be reserved for those which, whilst mainly surface vessels, can be brought to an awash or submerged condition. **1928** C. F. S. Gamble *Story North Sea Air Station* xiii. 224 A pilot might sight..a submarine and a surface-borne craft like a cruiser or destroyer. **1939** *Sun* (Baltimore) 17 Apr. 9/1 The North Haven surface ship to be used in transporting supplies, will carry 314,000 separate items. **1945** *Army & Navy Jrnl.* 18 Aug. 1534 *ASV, Airborne Surface Vessel Detection*, airborne radar devices used to locate surface vessels and surfacing submarines. **1954** *Ann. Reg. 1953* 337 *The Tirpitz*..a well-documented account of the career and sinking of the war-time surface raider. **1975** *Listener* 17 June 77/2 The 'Bismarck'..was later sunk by surface vessels. **1982** A. Melville-Ross *Trigger* ii. 33 You don't have enough surface ships left for you to hoist your admiral's flag.

(*e*) In reference to (chiefly, public) transportation at ground- or sea-level, as opp. to underground or air carriage (orig. *U.S.*); cf. *surface car*, sense 6 d in Dict. Also, *spec.* applied to mail or post, as *surface letter, parcel*, etc.; cf. *surface mail*, sense 6 d below.

1906 'Mark Twain' *Let.* 5 May in C. Clemens *Mark Twain* (1932) 156 My daughters are frequently robbed by conductors on the surface lines. **1909** *N.Y. Even. Post* (Semi-weekly ed.) 4 Mar. 1 On streets leading to these ferries surface travel was blocked by heavily laden vehicles stalled. **1927** *New Republic* 12 Oct. 208/2 Chicago, alas! despite the fact that it could undoubtedly solve its transportation difficulties by surface carriage,.. has decided to go in for subways. **1933** *Jrnl. R. Central Asian Soc.* Jan. 81 Surface transport conditions for the necessary stores and spares are bad. **1934** *Air Mail Service* (G.P.O. Green Paper 1), The actual cost incurred for handling, surface transmission, and air conveyance. **1951** *Overseas Air Mails* (G.P.O.) Feb. 1/2 The general regulations applicable to ordinary surface parcels..apply to air parcels. **1956** L. Zilliacus *From Pillar to Post* xiii. 163 An ordinary surface letter..takes a week or more... By air it takes two or three days. **1977** *National Observer* (U.S.) 1 Jan. 2 Adams is also a critic of several leading schemes for deregulation of airlines and surface carriers.

(*f*) *Linguistics.* Of or pertaining to the level of language at which normal communication exists, as opposed to the underlying level revealed by 'deep' semantic and syntactic analysis, esp. as *surface grammar.* See also *surface structure*, sense 6 d below.

1953 G. E. M. Anscombe tr. *L. Wittgenstein's Philos. Investigations* 1. 168e In the use of words one might distinguish 'surface grammar' from 'depth grammar'. What immediately impresses itself upon us about the use of a word is the way it is used in the construction of the sentence, the part of its use..that can be taken in by the ear.—And now compare the depth grammar, say of the word 'to mean', with what its surface grammar would lead us to suspect. **1958** C. F. Hockett *Course in Mod. Linguistics* xxix. 249 This most apparent layer constitutes, we shall say, ***surface grammar.*** Beneath it lie various layers of ***deep grammar***, which have much to do with how we speak and understand but which are still largely unexplored, in any systematic way, by grammarians. **1965** N. Chomsky *Aspects of Theory of Syntax* 199 In place of the terms 'deep structure' and 'surface structure', one might use the corresponding Humboldtian notions 'inner form' of a sentence and 'outer form' of a sentence... The terms 'depth grammar' and 'surface grammar' are familiar in modern philosophy in something roughly like the sense here intended. **1967** D. G. Hays *Introd. Computational Linguistics* viii. 155 Their system begins with a surface parser. **1972** *Language* XLVIII. 678 His general discussion of what syntax is all about deals exclusively with surface phenomena, chiefly the order of elements in a sentence. **1977** *Word 1972* XXVIII. 92 Yet the simplest solution superficially is not necessarily the best, and a surface-oriented approach to *tá* predicates is faced with problems, too. **1981** A. C. Thiselton in *Believing in Church* iii. 51 Language is said to determine the scope and limits of thought on the basis of vocabulary-stock or even surface-grammar.

c. locative, as *surface-sow* vb.; *surface-sowing, -sown* (all chiefly *N.Z.*), *-swimming* adjs. and sbs.; objective, as *surface skimmer*; *surface sterilization* (hence *surface-sterilize* vb., *-sterilized* ppl. adj.).

1748 Richardson *Clarissa* III. 145, I love to plague thee, who are..a surface-skimmer in learning, with out-of-the-way words and phrases. *a* **1911** D. G. Phillips *Susan Lenox* (1917) I. xiii. 213 We shallow surface-skimmers make such a..fuss. **1921** H. Guthrie-Smith *Tutira* xix. 163 The land is surface-sown with grass and clover seed. **1882** W. D. Hay *Brighter Britain!* I. viii. 197 In spite of..the rough ground, and the mere surface-sowing, our grass will carry four sheep per acre. **1950** *N.Z. Jrnl. Agric.* Apr. 309/2 The uncertain establishment of plants from the surface sowing of clover seeds. *Ibid.* Feb. 121/1 The more fertile surface-sown hill country of the North Island. **1954** Kirk & Othmer *Encycl. Chem. Technol.* XII. 914 Ultraviolet radiation exhibits extremely low penetration. Because of this the major applications have been in air sanitation and surface sterilization of food products, packaging materials.., and working spaces. **1978** *Canad. Jrnl. Bot.* LVI. 226/1 Close the open end of the syringe with a syringe nose cap to keep the seeds and sterilizing solution from being ejected during surface sterilization. *Ibid.*, After the seed is surface sterilized, remove the nose cap and affix a sterile 18-gauge needle to the syringe. **1956** *Nature* 17 Mar. 534/2 The adult female mosquito was surface-sterilized by immersion for 2 min. in a 0·5 per cent solution of mercuric chloride in 50 per cent ethyl alcohol. The surface-sterilized insect was transferred to insect Ringer solution. **1967** K. M. Smith *Insect Virol.* ix. 165 Pupae were surface-sterilized in 70% ethanol for 5 minutes. **1978** *Canad. Jrnl. Bot.* LVI. 225 (*heading*) Rapid, contamination-free sowing of surface-sterilized seeds and spores. **1925** J. T. Jenkins *Fishes Brit. Isles* 73 The coryphænidæ are tropical and sub-tropical fish of pelagic or surface-swimming habits. **1970** *Commercial Fisheries Rev.* Apr. 4/1 The government of American Samoa seeks to broaden the islands' economic base by harvesting surface-swimming tunas.

d. surface-active *a. Physical Chem.*, (of a substance) able to affect the wetting or surface tension properties of a liquid; hence **surface-activity; surface blow** *Engin.*, a device by which the surface water and scum in a steam boiler may be blown off; hence **surface blow-off**, the act of discharging this scum; **surface casing** *Oil Industry*, the length of casing in a bore-hole which is nearest the surface; **surface chemistry**, the study of the chemical processes occurring at the boundaries between different phases; **surface couching** *Embroidery*, a form of couching (Couch *v.*[1] 4 b) in which the couched thread is held flat on the surface of the fabric by stitches looped over it (cf. *underside couching* s.v. *UNDERSIDE b); so **surface couched** *pa. pple.*; **surface effect,** any effect associated with, or only encountered near, a surface; also *attrib.*, esp. designating an air-cushion vehicle in which the cushion is sealed by rigid sidewalls and flexible seals fore and aft (cf. *SIDEWALL 3 b); **surface mail,** a postal service for conveying mail by land or sea, contrasted with *AIRMAIL; the mail conveyed; **surface noise,** a background hiss heard on reproduction of a gramophone record owing to irregularities in the surface of the groove walls; **surface-road** (examples); **surface shelter**: in the war of 1939–45, an air-raid shelter at ground-level; **surface speed,** the speed of which a submarine is capable when moving on the surface; **surface structure** *Linguistics* (esp. in *Generative Grammar*), the syntactic elements forming an utterance or sentence, contrasted with the 'hidden' or not immediately recognizable logical form underlying such elements (the *deep structure*: see *DEEP *a.* IV. c); a string of such elements arranged with labels and brackets to show the relationship of the constituent parts.

1920 *Chem. Abstr.* XIV. 3256 The changes in the surface tension brought about by acid and alkali are so slight the titration with surface active substances as indicators cannot be significantly disturbing. **1978** P. W. ATKINS *Physical Chem.* viii. 240 The material described in this section is put to use in the study of surface-active agents (or surfactants). These agents include long chain molecules, such as soaps and detergents, which accumulate at the water–air interface and lower the surface tension. **1925** *Chem. Abstr.* XIX. 3094 It was proved that in certain diseases the surface activity of the urine not only deviates from its normal value in the quant. sense, but that in conditions such as *morbus meculosis* it suffers qual. changes. **1972** *Materials & Technol.* V. x. 273 (*heading*) Principles of surface-activity. **1859** W. J. M. RANKINE *Man. Steam Engine* III. iv. 453 Another blow-off cock is sometimes so placed as to discharge occasionally the scum, consisting of crystals of salt, which collects on the surface of the water: this is called the 'surface blow'. **1888** R. H. THURSTON *Man. Steam Boilers* xii. 446 When using sea-water in the boilers, frequently blowing off from the bottom or a continuous discharge from the 'surface-blow' or 'scum pipes' is essential to keeping the water so fresh as not to produce deposits or incrustation. **1888** *Lockwood's Dict. Mech. Engin.* 361 *Surface blow-off*, the blowing off of the scum which collects on the top of the water in a boiler. **1977** WOODRUFF & LAMMERS *Steam-Plant Operation* (ed. 4) v. 254 Surface blowoff is advantageous in skimming or removing oil from the boiler water. **1946** L. C. UREN *Petroleum Production Engineering* (ed. 3) I. xi. 388 Some varieties of surface casing are made of galvanized sheet steel. **1977** *Offshore Engineer* Aug. 28/2 A widely used drilling programme..using 30″ conductor pipe, 20″ surface casing. **1926** E. K. RIDEAL (*title*) An introduction to surface chemistry. **1951** A. E. ALEXANDER *Surface Chem.* p. v, The study of surface chemistry gives an unusually clear insight into the real existence and behaviour of molecules. **1975** *McGraw-Hill Yearbk. Sci. & Technol.* 174/2 Conductance monitoring of thin-film electrodes constitutes a powerful new approach to the study of surface chemistry and physics. **1938** A. G. I. CHRISTIE *Eng. Medieval Embroidery* 25 *Surface Couching.* The method of couching familiar to modern workers, that of securing one or more threads by passing another across them.., although well known in the Middle Ages, does not appear to have been extensively used. *Ibid.*, The medieval English embroidery, preserved in the Musée de Cluny,..is surface-couched throughout. **1963** *Opus Anglicanum* (V.&A. Mus. Exhib. Catal.) 14/1 Silver-gilt and silk thread in underside and surface couching and stem stitch. *Ibid.* 44/2 In the band with butterflies the metal threads are surface couched. **1905** R. C. H. HECK *Steam-Engine & Other Steam-Motors* I. iv. 109 The surface-effect.—Of the total interior surface of the cylinder, that part which may be called the clearance-surface—including the cylinder head and the piston-face, with the steam-passages. **1945** [see *mass effect* s.v. *MASS *sb.*² 10 d]. **1962** *Marine Engin./Log* Oct. 72/2 A surface-effect ship is being developed under a $370,000 MarAd contract. **1979** *Canad. Jrnl. Biochem.* LVII. 106/1 This preference [for phosphatidylcholine] is manifested in the ethereal system, in which surface effects are absent. **1935** *Post Office Mag.* Jan. 2/2 1928, new services introduced and direct air or combined air and surface mails to half the countries of the world. **1946** R. ALLEN *Home Made Banners* xii. 156 Pop's reply was so long that it came by surface mail. **1956** *B.B.C. Handbk. 1957* 247 It is published in a surface mail edition at an annual rate of 25 *s.* **1977** P. MOYES *To Kill Coconut* vi. 82 Look at the date. Three weeks old. Just arrived by surface mail. **1921** *Daily Colonist* (Victoria) 17 Mar. 7/7 The Sonora plays with a total absence of that 'surface noise' or record scratching which you had believed could not be eliminated. **1981** *Hi-Fi Answers* Sept. 87/1 The general idea was to boost high frequencies on recording, so that when an equal and opposite act was applied on play-back it cut out a lot of the surface noise. **1889** *Cent. Dict.*, Surface-road. **1903** *N.Y. Evening Post* 3 Sept. 6/4 The short-haul business is well provided for by the existing surface roads. **1940** *New Statesman* 19 Oct. 375 He is getting worried about his wife and children in their surface shelters. **1902** *Encycl. Brit.* XXXII. 576/2 With her original machinery the *Plunger* was to have had a surface speed of 15 knots. **1976** G. COOK *Silent Marauder* i. 58 The K-class steam-driven submarine...could produce a surface speed of twenty-four knots. **1964** N. CHOMSKY *Current Issues in Linguistic Theory* i. 10 Thus the syntactic component must provide for each sentence (actually, for each interpretation of each sentence) a semantically interpretable *deep structure* and a phonetically interpretable *surface structure*, and, in the event that these are distinct, a statement of the relation between these structures. **1969** *Neuphilologische Mitteilungen* LXX. 203 The distinction between 'surface' and 'deep' structures should be given up, since no such contrast exists: there are only structures and their meanings. **1971** *Archivum Linguisticum* II. 131, I shall use the traditional term *Article* to refer to *the, a, this*, etc. when I am characterizing them as surface-structure elements. **1975** *Ibid.* VI. 23 Even mutations which are determined by a lexical environment are not all triggered by the surface structure. **1977** E. VON GLASERSFELD in D. M. Rumbaugh *Language Learning by Chimpanzee* v. 103 In this context it must be said that Chomsky's introduction of the terms 'surface structure' and 'deep structure'..seemed a step in the right direction.

surface, *v.* Add: **3. b.** *fig.* To bring to public notice; *spec.* to produce or expose (a defector, spy, etc.). *U.S. colloq.*

1955 *N.Y. Times* 6 Mar. IV. 2/6 In Moscow last week the authorities 'surfaced' a brilliant British atomic scientist who had disappeared behind the Iron Curtain five years ago. **1963** J. JOESTEN *They call it Intelligence* I. iv. 45 Now and then secret agents are purposely 'surfaced'. **1973** *N.Y. Times* 20 May I. 64/1 Martin Tolchin, another Times reporter, surfaced one of the stories last October. **1974** *Anderson* (S. Carolina) *Independent* 23 Apr. 1B/2 Rep. Dan Marrett..surfaced the controversial issue.

4. a. (Examples of submarines and divers.) Also *fig.*

1935 *Jrnl. R. United Services Inst.* LXXX. 126 Diving and surfacing were carried out by filling or employing a number of goatskins. **1955** *Times* 18 Aug. 8/3 [The officer]..had an under-water swimming suit with breathing equipment. He failed to surface. **1959** *Listener* 9 Apr. 635/2 The *Skate* surfaced ten times during the voyage. **1965** M. SHADBOLT *Among Cinders* xxvi. 276, I swam down a gloomy passage..and surfaced in a gently lighted room. **1974** L. DEIGHTON *Spy Story* xviii. 192 Nuclear subs go faster submerged... When we surfaced they did the usual tests.

b. *fig.* Of persons: to become fully conscious or alert, esp. after sleep. Also, to come to general notice (after a period of seclusion), to appear in public view.

1959 H. HAMILTON *Answer in Negative* ii. 33 He was rather silent over the meal... It was only when they had returned to the drawing-room that he really surfaced and returned to the case. **1963** *Times* 11 Jan. 3/7 He went to bed early last night and did not feel well enough to surface today. **1968** 'R. SIMONS' *Death on Display* xii. 180 'Has there been any sign of that damned Tebaugh woman yet?' 'Afraid not... She still hasn't surfaced.' **1971** 'A. GILBERT' *Tenant for Tomb* v. 73 If there wasn't a reason he'd have—what's the word?—surfaced before this. **1975** *New Yorker* 21 Apr. 133/1 Members of revolutionary committees that were created by the Communists over the past several years in all South Vietnamese provinces have now surfaced.

c. Similarly, of something newly presented to public attention, esp. after being concealed.

1971 *Nature* 26 Feb. 590/1 The proposal surfaced last December with the report of a panel of consultants commissioned by Senator Ralph Yarborough. **1973** *Time* 5 Feb. 51/1 The dispute soon surfaced in the press. **1978** R. LUDLUM *Holcroft Covenant* xxvii. 318 She wanted me to be prepared if it ever surfaced, if anyone for any reason ever remembered and tried to use the information.

surfaced, *a.* Add: **2.** Provided with a (special) surface or surfaces. Esp. of paper treated on one side to receive a sharp printed impression. (Usu. without qualifying word.)

1888 *Paper & Printing Trades Jrnl.* Mar. 29/1 The use of highly surfaced super-calendered paper..is extending to this country. **1967** M. A. KHAN *Friends not Masters* iii. 23 The only good stretch of surfaced road that existed, to my knowledge, was somewhere in Pabna district. **1971** D. POTTER *Brit. Eliz. Stamps* vi. 68 All these stamps were issued on surfaced paper.

3. Of a submarine: that is afloat but not submerged.

1943 *Times* 6 Dec. 4/5 On the sixth day a Liberator attacked a surfaced U-boat near this convoy. **1974** L. DEIGHTON *Spy Story* xviii. 193 If London's reception is poor, surfaced subs in transit monitor for them.

surfacer. Add: **1. b.** *spec.* A woodworking machine for cutting and planing the surface of wooden boards.

1884 J. KANE *Shavings & Sawdust* xviii. 81 Small surfacers..used by cabinet and piano factories..should have all the four rolls driven. **1937** H. HJORTH *Machine Woodworking* v. 139 A single planer or surfacer planes only one side of a board at a time, while a double surfacer planes both sides at the same time.

3. A paint used to smooth any slight unevennesses of a surface before another coat is applied.

1927 *Automotive Manufacturer* July 13/2 For the first coat, use primer and surfacer, half and half, spraying on a medium coat... No sanding will be needed prior to spraying the coat of surfacer. **1954** A. ST. J. MASTERS *Do your own Spray Painting* viii. 75 For amateur use there is no doubt that the best plan is to continue with the cellulose surfacer as previously described. **1979** *Guardian* 30 May 5/3 (Advt.), The body is then given a surfacer, sprayed with a sealer and oven-hardened.

surface wave. SURFACE *sb.*] **a.** A wave of displacements propagated along the surface of a solid or a liquid.

1887 LD. RAYLEIGH in *Proc. Lond. Math. Soc.* XVII. 11 It is not improbable that the surface waves here investigated play an important part in earthquakes, and in the collision of elastic solids. **1900** *Nature* 4 Oct. 562/1 The earthquake wave takes about 110 minutes to travel from its origin to the opposite end of the earth's diameter, but whether it is propagated through the centre of the earth or as a surface wave cannot at present be decided. **1953** H. KOLSKY *Stress Waves in Solids* ii. 16 Where there is a bounding surface..elastic surface waves may also occur. These waves..are similar to gravitational surface waves in liquids. **1973** *IEEE Trans. Microwave Theory & Techniques* XXI. 176/1 Their size, design flexibility, and reproducibility make acoustic surface-wave devices excellent candidates for many important applications in radar and communication systems.

b. *Radio.* [tr. G. *oberflächenwelle* (A. Sommerfeld 1911, in *Jahrb. d. drahtl. Telegr.* IV. 166).] A radio wave propagated along the surface of the earth.

1913 [see *space wave* s.v. *SPACE *sb.*¹ 19]. **1943** [see *ground wave* s.v. *GROUND *sb.* 18]. **1971** [see *sky wave* s.v. *SKY *sb.*¹ 9].

surfacing, *vbl. sb.* Add: **1.** (Examples *spec.* of roads.)

1908 C. E. MORRISON *Highway Engin.* iii. 46 Gravel roads seem to occupy an intermediate place between those of earth and broken stone, in the tractive force required, character of surfacing, and cost of construction. **1937** *Times* 13 Apr. p. iii/2 Much that can make for safety lies in the expert designing, surfacing and lighting of the highways. **1954** *Gloss. Highway Engin. Terms* (*B.S.I.*) 31 *Surfacing*, the top layer or layers, comprising the wearing course and/or base course but not the base.

2. (Earlier example.)

1853 E. CLACY *Lady's Visit to Gold Diggings Austral.* vi. 85 The riches of Peg Leg Gully were brought to light through the surfacing of three men with wooden legs, who were unable to sink a hole in the regular way.

3. Of a submarine: rising to the surface of the water. Also *fig.* Cf. SURFACE *v.* 4 a in Dict. and Suppl.

1922 *Glasgow Herald* 27 Apr. 7 Submarine H 42 rose to the surface some 30 yards right ahead of the Versatile... The reason for her surfacing was not known. **1958** *Times* 18 Dec. 11/4 Surfacing is an effective word to indicate those friends who suddenly appear on the doorstep after touch has been lost with them for months. **1970** *Wall St. Jrnl.* 6 Nov. 1/1 The surfacing of high-school students' demands is relatively recent in its own right.

surfactant (sɜːɪfæ·ktănt). *Chem.* [f. initial elements of *surf*ace-*act*ive adj. s.v. *SURFACE *sb.* 6 d + -ANT¹.] A surface-active agent. Also *attrib.*

1950 *American Dyestuff Reporter* XXXIX. 379/3 A new word, Surfactants, has been coined by Antara Products, General Aniline & Film Corporation, and has been presented to the chemical industry to cover all materials that have surface activity, including wetting agents, dispersants, emulsifiers, detergents and foaming agents. **1959** *Times* 7 Dec. (Agric. Suppl.) p. vii/1 Since the war, various growth supplements have been recommended, including arsenic acid supplements, surfactants..hormones and antibiotics. **1967** *New Scientist* 28 Sept. 686/2 They propose that a process of solubilization takes place under the influence of a surfactant—a substance which lowers the surface tension of water. **1968** *Gloss. Formwork Terms* (*B.S.I.*) 25 *Surfactant* (surface-active agent, activating agent, deprecated), a chemical which lowers the surface tension of water. *Note.* Surfactants are used in mould oils to reduce the occurrence of blowholes in the concrete face. **1972** *Daily Colonist* (Victoria, B.C.) 27 Feb. 24/7 Doctors believe hyaline membrane..is an unwanted substitute for a totally or partially missing 'surfactant' membrane that in normal babies keeps the lungs from collapsing. **1979** *Enhanced Oil Recovery* (Shell Internat. Petroleum Co.) 5 Injection of water containing surfactants (soap-like chemicals) into the reservoir can lower the oil/water interfacial tension very substantially..and therefore mobilize the oil held by capillary forces.

surfacy (sɜ̆·ɹfĕsi), *a.* Also **surfacey.** [f. SURFACE *sb.* 1 b + -Y¹.] 'On the surface', without depth; superficial.

1887 W. ARMSTRONG in *Art Jrnl.* June 167/1 Titian fails to give the substance of flesh. His flesh is surfacy and without the variety of truth; it is, in fact, without texture. **1957** *Psychol. Rev.* LXIV. 139/1 When we are fixated upon the vase in the Rubin reversible figure, the background recedes, is less surfacy, and..seems to provide a less centrally adequate form of sensory input. **1975** *Citizen* (Ottawa) 3 Nov. 57/3 Neither he nor Dame Peggy wish to deliver glib, surfacy imitations. **1979** *Rydge's* (Sydney) Apr. 105/2, I would still be trying to select the one that had the fine edge, but I wouldn't be as surfacey as to select it on that one aspect.

surfari (sɜ̆ɹfā·ri). [Blend of SURF *sb.* and *SAFARI *sb.*: cf. *surf safari* s.v. *SURF *sb.* 3.] A journey made by surfers in search of good conditions for surfboarding; a group of surfers travelling to or around suitable beaches. Phr. *on surfari* (S. Afr.): cf. *on safari* s.v. *SAFARI *sb.* 1 a.

1963 *Pix* 28 Sept. 63 Driving in a surfari to the beach is just one point better than travelling 'Robinson Crusoe' (alone). **1965** J. POLLARD *Surfrider* ii. 21 Soon it will be too crowded, other 'surfaris', groups of surfers looking for a surf, are already on the beach. **1965** *S. Afr. Surfer* I. III. 27 Takkies has made it to the beach at Zinkwazi where he meets three stokies who are on surfari. **1968** *Surfer* IX. IV. 69 Ever since Endless Summer, surfers visiting Cape St. Francis have been disappointed, day after day, by fast unrideable, rock-riddled waves where Bruce found the best surf of his world surfari.

surfer (sɜ̄·ɹfəɹ). [f. SURF *sb.* or *v.* + -ER[1].] One who rides a surfboard; a surfboarder. Also *fig.*

1955 A. Ross *Australia 55* xv. 214 The heads of the surfers bob over several ignored undulations. **1962** M. MCLUHAN *Gutenberg Galaxy* 144 (*heading*) Peter Ramus and John Dewey were the two educational *surfers* or wave-riders of antithetic period. **1966** T. PYNCHON *Crying of Lot 49* vi. 147 What chance has a lonely surfer boy For the love of a surfer chick? **1970** A. TOFFLER *Future Shock* xiii. 255 Surfers display sores and nodules on their knees and feet as proud proof of their involvement. **1978** G. A. SHEEHAN *Running & Being* vi. 75 'Surfing is a spiritual experience,' says Michael Hynson, one of the world's top surfers.

surficial (sɜ̄ɹfi·ʃăl), *a. Geol.* [f. SURFACE *sb.*, after *superficial*.] Of or pertaining to the surface of the earth. Cf. SUPERFICIAL *a.* 1 a.

1892 J. D. DANA in *Amer. Jrnl. Sci.* CXLIV. 166 The outflow retains a thickness of 250 feet quite to its extreme western limit, which it could not have done if it had been a subaerial, or, using a much needed new word, a surficial flow. **1926** [see *HYPABYSSAL *a.*]. **1981** COSTA & BAKER *Surficial Geol.* ii. 25/2 Both surficial and bedrock geologic maps can be used to identify and classify materials, hazards, and resources.

Hence **surfi·cially** *adv.*, on the surface (esp. of the earth).

1895 J. D. DANA *Man. Geol.* (ed. 4) IV. 806 The trap was poured out surficially from fissures along the eastern margin of the area. **1918** [see *CREEP *v.* 10]. **1944** C. PALACHE et al. *Dana's Syst. Min.* (ed. 7) I. 799 The crystals..are often surficially bounded by a yellow or brown alteration shell. **1971** *Nature* 2 July 41/1 In the theory of plate tectonics convergent plate junctures are the loci of orogeny, marked surficially by arc-trench systems.

surfie (sɜ̄·ɹfi). *slang* (chiefly *Austral.*). [f. SURF *sb.* + -IE.] A surfer or surfboarding enthusiast, *spec.* characterized as one of a set of long-haired, sun-tanned young people on a beach. Also *attrib.*

1962 *Austral. Women's Weekly* 24 Oct. (Suppl.) 3/4 *Surfie*, a fond term for a good and keen surfer. **1963** *Sunday Mail* (Brisbane) 10 Nov. 23 He talk surfie talk.. 'cowabunga, wipe-out, I'm get stoked..yay gremmies'. **1967** *Coast to Coast 1965–66* 254 In one coffee-bar doorway stood the hoodlums..glowering at the pink and orange and green of the surfies going by. **1972** *Sunday Mail* (Brisbane) 26 Mar. 8/2 They have peddled the mushrooms to all-night trippers, located through surfie contacts. **1981** *Times Lit. Suppl.* 30 Jan. 110/5 He agrees to deliver a deal for this scruffy surfie and the plot is primed.

surfy, *a.* (Earlier example.)

1738 A. HILL *Let.* 11 May in G. Sherburn *Corr. Alexander Pope* (1956) IV. 98 The rushing of a watery sound—a kind of hollow, washy murmur, like the workings of a surfy tide.

surge, *sb.* Add: **2. c.** Also, a rapid increase in price, activity, etc., esp. over a short period.

1964 *Ann. Reg. 1963* 191 The final deficit for the fiscal year which ended on 30 June 1963 was $6,200 million, largely because of the surge in business spending and improved tax collection. **1976** *Yellowstone Explorer* July 7/2 The surge in the use of back-country areas is certainly as true here in Yellowstone as it is in other wild places across the country. **1980** *N.Y. Times* 18 Nov. B7/3 The population surge in the Sun Belt has been even greater than expected.

d. (Further examples.)

1911 W. N. SHAW *Forecasting Weather* iii. 72 The last of the charts to represent the classification of isobars.. are selected to show what Abercromby calls 'surge'—that is to say, a general alteration of pressure that seems to be superposed upon the changes related to a low pressure centre. **1936** *Discovery* Sept. 289/2 It is thus possible to study the passage of 'surges' travelling along the mission line at 186,000 miles a second. **1973** *Physics Bull.* Mar. 148/3 The high voltage cathode-ray oscillograph..was used to detect lightning discharges and other electrical surges in high voltage transmission lines. **1979** *Time* 8 Jan. 80/3 That includes..keeping a weather-eye on cold surges (masses of low-temperature air moving rapidly down from Siberia).

4*. *Naut.* A rhythmic motion forward and aft that is in addition to any steady speed of the vessel.

1949 K. C. BARNABY *Basic Naval Archit.* xvii. 255 A very uneven drive, such as that given by a single-cylinder paddle-wheel engine, will cause a perceptible surge. **1968** F. N. SPIESS in J. F. Brahtz *Ocean Engin.* xv. 566 Stability against horizontal oscillatory motion (surge and sway) and against roll and pitch can chiefly be achieved by providing horizontal extent comparable to or greater than a wavelength. **1977** *Offshore Engineer* May 44/3 During these tests, the data acquisition system recorded.. surge, sway and yaw of the lay barge.

5. surge chamber, tank *Civil Engin.*, a chamber (often open to the air) connected by a T-junction to a water pipe so as to absorb surges of pressure by filling and drops in pressure by emptying; **surge voltage** *Electr.*, the peak voltage produced in a transmission line by an electrical surge.

1928 *Daily Express* 10 Oct. 12 The pent-up waters sweep through a narrow tunnel to the surge chamber of a newly built power-house, driving the turbo-generators. **1974** *Encycl. Brit. Macropædia* XVIII. 770/2 To assist regulation with long pipelines, a surge chamber is often connected to the pipeline as near as possible to the turbine, thus enabling part of the water in the pipeline to pass into the surge chamber as the turbine is closed. **1909** *Trans. Amer. Soc. Mech. Engineers* XXX. 443 'Surge tank' is a term applied to a stand pipe or storage reservoir placed at the down-stream end of a closed aqueduct to prevent undue rise of pressure in case of a sudden diminution of draft, and to furnish water quickly when the gates are opened, without having to wait for the velocity in the long feeder to pick up. **1930** *Engineering* 3 Jan. 19/2 Each divided tunnel is provided with a separate surge tank. **1975** *North Sea Background Notes* (Brit. Petroleum Co.) 27 Injection water surge tanks, filters and pumps are located on this deck. **1904** E. B. RAYMOND *Alternating Current Engin.* ii. 76 The surge voltage is an entirely separate phenomenon from that of resonance. **1979** C. A. GROSS *Power System Analysis* iv. 118 Surge voltages provide the most stringent test and supply the rationale for the standard impulse voltage waveform.

surgent, *a.* (*sb.*) Add: **A.** *adj.* **1. c.** *Psychol.* A term used by the psychologist R. B. Cattell (b. 1905), in his factorial analysis of personality, to designate a type characterized by resourcefulness and responsiveness considered as a distinct source trait.

1933 R. B. CATTELL in *Brit. Jrnl. Psychol.* Jan. 326 The essence of the temperament is expressible by some term conveying the idea of 'leaping' or 'rising up' with facility. 'Repressed' and 'Unrepressed' convey more than we are entitled to infer at present... The word 'Surgent', from the Latin *surgo*, seems most aptly to express the quality which the tests reveal. **1940** J. BOWLBY *Personality & Mental Illness* v. 71 This division corresponds roughly to the division of surgent personalities into good- and bad-tempered. **1968** *Psychol. Abstr.* XLII. 68/2 Findings..gave more significance to the covariances between 'surgent' character traits and inventive factors.

Hence **su·rgency**, the attribute possessed by the surgent personality (see sense 1 c of the adj.).

1933 R. B. CATTELL in *Brit. Jrnl. Psychol.* Jan. 327 The amount of [trait] '*c*' possessed by any individual could be referred to as the degree of Surgency. **1940** J. BOWLBY *Personality & Mental Illness* v. 70 The hypomanic personality has much surgency. **1952** *Brit. Jrnl. Psychol.* May 153 The range covered is very comprehensive, including such recent words as..narcoanalysis, surgency and tele. **1973** R. B. CATTELL *Personality & Mood* i. 10 Intelligence, ego strength, surgency, and characterological anxiety..are source traits.

surgeon, *sb.* **1. b.** For 'army or the navy' read 'army, navy, or air force' and add: *surgeon-general* (earlier and later examples); also (*U.S.*), the senior medical officer of the Bureau of Public Health or similar state authority.

1706 G. FARQUHAR *Recruiting Officer* (ed. 2) IV. ii. 49 In short, the Operation will be perform'd with so much Dexterity, that with general Applause you will be made Surgeon General of the whole Army. **1777** *Jrnls. Continental Congress U.S.* (1907) VII. 162 There [shall] be a physician and Surgeon General with the main army. **1869** *Boyd's Business Directory* 111 Governor's Staff [N.Y. State]—..Surgeon-General, Jacob S. Mosher, of Albany. **1917** *Rep. Surgeon General, U.S. Navy* 16 The Surgeon General, as a member of the General Medicine Board, has participated in the work [for the Council of National Defense]. **1973** *Philadelphia Inquirer* (Today Suppl.) 7 Oct. 4 (Advt.), Warning: the Surgeon General has determined that cigarette smoking is dangerous to your health.

c. (Examples of fig. phr. *surgeon's knife.*)

1940 L. MACNEICE *Last Ditch* 22 Here she stands who was twenty and is thirty. The same but different and he found the difference A surgeon's knife without an anaesthetic. **1962** *Daily Tel.* 13 Sept. 1/1 Sir Alexander Bustamante said that the Treaty of Rome was a 'surgeon's knife thrust into the Commonwealth body'.

3. b. surgeon-fish, substitute for def.: a herbivorous, tropical, marine fish of the family Acanthuridæ, distinguished by sharp spines on either side of the tail; (examples); **surgeon's knot** (see quot. 1968).

1871 *Harper's Mag.* July 191/2 The terror of all, the surgeon-fish,..boldly swims in every quarter, opening and shutting his lancet. **1931** J. R. NORMAN *Hist. Fishes* v. 97 The Surgeon-fishes..of tropical seas derive their name from the presence of a lancet-like spine on either side of the fleshy part of the tail. **1974** *Environmental Conservation* I. 72 (*caption*) A Surgeon-fish..is prominent on right below. **1733** *Med. Ess. & Obs. Soc. in Edin.* I. 108 By the help of a needle, or a flexible eye'd probe, the surgeons knot is made with the thread. **1945** *Ann. Surg.* CXXI. 440 The artery was secured to the tube..by a No. 3 Deknatel ligature tied tightly behind the holding ridge, using a surgeon's knot. **1968** E. FRANKLIN *Dict. Knots* 27 *Surgeon's knot.* This is a variation of the reef knot in which an extra turn is taken at the start to help prevent the knot from tending to loosen while being completed. Used by surgeons for tying a ligature and by us [*sc.* Scouts] for parcels, etc.

surgeoncy (earlier example); **surgeoness** (earlier example).

1729 *Indenture of Apprenticeship* (Hammersmith Archives: PAF/1/272, Ref. 70), Mary Webb, daughter of John Webb, a poor child of the said parish, apprentice to Anne Saint of St. Leonard's Shoreditch in the County of Middlesex—surgeoness. **1792** *Dublin Even. Post* 18 Feb. 1/2 (Advt.), Wanted, a surgeoncy in a regiment of infantry.

surgery. Add: **1. d.** *Math.* The topological alteration of manifolds by conceptually removing a neighbourhood and replacing it by another having the same boundary; an instance of this.

1961 J. MILNOR in *Proc. Symp. Pure Math.* III. 39 Given any imbedding of $S^p \times D^{q+1}$ in a manifold W of dimension $n = p + q + 1$, a new manifold W' can be formed by removing the interior of $S^p \times D^{q+1}$ and replacing it by the interior of $D^{p+1} \times S^q$. This procedure will be called surgery. *Ibid.* 40 A surgery of type $(0, n+1)$ replaces W by the disjoint sum $W + S^n$. **1974** *Encycl. Brit. Macropædia* XVIII. 503/1 If M is an oriented manifold of dimension $n \geq 4$, one can, by a succession of surgeries of index 1, kill the whole fundamental group π_1 of M. **1979** M. A. ARMSTRONG *Basic Topology* vii. 162 The result is a surface homeomorphic to the torus. A further surgery will give us the sphere.

2. a. Also, the regular session at which a doctor receives patients for consultation in his surgery.

1938 F. B. YOUNG *Dr. Bradley Remembers* i. 1 Between six and eight..Dr. Bradley 'took' his evening surgery as usual. **1944** J. D. CARR *Till Death do Us Part* xi. 113 I've got to be back..for surgery at half-past ten. **1964** D. FRANCIS *Nerve* v. 73 I'm late for surgery... Those pills ought to keep him quiet. **1975** 'J. BELL' *Victim* ii. 23 Dr. Swallow was dealing with his morning surgery.

b. Hence, a session at which a Member of Parliament, local councillor, etc., is available to be consulted locally by his constituents, usu. on regular occasions. Also, the room or office at which this occurs.

1951 *Hansard* (Commons) 19 Feb. 966 It is a practice of mine..to call personally upon as many of my constituents as I can, and I find that by doing this a different set of problems is presented to me from those which my post-bag or even my weekly 'surgery' bring. **1957** *Times* 22 Apr. 7/7 On the question of surgeries, they are largely a self-imposed task about which MP's cannot complain since they are so often the chosen method of getting votes at the next election. **1964** G. E. NOEL *Harold Wilson & 'New Britain'* xiv. 111 As Prime Minister he intends, whenever humanly possible, to retain the system initiated in Ormskirk of personally visiting constituents who have reported problems instead of obliging them to attend 'surgeries'. **1968** *Times* 7 Nov. 11/5, I was at my 'surgery' near the hall when constituents called to complain that they could not gain admittance to the meeting. *a* **1974** R. CROSSMAN *Diaries* (1975) I. 258, I am going to have three successive days sitting on the front bench, followed on Friday by a full day of official visitations and a surgery in Coventry. **1982** P. TURNBULL *Dead Knock* vii. 126 Councillor Floyd..was holding a surgery in the Council Chambers.

c. A similar occasion when free advice is provided by lawyers, accountants, or others.

1973 *Observer* (Colour Suppl.) 18 Nov. 39/1 The law surgery..run by the Sheffield Free Legal Information Service. **1980** *Daily Tel.* 7 June 19/3 An increasing number of Citizens' Advice Bureaux have regular 'surgeries' chaired by volunteer local accountants. **1981** *Times* 4 Apr. 2/5 The Asian community is..providing census 'surgeries' for householders.

surgical, *a.* Add: **1. c.** Of garments: worn to cure, correct, or relieve an illness or deformity.

1896 *Woman's Life* 10 Oct. 200/2 (Advt.), Surgical hosiery, belts, etc. **1910** *Bradshaw's Railway Guide* May (Advt. facing p. xv), Bailey's surgical hose. **1955** W. GADDIS *Recognitions* I. i. 24 Her mother..done in by a surgical belt salesman from New York. **1974** D. RAMSAY *No Cause to Kill* I. 7 Painfully swollen legs encased in surgical stockings.

d. *fig.* or in fig. contexts.

1939 C. ISHERWOOD *Goodbye to Berlin* 68 The afternoon he came to say good-bye there was a positively surgical atmosphere in the flat. **1962** *Listener* 8 Mar. 400/2 Purchase tax—deliberately uneven and at times deliberately surgical in its effect.

e. Designating swift and precise military attack, esp. from the air. orig. *U.S.*

1965 T. C. SORENSEN *Kennedy* xxiv. 684 The idea of.. a so-called 'surgical' strike..had appeal to almost everyone first considering the matter, including President Kennedy. **1971** *Harper's Mag.* Nov. 55 Even the language of the bureaucracy—the diminutive 'nukes' for instruments that kill and mutilate millions of human beings, the 'surgical strike' for chasing and mowing down peasants from the air by spraying them with 8,000 bullets a minute—takes the mystery, awe, and pain out of violence. **1974** E. NEWMAN *Strictly Speaking* ii. 63 The war in Indochina produced a host of terms that media folks accepted at their peril: protective reaction strike, surgical bombing, free-fire zone. **1978** *Guardian Weekly* 5 Mar. 9/3 Moscow might be ready to undertake a surgical strike to take out China's nuclear installations.

2. *ellipt.* as *sb.* A surgical case or ward; † a surgical operation. *colloq.*

1828 W. SEWALL *Diary* 1 July (1930) 121/2 Sat off for home, accompanied by Reed's son, for the purpose of having a surgical on his foot. **1961** [see *KNIFE *sb.* 1 f]. **1976** C. STORR *Unnatural Fathers* i. 11 I'm awfully muddled, the way surgicals and medicals are mixed up here.

surgically *adv.*: also *fig.* (earlier and later examples).

1805 J. TAYLOR *Let.* 25 Jan. in *Minutes of Evidence* 200 in *Parl. Papers 1809* II. 1, The lad was brought to Dublin ..and was surgically rejected and dismissed before I received the letter. **1965** *Economist* 18 Sept. 1074/2 More surgically still, General de Gaulle calls for an 'interpretation' of the common market treaty which in fact violates it.

Surgicenter (sɜ̄·ɹdʒise:ntəɹ). *U.S.* Also **surgicenter.** [f. SURGI(CAL *a.* + CENTRE *sb.*] The proprietary name for a surgical unit where minor operations are performed on out-patients.

1969 FORD & REED in *Arizona Medicine* Oct. 801/2 The building to house the Surgicenter is under construction at 1040 East McDowell Road, Phoenix. *Ibid.* 804/2 The Surgicenter..is designed to provide quality surgical care to the patient whose operation is too demanding for the doctor's office, yet not of such proportion as to require hospitalization. **1971** *Official Gaz.* (U.S. Patent Office) 15 June TM183 Surgicenter, Inc., Phoenix, Ariz... *Surgicenter.* For providing facilities for doctors to perform surgical operations on patients... First use Feb. 12, 1970. **1973** *Americana Annual* 450 A trend toward development of more outpatient or ambulatory care services by hospitals was also evident in 1972. A noteworthy development was the emergence of 'surgicenters' where minor surgery can be performed on an out-patient basis. **1977** *Washington Post* 7 Nov. C7/4 The new facility will have 16 operation rooms, plus two 'surgicenters' for patients needing minor surgery that does not require hospitalization. **1981** *National Jrnl.* (U.S. Govt. Research Corp.) 20 June 1113/1 Surgicenters and other new services and programs that will be cultivated in a pro-competitive environment.

surging, *vbl. sb.* Add: **3.** *Electr.* The occurrence of surges in a current; also, a surge.

1904 E. B. RAYMOND *Alternating Current Engin.* ii. 75 On underground cables, where the ratio of *l* to *c* is much lower than in overhead wires, the tendency to puncture, due to surging, is much less. **1926** R. W. HUTCHINSON *First Course Wireless* vii. 105 The discharge consists, not of a steady flow, but of a number of rapid oscillations or surgings of electricity to and fro. **1966** *McGraw-Hill Encycl. Sci. & Technol.* XIII. 323/2 Surging in electric circuits corresponds to overshooting.

4. *Mech.* An increased action in a valve spring of an internal-combustion engine owing to its natural frequency of oscillation coinciding with the frequency of operation of the valve.

1931 H. R. RICARDO *High-Speed Internal-Combustion Engine* (ed. 2) viii. 227 Periodic vibrations in the spring itself ('surging'). **1975** M. J. NUNNEY *Automotive Engine* ii. 80 To lessen any tendency towards surging within the operating speed range of the engine, the valve springs are designed to have a high natural frequency of vibration.

‖ **surimono** (surimō·no). [Jap.] Pl. unchanged; (anglicized) **-s.** A print; *spec.* a small-sized Japanese colour print used to convey greetings or to mark a special occasion.

1899 C. J. HOLMES *Hokusai* 9 He..designed many *surimono*—the dainty cards used for festive occasions. *Ibid.* 15 The celebrated designer of *surimonos.* **1910** *Daily News* 16 May 4/5 It is worth while knowing what a surimono is. **1961** *Times* 7 Mar. 22/6 Two fine surimono by Kunisada. **1977** *Times* 18 July 10/3 The Japanese *surimono* was a wood-block print.

Surinam. Add: Also, in names of pidgin or creole languages spoken in Surinam, as *Surinam Negro-English, Taki-Taki*; cf. *SRANAN; **Surinam cherry,** (*b*) substitute for def.: an evergreen shrub or small tree, *Eugenia uniflora*, native to tropical America; also, its edible red fruit; (examples).

1895 'F. FRANCESCHI' *Santa Barbara Exotic Flora* 33 The Surinam Cherry..[is] growing too in Montecito. **1920** BRITTON & MILLSPAUGH *Bahama Flora* 304 *Eugenia uniflora*... Native of South America. Surinam Cherry. **1972** C. D. ADAMS *Flowering Plants Jamaica* 522 Surinam Cherry. Shrub to 2·5 m. high;..berries red, edible. **1934** *Amer. Speech* IX. 181 (*heading*) Surinam Negro-English. **1964** Surinam Negro-English [see *NEGRO 1 d]. **1967** R. I. MCDAVID in G. V. Bobrinskoy *Lang. & Areas* 86 A viable language in its own right—like Surinam Taki-taki.

Hence **Surina·mer** [-ER¹], a native or inhabitant of Surinam.

?**1943** *Holland carries On* (Netherlands Information Bureau, N.Y.) 27/1 The Surinamers are..far from being moulded..into a real national community. **1963** H. MITCHELL *Europe in Caribbean* xii. 119 Instruction is modelled on that of the Netherlands, where many Surinamers complete their studies. **1969** *Atlantic Monthly* Nov. 48/3 The border confrontation gave the Surinamers something new to talk about. **1976** *Daily Times* (Lagos) 26 Aug. 24/3 The black Surinamers (the former Dutch Guyanese in South America) could live with, and tolerate, the Indians, Japanese, Lebanese Jews, Ameri-Indians, Caribs, Arowaks and a salad of cultures over the century.

Surinamese (sʲūᵊrinæmī·z), *sb.* and *a.* [f. SURINAM + -ESE.] **A.** *adj.* Of or pertaining to Surinam or its people. **B.** *sb.* A native or inhabitant of Surinam; *pl.*, the people of Surinam.

?**1964** *Final Rep. Surinam–American Technical Co-operative Service* 37/2 Its objective was to supplement..training facilities provided for Surinamese technicians. **1972** *Guardian* 25 Mar. 12/6 The West Indians and Surinamese who have the luck to find a modern flat, cram it with friends and relations. **1979** *Dictionaries* I. 147 There are native speakers of Surinamese Dutch, and there is indigenous transmission of the language form from generation to generation. **1980** *Times* 18 Mar. 7/4 When it was announced that Mr Bruma would form the new Cabinet, many Surinamese were astonished.

surjection (sɜ̄ɹdʒe·kʃən). *Math.* [f. SUR-, after *INJECTION 4*.] An onto mapping.

1964 W. J. PERVIN *Found. Algebraic Topology* i. 11, *f* is a surjection or epimorphism. **1979** *Q. Jrnl. Math.* XXX. 358 The well-known surjection from tensor powers of P_{ab} to lower central factors of P.

Hence **surje·ctive** *a.*, that is a surjection.

1964 S.-T. HU *Elem. Gen. Topology* i. 7, $f:X \to Y$ is surjective if, for every point *y* in *Y*, there exists at least one point *x* in *X* such that $f(x) = y$. **1968** D. L. CLARKE *Analytical Archaeol.* ix. 360 The taxa of one aspect are related to the taxa of the other aspects as elaborate injective and surjective mappings. **1979** *Proc. London Math. Soc.* XXXVIII. 209 We recall some facts..about the abelian group $A(G)$... If *F* is a finite subgroup of *G*, then $A(G) \to A(F)$ is surjective.

surly, *a.* Add: **5.** *surly-looking* adj.

1904 W. H. HUDSON *Green Mansions* vii. 97 Two dogs ..They were surly-looking brutes. **1954** W. FAULKNER *Fable* 141 Followed by a thin wiry surly-looking private.

surmising, *ppl. a.* (Later example.)

c **1862** E. DICKINSON *Poems* (1955) I. 348 Sweeter—the Surmising Robins—Never gladdened Tree—Than a Solid Dawn.

‖ **sur place** (sür plas), *adv.* [Fr.] **1.** At the place in question; 'on the spot'.

1915 LADY R. CHURCHILL *Let.* 21 Nov. in M. Gilbert *Winston S. Churchill* (1972) III. Compan. II. 1284, I can understand that you want to study *sur place* this new phase of warfare. **1939** 'A. BRIDGE' *Four-Part Setting* xii. 157 You didn't stay and face the situation and the pain *sur place*, did you? **1976** *Listener* 28 Oct. 533/2 It is..exciting to read a regional novel *sur place*.

2. *Ballet.* Without leaving the place where one has been standing.

1930 CRASKE & BEAUMONT *Theory & Pract. Allegro in Classical Ballet* 87 *Relevez* sharply *sur place* on the *left pointe.* **1947** *Ballet Annual* I. 28 Her *fouettés* were *sur place*, and one never doubted her ability to complete the thirty-two. **1950** FRENCH & DEMERY *Advanced Steps in Ballet* 37 *Petits battements sautés.* These should be *sur place.*

surplus, *sb.* and *a.* Add: **A.** *sb.* **1. b.** *Polit.* In some systems of election by transferable vote: the votes which are transferred from a candidate who has attained the quota necessary for election to one who has not.

1926 HOAG & HALLETT *Proportional Representation* 345 The particular ballots of a candidate to be transferred as his surplus shall be those which have received certain serial numbers. **1950** THEIMER & CAMPBELL *Encycl. World Politics* 353/1 In successive counts by the electoral officials the candidates with most preferences are elected and their surpluses over the minimum quota necessary for election transferred according to the voters' preferences until all the seats are filled. **1973** *Irish Times* 2 Mar. 1/1 This was also the first striking example of Fine Gael votes transferring to Labour: Mr. Kyne was elected on the surplus of Mr. Eddie Collins.

B. *adj.* **2.** *surplus value* (Econ., esp. in Marxism), that part of the value of the results of human labour which accrues beyond the amount needed to reproduce the initial labour power.

1816 S. T. COLERIDGE in D. P. Calleo *Coleridge & Idea of Modern State* (1966) i. 12 The nearest approach to the realization of such a state is a colony, composed of 100 wealthy Planters, and a 100,000 Slaves, the surplus value of whose labor above the price of the scanty food and cloathing centers in the 100. **1887** [see sense B. 1 in Dict.]. **1904** W. T. MILLS *Struggle for Existence* xxv. 325 Labor produces more than the cost of its own reproduction. This product of labor in excess of the labor cost of producing labor is the 'surplus value' of Karl Marx. **1933** H. G. WELLS *Shape of Things to Come* I. §4.51 The entrepreneur, the capitalist, became the villain of his [*sc.* Marx's] piece, using the prior advantage of his capital to appropriate the 'surplus value' of production. **1944** G. B. SHAW *Everybody's Political What's What?* i. 1 He [*sc.* Marx] proved up to the hilt that capital in its pursuit of what he called Mehrwerth, which we translate as Surplus Value (it includes rent, interest, and commercial profit), is ruthless. **1966** T. PYNCHON *Crying of Lot 49* iv. 89 How can you be against a corporation that wants a worker to waive his patent rights. That sounds like the surplus value theory to me, fella, and you sound like a Marxist. **1975** *Chinese Econ. Stud.* VIII. IV. 60 Capitalist production is commodity production aimed at reaping surplus value.

3. Of a shop: that sells goods which are surplus to (chiefly, military) requirements.

1951 R. SENHOUSE tr. *Colette's Last of Chéri* 208 Jean de Touzac—is in the surplus store racket. What a set! **1970** A. FOWLES *Dupe Negative* xi. 140, I found a surplus store and bought a duffel bag. **1978** S. WILSON *Dealer's Move* iii. 40, I..drove down to a surplus shop in Hampstead Road, and bought a down-filled sleeping-bag.

Hence as *v. trans.* (U.S. Mil. colloq.), to dispose of (property which is surplus to requirements); also with *out.* Chiefly in *pass.*

1963 D. BROUN *Egypt's Choice* (1964) i. 12 The helicopter..used to belong to the United States Marine Corps. It was surplussed out a year ago. **1968** R. WEST *Sk. from Vietnam* i. 18 Many were 'surplused' during the following month.

surprise, *sb.* Add: **4. b.** Also, in phr. *the surprise of one's life*(*time*). Cf. *of one's life* s.v. *LIFE *sb.* 8 a.

1927 W. E. COLLINSON *Contemp. Eng.* 117 The surprise of his lifetime. **1931** *Daily Express* 15 Oct. 19/3 You will have the surprise of your life.

c. As *int.*: *surprise, surprise*: an exclamation indicating surprise. Sometimes parenthetically. Freq. in irony or sarcasm.

1953 B. GLEMSER *Dove on his Shoulder* vi. 111 'Roger!' Miss Marsh laughed. 'Surprise! Surprise!' **1962** *Times* 24 Nov. 4/6 The plum Monday spot finally went—surprise, surprise—to our old friend *Naked City.* **1970** A. PRICE *Labyrinth Makers* xiv. 178 Surprise, surprise! I didn't expect to see you. **1978** I. MURDOCH *Sea* 106, I gather you didn't even know Lizzie was living with Gilbert. Surprise, surprise. Everybody knew that. **1982** N. PAINTING *Reluctant Archer* vii. 124 At the end of the programme the identity of the 'mystery accompanist' was divulged. It was of course (surprise, surprise!) me!

5. *surprise weapon*; *surprise-free* adj.; **surprise-party** (earlier and later examples); (*b*) also, the celebration or function itself.

1968 *Listener* 20 June 791/1 Kahn and Wiener flatly deny that they're making 'predictions': they are merely sketching 'possible scenarios' for the future, based on what they call 'surprise-free projections'. **1858** H. D. THOREAU *Jrnl.* 9 Aug. (1906) XI. 86 There are also regattas and fireworks and 'surprise parties' and horse-shows. **1909** E. NESBIT *Daphne in Fitzroy St.* xvii. 272, I thought you'd like the surprise party. Was I wrong? **1969** N. W. PARSONS *Sagebrush Harp* xxi. 118 A vogue for surprise parties began among the English families in our community. **1946** *Rep. Internat. Control Atomic Energy* (Dept. of State, Washington) I. 4 This danger is accentuated by the unusual characteristics of atomic bombs, namely their devastating effect as a surprise weapon, that is, a weapon secretly developed and used without warning.

surprise, *v.* Add: **5. a.** Also *colloq.* as a retort: *you'd be surprised*, the facts are not as you would think.

1926 MAINES & GRANT *Wise-Crack Dict.* 16/2 *You'd be surprised*, admitting entire satisfaction with results. **1948** 'J. TEY' *Franchise Affair* x. 102 'What else could she have been doing?'..Robert bit back a 'You'd be surprised!' **1964** 'E. MCBAIN' *Ax* v. 82 'I don't think the boys would know without *your* knowing too.'..'Sometimes... You'd be surprised.' **1971** 'D. HALLIDAY' *Dolly & Doctor Bird* ii. 19 'The emergency situation is perhaps more frequent in medicine than in portrait-painting.' 'You'd be surprised,' said the man Johnson gently.

b. *intr.* for *pass.*

1943 *Mod. Lang. Notes* LVIII. 14 They wanted to surprise me, but I don't surprise so easy. **1978** *Guardian Weekly* 1 Jan. 20/4 You don't drive cabs in Harlem if you surprise easily.

surprisingness. (Later example.)

1962 N. STREATFEILD *Apple Bough* vi. 83 What never wore off was the surprisingness of Grandfather.

surra. Substitute for def. after 'countries,': caused by the flagellate *Trypanosoma evansi* and characterized by periods of increasingly severe fever and loss of weight, usually leading to death. (Earlier and later examples.)

1883 W. ROBERTSON *Textbk. Practice Equine Med.* xi. 235 Surra may be conveniently defined as a specific blood disease of the horse. **1932** RILEY & JOHANNSEN *Med. Entomol.* xviii. 300 They [*sc.* tabanids] transfer by direct inoculation certain trypanosomes of animals, such as *Trypanosoma evansi*, which causes the highly fatal surra of horses. **1962** GORDON & LAVOIPIERRE *Entomol. for Students of Med.* xxiv. 155 There are a number of species [of tabanid] which are vectors of diseases to domestic animals, such as surra.

surreal (sɜ̄rī·ăl), *a.* [Back-formation from *SURREALISM, *SURREALIST *a.* and *sb.* Poss. coined (as *surréel*) in Fr. Cf. *super-real* adj. s.v. *SUPER- 4 a (*a*).] Having the qualities of surrealist art; bizarre, dreamlike. So **surrea·lity, surre·ally** *adv.*

1936 D. GASCOYNE tr. *Breton's What is Surrealism?* vi. 66 As I said in the *Manifesto*: 'I believe in the future transmutation of those two seemingly contradictory states, dream and reality, into a sort of absolute reality, of surreality, so to speak.' **1937** *Burlington Mag.* Jan. p. xiv/1 Some 'surreal' influence haunts the regions of the Black Forest. **1952** *N.Y. Times Bk. Rev.* 4 May 26/5 I'll agree with that; however I didn't select the surrealism, the distortion, the intensity, as an experimental technique but because reality is surreal. **1956** *Time* 18 June 109/1 Author Gascar's power to evoke disgust, which he does by combining familiar objects in unfamiliar ways, until they become surreal and emetic. **1968** *New Yorker* 25 May 87/1 A surreally funny hour of film..which is goonish, rude, and altogether relieving. **1968** P. OLIVER *Screening Blues* vi. 199 A startling flight of sexual fantasy, it [*sc.* 'Coffee Blues']..extends to surreal associations which imply the sexual virtuosity of the singer. **1974** *Encycl. Brit. Micropædia* IX. 693/2 The world of dream and fantasy would be joined to the everyday rational world in 'an absolute reality, a surreality'. **1976** S. HYNES *Auden Generation* vii. 227 As the 'thirties moved on toward the end, there was only the surreal... Even the agents of order were surreal and terrifying. **1980** J. O'FAOLAIN *No Country for Young Men* xv. 319 Scale impresses him. He calls it 'art'. 'Surreality', if you please. **1982** *Times Lit. Suppl.* 21 May 549/1 Surreally hard-edged, the world *Child's Play* projects is one where details have a hallucinatory vividness.

surrealism (sɒ̆rī·ăliz'm). Also † in F. form ‖ **surréalisme,** and with capital initial. [ad. F. *surréalisme*, f. *sur-* super- + *réalisme* realism; the precise English equivalent would be *super-realism* (see *SUPER- 4 a (*b*)).] A movement in art and literature seeking to express the subconscious mind by any of a number of different techniques, including the irrational juxtaposition of realistic images, the creation of mysterious symbols, and automatism (q.v., sense *5); art or literature produced by or reminiscent of this movement.

The term *surréalisme*, coined by Guillaume Apollinaire (see quot. 1917), was taken over by the poet André Breton as the name of the movement, which he launched with his *Manifeste du Surréalisme* in 1924; his statement there of the term's meaning is given in quot. 1935.

[**1917** 'G. APOLLINAIRE' *Notes to 'Parade'* in *Table Ronde* (1952) Sept. 45 De cette alliance nouvelle, car jusqu'ici les décors et les costumes d'une part, la chorégraphie d'autre part, n'avaient entre eux qu'un lien factice, il este résulté, dans 'Parade', une sorte de surréalisme.] **1927** C. CONNOLLY *Let.* 21 Apr. in *Romantic Friendship* (1975) 294 His [*sc.* Brueghel's] realism with people, 'surrealisme' with places, is like Crabbe. **1931** [see *POPULISM b]. **1934** C. LAMBERT *Music Ho!* II. 78 Surrealism may conveniently be defined as the free grouping together of incongruous and non-associated images. **1935** D. GASCOYNE tr. A. Breton in *Short Survey Surrealism* iv. 61 *Surrealism*, pure psychic automatism, by which it is intended to express, verbally, in writing, or by other means, the real process of thought. **1952** R. BRYDEN in *Granta* 29 Nov. 8/1 Sometimes we find that neither subject suffers from juxtaposition, but that together they form a new kind of experience to Surrealism, which we rather admire. **1970** *Oxf. Compan. Art* 1115/1 Surrealism sought to explore the frontiers of experience and to broaden the logical and matter-of-fact view of reality by fusing it with instinctual, subconscious, and dream experience in order to achieve an absolute or 'super' reality. **1978** *Amer. Scholar* Summer 357 It is clear, from what people say about contemporary surrealism.., that such poetry is supposed to be terribly mysterious, profound stuff.

surrealist (sɒ̆rī·ălist), *a.* and *sb.* Also † in F. form ‖ **surréaliste** and with capital initial. [ad. F. *surréaliste*, f. *sur-* super- + *réaliste* realist.] **A.** *adj.* Of, pertaining to, or characteristic of, surrealism. **B.** *sb.* An adherent of surrealism. Also *transf.*

The adjective was coined by Guillaume Apollinaire (see quot. 1918), perhaps (according to Robert) in the sense of F. *surnaturaliste*, and was taken over by the movement founded by André Breton (see prec.).

[**1918** 'G. APOLLINAIRE' *Les Mamelles de Tirésias* (1946) 9 Pour caractériser mon drame, je me suis servi d'un néologisme qu'on me pardonnera car cela m'arrive rarement et j'ai forgé l'adjectif surréaliste qui..définit..une tendance de l'art.] **1918** *Egoist* Apr. 56/1 Surréaliste is the denomination M. Guillaume Apollinaire..has attached to his play, *Les Mamelles de Tirésias*... Thus he must be credited with the foundation of a successor to the *Unanimiste* and *Simultanéiste* schools. **1925** R. FRY *Let.* 1 May (1972) II. 567, I went yesterday..to see the works of the two great Sure-realist [*sic*] painters Miro and Masson. **1925** —— *Let.* 11 Nov. (1972) II. 584 That beastly young Surrealist Masson. **1929** A. HUXLEY *Do what you Will* i. 167 The Surréalistes..have presented us ..with the dream-like incoherencies which creative thought uses as its raw material. **1934** *Sun* (Baltimore) 25 Oct. 12/2 The Senator is the *surrealist* of politics—for surely he is above reality—or below it or to the right or left of it. **1936** D. GASCOYNE *Man's Life is this Meat* (verso title-page), With the exception of Nos. 1–6, the poems in this collection are Surrealist poems. **1940** L. TRILLING in *Kenyon Rev.* Spring 157 The Surrealists have, with a certain inconsistency, taken from Freud a kind of scientific sanction for their program. **1942** E. WAUGH *Put out More Flags* i. 39, I should have thought an air raid was just the thing for a surréaliste..limbs and things lying about in odd places. **1958** *Sunday Times* 26 Jan. 13/4 Behind the Empress, entirely dominating her..was the surrealist figure of Rasputin. **1964** M. MCLUHAN *Understanding Media* (1967) II. xvii. 180 The elders of the tribe ..had never noticed that the ordinary newspaper was as frantic as a surrealist art exhibition. **1978** K. J. DOVER *Greek Homosexuality* III. 133 'Surrealist' elements are very rare in Greek art, but an exception is the 'phallos-bird' which has the legs, body and wings of a bird but a neck and head in the form of a curved penis.

Hence **surreali·stic** *a.*, characteristic or suggestive of surrealism; **surreali·stically** *adv.*

1930 *Nation* 6 Dec. 326/1 The sheer absurdity of the characters' behaviour produced a sort of *surréalistic* poetry. **1934** WEBSTER, Surrealistically. **1958** *Spectator* 20 June 813/1 He produced Hauptmann's *Hannele* surrealistically as early as 1895. **1959** M. PUGH *Chancer* 36 Your eyes are so bloody bloodshot that they look like surrealistic marbles. **1979** *United States 1980/81* (Penguin Travel Guides) 129 You might hear along the way that Cleveland isn't the town it used to be, but surrealistically speaking, what place is? **1980** *N. & Q.* Dec. 505/2 As usual in De Quincey's surrealistic dream prose, several ideas coalesce in a single image.

Surrey[2] (sɒ̆·ri). The name of a county in southern England, used *attrib.* in **Surrey capon, chicken, fowl,** to designate a fowl specially fattened before being killed and prepared for cooking.

1874 L. WRIGHT *Bk. Poultry* xxii. 319 We have often been asked to describe the large 'Surrey' or 'Sussex' fowls which are so largely reared for the London market. **1910** J. T. BROWN *Encycl. Poultry* II. 459/1 'Surrey Fowls'. A trade description for the best produce of the Sussex fattening coops. **1938** [see *Light Sussex* s.v. *LIGHT *a.*[2] 3]. **1971** *Selfridge Xmas Food Catal.* 6/1 Surrey capons.. Plump full-breasted succulent birds. **1971** *Guardian* 27 Nov. 3/8 You tuck the quail into a poulet de bresse (a Surrey fowl would do).

surrogate, *sb.* (a). Add: **2. a.** Also as the second element of a Comb. Chiefly in *father-surrogate* s.v. *FATHER *sb.* 12, *mother-surrogate* s.v. *MOTHER *sb.*[1] 16 a.

1950 A. HUXLEY *Themes & Variations* 46 Not a trace of the divine or the eternal remains, and the notions of State, Nation and Party are therefore free to expand into vast and monstrous caricatures of God. In the service of this God-surrogate and of his prophet, Efficiency, totalitarian dictators find it right and proper to behave with systematic savagery. **1970** MASTERS & JOHNSON *Human Sexual Inadequacy* v. 147 *Partner surrogate* has been reserved to indicate the partner provided by the cotherapists for an unmarried man referred for treatment who has no one to provide psychological and physiological support during the acute phase of the therapy. **1979** [see *sex surrogate* s.v. *SEX *sb.* 5].

c. *spec.* A surrogate partner in sex therapy.

1975 M. COLE in S. Jacobson *Sexual Problems* 103 The use of male surrogates for the treatment of vaginismus and frigidity of various types has proved to be even more successful. **1976** T. SHARPE *Wilt* xii. 119 'I was a surrogate,' said Sally. 'A surrogate?' 'Like a sex counsellor.'

d. A woman whose pregnancy arises from the implantation in her womb of a fertilized egg or embryo from another woman.

1978 *Time* 5 June 59 The demand for surrogates remained strong... Despite potential legal problems, some have already opted for surrogate mothers. **1982** *New Scientist* 7 Oct. 16 This slippery slope would begin to steepen if the same technical procedure were to be applied to a non-donor who was not sterile but who acted as a surrogate ('foster mother') for the donor.

B. Now esp. in contexts where the substitute is intended to fulfil the emotional needs of a person. Also used in sense 2 d above.

1955 *Times Lit. Suppl.* 25 Feb. p. ix/1 Poe lived riotously in Dupin... Dupin was to him what Jim Hawkins was to Stevenson or Hadrian VII to Frederick Rolfe, a surrogate self living the life denied to the writer. **1977** *Time* 15 Aug. 50/3 In the life of the mind, Saville lives a surrogate boyhood. **1977** C. MCFADDEN *Serial* (1978) xliii. 92/2 His Surrogate Parent for the session made him drink a lot of lemon-grass tea. **1978** Surrogate mother [see sense 2 d above]. **1979** *Sci. Amer.* June 36/3 Will this research lead..to the use of 'surrogate parents', where, for example, rich women might pay poor women to carry their children? **1979** W. STYRON *Sophie's Choice* xi. 316 Sophie found herself acting as a kind of surrogate kin, a younger sister or daughter.

surround, *sb.* Add: **1.** (Earlier example.)

1825 in *N. Dakota Hist. Q.* (1929) IV. 35 The Mandans went out to kill Buffalo, by making whats called a surround, at 8 miles distant from fence.

3. The area or substance surrounding something; the vicinity, surroundings, or environment (*of* something).

1922 *Daily Mail* 11 Nov. 15/4 The inflammation often extends to the surround of the eye and to the wattles and throat [of poultry]. **1937** *Nature* 3 July 12/2 Large thermal inertia in the optical parts and small and slow changes in the surround of each instrument were required. **1939** *Country Life* 11 Feb. p. xxi/1 (Advt.), All types of Fencing and Tennis Court Surrounds are described in Catalogue 495. **1943** H. J. MASSINGHAM *Men of Earth* ii. 10 A country building..in relation to its matrix or surround. **1959** *Listener* 1 Jan. 13/1 It was the country, the flat agricultural surround, that so ravished me. **1962** *Which? Car Suppl.* Oct. 139/1 [There was] creaking noise from steering column surround. **1976** L. VAN DER POST *Jung & Story of Our Time* (1978) iii. 70 My own isolation in a great natural surround. **1978** *Nature* 14 Sept. 141/2 Bipolar cell responses to illumination of the surround have been thought to be mediated by horizontal cells.

surround, *v.* **I. 1.** For † *Obs.* read '*Obs.* exc. *dial.*' and add later example.

1877 S. B. J. SKERTCHLEY *Geol. of Fenland* ii. 17 In winter nearly all the peat-land was drowned, or as the old fen-men say 'surrounded'.

III. 6. The verb-stem in Comb., as **surround sound, surround-sound,** any of various systems of stereophony involving three or more speakers surrounding the listener so as to give a more realistic effect; *esp.* a four-, five-, or six-speaker system employing signal matrixing, with the aim of reproducing the original front-to-back, floor-to-ceiling, and side-to-side sound distribution. Also *attrib.*

1969 *High Fidelity Mag.* Sept. 63/1 Vanguard's initial offering in what it has termed 'Surround Sound' will include the Berlioz Requiem, which calls for four brass bands to be spread around the cardinal points of the hall. **1974** *Nature* 13 Dec. 535/2 The present upsurge of interest in surround-sound was in some measure triggered by engineers and producers playing back such four-track material directly into four amplifiers and loudspeakers distributed approximately in a square near to the corners of the monitor room. **1978** *Broadcast* 6 Mar. 18/3 In radio, engineers are experimenting with surround sound systems as the next step forward from stereophonic sound. **1981** *Hi-Fi Answers* May 58/1 Efforts were made in the mid seventies to market a system of surround sound which went by the name of quadraphonics. **1983** *Listener* 19 May 34/1 It can create a remarkable surround-sound effect.

sursassite (sɒ̆·ɹsăsəit). *Min.* [ad. G. *sursassit* (J. Jakob 1926, in *Schweiz. Min. und Petrogr. Mitt.* VI. 376), f. *Sursass*, name of the Oberhalbstein region in the Rhaeto-Romance dialect: see -ITE[1].] A hydrated silicate of manganese and aluminium, found as tufts and radial aggregates of reddish brown or yellow monoclinic crystals.

1928 *Chem. Abstr.* XXII. 45 (*heading*) Sursassite, a manganese silicate from Val d'Err. **1964** *Amer. Mineralogist* XLIX. 168 Various chemical formulae have been proposed for sursassite. **1973** *Mineral. Rec.* IV. 290/1 Recently braunite..and sursassite..have been found in Palos Verdes Hills, Los Angeles County, California... The only other occurrence of sursassite known in North America is in New Brunswick..Maine.

sursum- (sɒ̆ɹsɒ̆m-), formative element [f. L. *sursum* from below, up] used in terms in *Ophthalm.*, as **sursumdu·ction** [a. F. *sursumduction* (G. T. Stevens 1886, in *Arch. d'Ophtalm.* VI. 545): see DUCTION], vertical movement upwards of one eye alone; the degree to which this action occurs; **sursumve·rgence** [L. *vergentia* (f. *vergere* to bend, turn): see -ENCE], the simultaneous movement of one eye upwards and the other downwards, classified as *left* or *right* according to which eye moves upward; the degree to which this motion occurs; **sursumve·rsion** [L. *version-em*, f. *vertere* to turn: see -ION], the parallel upward movement of both eyes.

1893 G. E. DE SCHWEINITZ *Dis. Eye* ii. 76 Sursumduction, or the power of uniting the image of the candle flame, seen through a prism placed with its base downward before one eye, with the image of the same object as seen by the other eye, is ascertained by beginning the trial with a weak prism..and gradually increasing its strength. **1949** W. S. DUKE-ELDER *Text-bk. Ophthalm.* IV. xlv. 3814 Depending on whether the [eye] movement is in, out, up or down, the terms adduction, abduction, supraduction (sursumduction) and infraduction (deorsumduction) are employed. **1975** M. M. PARKS *Ocular Motility & Strabismus* xviii. 149/1 Dissociated double hyperdeviation is synonymous with alternating sursumduction which describes the upturning movement of each eye as the cover-uncover test is performed. **1897** A. DUANE *New Classification of Motor Anomalies of Eye* 38 The sursumvergence, i.e., the amount by which the eyes can diverge in a vertical plane, is determined by the strength of prism placed up or down before the eyes, which the latter can overcome when looking at a distant object. **1962** H. W. BROWN in G. M. Haik *Strabismus* (Symposium N. Orleans Acad. Ophthalm.) xii. 243 The normal limits of sursumvergence are small. **1974** BURIAN & VON NOORDEN *Binocular Vision & Ocular Motility* xiii. 207/2 In some texts the normal limits for distance fixation are given as..3Δ to 4Δ for sursumvergence and deorsumvergence. **1897** A. DUANE *New Classification of Motor Anomalies of Eye* 68 Explanation of the conditions..may be had by assuming a weakness of deorsumversion in the former case and of sursumversion in the latter. **1975** M. M. PARKS *Ocular Motility & Strabismus* ii. 14/2 Vertical versions are supraversion (sursumversion) and infraversion (deorsumversion).

Sursum corda (sɒ̆·ɹsɒ̆m kǭɹdă). [L. *sursum* upwards + *corda*, pl. of *cor* heart.] In Latin Eucharistic liturgies, the words addressed by the celebrant to the congregation at the beginning of the Eucharistic Prayer; in English rites, the corresponding versicle, 'Lift up your hearts'. Also *transf.* and *attrib.*

1559 T. BECON *Displaying of Popishe Masse* in *Works* (1563) III. 41b Before it was *Sursum Corda*, Lift vp your hearts vnto the Lord, but now is *Sursum Capita*, come in, Lift up your heads. **1744** [see *ANAPHORA 2]. **1837** J. ROMILLY *Diary* 2 Nov. (1967) 133 Crick made a long dull oration ending with 'Sursum corda'. **1889** H. M. LUCKOCK *Div. Liturgy* xxi. 176 The Gallican was almost alone among the ancient Liturgies in placing the prayers for the Church before the *Sursum Corda* ('Lift up your hearts'), which commenced the more sacred part, the Anaphora in the East, the Canon in the West. **1917** *Daily Chron.* 2 July 2/6 A fine speech ended finely on the sursum corda note. **1934** S. BECKETT *More Pricks than Kicks* 31 That.. is where I have sursum corda. **1955** W. GADDIS *Recognitions* II. i. 332 Thus called upon, he took courage: the sursum corda of an extravagant belch straightened him upright. **1971** N. FREELING *Over High Side* I. 6 Oranges.. smelt, like everything else, of plastic... Sursum corda, thought Van der Valk; get up off the floor.

surtax, *sb.* Add: *spec.*, an additional income tax at higher rates charged on personal incomes above a certain value; = *super-tax* sb. s.v. SUPER- 13 in Dict. and Suppl. Also *attrib.*

A surtax on personal income was introduced in the U.S. in 1913. In the U.K. the designation *surtax* officially replaced *super-tax* in 1929; this tax was abolished in 1973 when a new graduated system of income tax was established.

1916 *Yale Law Jrnl.* Apr. 427 The Tariff Act of 1913.. provides for levying, assessing and collecting an additional income tax. This additional tax is commonly known as a 'surtax'. **1927** *Rep. Comm. Nat. Debt & Taxation* 416 in *Parl. Papers* (Cmd. 2800) XI. 371 In view..of the already complicated character of the present Income Tax and Super-tax,..we think it might be found convenient to raise the additional revenue..by the introduction of a special graduated Sur-tax applicable to investment income alone. **1940** *Economist* 20 Apr. 718/2 The average surtax-payer will have about £2,650 left. **1954** *U.S. News & World Rep.* 19 Mar. 102/3 Other changes..are provided in the massive tax bill. The normal tax and the surtax on personal income are combined. **1970** *Money Which?* Mar. 4/1 The Surtax Office will work out how much surtax you have to pay, on the basis of the information you give your Tax Inspector for income tax. **1978** *Daily Tel.* 12 May 2/4 The amendment..raised the point at which 'surtax' starts from £7,000 to £8,000 of taxable income.

surtax, *v.* (Later examples in spec. sense of the sb.)

1934 G. B. Shaw *On Rocks* II. 237, I shall get three and a half per cent..and on that..I shall be income-taxed and surtaxed. **1950** —— *Farfetched Fables* 96 To substitute cost-of-production prices..for prices loaded with enormous rents for the proprietors of London land and Seaham mines, not equivalently surtaxed.

surucucu (*suruku·ku*). Also **sirocucu, surukuku.** [a. Tupi *surucucú*.] A large, venomous pit viper, *Lachesis muta*, native to tropical America and distinguished by black bands and blotches on a reddish-yellow skin; = *bush-master* s.v. Bush *sb.*[1] 11.

1845 *Encycl. Metrop.* XXV. 775/2 *Surukuku*,..probably the *Boschmeester*, or *Coenicoussi*, of the inhabitants of Surinam. **1910** R. L. Ditmars *Reptiles of World* IV. 339 This terrible creature is known under several titles—the Sirocucu, the Mapepire and the Bushmaster. **1967** *Times* 23 Nov. 10/7 The Indian girl..heard a surucucu coming through the undergrowth. It's the biggest poisonous snake in Brazil, and really very dangerous because it's aggressive.

surveil (sɒ̆ɹvē[i]·l), *v.* Also **surveille.** [Back-formation from Surveillance.] *trans.* To exercise surveillance over (someone), subject (someone) to surveillance. Also with a place or area as obj., and *absol.* Hence **survei·lled** *ppl. a.*, **survei·lling** *vbl. sb.*

1960 *Federal Suppl.* (U.S.) CLXXXII. 750/1 The plaintiff also stresses that the store as a whole, and the customer exits especially, were closely surveilled. **1966** *Harper's Mag.* Oct. 37/1 If the U.S. Central Intelligence Agency is as adroit in surveilling others as it is in escaping surveillance of itself, the Republic can relax. **1968** *Guardian* 6 Aug. 4/1 It was some time before I was being surveilled..with the full courtesy of a Home Office warrant. **1969** *New Scientist* 10 July 10/1 Night surveilling systems for railway marshalling yards. **1972** B. F. Conners *Don't embarrass Bureau* II. 123 'You'll have to conduct the surveillance.'..'I'm supposed to surveil her?' 'That's right.' **1975** O. Sela *Bengali Inheritance* xix. 169 'Where the hell is everybody?'..'Out... Surveilling. Big emergency.' **1980** N. Freeling *Castang's City* xvii. 111 A few hints are conveyed by the word 'light'. Not around twenty-four hours: that's 'intense' and needs three separate shifts... Light means not leaning on people: the surveilled aren't supposed to notice.

surveillance. Add: Also with pronunc. (sɒ̆ɹvē[i]·(y)ăns) (cf. the note s.v. Surveyance).

b. *attrib.*, esp. of devices, vessels, etc., used in military or police surveillance.

1947 *Aviation* Feb. 83/3 It recommended that surveillance radar be developed as an adjunct to airport traffic control... Surveillance radar could be used by control tower personnel to..locate planes [etc.]. **1958** *Times* 24 July 9/6 New methods of detection by surveillance drones, airborne and ground radar, [etc.]. **1960** *Signal* Mar. 41/1 BMEWS will have a long-range surveillance radar system which reportedly will detect ICBM's as they rise over the horizon at distances of several thousand miles. **1966** M. Woodhouse *Tree Frog* viii. 63 The Americans are putting up about one new surveillance satellite every fifteen days or so. **1968** *Globe & Mail* (Toronto) 3 Feb. 9/6 The USS Pueblo, the electronic surveillance ship seized by North Korea. **1975** D. Pitts *Target Manhattan* (1976) ii. 262 He switched on the surveillance cameras and looked at the street. **1976** *Honolulu Star-Bull.* 21 Dec. B-6/1 He was on a surveillance team which saw Scanlan and Maiava meet with the informer on different occasions. **1980** *Globe & Laurel* July/Aug. 199/2 Its initial appearance took E Coy—on surveillance duty—completely by surprise.

survey, *sb.* Add: **5. b.** A systematic collection and analysis of data relating to the attitudes, living conditions, opinions, etc., of a population, usu. taken from a representative sample of the latter; freq. = *poll *sb.*[1] 7 d. Also preceded by a defining word, as (*public*) *opinion survey*, *social survey*: see under the first element in Suppl.

1927 [see *social survey* s.v. *social *a.* 12]. **1935** *Fortune* July 65 (*heading*) Fortune applies to factual journalism the technique of the commercial survey. *Ibid.* 66/2 Fortune will present the results of independent surveys of national scope scientifically conducted. *Ibid.* 66/1 It seems obvious that the survey technique is not only as well adapted to journalistic use as to other uses but considerably better adapted. **1959** J. W. Krutch *Human Nature & Human Condition* vii. 127 One survey made by the Gallup Poll may reveal that 61 per cent of all adults could not remember having read one book during the year just passed. **1965** M. Frayn *Tin Men* xiii. 69 The crash survey showed that people were not interested in reading about road crashes unless there were at least ten dead. **1969** *Times* 7 Jan. 8/6 Both science and arts students believe in magic to an equal extent, according to a survey carried out at Ghana University. **1979** [see *sample *sb.* 2 d].

6. (Later examples.) Also in senses 4 and *5 b. **survey course** *U.S.*, an introductory academic course in which the significant features of a wide subject area are studied.

1911 *Daily Colonist* (Victoria, B.C.) 13 Apr. 14/2 An advertisement was published yesterday..calling for tenders for the purchase of the old survey ship, which formerly served in the war fleets. **1930** L. G. D. Acland *Early Canterbury Runs* 1st Ser. ix. 224 This was in 1852 when a few wooden buildings..were all there was of Christchurch, except survey pegs. **1941** C. Fadiman *Reading I've Liked* (1946) p. xxii, My brother, five years my senior and a student at Columbia College, was at the time taking a conventional survey course that used a sound standard anthology. **1951** M. McLuhan *Mech. Bride* (1967) 47/1 Survey techniques inevitably throw up images of normalcy. **1964** P. Meadows in I. L. Horowitz *New Sociol.* 450 Others exploited survey-questionnaire methods. Indeed, industrial society became in the 'thirties the land of the Gallup Poll—'Galluputia'. **1967** M. Argyle *Psychol. Interpersonal Behaviour* ix. 151 In fact the reliability of survey interviews is not very high. **1978** *N. & Q.* Feb. 82/1 Brief or survey treatment of major authors.

survey, *v.* Add: **1.** *spec.*, to examine the condition of a property on behalf of its prospective buyer.

1860 Geo. Eliot *Let.* 5 Sept. (1954) III. 342 It is a better house than I care to have..moreover, the place must be surveyed by a builder before we can come to a final decision.

5. Also (sɒ̆·ɹvei). To carry out a survey (sense *5 b)of (a group of people, or its beliefs, living conditions, etc.).

1953 Pohl & Kornbluth *Space Merchants* (1955) iii. 34 Survey the book-buyers, the repeat-viewers. **1958** M. Argyle *Relig. Behaviour* iv. 31 Beliefs have also been repeatedly surveyed by one or two investigators. *Ibid.* vi. 63 Kuhlen and Arnold..surveyed over 500 children grouped around the ages of 12, 15 and 18.

survey line. Also with hyphen. [f. Survey *sb.* + Line *sb.*[2]] **a.** A line along which the measurements and observations are made in a survey.

1889 G. W. Usill *Pract. Surveying* v. 139 The accuracy of a survey..will best be assured by arranging the survey-lines so that the offsets shall be as short as possible. **1930** S. W. Perrott *Surveying for Schools* i. 3 It frequently happens that the group or groups of survey lines..do not form triangles. **1981** J. Pettet *Site Surveying & Levelling* 9 Measurements can then be carried out between these points, or from the survey lines joining them, to complete the survey.

b. *Dentistry.* A line scribed on a cast of a tooth marking the place of greatest diameter with respect to the chosen line of insertion of the denture.

1949 V. R. Trapozzano *Comprehensive Rev. Dentistry* xx. 565 Draw the labial of a mandibular molar and indicate a typical survey line. **1954** Osborne & Lammie *Partial Dentures* vii. 80 If a carbon marking rod is substituted for the vertical plane and a tooth takes the place of the curved surface, then an actual line will be produced at the level of the maximum tooth bulge. This is known as the survey line. **1980** R. W. Blakeslee et al. *Dental Technol.* xi. 271 The resultant survey line shows those hard and soft tissues over which the removeable partial denture must pass when it is placed and withdrawn by the patient. The survey line also shows the height of contour of each tooth.

surveyor. Add: **6.** *Dentistry.* An instrument used to survey the casts of teeth, esp. to determine parallelism between surfaces on different teeth.

1928 W. E. Cummer in Turner & Anthony *Amer. Textbk. Prosthetic Dentistry* (ed. 5) ix. 326 The Ney surveyor, in addition to the vertical marking member, includes a tilting table to which the cast is attached. **1939** J. Osborne *Dental Mechanics for Students* ix. 97 A clasp surveyor is a useful instrument for determining the exact position of the clasps. **1980** R. W. Blakeslee et al. *Dental Technol.* xi. 267/2 A dental surveyor consists of a platform to which an adjustable vertical tool holder is attached so that it is perpendicular to the platform.

surview, *sb.* **3.** Delete *arch.* and add later examples.

1958 *Medical World* LXXXIX. 9 (*heading*) Surview of the National Health Service 1948–58. **1961** K. Tynan *Curtains* I. 118 Mr. Dallas' play, a scathing surview of the Trojan War, is acted with notable assurance. **1977** *Times Lit. Suppl.* 23 Dec. 1508/5 Dickens's imaginative achievement in creating a whole surview of the chaos that can be unleashed in a riot is masterly.

survivability. (In Dict. s.v. Survivable *a.*) Add: (Later examples.) Now esp., ability to survive military attack.

1964 *Financial Times* (Defence Survey) 23 Mar. 21/4 The solid fuel missile..which, when widely dispersed in underground silos.., offers reasonable survivability against any first strike. **1972** *Sci. Amer.* July 14/2 Methods of anti-submarine warfare that might eventually threaten the survivability of missile-launching submarines. **1976** *Ibid.* July 64/1 (Advt.), Computer-aided design is used to model..helicopter 'survivability' under the most turbulent conditions. **1980** D. Bloodworth *Trapdoor* xi. 62 This..Airborne Command Post is designed to improve communications and so increase survivability in case of sudden nuclear attack. **1981** *Times* 28 Feb. 15/3, I suggest that..the overriding problem is the flammability of aircraft fuel. If we can reduce this, many of the survivability problems will diminish.

survivable, *a.* Add: **1.** (Later examples.)

1973 *Washington Post* 13 Jan. A23/3 The only survivable..nuclear deterrent forces. **1982** *Daily Tel.* 17 Nov. 5/1 The sinking of the destroyer Sheffield, 3,500 tons, and of the Atlantic Conveyor, 14,946 tons, by Exocet missiles was seen by some as evidence 'that large surface ships are not survivable, or at least not in a cost effective manner'.

2. Capable of being survived (esp. of an accident); not fatal.

1961 in Webster. **1967** *Times Rev. Industry* Feb. 38/3 The attitude to safety in survivable accidents, while officially condoned, is indefensible. **1981** *Brit. Med. Jrnl.* 10 Oct. 963/1 The suggestion that a nuclear war may be survivable. **1982** *Observer* 14 Mar. 5/1 The report..published by the United States Transportation Safety Board in Washington..defines a 'survivable' accident as one in which the forces exerted on passengers do not exceed the limits of human tolerance and in which the aircraft structure remains substantially intact.

survival. Add: **3.** Also, used *spec.* in *Anthrop.* with ref. to a theory that from such surviving customs and observances the earlier stages in the evolution of a culture can be reconstructed.

1867 E. B. Tylor in *Proc. R. Inst.* V. 91 Their remnants have lingered on into a period of higher mental culture, and have become survivals. **1873** —— *Primitive Culture* (ed. 2) I. i. 16 Among evidence aiding us to trace the course which the civilization of the world has actually followed, is that great class of facts to denote which I have found it convenient to introduce the term 'survivals'. **1920** R. R. Marett *Psychol. & Folk-lore* v. 99 Folk-lore, usually defined as the study of survivals, needs to conceive its object in a dynamic, not a static way. **1937** R. H. Lowie *Hist. Ethnol. Theory* v. 41 Applying the principle of survivals, the author interprets mythological references to outstanding women as relics of a one-time gynaecocracy. **1944** B. Malinowski *Sci. Theory of Culture* iii. 29 The real harm done by the concept of survivals in anthropology consists in that it functions on the one hand as a spurious methodological device in the reconstruction of evolutionary series; and, worse than that, it is an effective means of short-circuiting observation in field-work. **1965** L. Mair *Introd. Social Anthrop.* ii. 26 Rivers was the last British field anthropologist to interpret usages that he actually observed as survivals of an earlier stage of society.

4. *attrib.* and *Comb.*, as *survival capsule, car, course, kit, machine, pack, rate, skill, suit, training*; **survival bag,** a large plastic bag used by climbers as a protection against exposure; **survival curve,** a curve showing how the number of survivors varies with the size of a radiation dose or with the length of time after a dose; **survival time** *Biol.*, the time for which a biological system survives after a given dose of a chemical or ionizing radiation; **survival value** *Biol.*, the property of any heritable or other character that renders the individuals possessing it more likely to survive and reproduce; also *transf.*; also, the ability to survive.

1971 *Guardian* 22 Feb. 10/2 Cheap, light plastic or plasticised 'survival bags' can be bought for a few shillings. **1977** *Navy News* Aug. 21/3 The party spent the night practically underwater in polythene survival bags. **1960** *Britannica Bk. of Year* 557/2 The phrase *survival capsule* was used to mean the pilot's detachable compartment in a manned rocket. **1962** *Amer. Speech* XXXVII. 272 *Survival car*,..a traffic patrol car equipped with all sorts of strapping and cushioning devices to insure survival of the driver in case of a high-speed collision or roll-over. **1961** D. Huff *Score* (1962) i. 2 Sometimes I wonder why my high school didn't give me a course in how to take tests. These days it would be a survival course. **1936** E. C. Smith in B. M. Duggar *Biol. Effects of Radiation* II. xxvii. 893 It has already been mentioned that deviations from the logarithmic type in the S-shaped survival curves have been attributed by many to other varying factors. **1947** *Radiology* XLIX. 322/2 Since the survival curves for the two radiations are very similar, it is possible to establish a standard base curve which represents the expected survival for any combination of added doses of beta rays and gamma rays. **1980** *Genetics* XCV. 281 After UV treatment, [mutant] *psor-1* in stationary phase is very sensitive and demonstrates an exponential survival curve. **1944** *Yank* 21 July 2/1 A plastic-boxed survival kit (fishhooks, dextrose tablets, first-aid materials and other stuff). **1962** D. Slayton in *Into Orbit* 24 He would have a survival kit attached to the raft, which included a mirror he could use to signal airplanes overhead, some packages of shark repellant and a knife for cleaning fish. **1973** *Times* 17 May 12/6 Compiled a kind of survival-kit beginning with instructions on how to write out a cheque. **1976** R. Dawkins *Selfish Gene* ii. 21 The replicators which survived were the ones which built survival machines for themselves to live in. **1970** 'B. Mather' *Break in Line* ix. 116 Compressed rations that had probably been stolen from American Air Force survival packs. **1953** E. Smith *Guide to Eng. Traditions & Public Life* 240 The increase of population was largely due not so much to a higher birth-rate as to a higher survival-rate. **1976** *National Observer* (U.S.) 6 Nov. 17/2 Such 'survival skills' as filling out a job application and using a telephone book. **1980** *Christian Sci. Monitor* (Midwestern ed.) 4 Dec. B32/1 Survival suits and inflatable life rafts must now be provided by the shipping companies. **1947** *Radiology* XLIX. 359/1 Survival time, which was one of the most sensitive responses, showed effects following daily exposures in the range of 0·1r of fast neutrons and 1r of gamma rays. **1980** *Amer. Jrnl. Hematol.* VIII. 290 The gamma model is so far the best among the nine recommended methods for calculating the mean survival time in ^{51}Cr-labeled platelet survival study. **1972** *National Observer* (U.S.) 27 May 1/1 Bondurant's school is one of a handful that offer this 'survival' training. **1912** J. S. HUXLEY *Individual in Animal Kingdom* i. 16 This..view of the individual, as a whole whose diverse parts all work together in such a way as to ensure the whole's continuance, or, as the evolutionist would say, whose structure and working have 'survival-value', cannot stand without some qualification. **1924** J. A. THOMSON *Sci. Old & New* xlvii. 280 The notable musical talent of birds..has its survival-value in connection with mating and as an expression of very vital emotion. **1944** A. L. ROWSE *Eng. Spirit* xvii. 142 The survival-value of the College must be rated extraordinarily high. **1965** J. D. CHAMBERS in Glass & Eversley *Population in Hist.* xiii. 313 The survival-value of the small man under the impact of enclosures should not be under-estimated. **1966** *Listener* 17 Mar. 385/2 This behaviour has great survival value. So long as the troop sticks together, the prospects of a predator getting a meal are slim.

survivalism (sɒ̆ɹvəi·văliz'm). *rare.* [f. SURVIVAL + -ISM.] **1.** A theory of survival (see *SURVIVAL 3).

1892 F. W. MAITLAND *Let.* 4 Sept. (1965) 104, I am putting into the L.Q.R. a protest against Mr. Gomme's 'survivalism'.

2. A policy of trying to ensure one's own survival or that of one's social or national group.

1952 *Round Table* Dec. 26 The persistence of the unceasing attack on 'survivalism'..argues that the Soviet critics recognize..the existence of a national pride. **1953** O. CAROE *Soviet Empire* xiii. 223 The minstrels sang of heroes of the resistance, and their original work is therefore banned as tainted with 'survivalism'. **1982** *New Musical Express* 30 Oct. 19/1 The survivalism of Jamaica's sufferers.

survivalist. For *nonce-wd.* read *rare* and add: **1.** (Later examples with ref. to *SURVIVAL 3.)

1893 F. W. MAITLAND in *Law Q. Rev.* IX. 44 Had the manner in which Coton Field was occupied in 1835 been brought to the notice of some of our 'survivalists', they would have pronounced it to be an interesting relic of archaic times. **1968** *Encycl. Brit.* IX. 519/2 The controversy between the diffusionists, who believed culture contacts to be the main explanation of peasant beliefs and customs, and the survivalists, who attributed them to the processes of folk memory and to oral tradition handed down through the ages.

2. One who succeeds in surviving; one who makes a policy of aiming to survive. Also *attrib.*

1922 *Glasgow Herald* 6 May 9/2 They cannot deprive the London Scot of his reputation as a dancer and his fame as the survivalist of an institution so noteworthy as the Royal Caledonian Ball. **1953** O. CAROE *Soviet Empire* xi. 177 That, however, is what Communists would nowadays call a feudal survivalist deviation. **1978** *Time* 17 Apr. 2/2, I admire politicians... They're the best of the survivalists. **1980** *Times Lit. Suppl.* 25 Apr. 476/2 As historians come to appreciate the strength of 'survivalist' Catholicism, so Protestantism seems to be less and less a pre-ordained and natural consummation, England's manifest destiny.

survivant, *a.* For † *Obs.* read *rare* and add later example.

1934 F. SCOTT FITZGERALD *Tender is Night* I. xix. 107 But they were frightened at his survivant will.

survive, *v.* Add: **3.** *intr.* and *trans.* In trivial use. Freq. in phr. *I'll survive.*

1902 KIPLING *Traffics & Discoveries* (1904) 30 'But it'll bore you to death,' he says... 'I'll survive,' I says, 'I ain't British. I can think,' I says. **1928** M. ARLEN *Lily Christine* xiii. 240 'All this trouble your silly husband has brought on you!' 'Oh, we'll survive that,' she said lightly. **1949** 'J. TEY' *Brat Farrar* xxxi. 278 The fact that we are making him part of the family..will take a lot of the fun out of it for the scandal-mongers. We'll survive, Nell. And so will he. **1958** C. S. FORESTER *Hornblower in W. Indies* 184 'I don't envy you, frankly.' 'No doubt I'll survive, sir.' **1971** 'F. CLIFFORD' *Blind Side* IV. ii. 157 'It's nice... Cosy.' 'No *fados*, I'm afraid.' 'I'll survive.'

survivor. Add: **1. c.** Special *Comb.*: **survivor syndrome**, the (freq. delayed) symptoms, such as disintegration of personality, nightmares, tension, and guilt, which are classed as a syndrome and can afflict someone who has survived a dehumanizing and degrading experience of terror.

1968 W. G. NIEDERLAND in H. Krystal *Massive Psychic Trauma* iv. 63 Only in this way can we understand, in our appraisal of these people, the mental condition from which they suffer today: this survivor syndrome which I have described as a clinical entity. **1979** B. BETTELHEIM *Surviving* 29 Unable to embark on the strenuous and hazardous task of integrating their personalities, such survivors suffer from a psychiatric disorder which has been named the concentration camp survivor syndrome.

3. *colloq.* One who has the knack of surviving afflictions unscathed.

1971 P. D. JAMES *Shroud for Nightingale* ix. 295 She would be earning a good living somewhere... The Mary Taylors of the world were natural survivors. **1978** J. ANDERSON *Angel of Death* xiv. 167 You're a survivor, Paul. People like you always come through.

survivorship. Add: **2. b.** The probability of surviving to a given age; the proportion of a population that does this.

1949 L. I. DUBLIN et al. *Length of Life* (ed. 2) ix. 178 With information available regarding the actual mortality and survivorship of the cohort born in 1890, it becomes possible to compute..the average years of life lived after any attained age. **1954** *Q. Rev. Biol.* XXIX. 105/1 These quantities are nicely summed up by the familiar life-table function, survivorship (l_x)..and by the age-specific birth rate. **1978** *Nature* 5 Oct. 466/1 In higher forms life span and survivorship can be expressed in terms of allometric and Gompertz equations.

4. Special Comb.: **survivorship curve**, a curve showing the proportion of a population surviving at different ages.

1953 E. P. ODUM *Fund. Ecol.* vi. 108 The resulting curve is called a survivorship curve. **1976** *Nature* 1–8 Jan. 12/2 Van Valen..has made a notable contribution in this respect by applying the survivorship curve technique of population biologists to the study of extinction rates for numerous fossil taxa.

sus, suss (sɒs), *sb. slang.* **1.** [Abbrev. of SUSPICION or SUSPICIOUS *a.*] Suspicion of having committed a crime; suspicious behaviour, esp. loitering; the sus law. Freq. in phr. *on sus.*

1936 'J. CURTIS' *Gilt Kid* xxv. 248 What you nick me for? Sus? **1963** T. & P. MORRIS *Pentonville* xv. 312 Men who are, in the prison idiom, 'done for sus', that is to say, prosecuted as 'suspected persons or reputed thieves loitering with intent to commit a felony'. **1970** G. F. NEWMAN *Sir, You Bastard* ii. 74 Chance nickings in the street, from anything on sus, to indecent exposure. **1978** G. WILLIAMS *Textbk. Criminal Law* xxxvii. 817 Another provision of the Vagrancy Act s.4 (as amended) allows the punishment on summary conviction of 'suspected persons' and 'reputed thieves' who 'frequent and loiter' in certain public places with intent to commit an arrestable offence. Persons 'found' committing the offence can be arrested. In police jargon, the man is 'picked up on sus'. **1981** *Times* 24 Aug. 3/8 The delight at the passing of 'sus' is, however, mitigated by a degree of apprehension about its replacement, the newly created offence of 'interference with vehicles'.

2. [Abbrev. of SUSPECT *sb.*[2] or SUSPECTED *ppl. a.*] A suspected person, a police suspect.

1936 'J. CURTIS' *Gilt Kid* xxix. 281 Yes, there was a bit of a coring match when they claimed me. Picked me up as a sus and then hung a screwing rap on me. **1967** K. GILES *Death in Diamonds* vi. 110 Sorry, old man, they found your chief sus. with his neck broken. **1970** R. BUSBY *Frighteners* viii. 80 He's going to go running to the law, because if he don't, he's the number one suss. **1977** *Evening Standard* 8 Mar. 8/2 'Sus' is an ugly word whose meaning is now known to nearly every young West Indian living in London. It is short for 'suspected person'. Its widespread and growing use by the police against black youngsters is coming to be regarded by many lawyers.. as a major scandal.

3. *attrib.* and *Comb.*, as *sus book, case, charge, offence*; **sus law**: until 1981, the law by which a person could be arrested on suspicion of committing a crime; effective since the Vagrancy Act (5 *Geo. IV* c. 83) of 1824.

1970 J. BOLAND *Big Job* xv. 124 The Sus book..was where lists of Suspected Persons were kept. **1977** *Morning Star* 19 Jan. 2/4 These limitations have serious impact in 'sus' (being a suspected person) and 'enclosed premises' charges. **1977** *Evening Standard* 8 Mar. 8/3 A study of a number of 'sus' cases shows that they all conform to a remarkably similar pattern. **1981** *New Statesman* 13 Feb. 3/1 The government is proposing to keep the 'Sus' laws in Scotland, even though they are being repealed in England and Wales. *Ibid.* The 'useful and necessary' provisions of the Vagrancy Act 1824 and the Burgh Police (Scotland) Act 1892 which define sus offences in Scotland. **1981** *Times* 24 Aug. 3/8 The controversial 'sus' law, under which people can be arrested on suspicion that an offence is likely to be committed, is no more. The Criminal Attempts Act, which comes into force today, abolishes section 4 of the Vagrancy Act 1824.

sus, suss (sɒs), *v. slang.* [Abbrev. of SUSPECT *v.*; cf. prec.] **1. a.** *trans.* To suspect (a person) of a crime (cf. *SUSS *sb.* 1). Also in general use.

Participles of the verb are usu. formed with a double final consonant in the stem. The form with final double *s* has now spread to the infinitive. The substantive, however, is still most commonly encountered with a single final consonant (*sus*).

1953 D. WEBB *Crime is my Business* x. 202 He turned to Hodge and said, 'Who's sussed for this job?' **1959** *Observer* 11 Oct. 21/4 Commercial artist..pursued by beat blonde he has never seen... Later heavily sus-ed of her murder at the beach house. **1960** [see *LOT *sb.* 2d]. **1966** C. ROUGVIE *Gredos Reckoning* iii. 49, I sussed a weirdie and asked: 'You queer or something?' **1970** R. BUSBY *Frighteners* ii. 25 You'll get sussed right off. The club boys'll mark you down for a copper the minute you walk through the door.

b. With obj. clause: to suspect, to imagine or fancy (something) as likely; hence, to feel or surmise.

1958 [see *GET *v.* 27d]. **1960** *Punch* 24 Feb. 284/2, I sussed that all the dodgy bookshops would soon be skint. **1969** *It* 4–17 July 14/1 It wasn't a situation too conducive to free, relaxed chat and one could suss that Mick was a bit fed up with having to reel out witty and intelligent quips for the voracious appetites of the human media. **1977** *Transatlantic Rev.* LX. 192 Mercurially sussing that the largest ingredient of the briefcase was dollar bills, [he] added: 'Were you aware..that the largest ingredient of bank-note paper was Indian Hemp?'

2. To work or figure *out*; to investigate, to discover the truth about (a person or thing). Also with obj. clause and without const.

1966 *Queen* 28 Sept. 28/3 Youth susses things out on its own. **1969** FABIAN & BYRNE *Groupie* xxix. 207 When chicks came round I enjoyed sussing them out, and trying to guess which one would last and which one would be dropped. **1971** *It* 2–16 June 18/2 Everybody seems to have at least two nicknames plus their birth-signs so every little chickie can think they've got it sussed. **1971** N. SAUNDERS *Alternative London* xxvii. 256 Talk to him to sus him out—if you're not sure of him, don't leave him out of your sight. **1975** *Daily Tel.* 20 Jan. 7/1 'If ever my members sussed out that I can't read, I'd be a gonner,' he said. **1976** P. CAVE *High Flying Birds* x. 105 Stay there a minute. I'll go and suss it out. **1977** *Daily Mirror* 10 May 17/1 It took me about half a day to suss out the industry and realise how easy it would be to move in. **1977** *Sounds* 9 July 30/5 Here we have a stylish axe/singer who's sussed the factors that made Benson such a universally popular guitarist. **1980** *Times Lit. Suppl.* 26 Sept. 1064/3 A morning's browsing in a book shop will suffice for you to suss out the market.

susceptance (sɒ̆se·ptăns). *Electr.* [f. SUSCEPT(IBLE *a.* + -ANCE.] In an alternating current circuit, the imaginary part of the admittance, as opposed to the real part or conductance.

1894 STEINMETZ & BEDELL in *Trans. Amer. Inst. Electr. Engineers* XI. 648 Admittance, conductance and susceptance are thus used as the inverse correspondents of impedance, resistance and reactance, and may be added as vector quantities. **1960** H. W. JACKSON *Introd. Electric Circuits* xiv. 307 Susceptance is the ability of an inductance or capacitance to pass alternating current. *Ibid.*, Capacitive susceptance is a $+j$ quantity. **1966** *McGraw-Hill Encycl. Sci. & Technol.* XIII. 330/1 Susceptance is a function involving both resistance and reactance. If resistance is negligible, the $B=$..the reciprocal of the reactance.

susceptibility. 2. a. (*b*) (Earlier example.)

1754 RICHARDSON *Sir Charles Grandison* IV. xxxiii. 228 Emily is a good girl; but she has susceptibilities already.

susceptible, *a.* Add: **B.** *sb. Med.* An individual capable of getting a disease because not immune.

1923 *Jrnl. Exper. Med.* XXXVII. 255 The massive lethal dose of a 1:200 dilution or less selects a relatively constant number of susceptibles. **1944** L. E. H. WHITBY *Med. Bacteriol.* (ed. 4) iii. 30 When the proportion of susceptibles is high the disease becomes epidemic until the endemic level of susceptibles is again reached. **1980** *Sci. Amer.* July 26/3 A graph shows the cases reported from 1950 on; there are peaks every four to seven years, time to accumulate a pool of new susceptibles 'following the high birth rate' in densely populated areas.

‖ **sushi** (su·ʃi). [Jap.] A Japanese dish consisting of small balls of cold boiled rice flavoured with vinegar and commonly garnished with slices of fish or cooked egg. Also *attrib.* Hence **sushiya** (suʃī·ya), in Japan, a shop which serves *sushi.*

1893 A. M. BACON *Jap. Interior* xi. 180 Domestics served us with tea and sushi or rice sandwiches. **1910** J. INOUYE *Home Life in Tokyo* vi. 77 The most common food taken on such an occasion is *sushi*, which is a lump of rice which has been pressed with the hand into a roundish form with a slight mixture of vinegar and covered on the top with a slice of fish or lobster, or a strip of fried egg, or rolled in a piece of laver. **1928** K. YAMATO *Shoji* vi. 77 His *sushi*, to afford the acme of succulence, had to be eaten at the stall. **1936** K. TEZUKA *Jap. Food* 74 *Sushi* has been made in many ways since olden times and is prized by rich and poor alike. **1967** D. & E. T. RIESMAN *Conversations in Japan* 282 We were standing at the *sushi* buffet of the train. **1968** P. S. BUCK *People of Japan* xiii. 158 Since sushi is nothing more than the equivalent of a sandwich, or fishy snack, the sushi bar can hardly be described as a den of iniquity. **1970** P. & J. MARTIN *Jap. Cooking* 53 The *sushiya*, or sushi shop, plays in Japan a role curiously similar to that of the pub in England.

Susian (sū·ziăn), *a.* and *sb.* [ad. L. *Sūsiānus*, Gr. *Σούσιος Σουσιανή* Susian, f. the name (*τά*) *Σοῦσα* Susa (cf. OPers. *Shush*): see -IAN.] **A.** *adj.* Of or pertaining to (Susa, the ancient capital of) Susiana (modern Khuzistan in Iran), its natives or inhabitants, or the language spoken by them. **B.** *sb.* **a.** A native or inhabitant of Susiana or its capital, Susa. **b.** The language of the Susians, known from inscriptions of the third millenium B.C., also known as Elamite (see *ELAMITE *sb.* and *a.*). Also **Susia·nian** *a.* and *sb.*

?**1552** W. BARKAR tr. *Xenophon's Cyropædia* IV. sig. Qiv, They had selected a moste goodly tente for Cyrus, and a Seusian woman. **1601** P. HOLLAND tr. *Pliny's Nat. Hist.* VI. xxvii. 138 It receiveth..the river Hedypnus..and one more out of the Susianes countrey. **1857** W. K. LOFTUS *Trav. Chaldæa & Susiana* xxviii. 372 The details of the Susian and Persepolitan structures. *Ibid.* xxx. 408 A much-defaced and weathered inscription, written in a language which M. Oppert terms 'late Susanian'. *Ibid.* 426 Pliny, referring to Susa, says that 'the Eulæus surrounded the citadel of the Susians'. **1874** A. H. Sayce in *Trans. Soc. Bibl. Archaeol.* III. 466 The Susians, or Susianians proper, who had their seat at Shushan. *Ibid.* 474 This plural in *-ib* (or *-be* after a consonant) meets us again in Susian. *Ibid.* 476 Susian or southern Susianian. *Ibid.* 484 The Susian and Accadian genitive follows the substantive which governs it. **1877** G. Rawlinson *Orig. of Nations* II. iv. 213 The primitive Babylonians and their neighbors and kinsmen, the Susianians. *Ibid.*, Babylonian and Susianian royal names. **1915** P. M. Sykes *Hist. Persia* I. iv. 57 In Elam there are found..proper names.. which belong to a language..known among scholars as Anzanite, Susian, or simply Elamite. *Ibid.* 58 The chief deity..was referred to as..the 'Susian'. *Ibid.* 54 There was a very ancient occupation of the Susian plain. **1948** W. W. Tarn *Alexander the Great* II. II. 311 It remains to consider the Susian satrapy mentioned above. **1965** W. Culican *Medes & Persians* v. 98 Besides Medes, Persians and Susians, R. D. Barnett has listed..Haraiva [*etc.*]. *Ibid.* 102 The tablets..are file-copies kept by the Susian scribes.

Susie-Q (sū·zi kiū). Also **Suzie-Q, Suzi-Q,** and without hyphen. [Origin unknown.] A modern dance of Negro origin; the step characteristic of this dance (see quots.).

1936 Davis & Coots (*song-title*) Doin' the Suzi-Q. *Ibid.* 4 A new dance hit the town, It's really gettin' 'round, It's lots of fun, I found, Doin' the Suzi-Q. **1937** L. Shomer *How to Dance* 37 The Suzi-Q is the latest and most intricate of Fox Trot Steps. To begin with, it combines the features of the tap-dance with the nimble Off-Beat Syncopated Running Steps and Turns. **1938** A. Murray *How to become Good Dancer* 188 Neither truckin' nor the Suzie-Q is a complete dance in itself. Both are skylarking steps that add variety. *Ibid.* 190 The Susie-Q is a solo dance. It is not danced with a partner. **1946** Mezzrow & Wolfe *Really Blues* xiii. 235 And from the old folks' shuffle to the Suzie Q and Sand, wasn't none of them steps new to grandpa—just the names were different. **1956** G. P. Kurath in A. Dundes *Mother Wit* (1973) 106/2 The Susie-Q and Truckin' are said to have developed in New York's Negro quarter, Harlem. **1963** *N.Y. Times Mag.* 27 Oct. 104/2 [The Negroes'] body rhythm and frank sensuality turned the formal European waltz into the closely clutched two-step and one-step,..the Susie Q. and the big Apple.

suspected, *ppl. a.* Add: **3.** *The Suspected,* a moth, *Parastichtis suspecta,* which has reddish-brown fore-wings and is found in Europe and northern Asia.

1908 R. South *Moths Brit. Isles* II. 7 The Suspected... Of this species there are two groups of forms—plain and variegated. **1948** W. J. Stokoe *Caterpillars Brit. Moths* I. 323 The Suspected... The chief British quarters of this species appear to be in Yorkshire. **1973** *Times* 5 May 12/8 The men who christen moths must be poets. Consider some of the enchanting names of those recorded in the garden..: Heart and Dart, Flame Shoulder, Nutmeg, Common Quaker, The Suspected, [etc.].

suspend, *v.* Add: **4. d.** *to suspend disbelief,* to refrain from being sceptical, or from doubting the truth of something. Cf. *suspension 3 b.

1963 *Listener* 28 Feb. 393/2 By the time he arrived at the cliff-hanging conclusion there was nothing for it but to suspend disbelief. **1979** *Amer. N. & Q.* Feb. 97/1 In suspending disbelief, poets could construct a fictitious transitional zone.

5. b. For *Obs.* (or *dial.*) read Now *rare* and add later example.

1962 *Listener* 27 Sept. 483/1 Dostoyevsky harrows and suspends his reader.

suspended, *ppl. a.* Add: **I. 3.** *suspended animation* (earlier example).

1795 *British Critic* VI. 533 The author having examined the causes of suspended animation in animals that are hanged, drowned, suffocated, or killed by noxious vapours, concludes that it is occasioned solely by the exclusion of vital air from the lungs.

4. b. *suspended sentence* (Law), a sentence which is imposed but remains in suspense provided that the offender commits no further offence within a stipulated period.

The suspended sentence was first introduced in Europe in the late nineteenth cent. Before this the phr. 'to suspend sentence' was used, esp. in the U.S., to denote the remission or commutation of a capital sentence (see quots. 1828, 1860). In Great Britain the suspended sentence became legal only in 1967 (see quot. 1967), and is commonly used in conjunction with the system of probation (see Probation 3).

[**1828** De W. Clinton in E. Cowen *N.Y. State Supreme Court Rep.* (1859) IX. 730 If the judiciary be exposed to sudden..attempts on its humanity..to suspend the sentence of the law, what must be the effect on the executive, when it comes before him, backed by judicial authority; a prevalent sentiment against the punishment of death. **1860** N. Howard *Practice Rep. Supreme Court State N.Y.* XX. 119, I have learned by newspapers that the recorder of this city occasionally suspended sentence upon verdicts or pleas of guilty. *Ibid.*, The court does not possess the power to suspend sentence indefinitely. The judge should recommend the prisoner to a pardon and not suspend sentence, in case he thinks no punishment ought to be inflicted.] **1884** *Chicago Legal News* XVI. 392/1 The same ruling might be held to apply as to the enforcement of suspended sentences..if the power of suspension existed. **1912** *Atlantic Reporter* LXXXII. 424/1 The term 'suspended sentence', as used in criminal law, refers to the suspension of the execution of a sentence already imposed, and not correctly to the suspending of a sentence. **1923** *Texas Law Rev.* I. 191 If anyone is to be given a suspended sentence and another chance to 'make good', surely it is the young man who has committed his first misdemeanor. **1947** *Survey* LXXXIII. 219/1 In 1940, 33 percent of our adult offenders were put on probation or granted suspended sentence. **1950** [see *box *v.*[2] 2 d]. **1950** *Times* 21 Oct. 3/3 Sir Leo Page had suggested to him that the probation system might be strengthened by the suspended sentence as used in France and other countries. **1957** *Alternatives to Short Terms of Imprisonment* (Home Office) 9 We understand from the Association of Chief Police Officers that there is strong support among the police for the courts being given power to impose a suspended sentence. **1967** *Act Eliz. II* c. 80 §39 A court which passes a sentence of imprisonment for a term of not more than two years for an offence may order that the sentence shall not take effect unless, during a period specified in the order..the offender commits in Great Britain another offence punishable with imprisonment.. and in this Part of this Act 'operational period', in relation to a suspended sentence, means the period so specified. **1971** L. Radzinowicz in M. Ancel *Suspended Sentence* p. vi., The suspended sentence is essentially a continental system. It began its meteoric career over seventy years ago, with the Belgian and French laws of 1888 and 1891... From there it made a *tour du monde*... It eventually reached Israel..in 1954, before entering the United Kingdom, as a very late immigrant, in 1967. **1972** J. Wilson *Hide & Seek* viii. 151, I got six months suspended sentence last time and fined twenty rotten quid. **1973** F. Rinaldi *Suspended Sentences in Australia* vi. 85 To every suspended sentence there should be added a supervision order. **1979** T. Skyrme *Changing Image Magistracy* x. 125 After the introduction of suspended sentences other forms of penalty, financial as well as custodial, diminished steadily.

c. *suspended participle* (Gram.), a participle in an absolute clause or phrase whose subject is omitted, resulting in ambiguity; a dangling participle.

1942 E. Partridge *Usage & Abusage* 93/1 *Confused participles*... Here will be treated what are variously known as disconnected or misrelated or suspended participles... Dr Onions cites the following additional examples:– *Calling upon him last summer,* he kindly offered to give me his copy. (Say: *When I called.*) **1972** R. D. Walshe in G. W. Turner *Good Austral. Eng.* 256 This lapse..has variously been called the..*isolated, suspended,* or *dangling participle* (or *phrase*).

d. *suspended disbelief*: see *suspend *v.* 4 d.

1965 *New Statesman* 20 Aug. 262/1 For a moment you forgot these were actors and participated..in the panic of..the St Valentine's day massacre... A moment later the curtain came down, the lights went up. The theatre has its own short way with suspended disbelief. **1977** *N.Y. Rev. Bks.* 26 May 13/4 If in the end I remain in a state of suspended disbelief, it is..because I find it hard to believe that there can be a single explanation for so complex a phenomenon.

II. 6. *suspended ceiling,* a ceiling fixed so as to alter the proportions of the room or to give sufficient space above it to accommodate services.

1933 *Archit. Rev.* LXXIV. 54/3 The suspended ceilings are built of steel, wire hangers, steel bars and expanded metal, and plaster. **1955** [see *insulation 3 a]. **1978** *Cornish Guardian* 27 Apr. 17/8 (Advt.), The County Council invite offers to submit fixed price tenders for.. the provision of a suspended ceiling.

B. *sb.* or quasi-*sb. ellipt.* for *suspended sentence,* sense 4 b above. *slang.*

1970 G. F. Newman *Sir, You Bastard* i. 34 The bird'll get a suspended, I don't doubt her old man's had a word somewhere. **1979** M. Page *Pilate Plot* ix. 130 If you cooperate, I can probably get you off with a £20 fine and a month's suspended—and no press publicity.

suspender. Add: **II. 4. b.** (Earlier examples.)

1878 *Queen* 13 July (Advt.), The new stocking suspender (Patent) worn by the leaders of fashion and strongly recommended by the medical profession. **1881** *Queen* 18 June 6/2 (*heading*) The New Stocking Suspender. .. A handsome pair of..suspenders, in a fancy box.

c. suspender belt, an undergarment used for holding up stockings, consisting of a belt and suspenders to which the tops of the stockings are clipped; a garter belt; **suspender clip, end,** the clip on a suspender belt.

1926–7 *Army & Navy Stores Catal.* 667/2 Suspender belts. White only..each 2/6. **1930** A. Huxley *Brief Candles* 303 And then that further humiliation of having to ask him to help her look for her suspender belt! **1976** *Vogue* 15 Mar. 79 Blue satin suspender belt, £6.90. **1973** T. Pynchon *Gravity's Rainbow* (1975) I. 127 Concentrating on gartering her nylons,..suspender-clips glittering silver under or behind her lacquered red fingernails. **1966** *Olney Amsden Price List* 36 *Suspender ends*..Nylon Fitting 6/8 dozen cards.

suspense, *sb.* Add: **3. e.** (Earlier example.)

1869 *Bradshaw's Railway Man.* XXI. 383 From this was deducted 31,383 *l.* transferred from suspense account.

II. Attributive uses and combinations. **6.** *attrib.* Of popular literature, etc.: characterized by the capacity to arouse suspense, excitement, or apprehension, as *suspense novel, story,* etc.

1952 *Spectator* 3 Oct. 452/2 Many of their 'suspense'—as opposed to 'detective'—novels are first-class. **1957** S. Beach in *This Week's Stories of Mystery & Suspense* 327 In the suspense story the focus..is fixed on the effort of a single individual to overcome danger. **1962** A. Lurie *Love & Friendship* xi. 220 It gave him a dissolute, suspense-movie look which Miranda rather liked. **1963** *Listener* 24 Jan. 158/2 Before compressionism could be taken seriously, suspense drama and the literature of confinement had to be brought together. **1972** J. Philips *Vanishing Senator* III. iii. 150 You said yesterday I should be writing suspense novels. Well, maybe I've read too many of them. **1977** *Amer. N. & Q.* XV. 76/2 Norman Donaldson, an authority on suspense fiction, has written a new introduction for this edition. **1980** D. Bloodworth *Trapdoor* xxix. 175 Enemy agents in suspense thrillers who were programmed by post-hypnotic suggestion.

7. *Comb.,* as *suspense-laden* adj.

1963 *Times Lit. Suppl.* 24 May 374/4 *Les Gommes*.. was conspicuous for..sharp characterization and suspense-laden plotting. **1964** *English Studies* XLV. 375 My chief reason for favoring four beats is therefore that the atmosphere seems more mysterious, suspense-laden, and, as it were, inhuman with four beats than with three.

suspension. Add: **I. 3. b.** (*willing*) *suspension of disbelief*: Coleridge's phrase for the voluntary withholding of scepticism on the part of the reader with regard to incredible characters and events. Now freq. in allusive or extended use.

1817 Coleridge *Biog. Lit.* II. xiv. 2 A semblance of truth sufficient to procure for these shadows of imagination that willing suspension of disbelief for the moment, which constitutes poetic faith. **1930** I. A. Richards *Practical Criticism* vii. 277 Coleridge, when he remarked that 'a willing suspension of disbelief' accompanied much poetry, was noting an important fact. **1962** N. Coghill in Davis & Wrenn *Eng. & Medieval Studies* 210 Here indeed is a call upon us for the suspension of our disbelief. **1962** *Listener* 6 Sept. 366/1 Willing suspension of disbelief doesn't exist for television. **1976** T. Sharpe *Wilt* (1978) ix. 98 Wilt looked desperately round the caravan and met the eyes of the police stenographer. There was a look in them that didn't inspire confidence. Talk about lack of suspension of disbelief.

12. suspension dot, one of a series of dots used to indicate an omission or an interval in a printed text; **suspension-feeder,** a bottom-dwelling aquatic animal which feeds on plankton, etc. found in suspension in the surrounding water; so **suspension-feeding** *ppl. a.* and *vbl. sb.*; **suspension period, point** = *suspension dot* above; **suspension polymerization,** polymerization in which the polymer separates out from a dispersion of the monomer in a liquid.

1949 G. Summey *Amer. Punctuation* viii. 109 Suspension dots or 'French dots' (*points de suspension*) occur in groups, usually of three, usually spaced but sometimes closed up. They mark preceding material as unfinished, or left dangling an instant for attention. They are used within sentences or as terminal points—sometimes in place of the usual sentence point, sometimes in addition. (Ellipsis dots, in the same form, are discussed in Chapter 9.) **1925** O. D. Hunt in *Jrnl. Marine Biol. Assoc.* XIII. 567 Those which feed by selecting from the surrounding water the suspended micro-organisms and detritus,..for want of a better term, may be termed Suspension-feeders. **1959** A. C. Hardy *Open Sea* II. v. 106 Most animals on rocks or stones will be suspension-feeders,..because little detritus can remain there. **1975** *Nature* 7 Aug. 521/1 As those samples included some typical 'suspension-feeders' (Porifera, Ectoprocta, Sabellida and so on), a water current able to transport the food items evidently exists and may explain the development of a rich bottom fauna under the Ross Ice Shelf. **1925** *Jrnl. Marine Biol. Assoc.* XIII. 575 The contents of their stomachs resembles closely that of the suspension-feeding molluscs. **1963** R. P. Dales *Annelids* ii. 53 They [*sc.* sabellids] are not the only ones that have adopted suspension-feeding. **1963** H. Shaw *Punctuate it Right!* xvi. 91 When ellipsis periods come at the end of a statement requiring a period, then four of these 'suspension periods' or 'suspension points'.. are occasionally used. **1969** G. Smith in *Lett. Aldous Huxley* 4 He often used suspension points (...) in place of commas or final stops when typewriting. **1972** *Computers & Humanities* VI. 152 Omit some parenthetic clauses of no importance to the context, and..replace them by suspension points. **1944** *India Rubber World* CXI. 173/1 More details on suspension polymerization will be given in another article on this same subject. **1973** *Materials & Technol.* VI. viii. 504 Suspension polymerization is more suited to batch operation and it is difficult to convert it into a continuous process.

suspensoid (sə̆spe·nsoid). *Physical Chem.* [a. G. *suspensoid* (P. P. von Weimarn 1908, in *Zeitschr. f. Chem. u. Industr. d. Kolloide* III. 27/2), f. *suspens-ion* Suspension: see -oid.] A lyophobic colloid from which the dispersed phase is readily (and often irreversibly) precipitated by the addition of an electrolyte.

1909, etc. [see *emulsoid]. **1927** [see *lyophobe *a.*]. **1936** *Jrnl. Faraday Soc.* XXXII. 1166 The variation of sulphur dioxide and black suspensoids during the fog of 23rd December, 1935, in London, is shown. **1954** [see *kern *sb.*[2] 3]. **1975** *Jrnl. Faculty Fisheries & Animal Husbandry* (Hiroshima Univ.) XIV. 24 Suspensoids were collected from the surface and bottom water samples at stations 3 and 13.

suspicion, *v.* For Now *dial.* (chiefly *north.*), *U.S.,* or *rare arch.* read *dial.* and *colloq.* (orig. *U.S.* and add: **a.** (Later examples.)

Quot. *a* **1637** in Dict. appears to be a fortuitous occurrence unrelated to later uses.

1916 H. L. WILSON *Somewhere in Red Gap* ii. 68 Wilbur says I'm too good, not suspicioning. I'm just being wily, so he says he'll write up and fix it. **1919** J. BUCHAN *Mr. Standfast* xxi. 386 If the Boche once suspicions how little he's got before him the game's up. **1937** C. S. FORESTER *Happy Return* xxii. 259 He is in need of distraction, I suspicion. **1938** S. BECKETT *Murphy* iii. 32 Intense Love nature prominent, rarely suspicioning the Nasty. **1946** S. J. PERELMAN in *New Yorker* 5 Jan. 21/3 Our nineteen-year-old son, which he's home from Yale on his midyears and don't suspicion that his folks are rifting. **1959** *Observer* 22 Mar. 23/6 The major is no fool, and he suspicions as quickly as the audience that the presumed Englishman is a wounded Hungarian on the run. **1961** R. P. HOBSON *Rancher Takes Wife* (1962) viii. 114, I quite often suspicioned this trait of Gloria's but when I found it out for sure it was almost too late. **1973** 'D. SHANNON' *No Holiday for Crime* (1974) vi. 88, I suspicioned what she was, but I didn't have no proof.

b. *absol.* or *intr.*

1905 KIPLING *Actions & Reactions* (1909) 40 An' d'you mean to tell me you never suspicioned? **1946** C. MCCULLERS *Member of Wedding* III. 173 In those bridge games..nobody ever drew a good hand, the cards were all sorry, and no high bids made—until finally Berenice suspicioned, saying: 'Less us get busy and count these old cards.'

Susquehannock (sɒskwəhæ·nǫk). Now only *Hist.* Forms: 7 **Sasquehanno, Sasquesahanock, -hanough, Sesquesahamock,** 8 **Susquehannah,** 9 **Susquehanno, Susquehanough; Susquehanna,** etc. [a. the name of this people in a neighbouring Algonquian language, lit. 'person (or people) of the Susquehanna River': the river flows from N.Y. State into Chesapeake Bay.] = *CONESTOGA 1. Also *attrib.*

1612 J. SMITH *Map of Virginia* 8 To proceed, 60 of those Sasquesahanocks, came to the discouerers with skins, bowes..and tobacco pipes for presents. *Ibid.*, The description of a Sasquesahanough. *Ibid.* 19 The people differ very much in stature,..some being very great as the *Sesquesahamocks*, others very little, as the Wighcocomocoes. **1676** *Rec. Court of New Castle on Delaware* (1904) 39 If the Sasquehannos should aply to you for anything, you are to use them kindly. **1751** in *New Jersey Archives* (1883) 1st Ser. VII. 598 The Susquahannah Indians only want leave from the Mohawks whom they call their Fathers in order to their accepting of a missionary. **1833** S. KERCHEVAL *Hist. Valley of Virginia* p. xxiv, He ran amongst his men, crying out..these are our friends the Susquehanoughs. **1845** *Encycl. Metrop.* XXV. 937/2 Thus Maryland was inhabited by the Susquehannoes, who were afterwards destroyed by the Iroquois assisted by four nations. **1898** *Contrib. Indian Hist. Lower Susquehanna Valley* (Hist. Soc. Dauphin County, Pa.) 39 Prior to 1600, but how long before is not known, the Susquehannocks were seated upon the river from which they have derived their name. **1910** *Encycl. Brit.* VI. 897/2 *Conestoga*, a tribe of North American Indians of Iroquoian stock... They were sometimes known as Susquehannas... The tribe suffered final extinction in the Indian wars of 1763. **1915** J. BUCHAN *Salute to Adventurers* v. 79, I was with Bacon in '76, in the fray with the Susquehannocks. I speak the Indian tongues. **1940** T. W. CLARKE *Bloody Mohawk* 36 The Iroquois, about 1660, turned their attention to the Andastes, or Susquehannocks of Pennsylvania and southern New York. **1957** *Encycl. Brit.* XII. 683/2 The Iroquoian family occupied three territories, a northern, southern, and southeastern. In the northern area there lived, besides the Iroquois proper, the Conestoga or Susquehanna in Pennsylvania. **1978** *Handbk. N. Amer. Indians* XV. 363/1 The term Sasquesahanough (Susquehannock) was first recited to Capt. John Smith by his Algonquian-speaking interpreter when he was visited by 60 Susquehannocks in 1608. **1978** J. A. MICHENER *Chesapeake* i. 4 The common warriors..felt that for a Susquehannock to pass more than a year in peace would be disgraceful. *Ibid.* 6 He would have to pass two Susquehannock villages to the south.

suss: see *SUS, SUSS *sb.*, *v.*

Sussex. Add: **a.** (Later examples of a breed of cattle; also *ellipt.*)

1886 J. MACDONALD *Pringle's Cattle* (ed. 3) vi. 117 The Sussex breed of cattle possesses several of the characteristics of the Devon, but is larger in frame. *Ibid.*, Some fine specimens of Sussex oxen are shown annually. **1919** K. J. J. MACKENZIE *Cattle* x. 144 Today the Sussex is essentially a beef-breed. *Ibid.*, The Sussex inherits some of the faults of the draught-cattle from which he springs. *Ibid.*, The Sussex bullock has to be thoroughly fattened before he is a really good butcher's animal. **1974** *Country Life* 7 Nov. 1396/1 Today the beef animal is supreme—Welsh Black, Sussex, Galloway.

c. Sussex spaniel, a long-coated, stocky, golden-brown spaniel belonging to a breed developed in Sussex and neighbouring counties; also *ellipt.*

1856 Sussex spaniel [in Dict., sense a]. **1859** [see *Norfolk spaniel* s.v. *NORFOLK b]. **1904** H. COMPTON *Twentieth Century Dog* II. 237 The Sussex spaniel is a smaller dog than the Clumber. **1981** C. I. A. RITCHIE *Brit. Dog* vi. 164 In spite of the popularity of land spaniels, such as the beautiful Sussex, the water spaniel was perhaps the favourite.

sussexite (sɒ·seksəit). *Min.* [f. *Sussex*, the name of a county in New Jersey + -ITE[1].] A basic borate of manganese and magnesium, $(Mn,Mg)BO_2OH$, found as white or yellowish orthorhombic crystals, isomorphous with szaibelyite.

1868 G. J. BRUSH in *Amer. Jrnl. Sci.* XCVI. 140 (*heading*) New borate from Mine Hill, Franklin, Sussex Co., New Jersey—sussexite. **1951** C. PALACHE et al. *Dana's Syst. Min.* (ed. 7) II. 375 The names sussexite and szaibelyite are applied to the halves of the series with Mn > Mg and Mg > Mn, respectively. **1954** [see *HULSITE]. **1974** *Encycl. Brit. Micropædia* IX. 699/1 Sussexite occurs as hydrothermal fibrous veinlets in the U.S. at Franklin, N.J., and Iron County, Michigan.

susso (sɒ·so). *Austral. slang. Obsolescent.* Also **Susso.** [f. SUS(TENANCE + *-O[2].] **a.** State government relief paid to the unemployed, *spec.* during the Depression. Also in phr. *on the susso.*

1941 BAKER *Dict. Austral. Slang* 51 *On the susso*, in receipt of unemployed sustenance. **1942** L. MANN *Go-Getter* 10 Five shillings were five shillings and a handsome help to the sustenance. 'We're on the Susso now.' That was the song they knew and did not sing. **1974** *Times Lit. Suppl.* 15 Feb. 155/4 We're on the Susso now. In the 1930s Melbourne schoolchildren grew up chanting this (to them) cheerful folk song—'Susso' being the state government sustenance available to the unemployed throughout Australia under varying conditions during the Depression.

b. One who draws this relief.

1947 V. PALMER *Cyclone* 8 He thinks it puts hair on his chest knocking about with the sussos. **1963** F. HARDY *Legends from Benson's Valley* 166 The very thought..of the contempt the respectable held for the sussos changed his mood to defiance.

sussy (sɒ·si), *a. slang.* [Shortened f. SUSPICIOUS *a.* or SUSPECTED *ppl. a.* + -Y[1]; cf. *SUS, SUSS *sb.*] Suspicious, suspect, suspected.

1965 L. J. CUNLIFFE *Having it Away* xiv. 97 It seemed a bit sussy to me. **1974** G. F. NEWMAN *Price* iii. 97 Sneed's questions were becoming more accusing; there was something sussy about Roger Dawes. **1978** N. MARSH *Grave Mistake* iii. 95 He's done porridge for attempted blackmail and he's sussy for bringing the hard stuff ashore.

sustain, *v.* **9. d.** Delete † *Obs.* and add later examples.

1884 *Encycl. Brit.* XVII. 88/1 It was in that very opera, *The Siege of Rhodes*, that Mrs. Colman, daughter-in-law of one of the composers, sustained the character of Ianthe. **1939** JOYCE *Finnegans Wake* 49 He may have been the utility man of the troupe capable of sustaining long parts at short notice. **1975** *U.S. News & World Rep.* 3 Mar. 39/2 Students of geopolitics assert that the U.S. has a near-perfect combination to sustain such a role. **1980** M. FONTEYN *Magic of Dance* 312 These ballets seem essential to theatre dance as a whole because they stretch the artist's interpretive powers to the limit in sustaining long roles. **1983** *Financial Times* 16 Feb. 13/4 The solid-voiced baritone Roland Herrmann sustained the killing role of Creon with burly resilience.

sustainable, *a.* Add: **3.** Capable of being maintained at a certain rate or level.

1965 *McGraw-Hill Dict. Mod. Econ.* 501 *Sustainable growth*, a rise in per-capita real income or per capita real gross national product that is capable of continuing for a long time. A condition of sustainable economic growth means that economic stagnation will not set in. **1971** *Nature* 9 July 80/2 The blue whale could have supplied indefinitely a sustainable yield of 6,000 individuals a year. **1976** *Times* 4 Aug. 3/8 The achievement of a sustainable, stationary population.

Hence **sustainabi·lity.**

1972 T. SOWELL *Say's Law* iii. 100 An increase beyond limits of sustainability existing at any given time would lead only to reduced earnings and subsequent contraction of the quantity supplied. **1980** *Jrnl. R. Soc. Arts* July 495/2 Sustainability in the management of both individual wild species and ecosystems..is critical to human welfare.

sustained, *ppl. a.* Add: **1. b.** *sustained yield* (orig. *Forestry*): the quantity that can be periodically harvested from a crop or population without depleting it in the long term; also *attrib.*

1919 RECKNAGEL & BENTLEY *Forest Management* xii. 124 By sustained yield is understood the yield or cut of timber from a forest which is managed in such a way as to permit the removal of an approximately equal volume of timber, annually or periodically, equal to the increment. **1980** PURDOM & ANDERSON *Environmental Sci.* ix. 219/1 Foresters are finding the sustained yield method, which produces a modest annual timber crop, increasingly more desirable. *Ibid.* x. 245/2 The goal of the fishing industry should be to establish a sustained yield. Closed seasons, catch quotas, nets with larger mesh size, and minimum fish size can help achieve a sustained yield.

c. *sustained-release* adj. (Pharm.): applied to a preparation that releases a substance slowly or intermittently into the bloodstream over a period so as to maintain a steady concentration of it, esp. by means of numerous tiny pellets with different coatings contained in and administered orally as a single capsule. Cf. *slow-release* adj. (*b*) s.v. *SLOW *a.* 16 d, *SPANSULE.

1956 *Jrnl. Pharmacy & Pharmacol.* VIII. 975 It was thought that these resins might provide suitable chemical carriers for drugs in sustained release preparations. **1974** SHOTTON & RIDGWAY *Physical Pharmaceutics* xii. 340 Sustained release products can be made by embedding the drug in a hydrophobic matrix from which it is leached out over a period of time. **1979** *Arizona Daily Star* 8 Apr. c10/1 (Advt.), Most products provide short-duration nutritional burst. *Heritage* sustained-release tablets work all day long, up to 12 hours, to release nutrients when you need them.

sustaining, *ppl. a.* Add: **c.** *sustaining pedal*, (*a*) (see PEDAL *sb.* 1 b); chiefly *U.S.*; (*b*) = *damper-pedal* s.v. DAMPER 7 a.

1889 in *Cent. Dict.* s.v. *Pedal.* **1911** H. E. KREHBIEL *Pianoforte & its Music* iii. 47 On some pianofortes there is a third pedal between the other two, called the Tone Sustaining Pedal, the action of which is to withhold the damper from the string or strings struck just before the depression of the pedal. **1922** A. H. LINDO *Pedalling in Pianoforte Music* I. 14 Students..are frequently told that it [*sc.* the right pedal] should be called, not the 'loud', but the 'sustaining' pedal. **1923** [see *ACCENTUATOR]. **1931** G. JACOB *Orchestral Technique* i. 2 In transcribing pianoforte music the effect of the sustaining pedal is often not taken into account. **1976** *Gramophone* Dec. 1016/2 The Gieseking is..an object-lesson..in how to do without the sustaining-pedal as a prop.

d. *sustaining programme*, a radio or television programme which is paid for by the broadcasting station. *U.S.*

1931 F. A. ARNOLD *Broadcast Advertising* 31 Sustaining programs are those which are prepared and paid for exclusively by the broadcasting station and in which the advertiser has no participation whatever. **1952** H. L. EWBANK *Broadcasting* viii. 128 A *sustaining* program is neither paid for by a sponsor nor interrupted by spot commercials. **1961** S. P. LAWTON *Mod. Broadcaster* 85 The network contracts themselves,..and the agreements for carrying sustaining programs, all play an important part in the make-up of schedules of affiliate stations. **1973** J. R. GRIMES *Mod. Radio Programming* xii. 173 *Sustaining*, non-sponsored.

sustentation. Add: **7. b.** *Aeronaut.* The action or condition of being aerodynamically supported either by the lift afforded from the motion of an aerofoil or by means of an air-cushion.

1907 [see *AEROFOIL]. **1939** *Nature* 18 Feb. 272/1 Most modern air transport is by means of the aeroplane, a body heavier than air, depending upon forward movement for sustentation. **1966** *McGraw-Hill Encycl. Sci. & Technol.* I. 197/2 Another form [of air-cushion vehicle] creates high air pressure beneath its structure for sustentation. **1977** T. K. S. MURTHY in *Proc. 2nd Internat. Waterborne Transportation Conf.* (1978) 308 The sustentation of the vehicle above the water surface is therefore partly due to the pressure of the air in the cushion and partly due to the hydrostatic buoyancy of the submerged hulls.

Susu[2] (so·so). Also † **Soosoo, Suzee.** [Native name.] (A member of) a Mande people inhabiting the north-west of Sierra Leone and the southern coastal regions of the Republic of Guinea in West Africa; also, the language of this people. Also *attrib.* or as *adj.*

[**1670** J. OGILBY *Africa* II. 368 The Kingdom of Bena and Sousos, deriving its Name from the inhabitants of its principal Town, which is named Sousos, stands situate about nine days Journey from..the Kingdom of..Serre-Lions.] **1786** J. MATTHEWS *Let.* 20 Feb. in *Voy. River Sierra-Leone* (1791) 13 The river Riopongeos..is..one of the principal rivers for trade... The natives are originally Suzeés. *Ibid.* 20 Nov. 95 The Suzeé language seems to be the root from which the Bagoe..sprung. **1803** T. WINTERBOTTOM *Acct. Native Africans Sierra Leone* I. i. 5 The Bulloms..possessed the whole of the river Kissee, from which they were driven by a nation called Soosoos or Suzees. **1845** *Encycl. Metrop.* XXIV. 579/2 The Súsús were well known to the learned and philosophical Arab historian of Africa. **1846** R. G. LATHAM in *Proc. Philol. Soc.* II. 221 The Susu, of which we have a grammar, is allied to the Mandingo. **1911** [see *MALINKE]. **1957** M. BANTON *W. Afr. City* vii. 127 The Susu and Yalunka (or Dyalonke) appear to be two branches of the same people. .. There are four Susu and three Yalunka chiefdoms. **1977** *Whitaker's Almanack 1978* 758 The southern half of Sierra Leone is inhabited by peoples whose languages fall into the Mende group; the northern half by the Temne, and smaller groups such as the..Susu.

susuhunan (sɒsūhūnā·n). [ad. Javanese *sesuhunan.*] The title of the monarchs of Surakarta (also called Solo) and of Mataram in Java.

1817 T. S. RAFFLES *Hist. Java* II. x. 157 The company and the *susuhúnan* should assist each other. **1831** *Canton Misc.* No. 2. 77 Solo, is the residence of the Susuhunan commonly called the Emperor, and whose ancestors in the 13th and 14th centuries reigned over the greater part of Java. **1915** D. M. CAMPBELL *Java* II. xix. 997 The sultan and susuhunan on state occasions frequently adorn themselves in the Dutch general's uniform. **1973** G. M. D. HOWAT *Dict. World Hist.* 1526/1 The Crown Prince of Mataram, later Susuhunan Amangkurat II (*reg.* 1677–1703).

susumber (sŭsɒ·mbəɹ). Also **sosuma, soushumber.** [perh. f. Ewe *súsume* or Twi *nsúsŭaa* an edible plant + Twi *mbá* young plants.] A prickly shrub, *Solanum torvum*, of the family Solanaceæ, native to the tropics, esp. America and the West Indies, and bearing clusters of white flowers followed by edible berries; also *attrib.*; = *macaw-bush* s.v. MACAW[2].

1814 J. LUNAN *Hortus Jamaicensis* II. 245 There are two varieties, both very common in Jamaica, the berries about the size of small cherries... They are..known by the names soushumber, cat-nail, Port-Morant tobacco, and macaw bush. **1839** B. M'MAHON *Jamaica Plantership* 27 He then ran after them, flogging, knocking them down, and tumbling them into the susumber bushes, full of thorns. **1913** W. HARRIS *Notes on Fruits & Veg. in Jamaica* 42 The soushumber is used mainly by the natives who..consider it a wholesome vegetable. **1929** M. W. BECKWITH *Black Roadways* 14 Salt cod cooked with..the sosuma berry, is a favourite breakfast dish even upon the tables of the whites. **1953** *Caribbean Q.* III. I. 10 Susumber berries..grow wild everywhere. **1972** C. D. ADAMS *Flowering Plants Jamaica* 656 *S[olanum] torvum*... Gully Bean, Susumber, Turkey Berry... Shrub 1–4 m high... General in the tropics.

susurrate, *v.* For † *Obs. rare*⁻⁰ read *rare* (chiefly *Lit.*) and add: (sⁱū·sɒrēⁱt, sⁱūsɒ·rēⁱt). *intr.* (Examples.)

1957 H. WILLIAMSON *Golden Virgin* III. xxvi. 395 While feet susurrated on the parquet floor made smooth.. by scatterings of french chalk. **1968** M. JONES *Day They put Humpty together Again* 45 The lining of her coat susurrated noisily. **1972** *New Yorker* 30 Sept. 6/3 In the Palm Court, violin music susurrates from five to seven.

susurrous, *a.* Add: Also, characterized by, or full of, whispering.

1886 in WEBSTER. **1946** M. PEAKE *Titus Groan* lxiv. 388 The long corridors were susurrous with rumour.

susurrus. (Earlier example.)

1826 *Blackw. Mag.* XX. 146/2 Through the..range of laughter, from faint susurrus to indomitable guffaw.

Sutherland (sɒ·ðəɹlǣnd). The title of Harriet Elizabeth Leveson-Gower, Duchess of *Sutherland* (1806–68), used *attrib.* in *Sutherland table*, a gate-leg table with rectangular leaves.

1879 *Designs Cabinet Furnit.* (Blyth & Sons) (Index) 2 Sutherland Tables. **1926** R. B. WHIFFEN *Pocket Compend. Furnit.* 99 *Sutherland Table*—A small table with a narrow top (useless when shut) and two large folding leaves, when these are let down it occupies but little space. **1952** F. G. ROE *Victorian Furnit.* xi. 93 The 'Sutherland Table', a Victorian recension of the old flap table with pull-out supports, its name a reminder of that Duchess of Sutherland who had been Queen Victoria's Mistress of the Robes, ..and was..Her Majesty's personal friend. **1979** 'J. GASH' *Grail Tree* xvii. 170 Just telling Jimmo here you're wanting a Sutherland table.

Suthu, Suto, varr. *SOTHO.

sut(t)ringee, var. SITRINGEE in Dict. and Suppl.

suture, *sb.* Add: **4.** *Geol.* In plate tectonics, the junction or line of junction formed by the collision of two lithospheric plates.

1971 *Nature* 18 June 418/2 Within the present continents there are several linear belts of distinctive oceanic and geosynclinal deposits which apparently mark the boundaries (sutures) between once separated continents. **1977** *Sci. Amer.* Apr. 32/1 Most of the sutures in Eurasia appear to be older than 200 million years.

suture *v. trans.*, (*b*) *Geol.*, to join (lithospheric plates) by means of a suture; often const. *together*; **suturing** *vbl. sb.* (further examples in *Geol.*).

1970 *Nature* 14 Nov. 659/1 If..continents are being joined, their suturing prevents further relative motion between the plates on which they ride. **1976** B. E. HOBBS et al. *Outl. Structural Geol.* x. 468 Depositional sites that are subsequently 'sutured' together by convergent plate motion. **1977** *Sci. Amer.* Apr. 32/1 When two continents collide, they suture themselves together to form a larger continent. **1979** *Nature* 6 Dec. 608/2 The act of complete suturing could trap basaltic crust and supracrustals between the two masses.

sux- (sɒks) (before a consonant also **suxa-**), formative element [repr. the sound of *succ-* (sɒks-) in SUCCINYL] in the names of drugs, as in *SULFASUXIDINE and *SUXAMETHONIUM.

suxamethonium (sɒ:ksămeþōᵘ·niɒm). *Pharm.* [f. *SUX- + *METHONIUM.] = *SUCCINYLCHOLINE. Also *suxamethonium bromide, chloride, iodide.*

1953 J. H. GADDUM *Pharmacology* (ed. 4) xi. 230 Suxamethonium iodide..also causes brief neuromuscular block. **1963** [see *DECAMETHONIUM]. **1977** *Lancet* 18 June 1305/2 Prolonged suxamethonium apnœa during a general anæsthetic occurred in a patient with Goodpasture's syndrome who had recently had plasmapheresis.

Suze (sūz, ‖ sǖz). [See quot. 1961.] The proprietary name of a yellow, gentian-based aperitif; also, a drink or glassful of this.

1950 D. AMES *Corpse Diplomatique* iii. 22 It..enables one to have another drink... I thought a Suze and a Cinzano? **1961** *Trade Marks Jrnl.* 5 Apr. 483 *Suze*... Aperitif wines having a gentian base. Distillerie de la Suze.., 11, Avenue de Général Leclerc, Maisons-Alfort (Seine), France. **1964** L. DEIGHTON *Funeral in Berlin* xxii. 124, I poured two Suzes into my face. **1974** N. FREELING *Dressing of Diamond* 72 He'd like a big Suze with lots of ice.

Suzie-Q, var. *SUSIE-Q.

Suzie Wong (sᵘ·zi wɒŋ). *slang.* Also **Susie Wong.** The name of the leading character in *The World of Suzie Wong* (1957), a novel by R. L. Mason, applied *transf.* to a woman, esp. a prostitute, in Hong Kong who consorts with visiting servicemen, etc.; also *sing.* used generically, and *attrib.*

1962 E. SNOW *Other Side of River* xxxvii. 274 What did happen to all these Suzie Wongs? **1965** *Guardian* 24 July 8/5 A teenage English blonde would be far safer in the Suzy Wong quarter of Hongkong than in a side street in Soho. **1971** *Nat. Geographic* Oct. 547/2 Sailors come to sport with Suzie Wong. *Ibid.* 571/2 The fleets of the world have indeed found this superlative anchorage, and the sailors have found Wan Chai, that traditional world of all the Suzie Wongs. **1977** 'J. LE CARRÉ' *Hon. Schoolboy* I. vii. 151 What's happened to Susie Wong since war-weary GIs..have ceased to flock in for rest and recreation? **1978** P. HARCOURT *Agents of Influence* iii. 60 What are you doing here..enjoying the delights of Suzie Wong land?

‖ **suzuribako** (suzuribā·ko). [Jap.] In Japan: a box (often, of finely-wrought lacquer-work) in which an inkstone, ink-stick, several brushes, and a small water container are kept; equivalent to an inkstand.

1967 *Times* 7 Mar. 21/6 A suzuribako by Shiomi Masanari. **1974** *Country Life* 6 June p. xii/2 Detail of a suzuribako decorated with a figure of Kajiwara Kagesuye ..Japanese 19th century. **1981** *Jrnl. R. Asiatic Soc.* I. 120 Eight *suzuribako* appear, one (No. 18) with a concealed *waka* poem.

svabite (svā·bəit). *Min.* [ad. Sw. *svabit* (H. Sjögren 1892, in *Geol. Föreningens i Stockholm Förhandl.* XIII. 789), f. the name of A. *Svab* (1703–68), Swedish mining official: see -ITE[1].] A fluoride and arsenate of calcium found as colourless or light-coloured prismatic crystals of the hexagonal system.

1893 *Jrnl. Chem. Soc.* LXIV. II. 420 Svabite is a new mineral of the apatite group from the Harstig mine. **1966** *Doklady Acad. Sci. USSR: Earth Sci. Sect.* CLXVI. 134/1 Svabite $Ca_5[AsO_4]_3(OH, F, Cl)$, the arsenical counterpart of apatite, is an extremely rare mineral.

Svan (svān). Also † (Pl.) **Ssuanes.** [Russ., cf. L. *Suani* (also used).] (A member of) a southern Caucasian people living in Svanetiya in western Georgia; also, the language of this people. Also **Sva·nian, Swa·nian.** Also *attrib.*

1601 P. HOLLAND tr. *Pliny's Nat. Hist.* I. VI. iv. 117 You meet with another river called Charien: upon which bordereth the nation of the Salæ, named in old time Phthirophagi and Suani... The river Cobus,..issueth out of Caucasus, and runneth through the country of the Suani abovesaid. **1814** F. SCHOBERL tr. *von Klaproth's Trav. in Caucasus & Georgia* xxiv. 298 The village of Chulam is inhabited by families of Ssuanes. *Ibid.* xxiv. 292 About six German miles to the south-west of the village of Ckaratschai lies the mountain Dshuman-taw, where commence the settlements of the Ssuanes. **1869** D. W. FRESHFIELD *Trav. in Central Caucasus* x. 292 Suanetia is the general name bestowed..on the upper valley of the Ingur, and is derived from the inhabitants, who from very ancient times have been called the Suani, or Suanetians. **1910** [see *SVANETIAN *a.* and *sb.*]. **1939, 1948** [see *LAZ]. **1959** B. GEIGER et al. *Peoples & Lang. Caucasus* iv. 15 Svan... English variants: Svan, Svanetians... The Svan language is a member of the S. Caucasian..language-family, to which belong..Mingrelo-Laz and Georgian, the latter languages forming one group as against Svan. **1962** D. M. LANG *Mod. Hist. Georgia* i. 10 The Svans were cut off for centuries from the main stream of Georgian civilization. *Ibid.* 18 Svanian and Mingrelo-Laz..are separate languages.

svanbergite (svæ·nbəɹgəit). *Min.* [f. the name of Lars F. *Svanberg* (1805–78), Swedish chemist: see -ITE[1].] † **a.** = PLATINIRIDIUM in Dict. and Suppl. *Obs.* **b.** [ad. Sw. *svanbergit* (L. J. Igelström 1854, in *K. Vetenskaps-Akad. Förhandlingar* XI. 156).] A basic phosphate and sulphate of aluminium and strontium, $SrAl_3PO_4SO_4(OH)_6$, found as translucent rhombohedral crystals.

1857 C. U. SHEPARD *Treat. Mineral.* (ed. 3) 303 *Svanbergite* (S.), Platiniridium, Svanberg... In small grains and rarely..cubes, with truncated angles. **1866** BRANDE & COX *Dict. Sci., Lit. & Art* II. 532/3 Pissophane. Svanbergite. Amblygonite. **1900** *Mineral. Mag.* XII. 252 Svanbergite is crystallographically very similar both to beudantite and also to hamlinite and florencite. **1979** *Mineral Abstr.* XXX. 422/2 The source of the Sr and P in the svanbergite was probably the basaltic lavas which covered northern Syria in the Quaternary.

Svanetian (svanī·ʃǎn), *a.* and *sb.* Also † **Suanetian.** [f. *Svanet(iya* (see *SVAN) + -IAN.] **A.** *adj.* Of or pertaining to the Svans. **B.** *sb.* = *SVAN.

[**1788** G. ELLIS *Mem. Map Countries between Black Sea & Caspian* 77 (*heading*) Georgian language. Carduel dialect. Imretian. Suaneti dialect.] **1854** A. VON HAXTHAUSEN *Transcaucasia* v. 159 His wife was the daughter of a Suanetian prince. *Ibid.* 162 The Suanetians have generally blue eyes and blond hair. **1896** D. W. FRESHFIELD *Exploration Caucasus* I. x. 221 The Suanetian language resembles Old Georgian. **1902** *Encycl. Brit.* XXVI. 619/2 The high valleys of the Caucasus are populated by..Svanetians, Ossets, Pshaves, and Khevzurs in the middle. **1910** *Ibid.* XI. 760/1 The Svanetians, Shvans, or Swanians, on the Upper Ingur. *Ibid.* 761/1 Both the Laz..and the Svanetian present..structural and verbal differences. **1951** W. K. MATTHEWS *Languages U.S.S.R.* v. 87 The rather more divergent Svanetian (Svan). **1959** [see *MINGRELIAN *sb.* and *a.*].

‖ **svara** (swa·ra). Also 8 **swara.** [Skr., lit. 'sound, voice'.] In Indian music, a note of a musical scale.

1792 W. JONES in *Asiatick Researches* III. 68 The first of these [notes] is emphatically named *swara*, or *the sound*, from the important office which it bears in the scale. **1891** [see *MURCHANA]. **1927** *Grove's Dict. Mus.* (ed. 3) II. 705/2 The second subject..with only two variations, and after these a *Svarā*, or sol-fa'ed passage, by way of a cadenza. **1968** *Indian Mus. Jrnl.* V. 28 He used to play the svara exercises on a single string. **1972** P. HOLROYDE *Indian Music* vi. 221 The svaras or notes are still used for vocal gymnastic exercises.

svarabhakti (swarab(h)a·kti, svara-). *Philol.* [Skr., vowel-separation, f. *svára* vowel + *bhaktí* separation.] The process by which a parasitic vowel is inserted between two consonants. Usu. *attrib.*, esp. as *svarabhakti vowel.*

1880 A. H. SAYCE *Introd. Sci. of Lang.* I. 317 The insertion..of vowels..goes under the technical name of *Swarabhakti*. This name was imported from the Hindu grammarians by Johannes Schmidt. *Ibid.* 318 Prosthesis, or prothesis..is another illustration of *Swarabhakti*. **1888** [see *INDETERMINATE *a.* (*sb.*) 2 e]. **1908** *Indogerm. Forsch.* XXIII. 254 The *-i-* of *pulisa-* and the second *-u-* of *puruṣa* are svarabhakti-vowels. **1942** *Amer. Speech* XVII. 100 A short vowel in E before *r* + a velar is lowered to [ɑ] in the dialect and a svarabhakti [ɪ] develops between the *r* and the velar. **1977** F. COLLINSON in Campbell & Collinson *Hebridean Folksongs* II. 257 The variation of rhythm or melody arising from the presence of a svarabhakti vowel is of constant occurrence in most of the songs.

Hence **svarabha·ktic** *a.*

1894 W. M. LINDSAY *Latin Lang.* 145 The inserted or 'parasitic' vowel (sometimes styled in the terminology of the Sanskrit grammarians 'svarabhaktic' vowel..) is often seen in the older Latin loanwords from Greek. **1965** *English Studies* XLVI. 174 We may here just possibly be ..taking..the *e* to be svarabhaktic.

‖ **svarita** (swa·rita). Also **Svarita.** [Skr. *svarita*.] A falling glide used in the recitation of Vedic texts (see quots.). Also in extended use.

1916 A. A. MACDONELL *Vedic Gram. for Students* 448 The Svarita is a falling accent representing the descent from the Udātta pitch to tonelessness. **1955** T. BURROW *Sanskrit Lang.* iii. 113 The accent of the syllable immediately following the udātta is termed *svarita-* and it is described by Pāṇini as a combination (*samāhāra-*) of udātta and anudātta. **1957** *New Oxf. Hist. Music* I. iv. 200 The way of chanting the Rigvedic hymns has definite musical importance, as the three accents employed, the *udātta*, the *anudatta*, and the *svarita*, denote a distinct difference in pitch. **1971** *Canadian Jrnl. Linguistics* XVII. 73 The sandhi-organization..is sufficient peculiar origin for Sanskrit svarita. **1973** A. H. SOMMERSTEIN *Sound Pattern Anc. Greek* v. 122 On the vowel following an acute-accented vowel, as also on the latter part of a circumflex-accented vowel, there was a falling glide. [*Note*] Hereinafter often referred to as *svarita*.

Svedberg (sve·dbǝɹg). *Biochem.* [The name of Theodor S. *Svedberg* (1884–1971), Swedish chemist.] Also *Svedberg unit.* A unit of time equal to 10^{-13} second used in expressing sedimentation coefficients. Symbol S (*S 4 d).

1942 *Ann. N.Y. Acad. Sci.* XLIII. 176 The members of the conference..indicated a desire to honor Professor The Svedberg... It was unanimously decided:..to adopt, as a convenient practical unit for sedimentation constants, the *Svedberg*, to be denoted by the letter *S* and equal to 10^{-13} times the absolute units, which are in seconds. **1944** *Jrnl. Biol. Chem.* CLII. 682 The average sedimentation constant of the iron hydroxide micelle was 150 Svedberg units. **1970** *Nature* 5 Sept. 1068/2 One can comprehend but not condone the biologist's affection for units such as Å, the Svedberg and mmHg. **1976** *Sci. Amer.* Aug. 63/1 It was the expected size (nine Svedberg units).

svelte. Delete ‖ and add: **b.** *transf.* Elegant, smooth, graceful.

1909 E. POUND *Personae* 43 And first the cities of north Italy I did behold, Each as a woman wonder-fair, And svelte Verona first I met at eve. **1967** *Listener* 30 Mar. 434/1 His earlier work, technically less accomplished, rougher, coarser in execution, left a way open—one felt one could break out of the paint. But now his handling is so skilful, svelte, that all other possibilities are closed. **1974** N. MARSH *Black as he's Painted* xi. 78 Is our svelte hired limousine at the door? **1977** *Gramophone* July 202/1 His rhythmic pungency..in the third piece and the svelte charm of the central waltz..suggest that he might be equally at home with Roussel's symphonic music.

Svengali (svengā·li). The name of *Svengali*, musician and hypnotist, a character in the novel *Trilby* (1894) by George Du Maurier, used *transf.* and allusively to designate one who exercises a controlling or mesmeric inluence on another, freq. for some sinister purpose. Also *attrib.* and *Comb.*

1914 KIPLING *Divers. Creatures* (1917) 145 I'm glad Svengali's back where he belongs [referring to a dog with a mesmeric stare]. **1919** C. MACKENZIE *Sylvia & Michael* v. 92 The juggler..passed into the category of the Svengalis, and became one of a long line of romantic impossibilities. **1934** B. DARWIN *Playing the Like* 121 He believes himself a new Svengali with a second Trilby. **1942** *Amer. Speech* XVII. 90/1 The word 'Svengali' shows the player's ability to keep his opponent so 'hypnotized' that he will not be aware of his trickery. **1962** N. FREELING *Love in Amsterdam* I. 40 He fascinated her. Svengali stuff. **1963** AUDEN *Dyer's Hand* 457 It is impossible to represent Christ on the stage. If he is made dramatically interesting, he ceases to be Christ and turns into a Hercules or a Svengali. **1966** N. MARSH *Black Beech & Honeydew* x. 231 A hideous Svengali-like face. **1972** *Maclean's Mag.* Mar. 41/2 He had a strange hypnotic power—not that he was a Svengali, but when he spoke people listened. **1978** M. DICKENS *Open Book* vi. 59 Charles Pick..already showed the infectious Svengali enthusiasm to which many writers beside me owe the fact that they have had the courage to go on writing.

Sverdrup (svɜ·ɹdrup). Also **sverdrup.** [Name of H. U. *Sverdrup* (1888–1957), Norwegian oceanographer and meteorologist.] Also *Sverdrup unit.* A unit of flow equal to one million cubic metres per second.

1963 G. L. PICKARD *Descr. Physical Oceanogr.* vii. 117 The most commonly used unit for volume transport is 'one million m^3/sec'..referred to as 'one sverdrup'. **1970** *Sci. Jrnl.* Mar. 58/2 Fifty Sverdrup units of flow approach the east coast of Mindanao in the Philippines and half of this volume turns north into the Kuroshio. **1977** J. D. MACDONALD *Condominium* xxxiv. 341 The..total flow of all the rivers of the world combined..is two sverdrups.

swab, *sb.*[1] (*a.*) Add: **1. c.** (Earlier U.S. example.)

1863 'MARK TWAIN' *Celebr. Jumping Frog* (1867) 73 A sheet was wound around me until I resembled a swab for a Columbiad [cannon].

d. Also † *transf.*, a naval officer. *Obs.*

1793 C. DIBDIN in *Britannic Mag.* I. 25/2 And there's never a swab but the captain knows the stem from the stern of the ship. **1850** H. MELVILLE *White Jacket* II. xliii. 289 Touch your tile whenever a swob (officer) speaks to you.

f. *Oil Industry.* A device in the form of a plunger with a valve, used to raise fluid in a well and induce a flow.

1904 *Dialect Notes* II. 391 *Swab*, n., a tool used in drilling... When water comes in faster than it can be got out by the sand-pump, the swab is run down. The fluid passes through it, and by it several hundred feet of fluid can be raised out of the hole at one run. **1916** A. B. THOMPSON *Oil-Field Devel.* x. 482 The early swab consisted of a hollow steel barrel, around which was wrapped sufficient hemp..to tightly fit the well casing when inserted. **1930** W. H. OSGOOD *Increasing Recovery of Petroleum* I. x. 169 Swabbing..may result in the forming of emulsions when the swab is run too low in the fluid and water is present. **1974** P. L. MOORE et al. *Drilling Practices Manual* ix. 241 Swab pressures are associated with fluid flow, caused by pulling equipment out of a liquid filled bore-hole.

swab, *v.*[1] Add: **II. 7.** *Oil Industry.* To introduce a swab (*SWAB *sb.*[1] (*a.*) 1 f) into (an oil-well) in order to induce a flow.

1916 A. B. THOMPSON *Oil-Field Devel.* x. 482 It was the local custom to swab wells at intervals. **1974** P. L. MOORE et al. *Drilling Practices Manual* ix. 245 This deceleration pressure indicates a well can be swabbed when running pipe into the hole.

swabber[1]. **1. b.** (Later example.)

1931 [see *roach-powder* s.v. *ROACH *sb.*[4] 4].

swabbing, *vbl. sb.* (Examples in the *Oil Industry.*)

1921 W. H. JEFFERY *Deep Well Drilling* xii. 338 Swabbing and agitating are sometimes effective in causing wells to resume flowing. **1930** [see *SWAB *sb.*[1] 1 f]. **1974** P. L. MOORE et al. *Drilling Practices Manual* xii. 302 When a viscous mud is being used, additional mud weight may be required because of swabbing.

Swabian, *a.* and *sb.* Add: **b.** *sb.* (Earlier example.)

1840 BROWNING *Sordello* I. 12 They laughed as they enrolled That name at Milan on the page of gold For Godego.., Loria, and every sheep-cote on the Swabian's fief.

c. The dialect of Swabia. Also *Comb.*

1866 J. MACGREGOR *Thousand Miles in Rob Roy Canoe* (ed. 2) v. 76 They were much delighted..and went back prattling their purest Suabian in a highly satisfied frame of mind. **1886** STRONG & MEYER *Outl. Hist. German Lang.* v. 74 Swabian-Alemanic, spoken in Bavaria as far as the Lech, and in Würtemberg. **1937** D. P. INSKIP tr. *E. Tonnelat's Hist. German Lang.* x. 210 It is difficult to draw a boundary between Swabian and Alemanic proper. **1961** R. E. KELLER *German Dialects* 10 Speaking of a certain dialect, e.g. Swabian, implies that such a dialect has an identity which distinguishes it more or less clearly from other dialects. **1981** R. MANNHEIM tr. *G. Grass's Meeting at Telgte* iv. 22 After thirty years of residence in London, the diplomat Weckherlin still spoke an unvarnished Swabian.

swacked (swækt), *ppl. a. U.S. slang.* [f. SWACK *v.*[1] in Sc. dial. sense 'to gulp, swill' + -ED[1].] Drunk, intoxicated.

1932 *Amer. Speech* VII. 436 A man drunk is 'limp', 'tight', 'swacked'. **1936** WODEHOUSE *Laughing Gas* ix. 93 My father used to drink till he saw the light, and he prided himself on being able to say anything at any time of the day or night, no matter how swacked he might be, without tripping over a syllable. **1965** H. KANE *Devil to Pay* (1966) iii. 17 I'm slightly swacked on champagne. **1977** J. WAMBAUGH *Black Marble* (1978) vi. 71 They said he was bombed, swacked, bagged. By noon? She wasn't sure if it was booze.

swaddy: now generally superseded by *SQUADDIE.

Swadeshi. Substitute for def.: Used chiefly *attrib.* to designate an Indian nationalist movement originating in Bengal, which advocated principally the support of indigenous industries using home-produced materials (esp. cotton), and the boycott of foreign goods. Now (since the partition of 1947) *Hist.* (Later examples.)

1925 S. BANERJEA *Nation in Making* 198 [Jogesh Chunder Chaudhuri] it was who first started an Industrial Exhibition of *Swadeshi* articles as an annexe to the Indian National Congress. That was in 1896. **1936** J. NEHRU *Autobiogr.* xxxv. 266 So far the Congress had thought along purely nationalist lines, and had avoided facing economic issues, except in so far as it encouraged cottage industries and *swadeshi* generally. **1941** L. S. S. O'MALLEY *Mod. India & West* xvi. 762 *Swadeshi* goods..are goods manufactured in India by Indian labour from Indian raw and basic materials under the guidance of concerns whose capital and management are predominantly Indian, with the proviso that foreign raw or basic materials may be used in cases where India cannot supply them. **1970** 'B. MATHER' *Break in Line* xii. 156 Big coloured Swadeshi towels warming..by the stove. **1975** E. SHILS in H. M. Patel et al. *Say not the Struggle Nought Availeth* 68 The Indian political movement..did not cavil at the European substance of higher education. The Swadeshi movement made an issue of it, but it was more concerned with the intentions which were said to underlie it rather than with the substance.

swag, *sb.* Add: **6. b.** *Theatr.* A festooned stage-curtain or drapery, fastened similarly. Also *transf.* and *attrib.*

1959 RAE & SOUTHERN *Internat. Vocab. Techn. Theatre Terms 58* 74 Swag border. **1961** J. OSBORNE *Entertainer* 11 Different swags can be lowered for various scenes to break up the acting areas. **1982** BARR & YORK *Official Sloane Ranger Handbk.* 136/3 Lots of pretty pelmets and a few swags, variations on the theme of stage curtains—not like those dreadful draped net affairs one sees from the bypass.

7. (Earlier U.S. example.)

1848 *Holden's Dollar Mag.* Aug. 475/2 A 'Swag' is often met with in the Western country. It is a concave spot, sunk in below the level by nature.

9. (Earlier example.)

1794 *Sessions Papers Central Criminal Court* Jan. 341/1 There are very few gentlemen here on the jury but what know what a *swag* is; the meaning is, a bundle of clothes that are stolen from any place.

10. Also *N.Z.* Freq. in colloq. phrases *to hump the swag*: see HUMP *v.* 2 in Dict. and Suppl.; *on the swag*: on one's travels.

1853 J. ROCHFORT *Adventurers of Surveyer* vi. 49 Disregarding the state of the roads,..we strapped on our 'swags', consisting of a pair of blankets and a spare pair of trousers, and started for the diggings. **1935** J. GUTHRIE *Little Country* xxi. 312 You shouldered your swag and left to seek the foot of another rainbow. **1941** BAKER *N.Z. Slang* v. 41 Such expressions as *to swag it* and *go on the swag* need no elaboration. **1947** D. M. DAVIN *Gorse blooms Pale* 76 Jack went off on the swag for a few years. **1966** J. K. BAXTER *Pig Island Lett.* 16 No books, no bread Are left in my swag. **1971** *N.Z. Listener* 19 Apr. 56/5 He had a compass in his swag but it was pukeroo'd.

11. (*Austral.* and *N.Z.* examples in former sense.)

1929 K. S. PRICHARD *Coonardoo* 49 A boy with a swag of ideas, Hughie was still, Mrs. Bessie realized. **1949** F. SARGESON *I saw in my Dream* ix. 75, I suppose you blokes get told a lot of yarns about a crook missis and a swag of kids. **1963** *Weekly News* (Auckland) 5 June 37/2 There was a big swag of fowls on the station running semiwild. **1973** *New Journalist* (Australia) July–Aug. 4/1 It is cheaper to buy a swag of aged situation comedies.. than to produce even the simplest studio-bound program in Australia.

12. a. swag lamp, light *N. Amer.*, an overhead light externally wired so that the flex hangs in a loop across the ceiling towards the power socket; **swagsman** (earlier examples); also *N.Z.*; now *Obs.*

1970 *Toronto Daily Star* 24 Sept. 28/6 (Advt.), Swag lamps; chromed chairs, easy chairs. **1966** M. M. PEGLER *Dict. Interior Design* (1967) 436 *Swag light*, a lamp or light fixture which is hooked into the ceiling with the electric cord..swagged from the hanging point to the nearest wall, and then down to the floor outlet where it is plugged in. **1869** in W. M. Hugo *Hist. First Bushmen's Club Austral. Colonies* (1872) 30 A swagsman, and not ashamed to own it. I have done the 'wallaby' for years past in search of a billet. **1874** A. BATHGATE *Colonial Experiences* xv. 212 One source of annoyance to the squatters is the 'swagsmen'..or men who travel about the country, professedly in search of work, but who do not in reality want it.

b. (Earlier example.)

1829 P. EGAN *Boxiana* 2nd Ser. II. 74 It is impossible to describe the applause bestowed upon Delay by the boys of the Blue Anchor, the Cock and Cross, and the Ship and Gun, near the *great swag* shop in the east.

swag, *v.* Add: **4.** Chiefly *Austral.* and *N.Z.* **a.** Also in extended use, to travel as a swagman (*up* a region). **b.** Also, to carry in a 'swag'; to wander about (the land) as a swagman.

1861 J. HAAST *Rep. Topographical Exploration Western Districts Nelson Province* i. 16 We again started, on the 11th of February, swagging part of the provisions, &c., down the Buller. **1875** J. JENKINS *Diary Welsh Swagman* (1975) 52 It is better than swagging the country..searching for work. **1883** W. S. GREEN *High Alps N.Z.* 247 We would be obliged..to obtain a sheep and 'swag' it up the glacier again. **1901** *Bulletin Reciter* (Sydney) 5 And swagging up the long divide that leads to Daybreak Range We came. **1914** A. A. GRACE *Tale of Timber Town* 116 You'll get the tucker..and you'll help swag it. **1939** J. D. PASCOE *Unclimbed N.Z.* 42 We left the hut in auspicious weather to swag up the Mingha riverbed. **1960** 'A. CARSON' *Rose by any Other Name* ix. 50, I was swagging my way up to the Northern Territory.

5. *Criminals' slang.* † **a.** To steal; to make away with (stolen property). *Obs.* **b.** To push (a person) forcefully, to 'shove'; to take or snatch away roughly.

1846 *Swell's Night Guide* 113/2 Bag, to take away, see pinch and swag. **1886** H. BAUMANN *Londinismen* 200/2 *Swag*..*v.*, plündern, rauben. **1958** F. NORMAN *Bang to Rights* I. 10 So when we got swaged into the meatwagon I asked another geezer the strength of him, and the strength was that he'd got nicked for ponceing. **1978** J. BARNETT *Head of Force* iii. 21 The object is to see if the Commissioner was swagged away by anyone during the demo.

swager[2] (swē[i]·dʒəɹ). Now *rare.* [f. SWAGE *v.*[3] + -ER[1].] One who swages metal.

1881 in *Instructions to Census Clerks* (1885) 91. **1921** *Dict. Occup. Terms* (1927) § 190 s.v., Agricultural machine knife swager. **1954** *Times* 9 Apr. 9/4 In my grandfather's lifetime the swager was a familiar figure in the West Country.

swagged, *a.* [f. SWAG *sb.* 6 + -ED[2].] Draped in swags; decorated with swags.

1959 *House & Garden* July 13 For curtains, we suggest ..swagged muslin. **1970** *Daily Tel.* 21 Oct. 15 Two Moroccan woollen belts, about 54in long,..bound and swagged with other bright wools.

swagger, *sb.*[1] Add: **2.** Also, short for *swagger bag, coat,* etc.: see *SWAGGER-.

1929 *Papers Mich. Acad. Sci., Arts & Lett.* X. 327/2 *Swagger* (hospital slang), a tunic for promenade occasions; 'square-push' tunic. **1939** [see *beaver lamb* s.v. *BEAVER[1] 6]. **1968** J. IRONSIDE *Fashion Alphabet* 38 *Swagger*, a jacket with a very full back, hanging loose in front. **1979** *Arizona Daily Star* 1 Apr. (Suppl.), In-fashion spring bags... Swaggers, shoulder-straps, double handles.

swagger-. Add: *swagger-bag*; **swagger coat,** a three-quarter-length ladies' coat cut with a loose flare from the shoulders (particularly fashionable in the 1930s).

1933 *Bulletin* (Glasgow) 14 Oct. 15/1 A swagger-coat with collarette and gauntlets of black astrakhan. **1938** 'J. BELL' *Port of London Murders* ii. 24 Her hands were pushed into the pockets of an old swagger coat. **1953** 'P. WENTWORTH' *Watersplash* ii. 8 The glove and its fellow had been thrust into the pocket of a blue swagger coat. **1974** *Index-Jrnl.* (Greenwood, S. Carolina) 23 Apr. 3/2 (Advt.), Special selection of baskets, swagger bags, totes, envelopes. **1980** B. BAINBRIDGE *Winter Garden* x. 74 She stood in the gutter in her swagger coat and allowed her teeth to chatter piteously.

swagging, *vbl. sb.* Add: **3.** *Austral.* and *N.Z.* Travelling as a swagman; carrying one's 'swag', back-packing.

1883 W. S. GREEN *High Alps N.Z.* xvi. 268 Descending to the lower camp..and doing the hard swagging work all over again. **1892** *N.Z. Alpine Jrnl.* I. 100 All our dirty work and heavy swagging will be done for us. **1940** W. S. GILKISON *Peaks, Packs & Mountain Tracks* xiii. 102 Swagging—or, if you prefer it, back-packing—is more or less an essential part of every climbing trip. **1960** 'A. CARSON' *Rose by any Other Name* ix. 50 Swagging is an honourable profession in Australia.

Swahili. (Earlier example of the language.)

1847 W. W. GREENOUGH in *Jrnl. Amer. Oriental Soc.* I. 263 The Sooahelee has been called a lingua franca.

Swahilian, *a.* (Example.)

1846 J. R. BROWNE *Etchings Whaling Cruise* xvi. 335 The Sowhelian language is the most generally spoken.

Swainson (swē[i]·nsən). The name of William *Swainson* (1789–1855), English naturalist, used in the possessive to designate birds named in his honour, as **Swainson's † buzzard, hawk,** a dark-coloured buzzard hawk, *Buteo swainsoni*, found in western North America; **Swainson's thrush,** an olive-backed thrush, *Hylocichla ustulata*, found in western North America; **Swainson's warbler,** a brown and white warbler, *Limnothlypis swainsonii*, found in swamp regions of south-eastern North America.

1858 S. F. BAIRD *Birds Pacific Railway Routes* 19 Swainson's Buzzard,.. more nearly related to a generic form of the Old World. *Ibid.* 252 Swainson's Warbler.. South Atlantic States. **1869** *Amer. Naturalist* III. 31 Swainson's Thrush... Common at Cœur d'Aleñe Mission. **1895** *U.S. Dept. Agric. Yearbk. 1894* 222 The food of Swainson's hawk..is of much the same character as that of the two preceding species. **1912** C. A. REED *Birds Eastern N. Amer.* 359 Swainson's Warbler is a comparatively rare species found in the Southeastern States. **1939** F. C. LINCOLN *Migration Amer. Birds* 79 Observers in the Great Plains saw large flocks of Red-tailed Hawks, Swainson's Hawks and Rough-legged Hawks wheeling majestically. **1972** *Islander* (Victoria, B.C.) 21 May 6/2 In the evening the sound of the Swainson's thrush. **1976** *National Observer* (U.S.) 31 July 5/2 Southern Swainson's warblers would no doubt agree. **1980** *Country Life* 3 July 46/2, I watched huge flocks of broad-winged hawks..and a few Swainson's hawks.

Swakara (swa·kara). [f. the initials of *S*outh *W*est *A*frica + *KARA(KUL.] The coat of a karakul lamb, bred in Namibia, valued as a fur. Chiefly *attrib.*

1966 *Fur Rev.* May 13/1 Selective breeding has improved the..qualities of S.W.A. Persian Lambskins and brought about a changeover..to a flat glossy pelt... In order to spread..the extended range of S.W. African merchandise, a publicity agent has..[come] up with the clever catchword '*Swakara*'. **1973** *Country Life* 1 Feb. 302/3 Slim little jackets in Swakara broadtail, dyed delectable shades of peach. **1978** *Lancashire Life* Sept. 110/1 Natural grey Swakara Persian lamb has a unique charm.

swale, *sb.*[3] Add: Also *U.S.*, a hollow between adjacent sand-ridges.

1894 *Dialect Notes* I. 334 *Swale*, low land between sand ridges on the coast beaches [of New Jersey]. **1945, 1976** [see *point bar* (*b*) s.v. *POINT *sb.*[1] D. 14].

swale (swē^{i}l), *sb.*[4] *South. dial. local.* [Origin uncertain: cf. SWEAL, SWALE *sb.*, and *swill* sb.[1] 10 in *Eng. Dial. Dict.*] A small broom or brush without a stick for a handle.

1949 K. S. WOODS *Rural Crafts of England* III. vii. 123 Some besoms are made without sticks. These are known as swales, an interesting word meaning 'a small bright fire enough to boil a kettle'. Swales are used to brush the flakes from steel-plate. **1968** J. ARNOLD *Shell Bk. Country Crafts* 100 Like the besom, it has a head of birch..but is without a handle and is called a swale.

Swaledale (swē^{i}·ldē^{i}l). The name of a region of North Yorkshire used *absol.* or *attrib.* to designate a long-woolled sheep of the hardy hill breed first developed in the area; also, the breed itself or the long coarse wool produced by a sheep of this kind.

1916 W. J. MALDEN *Brit. Sheep & Shepherding* vi. 58 Among the remaining breeds of the northern hills may be mentioned the Swaledale, a very hardy breed. **1944** G. HENDERSON *Farming Ladder* i. 24 The stock consisted of 650 Blackfaced mountain ewes, and thirty pedigree Swaledales. **1961** J. GUNSTON *Profit from Sheep* ii. 22 Swaledales..do very well in a wide range of hard-grazing and cold districts. **1971** *Farmers Weekly* 19 Mar. 43/3 Certain wool types such as Blackface, Devon and Swaledale have met a better market demand than others. **1980** *Times* 3 Mar. 16/2 A Pennine farmer..was saving 50 bales of hay a day among his Swaledale ewes.

swallow, *sb.*[1] Add: **1. d.** *ellipt.* for *swallow dive* below.

1902 *Encycl. Brit.* XXXIII. 121/2 The 'swallow' is one of the most thrilling dives. **1971** 'D. HALLIDAY' *Dolly & Doctor Bird* xi. 148 Sergeant Trotter himself nipped up the diving-board and executed a swallow and somersault.

e. *transf.* A woman employed by the Soviet intelligence service, who seduces men for the purposes of espionage. *slang.*

1972 D. BLOODWORTH *Any Number can Play* ix. 69 You have doubtless read about the..'swallows' of the KGB, the young ladies trained..to bed down intelligence targets, so that they can be comfortably and conveniently bugged and photographed in compromising..positions? **1976** 'M. BARAK' *Secret List H. Roehm* xii. 130, I need a swallow in America. One..who is sexually skilled and expert in obtaining information. **1979** P. WAY *Sunrise* i. 15 Had she been working for the KGB, Joanna would have been..called a 'swallow'. In the CIA she would have been a 'honeypot'.

4. swallow dive, a forward dive in which the arms are extended sideways, to simulate the outline of a swallow, until just before entry into the water; also *fig.*; so **swallow-diving**; hence **swallow-dive** *v. intr.*; **swallow fork** orig. *Amer.*, a forked cut used in marking cattle or sheep on the ear (see quot. 1966); hence **swallow-fork** *v. trans.*, to cut a swallow fork in (the ear); **swallow-forked** *ppl. a.*, shaped so as to cut a swallow fork; **swallow's nest:** also in *swallow's nest soup*, an oriental dish (see BIRD'S-NEST, BIRD-NEST *sb.* 1).

1898 *Swimming Mag.* Oct. 46/1 To Englishmen the term 'swallow' dive, not 'swan', would best convey the notion of this idealistic manner of reaching the water. **1971** 'D. HALLIDAY' *Dolly & Doctor Bird* xi. 148 Sergeant Trotter, reappearing at the top of the diving-board, swallow-dived efficiently. **1976** 'A. HALL' *Kobra Manifesto* xvi. 215 Sassine had come off his high in a swallow dive. **1897** *Encycl. Sport* II. 425/1 The most graceful is that termed 'swallow-diving', the body being shot out from the board [etc.]. **1636** *Plymouth* (Mass.) *Rec.* (1889) I. 1 Every mans marke of his Cattle... Christopher Wadesworth a swallow forke. **1869** *Overland Monthly* III. 126 An over-slope and a slit in the right, and a swallow-fork in the left. **1934** *Amer. Ballads & Folk Songs* xvi. 409 They cropped and swallow-forked his ears. **1966** *Publ. Amer. Dial. Soc. 1964* XLII. 16 *Swallow fork*, two slits run together to form a *W* or an *M*. **1972** P. NEWTON *Sheep Thief* xvi. 134 It was a pair of swallow-forked earmarkers. **1920** E. & P. SYKES *Through Deserts & Oases Central Asia* iv. 78 Swallows' nest soup is almost unprocurable nowadays. **1976** *Times* 14 Feb. 10/4 A real Thai Chinese restaurant..three colours swallow's nest soup..or even plain shark's fin soup.

swallow, *v.* Add: **1. b.** Also, *to swallow the anchor*, to retire from a sea-faring life; also *transf.*; *to have swallowed the dictionary*: see *DICTIONARY 1 c.

1907 J. MASEFIELD *Tarpaulin Muster* xii. 129 An old sailor..had 'swallowed the anchor' in Colon. **1931** A. R. L. GARDNER *Art of Crime* 253 We are glad to be able to quote these..words to..our readers who may entertain..fears lest the crook proper should one day 'swallow the anchor' and retire permanently from the stage. **1977** *Islander* (Victoria, B.C.) 22 May 6/1 But, now he had 'swallowed the anchor', he was a hard-headed business man.

swallower. 3. Delete † and add later example with *up*.

1855 MRS. GASKELL *Let.* Feb. (1966) 332 Meta's atelier is such a swallower-up of time.

swallow-tailed, *a.* **II. 6.** (Earlier example.)

1824 J. MORIER *Adventures of Hajji Baba* I. p. xl, I sighed for shaven chins and swallow-tailed coats.

swamp, *sb.* Add: **3. a.** *swamp-dweller* (earlier example), *forest, -jungle, land* (earlier examples), *meadow*; **swamp buggy** *N. Amer.*, a vehicle used in swampy regions; *spec.* a tracked vehicle which can pull a heavily loaded trailer; **swamp cooler** *U.S.* (see quot. 1950); **swamp fever,** (*b*) a contagious virus disease of horses, causing anæmia, emaciation, and usually death; **swamp fire** *Canad.*, methane burning in a swampy area; a will-o'-the-wisp (also used in metaphorical comparisons); **swamp plough** *N.Z.*, a type of plough with a large mould-board, for use on heavy soils; **swamp rock,** a type of rock music associated with the Southern U.S.; **swamp Yankee** *U.S. dial.* (see quot. 1963).

1941 *Nat. Geogr. Mag.* June 706 Their 'swamp-buggy' is a seagoing amphibious-looking vehicle. Its 10-foot high wheels are equipped with fat, fin-studded oversized tires which act as propellers; when the odd vehicle leaves the land and takes to water, it begins to swim. **1966** *North* July–Aug. 14/2 When the usually dependable swamp buggy breaks down, it's back to the dog team. **1973** *Globe & Mail* (Toronto) 3 Feb. 7/5 While the public sleeps, a Pandora's Box is opening to release a flood of hovercraft, dune buggies, swamp buggies, trail bikes, air sleds and airboats on the long-suffering landscape of crowded Southern Ontario. **1950** *Newsweek* 14 Aug. 51 In dry climates it is possible to rig up a primitive but highly effective cooling system, called a 'swamp cooler'. It consists simply of a fan blowing over an excelsior mat which is drenched with dripping water. **1979** *Tucson* (Arizona) *Citizen* (Weekender Mag.) 28 Apr. 9/1 A swamp cooler has maybe five moving parts; if it quits, you go up on the roof, look to see which part has quit moving, and replace it. **1890** Swamp-dweller [see *PINE LAND]. **1903** *Rep. Min. Agric. Canada 1902* 85 There has been known in the Red River Valley a peculiar and very fatal disease of horses... It is a disease of low lying and swampy country and it is therefore popularly known as swamp fever. **1975** *Daily Colonist* (Victoria, B.C.) 6 July 2/3 Swamp fever..equine infectious anemia—has ravaged almost half of..the little ponies. **1903** S. E. WHITE *Forest* 122 Like swamp-fire, it lured the imagination always on and on and on through the secret waterways of the uninhabited North. **1954** V. LYSENKO *Yellow Boots* 146 Behind them the swamp fire, like a gigantic Jack o'lantern, bumped and danced and ran around the sky, then finally, as it reached the ground, evaporated into the night air. **1982** H. LIEBERMAN *Night Call* iii. 12 Daughtry's reputation..traveled like swampfire. **1909** GROOM & BALFOUR tr. *Warming's Oecol. Plants* lx. 234 (*heading*) Littoral swamp-forest. Mangrove. **1955** P. A. BUXTON *Nat. Hist. Tsetse Flies* ix. 269 In places there are 'swamp forests'..the trees growing in a few feet of water at all seasons. **1964** G. B. SCHALLER *Year of Gorilla* (1965) viii. 215 The swamp forest that grows in the low country bordering the South China Sea. **1902** D. G. HOGARTH *Nearer East* 108 Torrential floods, which..support a dense swamp-jungle. **1662** in *Connecticut Hist. Soc. Coll.* (1912) XIV. 433 One Parcel of land.. being Swamp land. **1701** *Early Rec. Providence, Rhode Island* (1894) V. 125 A Certaine ffarme or tract of land consisting of upland swampe land & Meadow land. **1697** *Cambridge* (Mass.) *Proprietors' Rec.* (1896) 344 Four Rods of fence, Lyeing att the head of Samuel Hastings Swamp-meadow. **1880** *Harper's Mag.* June 80 Out in the swamp meadow the tall clumps of boneset show their dull white crests. **1951** R. P. HOBSON *Grass beyond Mountains* 41 We sat around..talking of range cows, and tough trails, slough grass and swamp meadows. **1930** L. G. D. ACLAND *Early Canterbury Runs* 1st Ser. iii. 42 They..spent a lot of money in cutting the scrub, crushing it down with rollers, and ploughing it in with swamp ploughs. **1973** *Massey Ferguson Rev.* (N.Z.) Mar.–Apr. 5/1 He..leaves it for two years before getting to work with a 19-inch swamp plough. **1970** *Guardian* 17 Apr. 10/2 Then Creedence. The band['s]..music, like that of Delaney and Bonnie, is called 'swamp rock', and identified with the Southern States of America. **1941** H. KURATH *Linguistic Atlas of New England* II. II. Map 450 The map shows a great variety of terms, largely derogatory and jocular, applied to a person who lives in the country—specifically to an old farmer who seldom visits the village or city. The following terms were recorded in more than one community: rustic,.. swamp Yankee, hayback, hayseed or hayseeder. **1963** *Amer. Speech* XXXVIII. 121 The term *swamp Yankee* may be defined as 'a rural New England dweller who abides today as a steadfast rustic and who is of Yankee stock that has endured in the New England area since the colonial days.' **1975** G. V. HIGGINS *City on Hill* iv. 104 That back country's full of swamp Yankees, guys..that impregnate their own daughters.

b. swamp deer: see also *BARASINGHA; (earlier example); **swamp rabbit,** either of two dark brown rabbits of the south-eastern United States, the cane-cutter, *Sylvilagus aquaticus*, or the marsh rabbit, *S. palustris*; cf. *swamp hare*; **swamp robin** (earlier and later examples); also, = TOWHEE; **swamp wallaby,** a large wallaby, *Wallabia bicolor*, which has reddish or greyish fur with darker markings; **swamp warbler** (earlier example).

1874 T. C. JERDON *Mammals of India* 254 The Swamp Deer... Horns very large and moderately stout. **1845** C. LYELL *Second Visit U.S.* I. 228, I had heard much of the swamp-rabbit, which they hunt near the coast in South Carolina and Georgia. **1875** *Fur, Fin & Feather* (ed. 3) 136/1 The 'swamp rabbit' inhabits the heavy timbered woodlands and river bottoms. **1938** M. K. RAWLINGS *Yearling* v. 51 The pair of black swamp rabbits was not new. **1964** W. H. BURT *Field Guide Mammals* (ed. 2) 223 Swamp Rabbit... This is a rich brownish-gray rabbit with coarse hair; feet rusty. **1769** R. SMITH *Jrnl.* 18 May in *Tour of Four Great Rivers* (1906) 41 The lively Note of the Swamp Robin, the Red Bird and other Birds from the earliest Dawn is entertaining. **1955** Swamp robin [see *JOREE]. **1896** Swamp wallaby [see *brush wallaby* s.v. *BRUSH *sb.*[1] 4]. **1970** W. D. L. RIDE *Guide Native Mammals Austral.* v. 47 The Swamp Wallaby..is usually placed in a separate genus *Wallabia*. **1859** THOREAU *Jrnl.* 30 Apr. in *Writings* (1906) XVIII. 167 This first *off-coat* warmth just preceding the advent of the swamp warblers (parti-colored, red-start, etc.) brings them out.

c. swamp ash (earlier example); **swamp azalea** (later example); **swamp blackberry,** a low-growing, semi-evergreen dewberry, *Rubus hispidus*, found near water and marshy ground in parts of Canada and northern and central U.S.A.; **swamp blueberry,** the high-bush blueberry, *Vaccinium corymbosum*, or its fruit; **swamp-cabbage** (later examples); also, the cabbage palmetto, *Sabal palmetto*; **swamp dewberry** = *swamp blackberry* above; **swamp hickory,** the water hickory, *Carya aquatica*, or the bitternut hickory, *C. cordiformis* (earlier and later examples); **swamp honeysuckle,** (*b*) a honeysuckle of eastern North America, *Lonicera oblongifolia*, with yellowish flowers and red berries; **swamp laurel,** substitute for def.: the sweetbay magnolia, *M. virginiana*; formerly, also the pale American laurel, *Kalmia polifolia*; (earlier and later examples); **swamp lily** (earlier example); (*d*) *Crinum americanum*, which bears white flowers and is native to the south-eastern United States; **swamp mahogany,** a gum tree, *Eucalyptus robusta*, native to coastal regions of eastern Australia; (earlier example); **swamp maple** (examples); **swamp pine** (later examples); **swamp rose** (examples); also, another wild N. Amer. rose, *Rosa palustris*; **swamp sumach,** for *venenata* read *vernix* (later examples); **swamp willow** (earlier example).

1794 W. CLARK *Jrnl.* 15 Sept. in *Mississippi Valley Hist. Rev.* (1914) I. 437 The face [of the land] is nearly covered with a thick groth of Shrubbery, Brush, some Beech, Swamp Ash. **1958** G. A. PETRIDES *Field Guide to Trees & Shrubs* 365 Swamp Azalea... A medium-sized to tall shrub with leaves glossy above. **1854** THOREAU *Jrnl.* 4 Aug. in *Writings* (1906) XII. 419 The swamp blackberry on high land, ripe a day or two. **1903** H. L. KEELER *Our Northern Shrubs* 161 Few trailing plants combine a better effect of flower and foliage than our Swamp blackberry. **1975** E. WIGGINTON *Foxfire 3* 285 Swamp blackberry is found in thickets in low, wet places. **1860** THOREAU *Jrnl.* 30 Dec. in *Writings* (1906) XX. 299 Some ten days later comes the high blueberry, or swamp blueberry, the commonest stout shrub of our swamps. **1917** E. S. BAILEY *Sand Dunes Indiana* 154 There is a chance to study all the sides of a small pond, with the shrub zone of plants in perfect type, such as swamp blueberry, cranberry [etc.]. **1949** *Pacific Spectator* Spring 223 You had to cross the river..to find the low swamp blueberries, lighter blue and sweeter than any other kind. **1880** *Harper's Mag.* June 66 The swamp-cabbage flower..peers above the ground beneath his purple spotted hood. **1938** M. K. RAWLINGS *Yearling* xx. 250 He pulled away layer after layer of the white cores and came at last to the hearts [of palms], crisp and sweet. He said, 'Now I want that fryin' pan, Mr. Penny, please, for my swamp cabbage.' **1942** S. KENNEDY *Palmetto Country* 3 Folks outside the region usually think of the palmetto as the tall palm which is locally called the swamp cabbage or cabbage palm. **1976**

National Observer (U.S.) 22 May 16-A/1 They were forced to subsist on a diet of unpolished rice, swamp cabbage, and tiny fish. **1924** C. Deam *Shrubs Indiana* 109 *Rubus hispidus* Linnaeus. Swamp Dewberry. **1942** L. R. Tehon *Fieldbk. Native Illinois Shrubs* 116 The Swamp Dewberry grows near lakes and marshes, especially at the base of wooded slopes. **1976** *Hortus Third* (L. H. Bailey Hortorium) 985/2 *Swamp dewberry, running blackberry, swamp b.*, slender, hispid, often glandular trailer, laying close to the ground, without prickles. **1806** in *Message from President of U.S., communicating Discoveries made in exploring the Missouri by Captains Lewis & Clark* 65 The growth, on the highest [places is] handsome oaks, swamp hickory, ash, grape vines, &c. **1912** I. S. Cobb *Back Home* 306 He was tough as swamp hickory. **1938** C. H. Matschat *Suwannee River* 161 They alus stuck togither tightern the bark on a swamp hickory. **1958** G. A. Petrides *Field Guide Trees & Shrubs* 47 Swamp Honeysuckle *Lonicera oblongifolia*... A more or less hairless honeysuckle. **1743** J. Clayton *Flora Virginica* 83 *Magnolia Laurifolia*,..Swamp-Laurel. **1869** J. G. Fuller *Uncle John's Flower-Gatherers* 138 The farmers around here call it [sc. *Kalmia*] 'Swamp-Laurel'. **1884** C. S. Sargent *Rep. Forests N. Amer.* 20 Sweet Bay..Swamp Laurel... A tree 15 to 22 meters in height. **1737** J. Brickell *Nat. Hist. N. Carolina* 21 Another Weed, vulgarly called the Swamp-Lillie..grows in the Marshes and low Grounds, and is something like our Dock in its Leaves. **1884** A. Nilson *Timber Trees New South Wales* 71 Swamp Mahogany.—A large tree..with a rough furrowed bark. **1810** Swamp maple [see *maple tree]. **1869** Mrs. Stowe *Oldtown Folks* xiv. 153 Here and there, a swamp-maple seemed all one crimson flame. **1936** E. B. White *Let.* 3 Sept. (1976) 141 Joe and I have gathered boughs of red swamp maple, to decorate the back porch. **1969** T. H. Everett *Living Trees of World* xxii. 221/1 The most important American soft maples are the red or swamp maple..and the silver maple. **1743** M. Catesby *Nat. Hist. Carolina* II. p. xxii, The Swamp Pine grows on barren wet land. **1851** J. S. Springer *Forest Life* 41 This difference is accounted for by..the tardiness with which the swamp Pine matures. **1958** G. A. Petrides *Field Guide Trees & Shrubs* 15 Swamp Pine..similar to Pitch Pine. **1785** H. Marshall *Arbustrum Americanum* 135 Swamp Pennsylvanian Rose..[rises] to a height of four or five feet. **1814** J. Bigelow *Florula Bostoniensis* 121 Swamp rose..grows in swamps and wet grounds. **1902** *Outing* June 272/2 The Carolina or swamp rose..is well known to us all. **1814** Swamp sumach [see *poison dogwood* s.v. *poison *sb.* 5 b]. **1945** H. T. Darlington *Higher Plants of Michigan* 25 Red maple and swamp sumac..may add to the brilliant effect. **1765** J. Bartram *Jrnl.* 31 July in *Trans. Amer. Philos. Soc.* (1942) XXXIII. 17/1 They have ye upland willow oak with A hoary leafe, & ye swamp willow with A narrow leafe.

swamp, *v.* Add: **5.** (Earlier and later examples.) Also with *out*. Also *Canad.*

1784 M. Patten *Diary* 18 Mar. (1903) 480, I swampt out 4 small oak logs the boys saved in cuting wood Ready for hauling out. **1851** J. S. Springer *Forest Life* 84 This is done by an experienced hand, who 'spots' the trees where he wishes the road to be 'swamped'. **1871** R. L. Dashwood *Chiploquorgan* viii. 104 A crew of lumberers have different occupations assigned to them;..the 'swampers', who 'swamp'—cut roads—to the felled trees, to enable the 'teamster' and his assistants to haul them on a 'Bob sled'. **1937** P. K. Devine *Devine's Folk Lore of Newfoundland* 50 To swamp a road or path is to build one with a bedding of boughs to be used in hauling slide loads of wood in winter. **1954** C. Bruce *Channel Shore* 27 [He] had swamped a hauling-road into the middle of the stretch that lay south of the shore road. **1974** D. Sears *Lark in Clear Air* iii. 40 Where the logs came from and who cut them and the names of the horses that swamped them out.

6. *intr.* To work as a bullock-driver's assistant (also casually, in return for having one's 'swag' carried); to make (*one's way*) by obtaining a lift from a traveller. Cf. *swamper 1 c, d. *Austral. slang.*

1926 K. S. Prichard *Working Bullocks* 101 Billy Williams the bullocky, and Ern Collins who was swamping for him, turned their team into the yards on the following Monday. **1937** E. Hill *Ports of Sunset* 96 In they came, across the jagged Leopolds, or up from the desert, 'swamping' with a bullocky, staggering behind a pack donkey, or on Shanks' pony. **1944** M. J. O'Reilly *Bowyangs & Boomerangs* 6 My duties were to help to load and unload, bring the horses in the morning, to harness up, help to corduroy bad patches on the track, [etc.]... Fortunately the chap I 'swamped' for was an exceptionally good sort. **1964** T. Ronan *Packhorse & Pearling Boat* 170 If I broke it for a tenner, I'd roll my swag and swamp my way back to Queensland.

swamper. Add: **1. b.** (Examples.) Also, an assistant to a cook.

1907 *Oregonian* (Portland) 13 Oct. 8/1 He was a swamper in a saloon. **1929** *Collier's* 5 Jan. 33/1 As a result it became pay dirt, and in later years the swamper actually had to pay for his job. **1939** P. A. Rollins *Gone Haywire* 65 Until the call was given, the average cook permitted nobody to approach the fire except the helper whom he rarely had, and who was known as the flunky, roustabout, swamper, or cook's louse. **1962** E. Lucia *Klondike Kate* iii. 81 The [theatrical] company had its own bartenders and swampers. **1979** D. Anthony *Long Hard Cure* ii. 20 He'd returned promptly to his apartment over the tavern. His Negro swamper bore him out.

c. An assistant to a driver of horses, mules, or bullocks. *slang.* (orig. *U.S.*).

1870 *Daily Territorial Enterprise* (Virginia City, Nevada) 21 Apr. 3/1 A 'swamper' is a man who goes with the driver of a 10, 12, or 14-mule team as his assistant—the driver being chief engineer and the swamper first-assistant. **1926** K. S. Prichard *Working Bullocks* i. 6 Red Burke shouted to the bullocks... His swamper yelled and danced. **1960** A. Downs *Wagon Road North* 43 Many drivers were accompanied by a 'swamper', who was usually a young fellow apprenticed to the teaming business. The swamper looked after the horses, including rounding them up in the morning, usually about four o'clock, and in general assisted the teamster with the over-all duties of freighting.

d. One who travels on foot but has his swag carried on a wagon; hence, one who obtains a lift. Cf. *swamp *v.* 6. *Austral. slang.*

1901 M. Vivienne *Travels in W. Australia* 284 A 'swamper' is a man tramping without his swag, which he entrusts to a teamster to bring on his waggon... While on foot the swamper will generally leave the track, and prospect. **1929** J. Raeside *Golden Days* 380 With many a swamper's swag on And many a billy black. **1966** T. Ronan *Once there was Bagman* i. 15 My..fellow swamper tossed his swag off [the mailman's truck] here; he was home.

e. An assistant to the driver of a lorry. *N. Amer. slang.*

1929 *Amer. Speech* IV. 345 *Swamper*, a helper on an auto truck. **1953** C. Armstrong *Catch-as-catch-Can* xiv. 114 The driver of this linen service truck, told his swamper ..to stay with it. **1963** *Sun* (Vancouver) 28 Feb. 1/5 A wood truck swamper was charged $25 each for two stolen kisses Wednesday. **1975** E. Iglauer *Denison's Ice Road* viii. 194 We don't have swampers, a second man on the truck, the way the oil-field men have.

2. (Earlier examples.)

[**1735** J. Belcher in *New Hampshire Provincial Papers* (1870) IV. 878 The B B's Pr—st is a jolly Fellow. I hear he stood Kick and Cuff upon the Road with some Swampeers.] **1775** *N. Carolina Gaz.* (New Berne) 24 Mar. 3/3 Fellow Dismalites and Swampers, are we not the Men whom God hath appointed to curb the Insolence of Britain. **1857** J. D. Long *Pictures of Slavery* xvii. 323, I made an appointment to deliver a temperance address to the 'swampers'.

swan, *sb.* Add: **2. c.** (Later examples with allusion to Shakespeare.)

1895 G. B. Shaw *Our Theatres in Nineties* (1932) I. 197 Everyone concerned..is full of earnest belief that the splendor of the Swan will be revealed at last, like the Holy Grail. **1922** Joyce *Ulysses* 186 Shakespeare..does not stay to feed the pen chivying her game of cygnets towards the rushes. The swan of Avon has other thoughts.

e. [f. *swan *v.*^{1} 2.] An apparently aimless journey; an excursion made for reconnaissance or for pleasure. *slang* (orig. *Mil.*).

1946 Visct. Montgomery *El Alamein* 45 A recurrence of what was then becoming known in the Eighth Army as the 'annual swan' between Egypt and El Agheila. **1958** *Spectator* 23 May 665/2 The General.., yielding to a very natural temptation to go for a 'swan' early in the battle, was away from his headquarters for over thirty-six hours. **1960** C. Achebe *No Longer at Ease* xvii. 153 But for an African like you, who has too many privileges as it is, to ask for two weeks to go on a swan, it makes me want to cry. **1968** *Listener* 22 Feb. 238/1 It [*sc.* a festival] has become an accepted 'swan' for the British correspondents. **1974** D. Hart-Davis *Peter Fleming* iv. 75 The trip as a whole was designed to be what he later called a 'swan'—a general look round. **1979** D. Clark *Heberden's Seat* vii. 150 'Reed and I may have to go to London for the day.'.. 'It's not just a swan is it?'

4. a. (Further chiefly *poet.* examples.) *swancomb* (fig.), *-flight, -meat, -plumage*; objective, *swan-delighting* adj.; instrumental, *swan-instructed* adj.; parasynthetic and similative, *swan-breasted, -bright, -feathered, -fledged, -soft* adjs.

1930 R. Campbell *Adamastor* 73 The great swan-breasted seraphs soar and sing. **1923** E. Sitwell *Bucolic Comedies* 35 The swan-bright fountains. **1922** Swancomb [see *high-reared* s.v. *high *adv.* 10 a]. **1936** Auden *Look, Stranger!* 41 The swan-delighting river. **1953** R. Graves *Poems* 17 Past either cheek Swan-feathered arrows whistle. **1862** G. M. Hopkins *Vision of Mermaids* (1929), And shake From wings swan-fledged a wheel of watery light. **1959** E. Pound *Thrones* xcviii. 38 The King's job, vast as the swan-flight. **1942** S. Smith *Magic Morning* in *Coll. Poems* (1975) 206 'Charley, Charley, Charley' cry the swan-instructed curlews. **1922** Joyce *Ulysses* 151 Wonder what kind is swanmeat. **1953** E. Sitwell *Gardeners & Astronomers* 37 And Cygnus who gave you all his bright swan-plumage. **1925** —— *Troy Park* 12 In the thick swan-soft fields.

b. swan dive *U.S.*, a swallow dive (see *swallow *sb.*^{1} 4); hence **swan-dive** *v. intr.*; **swan-drop,** (*b*) (earlier example); **swanproof** *a. nonce-wd.*, not susceptible to the influence of Shakespeare (cf. sense 2 c in Dict. and Suppl.); **swan-shot,** also used in angling as a weight; **swan-song:** hence, any final performance, action, or effort; **Swan Vesta,** the proprietary name of a make of match; cf. Vesta 4.

1898 *Swimming Mag.* Oct. 45/2 The diving..included forward headers,..somersaults and the 'Swan' dive from twenty, thirty, and forty feet. **1912** J. London *Son of Sun* ii. 53, I used to swan-dive a hundred and ten feet in the clear. **1932** E. Hemingway *Death in Afternoon* i. 21 As though a diver could control..[the] speed..of a swan dive. **1972** B. F. Conners *Don't embarrass Bureau* (1973) i. 7 Mrs. Green..executed her swan dive, flopping onto the water with the poise of a stricken bird. **1853** J. Palliser *Solitary Rambles* ii. 55 My own saddle-bags contained..powder and shot, and, by great good luck, some swan-drops. **1905** G. B. Shaw in *Shaw on Theatre* (1958) 103 Since Shakespear's words are still the basis of the dialogue, there are moments when the bard enjoys his own again; for all the players are not as completely swanproof as Mr Tree. **1856** 'Stonehenge' *Man. Brit. Rural Sports* 255/2 Swan-shot or lead, in some form, is required to sink the bait. **1971** *Angling Times* 10 June 6/2 Any float will do that a swan shot can't quite take under. **1976** *Monitor* (McAllen, Texas) 28 Nov. 11A/4 Rockefeller fairly bubbled with optimism during a recent swan song interview. **1978** G. Greene *Human Factor* vi. ii. 319 Ivan made his swan song as an interpreter in a building not far from the Lubianka prison. [**1907** *Yesterday's Shopping* (1969) 24/2 Swan White Pine Vestas. (Bryant & May's.)..Doz.. 0/3½.] **1908** *Trade Marks Jrnl.* 12 Aug. 1340 *Swan Vestas*... Matches. Bryant & May, Limited, Fairfield Works, Bow, London..; match manufacturers. **1958** J. Townsend *Young Devils* vii. 59, I collected..a number of loose Swan Vestas from the class. **1977** 'E. Crispin' *Glimpses of Moon* vii. 109 Ling gave his Swan Vesta box an experimental shake.

d. *swan-maiden* (earlier example).

1859 G. W. Dasent *Pop. Tales from Norse* p. lxi, Brynhildr and the Valkyries..became swan-maidens.

swan, *v.*^{1} Add: **1.** Also without *it*. Also *transf.*

1938 H. G. Wells *Apropos of Dolores* vi. 304 He began as an Osteopath but afterwards he became a Mind Healer —with Physical Exercises... He taught them to swan (!?) Swan, you know—like swans. Swanning exercises. Some of them swan now quite beautifully. **1962** *Listener* 13 Sept. 386/2 In his painting Andrea can be seen swanning through the water.

2. To move about freely or in an (apparently) aimless way (formerly, *spec.* of armoured vehicles); hence, to travel idly or for pleasure. Freq. with *about, around,* or *off. slang* (orig. *Mil.*).

1942 *Daily Tel.* 3 Sept. 6/6 Breaking up his armour into comparatively small groups of..tanks, he began 'swanning about', feeling north, north-west and east for them [*sc.* British tanks]. *a* **1944** K. Douglas *Alamein to Zem Zem* (1946) 24 It seemed crazy to go swanning off into the mist. **1945** *Times* 17 Mar. 4/2 [General Patton's armour] ..is 'swanning' more or less unchallenged amid the open moors of the Hunsrück plateau. **1947** C. Day Lewis *Poetic Image* 111 A few bold or bomb-happy types still swanning around outside. **1961** G. Egmont *Art of Egmontese* i. 15 Another excellent way of making contacts is, of course, 'swanning' on the Continent. **1971** *Petticoat* 17 July 28/1 You can't do that if you're swanning around making films all the time. **1980** D. Bogarde *Gentle Occupation* viii. 200 She swanned about at the party like the Queen Mother.

Swanee (swǫ·ni). Also **Swannee.** [Var. of *Suwannee*, the name of a river in Georgia and Florida.] **1.** *Swanee whistle*, a small woodwind instrument with a slide-plunger to vary the pitch, chiefly used as a toy. Also *Swanee flute*.

1926 S. T. Warner *Lolly Willowes* ii. 114 She bought a Swanee flute. **1930** R. Paget *Human Speech* 239 Various forms of mute for converting the whistle sound of a Swannee Whistle into a breathed sound. **1961** A. Baines *Mus. Instruments through Ages* ix. 235 The Swanee whistle, scored for by Ravel in *Les Enfants et les sortilèges*, is also made by Indian children as a bamboo bird-pipe. **1962** A. Nisbett *Technique of Sound Studio* x. 172 An object (or person) being thrown high into the air might be indicated by the use of a glide up and down on a swannee whistle (this is a whistle which has a slide piston to govern the pitch). **1978** *Times* 15 July 2/4 (*caption*) Pupils.. playing a Swanee whistle..and a Melodica, a wind keyboard. **1983** *Daily Tel.* 23 June 18/4 The piece, to be recited by the composer himself, is performed on toy clarinets, saxophones, rattles, swanee whistles, plastic hosepipes and paper-bags.

2. *to go down the Swanee* = *to go down the drain* s.v. *drain *sb.* 1e; to become ruined or bankrupt. Cf. *river *sb.*^{1} 3* c. *slang.*

1977 *Observer* 21 Aug. 1/3 A senior Leyland convener.. called on the Government to give Leyland 'latitude' in settling its pay problems. Without that, he said, the company 'would go down the Swanee'.

swank, *sb.*^{2} Add: **2.** = Swanker^2.

1913 V. Sackville-West *Let.* 15 Feb. in V. Glendinning *Vita* (1983) v. 54 [He is] a swank, more swank than you could ever dream of. **1923** 'R. Crompton' *William Again* v. 91 He was a pariah, outside the pale, one of the 'swanks' who lived in big houses and talked soft. **1949** W. C. Williams *Autobiogr.* xxxii. 190 We were not concerned with the moving-picture colony or the swanks.

swank (swæŋk), *a.*^{2} *colloq.* (chiefly *U.S.*). [f. Swank *sb.*^{2} or *v.*] Stylish; 'posh', 'classy'. (Freq. applied to shops, hotels, or apartments.)

1913 [see *swank *sb.*^{2} 2]. **1919** W. Deeping *Second Youth* xvii. 145 Look here, come for a ride. Had this new swank machine just a week. **1928** *Publishers' Weekly* 30 June 2578 From honor and riches to poverty and shame —from the swankest hunting set of England to a garret in the Latin Quarter of Paris. **1947** D. Riesman in *University Observer* Winter 20/1 John..refuses to angle for the mastership of..one of the swank Harvard Houses. **1957** L. Stern *Midas Touch* i. xii. 98 These were the women..who patronized the swank Michigan Avenue specialty shops. **1972** 'E. Lathen' *Murder without Icing* (1973) xx. 179 He was thrilled at having a swank apartment. **1981** R. Barnard *Mother's Boys* i. 12 Have you got a big box of chocks? Something real swank?

swank, *v.* Add: **1. b.** To boast.

1874 Hotten *Slang Dict.* 316 *Swank*, to boast or 'gas' unduly. **1914** G. B. Shaw *Fanny's First Play* iii. 211, I used to boast about what a good boy Bobby was. Now I swank about what a dog he is; and it pleases people just as well. **1950** *Sport* 7–13 Apr. 9/2 Lest I may appear to be swanking, let me hasten to add that all of the credit went to someone else. **1960** J. Rae *Custard Boys* I. vii. 80 'You think that I am swanking too much, John?' With his accent the slang word sounded very strange. **1980** *London Rev. Bks.* 17 Apr. 6/2 Anonymity..is no guarantee against a tendency on the part of informants to swank about their supposed religious experiences.

swankily (swæ·ŋkili), *adv. slang.* [f. Swanky *a.*² + -ly².] In a swanking or ostentatious manner; boastfully.

1924 D. Moore *Fen's First Term* viii. 87 Angela did it first, and did it swankily. **1940** E. F. Benson *Final Edition* xiii. 284, I swankily told my friend..that I had decided not to go to the Coronation but to give my place to someone else. **1951** *Sport* 6–12 Apr. 11/1 You are unfortunate in not..being able to play swankily to the gallery, not having the peculiar knack some players have of catching the eye.

swankiness (swæ·ŋkinės). *slang.* [f. Swanky *a.*² + -ness.] The quality of being swanky; swagger.

1920 *Christian World* 2 Sept. 4/2 The average American is free from swankiness. **1965** *Listener* 22 July 125/1 The 'swankiness' inside the school was matched in the streets outside. 'Grammar grubs', the secondary schoolboys shouted at us, and we passed by, noses lifted... We thought them the bottom.

swa·nking, *vbl. sb. slang.* [f. Swank *v.* + -ing¹.] = Swank *sb.*²

1900 [in Dict. s.v. Swank *v.* 1]. **1916** *Captain* June 231/1 (*heading*) The perils of swanking. **1918** *Daily Express* 2 Oct. 2/2 History will declare that by swanking the Hohenzollerns fell.

swa·nking, *ppl. a. slang.* [f. Swank *v.* + -ing².] That swanks; boastful, ostentatious, pretentious.

1918 *Daily Express* 2 Oct. 2/2 The swanking dustman is a nuisance. So is the swanking duke.

swankpot (swæ·ŋkpǫt). *slang.* [f. Swank *sb.*² + Pot *sb.*¹] An ostentatious or boastful person; one who is full of swank.

1914 *Picture Fun* 26 Dec. 1/6 Brimstone..and Billy kept the old swankpot nicely on the trot. **1927** H. Walpole *Jeremy at Crale* xii. 212 He's an awful swankpot. **1936** J. B. Priestley *They walk in City* v. 115 Silly swank-pot! **1959** I. & P. Opie *Lore & Lang. Schoolch.* xiii. 302 If a boy is under the necessity of coming to school in a new suit his fellows greet him with,..'Swank pot', 'Posh guy'.

swanky, *a.*² Add: Also, boastful. Of things: imposing, stylish, 'posh'.

1929 'R. Crompton' *William* i. 9 'I read that too,' interrupted Ginger, 'so you needn't be so swanky.' **1940** C. Day Lewis tr. *Virgil's Georgics* II. 49 No mansion tall with a swanky gate. **1959** *Spectator* 25 Sept. 406/3 An English producer and a London critic..in the swanky bar of the Excelsior. **1974** *Sunday Tel.* 8 Dec. 8/6 Swanky Christmas presents, beautifully wrapped in red and gold.

swan-neck. 2. (Later examples.)

1923 G. Sturt *Wheelwright's Shop* 223 *Swan-necks*, curved hooks fastened to the shafts of a dung-cart, for attaching the shafts to the body. **1935** *Discovery* Jan. 9/1 The adjustment of these beams was generally effected by bending the swan-necks in or out so as to alter the arm lengths. **1967** *Gloss. Sanitation Terms (B.S.I.)* 51 *Swan-neck*, a short bent delivery pipe attached to the outlet of a tap.

swan-necked, *a.* Add: **2.** (Earlier example.)

1745 W. Ellis *Mod. Husbandman* Aug. vii. 62 Their five-toothed, long, Swan-neck'd, wooden..Rake.

swanning (swǫ·niŋ), *vbl. sb. slang* (orig. *Mil.*). [f. Swan *v.*¹ + -ing¹.] The action of the verb (sense *2).

1951 E. Linklater *Campaign in Italy* v. 257 Some..were indulging in a favourite pastime of the army, known as swanning. The swan..has the habit of taking short flights that create appreciable commotion but have no serious purpose. Officers who spent their spare time in swanning had in a like manner no graver reason than a desire to watch some particular fragment of a battle, or to visit friends. **1960** *Times Lit. Suppl.* 16 Sept. 587/2 The 22nd Armoured Brigade was continually exercised in a swanning role, of the kind which had so often led to defeat in the past. **1975** *Bookseller* 12 Apr. 2095/1 Harold Latham, the Macmillan editor,..was on a casual swanning tour round Georgia.

swanny, *a.* **2.** (Later example.)

1871 G. M. Hopkins *Jrnls & Papers* (1959) 207 Clouds ..in burly-shouldered ridges swanny and lustrous.

swan-pan. (Examples with spelling *suan pan*, now the usual form.)

1836 J. F. Davis *Chinese* II. xviii. 296 A little apparatus called a *Suán-pân*, or 'calculating dish'. **1917** S. Couling *Encycl. Sinica* 1/1 *Suan p'an*, reckoning plate, the counting-board used by the Chinese. **1946** G. Stimpson *Bk. about Thousand Things* 207 Virtually all calculations were performed on the abacus, an apparatus resembling the Chinese *suan pan* or the bead-and-frame affairs now used in kindergarten work. **1973** T. R. Tregear *Chinese* vi. 128 A further six hours a week is devoted to arithmetic, when calculating with the abacus or *suan p'an* is learnt.

Swan River. The name of a river in Western Australia, used *attrib.* in **Swan River daisy,** an annual herb of the genus *Brachycome*, esp. *B. iberidifolia*, belonging to the family Compositæ, native to Western and South Australia, and bearing pinnate leaves and blue, violet, or white flowers resembling daisies.

[**1841** J. Lindley in *Edward's Bot. Reg.* XXVII. 9 Mr. Lowe, of Clapton, has also raised the Large Swan Daisy.] **1873** W. B. Hemsley *Handbk. Hardy Trees, Shrubs, & Herbacious Plants* 235 Swan River Daisy.—An erect glabrous annual about a foot high. **1915** W. Stevens *Let.* 25 July (1967) 184 Another new thing was what is called swan-river daisies from Australia. **1957** J. S. Dakers *Annuals* xiii. 92 Swan River Daisy..one of the most beautiful of all our annuals. **1962** R. Page *Educ. Gardener* xi. 302 The cypresses are underplanted with sheets of..the blue Swan River daisy.

Swanscombe (swǫ·nzkǝm). The name of a village in north-west Kent, used *attrib.* to designate a Middle Pleistocene fossil hominid, an early type of *Homo sapiens*, known from parts of a skull found in a gravel pit near Swanscombe in 1935 and subsequent years. Also *Swanscombe skull*.

1938 W. LeG. Clark in *Jrnl. R. Anthropol. Inst.* LXVIII. 58 (*title*) General features of the Swanscombe skull bones. **1940** *Nature* 13 July 51/2 Swanscombe man appears..in gravels heralding the third glacial stage. **1946** F. E. Zeuner *Dating Past* viii. 279 The view..is beginning to be held generally, and especially on the strength of the Swanscombe skull, that *H[omo] sapiens* evolved during the Penultimate Interglacial. *Ibid.* ix. 298 Swanscombe Man..is a member of the *sapiens* group. **1962** *Listener* 22 Nov. 878/2 For those who think Pleistocene is a substance, Mary Cathcart Boxer's *Mankind in the Making*..will prove a model of clarity that..sorts the jumble of prehistory in a manner that even those as thick of skull as Swanscombe Woman can grasp. **1973** B. J. Williams *Evolution & Human Origins* x. 169/2 The bone of the Swanscombe skull is thinner than that of Peking Man but thicker than in modern man's. **1975** J. G. Evans *Environment Early Man Brit. Isles* i. 1 Many dramatic environmental changes separate Swanscombe Man by more than 150,000 years from the development and eventual spread into Britain of farming communities.

Swansea (swǫ·nzi). The name of a city in South Wales, used *attrib.* and *absol.* to designate pottery and porcelain made at the Cambrian Pottery there from 1764 to 1870.

1863 W. Chaffers *Marks & Monograms on Pott. & Porc.* 151 *Swansea.* This china was introduced about 1800, and was remarkable for the beautiful delineation of birds, butterflies, and shells. **1879** M. E. Braddon *Vixen* II. ii. 19 Old Worcester teacups..or flowered Swansea. *Ibid.* vii. 107 The Swansea tea-set. **1895** *Wales* Aug. 372/2 The best Swansea china is exquisitely beautiful. **1904** [see *duck's egg d]. **1957** Mankowitz & Haggar *Encycl. Eng. Pott. & Porc.* 216/2 These [fakes], however, are mostly distinguishable from true Swansea as the style of decoration and often the forms and shapes are quite dissimilar. **1967** W. H. Boore *Cry on Wind* x. 95 An old, long-settled place..has its own surprising treasures..a bardic chair..some priceless Swansea porcelain [etc.]. **1976** *Western Mail* (Cardiff) 27 Nov. 16/3 (Advt.), Collector wishes to purchase Swansea Pottery and Porcelain.

swanskin. Add: **3. b.** *fig.* Soft and delicate, smooth like swanskin. (Only found in the work of E. Sitwell.)

1925 E. Sitwell *Troy Park* 38 Once, plumaged like the sea, his swanskin head Had wintry white quills. **1936** —— *Victoria of England* xvi. 197 Wild violets beneath their swan-skin leaves.

SWANU (swā·nu). [Acronym f. the initial letters of *S*outh *W*est *A*frica(n) *N*ational *U*nion.] An African nationalist organization in Namibia. Cf. *SWAPO.

1962 *Rep. U.N. Spec. Comm. S.W. Afr.* 14 Sept. 3 Mr. Kozonguizi explained that he represented the South West Africa Union (SWANU)... The aims of SWANU were to achieve independence for South West Africa. **1963** R. First *South West Afr.* v. iv. 200 The following month the South West African National Union, known as the 'First S.W.A.N.U.', was established. **1970** J. Woronoff *Organizing African Unity* iii. 265 Several nationalist groups were formed as of 1959. First was the South West African National Union (SWANU). **1973** *Black World* Oct. 35/2 Free the land FROLIZI. Swing in there SWANU.

swap, swop, *sb.* Add: The spelling *swap* is recommended. **II. 3.** *Finance.* In foreign exchange operations: an exchange of an amount of money at different rates (i.e. a 'spot' sale for a 'forward' purchase). More generally, an arrangement between the central banks of two countries for stand-by credit to facilitate the exchange of each other's currency. Chiefly *attrib.*

1963 *Economist* 14 Dec. 70/1 A permanent system of automatic swap-lines as opposed to the existing three-monthly swaps is favoured together with easier facilities for medium term credit. **1968** *Times* 9 Sept. 1/2 *Swap arrangements.* The 12 members of the Basle central bankers' club have made reciprocal arrangements to make short-term loans to each other in the event of any currency coming under severe pressure. **1970** Sloan & Zurcher *Dict. Econ.* (ed. 5) 425 Swap credits are used especially in periods of emergency when a particular country's currency..comes under pressure because speculators are selling it on the world markets. **1975** *Financial Times* 29 Oct. 7/1 A classic swap is a transaction in which a spot purchase of a given currency, is covered by a forward sale of the same amount. **1979** *Bank of England Q. Bull.* June 131 The Federal Reserve and the US Treasury again repaid some swap debt to other central banks.

4. Special combinations. **swap fund** *U.S. Stock Exchange*, a fund which investors enter by exchanging securities directly for shares in the fund, obtaining a diversified portfolio without selling stock, and thereby avoiding liability for capital gains tax on the sale of these securities; **swap meet** chiefly *U.S.*, a gathering at which enthusiasts discuss, exchange, or trade items of common interest; **swap shop**, an agency for putting people with articles to exchange or trade in touch with one another; also *fig.*

1966 *Economist* 23 July 380/1 The Revenue Service..will no longer permit investors to defer capital gains tax on the appreciation of stocks exchanged for shares of the special swap funds. **1973** *Daily Tel.* 25 Aug. 16/1 A market has been established in them [*sc.* bottles] and regular 'swop-meets' are arranged so that enthusiasts can buy and sell among themselves. **1976** *Billings* (Montana) *Gaz.* 11 July 3-B/1 The swap meet has become an annual event that attracts visitors from Canada and other states to exchange information about antique cars and parts, he said. **1976** *Milton Keynes Express* 18 June 27/6 (Advt.), Dishot Swop Shop. **1976** *Sunday Post* (Glasgow) 26 Dec., Just before half-time some fans not involved in the beer can 'swop-shop' took refuge on the park. **1977** *Skateboard Special* Sept. 2/1 If you want to take up our super Swap-Shop offer now's your chance. **1979** *Guardian* 5 July 4/4 Instead of handing down golden tablets..the Schools Council will become more of a swap shop for ideas.

swap, swop, *v.* Add: **II. 8. a.** Also *colloq.*, to give (something) to (a person) by way of exchange; *to swap horses in midstream*: see *horse *sb.* 17.

1934 D. Hammett *Thin Man* iii. 14 Right now I'd swap you all the interviews with Mayor-elect O'Brien ever printed..for a slug of whis——. **1940** W. Faulkner *Hamlet* I. ii. 38 The team Stamper had swapped him stopped now with their heads down. **1948** —— *Intruder in Dust* (1949) ix. 192, I swapped Crawford Gowrie a German pistol.

c. Also with indirect obj., to make an exchange of some specified item with (someone). *colloq.*

1976 *Evening Chron.* (Newcastle) 26 Nov., As Coun. Collins says this council work will suit a pensioner, if he will answer this letter and tell me how many council meetings he has in a week, I will swap him.

SWAPO (swā·pǝ). Also **Swapo.** [Acronym f. the initial letters of *S*outh *W*est *A*frica(n) *P*eople's *O*rganization.] An African nationalist organization in Namibia. Cf. *SWANU.

1962 A. K. Lowenstein *Brutal Mandate* vi. 117 SWAPO grew out of the Ovamboland People's Organization. **1970** C. P. Potholm *Four African Polit. Systems* iv. 100 In South West Africa, the South West Africa People's Organization (SWAPO) likewise undertook a modest policy of selective sabotage. **1973** *Times* 25 Aug. 5/1 The Swapo youth wing's statement..says that its protests at 'Boer' injustices in Namibia have been met with imprisonment, torture, brutality and other forms of oppression. **1976** *Plain Truth* Dec. 6/2 The South West Africa People's Organization (SWAPO), despite its terrorist activities and opposition to the conference, has been invited to be the proposed new government's political opposition.

swapping, swopping, *vbl. sb.* Add: **3.** *Finance.* The action or process of making a swap (sense *3).

1957 *Times* 19 Dec. 15/1 There was rather more outright buying of Dominion and Colonial stocks.., as well as a fair amount of swapping among Crown Colony loans. **1971** *Guardian* 8 Sept. 1/8 Of this inflow, £500 millions was used, indirectly, to support the dollar by 'swapping forward'—Britain actually claimed only a small proportion of the foreign currency due to her, and took the rest in foreign IOUs.

Swaraj (swarā·dʒ). *Indian Hist.* Also **swaraj.** [ad. Skr. *svarāj* self-ruling (*svarājya* own dominion), f. *sva* one's own + *rāj* to reign, rule.] Self-government (for India); the agitation in favour of this.

[**1845** *Encycl. Metrop.* XXI. 679/2 The Swa-ráj, or 'Own Sovereignty', secured to him all the territory possessed by Sivá-ji.] **1907** *Westm. Gaz.* 18 Dec. 1/3 The movement known as Swaraj. **1908** *Times* 27 Oct. 8/3 There is a good deal of talk going on in these days about 'swaraj', or the making of India a self-governing country. **1920** M. K. Gandhi *Non-Co-operation* 12 Aug. (1921) 2 Mr. Tilak lived for his country. The inspiration of his life was freedom for his country which he called Swaraj. **1945** R. Hargreaves *Enemy at Gate* 182 It was a deadlock..which forced the sponsors of *Swaraj* to try and 'save face' by endeavouring to shift the whole matter on to a basis of pacifism and 'appeasement'. **1965** J. K. Mittal in *University of Allahabad Studies: Law Section* 39 In 1927, the Swaraj Constitution, based on a declaration of rights, was framed to give momentum to the fight for *Swaraj* (i.e. Self-Government). **1977** C. ALLEN *Raj* x. 129/2 All Anglo-India knew that one day *swaraj* (home rule) must inevitably come.

Hence **Swara·jist**, one who advocated self-rule for India; also *attrib.*

1908 *Westm. Gaz.* 24 June 5/1 The family lawyer.. introduced him to two men..who were ardent Swarajists. **1923** *Glasgow Herald* 12 Dec. 8 Failing unconditional assent, the Swarajist intention is to obstruct every official measure coming before the Assembly. **1953** EARL WINTERTON *Orders of Day* x. 133 The Swarajists were very active..in India.

sward, *sb.* Add: **4.** *sward-land* (earlier example); **sward-cutter** (earlier example).

1744 W. ELLIS *Mod. Husbandman* Jan. i. 12 (*heading*) The Gloucestershire way of preparing and sowing sward-Land with corn. **1786** R. SANDILANDS (*title*) A description of the patent instrument called a sward-cutter.

swarf, *sb.*^{2} Add: **a.** Also, any fine waste produced by a machining operation, esp. when in the form of strips or ribbons. (Further examples.)

1917 *Yorkshire Post* 3 Jan. 4/6 Rough copper, copper ore, and copper scrap and swarf in the possession of or due under existing contract to a manufacturer. **1953** *Times* 23 Oct. 5/3 There's swarf—chips of wood, metal, etc.—grinding around in your expensive machinery and shortening its life. **1970** P. DICKINSON *Seals* ii. 41 Down the inside rim of the second key-hole there was..a thin curl of swarf still attached to the main brass. **1973** J. G. TWEEDDALE *Materials Technol.* II. vi. 142 In more ductile materials chips may remain partially bonded to each other to form continuous severely-work-hardened ribbons sometimes called swarf.

b. *spec.* The material cut out of a gramophone record as the groove is made.

1935 H. C. BRYSON *Gramophone Record* x. 275 When metal is recorded upon..it is often necessary to arrange for the removal of the swarf either by blowing..or by means of a small brush. **1947** *Jrnl. Inst. Electr. Engineers* XCIV. III. 288/2 By using a suction system to remove swarf continuously while recording, these troubles are avoided. **1977** *Times* 18 Apr. (Gramophone Suppl.) p. iv/7 For a long-playing record, this swarf, a strip narrower than a human hair, might be half a mile long.

Hence (*rarely*) as *v. trans.* with *up*, to make dirty with swarf; **swarfed** *ppl. a.*, dirtied with swarf, mucky. *colloq.*

1914 D. H. LAWRENCE *Widowing of Mrs. Holroyd* I. i. 4 A man in blue overalls, swarfed and greased. *Ibid.* 5 *Mrs. Holroyd*:..Here, take hold, and help me fold it. *Blackmore*: I shall swarf it up.

swarm, *sb.* Add: **2.** (*c*) *spec.* (i) of asteroids or meteors (cf. *meteor-swarm* s.v. METEOR 6 d); (ii) of earthquakes; cf. also *dike-swarm* s.v. *DIKE, DYKE *sb.*^{1} 10.

1929 J. JEANS *Universe around Us* iv. 242 The asteroids occur as a single swarm. **1958** C. F. RICHTER *Elem. Seismol.* I. vi. 71 Certain localities are..visited by earthquake swarms, long series of large and small shocks with no one outstanding principal event. Such swarms are common in volcanic regions. **1959** *Listener* 30 July 172/2 The Trojans, whose mean distances from the Sun are the same as that of Jupiter, so that they lie far beyond the main swarm [of asteroids]. **1962** F. I. ORDWAY et al. *Basic Astronautics* iii. 105 Many swarms of meteors orbit the Sun and some periodically intersect the orbit of the Earth causing meteor showers. **1979** *Nature* 25 Oct. 661/1 Earthquake swarms, consisting of many earthquakes of nearly equal magnitude within a small area, often occur in areas of recent or current volcanic or tectonic activity. **1981** I. RIDPATH *Young Astronomer's Handbk.* 197/1 At various times of the year, the Earth crosses the orbits of certain comets, encountering whole swarms of meteors.

(*e*) *Ecol.* = *hybrid swarm* s.v. *HYBRID *a.* 3.

1926 *Nature* 30 Oct. 624/1 Where a specific name has been given to a smaller group within the swarm..we may adopt this name for the minor group. **1963** DAVIS & HEYWOOD *Princ. Angiosperm Taxon.* xiv. 483 Hybrids.. may even become established and form large swarms many miles from either parent.

3. *swarm-formation.*

1946 *Nature* 21 Sept. 423/1 The most important biological attribute of an outbreak centre is to provide conditions for survival and multiplication of locusts at those times when their range of dispersal is at a minimum, and also to provide conditions necessary for an increase in that range of dispersal (by swarm-formation). **1953** J. S. HUXLEY *Evolution in Action* iii. 72 At least six species [of malaria-carrying mosquitoes] must be distinguished.. some mating without swarm-formation, others requiring the stimulus of swarming.

swarmed (swǭ·ɹmėd, swǭɹmd), *ppl. a. poet. rare.* [f. SWARM *v.*^{1} + -ED^1.] Of a place: crowded, thronged. Of people: assembled in a crowd, congregated, massed.

1885 G. M. HOPKINS *Poems* (1967) 98 How then should Gregory, a father, have gleanèd else from swarm-èd Rome? **1951** R. GRAVES *Poems & Satires* 37 Tormented by his progress he displays An open flank to the swarmed enemy.

swarmer^1. Add: **1.** Also, a swarmer cell.

1964 *Bacteriol. Rev.* XXVIII. 242/2 If the swarmer is to become a recognizable caulobacter cell, it must develop a stalk after cell division.

3. swarmer cell *Bacteriol.*, a flagellated motile cell produced by the stalked cell of certain species of stalked bacteria.

1950 *Biochimica & Biophysica Acta* V. 41 A study was made of the flagellation of swarmer cells of *Proteus vulgaris.* **1976** *Jrnl. Bacteriol.* CXXVIII. 456/1 The stalked cell [of *Caulobacter crescentus*] divides repeatedly to produce new swarmer cells, whereas the swarmer cell, which cannot divide, loses motility and develops into a stalked cell.

‖ **swart gevaar** (swart χəfā·r). *S. Afr.* [Afrikaans, lit. 'black peril', f. Du. *zwart* SWART, black + *gevaar* danger, peril.] The name given in South Africa to the threat to the Western way of life and white supremacy believed to be posed by the black races. Cf. *yellow peril* s.v. YELLOW *a.* 1 d.

[**1939** R. F. S. HOERNLÉ *S. Afr. Native Policy* 1 To protect White South Africa against 'the Native Danger' —*die donker gevaar* or *die swart gevaar*—is..the simple pole towards which the needle of Native Policy steadily points.] **1948** *Hansard S. Afr.* 20 Jan. 111 In a pathetic attempt to get into power they have dropped Republicanism and adopted the Swart Gevaar. **1970** *Cape Times* 28 Oct. 9/2 They introduce *swart gevaar* where it suits them. **1979** *Economist* 8 Sept. 59/1 Afrikaner Nationalists, brought up for more than half a century on the politics of *swart gevaar* (black danger).

swarth (swǭɹð), *v. poet. rare*$^{-1}$. [f. SWARTHY *a.*^{1}] *trans.* To make swarthy, to darken.

a **1889** G. M. HOPKINS *Poems* (1967) 180 His cheeks the forth-and-flaunting sun Had swarthed about with lion-brown.

swarthily, *adv.* Delete *rare*$^{-0}$ and add examples.

1955 J. THOMAS *No Banners* v. 40 De Laurière was a tall man, swarthily handsome. **1981** *Times Lit. Suppl.* 20 Feb. 198/4 A swarthily soulful young boy sitting all alone on a chair in a predominantly bare room.

‖ **swartwitpens** (swartvi·tpens). *S. Afr.* Also **swart witpenz, zwart wit pens.** [Afrikaans, f. *swart* black + *wit* white + *pens* belly.] = *sable antelope* s.v. SABLE *sb.*^{2} 5.

1869 T. BAINES *Diary* 31 Aug. (1946) I. 137 We saw a fine troop of *Zwart-wit-pens*..or Harris bucks. **1880** E. F. SANDEMAN *Eight Months in Ox Waggon* 254 We rode along..hoping to find..a swartwitpense [*sic*] feeding on the luxuriant grass. **1889** H. A. BRYDEN *Kloof & Karroo* xvi. 284 The Sable antelope, 'zwart wit pens'—i.e. black with white belly. **1939** S. CLOETE *Watch for Dawn* xx. 265 Game was abundant: eland, giraffe, wildebeeste, zebra, swart witpenz,..and innumerable rhinoceros. **1951** *Cape Argus* 8 Dec. 4/3 He and Conroy spotted a fine buck—a swartwitpens.

swarve, *v.*^{1} (Example of *active* form.)

1906 KIPLING *Puck of Pook's Hill* 250 Next floods the brook'll swarve up.

swash, *int.* or *adv.* and *sb.*^{1} Add: **A.** *int.* or *adv.* (Later example of spelling *swosh.*)

1927 J. MASEFIELD *Midnight Folk* 92 He swung Blackmalkin [*sc.* a cat] round his head and pitched him swosh into the mud.

B. *sb.* **I. 1.** † **b.** *transf.* Nonsense; worthless stuff. Cf. *HOG-WASH b. *slang. obs.*

1895 W. C. GORE in *Inlander* Nov. 65 *Swosh*,..nonsense; inferior work. **1924** GALSWORTHY *White Monkey* II. v. 162 Anyway sentiment was swosh! Cut it out!

5. b. *Physical. Geogr.* The rush of sea water up the beach after the breaking of a wave.

1919 D. W. JOHNSON *Shore Processes & Shoreline Development* x. 514 Since there are a variety of marks left on the sand by wave action, and the present feature is peculiarly a product of the swash, I have given it the name of 'swash mark'. **1934** *Geogr. Jrnl.* LXXXIII. 485 When the swash dies out the backwash of the wave returns directly down the steepest slope to the sea. **1976** P. D. KOMAR *Beach Processes & Sedimentation* ii. 14 The return flow of the swash collides with the incoming surf bores.

III. 9. (sense *5 b) *swash mark, -slope, -zone*; **swash-plate** *Engin.*, a disc mounted obliquely on the end of a revolving shaft, which can impart to a rod in contact with the edge of the disc a reciprocating motion parallel to the axis of the shaft.

1919 Swash mark [see sense 5 b above]. **1982** *Sci. Amer.* Aug. 130/2 Seaward of a swash mark on some beaches one is likely to find smaller diamond-shaped markings left by the backwash. *a* **1877** KNIGHT *Dict. Mech.* III. 2467/2 Swash-plate. **1913** W. E. DOMMETT *Motor Car Mech.* 158 The plungers are driven by a swash-plate mechanism. **1977** *Design Engin.* July 92/1 (Advt.), To obtain precise control in many fields, e.g. valves, or engine throttle position, or a pump swashplate, you need a remote position actuator. **1931** *Geogr. Jrnl.* LXXVIII. 134 They [*sc.* waves]..on nearing high-water mark were busily pushing forward shingle to the top of their swash slope. **1976** P. D. KOMAR *Beach Processes & Sedimentation* ii. 14 Schiffman ..defines a transition zone between the surf and swash zones.

swashbuckle, *v.* (Later examples.)

1939 W. FORTESCUE *There's Rosemary, There's Rue* vi. 41 One proud day I was promoted to study the part of Rosalind in 'As You Like It', and I swashbuckled round that flat in imaginary doublet and hose. **1979** R. BLYTHE *View in Winter* ix. 312, I knew a remittance man in Kenya ..swashbuckling about with a revolver in his belt.

swashbuckler. Add: **b.** A book, film, or other work portraying swashbuckling characters.

1975 *Daily Colonist* (Victoria, B.C.) 27 July 20/3 Clavell's most ambitious novel—an oldfashioned swashbuckler complete with all the popular ingredients. **1977** *Time* 30 May 42/2 *Star Wars* is a combination of *Flash Gordon, The Wizard of Oz*, the Errol Flynn swashbucklers of the '30s and '40s and almost every western ever screened.

swastika. Delete ‖ and add: Now usu. pronounced (swǫ·stikă). **2. a.** This symbol (with clockwise projecting limbs) used as the emblem of the German (and other) Nazi parties; = *HAKENKREUZ, HAKENKREUZ. Also, a flag bearing this emblem.

1932 'NORDICUS' *Hitlerism* ii. 17 Thousands flocked to his standard—the 'Hakenkreuz'—(swastika), the ancient anti-semitic cross in a color scheme of red-white-black in memory of the colors of the old army. **1933** [see *ARYAN *a.* 2]. **1941** G. ZIEMER *Educ. for Death* i. 4 A squad of Nazi youngsters in..brown shirts decorated with swastikas. *Ibid.* ii. 30 A luxury hotel managed by a Jew... The swastika over it fluttered gaily. **1951** L. HAGEN *Follow my Leader* i. 6 Most of the men in my Sturm wore at least part of a uniform, and all I could do was wear a swastika armlet. *Ibid.* vii. 266 Our compatriots..clung to their German ways and..flew the swastika on our national holidays. **1967** T. GUNN *Touch* 15 A silk tent of swastikas. **1977** E. HEATH *Travels* iv. 113 Along this street had stretched the Nazi columns... Gone, now, were the crowds and the bright-red banners flaunting their swastikas over the streets. **1979** J. BURMEISTER *Glory Hunters* i. 5 In addition to her national flag she [*sc.* a ship] also flew the Swastika.

b. *attrib.* and *Comb.*

1934 *Ann. Reg. 1933* I. 179 Minor acts of defiance towards the Austrian Government..such as..the lighting of Swastika fires and the daring hoisting of forbidden Swastika banners under the eyes of the police..and the hoisting of Swastika flags. **1940** H. G. WELLS *All Aboard for Ararat* iv. 101 As regards the olive branch incident, it is to be noted that the leaves were blood-stained and tied with a swastika ribbon. **1946** J. FLANNER in *New Yorker* 5 Jan. 46/1 Ten years ago, he [*sc.* Goering] was baying 'Heil' as he strutted the swastika-hung streets. **1957** T. GUNN *Sense of Movement* 36 The swastika-draped bed. **1960** *Jewish Chronicle* 8 Apr. 14/3 The recent swastika-daubings in this country.

Hence **swa·stika'd** *a.*, decorated with or wearing a swastika, esp. as a badge of Nazism.

1965 *New Statesman* 15 Oct. 552/3 Buckley has.. described the American Nazi Party as 'two dozen swastika-ed cretins who go about plying their pathology in the fever-swamps of the crazy-Right'. **1969** *Listener* 14 Aug. 225/3 Where do those swastika'd Hell's Angels types fit in?

Swat (swǫt), *sb.*^{3} [The name of a district in the Malakand Division of North-west Frontier Province, Pakistan.] = (and superseded by) *SWATI. Also *attrib.* or as *adj.*

1897 *Westm. Gaz.* 8 Sept. 2/2 The Afridi rising..was all a matter of wire-pulling on the part of..the Swat Fakirs. **1911** G. P. GOOCH *Hist. our Times* vii. 170 A rising began in 1897 among the Swats, Mohmands, and Afridis.

swat, *v.*^{1} Add: **2.** Restrict Chiefly *U.S.* to sense in Dict. and add: Also, to crush (a fly, etc.) with a blow. (Later examples.)

1916 A. HUXLEY *Let.* 29 Sept. (1969) 114 A poem.. which..is destined to become a cause of rupture in the world, dividing it up into..Monts and Caps, Mouldiwarpians and Swat-that-Moleites. **1942** *R.A.F. Jrnl.* 18 Apr. 9 The familiar white butterflies should be 'swatted' wholesale. **1958** R. K. NARAYAN *Guide* vii. 139 He repelled me with a back-stroke of his left hand as if swatting a fly. **1962** K. KESEY *One Flew over Cuckoo's Nest* (1973) 9 One swats the backs of my legs with a broom handle to hurry me past. **1976** *Times Lit. Suppl.* 12 Nov. 1414/2 Identical communities to Tolmers Square have been swatted from the urban map.

Swatantra (swatā·ntră). [Hindi, (one who is) self-determined or self-motivated.] In full, *Swatantra party.* A liberal conservative political party (the Freedom Party) in the Republic of India from 1959 to 1972. Also *attrib.*

1959 *Hindu* 8 June 1/5 Addressing a..public meeting in Royapettah last evening, Mr. C. Rajagopalachari explained the aims and policies that would be pursued by the new Opposition party, which he said, would be called the Swatantra Party. **1963** H. TINKER *Democratic Ideal in Asia* 23 C. R. Rajagopalachari, the veteran Swatantra statesman. **1966** *Economist* 24 Dec. 1319/3 The rajahs who joined Swatantra in droves were angry with Congress for having reduced them to commoners. **1979** V. L. PANDIT *Scope of Happiness* ii. 13 A merger of Congress (O), Swatantra party, Jan Sangh, and Bharatiya Lok Dal.

swatch, *sb.*^{1} For '*Sc.* and *north.*' read 'orig. *Sc.* and *north.*' and restrict *north.* to sense 1.

2. Hence, of other materials (see also *S.N.D.*). Also, a collection of samples bound together, a swatch-book. (Later examples.)

1953 *Times* 23 July 1/4 (Advt.), Duffle jackets and duffle coats... Swatches sent on request. **1973** *Sci. Amer.* June 119/2 Continue..until a piece of filter paper or swatch of cotton held close to the exit by means of long metal forceps begins to burn. **1982** *Daily Tel.* 2 Aug. 9/2 He wears swatches of the hats he is currently working on, hat-pinned to his tie for inspiration.

transf. (Later examples.)

1928 P. GREY *Making of King* 6 Ye'll mind an' bring a swatch o' yer wallpaper wi' ye. **1957** *Brit. Commonwealth Forest Terminol.* II. 192 *Swatch*, a sample sheet of veneer, usually 3 ft. long and the full width of the flitch. **1965** G. MCINNES *Road to Gundagai* iii. 38 One's wants were provided for by a swatch of neatly cut squares from the Hobart *Mercury* struck on a nail in the wall. **1973** *Sci. Amer.* Apr. 41/1 A swatch of inks as rendered by Kodak color slide films that maximize consumer satisfaction with the greenness of grass, the blueness of sky, and the healthy glow of complexions. **1981** N. GORDIMER *July's People* 54 She knew it was impossible that he could have made free of the still-thick swatch of notes, lying swollen as the leaves of a book that has got wet and dried again.

3. (Later examples.) Also extendedly (esp. without the notion of a sample), a portion, a clump.

1930 *Aberdeen Press & Jrnl.* 19 May 5/2 Swatches from Shakespeare... The miscellany consisted of excerpts from 'Henry IV',..the ghost scene in 'Hamlet', [etc.]. **1950** A. LOMAX *Mister Jelly Roll* 30 The hollows of his cheeks and temples showing dark against silvery skin, and up towards the ceiling a swatch of silvery hair. **1961** J. STEINBECK *Winter of our Discontent* 358 A swatch from Lincoln's Second Inaugural. **1963** *Punch* 31 July 165/1, I..consumed unbelievable swatches of it [*sc.* electricity]. **1972** J. MOSEDALE *Football* ii. 23 A swatch of astroturf in the Hall leads to the present. **1975** *Times Lit. Suppl.* 24 Oct. 1254/1 Mr Boston gives a fair selection: the life and death of the Admirable Crichtoun from *The Jewel*, a reasonable swatch of *Logopandecteision*.

4. Comb. **swatch-book**, a book of samples.

1956 *Archit. Rev.* CXIX. 286/1 One of the first firms to pin their colours to this mast is T. & W. Farmiloe Ltd., the manufacturers of Nine Elms Paints, who present the full range in the form of a truly magnificent swatch-book. **1978** *Times* 26 Jan. 13/5 Some of the collections were just dull... Why not just send for the swatch-book?

swatchel (swǫ·tʃəl). *slang.* Also 9 **schwassle.** [Perh. f. G. *schwätzeln*, frequentative form of *schwatzen* to chatter, tattle.] An older form of *SWAZZLE; also interpreted as the name for Mr. Punch in a Punch and Judy show. Freq. *attrib.*, as *swatchel box, cove* (see quots.).

1854 *Househ. Words* 24 Sept. 76/1 A Punch's show [is] a schwassle-box. **1864** HOTTEN *Slang Dict.*, *Swatchel-cove*, the master of a Punch-and-Judy exhibition who.. does the necessary squeak for the amusement of the bystanders. **1887** W. E. HENLEY *Villon's Good-Night* in J. S. Farmer *Musa Pedestris* (1896) 174 You swatchel-coves that pitch and slam. **1900** *Sat. Rev.* 19 May 613/1 Students of Romany..will find some interest in a list furnished to a friend who handed it on to me by a 'swatchel-cove' or peregrinating Punch-exhibitor. **1921** *Glasgow Herald* 24 June 7 'Swatchel' is Mr Punch, hence 'Swatchel-box' the show, and 'Swatchel cove' the patterer. *c* **1938** A. HAMBLING *Punch & Judy* 3 Wet the swatchel, and having fixed the thread, put it on the tongue crosswise. **1983** *Listener* 22 Sept. 14/3 The word 'swatchel' is Punch and Judy showmen's slang for the figure of Punch.

swath[1], **swathe.** Add: **3. c.** Now freq. *to cut a wide swath.*

1902 H. L. WILSON *Spenders* 348 You folks been cuttin' a pretty wide swath here in New York. **1929** *Amer. Speech* V. 119 [Maine] Someone conceited..'feels his oats', 'cuts a wide swath', 'is one of the big bugs'. **1960** I. WALLACH *Absence of Cello* (1961) 241 He was determined to cut a wide swath with the girls—no easy trick in Philadelphia.

5. *swath-width* (later example); **swath-board,** a slanting board attached to the cutter-bar of a mowing machine, designed to force the cut grass, etc., into a narrower swath; **swath-turner** (examples).

1952 J. W. DAY *New Yeomen of England* vii. 87 After mowing, the lucerne is tedded to remove the wad, left by the swathe board, and is then swept to the tripods and cocked. **1963** *Listener* 28 Mar. 552/1 The swathe-board.. of a grass-mower. **1922** JOYCE *Ulysses* 699 Grindstone, clodcrusher, swatheturner, carriagesack. **1958** *Times* 27 Oct. 15/4 A swath-turner was used to invert the swath and move it onto dry ground. **1970** G. F. BURNETT in H. W. Mulligan *African Trypanosomiases* xxiv. 506 When treating an area of woodland, the aircraft must pass over it on parallel runs at regularly spaced intervals, each of which is referred to as a 'swath width'.

swather[2]. (Later examples.)

1929 *Kansas City* (Missouri) *Times* 26 June, The swather, or windrowing machine, is proving almost as popular as the older combine, which it complements. **1958** *Times* 24 Nov. 15/4 There is still a great deal of room for improvement in the design of combine harvesters and swathers. **1976** *Billings* (Montana) *Gaz.* 17 June 6-F/2 (Advt.), Swather, with conditioner. 14' auger head, industrial gas engine.

Swati (swǫ·ti). Also † **Swa(u)tee, Swathi.** [f. *SWAT *sb.*[3] + *-I.] A member of a people inhabiting the district of Swat in Pakistan. Also *attrib.* or as *adj.*

1815 M. ELPHINSTONE *Acct. Kingdom of Caubul* II. xii. 319 The Swautees..appear to be of Indian origin... Swaut and Boonair, their last seats, were reduced by the Eusofzyes in the end of the fifteenth century. **1866** T. SEATON *From Cadet to Colonel* II. 202 Afreedees and Swatees, Affghans and Maguls. **1897** W. S. CHURCHILL in *Daily Tel.* 7 Oct. 11/1 The Swatis, Bonerwals, Mohmands and other frontier tribes with whom the Malakand Field Force is at present engaged are brave and warlike. **1927** *Rep. Admin. Border N.W.F.P. 1925–26* (Calcutta) 7 Extensive smuggling of *charas* into Peshawar which was known to be carried on by Swathi traders. **1955** *Times* 25 June 7/7 Swati politics are quite straight-forward. **1977** D. MURPHY *Where Indus is Young* 10 That battered bus, full of Swatis on their way home.

Swatow (swā·tau). The name of a port (now Shantou) in the province of Guandong, China, used to designate a type of porcelain produced in the Ming dynasty (A.D. 1368–1644) (see quots.).

1925 R. L. HOBSON *Later Ceramic Wares China* xii. 111 A type of coarse porcelain, distinguished by an iron-red biscuit and accretions of..grit in the base..known among Chinese dealers as Swatow ware. **1945** W. B. HONEY *Ceramic Art China* i. 21 The red-and-green and green-and-blue wares made for export in Southern China (the 'Swatow wares' of the English collector). *Ibid.* ii. 127 Plates and dishes of the Swatow class. **1953** S. JENYNS *Ming Pottery & Porcelain* 147 The so-called 'Swatow' plates, which we now believe..to have been made at, or near, Shih-ma in Fukien. **1970** *Oxf. Compan. Art* 235/1 The still unidentified makers of 'Swatow' porcelains, which are chiefly large dishes coarsely but attractively painted in red and green.

swatter (swǫ·təɹ), *sb.* [f. SWAT *v.*[1] + -ER[1].] An instrument for swatting flies. Also occasionally, one who swats flies (with a swatter).

1917 [see *fly-swatter* s.v. *FLY *sb.*[1] 11]. **1923** *Dundee Tel.* 21 July 3/3 We have tried fly-papers, swatters, formaline solution, and nets. **1926** *Glasgow Herald* 4 Oct. 8 Poultry food is made from the Mexican bluebottle, professional 'swatters' making a good living by catching them. **1947** J. STEINBECK *Wayward Bus* i. 8 The death of a fly by swatter, or slowly smothered in the goo of fly paper. **1967** O. WYND *Walk Softly, Men Praying* iii. 35 The Principal turned back to pick up a swatter on his desk, then lashed out.

S wave: see *S 6.

sway, *sb.* Add: **I. 9. b.** *Naut.* A rhythmic linear motion of a vessel from side to side (as distinguished from the rotatory motion of a roll).

1957 *Trans. Inst. Naval Architects* XCIX. 121/1 Sway accelerations were actually measured to a good approximation in the form of the displacement of the apparent vertical. **1968** RAWSON & TUPPER *Basic Ship Theory* xii. 427 Disturbances in the yaw, surge and sway modes will not lead to such an oscillatory motion..when the ship is in a seaway. **1977** *Offshore Engineer* May 44/3 During these tests, the data acquisition system recorded waves,.. sway and yaw of the lay barge, pull and length of mooring cables, and anchor positions.

12. (Later examples in *Thatching.*)

1949 K. S. WOODS *Rural Crafts of Eng.* IV. xiii. 203 The light timbers that support the thatch are 'flues' laid upward from eaves to ridge like rather thin rafters; 'sways' or long laths are laid horizontally across them at frequent intervals. **1966** *Punch* 10 Aug. (Advt. following p. 216), Hazel rods or 'sways' are used in conjunction with iron hooks to fasten the thatch to the roof timbers.

sway-. Add: **sway-bar,** (*b*) chiefly *N. Amer.*, a bar joining the suspension assemblies of corresponding wheels at either side of a motor vehicle so as to reduce rolling when cornering; an anti-roll bar; **sway-brace** *v.* (earlier example).

1973 *Hot Rod* Oct. 108/1 Also known as stabilizer bars, antiroll bars, or just plain sway bars, these little goodies ..can make so much difference you wouldn't believe it. **1979** *Tucson* (Arizona) *Citizen* 3 Oct. c. 14/5 (Advt.), 69 MGB... High performance sway bars, Monza exhaust system. **1894** W. H. WARREN *Engin. Construction* xix. 304 High trestle piers of timber present great varieties in design. They should be thoroughly sway-braced.

swayable, *a.* Add: (Later examples.) No longer *rare.*

1978 C. TOMLINSON *Shaft* 42 A wind is having its way with all swayable things, Combing through flag and steam, streaming-out hair. **1982** *Washington Post* 4 May C5/4 As hostess, you should generally give the impression of someone who has rules but is swayable.

‖ **swayamvara** (swa:yamvā·rā). *India.* Also **swayambara, swayamvar.** [Skr., lit. 'self-choice'.] A Hindu ceremony in which a woman chooses her husband from amongst several contenders; a symbolic representation of this, preceding an arranged marriage.

1831 H. H. MILMAN in *Q. Rev.* XLV. 17 A solemn assemblage, called the *Swayambara*, or self-election, where the princess is to designate the favoured suitor by throwing a wreathe of flowers round his neck. **1863** M. WILLIAMS *Indian Epic Poetry* 100 Draupadí was about to hold her swayamvara. **1932** J. NEHRU *Let.* 23 June in *Glimpses of World Hist.* (1939) 210 There is a long poem about one of these Chalukyan kings, and in this it is stated that he was chosen by his wife at a public swayamvar. **1970** *Times* 28 Feb. 6/1 The wedding began on Monday with the Swayamvara ceremony, in which the Hindu girl accepts her parents' choice of husband by garlanding him.

swayback, *sb.* Add: **1. a.** (Example of the condition in human beings.) Also, an instance of this.

1939 J. CARY *Mister Johnson* 156 She is a huge, lumbering woman... She has a sway back..and long heels like a hen. **1946** *Richmond* (Va.) *News-Leader* 14 Nov. 30 (*heading*) Swayback is figure fault. Exercises quickly correct.

b. A sway-backed horse or lamb. Also *transf.*, of a person.

1874 *Rep. Vermont Board Agric.* II. 402 The buckskin McClellan was a regular hollow or sway back. **1921** S. KAYE-SMITH *Joanna Godden* I. 35 'He'd three sway-backed lambs at Rye market on Thursday.' 'Sway-backs!' 'Three. 'Twas a shame.' **1934** S. BECKETT *More Pricks than Kicks* 68 A woman..is either: a short-below-the-waist, a big-hip, a sway-back, a big-abdomen or an average. **1974** M. LAURENCE *Diviners* iv. 80 Make pemmican out of the swayback which dropped dead of exhaustion on the Back Forty.

2. A copper deficiency disease affecting the nervous system of young lambs, causing paralysis. Cf. *RENGUERRA.

1938 *Nature* 5 Mar. 400/1 Swayback..accounts from time to time for many lambs. **1947** *Sci. News* V. 100 Research has been going on into a disease of newborn lambs called swayback. **1960** *Farmer & Stockbreeder* 1 Mar. 105/3 Injection of a copper preparation..into a ewe during pregnancy can prevent swayback in its lambs. **1970** 'J. HERRIOT' *If only they could Talk* xxv. 149 The diseases which beset the lambs themselves—swayback, pulpy kidney, dysentery. **1980** *Daily Tel.* 16 Feb. 12/6 Thousands of lambs may die from a nervous disorder called swayback.

sway-backed, *a.* Add: (Further *transf.* examples.)

1919 T. K. HOLMES *Man from Tall Timber* ix. 101 'Does seem a pretty springtime, after all,' Aunt Tabby ruminated, as she rocked in a swaybacked chair. **1950** *Audio Engin.* Sept. 30/2 If the *lows* and *lower highs* are both present to excess, the system is *sway-backed.* **1965** J. A. MICHENER *Source* (1966) 730 Shmuel Hacohen, a sway-backed Jew from Russia, sought an opposing judgment. **1976** H. MACINNES *Agent in Place* xviii. 197 It was a steep pull, the stone steps made sway-backed by centuries of..feet. **1977** D. HARSENT *Dreams of Dead* 49 On knees and palms, swaybacked like a stricken runner..she begged, 'Pleasure me, pleasure me.'

swayless (swēⁱ·lės), *a. poet. rare.* [f. SWAY *sb.* + -LESS.] Not swayed or swaying; unmoved, immovable.

1856 *Tait's Mag.* XXIII. 548/1 A gnarled tree, which.. free and swayless in the fresh air grew. **1897** F. THOMPSON *New Poems* 12 And with her magic singing kept she.. That garden of enchanting In visionary May; Swayless for my spirit's haunting.

Swazi (swā·zi), *sb.* and *a.* [ad. Nguni *Mswati*, the name of a former king of the Swazi.] **A.** *sb.* **a.** A (member of a) people of mixed stock, predominantly Nguni, inhabiting the kingdom of Swaziland (independent since 1968) and parts of eastern Transvaal in the Republic of South Africa. **b.** A dialect of Nguni spoken by the Swazi. **B.** *adj.* Of, pertaining to, or characteristic of this people.

[*a* **1857** J. SHOOTER *Kafirs of Natal & Zulu Country* 391 The Amaswazi partially shave their head [*sic*].] **1872** C. A. PAYTON *Diamond Diggings of S. Afr.* 142 A book of very great interest on new African sport and travel, entitled, I believe, 'Swazi Kafirs and Swazi Game'. **1878** A. AYLWARD *Transvaal of To-day* 182 The Swazis transferred the fidelity and love they bore him. **1884** K. JOHNSTON *Africa* xxvi. 461 The most..numerous..are the Bechuanas..cut off from the Zulus and Swazi by the Quathlamba range on the east. **1902** *Encycl. Brit.* XXXIII. 111/2 The Swazies are a branch of the Bantu family... Swazieland was first constituted a petty native state in 1843, when the Barabuza people under their chief, Swaze, rose against their Zulu oppressors, and according to custom took their name from the founder of their chieftaincy. **1910** J. BUCHAN *Prester John* xi. 193 There were tall Zulus and Swazis with *ringkops* and feather head-dresses. **1919** H. H. JOHNSTON *Compar. Study of Bantu & Semi-Bantu Languages* 298 The Zulu-Kafir Languages..Swazi..Tekele. **1937** N. J. VAN WARMELO in I. Schapera *Bantu-Speaking Tribes* iii. 51 Commencing with the increasing power of the Ngwane Chief Sobhuza (*ca* 1820), the 'Swazi' people gradually began to come into being. **1947** J. STEVENSON-HAMILTON *Wild Life S. Afr.* xxiii. 188 The man (a Swazi) entered, and almost immediately was attacked by the leopard. **1956** H. BLOOM *Episode* v. 72 She wagged her head and huffed her shoulders and muttered in Swazi. **1961** W. VAUGHAN-THOMAS *Anzio* ix. 197 The cheerful Swazi Pioneer..dashed around the football field in an enormous beret. **1973** 'S. HARVESTER' *Corner of Playground* III. ii. 181 A Swazi king in eighteen-fiftyfour raided the Tsonga to find boys and girls to sell to the Boers. **1982** *Times* 1 June 8/1 We [*sc.* the Zulus] are their countrymen, and yet they are prepared to sell us out to the Swazis in a clandestine deal.

swazzle (swǫ·z'l). Also **swozzle.** [Var. *SWATCHEL.] In a Punch and Judy show: an instrument consisting of two convex metal pieces bound together with a length of tape stretched from side to side between them, which is held in the mouth of the puppeteer and is used to produce the characteristic squeaking voice of Mr. Punch.

Mayhew's *call* (CALL *sb.* 6 e), described in *London Labour* (1861) III. 45/2.

1942 S. DE HEMPSEY *How to do Punch & Judy* 86 Amongst the professional Punch and Judy performers the gadget for the Punch voice is popularly known as a 'Swazzle'. **1951** G. SPEAIGHT in *Oxf. Compan. Theatre* 644/2 [Punch] spoke in a high squeak, formed by inserting a 'swazzle' or squeaker into the mouth of the speaker. **1959** *Times* 13 Aug. 10/6 My friend, removing his top and bottom dentures, put my swazzle in his mouth and gave an expert demonstration of the Punch voice. **1962** *Guardian* 31 Mar. 6/5 The swozzle—the hand-made reeded 'call' which the operator keeps in his mouth to reproduce the Punch squawk. **1973** G. SIMS *Hunters Point* ii. 13 Mr. Punch's high-pitched buzzing voice was.. achieved by using a 'swozzle', a piece of linen stretched between two flat pieces of silver, bound together with more linen, and placed at the back of Mr. Jackman's throat. **1983** *Daily Tel.* 11 Apr. 12/4 The swazzle, the flat metal instrument bound with black thread which the Punchinello keeps in his mouth (at some risk of swallowing) to make Mr Punch's nasal squeak.

swear, *v.* Add: **III. 17*. swear with—.** = sense 12 b. *rare.*

1789 H. WALPOLE *Let.* 2 July (1961) XXXI. 306, I do not propose putting your name.., as I think it would swear with the air of ancientry you have adopted in the signature and notes. **1976** C. OMAN *Oxf. Childhood* 101 It was decreed that she must wear a rose-pink robe which swore most horribly with her greatest asset.

IV. 21. swear off. c. (Earlier examples.) More recently, with obj. expressed. Chiefly *U.S.*

1839 *Spirit of Times* 16 Nov. 434/1 Like swearing off from liquor and going into a grog-shop. **1853** MRS. STOWE *Key to Uncle Tom's Cabin* 91/2 Well, after all, I suppose, Mr. Legree, you wouldn't have any objections to swarin' off? **1922** 'MARK TWAIN' in *Harper's Mag.* Mar. 457/1, I..swore off my taxes like the most conscienceless of the lot. **1960** R. ST. JOHN *Foreign Correspondent* v. 88 He became a newspaper reporter and swore off personal involvement in politics, at least for the time.

swearing, *vbl. sb.* **4.** (Later examples.)

1842 D. G. ROSSETTI *Let.* 1 Sept. (1965) I. 7 Uncle Henry's Swearing-book combines both Bible and Prayer-Book. **1899** Swearing-habit [see *drinking-habit* s.v. *DRINKING *vbl. sb.* 4 c]. **1939** JOYCE *Finnegans Wake* 524 Mr. Cockshott, as he had his assignation with, present holder by deedpoll and indenture of the swearing belt.

swearing, *ppl. a.* **2.** (Earlier example.)

1796 J. WOODFORDE *Diary* 10 Oct. (1929) IV. 312 My Boy, John Brand, left my Service to day, as he had proper Notice so to do, being the most saucy swearing Lad that ever we had.

sweat, *sb.* Add: **II. 3. a.** *cold sweat*: freq. in phr. *in a cold sweat* (also *fig.*) (later examples). Cf. sense 10 in Dict.

1840 LYTTON *Money* (ed. 2) III. vi. 94 'Poor fellow! He'll be ruined in a month.'..'I'm in a cold sweat.' **1941** C. MACKENZIE *Red Tapeworm* xii. 153 He would..have broken out in a cold sweat at the thought of what might have happened. **1966** C. AIRD *Relig. Body* xvii. 158 Cousin Harold must have been in a cold sweat in case his father died before he got to Cullingoak.

4. c. A long training run for schoolboys. *Public Schools' slang.*

1916 E. F. BENSON *David Blaize* xiv. 274 You brutes have been having an innocent happy sweat along the road. **1924** KIPLING *Debits & Credits* (1926) 93 For the juniors, a shortish course..while Packman lunged Big Side across the inland and upland ploughs, for proper sweats. **1983** W. BLUNT *Married to Single Life* iv. 62 Long melancholy 'sweats' (runs) over the downs [at Marlborough].

III. 9. b. *old sweat*: see *OLD *a.* D. 4.

10. b. *no sweat*: see *NO *a.* 5 d.

IV. 11. *sweat labour* (later example), *-stain*; *sweat-absorber*; *sweat-marked*, *-shining*, *-soaked*, *-stained* (examples), *-wet* adjs.; **sweat-band,** (*b*) in *Sport*, a strip of material worn around the (fore)head or wrist to absorb perspiration; **sweat-bath,** a steam-bath or hot-air bath, esp. among N. American Indians; cf. SWEAT-HOUSE 1; **sweat-box,** (*a*) (earlier and later examples); also *U.S.*, a room in which a prisoner undergoes intensive questioning (see quot. 1931); (*d*) *transf.* and *fig.*, *spec.* a heated compartment in which perspiration is induced, to encourage weight loss, etc.; **sweat cooling** *Engin.*, a form of cooling in which the coolant is passed through a porous wall and evenly distributed over the surface, which is cooled by its evaporation; hence **sweat-cooled** *ppl. a.*; **sweat equity** *U.S.*, an interest in a property earned by a tenant who contributes his labour to its upkeep or renovation; **sweat-hog** *U.S. slang*, a difficult student singled out in school or college for special instruction; **sweat-lodge** (later examples); **sweat pants** chiefly *U.S.*, trousers of thick cotton cloth worn by athletes, esp. before or after strenuous exercise; tracksuit trousers; **sweat-rag,** delete *Australian* and substitute for def.: any cloth used for wiping off sweat, or worn round the head to keep sweat out of the eyes; **sweat rug** a rug put on a horse after exercise; **sweat-shirt** orig. *U.S.*, a loose shirt; *spec.* a long-sleeved, high-necked pullover shirt of thick cotton cloth (usu. with a fleecy lining), worn by athletes to avoid taking cold before or after exercise (cf. SWEATER 7 b); hence **sweat-shirted** *a.*; **sweat-shop**: for *U.S.* read orig. *U.S.* and add earlier and further examples; also *fig.*; **sweat-suit** orig. *U.S.*, an athlete's suit consisting of a sweat-shirt and sweat-pants.

1956 S. BECKETT *Malone Dies* 93 A sweat-absorber for the armpit. **1956** R. H. APPLEWHAITE *Lawn Tennis* i. 12 Sweatbands..are worn round the wrist to prevent perspiration running down the arms into the hands. **1977** J. F. FIXX *Compl. Bk. Running* xii. 134 When I started running, I saw a lot of runners wearing sweatbands, so after sweat had dripped into my eyes a few times I went out and bought one. **1877** S. POWERS *Tribes of California* xxvi. 244 [The Shasta Indians] have no assembly chamber..; nothing but a kind of oven large enough that one person may stretch himself therein and enjoy a sweat-bath. **1921** J. HASTINGS *Encycl. Relig. & Ethics* XII. 128/2 When we turn to the Old World, we find a striking resemblance to the American customs in Herodotus's description of the use of the sweat-bath among the Scythians as a means of purification, after mourning. **1963** E. WAUGH *Let.* Sept. in C. Sykes *Evelyn Waugh* (1975) xxvi. 439, I have sat in a 'sweat-bath' and been severely massaged. **1965** S. G. LAWRENCE *40 Yrs. on Yukon Telegraph* xiv. 75 They [*sc.* some Indians] stayed over a day and all the old men took sweat baths. **1870** *U.S. Navy Gen. Orders & Circulars* (1887) 97 He was.. gagged and confined in a sweat-box of such dimensions that it was impossible to sit down. **1897** *Chicago Tribune* 10 July 1/4 The upper gallery commonly known as the 'sweat box' in regular theaters. **1901** 'J. FLYNT' *World of Graft* 102 He was copped out on suspicion. They put him in the sweat-box, made him cough, an' you know the rest. **1931** Z. CHAFEE et al. in *Rep. Nat. Comm. Law Observance & Enforcement* (U.S.) ii. 38 The original 'sweat box' used during the period following the Civil War..was a cell in close proximity to a stove, in which a scorching fire was built and fed with old bones, pieces of rubber shoes, etc., all to make great heat and offensive smells, until the sickened and perspiring inmate of the cell confessed in order to get released. **1973** 'H. HOWARD' *Highway to Murder* ii. 28, I ought to stick you in the sweat box until you told me the name of your client. **1974** J. ENGELHARD *Horsemen* vi. 38, I never go in a sweatbox... I lose all the weight I want playing tennis. **1948** *Technical Publ. Amer. Inst. Mining & Metall. Engineers* No. 2343. Class E. 1 In designing a sweat cooled part it is imperative to assure a given rate of flow of coolant. *Ibid.*, A less orthodox method consists of making the part to be cooled of a porous material, so that the cooling fluid can be forced through the pores... This method, referred to as 'sweat cooling', was proposed at the Jet Propulsion Laboratory in September 1944. **1969** E. C. ROBERTSON *Now Bks. Rocket Motors* iv. 29 Many devices have been tried to keep the walls of the chamber cool and techniques have ranged from sweat cooling..to the one that is most common today. **1973** *Time* 16 July 43 A group of poor, racially mixed tenants took over a nearby city-owned tenement, stripped the shabby interiors and are building modern apartments to replace the narrow, cold-water flats... In return for their 'sweat equity', the builder-residents will make payments as low as $80 per month and ultimately own the building as a cooperative. **1980** B. VILA *This Old House* v. 83/1 The calculations you make in a sweat equity job are different from those in a project in which you are employing professionals. **1976** *Senior Scholastic* 4 May 41 John Travolta..[is] back in the classroom..as the leader of the sweathogs in ABC's *Welcome Back, Kotter.* **1979** BROOKS & MARSH *Compl. Directory Prime Time Network TV Shows, 1946–Present* 673/1 Gabe's 'sweathogs' were the outcasts of the academic system, streetwise but unable or unwilling to make it in normal classes. **1970** *Islander* (Victoria, B.C.) 22 Nov. 5/1 Little by little they cleared each acre with axe and cross-cut saw. It was slow, sweat-labor. **1973** *New Society* 19 July 137/2 A 'sweat lodge', or hut fashioned from rocks, branches and a sacred blanket. The sauna-like action of a fire inside the hut helps purify his soul along with his body. **1977** *Rolling Stone* 7 Apr. 55/3 She learned of the sweat lodge and the sacred pipe ceremony and the Sun Dance while researching her Indian history book, and then began to understand them as part of the present. **1914** D. H. LAWRENCE *Prussian Officer* 20 His sweat-marked horse swishing its tail. **1957** H. ROOSENBERG *Walls came tumbling Down* v. 127 They had noticed that Nell's green skirt was badly worn—would she try on these sweat pants and see if they fitted? **1978** R. B. PARKER *Judas Goat* vi. 33 My blue sweat pants worn stylishly with the ankle zippers open. **1843** 'R. CARLTON' *New Purchase* I. xi. 73 This luxury..was used only as a 'sweat rag', and not 'as a nose-cloth'. **1930** *Aberdeen Press & Jrnl.* 28 Mar. 7/5 Making a swab with a sweat-rag, he attempted to stop the flow of blood. **1953** X. FIELDING *Stronghold* 256 The dirty old sweat-rag which he had worn round his head for the last three months. **1974** D. STUART *Prince of My Country* v. 32 Father puts down his knife and wipes his face with the sweatrag at his neck. **1971** M. BRANDER *Horseman's Vade Mecum* 439 *Sweat-rug*, a string rug put on under a reversed top rug when a horse has been sweating. **1978** 'F. PARRISH' *Sting of Honeybee* i. 11 She had taken off his saddle and put on a sweat-rug. **1923** D. H. LAWRENCE *Birds, Beasts & Flowers* 172 And dance, and dance, forever dance, with breath half sobbing in dark, sweat-shining breasts. **1929** *Sears, Roebuck Catal.* Spring/Summer 394 Every Man and Boy Wants A Sweat Shirt. **1938** E. HEMINGWAY *Fifth Column* (1939) 291 He'd pull on a rubber shirt over a couple of jerseys and a big sweat shirt over that. **1948** *Daily Express* 4 Sept. 2/5 (*caption*) The fluffy blonde in pale lemon sweat shirt. **1958** J. & W. HAWKINS *Death Watch* (1959) i. 16 She was wearing jeans, moccasins and a white sweat shirt. **1978** L. HEREN *Growing up on The Times* ix. 307 Another [young lad] exchanged his jeans and sweatshirt for a white dinner jacket and plum-coloured trousers. **1977** R. BARNARD *Blood Brotherhood* i. 14 The be-jeaned and sweat-shirted figure. **1892** *Charities Rev.* Jan. 115 What relaxation or excitement can a car-driver or a sweat-shop tailor get except by drinking? **1903** *Bond of Brotherhood* (Calgary, Alberta) 12 June 4/1 Healthy niggers sound in wind and limb well broke to handcuffs, two pair of genuine sweat shop overalls given with each piece of ebony. **1938** *Times Lit. Suppl.* 3 Dec. 767/2 The story of two Jews who, in youth, work in the same tailoring sweat-shop. **1959** *Daily Tel.* 17 Apr. 13/8, I cannot really think that he should want my job. Whitehall, and certainly Downing Street, is nothing but a sweatshop. **1972** *Bookseller* 4 Mar. 1476/1 If 28 jobs were costing only £6,000 a year..then the N.B.L. were running a sweat shop. **1944** K. LEVIS in Murdoch & Drake-Brockman *Austral. Short Stories* (1951) 429 Our shirts sweat-soaked under the midday sun. **1973** 'R. MACLEOD' *Burial in Portugal* i. 29 His sweat-soaked shirt was sticking to his back. **1973** R. BUSBY *Pattern of Violence* vi. 96 There was a dark sweat stain down the back of his shirt. **1932** W. FAULKNER *Light in August* ii. 28 Byron watched him standing there and looking at the men in sweat-stained overalls. **1975** H. R. F. KEATING *Remarkable Case* i. 3 His jacket and trousers were..worn and sweat-stained. **1930** L. W. OLDS *Track Athletics & Cross Country* i. 4 Sweat suits should be fleece-lined, washable and worn for warmth rather than a flashy appearance. **1951** I. SHAW *Troubled Air* x. 158 Archer lay on the mat in a sweatsuit. **1979** J. P. R. WILLIAMS *JPR* iv. 91 An Adidas sweat-suit keeping out the elements. *a* **1963** S. PLATH *Crossing Water* (1971) 58 Tangled in the sweat-wet sheets I remember the bloodied chicks.

sweat, *v.* Add: **I. 2. b.** In slang phrases *to sweat one's guts out* (later examples); also *to sweat blood*, (*a*) to exert oneself to the utmost; (*b*) to be terrified.

1911 G. S. PORTER *Harvester* xvii. 405 He just sweat blood to pacify her, but he couldn't make it. **1924** D. H. LAWRENCE in M. Magnus *Mem. Foreign Legion* 53, I sweat blood every time anybody comes through the door. **1937** 'G. ORWELL' *Road to Wigan Pier* xii. 228 It makes one sick to see half a dozen men sweating their guts out to dig a trench.., when some easily devised machine would scoop the earth out in a couple of minutes. **1950** 'J. TEY' *To love & be Wise* xiii. 163, I expect he sweats blood over his writing. He has no imagination. **1961** R. JEFFRIES *Evidence of Accused* v. 45 You sweated your guts out for months and finished your book, then the public looked the other way. **1973** W. M. DUNCAN *Big Timer* xxi. 138, I was sitting there sweating blood when those damned cops arrived.

d. With *off.* To (cause to) lose (weight, etc.) through strenuous exercise; *spec.* in *Boxing* (see quot. 1955).

1895 KIPLING *Day's Work* (1898) 347, I sweated the beef off 'em, and then I sweated some muscle on to 'em. **1899** —— *Stalky & Co.* 129 We've sweated a stone and a half off him since we began. **1955** F. C. AVIS *Boxing Dict.* 110 *Sweat off*, to lose weight through perspiration caused by vapour baths, etc., in an effort to bring the body to the poundage required for a given championship grade. **1976** *Southern Even. Echo* (Southampton) 12 Nov. 27/5 The..finalist outboxed his opponent, who was weakened after sweating off six pounds during the week.

4. c. *slang.* To subject (a prisoner, etc.) to close interrogation † or torture; to give the 'third degree' to (someone). Cf. *sweat-box* s.v. *SWEAT *sb.* 11.

1764 *Select Trials* I. 285, I..had heard him say, that Capt. Clark was a very great Rascal; and at Admiral Knowles's Trial, he would sweat Capt. Clark if he was examined, and if he could not sweat him there, he would sweat him another way. **1892** 'MARK TWAIN' *Amer. Claim.* xix. 194 It seems a piteous thing to sweat this poor ancient devil for a burglary he hadn't the least hand in. **1926** J. BLACK *You can't Win* xviii. 260, I wasn't taken out of my cell and 'sweated' or third-degreed, or beaten up. **1979** 'J. LE CARRÉ' *Smiley's People* (1980) xix. 237 Probably Mikhel intercepted and read it... We could sweat him, but I doubt if it would help.

II. 9. b. *trans.* With *out*, to await or endure anxiously or with unease. Esp. in phr. *to sweat it out. colloq.*

1876 'MARK TWAIN' *Tom Sawyer* xx. 200 Well, it's a kind of a tight place for Becky Thatcher... Just..let her sweat it out! **1942** E. COLBY *Army Talk* 229 *Sweat*..is a synonym for wait. You sweat a man out when you are waiting for him. You 'sweat out' a chow line while waiting for your turn for the sergeant to put your food in the mess kit. **1945** 'L. LEWIS' *Birthday Murder* (1951) xiii. 191, I haven't much time..but I'll sweat it out awhile. **1960** *News Chron.* 29 Sept. 1 Mr. Khruschev is just sweating it out in New York for an announcement of a manned flight in orbit. **1976** 'D. FLETCHER' *Don't whistle 'Macbeth'* 148, I had no intention of telling Hugo... Let him sweat that one out.

c. *intr.* With *on*, to await anxiously (an event or person); *spec.* in the game of lotto. Also *transf.*, to be close to attaining, as in phr. *to sweat on the top-line. slang* (chiefly *Austral.*) orig. *Mil.*

1917 A. G. EMPEY *From Fire Step* xix. 127 Sometimes you have fourteen numbers on your card covered and you are waiting for the fifteenth to be called. In an imploring voice you call out, 'Come on, Watkins, chum, I'm sweating on "Kelly's Eye".' *Ibid.* 252 *Sweating on leave.* Impatiently waiting for your name to appear in orders for leave. **1919** *Athenæum* 1 Aug. 695/2 'Sweating on the top line' is to be within an ace of obtaining what you want. **1959** S. J. BAKER *Drum* 150 *Sweat on*, to wait, usually to wait anxiously (for something to happen). **1968** S. L. ELLIOTT *Rusty Bugles* in E. Hanger *3 Austral. Plays* I. iv. 62 Wimpy sweats on me see..waits his chance..puts on a hut raid the other night and finds me mosquito net's not down and I lose my stripes.

d. *intr.* To experience discomfort through anxiety or unease (*colloq.*). In phr. *don't sweat it* (U.S. slang), don't worry.

1963 *Amer. Speech* XXXVIII. 271 *Don't sweat it* means 'don't worry about it'. **1973** R. HAYES *Hungarian Game* xxxix. 234 'Hold off for a moment. I want to watch him sweat.' 'The guy's about to faint from pain.' **1976** N. THORNBURG *Cutter & Bone* x. 238 Cutter reached over and covered her hand with his own, patted it. 'Don't sweat it, kid,' he said. 'It's nothing.' **1978** D. DEVINE *Sunk without Trace* ix. 92 No point in being early. Let him sweat.

III. 13. b. *Cookery.* To heat (meat or vegetables, etc.) in a pan with fat or water, in order to extract the juices.

1877 E. S. DALLAS *Kettner's Bk. of Table* 452 *Sweat, to,* is not a pretty phrase, but it expresses clearly..the act of making meat yield its juices by being heated in a pan with little or no water... The heat applied must be low and slow. **1942** [implied at *SWEATING *vbl. sb.* 3 c]. **1953** N. HEATON *Cassell's Cooking Dict.* 171 *Sweat,* to heat gently to extract flavour. **1972** *Guardian* 18 Aug. 11/3 Finely chop one large onion and two cloves garlic. Sweat these in a little oil in a thick saucepan.

Hence **swea·table** *a. rare,* capable of becoming sweated labour or a sweated labourer.

1922 G. B. SHAW in S. & B. Webb *Eng. Prisons* p. xlvi, The supply of sweatable labor. **1928** —— *Intelligent Woman's Guide* xli. 158 Our capitalist traders..were the enemies of every country, including their own, where there was a sweatable laborer to make dividends for them.

sweater. Add: **2. b.** A servant. *Winchester College slang.*

1900 J. S. FARMER *Public School Word-Bk.* 198 *Sweater* ..(Winchester), a servant. **1973** *Country Life* 19 July 147/1 This is a souvenir plaque..showing the famous painting of the 'Trusty Servant' at Winchester College.. or 'Sweater' as he is sometimes called.

5. (Earlier example.)

1846 *Manch. Guardian* 21 Mar. 7/4 A sort of middlemen, called 'sweaters', who get it [*sc.* tailoring work] by men and women at starvation prices.

6. (Earlier example.)

1845 *Currency Theory Reviewed* 69 It being obvious that the coinage, in the very nature of things, must be for ever, unit by unit, falling under depreciation by the mere action of ordinary and unavoidable abrasion—(to say nothing of the inducement which every restoration of the coinage holds out to the whole legion of 'pluggers' and 'sweaters').

7. b. Now also a similar garment in general informal use; a jumper or pullover.

1895 *Century Mag.* May 25/2 His brawny, muscular chest, which was covered only by a dark, close-fitting 'sweater', was that of an athlete. **1912** J. SANDILANDS *Western Canad. Dict. & Phrase-Bk., Sweater,* a woollen jacket, much worn in Canada during the winter both indoors and outdoors, and sometimes a somewhat gaudy article of wear. **1957** *Times Lit. Suppl.* 25 Oct. 640/1 A tall, bespectacled young man in turtle-necked sweater. **1981** G. SWIFT *Shuttlecock* i. 13 Martin has a red poloneck sweater and Peter a brown one and they both wear identical child's blue jeans.

9. *attrib.* and *Comb.*, as (sense 7 b) *sweater blouse, coat, dress, -suit;* **sweater girl** *U.S.*, a girl, esp. a model or actress, who wears tight-fitting sweaters; orig. a name applied to the American actress Lana Turner (b. 1921) who wore such a sweater in the film *They won't Forget* (1937), and in subsequent publicity photographs; **sweater-shirt,** (*a*) *U.S.*, a knitted garment that may be worn as a sweater or a shirt; (*b*) = *sweat-shirt* s.v. *SWEAT *sb.* 11.

1925 *Vogue* Early Mar. 60 (*caption*) This straight-line sweater blouse from Molyneux..is fashioned of fine dark-blue tricot covered with an all-over woven pattern in gold thread. **1954** *New Yorker* 27 Nov. 141/1 A wool jersey sweaterblouse, lavender or white, has cap sleeves and a scoop neck ornamented with gold thread and tiny pink felt buds. **1911** Sweater coat [see *LOVAT]. **1963** *Vogue* Dec. 190 Sweater-coat hand-knitted in Italy. **1965** *Harper's Bazaar* May 6 (Advt.), An enchanting cashmere sweater-dress. **1940** *Movie Mirror* June 9/1 (*caption*) Sweet and sophisticated sixteen: Lana Turner, at the time her face hit a thousand papers as the 'Sweater Girl'. **1941** *Life* 14 Apr. 33/2 Mr. Breen's letter left moviemakers wondering..what to do with their up-and-coming sweater girls. **1956** S. ERTZ *Charmed Circle* 71 Among all the 'sweater girls' she looked, in her unrevealing black dress, as if she had strayed in by mistake. **1971** D. MACKENZIE *Sleep is for Rich* iii. 66 Crying Eddie was getting plenty of attention from the sweater girls. **1964** *New Yorker* 12 Oct. 15 Sweater-shirt of pink cashmere. **1977** *Private Eye* 4 Mar. 20/2 (Advt.), American styled printed sweatshirts and T-shirts. **1929** M. LIEF *Hangover* 232 'You're looking fine,' said Whippet, admiring her..slim figure in a neat-fitting sweater-suit. **1964** *Glamour* Sept. 160 Town sweater-suits [are] booted for the summer.

Hence **swea·tered** *a.*, wearing a sweater; clothed in a sweater.

1901 S. E. WHITE *Claim Jumpers* i. 11 Two sweatered and white-ducked individuals. **1936** R. CHANDLER in *Trouble is my Business* (1954) 205 The sweatered man snatched the gun up. **1971** C. MCCULLERS *Mortgaged Heart* (1977) 74 His blue sweatered shoulders were shaking.

sweat-house. Add: **3.** (See quot.) Cf. *sweat-box* (*c*) s.v. SWEAT *sb.* 11. *rare.*

1882 *Harper's Mag.* Nov. 872/2 The grapes for raisin-making..are removed to an airy building known as a 'sweat-house', where they remain possibly a month, till the last vestiges of moisture are extracted.

sweating, *vbl. sb.* Add: **3. a.** Also with *out.* Cf. SWEAT *v.* 12.

1969 BENNISON & WRIGHT *Geol. Hist. Brit. Isles* iii. 43 The last major effect of the metamorphism was the 'sweating out' of synorogenic pegmatites which cross-cut some of the Inverian structures. **1971** I. G. GASS et al. *Understanding Earth* iii. 66/2 The present oceans and atmosphere of the Earth are secondary features due to the subsequent dewatering or 'sweating out' of the Earth's interior.

c. *Cookery.* The action or process of *SWEAT *v.* 13 b.

1942 C. SPRY *Come into Garden, Cook* xi. 137 Cook the sliced vegetables first in a little fat... This preliminary sweating of the vegetables draws out the flavour.

5. b. Extortion of a confession (from a prisoner, etc.) by close interrogation † or torture. Cf. *SWEAT *v.* 4 c.

1824 J. DODDRIDGE *Notes Settlement Indian Wars* II. xii. 122 The torture of sweating..that is of suspension by the arms pinioned behind the backs, brought a confession. **1904** *Cincinnati* (Ohio) *Enquirer* 21 Oct. 4 He confessed, under sweating, that he broke into several offices. **1949** *Amer. Speech* XXIV. 262 The device of *sweating* consisted of suspending the offender from the limb of a tree by his arms, and laying lashes on him.

6. sweating pen *Austral.*, a pen in which sheep are kept (formerly, to sweat so as to soften the wool) before shearing; = *holding pen* s.v. *HOLDING *vbl. sb.* 6 b.

1882 ARMSTRONG & CAMPBELL *Austral. Sheep Husbandry* xv. 176 On each side of the board are built the sheep pens, which are filled from a race on each side.. which is in its turn filled from the sweating pen. *c* **1929** H. B. SMITH *Sheep & Wool Industry in Austral. & N.Z.* (ed. 3) x. 73 After drafting, the sheep to be shorn are run up a ramp into the sweating pens of the shed. **1965** J. S. GUNN *Terminol. Shearing Industry* II. 29 *Sweating pen,* sometimes used in the same sense as 'holding pen', although there is no longer any suggestion of deliberately 'sweating' the sheep.

sweating, *ppl. a.* **2.** (Later examples.)

1976 K. BONFIGLIOLI in *Winter's Crimes 8* 44 The sweating heel of some nameless cheese. **1981** J. B. HILTON *Surrender Value* vi. 47 A sweating expresso machine.

sweaty, *a.* Add: **1. d.** Severe, demanding. *colloq.*

1919 A. LUNN *Loose Ends* iii. 27 'It's a sweaty house for new men.' Cliff shook his head sadly. 'Yes, it's a hard life for new men.' *Ibid.* xiii. 118 These Blues are sometimes rather sweaty. They think it lip if you cut your work for a man who's been a Blue. **1973** M. AMIS *Rachel Papers* 85 I'm not trying to be sweaty or anything, but, um—just out of interest—how long have you known De Forest?

sweatily *adv.*: also *fig.*, anxiously, feverishly.

1975 *Times* 4 Sept. 12/8 Men talking sweatily about the upcoming upcurve in house prices. **1978** W. F. BUCKLEY *Stained Glass* iii. 21 On the occasions when they found themselves trapped in his company at a dinner party, they would sweatily engage other members of the party.. in concentrated, often nonsensical, discussions.

Swede. Add: **4. swede-basher** *slang,* a farm worker; hence, a rustic (cf. *BASHING *vbl. sb.* 3); so **swede-bashing** *a.*

1936 J. CURTIS *Gilt Kid* iv. 40, I know you're not a swede-bashing judy. **1943** HUNT & PRINGLE *Service Slang* 63 *Swede-basher,* agricultural worker; country bumpkin. **1948** A. BARON *From City, from Plough* 84 There's a lot o' these swedebashers go down the farms every night. **1966** *New Statesman* 18 Mar. 363/1 Sir Gerald Nabarro is said to have remarked on TV that the fate of the nation depended on a few swede-bashers. **1976** J. GRENFELL *Joyce Grenfell requests Pleasure* (1977) xiii. 190, I tried to sing a song appropriate for the swede-bashers from Lincolnshire, the Cockneys, Scots.., and so on.

Swede (swīd), *a.* Chiefly *Canad.* [f. the sb.] = SWEDISH *a.*; *spec.* in *Swede saw,* a type of saw having a bow-like tubular frame and a sharp blade with many cutting teeth.

1934 G. BETTANY *Valley of Lost Gold* 29 I've been to the Swede settlement west of the hills. **1950** J. HAMBLETON *Abitibi Adventure* 120 It looked just like any other 'Swede saw', with its tubular metal frame, painted blue, and a thin, keen blade which was kept taut by a clamp. **1971** D. C. BROWN *Yukon Trophy Trails* ii. 39 Louis packed the axe and the Swede saw, and I carried the gun and lunch. **1981** *Nordic Skiing* Jan. 30/2 Lee saws firewood with the Swede saw and I get the honor of splitting it into burning size.

Swedenborgian, *a.* and *sb.* Add: **a.** *adj.* (Earlier and later examples.) **b.** *sb.* (Earlier and later examples.) **Swedenborgianism** (earlier examples).

1791 J. LACKINGTON *Mem.* xxv. 195 The *Swedenborgians,* or *New Jerusalemists,* are gaining ground very fast. **1807** SOUTHEY *Lett. from Eng.* III. lxii. 144 (*heading*) Account of Swedenborgianism. *Ibid.*, The New Jerusalem, or Swedenborgian chapel. **1842** C. FOX *Jrnl.* 6 June in *Memories of Old Friends* (1882) viii. 160 Thomas Carlyle came in..and we presently got, I know not how, to Swedenborgianism. **1856** *Spiritual Herald* June 147 The Lord may be better represented by an animated and intelligent orb..than by a Whewellite or Swedenborgian star. **1914** C. MACKENZIE *Sinister Street* II. III. ix. 682, I should love to be a sort of Swedenborgian with all sorts of fanciful private beliefs. **1920** M. BEER *Hist. Brit. Socialism* II. III. i. 12 William Hill, a Swedenborgian preacher and a grammarian. **1976** *Gramophone* June 32/1 Pitcairn wished to sponsor the promotion and recording of his fellow Swedenborgian's music.

swedge, *v.* Add: Also *intr.* To go *off* or depart without paying. *U.S. Naut. slang. rare.*

1897 KIPLING *Capt. Cour.* v. 124 'Seems kinder unneighbourly to let 'em swedge off like this,' Salters suggested, feeling in his pockets.

Swedish, *a.* and *sb.* Add: **A.** *adj. Swedish exercises* = *Swedish drill;* also *fig.*; *Swedish massage,* a system of massage combined with manipulation of the joints and muscles, first devised in Sweden; hence *Swedish masseur,* (fem.) *-euse,* one trained in the practice of Swedish massage; *Swedish modern* = *Danish modern* s.v. *DANISH *a.* (cf. *SCANDINAVIAN *a.* 2). Also with reference to persons living in Sweden, or of Swedish descent.

1799 MALTHUS *Diary* 27 July (1966) 191 The son-in-law told us that a Norway lap must not go into Sweden, nor a Swedish lap come into Norway. **1911** *Daily Colonist* (Victoria, B.C.) 8 Apr. 5/2 (Advt.), Swedish Massage, Medical Sick-Gymnastic, Electric Vibrations... Above treatments highly recommended by leading physicians. **1911** Swedish masseur [see *OPSONIST]. **1912** 'SAKI' *Unbearable Bassington* vii. 124 A sporting cat..watching the Swedish exercises of a well-spent..mouse. **1923** WODEHOUSE *Inimit. Jeeves* xi. 123 If she had knocked off starchy foods and done Swedish exercises for a bit, she might have been quite tolerable. **1948** A. H. RUTT *Home Furnishing* (ed. 2) xiii. 217 Swedish Modern is a favorite style which successfully combines native, Classical, Empire, and Modern ideas. **1958** 'S. MARLOWE' *Second Longest Night* iii. 26 The living-room was Swedish modern ..with black lacquered pieces and high-grained white ash. **1959** A. GLYN *I can take it All* ii. 30 'But you live in—' I was going to say Helsinki, but I remembered..that she was a Swedish Finn '—in Helsingfors?' **1966** J. MITFORD in *McCall's* Mar. 190/2 A splendid Swedish masseuse.. rubs you all over with cream. **1970** D. BAGLEY *Running Blind* vii. 156 The room was decorated in that generalized style known as Swedish Modern. **1975** C. YOUNG *Massage* ii. 16 In the beginning of the nineteenth century a Swedish fencing master, Peter Henrik Ling, introduced a system of movement that consisted of massage and exercises... This method..became the basis for..Swedish massage. **1979** J. TATE tr. *Martenson's Death calls on Witches* v. 33 Her parents were Swedish-Americans.

† **sweedle** (swī·d'l), *v. Obs. slang.* [Blend of SWINDLE *v.*[2] and WHEEDLE *v.*] *trans.* To swindle by wheedling. Hence **swee·dling** *vbl. sb.* and *ppl. a.*

1908 H. A. JONES *Dolly reforming Herself* IV. 94 I'm not going to be sweedled!—*Matt.* What is sweedled? *Harry.* Sweedling is sweedling! It's part swindling and part wheedling! **1908** *Westm. Gaz.* 4 Nov. 5/2 Dolly is a 'sweedling' extravagant little vixen. **1909** *Daily Chron.* 19 Jan. 4/4 He circumvented Isengrim the Wolf and 'sweedled' King Noble the Lion. **1914** *Angl. Forsch.* XLII. 20 The mind, hesitating between *swindle* and *wheedle,* compromises on *sweedle.* When the result pleases the coiners, it sometimes continues in family use, as *sweedle* in the case of a Nebraska family.

Sweeney (swī·ni). *slang.* Also **sweeney, Sweeny.** [f. the name of *Sweeney* Todd, a barber who murdered his customers, the central character of a play by George Dibdin Pitt (1799–1855), and of later plays.] **1.** In full *Sweeney Todd.* Rhyming slang for 'Flying Squad'. So, a member of the Flying Squad.

1936 J. CURTIS *Gilt Kid* xxii. 223 The slops had been turning up at the block of flats just as he was making his getaway. Yes, and coming along in a jam jar too. That made them look like Sweenies. **1938** F. D. SHARPE *Sharpe of Flying Squad* 333 *The Sweeney Todd,* the Flying Squad. **1956** J. D. CARR *Patrick Butler for Defence* xiii. 140 The Flying-Squad people are called sweenies, from Sweeny Todd. **1967** N. LUCAS *C.I.D.* xiii. 195 By the way, don't bother to call the Sweeny (Sweeney Todd—Flying Squad). **1971** R. BUSBY *Deadlock* I. v. 56, I was with the sweeney before this firm... The Sweeney Todd—crime squad... If you're an old sweeney man too, we'll get along all right. **1977** *Guardian Weekly* 17 July 10/1 Was designed—as they say in The Sweeney—to put the frighteners on Labour knockers.

2. A (nickname for a) barber.

1966 'L. LANE' *ABZ of Scouse* 104 I'm goin' ter Sweeny ter 'ave me hur cut. **1980** *Globe & Laurel* July/Aug. 217/2 It has been noted that a significant number of the ship's company now have a 'Sweeney' Barber special.

sweenied (swī·nid), *a. U.S.* Also **sweeneyed, swinneyed, swyneyed.** [f. next + -ED[2].] Suffering from sweeny. Hence *sweenied-looking* adj.

1861 *Harper's Mag.* Aug. 421/2 The people have been fed on buncombe, while a lot of spavined, ring-boned,.. swyneyed, split-headed..polleviled politicians have had their noses in the public crib. **1872** *Rep. Indian Affairs 1871* (U.S.) 554 The three mules were thin, and one of them lame in the right shoulder, 'sweenied'. **1872** *Borderer* (Las Cruces, New Mexico) 5 Oct. 2/4 God Almighty only knows the age of 'em!—three footed, one-eyed, sweeneyed, spavined, broken-down ex-livery stable stock, 'political hacks', and sway-backed horses. **1960** V. WILLIAMS *Walk Egypt* 188 Mule and tree had grown old and swinneyed together. *Ibid.* 240 He picked up a mule... It was a swinneyed-looking thing.

sweeny. (Earlier examples.)

1813 E. GERRY *Diary* 23 June (1927) 131, I answered he [*sc.* a horse] was foundered, but was informed that it was another complaint called the sweeney. **1832** J. P.

KENNEDY *Swallow Barn* II. i. 22 He professed to cure the colt's distemper, sweeny, and other maladies.

sweep, *sb.* Add: **I. 1. b.** Also *spec.* with reference to aircraft patrols, usu. offensive, but occas. also for reconnaissance purposes.

1940 *Sun* (Baltimore) 21 Feb. 1/6 In a daylight sweep over the Channel..British fighters set another Nazi E-boat afire. **1942** *Ann. Reg. 1941* 52 About the middle of June the Royal Air Force began to make what were called 'offensive sweeps'..seeking for enemy machines. **1959** R. COLLIER *City that wouldn't Die* x. 167 Some fifty day-fighters and thirty night-fighters had taken part in this spectacular sweep. **1973** 'R. LEWIS' *Blood Money* viii. 106 The helicopter seemed to have completed its sweeps... The shadows..had made spotting difficult.

d. *Sport.* Victory in all the games in a contest, tournament, etc., by one team or one competitor, or the winning of all the places in an event or competition. orig. and chiefly *U.S.*

1960 WENTWORTH & FLEXNER *Dict. Amer. Slang* 531/1 *Sweep n.*, the act or an instance of one athlete or team winning a tournament without losing an individual game or contest. **1974** *State* (Columbia, S. Carolina) 31 Mar. 5-D/4 The Gamecocks claimed all three places for a sweep of the 880 as John Brown rolled home with a time of 1:56.6 to best teammates Mike Sheley and Don Brown. **1977** *Hongkong Standard* 12 Apr. 12/7 John Mayberry also drove in two runs to help Royals complete a season-opening sweep of the three-game series against the Tigers. **1979** *Arizona Daily Star* 1 Apr. C1/1 James Frazier led an Arizona sweep in the high jump with a winning leap of 7-3¾, followed by Roger Curtis' 7-1¾.

5. b. *Cricket.* An attacking stroke made on the front foot, in which the batsman brings the bat across his body to hit the ball square or backward of square on the leg side.

1888 R. H. LYTTELTON in Steel & Lyttelton *Cricket* ii. 65 George Parr's leg hit..was the sweep to long leg off a shortish ball. **1920** D. J. KNIGHT in P. F. Warner *Cricket* 35 The sweep to leg is a very paying and useful stroke, although not elegant. It is effected by sinking almost down on the right knee and sweeping the ball right round in the direction of long leg. **1955** *Times* 9 May 15/1 He had played some good drives and sweeps. **1970** *Times* 19 Aug. 6/5 Most of the Yorkshire batsmen were obsessed by that ugly and risky stroke, the sweep.

6. d. *Electronics.* A steady movement across the screen of a cathode-ray tube of the spot produced by the electron beam; the moving spot itself, or the line it generates.

1924 *Wireless World* 5 Mar. 705/2 The approximate form of transient phenomena may also be indicated, if the frequency is low enough to enable a single sweep of the ray across the screen to be seen. **1946** *Radar: Summary Rep. & Harp Project* (U.S. Nat. Defense Res. Comm., Div. 14) 144/1 By making this motion rapid and continuous, the point of light becomes a line of light, and is called a sweep. **1958** *New Scientist* 10 Apr. 17/2 A ray of greenish-blue light—the sweep—pivots on the centre of the tube like the spokes of a wheel. **1966** M. WOODHOUSE *Tree Frog* xxi. 154 The bright scanning sweep swung around the orange tube face of the monitor like the seconds' hand of a stop-watch. **1975** G. J. KING *Audio Handbk.* v. 114 The oscilloscope's time-base is switched off and the horizontal sweep provided by high-level signal from the audio oscillator.

e. *Electronics.* A steady, usu. repeated, change in the magnitude or frequency of a voltage or other quantity between definite limits.

1930 *Proc. IRE* XVIII. 590 A single sweep, exposing each tone about 1/150th of a second was found sufficient to give a useful record. **1966** *McGraw-Hill Encycl. Sci. & Technol.* XIII. 336/1 Hyperbolic sweeps may be generated as a modification of the type of circuitry used in the generation of saw-tooth sweep waveforms. **1975** D. G. FINK *Electronics Engineers' Handbk.* XVI. 29 Circuits delivering a linear voltage sweep fall into two categories, the Miller time base and bootstrap time base.

8. b. *fig.* A comprehensive search, esp. in relation to crime investigation; *spec.* a search for electronic listening devices. *colloq.* (orig. *U.S.*).

1966 *Wall St. Jrnl.* 17 Feb. 1/4 In Burns' 'sweeps'.. specialists check furniture, light switches, air vents, drapes, rugs, telephones, pictures and walls with..detection gear. **1973** *Times* 18 June 2/7 One of the largest British-based international companies recently employed a security firm to conduct 30 anti-bugging 'sweeps' on its premises every month. **1974** *Union* (S. Carolina) *Daily Times* 20 Apr. 1/7 Police mounted a room-by-room sweep of hotels..in search of Dantzler. **1978** J. GARDNER *Dancing Dodo* xiii. 93 '*Overshoot?*' Dobson queried reflectively... 'Will you do a sweep of the files?'

II. 14*. *Aeronaut.* = *sweepback* s.v. *SWEEP- 3.

1914 *Aeroplane* 26 Mar. 358/2 (*caption*) Plan view of the Grahame-White biplane, showing sweep of wings. **1947** *Aircraft Engin.* June 180/2 As can be seen..the sweep is 38°..for the main plane and rather less for the tail plane. **1976** *Farnborough Internat. Exhibition* (Official Programme) 41 Studies indicate that, by adjusting the angle of sweep, fuel consumption..can be materially reduced.

III. 15. f. *Forestry.* The natural curve of a tree or log of wood.

1932 CHAPMAN & DEMERITT *Elem. Forest Mensuration* xi. 179 The extent of the actual loss of boards by reason of crook or sweep depends on the minimum length of a merchantable board. **1946** *Q. Jrnl. Forestry* XL. 52 Many of the trees had a severe 'sweep' which resulted in the very poor output of suitable telegraph pole material. **1957** *Brit. Commonw. Forest Terminol.* II. 192 *Sweep*, the natural bend of a log, generally applied to long gentle bends.

V. 26. (Later examples.)

1923 H. BELLOC *Sonnets & Verse* III. 119 The sweeps have fallen from Ha'nacker Mill. **1968** J. ARNOLD *Shell Bk. Country Crafts* 170 The original form of sweep consisted of a light framework mounted on each stock, or sail-arm, over which a canvas sail was set or furled according to the wind.

29. Also in mine-sweeping.

1915 *Chambers's Jrnl.* June 387/2 Those six small gray ships will return with..a fearsome tale of many mines caught in their sweeps and destroyed. **1923** *Man. Seamanship* (Admiralty) II. 172 The vessel..puts the end of the sweep on a slip somewhere on her quarter-deck. **1943** *His Majesty's Minesweepers* (Min. of Information) 8/1 The thud of the explosion as a mine, caught in a sweep, detonated under a trawler's counter.

33. b. (Examples.) Chiefly at Yale University. ? *Obs.*

1900 *Dialect Notes* II. 65 *Sweep, n.*, a care-taker of college rooms at Yale, where negro boys are employed. **1950** *Harvard Alumni Bull.* 22 Apr. 590/3 In early times, sweeper was in use instead of goody, and even now at Yale College the word sweep is retained.

VII. 34. (sense *6 d, e) *sweep amplifier, generator, oscillator, voltage*; (sense 19) *sweep-ticket*; **sweep-swinger** *U.S.*, an oarsman in a racing boat.

1947 R. LEE *Electronic Transformers & Circuits* i. 4 Make efficient transformers for the non-sinusoidal wave shapes such as are encountered in pulse, video, and sweep amplifiers. **1946** *Radar: Summary Rep. & Harp Project* (U.S. Nat. Defense Res. Comm., Div. 14) 144/1 *Sweep circuit* or *generator*, a circuit which produces at regular intervals an approximately linear or circular, or other form of movement (sweep) of the beam of the cathode-ray tube. **1975** D. G. FINK *Electronics Engineers' Handbk.* XVI. 29 Sweep generators may also be looked upon as integrators with a constant-amplitude input signal. **1939** H. J. REICH *Theory & Application Electron Tubes* xv. 596 Practical sweep oscillators do not furnish a voltage that satisfies the requirements for a perfect sweep voltage. **1967** *Electronics* 6 Mar. 2 (Advt.), All solid-state Hewlett-Packard 3211A sweep oscillators..meet virtually all of your swept frequency testing requirements. **1949** *N.Y. Times* 12 June 48/4 Hundreds of sweepswingers are sweating it out..on Connecticut's Thames River. **1971** L. KOPPETT *N.Y. Times Guide Spectator Sports* xviii. 234 A crewman is a 'sweepswinger'. **1930** *Daily Express* 23 May 3/4 Who sent out the Mayfair Luncheon Club's £20,000 sweep tickets? **1934** J. H. REYNER *Television* vii. 78 The spot can be shifted horizontally or vertically, as required, irrespective of the sweep or work voltages. **1962** SIMPSON & RICHARDS *Physical Princ. Junction Transistors* xvii. 443 The simplest sweep voltage is obtained by suddenly applying a d.c. voltage *V* to a resistor *R* and a capacitor *C* in series and taking the voltage across the capacitor as the output.

sweep, *v.* Add: **2. b.** *Cricket.* To hit (the ball) with a sweep (sense *5 b). Also *absol.* or *intr.*, to play a sweep.

1920 [see *SWEEP *sb.* 5 b]. **1958** D. BRADMAN *Art of Cricket* 80 An inviting half-volley comes along... The greater scoring medium would be to sweep it fine. **1963** *Times* 19 Feb. 4/2 He is a fine cutter and an enthusiastic sweeper. Today he swept only twice, lest the shot should get him into trouble, as it sometimes does. **1965** D. SILK *Attacking Cricket* iv. 60 The batsman must always try to sweep the ball along the ground. **1976** *Star* (Sheffield) 30 Nov., Fletcher eventually fell lbw sweeping at Eknath Solkar.

6. c. *to sweep* (a person) *off his feet*: to affect with overwhelming enthusiasm, to infatuate. Also *transf.* Cf. *to carry* (a person) *off his feet* s.v. FOOT *sb.* 27.

1913 F. L. BARCLAY *Broken Halo* xiv. 151, I remember being swept completely off my feet when I first met Jim. **1937** W. R. INGE *Rustic Moralist* I. ii. 46, I do not approve of concentration camps, or of Jew-baiting, or of sabre-rattling. I only want to understand a movement which has swept a great nation off its feet. **1977** *Daily Mirror* 16 Mar. 13/5 Mr. Lipscombe's daughter Gillian was swept off her feet by De Roth.

8. b. *U.S.* To win every event in (a series of sporting events, etc.), or to take each of the main places in (a contest or event).

[**1942** BERREY & VAN DEN BARK *Amer. Thes. Slang* § 650/7 *Phlanx, sweep the event*, to win all of the main events in all three first places in a meet.] **1960** WENTWORTH & FLEXNER *Dict. Amer. Slang* 531/1 *Sweep...v.t.*, to win a tournament without losing a game or contest. **1974** *Greenville* (S. Carolina) *News* 22 Apr. 15/1, I didn't think either team would sweep this series. **1979** *Tucson* (Arizona) *Citizen* 20 Sept. 8D/3 Montreal swept a double-header from New York, 3–1 and 4–1.

13. d. *fig.* To examine (premises, telephone lines, etc.) for electronic listening or recording devices. *colloq.* (orig. *U.S.*).

1966 *Wall Street Jrnl.* 17 Feb. 1/4 The companies also are having their offices regularly 'swept'—checked by professional sleuths to find any hidden transmitters. **1968** [see *SWEEPER 5 b]. **1970** K. BENTON *Sole Agent* xx. 210 This room's all right. It was 'swept' only a few weeks ago. **1979** J. BARNETT *Backfire is Hostile!* iii. 37 'How safely can we speak on this line?'..'The line is swept every fifteen minutes and it is very clean.'

14. b. *Ent.* To drag a net over the surface of (herbage, etc.) in order to catch insects. Cf. SWEEP-NET 2.

1826 KIRBY & SPENCE *Introd. Entomol.* IV. l. 517 For this last operation—sweeping the grass, &c.—..you will find a net invented by Mr. Paul..a very useful implement. **1926** A. H. HAMM in J. J. Walker *Nat. Hist. Oxf. District* 263 *Hemerodromia precatoria* Fln. and *H. raptoria* Mg. have been captured by sweeping water plants in 'Mesopotamia'. **1977** RICHARDS & DAVIES *Imms's Gen. Textbk. Entomol.* (ed. 10) II. III. 1205 The adults are most often obtained by sweeping or shaking the vegetation.

18. a. Also *fig.*

1957 W. S. CHURCHILL *Hist. English-Speaking Peoples* III. vii. 272 Although his generals and Ministers were reluctant and apprehensive a kind of delirium swept the martial classes of the Empire. **1958** P. H. GIBBS *Curtains of Yesterday* xix. 156 That was a gruesome sight! The whole country is swept by typhus. I guess some of us may be unlucky. It may be difficult to dodge.

b. To achieve widespread popularity throughout (a town, country, etc.). Also *spec.* in Politics, to gain control of by an overwhelming margin.

1892 *Times* 9 July 11/1 Mr Gladstone is not likely to 'sweep' the counties any more than he has 'swept' the boroughs. **1931** W. HOLTBY *Poor Caroline* vii. 278 Tell her that that C.C.C. is going to *sweep England.* **1950** *Times* 27 Apr. 4/3 Any party which, at the next election, pledged itself to forming a coalition Government no matter how big a majority it obtained would sweep the country. **1960** *Sunday Express* 14 Aug. 12/3 The short cut is sweeping the town. **1970** *Morning Star* 29 May 1 Ceylon's Left wing United Front led by Mrs Sirimavo Bandaranaike swept the polls here today. **1974** *News & Courier* (Charleston, S. Carolina) 10 Mar. 9-A/2 Sweep the Negro vote..and pick up enough whites to come out of the primary with something more than 50 per cent of the ballots.

19. Also *spec.* with an aircraft as subject.

1941 E. SHEPHERD *Mil. Aeroplane* 26 These aeroplanes have to sweep the seas and watch enemy harbours. **1959** R. COLLIER *City that wouldn't Die* iv. 56 At 9.35 p.m. the usual dusk patrol, a few day and night fighters, sweeping the raiders' normal routes. **1976** A. WHITE *Long Silence* vii. 53 We had picked up our fighter escort... Every so often, one or the other would peel off and sweep an observation circuit.

sweep-. Add: **1. sweep hand** = next; **sweep second(s (hand)** orig. *U.S.* = *centre-second(s* s.v. CENTRE, CENTER *sb.* and *a.* 19; hence *sweep-seconds watch.*

1948 *Wrist Watches, Pocket Watches & Clocks* iii. 185 Watch stops... This may be caused by..sweep hand rubbing on dial. **1967** R. MEYERS *Dolphin Rider* (1968) i. 22 Henries..listened while he watched the sweep hand of his watch. **1977** *Times Lit. Suppl.* 24 June 779/1 The sweep hand of my watch is there in order to make seconds easier to read. **1948** *Wrist Watches, Pocket Watches & Clocks* ii. 154 Remove sweep seconds hand. **1953** W. J. GAZELEY *Watch & Clock Making* iii. 48 Nowadays..we have what are termed sweep-seconds watches. At one time these were referred to as centre-seconds. **1962** E. BRUTON *Dict. Clocks & Watches* 170 *Sweep seconds*, American name for centre seconds. **1962** J. D. MACDONALD *Girl, Gold Watch, & Everything* viii. 101 Uncle Omar's gold watch..had an hour hand, a minute hand and a sweep second hand. **1969** *Guardian* 20 Aug. 7/1 All the clocks..have a sweep second hand. **1979** *Sci. Amer.* May 145/1 A sweep second hand on a wristwatch will also serve.

3. With advbs.: **sweepback** *Aeronaut.*, the form of an aircraft wing that is angled backwards, so that the part farther from the fuselage is aft of the nearer part; the angle made by such a wing with a line at right angles to the fuselage; **sweep-forward** *Aeronaut.*, the form of an aircraft wing that is angled forwards, so that the part further from the fuselage is forward of the nearer part; **sweep-out**, an act of sweeping out; (*U.S. colloq.*) a clearance or purge.

1914 *Aeroplane* 19 Mar. 308/1 Owing to the sweep back on the wings the side area of these struts may be regarded as taking the place of tail fins. **1918** H. J. STEPHENS *Gloss. Aeronaut. Words* (ed. 2) 36 *Sweepback*, the angle at which the planes slope backwards each side of the fuselage. **1939** *Aircraft Engin.* Apr. 159/3 The basic characteristic of sweepback on a rectangular wing would appear to be an early stalling of the tips which may or may not produce greater lateral stability. **1968** MILLER & SAWERS *Technical Devel. Mod. Aviation* vi. 204 The slightly greater sweep-back of the 707's wing means that it takes off at a greater angle of attack. **1977** *Jrnl. R. Soc. Arts* CXXV. 349/2 We can use the improved methods..to reduce wing sweepback (thus improving take-off and landing). **1932** *Technical Rep. Aeronaut. Res. Committee 1930–1* I. 39 Sweep-forward increases the maximum lift and considerably delays the stall. **1953** M. RAUSCHER *Introd. Aeronaut. Dynamics* ix. 378 A wing without pronounced sweep-back or sweep-forward. **1975** L. J. CLANCY *Aerodynamics* xvi. 532 Sweep forward would have a de-stabilizing effect. **1947** *Sun* (Baltimore) 16 Aug. 12/8 Governor Lane has ordered a sweep-out at the Board of Supervisors of Elections... About 30 places on the pay roll..are slated to be pulled out from under employés who are on the wrong side of the Democratic factional fence. **1978** *Detroit Free Press* 6 Apr. E 5/3 A total of 47 rookies won jobs this season, reflecting a lot of dead wood on the rosters. 'Next year', predicts our source, 'will see an even bigger sweep-out.'

sweeper. Add: **1. c.** (Later examples.) Now usu. short for *mine-sweeper.*

1915 S. H. CARDEN in M. Gilbert *Winston S. Churchill* (1972) III. Compan. I. 405 Battleships preceded by sweepers making way up towards Narrows. **1941** S. O'CASEY *Let.* 28 Apr. (1975) I. 886 Delighted to hear John [Allen]'s allright on a sweeper. **1979** D. GURR *Troika* i. 5 Losses of submariners trying to run the Baltic minefields without benefit of sweepers were appalling.

d. *Cricket.* A batsman who sweeps (sense *2 b).

1961 *Times* 21 Aug. 3/3 There can be few more effective sweepers. **1963** [see *SWEEP *v.* 2 b]. **1965** D. SILK *Attacking Cricket* iv. 60 The best sweepers bring the bat down on the ball from above as well as across.

e. *Assoc. Football.* One who plays as the last line of defence except the goalkeeper, across the width of the field (i.e. as opposed to a right or left back, etc., in other systems).

1964 *Times* 13 Apr. 4/1 Moore..played a giant part in his role as 'sweeper' of the rear. **1971** *Times* 15 Feb. 9/2 Of the other younger England [hockey] players Perry had a solid game as sweeper. **1973** *Daily Pennsylvanian* 9 Oct. 6 We knew they were using a sweeper, so we had to run to the corners to draw him out. **1976** *Denbighshire Free Press* 8 Dec. 24/2 Even with Bernie Welsh operating as sweeper behind a defensive line of four, Courtaulds were far from impressive at the back when the ball was in the air.

2. a. (Earlier example in *spec.* sense.) Also *attrib.* as *sweeper caste.*

1844 W. H. SLEEMAN *Rambles & Recollections Indian Official* I. viii. 64 The right of sweeping within a certain range is recognised by the caste to belong to a certain member... If any house-keeper..happens to offend the sweeper..none of his filth will be removed. **1859** MRS. R. M. COOPLAND *Lady's Escape from Gwalior* iii. 58 Matrané, a woman of the sweeper caste. **1909** J. HASTINGS *Encycl. Relig. & Ethics* II. 551/2 The sweeper or scavenger caste of Hindustan.

5. b. *colloq.* An electronic device for detecting listening or recording apparatus. Also, a person operating such a device.

1968 *Observer* 16 June 7/2 To help in the job of debugging, Mr. Johnson is having electronic 'sweepers' manufactured... Small ones can be operated by firms' security officers to keep a boardroom 'clean' after it has been 'swept'. It was with one of these 'sweepers' that an attempt to smuggle a bug into a boardroom in the bottom of a coffee pot was recently foiled. **1972** K. BENTON *Spy in Chancery* xi. 116 They sent a 'sweeper' team..and they went through the rooms in Chancery. **1979** F. FORSYTH *Devil's Alternative* x. 232 A secure room regularly checked by the 'sweepers' who are..looking for..listening devices.

6. (Examples.) Also, a partially fallen or drifting tree. *N. Amer.*

1888 S. M. ST. MAUR *Jrnl.* 19 July in *Impressions of Tenderfoot* (1890) vii. 95 We glided through the water at about ten miles an hour, sometimes rushing..within a few inches of a sweeper, as they call the trees which hang across the river. **1929** L. JOHNSTON *Beyond Rockies* 191 'Where are them sweepers, Charlie?' (sweepers being the river term for drifting trees, which may in a moment upset the craft of an unwary skipper). **1977** *New Yorker* 9 May 120/2 Over the cut bank a sweeper had recently fallen, a spruce whose trunk reached into the river... Sweepers tend to trap boats.

7. *Electronics.* A sweep generator or oscillator. *colloq.*

1967 *Electronics* 6 Mar. 2 (Advt.), The main frame of the 3211A contains everything you could hope to find in a sweeper. **1976** *Physics Bull.* Sept. 411/1 The hired equipment included spectrum analysers, signal generators, sweepers, oscilloscopes, [etc.].

sweeping, *vbl. sb.* Add: **3.** *sweeping-brush.*

a **1828** D. WORDSWORTH *Jrnl.* (1941) II. 329 Presently a Man enters with a sweeping brush, to '*arrange*'. **1922** JOYCE *Ulysses* 327 Gob, he'd adorn a sweepingbrush,..if he only had a nurse's apron on him.

sweet, *sb.* Add: **1. d.** (Earlier and later examples.) Now freq. *sing.*

1832 F. TROLLOPE *Domestic Manners Americans* II. xxviii. 131 They are 'extravagantly fond'..of puddings, pies, and all kinds of 'sweets'. **1954** J. BETJEMAN *Few Late Chrysanthemums* 95, I know what I wanted to ask you—Is trifle sufficient for sweet? **1968** [see *PUDDING *sb.* 6 a]. **1979** J. COOPER *Class* xii. 202 Everything from lemon water ice to jam roly-poly pudding, Caroline would call 'pudding'. She would never say 'sweet' or 'dessert'.

f. *pl.* Drugs, *esp.* amphetamines. *U.S. slang.*

1961 [see *HOLD *v.* 15 f]. **1979** S. SMITH *Survivor* xxi. 221 A whole load of minor drugs, mostly amphetamines—known as 'sweets', 'blues' and 'black bombers'.

5. b. *pl.* A woman's breasts. *poet.*

1817 KEATS *Poems* 49 Ah! who can e'er forget so fair a being? Who can forget her half retiring sweets? **1870** D. G. ROSSETTI *Poems* (ed. 2) 111 Your silk ungirdled and unlac'd And warm sweets open to the waist.

8. (sense 1 e) *sweet coupon, paper, ration, rationing*; (sense 1 d) *sweet course*; **sweet trolley,** a dining trolley from which a choice of cold sweet dishes may be offered in a restaurant.

1943 N. LAST *Diary* 25 Dec. in *Nella Last's War* (1983) 270 Not a flower, a card—or a sweet, although you had the sweet coupons in your pocket. **1974** G. MARKSTEIN *Cooler* xlvi. 164 Grace spent all the sweet coupons he had left on buying a bar of chocolate. **1892** *Girl's Own Paper* 23 Apr. 476/2 The sweet course can also be arranged for by having some stewed fruit..with a mould of rice or cornflour. **1981** P. VAN GREENAWAY *'Cassandra' Bell* vii. 83 The evening meal..lasted ten minutes... Cherry stabbed a fork at his once or twice, derided the sweet course, and went. **1964** *Guardian* 1 Feb. 8/3 An occasional sweet-paper flutters striped among the bushes. **1979** M. INGATE *Tomb of Flowers* xxi. 153 A few sweet papers, and one or two bottles. **1944** Sweet ration [see *RATION 3 c]. **1978** E. MALPASS *Wind brings up Rain* i. 11 She tried to take back the toffee—she *needed* her sweet ration. **1942** *Times* 24 July 2/6 As a prelude to the introduction of chocolate and sweet rationing..there is heavy selling at some retail shops. **1963** *P.M.L.A.* Dec. p. vii/2 [U.K.] sweet trolley: [U.S.] dessert cart. **1964** L. DEIGHTON *Funeral in Berlin* xv. 93 The steak was O.K. and I was strong-willed enough not to hit the sweet-trolley too hard. **1981** *Radio Times* 19–25 Sept. 21/1 It's irritating being pointed at in a restaurant, like a sweet trolley.

sweet, *a.* and *adv.* **A.** *adj.* **3. b.** Delete † *Obs.* and add later N. Amer. examples of *sweet butter.* See also SWEET WATER.

1925 *N.Y. Produce Rev.* 27 May 95 (Advt.), Specializing in sweet butter. **1952** M. SMALL *Special Diet Cook Bk.* 201 Grocers..catering to the Jewish trade usually carry sweet butter. **1971** S. WALKER *Highland Cookbook* 8 Scones are delicious with sweet butter, in Scotland called fresh butter.

e. (Later examples.) In mod. use also in the *Oil Industry,* of petroleum or natural gas: free from sulphur compounds, *esp.* hydrogen sulphide or alkyl mercaptans.

1863 *Edin. Rev.* Apr. 411 The 'sweetest' kinds of coal (the freest from sulphur) are reserved for the smelting furnace. **1911** *Rep. Brit. Assoc. Adv. Sci. 1910* 612 The Coal Measures include 'sweet', *i.e.,* non-sulphurous, coals at several horizons. **1919** E. W. DEAN *Motor Gasoline Properties* (U.S. Bur. Mines. Techn. Paper No. 214) 25 If the liquid remains unchanged in color and if the sulphur film is bright yellow or only slightly discolored.., the test shall be reported negative and the gasoline considered 'sweet'. **1950** [see *HYDRODESULPHURIZATION]. **1975** *Offshore Engineer* Sept. 44/3 The sweet gas is extracted through wells drilled by a Saipem rig. **1980** *Blair & Ketchum's Country Jrnl.* Oct. 6/3 Light, so-called 'sweet', crude yields a high percentage of automotive gasoline.

4. b. Hence, applied to music, esp. jazz, played at a steady tempo without improvisation, or to this style of playing and its exponents. Cf. *HOT *a.* 8 g. orig. and chiefly *U.S.*

1924 [see *HOT *a.* 8 g]. **1927** *Melody Maker* May 477/1 A really good saxophonist..must be able to render a sweet melody correctly phrased and as though his soul were in it, without a trend to exaggerate sloppy sentiment. **1933** *Fortune* Aug. 47/1 He is decidedly not a *sweet* trombonist—he doesn't play sentimentally with lots of *vibrato.* **1934** S. R. NELSON *All about Jazz* iii. 66 If it is of the melody type, and without much syncopation, the number is treated in the 'sweet' manner. **1956** A. HODEIR *Jazz: its Evolution & Essence* viii. 129 Both 'straight' jazz and 'sweet' music..make use of a sonority and a melodic and harmonic language that are exaggeratedly sugar-coated. **1981** *Oxford Times* 6 Feb. 13/1 The Dorseys' orchestra at this time was sweet rather than swinging, which will disappoint those like myself who prefer the jazzier side of Jimmy and Tommy Dorsey.

5. f. Used as an intensifier in certain slang phrases (often of a coarse nature) meaning 'nothing at all'. See also F.A. s.v. *F III. 3, *FANNY ADAMS 2, S.F.A. s.v. *S 4 a. Also *sweet nothing.*

1958 F. NORMAN *Bang to Rights* I. 28 You can do sweet B.A. about it. **1959** I. & P. OPIE *Lore & Lang. Schoolch.* xvii. 365 They stand on the field and they rave and they shout On subjects they know sweet nothing about. **1973** B. BROADFOOT *Ten Lost Years* ix. 95 The government provided sweet bugger all. Absolutely sweet bugger all. **1973** B. TURNER *Hot-Foot* vi. 43 What had I gained for my trouble? Sweet nothing, that's what.

6. c. (Further examples, with reference to mechanical or technical operations.)

1937 *Times* 11 Dec. 4/7 The engine is, in my opinion, more responsive and sweet than its predecessor. **1955** *Times* 10 May 7/6 The clutch is exceptionally sweet in operation, a point which helps to make the car easily manoeuvrable. **1975** *Washington Post* 25 Jan. A19/1 As J. Robert Oppenheimer said of the hydrogen bomb: 'It was so technically sweet, we had to do it.'

8. d. Also in phrs. *to bet one's sweet life, to take one's own sweet time, to go one's own sweet way,* and varr.

1889 KIPLING *From Sea to Sea* II. xxxii. 110 The younger ones [*sc.* Mormons]..*will* mix with the Gentile..and you bet your sweet life there's a holy influence working toward conversion in the kiss of an average Gentile. **1942** BERREY & VAN DEN BARK *Amer. Thes. Slang* § 54/3 Not hurry..take one's (own) sweet time. **1945** A. KOBER *Parm Me* 85 You betcha sweet life I'll give you a buzz. **1946** *Civil & Mil. Gaz.* (Lahore) 19 July 6/4 The station authorities..took their own sweet time in handing the driver the token for him to proceed on his journey. **1968** M. ALLINGHAM *Cargo of Eagles* iv. 52, I let him pass, making sure he'd turn off, but not on your sweet life. He was right with me all the way. **1970** 'D. HALLIDAY' *Dolly & Cookie Bird* vii. 105 You go your own sweet way, or so the evidence tells me. **1975** D. DELMAN *One Man's Murder* ii. 49 So you're finally here... You took your own sweet time about it. **1976** H. MACINNES *Agent in Place* xi. 120 Katie has complicated everything in her own sweet way. **1978** 'G. VAUGHAN' *Belgrade Drop* v. 33 If one single person's seen you get on this lorry..you can bet your sweet life they'll turn it inside out.

9. d. *to keep* (someone) *sweet*: to keep (someone) well-disposed towards oneself, *esp.* by complaisance or bribery.

1939 C. DAY LEWIS *Child of Misfortune* II. vi. 241 It was necessary to keep the wealthier parishioners sweet. **1944** 'N. SHUTE' *Pastoral* viii. 202 Mine won't worry, but I'd like to keep them sweet. **1965** N. GULBENKIAN *Pantaraxia* xi. 228 Mr. Sheets..had what he described as 'a wonderful idea' to keep the Russians sweet politically. **1972** G. BROMLEY *In Absence of Body* vi. 69 Joe Retford..helps to keep him sweet—wines him and dines him and all that. **1978** N. FREELING *Night Lords* iii. 17 The cops were capable of leaking the most dreadful nonsense if one didn't take pains to keep them sweet.

11. *Austral. slang.* Fine, in order, ready.

1898 *Bulletin* (Sydney) 17 Dec. (Red Page), *Sweet, roujig* and *not too stinkin'* are good. **1939** K. TENNANT *Foveaux* 312, 'I brassed a mug yesterday,' he told her, 'and everything's sweet again.' He flashed a roll of notes. **1949** L. GLASSOP *Lucky Palmer* 242 'Everything jake?' he asked. 'She's sweet,' said Max. **1962** S. GORE *Down Golden Mile* 120 Might as well be in it. We'll be sweet for getting back. **1975** X. HERBERT *Poor Fellow my Country* 353 Mossie came in..to say cheerfully, 'She's sweet.'

C. 1. a. sweetback *U.S. slang,* a woman's lover, a ladies' man; a pimp; also *sweetback man* (cf. *sweet man* below); **sweet band** orig. and chiefly *U.S.,* a band which plays sweet music; **sweet biscuit,** a biscuit flavoured with sugar; **sweet-bone(s** (later example); **sweet dreams** *int.,* a farewell to someone going to bed; **sweet Jesus** *int.,* used as an oath or exclamation (cf. *JESUS 1 b); **sweet life** = *DOLCE VITA; hence **sweet-lifer,** one who leads the sweet life; **sweet mama** *U.S. slang* (see quots.); **sweet man** *U.S. slang* = *sweetback* above; **sweetmouth** *v. trans. slang,* to flatter; **sweet music,** light instrumental music of a popular or conventional character (cf. *SWEET *a.* 4 b); also *fig.,* esp. in allusion to love-making; **sweet nothings** *colloq.,* sentimental trivia, endearments; **sweet papa** *U.S. slang* (see quot. 1970); **sweet spot,** the point on a bat, club, racket, etc., at which it makes most effective contact with the ball; cf. *MEAT *sb.* 3 f; **sweet-stuff:** now freq. in *pl.*; † also *euphem.,* gin (*obs.*); **sweet tooth:** also *transf.* and *fig.*

1929 in P. Oliver *Screening Blues* (1968) vi. 206 Had a man, good old sweetback. **1935** A. J. POLLOCK *Underworld Speaks* 117/2 *Sweet back,* a pimp. **1950** BLESH & JANIS *They all played Ragtime* ii. 39 The dapper, foppish 'macks' or 'sweet-back men'..got their gambling stakes from the girls. **1974** Sweetback [see *SUPERFLY *sb.*]. **1935** *Vanity Fair* (N.Y.) Nov. 71/2 Hot musicians look down on sweet bands, which faithfully follow the composer's arrangements. **1938** *Sat. Even. Post* 7 May 23/1 Art Hickman and the first wave of big sweet bands [were] calling the country's dance tunes. **1974** *Listener* 24 Oct. 532/1 Would Albert McCarthy..say that Glenn Miller's was the best dance/swing/'sweet' band? [**1926–7** *Army & Navy Stores Catal.* 6/2 Assorted biscuits. A choice selection of Plain, Sweet, and Fancy kinds.] **1929** W. FAULKNER *Sartoris* 168 Negroes lounged, skinning bananas or small florid cartons of sweet biscuits. **1941** *Ration Craft* 9 The present shortage of sweet biscuits is well known. **1977** *Lancashire Life* Feb. 19/1 Sweet biscuits were unknown until about sixty years ago. Before that the only biscuits made were ship's biscuits. **1969** C. DRUMMOND *Odds on Death* vii. 130 Sister has some Wiltshire sweetbones done under crisp suet crust. **1908** *Sears Roebuck & Co. Catal.* 198/1 Tenor Solos..Good Bye, Sweet Dreams, Good Bye. **1970** *New Yorker* 28 Feb. 70/2 Good night, sleep tight, sweet dreams. **1981** P. NIESEWAND *Word of Gentleman* xvii. 109 'I need some sleep.'..'Sweet dreams, then.' **1932** W. FAULKNER *Light in August* viii. 182 'Come on out,' the blonde woman said. 'For sweet Jesus,' Max said. **1955** F. O'CONNOR *Wise Blood* v. 95 Oh sweet Jesus, come on! **1973** 'D. JORDAN' *Nile Green* xxxiii. 157 Her voice so still, so soft, and I believed her, sweet Jesus, I believed her. **1962** *Sunday Express* 18 Feb. 13/5 Klaus was tired of being respectable and hungered for 'the sweet life'. **1974** M. CECIL *Heroines in Love* ix. 218 The sweet life was turning sour on heroines in the late 1960s. **1967** D. SKIRROW *I was following this Girl* iii. 16 I've been tailing that toffee-nosed sweet-lifer. **1950** A. LOMAX *Mister Jelly Roll* 19 Now these boys used to all have a sweet mama..they was what I would call, maybe a fifth-class whore. **1970** C. MAJOR *Dict. Afro-Amer. Slang* 111 *Sweet mama,* black female lover. **1942** BERREY & VAN DEN BARK *Amer. Thes. Slang* § 443/5 *Beau,*..sweet man. *Ibid.* § 508/3 *Pimp*..sweetman. **1952** S. SELVON *Brighter Sun* ii. 21 Look how Ah take up meself and leave sweetman life in town. **1959** [see *saga boy* s.v. *SAGA[1] 3]. **1972** J. MARYLAND in T. Kochman *Rappin' & Stylin' Out* 211 Damn, Rev., that's some real cruel shit, suggesting a sweet man [pimp] be iced. **1948** *Publ. Amer. Dial. Soc.* ix. 81 Employment [by the Gullahs] of groups of words for..verbs ..or other parts of speech (such as..*to sweet mouth* 'to flatter'). **1950** *Language* XXVI. 330 Not recorded in the Atlas but commonly considered to be of Negro origin are such metaphors as sweet-mouth 'to flatter' and bad-mouth 'to curse'. **1973** J. JONES *Touch of Danger* xli. 238 He went on sweetmouthing me, with his slippery mean eyes. **1967** *Guardian* 28 Sept. 4/5 If pop music should be a fad that passes he sees Radio One as becoming a 'sweet music' station. **1970** *Ibid.* 10 Mar. 1/3 A..choice between ..pop music on Radio 1 and 'sweet' music on Radio 2. **1971** R. GADNEY *Somewhere in England* xxi. 180 A small black girl..offered him 'some sweet music'. **1977** J. WAINWRIGHT *Day of Peppercorn Kill* 99 [They] should be making sweet music, every night of the week. **1981** H. R. F. KEATING *Go West, Inspector Ghote* iii. 29 Rock music, country music, sweet music, pop music—all or any of these..at the touch of a button. **1900** FAZL-I-HUSAIN *Diary* 20 May in A. Husain *Fazl-i-Husain* (1946) ii. 35 The sweet nothings so often talked of in the romantic descriptions. **1934** C. LAMBERT *Music Ho!* III. 212 The blues have a certain austerity that places them far above the sweet nothings of George Gershwin. **1973** M. AMIS *Rachel Papers* 119 Half the guests, including DeForest (after a minute of sweet-nuthins with Rachel), had wisely got the hell out as soon as dinner was over. *c* **1923** in *W. C. Handy's Coll. Blues* (?1925) 28 Ashes in my sweet pa-pa's bed So that he can't slip out. **1941** W. C. HANDY *Father of Blues* x. 141 The sweet papa who happened to be shining around the absentee prisoner's gal at the moment. **1970** C. MAJOR *Dict. Afro-Amer. Slang* 111 *Sweet papa*, a sugar-daddy and sweet man. **1976** *National Observer* (U.S.) 1 May 10/4 The sweet spot—the precise point of contact on the racket face where all the force of a swing goes into the ball without jarring the arm—was considerably farther from the center than anyone had ever suspected. **1976** *Golf International* 13–29 May 21/1 Because we use investment casting, the head weight is distributed over a wider area, increasing the sweet spot. We call this Perimeter Weighting. **1980** *Esquire* Mar. 78 Tennis players, of course, are accustomed to a long racquet, but they're also accustomed to a nice fluffy projectile and the luxury of a forgiving 'sweet spot'. **1835** DICKENS in *Even. Chron.* 7 Feb. 3/3 Wretched houses with..'sweet-stuff' manufacturers in the cellars. **1908** *Chambers's Jrnl.* Feb. 204/1 The scent for sweetstuffs is very strongly developed in the Customs officer, and he has found sugar in such an unlikely article as blacking. **1963** *Times* 18 May 9/4 We teach our students the harmful effects of the consumption of sweetstuffs between meals. **1899** J. LONDON *Let.* 29 July (1966) 45 If you're a sweet tooth you will not receive accommodation here except in the fruit line and the candy stores. **1946** DYLAN THOMAS *Deaths & Entrances* 14 Till the sweet tooth of my love bit dry. **1960** *Times* 5 July 16/5 A symphony for sweet-tooths.

b. *sweet locust* (earlier example), *orange* (earlier example); *sweet pepper-bush* (earlier and later examples); **sweet Alice**, sweet alyssum, *Lobularia maritima* (cf. ALYSSUM 2) or *Arabis alpina*, another small cruciferous herb with white flowers; **sweet bay**, (*b*) for *glauca* substitute *virginiana*; (later examples); **sweet-bough** *U.S.*, an early variety of apple or the tree that bears it; **sweet buckeye**, a yellow-flowered horse chestnut, *Aesculus octandra*, found in eastern North America; **sweet cane**: = *sweet flag*; (examples); **sweet chestnut**: for *vesca* substitute *sativa*; also, the fruit or timber of this tree; (later examples); **sweet corn** (earlier and later examples); **sweet flag** (earlier example); **sweet gum(-tree)** = LIQUIDAMBAR 2; **sweet melon** = *SPANSPEK; **sweet olive**, an evergreen shrub, *Osmanthus fragrans*, of the family Oleaceæ, native to eastern Asia and bearing clusters of small fragrant white flowers; **sweet pepper**, (*a*) = *PEPPER *sb.* 2 b; (*b*) = *sweet pepper-bush*; **sweet potato**, the edible tuber of a perennial vine, *Ipomœa batatas*, native to South America and widely cultivated elsewhere; (examples); **sweet scabious**, (earlier and later examples); also *E. philadelphicus*; **sweet willow**, (*a*) (examples); (*b*) (later examples).

1886 BRITTEN & HOLLAND *Dict. Eng. Plant-Names* 459 Sweet Alice. *Arabis alpina*, L... A corruption of Sweet Alison, which name belongs more properly to *Alyssum maritimum*, L. **1927** V. WOOLF *To Lighthouse* I. iv. 38 She was picking Sweet Alice on the bank. **1850, 1903** Sweet bay [see *laurel magnolia* s.v. *LAUREL *sb.*[1] 6]. **1938** M. K. RAWLINGS *Yearling* xviii. 217 The sweet bay was still in bloom, filling the sink-hole with its fragrance. **1958** G. A. PETRIDES *Field Guide to Trees & Shrubs* 303 Sweet-bay Magnolia... A large shrub or small tree with thick, rather leathery, elliptic leaves that are evergreen. **1850** *Rep. Comm. Patents: Agric. 1849* (U.S.) 281 Of summer apples, the best..are the early-harvest and early sweet-bough. **1906** *Harper's Mag.* Apr. 667 He halted under the sweet-bough and gave one branch a shake. **1815** D. DRAKE *Cincinnati* ii. 77 Sweet buckeye. **1943** R. PEATTIE *Great Smokies* 155 The sweet buckeye or horse chestnut is found here up to 125 feet in height. **1969** T. H. EVERETT *Living Trees of World* xxii. 224/2 The largest of the Americans is the sweet or yellow buckeye. **1611** Sweet cane [see CANE *sb.*[1] 2]. **1718** J. QUINCY *Compleat Eng. Dispensatory* II. i. 85 Sweet-Cane..is a spicy bitterish Root. **1822** J. CAMPBELL *Trav. S. Afr.: 2nd Journey* I. xx. 226 A constant succession of fresh visitants arrived, several of whom brought us presents of sweet cane. **1838** J. C. LOUDON *Arboretum & Fruticetum Britannicum* III. 1983 The term Sweet Chestnut is applied with reference to the fruit. **1909** ELWES & HENRY *Trees Gt. Brit. & Ireland* IV. 844 The Sweet or Spanish Chestnut..is..one of the largest trees in England. **1956** *Handbk. Hardwoods* (Forest Prod. Res. Lab.) 72 Sweet chestnut bears a close resemblance to oak but is more easily worked. **1977** *New Yorker* 4 July 22/2 If he could, he would supplement local bounty only with sweet chestnuts and Korean pears. **1981** G. KEYNES *Gates of Memory* xxix. 351 Nearer to us were glorious stands of trees,..sweet chestnuts hundreds of years old with twisted trunks. **1646** E. HOPKINS *Let.* 20 Mar. in *Coll. Mass. Hist. Soc.* (1863) 4th Ser. VI. 334 Wequash Cooks brother tooke from him..2 bushell of sweet corne. **1810** T. JEFFERSON *Garden Bk.* (1944) 424 [Sowed].. Sweet or shriveled corn in the N.W. corner. **1909** 'O. HENRY' *Roads of Destiny* 364 Cigarettes rolled with sweet corn husk were as honey to Buck's palate. **1917** WILL & HYDE *Corn among Indians* 118 The Upper Missouri tribes prepared this 'sweet corn' for winter use in two ways: by boiling it in kettles, and by roasting it in fires. **1974** A. PRICE *Other Paths to Glory* II. iii. 139 To the north..of the house there had been..a single tiny field of sweet corn. [**1640** J. PARKINSON *Theatrum Botanicum* xlviii. 139 This sweet smelling Flagge hath many flaggy long and narrow fresh greene leaves. **1728** R. BRADLEY *Dictionarium Botanicum* I. s.v., Calamus aromaticus Off. is also call'd Acorus, and in English, The sweet smelling Flag.] **1790** L. CASTIGLIONI *Viaggio negli Stati Uniti* II. 185 Acorus verus..Sweet-flagg. **1700** *Baltimore Rent Rolls* in *Maryland Hist. Mag.* (1924) XIX. 367, 127 acre Sur[veyed]..begun at a bounded sweet gum. **1709** J. LAWSON *New Voy. Carolina* 95 The sweet Gum-Tree, so call'd, because of the fragrant Gum it yields in the Spring-time, upon Incision of the Bark, or Wood. **1884** [see COPALM]. **1981** A. MITCHELL *Gardener's Bk. Trees* 101/1 For summer foliage and autumn colours the Sweet gum has few equals. **1819** Sweet locust [see *honey-locust* s.v. *HONEY *sb.* (*a*.) 7 b]. **1883** J. ROTH *Man. S. Afr. Gardening* 78 The Water Melons must not be ripped or cut, as required by Sweet Melons. **1970** *Rand Daily Mail* 28 Feb. 7/4 South Africans also speak of..'sweet melons'. [**1789** W. AITON *Hortus Kewensis* I. 14 Sweet-scented Olive. Nat[ive] of Cochinchina, China, and Japan.] **1861** S. K. HOLMES *Jrnl.* 15 Oct. in *Brokenburn* (1955) 61 Mrs. Carson gave Mamma plants of sweet olive..and purple magnolia. **1899** [see *CITRONELLE]. **1958** S. A. GRAU *Hard Blue Sky* iii. 122 There was..the winey odor of the sweet olive. **1785** J. WOODFORDE *Diary* 19 Apr. (1926) II. 185 To a Dozen of sweet Oranges to carry home p[d] 0. 1. 6. **1923** Sweet pepper [see *PEPPER *sb.* 2 b]. **1944** E. A. HOLTON *Yankees were like This* 84 The perfume of bush honeysuckle and sweet pepper from the swamps. **1969** *Oxf. Bk. Food Plants* 128/1 The larger-fruited kinds [of *Capsicum annuum*] are quite mild in taste and are known as 'sweet peppers'. **1972** *Country Life* 16 Mar. 625/3 Every garden that can provide lime-free soil ought to contain a bush of the Sweet Pepper, *Clethra alnifolia*. **1814** O. O. RICH *Synopsis Genera N. Amer. Plants* 50 Clethra. Sweet Pepper-Bush. **1901** C. T. MOHR *Plant Life Alabama* 652 Sweet Pepper Bush... Common in the coast plain on swampy banks of pine-barren streams. **1976** *Hortus Third* (L. H. Bailey Hortorium) 286/2 Sweet pepperbush... Summer to autumn. **1750** J. BIRKET *Some Cursory Remarks* 9 They have..abundance of..the Sweet Potatoe. **1775**, etc. [see POTATO 3 a]. **1832** [see BATATA]. **1972** Y. LOVELOCK *Veg. Bk.* I. 233 Sweet potato is now grown throughout the tropics. **1976** M. H. KINGSTON *Woman Warrior* (1977) 79 My mother liked to look at the ducks and plan how she would dig a pond for them near the sweet potato field. **1789** W. AITON *Hortus Kewensis* I. 137 Sweet Scabious. Nat[ive]. **1828** C. RAFINESQUE *Med. Flora* I. 162 *Erigeron Philadelphicum*... Vulgar Names—Skevish, Scabish, Sweet Scabious [etc.]. **1937** *Range Plant Handbk.* (U.S. Dept. Agric. Forest Service) W67 Annual wild-daisy (*E. annuus*) and Philadelphia wild-daisy, misnamed sweet scabious.. are other wild-daisies with similar properties. **1976** *Hortus Third* (L. H. Bailey Hortorium) 1014/1 Sweet scabious..naturalized in California. **1731** Sweet willow [see WILLOW *sb.* 2 a]. **1776** W. WITHERING *Bot. Arrangement Veg. Gt. Brit.* 610 Gale..Sweet Willow. Dutch Myrtle. In marshy barren ground. **1839** J. J. AUDUBON *Ornith. Biogr.* V. 288 A heavy growth of cotton-wood, ash, and sweet-willow. **1855** A. PRATT *Flowering Plants & Ferns Gt. Brit.* V. 56 Sweet Gale, or Dutch Myrtle..is called Sweet Willow.

c. *sweet-breathed* (later examples), *-faced* (later example), *-flavoured* (example), *-fleshed*, *-mannered*, *-souled* (later example), *-tasted* (later example), *-voiced* (later example).

1881 O. WILDE *Poems* 209 Most bounteous Spring! That cans't give increase to the sweet-breath'd kine. **1949** M. MEAD *Male & Female* xiv. 283 Life is a race that boys and girls must run clear-eyed, sweet-breathed, well bathed. **1981** M. WARNER *Joan of Arc* xiii. 267 The young Joan of Arc, the sweet-faced child of hagiography. **1952** A. G. L. HELLYER *Sanders' Encycl. Gardening* (ed. 22) 9 [*Actinidia*] *purpurea*, sweet-flavoured purple berries. **1923** D. H. LAWRENCE *Birds, Beasts & Flowers* 41 A rock-living, sweet-fleshed sea-anemone. **1887** G. M. HOPKINS *Let.* 25 Dec. (1956) 183 The youngest boy Leo is a remarkably winning sweetmannered young fellow. **1932** D. H. LAWRENCE *Etruscan Places* i. 12 Those pure, clean-living, sweet-souled Romans, who smashed nation after nation. **1913** J. MASEFIELD *Daffodil Fields* 31 Cropping sweet-tasted pasture. **1919** —— *Reynard the Fox* 11 John Pym..Gross and blunt-headed like a shrike. Yet sweet-voiced as a piping flute.

d. sweet-lip, any of several marine fishes with prominent mouths, esp. an Australian food fish, *Lethrinus chrysostomus*, or a brightly coloured tropical fish of the family Plectorhynchidæ.

1934 T. WOOD *Cobbers* xvii. 223 Sweet-lip, and barracouta, a slim silver sword. **1951** T. C. ROUGHLEY *Fish & Fisheries Austral.* (rev. ed.) 75 The best-known of the emperor breams is the sweet-lip or red-mouthed emperor. **1974** J. M. THOMSON *Fish of Ocean & Shore* xiii. 142 The sweetlip emperor, or simply sweetlip..is highly regarded for the table.

2. a. *sweet-sounding* (later example).

1910 W. DE LA MARE *Three Mulla-Mulgars* v. 71 When you hear my sweet-sounding..song.

b. *sweet-familiar*, *-sad* (examples).

1865 G. M. HOPKINS *Poems* (1967) 21 New-dated from the terms that reappear, More sweet-familiar grows my love to thee. **1946** A. HUTCHINGS in A. L. Bacharach *Brit. Music* xvi. 200 Parts were Arthur Blissy, and none the worse for that; parts were sweet-sad and Englysshe. **1962** R. PRAWER JHABVALA *Get Ready for Battle* ii. 97 There was music blaring out of various radios, sweet-sad music played at top volume.

3. sweet seventeen: see SEVENTEEN *a.* 2; now more usually, **sweet sixteen** (cf. SIXTEEN *sb.* 4); **sweet-throated**, sweet-voiced; **sweet-toothed** *a.* (later example).

1826 *Blackw. Edin. Mag.* XX. 138/1 A bright-eyed, round-limbed virgin of sweet sixteen. **1898** J. THORNTON (*song-title*) When you were sweet sixteen. **1977** *Grimsby Even. Tel.* 5 May 12/3 Unfortunately everybody can't be sweet 16 and there are many shops catering for the older woman. **1887** J. R. LOWELL *Credidimus* in *Atlantic Monthly* Feb. 251 Who knows but from our loins may spring (Long hence) some winged sweet-throated thing. **1928** W. B. YEATS tr. *Sophocles' King Oedipus* 5 What message of disaster from that sweet-throated Zeus? **1975** *Times* 31 May 7/2 The puddings, often a weakness in French restaurants from a sweet-toothed British customer's point of view.

Sweet Adeline (swīt æ·dèlain). *U.S.* A name in a popular close-harmony song (see quot. 1903), used in *pl.* to denote a group or organization of female barber-shop singers (cf. *BARBER-SHOP 2 b). Also *attrib.* in *sing.*

[**1903** ARMSTRONG & GERARD *You're the Flower of my Heart, Sweet Adeline* (song) 5 Sweet Adeline. For you I pine.] **1947** *Harmonizer* Nov. 37/1 The Sweet Adelines, women's quartet organization, held their first convention and contest in Tulsa in October. **1958** *Music Jrnl.* Nov.–Dec. 67/2 A Sweet Adeline Chapter..is a chorus and usually meets once a week. **1969** *Pitch Pipe* Summer 7/1 We as Sweet Adelines have a..responsibility to present ourselves as an 'in' group..capable of presenting.. choruses and performances. **1972** *Music Educators Jrnl.* Dec. 71/1 'The Sweet Adelines', an organization for women, have been largely responsible for keeping alive this style of singing. **1979** *Tucson* (Arizona) *Citizen* 20 Sept. (Old Pueblo Suppl.) 2/4 On the bill for the 5 p.m. show are the Arizona Opera Puppets..the Old Pueblo Sweet Adelines.

So as *v. intr.*, to sing in barber-shop style; hence **Sweet A·delin(e)ing** *vbl. sb.*

1949 *Educational Music Mag.* Nov.–Dec. 38/3 So—get fourboys 'Sweet Adelining' around the place if you want to start a real male section to your choir. **1961** *Pitch Pipe* Aug. 13/2 I've just completed one of the most fabulous weekends in my career of 'Sweet Adelining'. **1966** *Ibid.* Spring 6/1 Sweet Adeline-ing is almost as habit-forming as a drug!

sweet and sour, sweet-sour, *adj. phr.* [f. the adjs.] **1.** = SOUR-SWEET *a.* Also, alternatively sweet and sour.

1594, 1707 [in Dict. s.v. SWEET *a.* and *adv.* C. 2 b]. *c* **1879** G. M. HOPKINS *Poems* (1967) 179 When the air was sweet-and-sour of the flown fineflour of Those goldnails and their gaylinks that hang along a lime. **1909** E. B. TITCHENER *Text-Bk. Psychol.* I. xxxvii. 141 The mixed sweet-sour stimulus affects only the sour-sensitive bulbs. **1959** *Vogue* Dec. 120 This sweet-and-sour glimpse of the cultured Sahib chez soi continually excites by its freshness. **1967** P. D. JAMES *Unnatural Causes* III. iv. 211 Dalgliesh could smell his breath, the sweet-sour trace of too much drinking. **1975** *Chem. in Brit.* XI. 18/3 If it [*sc.* the chemical industry] is subjected to short term sweet-and-sour treatments of restraints, constraints, stimuli, and instant statute, it could very easily be damaged beyond repair.

2. *Cookery.* Cooked in or flavoured with sugar and vinegar or lemon. Now esp. of Chinese food. Also *absol.* as *sb.*

1723 J. NOTT *Cook's & Confectioner's Dict.* sig. L l 2, To make a sweet-sour-tart. Boil..Sugar in..Verjuice, or Lemon Juice. **1932** L. GOLDING *Magnolia Street* v. 103 Mrs. Emmanuel brought in some fish cooked in sweet-and-sour sauce. **1951** *Good Housek. Home Encycl.* 360/2 The soup should have a pleasant 'sweet-sour' taste. **1959** E. MANNIN *Blue-Eyed Boy* I. xi. 129 'A little more sweet-and-sour?' 'A lot,' said Len. He added, 'It's tasty, I must say.' **1961** [see *CHOW MEIN]. **1977** *Times* 7 May 9 The usual chow meins and sweet-and-sours can be had. **1978** *Texas Highways* Feb. 16/2 Hong Kong chicken in a sweet-sour sauce. **1982** C. THOMAS *Jade Tiger* 5 The German Chancellor's top adviser..struck down by sweet and sour pork.

sweeten, *v.* Add: **7.** Also with *up*.

1875 'MARK TWAIN' in *Atlantic Monthly* Aug. 195/1 Stephen sweetened him up and put him off a week. **1971** 'E. LATHEN' *Ashes to Ashes* x. 99, I know Unger is just trying to sweeten us up... Maybe we should be trying to sweeten him up.

8. e. *Oil Industry.* To free (petroleum products) from sulphur or sulphur compounds.

1924 *Industr. & Engin. Chem.* Nov. 1113 Although naphthas and kerosenes have been sweetened by the sodium plumbite method for many years, the process is entirely empirical. **1975** W. G. ROBERTS *Quest for Oil* (rev. ed.) ix. 92 The lighter distillates, liquid petroleum gas, gasolenes and kerosenes, can be sweetened by simple chemical treatments which either remove the sulphur compounds or turn them into harmless and non-smelly forms.

sweetened, *ppl. a.* (Further example.)

1924 *Industr. & Engin. Chem.* Nov. 1113 The reactions involved..have furnished explanations of the various complications which appear in sweetening, including.. the sourness developed in rerunning a sweetened oil.

sweetener. 2. c. Delete † and add: (Further examples.) Also, a bribe; a concession or appeasement (esp. in politics, business, etc.). Cf. DOUCEUR 3.

1829 P. EGAN *Boxiana* 2nd Ser. II. 415 As a reward, or sweetener for his numerous defeats,..the above unexpected victory has put Sampson once more into good humour with himself. **1847** A. HARRIS *Settlers & Convicts* vi. 89 The handsome 'sweeteners' (bribes) which old D—'s profits enabled him to give the constables. **1955** *Times* 24 May 16/2, I suggest that what you got from Carroll Levis was a sweetener or a bribe. **1959** *Economist* 28 Mar. 1176/1 The main attraction of the Kennedy Bill is its 'sweeteners' in the form of amendments, made to the order of the labour leaders, to the basic Taft-Hartley Act regulating trade union activities. **1960** *Wall St. Jrnl.* 26 Sept. 11 The State Department responded..by permitting the imports but removing the sweetener—the premium that other sugar suppliers enjoy in their sales to the U.S. **1975** *Times* 10 Apr. 8/2 Mr Nixon used the threat of renewed bombing as a sweetener to get the reluctant President Thieu to sign the agreements. **1979** G. HAMMOND *Dead Game* x. 138 Everybody gives 'sweeteners' of some kind or another, even if it's only a bottle at Christmas.

3. b. (Earlier example.)
1823 in *Spirit of Public Jrnls.* (1825) 508 Here the music of bidding grows loud and more loud—Here the sweetener is conning his hints for the day.

sweetening, *vbl. sb.* Add: **1. e.** *Oil Industry.* The process of freeing petroleum products of sulphur or sulphur compounds.
1924 *Industr. & Engin. Chem.* Nov. 1113 Sweetening consists in the removal of hydrogen sulfide and of alkyl mercaptans which are the only compounds responsible for sourness. **1959** H. M. Noel *Petroleum Refinery Man.* v. 153/1 Kerosene stocks which are too low in smoke point to be finished by simple sweetening. **1970** C. L. Thomas *Catalytic Processes & Proven Catalysts* xix. 199 Mercaptans in gasoline have an objectionable odor ('sour' gasoline). By converting them to disulfides which have less odor, a 'sweet' gasoline is produced; hence the term 'sweetening'.

sweet-field: see *sweet-veld.

sweet-grass. Add: **b.** *S. Afr.* = *sweet-veld.
1812 A. Plumptre tr. *Lichtenstein's Trav. S. Afr.* I. II. xv. 204 On the high hills, sweet grass grows in tolerable plenty. **1838** W. B. Boyce *Notes S. Afr. Affairs* 186 Men should be sent from..the sweet-grass and karoo farms. **1897** [see *num-num]. **1913** [in Dict.].
c. *N. Amer.* One of several scented grasses, esp. *Hierochloë odorata,* used in basket-making.
1926 *Daily Colonist* (Victoria, B.C.) 24 Jan. 20/1 From making sweet-grass baskets on the shores of the lake of Bays to singing before royalty in the Albert Hall is a far cry. **1968** E. Buckler *Ox Bells & Fireflies* xv. 227 Her contentment grows as the sweet-grass basket fills. **1973** A. H. Whiteford *North Amer. Indian Arts* 43 Sweet grass is widely used in coils.

sweetheart, *sb.* Add: **1.** Also used ironically or contemptuously.
1941 B. Schulberg *What makes Sammy Run?* iv. 51 (*addressing a man*) 'Hiya, sweetheart,' he said. **1977** F. Parrish *Fire in Barley* viii. 82 Try harder, sweetheart, or I'll plug you in the guts.
d. *N. Amer.* Anything especially good of its kind. Cf. *honey *sb.* (*a.*) 5 b.
1942 *Amer. Speech* XVII. 105/1 *Sweetheart,* piece of equipment which performs well. **1970** *Globe & Mail* (Toronto) 28 Sept. 27/7 (Advt.), 68 Renault R10, deluxe, radio, a little sweetheart. **1978** *Detroit Free Press* 2 Apr. 15F/4 (Advt.), Lovely 3 bedrm brick ranch, 1½ baths, re rm, a sweetheart for $45,900.
5. A variety of *Rosa wichuraiana* developed by M. H. Walsh about 1903 which bears clusters of small pink flowers; also = *sweetheart rose,* sense 6 b below.
1905 *Country Life Amer.* VII. 625 Sweetheart..delicate blush. **1920** R. Pyle *How to grow Roses* 106 Some roses have acquired new names... Sweetheart P. Mlle Cecile Brunner. **1955** H. van P. Wilson *Climbing Roses* v. 75 Sweetheart (1901)... Rose-pink buds open to very double, 2½-inch, white flowers that are richly fragrant.
6. a. *attrib.* or as *adj.* Designating a contract, agreement, etc., arranged privately (i.e. without genuine collective bargaining) by trade unions and employers which is beneficial to themselves but prejudicial to the interests of the workers; hence applied to persons, etc., prone to such collaboration. Also *transf. colloq.* (orig. and chiefly *U.S.*).
1959 *Washington Post* 5 Feb. A2/2 The Administration's ban..would stop an honest union from picketing a shop that had made a substandard 'sweetheart' deal, recognizing a racket union. **1962** N. S. Falcone *Labor Law* xi. 321 Some employers engaged in collusion with unions and paid union officials to get 'sweetheart' contracts. **1965** *Wall St. Jrnl.* (Eastern ed.) 23 Sept. 1/6 The mine manager is a 'sweetheart' operator... In the classic 'sweetheart' situation, corrupt union leaders accept or extort payoffs from employers in exchange for assuring labour peace or winking at contract violations. **1967** G. Tyler *Labor Revolution* xi. 243 The contract is a 'sweetheart agreement' to give the union heads an income, to give the employer relief from a real union, and to give the workers nothing. **1974** *Australian* 12 Nov. 3 Miss Martin said Mr Jones' description of the..award as a sweetheart agreement was farcical. The award had been decided by arbitration, not by negotiation between Qantas and the unions. **1975** *Publishers Weekly* 14 July 54/2 She takes us to three factors, one unorganized, a second with a sweetheart union, the third with an excellent local. *Ibid.* 24 Nov. 53/1 Caffery, a 35-year-old hockey star... Keeping his medical problem secret Caffery negotiates a sweetheart contract to jump league to Texas. **1977** *Time* 1 Aug. 32/2 William Safire..raised the question of whether the $3.4 million loan that was granted on Jan. 7, after Lance had accepted the sensitive OMB job, was a 'sweetheart oan'. **1979** *Times* 21 Nov. 20/3 What are known as 'sweetheart' transactions (when [supermarket] checkout operators reduce the bill for those they know). **1981** *Times* 30 Nov. 15/1 Mobil has accused US Steel of an illegal 'sweetheart deal' with Marathon board members at the expense of the shareholders.
b. Special Comb.: **sweetheart neck(line),** a heart-shaped neckline on a dress, blouse, etc. (see quot. 1968); **sweetheart plant,** either of two species of *Philodendron, P. cordatum* or *P. scandens,* epiphytic herbs of tropical America which have large heart-shaped leaves; **sweetheart rose** *U.S.,* one of several roses having small pink, white, or yellow flowers, particularly attractive as buds, esp. the climbing polyantha Cécile Brunner; see also sense 5 d above.
1965 *Housewife* Jan. 16/1 She has a great feeling for a return to the late forties. 'Wide shoulders, sweetheart necks.' **1968** J. Ironside *Fashion Alphabet* 54 *Sweetheart neckline,* a neckline cut in front in two almost semicircular curves, like a heart. **1974** *Country Life* 17 Jan. 106 Sweater with a sweetheart neckline. **1980** B. Bainbridge *Winter Garden* xvi. 129 Enid..sauntered through the cool reception hall in her pink summer dress with the sweetheart neck and emerged into the evening sunshine. **1981** *Daily Tel.* 21 May 17/2 The bride, of course, was a stunner —all demure in white broderie anglaise with a sweetheart neckline. **1963** *Reader's Digest Compl. Libr. of Garden* II. 658/1 *P[hilodendron] scandens* (sweetheart plant) origin: Puerto Rico, Panama. A popular and attractive climbing plant. **1981** *Times* 28 Mar. 11/4 A 6½ ft sweetheart plant..cost £29. **1936** J. H. Nicolas *Year in Rose Garden* xv. 72 Cécile Brunner (Sweetheart Rose): Light pink tea-like flowers. **1976** *Columbus* (Montana) *News* 27 May 6/4 She carried a bouquet of yellow sweetheart roses.

sweetie. Delete 'and chiefly' and add: **1. b.** *sweetie-shop.*
1928 J. Buchan *Runagates Club* ii. 85 Some biscuits which I bought at a sweetie shop. **1980** *Times* 11 Dec. 11/2 Cheery old Mrs Mutterance has a Battersea sweetie shop.
2. *colloq.* (orig. *U.S.*). **a.** A sweetheart, a lover; a lovable person. Also as a term of endearing address.
1778 [see Yankee 1 a]. **1925** F. Scott Fitzgerald *Great Gatsby* ii. 42 Tom's the first sweetie she ever had. **1932** Wodehouse *Hot Water* xv. 248 'I'll drop down off the balcony with the stuff.'..'You won't hurt yourself, sweetie?' **1949** A. Christie *Crooked House* vi. 34 The poor old Sweetie... He..was just on ninety. **1958** *Listener* 3 July 31/1 His *fiancée,* Julia, who is a sweetie. **1964** G. McDonald *Running Scared* i. 14 'Where is Dad?' 'He's in Washington, I think, Sweetie.' **1975** *Times* 19 Sept. 9/3 Karen Black as the steely sweetie on the way up. **1977** N. Marsh *Last Ditch* ii. 40 'Sweetie,' Julia cried extravagantly, 'you *are* such heaven!'
b. *Comb.,* as *sweetie-pie.*
1928 Wodehouse *Money for Nothing* iv. 76 'Hello, sweetie-pie,' said Miss Molloy. **1937** D. B. Wyndham Lewis in L. Russell *Press Gang!* 239 Follies show-girl Gladileen ('Sweetie-Pie') Kisse. **1955** Ld. Winterton *Fifty Tumultuous Years* 28 She is not his daughter; as I tell you, she his girl; how you say, his 'sweetie-pie'. **1957** E. Hyams *Into Dream* I. 77 'I think they're all perfect sweetie-pies,' Barbara said. **1977** 'L. Egan' *Blind Search* v. 83 He's..the kind of man who calls anything female 'honeybunch' and 'sweetie-pie'.

sweetikin. Delete '† *Obs. rare*$^{-1}$' and add later example. Also *sweetiekins.*
1974 I. Murdoch *Sacred & Profane Love Machine* 81 Oh my sweetikin, how can such a love as ours stop? **1978** C. MacLeod *Rest you Merry* (1979) vi. 56 Next time you drop one of your time bombs into the punch bowl, sweetiekins, you clean the bathrooms.

sweet John. Delete '? *Obs.*' and add later example.
1911 C. Mackenzie *Passionate Elopement* xxix. 257 The very heart of high June and hot July dwelt in that fragrant enclosure. Sweet Johns and Sweet Williams with Dragon flowers and crimson Peaseblossom.

sweetmeat, *sb.* Add: Now chiefly *arch.* **3.** *sweetmeat glass, shop* (example).
1897 A. Hartshorne *Old English Glasses* xviii. 299 The bowls of the cut sweetmeat glasses have the edges engrailed, vandycked, or faceted. **1971** *Country Life* 9 Sept. 639/2 Exquisite sweetmeat glasses with elaborately cut bowls and sturdy facet-cut stems were made between 1740 and the 1780s. **1857** Dickens & Collins in *Househ. Words* 10 Oct. 338/1, I see a sweetmeat shop.

sweetness. Add: **1. a.** *sweetness and light,* now usu. in trivial (freq. ironic) use, under influence of senses 6, 7: pleasantness, good will.
1927 Wodehouse *Meet Mr Mulliner* vi. 186 He had been all sweetness and light and had not done a thing to them. **1949** N. Balchin *Sort of Traitors* xi. 191 You know how it is when you've got to poke about round somebody else's work—it's not all sweetness and light as a rule. **1953** P. Wentworth *Anna, where are You?* vii. 45 A desire to spread sweetness and light. **1968** G. Jones *Hist. Vikings* II. iii. 106 Anskar, the monk of Corbey,..whose sweetness and light were probably much lightened and sweetened by his biographer Rimbert. **1974** *Times* 16 Jan. 16/5 When this Act was introduced it was done..to create sweetness and light between management and unions. **1982** *Sunday Tel.* 12 Dec. 14/5 Hell hath no fury like a peace-woman scorned, by comparison with whom even a Cruise missile becomes a soft symbol of sweetness and light.
b. *spec.* molasses. *Canad.*
1912 N. Duncan *Best of Bad Job* xxi. 143 T' beg a barrel o' flour an' a gallon o' sweetness. **1920** W. T. Grenfell *Labrador Doctor* viii. 164 The fact that we were without butter, and that 'sweetness' (molasses) was low, was scarcely even noticed.

sweet pea. Add: **b.** The scent of the sweet pea, esp. as used in cosmetics, etc.
1890–1 *T. Eaton & Co. Catal.* Fall & Winter 42/2 Colgate's perfumes—white rose, sweet pea, Cashmere bouquet. *c* **1938** *Fortnum & Mason Catal.* 54/1 Soaps.. sandal wood..sweet pea..verbena. **1972** [see *lilac 2 c].

sweet singer. Add: **2. a.** A religious poet.
1560, etc. [see Singer[1] 2]. **1892** J. Julian *Dict. Hymnol.* 1284/2 William Williams, of Pantycelyn, wa the Sweet Singer of Wales. **1933** *Sign* July 92/2 The swee singer, Christina Rossetti.
b. A popular, esp. sentimental, writer o singer.
[**1878** J. A. Moore (*title*) Sweet singer of Michigan. **1936** *New Statesman* 25 Jan. 113/2 Kipling..was a swee singer to the last. He could bring home the colours an savours of many distant places... But he was not faultless writer. **1958** *Listener* 4 Dec. 913/1 The lates hit of one of the sweet singers of Hong Kong, Li Li Hu or Yao Lee.

sweet-sour: see *sweet and sour, sweet sour *adj. phr.*

sweet-talk (swī·t tǭk), *v. colloq.* (orig. an chiefly *U.S.*). [f. (as) next.] **a.** *trans.* T cajole, flatter, persuade. Cf. *smooth talk *v.*
1936 M. Mitchell *Gone with Wind* xlvii. 836 Don't tr to sweet talk me. **1955** T. Williams *Orpheus Descendin* II. iv. 80 I'd say a peculiar slew-footer that sweet talk you while he's got his hand in the cashbox. **1965** *Listene* 27 May 791/1 There she worked her life away on the edg of poverty, sweet-talking her customers as she lathere them. **1970** J. H. Gray *Boy from Winnipeg* 199 The 'pul ler' would come out and sweet-talk them into the store **1981** *Observer* 17 May 19/6 Many have tried over the year to sweet-talk Walsh into selling, but he remained strongl independent until the last.
b. *intr.* To talk persuasively or flatteringly
1956 H. Gold *Man who was not with It* (1965) iv. 33, would just have to sweet-talk a little. **1968** L. Deighto *Only when I Larf* viii. 102 He'll switch on the charm an sweet-talk so hard that I am throwing my arms aroun him.
Hence **swee·t-talker; swee·t-talking** *ppl. a* and *vbl. sb.*
1946 Mezzrow & Wolfe *Really Blues* p. vi, To th sweettalkers, the gumbeaters, the highjivers. **1956** R Ellison in *New World Writing* IX. 230 Now he ain't lik that ole clarinet; clarinet so sweet-talking he just *ease* you in the dozens. **1966** J. B. Priestley *Salt is Leavin* vi. 81, I still say, my sweet-talking friend, that..you' have..forgotten me. **1979** *Arizona Daily Star* 1 Apr. H 1/ Why did he let himself be wheedled out of a lifetime job Some sweet-talker, that Lyndon Johnson. **1981** P Niesewand *Word of Gentleman* xxxii. 221 We tried dip lomacy and sweet talking.

swee·t talk, *sb. colloq.* (orig. *U.S.*). [Sweet *a.*] Endearment, blandishment, flattery.
1945 L. Shelly *Jive Talk Dict.* 35/1 *Sweet talk,* en dearing terms. **1968** S. Ellin *Valentine Estate* III. vii 163 'And stop calling me baby!' she said with sudde heat. 'It's not Tinpan Alley sweet talk, the way you sa it... It sounds full of contempt.' **1979** J. W. Wainwrigh *Tension* xlv. 142 A touch of sweet-talk and a winnin smile.

sweet-veld. Now the usual form of Sweet-field. Substitute for def.: In South Africa an area of land providing good nutritiou grazing; also, the vegetation of an area of thi kind. (Further examples.)
1852 M. B. Hudson *S. Afr. Frontier Life* I. 137 The sheep from the sweet veld fall sick on karroo. **1896** R Wallace *Farming Industries Cape Colony* 82 Animal brought from sweet veld suffer from what is termed vel sickness. **1937** *Handbk. Farmers S. Afr.* 381 The types o grass found in the sweet veld maintain their feed valu after maturity. **1948** H. V. Morton *In Search of S. Afr.* 8 There is sweet veld and sour veld, high veld and low veld **1972** *Even. Post* (Port Elizabeth) 19 Feb. (Weekend Mag. 2 Somerset East was, with its wonderful water supply an sweet veld, a choice place for men and beasts to rest.

swell, *sb.* Add: **3. a.** Also *spec.* in *Meteorol* and *Oceanogr.,* wave movement persistin after the wind causing it has dropped, or du to disturbance at a distance. Constraste with *sea *sb.* 5 d.
1930 *Meteorol. Gloss.* (Meteorol. Office) (ed. 2) 188 Swel is wave motion in the ocean persisting after the originatin cause of the wave motion has ceased or passed away **1957** *Encycl. Brit.* XXIII. 442A/1 When wind-raise waves travel out of a storm area they advance as 'swell' and after having travelled large distances become a serie of long, low and fairly regular undulations. **1977** [se *sea *sb.* 5 d].
4. a. Also, a similar feature on the sea bed a relatively elevated part of a lithospheri plate.
1963 G. L. Pickard *Descriptive Physical Oceanogr.* ii. 1 The characteristic features [of the deep-sea bottom] are. either basically long and narrow..or of roughly equa lateral extent (swells and basins). **1971** *Nature* 30 Apr 555/1 Many areas such as Kenya mark igneous province of characteristic per-alkaline magma..which are up swollen portions ('swells') of the African plate some 1,00 km across.
9. (Earlier example.)
1786 *Sessions Papers* 13 Dec. 92/2 Here is a *swell* coming. What is the meaning of that?—I do not know what meaning they give to it, without it is a gentleman.

swell, *a.* Add: Now chiefly *U.S.* **a.** (Late examples.) More recently, also in weakene use as a general expression of approval.

1926 MAINES & GRANT *Wise-Crack Dict.* 13/1 *Swell dish*, ery beautiful girl. 1951 M. MCLUHAN *Mech. Bride* (1967) o/2 He was a swell kid. 1977 I. SHAW *Beggarman, Thief* . iii. 141 That's great. She's swell, a real lady. What a ifference between her and some of the dames we had to ut up with on the boat.

b. Also similarly weakened: 'great', 'fine', tc.

1930 E. H. LAVINE *Third Degree* xi. 128 The swell ime he had with the swell broads in the swell musical omedy company. 1947 A. MILLER *All my Sons* II. 62 We're eating at the lake; we could have a swell time. 1952 . KAUFFMANN *Tightrope* viii. 142 A play like this, with swell part for her..all that may not come along again or five years. 1968 *Amer. Speech* XLIII. 223 It was a well date. 1978 J. KRANTZ *Scruples* iii. 77 All in all, a well arrangement, and Spider learned a great deal during he year he was Levy's assistant.

c. *swell mobsman* (earlier example). Now *Obs.* or *Hist.*

1843 *Sessions Papers* 6 Jan. 38, I have heard..that the risoner is a swell mob's man.

d. *predic.* Most pleasant or kind; very ffective; 'splendid'. *U.S.*

1926 *Scribner's Mag.* Aug. 198/2 He also knew that the eggs were not trained fur-thieves... 'They were swell n safes, but a bum would have showed better judgment n furs.' 1931 H. CRANE *Let.* 2 June (1965) 370 Moisés as been swell to me. 1942 WODEHOUSE *Money in Bank* 1946) ii. 16 You eat vegetables and breathe deep and ance around in circles. It's supposed to be swell for the oul. 1965 A. LURIE *Nowhere City* IV. xxi. 237 Yeah; hat'd be really swell, if you would.

e. *int.* As an expression of satisfaction.

1930 D. HAMMETT *Maltese Falcon* xvii. 201 'She's full f gas and ready to go.' 'Swell.' 1935 WODEHOUSE *Luck f Bodkins* xxii. 289 'Swell,' said Mabel, placing the docuent in her vanity-bag. 1976 *Daily Record* (Glasgow) 2 Nov. 10/3 My fellow Scot agreed that you could call it hat. 'Swell,' said the reporter.

swell, *v.* Add: **10.** (Earlier example with *it.*)

1841 *Punch* 23 Oct. 178/2 Father Thames..has been swelling it'..through some of the streets of the metroolis. As if to inculcate temperance, he walked himself own into public-house cellars, filling all the empty casks with water.

swell-. Add: *swell-head* (earlier U.S. examples).

1845 J. J. HOOPER *Some Adventures Simon Suggs* iv. 46 s for the present directory, they're all a pack of d—d well-heads. 1867 G. W. HARRIS *Sut Lovingood* 61 Wif an nintemitant attack of swell-head.

swelled, *ppl. a.* Add: **b.** *swelled head*: also, a erson affected with 'swelled head'.

1862 *Harper's Mag.* June 33/1 He was set down as a orn aristocrat and 'swelled head'. 1900 *Times* 7 July o/1 The Queen's-hall was filled with swelled heads, and, udging from your correspondent's note, the swelled heads lected one of their own body.

swellishness. (Earlier example.)

1863 W. H. KNIGHT *Diary of Pedestrian in Cashmere & Thibet* v. 186 One..group of Mahomedan exquisites.. ad, in addition to their heavy swellishness, an air of astern listlessness.

swelp. (Earlier and later examples.)

1894 [see *DICKEN, DICKIN *int.*]. 1937 N. MARSH *Vintage Murder* x. 112 It's true... S'welp me. 1981 J. BARNETT *Firing Squad* vii. 74 'Think again—harder.' Swelp me, Mr Smiff—.'

swept, *ppl. a.* Add: **1.** *swept-up*: *spec.* of air, brushed up towards the top of the head.

1948 'J. TEY' *Franchise Affair* xviii. 217 With her hair wept up and some make-up on, she would look quite ifferent. 1959 *News Chron.* 18 Aug. 6/7 Swept-up hair tyles which straggle down the neck. 1973 M. WOODHOUSE *Blue Bone* vi. 58 She was about five feet six, with buttery glasses and swept-up hair.

2. *Electronics.* Of (the frequency of) a ignal: increased (or decreased) through a ange of values, usu. rapidly and repeatedly.

1965 *Wireless World* Aug. 384/1 A random vibration esting technique which was similar to a swept sinewave requency test except that the single frequency was relaced by a narrow band of noise. 1980 *IEEE Trans. Microwave Theory & Techniques* XXVIII. 792/1 An utomated swept-frequency absorption spectrometer.

3. Special collocations: **swept-back** *a. Aeronaut.*, (of a wing) having its leading edge ngled backwards (cf. *sweepback* s.v. *SWEEP-, and *delta wing* s.v. *DELTA 4); also *transf.*; **swept valley** *Building* [VALLEY *sb.* 4] (see quot. 1964); **swept volume** *Mech.*, the volume hrough which a piston or plunger moves as t makes a stroke; **swept wing** *Aeronaut.*, a wept-back wing; freq. *attrib.*; also as *sb.*, a wept-wing aircraft.

1914 *Aeroplane* 26 Feb. 213/2 Swept-back wings with egative tips must always have their centre of side presure farther back relatively to their centre of lift than ormal wings. 1951 *Engineering* 20 Apr. 474/3 The third ype of British swept-back 'delta'-wing experimental airraft. 1959 *Ibid.* 16 Jan. 95/1 At each side of the column ust below the engine are 'swept back' service ducts xtending to the cell walls. 1976 B. JACKSON *Flameout* x. 69 Fast aircraft with swept-back wings are susceptible o dutch rolls. 1926 G. ALLEN *Smaller House of Today* i. 96 Swept valleys are very suitable for slated and stone roofs. 1951 N. WYMER *Village Life* iii. 64 A particularly unusual feature of the Cotswold roof is the 'swept valley'. 1964 J. S. SCOTT *Dict. Building* 326 *Swept valley*, a valley formed of shingles, slates, or tiles cut or made to a taper so as to eliminate the need for a flexible-metal valley. A tile-and-a-half tile is used and cut to shape so that its tail is narrower than its head. 1918 W. E. DOMMETT *Dict. Aircraft* 45 *Swept Volume.* The volume swept by the piston equals area of piston multiplied by the stroke. 1930 *Flight* 24 Jan. 144/2 The engine is of the fivecylinder radial type of 150 cub. ins. swept volume. 1971 B. SCHARF *Engin. & its Lang.* xiii. 193 Volumetric efficiency. This is the ratio of the actual volume discharged [from a pump] (capacity) to the displacement or swept volume of the cylinder(s). 1947 *Jrnl. R. Aeronaut. Soc.* LI. 15/2 Whether or not the delta wing is a better compromise than the swept wing..must await the verdict of appropriate researches. 1955 *Times* 25 June 6/2 The R.A.F.'s latest type of Hawker Hunter swept-wing fighter, the Mark IV, is being used for the first time. 1978 A. WELCH *Bk. Airsports* i. 9/2 In between are swallowtails, swept-wings without tails and even the occasional biplane.

swerve, *sb.* Add: *Cricket.* (Earlier example.) Also *attrib.*, as *swerve-bowler, -bowling.*

1900 A. W. PULLIN *Talks with Old Eng. Cricketers* 125 One hears occasionally of swerving balls, but the swerve depends very much on the air. 1930 C. V. GRIMMETT *Getting Wickets* iii. 67 In swerve bowling, like other branches of the art, it must be the bowler's object so to regulate his swerve that the ball will hit the wicket. 1944 E. BLUNDEN *Cricket Country* iii. 37 A large wrathful swerve-bowler using the wind..to the immediate..destruction of all.

swerve, *v.* Add: **7. b.** Also *intr.* Of a delivery, to deviate in the air. Of a bowler: to bowl with a swerve.

1894 *Cricket Field* 437 Lockwood was bowled by a ball that swerved considerably in the air. 1903 C. B. FRY *Let.* Sept. in P. F. Warner *How we recovered Ashes* (1905) ii. 15 Much will depend on how you work your bowlers. I wonder which of your 'swervers' will swerve best in Australia?

swerver. b. (Earlier cricketing example, of a bowler.)

1903 [see *SWERVE *v.* 7b].

swerving, *ppl. a.* Add: (Earlier example in *Cricket.*)

1900 [see *SWERVE *sb.*].

swidden (swi·dən). *Agric.* [f. *swidden*, var. SWITHEN *v.* (see *Eng. Dial. Dict.*: also, as a place-name element in Yorks.); in mod. use, a conscious readoption of the dialect word (see sense 2, quot. 1951).] **1. a.** An area of land that has been cleared for cultivation by slashing and burning the vegetation cover. Formerly only *north. dial.* (see quot. 1868).

1868 J. C. ATKINSON *Gloss. Cleveland Dial.* 514 *Swidden*, any place on the moor from which the Ling and other herbage has been burnt away, and which still shows signs of burning. 1957 *Proc. 9th Pacific Sci. Congress* (1958) XX. 127/1 They maintain permanent villages.., constructing temporary simple houses in their swidden, where at least part of the family lives during those times of the year when the swidden requires a great deal of care. 1961 *Current Anthropol.* II. 27/2 The specific form that a system of swidden agriculture may exhibit..depends on..the dispersal of swiddens... Swiddens may or may not be fenced. 1972 *Nature* 3 Mar. 41/1 In one case a specific tree is found growing in the new swidden.

b. *ellipt.* for *swidden cultivation.*

1955 *Proc. Prehistoric Soc.* XXI. 45 Even if *swidden* (clearance of woodland by burning) was not widely practised before Neolithic times, [etc.]. 1971 D. J. ROBINSON in Blakemore & Smith *Latin Amer.: Geogr. Perspectives* v. 191 Swidden appears to have formed the basis of the subsistence agriculture of..a part of the tropical zone. 1977 J. J. FOX *Harvest of Palm* i. 38 The Timorese have been forced..to rely even more heavily on swidden.

2. *attrib.* = *SLASH-AND-BURN *attrib. phr.* (The principal use.)

1951 K. G. IZIKOWITZ *Lamet Hill Peasants in French Indo-China* 7 This is a book about the Lamet, swidden cultivators in the northern part of Laos. [*Note*] The primitive system of farming which involves clearing and burning the forest... In English it is sometimes called 'shifting cultivation' or 'slash and burn'. There is no single word in ordinary English which covers the meaning, since the method is no longer used in England... In searching for an English word I have taken..a dialect word, *swidden.* 1957 *Proc. 9th Pacific Sci. Congress* (1958) XX. 127/1 We have swidden cultivators who are sedentary in Southeast Asia and other parts of the humid tropics. 1965 G. A. COLLIER *Fields in Tzotzil* iii. 60 Virtually all are subsistence corn farmers who utilize the slash-and-burn or 'swidden' system of agriculture. 1971 *Sci. Amer.* Sept. 101/2 There is a structural similarity between a swidden garden and a tropical rain forest. 1978 KUNSTADTER & CHAPMAN in P. Kunstadter et al. *Farmers in Forest* i. 3/2 Swidden fields are usually located at some distance from markets, generally on land that is considered marginal... Swiddening is often carried out primarily as a subsistence operation..rather than as a source of cash crops.

Hence (as a back-formation) *v. trans.*, to cultivate by the swidden method; **swi·ddener, swi·ddening** *vbl. sb.*

1971 *Sci. Amer.* Sept. 119/1 Between one month and four months after clearing begins..the felled litter on the site is burned. This is a step of considerable importance in the swiddening regime. 1975 J. NANCE *Gentle Tasaday* xvi. 282 Swiddeners did not uproot the growth, but burned it over and planted within it. 1978 KUNSTADTER & CHAPMAN in P. Kunstadter et al. *Farmers in Forest* i. 7/2 The land that is swiddened may or may not be claimed by a village unit as a whole.

Swiderian (swidīᵊ·riăn), *a. Archæol.* [ad. F. *swidérien*, G. *swiderien*, f. *Swidry*, the name of an archæol. site near Warsaw (see quot. 1936): cf. -AN.] Of, pertaining to, or characteristic of a (principally) mesolithic culture in Poland and neighbouring countries, or its artefacts. Also *absol.* as *sb.*

[1922 *Wiadomosci Archeologiczne* VII. 96 Dans la formation III on trouve des documents archéologiques se rapportant aux industries magdalénienne moyenne, swidérienne, azilienne.] 1936 J. G. D. CLARK *Mesolithic Settlement N. Europe* ii. 62 Two alternative names have been put forward..to label a culture..centering on the valleys of the Vistula and the Bug–Swiderian, after the site at Swidry..and Chlebowician... Numerous Swiderian sites are known from Poland. 1939 V. G. CHILDE *Dawn Europ. Civilization* (ed. 3) i. 4 The *Swiderian* culture, represented by assemblages of small flint tools collected from sand-dunes in Russia and Poland, sometimes under fossil turf-lines of Atlantic age, is characterized by small asymmetrically tanged-points..used presumably as arrow-heads. 1948 A. KROEBER *Anthropol.* (ed. 2) xvi. 270 *Swiderian*, Poland, Rumania; smallish, tanged blades; early Mesolithic—in fact apparently late Palaeolithic also. 1951 [see *LYNGBY]. 1960 C. WINICK *Dict. Anthropol.* 518/2 *Swiderian*, a culture found in Poland, with the tranchet ax a typical tool. Its remains, mostly kitchen middens, resemble the Campignian culture, which is found further south.

swift, *a.* (*adv.*) Add: **C.** Combinations, etc. **3.** *swift-darkening, -eddying, -falling, -flashing, -moving, -pursuing, -sprung, -striding.*

1933 W. DE LA MARE *Fleeting* 33 Even the wise..Have smiled with swift-darkening eyes. 1923 H. BELLOC *Sonnets & Verse* 13 Anchor hold against swift-eddying time. 1791 BLAKE *French Rev.* in *Compl. Writings* (1972) 141 Aumont, whose chaos-born soul Eternally wand'ring a Comet and swift-falling fire, pale enter'd the chamber. 1951 W. DE LA MARE *Winged Chariot* 38 Swift-falling flower, slowly fretting stone Clock on unheeded those who lie alone. 1855 W. WHITMAN *Leaves of Grass* 62 The great gay-pennanted..steamboat.., with her..delicate swift-flashing paddles. 1930 BLUNDEN *Summer's Fancy* 44 With swift-flashing hope. 1872 W. WHITMAN *As Strong Bird on Pinions Free* 4 Thee as another equally needed sun, America-radiant, ablaze, swift-moving, fructifying all. 1955 J. R. R. TOLKIEN *Return of King* v. i. 19 He wondered if he was..still in the swift-moving dream in which he had been wrapped. 1785 T. DWIGHT *Conquest of Canäan* VIII. 188 Once hast thou fled the swift-pursuing spear, But fled'st in vain. 1948 R. GRAVES *Coll. Poems 1914–47* 231 The swift-pursuing reed. 1935 KIPLING *King & Sea* in *Times* 17 July 19/4, I opened him all the guile of the seas—Their sullen, swift-sprung treacheries. 1929 —— *Poems 1886–1929* III. 341 One silent, swart, swift-striding camel, oceanward wending.

swift, *v.*² Add: (Later example.) Now only as *nonce-usage.*

1935 R. MACAULAY *Personal Pleasures* 195 There goes the Atalanta among cars; see how it swifts along, passing all others.

swifter, *sb.* Restrict *Naut.* to senses in Dict. and add: **2.** *N. Amer. Logging.* A cable or spar used to secure a raft of logs.

1870 *Overland Monthly* 5 July 58/1 In a 'square' raft, long, slender spars, called 'swifters', are placed. 1975 H. WHITE *Raincoast Chron.* (1976) 150/1 They were using a hand winch to pull the swifters across that locked the logs in place.

swiftie (swi·fti). Also **swifty.** [f. SWIFT *a.* + -Y⁶, -IE.] **1.** A fast-moving person: a rapid runner, a quick thinker. Also *ironically. colloq.*

1945 *Sun* (Baltimore) 24 Feb. 9/1 Dan Ferris..says that the Swedish swiftie's provisional entry still is among the 36 hopefuls in the 3-mile run. 1946 J. IRVING *Royal Navalese* 170 *Swifty*, a derisive nickname for any particularly lugubrious and slow-moving man. 1969 N. FREELING *Tsing-Boum* xvii. 126 Make no mistake about those feminine nails: a swifty.

2. An act of deception, a trick or sleight; = *ROUGHIE 3. Also in phr. *to pull a swiftie* (cf. *to pull a fast one* s.v. *FAST *a.* 11, and *PULL *v.* 19 e). *Austral. slang.*

1945 BAKER *Austral. Lang.* xv. 265 *Swiftie*..will..be heard in male conversation to describe a joke or trick that is either agreeable or disagreeable. 1953 'CADDIE' *Sydney Barmaid* 224 'You didn't work a swiftie on them, did you?' I asked suspiciously. For I was already aware that Bill was collecting three doles for himself. 1962 R. TULLIPAN *March into Morning* 43 If these mugs hadn't pulled a swifty they wouldn't have been working for me at all. 1969 *Sunday Truth* (Brisbane) 23 Mar. 28/4 Police ..arrested him for his Sydney swiftie. 1976 *Sydney Morning Herald* 9 Apr. 6 The Queensland Premier..is now worried that the Federal Treasury may be trying to pull a swiftie.

swig, *sb.*³ Add: **2.** (Earlier U.S. example: a punning use of SWIG *sb.*¹)

1849 H. MELVILLE *Redburn* I. ix. 94 Every once in a while, the men went into one corner, where the chief mate could not see them, to take a 'swig at the halyards', as they called it;.. 'to taper off'.

swig, *v.*[3] Add: **3.** Also *intr.*, to pull *on* a rope (see quot. 1961).

1917 A. T. Quiller-Couch *Mortallone & Aunt Trinidad* ix. 77 He had now to hoist sail; which he did very leisurably..swigging on the uphaul till he had it chock-a-block. **1939** A. Ransome *Secret Water* xxi. 250 'It's just the wind we want,' panted Daisy swigging on her halyard. **1961** F. H. Burgess *Dict. Sailing* 203 *Swig*, to swig on a rope is to take half a turn with one hand, whilst heaving and taking up the slack with the other.

swiggle, *v.* **2.** Delete ? *U.S.* and add later example.

1907 J. M. Synge *Playboy* II. 39 To think of you swaying and swiggling at the butt of a rope.

3. Also with vessel (spec. a beer glass) as obj.

1943 *Pub & People* (Mass Observation) vi. 185 Some people have a habit of what may be called 'swiggling' their glasses, which consists in moving them round and round in circles, either on the bar counter or table top, or up in the air.

Hence **swi·ggling** *vbl. sb.*

1948 L. A. G. Strong *Trevannion* xiii. 229 There was a wild splashing; Trevannion, craning forward, saw the gleam of a silver belly, and heard a madly energised swiggling and slithering. **1971** *Weekly Guardian* 2 Jan. 19/3 Such categories of pub behaviour as 'Swiggling'—the habit of moving a beer glass round and round between sips.

swile (swəil). *Newfoundland.* Also **swoil(e.** Irregular var. of Seal *sb.*[1] Cf. Soile.

1802 J. Murphy *Old Sealing Days* (1916) 2 [J]ars, Doaters and Gunswoils and many others brew upon the rocks. *c* **1845** in *Dict. Newfoundland Eng.* (1982) 450/2 When we got into the jam the swoiles were very thick. **1878** in C. Hallock *Hallock's Amer. Club List & Sportsman's Gloss.* p. xi/2 Swile. **1907** J. G. Millais *Newfoundland* ii. 39 Swoiles (seals) was much to us in the spring, for it meant 'bout what we lived on. **1924** F. Baird *Parson John of Labrador* iii. 64 It's t' good Lard as does it,.. as made t' harbours for we, an' sends t' fish, an' t' swiles. **1969** H. Horwood *Newfoundland* xii. 83 Seals on the north-east coast are called swiles, and the guns used for hunting them are swilin' guns. **1974** F. Mowat *Boat who wouldn't Float* vi. 58 A number of swile guns—longbarrelled, smooth-bore guns intended for killing seals.

Hence as *v. intr.* = Seal *v.*[3]; **swiling** *vbl. sb.*

c **1894** in *Dict. Newfoundland Eng.* (1982) 455/2 Ma shall have a new silk dress, When Da comes home from swoiling. **1897** B. Willson *Tenth Island* 110, I was no good for 'swilin'' any more. **1905** N. Duncan *Dr Grenfell's Parish* 40, I been swilin'..in these seas every spring for fifty-seven years. **1906** J. Lumsden *Skipper Parson on Bays & Barrens of Newfoundland* 90 If the Canadians come down here to take our country I'll get down my 'swiling gun', and we'll go out and meet 'em. **1969** [see the sb. above].

swiler (swəi·ləɹ). *Newfoundland.* [f. *swile *v.* + -er[1].] **1.** = Sealer *sb.*[2] 2.

1883 Hatton & Harvey *Newfoundland* 88 The roads.. begin to be enlivened by the appearance of the sealers, or, as they are called in the vernacular, 'silers', their enterprise being designated 'swile huntin''. **1927** in *Dict. Newfoundland Eng.* (1982) 455/1 We are swoilers fearless, bold. **1958** M. Harrington *Sea Stories from Newfoundland* 118 She sailed..with Skipper Ned Dower in command, and a crew of able 'swoilers'. **1976** *Globe & Mail* (Toronto) 27 Nov. 35/3 It's the swoilers of Newfoundland and the pea-soupers of Quebec, symbols of cultures that in their turn have been despised for different reasons.

2. = Sealer *sb.*[2] 1.

1897 B. Willson *Tenth Island* 110 When the 'swiler' came to start I give my place to another man. **1900** in Oliver & Burke *People's Songster* 46 The interest of all the people was centred on the 'swoilers'. **1959** in Ryan & Small *Haulin' Rope & Gaff* 70 You'll need no Daylight Bill When a 'swiler' first is sighted From the tower upon the 'Hill'.

swill, *sb.*[2] Add: **2. b.** *six o'clock swill*, the customary bout of hasty drinking in public houses at the end of the working day, occasioned by the former six-o'clock-closing regulations. *Austral.* and *N.Z. colloq.*

[**1951** A. W. Upfield *New Shoe* 93 It wanted ten minutes to the fatal hour of six, and the enforced National Swill was in full flood.] **1955** A. Ross *Australia 55* 81 This evening ritual, known amongst Australians as the 'six o' clock swill'. **1961** F. Hardy *Hard Way* 73 The [prison] yard was filling steadily, mostly with drunks, and a few victims of the six o' clock swill. **1970** D. Horne *Next Australia* 160 The 'six o'clock swill' before the lavatory-tiled bars closed was one of the continuing tests of masculinity.

3. *swill-barrel, -bucket, -pail* (earlier example); † **swill-milk** *U.S.*, inferior milk produced by cows fed entirely on swill (*obs.*).

1869 Mrs. Stowe *Oldtown Folks* xxxvi. 469 The wasteful excesses she had seen in the minister's swill-barrel. **1932** Kipling *Limits & Renewals* 311 Enoch sat helpless on a swill-bucket. **1975** *Country Life* 13 Mar. 666/1 Those happy-go-lucky swill-bucket days. **1853** *Hunt's Merch. Mag.* XXVIII. 684 The whole business [is] in the hands of the swill milk manufacturers. **1894** P. L. Ford *Hon. Peter Stirling* 72 The press began, too, a crusade against the swill-milk dealers. **1741** *Boston News-Let.* 12 Feb. 2/1 Taken up by John Morey, Esq...a Swill-Pale, otherwise called a Hog-Pale.

swiller[2]. *north. dial.* [f. Swill *sb.*[1] + -er[1].] One who makes swills or baskets.

1859 W. Dickinson *Gloss. Words & Phrases Cumberland* 116 *Swiller*,..a swill-maker. **1901** C. W. Bardsley *Dict. Eng. & Welsh Surnames* 522/2 In Ulverston registers to this day a maker of *swills* (i.e. baskets) is set down as a *swiller*. **1949** K. S. Woods *Rural Crafts of Eng.* iii. viii. 142 In Furness the baskets are known as swills, and the craftsmen as swillers. Whether the word is a form of scull or scuttle, or whether it means swaler, is not known. **1972** *Daily Tel.* 5 Aug. 9/4 The Lancashire mountains near Ulverston, home of the 'swillers', or basket-makers. *Ibid.*, With a short and very sharp knife the swiller slices his oak into ribs which he fixes across a hazel rim.

swim, *sb.* **5. a.** (Earlier example.)

1764 J. Wesley *Jrnl.* 16 Jan. (1914) V. 44 My mare lost both her fore feet, but she gave a spring, and recovered the causeway; otherwise we must have taken a swim, for the water on either side was ten or twelve feet deep.

10. a. Simple attrib. 'Worn while swimming', as *swim-cap, -pants, -shorts, -trunks, -wear.* Cf. *swimming *vbl. sb.* 6.

1964 *Harper's Bazaar* Nov. 102 Black and white felt, close as a swimcap. **1942** N. Last *Diary* 5 June in *Nella Last's War* (1983) 207 Arthur stripped off to a pair of swim-pants, to get sun-browned. **1977** J. D. MacDonald *Condominium* xxxiv. 328 He wore brief turquoise swim pants and large, very dark sunglasses. **1973** G. Beare *Snake on Grave* iv. 22 All he wore was swim-shorts and leather sandals. **1959** *Spectator* 21 Aug. 223/1 Several were wading about in the water. Two were braving it out in swim-trunks. **1979** G. Mitchell *Mudflats of Dead* iii. 35 He..put on his swim-trunks, and slung a towel around his shoulders. **1935** A. P. Herbert *What a Word!* iv. 115, I have been implored by many to attack 'neck-wear', 'foot-wear', 'sleep-wear', and 'swim-wear'. **1962** *Punch* 23 May p. xiii/1 Harvey Nichols have a new range of Californian swimwear. **1976** J. Archer *Not Penny more, not Penny Less* x. 104 I'll never get into the swimwear I'm..modelling next week.

b. Special combinations. **swim-feeder,** in coarse fishing: a short length of perforated plastic tube about an inch in diameter, used to contain maggots, which escape gradually once it is sunk in the water; **swimgloat,** Logan Pearsall Smith's term for the enjoyment of brief social success without becoming corrupted by it; **swim-hole** = *swimming hole* s.v. *swimming *vbl. sb.* 6; **swim-pool** = *swimming-pool* s.v. *swimming *vbl. sb.* 6; **swimsuit,** a (woman's) bathing costume; hence **swim-suited** *a.*

1958 F. Oates *Coarse Fishing Baits* ix. 68 Another method of ground baiting is by the use of a new gadget called a 'swim-feeder'. **1981** B. Walsh *Live Bait* v. 33, I used a paternoster rig, with a swimfeeder and a coffin leger to hold the bottom. **1943** J. Lees-Milne *Jrnl.* 5 Sept. in *Ancestral Voices* (1975) 236 He [*sc.* Logan Pearsall Smith] calls Stuart's social success a 'swimgloat'. **1974** *Times Lit. Suppl.* 11 Oct. 1112/3 Logan Pearsall Smith coined a word for the buoyant negotiation of the vanities and temptations of society..: 'swimgloat'. It is a term which suggests the eternal resilience of the picaresque hero. **1924** Kipling *Debits & Credits* (1926) 321 There was a wet ditch at the bottom that I had wanted..to dam up to make a swim-hole for Mrs. Bevin's ducks. **1958** J. Kerouac *On Road* i. i. 10 My boyhood in those dye-dumps and swim-holes. **1964** C. Barber *Ling. Change Present-Day Eng.* ii. 21 Recently I have seen..*swim-pool* in a high-class newspaper. **1970** *New Yorker* 10 Oct. 80/1 (Advt.), Two swim pools. **1977** *Lancashire Life* Mar. 115/1 Britain has some of the finest swim pool engineers in the world. **1934** *Times* 18 July 17/6 The one-piece swim-suits with attached skirt are still the most popular. **1948** J. Betjeman *Coll. Poems* (1958) 148 Don't hang swim-suits out on sills (A line has been provided at the back). **1980** B. Castle *Castle Diaries* 151 To the disapproval of the department I insisted on taking an hour off on my way to the office to try to buy a swimsuit for my holiday. **1955** *New Statesman* 16 July 66/2 Brutally honest was the Visual Arts float: the Visual Arts..were..represented by a number of swim-suited young women. **1979** 'J. Ross' *Rattling of Old Bones* iii. 32 She was all fresh and rosy and swimsuited.

swim, *v.* Add: **I. 1. c.** Also, *to swim against the tide.*

1705 Ld. Fermanagh *Let.* 18 Nov. in M. M. Verney *Verney Lett.* (1930) I. xiii. 229, I fancy Mr. Gape may lose it... Its hard Swimming against the Tyde. **1971** *Nature* 22 Oct. 515/3 The Sira Institute seems to be swimming against the economic tide.

II. 13. b. Delete † *Obs.* and add later examples.

1939 A. Ransome *Secret Water* xxvi. 315 You'll just have to lie on your back and keep still, and I'm going to swim you ashore. **1953** *Sun Mag.* (Baltimore) 25 Oct. 29/1 The gun fires and the bay dog is over with a splash. Exultantly he swims the dead game back to his master.

14. c. (Earlier example.)

1794 M. Parry *Jrnl.* 23 May in *Kentucky Hist. Soc. Register* (1936) XXXIV. 380 Forded Buffaloe Creek, at the mouth, which did not quite swim them [*sc.* the horses].

† **15.** To carry (a publication) to success. *Obs.*

1870 'Mark Twain' *Lett. to Publishers* (1967) 45 Launch a book right on our big tidal wave and swim it into a *success*. **1890** G. Meredith *Let.* 19 Nov. (1970) II. 1012 If clogged with the letter-press, I should have my doubts of success, even with his name to swim the book.

swimathon (swi·măþǫn). Also **swim-a-thon.** [f. Swim *v.* + *-athon.] A long-distance swimming race; a marathon (often sponsored) swimming event.

1968 *Telegraph* (Brisbane) 20 Dec. 2/2 Six Gold Coast girls will take part in a swimathon at Southport's Olympic Pool. **1976** *Estevan* (Saskatchewan) *Mercury* 23 June 16/3 A swim-a-thon will be held at Woodlawn Swimming Pool June 27... Proceeds will go toward the aquatic club.

swim-in (swi·min). [f. Swim *v.* + *-in[3].] A form of protest or recreation at which a number of people swim together. Cf. *sit-in *sb.* 1.

1960 *Daily Progress* (Charlottesville, Va.) 2/3 Other white bathers cleared out of the immediate vicinity of the swim-in. **1977** *Navy News* Sept. 25/2 Other events on the social programme have included a barbecue and a 'swim-in' at the local pool.

swimmable, *a.* Add: Also, suitable for swimming in. Also *swimmable-in*.

1963 P. McCutchan *Man from Moscow* ix. 91 The sea's swimmable-in, if you're a Spartan. **1966** *Telegraph* (Brisbane) 3 Feb. 18 (*caption*) Bare midriff camisole tops are the latest on the patio this summer. Worn with snug hip-hugger jams in nylon knit. Both are completely swimable. **1976** *National Observer* (U.S.) 13 Mar. 7/2 Congress poured money into it to help cities do their part in achieving 'swimmable, fishable' waters.

swimmer. Add: **7.** *slang.* A swimming costume. Now (*Austral.*) *pl.* const. *sing.* Cf *bather 3.

1929 *Daily Tel.* 3 June 7/1 Two coloured swimmer with brassiere attached. **1967** *Sunday Truth* (Brisbane) 23 July 1/1 Bikini girls at Parliament House..when a parade of new season's swimmers..will be on show. **1978** *Courier-Mail* (Brisbane) 22 Feb. 1/9, I am not an exhibitionist and if I go swimming on the main beach, I would wear swimmers.

8. Special combination. **swimmer's itch** *Med.*, a painful dermatitis caused by the cercaria of certain species of blood flukes, notably *Schistosoma mansoni*, which penetrate human skin (or mucous membrane) during swimming.

1928 *Minnesota Med.* XI. 573/1 There has been reported from several lake regions in Minnesota a peculiar type of skin eruption locally called 'swimmer's' itch. **1969** *Trans. R. Soc. Trop. Med. & Hygiene* LXIII. 557 Visitors to that camp suffered severe swimmer's itch when bathing in one of the rock pools.., and subsequently developed schistosomiasis.

swimming, *vbl. sb.* Add: **6.** *swimming costume, suit, trunks*; *swimming bath* (examples in *pl.*); **swimming hole** chiefly *U.S.*, *Austral.*, and *N.Z.*, a bathing place in a stream or river; **swimming pool,** an artificial pool designed for swimming in.

1868 A. J. Symonds *Let.* 29 July (1967) I. 828, I went.. to the Victoria Swimming Baths, as I occasionally do, to smoke my cigar & to learn the secrets of Form. **1982** *Financial Times* 9 Dec. 9/1 Proposals are being investigated for private sector school meals and cleaning, the running of swimming baths, [etc.]. **1904** R. Thomas *Swimming* 112 It is very difficult to get photographs of amateur ladies in swimming costume. **1962** F. C. Avis *Swimming Dict.* 95 *Swimsuit*, a superior or elegant swimming costume, with particular reference to the female bather. **1977** N. Slater *Crossfire* iii. 58 A twenty-nine-year-old married woman..who wore a bathing cap and a one-piece swimming costume. **1867** G. W. Harris *Sut Lovingood* 25 He wer aimin fur the swimin hole in the krick. **1912** J. H. Moore *Ethics & Educ.* 128 The boy's love for the water, his affection for the old swimming-hole. **1928** [see *bogy[2], bogey[2]]. **1975** D. Bagley *Snow Tiger* ii. 33 The bluff..projected into the river..and that was where they had their swimming hole. **1899** *Scribner's Mag. Advertiser* Jan. 26/2 You can enjoy..a plunge into the great marble swimming pool, where the water is tempered according to season. **1921** A. Huxley *Crome Yellow* iii. 19 The stone-brimmed swimming-pool. **1972** *Punch* 1 Mar. 266/3 Our goals are increasingly the same —a bigger car, an expense account, and a swimming-pool in every back garden. **1926** E. Hemingway *Sun also Rises* ii. xix. 245, I found my swimming suit, wrapped it with a comb in a towel. **1971** 'D. Halliday' *Dolly & Doctor Bird* vi. 83 My swimming-suit, helmet and towel **1943** *New Yorker* 22 May 26/1 He was big, stalwart, and dressed only in swimming trunks. **1978** I. Murdoch *Sea* 70 Shall I come and bring my swimming trunks?

swimmy, *a.* Add: † **b.** Graceful, elegant. *Obs. nonce-use.*

1827 Coleridge *Let.* 2 June (1971) VI. 687 A fine, tall, slim, swimmy, glidy lass.

c. Of the eyes: watery, tearful. Also, of tears.

1936 J. B. Priestley *They walk in City* vii. 178 She had a round moist face, with swimmy eyes. **1978** J Irving *World according to Garp* xvii. 358 The woman's.. face, dissolving before him in his own swimmy tears.

Swinburnian (swinbɔ̄·ɹniăn), *a.* [f. the name of the English poet Algernon Charles *Swinburne* (1837–1909) + -ian.] Of, pertaining to imitative or characteristic of Swinburne or his poetry. Hence **Swinbu·rnianism, Swi·nburnism.**

1867 E. B. Lytton *Let.* 25 Jan. in *Lett. R. Lytton* (1906 I. 207 The 'Gyges and Candaules' have some dangerou supersensual lines which I advise you to reconsider. I will not do for you to be 'Swinburnian'. **1868** A. J. Symonds *Let.* 24 Apr. (1967) I. 803 Courthope..is full of the gall of bitterness against the Apostles of Swinburnism. **1892** W. B. Scott *Autobiogr. Notes* I. xxii. 300 When the Swinburnian passion for French things..had infected nearly all our young writers. **1920** *Glasgow Herald* 30 Dec. 4 The 'Various' verses show now and then a Swinburnian touch. **1931** G. K. Chesterton *All is Grist* xxxviii. 212 Something that is connected not only with Swinburne but with Swinburnianism. **1949** A. Huxley *Let.* 6 Apr. (1969) 595 Any equivalent in English becomes automatically Swinburnian, that is to say rich without the weight ..which Latin imposes. **1960** J. Betjeman *Summoned by Bells* vii. 75, I was released Into Swinburnian stanzas with the wind. **1974** E. Hardwick *Seduction & Betrayal* 109 A Swinburnian mood of spankings and teasing degradation. **1976** *Times Lit. Suppl.* 26 Nov. 1495/2 [Gilbert Murray's] translations of Greek tragedies are still to be found on the shelves of college bookstores today, in spite of all the rude things that have been said about their Swinburnianism.

swindle, *sb.*[3] Add: **1. a.** (Earlier example.)

1883 in A. Bunn *Stage* (1840) I. 134 There was a universal cry of 'off-off'—'swindle-swindle'.

3. Special combination. **swindle sheet** *slang* (chiefly *U.S.*), an expense account; also (*joc.*) in extended use, of other documents which conceal (or reveal) fraudulence and other 'swindles', as a log-book or time sheet.

1923 *N.Y. Times* 9 Sept. vii. 2/3 *Swindle sheet*, the advance agent's expense account. **1934** J. O'Hara *Appointment in Samarra* ii. 42 The Apollo [hotel] got a big play from salesmen who had their swindle sheets to think of. **1936** *Times Lit. Suppl.* 15 Feb. 125/3 The 'swindle-sheet' for the average motor-car shows that 40 per cent of the fuel energy goes into the cooling water. **1960** H. L. Lawrence *Children of Light* v. 77 The fare's ten bob... Put it on the swindle sheet. **1971** M. Tak *Truck Talk* 161 *Swindle sheet*, the daily log book, mandatory for all drivers.

swindler. (Earlier example.)

1774 W. Hawke (*title*) The life, trial, &c. of William Hawke... To which is added a full description of the impositions and deceptions practiced by the swindlers, sharps, gamblers..in and about London.

swindlery. (Later example.)

1869 Dickens in *All Year Round* 2 Jan. 109/2 Swindlery in doubtful boots, on the sharp look-out for any likely young gentleman.

swindling, *vbl. sb.*[2] (Earlier example.)

1788 *Gentl. Mag.* LVIII. 1154/2 As *swindling* is a word that occurs not in our dictionaries, and yet we often meet with it in modern writers.., we should be obliged to any gentleman among your correspondents.., to define it; or..inform us what..distinguishes it from other modes of fraud and imposition.

swine. Add: **2. b.** Of a thing: = *pig *sb.*[1] 1 c. *slang.*

1933 Dylan Thomas *Let.* Oct. (1966) 31 This method of letter writing..is very satisfying, but it's a swine in some ways. **1938** N. Marsh *Artists in Crime* iii. 38 'It's a swine of a pose, Miss Troy.' 'Well, stick it a bit longer.' **1967** K. Giles *Death in Diamonds* ii. 41 The Inspector groaned. 'Could be heroin. That's a swine.' **1976** H. MacInnes *Death Reel* iii. 19 This car's..a swine to drive at slow speeds.

4. *swine-fat*; *swine-headed* adj. (later example).

1922 Joyce *Ulysses* 468 Her odalisk lips..smeared with salve of swinefat. **1922** Swineheaded [see *dog *sb.* 17 c].

5. a. swine-chopped *a.*, of a hound: having the lower jaw projecting forward of the upper one; so **swine-chop**, a malformation of this kind; **swine erysipelas**, an infectious, sometimes fatal, disease of pigs, caused by the bacterium *Erysipelothrix rhusiopathiæ*, and characterized by fever, reddish spots on the skin, and general debility; **swine flu** = *swine influenza* below; **swine-hound** *slang rare*, tr. G. *schweinehund* *schwein(e)hund (quot. in Mil. context); **swine influenza**, an infectious virus disease of pigs, esp. young ones, characterized by fever, coughing, and difficulty in breathing; also, influenza in man caused by the same (or a closely related) virus; **swine vesicular disease**, an infectious virus disease of pigs (similar to foot-and-mouth disease) characterized by mild fever and blisters round the mouth and feet.

1962 *Times* 9 June 11/4, I have seen..puppy show prizes awarded to young hounds with swine-chop. **1930** Kipling *Thy Servant a Dog* 20 Moore-man lifted Ravager's head and opened his mouth... 'Look, m'lord. He's swine-chopped.' **1965** D. Moore *Bk. Foxhound* ii. 29 The forehead and nose merge invisibly, giving always a rather stupid expression, and sometimes accompanying a swine-chopped mouth. **1898** M. M. Hayes tr. *Friedberger & Fröhner's Vet. Pathol.* 72 Swine erysipelas (or swine measles)..is a specific septicæmia produced by a minute bacillus. **1922** A. T. Kinsley *Swine Practice* xii. 338 Swine erysipelas is an infective disease of swine characterized by a high temperature, cerebral disturbances and discoloration of the skin. **1970** W. H. Parker *Health & Dis. in Farm Animals* x. 141 A disease which can easily be confused with swine fever is swine erysipelas. **1921** *Wallace's Farmer* 25 Feb. 371/1 So-called 'swine flu', a name which, while it became quite popular thru its association with the human disease, is nevertheless a misnomer, is primarily a bronchitis. **1976** *National Observer* (U.S.) 21 Aug. 2/2 The swine-flu insurance bill was signed by President Ford, clearing the way for mass inoculations in about six weeks. **1981** *Sci. Amer.* Oct. 46/2 Epidemiologists determined..that recipients of the swine-flu vaccine were developing Guillain-Barré syndrome at a rate several times the usual one. **1916** 'Boyd Cable' *Action Front* 245 'Sulky, eh, my swine-hound!' said the officer. 'But I think we can improve those manners.' **1922** *Jrnl. Amer. Vet. Med. Assoc.* LXI. 178 We must be able to differentiate between hog cholera, necrotic enteritis,..broncho-pneumonia or swine influenza, and many others. **1935** *Lancet* 11 May 1123/2 It seems to me..exceedingly probable that the virus of swine influenza is really the virus of the great [influenza] pandemic of 1918 adapted to the pig and persisting in that species ever since. **1969** C. W. Schwabe *Vet. Med. & Human Health* (ed. 2) vii. 216/2 Swine influenza was not known before the human influenza pandemic of 1918. **1976** *Globe & Mail* (Toronto) 26 Mar. 1/1 Ontario residents probably will be vaccinated against a deadly swine influenza virus, Alan Backley, Ontario's deputy health minister, said yesterday. **1972** *Guardian* 16 Dec. 1/8 The outbreaks of suspected foot-and-mouth disease in the Midlands have turned out to be a rare virus which affects only pigs. Its new name, invented by the Ministry of Agriculture yesterday, is swine vesicular disease. **1981** *Vet. Rec.* 30 May 468/3 The relative decline in the number of cases of swine vesicular disease this year suggests that the campaign against the disease is achieving worthwhile results.

swing, *sb.*[2] Add: **I. 6. d.** A swift tour or journey (*through* a place) involving a number of stops or visits. Now *spec.* a political campaign tour; also, *swing around the circle*, a campaigning tour of a constituency or larger area. Cf. *swing *v.*[1] 11 c. *U.S.*

1860 H. J. Hawley *Jrnl.* 22 Apr. in *Wisconsin Mag. Hist.* (1936) XIX. 330 Had a fine time a nice swing . saw sights and returned. **1905** *Springfield* (Mass.) *Weekly Republican* 6 Oct. 1 Will the appropriated money be available for campaigning swings around the circle? **1929** *Sun* (Baltimore) 23 Oct. 2/7 Mr. Hoover has undergone much strain on this swing and he showed it as he waved a weary adieu to the hospitable Ohioans. **1949** *Manch. Guardian Weekly* 1 Sept. 2 Before his recent swing around the Marshall countries. **1967** *Boston Globe* 5 Apr. 51/1 Dizzy Dean's wife once traveled with him on an Eastern swing by the Cardinals. **1972** *Even. Telegram* (St. John's, Newfoundland) 27 June 5/3 Senior citizens can call a number and a van will come by to pick them up on swings through the city. **1978** L. Heren *Growing up on The Times* iii. 92, I..was sharing a room..with Colin Reid of the *Daily Telegraph*, who was on a swing from Beirut.

e. A worker's rest period between duties; a shift system which incorporates such breaks. Also, time off work as leave, furlough. Cf. *swing-shift* s.v. *swing- 2 a. *U.S. slang.*

1917 D. C. Roper *U.S. Post Office* 353 *Swing*, period of time within the day's tour or 'trick' when an employee is temporarily off duty. **1918** *Outlook* (N.Y.) 17 July 443/2 [On a street railway] The 'swings', or free time between runs, are for the most part so arranged as to be inconvenient for going home. **1945** *Transit News* (Capital Transit Co., Washington, D.C.) 15 June, A 'Swing' works during the morning rush hour, and the operator is then off until time to start the evening rush hour. **1972** J. Mills *Report to Commissioner* 129, I went on my swing after that.

f. In colloq. phr. *to go with a swing*: said of a lively, successful party or other entertainment or undertaking.

1976 *Bridgwater Mercury* 21 Dec. 9/3 Families may soon be enjoying a tipple at the bar to make their parties held in the community centre go with a swing.

7. b. *Boxing.* A punch delivered with a sweep of the arm; a swinging blow. Also in gen. colloq. use, esp. in phr. *to take a swing at* (someone).

1910 [see *hook *sb.*[1] 13 b]. **1962** *Times* 28 Apr. 3/5 Barlow came rushing in attempting to land with right swings to the head. **1983** W. Winward *Last & Greatest Art* 211 If I stand here much longer I'm going to be tempted to take a swing at you.

8. g. *Cricket.* A curving deviation of a ball from a straight line of flight on delivery, occasioned by a combination of the angle of its seam and the relative smoothness of the leather each side of this.

1906 *Cricket* 29 Nov. 450/1 He and Raynor..were two of the best boy bowlers I have seen, and the latter had more break—not swing—in the air than anyone else I ever saw. **1920** Lyttelton & Wilson in P. F. Warner *Cricket* (ed. 2) 270 Baker did not swing too much..and he combined swing with length. **1976** J. Snow *Cricket Rebel* 101 It is not often in Australia that the atmospheric conditions encourage swing.

h. An observable movement in general opinion away from one position towards another. Hence *spec.* in *Pol.*, a change in the relative distribution of popular support for political parties, often measured in terms of percentage gains or losses by each party at a poll. Formerly also † *swing of the pendulum.*

1899, 1912 [in Dict., sense 8 a]. **1933** D. W. Brogan *Amer. Polit. System* x. iv. 368 The strength of American parties is, as a rule, too sectional, too much divorced from any current national controversies, for there to be anything like our 'swing of the pendulum'. **1940** *Economist* 5 Oct. 421/2 The swing in American public opinion has been such that the Nazis may well despair of keeping the United States out of a long war. **1945** *Times* 27 July 4/1 When the votes were counted..it was revealed that the Government formed by Mr Churchill on the break-up of the Coalition had been decisively beaten by a surging swing of opinion to the Left. **1955** *Times* 26 May 10/1 The absence of any pronounced 'swing' towards the Government. **1960** *Where?* III. 17 *'Swing', the*, jargon for the relatively recent tendency among sixth form pupils to specialize in science rather than arts subjects. *a* **1974** R. Crossman *Diaries* (1975) I. 493 It was only a 3·1 swing, and by God a 3·1 swing can become a 4·0 counter-swing very quickly indeed. **1976** H. Wilson *Governance of Britain* ii. 38 We had bad county council results in April, including Lancashire though with a favourable swing in Greater London.

i. *Electr.* An increase or decrease in the magnitude of a current or voltage, the difference between its greatest and smallest values.

1908 *Rep. Brit. Assoc. Adv. Sci. 1907* 622 These [oscillations]..are transferred..into a closed air-condenser circuit, which, when its swings reach a maximum, overflows into the coherer. **1957** *Practical Wireless* XXXIII. 562/1 It is possible to increase the anode voltage swing and the anode peak current. **1978** *Sci. Amer.* Dec. 54/1 Load-following generators are started daily and run most of the time to cope with daily swings in the load; they may be shut down at night.

j. *Psychol.*: see *mood swing* s.v. *mood *sb.*[1] 3 f.

k. *Bridge.* The difference between the total scores of two teams of two pairs playing the same deal at two tables, each team having north-south positions at one table and east-west at the other.

1945 S. J. Simon *Why You lose at Bridge* 24 In Room 1, North-South bid six Spades and made five. In Room 2, North-South stopped in 4 spades and declarer, playing for safety, made three. No swing! **1949** *Contract Bridge Jrnl.* Feb. 5/2 On the very next hand the Scots repaid the compliment; at this stage they were going great guns, and on Board 54 came the biggest swing to-date. **1961** *Listener* 10 Aug. 222/3 The swing on the board was 2,080, or 11 match points.

10. b. *Mus.* A quality of jazz, dance music, etc., that has a flowing but strongly compelling rhythm; since the mid-thirties (esp. for a decade), applied to a variety of big dance-band music played in this style. Cf. *swing- 2 d.

(*a*) **1899** H. H. Mincer (*song-title*) Virginia. Two-step & hot rag swing. **1917** *Sun* (N.Y.) 5 Aug. 3/7 Jazz is based on the savage musician's wonderful gift for progressive retarding and acceleration guided by his sense of swing. **1924** (*music-title*) Lou'siana swing [performed by Piron's New Orleans Orchestra]. **1932** 'Duke' Ellington (*song-title*) It don't mean a thing (If it ain't got that swing). **1939** —— in *Melody Maker* 15 July 8/3 No notes represent swing. You can't write swing because swing is the emotional element in the audience and there is no swing until you hear the note. **1954** *Grove's Dict. Music* (ed. 5) IV. 600/1 'Swing'..can only be said to designate the regular but subtle rhythmic pulsation which animates 4–4 time and must be present in every good jazz performance. Swing is essentially the performer's concern: it cannot be indicated in musical notation except implicitly.

(*b*) **1936** *Delineator* CXXIX. 10/1 This swing, it's nothing more or less than jazz, is it? **1937** L. Armstrong *Swing that Music* xiv. 117 Even now, thirty years after Swing was born, this book is the first history of swing music, and of the men who made it, to be published in the English language. **1943** D. Welch *Maiden Voyage* xiv. 110 'What kind of records have you got?' 'There's plenty of swing.' **1957** R. Hoggart *Uses of Literacy* v. 129 The emotional patterns bodied out by 'swing' are quite close to those of the older, waltz-derived, styles: in fact, 'swing' has been adapted and assimilated; a modern 'swing' song and an old-fashioned waltz tune live together with ease. **1973** J. Wainwright *Pride of Pigs* 61 It wasn't jazz. Not *real* jazz... Swing..that's what they'd called it, when [Artie] Shaw had introduced it in the 1930's.

II. 11. b. Colloq. phr. *to gain on the swings and lose on the roundabouts* and varr., according to which one's losses in one quarter balance one's gains in another. Also *allusively.*

1912 P. R. Chalmers *Green Days & Blue Days* 20 For 'up an' down an' round,' said 'e, goes all appointed things, An' losses on the roundabouts means profits on the swings! **1927** *Times* 24 Mar. 15/5 By screwing more money out of tax-payers he diminishes their savings, and the market for trustee securities loses on the swings what it gains on the roundabouts. **1944** G. B. Shaw *Everybody's Political What's What* xv. 121, I was taxed at a higher rate than my fellow capitalists who had smaller incomes. But then I had to pay at a lower rate than others who had bigger incomes. Whether I lost on the swings what I gained on the roundabouts I do not know. **1964** *English Studies* XLV. (Suppl.). 98 The more a word loses in meaning, the more it gains in functional, as distinct from semantic, importance. What we lose on the swings we win on the roundabouts. **1976** *Listener* 18 Nov. 641/1 There is a certain rough justice in charging for the possibility of using the [broadcasting] service... Swings and roundabouts.

12. d. Also *swing-steer.*

1869 [see *lead *sb.*[2] 11 b].

swing, *v.*[1] Add: **4.** Also, *to swing Kelly* (or *Douglas*), to wield an axe, to do axework. *Austral. slang.*

1945 BAKER *Austral. Lang.* i v. 78 *Kelly* and *douglas*, an axe (from the names of makers), with their derivatives *to swing kelly* or *douglas*, to do axework. **1966** 'J. HACKSTON' *Father clears Out* 98 The scholars..could have passed with honours in such subjects as milking, swinging Douglas, panning off.

7. a. Also, *to swing the lead*: see *LEAD *sb.*^{1} 6 b.

11. c. *to swing around the circle*, to make a political tour of a constituency or larger area. *U.S.*

1866 E. MCPHERSON *Polit. Man.* v. 58 We swing around the circle of the Union with a fixed and unalterable determination to stand by it. **1871** G. W. PECK *Adventures Terence McGrant* iv. 27 Until me Cousin Ulissis gets through swinging around the circle. **1887** *Chicago Tribune* 2 Oct., President Andrew Johnson originated the phrase 'swinging round the circle' on the occasion of his famous tour to Chicago..in September, 1866. **1910** *N.Y. Evening Post* 29 Oct. 2 To stem the rising tide against him, Col. Roosevelt is to swing around the circle in Brooklyn to-night.

d. *Cricket.* Of a bowler: to impart swing to the ball on delivery. Also with the ball as subj. Cf. *SWING *sb.*^{2} 8 g.

1900 P. F. WARNER *Cricket in Many Climes* 84 Morton ..has a beautiful natural action, and swings in the air with his arm. *Ibid.* 179 Rowe..has, too, a very good fast 'yorker' which swings in the air. **1952** *M.C.C. Cricket Coaching Bk.* ii. 37 The farther up the ball is pitched, the more 'room' it has in which to swing. **1977** *World of Cricket Monthly* June 30/1 Bowling medium-pace, he got the ball to swing in the heavy atmosphere.

e. Of a spacecraft: to pass *by* a planet using its gravitational field to change course.

1967 [implied at *swing-by* s.v. *SWING- 2 a]. **1970** *Nature* 1 Aug. 434/2 The spacecraft will be launched in the autumn of 1973, swinging by Venus at a distance of 3,000 miles. **1976** *Sci. Amer.* May 116/2 These two spacecraft are scheduled to be launched in 1977 and to swing by Jupiter in 1979.

12. c. (Earlier example.)

1819 J. G. LOCKHART *Peter's Letters* (ed. 2) III. lxix. 203 The balls..being swung to and fro in a terrific manner, by means of long queues with elastic shafts.

d. In fig. phr. *to swing it on* or *across* (someone) = *to put it across* s.v. *PUT *v.*^{1} 35* a (*b*).

1923 *Daily Mail* 16 June 11 Too experienced to let even a thundering smart girl swing it on him as easily as that. **1943** N. MARSH *Colour Scheme* iv. 64 You saw Questing swing it across me. **1950** T. E. LAWRENCE *Mint* 39 'Swinging it on the..rookies, they are, the old sweats' grumbled Tug.

e. *to swing the gate* (see quot. 1933). Cf. *DRAG *v.* 9 b and *swing-gate* s.v. SWING- 2 a. *Austral.* and *N.Z. slang.*

1933 L. G. D. ACLAND in *Press* (Christchurch, N.Z.) 16 Dec. 21/8 *Swing the gate*, to be the fastest shearer in the shed. **1941** [see *DRAG *v.* 9 b]. **1965** J. S. GUNN *Terminol. Shearing Industry* II. 12 A ringer is..said to 'swing the gate', presumably because he keeps the catching-pen gate swinging.

f. To turn a starting-handle in order to start (a motor vehicle, its engine). Also with *over*. *colloq.*

1927 R. LEHMANN *Dusty Answer* III. 164 It took ten minutes to get the car started, with Martin and Roddy madly swinging her by turns. *a* **1938** in T. E. Lawrence *Lett.* (1938) 495 S[haw] was asked to swing the car for the old boy. **1957** L. F. R. WILLIAMS *State of Israel* iv. 42 Two men break off for a moment from swinging the engine of a tractor. **1977** *Daily Tel.* 12 Jan. 10/2 Attempting to 'swing over' modern high-compression engines would tax the strength of all but the most muscular.

g. *Cricket.* Of a bowler: to bowl (the ball) with swing. Cf. *SWING *sb.*^{2} 8 g.

1948 [see *seam bowler* s.v. *SEAM *sb.*^{1} 10].

14. b. To bring (something uncertain) about; to contrive or manage; to 'wangle'. Freq. with *it*. *colloq.*

1934 E. POUND *Let.* 7 Jan. (1971) 250 A guy named Collis... Wants me to edit a mag again. I have replied that..I wd. edit an annual... If he swings it, I shd. want to see a batch of yr. mss. in say about 6 months' time. **1937** WODEHOUSE *Summer Moonshine* (1938) i. 14 'The idea is to get him to trim the thing a little.' 'How do you expect to swing that?' **1941** B. SCHULBERG *What makes Sammy Run?* vi. 104 And Julian actually has a real job?.. How the hell did you swing it? **1955** 'J. CHRISTOPHER' *Year of Comet* ii. 77 I'm not promising anything, but there's a chance I may be able to swing something useful there. **1962** 'K. ORVIS' *Damned & Destroyed* x. 71 Phil had gotten himself a white nest-egg. Now how..could a half-broke addict-musician have swung that? **1975** M. BRADBURY *History Man* viii. 138 You can't con me, but you might swing it with someone else.

16. *Mus.* **a.** *intr.* To play jazz music with swing (see *SWING *sb.*^{2} 10 b). Also, *to swing it.*

[**1918** (*music-title*) Swinging along. **1928** (*music-title*) Swing on the gait.] **1931** (*music-title*) Swing it. **1933** [see *GET *v.* 62 l]. **1934** *Esquire* Feb. 96/2 This still leaves a comfortable margin of popular acclaim for the boys who couldn't read it, but who, in the parlance of *hot*, knew how to *swing* it. **1935** *Swing Music* Nov.–Dec. 248/2 In the Duke's band the brass section may swing while the rhythm-section and reed-section provide a harmonic..background. **1937** L. ARMSTRONG *Swing that Music* xiii. 114 A lot of Americans in Paris came to hear me swing. **1955** in Shapiro & Hentoff *Hear Me Talkin' to Ya* xviii. 289 Don't let Benny scare you, you're a *piano player*, Johnny—and you *swing*. **1966** T. PYNCHON *Crying of Lot 49* iii. 48 The early crowd tends to dig your Radio Cologne sound. Later on we really swing. **1977** J. WAINWRIGHT *Do Nothin' till you hear from Me* viii. 125 He sometimes plays pure 'Palm Court'.., and without that extra lift which can make a band swing.

b. *trans.* To play (a tune) with swing.

1936 (*music-title*) Swingin' them Jingle Bells. **1938** *Times Herald* (Dallas) 1 Apr. III. 11 The Detroit station pull[ed]..Tommy off the air for 'swinging' Loch Lomond. **1947** *Penguin Music Mag. II* May 28 His instructions in the introduction to the score are that these are to be slightly 'swung', and he admits the influence upon his music of all Negro spirituals. **1954** *Grove's Dict. Music* (ed. 5) 600/2 A score can at most be more or less susceptible to being 'swung'. One band may swing an arrangement while another may play the same arrangement without a touch of swing. **1968** *Blues Unlimited* Nov. 23 The waltz, swung so gently and delicately by the cajuns, is in constant demand.

c. *intr.* To enjoy oneself, have fun, esp. in pursuit of what is considered fashionable or in a manner free of conventional constraints; to be up to date. Also of a place, to provide lively enjoyment.

1957 N. MAILER in *Dissent* Summer 288 Still I am just one cat in a world of cool cats, and everything interesting is crazy, or at least so the Squares who do not know how to swing would say. **1966** *Reporter* 24 Mar. 22/1 Surprising nightlife. Amsterdam *swings*. **1967** *Wall St. Jrnl.* 24 Jan. 30 He has to really swing: Motor-cycle racing, free-fall parachuting, [etc.]. **1975** D. LODGE *Changing Places* ii. 59 Jane Austen and the Theory of Fiction. Professor Morris J. Zapp... 'He makes Austen swing,' was one comment. **1983** *Times* 25 Oct. 10/1 The fashion collections..are supposed to have proved..that 'London swings again'.

d. To engage in (promiscuous) sexual intercourse; *spec.* to advocate or engage in group sex or swapping sexual partners. Also, *to swing both ways*, to enjoy both heterosexual and homosexual relations. *slang.*

1964 W. & J. BREEDLOVE *Swap Clubs* iii. 73 Almost everyone in the group knows one or more couples with which they swing who were not accepted by the recruitment committee. **1970** E. M. BRECHER *Sex Researchers* ix. 251 If only one-tenth of one percent of married couples (one couple in a thousand) swing, however, the total still adds up to some 45,000 swinging American couples. **1972** J. G. VERMANDEL *Last seen in Samarra* xxii. 153 As for the mystery that still surrounded Robin Aseltine's death, the police had picked up and questioned several former girl and boy friends, Robin having been found to swing both ways.

e. Of a party: to go with a swing (see *SWING *sb.*^{2} 6 f). *colloq.*

[**1963** *Amer. Speech* XXXVIII. 171 [Kansas University slang.] A particularly rough and noisy party..*swinger*.] **1975** D. LODGE *Changing Places* ii. 87 The party's beginning to swing. **1978** J. ANDERSON *Angel of Death* xii. 128 They were trying hard to make the party swing, but.. there seemed a forced air about the revelry.

swing-. Add: **1. c.** With advbs. forming attrib. phrases in sense 'that swings in the direction specified', as (hyphened) *swing-away, -down, -out.* See also sense 2 a below.

1965 *Wireless World* July 3 (Advt.), Swing-away, lift-off mounting (optional). **1949** *Archit. Rev.* CV. 241 A slightly less conventional example is the swing-down metal wash-basin with which the Viking is equipped. **1977** *Times* 29 Apr. 13/4 There are 156 A class cabins each with two sofa beds, swing-down bunks, lavatory and shower. **1967** K. M. SMITH *Insect Virol.* v. 103 In this gradient a discrete band was obtained after 60 minutes centrifugation in a swing-out (Spinco SW25) head at 24,000 rpm.

2. a. swing-back, (*b*) the backward swing of a body, weapon, etc.; back-swing; (*c*) a movement of reaction to(wards) a previous state; (*d*) applied *attrib.* to a style of coat or jacket cut to swing as the wearer moves; **swingball,** a game of table-skittles in which a suspended ball is thrown to hit the skittles on the return pass; also (*U.S.*), a larger-scale version of the game played in a doorway; see also quot. 1980; **swing bowler** *Cricket*, a bowler who makes the ball swing; also **swing bowling; swing-by,** a change of course made by a spacecraft by using a planet's gravitational field (see also quot. 1967); **swing-coat,** a fashionable coat cut to give a swinging motion when the wearer moves (cf. *swing-back* (*d*) above); **swing-gate** (earlier N.Z. example); **swing hand** *Bridge*, a hand which proves to be decisive for a team in the overall result of a rubber or match; **swing label** = *swing ticket* below; **swing man,** (*a*) *U.S.* = SWING *sb.*^{2} 12 e; (*b*) *Mus.*, a jazz musician who plays swing music (see also sense 2 d below); (*c*) *U.S. Sports slang*, a versatile player who can play effectively in different positions; (*d*) *slang*, a drug pedlar; **swing mirror** = *swing-glass*; **swing needle,** a sewing-machine needle which can move sideways to the direction of work to accommodate another needle or to form zigzag or patterned stitches; freq. *attrib.*; **swing-over,** a change to a contrastive state or opinion; **swing pass** *U.S. Football*, a short pass to a back running to the outside; **swing room** *U.S.*, a room in which employees may relax while (temporarily) off duty; **swing-round,** a striking change or reversal of direction (in quots., *fig.*); **swing set,** a set of children's play equipment, including one or more swings, supported by a rigid frame; **swing-shift** *U.S.*, a work shift between the standard day and night shifts, esp. from the afternoon to late evening; applied to other irregular shift arrangements; **swing-stoppered** *a.*, applied to a bottle whose stopper is clamped in place by a wire mechanism about the bottle-neck; **swing-tail,** restrict † to sense in Dict. and add: (*b*) *Aeronaut.*, a hinged rear section of a fuselage which can be swung to one side to facilitate the loading of large items of cargo; freq. *attrib.*; **swing-ticket,** a tag or label which carries a guarantee or other information, and hangs loosely from the article to which it is attached; **swing vote(r)** *U.S.*, the independent vote(r) that often decisively influences the result of a poll; also, a casting voter; **swing wing,** an aircraft wing whose sweep can be increased at high speeds to delay the development of shock waves and decreased at low speeds to provide more lift; freq. *attrib.* (with hyphen); cf. **variable sweep*.

1890 H. G. HUTCHINSON et al. *Golf* iv. 98 It is an effect of stretching after an artificially long swing back. **1924** *Public Opinion* 4 July 16/2 The swing-back to biblicism appears as an accomplished fact. **1945** *N.Y. Times* 12 Aug. IV. 6/2 Legislation will be necessary to tide over those men who are unemployed while the gigantic swing-back to peacetime industry is being accomplished. **1952** W. CUNNINGTON *Eng. Women's Clothes in Present Cent.* viii. 280 Coats were swing-back, flared or tiered [in 1945]. **1972** *Daily Tel.* 1 Mar. 5/1 The firm has charted a remarkable swing-back among its African personnel from rejection to timid acceptance. **1973** *Country Life* 15 Mar. 723/1 Swing-back jacket in showerproof Terylene/cotton twill. **1935** *Popular Mechanics* Dec. 925 (*heading*) 'Swing Ball' table top action game of skill. **1955** D. A. HINDMAN *Handbk. Indoor Games & Stunts* xii. 188 *Swingball bowling*... The player takes the ball and carries it any desired distance away from the doorway. **1977** *Sci. Amer.* Dec. 39/2 They range from simple board games [to].. indoor versions of miniature golf, swingball bowling (the ball is tethered to the top of a doorframe). **1980** *Trade Marks Jrnl.* 23 July 1316/2 Swingball... Games (other than ordinary playing cards) and playthings incorporating the use of balls. Dunlop Holdings Limited,..London, SW1Y 6PX; a holding company. **1958** *Times* 11 Nov. 15/2 He made an uppish defensive shot against medium-paced swing bowler, Strauss. **1953** *Times* 27 Aug. 3/7 Wind tunnel experiments at this university have shown that spin plays only a secondary part in swing bowling. **1963** A. ROSS *Australia* 63 iii. 87 This was swing bowling of the kind Statham does not often manage. **1967** *Britannica Bk. of Year 1966* 804/3 *Swing-by*, an interplanetary mission in which a space vehicle utilizes the gravitational field of a planet near which it passes for changing course (a *swing-by* through the gravitational field of Venus on the way to Mars). **1970** *Nature* 1 Aug. 434/2 The next opportunity to make a similar swing-by flight to Mercury will not occur until 1982. **1935** *Times* 4 Nov. 7/1 There is a new flat swing-coat in shower-proof Llamavel curl. **1939** *Country Life* 11 Feb. p. xxxvii/2 (Advt.), The three-quarter 'swing' coat of dyed baby sealskin obtainable in black, brown, or cafe. **1878** E. S. ELWELL *Boy Colonists* 214 This was something like a 'race' for drafting sheep, with a swing gate. **1960** T. REESE *Play Bridge with Reese* x. 41 Playing in a team-of-four match against strong opponents, I pick up this swing hand. **1968** J. IRONSIDE *Fashion Alphabet* 100 *Swing label*, the cardboard label hanging from a garment giving name of manufacturer, size, price, etc. **1903** A. ADAMS *Log of Cowboy* iii. 20 The herd trailed along behind the leaders..guarded by outriders, known as swing men. **1936** *Delineator* CXXIX. 10/3 There have been many other great *swingmen* whose names have become tradition. **1957** D. HAGUE in S. Traill *Concerning Jazz* 123 Many years ago the best alto player among the swingmen was Johnny Hodges—and to-day he is still tops! **1969** *Daily Progress* (Charlottesville, Va.) 6 Aug. A6/1 As the swingman last year the former Lane High All-Stater was used as a replacement for either of the Browns' starting offensive guards. **1972** T. A. BULMAN *Kamloops Cattlemen* xii. 72 Another rider, called the swing man, cut in about the middle of the bunch. **1972** *Sunday Sun* (Brisbane) 2 July 14/2 Now he [drug supplier] is called the connection, the bagman, the swing man, the dealer. **1973** J. WAINWRIGHT *High-Class Kill* 157 Tell us about all the dope he pushed... He was taking from *his* swingman. **1930** *Heal & Son Catal.: Matter of Taste in Furnit.* (1972) 11 Toilet Table with two drawers and oval swing mirror. **1978** *Cornish Guardian* 27 Apr. 10/4 (Advt.), Mahogany swing mirror. **1954** M. B. PICKEN *Singer Sewing Bk.* (ed. 2) 246/1 The twin needles provided for the Swing Needle Machine allow you to do beautiful double stitching, using two different-colour threads. **1959** R. P. GILES *Needlework* i. 6 The more recently introduced swing needle machines..are able to stitch automatically many embroidery stitches. **1961** *Observer* 28 May 33/1 Swing-needle (zigzag) machines ..range from £50 upwards. **1927** *Daily Tel.* 1 Nov. 13/5 Harden was twitted with the violence of his swing-over. **1977** G. CLARK *World Prehistory* (ed. 3) II. 56 The most striking change in respect of animals was a swing-over from heavy emphasis on gazelle to sheep and goat. **1960** *Washington Post* 3 Jan. C4/2 They prattle knowingly of splits and gaps,..of flare passes and swing passes. **1979** *Tucson* (Arizona) *Citizen* 20 Sept. 1D/1 The hardest thing on a linebacker is the swing pass. **1917** D. C. Roper *U.S. Post Office* xxv. 291 The modern 'swing' rooms of many large post offices..have been made ideal club rooms. **1973** 'E. McBain' *Hail to Chief* iv. 56 Patrolman Gomez..was watching television in the swing room on the ground floor. **1940** W. Empson *Gathering Storm* 71 The swing-round of the Trade Unions to rearmament. **1959** *Times* 16 Jan. 14/6 (*heading*) Swing-round in Paris markets. **1951** *Sears, Roebuck & Co. Catal.* Spring and Summer 958/2, 3-Stunt Swing Set. Non-tilt enameled wood swing seat..wood trapeze bar..metal trapeze rings, wood grips. **1978** J. Irving. *World according to Garp* xii. 230, I can travel across lawns, over porches, through swing sets. **1943** *Sun* (Baltimore) 26 Mar. 1/5 (*heading*) Swing-shift workers cross border for 15-cent highballs after California bars close. **1974** *Spartanburg* (S. Carolina) *Herald-Jrnl.* 20 Apr. B5/1 (Advt.), Baby sitter..needed for swing shift in Pacolet area. [**1957** *Encycl. Brit.* I. 225/1 Swing lever stoppered bottles.] **1972** E. Fletcher *Bottle Collecting* iii. 51 In 1894, swing-stoppered bottles were introduced for sterilized milk. **1959** *Wall St. Jrnl.* (Eastern ed.) 20 Feb. 12/2 Feature of the cargo planes is a 'swing tail', which permits the whole aft section of the fuselage to swing aside. *Ibid.*, Although there are other aircraft with rear-loading doors, the flight characteristics of the new swing-tail planes would be considerably better. **1963** *Economist* 21 Sept. 1013/2 The swing-tail version of the Bristol Britannia. **1980** *Jane's Encycl. Aviation* II. 370/1 Commercial Forty-Fours.. were built with swing-tails for straight-in loading as CL-44D4s. **1962** *B.S.I. News* July 10/1 Many of the chromium-plated goods on show carried the now familiar swing ticket indicating that the chrome conformed to British Standard. **1972** *Times* 27 June 11/4 Size and price can both go on swing tickets. **1970** *New Yorker* 12 Dec. 63/3 Sellers told him that Fong was one of the swing votes. **1978** H. Kemelman *Thursday Rabbi walked Out* (1979) iii. 21 Blair and Mitchener will vote for it... So that leaves Cunningham. He's the swing vote. **1966** *Economist* 5 Mar. 898/2 He is expected to join Mr Daane as a 'swing voter', leaving Mr Martin with only one conservative colleague. **1965** *New Scientist* 22 Apr. 217/1 One new project in view is the development..of a swing-wing aeroplane. **1976** *Farnborough Internat. Exhibition* (Official Programme) 8/1 Swing wings..permit Tornado to achieve its best performance in all sections of its flight. **1978** G. Vidal *Kalki* i. 5, I persuaded Boeing to drop the variable-geometry (or swing-wing) aircraft in favor of the fixed delta-shaped wing and tail plane.

d. *Mus.* The jazz sense of 'swing' (*swing *sb.*^{2} 10 b) used *attrib.* and in *Comb.*, as *swing band, craze, music*, etc.; *swing-minded* adj.

1933 *Fortune* Aug. 90/3 The best white ensembles usually compromise by playing both *sweet* and *hot* music. This is true of Ben Pollack's excellent *swing* band of Chicago (with Trombonist Teagarden and other crack soloists). **1935** (*title*) Swing music. **1937** L. Armstrong *Swing that Music* xiv. 117 People were beginning now to understand more clearly the difference between a swing orchestra and an ordinary popular orchestra. **1938** *Sat. Even. Post* 7 May 112/2 If any one musician brought about the Swing Age, it is Benny Goodman. **1939** A. Huxley *After Many a Summer* I. xiii. 178 Real romance, like in the pictures, with moonlight, and swing music. **1941** *Melody Maker* 12 July 4/2 Which would you say is the most swing-minded provincial town in the British Isles? **1945** Koestler *Twilight Bar* 11 The swing-band at the Ritz is also on strike, so they play for them. **1947** R. de Toledano *Frontiers of Jazz* v. 68 A combination of events set off the 'swing' craze. **1949** L. Feather *Inside Be-Bop* i. 3 The swing era brought jazz to the attention of the public in the 1930's. **1952** A. Lomax *Mister Jelly Roll* 292 Jelly Roll tried to compete with the swing bands. **1956** M. Stearns *Story of Jazz* (1957) xvi. 189 It was this style, made famous by Benny Goodman and brought to a peak by the Count Basie Band, that characterized the Swing Era. **1968** *Blues Unlimited* Nov. 23 It features a superb vocal with encouragement from someone in the band in the true hot western swing tradition of Bob Wills. **1976** A. Murray *Stomping Blues* vii. 107 (*caption*) The Savoy, the most famous ballroom in Harlem during the so-called Swing Era.

3. In *attrib.* or semi-adjectival use.

a. The electoral sense of 'swing' (*swing *sb.*^{2} 8 h) applied to a marginal constituency, state, etc.

1964 *Economist* 4 July 44/2 That interesting phenomenon, a 'swing' state. **1974** *Times* 2 Mar. 4/5 The two major parties have very efficient organizations, as would be expected in a swing constituency. **1980** *Washington Post* 19 Oct. A5/5 An effort to improve his chances of carrying the 26 electoral votes of that swing state.

b. Designating a nation that has the capacity to adjust oil production according to demand; also applied to the oil itself.

1973 *Synagogue Light* Sept. 76/2 U.S. Treasury Deputy Secretary William H. Simon has identified Saudi Arabia as the 'swing nation', capable of a huge increase in its oil production. **1975** *Offshore Engineer* Sept. 24/1 Acting as a 'swing producer', Saudi Arabia has absorbed the biggest drop in oil income. **1980** *Times* 5 Feb. 18/2 Oil is the present 'swing' or 'balancing' fuel. Its flexibility of marketing and supply allows it to be easily taken up or cut back according to demand.

swinger^{3}. Add: **I. 2. b.** See also *jim-swinger.

c. *Cricket.* A ball that swings in the air on delivery; an inswinger or outswinger.

1920 Lyttelton & Wilson in P. F. Warner *Cricket* (ed. 2) 266 He bowled a swinger, an off break, and a fast ball, which went with his arm. **1948** *Sporting Mirror* 21 May 2/3 Heath bowls medium fast swingers and opens the bowling. **1966** [see *cutter *sb.*^{1} 5 b]. **1977** *Listener* 11 Aug. 182/4 Waving at a late swinger outside the off stump.

d. A gramophone record with an eccentric spindle-hole.

1935 H. C. Bryson *Gramophone Record* vi. 147 The central hole has to be made perfectly true, for were it the least eccentric with the grooves, the records produced from it would be swingers. **1961** E. N. Bradley *Records & Gramophone Equipment* i. 22 The most likely cause of wow is a swinger—a record whose spindle hole is not exactly central and so turns eccentrically as a result. **1981** *Hi-Fi Answers* Apr. 74/2 If you press the grooves off-centre relative to the centre hole it sounds terrible. A swinger that would just be okay at 33 will not do at 45.

2*. a. *Mus.* A musician who plays jazz with swing.

1934 in B. Rust *Jazz Records 1897–1942* (1969) 1516 (recording artists) The Six Swingers. **1958** K. Goodwin in P. Gammond *Decca Bk. of Jazz* xiii. 151 There are some *real* swingers on the coast, among them a young coloured pianist—Hampton Hawes. **1962** *Sunday Times* (Colour Suppl.) 10 June 3 Unexcelled as a technician and swinger, Baker is said by some to lack a musical heart and personality of his own.

b. A lively person who keeps up with what is considered fashionable; one who is 'with it'.

1965 P. Kael *I lost it at Movies* 19, I think in treating indiscriminateness as a *value*, she has become a real swinger. **1966** *Economist* 11 June 1240/3 No attempt has been made to attract the wilder London 'swingers' of *Time*-fame. **1967** H. Kemelman *Nine Mile Walk* (1968) 149 In the parlance of the undergraduate..Professor John Baxter Bowman..was a swinger, with a taste and interest in clothes not usually associated with the professoriat. **1972** J. Gores *Dead Skip* (1973) xiv. 96 The Dukum Inn.. looked..like an aging swinger getting up in the morning with his teeth still in the water glass. **1977** M. French *Women's Room* (1978) i. 14 I'd meet some middle-aged swinger with a deep tan and sideburns.

c. A person who is sexually promiscuous; *spec.* one who advocates or engages in group sex or the swapping of sexual partners. Also, a homosexual. *slang.*

1964 W. & J. Breedlove *Swap Clubs* i. 37 We will on occasion utilize 'swinger' and 'swinging' to describe the advocate of sexual partner exchange and the exercising of that practice. **1966** T. Pynchon *Crying of Lot 49* vi. 147, I had a date last night with an eight-year-old, And she's a swinger just like me. **1972** G. Baxt *Burning Sappho* iii. 47 Flo pondered the invitation... 'You sure you ain't no swinger?' 'I assure you my dear,' said Lady Molly..'I am *not* a womaniser.' **1977** *Time* 4 July 38/2 Some operators have converted nudist colonies into 'swinger camps', the new rural retreats for the randy.

swinging, *vbl. sb.* Add: **5.** Indulgence in sexual promiscuity; *spec.* engaging in group sex or the exchanging of sexual partners. *slang.*

1964 [see *swinger^{3} 2* c]. **1967** W. & J. Breedlove *Swinging Set* v. 65 The act of prostitution is separate from 'swinging'. **1970** E. M. Brecher *Sex Researchers* ix. 250 What happened during the 1960's was that group sex in public—swinging—emerged from the brothels and became an established though minor feature of American urban and suburban life. **1973** *New Society* 24 May 437/1 'Swinging' is extra-marital sex by both spouses, at the same time and usually in the same place.

swinging, *ppl. a.* Add: **3. b.** *Mus.* Applied to a musician who plays jazz with swing; also, to the music itself. Cf. *swing *sb.*^{2} 10 b.

1955 in A. J. McCarthy *Jazzbook 1955* 31 It has been satisfying to witness the renewed success within the past two years of Count Basie's orchestra, as the swinging spearhead of coloured jazz. **1958** K. Goodwin in P. Gammond *Decca Bk. of Jazz* xiii. 153 Mel Lewis—.. easily the most swinging drummer ever to work with the Kenton band. **1956** B. Holiday *Lady sings Blues* (1973) xxiii. 189 They were the swingingest cats I ever heard.

c. Uninhibited, ignoring conventions; lively and up to date: applied to persons, places (*swinging London*), etc., and *spec.* to the 1960s (*swinging Sixties*). Also, as a general term of approval: fine, splendid, 'great' (temporarily contrasted with *dodgy*). *colloq.*

1958 *Publ. Amer. Dial. Soc.* xxx. 47 *Swingin'*, the highest term of approval. May be applied to anything a jazzman likes, or any person. **1959** *Manch. Guardian* 25 June 8/7 [She] informed him that she wants a large place 'in a swinging part of town'..so he is looking around in Chelsea and Knightsbridge. **1962** J. Baldwin *Another Country* (1963) II. iii. 299 'You feeling all right?'..'He's going to feel just swinging.' **1964** N. Vaughan in *T.V. World* 24 Sept. 48 When people ask me how I feel about the months ahead, I tell them: 'Sometimes it's a bit dodgy, but most of the time it's swinging!' **1965** *Weekend Telegraph* 16 Apr. 12/2 Diana Vreeland..editor of *Vogue* ..has said simply 'London is the most swinging city in the world at the moment'. **1966** *Time* 15 Apr. 11/3, I know this world, this swinging London... But I wouldn't describe myself as a swinger. **1967** *Listener* 19 Jan. 107/1 He does not fit into the *Zeitgeist* of the swinging 'sixties. **1967** F. Mullally *Prizewinner* iii. 41 The swinging London Percy had read so much about. **1971** H. Wilson *Labour Govt.* xxxvii. 766 The press publicized what they called the new swinging style of the Downing Street receptions. **1976** P. Cave *High Flying Birds* iii. 25 Young people from all over the world—draft-evading Americans, poker-faced Germans, swinging Swedes and the comic-clown Dutch. **1980** M. Sellers *Leonardo & Others* x. 56 Zuleika lived life to the full. She was a product of the swinging sixties. **1982** S. Brett *Murder Unprompted* v. 51 The British film industry..was committed to making zany films about Swinging London.

d. Of or pertaining to one who engages in promiscuous sexual activity (esp. group sex or the swapping of sexual partners). *slang.*

1964 W. & J. Breedlove *Swap Clubs* ii. 43 A 'swinging couple'. **1978** *Bulletin* (Sydney) 11 Apr. 6/2 'Swinging couples' are no longer addicted to square dancing but to the less innocuous pastime of wife-swapping.

4. swinging bridge, (*b*) (earlier Amer. example).

1708 in *Rec. Early Hist. Boston* (Boston Registry Dept.) (1883) VIII. 52 The way leading from Madam Butlers Corner..to the Swinging Bridg.

swingle (swi·ŋg'l), *sb.*^{2} *N. Amer. slang.* [Blend of *swinging *ppl. a.* 3 c, d and *single *sb.* 5 c.] A 'swinging' single or unaccompanied person; *spec.* one in search of a sexual partner.

1967 *Glamour* June 82 Hilton Swingles Week. We created a week for people like you: Swinging Singles. **1973** *Newsweek* 16 July 53 The sheer number of singles, meshed with the media's seductive imagery (singles who swing are jauntily dubbed 'swingles'), is gradually revising society's view of its unwed members. **1978** *Chatelaine* (Canada) Dec. 106/3 When she went out with her women friends for an evening, their husbands felt she was luring their wives into swingles bars and white slavery.

swingometer (swiŋǫ·mĭtəɹ). [f. *swing *sb.*^{2} 8 h + -ometer, after *barometer*, etc.] A device consisting of a dial with a movable pointer, used to demonstrate (esp. on television) how a likely or observable 'swing' should influence the outcome of an election. Also *transf.* and *fig.*

1965 *B.B.C. Handbk.* 36 (*caption*) Robert McKenzie demonstrating the Swingometer. **1969** D. Widgery in Cockburn & Blackburn *Student Power* 128 Eventually the 'swingometer' which the UCL NUS Committee had installed in their Gower Street office moved slowly in favour of the ISC and the Executive. **1974** *Daily Tel.* 22 Oct. 18 After five or six results, Robert McKenzie's famous swing-ometer accurately showed what was to be in the event a majority of 40 or so for Labour over Conservative. **1978** *Sunday Times* 19 Mar. (Weekly Rev.) 37 Guardians of the social swingometer..have been drawing attention to punk rock. **1979** H. Wilson *Final Term* v. 84 This figure headed the election night screens, until the 'swing-ometer' working on the first declarations rapidly moved into a much more moderate posture.

swingster (swi·ŋstəɹ). *slang.* [f. *swing *sb.*^{2} 10 b + -ster.] = *swinger^{3} 2* a.

1937 *Nebraska State Jrnl.* (Lincoln, Nebraska) 22 Aug. CD-9/4 Swingsters got the best touch of feet-itch of the season. **1946** *Jazz Writings* 19/2 Holmes' jazz is 'grown-up' jazz—as opposed to the 'adolescent' jazz of the swingsters. **1952** B. Ulanov *Hist. Jazz in Amer.* xxii. 307 It was an old war in jazz; it had not been declared by the swingsters or the boppers.

swingy (swi·ŋi), *a. colloq.* [f. Swing *sb.*^{2} + -y^{1}.] That swings; characterized by swing. In various senses. **1.** Of music: see *swing *sb.*^{2} 10 b.

1933 *Melody Maker* 25 Nov. 3/1 (*song-title*) Swingy little thingy. **1956** E. Delaney in S. Traill *Play that Music* 54 Do you remember the Gerry Mulligan sounds?—easy, swingy and very *quiet*. **1968** *Melody Maker* 30 Nov. 22/2 The arrangements are tight and swingy. **1973** J. Wainwright *Pride of Pigs* 46 The trombonist..improvised a tidy, swingy, four-bar lead-in.

2. Of garments, esp. skirts.

1937 *Evening News* 1 Feb. 1/3 Skirts will be shorter and swingier.., in keeping with swing music. **1960** *She* Dec. 8 It's the swingiest thing! Lister 'Crimplene' in party casuals. **1981** *Times* 28 Apr. 10/6 Chic tweed suits with swingy skirts.

3. Of movement, gait, etc.

1943 J. Steinbeck *Once There was a War* (1959) 22 A band of pipers marches out in kilts, with bagpipes and drums and the swingy march of pipers. **1944** D. Burley *Handbk. Jive* 85 You bend your knees halfway and rock back and forth on your heels and toes with a swingy sway.

Swinhoe (swi·nhǫ). The name of Robert *Swinhoe* (fl. 1862–3), British consul in Taiwan, used in the possessive, as **Swinhoe's pheasant** (occas. **kaleege** [Kaleege, kalij]), to designate *Lophura swinhoei*, a brightly coloured pheasant native to Taiwan, where he first collected it in 1862. Also *ellipt.* as **Swinhoe's.**

1863 *Proc. Zool. Soc.* 119 (*heading*) Swinhoe's pheasant. **1921** W. Beebe *Monogr. Pheasants* II. 78 We have no definite information as to the distribution of Swinhoe's kaleege, except that it is not found near the coast of Formosa, but only in the..interior. *Ibid.* 80 The price for the first pair of Swinhoes was between four and five thousand francs. **1951** J. Delacour *Pheasants of World* 162 Swinhoe's Pheasant has developed an interesting mutation in captivity. **1965** P. Wayre *Wind in Reeds* xv. 212 The male Swinhoe's is..magnificent.., his neck, underparts, rump and outer tail feathers being a dark metallic blue; a white crest tops his head and there is a white patch on his back; his scapulars are bright maroon. **1973** *Sci. Amer.* June 40/1 The birds are Swinhoe's pheasant, the mikado pheasant, [etc.].

swipe, *sb.*^{2} Add: **II.** [Miscellaneous senses of uncertain affiliation.] **4.** A groom or stable-boy. *U.S. slang.*

1929 S. Anderson in *Mercury Story Bk.* 221, I had taken a job as swipe with one of the two horses Harry was campaigning. **1954** W. Faulkner *Fable* 178 He hasn't got any money... What little there might have been, that cockney swipe threw away long ago on whores and whisky.

5. An objectionable person; also, such persons considered *collect.* *slang.*

1929 D. H. Lawrence *Pansies* 138 And do you think it's my business to be handing out money to a lot of inferior swipe? **1944** J. Devanny *By Tropic Sea & Jungle* xviii. 163 Some swipe has lost the fishing lines. **1951** R. Park *Witch's Thorn* xiv. 177 His tormentors leapt off him... 'Bloody little swipes!' said Mr Mate Solivich.

6. The penis. *slang* (*U.S. Blacks*).

1967 'I. Slim' in T. Kochman *Rappin' & Stylin' Out* (1972) 389 Slim, pimping ain't no game of love, so prat 'em and keep your swipe outta 'em.

swipe, *v.* Add: **2. c.** (Earlier example.)

1851 W. Clarke in W. Bolland *Cricket Notes* vii. 148 Some would shut their eyes at a fast one, but might perchance swipe away a slow one for four.

4. For *U.S.* read *slang* (orig. *U.S.*) and add earlier and later examples.

1889 *Seattle Post-Intelligencer* 5 Dec. 8/1 'By adopting this method,' said the merchant, 'we can stand back and laugh at their vain attempts to 'swipe' our goods.' **1936** Wodehouse *Laughing Gas* xxii. 238 You expect me, do you, not only to act as a stooge for you in front of the camera, but to sit smiling in the background while you horn in and swipe my interview. **1946** 'S. Russell' *To Bed with Grand Music* ii. 27 Is there another drink going before you swipe the lot? **1970** T. Roethke *Let.* (1970) 10 June 263 That beautiful Greek anthology you sent me some student swiped. **1982** *Verbatim* Autumn 3/1 The hero gallantly sets out to recover the item, which he does after much derring-do—climbing walls, crawling through windows, swiping addresses out of locked desk drawers.

swiping *vbl. sb.* (earlier example).

1833 in G. W. Ormerod *Ann. Teignbridge Cricket Club* (1889) 14 And when he's in the swiping mood, My stars! how Johnny works 'em!

swiper. 2. (Earlier example.)

1853 F. Gale *Public School Matches* 59 Swiper has the ball; now, if there is one ball which Swiper hits harder than any other, it is an on[-side] long hop rather wide to the leg.

swipey, *a.* (Earlier example.)

1821 P. Egan *Life in London* ii. ii. 181 If the latter are caught in any ways inclined to roosting from being swipy, the young buzzmen will make them pay dearly for the few winks they may enjoy.

swirl, *sb.* Add: **1. b.** A fairground roundabout with freely-pivoted cars drawn by a spider frame. *slang.*

1962 *Sunday Express* 4 Feb. 1/4 She had four rides on the merry-go-round, two trips on the ghost train, and rides on the 'swirl' and the dodgems. **1968** D. Braithwaite *Fairground Architecture* vi. 107 In the 1920's Savages of King's Lynn produced a ride known as the 'Womp'. This was a variant of the 'Whip'... Re-named the 'Swirl' by showmen, this ride was considerably refined by Thurston, Thurston and Lakin's Patents of 1929 and became one of the fastest rides on the fairground.

2. b. *Engin.* A circular motion imparted to the mixture entering the cylinder of an internal-combustion engine. Freq. *attrib.*

1926 *Engineering* 27 Aug. 279/1 It is possible with sleeve valve operation to provide a high degree of swirl in the cylinder, which..serves to bring the air to the fuel. **1940** C. B. Dicksee *High-Speed Compression-Ignition Engine* vii. 170 The swirl ratio, i.e. the ratio between the rate of air swirl and the rotational speed of the engine, varies in different designs. *Ibid.* The effect of the squish is..to increase the swirl already present. **1979** P. J. Bowyer *Boat Engines* ii. 48 The mixing of air and fuel is all important so that the design of the inlet and exhaust ports, as well as the combustion area, is arranged to cause phenomena such as 'squish' or swirl.

4. Special Comb.: **swirl chamber** *Engin.*, a chamber in an internal-combustion engine fashioned so as to impart a whirling motion to the mixture passing through it into the cylinder; **swirl skirt,** a skirt cut circular or with many gores, so as to swirl when the wearer walks.

1934 *Proc. Inst. Mech. Engineers* CXXVIII. 169 In some types of engine a very distinct improvement had been effected by making an additional passage from the cylinder head into the swirl chamber, so that the 'squish' was allowed to interfere..with the swirl. **1976** *Daily Tel.* 3 Nov. 12/3 The swirl chamber in the 2068cc Rekord engine is specially designed for the best mixture and combustion of the fuel. **1962** *Harper's Bazaar* Aug. 32 Dashing young suit with a swirl skirt. **1976** *Morecambe Guardian* 7 Dec., Wearing a Russian-style fur hat, boots and a warm-coloured burgundy coat with swirl skirt, the Princess was escorted..to the private dining room at Cartmel College.

swirly, *a.* Add: **2.** = Swirling *ppl. a.* 2. Also *fig.*

1912 W. R. Titterton *From Theatre to Music Hall* ii. i. 117 Viennese operetta, luscious and swirly. **1939** A. Ransome *Secret Water* xxvii. 317 The water would be a good deal higher.., and already felt swirly and strong. **1979** R. Jaffe *Class Reunion* (1980) i. ii. 38 Her favorite black taffeta dress with the swirly pleated skirt.

swish, *sb.*[1] Add: **1. c.** A rough hiss heard at each revolution of a faulty gramophone record.

1949 G. A. Briggs *Sound Reproduction* xxi. 130 A background noise of even volume..is much more tolerable than a sudden or changing sound such as the click of a damaged surface or the swish of a warped record. **1978** *Gramophone* Jan. 1307/1 Background noise can be at remarkably low levels on disc—though admittedly in only the best examples, and with an ever-present risk of warps, swishes and other annoyances.

5. A male homosexual; an effeminate man. *U.S. slang.*

1941 B. Schulberg *What makes Sammy Run?* iv. 71 If..that fat swish lets the producer know he did all the writing, you're dead. **1967** L. Forrester *Girl called Fathom* xiv. 178 'I think he's a swish.' A—what?' 'Faggot. Queer.' **1975** J. F. Burke *Death Trick* (1976) iv. 62 [He] dresses mod, and he talks like some kind of a swish.

6. *Cricket.* A rapid or careless attacking stroke. *colloq.*

1963 *Times* 25 Feb. 4/1 He resorted at last to the swish, an invitation to the disaster which presently befell him. **1977** *Daily Mirror* 15 Mar. 31/3 The striking sequence that whistled young Hookes from 36 to 56 was as follows: An enormous one-bounce slog over mid-off; a swish to long leg [etc.].

swish (swɪʃ), *a.* *colloq.* [Perh. f. Swish *int.* or *adv.* and *sb.*[1]] Smart, elegant, fashionable.

1879 *N. & Q.* 5th Ser. XI. 116 Provincialisms..in the neighbourhood of Lydford... *Bain't you swish?*=How smart you are. **1922** E. Raymond *Tell England* II. xi. 269 Really, under these conditions, the Peninsula, we felt, would be quite 'swish'. *Ibid.* xii. 273 'If I'm killed you can put those lines over me.'.. 'They are rather swish,' I murmured. **1933** Auden *Witnesses* in *Listener* 12 July (Suppl.) p. ii/1 He was born in a palace, his people were swish. **1960** *Guardian* 14 July 7/7 A party at a swish place with the best people. **1972** *Daily Tel.* (Colour Suppl.) 7 Jan. 7/1 He..is a lover of the sea, food, lilies, the Old Vic, and swish cars: he is contemplating the purchase of a £5,380 Mercedes 350SL Coupé. **1974** P. Dickinson *Poison Oracle* ii. 60 The architects..had made their name running up swish hotels in Beirut.

swish-swish: see Swish *sb.*[1] 1 b.

swishy, *a.* Add: **2.** *slang.* Characteristic of a male homosexual; effeminate. Also as *sb.*

1941 G. W. Henry *Sex Variants* II. 1177 *Swishy.* The reference is to the peculiarly effeminate walk of many male homosexuals. **1954** C. Isherwood *World in Evening* ii. 125 You thought it meant a swishy little boy with peroxided hair, dressed in a picture hat and a feather boa, pretending to be Marlene Dietrich? Yes, in queer circles, they call *that* camping. **1959** J. Osborne *World of Paul Slickey* i. v. 48 He's a cad... He's contrary, he's a swishy. **1968** *Globe & Mail Mag.* (Toronto) 13 Jan. 6/3 Though they ordinarily despise swishy gestures, even masculine homosexuals will sometimes camp (exhibit feminine mannerisms).

Swiss, *sb.* and *a.* **A.** *sb.* **2.** For *rare*$^{-0}$ read *rare* and add later example.

1949 J. C. Herold *Swiss without Halos* i. 15 There are several popular misconceptions concerning the language situation in Switzerland. Some believe that the Swiss speak a language called Swiss. **1972** L. P. Johnson in M. Pasley *Germany* i. 19 Alsatian, Swabian and Swiss are forms of Alemannic.

3. Short for *Swiss muslin.* Freq. *dotted Swiss.*

1895 *Montgomery Ward Catal.* Spring & Summer 19/1 Imported Curtain Swiss, white with woven coin spots. **1897** *Sears, Roebuck Catal.* 214/1 *Shirt*.. With wide pleated puff bosom of snow white dotted Swiss. **1909** *Public Ledger* (Philadelphia) 24 June 5/7, 50c. for 75c. to $1. Dressing Sacques: Lawns and Swisses. **1924** C. E. Mulford *Rustlers' Valley* vi. 68 He thought he could make out an oval face drawing back from the dotted Swiss. **1948** E. B. White *Let.* June (1976) 294 Mrs. Dow has just entered this room bearing fresh dotted Swiss curtains. **1978** J. Updike *Coup* (1979) iv. 157 An overheated room with..dotted Swiss curtains.

4. A tournament, usu. of bridge or chess, played in accordance with the Swiss system (see sense 1 b of the adj. below).

1953 *British Chess Federation Year Bk.* 1951–52 150 Do not expect the Swiss to do more than it is capable of doing. **1965** *Listener* 29 Apr. 651/2 It is usual, for publicity purposes, to pair the favourite with one of the local hopes in the first round of a Swiss. **1975** *Games & Puzzles* June 4/2 A 5-round Swiss would make an excellent final.

B. *adj.* **1. a.** Also *Swiss-French, -German* (later examples) adjs. and sbs., (designating) the dialect of French or German spoken in Switzerland, or a speaker of this. Cf. *French-Swiss, German-Swiss* at first element in Suppl.

1941 M. F. K. Fisher in *As they Were* (1983) 58 She.. stood close against the stone, saying, 'Oh, you are adorable, adorable'..in..Swiss-French. **1961** L. F. Brosnahan *Sounds of Lang.* vii. 166 [pf,ts] and [kx] are still almost exclusively characteristic of High German, the former two in the standard language, the last confined to a few of the Swiss-German dialects. **1964** M. A. K. Halliday et al. *Linguistic Sciences* 83 Germanic speakers in Switzerland regard themselves..as speaking a distinct 'Swiss-German'. **1969** R. Petrie *Despatch of Dove* i. i. 19 Her French was fluent, without the savoyard singsong you could so often detect in Swiss-French. **1970** *Guardian* 2 June 15/4 Mr Schwarzenbach is a Swiss-German. **1979** T. Barling *Olympic Sleeper* i. 17 Her accent could have been Swiss-French.

b. Designating a system of organizing tournaments, usu. of bridge or chess, under which each player or team is matched, in each round except the first, against an opponent with a similar score, but no two opponents may meet more than once.

1953 *Brit. Chess Federation Year Bk.* 1951–52 150 The Swiss system in the last few years..has become increasingly popular. **1964** Frey & Truscott *Official Encycl. Bridge* 599/1 *Swiss system* (for multi-session team-of-four events), a method which has been used successfully for many years in major chess tournaments. When insufficient time is available for a complete round robin, a partial round robin is played. **1965** *Listener* 29 Apr. 651/1 The most popular method of deciding a large tournament is now the Swiss system, a hybrid of the conventional all-play-all event and a knock-out. **1973** *Jewish Chron.* 19 Jan. 43/2 This is the first time the English Bridge Union have held a 'Swiss' teams event.

2. *Swiss chalet, clock, franc, lace* (earlier example), *milk* (earlier example), *muslin* (earlier examples), *watch*; **Swiss bank,** a bank in Switzerland, often chosen by international clients, whose anonymity and security are preserved by a system of numbered accounts (see *numbered *ppl. a.* 2); also **Swiss banker, banking; Swiss chard** = *silver beet* s.v. *silver *sb.* and *a.* 21 e; **Swiss cottage,** a chalet; hence, a type of tent; **Swiss cream,** a type of trifle; **Swiss file** (see quot. 1964); **Swiss Itch** *U.S. slang* (see quot. 1967); **Swiss steak** *U.S.*, a steak (usu. round) cooked by dipping in flour, pounding and braising, and served with vegetables; hence, a steak (usu. a less tender cut) suitable for cooking in this way.

1949 M. Cranston *Introd. Switzerland* v. 54 To have one's money in a Swiss bank is to have it somewhere secure against wars and revolutions. *Ibid.* Capital flowed into Switzerland during the two decades between the wars, and Swiss bankers were able to take advantage of this. **1962** Sayers & Linder in R. S. Sayers *Banking in Western Europe* 188 The Swiss banker does not regard bonds as a really attractive use of resources. **1981** P. O'Donnell *Xanadu Talisman* ix. 187 Your Swiss banker telephones confirmation of receipt. **1982** D. Wiltse *Wedding Guest* xvi. 215 The reputation of the entire Swiss banking community, depends on reliability in following procedures the client stipulates. **1879** I. L. Bird *Lady's Life in Rocky Mts.* v. 58 A small house, which bore a delightful resemblance to a Swiss châlet. **1970** 'D. Halliday' *Dolly & Cookie Bird* iii. 33 The story..about Diana doing her Swiss chalet housekeeping last winter. [**1731** P. Miller *Gardeners Dict.* s.v. *Beet*, The Swiss or Chard Beet.] **1832** Swiss chard [see Chard[2]]. **1900** L. H. Bailey *Cycl. Amer. Hort.* I. 289/1 This vegetable is also known as Sea-kale Beet and Swiss Chard. **1950** *N.Z. Jrnl. Agric.* Jan. 10/1 Silver beet also called Swiss chard and sea kale beet is grown for its foliage. **1980** *Times* 23 June 16/5 The Swiss chard, a spinach-like green, was developing brown dry spots on the leaves. **1897** M. H. Kingsley *Trav. W. Africa* i. 16 Manchester cottons and shawls, Swiss clocks, and.. vividly coloured china. **1982** R. Ludlum *Parsifal Mosaic* xix. 306 'Pretty punctual, huh?' 'Like a Swiss clock.' **1820** M. Wilmot *Let.* 1 Aug. (1935) 75 A beautiful Swiss Cottage, built in the most correct manner. **1884** T. H. Lewin *Fly on Wheel* iv. 117 The 'Swiss cottage' tent, on which I decided [in 1862], as it had the advantage of being divisible into two compartments, with, in addition, a small bathing-room, and large outer flaps which served as shelter for my servants. **1968** *Sat. Rev.* (U.S.) 27 July 40/1 Take the omnibus..to the Swiss Cottage—the play-chalet which Prince Albert designed for his children. **1971** A. D. Gorwala *Queen of Beauty* 70 In the snug well-lighted Swiss Cottage tent that was his itinerant home and office for weeks on end while on tour. *Ibid.* 77 There were quite a number of places at which the old Swiss Cottage proved useful. **1845** E. Acton *Mod. Cookery* xx. 527 (*heading*) Swiss cream, or trifle. (Very good.) **1861** Mrs. Beeton *Bk. Househ. Managem.* 748 *Swiss cream*.. ¼lb. of macaroons or 6 small sponge-cakes, sherry, 1 pint of cream, 5 oz. of lump sugar, 2 large tablespoonfuls of arrowroot, the rind of 1 lemon, the juice of ½ lemon, 3 tablespoonfuls of milk. **1903** Joyce *Let.* 26 Feb. (1966) II. 31 Today for dejeuner I had some cold ham, bread and butter, Swiss cream with sugar. **1960** E. L. Delmar-Morgan *Cruising Yacht Equipment & Navigation* xiv. 163 The Swiss files are most useful for repair jobs. **1964** S. Crawford *Basic Engin. Processes* i. 8 Needle files or Swiss files, small fine-cut files of various cross-sections, used for instrument work and in the match-making industry. **1934** Webster, Swiss franc. **1938** M. Muggeridge *In Valley* ix. 62, I wrote a cheque for twenty Swiss francs. **1973** 'G. Black' *Bitter Tea* i. 11 She had just made quite a killing..and had invested her take in Swiss francs. **1959** *Life* 7 Dec. 51/1 The technique..was ..old stuff to mature Americans who in Prohibition days had used it, complete with salt, as the safe way to take bathtub gin, then called 'Swiss Itch'. **1967** *Amer. N. & Q.* June 152/1 *'Swiss Hitch'*.., I believe the correct form is Swiss Itch, and I suspect that there is more than one recipe, but I have always heard the term applied to the process by which one places a pinch of salt on the back of the hand, then licks it off, and takes immediately a jigger of tequila, and follows *that* by immediately biting into a segment or a slice of lime. **1865** *Reading Industr. Exhib. Catal.* in *Reading Mercury* (1968) 17 Aug. 11 Swiss lace, tambour muslin, leno and every description of curtain materials. **1889** *Girl's Own Paper* Summer No. 13/1 A small tin, which everyone supposed was Swiss milk, but which proved to be a shilling tin of cream. **1832** T. S. Fay *Dreams & Reveries* I. 155 If I had anything to say about bobbinet or Swiss muslin collars, I should at least wait till he had reached some passage not particularly remarkable for beauty. **1932** E. Craig *Cooking with Elizabeth Craig* 175 Swiss Steak... Take a..2

pound slice of steak. Sprinkle thickly with flour. Pound. . . Brown steak on both sides. **1947** L. P. DE GOUY *Gold Cookery Bk.* vi. 345 Swiss Steak. The original name of this recipe was 'Schmor Braten.' It is three centuries old. **1973** *Black Panther* 12 May 10/1 Safeway was charged with . . mislabeling swiss steaks as round steak for an extra profit of ten cents per pound. **1885** C. M. YONGE *Two Sides of Shield* I. iii. 28 Her mother's little Swiss watch. **1977** H. KAPLAN *Damascus Cover* (1978) xvi. 174 The Colonel had honed the movements of the two Israeli agents with the precision of a Swiss watch.

Swiss cheese. **1.** (In Dict. s.v. SWISS *a.* 2.)

2. *fig.*, with reference to the pitted or honeycombed structure of some varieties of Swiss cheese. Freq. *attrib.*

1924 NOVAK & MARTZLOFF in *Amer. Jrnl. Obstetrics & Gynecol.* VIII. 387 We are accustomed to speak of the endometrium as presenting a 'swiss cheese' pattern in these cases. *Ibid.* 409 The glands are of the 'swiss cheese' pattern, large dilated glands being found side by side with glands which are small and narrow. **1929** HALL & NILES *One Man's War* i. 5 Passing out of the up-rush, I dropped into what was then known as a Swiss cheese section of air. **1949** *Bull. Geol. Soc. Amer.* LX. 1290/1 Collapsed pumice fragments, usually less resistant than the matrix, weather to give the rock a Swiss-cheese appearance. **1968** *Nature* 10 Feb. 513/2 Such a universe can be simulated by a 'swiss cheese' model in which spherical perturbations . . are distributed through space. **1970** J. R. LINCKE *Jenny was no Lady* vi. 81 The planes ran into 'Swiss-cheese' air, downdrafts . . and violent gusts. **1974** A. LURIE *War between Tates* i. 13 Their friendship now is full of Swiss-cheese holes in which sit things which cannot be discussed.

3. Special combination: **Swiss cheese plant,** an evergreen climbing plant, *Monstera deliciosa*, of the family Araceæ, native to central America and often cultivated as a house plant for the sake of its large ovate perforated leaves.

1946 M. FREE *All about House Plants* xviii. 267 One of the most interesting [aroids] is the . . Swiss Cheese Plant, because of the holes naturally formed in the much-divided leaves. **1955** W. E. SHEWELL-COOPER *Pot Plants* i. 15 *Monstera deliciosa* . . is usually called the Swiss Cheese plant. **1970** *Sunday Tel.* 3 May 19/2 A variation of the 'Swiss cheese plant' has golden marking besides the familiar 'holes' in the leaves. **1981** 'J. ROSS' *Dark Blue & Dangerous* xxiii. 130 An immense Swiss Cheese plant climbed a cement pillar.

switch, *sb.* Add: **I. 3. b.** (Earlier example.)

1865 W. H. PREECE *Railway Electric Signalling* 16 The instrument which is employed to raise and lower the signal is called a 'Switch'.

d. *fig.* or in fig. contexts, esp. with reference to railway or electrical switches. *U.S. colloq.*: *asleep at the switch*, etc., negligent of or oblivious to one's responsibility, off guard.

1898 G. B. SHAW *Let.* 16 Mar. (1972) II. 16, I am very cross and incommoded . . by having to adapt myself [to a new secretary] . . . For three sentences, I feel resentful . . and quite put out. At the fourth the switch operates and I am on to the new line as if I had never dictated to anybody else. **1906** H. GREEN *At Actors' Boarding House* 368 Snow . . awoke the startled Williams, asleep at the switch. **1932** W. FAULKNER *Light in August* viii. 161 Mind and body as if on the same switch, believing that he had seen a movement among the shadows. **1958** *Observer* 19 Oct. 18/4 [The television play], though a bit slow off the switch, scored well over half-marks for sincerity and realism. **1966** C. ACHEBE *Man of People* iv. 51 We must not let up. We just must not be caught sleeping on the switch again.

e. *Computers.* A program instruction that selects one or other of a number of possible paths according to the way it is set.

1951 M. V. WILKES et al. *Preparation of Programs for Electronic Digital Computer* 167 Numbers at one end of a permitted range can be detected by adding a constant and testing the sign, and then the result of the discrimination may be used to operate a multiway switch. **1962** R. S. LEDLEY *Programming & utilizing Digital Computers* vi. 227 The switch designator is of the form NAME[N] where NAME is the name of the switch corresponding to the switch declaration and N is an integer telling which label of the switch declaration to use. **1970** O. DOPPING *Computers & Data Processing* v. 89 A switch can consist of a branch instruction, the address part of which can be altered by the program.

4. (Earlier U.S. example.)

1870 L. M. ALCOTT *Old-Fashioned Girl* xi. 223 So much hair of her own, that she never patronized either rats, mice, waterfalls, switches, or puff combs.

7*. **a.** A change from one state or course to another; an alteration of position, policy, etc.

1920 ADE *Hand-Made Fables* 27 A switch had to be made. The Wholesaler . . wished him on to the Banker. **1941** *News Rev.* 14 Aug. 4/2 The Soviet's entry into the war against Nazi Germany meant a switch in the Communist Party's home policy as well as its foreign outlook. **1951** M. McLUHAN *Mech. Bride* (1967) 151/2 In the space of six months it recently shifted a large section of its enterprises from murder to love comics. The combined attacks of Dr. Frederic Wertham, Mr. G. Legman, and others suggested the advisability of a partial switch from Death to Love. **1960** *Economist* 15 Oct. 260/2 Large-scale cultivation of wheat in the new areas would make possible a switch to industrial crops in the older agricultural parts. **1977** 'E. CRISPIN' *Glimpses of Moon* viii. 151 If you're thinking I could have done some sort of a switch at some stage, you can put the idea out of your mind straight away. **1981** F. HOYLE *Ice* x. 158 It is satisfactory that both of the switches, to and from an ice-age condition, can arise from the same kind of cosmogonic event.

b. *Bridge.* A change of suit either in bidding or play. Cf. sense 7 b of the vb.

1921 A. M. FOSTER *Auction Bridge* 70 The take-out or switch. **1923** [see *ASSIST *sb.* a]. **1939** N. DE V. HART *Bridge Players' Bedside Bk.* iv. 38 It was a clever switch, and at once turned the hand into a difficult problem. **1952** I. MACLEOD *Bridge is Easy Game* xii. 141 Here you dare not concede the opening trick for a Heart switch will surely defeat you. **1980** R. MARKUS *Bridge-Table Tales* vi. 19 Declarer was forced to win East's king for fear of a spade switch.

c. An exchange; *spec.* a substitution which involves criminal deception. *colloq.* and *slang.*

1935 WODEHOUSE *Luck of Bodkins* xiv. 144, I plunged into . . your state-room . . and gave the sleeping figure . . a hearty wallop . . and it was Gertrude. . . 'What's the idea? Why the switch?' **1938** F. CHESTER *Shot Full* xxv. 302 Another of Lewis's rackets was to pose as a buyer of loose diamonds, and then substitute glass for the stones. . . This form of robbery is known as 'the switch'. **1955** W. GADDIS *Recognitions* II. ii. 369 Somebody pulled the old twenty-dollar-bill switch on her, Ellery said looking up from his magazine.

III. 8. *switch box*; **switch base** (see quot. 1940); **switch-blade,** (b) a pocket knife with a blade released by pressing a button or similar device on the handle (cf. *flick-knife* s.v. *FLICK *sb.*[1] 4); in full, *switch-blade knife*; **switch cane,** a large bamboo, *Arundinaria gigantea* subsp. *tecta*, native to southern N. America; **switch dealing** *Econ.*, purchase and resale, or sale and repurchase, of a commodity in order to profit by differential values of currency; repurchase or resale through a third party; hence **switch deal, dealer; switch dollar** *Econ.* (see quots.); **switch gear,** the assembly of switching devices and associated equipment used in the generation and transmission of electric power; **switch gene** *Genetics*, a gene whose presence or absence determines whether a group of other genes is expressed; **switch-girl** *Austral.* = *switchboard girl* s.v. *SWITCHBOARD b; **switch-hitter** *U.S. Baseball*, an ambidextrous batter; also *transf.* (colloq.) in sporting and gen. contexts; *slang*, a bisexual; also **switch-hitting** *ppl. a.* and *vbl. sb.*; **switch hook** *Teleph.*, the hook or support in a telephone set which operates the circuit switch when the receiver is placed upon or removed from it; **switch-knife** = *switch-blade* (b) above; **switch-light** *U.S.* = *switch-lamp, -lantern*; also *transf.* (see quot. 1960); **switch mechanism** *Genetics*, the mechanism by which a switch gene operates; **switch-reference** *Linguistics* (see quot. 1972); **switch-room** (earlier example); **switch selling,** a sales technique whereby cheap goods are displayed in order to lead the consumer to buy similar but more expensive items; also *transf.*; hence **switch-selling** *ppl. a.* and (as a back-formation) **switch-sell** *v. intr.*; **switch-tender** (earlier example); **switch-tower** (earlier example); **switch trading** *Econ.*, international trading in commodities conducted through media other than currency (cf. *switch deal* above); **switchyard** *U.S.*, (*a*) an area of a railway taken up by points, and in which trains are made up; also *transf.*; (*b*) an enclosed area of a power system which contains the switchgear.

1940 *Chambers's Techn. Dict.* 826/1 *Switch-base*, the insulating base on which a switch is mounted. **1967** M. CHANDLER *Ceramics in Mod. World* iv. 114 For telegraph or telephone insulation, as for domestic switch-bases, fuse-holders, bulb-sockets, and so on, almost any kind of insulating material will work. **1932** L. HUGHES *Negro Mother* 13 'Cause I carries a switch-blade And I swing it a-hummin', And if I don't get you goin', I'll cut you down comin'. **1950** PATTERSON & CONRAD *Scottsboro Boy* II. ii. 96 He put the shears in his pocket and went to his cell. I had a switch-blade knife. I went looking for him. **1957** *New Yorker* 5 Oct. 64/1 A fist fight between two champions, but there are emotional complications, and the switch-blade knives are put to work. **1975** P. THEROUX *Great Railway Bazaar* xxx. 342, I would have plotted myself into danger: Sadik would have had a switchblade and gold teeth. **1940** *Chambers's Techn. Dict.* 826/1 *Switch-box*, an enclosure housing one or more switches operated by means of an external handle. **1978** W. F. BUCKLEY *Stained Glass* xxii. 217 Blackford walked to the switch box. **1845** W. T. PORTER *Big Bear Arkansas* 132 They circled about among the switch-cane and priscimmon bushes a long time. **1954** W. FAULKNER in *Holiday* XV. 36/3 The Natchez doctor was clearing the land fast now, plowing under the . . switch cane of the creek and river bottoms. **1973** 'D. JORDAN' *Nile Green* xxi. 85 KK hovered in his office, too, doing a quick switch deal in forward dollars. **1967** *Economist* 14 Jan. 143/1 When the Russians don't wish to take up a consignment of Moroccan oranges to which they are committed under a bilateral trade agreement, they go to a specialist known as a switch dealer in one of Europe's financial centres, and he arranges a resale to someone else, at a discount. That, in a nutshell, is the mysterious art of switch trading. **1957** *Ibid.* 21 Dec. 1082/1 Commodity shunting in general virtually stops when the margin between transferable sterling and official sterling is a little less than three per cent. But 'switch' dealings in platinum are possible at a narrower margin. **1964** *Times Rev. Industry* Sept. 17/1 All purchases of foreign exchange for investment in non-Sterling Areas are subject to control. . . Direct investment projects . . may be financed . . either by borrowing abroad or by using the non-sterling currency proceeds of the sale of foreign securities . . ; i.e., so-called 'switch dollars'. **1978** J. PAXTON *Dict. European Econ. Community* (rev. ed.) 236 *Switch dollar market.* Investment in foreign securities by United Kingdom residents is not normally allowed . . , but existing holdings may be realised and the proceeds switched into (*i.e.* used to buy) other securities, or sold . . to other United Kingdom residents who wish to purchase foreign securities. For convenience, such funds, whatever the currency, are expressed in terms of United States dollars called Switch, security or investment dollars. **1901** Switch gear [in Dict.]. **1930** *Times* 29 Mar. 19/4 Our metal is now being adopted as a substitute for non-magnetic iron in many instances, such as in the large casings for metal-clad switchgear. **1958** *Optima* Sept. 130/2 The electrical industry uses platinum for switchgear contacts in such equipment as traffic lights, telephone exchanges, radio stations and generating stations. **1978** *Jrnl. R. Soc. Arts* CXXVI. 609/2 Continued improvements in control circuitry and microprocessors are likely to . . further increase the utilization of transformers, switchgear and circuits. [**1941** MATHER & DE WINTON in *Ann. Bot.* V. 310 The more rigorous the selection of illegitimacy to outbreeding conditions the more efficient it is as an inbreeding mechanism when the switching genes are changed.] **1942** *Nature* 14 Nov. 564/1 Mather and de Winton have recently spoken of such genes as 'switch genes'. **1968** R. D. MARTIN tr. *Wickler's Mimicry in Plants & Animals* vii. 82 Polymorphism is sometimes controlled by single genes, sometimes by groups of genes, and . . switch genes (as explained for *Papilio dardanus*) may also play a part. **1943** K. TENNANT *Ride on Stranger* xi. 120 Some of them would be asking for letters at the switch-girl's desk. **1969** *Southerly* XXIX. 93 The tea-lady panders to the biological necessities of life, the switchgirl makes communication easier. **1948** L. DUROCHER *Dodgers & Me* vii. 49 Cullenbine, a switch hitter, and Steve Rachunok . . were two athletes we had picked up . . from Detroit. **1956** H. KURNITZ *Invasion of Privacy* iii. 25 A free-swinging roundhouse slap . . landed high on his cheek. . . 'What do you know!' he said softly. 'A southpaw!' 'Wrong,' said the girl. 'A switch-hitter.' **1960** WENTWORTH & FLEXNER *Dict. Amer. Slang* 534/1 *Switch-hitter*, a bisexual person. **1972** *Pussycat* XXXIII. LIX. 8/1 The buddy would shove cock to me. I can still remember the first switch-hitter. **1938** *Philadelphia Rec.* 5 Feb. 15/6 A signed contract has been received from Emmett Mueller, switch-hitting rookie whom the Phils rescued from the Cardinal chain gang this winter. **1952** *Sun* (Baltimore) 25 Feb. (B ed.) 14/6 He also picked up a switch-hitting style from baseball. Gordie is the only player . . who has mastered the art of switching hands on his stick, so that he can shoot from either his right or left side without warning. **1970** *N.Y. Times* 16 Aug. II. 1/1 Chock full of scenes of what people apparently *want* to see today . . lesbianism, switch-hitting, group gropes. **1922** *Telegr. & Teleph. Jrnl.* VIII. 82/2 If a subscriber leaves his receiver off the switchhook . . the switching equipment is automatically released after a certain interval. **1975** D. G. FINK *Electronics Engineers' Handbk.* XXII. 4 In the *common-battery* [telephone] *set* . . a circuit closure, activated by the switch hook, serves to alert the central office. **1955** *Time* 6 June 27/3 They manufacture pistols, carry switchknives and use them. **1957** WODEHOUSE *Over Seventy* xv. 144 At Eightieth Street he produced a switch-knife. . . 'This is a stick-up', he announced. **1892** *Harper's Mag.* Dec. 80 He saw the station agent running down the tracks with the red switch-light. **1929** W. FAULKNER *Sartoris* IV. 350 Along the tracks green switch-lights were steady in the dusk. **1960** *Listener* 18 Aug. 250/2 When a hungry young boomer came in and demanded . . 'a couple of switch lights in the fog' . . what he really wanted was . . two fried eggs with the grease poured over them. **1941** *Ann. Bot.* V. 308 The switch mechanism at the S,s locus offers the possibility of a very different adjustment to changed breeding conditions. **1953** J. S. HUXLEY *Evolution in Action* I. 29 Some genetic differences act as a switch mechanism, turning on a whole battery of further processes. **1967** W. JACOBSEN in Hymes & Bittle *Stud. in Southwestern Ethnolinguistics* 238 This paper discusses a device for pronominal reference, denominated 'switch-reference', which is found, with considerable differences of detail, in three languages of the Hokan-Coahuiltecan group. **1972** D. HYMES in M. E. Smith *Stud. in Linguistics in Honor of G. L. Trager* 105 The use of separate forms of third person to keep track of discourse is best treated under the general heading of 'switch reference'. . . It may be preferable to abandon use of the term 'fourth person' altogether, speaking simply of 'inclusive', 'obviative' . . , and 'switch reference'. **1978** *Language* LIV. 220 The presence of switch-reference morphemes . . also appears to be an areal feature in parts of California. **1885** *List of Subscribers, Classified* (United Telephone Co.) (ed. 6) 8 Each subscriber is furnished with a set of instruments . . which is connected with a wire communicating with the Exchange or Switch Room nearest his address. [**1930** *Amer. Speech* VI. 128 To switch a customer is to quote to him a low price on an article to inspire him, and then to direct his interest to another article.] **1960** *Guardian* 30 Nov. 2/7 The practice of switch selling of sewing and other machines . . from misleading advertisements. **1965** E. GUNDREY *Foot in Door* ii. 20 The fast-talking, switch-selling, hard-pressing salesman. *Ibid.* xxxviii. 219 It should . . be made illegal to 'switch-sell'. **1971** H. WILSON *Labour Govt.* xix. 361 Mr Kosygin . . was escorted throughout the day by . . the Secretary of State, who had been told about the American exercise in switch-selling the night before and had been asked to watch out for any signs of reaction. **1853** *Putnam's Mag.* July 34/2 We went roaring, rushing, screaming, up the valley of the Susquehanna, occasionally passing a switch-tender with his white lights. **1897** KIPLING in *Scribner's Mag.* Aug. 146/1 They were at the far north end of the yard, now, under a switch-tower, and looking down on the four-track way of the main traffic. **1967** *Switch trading* [see *switch dealer* above]. **1974** *Harper's Mag.* Dec. 54 What Intertel does is . . advise on geopolitical 'switch-trading opportunities'.

1888 *Austin* (Texas) *Statesman* 1 Nov. 6/6 In the switch yards of the Chicago & Alton..nearly all the men reported for duty this morning. **1943** J. S. Huxley *TVA* 85 The transformers and switchyard..are not applied to a predetermined structure, they are part of it. **1956** H. Gold *Man who was not with It* (1965) x. 70, I was at the switchyards, still running, and then I was clambering in the coupling of a moving freight. **1969** *Daily Colonist* (Victoria, B.C.) 16 Oct. 40/7 Work is to begin immediately on placing the..generators at the underground powerhouse.. and the switchyard and central control building on the surface. **1971** *Sci. Amer.* June 60 Near the end of its trip the electron beam passes through a 'beam switchyard' before reaching the target areas.

switch, *v.* Add: **1. c.** *I'll be switched,* a mild indication of exasperation, denial, or surprise. *N. Amer. colloq.*

1838 *U.S. Mag.* I. 427, I'll be switched if I do. **1841** J. B. Jones *Wild Western Scenes* xiv. 178 I'll be switched if many folks lives in *higher* houses than I does. **1901** *Daily Colonist* (Victoria, B.C.) 4 Oct. 3/7 'Well, I'll be switched!' ejaculated the chatterer. **1941** L. I. Wilder *Little Town on Prairie* ix. 99 'Well, I'll be switched!' said Pa... It takes you to think up a chicken pie, a year before there's chickens to make it with.

6. b. (Earlier example.)

1853 'Mark Twain' *Let.* in *Iowa Jrnl. Hist.* (1929) XXVII. 413 Our train ran back half a mile and switched off another track, and stopped.

7. b. Substitute for def.: To change or transfer from one thing to another; to alter to another state or activity. Also with advbs. *spec.* in *Bridge,* to change to another suit in bidding or in play (see sense 7*b of the sb.) (Later examples.)

1921 A. M. Foster *Auction Bridge* 32 Your partner.. can support your call or switch into another bid. **1932** *Daily Tel.* 8 Oct. 15/5 At Contract he has the..duty of raising the opener's bid..and, if he switches, of deciding whether to make a pre-emptive bid or not. **1952** I. Macleod *Bridge is Easy Game* xiv. 189 Switching to Diamonds declarer made her contract. **1980** R. Markus *Bridge-Table Tales* iv. 16 West won and switched to a spade.

1923 H. Crane *Let.* 20 Jan. (1965) 117, I..urged him not to 'waste his time' on any magazine project. But after his visit here last summer I quickly switched about. **1930** H. Zink *City Bosses in U.S.* x. 207 He bolted the regulars and switched to reform groups. **1954** J. Steinbeck *Sweet Thursday* v. 34 He knows when high-school boys have switched from gin to marijuana. **1962** *Rep. Comm. Broadc. 1960* 239 in *Parl. Papers 1961–2* (Comnd. 1753) IX. 259 Viewers who did not switch would find themselves exposed at some time of the evening to informational material. **1978** M. Amis *Success* ix. 173 Some dead-end toiler asked to switch from one equally meaningless chore to another.

c. *trans.* To exchange (items), esp. with intent to deceive.

1897 *Columbus* (Ohio) *Dispatch* 18 June 5/2 An opportunity presented itself to 'switch' the bottles. **1917** *Dialect Notes* IV. 330 *Switch, v.t.,* to exchange, esp. surreptitiously. 'I thought I was getting title to this land, but they switched deeds on me in the office.' Neb. **1948** C. L. B. Hubbard *Dogs in Britain* iii. xv. 130 A business in which dogs have been 'switched' (and doped) and the results manipulated is questionable. **1978** F. Weldon *Praxis* x. 75 Praxis managed to switch envelopes so that an empty one was dispatched instead.

d. To change or alter (*from* one thing *to* another); to transfer. Also, with items involved in the change as plural obj.

1919 Wodehouse *My Man Jeeves* 157 It struck me that I'd no right to butt in on his secret sermons, so I switched the conversation. **1931** W. G. McAdoo *Crowded Years* x. 157 Sullivan switched the fifty-eight votes of Illinois from Clark to Wilson. **1957** A. C. Clarke *Deep Range* xxi. 188 The very idea of switching our entire herds to milking instead of slaughtering is just crazy. **1959** *Daily Tel.* 15 Oct. 12 Among those who have switched offices, Mr. Watkinson's is perhaps the most surprising translation. **1963** *Listener* 28 Feb. 363/2 The government was forced to switch the full campaign towards the less flexible statutory committees. **1975** D. Lodge *Changing Places* vi. 229 Philip switches channels until he hits the transmission of the Plotinus March.

8. a. More recently, also of a radio or television set, etc.; to turn *out* (an electric light). Also, to change the state of (a two-state device).

1935 *Radio Times* 13 Sept. 4/3 If you were to switch on your set..you would have no difficulty in distinguishing ..who was speaking or singing. **1954** I. Murdoch *Under Net* iii. 53, I didn't switch out the light, but covered the lamp up again with gauzy stuffs until it gave only a faint glow. **1960** Haley & Scott *Analogue & Digital Computers* vii. 188 The core is switched from the 1 to the 0 state. **1964** F. L. Westwater *Electronic Computers* iv. 79 This is..got round by first switching a wound core..and then allowing the read current in this core to be used to write in the appropriate row and column. **1983** J. Fuller *Convergence* xix. 210 It is no sweat. Easy as switching on the old FM.

(ii) *to switch in*: to bring into a circuit by the operation of a switch; similarly *to switch out.*

Cf. quot. 1891, sense 8 in Dict.

1957 *Practical Wireless* XXXIII. 734/1 A resistor could be switched in initially to limit the maximum possible current flowing to 10 mA. **1970** J. Earl *Tuners & Amplifiers* iii. 67 The loudness control filter..can be switched out allowing the volume control to work in the ordinary, uncompensated manner. **1978** *SLR Camera* Aug. 90/1 To switch in the automatic exposure control system all he need do is turn the shutter speed setting dial to the position marked 'Auto'.

(iii) *intr.* Of a two-state device: to pass to the other state. Of its state: to change.

1964 F. L. Westwater *Electronic Computers* iv. 77 The resulting change of flux as the core switches will cause an electromotive force in the read wire. **1981** J. D. Lenk *Handbk. Digital Electronics* ii. 41 Inputs cause the state of the circuit to switch, reversing the output.

b. *intr.* or *absol.* To turn *on* (or *off*) a radio or television set, or other device. Cf. *turn *v.* 73 h, 74 a.

1932 *Even. Standard* 21 Jan. 3/3 The best plan is to tell listeners what is going to happen and let them decide whether they switch off or not. **1951** 'J. Wyndham' *Day of Triffids* xi. 206, I could not hear above the noise of the engines. We both switched off. **1958** *Listener* 20 Nov. 849/3 Many viewers may have missed it by switching off in fatigue. **1975** *Ibid.* 9 Jan. 38/2 They do it because someone's just switched on. **1977** *Rep. Comm. Future of Broadcasting* (Cmnd. 6753) iii. 19 Viewers and listeners cannot ..express..disapproval, except by switching off.

c. *intr.* To change *over* to another state by means of a switch; *spec.* to alter the receiving channel of a radio or television set.

1937 *Discovery* Nov. 348/2 By switching over from white light to black an entire scene can be changed instantaneously. **1940** N. Mitford *Pigeon Pie* v. 85 It would be difficult to do better, for an account of the Wig Inquest than to switch over, as they say on the wireless, to the columns of the *Evening Runner*. **1958** *Sunday Times* 26 Jan. 6/5, 200 pages of mumbo-jumbo which would make anyone switch over to another programme. **1961** S. Price *Just for Record* i. 13 The phone hasn't rung all day because I've switched over to the answering service.

d. *trans.* To turn *off* (a television or radio programme, or its content).

1947 G. B. Shaw *How to become Musical Critic* (1960) 321 [The B.B.C.'s] worst concessions to popular bad taste..are very horrible. I switch them off so promptly that I am hardly qualified to condemn them. **1962** *Listener* 18 Oct. 633/3 The archness of the dialogue had to be heard to be switched off.

e. To direct (a telephone link) *through* to a subsidiary receiver by means of a switch.

1971 'S. Smith' *Grave Affair* xii. 181 The telephone had not been switched through to my study deliberately. **1976** J. Tate tr. *A. Bodelsen's Operation Cobra* xvii. 83 They switched the telephone through and went on up.

9. *transf.* and *fig.* **a.** To turn *on* or *off*, as if by means of a switch.

1929 W. J. Locke *Ancestor Jorico* viii. 111 Without great discourtesy one couldn't switch off Binkie. **1934** *Discovery* Sept. 259/2 In this way she succeeded in switching off any unpleasant dream. **1966** *Listener* 24 Mar. 426/1, I have always found it very easy to 'switch on' emotion. **1967** B. Patten *Little Johnny's Confession* 54 Those couples who Having been switched off permanently, Are so very still. **1980** *Nature* 27 Mar. 379/2 The prose style is guaranteed to switch off all but the most ardent student.

b. *intr.* for *refl.* With *off.* Of persons: to cease listening, to lose concentration; to become bored or inattentive.

1921 G. B. Shaw *Back to Methuselah* iii. 94 Dont switch off. Listen. This American has invented a method of breathing under water. **1928** [see *easy *adv.* 4 b]. **1955** *Times* 22 June 11/5 Does he seriously maintain that in a class of 24 boys, where 23 are working keenly and well, it is invariably the master who is to blame because No. 24 always 'switches off'? **1976** J. I. M. Stewart *Memorial Service* vii. 108 He was heavy alike with his years and his whisky and wine, and he may simply have switched off. **1980** D. Bloodworth *Trapdoor* xx. 121 For some reason he could not fathom she had switched off. Her love had died.

switchable (swi·tʃăb'l), *a.* [f. Switch *v.* + -able.] Capable of being switched between different positions or modes of operation. Freq. in *techn.* contexts.

1961 [see *dual-standard* s.v. *dual *a.* (*sb.*) 3]. **1970** J. Earl *Tuners & Amplifiers* vi. 142 Signal in the i.f. channel also operates the tuning meter, switchable to a.m. by the f.m./a.m. changeover switch. **1977** *Nature* 6 Jan. 92/1 The range is −0·05 to 1·999A with a switchable decimal point and double over-range indication. **1982** *Sunday Times* 31 Oct. 57/1 Switchable pension... Switching is allowed among six funds (corresponding text).

switchback, *a.* and *sb.* Add: **A.** *adj.* (Earlier example.) Also *fig.* and in extended *transf.* uses.

1887 R. Fry *Let.* 21 Nov. (1972) I. 117 Some of us went on a switchback railway (the sensation of which I thought very pleasant). **1908** F. W. Lanchester *Aerodonetics* 30 A magnificent flight, remarkable 'switch-back' flight path, distance, relative to the wind, probably over 600 yards. **1912** G. Mackenzie *Carnival* ix. 90 Jenny thought what horrible places they were, these sweeping moorland wastes..with switchback stone walls. **1961** *Daily Tel.* 5 Sept. 12/2 Where Mr Hill made much more sense was in criticising what he called the Government's 'switchback economies'. **1965** *Daily Mail* 28 Oct. 5/3 A dangerous 'switchback' course can build up as the plane descends. **1978** S. Wilson *Dealer's Move* vii. 116, I got hung up behind a couple of lorries... It was switch-back country and there was no way you could see what was coming.

B. *sb.* (Earlier U.S. and later *fig.* examples.) *transf.* (later examples); also applied in N. Amer. to a tight bend on an ascending road or trail.

1863 *Harper's Mag.* Sept. 465/1 We descend from our high elevation by gravity, changing our direction at various points by means of what is called a Switch-back. **1933** *Nat. Geogr. Mag.* Feb. 196 (*caption*) An excellent highway climbs by turns and switchbacks through natural timber to the top of the towering dome. **1934** [see *giant racer* s.v. *giant *sb.* 6]. **1965** *Daily Mail* 28 Oct. 5/3 If the Vanguard..was on the down-slope of a switchback when the talk-down was ended,..probably no further cause for the crash need be sought. **1969** *Islander* (Victoria, B.C.) 9 Nov. 7/1 Steep grades are not the only challenge on this road. Several of the switchbacks are so tight that much manoeuvring is required to get around them. **1976** J. Snow *Cricket Rebel* 61 Each time I was to find the county side at a lower ebb, with the team on a down slide of the switchback we rode in the 1960s.

switchback *v.* (later examples); **swi·tch-backed** *ppl. a.*, **swi·tchbacking** *vbl. sb.* and *ppl. a.*

1913 *Outing* Jan. 498/1 Switch-backing or zigzagging up a hill is simply striking off to the right, for instance, at an angle and then turning off to the left. **1930** J. Collier *His Monkey Wife* vi. 72 Electric light cables..switch-backed along the undulating coast. **1963** *Times* 16 Feb. 11/1 Another short drop leads to the edge of the lake with its bathing station and a surrealist structure built for high diving and switchbacking into the water. **1972** *Daily Tel.* (Colour Suppl.) 13 Oct. 86/2 A switchbacking lane over the heath to Studland. **1976** B. Bova *Multiple Man* (1977) vi. 65 My rented car climbed the switch-backed driveway.

switchboard. Add: **a.** (Earlier examples.)

1873 *Harper's Mag.* Aug. 349/2 The switch-board..is the central ganglion of the whole [telegraphic] system. **1879** *Nature* 11 Sept. 461/2 The switch-board at the central office.

b. *attrib.*, esp. as *switchboard girl, operator.*

1903 *P.O. Telephone Service* 77 The current from the 'busy-back' and 'don't answer' commutators is not led directly to the switchboard terminals. **1925** F. G. C. Baldwin *Hist. Telephone in U.K.* xi. 301 Switchboard cable containing 42 wires was employed between the test board and the first switch section. **1952** *Traffic* Apr. 34 (Advt.), Suppliers to the World for all Telecommunication products..Automatic telephone equipment for main and satellite exchanges..Telephone instruments and accessories. Switchboard lamps (Hivac Ltd.). **1961** M. Kelly *Spoilt Kill* ii. 105 He just wouldn't have anything to do with her. A girl from the works, the switchboard girl! **1967** N. Freeling *Strike out where not Applicable* 111 'All right,' said the switchboard girl indifferently. **1974** A. Morice *Killing with Kindness* ii. 18 The call came through a switchboard operator.

switched, *a.* and *ppl. a.* Add: **2.** Also, of an egg. *rare.*

1931 A. J. Cronin *Hatter's Castle* iii. ix. 602 I'm to have a switched egg.

3. a. Of a mechanism: turned *on* or *off* by a switch. Also *fig.*

1962 *Listener* 28 June 1131/1 His characters were understandably so permanently switched on that their moments of crisis were brought about by the small talk of others. **1968** P. Marlowe *Hire me a Hearse* vii. 101 He hung up the picture with the switched-off mike. **1968** *Listener* 25 July 127/2 The screen of a switched-on television. **1974** J. Wainwright *Evidence I shall Give* i. 9 The switched-on light would emphasise the possible importance of..the one room..with the light still burning. **1977** *Times* 15 Aug. 2/1 Switched-off heating in every unoccupied room.

b. *switched-on*: aware of all that is considered fashionable and up to date. Cf. *turned on* s.v. *turned *ppl. a.* 8. Less frequently, in contrast, *switched-off. slang.*

1964 *House & Garden* Nov. 78/2, I..want..to open a department store which caters for switched-on people. **1966** *Punch* 29 June 946/1 But nowhere have I come across a word of guidance for the 'out' crowd—the vast, non-swinging, switched off, palateless, utterly without-it lot who dominate the community. **1967** N. Fitzgerald *Affairs of Death* viii. 141 They must be more switched on than I gave them credit for being. **1970** D. Devine *Illegal Tender* ii. 25 Her mother wasn't switched on, she knew nothing of modern fashion. **1972** C. Weston *Poor, Poor Ophelia* xxv. 153 The fine beautiful free life. The switched-on scene. **1979** 'A. Hailey' *Overload* iv. iii. 302 She had delivered the tapes to that switched-on black woman who worked for a newspaper. **1982** *London Rev. Bks.* IV. xxiv. 7/2 What Amis's *sprezzatura* is saying is that most of his readers are out of touch, old fogies, Prufrock retreats, switched-off.

4. *a.* and *ppl. a.* Electr. Having a switch; obtained by switching; subjected to switching.

1961 *IBM Jrnl. Res. & Devel.* V. 93 A phase reversal data transmission system is described, capable of operating at 2000 bauds over private telephone lines and at 1200 bauds over switched networks. **1971** *Gloss. Electrotechnical, Power Terms* (*B.S.I.*) iii. vi. 12 Switched beam direction finder. **1971** *Physics Bull.* Oct. 612/3 The instrument can be used for checking all types of digital logic... Three switched frequency ranges are standard (0–50 kHz, 0–500 kHz, 0–5 MHz). **1974** Harvey & Bohlman *Stereo F.M. Radio Handbk.* v. 106 (*caption*) Mullard switched decoder.

switchel. a. For *U.S.* read *N. Amer.* and add earlier and further examples.

1790 P. Freneau in *Daily Advertiser* (N.Y.) 22 Mar. 3/1 Not wretched switchel and vile hogo drams. **1843** *Family Herald* 29 July 183/1 The drinks ain't good here;..no white noses..switchel-flip..or nothin', but that heavy, stupid, black, fat porter. **1925** *Dialect Notes* V. 344 [Newfoundland] *Switchel,* a drink of water and molasses. **1959** W. R. Bird *These are Maritimes* vii. 190 She kept the jug in the cellar and boy when you came in and had a mug of that switchel it was worth while. **1977** *New*

Hampshire Times 27 July vII. 20/3 Switchel was a concoction of cold water, sugar, ginger and vinegar, and..it was more or less thirst-quenching.

b. *Newfoundland.* (A drink of) tea, esp. amongst fishermen and sealers (see quots.).

1897 *Jrnl. Amer. Folklore* x. 211 *Switchel*, a mug of weak tea given to the sailors between meals when at the seal fishing. **1924** G. A. ENGLAND *Vikings of Ice* 50 Some were devouring beans and salt meat; others, gulping tea that steamed. 'Switchel', this tea was; that is, boiled-over tea whereto now and again fresh leaves are added. **1963** *Amer. Speech* XXXVIII. 300 *Switchel*, cold tea. **1974** *National Geographic* Jan. 114/2 [We] snugged down in the cabin for a 'cup o' switchel', as they call strong tea.

switcher. Add: **d.** One who changes or transfers something to another position; a person who exchanges items, or substitutes one for the other. *slang* and *colloq.* (orig. *U.S.*).

1914 [see *FLOPPER 2]. **1958** *Wall St. Jrnl.* 3 Nov. 1/1 Almost a third of the voters who plan to vote mostly for Republican candidates tomorrow are recent 'switchers', who until a few days ago either had planned to vote Democratic or were still undecided. **1978** *Economist* 1 Apr. 26/1 Singapore, South Korea and the Philippines as well as eastern European countries are said to be among the more determined switchers out of dollars.

switcheroo (switʃĕrū·). *colloq.* (chiefly *U.S.*). [f. SWITCH *sb.* + *-EROO.] = *SWITCH *sb.* 7*a, c; a change of position or an exchange, esp. one intended to surprise or deceive; a reversal or turn-about; *spec.* an unexpected change or 'twist' in a story. Also *attrib.*, reversible, reversed.

1933 *Forum* Dec. 372/2 We'll pull a switcheroo. We'll use olives instead [of cherries]. **1941** B. SCHULBERG *What makes Sammy Run?* iv. 81 All you gotta do to that story is to give it the switcheroo. Instead of the minister you got a young dame missionary, see. **1949** *Sun* (Baltimore) 22 Sept. 7 (Advt.), Girls' 'switcheroo' jacket. One side's red or green corduroy and..the other side's a gay..wool plaid. **1953** C. M. KORNBLUTH *Syndic* v. 52 Two strapping girls..began to tear *his* clothes off, laughing at their switcheroo on the year's big gag. **1961** *N.Y. Times Bk. Rev.* 21 May 6/3 In Chapter X, then, with a neat whodunit switcheroo, Radin puts the finger on that most obvious suspect who, it appears, was cleared in too much haste. **1970** 'A. GILBERT' *Death wears Mask* vi. 102, I ought to have suggested it was a switcheroo. You know—criminal makes the discovery and informs the police. **1980** *Fortune* (Chicago) 7 Apr. 44/3 The arbitrator..turned out to be Daniel Collins,..who had upheld Equity in the 1976 row... Collins this time came down on the side of management. It was one of those great switcheroo endings.

switchfoot (swi·tʃfut). *Surfing.* Pl. **-foots.** [f. *SWITCH *v.* 7 + FOOT *sb.*] (See quot. 1970.) Also **switch-footer.**

1970 *Studies in English* (Univ. of Cape Town) I. 30 The few surfers who are able to ride with equal skill with either right or left foot forward, are known as switchfoots. **1971** *Ibid.* II. 26 Finally, surfers differentiate among themselves between naturals,..goofies..and switch-footers, who can switch stance. **1978** G. WRIGHT *Illustr. Handbk. Sporting Terms* 147/4 *Switchfoot*, a surfer who can ride with either his left foot or right foot forward.

switching, *vbl. sb.* Add: **4. b.** Changing or transferring from one position to another; exchanging.

1904 'No. 1500' *Life in Sing Sing* 253/1 *Switching*, transferring; passing to another. **1957** *Publ. Amer. Dial. Soc. 1956* XXVI. 40 Precision would thus require us to distinguish three stages in diffusion: (1) *switching*, the alternate use of two languages, [etc.].

c. *Stock Exchange.* The purchase (or sale) of one stock, and the sale (or purchase) of another stock, at a stipulated price difference.

1932 *Literary Digest* 30 Jan. 49/1 (*title*) 'Switching' in a bear market. **1936** *Economist* 1 Feb. 248/2 The available evidence suggests that 'switching' has not greatly affected the past year's results. Some trusts..have increased their American holdings. **1960** *Ibid.* 15 Oct. 288/3 Buying in the gilt edged market increased..and demand from both home and continental buyers, including some switching and investment buying, remained high. **1981** *Times* 18 Aug. 18 The shares managed a 16p rise..with heavy switching from the ordinary into the NV.

5. (*b*) *switching yard* = *switchyard* (*a*) s.v. *SWITCH *sb.* 8; (*c*) Also, pertaining to the switching of electrical apparatus or electronic devices, as *switching centre, circuit, speed, station, theory, time.*

1894 *Daily Ardmoreite* (Ardmore, Okla.) 28 Mar. 1/8 There came very near being a disastrous collision..in the upper switching yards of the Santa Fe. **1939** H. J. REICH *Theory & Applic. Electron Tubes* xii. 459 Two high-vacuum amplifier tubes..are alternately overbiased by the voltage drop through the anode resistors of the switching circuit. **1959** J. M. PETTIT *Electronic Switching, Timing, & Pulse Circuits* iii. 73 The switching speed of a triode in ordinary circuits is impaired by capacitances rather than by transit time of electrons in the tube. **1960** *McGraw-Hill Encycl. Sci. & Technol.* XIII. 357/1 The bulk of switching theory is concerned with circuits made of binary (two-valued) devices, since these are most common. **1960** R. S. LEDLEY *Digital Computer & Control Engin.* xxi. 697 The value of R_c can be estimated by means of considerations concerning the switching time of the core, the time τ required to switch or flip a core. **1962** *B.B.C. Handbk.* 113 The EBU is responsible for the co-ordination of the programme, legal, and technical aspects of Eurovision, and operates the switching centre in Brussels. **1968** Switching station [see *FEEDER 10 a]. **1969** *Jane's Freight Containers 1968–69* 116/3 Progress has been made in reducing the time cars spend in switching yards. **1973** *Times* 30 Oct. 1/2 Engineers who man power stations and switching centres will refuse to turn out if a breakdown or other difficulty arises while they are off duty. **1977** *Sci. Amer.* Sept. 212/3 Switching theory, which was developed to help design the relay-operated switching networks of automatic telephone systems, provided guides that enabled a designer to formulate a network with the minimum number of relays for accomplishing some given logical operation. **1978** *Ibid.* Mar. 61/2 (*caption*) Supervisory and switching circuits in the central office connect the two sets for the conversation and disconnect them when the call is over.

swi·tch-off. [f. vbl. phr. *to switch off*: see SWITCH *v.* 8.] The turning off of an (electrical) power supply, television set, etc., by means of a switch. Also *attrib.* and *transf.*

1947 *Times* 11 Feb. 2/3 Liverpool electricity undertaking..reduced its load by about 55 per cent, during both the morning and afternoon switch-off periods. **1966** *Listener* 7 July 9/2 Television is continually at the mercy either of switch-off or switch-over. **1974** *Times* 15 Jan. 14/3 A mass switch-off of electrical appliances. **1978** *Nature* 5 Jan. 10/3 This suggests that the switch-off of interferon production is due to cessation of mRNA synthesis as well as to its inactivation. **1980** *Daily Tel.* 10 Mar. 13/2 The home viewer who cannot cope with BBC 2 or the switch-off button is going to feel swamped by the Olympics.

swi·tch-on. [f. vbl. phr. *to switch on*: see SWITCH *v.* 8.] The switching on of an (electrical) power supply, light, etc. Also *transf.*

1950 *Sun* (Baltimore) 4 Mar. 2/7 A new electric 'pick-proof' motor car lock which..permits switchon, and starts with a single key, is being manufactured in Stockholm, Sweden. **1976** *Sunday Mail* (Glasgow) 28 Nov. 11/6 Councillor Brian Meek..will attend the district council's tree switch-on. **1978** *Nature* 5 Jan. 10/3 Thus the switch-on of interferon synthesis requires new transcription.

swi·tch-over. [f. vbl. phr. *to switch over*: see *SWITCH *v.* 8 c.] A switch or change from one state or course to another; a change-over.

1928 *Daily Express* 12 Nov. 10/2 The opening left by America's switch-over to the 'talkies' can be brilliantly exploited. **1937** *Essays & Stud.* XXII. 148 The cross-currents, switch-overs, throw-backs, and quasi-automatic tags of *The Waste Land.* **1941** 'R. WEST' *Black Lamb & Grey Falcon* I. 159 He believes that any moment the whole process of life may make a slight switch-over and that every thing will be agreeable for ever. **1952** S. KAUFFMANN *Philanderer* (1953) iv. 66 So six months after we start, we've got the name of the book banged into the public's head, and maybe..we've held on to a lot of the confession readers in the switch-over. **1962** *Rep. Comm. Broadc. 1960* 210 in *Parl. Papers 1961–2* (Cmnd. 1753) IX. 259 *The method of changing the line standard*... It considered the possibility of 'a simultaneous change-over throughout the country'—that is, a 'switchover'. **1979** *Financial Rev.* (Sydney) 6 July 46/4 Each of the..pulse generators across Australia required manual switchover in the event of failure.

switzerite (swi·tsərait). *Min.* [f. the name *Switzer* (see quot. 1967) + -ITE[1].] A hydrated phosphate of manganese and iron, $(Mn, Fe)_3(PO_4)_2.4H_2O$, found as pink to brown monoclinic crystals.

1967 LEAVENS & WHITE in *Amer. Mineralogist* LII. 1595 The name switzerite is proposed for the mineral in honor of George Switzer, Chairman, Department of Mineral Sciences, Museum of Natural History, Smithsonian Institution. **1978** *Rocks & Minerals* LIII. 160 A number of new minerals..from the Quarry include switzerite, eakerite and brannockite.

swivel, *sb.* Add: **4. a.** *swivel rocker, -seat.*

1916 *Blackw. Mag.* Oct. 475/1 He walked unsteadily across the room and sat down on a swivel-seat. **1975** Swivel rocker [see *saddle brown* s.v. *SADDLE *sb.* 10].

b. swivel eye (earlier example, applied by synecdoche to a dog); **swivel hips** *Trampolining*, an exercise consisting of a seat drop followed by a half-twist into another seat drop (constr. *sing.*); also *transf.*

1765 S. CIBBER *Let.* 3 Oct. in *Private Corresp. David Garrick* (1831) I. 201, I hope you remember that I have lost poor little swivel-eye, that was blind, and also that you promised me a dog that could see. **1943** L. GRISWOLD *Trampoline Tumbling* 49 As the legs are swung through the vertical position, the twist is made to right or left and the hips are flexed to assume the sitting position for landing. The movement performed by the hips is called 'swivel hips'. **1948** —— *Ibid.* (ed. 2) vi. 46 This exercise—popularly called 'swivel hips'—consists of a seat-drop take-off, a half twist, and a seat-drop landing. **1964** *Trampolining* ('Know the Game' Series) 22/1 The first one [*sc.* bounce] to practise is the seat bounce with half twist known as the swivel hips. **1966** ROTE & WINTER *Lang. Pro Football* III. 141/1 *Swivel hips*, elusive ball carrier who fakes potential tacklers by shifting hips from side to side. **1980** *Sci. Amer.* Mar. 118/2 An astronaut in space could easily reorient himself in any direction with swivel hips and tuck drops.

swivel, *v.* Add: **4.** [For an equivalent change of initial *shr-* to *sw-*, compare U.S. dial. *swimp* shrimp.] *intr.* To shrivel. Also const. *up.* *U.S. dial.*

1898 'R. SANDERS' *Sk. Country Life* xxv. 155 Sometimes I think to myself if Christmas didn't come reglar onest a year..this old world would soon swivel and swink up and die out with the dry rots. **1957** W. FAULKNER *Town* (1958) vii. 103 Old hermits setting on rocks out in the hot sun..watching their blood dry up and their legs swivelling.

swivelled *ppl. a.* (examples in above sense).

1898 'R. SANDERS' *Sk. Country Life* viii. 53, I..filled my pockets full of scalybarks and peanuts and some swivelled up apples of my own raisin. **1938** M. K. RAWLINGS *Yearling* xvii. 204 The one we cain't spare was the one was takened... And him a swivveled, no-account thing, too. **1975** E. WIGGINTON *Foxfire 3* 258 It'll be a little bitty old swivelled up thing.

swivet (swi·vėt). *dial.* (chiefly *U.S.*). Also **swivvet, swi(v)vit.** [Origin unknown.] A state of agitation; a fluster or panic. Also, a hurry. Freq. in phr. *in a swivet.*

1892 *Dialect Notes* I. 232 *Swivet* (swivit),..'Don't be in such a swivet.' *a* **1904** in *Eng. Dial. Dict.* (1904) V. 893/2 What a swivit ee's in. **1913** H. KEPHART *Our Southern Highlanders* xiii. 294 When a man is..in a hurry, he is in a swivvet. **1917** *Dialect Notes* IV. 418 [N. Carolina] *Swivvit*, n., hurry. 'He's always in a swivvit.' Also La. **1933** I. S. COBB *Murder Day by Day* xvi. 209 And Hilda, so Verity said, was in quite a swivit over the prospect of being interviewed again. **1955** *N.Y. Sunday News* 27 Mar. 100/1 She does not get in 'swivets' or 'tizzies', either, and she does not often sulk. **1962** M. CARLETON *Dread Sunset* (1963) v. 81 'Don't get into a swivet,' Ellen soothed. **1978** C. MACLEOD *Rest You Merry* xxiv. 168 Jemina was always in a swivet about something.

swizz (swiz). *slang.* Also **swiz.** [Shortened f. *SWIZZLE *sb.*[2]] A disappointment or 'swindle.' Freq. in the exclamation 'What a swizz!'

1915 W. OWEN *Let.* 19 Mar. (1967) 328 What a swizz about Harold! **1921** V. BRITTAIN *Let.* Nov. in *Testament of Youth* (1933) x. 513 What a swiz for all the people who swore that there was nothing in it between Ramage and Cathleen Nesbitt. **1932** G. CLARK *Mistress* II. v. 186 They want us to go lunch. Just round the corner here... Bit of a swiz, isn't it? I did my best to get out of it. **1937** S. SMITH *Good Time was had by All* 38 The people say that spiritism is a joke and a swizz. **1959** R. FULLER *Ruined Boys* II. ix. 144 He's given him not out. What a sodding swiz. *a* **1974** R. CROSSMAN *Diaries* (1976) II. 208 We were drinking cheerfully when up came that phrase Quintin Hogg is always using: 'Really, it's only a swizz.'

Hence as *v. trans.*, to trick by swindling, to subject to disappointment (in quot., *pass.*).

1961 H. & M. WILLIAMS *Irregular Verb to Love* in J. C. Trewin *Plays of Year* XXIII. 84, I..felt I'd been swizzed —not just of sex though that was part of it.

swizzle (swi·z'l), *sb.*[2] *slang* (chiefly *School-children's*). [Prob. altered f. SWINDLE *sb.*[3]] = *SWIZZ.

1913 A. H. DAWSON *Dict. Eng. Slang & Colloquialisms* 139 *Swizzle.* (1) Any sort of drink. (2) A swindle, fraud. Also a verb in both senses. **1931** C. MACKENZIE *Buttercups & Daisies* v. 59 'What a swizzle you can't eat rats,' Roger sighed. *Ibid.* xviii. 229 What a swizzle it's so late. **1950** A. BUCKERIDGE *Jennings goes to School* i. 12 It was a rotten swizzle, sir, because we flew through low cloud and we couldn't see a thing. *a* **1976** A. CHRISTIE *Autobiogr.* (1977) IX. v. 476 This place is awful, Mother... As for those bathrooms,..it's an absolute swizzle! They're never used.

swizzle, *v.* Add: Hence **swi·zzled** *ppl. a.*, drunk, 'sozzled'; influenced or induced by heavy drinking.

1843 *Knickerbocker* XXII. 366 We were never 'groggy', ..'swizzled' or 'tight', but once. **1888** *Texas Siftings* 14 Jan. 8/2 Old Shep, with a swizzled intuition, would darkly imagine that the singers were alluding to his calcium nose. **1918** G. FRANKAU *One of Them* ix. 65 Some quaff th'embittered cocktail, or the rum Whose swizzled headaches heavy on to-morrow weigh. **1934** *Amer. Spectator* July 2/3 The editors of *The American Spectator* got somewhat swizzled one night last week and didn't feel so good the next day.

swi·zzler. *dial.* and *slang.* Now *rare.* [f. SWIZZLE *v.* + -ER[1].] **a.** A drunkard. **b.** A swindler.

1876 F. K. ROBINSON *Gloss. Whitby* 192/1 *Swizzler*, a drunkard. **1936** 'N. BELL' *Crocus* ix. 235 Oh, he didn't diddle me... I knew him for a swizzler from the word go. **1938** J. W. DAY *Dog in Sport* xvii. 233 Lights gleamed in a building ashore. The Cockney swizzlers were still at it.

swizzle-stick. (In Dict. s.v. SWIZZLE *sb.* b.) Add: **1.** (Earlier and later examples.) Also, a rod used to stir a mixed drink, or to flatten the effervescence of a cocktail, etc.

1879 J. W. BODDAM-WHETHAM *Roraima & Brit. Guiana* xii. 129 The revolutions of a peculiar instrument called the swizzle-stick. **1899** C. J. C. HYNE *Further Adventures Capt. Kettle* v. 135 Shout for your boy to bring the cocktail... Where's the swizzle-stick? **1951** *N.Y. Herald-Tribune* 9 Mar. 18/3 Under Otto Preminger's direction it is all as frothy and inevitable as the action of a swizzle stick in a champagne glass. **1964** WODEHOUSE *Frozen Assets* ii. 36 The way the mere sound of her voice got inside one and stirred one up as with a swizzle-stick. **1976** J. I. M. STEWART *Young Pattullo* iii. 69, I was being officiously counselled not to commit the solecism of using a swizzle-stick too soon.

2. *transf.*

1962 J. GLENN in *Into Orbit* 44 A simple little rod... It is ten inches long, has a hook on the end of it for pulling at levers and a stub for pushing at buttons. You grasp it in your glove if you know you are not going to be able to reach something with your fingers.. We call it, naturally, a 'swizzle stick'. **1977** *Lancet* 16 Apr. 836/2 The swizzlestick consists of a handle fastened to a small stainless steel circular platform to which is also fastened a stainless steel displacement probe having a diameter slightly less than the bore of a capillary tube and a volume equal to the volume of blood required for the assay.

3. *Comb.*, as **swizzle-stick tree**, a small aromatic evergreen tree, *Quararibea turbinata*, of the family Bombacaceæ, found in the W. Indies and tropical South America.

1943 RECORD & HESS *Timbers New World* 98/1 All specimens of *Quararibea* without distinct heartwood... Common names: Garrocho, swizzle-stick tree. **1951** E. MITTELHOLZER *Shadows move among Them* I. xvi. 153 Wild cacao and swizzle-stick trees and ferns..grew out of reddish sand.

swollen, *ppl. a.* Add: **2. c.** *swollen head*: excessive pride, or a person suffering from it; also, a hangover. *colloq.* Cf. SWELLED *ppl. a.* b.

1899 N. GOULD *Landed at Last* vi. 59 You have got a swollen head this morning... Had too much to drink last night. **1922** F. HAMILTON *P.J., Secret Service Boy* vi. 242 You don't strike me, somehow, as being liable to swollen head. **1928** *Daily Express* 23 July 9 British film-producers..are..annoyed with me for saying that their swollen-headed outlook was the root-trouble... I feel certain that the swollen heads will bring about many crashes in British film-production.

3. a. *swollen-eyed, -headed* adjs.

1930 E. POUND *XXX Cantos* xv. 67 'Ηέλιον τ' Ηέλιον blind with the sunlight, Swollen-eyed, rested. **1977** N. SAHGAL *Situation in New Delhi* xvi. 153 The girl raised her head, swollen-eyed. **1928** Swollen-headed [see sense 2 c above]. **1983** D. FRANCIS *Danger* i. 13 Chasing personal glory. Stupid, swollen-headed, lethal human failing.

b. Special combination. **swollen shoot**, a virus disease of cocoa trees, spread by mealy bugs and distinguished by swelling of the young shoots, leading to the death of infected trees.

1936 W. F. STEVEN in *Gold Coast Farmer* V. 144/1 A new disease of cocoa..has provisionally been named 'Swollen Shoot and Die-back'. **1950** *Times* 2 Feb. 9/2 We shall test our proposed method for the prevention of swollen shoot disease of cocoa in the Gold Coast, using systemic insecticides. **1972** P. F. ENTWISTLE *Pests of Cocoa* x. 170 At the time of discovery of swollen shoot disease planting in the Eastern Region was still expanding.

swollenness (swōᵘ·l'n,nės). [f. prec. + -NESS.] The state or appearance of being swollen.

1902 E. SELOUS *Thought Transference in Birds* (1931) 14 In a very little while..this swollenness subsides and there is the same average appearance of the birds.

swooner (swū·nəɹ). [f. SWOON *v.* + -ER[1].]

1. One who swoons or faints, or pretends to do so.

1911 K. D. WIGGIN *Mother Carey* xxx. 263 Nancy had secretly trained Peter so that he was the best swooner of the family. **1951** M. MCLUHAN *Mech. Bride* (1967) 28/2 There's no need to reassure the swooner that Lana is human flesh and blood. **1966** *New Statesman* 19 Aug. 269/3 Olga Ferri accepted the chance to appear more of a queen, less of a lyrical swooner.

2. *U.S.* One who sings in a manner which resembles crooning. Also (nonce-wd.) *swooner-crooner*.

1944 *Amer. Speech* XIX. 102/1 Swooner-crooner is a characterizing term in current use among journalists and humorists for the singer Frank Sinatra. It made its advent in late 1943. **1952** B. ULANOV *Hist. Jazz in Amer.* xxi. 268 His voice..never falls into the whispering faint that makes listening to the swooners and crooners so disturbing.

swoony, *a.* Add: **1.** (Example.)

1978 M. DICKENS *Open Book* (1980) ii. 26 For one of her heroes, in the style she originated as a swoony girl in Dulwich, Fanny wrote: [etc.].

2. Inducing a swoon; hence, distractingly attractive, delightful. *colloq.*

1934 in WEBSTER. **1960** WENTWORTH & FLEXNER *Dict. Amer. Slang* 534/2 *Swoony,..adj.*, attractive. Teenage use, *c*1940. More often in movies and stories about teenagers than used by teenagers. **1973** T. PYNCHON *Gravity's Rainbow* I. 57 Those eyes she could never quite see into were so swoony. **1974** 'R. TATE' *Birds of Bloodied Feather* ii. 26 Champers and strawberries and Ronald and swoony lanes on the way back. **1976** P. FLOWER *Crisscross* i. 11 Their kiss was long and deep and swoony.

Hence **swoo·niness**, a quality suggestive of a swoon.

1909 R. BRIDGES in R. W. Dixon *Poems* p. xxx, The faintness and swooniness is in some sort akin to the remoteness and misty atmosphere of antiquity.

swooping, *ppl. a.* Add: **2. b.** Of a surface: sloping sharply or steeply.

1956 G. DURRELL *My Family & Other Animals* viii. 103 One of the first to arrive was Zatopec, an Armenian poet, a short, stocky individual with a swooping eagle nose. **1979** *Jrnl. R. Soc. Arts* Nov. 744/1 The gently upturned, swooping roofs.

swoose (swūs). [Blend of SWAN *sb.* and GOOSE *sb.*] A bird that is the offspring of a swan and a goose. Also *transf.*

1920 *Daily Mail* 13 July 7/5 A bird prodigy of evil and hybrid character is the despair of a Norfolk farmer. It rejoices in the name of the 'swoose', a portmanteau word indicating its origin, for its father was a swan and its mother a goose. This ill-assorted pair had three children—three 'sweese'. **1927** *Daily Express* 12 July 8/4 The swoose is a cross between the goose and the swan. **1954** *Sun* (Baltimore) 27 Apr. 1/7 A Democratic swan..who fell in love with a common farmyard goose today became the father of a 'swoose'. **1964** *Sunday Mail* (Brisbane) 24 May 29/2 By salvaging parts from the damaged planes, airmen resurrected a few bombers like the Swoose. The name Swoose, for part-swan, part-goose, reflects the plane's patchwork rebirth. **1976** *Sydney Sun* 20 Aug. 16/2 Like the 'swoose' (a cross between a swan and a goose) the 'churkey' is a mythical bird.

swop (swǫp), informal contraction of 'so help': see S'ELP, SWELP.

1890 P. H. EMERSON *Wild Life* 46 Swop my bob. **1912** W. DEEPING *Sincerity* xxviii. 214 Swop me bob, somebody else will be callin' for the police.

sword, *sb.* Add: **1. e.** *pl.* One of the four suits in packs of playing-cards used in Italy and in Spanish-speaking countries, and in tarot packs. Cf. SPADE *sb.*[2]

1816 G. W. SINGER *Researches into Hist. Playing Cards* I. 17 The four suits, *Spade*, (swords,) *Coppe*, (cups,) *Denari*, (money,) and *Bastone*, (clubs,) adopted both by the Italians and Spaniards, were probably the suits of the Eastern game. **1848** W. A. CHATTO *Facts & Speculations on Origin & Hist. Playing Cards* iv. 191 The earliest writers who mention Tarocchi as a kind of cards, always speak of them as consisting of four suits,—Swords, Cups, Batons, and Money. *Ibid.* 227 The cards most commonly used in Italy in the latter part of the fifteenth century, were those which had..Swords, Cups, Batons, and Money,—as the marks of the suits. **1892** 'PAPUS' *Tarot of Bohemians* v. 44 When we consider the four colours of the Tarot, new deductions will be called forth... The Sword represents the union of the two by its crucial form. **1911** A. E. WAITE *Pictorial Key to Tarot* I. iv. 36 We must forbear from saying, for example, that the Conditions of Life correspond to the Trumps Major..and the conditions of life to Swords. **1934** J. D. CARR (*title*) The eight of swords. **1952** V. WILKINS *King Reluctant* III. iii. 230 He..produced two [tarot] cards... 'The King of Swords and the King of Cups!' he said. **1978** *Jrnl. Playing-Card Soc.* Feb. 90 It comprises 52 cards, with suits of Swords, Batons, Cups and Pomegranates.

2. b. *at the sword's point*: under pressure of a threat or an urgent demand; *at swords' points*: in a state of open hostility. Cf. DAGGER *sb.* 2.

1895 A. BEARDSLEY *Let.* Nov. (1970) 104 The dreadful thing was a blaze up with Lane-cum-Mathews, and a drawing to be produced at the sword's point. **1909** WEBSTER, At swords' points. **1963** M. MCCARTHY *Group* x. 214 Mrs Hartshorn and her dead husband had had a running battle over Wilson and the League, and now Priss and Sloan were at swords' points over Roosevelt and socialized medicine.

3. c. Contrasted with *ploughshare* (in allusion to Isaiah ii. 4 and Micah iv. 3), as types respectively of war and peace: see PLOUGHSHARE I. Esp. in phr. *to beat swords into ploughshares.*

1924 L. P. SMITH *S.P.E. Tract* XVII. 38 We must take them [*sc.* words] as they come to our hands; if they are ploughshares which have been beaten into swords, tools which have been made into battle-axes, they are tools nevertheless for which we have no substitutes. **1976** N. THORNBURG *Cutter & Bone* x. 242 You know the old phrase about beating swords into plowshares—well I think you've beaten your grief into a sword.

5. a. (Further examples.)

1942 R. DAVEY *Measurement of Trees* ii. 28 When a tree lies on the ground, there may be some difficulty in passing the tape beneath it. A flat piece of metal with a hook at one end, called a 'timber sword' may be used for this purpose. **1953** H. L. EDLIN *Forester's Handbk.* xiv. 213 Find the mid-point of the log, and pass a girthing tape around it; with large logs, the device called the timber-measurer's sword will be of assistance.

6. a. *sword-clash, -flash, -hate, -rust.* **c.** Objective, *sword-rusting* adj.; similative, *sword-keen* adj.

1946 R. CAMPBELL *Talking Bronco* 45 Amidst the sword-clash of the reeds. **1969** G. M. BROWN *Orkney Tapestry* 74 It was a long stern battle, hurling of missiles and sword-clash. **1874** R. BUCHANAN *Poet. Wks.* III. 228 Feeble as a maid who hides her face In terror at a sword-flash. **1912** E. POUND *Ripostes* 29 Disease or oldness or sword-hate Beats out the breath from doom-gripped body. **1901** KIPLING *Kim* viii. 209 He caught Mahbub's sword-keen glance. **1923** D. H. LAWRENCE *Birds, Beasts & Flowers* 54 Think of it, from the iron fastness Suddenly to dare to come out naked, in perfection of blossom, beyond the sword-rust. **1930** T. S. ELIOT tr. *St.-J. Perse's Anabasis* 47 In the mirror of our dreams, the sword-rusting sea.

d. *sword-mat* (earlier example); **sword-rattling** *a. fig.*, that threatens military action; aggressive, pugnacious; also as *sb.* = *sabre-rattling* vbl. sb. s.v. *SABRE *sb.* 4 a; **sword-work** = SWORD-PLAY I; also *fig.*

1851 H. MELVILLE *Moby Dick* II. v. 31 Queequeg and I were mildly employed weaving what is called a sword-mat, for an additional lashing to our boat. **1914** *Bulwark* June 84/2 No doubt the Germans will know how to make their Prince acquainted with the unpopularity of his sword-rattling swagger. **1955** *Times* 12 May 1 (*heading*) Afghan 'sword rattling'. *Ibid.*, I would like to ask my Afghan friends whether they really think such a sword-rattling and offensive attitude is going to help them. **1978** *Guardian Weekly* 29 Jan. 6/3 There are 1,500 British troops in Belize.., as the result of Guatemala's sword-rattling last July. **1913** *Nation* 28 June 484/2 Not only has he [*sc.* Sir John Simon] shown his greatest skill in this sword-work [etc.]. **1977** P. SCUPHAM *Hinterland* 58 Boughs come adrift Over the splayed sword-work of spring flowers.

e. sword-bean (earlier example); **sword-fern:** also, *Polystichum munitum*, native to western North America; (later examples).

1875 *Encycl. Brit.* III. 460/2 Beans or pulse, of no small importance as articles of diet, such as the..sword bean of India. **1899** E. COTES *Path of Star* i. 4 The bunch of sword-ferns..grew beside the door. **1932** J. STEINBECK *Pastures of Heaven* vi. 126 Swordferns grew rankly under the alders. **1976** *Islander* (Victoria, B.C.) 4 Jan. 5/1 Most of the park is forest, the damp coastal rain forest of huge sword-ferns and gigantic cedar trees.

swot, swat, *v.* Add: *intr.* Also, to 'bone *up*'. *trans.* (examples); more rarely, without *up*.

1901 *Chambers's Jrnl.* July 445/2 Dick was 'swotting' blue china for all he was worth, at the British Museum and elsewhere. **1913** *Wireless World* I. 37/2 There will be a chance for fellows like me, who have been swatting up Fleming's books. **1931** R. CAMPBELL *Georgiad* i. 18 All who..of despair have baulked the yawning precipice By swotting up his melancholy recipes For 'happiness'. **1955** *Times* 26 May 13/2 Mr. Forester must have 'swotted up' the subject of wartime Atlantic convoys just as he 'swotted up' the subject of the Navy in Nelson's time. **1967** K. GILES *Death in Diamonds* vi. 114 Been swatting the maps, I see. **1977** *N.Y. Rev. Bks.* 23 June 8/2 Our culture hound..swots up in the Encyclopedia before distinguished guests arrive.

swotter (swǫ·təɹ). *slang.* [f. SWOT *v.* + -ER[1].] = SWOT *sb.* 2. Also *swotter-up*.

1919 in *Cassell's New Eng. Dict.* **1925** *Times Lit. Suppl.* 26 Mar. 219/1 If we allow contempt to confuse thought, the 'swotter', for all his dullness, will have us on the hip. **1931** R. CAMPBELL *Georgiad* iii. 62 Swotters-up of philosophic blisses.

swotting (swǫ·tiŋ), *vbl. sb. slang.* [f. SWOT *v.* + -ING[1].] = SWOT *sb.* 1; hard work at one's studies.

1873 *Punch* 11 Jan. 19/2 For downright hard 'swotting' there's no place like School. **1959** I. & P. OPIE *Lore & Lang. Schoolch.* x. 179 'Swotting' or 'mugging up' is only considered good form if a person is on the point of taking an exam. **1974** 'J. HERRIOT' *Vet in Harness* v. 37 He had been blessed with the kind of brain which made swotting irrelevant.

swozzle, var. *SWAZZLE.

swung, *ppl. a.* Add: **3.** *swung dash*, a curved dash ~, used in dictionaries to stand for the headword of an entry or for a specified part of it.

In Oxford dictionaries first used in the first edition of *The Little Oxford Dictionary* (1930) but there called a tilde.

1951 *Conc. Oxf. Dict.* p. iii, In this edition..the swung dash has been freely employed. **1975** *Amer. N. & Q.* XIV. 60/1 *ER*, like most dictionaries, uses a swung dash to denote the entry word.

swy (swəi). *Austral. slang.* Also **swi.** [ad. G. *zwei* two.] **1.** Two; *spec.* a two-shilling coin or a two-year prison sentence.

1924 *Truth* (Sydney) 27 Apr. 6 *Swy*, two. **1941** BAKER *Dict. Austral. Slang* 75 *Swy*, the game of two-up. (2) A sentence of two years' gaol. (3) A florin. **1983** *Age* (Melbourne) 15 Dec. 13 (*caption*) Exhibition of used coin of the realm: bank notes, collector's items, swys, deaners, zacs, treys, brass razoos.

2. The game of two-up (see also quot. 1950). Also *swy-up*.

1940 *Bulletin* (Sydney) 17 Jan. 34/3 The crown-and-anchor seminary he avoids; When swi-up's on, a different direction He takes. **1950** K. S. PRICHARD *Winged Seeds* 63 What set the whole town agog, though, was their attempt to visit the 'swy': the famous two-up ring on a sand hill near the old Rising Sun Inn. **1953** R. BRADDON in I. Bevan *Sunburnt Country* 127 Swy is a game of chance, requiring the tossing of two or three pennies into the air and the betting of those who watch their rise and fall on whether they come down heads or tails. **1969** *Courier-Mail* (Brisbane) 24 Sept. 1/1 He said two-up (or swy) was Australia's national game. **1976** *Sunday Mail* (Brisbane) 24 Oct. 16/4 The police know they will never stop gold-fielders playing swy.

3. *Comb.*, as **swy game**, a game of two-up; **swy school**, a group of persons who have gathered to play two-up.

1950 *Austral. Police Jrnl.* Apr. 118 *Swi*, 2s., but a swi-game is a two-up game. **1953** K. TENNANT *Joyful Condemned* xxix. 284 There's all these little crims in the swi-game and the S.P. betting. **1969** *Telegraph* (Brisbane) 14 May 8/4 Otherwise they blow it at the pub, or at the swy game. **1921** *Aussie* 15 Mar. 54 Just done me last dollar up at the swi school. **1956** S. HOPE *Diggers' Paradise* 59 Neither shalt thou play two-up for lucre in the street, nor attend such swy schools in any private or public premises.

swyneyed, var. *SWEENIED *a.*

-sy. Add: In adjectival formations expressing a degree of mocking contempt, as *artsy-and-craftsy, artsy-fartsy, backwoodsy, bitsy, booksy, folksy, itsy-bitsy, teensy*, etc., the suffix may be considered to represent a nursery form (cf. -Y[6]), or the *pl.* (or even a singular ending) in *-s* + -Y[1].

sycon (səi·kǫn). *Bot.* [a. Gr. σῦκον fig.] † **1.** = Syconium. *Obs.*

1845 *Encycl. Metrop.* VII. 51/1 A sycon is a fleshy, concave receptacle surrounding the fruits.., which are numerous, small, and distinct. **1900** B. D. Jackson *Gloss. Bot. Terms* 262/1 Sycon..a multiple hollow fruit, as that of the fig.

2. [Adopted as a generic name by A. Risso, *Hist. Nat. Europe Méridionale* (1826) V. 368.] A calcareous sponge of the genus of this name; also, a stage in the development of sponges in which flagellated chambers are developed and lined with choanocytes.

1882 W. J. Sollas in P. M. Duncan *Cassell's Nat. Hist.* VI. 326 A transitional series of species can be shown to exist between a simple Ascon and a Sycon in which radiate buds have all united..to form a complex tubulated wall. **1912** *Phil. Trans. R. Soc.* B. CCII. 170 The normal young Sycon has a beautiful double ascular crown of long monaxons. **1932** Borradaile & Potts *Invertebrata* iii. 113 The three grades of sponge structure ..are known as the 'Ascon', 'Sycon', and 'Leucon' grades.

sycophantish, *a.* (Earlier example.)

1821 R. Lee *Diary* 20 Oct. (1897) 26 Mr. L. said that although he admired Sir W. Scott's talents, still there was something about him which he did not like—a sneaking, flattering, sycophantish manner.

Sydama, var. *Sidamo.

Sydenham (si·dĕnăm). *Path.* [The name of Thomas *Sydenham* (1624–89), English physician, who described the chorea in *Schedula Monitoria de Novæ Febris Ingressu* (1686).] *Sydenham's chorea*: a self-limited disorder of childhood or pregnancy that is a neurological manifestation of rheumatic fever, affecting the motor activities of the nervous system and characterized by involuntary movements.

1892 *Med. Record* (N.Y.) XLI. 285/2 There are many cases of Sydenham's chorea in which voluntary effort arrests the movements. **1954** *Handbk. for Mental Nurses* (ed. 8) vi. 162 Sydenham's Chorea. This, also known as St. Vitus's Dance, is..much commoner in girls than in boys. **1976** Smythies & Corbett *Psychiatry* vii. 128 Sydenham's chorea occurs in younger people, there is no family history, no dementia and the course is not progressive.

Sydnæan, var. *Sidneian *a.*

Sydney (si·dni). [The name of the capital city of New South Wales.] **1.** In *Austral.* colloq. phr. *Sydney or the bush*, all or nothing. Cf. Bush *sb.*[1] 9.

1924 *Truth* (Sydney) 27 Apr. 6 *Sydney or the bush*, all or nothing. **1930** E. Shann *Econ. Hist. Austral.* 365 'Sydney or the bush!' cries the Australian when he gambles against odds. **1970** R. Beilby *No Medals for Aphrodite* 34 'Here we go,' Turk murmured grimly, climbing in behind the wheel. 'It's Sydney or the bush! Keep your fingers crossed.'

2. Special combinations. **a. Sydney-side** [Side *sb.*[1] 15 b], Sydney and the surrounding area; also as *adj.*; **Sydneysider,** a resident or native of Sydney or of New South Wales.

[**1872** W. M. Hugo *Hist. First Bushmen's Club in Austral. Colonies* 108 Very frequently, however, they are not allowed to proceed so far as the city, but get 'bailed up', as they call it on the Sydney side, before they reach their destination.] **1888** 'R. Boldrewood' *Robbery under Arms* I. i. 1 My name's Dick Marston, Sydney-side native. **1928** 'Brent of Bin Bin' *Up Country* v. 67 She was..supposed to be..a descendant..of the famous Sydney-side sire 'Clifton'. **1941** Baker *Dict. Austral. Slang* 75 *Sydneyside*, originally the area which is now N.S.W. Later, especially the area of Sydney. **1865** H. Kingsley *Hillyars & Burtons* III. xiii. 144 The Sydney-siders' loss is considered by him to have been far greater. **1931** *Times Lit. Suppl.* 1 Oct. 738/1 A fear of its [*sc.* Melbourne's] writers..echoed the nationalist emotion, but in abstract terms that lacked the appeal of the Sydney-siders. **1980** N. Marsh *Photo-Finish* vii. 199 He was a self-made man, a Sydneysider.

b. *Nat. Hist.* In the names of plants or animals associated with the region, as **Sydney blue gum,** a flooded gum, *Eucalyptus saligna*; **Sydney golden wattle,** a shrub or small tree, *Acacia longifolia*; **Sydney silky** (also **silkie**), a small stocky terrier of the breed so called, with long, silky, grey-blue fur and tan markings.

1932 R. H. Anderson *Trees N.S.W.* v. 101 Sydney Blue Gum... A tall-growing, shaft-like species. **1933, 1965** Sydney blue gum [see *flooded *ppl. a.*]. **1909** A. E. Mack *Bush Calendar* 20 Flowers blooming [in September]. *Acacia longifolia*. Sydney golden wattle. **1976** *Hortus Third* (L. H. Bailey Hortorium) 6/1 Sydney golden wattle..flower heads in loose spikes. **1945** Sydney silky [see *Australian *sb.* 3]. **1965** *Austral. Encycl.* III. 265/2 The Sydney silky, classed as a toy dog,..has a coat of steel-blue, silky hair up to 6 inches long, with a tan face, legs and points. **1977** *N.Z. Herald* 8 Jan. 4-9/7 (Advt.), Sydney silkie dog pups, 6 wks old.

Sydnian, var. *Sidneian *a.*

Syenna, obs. var. *Siena.

syenodiorite (səi,ĕnodəi·ŏrəit). *Petrogr.* [f. *syeno-*, comb. form of Syenite + Diorite.] A plutonic rock of a kind intermediate between syenite and diorite, containing both alkali feldspar and plagioclase.

1917 A. Johannsen in *Jrnl. Geol.* XXV. 89 Syenodiorite, syenogabbro, and granogabbro are introduced as new terms. **1940** *Bull. Geol. Soc. Amer.* LI. 1592 The laccolith near the abandoned wax factory on Fresno Creek..is composed of a striking augite syenodiorite. **1977** A. Hallam *Planet Earth* 162/1 Color index rises to about 50 in the gabbros and is between 20 and 50 in the diorites and syenodiorites.

Sykes (səiks). The name of William Henry *Sykes* (1790–1872), English soldier and naturalist, used in the possessive in **Sykes'(s) monkey,** to designate *Cercopithecus albogularis*, a blue-grey guenon native to East Africa.

[**1831** *Proc. Zool. Soc.* 105 Major Sykes subsequently called the attention of the Committee to a Monkey presented by him to the Society.] **1864** *Ibid.* 709 Sykes's Monkey. **1905** [see Monkey *sb.* 1 b]. **1914** R. C. F. Maugham *Wild Game in Zambezia* xi. 252 Sykes' Monkey is a comparative rarity. **1932** S. Zuckerman *Soc. Life Monkeys & Apes* xi. 185 Loveridge found that Sykes' monkeys were plentiful at Morogoro in East Africa. **1963** A. Smith *Throw out Two Hands* xiii. 132 We had initially been concentrating on a group of Sykes's monkeys.

syllabic, *a.* and *sb.* Add: **A.** *adj.* **1. c.** (Earlier examples.)

1804 J. Barrow *Trav. in China* vi. 270 [The Manchu writing-system] is alphabetic, or, more properly speaking, syllabic. **1838** P. Du Ponceau *Chinese System of Writing* p. xii, Syllabic alphabets, besides, have considerable advantages over those that we make use of.

d. Of verse or metre: based upon or determined by the number of syllables in a line, etc.

1923 L. Abercrombie in *Times Lit. Suppl.* 12 Apr. 247/1 English metre, according to many theorists, is neither syllabic nor quantitative, but simply accentual. **1965** A. F. Scott *Current Lit. Terms* 282 The determining feature of syllabic verse is the number of syllables in the line, not the stress nor the quantity. **1970** G. S. Fraser *Metre, Rhyme & Free Verse* iv. 50 Purely syllabic metrics seems..not suitable to the prosody of English as a natural language.

B. *sb.* **4.** *pl.* Syllabic verse.

1964 *Times Lit. Suppl.* 16 Jan. 53/4 Syllabics are as legitimate a metrical device as any other. *Ibid.*, Syllabics accommodate speech rhythms... MacBeth and..B.S. Johnson, independently discovered this quality of syllabic metre a few years ago. **1977** *Ibid.* 8 Apr. 428/2 The line in Bridges's use of neo-Miltonic syllabics is fundamentally of twelve syllables.

syllabicate, *v.* Delete *rare*[−0] and add examples. Also *intr.*, to form or construct syllables; to divide a word or passage into syllables.

1654 J. Brooksbank *Plain, Brief, Rules for Syllabication Eng. Words* 27 To Syllabicate, which is to find out a word by its syllables. **1831** J. Boaden *Life of Mrs. Jordan* II. xx. 178 He did not syllabicate, his notion of a word was often caught from vulgar speakers. **1902** H. Bradley *Let.* 9 Jan. in *Corresp. Bridges & Bradley* (1940) 9 If the Greeks syllabicated like this..a syllable ending in *one* or more consonants is long. **1971** *Language* XLVII. 138 *Perpetual* is syllabicated as *per. pety. u. al.*

syllabication. Add: (Later examples.)

Tending to give way to *syllabification*.–Ed.

1933 L. Bloomfield *Language* vii. 121 The ups and downs of *syllabication* play an important part in the phonetic structure of all languages. **1971** *Language* XLVII. 138 The rule for the devoicing of liquids follows syllabication.

syllabicity (silăbi·sĭti). [f. Syllabic *a.* + -ity.] = Syllabicness.

1933 L. Bloomfield *Language* viii. 130 Syllabicity determined also by manner of articulation. **1944** L. M. Hartman in *Language* XX. 33 One of these [morphophonemic changes] is the loss of syllabicity either by this or by the preceding syllable. **1952** A. Cohen *Phonemes of Eng.* iii. 62 There does not seem to be any need for assuming a special phoneme of syllabicity. **1968** F. G. Lounsbury in J. A. Fishman *Readings Sociol. of Lang.* 53 What we have accomplished is to suppress from our transcription the representation of features of the acoustic stimulus (voicing, syllabicity, laryngeal order, and position of the accent) which do not serve as cues for differential responses on the part of the native subjects. **1977** *Archivum Linguisticum* VIII. 87 There is no experimental evidence for, and some experimental evidence against, the necessary presence of such pulses as physiological correlates of syllabicity.

syllabification. (Later examples.)

1972 *Webster's New World Dict.* (Delux Color ed.) p. x, The syllabifications used in this dictionary are in the main those in general use by printers since the 18th century. **1977** *Archivum Linguisticum* VIII. 87 Such questions, he states, are now 'reduced to practical matters of articulatory adjustment in particular languages'..—which would seem to imply that syllabification rules are part of particular phonologies. **1979** *Collins Eng. Dict.* p. x, Syllabification breaks are shown for all headwords. **1980** *Verbatim* Spring 19/1 Lexicography is not simply adding one good point to another to make an ideal dictionary, but balancing the saving of space against fullness of information, the amount of information against cost, a more exact pronunciation guide against added difficulty for some users, the addition of extra information (pronunciation or syllabification) in the headword at the expense of its clean appearance.

sylla·bify, *v.* Delete *rare*[−0] and add examples. Also *intr.*

1926 [see *syllabization]. **1954** F. G. Cassidy *Robertson's Devel. Mod. Eng.* (ed. 2) xii. 381 Though the American may syllabify more fully where the Englishman elides, he also slurs more. **1972** *Language* XLVIII. 357 If one assumes that ø is the alternative to syllabifying *-s*, then one can establish a graded gamut of markedness among the three alternants.

syllabiza·tion. [f. Syllabize *v.* + -ation.] = Syllabification.

1926 H. W. Fowler *Mod. Eng. Usage* 590/2 A verb & a noun are clearly sometimes needed for the notion of dividing words into syllables. The possible pairs seem to be..syllabify..syllabification [etc.]... The best thing would be to accept the most recognized verb *syllabize*, give it the now non-existent noun *syllabization*, [etc.]. **1929** *S.P.E. Tract* xxxiii. 436 Under *syllabize etc.* he [*sc.* Fowler] exposes a want in our vocabulary, which perhaps indicates a general lack of interest in *syllabization*. **1976** *Archivum Linguisticum* VII. 181 In Adrados's explanation, these forms without colouring of the vowel occur in a different syllabization.

syllabize, *v.* Add: **1.** Also **sy·llabized** *ppl. a.*

1957 A. Oras in N. Frye *Sound & Poetry* 112 Milton's growing dislike of syllabized *-ed* endings. **1969** *Computers & Humanities* III. 257 The latter is based upon successive scanning of the syllabized text in groups of four, three, two and one characters.

syllable, *sb.* Add: **1. c.** Colloq. phr. *in words of one syllable*, in simple language.

1922 F. H. Burnett *Head of House of Combe* xvii. 206 The French Revolution..—the cataclysms of agony—need not have been, but they *were*. To put it in words of one syllable. **1941** V. Woolf *Between Acts* 218 Let's talk in words of one syllable, without larding, stuffing or cant. **1966** 'E. Lathen' *Murder makes Wheels go Round* xxi. 166 'John,' he said breathlessly, 'would you please explain in words of one syllable.' **1970** *Guardian* 9 Mar. 24/1 Why don't they tell us precisely, in words of one syllable, how they would behave if they were in our place?

4. *syllable-count, stress; syllable-counting, -final, -initial* adjs.; **syllable-timed** *a.*, of or having a rhythm in which syllables occur at roughly equivalent time intervals; opp. *stress-timed* adj. s.v. *stress *sb.* 10; hence **syllable-timing.**

1969 *Language* XLV. 250 The text itself is composed in syllable-count verse forms. **1983** *Listener* 6 Jan. 21/3 Pop lyrics writers throw in an 'oh yeah' or a 'baby' wherever the syllable-count needs padding out. **1959** *PMLA* LXXIV. 588/2 This has been done on strictly accentual (plus syllable-counting) principles. **1978** *Early Music* Oct. 587/3 He describes in detail three kinds of relationship..between words and music in the period—the metrical..the accentual..the syllable-counting (the characteristic mode of Christian and much courtly poetry). **1964** B. Malmberg in D. Abercrombie et al. *Daniel Jones* 116 Many languages have an opposition between explosive (syllable-initial) and implosive (syllable-final) consonant. **1978** *Language* LIV. 23 Durand.. points out that the [t] in *petit orage* 'little storm' is syllable-initial, while the [t] in *petite orange* 'little orange' appears to be syllable-final for most speakers. **1924** H. E. Palmer *Gram. Spoken Eng.* i. 6 *Word-stress* (in the opinion of the author the term *syllable-stress* would be more appropriate). This term is used with reference to a syllable. **1964** W. S. Allen in D. Abercombie et al. *Daniel Jones* 14 These remarks on English verse are intended only to apply to the 'syllable-stress' metres. **1947** K. L. Pike *Phonemics* i. ii. 13/1 In English one tends to hear stress-timed rhythm in contra-distinction to a syllable-timed rhythm. In the syllable-timed type the syllables themselves tend to be more or less equally spaced... As a result of the syllable timing the vowels are likely to be clear cut. **1980** *English World-Wide* I. i. 108 This, as well as the syllable-timed rhythm, gives rise to the staccato impression often noticed by outsiders. **1964** M. A. K. Halliday et al. *Linguistic Sci.* 72 The English type of rhythm is known as 'stress-timing', by contrast with the 'syllable timing' of French.

syllabus. Add: **1. b.** *spec.* a statement of the subjects covered by a course of instruction or by an examination, in a school, college, etc.; a programme of study.

1889 *Rep. Higher Educ. in London* p. ix, in *Parl. Papers* (C. 5709) XXXIX. 323 The colleges having no *locus standi* to make representations to the authorities of the university either as to the settlement or alteration of the 'syllabus' by which the course of the examinations is regulated. **1955** E. Blishen *Roaring Boys* iii. 117 The history syllabus for the school had been drawn up by Mr Benson. **1972** *Daily Tel.* (Colour Suppl.) 1 Dec. 15 Schools should allow pupils to determine syllabi.

c. *fig.*

1938 Auden *Commentary* in *Journey to War* (1939) 290 And the young emerging from the closed parental circle, to whose uncertainty the certain years present their syllabus of limitless anxiety and labour.

syllid (si·lid), *sb.* and *a.* [ad. mod.L. family name *Syllidæ*, f. generic name *Syllis* (J. B. P. A. de M. de Lamarck *Hist. Nat. Animaux sans Vertèbres* (1818) V. 317) + -ID[3].] **A.** *sb.* A small errant polychæte worm of the family Syllidæ, distinguished by three tentacles on its head and found on rocky shores. **B.** *adj.* Of or pertaining to an animal of this kind. Also † **sylli·dian** *sb.*

1888 ROLLESTON & JACKSON *Forms Animal Life* (ed. 2) 607 The parent-form in these Syllidians remains non-sexual. **1910** *Encycl. Brit.* V. 793/1 There are even dimorphic forms among the Syllids. **1928** RUSSELL & YONGE *Seas* ii. 52 The little syllid worms break up..into fragments of a few segments, each of which..develops into a full-sized worm. **1930** *Q. Jrnl. Microsc. Sci.* LXXIII. 651 (*heading*) On a new Hermaphrodite Syllid. **1963** R. P. DALES *Annelids* i. 30 The nephridiostome remains as a recognisable notch or pocket in the larger coelomostome, as it does..in some syllids. **1971** *Oxf. Bk. Invertebrates* 96 Syllids usually cling to sea-vegetation or nestle in empty shells and crevices. *Ibid.* 96/2 *Syllis* shows well the typical syllid processes arising from the sides of the body.

Sylow (sī·lǫf). *Math.* The name of P. L. *Sylow* (1832–1918), Norwegian mathematician, used *attrib.* and in the possessive to designate concepts in group theory propounded by him (*Math. Annalen* (1872) V. 584), as **Sylow (p-)subgroup,** a subgroup whose order is the largest power of the prime *p* which divides the order of the group; **Sylow's theorem** (see quots. 1897, 1975).

1893 *Proc. Lond. Math. Soc.* XXV. 14 It is then shown that Sylow's theorem leads to relations between the numbers of operations of different orders which it is impossible to satisfy. **1897** W. BURNSIDE *Theory of Groups of Finite Order* vi. 91 We shall divide the proof of Sylow's theorem into two parts. First we show that, if p^α is the highest power of a prime *p* which divides the order of a group, the group must have a sub-group of order p^α; and secondly that the sub-groups of order p^α form a single conjugate set and that their number is congruent to unity, mod. *p*. **1905** *Messenger Math.* XXXV. 48 A group..all of whose Sylow subgroups are cyclical. **1975** I. STEWART *Concepts Mod. Math.* vii. 104 The best that can be said in general is Sylow's theorem; if *h* is a power of a prime and divides the order of a group *G*, then *G* has a subgroup of order *h*. **1976** *Nature* 20 May p. vii (Advt.), The classification of nonsoluble groups with abelian sylow 2-subgroups.

sylph. Add: **3.** *sylph-like* (earlier example).

1801 C. WILMOT *Let.* 13 Dec. in T. U. Sadleir *Irish Peer* (1920) 15 Madame, their Mother, was too much en bon point to have such a sylphlike appearance as her daughters.

Sylphon (si·lfǫn). Also **sylphon.** [Invented word.] A proprietary name (see quots. 1906, 1916, 1933) used esp. to designate concertina-like metal bellows and devices employing them.

1906 *Official Gaz.* (U.S. Patent Office) 3 Apr. 1643/1 Heat-regulators for use on boilers, furnaces, and stoves... *Sylphon.* **1916** *Ibid.* 25 July 1432/1 *Sylphon...* A hollow expansible and contractible corrugated tubular metal device. **1933** *Trade Marks Jrnl.* 2 Aug. 925/2 *Sylphon...* Valves, hot and cold water mixers and dampers all being parts of steam boilers... The Fulton Sylphon Company.., Knoxville, Tennessee. **1937** *Jrnl. Psychol.* IV. 281 The essential unit is a small capacity sylphon or thin-gauge metal bellows enclosed in an airtight metal housing. **1938** *Jrnl. R. Aeronaut. Soc.* XLII. 1072 The valves of these tanks may be operated by a sylphon bellows. **1945** H. D. SMYTH *Gen. Acct. Devel. Atomic Energy Mil. Purposes* x. 110 The pumps used were sylphon-sealed reciprocating pumps.

Sylvaner (silvā·nəɹ). Also **sylvaner.** [a. G. *silvaner, sylvaner*: cf. SYLVAN, SILVAN *sb.* and *a.*]

1. A variety of vine first developed in German-speaking districts, the dominant form bearing white grapes; a vine or grape of this variety. Also *attrib.*

1928 P. M. SHAND *Bk. French Wines* vi. 201 The Gutedel..Ortlieber, Burger, Sylvaner, and Klevner are grown besides [in Alsace]. **1963** *Times* 17 Jan. 4/6 It has the typical flavour of a wine made from Sylvaner grapes. **1965, 1976** [see *PINOT]. **1981** T. MCLEAN *Medieval Eng. Gardens* ix. 256 The Müller-Thurgau vine..is a cross between a Riesling and a Sylvaner.

2. The white wine made from the Sylvaner grape.

1958 A. L. SIMON *Dict. Wines, Spirits & Liqueurs* 152/2 *Sylvaner*, a free-bearing white-wine grape grown extensively in Germany and in Alsace. Much Alsation wine (white) made from Sylvaner grapes is marketed under the name of *Sylvaner.* **1961** *Spectator* 24 Nov. 756 [The wines] are labelled according to the grapes used, as in Alsace... The commonest names are Riesling..Sauvignon, Sylvaner, [etc.].

sylvatic, silvatic, *a.* Restrict *rare* to **silvatic** and sense in Dict. and add: **2.** *Med.* Also (*rare*) **selvatic.** Applied to certain diseases (as rabies, yellow fever, plague, and Chagas's disease) when contracted by wild rather than domesticated animals, and to the pathogens causing them. [ad. F. *selvatique* (R. Jorge *Les Rongeurs & leurs Puces dans la Propagation de la Peste* (1928) ii. 36); cf. L. *silvāticus* wild.]

1931 C. O. STALLYBRASS *Princ. Epidemiol.* ix. 310 In this way arise two types of epizoötic [plague]... One.. among wild rodents, spreading slowly from colony to colony, independent of man's lines of communication..; to this type of epizoötic Jorge (1928) has given the title selvatic plague. **1935** *Jrnl. Amer. Med. Assoc.* 17 Aug. 535/2 The invasion of sylvatic plague among the ground squirrels of the foothills of the Sierras and Cascade Mountains creates a widening menace in the United States. **1936** WU LIEN-TEH in Wu Lien-Teh et al. *Plague* vi. 195 Jorge..distinguished between the pandemic plague introduced..by..'domestic' rodents, and selvatic plague, dangerous to man only when he invades the remote endemic areas populated by wild rodents. **1970** *Sci. Jrnl.* Apr. 35/1 There has been a steady and alarming increase in rabies in wild animals—so-called sylvatic rabies. **1978** *Nature* 27 Apr. 820/1 We have identified distinct sylvatic and domestic strain-groups of *T*[*rypanosoma*] *cruzi*, apparently circulating independently and transmitted by different vector species.

sylvestrene (silve·strīn). *Chem.* [ad. G. *sylvestren* (A. Atterberg 1877, in *Ber. Deut. Chem. Ges.* X. 1203), f. L. *sylvestr-is* found in woods (f. *silva*: see SYLVA, SILVA), specific epithet of the Scots pine, *Pinus sylvestris*: see -ENE.] A liquid monocyclic terpene, $C_{10}H_{16}$, known in two optically active forms and formerly believed to be a natural constituent of pine oil, but now recognized as a product of the extraction process.

1877 *Chem. News* 6 July 7/1 A. Atterberg has examined the crude '*Wood-Spirit from Norwegian Pines*', and found in the higher boiling portions..a new turpentine, to which he assigns the name *sylvestrine.* **1931** [see *ISOPRENE b]. **1952** TURNER & HARRIS *Org. Chem.* xix. 317 Simonsen..showed that the precursor of sylvestrene is the naturally occurring (+)-Δ^3-carene.

Sylvian, *a.*[2] (Earlier example.) *fissure of Sylvius* (examples).

1828 J. QUAIN *Elem. Anat.* ix. 613 The angular part of the anterior lobe..is included between the internal termination of the fissure of Sylvius, the longitudinal fissure, and the commissure of the optic nerves. **1839–47** [see *ROLANDO a]. **1849** S. G. MORTON *Illustr. Syst. Human Anat.* 547 The insula [of Reil] consists of five or six small convolutions grouped and concealed within the Sylvian fissure. **1888, 1939** [see *REIL]. **1980** A. SILVERSTEIN *Human Anat. & Physiol.* xiii. 278/2 Viewed from the side, the cerebrum looks something like a large mitten, with the wrist at the back and the fingers at the front of the head. The 'thumb' of the mitten is separated from the remainder by another prominent groove, the lateral fissure or fissure of Sylvius.

sylvics, silvics. Add: (Further examples.) orig. and chiefly *U.S.* (The form *sylvics* is *rare*$^{-0}$.) Cf. *SILVICAL *a.*

1946 *Jrnl. Forestry* XLIV. 965/1 The forester's knowledge of the silvics of the species was pretty thin. **1948** H. J. OOSTING *Study of Plant Communities* (ed. 2) xii. 317 An important part of a forester's training is forest ecology, or silvics, in which he learns the scientific background upon which silvicultural practices are based. **1975** *Agriculture Handbk.* (U.S. Dept. Agric.) No. 486 (*title*) Quaking aspen: silvics and management in the Lake States.

sylvinite (si·lvinəit). *Min.* [ad. G. *sylvinit*, f. G. *sylvin* SYLVINE: see -ITE.[1]] A commercial name for a mixture of sylvite and halite (the form in which sylvite commonly occurs).

1896 A. H. CHESTER *Dict. Names Minerals* 263 *Sylvinite*, the commercial name for sylvite. **1962** *Economist* 31 Mar. 1274/3 The D'Arcy Exploration Company..found ..potash-bearing brine and sylvinite (a mixture of potassium chloride and salt) in a boring near Whitby. **1980** H. BLATT et al. *Origin Sedimentary Rocks* (ed. 2) xv. 558 Sylvinite is composed of sylvite (KCl) and halite (NaCl).

sym-. Add: **symphala·ngism** *Anat.* [L. *phalang-*: see PHALANX], a condition in which the middle phalanx of a finger or toe is properly developed in length but its proximal (or distal) joint is imperfect or absent; **sy·mphile** *Ent.*, an insect that lives with ants or other social insects as a guest in a relationship of symphilism; hence **symphi·lic** *a.*, pertaining to or being a symphile; also *fig.*; **symphilism,** add: [ad. G. *symphilie* (M. E. Wasmann 1896, in *3me Congr. Internat. Zool.* 412)]; **sy·mphylan, sy·mphylid** *adjs.* and *sbs. Ent.* [mod. L. *Symphyla*, name of a class of arthropods (J. A. Ryder 1880, in *Amer. Naturalist* XIV. 376), f. Gr. φυλή tribe: so called from their combining characteristics of several other classes] (of or pertaining to) an arthropod of the class Symphyla, the members of which resemble centipedes, having soft bodies and many legs; **sy·mport** *Biochem.* [after TRANSPORT *sb.*], flow of two substances through a membrane in the same direction in which the rate is increased by a cooperative effect.

1916 H. CUSHING in *Genetics* I. 91 This paper will present a much more complete family record of an inherited trait... The malformation will be designated symphalangism. **1943** *Jrnl. Heredity* XXXIV. 344/1 Similar reports of abnormalities of hands and feet including symphalangism, syndactylism, and polydactyly..seem to agree that many anatomical anomalies may be inherited as single dominant traits. **1965** *Arch. Internal Med.* CXV. 580/1 Symphalangism (congenital fusion of the phalanges) is occasionally associated with brachydactyly. **1910** Symphile [see *synœkete* s.v. *SYN-]. **1960** H. OLDROYD tr. *Jeannel's Introd. Entomol.* viii. 212 The greater number of symphiles are beetles, cherished by the ants, and carried with them wherever the nest is moved, but nevertheless terrible enemies of the colony because of the great damage they do to it. **1971** E. O. WILSON *Insect Societies* xx. 403/1 Many of the better-integrated symphiles dispense attractive substances to their hosts from epidermal glands. **1919** W. OSLER *Old Humanities & New Sci.* ii. 12 This attention is what our symphilic community—to use a biological term—bestows on you. **1927** H. ST. J. K. DONISTHORPE *Guests of Brit. Ants* p. xvi, They mostly possess characteristic or 'symphilic' colours and texture—a yellow-red, with an oily looking surface. **1971** E. O. WILSON *Insect Societies* xx. 403/2 A large percentage of the symphilic beetles..possess peculiar tufts of red or golden hairs. **1898** A. S. PACKARD *Text-bk. Entomol.* 21 He..believed that the Symphyla are the forerunners of the myriapods, and not of the insects, his genealogical tree representing the symphylan and thysanuran phyla as originating from the same point. **1964** U. LANHAM *Insects* i. 19 Two of these classes [of many-legged arthropods]—the pauropods and the symphylans—are small, obscure creatures... The other two—centipedes and millipedes—are larger, more conspicuous. **1979** W. D. RUSSELL-HUNTER *Life of Invertebrates* xvi. 301 In some structural features, symphylans resemble the centipedes and in others the apterygote insects. **1936** *Trans. Soc. Brit. Entomol.* III. 14 The contention that the opisthogoneate condition in insects has been derived from Symphylid stock. *Ibid.* 16 The heart, haemocoel, fat-body and anal glands have all been inherited from the Symphylids. **1973** *Nature* 16 Nov. 128/1 It is of interest that certain of the symphilids carry styli on the base of the second and third pairs of legs. **1974** *Encycl. Brit. Macropædia* XII. 771/1 Symphilid species are small, fragile, and lacking pigmentation. **1963** P. MITCHELL in *Biochem. Soc. Symp.* XXII. 148 Over a certain range of concentration, the asymmetry of distribution of the molecules of one substrate across the membrane gives rise to an increased flow of the second substrate in the same direction. We will call this type of coupled movement symport. **1978** *Nature* 2 Mar. 97/1 There are discussions of algal ion transport and of Na^+/organic solute cotransport (symport).

Symbionese (si:mbi,ǒnī·z), *a.* [f. SYMBIO(SIS + *-n-* + -ESE, after group and people names in *-nese* (*Chinese, Lebanese*, etc.): see quot. 1974.] *Symbionese Liberation Army*, the name adopted by a socialist revolutionary group active in the United States in the mid-1970s.

1973 *N.Y. Times* 10 Nov. 1/4 Two days ago, a group calling itself the Symbionese Liberation Army took the responsibility for the killing. **1974** *Black Panther* 23 Feb. 11/2 The Symbionese Liberation Army is made up of the aged, youth and women and men of all races and people. The name Symbionese is taken from the word symbiosis and we define its meaning as a body of dissimilar bodies and organisms living in deep and loving harmony and partnership in the best interest of all within the body. **1975** *Times* 20 Nov. 1/3 Miss Patricia Hearst, the runaway heiress..was arrested..[in] a routine check on the movements of people associated with the Symbionese Liberation Army (the SLA). **1976** M. J. LASKY *Utopia & Revolution* (1977) 603 Six leading American members..of the so-called Symbionese Liberation Army were killed in Los Angeles in a gun fight [in 1974] with the local police.

symbiose (si·mbəi,ǒᵘz), *v.* [Back-formation from next.] *intr.* To live as a symbiont.

1960 *McGraw-Hill Encycl. Sci. & Technol.* XI. 546/2 Strains of each species show marked host specificities in their abilities to symbiose with the plants within each group. **1971** M. ALEXANDER *Microbial Ecol.* xi. 266 A single fungus can apparently symbiose with dissimilar species of algae.

symbiosis. Add: Pl. **symbioses. 1.** Delete † *Obs. rare*$^{-1}$ and add later examples.

1910 *Spectator* 30 July 173/2 The savage with his.. sense of 'participation', of 'symbiosis'. **1920** *Q. Rev.* July 164 So long as the people concerned can talk freely together, they form one spiritual symbiosis, and their culture will be the same.

2. a. (Further examples.) Also more widely, any intimate association of two or more different organisms, whether mutually beneficial or not.

1909 tr. *Warming's Oecol. Plants* xxv. 84 Parasitism is a form of symbiosis. **1941** H. KIRBY in Calkins & Summers *Protozoa in Biol. Res.* xix. 891 De Bary..used symbiosis as a collective term, the subdivisions of which include parasitism and mutualism; he recognized two main categories, antagonistic and mutualistic symbiosis. **1953** [see *SYMBIOTE]. **1953**, etc. [see *MUTUALISM 2]. **1973** R. G. KRUEGER et al. *Introd. Microbiol.* xxxi. 748/1 Three or more different kinds of organisms are involved in some symbioses. **1977** R. L. SMITH *Elem. Ecol. & Field Biol.* x. 268/1 Mutualism is often termed symbiosis. Actually symbiosis..includes mutualism, commensalism, and parasitism.

b. *transf.* and *fig.*

1921 G. B. SHAW *Back to Methuselah* II. 79 Let the Creator say, if you like, 'I will establish an antipathetic symbiosis between thee and the female.' **1955** *Bull.*

Atomic Sci. Apr. 143/2 Two world wars predetermined the henceforth inevitable symbiosis of scientific activity and political decision. **1963** *Listener* 28 Feb. 386/1 The agreement between Castro and the Communist Party early in 1958..began the process of symbiosis which worried many of the more thoughtful *fidelistas*. **1967** M. J. RUGGLES in D. H. Perman *Bibliogr. & Historian* (1968) II. 22 A symbiosis between scholar and librarian is necessary. **1976** *New Yorker* 17 May 127/1 In the symbiosis that will link the candidates and the press throughout this election year, many representatives of each are out in Iowa. **1982** *Listener* 23 & 30 Dec. 29/2 The politician and the journalist exist in a state of uneasy symbiosis.

symbiote, (*b*) = SYMBIONT; also *fig.*; **symbiotic** *a.* (further examples); also *transf.* and *fig.*

1923 *Anat. Rec.* XXV. 2 Portier believes that the 'symbiotes' are especial microorganisms found in great abundance in nature. They are constantly entering and leaving the host organism. **1925** *Jrnl. Infectious Dis.* XXXVI. 94 The intracellular bacteria have been designated as 'symbiotes'. **1953** R. P. HALL *Protozoology* x. 528 Endoparasites which participate in symbiosis, an association involving mutual benefits to host and parasite, are known as symbiotes. **1953** [see *MUTUALISM 2]. **1970** *Times Lit. Suppl.* 14 Aug. 899/5 His suggestion of a future man as a bio-mechanical symbiote. **1951** R. FIRTH *Elem. Social Organization* i. 10 It is most evident in the case of an African tribe having its members living intermingled with those of other tribes and in symbiotic relationship with them. **1956** *Psychiatric Research Rep.* No. 3. 8 A therapeutic move of considerable importance in such a situation is for the physician to function as the other half of the patient's 'symbiotic' system. **1962** *Lancet* 19 May 1033/2 The human infant in its first year is more precariously placed than has hitherto been appreciated since mother and child form a symbiotic union. **1970** *Nature* 6 June 905/1 Throughout its auspicious history the Botanical Society of Edinburgh has had a symbiotic relationship with the Royal Botanic Garden. **1979** W. STYRON *Sophie's Choice* vi. 150 Höss eventually developed what might be called a fruitful—or at least symbiotic—relationship with the man who was to remain his immediate superior.

symbiotrophic (si:mbəi,otrōᵘ·fik, -trǫ·fik), *a.* *Ecol.* [f. SYMBIO(SIS + *-TROPHIC.] Obtaining nourishment through symbiosis.

1905 B. D. JACKSON *Gloss. Bot. Terms* (ed. 2) 358/1. **1974** D. H. LEWIS in Carlile & Skehel *Evolution in Microbial World* 386 Chemoheterotrophs, including animals, may derive nutrients in the free-living state (saprotrophic) or following intimate contact with other organisms (symbiotrophic). **1978** *Proc. Indian Acad. Sci.* B. LXXXVII. x. 243 Despite high salinity and acidity an acid sulfate soil harboured N_2-fixing symbiotrophic organisms with appreciable efficiency.

symbol, *sb.*[1] Add: **4.** *symbol-maker, -making, -object, -system, -user*; *symbol-making, -minded, -using* adjs.

1981 F. INGLIS *Promise of Happiness* iii. 85 The nineteenth-century novelists were the symbol-makers for a new order. **1953** R. LEHMANN *Echoing Grove* 28 Its one round turret, its weather-cock and flag-pole all supernaturally designed in the last sun's last symbol-making glow. **1962** W. NOWOTTNY *Lang. Poets Use* viii. 180 A kind of linguistic ambiguity..seems frequently to occur in poems bent on symbol-making. **1936** O. NASH *Primrose Path* 55 Still, I think, a pig's a pig—Ah, there, symbol-minded Sig! **1977** *N.Y. Times* 20 Jan. 4/3 Ever since he walked home from his inauguration, Mr. Carter has presented the country with a symbol-minded Presidency. **1913** L. BLOOMFIELD in C. F. Hockett *Leonard Bloomfield Anthol.* (1970) 43 This symbol-object is..the word: without it no concept of action, quality, or relation can exist. **1964** E. BECKER in I. L. Horowitz *New Sociol.* 119 Man..possesses both thing-objects, like all other animals; and, uniquely, symbol-objects. **1946** F. P. CHISHOLM in W. S. Knickerbocker *Twentieth Cent. Eng.* II. 183 The communication process involves both speakers and listeners, writers and readers, using a socially-constructed symbol-system, in whose structure 'reality' must be represented. **1964** R. H. ROBINS *Gen. Linguistics* 13 Among symbol systems language occupies a special place. **1946** F. P. CHISHOLM in W. S. Knickerbocker *Twentieth Cent. Eng.* II. 172 Our distinguishing human characteristic is that we are symbol-users. **1951** J. HOLLOWAY *Lang. & Intelligence* vi. 95 Intelligence displayed in a symbol-using planning sequence sometimes enables us to reduce the sequence of actions to a sequence of routines. **1977** R. HOLLAND *Self & Social Context* i. 18 Ethnomethodology..embraces a phenomenological concern for the experiencing, symbol-using self.

symbolic, *a.* (*sb.*) Add: **2. c.** *symbolic logic*, logic that employs a special technical notation of symbols; formal or mathematical logic (see *MATHEMATICAL *a.* 1 e). Hence *symbolic logician.*

1856 A. DE MORGAN in *Trans. Cambr. Philos. Soc.* IX. 83, I think it reasonably probable that the advance of symbolic logic will lead to a calculus of opposite relations, for mere inference, as general as that of + and − in algebra. **1881** [in Dict., sense 2 a]. **1903** B. RUSSELL *Princ. Math.* ii. 10 Symbolic or Formal Logic—I shall use these terms as synonyms—is the study of the various general types of deduction. The word *symbolic* designates the subject by an accidental characteristic, for the employment of mathematical symbols, here as elsewhere, is merely a theoretically irrelevant convenience. *Ibid.* vi. 74 By symbolic logicians..this will be felt as a reactionary view. **1933** C. A. MACE *Princ. Logic* iv. 64 The fact that symbolic logicians have not generally recognized this form compels us to introduce a symbol that is not in common use. **1941** [see *mathematical logic* s.v. *MATHEMATICAL *a.* 1 e]. **1958** *Times Lit. Suppl.* 19 Dec. 729/3 Professor Sparshott quotes the dying symbolic logician—'complete rigour at last!' **1968** *Brit. Med. Bull.* XXIV. 239/2 The final study to be reviewed concerns diagnosis by the computer using a combination of symbolic logic.. and similarity coefficients. **1973** *Sci. Amer.* Apr. 101/3 First Frege, then Peano and finally Russell turned to symbolic logic as a potential source of the fundamental notions necessary for a theory of natural number.

d. *symbolic address* (Computers), an address consisting of a symbol chosen by the programmer for its convenience; so *symbolic addressing.*

1953 *Trans. IRE Professional Group on Electronic Computers* Mar. 10/1 Programs for automatic calculators can be written with symbolic addresses instead of actual addresses. **1970** O. DOPPING *Computers & Data Processing* xix. 308 In automatic coding..each data item receives a name, or symbolic address. **1977** *Gloss. Terms Data Processing* (*B.S.I.*) VII. 13/1 Symbolic addressing. **1981** M. E. WALSH *Understanding Computers* iii. 48 This process of using mnemonic instructions..and symbolic addressing and having them translated into machine language is called assembling a program.

3. c. *symbolic interaction* (Social Psychol. and Sociol.), the sharing and use of common symbols in human communication; freq. *attrib.*; also *symbolic interactionist*, an adherent of the theory that the child is formed into a social being through learning the common meaning attached to symbols by its group; also *attrib.* or as *adj.*; hence *symbolic interactionism.*

1937 H. BLUMER in E. P. Schmidt *Man & Society* 153 The group of social psychologists who may be conveniently labelled 'symbolic interactionists'. *Ibid.* 174 It is clearly an instance of the symbolic interaction. *Ibid.* 191 The stimulus-response approach is interested in *reaction*; the symbolic interaction view in *action*. **1961** D. MARTINDALE *Nature & Types Sociol. Theory* xiv. 339 The symbolic interaction school took shape in America, primarily under the influence of pragmatism. **1967** *Sociol. Q.* VIII. 149 (*title*) On the edge of rapprochement: was Durkheim moving toward the perspective of symbolic interaction? **1969** H. BLUMER (*title*) Symbolic interactionism. *Ibid.* i. 1 George Herbert Mead who, above all others, laid the foundations of the symbolic interactionist approach. **1972** S. MENNELL in Cox & Dyson *20th-Cent. Mind* III. v. 160 Another kind of social action theory has also been influential, especially in the last decade. It is usually known as 'symbolic interactionism', and has deep roots in American sociology. **1977** J. A. KOTARBA in Douglas & Johnson *Existential Sociol.* ix. 272 The concept of illness as deviant behavior..is built upon the labeling theory of the symbolic interactionist perspective. **1979** *Human Relations* Sept. 803 Symbolic interaction stresses the personal definition of the situation, while frame analysis seeks to uncover the background assumptions within which interaction takes place. **1982** *Jrnl. Learning Disabilities* XV. 347 Using a symbolic interaction perspective, the study focused on the extent of agreement..in referring children..to a university clinic for psychoeducational assessment.

symboling: see SYMBOLLING *vbl. sb.* in Dict. and Suppl.

symbolist. 2. c. (Earlier example.)

1888 G. MOORE *Confessions of Young Man* vi. 147 Like a white flag fluttering faintly, Symbolists and Decadents appeared.

‖ **symboliste** (sæ̃bǫlīst). Also with capital initial. [Fr.: cf. SYMBOLIST.] = SYMBOLIST 2 c (*b*). Chiefly *attrib.*

1925 [see *CROCEAN *a.*[2]]. **1957** J. HOLLANDER in N. Frye *Sound & Poetry* 67 Professor Knight has elevated his rather *symboliste* construction of the word 'music' to the heights proclaimed in Verlaine's manifesto. **1966** *Listener* 17 Mar. 378/1 T. S. Eliot..found the clues he needed..in the French *Symbolistes* like Laforgue. **1980** A. ALPERS *Life K. Mansfield* vii. 135 A little *symboliste* prose-poem.

symbolled, *a.* (Example of spelling *symboled.*)

1935 DYLAN THOMAS in *New Verse* Aug.–Sept. 3 The invalid rivals, Voyaging clockwise off the symboled harbour.

symbolling, *vbl. sb.* Add: In U.S. usu. with spelling **symboling.** Also, the use of symbols in communication.

1974 H. G. BURGER in *Gen. Systems* XIX. 64/1 What appears to be non-language..is probably a precisely coded symboling of a non-standard dialect. **1977** —— in B. Bernardi *Concept & Dynamics of Culture* 419 Between the gross human ability of symboling, so well known, and the peculiarly human institutions, also well known, lie special symboling processes. **1977** *Dædalus* Summer 62 Process theory is no longer linked, as in its earlier heyday, with Gumplowicz's notion that 'man's material need is the prime motive of his conduct'; it now recognizes the critical importance of meaning and symboling.

symbolling, var. *SEMBLING.

symbolo-, combining form of Gr. σύμβολον SYMBOL *sb.*[1], as in **symbolo-fideism** (si:mbǒlofəi·di,iz'm) [F. *symbolo-fidéisme*], the theory that symbols are of the essence of religious dogma, and that the attitude of faith has priority over intellectual belief (see quot. 1921); hence **sy:mbolo-fi·deist,** one who holds this theory; **sy:mboloma·nia** *nonce-wd.*, excessive use of symbols.

[**1897** A. SABATIER *Esquisse d'une Philosophie de la Religion* III. vii. 406 En combinant les vues de M. Ménégoz et les miennes qui se complètent en effet réciproquement, on a pu baptiser la conception nouvelle de *symbolo-fidéisme*.] **1903** *Hibbert Jrnl.* I. 555 In these two principles,—the symbolic, pictorial character of all the concepts and terms of religion, and the distinction just mentioned between faith and belief,—we have the germs of Symbolo-fideism. The name appears to have been given to the school by an anonymous writer in 1894. **1921** *Encycl. Relig. & Ethics* XII. 151 Symbolofideism is the name given to the theology taught in the second half of the 19th cent. at the Protestant Faculty of Paris by Professors Auguste Sabatier and Eugène Ménégoz. **1949** E. L. MASCALL *Existence & Analogy* v. 93 Modern Roman Catholic theologians..under the stress of their controversy with symbolo-fideists and modernists of various kinds, have discussed the doctrine of analogy at great length. **1970** *Nature* 4 Apr. 47/2 Such a hornet's nest of symbols, wiggly lines,..and the like, that the reader, despairing of ever reaching the goodies obscured by the fog of symbolomania, may come to think that this new approach to mathematics is not worth while.

symbology. Add: **symbological** *a.*, **symbologist**: for *rare*$^{-0}$ read *rare*; (examples).

1924 *Glasgow Herald* 4 Apr. 13 Professor Stern returns to the attack upon this theory-mongering, always recalling the symbologists and complex-jargonists to a consideration of practical realities as a test of their deductions. **1976** *N.Y. Rev. Bks.* 15 Apr. 29/2 He considered the Papal Bull of 1950 declaring the Assumption of the Virgin an article of faith to be the most important symbological event since the Reformation.

symmachy. For † *Obs. rare*$^{-0}$ read *rare* and add example.

1911 C. PHILLIPSON *Internat. Law & Custom Ancient Greece & Rome* I. ix. 222 The relationship existing between those cities which constituted the military symmachy in Italy.

symmetallism (sim,me·tăliz'm). Also **Symmetallism.** *Econ.* [f. SYM- + BI)METALLISM.] A proposed monetary system based on the use of an amalgam of gold and silver as a standard (see quot. 1979). Hence **symmeta·llic** *a.*; **symme·tallist** *sb.* an advocate of symmetallism (also *attrib.* or as *adj.*).

1895 F. Y. EDGEWORTH in *Econ. Jrnl.* V. 443 The arrangement that there should be a *joint demand* for gold and silver money might, perhaps, be called *symmetallism*, to distinguish it from the arrangement that there should be a *composite supply* which is called bimetallism. *Ibid.* 444 Suppose England with India adopts one symmetallic ratio. **1897** *Daily News* 30 Nov. 4/6 [A man] may be a Symmetallist, and believe that standard coins should be made from a mixture of silver with gold. *Ibid.*, Whether a symmetallist coinage be possible or not, it is certain that we have a symmetallist Administration. **1923** A. MARSHALL *Money, Credit & Commerce* 64 Although coinage of gold and silver at a fixed ratio causes movements of prices to be governed chiefly by the production of gold and silver alternately, a plan can be devised which would make the two metals work together: it may be called Symmetallism. **1934** *Sun* (Baltimore) 24 May 10/2 It [*sc.* the President's proposal] does not involve either bimetallism or symmetalism [*sic*]. **1979** *Econ. Jrnl.* LXXXIX. 29 Consider now Marshall's..proposal for a 'stable bimetallism', which is usually called symmetallism. Under this system the central bank does not attempt to stabilise the price of either gold or silver separately, but rather pegs the price of a reserve unit that corresponds to a specified combination of the two metals. **1980** *Internat. Econ. Rev.* XXI. 675 Under a symmetallic standard..the monetary authority does not set prices for individual commodities.

symmetric, *a.* Add: **1. b.** Math. and Logic. *symmetric difference* (see quot. 1936); *symmetric group*, the group of all the permutations of a set of unlike entities.

1936 *Trans. Amer. Math. Soc.* XL. 38 The Union (modulo 2), or symmetric difference, of two classes is the class of objects belonging to one or the other, but not to both, of those classes. **1971** J. H. CONWAY in Powell & Higman *Finite Simple Groups* vii. 225 If some non-empty $\mathcal{C}$-set has fewer than five elements, every set of the same cardinal would be a $\mathcal{C}$-set,..and by taking symmetric differences we should obtain every two-element set..as a $\mathcal{C}$-set, which cannot be. **1897** W. BURNSIDE *Theory of Groups of Finite Order* viii. 139 The group of order $n!$ which consists of all the substitutions that can be performed on n symbols is called the symmetric group of degree n. **1955** L. MIRSKY *Introd. Linear Algebra* ix. 257 In addition to the symmetric group..there are other groups of permutations, all of them naturally subgroups of the symmetric group.

c. *Physics.* = *SYMMETRICAL *a.* 2 c.

1935 CONDON & SHORTLEY *Theory of Atomic Spectra* iii. 165 If the atom is at a certain moment in a symmetric state it will always remain in a symmetric state. **1965** H. MUIRHEAD *Physics Elem. Particles* ix. 369 It is apparent from this equation that parallel spin states..are symmetric. **1979** *Nature* 29 Mar. 404/2 Certain baryons.. contain three identical quarks with parallel spins in a state which is symmetric (the wave function does not change sign) to the interchange of a pair of quarks.

2. *Logic.* Of a binary relation: such that when two terms for which it is true are interchanged, it remains true.

1933 *Mind* XLII. 34 Not even God himself can make men into women by shifting words, or make what we call 'implies' symmetric by changing names. **1968** *New Scientist* 16 May 339/1 Equality is symmetric as well as being reflexive. **1979** K. J. DEVLIN *Fund. Contemp. Set*

Theory i. 14 A binary relation on a set is an equivalence relation just in case it is reflective, symmetric, and transitive.

symmetrical, *a.* Add: **2. b.** Also in *Logic*, = *SYMMETRIC *a.* 2.

1903, 1937 [see *REFLEXIVE *a.* 7]. **1954** I. M. Copi *Symbolic Logic* v. 141 Various symmetrical relations are designated by the phrases: 'is next to', 'is married to', and 'has the same weight as'. A symmetrical relation is one such that if one individual has that relation to a second individual, then the second individual must have that relation to the first. **1979** Georgacarakos & Smith *Elementary Formal Logic* ix. 329 When a relational expression has this property, we say that it is symmetrical.

c. In *Physics* also applied to a state represented by such a wave function.

1930 P. A. M. Dirac *Princ. Quantum Mech.* xi. 201 It is quite possible for only symmetrical or antisymmetrical states to occur in nature... One assumes the symmetrical states for photons. **1963** R. P. Feynman et al. *Feynman Lect. Physics* I. xi. 2 The laws of physics are symmetrical for translational displacements,..in the sense that the laws do not change when we make a translation of our coordinates. **1973** B. H. Bransden et al. *Fundamental Particles* iv. 79 The triplet spin state is symmetrical.

d. Math. and Logic. *symmetrical difference* = *symmetric difference* s.v. *SYMMETRIC *a.* 1 b.

1978 C. H. Greenstein *Dict. Logical Terms & Symbols* 172 Symmetrical difference. **1979** Kandel & Lee *Fuzzy Switching & Automata* ii. 53 The symmetrical difference (or Boolean sum) of two fuzzy sets.

symmetricalness. (*b*) (Earlier example.)

1858 W. Bagehot in *National Rev.* Oct. 460 The mode in which those opinions are expressed, and..the mode in which they are framed, affect us..with a sensation of symmetricalness.

symmetrize, *v.* **1.** For *rare*$^{-1}$ read *rare* and add earlier example.

1749 J. Cleland *Mem. Woman of Pleasure* II. 233 An air of becoming manliness..that symetriz'd [*sic*] nobly with that air of distinction..with which nature has stamped it [*sc.* his face].

2. Also *absol.*

1973 *Sci. Amer.* Jan. 111/2 This leaves one column and one row, with the poison piece at the vertex... From now on the first player 'symmetrizes'. Whatever his opponent takes from either line, he takes equally from the other.

Hence **sy·mmetrized** *ppl. a.*

1966 *Math. Rev.* XXXI. 36/1 (*heading*) Matrix applications of a quadratic identity for decomposable symmetrized tensors. **1979** *Nature* 29 Feb. 597/2 It is the interference between the two parts of the symmetrised wave-functions..that leads to the intensity interference.

symmetrodont (sime·trodǫnt), *sb.* and *a.* [f. mod.L. order name *Symmetrodonta* (G. G. Simpson 1925, in *Amer. Jrnl. Sci.* CCX. 560), f. Symmetr(y + Gr. ὀδούς, ὀδοντ- tooth, in allusion to the form of the teeth (see quot. 1979[2]).] **A.** *sb.* A fossil mammal of the order Symmetrodonta, known from remains found in North America and Europe. **B.** *adj.* Of or pertaining to an animal of this kind or the order including it.

1933 A. S. Romer *Vertebr. Paleont.* xii. 260 The symmetrodonts seem to have been somewhat off the main evolutionary line. **1950** *Nature* 21 Oct. 696/2 The specimen can easily be described as a lower symmetrodont cheek tooth. **1977** A. Hallam *Planet Earth* 223 Triconodont and symmetrodont mammals died out during the Cretaceous. **1979** R. C. Fox in Fairbridge & Jablonski *Encycl. Paleont.* 429/2 Symmetrodonts were small shrew-sized mammals, probably having insectivorous food habits. *Ibid.*, Symmetrodont molars are highly characteristic: both upper and lower crowns formed simple occlusal triangles... The lower molar triangles are reversed in respect to the uppers and occlusion was alternate in the sense that each molar occluded within the embrasure between two successive molars on the opposite jaw.

symmetry. Add: **3. b.** (*a*) More widely, a property by virtue of which something is effectively unchanged by a particular operation; an operation or set of operations that leaves something effectively unchanged; in *Physics*, a property that is conserved (cf. *symmetry operation*, sense 4 below). (Further examples.)

1908 H. Hilton *Theory of Groups of Finite Order* iv. 42 If a movement (other than identity) brings every point of a figure F into the position previously occupied either by itself or by some other point of F, F is said to possess symmetry. **1941** Birkhoff & MacLane *Survey Mod. Algebra* vi. 122 The algebra of symmetries has its genesis in the fact that we can multiply two motions by performing them in succession. **1965** R. P. Feynman et al. *Feynman Lect. Physics* III. xvii. 8 Symmetry with respect to displacements in time implies the conservation of energy; symmetry with respect to position in x, y, or z implies the conservation of momentum. **1967** *Physical Rev. Lett.* XIX. 1264/2 As far as we know, two of these symmetries are entirely unbroken: the charge Q..and the electron number N. **1968** M. S. Livingston *Particle Physics* xii. 201 One consequence of the translational symmetry of space is the invariance of physical laws under translation from one location to another. **1974** Frauenfelder & Henley *Subatomic Physics* vi. 154 Some of the symmetries are perfect even under closest scrutiny, and no breakdown in the corresponding conservation law has ever been found. Rotational symmetry and conservation of angular momentum are one example.

(*b*) Also in *Logic* (cf. *SYMMETRICAL *a.* 2 b).

1950 [see *REFLEXIVITY]. **1967** S. C. Kleene *Math. Logic* iii. 158 Sometimes 'equality' is used in a different sense, so that it possesses only the first three properties (reflexivity, symmetry and transitivity).

4. *attrib.* and *Comb.*, as *symmetry principle*, *property*; **symmetry-breaking** *ppl. a.* and *vbl. sb. Physics*, (causing) the absence of manifest symmetry in a situation despite its presence in the laws of nature underlying it; **symmetry group**, a group (Group sb. 5 a in Dict. and Suppl.) whose elements are all the symmetry operations of a particular entity; **symmetry operation** *Physics*, an operation or transformation that leaves something effectively unchanged.

1961 M. Gell-Mann in Gell-Mann & Ne'eman *Eightfold Way* (1964) We attempt..to treat the eight known baryons as a supermultiplet, degenerate in the limit of a certain symmetry but split into isotopic spin multiplets by a symmetry-breaking term. **1977** *Dædalus* Summer 29 As a result of this symmetry-breaking, the quanta of the weak interactions are predicted to acquire a mass approximately forty or more times heavier than that of a proton. **1981** *Nature* 10 Dec. 522/1 The usual analogy used for spontaneous symmetry breaking is ferromagnetism. Maxwell's equations are rotationally invariant; however, below the Curie temperature the rotational invariance of a ferromagnet is spontaneously broken when the magnetization chooses a specific direction. **1956** *Ibid.* 10 Mar. 458/1 To-day the instinctive reaction of every theoretical physicist, confronted with an unexplained regularity in the behaviour of elementary particles, is to postulate an underlying symmetry-group. **1975** I. Stewart *Concepts Mod. Math.* vii. 97 Every shape has a symmetry group. **1981** *Sci. Amer.* Apr. 50/2 The $SU(2) \times U(1)$ theory is only a partial unification because it still includes two distinct forces, each with its own symmetry group and its own coupling constant. **1952** H. Weyl *Symmetry* 27 For forms fixed to the bottom of the ocean the direction of gravity is an important factor, narrowing the set of symmetry operations from all rotations around the center P to all rotations about an axis. **1973** B. H. Bransden et al. *Fundamental Particles* iv. 56 The symmetry operations with which we are concerned are transformations of the dynamical variable that leave the Hamiltonian operator unaltered. **1968** M. S. Livingston *Particle Physics* xii. 201 It is possible that the number of such symmetry principles is limited and that they are interrelated. *Ibid.*, One of the most basic symmetry principles is that of the homogeneity of space and the associated symmetry of time. **1977** *Dædalus* Fall 31 Some theorists turned to the study of symmetry principles and conservation laws, which can be applied to physical phenomena without detailed dynamical calculations. **1935** Pauling & Wilson *Introd. Quantum Mech.* xiv. 388 The symmetry properties of molecular wave functions. **1968** M. S. Livingston *Particle Physics* iii. 58 The type of quantum statistics which applies to a system of particles (all of one kind) is related to the symmetry properties of the wave function describing this system of particles.

symmography (simǫ·grăfi). [f. Symm(etry + -ography.] = *string art* s.v. *STRING *sb.* 32. Also **sy·mmograph**, a pattern or picture made by symmography; **symmogra·phic** *a.*

1971 L. Kreischer *Symmography* 4 Symmography is an art form using yarn, wood, and nails as the media. *Ibid.* 5 The materials you need to begin a symmograph are basically quite simple. *Ibid.*, The nails I use for my symmographic creations are..bright steel wire. **1975** *String Art Encycl.* 9 Whereas originally string-craft creations were often symmographs—art works in which string was wound attractively and symmetrically around nails in a board—this book deals with string in other artistic forms as well.

Symondite (si·mǫndəit). Now *Hist.* [f. the name of Rear-Admiral Sir William *Symonds* (1782–1856): see -ite[1].] A small warship designed by Sir William Symonds in his capacity as surveyor to the Royal Navy.

1927 B. M. Chambers *Salt Junk* iv. 27 The *Eurydice* was what was known as a Symonite [*sic*] or Jackass frigate, i.e., something between a sloop and a frigate. **1932** A. H. Long *Round the Bill* 9 She was a good little boat, about seven feet beam, drew three feet six inches, and had a regular Symondite bottom, like the *America*. **1935** H. I. Chapelle *Hist. Amer. Sailing Ships* 156 As a class, the Symondites were very unsteady gun-platforms. **1957** *Mariner's Mirror* XLIII. 337 For rolling, pitching and lee-lurches the Symondites beat the lot.

sympathectomy. Add: (Later examples.)

1903 *Med. Record* LXIII. 875/2 So far as the question of choice of operation between hemisection and sympathectomy went, he believed that the Jennesco operation gave better results. **1936** *Q. Jrnl. Med.* XXIX. 438 Of all the 'sympathectomies' which have been proposed and tried, 'ganglionectomy' is the only one really worth doing. **1955** *Sci. News Let.* 22 Oct. 262/1 The nerve-cutting operation, called sympathectomy, is to dilate arteries that have been stopped. **1968** G. Maxwell *Raven seek thy Brother* ii. 29 There was no alternative, he said, to lumbar sympathectomy. **1979** *Molecular Pharmacol.* XV. 35 Microsomal preparations derived from several peripheral organs of cats or rabbits following chemical sympathectomy.

Hence **sympathe·ctomized** *a.*, that has undergone sympathectomy.

1928 *Amer. Jrnl. Physiol.* LXXXV. 493 Table 3 shows the changes produced in the relative mononuclear count in sympathectomized animals. **1970** H. Shands *Semiotic Approaches to Psychiatry* xxiii. 396 He [*sc.* the schizophrenic] thrives (relatively speaking) when, like Cannon's sympathectomized cats, he is never exposed to normally expectable variation.

sympathetic, *a.* (*sb.*) Add: **A.** *adj.* **1. e.** Also *spec.* in Mus., *sympathetic strings*: (see quot. 1960).

1884 F. Niecks *Dict. Mus. Terms* s.v. *Viola d'amore*, a bow stringed instrument a little longer than the viola, with seven (sometimes fewer) catgut strings about the fingerboard, and seven sympathetic wire strings below it. **1888** Hipkins & Gibb *Mus. Instruments* 53 In the beautifully carved and inlaid instrument here drawn, a perfect viola d'amore in form.., the sympathetic strings are absent. **1908** L. J. de Bekker *Stokes' Encycl. Mus. & Musicians* 706/2 The sympathetic strings give a beautiful effect. **1928** E. Blom *Romance of Piano* x. 178 In the treble, the sympathetic strings of the Blüthnor piano are tuned in unison with the ordinary strings. **1940** C. Sachs *Hist. Musical Instruments* xvi. 365 Sympathetic strings had come to England from the Near East, apparently in the sixteenth century. Praetorius related that the English used sympathetic viol strings. **1960** H. Hayward *Antique Coll.* 297/2 *Viola d'amore*, a musical instrument.. notable for its system of 'sympathetic' strings... Although out of reach of the bow and fingers these strings vibrate freely in sympathy with the notes played and produce a peculiarly ethereal effect. **1966** *Melody Maker* 7 May 10 The sympathetic strings [in a sitar] vibrate when the main strings are played, giving an answering drone. **1976** *Early Music* July 303 This viol still bore twelve wrestpins in the end block which would have originally carried sympathetic strings added in the 18th century. *Ibid.* 305 A viola bastarde..with six sympathetic strings beneath the six bowed strings.

2. b. Tending to elicit sympathy (senses 3 b, d) or to induce a feeling of rapport; also *loosely*, pleasant, likeable. Cf. *SYMPATHIQUE *a.*

1900 M. Beerbohm in *Sat. Rev.* 10 Mar. 295/2 The true Don Juan..is..not a 'sympathetic' part. **1926** Fowler *Mod. Eng. Usage* 590/2 Macbeth..is not made sympathetic, however adequately his crime may be explained & palliated, by being the victim of a hallucination. **1965** *Listener* 23 Dec. 1045/1 Being a lover of the south, I personally found it [*sc.* a novel] more sympathetic. **1976** A. Eden *Another World* iv. 54 It was not a sympathetic house and the furnishing and pictures were ugly.

3. b. *sympathetic strike*, a strike by workers in support of the action of strikers in another union, industry, etc.

1901 [in Dict.]. **1913** in J. O'Connor *Hist. Ireland 1798–1924* (1925) II. xvii. 192 They followed by a somewhat lame conclusion that the 'sympathetic strike was being met with the sympathetic lock-out.' **1958** *Times Rev. Industry* Aug. 7/2 The merest murmur of the words 'sympathetic strike' will command the dockers' attention.

sympatheticotonia, -ic: see *SYMPATHICOTONIA.

sympathico-: see *SYMPATHO-.

sympa:thicoto·nia. *Physiol.* Also anglicized as **sympa:thicoto·ny.** [f. *SYMPATHICO- + *-TONIA.] The state or condition in which there is increased influence of the sympathetic nervous system and heightened sensitivity to adrenalin. Also **sympathe:ticoto·nia, -to·nus,** in the same sense.

1916 J. P. Stewart *Diagnosis of Nervous Dis.* (ed. 4) xx. 356 Vago-tonus and sympathetico-tonus.—Individuals may be classified into two great vegetative types, according as their autonomic sensitiveness prevails over their sympathetic, or *vice versa*. **1923** *Handbk. for Mental Nurses* (Medico-Psychol. Assoc.) (ed. 7) ix. 375 The condition is then known as sympathetico-tonus or vagotonus, as the case may be. **1930** J. E. Nicole *Psychopathology* ix. 77 The characteristics of vagotonia might be due to the thymus and pituitary glands, while the adrenals and thyroid would account for sympatheticotonia. **1948** A. Brodal *Neurol. Anat.* xi. 371 Frequently persons are also met with in whom only one organ reveals a clear-cut parasympathetic or sympathetic dominance (local vagotonia or sympathicotonia). **1977** *Lancet* 12 Nov. 1027/2 During sympathicotony the organism is already making use of Nature's reserve supply of lachrymal fluid.

Hence **sympathe:ticoto·nic, sympa:thicoto·nic** *adjs.*, displaying or promoting sympathicotonia; also as *sbs.*, a sympathicotonic person.

1916 J. P. Stewart *Diagnosis of Nervous Dis.* (ed. 4) xx. 357 Sympathetico-tonic individuals are specially sensitive to adrenalin which exaggerates all their characteristics. **1930** J. E. Nicole *Psychopathology* viii. 70 The sympatheticotonics..have dry skins, prominent eyes, dilated pupils, and are possessed of great energy, both mental and physical. **1944** L. J. Bendit *Paranormal Cognition* iii. 47 She was of the sympathicotonic type, given to attacks of vomiting when emotionally upset. **1954** S. Duke-Elder *Parsons' Dis. Eye* (ed. 12) xxi. 235 It is seen particularly in those who are highly strung, anxious in disposition and sympatheticotonic in type. **1975** *Year Bk. Ear, Nose & Throat* 273 Sympathicotonic influences might cause hypertonicity of the cricopharyngeus muscle.

sympa:thicotropic (-trōu·pik, -trǫ·pik), *a.* *Pharm.* [f. *SYMPATHICO- + *-TROPIC.] Possessing an affinity for the sympathetic nervous system. Also **sy:mpathotro·pic** *a.*, in the same sense.

1914 *Jrnl. Amer. Med. Assoc.* 22 Aug. 619/2 Epinephrin ..affects especially the sympathetic... It is therefore spoken of as a sympathicotropic drug. **1964** *Internat. Jrnl. Neuropharmacol.* III. 217 When evaluating the effect of indirectly acting sympathotropic substances one must first ascertain whether the tissue stores endogenous catecholamines. **1975** *Acta Biol. Med. Germanica* XXXIV. 661 (*heading*) The action of sympathicotropic substances upon liver microsomes in vivo and in vitro.

sympathin (si·mpăþin). *Physiol.* [f. *SYMPATH(O- + -IN[1].] A hormone which acts as a mediator of nerve impulses at sympathetic nerve synapses; now effectively a disused synonym of *NORADRENALINE.

1931 CANNON & BACQ in *Amer. Jrnl. Physiol.* XCVI. 411 Because the substance is derived from structures under sympathetic control, when they are influenced by sympathetic impulses, we suggest that it be called sympathin. **1938** *Nature* 12 Feb. 266/2 The authors reject Bacq's rather factious criticisms of their theory of sympathins *E* and *I*. **1946** *Ibid.* 20 July 88/1 In Cannon's remaining active years he was largely concerned with evidence as to the nature of the sympathetic transmitter 'sympathin', which he believed to be not identical with adrenaline. **1971** *Ibid.* 2 Apr. 340/2 In an attempt to demonstrate this increase the transmitter 'sympathin' liberated from sympathetic nerve to the spleen was examined.

‖ **sympathique** (sæ̃patīk), *a.* [Fr.: see SYMPATHIC *a.*] Of a thing, place, etc.: agreeable, to one's taste, suitable. Of a person: likeable, en rapport with one, congenial. Cf. *SYMPATHETIC *a.* 2 b.

1859 QUEEN VICTORIA *Let.* 27 Apr. in R. Fulford *Dearest Child* (1964) 187 The sight of a professor or learned man alarms me, and is not sympathique to me. **1865** —— *Let.* 30 Dec. in *Ibid.* 52 Oh if only Antoinette was in Ali's place! She is so much more *sympathique* and *grande dame*. **1869** W. JAMES *Let.* 1 Nov. in R. B. Perry *Thought & Char. W. James* (1935) I. 308 England is evidently *sympathique* to you. **1897** A. BEARDSLEY *Let.* Apr. (1970) 305 The Baronne Dufour came to see us today... How sweet and sympathique she is. **1930** E. WAUGH *Vile Bodies* vii. 116, I do think, when you get to my age, dear, there is something *sympathique* about a wig, don't you? **1960** *Harper's Bazaar* July 25 A warm and *sympathique* personality. **1975** D. GRAY *Ride on Tiger* ii. 14, I find you *sympathique*.

‖ **sympathisch** (zümpā·tiʃ), *a.* Also *erron.* sympatisch. [Ger.: see SYMPATHIC *a.*] = *SYMPATHIQUE *a.*

1911 R. BROOKE *Let.* 13 Dec. (1968) 325, I find that Creative Artists are so particularly *sympathisch*. **1922** D. H. LAWRENCE *Let.* 25 Oct. (1932) 559 But it [*sc.* New Mexico] isn't *sympatisch* like Australia. **1937** AUDEN in Auden & MacNeice *Lett. from Iceland* viii. 100 You I find sympatisch, a good townee. **1976** P. HENISSART *Winter Quarry* I. vii. 72 Another lie? It's what makes you so *sympatisch*, isn't it? **1982** *N.Y. Times Mag.* 17 Oct. 100/5 The personality of the singer himself—warm, intelligent, *sympathisch*, recognizable.

sympatho- (si·mpăþo), combining form of SYMPATHETIC *a.* (*sb.*), used to form terms relating to the sympathetic nervous system; also **sympa·thico-**; **sy:mpathogonia** (-gō^u·nia) *sb. pl. Med.* [ad. G. *sympathogonien* (H. Poll 1906, in O. Hertwig *Handb. d. vergleichenden und exper. Entwickelungslehre d. Wirbeltiere* V. III. i. 460), f. Gr. γόνος offspring, begetting], undifferentiated embryonic cells of the sympathetic nervous system which give rise to sympathoblasts; also used as *sing.*; **sy:mpathogonio·ma, sympa:thicogonio·ma** [*-OMA], a malignant tumour composed chiefly of sympathogonia.

1934 *Jrnl. Path. & Bacteriol.* XXXIX. 28 The sympathogonia from which the medulla of the suprarenal takes origin, as first described by Wiesel (1902), began to invade the anlage of the adrenal cortex. **1966** *Pharmacol. Rev.* XVIII. 659 The common progenitor, called sympathogonia, is a small lymphocyte-like cell with a dense, chromatin-rich, spherical or pyriform nucleus and a scanty rim of clear, poorly-staining cytoplasm. **1934** *Jrnl. Path. & Bacteriol.* XXXIX. 28 Those formed of sympathogonia have been classified as sympathogoniomas. **1966** *Pharmacol. Rev.* XVIII. 659 Each of these three types of sympathetic cell may give rise to a tumor: the sympathogonia to a sympathogonioma; the sympathoblast to a sympathoblastoma; and the ganglion cell to a ganglioneuroma. **1974** *Oncology* XXIX. 521 Tumour biopsies of a..sympathicogonioma..were obtained when the tumours were removed surgically.

sy:mpatho-adre·nal, *a. Physiol.* [f. *SYMPATHO- + *ADRENAL *a.*] Pertaining to or involving the sympathetic nervous system and the medulla of the adrenal gland, and their activity. Also **sympa:thico-adre·nal** *a.*, in the same sense.

1928 *Amer. Jrnl. Physiol.* LXXXIV. 560 Previous investigations..have emphasized the emergency functions of the sympathico-adrenal mechanism. **1949** KOESTLER *Insight & Outlook* v. 59 The whole complex of sympathico-adrenal excitation which characterizes aughter is not only absent in crying, but is replaced..by parasympathetic excitation, or..by types of reaction, for example, fatigue, which are the direct opposites of sympathetic excitation. **1965** *Jrnl. Physiol.* CLXXIX. 290 Three drugs which are known to have various actions on the sympatho-adrenal system were tested. **1974** *Jrnl. Appl. Physiol.* XXXVI. 183/1 Sympathicoadrenal medullary secretion of catecholamines is increased during acute cold exposures. **1979** *Med. Hypotheses* V. 317 Some disorders in which excessive sweating..is a symptom are also characterized by increased sympatho-adrenal activity.

sympathoblast (si·mpăþoblæst). *Med.* [f. *SYMPATHO- + -BLAST.] A small, relatively undifferentiated cell formed in the early development of nerve tissue which develops into a sympathetic neurone. Also **sympa·thicoblast**, in the same sense.

1927 *Amer. Jrnl. Path.* III. 212 These lesions represent a tumor of a more primitive type of cell (sympathicoblast) than the sympathetic neuroblast. **1934** *Jrnl. Path. & Bacteriol.* XXXIX. 28 Different stages in development may be present in the same tumour *e.g.* sympathogonia, sympathoblasts and ganglion cells. **1966** *Experientia* XXII. 297 In the developing CNS [*sc.* central nervous system] and the spinal ganglia, only the sympathoblasts of the primary and secondary trunk of chick embryos contain a varying amount of catechol amine-containing granules.

Hence **sympa:thicoblasto·ma,** (less commonly **sy:mpathoblasto·ma**) [*-OMA], a malignant tumour composed chiefly of sympathoblasts.

1927 *Amer. Jrnl. Path.* III. 213 The sympathicoblastomas have often been described as consisting of two types of tissue. **1934** *Jrnl. Path. & Bacteriol.* XXXIX. 29 Sympathicoblastomata are the commonest sympathetic tumours found. **1960** *Hirosaki Med. Jrnl.* XII. 92 (*heading*) A case of sympathoblastoma, suspected to be Ewing's tumor. **1974** *Oncology* XXIX. 521 Tumour biopsies of a sympathicoblastoma..were obtained when the tumours were removed surgically.

sy:mpatholytic (-li·tik), *a. Med.* [f. *SYMPATHO- + *-LYTIC.] Annulling or opposing the transmission of nerve impulses in the sympathetic system. Also **sympa:thicoly·tic** *a.*, in the same sense.

1947, 1948 Sympathicolytic [see *ADRENO-]. **1951** Sympatholytic [see *DIOXAN]. **1952** *Acta Endocrinol.* IX. 116 The alarm reaction caused by adrenaline..can be counteracted by using a sympathicolytic agent. **1954** *Brit. Jrnl. Pharmacol.* IX. 236 The assay of sympatholytic (anti-adrenaline) drugs. **1961** *Lancet* 26 Aug. 475/1 Failures of wholly different origin are those due to administration of sympatholytic or ganglion-blocking drugs. **1977** *Ibid.* 19 Mar. 650/2 The medical treatment of essential hypertension is currently based almost exclusively on sympatholytic drugs of one kind or another on the assumption that the disease is caused by over-activity of the sympathetic nervous system.

sy:mpathomime·tic, *a.* (and *sb.*) *Pharm.* [f. *SYMPATHO- + MIMETIC *a.* (and *sb.*).] Producing physiological effects characteristic of the sympathetic nervous system (as raised blood pressure and rate and depth of breathing, decreased secretion and tone of smooth muscle) by promoting stimulation of sympathetic nerves. Also as *sb.*, a substance which does this. Also **sympa:thicomime·tic** *a.* (and *sb.*), in the same sense.

1910 BARGER & DALE in *Jrnl. Physiol.* XLI. 21 A term at once wider and more descriptive than 'adrenine-like' seems needed to indicate the type of action common to these bases. We propose to call it 'sympathomimetic', a term which indicates the relation of the action to innervation by the sympathetic system. **1949** KOESTLER *Insight & Outlook* xx. 281 In contrast to the sympathomimetic hormones, the vagus substance is rapidly destroyed. **1956** *Nature* 7 Jan. 44/2 The presence of sympathomimetic activity in adrenergic nerve tissue has been demonstrated. **1964** W. G. SMITH *Allergy & Tissue Metabolism* ix. 91 Sympathomimetic amines and theophylline are believed to work by a bronchodilator action. **1966** *Acta Physiol. Scand.* LXVII. 482 Peripherally they are generally classified as indirectly acting sympathomimetics, i.e. they depend on an intact sympathetic nervous system for their activity. **1958** *Dis. of Chest* XXXIII. 18 (*heading*) Depressed response to intravenous sympathicomimetic agents in humans during acidosis. **1970** PASSMORE & ROBSON *Compan. Med. Stud.* II. ix. 6/1 Many of the substances most useful in asthma, e.g. sympathomimetic drugs.., act not as specific agents but by producing an opposing, and often overriding, effect on the bronchi. **1973** *Brit. Jrnl. Hosp. Med.* IX. 21/1 Inhalation challenge using agents producing a type I skin response often induce immediate airways obstruction with asthma, reversible by sympathomimetics. **1983** *Amer. Rev. Respiratory Dis.* CXXVII. 413 Airway resistance..and lung volume were assessed before and after inhalation of a β2-sympathicomimetic.

sympathy. *sb.* Add: **4.** *Comb.* **sympathy card**, a printed card expressing condolence on a bereavement; **sympathy strike** = *sympathetic strike* s.v. *SYMPATHETIC *a.* 3 b; hence **sympathy striker.**

1967 'T. WELLS' *Dead by Light of Moon* (1968) x. 102 'Sympathy cards? Oh yes.' I remembered now. She wrote greeting card verses. **1976** *Billings* (Montana) *Gaz.* 27 June 3-D/4, I left it in a phone booth while I was writing a sympathy card to be mailed. **1937** *Sun* (Baltimore) 19 Mar. 2/3, 200 women in the South Unit sewing department..struck because of a wage dispute. Some 280 other women seamstresses in the North Unit staged a one-hour 'sympathy strike'. **1973** *Morning Star* 28 Aug. 3 (*heading*) Chrysler hit by sympathy strikers. **1981** *Sunday Tel.* 22 Mar. 6/6 The first sympathy strike by students of an American university has been organised in support of demands made by students on strike at a brother-campus in Britain.

sympatisch, erron. var. *SYMPATHISCH *a.*

sympatric, *a.* (In Dict. s.v. SYM-.) Substitute for def.: Occurring in the same geographical region, or in overlapping regions. Opp. *ALLOPATRIC *a.* (Further examples.)

1904 E. B. POULTON in *Trans. Entomol. Soc.* V. p. xc, Forms found together in certain geographical areas and not in other areas. Such groups may be called *Sympatric*. **1942** E. MAYR *Systematics & Origin of Species* vii. 149 The gaps between sympatric species are absolute, otherwise they would not be good species; the gaps between allopatric species are often gradual and relative. **1953, 1958** [see *ALLOPATRIC *a.*]. **1974** *Nature* 16 Aug. 540/1 The two species are sympatric throughout much of their range. **1978** *Ibid.* 21 Sept. 256/1 White makes a good argument for sympatric speciation on small oceanic islands with many species and also for allochronic speciation.

Hence **sympa·trically** *adv.*; **sympatry**, substitute for def.: the occurrence of sympatric species or forms; (further examples).

1904 E. B. POULTON in *Trans. Entomol. Soc.* V. p. xc, The occurrence of forms together may be termed Sympatry, and the discontinuous distribution of similar forms Asympatry. **1968** *Amer. Mus. Novitates* No. 2349. 6 The grasslands of this region are generally similar to those of the area of sympatry west of Bahía Blanca. **1970** *S. Afr. Jrnl. Sci.* LXVI. 392/1 The two species have been found to occur sympatrically over a depth range of 14 to 33 metres. **1973** *Nature* 9 Feb. 406/2 The planting of dense agricultural stands of larval foodplants..[is] believed to have affected the species' geographical ranges and abundances, causing extensive sympatry over much of the eastern United States. **1975** *Jrnl. Zool.* CLXXVII. 330 True polymorphism is thus restricted to multiple forms of a species which regularly occur sympatrically (and synchronically) within a population.

symphonette (simfǒne·t). *rare.* [f. SYMPHON(Y + -ETTE.] A popular musical composition in classical symphonic form (cf. *symphonic jazz* (*a*) s.v. *SYMPHONIC *a.* (*sb.*) 3); a short symphony.

1947 A. EINSTEIN *Mus. Romantic Era* xi. 131 *Overture, Scherzo, and Finale*.., a work that Schumann in all seriousness wanted to bring out as his Second Symphony, or at least as a 'Symphonette'. **1955** L. FEATHER *Encycl. Jazz* 201/1 Completed mambo symphonette in three movements, March 1955.

symphonic, *a.* (*sb.*) Add: **3.** (Further examples.) *symphonic ballet*, a ballet choreographed to the music of a symphony, with an emphasis on pattern rather than plot; *symphonic jazz*, (*a*) jazz influenced by the form and instrumentation of classical music; (*b*) classical music scored and performed in jazz style.

1886 A. L. ALGER tr. *Reissman's Life & Works R. Schumann* iii. 57 Schumann took an important step forward in the path of his progress... Thus arose: 'The Carnival'.., the 'Symphonic Studies' (Op. 13, 1834) [etc.]. **1913** *Times* 3 Oct. 8/5 The two new works—Sir Edward Elgar's symphonic study for orchestra, *Falstaff*, and Mr. Hamilton Harty's setting..of..'The Mystic Trumpeter'. **1926** WHITEMAN & MCBRIDE *Jazz* iii. 58 Symphonic jazz had proved so successful that the Alexandria's cover receipts had risen from $300 to $1200 a day. **1929** *Metronome* Jan. 32/1 Whiteman put jazz in its Sunday dress and made it respectable. He applied the jazz treatment to the classics and established symphonic jazz which could be scored on paper. **1934** S. R. NELSON *All about Jazz* v. 101 Grofé has added 'Grand Canyon Suite'..to his personal contribution to the field of symphonic Jazz. **1936** *Times* 24 June 14/3 'Les Presages'. M. Massine's first symphonic ballet..was revived at Covent Garden last night. **1947** W. MELLERS *Stud. Contemp. Mus.* xi. 176 The string quartet Variations, and even Rawsthorne's biggest and most important work, the Symphonic Studies, are more freely based on the same notion of the variation of form. **1958** G. LASCELLES in P. Gammond *Decca Bk. Jazz* viii. 104 Paul Whiteman absorbed the nucleus of the Goldkette Orchestra into his own symphonic jazz group. **1964** RAFFÉ & PURDON *Dict. Dance* 487/1 Most choreographers who have attempted symphonic ballet have..used the music as a basis for vague generalisations by way of theme, while avoiding the technical aridity of 'abstract ballet'. **1976** *New Yorker* 26 Jan. 96/3 The big symphonic ballet in the Allegretto is a space-filling geometrical composition.

symphonically (simfǫ·nikăli), *adv.* [f. SYMPHONIC *a.*: see -ICALLY.] In a symphonic manner; as or like a symphony. Also *transf.*

1854 H. F. CHORLEY *Mod. German Mus.* v. 274 We may arrive at some canons of dramatic orchestral effect, not easy to reconcile with the practice of those writers who have treated Opera symphonically. **1923** G. SAINTSBURY in *Times Lit. Suppl.* 4 Jan. 2/1 There undoubtedly is room for ametric and unrhymed but symphonically rhythmed verse. **1927** R. VAUGHAN WILLIAMS in *Radio Times* 3 June 440/3 The words as well as the music are treated symphonically. **1929** *Sunday Dispatch* 13 Jan.

16 Paul Whiteman records have a wonderful following—chiefly because he can treat jazz symphonically. **1972** *Human World* Feb. 3 Hence the aptness of the symphonically deployed arch-motif in the imagery [of Racine's *Phèdre*]—the repeated reference to monsters. **1977** *Gramophone* Mar. 1457/1, I like both symphonies very much indeed even though I am not sure that they work symphonically.

symphonism (si·mfŏniz'm). [f. SYMPHON(Y + -ISM.] Music of a symphonic kind; symphonies collectively.

1965 *Listener* 27 May 805/2 Operatic music, which has to encompass drama and accommodate it as a further musical element, needs a more flexible technique than the pure music of symphonism. **1973** *Radio Times* 15 Nov. 60 A series of 13 concerts. 7: 'Cyclic' Symphonism.

symphonist. 2. Restrict † *Obs.* to sense in Dict. and add: Also, a player in a symphony orchestra. *rare.*

1964 M. McLUHAN *Understanding Media* (1967) II. xxiii. 378 The satisfactions are just as few for the.. symphonists, since a player in a big orchestra can hear nothing of the music that reaches the audience.

symphonize, *v.* Restrict 'Now *rare* or *Obs.*' to sense 1–3 and add: **3. b.** *trans.* To accompany musically.

1801 C. WILMOT *Let.* 29 Nov. in T. U. Sadleir *Irish Peer* (1920) 4 During the dinner..we were symphoniz'd by republican tunes, play'd outside the window. **1802** —— *Let.* 19 Oct. in *Ibid.* 103 A Gothic Castle..symphonis'd by the music of the waters.

4. To give the character or style of a symphony to (a piece of music), to render symphonic.

1932 *Amer. Speech* Apr. 241 Jazz is meant for the mass, it isn't meant to be symphonized, and all attempts at symphonization have been no more than negligible.

Hence **symphoniza·tion**; **sy·mphonized** *ppl. a.*, composed in the manner of a symphony.

1932 Symphonization [see sense 4 of the vb. above]. **1946** R. BLESH *Shining Trumpets* i. 14 A spate of symphonized jazz and pseudo-jazz master-works.

symphony. Add: **5. d.** *ellipt.* for 'symphony orchestra'.

1926 WHITEMAN & McBRIDE *Jazz* xiv. 287 The unknown composer has to pay to get his compositions played by a good symphony. **1934** S. R. NELSON *All about Jazz* v. 87 Symphony work, although of the highest *ton*, is not very lucrative, and most players have additional sources of income. **1968** *Globe & Mail* (Toronto) 17 Feb. 23/4 The former manager of the Vancouver Symphony. **1977** *Times* 23 Apr. 11/3 The seven arias skimpily supported by the Barcelona Symphony.

6. *attrib.* and *Comb.*, as (sense 5 b) *symphony concert, form, orchestra.*

1863 *Dwight's Jrnl. Mus.* XXIII. 110/3 Our concern now is with the concerts... To begin with the most important, those of the Orchestra, the so-called 'Philharmonic', or Symphony concerts. **1919** *Daily Mail Year Bk.* 200/1 Conductor of the Promenade Concerts since 1895, the Queen's Hall Symphony Concerts. **1956** A. H. COMPTON *Atomic Quest* ii. 68 On one occasion, Mrs. Edward Ryerson saw me as I was seeking a little relaxation at a symphony concert. **1911** *Contemp. Rev.* May 615 The idea that the symphonic poem is a further development of the symphony form. **1881** in Grove *Dict. Mus.* (1884) IV. 43/1 Orchestra to be permanent, and to be called The Boston Symphony Orchestra. **1932** *Daily Tel.* 8 Oct. 1/6 London Symphony Orchestra. **1978** *Ann. Reg.* *1977* 404 Their success went a good way towards discounting the much-publicized theory that the conventional symphony orchestra now exists only for the purpose of playing music from the past.

symplasm (si·mplæz'm). *Biol.* [f. SYM- + PLASM.] **a.** *Bacteriol.* A group of bacterial cells that have coalesced into one amorphous mass. ? *Obs.*

1916 LÖHNIS & SMITH in *Jrnl. Agric. Res.* VI. 680 Type D is in most cases the dissolution product either of the large forms [of *Bacillus azotobacter*]..or of the small cells. .. As it is made up by a thorough mixing or melting of a frequently large number of cells, spores, or gonidia, the term *symplasm* or *symplastic stage* seems to be a correct and convenient name. **1923** *Anat. Rec.* XXVI. 69 The bacteria coalesce and resolve into a sort of plasmodium. This plasmodium is the symplasm. Later, in the completion of the life-cycle, bacteria are again formed by the breaking up of the symplasm. **1934** A. T. HENRICI *Biol. Bacteria* ix. 153 Such symplasms are found in old cultures and they probably represent masses of gum secreted by the bacteria, or more likely, masses of débris formed from dead and dissolved bacterial cells.

b. *Bot.* The cytoplasm of a symplast (sense *b); an interconnected mass of cytoplasm.

1948 *Recueil d. Travaux botaniques Néerlandais* XLI. 5 Up until now, only a few publications have dealt with estimations as to what extent the symplasm is permeable for solutes. **1954** *Nature* 31 July 223/2 The transport in the cytoplasm from cell to cell..without loss to the outer solution indicates that plasma connexions between the cells must exist. The cells behave like a 'symplasm'. **1973** *Planta* CXII. 293 Stelar tissues only accumulate ions when these are supplied through the root symplasm.

Hence **sympla·smic** *a.*, of or pertaining to (a) symplasm.

1923 *Anat. Rec.* XXVI. 70 The symplasmic stage in the life-cycles of bacteria appear[s] to be universal. **1971** *Protoplasma* LXXII. 315 The concept of symplasmic transport between plant cells must take account of the possible role of plasmodesmata.

symplasma (simplæ·zmă). *Med.* Pl. **-plasmata.** [mod.L., coined in Ger. (R. Bonnet 1903, in *Monatsschr. f. Geburtshülfe u. Gynaekol.* XVIII. 8): see SYM- and PLASMA.] A mass of cell nuclei and cytoplasm regarded as formed by the breaking down of the cell walls of the outer layer of the placenta.

1908 *Q. Jrnl. Microsc. Sci.* LIII. 134 The maternal tissue..is universally recognised to undergo catalytic changes, and to pass into a symplasma, towards the composition of which superficial epithelium, proliferated epithelium of crypts and glands, subepithelial connective tissue, leucocytes, and blood have all largely contributed. **1910** F. H. A. MARSHALL *Physiol. of Reproduction* x. 414 After the destruction of the epithelium, the villi penetrate into the deeper tissues of the mucosa by gradually absorbing the symplasmata, and branch to form secondary and tertiary villi. **1923** *Q. Jrnl. Microsc. Sci.* LXVII. 146 A degenerating syncytium is called a symplasma.., a term which can be correctly applied only to maternal structures of a degenerate nature contained in the plasmodium. **1973** BOVING & LARSEN in Hafez & Evans *Human Reproduction* vii. 149/1 By this stage, the rabbit uterine epithelium has become converted into a 'symplasma' or multinucleated syncytium through the disappearance of the cell membranes between the epithelial cells.

symplasmatic (simplæzmæ·tik), *a.* [f. prec. after *plasma, plasmatic.*] **a.** *Med.* Of or pertaining to a symplasma. **b.** *Bot.* = *SYMPLASMIC *a.*

1923 *Q. Jrnl. Microsc. Sci.* LXVII. 156 In the symplasmatic zone of the diploplasma are to be found remains of maternal nuclei, maternal blood corpuscles and various granules. **1974** *Planta* CXIX. 47 Transients are observed in mutated cells when the illuminated green leaf sample also comprises normally green cells and there is a symplasmatic connection between the 2 types of cells.

symplast (si·mplɑst). *Bot.* [f. SYM- + -PLAST.] † **a.** [ad. G. *symplast* (J. von Hanstein 1880, in *Bot. Abh.* IV. II. 9).] A multinucleate cell created either by the fusion of cells into one cytoplasmic mass, or by the division of the nucleus of a single energid. *Obs.*

1894 *Jrnl. R. Microsc. Soc.* 376 Klemm objects to the term 'unicellular' as applied to *Caulerpa prolifera* and similar organisms. They should be regarded rather as 'symplasts', composed of a number of energids. **1900** *Ibid.* 475 When the polyplasts are so completely fused together that their cytoplasms form a single mass in which a number of nuclei are imbedded, Hanstein's term 'symplasts' may be applied. **1912** L. A. BORRADAILE *Man. Elem. Zool.* vi. 116 Groups of similar, unseparated energids are known as syncytia. They may be plasmodia, formed by the union of free energids, or symplasts, formed by the division of the nucleus of a single energid.

b. [ad. G. *symplast* (E. Münch *Die Stoffbewegungen in der Pflanze* (1930) 73).] A continuous network of interconnected plant cell protoplasts.

1938 *Amer. Jrnl. Bot.* XXV. 529/2 Studies on the occurrence of plasmodesmata in living tissues show that where pits occur the protoplasts are commonly connected by these strands. Consequently the 'symplast'..of the root must constitute an interconnected protoplasmic unit. **1976** B. E. S. GUNNING in Gunning & Robards *Intercellular Communication in Plants: Studies on Plasmodesmata* I. 2 Following the evolution of plasmodesmata, the plant body is..composed of two major compartments, for which the terms apoplast and symplast are convenient (Münch, 1930)... The term symplast refers to the interconnected protoplasts, all bounded by a continuous plasmalemma.

Hence **sympla·stic** *a.*, of or pertaining to a symplast or symplasm; *symplastic growth*, the expansion of a common wall between adjacent plant cells during cell enlargement.

1916 [see *SYMPLASM a]. **1930** J. H. PRIESTLEY in *New Phytologist* XXIX. 132 It is proposed to call this alternative method of growth now described symplastic growth. **1981** J. R. BARNETT *Xylem Cell Devel.* ii. 63 This symplastic growth hypothesis..could not explain satisfactorally the type of growth in which an enlarging cell, such as a fibre, increases the number of cells with which it is in contact as it grows.

symplectic, *a.* and *sb.* For **a, b** read **A, B** and add: **A.** *adj.* **2.** *Petrol.* Of a rock or its texture: exhibiting an intimate intergrowth of two different minerals, esp. one where one mineral has a vermicular habit within the other as a result of secondary action. [ad. G. *symplektisch* (C. F. Naumann *Lehrb. der Geognosie* (1850) I. 667).]

1916 J. J. SEDERHOLM in *Bull. de la Comm. Géol. de Finlande* No. 48. 46, I..take the liberty of proposing that the term symplektic, or symplektitic should be used preferably as a designation of secondary intergrowths of two different minerals. **1949** F. H. HATCH et al. *Petrol. Igneous Rocks* (ed. 10) iv. 281 A characteristic feature of certain noritic rocks is the development of symplectic intergrowths along intercrystal boundaries. **1971** *Nature* 3 Dec. 251/3 The decomposition of a fayalitic olivine (Fe_2SiO_4) to symplectic metallic iron and cristobalite provides confirmation of a very low oxygen fugacity.

Hence **symple·ctite**, an intergrowth of this kind; **symplecti·tic** *a.*

1916 J. J. SEDERHOLM in *Bull. de la Comm. Géol. de Finlande* No. 48. 46, I..propose to use for these intergrowths of two minerals plaited together, and generally of second origin, the common designation symplektites (or symplectites). **1949** F. H. HATCH et al. *Petrol. Igneous Rocks* (ed. 10) iv. 282 (*caption*) Myrmekite-like symplectites of orthopyroxene and plagioclase are lobed into the labradorite. **1976** *Nature* 22 Apr. 673/2 Rare symplectites of spinel and pyroxene may result from the dehydration of amphibole. **1979** *Ibid.* 5 Apr. 512/2 Symplectitic diopside is not different from coarser, recrystallised diopside.

symplesite (si·mplĕzəit). *Min.* [ad. G. *symplesit* (A. Breithaupt 1837, in *Jrnl. f. prakt. Chem.* X. 501), f. Gr. πλησ-ιάζειν to bring together (in allusion to its relations to other minerals): see SYM- and -ITE[1].] A hydrated ferrous arsenate, $Fe_3(AsO_4)_2.8H_2O$, found as green triclinic crystals (altering to blue), usu. in aggregates having a coarsely fibrous radial structure.

1844 J. D. DANA *Syst. Min.* (ed. 2) VI. 532 Symplesite...Occurs at Lobenstein in Voigtland, with cobaltic pyrites and dolomite. **1968** I. KOSTOV *Mineralogy* 453 Symplesite is found in spherical aggregates, light green to indigo-blue when oxidized.

symploce. Add: Also **symploke** (-ŏkī). (Later example.)

1952 J. D. DENNISTON *Gr. Prose Style* v. 90 Occasionally repetition occurs both at beginning and at end of clause, anaphora being combined with antistrophe. This is the figure known as symploke.

symposiast. 2. (Later examples.)

1930 *Time & Tide* 16 May 638 This new sally is directed against the Religious Symposiasts of the popular press, against the well-known writers who take part in those series called 'Is Prayer Answered?' [etc.]. **1978** *Social Sci. & Med.* XII. 185 The symposiasts insist that their analyses are stimulated by the cultural science, yet cannot specify just how.

symposium. Add: **2. b.** A book consisting of essays on various aspects of a subject contributed by a number of different authors.

1946 *Nature* 19 Oct. 534/1 Advances in biological sciences in the U.S.S.R. within the recent 25 years, 1917–1942. Symposium. Editor-in-chief: L. A. Orbeli. (In Russian.) Pp. 356. **1969** *Listener* 15 May 696/1 A symposium on 20th-century music, published in 1960, contained a fulsome and over-extended reference to a then almost unknown French composer. **1972** *Daily Tel.* 30 Mar. 6 This generously illustrated symposium, by contributors of different denominations, covers a worldwide range of Christian art and architecture. **1979** *Nature* 1 Mar. 102/1 Symposia are at present, perhaps, an over-popular form of publication: in many of them the thread of supposed common interest which binds the essays together is far too tenuous, and indeed, in the case of some complimentary volumes such as this, completely non-existent.

sympotic (simpǫ·tik), *a.* [f. as next.] = SYMPOTICAL *a.*

1972 P. M. FRASER *Ptolemaic Alexandria* I. x. 565 In other fields Asclepiades shows himself an innovator in his adaptation of existing poetical genres to the epigram. This is clearly shown in his sympotic epigrams, which form a main category of his work. **1981** *Times Lit. Suppl.* 6 Nov. 1307/5 The archaic age was the great age of sympotic pottery: potters and painters became rich and famous, producing shapes and painting designs which echoed the sympotic preoccupations of their aristocratic patrons.

sympotical, *a.* For *rare*$^{-1}$ read *rare* and add later example.

1981 *Times* 5 Aug. 12/6 The sympotical form is still quite distinctive of British culture from pubs to clubs.

symptom, *sb.* Add: **1. a.** (Further examples.) Esp., in mod. use, a subjective indication, perceptible to the patient, as opposed to an objective one or sign (*SIGN *sb.* 7 e).

1842, etc. [see *SIGN *sb.* 7 e]. **1869** S. FENWICK *Med. Diagnosis* i. 2 Diseases are distinguished from each other either by such alterations in the organs themselves, or their secretions, as can be ascertained by the senses of the observer (physical signs); or by changes in the functions of the parts affected (symptoms). **1922** *Amer. Jrnl. Med. Sci.* CLXIV. 684 The first sign noticed was cyanosis and the first symptom shortness of breath on exertion.

b. Also *Comb.*, as *symptom-free* adj.

1962 *Lancet* 27 Jan. 212/2 Most remain symptom-free, apart from aching calves, thighs and backs. **1980** *Recent Advances in Surgery* X. 396 Only about 45 per cent of patients achieve a perfect, symptom-free, Visick grade I result.

syn-[1]. Add: **1. synanthro·pic** *a.* [ANTHROPIC *a.*], living in habitats made or altered by man; **syna·pomorphy** *Taxonomy* [f. *apomorphy*, f. APO- + Gr. μορφή form], the possession by two organisms of some character (not necessarily the same in each) that is derived from one character in an organism from which they both evolved; also = next; so **syna·pomorph,**

any such derived character; **syncyano·sis** *Bot.* (pl. **-o·ses**) [ad. G. *syncyanose* (A. Pascher 1914, in *Ber. d. Deutsch. Bot. Ges.* XXXII. 340)], the relationship between a unicellular blue-green alga and a host within which it lives symbiotically; also *concr.*, the organisms themselves; **syne·chthran** *Ent.*, an insect that lives with ants or other social insects as an unwelcome guest in a relationship of synechthry; **synechthry,** add: [ad. G. *synechthrie* (M. E. Wasmann 1896, in *3ème Congr. Internat. Zool.* 412)]; **sy·nform** *Geol.*, a fold that is concave upwards, irrespective of the chronological sequence of the strata; cf. SYNCLINE in Dict. and Suppl.; **synkinema·tic** *a. Geol.*, formed or occurring when moving or as an accompaniment to motion; **synneu·sis** *Petrol.* [Gr. νεῦσις swimming], the clustering together of crystals of a mineral in a rock; freq. *attrib.* in *synneusis texture*; **synœkete** (sinī·kīt) *Ent.* [ad. Gr. συνοικέτης house-fellow, f. συνοικεῖν to live together (f. οἶκος house): cf. G. *synœkie* (M. E. Wasmann 1896, in *3ème Congr. Internat. Zool.* 412)], an insect that lives with ants or other social insects without either benefiting or harming them; **synoroge·nic** *a. Geol.* [cf. G. *synorogenese* sb. (H. Stille *Grundfragen d. vergleichenden Tektonik* (1924) 16)], formed or occurring during a period of orogenesis; **sy:nsedime·ntary** *a. Geol.*, formed or occurring at the time of deposition of (the) sediment; **sy:ntecto·nic** *a. Geol.*, formed or occurring during a period of tectonic activity; hence **syntecto·nically** *adv.*; **sy·nteny** *Genetics* [Gr. ταινία band, ribbon], the condition (of genes) of being on the same chromosome; hence **synte·nic** *a.*

1936 *Discovery* Mar. 89/2 There can be no question of post-glacial colonisation of Iceland by other than synanthropic insects. **1971** *Countryman* Summer 187/1 This is probably a yellow slug, *Limax flavus*, a synanthropic species, which lives in and around houses, cellars and old garden walls. **1969** E. MAYR *Princ. Systematic Zool.* x. 202 Derived characters (synapomorphs of Hennig) shared with a more recent ancestor. **1966** DAVIS & ZANGERL tr. *Hennig's Phylogenetic Systematics* ii. 90 It makes no difference whether the synapomorphy consists in the fact that an apomorphous character (a′) is present identically in all species..or whether it is present in different derived conditions (a′ and a″). **1979** *Nature* 18 Jan. 176/1 This inference is drawn from the fact that lungfish and cows share derived characters (synapomorphies such as internal nostrils, an epiglottis, a two-chambered auricle and so on..) not found in salmon. **1945** F. E. FRITSCH *Structure & Reproduction of Algae* II. 878 A different relation is seen in the association of certain Myxophyceae of small dimensions with Monads or Bacteria (syncyanoses of Pascher). **1967** *Jrnl. Phycol.* III. 37/2 *Cyanophora* is one of the few forms among the syncyanoses thus far found which has been thoroughly studied. **1978** *Bio Systems* X. 74/2 Lee suggested that members of the group originated from the union of a non-photosynthetic cryptomonad stock with cyanobacteria, resulting in an early 'syncyanosis' similar to that seen in *Cyanophora paradoxa* today. **1910** W. WHEELER *Ants* xxi. 382 In the United States *Megastilicus formicarius*.., which is not uncommon in the large mound nests of *Formica exsectoides*, is..a typical synechthran. **1967** J. H. SUDD *Introd. Behaviour Ants* vi. 127 Synechthrans are always treated with hostility by the ants and usually they, in turn, prey on the ants. **1937** BAILEY & MCCALLIEN in *Trans. R. Soc. Edin.* LIX. 81 In the following pages: Antiform means a fold that closes upwards. Synform means a fold that closes downwards. **1978** *Nature* 12 Oct. 539/1 Preserved in a large secondary synform, there occurs a sequence, several hundred metres thick, consisting of ribbon cherts, bedded jasperites, [etc.]. **1932** *Mineral. und Petrogr. Mitt.* XLII. 475 The older Archaean granites of Fennoscandia.. belong to characteristically synkinematic intrusive complexes from an early stage of an orogenic cycle. **1952** T. F. W. BARTH *Theoret. Petrol.* III. 243 Synkinematic granitization is probably responsible for the majority of the large granodiorite and granite batholiths. **1973** J. T. RENOUF tr. *Didier's Granites & their Enclaves* 7 The orogenic granites are classically divided into synkinematic (= synorogenic or syntectonic) and post-tectonic types. **1921** J. H. L. VOGT in *Jrnl. Geol.* XXIX. 321 The individuals of a mineral, segregated from a magma at an early stage, frequently swam together to assemblings or aggregates, the result of which is a structure, for which I propose the term together-swimming structure or synneusis structure. **1959** W. W. MOORHOUSE *Study of Rocks in Thin Section* xi. 241 Probably related to the banded character of the basic complexes is a texture, sometimes called 'synneusis' texture, in which the dark minerals.. tend to occur as lenticular clumps or aggregates. **1967** *Amer. Mineralogist* LII. 529 The preferential character of synneusis for several common individual minerals and mineral pairs. **1973** J. T. RENOUF tr. *Didier's Granites & their Enclaves* xiv. 368 When two rocks contain the same volumetric percentage of phenocrysts, synneusis is greatest in that with the smaller crystals and thus with the greatest number. **1910** W. WHEELER *Ants* xxi. 381 The symphiles represent the élite,..and number hardly more than 300 to 400 species, whereas the synœketes are much more numerous. **1971** E. O. WILSON *Insect Societies* (1972) xx. 390/2 Most of the time..the *Cremastocheilus* have the status of synoeketes, that is, they are simply ignored and allowed to wander through the nest without interference. **1936** *Bull. Amer. Assoc. Petroleum Geologists* XX. 853 Synorogenic movements dating from this time are to be recognized everywhere in this continent. **1971** I. G. GASS et al. *Understanding Earth* xx. 292/1 The synorogenic sediments that accompany mountain building. **1974** *Nature* 4 Oct. 382/2 In Africa the Kibaran belt experienced major tectonism about 1,300 Myr BP..with the subparallel Irumide belt undergoing synorogenic events about 1,100 Myr ago. **1960** *Gloss. Geol.* (Amer. Geol. Inst.) (ed. 2) Suppl. 65/1 Synsedimentary. **1976** *Jrnl. Geol. Soc.* CXXXII. 124 In sheet III the lower contact is a sharp, curved slide plane with occasional synsedimentary striations. **1979** *Nature* 9 Aug. 483/2 This sealing apparently results from a synsedimentary permineralisation caused by colloidal silica. **1942** M. P. BILLINGS *Structural Geol.* xv. 297 Syntectonic intrusives are always forcefully injected bodies, because the magma was moving under the influence of orogenic pressures. **1974** *Nature* 22 Mar. 325/2 In coastal Liberia the geological evidence of actual faulting that could definitely be said to be syntectonic with rifting is lacking. **1956** L. V. DE SITTER *Structural Geol.* xxvi. 392 The syntectonically metamorphosed mica-schists and migmatites. **1979** *Nature* 25 Jan. 290/1 A phase of upright asymmetric folding..with the steep limbs overturned to the northwest took place syntectonically with major brittle thrusting..of all units. **1971** J. H. RENWICK in *Ann. Human Genetics* XXXV. 80 If the inversion and a marker locus studied in the pedigree are syntenic (lying on the same chromosome pair), the marker may be on either side of either breakpoint and the linkage..to one of them may be close and may have a good chance of being detected. **1978** *Nature* 13 July 161/1 Five genes in the mouse..are syntenic and their human homologues have been assigned to human chromosome 1. **1971** J. H. RENWICK in *Ann. Human Genetics* XXXV. 83 The prior probability of the hypothesis of synteny—i.e. that the autosomal marker locus is somewhere on the chromosome pair that bears the inversion—is A/T. **1974** *Sci. Amer.* July 39/1 Assaying a number of clones for various human enzymes therefore provides information on the synteny of genes.

2. *Chem.* Designating geometrical isomers of organic compounds containing C=N or N=N in which the principal atoms or groups attached to the doubly bonded atoms are on the same side of the plane of the double bond; usu. italicized. Also without hyphen as an independent word. [Introduced in Ger. by A. Hantzsch 1894, in *Ber. Deut. Chem. Ges.* XXVII. 1702.]

1894 *Jrnl. Chem. Soc.* LXVI. I. 454 Such diazo-compounds as exist in the form of rings, due to the formation of inner anhydrides..must be syn-compounds. **1913** T. H. POPE tr. *Molinari's Treat. Gen. & Industr. Org. Chem.* 568 It forms a mixture of phenyldiazonium hydroxide..and syn-diazobenzene hydroxide. **1938** R. L. SHRINER et al. in H. Gilman *Org. Chem.* I. iii. 385 The amine oxide structure does not aid in accounting for the *syn* and *anti* forms of these oximes, but is necessary to account for the tautomerism of these isomers. **1978** *Nature* 9 Feb. 494/2 The intense sweetness of the *α-syn*-oxime of perillartine was first reported in 1920.

syn-[2] (sin), comb. form of SYNTHETIC *a.*, used to form words denoting synthetic products, as **sy·ncrude**, a synthetic product made from coal in imitation of crude oil; also as *adj.*; **sy·nfuel**, any fuel made from coal, oil shale, or the like as a substitute for a petroleum product; **sy·ngas**, a mixture of carbon monoxide and hydrogen, esp. when produced from coal; **sy·njet**, jet fuel derived from synthetic crude oil (syncrude); **sy·noil**, synthetic oil; **sy·nroc** [Roc(K *sb.*[1]], any of various synthetic crystalline materials composed chiefly of oxides of metals and semimetals and devised as sufficiently stable to contain radioactive waste in solid solution deep underground.

1971 *Kirk-Othmer Encycl. Chem. Technol.* (ed. 2) Suppl. 189 Both oils are subsequently hydrotreated to produce a syncrude oil. **1976** *Times* 9 Dec. 27 Looking at the alternative power sources for private transport, the survey reckons that the most likely ones are a synthetic liquid fuel (such as methanol or syncrude) derived from coal, or electricity stored in batteries. **1980** *McGraw-Hill Yearbk. Sci. & Technol.* 303/2 Salable by-products of ammonia, sulfur, and phenols are produced by several of the SNG and syncrude processes. **1976** *Dallas Morning News* 22 Sept. 2-D/3 Whatever has happened to all the synthetic fuel we were supposed to get to ease the oil and gas shortage? Now, three years later, we've still done very little towards the development of 'synfuels'. **1980** *Science* 16 May 740 Certain processes for developing some U.S. oil shales may generate more CO_2 per unit of usable energy produced than any other synfuel development. **1982** *Sunday Times* 9 May 54/6 Multi-billion investment—the basic fee to gain entry to the synfuels game—cannot be justified. **1975** *N.Y. Times* 24 Mar. 20/2 Much of the Western coal has been planned for conversion at the mine to synthetic pipeline gas... The 'syn-gas' is to replace natural gas from wells, the fuel that is expected to be in the most critical depletion by 1985. **1980** *Prospects for Petrochemicals in W. Europe* (Shell Internat. Petroleum Co.) 8 By the middle of next century it is possible that the petrochemical industry could even be sustained very largely, if not entirely, on syngas and methanol derived from coal and methane. **1983** *New Scientist* 28 Apr. 207/2 Syn-gas is also made from natural gas..by the related reaction $CH_4 + H_2O = CO + 3H_2$. **1979** *Ibid.* 7 June 818 In the long term, the choice must be between jet fuel derived from synthetic crude (synjet) or a wholly new type of fuel. **1980** *Times* 21 Feb. 20/4 The quick and easy solution, which is 'synjet'—kerosene made from coal, shale or tarsands. **1976** *Time* 1 Mar. 47 So far several plants have been..designed to turn 2,700 tons of high-sulfur Illinois coal into 22 million cu. ft. of 'syngas' and 3,000 bbl. of 'synoil' each day. **1978** *Nature* 3 Aug. 413/1 Whereas glassified waste may devitrify when exposed to ground water at high temperature and pressure, thus exposing a large surface area for the dissolution of the radionuclides in the glass, the new mineral—'synroc'—should be as stable as a natural rock. **1980** *New Scientist* 3 July 9/2 In the Synroc process the radioactive wastes are trapped in the crystal lattices of the minerals of the synthetic rocks and so are completely immobilised. **1982** *Nature* 9 Dec. 470/3 The plant..will make Synroc-C, which consists of 60 per cent titanium dioxide, with an admixture of barium oxide, calcium oxide, zirconia and alumina.

synæresis. Add: **2.** *Physical Chem.* The contraction of a gel accompanied by the separating out of liquid.

1864 T. GRAHAM in *Proc. R. Soc.* XIII. 336 In the jelly itself, the specific contraction in question, or synæresis, still proceeds. **1937** *Jrnl. R. Aeronaut. Soc.* XLI. 535 The material in tension might be explained by assuming (in accordance with the phenomenon of syneresis) that the solid portion of the isogel is in a state of contraction relative to the less condensed portions. **1974** *Encycl. Brit. Macropædia* IV. 857/2 A flocculated paste, or suspension of very fine particles, often behaves as a gel... The systems are often thixotropic... They show syneresis.

synæsthesia. Add: **1. c.** (Further examples.)

1895 *Amer. Jrnl. Psychol.* VII. 90 The study of the varying forms of persisting abnormal association, usually known as 'colored-hearing' and 'forms', but grouped together by Theodore Flournoy, under the convenient name *Synæsthesia*, has hardly..completed the stage of scientific observation. **1935** *Brit. Jrnl. Psychol.* XXV. 31 The most interesting phase of M's synaesthesia is the tendency to see the features of people in different colours. Her acquaintances were not only assigned particular colours, but they were remembered in terms of this colour. **1958** *New Scientist* 6 Feb. 29/3 Synaesthesia is not a commonly reported psychiatric symptom. **1971** *Daily Tel.* 21 Aug. 7/3 Synaesthesia (in his case 'colour-hearing') was observed among his blind patients by an English oculist. **1979** C. PRIEST *Infinite Summer* 40 In the morning my synaesthesia seemed to have receded again.

2. *Lit.* The use of metaphors in which terms relating to one kind of sense-impression are used to describe sense-impressions of other kinds; the production of synæsthetic effect in writing or an instance of this.

[**1901** H. OERTEL *Lect. Study of Lang.* v. 327 The second class of metaphors which ought to receive an exhaustive treatment is the transfer of terms from one sense sphere to the other. These..are illustrated by phrases like 'a sharp tone', 'loud colors'... The phenomenon of synaesthesia has received rather full treatment at the hand of the psychologists, but its reflection on language has not yet received adequate treatment by lexicographers.] **1932** G. STERN in *Göteborgs Högskolas Årsskrift* XXXVIII. I. 323 Synaesthesia is especially common among adjectives ..but there are numerous instances of nouns..: *The sound and light of sweeter songs* (Swinburne). **1936** W. B. STANFORD *Gr. Metaphor* 59 Synaesthesia..amongst certain schools of poetry became almost a major element in the technique of sense-expression. **1960** E. H. GOMBRICH *Art & Illusion* x. 366 What is called 'synesthesia', the splashing over of impressions from one sense modality to another is a fact to which all languages testify. **1977** *N.Y. Rev. Bks.* 24 Nov. 11/1 No child who has attempted a list like Whitman's or a synesthesia like Rimbaud's or a colloquy with the sun like Frank O'Hara's is likely to forget the parent-poem. **1978** *Times Lit. Suppl.* 1 Dec. 1406/4 Synaesthesia is a common technique, even a theme, in his work. **1982** *N. & Q.* June 194/2 The 'inevitable' complement to the serene synaesthesia of passages like the Hawkshead dedication.

3. *Linguistics.* **a.** The expression of more than one kind of sense-impression in the same word. **b.** The transfer of the meaning of a word from one kind of sensory experience to another. **c.** The relationship between speech sounds and the sensory experiences that they represent.

1946 A. G. ENGSTROM in *Philological Q.* XXV. 10 Traces of synaesthesia are as clear in language as in laboratory records... Hornbostel cites a Negro tribe that has a separate word for seeing, but employs a common term for hearing, tasting, smelling, and touching. **1946** S. D. ULLMANN in *Word* II. 114 What Wundt and his disciples term 'complicative change of meaning' is known to the vast majority of other students as 'synesthesia'. **1956** J. WHATMOUGH *Language* x. 191 There is some evidence to indicate that synesthesia such as associates the meanings of colour and sound under a single word may extend to smaller linguistic units. **1957** S. POTTER *Mod. Linguistics* vii. 154 By *synaesthesia* or *intersensory transfer* a word may be given a new sense. **1972** HARTMANN & STORK *Dict. Lang. & Linguistics* 229/1 *Synaesthesia*, the association of a particular sound or group of sounds with a particular meaning, e.g. *fl-* in *flare, flicker, flame*, [etc.]. **1977** *Word 1972* XXVIII. 309 Phonetic symbolism, described as the appropriateness of some phonemes to nonauditory experience, falls under the general heading of synaesthesia or, in psychological terminology, crossmodal association. *Ibid.*, As a result of the clustering, forced-choice testing yields congruent information not only in synesthesia studies but in phonetic symbolism and semantic differential tests as well.

synæsthesis. Add: **b.** (See quots.)

1922 C. K. OGDEN et al. *Foundations of Aesthetics* 76 Synaesthesis..covers both equilibrium and harmony.

1923 Ogden & Richards *Meaning of Meaning* vii. 267 We cannot enter here into the details of what, from the standpoint of more or less conventional psychology, may be supposed to happen in these states of synaesthesis. **1943** J. T. Shipley *Dict. World Lit. Terms* 327/2 *Synæsthesis*, the harmonious and balanced concord stimulated by art, as posited in the definition of beauty advanced by Ogden, Richards, and Wood in The Foundations of Aesthetics. **1949** Wimsatt & Beardsley in *Sewanee Rev.* LVII. 40 Among these [types of aesthetic theory] the theory of synaesthesis (Beauty is what produces an equilibrium of appetencies) was the one they themselves [*sc.* Ogden, Richards, & Wood] espoused.

synæsthetic (sinīsþe·tik) *a.* (*sb.*) Also **synesthetic.** **1.** [f. Synæsthesia, after *anæsthetic.*] Of, pertaining to, or exhibiting synæsthesia. Also *absol.* or as *sb.*, a synæsthetic person. So **synæsthe·tically** *adv.*

1910 *Mind* XIX. 296 Sense-experiences synaesthetically aroused. **1920** R. H. Wheeler *Synaesthesia of Blind Subject* 54 Synaesthetic phenomena in the field of imagery..reveal the same characteristics as do the same phenomena in the field of perception. **1925** *Amer. Jrnl. Psychol.* XXXVI. 530 The process of perceiving a synaesthetically colored month as an emotion,—by which we mean that the emotional response is represented in the various qualities of the colored imagery. **1935** *Brit. Jrnl. Psychol.* XXV. 37 Every case of synaesthesia..consists essentially of a parallel arrangement of two gradient series. They may be series of pitches, intensities..or anything else in keeping with the interests..of the synaesthetic. **1936** W. B. Stanford *Gr. Metaphor* 47 We shall call..transferences from the sphere of one sense to that of another *synaesthetic* or intersensal metaphor. *Ibid.* 61 Writers like Poe..and..Ayala affect the same kinds of synaesthetic phrases. Edith Sitwell has 'creaking light' and 'dawn...whining'. **1942** *Jrnl. Gen. Psychol.* XXVI. 213 Such results emphasize the continuity between synesthetic phenomena and more general phenomena of language and thinking. **1949** Koestler *Insight & Outlook* xxiii. 320 It is obvious that such 'synaesthetic' metaphors greatly facilitate the sharing by the reader of the teller's vision. **1951** S. D. Ullmann *Princ. Semantics* iv. 219 Gombocz developed these distinctions..redefining the essence of synaesthetic transfer which, contrary to Wundt and Roudet, he included among cases of affective sense-similarity. **1977** *Word 1972* XXVIII. 306 On investigation, a group of phonetic-symbolism, synesthetic, and semantic-differential studies was shown to have produced two groups of semantic qualities which were internally coherent and mutually exclusive. **1979** C. Priest *Infinite Summer* 39, I was still affected by the enemy's synaesthetic gas I had inhaled. My perception was disturbed.

2. [f. Synæsthesis, after *æsthetic.*] Of or pertaining to synæsthesis.

1922 C. K. Ogden et al. *Foundations of Aesthetics* 91 What we have called the synaesthetic character of the experience.

synagogue. Add: Also (*U.S.*) **synagog.**

1929 *Lit. Digest* 2 Nov. 24/1 New York now has..the largest synagog in existence—the new Temple Emanu-El on a site overlooking Central Park. **1963** R. I. McDavid *Mencken's Amer. Lang.* 491 The 1962 Style Book, p. 63 specifies the following:..synagog. **1976** *National Observer* (U.S.) 22 May 16-A/5 Usually he was paid by the synagog and served in various capacities as rabbi, cantor, or schoolteacher.

Synanon (si·nănǫn). [See quot. 1965[2] for the supposed origin.] The name of a U.S. foundation concerned chiefly with the rehabilitation of drug addicts through group therapy; also (with small initial) the method of psychotherapy practised in its centres (see also quot. 1963). Freq. *attrib.*

1961 *Time* 7 Apr. 33/1 Synanon offers more than a few cures. *Ibid.*, The Synanon system cannot work until the addict really decides..to kick the habit. **1963** *Amer. Jrnl. Sociol.* LXIX. 135/1 The free, unrestricted interaction in small groups called 'synanons'. **1965** L. Yablonsky *Tunnel Back* p. viii, Synanon is a community of former addicts and criminals. *Ibid.*, The word 'synanon' originated with a newly arrived addict... In his attempt to say two 'foreign' words, 'symposium' and 'seminar' in the same breath, he blurted out 'synanon'. *Ibid.* vi. 137 The small-'s' synanon is the group psychotherapy of the total Synanon social structure. **1969** *Guardian* 16 Aug. 7/3 Synanon's communities are not unlike Socialist communes... Everything is free, everyone 'mucks in'. *Ibid.* 21 Aug. 8/4 Spinrad's latest novel..examines the process by which psychotherapy has become a religious experience, spawning synthetic cults like scientology..and the Synanon game. **1976** J. Rowan *Ordinary Ecstasy* iv. 44 The essence of the Synanon approach is direct aggressive confrontation of the one group member by one or more other members.

synaphe. (Earlier example.)

1740 J. Grassineau *Mus. Dict.* 250 *Synaphe*, a Greek term which signifies, according to Boëtius..conjunction; a chord is said to be conjoint, when so placed between two fourths.

synapomorphy: see *syn-[1] 1.

synapse (sinæ·ps), *v. Anat.* [f. the sb.] *intr.* Of a nerve-cell or axon: to form a synapse.

1910 *Practitioner* July 98 The rubro-spinal portion (Monakow's bundle) connects the red nucleus with the opposite side of the spinal cord, probably terminating by synapsing round the anterior horn cells. **1963** R. P. Dales *Annelids* vi. 119 The axon is T-shaped, the cell body lying ventrally or ventro-laterally at the bottom of the T and the tips of the arms synapsing with those of the next neuron. **1979** *Sci. Amer.* Sept. 84/1 Many such cells do not themselves make contact with a motor neuron; they synapse instead on yet other neurons of the great intermediate net.

Also **syna·psed** *ppl. a. Genetics* [cf. Synapsis 2 in Dict. and Suppl.], (of chromosomes) in a state of synapsis.

1931 *Amer. Jrnl. Bot.* XVIII. 370 The synapsed spireme strands traverse the nucleus freely. **1946** *Nature* 21 Dec. 912/1 Perhaps such chemical agents in the egg help in separating the synapsed X-chromosomes. **1974** *Ibid.* 12 Apr. 566/2 The X element contains three synapsed chromosomes.

synapsid (sinæ·psid), *a.* and *sb.* [a. mod.L. *Synapsida* (H. F. Osborn 1903, in *Mem. Amer. Mus. Nat. Hist.* I. 455), f. Syn- + Gr. ἁψίς, ἁψιδ- arch: see -id[3].] **A.** *adj.* Of or pertaining to the subclass Synapsida, which includes fossil reptiles having a single temporal opening on each side of the skull. So **syna·psidan** *a.* **B.** *sb.* A fossil reptile of the subclass Synapsida, showing a skull structure with some mammalian characteristics.

1903 *Mem. Amer. Mus. Nat. Hist.* I. 460 In all Synapsidan types above the Cotylosauria the squamosals and pro-squamosals early coalesce. **1910** *Bull. Amer. Mus. Nat. Hist.* XXVII. 114 The Synapsid reptiles..may conveniently be approached by a cursory review of the reptilian orders. **1933** A. S. Romer *Vertebr. Paleontol.* vi. 128 Forms with one opening (in which it was presumed that the two openings had fused into one), [were termed] 'synapsid' (fused-arched) reptiles. **1956** —— *Osteol. Reptiles* ii. 473 The mesosaurs..are associated with the synapsid orders. *Ibid.* 474 The synapsids..seem to be a very natural assemblage. **1974** D. & M. Webster *Compar. Vertebr. Morphol.* v. 102 The presence of this bone in both monotremes, where it is apparently functionless, as well as in metatherians is particularly confusing since there is no indication of a marsupial bone in synapsid reptiles. **1980** *Nature* 24 Jan. 378/2 The mammals arose from advanced synapsids in the Upper Triassic. *Ibid.*, An alternative view of the origin of the synapsid skull is that the ancestral condition of the temporal region consisted of a large supratemporal bone which was in contact anteriorly with the postorbital.

synapsis. Add: **2.** Substitute for def.: orig. (see quots. 1895, 1905); in mod. use, chromosomal pairing during the zygotene stage of meiosis.

Delete 1892 reference in Dict. (which is spurious). Quot. 1900 there represents a misunderstanding.

1895 J. E. S. Moore in *Q. Jrnl. Microsc. Sci.* XXXVIII. 296 The transformation of the cells of the first spermatogenetic period into those of the second, which I have termed the synapsis,..is marked by a peculiar evolution in the chromatin with the formation of peculiar nucleoli..and by the formation of an archoplasmic constituent round the centrosomes. **1905** —— in *Ibid.* XLVIII. 490 Synapsis represents that series of events which are concerned in causing the temporary union in pairs of premaiotic chromosomes, previously to their transverse separation and distribution, in their entirety, between two daughter nuclei. **1912** *Jrnl. Exper. Zool.* XIII. 348 A number of writers have suggested that the term synapsis..should be abandoned in favour of some less ambiguous word (such as Haecker's term 'syndesis') because it has so frequently been applied to the contraction-figure ('synizesis' of McClung). I am, however, in favor of the retention of the word, for the ambiguity has arisen simply through a misunderstanding of Moore's meaning. He applied the term 'synaptic phase', or 'synapsis', to the series of changes following the last diploid division..in the course of which the apparent number of chromosomes is reduced to one-half. **1960** L. Picken *Organization of Cells* iv. 137 Given the mitotic apparatus, the special features of meiosis might follow from the one act of synapsis—the pairing of homologues. **1978** M. W. Farnsworth *Genetics* vi. 123 During the zygotene stage homologous chromosomes begin to pair lengthwise with one another, a process called synapsis.

† **synaptenic** (sinæptī·nik), *a. Cytology. Obs.* Also **-tænic.** [ad. F. *synaptène* (H. von Winiwarter 1900, in *Arch. de Biol.* XVII. 54), f. Gr. συν- Syn-: see *-tene, -ic.] Epithet of the stage of meiosis now known as zygotene.

1900 *Jrnl. R. Microsc. Soc.* 654 The reticulum gives rise to a chromatic thread (deutobroch stage), which at first fills the nuclear cavity (leptotænic stage), and later forms a central dense mass (synaptænic stage). **1922** F. H. A. Marshall *Physiol. of Reproduction* (ed. 2) iv. 155 The nucleus enters upon the synaptenic condition, which extends over a somewhat longer time.

synaptic, *a.* (Examples in *Anat.* and *Cytology.*)

1895 J. E. S. Moore in *Q. Jrnl. Microsc. Sci.* XXXVIII. 287, I therefore propose the term Synaptic phase to denote the period at which this most important change appears in the morphological character of reproductive cells. **1974** D. & M. Webster *Compar. Vertebr. Morphol.* ix. 182 Each terminal bouton contains mitochondria and submicroscopic, membrane-bound spheres called synaptic vesicles. **1976** Smythies & Corbett *Psychiatry* iv. 42 When a nerve-impulse passes down an axon and reaches the terminal a chemical is released which crosses the synaptic cleft and causes depolarization of the next neurone. **1981** *Sci. Amer.* Oct. 122/2 The active form of the transmitter molecule is stored in the sacs called synaptic vesicles until the nerve cell is called on to release it.

synaptinemal, var. *synaptonemal *a.*

synapto- (sinæ·pto), ad. Gr. συναπτ-ικός, connective, used as comb. form of Synapse, in various terms in *Physiol.*, as **synaptoge·nesis**, the formation of synapses between nerve cells; **synapto·logy**, the study of the structure and operation of synapses; **syna·ptosome** [*-some[4]], a presynaptic nerve ending which, when isolated, seals up to form an intact sac; hence **synaptoso·mal** *a.*

1967 D. P. Purpura in A. Minkowski *Regional Devel. of Brain in Early Life* 131 We started this morning with looking at myelinogenesis, moved to cytoarchitectonics, and started talking about the probable growth of dendrites. You have now moved us into a fourth area of maturational considerations—that of synaptogenesis. **1979** *Experientia* XXXV. 207/1 Intracerebellar connections are gradually established as the synaptogenesis proceeds. **1962** *Anat. Rec.* CXLII. 332/2 (*heading*) An electron microscope study of the stratum radiatum of the rat hippocampus..with emphasis on synaptology. **1965** *Sci. Amer.* Jan. 56/3 Sir Charles Sherrington..laid the foundations of what is sometimes called synaptology. **1975** *Nature* 8 May 176/2 There have been great advances in knowledge of synaptology from electron microscopic studies of the retina. **1970** *Neurosciences Res.* III. 6 There is more than a sixfold increase in the ATPase activity of the rat brain nerve-ending fraction from prenatal to the 10-day-old animal, the enzyme apparently residing in the synaptosomal limiting membrane. **1978** *Nature* 17 Aug. 706/2 The crude synaptosomal pellet was resuspended in 0·32 M glucose..and equilibrated..in a rotary waterbath. **1964** V. P. Whittaker et al. in *Biochem. Jrnl.* XC. 293/1 The club-like presynaptic nerve endings resist disruption and are snapped or torn off from their attachments to form discrete particles (nerve-ending particles) in which all the main structural features of the nerve ending are preserved. For these particles we propose the name 'synaptosomes' in order to emphasize their relative homogeneity and their resemblance in physical properties to other subcellular organelles. **1973** *Nature* 9 Mar. 122/1 Isolation of intact synaptic nerve endings (synaptosomes) has made it possible to investigate transport across synaptic membranes.

synaptonemal (sinæptonī·măl), *a. Cytology.* Also **synapti-.** [f. Gr. συναπτι-κός connective or *synapto- + Gr. νῆμα thread.] *synaptonemal complex*: a set of several parallel threads seen adjacent to and coaxial with pairing chromosomes in meiosis.

1958 M. J. Moses in *Jrnl. Biophysical & Biochem. Cytol.* IV. 637/1 The term 'chromosomal core' was applied to the axial complex when it was first described... A more precise term would..indicate that the structure is associated specifically with chromosome pairing, and that it is thread-like. Unwieldy though it is, *synaptinemal complex* is more accurately descriptive. **1969** —— in *Genetics* LXI. Suppl. 50 It is proposed that 'synaptonemal complex', because it is similar to the original term and has been employed in the literature to refer to the structure in meiotic bivalents, henceforth be used in place of 'synaptinemal complex'. *Ibid.*, The synaptonemal complex (SC) is a regularly occurring, coplanar set of parallel strands (usually three), coaxial to meiotic bivalent chromosomes. Presence of this linear complex is prerequisite to, but not alone sufficient for chiasma formation (and hence, crossing-over). **1971** *Nature* 3 Sept. 48/1 Chromosome synapsis mediated by the synaptonemal complex seems to be non-specific, for it can also pull together non-homologous chromosomes. **1978** *Bio Systems* X. 111/1 A clear prediction of my phylogeny is that meiotic synaptinemal complex proteins should be homologous in all organisms.

sync, synch (siŋk). orig. *U.S.* Also **sink.** Colloq. abbrev. of Synchronism, Synchronization, Synchronize *v.*, etc. in Dict. and Suppl. Cf. *lip-sync(h)* s.v. *lip *sb.* 7. **a.** In technical senses, esp. in *Cinematogr.* and *Television.* Cf. *post-sync(h.

1929 *Photoplay* Apr. 31/2 *In sink*, in synchronism; picture and sound perfectly timed together. **1939** *Reader's Digest* Mar. 41/1 When your [television] set is out of synchronization the image sort of bobs and weaves; it is then 'out of sync'. **1943** *Gloss. Terms Telecomm.* (*B.S.I.*) 77 *Synchronising signal* (*Sync pulse*), a signal sent out periodically by the transmitter in order to keep the receiving system in synchronism. **1945** F. Hamann *Air Words* 52 *Synch, to*, to synchronize. **1954** *Proc. IRE* XLII. 106/2 With a strong (clean) sync signal, the color-carrier reference signal may be maintained as closely accurate as desired, independent of other factors. *Ibid.* 116/1 The composite system functions as a form of automatic frequency control system when out of sync and as an automatic phase control system when in sync. **1960** *How TV Works* 16/1 A 'line sync' is..the jargon for the timing signal which is given at the end of each separate line of a television picture. **1962** A. Nisbett *Technique Sound Studio* xii. 219 Mixing the output of two gramophone records or tapes playing almost in sync. **1963** Maley & Earle *Logic Design of Transistor Digital Computers* x. 275 If they [*sc.* pulsed-circuit flip-flops] are synced with a clock and thus with each other. **1965** *Wireless World* Aug. 389/1 The conditions for direct sync can now be examined. **1966** *Listener* 4 Aug. 160/1 The introduction of new lightweight sync-sound equipment. **1972** M. Muggeridge *Green Stick* ii. 69 The sync frequently went awry, with the words of the song and the movements of the singers lips not tallying. **1973** C. Bonington *Everest* xv. 238 Graham and I played with the little synch-sound super 8 mm. cine camera, trying to make a documentary of what life was like at Camp 4. **1977** *Rolling Stone* 5 May 31/1 It was Mercury who would blow a fuse if the lights were out of sync or the PA system malfunctioned. *Ibid.* 16 June 12/3 They wanted it synched to within one frame. **1978** *SLR Camera* Aug. 88/2 For electronic flash the camera is in sync at all speeds from 1/25th sec downwards and with expendable flash bulbs, at all speeds from 1/30th down. **1979** *Mod. Photogr.* Dec. 192/1 Connect an electronic flash to the camera with the proper sync terminal.

b. *gen.* Esp. in phrs. *in sync, out of sync.* Also *fig.*

1961 J. STEINBECK *Winter of our Discontent* II. xiv. 278 Something's going on... I just feel it... Everybody's a little out of synch. **1964** 'R. MACDONALD' *Far Side of Dollar* (1965) xxvi. 225 We could step up our schedule and synch our watches, eh? **1966** E. WEST *Night is Time for Listening* vi. 200 No cops, no State Department. Are we in sync? **1968** T. WOLFE *Electric Kool-Aid Acid Test* xi. 147 Somehow this ties in, *synchs*, directly with what Kesey has just said. **1974** *Times Lit. Suppl.* 8 Nov. 1247/4 Worldly success depends on being, as it were, in sync with the contemporary scene, and it was at this point that Fleming began to get out of sync, never to get properly in again. **1977** *Time* 17 Oct. 42/3 The next thing will be to bring the players' uniforms into sync with the floor design. **1978** J. IRVING *World according to Garp* xvii. 352 His watch..was several hours out of sync with the United States; he had last set it in Vienna. **1978** *English Jrnl.* Dec. 50/1 Or is the teaching 'out of synch' with the cognitive development..and the intentions of the learner? **1982** M. MILLAR *Mermaid* x. 110 She..sensed his uneasiness, his awareness that he was out of sync, out of tune.

syncategorematic, *a.* Add: (Later examples.) Also in extended uses in linguistic analysis.

1931 [see *AUTOSEMANTIC *a.* (*sb.*)]. **1957** G. RYLE in M. Black *Importance of Lang.* (1962) 159 This is what Mill had said of the syncategorematic words. **1966** J. J. KATZ *Philos. Lang.* v. 312 Since the meaning of 'good' cannot stand alone as a complete concept, we shall say that the meaning of 'good' is *syncategorematic.* **1972** *Language* XLVIII. 351 Syncategorematic features such as abrupt/non-abrupt and strident/mellow... By this term I mean features which necessarily occur only in conjunction with certain other features. Besides the abrupt/continuant vs. strident/mellow example, voiced/voiceless vs. tense/lax appear to be syncategorematic, as do compact/non-compact vs. diffuse/non-diffuse in vowels. **1975** *Ibid.* LI. 32 Russell's contextual or syncategorematic definition of definite descriptions is equivalent to the conjunction of three propositions, one of which embodies a uniqueness claim.

syncategorematical, *a.* Delete † *Obs.* and add later example.

1935 H. STRAUMANN *Newspaper Headlines* 72 The distinction resembles that of E. Husserl's (categorematical and syncategorematical words).

syncategorematically *adv.* (later example).

1975 *New Left Rev.* Nov.–Dec. 55 Philosophy has no object, in that it is its task to analyse concepts which can only be used syncategorematically, i.e. under some particular description, in science.

synch: see *SYNC, SYNCH.

synchisite. Add: Also **synchysite** and with pronunc. (-zəit). (Earlier and later examples.) [ad. G. *synchisit* (G. Flink 1901, in *Bull. Geol. Inst. Univ. Upsala* V. 82).]

1901 *Jrnl. Chem. Soc.* LXXX. II. 663 Synchysite.—This new name is applied to a mineral from Narsarsuk, in South Greenland. **1965** *Bull. Geol. Survey Dept. Malawi* No. 15. 124 Concentrations of bastnaesite and synchysite occur in the central core of sideritic carbonatite at Chilwa Island. **1975** [see *SYNTAXY].

synchro (si·ŋkro). [f. SYNCHRO(NOUS *a.*] = *SELSYN. Freq. *attrib.*

1943 *Appl. Electronics* (Mass. Inst. Technol. Dept. Electr. Engin.) vi. 316 When designed so that the rotor may turn or be turned freely, the device is given various trade names, such as *Selsyn, Synchro,* or *Autosyn.* **1958** W. G. HOLZBOCK *Automatic Control* vii. 122 There are different synchro components, such as the synchro transmitter, synchro receiver, synchro control transformer, etc., which are combined in control circuits in various ways. **1980** J. D. LENK *Handbk. Controls & Instrumentation* x. 289 A receiver synchro is limited to light loads such as moving a pointer across a scale to indicate the angular displacement of some device operating a transmitting synchro.

synchro- (si·ŋkro), comb. form repr. SYNCHRONOUS *a.* and related words, as in **sy·nchroflash** *Photogr.*, a flash whose operation is synchronized with the opening of the shutter; **sy:nchro-su·nlight** *Photogr.*, used *attrib.* to designate the use of flash to supplement sunlight; **sy·nchro-swim(ming)** = *synchronized swimming* s.v. *SYNCHRONIZED *ppl. a.*; also *ellipt.* as **synchro.**

1940 A. L. M. SOWERBY *Dict. Photogr.* 626 *Synchro-flash photography*, the taking of photographs with a flashbulb synchronised to the shutter of the camera. **1952** *Sci. News Let.* 24 Dec. 416/1 Synchroflash testing device enables both the professional and amateur photographer to check his equipment. **1974** *Encycl. Brit. Macropædia* XIV. 324/1 In the early days of *Life* and *Look*, photographers made great use of so-called synchroflash. **1940** F. J. MORTIMER *Wall's Dict. Photogr.* (ed. 15) 316 Synchro-sunlight technique is chiefly of use in connection with figure subjects, where it gives a well-lit figure against a much less well-lit background. **1981** G. L. WAKEFIELD *Beginner's Guide Photogr.* vii. 137 Synchro-sunlight photography has to be done carefully because if the amount of extra fill-in is excessive the flash takes over from the sunshine and the effect is completely false. **1968** G. RACKHAM *Synchronized Swimming* i. 27 Being so diverse in character Synchro provides a wide field of related activities. **1974** *Observer* (Colour Suppl.) 17 Mar. 75/1 A member of the Great Britain Synchronised Swimming Team..has been doing synchro for 11 years. **1976** *Star* (Sheffield) 3 Dec. 28/7 Eight Nalgo SC swimmers passed their respective synchro-swim grade examinations at Heeley Baths last night. **1976** *Milton Keynes Express* 11 June 11/1 It is hoped to bring both synchro-swimming and water polo to the city in the near future.

synchrocyclotron (si:ŋkro,səi·klǒtrǫn). *Physics.* [f. *SYNCHRO- + *CYCLOTRON.] A particle accelerator similar to a cyclotron in which the frequency of the accelerating electric field is decreased as the particles gain energy so as to allow for the concomitant increase in mass and enable greater energies to be achieved.

1947 *Times* 7 July 3/3 One machine being considered for Brookhaven National Laboratory on Long Island, New York, is a huge synchro-cyclotron. **1956** *Nature* 3 Mar. 397/2 These exchanges of views led to the decision to fix the energy of the proposed synchro-cyclotron for the international laboratory at 600 MeV. and that of the proton-sychrotron at greater than 25 GeV. **1971** *New Scientist* 2 Sept. 510/1 The University of Chicago synchrocyclotron..has been shut down. **1973** L. J. TASSIE *Physics Elem. Particles* 221 In circular accelerators, such as synchrocyclotrons and synchrotrons, the particles are confined to circular or spiralling paths by magnetic guide fields so that they pass one or several radiofrequency sources a large number of times.

synchromesh (si·ŋkromeʃ). *Mech.* Also **syncro-**. [f. *synchronized mesh.*] **a.** A mechanism that facilitates gear-changing in a motor vehicle by automatically causing gear-wheels to rotate in synchronism before they engage. Freq. *attrib.*

1929 *Amer. Motorist* Oct. 35/2 (Advt.), Syncro-mesh silent shift transmission. **1931** *Automotive Industries* 24 Oct. 644/1 Constant-mesh gears made synchro-mesh transmissions and free wheeling feasible. **1932** *Oxford Times* 23 Sept. 22/3 Free-wheeling and syncro-mesh gears have for some time been almost universal on cars built in the United States. **1933** *Motor* 10 Oct. 525/3 The Citroën Co. was also early in the field with synchromesh. **1950** *Engineering* 22 Sept. 255/3 Synchromesh engagement is provided for second, third and top gears. **1962** *Which? Car Suppl.* Oct. 129/2 These two cars had no synchromesh on first gear. **1976** P. R. WHITE *Planning for Public Transport* iii. 59 A synchromesh or semi-automatic transmission is quite adequate, as steady running replaces the frequent stopping and starting of urban operation.

b. *fig.*

1966 *Listener* 11 Aug. 204/2 They are vision, sound, decor, lighting, and a sense of style. When all these are in synchromesh, as in a well designed gearbox, the show may be a success. **1977** *Guardian* 5 May 14/2 Somewhere, somewhere, waits the perfect partner, the soul-mate, the sexual syncromesh. **1982** *Church Times* 23 Apr. 7/3 *The Flowers and Fruits of the Bible*..is a lovely book, if slightly out of syncromesh.

Synchromism (si·ŋkrǒmiz'm). [f. SYN- + Gr. χρῶμα colour + -ISM]. A movement in art resembling Orphism, founded by the U.S. painters Stanton Macdonald-Wright (b. 1890) and Morgan Russell (1886–1953), with emphasis on the abstract use of colour. Also, *loosely* = *ORPHISM 2. Cf. *SYNCHRONISM 4.

1912 M. RUSSELL in G. Levin *Synchromism & Amer. Color Abstraction 1910–1925* (1978) ii. 20 This is cubisme, Futurisme, Synchromisme and any isms possible for many years, perhaps centuries. **1913** *Forum* Dec. 768 This brings us to the latest phase of this chaotic and polyglot age of painting—Synchromism, sired by two Americans, S. Macdonald-Wright and Morgan Russell, which seems destined to have the most far-reaching effects of any art force since Cézanne. **1923** J. GORDON *Mod. French Painters* xiv. 149 Synchromism, Simultaneism..and so on, are merely various more or less pretentious methods adopted by artists..to say that they are going to do just as they like. **1937** T. H. BENTON *Artist in America* ii. 38 My old friend Wright came back to America before the gathering of the war clouds in Europe. He came back, the founder of a new school, synchromism, which he had flung in the face of Paris. **1958** M. L. WOLF *Dict. Painting* 288 Synchromism usually displayed its purposes in pictures of huge size, the colors forming prismatic patterns. **1978** G. LEVIN *Synchromism & Amer. Color Abstraction 1910–1925* ii. 20 The fact that the Delaunays had used closely related terminology, possibly at a slightly earlier date, does not, of course, make Synchromism a direct outgrowth of their art.

Hence **Sy·nchromist** *sb.* and *a.*, **Synchromi·stic** *a.*

1913 *Forum* Dec. 769 The Synchromists claim to have discovered the secrets of color. **1916** *Ibid.* Apr. 461 His later paintings have undergone somewhat the Synchromistic vision. **1923** [see *SIMULTANEIST]. **1936** *Cubism & Abstract Art* (N.Y. Mus. Mod. Art) 74 The first large Synchromist exhibition was held in Munich in June 1913. **1958** M. L. WOLF *Dict. Painting* 202 Known also as the Synchromist School, it [*sc.* Orphism] was essentially an abstract style. **1970** *Oxf. Compan. Art* 1118/2 Arthur Burdett Frost..helped to spread the ideas of the Synchromists in America. **1974** *Encycl. Brit. Micropædia* VI. 439/3 Although he [*sc.* Macdonald-Wright] denied any connection, his Synchromist theories were also influenced by the contemporary Parisian movement of Orphism.

Synchromy (si·ŋkrǒmi). Also **synchromy.** [f. as prec. + -Y[3], after *symphony.*] An abstract painting of a type characteristic of Synchromism.

1916 *Forum* Feb. 213 Why not hang a Pre-Raphaelite-Moreau work of Claude Buck beside an ultra-modern Synchromy. **1936** *Cubism & Abstract Art* (N.Y. Mus. Mod. Art) 74 The first purely abstract 'Synchromy' was not shown until the exhibition in Paris in the autumn of that year [*sc.* 1913]. **1974** *Encycl. Brit. Micropædia* IX. 737/3 The two artists were living in Paris, painting abstract works they called 'synchromies'.

synchroneity (siŋkrǒnī·iti, -ē·iti). Chiefly *Geol.* [f. SYNCHRON(OUS *a.* + *-eity*, after *simultaneity, spontaneity,* etc.] = SYNCHRONISM 1 a.

1909 *Cent. Dict.* Suppl., *Synchroneity*, synchronism; the character or fact of being synchronous; specifically, in *geol.*, supposed synchronism in time of deposition of strata. **1945** *Bull. Amer. Assoc. Petroleum Geologists* XXIX. 427 Facts bearing on synchroneity. **1968** R. G. WEST *Pleistocene Geol. & Biol.* xii. 286 There remain very many problems of chronology, in particular the synchroneity of pollen zones. **1979** *Nature* 11 Oct. 431/1 Their data indicate an approximate synchroneity of dinosaur and foram extinctions just below anomaly 29, the maximum error being about 100,000 years.

synchronic, *a.* Restrict *rare* to senses in Dict. and add: **3.** *Linguistics.* [tr. F. *synchronique* (F. de Saussure *a* 1913, in *Cours de linguistique générale* (1916) iii. 117).] Pertaining to or designating a method of linguistic study concerned with the state of a language at one time, past or present; descriptive, as opposed to historical or diachronic. Also *transf.* in Anthropology, etc.

1922 L. BLOOMFIELD in *Classical Weekly* 13 Mar. 142/1 One is glad to see, therefore, that Dr. Sapir deals with synchronic matters (to use De Saussure's terminology) before he deals with diachronic. **1927**, etc. [see *DIACHRONIC *a.* 2]. **1937** [see *SAUSSUREAN *a.*]. **1946** [see *ONOMATOPY]. **1954** [see *PROCESS *sb.* 5 b]. **1968** *Jrnl. Assoc. Teachers of Russian* XVII. 8 A synchronic study of a language studies the language of a particular period without reference to what went before or came after, and in practice the period in question is generally our own. **1975** *Listener* 20 Mar. 367/3 Though the 'synchronic' approach of the semiologists is for the moment more fashionable, it is impossible not to be interested in the history of social myths.

synchronical, *a.* Add: **3.** *Linguistics.* = *SYNCHRONIC *a.* 3.

1949 *Oxf. Classical Dict.* 971 If we accept J. B. Hofmann's distinction of the 'diachronical' and the '(idio)-synchronical' types of grammar..then Kühner-Blass belongs to the synchronical. **1956** *Archivum Linguisticum* VIII. 174 Particularly out of place in a synchronical book are some assumptions concerning Old Polish.

synchronically *adv.* (later examples relating to sense *3 of the adj.).

1935 *Year's Work in Eng. Stud. 1933* XIV. 48 The seven explanatory aspects include semasiology and morphology treated synchronically or diachronically, and also diachronic phonology. **1947** *Essays & Studies* XXXII. 79 There is, however, one grammar..that feels the need of changing the method, of recording the facts first synchronically, then, in the second part, diachronically. **1968** J. LYONS *Introd. Theoretical Linguistics* i. 46 It does not matter by what route (the number, nature or order of the moves) the players have arrived at the particular state of the game: this state is describable *synchronically* without reference to the previous moves. **1979** *Dictionaries* I. 6 One may wonder whether words like *fro* or synchronically unproductive suffixes like *-ure*..are really indispensable elements of the defining vocabulary.

synchronicity (si:ŋkrǒni·siti). [f. SYNCHRONIC *a.* + -ITY.] The name given by the Swiss psychologist, C. G. Jung (1875–1961), to the phenomenon of events which coincide in time and appear meaningfully related but have no discoverable causal connection.

1953 *Jrnl. Soc. for Psychical Res.* XXXVII. 28 Synchronicity, he [*sc.* Jung] explains, is not just synchronousness. In a 'synchronicity phenomenon', as he uses the phrase, two contemporaneous events are linked together in a meaningful manner. **1955** R. F. C. HULL tr. *Jung & Pauli's Interpretation of Nature & Psyche* i. 27, I have picked on the term 'synchronicity' to designate a hypothetical factor equal in rank to causality as a principle of explanation. **1963** *Punch* 25 Dec. 910/2 Hauntings..magical coincidence ('synchronicity') the lot. **1974** *Sci. Amer.* Jan. 113/2 The Wilhelm-Baynes volume includes the famous foreword by Jung in which he explains the oracular power of the *I Ching* by his theory of 'synchronicity'. **1980** C. FITZGIBBON *Rat Report* vi. 112 A thought-transference has also no mass, but very considerable energy and therefore 'travels'..through the time element called synchronicity.

synchronism. Add: **3. b.** *spec.* in *Cinematogr.* and *Television.* Cf. *SYNCHRONIZE *v.* 2 c.

1904 *Billboard* 27 Aug. 13/4 The motor of the cinematograph is absolutely dependent on the movement of the phonograph axle, and perfect synchronism must be had..in order to render the illusion as perfectly lifelike as possible. **1928** Television Mar. 37 Thus ensuring synchronism between the transmitter and the receiver. **1957** Manvell & Huntley Film Music iii. 75 Nothing..can be more vulgar than music synchronism in films. **1967** Electronics 6 Mar. 78/2 (Advt.), The display cathode ray tube on which this output is viewed is scanned in synchronism.

4. = *Synchromism. Cf. *Simultaneism 1.

[**1914** M. Russell Let. 12 Mar. in G. Levin Synchromism & Amer. Color Abstraction 1910–1925 (1978) ii. 20 Please don't say Synchronisme which does not apply to painting, the termination is 'chrome', 'color'.] **1961** M. Levy Studio Dict. Art Terms 109 Synchronism, an alternative expression for Orphism. **1972** C. W. E. Bigsby Dada & Surrealism ii. 10 In some ways it was a part of that artistic re-examination which spawned such schools as impressionism, cubism, futurism and, more exotically, suprematism, rayonism, plasticism, vorticism and synchronism.

5. Linguistics. = *synchrony 2.

1962 [see *diachronism 2].

synchronistic, a. Add: **2.** Linguistics. = *synchronic a. 3.

1937 J. Orr tr. Iordan's Introd. Romance Linguistics 284 Internal linguistics is static or synchronistic. **1949** Archivum Linguisticum I. 127 On the synchronistic plane, homonymy seems..to preclude the existence of any intrinsic link between form and meaning. **1951** [see *diachronistic a.]. **1962** L. J. Cohen Diversity of Meaning i. 12 Synchronistic and diachronistic enquiries—studies of a single period and studies through several periods, respectively—can and should complement each other.

3. Pertaining to or having the quality of synchronicity.

1955 R. F. C. Hull tr. Jung & Pauli's Interpretation of Nature & Psyche i. 40 Synchronistic events rest on the simultaneous occurrence of two different psychic states. **1972** Koestler Roots of Coincidence iii. 95 Thus precognitive experiences are 'evidently synchronistic..since they are experienced as psychic images in the present as though the objective event already existed'. **1979** G. Adler Dynamics of Self 10 Synchronistic phenomena, and in particular those of ESP, convinced Jung of the existence of a transcendental 'absolute knowledge'.

synchronistically adv.: also, in accordance with synchrony (sense *2) or synchronicity.

1949 Archivum Linguisticum I. 128 Is there any intrinsic and synchronistically valid reason for it [sc. a name] to have that form and no other? **1980** C. Fitzgibbon Rat Report vi. 112 My communication reaches you synchronistically at the same time as all the other rat reports which have been sent out every five hundred years.

synchronization. Add: spec. in Electr. Engin. and in other technical uses. Cf. *synchronize v. 2 c.

1913 N.Y. Times 18 Feb. 3/1 Mr. Edison was looking for perfect synchronization of record and film. **1922** Radio News (U.S.) Nov. 867/1 Mr. de Forest has solved the secret of the 'talkie movie' with perfect synchronization. **1928** Manch. Guardian Weekly 17 Aug. 134/4 The sound is transformed into light and recorded on the margin of the film in automatic synchronisation with the movement of the lips. **1932** Discovery July 215/1 Lodge had shown the importance of tuning or 'synchronization'. **1940** Amateur Radio Handbk. (ed. 2) xix. 274/1 When the vision signals are..subject to serious interference which tends to upset synchronisation. **1958** Newnes Compl. Amat. Photogr. 37 Shutter synchronisation. Ibid., The flash synchronisation may have only an X setting. **1962** S. A. Choudhury in G. A. T. Burdett Automatic Control Handbk. iv. 36 If, before the supply is switched on, the rotors are 180 degrees displaced, no synchronisation will take place when the excitation is applied.

synchronize, v. Add: **2. c.** In technical senses: to cause to coincide in time; to operate simultaneously or in synchronization. Also intr.

1910 Chambers's Jrnl. Mar. 206/1 The movements of the mouths of the characters on the scene synchronise with the utterance of the phonograph. **1922** Radio News (U.S.) Nov. 867/1 (heading), De Forest demonstrates his invention for synchronizing speech with movies... You.. heard the tone which, to a musically trained ear, synchronized perfectly with every movement of the violin bow. **1934** C. Lambert Music Ho! iii. 196 René Clair would not dare to synchronize one of his scenes with the sound of a real bal-musette band. **1940** F. J. Mortimer Wall's Dict. Photogr. (ed. 15) 315 Focal-plane shutters can be well synchronised with the flash on small cameras. **1956** Focal Encycl. Photogr. 492/1 The duration of electronic flash discharge is always shorter than the fastest shutter speed with which it can be synchronized. **1957** Encycl. Brit. XXI. 912 D/1 It [sc. a video signal]..must have added to it the timing pulses needed to synchronize the receiver. **1962** S. A. Choudhury in G. A. T. Burdett Automatic Control Handbk. iv. 39 A recent development which enables the receiver to accelerate from rest and automatically synchronise by simply putting the excitation on the selsyns through a three-pole switch. **1977** J. Hedgecoe Photographer's Handbk. 34/2 Cheaper cameras which only take bulbs or cubes are synchronized at low speeds, usually around 1/25 sec.

3. gen. To combine or co-ordinate.

1973 N.Y. Law Jrnl. 3 Apr. 4/5 The law is probably the only profession that must be synchronized with another profession—writing. **1976** Time 27 Dec., facing p. 36 (Advt.), Both media synchronize national interests with multinational scope. **1977** N.Y. Rev. Bks. 14 July 33/2 Silberman quotes an unreported speech given by the foreign minister, Milos Minic, which alleges not only that Western intelligence is involved with fascist exiles but also that Western press coverage of Yugoslavia is synchronized to discredit the country.

synchronized, ppl. a. Add: (Examples.) synchronized swimming, a form of swimming which involves a display of ballet-like routines performed to music (often as a competitive sport); hence synchronized swimmer.

1927 N.Y. Times 28 Aug. vii. 4/1 During the other portions of the reel there will be a synchronized orchestral score. **1932** New Yorker 9 Apr. 51/1 The new Ford has synchronized gear-shifting and a silent second-speed. **1942** R.A.F. Jrnl. 16 May 15 The normal armament is two 7·7 mm. synchronised guns. **1950** B. Spears (title) Beginning synchronized swimming. **1960** C. H. Gibbs-Smith Aeroplane xii. 89 Fokker's monoplane..with its fixed synchronised gun. **1968** Courier-Mail (Brisbane) 1 Feb. 11/8 Both women returned to Brisbane last week from the New South Wales synchronised swimming championships... Synchronised swimming is the initiate's term for water ballet. **1975** Oxf. Compan. Sports & Games 1014/1 As well as having the endurance of a trained racing swimmer, the synchronized swimmer must have the skill and artistry of a ballet dancer, and the grace, rhythm, and acrobatic ability of the gymnast. **1979** A. Fraser King Charles II (1980) iii. xii. 193 There were no fewer than seven clocks in his bedroom (their ill-synchronized chiming drove his attendants mad). **1981** J. Barnett Firing Squad xvi. 221 A synchronized rattle of rifle bolts. **1984** New Yorker 19 Mar. 114/2 It is normally very difficult to get a new sport accepted for the Olympics. Synchronized swimming will be on the docket this summer.

synchronizer. Add: Also in other technical senses, esp. in Cinematogr. and Photogr. Cf. *synchronize v. 2 c.

1924 S. R. Roget Dict. Electr. Terms 253/2 Synchroniser. Apparatus for indicating whether two alternating current machines or circuits are in synchronism. **1931** B. Brown Talking Pictures i. 5 The synchronizer itself consisted of a box having a transparent disc, bearing an indicating spot, and coupled by gearing to the mechanism of the cinema projector. **1940** F. J. Mortimer Wall's Dict. Photogr. (ed. 15) 314 A sharp distinction should be drawn between the flashgun and the simpler so-called 'synchronisers' which open the shutter, set at 'Bulb' or a slow snapshot speed, before the flash begins, and allow it to remain open till the flash is over. **1949** Proc. Inst. Mech. Engin., Automobile Div., 1947–8 III. 98/2 Constant load synchronizers are generally used, except for Vauxhall ..who use the baulked synchronizer. **1957** Manvell & Huntley Film Music i. 17 Throughout the silent period various gramophone synchronizers were developed for use with films. **1970** K. Ball Fiat 600, 600D Autobook vi. 53/1 This shaft carries the fourth-speed driven gear and synchronizer ring. **1972** Times Educ. Suppl. 21 July 27 The sound..is first recorded in the usual way. The tape is then passed through the recording head of the synchronizer... Subsequently, when the tape is played back, the control pulses are passed..to the projector.., and each automatically initiates a change of slide at the predetermined point.

synchronizing, vbl. sb. and ppl. a. (Later examples in technical senses.)

1926 Encycl. Brit. III. 136/1 In the latter case the synchronising signals must be transmitted over a channel separate from the picture channel [in phototelegraphy]. **1928** C. F. S. Gamble Story N. Sea Air Station iv. 68 The 'synchronizing gear', enabling a machine-gun to fire through the tractor air-screw. **1931** B. Brown Talking Pictures i. 3 The earliest practical attempts at synchronizing, i.e. keeping speech and gesture perfectly in phase. **1943** Gloss. Terms Telecomm. (B.S.I.) 35 Synchronising, the adjustment of the frequency of the time base to bear an integral relationship to the frequency of the phenomenon under investigation. **1961** G. Millerson Technique Television Production ii. 20 (caption) The component parts of the video signal..synchronizing level.

synchronous, a. Add: **2. a.** (Further examples.) Cf. sense 2 d below.

1972 Sci. Amer. Apr. 45/1 In all cases where this effect is significant these same tides will have 'despun' the satellite to synchronous rotation, that is, the satellite's period of rotation around its own axis equals its period of revolution around the planet and it always presents one face to the planet.

b. (Earlier and later examples.)

1897 A. Hay Princ. Alternate-Current Working vi. 88 By a synchronous motor is meant one whose speed bears a definite ratio to the periodicity of the alternating current. **1920** Whittaker's Electr. Engineer's Pocket-bk. (ed. 4) 219 If..the converter is in parallel with other synchronous machinery. **1930** Engineering 25 Apr. 534/3 (heading) Hydrogen-cooled synchronous condenser. **1962** J. Bell in G. A. T. Burdett Automatic Control Handbk. iv. 7 Torque synchros or synchronous links (Magslips).

c. Computers and Telecommunications. Of apparatus or methods of working: making use of equally spaced pulses that govern the timing of operations.

[**1947** A. W. Burks et al. in J. Von Neumann Coll. Wks. (1963) V. 68 Since the timing of the entire computer is governed by a single pulse source, the computer circuits will be said to operate as a synchronized system.] **1954** Trans. IRE Prof. Group Electronic Computers June 14/2 Because the system being designed was centrally synchronous, over-all timing considerations now came to the fore. **1962** Y. Chu Digital Computer Design Fundamentals v. 161 The binary state of the signals in logic circuits can be represented by either of two voltage levels or by pulses... A synchronous computer also requires clock pulses. **1971** I. H. Gould IFIP Guide Concepts & Terms Data Processing 76 Synchronous working and asynchronous working often coexist in different parts of a computer system. For example, in many computers the central processor is synchronous, but the operation of peripheral equipment is only initiated by signals from the central processor and thereafter proceeds asynchronously. **1982** Heap & Martin Introd. Digital Electronics iii. 73 In the worst case the problem of interfacing two independent synchronous systems which are operating at different clock rates may occur.

d. Of a satellite: rotating round the parent planet at the same rate as the planet rotates. Of an orbit: such that a satellite in it is synchronous.

1961 N.Y. Times 30 July iv. 9/8 Synchronous satellites will require bigger boosters to reach their higher altitudes. **1964** Daily Tel. 4 Mar. 14/6 Three satellites in this synchronous orbit would give a complete global system of communications except for small regions round the North and South Pole. **1967** Technology Week 20 Feb. 4/2 There is substantial agreement that a synchronous satellite is desirable for air traffic control. **1970** Nature 9 May 503/1 Only one orbit exists which is at the same time equatorial, circular and synchronous. **1978** Daily Tel. 11 July 2/5 'Charon', which brings to 33 the number of known moons in the solar system, appears to have a synchronous orbit around Pluto of 12,000 miles, which means that it always stays over a fixed spot over Pluto.

3. Linguistics. = *synchronic a. 3.

1936 [see *diachronous a. 2].

synchronously, adv. Add: **3.** Linguistics. According to the methods or conclusions of synchronic linguistics.

1923 L. Bloomfield in Mod. Lang. Jrnl. VIII. 318 At any given time ('synchronously'), the language of a community is to be viewed as a system of signals.

synchrony. Add: **2.** Linguistics. A synchronic method of linguistic study; synchronic treatment.

1931 L. H. Gray in Amer. Jrnl. Philol. LII. 77 Synchrony must determine the nature of these categories. **1955** Word XI. 630 The Saussurean antinomy between synchrony and diachrony. **1959, 1963** [see *diachronic a. 2]. **1972** Language XLVIII. 438 It has recently been claimed that Georg von der Gabelentz anticipated a number of Saussurean concepts, in particular his dichotomies of langue-parole and synchrony-diachrony.

synchroscope (si·ŋkrǫskōᵘp). [f. *synchro- + -scope.] **1.** Electr. Engin. An instrument for indicating any difference in frequency or phase between two alternating voltages.

1908 V. Karapetoff Exper. Electr. Engin. xxi. 494 It only remains..to bring the machine into phase with the voltage at the bus-bars. This is done either by means of properly connected incandescent lamps..or special instruments, so-called synchroscopes. **1952** H. F. Banks Electricity I. xvii. 268/2 A..usually adopted method of paralleling two alternators is by means of the rotary synchroscope. **1981** T. Wildi Electr. Power Technol. xix. 364/2 Observe the phase angle between E_0 and E by means of a synchroscope.

2. Electronics. (See quot. 1945.)

1945 Electronic Industries Sept. 226 Synchroscope, an oscilloscope on which recurrent pulses or wave-forms may be observed, which incorporates a sweep-generator that produces one sweep for each pulse, regardless of frequency, thus allowing no more than one cycle to be viewed on the screen. **1947** R. Lee Electronic Transformers & Circuits ix. 257 This curve is observed by connecting the vertical plates of a synchroscope..across the transformer output winding. **1953** Electronic Engin. XXV. 229/1 Another specialised oscilloscope (synchroscope) is provided to display all details of the television waveform.

synchrotron (si·ŋkrotrǫn). Physics. [f. *synchro- + *-tron.] An accelerator in which electrons or protons gain energy from an alternating electric field as they travel round a closed orbit in a magnetic field, the strength of this field (and in the case of protons, the frequency of the electric field) being increased to keep the radius of the path constant as the particles gain mass relativistically. Also transf.

1945 E. M. McMillan in Physical Rev. LXVIII. 143/2 (heading) The synchrotron—a proposed high energy particle accelerator. **1947**, etc. [see proton synchrotron s.v. *proton 3]. **1950** Engineering 24 Mar. 332/2 A new electron synchrotron..at work on problems of photo-disintegration and pair production. **1971** Sci. Amer. July 79/1 The Crab Nebula is a cosmic synchrotron, permeated by electrons with energies of 1,000 billion electron volts or even higher. **1977** J. D. Lawson Physics of Charged-Particle Beams ii. 79 Large synchrotrons consist of a sequence of magnets arranged in a ring separated by 'straight sections', which may not all be of the same length.

2. attrib. and Comb., as synchrotron emission, mechanism, process; **synchrotron radiation,** polarized radiation emitted by a charged particle as it spirals at high speed in a magnetic field, as in a synchrotron; the emission of this.

1962 C. Susskind Encycl. Electronics 275/2 The visible continuum of the Crab nebula has been accepted as synchrotron emission. **1978** Pasachoff & Kutner University Astron. xxiv. 594 Continuum radio radiation can be generated by any of several processes. One of the most important is synchrotron emission, the process that produces the radiation from Taurus A. **1956** Astrophysical Jrnl. CXXIII. 550 The synchrotron mechanism..beautifully explains the radiation and polarization of the continuum of the Crab Nebula. **1962** C. Susskind Encycl. Electronics 275/2 As few as 10^{-4} relativistic electrons per cubic centimeter, emitting by the synchrotron process in a field of 10^{-6} gauss, can explain the observations. **1975** *Sci. Amer.* Dec. 38/1 When the electrons spiral along the lines of force of the star's magnetic field, they radiate by means of the synchrotron process, emitting radio waves, visible light and X rays. **1956** *Astrophysical Jrnl.* CXXIV. 416 (*heading*) On synchrotron radiation from Messier 87. **1981** J. B. ADAMS in J. H. Mulvey *Nature of Matter* vii. 165 The large size of LEP [*sc.* a synchrotron] is due not to its particle energy but to the need to reduce synchrotron radiation losses and to economize on electrical power consumption.

syncline. Add: (See also quot. 1972.) Cf. *synform* s.v. *SYN-[1] 1.
1937 *Trans. R. Soc. Edin.* LIX. 81 In common tectonic practice, an anticline has come to be understood as a fold with a core of previously underlying rocks, and a syncline as a fold with a core of previously overlying rocks. **1972** *Gloss. Geol.* (Amer. Geol. Inst.) 718/2 *Syncline*, a fold, the core of which contains the stratigraphically younger rocks; it is concave upward.

syncopate, *v.* Add: **3.** Also *transf.*
1928 *Sunday Express* 27 May 15 Her eager feet, that used to patter back and forth in happy household duties, now syncopate to the beat of drums and the clashing of cymbals. **1966** *Listener* 28 July 142/3 At the back of Albéniz's mind there is generally..a dancer whose castanets are always syncopating against each other. **1983** P. INCHBALD *Short Break in Venice* xx. 190 They passed a lighthouse syncopating white above with green below.

syncopated, *ppl. a.* Add: **2. b.** Applied to modern popular music played or composed in the manner typical of ragtime and jazz.
1908 *Catal. Copyright Entries* (U.S. Libr. Congress) 1069/2 Floreine waltz; syncopated, by Ernest J. Schuster. **1929** W. THURMAN *Blacker the Berry* 120 They muddled their words and seemed to impregnate the syncopated melody with physical content. **1969** E. ROTH *Business of Music* x. 247 Apart fron syncopated rhythms, jazz proved unfruitful ground for serious music.

c. Designating an orchestra, composer, etc., associated with popular syncopated music.
1927 [see *cross-rhythm* s.v. *CROSS- B]. **1928** *Grove's Dict. Mus.* (ed. 3) V. 243/1 Dance bands are frequently spoken of as 'Syncopated Orchestras', less because their music employs syncopation than because their constitution with saxophones, percussive instruments, etc., is designed to emphasize the effects essential to dance music of the American type. **1934** C. LAMBERT *Music Ho!* III. 222 The composer of highbrow jazz must obviously extend his harmonic vocabulary beyond the somewhat narrow range of the syncopated kings.

d. *fig.*
1924 WODEHOUSE *Bill the Conqueror* iii. 62 The breeze was stronger now, and it ruffled the surface of the water, so that the goldfish had for the moment a sort of syncopated appearance. **1950** 'D. DIVINE' *King of Fassarai* xvi. 128 A regular syncopated pattern of shifting light. **1964** E. J. HOBSBAWM *Labouring Men* 133 The oddly syncopated rhythm of the European trade-union 'leaps' between 1889 and 1914. **1974** M. CECIL *Heroines in Love* vi. 155 Eventually Jizabel awoke from her syncopated dreamland. **1979** *Jrnl. R. Soc. Arts* Nov. 751/2 This last element [*sc.* a colonnade] modulates back and forth in a rather jerky and syncopated manner.

syncopation. Add: **3. b.** Music characterized by a syncopated rhythm, *spec.* dance music influenced by ragtime.
1921 *Chambers's Jrnl.* Jan. 23/1 The pulsating sound [of the drum] heightens excitement to the verge of frenzy, and indicates the direct origin of the orgiastic African syncopation to which the wives and daughters of the conquering Anglo-Saxon race dance with their men-partners, retained by arrangement, in the aristocratic dance-clubs of London and New York. **1928** *Grove's Dict. Mus.* (ed. 3) V. 243/1 Syncopation has become a general term for all that class of 20th-century dance music which has sprung from the American adoption of rag-time. **1962** CHARTERS & KUNSTADT *Jazz* vi. 73 Even the Clef Club Orchestra was advertised as a jazz band, with '50 Joy Whooping Sultans of High-Speed Syncopation'. **1968** P. TAMONY *Americanisms* (typescript) No. 23. 4 *Syncopation* described 'Alexander's Ragtime Band' and other printed music in the first decade or so of this century, *ragtime* becoming old shoe and pejorative.

c. *fig.*
1979 *Jrnl. R. Soc. Arts* Nov. 777/1 The stained glass and colour syncopations in blues and greens.

syncopator (si·ŋkŏpēⁱtə̆ɹ). Also **syncopater.** [f. SYNCOPATE *v.* + -OR.] One who performs syncopated jazz music, usu. in a dance band. Freq. *pl.*, in the name of a band.
1926 *Daily Colonist* (Victoria, B.C.) 13 Jan. 6/3 With Professor Hunt's syncopators providing the dance music programme. **1927** *Daily Tel.* 22 Feb. 12/1 You may see (and hear) the first 'Lady Syncopators',..cutting rhythm into jazz patterns with the best of mere male 'syncopators'. **1930** *Dancing Times* Oct. 117/2 The White Star Syncopators, the Cunard Dance Band. **1952** B. ULANOV *Hist. Jazz in Amer.* (1958) ix. 94 The swinging Vendome syncopaters took over the stage. **1970** P. OLIVER (*title*) Savannah syncopators.

syncope, *sb.* **2.** Delete *rare* and add later examples. Also *attrib.* and in *Comb.*
1953 K. JACKSON *Lang. & Hist. in Early Britain* II. 614 A Pr[imitive] W[elsh] syncope-form **Car'dig.* **1972** *Language* XLVIII. 350 The same syncope rule which is optional in Russian /stl/ and /stk/ clusters is obligatory in /stn/ and /zdn/ clusters. *Ibid.*, Maximal distinctiveness, hence retention of the consonant, is manifested in the explicit subcode of contemporary standard Russian; whereas partial absence of distinctiveness, hence syncope of the consonant, is manifested in the elliptic subcode.

syncretic, *a.* Add: **2.** *Psychol.* Relating to or characterized by the fusion of concepts or sensations. Cf. *SYNCRETISM 3.
1932 M. GABAIN tr. *Piaget's Moral Judgment of Child* ii. 192 Since every word obtains its meaning as a function of these syncretic schemas, words end by acquiring a substance of their own independently of reality. **1952** WERNER & KAPLAN *Acquisition of Word Meanings* ii. 48 The conclusion can be drawn..that syncretic concepts are more characteristic of the younger children. **1962** I. SARNOFF *Personality Dynamics & Devel.* vi. 126 One variety of syncretic perception..involves a synthesis of sensations that pertain to several different sense modalities. **1969** T. FREEMAN *Psychopathol. of Psychoses* viii. 126 This thinking defect consists in the re-emergence of condensing or syncretic trends, fusing concepts that in normal circumstances are discrete and autonomous.

syncretically (sinkre·tikăli), *adv.* [f. SYNCRETICAL *a.* + -LY[2].] In a syncretic manner.
1900 W. JAMES *Let.* 10 June in R. B. Perry *Tht. & Char. W. James* (1935) I. 647 Assuming no duality of material and mental substance, but starting with bits of 'pure experience', syncretically taken. **1957** *Times Lit. Suppl.* 27 Dec. 781/3 But he manages to square his religious views..with a staunch advocacy of anthropology and sociology as ancillary techniques in historical method. To say that this position is syncretically achieved would be something of an understatement.

syncretism. Add: **2.** *Philol.* The merging of two or more inflectional categories.
1909 in WEBSTER. **1933** L. BLOOMFIELD *Language* xxi. 388 Homonymy and *syncretism*, the merging of inflectional categories, are normal results of sound-change. **1949** C. E. BAZELL in E. P. Hamp et al. *Readings in Linguistics II* (1966) 225 It may not always be possible to draw a fast line between syncretism proper and the neutralisation of a morphemic opposition. **1957, 1963** [see *DEFECTIVATION]. **1968** W. J. SAMARIN in J. A. Fishman *Readings Sociol. of Lang.* 664 Planned languages reveal many of the features of pidgin languages, namely, lexical syncretism and reduction of redundancy. **1979** [see *SYNTAGMA 4].

3. *Psychol.* The process of fusing diverse ideas or sensations into a general (inexact) impression; an instance of this.
1926 M. WARDEN tr. *Piaget's Lang. & Thought of Child* iv. 130 We can discern in this activity of understanding and invention on the part of the child several of those schemas of analogy, of those leaps to conclusions which are the outstanding characteristics of verbal syncretism. **1963** T. R. & E. MILES tr. *Michotte's Perception of Causality* xvii. 276 It is probable that an extreme 'syncretism' (i.e. an undifferentiated blending) holds sway at this time. **1967** A. L. BALDWIN *Theories Child Devel.* xvii. 501 An example of syncretism in normal adult functioning can be seen in the close relationship between taste and smell.

syncretistic, *a.* Add: Also = *SYNCRETIC *a.* 2.
1926 M. WARDEN tr. *Piaget's Lang. & Thought of Child* iv. 132 To this childish form of perception M. Claparède has given the name of *syncretistic perceptions*, using the name chosen by Renan to denote that first 'wide and comprehensive but obscure and inaccurate' activity of the spirit where 'no distinction is made and things are heaped one upon the other'. **1976** S. ARIETI *Creativity* ix. 195 The artist or viewer has a syncretistic grasp of the total object. He abandons precise visualization and experiences an unclear vision of the whole.

syncromesh, var. *SYNCHROMESH. **syncrude:** see *SYN-[2]. **syncyanosis**: see *SYN-[1] 1.

syncytium. Add: Hence **syncy:tiotro·phoblast,** the outer, syncytial layer of the trophoblast; also, one of the cells that make up this layer; **syncy:tiotrophobla·stic** *a.*
1926 *Jrnl. Anat.* LXI. (*Proc. Anat. Soc.*) 77 The trophoblast consists of a thick folded cellular layer (cytotrophoblast), on the outer surface of which an irregular and as yet thin deeply staining layer of syncytio-trophoblast is in process of differentiation. **1961** *Nature* 29 July 510/1 In human beings, the syncytiotrophoblasts are the fœtal cells in direct contact with the maternal bloodstream. *Ibid.* 511/1 The evidence favours the interpretation of the binding of tagged globulin from post-partum sera by the syncytiotrophoblastic cytoplasm as an immune phenomenon. **1980** *Sci. Amer.* Aug. 82/2 (*caption*) As the invasion proceeds the trophoblast differentiates into two layers, the outer syncytiotrophoblast, which leads the advance into the endometrium, and the cytotrophoblast, which forms a complex system of projections that eventually push through the syncytiotrophoblast into the pools of maternal blood.

† **syndesis** (sindī·sis). *Cytology. Obs.* [a. G. *syndesis* (V. Häcker 1904, in *Zool. Jahrb.* VII. 200), f. Gr. συν- SYN- + δέσις binding together (f. δεσμός bond, connection).] The pairing of chromosomes in mitosis or meiosis. Cf. *SYNAPSIS 2.
1909 *Ann. Bot.* XXIII. 49 Haecker has proposed the word *Syndesis* to apply to the conjugation or association of the homologous parental chromosomes.. **1912** [see *SYNAPSIS 2]. **1925** E. B. WILSON *Cell* (ed. 3) vi. 503 It is now widely held that reduction is initiated by a preliminary process or synapsis or syndesis in the course of which the chromosomes conjugate.

syndesmo-. Add: **synde·smophyte** [-PHYTE], a bony outgrowth from an injured joint or vertebra.
1957 in *Dorland's Med. Dict.* (ed. 23). **1966** E. W. BOLAND in J. L. Hollander *Arthritis* (ed. 7) v. xxxix. 648/1 In contrast to the marginal, heavy osteophytes of degenerative disease of the spine, the syndesmophytes of ankylosing spondylitis begin as linear, poorly defined calcifications adjacent to the margins of the vertebral bodies. **1980** BLUESTONE & KATICH in R. Bluestone *Rheumatology* xxiii. 284 (*caption*) Note mature syndesmophytes outlining annulus of several disks and bridging vertebral bodies.

syndetic, *a.* Add: **b.** *Librarianship.* Pertaining to or designating a catalogue, index, etc., which uses cross-references to indicate links between entries. Also used in automatic data-processing.
1876 C. A. CUTTER *Rules for Printed Dict. Catal.* 15 *Syndetic*, connective, applied to that kind of dictionary catalogue which binds its entries together by means of cross-references so as to form a whole. **1958** T. LANDAU *Encycl. Librarianship* 299/2 *Syndetic*, applied to an alphabetical subject catalogue or dictionary catalogue which includes cross-references as connecting links between subjects. *Ibid.*, Systematic catalogues have no need of such a syndetic apparatus. **1968** T. C. HINES *Vocab. Control in indexing Lit. of Librarianship & Information Sci.* (ERIC doc. No. ED050742) 16 Perhaps because of the concurrent use of shelf classification, library heading lists (although they include a syndetic apparatus which serves some of the same purposes) do not include the kind of classification of the headings themselves found in some thesauri expressed as 'broader terms'. **1974** *Encycl. Brit. Macropædia* X. 869/1 Provision is made for cross-references from unused terms and from one term to a related one. A catalog containing these entries is known as a syndetic catalog. **1977** A. P. JENSEN et al. (*title*) An instructional and research laboratory for syndetic analog-digital computation in science and engineering education. **1981** *Resources in Educ.* Oct. 138/2 This module describes the main subject heading, LC classification numbers which accompany the headings, 'see' references, 'see also' references, subheadings, and other syndetic features of the LC headings.

syndeton (si·ndĭtǫn). *Gram.* [Back-formation from ASYNDETON and POLYSYNDETON: cf. SYNDETIC *a.*] (See quots. 1954, 1972.)
1954 PEI & GAYNOR *Dict. Linguistics* 210 *Syndeton*, a phrase or construction in which the elements are linked together by connecting particles. **1971** *Computers & Humanities* V. 262 The frequency distribution enabled us to see also the amount of initial syndeton..in each sample. **1972** HARTMANN & STORK *Dict. Lang. & Linguistics* 230/1 *Syndeton*, a construction, parts of which are linked together by means of conjunctions or joining words, e.g. in *He came and went again.*

syndical, *a.* Add: **b.** In other collocations: of or relating to syndicalism; organized in unions.
1907 I. ZANGWILL *Ghetto Comedies* 411 Your only remedy is a general strike. You must join the Syndical Anarchists. **1943** G. BRENAN *Spanish Labyrinth* xii. 271 The real strength of the C.N.T. lay..in their powers of syndical resistance. **1955** *Times* 5 Aug. 8/3 General Perón said that the syndical organization of the people fought for ideals and interests.

syndicalist. For 'Also *attrib.*' read 'Also *attrib.* passing into *adj.*' and add later examples.
1962 V. NABOKOV *Pale Fire* 77 We find him next.. printing peevish pamphlets, acting as messenger for obscure syndicalist groups. **1974** J. WHITE tr. *Poulantzas's Fascism & Dictatorship* III. iii. 132 At the same time there was the first rupture with the 'left' syndicalist wing of the movement. **1976** *New Yorker* 3 May 89/1 Marcos has said that he wants to encourage trade unionism, but the fact is that, while his government countenances unions, it appears in some ways to be moving toward the creation of a syndicalist state not unlike Mussolini's Fascist corporate state. **1979** *Jrnl. R. Soc. Arts* Nov. 775/2 Here we have then a typical 'vest-pocket utopia' a form of syndicalist and local organization being collaged into the existing fabric, both formally and politically.

Hence **syndicali·stic** *a.*
1912 *Daily News* 20 Mar. 1 There was nothing particularly syndicalistic about a request for a minimum wage. **1919** M. BEER *Hist. Brit. Socialism* I. II. x. 286 The organized working class turned syndicalistic.

‖ **Syndicat d'Initiative** (sæ̃dika dinisyatīv). Also with small initials. [Fr.] In France, an association for promoting tourism; a tourist information office.
1911 W. J. LOCKE *Glory of Clementina Wing* ix. 128 The quarter of the town on which the Syndicat d'Initiative prides itself. **1926** E. HEMINGWAY *Sun also Rises* II. x. 92 We went..to the local Syndicat d'Initiative office. **1965** *Harper's Bazaar* Jan. 73/2 The local tourist offices—the *syndicats d'initiative* in France. **1968** F. WHITE *Ways of Aquitaine* 170 Almost all towns and many villages have *syndicats d'initiative*. These are information offices, which will give the tourist local lists of hotels and places of interest. **1972** D. LEES *Zodiac* 85 It's not the sort of thing the Syndicat d'Initiative likes to have get around but it does rain in Antibes every now and again. **1981** C. WATSON *Bishop in Back Seat* xxxvi. 208, I would go to the Gendarmerie, the Syndicat d'Initiative.

syndicate, *sb.* Add: **3. a.** Also, an association of people joined in a gambling or betting enterprise. In Gameshooting, a group of sportsmen who share rented shooting rights; also in Angling.

1934 D. Teilhet *Talking Sparrow Murders* ix. 138 La Roc? He's with von Lindbrulle in a betting syndicate. **1961** C. Willock *Death in Covert* i. 25 The game book for the past three seasons showed an average of 1,200 pheasants, 75 woodcock,..160 hares,..and 30 partridges per season... To hell with any qualms he felt about the members of the syndicate individually. **1964** *New Statesman* 3 Apr. 525/1 The fashion for office syndicates and 'sweeps' for charity. **1978** *Country Life* 27 July 272/1 The syndicates that form the basis of many shoots. **1979** *Angling* July 54/1 Catching good fish from strictly private or syndicate waters would prove nothing.

b. *spec.* (freq. with def. article and capital initial). In the U.S., a network of criminals controlling racketeering and other organized crime; also = *Cosa Nostra. Cf. *The Mob* s.v. *mob *sb.*[1] 5 b.

1929 Hostetter & Beesley *It's a Racket!* i. 4 Beer and alcohol running, bombing, bank robbery, murder for pay, window smashing, and a score of other crimes that can be carried on successfully only by organized groups or 'syndicates', are all rackets to the police. **1948** E. L. Irey *Tax Dodgers* xiv. 271 The Syndicate was the remnant of the Al Capone mob. **1952** [see *organized *ppl. a.* 4]. **1962** J. D. MacDonald *Key to Suite* (1968) i. 7 The smut-shadow of beard gave him somewhat the look of imported syndicate muscle. **1963, 1964** [see *Cosa Nostra]. **1969** *Guardian* 24 Jan. 7/6 The Syndicate is increasingly entering legitimate business. **1980** S. Allan *Dead Giveaway* iv. 38 The Syndicate had not been slow in learning of his involvement..and using it. **1982** *Amer. Speech* LVII. 244 Some successful criminals escape getting a monicker, for they, especially top-notch con men and syndicate members, think it adds 'class' to be without one.

c. *Syndicate of Initiative* = *Syndicat d'initiative.

1930 Kipling *Limits & Renewals* (1932) 325 A syndicate of Initiative has, indeed, approached me to write on the attractions of the district, as well as on the life of Saint Jubanus.

syndicate, *v.* Add: **2.** Also *spec.* in *Horse-racing*, to sell (a horse) to a syndicate.

1973 *Country Life* 6 Dec. 1897/3 American racing seems to have had a prosperous season with..the prices of bloodstock up. Secretariat was syndicated at $190,000 a share. **1979** D. Francis *Whip Hand* xiii. 161 He buys quite good horses...Then he syndicates them.

syndicated, *ppl. a.* Add: (Examples in the context of journalism.) Similarly in Broadcasting. *syndicated crime*, criminal activities organized by a syndicate (sense *3 b).

1928 [see *gramophone *v.*]. **1959** *Times Lit. Suppl.* 11 Dec. 719/2 Mr. Marquis Childs, the well-known syndicated columnist, formerly of the even better-known *St. Louis Post-Dispatch*. **1968** *Globe & Mail* (Toronto) 13 Feb. 8/3 The Roach report..drew a fine distinction between organized crime and syndicated crime. **1972** *Amer. Speech 1968* XLIII. 211 Van Johnson is quoted in Hedda Hopper's nationally syndicated column. **1974** *Howard Jrnl.* XIV. 108 (Advt.), An exposition of the many problems of organized, syndicated or corporate crime. **1976** *Liverpool Echo* 7 Dec. 17/3 The week gave me new experiences of writing. A syndicated article for the country's local newspapers, a particularly difficult article for a sports journal. **1980** *TWA Ambassador* Oct. 85/1 William R. Allen, professor of economics at UCLA, is known nationally for his syndicated radio commentaries.

syndication. Add: **3.** Publication or ownership by a syndicate. Freq. *attrib.*

1925 A. Huxley *Let.* 21 Apr. (1969) 247, I am trying to arrange for syndication of articles in America. **1955** *Times* 2 Aug. 2/5 Syndication is a nuisance to breeders. They have to guess at a horse's ability as a stallion when they take a share in him at the end of his racing days. **1959** R. Condon *Manchurian Candidate* (1960) ix. 137 The paper..offered Raymond fifty per cent of the syndication money. **1973** K. Giles *File on Death* iv. 97 Once the first instalment hits the street and the syndication rights have been arranged..the Establishment will be chary of proceeding. **1980** *Daily Tel.* 20 Mar. 24/5 (Advt.), Syndication Manager of the Daily Telegraph is looking for a secretary.

syndiotactic (sindəiotæ·ktik), *a. Chem.* Also (more correctly) **syndyo-**. [f. Gr. σύνδυο two together + τακτ-ός arranged, ordered + -ic.] Having or designating a polymer structure in which the substituent groups alternate on either side of the backbone of the molecule.

1956 Natta & Corradini in *Jrnl. Polymer Sci.* XX. 262 We propose to call all vinyl polymers with alternating D- and L-configurations of their substituents (like 1,2-polybutadiene) 'syndyotactic' polymers. **1966** *McGraw-Hill Encycl. Sci. & Techn.* X. 478/2 Isotactic and syndyotactic (stereoregular) polymers are formed in the presence of complex catalysts. **1972** *Physics Bull.* Nov. 668/3 The cellulose molecule..is syndiotactic and hence able to crystallize. **1978** *Nature* 9 Feb. 508/2 Commercial atactic polystyrene. is 70% syndiotactic.

Hence **sy:ndiota·ctically** *adv.*; **sy:ndiotacti·city**, the property or state of being syndiotactic.

1959 *Jrnl. Polymer Sci.* XXXIV. 9 Syndiotacticity is the corresponding arrangement. We can think of it as composed of positional and structural arrangements identical to those of isotacticity (repetition arrangements) and of a tacticity opposite to that of isotacticity (inversion tacticity). **1964** *Ibid.* B. II. 319 Predominantly isotactic addition may occur on heterogeneous surfaces, accompanied by conversion of the active complexes to form different..catalyst sites, which propagate predominantly syndiotactically. **1974** *Nature* 26 Apr. 758/1 If there is a high degree of syndiotacticity, a structure incorporating four monomer units per fibre repeat may be present.

syndrome. Delete || and add: Now only with pronunc. (si·ndrōᵘm).

2. Restrict † *Obs.* to sense in Dict. **b.** In recent use, a characteristic combination of opinions, behaviour, etc.; freq. preceded by a qualifying word.

1955 A. Huxley *Genius & Goddess* 26 She took a professional interest in caterpillars... It was part of the Gloom-Tomb syndrome. Caterpillars were the nearest approach, in real life, to Edgar Allen Poe. **1958** C. P. Snow in *Times Lit. Suppl.* 15 Aug. p. iii/2 There is a syndrome of attitudes in literature, nearly all quite modern, apparently unconnected, which spring from the same root. **1965** *Harper's Mag.* Feb. 74 A student..explained Albuquerque's all-enveloping friendliness in terms of the Luke Short syndrome. Typically in a Luke Short novel, a cowboy, footsore and weary, comes into town carrying a saddle over his shoulders. Nobody asks any questions. Friendliness is simply his for the asking. **1971** C. M. Kernan *Lang. Behavior in Black Urban Community* i. 16 The demographic statistics of this community, although depicting accurately a cluster of traits which might be labeled those comprising a lower-class poverty syndrome, do somewhat of an injustice to the social structure of the community. **1976** *Globe & Mail* (Toronto) 21 Dec. 7/1 They were working under the old syndrome that we couldn't do anything—the Government would always block us. **1976** J. I. M. Stewart *Memorial Service* xi. 177 His reclusive side—the withdrawn scholar syndrome, it might be called—remained on top. **1980** *West Lancs. Even. Gaz.* 23 Oct. 13 The falling roll syndrome [in schools] was a problem of the greatest magnitude and one never experienced before.

syndrum (si·ndrɒm). [f. Syn(thesizer + Drum *sb.*[1]] A drum designed with electronic means of amplification or alteration of pitch, etc.

1979 *Oxford Times* 28 Sept. 22 The drummer used syndrums more inventively than most disco arrangers. **1980** *Musicians Only* 26 Apr. 13/6 There's a Sonor drumkit, syndrums, and a whole range of Latin percussion. **1981** *Guardian* 13 July 9/1 They dressed up the reggae beat with subtle use of electronic 'syn drums' borrowed from the disco world.

synechism (si·nekiz'm). *Philos.* [f. Gr. συνεχής continuous + -ism: cf. Synechia.] The doctrine that continuity is one of the most important principles in scientific explanation. Hence **sy·nechist**, an adherent of this doctrine.

1892 C. S. Peirce in *Monist* II. 534 The tendency to regard continuity, in the sense in which I shall define it, as an idea of prime importance in philosophy may conveniently be termed *synechism*. **1902** J. M. Baldwin *Dict. Philos. & Psychol.* II. 657/1 The synechist maintains that the only..justification for..entertaining a hypothesis, is that it affords an explanation of the phenomena. **1909** W. James *Pluralistic Universe* 398 Peirce meets this objection by combining his tychism with an express doctrine of 'synechism' or continuity. **1937** *Mind* XLVI. 394 Book i sets forth the doctrines of *Tychism*, *Synechism*, and *Agapism*: that is to say, it attempts to explain the universe by the use of Pure Chance, Continuity, and psychological categories. **1976** *Internat. Philos. Q.* XVI. 228 This difficulty is also found in Peirce's notions of tychism and synechism.

synechthran, -echthry: see *syn-[1] 1.

synecology (sinīkǫ·lŏdʒi). Also † **synoekology.** [ad. G. *synökologie* (Schröter & Kirchner *Die Vegetation des Bodensees* (1902) II. ii. 63), f. Syn- + *ecology.] The study of plant or animal communities.

1910 *Proc. 3rd Internat. Bot. Congr.* I. 266 M. Shull... Synoekology of particular regions. **1911** A. Tansley *Types Brit. Veg.* 3 The study of synecology is considerably in advance of autecology. **1936** *Nature* 4 Apr. 565/1 Synecology cannot..be properly studied without a good taxonomic knowledge of the local flora. **1957** [see *biocœnology]. **1977** A. Hallam *Planet Earth* 245 As in ecology, the concern is first with the individual or individual species (autecology), and then investigation proceeds to the assemblage as a whole (synecology).

Hence **synecolo·gical** *a.*; **syneco·logist**, a student of synecology.

1922 *Jrnl. Ecol.* X. 14 Up to the present time most ecological work has been of an extensive (synecological) nature. **1938** *Nature* 17 Dec. 1056/1 The synecologist has to name and ecologically to describe and classify the species components of the vegetation. **1940** E. J. Salisbury in J. S. Huxley *New Systematics* 336 Each [species] has its value for synecological diagnosis. **1974** *Nature* 7 June 599/2 Autecological studies pour out increasing quantities of details for synecologists to work on. **1976** *Ibid.* 22 July p.x (Advt.), Duties: To carry out..synecological studies of aquatic plants in irrigation systems.

synectics (sine·ktiks). orig. *U.S.* Also **Synectics.** [f. Synectic *a.*, perh. after *dialectics*.] A method of problem-solving, esp. by groups, which seeks to illuminate and utilize the factors involved in creative thinking.

A proprietary term in the U.S. (see quot. 1966).

1961 W. J. Gordon *Synectics* ii. 34 Synectics is an attempt to describe those conscious, preconscious and subconscious psychological states which are present in any creative act. **1965** *Times* 11 Aug. 11 A new philosophy, 'synectics', which is said to liberate the creative instinct and so stimulate inventiveness, is gaining a following among big corporations. **1966** *Official Gaz.* (U.S. Patent Office) 25 Oct. 191 *Synectics*, for teaching services —namely, the teaching to individuals and groups, techniques for arriving at creative new concepts, products and solutions; and advising businesses and individuals [etc.]. **1973** *Times* 22 Jan. 20/7 Synectics, a widely used technique for problem-solving in small groups. **1975** R. H. Rimmer *Premar Experiments* i. 128 The basic thrust of Synectics is joining people together into problem-stating and problem-solving groups. **1976** S. Arieti *Creativity* xvi. 376 The synectics method started as a group method. But..the occurrence of analogy—that is, the recognition of similarities—is one of the main processes of individual creativity.

synergetic, *a.* Delete *rare* and add: In mod. use, of or pertaining to synergy (sense *c); = *synergistic *a.* 3. Cf. *synergetical *a.*

1960 R. W. Marks *Dymaxion World of B. Fuller* 8/1 An illustration of the synergetic effect is the behavior of metallic alloys. **1969** R. Buckminster Fuller *Operating Man. Spaceship Earth* v. 73 Universe is synergetic. Life is synergetic. **1975** J. De Bres tr. *Mandel's Late Capitalism* viii. 251 The so-called synergetic model of company planning—in which the overall result of various programmes exceeds the sum of the partial results foreseen for each individual programme—is..derived from military programmes.

synergetical, *a.* For † *Obs.* read *rare* and add: Also in *gen.* use. Hence **synerge·tically** *adv.* Cf. *synergistic *a.* 3, *synergistically *adv.*

1960 R. W. Marks *Dymaxion World of B. Fuller* 166 Thus the system joins together 'synergetically' to distribute and inhibit the loads. [**1969** R. Buckminster Fuller *Operating Man. Spaceship Earth* vi. 77 The patron's supine concessions to the nonsynergetical thinking.] *Ibid.* 109 It produced billions of dollars of new wealth through the increased know-how and intelligence thus released, which synergetically augmented the spontaneous initiative of that younger generation.

synergic, *a.* Add: Also in *Chem.*, with reference to the mutual strengthening of sigma and pi bonds.

1960 L. E. Orgel *Introd. Transition-Metal Chem.* ix. 137 We have discussed σ and π bonding independently. While this gives a satisfactory qualitative picture, the synergic interaction between them is most important. **1974** *Encycl. Brit. Macropædia* XVIII. 606/2 Carbon monoxide is able to form carbonyls with transition metals because the bonding of those metals to the carbon monoxide molecule is of a dual or synergic nature.

synergism. Add: **2. a.** The combined activity of two drugs or other substances, when greater than the sum of the effects of each one present alone.

1910 A. R. Cushny *Textbk. Pharmacol. & Therapeutics* (ed. 5) 29 Other examples of synergism are offered by the anæsthetics, for..a mixture of two of these may induce anæsthesia when administered in a dilution far below that necessary if either is employed alone. **1938** [see *antagonism 1 d]. **1961** *Lancet* 12 Aug. 375/2 Combined chemotherapy of acute leukæmia with 6-mercaptopurine plus corticosteroids gave a higher remission-rate than that observed for either of these administered alone... Synergism was not observed with other drug-combinations given for malignant blood diseases. **1972** *Materials & Technol.* V. x. 313 Products of this type are widely used for their ability to work together with other surfactants (synergism), as clarifying and emulsifying agents. **1979** *Buffalo Evening News* 18 May ii. 23/2 By combining 2,4-D and silvex, the weed killer became more effective... This is known as synergism.

b. *transf.* and *fig.*

1925 J. Laird *Our Minds & Their Bodies* ii. 26 These various arguments..are often so closely allied as scarcely to be distinguished. There is synergism in all their ramifications... Nevertheless, we must try to discriminate between the different steps and stages in these converging arguments. **1941** Beigel & Kurth tr. *Reik's Masochism in Mod. Man* i. 30 Freud dropped his attempt to reduce masochism to the assumption of a sexual synergism of pain and discomfort in the infantile organism. **1970** *Nature* 4 July 71/1 We wish to describe synergism between two distinct populations of cells in the production of cellular immunity. **1971** K. Chin Wu in W. O. Dingwall *Survey Linguistic Sci.* (1978) vii. 159 Articulating speech was..a function involving a rather delicate synchronization, synergism to use a more technical term, of many muscular activities that had to be learned. **1974** *Jrnl. Amer. Med. Assoc.* 15 Apr. 290 Thus, it seems that the synergism obtainable by a working together of both professions would, most of all, aid the physicians who read the journals. **1977** *New Scientist* 30 June 767/2 We've done some experiments on cells in culture and you don't get any synergism, you get addition. **1978** *N.Y. Times* 30 Mar. D3/2 (Advt.), The result: a synergism where the results are greater than the sum of the parts.

synergist. 2. (Further examples.)

1938 *Brain* LXI. 322 This is not necessarily true for contraction of synergists. **1959** *New Scientist* 13 Aug. 174/3 Chemical research has already provided 'synergists', cheaper materials which, while not insecticidal themselves, are able to make the pyrethrins more effective in greater dilution. **1969** N. W. Pirie *Food Resources* ii. 67 Substances (called synergists) are added which, though not themselves effective insecticides, prevent those metabolic changes taking place which confer resistance.

synergistic, *a.* Add: **2.** (Further examples.) Also more widely.
1962 *New Scientist* 10 May 263/2 Fucidin is 'synergistic' with penicillin and erythromycin—that is, the activity of a mixture is greater than the sum of the individual antibiotics. **1976** *Sci. Amer.* Feb. p. iv/2 (Advt.), The synergistic effect of mixing finely divided titanium dioxide with opacifying dyes permitted us to use a lesser quantity of dyes than if we had used the dyes alone.

3. *gen.* Co-operative, interacting, mutually stimulating.
1965 H. I. Ansoff *Corporate Strategy* v. 76 This step certainly provides for some of the synergistic interactions. *Ibid.* 83 The synergistic effect can be measured in either of two ways. **1970** *Nature* 26 Dec. 1261/2 The synergistic creativity of Wordsworth and Coleridge which produced *The Lyrical Ballads* in 1798 and began the romantic movement in poetry was over by 1805. **1972** M. Crichton *Terminal Man* i. iii. 30 Designing electronic components to be synergistic with the human brain. **1975** J. A. Argüelles *Transformative Vision* i. 7 The ancient *t'ai-chi* of the Chinese..symbolizes not only the synergistic totality of the two modes of consciousness, but also the interaction of day and night, life and death [etc.]. **1980** *Jrnl. R. Soc. Arts* July 497/2 It was intended that..it should consider the synergistic interactions between the different factors.

synergistically *adv.* (later examples in sense *3 of the adj.).
1968 *N.Y. Times* 8 Jan. 141 By this he meant that science and technology had come to the point where the parts fed upon each other continuously and synergistically to enlarge the whole. **1979** *Logophile* II. v. 8/2 Do the 'principles of acceptance' identified in this study operate synergistically?

synergize, *v.* (In Dict. s.v. Synergist 2.) Add: (Examples.) Hence **sy·nergizing** *ppl. a.*
1954 *Times Lit. Suppl.* 12 Nov. 721/1 The illuminating, synergizing word here, without which the rest is nothing but maundering, is..the word sighs. **1962** *Endocrinology* LXXI. 219/1 Prolactin is well known to synergize with growthhormone in the tibial growth test. **1973** *Nature* 13 Apr. 477/2 Progesterone..synergizes with oestrogen to enhance sexual receptivity.

synergy. Add: **c.** Increased effectiveness, achievement, etc., produced as a result of combined action or co-operation.
1957 R. B. Cattell *Personality & Motivation* xvii. 791 Immediate synergy through group membership..expresses the energy going into the group life as a result of satisfaction with fellow members. **1960** R. W. Marks *Dymaxion World of Buckminster Fuller* 8/1 Fuller refers to the integrated behavior patterns as synergy. **1965** H. I. Ansoff *Corporate Strategy* v. 75 We begin to explore *synergy*... It is frequently described as the '2+2=5' effect to denote the fact that the firm seeks a product-market posture with a combined performance that is greater than the sum of its parts. **1974** M. B. Brown *Economics of Imperialism* ix. 228 The world-wide 'synergy' of the trans-national company is..the logical conclusion of a long historical process of capital accumulation and territorial assimilation. **1981** *Economist* 28 Nov. 19/2 Others, through mergers (eg, research houses into retail brokerage houses), have demonstrated that there is something to be said for synergy.

synesthesia, var. Synæsthesia in Dict. and Suppl. **synesthetic,** var. *synæsthetic *a.* (*sb.*). **synezesis,** erron. var. *synizesis 3. **synform:** see *syn-[1] 1. **synfuel:** see *syn-[2].

syngameon (singæ·miǫn). *Genetics.* [f. Syngamy + *-on[1].] A cluster of species and subspecies between the members of which natural hybridization occurs.
1922 J. P. Lotsy in *Rep. Brit. Assoc. Adv. Sci. 1921* 453 Nature consists of individuals; similar individuals form syngameons, and these have been mistaken for species. **1930** *Svensk Bot. Tidskr.* XXIV. 386, I have..used Lotsy's term 'syngameon' in a rather wide sense, i.e. as a..handy term for any intercrossing population not divided by distinct lines or zones of discontinuity. **1970** *Brittonia* XXII. 335 We realized that syngameon complexes..were currently contributing to the establishment of additional tetraploid populations in neighbouring areas.

syngas: see *syn-[2].

syngen (si·ndʒěn). *Microbiology.* [f. Syn- + Gen(erate *v.*] A group of organisms, esp. protozoans, capable of breeding together.
1957 T. M. Sonneborn in E. Mayr *Species Problem* 201, I propose the term 'syngen' for the potentially common gene pool, for organisms capable of 'generating together'. **1977** *Jrnl. Protozool.* XXIV. 18/1 We have learned so far that there are 'isozymes' of the epiplasmic proteins in *Tetrahymena*; the molecular weights of proteins B and C vary according to species (including syngens).

syngeneic (sindʒenī·ik, -ēi·ik), *a.* *Immunol.* [f. Syn- + Gr. γενε-ά race, stock + -ic.] Immunologically compatible; (of a group of organisms) so closely related that their tissues do not act as antigens when transplanted to one another; = *isogeneic *a.*
1961 P. A. Gorer et al. in *Nature* 25 Mar. 1025/1 We suggest the introduction of 'syngeneic' as a synonym for 'isogenic'. If one does not wish to refer to 'intra-strain immunity' one could then use 'syngeneic immunity'. **1977** *Lancet* 8 Oct. 743/2 Some syngeneic grafts have failed, sometimes because they were undertaken when the patient was already seriously ill. **1978** *Nature* 17 Aug. 697/2 When tumour cells are inoculated into syngeneic mice their establishment and growth is subject to regulation by the host animal.

Hence **syngene·ically** *adv.*
1971 *Nature* 18 June 449/2 The tumour..has been maintained syngeneically as a solid as well as an ascites tumour.

syngenetic, *a.* Add: **2.** (Examples.) More widely, characterized by or pertaining to a formation contemporaneous with the enclosing or surrounding rock.
1905 J. Geikie *Struct. & Field Geol.* xvi. 225 Ore-formations may be grouped under these two main divisions:—1. Syngenetic or Contemporaneous, and 2. Epigenetic or Subsequent... Syngenetic ore-formations..are formations of the same age..as the rocks in which they occur. **1914** [see *epigenetic *a.* 2]. **1962** *Geografiska Annaler* XLIV. 382/2 The ice-wedges..are clearly 'syngenetic'..i.e. the frost cracks have extended upwards successively as new sediments were deposited on top. **1971** *Nature* 12 Mar. 108/2 It remains to be seen whether the small amounts of racemic amino-acids were syngenetic with the meteorite parent body or were synthesized later. **1978** S. S. Peng *Coal Mine Ground Control* v. 117 Syngenetic anisotropy originates during the formation processes of rock materials. Bedding planes and preferred alignment of pores or mineral grains are examples.

Hence **syngene·tically** *adv.*
1951 *Bull. Amer. Assoc. Petroleum Geologists* XXXV. 2226 Apparently the oölites of hematite formed both syngenetically and epigenetically. **1978** *Nature* 19 Oct. 641/1 The Brioverian unicells and colonies are *bona fide* Precambrian fossils:..they were deposited syngenetically with Precambrian sedimentation.

synizesis. Add: **3.** *Cytology.* Also (*erron.*) **synezesis.** A stage of meiosis in some species in which all the chromosomal material is seen tightly contracted into a clump. Hence **synize·tic** *a.*
1905 C. E. McClung in *Biol. Bull.* IX. 329, I would suggest that..a new descriptive word be applied to the condition of the nucleus in which the chromatin is found massed at one side of the vesicle, without regard to whether it is a normal phenomenon or not. To carry out this idea I shall call this stage the 'synizesis' of the chromatin. **1921** *Ann. Bot.* XXXV. 367 In this paper the term synizesis is adopted for the tightly contracted phase of the nucleus, following the usage which has become customary in the literature of animal cytology. **1931** *Jrnl. Exper. Zoöl.* LVIII. 299 Synezesis stages were present, but mixed with secondary spermatocytes. **1931** *Amer. Jrnl. Bot.* XVIII. 370 The next stage involves a very rapid shortening of the spireme, the opening out of the spirals, and the transition to an interwoven thread system, which ..persists until toward the climax of synizetic sensitiveness. **1933** *Cytologia* IV. 270 By the use of the methods employed in the studies reported here, the chromatin is drawn into a tight knot (synizesis) at the stages at which synapsis takes place. *Ibid.* 271 Synizetic stages were studied in asynaptic plants which showed little associations of homologous chromosomes at metaphase. **1979** *Hereditas* XCI. 87/1 In the zygotene of the arctic brambles there is a polarised stage called a synizesis. The synizesis is a zygotene bouquet in which mass contraction has occurred.

synjet: see *syn-[2]. **synkinematic, synneusis:** *syn-[1] 1.

synodsman. Add: **2.** Also in other Anglican churches, esp. a member of the General Synod of the Church of England.
1970 *Church Times* 6 Nov. 20/3 Sir John Guillum Scott ..read the gospel—the familiar Beatitudes from St. Matthew containing good advice to all synodsmen. **1972** *Times Lit. Suppl.* 20 Oct. 1261/3 Quite beyond the reach of the average synodsman or lay communicant. **1980** *Times* 23 June 18/2 The synodsmen were concerned to see that the new Anglican Liturgy accurately reflected the contemporary face of Anglicanism.

synœkete: see *syn-[1] 1. **synoil:** *syn-[2].

synonym, *sb.* Add: **5.** *Comb.*, as (sense 1) *synonym-pair*; **synonym-compound** (see quot. 1923).
1923 B. Karlgren *Sound & Symbol in Chinese* iii. 32 The additions were of various kinds, the commonest and by far the most important of which was the formation of what may be called synonym-compounds. This consists in coupling together two simple words with the same or at least analogous meanings, words that formerly had been used alone. **1964** *Language* XL. 104 The Chinese..invented tones to keep the monosyllables apart, and then synonym-compounds, further to clear up the difficulties they were now experiencing with their own language. **1980** *Logophile* IV. i. 28, I have been working for some time on an article about the curious existence in English and French of synonym-pairs.

synonymic, *sb.* (Examples of form *synonymics.*)
1939 W. E. Collinson in *Trans. Philol. Soc.* 54 (*title*) Comparative synonymics: some principles and illustrations. *Ibid.* 58 The first principle I venture to set up in synonymics..[is that] 'one must never be content with studying synonyms as isolated items'. **1962** H. M. Hoenigswald in Householder & Saporta *Probl. Lexicogr.* 103 Some works, like Dornseiff's monstrous *Wortschatz* or like other thesauri of synonymics are arranged according to semantic areas.

synonymize, *v.* Restrict *rare* to senses in Dict. and add: **5. a.** To be synonymous with (a concept, phrase, etc.).
1938 S. Leslie *Film of Memory* v. 144 The old Baroness was very popular with the crowd and synonymised Victorian charity. **1947** Partridge *Usage & Abusage* 44/2 *As to* in such senses..is defensible when it synonymizes *in respect of* or *in the matter of.*

b. To regard (terms, concepts, etc.) as synonymous.
1970 *Nature* 5 Sept. 1065/1 Hill's classification is not wholly in line with recent trends in primate systematics, which is to synonymize the species of *Papio*. **1976** *Ibid.* 5 Feb. 360/2 If we were now to start referring to cyanophytes as 'blue-green bacteria', we would implicitly synonymise the words 'prokaryota' and 'bacteria'.

synopsis. 2. (Earlier example.)
1844 J. Cowell *Thirty Yrs. passed among Players* i. xxi. 51/2 Snuffed two tallow-candles, and took a synopsis of the floating apartment.

synopsize, *v.* For (*U.S.*) read (orig. *U.S.*) and add later examples.
1959 J. Gill *Council of Florence* p. xv, Very many long speeches occur in the main sources, which I have synopsised. **1974** *Times Lit. Suppl.* 20 Sept. 1018/5 The 'avowal' here is..that of the editors of the volume, in a short preface in which they attempt to synopsize its contents. **1982** *Daily Tel.* 6 Feb. 11/4 Plot is the very least of Hardy. If you were to synopsise the events of this early novel..you would be a laughing-stock.

synoptic, *a.* (*sb.*) Add: **1. a.** *spec.* Depicting or dealing with weather conditions over a large area at the same point in time.
[**1861** F. Galton (*title*) Synchronous weather chart of England.] **1868** *Symons's Monthly Meteorol. Mag.* III. 144 It is now fourteen years since, impressed with the importance of synoptic weather charts,..I attempted to bring out a series of such charts [of the Indian Ocean]. **1887** [in Dict.]. **1909** A. C. Scott *Notes Meteorol. & Weather Forecasting* 1 Within the last 40 years the Synoptic method of weather-charting has been introduced, which has changed the whole aspect of Meteorology. **1939** *Geogr. Jrnl.* XCIV. 135 Synoptic meteorology (i.e. the science of synchronous weather charts). **1963** G. L. Pickard *Descriptive Physical Oceanogr.* vi. 74 It is.. impracticable to obtain a truly simultaneous picture of the ocean, and the synoptic oceanographer has to make the assumption that when he analyses them the data from his cruise or cruises may be considered as simultaneous. **1974** *Nature* 1 Mar. 87/3 Synoptic climatology is essentially a practical subject.

synoptist. 1. (Earlier example.)
1846 Geo. Eliot tr. *Strauss's Life of Jesus* II. ii. vi. 135 The mode in which the synoptists arrange the sayings of Jesus.

synoptophore (sinǫ·ptofoᵊɹ). *Ophthalm.* Also **-phor.** [Syn- + Opto- + -phore.] An instrument for measuring the deviations of the visual axes of eyes not properly coordinated for binocular vision.
1934 M. L. Hine *May & Worth's Dis. of Eye* (ed. 7) xxvii. 416 The synoptophore..is an elaborate development of Worth's original amblyoscope. **1955** P. D. Trevor-Roper *Ophthalmol.* xviii. 281 Various major amblyoscopes are marketed. The pattern that is perhaps the most generally serviceable is the 'Moorfields Synoptophore'. **1975** *Nature* 17 Apr. 613/2 Binocular interaction was tested on the synoptophor.

synorogenic: see *syn-[1] 1.

synovectomy (sinǒve·ktǒmi). *Surg.* [f. Synov(ia + *-ectomy.] Total or partial excision of the synovial membrane of a joint, esp. the knee, or of a tendon sheath, esp. to relieve pain.
1903 *Buck's Handbk. Med. Sci.* (rev. ed.) VI. 519/1 The procedures ordinarily employed are *évidement* of the focus, and in the later cases..ablation of the patella, with synovectomy or arthrectomy when necessary. **1923** *Jrnl. Amer. Med. Assoc.* 10 Nov. 1579/1 Synovectomy..was originally recommended as a surgical treatment for synovial tuberculosis. **1940** B. I. Comroe *Arthritis & Allied Conditions* xvii. 222 Synovectomy of the knee is the removal of the synovial tissue of the knee. **1976** *Proc. R. Soc. Med.* LXIX. 930/2 The indications for synovectomy or patellectomy in either rheumatoid or osteoarthritis of the knee are well known and differ little in the elderly.

synroc: see *syn-[2]. **synsedimentary:** *syn-[1] 1.

synsemantic (sinsimæ·ntik), *a.* *Philol.* [ad. G. *synsemantisch* (A. Marty *Untersuchungen zur Grundlegung d. allgemeinen Grammatik und Sprachphilosophie* (1908) ii. i. 206): see Syn-, Semantic *a.*] Of a word or phrase: having no meaning outside a context; meaningless in isolation; syncategorematic; opp. *autosemantic.* See also note s.v. *autosemantic *a.* (*sb.*).

1929, etc. [see *AUTOSEMANTIC *a.* (sb.)]. **1954** *Archivum Linguisticum* VI. 18 These 'synsemantic' words 'adsignify' or contribute only to the sense of the whole group to which they belong. **1960** *Analysis* XXI. I. 3 According to Brentano 'Paris' is not a genuine constituent of 'I am thinking-of-Paris'. It is in this context, as he sometimes says, a synsemantic expression. As such, it does not refer to anything. **1965** B. COLLINDER in Bessinger & Creed *Medieval & Linguistic Stud.* 28 The definite article is a synsemantic demonstrative pronoun.

syntactic, *a.* Add: **1.** (Earlier examples.) Also *Comb.*, as *syntactic-semantic* adj.

1807 R. KIRWAN *Logick* IV. i. 531 We learn to ascertain the relation of these different parts to each other, according to the syntactic rules peculiar to each language. **1816** P. S. DUPONCEAU *Let.* 31 July in *Trans. Hist. & Lit. Comm. Amer. Philos. Soc.* (1819) I. 402 As I have given to the Chinese and its kindred dialects, the name of *asyntactic*, the opposite name, *syntactic*, appears to me that which is best suited to the languages of the American Indians. **1972** G. LAKOFF in *Language* XLVIII. 291 Anaphora..is a syntactic-semantic phenomenon which can, and must, be specified independently of lexical idiosyncrasies. **1978** *Archivum Linguisticum* IX. 79 We will assume that if such commensurability could be established, we would have strong evidence for the existence of a syntactic-semantic component in our overall grammar, rather than separate syntactic and semantic components.

2. Exhibiting or characterized by syntaxy; *syntactic foam*, a plastic foam made by introducing small hollow spheres into a liquid matrix which then solidifies.

1955 *Sci. News Let.* 2 Apr. 213/3 Called 'syntactic foam', by its developer, the Bakelite Company of New York, the new lightweight material is produced by bonding microscopic hollow spheres made of phenolic resin together with phenolic, epoxy or polyester resins. **1970** *Adv. Chem. Ser.* XCII. 150 Syntactic foams..consist of a dispersion of small hollow glass spheres in a continuous phase or matrix. **1974** *Petroleum Rev.* XXVIII. 675/1 Syntactic foam blocks attached to the top of the frame produce a slight positive buoyancy. **1975** C. A. HARPER *Handbk. Plastics & Elastomers* VII. 44 Syntactic foams, like syntactic crystalline polymers, are characterized by their high degree of order or structure.

B. as *sb. pl.* (const. *sing.*). *Linguistics.* C. W. Morris's term for that branch of linguistics which is concerned with the formal relations of signs to each other.

1937 [see *PRAGMATIC *sb.* 4]. **1938** C. W. MORRIS in *Internat. Encycl. Unified Sci.* I. II. 14 Syntactics is, then, the consideration of signs and sign combinations in so far as they are subject to syntactical rules. **1941** A. TATE in *Southern Rev.* VI. 636 The role of syntactics in the semiotic science remains somewhat obscure; it seems to consist in a number of 'transformation rules'—that is, in formulas by which given expressions in words, numbers, or symbols can be changed into equivalent but formally different expressions. **1945** [see *intra-linguistic* s.v. *INTRA- 1]. **1964** E. A. NIDA *Toward Sci. Transl.* iii. 35 While semantics deals with the relationship of symbols to referents, syntactics is concerned with the relationship of symbol to symbol; for the meaning of expressions is not to be found merely in adding up symbols, but also in determining their arrangements, including order and hierarchical structuring. For example, the constituents *black* and *bird*, when occuring in juxtaposition, may have two quite different meanings. **1969** [see *PRAGMATIC *sb.* 4].

syntactical, *a.* Add: Also *transf.* in reference to logic (see *SYNTAX 2 d).

1937 A. SMEATON tr. *Carnap's Logical Syntax of Lang.* 2 The difference between syntactical rules in the narrower sense and the logical rules of deduction is the only difference between formation rules and transformation rules, both of which are completely formulable in syntactical terms. **1954** I. M. COPI *Symbolic Logic* vi. 184 To characterize the criterion as 'purely formal' is to say that it is syntactical rather than semantical. **1978** *Jrnl. Symbolic Logic* XLIII. 511 We need first two syntactical transformations on formulae.

syntactically, *adv.* Add: Also *transf.* in reference to logical syntax.

1940 W. V. QUINE *Math. Logic* vii. 286 The fact that 'Vbl'.., and 'LFmla' are definable in this syntactical notation is perhaps best expressed..by speaking of them as *syntactically definable.* **1967** *Encycl. Philos.* V. 23/1 Deductive systems for sentential logic..serve to characterize logic syntactically. **1971** G. HUNTER *Metalogic* III. 116 PS is syntactically complete..iff no unprovable schema can be added to it..without inconsistency.

syntactician. Add: **1.** (Later examples.)

1904 *Amer. Jrnl. Philol.* XXV. 355 President Wheeler has not been harder on syntacticians than Piron was on grammarians. **1926** [see *rhythm-deaf* s.v. *RHYTHM *sb.* 9 a]. **1935** *Punch* 9 Oct. 406/2, I remind myself that the budgerigar is that spiteful little creature known..as the 'lovebird'. I recommend it to future Latin syntacticians as an example of the *lucus a non lucendo.* **1970** *Eng. Stud.* LI. 52 On the whole, present-day syntacticians tend to pay too little regard to the patterning of paradigmatic variables, focusing their attention on syntactic structure on the basis of the theory of grammaticality. **1982** *N. & Q.* Oct. 386/2, I hope the compilers will find a title to express the importance for syntacticians and others of what it will contain.

† **2.** = SYNTAXIAN. *Obs.*

1774 H. T. BLOUNT *Diary* in *Publ. Cath. Rec. Soc.* (1972) LXIII. 358 On the 9th August Jas. Hart, Syntactician, went to England.

syntacticist (sintæ·ktisist). [f. SYNTACTIC *a.* + -IST.] = SYNTACTICIAN 1.

1889 W. G. HALE in *Classical Rev.* III. 168/2 The very phrases comparative grammar and comparative philology are commonly used in a way to leave the syntacticist outcast and alien. **1944** *Mind* LIII. 243 What the syntacticist is interested in is, that..these isomorphs are themselves analytic. **1977** *Daily Tel.* 10 Feb. 12/6 Syntacticists, linguists and psycholinguists are turning greedily to the poetics of fiction in 'Winnie the Pooh' and the psychological processes in the reading of 'Alice'.

syntacto- (sintæ·kto), used as combining form of SYNTACTIC *a.*, as **syntacto-semantic** *a.* = *syntactic-semantic* adj. s.v. *SYNTACTIC *a.* 1; **syntactostyli·stics** *sb. pl.* (const. *sing.*), the study of the stylistic implications of syntactic variation.

1972 *Archivum Linguisticum* III. 7 In particular, I shall show how an adequate grammar must indicate not only a variety of syntacto-semantic features of the noun (such as humanness and inherent duality), but also features of any numeral preceding the noun phrase and certain morphological features of both nouns and adjectives. **1977** *Canad. Jrnl. Linguistics 1976* XXI. 84 The second and third axes represent an arbitrary division of the syntacto-semantic domain of the signal, the motivation for which is discussed below. **1969** Syntactostylistics [see *PHONOSTYLISTICS *sb. pl.*].

syntagm. Restrict † *Obs.* to sense in Dict. and add: **2.** *Linguistics* = *SYNTAGMA 4. Also *transf.* and *fig.*

1947 R. S. WELLS in *Word* III. 8 A compound sign, i.e. an interrupted sequence of morphemes (no two of which occur simultaneously) is called a syntagm. **1959** W. BASKIN tr. *F. de Saussure's Course in General Linguistics* (1960) II. v. 123 In discourse,..words..are arranged in sequence on the chain of speaking. Combinations supported by linearity are *syntagms.* The syntagm is always composed of two or more consecutive units. **1970** E. LEACH *Lévi-Strauss* iii. 48 The term *syntagm*, as applied to an assemblage of non-verbal signs, corresponds to *sentence* in a verbal language. **1973** D. MATIAS tr. C. Metz in *Screen* Spring/Summer 77 The film-maker at each point in the film..has a choice between a limited number of *basic* combinations..the alternating syntagm, the episodic syntagm, the descriptive syntagm, the 'single shot', [etc.]. **1976** *Times Lit. Suppl.* 19 Nov. 1458/3 The syntagm *il ne va pas* is no longer almost identical with *il ne va un pas.* **1978** 'A. BURGESS' *1985* 99 Separate the sexual act from love, and the language of love is devalued. An aspect of our freedom is our right to debase the language totally, so that its syntagms become mere noise.

syntagma. Restrict ‖ to senses in Dict. and add: **4.** *Linguistics.* [ad. F. *syntagme* (F. de Saussure *a* 1913, *Cours de Linguistique Générale* (1916) II. v. 176).] A syntactic unit comprising two or more linguistic signs or elements. Also *transf.*

1937 J. ORR tr. *Iordan's Introd. Romance Linguistics* iv. 286 A syntagma is composed of at least two units in sequence. **1946** *Word* II. 117 To the best of our knowledge, there are three such ultimate and irreducible signs: the phoneme, the word, and the construction or syntagma. *Ibid.* 118 The *syntagma* is defined as the sign of the relations into which the referents of words, enter. **1967** *Ibid.* XXIII. 380 As all composites are syntagmas, i.e., grammatical entities, they must be explainable from an underlying sentence whose syntactic relations they mirror. **1974** M. TAYLOR *Metz's Film Lang.* p. x, A *syntagma* is, consequently, a unit of actual relationship, while a *paradigm* is a unit of potential relationship. **1979** *Trans. Philol. Soc.* 82 The Latin noun declensions provide more than sufficient illustration of syncretism within word paradigms..with the burden of disambiguating relevant properties then being shifted to the syntagma.

syntagmatic (sintægmæ·tik), *a. Linguistics.* [ad. F. *syntagmatique* (F. de Saussure *a* 1913, *Cours de Linguistique Générale* (1916) II. v. 177).] Of or pertaining to the syntactic relationship between linguistic units. Also *transf.*

1937 J. ORR tr. *Iordan's Introd. Romance Linguistics* iv. 333 To the study of the combinations of linguistic signs ..he [*sc.* Sechehaye] gives the name of syntagmatic grammar. **1948** J. R. FIRTH in *Trans. Philol. Soc.* 129 We generalize syllabic structure in a new order of abstraction eliminating the specific paradigmatic consonant and vowel systems as such, and enabling the syntagmatic word structure of syllables..to be stated systematically. **1959** W. BASKIN tr. *F. de Saussure's Course in General Linguistics* (1960) II. v. 123 The syntagmatic relation is *in praesentia.* It is based on two or more terms that occur in an effective series. **1966** T. BENDOR-SAMUEL in C. E. Bazell *In Memory of J. R. Firth* 37 In the grammatical description, as in the phonological, it is not sufficient to speak of units as comprising a structure of elements arranged in place since there are also syntagmatic features whose domain of relevance extends beyond any of the elements of the structure. **1973** MATIAS & WILLEMEN tr. M. Cegarra in *Screen* Spring/Summer 144 Because to Metz, the organisation of the cinema is 'manifestly syntagmatic'.. his criticism of the montage films is in fact no more than reproaching them for being syntagmatically bad. **1981** *Word 1980* XXXI. 243 A hierarchy of phonology, morphology, syntax, and semantics related to each other by paradigmatic and syntagmatic rules.

Hence **syntagma·tically** *adv.*

1937 J. ORR tr. *Iordan's Introd. Romance Linguistics* iv. 286 The constituent elements of human language, considered at a particular moment,..are related to each other syntagmatically and associatively. **1951** *Essays & Studies* IV. 126 Throughout his poetry Swinburne lays general constructions alongside each other, syntagmatically parallel collocations are a feature of verse-form and stanza-form. **1961** Y. OLSSON *Syntax Eng. Verb* ii. 27 Both collocation and colligation operate syntagmatically, that is, along the line one-after-another. **1973** [see *SYNTAGMATIC *a.*]. **1977** *Word 1972* XXVIII. 261 Examples of the alveolarization of the /t/ in word-initial position could be explained syntagmatically (i.e., it might be attributable to the presence of an alveolar consonant in the preceding word).

syntagmeme (sintæ·gmīm). *Linguistics.* [f. SYNTAGM(A + *-EME.] In tagmemics, a group of tagmemes of one structural level which represents a tagmeme of a higher level (see also quot. 1964).

1958 K. L. PIKE in *Jrnl. Amer. Linguistics* XXIV. 273/2 We have..abandoned the term grammeme and replaced it with Bloomfield's term 'tagmeme'. It also appears probable that we should replace the term 'uttereme' (for 'utterance-eme') with 'syntagmeme'. **1962** E. F. HADEN et al. *Resonance-Theory for Linguistics* iii. 41 This complex of slot and filler constitutes a syntagmeme. **1964** R. E. LONGACRE *Grammar Discovery Procedures* 17 Syntagmemes of one structural level manifest tagmemes of the next higher level; e.g., words manifest phrase level tagmemes. But a syntagmeme may manifest a tagmeme of another syntagmeme on the same level; e.g., one phrase may occur imbedded within another phrase... On occasion, a syntagmeme of a higher level may manifest a tagmeme of a lower level; e.g. a subordinate clause may occur within a phrase. **1971** *Language* XLVII. 739 Syntagmemes are charted for five levels, according to four features: internal constituents, prosody, nucleus and juncture.

syntax. 1. a. Delete † *Obs.* and add later examples.

1959 J. D. EVANS *Malta* ii. 67 The decoration [of certain pottery]..derives its general syntax fairly exactly and its patterns in a more general way from the repertoire of the preceding phases. **1965** *Listener* 9 Dec. 965/2 We have to work to reconcile the shiny shoe with the flat red floor or with the absurd loopy shapes of the legs, or the crushed, pulpy mask of the head. For not only is the syntax of the paint disconnected and inconsistent, but the degree of distortion is too. **1967** G. STEINER *Lang. & Silence* 380 A young East German might come to be more at home, in the syntax of his politics and feelings, in Peking or Albania than in Cologne.

2. a, b. Also with reference to programming languages.

1958 *Communications Assoc. Computing Machinery* Dec. 11 In the sequel explicit rules—and associated interpretations—will be given describing the syntax of the language. **1980** P. CRESS et al. *Structured Fortran with WATFIV-S* i. 8 WATFIV-S not only compiles the FORTRAN program, but detects errors in syntax while doing so. **1981** R. D. TENNENT *Princ. Programming Languages* ii. 25 An abstract syntax tells us what syntactic structures are available in a language, but does not specify which strings of characters are well-formed program texts, nor their phrase structures.

d. *transf.* in *Logic.* The order and arrangement of the words or symbols forming a logical sentence; the rules operating in formal systems. (See quots.)

1922 tr. *Wittgenstein's Tractatus* 59 The rules of logical syntax must follow of themselves, if we only know how every single sign signifies. **1937** A. SMEATON tr. *Carnap's Logical Syntax of Lang.* 1 By the logical syntax of a language, we mean the formal theory of the linguistic forms of that language—the systematic statement of the formal rules which govern it together with the development of the consequences which follow from these rules. *Ibid.* 2 Thus we are justified in designating as 'logical syntax' the system which comprises the rules of formation and transformation. **1937,** etc. [see *METALOGIC]. **1940** W. V. QUINE *Math. Logic.* vii. 286 Discourse which is 'formal' in this sense, and hence translatable into the notation just now described, is called metamathematics, formal syntax, or briefly syntax. **1955** A. N. PRIOR *Formal Logic* iii. 70 But as it happens—this can be shown from outside the system—no set of axioms and rules for a system containing its own syntax ever *is* 'complete'. **1979** J. A. ROBINSON *Logic: Form & Function* ii. 8 The predicate calculus has a simple, systematic basic *syntax*, whose principal feature is the characterization of the class of expressions that are its *formulas.*

3. *attrib.* and *Comb.*, as *syntax diagram, table*; *syntax-directed* adj.; **syntax language,** the language used to refer to the syntactical forms of an object language; a metalanguage.

1980 L. V. ATKINSON *Pascal Programming* i. 10 The syntax of a programming language can be conveniently illustrated by 'syntax diagrams'. **1961** *Communications Assoc. Computing Machinery* IV. 51 (*heading*) A syntax directed compiler for ALGOL 60. **1972** J. J. DONOVAN *Systems Programming* vii. 228 A syntax-directed compiler uses a data base containing the syntactical rules of a source language to parse..the source-language input. **1935** Syntax language [see *OBJECT LANGUAGE 1]. **1956** A. CHURCH *Introd. Math. Logic* 58 The meta-language used in order to study the logistic system..is called the syntax language. **1961** *Communications Assoc. Computing Machinery* IV. 55/1 The descriptions are added to the syntax tables used for the second phase, which invokes DIAGRAM to output the assembly language program.

syntaxic (sintæ·ksik), *a.* **1.** *Cryst.* [f. *SYNTAXIS 3 or *SYNTAXY + -IC.] = *SYNTAXIAL *a.*

1944 [see *SYNTAXIS 3]. **1972** *Acta Crystallogr.* A. XXVIII. 509/1 The syntaxic intergrowths of the rare-earth carbonates.

2. *Psychol.* [f. SYN- + TAX(IS + -IC.] A term orig. used by the American psychiatrist

H. S. Sullivan (1892–1949), to designate a mode of experiencing or communicating in which objectivity and the use of consensually validated symbols have replaced subjectivity. Cf. *PARATAXIC, *PROTOTAXIC *adjs.*

1945 P. MULLAHY in *Psychiatry* VIII. 185/2 Consensually validated symbol activity has more recently been called 'syntaxic' thinking by Sullivan. It involves an appeal to principles which are accepted as true by the hearer. *a* **1948** H. S. SULLIVAN *Interpersonal Theory of Psychiatry* (1955) ii. 28, I shall offer the thesis that these modes are primarily matters of 'inner' elaboration of events. The mode which is easiest to discuss is relatively uncommon—experience in the syntaxic mode. *Ibid.* xi. 183 Syntaxic symbols are best illustrated by words that have been consensually validated. **1969** A. NEEL *Theories of Psychol.* xx. 248 The appearance of the syntaxic or reality-oriented period was greatly aided by acquisition of language skills. **1972** L. SALTZMAN in Freedman & Kaplan *Interpreting Personality* vi. 176 Obviously, the capacity for syntaxic thinking requires comfortable amounts of self-esteem. **1975** *Psychol. Abstr.* LIV. 141/1 Sullivan's theory of syntaxic mode is compared with Peirce's concept of symbolic interaction.

syntaxis. Restrict † *Obs.* to sense in Dict. and add: Pl. **syntaxes** (-tæ·ksīz). **2.** *Geol.* An arrangement of fold axes or mountain ranges showing convergence towards a common point. [tr. G. *schaarung* (E. Suess).]

1909 H. B. C. & W. J. SOLLAS tr. *Suess's Face of Earth* IV. 289 In the direction of the syntaxis, i.e. towards the west, their strike bends back in an arc. **1933** W. H. BUCHER *Deformation of Earth's Crust* iv. 84 The abrupt deflections and the repeated syntaxes of the Alpine system of southern Europe and western Asia. **1952** *Q. Jrnl. Geol. Soc.* CVIII. 23 The Upper Assam valley..terminates in one of the most impressive examples of syntaxis which our fascinating world can offer.

3. *Cryst.* = *SYNTAXY.

1944 *Amer. Mineralogist* XXIX. 267 Ungemach..has introduced the term *syntaxie* to describe the coalescence of polyptic substances... The best English equivalent is probably 'syntaxis', the adjective being 'syntaxic'. **1951** *Phil. Mag.* XLII. 1020 The commonly observed coalescence or 'syntaxis'..of various types of carborundum.

syntaxy (si·ntæksi). *Cryst.* [ad. F. *syntaxie* (H. Ungemach 1935, in *Bull. de la Soc. Française de Minéral.* LVIII. 187): see SYNTAXIS and -Y³.] Crystal growth or intergrowth in which the new material has the same orientation as the parent, although it may differ chemically.

1952 M. I. GOLDMAN in *Mem. Geol. Soc. Amer.* L. 7 Although Royer uses 'epitaxie' to designate continuous crystallographic orientation between added material and its nucleus, etymologically it means merely 'orientation upon'. It is desirable to distinguish between the relation of added crystalline material with the same orientation as the nucleus, for which I propose *syntaxy* and *syntaxial*. **1953** G. & J. D. H. DONNAY in *Amer. Mineralogist* XXXVIII. 939 Ungemach's definition of syntaxic intergrowth seems to be unduly restrictive, as this kind of intergrowth is found to occur also with constituent substances that are chemically different. We therefore propose to abandon the condition of identity of chemical compositions. Henceforth we shall use the term *syntaxy* in this extended meaning. **1973** *Jrnl. Solid State Chem.* VI. 396 Ordered syntaxy and polytypism..give a regular repetition of structural or chemical elements over very long crystalline distances. **1975** *Amer. Mineralogist* LX. 351 Intimate syntaxy between parisite, synchisite, roentgenite, and bastnaesite was quite commonly observed even on a very fine scale.

Hence **synta·xial** *a.*; **synta·xially** *adv.*

1952 Syntaxial [see *SYNTAXY]. **1958** *Liverpool & Manch. Geol. Jrnl.* II. 15 A mosaic of grains can grow by the deposition of material in lattice-continuity with, or syntaxially with..pre-existing free crystal faces. *Ibid.* 27 The syntaxial rim resembles superficially a cement rim. **1972** H. BLATT et al. *Origin Sedimentary Rocks* xiii. 463 Syntaxial overgrowths are large crystals of calcite that have grown in optical continuity with original single crystal grains.

syntectonic to **synteny**: see *SYN-¹ 1.

syntexis (sinte·ksis). *Petrol.* [a. Gr. σύντηξις, f. συντήκειν to fuse together, f. τήκειν to melt: see SYN-.] The alteration of magma by the melting or assimilation of another rock.

1911 F. LOEWINSON-LESSING in *Geol. Mag.* VIII. 295 When the re-melted portion of the crust is composed of different rocks, eruptive, or sedimentary,..the process is rather a 'syntexis', as I have called it, an assimilation which is followed by liquation and differentiation. **1932** F. F. GROUT *Petrogr. & Petrol.* III. 230 Syntexis has been appealed to in explaining how the more siliceous and the more alkalic rock clans can be derived from primary basaltic magma. **1966** *McGraw-Hill Encycl. Sci. & Technol.* X. 84/1 In some instances such endomorphic effects are sufficiently intensive to result in modification of the composition of the magma (syntexis).

synth (sinþ), colloq. abbrev. of *SYNTHESIZER 2 (in sense of musical instrument).

1976 *Liverpool Echo* 24 Nov. 5/4 (Advt.), Crumar String Synth, only one year old, perfect working order, cost nearly £500, accept £270 o.n.o. **1977** *Sounds* 9 July 31/6 They range from a scat slant on 'I Got The Music In Me' through Inter City Disco 'Touch Me Up' to the title cut—a seven minute mutha with heavy southern overtones; brassy, rather stringy, not a synth in sight. **1983** *Yellow Advertiser* (Basildon) 4 Mar. 14/3 Singer-songwriters or synth bands.

synthalin (si·nþălin). *Pharm.* [a. G. *synthalin* (E. Frank et al. 1926, in *Klin. Wochenschr.* 5 Nov. 2101/1), f. *synth-etisch* SYNTHETIC *a.* + *-a-* + *insu-lin* *INSULIN.] A synthetic but toxic aliphatic diguanidine which has the hypoglycæmic effect of insulin when taken orally; decamethylene-diguanidine, $H_2N\cdot C(NH)\cdot NH\cdot (CH_2)_{10}\cdot NH\cdot C(NH)\cdot NH_2$; also called *synthalin A*; *synthalin B*, an analogous compound in which $—(CH_2)_{10}—$ is replaced by $—(CH_2)_{12}—$.

1927 *Chem. Abstr.* XXI. 772 To produce a molecule of min. toxicity and max. insulin activity, further changes were made in the mol...which resulted finally in a deriv. that is called Synthalin. **1936** HILL & HOWITT *Insulin* ix. 190 The decided differences between the action of both synthalin and synthalin-B and insulin render even these substances doubtful as effective substitutes for the hormone. **1952, 1961** [see *DIGUANIDINE]. **1980** J. CROSSLAND *Lewis's Pharmacol.* (ed. 5) lvi. 878/1 In the early 1920's..it was found that a number of aliphatic diguanidines such as the Synthalins A and B..produced hypoglycaemia in man.

synthase (si·nþēiz). *Biochem.* [f. SYNTH(ESIS + *-ASE.] Any enzyme that catalyses the addition of a group to carbon atoms joined by a double bond, or the converse reaction; also, a synthetase.

1954 COHEN & HIRSCH in *Jrnl. Bacteriol.* LXVII. 182/2 This paper describes an enzyme system synthesizing threonine from homoserine; we have called it threonine synthase. **1961** *Rep. Commission on Enzymes* v. 37 Enzymes removing groups from substrates non-hydrolytically, leaving double bonds (or adding groups to double bonds) will be called 'lyases'... 'Synthetase' will not be used for any enzymes in this class; where it has been customary, 'synthase' will be used instead. **1976** *Ann. Rev. Microbiol.* XXX. 212 An alternate view is that cyst-specific RNA synthesis during encystment is not necessary for the formation of cellulose synthase. **1979** *Science* 7 Dec. 1149/3 The ATP synthase is a chemiosmotic membrane-located reversible ATPase.

synthesis. Add: **1. b.** In philosophical systems influenced by Hegelian ideas, the final stage of a triadic progression in which an idea is proposed, then negated, and finally transcended by a new idea that resolves the conflict between the first and its negation.

The process is often represented as that of thesis, antithesis, and synthesis, although the terms are not Hegel's. The term is freq. used in relation to the political philosophy of Marx, where this process is seen as exemplified in the history of man's social development (see *dialectical materialism* s.v. *DIALECTICAL *a.* 1 b).

1896 J. MCTAGGART *Stud. in Hegelian Dialectic* i. 2 This idea of the synthesis of opposites is perhaps the most characteristic in the whole of Hegel's system. It is certainly one of the most difficult to explain. **1904** N. I. STONE tr. *Marx's Introd. Critique Pol. Econ.* 288 The two systems by mutually modifying each other may result in something new, a synthesis (which partly resulted from the Germanic conquests). In all of these conquests the method of production..determines the nature of the new distribution which comes into play. **1936** S. HOOK *From Hegel to Marx* i. 68 A dialectical synthesis is all this and more. Thesis and antithesis are resolved in such a way that..aspects of each are retained or *conserved* in every new whole or situation; and are reinterpreted or *elevated*. *Ibid.*, For Marx..the manner of synthesis depends..upon the shifts and realignments of human interests in time. **1958** P. HEATH tr. *Wetter's Dialectical Materialism* I. i. 4 This third phase then figures in turn as the first step in a new dialectical process, leading to a new synthesis. **1963** F. J. COPLESTON *Hist. Philos.* VII. ix. 177 We have used the word 'synthesis' for the moment of identity-in-difference in the dialectical advance. But..the terms 'thesis', 'antithesis' and 'synthesis' are more characteristic of Fichte than of Hegel. **1978** P. S. FALLA tr. *Kolakowski's Main Currents Marxism* I. vii. 152 As private property develops it necessarily creates its own antagonist; this negative force is itself dehumanized, and as its dehumanization progresses it becomes the precondition of a synthesis that will abolish the existing opposition together with both its terms.

8. Special Comb.: **synthesis gas**, a gas used as a feedstock in the industrial synthesis of a chemical, *esp.* a mixture of hydrogen and carbon monoxide.

1941 *Thorpe's Dict. Appl. Chem.* (ed. 4) V. 503/1 Synthesis Gas.—There is required for the synthesis of methanol or the Fischer synthesis of hydrocarbons, a gas in which the ratio of carbon monoxide to hydrogen is 1:2. The ratio of CO/H_2 in normal blue water-gas is 1:1·25. **1965** M. SITTIG *Nitrogen in Industry* ii. 31 Synthesis gas, as the term is used here, is the gaseous mixture of one part nitrogen and three parts hydrogen used as a feed material for ammonia manufacture. **1972** *Sci. Amer.* Oct. 28/1 Lurgi has built more than 50 units to provide town gas (for domestic use) or synthesis gas (for making gasoline). **1980** *Prospects for Petrochemicals in W. Europe* (Shell Internat. Petroleum Co.) 8 A more speculative, but nonetheless plausible, prospect..would be the development of a petrochemicals industry based on synthesis gas.

synthesizer. Add: **1.** (Example in sense b of the vb.)

1980 *Sci. Amer.* Apr. 27/1 The fibrous texture of jade may daunt the synthesizers.

2. *spec.* in *Electronics*, one of various types of instrument for generating and combining signals of different frequencies; esp. a computerized instrument used to create music electronically.

1909 [in Dict.]. **1939** H. DUDLEY *U.S. Patent 2,151,091* 21 Mar. 13/2 Control currents are then passed to the speech synthesizer. *Ibid.*, In the synthesizer described in detail above, the element equivalent to the vocal system is entirely electrical. **1943** H. J. FINDEN in *Jrnl. Inst. Electr. Engineers* XC. III. 165 (*heading*) The frequency synthesizer. *Ibid.* 167/2 There is a demand for a precise frequency generator which will give any desired frequency with a pure output. The frequency synthesizer is an attempt to realise this. **1947** *Jrnl. Appl. Physics* July 601 An electronic synthesizer is described for determination of atomic positions in crystals. **1957** *Sat. Rev.* (U.S.) 26 Jan. 56/2 The American school has not yet, so far as I know, made use of the RCA Electronic Music Synthesizer. *Ibid.* 56/3 The perforated tape operates the music synthesizer in much the same way that a music roll 'plays' a player piano. **1958** E. FISCHER-JØRGENSEN in Saporta & Bastian *Psycholinguistics* (1961) 117/2 Of particular interest to the linguist are the various speech *synthesizers* which have been built recently. **1965** *Wireless World* July 62 (Advt.), The new range of MST transistorized receivers uses synthesizers to provide accurate selection of 250,000 frequencies. **1969,** etc. [see *MOOG]. **1973** *Melody Maker* 25 Aug. 27 Baker (electronics, bass) came to London from Australia. He's been working with electronics for ten years, concentrating on solo synthesiser performances. **1975** *New Yorker* 5 May 45/1 The synthesizer can produce a ceaseless kaleidoscope of shapes and colors on the screen. **1981** *Oxford Times* 20 Feb. 13/1 He plays acoustic piano as well as imitating steel drums on his synthesiser.

synthetase (si·nþĕtēiz). *Biochem.* [f. SYNTHET(IC *a.* + *-ASE.] = *LIGASE; also, a synthase.

1947 COHEN & MCGILVERY in *Jrnl. Biol. Chem.* CLXXI. 132 We wish to suggest the term 'synthetase' for those enzymes creating a new molecule by the elimination of water between two substrate molecules, excluding the formation of phosphote esters and anhydrides. **1961** [see *LIGASE]. **1961** [see *SYNTHASE]. **1972** *Nature* 15 Dec. 377/1 Aspirin and aspirin-like drugs inhibit..the synthetase which synthesizes prostaglandins from the unsaturated fatty acid, arachidonic acid. **1979** *Sci. Amer.* May 78/2 Interferon also induces the manufacture of a second enzyme, a synthetase that catalyzes the polymerization of adenine nucleotides into a long chain of adenine units called 2,5-oligoadenylic acid.

synthetic, *a.* Add: **A.** *adj.* **2. b.** Of a substance: made by chemical synthesis in imitation of a natural product (cf. *SYN-²). Also, esp. of a man-made fibre or fabric: made from synthetic materials rather than natural ones (cf. *MAN-MADE *a.*).

1874 *Chem. News* 12 June 265/1 (*heading*) Synthetic cymol obtained from normal bromide of propyl and crystalline bromtoluol. **1907** *Chem. Abstr.* I. 1179 (*heading*) Synthetic resins. **1907** *Nature* 25 Apr. 614/2 Since 'synthetic' indigo was put upon the market in 1897, some uncertainty has existed regarding its tinctorial value as compared with the natural dyestuff. **1909,** etc. [see *RESIN *sb.* 2*]. **1932** B. HEDWORTH *Foolish Pelican* II. iv. 136 She had discovered..that synthetic stockings wore better than pure silk. **1941** [see *RUBBER *sb.*¹ II a]. **1946** A. J. HALL *Stand. Handbk. Textiles* i. 66 The du Pont company..commenced the manufacture of a synthetic fibre which has since become known..as nylon. **1955** J. G. DAVIS *Dict. Dairying* (ed. 2) 1005 Synthetic or imitation cream. **1955, 1966** [see *MAN-MADE *a.*]. **1973** *Materials & Technol.* VI. 485 The cleaning of man-made fibres is usually a relatively simple operation which involves a treatment with a mild soap or a synthetic detergent solution. **1983** *Sci. Amer.* Apr. 73/3 In the 19th century, before the boom in organic chemistry that followed the discovery of synthetic dyes, many prominent chemists had undertaken analyses of inorganic natural substances.

c. *fig.* Artificial, imitation, invented.

1930 *Daily Express* 16 Oct. 10/5 With the synthetic idiot, Harpo, you must have a vein of the ridiculous in your laughter gland if boredom is to be kept at bay. **1932** *Sun* (Baltimore) 29 Aug. 8/2 A printing press upon which were struck off bogus service certificates for 'synthetic veterans'. **1934** *Amer. Speech* IX. 101/2 Even when launched in a preliminary fashion, with say fifty or a hundred users, the synthetic language will not grow of itself. **1948** 'N. SHUTE' *No Highway* iv. 92 The synthetic, phoney film business. **1948** *Newsweek* 10 May 34/2 He has been in London long enough to achieve a synthetic British appearance. **1949** *Hansard Commons* 12 Dec. 2417, I have seldom heard such an outburst of indignation... It seemed to me a little synthetic. **1976** E. FROMM *To have or to Be?* (1979) II. iv. 92 The learned, synthetic smile of the marketplace.

d. *Aeronaut.* Of training, exercises, etc.: simulating on the ground what is performed in the air; also *ellipt.* Similarly of equipment used in such training.

1942 *Tee Emm* (Air Ministry) II. 93 All sorts of gadgets and synthetic devices are used..from the cine-film assessor..to the Fisher trainer. **1944** *Horizon* Jan. 49 We are now in the middle of 'synthetic'—i.e. doing things on the ground as they will be done from the air. **1948** *Hansard Commons* 15 Mar. 1808 If people can go for an hour or two in the evenings for synthetic training. **1949** *Aircraft Engin.* Apr. 122/2 There is ample mathematical and electric knowledge in existence to-day to construct 'synthetic aircraft' to simulate the flight of any proposed aircraft from the design data. **1956** *U.S. Air Force Dict.* 504/2 *Synthetic*,..artificial or simulated, as in *synthetic combat mission, synthetic training device*, etc. **1976** R.

HURST *Pilot Error* 260 Complementary process of behavioural engineering and the selection and training of pilots..Performance prediction. Synthetic flight training. Performance assessment.

6. (Earlier example.)

1816 P. DUPONCEAU in *Trans. Hist. & Lit. Comm. Amer. Philos. Soc.* (1819) I. 401 The third class [of languages] would..be that in which the principal parts of speech are formed by a synthetical operation of the mind, and in which several ideas are frequently expressed by one word. Such are what are called the Oriental languages, with the Latin, Greek, Slavonic, and others of the same description. These I would call *synthetic*.

9. Special collocations: *synthetic aperture*, 'a simulated aperture obtained by moving an aerial or detector transversely during reception so as to increase its effective length; usu. *attrib.*, esp. designating radar employing this; *Synthetic Cubism*, that type of Cubism which involves the combination or reorganization of forms, rather than their analysis (see *CUBISM); hence *Synthetic Cubist* adj.

1962 *IRE Trans. Military Electronics* VI. 111 (*heading*) Some early developments in synthetic aperture radar systems. *Ibid.* 113/2 Differences between physical and synthetic apertures. **1977** *Sci. Amer.* Oct. 89/1 Since resolution is proportional to the length of the antenna but inversely proportional to the range, for synthetic-aperture radar the two effects compensate for each other... Synthetic-aperture radar thus makes it possible to obtain high-resolution images of terrain many miles away. **1979** *McGraw-Hill Yearbk. Sci. & Technol.* 224/2 Holography has also been applied, in the form of synthetic-aperture techniques, to the B-scan acoustic reflection systems to provide greater detail in the body areas located near the acoustic transducer. **1947** D. COOPER tr. *Kahnweiler's Juan Gris* II. vi. 89 Synthetic Cubism was built on a lasting foundation. Gris..finally gave up presenting the beholder with a great variety of information..about the objects which he displayed. He now offered a *synthesis*: that is to say, he packed his knowledge into one significant form, an emblem. **1981** *Times Lit. Suppl.* 9 Jan. 24/3 When constructed sculpture came, along with Synthetic Cubism in 1912, it did so with suddenness, *éclat*, and in quantity. *Ibid.* 24/4 It is often forgotten that Synthetic Cubist space without collage was potentially the most flexible and exciting pictorial space since the Baroque.

B. *sb.* A product obtained by artificial synthesis rather than from natural sources; esp. a synthetic fibre or fabric. Chiefly *pl.*

1934 in WEBSTER. **1940** *New Statesman* 16 Mar. 361/1 The scientists could see in such synthetics [*sc.* plastics].. the threat of maladjustments in industry. **1943** *Sun* (Baltimore) 10 Feb. 4/2 The company built the new plant at its own expense in an effort to increase supplies of the badly needed synthetic. **1951** P. Z. BEDOUKIAN (*title*) Perfumery synthetics and isolates. **1957** *Times* 12 Nov. (Canada Suppl.) p. v/3 Trapping becomes less and less profitable as synthetics displace furs. **1972** D. BLOODWORTH *Any Number can Play* ii. 10 Lightweight suits cut from one of those shiny Japanese synthetics. **1982** *Sunday Times* 9 May 54/5 There was a sudden scramble to get out of synthetics—those expensive 'fuels of the future'.

synthetical, *a.* **3.** (Earlier examples.)

1796 F. A. NITSCH *Gen. View Kant's Princ. concerning Man* 76 This act may be called a synthetical act of the reproductive imagination. *Ibid.* 89 A synthetical judgment *à priori*.

synthol (si·nþǫl). [a. G. *synthol* (Fischer & Tropsch 1923, in *Brennstoff-Chem.* IV. 281/1), f. *synth-etisch* SYNTHETIC *a.*: see -OL.] (See quot. 1938.)

1924 *Chem. Abstr.* XVIII. 459 The preparation of synthetic oil mixtures (synthol) from carbon monoxide and hydrogen. **1926** J. JOYCE *Let.* 5 Mar. (1966) III. 138 He is now using some kind of new chemical stimulant (not chemical but acting by purely physical means, recently discovered here [in France], I understand, synthol for massaging the temples and brow). **1938** *Thorpe's Dict. Appl. Chem.* (ed. 4) II. 350/2 Using mixtures of carbon monoxide with excess hydrogen..Fischer..obtained a mixture which he termed 'Synthol', consisting of alcohols.., ketones, aldehydes, acids.., and various esters. *Ibid.* 425/2 If, instead of zinc-chromium oxides, an alkalised iron catalyst is employed, the liquid product, 'synthol', obtained is a mixture of alcohols, ketones and hydrocarbons containing from 2 to about 8 carbon atoms per molecule.

synthon (si·nþǫn). *Chem.* [f. SYNTH(ETIC *a.* + I)ON; cf. *-ON[1].] A constituent part of a molecule to be synthesized which readily lends itself to an operation of synthesis.

1967 E. J. COREY in *Pure & Appl. Chem.* XIV. 22 The term 'synthon' is suggested [for such units]. These are defined as structural units within a molecule which are related to possible synthetic operations. **1977** *Jrnl. Chem. Soc.: Chem. Communications* 497 (*heading*) A synthon for epoxyolefin cyclisation. **1980** *Jrnl. Amer. Chem. Soc.* CII. 5979/1 (*heading*) Allyl sulfones as synthons for 1,1- and 1,3-dipoles via organopalladium chemistry.

syntone[2] (si·ntōun). *Psychiatry.* [Back-formation from *SYNTONIC *a.*[2] 2.] A person having a syntonic temperament.

1940 J. BOWLBY *Personality Types & Mental Illness* ii. 23 Syntones therefore are far from having the 'frank open personalities' commonly attributed to them.

syntonic, *a.*[1] Add: *syntonic comma* (examples).

1944 W. APEL *Harvard Dict. Mus.* (1946) 166/2 The *Didymic* (Didymos, Greek theorist, b. 63 B.C.) or *syntonic comma* which indicates the difference between E as the fourth tone of the circle of fifths..and the E of just intonation. **1954** *Grove's Dict. Mus.* (ed. 5) IV. 523/1 The comma of Didymus (commonly called a *comma* without qualification, and sometimes a syntonic comma). **1979** *Early Music* Apr. 239/2 The major third produced by tuning four successive perfect fifths..is wider than the pure interval..by a syntonic comma.

syntonic, *a.*[2] Restrict *Electr.* to sense in Dict. and add: **2.** *Psychiatry.* [f. *SYNTONY 2 + -IC.] Denoting the responsive, lively type of temperament which is liable to manic-depressive psychosis.

1925 A. A. BRILL in *Amer. Jrnl. Psychiatry* LXXI. 592 Bleuler proposed for this reaction the name syntonic. *Syntonic* not only signifies 'equally toned' but also means to be 'attuned' and in 'harmony'... If a person is neither exclusively schizoid, nor entirely syntonic, one can only say that he is preponderatingly schizoid or preponderatingly syntonic... Thus, if a person shows a manic attack, it means that the syntonic components predominate qualitatively and quantitatively to a morbid degree. **1927** [see *CYCLOID *sb.* 3]. **1933** *Brit. Jrnl. Psychol.* July 30 Our results would indicate that the connection of cyclothyme or syntonic type with low perseveration..has no experimental support. **1948** NOYES & KOLB *Mod. Clinical Psychiatry* (ed. 3) vi. 98 Bleuler preferred the term 'syntonic' to Kretschmer's 'cycloid' to describe a personality tendency opposed in characteristics to the schizoid. **1969** H. J. & S. B. G. EYSENCK *Personality Structure & Measurement* iv. 23 The large number of persons in the centre of the distribution he would call *syntonic* if they were on the cyclothymic side.

syntonically *adv.* (example in sense *2 of the adj.).

1925 A. A. BRILL in *Amer. Jrnl. Psychiatry* LXXXI. 592 The affectivity of the person reacting for the most part syntonically harmonizes with the people of his environment.

syntony. Restrict *Electr.* to sense in Dict. and add: **2.** *Psychiatry.* [ad. G. *syntonie* (E. Bleuler 1922, in *Zeitschr. f. d. gesamte Neurol. u. Psychiatrie* LXXVIII. 373).] A syntonic state or condition (see *SYNTONIC *a.*[2] 2).

1925 A. A. BRILL in *Amer. Jrnl. Psychiatry* 598 Translating..syntony into Freudian terms we can say that every transference neurotic has also a fragment of narcistic [*sic*] libido.

3. *transf.* and *fig.*

1958 F. BERRY *Poets' Gram.* ii. 20 [The Towneley pageant] is not a work wherein 'anachronisms' occur but a poetic drama where syntony, or multiplicity of tenses running together, is basic to its conception. **1973** D MATIAS tr. C. Metz in *Screen* Spring/Summer 55 Pierre Schaeffer's specific propositions towards a classification of the possible interactions between music and image into four categories ('masks', 'opposition', 'synchronism', 'syntony'.) **1978** J. WAINWRIGHT *Jury People* l. 177 There was a link. A basic syntony which each felt for the other. They each recognised in the other a man proud of his own particular skill.

syntrophy (si·ntrŏfi). *Biol.* [ad. G. *syntrophie* (E. Wasmann 1897, in *Zool. Anz.* XX. 173), f. Gr. συν- SYN- + τροφή nourishment.] The continuing relationship between the individuals of two different species or strains of organisms in which one, or more usually both, benefit nutritionally from the presence of the other; *spec.* that between two bacterial strains which are dependent on each other for their proliferation. Also **sy·ntrophism**, in the same sense. Hence **syntro·phic** *a.*

1897 *Jrnl. R. Microsc. Soc.* 283 Wasmann also speaks of the 'syntrophy' of *Lælaps oophilus* Moniez, [a mite] which occurs freely on the surface of the eggs of ants.., but without doing them any damage, apparently depending on the salivary secretion of the ants, which are always licking their eggs. **1946** *Jrnl. Bacteriol.* LII. 503/2 Syntrophism. This is defined as the growth of two distinct biochemical mutants in mixed culture as a result of the ability of each strain to synthesize the growth factor required by the other... Mutants blocked at different steps in the synthesis of the same factor show syntrophism. **1950** *Experientia* VI. 42/2 Other possible explanations of the requirement of intermediate cultivation in the penicillin method include segregation of mutant and non-mutant nuclei from a multinucleate cell, and a syntrophic effect of the non-viable irradiated bacteria, which would promote sterilization of mutants by penicillin. **1971** M. ALEXANDER *Microbiol. Ecol.* x. 242 Mutual feeding by dissimilar auxotrophs is termed syntrophism, a relationship in which two or possibly more populations are able to develop in nutrient-deficient circumstances not suitable for the proliferation, or allowing for the poor development at best, of either. *Ibid.* 243 The extensive distribution of bacteria both exporting and importing growth factors suggests a widespread occurrence of syntrophy in nature.

synusia (sin[1]ū·siă). *Ecol.* Pl **-iae.** [mod.L., ad. G. *synusie* (H. Gams 1918, in *Viertel-jahrsschr. der Naturforsch. Ges. in Zürich* LXIII. 428), f. Gr. συνουσία society, company.] A group of organisms (usu. plants) of one or more species which have similar life-forms, occupy the same ecological niche, and play a similar role in the community which they form. Also **synu·sium.**

1924 *Jrnl. Ecol.* XII. 15 An aggregation of plants which belong to the same 'life-form' and make similar demands upon a similar habitat constitutes Gams' conception of a synusium. **1926** TANSLEY & CHIPP *Study of Vegetation* ii. 25 The individuals composing a synusia may belong not only to different species but to different families or even different higher groups. **1930** *Svensk Bot. Tidskrift* XXIV. 496 The method of dividing each sociation into its elementary one-layered units, or synusiae, and grouping the synusiae of each layer independently of those of the other layers to synusiae of higher rank. **1932** FULLER & CONARD tr. *Braun-Blanquet's Plant Sociol.* xii. 302 A cover of crustose lichens, a pure carpet of moss or of dwarf shrubs, the tree layer of a fir stand are ecological synusiae. **1960** [see *NICHE *sb.* 3 c]. **1965** B. E. FREEMAN tr. *Vandel's Biospeleology* xvii. 285 Each biotope contains an animal population which is called the synusium. **1975** T. C. WHITMORE *Trop. Rain Forests Far East* ii. 12 Species of very diverse taxonomic affinity make up the synusiae.

syph (sif). *slang.* Also **siph.** Abbrev. of SYPHILIS. Also with def. article. Cf. *SIFF.

1914 *Dialect Notes* IV. 113 *Syph, abbrev.*, syphilis. **1925** *Amer. Speech* I. 24/2 For 'syphilis', 'pox' was used wiedly many years ago, but has given place more recently to the simple abbreviation 'syph'. **1930** J. DOS PASSOS *42nd Parallel* I. 108 He got the siph off 'n her. **1947** *Horizon* Sept. 202 We're going to get the syph. **1960** D. LYTTON *Goddam White Man* i. 15 Everybody dies of the cough... Or you get syph as well... They say you scream like a hound when you have the syph and the cough together. **1969** P. ROTH *Portnoy's Complaint* 129 I'll come down with the syph from just touching the ticket. **1980** 'D. KAVANAGH' *Duffy* viii. 149 He goes down to the clinic..and finds he's got the worst case of syph they've seen in years.

syphilide. (Earlier example.)

1829 *Glasgow Med. Jrnl.* II. 327 By syphilide is understood every eruption produced on the skin, by the action of the syphilitic virus.

syphilo-. Add: **syphilo·logy**, the study of syphilis; hence **syphilolo·gic, -lo·gical** *adjs.*; **syphilo·logist**, a specialist in syphilology.

1944 J. H. STOKES et al. *Mod. Clin. Syphilol.* (ed. 3) p. iii, The enormous increase in syphilologic knowledge.., and the earthquake of penicillin have made the revising of a book at this moment a hazardous undertaking. **1908** E. L. KEYES *Syphilis* p. v, The facts upon which the volume rests are the classified cases from the private office books covering forty years of continuous work by myself along syphilological lines. **1890** *Lancet* 13 Dec. 1307/1 The Russian Government has appointed a committee, consisting of Professor Tarnovski and other syphilologists. **1910** *Practitioner* Feb. 231 Few..syphilologists..would now venture to give an opinion on a ..lesion without previously examining a scraping. **1890** WEBSTER, Syphilology. **1893** P. A. MORROW et al. (*title*) A system of genito-urinary diseases, syphilology and dermatology. **1969** J. L. SMITH *Spirochetes in Late Seronegative Syphilis* ii. 9/2 Many practitioners are not aware of even the basic doctrines of classic syphilology.

syreen, var. *SIREEN.

Syrette (sire·t). Also **syrette.** [f. SYR(INGE *sb.* + -ETTE.] The proprietary name of a disposable injection unit, comprising a collapsible tube with an attached hypodermic needle and a single dose of a drug (esp. morphine).

1941 *Official Gaz.* (U.S. Patent Office) 9 Sept. 280/2 E. R. Squibb & Sons, New York, N.Y. Filed July 29, 1939. Syrette for injection units containing narcotic, hypnotic, sedative, analgesic, and vasoconstrictive preparations. **1947** *Sun* (Baltimore) 7 June 5/5 Morphine-containing Syrettes, used by the armed forces during the war to relieve wounded men, are finding their way into illegal narcotic channels. **1953** *Trade Marks Jrnl.* 12 Aug. 718/2 *Syrette*... Pharmaceutical preparations in collapsible tubes fitted with a hypodermic needle. **1953** [see *SHOOT *v.* 23 h]. **1962** L. DEIGHTON *Ipcress File* vi. 40 Dalby put the used morphia syrette tube into a matchbox. **1976** *Interdisciplinary Sci. Rev.* I. 179/1 It would be simple to mass-produce disposable syrettes containing one unit of the anti-soma.

Syrian, var. *ZYRIAN *sb.* and *a.* **Syrianian,** var. *SIRYENIAN *sb.* and *a.*

syringa. Add: Also = LILAC 1 a, b. (Later examples.)

1946 T. C. MANSFIELD *Shrubs* 244 Syringa is the botanical name for Lilac. **1974** R. L. FOX *Variations on Garden* 75 The old still try and call it [*sc.* philadelphus] *Syringa* which, of course, is the proper name for lilac.

syringe, *sb.* Add: **3. syringe passage** a technique for maintaining a strain of micro-organisms or parasitic protozoans by transferring them through generations of laboratory animals by inoculation with a syringe; also (with hyphen) as *v. trans.*, to subject to this technique; **syringe-passaged** *ppl. a.*

1946 *Ann. Trop. Med. & Parasitol.* XL. 270 All the strains [of *Trypanosoma*] having been maintained by syringe passage through small laboratory animals. **1947** *Ibid.* XLI. 29 It is shown from the literature that a strain which is syringe-passaged through mice gradually increases in its sensitivity to arsenicals. **1970** P. J. WALKER in H. W. Mulligan *African Trypanosomiases* v. 89 Syringe passage has certain inherent defects. **1980** *Jrnl. Infection* II. 106 They [*sc.* trypanosomes] had been syringe-passaged from rodent to rodent in the laboratory. **1947**

Ann. Trop. Med. & Parasitol. XLI. 27 All the trypanosomes present in the syringe-passaged strain were the long heterozygous form of *T[rypanosoma] rhodesiense.* **1971** P. C. C. GARNHAM *Progr. Parasitol.* iii. 28 Such trypanosomes lose their polymorphic morphology, just as they do in syringe-passaged strains in the laboratory.

syringo-. Add: **syringobu·lbia,** [L. *bulbus* onion, bulb], the formation of abnormal cavities in the medulla oblongata of the brain (usu. extensions of those of syringomyelia), resulting in symptoms such as paralysis of the palate, pharynx, and larynx.

1908 *Jrnl. Med. Res.* XVIII. 127 The pathological findings have an important bearing upon the explanation of the bulbar symptoms in cases of syringomyelia and syringobulbia. **1964** S. DUKE-ELDER *Parsons' Dis. Eye* (ed. 14) 545 In syringomyelia cavities form around which secondary gliosis develops in the cervical and upper dorsal cord; in syringobulbia the process extends up to the medulla. **1975** *Neurology* XXV. 875/1 Syringobulbia is an uncommon lesion of the central nervous system, and is particularly rare in children.

Syrjenian, var. *SIRYENIAN *sb.* and *a.*

Syro-. Add: *Syro-Arabian* (earlier examples), *-Chaldaic* (earlier examples), *-Egyptian, -Hittite, -Palestinian.*

1841 J. C. PRICHARD *Res. Physical Hist. Man* (ed. 3) III. 6 The name of Syro-Arabians, formed on the same principle as the now generally admitted term of Indo-Europeans, would be a much more suitable expression. *Ibid.*, The Syro-Arabian tribes lost, at an early period, their ascendancy among the civilized nations of the world. **1835** *Q. Rev.* Sept. 307 A remarkable Syro-Chaldaic lectionarium in the Vatican library. **1836** N. WISEMAN *Lect. Doctr. Cath. Ch.* II. xiv. 152 In Syro-Chaldaic there is no expression for to accuse or calumniate. **1964** P. F. ANSON *Bishops at Large* vii. 217 Rites and ceremonies were performed like those of the Syro-Egyptian church. **1931** *Times Lit. Suppl.* 5 Mar. 176/2 Syro-Hittite seals. **1962** D. HARDEN *Phoenicians* xiii. 180 Those cylinder-seals and stamp-seals often termed Syro-Hittite, whose motifs and style are so obviously derived from those of Assyria and Babylonia. **1939** L. H. GRAY *Foundations of Lang.* 364 [Arabic] was divided into several dialects, of which only that of Mekkah has survived, this being the parent of a large number of modern vernaculars, notably Arabian.., Irāqian.., Syro-Palestinian.., Egyptian [etc.]. **1976** *Times* 31 Jan. 13/2 Israeli intervention?.. The mere threat of it headed off Syro-Palestinian intervention in the Jordanian civil war of 1970.

syrup, *sb.* Add: **2.** *syrup of violets* (later example); **syrup of figs,** an aperient prepared from dried figs, usu. with senna and carminatives.

1849 J. RUSKIN *Diary* Apr. in M. Lutyens *Ruskins & Grays* (1972) xxi. 188 The landlady, who noticed my illness, made me some syrup of violets. **1897** *Sears, Roebuck Catal.* 29/2 Sears' fig laxative (a pleasant syrup of figs for constipation.) **1939** A. HUXLEY *After Many a Summer* II. iii. 206 The Baby was acting strange... Acting for all the world like one of those advertisements for Sal Hepatica or California Syrup of Figs. **1981** T. BARLING *Bikini Red North* i. 29 A special diet of laxative chocolate... And syrup of figs.

Syryane, Syryen, varr. *ZYRIAN *sb.* and *a.*
Syryenian, var. *SIRYENIAN *sb.* and *a.*

sysertskite (si·sǝɹtskǝit). *Min.* Also **sis(s)erskite.** [ad. G. *sisserskit* (W. von Haidinger *Handb. der bestimmenden Min.* (1845) IV. 558), f. *Sysert*, name of a city near Sverdlovsk in Russia: see -ITE[1].] A native alloy of osmium and iridium; iridosmine; (see also quots.).

1850 J. D. DANA *Syst. Min.* (ed. 3) 547 At a high temperature the Sisserskite gives out osmium, but undergoes no further change. **1938** *Mineral. Abstr.* VII. 162 The natural alloys are divided into three groups: (1) iridium group with 0–35% Os, cubic; (2) nevyanskite with 35–50% Os; (3) sysertskite with 50–70% Os. **1963** [see *NEVYANSKITE]. **1965** G. J. WILLIAMS *Econ. Geol. N.Z.* x. 155/1 In the other [fraction] consisting of flattened grains of light steel-grey colour, Os was found in excess of Ir, and the Ru proportion is higher—siserskite or ruthenian siserskite. **1973** S. E. LIVINGSTONE in J. C. Bailar et al. *Comprehensive Inorg. Chem.* III. xliii. 1165 Alloys of osmium and iridium occur in placer deposits. These are known as osmiridium or sysertskite—with less than 60% (usually *ca.* 50%) iridium and *ca.* 35% osmium—and iridosmium or nevyanskite—with over 60% (usually *ca.* 70%) iridium and *ca.* 20% osmium.

systatic, *a.* (*sb.*) **3.** For *rare*⁻⁰ read *rare* and add examples.

1947 G. EVERY *Byzantine Patriarchate* xiii. 177 The synod decided to ask the Pope for a 'systatic letter'. **1955** S. RUNCIMAN *Eastern Schism* ii. 32 His successor, Sergius IV, sent a Systatic Letter to Constantinople.

system. Also with pronunc. (si·stĕm).
I. 1. c. With *the*: (*a*) The prevailing political, economic, or social order, esp. regarded as oppressive; the Establishment; any impersonal, restrictive organization. Freq. with capital initial.

1806 C. WILMOT *Let* 23 Mar. in Londonderry & Hyde *Russ. Jrnls.* (1934) II. 223 Dozens of Slaves are waiting.. to greet the Princess... Her Lenity makes their Lot better perhaps than that of others, but that's saying very little for the System. **1855** *Mechanics' Mag.* LXIII. 542 (*heading*) It is the system. *Ibid.*, I have not heard anything of it from that day to this, and must therefore infer that his Lordship was *instigated* by the 'system'. **1906** U. SINCLAIR *Jungle* xxx. 384 These Western fellows were just 'meat' for Tommy Hinds—he would get a dozen of them around him and paint little pictures of 'the System'. **1911** H. WALPOLE *Mr. Perrin & Mr. Traill* ix. 178 She suddenly..had a revelation..that it wasn't really any one's fault at all—that it was the system, the place, the tightness and closeness and helplessness that did for everybody. **1965** G. JACKSON *Let.* June in *Soledad Brother* (1971) 78 It's frayed nerves, caused by the harsh terms that defeat brought when they went against the system, the same system that runs this place. **1973** *Ottawa Jrnl.* 18 May 16/1 It is the deeply moving, contemporary story of a young man who wouldn't surrender to the System..and the girl who always stood beside him. **1977** *Gay News* 24 Mar. 20/1 No, I accepted the system wholeheartly—the suit, white stiff collar and tie, night school, the lot. **1981** 'A. CROSS' *Death in Faculty* vi. 65 If I hadn't made it quite to Harvard, I might still have thought there was a chance for me in the system. But Harvard—the oxygen was too pure.

(*b*) *spec.* (See quot. 1945.) *Austral. Hist.*

1874 M. CLARKE *His Natural Life* (1875) III. IV. vii. 194 'You have a future to live for, man.' 'I hope not,' said the victim of the 'system'. **1934** B. PENTON *Landtakers* (1935) I. v. 42 Joe's..not the same as other lags... The System soon breaks them up, but Joe it just sets on fire and leaves him as hard as brick. **1945** BAKER *Austral. Lang.* ii. 43 The prison at Fremantle was the *establishment*, a term which is fit to rank with *the System*—as transportation in general and the maltreatment of prisoners in particular became known—as notable examples of understatement.

3. c. In fig. phr. *to get* (something) *out of one's system* and varr.: to rid oneself of some preoccupation or obsession, esp. by indulging in it to a point of satiety. Cf. quot. 1908, sense 3 b in Dict.

1900 H. A. JONES *Mrs. Dane's Defence* IV. 80 I'm rather glad he has taken it [*sc.* a disappointment in love] so violently... It means that in six months it will be out of his system. **1911** G. STRATTON-PORTER *Harvester* xviii. 430 Let me finish... Let me get this out of my system. **1962** P. GREEN tr. *S. de Beauvoir's Prime of Life* iii. 129 She still saw him occasionally, trying, at one and the same time and with equal lack of success, to win him back and get him out of her system. **1970** *New Yorker* 17 Oct. 39/1 By the time I put a couple of drinks under my belt, I worked the whole thing out of my system. **1974** J. GARDNER *Return of Moriarty* 28 We had stayed silent, it was better to let the young fool get it out of his system.

4. c. *Geol.* A major stratigraphic division, composed of a number of series and corresponding to a period (PERIOD *sb.* 4 b) in time; the rocks deposited during any specific period.

1829 A. SEDGWICK in *Trans. Geol. Soc.* III. 121 The previous statements seem to show, that the system of the new red sandstone could not have been produced by any sudden and transitory agency. **1835** —— in *Ibid.* IV. 70 The lowest beds of the carboniferous system of this region. **1835** R. I. MURCHISON in *Phil. Mag.* VII. 48, I venture to suggest..the term 'Silurian system' should be adopted as expressive of the deposits which lie between the old red sandstone and the slaty rocks of Wales. **1839** —— *Silurian System* xiv. 169, I venture..to apply to it [*sc.* the Old Red Sandstone] the term system, in order to convey a just conception of its importance in the natural succession of rocks. **1882** A. GEIKIE *Text-bk. Geol.* 636 The Geological Record is classified into five main divisions... These divisions are further ranged into systems, each system into series..or formations, each formation into groups or stages. **1898, 1927** [see *GROUP sb. 4 b (iii)]. **1944** A. HOLMES *Princ. Physical Geol.* vii. 103 Pebbles of Shap granite..occur in the conglomerates at the base of the Carboniferous system in Westmorland. **1961** *Bull. Amer. Assoc. Petroleum Geologists* XLV. 658/2 The system is the fundamental unit of world-wide time-stratigraphic classification of Phanerozoic rocks... In the Precambrian, systems still have only local significance. **1971** *Nature* 12 Feb. 480/2 In historical geology, the subdivision of periods into epochs and ages (or systems into series and stages) is usually defined by unconformities.

d. The set of the various phases that two or more given metals are capable of forming at different temperatures and pressures. Usu. with qualifying term, as *alloy system.*

1911 *Jrnl. Inst. Metals* V. 127 In the year 1897 the late Sir William Roberts-Austen..published the complete freezing-point curve of the copper-zinc alloys... This diagram was the first attempt to construct what would in present-day terminology be the Equilibrium Diagram of the Copper-Zinc System. **1922** *Encycl. Brit.* XXXI. 927/2 In non-ferrous alloys, considerable attention has been given to the alloys of zinc, a portion of the ternary system copper-aluminium-zinc. **1967** A. H. COTTRELL *Introd. Metallurgy* xv. 233 Many alloy systems are complicated by the appearance of several intermediate phases. **1977** *Sci. Amer.* July 82/3 Both cements are based on the ternary system of oxides of calcium, silicon and aluminum ($CaO–SiO_2–Al_2O_3$).

e. *Linguistics.* A group of terms, units, or categories, in a paradigmatic relationship to one another.

1953 R. H. ROBINS in *Trans. Philol. Soc.* 109 Professor J. R. Firth has recently suggested that the terms 'Structure' and 'System' be kept distinct in the technical vocabulary of linguistic description. 'Structure' might be used to refer to undimensional, linear abstractions at various levels from utterances or parts of utterances... When..categories have been devised by means of which the utterances of the language can be successfully described and analysed, closed systems are formed of these categories. **1956** J. R. FIRTH in *Trans. Philol. Soc. 1955* 91 Neither the Americans nor the Scandinavians have controlled and distinguished the use of *system* and *structure* as we have in the linguistics group at the School of Oriental and African Studies. **1961** Y. OLSSON *Syntax Eng. Verb* ii. 27 Values for the elements are given by *terms* which commute, that is, operate along the line one-instead-of-another; terms constitute *systems.* **1964** R. H. ROBINS *Gen. Linguistics* ii. 49 It is useful to employ *structure*..specifically with reference to groupings of syntagmatically related elements, and *system* with reference to classes of paradigmatically related elements. **1977** *Canad. Jrnl. Linguistics 1976* XXI. II. 196 Throughout the late 'fifties and early 'sixties he [*sc.* M. A. K. Halliday] extended J. R. Firth's concepts of 'system' and 'structure' and 'modes of meaning' into what came to be known as scale and category linguistics.

f. *Computers.* A group of related programs; *spec.* = *operating system* s.v. *OPERATING *vbl. sb.* b.

1963 L. SCHULTZ *Digital Processing* xiii. 271 In applications such as were described in Chapter 6, a system of programs rather than a single program is necessary. **1972** *Computers & Humanities* VII. 82 If a package of programs is so tightly integrated that output from one program is automatically input to another program, then it is frequently called a system. **1978** LYNCH & RICE *Computers* ix. 407 A system..handles the manipulation of source programs, language translators, input-output and so on.

g. With reference to business and social organizations and the operations or interactions they involve (see also quot. 1967[2]).

1963 *Brit. Jrnl. Sociol.* XIV. 38 The idea of 'system' has been used to imply that its parts (organizations or institutions) are interdependent with each other: that the performances of the parts have consequences or functions, consequences for the 'performing' part, consequences for other 'parts', consequences for the whole system. **1965** H. I. ANSOFF *Corporate Strategy* (1968) ix. 166 The term 'systems' is becoming popular for describing large-scale non-military industrial projects. **1967** R. WHITEHEAD in Wills & Yearsley *Handbk. Managem. Technol.* iv. 70 The health of the nation is made possible by a number of systems: doctors, nurses, hospitals, pharmaceutical companies, chemists, and, of course, patients. These are not isolated systems but interacting parts of a large and exceedingly complex whole. *Ibid.* iv. 54 The typewriter may be a relatively simple machine but in this context it is a system with a person and a machine coupled together, both interrelated and interacting. **1969** D. C. HAGUE *Managerial Econ.* i. 17 We have been considering models for analysing business problems. These seek to state the set of relationships—what we shall call the system—within which and about which business decisions have to be taken.

h. Colloq. phr. *all systems go*: everything functioning correctly, ready to proceed; everything fully operational. Chiefly *fig.* (orig. *U.S.*).

1962 [see *GO *a.* 1]. **1967** A. LURIE *Imaginary Friends* i. 8 The Seekers were looking for new members, and we should have no trouble making contact. As McMann put it, all systems were Go. **1969** *Times* 22 July (Moon Rep. Suppl.) p. i/1 Neil Armstrong on the porch of the Eagle at 109 hours 19 minutes and 30 seconds to L.O.S., all systems go, over. **1977** *Listener* 7 Apr. 450/1 It was *sportsfest* time again for the BBC last week—all systems go.

i. A prefabricated construction unit used in system building (see sense 11 d below).

1963 [see *INDUSTRIALIZED *ppl.a.*]. **1969** H. A. FREY tr. *Schmid & Testa's Syst. Building* 26/2 Building with systems is naturally more compatible with team thinking than with the approach of the isolated independent architect. **1974** *Encycl. Brit. Macropædia* III. 455/2 Basically a modular volumetric unit composed of some combination of walls, roof, and/or floor, the box system is usually prefabricated in a plant.

II. 9. d. Any method devised by a gambler for determining the placing of his bets.

1850 THACKERAY *Pendennis* II. xxvi. 262, I won a good bit of money there, and intend to win a good bit more... I've got a system. I'll make his fortune. **1896** [in Dict., sense 9 a]. **1908** CHESTERTON *All Things Considered* 47 His vanity..remains a mere mistake of fact, like that of a man who..thinks he has an infallible system for Monte Carlo. **1965** J. SYMONS *Belting Inheritance* iii. 54 He had all sorts of bright ideas that were going to make a fortune. One was..a racing system, something to do with backing second favourites.

e. *System D* [tr. F. *Système D* (also used)], (see quots. 1918, 1970). *slang.*

1918 in C. A. Smith *New Words Self-Defined* (1919) 185 'System D' is coming into play in the United States Army. 'System D' is a bit of French slang. It means to unmix, to disentangle, to go straight through... It comes from the initial letter of the word 'débrouiller'. **1947** M. LASKI in *Vogue* Oct. 63/1 That method called by the French *System D*, the phony medical certificate, the faked-up business journey. **1970** N. FREELING *Kitchen Bk.* v. 45 He was a master of the short cut, the easy way out, the system D. D. stands for dé as in débrouiller or démerder —to extricate, and I suppose that in English it is 'I'm all right, Jack'. **1973** 'TREVANIAN' *Loo Sanction* (1974) 78 MI-6..muddled their way through the Second World War, relying largely on the French organizational concept, 'système D'.

III. 11. a. (sense *4 g), as *system library, technology*, etc.

1952 T. PARSONS *Social System* 7 The moment even the most elementary system-level is brought under consideration a component of 'system integration' must enter in. **1962** J. RIORDAN *Stochastic Service Systems* iv. 70 As noted previously, this is a system with limited waiting capacity. If the waiting capacity is K − 1, the system capacity is K. **1962** E. GODFREY *Retail Selling & Organization* xi. 120 Many firms now recognize that system training needs to be interspersed with periods of practical selling. **1970** *Gloss. Aeronaut. & Astronaut. Terms* (*B.S.I.*) x. 4 *System capacity*, the total power available from the power sources under the prescribed operating and environmental conditions in the aircraft. **1973** C. W. GEAR *Introd. Computer Sci.* iv. 156 These built-in subroutines.. form part of what is called the system library. **1976** *Time* 20 Dec., facing p. 2 (Advt.), This new aid for a communication-saturated world is one more example of Toshiba's sophisticated system technology, which brings together technology from many different fields to solve complex problems of today. **1978** J. MCNEIL *Consultant* ix. 108 The details of his past career..appeared to have involved Webb in the study of system efficiency.

b. (i) *system-builder* (earlier example), *-building* (examples), *-mongering*; also in sense *4 g, as *system contradiction, integration* (so *system-integrative* adj.); (ii) in appositive use, as *system-structure*.

1761 STERNE *Tristram Shandy* IV. xvii. 125 But what it is, I leave to system builders and fish pond diggers betwixt 'em to find out. **1911** J. DRUMMOND *Paul* vi. 79 There is no attempt at system-building. **1969** A. MAUDE *Common Problem* v. 94 The difference between this process [*sc.* the construction of a system by a political philosopher] and the determinist system-building of social scientists today is concerned with the making of ethical choices about ends. **1977** A. GIDDENS *Stud. in Social & Polit. Theory* ii. 127 By 'system contradiction' I mean a disjunction between two or more 'principles of organization' or 'structural principles' which govern the connections between social systems within a larger collectivity. **1952** System integration [see sense 11 a above]. **1977** A. GIDDENS *Stud. in Social & Polit. Theory* ii. 123 While the notion of function is redundant to the theory of structuration, that of 'social integration' can still be regarded as a basic one—together with the further one of 'system integration'. **1953** System integrative [see *POLAR *a.* 7 b]. **1940** *Mind* XLIX. 120 Hegel was wrong in his formal system-mongering which reflects the influence upon his thought of Christian theology. **1978** *N.Y. Rev. Bks.* 23 Feb. 6/1 [Matthew] Arnold frowned on dogmatic religion, puritanism, and system-mongering. **1964** P. STREVENS in D. Abercrombie *Daniel Jones* 125 Such disparate bodies of grammatical theory as those which lie behind phoneme-morpheme-syntax grammar..and system-structure grammar. **1975** M. A. K. HALLIDAY in S. Rogers *Children & Lang.* IV. 225 Prague theory, glossematics, system-structure theory, tagmemics, stratification theory and the later versions of transformation theory are all variants on this theme.

c. In pl. *systems*, used esp. in sense *4 g, as *systems approach, manager, theory*, etc. Cf. also sense 11 d below.

1952 *N.Y. Certified Public Accountant* Oct. 604/2 Principles for acquiring specialized knowledge and experience in the systems field. *Ibid.* 605/2 You can rely on a systems consultant whose business it is to devote more time..than you..can afford to give. **1959** *Economist* 11 Apr. 139/1 The American department is relying increasingly on prime contractors (called 'systems managers') to combine the works of many sub-contractors. **1967** *Ibid.* 28 Jan. 328/3 Airlines in general are shifting toward a 'systems concept' which takes charge of the traveller from door to door, not simply between departure and arrival lounges. **1968** *Sat. Rev.* (U.S.) 23 Nov. 32/3 General Motors and Ford can use a 'systems' approach to their global investments. **1969** *Times* 30 Apr. 23/4 (Advt.), In advanced technology. Systems evaluation engineers. Systems trials engineer. Systems test engineers... We require a number of engineers experienced in the assessment, evaluation and/or trials of complex defence weapon systems. **1970** T. LUPTON *Managem. & Social Sci.* (ed. 2) iii. 80 An example of a practical application of a systems theory of organization. **1975** *Modeling & Simulation* VI. 795 (*heading*) Are systems scientists not scientists? **1976** J. LUND *Ultimate* i. 11 Fernandos was a systems consultant to a group of supermarket owners. **1977** *R.A.F. News* 22 June–5 July 9 (Advt.), Systems test engineers £3,500–£4,000. **1977** A. GIDDENS *Stud. in Soc. & Polit. Theory* ii. 115 Von Bertalanffy counterposes the 'mechanistic' views characteristic of nineteenth-century physical science with the twentieth-century perspective of systems theory. **1978** *Times* 2 Oct. 6/8 A new industry, or sub-industry, has emerged, formed on 'systems houses' which buy in the micro components and other hardware, write the software, and design and market the complete systems. **1978** J. MCNEIL *Consultant* ix. 109 You might have a bit of trouble with my Systems Manager.

d. Special Comb., as **systems** (or † **system**) **analysis**, the rigorous, often mathematical, analysis of complex situations and processes as an aid to decision-making or preparatory to the introduction of a computer; so **systems analyst**; **system building** *vbl. sb.*, a method of construction using standardized prefabricated components (see sense 4 i above); hence **system builder**; **system-built** *ppl. a.*; **system(s) design**, the process or task of matching a computer to the situation into which it is to be introduced and determining the procedures that are to be used; **systems engineering**, the investigation of complex, man-made systems in relation to the apparatus that is or might be involved in them; so **systems engineer**; **system(s) program** *Computers*, a program forming part of an operating system; so **system(s) programmer, programming**; **system(s) software** *Computers*, system programs collectively.

1950 in J. H. Batchelor *Operations Research* (1959) 769 Notes on ($m \times 2$) evaluation matrices for special system analysis applications. **1953** *Jrnl. Operations Res. Soc. Amer.* I. 191 Sometimes this broad type of operations research is called 'systems analysis', 'systems planning', or 'market research'. **1966** A. BATTERSBY *Math. in Management* i. 26 This field of application of mathematics has been defined as 'systems analysis', which considers the thing-being-managed as a system subject to control and operating within an environment with which it interacts. **1977** *Time* 4 Apr. 50/1 Systems analysis, which is really good common sense on a grand scale, combines the knowledge of mathematical probabilities with the aim of dealing with problems in their entirety rather than just piecemeal. **1955** *Operations Research* III. 470 How does the systems analyst choose the preferred strategy? **1967** D. WILSON in Wills & Yearsley *Handbk. Managem. Technol.* 47 The macro block-diagrams show the main logic for a particular program and may be prepared by the systems analyst. **1982** M. DUKE *Flashpoint* xxvii. 205 From computer programmer to systems analyst. Quite an achievement. **1965** *Times* 4 Dec. 5/7 If you want to give the system-builder a fair chance of developing his system you have got to have continuous production for a number of years. **1973** *Architect* Jan. 4/1 If you require the services of a good system builder... We can manufacture to your own particular design or in a manner which allows the best use of our standard components. **1964** R. M. E. DIAMANT *Industrialised Building* I. p. viii, System building is particularly well suited to the rapid erection of tall, low-cost blocks of flats. *a* **1974** R. CROSSMAN *Diaries* (1975) I. 80 A brilliant group of young men and women actively at work developing two methods of system-building, 5M and 12M. **1968** *Guardian* 13 Nov. 1/4 The Minister of Housing..made strenuous efforts to halt the collapse of confidence in system-built blocks. **1973** *Archit. Assoc. Q.* V. IV. 8/2 Later models [of bungalow] were supplied with what would appear to be system-built furniture. Described by the architect as 'chair-furniture', it consisted of various components which could be assembled into chairs, stools, tables, etc. **1954** *Trans. IRE Prof. Group Electronic Computers* June 8/2 The necessity for effecting compromises and avoiding conflicts of this kind between the rival claims of operational effectiveness and engineering reliability and economy strongly influenced the system design of the SEAC and DYSEAC. **1960** GREGORY & VAN HORN *Automatic Data-Processing Systems* xi. 380 Some analysts with an accounting and systems-design background suggest the straightforward approach—simply asking management people what they must have to control operations. *Ibid.* 396 System design is discussed here in terms of fact finding, developing specifications, meeting specifications, and matching equipment with the system. **1980** *Jrnl. R. Soc. Arts* Feb. 147/1 With the advent of micro-electronics and the growth in the field described nowadays as systems design, there is some danger that.. the manager will fail to appreciate the real importance of the design element. **1980** J. MCNEIL *Spy Game* i. 22 You're the best systems designer in his Division. *Ibid.* 28 Stick to systems design... You make a lousy financial expert. **1955** *Business Week* 15 Jan. 164/3 Nowadays, the systems engineer starts a project by wrestling with the abstruse questions of what elements in the system need accurate measurement, which ones are important to control. **1974** *Encycl. Brit. Macropædia* XVII. 972/1 The first task of the systems engineer is to develop as clear a formulation of objectives as possible. **1952** W. H. MARTIN in *Proc. 5th Ann. Conf. Administration of Research 1951* 8/1 In our organization [*sc.* Bell Telephone Laboratories] extensive use is made of an analytical procedure which we call Systems Engineering. **1962** A. BATTERSBY *Guide to Stock Control* i. 9 Two types of specialists concern themselves with the study of these communications networks: we may say broadly that the Organization and Methods experts are responsible for the general layout of the network, whereas the accountants are concerned with the messages which flow along them. The two functions are combined in the new specialism called Systems Engineering. **1973** GOTTFRIED & WEISMAN *Introd. Optimization Theory* i. 5 The techniques of systems engineering (of which optimization techniques constitute an important subclass) are applicable to a very wide variety of physical problems. **1958** *Communications Assoc. Computing Machinery* Aug. 12 A minimum of 'system programming' should be required to produce the system initially. *Ibid.* 16 System programmers writing in UNCOL can use an existing translator to produce their ML system programs. **1960** *Ibid.* III. 537 (*heading*) A list of computer systems programs for the IBM 650, DATATRON 205, and UNIVAC-SS80. **1970** O. DOPPING *Computers & Data Processing* v. 92 Nowadays, only some very specialized 'system programmers' write programs in machine code. **1973** ABRAMS & STEIN *Computer Hardware & Software* iii. 14 Software may be divided into..applications programs, which are written to solve users' problems, and systems programs, which are concerned with operating the computer service. **1973** C. W. GEAR *Introd. Computer Sci.* ii. 53 These programs, called system programs, will read in our program after it has been punched on cards in a suitable form and arrange for the instruction counter to be set to the address of the first instruction in our program. **1979** R. BORNAT *Understanding & Writing Compilers* xiv. 240 Most system-programming languages allow stack pointers to be used with even more freedom than in ALGOL 68. **1971** B. DE FERRANTI *Living with Computer* 89 *System software*, those programs, usually prepared by the hardware manufacturer, that provide the link between the programs of the user and the hardware. **1980** PALMER & MORRIS *Computing Sci.* viii. 283 Systems software is written to schedule the various stages in running a program..at the same time making efficient use of the hardware.

systematic, *a.* and *sb.* Add: **A.** *adj.* **3. a.** (Earlier example.)

1789 *Loiterer* 13 June 8 Armour was rarely used in battles where artillery alone could decide..the Day. ..There was seldom any opportunity of signalizing personal courage amidst the regularity of systematic murder.

c. *systematic ambiguity* (Philos.) (see quot. 1933). Cf. *systematically ambiguous* adj. phr. s.v. *SYSTEMATICALLY *adv.* 1 c.

1910 B. RUSSELL in Whitehead & Russell *Principia Math.* I. Introd. iii. 45 This is due to a systematic ambiguity in the meanings of 'not' and 'or', by which they adapt themselves to propositions of any order. **1933** L. S. STEBBING *Mod. Introd. Logic* (ed. 2) ix. 161 When the same words are used in sentences which express different kinds of propositions, yet in each case the usage is significant, then these words are said to have 'systematic ambiguity'... This ambiguity is *systematic* because it can be formulated according to a rule. **1952** W. V. QUINE *Methods of Logic* p. xi, Systematic ambiguities..are essential to the nature of language. **1979** *Proc. Amer. Cath. Philos. Soc.* LIII. 78 In this paper, I want to argue that there is a systematic ambiguity in the concept of person which explains why it has often been used to favor sexist discrimination.

d. *systematic error*, an error with a non-zero mean, so that its effect is not reduced when observations are averaged.

1925 R. A. FISHER *Statistical Methods for Research Workers* vi. 169 It is worth while to consider the effects of two classes of systematic errors, which, although of little or no importance when single values only are available, become of increasing importance as larger numbers of samples are averaged. **1981** *Astrophysical Jrnl.* CCXLVIII. 34/2 Although there is a statistically significant deviation from a Planck spectrum, there are serious limitations to the statistical analysis where systematic errors are likely.

7. *Chem.* Of the name of a chemical species: constructed in accordance with an agreed set of rules so as to represent the detailed chemical structure of the named species (e.g. *N-methylpent-2-ylamine*); so *systematic nomenclature*. Cf. *TRIVIAL *a.*

1858 *Rep. Brit. Assoc. Adv. Sci. 1857* II. 45 The classification on which the author proposes to base a systematic nomenclature for organic compounds, is a modification of that employed by Gerhardt. **1879** WATTS *Dict. Chem.* Suppl. I. 705 A systematic nomenclature for the hydrocarbons, which are the fundamental compounds of organic chemistry, is a great desideratum. **1892** *Nature* 19 May 57/2 It is clearly an absolute necessity of the times that every compound should bear a systematic name of such a character that it can be at once translated into the corresponding formula. **1959** R. S. CAHN *Introd. Chem. Nomenclature* iii. 39 There is a fundamental distinction between the use of trivial and systematic names: trivial names refer to compounds, systematic names to structures. **1978** *Nature* 31 Aug. 929/2 Natural products with particular molecular features cannot normally be located by the keyword approach, as such compounds usually have trivial, rather than systematic, names. **1982** J. E. FERNANDEZ *Org. Chem.* iv. 59 An international, systematic nomenclature system now exists and is used by organic chemists throughout the world.

B. *sb.* **2.** Substitute for def.: = TAXONOMY. (Earlier and later examples.)

[**1840** W. WHEWELL *Philos. Induct. Sci.* I. VIII. ii. 468 A department of the philosophy of natural history which has been termed by some writers (as Decandolle,) Taxonomy..by some Germans..has been denominated *Systematik*; if we could now form a new substantive after the analogy of the words Logic, Rhetoric, and the like, we might call it Systematick.] **1940** J. S. HUXLEY *New Systematics* 1 To-day..systematics has become one of the focal points of biology. **1951** G. H. M. LAWRENCE *Taxon. Vascular Plants* i. 3 In this text the taxonomy of vascular plants includes the systematics of the taxa known as pteridophytes, gymnosperms, and angiosperms. **1969** E. MAYR *Princ. Systematic Zool.* p. vii, Systematics has had a remarkable renaissance during the last generation.

systematically, *adv.* Add: **1. c.** *systematically ambiguous* adj. phr. (Philos.), having an ambiguity that is systematic (see *SYSTEMATIC *a.* 3 c).

1929 C. I. LEWIS *Mind & World-Order* i. 11 The adjective 'real' is systematically ambiguous and can have a single meaning only in a special sense. **1943** I. A. RICHARDS *How to read a Page* iii. 52 There are few important words which are not in varying patterns systematically ambiguous; *say* is typical. These *regular* shifts of sense as a rule give us little trouble in reading. **1967** *Philos.* XLII. 208 'Reality' may be systematically ambiguous.

systematicity (sistĕmăti·sĭti). [f. SYSTEMATIC *a.* + -ITY.] The quality or condition of being systematic; systematicness.

1970 CAMPBELL & WALES in J. Lyons *New Horizons in Linguistics* 257 The child first of all does something 'correctly' and then, with every appearance of systematicity, later proceeds to do it 'wrongly'. **1974** R. A. HALL *External Hist. Romance Languages* 239 Meyer-Lübke's work was characterised by sobriety and balance, with exceptional solidity in detail but with an over-all sense of systematicity. **1977** *Language* LIII. 883 He has little time or inclination to follow through his concept of music theory with any thoroughness or systematicity.

systematy (si·stĕmăti). [f. Gr. σύστημα, -ατ- SYSTEM + -Y³.] Systematic classification; = TAXONOMY.

1912 W. L. BALLS *Cotton Plant in Egypt* 5 In this brief summary of the few available historical facts, it has seemed advisable to evade systematy. **1921** *Oxf. Bot. Mem.* XI (*title*) Elementary notes on the systematy of Angiosperms. **1929** E. M. NICHOLSON *Study of Birds* 20 Mechanical and unfruitful as systematy inevitably is, ornithologists ought to be grateful to those who have plodded through it.

‖ **Système International** (sistẹ̄m æ̃ntẹrnasyonal). Also (*erron.*) **-nationale.** [Fr.] In full *Système International d'Unités.* The International System of Units (see *INTERNATIONAL *a.* 1 c).

[**1957:** see *INTERNATIONAL *a.* 1 c.] **1969** *Symbols, Signs, & Abbreviations* (R. Soc.) 21 (*heading*) The International System of Units (Système International d'Unités —SI). **1971** [see SI s.v. *S 4 a]. **1972** *Physics Bull.* Aug. 461/3 If the precision of the measurement system can lead us to parts in 10⁹, it might be possible to change the way in which the electrical units are defined in the Système Internationale.

systemic, *a.* Add: **1. c.** Of a herbicide, insecticide, or fungicide: entering the system of a plant or animal and freely transported within its tissues. Also as *sb.*, a systemic agent.

1949 *Ann. Appl. Biol.* XXXVI. 160 The term 'systemic insecticides' refers only to chemical substances which are absorbed by the plant and translocated to all parts of it, rendering it insecticidal. **1961** *New Scientist* 5 Jan. 50/2 The animal systemics ronnel..and CoRal have been in commercial use for some time. **1964** *Which?* Apr. 114/1 Dimethoate and menazon are unlike the other insecticides in being systemics, i.e. they are absorbed into the plant instead of just being deposited on it. **1971** *Exper. Agric.* VII. 2 Four different systemics were used. **1979** *Radio Times* 5–11 May 13/4 The best control is to spray young foliage thoroughly with Benlate systemic fungicide.

2. Delete *rare*⁻⁰ and add examples.

1946 C. MORRIS *Signs, Lang. & Behavior* 104 In the systemic use of signs the aim is simply to organize sign-produced behavior. **1952** A. COHEN *Phonemes of English* 54 It is not as loans, but as residual structural irregularities, which might rather be called 'systemic fragments' than 'coexistent systems'. **1966** S. BEER *Decision & Control* xvii. 439 They will demand that systemic qualities be measured which no-one as yet knows how to measure. **1975** *Times Lit. Suppl.* 17 Oct. 1233/5 A tradition of American political and social thought..that demands social justice without labelling injustice a systemic product. **1977** *Dædalus* Summer 55 Many scholars, especially those whose level of analysis is systemic, implicitly write as if they were addressing themselves to a world government.

3. *systemic grammar*, a method of linguistic analysis developed by M. A. K. Halliday in 1961 in *Word* XVII, based on the ideas of J. R. Firth and others. Similarly *systemic linguistics*. Cf. *SYSTEM 4 e.

1968 *Computers & Humanities* II. 147 The linguistic description I adopted for my study was systemic grammar. **1971** D. CRYSTAL *Linguistics* iv. 215 More recently, Halliday has developed out of this a concept of *systemic* grammar. **1975** M. BERRY (*title*) Introduction to systemic linguistics. **1978** *Language* LIV. 351 The grammar that assigns to sentences structures like the one in Fig. 1 is generative fusion of elements of American-style immediate-constituent analysis (cf. Nida 1960), European-style dependency theory (cf. Tesnière 1959), and British-style systemic grammar (cf. Halliday 1961).

systoflex (si·stofleks). *Electr. Engin.* [f. *systo-*, of unknown origin + *FLEX *sb.*²] Flexible sleeving for insulating electric wires.

1922 *Wireless World* X. 556/1 One may lose much time trying to push No. 18 wire into systoflex intended for No. 20. **1968** M. WOODHOUSE *Rock Baby* ix. 93 His study ..smelled..of soldering fluid, swarf, oil, charred systoflex sleeving..the indefinable smell of home-made electronic gear.

systole. Add: **1. c.** Also *Comb.*, as *systole-diastole.*

1924 C. GRAY *Survey Contemp. Music* 260 The immediate future..will witness a return to tradition... So it always has been... It is the *systole-diastole* of the world of art. **1946** M. LOWRY *Let.* 2 Jan. (1967) 74 Here we come to the heart of the book which..returns..to the uneasy, but healthy, systole-diastole of Hugh.

systrophe (si·strofi). *Biol.* [ad. G. *systrophe* (A. F. W. Schimper 1885, in *Jahrb. f. wiss. Bot.* XVI. 221), f. SYN- + Gr. στροφή, turning.] The clumping together of chloroplasts in a cell when exposed to bright light.

1886 *Jrnl. R. Microsc. Soc.* VI. 642 Very strong irritation of light causes the chlorophyll-grains to collect into one or two lumps, a phenomenon for which Schimper proposes the term systrophe. **1936** *Geogr. Jrnl.* LXXXVIII. 48 Diatoms..sink deeper and display the phenomenon of systrophe. **1966** E. J. STADELMANN in D. M. Prescott *Methods Cell Physiol.* II. vii. 206 Systrophe is a typical and reversible response reaction of the living protoplasm to a variety of stimuli.

Szechuan (setʃwā·n). Also **Szechwan.** [ad. Chin. *Si-chuān.*] The name of a province in south-western China, used *attrib.* (with reversed stress) to designate the distinctively spicy cuisine originating there. Also *Comb.*, as *Szechuan-style* adj. Also *transf.*

1956 BUWEI YANG CHAO *How to cook & eat in Chinese* I. i. 30 Szechwan cooking has a fine balance of flavours except that hot pepper is added freely. **1974** *Times* 23 Aug. (Hongkong Suppl.) p. x/7 The Chinese food in Hongkong is superb..Peking duck and Szechwan smoked duck. **1977** *Harpers & Queen* Nov. 30/2 A new restaurant serving Szechaun food. **1979** *United States 1980/81* (Penguin Travel Guides) 179 Honolulu also has several Mandarin or Szechwan-style Chinese restaurants. **1980** E. BEHR *Getting Even* vii. 89 There was the smell of real Szechuanese cooking, chillies and hot sesame oil... Waiters began serving an elaborate Szechuan meal.

Szechuanese (setʃwanī·z), *a.* and *sb.* Also **Szechwanese.** [f. as prec. + -ESE.] **A.** *adj.* Of, pertaining to, or characteristic of Szechuan or its people, or of the Chinese spoken there. **B.** *sb.* **a.** An inhabitant of Szechuan. **b.** The dialect of Szechuan.

1918 *North-China Herald* 19 Jan. 115/2 Szechuanese invasion of Yunnan... It is reported that the Szechuanese have invaded Yunnan. **1937** E. SNOW *Red Star over China* v. 199 The Szechuanese are sentimental about their few bridges. **1947** J. BERTRAM *Shadow of War* x. 336 We gathered for supper at a Szechwanese restaurant and.. tasted..the roast duck of Chengtu. **1947** N. C. SCOTT in *Bull. School Orient. & African Studies* XII. 197 (*heading*) The monosyllable in Szechuanese. **1966** R. & D. MORRIS *Men & Pandas* iv. 65 He not only spoke good English, but also knew the Szechuanese dialect. **1972** 'M. HEBDEN' *Killer for Chairman* II. i. 127, I could hear voices talking in..a Szechwanese dialect... The Szechwanese had a reputation for bloody-mindedness. **1978** A. GREY *Chinese Assassin* xvii. 174 Your Szechuanese accent is a dead give-away. **1980** [see prec.].

Szekel (sē·k'l), *sb.* (*a.*) Also in Ger. form **Szekler.** [ad. Hungarian *Székely* (also used).] (A member of) a Magyar people living in eastern Transylvania. Also *attrib.* or as *adj.*

1843 *Penny Cycl.* XXV. 164/2 The nation [of Transylvania] in the political sense of the word is composed of three bodies or 'nations', the Hungarians, the Szeklers, and the Saxons, who have the collective name of the 'Uniti'. *Ibid.*, When a Hungarian or Szekler nobleman of Transylvania settles in Hungary, he is entitled to all the privileges of noblemen in Hungary. **1869** A. J. PATTERSON *Magyars* II. xxxi. 354, I started for the little hamlet..accompanied by a Székel. **1888** E. GERARD *Land beyond Forest* II. xxxviii. 151 The Szekel villages, of a formal simplicity, are as far removed from the Roumanian poverty as from Saxon opulence. **1910** *Encycl. Brit.* X. 392/2 The isolated groups of Hungarians now found in Transylvania and called Szeklers are considered the purest descendants of the invading Magyars. **1920** *Glasgow Herald* 23 Apr. 8 At the very most 1,900,000 Magyars are lost, of whom over 900,000 (including the Szekels) are in Transylvania. **1934** R. W. SETON-WATSON *Hist. Roumanians* ii. 20 Already Koloman and Stephen II in the first three decades of the Twelfth century began to settle Magyar colonists—the so-called Székelys or Siculi. *Ibid.* 21 Transylvania falls into three distinct political groupings—finally crystallised by the events of 1437 into three privileged nations, the Magyars, the Székels and the Saxons. **1956** F. S. PISKY in S. Fischer-Galati *Romania* iii. 54 Although there are no ethnic or linguistic differences, Hungarians make a distinction between the *Szekelys* and *Magyars*. The *Szekelys*, descendants of the free frontiersmen in Transylvania, populate the Odorhei, Cius and Trei Scaune districts. **1974** *Encycl. Brit. Micropædia* VI. 496/3 The Szeklers, meaning Frontier Guards, received their name, it seems, because they were Magyars sent to Transylvania to protect the eastern flank. *Ibid. Macropædia* IX. 31/1 Colonies of Szekels, a people akin to the Magyars who had preceded the latter into the central plains, were settled behind its eastern passes.

Sze Yap (sī yæp). Also **Sze-Yap, Szeyap.** [Chinese.] The name of an area made up of four counties in the south of Guangdong Province in China (see quot. 1973) used *attrib.* and *absol.* to designate the Chinese dialect spoken there.

[**1948** R. A. D. FORREST *Chinese Lang.* x. 200 Cantonese, with reference also to the dialect of Sze-Yap, to the west of the Canton River delta, generally regarded as a minor variety of Cantonese.] **1964** *Asia Mag.* 12 July 22/3 The Chinese [in Hong Kong]..speak no less than seven tongues —Cantonese, Hoklo, Sze Yap, [etc.]. **1971** K. HOPKINS *Hong Kong* 235 Cantonese is very much the predominant language but there are minorities who speak..Sze Yap. **1973** R. A. D. FORREST *Chinese Lang.* (ed. 3) xi. 235 Usually reckoned a sub-dialect of Cantonese, though, in the opinion of the present writer, showing enough distinctive features to warrant its separation, is the dialect of Sze-Yap, the 'Four Towns', spoken on the west of the Canton River delta... Like most varieties of Cantonese, Sze Yap has lost all distinction of *s-* and *ʃ-*. *Ibid.* 328 The Sze Yap dialect has regularly *h-* for *t'-*. **1982** *English World-Wide* III. I. 48 Other varieties of Chinese spoken include Szeyap, Chiuchow, Shanghainese, Hokkien and Hakka.

‖ **szlachta** (ʃla·χta). *Hist.* [Polish.] The aristocratic or land-owning class in Poland before 1945.

1885 *Encycl. Brit.* XIX. 285/2 We soon find the following divisions of society among the Poles:— (1) the nobility, *szlachta*, who throughout Polish history constitute the nation properly so-called. **1905** *Cambr. Mod. Hist.* (1907) III. iii. 76 Poland was at this time on the threshold of a period of political transition of an almost revolutionary character, the most remarkable feature of which was the elevation to power of the Polish *szlachta*, or gentry. **1969** P. ANDERSON in Cockburn & Blackburn *Student Power* 264 Bronislaw Malinowski, a Polish aristocrat from the Galician szlachta. **1978** W. B. LINCOLN *Nicholas I* iv. 136 The more substantial portions of the Polish *szlachta* (nobility) had done relatively well under fifteen years of Russian rule.

T

T. Add: **I. 1. b.** (Earlier example.)

1849 [see CROSS *v.* 7 a].

c. (Later examples of *to a tee.*)

1873 K. H. DIGBY *Last Year's Leaves* viii. 302 Then should you scorn such feasts, like me, We've what will suit you to a tee. **1922** JOYCE *Ulysses* 58 Simon Dedalus takes him off to a tee with his eyes screwed up. **1966** *Listener* 29 Sept. 480/1 John Hollis had Walter off to a tee. **1973** *Brit. Printer* May 62/3 Edwin Snell of Yeovil has the direct mail touch to a tee.

2. b. *Electr.* A network of three impedances that can be represented diagrammatically as a T in which the stem and each arm is an impedance. Freq. *attrib.*; so *T-connected* adj.

1909 BEDELL & PIERCE *Direct & A.C. Testing* vii. 248 Transforming from a 2-phase primary circuit to two sets of T-connected secondaries. *Ibid.* 249 The line voltage, thus obtained by the *T*-connection, is accordingly the same as would be obtained by three 3-phase generator coils..in delta. **1934**, etc. [see *LATTICE *sb.* 2 d]. **1947** R. LEE *Electronic Transformers & Circuits* vi. 150 In the 'low pass' filter T-section of Fig. 115, the inductance arms shown as *L*/2 and the capacitance *C* are made with losses as low as possible. **1973** J. R. NEUENSWANDER *Mod. Power Systems* iii. 32 For a line of medium length, a better approximation is arrived at through either the π or the *T* connection. **1975** D. G. FINK *Electronics Engineers' Handbk.* XIII. 30 While many null network configurations are useful (including the bridged-T and twin-T), the Wien bridge design predominates.

c. *Naut.* In phr. *to cross the T*: of a fleet or ship, to cross ahead of another (enemy) fleet's or ship's line of advance approximately at right angles, thus securing tactical advantages.

1916 'TAFFRAIL' *Pincher Martin* xvii. 323 Sir David Beatty..altered course to the east and crossed the enemy's T,..inflicting terrible damage with his heavy fire. **1953** *Hist. Today* Feb. 114/1 The Japanese main force was able to steam across the head of the Russian line... This manoeuvre, known as 'crossing the T', has been the dream of all admirals once steam tactics were introduced. **1968** D. THOMAS *Battle of Java Sea* x. 143 The destroyer *Oshio*..had crossed the Dutch cruisers' T and exchanged a rapid but ineffectual fire with *Java*. **1976** *Oxf. Compan. Ships & Sea* 213/2 The fleet 'crossing the T' has a considerable gunnery advantage.

3. a. *T-bandage* (later example), *-head* (examples), *-joint* (earlier example).

1885 W. H. COLEMAN *Hist. Sketch Bk. New Orleans* xviii. 187 The Chevalier appeared in the streets wearing what the surgeons call a T bandage about his face and jaw. **1913** W. E. DOMMETT *Motor Car Mech.* 42 The arrangement shown at E is the most extensively used, the cylinder being said to have a T-head. **1969** *Jane's Freight Containers 1968–69* 179/3 A new Oil Jetty running 217 m.. out into Harwich Harbour.., and having a minimum depth of 33 ft alongside the T-head. **1889** *Cent. Dict.*, T-joint.

b. T account *U.S. Book-keeping*, a standard form of ledger account (see quot. 1976), or a simplified version of this; **T-bar,** a metal bar with a T-shaped cross-section; a T-shaped fastening on a shoe (cf. *T-strap* below); *spec.* a type of ski-lift consisting of a series of T-shaped bars whereby skiers are towed uphill; **T-bone steak** orig. *U.S.*, a beef-steak cut from the sirloin and containing a T-shaped bone; also *ellipt.* as *T-bone*; **T-formation** *U.S. Football*, a T-shaped offensive formation of players (see quot. 1978); **T-junction,** a T-shaped intersection (of pipes, etc.); *spec.* a T-shaped road junction; † **T-light** *Theatr.*, a type of gas lighting-device utilizing a pipe in the shape of a letter T (*obs.*); **T-strap,** a T-shaped instep strap on a shoe; freq. *attrib.*; also *absol.*, a shoe with such a strap; cf. *T-bar* above. See also *T-SHIRT.

1936 OWENS & KENNEDY *Accounting* v. 49 Sometimes 'skeleton' or 'T' accounts are used instead of the regular accounts. **1941** L. O. FOSTER *Introd. Accounting* x. 181 T accounts are accounts without rulings and are used in classroom discussions because of the simplicity of their structure. **1976** D. W. MOFFAT *Econ. Dict.* 270/1 *T account.* In double-entry book-keeping, each account has the name of the account on a horizontal across the top, and then a vertical line separates the debit entries from the credit entries. The lines form a T. **1889** *Cent. Dict.*, T-bar. **1940** [see *chair-lift* s.v. *LIFT *sb.*[2] 10 b]. **1956** [see *SECTION *sb.* 2 p]. **1964** *Woman* 18 Jan. 13 Today's chair-lifts and T-bars mean you'll be sitting as much as ski-ing. **1966** A. W. LEWIS *Gloss. Woodworking Terms* 78 (*caption*) T-bar sach cramp. **1972** *Daily Tel.* 24 Jan. 11/7 The little girl's T-bar beach-shoe. **1979** *United States 1980/81* (Penguin Travel Guides) 648 Excellent skiing facilities including a chair lift,..T-bar, beginners' lift, and various snack bars. **1916** *Dialect Notes* IV. 270 *T-steak* or *T-bone-steak*,..so called from the shape of the bone. **1923** N. ANDERSON *Hobo* I. iii. 34 These bills of fare..displayed.. T-Bone Steak. **1934** E. NEWHOUSE *You can't sleep Here* xii. 144 When it's a toss-up between buzzards' gizzards and a t-bone.., me for the t-bone. **1959** *Times* 27 Apr. 7/4 Fillet and T-bone steaks were the order of the hour. **1979** R. RENDELL *Make Death love Me* xi. 98 He got Marty to fetch in three great hunks of T-bone because Joyce said she liked steak. **1930** R. C. ZUPPKE *Coaching Football* vii. 208 The 'T' formation..is at its core a strong formation. **1942** L. O. WALDORF *How to play Football* ix. 112 In 1940, Stanford University used the T formation with great success. **1978** G. WRIGHT *Illustr. Handbk. Sporting Terms* 85/3 *T-formation*, one of the basic offensive formations with the quarterback behind the center and the other three backs behind in a row parallel to the line of scrimmage. **1954** *Gloss. Highway Engin. Terms* (*B.S.I.*) 56 *T junction*, a junction shaped like a T. **1956** *Nature* 24 Mar. 561/1 The study of the stresses in the T-junction of a branched pipe. **1958** *Listener* 20 Nov. 835/3 The first T-junction that comes along without a signpost of any kind. **1969** E. H. PINTO *Treen* 380/2 The method of making a right-angle turn, or a T junction, is shown in Plate 408, where the tapered short section is driven into a cone socket in the side of the longer length of elm pipe. **1982** S. SPENDER *China Diary* 104 He jumped out of the car..and walked..till he came to a T-junction where the [traffic] blockage seemed to originate. **1898** A. W. PINERO *Trelawny of 'Wells'* IV. 171 Just below the footlights is a T-light, burning gas. **1911** [see *DU THÉÂTRE]. **1933** J. MARTIN-HARVEY *Autobiogr.* iv. 43 The gloomy underground stage unlit by anything but the 'T' light on which a single jet of gas literally made darkness visible. **1963** *Times* 1 Feb. 14/5 Some shoes had..slender T-straps. **1963** *Harper's Bazaar* Apr. 75 The T-strap sandal shown here in patent leather. **1969** *Sears Catal.* Spring/Summer 7 Dashing T-strap with sparkling patent vinyl upper. **1974** *Country Life* 21 Mar. 687/2 A brogued court with T-strap. **1978** *Detroit Free Press* 5 Mar. A19 (Advt.), Popular T-strap slings with open or closed backs and espadrilles.

II. 4. T-model (Ford) = *Model T* s.v. *MODEL *sb.* 7 e.

1932 [see *MODEL *sb.* 7 e]. **1942** Z. N. HURSTON in A. Dundes *Mother Wit* (1973) 28/1 Way after a while a T-model Ford came along full of Negroes. **1962** *John o' London's* 11 Jan. 43/3 Driving a T-model Ford over the roof-tops.

6. a. T (*Physics*) = *TERA-; T (*Physics*) = *TESLA; *t* (Physics), top or truth, a quark flavour; T (*Physics* and *Chem.*) = *TRITIUM; TA (*U.S.*), teaching assistant; T.A., Territorial Army (see also note s.v. TAVR below); T.A. (*Psychol.*), transactional analysis; T.A.B. (*Austral.* and *N.Z.*), Totalizator Agency Board; T.A.B. (*Med.*), a vaccine against typhoid, paratyphoid A, and paratyphoid B; usu. *attrib.*; T. & A., T and A (*U.S.*), tonsils and adenoids; tonsillectomy and adenoidectomy; t. and g., t. & g., (*Woodworking*), tongued and grooved; TAT (*Psychol.*), thematic apperception test; TAVR, Territorial and Army Volunteer Reserve (the name given to the restructured Territorial Army in 1967, but replaced by the name 'Territorial Army' in 1979); T.B., torpedo-boat; T.B., Treasury Bill (cf. *T-Bill*, sense 6* below); T.B., t.b., tuberculosis; *T.B.-tested* adj., (of an animal) tested to establish the absence of tuberculosis; also (*U.S. slang*), a confidence trickster (see quot. 1930); T.B.D., t.b.d., torpedo boat destroyer; tbs., tbsp., tablespoon(ful); TBS, *t*alk *b*etween *s*hips, a short-wave radio apparatus used for verbal communication between ships at sea; TCA trichloroacetic acid (a herbicide); TCB (*U.S. Black slang*), (to) take care of business; T.C.D., Trinity College, Dublin; TCDD = *tetrachlorodibenzodioxin* s.v. *TETRA- 2 a; TCNQ (*Chem.*) [f. T(ETRA- + CN, chemical formula of the cyano group + Q(UINONE], 7,7,8,8-tetracyano-*p*-quinodimethane, an organic compound forming salts of unusually low resistivity; T.C.P., the proprietary name of a disinfectant; TCP (*Physics*), time (reversal), charge (conjugation), and parity (conservation); T.D. [Ir. *Teachtaí Dála*], a member of Dáil Éireann, the lower house of the Irish parliament; T.D., Territorial Decoration (in the Territorial Army); TD (*U.S.* and *Canad. Football*), a touchdown; T.D.C., Temporary Detective Constable; TDC (*Mech.*), top dead centre; TDE [f. T(wo *numeral a.* + *d*ichlor*e*thane], an organochlorine insecticide (see quot. 1946) formerly used on fruit and vegetables; T.D.R., Treasury Deposit Receipt; t.d.s. (*Med.*) [L. *ter die sumendus*], to be taken three times a day; TEE, Trans Europ (also Europe, European) Express (train); TEFL, Tefl (tefl), Teaching of English as a Foreign Language; TESL (tesl), Teaching of English as a Second Language; TESOL (te·sǫl), Teachers of English to Speakers of Other Languages; TeV, tera-electron volt; T.G., temporary gentleman (see *TEMPORARY *a.* 1 b); T.G., thank God (cf. D.G. s.v. D III. 3); TG (*Linguistics*), transformational-generative (grammar) (see *TRANSFORMATIONAL *a.*); TGV [F. *train à grande vitesse*], a type of high-speed French passenger train; T.G.W.U., Transport and General Workers' Union; THC, tetrahydrocannabinol; t.i.d. (*Med.*) [L. *ter in die*], three times a day; T.I.G., Tig (*Engin.*), tungsten inert gas (with reference to welding with a tungsten electrode in an atmosphere of an inert gas); TIR [F. *transport international routier*), international road transport (with reference to an international customs agreement: see quot. 1969); TKO, t.k.o., (chiefly *N. Amer.*), in Boxing, a technical knock-out; also *fig.* and as *v. trans.*; TL, thermoluminescent (dating technique); also *TL-dating*; TLC (*colloq.*), tender loving care; TLC, t.l.c. (*Chem.*), thin-layer chromatography; TLR (*Photogr.*), twin-lens reflex (camera); T.L.S., *The Times Literary Supplement*; TM, trade mark; TM, transcendental meditation; T.M., trench mortar (cf. *TOC EMMA); TMV, tobacco mosaic virus; T.N.T. = *TRINITROTOLUENE; T.O., turn over (cf. P.T.O. = 'please turn over' s.v. P II in Dict. and Suppl.); TOEFL, Test(ing) of English as a Foreign Language; TOFC (orig. *U.S.*), trailer on flatcar (with reference to a type of freight container); TOW, *t*ube-launched, *o*ptically tracked, *w*ire-guided (missile); T.P.R. (*Med.*), temperature, pulse, and respiration; TR (*Electronics*), transmit–receive; usu. *attrib.*; TRF, TRH (*Biochem.*) = *thyrotropin-releasing factor* or *hormone* s.v. *THYRO-2; tRNA (*Biochem.*), transfer RNA; also † T-RNA; T.S. (*U.S. Forces' Slang*), tough shit (also situation, stuff); also used *attrib.* to designate a (real or imaginary) card, etc., allowing the recipient an interview to discuss his grievances with the chaplain; TS (*pl.* TSS), typescript; TSA, Training Services Agency; TSH (*Biochem.*), thyroid-stimulating hormone (cf. *THYROID *sb.* 2 b); tsp., teaspoon(ful); TSS, twin-screw steamer; TSS (see *TS* = typescript above); T.T., t.t., teetotal, a teetotaller; T.T. (*Comm.*), telegraphic transfer; T.T., Tourist Trophy (freq. used *ellipt.* for *Tourist Trophy Race*); T.T. = *tuberculin-tested* ppl. adj. s.v. *TUBERCULIN b; also *transf.*; T.T.F.N. (*colloq.*), 'ta-ta for now' (a catch-phrase popularized by the 1940s BBC radio programme *Itma*); T.T.L. (*Photogr.*), through-the-lens (metering); TTL (*Electronics*) = **transistor-transistor logic* s.v. *TRANSISTOR *sb.* 3 b; TV (*colloq.*, orig. and chiefly *N. Amer.*), a transvestite; T.V.A. [Fr., *taxe á la valeur ajoutée*] = *V.A.T.; T.V.A. (*U.S.*), Tennessee Valley Authority; TVP, textured vegetable protein (proprietary name); see *TEXTURED *a.*; TWA (*U.S.*), Trans World Airlines (formerly, until 1950, Transcontinental and Western Air). See also *TAM, *TANU, *TASS[1], *TEWT, *TIM, *TOPS, *T.U.C., *TV.

1951 *Symbols, Signs & Abbreviations* (R. Soc.) 15 Tera ($\times 10^{12}$) T. **1978** *Guardian Weekly* 27 Aug. 13/3 Sweden's energy requirements..—125 Twh in 1985. **1964** *Internat. System (SI) Units* (*B.S.I.*) 8 The tesla (symbol T) is the name given to this unit in Continental literature. **1973** *Physics Bull.* Sept. 555/3 He used pulsed magnetic fields as high as 30 T. **1978** *Nature* 2 Feb. 407/1 This new quark pair is labelled t and b for 'top' and 'bottom'. *Ibid.* 407/2 The prudish may care to note that t and b are said to stand for truth and beauty, rather than top and bottom, by some physicists. **1984** *Daily Tel.* 5 July 36/4 Discovery of a sub-atomic particle labelled the 'T-top' quark has been announced by scientists at Cern. **1948** GLASSTONE *Textbk. Physical Chem.* (ed. 2) ii. 172 The ^{3}H isotope, called tritium, symbol T, has also been obtained by the bombardment of nitrogen by neutrons.

1973 *Nature* 3 Aug. 257/1 The square-root law of mass-dependence does not apply to isotopic variants HDO and HTO. **1969** C. Davidson in Cockburn & Blackburn *Student Power* 357 These considerations make the organization of a radical trade union of TAs a crucial part of any strategy for change. **1980** *Berkeley Graduate* Oct. 3/4 Matthew Soyster, a Comparative Literature graduate student, is currently a TA in the Rhetoric Department. **1924** *Regulations for Territorial Army* I. iii. 33 An officer appointed to command a brigade..will..be granted such rank in the T.A. temporarily. *Ibid.* iv. 53 The senior T.A. officer in the locality. **1939** W. S. Churchill *Let.* 30 Aug. in M. Gilbert *Winston S. Churchill* (1976) V. liii. 1106 Would it not be helpful to call up the reserves and mobilize the TA? **1980** *Whitaker's Almanack 1981* 473/2 The Territorial Army (TA) is designed to provide a reserve of highly trained and well equipped units and individuals. **1972** *N.Y. Times Mag.* 19 Nov. 42 Initial capitals are common in the vocabulary of Transactional Analysis, or T.A. **1976** *S. Wales Echo* 25 Nov. 16/7 In the group therapy of TA members can see a wider range of ego states than they could on their own, and the collective framework is thought to aid analysis and change. **1957** *Press* (Christchurch, N.Z.) 19 Nov. 16/1 If people want things like the T.A.B., alcohol and cigarettes. **1969** *Sydney Morning Herald* 24 May 27/1 (*heading*) The Moorebank Handicap, second leg of the TAB double. **1977** *Herald* (Melbourne) 17 Jan. 6/8 A spokesman for the TAB head office. **1929** *Lancet* 9 Feb. 288/1 These T.A.B. vaccine injections..caused remission in the course of general paralysis. **1970** *Guardian* 24 Jan. 17/3 The Department of Health advises *all* travellers abroad to take the precaution of a TAB vaccination. **1981** *Brit. Med. Jrnl.* 18 Apr. 1313/1 We all lined up, hand on hip, to receive the dreaded TAB. **1942** Berrey & Van den Bark *Amer. Thes. Slang* §532/1 *T.&A.*, tonsils and adenoids. **1960** in *Arch. Otolaryngology* Aug. 183/1 Tonsilloadenoidectomy (T and A) is often classified as minor surgery. *Ibid.* 186/1 Immediate hemorrhage in the first 24 hours post T and A continued to be approximately 3%–4%. **1976** *Amer. Speech 1973* XLVIII. 204 Relatively simple operations like a *T and A*..are considered routine procedures on the hospital's *OR* (operating room) *schedule.* **1948** *Archit. Rev.* CIII. 133 Exterior walls are of two by four studs, four by four posts, faced externally with wood sheathing and t. and g. vertical boarding. **1949** *Gloss. Terms Timber* (*B.S.I.*) 41 *t. & g.*, tongued and grooved. **1946** *Jrnl. Presonality* XV. 70 The Thematic Apperception Test (TAT)..is a projective device which purports to reveal the basic personality characteristics of individuals. **1952** [see *global *a.* 2]. **1964** M. Argyle *Psychol. & Social Probl.* iv. 49 There are various ways of scoring TAT stories for aggressiveness. **1972** *Jrnl. Social Psychol.* LXXXVIII. 191 The standard Murray TATs.. were not considered appropriate. **1967** *Army Q.* XCIV. 36 T.A.V.R. I and II will be adequately equipped with modern weapons and equipment. **1977** *R.A.F. News* 22 June–5 July 18 (*caption*) The Wapinschaw..attracts entries from many regular and TAVR units in the North of Scotland. **1897**, etc. T.B. = torpedo boat [implied at T.B.D. below]. *a* **1912** W. T. Rogers *Dict. Abbrev.* (1913) 187/1 *T.B.*,..torpedo boat. **1925** R. H. Bacon *Naval Scrap-bk.* x. 144 In the 1895 manœuvres, when I was a Lieutenant of just under twelve years' seniority, I was appointed in command of *No. 94 T.B.* **1938**, etc. [see M.T.B. s.v. *M 5 a]. **1977** Preston & Brown tr. *Jentschura's Warships Imperial Jap. Navy, 1869–1945* ix. 124 TBs. *1–4* were modelled by Sir Edward Reed on the RN 100ft type. They were assembled in Japan. **1936** *Financial Times* 20 Nov. 1/1, 3 months T.B.—*£0 10 6·24 pc. **1971** *Financial Mail* (Johannesburg) 26 Feb. 661/1 National has about R25m of TBs on its book. **1912** D. Lowrie *My Life in Prison* iv. 33 He's doin' 35 years an' has the T.B. **1921** A. Mason *Flying Bo'sun* ii. 19 Their mother died two years ago... The doctor said it was T.B. **1930** J. Lait *Big House* i. 7 A confidence (or 'con') man is a 'T.B.', ('con' is short and slang for consumption, and 'T.B.' is ditto for tuberculosis). **1932** U. Sinclair *Candid Reminiscences* x. 88 The old captain was ill of TB. **1942** C. Himes *Black on Black* (1973) 176 Men..of all stages of deterioration—drifters and hopheads and tb's and beggars and bums and bindle-stiffs and big sisters. **1951** J. Cannan *And all I Learned* x. 180 We've our own cows, T.B. tested and so beautifully kept. **1957** S. Smith *Coll. Poems* (1975) 336, I lay with my young bride in my arms, A girl with t.b. **1974** M. Butterworth *Man in Sopwith Camel* ii. 26 They wouldn't take me 'cos I'd had a touch of TB. **1897** Kipling *Let.* Aug. in C. Carrington *Rudyard Kipling* (1955) xi. 268 Ref: t.b.d. trials. My attention is at present taken up by one small craft recently launched from my own works. **1902** —— *Traffics & Discoveries* (1904) 182 The chief engineer o' the *Djinn*, 31-knot T.B.D. **1919** C. P. Thompson *Cocktails* 249, I passed an enjoyable day giving a T.B.D. lieutenant a headache. **1978** H. Wouk *War & Remembrance* xx. 200 The TBD is a lot slower. **1950** *Good Housek. Picture Cookery* 170/2 Coffee Glacé Icing. 8 oz. icing sugar 2 tbsps. water. Coffee essence to taste. **1974** J. Paxton *Everyman's Dict. Abbrev.* 338/1 *tbs., tbsp.*, tablespoon; tablespoonful. **1977** *Times Lit. Suppl.* 1 Apr. 391/2, I only wish my dog *liked* his food sprinkled with the recommended 2 tbs of the product every day. **1944** TBS [see *gravelly *a.* 5]. **1946** *Sat. Even. Post* 26 Oct. 66/3 The astounded admiral grabbed the TBS radio and shouted. **1978** H. Wouk *War & Remembrance* xv. 153 Rear Admiral Spruance, issuing order after order on the TBS, finally regained a semblance of control. **1960** *Farmer & Stockbreeder* 22 Mar. 136/3 After T.C.A. treatment 8 weeks should elapse before planting potatoes. **1971** *Arable Farmer* Feb. 15/2 A pre-planting application of TCA to peas may reduce the waxiness of the crop foliage, leading to unexpected damage from dinoseb applied subsequently. **1969** S. E. Henderson in Cook & Henderson *Militant Black Writer* 78 These poems were not intended for white readers and white audiences..their purpose was direct address to the black community, to get us together to TCB. **1973** *New Times* 2 Nov. 41 Where he is always to be found TCB'ing (takin' care of business, an old ghetto phrase which originally meant to copulate). **1831** M. C. Taylor *Let.* 22 June in J. J. Auchmuty *Sir T. Wyse* (1939) ix. 134 The Scholars of T.C.D. do not afford a Protestant, a learned or an independent constituency. **1916** H. Plunkett *Jrnl.* 29 Apr. in M. Digby *Plunkett* (1949) ix. 212 The firing from the other side of the T.C.D. guards was so fierce that we had to turn back. **1939** Joyce *Finnegans Wake* 424 Go o'er the sea, haythen, from me and leave your libber to TCD. **1979** J. Sheehan in J. J. Lee *Ireland 1945–70* 67 A UCD/TCD merger or co-ordination of some sort. **1971** *New Yorker* 14 Aug. 57 The only real question concerning the safety of 2,4,5-T has to do with the TCDD dioxin with which it is contaminated. **1981** *McGraw-Hill Yearbk. Sci. & Technol.* 199/2 It is impossible to substantiate the charge that TCDD has led to an increase in the number of malformed children in Vietnam. **1960** *Jrnl. Amer. Chem. Soc.* LXXXII. 6408/1, 7,7,8,8-Tetracyanoquinodimethane (TCNQ) has been synthesized and found to yield a series of stable anion-radical derivatives. **1979** *Sci. Amer.* Oct. 48/2 Many salts in which TCNQ is combined with other atoms or molecules form linear-chain solids. **1934** *Trade Marks Jrnl.* 22 Aug. 1084/1 *T.C.P.*... Antiseptic and germicide solutions (being disinfectants). British Alkaloids Limited, 104, Winchester House, Old Broad Street, London, E.C.2; manufacturing chemists. **1947** J. Lees-Milne *Diary* 22 Jan. (1983) 128 Cut my mole shaving this morning and thought it would never stop bleeding. T.C.P. finally staunched it. **1959** I. & P. Opie *Lore & Lang. Schoolch.* ix. 171 Earnestly applying T.C.P...in the privacy of their bedrooms. **1981** G. Kaye *Day after Yesterday* ii. 22 You cried when you only scraped your knee..a little scrape and a bit of TCP. **1957** *Physical Rev.* CVI. 385/1 According to a general theorem, invariance with respect to the product *TCP* follows for a wide class of field theories from invariance with respect to the proper Lorentz group alone. **1974** Frauenfelder & Henley *Subatomic Physics* ix. 223 When violation of parity became a possibility the *TCP* theorem suddenly acquired more meaning. **1979** J. C. Polkinghorne *Particle Play* iii. 47 We do not know how to write down any theories which are not invariant under TCP. **1947** S. Malone *Notes on Procedure in Houses of Oireachtas* p. vii, Members of Daíl Eirann (Teachtaí Dála)—referred to as T.D.'s or Deputies. **1959** B. Chubb in D. E. Butler et al. *Elections Abroad* iii. 187 TD—Teachta Dála; the Irish equivalent of Member of Parliament. TDs are addressed as 'Deputy'. **1979** M. Manning in J. J. Lee *Ireland 1945–70* 51 Its TDs tended to act more as independents than as members of a political party. **1924** *Regulations for Territorial Army* I. x. 145 The letters 'T.D.' will be inserted in the Army List after the name of the officer on whom the decoration is conferred. **1981** *Whitaker's Almanack 1982* 248 *Alport*, Cuthbert James McCall Alport, P.C., T.D. **1953** Berrey & Van den Bark *Amer. Thes. Slang* (1954) §692/2 Touchdown,..*TD, touch.* **1969** *Eugene* (Oregon) *Register-Guard* 3 Dec. 2D/1 Nyseth scored three TDs en route to 137 yards. **1970** *Globe & Mail* (Toronto) 25 Sept. 33/3 Another fumble set up Riverdale's second TD when Bob Nichols recovered the ball in Lions' end zone. **1977** *Detroit Free Press* 11 Dec. 10-D/4 TD passes, home runs, goals or point averages. **1970** G. F. Newman *Sir, You Bastard* ii. 45 TDC Sneed and DC Lambert to watch on Sloane Square to investigate shoplifting complaint. **1978** B. Norman *To nick Good Body* ii. 9 A temporary detective constable..had just brought in the Guv'nor's tea... The Guv'nor waved the T.D.C. **1938** *Jrnl. R. Aeronaut. Soc.* XLII. 888 T.D.C. or any other reference marks are marked by the discharge flash of a thyratron circuit, controlled by suitable contacts on the engine crankshaft. **1976** *New Motorcycling Monthly* Oct. 34/2 With piston at TDC, pull barrel up mounting studs. **1946** *Nature* 6 July 22/1 'D.D.D.' or 'T.D.E.' The compound 2.2-*bis*(*p*-chlorphenyl)1,1-dichlorethane..has been shown to be about as toxic as D.D.T. to mosquito larvæ in laboratory tests. **1970** *New Scientist* 1 Jan. 16/1 Much of this case also applies..to the other 'hard' organochlorine insecticides: aldrin,..BHC and TDE (Rhothane). **1948** G. Crowther *Outl. Money* (ed. 2) ii. 37 There are four main types of bank assets, which are..bills.., Treasury Deposit Receipts (usually known as TDRs), investments and loans. **1965** J. L. Hanson *Dict. Econ. & Commerce* 383/1 By 1945 T.D.R.s had reached a total of over £1,800 million. **1899** P. G. Lewis *Nursing* ii. 18 Medicines are ordered to be taken either statim (immediately), or t.d.s. = ter die sumenda (to be taken three times a day). **1919** *Jrnl. R. Naval Med. Service* V. 93 He was given quinine 15 gr. t.d.s. **1961** *Lancet* 29 July 238/1 The response of our patients to a course of 20 electroshock treatments or to chlorpromazine 100–400 mg. t.d.s. **1963** *Times* 23 May 13/7 TEE trains now link 90 European cities. **1967** R. Sawkins *Snow in Paradise* iii. 29 The TEE is just about as quick as the plane. **1977** J. Paxton *Dict. Europ. Econ. Community* 246 *Trans-Europ-Express* (*T.E.E.*). Trans-Europ-Expresses connect major cities in nine European countries by a network of very fast and comfortable trains for which frontier formalities have been reduced to a minimum. **1963** *Language Learning* (Univ. of Michigan) XIII. 225 (*heading*) Reflections on Preparation for TEFL. **1968** *Language* XLIV. 206 Any gathering of TEFL leaders today will be sure to include a large number who received their initial experience at Michigan. **1977** P. Strevens *New Orientations Teaching of English* v. 56 The American terms TEFL, TESL, TESOL, TESOLD have no precise counterparts in British usage. **1981** *Guardian* 14 Apr. 21/4 (Advt.), Applications are invited from candidates who have experience in..Tefl. **1967** *Sat. Rev.* (U.S.) 16 Sept. 83 Though a major curriculum emphasis is developing fluency in the English language using the linguistic approach of TESL (Teaching English as a Second Language), the knowledge of Navaho is still essential to many jobs on the reservation. **1980** *Verbatim* Spring 20/1 A dictionary or international English might have remembered TESL and TEFL 'teaching of English as a Second (or Foreign) Language', however. **1969** *Language* XLV. 171 The two halves of the collection, articles on the description of English and articles on TESOL, reflect the sad dichotomy between descriptive linguists and language-teaching methodologists the world over. **1956** *Proc. CERN Symposium* I. 64/2 These machines would have equivalent energies of 1340 Gev, or 1·3 Tev. **1980** *Sci. Amer.* Jan. 32/3 Completion of the full lower ring is now expected toward the end of 1981, and protons at 1 TeV should be delivered to the experimental areas in 1982. **1916** N. Mitchison *Jrnl.* in *All Change Here* (1975) xv. 147 Last night about half a dozen[officers] came into the salon and started a conversation... They were awful TGs mostly... Here am I, sitting..in the middle of the stuffy salon of a third-rate French hotel, being as charming as I can to an audience of TGs, all to give them the memory of a pleasant evening to take back to the trenches at Givenchy. **1934** J. Rhys *Voyage in Dark* I. i. 17 'Only three more weeks of this damned tour, T.G.,' Maudie said. 'It's no life.' **1978** D. Murphy *Place Apart* xi. 226 Isn't it a tough world to be tryin' to raise twelve boys in? But T.G. so far they're good lads. **1968** B. M. H. Strang *Mod. Eng. Structure* (ed. 2) 200 The most eminent TG thinkers are still evolving and modifying parts of their theory. **1971** *Archivum Linguisticum* III. 64 Of recent years it is transformational-generative grammar (TG) that has undoubtedly called the tune. **1977** *Trans. Philol. Soc. 1975* 8 General linguists unsympathetic to TG. **1978** *English Jrnl.* Dec. 52/1 On the other hand, we should not jump indiscriminately into transformational-generative grammar. A full-blown TG grammar is complex. **1980** *N.Y. Times* 19 Nov. 17/1 Among the trains being studied as possible models for Ohio is the French TGV. [**1924** G. D. H. Cole *Organised Labour* II. i. 20 The Transport Workers' Federation, which..has lost much of its importance since the formation of the T. and G.W.U.] **1955** *Times* 2 May 12/6 He became general secretary of the T.G.W.U. in 1945. **1957** *Economist* 26 Oct. 292/1 Last July the TGWU, together with the other unions involved, called an official strike of the provincial busmen. **1977** M. Walker *National Front* vi. 157 It was an American executive who flew to secret talks with the TGWU union negotiators at Llandudno. **1968** *Time* 19 Apr. 79 At a Chicago conference on psychedelic drugs, Dr. Donald R. Jasinski..reported that he had produced LSD-like symptons with tetrahydrocannabinol (THC), one of the purified active ingredients of cannabis. **1974** *Times Lit. Suppl.* 8 Mar. 240/5 Marijuana smokers in the United States are 'playing at cannabis use'—in that their daily ingestion of THC is only one-fifth of that of users in India, Egypt or Morocco. **1885** C. S. Weeks *Textbk. Nursing* vii. 105/2 *T.i.d.*, *ter in dies*, three times a day. **1941** *Jrnl. R. Naval Med. Service* XXVII. 301 The course of atebrin tablets, one t.i.d. **1976** *Amer. Speech 1973* XLVIII. 198 Referring to the exact times a patient must have a certain medication are *b.i.d.* for *bis in die* 'twice daily', *t.i.d.* for *ter in die* 'three times a day', [etc.]. **1960** *McGraw-Hill Encycl. Sci. & Technol.* XIV. 467/2 Inert gas shielding is essential with tungsten electrodes, hence the term Tungsten Inert Gas (TIG) welding. **1969** D. K. Allen *Metallurgy Theory & Practice* xix. 612 (*caption*) Photomicrograph of a Tig weld with low voltage electron beam weld in center of Tig nugget to show relative width of heat affected zone in each process. **1975** Bram & Downs *Manuf. Technol.* ii. 55 The T.I.G. process differs from the manual metal-arc technique in as much as the electrode is virtually non-consumable. **1968** E. Pugh *Dict. Acronyms & Abbrev.* 169 *TIR*, Transports Internationale Routiers [*sic*]. **1969** *Jane's Freight Containers 1968–69* 141/1 For road transport, the so-called 'TIR' Convention, concluded under the auspices of the ECE, allows the transport of goods under Customs seal in lorries from the Customs office of departure to the Customs office of arrival. **1980** K. Hagenbach *Fox Potential* xii. 119 We passed a couple of big TIR trucks, each pulling a trailer. **1942** Berrey & Van den Bark *Amer. Thes. Slang* §704/1 Technical knockout,..*T.K.O.* **1956** 'T. Betts' *Across the Board* xxi. 296 Endocrinology TKO's Freud in the second round. **1968** M. Richler in R. Weaver *Canad. Short Stories* 2nd Ser. 164 'You lost by a TKO,' my father said. 'Thanks,' my mother said. **1971** *Weekend World* (Johannesburg) 9 May 1/3 Tulwana's fly weight title which Dlamini took on a third round t.k.o. **1975** J. Gores *Hammett* (1976) iii. 28 Revani TKO'd his Filipino opponent after..using his gut as a workout bag in the fourth [round]. **1972** *Oxf. Univ. Gaz.* CII. Suppl. II. 12 Development and application of TL at the National Museum, Edinburgh. **1978** *Times* 11 Nov. 3 TL-dating was developed in the 1960s for dating pottery and other fired materials from archaeological sites. **1960** I. A. Stanton *Dict. for Medical Secretaries* 149/1 *T.L.C.*, abbreviation for tender, loving care. **1973** *Publishers Weekly* 19 Nov. 55/1 The contagious potential of his TLC when he launches a yarn. **1977** *Listener* 12 May 605/3 It is in a nurse's nature and in her tradition to give to the sick what is well called 'TLC', 'tender loving care'. **1961** *Jrnl. Amer. Oil Chemists Soc.* XXXVIII. 316/1 TLC has a number of features which make it an ideal technique for the analysis of these compounds. **1975** Williams & Wilson *Biologist's Guide to Princ. & Techniques Pract. Biochem.* iii. 58 Adsorbents used in t.l.c. differ from column adsorbents in that they may contain a binding agent such as calcium sulphate. **1980** *Nature* 8 May 105/1 To determine the sequence of the two amino acids, the active sample was dansylated, hydrolysed and the dansyl derivative examined by TLC. **1965** M. J. Langford *Basic Photogr.* 376/1 (Index), TLR. **1978** *SLR Camera* Sept. 61/1 Rollei..originally only manufactured top quality TLR cameras. **1979** *Amat. Photographer* 10 Jan. 110/2 I'd recommend the TLR every time if monochrome prints are the objective, more so when the prints are to over 10×8in. **1953** R. Crawshay-Williams *Let.* 1 Aug. in B. Russell *Autobiogr.* (1969) III. ii. 91 There are a nice lot of sly digs..the T.L.S. pastiche. **1967** E. Coxhead *Thankless Muse* i. 18 A little advance something in the TLS never comes amiss, does it? **1977** *Bookseller* 4 June 2704/2 The *Times Literary Supplement* (never called the *T.L.S.* then [in 1952]). **1961** Webster, TM, trademark. **1964** *Trademarks in Marketplace* (U.S. Trademark Assoc.) 64 We use the term 'trademark' right under the selected word, or we put a little 'TM' in the place where you normally would put the ®. **1980** *Sci. Amer.* Oct. 138/1 (Advt.), The Clan of the Cave Bear, Earth's Children™, a novel by Jean M. Auel. **1967** *Listener* 7 Sept. 299/1, I hear you're hostile to drugs now and have taken to TM. **1977** E. V. Cunningham *Case of One-Penny Orange* (1978) ix. 110 Topanga Canyon.. had..sensitivity centers and nudist camps and TM temples. **1980** *Times* 27 May 1/8 The Home office does not approve the use of TM in borstals or prisons. **1925** Fraser & Gibbons *Soldier & Sailor Words* 275 T.M. batteries were created for trench warfare and T.M. schools of instruction were established. **1930** Brophy & Partridge *Songs & Slang 1914–1918* 173 When a T.M.

battery had fired a few shots it departed with speed. **1960** *Proc. Nat. Acad. Sci.* XLVI. 636 (*heading*) The amino acid composition and C-terminal sequence of a chemically evoked mutant of TMV. **1974** W. K. Joklik in Carlile & Steehel *Evolution in Microbial World* 298 The fascinating work of Klug and his colleagues with TMV. **1915** D. O. Barnett *Let.* 4 July 203 The yellow muck doesn't choke you, though, like the black greasy smoke (T.N.T.) which they generally have in the 6 and 8-inch shells. **1962** E. Snow *Other Side of River* (1963) xxix. 217 A responsible Western physicist's estimate that the world then possessed a nuclear weapons stockpile roughly the equivalent of forty tons of TNT for each person alive. **1979** O. Sela *Petrograd Consignment* 53 The casing contains a pound of TNT and it can be attached to a timing device. **1853** Mrs. Gaskell *Cranford* v. 68 However, at the foot of the page was a small 'T.O.', and on turning it over, sure enough, there was a letter to 'my dear, dearest Molly'. **1889** E. C. Dowson *Let.* c 23 Jan. (1967) 29 When we will proceed to Pinoli or where you will. T.O. Act à votre discretion in the matter of booking seats. **1981** *Oxf. Dict. for Writers & Editors* 412/2 *TO*, turn over. **1964** *Overseas* Jan. 22 On February 17, 1964, a new English-proficiency test for foreign students will be administered overseas. Called TOEFL for short, this Test of English as a Foreign Language is designed to help..assess the language competence of foreign students. **1972** J. L. Dillard *Black English* 272 It is of primary importance that all such materials, like all TOEFL materials, take the student's native language (here, dialect) into full account. **1954** TOFC [see *pick-a-back *adv. phr.* (*a.*, *sb.*) b]. **1964** *Economist* 26 Sept. 1243/1 The [US] railways have introduced TOFC service—trailer-on-flatcar, better known as Piggyback. **1969** TOFC [see *kangaroo *sb.* 3 h]. **1972** *Guardian* 22 Aug. 3/1 The missiles [are] called TOWs... TOW stands for tube-launched, optically tracked, and wire-guided. **1976** *N.Y. Times* 28 Mar. 1 The TOW missile can be used offensively from jeeps or armed cars. **1917** V. Brittain *Let.* 5 Dec. in *Testament of Youth* (1933) viii. 395 Morning work—i.e. beds, T.P.R.s (temperatures, pulses, respirations), washings, medicines, etc. **1976** *Amer. Speech 1973* XLVIII. 197 His *vitals* 'vital signs' such as temperature, pulse, and respiration (*TPR*). **1945** *Electronic Industries* Sept. 226 *T R switch*, transmit–receive switch. A switch which prevents the transmitted energy from getting to the receiver, but allows the received energy, which is much weaker, to reach the receiver without appreciable loss. This is necessary when the same antenna is used for both transmission and reception. **1975** D. G. Fink *Electronics Engineers' Handbk.* IX. 23 Such limiters are replacing TR gas discharge tubes in radar. **1959** K. Shibusawa et al. in *Endocrinol. Jap.* VI. 31 We found a thyroid stimulating neurohumor in the hypothalamus... It was provisionally designated by us as TRF (Thyrotropin Releasing Factor). **1972** *Clin. Endocrinol.* (1973) (B.M.A.) 47 Thyrotrophin-releasing factor (TRF), has recently been synthesized. **1968** A. V. Schally et al. in *Rec. Progr. Hormone Res.* XXIV. 449 (*table*) Present name... Thyrotropin-releasing factor. TRF... Proposed name... Thyrotropin-releasing hormone. TRH. **1977** *Proc. R. Soc. Med.* LXX. 698/1 The chief value of the thyrotrophin releasing hormone (TRH) test has been the diagnosis of dysthyroid eye disease. **1962** *Cold Spring Harbor Symp. Quantitative Biol.* XXVIII. 559 The system consisted of *E. coli* ribosomes and high speed super natant which contained transfer RNA (T-RNA), the amino acyl-T-RNA synthetases, and the enzymes involved in the final steps of the synthesis of the polypeptide chain. **1966** *Ibid.* XXXI. 587/1 The elution profiles of noninfected-cell and infected cell arginyl tRNA exhibit unambiguous major differences. **1977** *Time* 4 Apr. 39/2 Aaron Klug..first determined the crystalline structure of transfer RNA (tRNA), the molecule that brings amino acids to the ribosome for assembly into protein. **1944** A. M. Taylor *Lang. World War II* 69 TS Cards: Beachhead chaplains are carrying a special 'tough stuff' ticket these days which they issue to guys with complaints about which nothing can be done. **1944** *Yank* 18 Aug. 16/2, I..will be ever grateful for any possible solution, for I have tried everything I know, even prayer. Still TS. **1946** *Amer. Speech* XXI. 249 A *T.S. ticket* is an imaginary form entitling the bearer to sympathy and nothing else. 'All I can do is punch ya T.S. ticket (or slip) for ya.' **1946** *Amer. Jrnl. Sociol.* Mar. 422 One such expression is 'TS' or 'tough s—'... 'TS', resigned acceptance, said with a bitter smile. **1966** *Sunday Times* (Colour Suppl.) 4 Dec. 73/4 [GI Jargon] *TS*, tough situation. **1942** Partridge *Dict. Abbrev.* 97/1 *t.s.* or *ts.* or *ts*; also *T.S.*, etc., typescript. **1975** *Record* (Oxf. Univ. Press) xx. 24/1, 11 unsolicited poetry TSS in one week. **1975** *Petroleum Rev.* XXIX. 399/2 The TSA has been very active since its inception. **1976** *Even. Post* (Nottingham) 15 Dec. 12/7 The TSA's direct training services which include the provision of specially tailored courses to meet individual requirements. **1941** *Trans. Amer. Assoc. Study Goiter* 161 Media, which originally contained TSH in a concentration equivalent to one unit per cubic centimeter were found to have lost about seven-eighths of their activity. **1983** *Oxf. Textbk. Med.* I. x. 12/2 Hypothyroidism due to TSH deficiency is often mild and easily overlooked. **1950** *Good Housek. Picture Cookery* 161/1 Unboiled fondant. 1 lb icing sugar..tartar ..1 tsp. lemon juice..1 egg white. **1955** R. J. Schwartz *Compl. Dict. Abbrev.* 178/1 *tsp*, teaspoon. **1973** Rubinstein & Bush *Penguin Freezer Cookbk.* 211, ½ lb. tomatoes, 1 tsp. allspice, 1 tsp. pine kernels. **1935** Duckworth & Langmuir *West Highland Steamers* ii. 107 T.S.S. 'Flowerdale'..came into Mr. MacBrayne's hands as his first twin screw sea-going steamer. **1981** 'J. Ashford' *Loss of 'Culion'* viii. 52, I understand you've some information on the sinking of the TSS *Culion*..in the Indian Ocean. [**1841** *Niles' Reg.* 21 Feb. 400/3 TTT. They have temperance wagons in the west, marked with three Ts, to denote that the owner is a tee-to-taller.] **1922** Joyce *Ulysses* 159 Selfish those t.t's are. Dog in the manger. **1936** *Punch* 22 July 97/2 Every birthday he gets a magnificent..Gift Of wine... It is sad To add I've brought him up to be T.T. **1975** J. Symons *Three Pipe Problem* v. 35 Can't offer you a beer, strict TT. **1893** R. Bithell *Counting-House Dict.* (rev. ed.) 292 *T.T.*, telegraphic transfer. **1927** *Financial Times* 3 May 1/4 Kobe, T.T. Yen 24·58d. **1940** *Economist* 11 May 862/2 This compares with..⅛ per cent. for T.T. redemptions from Palestine. **1966** A. Gilpin *Dict. Econ. Terms* 201 (*heading*) Telegraphic Transfer ('T.T.'). **1913** W. T. Rogers *Dict. Abbrev.* 192/1 *T.T.* (motor), Tourist Trophy machine *Ibid.*, *T.T. Race* (motor), Auto-Cycle Tourist Trophy Race. **1914** *Autocar* 16 May 948/2 (*heading*) The T.T. race. **1929** *Motor* 2 July 1060/1 A driver who has, after all, driven at Le Mans and in the T.T. **1976** *Southern Even. Echo* (Southampton) 17 Nov. 21/5 The Isle of Man programme will include the usual classic TT. **1927** *Field* 15 Sept. 413/1 There are now a larger number of farmers producing Grade A (T.T.) milk. **1958** *Times* 28 July 11/5 A T.T. dairy farm. **1970** A. Jenkins *Drinka Pinta* x. 105 Scots were particularly keen that it should be Grade 'A' (T.T.) milk. **1948** F. Worsley *ITMA* 21 The beloved Cockney Charlady, Mrs. Mopp (played by Dorothy Summers)..did not make her first appearance..until 10th October, 1941... Another of her famous sayings were the letters 'T.T.F.N.'—a contraction of 'Ta-ta for now' with which she made her exit. **1966** A. Hall *Frost* 19 'See you soon then.' 'T.T.F.N.' **1976** *Observer* 11 Apr. 2/6 JY [*sc.* Jimmy Young] said TTFN to Mr Healey. **1963** *Electronics* 22 Mar. 54/1 Transistor-transistor logic (TTL) offers a saturated-transistor logic that is simple, compact, and has a high degree of design flexibility. **1967** *Ibid.* 6 Mar. 123/1 Litton Industries Inc. had developed the 'Phoenix gate' TTL for the Phoenix missile. **1977** *Sci. Amer.* Sept. 79/3 Compared with the previous family of RTL gates, TTL circuits provide greater output power (so that more gates in the next stage of an array can be driven), less stringent tolerances in manufacturing and greater immunity to spurious voltages. **1968** *Amateur Photographer* 24 Apr. 4/2 (Advt.), The most sought after T.T.L. camera! **1978** *Ibid.* 2 Aug. 101/1 Landscapes with a lot of sky detail in the shot can often be wrongly exposed, particularly if the camera has TTL metering. **1965** *Realist* Mar. 24 TVs are not as feminine as they themselves think they are. **1979** J. Hansen *Skinflick* (1980) x. 81 Spence doesn't want to be fooled. He knows I'm a TV. **1983** *The Magazine* Apr. 24/3 We get a lot of TVs in and a few of the leather boys of course. **1963** *Times* 2 Feb. 9/5 When we enter the Common Market,.. a T.V.A. (tax value added) tax will have to be substituted for purchase tax. **1963** *Economist* 17 Aug. 567/2 The probable impact of a TVA tax on different types of industries. **1965** *Listener* 22 Apr. 585/2 The added-value tax is commonly known as the TVA. **1935** *Harvard Law Rev.* XLVIII. 806 It would seem that if the TVA is in fact unconstitutional, the contracts are subject to rescission. **1936** *N.Y. Herald Tribune* 4 June 36/8 The T.V.A. development. **1943** J. S. Huxley *TVA* 7 TVA stands for Tennessee Valley Authority, and the Tennessee Valley Authority is the outstanding example of democratic planning. **1965** Mrs. L. B. Johnson *White House Diary* 7 Apr. (1970) 256 Lyndon talked about the vast Mekong River project which can provide food and water and power on a scale to dwarf even our own TVA. **1968** *Guardian* 4 July 7/6 What TVP has been created from is mercifully not revealed. **1969** *Official Gaz.* (U.S. Patent Office) 18 Mar. 120/2 *TVP*... For unflavored and meat and poultry flavored vegetable protein food... First use on or before May 2, 1966. **1974** *Observer* (Colour Suppl.) 24 Feb. 14/1 High-protein mock-meat has been in use in a fairly small way for some years... Known as tvp—textured vegetable protein—it comes in 'extruded' chunks, or minced. **1975** *Trade Marks Jrnl.* 21 May 1049/1 *TVP*... Foods prepared from soya bean derivatives and included in Class 9. Archer Daniels Midland Company.., Decatur, Illinois, United States of America; manufacturers and merchants. **1976** *Times Lit. Suppl.* 13 Feb. 166/1 The chunks of fictionalized, texturized social history (which are to drama as TVP to steak). **1933** *Meccano Mag.* Apr. 270/2 T.W.A. state that most of the transcontinental air mail is carried by their machines. **1941** B. Schulberg *What makes Sammy Run?* vi. 93 They were flying back again via TWA. **1960** [see *red carpet* s.v. *red *a.* 19 a]. **1976** *National Observer* (U.S.) 17 Apr. 20/5 Pressed by banks that had lent TWA millions, he sold his TWA stock for $546,549,171.

b. *Biol.* T designates lymphocytes that are derived from or have been processed by the thymus, which are responsible for cellular immune reactions.

1970 *New Scientist* 7 May 271/1 Some of the lymphocytes ..'stray' into the thymus gland, where they are converted ..into a new sort of lymphocyte, called a T cell. **1973** *Sci. Amer.* July 58/1 *T* cells and *B* cells cannot be distinguished by their form. **1974** *Nature* 8 Feb. 387/2 T lymphocytes in human peripheral blood may be identified by their ability to form rosettes *in vitro* with untreated sheep erythrocytes. **1976** *Path. Ann.* XI. 437 During famine the severity and frequency of diseases kept in check by T-cell function, such as tuberculosis, will increase. **1982** Arms & Camp *Biology* (ed. 2) xxxiv. 541 Lymphocytes may be divided into two major groups, T lymphocytes and B lymphocytes.

6*. In combinations containing the abbrev. T (or extension, as T.D.) followed by a word, as **T-Bill** [Treasury sb.] = *treasury bill* s.v. Treasury *sb.* 6 (cf. *T.B.*, sense 6 a above); **T.D. pipe** *U.S.* [see quot. 1889], a kind of clay pipe; **T-group** *Psychol.* [Training *vbl. sb.*], a sensitivity-training group (see *sensitivity 4); **T-man** *U.S. colloq.* [Treasury *sb.*: cf. *G-man b], a law enforcement officer of the Treasury Department; **T-rule** *Linguistics* [Transformational *a.*] = transformational rule (see *transformational *a.*); **T scale, score** *Psychol.* [Thorndike-Terman (see quot. 1922)], a method of scaling or scoring a psychological test; **T stop** (*Photogr.*) [Transmission], a measured point on a scale of aperture values based on the actual light transmitted through the lens of a camera; similarly *T number*; **T-unit** *Linguistics* [Terminable *a.*], a minimal terminable unit (see quot. 1965).

1982 *Daily Tel.* 27 Sept. 18 Examples..occur in financial futures, with the difference between the futures price and the price of its underlying cash instrument (cf. gold futures and the bullion price, or T-Bill futures and cash T-Bills). **1880** *Harvard Lampoon* 19 Mar. 26/2 So, after he had taken his breath of fresh air, he filled his T.D. pipe. **1889** *Amer. N. & Q.* II. 114 'T.D. Pipes'.. It is said that they took their name from Timothy Dexter, an eccentric capitalist, who in his will left a large sum of money to be expended in the erection of a factory where cheap clay pipes, such as those that now bear the name of 'T.D.'s', were to be manufactured. [**1947** E. H. Paul *Linden on Saugus Branch* 27 Deacon Parker, known to the boys as T.D., because he smoked the one-cent clay pipes of that name.] **1950** *Jrnl. Social Issues* VI. ii. 3 Most of the core staff goes through a 'Practicuum in Group Membership' seminar worked out along the lines of the 'T' group training program at the National Training Laboratory in Group Development. **1967** M. Argyle *Psychol. Interpersonal Behaviour* x. 193 T (training)-groups were first developed in the National Training Laboratories at Bethel, Maine, in 1947... The members of a T-group spend their time studying the group and the processes of social interaction that take place in it. **1977** *N.Y. Times* 15 July c 22/2 We already spend far too much time practicing artificial modes of sociability, such as group encounters, sensitivity training, 'T' groups, Rolfing and the like. **1938** *Sun* (Baltimore) 12 Mar. 10/7 Comparatively little has been heard in late times about the Treasury Department's 'T-men'. **1952** *Daily Progress* (Charlottesville, Va.) 6 Feb. 1/5 T-man William Frank says backdating of tax returns is the major irregularity he found. **1951** G. H. Sewell *Amateur Film-Making* (ed. 2) iii. 32 The T number indicates the actual light transmission obtained by measuring instruments. **1961** G. Millerson *Telev. Production* iii. 38 Modern lenses are sometimes marked in 'T' numbers rather than f-numbers. **1964** E. Bach *Introd. Transformational Gram.* iv. 60 The difference between PS rules and T rules can be made clearer.. by the following remarks. **1976** *Language* LII. 108 In 1962, Wolfgang Motsch proposed a T-rule for a class of German adjectives. **1922** W. A. McCall *How to measure in Educ.* x. 299 It is a tribute to their genius to call the proposed unit..a Thorndike–Terman, or, for brevity, a T... Every product scales [*sic*] may be transmuted into T scales, thereby making all scales performance scales. **1954** A. Anastasi *Psychol. Testing* iv. 83 If the normalized standard score is multiplied by 10 and added to or subtracted from 50, it is converted into a *T-score*, a type of score first proposed by McCall. **1970** F. G. Brown *Princ. Educ. & Psychol. Testing* vii. 173 *T* scores were originally defined..with reference to a particular norm group. .. However, as used today, the *T*-score designation generally applies to any normalized standard score system with $\bar{X} = 50$ and $s = 10$. **1956** J. J. Rose *Amer. Cinematographer* (ed. 9) 133 The new method of calibration will be known as the 'T' Stop system, the T denoting transmission of light and the 'T' stops representing absolutely accurate light measurement. **1977** J. Hedgecoe *Photographer's Handbk.* 344 *'T' stops*, more accurate measurement of light entering a lens than 'f' numbers. **1965** K. W. Hunt *Gram. Structure written at Three Grade Levels* iii. 21 These units might be christened 'minimal terminable units', since they would be minimal as to length, and each would be grammatically capable of being terminated with a capital letter and a period. For short, the 'minimal terminable unit' might be nicknamed a 'T-unit'... T-unit will be the name used for it in this investigation. **1975** *Language for Life* (Dept. Educ. & Sci.) iii. 39 Writing of high quality can employ a simple style that would not necessarily yield a high score as measured by the T-unit. **1977** *Publ. Amer. Dial. Soc. 1974* LXI/LXII. 30 The transcripts of these interviews (exclusive of garbles and false starts) were marked off into T-units and the mean length of T-units was computed for each informant.

6.** Used as a symbol. **a.** *Physics.* [Adopted as being the next letter after S alphabetically (cf. *S 7).] *T* is the symbol of the quantum number of iso-spin; = *I 7 b.

1937 E. Wigner in *Physical Rev.* LI. 110/1 The quantum numbers S_z, T_ζ, Y can be called magnetic quantum numbers. They determine..the μ uniquely. *Ibid.* 117/1 A total isotopic spin T will be a term with the same binding energy for all nuclei with isotopic numbers from −T to T. **1974** *Encycl. Brit. Macropædia* XIII. 339/2 Isospin-equal-one states can exist in the three isobars $^6_2$He, $^6_3$Li, and in $^6_4$Be, whereas the $T = 0$ state can exist only in $^6_3$Li.

b. *Bacteriology.* [Initial letter of *type*.] T followed by a numeral is the designation of certain strains of phages of the bacterium *Escherichia coli* that have been much used experimentally. So *T-even*, designating the strains for which the numeral is even.

1944 *Proc. Nat. Acad. Sci.* XXX. 398 The viruses used were the strains α and γ described by Delbrück and Luria and a new strain..which has been determined to be identical with strain *T7* of Demerec and Fano [*reference given to paper* 'in press', *quoted next*:] **1945** Demerec & Fano in *Genetics* XXX. 119 The materials used in our experiments consisted of the same bacterial strain—*E. coli* B—previously used by Luria and Delbrück.., of seven phage strains active on B, and of various strains of bacteria.. resistant to one or more of the phages. The phage strains were indicated as type 1 to type 7 (T1 to T7). **1960** *New Biol.* XXXI. 78 One group of the larger phages..has become the best understood of any kind of virus. These are the closely related T2, T4 and T6, known collectively as the T-even phages. **1968** H. Harris *Nucleus & Cytoplasm* iii. 46 It was known at the time that this work was undertaken that when *E. coli* cells were infected with the T-even bacteriophages net synthesis of bacterial RNA was rapidly inhibited. **1973** R. G. Krueger et al. *Introd. Microbiol.* xiv. 410/2 Studies of T4 mutants have gone a long way towards elucidating the steps by which biological structures, such as the head and tail of the virus, are assembled.

c. *Astronautics.* [Initial letter of *time.*] T represents the time at which a spacecraft is due to be launched.

1959 *Manch. Guardian* 3 Jan. 5 'T-time' is the moment the firing switch is closed to set off a missile. **1970** N. ARMSTRONG et al. *First on Moon* ii. 32 Only in the latter stages of the final countdown does the nomenclature change to T minus hours and minutes.

IV. 9. 2,4,5-*T*: a selective herbicide used esp. for controlling brushwood; 2,4,5-trichlorophenoxyacetic acid, $C_6H_2Cl_3{\cdot}O{\cdot}CH_2COOH$.

1947 *Bot. Gaz.* CIX. 194/2 The use of 2,4-dichlorophenoxyacetic acid (2,4-D) has been emphasized in nearly all investigations.., although the possible use of 2,4,5-trichlorophenoxyacetic acid (2,4,5-T) for similar purposes was recognized by Hamner and Tukey. **1956** *Nature* 3 Mar. 418/1 An investigation into the effect of the arboricide 2,4,5-T on freshly cut stumps of thicket suggests that this substance may be of practical value in preventing regeneration. **1977** *New Yorker* 25 July 37/2 The military had withdrawn huge stocks of Agent Orange—a fifty-fifty mixture of 2,4,5-T and 2,4-D, which was principally used in its herbicidal operations—from Vietnam.

't², dial. shortened form of THAT *relative pron.* or *conj.* Cf. AT, 'AT *rel. pron., adv., conj.*

1867 *Our Young Folks* Mar. 130 Jest show me that! Ur prove 't the bat Hez got more brains than's in my hat. **1871** W. ALEXANDER *Johnny Gibb* xv. 108, I ance was neepours wi' a chap 't could 'a deen that. **1887** R. T. COOKE *Happy Dodd* xxvii. 286, I didn't feel real cherk this week, so't I didn't go to sewin' s'ciety.

ta, *int.* Add: Now also commonly in colloq. adult use.

1931 A. POWELL *Afternoon Men* xxx. 252 'Will you give him this, Sophy?'..'What did he say?' Sophy said: 'He just said, "Tar".' **1946** K. TENNANT *Lost Haven* (1947) iii. 47 Grandfather Starbrace shovelled great handfuls of pink prawns... 'Ta, Nathe,' Mr. Thorne said. **1970** 'R. GORDON' *Doctor on Boil* xxiii. 164 'Ta,' he said, slipping the card into the back pocket of his jeans. **1981** D. CLARK *Longest Pleasure* vi. 136 'You know your way, don't you?' 'Ta, love.'

taaffeite (tā·fəit). *Min.* [f. the name of Edward Charles Richard *Taaffe* (1898–1967), Bohemian-born Irish gemmologist + -ITE¹.] A mauve gemstone similar to spinel, having the composition $BeMgAl_4O_8$ and a hexagonal crystal structure.

1951 B. W. ANDERSON in *Gemmologist* XX. 76/2 One of the 'spinels' gave a rather high refractive index reading and seemed to show double refraction... The second 'Taaffeite' was found! **1951** —— & CLARINGBULL in *Mineral. Mag.* XXIX. 765 The new mineral..has been named taaffeite in honour of its discoverer. **1967** *Rocks & Minerals* XLII. 803/1 The world's fourth known cut taaffeite was discovered in August of this year. **1974** *Jrnl. Gemmology* XIV. 104 The discovery of the new gem mineral Taaffeite reads like a gemmological fairy tale.

taaibos (tāi·bɒs). *S. Afr.* Also 9 **ta(a)ybosch; taaibosch.** [Afrikaans, f. Du. *taai* tough + *bos(ch)* bush.] Any of several shrubs or trees with strong, pliable branches, esp. any of several species of *Rhus.*

1821 C. L. LATROBE *Jrnl. Visit S. Afr.* 559 Taaibosch—a species of Rhus, of which genus several bear the name of Taaibosch. **1833** *S. Afr. Almanac & Directory* p. xlviii, One of the Cape sumachs (Taaybosch) has been recommended for culture. **1834** *Cape Good Hope Lit. Gaz.* Mar. 41 The extract may be procured..if the tree is treated as recommended for the colonial Taybosch. **1905** F. G. STOW *Native Races S. Afr.* v. 93 They [*sc.* fish baskets] were composed of reeds and twigs of the taaibosch. **1948** *Cape Times* 5 Aug. 8/7 The safer and more effective plants are reeds and many-stemmed shrubs, such as taaibos. **1974** *Stand. Encycl. S. Afr.* X. 396/1 Taaibos. Name generally applied to plants with tough branches and bark, such as *Passerina vulgaris*..but particularly to shrubby *Rhus* species.

taakhaar, var. *TAKHAAR.

tab, *sb.¹* Add: **I. 1. f.** = *pull-tab* s.v. *PULL-2: used to open a can of beer, etc.

1963 *Wall St. Jrnl.* 1 Oct. 16/1 The beer drinker opens the can by pulling off the tab. **1978** O. WHITE *Silent Reach* xi. 108 The fat man..pulled the tab from a can.

2. d. A coloured tab, esp. a red tab or gorget patch, worn by a senior or staff Army officer; hence formerly, in *Army slang,* such an officer.

1916 J. BUCHAN *Greenmantle* i. 2 'Try my tailor,' said Sandy. 'He's got a very nice taste in red tabs.' **1917** *B.E.F. Times* 20 Jan. 4/2 Realising Men must laugh, Some wise Man devised the Staff: Dressed them up in little dabs Of rich variegated tabs. **1925** FRASER & GIBBONS *Soldier & Sailor Words* 275 *Tab, a,* a Staff Officer. **1948** PARTRIDGE *Dict. Forces' Slang* 154 *Red tabs,* red gorget patches, worn by Colonels and above. 'Red-tab' was sometimes used for an officer who wore them. **1977** D. JAMES *Spy at Evening* vii. 51 He had red tabs on his collar. He had authority even over my father.

4. c. *Aeronaut.* A usu. hinged part of a control surface that serves to modify the action or response of the surface.

1934 *Flight* 25 Jan. 75/1 The word 'tab' has been approved by the [U.S.] Department of Commerce as the name for auxiliary control flaps. **1942** 'B. J. ELLAN' *Spitfire!* p. x, Winding the bias control one way or the other moves the tab and gives port or starboard bias. **1965** C. N. VAN DEVENTER *Introd. Gen. Aeronautics* iv. 95/2 Controllable or fixed tabs may be attached to any of the control surfaces—the elevators, the ailerons, or the rudder. **1983** D. STINTON *Design of Aeroplane* xi. 397 Often trimming is achieved on the ground by bent plate tabs.

5*. An ear. *dial.* and *slang.*

1866 J. E. BROGDEN *Provinc. Words Lincs.* 202 *Tab,* a piece of leather in the front of a boot, a latchet, the ear. **1959** *New Statesman* 26 Dec. 904/2 Dad was sitting by the fire, behind his paper with one tab lifted. **1977** SCOLLINS & TITFORD *Ey up, mi Duck!* III. 15 Ah gorra bile be'int me tab.

II. 6. For *U.S. colloq.* read *colloq.* (orig. *U.S.*). (Further examples.) Also, a bill or charge (chiefly *N. Amer.*): see also *to pick up the tab* s.v. *PICK *v.¹* 20 r. *to keep (a) tab*: now chiefly current in fig. phr. *to keep tabs (on).* Also *fig.*

1890 B. HALL *Turnover Club* 19 They knocked off and filed out into the deserted streets, while the Purveyor figured up the 'tabs'. **1924** [see *TAB *v.* 2]. **1929** 'E. QUEEN' *Roman Hat Mystery* iii. 37 We got to keep pretty close tabs on the time, and I know it was ten minutes because..it was just the part on the stage when [etc.]. **1932** D. L. SAYERS *Have his Carcase* xxvi. 348 The one person..likely to have kept tabs on Mr Perkins..was old Gaffer Gander. **1946** J. O'HARA in *New Yorker* 23 Mar. 25/1 You signed a small tab, sir. **1952** S. KAUFFMANN *Philanderer* (1953) iii. 52 So all those old ideas are finished and God is dying. There's nobody in Heaven keeping tabs. And there's just going to be less for people to hang on to? **1954** E. B. WHITE *Let.* 9 July (1976) 395, I did a little haying yesterday..and..I am spending today indoors paying the tab. **1963** T. PARKER *Unknown Citizen* v. 138 He's antagonistic to anything or anybody who represents authority... He thinks that our main purpose is to keep tabs on him while he's out. **1976** M. MACHLIN *Pipeline* xii. 144 He started to reach into the pocket of his Arctic down pants for his wallet, but Nick had already paid the tab. **1978** M. PUZO *Fools Die* ii. 18 Jordan knew that Merlyn the Kid kept tabs on everything he did.

7. A cigarette. *north. dial.* and *slang.*

1934 P. ALLINGHAM *Cheapjack* iii. 24 ''Ave you got a tab on yer?' The only tabs I knew were connected with the theatre, but I discovered later that 'tab' is a common name in the north for a cigarette. **1948** A. BARON *From City, from Plough* i. 10 'Gie us a tab, Lanky.' He passed his cigarettes round the carriage. **1968** B. HINES *Kestrel for Knave* 71 From various pockets Gryce collected two ten-packets, which rattled when he shook them, a handful of tabs, three lighters and a box of matches. **1980** C. ROSS *Case for Compensation* xiv. 68 'Tab?' Duncan looked blank. 'Cigarette?' he said. Duncan accepted. **1983** *New Society* 2 June 333/1 £13.65 a week to pay for..clothes, 'snake bites' (cider and lager), 'tabs' (cigarettes).

8. A tablet or pill, *spec.* one containing LSD or another illicit drug. *slang.*

1961 in WEBSTER. **1968–70** *Current Slang* (Univ. S. Dakota) III–IV. 123 *Tab,* a tablet of sugar or saccharine impregnated with LSD. (Drug users' jargon.) **1971** *Daily Tel.* 18 Sept. 12 Whenever anybody had any money it nearly always went on drugs, with LSD at £1 a 'tab' (tablet). **1973** 'J. MARKS' *Mick Jagger* (1974) 137 He presses his palm to his mouth and swallows the tab. **1978** M. WALKER *Infiltrator* xii. 136 An order for two tabs of acid.

III. 9. Special combination. **tab collar,** (*a*) a shirt collar whose points are held down by buttons or other fastenings (cf. *button-down* adj. s.v. *BUTTON *sb.* 12); (*b*) (see quot. 1957).

1928 *Men's Wear* 21 Nov. II. 5/1 The tab collar is being worn by quite a few of the best dressed eastern university students. It should prove to be an important feature. **1942** B. G. CHAMBERS *Color & Design in Apparel* xv. 498 *Tab collar.* The fronts have loops on the under side with button-holes which fasten on buttons or small rigid stays, that help keep the tie in place at the top of the collar. **1957** M. B. PICKEN *Fashion Dict.* 75/2 *Tab c[ollar],* collar cut in tabs, often with two at front. **1979** *Time Out* 4 May 65 The Mod revival hits London in force: each day offers a gig at which parkas, tab collars and fox-tailed Lambrettas would be acceptable.

tab (tæb), *sb.²* *slang.* [Abbrev. of TABBY *sb.* 3.] **a.** An elderly woman. **b.** *Austral.* A young woman or girl.

1909 J. R. WARE *Passing Eng.* 239/1 *Tabs* (*Theatrical*), ageing women. **1932** H. SIMPSON *Boomerang* x. 276 We don't need to go mackin' round with Chinks and wimmen's earnings. We pay our tabs..when we want 'em, and tell 'em to get to hell out of it when we don't. **1971** [see *MA-IN-LAW].

Tab (tæb), *sb.³* *University slang.* [Short for CANTAB.] A member of the University of Cambridge.

1914 C. MACKENZIE *Sinister Street* II. III. iii. 555 He will get his blue next term and show the Tabs that he's a jolly good fellow. **1930** A. ALINGTON *Slowbags & Arethusa* i. 4 Then the morning's play is discussed, the loathly Tabs reviled—for the Slows are Oxford to a man.

tab (tæb), *sb.⁴* *Theatr. slang.* Abbrev. of *tableau curtain* s.v. *TABLEAU 6.

1929 J. B. PRIESTLEY *Good Companions* II. vii. 447 The girls here follow him round with their tongues hanging out, as usual—but away from the tabs he's the same as ever. **1936** N. ROYDE-SMITH *All Star Cast* 44 The tab curtains fell together as the girl and the man stood at arm's length from one another. **1946** 'BRAHMS' & 'SIMON' *Trottie True* vii. 164 Down came the crimson tabs. Up went the shouting and the cooing. Out tottered Marie [Lloyd] to the public that idolized her. **1957** P. FRANKAU *Bridge* 59 The dark stage-hand..came through the tabs. **1983** *Listener* 22/29 Dec. 28/1 When she did the last song, she used to do it in front of the tabs.

tab (tæb), *sb.⁵* *Typewriting* and *Computing.* [Abbrev. of TABULATOR b, TABULAR *a.,* etc.] A tabulator (key); a tabular stop, used to preset the movement of the carriage, cursor, etc., under the direction of the tabulator.

1916 H. ETHERIDGE *Bar-Lock Typewriter Manual* 45 The Tab. key acts exactly in the same manner as the carriage release lever. *Ibid.,* On releasing the Tab. key the carriage remains at the number on the scale where the first stop has been fixed. **1969** *Sears, Roebuck Catal.* Spring/Summer 1195/2 Automatic key-set tabs, clear key. **1982** HARRIS & CHAUHAN *So You want to Buy a Word Processor?* v. 65/1 Not only do tabs have to be set up at appropriate positions, but the facility needs to be reactivated when any of the text involved is subsequently edited.

tab, *v.* Add: **2.** To identify, name, or 'dub'; to label or record. Also, to watch, 'keep tabs on' (formerly also with *up*). *colloq.* (chiefly *U.S.*).

1924 G. C. HENDERSON *Keys to Crookdom* 420 *Tab,* to name. *To keep tabs on,* to keep in touch with. **1926** J. BLACK *You can't Win* xix. 283 You are a burglar; you have put in a week 'tabbing up' a residence. **1946** *Sun* (Baltimore) 18 Feb. 11/5 The Navy has tabbed entertainment with the high-sounding name liaison unit. **1954** 'J. CHRISTOPHER' *Twenty-Second Cent.* 86 The doctors have it all tabbed. It's what they call cumulative stress. **1969** *Eugene* (Oregon) *Register-Guard* 3 Dec. 1D/2 Ken Wiedemann of Cal, tabbed as the best defensive back, was sidelined for a major part of the season with a bad knee. **1978** M. PUZO *Fools Die* ii. 33 He had Jordan tabbed as a degenerate gambler.

tabac, *a.* Add: (Earlier example.) Also as *sb.*

1881 *Queen* 18 June 8/1 *Best felt hats.* For Ladies and Gentlemen. The new 'Vicuna' 'Tabac' Brown, and all Colours. **1886** *Graphic* 30 Jan. 123/2 Colours are Black, Brown, Gold, Geranium, and Tabac. **1922** *Daily Mail* 18 Dec. 1 (Advt.), In shades of Coral, Champagne,..Tabac.

‖**tabac** (tabak), *sb.* [Fr.] In French-speaking countries: a tobacconist's shop.

1918 'K. MANSFIELD' *Let.* 11 Jan. (1928) 96 The *tabac* woman did not know me and had no tobacco. **1934** H. MILLER *Tropic of Cancer* 52 We sat in the back of the little *tabac* called *L'Eléphant.* **1965** P. O'DONNELL *Modesty Blaise* vii. 75 He left the boules with the lady who ran the *tabac.* **1980** 'M. HARRIS' *Treasure of Sainte Foy* ii. 18 There is a boulangerie-pâtisserie, a tabac, and the milk bar.

tabanid, *a.* and *sb.* After 'Linnæus' in etym. add: (1736, in *Acta Soc. R. Scient. Upsaliensis* 31). (Further examples.)

1892 *Insect Life* V. 59 An examination showed it to be a true Tabanid. **1931** K. M. SMITH *Textbk. Agric. Entom.* xi. 163 Tabanid larvae are whitish and occur in the water or soil. **1967** V. NABOKOV *Speak, Memory* vi. 137 Because of our ferocious Russian tabanids, one could not leave a horse haltered in a wood for any length of time.

tabard. Add: **3. b.** A fashionable slimly cut ladies' jerkin or similar garment with short (or no) sleeves; *spec.* one used as a beach-robe.

1923 in C. W. Cunnington *Eng. Women's Clothing in Present Cent.* (1952) v. 175 Evening dress with tabard top. **1959** *Housewife* June 49 A beach tabard in..cotton, over a bikini and bra. **1977** P. D. JAMES *Death of Expert Witness* II. xii. 106 She wore a dress in fine fawn wool, topped with an elaborately patterned, short-sleeved tabard. **1983** *Times* 11 Mar. 8/4 An odd, misshapen tabard, worn with a long slim suede skirt.

tabardillo (tæbă.ɪdi·lo, ‖tabardi·lʸo). *Path.* [Sp. *tabardillo* (see quot. 1980).] A fever common in Mexico and S. America; now *spec.* a murine typhus (cf. *MURINE *a.* b) found in Mexico which, unlike most forms of murine typhus, can occur as an epidemic.

[**1598** W. PHILLIP tr. *Linschoten's Voy. E. & W. Indies* I. i. 2/1 Hee fell sicke of a disease called *Tauardilha.*] **1624** W. ASTON *Let.* 10 Dec. in *Cabala: sive Scrinia Sacra* (1654) I. 166 He hath been held divers dayes with a terrible Calenture, which proved at last a *Tabardillo.* **1853** W. L. HERNDON *Exploration Valley of Amazon* I. v. 113 The most common diseases are pleurisies, rheumatisms, and a putrid fever called *tabardillo.* **1944** R. A. MOORE *Textbk. Path.* xlii. 459 It was shown before 1930 that Brill's disease, tabardillo of Mexico, and endemic typhus of the southeastern United States are all transmitted by the rat flea..and by the rat louse. **1980** A. L. SMITH *Microbiol. & Path.* (ed. 12) I. xxv. 300/2 The endemic typhus fever of Mexico is known as *tabardillo* (from the Spanish word *tabardo,* meaning a coloured cloak, to designate the mantlelike spotted rash of the disease).

tabaret. (Earlier example.)

1790 P. A. ROBB *Let.* in M. Dunsford *Hist. Mem. Tiverton* IV. 235 This year [*sc.* 1752] was introduced to Tiverton the manufacture of..camblets, tarborates, damasks.

Tabasco. Add: A proprietary name. (Earlier and further examples.) *fig.*: delete 'a story "highly-spiced".'

1876 J. MILLER *First Fam'lies Sierras* 126 The following popular drinks..were all made from the same decoction of bad rum, worse tabasco, and first-class cayenne pepper. **1878** *Let. to E. McIlhenny* (E. S. Hyatt & Co.) 16 Dec. (MS.), Please send us by return mail your lowest prices and terms on your Tabasco pepper sauce. **1879** E. C. HAZARD *Let. to E. McIlhenny* 30 July (MS.), Would you agree to sell us your entire packing of tabasco sauce? **1902** *Trade Marks Jrnl.* 3 Sept. 1010 Tabasco pepper sauce. Pepper Sauce made from Tabasco Pepper. Edward Avery McIlhenny, . . Sauce Manufacturer.—25th July 1902. Mark has been used in respect of the said Goods by the applicant and his predecessors in business since five years before the 13th August 1875. **1923** WODEHOUSE *Inimitable Jeeves* iv. 41 Little as he might look like one of the lads of the village, he certainly appeared to be the real tabasco and I wished he had shown me this side of his character before. **1924** *Trade Marks Jrnl.* 18 June 1385 Tabasco. 439,246. Pepper Sauce made from Tabasco Pepper. McIlhenny Company... 21st July 1923. **1949** *Amer. Speech* XXIV. 34 Tabasco sauce is acid used in breaking a limestone formation. **1979** *Guardian* 19 July 12/3 Fred Jackson in among the saxophones to add a tabasco spice to the disco bids.

Tabassaran (tæbäsärā·n), *sb.* (and *a.*). Also **Tabasaran.** [Native name for a district in S. Daghestan.] A North Caucasian, Lesghian language of Daghestan, known in both written and spoken forms. Also *attrib.* and as *adj.*

1951 W. K. MATTHEWS *Languages U.S.S.R.* v. 89 Agul has twenty-five, Awar thirty, and Tabassaran thirty-five cases. **1968** [see *LESGHIAN *sb.* and *a.*]. **1971** [see *LAK]. **1977** C. F. & F. M. VOEGELIN *Classification & Index World's Lang.* 96 Eleven members of the Caucasian groups have official status as literary languages: . . Tabasaran (35,000).

‖ **tabbouleh** (tabū·le). Also **tabbouli, tabbuuli.** [ad. Arab. *tabbūla.*] An Arabic vegetable salad made with crushed wheat.

1955 J. GULICK *Social Structure & Culture Change in Lebanese Village* 42 The other is *tabbuuli.* This has nearly the same ingredients as the salad, but they are chopped up very fine and mixed with cracked wheat which has been soaked in water. **1958** F. COPELAND *Land between: Middle East* ix. 99 No picnic is complete without a special salad called *tabbouleh.* **1965** *Times* 31 May 13/6 Tabbouleh is a salad made from crushed wheat known as bourghul, with chopped parsley and mint. **1968** C. RODEN *Bk. Middle Eastern Food* 57 *Tabbouleh* is traditionally served in individual plates lined with boiled vine leaves. **1977** C. MCFADDEN *Serial* (1978) lii. 110/2 Marlene must have cooked her head off. The tabbouleh, all that whole-wheat lasagne, . . the brown rice and veggies.

tabby, *sb.* and *a.* Add: **A.** *sb.* **3. b.** An (attractive) young woman or girl; = *TAB *sb.*[2] b. *slang.*

1916 C. J. DENNIS *Moods of Ginger Mick* 20 Then the tabbies took to screamin'. **1925** FRASER & GIBBONS *Soldier & Sailor Words* 275 *Tabby, a,* a girl. **1935** A. J. POLLOCK *Underworld Speaks* 118/1 *Tabby,* an attractive girl. **1958** J. WAIN *Contenders* iv. 88 'I said, is it true what Joe says that you've got yourself fitted out with a tabby?' 'My humble roof,' said Robert . . 'is shared by a distinguished actress.'

c. tabby weave *Textiles* = *plain weave* s.v. *PLAIN *a.*[1] and *adv.* C. c.

1906 H. NISBET *Gram. Textile Design* ii. 6 The 'plain' . . or 'tabby' weave . . is the most simple and elementary combination of two series of threads employed in the construction of textile fabrics. **1957** SIMPSON & WEIR *Weaver's Craft* vii. 77 We may weave a binder thread (a row of plain or tabby weave) of very fine material in between the rows of pattern.

Tabele, var. *TEBELE.

tabi. Add: Also 9 **tapie;** (anglicized pl.) **tabis.** For def. read: Thick-soled Japanese ankle-socks with a separate stall for the large toe, worn by both sexes. Also *attrib.* (Earlier and later examples.)

1616 R. COCKS *Diary* 23 Jan. (1883) I. 102, 2 peare *tabis* for Jeffrey. **1822** F. SHOBERL tr. *Titsingh's Illustrations of Japan* I. 130 The men leave off the *tapie* on the 1st of the third month, but the women wear them all the year round. **1880** I. L. BIRD *Japan* I. xiii. 131 On her little feet she wears white *tabi,* socks of cotton cloth, with a separate place for the great toe. **1892** H. NORMAN *Real Japan* 193 The costume is completed by a pair of *tabi.* **1938** *N. & Q.* 21 May 361/1 The Japanese private . . used to put on his *tabis* and get to work on his arms. **1963** R. GODDEN *Little Plum* 17 'Why, you have made them tanzen—proper Japanese coats—and tabi,' he said, touching the socks. **1975** J. CLAVELL *Shōgun* II. xi. 229 He wore a belted kimono of the Browns and tabi socks and military thongs.

tabid, *a.* Add: **1.** (Later example.) Also *fig.*

1914 C. MACKENZIE *Sinister St.* II. iv. v. 964 He was disappointed to see no cab . . merely a tabid woman clothed in a cobweb of crape, asleep over her tray of matches. **1947** M. LOWRY *Under Volcano* ii. 58 Outside . . in the backwash of tabid music from the still-continuing ball.

‖ **tabl** (tāb'l). Also **teboul.** [Arab.: see ATABAL.] In the Arab world: a drum (usu. played with the hand).

[**1777** J. RICHARDSON *Arab. & Pers. Dict.* p. xlv, *Tebl* is a drum, *Teblek* a small drum. **1836** E. W. LANE *Acct. Manners & Customs Mod. Egyptians* II. v. 75 Several kinds of drums, of which the most common kinds are the *tub'l bel'edee* (or country drum, that is, Egyptian drum), and the *tub'l Sha'mee* (or Syrian drum).] **1876** STAINER & BARRETT *Dict. Mus. Terms* 415/1 *Tabl,* an Egyptian drum formed from a hollow block of wood, or made of earthenware, with a skin stretched over one end. **1923** *Chambers's Jrnl.* Apr. 307/1 White-collared gentlemen . . play strange instruments—a big guitar, a big drum called a *teboul.* **1976** *Guardian* 16 Dec. 16/3 (Advt.), The *tabl,* the larger wooden drum, probably came [to Qatar] from Africa, though there are obvious etymological links with the Persian *duhul* and the Indian *tabla.*

‖ **tabla** (ta·bla). Also 9 **tubla.** [Hind., ad. Arab. *ṭabl* (see prec.).] A pair of drums used in Indian music (esp. that of the northern region), of which the left-hand (bass) head is larger than the other (tenor) head; either of these drums separately (see quot. 1969). Also *absol.,* a tabla-player. Cf. *MRIDANGAM, *PAKHAWAJ.

1865 *Proc. R. Irish Acad.* IX. I. 117 (*Tubla*). These drums, tenor and bass, rank with the pukhraj... The *tubla* drums are made of copper. **1888,** etc. [see *MRIDANGAM]. **1914** A. H. F. STRANGWAYS *Mus. Hindostan* ix. 227 The tubla, left and right, are of the shape of a giant tea-cup and coffee-cup respectively. **1927** *Observer* 12 June 14/5 The Hindu drummer's saying that 'the left *tabla* (hand drum) is like the sleeve of my coat, and the right like such embroidery as I may put on it'. **1955** R. P. JHABVALA *To whom she Will* xiii. 92 The musicians . . played with placid expressions . . only the tabla-player smiled. **1969** R. SHANKAR *My Music* i. 40/2 Of the multitude of drums that are found throughout India today, the most popular variety in the North is the *tabla,* which is actually two drums, each with one skin stretched across the top. The smaller of the two drums is the right-hand *tabla,* and the bass, left-hand drum is called the *bonya,* though the two are called collectively *tabla.* **1973** 'D. JORDAN' *Nile Green* xxiv. 99 'No evening Raga tonight?' I asked. 'The tabla has got flu so it's postponed.' **1975** I. MURDOCH *Word Child* 3 Christopher was learning to play the 'tabla', a dreary little oriental drum.

tablature. 1. For *Obs.* exc. *Hist.* read 'Now chiefly *Hist.*' and add later examples drawn from the revived study and performance of early music.

1969 *Daily Tel.* 12 Nov. 14/4 The procuring of music for the lute presented the greatest difficulty: it is not written in staff notation but in tablature, so Dolmetsch had to decipher this from old MSS in the British Museum. **1977** *Listener* 15 Dec. 796/3 Tablatures . . semi-diagrammatic signs that belong to a specific instrument and make no sense in the abstract. **1980** *Early Music* Apr. 250 Our edition includes voice and tablature as well as voice and transcription.

table, *sb.* Add: **I. 5. b.** (Examples of *on the table.*) *to lay on the table* (examples); also, to present for immediate discussion; *to lie on the table* (earlier examples). Cf. sense 4 a of the vb. in Dict. and Suppl.

1730 E. KNATCHBULL in *Camden Soc.* (1963) 3rd Ser. XCIV. 106 So a division for it [*sc.* a Petition] lying on the table, carried by 163 against 144. **1733** in *15th Rep. R. Comm. Hist. MSS.* App. VI. 107 in *Parl. Papers 1897* (C. 8551) LI. 1 The majority, for laying the Petition on the Table . . and not hearing it by counsel, was only seventeen. **1744** *Archives New Jersey* (1882) 1st Ser. VI. 191 The House of Representatives . . would not commit it [*sc.* a bill] but ordered it to lie on the table. **1855** MACAULAY *Hist. Eng.* IV. xix. 343 Shrewsbury laid on the table of the Lords a bill for limiting the duration of Parliaments. **1915** J. LONDON *Let.* 25 Aug. (1966) 458 It is . . on the table whether or not we shall say 'it is I' or 'it is me'. **1923** H. M. ROBERT *Parl. Law* (U.S.) 63 It is in order for a mere majority to lay on the table the questions that have not been disposed of. **1958** [see *PRAYER[1] 5]. **1977** *Times* 14 Apr. 1/3 While stating that those proposals should 'remain on the table', he [*sc.* Ian Smith] is now prepared to listen to new ideas.

c. *spec.* The table which stands before the Speaker's chair in the House of Commons, at which the Clerk of the House and his assistants receive motions and questions to ministers, etc., and at which new members are sworn in (cf. also prec. sense).

1675 *Grey's Debates* (1769) III. 129 Mr Stockdale, and some others, setting their feet upon the mace, which lay below the table, in the usual place at Grand Committees. **1771** *London Even. Post* 28 Feb.–2 Mar. 3/1 Upon which Mr. Byng and Mr. Buller, seized him by the collar, and brought him up to the table. **1885** *Encycl. Brit.* XVIII. 312/1 Having first taken the oath himself, he [*sc.* the Speaker] is followed by other members, who come to the table to be sworn. **1958** *Spectator* 11 July 47/1 Mr. Gaitskell's head wagged up and down as if he wanted to punch a hole in the Table with his nose.

d. A surgeon's operating-table; also, a table or slab on which a body is laid for post-mortem examination.

1917 T. S. ELIOT *Prufrock* 9 Like a patient etherized upon a table. **1936** G. B. SHAW *Millionairess* II. 166, I should have cut my patients entirely away if the nurse had not stopped me before they died on the table. **1941** A. HUXLEY *Let.* 17 Nov. (1969) 470 The patient will die on the table if operated—off the table, if not operated. **1977** P. D. JAMES *Death of Expert Witness* IV. 226 As for the cause of death . . well, you'll have to wait till I get her on the table.

e. Attrib. phr. *under-the-table*: kept secret, hidden, esp. of clandestine deals or payments. Also (unhyphened) used predicatively and as advb. phr. Cf. *under the counter* s.v. *COUNTER *sb.*[3] 4 b.

1949 *Sun* (Baltimore) 25 Feb. 19/3 Two home purchasers told a Federal Court jury . . that they were required to make under-the-table payments to purchase housing accommodations. **1973** W. H. HALLAHAN *Ross Forgery* vi. 115 Under-the-table freight rebates reached absurd proportions. **1976** *Listener* 5 Feb. 144/1 Some of the sports do check people's bank accounts to see that they have not got too much money under the table. **1976** G. SEYMOUR *Glory Boys* vii. 85 This bomb that the Israelis keep so much under the table . . what state is that in? **1980** *Times Lit. Suppl.* 25 July 839/3 The Rheinmetal company for long refused to pay anything, but eventually arranged for an under-the-table payment of DM2,500,000 (which provided $425 for each of its former slaves).

f. A table around which parties (esp. in an industrial dispute) sit to discuss points at issue; a negotiating table. *round-the-table* adj. phr., designating such discussions; (*up*)*on the table*: see sense 5 b.

1963 [see *RECREATIONIST]. **1976** *West Lancs. Evening Gaz.* 15 Dec. 1. 9/4 Transport and General Workers' Union officials want round-the-table talks with the management. **1980** *Times* 6 Feb. 1/1 We hope to get our negotiators around the table as soon as possible.

6. c. Also *the pleasures of the table* [tr. F. *les plaisirs de la table*], good food and drink, considered as a source of enjoyment.

1769 F. BROOKE *Hist. Emily Montague* IV. 146, I love the pleasures of the table. **1825** SCOTT *Talisman* in *Tales of Crusaders* III. xi. 212 Richard . . despised the inclination of the German for the pleasures of the table. **1845** [see *SARD *sb.*[2] 1]. **1942** G. M. TREVELYAN *Eng. Social Hist.* xiii. 408 Eighteenth Century Englishmen were much addicted to the pleasures of the table. **1981** T. FITZGIBBON (*title*) The pleasures of the table.

d. Slang phr. (*to put,* etc.) *under the table,* (to make) drunk to the point of insensibility.

1921 W. S. MAUGHAN *Trembling of Leaf* 28 Walker had always been a heavy drinker, he was proud of his capacity to see men half his age under the table. **1924** D. MARQUIS *Old Soak's Hist. World* vi. 32 By three therty everybody was under the tabil. **1936** V. W. BROOKS *Flowering of New England* v. 95 He was far from sober, or would have been if two tumblers of brandy had been enough to put him under the table.

9. b. *to lay, put* (or *play with*) (*all*) *one's cards on the table*: see *CARD *sb.*[2] 2 d.

c. *Bridge.* The hand belonging to dummy.

1959 *Listener* 7 May 808/2 The lead of the Queen from the table allows East's K 9 x to be smothered. **1960** T. REESE *Play Bridge with Reese* 127, I play low from table. **1974** *Country Life* 28 Feb. 453/2 South won with the Ace, crossed to the Spade Ace on the table, and led a Club.

10. f. = *league table* s.v. *LEAGUE *sb.*[2] 4.

1951 *Sport* 6–12 Apr. 10/4 Mr. Drake has been the guiding light behind a remarkable revival that has taken the club soaring up the table. **1972** G. GREEN *Great Moments in Sport: Soccer* v. 62 Around Christmas, they had begun to catch a tide of success as they crept slowly up the table. **1976** *Western Mail* (Cardiff) 27 Nov. 20/2 Newcastle, third in the table thanks to their midweek win over Everton.

III. 21. a. In sense 5, 'of a table': *table-edge*; in sense 6, 'of the dinner-table': *table-waiter*; 'of implements, etc. used at table': *table cutlery, decoration, fork* (earlier example), *mat, runner*; 'for consumption at table': *table fish* (earlier examples), *-grape*; in sense 10: *table look-up* (*LOOK-UP 2). **b.** *table-thumping* adj. and sb. **c.** *table-piano*(*forte*).

1861 *Chicago Tribune* 10 July 1/9 Crockery Ware, Table Cutlery, Plated Ware, &c. **1946** A. CHRISTIE *Come, tell me how you Live* vii. 116 Civilisation's invention of table cutlery presents a perpetual headache to a worried house-boy. **1937** C. SPRY *Flowers in House & Garden* 169 Your choice of table decorations is bound to be influenced by . . your guests. **1979** I. WEBB *Compl. Guide Flower & Foliage Arrangement* vii. 97/2 'Frensham' roses and ivy berries combine to make an arresting table decoration. **1935** H. H. BASHFORD *Lodgings for Twelve* 87 George Gedge's Wiltshire guile and a miraculous succession of table-edge strokes. **1977** F. ORMSBY *Store of Candles* 30 Resumes his beat from table-edge to door, From door to table. **1770** *Boston Gaz.* 15 Jan. 2/3 *Table fish* warranted the very best, To be Sold at the Store the Corner of Kilby-Street. **1872** F. F. VICTOR *All over Oregon* 63 Besides the salmon of commerce, the Columbia furnishes a great many other species of edible fish . . all of which are excellent table-fish in their proper seasons. **1785** *Daily Universal Reg.* 1 Jan. 3/2 Ivory table knives and forks. **1926** *Zionist Rev.* Apr. 144/2 Splendid prospects exist for good table-grapes in those parts of Palestine where the Jewish urban population is growing. **1979** *Tucson Mag.* Apr. 20/2 An attractive feature . . is the possibility that vineyards will be a 'dryland crop', using considerably less water than table grapes. **1957** D. D. MCCRACKEN *Digital Computer Programming* xvii. 200 The code number is placed in one of the arithmetic registers and a table look-up instruction given. **1967** COX & GROSE *Organization & Handling Bibl. Rec. by Computer* VI. 142 These will be linked with 'table-look-ups' within the output programs to translate each symbol into a full form. **1779** in *Dict. Amer. Eng.* (1938) s.v. *Table* n., Table mat. **1834** DICKENS *Bloomsbury Christening* in *Monthly Mag.* Apr. 380 A front drawing-room, very prettily furnished with a plentiful sprinkling of little baskets, paper table-mats, [etc.] . . on the different tables. **1965** A. NICOL *Truly Married Woman* 5 She remembered the wine glasses and the beer-advertising table-mats in time and put those under the sofa. **1911** *Daily Colonist* (Victoria, B.C.) 27 Apr. 11/7 The hotel furniture consists of . . blankets, sheets, spreads, pillows, toilet sets in 60 rooms, 1 table piano, card tables, [etc.]. **1952** J. GLOAG *Short Dict. Furniture* 468 Table pianos were designed to conceal the fact that they were musical instruments:

when closed they looked like clumsy and ill-proportioned tables. **1976** *Early Music* Oct. 483/1, I find the choice of cover picture oddly revealing: a small table-piano ordered by an aristocrat for his children. **1851** *Official Catal., Gt. Exhib.* III. 1225/1 Patent square and console piano-fortes; square and hexagonal table pianofortes. **1889** Table runner [see *RUNNER 14 c]. **1939** W. FORTESCUE *There's Rosemary* xliv. 259, I cut lengths of brocatello, designed cushions and table-runners, &c. **1967** E. SHORT *Embroidery & Fabric Collage* iii. 63 Small mats, table runners, *Radio Times* covers are quite unnecessary. **1963** *Time* 2 Aug. 17/2 The changeover from Stalin, the 'oriental despot', to Khruschev, the table-thumping but jolly politician. **1964** A. BATTERSBY *Network Analysis* ix. 137 The Esso team..do claim with confidence that resources are utilized more effectively than before,..and that, in general, there is less table-thumping. **1928** D. H. LAWRENCE *Woman who rode Away* 15 The sister was all that could be desired as..an upper parlour-maid, and a table-waiter. **1975** *Budget* (Sugarcreek, Ohio) 20 Mar. 1/4 Tablewaiters were David F. Yoder, Susie Bontreger, [etc.].

d. Designed to stand on a table, as *table lamp, lighter, model, stand.*

c **1849** J. S. COYNE *How to settle Accts. with your Laundress* 3 Table at back, L., on which is a table lamp. **1854** C. M. YONGE *Heartsease* I. II. i. 102 A pretty little rosewood work-table, on which was..a table-stand of books. **1907** *Yesterday's Shopping* (1969) 1150/3 Folding Music Stands... Table stand... Brass 7/6. **1922** A. BENNETT *Lilian* II. vii. 119 It was the silver table-lamps..that impressed her. **1929** *Radio Times* 8 Nov. 437/1 The table model Columbia is..the most advanced radio of the day. **1951** *Catal. Exhibits, South Bank Exhib., Festival of Britain* 147/2 Shagreen table lighter. **1954** 'N. BLAKE' *Whisper in Gloom* I. vii. 99 Applying his cigar to a massive table-lighter. **1962** A. NISBETT *Technique Sound Studio* i. 30 There are four types of microphone mounting. These are: (i) The table stand, [etc.]. **1967** P. CHAMBERS *Bad die Young* i. 11 A grateful client had given me a heavy bronze table lighter. **1976** 'W. TREVOR' *Children of Dynmouth* iii. 60 Only a table-lamp burned, its weak bulb not up to the task of fully illuminating the room. **1977** D. E. WESTLAKE *Nobody's Perfect* 10 He'd cased that TV repair shop—he'd even brought in a perfectly good Sony table model and let them charge him for six new tubes.

e. Designating various games played on a table, which simulate more or less closely the action of some sport, as *table football, hockey,* etc. See also *table-tennis,* sense 22 in Dict. Cf. *table game,* sense 22 below.

1907 *Yesterday's Shopping* (1969) 1032/2 Wibley Wob or Table Football. A game for 2 or 4 players, to be placed upon an ordinary dining table. **1948** *Sporting Mirror* 21 May 10/3 (Advt.), Send 3d. stamp for full details of *Subbuteo* the game of Table Soccer... Played with 22 miniature men, ball and goals. **1949** S. F. COLLIS (*title*) Proper channels for the distribution of 'table hockey'. **1956** H. & L. EIZENBERG *Omnibus of Fun* xvii. 343 Table Hockey. This ping-pong blow game can have four teams on rectangular table. **1976** DEAKIN & WILLIS *Johnny go Home* i. 27 The biggest amusement arcade he had ever seen..the metropolitan mecca of pinball and table football.

22. table bed (earlier example); **table bell** (earlier examples); **table carpet,** delete † and add: also, a decorative table-cloth of other material (now *Hist.*); **table centrepiece,** a decorative piece placed at the centre of a table, esp. one arrayed with flowers, etc.; **table-chair** = *chair table* s.v. *CHAIR *sb.*[1] 15; **table cover** (earlier example); **table-decker,** delete † and add later example of use in the Royal Household (now *rare*); **table desk,** (*a*) a desk with a broad, flat top; (*b*) a kind of folding writing-box that opens to provide a sloping desk-top, for use on a table; **table game,** a game played on a table or similar surface, usu. with balls, counters, or other pieces (and sometimes distinguished from card- or board-games); **table hand,** (*a*) *N.Z. Sheep-shearing*: in a wool-shed, one who helps the fleece-picker to skirt and roll the fleeces; (*b*) *Printing,* a bindery assistant; **table-hop** *v. intr. U.S. colloq.,* to go from table to table in a restaurant, meeting the diners (cf. *island-hop* s.v. *ISLAND *sb.* 4); also **table-hopping** *vbl. sb.*; **table jelly,** a flavoured jelly served at table as a sweet; a commercial preparation for making this; **table-maid** (earlier example); **table manners** *sb. pl.* orig. *U.S.,* behaviour or deportment at table, judged according to accepted standards of propriety; **table-money,** (*a*) (earlier example); (*b*) (earlier example with reference to dining charges on board ship); **tablemount** *Oceanogr.* = *GUYOT; **table napkin** (later examples); **Table Office:** in the House of Commons, the office in which the civil servants work whose duties include the preparation of the Notice Paper and the Order Book; by extension, the Office personified by its clerks; **table officer** *Canad.,* any of the principal officers in an organization (cf. BOARD *sb.* 8); **table-plan,** a seating plan for those attending a formal meal; **table rock** (earlier example); **table-screen,** (*a*) a trestle table in a wool-shed; (*b*) *Chinese Ceramics* (see quot. 1974); **table-service,** (*c*) (earlier examples); **table-setting,** (*a*) the activity of setting a table: see sense 21 b in Dict.; (*b*) the cutlery, napery, etc., required to set a place at table; **table stake** *Poker* (see quot. 1885); **table tape** *Computers,* a magnetic tape containing tabulated numerical information for use in computations; **table-tennis** (earlier and later examples); now an international sport rather than just a parlour game; **table wine,** wine suitable for drinking with a meal, esp. plain wine which is not fortified or sparkling; a wine of this class; cf. *TAFELWEIN, *vin de table* s.v. *VIN 3.

1714 E. POSTLETHWAYT *Let.* 5 Mar. in E. Pyle *Mem. Royal Chaplain* (1905) 33 Pray take care of putting up the Table Bed, put nothing in but what belongs to it. **1779** in *Dict. Amer. Eng.* (1938), Table bell. **1832** *Chambers's Edin. Jrnl.* I. 236/2 This minikin table-bell, which I must have unconsciously pocketed. **1967** E. SHORT *Embroidery & Fabric Collage* iii. 74 Great families worked their own table carpets in tent stitch on canvas sometimes incorporating their coats of arms into the design. **1917** *Harrods Gen. Catal.* 882 Table centre pieces and vases. Finest English hand-made cut crystal. **1979** E. TAYLOR in I. Webb *Compl. Guide Flower & Foliage Arrangement* viii. 104/3 The table centre-piece holds Norway spruce, variegated holly and berries, pine cones and red ribbons. **1671** in *Farm & Cottage Inventories of Mid-Essex 1635–1749* (1950) (Essex Record Office Publ. No. 8) 120 In The Hall—..one Table-chaire. **1836** S. S. ARNOLD in *Proc. Vermont Hist. Soc.* (1940) VIII. 125 Father gave me his old table-chair. **1962** 'K. ORVIS' *Damned & Destroyed* v. 35 Shabby men and women sat in white table-chairs. **1848** C. H. HARTSHORNE *Eng. Med. Embroidery* 126 The manner commonly used in braiding table covers. **1983** *Daily Express* 18 Oct. 22/2 Specially trained 'table-deckers' set the places at State banquets. **1904** M. CORELLI *God's Good Man* 503 Placed below this, and slightly towards the centre of the room, was the Bishop's table-desk and chair. **1933** 'A. ARMSTRONG' *Ten-Minute Alibi* I. 9 Right centre is a flat table-desk with two drawers. **1933** *Burlington Mag.* June p. xviii/2 The acquisition from the funds of the Murray Bequest of the table-desk associated with Henry VIII. **1965** J. A. MICHENER *Source* 799 Gottesmann was surprised, therefore, when this frail child slammed shut the folding table-desk used by the Palmach as its headquarters. **1864** *Amer. Boy's Bk. Sports & Games* 455 (*heading*) Table and toy games. **1905** W. FISKE *Chess in Iceland* 357 We have, as stated, confined ourselves wholly to table-games, that is those which are played on a board or other surface, on which some peculiar design is drawn. **1976** E. WARD *Hanged Man* xxviii. 180 Burnett..felt helplessness, a toy rabbit running on the magnetized tracks of a table game made for children. **1950** *N.Z. Jrnl. Agric.* Oct. 311/2 Pressing the fleece wool with all the skirtings, bellies, stains, [etc.]..still adhering..costs the farmer far more.. than if he had hired one or two table hands at shearing to skirt his fleece wool for him. **1955** G. BOWEN *Wool Away!* vii. 92 A common fault is for a wool-table to be too high, which makes harder work for the table hands and the 'fleeco'. **1972** *Classification of Occupations* (Dept. Employment) III. 172/2 *Bindery assistant.* Performs, by hand or machine, folding, gathering, collating and/or sewing tasks in binding books, periodicals or stationery and assists bookbinders... Other titles include..Table hand. **1979** *West Lancs. Even. Gaz.* 12 Oct. 24 (Advt.), Fully experienced tablehand (SOGAT) required in our Bindery. **1958** *Time* 6 Oct. 16/1 He table-hopped to shake hands. **1977** *Time* 28 Mar. 28/2 In Charleston, he table-hopped through the cafeteria at the West Virginia State Capitol. **1967** *N.Y. Times Mag.* 20 Aug. 33 The writers' club..is a place for gossip, banter, flirtation, shoptalk, confidences and compulsive table-hopping. **1895** *Army & Navy Co-op. Soc. Price List* 16 Table jelly powder. **1917** *Harrods Gen. Catal.* 1224/2 Table jellies (Spring's). **1975** in T. Steel *Life & Death of St Kilda* (1977) xi. 176 She had a few table jellies left. **1862** J. BINNY in H. Mayhew *London Labour* Extra vol. 355/2 Table-maids in aristocratic families or at first-class hotels. **1867** *Harper's Mag.* Sept. 470/1 That upright position which belongs no less to table-manners than to hygiene. **1904** [in Dict., sense 21 a]. **1949** M. MEAD *Male & Female* ix. 187 In cultures where table-manners are the insignia of humanity people may be unable to eat their food at the table with some one who eats differently. **1835** J. E. ALEXANDER *Sketches in Portugal* vi. 148 A contract was entered into with them.., that they should receive British pay and table-money during the continuance of the war. **1842** G. PARBURY *Hand Bk. for India & Egypt* (ed. 2) 383 Table money, say 25 days, at 3 rupees per diem. **1952** *Procès-Verbaux Assoc. d'Oceanogr. Physique* v. 71 The term guyot seems unnecessary in view of the more satisfactory term table mount. **1959** Tablemount [see *GUYOT]. **1882** CAULFIELD & SAWARD *Dict. Needlework* 468/1 Tablecloths, table napkins, tray ditto [etc.]. **1917** *Harrods Gen. Catal.* 1448/3, 1 doz. Table Napkins £1 7s. 6d. **1938** *John o' London's Weekly* 18 Mar. 991/3 To plant palm trees and pampas grass on the Devon hills is like calling a table napkin in an Englishman's dining-room a serviette. **1970–1** *Kay's Catal.* Autumn–Winter 585 White cotton tablecloth... Matching table napkins available. **1946** *2nd Rep. Sel. Comm. on Procedure* p. iv, in *Parl. Papers 1945–46* IX. 161 Questions received at the Table Office before the hour of sitting of the House shall be deemed to have been received the day before. **1950** *Erskine May's Law of Parl.* (ed. 15) xii. 243 The Table Office assists the Clerks at the Table particularly in the preparation of the Notice Paper and the Order Book. **1973** *Times* 15 May 7/2 The table office at the House refused, after taking advice, to accept the questions. **1968** *Daily Colonist* (Victoria, B.C.) 9 Nov. 1/6 John Laxton..confirmed that a..meeting of the caucus of MLA's and the provincial table officers..had agreed on the convention date. **1973** *Globe & Mail* (Toronto) 8 Sept. 8/5 He's been involved in some of the most complex bargaining in that field..and was one of the table officers when construction workers two years ago rejected a back-to-work order. **1911** W. J. LOCKE *Glory of Clementina Wing* xxiii. 345 Quixtus at the end of the table... Clementina had thus arranged the table-plan. **1948** G. V. GALWEY *Lift & Drop* v. 93 Dance was..fretting over..the way his table plan had been upset. **1982** K. FOLLETT *Man from St. Petersburg* xiv. 252 She sent for Pritchard and made the table plan with him. **1817** in *Minnesota Hist. Soc. Coll.* (1860) II. 36 The mode I adopted to ascertain the height of the cataract, was to suspend a line and plummet from the table rock on the south side of the river. **1881** Table screen [in Dict., sense 21 c]. **1971** *Country Life* 10 June 1425/3 Several table screens are on view. A rare example ..is made of turquoise matrix carved with an eastern scene. **1972** *Trans. Oriental Ceramic Soc.* XXXVIII. 112 Table screen painted in blue... Chêng-tê period, 1506–21. **1974** SAVAGE & NEWMAN *Illustr. Dict. Ceramics* 282 *Table-screen,* a small rectangular porcelain plaque or tile, usually decorated on both sides, mounted vertically on a stand, and intended to be placed on the scholar's table, probably to protect his work from unwanted sunlight. **1765** J. WEDGWOOD *Let.* 25 July (1965) 36 Your Brother Josiah's Pottworks were the subject of conversation for some time, the Cream colour Table services in particular. **1885** *List of Subscribers, Classified* (United Telephone Co.) (ed. 6) 229 (Advt.), Crystal and Demi-Crystal Table Services and Ornaments. **1955** *House & Garden* June 74/2 Table mats are a most practical form of table setting. **1967** E. SHORT *Embroidery & Fabric Collage* iii. 66 A tablecloth designed with the table setting in mind will enhance the general effect rather than confuse it. **1885** *Encycl. Brit.* XIX. 283/1 The modern usage is to play *table stakes*; i.e., each player puts up such an amount as he pleases at the commencement of each deal, and he cannot be raised more than he has on the table; but he has the option of making good from his pocket a previous raise which exceeds his table stake. **1973** T. PYNCHON *Gravity's Rainbow* I. 7 Routine: plug in American blending machine won from Yank last summer, some poker game, table stakes, B.O.Q. somewhere in the north. **1948** Table tape [see *problem tape* s.v. *PROBLEM 7]. **1956** G. A. MONTGOMERIE *Digital Calculating Machines* x. 213 Numbers may also be taken from the table tapes as required. **1887** in *75 Years of Fun* (Parker Bros., Inc.) (1958) 19 Table Tennis... This game is laid out like a lawn tennis court, played and counted just the same, all the rules being observed. **1977** *World Book Encycl.* XIX. 4/2 A British firm manufactured table tennis equipment and registered the name *Ping-Pong* in England in 1900 and in America in 1901. Soon afterward it sold the American rights to Parker Brothers of Salem, Massachusetts. The monopoly of the game by these two companies and their dictation of rules and equipment led to a revolt by internationally organized players in 1921. As a result, the unpatented name *Table Tennis* was adopted. **1673** J. RAY *Observations Journey Low-Countries* 340 The red Florence wine is most commended for a table wine of any in Italy. **1827** DISRAELI *Vivian Grey* III. v. iv. 73 Very fair table-wine, I think. **1978** J. SYMONS *Blackheath Poisonings* I. 40 Roger poured a red table wine that had been decanted.

table, *v.* **4. a.** For *U.S. Congress* read *U.S. Pol.,* and add later examples.

1916 J. B. THOBURN *Stand. Hist. Oklahoma* II. 715 [The bill] was sent to the council where it was considered, amended, and finally tabled. **1931** H. F. PRINGLE *Theodore Roosevelt* I. vi. 71 The resolution had no sooner been offered than..members were..demanding that it be tabled. **1950** W. S. CHURCHILL *2nd World War* III. II. xxxvi. 609 The British Staff prepared a paper which they wished to raise as a matter of urgency, and informed their American colleagues that they wished to 'table it'. To the American Staff 'tabling' a paper meant putting it away in a drawer and forgetting it. **1974** *Sumter* (S. Carolina) *Daily Item* 22 Apr. 5A/7 Various plans for fundraising were discussed but it was decided to table any such plans until the fall.

tableau. Add: **2. c.** Also (*Theatr.*), a representation of the action at some stage in a play, created by the actors suddenly holding their positions or 'freezing', esp. at a moment critical to the plot, or at the end of a scene or act. Also, as a stage direction.

c **1863** T. TAYLOR *Ticket-of-Leave Man* I. 22 Brierly is overpowered and handcuffed—Guests rush in and form Tableau. **1866** *Black ey'd Susan* ii. 9 fo. 30 The door opens. William enters C. *Susan.* Ah. William! Alive! (*Tableau*). **1881** P. FITZGERALD *World behind Scenes* I. 46 The tableaus at the end of each act..were brought about with admirable simplicity. **1982** C. CASTLE *Folies Bergère* vi. 221 There are some 45 sets and tableaux.

d. *Cards.* The arrangement formed by the cards laid out on the table in the game of patience.

1875 A. CADOGAN *Illustr. Game Patience* (ed. 2) 1 Having placed the tableau, take any aces that may appear on the surface of the packets and play them in their allotted spaces. **1913** 'L. HOFFMANN' *Sel. Patience Games* 5 The first step, in the case of most Patience games, is to arrange a certain number of cards face upwards on the table. The cards thus arranged are known as the 'lay-out', or tableau. **1975** *Way to Play* 147/4 Spaces in the tableau (caused by the removal of an entire fan) remain unfilled.

5. = *simplex tableau* s.v. *SIMPLEX *sb.* 4.

1953 A. CHARNES in W. W. Cooper et al. *Introd. Linear Programming* II. vi. 67 The coefficients of the ϵ-polynomial multiplying P_i..are given in due order by the entries in the P_i row of the tableau. **1971** D. C. HAGUE *Managerial Economics* ix. 186 The rule in the Simplex method is that any variable—that is, any x or any s—which appears on the left-hand edge of the tableau..has a positive value. **1980** A. J. JONES *Game Theory* iii. 165 The artificial variables have performed their function, and we can now drop the columns of the tableau associated with a_5 and a_6.

6. Special combination. **tableau curtain** *Theatr.* (see quot. 1967); cf. *TAB *sb.*[4]

1881 W. H. RIDEING *Dramatic Notes* 45 It may here be worth mentioning that the handsome 'tableau curtain' made for this occasion..cost £740. **1967** *Oxf. Compan. Theatre* (ed. 3) 932/1 Tabs (short for Tableau Curtain), used originally of an act-drop which parted and rose sideways towards the outer top corners, and by extension to any front curtain or, mistakenly, to curtain settings on the stage.

table-book. **1.** For † *Obs.* read *Obs.* or *rare* and add later examples.

1852 THACKERAY *Henry Esmond* II. v. 76 We were off Finisterre on the 31st of July, so Esmond's table-book informs him. **1937** BLUNDEN *Elegy* 11 Might Machiavel Now from his table-book communicate Precept or paradox that could do well In the nerve centres of a modern state?

tabled, *a* Add: **1. b.** Seated at table. *rare*$^{-1}$.

1922 JOYCE *Ulysses* 167 He gazed round the stooled and tabled eaters.

tableful. Add: **b.** (Earlier example.) Also, as many (things) as a table is holding, all that is on the table.

1868 H. A. VAUGHAN *Let.* 26 Dec. in *Lett. to Lady Herbert* (1942) 134 Mrs. Vaughan gave us tablefuls of excellent food. **1872** GEO. ELIOT *Middlemarch* II. IV. xxxvi. 228 Lydgate's tableful of apparatus and specimens. **1977** *Zigzag* June 15/2 He was so pleased to see me that he threw a tableful of drinks over..like in the movies!

tabler[2]. Add: **4.** (Example in sense 4 a of the vb.)

1976 H. WILSON *Governance of Britain* vii. 141 If the tablers of each of these questions are called by Mr Speaker, no other question is called.

5. With initial capital. A member of the Round Table organization; a Round-Tabler.

1955 [see *SOROPTIMIST *a.* and *sb*]. **1973** *Scotsman* 21 Feb. 8/4 During lunch with some executives in Rotary and the Round Table..the prominent young Tabler from Lower Yarrow..suggested [etc.]. **1977** *Abingdon Herald* 10 Mar. 2/5 Between them, the 1,215 Tablers are buying an off-shore lifeboat.

table-rapping. Add: (Earlier and later examples.) Also as *adj.*, and **ta·ble-rapper,** one who practises table-rapping.

1856 *Spiritual Herald* Apr. 73 The matter has been explained to us thus... Table-turning and table-rapping are designed to call attention to the existence and presence of super-human powers. **1893** *Harper's Mag.* Feb. 377/1, I could not ring a bell when there was none to ring, as spirits do in table-rappers' closets. **1936** M. FRANKLIN *All that Swagger* x. 89 Familiar association with bogus lords and parsons, soothsayers, table-rappers, medical quacks, [etc.]. **1973** T. PYNCHON *Gravity's Rainbow* I. 55 The young statistician is devoted to number and to method, not table-rapping or wishful thinking.

table-spoon. Add: Also *loosely*, = TABLESPOONFUL.

1960 E. DAVID *Fr. Prov. Cooking* 506 For 2 lb. of fruit add 6 tablespoons of vanilla sugar. **1981** *Sunday Tel.* 8 Mar. 11/2 Cucumber soup. 1 small onion; 1 clove garlic; 2 tablespoons sunflower oil; [etc.].

tablespoonful. Add: Also *fig.*

1880 [see *CONTINUED *ppl. a.* 3 b].

tablet, *sb.* Add: **1. d.** Also, a plaque of pottery; *spec.* one forming the central part of a chimney-piece. Cf. *BLOCK *sb.* 12 c.

1768 J. WEDGWOOD *Let.* 6 Nov. (1965) 68, I have lately had a Vision by night of some new Vases, Tablets &c with which Articles we shall certainly serve the *whole World!* **1775, 1875** [see *BLOCK *sb.* 12 c]. **1970** G. SAVAGE *Dict. Antiques* 462/2 The year 1773 saw the first catalogue of ornamental wares, which included..tablets for chimney-pieces and furniture-mounts.

e. *U.S.* = PAD *sb.*[3] 4. Cf. WRITING TABLET in Dict. and Suppl.

1880 *Geyer's Stationer* 12 Aug. (Advt.), The M. & H. Blotter Tablet... Beware of tablets sold by J. C. Blair, as he is manufacturing without a legal right. **1897** *Sears, Roebuck Catal.* 349/2 Everything from a 400 page tablet of fair paper for 4 cents, to one of fine cream laid paper. **1934** *Chain Store Age* (Gen. Merchandise ed.) Jan. 57/2 The customer does not notice that there are three sheets less in a tablet. **1977** *Chicago Tribune* 2 Oct. XII. 39/1 Cadillac boasts in its 1978 Seville that it has made 'provision for a phone installation, writing pad, and pen'. But it's only a provision—you have to supply the phone, pen, and tablet.

f. A small metal disc similar in function to a 'staff' (*STAFF *sb.*[1] 9 f), and used for working single-track railways.

1897 W. E. LANGDON *Applic. Electr. to Railway Working* vi. 129 When the instruments are in their normal condition, all tablets being in, the very first ring from the station of whom the permission to withdraw a tablet is made..would..be equally serviceable for the purpose. **1950** O. S. NOCK *Brit. Locomotives from Footplate* 183 This train was booked non-stop between Arrochar and Crianlarich, but the slack for tablet exchange made it necessary to pass very slowly through Ardline. **1969** *Railway Mag.* Feb. 88 (*caption*) The single-line tablet for the section to Kingussie is being given by the signalman to the driver.

g. A rigid card used in tablet-weaving (see sense 8 below).

1921 M. & H. PEACH tr. *Pralle's Tablet Weaving* 6 The earliest examples found of the little tablets for the weaving were of thin polished wood. **1964** H. HODGES *Artifacts* x. 137 The tablets were generally oval or rectangular with a hole, or a pair of holes, at each end. **1970** J. P. WILD *Textile Manuf. in N. Roman Provinces* vii. 73 Each tablet governs the four (or three) warp-threads which are threaded through its holes..; and the pack of tablets is held in the hand like a pack of cards.

3. b. For *Sc.* read orig. and chiefly *Sc.* and add earlier and later examples. Also, a piece of this. Orig. a type of candy, but now a type of fudge.

1736 MRS. MCLINTOCK *Receipts for Cookery* 35 (*heading*) To make Orange Tablets with the Grate. **1850** MRS. DALGAIRNS *Practice of Cookery* 347 Ginger tablet may be made in this way. **1897** *Private Life of Queen* xvii. 140 Among the favourites of the Queen..are..tablets, *petits fours*,..pralines, almond sweets. **1922** 'R. WEST' *Judge* I. ii. 56 Here's some taiblet for you, lassie. **1948** *Good Housek. Cookery Bk.* 643 *Ginger Tablet*, use the same ingredients as for Hazel Tablet, but omit the nuts and vanilla essence and add ½ oz. of ground ginger. **1973** *Times* 13 Dec. 12/2 Tablet, for those who don't know, is a delicious, crumbly fudge that melts in your mouth—it's a Scottish speciality.

c. A piece of compacted powder of standard size, shape, and composition, ready for subsequent moulding.

1935 [see *PREFORM *sb.* 1]. **1936** H. W. ROWELL *Technol. of Plastics* xx. 148 A 'tablet' is of the correct weight and density required and is made of suitable diameter and thickness to fit the mould. It is made in a stock size of die and is not preformed to the approximate shape of the moulding. **1947** R. L. WAKEMAN *Chem. Commercial Plastics* v. 76 Tablets and preforms fit freely inside the mold ultimately employed. **1974** *Gloss. Packaging Terms* (*B.S.I.*) III. 9 *Tablet*, a compressed mass of moulding material of prescribed form and mass.

6. (Earlier example.)

1788 [see *GOBELIN 1].

8. tablet paper *U.S.*, notepaper taken from a writing-pad; **tablet-weaving,** an early method of weaving, in which warp-threads are passed through holes in a number of parallel tablets, which are then rotated to form sheds.

1964 MRS. L. B. JOHNSON *White House Diary* 25 Feb. (1970) 73 The file..marked 'particularly appealing'. Those were the letters that were taken to Mrs. Kennedy to read. They came written in poetry, they came in barely legible pencil on tablet paper. **1921** M. & H. PEACH tr. *Pralle's Tablet Weaving* 6 Tablet weaving.. is considered the origin of all weaving. *Ibid.*, In the Museum at Copenhagen..is a belt which must have been woven by this tablet-weaving method. **1950** *Proc. Prehist. Soc.* XVI. 130 The archaeological material..is then reviewed, with a special note on the curious technique of tablet-weaving. **1979** B. CUNLIFFE *Celtic World* 60/2 Finer weaving to make braid and a form of tablet weaving are also attested.

tablet, *v.* Add: **2.** (Examples of *trans.* use.)

1936 H. W. ROWELL *Technol. of Plastics* xx. 148 Tableting or preforming or pelleting a powder is generally done on automatic machines. **1963** *Times* 4 May 11/5 In an article in a medical journal some time ago describing the clinical trial of a drug, reference was made to the manufacturer who 'tableted and distributed' the drug. **1973** R. PARKES *Guardians* ii. 59 This heroin is comparable in quality to that being sniffed by U.S. troops in Vietnam and far superior to that being tableted for U.K. distribution.

Hence **ta·bleted** *ppl. a.*, **ta·bleting** *vbl. sb.* and *ppl. a.* (examples in sense 2 of the vb.).

1889 [see sense 2 in Dict.]. **1936** H. W. ROWELL *Technol. Plastics* xx. 148 Tableting machines measure the charge in this way. **1937** *Mod. Packaging* Oct. 110/1 Small powdered, tableted and similar products. **1947** R. L. WAKEMAN *Chem. Commercial Plastics* v. 76 In compression operations, recourse is often had to tableting and preforming in order to speed up molding. **1972** *Materials & Technol.* V. xxi. 763 The tabletting process consists of feeding free-flowing granules into a ..die, and compressing the material. **1983** *Glaxo Group News* Sept. 4/3 The accuracy and efficiency of single punch tabletting machines have been monitored by strain gauges.

ta·ble-top, *a.* Also **table top, tabletop.** [f. *table-top* sb. (see TABLE *sb.* 22).] **1.** Of, pertaining to, or designating photography of subjects which can be contained within the area of a table-top; *spec.* applied to photography of small-scale models which gives the illusion of a larger subject.

1914 S. C. JOHNSON *Saturday with my Camera* xliv. 368 We can all enter the lists of table-top photography,..and spend our winter evenings counterfeiting, at leisure, many of the most attractive sights of the world. **1923** *Kodak Mag.* Apr. 58 (*heading*) Home-made landscapes—a few words on table-top photography. **1935** *News Chron. Amat. Photogr.* xiv. 176 Flashlight has special application to table-top photography, now becoming so popular, as the illumination is under complete control, and all the work can be done in the evening. **1956** *Focal Encycl. Photogr.* 1151/1 There are three different branches of photography open to the photographer who chooses to work within the limits of a table top studio: still life studies, photography of small scale models and creative composition. The last is the true 'table top photography'. *Ibid.* 1152/2 Most table-top pictures fail either because they include too many items or because they try to represent the subject accurately and in detail instead of simply suggesting it in a broad effect.

2. That is or can be placed, or that takes place, on a table.

1945 F. BROWN in *Astounding Sci. Fiction* Jan. 133/1 There was a boom market in portable and table-top receivers. **1962** *Guardian* 9 July 5/3 He made table top models of the machines. **1971** *Physics Bull.* Sept. 513/2 The total number of installed computers, including table top computers, is expected to be 60 000 in 1975 and 96 500 in 1980. **1979** *Guardian* 31 Oct. 1/8 Fagging.. includes..retrieving the little red ball when it goes under chairs during games of table-top cricket.

tableware. (Earlier example.)

1772 J. WEDGWOOD *Let.* 10 Sept. (1965) 134, I think he might by that means sell now and then a sett of it in Tableware.

Tabloid. Add: **1. a.** (Examples of the proprietary term.) Also *loosely*, (with small initial), a small (medicinal) tablet.

1884 *Trade Marks Jrnl.* 23 Apr. 334 *Tabloid*... Burroughs, Wellcome & Company, Snow Hill Buildings, Holborn Viaduct, London, E.C... Chemical substances not included in Class I, used in Medicine and Pharmacy. **1894** *Murray's Handbk. India* (ed. 2) p. xx, For medicine, plenty of quinine in 2 or 4 grain 'tabloids' or pills. **1895** *Army & Navy Co-op. Soc. Price List* 695/1 Tabloids—Ichthyol per bott. 0/7½... Tea per tin 0/5. **1904** *Official Gaz.* (U.S. Patent Office) 18 Oct. 1743/2 Drugs and chemicals for human and veterinary use... *Tabloid.* **1916** 'TAFFRAIL' *Pincher Martin* ix. 161 Morphia tabloids were served out to all the officers of quarters for administration to badly injured men. **1938** E. J. G. FORSE *Ceremonial Curiosities* xxix. 149 It is wise to carry a few simple tabloids with you. **1978** *Daily Mirror* 19 Apr. 24/1, I found a metal box which used to contain 'Tabloid' tea.

b. *fig.*, etc. (Later examples.)

1909 *Westm. Gaz.* 22 Oct. 5/2 While in literature the trend of taste is all in the direction of tabloids, composers seem ashamed of anything approaching terseness. **1920** R. MACAULAY *Potterism* VI. iii. 232 People might like their science in cheap and absurd tabloid form... The Potter press exulted in scientific discoveries made easy. **1928** *Melody Maker* Feb. 145/2 Mr. Harold Craxton's playing on the piano of the 'Three Blind Mice'..as a tabloid Hungarian Rhapsody by Liszt. **1935** *Brit. Jrnl. Psychol.* July 27 Statements of a vague character, which are condensations of complex propositional wholes... To such propositions I have elsewhere given the name 'tabloids'.

2. a. *R.A.F. slang.* A small Sopwith biplane. (*Disused.*)

1913 *Aeroplane* 11 Dec. 635/2 The small speedy Sopwith biplane has been nicknamed the 'Tabloid' because it contains so many good qualities in such small compass. **1915** *War Illustr.* 20 Feb. 22/2 The 'Tabloid's' supreme value lies in its speed and climbing power. **1925** FRASER & GIBBONS *Soldier & Sailor Words* 275 *Tabloid, a*, an Air Force nickname for a type of small Sopwith biplane of high speed and rapid climbing powers, a special favourite from its numerous good points, its, as it were, concentrated excellencies. **1928** C. F. S. GAMBLE *North Sea Air Station* x. 149 In addition to its maximum speed of 92 miles an hour the 'Tabloid' was remarkable in those days for its great speed range.

b. In full *tabloid cruiser*. A small cruising yacht.

1930 *Yachting Monthly* XLIX. 428/1 T's ship, Honora, is, except for her draught, a 'tabloid' cruiser: 19 ft. LOA, with 5 ft. 9 in. beam. **1937** *Ibid.* LXIV. 17/1 Reflections on an unusual little tabloid. **1938** *Ibid.* 452/2 A tabloid cruiser that goes foreign ought to be registered.

3. a. A popular newspaper which presents its news and features in a concentrated, easily assimilable, and often sensational form, esp. one with smaller pages than those of a regular newspaper.

1918 W. E. CARSON *Northcliffe* x. 304 Since 1908 Alfred Harmsworth, like his famous 'tabloid', has disappeared from view. **1926** *Encycl. Brit.* II. 1055/2 The introduction of tabloids may be explained..by the passing remark of Lord Northcliffe, 'If some American does not start one I shall have to come over to do it.' **1928** *Observer* 5 Feb. 18/1 The..chain now includes 26 papers, in most cases 'tabloids' or papers with a popular appeal. **1934** A. WOOLLCOTT *While Rome Burns* 100, I remembered how confidently, but how inaccurately, the tabloids had prophesied the..divorce. **1949** [see *ANGEL *v.* 1]. **1957** *Listener* 31 Oct. 683/2 Newspapers have been allowed to transform themselves into tabloids with gossip columns, adulation of film stars, beauty contests and other requisites of the popular press of the West. **1970** G. F. NEWMAN *Sir, You Bastard* vi. 174, I presume you've read the tabloids? **1978** *Time* 3 July 12/1 The *National Enquirer*, the Florida-based tabloid, dispatched ten reporters and photographers to scour the Riviera in quest of informants on the courtship.

b. *attrib.*, esp. as *tabloid newspaper*.

[**1901, 1902**: in Dict.] **1918** W. E. CARSON *Northcliffe* x. 299 The New York *World* made its appearance. Harmsworth had issued the paper in what he called 'tabloid form'. **1926** *Amer. Mercury* Dec. 462/1 A tabloid weekly theatrical newspaper, published in New York, and filled with ugly type, heavy black advertisements and the most atrocious English ever put into print, was named as co-respondent by his wife. **1938** [see *JAZZ *sb.* 6]. **1949** KOESTLER *Promise & Fulfilment* II. ii. 232 To the distant reader of the tabloid Press..it looked as if history had at last met Metro-Goldwyn-Mayer's most ambitious dream. **1962** V. NABOKOV *Pale Fire* 22 He was back in the car, reading a tabloid newspaper which I had thought no poet would deign to touch. **1977** *New Yorker* 19 Sept. 31/1 Next day, the tabloid *Daily Mail* gave the hearing its entire front page, but the *Guardian* didn't mention it at all.

Hence as *v. trans.*, to express briefly or concisely; to condense. *rare.*

1933 PARTRIDGE *Slang To-day & Yesterday* I. iv. 36 Much of the best wit, the most delectable humour is couched in slang; for, slang offers no compulsion to think *how* the happy thought is phrased or, perhaps, tabloided into an expressive adjective, or a second-sighted noun, an unravelling or illuminating verb. **1934** *Punch* 21 Mar. 329/2 Also there is a certain sketchiness in the tale as tabloided for the two hours' traffic of our stage, and some of the connecting-links seem to have got lost in the process.

tabnab (tæ·bnæb). *Naut. slang.* [Origin obscure.] A cake, bun, or pastry; a savoury snack.

1933 M. LOWRY *Ultramarine* v. 212 Perhaps he would be able to speak to Andy when he gave him the tabnabs. **1947** —— *Under Volcano* vi. 172 What the bosun called, with unction, 'afternoon tea'. With tabnabs. The tabnabs were delicate and delicious little cakes made by the second cook. **1962** *Punch* 10 Jan. 98/1 Tea and tabnabs (seafaring for cake). **1978** K. BONFIGLIOLI *All Tea in China* viii. 111 These 'tabnabs' were little gullet-tickling confections... My favourite 'tabnab' was..a little fried potato-cake with a morsel of kari'd mutton inside.

tabo- (tē¹·bo), comb. form of TABES, as in **tabopara·lysis** *Med.* (see quot. 1972); **tabopare·sis** = prec.

1910 F. W. MOTT in Power & Murphy *System of Syphilis* IV. x. 328 An important point to remember is the frequency with which optic atrophy is followed by taboparalysis. **1972** R. A. & A. T. WILLIS *Princ. Path. & Bacteriol.* (ed. 3) xvi. 201 The quaternary syphilitic diseases are (1) general paralysis of the insane or dementia paralytica, and (2) locomotor ataxia or tabes dorsalis. A combination of the two, taboparalysis, also occurs. **1910** *Med. Rec.* (N.Y.) LXXVII. 219/1 (*heading*) The pathological prodromes of taboparesis. **1932** W. BOYD *Textbk. Path.* xxx. 829 There is sometimes a combination of tabes and paresis (taboparesis), with degeneration of the posterior columns [of the spinal cord]. **1980** A. KING et al. *Venereal Dis.* (ed. 4) v. 89 This suggests that there is an element of tabes present (taboparesis).

taboo, tabu, *a.* and *sb.* Add: **B.** *sb.* **1. c.** *Linguistics*, a total or partial prohibition of the use of certain words, expressions, topics, etc., esp. in social intercourse.

1933 [see sense 3 b below]. **1962** S. ULLMANN *Semantics* viii. 205 Taboo is an important cause of semantic change. Language taboos fall into three more or less distinct groups according to the psychological motivation behind them. **1980** R. A. HUDSON *Sociolinguistics* ii. 53 The distinction between conventional and necessary social restrictions is also interesting in view of the strength of feeling which the former arouse. This is particularly clear in the case of *linguistic taboo*, such as the so-called 'four-letter words' of English.

3. b. *Linguistics.* With reference to an expression or topic considered offensive and hence avoided or prohibited by social custom.

1933 L. BLOOMFIELD *Language* xxii. 396 In America, *knocked up* is a tabu-form for 'rendered pregnant'; for this reason, the phrase is not used in the British sense 'tired, exhausted'... In such cases there is little real ambiguity, but some hearers react nevertheless to the powerful stimulus of the tabu-word. **1978** *Amer. Speech* LIII. 16 It may be that taboo terms form a group which is logically akin to, yet separate from, true slang, since many taboo terms are the only ones available to non-academic speakers. **1980** *Scottsdale* (Arizona) *Progress* 9 Feb. 12 We now have a set of taboo expressions relating to ethnic groups and individuals.

taboo·ness, the state or condition of being taboo.

1974 *Verbatim* I. 1. 4/1 The tabooness of *fuck.* **1978** *Maledicta 1977* I. 236 Tabooness focuses on the speaker and his/her decision about what can or cannot be said in a given context.

‖ **taboot**[1] (tābū·t). Also **tabut.** [Hindi, a. Arab. *tābūt* coffin, box, Ark of the Covenant.] A sacred box or coffin; *spec.* a box, representing the tomb of Husain, which is carried in procession through the streets during the Muslim festival of Muharram.

1622 in W. Foster *Eng. Factories India 1622–3* (1908) 94 This daye is heere aryved Sultan (Khus) roues taboots [*sic*] from Brampore, (which to-) morrowe is to bee dispeeded to H(elobass?) there to bee intered by his mother. **1862** MRS. J. B. SPEID *Our Last Yrs. in India* 230 Taboots, or tazzias, the representation of Hosain's mausoleum at Kurbulla. **1879** L. PELLY *Miracle Play of Hasan & Husain* p. xvii, Against the side of the Imambarrah, directed towards Mecca, is set the *tabut.* **1891** *Daily News* 9 Sept. 5/4 Immense sums of money are spent upon the *taboots*..that, carried in these processions, are broken to pieces and buried at the end of the ceremony. **1958** G. E. VON GRUNEBAUM *Muhammedan Festivals* v. 89 The *ta'ziya*, or Passion play..became the real climax of the Shī'ite Tenth of Muharram celebrations. The stage requires few properties besides a large *tabut* (coffin),..and Husain's arms and banner. **1975** *Indian Express* 15 Jan. 5/1 Taboot processions with music will be allowed only on the last day of the Moharrum.

‖ **taboot**[2] (tā·būt). Also **tabut.** [Arab., abbrev. of *tābūt raf' al-miyāh* Archimedes screw, or of *tābūt al-sāquiya* scoop wheel: see prec. entry.] A form of water-wheel used in Egypt.

1836 E. W. LANE *Acct. Manners & Customs Mod. Egyptians* II. 25 There is a third machine, called *taboot*, used for the irrigation of lands in the northern part of Egypt. **1841** J. KITTO *Phys. Hist. Palestine* vii. p. ccxcvii, Another machine used for the irrigation of lands, when it is only necessary to raise the water a few feet..is called the *Taboot.* **1877** *Encycl. Brit.* VII. 708/1 The tâboot..differs from the sâkiyeh principally in having a hollow wheel instead of the wheel with pots. **1924** *Countries of World* III. 1757/1 The primitive but still effective apparatus known as the 'sakieh', the 'shaduf', and the 'tabut'.

‖ **tabot** (tabǫ·t). [Ge'ez: cf. *TABOOT[1].] A box, representing the Ark of the Covenant, which stands on the altar in an Ethiopian church.

1682 J. P. GENT tr. *Ludolphus's New Hist. Ethiopia* III. vi. 294 In the Sanctuary stands the Holy Table, which they call..*Manbar*... Upon this they place the sacred vessels. First the *Tabot*, or Chest..an Oblong Quadrangular Table, upon which the Dish and Cup are set. **1710** F. TELLEZ *Trav. Jesuits in Ethiopia* III. x. 242 We restore you the Faith of your Fore-Fathers. The former Clergy-Men may return to their Churches, put in their *Tabotes*, and say Masses. **1834** S. GOBAT *Jrnl. Three Years' Residence in Abyssinia* ii. 243 A church, when there is no 'tabot' in it, is no more to them than a common house. **1923** *Blackw. Mag.* Aug. 256/2 It [*sc.* the Abyssinian Church] venerates an object called the *tabot*, which is the replica of the Ark of the Covenant. **1968** E. ULLENDORFF *Ethiopia & Bible* ii. 83 Criticisms levelled against the Ethiopians on account of their *tabot*-centred worship.

tabouret. Add: **2. b.** *U.S.* A small table, esp. one used as a stand for house-plants; a bedside table.

1916 *Sears, Roebuck & Co. Catal.* Fall 1244/2 Tabourets or jardinier stands. **1968** J. UPDIKE *Couples* iii. 228 One of his flippers kicked over a tabouret holding a crammed ashtray and a small vase of asters. **1984** M. BABSON *Trail of Ashes* iii. 33 Look in the bedside tabouret for a little nightcap.

Tabriz (tăbrī·z). The name of a city in north-western Iran, used *attrib.* and *absol.* to designate carpets and rugs made there, the older styles of which often show a rich decorative medallion pattern.

1900 J. K. MUMFORD *Oriental Rugs* xi. 168 The model on which the Tabriz rugs were really designed is the ornamental and richly colored fabric of Kirman in southern Persia. **1911** G. G. LEWIS *Pract. Bk. Oriental Rugs* II. 184 With the Kirman the Tabriz shares the reputation of having the most graceful floral designs. **1931** A. U. DILLEY *Oriental Rugs & Carpets* iv. 104 Modern Tabriz rugs constitute a..revival of weaving that began at least as early as the Caliphate. **1946** *Lancet* 2 Mar. 322/1 The bedside carpet is important and must be gratifying to the bare feet... A subdued Shiraz will fulfil most people's requirements, though leptoforms may require something with a more stimulating pattern, say a Tabriz. **1962** N. FREELING *Love in Amsterdam* II. 79 He bought books and pictures, and had a treasured Tabriz carpet. **1978** S. WILSON *Dealer's Move* iii. 42 A superb Tabriz hung on the wall.

tab show. *U.S. slang.* [f. TAB(LOID + SHOW *sb.*[1]] A short version of a musical, esp. one performed by a travelling company.

1951 GREEN & LAURIE *Show Biz* 571/2 *Tab show*, tabloid version of a musical. **1953** *Sun* (Baltimore) 30 Sept. 38/6 He traveled in 'tab shows'—vaudeville and musical comedy—through the South. **1983** *N.Y. Times* 12 June XXI. 10/4 Most Broadway musicals are simply streamlined for travel, ranging from the 'tab shows' (short for tabloid) that are the trademark of some resorts, to abridged versions in stock or dinner theaters.

tabular, *a.* Add: **1. c.** Geol. *tabular* (*ice*)*berg*, a flat-topped iceberg which has broken away from an ice shelf.

1840 C. WILKES *Jrnl.* 20 Jan. in *Narr. U.S.A. Explora-tion Exped.* (1844) II. ix. 315 These tabular bergs are like masses of beautiful alabaster. **1848** C. TOMLINSON *Summer in Antarctic Regions* iv. 114 Westward of this point the *Vincennes* met a remarkable collection of tabular icebergs. **1905** R. F. SCOTT *Voyage of 'Discovery'* I. iv. 118 Cook preserves the name of Ice Island in describing the long tabular berg so typical of the Southern Regions. **1958** [see *ice-shelf* s.v. *ICE *sb.* 8]. **1979** C. KILIAN *Icequake* viii. 133 Drifting snow and falling ice masked much of the cliff face, but it did not look like the side of a tabular berg.

tabulating, *vbl. sb.* (Later examples.)

1921 J. A. V. TURCK *Origin Mod. Calculating Machines* 124 The carriage in the Ludlum machine..offered no solution to the feature of tabulating. **1979** *Washington Post* 9 June F3 Citizens in West Germany, France, Italy, Belgium and Luxembourg vote Sunday and tabulating begins that night.

tabulator. b. For 'also' read: a part of the mechanism of a typewriter (formerly, a separate attachment) for controlling the movement of the carriage in tabular work, indentation, etc. (Later examples.) *spec.* in *Computing*, a machine that produces lists, tables, or totals from the information in a data storage medium, esp. punched cards or tape.

1917 L. R. DICKSEE *Office Machinery* viii. 96 A complete installation, consisting..of three Punches, one Sorter, and one Tabulator, would involve the employment of four operators, none of whom need be skilled accountants. **1922** F. W. PIXLEY *Accountant's Dict.* II. 723/1 Accountants should..consider both systems.. The choice will generally depend on the form in which the data is finally required; in other words, the tabulator will usually govern the system adopted. **1949** [see *INTERPRETER 5 a]. **1970** O. DOPPING *Computers & Data Processing* iv. 73 A tabulator usually prints around 150 lines per minute, while a normal speed for a computer line printer is 1,000 lines per minute. **1978** J. KELLOCK *Elements of Accounting* xii. 214 The next step is to feed the cards into a tabulator.

Tabun (tā·bun). Also **tabun.** [Ger., of unkn. origin.] The name of an organophosphorus nerve gas, $(C_2H_5O)(CN)((CH_3)_2N)PO$.

1951 *Acta Physiol. Scandinavica* Suppl. No. 90. 11 The writer's aim has been to synthesize tabun and some of its homologues. **1953** [see *SOMAN]. **1967** *New Scientist* 26 Jan. 196/1 The nerve gas Sarin, known as GB, is said to be four times as toxic as the German Tabun of World War II. **1968** [see *SARIN]. **1978** A. MELVILLE-ROSS *Blindfold* iv. 26 A single 'Sarin' or 'Tabun' shell of British manufacture found its way to Egypt. **1980** *Sci. Amer.* Apr. 35/1 The first of these compounds, called tabun, was discovered in Germany in 1936 in the course of research on insecticides.

tacan (tæ·kăn). Also **Tacan, TACAN.** [f. the initial letters of *tac*tical *a*ir *n*avigation.] A navigational aid system for aircraft which measures bearing and distance from a ground beacon. Freq. *attrib.*

1955 *Times* 17 Aug. 6/4 The Defence Department has removed security restrictions from the technical details of Tacan (tactical air navigation system) and the Air Navigation Development Board will reveal them in an announcement on August 19. **1956** *Electrical Communication* Mar. 3/1 Tacan is a system that provides both bearing and distance information on direct-reading instruments in an airplane within 200 nautical miles of a selected ground station. *Ibid.* 26/1 A tacan ground-installed beacon consists of a receiver-transmitter..and either a shipboard or a shore antenna. **1966** [see *SHORAN]. **1977** P. WAY *Super-Celeste* III. 129 A small, slim fin broke the smooth underbelly of the plane... 'That's either a UHF antenna or a TACAN aerial,' said Bridge.

tacenda, *sb. pl.* (Earlier examples.)

1843 CARLYLE *Past & Present* II. x. 125 Willelmus Sacrista, and his bibations and *tacenda* are..softly yet irrevocably put an end to. **1870** S. H. HODGSON *Theory of Practice* I. ii. 217 A greater number of things are classed among tacenda... The French term pudeur seems exactly to express the feeling which is called out painfully or wounded by an lifting of the veil of the tacenda.

tach (tæk), U.S. colloq. abbrev. of TACHOMETER. Cf. *TACHO, *TACK *sb.*[8]

1966 *Publ. Amer. Dial. Soc. 1964* XLII. 9 *Tach..*, abbreviation of tachometer. **1974** R. M. PIRSIG *Zen & Art of Motorcycle Maintenance* I. iii. 36 The speedometer needle swings back and forth but the tach reads a steady nine thousand. **1980** *Family Handyman* Sept. 98/2 If you've used a tach/dwell meter for the point adjustment, leave it in place, and attach a timing light.

Tachai (da·dʒai). Also **Dazhai.** The name of a village in the Shansi Province of the People's Republic of China, used *attrib.* to designate its model commune or the methods of work, etc., associated with it. Also *Comb.*, as *Tachai-type* adj.

1969 *Observer* 16 Mar. 2/7 Under the 'Tachai' system, not only are peasants being rewarded with work points instead of hard cash, but the schoolteachers and the 'barefoot doctors' in the communes are also to be paid principally in work points. **1973** J. S. AIRD in Yuan-Li Wu *China Handbk.* I. xviii. 463 Even in the Tachai production brigade in Shansi, the family planning propaganda program at first elicited 'little positive response'. **1975** A. WATSON *Living in China* i. 22 The Communist Party almost always introduces its new policies and goals by putting forward examples for others to copy. One of the most famous of these is Dazhai Commune. **1977** *China Now* June 1 Myriads of such Tachai-type people, Tachai-type cadres, their outlook constantly broadened and deepened by Marxist science. **1979** *Ibid.* Mar./Apr. 3/1 The movement to spread 'Dazhai-type counties' throughout the country is lagging.

tacharanite (tæ·kărănəit). *Min.* [See quot. 1961 and -ITE[1].] A monoclinic hydrated silicate of calcium, magnesium, and aluminium found as white aggregates or masses.

1961 J. M. SWEET in *Mineral. Mag.* XXXII. 750 It is thought that this mineral is sufficiently distinctive to deserve a name of its own and that tacharanite..from the Gaelic *tacharan* (a changeling) would be suitable, both from the nature of its behaviour and the wealth of folklore associated with the island [*sc.* Skye] in which it occurs. **1975** *Ibid.* XL. 113 Tacharanite has been re-examined... The composition approximates to $Ca_{12}Al_2$-$Si_{18}O_{69}H_{36}$. **1978** *Ibid.* XLII. 383/1 Tacharanite in fractures in metagabbroic rocks filled by zeolitic assemblages has been found in the Gruppo di Voltri, Ligurian Alps.

tache, *sb.*[1] **1. c.** *spec.* in Art, a spot or dash of colour. Also *fig.* Cf. *TACHISM.

1957 *Observer* 3 Nov. 14/6 The 'tache' is the mark the painter makes on the canvas with his paint-loaded brush, and an emphasis on the freedom and spontaneity of the creative act itself and on extreme sensitivity towards the actual materials of painting is characteristic of the tachists. **1967** J. N. Barron *Lang. Painting* 188 *Tachisme* .., a term used to describe a style of painting in which the color is applied in splotches or blots (*taches*) of color. **1978** G. Greene *Human Factor* II. ii. 67 The simple precise words, with the single tache of colour reminded Castle of the local background so often to be found in primitive paintings.

tache, *sb.*[3] Add: Forms: 8–9 **teach.**

1. (Further examples.)

1788 P. Marsden *Acct. Island Jamaica* 26 The smallest and last copper is called the teach. **1835** in J. H. Ingraham *South-West* I. 240 In the last kettle—the *teach* as it is termed..the sugar is concentrated to the granulating point. **1862** *Illustr. Catal. Internat. Exhib., Industr. Dept., Brit. Div.* II. No. 6139 Stoves, ranges, sugar pans, teaches, or boilers to any pattern or make. **1887** *Encycl. Brit.* XXII. 626/1 The [cane sugar] juice..is passed from the one [pan] into the other till it reaches the last of the series, the striking teach. **1949** *Caribbean Q.* I. i. 9 The juice, now reduced to a syrup, was ladled into a final copper, the teache, for a last boiling.

'tache, var. *TASH.

tachinid (tæ·kinid), *sb.* and *a.* *Ent.* [a. mod.L. family name *Tachinidæ*, f. generic name *Tachina* (J. M. Meigen 1803, in *Mag. für Insektenkunde* II. 280), f. Gr. ταχινή, fem. of ταχινός swift: see -ID[3].] **A.** *sb.* A small hairy fly of the family Tachinidæ, the larvæ of which are parasitic on other arthropods. **B.** *adj.* Designating an insect of this family.

1888 *Insect Life* I. 44 We also reared an undetermined Tachinid. **1901** *Knowledge* Oct. 234/2 The ants..protect the caterpillars from the attacks of Ichneumon and Tachinid flies. **1925** R. W. G. Hingston in E. F. Norton *Fight for Everest* 285 Tachinids were common at the edge of a torrent at 17,000 feet. **1954** Borror & DeLong *Introd. Study of Insects* xxvii. 636 Tachinid Flies... All the tachinids are parasitic on other insects. **1972** *Nature* 21 Jan. 135/3 Such long-established successes of biological control as that of the..coconut moth in Fiji by the tachinid parasite. **1979** *New Scientist* 3 May 380/2 Rettenmayer watched the behaviour of the tachinid and conopid flies.

tachist (tæ·ʃist), *sb.* (and *a.*). Also ‖**tachiste** (taʃist). *Art.* [ad. F. *tachiste*, f. *tache* stain, spot + *-iste* -IST.]

† **1.** One who paints by juxtaposing small patches of unmixed colour. *Obs.*

1891 [see *plein-airiste* s.v. *PLEIN-AIR]. **1909** C. E. Hallé *Notes from Painter's Life* xi. 234 We have even schools which take their names from the manner of using the brush. We have 'Tachists', 'Vibrists', and Heaven knows how many more.

2. a. One who practices tachism (see below).

1954 *New Yorker* 4 Dec. 99/1 Negatively, it can be said that the unknowns are certainly not Cubists and not *tachistes*, and not Mondrianesque or Braqueish either. **1957** [see *TACHE *sb.*[1] 1 c]. **1960** *Guardian* 22 Apr. 9/4 The young English tachistes for whom freedom is an engrossing obsession.

b. *attrib.* or as *adj.*

1955 *New Yorker* 31 Dec. 40/3 The car, maybe the vegetables, and certainly the hope of sharing as an artist in the dubious kudos have all been attributed to a *tachiste* French painter. **1956** *Archit. Rev.* CXX. 186/1 In his delectable paintings of trout hovering in light-stained water he uses tachist techniques with a consummate professionalism. **1966** 'H. MacDiarmid' *Company I've Kept* iii. 103 People should not look at his [*sc.* William Johnstone's] paintings with any preconceived ideas and seek for elements in them which can be labelled..'tachist', and the like. **1972** R. Quilty *Tenth Session* I. 123 An aggressive twenty square feet of tachist canvas. **1982** S. Spender *China Diary* 118 The Western artist looks at the model... The first object of his attention is usually the image, even if this is abstract (except for *tachiste* painting).

Hence **ta·chism** [cf. F. *tachisme* (also used)] a style of modern painting in which spots or dabs of colour are arranged in apparently random manner to evoke an emotion, scene, etc.; cf. *action painting* s.v. *ACTION sb. 16.

1956 *Archit. Rev.* CXX. 333/1 The same Cézanne picture, considered simply as a painted surface, is one of the finest examples of 'tachism' in the history of art. **1957** *Times* 28 Nov. 3/4 The Canadian artist, Mr. Austin Cooper can claim to have been among the first in this country to practise what is now generally known as *tachisme*. **1960** J. Cohen *Chance, Skill & Luck* ii. 42 Nealces may deserve to be described by the historian of art as the founder of Tachism. **1978** *Jrnl. R. Soc. Arts* CXXVI. 696/1 Abstract expressionism and tachisme, dead on time, and an explosion of hard-edged colour, produced, he told me, under the razzamataz influence of New York. **1979** E. H. Gombrich *Sense of Order* ii. 62 Any number of Ph.D. theses await being written about the influence of Cubism, of Tachism, of Op or Pop art on fabrics and wall paper.

tachistoscope. Add: (Earlier and later examples.) Hence **tachistosco·pic** *a.*; **tachistosco·pically** *adv.* (also *fig.*).

1890 Billings *Med. Dict.* II. 641/1 Tachistoscope. **1903** *Psychol. Rev.* X. 393 (*heading*) Tachistoscopic experiments. *Ibid.* 394 The number of separate objects that can be apperceived at once with the tachistoscope is given as varying from four to five. **1917** *Arch. Psychol.* XL. 3 The material was presented tachistoscopically with a fixed tempo of presentation. **1931** *Brit. Jrnl. Psychol.* XXII. 67 The instrument..embodies an attempt to meet the many theoretical requirements of the perfect tachistoscope by constructing one without moving parts. **1949** *Jrnl. Personality* XVIII. 24 Present tachistoscopically a picture of a love scene, a handsome young Arab leaning yearningly over his beloved on a couch in a Moorish setting. **1969** J. Brunner *Plague on Both your Causes* xix. 141, I saw a tachistoscopically rapid glimpse of one of the half-tracks [from a helicopter]. **1979** R. Hawkey *Side-Effect* vii. 54 I'd like to..have you take the tachistoscopic perception test... Look at a series of images we'd put up on a tachistoscope.

tacho (tæ·ko), colloq. abbrev. of Tachometer. Cf. *TACH, *TACK *sb.*[8]

1964 *Motor* 13 June 9/1 (*heading*) Japanese tachos. **1975** G. J. King *Audio Handbk.* viii. 195 Now, should the motor speed tend to decrease, owing to an increasing load for example, the tacho output also decreases. **1979** *Truck & Bus Transportation* May 26/1 On the open roads, the rear axle ratio of 4·33:1 made 100 km/h a comfortable cruising speed with a tacho reading of around the 2800 rpm mark.

tacho-ge·nerator (tæ:ko-). [f. *tacho(meter)-generator* s.v. *TACHOMETER 2.] An instrument that generates a voltage accurately proportional to the rate of rotation of a shaft or the like.

1952 *Electronic Engin.* XXIV. 382/1 Factors affecting the linearity of response with speed of D.C. tacho-generators. **1958** *New Scientist* 4 Sept. 751/1 One such piece of apparatus for keeping watch on the rpm of engines in flight is actuated by a small tacho-generator to measure the rate of rotation and communicate its warning if overspeeding occurs. **1976** *Gramophone* Sept. 510/1 Speed accuracy is controlled by a new system using a tacho-generator.

tachograph (tæ·kograf). [f. Gr. τάχο-ς speed + -GRAPH.] A device in a motor vehicle for recording its speed, travel time, and other information automatically.

[**1903** *Nature* 26 Nov. 95/2 On the use of the Schrader tacheograph in hydrographic work.] **1909** *Cent. Dict.* Suppl., *Tachograph*, a recording tachometer applied to shafting or wheels to register rotation-speed; a speed indicator. [*With reference to prec. source.*] **1941** F. D. Jones *Engin. Encycl.* II. 1258 Some of these recording tachometers or tachographs have a dial in addition to the recording charts. **1968** *Guardian* 1 Oct. 5/2 Road tanker drivers..are protesting against the proposal..to install a tachograph in lorries—a device which records speeds, length of time taken on journeys, and periods when the vehicle is stationary. **1976** *Citizen* (Ottawa) 8 Jan. 1/6 The 10 ambulances in Ottawa are equipped with a tachograph that records the speed of the vehicle. **1980** *Times* 24 Jan. 2/3 The Road Haulage Association acknowledged last night that the tachograph, which records speed, mileage travelled, stopping time and the use of brake and accelerator, could open the way to productivity deals if drivers could show that they were operating more efficiently.

tachometer. Add: **1. a.** *spec.* One that indicates the speed of an engine in r.p.m. (Further examples.)

1918 *Bull. U.S. Naval Consulting Board* No. 3. 10 Many new instruments have been devised for aircraft. These include..tachometers, which indicate the engine speed. **1953** C. A. Lindbergh *Spirit of St. Louis* II. vi. 187 The tachometer needle shows 1825 r.p.m. **1975** *Drive* New Year 88/1 This is an important job performed by the rev-counter, or tachometer.

2. Special Comb.: **tachometer generator** = *TACHO-GENERATOR.

1946 *Shell Aviation News* No. 103. 24/1 The gearbox is of Rolls-Royce design... It is mounted on the bulkhead and provides drives, on the forward side, for the air pump and the generator, and on the rear side for the tachometer generator. **1958** W. D. Cockrell *Industr. Electronics Handbk.* II. 254 Tachometer generators are used in systems to generate feedback signals in servoloops or used directly with an indicating instrument.

Hence **tachome·tric** *a.*

1931 S. R. Roget *Dict. Electr. Terms* (ed. 2) 341/1 Tachometric electrometer. **1967** O. I. Egerd *Control Syst. Theory* vii. 238 Tachometric feedback.

‖**ta chuan** (da dʒwan). Also **ta tchuen.** [Chinese *dàzhuàn*, f. *dà* big + *zhuàn* seal character.] In Chinese calligraphy, an early form of script used during the Chou dynasty (*c* 1028–221 B.C.); 'large seal script'.

1894 T. de Lacouperie *Beginnings of Writing in Central & Eastern Asia* 194 The Chinese writing exhibits in its history eight successive styles, viz:..(2) *Ta tchuen* of 820 B.C. **1910** *Encycl. Brit.* VI. 220/1 Authentic specimens of the..*ta chuan*, older or Greater Seal writing, are exceedingly rare. **1958** W. Willetts *Chinese Art* II. vii. 566 Those [characters] then substituted..were what Han scholars called *ta chüan* or 'Great Curly', and sometimes *chou wên* after the name of the supposed Annalist. **1966** C. Ch'en *Chinese Calligraphers & their Art* iii. 24 Scholars of a later day have chosen to group all the different scripts before Li Ssŭ's time as the *ta chuan*. **1973** T. C. Lai *Chinese Calligraphy* 12 (*caption*) A ceremonial basin *ta chuan* script.

tachy-. Add: **tachymeta·bolism** *Zool.* (see quot. 1973); hence **ta:chymetabo·lic** *a.*; **ta:chyphyla·xis** *Pharm.* [mod.L., ad. F. *tachyphylaxie* (Champy & Gley 1911, in *Compt. Rend. Soc. de Biol.* LXXI. 161), f. Gr. φύλαξις protection], a rapidly diminishing response to successive doses of a drug; **tachypnœ·ic** *a. Med.*, exhibiting tachypnœa; **tachyzo·ite** *Zool.* [*-ZOITE], one form of the protozoon toxoplasma (see quot. 1973).

1974 *Nature* 13 Sept. 143/2 Already at this early age the dog is tachymetabolic. **1978** *Ibid.* 5 Oct. 441/1 The central nervous system (CNS) is very sensitive to elevated temperatures, and consequently, both bradymetabolic and tachymetabolic terrestrial vertebrates have evolved physiological mechanisms which effect localised cooling of the brain. **1973** Bligh & Johnson in *Jrnl. Appl. Physiol.* XXXV. 954/2 *Tachymetabolism*: The high level of basal metabolism of birds and mammals relative to those of reptiles and other nonavian and nonmammalian animals of the same body weight and at the same tissue temperature... Synonym: *Warm-Blooded.* Antonym: *Bradymetabolism, Cold-Blooded.* **1911** *Index Medicus* IX. Index of Subjects 214/2 Tachyphylaxis. **1947** F. K. Oldham et al. *Essent. Pharmacol.* xi. 132 Its [*sc.* ephedrine's] disadvantages include..the lessened effect of repeated doses (tachyphylaxis). **1979** *Nature* 29 Nov. 515/2 The response to DAEA showed neither desensitisation during a 3-min exposure period nor tachyphylaxis with repeated applications. **1961** Webster, Tachypneic. **1976** *Lancet* 13 Nov. 1083/1 He was not cyanotic or tachypnœic. **1973** J. K. Frenkel in Hammond & Long *Coccidia* 344/1, I am introducing two other terms: 'tachyzoites' for the rapidly multiplying forms of the acute infection, previously called trophozoites, aggregations, and proliferative forms; and 'bradyzoites' for the slowly multiplying encysted forms characteristic of chronic infection, which have been variously called merozoites or just zoites. **1979** *Biol. Abstr.* LXVIII. 7579/1 Probably most toxoplasmosis infections involve the ingestion of cat feces bearing cysts and oocytes rather than contact with tachyzoites.

tachygraph. Add: **2.** Also, a tachygraphic sign.

1965 E. V. K. Dobbie in *Language* XLI. 153 The inventory of the allographs (including nonalphabetic allographs, such as tachygraphs).

tachyon (tæ·ki,ǫn). *Physics.* [f. Tachy- + *-on[1].] A hypothetical particle that travels faster than light and has imaginary mass. Hence **tachyo·nic** *a.*

1967 G. Feinberg in *Physical Rev.* CLIX. 1090/1 One description is presented..for noninteracting faster than light particles, which we call tachyons. **1970** *Sci. Amer.* Feb. 70/2 Hence a tachyon that was losing energy by interacting with matter or by radiating light would speed up, whereas a tachyon that was gaining energy from some outside source would slow down, and its speed would approach *c* from above rather than below. **1970** *Physical Rev. D* II. 265/2 (*caption*) *A* and *B* use tachyonic antitelephones to communicate backwards in time. **1974** *Globe & Mail* (Toronto) 13 Apr. 5/1 The pursuit of the elusive tachyon lures scientists into the realm of complex mathematical abstraction and high-flown theoretical physics. **1978** Pasachoff & Kutner *University Astron.* xxvii. 695 So far, there is no experimental evidence that tachyons exist.

tachysterol (tækistī°·rǫl, -ste·rǫl). *Biochem.* [ad. G. *tachysterin* (A. Windaus et al. 1932, in *Ann. d. Chem.* CCCCXCIX. 188): see Tachy- and *STEROL.] An oily isomer of ergosterol and lumisterol, $C_{28}H_{43}OH$, which will form calciferol when irradiated with ultraviolet light.

1933 *Chem. Abstr.* XXVII. 729 The addn. compd. from irradiated ergosterol and citraconic anhydride (20 g.) and 75 cc. Ac_2O, warmed 2 hrs., give [*sic*] 7 g. of tachysteryl acetate citraconic anhydride... Tachysterol..has not been crystd. **1954** A. White et al. *Princ. Biochem.* l. 1053 Of the series of compounds obtained from the irradiation of ergosterol only calciferol (vitamin D_2) possesses antirachitic activity. However, one of the series, tachysterol, may be catalytically reduced to dihydrotachysterol.., which is antirachitic. **1976** H. Campion et al. in B. E. C. Nordin *Calcium, Phosphate & Mineral Metabolism* xii. 445 Lythgoe has reported the synthesis of a closely related isomer, tachysterol, by a nonphotochemical pathway.

tack, *sb.*[1] Add: **I. 2. a.** Also in colloq. phr. *to come* (or *get*) *down to brass tacks*: see *BRASS *sb.* 5 b. See also *TIN-TACK b.

3. c. *Basket-Making.* A size of willow rod, usu. 3 ft. long.

1912 T. Okey *Art of Basket-Making* ii. 6 White and buff rods are sorted into tacks from 2 ft. 6 in. or 3 ft. to 3 ft. 6 in. **1953** [see *long-small* s.v. *LONG *a.*[1] A. 18]. **1961** L. G. Allbon *Basic Basketry* ii. 11 Willow is sold by the bolt... The rods are sorted..on the farm into lengths... Local usage often gives special names to the sizes.., such as Tack or Short Smalls (3ft.), Smalls (4 ft.),..and so on. **1973** B. Maynard *Mod. Basketry from Start* 171 *Tacks*, term used for 3 ft willow rods.

IV. 10. b. (Later examples.) Used esp. in *Printing.*

1939 *Printing* Feb. 27/1 Where excess *tack* is attributed to these rollers, it is frequently found that the complainant is..referring to natural rubber rollers rather than synthetics. **1967** E. Chambers *Photolitho-Offset* xvi. 243 Ink of low tack fills in shadow areas more readily, whilst high tack may pull the surface of a coated paper, if the separation is quick. **1971** *Engineering* Apr. 17/1 A suitable adhesive..to give a reasonable tack. **1972** *Physics Bull.* Nov. 665/3 *Tack*, with prepreg materials, the degree of stickiness of the resin. **1979** G. A. Glaister *Gloss. Bk.*

(ed. 2) 469/1 If an ink has insufficient tack it will not print sharply.

V. 12. a. tack-hammer (earlier example); also as *v. trans.*
1865 *Atlantic Monthly* June 736/2 If she absolutely cannot get a tack-hammer with a claw on one end, she can take up carpet-nails with an iron spoon. **1908** KIPLING *Bk. of Words* (1928) 36 The meanest collection of packing-cases that was ever tack-hammered together.

c. in sense 4: **tack weld** *v. trans.*, to join (materials) at intervals with provisional welds in order to hold them in position for subsequent work; hence as *sb.*
1919 *Chambers's Jrnl.* Jan. 60/2 Up the sides the seams were only welded at intervals, or 'tack welded', as it is called. **1950** B. R. HILTON *Welding Design* ii. 42 If tack welds are not to be removed as the welding proceeds, their section should be equivalent to that of the first weld run. **1964** S. CRAWFORD *Basic Engin. Processes* iii. 82 A tack weld is made by applying the flame to the metal until it melts and then adding a little welding rod. **1979** *Financial Times* 22 Jan. 9/7 The top is tack welded, then the bottom, followed by the sides. Clamps and devices are removed and the weld completed.

d. in sense 10: **tack coat** (see quot. 1954); **tack rag** *U.S.*, an impregnated cloth used for cleaning a surface prior to painting or varnishing.
1949 *Sun* (Baltimore) 17 Oct. 26/3 Workmen spread a 'tack coat' of asphalt on the old pavement. **1954** *Gloss. Highway Engin. Terms* (*B.S.I.*) 28 *Tack coat*, a coat of liquid (such as bitumen, road tar, or an emulsion thereof) applied as a thin film to a surface to improve the adhesion of a course laid thereon. **1979** *Civil Engin.* Nov. 27/1 The painting on of a grid of levels on the tack coat by engineers. **1958** *Washington Post* 16 Aug. B 3/6 So-called 'tack' rags are used in factories where dust particles are likely to mar freshly painted surfaces. **1979** P. WALLAGE *Restoration Post-W.W.II Cars* ii. 25/2 Go over it with a tack rag.

tack, *sb.*[4] (Later example.)
1826 J. O'KEEFE *Recollections* I. vii. 268 The young nobleman..when he was the striker, took the nicest pains to place his tack in such a manner, that to hold his adversary's ball seemed a matter of course.

tack, *sb.*[7] Abbrev. of TACKLE *sb.* † **a.** In sense 1. *dial. Obs.*
1777 in *Eng. Dial. Dict.* (1905) VI. 3/2. **1879** G. F. JACKSON *Shropshire Word-bk.* 428 My tacks bin at Newport, or I'd soon ketch them rots. **1893** J. SALISBURY *Gloss. Words & Phr. S.E. Worcs.* 41 *Tack*,..a collection of tools; a razor-grinder's machine is his tack; a smith's box of tools for shoeing horses is his 'shoeing tack'.

b. In sense 6. Also *Comb.*, as *tack room.*
1924 I. MADDISON *Riding Astride for Girls* xiv. 226, I will now give a few hints on tack..in the show ring. The tack on a saddle-horse should be as light as possible. **1933** A. BLEWITT *Ponies & Children* iii. 34 Any prize rosettes they win are stuck up on their tack-room wall. **1940** *Evening Sun* (Baltimore) 15 Apr. 21/4 Tack is the name for a rider's equipment—saddle, whip, boots, etc., apparently derived from tackle. **1950** J. CANNAN *Murder Included* iv. 65 Patricia..was cleaning tack in the stable. **1964** D. FRANCIS *Nerve* xi. 147 It was a tack-room. Every stable has one..the place where the saddles and bridles are kept. **1975** F. KENNEDY *Alberta was my Beat* ix. 111 He stood there like a broke saddle horse as we put the tack on him. **1979** J. JOHNSTON *Old Jest* 100 There was a boy who kept the tack, polished the lovely shiny boots. There was a smell of saddle soap and horse dung. The saddles are flaking now, out in the damp tack room.

tack, *sb.*[8] U.S. colloq. abbrev of *TACHOGRAPH, TACHOMETER. Cf. *TACH, *TACHO.
1963 *Amer. Speech* XXXVIII. 46 *Tack*,..the device in the cab which automatically records miles driven, number of stops, speed, and so on, during a trip; short for *tachometer*. **1971** M. TAK *Truck Talk* 162 *Tack*, short for tachometer or tachograph.

tack, *v.*[1] Add: **5.** Also const. *on.*
1908 L. M. MONTGOMERY *Anne of Green Gables* viii. 83 Marilla was as fond of morals as the Duchess in Wonderland, and was firmly convinced that one should be tacked on to every remark made to a child. **1960** C. DAY LEWIS *Buried Day* i. 17 My father's family name was originally Day, the Lewis being tacked on by a man who adopted his grandfather or great-grandfather.

tack, *v.*[5] *trans.* Abbrev. of TACKLE *v.* 3. Usu. with *up*. Also *absol.* Cf. *TACK *sb.*[7] b.
1946 M. C. SELF *Horseman's Encycl.* 395 To tack up a horse means to put the saddle and bridle on him. **1962** W. FAULKNER *Reivers* viii. 178 So we..tacked up and..led the way. **1972** *Islander* (Victoria, B.C.) 26 Mar. 13/1 In addition to being taught how to groom a horse, the new student must learn how to tack-up (that's putting a saddle and bridle on). **1977** *Sunday Tel.* (Colour Suppl.) 1 May 22/3 It is not a bad idea either to acquire a creature that will come when it is called or will at least stand still long enough to get it tacked up for a bit of a ride.

tacketed, *ppl. a.* (Earlier example.)
1864 J. BROWN *Let.* Dec. (1912) 234 To-morrow I meant in a pair of tacketed shoon to have explored some Grampian.

tackie (tæ·ki). *S. Afr.* Also **takkie.** [Origin uncertain: perh. rel. to TACKY *a.*[2] App. not Afrikaans.] A rubber-soled canvas shoe; a plimsoll or sand-shoe. Also, a track shoe with a rubber sole. Usu. *pl.*
c **1902** I. VAUGHAN *Diary* (1958) 60 We all have to wear..white tackies on the feet. **1913** C. PETTMAN *Africanderisms* 491 *Tackies*, in the border towns of the Eastern Province this is the name given to rubber-soled sand-shoes. **1924** *Ann. Mountain Club S. Afr.* No. 27. 46 Ye who scale with ropes and 'tackies' Cliffs of awe-inspiring grandeur. **1946** *Amer. Speech* XXI. 59 What are known as 'sand shoes' or 'tackies' in English are the same articles which I still backslide into calling 'sneakers'. **1953** M. MURRAY *Fire-Raisers* xi. 108 He padded over the rocks on his tackies. **1955** D. JACOBSON *Trap* I. 20 He wore canvas *takkies* on his feet, his toes poking through the ends. **1961** *Personality* 16 May 27, I have yet to discover why tennis shoes, which are known in England as plimsoles, are called 'tackies' in South Africa. **1981** A. PATON *Towards Mountain* xvii. 134 Hofmeyr was a camper of the first water. He wore an ancient canvas hat, a khaki shirt and shorts, and discoloured sandshoes, known as tackies.

tackifier (tæ·kifəi,əɹ). [f. TACKY *a.*[2] + -FY + -ER[1].] A substance that makes something sticky; an adhesive agent or ingredient.
1942 *Science Illustr.* Apr. 4/2 As processing aids, naval stores products are numbered among the many plasticizers, softeners, and tackifiers. **1958** *New Scientist* 23 Oct. 1110/2 This pressure-sensitive thermoplastic..is so sticky that a tackifier such as resin need not be added. **1963** H. R. CLAUSER *Encycl. Engin. Materials* 449/2 The liquid nitrile polymer finds use as a tackifier..in molded rubber parts, cements, friction and calendered stocks. **1970** *New Scientist* 5 Nov. 275 (Advt.), Sometimes it's [*sc.* Lorival liquid rubber] a tackifier in ebonite grinding wheels.

tackily (tæ·kili), *adv.*[1] [f. TACKY *a.*[2] + -LY[2].] In a slightly adhesive or sticky manner. (In quot. 1903, *fig.*)
1903 KIPLING *Traffics & Discoveries* (1904) 124 The sea..drummed tackily to gather my attention, coughed, spat, cleared its throat. **1971** *Sunday Times* 20 June 42 For every loving Mum who has ever wished there was an easier way of preventing nappy-rash than smearing on..petroleum jelly, Johnson & Johnson is introducing..a melt-on-contact Baby Gel which does the job less tackily.

tackily (tæ·kili), *adv.*[2] *colloq.* [f. TACKY *a.*[1] + -LY[2].] In a tasteless or vulgar style; shabbily, dowdily.
1936 M. MITCHELL *Gone with Wind* IV. xxxii. 544 She was ugly and dressed tackily. **1979** P. DRISCOLL *Pangolin* I. xiv. 115 A square little hovel tackily partitioned into two rooms.

tackiness[2] *colloq.* (f. TACKY *a.*[1] + -NESS.] The quality of being cheap or in poor taste.
1977 *Washington Post* 26 Mar. B5 Their visual craftsmanship and polish are compromised by the manifest tackiness of the story material. **1982** J. FOX *White Mischief* i. 19 A provincial tackiness..pervades the residential suburbs of Nairobi.

tacking, *vbl. sb.* Add: **d.** *Comb.*, as **tacking iron** *Photogr.*, a tool used for attaching tissue to a print or mount by the application of heat at chosen points.
1973 *Bodl. Libr. Rec.* IX. 2 The work bench is equipped with tacking irons and a pH meter. **1977** J. HEDGECOE *Photographer's Handbk.* 309 (*caption*) Using an electric tacking iron gently touch the center of the tissue, sticking it to the print.

tackle, *sb.* Add: **2.** In this sense freq. with pronunc. (tēi·k'l).

4. b. *to stand to one's tackle* (later example).
1841 C. BRONTË *Let.* 1 July in Wise & Symington *Brontës* (1932) I. 234 Mrs. White offered me a week..but I demanded three weeks, and stood to my tackle with a tenacity worthy of yourself.

9. Restrict *Football* to senses in Dict. **a.** (Earlier example.) Also in *U.S. Football.*
1876 in P. H. Davis *Football* (1911) 462 A tackle is when the holder of the ball is held by one or more players of the opposite side. **1898** A. SPURLING in W. A. Morgan *'House' on Sport* 170 If you are running after an opponent who has the ball, and find he is gaining on you, don't give up, as he may be checked, and you have the pleasure of making a good tackle.

b. (Earlier example.)
1891 W. CAMP *Amer. Football* 41 The tackle is an assistant to both end and guard.

c. The act of tackling in other sports. Cf. *TACKLE *v.* 5 (*c*).
1930 M. POLLARD *Hockey for Women* viii. 106 A defence player can run towards the tackle, but she should never run into it. **1967** J. POTTER *Foul Play* x. 120 Basil was out of the goal in a lightning flash, cutting off the pass with a sliding tackle.

10. *tackle-box* (earlier example), *-maker* (earlier example); **tackle-room,** a room in which horse tackle is stored; cf. *tack room* s.v. *TACK *sb.*[7] b.
1902 *Chambers's Jrnl.* Oct. 702/2 This will render carrying a tin tackle-box unnecessary. **1832** *Chambers's Edin. Jrnl.* 7 Apr. 87/1 The lines of the angler may be bought from the tackle makers. **1951** *Chambers's Jrnl.* Oct. 587/1 You enter the tackle-room, where surgical harness is stored. **1962** A. FRY *Ranch on Cariboo* v. 53 Like all cabins, [it] was kitchen, dining and living all rolled into one, sometimes even tackle room.

tackle, *v.* Add: **4. c.** Also *transf.*
1920 *Blackw. Mag.* Jan. 105/2 The sort of road that even a Ford would hesitate to tackle.

d. (Earlier example.)
1884 'MARK TWAIN' *Huck. Finn* xxx. 313 So the king sneaked into the wigwam, and took to his bottle for comfort; and before long the duke tackled *his* bottle.

5. Restrict *Football* to senses in Dict. (*a*) Also in *U.S. Football.* (*c*) In other sports, to obstruct or accost (an opponent) in order to deprive him of the ball or other object of play.
1895 H. F. P. BATTERSBY *Hockey* 98 In defence, they [*sc.* the halves] must tackle everything, and stick to it. **1935** *Encycl. Sports* 701 The referee may also penalise a side if any of the players holds the ball under the water when tackled. **1959** M. BOYD *Lacrosse Playing & Coaching* vi. 70 As soon as their opponents get the ball, attack players must tackle back onto them. **1975** *Oxf. Compan. Sports & Games* 320/2 The supporting backs and line-backers are prepared to tackle the carrier.

tackler. Add: **c.** Also in other sports.
1955 DOYLE & SMITH *Lifetime in Hurling* xx. 144 A quick hitter..and a fearless tackler.

tackling, *vbl. sb.* Add: **6. tackling bag** *U.S.* and *Rugby Football*, a stuffed bag suspended and used for practice in tackling; **tackling dummy** *U.S. Football* = *tackling bag* above.
1892 *Outing* (U.S.) Jan. 279/2 Their one special piece of apparatus is..the tackling bag, and this is..necessary to the indoor practice of a football team. **1978** *Rugby World* Apr. 25 (Advt.), Order now for 1978–79 pre-season training the new Allander tackling bag. **1904** *Outing* (U.S.) Dec. 367/2 The tackling dummy was used by many squads. **1959** N. MAILER *Advts. for Myself* (1961) 51 The Japs looked like bushes, or like tackling dummies in the evening when practice was over.

tacky, *sb.* and *a.*[1] Delete *local* and add: Also **tackie. A.** *sb.* **a.** (Earlier examples).
1800 W. TATHAM *Agric. & Commerce* 81 A horse, a cow, or a little *tackie*, &c. (which last term signifies a poney or little horse of low price). **1839** C. F. HOFFMAN *Wild Scenes* 117 The land pirates had disappeared, without molesting my tackey.

B. *adj.* For *U.S. colloq.* read *colloq.* (orig. and chiefly *U.S.*). Also, in poor taste, cheap, vulgar. (Earlier and later examples.) Also *Comb.*, as *tacky-looking* adj.
1862 K. STONE *Jrnl.* 16 Feb. in *Brokenburn* (1955) 89 What a weary, bedraggled tacky-looking set they were. **1883** I. M. RITTENHOUSE *Maud* 262 Two little cards (with his name printed on them in gilt. Tackey? Ugh). **1937** HART & KAUFMAN *You can't take it with You* III. 180 An extremely tacky-looking evening wrap. **1957** M. KENNEDY *Heroes of Clone* III. i. 158 He went again to the window to watch for the arrival of the tacky little car. **1967** N. MAILER *Cannibals & Christians* I. 16 All the tacky doings of each small town. **1971** 'O. BLEECK' *Thief who painted Sunlight* (1972) iii. 30 A tacky-looking bulletin board. **1983** *Listener* 10 Feb. 29/3 They were really very good, putting together a fast and lively show, full of cheerfully dreadful jokes and inventively tacky songs.

taco (tā·ko, tæ·ko). Chiefly *N. Amer.* [Mex. Sp.] **a.** A Mexican snack comprising a fried, unleavened cornmeal pancake or tortilla filled with seasoned mincemeat, chicken, cheese, beans, etc.
1949 *Amer. Speech* XXIV. 235/2 The *touristas* almost always eat in a Mexican restaurant and bravely attempt to order their meals in Spanish. Such meals are (1) [tækoz], a mispronunciation of the Spanish word *tacos* [takos]. **1957** J. KEROUAC *On Road* (1958) xiii. 93 We went into a Mexican restaurant and had tacos and mashed pinto beans. **1965** *Austral. Women's Weekly* 20 Jan. 25/1 She would serve up a traditional Mexican dish of unsurpassable excellence, the white meat..rolled up in a delicate crisp pancake, or taco. **1966** *Listener* 4 Aug. 164/2 *Tacos*..are *tortillas* rolled round shredded meat or bird and fried in oil. **1971** *Islander* (Victoria, B.C.) 4 July 2/4 Friends in San Diego had introduced us to tortillas and tacos. **1978** S. WILSON *Dealer's Move* vi. 107 Washing the food down with two strong cups of tea and mopping up with South London's answer to tacos, sliced white loaf.

b. *attrib.*, as *taco joint, sauce, stand.*
1967 *Trans-Action* Apr. 8/1 Time is alive when and where there is action... During the regular school year it may pick up for an hour in the afternoon when the 'broads' leave school and meet with the set at a corner taco joint. **1977** *Time* 28 Nov. 58/1 Some have about as much feeling for a community's sense of itself and its needs as does the imported manager of a franchised taco joint on the highway outside town. **1976** *Punch* 11 Aug. 227/1, I took to enchilada mix, tortillas, taco sauce, and all those Mexican delicacies. **1977** *Daily News* (Perth, Austral.) 19 Jan. 13 (Advt.), Taco—a crisp tortilla filled with beef, onions, lettuce, taco sauce and cheese. **1969** D. MACKENZIE *Night Boat to Puerto Vedra* (1970) 172 A few seamen were at the taco stands... He bought himself a cone of maize flour filled with peppered ground meat. **1979** R. L. SIMON *Peking Duck* ii. 18 Jogging behind a gas station and a taco stand to a nondescript stucco gate.

Taconic, *a.* Add: [f. the name of the *Taconic* Mountains in New England and New York State.] **a.** (Earlier example.)
1842 E. EMMONS in *Geol. N.Y.* II. vii. 135 It has been deemed advisable to annex to the general account of the group of rocks of the northern district, a brief sketch of the services which constitute the Taconic System.

b. Epithet of an orogeny that occurred in Ordovician times in eastern North America.

1908 *Bull. Geol. Soc. Amer.* XX. 503 The other three [emergences]..were of long duration and of great significance. These are: (1) The Taconic revolution..; (2) the Appalachian revolution.., and (3) the Laramide revolution. **1980** *Sci. Amer.* Oct. 136/1 The southern Appalachians have evolved in a series of collisions of fragments of continental or island-arc material at the eastern edge of North America in the Taconic, the Acadian and the Alleghenian orogenies.

taconite (tæ·kŏnəit). *Geol.* [f. TACON(IC *a.* in Dict. and Suppl. + -ITE[1].] **a.** A type of chert used as an iron ore in parts of N. America.

1905 *Econ. Geol.* I. 48 In the Mesabi district the local name 'taconite' is applied to the ferruginous chert. **1951** *Engineering* 22 June 761/2 To be able to take a hard ore, such as taconite, separate the magnetite and silica by grinding the material down to pass a 300-mesh sieve, and agglomerate the concentrates by pelletising, at a price to compete with imported ores, was no mean achievement. **1981** D. R. COATES *Environmental Geol.* v. 104/1 Taconite is a low-grade ore of iron which is the source of most current U.S. iron production.

b. *attrib.*, as *taconite mine, ore, pellet, tailing.*

1974 *Sumter* (S. Carolina) *Daily Item* 23 Apr. 7B/7 Reserve, which..produces 15 per cent of the iron ore used in the nation's steelmaking blast furnaces, also closed its taconite mine at Babbitt. **1975** *Sci. Amer.* Nov. 52/3 The place of the high-grade ores was then taken by taconite ores containing iron in the form of finely disseminated magnetite. **1958** J. SZARKOWSKI *Face of Minnesota* 270 By 1948 the first mass-produced taconite pellets reached the blast furnaces. **1975** *Telegraph* (Brisbane) 18 Mar. 12/4 The refinery's discharge of taconite tailings.

tacouba (tăkū·bă). Also **tacooba, tacuba.** [Origin unknown, perh. an Arawakan word.] In Guyana, a tree which has fallen across a river forming a bridge or obstruction. Also *fig.*

1934 E. WAUGH *92 Days* ii. 55 In the wet season..you had to crawl across a tacuba leading a swimming horse. **1951** E. MITTELHÖLZER *Shadows move among Them* II. iv. 196 'What's a *tacooba?*' 'Indian word. Means a fallen tree or any sort of obstruction in a river or creek that constitutes a menace to navigation.' **1959** P. CAPON *Amongst those Missing* 124 He had expected rapids every few miles, numerous tacoubas and a cataract or two. **1965** 'LAUCHMONEN' *Old Thom's Harvest* v. 58 He was a squat negro, a stumpy little piece of a man, a knotty old tacuba tree-stump. **1974** H. MACINNES *Climb to Lost World* vi. 73 The walking itself wasn't difficult, but there were plenty of streams to cross, some of them bridged by slippery tacoubas, or tree jams.

tact. Add: **II. 5.** *Psychol.* [Final element of *con)tact.*] B. F. Skinner's term for an utterance which is evoked by an object, event, etc., and reinforces the learning of a response. Hence as *v. trans.*, to respond to (a stimulus) with an utterance; as *v. intr.*, to utter words or sounds in this way; so **ta·cted** *ppl. a.*; **ta·cting** *vbl. sb.* Cf. *MAND.

1954 *Brit. Jrnl. Psychol.* Aug. 181 Skinner..describes how a child learns to emit 'tacts' (i.e. verbal responses controlled by properties of objects or situations) under the influence of 'generalized reinforcers', particularly approval. **1957** B. F. SKINNER *Verbal Behavior* v. 81 There is no suitable term for this type of operant... The invented word 'tact' will be used here. The term carries a mnemonic suggestion of behavior which 'makes contact with' the physical world. A tact may be defined as a verbal operant in which a response of given form is evoked (or at least strengthened) by a particular object. **1959**, etc. [see *MAND]. **1964** A. W. STAATS *Human Learning* iii. 73/2 The child learns in this manner to tact environmental events as well as objects. **1969** B. F. SKINNER *Contingencies of Reinforcement* viii. 254 The close relation between the topography of behavior and the tacted stimulus. **1977** *Listener* 5 May 597/2 What is nowadays called 'tacting' (i.e., verbal behaviour controlled primarily by its antecedents—in this case the sight of the milk)... Victor was evidently conditioned only to tact.

tactic, *a.*[1] Add: **3.** *Linguistics.* Of or pertaining to taxemes, their arrangement or order. Cf. *TACTICS 3.

1933 L. BLOOMFIELD *Language* x. 166 Combinations of taxemes, or, quite frequently, single taxemes, occur as conventional grammatical arrangements, *tactic forms.* **1962** E. F. HAYDEN et al. *Resonance Theory for Linguistics* iii. 24 Like beads on a string, each entity in phonotactics has a distinct Form, since no two beads can occur in the same place on the string. This is the tactic form, i.e. the structural form in the sequence. **1966** S. M. LAMB *Outl. Stratificational Gram.* 5 This process of isolating recurrent partial similarities is the basis of tactic analysis. *Ibid.* 54 Thus the analysis (*un true*) (*ly*) fits the simplest tactic description. *Ibid.* 58 The description of a stratal system is probably most conveniently presented in two parts: the tactic description and the realizational description. **1968** P. M. POSTAL *Aspects Phonol. Theory* viii. 198 There are four distinct strata, each of which is an independent system with its own generative rules (tactic rules)... The four current properly linguistic strata are..the sememic, the lexemic, the morphemic, and the phonemic. It is apparently the function of the tactic rules on a particular stratum X to generate both the class of X-emes and the possible combinations of X-emes. **1969** *Language* XLV. 303 This tactic fact is that..the low vowels /e a o/ can occur only if accompanied by stress; therefore the only unstressed vowels are /i ə u/.

tactical, *a.* Add: **1. b.** Applied to aircraft, bombing, etc., employed in direct support of ground forces. Cf. *strategic bomber, bombing* s.v. *STRATEGIC *a.* 4.

1916 F. W. LANCHESTER *Aircraft in Warfare* vii. 69 The tactical scout or machine for local reconnaissance will require to be furnished..with both offensive and defensive armament. **1922** *Flight* 24 Aug. 488/1 Tactical bombing and 'trench-strafing', etc., in battles in accordance with the plans and under the command of the naval or military officer in charge of the operations. **1941** A. O. POLLARD *Bombers over Reich* xv. 208 Tactical bombing replaces..the long-range attacks on objectives far behind the lines. **1942** *R.A.F. Jrnl.* 3 Oct. (*recto rear cover*), The transition to low wing monoplane trainers and tactical ships of advanced type. **1955** *Bull. Atomic Sci.* May 192/2 One of the pitfalls of the atomic age is the use of words that becloud important meaning, rather than clarify it. Take the words 'tactical' and 'strategic', in defining two kinds of bombing. **1958** *Listener* 11 Sept. 376/2, I believe that the initiation by the West of the use of small tactical bombs on a battlefield in Europe would prove disastrous to NATO forces. **1977** *R.A.F. News* 11–24 May 6 (Advt.), A two-seater all-weather tactical interdictor and attack bomber.

c. Designating nuclear weapons intended for short-range use against an enemy's forces. Opp. *STRATEGIC *a.* 2.

1957 [see *STRATEGIC *a.* 2]. **1968** *Observer* 31 Mar. 25/1 Consider the weapons that have become operational for the first time in the past 20 years. They include the H-bomb and the so-called 'tactical' A-bombs. **1970** *Toronto Daily Star* 24 Sept. 22/5 It is estimated that about 20 lbs. or so would be sufficient for one atomic bomb in the one kiloton range, a so-called tactical bomb with mainly localized effects. **1976** LD. HOME *Way the Wind Blows* xii. 167 The balance of argument through the years moved towards a substantial conventional force, but it was gradually rendered somewhat academic by the introduction of the tactical nuclear weapon. **1979** N. CALDER *Nuclear Nightmares* ii. 35 This definition is..not as sharp as the cynic's version: 'A tactical nuclear weapon is one that explodes in Germany.' *Ibid.*, 'Tactical' nuclear weapons can be let off without necessarily signalling a 'strategic', all-out exchange between the Soviet Union and the United States.

tacticity (tækti·sĭti). *Chem.* [f. TACTIC *a.*[1] + -ITY.] The stereochemical arrangement of the units in the main chain of a polymer.

1959 NATTA & DANUSSO in *Jrnl. Polymer Sci.* XXXIV. 4 The rule, or *taxis*, which characterizes an arrangement partially or completely ordered, or tacticity, may be simple or composed by few simple rules. **1967** MARGERISON & EAST *Introd. Polymer Chem.* ii. 63 The tacticity of the chain. **1975** *Nature* 24 Apr. 696/1 Fibrocytes react to some microarchitectural or 'tacticity' difference between homologous copolymeric substrata.

tactics. Add: **3.** *Linguistics.* C. F. Hockett's term for the study of the relation and arrangement of linguistic units, esp. the study of the arrangement of morphemes.

1947 C. F. HOCKETT in *Language* XXIII. 274 We should therefore expect to find the following topics treated in his book..; (4) tactics—stating the arrangements of morphemes... This term seems simpler than 'taxemics' or 'tagmemics' which one might derive more directly from Bloomfield's labels. **1953** F. G. LOUNSBURY in *Yale Univ. Publ. in Anthropol.* XLVIII. 18 Statements describing the occurrences of morphemes constitute the portion of a grammar called *tactics*... Tactics is not concerned with the phonemic forms of morphemes, whether they are constant or variable. **1966** S. M. LAMB *Outl. Stratificational Gram.* 1 Each of these systems has its own syntax or tactics, so that a linguistic structure as a whole has a series of tactic components rather than just one.

tactile, *a.* Add: **2. a.** Also, characterized or influenced by the sense of touch. Hence *absol.* as *sb.*, one for whom the sense of touch predominates over the other senses.

1892 [see *MOTILE *a.*]. **1917** [see *AUDILE *sb.*]. **1956** [see *AUDILE *a.*]. **1971** A. MONTAGU *Touching* v. 169 Children who are highly tactile but have no accompanying sexual interest in others.

c. Art. *tactile value*: B. Berenson's term for the illusion of tangibility which a painter can create with regard to the figures and objects he represents; the attribute or impression of a tangible quality. Also *transf.*

1896 B. BERENSON *Florentine Painters of the Renaissance* ii. 4 Every time our eyes recognise reality we are.. giving tactile values to retinal impressions. **1907** —— *North Italian Painters of Renaissance* 146 In figure painting, the type of all painting, I have endeavoured to set forth that the principal..sources of life-enhancement are *tactile values, movement*, and *space composition*, by which I mean ideated sensation. **1908** E. M. FORSTER *Room with View* ii. 22 The traveller who has gone to Italy to study the tactile values of Giotto, or the corruption of the Papacy. **1919** A. N. WHITEHEAD *Princ. Nat. Knowl.* 88 This property of 'conveying' an object..is already well-known in the theory of art-criticism, as is evidenced in such phrases as 'tactile-values'. **1938** R. G. COLLINGWOOD *Princ. Art* vii. 146 Mr. Berenson..taught his pupils..to look in paintings for what he called 'tactile values'. **1962** *Listener* 15 Nov. 832/1 It [*sc.* a play] is remarkable because of what one might call, after Berenson, its tactile values. **1970** *Oxf. Compan. Art* 1120/1 Berenson was notoriously incapable of appreciating those schools of modern—and ancient—art which subordinate tactile values to other qualities of pictorial design.

d. *Comb.*, as *tactile-visual* adj.

1969 *New Scientist* 27 Mar. 678/1 A tactile-visual system..should provide valuable information concerning such psychological questions as the nature of sensory processing. **1978** *Verbatim* May 16/1 My point is that the oral-aural mode is intricately combined with the tactile-visual mode.

Hence **ta·ctilely** *adv.*

1953 A. C. KINSEY et al. *Sexual Behavior Human Female* xiv. 578 Some areas which are tactilely sensitive.. are of no especial importance as sources of erotic response. **1977** *Verbatim* Feb. 8/1 It takes some talent and not much money to design and manufacture a book artistically, one that provides as much aesthetic pleasure visually and tactilely as it does in its reading.

tactily (tæ·ktĭli), *adv.* [Irreg. f. TACT + -LY[2].] = TACTFULLY *adv.*

1895 G. MEREDITH *Amazing Marriage* I. iv. 37 She had to warn her brother to preserve his balance. He tactily did so, aware of the necessity. **1929** M. LOWRY *Let.* 13 Mar. (1967) 5 The bewildered parent..would be willing to pay you 5 or 6 guineas a week (I should say six personally, but tactily) if you would tolerate me for any period..as a member of your household.

† **tactism** (tæ·ktiz'm). *Biol. Obs.* [f. L. *tact-*, stem of *tangĕre* to touch + -ISM.] The motile response of a living organism to an external stimulus.

1902 *Fortn. Rev.* June 1013 By his revelations of the *rôle* of the 'trophisms' and 'tactisms' Dr. Loeb drove boldly into the domain of mental phenomena. **1912** A. TRIDON tr. *Delage & Goldsmith's Theories Evol.* 164 Others..attribute differentiation to the influence of the various tropisms and tactisms.

tactoid (tæ·ktoid). *Physical Chem.* Also † **taktoid.** [a. G. *taktoid* (Zocher & Jacobsohn 1929, in *Kolloidchem. Beihefte* XXVIII. 167), f. Gr. τακτ-ός ordered (see TACTIC *a.*[1]): see -OID.] A small anistropic, birefringent region in a dilute, isotropic sol, consisting of an aggregate of rod-like particles or macromolecules aligned parallel to one another.

1929 *Chem. Abstr.* XXIII. 2868 In these taktosols..the individual microscopic particles are called taktoids. **1939** *Nature* 14 Jan. 82/1 The formation of tactoids from thixotropic sols,..and the crystallization of proteins are regarded as being typical of unipolar coacervation. **1952** J. T. G. OVERBEEK in H. R. Kruyt *Colloid Sci.* I. viii. 327 The concentrated phase in the tactoids still contains a great deal of dispersion medium which implies that the particles are comparatively far apart. **1953** S. E. LURIA *Gen. Virol.* v. 94 In the liquid phase, the rod-shaped [virus] particles orient themselves sidewise into 'tactoids' which then settle into the liquid crystalline phase. **1978** *Nature* 14 Dec. 666/3 Minton has applied fundamental models for the entropically driven formation of tactoids from long rod-like molecules or particles to the haemoglobin S system.

So **ta·ctosol** [ad. G. *taktosol* (Zocher & Jacobsohn, *loc. cit.*)], a sol containing tactoids.

1929 [see *TACTOID]. **1959** *Lancet* 3 Oct. 513/1 Tactosols are colloidal solutions containing non-spherical particles ('tactoids') which are capable of orienting themselves.

‖ **tactus** (tæ·ktŏs). *Mus.* [L.: see TACT.] = TACT 4.

1740 J. GRASSINEAU *Mus. Dict.* 130 *Metron*, Tactus, Mensura, Battuta,—the beating or measuring the time by a motion of the hand or foot. **1786** BUSBY *Compl. Dict. Mus.* s.v. *Tactus*,..when the time consisted of a breve in a bar, the time-stroke was called *Tactus-Major*; and when of a semibreve in a bar, *Tactus-Minor.* **1959** *Collins Mus. Encycl.* 644/1 A term used for 'beat' by the theorists of the 15th and 16th cent... The semibreve was the normal *tactus* in the 15th cent.; in the course of the 16th cent. the minim became the normal... With the introduction of bar-lines the semibreve became the unit of a bar and the measuring *tactus* was replaced by the metrical beat. **1980** *Early Music* July 310/2 To sing the passage to a tactus, however, is to miss its *raison d'être* and obliterate the most vital element of the madrigal's expressive scheme.

tacuba, var. *TACOUBA. **Tacully,** var. *TAKULLI.

tad (tæd). *colloq.* (orig. and chiefly *N. Amer.*) [Orig. uncertain; perh. f. TADPOLE[1].] † **1.** (See quots.) *Obs.*

1845 in C. Cist *Cincinnati Misc.* I. 240 Among a certain class in the eastern cities,..the word *Tad*, is applied to one who don't nor won't pay. **1851** B. H. HALL *College Words* 297 At Centre College, Ky., there is a society.. composed of the very best fellows of the College, calling themselves Tads. **1890** E. B. CUSTER *Following Guidon* 213 These youths [*sc.* graduates from West Point] were called 'tads' and 'plebes'.

2. A young or small child, esp. a boy. Occas. used *joc.* of old men.

1877 BARTLETT *Dict. Amer.* (ed. 4) 688 Tads, *little tads*, small boys. *Old tads*, graybeards, old men. **1896** ADE *Artie* xi. 98 Oh, he's a great old tad. **1901** F. NORRIS *Octopus* I. v. 197 There's a little tad that was just born to be a lady. **1904** W. D. NESBIT *Trail to Boyland* 49 That handle has been broken since he was just a tad. **1928** S. LEWIS *Man who knew Coolidge* I. 55 One of the bell-boys at the hotel, cute little tad, knew the town like a book. **1935** H. DAVIS *Honey in Horn* xxii. 370 I've handled more horses than this tad ever heard of. **1949** O. NASH *Versus* 131 The sea lion loves a loveable lad, An urchin, a gamin, a tyke, a tad. **1974** W. GARNER *Big Enough Wreath* vii. 93 Nowadays young tads think they know it all. **1983** *Sunday Times* 3 Apr. 33/2 The nuns picked me out when I was still a tad, groomed me for a scholarship.

3. A small amount; freq. used *advb.* in the expression *a tad*, a little, slightly.

1940 *Amer. Speech* XV. 448/1 *Tad*, a very small amount. 'I want to borrow a tad of salt.' **1969** L. MICHAELS *Going Places* 159, I tried to smile. 'You come back later, baby. I'm a tad indisposed.' **1976** *Time* 27 Sept. 39/2 'Pull 'er up a tad, please, mister,' said the nonchalant teen-ager pumping gas. **1977** *Time* 14 Mar. 28/3 White House watchers also think they can glimpse a tad of arrogance showing through the good ole boy pose. **1977** *Globe & Mail* (Toronto) 15 Dec. 8/2 Things are a tad hectic. **1979** D. ANTHONY *Long Hard Cure* xv. 116 Why don't we sit here on the veranda? There's a tad of breeze. **1980** *N.Y. Times* 12 Aug. A18/1 The Mayor's pitch is a tad exaggerated both on the law's certainty and on the roominess of New York's prisons.

taddy (tæ·di). *Sc.* Also **Taddy.** The name of *Taddy* and Co., of London, used *attrib.* and *absol.* to designate snuff manufactured by them. Also *Comb.*, as **taddy-box,** a snuff-box.

1869 A. MACDONALD *Love, Law & Theology* viii. 118 Tapping his box, and inhaling a large pinch of his favourite Taddy. **1870** J. NICHOLSON *Idylls* 46 Some tea to the auld folk, tobacco or taddy. **1872** 'R. F. BARDINARUS' *Arn at Flail* 9 But John took up the Taddy pouder. **1881** R. FORD *Humorous Sc. Readings* 67 Three or four heapit ladlefu's o' London taddy. **1897** J. WRIGHT *Scenes Sc. Life* 5 Irish blackguard and taddy snuff mixed. **1907** N. MUNRO *Daft Days* xxxiv. 278 The Provost, who had just stepped into P. & A.'s for his Sunday sweeties, smiled tolerantly and passed his taddy-box. **1939** J. M. DALLAS *Toakburn* 11 He got his best 'sneeshin'' from Johnnie Bickles, who kept the genuine 'taddy'.

Tadjik, Tadzhik, varr. *TAJIK.

‖ **tædium vitæ** (tī·diŏm vəi·ti, vī·təi). Also **tedium vitæ.** [L.: cf. TEDIUM.] Weariness of life; extreme ennui or inertia, sometimes regarded as a pathological state.

[**1618** J. CHAMBERLAIN *Let.* 14 Oct. (1939) II. 170 The Lord Clifton..tooke his paterne from your Secretarie of Utrecht to stab and mangle himself with a penknife.. without any other shew of reason or cause, but even *vitæ tædio* (as he saide himself).] **1759** E. YOUNG *Conjectures on Original Composition* 8 Both These are happy in *this*, that by fixing their attention on objects most important, they escape numberless little anxieties, and that Taedium Vitae which often hangs so heavy on its evening hours. **1796** T. JEFFERSON *Let.* 24 Apr. (1926) 86 My health has suddenly broken down, with symptoms which give me to believe I shall not have much to encounter of the *taedium vitae*. **1803** S. OWENSON *St. Clair* xxi. 89 The dreadful oppression of the *tedium vitae*. **1826** *Reg. Deb. Congress U.S.* 30 Mar. 402 *Tedium vitæ* appears in Sunday Schools. **1855** *Newsp. & Gen. Reader's Compan.* 156 That *taedium vitae*, which springs from a consciousness of talents abused and opportunities lost. **1883** T. S. CLOUSTON *Clin. Lect. Mental Dis.* xvii. 560 A cloud of vague depression rests on the man, who shuns society, falls off in fat, becomes restless and hypochondriacal, and feels strongly the *tedium vitæ*. **1891** O. WILDE *Pict. Dorian Gray* xi. 216 That ennui, that terrible *tædium vitæ*, that comes on those to whom life denies nothing. **1920** J. HUNEKER *Painted Veils* vi. 251 Her languour had not been dissipated; 'tædium vitæ', the doctor named it. **1940** 'G. ORWELL' *Inside Whale* 159 Everyone with a safe £500 a year..began training himself in *taedium vitae*. **1958** L. DURRELL *Mountolive* ix. 187 Even these simple motions of joining with the ordinary world of social habit and pleasure, of relieving the *taedium vitae* of his isolation, were all infected by the new knowledge. **1977** V. S. PRITCHETT *Gentle Barbarian* xii. 201 He..is suddenly attacked by the *taedium vitae*, the disgust with life, as a man who talks too well may easily be.

‖ **tae kwon do** (tē¹, tai kwǫn dō). Also **Tae Kwon Do, taekwondo,** etc. [Korean: see quot. 1967.] A Korean system of unarmed combat resembling karate.

1967 *Karate & Oriental Arts* Sept./Oct. 2 Taekwondo, which is just starting in this country..will be open to the same abuse as karate. *Ibid.* 27/1 Breaking the word Taekwondo down into its three parts we get: Tae—kick, Kwon—fist, Do—art, way, method. **1969** *Melbourne Truth* 12 July 9/4 Rozinsky gained his Black Belt in Tae Kwon Do at the Jidokwan, Seoul, South Korea. **1972** *Sunday Times* (Kuala Lumpur) 18 June 16/7 To unwind and also to keep fit, he sweats it out at tae-kwon-do classes. **1972** C. WESTON *Poor, Poor Ophelia* (1973) xvi. 94 The newcomers to whom Tae Kwon Do seemed an impossible skill. **1976** *Eastern Even. News* (Norwich) 9 Dec. 2/6 Taekwondo (Korean karate) training, Duke Street Centre. **1979** *Sci. Amer.* Apr. 110/1 Karate is just one of a wide variety of martial arts that have evolved in the Orient, including tae kwon do, kempo and kung fu.

tael. Add: Also **tahil. 1.** (Further examples.)

1902 *Encycl. Brit.* XXXIII. 813/1 Tahil..Straits Settlements 1⅓ oz. av. = 10 chee = 100 hoon. **1947** R. O. WINSTEDT *Malays* vi. 112 Soon after the founding of Malacca Chinese annals under 1416 record..that, 'tin.. is cast into small blocks weighing 1 *kati* 8 *tahil* or 1 *kati* 4 *tahil* official weight... They use these pieces of tin instead of money.' **1972** *Straits Times* 25 Nov. 15/1 The gold bars, weighing 15 katis seven tahils.

2. b. A Chinese gold coin based on the value of a tael of silver.

1926 E. KANN *Currency China* I. i. 13 Taiping tael gold coin... During the rule of the T'aipings in Nankin a gold coin was issued there..supposed to represent 25 taels of silver. **1962** R. A. G. CARSON *Coins* 543 A rare tael in gold was also struck in this issue. **1979** *Courier-Mail* (Brisbane) 9 July 4/3 Some Chinese had sufficient savings tucked away in gold taels, the traditional, and sensible, way of saving adopted by many East Asian societies, to bribe officials or simply to pay for the right to escape.

tænii-. Add: Also (*U.S.*) **tenii-; tæni·asis** (pl. **-iases**) *Path.* and *Zool.* [*-IASIS], infestation with tapeworms, esp. adult worms in (or formerly in) the genus *Taenia*.

1896 F. W. GAMBLE in *Camb. Nat. Hist.* II. iii. 82 The Jewish observance with regard to swine is the surest preventive measure against taeniasis. **1900** DORLAND *Med. Dict.* 675/1 Teniasis. **1969** EDINGTON & GILLES *Path. in Tropics* iii. 173 Taeniasis may occur in all countries where beef or pork are eaten. The beef tapeworm—*Taenia saginata*—has a cosmopolitan distribution... The pork tapeworm—*T. solium*—is also widely distributed and its larval stage..produces cysticercosis in man. **1971** R. A. MARCIAL-ROJAS *Path. Protozoan & Helminthic Dis.* xxxi. 618/1 The pathology and symptomatology of the taeniases in man vary according to the evolutionary stage of the parasite affecting him.

tæniodont (tī·niˌodǫnt). [f. mod.L. order name *Tæniodonta* (E. D. Cope 1876, in *Proc. Acad. Nat. Sci. Philadelphia* XXVIII. 39), f. TÆNIO- + Gr. ὀδούς, ὀδοντ- tooth.] A fossil mammal of the order Tæniodonta, related to the edentates and known from remains found in North America.

1933 A. S. ROMER *Vertebr. Paleontol.* xiv. 278 Taeniodonts..were seemingly never common. **1949** B. PATTERSON in G. Jepsen et al. *Genetics, Paleontol. & Evolution* xiii. 243 (*title*) Rates of evolution in taeniodonts. **1979** M. J. NOVACEK in Fairbridge & Jablonski *Encycl. Paleontol.* 441/1 The taeniodonts..evolved long-clawed feet; ever-growing cheek teeth; short, broad skulls; and deep jaws.

tæniolite (tī·niˌōᵘləit). *Min.* Also **tainiolite.** [f. Gr. ταινία band, ribbon + -O + -LITE.] A rare colourless mica containing lithium and magnesium but without essential aluminium.

1899 G. FLINK in *Meddelelser om Grønland* XXIV. 116 The name of tainiolite that I have given the mineral is derived from the Greek word ταινία, a band or strip, because the crystals always have the form of bands or strips. **1900** *Amer. Jrnl. Sci.* CLX. 324 Tainiolite (tæniolite) is a kind of mica occurring in elongated colorless crystals. **1938** *Amer. Mineralogist* XXIII. 110 Because of the absence of essential aluminum, taeniolite is unique among the micas. **1962** W. A. DEER et al. *Rock-Forming Minerals* III. 89 A very rare mica, taeniolite (ideal formula $K_2Mg_4Li_2Si_8O_{20}F_4$), has no aluminium... It may be regarded as a magnesian lepidolite although it could be classed also as a lithian phlogopite. **1968** I. KOSTOV *Mineralogy* 361 Tainiolite.

‖ **Tafelmusik** (tā·fəlmuzīːk). Also **tafelmusik, tafel musik.** [Ger., lit. 'table music'.] **1.** Music so printed that parts can be read from the same page by two or more persons seated on opposite sides of a table.

1876 STAINER & BARRETT *Dict. Mus. Terms* 420/1 *Tafelmusik*,..table music. **1907** [see sense 2 below].

2. Music intended to be performed at a banquet or a convivial meal, esp. popular in the eighteenth century.

1880 GROVE *Dict. Mus.* II. 400/1 The Tafelmusik, Nachtmusik, etc., [of Mozart] for wind instruments.. often present the most extraordinary combinations. **1907** T. S. WOTTON *Dict. Foreign Mus. Terms* 193 *Tafelmusik*, ..(1) Music intended to be sung or played at meal times. (2) Music so arranged that two persons seated at opposite sides of a table can sing from the same page. **1961** *Times* 13 Mar. 3/1 Like the more aimlessly gossipy *Tafelmusik* of an eighteenth-century composer. **1969** *Times* 29 May 8/5 The analogy was with contemporary *tafel musik* rather than the wilder shores of radicalism. **1971** G. STEINER *In Bluebeard's Castle* iv. 92 Much of this [eighteenth-century] music was, in fact, conceived as *Tafelmusik* and aural tapestry around the busy room. **1980** *Early Music* July 300/1 If you seek in your Italian madrigal an escape to remote and perhaps picturesque sonorities, then the last thing you want is to understand it well enough to know why it is different from, say, Gregorian chant or rococo *Tafelmusik*. **1980** *Times* 19 Aug. 7/3 One of Telemann's many pieces of *tafelmusik*.

‖ **Tafelwein** (tā·fəlvəin). Also **tafelwein.** Pl. **-e.** [Ger., lit. 'table wine'.] Wine of less than middle quality, suitable for drinking with an ordinary meal; = *table wine* s.v. *TABLE *sb.* 22. Cf. *vin de table* s.v. *VIN.

1972 *Times* 27 Nov. (Wines & Spirits Suppl.) p. iii/5 There will be three categories of wine: *tafelweine* for all the *vins ordinaires*; *qualitätswein* for middle quality wines..; and *qualitätswein mit prädikat*. **1978** W. F. BUCKLEY *Stained Glass* xix. 186 He flashed his light down and saw a half-empty case of white Tafelwein. **1980** A. SCHOLEFIELD *Berlin Blind* III. 183 A bottle of *tafelwein* half empty.

Taff (tæf). Abbrev. of TAFFY². Occas. applied also to women.

1929 F. BOWEN *Sea Slang* 137 *Taff or Taffy*, any Welsh seaman, or one with a Welsh surname. **1943** [see *ASDIC]. **1973** M. AMIS *Rachel Papers* 81 She, Nanny, wasn't too bad: a red-faced, fat but strong-looking woman of about sixty-five or seventy. A Taff all right. **1977** *Listener* 25 Aug. 235/1 Taffs and Geordies and Scouses who were barely intelligible.

taffeta, taffety. Add: **B.** *attrib.* and as *adj.* **2.** *taffety cream*, substitute for def.: A dish of cream and eggs. (Earlier example.)

1723 J. NOTT *Cook's & Confectioner's Dict.* sig. L1, *Taffaty Cream.* Beat the Whites of eight Eggs..with Rose-water,..put it into a Quart of cream.

taffy¹. Add: **1.** (Later examples.) Freq. used in comparisons as a type of something which yields to pressure or can be stretched out into lengths.

1960 R. W. MARKS *Dymaxion World of B. Fuller* 127/2 The wood die rises, actuated by the console controls, while the universal-jointed giant fists stretch the metal gutter piece like *taffy* around the wooden die's elliptical groove perimeter. **1974** K. MILLETT *Flying* (1975) v. 474 Each wonderful swatch of hair like a chunk of taffy stretched. **1979** *Sci. Amer.* Oct. 117/2 Below the interface the lava is a fluid that yields like taffy when a drill probe is pushed into it.

2. (Earlier example.)

1878 E. L. WHEELER *Buckhorn Bill* 2/1 Don't try to stuff that kind of taffy down me. *I* know better.

3. *taffy-coloured* adj.; **taffy apple,** a toffee-apple; **taffy pull, pulling,** an occasion on which young people assemble to make taffy.

1967 MRS. L. B. JOHNSON *White House Diary* 12 Sept. (1970) 567 Stands dispensing hot dogs, Coca Cola, taffy apples, popcorn, and cotton candy. **1978** A. MALING *Lucky Devil* xxiii. 122, I threw the taffy apple stick away. **1939** L. M. MONTGOMERY *Anne of Ingleside* xxxii. 232 Young Mrs David Ransome, with her taffy-coloured hair. **1970** J. HANSEN *Fadeout* (1972) xi. 89 A taffy-colored cocker spaniel. **1883** I. M. RITTENHOUSE *Jrnl.* in *Maud* (1939) 159 We're going to have a taffy pull at our Y.P.T.A. Friday night. **1926** *One Big Union Bulletin* (Winnipeg) 19 Aug. 5/6 We had planned a taffy pull but the ball game was so prolonged that we only succeeded in making fudge. **1982** S. B. FLEXNER *Listening to America* 138 The taffy pulls..were a suitable face-to-face pastime for courting couples. **1863** M. B. CHESNUT *Diary* 18 Dec. in C. V. Woodward *May Chestnut's Civil War* (1981) xx. 507 General Hood..wanted me to go to a taffy pulling at the Prestons'. **1912** *Out West* Mar. 166/2 He wrote with beautiful flourishes, little notes of regret..declining all socials, taffy pullings and croquet parties. **1959** R. CAMPBELL *I Would do It Again* ii. 7 There was taffy pulling and all the other fun that goes with a picnic.

tafia. (Earlier example.)

1763 tr. *Le Page du Pratz's Hist. Louisiana* II. IV. iv. 266 At night you shall have a cup of *Tafia* (or rum) to give you strength and spirits.

tafoni (tæfōᵘ·ni), *sb. pl. Geol.* [a. G. *tafoni* pl. (F. C. A. Penck *Morph. d. Erdoberfläche* (1894) I. 214), a. Corsican dial. *tafóni* pl., holes, hollows.] Shallow rounded hollows in rock produced by weathering.

1942 C. A. COTTON *Climatic Accidents in Landscape Making* i. 9 Rarely or never are positive signs of sand-blasting found in association with typical tafoni. **1968** R. W. FAIRBRIDGE *Encycl. Geomorphol.* 1103/1 Smaller rounded depressions may diversify the larger tafoni. **1970** R. J. SMALL *Study of Landforms* ix. 294 Cavity weathering, leading to the formation of rounded hollows ('tafoni') in granite, may also be due to chemical decay, since it occurs commonly in shaded areas where moisture is likely to linger.

tafrogenesis, var. *TAPHROGENESIS.

taft, *sb.* Add: Also Comb.: **taft joint,** a joint between two pipes, made by tafting one pipe, shaping the other to fit into it, and soldering them.

1891 S. S. HELLYER *Plumbing* xvii. 91 There is no form of wiped soldered joints so easy to make as a *taft joint*. **1906** GOODCHILD & TWENEY *Technol. & Sci. Dict.* 742/1 *Taft joint*, a blown joint. **1945** W. J. WOOLGAR *Pract. Plumber* iv. 102/2 The taft joints are seldom used in plumbing, because of the low tensile strength. **1972** J. HASTINGS *Plumber's Compan.* 146 A taft joint..requires little skill in the making. **1976** *Pract. Householder* Nov. 46/1 Plumber's solder can, of course, be used especially with the taft joint and finger wipe joint.

tag, *sb.¹* Add: **8. a.** Also *fig.* = TAB *sb.¹* 6 in Dict. and Suppl.

1961 *Times* 5 Jan. 4/3 After the interval Surrey drafted in extra men to help Prosser keep a tag on Farooq.

c. *Electronics.* A small metal projection to which a wire may be soldered or attached.

1919 R. MORDIN *Strowger Automatic Telephone Exchange* ii. 34 The tags are arranged in ten sets of three rows, and pass completely through holes in the tag board, so that it is possible to wire the tags on either or both sides of the board. **1958** *Practical Wireless* XXXIV. 63/2 All earth leads on the pre-amplifier are taken to one point, actually to a soldering tag on the input coaxial socket. **1971** *Hi-Fi Sound* Feb. 71/1 Never, under any circumstances, solder connections to the tags with them already on the cartridge.

d. (See quot. 1935.) *N. Amer. slang.*

1935 A. J. POLLOCK *Underworld Speaks* 118/1 *Tag*, an automobile license plate. **1971** *Maclean's Mag.* Sept. 34/1 The license plates ('tags'), laws unto themselves, somehow manage to contradict and complement each other at the same time. **1976** *Billings* (Montana) *Gaz.* 18 June 7c/3 [They] observed a Thunderbird with Louisiana tags circling the block.

e. *Computers.* A character or set of characters appended to an item of data in order to identify it.

1948 *Theory & Techniques for Design of Electronic Digital Computers* (Moore School of Electr. Engin., Univ. of Pennsylvania) IV. xxxix. 1 To introduce..a new element called a stop order tag which may be attached to the words stored in the memory. **1961** Leeds & Weinberg *Computer Programming Fund.* v. 151 Bits 0, 1, and 2 (often called the prefix of the word) and bits 18 to 20 (called the tag) specify the operation. **1963** *IBM Jrnl. Res. & Devel.* VII. 337/2 If it is desired to translate the text with the aid of a microglossary, the text is preceded by a tag specifying the pertinent field. **1978** J. P. Hayes *Computer Archit. & Organization* iii. 149 The processor merely has to inspect the operand tags to determine the specific type of operation to be performed, e.g., a fixed-point double-precision addition.

f. An epithet; a label or popular designation. *colloq.*

1961 in Webster. **1972** *Times* 7 Aug. (Jamaica Suppl.) p. iii/4 The lost goodwill..and the loss of the tag of still being the safest Caribbean country for investment. **1976** *Daily Tel.* 20 July 3/2 The Black Panther tag, probably coined by the press, was the worst of it. **1982** *Oxford Star* 4–5 Feb. 3/2 Cassells doesn't let the tag of Third Division top scorer bother him too much.

g. A price (cf. *price-tag* s.v. Price *sb.* 14); hence, an account or bill. Cf. Tab *sb.*[1] 6 in Dict. and Suppl.

1968 *Globe & Mail* (Toronto) 3 Feb. B2/3 (*heading*) Petrofind raises fuel oil price, bulk gas tag. **1977** *Modern Railways* Dec. 474/2 BR stresses, too, that if there's a gulf between the price of the basic, low-cost vehicles customers have been using in old-style wagonload working and the tag on a late-1970s air-braked, 75 mile/h vehicle, there's a comparable contrast in the service obtainable. **1979** D. Meiring *Foreign Body* xviii. 197 Even if they went broke, the bank would pick up Sagr's crude-oil tag and pay it.

9. c. (Earlier examples.)

1717 J. Gay et al. *Three Hours after Marriage* i. 25 The tag of the Acts of a new Comedy. **1755** C. Charke *Life* 205 Concluding the Play with Jane Shore's Tag, at the End of the first Act of that Tragedy.

d. A musical phrase added to the end of a piece in composition or performance (see also quot. 1978). Esp. in *Jazz.*

1929 *N.Y. Times* 20 Oct. ix. 8/6 *Tag*, ending added to a musical composition. **1932** *Melody Maker* June 507/3 The tag..implies that this is a band record. **1943** *Riverboat Jazz* (Brunswick Records) 7 He comes in to play a tag—just a few notes. **1958** P. Tanner in P. Gammond *Decca Bk. Jazz* xi. 130 A tradition has grown up..of concluding with a short drum break and a tag ensemble coda. **1960** H. O. Brunn *Story Original Dixieland Jazz Band* v. 59 The Dixieland Band's stock ending, the 'dixieland tag', faithfully concluded every number. **1978** *Amer. Speech 1975* L. 301 *Tag*, added ending of a song, often repeating the final words and designed to make a complete and satisfying arrangement.

e. *Linguistics.* An interrogative formula used to convert statements into questions. Cf. *tag question*, sense 13 below.

1957 *Publ. Amer. Dial. Soc.* xxviii. 17 An understanding of tags implies an understanding of sentence order and the role of accent. **1963** F. T. Visser *Hist. Syntax* I. ii. 175 *The type* 'oh, Biffin told you, *did he?* (or *He did?*)'. This type differs from that illustrated in the preceding section in the fact that statement and tag with *to do* are either both positive or both negative. **1977** *Language* LIII. 742 An auxiliary verb typically can appear in the tag of tag questions. **1973** *Archivum Linguisticum* IV. 69 Tag constructions can convey much to the discriminating listener.

12*. *slang.* A person who follows another as a detective or spy. Cf. *Tag *v.*[1] 4 b, *Tail *sb.*[1] 6 b.

1966 'A. Hall' *9th Directive* vii. 62 Who were the tags? The thin one, and the one with the splay-footed walk? **1972** J. D. Buchanan *Professional* v. 62 Guerin realized he had a tag... Guerin would walk and stop, the tag would do the same. **1979** 'A. Hall' *Scorpion Signal* xii. 139 Ignator went through the lights at yellow... I don't think he was going through on the yellow because he'd discovered the tag.

13. tag axle *N. Amer.*, a non-powered set of wheels on a truck, etc., attached so as to support extra weight; **tagboard,** (*a*) *U.S.*, a type of strong cardboard, used esp. for making luggage labels; (*b*) *Electronics*, a board of insulating material containing two or more parallel lines of tags (sense 8 d above), so that a component can be mounted between each pair; **tag day** *N. Amer.* = *flag-day* (*b*) s.v. *Flag *sb.*[4] 7; **tag-end** (earlier example); **tag line** *U.S.* = *Punch line; **tag-phrase,** an automatically repeated or over-used phrase; **tag question** *Linguistics*, a question formed by the appendage of an interrogative formula to a statement; a formula used in this manner (cf. sense 9 e above); **tag strip** *Electronics*, a strip of insulating material on which are mounted a line of tags (sense 8 c above); **tag-tail** (example of sense 'a parasite, a hanger-on').

1971 M. Tak *Truck Talk* 163 *Tag axle*, the hindmost axle of a tandem-axle tractor if that axle serves only to support additional gross weight. **1977** *Telegraph-Jrnl.* (St. John, New Brunswick) 1 June 3/5 He said in an interview that the Motor Vehicles Branch no longer allows extra weight when a third 'tag axle' is added to tandem drive trucks. **1912** *Walden's Directory of Papers* (Eastern ed.) p. liii, Paper and card board..translucents, tag boards, etc. **1952** E. J. Labarre *Dict. Paper* (ed. 2) 301/1 *Tag paper* or board is a very strong and tough product made on the Fourdrinier (Bristol), used for making the well-known luggage and shipping tags. **1956** *Wireless World* Mar. 125/1 A plain tagboard, carrying resistors and capacitors. **1973** G. Davey *Fun with Hi-Fi* iii. 25 (*caption*) Layout and tagboards of Mullard 510 amplifier. **1976** *National Observer* (U.S.) 23 Oct. 20/1 (Advt.), Each issue is 42 or more pages long, bound in sturdy tagboard. **1908** Tag day [see sense 8 a in Dict.]. **1916** *Daily Colonist* (Victoria, B.C.) 4 July 6/3 Friday, August 4, is to be tag day for the Italian Red Cross Society. **1949** *Courier-Journal* (Louisville, Kentucky) 3 Sept. 10/1 The conference agreed [upon]..a tag day on which Boy Scouts and Girl Scouts will solicit funds during the Kentucky State Fair. **1807** C. Wilmot *Let.* 15 May in *Russ. Jrnls.* (1934) ii. 245, I believe..we have been solemnising..the Tag end of those very May Day ceremonies which scandaliz'd *ould Cato* near two thousand years ago. **1926** G. Ade *Let.* 14 Sept. (1973) 113 The prosecutor asks: 'Do you know him?' She studies him carefully and then pulls the tag line: 'No, I don't recognize him at all.' **1941** B. Schulberg *What makes Sammy Run?* iii. 44 One of those long dirty stories for which the only justification would be the tag line at the climax. **1982** *Fortune* 6 Sept. 53/1 One recent ad. shows a stunning model wearing nothing but a solitaire diamond necklace. 'She can't flaunt a fur on the Côte d'Azur,' reads the tagline. **1933** R. Tuve *Seasons & Months* iv. 110 All these uses of the seasons-introduction appear and reappear, sometimes elaborately, sometimes in a mere conventional tag-phrase. **1963** Tag-phrase [see *goon-like* adj. s.v. *Goon 5]. **1933** O. Jespersen *Essentials Eng. Gram.* xxviii. 304 Note especially tag-questions..like: He was angry, wasn't he? **1957** R. W. Zandvoort *Handbk. Eng. Gram.* v. ii. 224 A certain type of compound sentence, consisting of a statement followed by an *appended question* (or 'tag question') modelled on the main clause... You are not ill, are you? **1982** *Amer. Speech* LVII. 95 Lakoff..considers tag questions (*He can work, can't he?* and *He is honest, isn't he?*) as declaratives—assertions. **1942** *Electronic Engin.* XV. 238/2 Such tag strips are found in medium wave receivers, as well as in short wave apparatus. **1960** *Practical Wireless* XXXVI. 405/1 A tag-strip provides a convenient anchoring point for leads. **1834** C. A. Davis *Lett. J. Downing* 311 You are surrounded by such a raft of snuffle-nose, scabby set of tag-tails, that I can't have nothing more to do with you.

tag, *sb.*[2] Add: **2.** *Baseball.* The act of putting out a runner by touching him with the ball (or with the gloved hand holding the ball) while he is off base. Also *tag-out.* Cf. *Tag *v.*[2] 2 a.

1941 *Baseball Mag.* Sept. 439/1 A big league infielder.. confessed..'I've made the tag with the empty glove outstretched.' *Ibid.* 439/3 Some stars..use a two-handed tag. **1952** *N.Y. Herald-Tribune* 16 Aug. 11/1 Only Lockman's cut-off of Hartung's throw and the subsequent tag-out of Mathews at third averted further damage to the home forces. **1971** L. Koppett *N.Y. Times Guide Spectator Sports* i. 21 The rules forbid a runner to leave the 'base-path'—an imaginary direct line between bases—to avoid a tag.

B. as *adj.* Of, pertaining to, or designating a form of professional wrestling between single alternating representatives of two teams (usu. of two men each).

One team-member cannot enter the ring until the other tags or touches hands with him on leaving it.

1955 *Sun* (Baltimore) 16 May 16/7 (*heading*) 6-man tag bout tops mat card. *Ibid.* For the first time in the history of wrestling, a six-man tag team bout will be staged. **1963** *Economist* 7 Sept. 819/1 The confused spectacle of tag wrestling (four in a ring). **1966** *Times* 28 Feb. (Canada Suppl.) p. xiv/7 The average card in Canada has a tag match (two-man teams with the members taking turns to maul each other). **1972** J. Mosedale *Football* viii. 115 He teamed with his old idol Nagurski in tag team matches. **1974** *Greenville* (S. Carolina) *News* 23 Apr. 8/2 In other bouts, Sandy Scott and Johnny Weaver downed Gene Lewis and Bill White in a special tag team event.

‖**Tag** (tāk), *sb.*[3] [Ger.] = *Day *sb.* 9 c. Usu. *der Tag.*

1914, etc. [see *Day *sb.* 9 c]. **1914** J. M. Barrie (*title*) Der Tag. **1916** O. Seaman *Made in England* 35 For now the psychologic *Tag* has come To put the final lid on Christendom. **1918** *Times* 9 Dec. 9/3 The wonderful day, the great Der Tag, Which Prussians had vow'd with unmannerly brag Should see Old England lower her flag. **1924** J. Buchan *Three Hostages* ix. 125 We'll fix the 10th of June for *Der Tag*... The round-up of all must be simultaneous. **1939** C. Day Lewis *Child of Misfortune* iii. iii. 290 You're saving it up for Der Tag... A time will come when those persons will be very sorry. **1966** P. Flower *Fiends of Family* xvi. 187 '*Der tag*,' Maggie said. 'At long last, the day of the great adventure.' **1975** tr. *Melchior's Sleeper Agent* ii. 133 When *der Tag* comes, when his usefulness is Kaput, we'll slap him in detention.

tag, *v.*[1] Add: **1. b.** Also *spec.*, to mark and record (animals) so that their migrations can be traced. (Later examples.)

1953 Scott & Fisher *Thousand Geese* vi. 58 The expedition was confined to camp, except for short dashes.. to tag a few whooper cygnets. **1974** *Nature* 19 Apr. 642/2 Anglers tagged 954 bass..on the coast of Devon.

d. *Biol.* and *Chem.* = *Label *v.* 2.

1939 *Amer. Jrnl. Physiol.* CXXVII. 557 The radioactivity 'tags' the atoms. **1947** *Ann. Rev. Microbiol.* I. 271 The foregoing method is..not limited to 'tagging' the antigen by means of glucosamine analyses. **1969** *Times* 9 Apr. 7/2 DNA sub-units tagged with radioactive marker atoms were fed to bacteria. **1977** *Sci. Amer.* July 46/3 The antigens were first visualized by tagging their antibodies with a fluorescent dye that could be seen under ultraviolet radiation.

e. *Computers.* To label (an item of data) in order to identify it for subsequent processing or retrieval.

1959 M. H. Wrubel *Primer of Programming for Digital Computers* iii. 56 We must..tag the instructions to be modified..so that those instructions and no others will be modified by adding the contents of the loop box. **1971** *Computers & Humanities* VI. 43 It is a simple matter to enter and tag automatically categories of information indicated by font and/or format... Such tagging is a part of the Dissly service. **1983** *Trans. Philol. Soc.* 33 This is a program which identifies and tags idioms which it finds in an Idiom list.

2. Also with *on.*

1916 T. MacDonagh *Literature in Ireland* 150 The first two verses of the better version..are essential poetry; the three that are tagged on in the song-books are no such thing.

4. a. (Further examples.) Freq. const. *after, along, (a)round, on.* Also *fig.*

1822 G. F. Cooper *Spy* II. xii. 307 Pooh! Pooh!..if you tag after a troop of horse, a small bit of a joke must be borne. **1897** Kipling *Captains Courageous* ix. 214 Don't go taggin' araound after them whose eyes bung out with fatness. **1900** Ade *More Fables in Slang* (1902) 113 The men..wanted to Tag along, but Clara drove them back. **1930** J. Dos Passos *42nd Parallel* ii. xi. 164 She followed his talk breathless the way she used to tag along after Joe and Alec down to the carbarns when she was little. **1933** D. L. Sayers *Murder must Advertise* iii. 41 He used to tag round with that de Momerie crowd. **1946** 'P. Quentin' *Puzzle for Fiends* (1947) ix. 70 So you're ready to tag along with me, eh, Gordy? **1948** C. Day Lewis *Otterbury Incident* 43 Toppy's kid sister..tagged on, which was rather a bore. **1957** *Economist* 23 Nov. 661/2 There is a Yemeni home public. Its upper crust has been most critical of the recent tendency to tag along with Egypt and do deals, including an arms deal, with Russia. **1960** S. Barstow *Kind of Loving* i. vi. 126 Two or three more people sitting outside the room where they actually take the blood. Me and the Old Man tag on to the line. **1960** L. Cooper *Accomplices* i. iv. 37 He was sick of the sight of those damned Batemans... Couldn't we ever go anywhere without them tagging on? **1960** C. Day Lewis *Buried Day* ii. 44, I would tag around with him, hardly understanding a word he said because of his thick East-Anglian dialect. **1973** J. Pattinson *Search Warrant* v. 80, I guess I'll tag along. Just for the ride.

b. Also *spec.*, to follow as a detective or spy. Cf. *Tag *sb.*[1] 12*, *Tail *v.*[1] 5 b.

1966 'A. Hall' *9th Directive* vii. 63 Why did you tag me here? **1975** —— *Mandarin Cypher* viii. 123 If I thought I was tagged here because Chiang had blown me I was wrong.

6. (Further examples.)

1853 T. D. Price *Diary* 17 Mar. (MS.), Tagged the ewes in the forenoon. **1863** H. S. Randall *Pract. Shepherd* iii. 141 Tagging sheep before they are let out to grass.

tag, *v.*[2] Add: **1.** (Examples.)

1878 F. H. Hart *Sazerac Lying Club* 166 One of them, who had been 'tagged' seven times in succession, got tired, and proposed to change to playing house. **1891** *Jrnl. Amer. Folk-Lore* IV. 222 One player, who is 'it', attempts to tag, or touch, one of the other players. **1969** I. & P. Opie *Children's Games* ii. 64 In Monmouthshire, Gloucestershire, and Oxfordshire, they speak of 'tagging' each other.

2. *Baseball* and *Softball.* **a.** To put out (a runner) by touching him with the ball (or with the gloved hand holding the ball) while he is off base. Also with *out.* Cf. *Tag *sb.*[2] 2.

1907 'B. L. Standish' *Dick Merriwell's Magnetism* xxxviii. 243 He tagged Spratt, and this made the second man out. **1944** E. S. Gardner *Case of Black-Eyed Blonde* 64 Keep cutting corners, Mason, and I'm going to catch you off first base one of these days, and then I'll tag you out. **1971** L. Koppett *N.Y. Times Guide Spectator Sports* i. 21 No one is attempting to tag him. **1976** *Billings* (Montana) *Gaz.* 28 June 1-c/2 (*caption*) Dave Konzen, of Buck's Bar slow pitch softball team, is tagged out as he slides against Heidelberg of Tacoma, Wash. **1982** S. B. Flexner *Listening to America* 34 Someone had the bright idea of forcing the runner out by throwing the ball to the base ahead of him or by tagging him with the ball rather than throwing the ball at him.

b. intr. *to tag up*: of a runner to (return to and) touch one's base after a fly ball is caught.

1942 *Baseball Digest* Dec. 52 Fletcher tagged up at third after the catch and then started for the plate. **1971** L. Koppett *N.Y. Times Guide Spectator Sports* i. 20 The runner 'tags up', waits at his base until the ball is caught, and still beats the throw to the next base. **1978** G. Wright *Illustr. Handbk. Sporting Terms* 89/2 If the ball is caught..the base runners, unless tagging up.., may not advance.

c. *trans.* To make a hit or run off (a pitcher).

1961 in Webster. **1974** *Greenville* (S. Carolina) *News* 23 Apr. 8/5 Seaver was taken out of the game after being tagged for hits by the first two batters in the Pittsburgh sixth.

Tagalog (tăgā·lǫg), *sb.* and *a.* Also † **Tagal, -la, -lian, -lic, -loc.** [Tagalog, f. *tagá* native to + *ilog* river; cf. Sp. *tagalo.*] **A.** *sb.* **a.** (A member of) a people living in the neighbourhood of Manila in the Philippine Islands. **b.**

The Austronesian language spoken by this people, an official language of the Republic of the Philippines.

1704 tr. *Careri's Voy. round World* in A. & J. Churchill *Coll. Voy. & Trav.* IV. 430/2 From these are descended the Tagalians, which are the Natives of Manila and the Country about it. *Ibid.* 446/1 The Languages are so numerous, that there are six in the only Island of Manila, which are Tagalian, Pampangan, [etc.]. **1808** *Asiatick Researches* X. 207 The Tagala or rather Tă-Gála or the Gala language is among the Philippines, what the Malayu is in the Malay islands. *Ibid.* 213 With respect to the original literature of the Tăgalás, the accounts of the Spanish missionaries are rather discordant. **1814** J. Maver *Martinez de Zuñiga's Hist. View Philippine Islands* I. p. xi, In respect to the aboriginal language, or Tagalic, very slight attempts have been made to trace it beyond the quarter in which it was found to prevail. Our author..draws the conclusion that the Tagalic language and original population of all the islands westward of the coast of South America derive from that continent. **1834** W. Marsden *Misc. Wks.* 39 Of these dialects six are considered as meriting distinction..; they are the *Tagala* or *Tagalog* [etc.]. **1840** *Penny Cycl.* XVIII. 88/2 The Malays are divided into a great number of tribes, of which that called Tagala occupies the neighbourhood of Manila. **1885** *Encycl. Brit.* XVIII. 753/1 First among these rank the Tagals... Their language (Tagalog) especially has made extensive encroachments on the other Philippine tongues since the conquest. **1919** F. R. Blake in C. F. Hockett *Leonard Bloomfield Anthol.* (1970) 82 This work contains an extended treatment of Tagalog, the most important native language of the Philippine Islands. **1933** L. Bloomfield *Language* vi. 105 Even simpler is the *three-vowel* system which appears in some languages, such as Tagalog. **1974** *Encycl. Brit. Micropædia* IX. 764/3 Most Tagalogs are farmers. **1976** 'G. Black' *Moon for Killers* vi. 83 A verbal exchange..starting in English, shifting to Spanish, and then apparently getting down to the real obscenities in Tagálog.

B. *adj.* Of or pertaining to this people or their language.

1808 *Asiatick Researches* X. 208 The Tăgála alphabet consists of seventeen letters. **1814** [see the sb. above]. **1859** J. Bowring *Philippine Islands* xiii. 219 What is the Tagáloc language? **1906** *Jrnl. Amer. Folk-Lore* XIX. 191 (*heading*) Philippine (Tagalog) superstitions. **1959** N. Mailer *Advts. for Myself* (1961) 131 Miguel said something to the other Filipinos in the Tagalog language. **1978** M. B. Hooker *Conc. Legal Hist. South-East Asia* viii. 215 The *Maragtas* text..is found in a recension dated A.D. 1650 written in the Tagalog script.

ta·g-along, *a.* and *sb. N. Amer. colloq.* Also **tagalong.** [f. vbl. phr. *to tag along*: see Tag *v.*[1] 4 a in Dict. and Suppl.] **A.** *adj.* **a.** Designating that which is towed or trailed behind something else. **b.** Applied to an uninvited follower.

1944 *Sun* (Baltimore) 21 Jan. 2/3 Evidence of trailed, or 'tag-along', bombs still is scanty. **1960** *Newsweek* 20 June 91/1 The tag-along highway trailers are delivered to..the bus terminals. **1973** *Islander* (Victoria, B.C.) 10 June 16/1 The small trailer snug beside it like a tagalong pup. **1974** *Spartanburg* (S. Carolina) *Herald-Jrnl.* 21 Apr. C9 (Advt.), Also all types of trucks and truck tractors, all types of trailers including low-boy and tag-A-long.

B. *sb.* An unwelcome, uninvited, or neglected companion.

1961 in Webster. **1967** *Boston Sunday Herald* 2–8 Apr. 45/1 The whole family suffers when Ernie becomes a dreadful tagalong. **1974** *Publishers Weekly* 28 Oct. 46/1 Seems to have spent most of her life as a 'tagalong' to a man who, as test pilot and astronaut, was seldom home. **1977** *Islander* (Victoria, B.C.) 16 Jan. 8/1 (*heading*) Are Victoria women just tag-alongs in motor sports?

tagetes (tădʒī·tīz). [med.L. (L. Fuchs *De Historia Stirpium* (1542) 48), f. *Tages*, name of an Etruscan deity.] An annual or perennial herb of the genus of this name, belonging to the family Compositæ and native to South and Central America; esp. = Marigold 1 b.

1792 *Curtis's Bot. Mag.* V. 150 (*heading*) Spreading Tagetes, or French Marigold. **1895** W. Robinson *Eng. Flower Garden* (ed. 4) 780/2 There are also perennial Tagetes, but they are not hardy enough to make satisfactory plants out-of-doors. **1926** *Contemp. Rev.* Feb. 233 A thick mass of petunia and tagetes..in blossom. **1962** R. Page *Educ. Gardener* vii. 220 French gardeners are used to cultivating huge batches of..several varieties of tagetes. **1975** *Country Life* 13 Feb. 388/2 Tagetes marigolds are not at all bad in shade. **1980** L. Mantell *Murder or Three* ii. 23 Small shrubs..and an edging of velvety gold and brown Tagetes.

tagged, *ppl.* a. Add: **1.**

d. Of an animal: marked to help study of its habits or migrations.

1927 *Zoologica* IX. 204 Every tagged frog was given a new page. **1979** *Fisherman's Weekly* 21 June 4/3 More than 400 of the tagged brown and rainbow trout released into Draycote Water by fisheries officers of the Severn-Trent Water Authority have already been notified.

e. Fastened *on*, appended. Cf. *Tag *v.*[1] 2.

1982 *N. & Q.* Feb. 80/1 A tagged-on chapter on 'Critical History' runs only to six pages.

f. *Computers.* Marked or labelled with a 'tag' (*tag *sb.*[1] 8 e).

1983 *Trans. Philol. Soc.* 29 A tagged corpus..provides a head start for anyone undertaking more advanced linguistic analyses of the corpus.

6. *Biol.* and *Chem.* = *Labelled *ppl. a.* d.

1945 *Jrnl. Sci. Instruments* XXII. 23/1 Tagged atoms are used to enable the investigator to see where the rest of his material is going. **1955** *Sci. News Let.* 2 July 15/1 When a plant is supplied with isotopically labeled nitrate ..the 'tagged' element rapidly spreads throughout the tissues and is incorporated into all the major nitrogen fractions.

taggeen (tăgī·n). *Anglo-Ir.* [ad. Ir. *taidhgín.*] A small cup or glass (of spirits); a 'dram'.

1899 Somerville & 'Ross' *Some Experiences Irish R.M.* i. 10 'There's no bath in the house, sir.. but..would ye like a taggeen?' This alternative proposal proved to be a glass of raw whisky. **1936** M. Franklin *All that Swagger* iii. 35 Doing the dirty work of some cowardly crawler, who's bought you for a plug of tobacco and a taggeen of rum.

tagger[1]. Add: **4.** Now also *sing.*, chiefly in *attrib.* use.

1938 *Shelf Appeal* July 26/1 The tagger-top in its present form, with a cutter in the lid. **1959** *Gloss. Packaging Terms* (*B.S.I.*) 55 *Lever ring and tagger*, a lever type closure comprising a diaphragm of tagger tinplate or aluminium secured (together with the ring) to the body... *Cutter lid*, an outer lid containing a steel cutter with which the thin tagger tinplate top of the body is pierced and cut away.

tagger[2]. (Example.)

1969 I. & P. Opie *Children's Games* i. 23 One person is the tagger and has to count to thirty.

tagging, *vbl. sb.* Add: **a.** Also *spec.* (*a*) the marking of animals as an aid to study of their migrations; (*b*) *Computers*, the action of *Tag *v.* 1 e.

1927 *Zoologica* IX. 201 (*title*) Frog tagging: a method of studying anuran life habits. **1953** Scott & Fisher *Thousand Geese* vi. 65 We worked away in camp at journals, nest records, tagging data. **1960** *Guardian* 25 Oct. 8/4 To study the movement and growth rates there is an elaborate system of fish tagging carried out at sea. **1972** *Even. Telegram* (St. John's, Newfoundland) 24 June 11/1 Tagging studies have shown most salmon intercepted are headed for the northern river spawning beds.

1948 *Theory & Techniques for Design of Electronic Digital Computers* (Moore School of Electr. Engin., Univ. of Pennsylvania) IV. xxxix. 20 This tagging is done by the little cycle..until the sentinel..trips on a coincidence and causes the control to go on to the next stage of computation. **1972** *Computers & Humanities* VII. 5 The study of *Automatic Grammatical Tagging of English*.. describes the theory and method of parts-of-speech tags, procedures used in tagging, and the context frame test employed. **1983** *Trans. Philol. Soc.* 33 The tagging of the LOB Corpus is due for completion by September 1983.

Taghairm (tŏ·γėrm, tŏ·'ėrm). *Sc.* [Gael.] A method of divination formerly practised in the Scottish Highlands (see quots.).

1774 T. Pennant *Tour in Scotl. & Voy. Hebrides 1772* 311 A vast cataract, whose waters falling from a high rock, jet so far as to form a dry hollow beneath... One of these imposters was sowed up in the hide of an ox, and.. was placed in this concavity: the trembling enquirer was brought to the place, where the shade, and the roaring of the waters, encreased the dread of the occasion. The question is put, and the person in the hide delivers his answer, and so ends this species of divination styled *Taghairm*. **1810** Scott *Lady of Lake* iv. iv. 146 Brian an augury hath tried, Of that dread kind which must not be Unless in dread extremity, The Taghairm call'd; by which, afar, Our sires foresaw the events of war. **1906** *Athenæum* 2 June 668/3 Another saying, 'Keep the cat turning', refers to the horrid practice of the Taghairm, or divination by the cat. **1953** *Scots Mag.* Dec. 223 Taghairm was, indeed, a magical means of compelling spiritual presences to grant desirable and valuable boons to the sorcerer who invoked them.

tagliarini (talʸarī·ni). [ad. It. *taglierini* sb. pl. (also used); cf. *Tagliatelle.] Egg noodles cut into very narrow strips.

1846 [see *ravioli]. **1899** J. Ross *Leaves from our Tuscan Kitchen* 69 Repeat the alternate layers of tagliarini, cheese and butter, until the dish is full. **1943** A. Simon *Conc. Encycl. Gastron.* IV. 64/1 Italian pastes..known.. by different names such as Macaroni, Vermicelli,.. Tagliarini, Tagliatelle, [etc.]. **1964** E. H. & M. O. Knopf *Food of Italy* ii. iii. 184 To make tagliarini. Proceed as for lasagne. **1982** G. Bugialli *Classic Techniques Italian Cooking* vi. 138 The finely cut pasta, *taglierini* almost as fine as angel's hair, is appropriate to very delicate sauces and to broths and soups.

tagliatelle (talʸate·le). Also **tagliatelli** (-ī). [It., sb. pl., f. *tagliare* to cut.] Egg noodles cut into ribbons. Also *fig.*

1899 J. Ross *Leaves from our Tuscan Kitchen* 69 (*heading*) Tagliatelle with ham. **1926** R. Hall *Adam's Breed* i. iii. 21 There were paste from Naples..Tagliatelle, Gnocchi, [etc.]. **1934** [see *pasta]. **1957** G. Smith *Friends* 9 In Rome, where the *tagliatelli* had disagreed with him. **1967** [see *rigatoni *sb. pl.*]. **1977** *Times Lit. Suppl.* 4 Feb. 120/2 All those tapes, those monstrous forkfuls of magnetized tagliatelle..would lead to definite strangulation. **1980** T. Holme *Neapolitan Streak* 100 She ladled *tagliatelle*..on to the plates of her family. **1983** *Listener* 13 Jan. 5/2 That sentence would have wound up on the cutting-room floor, another piece of inedible Grundig tagliatelle.

tagma. Add: **2.** *Zool.* Each of the morphologically distinct regions, comprising several adjoining segments, into which the bodies of arthropods and some other metamerically organized animals are divided. Chiefly *pl.* Hence **tagmo·sis**, the formation of tagmata.

1902 E. R. Lankester in *Encycl. Brit.* XXV. 691/2 It is convenient to have a special word for..regions of like meres, and we call each a tagma (ταγμα, a regiment). The word 'tagmosis' is applicable to the formation of such regions. **1935** R. E. Snodgrass *Princ. Insect Morphol.* iv. 80 Tagmosis is more variable in the Crustacea [than in insects]; in the Chilopoda and Diplopoda it results only in the formation of a head, including the gnathal segments, and a body. **1980** C. Gillott *Entomol.* iii. 54 The basic segmental structure is frequently obscured as a result of tagmosis. In insects three tagmata are found: the head, the thorax, and the abdomen.

3. *Linguistics.* **a.** A feature of grammatical arrangement or syntax.

1949 *Archivum Linguisticum* I. 1 Such distinctions as that of morpheme and 'tagma' as the constituents of the syntagm provide the necessary correction. But there is a different sense in which morpheme and tagma may share in the expression of the meaning of a syntagm: a feature of meaning may be distributed over both.

b. In tagmemics, the smallest meaningful unit of grammatical substance (contrasted with tagmeme).

1964 R. E. Longacre *Grammar Discovery Procedures* i. 46 Copy the data from the filing slips onto charts: (a) There should be a column for each tagma, i.e. for each tentatively identified function-set correlation. **1969** W. A. Cook *Introd. Tagmemic Analysis* vii. 187 Tagmemics is a grouping process, which involves human judgment, an attempt to group tagmas into units essential to the language, as the language appears to the native speaker.

tagmeme (tæ·gmīm). *Linguistics.* [f. Gr. τάγμα arrangement (see Tagma) + *-eme.]

1. The smallest meaningful unit of grammatical form.

1933 L. Bloomfield *Language* x. 166 In the case of lexical forms, we have defined the smallest meaningful units as morphemes, and their meanings as sememes; in the same way, the smallest meaningful units of grammatical form may be spoken of as tagmemes, and their meanings as episememes. **1950** S. Potter *Our Language* 86 Beginning with the phoneme, philologists pass on to speak about morphemes, taxemes or tagmemes.

2. The correlate of a grammatical function and the class of items which can perform it.

1943 K. L. Pike in *Language* XIX. 69 Somewhat diffidently I suggest the following classifications and relabelings as perhaps being a bit easier to handle than Bloomfield's... *Tagmeme*, a composite view of the basic composite taxemes of a linguistic form, at any one specific layer of structure. E.g. the total arrangement features of the form *duchess* considered as a single entity. **1957** —— in *General Linguistics* III. 29 In future work, therefore, we are adopting the term *tagmeme*. It should be noted, however, that our definition of this term is sharply different from Bloomfield. **1968** *Language* XLIV. 190 Another basic concept in tagmemic analysis is the consistent distinction observed between obligatory and optional tagmemes. **1969** S. Potter *Changing English* viii. 163 Every sentence is a frame into which syntactic units, or tagmemes, are fitted. When a word is forced into an unusual tagmemic slot, it is said to undergo grammatical conversion or functional shift. **1973** *Amer. Speech 1970* XLV. 135 The highest level tagmeme operates at the level of the T-unit. **1981** *Word 1980* XXXI. 232 The infrastructure of English contains seven slots or tagmemes and that of German six.

tagmemic (tægmī·mik), *a. Linguistics.* [f. *tagmeme + -ic.] Of or pertaining to tagmemes or tagmemics.

1958 K. L. Pike in *Internat. Jrnl. Amer. Linguistics* XXIV. 275 In order to demonstrate another crucial difference between our tagmeme and that of Bloomfield it is necessary to indicate the manner in which slot and distribution class are relevant to our tagmemic view. **1964** R. H. Robins *Gen. Linguistics* p. xx, P. Postal..sets out a vigorous criticism of both immediate constituent and tagmemic analysis. **1968** *Language* XLIV. 190 Tagmemic theory provides a tight hierarchical scheme for grammatical description. **1969** [see *tagmeme 2]. **1978** *English Jrnl.* Dec. 66 A clause analysis technique reflecting a sketch of the core grammatical system of English based on a tagmemic model. **1981** *Word 1980* XXXI. 231 He.. adopts the generative tagmemic approach as the basis of his work.

tagmemicist (tægmī·misist). *Linguistics.* [f. *tagmemic(s + -ist.] A student or exponent of tagmemics.

1965 *Language* XLI. 640 It would be easy to go farther and say that transformationists represent the extreme of preoccupation with linguistic theory, while tagmemicists represent the extreme of practical concern. **1972** *Times Lit. Suppl.* 22 Sept. 1116/2 Like the units of the tagmemicists, Šaumjan's categories are a combination of form and function. **1977** *Language* LIII. 247 The linguistic study of discourse or intrasentential relations has been carried out by such diverse scholars as..tagmemicists (e.g. Pike 1967).

tagmemics (tægmī·miks), *sb. pl.* (const. as *sing.*). *Linguistics.* [f. *tagmeme: see -ic 2.] The study and description of language in terms of tagmemes; *spec.* a school of linguistic analysis, based on the work of Kenneth L. Pike (b. 1912), which stresses the functional and structural relations of grammatical units.

1947 C. F. Hockett in *Language* XXIII. 274 This term [sc. *tactics*] seems simpler than 'taxemics' or 'tagmemics', which one might derive more directly from Bloomfield's labels. **1958** K. L. Pike in *Internat. Jrnl. Amer. Linguistics* XXIV. 273 Tagmemics, as I see it, should work with neither of these schematic views by itself. **1964** *Language* XL. 314 The similarity of Firthian linguistics to American slot-and-filler grammatical description, notably tagmemics, has already been noted. **1967** R. H. Robins *Short Hist. Linguistics* viii. 212 In thus employing semantics diagnostically, and in severely modifying immediate constituent structures in syntax, tagmemics marks its major divergencies from 'Bloomfieldian' grammatical analysis. **1975** M. A. K. Halliday in S. Rogers *Children & Lang.* iv. 225 With the now general recognition of the basically tri-stratal nature of the linguistic system (and Prague theory, glossematics, system-structure theory, tagmemics, stratification theory and the later versions of transformation theory are all variants on this theme), the semantic perspective has been restored. **1981** *Word 1980* XXXI. 230 He makes use of the slot-and-filler infrastructure, characteristic of tagmemics.

tag-rag, *sb.* **a.** (Later example.)
1870 J. Patrick *Let.* 10 Nov. in D. O. Hunter *Life Marquess of Bute* (1921) v. 96 At the funeral the Rothesay tag-rag outside cheered me as I left the churchyard.

‖ **taharah** (tahară·). Also 9 **tohoro; tahara.** [a. Heb. *ṭohŭrāh* purification, cleansing.] A Jewish ceremony of washing a corpse before burial.
1819 L. Alexander *Hebrew Ritual* 188 Those who are drawn by lot..to attend, in order to wash the corpse, put on the shrouds... This ceremony is called..*Tohoro*, that is, the cleansing. **1902** *Laws & Bye-laws Burial Soc. United Synagogue* 49 (Index), Tahara men, dismissal of... Tahara women. **1932** C. Roth *Hist. Marranos* vii. 190 The traditional *taharah*, or ritual laving of the body. **1964** H. Rabinowicz *Guide to Life* iii. 38 The utmost respect must be shown to the body during *Taharah*... The body is laid on the *Taharah* board... Warm water..must then be poured down the body. **1974** *Jewish Chron.* 1 Nov. 10/1 (*heading*) Tahara helpers required. *Ibid.*, The ministers.. had expressed their willingness to be trained in tahara and to help out.

tahil, var. Tael in Dict. and Suppl.

‖ **tahina** (tahī·nă). Also **tahine, tahini,** etc. [Arab., f. *ṭaḥana* to grind or crush.] A paste or sauce made of sesame seeds, much eaten in the Middle East.
1950 E. David *Bk. Mediterranean Food* 146 *Tahina* is a thick white oil made from pounded sesame seeds. It is served in a bowl and eaten by dipping bread... You buy the white *tahina* from the grocer, and it is then thinned with water. **1968** C. Roden *Bk. Middle Eastern Food* 35 *Tahina* itself is a paste made from sesame meal, and can be found in all Greek stores. *Ibid.*, Serve the *tahina* cream in a bowl. **1971** W. Tucker *This Witch* (1972) ii. 14 The Arab cook had added a small dish of taheena to whet my appetite. **1972** *Vogue* Feb. 33/1 Moroccan tahine dishes with cone lids for couscous, £1.10. **1976** *Ibid.* Jan. 88/2, I like them [*sc.* chick peas] best made into *hummus*, mixed to a smooth paste with *tahini*, lemon juice and garlic. **1976** *Islander* (Victoria, B.C.) 1 Aug. 5/1 They saw a tahina factory where sesame oil is made, the peanut butter of the Middle East. **1979** *Guardian* 8 June 9/4 In Morocco it is either couscous or tajine. **1980** C. Smith *Cut-Out* xvi. 120 Both Palestinians ate sparingly..mining modestly into the *hommas* and *tehineh* dips with their *pitta* bread.

Tahiti (tahī·ti). The name of an island in Polynesia used *attrib.* in **Tahiti arrow-root,** a starchy powder made from the tubers of *Tacca pinnatifida*; **Tahiti chestnut** = *ivi.
1861 Tahiti arrow-root [see *Otaheitean *a.* and *sb.*]. **1884** *Encycl. Brit.* XVII. 664/2 Tahiti chestnut. *Inocarpus edulis.* S. Sea Islands. **1974** G. Usher *Dict. Plants used by Man* 319/1 Polynesian Chestnut, Tahiti Chestnut... The seeds are..eaten raw or cooked. *Ibid.* 564/1 The tuber yields a rather indigestible arrowroot (Fiji Arrowroot, Tahiti Arrowroot,..).

Tahitian (tahī·ʃăn, tahī·ti,ăn), *a.* and *sb.* Also **Tahitan,** † **Taitian,** † **Taitienne.** [f. *Tahiti + -an; cf. *Otaheitean *a.* and *sb.*] **A.** *adj.* Of or pertaining to Tahiti, its inhabitants, or their language.
1822 tr. *Malte-Brun's Universal Geogr.* I. xxiii. 572 Tagalic, Taitienne languages, &c... The Taitian is distributed through all the small islands of the Great Ocean. **1825** W. Ellis *Jrnl. Tour Hawaii* 244 Both in the Hawaiian and Tahitian languages, every syllable, and every word, ends with a vowel. **1847** *Dublin Rev.* Dec. 357 Numerous other matters of European manufacture.. were strewn about among..the ordinary furniture of a Tahitian dwelling. **1852** J. Crawford *Gram. & Dict. Malay Lang.* I. p. cclix, The names of the three plants are exactly according to the Tahitian pronunciation. **1921** tr. *Rathenau's New Society* iv. 26 When a European artist writes or paints in Tahiti, what he produces is not a work of Tahitian culture. **1958** [see *cargador]. **1980** *London Mag.* July 23 The ochre Tahitian soil of Gauguin's paintings.
B. *sb.* **a.** A native or inhabitant of Tahiti. **b.** The Polynesian language spoken in Tahiti.
[**1822**: see the adj. above.] **1825** W. Ellis *Jrnl. Tour Hawaii* 49 He [*sc.* Ellis] could not help stating to them the striking identity between theirs [*sc.* their traditions] and those of the Tahitians. **1854** J. Crawfurd in C. Bunsen *Outl. Philos. Universal Hist.* I. 427 A sentence in the Maori and Tahitian can be written in words common to both. **1859** N. Wiseman *Twelve Lect. Sci. & Rev. Relig.* (ed. 6) I. 186 Charlevoix observed it among the Esquimaux,.. Wallis among the Tahitans. **1914** R. Brooke *Let.* Apr. (1968) 572 My Greek is something rusty. Had it been Tahitian now, or Fijian. **1918** L. Huxley *Life Sir J. D. Hooker* II. 483 He gratified Banks's philanthropic zeal by leaving in his care two Tahitians and two Maoris. **1957** P. Worsley *Trumpet shall Sound* i. 30 Sects including more or less of these elements have also appeared amongst the Tahitians. **1969** J. H. Vance *Deadly Isles* (1970) iii. 22 He would forget the songs and his few words of Tahitian. **1980** *London Mag.* July 24 Stevenson..and two Tahitians lolling among a pile of coconuts.

tahr (tāɹ). Now the usual spelling of Tehr. Substitute for def.: A wild goat of the genus *Hemitragus*, found in mountainous regions of southern Asia or Arabia, esp. *H. jemlahicus*, which has long brown fur and is native to the Himalayas. (Later examples.)
1902 *Little Folks* Apr. 282/1 The tahrs are true goats, though..they have no beard. Their home is..high up in the Himalaya Mountains. **1939** *Proc. Prehistoric Soc.* V. 52 A muscular development and agility in the feet commonly met with in the chamois,..the tahr and others of their kind. **1959** W. Thesiger *Arabian Sands* xiii. 256 The Arabian tahr had never previously been seen by a European. **1972** T. McHugh *Time of Buffalo* xvii. 200 And goats, sheep, and Himalayan tahrs stamp their front hoofs under similar circumstances [*sc.* in rut].

‖ **tahsil** (tāsī·l). Also **tehsil,** † **tuhseel.** [Urdu; cf. Tahsildar.] In India and Pakistan, an administrative division comprising several villages; formerly *spec.* a division made for purposes of revenue administration.
1846 *Directions for Collectors of Land Revenue N.W. Provinces* (India) App. VI. p. xxx, Comparing the tuhseel monthly accounts..with the cancelled dustuks. **1881** *Encycl. Brit.* XII. 769/2 Broadly speaking, the subdivision is characteristic of Bengal..and the *tahsil* of Madras. **1921** *Glasgow Herald* 19 Dec. 12 All district Congress Committees..must send out parties of about 20 Volunteers as a patrol daily in every town, tahsil, and village. **1944** Visct. Wavell *Let.* 7 Mar. in *Transfer of Power in India* (Foreign & Commonw. Office) (1973) IV. 784 Whilst I was at Nagpur I visited a village, a rural tahsil office, and a small irrigation work. **1954** O. H. K. Spate *India & Pakistan* p. xxiii, The States of India are divided (if large enough) into Divisions and these into Districts... Districts are subdivided into *taluks* (*taluqs*) or *tahsils* (*tehsils*) normally from 3 to 8 to a district. **1962** *Courier-Mail* (Brisbane) 14 Aug. 2/7 The four-tier scheme of basic democracies—at the village, tehsil, district and division levels. **1968** N. Mitchell *Sir G. Cunningham* v. 100 From 14th to 18th November he was touring on horseback in the Nowshera and Swabi Tahsils. **1971** *Illustr. Weekly India* 18 Apr. 7/2 A very senior and respected elder of our *tehsil* tried to stop me to ask me something. **1975** *Bangladesh Observer* 25 July 4/1 (Advt.), For Tahsil copy in the left hand side of the volume there will be a pocket.. for keeping maps.

tahsildar. Add: Now freq. with spelling **tehsildar.** (Later examples.) Also, the chief official of a tahsil.
1940 *Geogr. Jrnl.* XCV. 426 Khan Sahib Afraz Ghul Khan..is now tehsildar at Gilgit. **1954** J. Masters *Bhowani Junction* xxii. 191 That was a message from the tehsildar in Pathoda. **1972** *Times of India* 28 Nov. 1/2 The Mulki rules will apply only to non-gazetted posts and posts of tahsildar and civil assistant surgeons in the Telengana region. **1978** 'M. M. Kaye' *Far Pavilions* vi. 101 Ash had been given lodging for the night in the house of the *tehsildar*.

Tahunian (tahū·niăn), *a.* Also **Tahounian.** [ad. F. *Tahounien* (R. Neuville 1934, in *Revue Biblique* XLIII. 255), f. the place-name *Tahouneh*: see -ian.] Of, pertaining to, or designating a neolithic culture of Palestine represented by remains found at Tahouneh. Also *absol.*
1936 J. Garstang in *Annals Archaeol. & Anthropol.* XXII. 168 There seems to be no doubt that we are in the presence of a distinctive culture of the neolithic period. Whether it will be classed finally as Tahunian II is a matter for experts; meanwhile, as the Tahunian specimens are surface finds..we propose the more descriptive title 'Neo-Tahunian'. **1949** [see *Maglemosian *a.* and *sb.*]. **1952** V. G. Childe *New Light on Most Ancient East* xi. 225 By 1934 assemblages of flints from caves..had enabled Neuville to define a 'Tahunian' industry which could be classified as Neolithic. **1960** K. M. Kenyon *Archæol. in Holy Land* ii. 46 The flint industry which has for long been accepted as the classic Neolithic industry of Palestine is called the Tahunian. **1961** G. Clark *World Prehist.* iv. 82 The lithic industry in the upper Jericho level, with its pressure-flaked tanged arrowheads.. compares closely with that of the Tahounian. **1977** *Ibid.* (ed. 3) ii. 51 The Tahunian lithic component shows marked continuity, but one notable innovation in the form of flake arrows with side-notches.

tai (tai), *sb.*[1] [Jap.] Also † **tay.** A Pacific sea bream, *Pagrus major*, of the family Sparidæ, eaten as a speciality in Japan.
1620 R. Cocks *Let.* 10 Mar. in *Diary* (1883) II. 311 Dried fish lyke a breame, called heare *tay*, in aboundance. **1727** J. G. Scheuchzer tr. *Kæmpfer's Hist. Japan* I. i. 135 *Tai*, is what the Dutch in the Indies call *Steenbrassem*. This is very much esteem'd by the Japanese as the King of Fish. **1795** tr. *Thunberg's Trav.* IV. 39 Among their valuable fishes is what they call the *tay*. **1884** tr. *Rein's Japan* I. vii. 192 The Tai proper is a beautiful deep-red to brown-red gold-bream. **1920** [see *sashimi]. **1965** W. Swaan *Jap. Lantern* iii. 41 The deep red and rather bloody-looking *tai* (a type of sea bream).

Tai (tai), *sb.*[2] and *a.* Also **T'ai.** [Native name.] **A.** *sb.* **a.** (A member of) a group of peoples of southeast Asia which includes the Lao, Shan, and Thai; also *spec.* = *Thai *sb.* b. **b.** A group of languages including Thai (Siamese), Lao, Shan, and other languages of southeast Asia, regarded by some as belonging to the Sino-Tibetan family; also *spec.* = *Thai *sb.* a. Also *Comb.*, as *Tai Dam, Tai-Shan, Tai-Chinese* adj. and sb., *Tai Yai.*
1693 A. P. tr. *S. de la Loubère's New Hist. Relation Kingdom of Siam* I. i. ii. 6 The Siameses give to themselves the name of *Tai*, or free, as the word now signifies in their language. **1798** *Asiatick Researches* V. 227 The first dialect is that of the kingdom of Siam, the most polished people of eastern India. They called themselves to me simply Tai. **1811** *Ibid.* X. 241 He divides them into two races, the Tai and the Tai Yai. **1837** *Jrnl. Asiatic Soc. Bengal* VI. 18 The Ahom is a branch of the Tai language, which is spoken, with some variations, by the Khamtis, the Shyáns, the Láos, and the Siamese, all of whom designate themselves by the general appellation of Tai. Among the Ahoms, or the portion of the Tai race inhabiting *Assám*, the language is nearly extinct. *Ibid.*, The sound of the French *u*..is..common in the Tai. **1844** *Chinese Repository* XIII. 169 The inhabitants of this country are not called Siamese but T'ai. **1887** Tai-Shan [see *Mon-Khmer]. **1902** *Census of India 1901* XII. viii. 119 We are..practically where we were ten years ago in respect of our acquaintance with the early beginnings of the Tai. **1934** Webster, Tai-Chinese, *adj.* **1939** L. H. Gray *Foundations of Lang.* 389 The group [*sc.* Sino-Tibetan] falls into three great divisions: Yenisei-Ostyak, Tibeto-Burman, and Tai-Chinese. *Ibid.* 390 The other members of the Tai-Chinese family are Si-lo-mo.., Karen .., and Tai, the latter sub-divided into south-eastern, eastern, and northern. To the south-eastern division belong Siamese, Lao, Lü, and Khün. **1948** R. A. D. Forrest *Chinese Lang.* v. 100 There is evidence that T'ai in an older phase used a system of prefixes and infixes in word formation. **1956** J. Whatmough *Language* ii. 32 Note also Tai (Siamese). **1977** Tai Dam [see the adj. below]. **1978** *Amer. Poetry Rev.* Nov./Dec. 15/1 Judith Gautier's informant and lover was a Tai and often himself did not understand the Chinese.
B. *adj.* Of or pertaining to the Tai peoples or languages.
1837 [see the sb. above.] **1883** A. P. Phayre *Hist. Burma* i. 12 People of the Tai race were..in the country of the..river..Sâlwin; and there is evidence of an irruption of that people into the country of the Irâwadi. **1892** *Census of India 1891* IX. viii. 167 The Tai language, of which there are numerous dialects, is essentially a Polytonic language. *Ibid.* 202 A great wave of Tai migration descended. **1902** *Census of India 1901* XII. viii. 119 The classification of the Tai races is a task of far greater magnitude than appeared when the last census was taken. **1933** L. Bloomfield *Language* iv. 69 The second branch of Indo-Chinese is the *Tai* family, which includes *Siamese*. **1948** R. A. D. Forrest *Chinese Lang.* v. 98 The T'ai languages are remarkably uniform over their wide area. **1977** *New Yorker* 5 Sept. 40/3 Of the three groups..the best off were the Tai Dam..members of a Tai racial group that had settled in China many years ago.

‖ **taiaha** (ta,ī·aha). *N.Z.* [Maori.] A long-handled Maori club with a sharp tip. Also *fig.*
1845 E. J. Wakefield *Adventure N. Zealand* I. 140 The *taiaha* is rather a long-handled club than a spear. It ..is about six feet long. **1863** A. S. Atkinson *Jrnl.* 8 Sept. in *Richmond-Atkinson Papers* (1960) II. 61 The first of them was an old man with a handsome taiaha. **1894** *Westm. Gaz.* 29 Aug. 2/1 He looked his best in a picturesque native robe, with lurid feathers in his hair, and a 'taiaha', or spear, in his hand. **1938** R. D. Finlayson *Brown Man's Burden* 10 'Ae, we are one people!' he cries, brandishing a taiaha. **1949** P. Buck *Coming of Maori* (1950) ii. xi. 280 The *taiaha* head with its projecting tongue functioned as a stabbing point. **1963** S. Ashton-Warner *Teacher* 110 How can I protect my beautiful Matawhero from the taiaha of prejudice? **1974** *N.Z. Listener* 20 July 13/4 The Maori bus driver was 'threatened' with a friendly poke of the taiaha carried by another Maori.

‖ **T'ai Chi** (tai tʃī). Also **Tai Chi, t'ai chi,** etc. [ad. Chinese *tàijí*, f. *tài* extreme + *jí* limit.]
1. In Taoism and Neo-Confucianism, the Supreme Ultimate (see quot. 1955). Also, the symbol which represents this.
1736 R. Brookes tr. *Du Halde's Gen. Hist. China* III. 54 They give the first Principle of all things the Name of *Tai ki.* **1845** *Encycl. Metrop.* XVI. 568/2 *T'haï-kĭ* (the Great Summit) the soul of the universe, when in motion.. produced *Yang*, the living principle; when at rest, *Yn*, the dead principle, the one perfect and male, the other imperfect and female; from the union of which the elements sprang. **1914** D. T. Suzuki *Brief Hist. Early Chinese Philos.* 161 The term, *T'ai Chi*, first appears in one of the Confucian Appendices to the 'Yi Ching'. 'In the system of the Yi there is the Great Ultimate (or source or limit, *t'ai chi*).' **1931** A. U. Dilley *Oriental Rugs & Carpets* (caption to Pl. 63), The centre circle or Tae-keih (Great All) contains Yin (female) and Yang (male). **1955** E. Herbert *Taoist Notebk.* 3 *T'ai Chi* was presented as the starting-point, which was also the finishing-point, of a cosmic process: a cyclic process of constant change, in the course of which were produced in turn the linked principles of *Yang* and *Yin*..the *Wu Hsing* or Five Elements ..and all forms and existences in the material world. **1960** C. Winick *Dict. Anthropol.* 523/1 *T'ai chi*, in Chinese

art, the symbol of the Great Absolute. It consists of a wavy or double curved line bisecting a circle, one half of which is red..and the other black. **1962** E. SNOW *Other Side of River* (1963) l. 338 Tao is the Absolute that contains the total life force, or T'ai Chi.

2. In full *T'ai Chi Ch'uan* [Chinese *quán* fist], a Chinese martial art, believed to have been devised by a Taoist priest in the Sung dynasty (960–1279), promoting meditative as well as physical proficiency.

1962 E. SNOW *Other Side of River* (1963) ii. 24 Servants don't spend their idle time playing mah-jongg now but sit by the bell boards studying English or Russian, or other textbooks, getting ready for after-hours classes; or they do t'ai chi ch'uan calisthenics. **1968** *Times* 22 Nov. 9 Embrace Tiger and Return to Mountain it is called, this being the name of one exercise in T'ai-chi, a Chinese system of callisthenics claimed to produce pliability, health and peace of mind. **1972** DA LIU *T'ai Chi Ch'uan & I Ching* p. v, The movements of T'ai Chi Ch'uan and the hexagrams upon which they are based are both methods of describing the circulation of psychic energy in the body of the meditator. **1979** P. DRISCOLL *Pangolin* I. xx. 147 Kids were doing Tai Chi exercises and playing soccer.

Taig: see *TEAGUE 2.

taiga (tai·gă). [Russ.] The swampy coniferous forest area of Siberia; also, the zone of temperate coniferous forest stretching across Europe and North America.

1888 *Encycl. Brit.* XXIII. 70/2 They [*sc.* the Altai] are chiefly hunters, passionately loving their *taiga*, or wild forest. **1920** J. RITCHIE *Animal Life Scotl.* vi. 329 The typical pine forest region, or taiga. **1946** F. E. ZEUNER *Dating the Past* III. v. 122 Stunted forest of the taiga type may have played a larger part in preglacial Europe than is commonly assumed. **1957** *Times* 12 Nov. (Canada Suppl.) p. xvi/1 Northward..the timber attenuates into sub-Arctic forest (taiga) and finally gives way to the true Arctic tundra. **1964** *Listener* 12 Nov. 747/1 A huge artificial lake has been created, inundating thousands of square acres of the Siberian taiga, the endless forest of birches and firs and pines that covers southern Siberia. **1969** *Beaver* Summer 5/1 Stunted taiga forest, lakes, yellow-green marshes. **1974** T. P. WHITNEY tr. *Solzhenitsyn's Gulag Archipelago* I. I. ii. 24 *Before* it came the wave of 1929 and 1930, the size of a good River Ob, which drove a mere fifteen million peasants, maybe even more, out into the taiga and the tundra. **1980** *Jrnl. R. Soc. Arts* Feb. 140/1 These are generally described in terms of bioclimatic zones—arctic, tundra, taiga, boreal forest, temperate deciduous forests, prairies, desert savanna, and rain forest.

‖ **taihoa** (ta,iho·a), *int. N.Z.* Also **taiho.** [Maori.] Wait a bit; by and by; presently. Occas. *attrib.*

1842 W. R. WADE *Journey in N.Z.* iii. 66 'Taihoa.' This word has been translated, By and by; but in truth it has all the latitude of directly,—presently,—by and by,—a long time hence,—and nobody knows when. **1851** J. C. RICHMOND *Let.* Apr. in *Richmond-Atkinson Papers* (1960) I. ii. 90 Glad we were to pay off our Maori lad & be done with their provoking 'taiho!' 'waiho' (*presently wait*). **1881** J. L. CAMPBELL *Poenamo* v. 87 That irritatingly provoking word, 'taihoa'. **1905** J. M. THOMSON *Bush Boys N.Z.* xii. 170 Taisho, Mac. I'll be there in a minute. [Note] The bush-boy corruption of the Maori 'Taihoa', 'Wait a bit'. **1910** A. A. GRACE *Hone Tiki Dialogues* 4 There is too much taihoa about you Maoris. **1921** H. FOSTON *At Front* 188 Taking twelve years instead of five... It was described as a Taihoa policy. **1965** S. T. OLLIVIER *Petticoat Farm* i. 3 'Taihoa,' Harry said (it was the only Maori word he knew). 'Taihoa, I've not the money yet: wait until I have the money.'

tail, *sb.*[1] Add: **2. m.** The rear part of an aeroplane or air-balloon.

Except in the case of quot. 1804, the 19th-century examples refer to projected not actual aircraft.

1804 G. CAYLEY in C. H. Gibbs-Smith *Sir George Cayley's Aeronautics* (1962) vi. 18 This rod..supported a tail, made of two planes crossing each other at right angles... The tail could be set to any angle. **1835** *Nautical Mag.* IV. 612 An internal balloon is fitted for the purpose of ascending and descending at will, and the whole is intended to be propelled by fins, paddles, or wings we may call them... Finally the creature enjoys the important appendage of a tail abaft. **1848** *Chambers's Edin. Jrnl.* 6 May 302/2 There was also a tail, which, turning on a joint, was to direct the Ariel's flight. **1909** [see *FEATHERING *ppl.a.* c]. **1913** A. H. VERRILL *Harper's Aircraft Bk.* xi. 120 The parts of an aeroplane are mainly the frame, or 'chassis'; the body, or 'fuselage'; ..the rudder and tail;..and the control system. **1915** D. O. BARNETT *Let.* 13 June 176 Up went his tail, and he began going down in spirals. **1959** *Chambers's Encycl.* I. 99/1 Streamlining eliminates this feature of bluff sections, a narrow wake forming only as the tail is approached. **1978** J. GARDNER *Dancing Dodo* iv. 24 One [body] had been found towards where the tail and elevators should have been... The other had been taken from..the wreckage of the tail cone.

n. *Math.* An extremity of a curve, esp. that of a frequency distribution, as it approaches the horizontal axis of a graph; the part of a distribution that this represents.

1895 K. PEARSON in *Phil. Trans. R. Soc.* A. CLXXXVI. 397 We require to have the 'tail' as carefully recorded as the body of statistics. Unfortunately the practical collectors of statistics often..proceed by a method of 'lumping together' at the extremes of their statistical series. **1930** E. RUTHERFORD *Coll. Papers* (1965) III. 235 It is seen that the curve is very nearly symmetrical, but that there is a small 'tail' on the low-velocity side. **1980** K. RANDSBORG *Viking Age in Denmark* vii. 157 The Russian and Scandinavian finds of the ninth century have long tails of older coins.

3. Also (in *sing.* or *pl.*), the back part of a man's shirt that reaches below the waist. Also, in *pl.*, a tail-coat; a dress suit with tail-coat.

1845, etc. [see *shirt-tail* s.v. *SHIRT *sb.* 5 c]. **1857, 18..** [in Dict.]. **1915** MRS. H. WARD *Eltham House* ii. 23 You made up your mind from the time you got into tails at Eton. **1932** S. GIBBONS *Cold Comfort Farm* i. 10 Charles looked well in tails. **1958** B. NICHOLS *Sweet & Twenties* 110 Young men wore tails and white ties as a matter of course. **1960** *Guardian* 16 Dec. 8/3 At balls, even in the London season, tails are not uncompromisingly de rigueur. **1965** R. P. JHABVALA *Backward Place* iii. 166 He ran after her into the street, the tails of his crumpled shirt flying as he ran.

4. c. Also *spec.*, the non-combatant personnel of an armed service or of a military unit.

1946 *Hansard Commons* 30 Oct. 690 Our job must be to secure an efficient fighting force in which the tail is kept as short as possible, and the teeth as long and as keen as possible. **1950** *Ibid.* 26 July 555 If one is to provide an operational division,..the tail cannot be avoided, otherwise the division is not operational at all. **1961** B. FERGUSON *Watery Maze* vii. 159 As 'Teeth' troops (to use a phrase which was then [*sc.* in 1942] both new and picturesque, but has long since become a *cliché*) there was little to equal them; but they lacked a 'Tail'—those ancillaries which in modern war virtually wag the dog **1972** D. BLOODWORTH *Any Number can Play* xiii. 116 When a soldier moves, all his basic needs are looked after by a vast administrative tail that..clothes him, feeds him, transports him. **1977** *R.A.F. News* 30 Mar.–12 Apr. 7/2 It is possible to continue trimming the so-called 'tail' by successive cuts in defence expenditure.

† **m.** A small evening party, subsequent to a dinner or a ball. *Obs.*

1837 C. RIDLEY *Let.* in *Cecilia* (1958) 26 We went to Lady Domville's—the nicest ball I have been at this year. .. We afterwards went to a tail where we saw a collection of unwashed uncombed philosophers. **1912** G. W. E. RUSSELL *One Look Back* viii. 164 'Tails', as the name implies, were little parties tacked on to the end of big dinners, where a few people looked in, rather cross at not having been invited to dine, or else in a desperate hurry to get on to a larger party or a ball.

n. *Phonetics.* (See quot. 1922.)

1922 H. E. PALMER *Eng. Intonation* iv. 10 Any syllable or syllables following the nucleus in the same Tone-Group is termed the 'Tail' of the group. The Tail-syllable or group of syllables following the Falling Nucleus..is pitched on the low level. **1965** *Amer. Speech* XL. 72 Word order affects intonation in the tail, head, and nucleus.

o. The rear part of a motor vehicle.

1928 E. WALLACE *Double* xiii. 187 Outside he saw five police cars parked bonnet to tail. **1975** *Drive* New Year 106/3 The car's tail tends to drift out of corners at lower speeds than earlier models.

5. a. Also in U.S. dial. and colloq. use.

1935 J. T. FARRELL *Judgment Day* in *Studs Lonigan* (1938) iv. 86 This idea of sweating your tail off with work ..is the undiluted crap. **1942** W. FAULKNER *Go down, Moses* 229 This is the first time you've had your tail out of that kitchen since we got here except to chop a little wood. **1969** *New Yorker* 14 June 72/3 Go out there and work your tail off. Don't wake up tomorrow morning regretting that you didn't give a hundred per cent. **1976** *Billings* (Montana) *Gaz.* 1 July 4-E/1, I worked my tail off to help win a pennant for the Dodgers.

c. (Later examples.)

1972 F. WARNER *Lying Figures* III. 17 Give her her head..and she'll give you her tail. **1977** *Transatlantic Rev.* LX. 78 He had been after her tail for months, but Judy, being an old-fashioned girl, declined his advances.

d. *slang.* † (i) a prostitute (*obs.*); (ii) women regarded collectively (by men) as a means of sexual gratification; sexual intercourse; a sexual partner. Freq. in phr. *a piece* (or *bit*) *of tail.* Cf. *PIECE *sb.* 3 d.

1846 *Swell's Night Guide* 58, I takes my pitch last night on Fleet pave, then..a swell was sweet on me for a tail. **1869** F. HENDERSON *Six Yrs. in Prisons of Eng.* vii. 76 He meant a 'flash-tail', or prostitute who goes about the streets at nights trying to pick up 'toffs'. **1933** M. LOWRY *Ultramarine* ii. 67 It's not as though you were a bloody man who'd been having a bit of tail. **1942,** etc. [see *PIECE *sb.* 3 d]. **1951** J. D. SALINGER *Catcher in Rye* xiii. 109 Innarested in a little tail t'night? **1953** H. MILLER *Plexus* (1963) xi. 391 He's at loose ends. Hates his work, loathes his wife, and the kids bore him to death. All he thinks of now is tail. And boy, does he chase it! **1967** J. POTTER *Foul Play* xiii. 157 Where's all the tail today? No Hermione, no Bunty, no Christabel. **1976** 'R. GORDON' *Doctor on Job* vi. 59 Even if it was deciding whether to go out on the booze at night or have a bit of tail off of the wife. **1977** *Transatlantic Rev.* LX. 39 He would yell, 'How y'all doin, chief? Gettin much tail?'

6. b. A person (as a detective or spy, etc.) who secretly follows and observes another. Also *collect.*, people in the act of following. Cf. *TAG *sb.*[1] 12*, *TAIL *v.*[1] 5 b. *colloq.* (orig. *U.S.*).

1914 [see *TAIL *v.*[1] 5 b]. **1933** A. MERRITT *Burn Witch Burn!* (1934) xii. 181 One of the tails—one of the lads who's been looking—meets up with me. **1940** R. STOUT *Over my Dead Body* xiv. 215 'Yes, we were having Miss Lovchen followed?' 'Yes, a double tail... Their instructions are to report in every two hours.' **1955** J. CANNAN *Long Shadows* iii. 63 I'd like to put a tail on the lady. **1962** 'K. ORVIS' *Damned & Destroyed* v. 42, I realized almost at once I'd picked up a tail. The two shadowing me..were..obvious. **1978** M. H. CLARK *Stranger is Watching* xxvi. 112 We'll have a loose tail on you—an agent following you from a distance.

8. a. *spec.* in *Cricket*, the lower end of the batting order, comprising the weaker batsmen in a team; (earlier and later examples). Also *fig.*

1851 J. PYCROFT *Cricket Field* xi. 221 Never put in all your best men at first, and leave 'a tail' to follow. **1879** *James Lillywhite's Cricketers' Ann.* 17 The tail was again weak, the last five wickets only adding 16 runs. **1913** J. B. HOBBS *How to make Century* xii. 82 The fast bowler.. was bowling far too accurately for 'tail' batsmen to do much with him. **1926** C. E. MONTAGUE *Rough Justice* III. ix. 125 They seemed to be talking about the conflict then arising between the House of Lords and the..House of Commons. 'If it comes to a Test Match,' said Wynnant, 'we'll lose. Too long a tail to our team.' **1955** *Times* 4 July 3/2 Due..to the obstinate wriggling of the tail, the last four Cambridge wickets more than doubled the score. **1977** J. LAKER *One-Day Cricket* 67 Marsh, with no support at all from the tail, was left high and dry with 52 not out.

11. b. (Earlier *fig.* example.)

1842 F. A. KEMBLE *Let.* 6 May in *Rec. Later Life* (1882) II. 218 She has scornfully..departed with her tail over her shoulder, leaving the behind scenes of Her Majesty's Theatre with their tails between their legs.

e. *to get one's tail down* and varr., to become dispirited; *to have one's tail up* and varr., to be in good spirits.

1853 'P. PAXTON' *Stray Yankee in Texas* 97 To use an expressive Westernism, 'Dave's tail was up', and every possible preparation was made to preclude a failure. **1874** HOTTEN *Slang Dict.* 318 *Tail-down*, 'to get the tail down', generally means to lose courage. When a professional at any game loses heart in a match he is said to get his *tail down*. 'His *tail* was quite *down*, and it was all over.' **1917** G. S. GORDON *Let.* 26 Apr. (1943) 75 We were getting jaded till this touch of spring came, and now we have our tails up again, and are prepared to attack anything. **1921** *Punch* 12 Jan. 23, I must try and keep my tail up. **1923** GALSWORTHY *Captures* 190 He was a Northumbrian.. and his 'tail still up', as he expressed it. **1928** *Sunday Dispatch* 15 July 14, I sincerely hope that..standard producers..will not get their tails down over this 'cheap record boom'. **1933** WODEHOUSE *Mulliner Nights* iii. 93 'Tails up, Uncle Theodore, tails up!' 'Tails up!' repeated the Bishop dutifully, but he spoke the words without any real ring of conviction in his voice. **1941** C. MORGAN *Empty Room* II. 88 May be a snag somewhere. Usually is when one gets one's tail up about an idea. **1960** [see *BALANCE *sb.* 15 c]. **1978** R. MARK *Office of Constable* xv. 187 Nevertheless, in dealing with the worst forms of crime our tails were well up.

f. *two shakes of a lamb's tail* (and varr.): see *SHAKE *sb.*[1] 2 h.

a **1855** J. F. KELLY *Humors of Falconbridge* (1856) 137 In the wag of a dead lamb's tail. **1901** *Dialect Notes* II. 142 'I'll do it in three jerks of a lamb's tail,' i.e., very quickly. *Ibid.* 429 She got all cleared up in the whisk of a lamb's tail. **1917** *Ibid.* IV. 402 *Two jerks of a lamb's tail*, *n. phr.*, an instant, a jiffy.

g. *the tail wags the dog*, the less important or subsidiary factor dominates the situation; the proper roles are reversed.

[**1907** M. A. VON ARNIM *Fräulein Schmidt* xxvi. 84 Isn't it rather weak to let yourself be led round by the nose..? It is as though instead of a dog wagging its tail the tail should wag the dog.] **1935** F. SCOTT FITZGERALD *Let.* 11 Mar. (1964) 260 This letter is a case of the tail (the parenthesis) wagging the dog. **1945** *Jrnl. R. Aeronaut. Soc.* XLIX. 463/1 The aeroplane developing an undamped short period oscillation in which rapid movement of the rudder from side to side plays an essential part—the tail wagging the dog. **1956** W. H. WHYTE *Organization Man* ii. 19 The tail wagged the dog in this case and it still often does. **1968** *Listener* 4 Jan. 23/3 Most producers are going to continue resisting..indulgence in an academic exercise. There's a danger of the tail wagging the dog. **1980** *Truck & Bus Transportation* (Surry Hills, New South Wales) Feb. 26/2 Tractor response during a lane-change manoeuvre shows how the externally-applied force through the fifth wheel induces tractor lateral motion. This is better known as 'tail wagging the dog'.

h. *to be on someone's tail* and varr., to follow or pursue someone closely (see also quot. 1925). Also *fig.*

[**1865** 'L. CARROLL' *Alice's Adventures in Wonderland* x. 151 There's a porpoise close behind us, and he's treading on my tail.] **1925** FRASER & GIBBONS *Soldier & Sailor Words* 275 *Tail, to get on the*, an Air Force expression for an attack on the rear of an opponent. **1937** PARTRIDGE *Dict. Slang* 860/2 *Tail, be*—gen. *shall* or *will be—on a person's*, to look for, to pursue, a person with a view to punishing or severely scolding him: C. 20. **1962** 'J. LE CARRÉ' *Murder of Quality* iv. 54, I rather gathered ..that his Chief Constable was treading on his tail, urging him to scour the country for tramps. **1971** B. MALAMUD *Tenants* 71, I wouldn't want anybody else on my tail or in my hair, with or without cause. **1971** M. TAK *Truck Talk* 154 *Stay on his tail*, to follow another truck closely. **1981** *Sunday Times* 1 Feb. 63/5 Sir Hugh thought the Lonrho boss had put a private eye on his tail.

i. *to chase one's tail*, to indulge in a futile pursuit; to go round in circles.

1963 *Times* 14 May 8/4 'We have been chasing our tails overlong,' he said. 'Given a Labour Government committed to the principles of equity and justice, a coordinated wages policy may be possible.' **1973** *Archivum Linguisticum* IV. 35 Is anything indeed to be gained from hunting for some notion embodying the cumulate surface exponency of..transitive and perfective..? It is all too easy at times to chase our conceptual tail.

12. a. *tail half* (later example), *-wind* (later *Aeronaut.* examples).

1970 T. HUGHES *Crow* 15 He stuffed the head half head-first into woman And it crept in deeper and up to peer out through her eyes Calling its tail-half to join up quickly. **1927** C. A. LINDBERGH *We* iii. 39, I left Tex-arkana with a strong tail wind. **1976** *Evening Times* (Glasgow) 1 Dec. 5/3 Tail winds across the Atlantic knocked up to an hour off the flying times of some trans-atlantic flights.

13. a. *tail-tuft*; **b.** *tail-buffeting, -chasing* (examples), *-dangler, -wagger*; **c.** *tail-down* adj. and adv.; *tail-first*: also as adj.

1931 *Flight* 30 Jan. 90 To the new phenomenon the sub-committee gives the name 'tail buffeting'. **1947** *Times* 8 Feb. 2/5 There was tail-buffeting within a certain speed range in very bumpy conditions. **1921** J. D. M. RORKE *Musical Pilgrim's Progress* III. 49 The excitement and tail-chasing demonstrations of a dog at the home-coming. **1957** R. H. SMYTHE *Conformation of Dog* 123 Tail-chasing, spinning and walking in circles. **1922** JOYCE *Ulysses* 646 It [*sc.* a horse] was a..taildangler, a headhanger. **1916** H. BARBER *Aeroplane Speaks* 87 An inclinometer..which will indicate a nose-down position by increase in air speed, and a tail-down position by decrease in air speed. *Ibid.* 113 If the angle of incidence..is too great, it will produce an excess of lift, and that way..result in a tendency to fly 'tail-down'. **1935** P. W. F. MILLS *Elem. Pract. Flying* vii. 103 When brought too quickly into tail-down attitude their wings retain an uncomfortable degree of buoyancy for some little time. **1914** H. M. BUIST *Aircraft in German War* v. 101 The latter quality lead to the original example of this tail-first machine being purchased by the Ruman-ian Army. **1945** *Sun* (Baltimore) 7 Feb. 7-0/4 (*heading*) New 'tail-first' fighter plane appears to fly backward. **1910** W. DE LA MARE *Three Mulla-Mulgars* xvii. 224 They sat, with tail-tufts over their shoulders. *a* **1930** D. H. LAWRENCE *Last Poems* (1932) 260 The two lions who devoured one another, and left the tail-tufts wagging. **1948** B. VESEY-FITZGERALD *Bk. of Dog* I. 114 Organisa-tions, such as the Tail Waggers Club, undertake to provide discs that can be attached to the collar. **1952** *Chambers's Jrnl.* Apr. 239/1, I reckon that about 3,000,000 folk would have to look elsewhere for their bread and butter if there were no trawlermen—or fish. We mustn't forget the tail-waggers. **1982** L. CODY *Bad Company* iii. 26 'What's this then? The Tail-Waggers Club? he asked as he..fended off the retriever's enthusiastic welcome.

14. tail-area *Statistics*, an area under the curve of a frequency distribution lying be-tween one end of the curve and any ordinate on the same side of the mode; **tail assembly** [*ASSEMBLY 1 c] *Aeronaut.* = *EMPENNAGE; cf. *tail unit* below; **tailback:** in U.S. football, the player stationed farthest from the for-wards; **tail boom** *Aeronaut.*, one of the main spars of the longitudinal framework carrying the tail of an aeroplane when not supported by the fuselage; **tail comb,** a comb with a tapering tail or handle used in styling to lift, divide, or curl the hair; **tail cone** *Aeronaut.*, the conical rear end of the fuselage of an air-craft; **tail-dragger** *Aeronaut.*, an aeroplane that lands and taxis on a tail wheel or tail skid, its nose off the ground; **tail fin,** (*a*) the caudal fin of a fish; (*b*) *Aeronaut.* (see quot. 1940); (*c*) an upswept ornamental projection forming a continuation of the fender line at the rear of a motor vehicle; **tail-flap,** (*a*) the tail of a crustacean; (*b*) *Aeronaut.*, an adjust-able control surface on the tail of an aircraft; **tail gas** (see quot. 1967); **tail gunner** = *rear gunner* s.v. *REAR *sb.*[3] (and *a.*[1]) 9; **tail-heavy** *a.*, of a motor vehicle, boat, etc.: having a tendency for the rear end to bear down more than the front; hence **tail-heaviness** (used esp. with reference to aircraft); **tail-light** (examples with reference to motor vehicles and aircraft); **tail parachute** *Aeronaut.*, a deceleration parachute attached to the tail of an aircraft; **tail-pin,** (*d*) *Mus.* (i) (see quot. 1961); (ii) a metal spike attached to the cello and other instruments to support them at the correct height from the ground; **tailplane** *Aeronaut.*, the horizontal stabilizing surface of the tail of an aircraft; **tail-pole,** a wooden lever or turning beam by means of which a post- or windmill is turned to the wind; **tail-rime, -rhyme** (examples); **tail rotor** *Aeronaut.*, an auxiliary rotor at the tail of a helicopter designed to counterbalance the torque of the main rotor; **tail-shaft** (earlier example); †**tail-shot** = *tail-ill* (*obs.*); so †**tail-shotten** *a.*; **tail skid** [*SKID *sb.* 2 f] *Aeronaut.*, that part of an aircraft's landing gear which supports its tail; **tail-slide** *Aeronaut.* (see quot. 1969); **tail-twisting,** (*c*) in gen. *fig.* use, harassment or malicious annoyance; **tail unit** *Aeronaut.* = *EMPEN-NAGE; **tail-walking,** the movement of fish over the surface of water by means of pro-pulsion with the tail; hence (as a back-formation) **tail-walk** *v. intr.*; **tail wheel** *Aeronaut.* = *tail skid* above.

1957 KENDALL & BUCKLAND *Dict. Statistical Terms* 290 Tail area (of a Distribution). **1971** D. C. HAGUE *Mana-gerial Economics* vii. 153 If we want to take the probability of there being less than 2 in of rain, we take the area of the first two bars [of the histogram], and so on. If we do this, we are said to be considering tail areas. **1968** *Globe & Mail* (Toronto) 3 Feb. 1/2 The wreckage was a compacted heap of rubble... Only the tail assembly was intact. **1977** J. CLEARY *High Road to China* iv. 128 The plane quivered.. then the nose came up, the quivering slid out through the tail-assembly. **1930** R. C. ZUPPKE *Coaching Football* vii. 208 The tail-back is four and one-half yards back of the scrummage line and directly back of the fullback. **1980** *Washington Post* 10 Oct c6/5 Of the six Rattler touch-downs Keith pointed out FAMU 'earned' only one: the 69-yard first-quarter run by tailback Archie Jones. **1913** *Flight* 23 Aug. 927/1 One of our sketches shows the method of joining the struts to the tail booms. **1969** K. MUNSON *Pioneer Aircraft 1903–14* 142/1 The three tubular steel tailbooms formed a triangular section, and the tail control wires were led through the uppermost boom, which also acted as a propeller bearing. **1782** J. WOOD-FORDE *Diary* 24 Apr. (1926) II. 19 To a Tail Comb and another Comb for Nancy of Baker pd. 0. 0. 10. **1855** F. DUBERLY *Let.* 22 July in E. E. P. Tisdall *Mrs. Duberly's Campaigns* (1963) v. 153 Oh, please will you send me a tail comb in the box. **1907** *Yesterday's Shopping* (1969) 110/1 Tail or curling combs—buffalo horn. **1930** V. SACK-VILLE-WEST *Edwardians* i. 38 Don't drag my hair back... Give me the tail comb... It wants more fullness at the sides. **1976** J. GRENFELL *Joyce Grenfell requests Pleasure* xvii. 246 Her dark hair was kept neat in a fine net... A tail-comb raised the waves. **1944** H. F. GREGORY *Any-thing a Horse can Do* xxi. 216 The tail rotor and approxi-mately the last four feet of the tail cone were broken completely. **1978** Tail cone [see sense 2 m above]. **1971** *Flying* Apr. 39/2 If you trace the 172 back to the rag-wing 170 taildragger of 1948. **1981** *R.A.F. News* 14 Jan. 12/3 The Chipmunk is well suited to the unit's role be-cause, as a taildragger, it introduces characteristics that 'sort out the men from the boys'. **1681, 1835–6** Tail fin in Dict., sense 13 a]. **1940** *Chambers's Techn. Dict.* 333/1 *Fin*, in an aeroplane, a fixed vertical surface giving lateral stability of motion; usually placed at the tail, then sometimes called a tail fin. **1945** W. LANGEWIESCHE *Stick & Rudder* vii. 115 The purpose of the horizontal tail fin is not to hold the tail up, but to hold it down; it is a sort of wing, but a wing set at a negative Angle of Attack. **1954** *Wall St. Jrnl.* 22 Oct. 16/6 Its [*sc.* the car's] high fender-line sweeps backward in a straight line but is slightly lower at the tail fins than at the headlights. **1974** P. DICKINSON *Poison Oracle* i. 22 The plane lay still... The symbol of the rising sun stared from the tall tail fin. **1982** *Quarto* Mar. 7/4 The American family car was a 425-horsepower, twenty-two-foot-long Buick Electra with tail fins in back. **1847–8** Tail-flap [in Dict., sense 13 a]. **1913** A. E. BERRIMAN *Aviation* p. xxiv, The glide..as the pilot switches on at the last moment and cocks up the tail flap to flatten out ere touching the ground. **1980** J. DITTON *Copley's Hunch* II. i. 115 The tail-flaps were working all right, because he zoomed up and over to gain height. **1948** *Economist* 31 July 193/2 Tail gases..carried ..by pipe-line..will replace some of the coke at present used..for the production of ammonia, methanol and petrol. **1967** *Gloss. Terms Gas Industry* (*B.S.I.*) 12 *Tail gas*, refinery gas which is not required for further pro-cessing in the refinery. **1939** *War Illustr.* 29 Dec. 539/2 The tail gunner reported 'Fighters on our tail'. **1971** P. O'DONNELL *Impossible Virgin* xii. 246 A bloke called Worsfold, tail-gunner in a Lancaster during the war..fell over seven thousand feet... Only broke a leg and a few ribs. **1919, 1930** Tail-heaviness [see *nose-heaviness* s.v. *NOSE *sb.* 18]. **1977** D. BEATY *Excellency* vi. 83 The tail-heaviness had been deliberate..this ingenious way of getting rid of him. **1916** H. BARBER *Aeroplane Speaks* 110 The aeroplane will, in flight, be nose-heavy or tail-heavy. **1923** G. STURT *Wheelwright's Shop* 223 *Tail-heavy*, the opposite fault to fore-heavy. In a tail-heavy cart the tendency was to lift the horse off the ground. **1957** [see *SCORCH *v.*[1] 3]. **1978** R. V. JONES *Most Secret War* xvi. 131 The weight of two cameras, about 120 lbs., would pull back the centre of gravity of the aircraft making it 'tail heavy' and dangerous to fly. **1937** *Esquire* Jan. 64/3 He turned and watched the red tail-light sink into the distant darkness. **1946** R. A. MCFARLAND *Human Factors in Air Transport Design* xii. 610 The pilot..had.. mistaken the taillight of the stationary D.C.-3 for one of a row of ..boundary lights. **1978** S. BRILL *Teamsters* vii. 286 Only one man was working the night shift, replacing some tail lights on a trailer. **1937** *Jrnl. R. Aeronaut. Soc.* XLI. 731 The Russian plane A.N.T.6 which was the first to land at the pole was provided with a tail parachute, which was released as soon as the skis touched the ice. **1978** A. WELCH *Bk. of Airsports* ii. 29/2 Tail parachutes are 'one-shot' drag producers and are more useful as an emergency aid. **1884** E. HERON-ALLEN *Violin-Making* xi. 195 The *Tail-pin*..is the peg of ebony or box-wood, which is firmly fixed into the bottom block..to which is fastened the loop..of the tail-piece. **1923** E. VAN DER STRAETEN *Technics Violoncello Playing* (ed. 4) iii. 18 The use of the tail pin is now generally adopted, and offers the double advantage of steadying the instrument and strengthening its tone. **1946** R. ALTON *Violin & 'Cello Building* vii. 60 The tail-rest..over which the tail-gut passes on its way to the tail-pin, must now be inserted. *Ibid.* xv. 147 With a tapered reamer fit the tail-pin into its place, gradually enlarging the hole until the tail-pin fits. **1961** A. BAINES *Mus. Instr. through Ages* 358 *Tailpin*, the button let into the bottom block of a violin, etc., to which the tailpiece is attached by a gut loop. **1978** *Early Music* Oct. 530/2 My own contribution to this debate..is concerned with thicknesses and struttings, lengths and positions of necks, bridge heights and string angles and tailpin hitches. **1909** A. BERGET *Conquest of Air* II. iv. 189 Tail planes. **1911** [see *EMPENNAGE]. **1948** 'N. SHUTE' *No Highway* i. 8 It had only been necessary to break one of these expensive tailplanes for the strength tests for the airworthiness of the machine. **1979** D. KYLE *Green River High* xvii. 219, I tested the tailplane's firmness to be sure it would take my weight. **1945** *Archit. Rev.* XCVIII. 71 This 'winding' of the mill was first accomplished by push-ing the whole body of a post mill round by means of the 'tail pole', which projected downwards through the ladder. **1968** J. ARNOLD *Shell Bk. Country Crafts* 170 The problem of keeping the sweeps or sails into the wind was originally met by manual labour at the 'tail-pole', or turning beam. **1838** E. GUEST *Hist. Eng. Rhythms* II. IV. i. 289 This, like the interwoven and tail-rhime, seems to have been first used by the Latinist. **1916** J. E. WELLS *Man. Writings Middle Eng.* I. 86 Lines 3411 to the end are in tail-rime stanzas. **1945** Tail-rhyme [see *RIME *sb.*[1] 2 e]. **1982** *N. & Q.* June 242/2 With certain common patterns, of couplets, quatrains, and versions of the tail-rhyme stanza, predominating. **1944** H. F. GREGORY *Any-thing a Horse can Do* x. 107 The control stick..would decrease the pitch of the blades on the right horizontal tail rotor. **1979** *Jrnl. R. Soc. Arts* CXXVII. 571/1 The helicopter for replacement of Sea King is rather a noisy beast, in that it has a tailrotor. **1888** KIPLING *Day's Work* (1898) 277 When d'ye ship a new tail-shaft? **1790** J. WOODFORDE *Diary* 5 Feb. (1927) III. 169 My poor Cow rather better this morning, but not able to get up as yet, she having a Disorder which I never heard of before or any of our Somersett Friends. It is called Tail-shot, that is, a separation of some of the Joints of the Tail about a foot from the tip of the Tail, or rather a slipping of one Joint from another. **1798** *Ibid.* 1 Aug. (1931) V. 130 She is tail-shotten, & hath something of the Gargut. **1913** A. E. BERRIMAN *Aviation* iii. 25 The tail-skid is com-paratively an insignificant member of the design: provided it serves its purpose as a protection. **1973** J. D. R. RAWLINGS *Pictorial Hist. Fleet Air Arm* ii. 18 The fourth broke his tailskid and had to abort the sortie. **1916** H. BARBER *Aeroplane Speaks* ii. 73 Should the surface tend to assume too large an angle..the pressure D decreases, with the result that C.P. moves forward and pushes up the front of the surface, thus increasing the angle still further, the final result being a 'tail-slide'. **1969** *Gloss. Aeronaut. & Astronaut. Terms* (*B.S.I.*) II. 2 *Tail slide*, rearward motion of an aircraft along its longitudinal axis from a vertical or near vertical, stalled attitude. **1887** KIPLING *Plain Tales* (1888) 77 The Colonel's Wife..went away to devise means for 'chastening the stubborn heart of her husband'. Which, translated, means, in our slang, 'tail-twisting'. **1937** E. LINKLATER *Juan in China* ii. 58 He had no reason to feel friendly..and the idea of a little tail-twisting was pleasant. **1982** W. J. BURLEY *Wycliffe's Wild-Goose Chase* vi. 110 If there is any attempt at tail twisting you can rely on me to see 'em off. **1926** *Chambers's Jrnl.* Aug. 580/1 In every aeroplane the tail unit..comprises the rudder [etc.]. **1977** D. BEATY *Excel-lency* i. 8 A lot of junk..six DC6 wheels, a Viscount tail unit. **1971** W. HILLEN *Blackwater River* viii. 72 The trout leaped, tail-walked, shook himself, leaped again, and ran past the raft for deep water. **1979** *Angling* July 53/2 A fish hits the bait. It runs, leaps, tail-walks. **1946** *Rich-mond* (Va.) *Times-Dispatch* 16 June 12-B/2 Oh yes, there are certain salt-water fish which do a certain kind of tail-walking, but the way the bass performs these antics is peculiar to himself. **1970** *Islander* (Victoria, B.C.) 25 Oct. 3/3 Out in the salt-chuck where he [*sc.* a salmon] has a whole ocean to play in you can expect to see some fancy tail-walking. **1910** R. FERRIS *How it Flies* xx. 472 *Tail wheel*, a wheel mounted under the rear end of an aero-plane as a part of the alighting gear. **1933** *Jrnl. R. Aeronaut. Soc.* XXXVII. 29 But with the advent of tail wheels, that difficulty should not arise. **1981** *Pilot* Jan. 12/2 A 110 hp tailwheel model.

tail, *sb.*[2] Add: **3. b.** *tail male, female*: also *transf.*, the line of descent of dogs or horses, considering either the male or female ances-tors.

1926 EARL BATHURST *Breeding of Foxhounds* vii. 96 The top line perhaps may be considered important, for it represents the descent in tail-male. *Ibid.* 99 The Bruce-Lowe system..is..the importance of the female line, or 'tail-female'. **1931** *Times Lit. Suppl.* 23 Apr. 325/2 His blood is to be found in most of our 'classic' winners, and in tail female it never waned. **1957** C. LEICESTER *Blood-stock Breeding* ix. 144 This..leaves untouched the tail female line, i.e. the dam, grandam, etc. of the animal under investigation. **1972** *Country Life* 10 Feb. 332/1 One of Whipcord's descendants was the famous Four Burrow Pleader '38, whose ancestry can be traced..on his tail female to Mr. Darley's Damsel..and on tail male (through Whipcord) to the Brockelsby Bumper, 1748.

tail, *v.*[1] Add: **I. 5. a.** Also in N.Z. and with reference to horses.

1852 J. R. CLOUGH *Jrnl.* 29 Feb. in J. Deans *Pioneers of Canterbury* (1939) 291, I have had to tail the cattle on foot this five weeks as I have had no saddle. **1871** C. L. MONEY *Knocking about in N.Z.* ix. 133 The horses, after being 'tailed', or shepherded, all day by one of us.., were tied in rows..for the night.

b. To follow someone closely; *spec.* to follow secretly as a detective or spy, etc. Cf. *TAG *v.*[1] 4 b, *TAIL *sb.*[1] 6 b. *colloq.* (orig. *U.S.*).

1907 *Everybody's Mag.* Mar. 341/2 Detectives were assigned to 'tail' him. **1914** JACKSON & HELLYER *Vocab. Criminal Slang* 83 *Tail, verb.* General circulation. To trail; to follow. Used as a noun in the same sense. **1925** E. WALLACE *Strange Countess* ix. 81 'What's your idea in tailing me?'..' "Tailing"? Oh, you mean following you, I suppose?' **1950** D. HYDE *I Believed* viii. 88 For some months I was tailed by a curious assortment of police agents. **1956** S. PLATH in *Granta* 20 Oct. 22/2 Ben tailed us out to the kitchen, where the black old gas stove was, and the sink, full of dirty dishes. **1966** T. PYNCHON *Cry-ing of Lot 49* v. 130 Oedipa gave him half a block's start, then began to tail him. **1978** S. BRILL *Teamsters* iv. 127 I'm not gonna let you tail me like some kinda cop. **1978** G. GREENE *Human Factor* v. iii. 278 Castle led the way down the stairs to the cellar. Buller followed him and Mr Halliday tailed Buller.

9*. *slang.* To copulate with (a woman).

1778 in Weis & Pottle *Boswell in Extremes* (1971) 248

When we talk of *pleasure*, we mean sensual pleasure. When a man says he had pleasure with a woman, he does not mean conversation, but that he *tailed* her. **1846** *Swell's Night Guide* 133/2 *Tail*, to cohabit with women. **1973** J. Wainwright *Devil you Don't* 51 So, I tailed his wife... So what?

III. 19. c. (Earlier example.)

1830 A. Sedgwick *Let.* 21 Nov. in J. W. Clark *Life A. Sedgwick* (1890) I. 366 Many men will tail off, if they have an excuse.

21. The vb.-stem in Comb. **tail-back**, a queue of stationary or slowly moving motor vehicles; **tail-off** *colloq.*, a decline or tapering off of demand, etc.; a period of this.

1975 D. Lodge *Changing Places* v. 188 They hit a tailback of rush-hour traffic in the Midland Road. **1978** *Times* 26 July 8/3 One of the worst traffic jams in living memory with tailbacks of several miles. **1975** D. Francis *High Stakes* vii. 109 There would be at first a patch of sporadic success..and then a long tail-off with no success at all. **1984** *Times* 15 Feb. 20/7 Laurie Millbank does not envisage any tail off in demand.

tail, *v.*[3] (Earlier Canad. example.)

1770 G. Cartwright *Jrnl.* 27 Aug. (1792) I. 30, I tailed a couple of traps for otters, but did not find many rubbing places.

tail-end. Add: **1. a.** (Earlier and later examples.)

1747 H. Glasse *Art of Cookery* ix. 92 Take a large Eel, ..cut it into four Pieces, take the Tail-end, [etc.]. **1917** 'Contact' *Airman's Outings* viii. 214 V., my pilot and flight-commander, was given to a quick dive at the enemy,..and another dash to close grips from an unexpected direction, while I guarded the tail-end.

d. *Cricket.* = *tail *sb.*[1] 8 a. Freq. *attrib.*

1888 A. G. Steel in Steel & Lyttelton *Cricket* iii. 176 The tail end of a team are usually victims to a good straight fast bowler. **1904** [in Dict., sense 1 a]. **1930** *Morning Post* 16 July 11/5 He had batted on three different days, and had shown ability and courage. He can never in future be regarded as a tail-end batsman. **1955** *Times* 13 July 3/2 With the first ball of his next Smales bowled Smith, who had..looked the one man likely to deprive Nottinghamshire of a win with tail-end wickets falling fast. **1976** *0–10 Cricket Scene* (Austral.) 15/1 He.. then routed Victoria's tail-end to win another close encounter.

4. tail-end Charlie, a tail-gunner; the last aircraft in a flying formation (*Services' colloq.*); also *transf.* and *fig.*, one who comes last or behind, a tail-ender.

1941 *Illustr. London News* CXCIX. 579 (*caption*) The 'tail-end Charlie' of a 'Halifax' gives the 'thumbs up' sign just before his machine takes off. **1942** *Sun* (Baltimore) 8 Aug. 3/1 Lessig crossed the channel with the RAF, flying a Spitfire in the 'tail end Charlie' position—the last plane in a flight of four. **1956** P. Scott *Male Child* I. ii. 40 My brother..was killed in the war... A tail-end Charlie. **1961** *Times* 7 June 5/7 The Spaniard, Goyeneche was *lanterne rouge*, the cyclists' equivalent of tail-end-Charlie. **1976** *Daily Mail* 4 Oct. 3/3 The average lifespan of a 'Tail-end Charlie' was reckoned as ten 'ops.'

transf. and *fig.* **1962** A. Sampson *Anat. of Britain* xxxiv. 550 The essential services may, as in America, become regarded as the tail-end Charlies, the forgotten drudges under the pavements and pit-heads. **1969** *Daily National* (Nairobi) 31 Oct. 35 (Advt.), Congratulations to Joginder Singh and Ken Ranyard on their magnificent drive in car No. 46, starting as 'tail end Charlie'. But finishing with the major honours. **1973** *Listener* 15 Nov. 661/3 On tours, when I used to go with my parents..a sort of tail-end Charlie. **1978** A. Price *'44 Vintage* x. 131 The jeep behind them was closing up... The Sergeant was taking his tail-end Charlie role..seriously. **1980** *Outdoor Life* (U.S.) (North-east ed.) Oct. 53/3, I found myself on a hillside where the birds were flushing below, but then there was one tail-end Charlie who went up the hill.

tail-ender. Add: (Further examples.) Now used esp. in Sport.

1885 *Sydney Mail* 28 Feb. 451/4 Garrett and Evans, the 'tail-enders', established themselves..firmly at the wickets. **1915** *Lit. Digest* 21 Aug. 360/3 The St. Louis Cardinals, whom the writer designates as 'almost chronic tail-enders', are, in regard to the amounts spent for new players, just about the same. **1955** *Times* 23 June 17/1 It has certainly been focused so far on the leaders rather than the tail-enders in the various markets. One possible brake on the rise..is an increase in the corpus of securities **1961** *Sunday Express* 7 May 1/6 Both men were lapping the tailenders now. **1977** *World of Cricket Monthly* June 24/2 Eric was also the better batsman, Alec being more of the hard-hitting tailender type. **1980** A. Crawley *Dial 200-200* ix. 98 'You might have been killed yourself.' 'Not much chance; the raid had already gone past us. It would have had to be a tail-ender, like the one that got the maid.'

tailer. Restrict *Angling* to sense in Dict. and add: † **2. a.** A follower or hanger-on. **b.** *spec.* on the U.S. Stock Exchange (see quot. 1900). *Obs.*

1838 Disraeli *Let.* in Monypenny & Buckle *Life Disraeli* (1912) II. i. 20 Two of the greatest ruffians in the House... They are 'Tailers'. **1899** G. B. Shaw *Let.* 30 Dec. (1972) II. 127 Though the old favorites would get in on both sides, there would be a real contest between the outsiders and tailers. **1900** S. A. Nelson *ABC Wall St.* 161 Tailer. Big operators have a following of little traders who tail-on a bull or a bear movement on the theory that to make money it is a good thing to follow in the wake of the successful men. **1903** F. Norris *Pit* viii. 269 The 'tailers'—the little Bulls—were radiant.

3. *Austral.* One who follows, drives, or tends sheep or cattle; also, a straggling animal.

1893 K. Mackay *Out Back* (ed. 2) III. iii. 233 Fitzspats was absent, having gone out with the 'tailers' that morning. **1927** M. M. Bennett *Christison of Lammermoor* xxvi. 237 The cattle that had come in were watered and handed over to the tailers' mob. **1959** J. Wright *Generations of Men* (1960) ix. 107 Silent dogs at the heels of the tailers.

4. A device with a metal loop used for landing large fish by the tail.

1962 *Times* 31 Mar. 11/5 Some fishermen prefer the tailer to the gaff at all times. **1974** *Country Life* 14 Mar. 599/3, I was not optimistic enough to bring with me a tailer or gaffe or net, but..my fly was taken by an eight-pounder.

5. tailer-out, one who guides timber as it comes off a saw. *Austral.* and *N.Z.*

1907 G. B. Lancaster *Tracks we Tread* vi. 87 The bench sawyers felt it, and the trolley-men; and each tailer-out and engine driver. **1930** W. Smyth *Wooden Rails* ii. 32 She came upon the sawyer and his mate, the tailer-out. **1950** *Landfall* IV. 125 The planer..spits out faced boards for the tailer-out to stack by the goose-saw. **1971** *N.Z. Listener* 8 Nov. 15/4 He worked all day as a tailer-out in the mill.

taileron (tēⁱ·lĕrǫn). *Aeronaut.* [Blend of Tail *sb.*[1] and *aileron.] A horizontal control surface on an aircraft which can function as both elevator and aileron, moving either in unison with its partner or in opposition to it.

1966 D. Stinton *Anat. Aeroplane* viii. 163 The tailerons of the BAC-TSR 2..were slab surfaces that moved either together, as pitch controls, or independently for additional control in roll. **1975** *Flight* 16 Oct. 569 Roll and pitch stabilisation operates by moving the tailplane surfaces as tailerons, leaving the lateral spoilers and ailerons purely under the pilot's control.

tail-gate. 1. (In Dict. s.v. Tail *sb.*[1] 14, sense (*a*).) (Later example.)

1983 G. Swift *Waterland* v. 29 The lighters are approaching. Dick is opening the tail-gates.

2. (In Dict. as above, sense (*b*).) Also, a tail-board or back on a lorry, etc., hinged or removable to facilitate the loading of goods; a hatchback door on a car. orig. *U.S.*

1868 *Oregon State Jrnl.* 28 Nov. 2/3 The whole charge.. [passed] through the tailgate of the wagon. **1886** [in Dict. s.v. Tail *sb.*[1] 14]. **1909** Webster, *Tail gate*,..a heavy wooden panel pivoted to the end of a railroad car to form an incline from the car bottom to the rails. **1940** W. Faulkner *Hamlet* IV. i. 246 The wagon moved gradually backward until the head of the first horse was snubbed up to the tail-gate. **1956** *New Yorker* 1 Dec. 196/2 This year's crop of friction-motor automobiles includes..a ten-inch Country Squire station wagon, with a tail gate that can be opened and closed. **1963** *Guardian* 13 Mar. 5/4 The one-piece tailgate, which is counter-balanced, rises to 5 ft. 10 in. from the ground, providing protection for both load and loader against the rain. **1967** *Financial Times* 21 Apr. 9/8 Hi-pope vertical tailgate equipment for fitting to lorries. **1974** *Daily Tel.* 22 Oct. 10/7 The styling is angular, but pleasant, and features a large rear tailgate for access to the luggage compartment behind the rear seats. **1978** J. Irving *World according to Garp* xv. 309 She felt her way along the truck toward the tailgate. **1980** *Times* 28 May 3/1 BL's long-awaited new small car, the Mini Metro,..is a front-wheel-drive model with two side doors and a tailgate.

B. *attrib.* or as *adj.* **1.** Used to designate a style of jazz trombone playing characterized by improvisation in the manner of the early New Orleans musicians. [From the traditional position of the trombonist at the rear of the wagon in parades, etc.]

1946 R. Blesh *Shining Trumpets* ii. 32 Long glissandi.. heard in the 'tailgate' or circus-style trombone of jazz. **1959** 'R. Gant' *World in Jug* 26 Vic was our trombonist... He had a real tailgate style—that comes from the days when the trombonist sat at the back of the wagon so that he did not push out the eyes of the other bandsmen. **1973** *Times* 25 Jan. 18/6 It needed the utmost in timing and execution, as many would-be tailgate trombonists have since proved by default.

2. Applied to refreshment stops, etc., made during the course of a journey or outing and arranged at the open tail-gate of a parked car.

1970 [see *potlatch b]. **1980** L. Birnbach et al. *Official Preppy Handbk.* 102/2 Tailgate picnics, whiskey sours in the stadium, and the general complexity of the sport guarantee that nobody knows what is going on.

ta·il-gate, *v.* *colloq.* (orig. *U.S.*) Also unhyphened. [f. the sb.] **1.** *intr.* To drive too close behind another vehicle.

1951, 1955 [implied in *vbl. sb.* below]. **1962** 'F. & R. Lockridge' *Murder has its Points* xiv. 160 The police car they followed knew its way, and Weigand tail-gated. **1964** *Punch* 23 Sept. 442/3 'Don't tailgate!'..meaning don't drive on the other man's tail. **1976** *Good Motoring* May 32/1 In the dangerous sphere of motorway driving, for example, they would not tailgate at speeds where if the man in front stopped suddenly they could not..help but stop in exactly the same place on the road.

2. *trans.* To follow (a motor vehicle) excessively closely in another vehicle.

1967 *Lebende Sprachen* XII. 73/2 The use of the verb (which is a recent accession) no longer requires that the car ahead does in fact have a tailgate. One can tailgate a VW. **1968** *National Observer* (U.S.) 8 Apr. 5/4 Negro cabbie John W. Smith, whose arrest for 'tailgating' a police car..helped spark five days of rioting.., was found guilty of assaulting a policeman. **1970** *Daily Tel.* (Colour Suppl.) 9 Oct. 25 The cruise cars are programmed on an intricate shuttle, one tailgating the other, so that no more than 20 seconds can..pass between a radio alarm and the arrival of a car. **1982** H. Kissinger *Years of Upheaval* vii. 228 We took off in a motorcade traveling at a speed of close to 100 miles per hour with cars tailgating each other.

3. *fig.*

1977 *Times Lit. Suppl.* 20 May 618/3 Pictures tailgate each other, wall to wall, and floor to ceiling, in the authentic eighteenth-century manner. **1978** *Saturday Night* (Toronto) Apr. 5/2 One takeover scenario has tailgated another: in 1969 it was Time Inc. muscling in.

Hence **tai·lgater; tai·lgating** *vbl. sb.*

1951 *Amer. Speech* XXVI. 309/1 *Tail-gating, part. phr.*, a bad practice of following too close to the tail gate of the truck ahead. **1955** *Ibid.* XXX. 93 Twenty-two..[lorry] drivers agreed that tailgating means riding too closely behind the vehicle ahead. **1957** *How to Drive* (Amer. Auto. Assoc.) viii. 71 Expressway 'tailgating' is suicidal. **1968** H. McCloy *Mr. Splitfoot* (1969) xvii. 195 Another car passed him and slipped in between his car and Folly's. One of those eager tailgaters who cannot bear to see a few inches between two cars ahead of them. **1970** V. Johnston *Phantom Cottage* xxi. 160 'So if you will just let me keep following your car—.'..'All right. But no tailgating.' **1976** *National Observer* (U.S.) 13 Mar. 8/6 In informal testing by The Observer, a Cyberlite appeared to reduce 'tail-gating' behind the test vehicle. **1978** *Telegraph* (Brisbane) 18 Jan. 2/1 A spider on the boot is a lot less dangerous than a tailgater on the bumper bar. **1980** *West Lancs. Evening Gaz.* 21 May 1/1 In a statement today the AA said poor driving, including the 'often fatal practice of "tailgating" ', was responsible for a big increase in serious accidents.

tailing, *vbl. sb.*[1] Add: **1.** (Further example.)

1848 H. W. Haygarth *Recoll. Bush Life Australia* vi. 56 When cattle are first brought to a new country they are subjected to a process called 'tailing', which consists in watching them with horsemen by day, and driving them into their enclosures every night.

5. *tailing ground, pile, yard.*

1878 E. S. Elwell *Boy Colonists* 67 He had caught sight of a native hanging about the 'tailing-ground'. **1897** 'Mark Twain' *Following Equator* lxviii. 687 The gold fields of the world now deliver up to fifty millions dollars' worth of gold per year which would have gone into the tailing-pile under the former conditions. **1934** I. W. Hutchison *North to Rime-Ringed Sun* vi. 54 Across the entrance of the valley..stretched the heaped 'tailing-piles', tippings of the huge gold-dredges. **1930** A. W. Groom *Merry Christmas* xx. 158 The cattle could be seen moving quietly to the tailing yards. **1963** W. E. Harney *To Ayers Rock & Beyond* v. 45 During my early cattle days all mustering was done into drafting yards... They did not alter the method until the drafting-yards was superseded by the 'tailing-yard' with bronco-panels and twisted greenhide ropes with a leather 'hoonda' for the ring.

tailism (tēⁱ·liz'm). *Pol.* [f. Tail *sb.*[1] + -ism.] In Communist jargon, the fault of accommodating policy to the wishes of the masses, thereby following in their wake rather than taking an active revolutionary role.

[**1933** tr. *Lenin's What is to be Done?* ii. 52 It would be more correct to describe its tendency not as opportunism, but *khvostism* (from the word *khvost*)... [Note] *Khvost* is the Russian word for tail.] **1948** J. Towster *Political Power in U.S.S.R.* ix. 180 A double injunction against either 'commanding' or 'tailism' (following, instead of showing initiative). **1957** *Economist* 26 Oct. 320/1 After three months, all the crimes in the jargon book of communist heresy—including such esoteric offences as.. 'tailism' ('refusal to lead the masses')—have been hurled at the hundreds of eminent non-party rightists uncovered or named during..the recent disharmony. **1966** tr. *Quotations from Chairman Mao Tsetung* xi. 124 The reason why such evils as dogmatism, empiricism, commandism, tailism, sectarianism, bureaucracy and an arrogant attitude in work are definitely harmful..is that they alienate us from the masses. **1971** R. MacFarquhar in S. E. Fraser *Educ. & Communism in China* vi. 352 They read aloud the slogans... 'Do you listen to Chairman Mao, or to doctrinairism? Shameful tailism!'

taille. Add: **3.** *Mus.* (See quot. 1944.)

1842 J. A. Hamilton *Dict. Two Thousand Musica Terms* 85 *Taille* (French), the tenor voice or part. **1876** Stainer & Barrett *Dict. Mus. Terms* 420/1 *Taille* (Fr.), (1) the tenor voice or tenor part, (2) the tenor violin, the viola. **1889** Grove *Dict. Mus.* IV. 52/2 The tenor violoncello clef was originally appropriated to the Taille. **1932** C. S. Terry *Bach's Orchestra* v. 98 His players were certainly never provided with an instrument capable of sounding g, except the taille. **1944** *Harvard Dict. Mus.* 731/2 *Taille* [F.], old name for a middle voice, particularly the tenor. The term was also used for instruments performing such parts, e.g., *taille de basson*, tenor oboe; *taille de violon* or simply *taille*, viola.

taille-douce. Delete *Obs.* and add later examples.

1897 O. Firth *Postage Stamps* ii. 7 The original example of line-engraved stamps, or stamps 'engraved in *taille-douce*'. **1924** F. J. Melville *Compl. Philatelist* vi. 83 Most of the stamps produced after this portrait were surface-printed, but the Falkland Islands and the Turks and Caicos Islands presented it in *taille-douce* engraving. **1955** Boggs & Strange *Foundations of Philately* xi. 128 Line engraving is a classic process which was used for the first adhesive stamps issued in Great Britain in 1840... This process is also known as intaglio, recess printing, or *taille douce.* **1969** F. L. WILDER *How to identify Old Prints* v. 77 Line-engraving (taille-douce) had become the principal form of engraving in France and it was said that the art was almost born and died with him [*sc.* Jacques-Philippe Le Bas], shortly before the Revolution. **1975** W. FINLAY *Illustr. Hist. Stamp Design* ii. 21/2 The paper usually has to be dampened..and then is laid on top of the plate and forced down under great pressure, so that the plate bites into the paper. The paper squeezed into the grooves picks up the ink; this is what gives stamps and banknotes printed in this fashion their characteristic ridged surface. This process is known as *intaglio, taille douce*, recess printing or direct plate printing. Philatelists often use the term 'line engraving'.

‖ **tailleur** (taiyör) [Fr.] A woman's tailor-made suit.

1923 *Weekly Dispatch* 29 Apr. 15 New, indeed, is the sunshade composed of chrome leather, designed specially for use with the morning *tailleur*. **1945** N. MITFORD *Pursuit of Love* xviii. 158 The spring *tailleurs*, the summer *imprimés*, the autumn *ensembles*, and the winter furs. **1982** T. FITZGIBBON *With Love* I. ii. 18, I pressed the black *tailleur*, bought a gay scarf..and went off to look for a job.

tailor, *sb.* Add: **5.** *tailor-man* (earlier example), *-shop*.

1882 'MARK TWAIN' *Prince & Pauper* xiii. 154 Noble large stitches..that do cause these small stingy ones of the tailor-man to look mightily paltry. **1916** G. FRANKAU in *Wipers Times* 3 July 7/2 Oh! where is Caw-Caw the Captain bold, The pride of the tailor-shop? **1979** *Maledicta* III. 20, I played a lot with Mezzrow. And with Sidney Bechet in his tailorshop in Brooklyn.

6. a. tailor-fashion *adv.* = *tailor-wise* adv. below; **tailor tack(ing)** = *tailor's tack*, sense 6 b below; **tailor-wise** *adv.*, in a cross-legged position.

1877 RUSKIN *St. Mark's Rest* II. iv. 45 A curly-haired personage..sitting in an absurd manner, more or less tailor-fashion. **1902** R. P. BROWNE *Pract. Work of Dressmaking & Tailoring* iii. 80 '*Tailor Tacking*'—This stitch is used to trace the seams, &c., through to the second side of the cloth—following the lines which have been marked with tailor's chalk. **1979** M. MCCRIRRICK *Better Dressmaking* iv. 35 *Tailor tacker*, for working quantities of tailor tacks on a thick pad of foam rubber... *Marking set*, for transferring single pattern marks to both sides of fabric at the same time as an alternative to tailor tacking. **1885** Tailor-wise [see TUCK *v.*[1] 6]. **1913** W. DE LA MARE *Peacock Pie* 20 To see them squatting tailor-wise Around a keg of rum. *c* **1973** J. CHOLERTON *Acrobatic Enchainements* (Assoc. Amer. Dancing) (ed. 7) 3 Lower (side view) to tailor-wise sit.

b. (Occas. *tailors'*.) **tailor's chalk,** hard chalk or soapstone used in tailoring, etc. to make eradicable marks on fabric as a guide to fitting; **tailor's dummy** (lit. example); **tailor's tack** (see quot. 1975); usu. in *pl.*; similarly **tailor's tacking** (cf. *tailor tack(ing)*, sense 6 a above); **tailor's twist** (example).

1881 C. C. HARRISON *Woman's Handiwork* III. 167 Grass and iris were sketched on the blue surface with tailor's chalk. **1932** D. C. MINTER *Mod. Needlecraft* 107/2 Almost indispensable to successful dressmaking are..a yard stick, tailors' chalk. **1966** *Olney Amsden & Sons Ltd. Price List* 36 Tailor's chalk.. Loose boxes of 100 pieces square or triangle. **1977** A. SCHOLEFIELD *Venom* v. 204 A maze of sewing machines and tailors' dummies. **1927** *New Butterick Dressmaker* x. 98 *Tailors' tacks*,—after cutting out a garment..mark with tailors' tacks the perforations at 'Outlet' or 'Let-Out' seams. **1964** *McCall's Sewing* ii. 32/2 *Tailor's tack*, method of marking pattern symbols. **1975** C. CALASIBETTA *Fairchild's Dict. Fashion* 488/2 *Tailor's tacks*, large stitches taken through two thicknesses of fabric with a loop left between the layers which are later cut apart, leaving tufts in each piece; used for guide marks in tailoring. **1952** E. KING *Successful Home Dressmaking* iv. 22 *Tailor's tacking*, suitable for all fabrics, but specially for woollens, crêpes, lace, velvets and loosely-woven or flimsy goods. **1873** *Young Englishwoman* Mar. 150/2 Work the button-holes with tailors' twist, which is sold..at one penny per dozen lengths of one yard.

tailor, *v.* Add: **5.** *fig.* To design or alter (something) to suit specific needs; to adjust or make suitable. orig. *U.S.*

1942 *Sun* (Baltimore) 23 Oct. 6/2 Maryland farmers will tailor next year's crops to a size which can be worked by their individual families. **1950** *Engineering* 9 June 655/3 To secure maximum performance the apparatus should be 'tailored' for each application. **1951** M. MCLUHAN *Mech. Bride* (1967) 98/2 To the mind of the modern girl, legs, like busts, are power points wich she has been taught to tailor. **1959** *Listener* 2 July 35/1 A writer who soberly tailors a piece to fit into sixty minutes. **1961** *New Scientist* 23 Feb. 484/1 Derivatives containing carbon can be 'tailored' to have suitable handling properties. **1964** *Observer* 28 June 23/3 Of course, the story of 'Hiroshima Pilot as Mental Patient' was at once tailored to fit the headlines. **1982** G. F. NEWMAN *Men with Guns* p. vi, The shotguns..the pair of Luigi Franchi double twelve-gauge..he had had tailored in London.

tailored, *ppl. a.* (In Dict. s.v. TAILOR *v.* 2.) Add: **b.** *fig.* Made to suit particular needs; adjusted. orig. *U.S.*

1942 *Sun* (Baltimore) 12 Aug. 5/4 Gasoline rationing officials..said that motorists coming into a rationed area from a non-rationed area on a pleasure trip can be supplied with a 'tailored' ration book to fit their needs. **1954** *Economist* 10 Apr. 141 A specially tailored compound containing the radio-active element. **1956** *B.B.C. Handbk. 1957* 38 The *North American Service* produces specially 'tailored' programmes to be rebroadcast by American and Canadian stations and networks. **1963** *Daily Tel.* 14 Mar. 15 (*heading*) 'Tailored' driving for Sunbeam Alpines.

tailoring, *vbl. sb.* Add: **d.** *fig.* The act of adjusting or producing to suit specific needs. orig. *U.S.*

1943 *Sun* (Baltimore) 5 Feb. 4/5 Thirty-seven ration boards in the State now are completing the tailoring of ration books. **1951** *Times* 21 Sept. 1/5 (Advt.), High-polymer chemist for applied research on the 'tailoring' of linear macromolecules required by an important, very modern works in S.W. England. **1979** *United States 1980/81* (Penguin Travel Guides) p. xii, Very precise editing and tailoring keeps our text fiercely subjective.

tailorless, *a.* (Earlier example.)

1876 J. A. H. MURRAY *Let.* in K. H. E. MURRAY *Caught in Web of Words* (1977) x. 192 We are not quite *tailorless* and so not obliged to go *trouserless*.

tailor-made, *a.* Add: Also **tailormade. 1.** (Later examples of the sb.)

1932 AUDEN in *Rev. Eng. Stud.* (1978) Aug. 284 She's been having her tailormades altered. **1981** A. LURIE *Lang. Clothes* viii. 222/1 The ordinary woman..might wear..a..wool or linen suit (the 'tailor-made') with a shirtwaist.

3. Made to answer a specific demand or requirement; perfectly suited *for* a particular purpose.

1896 G. B. SHAW in *Sat. Rev.* 7 Nov. 494/1 The public were tired of tailormade plays, and were ripe for a revival of colour and costume. **1897** —— in *Ibid.* 1 May 470/2 A theatre which is panelled, and mirrored, and mantelpieced like the first-class saloon of a Peninsular and Oriental liner..is no place..for anything except tailor-made drama and farcical comedy. **1938** *Cine-Kodak News* Aug. 10/1 (*heading*) Tailor-made showings. **1946** *Richmond* (Va.) *Times-Dispatch* 24 Nov. 12B The work is another venture in the science of redesigning plants and animals through genetics to bring forth 'tailor-made' species. **1953** *Economist* 30 May (Suppl.) 9/1 The tailormade molecules which form the long fibres used in weaving Terylene. **1958** *Spectator* 14 Feb. 194/3 A seat tailor-made..for the Liberals to dance further fandangoes on the carefully laid plans of their rivals. **1963** [see *PEG *sb.*[1] 1 e]. **1970** G. F. NEWMAN *Sir, You Bastard* i. 14 It's a job almost tailor-made for you. **1972** [see *INSIDE *a.* d]. **1980** *Jrnl. R. Soc. Arts* Mar. 185/2 The tailor-made building had arrived.

4. Designating a ready-made (as opp. hand-rolled) cigarette. Freq. *ellipt.* as *sb. slang* (orig. U.S.).

1924 'DIGIT' *Confessions 20th Cent. Hobo* 12 *Tailor-mades*, ordinary ready-made cigarettes. **1930** J. DEVANNY *Bushman Burke* 88 He smoked 'tailor-mades' now. **1945** *N.Z. Geographer* I. 23 The background of all this is tobacco. There are but few pipes, and 'tailor-made' cigarettes are only a luxury. 'Roll your own' is on most lips. **1952** E. WILSON *Equations of Love* 29 Just a match. .. I don't smoke tailor-mades. **1955** *People* (Austral.) 1 June 8/1 Leopold..was..told he had been reported for possessing contraband, a 'tailor-made' cigarette. Leopold didn't even know what a 'tailor-made' cigarette was. **1962** N. FREELING *Love in Amsterdam* III. 145 Martin stayed quiet after distributing his last tailormades. **1974** D. SEARS *Lark in Clear Air* iii. 40, I went and bought a package of Turret tailor-made cigarettes and I lit one.

tai·lor-make, *v.* orig. *U.S.* [Back-formation f. *TAILOR-MADE *a.* 3.] *trans.* To design (something) according to specific requirements.

1946 *Sun* (Baltimore) 1 July 8/2 Under ideal weather conditions that seemed to have been tailor made for the occasion, the atom bomb was successfully exploded. **1953** *Ibid.* 14 Apr. 3/4 It may be possible to tailor-make drugs which would prevent each type of dangerous virus from getting the electrical charges it needs in order to attack the target cell. **1959** *Listener* 18 June 1052/2 What will happen when Franco does disappear from the political scene? Some think he is trying to tailor-make a monarchy. **1967** M. CHANDLER *Ceramics in Mod. World* vi. 168 Alumina ceramics can be tailor-made to meet a wide range of industrial requirements. **1973** *Daily Tel.* 9 Aug. 3 (Advt.), If you haven't yet got central heating, an Esso Chartered Installer will tailor-make a complete system to suit your needs. **1981** *Arts Alert* Oct. 3/1 We were asked to tailor-make the hall for the LSO's needs.

tail-piece. 1. (Further examples.)

1723 J. NOTT *Cook's & Confectioner's Dict.* sig. KK3v, Draw your Sturgeon;..cut your first and second Rand very fair, cutting the Tail-piece least. **1786** BUSBY *Dict. Mus.* s.v. *Tail-piece*, the thin, broad piece of ebony horizontally suspended over the lower end of a violin, and to which one end of the strings is attached.

tail-pipe. Add: Also **tailpipe. 2. a.** *Aeronaut.* (See quot. 1933.) Chiefly *U.S.*

1922 L. S. MARKS *Airplane Engine* xvii. 423 For durability the muffler should be attached to the end of a tail pipe 6 or 8 ft. long which will cool the gases sufficiently **1933** *Brit. Standards Inst. Specif.* CLXXXV (Gloss. Aeronaut. Terms) vi. 53 *Tail pipe*, a pipe which leads exhaust gases away from a manifold. **1956** C. W. SMITH *Aircraft Gas Turbines* viii. 167 The exhaust gas pipe from the turbine is conducted to the propulsion nozzle through a duct (often called *tailpipe*). **1956** [see sense 2 b below]. **1973** *Physics Bull.* Dec. 728/1 This difference is often referred to as 'excess' or 'tailpipe' noise. Work to date has identified this noise source as being associated with the aerodynamic environment in the core exhaust system.

b. *U.S.* The exhaust-pipe of a motor vehicle.

1956 W. A. HEFLIN *U.S. Air Force Dict.* 511/1 *Tail-pipe*.., an exhaust pipe for escape of gases generated in an internal combustion engine; specif. in a jet engine, the pipelike structure aft of the exhaust nozzle. **1961** E. A. VENK *Automotive Fundamentals* (ed. 2) xi. 179/2 The tail pipe is a long winding pipe which is connected to the muffler... Two tail pipes are used in a dual exhaust system. **1964** S. BELLOW *Herzog* 121 Unless you remembered to bear right the tailpipe would scrape on the rocks. **1973** *Sunday Bulletin* (Philadelphia) 14 Oct. (Parade Suppl.) 16/3 Unfortunately the tailpipe didn't clear the underside of the car. **1979** D. ANTHONY *Long Hard Cure* iv. 33 Lorraine's car was parked..with the tailpipe backed into a hedge.

tail-race. Add: **b.** (Earlier examples.)

1863 *App. Jrnls. House Reps. N.Z.* D. vi. 14 Where the water is heavy, and there are no means of cutting a tail-race, water-wheels have been erected, with Californian pumps attached. **1874** [see *PADDOCK *sb.*[2] 3].

c. The watercourse leading from the turbine of a power-station or dam, etc.

1953 *Times* 4 Aug. 3/4 An electric screen has been devised which is successful in preventing salmon and sea trout from swimming into the tailrace (the outflow from a water turbine) of a power station. **1974** *Progress* (Easley, S. Carolina) 24 Apr. 11. 10/2 Rainbows are the most common species stocked into tailrace waters. **1978** *Texas Parks & Wildlife* July 13/3 We've dealt mainly with tailraces below large flood-control and power-generating dams.

tail-rope. 2. a. Delete † *Obs.* and add later N. Amer. examples.

1916 F. W. WALLACE *Shack Locker* (1922) 81 Make th' tail rope fast. *a* **1932** L. S. TAWES *Coasting Captain* (1967) 27 We had a long tail rope to slack the staysail over with. **1942** *Amer. Neptune* II. 234 'Tail rope' is a short line made fast to the after end of the fore-staysail boom for the express purpose of backing the jumbo.

tailspin (tē¹·lspin), *sb.* Also **tail spin, tail-spin.** [Cf. SPIN *sb.*[1]] **a.** *Aeronaut.* A downward movement of an aircraft in which the tail describes a spiral.

1917 V. W. PAGE *Gloss. Aviation Terms* 23 Tail spin. **1919** in C. A. Smith *New Words Self-Defined* 201, I remember when I thought it was time to try a *vrille* or tail-spin. **1926** *Daily Colonist* (Victoria, B.C.) 17 Jan. 2/5 Collison's airplane went into a tail spin when his motor failed to work. **1953** C. A. LINDBERGH *Spirit of St. Louis* II. vi. 263 He'd tried to land out of a tailspin—that was asking for a crash.

b. *fig.* A state of chaos, panic, or loss of control.

1928 R. E. BYRD *Let.* 24 July in *K. W. Rendell Autograph Catal. No. 34* (Kingston Galleries) (1968) 2, I am pretty much in a tail spin which I don't expect to get out of before the main part of the expedition leaves. **1929** *Times* 2 Nov. 12/6 The cyclic tailspin which has occurred in the 11th year of each of the four great previous periods of commercial prosperity. **1935** WODEHOUSE *Luck of Bodkins* xv. 183 A dashed shame, he considered, that things had gone into a tail spin for him like that. **1954** A. HUXLEY *Let.* 5 Dec. (1969) 717 A child stoked with fats will find it hard, because of adrenalin, to digest and will probably go into a bad psychological tailspin in consequence. **1967** E. S. GARDNER *Case of Queenly Contestant* vii. 84 [He] went into a tailspin. He was afraid of the responsibility. He was afraid his father would find out. *a* **1974** R. CROSSMAN *Diaries* (1977) III. 867 After my denial of the story that appeared in his Manchester lecture, the poor man came along in a terrible tail-spin to see me. **1982** *Daily Tel.* 16 June 19 The Argentine economy was already in a tail-spin before the Falklands invasion.

tai·lspin, *v.* Also **tail-spin.** [f. the sb.] *intr.* To perform or go into a tailspin.

1927 [see *barrel roll* s.v. *BARREL *sb.* 11]. **1936** F. CLUNE *Roaming round Darling* xvii. 167 We slithered in the mud, barrel-rolled, tail-spinned, sank to our hocks, and became part of the everlasting scenery. **1972** M. J. BOSSE *Incident at Naha* iv. 204, I had never seen Virgil so moved or so bitter. It was unlike him to tailspin into such a downer. **1973** *Daily Colonist* (Victoria, B.C.) 21 June 1/5 The red and white air craft was about 400 feet in the air a mile from the airport when it suddenly went into a nose dive, then tailspun to the pavement.

tainiolite, var. *TÆNIOLITE.

taint, *sb.* Add: **C. 1. c.** An unpleasant scent or smell. Cf. *TAINT *v.* C. 4 c.

1927 H. WILLIAMSON *Tarka the Otter* i. 5 Mingled with the flower odours..was the taint that had given her a sudden shock..; the taint most dreaded by the otters..—the scent of Deadlock, the great pied hound. **1951** 'J. WYNDHAM' *Day of Triffids* xi. 205 On the higher ground there was still little taint in the fresh air.

taint, *v.* Add: **C. 4. c.** *trans.* To drive *out* (rabbits) from their burrows by the introduction of an offensive smell.

1909 O. JONES *Ten Years Game-Keeping* ii. 22 Gipsies are a help to the keeper..when he has a difficulty in tainting out a colony of rabbits. **1972** *Young's Sporting Appliances* (S. Young & Sons Ltd.) II. 13 Proved to be best after exhaustive tests over many years for tainting out rabbits to lie out for shooting.

'taint (tē¹nt), *v.* Also **taint, t'ain't,** etc. Dial. and vulg. contraction of *it ain't*: see AIN'T *v.*; 'T.

1839 [see *SNUM *v.*]. **1859** A. J. SYMONDS *Let.* Sept. (1967) I. 206 You will think I am fallen desperately in love. Yet it taint so. **1919** W. DEEPING *Second Youth*

xxiii. 194 'Taint like 'im. 'E used to be sensible. **1942** Z. N. HURSTON in A. Dundes *Mother Wit* (1973) 225/1 'T'ain't nothing to you, nohow. **1974** H. R. F. KEATING *Underside* viii. 77 'I'm sure whatever they say's undeserved.' 'No, t'ain't. You ninny.'

taintless, *a.* Add: Hence **tai·ntlessness**, the quality of being taintless.
1811 SHELLEY *Let.* 26 Nov. (1964) I. 144 The first words you spoke to me..are eternal earnests of your taintlessness and sincerity. **1963** *English Studies* XLIV. 22 Taintlessness and incorruptibility seem to depend not so much on the predominance of blood stains as on outlook.

‖ **tai-otoshi** (tai͵otǫ·ʃi). *Judo.* Also **Tai-otoshi, tai-o-toshi,** etc. [Jap., f. *tai* body + *otoshi* the act of dropping.] The body drop throw.
1950 E. J. HARRISON *Judo* iii. 39 The most suitable moment for attempting the Taiotoshi is when your opponent with unbent legs, his body somewhat stiff, has leaned forward a little with his weight resting on his right leg. **1957** TAKAGAKI & SHARP *Techniques Judo* iii. 24 If *tai-otoshi* fails and the opponent pulls back. **1964** LEGGETT & WATANABE (*title*) Championship judo: tai-otoshi and o-uchi-gan attacks. **1978** D. STARBROOK *Judo* iv. 40/2 The tai-o-toshi is a hand throw, and its great advantage over so many other throws is that it can be performed against opponents who are either stationary or moving.

taipan[1] (tai·pæn). Also 9 **taepan, typan.** [Dial. var. of Chinese *dàbān*.] **a.** A foreign merchant or businessman in China. **b.** The (foreign) manager or head of a firm in China, esp. Hong Kong. Also *fig.* Hence **tai·panism.**
1834 *Canton Reg.* 28 Oct. 170/2 The election of a temporary Chief for the Superintendence of British affairs, until the appointment of one from England, who must be a *taepan* or Merchant, as before and not a Government Officer. **1892** in K. Lentzner *Dict. Slang-English Austral.* 91 My *typan* must make fun of me, When all his crowd can see—Ah! well, perhaps they do not care For a little clerk like me. **1921** *North-China Herald* 24 Dec. 815/1 What is 'Taipanism as seen in China', which Mr. Ku discusses in a recent issue of the 'Evening Standard'?.. Mr. Ku finds that 'Taipanism' is the spirit of respect for the sacred rights of property and vested interest. **1922** W. S. MAUGHAM *On Chinese Screen* xv. 63 With the elderly, but single, taipan of an important firm, what she simply loved was a game of golf. **1957** R. MASON *World of Suzie Wong* I. i. 9 Chinese taipans, who made the richest Europeans seem like paupers. **1972** *Times* 21 Oct. (Hongkong Suppl.) p. i/4 Opium can no longer be indulged in as it was with restraint by the *taipans*, or merchants, in old Shanghai. **1977** W. TUTE *Cairo Sleeper* i. 14 Ambassadors..mingled with other taipans of the higher civil service... Most members of the club worked in Whitehall. **1983** *Sunday Tel.* 10 Apr. 20/6 The Keswicks of Dumfries married into the Jardines in the middle of the last century. Four of them, including Henry, became *taipan* or head of the house.

taipan[2] (tai·pæn). Also **Taipan.** [Aboriginal name.] A large dark brown venomous snake, *Oxyuranus scutellatus*, of the family Elapidæ, native to northern parts of Australia.
1933 D. F. THOMSON in *Proc. Zool. Soc.* 858 The name 'taipan', by which *O. scutellatus* is known to the aborigines of Cape York Peninsula, is an excellent vernacular name for the species. *Ibid.*, The taipan frequents the open country of the coast, as well as the inland plains and savannah forests. **1953** P. BRICKHILL in I. Bevan *Sunburnt Country* 96 The long-fanged taipan..grows eleven feet long, and nearly as thick as a man's arm... Only two men are known to have survived a taipan bite. **1966** G. DURRELL *Two in Bush* v. 159 To have kept and bred something as rare and shy as a Taipan is a very great triumph. **1982** *Daily Tel.* 18 Feb. 3/1 A western taipan—one of the world's deadliest snakes—was bitten by a mouse and is fighting for its life in the Darwin Museum, Australia.

tai-ping. (Earlier example.)
1853 *North-China Herald* 7 May 158/1 'Conquering the rivers and mountains', the expression by which the 'holy warriors' of Tae-ping designate their enterprise.

‖ **taipo** (tai·po). *N.Z.* Also **taepo, Taipo, typo.** [Origin uncertain: see quots. 1891, 1946.]
1. An evil spirit.
1848 R. TAYLOR *Leaf from Nat. Hist. N.Z.* 43 (Morris), *Taipo*, female dreamer; a prophetess; an evil spirit. **1883** W. COLENSO in E. E. Morris *Austral Eng.* (1898) 454/2 Taepo means to visit or come by night,—a night visitant, —a spectral thing seen in dreams,—a fancied and feared thing, or hobgoblin. **1886** *N.Z. Country Jrnl.* X. 262 His wife became seriously affected, declaring that *Taipo* had entered into her. **1891** E. TREGEAR *Maori-Polynesian Comparative Dict.* 440/1 *Taepo*, a goblin, a spectre. Cf. *tae*, to arrive; *po*, night. **1921** H. GUTHRIE-SMITH *Tutira* xi. 91 This crossing has always been known in my time as the 'Taipo'—goblin—crossing, a name probably given because of a totara block which used to lie there hewn roughly to the similitude of a man's head. **1946** *Jrnl. Polynesian Soc.* June 150 *Taipo*, supernatural being; goblin: used by the Maori believing it to be Pakeha, and by the Pakeha believing it to be Maori; often spelt taepo, which also is not a Maori word: so taipo is a word coined by no one knows whom. **1968** *N.Z. Listener* 15 Mar 6/5 He hurriedly looked both ways and took to the scrub as if a taipo were after him. **1971** *Ibid.* 1 Mar. 13/2 As for dreaded taniwhas and taipos, why, I could take you to the home of some.

2. = *WETA.
1928 J. DEVANNY *Dawn Beloved* I. vii. 47 The very apogee of excitement would be reached when a 'typo' was discovered. Especially if it happened to be a big fat male. **1946** F. SARGESON *That Summer* 176 But the wetas come out at night... The Maoris call them taipos. **1966** *Encycl. N.Z.* III. 636/2 The tree or ground wetas and the 'taipos' of the West Coast of the South Island, the name of which to the Maori means 'the devil who comes by night'.

tairoa, var. *TOHEROA.

tait (tēⁱt), *sb. Austral.* [Aboriginal name.] = *honey possum* s.v. *HONEY *sb.* (*a.*) 7.
1894 R. LYDEKKER *Hand-bk. Marsupialia* 121 Known to the natives by the name of Tait, and Nulbenger, the Long-snouted Phalanger..is generally found..from Swan River to King George's Sound. **1941** E. TROUGHTON *Furred Animals Austral.* 81 The quaint little animal had quite a variety of names in the native vocabularies.., the one favoured as a popular name being 'Noolbenger', and others including 'Ait' [*sic*] and 'Deed'.

Taittinger (ta·tæn̄ʒe). Also *erron.* **Tattinger.** The proprietary name of a champagne manufactured and shipped by the firm of Taittinger in Rheims.
1949 *Trade Marks Jrnl.* 6 Apr. 304 Taittinger... Champagne. Etablissements Taittinger Mailly & Cie (a Societe Anonyme organised under the laws of France). **1964** A. LAUNAY *Caviare & After* xv. 106 Unlike other wines, Champagne is known under the name of the shipper... The best known are Boulinger.., Pommery, Taittinger and Veuve Clicquot. **1967** A. ARENT *Gravedigger's Funeral* xii. 189, I will buy you a jereboam of Tattinger. **1971** R. TEMPLE *Schulsinger Affair* i. 12 A bottle of Taittinger Blanc de Blancs, well iced. **1978** R. B. PARKER *Judas Goat* xii. 77 Hawk had filled the sink with ice and put..another bottle of Taittinger champagne in to chill. **1978** D. A. STANWOOD *Memory of Eva Ryker* xxv. 238 A magnum of Tattinger '05.

Taiwanese (taiwănī·z), *sb.* and *a.* [f. *Taiwan*, the name of a large island off the south-east coast of China + -ESE.] **A.** *sb.* A native or inhabitant of Taiwan. **B.** *adj.* Of or pertaining to the island of Taiwan or its inhabitants.
1942 A. J. GRAJDANZEV *Formosa Today* iv. 53 A rise in the price of Taiwanese rice. *Ibid.* vi. 86 The Taiwanese are a fish-eating people. **1962** E. SNOW *Other Side of River* (1963) lxxi. 549 People talk about giving the Taiwanese a plebiscite on whether they want to join China or not. **1969** *Times* 9 Dec. (Taiwan Suppl.) p. v/8 Sixty-three per cent of local government officials are natives of Taiwan. All local magistrates are Taiwanese. **1970** D. DODGE *Hatchetman* i. 22 We've got Army liaison..Taiwanese liaison, British liaison, Old China hands. *Ibid.* ix. 109 Attempts have been made on my life before, but by Taiwanese; my people, not yours. **1978** *Chicago* June 225/1 The simple storefront does a great job with a menu that includes..unusual Taiwanese squid and cuttlefish dishes. **1979** *Pacific Affairs* LII. 455 There was almost no contact between Red Army units and Taiwanese in this period.

taj (tādʒ). Also **tuj.** [Arab. (Pers.) *tāj* crown.] A crown or head-dress of distinction (see also quot. 1877).
1851 *Illustr. Catal. Gt. Exhib.* IV. i. 918/2 Crown, or tuj, as worn by the King of Oude; without jewels. **1877** *Encycl. Brit.* VII. 113/2 The tâj, or white cap, with the proper number of terks, or sections, belonging to the order [of dervishes]. **1886** J. ATKINSON tr. *Firdausi's Shâh Nâmeh* 92 He also gave him a taj, or crown of gold, which kings only were accustomed to wear.

Taj: see *TAJ MAHAL a.

Tajik (tādʒī·k), *sb.* and *a.* Also **Tadjik, Tadzhik,** etc. [a. Pers. *tājik* one who is neither an Arab nor a Turk, a Persian.] **A.** *sb.* **a.** A people of Iranian descent inhabiting Afghanistan and the Turkistan region of Central Asia; now also *spec.* a native or inhabitant of the Tajik S.S.R. **b.** The Persian dialect spoken by this people. **B.** *adj.* Of, pertaining to, or designating this people.
1815 [see *HINDKI]. **1836** *Penny Cycl.* V. 71/2 The Tadjicks consider themselves as the aborigines of the country [*sc.* Bokhara], and as the descendants of the ancient Sogdi and Bactrians. **1871,** etc. [see *SART *sb.*[2] and *a.*]. **1911** *Encycl. Brit.* XXVI. 365/1 The Tajik population of the richly-cultivated districts north of Kabul. **1920** *Christian World* 26 Aug. 9/2 The fanatical Tadjiks and Sarts of that portion of Turkestan. **1949** F. MACLEAN *Eastern Approaches* I. x. 152, I had no sooner got to sleep than they dug me in the ribs and introduced themselves as Tajiks. **1953** O. CAROE *Soviet Empire* iii. 33 With sedentary and town populations speaking Tajik it can as safely be accepted that they are of Iranian stock-origin. **1959** E. H. CARR *Socialism in One Country* II. xx. 268 The Tajik population, the only non-Turki-speaking group in the area. **1964** H. H. PAPER tr. *Shafeev's Short Gram. Outl. Pashto* 1 Until 1936 the official language of Afghanistan was Kabuli, one of the dialects of Tajik. **1970** *Times* 24 Mar. 7/1 The least emancipated women seem to be found among the Tadjiks, an Iranian people living in the wild mountainous regions at the Soviet Union's extreme south-eastern tip. **1974** *Listener* 17 Oct. 494/2 Travelling through the Hindu Kush..with three Tajik tribesmen. **1977** YIN MING *United & Equal* 4 There is hardly any place along China's long border without its communities of minority nationalities. Among them are..the Kazakhs, Uighurs, Khalkhas and Tajiks in Sin Kiang. **1978** *Times* 18 Oct. 16/8 [In] Uzbekistan.. many..speak Tadzhik..and other Asian languages. **1979** A. HENNING tr. *Myrdal's Silk Road* i. 5 Our hosts..are Tadzhiks... This is the Tashkurghan Tadzhik Autonomous County in the far west of China. *Ibid.* 8 We are sitting on the starkly beautiful, thick, Tadzhik carpet of felted wool. **1980** G. RICHARDS *Red Kill* xxv. 204 Children had come from all corners of the Soviet Union... Azerbaijanis, Tadjiks, Ukrainians.

Taj Mahal (tādʒ, tāʒ mähā·l). [perh. a corruption of *Mumtaz Mahal* (see below) under the influence of *TAJ; cf. MAHAL.] The name of a mausoleum built at Agra by Shah Jahan in memory of his wife known as Mumtaz (Pers. 'chosen one') Mahal (d. 1631), used: **a.** *ellipt.* as **Taj.**
1858 W. H. RUSSELL *Diary* 14 Oct. (1860) II. 279, I had seen that Pearl of architecture, the wonder of the world—The Taj of Agra. **1887** KIPLING *Lett. of Marque* (1891) i. 2 He saw from the train the Taj wrapped in the mists of the morning. **1912** E. LUTYENS *Let.* May in M. Lutyens *Edwin Lutyens* (1980) vii. 104 The Taj and some other of the tombs have charm. **1978** 'M. M. KAYE' *Far Pavilions* xiv. 225 Shah Jehan's Empress the lady of the Taj.
b. *fig.* denoting that which is excellent or surpassing of its kind. Also occas. in *transf.* use.
1895 *Q. Rev.* Apr. 353 Stevenson has set up and decorated with every precious stone a building so magnificent, that it deserves to be called the Taj Mahal of our prose literature. **1950** PARTRIDGE *Name into Word* 429 One not seldom meets with such phrases as 'the Taj Mahal of architectural elegance' or 'the Taj Mahal of romantic architecture'. **1980** D. POWNALL *Between Ribble & Lune* i. 20 In 1906..his lordship ordered the structure as a Taj Mahal for his dead wife.

taka (ta·kă). Also **Taka**; pl. **-(s).** [Bengali *ṭākā*.] The basic monetary unit of Bangladesh, equivalent to one hundred paise; also, a banknote of this value.
Quot. 1975 illustrates the idiomatic use of *taka* with *crore* (= 10 million).
1972 *Guardian* 22 Aug. 10/4 The Bangladesh taka, officially at par with the Indian rupee, is being freely offered..at 40 per cent discount. **1975** *Bangladesh Times* 21 July 1/3 He said if the factory could produce..30,000 tons of pulp annually that would meet the home demand as well as fetch about Taka six crore in foreign exchange by exporting pulp abroad. To meet the home demand.. Bangladesh now had to import pulp worth seven to eight crore Taka annually. **1976** M. S. HOQUE *Hunger* I. i. 7 Nuribow opens the knot at the corner of her sari, takes a Taka therefrom and pays. **1976** *Sci. Amer.* Oct. 32/1–2 (*caption*) The Bengali writing offers a '250-taka prize' (about $17) to anyone who reports a smallpox case to a health office. **1979** *Church Times* 26 Oct. 13/1 Until two years ago, the family's income consisted entirely of Appavo's wage—a princely thirty takas a week (about a pound).

Taka-diastase (tækă͵dəi·ăstēⁱz). Also **taka-.** [f. the name of J. Jokichi *Taka*(*mine* (1854–1922), Japanese-born biochemist and industrialist + DIASTASE.] A preparation containing a variety of enzymes which is obtained after the treatment of rice or bran with the mould *Aspergillus oryzæ*; now a proprietary name.
1896 *Jrnl. Amer. Med. Assoc.* XXVII. 374 Notes on taka-diastase. **1928** [see *PYROPHOSPHATASE]. **1928** *Official Gaz.* (U.S. Patent Office) 6 Nov. 10/2 Takamine Ferment Company, New York... *Taka-diastase*... For koji, moyashi, diastase, ferments, and converting agents. Claims use since 1895. **1955** *Trade Marks Jrnl.* 9 Mar. 258/2 *Taka-diastase*... Diastase for pharmaceutical purposes. **1960** [see *KOJI]. **1969** G. SMITH *Introd. Industr. Mycology* xv. 312 Takamine introduced into commerce.. products of high enzymic activity, particularly suitable for the dextrination of starch and the desizing of textiles. These products have been sold under the names 'Taka-diastase'..and 'Oryzyme'. **1976** *Ann. Rev. Microbiol.* XXX. 8 During our studies of adenylate deaminase, we observed that the enzyme from Takadiastase..would deaminate approximately 50% of the adenylate added to the reaction vessel.

takahe (ta·kahi). Also **Takahe.** [Maori.] = *NOTORNIS.
1851 G. MANTELL *Petrifactions* ii. 128 No one had seen such a bird, but all agreed that it was the traditional Moho or Takahé, which they believed was utterly extinct. **1898** *Daily News* 22 Oct. 2/2 The other day a specimen of the takahe..was found in the South Island. **1915** *Chambers's Jrnl.* May 318/2 There are the flightless kiwi, weka, and kakapo parrot; also the very rare takahe. **1966** G. Durrell *Two in Bush* iii. 103 Then, quite suddenly, from behind a large clump of snow grass, a Takahe appeared... I was imagining something about the size of an English Moorhen..but there stood a bird the size of a large turkey. **1978** *Nature* 9 Feb. 507/2 Take, for example, the takahe (*Notornis mantelli*), a flightless gallinule endemic to New Zealand.

Takali, var. *TAKULLI.

takapu (ta·kăpu). *N.Z.* [Maori.] The Australian gannet, *Sula serrator*.
1842 W. COLENSO in N. M. Taylor *Early Travellers N.Z.* (1959) 54 The natives often take this bird... They call it Takapu. **1882** W. L. BULLER *Man. N.Z. Birds* 91 (*heading*) Gannet. Takapu. **1966** R. A. FALLA *Field Guide Birds*

N.Z. 60 Australian Gannet..Local name: Takapu... Mainly white; crown and nape pastel yellow.

Takayasu (takaya·su). *Path.* [The name of Michishige *Takayasu* (1872–1938), Japanese ophthalmologist, who described the disease in 1908.] *Takayasu's disease*: a chronic arteritis leading to obstruction of blood-flow, esp. in the vessels arising from the aortic arch; pulseless disease.

1952 *Amer. Heart Jrnl.* XLIV. 629 Pulseless or Takayasu's disease is considered by Japanese ophthalmologists to be a rare but definite clinical entity. **1969** Edington & Gilles *Path. in Tropics* viii. 335 At one time Takayasu's disease was thought to affect only young females and the pathological lesions to be restricted to the aortic arch and its major branches. **1978** *Central African Jrnl. Med.* XXIV. 144/2 Takayasu's disease (pulseless disease) is a disease of unknown aetiology first described in Japan.

take, *v.* Add: **II. 2. a.** Also in *Criminals' slang*, to break into in order to burgle, to rob.

1926 J. Black *You can't Win* xxi. 331 After gathering every scrap of information available, I was sure I could 'take' the spot if I got a fair break on the luck. **1930** D. Runyon in *Liberty* 8 Nov. 24/2 Someone takes a jewellery store in the town.

e. (Earlier examples.)

1846 W. Denison *Cricket* 71 The greatest number of wickets he succeeded in taking in one match was 11. **1870** *Times* 11 July 10/5 Mr. Law was taken easily at the wicket with the score at 22.

6. a. Also, in *Med.*, of animal tissue, etc.: to continue in a healthy state after being transplanted.

1875 *Lancet* 23 Jan. 124/2 The transplanted pieces of skin..were found to have 'taken' remarkably well. **1936** *Anat. Rec.* LXIV. 167 Young donors supply material that is more likely to 'take'. **1977** *Time* 7 Mar. 43/2 Odds that a transplanted cadaveric kidney will 'take' are usually no better than 50%.

c. Of ice: to form (esp. in a lake, river, etc.). Cf. sense 44 d below. *dial.* and *N. Amer.*

1825 *Kingston* (Upper Canada) *Chron.* 4 Feb. 3/2 On Saturday night last, the ice took between Kingston and Long Island. **1877** E. Leigh *Gloss. Words used Dial. Cheshire* 206 'The ice is taking' means it is beginning to freeze. **1881** *Edmonton Bull.* 28 Mar. 1/2 Ice took in the Saskatchewan on the 19th of November. **1931** G. L. Nute *Voyageur* 79 Seines were set in the water just before the ice 'took' on the lake or river.

d. Of a lamb: to be accepted by a foster mother in place of her own dead lamb.

1874 Hardy *Far from Madding Crowd* I. xviii. 204 Mistress and man were engaged in the operation of making a lamb 'take', which is performed whenever an ewe has lost her own offspring, one of the twins of another ewe being given her as substitute.

8. c. *slang.* To swindle, cheat, or deprive of money by extortion. Freq. const. *for*.

1927 [see *clip *v.*[2] 9]. **1930** D. Hammett *Dain Curse* xii. 122 They landed Mrs Rodman... They took her for one of her apartment buildings. **1956** S. Bellow *Seize Day* i. 9 They make millions. They have smart lawyers... Whereas I got taken. **1968** 'L. Marshall' *Blood on Blotter* xxvii. 183 'How much did you take him for?' 'Slade? Plenty.' **1970** *Washington Post* 30 Sept. B12/4 It looks to me like yo're fixin' to git took for the dollar an' thirty cents, Shuffy. **1978** J. B. Hilton *Some run Crooked* ix. 86 It wasn't enough for Julie just to admit she'd been taken. **1982** 'E. Lathen' *Green grow Dollars* xiv. 112 'I told Mary to take them for every penny she could get,' he said stoutly.

d. *Motor-racing.* To overtake (a competitor).

1977 *Custom Car* Nov. 14/2 Jimmy Smith..finally took Falcone, who had developed trouble, and stayed ahead to win the race. **1978** *Guardian Weekly* 12 Mar. 23/5 The South African Grand Prix... Peterson (Lotus) shadowed the leader right to the end, taking him on a bend in the last lap for victory.

10. b. Also without const.

1969 'E. Ferrars' *Skeleton Staff* iii. 61 'Not enormously taken, are you?' 'Not bowled over.' **1978** P. H. Johnson *Good Husband* iii. 24 But about Ann...you were very taken, weren't you?

c. (Later examples.)

1842 J. A. Kasson *Let.* 22 Nov. in *Virginia Mag. Hist. & Biogr.* (1948) LVI. 418 A person, male or female, that relishes society and can *talk*, will take well. **1858** G. Meredith *Let.* 28 Apr. (1970) I. 35 Translate that placard. It would take. **1963** *Listener* 14 Mar. 457/1 Jazz has 'taken' in Africa. **1981** D. Martin in Martin & Mullen *No Alternative* ii. 19 The appeal to primitive practices can obscure the pressures of today which make such practices 'take' with a section of the clergy.

11. a. Delete now *rare*. (Later examples.)

1941 B. Schulberg *What makes Sammy Run?* xi. 203 She was married... The year she came out. But it didn't take. **1978** D. Bloodworth *Crosstalk* xv. 123 [Operation] Crosstalk can do no good whatsoever unless it takes, and ..this move against Sviridov..shows it has taken.

c. Also *fig.*

1906 E. Dyson *Fact'ry 'Ands* iii. 29 Fuzzy's love was the mysterious and unhallowed growth of a moment. Sarah..had beguiled him with her Ethiopian grin and glances of matured coyness... In the words of Benno the wise, 'It took like er vaccination'. **1951** G. Greene *End of Affair* v. iv. 201 'He did it there and then.'..'Did what?' 'Baptized her a Catholic... I always had a wish that it would 'take'. Like vaccination.'

III. 14. c. To possess sexually.

1915 D. H. Lawrence *Rainbow* i. 14 Whether he were going to take her out of inflamed necessity. *Ibid.* viii. 216 Even if he did not take her, he would make her relax, he would fuse away her resistance. **1930** A. Huxley *Brief Candles* 280 She kissed him again. 'Take me.' **1948** G. Vidal *City & Pillar* i. vi. 133 He wanted to throw her on a bed and take her against her will, violently. **1962** I. Murdoch *Unofficial Rose* xiii. 122 'Well, it's up to you too, my queen,' said Randall. 'You want to be—taken, don't you?' **1978** T. Allbeury *Lantern Network* viii. 110 She lay with her eyes open as he took her.

15. d. (Earlier example referring to a newspaper.)

1798 J. Woodforde *Diary* 6 Jan. (1931) V. 92 Crouse's Norwich Paper which we used to take, did not arrive.

17. b. *to take the Fifth Amendment* (U.S.): to appeal to Article V of the ten original amendments (1791) to the Constitution of the United States, which states that 'no person.. shall be compelled in any criminal case to be a witness against himself'; hence, to decline to incriminate oneself. Usu. *ellipt.*, *to take the Fifth.*

1955 *U.S. News & World Report* 22 July 36/2 In the armed services, let a man take the Fifth Amendment and his military career is virtually doomed. **1967** *N.Y. Times* 22 Jan. iv. 10/1 (*heading*) Law: taking the Fifth and making a living. **1972** J. G. Vermandel *Last seen in Samarra* xx. 133 'You can hardly have in mind to cast me as a villain because of that.'..Alex nodded. 'Right... If you want to take the Fifth, maybe Derek will settle it for us?' **1976** *Times Lit. Suppl.* 12 Nov. 1413/2 To do what I did not want to do: take the Fifth Amendment. **1978** S. Brill *Teamsters* Pl. 4 (*caption*) The former gym teacher took the Fifth Amendment when asked about the millions of dollars in insurance he had sold to the Teamsters health and welfare funds.

19. a. Also, to answer (a telephone call).

1970 P. Moyes *Who saw her Die?* iii. 37 The shrilling of the telephone provided a welcome release... Dolly said, 'I'll take it.' **1976** G. Sims *End of Web* i. 13 'Sorry, I'll have to take it. Might be a friend I was trying to contact this morning.'..He picked up the phone. **1979** C. MacLeod *Luck runs Out* iv. 37 The telephone rang. 'I'll take it,' said Shandy.

IV. 25. d. *intr. to take and* = *to go and* s.v. Go *v.* 32 c. *dial.* and *U.S. colloq.*

1836 *Southern Lit. Messenger* II. 388/2 If you do so I will take and tell father. **1859** T. Hughes *Scouring of White Horse* vi. 129 This here..maypowl wur the last in all these parts..but..the Uffington chaps cum up, and tuk and carried 'un down ther'. **1876** 'Mark Twain' *Tom Sawyer* i. 8 I'll take and bounce a rock off'n your head. **1901** J. Barlow *From Land of Shamrock* 17 Her cherished Nellie 'took and died on her' of some mysterious malady. **1925** W. Faulkner *As I lay Dying* 44 'She's gone,' Cash says. 'She taken and left us,' pa says. **1977** 'L. Egan' *Blind Search* viii. 133 Poor soul, this awful cancer. She took and died inside of three months.

26. e. *slang.* To confront, attack; to overcome, defeat; to kill.

1939 'E. Queen' in *Blue Bk.* Oct. 17 Seems to me the champ ought to take this boy Koyle. **1956** E. L. Perry in A. Hitchcock *Stories for Late at Night* (1962) 273 Let's take him... That fat guy looks really loaded. **1963** D. Cory *Hammerhead* xi. 161 There were two men now in the doorway, both with pistols... One of them Fedora might have taken; but not, he reluctantly decided, both. **1965** I. Fleming *Man with Golden Gun* vii. 97 It had been damned fine shooting... How in hell was Bond going to take him? **1976** *Publishers Weekly* 1 Mar. 93/3 They broke their tie with the Giants and went on to take the Tigers in seven wild World Series games. **1979** E. Bercovici *Wolftrap* 41 The man who tried to take me was Martinez... Next time I am going to kill him.

28. a. *to take* (*one's*) *time* (later examples).

1788 W. Cowper *Let.* 18 Aug. (1904) III. 303, I took my own time to return, and did not reach home till after one. **1796** [see Time *sb.* 8 a]. **1873** Hardy *Pair of Blue Eyes* III. i. 21, I don't press you for an answer now, darling... Take your time. **1912** W. B. Yeats *Land of Heart's Desire* (ed. 7) 11 It's precious wine, so take your time about it. **1925** W. Faulkner *As I lay Dying* 246 'Let him take his time,' I said. 'He ain't as spry as you, remember.' **1946**, etc. [see *sweet *a.* 8 d]. **1966** A. Higgins *Langrishe, go Down* iii. 28 Taking her time, Helen cycled slowly by the wall of the Charter School. **1981** 'E. Ferrars' *Experiment with Death* iv. 68 Emma suggested that Sam had probably gone to the lavatory. 'If so, he's taking his time,' Roger said.

c. *to have* (*got*) *what it takes*: to possess the necessary attributes or qualities, esp. those needed for success. *colloq.* (orig. *U.S.*).

1929 *Amer. Speech* IV. 357 To avoid using the word *money*, the well-informed user of slang may use..*the needful, the wherewithal*,..or *what it takes.* **1933** F. Baldwin *Innocent Bystander* ix. 186 Angela, who has planty of what it takes, is the White Hope of the arty crowd which gathers at her penthouse. **1944** M. Laski *Love on Supertax* iv. 49 Only maturity's got what it takes. **1947** D. M. Davin *For Rest of our Lives* 335 The cheap verses had everything it takes to make a soldier's song. **1956** B. Holiday *Lady sings Blues* (1973) iv. 41 Sometimes I wonder how we survived. But we did. If we didn't have what it took at the beginning, we picked it up along the way. **1972** J. Wambaugh *Blue Knight* (1973) xiii. 225 He's got everything it takes but guts. **1977** *Zigzag* Apr. 26/1 They've got the right idea and what it takes.

d. *it takes all sorts to make a world*: see *sort *sb.*[2] 11 d.

e. *to take one all one's time*: see *time *sb.* 8 d.

29. b. *to take it from there*: to take over or continue from the point or situation described.

[**1948** *Radio Times* 19 Mar. 5/3 A new weekly comedy series, *Take It From Here*, will make its appearance..on Tuesday evening.] **1959** *Internat. Celebrity Reg.* 430/1 Miss Shearer informed the studio of her find. They took it from there. **1960** Wodehouse *Jeeves in Offing* xix. 188 His future hangs on this speech, and we've got it and he hasn't. We take it from there. **1973** *Ottawa Jrnl.* 14 July 24/3 They interrupt each other and talk until the breath gives out and then another one cuts in and takes it from there. **1975** N. Luard *Travelling Horseman* vi. 167 I'd tell him what I'd found out and then he could take it from there.

V. 33. a. Also in phr. *to take a letter*: to write a letter down in shorthand from another's dictation.

1943 K. Tennant *Ride on Stranger* x. 110 He seated himself at his table... 'Will you take a letter, please?'.. Her pencil travelled quite speedily after his words. **1961** *Times* 7 June 2/5 Director of general publishing house.. needs an assistant-cum-secretary. Will be expected to 'take letters'.

b. Also with reference to cinematographic filming. Occas. *intr.* Cf. *take *sb.* 9 a.

1917 *N.Y. Times* 25 Feb. 4/1 Two thousand persons participated in the coronation, which required two full days to 'take', despite the fact that it remains on the screen only three minutes. **1929** H. B. Abbott *Motion Pictures with Baby Ciné* ii. 4 It has already been stated that the motion picture is made, or 'taken', in a special camera, and that the medium upon which the picture is made is a celluloid film coated with a sensitive emulsion. **1954** N. Bau *How to make 8mm. Films* 99 (*caption*) Hold the camera absolutely steady while taking. *Ibid.* 100 If you are taking a hand-held shot, hold the camera as steady as possible. **1974** *Daily Tel.* 2 May 3/4 Using a friend's projector and screen, he ran a short colour film taken at the wedding.

VI. 34. d. *take that!*: (*a*) said as an accompaniment to the delivery of a blow; (*b*) used, with a suggestion of challenge or defiance, to emphasize a foregoing statement.

a **1425** [in Dict., sense 34 b]. **1805** C. Wilmot *Let.* 7 Dec. in *Russ. Jrnls.* (1934) II. 209, I don't pity you in the least. Take that for asking me to write you 'beautiful Russian storys'. **1846** [in Dict., sense 34 c]. **1932** Kipling *Limits & Renewals* 81 'Then take that!' and he smacked the brute's head. **1942** Berrey & Van den Bark *Amer. Thes. Slang* § 158/8 Take that and see how you like it! **1983** A. Olcott *May Day in Magadan* xiv. 249 His pride was stung. 'They want me..' he said, with an unthinking 'take that!' tilt of his nose.

39. a. Freq. in phr. *take it or leave it* and varr., expressing indifference or a refusal to bargain, compromise, etc. Cf. *take-it-or-leave-it* adj. s.v. Take-.

[**1576** W. Lambarde *Perambulation of Kent* sig. 2D3ᵛ, I..doe leaue the Reader to his free choice, to take or leaue the one, or the other.] **1664** T. Killigrew *Thomaso* in *Comedies, & Tragedies* I. iv. ii. 361 That is the price, and less I know, in curtesie you cannot offer me; take it or leave it. **1762** J. Wesley *Let.* 21 May (1931) IV. 182 As to that particular expression, 'Dying at the feet of mercy', I have only farther to add, I do not care as it is not a scriptural phrase, whether anyone takes or leaves it. **1809** B. H. Malkin tr. *Le Sage's Gil Blas* x. x. 39, I will give forty [pistoles] at a word; take them or leave them. **1898** W. S. Churchill in R. S. Churchill *Winston S. Churchill* (1967) I. Compan. II. 917 The tremendous & unchallenged power of the Trust—enabled it to dictate wages to its workmen & prices to its customers. 'Take it or leave it' it said 'This is a free country.' Thereat the oil-mechanic had to accept the offered wage or find another trade and the customer to buy the oil at the offered price or wait in the dark. **1929** D. H. Lawrence in *Forum* Jan. p. L/3 The hen knows she is unanswerable. ..There it is, take it or leave it! **1953** A. Upfield *Murder must Wait* xi. 105, I cock a snook at you... You can take it or leave it. **1962** Wodehouse *Service with Smile* x. 151 Her air was that of somebody who, where Ickenhams were concerned, could take them or leave them alone. **1977** P. G. Winslow *Witch Hill Murder* II. xv. 206, I didn't want to..say I'd gotten married and he could take it or leave it, because I was afraid he'd leave it.

b. In extended use, of a woman. *rare.*

1932 W. Faulkner *Light in August* x. 212 There were white women who would take a man with a black skin. **1941** N. Mailer *Advts. for Myself* (1961) 36 When I take a man, and I may take him for a lot of reasons, in back of it all is the feeling..that that is something I can do better than any other woman.

41. b. Freq. in phr. *take it from me*: believe me, take my word for it, be assured.

1672 Wycherley *Love in Wood* (Dedication) sig. A2ᵛ, Madam, take it from me, no man..is more dreadful than a Poet. **1829** G. Griffin *Collegians* I. v. 101 Who should walk in the doore to him, only his dead wife..! Take it from me he didn't stay long where he was. **1889** [in Dict.]. **1902** H. James *Wings of Dove* i. 20 You may take it from me once for all that I won't hear of any one of whom *she* won't. **1938** A. Christie *Death on Nile* II. xvii. 178, I think you must take it from me, Mr. Pennington, that we have examined all the possibilities very carefully. **1957** D. Robins *Noble One* xix. 177 You can take it from me that I don't believe a word of it.

42. a. *to take it on the chin*: see *chin *sb.*[1] 1 d; *to take it lying down*: see Lie *v.*[1] 21 d; *to take it in one's stride*: see Stride *sb.* 3 d.

b. *to take things as one finds them* (earlier examples); also *to take* (people) *as one finds them*: to judge people without preconceptions; to accept people as they are, esp. by expecting no special preparations for one's entertainment, etc.

[**1548** E. Hall *Union Lancaster & York* fol. ccxliiᵛ, Myne aduise is, let all men trust them, as thei fynde them.] **1580** A. Munday *Zelauto* sig. H2ᵛ, In the meane whyle, take as you finde. **1596** J. Harington *Metamorphosis of Ajax* sig. B4ᵛ, We must now take him as we finde him, with all his faults. **1638** W. CHILLINGWORTH *Relig. Protestants* I. v. 241 But reall externall deeds doe take things in grosse as they find them, not separating things which in reality are joyned together. *c* **1807** J. AUSTEN *Watsons* (1954) 351, I am one of those who always take things as they find them. I hope I can put up with a small apartment for two or three nights. **1825** in H. Wilson *Mem.* I. 147, I could have been a little romantic about you, it is true; but I always take people as I find them. **1868** DICKENS in *Our Young Folks* May 260 We have but a simple joint..but if you will take us as you find us it will be *so* kind! **1886** G. B. SHAW *Cashel Byron's Profession* xiv. 148 You can either take me as you find me, or let me alone. **1903** A. BENNETT *Leonora* ii. 47 She's gotten sausages for you..though I told her you'd take us as you found us. **1912** A. LANG *Shakespeare, Bacon & Great Unknown* xii. 247, I am only taking Ben as I find him and as I understand him. **1943** K. TENNANT *Ride on Stranger* vi. 49 All these go by wearing the peevish expression of a housewife who, not having time to make the beds, grumbles: 'You must take us as you find us.' **1980** T. BARLING *Goodbye Piccadilly* vii. 129 'Do we phone ahead in the name of protocol?' 'Hell, no. We take them as we find them.'

c. *to take a joke*: to be able to bear teasing or amusement at one's expense; usu. in negative.

1780 J. WOODFORDE *Diary* 28 Mar. (1924) I. 276 Poor Sam cant take a Joke. I forgot what I said to disoblige him. **1838** C. FOX *Jrnl.* 4 Apr. in *Memories Old Friends* (1882) iv. 27 Speaking of Dr. [John] Dalton, he said he could not take a joke at all. **1863** M. B. CHESNUT *Diary* 14 Dec. in C. V. Woodward *M. Chesnut's Civil War* (1981) xx. 505 When he saw how angry I was, he said, 'Can't you take a joke?' **1921** E. O'NEILL *Diff'rent* I. 223 *Mrs. Crosby*... Shet up your foolin', Jack. *Jack*... Nobody in this house kin take a joke. **1972** D. DELMAN *Sudden Death* (1973) ii. 59 It was a joke. Hell with anybody who can't take a joke.

d. *to (be able to) take it*: to have the capacity to endure punishment, affliction, etc.

1862 in H. Mayhew *London Labour* (ed. 2) III. 387/2 That first flogging made me ripe. I said to myself, 'I can take it like a bullock.' **1914** O. W. HOLMES *Let.* 24 Sept. in *Pollock-Holmes Lett.* (1942) I. 222, I value everything that shows the quiet unmelodramatic power to stand and take it in your people. **1941** W. S. CHURCHILL in *Unrelenting Struggle* (1942) 190 If the storm is to renew itself, London will be ready, London will not flinch, London can take it again. **1952** *Chambers's Jrnl.* Apr. 196/2 But as soon as I hadn't got Derek—well, I just couldn't take it. **1976** C. BERMANT *Coming Home* I. vi. 87 A slogan, like 'Britain can take it'.

e. *to take things* (or *it*) *as they* (or *it*) *come(s)*: to deal with events as they arise, without anticipating difficulties.

1509 A. BARCLAY tr. *Brandt's Ship of Fools* fo. 266 *recto*, That man folowes hye wysdome Whych takys all thynges lyke as they come. **1611** J. DAVIES *Scourge of Folly* 170 Take all things as they come, and bee content. So many whores do, and yet pay their Rent. **1863** 'OUIDA' *Held in Bondage* I. ix. 203 The true secret is to take things as they come. **1926** [see *BOTTOM *sb.* 11 c]. **1979** V. KELLEHER *Voices from River* iii. 34, I was trying not to think... I kept telling myself, take it as it comes.

43. (Later examples with reference to motor transport.)

1972 M. KENYON *Shooting of Dan McGrew* xxii. 184 He took the corner like a rally driver. **1976** 'B. SHELBY' *Great Pebble Affair* 181, I took the lakeshore S curve designed for thirty mph at fifty-five.

44. d. (N. Amer. examples in sense 'to become frozen'.) Occas. *pass.* Cf. sense 6 c above.

1781 *Quebec Gaz.* 11 Jan. 2/1 It has not been known to take so early as the month of December. **1820** G. SIMPSON *Jrnl. Occurrences in Athabasca Dept.* (1938) 100 This is an unusual late season as the Lake usually takes from the 15th to the 20th Oct. **1830** J. MACMILLAN Let. 15 Dec. in G. P. T. Glazebrook *Hargrave Corr. 1821–43* (1938) 58 We had a very mild fall. The river was not taken before 6th of Decr. **1871** *Scribner's Monthly* II. 458 When the rivers are beginning to 'take' or freeze.

VII. 46. a. *to take (someone's) point* (and variants): see *POINT *sb.*[1] 28 c.

47. e. *to take* (something) *as done*: to consider an omission not to have occurred; *to take* (something) *as read*: see *READ *v.* 11 e.

1893 E. F. BENSON *Dodo* I. i. 9 You haven't congratulated me. Never mind, we'll take that as done.

48. a. Freq. in phr. *what* or *who(m) do you take me for?* said as a challenge to a derogatory implication, as of foolishness, dishonesty, etc.

1847 A. & H. MAYHEW *Greatest Plague* vii. 87, I wanted to ask her who the dickens she took me for. **1892** KIPLING & BALESTIER *Naulahka* xvii. 202 'You won't get the chance,' said Tarvin unshakenly... 'What do you take me for?' **1912** C. MACKENZIE *Carnival* xxx. 293 'What do you take me for?' enquired Irene. 'I take you for what you are—a rotter.' **1921** W. J. LOCKE *Mountebank* xiii. 164 'You haven't given me away?' 'My good girl,' I protested, 'what do you take me for?' **1927** W. S. MAUGHAM *Constant Wife* III. 186 But, my poor John, whom do you take us for? Am I so unattractive that what I'm telling you is incredible? **1939** G. B. SHAW *Geneva* II. 32 Then you went to school, did you? *Begonia.* Well, of course: what do you take me for? **1983** 'R. B. DOMINIC' *Flaw in System* xx. 129 What do you take me for? A simp?

51. c. *to take care of*: see also CARE *sb.*[1] 4 b in Dict. and Suppl.

VIII. 52. c. *to take five* (or *ten*): to have a five- (or ten-) minute break. Also *loosely*, to relax. *U.S. colloq.*

1929 *Amer. Speech* V. 147 If the miner craves a rest while on the job, he *takes five*, a long enough period for a smoke. **1943** *Yank* 7 May 3 Six members of a reconnaissance group 'take 10' at a railroad station. **1961** G. T. SIMON *Feeling of Jazz* 30 Man, I'm glad they said to take five, because this next arrangement looks rough. **1973** W. SHEED *People will always be Kind* vi. 60 'Could you go a little faster, Fatman?'..It was difficult making jokes... 'O.K. Fatstuff, take five, I was only kidding.'

d. *to take a fall* (U.S.): (*a*) *slang*, to be arrested or convicted of a crime (cf. *FALL *v.* 23 f, g); (*b*) *colloq.*, to suffer a fall; similarly *to take a spill*; also *fig.*, to fall for (cf. *FALL *v.* 59*).

1942 BERREY & VAN DEN BARK *Amer. Thes. Slang* § 353/7 Fall in love... take a fall. *Ibid.* § 500/6 Be arrested... take *or* have a fall. **1953** W. BURROUGHS *Junkie* iii. 34 Jack had taken a fall on a safe job and was in the Bronx County jail awaiting trial. **1958** S. J. PERELMAN *Most of S. J. Perelman* 35, I took a rather nasty fall over a wastebasket. **1962** D. LESSING *Golden Notebk.* IV. 474 Molly rang late—says that Jane Bond has 'taken a fall over' Mr Green. **1968** *Globe & Mail* (Toronto) 15 Jan. 29/6 Even the best skier can take a spill. **1973** *Times* 9 Feb. 12/2 Michael Fish took a couple of falls.

IX. 57. a. Also with *over*, to conduct through or show around (a building, garden, etc.).

c **1810** W. HICKEY *Mem.* (1918) II. xix. 251 She..took me over the house, which was as complete a one as ever I saw. **1837** C. FOX *Jrnl.* 15 May in *Mem. Old Friends* (1882) iii. 16 Took them all over the Grove Hill gardens. **1880** TROLLOPE *Duke's Children* III. xix. 215, I want to take her all over the house. **1911** *Rep. Labour & Social Conditions in Germany* (Tariff Reform League) III. 166 [He] was able yesterday to take a small deputation..over the 'Triumph' works.

d. In colloq. phr. *you can't take it with you*, in allusion to the impossibility of benefiting from earthly wealth after death.

1841 MARRYAT *Masterman Ready* II. ii. 22 He was very fond of money; but that they said was all the better, as he could not take it away with him when he died. **1923** G. ARTHUR *Let.* 16 Sept. in *Further Lett. Man of no Importance* (1932) 153 Mr. Gladstone, when a dead millionaire was held up for his admiration because he had left large sums for charities, said, 'Thank him for nothing; he was obliged to leave it somewhere as he couldn't take it with him.' **1937** KAUFMAN & HART (*title*) You can't take it with you. **1952** A. CHRISTIE *Mrs. McGinty's Dead* vii. 48 'They inherited a little money when Mrs. McGinty died.'..'Well, that's natural enough... You can't take it with you.' **1977** J. PORTER *Who the Heck is Sylvia?* x. 87 You're not short of the odd penny... And you can't take it with you, can you?

58. b. Also, *to take one's (own) life*: to kill oneself, commit suicide.

1920 D. H. LAWRENCE *Women in Love* xv. 211 It was not a question of taking one's life—she would *never* kill herself. **1965** *Amer. Speech* XL. 301 This person may indeed take his own life. **1981** *Daily Tel.* 18 June 19/2 A note left by them made it clear that they wanted to take their own lives and also wished to be buried in the same grave.

c. (Further examples.) Also *euphem.* in *pass.*, to die.

1749 GRAY *Let.* 7 Nov. (1900) I. 204 He who has preserved her to you so many years..has taken her from us to Himself. **1809** J. PORTER *Scottish Chiefs* xxxiv. 257 If all whom I love be lost to me here, take me then to thyself, and let my freed spirit fly to thy embraces in heaven! **1920** E. O'NEILL *Beyond Horizon* II. i. 69 It was God's will that he should be taken. **1977** [see *PASS *v.* 65 c].

XI. 74. take to—. h. *N.Z. slang.* To attack, usu. with fists.

1911 'KIWI' *On Swag* iii. 9 Take to him, Bill. **1960** N. HILLIARD *Maori Girl* II. xiv. 159 When we got home he really took to me. That was when I lost a lot of my teeth.

XII. 76. take aback. (Earlier *fig.* example.)

1829 F. MARRYAT *Frank Mildmay* I. ix. 266, I was so taken aback with the sudden appearance and address of this beautiful vision, that I knew not what to say.

76*. take about. *trans.* To conduct on a round of sight-seeing or on excursions, etc.

1823 P. PANAM *Mem. Young Greek Lady* 117 If you wish for any thing speak to him; he will take you about everywhere. **1894** E. FAWCETT *New Nero* Proem 8 He.. took him about for almost an hour, showing him a good many places. **1903** A. W. PATTERSON *Schumann* 113 He seems to have taken the Laidlaw ladies about a good deal.

77*. take apart. *trans.* **a.** To dismantle or take to pieces; also *fig.*, to search thoroughly; to demolish or wreck.

1936 C. SANDBURG *People, Yes* 60 Let's take it apart to see how it ticks. **1958** M. ALLINGHAM *Hide my Eyes* xv. 150, I am going to take this shed apart if it costs me my ticket. **1968** 'E. PETERS' *Grass Widow's Tale* xi. 140 It has to be somewhere here. Stands to sense. Go take that little front room apart, Skinner. **1969** *Oz* Apr. 25/1 There will be a lobby of Parliament which far from pleading with MPs will probably take Whitehall apart. **1974** D. SEAMAN *Bomb that could Lip-Read* xxiv. 243 There is going to be one God-awful search for the man... They will take this hamlet apart. **1978** M. PUZO *Fools Die* xv. 161 The new kids were wilder and started taking everything apart.

b. To thrash or beat soundly; also *fig.*, to attack with argument or criticism.

1942 N. BALCHIN *Darkness falls from Air* v. 94 Supposing I went round and took him apart? **1963** *Listener* 21 Feb. 350/3 The Labour Party's new leader was taken apart with the sort of cheerful and dedicated venom hitherto reserved for Tory Cabinet ministers. **1969** 'J. ASHFORD' *Prisoner at Bar* xii. 117 And don't get funny with Bladen..or he'll take you apart at the seams. **1971** S. E. MORISON *European Discovery Amer.: Northern Voy.* vii. 242 Manuel C. Baptista de Lima..has politely taken me apart and argued for the 1492 date. **1976** *Birmingham Post* 16 Dec. 12/2 League leaders Liverpool were taken apart by the speed, skill and determination of the entire Villa side.

78. take away. a. Also = *put away* s.v. *PUT *v.*[1] 38 f (*b*). *U.S.*

1919 E. O'NEILL *Where Cross is Made* in *Moon of Caribbees* (1923) 16 They say for his own good he must be taken away.

d. (Earlier example.)

1838 C. WATERTON *Ess. Nat. Hist.* p. xxv, After eluding him in cover for nearly half an hour, being hard pressed, I took away down a hedgerow.

80. take down. b. (*e*) (Earlier example.)

1840 M. EDGEWORTH *Let.* 30 Dec. (1971) 573 Sir John Campbell took me down to dinner and I was seated of course beside him.

c. *to take* (a person) *down a peg*: see PEG *sb.*[1] 3.

e. Also, with person as obj.: to write down the words of, to take dictation from.

1883 'MARK TWAIN' *Life on Miss.* xxii. 247, I enlisted a poet for company, and a stenographer to 'take him down'. **1928** D. H. LAWRENCE *Woman who rode Away* 18 She certainly didn't want to take him down in short hand.

f. *spec.* To record a contentious statement made in a legislative assembly with a view to invoking disciplinary procedure.

1784 *Universal Mag.* Jan. 45/1 Gen Conway said that he was ready to maintain what he had said. Let the right hon. gentleman move to take down his words, and he would make his charge. **1863** *Illustr. Times* 20 June 422/2 Mr Cox had..insinuated that..Lord Ranelagh wished to have power to flog volunteers; and on Monday Mr. Ormsby Gore rose and denounced these words as 'scandalous and unfounded'. Whereupon Sir Robert Jackes Clifton jumped up and moved that the words were taken down. **1934** *Sun* (Baltimore) 3 May 1/4 Representative Pettingill ..threatened to invoke disciplinary procedure against Mr. Britten by means of what is known in the House as 'taking down' his words.

g. To cheat, trick, swindle. *Austral. slang.*

1895 *Argus* (Melbourne) 5 Dec. 5/2 [The defendant] accused him of having 'taken him down', stigmatised him as a thief and a robber.

82. take in. e. Also *spec.*, to lead in (to dinner). (Further examples.) Cf. sense 80 b (*e*), *85 c.

1863 A. J. MUNBY *Diary* 3 June in D. Hudson *Munby* (1972) 165 The new Lord of the Admiralty..and his wife: whom I took in to supper. **1887** M. MONKSWELL *Jrnl* fo. 266 *recto*, 25 May in *Victorian Diarist* (1944) 132 We dined with the Dean [of Hereford] that very evening. He took me in.

k. (Earlier and later examples in sense 'to include in a journey or visit'.) Also *loosely*, to go to. No longer restricted to the U.S.

1755 in *Essex Inst. Hist. Coll.* (1916) LII. 80 In our way by the Skuylkill rd. took in ye prop[rieto]rs Gardens. **1880** 'MARK TWAIN' *Tramp Abroad* iii. 42 An owl that come from Nova Scotia..took this thing in on his way back. **1925** *New Yorker* 7 Mar. 19/1 There's no use me asking you if you took in all the revues. **1940** 'N. SHUTE' *Landfall* 26 He might pick up Matheson or Hooper and take in a movie. **1968** *Globe & Mail* (Toronto) 17 Feb. 32 (Advt.) Even take in breakfast at Le Drugstore..and head home again on the return flight. **1977** D. BAGLEY *Enemy* i. 12 We took in more theatres, an opera, a couple of ballets.

p*. *Stock Exchange.* To receive contango on (stocks or shares); to accept (stocks, etc.) as security for a loan. Cf. *give on* b s.v. *GIVE *v.* 61.

1893 R. BITHELL *Counting-House Dict.* (ed. 2) 292 The term [taken in stock] is applied solely to stocks taken in for fortnightly or monthly loans on the Stock Exchange. **1911** W. THOMSON *Dict. Banking* 503/1 In connection with the Stock Exchange settlements, a 'taker-in' is a broker who lends money against stock (i.e. 'takes in' stock) to a broker who requires to pay for a purchase. **1912** *Q. Rev.* July 102 The dealer says that he will 'take them in', which means that he will lend the money until the settlement following that for which the original bargain was effected. **1928** *Morning Post* 19 Nov. 3/3 If the other man..prefers to take a rate of money rather than to accept the cash which delivery of the shares would produce, he will 'take them in'—the opposite operation to 'giving on'. **1934** F. E. ARMSTRONG *Bk. Stock Exchange* vi. 108 When no 'takers' can be found someone has to provide the cash, and firms known as money brokers frequently agree to 'take in' the securities purely as a money-lending proposition. **1955** *Beginners, Please* (Investors' Chron.) ii. 44 In normal market conditions it is probably easier to 'take-in' shares, i.e., carry over a sale to the next settlement, than to 'give on' shares, i.e., carry over a purchase. This is because generally there are more bulls than bears. Under such conditions the 'giver' pays a rate of interest to the 'taker' for the accommodation provided.

p.** *slang.* To take into custody, arrest. Cf. *pull in* s.v. *PULL *v.* 25 e.

1942 BERREY & VAN DEN BARK *Amer. Thes. Slang* § 500/5 Arrest..take, take in or up. **1978** J. B. HILTON *Some run Crooked* xiv. 138 You can tell me now, or I'm taking you in to help. **1979** J. VAN DE WETERING *Maine Massacre* iii. 26 You're not taking me in, sheriff.

s. *N. Amer. dial.* To open, begin, *esp.* of a school term. Cf. sense 90 r below.

1876 'MARK TWAIN' *Tom Sawyer* 162 She could hardly wait for school to 'take in'. **1906** *Dialect Notes* III. 160 School takes in early and takes out late, seems to me. **1942** *Post* (Morgantown, W. Va.) 14 Sept. 4 An obligation ..upon drivers to be careful of children, esp. in the hours that school takes in and lets out. **1956** W. R. Bird *Off-Trail in Nova Scotia* iii. 99 One girl turned to me and declared she had seen him with it before school took in.

83. take off. a. (*e*) *U.S. Blacks.* To rob or burgle; to 'hold up'. Cf. *to rip off* (ii), (iv) s.v. *rip *v.*² 4**.

1970 C. Major *Dict. Afro-Amer. Slang* 113 *Take off*,.. to rob or hurt. **1972** J. Hudson in T. Kochman *Rappin' & Stylin' Out* 413, I can't go no place expecting to take off some fat sucker if I look like a greaseball. **1973** *Black World* Jan. 56/1 He and Cecil B were to take off a supermarket in San Jose.

c. (Earlier example.)

1836 Dickens *Pickw.* (1837) ii. 7 Here, No. 924, take your fare, and take yourself off.

e. Also in *Cricket*, to remove (a bowler) after a spell of bowling in order to replace him.

1851 W. Bolland *Cricket Notes* iv. 75 Do not..refuse to bowl any more; neither grumble nor growl if you are taken off. **1921** G. R. C. Harris *Few Short Runs* xi. 280 Don't turn sulky because after bowling five consecutive maidens you are taken off. **1977** *Times* 17 Jan. 7/1 When Greig took him off after 95 minutes his figures for the morning were 10–5–7–1.

n. (*a*) (Later examples in sense 'to go off', etc.)

1959 I. & P. Opie *Lore & Lang. Schoolch.* x. 193 Juvenile language is well stocked..with expressions inviting a person's departure, for instance:..take off, [etc.]. **1968** *Listener* 19 Dec. 809/3 I'm not stopping here,..no matter what they say or do... I'm taking off tonight. **1972** J. Philips *Vanishing Senator* (1973) iii. iii. 147 You'd better take off. I've just got to get some sleep. **1978** M. Duffy *Housespy* vii. 178 Danny Oldfield's taken off. I'll let you know when I find her.

(*d*) *Aeronaut.* Of a pilot, plane, etc.: to perform the operations involved in beginning flight; to become air-borne. Also *transf.* of a bird.

?**1849** G. Cayley *Let.* in C. H. Gibbs-Smith *Sir George Cayley's Aeronautics* (1962) xlii. 136 It is absolutely necessary that the tail be securely braced up a little, and that the centre of gravity be made to act steadily on the bulk of the surfaces so that when weighed up to the weight of the person trying the wings—should it take off, they would skim and not either rise up hill or sink down hill. **1918** *Punch* 3 Apr. 222/2 Yes, he crashed a few days ago—in his first solo flip, taking off. **1927** C. A. Lindbergh *We* ii. 19, I taxied to one end of the field, opened the throttle and started to take off. **1936** G. B. Shaw *Simpleton* ii. 69 All I want is a parapet to take off from. **1951** A. C. Clarke *Sands of Mars* i. 1, I once took-off standing up, just for a bet. **1973** *Sci. Amer.* Dec. 102/1 If the birds are pursued, they take off, but they do not fly far before they land again.

(*e*) *fig.* Of prices, costs, etc.: to rise steeply or suddenly. Of a scheme, project, etc.: to be launched (successfully), to become popular.

1963 J. N. Harris *Weird World Wes Beattie* (1964) xv. 184 Minerva took off, as we say, on a famous Friday the thirteenth... The stock rose from nineteen cents to over a dollar in the last half-hour of trading. **1970** *Melody Maker* 12 Sept. 33/3, I shall be pretty sick if Andy Williams' record takes off and mine dies. **1971** *Physics Bull.* Oct. 590/2 Prof. E. C. Cherry..devised an arrangement which resulted in reduction in bandwidth requirements... This likewise has not taken off so far although much more interest is now being show in it. **1976** *Ibid.* Sept. 401/1 Production and salary costs 'took off'. **1978** *Detroit Free Press* 5 Mar. B 12/2 They had best seller hopes for the book, but it hasn't really taken off. **1981** *Church Times* 10 Apr. 9/5 Frank Scuffham has hopes of his committee, but acknowledges that it has not taken off yet. **1983** *Times* 20 Jan. 15/3 Sales of existing properties have taken off during the last few months.

o. *U.S. dial.* To absent oneself from work, school, etc.

1935 W. Faulkner *As I lay Dying* 115 You take off and stay in the house today. **1936** W. Greene *Death in Deep South* (1937) 61 She thought she'd be off in the afternoon and she said she'd take off anyway if she wasn't.

84. take on. d. (*b*) To engage (someone) in a fight, contest, argument, etc.

1885 [in Dict.]. **1915** E. Corri *30 Yrs. Boxing Ref.* 150 Instead of going for what the boxers call the 'easy money', Basham took on Matt Wells. **1928** *Daily Tel.* 24 Apr. 12/6, I saw the Sopwith take him on, and whilst I was changing drums I was attacked again in front by a Roland. **1930** G. B. Shaw *Apple Cart* i. 26 In this conflict we are the challengers. You have the choice of weapons. If you choose scandal, we'll take you on at that. **1976** *Morecambe Guardian* 7 Dec. 8/3 Micky Taylor earned the spotlight with a brilliant, cheeky dribble in which he took on and beat four men.

f. Restrict † *Obs. rare* to sense in Dict. and add: (*b*) To pretend, affect.

1858 Dickens in *Househ. Words* Xmas No. 20/1 This gent took on not to know me.

85. take out. c. Also, to lead (a woman) in (to a formal dinner). Cf. sense 80 b (*e*), 82 e in Dict. and Suppl.

1876 Trollope *Prime Minister* III. x. 166 John Fletcher took her out to dinner and Arthur did not sit near her. **1880** —— *Duke's Children* ii. xx. 240 It was of course contrived at dinner that Lord Popplecourt should take out Lady Mary. **1905** J. H. Choate *Let.* 27 Jan. in E. S. Martin *Life J. H. Choate* (1920) II. viii. 272 The King took Mama out to dinner. **1913** in C. Seymour *Intimate Papers Col. House* (1926) I. vii. 188 He considered taking a duchess or royalty out to dinner was hard sledding.

j. *intr.* To go away, make off, start out. *U.S.*

1855 in *Montana Hist. Soc. Contrib.* (1940) X. 137, I took out in order to give them the slip. **1896** 'Mark Twain' in *Harper's Mag.* Aug. 355/1 Out jumps four men and took out up the road as tight as they could go. **1929** W. Faulkner *Sound & Fury* 310 They'll have to hitch up and take out to get home by midnight. **1938** M. K. Rawlings *Yearling* i. 11 How come you to take out such a fur piece?

k. *Bridge.* To remove (one's partner) from his situation in the auction by changing the suit of the probable contract or by bidding in response to his double. Also *into* (the fresh suit), with bid as obj., and *absol.*

1917 E. Bergholt *Royal Auction Bridge* (1918) 88 How am I to know..whether you are taking me out from strength or from weakness? **1921** A. M. Foster *Auction Bridge* 38 If your partner takes you out from weakness into a suit call you are likely to be fined. **1956** Mollo & Gardener *Bridge for Beginners* vii. 75 Responder may have a feeble five or six-card suit and nothing else. Then he takes out the double. **1977** *Homes & Gardens* Feb. 17 If..you held hand II, then it would be correct to take out into Two Hearts. *Ibid.* 14 Most players would take their partners out into Four Hearts on both of these hands.

l. To kill, murder; to destroy or obliterate (a specific target). *slang.*

1939 R. Chandler *Big Sleep* ii. 26 I'll take him out... He'll think a bridge fell on him. **1955** *Times* 28 June 4/4 The purpose of the attack was to 'take out'—as the strategist's jargon has it—the docks. **1962** L. Deighton *Ipcress File* xviii. 109 In terms of destructive area, this is a bomb that would take out a whole city. **1967** J. M. Fox *Dead Pigeon* 170 'He took out two people who could have involved him.'.. 'Took out? You mean he killed them?' **1977** *Times Lit. Suppl.* 15 Apr. 464/4 A sudden air attack, which would take out London, on a scale comparable with the attacks on Dresden or Hiroshima in 1945. **1978** M. Duffy *Housespy* v. 124 He was taken out yesterday... They ran him down. **1982** *Daily Tel.* 14 June 4/8 For several hours, as a commanding officer and his officers tried to 'take out' the sniper with machine gun, rifle and artillery fire, his bullets ricochetted off rocks above our heads.

m. *Austral.* and *N.Z. colloq.* To accept as a punishment, reward, etc.; to win.

1943 K. Tennant *Ride on Stranger* xvi. 176 George Benson told her briefly he would see her husband had a lawyer. He would probably get a month at the most and he'd better 'take it out'. **1976** *Australian* 15 July 2 Helen Morse..takes out the Australian Film Institute's top actress award tomorrow night. **1977** *N.Z. Herald* 8 Jan. i. 6/8 The Games we play..can't..end, till Someone takes them out.

86. take out of. g. *to take one out of oneself*: to distract one's attention from one's own concerns; to amuse, divert or occupy (a person).

1848 G. Jewsbury Let. 4 Oct. in *Lett. to Jane W. Carlyle* (1892) 257 There are no bothering algebraical calculations as far as I went, but glimpses, as it were, into the 'everlasting universe of things', till one is taken out of oneself completely. **1908** A. Bennett *Old Wives' Tale* iv. iv. 531 Dr. Stirling wished to practise his curative treatment of taking the sisters 'out of themselves'. **1929** J. B. Priestley *Good Companions* ii. iii. 301, I haven't enjoyed anything so much, I don't know when..they're so good they've taken me right out of myself. **1941** A. Christie *Evil under Sun* xii. 218 Poirot had..dwelt on the advantage it would be to Linda to have something to take her out of herself. **1958** P. Marris *Widows & their Families* ii. 21 My sister..took me out for walks. It's wonderful how it takes you out of yourself. **1974** [see *outside interest* s.v. *outside B. 6].

86*. take out on. *trans.* In phr. *to take it out on* (someone or something): to vent one's anger, frustration, etc., on an object other than the cause of it.

1840 H. Cockton *Valentine Vox* xxi. 158 P'r'aps you'd like to take it out on me, 'cos if yer would, yer know, why ony say so. **1903** 'C. E. Merriman' *Lett. from Son* vi. 72 Milligan..came around to take your cussing of him out on me. **1926** G. Hunting *Vicarion* xviii. 311 Make some records of me, and take it out on them. **1947** A. Huxley *Let.* 9 Mar. (1969) 567 He can't associate sex with respectability, but he has to take it all out on tarts or housemaids. **1958** *Daily Sketch* 2 June 12/6 You may be irritable at work, but don't take it out on your colleagues. **1967** *Listener* 11 May 611/2 The country took out its frustrations on Congress. **1978** P. Marsh et al. *Rules of Disorder* ii. 39 My brother..was a troublemaker and now they're taking it out on me.

87. take over. b. Also *absol.* Also *to take over from*: to relieve, take the place of, succeed.

1916 'Boyd Cable' *Action Front* 182 The colonel was severely wounded and had sent for the second in command to take over. *Ibid.* 234 Riley..explained the position to the subaltern who took over from him. **1946** D. C. Peattie *Road of Naturalist* i. 20 A ranker, branching dandelion took over from the desert dandelions. **1978** J. Gardner *Dancing Dodo* xiv. 101 Terry Makepiece was not going to take over on this. He would see it through himself.

90. *take up.* **c.** (*a*) (Further examples.) Also, † to make (a further hole) in order to shorten a strap. To shorten or tighten (a garment, pattern, etc.), esp. by hemming or tucking.

1818 C. Brown *Let.* 7 Aug. in *Lett. J. Keats* (1958) I. 361, I must have another hole taken up in the strap of my Knapsack. **1916** L. I. Baldt *Clothing for Women* ix. 186 To shorten pattern... Lay fold at same point, to shorten length, unless a great deal has to be taken up, in which case some could be taken from the bottom. **1937** P. H. Richards *Dress Creation* xiii. 113 The quantity taken up in the tucks should amount in all to the distance between A and C. **1972** A. Ross *London Assignment* 28 The trousers were a fraction long, and would need to be taken up.

d. (*a*) Also, to apply for or claim. Cf. *take-up *sb.* (*a*.) 6.

1971 *Guardian* 15 Apr. 1/1 A major campaign to persuade people to take up their welfare and social security benefits has been launched by the Government.

(*c*) (Earlier example in sense 'to subscribe for (shares)'.)

1869 *Bradshaw's Railway Man.* XXI. 402 Of 100,000 new 10*l.* shares..84,837 have been taken up.

(*d*) (Earlier examples.) Also *fig.*

1849 E. Davies *Amer. Scenes* 42 While they were singing Brother such-a-one would 'take up the collection'. **1880** 'Mark Twain' *Tramp Abroad* ix. 88 She became a sort of contribution box. This dear young thing in the theatre had been sitting there unconsciously taking up a collection [of fleas].

f. (*a*) Also *absol.* (see quot. 1974).

1960 E. L. Delmar-Morgan *Cruising Yacht Equipment & Navigation* vii. 86 The planks and timbers will dry out... When they are once again waterborne they will leak until the wood 'takes up'. **1974** J. Keats *Of Time & Island* xi. 177 The [fibreglass] boats did not have to be put into the river to soak, or take up, as the people said.

(*b*) *Engin.* To accept, absorb, or assimilate (by gearing, etc.).

1921 *Conquest* Oct. 510/2 It appears to have solved the problem generally of how gradually and smoothly to take up and transmit the power of a prime mover or motor. **1966** *Listener* 24 Nov. 773/1 Although the paint is applied neatly, there are slight irregularities... These slight irregularities help the colours to engage with each other,.. rather as the slightly abrasive surface of a clutch-plate takes up the transmission.

h. (*c*) *to take* (a person) *up on* (something): to accept an offer, invitation, etc. *colloq.*

1914 S. Lewis *Our Mr. Wrenn* v. 63 'We'll go Dutch to a lodging-house.'.. 'All right, sir; all right. I'll take you up on that.' **1948** 'N. Shute' *No Highway* vii. 192 It's just an estimate... I didn't want people to take me up on it like this. **1961** J. Stroud *Touch & Go* iv. 45 'Tell her not to hesitate to ask.' 'Thank yc ı... I might take you up on that.' **1974** 'E. Ferrars' *Hanged Man's House* xv. 149 I'll go over to see Mrs Bayne and take her up on her invitation to lunch. **1979** B. Parvin *Deadly Dyke* xxiv. 134, I must be going. I'll take you up on that coffee later.

n. (*a*) For *Obs.* exc. *dial.* read: Now *U.S.*, of a horse. Also *intr.* of a rider, to rein in.

1942 *Sun* (Baltimore) 20 Oct. 15/1 Fogoso..cut sharply in front of Sunset Boy, causing Jimmy Berger to take up. **1946** *Ibid.* 2 Oct. 15/2 Red Tag ran into tight corners at the head of the stretch and was forced to take up. **1950** *Ibid.* 20 May 11/1 Queen May, ridden by Joe Culmone, was not to get through... Culmone was forced to take up.

r. For † *Obs.* read: *Obs.* exc. *intr.* in *U.S.*, (esp. of a school term) to begin, start up. Cf. sense 82 s above.

1871 E. Eggleston *Hoosier Schoolm.* xii. 104 Meetin's took up. **1903** J. Fox *Little Shepherd* iii. 42 When school 'took up again', Chad was told to say them aloud in concert with the others. **1949** 'J. Nelson' *Backwoods Teacher* 51 Four other children..trooped in, having belatedly heard that school was taking up today. **1961** M. Beadle *These Ruins are Inhabited* (1963) iii. 46 Red's school took up in two days.

x. (Later examples.)

1936 M. Mitchell *Gone with Wind* xii. 234, I knew you were doing it just to take up for me. **1977** *New Yorker* 6 June 85/1 'Wouldn't it embarrass *you*, hearing that *your* daddy spent a night in jail?' And Henry said no, it wouldn't—not if he knew his daddy had been taking up for someone.

z. (*a*) Also, to become friendly with, to form a relationship with.

1957 R. Hoggart *Uses of Literacy* iii. 76 The woman he 'took up with' was likely enough to be married herself and of roughly the same age as his own wife. **1963** *Australasian Post* 14 Mar. 44/1 Miss Dolly has 'taken up' with a poor but respectable cabinet-maker and his wife... She sells her stolen nag to help them out. **1977** *Daily Express* 29 Jan. 7/2 The story is of a poor but pretty girl..who breaks her engagement to a morose butcher..and takes up instead with a feckless punter.

XIII. 91. *take* and 25 d, *t* as it comes 42 e, *t* as done 47 e, *t* as one finds 42 b, *t* a fall 52 d, *t* the Fifth Amendment 17 b, *t* five 52 c, *t* it 42 d, *t* it from me 41 b, *t* it from there 29 b, *t* a joke 42 c, *t* or leave 39 a, *t* a letter 33 a, *t* one's life 58 b, *t* over 57 a, *t* a spill 52 d, *t* ten 52 c, *t* that 34 d, *t* with one 57 d.

take, *sb.* Add: **2. a.** (Further examples.) Also *spec.*, personal income or earnings (*U.S. colloq.*).

1850 N. Wiseman *Let.* 9 Dec. in *Dublin Rev.* (1919) Jan. 9 On Sunday the church was open... You may judge of the crowds when I tell you that the *take* was £94. **1937** *Sun* (Baltimore) 9 Feb. 11/2 There is the case of the checkroom girl in a hotel, who receives tips for each garment checked, but turns her 'take' over to the management. **1943** *Ibid.* 25 Feb. 12/1 They will seek to increase their take by selling whisky on the side. **1966** P. O'Donnell *Sabre-Tooth* v. 83 It was a big enough take for her to make a once-only comeback from retirement. **1970** 'B. Mather' *Break in Line* v. 59 The luggage coolies..who kicked back half of their take to the Pathan hall porter. **1978** *Detroit Free Press* 5 Mar. B7/6 Isley will have to make do with his take from the Tractor Pull.

b. *Criminals' slang* (chiefly *U.S.*). Money acquired by theft or fraud.

1888 J. Greenwood *Policeman's Lantern* 69 A tidyish 'take' brought about by what he called the 'sweetstuff lay'. **1927** C. F. Coe *Me—Gangster* xiii. 228 After the stick-up..Carrots..can watch the take till I send the porter over after it. **1934** *Sun* (Baltimore) 14 July 3/5 A self-confessed confidence man..testified that he always handed his take to Graham, who..kept fifteen per cent for providing police protection. **1955** *Publ. Amer. Dial. Soc.* xxiv. 194 The day's *take* is the *knock up*, and the mob usually pools expenses for the day..and this amount is taken off the *top* (the total *take*). **1963** G. J. McCall in A. Dundes *Mother Wit* (1973) 422 The multimilliondollar 'take' of the hoodoo complex.

c. *U.S. colloq.* A percentage of a sum of money which is deducted, as for tax or other levies.

1935 *Sun* (Baltimore) 18 Jan. 14/7 Once the mutuel 'take' is raised over 7½ per cent. Maryland no longer can compete with other Eastern tracks. **1942** *Ibid.* 20 Mar. 14/2 What is the whole take of the Lewis dues collectors? How much of that take is a compulsory tribute through strong-arm imposition of closed-shop contracts? **1975** *Lamp* (Exxon Corporation) Winter 11/2 A recent act of Parliament imposes a special tax on revenues from British fields; combined with royalties and corporate income taxes, it raises total government 'take' to as much as 75 per cent, depending on the size of the field.

7. (Earlier examples.)

1847 J. S. Robb *Streaks of Squatter Life* 54 Here was a '*take*' in the book of human nature, which was most 'fair copy'. **1853** 'Mark Twain' *Let.* 26 Oct. (1917) I. i. 26 When one gets a good agate take, he is sure to make money.

8. a. *Med.* A successful inoculation with a vaccine. **b.** *Agric.* Successful germination and growth of seed. **c.** *Med.* An acceptance by the body of tissue foreign to the site or to the individual.

1909 in *Cent. Dict.* Suppl. **1914** *Q. Jrnl. Med.* VII. 284 Revaccination on an individual who has been vaccinated many years previously usually results in what might be termed a genuine 'take'. **1921** H. Guthrie-Smith *Tutira* xix. 165 Between the isolated plants of the miserable 'take' of seed there was ample space left for the germination of undesirables. **1924** *Surg., Gynecol. & Obstetr.* XXXVIII. 101/2 A temporary take [of grafted skin] occurred but did not thrive well. **1940** R. G. Stapledon *Re-grassing* 21 In cases where the 'take' had been exceptionally good, and where there has been no immediate return of undesirable species, excessive early growth is far from disastrous. **1965** *Nursing Times* 5 Feb. 180/1 Persistent negative nitrogen balance results in..poor graft take. **1977** *Lancet* 13 Aug. 356/2 In studies with live vaccines patients showing serological or virological evidence of virus 'take' are usually compared with the placebo group and/or with vaccine recipients who show no evidence of infection.

9. a. *Cinematogr.* A continuous section of film photographed at one time; an instance of such filming. Also preceding a numeral to distinguish individual sections of film. (In quot. 1922 used *collect.*) orig. *U.S.*

1922 *Opportunities in Motion Picture Industry* (Photoplay Research Soc.) 50 When the daily 'take' is handed in, does Mr. Director look for 'action'; does the technical man look to see how his pet scene photographed? **1928** *Sunday Dispatch* 2 Sept. 5/4 Notwithstanding the fact that the director knows that certain 'takes' are useless and need not be printed. **1937** H. G. Wells *Brynhild* ix. 144 Very few of the players..realized that a movie take was afoot outside the marquee. **1947** *People* 22 June 5/3 Micky and..Dave Crowley did the same fight 25 times before the final take was okayed. **1962** *Movie* Sept. 19/1 This conversation occupies part of a long take in a medium shot which favours neither point of view. **1972** *Listener* 21 Dec. 852/1 Sequence of calls before a shot. Production Assistant: 'Quiet. Going for a take.'.. First Assistant: '245, Take 5.' **1976** H. R. F. Keating *Filmi, Filmi, Inspector Ghote* vi. 53 The scrawled chalk figures on the black board must indicate which scene and 'take' this was.

b. A sound recording; the act of making such a recording. orig. *U.S.*

1926 Whiteman & McBride *Jazz* xii. 248 At 12, a rehearsal or phonograph take. **1946** R. Blesh *Shining Trumpets* ix. 209 The results are..a tribute to the recording engineer who supervised the 'take'. **1965** *Melody Maker* 3 Apr. 10 Of added interest is the fact that these takes..have not been issued in Britain before. **1972** *Daily Tel.* (Colour Suppl.) 17 Nov. 9/3 Barkworth once had a one-word voice-over: 'Maltesers', which required 42 takes. Listening to the playback of the tape, he got the giggles. **1977** *Rolling Stone* 13 Jan. 48/2 Still such gems as 'All the Way from Memphis' and 'All the Young Dudes', along with a different take of 'Roll Away the Stone' and two previously unheard cuts,..give this absorbing group a belated last testament.

10. *on the take*: taking bribes; capable of being suborned. *slang* (orig. *U.S.*).

1930 *Liberty* 29 Nov. 70/1 There are men and women ready to boost the thief's game. The steer guy finds him work, dicks on the take protect him. **1935** J. O'Hara *Appointment in Samarra* i. 27 There was a conductorman who was not on the take. Ed for some reason hadn't been about to get to him with a dime, not a dime. **1942** Berrey & Van den Bark *Amer. Thes. Slang* §374/5 *Bribable*, approachable, fixable, on the take. **1956** B. Holiday *Lady sings Blues* (1973) xxi. 169, I had heard of city cops taking plenty of money, but I never heard of a Treasury agent on the take since long before my time. **1967** *Boston Sunday Globe* 23 Apr. 18/5 In an unguarded public moment [he]..said, 'Half the people in Philadelphia are on the take.' **1975** *Listener* 16 Jan. 67/1 No matter how many Government departments were on the take, it was also evident that..the law enforcers themselves were bent. **1980** R. L. Duncan *Brimstone* v. 90 'I'm not on the take,' he said.

take-. Add: **take-all,** substitute for def.: a disease of wheat and other cereals caused by the fungus *Ophiobolus graminis*, which produces a foot rot, yellowing of the plants, and stunted growth; (later examples); **take-apart** *a.*, capable of being taken to pieces and reassembled; **take-charge** *a. colloq.* (orig. and chiefly *N. Amer.*), pertaining to or characterized by leadership or authority; cf. *take-hold* adj. below; **take-down,** (*a*) (later examples); (*b*) (a rifle with) the capacity to have the barrel and magazine detached from the stock; usu. *attrib.* or as *adj.*; (*c*) *Austral. slang*, a deceiver, cheat, or thief; **take-hold** *a.* (*U.S. colloq.*) = *take-charge* adj. above; **take-home** *a.* (orig. *U.S.*), that may be taken away home; esp. as *take-home pay*, that portion of a person's earnings which is left after deductions of tax, insurance, etc.; **take-it-or-leave-it** *a.*: also as *sb.* in various senses (cf. *take it or leave it* s.v. *Take *v.* 39 a); **take-with** *a.* (*U.S. colloq.*), that may be taken along with one; *spec.* (see quot. 1941); also applied to prices; cf. *cash and carry* s.v. *Cash *sb.*[1] 2 g.

1912 *Bull. Misc. Inf. R. Bot. Gardens Kew* 436 In the condition known as 'Take-all', the plants are attacked seriously at an early stage of growth and become yellow, and often die before the stem is formed. **1950** H. J. Massingham *Curious Traveller* viii. 150 The weather.. has certainly nursed the spread of take-all. **1978** *Times* 7 Aug. 3/2 'Take-all'..can make a wheat plant yield a stunted and useless ear. **1966** J. S. Cox *Illustr. Dict. Hairdressing & Wigmaking* 147/1 Take-apart wig. **1979** *Nature* 5 July p. viii/3 Equipment is housed in a practical, take-apart cabinet that provides a support surface and slip-fit vacuum connection for various manifold arrangements. **1954** *Sun* (Baltimore) 1 Apr. 20/4 [The team] lacks a take-charge guy... Neither..players..have those take-charge qualities. **1965** *Economist* 23 Jan. 339/1 Mr Wilson and Mr George Brown, the two take-charge men. **1970** [see *pivot *sb.* 3 c]. **1976** M. Machlin *Pipeline* xliii. 456 Usually that take-charge tone of voice would send the adrenalin racing through Larry's system, setting up deep currents of psychological resistance. **1897** *Sears, Roebuck Catal.* 578/2 All rifles of this model can be furnished with pistol grip, with take down and all other extras. *Ibid.* 579/2 No other lengths made in Take Down style. **1901** *Kynoch Jrnl.* Aug.–Sept. 136/1 This is not a 'take-down'..but the barrel is detachable in the true sense of the word. **1905** A. M. Binstead *Mop Fair* vii. 144 There are more takedowns at this game of racing than are suspected. **1906** E. Dyson *Fact'ry 'Ands* xi. 143 Well, iv she ain't a fair take-down! **1920** G. Burrard *Notes Sporting Rifles* 15 A rifle on this principle cannot be cleaned from the breech unless it is a take-down model. **1926** J. Doone *Timely Tips for New Australians* 19 *Take-down*, a slang word for thief. A cheat. **1934** *Bulletin* (Sydney) 31 Jan. 42/2, I could learn something from a cool-headed young take-down like you. **1971** L. Koppett *N.Y. Times Guide Spectator Sports* xix. 240 A 'takedown' gives 2 points to the wrestler who puts the other down. **1976** *Shooting Times & Country Mag.* 16–22 Dec. 7/2 (Advt.), Beautiful supple quality leather take down style gun cover... Barrels and action in separate compartments inside. **1977** *Rolling Stone* 24 Mar. 67 It survives the knocks and rough handling of countless loadings, unloadings, road bumps, set-ups, and take-downs. **1973** *N.Y. Law Jrnl.* 2 Aug. 16/3 (Advt.), Top salary, benefits for take-hold person with excellent skills, initiative. **1977** I. Shaw *Beggarman, Thief* i. ii. 21 Your brother Rudy is one hell of a man. A take-hold guy. **1943** *Sun* (Baltimore) 4 Dec. 12/1 (*heading*) Steel workers 'take home' pay rises 55%. **1951** *Manch. Guardian Weekly* 8 Feb. 15/4 It used to be that trainmen were classed first or second in take-home pay. **1968** J. D. Watson *Double Helix* xvi. 111 Though the theoretical basis for many of their conclusions was shaky, the take-home lesson was obvious. **1973** *Times* 15 Mar. 23/6 Licences should be granted to 'any retailer whose character and premises satisfy certain minimum standards, at least as far as the take-home trade is concerned.' *Ibid.* 23/7 Take-home beer sales. **1976** *National Observer* (U.S.) 28 Aug. 6/3 A total of 823 cadets took the take-home exam.., and many cadets, their attorneys, and others suspect that as many as half the class collaborated. **1977** *R.A.F. News* 11–24 May 1/3 Between £1.68 and £5.29 a week is added to the take-home pay of married men with two children. **1933** Wodehouse *Heavy Weather* xvi. 280 The gallant nonchalance of that take-it-or-leave-it of his..had sent Lord Tilbury scrambling for his cheque-book. **1940** C. Morgan *Voyage* iii. v. 267 [He] was a little distinguished among Thérèse's..adorers..by..his attitude of take-it-or-leave-it even towards Thérèse herself. **1942** 'G. Orwell' *War-Time Diary* in *Coll. Essays* (1968) II. 415, I believe, however, that in spite of the 'take it or leave it' with which our government started off, the terms will actually be modified. **1972** *Adoremus* Jan. 19 Devotion to her..is more than a matter of personal taste, a take-it-or-leave-it of the Christian religion. **1930** Godley & Kaylin *Control Retail Store Operation* xviii. 214 For a 'cash-take-with' register transaction, no salescheck is used. **1941** Duncan & Phillips *Retailing Princ. & Methods* xx. 720 Sometimes the terms 'take transaction' or 'take-with' are used to identify those sales in which merchandise is given to the customer at the close of the sale rather than having the goods delivered by the store. **1970** *Redbook* Jan. 97/2 Another feature..of the..Diet is take-with lunches for the working woman... For five days of each week's menu there are lunches that can be eaten at home or packed to take along to work. **1977** *Chicago Tribune* 2 Oct. ix. b (Advt. Suppl.) 2/2 Chain saws are take-with priced.

ta·ke-away, *sb.* and *a.* Also **Take-away, takeaway.** [f. vbl. phr. *to take away*: see Take *v.* 78.] **A.** *sb.* **1.** *U.S.* (See quot.) *rare.*

1931 *Amer. Speech* VII. 52 The train that takes the logs to the mill is the 'takeaway'.

2. *Golf.* The initial movement of the club at the beginning of a backswing.

1961 [see *lightning-quick* s.v. *Lightning 3 c]. **1976** *Sunday Mail* (Glasgow) 21 Nov. 39/5 Jack Nicklaus.. gives his advice today on another part of a good golf swing—the take-away.

3. A shop which sells take-away food (see sense 1 of the adj. below).

1970 *Cape Times* 28 Oct. 18/1 (Advt.), Are you interested in a take-away..or supermarket? **1974** *Times* 7 Oct. 8/6 There is just as likely to be a chop suey bar or a chippy or a take-away in..Bognor Regis..as in any big city. **1976** J. Fraser *Who steals my Name?* xi. 134 [He] drove to the Chinese Take-Away on the outskirts. **1981** M. Hardwick *Chinese Detective* xiv. 134 Proprietor of..a small string of burger eateries and takeaways.

B. *adj.* **1.** That may be taken away; *spec.* designating cooked food sold to be eaten away from the premises of sale.

1964 *Punch* 15 Apr. 572/3 Posh Nosh..was serving take-away venisonburgers. **1970** *Final Exam. Hons. Eng. Lang. & Lit.* (Univ. Newcastle upon Tyne) 1 (*heading*) Take-away paper. **1971** *Guardian* 27 Mar. 11/1 We sent out to the Chinese restaurant for a Chinese take-away curry. **1974** *Times* 7 Oct. 8/5 British people buy their take-away meals with convenient regularity. **1975** *Times* 18 Aug. 2/4 Second-class travellers will be able to buy a full meal on a take-away tray which will not slip off the tables in their saloons. **1976** *Nature* 18 Mar. 213/2 The takeaway message of the Dunbars' monograph is that superficially similar social systems may be the product of different behavioural arrangements. **1982** *London Rev. Bks.* IV. xxiv. 3/2 As a takeaway sample of what he had in mind, Alvarez contrasted the horses of Larkin's poem 'At Grass'..with the 'urgent' horses of Ted Hughes's 'A Dream of Horses'.

2. Of, pertaining to, or characterized by the selling of cooked food to be taken away.

1971 *Guardian* 18 June 11/5 Every take-away pieshop and baker sell a Cornish pasty. **1973** *Times* 3 Feb. 13/5 Leslie's also do a take-away service. **1977** *N.Z. Herald* 5 Jan. 2–15/8 (Advt.), Takeaway bar. **1978** *Cornish Guardian* 27 Apr. 14/4 (Advt.), Lucrative beach café.. good take-away business, ice cream servery. **1981** B. Knox *Killing in Antiques* vii. 157 [They] made an expedition..to the nearest Chinese take-away restaurant and brought back enough food.

Takelma (tǎke·lmă), *sb.* and *a.* Also 9 **Takilma.** [ad. Takelma *dāᵃgelmáʼn* those dwelling along the river.] **A.** *sb.* **1.** A Penutian language (now extinct) of south-western Oregon. **2.** The North American Indian speakers of this language. **B.** *adj.* Designating this people or their language.

1882 *Mag. Amer. Hist.* Apr. 258 Phonetically, Takilma is more..vocalic than Kúsa. **1891** J. W. Powell *Indian Linguistic Families* 121 The Takilma formerly dwelt in villages along upper Rogue River, Oregon... They are now included among the 'Rogue River Indians'. **1907** E. Sapir in *Jrnl. Amer. Folklore* Jan.–Mar. 33 The following notes regarding the ideas of the supernatural world held by the Takelma Indians were obtained..from..one of the very few full-blood survivors of the Takelmas. **1909** *Publ. Pennsylvania State Univ.: Anthropol.* II. i. 5 The Takelma language represents one of the distinct linguistic stocks of North America. It is..a source of congratulations that enough of the folk-lore of the Takelmas could be obtained to enable one to assign these Indians a definite place in American mythology. **1912** E. Sapir (*title*) The Takelma language of southwestern Oregon. **1941** C. F. Voegelin in L. Spier et al. *Lang., Culture & Personality* 23 When Sapir studied Takelma in 1906 there were only a few speakers of the language remaining. **1965** *Canad. Jrnl. Linguistics* Spring 124 Some statement should also be made concerning languages for which no speakers were found... Inland, no..Takelma, Molale, or Cayuse were found. **1974** *Encycl. Brit. Micropædia* VII. 859/2 Six of these [Penutian] languages—Costanoan, Cayuse, Molala, the Yakonan languages..and Takelma—are extinct.

taken, *ppl. a.* **b.** *taken-for-granted* (earlier example).

1895 G. B. Shaw in *Liberty* 27 July 2/1 The Impressionist movement..was evidently destined to improve pictures greatly by substituting a natural, observant, real style for a conventional, taken-for-granted, ideal one.

take-off, *sb.* and *a.* Add: Also **takeoff. A.** *sb.* **2.** Freq. in literary or theatrical use, a skit or parody. Const. *of* or (chiefly *U.S.*) *on*. (Earlier and later examples.)

1846 *Knickerbocker* XXVII. 457 Whittier will smile at the following 'take-off' of his spirited 'Songs of Labor'. **1930** C. Wittke *Tambo & Bones* iv. 157 The take-offs on theatrical stars..often displayed rare powers of mimicry. **1951** *Manch. Guardian Weekly* 4 Jan. 15/4 Finely written take-off on New York theatre society. **1967** J. Philip et al. *Best of Granta* ii. 103 A favourite ploy was to devote a whole issue to a take-off of a national magazine. **1976** *New Yorker* 15 Nov. 4/2 This musical, with the indicated twist, is a foolish takeoff on foolish musicals of the thirties. **1983** *Listener* 30 June 14/3 As well as being a take-off of Italian opera..*The Beggar's Opera* is a parody of the pastoral mode.

3. a. (Further examples in Sport.)

1887 M. Shearman *Athletics & Football* v. 153 If the 'take-off' is..so slippery as to make the jumper nervous of falling, he may..jump into the bar instead of over it. **1904** R. Thomas *Swimming* (ed. 2) 50 *Takeoff*, the board, side of bath or any standing place whether free from spring or not, from which a leap, header, feet first or other spring into water is made or taken. *Ibid.* 409/2 The one 'ready to dive' should have his feet over the edge of the takeoff. **1920** Naylor & Temple *Mod. Physical Educ.* 189 The 'take-off' may be made from one foot. **1951** *Times* 3 Jan. 4/5 Search the rinks of today for a take-off of beauty such as that of Bernard Adams..and you seek in vain. **1951** *Swimming* (E.S.S.A.) iii. 49 The take-off in the back-crawl is immediate, since there is no over-balancing to contend with as in the front-crawl or the breast-stroke. **1977** *Arab Times* 14 Dec. 10/3 Both high and long jump events were noticeable for their absence of the basic essentials; in the former, jumpers threw themselves at the bar with gay abandon without the slightest modicum of lift at take-off.

b. *Aeronaut.* The act of becoming airborne (see *Take *v.* 83 n (*d*)). Also *transf.*

1904 *Aeronaut. Jrnl.* VIII. 56/1 The incline is one in two, the lower end forming a curve... The 'take-off' is on an upward incline of one in ten. **1914** in C. F. S. Gamble *Story North Sea Air Station* (1928) 70 That take-off of his was worth going a long way to see. **1918** in *Ibid.* xx. 353 The boat..taxied slowly along the water until the desired position for the 'take-off' was reached. **1929** *Sat. Even. Post* 14 Dec. 13/2 A group of news camera-men were setting up to catch the take-off of the seaplane. **1942** [see *briefing *vbl. sb.* 2]. **1951** [see *blast-off]. **1966** *Electronics* 17 Oct. 107 Lengthy preflight tests increase the probability that the equipment will fail before takeoff. **1974** *Daily Colonist* (Victoria, B.C.) 28 Dec. 4/3 When the [hydrofoil] boat rises on its struts, it is called 'take-off'. **1977** D. Anthony *Stud Game* xii. 69, I have a witness who says you couldn't have made the aeroplane ride... Grant's take-off that night is a matter of record.

5. *fig.* The act of starting off (on a journey, etc.); a departure.

1928 H. Crane *Let.* Dec. (1965) 332 [I] think I'm going to like London entirely too well for an early take-off to Spain. **1965** J. Pollard *Surfrider* ii. 20 Another thing you have to watch is the 'late take-off', catching a wave at the last minute as it begins to break. **1973** *Black Panther* 13 Oct. 17/1 The little green Fiat conveniently parked on the corner for what was to have been a speedy take-off.

6. *fig.* The beginning of (a new phase of accelerated or increased) growth or development. *spec.* in *Econ.*

1953 W. W. Rostow *Process Econ. Growth* i. 17 The term 'take-off' is here used to describe the transition of a society from a preponderantly agricultural to an industrialized basis, or, more generally, a sustained rate of increase in output *per capita*. **1957** *Listener* 10 Oct. 554/2 Development capital and trading conditions which facilitate their take-off into industrialisation. **1964** M. McLuhan *Understanding Media* (1967) II. xiv. 147 'Backward' countries take a long time to reach economic 'take-off'. **1973** *Daily Tel.* 26 Feb. 17/6 The long-expected take-off in the sale of telephone facsimile machines will not happen before next year at the earliest. **1979** *Dædalus* Spring 1 In a country like France, where the postwar 'take-off' was particularly painful.

7. See *power take-off* s.v. *Power *sb.*[1] 18 f.

B. *attrib.* or *adj.* **1. b.** In sense *3 b of the *sb.*, as *take-off area, run, speed*, etc.

1943 *Yank* 16 July 10 The planes..proceed down the roadway to the take-off strip. **1958** *Chambers's Techn. Dict.* Add. 1019/1 *Take-off rocket*, a rocket, usually jettisonable, used to assist the acceleration of an aeroplane. **1958** [see *right of way 3 a]. **1960** *Guide to Civil Land Aerodrome Lighting* (B.S.I.) 7 *Take-off area*, an area on the ground of specified dimensions which abuts the end of a strip. **1968** Takeoff area [see *sand-bar* s.v. *Sand *sb.*[2] 10 a]. **1969** *New Yorker* 12 Apr. 100/2 The experiments, after they are set up, will be out of range of the blast of the LM's takeoff rocket. **1973** D. Kyle *Raft of Swords* (1974) II. xv. 162 He made take-off speed bumping disconcertingly. **1976** P. Cave *High Flying Birds* iii. 37 Before strapping in, I walked to the edge of the take-off area and cast my eyes around for any possible snags. **1981** C. Potok *Bk. of Lights* (1982) v. 129 They landed in late afternoon... As they walked, a huge aircraft went into its takeoff run.

c. Of or pertaining to a starting-point or point of development, increase, etc. Cf. senses 5, 6 of the sb.

1947 *Radiology* XLIX. 304/2 Prior to death, the heart may be injured, as shown by a lowering of the take-off level of the T-wave. **1962** M. McLuhan *Gutenberg Galaxy* 79 The great medieval invention of typography that was the 'take-off' moment into the new spaces of the modern world. **1962** E. Snow *Other Side of River* (1963) xxiii. 172 By 1962 natural catastrophes and disastrous mistakes in take-off phases of the communes had cruelly combined to expose fantastic overclaims for agricultural output in 1958. **1965** J. A. Michener *Source* (1966) 840 At eight o'clock all units were in take-off position. **1968** B. Magee *Aspects of Wagner* i. 21 This combination of poetry and symphony that provided the take-off point for Wagner. **1974** *Times* 21 Jan. 6/2 Nineteen sixty-six was the take-off year for population.

2. a. Also used of an appliance which removes something.

1945 *Richmond* (Va.) *Times-Dispatch* 8 June 13 For hair-free and satin smooth legs, use take-off hair pads.

b. That may be taken off; designed to be readily put on and taken off.

1950 *N.Y. Times* 29 Nov. 42/6 (*heading*) Take-off attire for spring shown. Bathing suits, town costumes and evening gowns have parts to be removed. **1977** *Lancashire Life* Feb. 20/2 Minty (..showing their latest range of suites with take-off covers).

ta·ke-out, *a.* and *sb.* Also **take out, takeout.** [f. vbl. phr. *to take out*: Take *v.* 85.] **A.** *adj.* **1.** Chiefly *N. Amer.* Designed or made to be taken out. **a.** Applied to a mechanical device that may be pulled or folded out as required.

1908 *Sears, Roebuck Catal.* 94 Our new model long body runabout... Very large, roomy seat, small take out seat in rear. **1982** *Motor* 3 July 55/1 A glass tilt or take-out sunroof.

b. Applied to prepared food sold for consumption elsewhere. Cf. *take-away *a.* 1.

1968 *Globe & Mail* (Toronto) 17 Feb. 47/4 (Advt.), Soft ice cream and take out food. **1970** *Times* 29 Jan. 27/3 One of New York's finest restaurants will provide gourmet 'take-out' lunches for the hard-pressed executive. **1972** B. Garfield *Line of Succession* (1974) I. 73 Lunch in the office..had been dreary with takeout food. **1975** *New Yorker* 21 July 83/2 Ken and Eve do a pretty good take-out-sandwich business at noon with people who work in the neighbourhood.

2. Of, pertaining to, or characterized by the sale of prepared food for consumption elsewhere. Cf. *take-away *a.* 2. orig. *U.S.*

1941 J. M. Cain *Mildred Pierce* ix. 177 Pies she hoped to sell to the 'take-out' trade. **1947** *Sun* (Baltimore) 2 July 30/1 One chain of sandwich shops, which does a large volume of 'take out' business. **1962** *Advance* Mar. 7/1 If you deliver take-out orders for restaurants, the pay is $20 a week and two meals a day. **1970** *New Yorker* 15 Aug. 22/1 Dialogue overheard in the take-out line of a mid-town coffee shop. **1972** J. Wambaugh *Blue Knight* (1973) xi. 183 He boxed some chicken..for a take-out customer. **1975** *Times* 8 Feb. 7/1 Simple fish-and-chip shops with a take-out counter and a few tables. **1977** *Belfast Tel.* 17 Jan. 15/7 (Advt.), Capable person to organise and run Safari Take-Out Cafe.

3. *Bridge.* Designating a bid or call that takes the bidder's partner out (see *Take *v.* 85 k); *take-out double* = *informatory double* s.v. *Informatory *a.* b.

1945 Phillips & Reese *How to play Bridge* 62 When a double is made for that reason it is called an 'informatory' or 'take-out' double. **1959** *Listener* 15 Jan. 146/2 A take-out bid might induce partner to bid too many diamonds. **1962** *Ibid.* 3 May 790/2 The take-out call. **1964** [see *informatory *a.* b]. **1967** R. L. Frey et al. *Bridge Players' Encycl.* 298/2 Negative double, the original name for a take-out double, in general use from 1915 to 1930, about which time the term 'informatory' became current. **1972** *Times* 23 Sept. 9/4 East read more in North's take-out double than in his partner's show of strength.

B. *sb.* **1.** *Bridge.* An act of taking out (see *Take *v.* 85 k).

1917 E. Bergholt *Royal Auction Bridge* (1918) 88 The 'weakness take-out' or 'rescue' is obligatory in all suits, but the 'strength take-out' only in hearts or spades. **1927** [see *denial 6]. **1945** Phillips & Reese *How to play Bridge* 62 If partner has not spoken, or has simply passed, a double of One or Two of a suit is for a take-out. **1962** *Times* 14 Nov. 17/2 The Double which may be either for a penalty or a take-out. **1977** *Times* 10 Dec. 13/4 Opponents double for a take-out whenever they can afford the risk.

2. *U.S.* A tax deducted from winnings on a horse-race.

1946 *Sun* (Baltimore) 18 Aug. 8/3 In some states as much as twelve per cent is deducted from every dollar won to cover breakage, track takeout and state and Government taxes. **1954** *Ibid.* 17 Feb. 20/5 With the present 10-cent take-out Maryland mile tracks are producing the highest revenue in proportion to the population in the area of any state in the nation. **1971** L. Koppett *N.Y. Times Guide Spectator Sports* x. 183 There is a 'take-out'—a tax—that is removed from the pool before winnings are returned. **1978** *N.Y. Times* 30 Mar. D17/4 Plans to reduce the parimutuel takeout at New York Racing Association tracks.

3. In *Bowls*, the knocking of an opponent's wood away from the jack; in *Curling*, the striking of an opponent's stone out of play.

1959 *Times* 19 Aug. 4/5 Either by direct scoring, or through judicious take-outs, he swung the outcome by 15 shots on six of the seven ends. **1961** J. S. Salak *Dict. Amer. Sports* 441 *Take out* (curling), striking a stone hard enough to remove it from rings. **1962** *Times* 16 Aug. 3/5 A. R. Allen..successfully essayed take-outs of varying strengths. **1964** [see *Canuck].

4. *U.S.* A special article in a newspaper or journal printed without a break in successive columns or pages so that it can be easily removed.

1961 in Webster. **1980** Collins & Lapierre *Fifth Horseman* I. 37 When..doing a major take-out on violent crime in the city. **1981** B. Granger *Schism* xv. 135 The phenomenon is the story here. UPI already has quite a long takeout on it.

5. A shop selling prepared food or drink for consumption away from the premises. Cf. *take-away *sb.* 3. orig. and chiefly *N. Amer.*

1970 *Globe & Mail* (Toronto) 25 Sept. 36/7 (Advt.), Chicken takeout and snack bar, close to city. **1972** *Even. Telegram* (St. John's, Newfoundland) 29 June 22/6 (Advt.), Commercial site. Formerly used as a Pizza Take-Out. **1972** *Guardian* 5 Sept. 17/6 Pizza parlours in Paddington and chop-suey 'takeouts' in Chorlton-cum-Hardy. **1978** *Detroit Free Press* 16 Apr. F 8/10 (Advt.), Bar & Grill. Liquor, beer & wine takeout.

ta·ke-over. orig. *U.S.* Also **take over, takeover.** [f. vbl. phr. *to take over*: see Take *v.* 87.] **1.** An act of taking over (see Take *v.* 87 b in Dict. and Suppl.). Also, that which is adopted or transferred.

1917 *Acts State New Jersey* xiv. 33 *Take Over*, the action by the department in assuming the control and maintenance of any part or parts of the State Highway System. **1921** W. S. Churchill *Let.* 1 June in M. Gilbert *Winston S. Churchill* (1977) IV. Compan. III. 1489 The whole principle of the 'take over' was to show the actual net cost of Mesopotamia in one vote. **1928** *Amer. Jrnl. Psychiatry* VII. 885 The accessory left ear movement may be a takeover of the same activity during nursing. **1930** J. B. Priestley *Good Compan.* III. i. 479 They want four thousand, lock, stock, and barrel, except the usual take-overs. **1932** M. Joynt tr. *Gougaud's Christianity in Celtic Lands* iii. 63 A direct take over of the monastic doctrines of the East. **1946** *Sun* (Baltimore) 10 Aug. 4/7 Special consideration was being given to the planning of a smooth take-over of UNRA facilities. **1954** *Newsweek* 11 Oct. 66/1 A solid hour without the relief of a teammate's take-over..seemed..a strain at times. **1964** M. McLuhan *Understanding Media* (1967) I. v. 64 Joyce's Bloom is a deliberate takeover from [Charlie] Chaplin. **1968** *Times* 16 Dec. 7/1 An attempt at a Ministry take-over and a threat to a much valued independence. **1980** *News & Observer* (Raleigh, N. Carolina) 28 Oct. WA-5/8, 3 bedrooms, 1½ baths, good loan takeover, nice patio overlooking woods.

2. A (usu. forcible) assumption of power or government; a military coup.

1957 *Economist* 28 Sept. 1023/2 The change in military personnel in Syria has not been followed yet by any complete communist take-over. **1966** *Listener* 10 Mar. 339/1 It is just over a week since the military take-over in Ghana and the dismissal of Dr Nkrumah. **1977** *Arab Times* 14 Dec. 3/1 The black takeover in Zambia. **1980** *Sunday Times* 21 Sept. 18/1 The military takeover in Turkey nine days ago.

3. *Econ.* The assumption of control or ownership of a business concern by another company, esp. by the acquisition of the majority of its shares, either by agreement or after a take-over bid.

1958 Bull & Vice *Bid for Power* 13 A take-over is intelligible only in the light of subsequent developments. **1959** *Punch* 16 Sept. 177/2 A surge of sentiment for Harrods has set in since the Fraser take-over. *a* **1974** R. Crossman *Diaries* (1976) II. 201 This afternoon Tony Wedgwood Benn made a Statement on the Chrysler take-over of Rootes. **1980** D. Williams *Murder for Treasure* xvi. 156 The alarms and excursions that could attend the last stages of a take-over.

4. a. *attrib.*, as *take-over activity, battle, plan*, etc.

1946 *Sun* (Baltimore) 25 Sept. 12/1, I am giving this 'take-over' plan the pitiless publicity it deserves. **1948** *Times* 13 Mar. 7/2 The discount on the shares narrowed slightly to 2½ per cent. to 2 per cent. below take-over values. **1954** R. Sutcliff *Eagle of Ninth* i. 11 After the formal take-over ceremony in the forum, the old garrison marched out. **1957** *Economist* 28 Dec. 1150/2 This is a legitimate dramatic view of a takeover struggle. **1972** *Accountant* 17 Aug. 211/1 Take-over activity serves a dual purpose. **1981** *Times* 13 Oct. 16/4 Takeover fever produced some bright spots in banks.

b. Special Comb.: **take-over bid,** an attempt or offer to gain a controlling interest in a business concern sufficient to take it over (Take *v.* 87 b); also *transf.* and *fig.*; hence **take-over bidder.**

1953 *Times* 10 Nov. 5/9 A certain type of financial operation described in general terms by Lord Hacking—the recent epidemic of 'take-over bids'. **1959** *Listener* 24 Sept. 501/1 The take-over bid [for the television audience] was made by A.B.C. who put back their usual production time by an hour. **1965** E. F. Russell *Somewhere a Voice* 88, I could make a takeover bid for the chief of police and preside over the search for myself. **1979** L. Meynell *Hooky & Villainous Chauffeur* ii. 27 A whole series of trusts, transfers, holding companies and take-over bids had put him close to his million [pounds]. **1982** *Times Lit. Suppl.* 19 Nov. 1281 There is, after all, no limit to the potential fissiparity of national feeling in a world where the United Nations exists to discourage takeover bids. **1958** *Punch* 27 Aug. 287/1 The voice of the take-over bidder has recently been heard loud, clear and sometimes discordant over the market. **1966** *Observer* 13 Nov. 7/6 With take-over bidders out in force last week, the stock market had more excitement than for some time past.

taker. Add: **2. f.** Also in extended use, one who accepts an offer, suggestion, etc.

1897 'Mark Twain' *Following Equator* xxxvii. 333 A youth staked out a claim and tried to sell half for £5; no takers. **1968** *Listener* 25 July 107/3 'If anybody fancies he's better off jumping, he'd better go now.' There were no takers. **1979** J. Thomson *Deadly Relations* vi. 76 Whoever killed her must have..laid her down fairly carefully. Any takers so far?

h. *Stock Exchange.* (See quot. 1979.)

1934, 1955 [see *take *v.* 82 p*]. **1979** G. Cummings *Investor's Guide to Stock Market* 104 *Taker/Taker-In*, a seller of shares previously paid for who is prepared to 'take-in' the shares and receive a rate under a contango instead of delivering in the normal way and receiving payment. Also a speculator who has sold short and is not able to cover his position by the end of the Stock Exchange account by making delivery, and who is ready to take a contango rate from a 'giver'.

4. a. taker-in (examples in Stock Exchange use).

1911 [see *take *v.* 82 p*]. **1928** *Morning Post* 19 Nov., The operation can be repeated as long as the client, the broker and the taker-in mutually consent. **1979** [see sense 2 h above].

take-up, *sb.* (*a*) Add: **3. a.** (Earlier example.)
1850 *Rep. Comm. Patents 1849* (U.S.) 186 Improvement in the delivery and take-up motion of Looms.

b. *Cinematogr.* The apparatus for gathering up film after exposure in a projector or camera.
1915 B. E. Jones *Cinematograph Bk.* 162 The take-up or driving mechanism of the bottom spool. **1931** B. Brown *Talking Pictures* 181 This is threaded through the projector..and down to the take-up. **1940** *Chambers's Techn. Dict.* 832/2 *Take up, take up reel* (Cinema), the drive and the reel which is necessary to accept the cinematograph film after exposure in the gate of a camera or projector.

5. *Engin.* The action or process of taking up (see *TAKE *v.* 90 f (*b*)).
1912 [see *CLUTCH *sb.*[1] 6 a]. **1927** *Daily Tel.* 21 June 7 The clutch too is light in action and positive,..its 'take-up' is smooth and without jerk.

6. The acceptance of something offered; *spec.* the claiming of benefits provided by the Welfare State. Cf. *TAKE *v.* 90 d (*a*).
1961 *Economist* 22 Apr. 347/3 Recent studies have suggested a similar social gradient in the use of certain infant welfare services and in the 'take-up' of welfare foods. **1971** *Times* 23 Jan. 18/5 The same low take-up has been shown to apply to free prescriptions. **1975** *Language for Life* (Dept. Educ. & Sci.) xxv. 371 The take-up of longer courses in our sample was very low. **1981** *Daily Tel.* 14 May 36/3 Mr Norman Buchan..put to his 'favourite social services minister'..that not one welfare benefit had 'a take-up' of more than 80 per cent.

7. *spec.* in *Finance*, the action of paying in cash for stock originally bought on margin.
1976 *Glasgow Herald* 26 Nov. 11/9 The market also faced repayment of moderate Bank of England loans.., Treasury Bill take-up, maturing local authority bills in official hands. **1979** *Irish Times* 28 Sept. 15/4 The market had a small net take-up of Treasury Bills to finance.

8. *attrib.*, as *take-up lever, reel, spool*, etc.
1884 Take-up motion [in Dict., sense 3]. **1904** *Dialect Notes* II. 391 *Take-up screw*,..a kind of screw for iron pull-rods or wire rope. **1927** T. Woodhouse *Artificial Silk* 123 Then the cloth goes over the emery take-up roller, and finally on to the cloth beam. **1931** B. Brown *Talking Pictures* 133 Only one spool-carrying spindle is employed, which takes both feed and take-up spools side by side. **1940** Take-up reel [see sense 3 b above]. **1943** *Gloss. Terms Telecomm.* (*B.S.I.*) 85 *Take-up reel*, [on a fire-alarm] a clockwork driven reel, which maintains the tension and winds-up the tape released by the register. **1954** *Trans. IRE Audio* II. 15/1 The tape is fed over another non-rotating tape guide combined with a compliance arm and fed to the take-up reel. **1961** *Which?* Nov. 277 (*caption*) Take up lever. **1972** *Sci. Amer.* Jan. 8/3 The new camera takes the film in a direct line back to the take-up magazine, thus providing an instrument that has only one turn for the film. **1977** J. Hedgecoe *Photographer's Handbk.* 12 The cassette is loaded into a compartment, and film threaded across the back of the camera into a take-up spool. **1978** D. A. Stanwood *Memory of Eva Ryker* I. xx. 191 The last of the seven hours of tape flipped onto the take-up reel of the recorder.

takhaar (tā·khāɹ). *S. Afr.* Also **taakhaar, takhar**, and with capital initial. Pl. **-e** or **-s.** [Afrikaans, f. Du. *tak* branch + *haar* hair.] A rustic or unsophisticated person (with derog. implication of unkempt appearance). Also *attrib.* or as *adj.* and in *transf.* use.
1899 *Graaff Reinet Advertiser* 20 Nov. (Pettman), There are several other poems, one of which urges the Takhaar Boers to 'Fight, fight, fight!' **1906** A. R. Colquhoun *Afrikander Land* 217 With the passing of the old *Taak haare* the little bit of picturesqueness will be gone. **1910** J. Buchan *Prester John* ii. 44 The place..gives the ordinary man the jumps... It may be the natives, or it may be the *taakhaars*, or it may be something else. **1931** T. J. Haarhoff *Vergil in Exper. of S. Africa* 15 The early consuls were described as *capillati*, and the trekkers as *takhare*. **1931** *Times Lit. Suppl.* 3 Dec. 979/2 This motive leads him [*sc.* Haarhoff] to look for special points of resemblance..between the *capillati consules* and the *takhaar* Voortrekkers. **1942** S. Cloete *Hill of Doves* xxvii. 378 A couple of Takhaars. Two backvelders who said I was a spy. **1971** *Rand Daily Mail* 25 May 11 Commentator X (well known for his scathing comments on British 'takhare'). **1972** *Het Suid-Western* 16 Mar. 2 A political meeting of takhare in the deep north.

‖**takht** (takt). [Pers.] A sofa or bed. So **takhtrawan** (also **taktrevan**) [*rawān* pres. pple. of *raftan* to proceed, travel], a litter or Sedan chair.
1786 S. Henley tr. *Beckford's Vathek* 97 Four of the most amiable, placed the Caliph, on a magnificent takt-revan. **1870** R. Anderson *Hist. Missions Amer. Board* III. xi. 171 Had not divine mercy stayed them just there, takhtrawan, bearers, and occupant would have been dashed down the precipice. **1979** V. L. Pandit *Scope of Happiness* vi. 43 There were also low divans called *takhts* in the living rooms. **1981** S. Rushdie *Midnight's Children* I. 19 She sips fresh lime water, reclining on a takht.

Takilma, var. *Takelma.

taking, *vbl. sb.* Add: **6.** *taking in* (later examples), *out* (later example), *over*.
1902 E. Banks *Newspaper Girl* 193 They prosper exceedingly and their takings-in at the end of the week are apt to be very large. **1983** *Sunday Tel.* 21 Aug. 11/8 Detection first determines a garment's original shape through successive takings-in and lettings-out. **1924** R. Macaulay *Orphan Island* xiii. 160 'If you have nothing to contribute, sir,' he whispered, 'kindly pass the plate, which is for puttings in, not takings out.' **1917** *Acts State New Jersey* xiv. 29 For any road in the State Highway System prior to its taking over as a State Highway [etc.].

7. *taking lens* (see Take *v.* 33 b in Dict. and Suppl.).
1951 [see *finder 3 d]. **1961** G. Millerson *Telev. Production* iii. 28 (*caption*) Small viewfinder kinescope showing TV picture (optically magnified) seen through taking lens. **1962** M. L. Haselgrove *Photogr. Dict.* 187 *Taking lens*, the lower lens of a twin-reflex camera, which forms the image actually falling on the film.

takkie, var. *tackie.

takovite (tæ·kovəit). *Min.* [ad. Serbo-Croat *takovit* (Z. Maksimović 1957, in *Zapisnici Srpskog Geol. Društva za 1955 God.* 219), f. *Takovo*, name of a place in Serbia: see -ite[1].] A bluish green clay-like mineral that is a rhombohedral hydrated basic aluminate and carbonate of nickel.
1957 *Zapisnici Srpskog Geol. Društva za 1955 God.* 224 (*heading*) Takovite, hydrous nickel aluminate, a new mineral... This occurs in Takovo, Serbia, on the contact of limestone and metamorphosed serpentinite. **1977** *Amer. Mineralogist* LXII. 463/1 The formula of the Australian takovite, for which only kaolinite is a significant impurity, is established with greater certainty.

Takulli (tăkɒ·li). Also 9 **Tacully, Takali** etc. [a. Carrier *dakełne* (pl. of *dakeł*) Carriers, Indians; lit. 'people who go by boat on the water.'] A name used for the Carrier Indians of British Columbia: at first used only for the eastern Carrier, but later extended to include the Babine Indians of Babine Lake and the Bulkley River.
1820, etc. [see *Carrier 2 b]. **1846** H. Hale *Ethnol. & Philol.* 201 The country of the *Tahkali* (or Tacullies) includes the region north of the Oregon Territory, termed by the English New Caledonia. **1932** D. Jenness *Indians of Canada* xxii. 363 The Carrier..had no common name for themselves, only names for the independent subtribes into which they were divided. In the nineteenth century, however, they adopted for themselves the obscure title Takulli, bestowed on them apparently by Europeans. **1974** *Encycl. Brit. Micropædia* II. 590/3 They [*sc.* the Carrier] also assumed the name of Takulli (People Who Go Upon the Water), a name of obscure origin.

takyr (tā·kiᵊɹ). Also **takir.** [a. Turki, Chagatai *takir* f. *tak* smooth.] In Russian Central Asia, any of the wide expanses of clay which are covered with water in the spring and are dry in summer.
1864 A. Vámbéry *Trav. Central Asia* 91 By degrees the sand disappeared, and about midnight we had so firm a clayey soil under us, that the regulated tread of the distant camels echoed as if some one was beating time in the still night. The Turkomans name such spots Takir. **1902** *Encycl. Brit.* XXIII. 511/2 Large areas amidst the sands are occupied by *takyrs*. **1961** L. D. Stamp *Gloss. Geogr. Terms* 444/2 *Takyr*.., area of barren alkaline soil with heavy unstructural clay soil.

‖**tala** (tā·lă). *Indian Mus.* Also **tal.** [Skr. *tāla*, Hindi *tāl* hand-clapping, musical time.] Musical time or rhythm; one of a series of traditional metrical patterns.
1891 [see *jati, jâti]. **1921** [see *dhrupad]. **1927** *Grove's Dict. Mus.* (ed. 3) II. 704/2 The principle of the time-units within the bar follows the varieties of prosodic feet. These are of one, two, three, or four syllables, and the times (*tāl*) are decided by the number of units (*mātra*) in each syllable (*akshara*) or beat (*tāl*). **1961** '*Gramophone*' *Long Playing Classical Record Catal.* Sept. 212/2 *Indian Music..Ragas and Talas.* Indian Instrumentalists. **1967** Singha & Massey *Indian Dances* v. 65 While the musicians play the syllabic beats, the dancer executes patterns within the tal or time-measure (pronounced 'taal'). **1977** Y. Menuhin *Unfinished Journey* xii. 258 The *tala* is the rhythm. Dozens exist.

Talaing (talai·ŋ), *sb.* and *a.* Also 8–9 **Talain;** 9 **Talien.** [Native name.] = *Mon *sb.*[2] and *a.* Cf. *Peguan *sb.* and *a.*
1798 F. Buchanan in *Asiatick Researches* V. 235 This people are named *Talain* by the *Burmas* and *Chinese* of *Yunan*. **1800** M. Symes *Embassy to Ava* v. 183 He has abrogated some severe penal laws imposed by his predecessors upon the Taliens, or native Peguers. **1835** *Penny Cycl.* IV. 438/1 Here and there, on the immediate banks of the river, are a few villages of Talain fishermen. **1844** *Jrnl. Asiatic Soc. Bengal* XIII. 43 The city of Puggan was taken, the Talaings were overawed. **1854** *Jrnl. Amer. Oriental Soc.* IV. 282 In its vocables, the Talaing is the most isolated language in Farther India. **1881** C. J. F. S. Forbes *Compar. Gram. Lang. Further India* iv. 51 The British province of Pegu, representing the old Mon or Talaing kingdom, has become practically as Burman..as Ava itself. **1904** G. A. Grierson *Linguistic Survey India* II. 1 The Mōn or Talaing spoken in Pegu. **1948** D. Diringer *Alphabet* vii. 408 When the ancestors of the modern Burmans came to the Irrawaddy basin, they found the people whom they call Talaings well established in southern Burma. **1957** *Encycl. Brit.* XXI. 759/1 From the Telingas, whose culture they [*sc.* the Mon] took and whose foreign blood they absorbed into their own stock, came the name Talaing. **1973** [see *Peguan *sb.* and *a.*].

‖**talak** (talā·k). Also **talaq.** [a. Arab *ṭalāq* divorce.] In Muslim law: (a method of) divorce by the husband's mere verbal repudiation of his wife in a set form of words (see quots.). Cf. *get *sb.*[3].
1791 C. Hamilton tr. *Hedàya* I. iv. 200 Talâk, in its primitive sense, means *dismission:*— in law it signifies the dissolution of a marriage, or the annulment of its legality, by certain words. **1861** in E. F. Moore *Rep. Cases Appeal from E. Indies* VIII. 395 A divorce by *Talâk* is the mere arbitrary act of the husband, who may repudiate his wife at his own pleasure, with or without cause. **1917** *Law Rep. King's Bench Div.* I. 649 In my judgment Dr. Mir-Anwaruddin has made such a marriage, as he was legally entitled to do, to which Talak has no application. **1931** S. Vesey-Fitzgerald *Muhammadan Law* ix. 73 Talaq..is a generic name for all divorce, but is specifically applied to repudiation by or on behalf of the husband. **1962** *Times* 2 Feb. 3/6 A husband domiciled in a Mohammedan country could validly divorce by talak a wife whom he had married in England. **1970** *Daily Tel.* 31 Oct. 3/3 A Pakistani doctor's 'Talaq' divorce was held.. to be valid in England. Talaq is the Moslem form which involves saying 'I divorce you' three times... The Talaq was contained in a letter.

talayot (tălā·yǫt). *Archæol.* [a. Cat. *talaiot* small watch-tower, ad. Arab. (Muslim Spain) *ṭāli'āt*, pl. of *ṭāli'a* watch-tower; cf. Arab. *ṭalī'a* with similar meaning.] A Bronze Age stone tower found in the Balearic Islands, usu. circular with a corbelled roof, used for residential or defensive purposes. Hence **talayo·tic** *a.* Cf. Nuragh.
1893 *Athenæum* 2 Sept. 328/1 Like the Sardinian nuragh, the talayot is essentially a vaulted tower of extra-massive proportions. **1927** *Daily Tel.* 12 July 5/4 The Talayots are round mounds, which appear to have served as sepulchres. **1932** M. Murray *Cambr. Excav. in Minorca: Trapuco* I. 6 Taulas are always found in connection with *talayots*, circular buildings of rough masonry. **1939** V. F. Childe *Dawn Europ. Civilization* (ed. 3) xiv. 249 There is no obvious break between the 'Copper Age' culture represented in the rock-cut tombs and that represented in the 'talayots'. **1950** *Antiquity* XXIV. 154 'Taulas'..occur in association with the strong circular towers known as 'talayots'. **1974** *Encycl. Brit. Macropædia* XIX. 279/1 In the Balearic Isles the Bronze Age corresponds to the 2nd millennium BC and is designated 'talayotic' from the name of the talayot, a megalithic monument in the form of a round or quadrangular tower. **1979** Service & Bradbery *Megaliths* vii. 131 In Majorca, the talayotic site called Ses Paisses..includes a central talayot tower, outer walls and four megalithic gateways around the dwellings in the enclosure.

Talbot (tǫ·lbǫt). *Optics.* [The name of W. H. Fox *Talbot* (1800–77), English polymath: cf. Talbotype.] *Talbot's law*, the law that a flickering source of light, varying in either colour or intensity, will be perceived as if it were a constant light source exhibiting the mean value of the varying quantity, provided that the frequency of flickering exceeds the flicker fusion frequency of the eye; also called the *Talbot–Plateau law* [J.A.F. *Plateau* (1801–83), Belgian physicist].
1895 E. C. Sanford *Course Exper. Psychol.* I. vi. 146 (*heading*) The Talbot-Plateau law. **1906** *Bull. Bureau of Standards* (U.S.) II. 2 Talbot's law is thus a statement of physiological rather than of physical phenomena, and depends for its explanation on the action of the eye. **1929** L. T. Troland in C. Murchison *Found. Exper. Psychol.* iv. 187 The Talbot-Plateau law..has been established very accurately. **1943** C. T. Morgan *Physiol. Psychol.* x. 198 As the [flicker] rate is lowered, the subjective brightness of a flickering light may considerably exceed that expected from Talbot's law. **1974** *Sci. Amer.* Apr. 93/1 The law of color fusion, also known as Talbot's law (although it actually goes back to Isaac Newton), enables us to predict what color will be perceived when two colors are mixed.

Talbotype, *sb.* (Earlier example.)
1844 *Times* 9 Sept. 1/3 (Advt.), Claudet's Daguerrotype and Talbotype Portraits... Mr. Claudet continues to take portraits by both the above processes... In Talbotype.. persons may be furnished with any number of copies on paper.

talc, *sb.* Add: **2. d.** [*ellipt.* for *talcum powder* s.v. Talcum.] Talcum powder, esp. as a cosmetic and toilet preparation. *colloq.*
1938 *Vogue Beauty Bk.* 16 Feb. 24/2 Sifter top talc, 3 at 1s. 6d. **1949** *Heiress* Aug. 82 (Advt.), Fragrant talc cool-silky-perfumed by the master Goya. **1966** P. O'Donnell *Sabre-Tooth* vii. 105 Two small bars of soap, a tin of talc, and some body mist. **1977** D. Cory *Bennett* ii. 37 Hunter contrived to take a shower..to apply to himself..a dusting of powdered talc.

talc, *v.* Add: Also, to dust (the skin) with talcum powder. **talced** (tælkt) *ppl. a.* (later example).
1976 M. Nelson *Crusoe Test* iii. 40 She sprayed and talced her body. **1976** L. Deighton *Twinkle, twinkle, Little Spy* xvii. 175 His..face talced like a..cottage-loaf.

talcky, *a.* Add: The usual form is now *talcy.* **a.** (Later example.)

1965 G. J. WILLIAMS *Econ. Geol. N.Z.* x. 162/2 A large land-slip extends over a good deal of the lens, and material in the slip contains large blocks of talcy serpentine.

b. Of or pertaining to talcum powder, in toilet and cosmetic use. Cf. *TALC *sb.* 2 d. *colloq.*

1972 *Daily Tel.* 11 July 13 The faint, talcy smell of babies in the bathroom.

talcum. Delete ‖ and add: *talcum powder*: now *spec.* applied to perfumed or medicated talc for general cosmetic and toilet use. Also used *absol.*

1908 *Sears, Roebuck Catal.* 797 Violet and white rose talcum powder. *Ibid.*, Just the thing for holding your face powders or talcums. 1927–28 *T. Eaton & Co. Catal.* Fall & Winter 367 Djer-Kiss Talcum Powder is low-priced. *Ibid.*, Pompeian Talcum is a fine white powder with the pleasing Pompeian odor. 1949 *Heiress* June 41 (Advt.), For cool, satin-like Comfort Dubarry Talcum is the dainty woman's necessity. 1968 [see *bath oil* s.v. *BATH *sb.*[1] VI]. 1981 *Good Housekeeping* Apr. 166/2 *Talcum powder* is closely related to face powder; the components are similar but the aim of body powder is to provide 'slip', a cooling effect and good absorbency.

Hence as *v. trans.*, to treat with talcum powder; **ta·lcumed** *ppl. a.*

1923 H. JEROME *Secret Woman* ix. 106 It is only the American man who smells sweet and soapy, as though he had just been shampooed and talcumed. 1943 G. GREENE *Ministry of Fear* I. iii. 47 Her face was talcumed and wrinkled. 1952 C. ARMSTRONG *Black-Eyed Stranger* vi. 47 Charles Salisbury had a clean and 'talcumed' look. 1970 *Daily Tel.* 9 Nov. 18/6 Researchers..concluded that the entire traditional marketing approach to toilet paper was wrong. The result is the soft, talcumed, flower-scented creation now on offer.

talcy: see TALCKY *a.* in Dict. and Suppl.

tale, *sb.* Add: **3. c.** Proverbial phr. *dead men tell no tales* (earlier and later examples).

[1560 T. BECON *Wks.* II. 97 He that hath his body laden with meat & drinke is no more mete to prai vnto god then a dead man is to tel a tale.] 1664 J. WILSON *Andron. Comn.* I. iv. 14 'Twere best To knock 'um i' th head, and give it out The Soldiers did it... The dead can tell no tales. 1681 DRYDEN *Span. Fryar* IV. i. 48 There is a Proverb..which saies, that Dead-men tell no Tales; but let your Souldiers apply it at their own Perils. 1702 G. FARQUHAR *Inconstant* v. 76 Ay, ay, Dead Men, tell no Tales. 1850 C. KINGSLEY *Alton Locke* I. iv. 67 Where are the stories of those who have not risen..who have ended in desperation?..Dead men tell no tales. 1974 'M. INNES' *Appleby's other Story* xv. 122 'There was only one sure way to do it.' 'To kill him?'..'Yes. Dead men, they say, can tell no tales.'

e. *tale of woe*: see *WOE *sb.* 1 a.

III. 10. *tale-writer* (earlier example).

1845 POE in *Broadway Jrnl.* 7 June 354/2 If we except.. Mr. Hawthorne..and..one or two others..there is not even a respectably skilful tale-writer on this side the Atlantic.

‖ **talea** (tā·lia). *Mus.* Pl. **taleæ.** [L., lit. stick, cutting.] A repeated rhythmic pattern in late-medieval isorhythmic motets.

1944 W. APEL *Harvard Dict. Mus.* 367/1 The repeated scheme of time-values which is used in the sections A, B, C and..in D, is called *talea* in 14th-century treatises. 1960 *New Oxf. Hist. Music* III. v. 145 The rhythmical pattern of the first section or *talea* serves to determine the formal structure of the whole... The melodic development of the individual *taleae* is now entirely subordinate to a rigid framework dictated by rhythm. 1963 *Listener* 17 Jan. 141/1 The structural skeleton of the movement is sixteen rotations of the melody, containing fifteen rotations of the rhythmic pattern or *talea.* 1974 *Early Music* Oct. 220 In some [motets] the isorhythmic voices are constructed not only with a *talea* (the rhythmic pattern) but also a *color.*

Talensi, var. *TALLENSI.

talent, *sb.* Add: **III. 6. d.** No longer rare as sing. (later examples.). (*Administration of*) *All the Talents* (earlier examples).

1928 E. BLOM *Limitations of Music* 139 Honegger is a Swiss and a great talent to boot. 1958 *Spectator* 4 July 14/1 The studio, with its presiding talent, Lee Strasberg. 1977 *Rolling Stone* 24 Mar. 74/1 The record's not great, but the lady's a real talent.

1807 *All Talents in Ireland!* 10 The general impression upon the public mind, relative to the recent change in administration, seems to be, that the downfall of 'All the Talents' was occasioned by the unbending perverseness of my Lord H-w-k..and the deference which Lord G-n-lle paid to Lord H-w-k. 1837 G. W. COOKE *Hist. Party* III. xviii. 460 The administration, which was ironically designated by its opponents as 'All the Talents'.

e. Frequenters of the underworld. *Austral. slang.* Now *Obs.* or *rare.*

1882 [see *FORTY *sb.* 7]. 1928 'BRENT OF BIN BIN' *Up Country* x. 151 The elder won by telling his son he could use the Waterfall stallion as a saddle-horse in the off season, and have him for his own in place of Black Belle, on condition that he left the talent of Eagle Hawk Gullies strictly alone. 1953 D. CUSACK *Southern Steel* 31 He'd learn responsibility quicker married than he would knocking about the ports with the rest of the talent.

f. The women of a particular locality collectively (as *sing.*), judged according to attractiveness and sexual promise, esp. as *local talent* (see *LOCAL *a.* 2 d). Also applied occas. to men. *slang.*

1947 [see *local talent* s.v. *LOCAL *a.* 2 d]. 1950 J. CLEARY *Just let Me Be* 115 [He] looked after her, and Harry grinned at him. 'Not bad, eh?' he said... 'That's a bit of the local talent.' 1963 *Sunday Times* (Colour Suppl.) 1 Sept. 8 You can take a turn on the [sea-]front and see what the talent is like. 1969 J. FOWLES *French Lieut.'s Woman* xxxix. 292 Far duller the customers—the numerically equal male sex, who, stick in hand and 'weed' in mouth, eyed the evening's talent. 1972 'M. YORKE' *Silent Witness* ii. 24 No chance had come her way... 'Your charms are waning,' Liz had said dryly. 'There isn't any talent,' Sue had answered.

8. talent agency, an organization which seeks to place talented amateurs in the world of professional entertainment; **talent money** (earlier example); **talent scout** = *SCOUT *sb.*[4] 2 e; so **talent-scouting** *vbl. sb.*; **talent show,** a show or competition consisting of performances by a series of promising entertainers, esp. ones seeking to enter show business professionally; **talent-spotter** = *talent scout* above; also **talent-spot** *v. trans.* and *intr.*, **talent-spotting** *vbl. sb.*

1956 B. HOLIDAY *Lady sings Blues* viii. 95 Nobody was in a position to push a hotel chain, a broadcasting network, and the talent agency around. 1977 *Rolling Stone* 24 Mar. 48/5 Christine and a girlfriend/singing partner snuck away from their strict parents in Birmingham and visited every talent agency they could find in London. 1859 *Bell's Life* 14 Aug. 8/2 When the time arrived for drawing the stumps. Both [players]..were loudly cheered during the presentation of the 'talent' money. 1936 *New Republic* 28 Oct. 351/2 Paramount's 'Big Broadcast of 1937'..(Paramount talent-scouts: there's a joker here somewhere.) 1939 N. MONSARRAT *This is Schoolroom* III. xvii. 383 He was appraising the women present, as if he were a talent scout who only recognised one talent. 1952 WODEHOUSE *Pigs have Wings* x. 202, I understand that he's always being approached with flattering offers by the talent scouts of Colney Hatch and similar institutions. 1976 A. POWELL *Infants of Spring* x. 170 Lyall worked intermittently as a film actor, consequence of a talent-scout seeing him making faces in a restaurant. 1934 M. H. WESEEN *Dict. Amer. Slang* 154 *Talent scouting*,..seeking new actors. 1955 F. G. PATTON *Good Morning, Miss Dove* 70 She had won a talent show and gone to New York. 1977 *Detroit Free Press* 11 Dec. 11-B/3 After that he landed parts in theater productions, ice shows and talent shows. 1937 *Boy's Own Paper* 2 Nov. 80/2 When talent-spotting, the thing he looked out for in a half-back was the ability to deliver an artistic pass. 1968 'D. TORR' *Treason Line* 69 He had also to prod her into making the best of her mother's party to talent-spot possible agents. 1979 A. BOYLE *Climate of Treason* x. 324 George Blake, a Royal Navy lieutenant whom he had 'talent-spotted' as a possible SIS recruit for counter-espionage work in Germany. 1944 *Gen* 15 Jan. 27/2 The B.B.C. talent-spotter is touring the Midlands. 1954 I. MURDOCH *Under Net* xiv. 197, I hope that the eye of the talent-spotter has lighted favourably upon you. 1978 L. MEYNELL *Papersnake* vii. 88 It's punk..no action, what you keep these lousy talent-spotters for I can't imagine. 1957 *Observer* 3 Nov. 9/5 Competitions are an effective method for talent-spotting, an encouragement to architects and a means, sometimes, of acquiring a masterpiece. 1978 J. PEARSON *Façades* iv. 69 Thanks to the talent-spotting skill of Richard Jennings..'Drowned Suns' was published in the London *Daily Mirror.*

Talgai (tælgai·). The name of a farm in Queensland, Australia, used *attrib.* in **Talgai boy, man, skull,** etc., to designate the fossil remains of a form of *Homo sapiens* found there in 1884.

The remains were presented to the University of Sydney in 1914.

1918 S. A. SMITH in *Phil. Trans. R. Soc.* B. CCVIII. 355 A comparison of these radiographs with those of the Talgai skull show that..an exposure..was only just sufficient for the bone. *Ibid.* 370 The palate of the Talgai boy approaches that of the reconstructed *Eoanthropus.* 1931 A. KEITH *New Disc. Antiquity of Man* xix. 303 The exact antiquity of the Talgai skull is still a moot point. *Ibid.*, The Talgai canines projected beyond the level of their neighbours. 1931 *Times Lit. Suppl.* 23 Apr. 317/1 Australia, having scored once with the help of the Talgai man, looks..for a no less successful second innings. 1977 G. CLARK *World Prehistory* (ed. 3) xi. 459 The Talgai group,..although clearly sapient, retains a number of archaic features.

talh(a) (tæl, tæ·lă). [a. Arab. *ṭalḥ*, collect. pl. of *ṭalḥa*: see TALCA GUM.] A small flat-topped spiny tree, *Acacia seyal*, of the family Leguminosæ, native to north-eastern parts of Africa; also, the exudate of this tree, used as a substitute for gum arabic. Also *attrib.*

1857 H. BARTH *Trav. & Disc. N. & Central Afr.* II. xxvii. 224 The forest..here consisted principally of.. talha-trees. 1867 [see TALCA GUM]. 1875 [see *ITHEL]. 1920 *Nature* 12 Aug. 757/1 The reports..have references to..distillation trials with talh wood (*Acacia Seyal*) from the Sudan. 1977 *Time* 3 Jan. 50/1 We bumped along in darkness looking for spots where talha trees or hills would provide protection.

‖ **taliq** (talī·k). Also **talik, ta'liq,** etc. [Pers., Arab. *ta'līq*, lit. 'hanging'.] A medieval Persian cursive script characterized by sloping rounded forms and exaggerated horizontal stroke, replaced by *NASTALIK in the fourteenth century.

1771 [see *NASKHI *sb. pl.*]. 1795, etc. [see *NASTALIK]. 1849 F. MADDEN tr. *Silvestre's Universal Palæogr.* I. 52 In general, especially in fine copies of poetical works, this writing takes a sloping direction, whence it has obtained the name of *taalik.* 1885 T. P. HUGHES *Dict. Islam* 690/2 We now turn to the Oriental style, where we meet again with a bipartition, viz. into the Eastern Naskhī, as it is written in Arabia itself, Egypt, and Syria, and the..Ta'liq, current in Persia, India, and Central Asia, 1962 D. DIRINGER *Writing* vi. 143 In the course of time the Naskhi script became the parent of innumerable styles and varieties including the *ta'liq* (with its seventy or so secondary forms). 1978 Y. H. SAFADI *Islamic Calligr.* 27 Ta'līq..became established as a defined script after the invention of Riyāsī in the ninth century.

Talisker (tæ·liskəɹ). The name of *Talisker* on the island of Skye, used to designate a variety of Scottish malt whisky manufactured at the distillery there, founded in 1831–32. Also, a drink or glass of this.

1883 *Trade Marks Jrnl.* 9 May 254 Talisker. Roderick Kemp & Co., Talisker Distillery, Skye... Whisky. 31,901. 2nd Apr. 1883. 1926 A. A. MACGREGOR *Over Sea to Skye* xiv. 102 Carbost with its far-famed Talisker distillery is in Bracadale. 1951 R. B. LOCKHART *Scotch* I. ii. 27 He feels..unable to decide between Talisker and Clynelish, each of which would be put first by its devotees. 1977 D. BAGLEY *Enemy* xxxiv. 278, I ordered two large Taliskers.

talk, *sb.* Add: **I. 1. c.** An informal lecture or address; *spec.* = *radio talk* s.v. *RADIO *sb.* 5 b.

1859 A. J. MUNBY *Diary* 2 May in D. Hudson *Munby* (1972) 32 Went to the W. M. College to hear Ruskin's 'talk' about Switzerland... His lecture was historical & geographical chiefly—without book, he standing before the fire. 1900 S. HALE *Let.* 25 Mar. (1919) x. 360 She is giving three 'talks' here in Syracuse. 1923 *Radio Times* 28 Sept. 9/3, 8.45.—A Short Talk by the Rev. W. A. Studdert-Kennedy. 1942 E. WAUGH *Put out More Flags* i. 58 He had..given the first in what was intended to be a series of talks for the B.B.C. 1962 A. NISBETT *Technique Sound Studio* 273 A 'talk' is a programme or programme segment which consists of one person talking at the microphone, usually from a script. 1977 *Rep. Comm. Future of Broadcasting* (Cmnd. 6753) ii. 12 Radio 3 continued to broadcast some specialised drama, poetry and talks in the evenings.

d. *pl.* Applied *attrib.* to a department of the B.B.C. concerned with the production of radio talks; also to its officials, programmes, etc., and *ellipt.*, the Talks department (with initial capital as a title).

1927 *B.B.C. Handbk. 1928* 124/1 The Talks Department is responsible for the news service, the S.O.S. service,.. Government department talks, and all the sporting, humorous, travel, literary, and general talks. *Ibid.* 125/2 We have evidence..of an increasing demand for the Talks programme and the Talks pamphlet. 1933 J. REITH *Diary* 5 May (1975) ii. 159 He might have done as a talks director.., but not for the big job. 1938 *Times* 5 Feb. 10/3 Two talks studios, music library, listening hall, [etc.]. 1940 R. S. LAMBERT *Ariel* ii. 49 After the 'hiving off' of Talks, Adult Education and even School Broadcasts, he was left with..Religion and the Children's Hour. 1942 'G. ORWELL' *Let.* 16 Oct. in *Coll. Essays* (1968) II. 246 Yours sincerely, (Geo. Orwell) Talks Producer Indian Section. 1954 W. K. HANCOCK *Country & Calling* vii. 189 She became a talks producer on the Overseas Service of the B.B.C. 1962 A. NISBETT *Technique Sound Studio* i. 31 Talks studio tables often have perforated, i.e. acoustically transparent, surfaces. 1978 F. MACLEAN *Take Nine Spies* vii. 228 Guy Burgess..was appointed to the Talks Department of the BBC. 1980 P. FITZGERALD *Human Voices* ii. 35 No-one could have any [brandy]—a disappointment to everybody except Talks, whose allocation..had already run out.

2. a. Also *spec.* in *pl.*, formal discussions, as between representatives of different countries, or between both sides in an industrial dispute; *talks about talks*: preliminary discussions held before entering into formal negotiations.

1952 *Ann. Reg. 1951* 202 The talks broke down on 21 June when it became clear that no agreement was possible. 1971 H. WILSON *Labour Govt.* vi. 78 This time they were more wary, and after some weeks were ready, more for appearances' sake it seemed, to enter into 'talks about talks'. 1977 *Whitaker's Almanack 1978* 590 Greek and Turkish officials began talks in London to try to settle their dispute over rights in the Aegean.

4. Also *talk of the town* = TOWN-TALK.

1624 J. CHAMBERLAIN *Let.* 5 June (1939) II. 561 The disgrace that would follow in beeing made *fabula vulgi* and the talke of the towne. 1912 J. N. MCILWRAITH *Diana of Quebec* xiv. 205 But it would be the talk of the town within twenty-four hours, should even one person chance to see me in pursuit. 1983 *N.Y. Times* 4 Sept. VI. 18/2 The talk of the town this summer, the advertisement was more a lecture than a letter.

II. 5. *big talk* (earlier example).

1860 J. G. HOLLAND *Miss Gilbert's Career* x. 173 He sort o' stands round, and spreads, and lets off all the big talk he hears.

7. † **talk-film** *temporary* = *TALKIE; **talk-master** *U.S. colloq.*, one who hosts a talk show on radio or television (cf. *quiz-master* (*b*) s.v. *QUIZ *sb.*[2] 2 b); **talk shop** *colloq.* = *talking shop* s.v. *TALKING *vbl. sb.* b; **talk show** chiefly *U.S.*, a television programme in which guests are interviewed by the host or 'talk-master'; a television discussion or 'chat' show; also (more *rarely*), a similar programme on radio.

1929 *Morning Post* 24 May 12/7 He had been booked.. for a talk-film on his voice alone. **1932** *Oxford Times* 23 Sept. 22/5 After a good deal of experimenting I have come to the conclusion that...the best needles to use with a pick-up are those designed for talk-film operation—'talkie' needles. **1975** *Publishers Weekly* 1 Dec. 60/2 Tom Westbrook is the master of radio talkmasters. **1958** *Times* 12 Aug. 7/7 Many Doubting Thomases who regard the United Nations as a mere 'talk shop'. **1973** C. MULLARD *Black Britain* xi. 133 They have broken away from the c.r.c., believing that it is a white man's talk-shop about black immigrant problems. **1965** *Times Lit. Suppl.* 25 Nov. 1042/2 There are now literally thousands of talk-shows. **1977** R. LUDLUM *Chancellor Manuscript* vi. 78 They don't want you giving those interviews or going on talk shows.

talk, *v.* Add: **I. 1. a.** *talk about* (earlier and later examples of colloq. use); *don't talk to me about* (something), an exclamation against some new topic of conversation of which one has bitter personal experience.

1863 *Fraser's Mag.* Nov. 667 'Talk about women talking!' says a lady of our acquaintance, herself by no means deficient in eloquence. 'Why, look at the debates in the House of Commons, the public dinners, the vestry meetings, and, above all, the gossip, gossip, gossip at those horrid clubs!' **1885** F. ANSTEY *Tinted Venus* xiv. 167 *Well*, Miss Collum, talk about jealousy! **1940** WODEHOUSE *Quick Service* xii. 134 Did she mention her views on poor relations?..She believes in treating them rough. Talk about oppressed minorities. **1958** P. MARRIS *Widows & their Families* viii. 118 'Don't talk to me about shoes,' said the mother of two small children ruefully. 'My little boy just ripped the sole off one pair.' **1973** W. M. DUNCAN *Big Timer* xxi. 134 Talk about trouble! Goodness knows what Frank will say. **1980** R. HILL *Spy's Wife* vi. 33 'We've had a lot of rain,' said Molly. 'Don't talk to me about rain! You should have been here... I've never seen rain like it.'

c. Of a ship, etc.: to communicate by radio.

1912 *Chambers's Jrnl.* Jan. 61/2 When several ships are 'talking' to the shore-station, some delay may arise in getting a message through. **1927** *Pictorial Weekly* 3 Mar. 117/1 Ships of all nationalities 'talking' with shore stations.

2. *talk of*: also, = *talk about* in colloq. use, sense 1 a in Dict.; *talking of..*: also *joc.* introducing an unconnected subj. (earlier examples).

1831 M. EDGEWORTH *Let.* 30 Apr. (1971) 531 'Talking of coincidencies' as Mr. Ward would say..that was something of a coincidence. **1840** *Spirit of Times* 23 May 133/2 By the way, 'talking of guns', we shall take it as a great favor if our correspondents will send their orders for English Magazines, papers, etc., direct to Messrs. Wiley and Putnam, instead of ordering them from this office. **1851** E. B. BROWNING *Let.* 12 Nov. (1897) II. vii. 29 Talk of English comforts! It's a national delusion. **1876** *Atlantic Monthly* Dec. 684 This gives Pulcheria time to murmur, 'Talk of snub-noses!' **1950** F. STARK *Traveller's Prelude* xv. 191 She..asked: 'Were you in a very *small* hospital?' 'I thought so.' Talk of cats!

3. a. *to talk to* (earlier example in sense 'to rebuke, scold'); (*U.S.*) *dial.*, to court or woo (a woman); also *to talk up to*. Of a woman: to accept a man's attentions.

1860 E. M. COWELL *Diary* 17 Feb. in M. W. Disher *Cowells in Amer.* (1934) 18 Arrived there, we were set upon by sleigh conductors, one of whom Sam had also to 'talk to' for using bad language. **1895** *Dialect Notes* I. 374 Judge Jackson's has been talkin' to my daughter nigh on a year. **1905** in *Eng. Dial. Dict.* VI. 22/2 Pat is talking to Kate this six months, they'll soon be married. **1906** *Dialect Notes* III. 160 *Talk up to, v. phr.*, to court, to woo. 'Bud's talkin' up to her.' **1951** L. CRAIG *Singing Hills* xii. 110 The old man and me are powerful glad Ikey's made up his mind to talk up to a woman. We've been scared he'd be an old bachelor-man. **1951** H. GILES *Harbin's Ridge* xviii. 157 She mentioned that Faleecy John was talking to Jenny Clark a right smart. *Ibid.* 159 I'd not heard of her talking to anybody but Faleecy John.

c. *to talk big*: see also BIG *a.* 8 b; *to talk down* (*to*) (examples); also *transf.* (in quots., of writers); *to talk through one's hat*: see *HAT *sb.* 5 c; *to talk through* (*the back of*) *one's neck*: see *NECK *sb.*[1] 3 e; *to talk turkey*: see TURKEY[2] 2 d in Dict. and Suppl.

1856 C. M. YONGE *Daisy Chain* II. xiv. 498 'Say it again—what you said about the sea,' said Mary, more comforted than if Ethel had been talking *down* to her. **1919** H. WALPOLE *Jeremy* ii. 43 He always talked down to us as though we were beings of another and inferior planet. He called it, 'Getting on with the little ones.' **1954** M. F. RODELL *Mystery Fiction* i. 1 This does not mean that mystery fiction need be hack work; nor that the authors of it must 'talk down' to their audiences. **1970** *Sci. Jrnl.* Apr. 84/2 The authors for future titles all seem to be practising scientists. The problem will be whether they can achieve the necessary clarity of style without 'talking down' to their new audiences.

d. *to talk at* (earlier example); also, *to talk over* (another person): to override or talk simultaneously with (another speaker) on a tape recording, broadcast programme, etc.

1789 *Loiterer* 14 Feb. 11 Sometimes they talk to me, and sometimes at me. **1962** A. NISBETT *Technique Sound Studio* vii. 126 Superimpositions. Two people talking over each other are irritating. **1975** D. PITTS *Target Manhattan* (1976) xxviii. 111 Would you please announce your name and station first and try not to talk over other people.

e. To say something to the purpose, esp. in colloq. phr. *now you're talking*. Also *fig.* of money: see *MONEY *sb.* 6 a.

1841 DICKENS *Barnaby Rudge* lii, in *Master Humphrey's Clock* III. 238 That's the kind of game... Now you talk, indeed! **1884** J. HAY *Bread-Winners* x. 149 Now you're talkin'. **1920** 'O. DOUGLAS' *Penny Plain* ii. 21 'I'm going to Scotland.' 'Ah,' said James Lauder, 'now you're talking.' **1936** L. HELLMAN *Days to Come* I. 26 'I was in Akron.' That's the job I wanted. 'Now we're talking... That's money for you.' **1952** A. CHRISTIE *Mrs. McGinty's Dead* viii. 59 'A few days later Mrs. McGinty was murdered.' 'Now you're talking.' **1974** M. HASTINGS *Dragon Island* xix. 174 'Now you're talking.' Jukes said approvingly... 'That's the best bit of sense you've spoke today.'

f. In various colloq. phrases stating or implying that someone is in no position to criticize another, exemplified by the types: *you can't talk!*; (*look, hark*) *who's talking!*; *who am I to talk?*; *I should talk!*

1847 THACKERAY *Van. Fair* (1848) xli. 371 A person can't help their birth... I am sure Aunt Bute need not talk: she wants to marry Kate to young Hooper, the wine-merchant. **1895** KIPLING *Day's Work* (1898) 200 'All you other men think of is to give him an absurd nickname.'..'Well, *you* can't talk, William. You christened little Miss Demby the Button-quail.' **1938** N. MARSH *Artists in Crime* ii. 24 You're paying his fare Home, of course. Well, I suppose I can't talk as you've given me the run of your house. **1945** A. KOBER *Parm Me* 62 'Look who's talking!' said Pa Gross, glaring at his wife. **1949** D. SMITH *I capture Castle* ii. 12 She has had that dressing-gown so long that I don't think she sees it any more... But who am I to talk—who have not had a dressing-gown at all for two years? **1962** J. CANNAN *All is Discovered* i. 11 Anyway Daddy can't talk. Whenever she's out he..spends hours with Maria. **1968** M. ROSS *Gasteropod* iv. 99 'You should have hated me... Most men would have done.' Max laughed. 'Hark who's talking! What did you do?' **1979** D. GURR *Troika* viii. 55, I was rough on you... And stupid—I should talk!

g. *to talk back*: to answer back; to indulge in 'back-chat'. *N. Amer. colloq.*

1869 'MARK TWAIN' *Innoc. Abr.* xii. 112 There was no 'talking back', no dissatisfaction about over-charging. **1939** L. M. MONTGOMERY *Anne of Ingleside* iv. 22 Dad would never let anyone 'talk back' to Aunt Mary Maria. **1955** L. HUGHES in *Oliphant Q.* Apr.–June 136 All over the world today folks with not even *Mister* in front of their names are raring up and talking back to the folks called *Mister*. **1977** M. FRENCH *Women's Room* (1978) ii. 117, I can't stand it when they start to talk back, be fresh.

h. With alcoholic drink as subj.: used to excuse or explain uncharacteristic sentiments supposedly brought on by the drink consumed. Chiefly in *pres. pple. colloq.*

1922 JOYCE *Ulysses* 742 Paying his compliments the Bushmills whisky talking of course. *a* **1953** E. O'NEILL *Touch of Poet* (1957) I. 42 But you understand, it was the liquor talking, if I said anything to wound you. **1982** R. LEWIS *Gathering of Ghosts* iii. 102 It was all a bit stupid, you know. Beer talking, you know how it is.

i. To disclose information, *spec.* to the police (or another authority), esp. incriminating oneself or others; to confess; to turn informer or 'squeal'. *slang.*

1924 G. C. HENDERSON *Keys to Crookdom* 420 Talk. See squeal, beef, spiel, chew rag. **1952** M. ALLINGHAM *Tiger in Smoke* xv. 216 They've been through it today, but they're not talking. Why should they? **1959** W. GOLDING *Free Fall* vii. 144 'I wont' talk. I know nothing.' 'Talk. Yes, that is the word. At some point, Mr. Mountjoy, you will talk.' **1976** *Times Lit. Suppl.* 21 May 605/3 He is, as they say, not talking, and refused to be interviewed by the authors of this book.

j. With advb. accusative. *to talk one's way in*: to gain admission by persuasion. Similarly with *out*.

1973 *Ottawa Jrnl.* 3 Feb. 6/1 Their length of hospital stays, during which they tried to talk their way out, ranged from seven to 52 days; the average stay was 19 days. **1978** 'D. KYLE' *Black Camelot* xv. 237 If Rasch could talk his way in..the task would be simple.

5. (Earlier example, of a boat.) Also, of an anchor which is dragged (see DRAG *v.* 1 c).

1793 WORDSWORTH *Evening Walk* 319 The talking boat that moves with pensive sound. **1914** 'BARTIMEUS' *Naval Occasions* xxiii. 224 'I think the starboard anchor is "talking".'.. A dull metallic sound detached itself from the sibilant rushing of water. **1917** J. S. MARGERISON *Sure Shield* 86 It was the ring chain that had worked slightly loose and which was allowing the five-ton mass of cast iron to slide three inches each way as the ship rolled or pitched, and the creaking sound of which had given rise to the phrase 'the anchor's talking'. **1962** W. GRANVILLE *Dict. Sailors' Slang* 118/1 A ship's anchor is said to come home, or 'talk', when it is dragging.

II. 7. *to talk a good game*: to discuss a topic convincingly (with implication that no action is taken). Also, *to talk a great ball game*. *U.S. colloq.*

1972 'H. PENTECOST' *Birthday, Deathday* iv. 39 Hollywood address... Talks a great ball game to the hotel people out there about his big film deals. **1973** *Philadelphia Inquirer* (Today Suppl.) 14 Oct. 171 She still talks a good game. To hear her tell it, she's the Henry Kissinger of consumerism. **1977** *New Yorker* 18 July 52/1 While they talk a good game, their considerations are consolidating their power around the world.

8. (Further examples.)

1711 POPE *Ess. Crit.* 36 No Place so Sacred from such Fops is barr'd,.. Nay, run to Altars; there they'll talk you dead. **1738** JOHNSON *London* 4 And here a female Atheist talks you dead. **1920** R. MACAULAY *Potterism* v. iii. 175 He..used to talk one sick about how little scope he had in his parish.

9. a. *to talk down*, (*a*) (earlier example, with impersonal obj.); (*b*) to reduce or diminish by talking; to denigrate or belittle; (*c*) *Econ.*, to depress the value of (a currency) or the price of (a commodity) by making tactical public statements; similarly, *to talk lower*; (*d*) see sense 9 d below; *to talk out of*: also, to extract from (a person) by persuasion; *to talk over* (earlier example); *to talk* (a person) *through* (something), to provide with a commentary on (some event); to take through with helpful explanation; *to talk up*, (*a*) (later example); (*b*) to discuss favourably; to stimulate interest in by talking, esp. exaggeratedly; to praise or advocate (chiefly *U.S.*).

1814 JANE AUSTEN *Mansfield Park* I. xiii. 269 She started no difficulties that were not talked down in five minutes. **1832** J. S. MILL *Let.* 25 Jan. in *Wks.* (1963) XII. 94 Most men in this country have a strong prejudice against any attempt to *talk them over* as the vulgar say. **1863** TROLLOPE *Rachel Ray* I. viii. 151 Mrs. Butler Cornbury..talked her young friend up to the top of the tree. **1872** *Rep. Vermont Board Agric.* I. 679 This little conversation led me to talk the matter up with the marble dealers. *a* **1882** TROLLOPE *Autobiogr.* (1883) I. v. 108, I received £20... The money had been 'talked out of' the worthy publisher by..my brother, who made the bargain for me. **1931** *Daily Express* 5 Sept. 10/5 Amsterdam is taking a bearish view of Royal Dutch and is 'talking' the shares £2 lower. **1932** W. FAULKNER *Light in August* iii. 56 The old men and the old women trying to talk down his gleeful excitement. **1933** *Sun* (Baltimore) 12 July 3/2 Thus far the dollar has been 'talked down'. **1938** *Richmond* (Va.) *Times-Dispatch* 10 Nov. 1/7 (*heading*) Victorious Taft talks down 1940 chances. **1956** H. GOLD *Man who was not with It* (1965) ii. 17 You talk it up like a longtime grifter. **1962** *Spectator* 28 Dec. 999/3 Most professionals [on the Paris Stock Exchange] are talking their market lower. **1967** *Economist* 4 Mar. 797/2 The nonmandatory system..will allow the Government, in American style, to 'talk down' a price. **1970** NEW ENG. BIBLE *Prov.* xix. 26 He who talks his father down vexes his mother. **1976** J. SNOW *Cricket Rebel* 27 A year later when I made my Test debut against New Zealand at Lord's. Ted [Dexter] virtually talked me through the game. **1978** *Daily Tel.* 16 Mar. 11/1, I am fed up with people talking down the NHS, failing to put things into perspective by pointing to the successes as well as the difficulties. **1980** *Times* 28 Jan. 19/2 For years the Silver Users Association..has been successfully talking the price of silver down. **1982** *Nature* 13 May 91/1 True, the Western media are delighted to talk up 'Star Wars' fantasies, the US shuttle, Ariane or Soviet space weapons. But they have overlooked the main substance of the Soviet [space] programme.

d. *to talk down*: to provide (an aircraft) with directions by radio communication which enable it to land, esp. in overcast or emergency conditions. Also with *in*: chiefly applied to ships seeking landfall. Hence with the pilot or navigating officer as subj. Occas. with other advbs. and preps.

1943 *Plane Talk* June 28/3 The bombardier talks the pilot 'in', telling him which way to turn. **1945** *Sci. News Let.* 25 Aug. 127/1 A blindfolded pilot..was 'talked-down' to the runway by a control operator. **1946** *Jrnl. Inst. Electr. Engin.* XCIII. III. A. 1–4 124/2 If we make these aircraft carry simple radio receivers, and pin-point them with our accurate radar, it is quite possible to 'talk them down' by giving detailed instructions to the pilot. **1955** *Sun* (Baltimore) 12 June (B ed.) 3/4 The ground controlled approach equipment—through which a plane is 'talked in' to a landing. **1957** *Times* 24 Aug. 4/1 From information telephoned to Ford by police officers it [*sc.* the helicopter] was 'talked' to where two young girls and a young man were clinging to an overturned dinghy. **1960** 'N. SHUTE' *Trustee from Toolroom* 97 They get us on the radar screen and talk us down on to the runway. **1962** J. DILL in *Into Orbit* p. xviii, Shephard was seated before a console..ready to talk John Glenn back to earth. **1967** *Observer* 2 Apr. 10/6 Ships could be advised of optimum routes and speeds as they approach port, and even 'talked in' through fog. **1970** *Daily Tel.* 21 Dec. 2/6 It is a 'blind landing system' in which a ground controller talks down an airliner in bad weather by watching its approach on a radar screen.

10. Colloq. phrases. *to talk the hind leg off a donkey* (*horse*, etc.), applied to one who: (*a*) talks with unflagging and wearying persistence, or: (*b*) is said to have the power to persuade another by eloquent or charming speech; *to talk* (someone's) *ear off*: to talk incessantly or until one is tired of listening (*U.S.*).

1808 *Cobbett's Weekly Pol. Reg.* XIII. II. 47 The old vulgar hyperbole of 'talking a horse's hind leg off'..will find its verification in the American Congress. **1861** *Temple Bar* I. 414 One has heard of persons who could 'talk a donkey's hind leg off'. **1879** TROLLOPE *John Caldigate* III. ix. 122 She'd talk the hind-legs off a dog, as we used to say out there [*sc.* in Australia]. **1915** W. S. MAUGHAM *Of Human Bondage* lxxxviii. 459 'Doesn't she look like Rubens' second wife?' cried Athelny. 'Wouldn't she look splendid in a seventeenth-century costume? That's the sort of wife to marry, my boy. Look at her.'

'I believe you'd talk the hind leg off a donkey, Athelny,' she answered calmly. **1935** G. & S. LORIMER *Heart Specialist* i. 9 An American will talk your ear off about his sport with a little encouragement. **1942** G. H. D. & M. COLE *Toper's End* IV. ix. 138 You can talk the 'ind leg off any donkey. **1976** *National Observer* (U.S.) 10 Apr. 9/5 Heck! I could talk your ear off. But let me just say that in all my 40 years of organizing and escorting tours, I haven't found a better one than this one.

talkable, *a.* Add: **b.** (Later examples.) *rare.*
1859 MRS. GASKELL *Lett.* (1966) 546 If Papa gets over-busy; & not talkable as to-day! **1899** H. VAN DYKE *Fisherman's Luck* III. i. 54 A person who has the rare merit of being talkable. 'Talkable' is not a new adjective. But it needs a new definition, and the complement of a corresponding noun... *talkability.* **1963** R. SYMONS *Many Trails* iii. 31 A grown woman yearns for somebody more 'talkable' than a thirteen-year-old.

talkathon (tǭ·kăþǫ̆n). *colloq.* (orig. *U.S.*). [f. TALK *v.* + *-ATHON, after *walkathon.*] **1.** An interminable session of talk or discussion; *spec.* a prolonged debate in a legislature or similar body, a filibuster.
1934 *Amer. Speech* IX. 76/2 Apropos of the walkathons, ..a contributor suggests that talkathons will be longer lived, especially in legislative halls. **1948** *Times-Dispatch* (Richmond, Va.) 3 Aug. 1/2 Filibustering Dixie Senators won a major round today in their effort to talk the anti-poll tax bill to death. The presiding officer..decided that an effort to curb the debate was in conflict with Senate rules, and so the talkathon continued. **1957** *Economist* 7 Sept. 820/2 The regular Assembly session..will begin with the annual talkathon, oddly styled the general debate. **1969** *Daily Colonist* (Victoria, B.C.) 3 May 2/7 Rene Matte..dashed any hopes of government supporters that the Creditistes were tiring of their talkathon. **1978** D. A. STANWOOD *Memory of Eva Ryker* xix. 181 No talkathons tonight, Eva... We'll get a fresh start in the morning.
2. A prolonged broadcast in which a political candidate is interviewed or questioned (*U.S.*). Also applied *transf.* to a lengthy radio or television discussion programme or 'talk show'. Cf. *RADIOTHON.
1952 *Economist* 6 Sept. 555/2 The latest American political novelty, the radio 'talkathon', in which..[Mr. Schmitt] answers questions for 25 hours at a stretch. **1961** *N.Y. Times Mag.* 29 Oct. 24/1 (*heading*) Political walkathons and talkathons. **1965** *Punch* 4 Aug. 176/1 The three-hour and twenty-five minute talkathon on BBC 2, was held by chance on the very day that Mr. Callaghan most heavily stamped on the economic brakes.

talkation. (Earlier example.)
1781 H. WALPOLE *Let.* 9 Sept. (1955) XXIX. 152 This is the sum total of what I can learn; matter enough to dissert upon if such were my propensity! but besides not loving talkation, it is painful for me to write.

talk-back (tǭ·kbæk). Also **talkback, talk back.** [f. TALK *v.*] **A.** *attrib.* Designating apparatus and facilities for two-way communication by loudspeaker, usu. between one who gives and one who receives instructions; *spec.* that connecting a studio and a control room.
1933 *B.B.C. Yearbk. 1934* 402 The 'talk back' facilities need setting up to suit the particular conditions of studio, listening point, etc., whereby the person listening to the rehearsal may speak over a microphone circuit and by means of a loudspeaker give instructions to those rehearsing. **1959** H. BARNES *Oceanogr. & Marine Biol.* 197 During the descent instructions are always relayed from the lower laboratory to a man at the winch by a microphone and talk-back system, and particular care is taken when nearing the bottom. **1971** M. LEE *Dying for Fun* xxiii. 107 The sound radio producer..put down his talk-back key and said: 'We won't start till you're ready.' **1982** J. SHERWOOD *Shot in Arm* xiii. 126 He pressed the talk-back key. 'Anthea..could you make it a bit lighter and more informal?'
B. *sb.* A talk-back system.
1957 *Listener* 11 July 53 Large numbers mean more widespread buildings and (in spite of a public address system, talkbacks, and so on) it is not always easy to get the people or things one wants as quickly as one wants them. **1962** A. NISBETT *Technique Sound Studio* vi. 107 The studio manager announces over the studio talk-back (which also goes to the recording room), 'We'll be going ahead in ten seconds from... now!' **1979** *Daily Tel.* 23 Apr. 14/4 Next door again is the studio, with Robin Day, that morning's speaker and, between them, a girl wearing headphones who passes on the caller's name and location over the talk back from the cubicle.

talk-down. [f. vbl. phr. *to talk down*: see *TALK *v.* 9 d.] The action or process of talking down an aircraft or a pilot. Chiefly *attrib.*
1946 *Engineering Jrnl.* Apr. 233/1 It is felt that the 'talk down' feature will not be well received in airline work. **1948** *Shell Aviation News* No. 123. 11/2 G.C.A. is a 'talk down' system and where such installations are available.. no equipment in the aircraft is needed other than efficient radio telephony. **1955** *Times* 20 June 3/5 The more complicated problems of refuelling in mid-air, baling out on to snowy tundra slopes, and landing at night by 'talk-down'. **1959** K. HENNEY *Radio Engin. Handbk.* (ed. 5) xxvi. 91 (*caption*) Information displayed to operators of precision indicators of GCA 'talk-down' radar landing system. **1963** L. DEIGHTON *Horse under Water* xx. 89 A Viscount came down the GCA talkdown, its white, red and green lights peep-boing the traffic pattern.

talked, *ppl. a.* Add: **2.** *talked-about* (chiefly with qualifying advb.): discussed.
1919 C. S. PARKER *Amer. Idyll* xvi. 178 He was the most talked-about man at the Convention. **1928** *Manch. Guardian Weekly* 7 Sept. 184/3 A striking proof of the reality and significance of the much-talked-about new entente. **1951** *Rochester* (N.Y.) *Democrat & Chron.* 12 Sept. 14/1 The fight, one of the most talked-about in years, will not be on television or radio. **1968** J. D. WATSON *Double Helix* ix. 65 The wine turned the conversation to the currently talked-about Cambridge popsies. **1982** J. FOX *White Mischief* v. 59 She was already a talked-about social success.

talkee-talkee. Add: Also *spec.* (usu. spelt *Taki-Taki*; also with small initials) an English-based creole language of Surinam; = *NINGRE TONGO, *SRANAN.
1932 A. G. BARNETT in *Amer. Speech* VII. 394 In Paramaribo, this speech of former slaves has degenerated into 'Talkee-talkee', which is loaded with a heavy percentage of Dutch. **1933, 1939** [see *NINGRE TONGO]. **1955** *Caribbean Q.* IV. II. 167 Translation in the Rural Creole of Surinam (Taki Taki) by Albert Helman. **1961** F. G. CASSIDY *Jamaica Talk* i. 8 It [*sc.* Macca] got into the common speech and has remained in Taki-taki and in Jamaican. **1970** *Language* XLVI. 409 Saramaccan..is only partly intelligible to speakers of Sranan or Taki-taki.

ta·lkfest. *slang* (chiefly *U.S.*). [f. TALK *sb.* or *v.* + *FEST.] A session of lengthy discussion or conversation, a 'talkathon'. Cf. *GABFEST.
1906 S. FORD *Shorty McCabe* ii. 36 Perhaps it'll be the grand annual ball of the Truck Drivers' Association, or just one of them Anarchist talkfests in the back room of some beer parlor. **1928** W. A. WHITE *Masks in Pageant* 247 He stepped naturally into supremacy at that talkfest [*sc.* a political convention] because he had been training for his famous speech. **1948** *Sun* (Baltimore) 18 June 19/4 (*heading*) County boy, girl win in 4-H 'talkfest'. **1961** B. PIKE *Robert Musil* viii. 167 Action is somehow made to seem irrelevant and trivial in this enormous talkfest. **1972** J. POTTS *Trouble-Maker* vii. 50 She wanted no part of the talkfest that was sure to occupy her fellow guests.

talkie (tǭ·ki). *colloq.* (orig. *U.S.*). Now *Hist.* [f. TALK *v.* + -IE, after *MOVIE.] **a.** A talking film, as opp. to a silent film. Freq. in *pl.* (esp. *the talkies*). Cf. *SPEAKIE.
1913 *Writer's Bull.* Mar. 9 The silent 'Movies', so popular to-day, will become tame in comparison with the 'Talkies'. **1921** *Daily Colonist* (Victoria, B.C.) 2 Apr. 12/2 All have seen the movies, now people are to have the opportunity of seeing and hearing the 'Talkies'... The author..of the remarkable speaking photoplay, 'Shell Shocked' is in the city. **1928** *Daily Express* 6 June 3/1 Marvel of the 'talkies'. **1930** E. WAUGH *Vile Bodies* vi. 94 She said, 'You're much later than you said. It's so boring to be late for a talkie.' **1939** M. S. RICE *Working-Class Wives* v. 110 Another Leeds woman says 'never get out except to shop; have never been to the talkies'. **1955** *Times* 25 May 5/5 It was not until the talkies came that the cinema divorced itself from reading. **1962** *Movie* Dec. 31/3 Part talkie with music and sound effects. **1978** E. MALPASS *Wind brings up Rain* xix. 184 It was about this time that the first Talkies came to Ingerby: a fact that gave Benbow the courage..to ask Ulrike to go to the pictures with him.
b. *attrib.*
1913 *Technical World Mag.* Aug. 815 One hundred other 'talkie-parties' are beginning in different parts of the city. **1922** *Radio News* (U.S.) Nov. 867/1 Mr. de Forest has solved the secret of the 'talkie movie' with perfect synchronization. **1932** L. GOLDING *Magnolia St.* III. iii. 512 An engagement at a talkie-theatre was about all Wilfred could hope for. **1936** AUDEN *Look, Stranger!* 34 By cops directed to the fug Of talkie-houses for a drug. **1960** *Times* 19 Feb. 5/1 In 1936 he had again the chance to make a feature film—a rather conventional 'talkie' adaptation of a stage success.

ta·lk-in. [See *-IN³.] **a.** A gathering or meeting for discussion; a conference.
1966 *N.Y. Times* 5 Oct. 46 LeRoi Jones, poet, playwright and polemicist, sustained each aspect of his reputation..at a reading at the Village Theater... It was the second in a series of talk-ins presented at that house. **1970** *Times* 7 Sept. 18 At the end of this month the insurance industry starts its talk-in with the Monopolies Commission over fire insurance. **1976** *Cumberland News* 3 Dec. 18/5 Members..attended a very interesting and comprehensive 'talk-in' on the best way to prepare and present exhibits for showing. **1980** J. DRUMMOND *Such a Nice Family* ii. 16 It's for the patients themselves to choose. Why don't you ask them tonight, at the talk-in?
b. *spec.* as a form of political protest (esp. by students) in which the matter at issue is discussed.
1967 *Time* 30 June 28 Last week 180 Free University students staged a 45-hour hunger strike and talk-in..to demand the release of a jailed anti-Shah demonstrator. **1977** D. JAMES *Spy at Evening* xx. 159, I was in a student meeting... It was a talk-in on Vietnam.
c. A radio or television discussion programme, esp. one broadcast live, and in which the audience may participate.
1971 *Guardian* 14 Dec. 2 Part Two of the Tuesday doomwatch..charts the putative dangers of spreading nuclear power: then a talk-in asks if we should all keep quiet about it. **1977** D. PARKER *Radio* 154 The first few months of Capitol Radio and LBC (a station mainly concerned with news, but actually including every kind of 'chat' from author-interviews to interminable talk-ins and phone-ins) were dreadful beyond recall.

talking, *vbl. sb.* Add: **a.** *talking to* (earlier example). Also in colloq. phr. *to do the talking.*
1873 HARDY *Pair of Blue Eyes* III. iv. 91 Knight did most of the talking along the journey. *c* **1875** 'BRENDA' *Froggy's Little Brother* (new ed.) iii. 35 I'd give him such a talking-to as never he had in his life before! **1903** *Red Book* Aug. 367/2 The girl did the talking, but for nearly an hour the head of the detective bureau sat silent, impassive as the sphinx. **1948** G. VIDAL *City & Pillar* x. 303 Bob did most of the talking and Jim listened.
b. talking blues, a blues song in which the lyrics (usu. narrative) are articulated in a rhythm approaching that of speech; **talking cure,** colloq. name for psychoanalysis or psychotherapy which relies on verbal interaction; **talking point,** a topic suitable for or inviting discussion or argument; **talking-shop,** a centre for idle and unconstructive talk; (derog.) applied to a parliament, *spec.* the House of Commons.
1969 *New Yorker* 1 Nov. 25/1 Alice's Restaurant—Arthur Penn's extension of Arlo Guthrie's talking-blues record. **1979** M. BOYCE *I was There!* 10/2 My first attempt at song writing took the form of humorous verse (in 'talking Blues' fashion). **1910** tr. *Freud's Outl. & Devel. Psychoanal.* in *Amer. Jrnl. Psychol.* XXI. 184 The patient herself, who at this time of her illness..spoke only English, gave this new kind of treatment the name of 'talking cure'. **1977** R. HOLLAND *Self & Social Context* viii. 240 At first sight nothing would seem more obvious than the dominant role of language in therapy—the talking cure. **1922** S. LEWIS *Babbitt* iv. 47 A broker..who understood Talking Points, Strategic Values, Key Situations, Underappraisals. **1979** B. PARVIN *Deadly Dyke* vi. 28 Quite a change of climate..but a talking point. **1912** C. MACKENZIE *Carnival* xliv. 385 Village! Talking-shop, I should say. **1922** A. M. HYAMSON *Dict. Eng. Phrases* 337/1 *Talking mill* (*shop*), *the*, (contemptuously) the House of Commons. **1942** R. G. COLLINGWOOD *New Leviathan* 213 Contemptuous language about the 'talking-shop at Westminster'. **1944** F. A. HAYEK *Road to Serfdom* v. 46 Parliaments came to be regarded as ineffective 'talking shops'. **1963** V. GIELGUD *Goggle-Box Affair* v. 49, I was an M.P. then... God knows why, damned talking-shop! **1979** R. BLYTHE *View in Winter* i. 72 The forge is the classic talking-shop of the village.

talking, *ppl. a.* Add: **2.** Comb. *talking book* (orig. *U.S.*), a sound recording of a book, for use by the blind; *talking clock* = *speaking clock* s.v. *SPEAKING *ppl. a.* 1; cf. *TIM; *talking doll*, a doll capable of emitting elementary sounds or words when activated; also *transf.* (of a person); *talking drum*, one of a set of drums, each pitched differently, which are beaten to transmit the words of a message in a tonal language, chiefly in W. Afr. (usu. in *pl.*); *talking head* (slang), a television presenter or interviewer who is shown on the screen talking directly in close-up to the camera; freq. in *pl.*; also *transf.*; *talking machine* (chiefly *U.S.*), (*a*) a machine designed to imitate human speech; *spec.* (the vocal mechanism of) a talking doll (*rare*); also *fig.*; (*b*) a phonograph; a gramophone which reproduces human speech (now only *Hist.*); *talking phonograph*: see PHONOGRAPH *sb.* 3 a.
1932 *Ann. Rep. Amer. Foundation for the Blind* 2 The development of books on phonograph records, or 'Talking Books', will be one of the greatest boons ever conferred on the blind. **1960** *Guardian* 22 July 3/4 The blind in Britain are to have 'talking books' incorporating the most advanced tape recording and play-back techniques... The present talking-books are long-playing records. **1978** D. BLOODWORTH *Crosstalk* xxi. 168 Extra-large cassettes ..from the library of the National Institute for the Blind. .. He examined the talking books. **1936** *Discovery* Oct. 315/1 The 'talking-clock' from which, merely by dialling T-I-M, every telephone user can now learn the exact time. **1969** N. FREELING *Tsing-Boum* xix. 94 One could phone the talking clock. **1925** C. MORLEY *Thunder on Left* xix. 241 There was the bleat of one of the talking dolls. '*Maaa-Maa!*' it cried. **1974** H. R. F. KEATING *Underside* vii. 66 He had been able to regard her completely in the light of some talking doll, irritating but unconnected..with the reality of life. **1977** *Detroit Free Press* 11 Dec. 15-A/3 (Advt.), The many phrases this big, beautiful talking doll 'Baby Sez' will make your daughter the happiest kid on the block. **1897** M. KINGSLEY *Trav. W. Afr.* vi. 114 In the street one sees the characteristic standing drum..and one or two talking-drums besides. **1923** R. S. RATTRAY *Ashanti* iii. 104 The big talking drums were immediately behind him and beat out: The King has sat down. **1966** C. ACHEBE *Man of People* xiii. 166 These were the same people that only the other day.. praise-singers followed with song and talking-drum. **1977** *Rolling Stone* 24 Mar. 48/2 Even drummer Mick Fleetwood finally ventured out from behind his drum kit to play the African talking drum on 'World Turning'. **1983** *Guardian* 19 July 9/4 A talking drums player from Ghana who seemed to have wandered on stage uninvited. **1968** *Punch* 24 Apr. 617/3 Indifference to people who weren't talking-heads?..If they were so monumentally unmemorable shouldn't they have been skipped altogether? **1976** *Listener* 15 Jan. 52/1, I begin to get very tired of the 'important' interview—indeed, of all talking heads—on television. **1980** *Ibid.* 4 Sept. 299/1, I looked at the talking heads, telling their stories directly to the camera. **1844** *Quincy* (Illinois) *Herald* 9 Feb. 3/2 A German, named Faber,..in New York, has invented and

brought to perfection a talking machine. It is played on by keys like a piano, and can be made to say any thing, in any language, that its inventor desires. **1844** *Picayune* (New Orleans) 18 Mar. 38/2 Why *don't* you go see the Talking Machine, and take little Matilda along with you? **1846** N. P. WILLIS *Compl. Works* III. 674/2, I had a half-hour's interview with the *talking machine* this morning, and found him a more entertaining *android* than most of my wooden acquaintances. **1850** CARLYLE *Latter-Day Pamph.* No. I. 52 A redtape Talking-machine and unhappy Bag of Parliamentary Eloquence. **1891** *Appleton's Ann. Cycl. 1890* 709/1 In 1886, J. S. Taintor, working along the lines followed by Mr. Edison, produced a talking machine, which was called the graphophone, or phonograph-graphophone. **1897** R. STUART *In Simpkinsville* 110 The little talkin' machine inside it has got out o' fix ..an' it don't say 'papa' an' 'mama' any more. **1930** W. FAULKNER *As I lay Dying* 181 Cash aimed to buy that talking machine from Suratt with that money.

b. *talking film, movie, picture* (now *Hist.*) = *TALKIE a; also formerly *talking photograph.*

1904 *Science Siftings* 26 Mar. 353/1 The inventor believes that in a short time these talking photographs will supersede the phonograph. **1908** *Variety* 16 May 11/3 (*heading*) Natural voice talking pictures... The idea is to have a capable company behind the screen and take up the cue as each character comes in view. **1921** [see *CINEPHONE]. **1927** *N.Y. Times* 28 Aug. VII. 4 If a 'talking movie' throughout were being made, it would be necessary to film a thousand feet at a time. **1978** *Lancashire Life* Oct. 97/3 Talking-pictures were introduced under the management of the late Ignatius Cullen, whose daughters continue to run the Civic Hall Cinema..showing 'wholesome family films' only.

ta·lk-out. *colloq.* [f. vbl. phr. *to talk out*: see TALK *v.* 9.] **a.** A 'talking out' of a bill in Parliament, a filibuster. (In quot., with pl. *talks out.*) *rare.*

1884 E. W. HAMILTON *Diary* 25 Mar. (1972) II. 583 One cannot help thinking that the Speaker..has missed an opportunity of applying the closure to prevent those purely obstructive 'talks out', which morning sittings are so well adapted to promote.

b. An exhaustive discussion, in which a matter is 'talked out'.

1965 *Listener* 16 Sept. 431/1 The series contained a fair number of..'talk-outs', as I must shudderingly report I have heard them called, on music, drama, poetry. **1967** *Telegraph* (Brisbane) 10 Apr. 7/6 A 'marathon talk-out' or similar scheme for mass support would pressure the Government to solve the present education problem in Queensland. **1978** *New York* 3 Apr. 58/2 At the conclusion of every Wednesday talkout, I was shocked, saddened, and dismayed.

talky, *a.* Add: *colloq.* **a.** (Earlier example.)

1815 BYRON *Let.* 31 Oct. (1975) IV. 326 Like other [dinner] parties..it was first silent, then talky, then argumentative,..then drunk.

b. Of a play, book, etc.: wordy, long-winded; containing verbose or tedious dialogue.

1937 *Partisan Rev.* Dec. 54 The producers, apparently still under the spell of the old superstition that a play cannot be 'talky', proceeded to excise almost all of the hero's connected conversation. **1967** *Times* 23 Nov. 8/7 The action scenes..do a lot to make up for a slow and talky opening. **1976** *Publishers Weekly* 23 Aug. 60/1 Once past the rather talky and confusing opening, readers will find Price's spy novel a corker.

talky-talky *sb.*, trivial conversation; loquacity; similarly, **talky-talk, talki-talk,** trivial conversation, talk for talking's sake.

1870 *Punch* 22 Oct. 173/1 Perhaps this Lighthearted Gallant doesn't have no end of talky-talkies with all the.. six-foot nothings in jack-boots all over the shop. **1884** 'MARK TWAIN' *Huck. Finn* xxvi. 258 All that kind of humbug talky-talk, just the way people always does at a supper, you know. **1907** G. B. SHAW *John Bull's Other Island* IV. 110 Why cant you say a simple thing simply, Larry, without all that Irish exaggeration and talky-talky? **1928** *Daily Express* 16 July 10/2 A..narrative in which motives and character are revealed in deeds and not in talky-talk. **1937** G. M. YOUNG *Daylight & Champaign* 134, I heartily agree that a large part of the talki-talk about influences and relationships could be with great advantage thrown into a single book. **1938** J. CARY *Castle Corner* 546 The poor child had been upset by all the talky-talky. **1953** W. REICH *Murder of Christ* xii. 111 The admirers feel uncomfortable.., not being free..to engage in small chit-chat and talki-talk. **1965** 'W. HAGGARD' *Hard Sell* xvi. 177 Away with this talky-talk, this stylized sparring between..officials.

tall, *a.* Add: **II. 6. a.** Also in proverbial phr. *tall, dark, and handsome*, denoting a type of attractive man (see also quot. 1965).

1906 R. E. KNOWLES *Undertow* xi. 135 He was tall—and dark—and handsome. **1940** *Chatelaine* Dec. 55/3 One Squadron Leader tells of filling an 'order' for 'three tall, dark and handsomes to go dancing'. **1958** M. STEWART *Nine Coaches Waiting* vii. 93 Tall, dark and handsome—the romantic cliché repeated itself in my head. **1965** T. WOLFE *Kandy-Kolored Tangerine-Flake Streamline Baby* (1966) ix. 178 It was Cary Grant that Mae West was talking about when she launched the phrase 'tall, dark and handsome' in 'She Done Him Wrong' (1933). **1978** 'H. CARMICHAEL' *Life Cycle* v. 64 If she felt like leaning on his shoulder it was certainly not because he was tall, dark and handsome.

7. a. (Later examples of ships, *spec.* square-riggers.)

1715 POPE tr. *Homer's Iliad* I. III. 192 When thy tall Ships triumphant stem'd the tide. **1726** —— tr. *Homer's Odyssey* I. IV. 201 From his tall ship the King of men descends. *a* **1865** SMYTH *Sailor's Word-bk.* (1867) 674 *Tall ship*, a phrase among the early voyagers for square-rigged vessels having topmasts. **1902** J. MASEFIELD *Salt-water Ballads* 59 All I ask is a tall ship and a star to steer her by. **1916** JOYCE *Portrait of Artist* (1969) v. 252 The spell of arms and voices; the white arms of roads..and the black arms of tall ships that stand against the moon. **1975** *Times* 4 July 4/8 The Admiralty Court yesterday granted ..an order that the tall ship, Regina Maris, be appraised and sold by the Admiralty marshal to pay a debt... The 137ft-long ship..competed in last year's Tall Ships Race.

b. *tall copy* (earlier example).

1807 SOUTHEY *Lett. from Eng.* I. xxi. 237 The size of the margin is of great importance. I could not conceive what was meant by *a tall copy*, till this was explained to me. If the leaves of an old book have never been cut smooth, its value is greatly enhanced.

c. (Earlier and later examples.) Cf. *tall-grass* adj., sense C below.

1789 *Ann. Agric.* XII. 441, I was surprized to see no tall oat grass there, the best and most useful of the grasses which meadows can be laid down with. **1979** *United States 1980/81 (Penguin Travel Guides)* 763 Now scarcely 1% of the original 400,000 square miles of tallgrass remain.

e. *tall timber* (N. Amer.), uninhabited forest. Usu. in phr. *to break* (*strike*, etc.) *for* (*the*) *tall timber*; also *transf.*, to run away, escape. Hence *tall-timbered* adj.

[**1831** *Boston Transcript* 24 June 2/4 Why didn't Van just go and *tell* the old man he wanted to *break for high timber*?] **1845** *St. Louis Reveille* 22 Jan. 1/6 Knowing the direction of the trees that stood in the grove, I 'broke for the tall timber'. **1877** J. M. BEARD *K.K.K. Sketches* 166 The panic-stricken darkies broke across the landscape with a yearning desire for tall timber that was eloquently depicted on every motion of the supple limbs. **1904** [see *SCRATCH *v.* 5 c]. **1914** D. W. ROBERTS *Rangers & Sovereignty* 128 The 'bad men'..began to strike for 'tall timber'. **1921** *Daily Colonist* (Victoria) 22 Mar. 13/1 The northern correspondent of The Colonist has just emerged from the tall timber, where he has been living under canvas for the past two years. **1949** *Skyline Trail* Oct. 18/1, I fell off *three times*; finally the disgusted critter took to the tall timber, leaving me to hike onward and to get across the frigid stream as best I could. **1966** *Times* 28 Feb. (Canada Suppl.) p. ii, Canada is a tall-timbered..rod-and-gun of a country.

f. Of game birds: high-flying. Occas. applied *transf.* to a shot at such a bird.

1913 R. PAYNE-GALLWEY *High Pheasants* iv. 37 The tallest pheasants I know of are at Harpton. *Ibid.* v. 45 These high birds..afford most sporting and tall shots. **1922** H. S. GLADSTONE *Record Bags & Shooting Rec.* 197 Correct judgment of distance is essential for accurate shooting..hence the tall stories of tall birds. **1952** J. W. DAY *New Yeomen of England* xi. 125 It was all done in the sacred service of King Pheasant, by men who laid out their woods in order to show tall birds. **1962** *Times* 28 Apr. 11/4 But equally tall pheasants can and do come over at shoots on ground as flat as a billiard table. **1976** *Shooting Times & Country Mag.* 18–24 Nov. 28/2 Half a dozen superb tall birds came over the gate.

8. d. (Earlier and later examples in *Cricket.*) *tall order* (later examples). Cf. *big* (*large*, *strong*) *order* s.v. ORDER *sb.* 24 c in Dict. and Suppl.

1864 F. LILLYWHITE *Guide to Cricketers* 95 The..match ..between Surrey and Thirteen of Cambridge University, ..owing to the 'very tall' scoring, was also unfinished. **1891** W. G. GRACE *Cricket* iv. 19 The season, so far, had been dry, and favourable for tall scoring. **1920** C. A. W. MONCKTON *Some Experiences New Guinea Resident Magistrate* xviii. 201, I..told the police we would make the attempt; clearly they thought we were taking on a devil of a tall order. **1946** *Civil & Milit. Gaz.* 26 May 15 (*heading*) Tall scoring by Indians at Lords. **1950** H. READ *Educ. for Peace* iv. 51 It is, to use our slang expression, 'a tall order', but it has been attempted before. **1976** *Norwich Mercury* 19 Nov. 2/1 'You do not by any chance know of anybody with an old lion's skin?' she asked. A tall order indeed.

B. quasi-adv. *to walk tall*: also, to have dignity or self-respect; *to sit tall*, to sit erect, with a straight back (in quot. *fig.*).

1970 *Guardian* 3 June 20/6 Officials gave the doctors folders entitled, 'Walk Tall in Australia'. *Ibid.* 6 Aug. 9/1 Walk tall, sisters... One woman's distinction adds a tiny bit to the stature of every other woman. **1976** *Billings* (Montana) *Gaz.* 6 July 3D/6 'We need to sit tall in the saddle and ride like hell in the right direction,' the governor added. **1980** *Times* 15 Feb. 16/8 'Walk tall,' say the television commercials [in Hongkong], 'report corruption.'

C. *Comb.*: *tall-hatted, -masted* (example), *-stemmed, -wheeled* (example); **tall-grass** *a.*, (esp. of a prairie) characterized by tall grasses (TALL *a.* 7 c); **tall poppy**: see *POPPY *sb.* 1 b.

1825 J. G. WHITTIER *Poet. Wks.* (1898) 522/2 With tall-masted ships on their broad bosoms riding. **1885** KIPLING *Departmental Ditties* (1886) 33, I drive no tall-wheeled traps. **1920** *Carnegie Inst. Washington Publ.* No. 290. 256 The tall-grass prairies are typical of regions in which humid farming prevails. **1922** JOYCE *Ulysses* 250 H. halted and four tallhatted white flagons halted behind him. **1925** J. FERGUSON in *Oxf. Poetry* 18 The tall-stemmed candles brighten. **1951** *Dict. Gardening* (R. Hort. Soc.) II. 921/1 In the tall-stemmed section, such as *G*[*rammatophyllum*] *speciosum*, there are probably six species. **1972** T. MCHUGH *Time of Buffalo* ii. 16 On the lush eastern half of the tall-grass prairie, one buffalo could have lived for a year on about ten acres. **1972** D. LEES *Zodiac* 27 A tall-hatted chef [was] serving a cold lunch. **1980** *Outdoor Life* (U.S.) (Northeast ed.) Oct. 97/1 Oak thickets, tall-grass ridges,..and aspen groves.

Tallensi (tǎle·nsi), *sb.* (and *a.*) Also **Talensi, Talenssi,** etc. [Native name.] **a.** An African people of Northern Ghana. **b.** The language spoken by this people, belonging to the Voltaic or Gur group of the Niger-Congo languages. Also *attrib.* or as *adj.*

1920 A. W. CARDINALL *Natives N. Territories Gold Coast* I. 1 The area..is peopled by mixed races, of which the principal tribes are Nankanni, Nabdam, Talansi..and Builsa. **1936** *Discovery* June 169/1 A Talenssi tribesman of the Gold Coast. **1949** M. FORTES *Web of Kinship among Tallensi* i. 1 The Tallensi are typical of the great congeries of Mole-Dagbane-speaking peoples that occupy the basin of the Volta rivers in the French Ivory Coast. **1951** R. FIRTH *Elem. Social Organization* vi. 207 In Tallensi ideology filial piety is an important moral principle. **1952** WESTERMANN & BRYAN *Lang. W. Afr.* v. 65 *Talensi*, own name talene. Language. Spoken by: Talensi (Tallensi, Tallense, Talansi, Talense), call themselves talis, talensi (Sing. talenja, talenga). Where spoken: Gold Coast, Zuarungu District. **1958** D. EMMET *Function, Purpose & Powers* ii. 33 In the West African Tallensi society..the important relations in terms of which behaviour is directed are kinship relations. **1963** *Internat. Jrnl. Amer. Linguistics* XXIX. I. 8 An enumeration of the membership of the Niger-Congo family by tentative genetic subfamilies follows..*Gur*:..Talensi. **1972** J. GOODY in P. Laslett *Household & Family* 106 The Tallensi and the Ashanti of Ghana.

tallied, *ppl. a.* Add: **1. b.** Counted, numbered.

1830 *Dublin Even. Post* 17 July 3/2 Not by 'tallied votes' but by acclamation.

Tallman, var. *TOLMAN.

tallow, *sb.* Add: **4.** (Earlier and later examples.)

1819 M. WILMOT *Let.* 21 Dec. (1935) 42 Wax candles are both bad, and dear. We use them of course, and *tallows* in the nursery and Kitchen. **1980** *Times Lit. Suppl.* 22 Aug. 929/3 He would blow out his tallow behind Coloured glass.

5. c. tallow-bush *U.S.* = *tallow shrub*; **tallow-nut** (examples); **tallow pot** *U.S.* and *Austral. slang*, the fireman on a locomotive engine; **tallow shrub** (earlier example); **tallow-wood** (earlier example).

1835 W. G. SIMMS *Partisan* 387 The prisoners..had been made to file into the groves of tallow bushes. **1791** W. BARTRAM *Trav. N. & S. Carolina* 94 These shelly ridges have a vegetable surface of loose black mould, very fertile, which naturally produces..Tallow-nut, or Wild Lime, and many others. **1884** C. S. SARGENT *Rep. Forests N. Amer.* 34 Wild Lime. Tallow Nut... Common and reaching its greatest development in Florida. **1914** *Dialect Notes* IV. 164 *Tallow pot*,..the fireman of a locomotive. **1929** *Bookman* July 524/1 I'm surprised to find a student tallow-pot up in the cab takin' orders from the bakehead. **1960** *Listener* 18 Aug. 250/2 Firemen are 'tallowpots' or 'bakebrains'. **1968** *Amer. Speech* XLIII. 289 *Tallow pot*, ..originally, before the days of lube oil, a fireman was so-called because he had to get out onto the steam chest of the engine with a can of tallow and hold it so the lubricant would be drawn into the cylinder. **1770** J. R. FORSTER tr. *Kalm's Trav. N. Amer.* I. 192 Tallow shrub, or Candleberry Tree. **1884** A. NILSON *Timber Trees N.S.W.* 67 Tallowwood; Mahogany.—A tall tree, with a persistent furrowed fibrous bark.

tallow-chandlery. a, b. (Earlier examples.)

1815 *Niles' Reg.* VIII. 141 There are..6 tallow chandleries [in Pittsburgh]. **1846** H. MELVILLE *Typee* xxv. 203 Mehevi..looking as if he had..undergone the process of dipping in a tallow-chandlery.

tallower. For *rare*⁻⁰ read *rare* and add example in sense 'a tallow-chandler'.

1946 E. ST. J. BROOKS *Sir C. Hatton* ii. 26 She married.. John Farrington, a tallower of the same town.

tally, *sb.*¹ **2. a.** Restrict † *Obs.* to sense in Dict. and add: Also, the record of a number.

1951 'J. WYNDHAM' *Day of Triffids* xi. 201 He had taken a tally of the livestock and the number of blind among it. **1976** H. WILSON *Governance of Britain* iii. 55 The prime minister usually keeps a tally of those for and against.

d. *spec.* in sporting use, a total score; also in *Baseball*, a single run.

1856 *Spirit of Times* 27 Dec. 276/3 One of these swiftly-delivered balls, when stopped by a skillful batsman, is sure to give the..striker time to go his rounds in safety, and score one tally as he reaches home. **1868** H. CHADWICK *Game of Baseball* 46 *Tally*, this term applies to the total score of the single innings played, or of the even innings, or of the totals at the close of the match. **1875** *Chicago Tribune* 29 July 5/4 [They] were only two tallies behind at the beginning of the ninth inning. **1949** *Marshfield* (Wisconsin) *News-Herald* 19 July 9/1 Phil Satkowiak homered with none on in the fourth and his teammates added two more tallies. **1976** *Liverpool Echo* 23 Nov. 17/1 Ainsdale marksman Alex Blakeman took his tally to nine goals from his last four games with a brilliant hat-trick. **1977** *Guernsey Weekly Press* 21 July 8/5 They shocked their opponents by scoring four runs on four hits in the top of the first and..holding the red-and-blacks to only one tally in the bottom half.

e. *Austral.* and *N.Z.* (See quot. 1965.)

1881 A. BATHGATE *Waitaruna* xii. 173 There was a rivalry among them [*sc.* shearers] as to who would have the biggest tally. **1908** D. FERGUSON *Bush Life Austral. & N.Z.* (ed. 4) v. 39 Not only did his tallies of 170, 180, and even 190 place him beyond the reach of the keenest competitor, but the quality of his work was far above that of shearers in ordinary. **1930** L. G. D. ACLAND *Early Canterbury Runs* 1st Ser. vii. 170 The combined shearing tally was..115,000 sheep. **1965** J. S. GUNN *Terminol. Shearing Industry* II. 31 *Tally*, a specialised alternative term for a number of sheep. Each shearer has his personal tally for..the day, progressively to date, and his final tally for the shed... At one time a notch was cut on a tally stick on the call of 'tally' or 'hundred', which indicated a hundred sheep counted.

3. a. (Later example.)

1950 J. AGEE *Morning Watch* (1951) II. 61 Hell of a saint I'd make, he said to himself; and added with cold and level weary self-disgust to the tally of the sins he must soon confess, I swore in Lady Chapel in the presence of the Blessed Sacrament.

4. b. (Earlier examples.)

1864 HOTTEN *Slang Dict.* 253 *Tally*, 'to live *tally*,' to live in a state of unmarried impropriety. **1867** B. BRIERLEY *Traddlepin Fold* 174 Aw'd advise thi t'live tally..if theaw con mak' it reet wi' some owd damsel.

7. a. (Earlier example.)

1851 H. MELVILLE *Moby Dick* I. xli. 303 Tying a lettered leathern tally round its neck.

e. *Naut. slang.* (See quots 1929, 1946.) Also *cap-tally* = *tally ribbon*, sense 9 c below.

1929 F. C. BOWEN *Sea Slang* 138 *Tally*, a name or name-plate of any description. **1945** 'TACKLINE' *Holiday Sailor* i. 9 We queued-up before him to have our cap-tallies—*not* cap-ribbons, we now discovered—secured about our caps with the authentic sailor's-knot. **1946** J. IRVING *Royal Navalese* 172 *Tally*, a sailor's name is his 'tally'—e.g. 'Answer your tally!'

9. a. *tally-book* (examples, also from *2 e), *-keeper* (earlier example). **b.** *tally-system* (earlier example). **c. tally band** *Naut.* = *tally ribbon* below; **tally card** *U.S.*, a score-card; **tally ribbon** *Naut.*, a sailor's cap-ribbon bearing the name of his ship (cf. sense 7 e above); **tally-stick** (earlier U.S. examples).

1977 *Times* 7 Jan. (Royal Navy Suppl.) p. ii/6 That dear little pancake hat with its silk tally band;..I believe that it was because of that little hat that I had joined the WRNS in the first place. **1965** J. S. GUNN *Terminol. Shearing Industry* II. 31 *Tally book*, the official record of what every man has shorn in each run of the day. **1972** T. A. BULMAN *Kamloops Cattlemen* xxxi. 178 Our tally books showed that we were short a bull and six head of cattle. **1909** *Cent. Dict.* Suppl., Tally card. **1928** *Publishers' Weekly* 14 July 172 Allied with these are tally cards, playing cards, novelties and party favors. **1880** 'MARK TWAIN' *Tramp Abroad* v. 55 The tally-keeper..tallied one for the opposition in his book. **1919** W. LANG *Sea Lawyer's Log* 14 Those three caps, too, look very smart, with the neat, white canvas cover which we wear during the summer months, and the tally ribbon with its tricky little bow on the left side. **1830** *Virginia Lit. Museum* 27 Jan. 526/2 A 'negro boy, with a talley stick was a statesman complete in his school'. *a* **1861** T. WINTHROP *Canoe & Saddle* (1863) vii. 153 She could not tell how many [years], having dropped her tally-stick in the fire..that very day. **1850** J. R. PLANCHÉ *Island of Jewels* II. i. 21 Is it all a trick, you make this mighty splash on, Or, is the tally system here in fashion?

tally, *v.*[1] Add: **I. 1. d.** *Sport* (chiefly *N. Amer.*). To score (a run, goal, etc.). (*a*) *intr.*

1867 *Ball Players' Chron.* 14 Nov. 2/4 Taylor took his first on a muff by Banker and tallied on passed balls. **1903** *N.Y. Times* 18 Aug. 5/2 The home players tallied only five times during the entire contest. **1931** *Randolph Enterprise* (Elkins, W. Va.) 9 July 5/3 The nine from Randolph had tallied five times in the same frame. **1947** *Sun* (Baltimore) 8 Nov. 12/2 The visitors tallied for the first time in the opening minutes of the game when Ann Worthington sent a hard shot into the corner of the cage. **1968** [see *PERIOD *sb.* 4 f]. **1974** *Cleveland* (Ohio) *Plain Dealer* 13 Oct. C.2/3 Terell tallied on a two-yard run and took a pass from Jeff Starrett 70 yards for a second score.

(*b*) *trans.*

1875 *Chicago Tribune* 24 Aug. 5/6 A furious overthrow by Beals at second..tallied three unearned runs. **1966** *Telegraph* (Brisbane) 22 Jan. 5/2 He started racing in November, and in five starts has tallied a win, second, and a third. **1976** *Billings* (Montana) *Gaz.* 6 July 1-c/6 The Angels tallied their fifth run in the third inning as Bob Brenly came on a Young single to short center.

tally-ho, *int.* and *sb.* Add: Also † **tally-oh.**

1. b. Also *fig.*

1955 *Times* 9 Aug. 9/2 Even the eminent scholar and social worker Liang Shu-ming has been cast out... Throughout China the tally-ho of the party hacks is echoing.

c. (Earlier and later examples.)

1825 H. WILSON *Mem.* (ed. 2) III. 96 A drunken man, in a dashing light green coat, a red waistcoat, and large tally oh! pin in his shirt. **1922** JOYCE *Ulysses* 571 A pack of bloodhounds led by Hornblower of Trinity brandishing a dogwhip in tallyho cap, and an old pair of grey trousers, follows from far.

tallyman. Add: **2.** (Earlier U.S. examples.)

1857 *Spirit of Times* 23 May 190/3 The tallymen were: Olympic, E. W. Cody; Bay State, W. W. Bragg, jr. **1867** 'T. LACKLAND' *Homespun* ii. 155 It may be the vote is very close; in that case the outside counters and tallymen are as much in the dark as the rest.

3. (Earlier example.)

1876 J. READ *They all do It* (song) 3 Mrs Brown says it's a sin, that Mrs Smith drinks gin And harbours tallymen from day to day.

talma. (Earlier example.)

1852 P. S. G. TEN BROECK *Let.* 1 Apr. in T. Donaldson *Moqui Pueblo Indians* (1893) 26 The most beautiful part of their dress is a talma.., which is thrown over the shoulders, fastened in front, and, hanging down behind, reaches halfway below the knee.

talmessite (tælme·səit). *Min.* [a. F. *talmessite* (Bariand & Herpin 1960, in *Bull. de la Soc. franç. de Min. et Crist.* LXXXIII. 120/1), f. *Talmessi*, name of a mine near Anarak, Iran: see -ITE[1].] A hydrated arsenate of calcium, magnesium, and barium, $Ca_2(Mg, Ba)(AsO_4)_2.2H_2O$, found as triclinic crystals.

1961 *Chem. Abstr.* LV. 8186 Analysis of an arsenate of Ca and Mg discovered in 1955..permits the definition of this new mineral as an isomorph of β-roselite... The name talmessite is proposed for the mineral. **1977** *Mineral. Abstr.* XXVIII. 229/2 White fibrous radiating aggregates of talmessite occur linked with the baryte.

‖**Talmid Chacham** (ta·lmid χǭ·χăm). Also **talmid chocham, hakham,** etc., and with small initials. [Heb., lit. 'disciple of a wise man'.] One well versed in the Jewish Law; a wise man (see also quot. 1962[1]). Cf. *HAHAM.

1863 *Chambers's Encycl.* V. 720/2 *Rabbi* (Master), *Talmid Chacham* (Disciple of Wisdom), were titles of honour given to those expert in a knowledge of the law. **1905** *Jewish Encycl.* XI. 678/2 *Talmid Ḥakam*..Honorific title given to one well versed in the Law... The talmide ḥakamim formed in Jewish society a kind of aristocracy having many privileges. **1959** D. D. RUNES *Conc. Dict. Judaism* 217/1 *Talmid Chakham*, student of true knowledge as interpreted by the Talmudic sages. **1962** *New Jewish Encycl.* 475/1 *Talmid Ḥakham*, originally this Hebrew term referred to a disciple of a learned man (that is, a teacher of the Oral Law), as its literal meaning implies. Later it applied to any Talmudic scholar of high reputation, and in its present usage it applies to any individual of high Jewish scholarship. **1962** B. ABRAHAMS tr. *Life of Glückel of Hameln* ii. 22 God...does not desert a Talmid Cocham. [*Note*] A wise and clever man, one well versed in the Torah and Talmud. **1973** *Jewish Chron.* 19 Jan. 42/3 A native of Czechoslovakia, he studied at Miskolc, Galanta, and other yeshivot, and was a man of scholarship—a *talmid chacham* in the truest sense of the word.

talmudism. Add: **2.** *fig.* in *Pol.* use [tr. Russ. *talmudizm*], (see quot. 1957). Cf. next.

1957 R. N. C. HUNT *Guide to Communist Jargon* xviii. 65 Dogmatism—or Talmudism, as Stalin at times called it—is defined..as 'the uncritical acceptance of dogma without considering the conditions of its application'. **1965** P. O'DONOVAN et al. *United States* iii. 56/1 Is this the victory of pragmatism over Constitutional talmudism?

talmudist. Add: **2.** *fig.* in *Pol.* use (see quot. 1957). Cf. prec.

1957 R. N. C. HUNT *Guide to Communist Jargon* xviii. 65 The second edition of the *Large Soviet Encyclopædia*.. defines *Talmudist* (figuratively) as 'a pedant, dogmatist, formalist, doctrinaire'. **1965** *New Statesman* 14 May 772/2 Soviet Russia is described as a 'filthy shed'... Its inhabitants are 'slaves' and its rulers 'blockheaded talmudists'.

talmudize, *v.* Add: (Later example.) Hence **talmudiza·tion.**

1927 V. BURCH *Jesus Christ & his Revel.* 13 If the Talmud depraves the values of Jesus Christ with cynicism, and the Kûran talmudises Him so that he becomes an inferior Jewish prophet, then we are guilty of a double talmudisation of the One we are said to follow. **1931** *Times Lit. Suppl.* 19 Mar. 228/2 Extraneous influences, historical development, Talmudization, do not trouble him.

‖**Talmud Torah** (ta·lmūd tōu·rŏ, tōə·rä). [Heb., 'study of the (Jewish) Law'; cf. TALMUD, TORAH.] The study of the Jewish Law. Also freq. used *attrib.* and *absol.* to designate a school run by the community for the instruction of children in the Jewish religion (see also quot. 1962). Cf. *CHEDAR.

1844 *Jewish Chron.* 18 Oct. 7/1 Mr. L. A. Green.. received the rudiments of his education at the 'Talmud Torah School', Bell Lane, Spitalfields. **1881** *Encycl. Brit.* XIII. 686/2 Besides the schools of the Alliance, there are 2287 pupils in the wretched Talmud Torah schools. **1907** I. ZANGWILL *Ghetto Comedies* 387 'We can meet and practise in your Talmud-Torah Hall!' 'The holy hall of study!' gasped the Rabbi. **1932** C. ROTH *Hist. Marranos* 391 A secret society for the purpose of studying the Law—*Talmud Torah.* **1960** L. P. GARTNER *Jewish Immigrant in Eng. 1870–1914* viii. 221 The Jews' Free School in Spitalfields... In its early days..was a Talmud Torah.. for poor children. **1962** *New Jewish Encycl.* 477/1 *Talmud Torah*, the literal meaning of this Hebrew term is 'the study of the Torah' or the 'teaching of the Torah', but it is commonly used as a designation for an elementary Hebrew school. Whereas the traditional *Ḥeder* was a private religious school, the *Talmud Torah* was a public institution maintained and administered by the community in order to provide education for orphans or children of parents who could not afford private teaching. In America, Talmud Torah generally refers to a school which meets in the afternoon after the secular school session is over. Its curriculum includes the study of the Bible, Hebrew, Jewish history, customs and ceremonies, and other phases of elementary Jewish knowledge. **1964** W. MARKFIELD *To Early Grave* (1965) ix. 151 When he wanted he had a marvellous head for Talmud Torah, except that he very seldom wanted and gave the *rebbe* trouble. **1968** M. RICHLER in R. Weaver *Canad. Short Stories* 2nd Ser. 155 My mother came home from her Talmud Torah meeting. **1976** B. WILLIAMS *Making of Manchester Jewry* xii. 322 The ten Corfiote families..contribute[d] collectively in 1872 to the languishing Talmud Torah of their home town.

talnakhite (tælnæ·kəit). *Min.* [ad. Russ. *talnakhit* (Bud'ko & Kulagov 1968, in *Zap. Vsesoyuznogo Min. Obshchestva* XCVII. 63), f. *Talnakh*, name of a locality near Dudinka in northern Siberia: see -ITE[1].] A sulphide of copper and iron, $Cu_9Fe_8S_{16}$, found as yellow, usu. iridescent, crystals of the cubic system.

1969 *Mineral. Abstr.* XX. 148/1 (*heading*) The new mineral talnakhite—the cubic variety of chalcopyrite. **1978** *Canad. Mineralogist* XVI. 29 The talnakhite structure has a broad range of possible compositions including both $Cu_9Fe_8S_{16}$ and $Cu_9Fe_9S_{16}$... The relatively restricted compositions found for natural talnakhite are the result of a change in kinetics of the ordering transformations with composition.

talo-. Add: **talocalcaneal** *a.* (example); also **talocalca·nean** *a.*; **ta:localca:neonavi·cular** *a.*, applied to the joint comprising the rounded head of the talus and the corresponding concavity formed by the navicular bone and calcaneus; **talofibular** *a.* (example); **talonavi·cular** *a.*, applied to the ligament joining the talus and navicular bone, and also to the joint between these bones (part of the talocalcaneonavicular joint).

1979 *Brit. Med. Jrnl.* 15 Dec. 1594/2 Simple rigidity of the talocalcaneal joint increases oxygen consumption during walking by up to 20%. **1900** DORLAND *Med. Dict.* 668/1 Talocalcanean. **1962** *Gray's Anat.* (ed. 33) 559 The lateral talocalcanean ligament..passes downwards and backwards from the lateral process of the talus to be attached to the lateral surface of the calcaneus. **1913** *Ibid.* (ed. 18) 402 (*heading*) Talocalcaneonavicular articulation. **1977** *Bone & Joint Diseases* (Brit. Med. Assoc.) 113 Talipes equinovarus or clubfoot is a limb anomaly that is best regarded as a congenital dislocation at the talocalcaneonavicular joint. **1979** R. H. FREIBERGER et al. *Arthrography* xi. 238/1 The most commonly injured of the lateral supporting ligaments of the ankle is the anterior talofibular ligament. **1907** MORRIS & MCMURRICH *Treat. Human Anat.* (ed. 4) III. 304 The articulations of the anterior and posterior portions of the tarsus..consist of two separate joints, viz., (i) an inner, the talo-navicular, which communicates with the anterior talo-calcaneal articulation; and (ii) an outer, the calcaneo-cuboid. **1977** *Bone & Joint Diseases* (Brit. Med. Assoc.) 3 The talonavicular joint has been replaced experimentally.

talon, *sb.* Add: **II. 4. a.** (Examples.)

1862 C. C. MEEHAN *Law & Practice of Game of Euchre* v. 86 *Talon*, the eleven cards remaining in the pack after the dealer has distributed five to each player and turned up the twenty-first card for the trump. **1921** M. C. WORK *Auction for Two or Three* III. 78 *Talon*..is, in fact, a sort of secondary *Stock* in Russian Bank and a distinguishing term must be used to describe it. **1977** *Jrnl. Playing-Card Soc.* May 25 When the discard is complete, everyone should have 11 cards and the four face-down cards remaining are called the talon.

b. (Later examples.)

1932 *Daily Tel.* 8 Oct. 2/3 Provision was made on May 3 for the conversion of the Austrian share of liability.. into new 4 per cent. bonds. Bonds, Talons, or coupons must now be presented at the Staatszentralkasse, Singerstrasse 17, Vienna, before Dec. 31. **1964** *Lebende Sprachen* IX. 99/2 A *coupon sheet*, consisting of *dividend coupons* and a *talon*, is attached to each share warrant. The dividend coupons are used by the holder to collect dividends. When the last coupon has been cashed, the talon is exchanged for a new coupon sheet. **1979** *Daily Tel.* 26 Nov. 24/6 The Bank of England give notice that new *coupon* sheets for the above-mentioned Loan will be available on and after 17th January 1980 in exchange for *talons.*

5. *talon-like* (earlier example).

1883 'MARK TWAIN' *Life on Mississippi* xxxi. 339 His hand..was talon-like, it was so bony and long-fingered.

talonid (tæ·lǫ̆nid). *Zool.* [f. TALON *sb.* 3 f + *-ID[5].] A flattened cusp on a mammalian lower molar tooth, corresponding to the talon on an upper molar.

1897 H. F. OSBORN in *Amer. Naturalist* XXXI. 1002 It [*sc.* the talon] invariably appeared first in the lower molars (where we may distinguish it as the 'talonid'). **1919** [see *HYPOCONID]. **1922** W. K. GREGORY *Orig. & Evol. Human Dentition* I. 38 The premolars..already possessed incipient talonid spurs. *Ibid.* 39 The talonids had not yet acquired basins or fossæ. **1968** [see *HYPOCONID]. **1979** *Nature* 20 Sept. 213/2 The isolated lower second molar of the right side..has the basic tribosphenic pattern with an elevated trigonid and a low talonid.

talpa[2] (tæ·lpă). *U.S.* Var. CATALPA.

1926 J. MASEFIELD *Odtaa* xvii. 283 Hi could see the fronds of the talpas moving above him. **1933** *Amer. Speech* VIII. 53/1 Talpa, n. Catalpa. This tree..has been planted in some Ozark towns.

tal qual (tæl kwæl), *adv. phr. Newfoundland.* Also **talqual.** [Shortened from L. *talis qualis* such as, of which sort or quality.] 'Just as they come': used with reference to fish sold without sorting.

1732 in *Calendar State Papers, Amer. & W. Indies* (1939) 282 And by carrying a mixt cargoe which is all sold at markett for marchantable fish, when it's only (what in the stile of the fishermen is called Tal Qual) to the shoarmen. *c* **1894** in *Dict. Newfoundland Eng.* (1982) 557/1 Tal qual, sometimes called *all qualls*, fish bought without culling is clearly the Latin *talis qualis*, 'such as it is'. **1928** in *Ibid.* 557/1 [He] said that tal qual fish was $8.20. **1930** W. F. Coaker *Hist. Fishermen's Protective Union of Newfoundland* 30 Fish would not have advanced beyond $5.30 taqual [*sic*] this season if the F.P.U. did not exist. **1934** *Rep. Newfoundland R. Comm.* 105 in *Parl. Papers 1933–4* (Cd. 4480) XIV. 357 During the war years, quantity rather than quality became the ruling consideration; the 'cull' was therefore dispensed with and fish were bought on what is known as the 'talqual' system, viz., an average price was fixed for the whole of a fisherman's catch without any exact regard to the varying qualities of the fish comprising the catch.

taluk, taluq. Add: Also **taluka.** (Earlier and further examples.)

1793 *Bengal Permanent Settlement Reg.* in *Bengal Code* (1913) I. 9 Dependent *taluk.* **1891** *Rep. Administration Local Boards in Bombay Presidency 1889–90* 1 There are ..39 Taluka Local Boards, presided over by the Assistant and District Deputy Collectors in charge of the tálukas. **1931** *Times Educ. Suppl.* 4 Apr. 123/2 The local municipal *taluka* or district board. **1977** *Lancet* 2 July 39/2 We have in fact already prepared a plan for the treatment of rabies in the taluka (somewhat bigger than a village).

talukdār, taluqdār. (Earlier example.)

1793 *Bengal Permanent Settlement Reg.* in *Bengal Code* (1913) I. 9 Dependent *talukdar.*

talweg, var. Thalweg in Dict. and Suppl.

TAM (tæm). Also **Tam,** etc. [f. the initial letters of *t*elevision *a*udience *m*easurement (see below).] Used in *Comb.*, usu. as *TAM rating*, to denote a measure of the number of people watching a particular television programme as estimated by the company Television Audience Measurement Ltd. Also *absol.*, the company itself.

1958 *Observer* 14 Dec. 15/1 In the telly-dominated world, where everybody from a philosopher to a flat-catcher is judged by his tam-rating, it was encouraging to see originality break through the crust of diffidence. **1959** *Listener* 24 Sept. 501/1 Head-hunting rivalry is understandable, but why does the type of head matter? Egg-shaped or with forehead villainous low, all are equal in the sight of TAM. **1960** *Spectator* 14 Oct. 565 Processed and packaged..down to strip-cartoon versions compatible with the maximum Tam ratings. **1963** *Daily Tel.* 17 Oct. 16/2 According to TAM figures published last Friday, [etc.]. **1966** *Punch* 24 Aug. 302/3 The first episode topped the Tamratings. **1975** Ld. Hailsham *Door wherein I Went* xxv. 158 They have their own fish to fry, their TAM ratings, their circulations, their Charters, their editorial policies, even their advertisers.

Tamachek, var. *Tamashek; **tamain,** var. *tamein.

tamanoir. (Earlier example.)

1785 T. Jefferson *Notes on Virginia* vi. 85 Aboriginals of..America..Tamanoir.

tamarack. Add: Also 9 **tamerack, temerack.** Substitute for def.: **a.** Any of several North American larches, esp. the red larch, *Larix laricina*; = Hackmatack. **b.** The shore pine, *Pinus contorta*, or the lodgepole pine, *P.c.* var. *latifolia*, of western North America; also, the timber of any of these trees. (Earlier and later examples.)

1805 W. Clark *Jrnl.* 14 Sept. in *Orig. Jrnls. Lewis & Clark Exped.* (1905) III. 66 The Mountains..thickly Strowed with falling timber & Pine Spruce fur Hackmatak & Tamerack. **1810** F. A. Michaux *Histoire des Arbres Forestieres* I. 29 American larch..Hacmatack..Tamarack par les Hollandois du New-Jersey. **1817** W. Keyes *Jrnl.* 25 Aug. in *Wisconsin Mag. Hist.* (1920) III. 351 Crossed a large meadow, a temerack swamp &c. **1894** *Outing* XXIV. 94/1 By vigorous working of three paddles we got up a 'tamarack breeze' that carried us rapidly along. **1947** R. Peattie *Sierra Nevada* 160 Lodgepole pine..is plain tamarack to many Californians. **1979** J. van de Wetering *Maine Massacre* xix. 225 The only decorations, hanging from hooks on the low, handhewn tamarack beams, were tools and weapons.

tamari (tamā·ri). [Jap.] A Japanese variety of rich soy sauce. Freq. *attrib.*, as *tamari (soy) sauce.*

1977 *Spare Rib* Jan. 36/3 For protein use soya bean paste (miso) or tamari soy sauce. **1978** G. Duff *Vegetarian Cookbk.* 14 Tamari is the genuine traditional Japanese soy sauce made only by natural methods from a mixture of wheat and whole soya beans. **1981** *Times* 22 Jan. 10/8 Root vegetables can be stir-fried..and flavoured with..soy or tamari sauce.

tamarillo (tæmări·lo). *N.Z.* [Artificial name (see quot. 1966); cf. Sp. *tomatillo*, dim. of *tomate* Tomato.] = *tree tomato* s.v. Tomato 2 b.

1966 *N.Z. Herald* 6 Sept. 5 The familiar tree tomato will go under the name of tamarillo after January 31, next year. *Ibid.*, It is hoped that export markets for both raw and processed fruit may be more successful with the use of this new, sub-tropical-sounding name. **1969** *N.Z. News* 23 July 4/5 Oranges, lemons,..tamarillos and chinese gooseberries are now in their shortest supply for several years. **1979** *Times* 17 Nov. 26/4 Specialities from New Zealand, including..tamarellos [*sic*].

tamarugo (tæmărū·go). Also *erron.* **tamarugal.** [Chilean Sp.] A small evergreen tree, *Prosopis tamarugo*, of the family Leguminosæ, native to the salt deserts of northern Chile and used to provide fodder in arid regions.

1972 *World Crops* XXIV. 297/1 The tamarugal is a thin-branching tree of 20–25 ft average height, yielding a leaf and a seed which are both nutritious and palatable. **1975** *Underexploited Trop. Plants* (Nat. Acad. Sci., U.S.) 128 In salt-devastated regions of suitable climate, tamarugo, an evergreen plant, could become a year-round fodder supply. *Ibid.* 129 Tamarugo pods need extensive leaching before they can be eaten by humans. **1977** *New Scientist* 17 Mar. 638/1 The leguminous tamarugo tree from Chile..can supply forage in dry, salty regions. **1980** *Times* 5 June 26/9 Where few economic plants could grow, the Tamarugo flourishes and provides good fodder all the year round.

tamasha. Add: **2.** *transf.* A fuss, a commotion.

1882 F. M. Crawford *Mr. Isaacs* x. 213 Mr. Ghyrkins ..wanted to know 'what the deuce all this *tamâsha* was about'. **1923** Kipling *Land & Sea Tales* 226 Why is there this *tamasha* (fuss)? **1964** A. Swinson *Six Minutes to Sunset* ii. 24 Stewart..asked 'What's all the *tamasha* about?' **1981** S. Rushdie *Midnight's Children* i. 30 Enough of this tamasha! No more of this..tomfoolery!

Tamashek (ta·mǎʃek). Also **Tamachek.** [Berber: see quot. 1896.] The Berber language spoken by the Tuaregs.

1885 *Encycl. Brit.* XVIII. 778/2 The principal dialects [of Berber] are the Kabyle, the Shilha, and the Tuarek or Tamashek, corresponding nearly to the ancient Numidian, Mauretanian and Gætulian respectively. **1896** A. H. Keane *Ethnol.* xiv. 384 This word [sc. *Tamahu*] still exists under various dialectic forms (*Tamahéeg, Tamashek, Tamazigt*) applied collectively to the Hemitic languages of the Sahara and Mauritania. The form T-amazig-t, when stripped of its fem. prefix and postfix particle *t*, is seen to be identical with the *Maxyes* of Herodotus (later *Masices, Mazices*), i.e. Amzigh, pl. Imazighen, 'freemen', the most general name of the Mauritanian Berbers. **1908** T. G. Tucker *Introd. Nat. Hist. Lang.* 173 Thus old Egyptian *annuk*..='I', for which the Berber Tamashek has *nek*... 'He' is in old Egyptian *entuf*, in Tamashek it is *enta*. *Ibid.* 174 Berber languages are still spoken in the Western Sahara (where is to be found the *Tamashek*, which is usually treated as the most representative dialect). **1974** *Encycl. Brit. Macropædia* VIII. 596/2 Tamashek has several verbal tenses. **1978** D. Bagley *Flyaway* xiii. 94 Assekrem is a Tamachek word—it means, 'The End of the World'.

tambala (tæmbā·lă). Also **tambola**; pl. **tambala, -s.** [Nyanja, lit. 'cockerel'.] A currency unit in Malawi, equal to 1/100 of a kwacha. Also, a coin of this value.

1970 *Compton Yearbk.* 188 Malawi's decimal currency was to be introduced in March 1971; the new unit, the kwacha, is divided into 100 tambolas. **1970** *Whitaker's Almanack 1971* 982 Malawi. *Malawi Kwacha* of 100 *Tambala* (from Feb. 15, 1971)... [Coins] *Tambala* 20, 10, 5, 2, 1. **1983** *Times* 19 Dec. 11/2 The Africans think we're mad..but really it wouldn't seem right without.. the five-tambala pieces in the pudding.

† **Tambaroora** (tæmbărūᵊ·rǎ). *Austral. Obs.* The name of a town in New South Wales, used to designate a bar game in which the winner buys drinks for the players. Also in *Comb.*, as *Tambaroora muster.*

1882 A. J. Boyd *Old Colonials* 63 It may be that the exciting game of Tambaroora is not familiar to all my readers... Each man of a party throws a shilling, or whatever sum may be mutually agreed upon, into a hat. Dice are then produced, and each man takes three throws. The Nut who throws highest keeps the whole of the subscribed capital, and out of it pays for the drinks of the rest. The advantage of the proceeding lies in this: Where drinks are charged at sixpence, the subscription is double that amount for each... Thus if ten Nuts go in for a Tambaroora, with nobblers at sixpence, the winner pockets five shillings by the transaction. **1895** C. Crowe *Austral. Slang Dict.* 84 *Tambaroora*, a game of a shilling each in the hat and the winner shouts. **1897** *Bulletin* (Sydney) 18 Dec. (Red Page), The essence of a present-day tambaroora is a sweep for the purchase of drinks—frequently on the principle that more liquor can be purchased wholesale for 1s. 6d. than six thirsty people can buy for 3d. each. Hence 'tambaroora muster', when the droughty party musters all the coin it's possessed of, and one individual goes and bargains for the beer. **1901** *Bulletin Reciter* (Sydney) 202 (*poem-title*) Tambaroora. **1945** Baker *Austral. Lang.* ix. 172 Just as the *shout* is an institution in this part of the world so are the..*Tambaroora muster* and a few other variations on the theme, all of which concern the creation of a jack-pot, usually with the object of buying drinks. The *Tambaroora*—taken from the name of an eastern township—dates from the early 1880s. The idea behind these expressions..is that everyone pays for himself.

tamber (tæ·mbəɹ), var. Timbre *sb.*[3]

[**1920** *S.P.E. Tract* iii. 11 Our English form of the French sound of the word would be approximately *tamber*; and this would be not only a good English-sounding word like *amber* and *clamber*, but would be like our *tambour*, which is *tympanum*, which again is *timbre*.] **1923** *Ibid.* xii. 60 Those enchanting qualities, the rhythm, the phrasing, the tamber, and accent of the living voice. **1937** J. R. Firth *Tongues of Men* iii. 36 In chiming reduplications you get..likeness of repeated articulation with difference of vowel quality or *tamber difference*—e.g., *see-saw*. **1950** D. Jones *Phoneme* iii. 12 An alphabetic system of phonetic transcription consists of letters representing sound-qualities (tambers) or phonemes. **1973** J. C. Wells *Jamaican Pronunc. in London* iv. 56 The tamber of nonprevocalic /l/ has been shown only when 'dark'. *Ibid.* 130 Chomsky and Halle call this feature 'tense' rather than 'long', thereby emphasizing the tamber differences.

tambo[1]**.** Add: (Earlier example.) Also, the tambourine played by such a musician.

1848 *New Negro Forget-me-not Songster* 32 We plaid dis song, 'on de banjo', Wid de fiddle and de bones, and ole tambo. **1870** T. A. Brown *Hist. Amer. Stage* 70/1 George Christy took the bone end, with Lansing Durand as tambo. **1952** [see *quill *sb.*[1] 1 c]. **1958** P. Oliver in *Decca Bk. Jazz* i. 22 The 'nigger minstrel' troupes comprising banjo players and 'end men' playing 'tambo and bones' being popular in the North throughout the nineteenth century.

‖ **tambo**[2] (tæ·mbo). [Sp., ad. Quechua *tampu* wayside hostelry.] In the Andean countries, esp. Peru, a lodging house or inn.

1830 E. Temple *Trav. Var. Parts Peru* ii. 65, I went from *tambo* to *tambo* in search of a lodging. **1854** W. L. Herndon *Amazon* i. 60 We stopped, at four, at the tambo of Acchahuarcu. **1902** *Encycl. Brit.* XXV. 377/1 One of the most interesting topics of study is the trails along which the seasonal and annual migrations of tribes occurred, becoming in Peru the paved road, with suspension bridges and wayside inns or tambos. **1959** G. Woodcock *Incas & Other Men* i. iii. 45 Primitive shelters, still called tambos, which were maintained..where no hotels existed. **1978** D. P. Werlich *Peru* ii. 36 The Incas constructed granaries to supply the army..and maintained *tambos* to serve travellers.

Tamboekie, var *Tambookie *sb.* and *a.*, Tambouki *a.* in Dict. and Suppl. **tamboetie,** var. *tamboti(e. **tambola,** var. *tambala.

tamboo[1] (tæmbū·). *Mil. slang.* Also **tambu.** [ad. Pers., Hindi *tambū* tent.] In the war of 1914–18, a temporary rough shelter in a trench.

1916 *Sphere* 19 Feb. 188 *b*/1 The 'Tamboo', as the sleeping apartment [in a dug-out] is called. **1918** W. Owen *Let.* 28 Sept. (1967) 579 Am still sitting on straw under our Tamboo, for it is raining again. *Ibid.* 10 Oct. 582 The corrugated iron wall of my Tamboo. *Ibid.* 31 Oct. 591 My servant & I ate the chocolate in the cold middle of last night, crouched under a draughty Tamboo, roofed with planks. **1925** [see *bivvy, bivy].

tamboo[2] (tæ·mbū). Also **tambou.** [Blend of Tambo or Tambour *sb.* + Bamboo *sb.*] In full *tamboo-bamboo.* In the West Indies, a small drum made of bamboo. Freq. *attrib.* Hence **tamboo-bambooist,** one who plays the tamboo.

1942 H. C. Gordon *West Indian Scenes* ii. iii. 57 The chief of these [instruments] for beating time was the *tambou*, a small drum. **1955** *New Commonwealth* 28 Nov. Suppl. p. xviii/2 They were not..allowed to make tambour (tamboo) bamboo bands. **1956** *Caribbean Q.* IV. iii. & iv. 195 Five to twenty stickmen formed a band.. accompanied by drummers and/or tamboo bamboo bands. **1959** W. A. Simmonds *'Pan'—Story of Steelband* 8 'Hell-yard', traditional headquarters of the Tamboo-bambooists of downtown Port-of-Spain. **1960** *Times* 17 Sept. 7/6 The three major influences on the development of the modern steel orchestra of Trinidad are the 'tamboo-bamboo' drum, the 'bottle and spoon', and the Indian drum and music of the Hosein festival. *Ibid.*, The tamboo-bamboo requires careful fashioning.

† **Tambookie** (tæmbū·ki), *sb.* and *a. Obs.* Also **Tamboekie, Tambouki, Tambuki,** etc. [f. as Tambouki *a.*] **A.** *sb.* The Tembu people. Cf. *Tembu *sb.*

1786 G. Forster tr. *Sparrman's Voy. Cape of Good Hope* II. 147 On the other side of Zomo dwells another nation, who, by the Snese-Hottentots, are called Tambukis. **1792** E. Riou tr. *J. van Reenan's Jrnl. Journey from Cape of Good Hope* 24 The country of the Tamboekies. *Ibid.* 42 The country of Captain Joobie the Tambookie. **1801** J. Barrow *Trav. Interior S. Afr.* I. iii. 201 With the Tambookies they live on friendly terms. **1824** [see *Amapondo]. **1874** *Friend* (Bloemfontein) 2 Apr., We were not sure but that the Tambookies would join the confederacy against us. **1902** *Encycl. Brit.* XXX. 3/1 The Ama-Tembu nation, popularly called Tambookies.

B. *adj.* Designating or pertaining to the Tembu people. Cf. *Tembu *a.*

1827 G. Thompson *Trav. S. Afr.* (ed. 2) II. 336 The *Tambookie* or *Amatymba* tribe. **1835** N. Adams *Let.* 5 June in D. J. Kotzé *Lett. Amer. Missionaries* (1950) 75 There is a good waggon road to Natal through the Tambookie country. **1846** J. C. Brown tr. *Arbousset & Daumas's Explor. Tour N.E. Colony Cape of Good Hope* xii. 93 Lekoro..undertook a military expedition to the Tambuqui country. **1860** W. Shaw *My Mission in S.-E. Afr.* 486 The Rev. John Ayliff, the resident Missionary, was constrained to escape with his family, accompanied by the native inhabitants of the Mission village, and take refuge in the Tembookie country. **1875** *Handbk. S. Afr.* (S. W. Silver & Co.) 460 *Tambookieland*, the country formerly inhabited by the Tambookie tribes of Kaffirs.

tamboora, var. TAMBOURA in Dict. and Suppl. **tamboritsa,** var. *TAMBURITZA.

tamboti(e (tambu·ti). *S. Afr.* Also **tamboetie, tambootie,** etc. [ad. Xhosa *umThombothi.*]

1. A deciduous tree, *Spirostachys africana,* of the family Euphorbiaceæ, native to southern Africa and with dark, rough bark and short spikes of tiny flowers. Freq. *attrib.*

1852 J. S. CHRISTOPHER *Natal* 32 The yellow, assegai, iron,..and Tamboote wood, grow in abundance. **1859** R. J. MANN *Colony of Natal* 157 A dark brown, very hard wood, distinguished by the Kafirs as 'tamboti-wood'..is employed in the construction of axles. **1871** J. MACKENZIE *Ten Years N. Orange River* xxiv. 460 The tall and resinous tambootie tree, which I selected for beams and rafters, was easily split. **1951** *Cape Argus* 27 Oct. (Mag. Sect.) 2/4 Our site was pitched in the shade of a glorious tambotie tree. **1963** H. C. BOSMAN *Unto Dust* 43 Inside were tamboetie wood trestles for the coffins. **1973** PALMER & PITMAN *Trees S. Afr.* II. 1157 The tamboti is widely known for three reasons—its fine wood, its toxic properties, and its 'jumping beans'.

¶ **2.** *tambotie grass* = *tambouki grass* s.v. TAMBOUKI *a.* in Dict. and Suppl.

1866 T. GEAST *S. Afr. Diaries* 42, I observed that almost every stem of the long tambootie grass had a silken filament flying from it. **1899** [see TAMBOUKI *a.*] **1939** tr. *E. N. Marais's My Friends the Baboons* iii. 31 The footpath here passed through a stretch of high tambotie grass.

tambou, var. *TAMBOO².

Tambouki, *a.* Add: Also **Tamboekie, Tambuki,** etc., and with small initial. Substitute for def.: *tambouki grass,* one of several tall coarse grasses of southern Africa, esp. one of the genus *Cymbopogon* or *Hyparrhenia; tambouki wood,* tamboti wood (see *TAMBOTI(E 1). (Earlier and later examples.)

1837 J. KIRKMAN in F. Owen *Diary* (1926) 158 The mother and child had hidden under the long Tamboukie grass. **1910** J. BUCHAN *Prester John* xiv. 230, I was..into a piece of parkland with long, waving tambuki grass. **1963** H. C. BOSMAN *Unto Dust* 119 Her hair was bleached the yellow of tamboekie grass in winter.

tambour, *sb.* Add: **4. c.** (Earlier example.)

1848 [see *PASSING *vbl. sb.* 3].

6*. A sliding, flexible shutter or door on a piece of furniture, made by sticking narrow strips of wood to a backing of canvas.

1940 *Chambers' Techn. Dict.* 833/1 *Tambour* (*Furn.*), a panel of slat-work or pleated textile material. **1952** J. GLOAG *Short Dict. Furnit.* 469 The tambour is used for desk tops and occasionally for doors. **1970** D. ASH *Dict. Eng. Antique Furnit.* 147/1 Tambours were introduced from France where they had been in use since about 1750, and were chiefly popular in England in the last quarter of the 18th century.

7. (in sense *6*) *tambour construction, cupboard, desk, door, front, shutter, slide, top, writing-table; tambour-fronted* adj.; **tambour-frame** (earlier examples); **tambour hook** = *tambour needle;* **tambour-stitch** (examples).

1934 *Burlington Mag.* Sept. 213/2 The origin of the tambour construction of doors, roll-tops, etc., which appeared in Europe about the middle of the eighteenth century; the bamboo sticks were split and the halves fastened on a piece of strong canvas, the whole being fitted into grooves. **1918** *Heal & Son Catal.: Cottage Furnit.* 26 Mahogany Inlaid Sideboard, bow front with tambour cupboard in centre. **1797** *Prices Cabinet Work* 57 A Tambour Desk, Three feet long, four long drawers in front. **1803** T. SHERATON *Cabinet Dict.* 316 Tambour doors are often introduced, in small pieces of work, where no great strength or security is requisite, as in night tables, and pot cupboards. **1973** 'K. ROYCE' *Spider Underground* ix. 139 The room was a library with an incongruous television set in one corner... Tambour doors were pulled across the ugly eye of the screen. **1781** in H. M. Brooks *Olden Time Series* (1886) IV. 52 Isaac Greenwood..makes Flutes,..Tea-Boards, Bottle-Stands, Tamboy [*sic*] Frames. **1782** J. BYNG *Jrnl.* 24 Aug. in *Torrington Diaries* (1934) I. 74 The long gallery is furnish'd with modern frippery, as tambour frames, &c. **1952** J. GLOAG *Short. Dict. Furnit.* 469 A tambour front is shown on the Harlequin Table illustrated on page 283. **1979** *Country Life* 30 Aug. 589/1 The compartment below, tambour-fronted, contains two drawers. **1880** L. HIGGIN *Handbk. Embroidery* v. 52 Irish or Limerick lace..is made on nèt in the old tambour frames, and with a tambour or crochet hook. **1962** *V. & A. Mus. Internat. Art Treasures Exhib.* 18/2 A George III satinwood secretaire bookcase banded with tulip and kingwood..in the centre a writing desk enclosed by a tambour shutter. **1973** *Country Life* 11 Jan. 91/3 Early-19th-century satinwood bedside cupboard..[with] tambour shutters. **1975** *Ibid.* 9 Oct. (Suppl.) 42/1 Sheraton Period Mahogany Work Table... The top section..is fitted with..two Tambour slides. *c* **1840** LADY WILTON *Art of Needlework* xx. 317 There are tambour-stitch, satin—chain—and queen-stitches. **1953** M. POWYS *Lace & Lace-Making* xi. 179 The outline may be made with tambour or chain stitch. **1797** *Prices Cabinet Work* 57 A Library Writing Table with Tambour Top. **1944** G. HEYER *Friday's Child* vi. 68 They laid the foundations of their future home by purchasing..a tambour-top writing-table, a crystal lustre, and a shaving-stand. **1794** *Cabinet Maker & Upholsterer's Guide* (ed. 3) pl. 69 (*caption*) Tambour Writing Table and Bookcase.

tamboura. Add: Also **tamboora, tambur(a), tanpoora,** etc. Substitute for def.: **a.** A long-necked lute of the Near East and Balkans, with a pear-shaped body and a fretted neck. (Later examples.) Cf. PANDORA², *TAMBURITZA.

1909 M. E. DURHAM *High Albania* vi. 141 A man.. came in with a tamboora and played.., his fingers plucking strange trills..from the slim, tinkling instrument. **1937** P. THORNTON *Dead Puppets Dance* i. 19, I contented myself with drumming on the floor..and clapping the rhythms of the tambora players. **1975** L. PICKEN *Folk Musical Instruments of Turkey* III. 220 This orientation..corresponds to one of the orientations adopted in preparing blocks of wood for Bulgarian *tambura.* **1983** *Listener* 20 Oct. 29/1 Saturday night's programme of Turkish music..was a continuous performance by the burbling, throaty flute called *ney* and the harsh, plucked instrument called the *tanbur.*

b. A long-necked fretless instrument of the lute family with a round body and usu. four wire strings plucked by the fingers, and used to provide a drone accompaniment in Indian music.

1864 [in Dict.]. **1875** ENGEL *Musical Instruments* v. 47 The Hindus..have also the divinity Ganesa, the god of Wisdom, who is represented as a man with the head of an elephant, holding a *tamboura* in his hands. **1891** C. R. DAY *Music & Mus. Instruments S. India* vii. 103 The vina, the tamburi or tamburu-vina, and the kinneri still remain just as they are described in the ancient books. **1921** H. A. POPLEY *Mus. India* vii. 110 The *Tambūr* is perhaps the most common stringed instrument in India. **1966** *Punch* 23 Nov. 770/2 The uncanny buzzing drone of a tambura, a four-stringed Indian instrument that looks like a bloated outsize wooden barometer. **1970** *Daily Tel.* 21 Sept. 9/1 She was singing..meanwhile plucking steadily at the drone-strings of her tanpoora. **1971** *Illustr. Weekly India* 25 Apr. 35/1 With Lata Mangeshkar sitting holding the *tanpura,* these inspirations would be shaped and sung and recorded. **1977** *N.Y. Times Mag.* 4 Dec. 41/3 Ram Dass had disembarked barefoot, wearing a long white robe and carrying a tambora for chanting. **1980** A. DESAI *Clear Light of Day* iv. 178 The *tanpura* player.. strummed the *tanpura* strings as if in a mesmerised state. **1981** LD. HAREWOOD *Tongs & Bones* xvii. 264 He was surrounded by two other vocalists (one also playing the tambura).

tambourer. (Earlier example.)

c **1810** MALTHUS in *Trav. Diaries* (1966) 225 Much deb.[auchery] prevails among the weavers, tambourers and master manufacturers.

tambourinate (tæmbŭrī·nēɪt), *v.* [f. TAMBOURINE *sb.* + -ATE³.] *trans.* To beat (a rhythm) as on a tambourine. (Only in the works of C. Mackenzie.)

1913 C. MACKENZIE *Sinister Street* I. I. iv. 47 He tambourinated upon the window-pane a gay little tune. **1928** —— *Extremes Meet* 63 Waterlow tambourinated with his knuckles on the shop-door the rhythm of the soldier's chorus from *Faust.*

tambu, var. *TAMBOO¹. **Tambuki,** var. *TAMBOOKIE *sb.* and *a.*; TAMBOUKI *a.* in Dict. and Suppl. **tambur(a,** var. TAMBOURA in Dict. and Suppl.

‖**tamburitza** (tæmbu·ritsǎ). Also **tamboritsa, tamburica,** etc. Pl. **-n, -s.** [Serbo-Croat.] A stringed musical instrument of the Balkans resembling a guitar or mandoline. Cf. TAMBOURA a.

1941 N. BESSARABOFF *Anc. Europ. Mus. Instruments* IV. 219 The *Tanbourica,* as used by the southern Slavs, belongs to a family of instruments similar to the Arabian-Persian *tanbur.* **1961** A. BAINES *Mus. Instruments* ix. 212 The pandoura, or 'long-necked' lute, remains a popular instrument from Persia..to the Balkans (*tamboritsa*). **1969** *Daily Tel.* 5 Nov. 13/6 Dancers from the Northern region of Barania..danced with joyful abandon to the music of tamboritzan—plucked instruments resembling guitars and mandolines. **1970** *Daily Colonist* (Victoria, B.C.) 14 Nov. 22/4 She first played on tamburitzas, Balkan instruments made by her father. **1972** DEAN & SMITH *Wisconsin* 32/2 Then the band starts banging on tamburitzas, and the patrons explode into an intricate folk dance. **1972** *Times* 21 Oct. 7/4 A choir sang Slavonian songs accompanied on the national instruments, *prim* and *tamburica,* like small mandolines. **1979** *United States 1980/81* (Penguin Travel Guides) 263 This is a Serbian restaurant where you can dine to the tune of tinkling tamburitzas.

tame, *a.* **2.** For '*Obs.* in ordinary use since *c* 1650' read 'Now restricted to U.S. use' and add further examples; *tame hay* (examples).

1838 H. W. ELLSWORTH *Valley Upper Wabash* iv. 39 It is very desirable..to get the tame grasses..set as soon as possible. **1857** *Trans. Illinois Agric. Soc.* II. 382 Where tame pasture is resorted to something more needs to be done. **1881** *Rep. Indian Affairs* (U.S.) 107 Some few have raised tame grapes. **1936** *Sun* (Baltimore) 15 Sept. 26/8 Tame hay production..is estimated at 355,000 tons. **1962** A. FRY *Ranch on Cariboo* x. 106 In conjunction with his store, he..put up a big field of good tame hay. **1976** *Billings* (Montana) *Gaz.* 20 June 8-D/8 (Advt.), 320 acres, 148 tillable now in tame grass.

‖**tamein** (tamǝi·n). *Burma.* Also 9 **tamehn, te-mine; tamain.** [Burmese.] A draped garment resembling a sari, worn usu. by women.

1839 H. MALCOLM *Trav. S.-E. Asia* I. II. iii. 214 Women universally wear a te-mine, or petticoat. **1858** C. T. WINTER *Six Months Brit. Burmah* vii. 56 The *te-miné* is a very scant garment. *Ibid.* viii. 73 The woman's tamehn is a simple piece of cotton or silk. **1863** *Leisure Hour* Oct. 667/1 With their shaven heads..and their scant tameins (petticoats). **1888** *Bow-Bells Weekly* 11 May 293/2 Burmese women..wear of evenings or when visiting religious places, gay-coloured silk 'tameins'. **1908** LADY R. CHURCHILL *Reminisc.* (1973) xiii. 272 As we drove by I saw half a dozen priests in their yellow 'tamains', or robes. **1926** *Chambers's Jrnl.* Feb. 66/1 An old *tamein* of blue cotton check..covered her from armpit to calf. **1950** J. H. WILLIAMS *Elephant Bill* x. 164 She wore her blue *tamain* girdled above her breasts, leaving her beautiful pale shoulders bare. **1984** J. COLENBRANDER *Portrait of Fryn* ix. 133 Mademoiselle Denigré, the blind French silk-weaver of the Royal *tameins.*

tameletjie (tamǝle·kʸi, -tʃi). *S. Afr.* Also **tammeletje, tommelaitje,** etc. [perh. f. Afrikaans *tabletje* small cake of chocolate, sugar, etc.] A hard toffee, sometimes containing pine nuts.

1838 T. SHONE *Diary* 6 Aug. in *Voorloper* (1976) 788 In the evening I made the Children some tommelatche as a treat on my birthday. **1862** —— 18 June in *Ibid.*, Made some Tommy Larche for the children. **1862** —— 17 July in *Ibid.*, Mrs. K. gave me a bason of sugar, to make Tomelah. **1904** H. DUCKITT *Hilda's Where is It? of Recipes* 237 *Tamelijtjes* (a favourite Cape sweet). **1926** P. SMITH *Beadle* (1929) 181 Jantje brought with him, secreted about his person, a horrible sticky mess of almond tommelaitjes. **1947** L. G. GREEN *Tavern of Seas* 65 For the children there would always be tameletjies, the sweets made of sugar, water, eggs, naartjie peel and dennebol pits—sweets that were typical of an earlier Cape Town, but which are not made so often now. **1953** *Cape Argus Mag.* 28 Feb. 3/7 Under a large oak in the main avenue sat a friendly, fat Coloured woman selling sweets —the 'Tammeletje Woman' we called her. **1974** *Cape Times Weekend Mag.* 12 Jan. 7 We searched among the pine needles for pips and collected cones. The highlight of our excursions was the tameletjies, a delicious sweet made with butter, brown sugar, syrup, vinegar and water, and the addition of the pips, which my elder sister made for us.

tamerack, obs. var. TAMARACK in Dict. and Suppl.

Tamil, Tamul. Add: The form *Tamil* is now standard. **a, b.** (Later examples of *attrib.* and adjectival use.)

1869 *Chambers's Encycl.* IX. 285/1 The earliest history of the Tamil' country is still involved in obscurity. **1911** *Encycl. Brit.* XVII. 478/2 There has been a great development in agricultural enterprise,..the estates being mainly in the hands of Europeans, and the labour mostly Tamil. **1971** *Ceylon Daily Mirror* 4 Oct. 2/2 There should be healthy rivalry and peaceful co-existence of political parties in Tamil areas.

Tamilian *a.* and *sb.* (later examples of the adj. and earlier and later examples of the sb.); **Tamulic** *a.* (earlier example).

1788 *Asiatick Researches* I. 146 The *Tamulians* (or *Malabars*) having no *h* in their alphabet. *Ibid.*, In their language, which is the *Tamulic*..the place is called *Mâvalipuram.* **1854** [see *MUNDA *sb.* and *a.*]. **1856** [see *MALAYALI]. *a* **1881** [see *BANDYMAN]. **1959** V. CRONIN *Pearl to India* vi. 89 Among the Tamilians *Vēdam* means both the three collections of hymns known as the Vedas, and also religion in general. **1968** P. LAL *Indian Recipes* 57 Pongal..is the Tamilian New Year. **1971** *Illustr. Weekly India* 25 Apr. 4/2 The Tamilian is well known for his remarkable adaptability to his surroundings.

‖**tamizdat** (tæ·mizdæt). [Russ., f. *tam* there + *izdat,* abbrev. of *izdat'el'stvo* publishing house, after *SAMIZDAT.] Russian writings which are published abroad and smuggled back into the U.S.S.R.; also this system of publication.

1974 MOORE & PARRY *Twentieth-Cent. Russ. Lit.* viii. 157 *Tamizdat,* a Russian word of later coinage and less spread than *samizdat*..refers to printed (not typed) material smuggled into the USSR from outside. *Ibid.* viii. 161 Plain mail is frequently used by people sending *samizdat* items out of the Soviet Union and *tamizdat* literature being sent into that country. **1975** *Economist* 11 Oct. 60/1 The volume of *samizdat* (unofficial and uncensored literature) has diminished, but this has been compensated for by the brisk circulation of publications known as *tamizdat* (from *tam,* 'there') printed abroad. **1978** *Observer* 1 Jan. 4/7 The era of *samizdat* is ending, he [*sc.* Georgy Vladimov] says. In its place has arrived the era of what he calls '*tamizdat*'—publication abroad of Russian writings that are then smuggled back into Russia. **1982** *Times Lit. Suppl.* 3 Sept. 950/1 It is thus a combination of *samizdat* and *tamizdat* (i.e., both unofficial Soviet and émigré publications).

tamka, var. TANGA¹ in Dict. and Suppl.

Tamla Motown (tæ·mlǎ mōᵘ·taun). The name of two U.S. record labels, *Tamla* and *Motown,* launched in 1960 by Berry Gordy Jr., used *attrib.* and *absol.* to designate a style of music characterized by a heavy beat and influenced by gospel music, which was made popular by the Black artists he employed. Also *ellipt.* as **Tamla.** Cf. *MOTOWN.

[**1964** *Melody Maker* 6 June 13/6 So far, the Tamla-Motown operation has subsisted almost entirely on single record hits.] **1968** P. OLIVER *Screening Blues* ii. 46 Rhythm and blues, rock 'n roll, the Tamla-Motown sound and the techniques of the gospel singer. **1970** *Melody Maker* 3 Oct. 25/1 The new record is directly in between reggae and Tamla Motown. *Ibid.* 25/2 I've always wanted to try to get a Jimmy Cliff sound, so I am bound to aim in a Tamla direction. **1977** *Time Out* 28 Jan.–3 Feb. 62/1 (Advt.), All types of sounds wanted—progressive/rock/oldies/middle of the road/jazz/blues/tamla-soul/classical/easy listening/films/shows/budget.

Tammany. Add: **a.** Also applied *transf.* to any similarly corrupt political organization or situation.

1901 'MARK TWAIN' *Speeches* (1910) 114 Great Britain had a Tammany and a Croker a good while ago. **1910** *Encycl. Brit.* II. 142/2 The spectacle of a Clerico-anti-Semitic tammany in Vienna had strengthened the resistance of the better elements in the country. **1980** J. BARNETT *Palmprint* xiii. 137 You're been out in the Caribbean before... Politics here are pure Tammany Hall circa 1900.

b. Tammany tiger, the symbol of the New York Tammany Society.

1871 [in Dict.]. **1953** *Manch. Guardian Weekly* 12 Nov. 2 Wagner, son of the late New Dealer swallowed up his opponents..leaving a broad smile on the face of the Tammany tiger.

tammar (tæ·măɹ). Also **tamma.** [Aboriginal name.] A greyish-brown scrub wallaby, *Thylogale eugenii*, found in south-western parts of Australia. Cf. PADDYMELON.

[**1892** A. ZIETZ in *Trans., Proc., & Rep. R. Soc. S. Austral. 1891–92* XV. 18 *Macropus eugenii.* Dama or Kangaroo Island Wallaby. **1924** F. W. JONES *Mammals S. Austral.* II. 240 The Dama Wallaby group was widely spread over the southern portion of Australia.] **1926** K. S. PRICHARD *Working Bullocks* iii. 27 The great days they had spent together, as youngsters, hunting.. tammas, in the Paper Bark swamps. **1941** E. TROUGHTON *Furred Animals Austral.* 193 Dama Pademelon; Tammar. **1970** W. D. L. RIDE *Guide Native Mammals Austral.* v. 48 Tammars are able to survive on food containing little water. **1979** *Nature* 5 Apr. 549/2, I therefore examined the role of the neural pathway from the mammary gland in tammar wallabies carrying diapausing embryos.

tammeletje, var. *TAMELETJIE.

Tammuz: see THAMMUZ, TAMMUZ. **tamongoong,** var. *TEMENGGONG. **tamoure,** var. *TAMURE.

tamoxifen (tămǫ·ksifen). *Pharm.* [f. *t* (perh. f. *T(RANS) + AM(INE + OXY- + PHEN(OL, with alteration of *y* and *ph.*] An œstrogen antagonist, $(CH_3)_2N(CH_2)_2{\cdot}O{\cdot}C_6H_4{\cdot}(C_6H_5)C{:}C(C_6H_5){\cdot}CH_2CH_3$, used to treat breast cancer and infertility in women.

1972 *Approved Names 1970* (Brit. Pharmacopœia Comm.) Suppl. IV. 6 Tamoxifen. **1972** *Clin. Endocrinol.* I. 275 A derivative of triphenylethylene was examined by Harper & Walpole (1967a,b) for its anti-oestrogenic activity in rats. This compound..was subsequently named tamoxifen. **1980** *Brit. Med. Jrnl.* 29 Nov. 1459/1 Lung metastases then enlarged and tamoxifen was substituted but discontinued after only two months because of progressive disease.

tamp, *v.* Add: **3. b.** To pack or consolidate tobacco in (a pipe or cigarette) by a series of light taps. Also with tobacco as obj. and const. *down.* orig. *U.S.*

1920 in WEBSTER. **1939** R. P. WARREN *Night Rider* ii. 42 The Captain took out his pipe, tamped it, and with an excess of care lighted it. **1940** *Sun* (Baltimore) 14 Aug. 8/6 The pipe stoppers used to tamp tobacco in the pipe bowl will be on view. **1941** 'A. MACDONALD' in *Astounding Sci. Fiction* Oct. 18/2 The man..took out another cigarette, tamped it on one end, turned it and tamped the other. **1959** J. CARY *Captive & Free* xxx. 134 Syson settled himself more comfortably and tamped his pipe with the end of a pencil. **1979** *PN Rev.* No. 9. 35/1 A pipe-smoker Tamps tobacco Down to the base of the pipe bowl. **1981** *Guardian* 12 Oct. 10/4 A local soul, resting from his labours, tamping the dottle in his pipe.

3*. *transf.* and *fig.* To oppress or constrict as by ramming; to subdue or contain by force. Also const. *down. U.S.*

1959 N. MAILER *Advts. for Myself* 19 We've all been flattened by the dead air of this time, dinched and tamped into a flat-footed class. *a* **1963** S. PLATH *Ariel* (1965) 74 Perfection... Cold as snow breath, it tamps the womb. **1976** *Time* 27 Sept. 27/2 While inflation has been tamped to just over 6%, unemployment is still high. **1977** *Time* 18 Apr. 53/2 Carter may be gambling that..he can tamp down the debate over the safety of nuclear power.

tampan. Substitute for def.: A blood-sucking tick of the genus *Ornithodorus*, esp. *O. moubata*, the vector of African relapsing fever. (Earlier and later examples.)

1861 D. LIVINGSTONE *Pop. Acct. Trav. S. Afr.* viii. 120, I dreaded the '*tampans*', so common in all old huts. **1937** *Handbk. for Farmers S. Afr.* 522 The fowl tick, often called 'tampan', is an oval-shaped, slate-coloured tick with light yellow legs. **1971** D. J. POTGIETER et al. *Animal Life S. Afr.* 222/1 To control the tampan, the floors of native huts should be well dusted with BHC powder.

Tampax (tæ·mpæks). Also **tampax.** The proprietary name of a sanitary tampon for women; also applied *loosely* to any variety of tampon, and in fig. contexts. Cf. *TAMPON *sb.* 1.

1932 *Official Gaz.* (U.S. Patent Office) 29 Mar. 1063/2 Tampax. For sanitary absorbent tampons. **1935** *Trade Marks Jrnl.* 13 Feb. 187/1 Tampax... Sanitary absorbent tampons. **1955** W. GADDIS *Recognitions* III. v. 884 When we launched the customs almost arrested me, they thought my Tampax was incendiary bombs. **1975** J. MCCLURE *Snake* iii. 35 '*Ach*, come on, Klip—what's got your Tampax in a twist?'..'It's nothing,' he muttered..'I'm just pissed off.' **1977** M. DRABBLE *Ice Age* II. 159 She went to the lavatory: there, for the first time for weeks, she found a Tampax machine. **1979** [see *TAMPON 1].

tamper, *sb.* Add: **1.** Also, an instrument or machine used for tamping. (Examples.)

1954 *Highway Engin. Terms* (*B.S.I.*) 49 *Tamper*, a wooden or metal template, beam or frame used for compacting road materials and for shaping the surface. It is manipulated by hand and may or may not carry mechanical means for tamping or vibrating. **1956** *Railway Mag.* May 344/2 It is a four-wheel caravan, painted yellow, providing living accommodation for the two men who operate the Matisa ballast tamper. **1967** *Boston Sunday Globe* 23 Apr. B 63/1 You will also need..a tamper that you can make by nailing handles to a short section of a log. **1976** *Jrnl.* (Newcastle) 26 Nov. (Advt.), Welding equipment, bench drill, bench grinder, wacker tampers, traffic light set.

2. A casing around an atomic bomb which increases its efficiency and decreases the critical mass required for an explosion.

1945 H. D. SMYTH *Gen. Acct. Devel. Atomic Energy Mil. Purposes* xii. 126 While the effect of a tamper is to increase the efficiency both by reflecting neutrons and by delaying the expansion of the bomb, the effect on the efficiency is not as great as on the critical mass. **1961** *New Scientist* 26 Oct. 231/1 A tamper, a heavy casing whose inertia resists dispersion in the early stages. **1977** N. FREELING *Gadget* II. 75 If the criticality isn't right then your whole exercise in cores and tampers..stays the way it is.

ta·mperproof, *a.* Also **tamper-proof.** [f. TAMPER *v.*[1] + PROOF *a.*] Proof against being tampered with; not susceptible to misuse. Esp. of mechanism.

1886 *Time* July (Advt., rear cover), An indicator which records the hours your day or night watchman remains on duty, and is absolutely tamperproof. **1954** *Federal Suppl.* (U.S.) CXVIII. 182/2 Armstrong in part claims a tamper-proof feature on Cel-O-Seal bands since they must be destroyed before being taken off the bottle. **1960** *Times* 3 Oct. (Advt. Suppl.) 1/2 A tamper-proof seal. **1967** D. C. COOKE *c/o American Embassy* (1968) xiii. 129 Timber locks are virtually tamperproof. **1970** *New Yorker* 3 Oct. 41/1 Not altogether tamperproof waiting lists. **1979** C. MCCARRY *Better Angels* IV. xv. 310 The computer had been designed to be absolutely tamper-proof.

tampon, *sb.* Add: **1.** (Earlier and later examples.) Esp. one inserted into the vagina; now *spec.* one made commercially and bought to provide sanitary protection during menstruation.

1848 C. D. MEIGS *Females & their Diseases* xxxiii. 432 Having confidence in the power of the tampon to suppress *such* a flooding [*sc.* menorrhagia], I would let her go very far towards a dangerous state rather than subject her to the mortification of the surgical intervention. **1921** B. M. ANSPACH *Gynecology* xxxix. 709 Tampons are made by placing over a strip of absorbent cotton a smaller strip of lamb's wool, and binding them together. **1932, 1935** [see *TAMPAX]. **1957** T. N. A. JEFFCOATE *Princ. Gynaecol.* xliii. 635 Proprietary tampons of various kinds are available but this method of applying antiseptics [to the vagina and cervix] is now rarely used. **1964** *Which?* Mar. 84/1 Medical opinion has always been divided over the use of tampons instead of external towels. **1970** G. GREER *Female Eunuch* 50 The success of the tampon is partly due to the fact that it is hidden. **1979** *Guardian* 27 Mar. 9/4 The tampon market is worth about £14 millions a year. Tampax has 62 per cent.

tamponade. Add: **2.** *Path.* Interference with the action of the heart by an excessive accumulation of blood or other fluid in the pericardial sac.

[**1930** BECK & COX in *Arch. Surg.* XXI. 1039 The tamponade effect produced by atmospheric pressure may be excited in various types of operation... In the selection of cases for operation, the heart should possess a certain reserve power capable of withstanding this tamponade effect.] **1932** *Southern Med. Jrnl.* (U.S.) XXV. 785/1 Blood is trapped in the pericardial sac, producing heart tamponade. **1962** *Lancet* 8 Dec. 1195/2 In view of the poor response to external massage and the probability of cardiac tamponade, left anterior thoracotomy was undertaken. **1974** THORNTON & LEVY *Techniques Anaesthesia* vi. 170 Tamponade may develop following open heart surgery.

tam-tam (tæ·mtæm). *Mus.* [Echoic, app. of Creole origin: cf. Fr., Ger. *tam-tam.*] A metal gong of oriental origin, *spec.* a Chinese gong, now used in western orchestras.

1839, etc. [in Dict., s.v. TOM-TOM *sb.* 1 b]. **1900,** etc. [see *GONG[2]]. **1933** M. D. CALVOCORESSI tr. *H. Scherchen's Handbk. Conducting* iii. 132 The tone of the gong does not differ from that of the tamtam but is definite in pitch. Sometimes composers prescribe a gong when they obviously mean a tamtan. **1947** *Penguin Music Mag.* May 85 There is a passage for tubular bells, cymbal, tam-tam, triangle. **1951** E. PAUL *Springtime in Paris* vii. 131 The gyrations of a near-eastern dance, to the beat of inaudible tam-tams. **1961** *Radio Times* 20 July 18/3 Six players, their instruments including bongos and maracas..a whip, temple block, four tam-tams, and crotales. **1978** P. GRIFFITHS *Conc. Hist. Mod. Music* xi. 164 A large tam tam (a kind of gong) is activated by two performers with various objects. **1983** *Listener* 15 Sept. 31/4 His orchestra (enlarged by two harps, piano, organ, celesta and a big percussion battery including tam-tam and bells) is handled with extreme refinement and virtuosity.

‖ **tamure** (tamū·re). Also **tamoure.** [Tahitian.] A Tahitian dance, the *ori Tahiti.*

1964 *Wanganui Photo News* 4 July 5 (*caption*) Nurse Anna Paotonu danced the tamoure for the floor. **1970** J. H. VANCE *Deadly Isles* iii. 25 Ah! the *tamure*! which was to the hula as whisky to milk. **1976** *Sat. Rev.* (U.S.) 30 Oct. 30/2 Palm trees and girls dancing the sexy *tamure.*

Tamworth (tæ·mwɒ̈ɹþ). The name of a town in Staffordshire, used *absol.* or *attrib.* to designate a pig of the breed of this name, usually red or brown in colour, lean and large in build, and used to produce bacon; also, the breed itself, first developed in the area.

1860 S. SIDNEY *Youatt's Pig* (ed. 2) iii. 34 The cross of the Berkshire with the Tamworth produces the most profitable bacon pigs in the kingdom. *Ibid.*, The Tamworth Breed is a red, or red-and-black pig,—hardy, prolific,..but slow in maturing. **1886** J. LONG *Bk. Pig* ix. 161 A cross between the Tamworth and the Berkshire was considered most valuable. **1897** S. SPENCER *Pigs* i. 17 The mahogany or grizzled pig..has acquired the name of the Tamworth. **1950** CARROLL & KRIDER *Swine Production* vi. 83 The Tamworth is a strictly bacon breed and the oldest of domesticated breeds of hogs. *Ibid.* 84 Tamworths are large, rugged hogs. **1967** M. KENYON *Whole Hog* viii. 93 Most of your Tamworths you call Duroc. They're the red ones—reddish-brown. **1977** *Jrnl. R. Soc. Arts* CXXV. 702/2 Tamworth pigs.., although still relatively scarce, have increased in numbers dramatically. *Ibid.* 704/2 The Tamworth..can adapt itself to a wide range of climatic conditions.

tan, *sb.*[1] (*a.*) Add: **II. 3. b.** (Earlier example.)

1749 J. CLELAND *Mem. Woman Pleasure* II. 233 The tan of his travels, and a beard..had..given it [*sc.* his face] an air of becoming manliness.

c. *pl.* Short for *Black and Tans* (see *BLACK *a.* 14 c). Also *sing.*, a member of this organization. Usu. with capital initial.

1932 S. O'FAOLÁIN *Midsummer Night Madness* 19 The Tans in their roaring Lancia patrol cars. *Ibid.* 227 'Shut up, you,' said the Tan angrily. **1951** C. LYNCH-ROBINSON *Last of Irish R.M.s* x. 161, I am sure that even amongst this class of the Tans..there were a number of quite decent fellows. **1962** E. O'BRIEN *Lost Girl* xii. 132 God Almighty, it reminded me of the tans..the night they burst the door in. **1978** F. BURTON *Politics of Legitimacy* iii. 69 Mrs Johnson sees the British troops of today..as latter-day Tans.

B. *adj.* Also, bronzed, sunburnt. Also *euphem.* (*rare*), black, negro.

1950 *Sun* (Baltimore) 13 Sept. 14/2 He has written an article in the 'tan' national magazine *Ebony.* **1963** *Pix* 28 Sept. 63 Her hair should be blonde and bunched and her figure trim and tan. **1974** S. SHELDON *Other Side of Midnight* xiv. 275 He looked tanner and leaner than when she had last seen him.

C. *attrib.* and *Comb.* **1. tan-pot** (see quot. 1978); **Tan war** *Ir. Hist.*, the conflict between the Black and Tans and the Irish Republican Army in 1921; **tan-yard** (later examples).

1946 K. TENNANT *Lost Haven* (1947) vii. 96 They could mend nets, boil tan-pots, play football. **1978** *Regional Lang. Stud.-Newfoundland* VIII. 18 A tan-pot or barking kettle is a large cauldron used for 'barking' a fisherman's nets with tan to prevent them from rotting in the salt water. **1968** 'N. BLAKE' *Private Wound* iii. 41 Flurry and I'd had enough of it after the Tan war. **1981** J. WRIGHT *Devil's Parole* ii. 27 His tales of the Tan War ..his often cruel sketches of the Irish. **1878** Tan-yard [see *hound-pup* s.v. *HOUND *sb.*[1] 7 a]. **1911** J. MASEFIELD *Everlasting Mercy* 18 The tan-yards stank of bitter bark.

‖ **tan** (tan), *sb.*[3] [Jap.] A Japanese unit of arable land or forest, equal to 300 *bu*; in modern use equivalent to approximately 0·245 acres (9·92 ares).

1871 A. B. MITFORD *Tales of Old Japan* II. 2 Rice land is divided into three classes; and,..it is computed that one *tan* (1,800 square feet)..should yield to the owner.. five bags of rice per annum. **1914** F. BRINKLEY *Hist. Jap. People* xxxvi. 527 In Hideyoshi's system,..the rule of 360 *tsubo* to the *tan* (a quarter of an acre) was changed to 300 *tsubo.* **1931** G. B. SANSOM *Japan* I. v. 98 The area was two *tan* (1 *tan* is 1,000 square yards). **1964** *Japan* (Unesco) (rev. ed.) i. 19/2 The Imperial Proclamation of the Taika Reformation was announced at the end of the year 646... Taxes shall comprise two large bundles and two small bundles of rice crop on one *tan* (about 0.245 acre). **1970** J. W. HALL *Japan* vi. 54 Strips of one *tan* each (at that time approximately .3 acres).

‖ **tan** (tan), *sb.*[4] [Jap.] A Japanese unit used for measuring cloth, equivalent to about ten yards in length and just over one foot in width; also, a piece of cloth of this size.

1876 W. E. GRIFFIS *Mikado's Empire* (1877) II. 609 A *tan*, or piece of cloth, varies in length from 25 to 30 or more feet. **1909** *Westm. Gaz.* 23 Oct. 13/1, I sentence each one to bring within three days one tan (about twenty-five yards) of cotton cloth. **1931** G. B. Sansom *Japan* III. x. 187 Princes of the blood and ministers of the first rank were restricted to 500 *tan* of cloth. *Ibid.*, One *tan* is about ten yards.

‖ **tan** (dan), *sb.*[5] Also **dan.** [Chinese.] A female character in a Chinese drama or opera; an actor of such a role.

1886 *Jrnl. R. Asiatic Soc.* (N. China Branch) XX. 208 *Tan* is a female character, and varies also according to age and..circumstances. **1917** S. Couling *Encycl. Sinica* 149/1 There are five classes of characters in a play..*shêng* ..*tan*..*ching*..*mo*..and..*ch'ou*. **1937** Arlington & Acton *Famous Chinese Plays* p. xxiv, *Tan*, subdivided into *laotan*, elderly dames with orange bandeau but no make-up; *ch'ing-i*, virtuous maidens and dutiful matrons; and *hua-tan*, vivacious and temperamental—often a courtesan or a piquante little maidservant. **1973** R. F. S. Yang in Yuan-li Wu *China* 739 The 'four great *tan* actors', namely, Mei Lan-fang, Ch'eng Yen-ch'ui, Shang Hsiao-yün, and Hsün Hui-sheng (all were female impersonators). **1975** C. P. Mackerras *Chinese Theatre in Mod. Times* xii. 199 The list of actors who took part in the festival of 1959 is an impressive one. Among exponents of the Peking Opera were three of the 'four great *tan*'. **1978** *Nagel's Encycl.-Guide: China* 201 There exist series of *dan*, or feminine roles, *sheng*, or chief masculine roles, *jing*, or heroic characters with painted faces, and *zhou* or fools.

‖ **tan** (dan), *sb.*[6] [Chinese.] A Chinese unit of weight equivalent to approximately 110 lb. or 50 kg. (formerly approximately 133 lb., 60 kg.)

1911 *Encycl. Brit.* XXVIII. 494/1 *Tan*, China = 25 gallons. Also 133⅓ lb. weight. **1965** T. R. Tregear *Geogr. of China* iii. 108 In terms of food this meant a loss of 250 million *tan* (1 *tan* equals 133 lb.) since one *mow* produces an average of 2½ *tan*. **1973** *Genius of China* 104/2 It is calculated that the price recorded..would in the reign of Wu Ti be approximately the equivalent of over 20 *tan* of grain.

tan, *v.* Add: **2. a.** *fig.* (Later example.)

1979 *Internat. Jrnl. Sociol. of Law* VII. 230 Ehrlich was not interested in the social life but in the 'legal life' of the Bukowina and..his picture of 'legal life' is heavily tanned by the traditional pattern of the Bukowinian society.

3. (Earlier example with person as obj.) Occas. *intr.*

1862 Mrs. H. Wood *Channings* II. ix. 137 'I'll tan you too, Mr. Bywater.'..'Tan away,' coolly responded Bywater. 'I can tan again.'

4. *Photogr.* To harden (gelatin) chemically in proportion to the amount of exposure.

1899 C. F. Townsend *Chem. for Photographers* (ed. 2) iv. 75 Formaldehyde is not the only aldehyde capable of tanning gelatine. **1957** R. W. G. Hunt *Reproduction of Colour* v. 43 Gelatin, in its usual state, is soluble in hot water. But by suitable chemical treatment it can be hardened, or tanned, so that it becomes insoluble. **1979** G. Haist *Mod. Photogr. Processing* I. v. 225 Images produced in the presence of such oxidation products are also tanned.

tana[1]. Add: **b.** Now usu. in form *thana* (see quot. 1961).

1936 W. H. Saumarez Smith *Let.* 5 Dec. in *Young Man's Country* (1977) ii. 45, I am making a tour of all the thanas this fortnight. **1961** L. D. Stamp *Gloss. Geogr. Terms* 450/2 *Thānā*, a political division of a district which is under the jurisdiction of a single police-station so that a thana is really a police-station area. **1975** *Bangladesh Times* 19 July 3/2 Besides forty three members of Jessore district and thana units of the defunct organisation have applied for the membership of BKSAL. **1977** *Ibid.* 19 Jan. 12/3 He made a plea for the abolition of..divisions, districts, sub-divisions and thanas because they are.. ineffective for today's needs.

Tanagra (tæ·năgră). The name of a city of Boeotia in ancient Greece, used *attrib.* and *absol.* to designate terra cotta statuettes of the 5th to 3rd centuries B.C. found in the neighbourhood. (See also quot. 1899.)

1878 C. Schreiber *Jrnl.* 29 Aug. (1911) II. 195 M. Grean was resettling some of his Greek (Tanagra) specimens. **1890** O. Wilde *Pict. Dorian Gray* (1891) 112 She had all the delicate grace of that Tanagra figurine that you have in your studio. **1899** C. A. Hutton *Greek Terracotta Statuettes* ii. 17 That aspect of individuality which is the great charm of the Bœotian statuettes from the Tanagra district, and which is so characteristic of them that any specially pretty figure, whatever its provenance, is popularly known as a 'Tanagra'. **1915** V. Horsley in S. Paget *Sir V. Horsley* (1919) 309 Some wonderful Greek sculptures small scale, and large Tanagras. **1927** *Glasgow Herald* 22 June 10 The style of the Tanagra heads of ancient Greece. **1960** R. G. Haggar *Conc. Encycl. Continental Pott. & Porc.* 469/1 Tanagra figures have been much admired..and much faked,—many of the fakes appearing..in the late 1870s and early 1880s not many years after the first discoveries of genuine Tanagra statuettes. **1978** 'M. M. Kaye' *Far Pavilions* II. xv. 240 Shushila-Bai was as small and exquisite as a Tanagra figurine.

tanaiste (tǭ·niʃtə). [a. Ir. *tánaiste*: see Tanist.] The deputy prime minister of the Republic of Ireland.

1938 *Éire: New Irish Constitution: Citizen's Manual* 22 The Taoiseach nominates a member of the Government as Tánaiste to act in his place for all purposes, should the Taoiseach die or become permanently incapacitated, or be temporarily absent. **1975** *Irish Times* 10 May 5/4 A tribute to the work of the former members..was paid by the Tanaiste and Minister for Health, Mr. Corish. **1982** M. Wallace *Brit. Govt. in N. Ireland* v. 94 The Labour *Tanaiste* or Deputy Prime Minister.

tanalized (tæ·nălәiz'd), *a.* [f. *Tanal(ith*, proprietary name of a water-borne preservative for wood + -ize + -ed[1].] Of timber, treated with Tanalith preservative or a similar compound.

1964 *Weekly News* (Auckland, N.Z.) 29 July 42/4, I built in tanalised or creosoted exotic timber which is everlasting and grown for the purpose by our Forest Service. **1967** *Daily Tel.* 15 Apr. 19/7 (Advt.), Garden frames. Made from tanalised timber, never need painting or maintenance. **1980** *Amateur Gardening* 18 Oct. 10/1 To this end, one of the most useful stock items you can keep is a bundle or two of tanalised batten.

Tancook (tæ·nkuk). Now *Hist.* The name of an island at the mouth of Mahone Bay, Nova Scotia, used *attrib.* in *Tancook whaler*, a double-ended schooner, about 45 feet long of a type formerly built there. Also *Tancook schooner*.

1933 *Yachting* Feb. 102/2 It will be the last model of a real Tancook whaler made in Nova Scotia. **1947** *Sun* (Baltimore) 18 Sept. 23/7 The Scotia schooner built to slide over rocks is Nicholas G. Schlegel's Windstark. The type is called a 'Tancook schooner', from the locality in Nova Scotia where she was built. **1951** H. I. Chapelle *Amer. Small Sailing Craft* iii. 166 The Tancook whaler was one of the most handsome of the double-enders used on the Atlantic Coast. **1967** H. F. Pullen *Atlantic Schooners* 33 The Tancook whaler was somewhat similar to the pinky, but with much sharper lines.

tandava (tā·ndăvă). Also **tandav.** [a. Skr. *tāṇḍava*.] The dance of Shiva; a traditional style of dancing in India, of a vigorous and masculine character. Cf. *lasya.

1924 Ld. Ronaldshay *India: Bird's-Eye View* xxi. 272 A dance of Shiva called Tandava, performed in cemeteries and burning-grounds. **1937**, etc. [see lasya]. **1967** Singha & Massey *Indian Dances* 22 Tandav was first danced by the god Shiva, Lord of the Dance, who then conveyed this art to mortals through his disciple Tandu. Shiva is the symbol of procreation and it is because of this that tandav is often regarded as a male dance. **1969** *Weekly Mail* (Madras) 26 July 10/4 The same movements performed with the vigour of males is tandava while it becomes lasya when performed by women possessing feminine grace. **1978** G. Vidal *Kalki* vii. 162 Indeed, there is a legend that the end will come when Siva begins the Tandava Dance, or dance of eternity.

tandem, *sb.*[1] and *adv.* Add: **B.** *adv.* Also *in tandem*, arranged one behind the other; also *fig.*, together, in partnership.

1930 [see *Corliss]. **1949** [see *scaling *vbl. sb.*[3] 2]. **1957** I. Asimov *Naked Sun* (1958) ii. 30 There were two seats in tandem, each of which could hold three. **1964** S. Lieberson in J. A. Fishman *Readings Sociol. of Lang.* (1968) 553 These measures, used in tandem, provide an instrument for a quantitative approach to a basic socio-linguistic problem. **1974** *News & Press* (Darlington, S. Carolina) 24 Apr. 8/7 Management and labor are learning to work in tandem, as has been evidenced by the sharp drop in strikes.

C. 1. a. *attrib.* and *Comb.* as **tandem axle** (see quot. 1969); usu. *attrib.*; **tandem bicycle** (earlier example); **tandem canoe** (example); **tandem duplication** *Genetics*, an atypical form of duplication (*duplication 1 e) in which the repeated segments lie immediately adjacent to one another on the same chromosome; **tandem formation** *Tennis*, the position of partners in a doubles match in which server and netman occupy the same half of the court at service; **tandem garage**, a garage with space for two vehicles to be parked one behind the other rather than side by side; **tandem-paced** *a.*, in cycle-racing: involving the use of a tandem for pacing.

1956 in E. Molloy *Automobile Engineer's Ref. Bk.* xxx. § 7 The Eaton type tandem axle unit has been developed as a method of increasing the proportion of payload to gross vehicle weight. **1969** Baker & Stebbins *Dict. Highway Traffic* 230 *Tandem* (*axles*),..an assembly of two axles for the support of the rear of a truck trailer. **1977** 'D. Rutherford' *Return Load* ii. 29 I'd suggest you have one of these new tandem axle Taskvans... They have air-bellow suspension. **1896** G. B. Shaw *Let.* 5 July (1965) I. 634, I will get a tandem bicycle; and we shall ride along over the celestial plains. **1867** J. MacGregor *Thousand Miles in Rob Roy Canoe* (ed. 5) ii. 37 In the Canoe Club we have three 'tandem' canoes, each for two paddles. **1959** C. M. M. Begg *Introd. Genetics* x. 137 A tandem duplication can result from unequal crossing over. **1981** L. L. Mays *Genetics* xii. 529 Tandem duplication of a short region of one chromosome is thought to result from inaccurate crossing over processes. **1967** P. Metzler *Advanced Tennis* ix. 116 When first confronted with the tandem formation..the left-hander is likely to continue hitting his return in its usual direction. **1976** *Tennis Today* Oct. 12/1 The American juniors played the whole match using what they call the Tandem Formation, more normally referred to as the Australian Formation in this country. **1968** *Globe & Mail* (Toronto) 3 Feb. 41/2 (Advt.), Executive home. Seven room solid brick bungalow with tandem double garage. **1974** *Country Life* 7 Mar. (Suppl.) 32 *l*, 2 reception rooms, kitchen/breakfast room. Tandem garage. **1929** *Star* 21 Aug. 17/1 F. W. Southall is expected to make an attack on the one mile tandem-paced record. **1955** *Times* 11 July 5/7 D. Marsh (Shaftesbury C.C.) won the 12-hour tandem-paced cycle race at Herne Hill on Saturday.

b. With reference to systems of work, machines, etc., which involve the use of two or more elements operating together or in series.

1921 *Telegr. & Telephone Jrnl.* VII. 79/2 With a machine switching tandem exchange large groups..can be established between each local exchange and the tandem exchange. **1923** Harbord & Hall *Metallurgy of Steel* II. xiv. 290 Splitting up the mill into a breaking-down mill, which is placed in front of, and feeds, the smaller finishing mill (the arrangement being usually known as a tandem mill) is preferable where there is a sufficient output to justify employing two sets of men. **1924** W. Aitken *Automatic Telephone Systems* III. 79 Tandem working through a tandem office will be introduced into London as quickly as possible. **1933** K. B. Miller *Telephone Theory & Pract.* III. iv. 243 In large cities..tandem operation is especially useful. *Ibid.*, The cost and inconvenience of using the tandem routing must be balanced against the trunk saving which it produces. **1955** *Archit. Rev.* CXVII. 141/2 A motor assembly known as a Two-speed Tandem Motor combines a squirrel cage and slip-ring motor within a single frame. **1959** *Wall St. Jrnl.* 3 July (Eastern ed.) 5/5 The New York State Thruway Authority has approved the use of tandem-trailers over its 559-mile highway system. The tandem vehicles—which consist of a heavy duty truck tractor hitched to two regular size trailer units—have been in experimental use. **1967** *New Scientist* 16 Feb. 397/1 Although the majority of larger telephone exchanges in Britain have direct connections with all other exchanges, many have to route their outgoing calls through central switching exchanges known as tandem exchanges. **1970** *Gloss. Aeronaut. & Astronaut. Terms* (*B.S.I.*) vi. 2 *Tandem boost*, a boost rocket motor assembly which is located at the rear of the missile and co-axially with it. **1971** W. K. V. Gale *Iron & Steel Industry: Dict. Terms* 54 *Continuous mill* (*tandem mill*), any rolling mill in which the stands are arranged in tandem. **1976** *NBR Market-place* (Wellington, N.Z.) III. 3/4 Tandem blades clog up with shaving foam and don't give as even a shave as the single blade. **1978** *Detroit Free Press* 14 Apr. 16D/2 Carrying 22 extra bolts and a new coupling device, a tandem tanker rumbled down a test track.

2. Passing into *adj.* **a.** In various uses with reference to the occurrence of one thing behind or after another.

1926 *Daily Tel.* 7 Aug. 7/4 Someone has given the appropriate name 'tandem' system to a form of curriculum in which students were limited to one main subject, and one subject only, at a time. **1952** *Mind* LXI. 356 Is minding what one is doing, then, after all, a tandem occurrence? **1968** E. A. Powdrill *Vocab. Land Planning* iii. 54 Two-tier, or tandem, development is merely the utilisation of backland to place one or more houses behind another. **1980** *Archaeology* Nov.–Dec. 37 We took a series of tandem camera exposures from the 300 meter level.

b. Co-operative, joint, dual; involving two persons, organizations, etc.

1962 *Economist* 24 Mar. 1094/1 The future is seen..in terms of a 'tandem' economic partnership between two continental common markets. **1963** *Times Lit. Suppl.* 18 Jan. 44/4 The tandem authors of this study merely add to the confusion. **1976** *National Observer* (U.S.) 21 Feb. 1/5 These tandem operations, Totera and Schuler explain, involve every aspect of IRS forms. **1977** *Time* 26 Sept. 37/3 Kepesh recalls a tandem tantrum he had with his wife.

tandemly (tæ·ndĕmli), *adv.* Chiefly *Genetics.* [f. Tandem *sb.*[1] and *adv.* + -ly[2].] End to end.

1968 *Jrnl. Molecular Biol.* XXXII. 328 Cairns' (1966) hypothesis that the long DNA fibers are composed of many tandemly joined replication sections is proved. **1974** [see *replicon]. **1978** *Nature* 5 Oct. 364/3 The histone genes of *Drosophila* represent a tandemly repeated gene family. **1980** *European Jrnl. Cell Biol.* XXII. 430 As Hensen's node regresses, paraxial somitomeres are added tandemly.

tandoori (tændūᵉ·ri), *a.* (*sb.*) Also **tanduri.** [f. as next.] Of, pertaining to, or designating food cooked in a tandour, or this style of cooking. Also *absol.* as *sb.*

1958 R. Howe *Cooking from Commonwealth* 484 Since partition the most popular form of restaurant cooking in India's capital, Delhi, has been tanduri cooking. *Ibid.* 540 Tanduri chicken is always eaten with the fingers. **1961** Mrs. B. Singh *Indian Cookery* 1. 18 A tandoor is used for the preparation of tandoori chicken, tandoori fish, seekh kabab, tandoori roti, nan, sheermal etc. **1966** *Daily Tel.* 24 Oct. 11/3 The fabulous *tandoori* cooking from the north-west of India: charcoal-heated clay-oven cooking which ensures food of distinction. **1969** *Guardian* 2 Oct. 17 The restaurant specialises in exclusive Indian cuisine: Tandoories—meat and chicken grilled in clay ovens over a charcoal fire. **1969** *Enact* (Delhi) Nov. 18/2 Bring out the *tanduri* fish. **1970** D. Singh *Indian Cookery* 30 *Tandoori* is food cooked on the spit in a clay oven. *Ibid.* 32 The various kebabs and kaftas used in tandoori, grills and roasts. **1975** *Indian Express* 1 Aug. 4/4 Multi-purpose gadget for tandoori cooking. **1977** D. James *Spy at Evening* viii. 53 Dinner..at..my favourite Tandoori house on Sidney Street. **1979** *Daily Tel.* 11 June 8/8 More rice is being eaten in Britain. Not in the old-fashioned rice pudding, but with curry, chop-suey and tandoori dishes.

tandour. Add: Also **tandoor, tandur. 2.** The form **tandoor** is usual in this sense.

[Urdu or Panj. *tandūr* oven.] A clay oven used in northern India and Pakistan; a shop that sells food cooked in this. Also *Comb.*, as *tandoor-cooked* adj.

1840 [in Dict.]. **1925** M. L. Darling *Punjab Peasant* viii. 166 A significant change is that, when the cultivator goes to town, he is not as content as he was with the low-class *tandur*, but has begun to put up at the hotel. **1947** *Civil & Milit. Gaz.* 8 Apr. 11/1 Some 'tandur' shops were partially affected by the fire. **1957** C. Rand *Twain shall Meet* 77 They complain too that there is no room for *tandoors*, special jarlike ovens for baking *chapatis*—wheat pancakes—a Punjab staple. **1967** *Guardian* 8 Dec. 6/4 North Indian or Pakistani [cooking] depends on the clay oven called a tandoor, into which kebabs, chickens marinated in yoghourt and spices, and the special bread called nan are lowered and rapidly cooked. **1974** [see *nan[3]]. **1977** *Sunday Times* (Colour Suppl.) 27 Nov. 35/3 The tandoor is the traditional oven used in Indian villages. It is fashioned out of clay and left to dry for two days. Then it is seasoned with yoghurt, spinach and oil to smooth it and prevent it from cracking. It is this, combined with the tremendous even heat of the burning coals, that gives tandoor-cooked meat its mild aromatic flavour.

tanewa, obs. var. *taniwha.

tang, *sb.*[1] Add: **I. 2. a.** Also in certain fire-arms.

1805 C. James *Milit. Dict.* (ed. 2), *Tang*, the upper part of the plug, or breech pin. **1869** V. D. Majendie *Milit. Breech-Loading Rifles* 62 The locking arrangements consists of the following parts:— Steel bolt.. Recess in breech tang for bolt. **1909** *Text Bk. Small Arms* I. iv. 35 The rear end of the body is in the form of a tang with sides. **1918** E. S. Farrow *Dict. Milit. Terms* 605 *Tang*, the projecting portion of the breech of a musket, by which the barrel is secured to the stock. **1929** *War Office Textbk. Small Arms* i. 12 On the underside of the cocking-piece is a projection..which travels in a groove, cut for it in the tang of the body. **1965** H. L. Blackmore *Guns & Rifles of World* 100 Butt tang engraved with Royal arms of France. **1976** *Shooting Mag.* Dec. 61/1 (Advt.), Model 801 Luxus O/U shotgun..10 mm wide ventilated barrel rib, sling swivels, top tang safety, double trigger.

3. Substitute for def.: = *surgeon-fish* s.v. Surgeon *sb.* 3 b in Dict. and Suppl. (Later examples.)

1925 D. S. Jordan *Fishes* (rev. ed.) xxxviii. 618 In the next family, *Acanthuridæ*, the surgeon-fishes or tangs, the scales remain small. **1965** Mrs. L. B. Johnson *White House Diary* 3 June (1970) 281 These were lots of little bright yellow fish, young blue tang, they called them—as they grow up they change color. **1980** R. E. Thresher *Reef Fish* xx. 147 The surgeonfish, or tangs, are high-bodied, laterally compressed fish.

4. Restrict *Stereotyping* to senses in Dict. **c.** *Typefounding.* The projection at the bottom of a piece of type which is formed by superfluous metal cooling in the opening of the mould.

1908 *Proc. Institution Mechanical Engineers* Dec. 1034 The gate through which the metal passes into the mould becomes also filled with type-metal and forms a projecting *tang* which must be broken from the type. **1921** W. H. Slater *What Compositor should Know* I. 23 Finishing means breaking off the 'tang' or 'jet' left at the bottom of each letter when this is not done on the machine. This tang occurs on all types cast by hand and all large sizes cast by machine. **1951** S. Jennett *Making of Bks.* ii. 32 When type is cast a fragment of metal, the tang, is left adhering at the base from the orifice in the mould through which the molten metal is injected. This tang is broken off and the resulting roughness of the fracture ground down.

Tang (tæŋ), *sb.*[5] Also **T'ang, Tanga.** [Chinese *táng*.] **a.** The name of a dynasty which ruled in China from A.D. 618 to *c* 906; a ruler belonging to this dynasty.

1669 J. Ogilby *Nieuhoff's Embassy from E.-India Co. to Emperor of China* I. xviii. 282 At last having miserably worried and weakened each other, they were all subdued by the seventh Race called *Tanga*, which seized upon the whole Empire, and reigned with his Posterity till the Year of Christ 618. **1738** J. B. Du Halde *Descr. Empire China & Chinese Tartary* I. 194 (*heading*) The Thirteenth Dynasty, call'd Tang, which had Twenty Emperors, in the Space of Two hundred eighty nine Years. **1788** tr. *Grosier's Gen. Descr. China* II. vi. iii. 209 Under the *Tang*, this superstition still continued. **1837** *Penny Cycl.* VII. 81/1 Ly-yuen..in A.D. 622 founded the dynasty of Tâng. **1925** B. Rackham in R. Fry et al. *Chinese Art* 15 When the classic period of T'ang is reached, the potters are working with the easy mastery of artists in their craft. **1940** E. Pound *Cantos* xiv. 41 Tang rising. And the first Tang was Kao Tseu, the starter. **1979** Mills & Mansfield *Genuine Article* iii. 62 Ming, Sung and T'ang have become names synonymous with the finest ceramics. T'ang was the dynastic name of the pottery of China in the eighth century AD.

b. *attrib.* or as *adj.* Freq. used to designate artefacts, etc., of this period.

1831 *Canton Miscellany* iv. 246 The Tang Dynasty was founded at the commencement of the Seventh century. **1854** *North-China Herald* 17 June 184/1 The first emperor of the T'ang dynasty. **1910** *Encycl. Brit.* VI. 213/2 It is in fact from the early religious schools of Japan that we can best conjecture the grandeur of the T'ang style. **1924** M. Borden *Three Pilgrims & Tinker* ii. 21 The van was full of the favourite belongings of each member of the family: their mother's Tang horses. **1935** *Burlington Mag.* Jan. p. xiii/2 The T'ang and Sung ceramics..should arouse much interest. **1943** D. Welch *Maiden Voyage* xviii. 153 Chou bronzes, T'ang grave figures and Sung porcelain. **1955** *Times* 6 Aug. 7/6 Eight Bodhisattvas, typical of early T'ang painting, and clearly owing their inspiration to Indian models. **1962** E. Snow *Other Side of River* (1963) xviii. 130, I..remembered the description of the scene by the T'ang poet Chen Chang. **1976** 'M. Delving' *China Expert* xiii. 179 How many T'ang horses ..really came from T'ang graves? **1980** *Times* 1 Mar. 13/6 Two hours' drive north-west of Xian is the tomb complex of the Tang emperor.

tanga[1]. Add: Also 9 **tank; tamka, tangka, tenga. b.** (Further examples.)

1876 C. Markham *Narr. Mission George Bogle to Tibet* xiii. 129 The following memorandum of weights used in Tibet is among Mr. Bogle's papers..5 *tanks* make one *nega*. **1889** G. N. Curzon *Russia in Central Asia* vi. 189 At the time of my visit the silver *tenga* was worth about fivepence. **1892** W. W. Rockhill *Jrnl.* 23 July (1894) iv. 253 The chief inquired if I had any Chinese silver or rupees to exchange for Lh'asa tankas. **1904** A. T. de Mattos tr. *Grenaud's Tibet* viii. 301 The commonest coin within the limits of the kingdom of Lhasa is the tangka. **1924** *Glasgow Herald* 30 June 12 Every time I rode through the city [of Bokhara] one of the Cossacks carried a purse with silver 'tengas' (a metal coin worth about sixpence), and distributed them to the..poor. **1970** R. D. Taring *Daughter of Tibet* iv. 44 The *tamka* was then worth about ninepence. **1972** G. Muller tr. *Schön's World Coin Catal. Twentieth Cent.* 826 Tibet..15 skarung = 1 tangka..3 tangka = 1 Indian rupee. **1974** D. Norbu *Red Star over Tibet* i. 34, 670 silver coins called *tamka*.

tanga[2] (tæ·ŋgă). [a. Pg., ad. Quimbundo *ntanga* loincloth.] **a.** (See quot. 1960): the garment is also worn by men. **b.** A bikini made of triangles of material joined by thin ties; *spec.* the lower half of this. Cf. *string *sb.* 6 c.

1912 T. A. Joyce *S. Amer. Archeol.* xii. 265 The so-called *tangas*.., triangular in shape, and convex in section,..are found in the burial-urns of women... It has been suggested that they are the 'translations' into pottery of the small triangular leaf coverings worn by many of the women of primitive Brazilian tribes in historical times. **1921** *Museum Jrnl.* (Univ. of Pennsylvania) Sept. 146 Nothing whatever was found on the inside of the burial urns except the so-called 'tangas' or fig leaves supposed to have been worn by the women... The tangas were always well made, hard burned, highly polished, and either in bright red monochrome or painted designs. **1948** B. Meggars in J. H. Steward *Handbk. S. Amer. Indians* III. 157 Tangas, which are found in abundance, are thought to have been worn by the women as a pubic covering. **1948** A. Métraux in *Ibid.* 670 Women..wore a short apronlike (tanga) cotton fringe.. or a cotton skirt. **1960** C. Winick *Dict. Anthropol.* 525/1 *Tanga*, a pubic covering worn by Indian women, especially in tropical South America and the West Indies. The most common form of tanga today is a beaded apron. Others consist of a small triangle of inner bark. **1975** *Times* 5 June 12/1 Nylon jersey tanga (or string). **1976** R. Condon *Whisper of Axe* I. x. 60 She had the sort of body that should not..wear anything but a *tanga*, that wonderful Brazilian string bikini.

tangana (tæŋgā·nă). Also **Tangana.** [Origin unknown.] A type of rhythm used in jazz music (see quot. 1952).

1926 A. Niles in W. C. Handy *Blues* 24 The Habañera or tango rhythm... Both the justification for its use in Negro music, and the explanation of its subsequent popularity among the Negroes themselves, are supplied on acceptance of the plausible theory that this is an African rhythm (the native word is *tangana*) and Spanish only by adoption through the Moors. **1952** B. Ulanov *Hist. Jazz in Amer.* (1958) iv. 31 In 1914 Handy published his 'St. Louis Blues' with its provocative Tangana rhythm, which is a kind of habanera or tango beat consisting of a dotted quarter, an eighth-note, and two quarter-notes. **1959** 'F. Newton' *Jazz Scene* iii. 41 An admixture of certain rhythms such as the tangana, or the habanera which..roused a particularly vivid response among continental negroes.

Tanganyikan (tæŋgănyī·kăn), *a.* (*sb.*) [f. *Tanganyik(a* (see below) + -an.] Of or pertaining to Tanganyika, now the continental part of the E. African republic of Tanzania. Also as *sb.*, a native or inhabitant of Tanganyika. Cf. *Tanzanian *sb.* and *a.*

1905 *Rep. Brit. Assoc. Adv. Sci.* 430 The total number of Tanganyikan species of fishes amounts to eighty five. **1957** *African Affairs* LVI. 304 He went on to ask.. whether the tsetse fly experiments were providing a hope that the scourge of the fly would be overcome... It would make for a great development in Tanganyikan agriculture. **1962** *Sunday Express* 21 Jan. 5/8 We who live in Tanganyika must think of ourselves as Tanganyikans and work for our country. **1971** *Standard* (Dar es Salaam) 7 Apr. 4/5 They could not cope with the then Tanganyikan education curriculum.

‖ **tangata** (ta·ŋata). [Maori: see Kanaka.] **a.** In Maori parlance, a person, a human being. **b.** *tangata whenua* (fenu·a), lit. 'people of the land', local people (e.g. as opp. to *nga manuhiri* the visitors).

1840 W. Deans *Let.* 30 Oct. in J. Deans *Pioneers of Canterbury* (1939) 29 He says they will take no other white man with them and they all want me to go and live there, calling me the *tangata* Widerup or the proprietor of it. **1949** P. Buck *Coming of Maori* (1950) I. v. 65 The Maori people who were in occupation of New Zealand at the time of European contact were the descendants of the intermixture of three successive groups of immigrants: the moa-hunters and the early *tangata whenua* [etc.]. **1974** *N.Z. Listener* 20 July 13/1 The body was lying in state on the stage at the end of the hall and the tangata whenua were seated. **1974** [see *moa-hunter].

tangeite (tæ·ŋgeˌəit). *Min.* [ad. Russ. *tangeit* (A. Fersman 1925, in *Priroda* No. 7–9. 239), f. the name of the *Tange* Gorge, Tyuya-Muyun, Fergana, central Asia: see -ite[1].] An orthorhombic basic vanadate of copper and calcium, $CuCa(VO_4)(OH)$, that is a secondary mineral found as green or greenish yellow crystals; calciovolborthite.

1927 *Mineral. Abstr.* III. 234 For the crystalline varieties the name tangeite, from the Tange gorge, is proposed, and for the colloidal variety the term 'Turkestan volborthite' is retained. **1951** C. Palache et al. *Dana's Syst. Min.* (ed. 7) II. 816 Tangeite appears to be identical with calciovolborthite. **1971** *Mineral. Mag.* XXXVIII. 488 The writers..now place on record an occurrence in Leicestershire of tangëite, $CuCaVO_4OH$, and volborthite, $Cu_3(VO_4)_2.3H_2O$, not hitherto described from Britain.

tangelo (tæ·ndʒĕlo). [f. Tang(erine *sb.* 2 a + Pom)elo.] A hybrid citrus fruit resembling a thick-skinned orange, produced by crossing the tangerine, *Citrus reticulata*, and the pomelo, *C. grandis*; also, the tree bearing this fruit.

1904 *Cosmopolitan Mag.* XXXVII. 262 Under the auspices of the United States Department of Agriculture has been evolved the 'tangelo'. **1905** Webber & Swingle in *Yearbk. U.S. Dept. Agric. 1904* 235 The term 'tangelo' is suggested by the writers as a name for this group of loose-skinned fruits, which lie midway between the pomelo and tangerine. **1932** Swingle & Robertson in *Proc. 6th Internat. Congr. Genetics* II. 385 The exhibit shows..tangelo fruits preserved in fluid. **1939** *Times* 23 Feb. 17/4 The basket [of Jamaican fruit] contained uglis, tangelos, grapefruit, oranges, [etc.]. **1969** *Oxf. Bk. Food Plants* 88/2 Tangelos are hybrids between the tangerine and grapefruit. **1970** *Harrod's Summer Food News* 8/1 Canadian tangelo juice. **1977** *N.Z. Herald* 8 Jan. 1-5/6 (Advt.), Fruit trees..tangelos.

tangent, *a.* and *sb.* Add: **A.** *adj.* **1. a.** Also as quasi-*adv.*

1936 A. W. Clapham *Romanesque Archit.* viii. 167 The subsidiary towers..at Mainz and Laach..are set axially and tangent at the ends of the transept. **1977** *Sci. Amer.* Aug. 37/1 The radiation is emitted tangent to these trajectories.

B. *sb.* **1. b.** *spec.* in *Surveying*, a tangent to a curve at a point (*tangent point*) where the curve starts or finishes; freq. *attrib.*, as *tangent distance, length*, the length of such a tangent from the tangent point to its intersection with the other tangent.

1850 T. Baker *Rudimentary Treat. Land & Engin. Surveying* II. ii. 171 Find the radii, as BO, CO'; the tangent point, as C'; and the junction point, as C, with the position of the common tangent at the junction point. **1862** W. J. M. Rankine *Man. Civil Engin.* I. v. 111 The places where permanent marks of the course of the line are chiefly required are on the tangents of curves. **1902** R. E. Middleton et al. *Treat. Surveying* II. v. 61 Find length of tangent for a 3° curve with central angle of 35° 42'. **1978** J. G. McEntyre *Land Survey Systems* x. 329 An easement curve is a transition curve utilized to increase the degree of curvature gradually from the tangent point to the circular portion of a curve. **1983** J. C. McCormack *Surveying Fundamentals* xxi. 384 The tangent distances are taped from the *P.I.* [*sc.* point of intersection] down both tangents to locate the *P.C.* and *P.T.*

ta·ngent, *v. rare.* [f. the sb.] *intr.* To go off or away at a tangent (see Tangent *sb.* 1 c); to fly off at an angle.

1920 F. Niven *Tale that is Told* vii. 44 They are always tangenting away, not from what I have said, but from what they imagine I have said. **1940** 'Gun Buster' *Return via Dunkirk* II. i. 85 The empty sardine tin that the Babe pitched, tangented off the side of his tin hat into the long grass. **1974** K. Millett *Flying* (1975) II. 201 She chuckles and then tangents off to some article.. she read.

tangential, *a.* Add: **1. d.** (*c*) Of the pick-up of a record-player: so mounted that it is kept at a tangent to the groove by a rectilinear motion of the arm.

1937 *Electronics* X. 9/2 The whys and wherefores of the 'tangential' type pick-up mount and its effects on distortion and record wear. **1977** *Time* 10 Oct. 43/1 (Advt.), The Beogram 4002 has an electronically controlled tangential arm which plays records in the same way that they were cut: tracing a straight line from the edge of the record to its centre instead of tracing an arc.

2. c. *tangential energy*: in the writings of P. Teilhard de Chardin, the form of energy that is manifest in the workings of the physical world and is described by the laws of thermodynamics. Cf. *radial energy* s.v. *radial *a.* 6. [tr. F. *énergie tangientielle*, introduced *c* 1938 by P. Teilhard de Chardin (*Le Phénomène Humain* (1956) I. ii. 62).]

1959, 1965 [see *radial *a.* 6]. **1969** A. Richardson *Dict. Christian Theol.* 332/2 Tangential energy links units at the same level of organization.

tanger (tæ·ŋəɹ). Also **tenger.** [f. TANG *v.*[1] + -ER[1].] **1.** *dial.* A person who has a noticeable effect on another (see also quot. 1886).

1886 W. CUDWORTH *Rambles round Horton* 237/1 *Tenger*, a deceiving person. **1914** D. H. LAWRENCE *Prussian Officer* 221 She looked a tanger sitting there, all like statues, her and the geese. **1922** —— *England, my England* 269 She's a tanger—'s driven the gel to what she is.

2. [TANG *sb.*[1] 2.] One who furnishes implements with a tang.

1921 *Dict. Occup. Terms* (1927) § 279 *Tanger, saw tanger*, places saw blade against gauge in semi-automatic machine, which marks and purchases tang hole in blade and rivets on tang. **1960** *Classification of Occupations* (Gen. Register Office) Index 107/2 Tanger—*cutlery mfr... razor mfr...saw mfr.*

tangerine, *sb.* Add: **2. b.** Also *Comb.*, as *tangerine-coloured* adj.

1977 M. KENYON *Rapist* iii. 31 Shovelling sugar into his tangerine-coloured tea.

tangi[1]. Add: (Earlier and later examples.) Also *transf.* and *fig.*

1836 J. A. WILSON *Missionary Life & Work in N.Z.* (1889) III. 34 Here we found many wailing over a dead body... As we passed some left the *tangi* and joined us. **1844** S. SELWYN 10 Apr. in A. Drummond *Married & Gone to N.Z.* (1960) 113 Nothing to disturb us but the incessant tangi of the children at night. **1905** W. BAUCKE *Where White Man Treads* 278 Our college graduate arrives; the home-coming tangi and nose-greeting is over; the guest meal set out on the floor. **1941** BAKER *N.Z. Slang* vi. 56 When we refer to *holding a tangi* about a setback or problem we are putting another Maori term into colloquial use. **1959** TINDALE & LINDSAY *Rangatira* xviii. 172 The tangi mourning ceremonies. **1963** B. PEARSON *Coal Flat* ii. 42 She said to me, 'Come on Joe, we'll have a *tangi* together.'

Hence as *v. intr.* to lament, to mourn; also *transf.* and *fig.*

1844 M. WILLIAMS 17 Oct. in A. Drummond *Married & Gone to N.Z.* (1960) 39, I could not think how I had consented, and tangied over his preparations. **1864** A. S. ATKINSON *Jrnl.* 19 Apr. in *Richmond-Atkinson Papers* (1960) II. 107 She sat down, began tangi-ing,.. & so they remained for some minutes. **1873** J. H. H. ST. JOHN *Pakeha Rambles through Maori Lands* x. 168 The old man,..enumerating the different degrees of relationship he stood in to the deceased, and his appreciation of his virtues, '*tangiéd*' again to such an extent, that another relation, affected at his extreme grief, presented him with a horse. **1881** J. L. CAMPBELL *Poenamo* vii. 201 Those who had *tangied* over Ngatai had to come and *tangi* over Te Pirete. **1943** N. MARSH *Colour Scheme* xiii. 224 'She's going to *tangi*.' 'To wail..to lament the dead.'

‖ **tangi**[2] (ta·ŋgi). [Pashtu *tangai*, pl. *tangī*, f. (Pers.) *tang* narrow, *tanga* mountain pass.] A gorge or defile in north-western Pakistan.

[**1854** *Q. Jrnl. Geol. Soc.* X. 467 Mr. Loftus..explains the great clefts or 'Tangs' (as they are termed in Persian) which pass through the elongated limestone saddles. These tangs are very numerous.] **1901** *Mem. Geol. Survey India* XXXI. 188 Narrow gorges or rifts locally called 'tangi'. **1923** *Blackw. Mag.* Feb. 221/2 The river emerged through a narrow Tangi in the hills. **1954** O. H. K. SPATE *India & Pakistan* xvi. 425 Tangis or transverse clefts, often only a few yards wide, by which the streams penetrate the longitudinal ridges. **1983** J. MASTERS *Man of War* x. 125 The Wazirs will try to ambush us... I've been marking my map with every likely gully and *tangi*.

tangible, *a.* Add: **1. b.** *tangible assets*, physical and material assets which can be precisely valued or measured.

1930 [see *INTANGIBLE *sb.*]. **1977** *Time* 8 Aug. 39/3 Recognizing that shares of many companies are selling at far less than the replacement value of their tangible assets, a number of chief executives have been using corporate cash to buy the assets of other companies at a discount. **1982** *Daily Tel.* 2 Sept. 19/2 Alexander Howden's net tangible assets were overstated..according to the audit of the British insurance company.

B. as *sb.* A thing that may be touched; something material or objective. Also *fig.*

1890 W. JAMES *Princ. Psychol.* II. xix. 77 Those things are *tangibles*; their real properties, such as shape, size, mass, consistency, position, reveal themselves only to touch. **1962** Y. MALKIEL in Householder & Saporta *Probl. Lexicogr.* 5 Range, i.e. the volume and spread of the material assembled, represents..the most obvious criterion [for classifying dictionaries]; it is also the most objective, involving by definition tangibles alone. **1965** *Economist* 21 Aug. 697/2 He also had some tangibles to offer, in particular a request to Congress to eliminate the import fee on sugar. **1980** I. ST. JAMES *Money Stones* II. i. 39 Financial operators like me deal in paper and rarely have first-hand contact with tangibles..reducing..a new jumbo jet or a sugar crop to one common denominator.. Money.

tangiwai (tæ·ŋiwəi). *Min.* [Maori, = tear-water.] A translucent kind of bowenite serpentine found in New Zealand that has droplet-shaped markings when polished.

1863 F. E. MANING *Old New Zealand* 321 This particular *mere* must have been made of the lovely translucent *tangiwai*. **1880** [see *KAWA-KAWA[1] 2]. **1911** [see *BOWENITE]. **1935** *Trans. & Proc. R. Soc. N.Z.* LXV. 201 All the talc-epidote-bearing serpentines examined by the writer are typical *tangiwais*.

tangka, var. TANGA[1] in Dict. and Suppl.

tangle, *sb.*[1] Add: **3. tangle-weed** (earlier and later examples).

1825 G. F. LYON *Brief Narr. Attempt to reach Repulse Bay* 65 The sea was much agitated, a great quantity of tangle weed floating about. **1870** J. LAUDER *Warblings of Caged Bird* 37 Whaur the stanes are green wi' moss And the tangle weeds are plenty.

tangle, *sb.*[2] Add: **1. b.** (Earlier example.)

1882 D. C. BEARD *Amer. Boy's Handy Bk.* xi. 88 The Tangle, a name given to tassels of hemp that are often attached to the bottom of the dredge itself or used separately.

3. *tangle-headed* adj. (earlier *fig.* example).

1884 'MARK TWAIN' *Huck. Finn* xv. 131, I think you're a tangle-headed old fool, Jim.

tangle, *v.*[1] Add: **5. c.** *transf.* To fight, to engage in conflict or argument (*with* or *up with*); also *fig.* and *loosely*, to associate or become involved with. *colloq.* (orig. *U.S.*).

1928 *Amer. Speech* III. 29 Fistic action in large and copious quantities is expected..tonight when Dave Shade tangles with Maxie Rosenbloom. **1929** D. HAMMETT *Red Harvest* xxiv. 242 While we're tangling, them bums will eat us up. **1929** D. RUNYON in *Hearst's Internat.* July 58/2, I remember reading in the paper about a lot of different guys who are considered very sensible until they get tangled up with a doll. **1942** *Sun* (Baltimore) 13 May 15/4 (*heading*) Preakness victor will tangle with old rivals if he runs at Belmont. **1945** L. R. GRIBBLE *Battle Stories of R.A.F.* xxv. 64 There's no better fun in the world than tangling with the Hun. **1953** E. S. GARDNER *Case of Green-Eyed Sister* (1959) ii. 17 You tangle up with Brogan..and you'll learn something about the noble art of shake-down. **1957** R. LAWLER *Summer of Seventeenth Doll* I. i. 17, I dunno why I always have to get tangled up with little men, just the same. Even Wallie, he was shorter than me. **1958** B. BEHAN *Borstal Boy* III. 185, I don't like tangling with anyone, but Ickey Summers was the sort of little bastard that would pick a fight with you until he lost and the best thing to do with him was to make sure that he lost the first time. **1960** M. STEWART *My Brother Michael* ix. 118, I didn't particularly want to tangle with Danielle. **1966** P. O'DONNELL *Sabre-Tooth* xviii. 244, I fancy we'll tangle in the long run, Willie. But not for a while. **1978** J. B. HILTON *Some run Crooked* xi. 116 There were men here who had nothing particular to hide, but who had learned ..that it was better not to tangle with Kenworthy. **1982** *Times* 10 Dec. 11/5 The mood of the House was sombre, and he had no desire to tangle with the Secretary of State.

tango (tæ·ŋgo), *sb.*[1] Pl. **tangoes, tangos** (*preferred*). [Sp., orig. a Negro or gypsy dance festival.] **1. a.** A Spanish flamenco dance.

1896 H. C. C. TAYLOR *Land of Castanet* 103 The girls.. dance again, not the vulgar flamenco or tango, but the charming dance of the province. **1931** [see *FARRUCA]. **1967** 'LA MERI' *Spanish Dancing* (ed. 2) vi. 83 The Tango (Tango Gitano, Tango Flamenco) is of Arabic origin... It might be well to observe here that the Tango Gitano has nothing whatever in common with the Argentine tango save the name.

b. A syncopated ballroom dance in 2/4 or 4/4 time introduced into Europe and N. America from Argentina, related to the Cuban Habanera but probably of African origin, characterized by a slow gliding movement broken up by pointing positions; a piece of music for this dance.

1913 G. GROSSMITH in *Daily Graphic* 12 May 9/1 'A Peeress' talks about the Tango. This is a most graceful and beautiful dance. **1915** T. BURKE *London Nights* 254 Music, gaiety, sparkle, fine dresses, costume songs, tangos, smart conversation and faces, and all the rest of it. **1921** *Spectator* 19 Feb. 236/3 Instead of a stately waltz at an even pace, Myers had no sooner taken the magnificent lady round the waist, than they were covering the floor with a glorified tango. **1925** C. CONNOLLY *Let.* 8 Apr. in *Romantic Friendship* (1975) 67 Someone is playing tangoes on a guitar. **1947** [see *GUAJIRA]. **1962** *Melody Maker* 7 July 7/5 Kid Thomas..leads his septet through standards, pops and tangoes. **1976** BOTHAM & DONNELLY *Valentino* iv. 34 This arrogant and deliciously handsome Continental who danced the tango as though it had been invented for him. **1981** E. NORTH *Dames* viii. 138 The music..played..a tango... He regarded better dancers tangoing.

2. *attrib.* and *Comb.*, as (sense 1 b) *tango band, -dancer, -dancing, foxtrot, music, rhythm, step*; **tango tea**, a thé dansant, usu. at a hotel or other gathering place, arranged for the purpose of dancing the tango (*disused*).

1927 C. CONNOLLY *Let.* 13 Feb. in *Romantic Friendship* (1975) 255 This is a very grand hotel, all lights and carpets and a melodious tango band. **1932** Tango band [see RUMBA *sb.* 1 a]. **1974** M. BUTTERWORTH *Man in Sopwith Camel* I. 11 Norman the demon tango-dancer of the Palais. **1918** G. FRANKAU *One of Them* xxxi. 243 She.. knew how wise she'd been to countermand Breastplate and shield which, though they looked entrancing, Would both have been a bore for tango-dancing. *c* **1925** 'H. NICHOLLS' (*music title*) Sunny Havana: tango foxtrot. **1913** *Sheffield Daily Tel.* 5 Sept. 6/4 Tango music is also expected to rival the popularity of ragtime. **1966** A. CAVANAGH *Children are Gone* II. v. 45 The Muzak was dispensing tango rhythms, loud and sinuous. **1977** 'F. CLIFFORD' *Ten Minutes on June Morning* 90 The music came again, tango rhythm. **1981** E. WARD *Baltic Emerald* ix. 64 A new tango step. **1913** *Punch* 6 Aug. 125 No tango-teas shall be given in *this* drawing-room. **1918** G. FRANKAU *One of Them* I. 14 What time we sang of guns and gore and trenches, Instead of oysters, tango-teas and wenches.

tango (tæ·ŋgo), *sb.*[2] (*a.*) [f. TANG(ERINE *sb.* 2 + *-O[2], perh. influenced by prec. sb. or by TAN *sb.*[1] 3.] A colour shade of deep orange.

1913 *Vanity Fair* Sept. 59/3 The one shown is of sand color and tango. **1933** *Archit. Rev.* LXXIII. 70 The colour scheme of the shopfront is tango-red throughout. **1958** B. NICHOLS *Sweet & Twenties* x. 126 Jade green, cerise, tango. **1976** *Burnham-on-Sea Gaz.* 20 Apr. 18/3 (Advt.), 1974 Hillman Hunter GLS 4-door saloon, tango.

ta·ngo, *v.* [f. *TANGO *sb.*[1]] *intr.* **a.** To dance the tango.

1913 *Punch* 10 Dec. 486/1 'Do you tango?' she asked me as soon as we were comfortably seated. **1925** C. DODD *Farthing Spinster* III. iii. 299 Young Jellis tangoed up to the two ladies. **1941** B. SCHULBERG *What makes Sammy Run?* xi. 206 Sammy didn't know how to tango. **1952** M. LASKI *Village* ii. 42 She..watched her father tangoing ..with Daisy Bruce. **1975** *Times* 4 Sept. 14/6 You have to count anxiously like one learning to tango. **1981** [see *TANGO *sb.*[1] 1 b].

b. *fig.* Freq. in proverbial phr. *it takes two to tango.*

1952 HOFFMAN & MANNING *Takes Two to Tango* (*song*) 2 There are lots of things you can do alone! But, takes two to tango. **1965** *Listener* 24 June 923/2 The President would like to know whom to negotiate with... On this score, the President has a firm, and melancholy, conviction: it takes two to tango. **1970** B. CONACHER *Hockey in Canada* (1972) x. 116 Despite all the problems I had had with Imlach, and believe it or not I realize it takes two to tango, I wouldn't have missed playing in the best league in the world. **1973** *Houston* (Texas) *Chron.* (Texas Mag.) 14 Oct. 2/1 An upcoming film of such explicit sexuality it'll have to tango with the new pornography rulings. **1977** *Time* 31 Oct. 48/1 Ellis Rabb can tango with words and he is a sly devil at milking an audience dry of laughter. **1979** *Guardian* 4 Apr. 12/3 It takes two to tango... Mrs Thatcher has turned Mr Callaghan down.

Hence **ta·ngoing** *vbl. sb.*; **ta·ngoist**, an exponent of the tango.

1913 G. B. CROZIER *Tango & How to dance It* i. 8 The Parisian version of the Tango..has so much to recommend it that one may..predict for it a permanent place in our affections long after the present craze for 'Tangoing' is over. *Ibid.* ii. 28 Embryonic 'Tangoists' cannot do better than bear that graceful animal [*sc.* the tiger] in mind while attempting to follow their advice. **1928** *Daily Express* 6 July 3/3 This tango is so slow, so smooth, so syrupy. Caterpillars skating over egg-shells could not move more gracefully, more softly, than the contemporary tangoists. **1976** U. HOLDEN *String Horses* vii. 81 They'd show the Camp what real tangoing was.

tangoreceptor (tæ·ŋgorise:ptǫɹ). *Zool.* [f. L. *tang-ĕre* to touch + -O + RECEPTOR.] A sensory receptor which responds to touch or pressure.

1906 C. S. SHERRINGTON *Integrative Action Nervous Syst.* ix. 335 The sessile creature retains..only some gustatory (?) receptors round the mouth, and some tangoreceptors..in the tegument. **1937** L. V. HEILBRUNN *Outl. Gen. Physiol.* xl. 506 In man and mammals, in addition to ordinary free nerve endings, special types of tangoreceptors are found in the skin and in the viscera. **1980** L. H. CHAPPELL *Physiol. Parasites* ix. 165 The sensory papillae of cercariae are thought to be tangoreceptors.

‖ **tangpu** (daŋbu). Also **Tang Pu.** [Chinese *dǎngbù*, f. *dang* party + *bù* office.] The headquarters of the Kuomintang at the central, and various local, levels.

1941 E. SNOW *Scorched Earth* VI. ii. 206 The *tangpu* system in China is a product of 'natural' political evolution. **1943** J. T. PRATT *War & Politics in China* xii. 200 Borodin impressed upon Dr. Sun the importance of securing the assent of the people at large to the revolutionary programme... This was to be effected by organizing local branches of the Kuomintang—Tang Pu—and by systematic propaganda. **1972** A. DESTENAY tr. *Guillermaz's Hist. Chinese Communist Party 1921–1949* vi. 79 Party offices (Tangpu) existed at the provincial, district and local levels.

Tangut (tæ·ŋgut), *sb.* (and *a.*). Also 8–9 **Tangout.** [App. a. Mongol, f. Chinese *Tang-hsiang* (tribal name): (see also quot. 1979).] A Tibetan people who inhabited north-western China and western Inner Mongolia, and formed the independent kingdom of Hsi Hsia from the eleventh to the thirteenth centuries A.D.; the country or language of this people. Also *attrib.* or as *adj.* Also **Tangu·tan** *a.* and *sb.*

1598 HAKLUYT tr. W. de Rubruquis in *Voy.* I. 116 Between the foresaid mountaines Eastward inhabiteth the nation of Tangut, who are a most valiant people. **1613** PURCHAS *Pilgrimage* IV. ix. 337 There were of them divers nations, called by one common name Mogli, which were divided into seven principal tribes, whose names were Tatar, Tangut, Cunat, Talair, Sonich, Monghi, Tebeth. **1795** W. WINTERBOTHAM *Hist. & Geogr. View Chinese Empire* 182 Thibet is known under different names, the Chinese call it Tsang; the Tartars, Barantola, Bouttan, and Tangout. **1827** H. E. LLOYD tr. *Timkowski's Trav. through Mongolia to China* I. xii. 442 Tangout is a Mongol word, designating the country which at present forms the whole of the western frontier of China, and is inhabited by the eastern Tibetans. **1876** H. H. HOWORTH *Hist. Mongols* I. i. 5 This town [*sc.* Ninghia]..was called in the Tangutan language Eyirkai. **1876** E. D. MORGAN tr. *Prejevalsky's Mongolia, Tangut*

Country & Northern Tibet II. iv. 109 The Tangutans, or the Si-fan as the Chinese call them, are of the same race as the Tibetans. *Ibid.* 119 In the Tangut country..the price of brick tea has considerably risen. **1888** *Encycl. Brit.* XXIII. 343/2 The Tang-chang and Peh-lang tribes boasted also of being descended from a monkey; they were the two great divisions of the Tang-hiang or Tangut, offsets of the same Sien-pi stock as that of the conquerors of Tibet. **1908** J. Curtin *Mongols* iv. 75 The subjection of the Kirghis and this new victory over Tangut secured the position of Jinghis in Northeastern Asia. **1934** K. S. Latourette *Chinese* I. iv. 159 The Later Chao was succeeded in the Northwest by a state established by a Mongol people, formerly supposed..to be Tanguts. **1954** Pei & Gaynor *Dict. Linguistics* 214/1 *Tangut*, an Asiatic language, a member of the Eastern group of the Mongol branch of the Altaic sub-family of the Ural-Altaic family of languages. **1979** L. Kwanten *Imperial Nomads* v. 72 This fails to explain how and when the inhabitants of Hsi Hsia became known as Tangut. *Ibid.*, Most scholars remain convinced that the Tangut language is a member of the Sino-Tibetan linguistic family, although..recent linguistic research indicates that there is a distinct possibility that Tangut is either a Turkic dialect or a language heavily influenced by a Turkic dialect.

tangy (tæ·ŋi), *a.* Also † **tangey.** [f. Tang *sb.*[1] + -y[1].] **a.** Having a sharp, distinct, or spicy taste. Also, characterized by a disagreeable tang or flavour (*rare*).

1875 *Ure's Dict. Arts* (ed. 7) III. 189 There is a perceptible deficiency in that fine, clean flavour, which is the perfection of a glass of good beer, its place being usurped by a flavour coarse and tangey. **1931** B. Starke *Touch & Go* xii. 193 The meal was strong and tangy and tough and stringy. **1946** C. S. Forester *Lord Hornblower* iii. 37 A bite of red cheese, tangy and seasoned. **1958** *People* 4 May 7/4 (Advt.), You will find Tango the tastiest, tangiest whole orange drink ever! **1966** *Woman's Own* 22 Jan. 29/1 What all my friends like is its sharp, tangy flavour. **1976** *National Observer* (U.S.) 17 July 1/3 After a tangy dinner of sausage creole, everybody is lounging about the living room. **1979** J. Wainwright *Home is Hunter* xxi. 71 The iced cider was a pleasant surprise; tangy, cool.

b. *transf.* and *fig.* Cf. Spicy *a.* 7.

1948 *Sun* (Baltimore) 3 Dec. 14/2 (*heading*) The tangy story of the frozen-orange juice industry. **1953** J. Masters *Lotus & Wind* x. 137 This was heavier, tangier stuff, and it reminded him more of animals than of flowers. **1967** *Punch* 4 Oct. 520/2 Despite a twinkly fondness for waggish puns..his style isn't exactly tangy. **1978** H. Wouk *War & Remembrance* viii. 78 She knew a tangy tale or two about Madge Knudsen!

tanh (tæn,ēi·tʃ). *Math.* Abbrev. of *hyperbolic tangent.*

1879 *Encycl. Brit.* IX. 819/2 Similarly we have the hyperbolic tangent tanh *x*, &c. **1968** E. T. Copson *Metric Spaces* vii. 107 The restriction..can be removed by considering for example the function tanh *f*(*x*).

tania, tanier, tannier. Add: Also **tannia.** (Later examples.)

1953 *Caribbean Q.* III. ii. 103 In 1811, Charles Edmonson..reported..: 'The quantity of rice the Bush Negroes have just rising out of the ground is very considerable independent of yams, tannias, plantains, tobacco, &c.' **1955** *Ibid.* IV. ii. 112 Grated tannia fritters..fried in deep fat on a coalpot. **1968** [see *dasheen]. **1979** *West Africa* 8 Jan. 51/1 In Cameroon..the other, *tannia* sort [of cocoyam] is called *macabo.*

tanister. For † Obs. *rare*[−1] read *rare* and add later example.

1937 *Burke's Landed Gentry* (ed. 15) 1496/1 Hugh Vernon Macleod, 11th Chieftain of Talisker, and apparent Tanister of Macleod of Macleod.

‖ **taniwha** (tæ·niwā, ‖ tanifa). *N.Z.* Also † **tanewa, taniwoa,** and with capital initial. [Maori.] A mythical monster supposed to reside in deep water.

1840 J. S. Polack *Manners & Customs New Zealanders* II. xiii. 126 The additional name of *Taniwoa* is added, (a water god). **1842** W. R. Wade *Journey in N.Z.* i. 34 One of our boatmen quickly repeated that the place was tapued for the tanewa (a water demon). **1863** F. E. Maning *Old N.Z.* ii. 26 Down, villain! down to..the Taniwha cave! **1882** W. D. Hay *Brighter Britain!* II. 214 They [*sc.* the Maori] have a tale of these taniwha..somewhat parallel to our nursery stories of dragons. **1905** [see *ngarara]. **1921** H. Guthrie-Smith *Tutira* x. 70 They felt the net being dragged away from them by the *taniwha* known to haunt the bay. **1938** R. Finlayson *Brown Man's Burden* 66 The carved taniwha monsters of the meeting-house. **1948** J. K. Baxter *Blow, Wind of Fruitfulness* 37 Riding the logs upstream, and waiting for the taniwha. **1966** *Encycl. N.Z.* I. 48/2 Places along the sea shore were feared because they were the haunts of the *taniwha*, awesome water monsters with man-killing tendencies.

tank, *sb.*[1] Add: **1. a.** Also in Australia, an artificial reservoir designed to hold water for livestock; *U.S. dial.*, an artificial pond or lake.

1898 D. Carnegie *Spinifex & Sand* 81, I append a table showing cost and contents of Government tanks excavated at the base of granite rocks between Southern Cross and Coolgardie. **1903** 'T. Collins' *Such is Life* 265 On a well-managed station..a tank is, whenever possible, excavated on the margin of a swamp. **1911** C. E. W. Bean *'Dreadnought' of Darling* i. 7 There is only one boundary rider's hut in it and one 'tank' of water. The tank may have dried up. **1915** *Dial. Notes* IV. 229 *Tank*, an artificial lake. 'Most west Texas towns get their water from *tanks*.' **1936** F. Clune *Roaming round Darling* xiv. 121, I strongly object to the back country habit of calling holes scooped out of the ground tanks. **1955** W. Foster-Harris *Look of Old West* ix. 273 Tank is cow country [language] for a small pond, made by damming a ravine or fixing a hollow to catch and hold rain water. **1965** *Austral. Encycl.* I. 133/2 In Australia, every farmer is interested in constructing and maintaining tanks and dams.

2. a. Also *spec.* a water receptacle (with transparent sides) in which to keep fish; an aquarium.

1854 P. H. Gosse *Aquarium* i. 3 The tanks in the new Fish House just erected in the [Zoological] Society's Gardens in the Regent's Park. **1890** G. C. Bateman *Fresh-Water Aquaria* i. 6 The ordinary oblong tank..containing four glass sides, is both ornamental and useful. **1936** M. G. Elwin *First Steps in Aquarium Keeping* iv. 27 The tank will look unfinished without a couple of the beautiful Angel fish. **1971** R. F. O'Connell *Freshwater Aquarium* 127 The breeding tank should be cleaned thoroughly and filled with seasoned water to a depth of 8 inches. **1982** I. Petrovický *Trop. Aquarium Fishes* 13 If an aquarium is to be purely ornamental, it is better to select one larger tank.

b. The fuel container of a motor vehicle.

1902 A. C. Harmsworth *Motors & Motor-Driving* vii. 117 With the gravity-fed carburetter the tank is fitted in the body of the car. **1944** L. D. Kitchin *Road Transport Law* 19/1 Not more than 60 gallons of petroleum spirit, including that contained in any vehicle fuel tank, may be kept in any one storage place. **1978** K. Amis *Jake's Thing* xxiv. 244 'Are we low on petrol, Ivor?' 'No, I had a full tank when I picked you up.'

3*. *U.S. slang.* A cell in a police station, *spec.* one in which several prisoners (esp. drunks) are held.

1912 D. Lowrie *My Life in Prison* iii. 30, I glanced at the number on the cell door. It was..34 Tank. **1933** 'J. Spenser' *Limey* xvii. 256 In our tank..there were three Chicago gangsters waiting to be returned to that city. **1947** A. R. Bosworth *San Francisco Murders* 264 The day a police reporter had to pick him out of the collection in the drunk tank. **1951** *Life* 8 Jan. 24 (*caption*) Still relatively blissful but due for an unhappy awakening, some of the 1,200 Angelenos charged with drunkenness sleep it off in the tank. **1964** Wodehouse *Frozen Assets* iii. 50 It gets boring after a while being thrown into the tank, always with that nervous feeling that this time the old man won't come through with the necessary bail. **1981** L. Deighton *XPD* xxv. 210 And then tossed into the drunk tank like a common criminal.

4. (sense 2 a) *tankhouse, -ship, -truck* (later U.S. example); **tank bag,** a receptacle for carrying luggage which fits on to the petrol tank of a motorcycle; **tank circuit** *Electronics*, a resonant circuit placed in the anode circuit of a valve oscillator in order to supply energy to an aerial for transmission; **tank farm** orig. *U.S.*, a collection of tanks for the large-scale storage of oil; **tank furnace:** substitute for def. (see quot. 1970); (examples); **tankstand** *Austral.* and *N.Z.*, a stand or support for a tank in which water is stored; **tank suit** *U.S.*, a (ladies') one-piece bathing-suit with scooped neck (cf. *maillot 2); **tank top,** a sleeveless upper garment with round neck and deep armholes, freq. of knitted material and similar to the top of a one-piece bathing-suit, worn by men or women; cf. *tank suit* above; **tank town** *U.S.*, a small, unimportant town, orig. one at which trains stopped to take on water.

1974 *Cycle World* June 24 (Advt.), Rain-proof cycle luggage... Tank bag—straps to gas tank. **1980** *Guardian* 28 Apr. 8/6 A set of good bike luggage—panniers and top box—is the best solution... A cheaper alternative is a pair of carriers to sling over the seat and a good tank bag. **1928** L. S. Palmer *Wireless Princ. & Pract.* vi. 183 A slightly different method is that of using a 'tank' circuit, which consists of a low impedance oscillatory circuit connected from the earth end of the aerial inductance to earth. **1959** K. Henney *Radio Engin. Handbk.* (ed. 5) xviii. 14 Resonant tank circuits are used in..power amplifiers to remove the effects of tube and circuit stray capacitances. **1971** *Gloss. Electrotechnical, Power Terms* (*B.S.I.*) iii. vii. 22 *Tank circuit*, tuned circuit in the anode circuit of the final stage of a transmitter which supplies the radio-frequency energy to the aerial or aerial feeder. **1932** *Amer. Speech* VII. 271 *Tank-farm*, a group of storage tanks. **1941** *Sun* (Baltimore) 7 Nov. 17/1 Chemical flames prevented anyone from getting into the explosion area, which Sears described as a 'tank farm', the storage area of the vinylite or plastics producing section. **1974** *Daily Tel.* 30 May 8/6 Huge 'tank farms' may be needed in parts of Scotland to store the oil. **1879** *Encycl. Brit.* X. 659/1 Mr Archibald Stevenson of Glasgow has patented a tank furnace fired by common coal from one end, with working holes on the other three sides. **1908** W. Rosenhain *Glass Manufacture* iv. 72 The tank furnace utilises the heat of the flame more efficiently. **1970** *Gloss. Industrial Furnace Terms* (*B.S.I.*) 20 *Tank furnace*, a furnace in which glass is melted in a refractory bath. **1941** *Sun* (Baltimore) 15 Oct. 19/2 It is an unwatched light showing quick red flashes,..28 feet above water, on a white skeleton tower and tankhouse on concrete piers. **1978** *Jrnl. R. Soc. Arts* CXXVI. 693/1 An important application is that of titanium blanks for the production of the starting sheets used in copper refinery tankhouses. **1945** *Sun* (Baltimore) 23 Aug. 9-0/1 More than 100 tankships, many of which had been torpedoed..have been cleaned and made free of gas. **1978** M. Dewis *Law Health & Safety at Work* i. 5 The crew of a British tankship. **1941** *Coast to Coast* 146 Then she crept off the veranda and went down under the tankstand. The soil under the tank was a rich chocolate brown, and there were drips of water coming from the tap. **1965** S. T. Ollivier *Petticoat Farm* v. 66 Emma carefully retraced her steps down the windmill until she reached the..corner of the tank-stand. **1977** C. McCullough *Thorn Birds* vi. 116 A drover whose cross said only *Tankstand Charlie he was a good bloke.* **1959** P. Roth *Goodbye Columbus* ii. 20 She wore a black tank suit and went barefooted. **1979** *Dancemagazine* Feb. 108/3 In *Moth Dance*, the lines of Hermans' tensed, slender body, in tanksuit and reflecting sunglasses, become clearer as the semidarkness grows lighter. **1968** *New Yorker* 27 Jan. 25 Miss Farrell—a tall, pretty ballerina dressed in a purple tank top and baggy rubber warm-up pants. **1971** *Observer* 1 Aug. 22/3 A favourite Paris idea is to put little woolly vests or tank tops over shirts and under suit jackets. **1977** Miller & Swift *Words & Women* 157 Even the latter have given up whalebone corsets and starched winged collars without assuming they have to switch to miniskirts or tank tops. **1906** J. F. Kelly *Man with Grip* 11 Tank towns are big ones, compared to our route. **1940** R. Chandler *Farewell, my Lovely* v. 38 You would find them in tanktown vaudeville acts. **1978** *Times* 25 Mar. 14/4 When vaudeville was in its final death throes, young Donald O'Connor was..going—as the show biz legend decreed he should—from 'one tank town to another'. **1976** *New Yorker* 9 Feb. 66/8 It was solved by designing a tank truck that intermittently travelled around the array and sprayed the mirrors with a cleaning solution.

tank, *sb.*[7] [Special use of Tank *sb.*[1] adopted in Dec. 1915 for purposes of secrecy during manufacture.] **1. a.** An armoured military vehicle moving on a tracked carriage and mounted with a gun, designed for use in rough terrain.

First put into commission on 15 Sept. 1916.

1916 *Times* 18 Sept. 9/6 'Tanks' is what these new machines are generally called, and the name has the evident official advantage of being quite undescriptive. **1917** A. Machen *Terror* i. 19 Last summer there were very few people outside high official circles who knew anything about the 'Tanks', of which we have all been talking lately. **1918** *Review of Reviews* (N.Y.) Oct. 383 The British tanks, as first produced, were of two types, male and female. The male tank was armed with two six-pounder, rapid-fire Hotchkiss guns, and four Lewis machine guns... The female type carried a lighter armament. **1926** *Daily Colonist* (Victoria, B.C.) 10 Jan. 5/2 Voltaire is said to be the real inventor of the armored war tank. In 1756 he designed what was called the 'Assyrian Chariot', which was armed like the tank. **1940** *Richmond* (Va.) *Times-Dispatch* 10 Aug. 1 (*heading*) Army irked as news leaks of plans for monster tank. **1957** *Encycl. Brit.* XXI. 791/2 In 1940..the French alone possessed about 3,600 tanks..superior in armour and fire power to those of the Germans. **1970** *Sunday Times* (Colour Suppl.) 16 Aug. 13/4 For security purposes the cumbersome metal machines needed a code-name: 'water carriers' was rejected in favour of 'tanks'. **1977** C. McCullough *Thorn Birds* xv. 344 Went through them big buggers of tanks like a dose of salts.

b. In pl., *ellipt.* for Tank Corps.

1943 J. B. Priestley *Daylight on Saturday* iv. 21 Her husband was abroad, in the Tanks. **1967** L. Deighton *Only when I Larf* (1968) vii. 85, I could see that the war had to come, so I..got a commission in the tanks. **1981** A. Price *Soldier no More* vii. 97 He was in the tanks during the war.

2. *attrib.* and *Comb.*, as *tank battle, Corps, crew, driver, officer, raid, warfare*; *tank-like* adj.; also used of naval vessels designed to transport and put ashore tanks, as *tank-landing craft*, etc. (cf. *landing craft, ship* s.v. *landing *vbl. sb.* 8); **tank buster** *slang*, an aircraft or other device designed to combat tanks (cf. *-buster); also *fig.*; **tank-destroyer** *U.S.*, a highly-mobile armoured fighting vehicle equipped with a field gun, designed to combat tanks; **tank-man,** a member of a military tank crew; **tank transporter,** a wheeled vehicle for the transportation of a tank; **tank trap,** an obstacle placed or constructed so as to impede or prevent the progress of a tank; **tank turret,** the rotating structure on a tank on which the gun is mounted; **tank watch,** a gold watch designed by Cartier of Paris, decorated with gemstones, and usu. regarded as a status symbol [designed in 1917; the gold side-panels were held to resemble the wide tracks of the new armoured tanks (see sense 1 a)].

1944 C. Milburn *Diary* 7 June (1979) 217 A tank battle was raging in one spot and an air battle not far away. **1978** A. Melville-Ross *Blindfold* xxii. 130 The great tank battles of the Second World War. **1941** *Illustr. London News* 29 Nov. 691/1 The Hawker 'Hurricane' is..proving its superiority in the battle of the Libyan Desert..as a dive-bomber and 'tank-buster'. **1942** J. Sweeney in Murdock & Drake-Brockman *Austral. Short Stories* (1951) 384 No sooner does the gong go for the third than Irish walks into..a rip-snorting tank-buster that Big Joe had been saving up for a secret weapon. **1967** *Electronics* 6 Mar. 311/2 (Advt.), Tiny tankbuster. **1917** *Army Order 239* 28 July, We deem it expedient to authorize the formation of, and to provide rates of pay for, a corps to be entitled 'Tank Corps'. **1976** *Listener* 20 May 633/3 He had joined the Tank Corps... He was lying in bed in barracks one night, listening to the flow of unremitting obscenity from his fellow tankmen. *a* **1944** K. DOUGLAS *Alamein to Zem Zem* (1946) 14 As soon as this was finished I began to make the acquaintance of my tank crews. **1973** A. PRICE *October Men* v. 71 Tales of stranded tank crews parboiled. **1941** *Sun* (Baltimore) 28 Aug. 24/1 The army today demonstrated..the type of unit it hopes is the answer to *panzer* attack, a 'tank-destroyer' battalion of fast-moving, self-propelled field guns protected to a certain extent by armor. **1961** W. VAUGHAN-THOMAS *Anzio* v. 76 The American 894th Tank-Destroyer Battalion..attacked again. The tank-destroyers advanced line ahead like battleships of old. **1928** Tank driver [see *CATERPILLAR *v.*]. **1980** J. DITTON *Copley's Hunch* I. ii. 42 'You [*sc.* the RAF] go into action sitting down.' 'So do tank drivers.' **1917** W. S. CHURCHILL in M. Gilbert *Winston S. Churchill* (1977) IV. Compan. I. 87 In addition a number (say) 50 tank-landing lighters would be provided, each carrying a tank or tanks. **1945** Tank landing ship [see *LANDING *vbl. sb.* 8]. **1969** *Listener* 4 Sept. 304/2 In January 1956 I thought I was going to a reserve fleet, but rather to my delight I was appointed to another command. This was to a tank landing-craft called *HMS Redoubt* in Malta. **1977** *Navy News* June 23 Audemer, a Royal Corps of Transport tank landing craft, is in the Review lines. **1916** E. MONTAGU *Let.* 31 Oct. in M. Gilbert *Winston S. Churchill* (1972) III. Compan. II. 1580 Cannot the idea of the Tank be so extended as to use a Tank-like machine to protect our Infantry. **1977** C. FREMLIN *Spider-Orchid* xvii. 111 A sort of monstrous arrogance..driving tank-like over all concerns other than its own. **1934** *N. & Q.* CLXVI. 73/2 In the tank-man we shall have the steel-clad mediaeval knight back again. **1976** Tankman [see *Tank Corps* above]. **1949** R. CHANDLER *Let.* 24 Jan. (1981) 145 At one [table] sat..a demobbed tank officer with his mother. **1978** A. PRICE *'44 Vintage* xi. 136 He certainly didn't intend to let any bloody tank officer..out-crawl him. **1917** 'CONTACT' *Airman's Outings* 135 Farther along the road was the scene of the first tank raids. **1943** *Times* (Weekly ed.) 24 Nov. 6 'Tank Transporter.' To save wear and tear of tracks and to save petrol, tanks are transported over hard roads by huge tank-carrying lorries. **1972** D. BLOODWORTH *Any Number can Play* xvi. 149 A respray job... What ran into it, a tank-transporter? **1925** *Scribner's Mag.* Sept. 234/1 Tank traps, trenches so wide that the little fellows went nose-down into them and stuck, and direct fire from Boche artillery stopped the most of them. **1977** *Time* 10 Jan. 22/2 The Chileans, bracing for a possible invasion, are mining the desert, implanting tank traps and building fortifications. **1946** E. LINKLATER *Private Angelo* xi. 131 Romans..tossed flowers into jeeps and tank-turrets. **1979** D. GRAHAM in K. Douglas *Alamein to Zem Zem* 10 Sufficient of its character remained, however, for it to move into action..with tank turrets open and umbrellas up. *a* **1944** K. DOUGLAS *Ibid.* (1946) 14 It is low-built, which in..tank warfare, is a first consideration. **1977** B. FREEMANTLE *Charlie Muffin* ii. 29 His absorption in the history of tank warfare. **1976** *Vogue* Dec. 216 Cufflinks and watches all from Cartier... Tank watch edged with diamonds, £1,800. **1978** T. GIFFORD *Glendower Legacy* (1979) 119 She looked at her Cartier tank watch with the sapphire on the stem.

Hence **ta·nker**[2] *colloq.* = *tank-man*, sense 2 above.

1919 *W.R.A.F. on Rhine* July 27 Little boys with.. tanks..asking the girls to come and play... What jolly boys those Tankers were! **1940** *Sun* (Baltimore) 23 Sept. 11/4 There are tankers who long ago served in the same regiment when it was fully horsed. **1961** W. VAUGHAN-THOMAS *Anzio* v. 79 Italian geography is unfriendly to the tank, and there were moments when tankers must have felt that the whole country was one enormous, endless anti-tank ditch. **1974** C. RYAN *Bridge Too Far* III. ix. 187 Taylor had hoped for the support of the tankers' guns along the fifteen-mile stretch of corridor the Screaming Eagles must control.

tank, *sb.*[8] *slang.* [Prob. abbrev. of TANKARD.] The amount held by a drinking-vessel; hence *loosely*, a drink (usu. of beer). Cf. *JAR *sb.*[2] 2 c, *TANK *v.*[1] 5 a.

1936 O. NASH *Primrose Path* 46 What can a man.. Ask..More than a pipe..And a modest tank of beer? **1941** BAKER *Dict. Austral. Slang* 75 *Tank*, a pint of beer. **1958** *Spectator* 7 Feb. 171/1 Their carousals over a few friendly tanks at the neighbouring Whitehall milk bar.

tank, *v.*[1] Add: **2.** Also, to put into a tank.

1960 KOESTLER *Lotus & Robot* I. i. 42 The driver-owners are so poor that they only tank one or two gallons at a time.

3. (Example.)

1906 U. SINCLAIR *Jungle* iii. 43 To another room came all the scraps to be 'tanked', which meant boiling and pumping off the grease to make soap and lard.

5. Chiefly *to tank up.* **a.** *intr.* for *refl.* To fill oneself with drink, to drink heavily. Also *refl.* Cf. *TANKED *ppl. a.* 1. *slang.*

1902 A. H. LEWIS *Wolfville Nights* xv. 236 Bowlaigs would reepair back ag'in to the Major [with the bottle], when they'd both tank up ecstatic. **1920** C. L. STAGG *High Speed* viii. 142 Both of 'em are tankin' up next door, and layin' for you and the whole bunch. **1925** F. SCOTT FITZGERALD *Great Gatsby* (1926) ii. 28, I think he'd tanked up a good deal at luncheon, and his determination to have my company bordered on violence. **1939** A. HUXLEY *After Many a Summer* II. iii. 208 She..made him feel good, like you felt when you'd tanked up a bit on Scotch. **1951** W. C. WILLIAMS *Autobiogr.* xxv. 148 Perhaps he was insubordinate or tanked himself up or did something otherwise improper. **1959** A. CHRISTIE *Cat among Pigeons* 18 On Sports Day..Lady Veronica arrived completely sober... But there were times when Lady Veronica tanked herself up. **1974** D. RAMSAY *No Cause to Kill* II. 132 Jessie's a lush... Hardly ever leaves the house.. except to tank up at the neighbourhood hangouts. **1980** I. HUNTER *Malcolm Muggeridge* xii. 216 Behan arrived for the interview 'somewhat full' and proceeded to tank up further in the BBC hospitality room.

b. *trans.* To fill the tank of (a vehicle) with fuel; to refuel. Also *absol.*, and *intr.* for *pass. colloq.*

1933 [implied in *TANKING *vbl. sb.*[1]]. **1944** 'N. SHUTE' *Pastoral* ii. 37 The Bowser was waiting to tank up the Wellington. **1948** —— *No Highway* ix. 244, I guess we'll make Ivanhoe by sundown... Tank up there, 'n have plenty up at the lake. **1959** HALAS & MANVELL *Technique Film Animation* v. 65 A cartoonist may want to give an automobile the characteristics of a dog in its attitude to the fuel that its owner offers it... It shakes its shaggy head in refusal to tank up with the wrong brand of spirit. **1963** D. IRVING *Destruction of Dresden* III. iii. 139 The whole force [of aircraft] had been tanked up with maximum fuel loads, 2,154 gallons of petrol each. **1977** N. FREELING *Gadget* I. 5 The four cars..stopped once to tank up. **1978** —— *Night Lords* xxx. 140 At the edge of the service area he stopped..while the car was tanked.

c. *transf.* and *fig.*

1942 *Tee Emm* (Air Ministry) II. 145 It's no good tanking up on them [*sc.* vitamins] and hoping you'll be able to detect a black cat at midnight in a Bremen cellar from 10,000 feet. **1959** *Word Study* Oct. 2/2 We are grateful for them, 'tank up' on their detailed and highly useful messages, and perhaps put them away for future reference. **1975** R. BUTLER *Where All Girls are Sweeter* ii. 15 She was twiddling the empty glass... I tanked her up and waited.

6. *intr.* In Lawn Tennis, to lose or fail to finish a match deliberately; to default. *slang.*

1976 *Times* 30 Sept. 11/5 Too many..singles players do not enter for the doubles. Either that, or they scratch or 'tank' (in boxing parlance, 'take a dive'). **1979** *Guardian* 13 Jan. 11 But it is ironic that Connors, a player generally considered too honest to 'tank' to anyone, should be the one to suffer.

Hence **ta·nker**[3], a heavy drinker; **ta·nking** *vbl. sb.*[1] (in the senses of the vb.).

1891 Tanking [in Dict. s.v. TANK *v.* 3]. **1918** H. BINDLOSS *Agatha's Fortune* iv. 40 When you get the tanking habit such things happen. **1930** *Aberdeen Press & Jrnl.* 31 Jan. 7/5 Tanking consists of salting ungutted herrings into big tanks for future use. **1932** H. CRANE *Let.* 16 Feb. (1965) 400 Especially with Luz around, who Lisa says is a great little tanker. **1933** *Flight* 16 Feb. 157/1 Petrol-filling installations, *i.e.* hand pumps, are now available on all important aerodromes, and the average time spent in tanking is only 45 min. **1935** J. O'HARA *Appointment in Samarra* ii. 49 But the rest of them! God, what a gang of tankers they were.

tank, *v.*[2] [f. *TANK *sb.*[7]] **1.** *intr.* To proceed or make one's way in a tank. Also *fig.*

1939 H. G. WELLS *Holy Terror* III. ii. 271 The city crowds cheered, the armies went tanking forward. **1945** A. THIRKELL *Miss Bunting* ix. 192 He tanked right over her without so much as noticing her. **1972** R. POOLE *Towards Deep Subjectivity* i. 4 The Russians..shot their way in, they tanked their way in.

2. *trans.* To defeat convincingly, to beat, thrash, or overwhelm. Hence **ta·nking** *vbl. sb.*[2] Cf. *TONK *v. Sc. dial.*

1973 'J. PATRICK' *Glasgow Gang Observed* vi. 60 We were to play football... ('Uzz Young Team always tank them.'). **1976** *Sunday Mail* (Glasgow) 26 Dec. 2/1 They.. had just come from a party for Rangers F.C., who tanked the local Clachnacuddin side 8–0. **1982** P. TURNBULL *Dead Knock* iii. 56 Glasgow..[is] a good city... The reputation for violence comes from the gangs who give each other tankings.

‖ **tanka**[2] (tæ·ŋkă). Also **Tanka.** [Jap., f. *tan* short + *ka* song.] A form of Japanese verse which consists of thirty-one syllables, the first and third lines containing five and the other three lines seven syllables.

1877 W. G. ASTON *Gram. Jap. Written Lang.* (ed. 2) x. 197 *Tanka*..or *mijika-uta*, i.e. 'short poetry', so-called to distinguish it from *naga-uta* or 'long poetry', is by far the commonest Japanese metre. **1899** —— *Jap Lit.* I. ii. 29 The Tanka is the most universal and characteristic of the various forms of poetry in Japan. **1923** JUN FUJITA (*title*) Tanka; poems in exile. **1940** W. DE LA MARE *Pleasures & Speculations* 201 A Japanese tanka..on the prolification on the exquisite little cups of the lichen. **1968** *Encycl. Brit.* XII. 886/1 From the raw material of Chinese poetry came the exquisite haiku and tanka forms. **1982** *PN Rev.* No. 26. 60/1, I do not think that haiku and tanka are translatable... Fortunately, there is a great deal more to Japanese poetry than tanka and haiku.

‖ **tanka**[3] (tæ·ŋkă). Also **thang-ka, thanka,** etc. [a. Tibetan *t'aṅ-ka, t'aṅ-ga* image, painting.] A Tibetan religious (scroll-)painting on woven material, hung as a banner in temples and carried in processions.

1925 G. ROERICH *Tibetan Paintings* 17 The most characteristic production of Tibetan pictorial art is the so-called thaṅ-ka, a word which is commonly interpreted as 'banner'. **1928** 'GANPAT' *Magic Ladakh* vii. 129 From the beams of the flat ceiling depend painted banners of silk—the gift of various donors. These *tankas*, as they are called, are often very beautiful. **1939** M. PALLIS *Peaks & Lamas* I. vi. 68 We were also shown a scroll-painting of the type found universally in Tibet, and called a *t'hanka.* **1952** A. K. GORDON *Tibetan Relig. Art* 15 Thang-kas are paintings or, occasionally, embroidered pictures, usually called 'banners'. They..are hung in the temples and at family altars in homes... They portray a deity..or scenes from the life of Buddha. **1969** R. FARRE *Beckoning Land* xx. 242 Thankas are similar to Chinese scroll paintings but the Tibetan ones are always on some religious theme. **1979** *Financial Times* 7 July 2/2 The imposing Potala Palace is uninhabited with its thousands of priceless gold Buddha statues, rare 'tankas', innumerable Buddhist scrolls and scrips.

tankage. Add: **4.** The fuel-carrying capacity of an aircraft.

1942 W. S. CHURCHILL in *Second World War* (1951) IV. I. vii. 114 We intend to increase petrol tankage of some Liberator aircraft to give an operational range of 2,300 sea-miles. **1950** *Times* 17 Feb. 8/5 The maximum still air range with full tankage of 300 gallons and 1,750 lb. of payload will be 1,250 miles and the practical stage length about 850 miles. **1966** M. WOODHOUSE *Tree Frog* v. 38 'What really shook me was the tankage.'..'How much fuel does that thing hold?'

tankard. 4. tankard turnip (earlier example).

1744 W. ELLIS *Mod. Husbandman* Jan. ii. 34, I saw a Farmer transplanting his biggest green tankard Turneps.

tankdrome, var. *TANKODROME.

tanked (tæŋkt), *ppl. a.* [f. *TANK *v.*[1] 5 + -ED[1].] **1.** *slang.* Filled with (alcoholic) drink; intoxicated; occas. *transf.*, drugged. Freq. with *up*. Also in phr. *tanked to the wide* (cf. *WIDE *sb.*) and in developed uses: completely intoxicated.

1893 [see *PUB *sb.* 1]. **1899** A. M. BINSTEAD *Gal's Gossip* 97 When my male parent, who was a free and frequent librator [*sic*], came home tanked up. **1917** [see *BLOTTO *a.*]. **1932** H. SIMPSON *Boomerang* ix. 183 Dawlish wrote poetry, and caused acute discomfort by reciting it aloud on starry nights when he was tanked up. **1964** WODEHOUSE *Frozen Assets* iv. 77 If a fellow raised from rags to riches at the breakfast table isn't tanked to the uvula by nightfall, it simply means he hasn't been trying. **1968** [see *EYEBROW 1 d]. **1977** J. MCCLURE *Sunday Hangman* xv. 178 He'd arrived half-tanked already.

2. *colloq.* Filled *up*, fuelled. Also *fig.*

1954 A. HUXLEY *Let.* 5 Dec. (1969) 717 A child tanked up with sugar or glucose is likely to get through a party without untoward incidents. **1968** R. CLAPPERTON *No News on Monday* v. 49, I got the Riley tanked up and started the long haul from Sydney. **1973** J. DRUMMOND *Bang! Bang! You're Dead* xxxi. 107 We may need the trucks at any time, keep them tanked up.

tanker[1]. Delete *colloq.* and substitute for def.: **1. a.** A sea-going vessel fitted with tanks for carrying oil or other liquids in bulk. Cf. *tank-boat, -steamer, -ship* s.v. TANK *sb.*[1] 4 in Dict. and Suppl. (Earlier and later examples.)

1900 *Boston Herald* 17 Jan. 1/3 The wreck was a tanker. **1920,** etc. [see *OIL *sb.*[1] 6 e]. **1923** R. D. PAINE *Comrades of Rolling Ocean* iv. 73 There was only four of us floated ashore on a capsized boat after the blessed tanker turned turtle. **1950** *Sun* (Baltimore) 19 Oct. (B ed.) 4/3 It was in 1878 that he [*sc.* Gustav Conrad Hansen] first put his idea into practice, converting two sailing ships into tankers. **1962** R. H. BROWN *Dict. Marine Insurance Terms* 281 A loaded tanker is usually low in the water. **1977** *R.A.F. News* 11–24 May 4/4 Two..dinghies attended by a Swedish tanker.

b. A road or rail vehicle with a container designed for transporting fluids in bulk. (Freq. with qualifying word.) Cf. *tank-truck, -wagon* s.v. TANK *sb.*[1] 4.

1927, etc. [see *OIL *sb.*[1] 6 e]. **1947** *Times* 8 Mar. 4/2 Milk tankers carrying supplies for 400,000 Londoners from creameries in Shropshire. **1951** 'J. WYNDHAM' *Day of Triffids* xvii. 300 With a hose from the tanker which held our main petrol supply I filled the half-track's tanks to overflowing. **1960** *Farmer & Stockbreeder* 2 Feb. 74/1 [He] received fatal injuries..when his car was involved in a collision with a petrol tanker. **1978** J. SHERWOOD *Limericks of Lachasse* iii. 35 There were two big road tankers..in the car park. It was used as a safe overnight compound for tankers.

c. An aircraft used for carrying fuel in bulk, esp. for the aerial refuelling of other craft.

1931 *Jrnl. R. Aeronaut. Soc.* XXXV. 1145 It is.. possible that aircraft which had become obsolete as passenger carriers might be utilised as tankers..although ..recent experiments indicate that refuelling in the air will best be accomplished by the use of tankers specially designed for their duty. **1950** C. H. LATIMER-NEEDHAM *Refuelling in Flight* i. 1 Two aircraft were equipped as tankers..and...were fitted with a 50-ft. length of hose. **1979** J. BARNETT *Backfire is Hostile* xiii. 145 The Russian carrier *Kiev* has flown off a number of strike aircraft at present refuelling from aerial tankers at low level.

2. a. *attrib.* and *Comb.*, as *tanker aircraft, load, train*, etc.

1938 *Jrnl. R. Aeronaut. Soc.* XLII. 389 The aeroplane would then take off with a small quantity of fuel in the tanks..and the tanks would be filled in the air from the tanker aircraft. **1945** G. MILLAR *Maquis* iv. 57 What they don't booze they send off to their factories in tanker wagons to make explosives with. **1953** *Times* 31 Oct. 11/1 The tanker drivers' strike is out of the way. **1958** *Ann. Reg. 1957* v. i. 360 The rise in tanker freights, and the greater use of the Cape route. **1965** D. FRANCIS *Odds Against* xi. 150 We might not find Smith, the tanker driver. **1973** *Country Life* 29 Mar. 873/3 A 3,000-hen battery laying unit produces weekly a 600-gallon tanker load of cage manure. **1978** *Times* 16 Aug. 2/6 The tanker train ran out of control. The tanker guard is blamed. **1981** 'D. RUTHERFORD' *Porcupine Basin* vii. 126 Two tanker-loading jetties pushed their long arms..out into the water. **1982** *Daily Tel.* 15 Dec. 24/4 Six TriStar aircraft are to be ordered from British Airways for use as strategic tanker aircraft for the RAF.

b. Special Comb.: **tanker man**, a seaman who is a member of the crew of a tanker (sense 1 a above).

1932 *Times* 9 Mar. 15/6 What can be done to help these tanker-men to bear or to enrich their isolation? **1974** J. Dyson *Prime Minister's Boat* xxx. 179 Come sun-up, the tanker men could pick them off at their leisure.

Hence as *v. trans.*, to transport in tankers; **ta·nkering** *vbl. sb.*, the putting (of oil, etc.) into tankers.

1928 *Daily Express* 20 Feb. 13 Port Said, where the tankering costs the..Company £1,000,000 annually. **1980** *Times* 8 Jan. 15/4 Airlines..use a complicated logistics operation to 'tanker' fuel around the world to avoid particular airports where it is scarce and expensive.

tankette (tæŋke·t). *Mil. disused.* [f. *Tank *sb.*⁷ + -ette.] A small armoured vehicle designed to facilitate the movement of infantry across rough country.

1927 [see *dragon¹ 10]. **1927** *Observer* 13 Nov. 19/5 The War Office sent a few tanks, tankettes and six-wheelers to perform. **1931** G. le Q. Martel *In Wake of Tank* xi. 120 He produced a two-man machine with armour protection... These machines were called Tankettes at this time, and they were required to act as scouts. **1942** *Times* (Weekly ed.) 2 Dec. 12 German barbarians pillaged Mikhailskoye collective farm, while they tied its chairman, an ardent Soviet patriot, to tankettes and tore him to pieces.

tankful. Add: Now usu. with reference to the fuel tank of a car.

1968 'E. Trevor' *Place for Wicked* ii. 23 He'd..taken her away with the seat-belt on and a warm engine and half a tankful on the dial. **1971** A. Price *Alamut Ambush* viii. 96 Give him a car and a tankful of petrol. **1978** *Detroit Free Press* 5 Mar. (Parade Suppl.) 26/1 The result is your average miles per gallon for the previous tankful. The cumulative average, after a few tankfuls, will be an accurate measure of your car's mileage efficiency.

† **tankodrome** (tæ·ŋkodrōᵘm). *Obs.* Also **tankdrome, tanko-drome.** [f. *Tank *sb.*⁷ + -o + *-drome, after *aerodrome 2 b.] An area where military tanks are kept.

1918 *Illustr. London News* 27 July 98 A 'tankdrome' on the Western Front. **1919** C. P. Thompson *Cocktails* 250, I left the tankodrome and went down with him to the machine. **1920** J. C. Fuller *Tanks in Great War* 58 A tankodrome (Tank Park) was established at Acheux.

tanky (tæ·ŋki). *Naut. slang.* Also **tankie.** [f. Tank *sb.*¹ + -y⁶, -ie.] The navigator's assistant; the captain of the hold (see quot. 1945).

1909 J. R. Ware *Passing Engl.* 241/1 Tanky (Navy), foreman or captain of the hold—which looks like a tank. **1921** *Blackw. Mag.* July 50/1 I'm hanged if I do Tankie any more. **1944** J. Mallalieu *Very Ordinary Seaman* vi. 91 Draw the meat, spuds, bread, butter, and vegetables from Tanky. **1945** *Times Lit. Suppl.* 9 June 271/3 The nickname 'Tanky' belonged to his [*sc.* a navigator's] Yeoman and derived from this man's incidental duty of looking after the freshwater tanks... When refrigerated storage for meat was introduced..it was the practice..to turn the care of these spaces over to 'Tanky'... Thus the lower deck came to connect 'tanky' with fresh meat... There are now, in consequence, at least two 'Tankies' in most ships: the officers' 'Tanky' who provides their bath-water and..the matlows' 'Tanky' who issues the meat and spuds. **1956** H. Tunstall-Behrens *Pamir* ix. 114 The sharp-witted Amigo had the job of Mate's Tanky.

tanna (ta·nă). Also with capital initial. Usu. in pl. **tannaim** (tanǫ·im); also † **tanaim, tannain.** [Aramaic, = teacher, f. *tĕna* to repeat, learn, cogn. w. Heb. *šānāh*: see Mishnah, mishna.] One of the Jewish doctors of the law of the first two centuries a.d. whose opinions are recorded in the Mishnah and Baraita. Occas. as **tannaite** (tā·neˌəit) (also as adj., = next); **tannaitic** (tā·neˌi:tik, ta:neˌi·tik) *a.*, of or pertaining to the tannaim.

1718 [see Mishnical *a.*]. **1845** *Encycl. Metrop.* IX. 639/2 He [*sc.* Antigonus of Socho] was the founder of the school of the tannain or mishnical doctors, by which name all the doctors of the Jewish law are distinguished, who lived between the death of Simon [the Just] and the middle of the second century after Christ. **1888** *Encycl. Brit.* XXIII. 36/1 The Mishnic doctors..were and are called *Tannaim.* **1905** *Jewish Encycl.* X. 633/1 In rabbinical literature careful discrimination must be made between the tannaitic period and that of the Amoraim. **1911** *Encycl. Brit.* XXVI. 399/1 The term *tanna* is used in the Talmud of those teachers who flourished in the first two centuries of the Christian era. **1919** H. A. A. Kennedy *Theol. Epistles* i. 17 These were due to the wisdom of many teachers, of whom the most famous were the so-called Tannaites. **1941** G. G. Scholem *Major Trends in Jewish Mysticism* ii. 51 The tradition of Tannaitic mysticism and theosophy was really alive among them [*sc.* the later Merkabah mystics]. **1950** L. S. Thornton *Revelation & Mod. World* ix. 283 The rabbinical teacher was known as a *tanna*, that is a 'repeater' of the tradition. *Ibid.*, There was a '*tannaite*' succession of teachers which traced its genealogy back through successive pairs of rabbis to the men of the Great Synagogue. **1957** *Encycl. Brit.* XV. 458/1 The Midrash of the schools, often called Halakhic or Tannaite (i.e. Mishnaic) Midrash. **1969** D. Daube *Roman Law* iii. 158 Tannaitic law, that is to say, the early Talmudic law of, say, 100 BC to AD 200. **1977** *New Yorker* 17 Oct. 48/3 Rabbi Gabriel used to remind her that, even according to the strictest letter of the law, kissing and embracing are permitted and that tannaim and amoraim frolicked with their spouses in bed.

tannase (tæ·nēⁱz). *Biochem.* [a. F. *tannase* (A. Fernbach 1900, in *Compt. Rend.* CXXXI. 1214): see Tannin and *-ase.] An enzyme that hydrolyses ester linkages in tannins.

1901 J. R. Green *Soluble Ferments* (ed. 2) x. 169 Tannase attacks not only tannin but the compound of tannin and gelatin, as well as other tannates. **1929** R. P. Walton tr. *Waldschmidt-Leitz's Enzyme Actions & Properties* 122 Tannase..must be regarded as a specific esterase having a special affinity for the esters of phenol carboxylic acids. **1979** *Jrnl. Chromatogr.* CLXX. 446 The use of tannase (tannin acylhydrolase..) in localization procedures for enzymatic activity has never been studied.

tanned, *ppl. a.* Add: **5.** Immunol. *tanned-(red-)cell*, used *attrib.* to designate a test in which antibodies can be detected by observing the agglutination of red blood cells that have been coated with tannic acid which has then bound with the appropriate soluble antigen.

1956 *Jrnl. Immunol.* LXXVI. 409/1 The tanned cell hemagglutination test..was also applied to the problem. **1962** *Lancet* 5 May 951/2 In a series of 78 patients with pernicious anæmia, the tanned-red-cell agglutination test was positive in 24% of males. **1980** *Canad. Jrnl. Zool.* LVIII. 245 One group [of cattle] infected with only *H[ypoderma] lineatum* was followed using the tanned-cell hemagglutination technique.

tanner¹. Add: **2.** [f. Tan *v.* 2 a.] A lotion, cream, etc., designed to promote a sun-tan when applied to the skin on exposure to the sun; *artificial, man-made tanner*, one which colours the skin brown without the aid of the sun.

1969 *Daily Tel.* 2 July 15/8 People with sensitive.. skins should be wary of all artificial tanners. It's advisable to try any man-made tanner on a small patch of skin. **1972** *Vogue* June Special 40/2 The new tanners: something here for every kind of skin... Rub your tanner right up into the hairline. **1979** *Country Life* 31 May 1776/1 There are many artificial tanners on the market; the Charles of the Ritz Self Tanning Foam, £3.95, claims to.. tan the skin in a similar way to the sun.

tannia: now the usual form of Tania in Dict. and Suppl.

tannie (ta·ni). *S. Afr. colloq.* Also **Tannie.** [Dim. of Afrikaans *tante*: see *tante 2.] **a.** An informal mode of address used to an aunt or any older woman. **b.** A prim elderly woman. Also *transf.*

1958 L. van der Post *Lost World Kalahari* i. 16 'Old tannie sea-cow' was our endearing way of naming the hippopotamus, so called because it was there in the surf of the sea to welcome my people when they first landed in Africa. **1958** R. Collins *Four-Coloured Flag* 16 'Good afternoon, Tannie,' he mumbled, from a distance of twenty feet. **1958** *Cape Times* 10 Dec. 11/3 The radiologist told him of the shrieks from alarmed *tannies* in from the country when they found themselves being elevated on high. **1969** I. Vaughan *Last of Sunlit Years* ix. 77, I am finding that most Afrikaans children call one 'Aunty', or 'Tannie', and are most charmingly co-operative. **1980** *Rand Daily Mail* 15 Apr. 8/3 So tasteful one feels sure one's most uptight Victorian tannie from Tweetackie-slippersfontein would be pleased to receive her.

tanning, *vbl. sb.* (Later examples.)

1887 J. E. Taylor *Tourist's Guide Suffolk* 61 Combs.. is distant 1 m., well known for the extensive tanning-works of Messrs. Webb. **1899** C. F. Townsend *Chem. for Photographers* (ed. 2) iv. 75 The 'tanning' of the gelatin or rendering it insoluble. **1935** *Discovery* July 190/1 Wash-out gelatine relief by development tanning, used for making matrices for obtaining 'imbibition'. **1944** J. S. Huxley *On living in Revolution* 70 Lamarckism.. the inheritance of characters acquired by an individual as a result of changes in the environment, like tanning due to sun. **1963** *Listener* 17 Jan. 138/1 From winter resort patronized by the pre-1914 crowned heads of Europe to tanning-factory for bikini-clad campers. **1980** B. H. Carroll et al. *Introd. Photogr. Theory* xi. 227 Tanning development involves the formation of an image in the form of insolubilized gelatin.

tanning, *ppl. a.* Add: **b.** *spec.* in *Photogr.* Cf. *tan *v.* 4.

1930 G. E. Brown *Clerc's Photography* xxviii. 224/2 The localized tanning of the gelatine gives rise to unequal contractions of the film during drying... Tanning developers are not used in astronomical work. **1959** *Chambers's Encycl.* X. 686/2 Most fixing solutions also contain a tanning or hardening agent which unites with the gelatin of the emulsion layer, increases its melting-point and reduces its swelling in water. **1973** D. A. Spencer *Focal Dict. Photogr. Technol.* 617 A typical tanning developer contains little if any sulphite.

tannish (tæ·niʃ), *a.* [f. Tan *a.* + -ish¹.] Somewhat tan-coloured.

1935 J. T. Farrell *Judgment Day* xiii. 287 He glanced at a squat fellow in a crimson jersey and tannish knickers. **1947** D. M. Davin *Gorse blooms Pale* 53 It [*sc.* the calf] had Rosy's colouring, only at the ends the hair deepened into the Jersey's tannish black. **1961** M. Beadle *These Ruins are Inhabited* (1963) iii. 40 We ambled into..a tiny Saxon church. Of tannish stone..it was thick-set..and sheltering. **1965** *Amer. Philos. Q.* II. 320/2 A deep olive green..would be more beautiful..against a tannish pink.

Tannoy (tæ·noi). Also **tannoy.** A proprietary name for electrical apparatus concerned with sound reproduction and amplification. Now used generally, esp. to denote a form of public address system.

1928 *Trade Marks Jrnl.* 18 Apr. 605 Tannoy 488,958. Electrical Instruments and Apparatus for use in connection with Wireless Telegraphy and Telephony and Electrical Conductors... Guy Rupert Fountain, trading as the Tulsemere Manufacturing Co... 28th February 1928. **1942** *Ibid.* 21 Oct. 433/1 Tannoy. Electric signalling and alarm apparatus, telephone systems..television..radio apparatus,..sound reproducing and sound amplifying instruments..; public address apparatus; electric amplifiers. **1944** 'N. Shute' *Pastoral* ii. 36 He was lighting his pipe..when the Tannoy sounded metallically above his head. **1954** G. Smith *Flaw in Crystal* xx. 215 The tannoy blared, telling the passengers to go aboard. **1958** M. K. Joseph *I'll soldier No More* ix. 158 A tannoy-loudspeaker on the deck brought them the hourly news bulletins. **1969** A. Glyn *Dragon Variation* i. 11 Above them the hoarse voice of the muezzin crackled through the Tannoy, calling the faithful to prayer. **1977** G. Scott *Hot Pursuit* iii. 34 A call in the Tannoy system drowned my words. **1980** *Daily Tel.* 12 Nov. 19/3 They were furious after missing a train because of a wrong announcement on the station tannoy.

Hence as *v. trans.*, to call (someone) by public address system; *intr.*, to use a public address system; **ta·nnoyed** *ppl. a.*, transmitted by public address system; **ta·nnoying** *ppl. a.*

1966 *Punch* 20 Apr. 564/1 The President spoke, and his tannoyed voice boomed back off the blighted trees and the peeling architecture. **1970** B. Turner *Another Little Death* ii. 14 He held the line while Chief Inspector Rillie was Tannoyed out of the basement. **1976** *Times* 24 Apr. 4 The Portuguese Socialist leader arrives behind a convoy of tannoying cars and almost bounces into the crowd. **1978** *Times* 2 Oct. 4/3 A great crowd..being ordered around by Tannoyed voices.

Tanoan (tănōᵘ·ăn), *sb.* and *a.* [f. Sp. *Tano*, ad. Southern Tewa self-designation *tʰá·nu*, + -an.] **A.** *sb.* A family of languages spoken in parts of New Mexico and Arizona by Pueblo Indians; also, the group of people which speaks these languages. **B.** *adj.* Of, pertaining to, or designating this linguistic group.

1891 J. W. Powell *Indian Linguistic Families of Amer.* 121 Tañoan. **1909** *Amer. Anthropologist* XI. 564 The Keres (Queres) are introduced among tribes speaking languages of the Tanoan family. **1925** [see *Keres]. **1928** J. P. Harrington *Vocab. Kiowa Lang.* 1 A brief text [has]..been included, as well as Tanoan etymologies taken from the Tewa dialect spoken at San Juan Pueblo near Santa Fe, New Mexico. *Ibid.* 11 In the Tanoan languages, several of the consonants have a hard and a soft form. **1941** C. F. Voegelin *Language, Culture & Personality* 28 Only fragmentary notes and word lists for Tanoan were available. Taos was taken as a type for Tanoan phonetics and morphology. **1950** F. Eggan *Social Organization of Western Pueblos* 314 The Tanoan groups in the Rio Grande. **1959** G. L. & E. L. Trager in *Amer. Anthropologist* LXI. 1078 (*title*) Kiowa and Tanoan. **1974** *Encycl. Brit. Micropædia* IX. 810/2 *Tanoan languages*, the family of Aztec-Tanoan languages spoken in the valley of the Rio Grande in..New Mexico, U.S., including Northern Tiwa, Southern Tiwa, Piro, Tewa, Tano (the type language), and Towa; spoken by about 5,000 people (24,500 in 1680).

tanpoora, tanpura, varr. Tamboura in Dict. and Suppl.

‖ **tansu** (ta·ns*u*). [Jap.] A Japanese chest of drawers.

1886 E. S. Morse *Japanese Homes & their Surroundings* iv. 196 The *tansu*—a chest of drawers not unlike our bureau—is often placed within the closet. **1936** K. Nohara *True Face of Japan* x. 141 The *tansu*, or chest, consists of two, three, or at the most four drawers above each other, which fit exactly into the wall recesses. **1958** M. Joya *Things Japanese* iii. 82 There are unpainted *tansu* or chests, tables, trays and boxes. **1970** P. Zelver *Honey Bunch* (1971) iv. 16 There was a good modern couch, a Japanese tansu, the art nouveau desk. **1977** *South China Morning Post* (Hong Kong) 15 Apr. 31/7 Happy Joss has just received a new shipment of tansu, Imari, hibachi and fabrics from Japan.

tansy. Add: **5.** *tansy tea* (examples).

1893–4 R. O. Heslop *Northumberland Words* II. 718 *Tansy-tea*, an infusion of the herb. **1902** *Spectator* 12 Apr. 546/1 Patent pills and soothing syrups have taken the place of calamint and tansy tea. **1965** M. Thomas *Grannies' Remedies* 26 Hysterics... Strong tansy tea, taken cold and in small quantities, is good.

tant, tanta, varr. *tante 2.

tantadlin, tantoblin. Add: Also **tantaf(f)lin. 1.** (Later examples.)

1905 in *Eng. Dial. Dict.* VI. 29/1 (S. Not.) She made cakes an' tantaflin sorts o' things. A bit o' that beef for me; a don't care for non o' yer tarts an' tantaflins. **1911** D. H. Lawrence *White Peacock* iii. 38 I'm sure you like tantafflins, don't you, Georgie?

tantalian (tæntē̍·liăn), *a. Min.* [f. TANTAL(UM + *-IAN 2.] Of a mineral: having a (small) proportion of a constituent element replaced by tantalum.

1930 W. T. SCHALLER in *Amer. Mineralogist* XV. 572 Tantalum—tantalian. **1959** [see *FERRIAN *a.*].

tantalization. (Later examples.)

1849 C. BRONTË *Shirley* I. viii. 225 Rose had no idea of tantalization, or she would have held him awhile in doubt. **1931** H. S. WALPOLE *Judith Paris* IV. 678 From that misery of tantalization he had died. **1983** *Listener* 28 July 32/3 The human frame is just not conditioned to support such stupendous tantalisation.

tantalus. 2. (Earlier example.)

1888 G. GROSSMITH *Society Clown* 178, I sent him a small souvenir in the shape of a 'Tantalus'.

‖ **tant bien que mal** (taṅ bi̯ęṅ kə mal), *adv. phr.* [Fr., lit. 'as well as badly'.] With indifferent success; moderately well, after a fashion.

1765 LD. CHESTERFIELD *Let.* (1774) II. 490 They amuse me, *tant bien que mal*, for an hour or two every morning. **1843** THACKERAY *Irish Sk.-Bk.* II. v. 97 Sketching, *tant bien que mal*, the bridge and the trees..the writer became an object of no small attention. **1890** W. JAMES *Princ. Psychol.* II. xxvi. 494 We explain the mystery *tant bien que mal* by our evolutionary theories. **1939** *Scrutiny* VIII. 42 Thus his fleshly desires are satisfied, *tant bien que mal*.

‖ **tante** (taṅt, ta·ntə). Also **Tante. 1.** [Fr., Ger.: cf. AUNT.] An aunt; also, an older woman who stands in a close relationship. Freq. prefixed to a proper name or as a form of address.

1815 F. BURNEY *Let.* 13–18 May (1980) VIII. 129 'My tante' made me a long agitated visit. **1929** E. M. BRENT-DYER *Rivals of Chalet School* i. 18 It was a smiling small face..that was raised to 'Tante Marguérite's' when Mrs Russell drew her close for a kiss. **1932** G. HEYER *Devil's Cub* i. 15 Aunt Fanny has already warned Tante against your nobody. **1935** Z. N. HURSTON *Mules & Men* II. vi. 287 Ah don't have five nickels, Tante Celestine, but Als'll send a boy to get them. **1941** M. TREADGOLD *We couldn't leave Dinah* viii. 130 I lived in Nuremberg... Grandmother and Tante Anna and Tante Frieda were very good to me. **1943** H. T. KANE *Bayous Louisiana* viii. 166 A nonc and tante..seem far closer than the usual American uncle and aunt. **1964** S. BELLOW *Herzog* 146 Come here, little Moses, and sit on your old *tante's* knee. **1981** B. DE BREFFNY *My First Naked Lady* III. 147 Anna's mother, tante Rachel, was Turkish.

2. *S. Afr.* With pronunc. (ta·ntə). Also **Tant** (usu. preceding a proper name which begins with a vowel), **tanta.** [Afrikaans, from Du.] = sense 1 above. Also more widely, a term of respect for any elderly woman. Cf. *TANNIE.

1845 S. DENNISON *Let.* 12 Apr. in D. R. Edgecombe *Lett. Hannah Dennison* (1968) 205 Pray give my love to Miss Gush and Mrs G and remember me kindly to your good Tant. **1871** H. H. DUGMORE *Reminisc. Albany Settler* (1958) iii. 33 Powers of persuasion had to be employed with oude Tante Nieuwkerk. **1872** *Cape Monthly Mag.* Sept. 230 And then, does it not sometimes guard the slumbers and share the dreams of our beloved 'tantas'? **1883** [see *OOM]. **1900** H. BLORE *Imperial Light Horseman* 162 If a Boer were to be presented at Court he'd offer to shake hands with Queen Victoria, and address her as 'Tante'. All women to whom one wishes to pay respect are called 'Tante'. **1923** O. SCHREINER *Thoughts on S. Afr.* vii. 260 Oom and Tante, I will whisper to you a secret! **1937** C. R. PRANCE *Tante Rebella's Saga* 63 Each homestead on a circuit has its own special call..so that every Tante on the line knows..if..someone has something to say to Tant' Emmerentia. **1950** *Cape Times Mag.* 5 Aug. 3/3 Tanta Theodora thought that her kettle..was not as dazzling as it might be. **1969** *Personality* 5 June, Always there is the contrast between past and present..the austere black dress of the old tante and the bright miniwear of a visiting granddaughter. **1974** *Panorama* Apr. 21 Imagine the surprise of old Tant Alida Prinsloo at finding the contents of her voorhuis (living room) described.

tanteuxenite (tæntyū̆·ksĭnəit). *Min.* [f. TANT(ALUM + EUXENITE.] A titanotantalate of yttrium, $Y(Ta, Ti)_2O_6$, found as brownish or black, tabular or prismatic, orthorhombic crystals.

1928 E. S. SIMPSON in *Jrnl. R. Soc. W. Austral.* XIV. 45 Whilst normal euxenite..is a titanoniobate of yttrium, the mineral here described differs from it in being essentially a titanotantalate of yttrium... A new name being required for the species, Tanteuxenite is suggested. **1970** *Neues Jahrb. für Mineral.: Abhandl.* CXII. 131 Tanteuxenite has been found in rough flat prisms in the alluvials of Liha, together with columbite, euxenite and uranium microlite. **1974** [see *STRUVERITE 2].

‖ **tantième** (taṅti̯ɛ̄m). *rare.* [Fr., f. *tant* so much + *-ième*, ending of Fr. ordinal numerals.] A percentage or share, esp. of profits, royalties, etc.

1897 G. B. SHAW *Let.* 8 Sept. (1965) I. 804 You would simply be robbing the deserving poor if you cut off my tantième. **1911** —— *Lett. to Granville Barker* (1956) 175 Where should I be if I had to live on my tantiemes.

‖ **tant mieux** (taṅ mi̯ö). [Fr.] So much the better. Cf. next.

1754 LD. CHESTERFIELD *Let.* 8 Mar. (1774) II. 354, I really believe [he] will be your friend upon my account; if you can afterwards make him yours, upon your own, *tant mieux*. **1791** H. WALPOLE *Let.* 26 May (1944) XI. 272, I am rich in letters from you... You tell me mine entertain you; *tant mieux*; it is my wish, but my wonder. **1830** M. EDGEWORTH *Let.* 8 Dec. (1971) 444 He..promised to do all he can for him... If that should be while I am here—tant mieux. **1876** C. M. YONGE *Three Brides* I. xii. 188 'She seems absolutely repellent.' '*Tant mieux*,' muttered Raymond. **1929** [see next]. **1972** M. KAYE *Lively Game of Death* (1974) xiii. 74 If your boss can pin his death on somebody, *tant mieux*.

‖ **tant pis** (taṅ pi). Also **tant-pis.** [Fr.] So much the worse. Cf. prec.

[**1768** STERNE *Sentimental Journey* I. 92 *Tant pis* and *tant mieux* being two of the great hinges in French conversation, a stranger would do well to set himself right in the use of them.] **1782** H. WALPOLE *Let.* 25 Mar. (1955) XXIX. 207 The new cabinet are to be Lord Thurlow, Chancellor, (*tant pis*), [etc.]. **1855** A. THACKERAY *Jrnl.* 10 June in H. Ritchie *Lett. A. T. Ritchie* (1924) v. 68 But tant-pis, when I'm older I hope I shall do it better. **1929** A. HUXLEY *Let.* 24 Nov. (1969) 319 If you happen to find people constituted like yourself, tant mieux. If you find them differently constituted, tant pis. **1979** N. SLATER *Falcon* ix. 160 If Hudson wouldn't play ball when the crunch came, then—*tant pis*. Too bad.

Tantric, *a.* Add: Also **tantric, tantrik.** (Later examples.) Also, characteristic of Tantrism. In Western use, also *loosely* denoting the association of spiritual and erotic practices. Occas. as *sb.* (in form *Tantrik*), (*a*) a practitioner of Tantrism; (*b*) a Tantra.

1920 WEBSTER, Tantrik. **1927** A. HUXLEY *Proper Studies* 181 The Tantric reformation introduced worship of goddesses, together with a rich collection of magical and erotic rites. **1937** M. COVARRUBIAS *Island of Bali* (1972) vii. 174 It was Erlangga who instituted Javanese as the official language of Bali. Tantric black magic seems to have played an important part in Erlangga's time. **1954** W. NOYCE *South Col* iv. 61 Erotic paintings of tantric gods and goddesses adorn the walls. **1956** A. HUXLEY *Adonis & Alphabet* 59 The Tantriks of northern India and Tibet. **1959** *Times Lit. Suppl.* 20 Feb. 96/2 It contains elements..which belong to the Tantric Buddhism of India. **1961** A. HUXLEY *Let.* 8 Jan. (1969) 902 Pure perceptual receptivity is the basis, incidentally, of many Tantrik exercises. **1966** L. COHEN *Beautiful Losers* III. 241 An entire cult of Tantric lore perfectionists turned exocentric in their second chance at compassion. **1969** *Cultural News from India* Nov. 16 But his oils showed an innate understanding of Tantric motifs as well as the..use of material within an arbitrarily fixed boundary. **1977** *Time Out* 28 Jan.–3 Feb. 65/2 (Advt.), Student of energy release, seeks tantric adept, female. **1977** *It* May 17/1 The Vak..develops in the course of its manifestation into the seed-sounds of the Tantriks. **1980** *Dædalus* Spring 103 Repressed Hindus rejoice in myths of extreme forms of..erotic Tantric orgiasticism.

Tantricism (tæ·ntrikiz'm). [f. prec. + -ISM.] = TANTRISM; also *spec.* Tantric yoga.

1959 *Times Lit. Suppl.* 20 Feb. 96/2 The secret of Tantricism lies in the control of nervous centres. **1969** *Newslet. Tibet Soc. U.K.* June 2 Gyudto and Gyudmed, the Upper and Lower Colleges of Tantricism, in its reorganised form.

Tantrism. (Earlier example.)

1877 [see *SAKTA].

tantrum. For 'Mostly' read 'Freq.' and add: (Earlier and later examples.) Now often *spec.* a fit of bad temper in a young child.

1714 E. VERNEY *Let.* 30 Oct. in M. M. Verney *Eighteenth Cent. Memoirs* (1930) II. xxi. 18 Our lady has had some of her tanterums as Vapors comeing out etc. **1927** A. CONAN DOYLE *Case-Bk. Sherlock Holmes* xi. 283 Sir Robert was in one of his tantrums. **1966** M. FRAYN *Russian Interpreter* xxii. 103 'Let's put all these books away in the case again,' she said coaxingly, as if Proctor-Gould had thrown his toys about in a tantrum. **1979** N. GORDIMER *Burger's Daughter* 329 If we'd still been children, I might have been throwing stones at him in a tantrum.

Tantum ergo (tæ·ntǝ̆m ɔ̄·ɪgo). [First two words of the penultimate stanza, which begins 'Tantum ergo sacramentum Veneremur cernui' (Therefore we, before him bending, This great sacrament revere), of the hymn of St. Thomas Aquinas 'Pange lingua gloriosi Corporis mysterium'.] The last two stanzas of this hymn sung at Benediction; also, a setting of these.

1709 A. BUSBY in B. Jarrett *Eng. Dominicans* (1921) ix. 188 Tantum ergo was sung by the Cannons accompanied with Musick wich fild our hearts with joy. **1897** ADDIS & ARNOLD *Cath. Dict.* (ed. 5) 84/1 Next the Te Deum..or some other canticle..is sung, followed by the 'Tantum Ergo'. **1905** J. H. HARTING *Hist. Sardinian Chapel* 38 A *Tantum Ergo* was composed by Alessandro De Angioli for the Sardinian Chapel. **1922** JOYCE *Ulysses* 355 Then they sang the second verse of the *Tantum ergo*. **1976** N. ROBERTS *Face of France* vii. 82 The procession to the Altar of Repose, when the *Tantum Ergo* comes rolling out in Gregorian and sonorous Latin.

TANU (tā·nu). Also **Tanu.** [Acronym f. the initial letters of *T*anganyika *A*frican *N*ational *U*nion.] The name of a former political party in Tanganyika (now Tanzania).

1957 *Times* 15 Feb. 7/2 Speeches made recently by the president of the T.A.N.U. **1957** J. NYERERE *Let.* in *Times* 18 Sept. 9/4 For the last three years T.A.N.U. has been trying to get from the administering authority a statement that it intends to develop Tanganyika to become a democratic African state. **1959** *New Statesman* 12 Sept. 300/1 TANU now has 800,000 members, each of whom pays two shillings entrance fee and six shillings a year. **1967** *Economist* 18 Feb. 613/1 The constitution of the Tanganyika African National Union (Tanu) lays down [etc.]. **1971** *Standard* (Dar es Salaam) 7 Apr. 1/4 He asked all members of the corporation to study well the new Tanu Guidelines during their discussions. **1977** *Jrnl. Commonwealth & Compar. Politics* XV. 247 TANU and the Afro-Shirazi Party of Zanzibar officially merged in February 1977 to form Chama cha Mapinduzi (the Revolutionary Party of Tanzania), abbreviated to CCM. **1978** S. NAIPAUL *North of South* II. iii. 163 The peasants here displayed little or no understanding of TANU policies.

Tanzanian (tænzănī·ăn), *sb.* and *a.* [f. *Tanzania* (see below) + -AN, -IAN.] **A.** *sb.* A native or inhabitant of Tanzania, an E. African state formed in 1964 by the union of the republics of Tanganyika and Zanzibar. **B.** *adj.* Of or pertaining to Tanzania.

1965 *Economist* 23 Jan. 332/3 Mr Nyerere..apparently decided he must at any cost assert Tanzanian independence from this supposed American intrigue. *Ibid.* 6 Feb. 519/1 Whatever in the world, Tanzanians are asking, have they done. **1970** *Drum* (E. African ed.) Feb. 22/3 A gradual increase in standards of health, education and housing..will mean in the end healthier, wealthier, better-fed and happier Tanzanians. **1973** *Listener* 6 Sept. 301/1 The Chinese-built Freedom Railways reached the Zambian border, its Tanzanian section having been completed. **1978** S. NAIPAUL *North of South* II. ii. 158, I watched the Swedish girl weighing the babies... 'We cannot get well-off and educated Tanzanians to come and help us out.' *Ibid.* vi. 248 The Immigration Officer (Tanzanian) poked a grinning head through the doorway.

tanzanite (tæ·nzănəit). *Min.* [f. as prec. + -ITE[1].] A highly pleochroic violet-blue gemstone that is a variety of zoisite in which some of the aluminium is replaced by vanadium.

1968 *Wall St. Jrnl.* 14 Oct. 4/1 Tiffany & Co. disclosed discovery of a rare gemstone that the firm's vice president, Henry B. Platt, has named tanzanite. The gem, discovered last year in Africa's Tanzania, has the blue coloring and relative transparency of a sapphire. **1975** *Nat. Geographic* Apr. 490/1, I take a dusty detour to see the mining of glorious gems of transparent purplish blue. Tiffany's has named them tanzanites.

‖ **tao** (tau, d-). Also **Dao, Tao, taou, tau.** [Chinese *dào* road, way.] **1. a.** In Taoism, an absolute entity which is the source of the universe; the way in which this absolute entity functions.

1736 R. BROOKES tr. *Du Halde's Gen. Hist. China* III. 30 Among the Sentences [of Laò Kiun] there is one that is often repeated..: Tao, says he, or Reason, hath produced one, one hath produced two, two have produced three, and three have produced all things. **1797** *Encycl. Brit.* IV. 676/1 *Tao* is one by nature: the first begot the second; two produced the third; the three created all things. **1868** J. CHALMERS *Lau-Tsze's Specul. Metaph.* p. xii, Existence is..said to be produced from nonexistence, and *Tau* is the union of the two. **1904** W. G. OLD tr. *Laotze's Simple Way* iv. 30 Tao is without limitation; its depth is the source of whatever is. **1934** A. D. WALEY *Way & its Power* 50 *Tao* is the way that those must walk who would 'achieve without doing'. But *tao* is not only a means, a doctrine, a principle. It is the ultimate reality in which all attributes are united. **1950** A. HUXLEY *Themes & Variations* 172 In China and Japan mountains were taken more seriously. The aspiring artist was advised..to contemplate them lovingly until he could understand the mode of their being and feel within them the workings of the immanent and transcendent Tao. **1957** J. KEROUAC *On Road* (1958) 251 He was reaching his Tao decisions in the simplest direct way. **1963** D. C. LAU *Lao Tzu* 23 In the *Lao tzu*, the *tao* is no longer 'the way of something', but a completely independent entity, and replaces heaven in all its functions. But the *tao* is also the way followed by the inanimate universe as well as by man. **1971** F. MANN *Acupuncture* (ed. 2) iv. 47 The root of the way of life (Dao or Tao), of birth and change is Qi. **1980** M. H. KINGSTON *China Men* (1981) 96 Bak Goong thought he understood the Tao, which is everywhere and in everything, even in our excrement.

b. = TAOISM, TAOIST *a.*

1745 tr. J. F. Gemelli Careri in A. & J. Churchill *Coll. Voy. & Trav.* (ed. 3) IV. II. iv. 313/2 In some of these *Pagods*, religious men and women live in community to serve them; of which there are two sorts, the one of the sect of *Foe*, and the other of that of *Tao*. **1747** *New Gen. Coll. Voy.* IV. I. v. 214/1 The Sectaries say..that the great Doctrine of *Fo* and *Tau* swallows up all in nothing. **1831** *Canton Miscellany* I. 28 Hwuy-tsung, an Emperor of the Sung Dynasty, was fond of being a Priest of the Taou Sect. **1959** *Listener* 26 Feb. 388/2 Tao and Zen. **1980** *Jrnl. R. Soc. Arts* Feb. 137/2 The garden was seen as the most powerful metaphysical symbol for Tao, Shinto and Zen.

2. In Confucianism and in extended uses, the way to be followed, the right conduct; doctrine or method.

1934 A. D. WALEY *Way & its Power* 30 Each school of philosophy had its *tao*, its doctrine of the way in which life should be ordered. **1943** C. S. Lewis *Abolition of Man* iii. 30 In the older systems both the kind of man the teachers wished to produce and their motives for producing him were prescribed by the *Tao*—a norm to which the teachers themselves were subject and from which they claimed no liberty to depart. **1966** F. Schurmann *Ideology & Organization in Communist China* i. 50 The Chinese Communists speak of the forces of world history which are universal and cosmic. Though this belief clashes with traditional Confucian beliefs of *tao* (something akin to 'natural law'), it bears certain similarities to the Taoist belief in Heaven as a real force. **1970** H. G. Creel *What is Taoism?* i. 2 Tao at first meant 'road' or 'path'. From this it developed the sense of a method, and of a course of conduct. As a philosophical term it appears first in the Confucian *Analects*. For the Confucians *tao* is the way, the method, of right conduct for the individual and for the state. **1972** F. Fitzgerald *Fire in Lake* i. 11 In analyzing these disasters the emperor blamed them on his deviation from Tao, the traditional way, which was at once the most moral and the most scientific course. **1980** *Dædalus* Spring 34 A Tao of Physics in which the details of modern macrophysics and microphysics are matched to those of the mystical tradition.

Taoiseach (tī·ʃəχ,-aχ). [a. Ir., lit. 'chief, leader'.] The Prime Minister of the Republic of Ireland.

1938 *New Irish Constitution: Citizen's Man.* 17 Dail Eireann is dissolved by the President on the advice of the Taoiseach. **1941** G. B. Shaw *Matter with Ireland* (1962) 285 The Irish Taoiseach (Premier), Mr de Valera, made no move. *a* **1966** 'M. Na Gopaleen' *Best of Myles* (1968) 128 You pick up the receiver and say 'Who? The Taoiseach? Oh very well. Put him on.' **1973** *Irish Times* 2 Mar. 9/1 Whoever is going to be Taoiseach is going to have to sweat and work every minute of every day. **1981** *Listener* 1 Jan. 4/2 Mrs Thatcher..permits herself to follow very much the kind of approach the Taoiseach, Mr Charles Haughey, was hoping for.

Taoism. Add: Also **Daoism** and with pronunc. (dɑu·iz'm). (Earlier and later examples.)

1838 Gützlaff & Reed *China Opened* II. xv. 209 (*heading*) Taouism. **1948** *Mind* LVII. 535 Dr. Fung.. shows how Buddhist philosophy..influenced both Confucianism and Daoism. **1981** *Times* 22 June 6/8 It is not the Vatican which bothers China's leaders most in religious matters—but Daoism (formerly known as Taoism), the only religion truly native to China. *Ibid.* 11 Nov. 6/7 The ancient Chinese religion of Daoism.

Taoist, *sb.* (*a.*) Add: Also **Daoist** and with pronunc. (dɑu·ist). **a, b.** (Earlier and later examples.)

1838 Gützlaff & Reed *China Opened* II. xv. 209 Such are the better description of Taouists in China. **1971** *Ink* 12 June 8/3 There were many non strict Daoist farmers there who could have been VC. **1981** *Times* 22 June 6/8 Unlike the Buddhists, the Daoists have been granted no licence to continue or revive their practices.

Tao Kuang (dɑu gwaŋ). Also **Daoguang.** The title of the reign of Xuan Zong (Min-Ning), emperor of China 1821–50, used *attrib.* and *absol.* to designate the period of his reign or pottery and porcelain made at this time.

1927 W. B. Honey *Later Chinese Porcelain* 59 A considerable part of Tao Kuang porcelain was made in revived Yung Chêng patterns. **1951** R. S. Jenyns *Later Chinese Porcelain* ii. 20 A series of 1662 to 1675 wares, often with K'ang Hsi marks, and some marked Shên-tê t'ang, a hallmark which does not occur only on Tao Kuang pieces. **1960** H. Hayward *Antique Coll.* 277/1 *Tao Kuang period*, (1821–50). Characteristic Chinese porcelain wares of this reign are those minutely painted in *famille rose*..style, employing low-toned enamels, and *graviata*, coloured grounds. **1973** *Country Life* 7 June 1680/2 A pair of reticulated ruby ground hexagonal vases..famille rose 19⅜ in, Tao Kuang. **1976** Scott & Koski *Walk-In* (1977) ii. 16 A shabby reproduction, made..in Hong Kong, of a Tao Kuang teapot. **1980** *Catal. Fine Chinese Ceramics* (Sotheby, Hong Kong) 90 Seal mark and period of Daoguang (Tao Kuang).

Taos (tɑus, tā·os). The name of a town in New Mexico, used *attrib.* (occas. *absol.*) to designate members of a Pueblo Indian tribe living there, or the language of this tribe, a variety of Tiwa.

1844 J. Gregg *Commerce of Prairies* I. 86 A Taos Indian who formed one of the Mexican escort, seeing a gun levelled at his commander, sprang forward and received the ball in his own body, from the effects of which he instantly expired! **1887** *Scribner's Mag.* II. 510 Then the saddle-blanket is laid over his withers, with sometimes a *tilpah*, or parti-colored rug, woven and dyed by the Navajo or Taos Indians. **1939** *Language* XV. 51 The Taos language forms with that of Picurís..the northern branch of Tiwa. *Ibid.*, The old people..speak Taos and Spanish. **1944** B. Johnson *As much as I Dare* 287 Adobe walls around the garden and various nooks and vistas were being built by Taos Indian labor. **1964** *Language* XL. 202 He has published an article describing the application of his system to the Taos language and culture. **1973** A. H. Whiteford *N. Amer. Indian Arts* 28 Taos and Picuris make only unpainted gold-tan pottery. **1978** *Language* LIV. 233 'About the nearest he ever came to having fun' was making charts of the Taos pronoun. **1978** G. A. Sheehan *Running & Being* viii. 111 A Taos Indian chief had once told him that white men were covered with wrinkles because they were crazy.

‖ **taotai** (tɑu·tai, d-). *Hist.* Also **Taotai, tautai,** etc. [Chinese *daòtái.*] The title given to the Chinese provincial officer responsible for the civil and military affairs of a district, abolished shortly after the establishment of the Republic in 1911.

1747 *New Gen. Coll. Voy.* IV. i. vi. 253 To every District there also belongs a Mandarin, called Tau-ti. **1835** *Chinese Repository* Oct. 279 The class of officers next in rank to these are called taou or taoutae: they are not under the orders of the 'two sze', but of the governor and lieut.-governor, and it is their duty to take part in the 'protection' and 'circuit-supervision' of portions of the province. **1848** S. W. Williams *Middle Kingdom* I. vii. 345 The gabel and commissariat are mostly under the direction of officers called *tau*, or *tautai*, sometimes termed intendants of circuit, who have other functions in addition. *Ibid.* 346 The *tautai*..are a kind of deputy of the governor-general and lieutenant-governor, residing in the *tau*, or circuits, into which each province is divided. **1895** *Daily News* 19 Jan. 6/6 A number of Chinese guerilla troops recently tried to enter Neuchwang. The taotai of the city closed the gates, and offered an armed resistance to their entry. **1926** *Blackw. Mag.* Nov. 629/1 A mandarin named Liang was sent to the island as Taotai. **1943** J. T. Pratt *War & Politics in China* xii. 193 When the Revolution came to Shanghai the Taoti—the chief Chinese official—requested the consular body to take temporary charge of the court. **1959** P. Fleming *Siege at Peking* iii. 42 Henceforth Bishops would rank with Governors-General and Governors, Provicaires with Treasurers, Judges and Taotais, and so on down the respective hierarchies.

‖ **t'ao t'ieh** (tɑu tyə). Also **taotie, tao-tieh.** [Chinese *tāotiè.*] The name of a mythical monster, or a mask-design showing its face, found esp. on metalware of the Chou period (1122–221 B.C.). Freq. *attrib.*

1915 R. L. Hobson *Chinese Pottery & Porcelain* II. xvii. 290 This is the face of the t'ao t'ieh (the gluttonous ogre) supposed originally to have represented the demon of the storm. **1933** *Illustr. London News* 9 Dec. (Suppl.) p. i/1 This bell has a *t'ao-t'ieh* design on the upper part. **1958** W. Willetts *Chinese Art* I. iii. 161 *T'ao-t'ieh*..is a device in which two confronting zoomorphs in profile form the left and right sides of an animal mask seen in full face. *Ibid.* 162 Karlgren analyses the *t'ao-t'ieh* motive into six different types. **1965** *New Statesman* 20 Aug. 257/1 Eloquent prose passages like René Grousset's dramatic evocation of the *t'ao-t'ieh* on the sides of Chou vessels. **1973** *Genius of China* 47/2 It is notable that the convention of the face painted on this bowl shows no relation to the *t'ao-t'ieh*, an evil-averting monster mask which pervades the later bronze-age art of central China. **1978** *New Archaeol. Finds in China* II. 29 Some broken pieces of the outer coffin remain; they are carved with a *tao-tieh* (ogre-mask) design in the form of an ox head. **1980** *Catal. Fine Chinese Ceramics* (Sotheby, Hong Kong) 80 A further frieze of upright acanthus leaves around the neck.., the shoulders set with moulded *taotie* (*t'ao t'ieh*) mask and ring handles.

‖ **taovala** (tɑuvala). [Tongan.] In Tonga, a piece of fine matting worn round the waist over a *vala* or Tongan kilt (and without which one is not considered properly dressed).

Traditionally worn by the male (with the exception of the Queen as monarch). It should be torn in several places, to show that the wearer does not set himself above his fellows.

1947 *Pacific Islands Monthly* Sept. 60/3 (*caption*) He wears the 'Taovala' (mat tied with coconut fibre) which is a 'must' with all Tongans who would show respect to their chiefs. **1953** *News Chron.* 2 June 7/1 With him rides a Queen—Queen Salote Tupon of the Tonga Islands. Her ceremonial dress includes a loose blouse and ankle-length skirt, round which is draped a tao-vala—a mat made from brown pandana leaves. **1977** *Daily Tel.* 15 Feb. 17/4 Pretty Tongan girls in white with the Taovala (traditional belts made from tree bark) round their waists kept the Royal party as cool as they could with fans made from the prickly-leaved pandanus tree.

tap, *sb.*[1] Add: **1. c.** *on tap* (later *fig.* examples). Also *spec.* in *Stock Exchange* use, applied to securities which are the subject of a large issue. Cf. quot. 1907, sense 1 b in Dict.

1890 R. L. Stevenson *Vailima Lett.* (1895) 35 The moon is on tap again. **1908** [see *concertina *v.*]. **1923** *Westm. Gaz.* 8 Jan. 4/2 It is some time since 'additional' Treasury Bills have been on 'tap' at so low a rate as.. 1⅞ per cent. **1926** L. R. Robinson *Investm. Trust Organization & Managem.* 71 Whether the investment trust should raise its funds by keeping 'on tap' its offerings to the public and 'feeding' them out in response to demand..depends upon a number of factors. **1931** J. Greenhill in *Westm. Bank Guild Lectures 1930–1* III.105 We have not seen Bills 'on tap' for some considerable time past. **1935** A. Huxley *Let.* 5 June (1969) 396 His own left organizations in France will of course be on tap. **1958** *Times* 2 Oct. 3/3 Anything offered by television is on tap. **1965** J. L. Hanson *Dict. Econ. & Commerce* 371/2 Securities are said to be on 'tap' when they are issued in unlimited quantities (though the amounts permitted to each individual may be restricted) and are available for purchase direct from the issuing authority at any time. **1975** J. F. Burke *Death Trick* (1976) v. 82 We'll look into those alibis. Meanwhile, I want you both on tap. Understand?

d. *Electr. Engin.* = *tapping *vbl. sb.*[1] 2 b.

1900 M. A. Oudin *Standard Polyphase Apparatus & Systems* ix. 173 The secondary of each interchangeable transformer has two taps, giving 50 per cent and 86·7 per cent of the full voltage, so that either transformer can serve as the teaser, or supplementary one, by using the proper terminals. **1947** R. Lee *Electronic Transformers & Circuits* viii. 214 To improve the closeness of voltage control, a variable autotransformer has been developed in which the moving tap is a carbon brush which slides over exposed turns of a winding. **1974** C. C. Woodward *Cable Television* vi. 121 A complete new installation.. from the tap to the subscriber's television set.

e. *Stock Exch.* A security which is available 'on tap' (see sense 1 c above).

1948 *Economist* 8 July 772/2 £24½m...was perhaps acquired by original conversion of Local Loan or through the tap; but the additional £55m. was presumably bought on the market. **1960** *Ibid.* 8 Oct. 167/2 The issue price is nominal, since no one expected more than a small fraction of Wednesday's issue of £500 million would be taken by the public. The rest goes into the official tap, and the tap price can of course be adjusted as events dictate. **1967** *Ibid.* 4 Feb. 444/1 Supplies of the long tap (Treasury 6¾% 1995/98), issued only last October 28th, had already run out. **1976** *Southern Even. Echo* (Southampton) 12 Nov. 24/6 Gilts managed to push forward by ¼ to ⅜ taking the new Treasury 14 per cent. 1982 'tap' up 1/16 to 98 5/16. But the new long 'tap' Treasury 15¼ 1996 stays at 97½. **1980** *Times* 15 Jan. 18 It would not surprise them to see the authorities issue another tap at the end of this week.

2. a. (Later examples.) Also *spec.* at *Eton College*: († *the*) *Tap*, a place where beer is sold to pupils at Eton.

1865 *Etoniana* 23 The 'Tap' and the Christopher had their earlier prototypes. **1917** A. Huxley *Let.* 30 Sept. (1969) 134 They were regrettably caught at the time just entering Tap. **1980** *Sunday Times* (Colour Suppl.) 14 Dec. 94/3 On the other days I'm free and I go for a drink to Tap.

5*. a. A device by means of which a telephone conversation may be listened to secretly by a third party. Cf. Tap *v.*[1] 2 c.

1923 E. Wallace *Missing Million* xxiii. 181 How did you know where the 'tap' was? **1959** *Washington Post* 26 Oct. A2/1 Law enforcement agencies use the taps even where prohibited by law. **1967** *Times Rev. Industry* Aug. 76/1 Telephones can be tapped so that it is virtually impossible for physical search to locate the tap, and if a searcher came near to it, the tap would automatically destroy itself without trace.

b. The act of listening secretly to a telephone conversation by means of a connection to the wire. Cf. *phone-tap* s.v. *phone *sb.*[2] 3; *telephone tap* s.v. *telephone *sb.* 3.

1950 *Sun* (Baltimore) 24 Jan. 12/3 The Holmes view has been accepted by the Supreme Court in a series of decisions steadily narrowing the use to which wire-tap material may be put in court. But there is still a shadow-land within which the Justice Department feels safe in authorizing use of the wire tap. **1968** W. Garner *Deep, Deep Freeze* iii. 35 He'd made a phone tap, a successful tap, and overheard a reference to an agent..who was being sent to England. **1973** B. Murphy *Business of Spying* viii. 134 As well as being 'bugged', a telephone can be 'tapped'. This permits the recording and/or monitoring of both sides of the conversation. The most basic and easy way to monitor a telephone conversation is to carry out a direct line tap. **1979** *Guardian* 1 Mar. 1/3 There had to be good grounds for suspecting that a tap would be productive.

c. A recording made secretly from a telephone conversation.

1969 L. Sanders *Anderson Tapes* (1970) xxix. 73 Tape SEC. 25 JUN 68... This is a telephone tap. **1978** S. Brill *Teamsters* ii. 62 Telephone taps were played on tape recorders in court.

5.** *on the tap*, begging, making requests for loans. Cf. Tap *v.*[1] 3 in Dict. and Suppl. *slang.*

1932 A. Gardner *Tinker's Kitchen* iii. i. 217 Bob the journalist was, like everyone else at the Cross,..out to get what he could.., in plain words 'on the tap'. **1977** P. Carter *Under Goliath* xii. 61 She was a real moaner and always on the tap, borrowing sugar and milk.

6. (sense *1 e) *tap bill, bond, issue, price, rate, sale, stock*; **tap-changing** *Electr. Engin.*, the process of changing the connection to a transformer from one tap to another so as to vary the turns ratio and hence control the output voltage under a varying load; so **tap-changer**, an apparatus for accomplishing this; † **tap-waiter**, a waiter in a tap-room or tap-house (*obs. rare*); **tap wrench** (later examples).

1957 A. C. L. Day *Outl. Monetary Econ.* xxxv. 443 The British Exchange Equalization Account started operations with large quantities of sterling assets, which it holds in the form of 'tap' Treasury bills. **1942** *Sun* (Baltimore) 9 May 16/1 (*heading*) About $4,500,000 'tap' bonds sold here. **1931** S. R. Roget *Dict. Electr. Terms* (ed. 2) 342/2 Tap changer. **1962** *Newnes Conc. Encycl. Electr. Engin.* 748/2 Where possible, the tap-changer has minimum voltage to earth, and on most high-voltage line transformers it is at the neutral point. **1979** *Railway Gaz. Internat.* Jan. 49/1 As compared with the equivalent ..tap-changer loco, maintenance was halved. **1929** W. T. Taylor *Electr. Supply Transformer Systems* ii. 21 For station and distribution types of transformers, voltage control is now effected by tap-changing on load; several satisfactory designs have been produced which enable tap-changing to be carried out directly on tappings from the main transformers. **1962** *Newnes Conc. Encycl. Electr. Engin.* 748/1 Tap-changing may be done when the transformer is out of circuit. **1926** L. R. Robinson *Investm. Trust Organization & Managem.* 71 'Tap issues' are better fitted for a market in which the investor is learning for the first time the advantages of participation in investment trusts. **1973** *Daily Tel.* 3 Feb. 21/1 During the past fortnight, despite the exhaustion of two sizeable tap issues and the successful launching of a new 9½ p.c.

long-dated stock, the [gilt-edged] market has lacked impetus. **1958** *Times* 21 June 11/3 The strong demand for Funding Five-and-a-Half per Cent., 1982–84,..enabled the 'tap' price (the price at which Government departments are prepared to sell the stock they took up when the original issue was made) to be raised by 1–16 twice during the day. **1922** *Daily Tel.* 12 June 2/1 New second-hand Treasuries were dealt in at $2\frac{1}{4}$ per cent., the 'tap' rate now being $2\frac{1}{8}$ per cent. **1926** L. R. Robinson *Investm. Trust Organization & Managem.* 71 'Tap' Sales, and occasional flotations. **1958** *Times Rev. Industry* Dec. (London & Cambridge Econ. Bull.) p. x/2 Tap sales have reduced bank liquidity. **1966** *Punch* 9 Nov. 710/3 The Bank will not allow anything like a boom in gilt-edged to develop—and it has tapstocks of its own to sell. **1980** *Times* 15 Jan. 15 Without tap stocks to deter them, gilts climbed briskly. **1835** Dickens *Sk. Boz* (1836) 1st Ser. II. 179 You leave your bag and repair to 'The Tap'... The tap-waiter finds himself much comforted by your brandy-and-water. **1956** H. Townsend in D. L. Linton *Sheffield* xvi. 299 Sheffield plays a large part in the production of drills and tipped cutters,..bit gauges, tap wrenches, pin vices,..and so on. **1964** S. Crawford *Basic Engin. Processes* i. 26 As its name implies the tap-wrench is required to provide a convenient method of revolving the tap in the drilled hole.

tap, *sb.*^{2} Add: **1. c.** = *tap-dancing.

1944 N. Streatfeild *Curtain Up* viii. 97 The same sandals do for everything except tap. **1950** Blesh & Janis *They all played Ragtime* (1958) iii. 57 Chauvin had a fine tenor voice and sang and danced superbly, buck and wing, regular and eccentric tap. **1952** A. Lomax *Mister Jelly Roll* v. 202 Well, I did my tap numbers in a lot of shows after that. **1972** *Guardian* 13 Dec. 9/1 It was quite bad enough doing tap—all the kids at school used to tease me.

d. *Phonetics.* A single momentary contact between vocal organs in the production of a speech sound; the sound produced by such contact.

1952 [see *one-tap* s.v. *one *a.* 32 a]. **1954** Pei & Gaynor *Dict. Linguistics* 214 The Spanish *pero* is pronounced with a *tap r*, but *perro* with a *trill r*. **1964** W. Jassem in D. Abercrombie et al. *Daniel Jones* 339 The assumption that two 'taps' are sufficient for a sound to be labelled 'rolled'. **1977** *Language* LIII. 861 The individual closures of a trill are much more rapid than the single closure of a tap.

e. In fig. phr. *a tap on the wrist*, a mild reprimand. Cf. *slap *sb.*^{1} 2 a.

1973 *Black Panther* 20 Oct. 2/1 Forty pages of charges gathered by the Justice Department, and he gets off with a tap on the wrist for income tax evasion. **1974** *Anderson* (S. Carolina) *Independent* 23 Apr. 4A/1 Disrespect for the law and the courts stems from instances..in which the accused have been found not guilty or have received a mere tap-on-the-wrist sentence when it was obvious that all evidence pointed to guilt.

2. (Earlier example.) Also *fig.*, the end.

1824 *H. R. Doc. 18th U.S. Congress 1 Sess.* No. 111. 35 It is his [*sc.* the orderly's] duty..to visit his rooms, at the taps; see that the lights are extinguished; the fires properly secured; the occupants present, and in bed. **1917** A. G. Empey *Over Top* 258 Then it was taps for me.

3. (Further examples.)

1743 J. Hempstead *Diary* 12 Dec. (1901) 418 Nailed on a pr of Tapps on a pr of New Shoes for adam. **1954** J. Steinbeck *Sweet Thursday* 33 Brown calf shoes (heel taps a little run over). **1965** E. Tunis *Colonial Craftsmen* iv. 107 The thick leather for the tap (sole) soaked all day in water. **1976** *National Observer* (U.S.) 6 Mar. 14/6 Amazing polyurethane taps keep heels perfect for months. Attach in seconds to any heel, and no one can tell you're wearing taps.

3*. In negative context: the slightest amount *of work*. Cf. Stroke *sb.*^{1} 11 a. *colloq.*

1887 *Lantern* (New Orleans) 22 Jan. 2/2, I understand that Eddie never done a tap of work in his life. **1946** F. Sargeson *That Summer* 185 For several weeks Jack hadn't done a tap of work in the garden. **1952** E. O'Neill *Moon for Misbegotten* I. 10 He's nothing but a drunken bum who never done a tap of work in his life.

4. tap-in *Basketball*, a goal scored by tapping the ball into the basket, usu. when following up an unsuccessful shot; **tap-kick** *Rugby Football*, a light kick given to the ball whereby play is re-started from a penalty and possession retained; also as *v. trans.*; **tap pants** *U.S.*, a type of fashionable ladies' knickers; **tap penalty** *Rugby Football*, a penalty taken with a tap-kick; **tap shoe**, a shoe worn for tap-dancing, having a specially hardened sole or attached metal plates at toe and heel to make a tapping sound.

1948 *Daily Progress* (Charlottesville, Va.) 4 Feb. 9/3 Counting a tap-in one point would help equalize the height advantage, he said, but as in the case of the delayed whistle, what would constitute a tap-in? **1976** *Cumberland & Westmorland Herald* 4 Dec. 12/5 Coward netted a brace with a powerful long-range shot and a tap-in from Martin's cross. **1960** T. McLean *Kings of Rugby* xi. 120 When Hewitt after a tap-kick penalty in the Lions' 25 set off with a tremendous burst of speed..the audience rose to him in wonderment and delight. **1978** *Rugby World* Apr. 6/1 After he had given an indirect free-kick against the French, the Scotland captain, Doug Morgan, dropped a goal direct from hand, without bringing it into play with a tap-kick first. *Ibid.*, Mr Thomas's explanation was that he had been telling the French why the kick had been awarded and that his back was half-turned when Morgan began the run-up to his kick. 'I assumed Morgan had tap-kicked the ball first,' he said. **1977** Tap pants [see *teddy 3]. **1982** *Penthouse* July 26, I..have bought pretty tap pants and knickers from various lingerie establishments. **1976** *Sunday Post* (Glasgow) 26 Dec. 36/3 It only took Gala five minutes to score. From a tap penalty Dickson tore a gash in the defence, and Telfer accepted his scoring pass in the corner. **1978** *Rugby World* Apr. 33/1 He..carries particularly fond memories of the six tries he recorded last season, almost all from tap penalties at close range. **1932** *Boot & Shoe Recorder* 20 Feb. 62/3 A four style range of toe, ballet, acrobatic and tap shoes covers the usual store's requirements. **1936** 'Isolde' *Tap Dancing Made Easy* 9 You can practise in an ordinary pair of shoes, but much better results can be obtained when wearing proper Tap shoes. **1980** *Daily Tel.* 10 Mar. 12/6 The musical.. brings out the best in the most bashful of bathroom singers and puts imaginary tapshoes on confirmed wall-flowers everywhere.

tap, *v.*^{1} Add: **2. c.** (Earlier and later examples.) So *to tap a call, line, message, telephone*, etc.

1869 *Cornh. Mag.* XIX. 759 A favourite plan of the raiders was to 'tap' the wire. **1871** *Q. Jrnl. Sci.* I. 117 For days the unconscious French were sending [telegraphic] messages, which were 'tapped' by the Prussians. **1874** J. H. Bunnel in J. E. Smith *Man. Telegraphy* (ed. 10) p. xv, The means employed to 'tap' a Telegraph line..are very simple. **1878** A. Pinkerton *Strikers, Communists, Tramps & Detectives* xvi. 199 The strikers certainly had some experienced telegraphers..capable of tapping the lines. **1909** G. B. Shaw *Press Cuttings* 3 Why didnt you telephone? *Balsquith.* They tap the telephone. **1911** *World's Work* XVIII. 588/2 Hundreds of amateur installations erected in the vicinity of either station, whereby messages might be tapped or confused. **1957** *Times* 7 June 10/5 (*heading*) Calls tapped on barrister's telephone. Home Secretary questioned. **1972** *Times* 19 Dec. 2/7 He could not prove beyond all reasonable doubt that the call he made to Mr Hope on December 1 had been tapped. **1978** G. A. Sheehan *Running & Being* ii. 32 There is no need to tap my phone or open my mail.

3. (Further examples.) Also *absol.*

1879 A. Pinkerton *Criminal Reminiscences* xiii. 212 In the act of 'tapping' the till of a North Side [of Chicago] German grocery. *c* **1926** [see *marble *sb.* 4 c]. **1929** W. R. Burnett *Little Caesar* i. 10 They only bank once or twice a week. They're careless, get that; because they've never been tapped. **1931** T. Horsley *Odyssey of Out-of-Work* xxiii. 247 We'll tap these mansions. **1931** 'G. Orwell' *Coll. Ess.* (1968) I. 57 Ginger tapped the local butcher, who gave us the best part of two pounds of sausages. **1935** —— *Clergyman's Daughter* ii. 105 They were begging..'tapping' at every..likely-looking cottage. **1939** J. Worby *Spiv's Progress* iii. 17 Every night he would put on his plimsolls and go tapping. **1979** *Tucson* (Ariz.) *Mag.* Mar. 46/1 Many of the big plush resorts that tap you for \$80 to \$100 a day.

tap, *v.*^{2} Add: **1. a.** Also *to tap out*, to mark or signify by a tap or series of taps; to cause to be produced thus; *spec.* to type out (a letter, etc.).

1903 R. Langbridge *Flame & Flood* i. 4 He was tapping out a cautious progress towards the women with a stick, letting himself down with a surprised bump upon each step. **1912** *Red Mag.* Mar. 427/2 The clock of the Royal Exchange began to tap out the hour of nine. **1944** in B. A. Botkin *Treas. S. Folklore* (1949) III. i. 447 He.. tapped out '73', which is the telegrapher's traditional symbol for goodby. **1952** M. Laski *Village* xviii. 248 Gerald tapped out a formal letter on the old typewriter. **1976** J. McClure *Rogue Eagle* ii. 27 Buchanan put down his cup where the writer carriage wouldn't bump it.. and..tapped out the name of his freelance agency.

c. To arrest (someone). Also in phr. *to tap on the shoulder. slang.*

[**1785** Grose *Dict. Vulgar T.* sig. Z3, *A tap on the shoulder*, an arrest.] **1859** G. W. Matsell *Vocabulum* 89 *Tap*, to arrest. **1894** J. G. Littlechild *Reminiscences of Chief-Inspector Littlechild* xix. 193 We instructed him.. to hint darkly that he was going to be 'tapped'—i.e. taken into custody on charges connected with the forged cheques. **1968** [see *do *v.* 11 m].

2. a. Also in reduplicated form **tap-tap** and varr., to tap repeatedly (usu. as pres. pple.).

1922 Joyce *Ulysses* 284 A stripling, blind, with a tapping cane, came taptaptapping by Daly's window. **1977** *New Yorker* 6 June 38/2 Two reels of thread escaped from it, rolled along the landing, and went tap-tapping down the stairs. **1982** R. Timperley *Face in Leaves* iv. 34, I heard her typewriter tap-tap-tapping.

d. To sound, esp. as a signal.

1887 A. J. Wilson *At Mercy of Tiberius* xxxiii. 576 Somewhere in the apartment, a bell tapped. *Ibid.* 577 The time has come; the drum taps, I must march away. **1915** C. Johnson *Battleground Adventures* liv. 419 A bell would tap for a waiter to come and take the team.

3. (Earlier and further examples.) Also *absol.*

1746 J. Hempstead *Diary* 1 Jan. (1901) 453, I tapt & nailed Jont. Pierpoints Shoes. **1781** in *Narragansett Historical Reg.* (1882) I. 284 Tapped a pair of shoes. **1852** *Knickerbocker* XL. 149 There is also the shoemaker..who 'taps' for half the city price.

4. To designate or select (a person) for a task, honour, or membership of an organization. *U.S. colloq.*

1952 E. O'Neill *Moon for Misbegotten* I. 55 He was tapped for an exclusive Senior Society at the Ivy university to which his father had given millions. **1972** J. Mosedale *Football* ii. 13 *Sports Illustrated* magazine tapped him..as its 'Sportsman of the Year'. **1977** *Time* 23 May 13/3 Britain's youthful Foreign Secretary David Owen announced last week that he had tapped Jay, at 40, to serve as Ambassador to Washington.

‖ **tapa**^{2} (ta·pă). [Sp., lit. 'cover, lid'.] Usu. *pl.* In Spanish bars or cafés, a savoury snack or hors d'œuvre of sausage, cured ham, seafood, potato salad, etc., typically served with glasses of wine or sherry.

The slices of sausage, etc., were originally put on top of the glasses as 'lids'.

1953 C. Salter *Introducing Spain* iv. 36, I should like to draw attention to..the admirable habit of the 'tapa'. In Spain, when you order a drink in a bar.., you will always be given..something to eat. **1959** W. James *Word-bk. of Wine* 186 *Tapas*, small dishes served gratis in boat-shaped saucers with every glass of wine ordered.. in a Spanish bodega or café. **1964** C. Rougvie *Medal from Pamplona* vi. 79 Must be a pub there with tapas..these bits of food they give you free with the booze. **1978** J. Hyams *Pool* vi. 74 She had *tapas* and white wine at Café Monaco with a friend. **1982** D. Serafín *Madrid Underground* 63 It was the hour to take *tapas* or pre-dinner snacks.

tapadero. Add: Also 9 **-daro.** (Earlier and later examples.) Also used elsewhere in North America.

1844 J. Gregg *Commerce of Prairies* I. 213 The stirrups ..over which are fastened the tapaderas or coverings of leather to protect the toes. **1872** 'Mark Twain' *Roughing It* xxiv. 178 It was a Spanish saddle, with ponderous *tapidaros*. **1879** *Cimarron* (N. Mexico) *News & Press* 20 Nov. 3/4 New Saddler Shop... Stirrups, Tapaderos, Saddle Bags, etc. **1933** J. Steinbeck *To God Unknown* xxv. 321 Joseph lifted the heavy saddle, and as the tapadero struck the horse's side, it reared. **1975** F. Kennedy *Alberta was my Beat* p. vi, It [*sc.* a saddle] was complete with Tapadero covered stirrups.

‖ **tapas** (ta·pās). [Skr., lit. 'heat'.] In Hinduism and Jainism, (the practising of) religious austerity or bodily mortification. Also **tapasya**· [Skr., religious austerity].

1810 J. Malcolm in *Asiatic Res.* XI. 267 Na'nac was celebrated for the manner in which he performed *Tapasa*, or austere devotion. **1815** M. Elphinstone *Acct. Kingdom of Caubul* II. xii. 318 The Tapasya, or ascetic devotion of Gurug. **1924** W. B. Selbie *Psychol. Relig.* 50 The ascetic methods of tapas and yoga, physical practices which belong to a debased mysticism not far removed from magic. **1962** A. Huxley *Island* ix. 137 The real thing only comes to people after years and years of meditation and *tapas* and..well, you know—not going with women. **1969** *Indo-Asian Culture* Oct. 53 In this art form..there is less of the austerity of *tapasya* in the artist's way of working. **1974** *Encycl. Brit. Macropædia* II. 137/1 In India, in the late Vedic period.., the ascetic use of *tapas* ('heat', or austerity) became associated with meditation and *yoga*, inspired by the idea that *tapas* kills sin.

ta·p-dancing. [f. Tap *sb.*^{2}] A form of exhibition dancing characterized by rhythmical tapping of the toes and heels.

1928 *Daily Express* 27 June 9 The inventor of tap dancing. **1934** *Evening News* 1 Mar. 11/2 If the working girl doesn't do her bending and stretching, then she joins a tap-dancing class. **1953** R. Lehmann *Echoing Grove* 33 She wished to study tap-dancing, and to broaden the mind. **1972** *Guardian* 29 Jan. 9/4, I started as a dancer: tap dancing, acrobatic dancing, funny dancing. **1977** D. MacKenzie *Raven & Ratcatcher* ii. 19 Tap-dancing schools.

Also **ta·p-dance** *sb.*; also *fig.* and as *v. intr.* (occas. *trans.*); **ta·p-dancer.**

1927 *New Republic* 12 Oct. 210/1 That fair singer, good tap-dancer, born-to-the-purple, bred-in-the-bone, works-while-she-sleeps comedian, the plump May Barnes. **1929** D. Runyon in *Hearst's Internat.* July 56/2 Miss Billy Perry is worth a few peeks, especially when she is out on the floor of Miss Missouri Martin's Sixteen Hundred Club doing her tap dance. **1931** G. Cadwell (*title*) How to tap dance. **1941** *Penguin New Writing* X. 17 The sergeant.. had been a tap-dancer in civilian life. **1946** R. Campbell *Talking Bronco* 25 The tap-dance of the morning stars. **1950** J. D. MacDonald *Brass Cupcake* (1955) i. 11 He stood up and tap-danced me out to the gate. **1963** A. Lubbock *Austral. Roundabout* 100 The moths tap-danced on the fly-screens. **1972** *Guardian* 28 Jan. 9/1 The lacquered, ringletted monsters who tap-danced their way into the weepies. **1974** *Listener* 17 Jan. 92/2 Old-fashioned, out-dated routines: middle-aged black tap-dancers, a middle-aged blonde. **1977** N. Adam *Triplehip Cracksman* xvii. 171 A larger one [*sc.* table] which would have made a good one-shot tap-dance floor. **1978** W. F. Buckley *Stained Glass* xxi. 209 He could be tap dancing on it and still he'd be a goner.

tape, *sb.*^{1} Add: **1. c.** Also used *lit.* or *fig.* in phrases: *to breast the tape*, to reach the finishing-line in a race; *on the tape*, at the very end of a race. Also in *Horse-racing*, a tape or set of tapes suspended across the course at the starting-point of a race; also *fig.*

1903 *Punch* 11 Feb. 103/1 Though a toughish task remains Before I breast the tape, J. Chamberlain, of Birmingham, Will round (or square) the Cape. **1916** J. B. Cooper *Coo-oo-ee* xvii. 270 'They've got me on the tape!' he cried; 'but I'm satisfied.' **1922** Joyce *Ulysses* 608 Judge of his astonishment when he finally did breast the tape and the awful truth dawned upon him anent his better half, wrecked in his affections. **1937** 'P. Wentworth' *Case is Closed* vii. 72 He was running in his school sports, winning the hundred yards again, breasting the tape, hearing the applause break out. **1955** *Times* 13 Aug. 4/2 Wheeler..regained the ground he had lost and just robbed the Hungarian of victory on the tape. **1957**

D. FRANCIS *Sport of Queens* vi. 122 The six or seven stranded starting tapes familiar in flat racing are not used for National Hunt racing. A single strand across the course is pulled down to a catch at shoulder level, and when this is released..the tape flies up at an oblique angle. **1963** *Times* 21 Feb. 4/5 They were described by an official observer after the last N.E.D.C. meeting as 'just coming up to the tapes'.

d. *Army* and *R.A.F. slang.* A chevron indicating rank worn by a non-commissioned officer on the upper part of the coat-sleeve; a stripe (STRIPE *sb.*[3] 2).

1943 HUNT & PRINGLE *Service Slang* 64 *Tapes*, the stripes worn by Corporals, Sergeants, and Flight Sergeants in the R.A.F. and by Lance-Corporals or Lance-Bombardiers, Corporals or Bombardiers, and Sergeants in the Army. **1944** *Gen* 15 Jan. 9/2 That binder's working for his tapes. **1944** *R.A.F. Jrnl.* Aug. 258, I wouldn't leave this unit for three tapes.

2. b. Also used in computing and data processing; = *paper tape* s.v. *PAPER *sb.* 12.

1945 J. VON NEUMANN in B. Randell *Origins of Digital Computers* (1973) 355 These instructions must be given in some form which the device can sense. Punched into a system of punchcards or on teletype tape, magnetically impressed on steel tape or wire, [etc.]. **1948** *Math. Tables & Other Aids Computation* III. 8 Orders to the machine.. are represented on tape by all combinations of three holes out of six. **1960** M. G. SAY et al. *Analogue & Digital Computers* ix. 266 The only problem in fast photoelectric reading arises when the tape has to be set in motion and stopped so rapidly that [etc.]. **1978** D. D. SPENCER *Data Processing* v. 105 Data are often hand-sorted before being punched into the tape.

c. = *magnetic tape* s.v. *MAGNETIC *a.* 5. Cf. *steel tape* (*b*) s.v. *STEEL *sb.*[1] 18.

1932 *Radio Times* 29 July 239/3 The Blattnerphone is an invention for recording magnetically upon steel tape. **1942** *Jrnl. R. Aeronaut. Soc.* XLVI. Abstr. Sci. & Technical Press 68 It consists of recording a sound pattern magnetically on steel tape. The signal is picked up from the tape at frequent split-second intervals. **1953** *Newsweek* 11 May 28/1 It was recorded on tape and was broadcast later that day. **1964** M. MCLUHAN *Understanding Media* xviii. 295 Tape and the l.p. record suddenly made the phonograph a means of access to all the music and speech of the world. **1982** *Times* 26 Oct. 15/7 Access to specific pieces of information is far faster on a compact, rapidly spinning disk than on a long ribbon of tape.

d. A length or reel of (magnetic or paper) tape; a recording on tape.

c **1946** [see *SUBROUTINE]. **1952** W. STEVENS *Let.* 13 May (1967) 750, I read at Cambridge a week or two ago and apparently someone in the audience took a tape. **1956** G. A. MONTGOMERIE *Digital Calculating Machines* x. 213 The instructions are punched in the tapes in a very simple notation. **1966** *Listener* 25 Aug. 287/2 This production came via a tape from the Holland Festival. **1977** *New Yorker* 22 Aug. 56/3 Most thefts of computer tapes are probably not reported to the police. **1978** D. D. SPENCER *Data Processing* v. 105 Both the tapes and the tape-producing equipment require less space than punched cards and card-producing equipment. **1983** D. DUNNETT *Dolly & Bird of Paradise* v. 54 Kim-Jim loved telly films... I had brought a lot of tapes with me.

e. Used in names designating (paper, transparent film, etc.) tape coated with adhesive and used for fastening packages, etc.; usu. as the final element of a Comb., as *adhesive tape, Scotch tape, Sellotape, sticky tape*: see under first element in Suppl.

1966 A. W. LEWIS *Gloss. Woodworking Terms* 99 *Tape*, gummed paper strip used to hold the edges of veneer together while the glue dries.

4. (In sense 2 b) *tape boy, price* (earlier example); (in senses *2 c, d) *tape editing, editor, eraser, head* [*HEAD *sb.* 11 g], *speed, splicing*; *tape-controlled, -playing* adjs.; (in sense *2 e) *tape dispenser*; **tape cartridge** = next (see also quot. 1983); **tape cassette** = *CASSETTE d; **tape-check** *Mus.*: in an upright pianoforte, a type of check (CHECK *sb.*[1] 10 d) developed by Robert Wornum (1780–1852) and incorporating a tape; also *attrib.* in *tape-check action*; **tape deck** (see *DECK *sb.*[1] 3 f); **tape-delay**, the use of a tape recorder to introduce an interval between recording and playing back or transmitting (cf. *DELAY *sb.* 1 c); **tape drive**, a tape transport or tape deck for use in computing; **tape guipure** *Lace-making* (see quots. 1865, 1881); **tape hiss**, extraneous high-frequency background noise during the playing of a tape recording; **tape loop** = *LOOP *sb.*[1] 4 k; **tape-measure** (earlier example); also as *v. trans.*, to measure with a tape-measure; hence **tape measurement; tape player**, a machine for playing (cassette) tape recordings; cf. *record player* s.v. *RECORD *sb.* 14; **tape punch** *Computers*, a device which punches holes in paper tape in patterns that represent coded information; also **tape-punching; tape reader** *Computers*, a device for sensing information recorded by sequences of holes or magnetized areas on computer tape (see *READER 7); also **tape reading; tape reproducer**, a machine that plays or reads tapes but does not record or punch them; **tapescript** [after *transcript, typescript*, etc.], a tape recording of the spoken word, esp. in the form of a lesson, interview, etc.; a transcript or text of this; **tape transport**, a mechanism which controls the movement of recording tape past a stationary head; also, a tape deck. See also *TAPE RECORDER.

1969 *Listener* 2 Jan. 12/1, I was in the Newsroom:.. where..tape boys..bore in huge foaming trays of paper strip to the duty editors. **1961** *High Fidelity Trade News* Sept. 55/3 Foley Electronics offers..an automatic tape cartridge playback unit employing the endless loop principle. **1972** *Observer* (Colour Suppl.) 22 Oct. 53/2 Tape cartridges are plentiful, even if cassette material is strangely lagging. **1983** D. H. SANDARS *Computers Today* vi. 159 (*caption*) Magnetic tape cartridges are used in minicomputers and data entry stations. This tape is ¼ inch wide and varies from 140 to 450 feet in length... Magnetic tape cassettes are used in microcomputers and data entry stations. This tape is either 150 or 300 feet long. **1972** G. V. HIGGINS *Friends of Eddie Coyle* xv. 88 He opened the glove compartment and removed a tape cassette. **1983** Tape cassette [see *tape cartridge* above]. **1929** *Evening News* 18 Nov. 2/6 Pianette... Iron frame. Tape check action. **1954** *Grove's Dict. Mus.* (ed. 5) VI. 739/1 We must now turn our attention to an action known as the 'tape-check'. **1966** W. L. SUMNER *Pianoforte* iii. 66 A later model anticipated the tape-check action, which prevented the hammer from giving unwanted repetition. **1962** *Gloss. Terms Automatic Data Processing* (*B.S.I.*) 98 Tape-controlled carriage. **1949**, etc. Tape deck [see *DECK *sb.*[1] 3 f]. **1967** *Oxf. Computer Explained* 7 A new configuration..consisting of twelve 30 kc tape decks, a high speed printer, a paper-tape reader, and a monitor printer. **1977** 'E. CRISPIN' *Glimpses of Moon* xii. 242 His stereo tape-deck only a few seconds away from the enormous climax of *Also Sprach Zarathustra*. **1968** *Listener* 12 Dec. 802/3 The music dissolves again, surmounted by quiet seagull sounds produced by high squeaks of feed back multiplied by means of tape-delay. **1983** *Ibid.* 18 Aug. 27/1 The catalyst which sets *Clocks and Clouds* in motion is the gradual de-synchronisation of identical melodic patterns—the classic 'tape-delay' device of electronic music. **1975** *New Yorker* 10 Mar. 31/1 An automatic tape dispenser. **1952** *Proc. Electronic Computer Symp., Los Angeles* (IRE Prof. Group Electronic Computers) 4 (*heading*) Survey of tape drive systems. **1978** J. MCNEIL *Consultant* x. 114 The computers..showed little signs of life beyond the occasional twitch from the tape drives. **1983** D. H. SANDARS *Computers Today* vi. 163 Before the data on a magnetic tape can be processed by a computer, the tape must be placed in a machine called a tape drive or tape transport. **1961** *Times* 17 Apr. 3/1 Knowledge of radio-production and tape-editing. **1973** G. TALBOT *Ten Seconds from Now* xix. 239 A wonderland of recording rooms and tape-editing suites. **1959** 'F. NEWTON' *Jazz Scene* x. 169 Recording supervisors, sound engineers and tape editors. **1958** *Oxf. Mail* 27 Aug. (Suppl.) 4/6 (Advt.), The..tape eraser will erase the contents of a spool of tape of any size up to ten inches at one operation. **1865** F. B. PALLISER *Hist. Lace* iii. 35 In that class called by the lace-makers 'tape guipure', the outline of the flowers is formed by a pillow or hand-made braid about the eighth of an inch in width, the middle filled in with the needle. **1881** C. C. HARRISON *Woman's Handiwork* 1. 94 Tape-guipure, made of linen tape twisted and folded into a pattern, held together with bars and then filled in and enriched with needlework. **1882** CAULFEILD & SAWARD *Dict. Needlework* 246/2 An embroidery worked in imitation of the Tape Guipure Laces. **1960** *Practical Wireless* XXXVI. 401/2 (Advt.), Luxury model with press-button inputs to suit any pick-up or tuner and most tape-heads. **1980** *Sunday Times* 24 Aug. 14/7 Magnetic patterns on the tape are translated by a tape-head into electrical impulses. **1962** A. NISBETT *Technique Sound Studio* ii. 38 There may be tape hiss due to setting the gain too low. **1977** *Gramophone* Oct. 638/2 The tape hiss seems now to be higher too. **1962** Tape loop [see *LOOP *sb.*[1] 4 k]. **1976** W. H. CANAWAY *Willow-Pattern War* xx. 199 The signal would be going out from a tape-loop. **1873** *Young Englishwoman* Mar. 151/2 Pin your tape-measure down on one of the fronts. **1962** L. DEIGHTON *Ipcress File* xxv. 158 Birth marks..were photographed and tape measured. **1971** LAVER & COLLINS *Educ. Tennis Player* i. 19 Dave Anderson..tape-measured me..and reported that my left forearm is twelve inches around. **1922** JOYCE *Ulysses* 523 Tape measurements will be taken next your skin. **1961** *High Fidelity Trade News* Sept. 55/3 (*heading*) Foley presents 'endless loop' tape player. **1977** *New Yorker* 24 Oct. 112/3 Such misdeeds as..having a tape player on too loud. **1962** *Times* 5 July 15/6 Tape-playing equipment to the value of some £160 altogether was being used. **1889** *Hints to Speculators* (G. Gregory & Co.) (ed. 5) 20 Deal at tape prices. **1947** [see *tape reader* below]. **1967** A.BATTERSBY *Network Analysis* (ed. 2) viii. 134 The sheets are then passed to a tape-punch operator who converts the information on them into a punched tape. **1951** M. V. WILKES et al. *Preparation of Programs for Electronic Digital Computer* 42 (*heading*) Tape punching and editing facilities. **1947** *Math. Tables & Other Aids to Computation* II. 355 In addition to these parts there are.. a drum commutator for operating the relays, a tape reader and a tape punch. **1964** C. DENT *Quantity Surveying by Computer* iii. 26 The program is all ready to be read by the input tape-reader at 300 characters per second. **1972** M. WOODHOUSE *Mama Doll* x. 143 It's frequency-coded for a tape-reader. **1970** O. DOPPING *Computers & Data Processing* xv. 237 Tape reading and tape writing can go on partly simultaneously, if the design of the computer allows it. **1961** Tape reproducer [see *REPRODUCER 2]. **1962** *Gloss. Terms Autom. Data Processing* (*B.S.I.*) 97 *Tape reproducer*, a machine used to copy and edit paper tape. **1962** A. NISBETT *Technique Sound Studio* 246 *Control cubicle* (BBC), the soundproof room equipped with control desk, gramophone and tape reproducers and high quality loudspeaker. **1961** J. S. HOLTON et al. *Sound Lang. Teaching* 248 *Tapescript*, term used to describe the written program (exercises and instructions) that the teacher has prepared for recording a language laboratory lesson. **1969** *John Edwards Mem. Foundation Q.* V. 1. 10 These tapescripts..are resumés of interviews of artists. **1983** *Financial Times* 16 Apr. 14 It is telly docu-drama at its most truth-honouring; based on real tapescripts, speeches and official records. **1954** *Gramophone Record Rev.* Jan. 139/1 With a tape speed of 7½ ins. per second the capstan thus makes about 80 revolutions per second. **1956** *Language* XXXII. 281 These experiments served as a test for two tape-splicing techniques. **1954** *Trans. IRE Audio* II. 23/1 The overall design of a tape transport for a professional tape recording system is very complex. **1981** *Hi-Fi Answers* Nov. 117/1 The tape transport is press button controlled, and operation appears to be achieved by a combination of mechanical and electrical means. **1983** Tape transport [see *tape drive* above].

tape, *v.* Add: **1. a.** Also, to affix or fasten (*up*) with adhesive tape.

1956 A. H. COMPTON *Atomic Quest* iv. 259 Alvarez taped three copies of this note to instrument boxes. **1972** *Daily Colonist* (Victoria, B.C.) 18 Jan. 17/1 Every girl.. should clip it out and tape it to her bedroom mirror. **1979** R. JAFFE *Class Reunion* (1980) I. i. 36 Daphne had taped up small museum reproductions of famous paintings and prints.

b. *spec.* to bind or gag (a victim, etc.) with adhesive tape. Also with *up*.

1932 'SPINDRIFT' *Yankee Slang* 60 *Tape a guy*, gag a victim with adhesive plaster. **1950** 'P. QUENTIN' *Follower* xix. 135 Once they'd taped his wrists, all hope would be gone. **1962** 'H. HOWARD' *Double Finesse* vi. 69 It shouldn't take Alan longer than that to tape the night-watchman's mouth. **1977** D. ANTHONY *Stud Game* xiv. 84 He knocks you out..tapes you up neatly, and calls us to come and get you. **1981** P. MALLORY *Killing Matter* xv. 157 Tie her and tape her.

2. b. *Gunnery.* To get the range of (a position), by means of a tape-line used in conjunction with a range-finder; hence, to hit and silence (a target).

See also sense 5 below.

1917 A. G. EMPEY *From Fire Step* xi. 65 Our artillery had taped or silenced them [*sc.* the trench mortars]. *Ibid.* xxi. 146 The German artillery..had us taped (ranged) for fair; it was worth your life to expose yourself for an instant. **1919** J. B. MORTON *Barber of Putney* iii. 45 There's a sniper got that corner taped. **1919** G. K. ROSE *2/4th Oxf. & Bucks L.I.* 36 The Pozières ridge, whose crest was well 'taped' by the German guns. **1927** E. THOMPSON *These Men thy Friends* iii. 70 'He tried them at sixteen hundred yards, and got nowhere near them—lengthened the range a thousand, and was still short. But Johnny [Turk] had *us* taped' he added. 'No bothering about mirage for him. He knew the land and the distance of every blotch and pimple on it.'

5. Colloq. phr. *to get* or *have* (someone or something) *taped*: to size up, ascertain, or understand fully (someone or something).

The development of this phrase is unclear. It may have arisen as a figurative use of sense 1 with the idea of 'tying up, having under control or in order' (cf. quot. 1854 in Dict.) or of sense 2 with the idea of 'measuring, assessing'.

1914 JOYCE *Dubliners* 210, I never saw such an eye in a man's head. It was at much as to say: *I have you properly taped, my lad.* He had an eye like a hawk. **1919** *War Slang* in *Athenæum* 18 July 632/2 'I got you taped,' an N.C.O. may say to a man, meaning 'I know what you are up to.' **1929** J. B. PRIESTLEY *Good Companions* I. iv. 114 We've made a 'ell of a bad break if we tell 'er oo we are and then there's nothing doin'. Got us taped then. **1944** A. E. COPPARD in *Wine & Food* XLIII. 153, I want to get off the land. Can you find a boat? Not a motor-boat, that's noisy and they've got the harbour taped for sure. **1959** *Times Lit. Suppl.* 13 Mar. 142/4 The main part of the book, with its cold effort to get Mencken 'taped'. **1977** *Evening Post* (Nottingham) 27 Jan. 6/5 And so say all of us. Let's hope Portland have illiteracy 'taped'.

6. To record on (magnetic) tape; to make a tape recording of. Also *absol.*

1950 *Senior Scholastic* 1 Mar. 25T (*heading*) We tape it. Recorders produce a transformation in the classroom. **1958** S. ELLIN *Eighth Circle* (1959) II. ii. 41 He's being taped Sunday, so have one of the girls make a transcript of the tape. **1960** *Guardian* 9 Nov. 11/1 One [teenager] with a tape recorder can tape a pile of 'pop' records. **1966** E. MCGIRR *Funeral was in Spain* 40 Okay, men, let's hear his verbal run through. I understand you didn't tape. **1975** R. H. RIMMER *Premar Experiments* (1976) i. 130 I've tried taping sober, high on alcohol, and stoned on grass. **1978** R. NIXON *Mem.* 501, I was not comfortable with the idea of taping people without their knowledge.

taped *ppl. a.* (examples in sense *6); also with *out*, measured or sized up; fully ascertained (cf. senses *2 b, *5); **taping** *vbl. sb.* (examples).

1929 *Papers Mich. Acad. Sci., Arts & Lett.* X. 329/1 *Taped out*, an expression applied to a strip of land upon which the German gunners had accurately registered distances. **1933** WODEHOUSE in *Sat. Even. Post* 30 Dec. 58/2 Didn't I tell you that I had everything taped out? **1953** POHL & KORNBLUTH *Space Merchants* (1955) v. 55 What..have you got to back that statement up with? Letters? Memos? Taped calls? **1955** I. A. RICHARDS *Speculative Instruments* x. 122 The study of language, even in the most elementary stages, has to be a dependant of that highest generic taping which may be called ethics. **1960** *Daily Mirror* 23 Apr. 18/3 Bobby Darin..left behind a taped Saturday Spectacular... This will be shown on ITV tonight. **1968** H. WAUGH *Con Game* xii. 109 A few of the people connected with the show had got together after the taping. **1972** R. PRAWER JHABVALA *New Dominion* I. 58 He kept turning on the taped music and the concealed lighting.

‖ **tapénade** (tapenad). Also **tapenade.** [Fr., f. Prov. *tapéno* capers.] A Provencal dish, usu. served as an hors d'œuvre, made principally from black olives, capers, and anchovies.

1952 G. MAUROIS *Cooking with Fr. Touch* iii. 56 Here is a southern (Nice) recipe for *tapenade*, which uses eggs, olives, and anchovies. *Ibid.*, *La tapenade* used always to figure on the list of hors d'œuvres at the old Hotel Victoria in Cannes. **1960** E. DAVID *Fr. Provincial Cooking* 142 To make the *tapénade*, called after the capers (*tapéno* in Provençal) which go into it. *Ibid.*, The *tapénade* is served pressed down into little deep yellow earthenware pots, like a pâté. **1966** P. V. PRICE *France: Food & Wine Guide* 299 Tapenade or tapanda. Pounded black olives, served on toast or as an *hors d'œuvres.* **1978** *Times* 20 May 10/2 Regular dishes such as tapénade (a Provençal purée of capers, black olives, anchovies, and sometimes tunny fish).

taper, *sb.*¹ Add: **2.** *taper-candlestick*, *-light* (later example), *-stick* (later examples, as an antique).

1847 GOUGH & PARKER *Gloss. Terms Heraldry* 70 The *taper-candlestick*, borne in the arms of the Founders' Company..has a spike, or..a pricket, upon which the taper is placed. **1913** W. DE LA MARE *Peacock Pie* 119 Lantern-light, taper-light, Torchlight. **1956** G. TAYLOR *Silver* v. 114 *Taper Sticks.* Examples do not occur in silver until the later part of the period, and are generally miniature candlesticks. **1982** *Nat. Art-Coll. Fund Ann. Rep. 1981* 39/2 Taper-sticks were made to hold tapers for lighting candles or pipes, and generally have flat circular bases and narrow sockets.

taper, *sb.*² Add: **II. 2.** *spec.* in *Forestry* (see quot. 1957).

1893 P. J. CARTER *Treatise Mensuration Timber* i. 5 Long logs should be measured in two or more sections.. the sections increasing..with the taper of each log. **1945** G. B. GRUNDY *Fifty-Five Years at Oxford* vii. 132 A scale of taper which means the number of inches a tree decreases in girth between its base..and a point in its circumference ten or twenty feet above that. **1957** *Brit. Commonwealth Forest Terminol.* II. 194 *Taper*, the decrease in diameter of a tree bole or log from the base upwards.

4. Taper-Lock, taper-lock *Mech.*, a proprietary name in the U.S. for a type of tapered bush (BUSH *sb.*² 1 b) inserted into a pulley, sprocket, etc., to enable it to be mounted rigidly on a shaft; **taper tap** *Mech.*, a tap (TAP *sb.*¹ 4) tapered lengthways for about two thirds of its length, used to begin the process of cutting a screw thread in a hole.

1954 *Official Gaz.* (U.S. Patent Office) 4 May 31/1 Dodge Manufacturing Corporation, Mishawaka... *Taper-Lock*... For machine elements to be mounted on shafts and bushings therefor. **1971** *Engineering* Apr. 4/2 Pulleys..complete with Taper-Lock bushes for fast, easy fixing. **1971** *Power Farming* Mar. 75/2 The new pulley illustrated incorporates the quick-fit taper-lock centre. *a* **1877** KNIGHT *Dict. Mech.* III. 2495/1 The process of screw-cutting was greatly improved by Maudslay, who introduced the practice of having three cutting edges, and using three taps, the entering taper tap, the middle tap, and the plug tap. **1964** S. CRAWFORD *Basic Engin. Processes* i. 24 The taper tap has a chamfer or tapered lead for a length of 8–10 threads.

taper, *sb.*³ Add: **a.** (Earlier example.)

1881 *Instructions to Census Clerks* (1885) 68 *Looming and Taping Room* [in Cotton Manufacture]:..Taper. Beam Flanger. Beamer.

b. One who tapes or deals with tape in other occupations.

1921 *Dict. Occup. Terms* (1927) § 304 Coil taper,.. binds coils with tape. **1927** *Daily Express* 2 Dec. 2/4 Taper,..[an] operator in charge of the insulation of armature.

taper, *a.* Add: **b.** † Also, of a person: reduced in funds, short (of money). (Earlier example.)

1789 J. BYNG *Torrington Diaries* (1935) II. 88 So now, being taper of the said necessary commodity [*sc.* cash], I was obliged to recruit from M. Oliver.

c. *taper roller bearing*, a roller bearing in which the rollers are tapered slightly and lie at an angle to the axis of the bearing, so as to provide resistance to thrust along the axis as well as at right angles to it.

1930 *Engineering* 7 Feb. 169/3 The driving wheels..are mounted on taper-roller bearings. **1971** *Power Farming* Mar. 50/1 The Benedict Soilmaster takes care of seed bed cultivations—and your tractor... No gears, no cranks and adjustable taper-roller bearings result in minimal maintenance.

taper, *v.* Add: **2. b.** (Earlier *colloq.* example.) Also const. *down.*

1848 J. F. COOPER *Oak-Openings* I. iv. 66 It's hard to give up old habits, all at once. If I could only taper off on a pint a day, [etc.]. **1960** *Wall St. Jrnl.* 18 Nov. 13/1 Carloadings 'taper down' starting in mid-November, when the bulk of Christmas shipping has been completed. **1971** *Daily Tel.* 4 Aug. 2/7 The deal is worth nearly £4-a-week more to the lower grades tapering down to £2 at the top end.

3. b. (Later example.) Also const. *down.*

1971 *Daily Tel.* 2 Aug. 7/8 There is speculation that the Government investment..in tracked hovercraft is to be tapered off. **1977** *Lancet* 23 Apr. 909/2 Oral prednisolone, 1 mg/kg/day, was resumed and rapidly tapered down to 0·5 mg/kg/day.

tape re·cord. *rare.* [f. TAPE *sb.*¹ + RECORD *sb.*] A record(ing) on magnetic or other tape.

1905 *Talking Machine News* III. 57/1 A tape record could be made to be reproduced by either the cylinder of [*sic*] disc type of machine. **1914** *Sci. Abstr.* B. XVII. 372 The author submits some tape records which are reproduced. **1961** Y. OLSSON *Syntax Eng. Verb* ii. 17 Speech in its natural environment or in tape-record tapping. **1968** *Listener* 6 June 733/2 Fuzzy telephones or muzzy tape records.

ta·pe-record, *v.* [Back-formation from next.] *trans.* To record (sounds, etc.) on magnetic tape by means of a tape recorder.

1950 *Aviation Week* 6 Mar. 35 (*heading*) Plane-tower talk tape-recorded. **1955** E. WARNER *Trial by Sasswood* ix. 177 As though your thoughts..had been tape-recorded and played back to you. **1967** A. HENRI in *Penguin Mod. Poets* X. 25, I sit here..trying to taperecord the sound of windflowers and celandines. **1978** N. J. CRISP *London Deal* vii. 110 Could we tape record this?

Hence **ta·pe-recorded** *ppl. a.*

1951 *Time* 25 June 23/2 Testimony continued—part of it played scratchily from long, tape-recorded interviews with addicts. **1973** S. TRUEMAN *Fascinating New Brunswick* xvi. 125 Her tape-recorded folksongs have left a priceless heritage to New Brunswick.

ta·pe reco:rder. Also with hyphen. [f. TAPE *sb.*¹ + RECORDER¹.] † **1.** A device which records data on 'ticker' tape. *Obs.*

1892 W. P. LOMBARD in *Jrnl. Physiol.* XIII. 4 The labour of measuring the curves and of computing the total work was so great..that it was found necessary to devise an apparatus which would record automatically the total height to which the weight was lifted. This apparatus, which may be called a tape recorder, consisted of an endless tape. **1922** *Science & Invention* Feb. 935 The accompanying diagram shows a very interesting special arrangement with relay for operating a tape recorder, klaxon or telegraph sounder.

2. An apparatus for recording sounds, etc. on magnetic tape and afterwards reproducing them.

1932 *B.B.C. Techn. Tables & Gloss.* 65/2 Steel Tape Recorder. **1949** *Consumer Reports* Feb. 68/2 The three tape models all proved..substantially more convenient than earlier tape recorders and better than..the wire recorders tested. **1949** *Electronic Engin.* XXI. 369 There will be a selection from the very wide range of G.E.C. sound equipment..and the new G.E.C. Tape Recorder. **1953** M. MCCARTHY *Groves of Academe* xiii. 252 The psychology student with the tape-recorder. **1964** M. MCLUHAN *Understanding Media* (1967) v. 63 Radio and gramophone and tape recorder gave us back the poet's voice. **1978** J. A. MICHENER *Chesapeake* 854 From the moment Amos discovered what those newfangled tape recorders could do, he was satisfied that his..problems were solved.

Also **tape recordist**, one who makes tape recordings.

1960 *Guardian* 9 Nov. 11/1 The tape recordists were clearly making money out of their activities. **1970** J. EARL *Tuners & Amplifiers* iii. 70 If you are a keen tape recordist then the amplifier should certainly be equipped with at least source sockets for tape replay.

ta·pe reco:rding, (*vbl.*) *sb.* [f. TAPE *sb.*¹ + RECORDING *vbl. sb.*, after prec.] A record (of sounds, etc.) on magnetic tape; the process of making such a recording.

1940 *Electronics* May 16 (*heading*) Photo-electric tape recording. *Ibid.* 17/1 The editor of such tape recordings has considerable freedom in arranging the material. **1946** *Electronic Engin.* XVIII. 54 (*heading*) German tape-recording equipment. **1954** A. HUXLEY *Let.* 12 Dec. (1969) 718, I listened to the tape recording and the foreign language certainly doesn't sound like the gibberish of ordinary glossolalia. **1962** A. LURIE *Love & Friendship* xiv. 286 His voice sounded funny to him, like a tape-recording. **1977** P. STREVENS *New Orientations Teaching Eng.* xiii. 163 A set of specialized tape recording/replay machines.

tapering, *vbl. sb.* Add: Also *tapering-off.*

1890 W. JAMES *Princ. Psychol.* I. iv. 124 The question of 'tapering-off', in abandoning such habits as drink and opium-indulgence, comes in here. **1955** KOESTLER *Trail of Dinosaur* 136 The Jews alone among the varied European immigrant population have resisted this 'tapering off' process.

tapestry, *sb.* Add: **1. c.** Now freq. applied to (pieces of) canvas embroidery executed typically with wool in tent stitch.

1882 CAULFEILD & SAWARD *Dict. Needlework* 473/2 Tapestry worked by the needle..differs but slightly from Embroidery. The stitches are made to lie close together, so that no portion of the foundation is visible. **1955** *Stitchcraft* Mar. 9 The design [for a picture] is worked in tent-stitch by the counted thread..; the chart includes instructions for tent-stitch and hints on stretching tapestry. **1971** *Harrods Magical Christmas* 9 Tapestry Cushion Pack of tramme canvas, wools and needle. *Ibid.*, If desired, we will stretch and mount the finished tapestry on velvet. **1976** P. CLABBURN *Needleworker's Dict.* 263/3 Nowadays in Britain, any piece of canvas work, large or small, is called tapestry work, which is a misnomer, while America, although not falling into that particular trap, calls canvas work needlepoint, which is also confusing as that word should apply to lace made with a needle.

2. Also short for *tapestry needle*, sense 3 below.

1895 *Montgomery Ward Catal.* Spring & Summer 88/1 Needle Case... Contains—..Crewel..Tapestry..Bodkin. **1968** J. IRONSIDE *Fashion Alphabet* 94 *Tapestry*, a needle which has a blunt point and large eye, used for embroidery with wool.

3. *tapestry room* (examples), *wool*; **tapestry needle,** a blunt needle with a large eye used in tapestry-making and canvas embroidery.

1888–9 *T. Eaton & Co. Catal.* Fall & Winter 64/2 The Household Needle Case contains darners, glovers, square-carpet, yarn, chenille, tapestry,..and crewel needles. **1967** E. LEMARCHAND *Death of Old Girl* xvii. 196 Tim Pollard watched her..as she plied a tapestry needle. **1817** M. EDGEWORTH *Harrington* xviii. 496 Mr. Montenero.. asked, in particular, about a tapestry room,—a picture of Sir Josseline. **1977** R. PLAYER *Month of Mangled Models* vi. 105 The casements of the Tapestry Room were wide span, and the Camelot curtains had been pulled back. **1880** L. HIGGIN *Handbk. Embroidery* i. 4 *Tapestry Wool* is more than twice the thickness of crewel... Tapestry wool is not yet made in all shades. **1960** G. LEWIS *Handbk. Crafts* 36 The most usual wool for this work is that with a slight twist to it called 'tapestry' wool, but other kinds may be used according to the mesh of the canvas.

tapestry-worker. (Later example.)

1908 H. PENTIN *Judith* iv. 77 'Judith and Holofernes' was also a favourite subject for tapestry-workers.

‖ **tapette** (tapet), *sb.* (and *a.*). [F. *tapette* pederast, homosexual (*slang*), f. *taper* to tap, hit + *-ette*, fem. suffix.] A passive male homosexual; an effeminate man or 'pansy'. Also as *adj.*

1930 E. WAUGH *Vile Bodies* ii. 22 My dear, he looks terribly *tapette.* **1936** 'R. WEST' *Thinking Reed* xiii. 455 'It will make my room look as if I were a *tapette*!' exclaimed Marc. **1949** A. WILSON *Wrong Set* 174 She replied '..you do look madly tapette when you're drunk.' **1960** J. BALDWIN *Another Country* (1963) II. i. 183 Yves had lived by his wits in the streets of Paris, as a semi-*tapette*, and as a *rat d'hôtel.* **1978** J. SHERWOOD *Limericks of Lachasse* xv. 181 My mother..wondered if you were perhaps *tapette*, but my brothers assured her that..you were perfectly masculine.

taphonomy (tæfǫ·nǒmi). *Palæont.* [f. Gr. τάφος grave + -NOMY.] The study of the processes by which animal and plant remains become preserved as fossils. Hence **tapho-no·mic, -ical** *adjs.*; **tapho·nomist**, a specialist in taphonomy.

1940 J. A. EFREMOV in *Pan-Amer. Geol.* LXXIV. 93, I propose for this part of palaeontology the name of 'Taphonomy', the science of the laws of embedding. *Ibid.*, Taphonomical research allows us to glance into the depth of ages from another point of view. **1971** *Nature* 8 Oct. 391/2 There seem to be neither palaeoecological nor taphonomical features of the formation that would preclude *Hipparion* being represented in the assemblage. **1974** *Times* 2 Mar. 14/2 Russian scientists have brought together a team of geologists..and a group of taphonomists: the last belong to a speciality created in Russia for studying the way animals and plants are preserved in their burial sites. **1974** *Nature* 8 Mar. 100/3 Sessions were devoted to..patterns of diversity and implications of taphonomic evidence for behaviour patterns. **1977** LEAKEY & LEWIN *Origins* i. 12/2 Any scientific meeting on our origins nowadays might be attended by archeologists..[and] taphonomists. **1981** *Nature* 10 Dec. 598/3 Palaeontologists are..bringing their subject out of the museum through studies of the processes by which the fossil record forms (taphonomy). *Ibid.*, Much of the book concentrates on the principles, methods of study and results of taphonomic studies of (mainly) African vertebrates.

taphrogenesis (tæfrodʒe·nėsis). *Geol.* Also **tafro-.** [ad. G. *tafrogenese* (E. Krenkel *Die Bruchzonen Ostafrikas* (1922) v. 181), *taphrogenese* (—— *Geologie Afrikas* (1928) II. 636), f. Gr. τάφρος pit: see -GENESIS.] The formation of large-scale geological structures by high-angle or block faulting, esp. as the result of tensional forces in the crust. Hence **taphroge·nic** *a.*

1923 *Bull. Geol. Soc. Amer.* XXXIV. 200 Faulting through tension [in East Africa] has gone on in compensation for the orogeny elsewhere. Therefore tafrogenesis (from the Greek for rifts or graben) is the counterpart of orogenesis, and East Africa is the type area for tafrogenic structures. **1963** E. S. HILLS *Elem. Structural Geol.* xi. 315 Taphrogenic movements—The necessity to recognise a third type of movement is indicated by the tectonic importance of major belts of block faulting, notably the rift valley and graben zones... The term was coined for the East African rifts, and is largely descriptive. In general, however, it implies tensional forces as opposed to horizontal compression for orogeny and differential vertical movements for epeirogeny. **1978** *Nature* 9 Mar. 158/2 Sedimentation has been controlled by NW–SE trending faults in close relationship to the taphrogenesis of the SW–NE trending Benue trough. **1979** *Ibid.* 7 June 478/3 There may be a long time interval between initial taphrogenic activity ('rifting') and creation of ocean floor by spreading ('drifting').

tapidaro, tapidero, varr. TAPADERO in Dict. and Suppl.

tapioca. Add: Also 9 **tabiaca.** (Earlier examples of *tapioca pudding*.)

1837 W. TAYLER *Diary* 14 May in J. Burnett *Useful Toil* (1974) II. 181 They had two soles fried with saws.. a tabiaca pudding, cheese and butter. **1859** D. BUNCE *Travels with Dr. Leichhardt* 107 Christmas day..tapioca pudding, each man having as much as he could eat.

tapis, *sb.* Add: ‖ **c.** *tapis vert*, a long strip of grass-covered ground; a grass walk. Cf. CARPET *sb.* 3.

1960 O. MANNING *Great Fortune* III. 215 They were walking down the main path beside the *tapis vert.* **1965** MRS. L. B. JOHNSON *White House Diary* 9 Mar. (1970) 248 He wants to..preserve the tapis vert, the long green ribbon that stretches..from the Capitol to the Lincoln Memorial. **1976** D. WOOD *Pract. Garden Design* ii. 42 Two steps down..to the enclosed gardens on either side of the *tapis vert*—'green carpet'.

Tapleyism (tæ·pli,iz'm). [f. the name of Mark *Tapley*, a character in Dickens's *Martin Chuzzlewit* (1843–4) + -ISM.] Optimism in the most hopeless circumstances, as expressed by Tapley's determination always to remain 'jolly'. Also **Ta·pleyan** *a.*

1857 B. SMITH *Let.* in W. James *Mem. & Stud.* (1911) ix. 246, I have a good share of Tapleyism in me and come out strong under difficulties. **1900** F. W. MAITLAND *Let.* 22 Jan. (1965) 209 Your letter..told me more than I had learned from any newspapers about the gloom of England, though I had read something between lines which seemed to me Tapleyan. **1972** *Scots Observer* 12 Mar. 2/2 What impressed me..was the grim way they held on to optimism... If that is Tapleyism..then Tapleyism is a fine thing.

tapped, *ppl. a.*[1] (In Dict. s.v. TAP *v.*[1]) (Examples in sense 2 c of the vb.)

1925 P. J. RISDON *Crystal Receivers & Circuits* 9 In the case of a tapped inductance coil, the wire is tapped at every turn for so many turns, for fine adjustment, and then once every few turns for coarse adjustment. **1964** L. DEIGHTON *Funeral in Berlin* v. 37 Transcripts of tapped phone calls. **1978** D. MURPHY *Place Apart* ii. 22 He called in a disguised message over the tapped phone that he would be over that evening.

tapped, *ppl. a.*[2] [f. TAP *v.*[2] + -ED[1].] **a.** *Phonetics.* Pronounced with a tap (see *TAP *sb.*[2] 1 d). **b.** *tapped penalty* (Rugby Football), a penalty taken with a tap-kick (see *TAP *sb.*[2] 4).

1964 R. H. ROBINS *Gen. Linguistics* 101 A flapped or tapped /r/..when the tongue tip lightly and momentarily touches the alveolar ridge is common between two vowels (as in *merry*). **1966** R. E. ASHER in C. E. Bazell *In Memory of J. R. Firth* 17, *r* is a tapped alveolar consonant. **1977** *Observer* 22 May 23/3 Bevan took a tapped penalty 15 yards from his own line.

tapper[1]. Add: **2. b.** One who 'touches' another for money; a beggar. Cf. TAP *v.*[1] 3 in Dict. and Suppl. *slang.*

1930 G. SMITHSON *Raffles in Real Life* xiv. 189 He was a hanger-on, a common cadger, a 'tapper'. **1939** J. WORBY *Spiv's Progress* iv. 32, I didn't have time to light a cigarette before I was accosted by a tapper. **1962** *John o' London's* 25 Jan. 82/2 One who lives by cadging or begging is a *bummer*, *knocker* or *tapper*.

c. One who taps (TAP *v.*[1] 2 c) telegraph or telephone wires; a phone-tapper, a wire-tapper.

1973 P. TAMONY *Americanisms* (typescript) No. 33. 7 Thirty three states legislated total wiretap bans.., while six created partial bans which allowed police to tap.., but forbidding private tappers under any conditions. **1976** *Time* 27 Dec. 42/2 Halperin..was furious at learning that the FBI had tapped his telephone... Last week Morton Halperin won a resounding victory that could cost his tappers, starting with President Nixon, nearly $1 million in damages. **1980** E. BEHR *Getting Even* xv. 170 He delivered an oblique message in Chinese... The tappers might not even tell the difference.

Tappertitian (tæpərti·ʃən), *a. rare.* [f. the name of Simon *Tappertit*, a conceited apprentice in Dickens's *Barnaby Rudge* (1841) + -IAN.] Characteristic of or resembling Tappertit, esp. in his amorous approaches to Dolly Varden.

1895 G. B. SHAW in *Sat. Rev.* 19 Jan. 94/1 One's gorge rose at the Tappertitian vulgarity and infamy of the thing. **1903** —— *Man & Superman* p. xxviii, I have been proof against the garish splendors and alcoholic excitements of the ordinary stage combinations of Tappertitian romance with the police intelligence. **1949** ST. J. ERVINE *Craigavon* II. lxi. 287 Had they been, there would not have been any procession of Tappertitian playboys.

tapping, *vbl. sb.*[1] Add: **2.** (Examples in senses 2 c, 3 of the vb.)

1931 T. HORSLEY *Odyssey of Out-of-Work* xxiii. 243 You do the tapping; I'll wait for you at the gate. **1955** 'E. CRISPIN' *Fen Country* (1979) 54 A line from your special switchboard..could be made safe from tapping. **1966** *Times* 14 Nov. 10/6 Mr. Russell Kerr..is to ask the Home Secretary..on how many occasions warrants have been issued for the tapping of M.P.s' private telephones.

b. *spec.* in *Electr. Engin.*, an intermediate connection made in a winding.

1903 K. EDGCOMBE *Whittaker's Electrical Engineer's Pocket Bk.* 244 The secondary of one of the transformers is wound to give a voltage equal to the required three-phase line-to-line voltage, and is divided into two equal parts by a middle tapping. **1934** *Discovery* Oct. 301/2 Twelve tappings are fitted to give an impedance range of 1·6 to 25,000 ohms. **1950** *Engineering* 22 Sept. 245/3 Tappings from the secondary and filament windings are connected to the electrodes. **1975** G. J. KING *Audio Handbk.* iii. 71 A tapping on the resistive element facilitates coupling of the loudness filter.

c. (sense *2 b) *tapping point*; **tapping coil** *Electr. Engin.*, a coil which acts as a tapping.

1933 P. KEMP *Alternating Current Electr. Engin.* (ed. 4) xiv. 188 In order to permit of a slight variation in the secondary terminal voltage, it is usual to provide a number of tapping coils in the L.T. winding. **1958** J. SHEPHERD et al. *Higher Electr. Engin.* xiv. 344 The tapping coils are placed physically in the centre of the transformer limb to avoid unbalanced axial forces acting on the coils. *Ibid.* 343 If..contact with position 2 is made before contact with position 1 is broken, the coils connected between these two tapping points are short-circuited, and will carry damagingly heavy currents.

tapping, *vbl. sb.*[2] Add: **a.** Also *spec.* tap-dancing.

1944 J. JOHNS *A.B.C. Tap Dancing* 2 'Tapping' has few stable rules but limitless variations.

c. tapping key *Electr.* = KEY *sb.*[1] 12 a.

1916 'BOYD CABLE' *Action Front* 173 These [orderlies]..brought them long screeds to be translated to the tapping keys. **1938** *Brit. Jrnl. Psychol.* XXIX. 41 Two tapping keys..were placed below the handles.

tapsell (tæ·ps'l). [Origin uncertain.] *tapsell gate*, a type of churchyard gate peculiar to Sussex, which turns about a central post.

1922 H. ALLCROFT *Downland Pathways* 114 You approach the building through a 'tapsel-gate'. **1947** E. MEYNELL *Sussex* vi. 134 One of those curious gates, swinging on a central post, known as tapsell gates. **1957** H. HALL *Some Sussex Sayings & Crafts* 181 *Tapsell gate*, this ingenious gate is peculiar to Sussex, but nothing is known of its origin or its designer. Its special use is to prevent cattle entering churchyards and to make room for coffin bearers to pass through easily... Today there are only six in the country. **1969** *Daily Tel.* 27 Feb. 21/8 Tapsell gates sometimes have a hook or spring-catch or even are chained and padlocked. **1979** *Country Life* 15 Mar. 726 Tapsell gates, which turn on a central pivot, are peculiar to Sussex. It has been suggested that they are so-called after one Tapsell, a Sussex iron-master.

tap-tap, tap-tapping: see also *TAP *v.*[2] 2.

tapu (tā·pū), var. TABOO, TABU *a.* and *sb.* (Largely a regional variation, esp. in *N.Z.*: see note at the dominant form.) **A.** *adj.* **a.** = TABOO *a.* Also (*rarely*) *fig.*

1832 H. WILLIAMS *Jrnl.* 18 Jan. in H. Carleton *Life H. Williams* (1874) 114 The canoe was *tapu*, having conveyed the body of Heagi..to his former place. **1849** W. T. POWER *Sketches in N.Z.* p. xliv, A barbarous murder was committed by some of the natives under the protection of Rangihaeta, who refused to give them up; moreover, making the road 'tapu' which communicated between the coast and Wellington. **1873** [see TABOO, TABU *a.* a]. **1902** G. B. SHAW *Mrs. Warren's Profession* p. xiii, Mrs Warren's profession must be either tapu altogether, or else exhibited with the warning side as freely displayed as the tempting side. **1936** *Discovery* Jan. 14/1 The Maoris had found out that the Morioris were a very *tapu* people. **1967** A. & D. REID *Paddle Wheels on Wanganui* iv. 33 The bodies were recovered and laid in the old house which was then declared tapu. **1978** P. GRACE *Mutuwhenua* ix. 56 Those hills, there are tapu places in them.

B. *sb.* = TABOO, TABU *sb.* 1 a. Also (*rarely*) *fig.*

1833 H. WILLIAMS *Let.* July in H. Carleton *Life H. Williams* (1874) 134 Some proposed Paihia, but this we declined, fearing it might bring the *tapu* upon a considerable portion of the land. **1851** [see TABOO, TABU *sb.* 1 a]. **1872** A. DOMETT *Ranolf & Amohia* 89 His sole 'tapu' a far securer guard Than lock and key of craftiest notch and ward. **1902** G. B. SHAW *Mrs. Warren's Profession* p. xiii, Each nation has its particular set of tapus in addition to the common human stock. **1938** R. FINLAYSON *Brown Man's Burden* 41 Uncle Tuna..disapproved of joking about matters of tapu. **1971** *N.Z. Listener* 29 Mar. 11/1 In old New Zealand there were two main causes of sickness and disease. One was the violation of tapu or a tapu place.

Also as *v. trans.* = TABOO, TABU *v.* 1. Now *rare.*

1837 in R. McNab *Old Whaling Days* (1931) xxi. 335, [I] tapued a piece of land of the proprietors, two respectable chiefs, for some blankets and fish-hooks. **1851** V. LUSH *Jrnl.* 16 Dec. (1971) 94 A native burial place which the Tryces had been obliged to fence in before the natives would allow them to dwell in peace—so great is the natives' dread lest a spot they have *tapued* should be desecrated by man or beast. **1863** F. E. MANING *Old New Zealand* i. 14 A good gun... I must have this; I must *tapu* it before I leave the ship. **1890** *Jrnl. Anthrop. Inst.* XIX. 100 Tapu is an awful weapon. I have seen a strong young man die the same day he was tapued.

Tapuia (tăpū·yă), *sb.* (and *a.*). Also 7 **Tapui;** 9 **Tapuio; Tapuya.** [a. Pg. *Tapuia*, Sp. *Tapuya*, ad. Tupi-Guaraní *tapua* savage, slave.] (A member of) a Brazilian Indian people not of Tupi stock. Also *attrib.* or as *adj.*

1613 PURCHAS *Pilgrimage* IX. vi. 712 Towards the East dwell the Itatini people, which call themselves Garay, that is, Warriours; and others, Tapuis or Slaues. **1860** MAYNE REID *Odd People* 44 Farther down the river, the 'Indio manso' is a 'tapuio', a hireling of the Portuguese, or, to speak more correctly, a *slave*. *Ibid.* 46 By such name is his house (or village rather) known among the *tapuios* and traders of the Amazon. **1910** *Encycl. Brit.* I. 783/2 The name Amazonas arises from the battle he had with a tribe of Tapuya savages. **1944** S. PUTNAM tr. *E. da Cunha's Rebellion in Backlands* i. 44 The hiding-places of the Tapuia. *Ibid.* ii. 83 The predominance of Tapuia terms in the geographic names of these places—terms that have resisted absorption by the Portuguese and Tupi languages.

tar, *sb.* Add: **1. a.** Also formed in the combustion of tobacco, etc.

1921 *U.S. Patent 1,398,734* 2/1 The catch basins..are adapted to concentrate the heavier particles of tar from smoke. **1932** *Amer. Jrnl. Cancer* XVI. 1513 The tar of cigarette smoke contains nicotine, phenolic bodies, pyridine bases, and ammonia. **1974** M. C. GERALD *Pharmacol.* viii. 155 Some of these are polycyclic hydrocarbons, commonly referred to as 'tars', and are undoubtedly responsible for the disproportionately greater incidence of lung cancer among cigarette smokers.

d. *to beat* (*knock*, etc.) *the tar out of*: to beat unmercifully, to reduce to a state of helplessness. Cf. *SHIT *sb.* 1 g. *U.S. slang.*

1884 *National Police Gaz.* 6 Sept. 11/1 (*heading*) The celebrated New York dubs get the tar knocked out of them. **1916** 'TEXAS' *Trav. Tourist 'Typo'* 46 The newsboy..whose chief occupation is..to wallop the tar out of smaller newsboys. **1939** D. TRUMBO *Johnny got his Gun* ii. 35 Naturally you..wanted Germany to get the tar kicked out of her. **1973** WODEHOUSE *Bachelors Anonymous* vii. 80 She is a fine upstanding woman, fully capable of beating the tar out of you.

e. Colloq. abbrev. of TARMAC or TAR MACADAM; a road surfaced with this.

1934 DYLAN THOMAS *18 Poems* 26 Nor city tar and subway bored to foster Man through macadam. **1971** *E. Afr. Standard* (Nairobi) 13 Apr. 6/5 He thought the tarmac was dangerous anywhere. Next year he wanted to see less tar and higher speeds elsewhere. **1980** G. LORD *Fortress* iii. 26 Both roads were dirt... The tar ended miles back.

4. a. That contains tar: *tar-pill* (earlier example); used for holding, or in making, tar: *tar-bucket* (examples). **b.** Objective, instrumental, etc.: *tar-brand* vb. (earlier example), *-mark* vb., *-painted* (example), *-smelling*, *-streaked* adjs. **c. tar acid,** any of numerous phenolic constituents of coal-tar distillates that react with dilute caustic soda to give water-soluble salts; **tar and feathers** *U.S.* (with reference to the practice of tarring and feathering: see TAR *v.*[1] b); **tar-baby,** (*a*) the doll smeared with tar, set to catch Brer Rabbit (see quot. in Dict.); hence *transf.*, *spec.* an object of censure; a sticky problem, or one which is only aggravated by attempts to solve it (*colloq.*); (*b*) a derog. term for a Black (*U.S.*) or a Maori (*N.Z.*); **tar ball,** (*a*) (in Dict., sense 4 a); (*b*) a ball of crude oil found in or on the sea; **tar base,** any of numerous cyclic, nitrogen-containing bases present in coal-tar distillates; **tar-boiler,** (*a*) (in Dict., sense 4 a); † (*b*) *U.S. slang* = TARHEEL (*obs.*); **tar-boy** *Austral.* and *N.Z.*, an assistant hand in a shearing shed who treats injured sheep with tar or other disinfectants; **tar-bush,** one of several aromatic shrubs of western N. America, esp. one of the genus *Eriodictyon*, of the family Hydrophyllaceæ, which includes several sticky or tomentose evergreens; **tar kiln** (later example); **tar-paper** chiefly *N. Amer.* (in Dict., sense 4 a): often used as a building material; freq. *attrib.*; (earlier and later examples); **tar-pavement, -paving,** a form of surfacing for roads, pathways, etc., composed mainly of tar; **tar-pot,** (*c*) an opprobrious name for a Black (*U.S.*), or a Maori (*N.Z.*) (cf. *tar-baby* (*b*) above); **tar-sand,** a deposit of sand impregnated with bitumen.

1909 *Chem. Abstr.* III. 1079 (*heading*) Hydrocarbons obtained from the tar acids of petroleum. **1951** M. MCLUHAN *Mech. Bride* (1967) 91 (Advt.), Coal-Tar Chemicals—Benzol, toluol, naphthalene, tar acids, tar bases, solvents, [etc.]. **1974** Tar acid [see *tar base* below]. **1775** P. V. FITHIAN *Jrnl.* 8 June (1934) II. 25 He hears many of his Townsmen talking of Tar and Feathers—These mortifying Weapons. **1834** *Southern Lit. Messenger* I. 87 If he remained longer, he was in danger of tar and feathers. **1954** J. STEINBECK *Sweet Thursday* xxxviii. 261 He left town, and just as well. There was talk of tar and feathers. He must have heard. **1982** W. MANKOWITZ *Mazeppa* vi. 97 The Vigilance Committees..had asserted law summarily with fast necktie parties, rail-rides and tar and feathers. *a* **1910** 'MARK TWAIN' *Autobiogr.* (1924) II. 18 For two years the *Courant* had been making a 'tar baby' of Mr. Blaine, and adding tar every day—and now it was called upon to praise him. **1924** KIPLING *Debits & Credits* (1926) 97 Number Five Study..were toiling inspiredly at a Tar Baby made up of Beetle's sweater, and half-a-dozen lavatory towels;..and most of Richard's weekly blacking allowance for Prout's House's boots. **1948** S. LEWIS *Kingsblood Royal* 334 'I didn't know she was a tar-baby.'..'Don't be so dumb. Can't you see it by her jaw?' **1959** M. SHADBOLT *New Zealanders* 140 'What a hide, though—' 'Those tar-babies and that fellow in the sweater.' **1976** *National Observer* (U.S.) 29 May 15A/3 The troubled U.S. Postal Service is fast becoming the political tar baby of the year. **1978** J. UPDIKE *Coup* (1979) iv. 135 She was one of those white women who cannot leave black men alone... Some questing chromosome within holds her sexually fast to the tarbaby. **1972** *Science* 16 June 1258/2 Crude oil lumps ('tar balls') are now universal constituents of the surfaces of the world oceans. **1921** *Jrnl. Amer. Chem. Soc.* XLIII. 1936 Crude coal tar bases vary greatly..in the nature and in the proportion of the bases which they contain. **1951** [see *tar acid* above]. **1974** *Encycl. Brit. Micropædia* II. 1017/2 Tar bases are the basic constituents of the distillate oils, present after tar acids have been removed. **1845** *Cincinnati Misc.* I. 240 The inhabitants of..N. Carolina [are called] Tar-boilers. **1885** W. WHITMAN in *N. Amer. Rev.* Nov. 433 Among the rank and file..[in the Civil War] it was very general to speak of the different States they came from by their slang names. Those from..North Carolina [were called] Tar Boilers. **1888** 'R. BOLDREWOOD' *Robbery Under Arms* I. x. 123 There wasn't a man of the lot in the shed, down to the tarboy, that wouldn't have done the same. **1936** A. RUSSELL *Gone Nomad* iii. 19 Then I found myself a tar-boy in the shearing-shed. **1956** G. BOWEN *Wool Away!* (ed. 2) 157 *Tar-boy*, the hand who walks the board where sheep are subject to the fly and who puts a smear of tar on the cuts made on sheep. **1977** C. MCCULLOUGH *Thorn Birds* x. 231 Luke took himself off on the shearing circuit as a tar boy, slapping molten tar on jagged wounds if a shearer slipped and cut flesh as well as wool. **1878** E. S. ELWELL *Boy Colonists* 205 It took a good month to muster and tar-brand all the sheep. **1723** *Amer. Weekly Mercury* 23–30 May 2/1 The forced Men..carryed the Brigantine into Curacao, with the Captains Head in a Tarr Bucket. *a* **1909** *Joseph W. Caldwell: Mem. Vol.* (1909) 66 There was a brindled cur dog under the wagon, keeping company with the tar bucket that swung from the coupling pole. **1931** *Sun* (Baltimore) 28 Oct. 13/4 Tall 'tar-bucket' helmets with the black plumes. **1884** W. MILLER *Dict. Eng. Names Plants* 134/2 Tar-bush, Californian. *Eriodictyon californicum.* **1902** *Out West* Oct. 452 There were the innumerable cacti with their brilliant flowers, and the tar bush. **1949** *Chicago Tribune* 20 Feb. 30/3 Cedar and mesquite alone are costing Texas ranchers 115 million dollars a year. Add the..blue oak, creosote, tarbush.. and prickly pear and the toll is terrific. **1943** H. PARKES in C. Goerch *Down Home* xx. 99 Any one who has ever seen a tar kiln in operation or been around a turpentine distillery will realize what sticky and dirty work it is. **1825** JAMIESON Suppl. II. 86/1 An old Angus laird,..on observing that one of the young ladies had both earrings and patches, cried out..in obvious allusion to the means employed by store-farmers for preserving their sheep; 'Wow, wow! Mrs. Janet, your father's been michtilie fleyd for tyning you, that he's baith *lug-markit* ye and tar-markit ye.' **1918** *Chrons. N.Z.E.F.* 30 Aug. 61 Tar-marking and branding cattle. **1787** P. F. FRENEAU *Journey from Philadelphia* ii. 14 You tar-painted [*Poems* (1795) vii. 343: Tar-smelling] monster!.. If Snip should be drownded, and lost in the sea, You never once think what a loss it would be! **1891** H. CAMPBELL *Darkness & Daylight* xxxi. 611 If he ventures to charge more, except for a dress..or for tar-paper..he is liable to lose the license. **1919** S. LEWIS *Free Air* 122 Then a lonely, tight-haired woman in the doorway of a tar-paper shack waved to her. **1966** D. F. GALOUYE *Lost Perception* ix. 89 The plane.. taxied up to a frame building with a tarpaper roof. **1978** R. LUDLUM *Holcroft Covenant* xxxii. 370 The tar paper.. bulged slightly next to the wall. **1883** *Proc. Assoc. Municipal Engin.* X. 53 My first experience in tar pavement was in 1850. *Ibid.*, Tar paving had been used to some extent for footways previous to..March 1881. **1967** *Gloss. Highway Engin. Terms* (*B.S.I.*) 47 *Tar paving*, a surfacing of tarmacadam laid in one or two courses for footpaths, playgrounds, and similar areas for pedestrian or very light vehicular traffic. **1728** E. SMITH *Compl. Housewife* (ed. 2) 304 *The Tar Pills for a Cough.* Take Tar and drop it on Powder of Liquorish, and make it up into Pills. **1944** H. L. MENCKEN in *Amer. Speech* XIX. 174 *Pickaninny* was..used..affectionately. So..was *tar-pot*..signifying a Negro child. **1949** F. SARGESON *I saw in my Dream* xiii. 120 He'd never let the tarpots inside the shed with their lousy sheep. **1899** *Nature* 15 June 159/1 Great trouble has been experienced in the effort to penetrate the 'tar-sands' at the base of the Cretaceous strata. **1978** *Ibid.* 29 June 703/3 The heavier oils will also have to be used as chemical feedstocks in the future: for example, Canada's 'tar sands', now the subject of a multi-million dollar project in Alberta. **1973** R. ADAMS *Watership Down* (ed. 2) xxiv. 173 He sat..on the bank above the tar-smelling road. **1782** J. TRUMBULL *M'Fingal* IV. 70 Adown his tar-streak'd visage, clear Fell..th'indignant tear. **1939** S. SPENDER *Still Centre* IV. 94 You stood once In the tar-streaked drizzling street.

‖ **tar** (tāɹ), *sb.*[2] *Anglo-Ind.* [Hindi *tār.*] A telegram.

1893 KIPLING in *Harper's Weekly* 30 Dec. 1246/3 My father is at the *tar*-house sending *tars.* **1901** —— *Kim* xi. 286 Therefore I did not send a *tar* (telegram) to any one saying where the letter lay. **1978** 'M. M. KAYE' *Far Pavilions* IV. xxviii. 411 It would have been a simple matter for the Rana..to arrange for a *tar* (telegram) to be dispatched.

tar, *v.*[1] Add: **b.** (Earlier and later examples.) Also *fig.*

1769 *Boston* (Mass.) *Chron.* 30 Oct. 3/2 A person..was stripped naked, put into a cart, where he was first tarred, then feathered. **1925** A. HUXLEY *Those Barren Leaves* II. iii. 113 Miss Carruthers, who has a short way with dissenters, would like to see them tarred and feathered—all except pacifists, who, like strikers, could do with a little shooting. **1960** N. ANNAN in *Victorian Stud.* June 331 The individualist, the eccentric, the man who offends against the trivial rules of the club, are tarred and feathered with gleeful brutality. **1977** *Daily News* (Perth, Austral.) 19 Jan. 6/5 The victims were stripped naked, tarred and shorn of their hair. **1981** A. PRICE *Soldier no More* 161 The Russians..wouldn't have cared less if we'd tarred and feathered Nasser and run him out of Suez on a rail.

tara, *int.* (Later examples.)

1922 JOYCE *Ulysses* 166 Tara tara. Great chorus that. Tara. Must be washed in rainwater. Meyerbeer. Tara: bom bom bom. *Ibid.* 503 Exercise your mnemotechnic. *La causa è santa.* Tara. Tara.

tara (tărā·), *int.*[2] Also **tarra(h**, etc. Colloq. (mainly North.) alteration of TA-TA, in familiar use.

1958 A. SILLITOE *Saturday Night & Sunday Morning* ii. 27 'See yer't dinnertime, Arthur.' 'Tarr-ar, Dad.' **1967** E. WILLIAMS *Beyond Belief* I. i. 6 They are off arm in arm to Belle Vue. Ta-ra-for-now, they call out, the warm casual Lancashire way of saying goodbye, 'ta ra!' **1973** B. BAINBRIDGE *Dressmaker* iii. 39 'Tarrah, Valerie!' called Rita up the stairs. 'Thank you very much for having me.' **1981** B. HINES *Looks & Smiles* 121 'I'm off now, Mum, ta-ra.' 'Ta-ra, love. See you tonight.'

tarabagan, var. *TARBAGAN.

‖ **tarada** (tarā·dă). [ad. Arab. *ṭarrāda* cruiser, swift war canoe.] A canoe used by the Marsh Arabs of Iraq.

1960 G. MAXWELL *Ring of Bright Water* I. vi. 75 We spent the better part of those two months [in Southern Iraq] squatting cross-legged in the bottom of a *tarada* or war canoe. **1964** W. THESIGER *Marsh Arabs* iii. 23 The top part of the ribs was..studded with five rows of flat, round nail-heads two inches across. These decorative nails were the distinguishing mark of a *tarada*..which only a sheikh may own. Years later, in Oslo, I saw the Viking ships preserved there and was at once reminded of the *taradas* in the Marshes. **1974** *Blackw. Mag.* Oct. 341/1 There is a bigger canoe called a *tarada*, graceful and swift, with a fine upswept prow.

Tarahumara (ta:răhumā·ră), *sb.* and *a.* Also **Tarahumar(e.** [a. Sp., of uncertain origin.] **A.** *sb.* **a.** (A member of) an Uto-Aztecan people of north-western Mexico. **b.** The language of this people. **B.** *adj.* Of, pertaining to, or designating this people.

1874 H. H. BANCROFT *Native Races Pacific States* I. v. 609 The *Tarahumares* inhabit the district of Tarahumara in the state of Chihuahua. *Ibid.* III. v. 666 The Tarahumara, which is a more polished language than its neighbors, contains words similar to the Aztec. **1911** J. G. FRAZER *Golden Bough: Magic Art* (ed. 3) I. iii. 150 The Tarahumares of Mexico are great runners. **1912** C. LUMHOLTZ *Unknown Mexico* I. viii. 168 Tarahumare pottery is exceedingly crude. **1934** A. L. KROEBER *Uto-Aztecan Lang. Mexico* 13 Varohío..is in all most similar to Tarahumar. But it can hardly be..merely a provincial dialect of Tarahumar. **1963** C. W. PENNINGTON *Tarahumar of Mexico* i. 5 Zapata's résumé of the Tarahumar missions in 1678..indicate that Coyáchic..was an important Tarahumar center. **1964** E. A. NIDA *Toward Sci. Transl.* iii. 35 The Tarahumara in northern Mexico have five basic color words, including one term *siyonomi*, which covers both green and blue. **1975** *Language* LI. 798 In Tarahumara, *-tu/-ru* retains the sense 'become' in its use as a derivational suffix. **1979** *Tucson* (Ariz.) *Mag.* June 48/2 Several Tarahumara dwellings and farm buildings have been reconstructed for the exhibit.

tarakihi (taraki·hi). *N.Z.* Also **terakihi** (te·rakī). [Maori.] A marine fish, *Cheilodactylus macropterus*, silver in colour with a black band behind the head, belonging to the morwong group and found off the coasts of New Zealand.

1873 J. H. H. ST. JOHN *Pakeha Rambles through Maori Lands* II. x. 173 Our best fish are the tarakihi, patiki or sole, and whitebait. **1937** *Nature* 7 Aug. 223/1 Tarakihi.. flesh was found to contain appreciable amounts of vitamin A. **1959** A. H. MCLINTOCK *Descr. Atlas N.Z.* 48 Tarakihi ..second only in importance [as a commercial catch] to snapper, is trawled off the east coast..[and] also caught in quantity in deep water along the west coast. **1960** N. HILLIARD *Maori Girl* II. v. 96 She..was preparing to fry a piece of *terakihi* for their tea.

taramellite (tærăme·ləit). *Min.* [a. It. *taramellite* (E. Tacconi 1908, in *Atti dell' Accad. Naz. dei Lincei: Rendiconti, Classe di Sci. Fisiche*, etc. XVII. I. 814), f. the name of T. *Taramelli* (1845–1922), Italian geologist: see -ITE[1].] An orthorhombic borosilicate of barium and other metals, chiefly iron and titanium, and usu. containing some chlorine.

1908 *Jrnl. Chem. Soc.* XCIV. II. 863 The author describes a new mineral, taramellite, occurring in radiating, fibrous, acicular aggregates or slender veins in the calcareous zone of Candoglia-Ornavasso (Val Toce). **1973** *Mineral. Abstr.* XXIV. 433/2 More than 50 minerals have been identified in rocks of this quarry of the Pacific Limestone Products Co. [in California]. They include.. 15 silicates three of which, celsian, pabstite, and taramellite, are Ba-bearing.

taramosalata (ta:rămŏsăla·tă). Also **taramasalata.** [a. mod.Gr., f. ταραμᾶς preserved roe (ad. Turk. *tarama* soft roe, red caviare) + σαλάτα SALAD.] A Greek fish pâté made (traditionally) from the roe of the grey mullet or from smoked cod's roe, mixed with garlic, lemon juice, olive oil, etc. Also *ellipt.* as **tarama.**

1910 Z. D. FERRIMAN *Home Life in Hellas* iv. 181 Red caviar..is pounded with garlic and lemon juice into what is called *tarama salata.* **1958** R. LIDDELL *Morea* II. iii. 70 A vinegary *taramosalata*, a preparation of salted fish eggs and oil, which is always Lenten food in Greece. **1964** *Spectator* 8 May 645/1 A Greek fish pâté, *taramasalata.* **1972** *Harper's & Queen* Apr. 92/1, I quite often add tarama to go with the avocado. **1978** *Chicago* June 233/1 Dinnertime favorites include saganaki,..taramosalata, red caviar, etc.

Taranaki (tærănæ·ki). The name of a province in New Zealand, used *attrib.* in **Taranaki gate,** a gate made of wire strands attached to upright battens (see quot. 1966).

1937 M. E. C. SCOTT *Barbara Prospers* 27 She..had the 'Taranaki' gate open in a twinkling. **1948** R. FINLAYSON *Tidal Creek* 205 Mind you get the taranaki gate properly up. **1953** J. W. BRIMBLECOMBE *Shear Nonsense* 110 He can now open a Taranaki gate without rolling himself up in it. **1966** G. W. TURNER *Eng. Lang. Austral. & N.Z.* ii. 31 The province gives its name to the *Taranaki gate*, a moveable piece of a wire fence held by a loop of wire at one end to form a makeshift gate. **1968** *Landfall* XXII. 390 Sure enough, we found someone had taken down the Taranaki gate on the side that led to the Oteranika Road.

taranakite (tærănā·kəit). *Min.* [f. prec.: see -ITE[1].] A hydrated basic phosphate of potassium (partly replaced by ammonium) and aluminium, found as a soft, whitish or grey clay-like substance composed of minute rhombohedral crystals.

1866 HECTOR & SKEY in *Rep. & Awards of Jurors N.Z. Exhib., 1865* 423 Taranakite, a new Phosphatic mineral.. presented by H. Richmond... This singular mineral was mistaken for Wavellite. **1882** *Trans. N.Z. Inst.* XV. 385 Taranakite..a double hydrous phosphate of alumina and potash, part of the alumina being replaced by ferric oxide, was first discovered by H. Richmond, Esq., at the Sugar Loaves, Taranaki. **1976** *Mineral. Abstr.* XXVII. 256/2 Aluminian strengite.., vivianite.., and taranakite ..(small yellowish white aggregates) from the Castellane caves, Apulia, southern Italy, occur embedded in small 'terra rossa' deposits, near the contact with superimposed layers of bat guano.

tarantula. Add: **5. tarantula-hawk**: substitute for def.: any of several species of spider wasp of the genus *Pepsis* that occur in the south-western U.S. and kill tarantulas; (examples); **tarantula-juice** *U.S. slang,* inferior whisky; **tarantula-killer** (earlier example).

1861 *Harper's Mag.* Jan. 147/2 Little to drink, except old-fashioned tarentula-juice, 'warranted to kill at forty paces'. **1867** *Amer. Naturalist* I. 137 The large, red-winged 'Tarantula Killer'..is, as far as I know, the largest of the dauber group. **1878** B. F. TAYLOR *Between Gates* 198 The tarantula hawk..pounces upon his victim and makes a needle-cushion of him. **1932** *Sun* (Baltimore) 8 June 9/1 A large wasp, known..as a 'tarantula hawk', was victor over a tarantula in a battle. **1980** F. H. WAGNER *Wildlife of Deserts* 148 Formidable as the tarantula is, it has its own enemies. The large tarantula hawk wasp (*Pepsis*) feeds the spiders to its young. **1939** C. W. TOWNE *Her Majesty Montana* 38 In the saloons, poisonous liquors are vended to all comers under the name of 'tangleleg', 'forty-rod', 'lightning', 'Tarantula-juice', etc.

† **Tarantulle** (tærăntu·l). *Obs.* [Cf. TULLE.] The proprietary name of a kind of cotton fabric.

1890 *Trade Marks Jrnl.* 3 Sept. 878 Tarantulle 89,034. Cotton piece goods of all kinds. Tootal Broadhurst Lee Company..Manchester..Manufacturers.—10th April 1889. **1915** *Official Gaz.* (U.S. Patent Office) 16 Mar. 1033/1 Tarantulle... Cotton piece goods—viz. Nainsooks, Cambrics, and Madapolams. **1923** *Daily Mail* 9 Jan. 1 (Advt.), Ladies' Night-dress, in standard Tarantulle, trimmed strong Embroidery. **1932** D. C. MINTER *Mod. Needlecraft* 253/2 Tarantulle. Dorcas cambric or fine longcloth.

tarara (tără·ră). Also *redupl.* [Echoic.] = TARATANTARA I.

1891 KIPLING *Light that Failed* ii. 18 Ridin', ridin', ridin', two an' two, Ta-ra-ra-ra-ra-ra-ra, All the way to Kandahar. **1892** —— *Barrack-Room Ballads* 57 You can't refuse when you get the card And the widow gives the party. (*Bugle:* Ta—rara—ra-ra-rara!) **1980** D. BLOODWORTH *Trapdoor* v. 25 The situation was..saved in the nick of time—tarara, *tarara*—by a little old lady.

Tarascan (tăræ·skăn), *sb.* and *a.* [f. Sp. *Tarasco*, name of a Meso-American Indian language of S.W. Michoacán, Mexico + -AN.] **A.** *sb.* **a.** A member of an Indian people of the mountain area about lake Pátzcuara in Michoacán. **b.** Their language. **B.** *adj.* Of or pertaining to this people or their language.

[**1874** H. H. BANCROFT *Native Races Pacific States* I. vi. 643 The Michoacagues or Tarascos are warlike and brave. *Ibid.* III. x. 744 The Tarasco, the principal language of Michoacan, can be placed almost upon an equality with the Aztec, as being copious and well-finished.] **1911** C. THOMAS *Indian Lang. Mexico & Central Amer.* 51 The Tarascan language is now well known as constituting a separate family. **1914** R. J.

MacHugh *Mod. Mexico* i. 2 One hundred and thirty-three separate Indian tribes recognized in Mexico..are arranged under sixteen language groups—the Athapascan..Piman, Tañoan, Tarascan, [etc.]. **1931** S. Chase *Mexico* ii. 31 There was only one basic culture in Mexico and Central America, in which the Mayas, the Toltecs, the Aztecs, the Tarascans, the Zapotecs and various other nations shared. **1948** R. C. West (*title*) Cultural geography of the modern Tarascan area. **1964** E. A. Nida *Toward Sci. Transl.* v. 94 Tarascan, a language of Mexico which has a number of metaphors, does not readily admit new ones. **1974** *Encycl. Brit. Macropædia* XII. 164/2 The relative isolation created by the mountains permitted the Tarascans to work out their own cultural variant.

tarbagan (tā·ɹbăgăn). Also **tarabagan.** [a. Russ. *tarbagán.*] A large long-haired marmot, *Marmota bobak* or *M. sibirica*, found in the steppes of eastern and central Asia; also, the pelt of this animal.

1928 in *Funk's Stand. Dict.* **1930** M. Bachrach *Fur* xii. 156 The other variety [of marmot pelts] is called Tarbagans, or Tarbaganas. **1947** *New Biol.* II. 11 It [*sc.* the germ of plague] is present..in..tarabagans in China. **1951** Whitby & Hynes *Med. Bacteriol.* (ed. 5) xviii. 303 The more important reservoirs of sylvatic plague include ..tarbagans in China. **1962** P. Manson-Bahr *Patrick Manson* xix. 168 The giant marnot..was being hunted for its fur, known as tarabagan skins. **1971** P. C. C. Garnham *Progress in Parasitol.* iii. 32 The infection primarily occurs in a variety of wild rodents..such as the tarabagan in Mongolia.

tar-brush. Add: **b.** (Earlier and later examples.)

1796 Grose *Dict. Vulgar Tongue* (ed. 3), *Blue-skin*,.. any one having a cross of the black breed, or, as it is termed, a lick of the tar brush. **1899** C. J. Cutcliffe Hyne *Further Adv. Capt. Kettle* viii. 189 Those snuff-and-butter coloured ladies..ignore their own lick of the tar-brush. **1928** J. Buchan *Runagates Club* i. 18 The Du Preez family had lived..close up to the Kaffir borders, and somewhere had got a dash of the tar-brush. **1970** D. M. Davin *Not Here, Not Now* vii. iii. 340 If he hadn't been an Irishman you'd think he had a touch of the tar-brush himself. **1975** 'S. Marlowe' *Cawthorn Jrnls.* (1976) xix. 163 She was beautiful... High yellow. Some places they would have said she had just a touch of the tar-brush.

Tarbuck knot (tā·ɹbʊk nǫt). *Mountaineering.* [f. the name of the British mountaineer Kenneth *Tarbuck* (b. 1914), who invented it.] An adjustable loop knot (see quots.).

1947 K. Tarbuck in *Wayfarers' Jrnl.* No. 8. 52 The practical advantages of the Tarbuck knot lie in its adjustability. It can easily be slid up or down the standing rope by hand in order to vary the size of the loop. **1950** tr. *Mountaineering Handbk.* (Assoc. Brit. Members Swiss Alpine Club) App. 167 The end of the rope..is tied..with a Tarbuck knot... Although in its general action this knot is similar to the Prusik knot, it has in addition a remarkable shock-absorbing run when subjected to a severe shock load. **1968** P. Crew *Encycl. Dict. Mountaineering* 114/2 Most knots bend the rope into a sharp angle, which reduces the strength of the rope by quite a high percentage—this is avoided in the Tarbuck knot.

tarbuttite (tā·ɹbɒ̆təit). *Min.* [f. the name of P. C. Tarbutt (1874–1943), English mining engineer + -ite[1].] A basic zinc phosphate, Zn_2PO_4OH, found as faintly coloured or colourless triclinic crystals.

1907 *Nature* 27 June 215/1 L. J. Spencer exhibited a suite of beautifully crystallised minerals, presented to the British Museum by Mr. Percy C. Tarbutt, from the Rhodesia Broken Hill mines in north-western Rhodesia... The crystals of this new species, for which the name *tarbuttite* is proposed, are anorthic. **1955, 1974** [see *parahopeite* s.v. *para-[1] 2 c].

Tardenoisian (tāɹdĕnoi·ziăn), *a.* *Archæol.* [ad. F. *Tardenoisien*, f. *Tardenois* (see below): see -ian.] Of, pertaining to, or resembling the mesolithic culture remains of which were first discovered in Tardenois, dept. of Aisne, France. Also *absol.*, this culture.

[**1912** R. Munro *Palæolithic Man* xi. 277 (*heading*) *Tardenoisien* flint industry.] **1921** *Glasgow Herald* 16 Feb. 13 Tribes..characterized in their industry by little geometric flints called Tardenoisian. **1939** C. S. Coon *Races of Europe* iii. 56 The cultures of the Mesolithic period may be divided into two elements... One was the intrusive Tardenoisian with its advanced microlithic technique, which came in from the south across the straits of Gibraltar. **1948** A. L. Kroeber *Anthropology* (ed. 2) xvi. 633 As early as 1887, Piette discovered an Azilian period after the Magdalenian, and in 1896 de Mortillet added the Tardenoisian to this. **1951** *Field Archaeol.* (Ordnance Survey) (ed. 3) 13 'Pigmy' flints of the type known as Tardenoisian from the site at Fère-en-Tardenois in Northern France. **1975** J. G. Evans *Environment Early Man Brit. Isles* v. 103 Features of a third group, considered to reflect the continental Tardenoisian, were also incorporated, in particular the use of the chisel-ended.. arrowhead.

tardiness. Add: **c.** Lateness in arriving, esp. at a meeting or assembly, a class or school, etc. *U.S.*

1828 Webster, *Tardiness*,..lateness; as, the tardiness of witnesses or jurors in attendance; the tardiness of students in attending prayers or recitation. **1902** J. Corbin *American at Oxford* 17 All this brings recollections of the paternal roof, where tardiness at breakfast meant the loss of dessert. **1930** *Randolph Enterprise* (Elkins, W. Va.) 2 Oct. 5/4 No business enterprise would tolerate the percentage of absence and tardiness experienced in the schools.

tardive, *a.* Add: **b.** Path. *tardive dyskinesia*, a neurological disorder, usu. a late-developing side-effect of long-term treatment with anti-psychotic drugs, which is characterized by involuntary movements of the face and jaws.

1964 A. Faurbye et al. in *Acta Psychiatrica Scandinavica* XL. 12 Tardive dyskinesia is first and foremost characterized by the occurrence of dyskinetic movements. **1979** *Nature* 1 Mar. 59/1 Of all the side effects of drugs used to treat psychotic illness such as schizophrenia, chronic tardive dyskinesias are the most disturbing.

tardon, var. *tardyon.

tardy, *a.* (*adv.*). Add: **1. c.** Late for a meeting, assembly, class, school, or appointment. *U.S.*

1638 in *Archives of Maryland* (1883) I. 6 Such as did appeare thoughe tardie should be pardoned. **1843** *Yale Lit. Mag.* VIII. 240 We were '*tardy*' at our matins. **1904** *Minneapolis Times* 29 May 6 Don't shoot your husband when he is two hours tardy for supper. **1948** *Daily Ardmoreite* (Ardmore, Okla.) 4 July 21/4 During this time he had been neither absent nor tardy.

tardy, *v.* (*arch.* example.)

1972 Auden *Epistle to Godson* 10 We've had it, are in for a disaster that no four-letter words will tardy.

tardyon (tā·ɹdi,ǫn). *Physics.* Also **tardon** (tā·ɹdǫn). [f. Tardy *a.* (*adv.*) + *-on[1].] A sub-atomic particle that travels at less than the speed of light.

1969 Bilaniuk & Sudarshan in *Physics Today* May 47/2 Let us refer to all subluminal particles as tardyons. **1970** *New Scientist* 10 Sept. 521/1 The number of tachyons in a system may vary from observer to observer—yet another deviation from the conventional world of tardons. **1972** *Nature* 7 Jan. 10/3 This assumes that 'ordinary' particles (called tardyons in this sort of discussion) have a mass *m* such that m^2 is greater than zero. **1975** J. Taylor *Superminds* (1976) vi. 114 Tardons (slower-than-light particles) and tachyons can never interchange roles.

tare, *sb.*[1] Add: **2. c.** *Angling.* (See quot. 1971.)

1971 *Angling Times* 10 June 12/1 Tares: a cereal bait used for roach fishing. **1976** *Reading Chron.* 19 Nov. 26/7 Kennet-style hemp groundbait and caster on the hook failed to get him a bite for the first 90 minutes. Then he switched to floated tares and the roach came thick and fast.

tare, *sb.*[2] Add: **a.** *tare weight* (later examples); also with reference to aircraft.

1944 C. A. Zweng *Aviation Dict.* 329/1 In weighing an aircraft..the weight of any incidental equipment needed, and whose weight is included in the final weight, must be subtracted to obtain the correct weight. This is called the tare weight. **1950** *Gloss. Aeronaut. Terms* (*B.S.I.*) i. 43 *Tare weight*, for design purposes: the standard weight of a type of aircraft complete in flying order but without crew, fuel, oil, removable equipment or payload. **1967** *Times Rev. Industry* May 78/2 Reductions of more than 50 per cent in tare weight..can often be made by using a particular new material. **1977** *Mod. Railways* Dec. 480/2 All timing loads in the working timetables are now calculated for tare weights in tonnes.

tare (in phr. *tare and ages, wounds*): see Tear *sb.*[2] 3 d.

tarentaal (tarĕntā·l). *S. Afr.* Also **tarantal(l).** [a. Afrikaans.] Either of two guineafowl of the family Numididæ, the crowned guinea-fowl, *Numida meleagris*, or the crested guinea-fowl, *Guttera edouardi*, both found in southern Africa.

[**1822** W. J. Burchell *Trav. Interior S. Afr.* I. xv. 364 The missionaries have a few domestic fowls..and Guinea hens or Pintadoes, which are called by the quaint name of *Jan Tadentaal*.] **1827** T. Philipps *Scenes & Occurrences in Albany* 99 Ten guinea-fowl..called here, by the Hottentots, *tarentalls*. **1906** W. L. Sclater *Birds S. Afr.* IV. 228 Crowned Guinea-fowl... 'Tarantal' of Dutch. **1948** H. V. Morton *In Search of S. Afr.* ix. 282 We would walk over the veld watching the guinea-fowl, the tarentaal, pour away into the mealies. **1953** U. Krige *Dream & Desert* vii. 187 Great Oupa, whose ear was so acute he could hear from the front stoep the call of a tarentaal against the ridge, slowly opened his eyes. **1958** McLachlan & Liversidge *Roberts' Birds of S. Afr.* (rev. ed.) 100 Crowned Guinea-Fowl. Tarentaal. *Numida meleagris*.. The only Guinea-fowl in our area with a casque on the head.

Tarentine, *a.* (*sb.*) Add: **c.** *sb.* A native or inhabitant of the ancient city of Tarentum (now Taranto), in SE Italy.

1579 T. North tr. *Plutarch's Lives* 443 Pyrrhus.. arrived at the length in the city of Tarentum, with twenty thowsand footemen..ioyning thereto to the choycest pyked men of the Tarentines. **1720** H. Eelbeck tr. *Cicero's First Oration Archias* 11, I am of Opinion that the Rheginians, or..the Tarentines, would not have refused the Privilege to this Poet. **1812** C. Kelsall tr. *Cicero's Last Pleadings against Verres* 97 What remuneration.. could compensate..the Tarentines, if they were to lose their Europa on a bull..and other works [of art]? **1978** M. Grant *Hist. Rome* iii. v. 77 The Tarentines were governed by a democracy, which..displayed..relative stability.

target, *sb.*[1] Add: **3. a.** Also *transf.*, *spec.* (*a*) a place or object selected for military attack, esp. by aerial bombing or missile assault; (*b*) a part of the body at which a boxer directs his attack.

1902 *Encycl. Brit.* XXXIII. 380/2 Taking range and size of target together, the most advantageous position is to be on the bow of the enemy while he bears abaft your beam. **1914** Hamel & Turner *Flying* xvi. 285 A pilot will have to make three or four attempts before..a bomb can be released in any hope of getting near the target. **1921** J. Driscoll *Text-bk. Boxing* 70 The 'jaw' target is ..preferable, if it should happen to be exposed. **1958** F. C. Avis *Boxing Ref. Dict.* 112 *Target*, that part of the boxer's body which may properly be punched, namely, the entire front and side parts of the body above the belt and the head. **1959** *Chambers's Encycl.* XIII. 430/1 The bomber force was sent out and so timed as to converge upon the target and complete the entire attack within a few minutes. **1971** H. Macmillan *Riding Storm* viii. 272 The R.A.F. carried out a number of rocket attacks on military targets.

d. *Physics.* The object or material at which a beam of atomic or sub-atomic particles is directed, as in a cathode-ray tube or particle accelerator.

1915 *Chambers's Jrnl.* Sept. 593/1 This anti-kathode (or target), enabling us to focus the rays, was introduced by Herbert Jackson. **1932** *Proc. R. Soc.* A. CXXXVII. 230 A target, A, of the metal to be investigated is placed at an angle of 45 degrees to the direction of the proton stream. **1953** Amos & Birkinshaw *Television Engin.* I. x. 217 The action of television camera tubes is dependent on an electron beam which is focused on the target and deflected so as to cover it in a series of scanning lines. **1961** G. R. Choppin *Exper. Nuclear Chem.* viii. 111 In a cyclotron, only one target at a time may be irradiated. **1975** D. G. Fink *Electronics Engineers' Handbk.* xi. 61 The target becomes positively charged in proportion to the light intensity.

e. *Biol.* and *Med.* A region in a cell which is especially sensitive to radiation.

1936 D. E. Lea et al. in *Proc. R. Soc.* B. CXX. 56 The hypothesis that the bacterium is uniformly sensitive to radiation throughout its volume raises..difficulties, and attention will therefore be turned to the alternative hypothesis that a target exists which is specially sensitive. **1968** *Brit. Med. Bull.* XXIV. 244/2 The curve can be represented by a model in which each of several targets in the organism must interact with radiation. **1979** I. M. Leahy et al. *Nurse & Radiotherapy* iii. 30 Targets are necessarily very small and are usually assumed to be within the nucleus or the DNA material itself.

f. *colloq.* An amount set as a (minimum) objective, esp. in fund-raising; a result (i.e. a figure, sum of money, etc.) aimed at. Phr. *on target*, on the right track, as forecast. Hence *loosely*, any goal which one strives to achieve.

1942 *N. & Q.* CLXXXIII. 256/1 *Target.* Who invented the ingenious use of this word for the amount aimed at in a public subscription? I think the use has been extended to things like coal consumption. **1943** *Ann. Reg. 1942* 307 The London Warship Week resulted in 146,065,225*l.* being raised as against the original target of 125,000,000*l.* **1951** E. Gowers *ABC of Plain Words* 133 If target was to have all the stimulating force it was capable of, it would not do to treat it as a live metaphor, and exhort people to do nothing more exciting..than merely to hit it. So we were offered a great variety of things that we might meritoriously do to our targets. We might reach them, achieve them, attain them or obtain them; we were to feel greatly encouraged if we came in sight of the target to which we were trying to do whatever we were trying to do, and correspondingly depressed if we found ourselves either a long way behind it or (what apparently amounts to the same thing) a long way short of it. **1952** *Sat. Rev.* 20 Sept. 9/2 There are legislative targets, crop targets, charity targets, gross national product targets. **1964** F. Chichester *Lonely Sea & Sky* xxxii. 333, I had failed to beat my 30 day target by 3 days, 15 hours, 7 minutes. **1967** *Time* 18 Aug. 88 Diddy is sure he did it; yet a blind girl near by who hears all and who proves to be on target about everything else, says he never left his seat. **1977** *Times* 10 Aug. 5/5 There has been unrealistic targeteering; the 1960s building target of 500,000 was never required. **1981** *Times* 23 Oct. 22/1 First-half results from Jeavons Engineering are on target at £306,000 pre-tax.

g. *Linguistics.* = *output *sb.* 1 e.

1970 J. Hill in *Linguistic Inquiry* I. 539 The formal statement of the HAB formation rule of Cupeño..is not going to be like the usual..rule involving description of input..; it can instead be visualized as involving first a statement of the target or output, and then a statement for reaching the target. **1977** *Language* LIII. 209 This constraint is a target; i.e., a number of rules of various types conspire to keep the verb in sentential second position.

5. (sense 3) *target-practise* vb., *-seeking*, *-shooting* (example); (appositively) designating an object of attack, as *target area, boat, vehicle*, etc.; (see also *target ship* in Dict.); *transf.*, esp. of a particular group over which influence is sought, as *target audience, company, group, population*; (sense *3 d) *target nucleus, volume*; (sense *3 f, passing into adj.) by which the desired goal is specified, as *target date, figure, output, prize, size*, etc.; **target**

cell *Biol.* and *Med.*, an abnormal form of red blood cell which appears as a dark ring surrounding a dark central spot in stained blood films; hence *target cell anæmia*, descriptive of any anæmia in which target cells are abundant; **target dialect,** the variety of a language learned as a second dialect; **target indicator,** an object, as a flare, dropped in order to illuminate or delimit a target for aerial bombing; **target man,** (*c*) *Assoc. Football* (see quot. 1978); **target organ** *Biol.*, any organ which responds to a particular hormone or hormones in the body (cf. *target tissue* below); **target program** *Computers* = *object program* s.v. *OBJECT *sb.* 10; **target theory** *Biol.* and *Med.* (see quots. and cf. sense 3 e above); **target tissue** *Biol.*, any tissue which responds to a particular hormone or hormones within an organism (cf. *target organ* above).

1936 *Proc. R. Soc.* B. CXX. 57 To prove that the target is a biological reality..the obvious experiment..is to use several different intensities of alpha rays and beta rays and to calculate the target area in each experiment. **1939** W. S. CHURCHILL in *New Statesman* 7 Jan. 6/2, I think a great mistake has been made in spreading our A.R.P. efforts over the whole country, instead of concentrating on what I should call the target areas. **1958** F. C. AVIS *Boxing Dict.* 77 *Off the target*, not connecting the opponent in the target area. **1980** J. MCCLURE *Blood of Englishman* xxv. 232 'Target area coming up,' he said, picking up the line of a wriggling dirt road... They were down to about 600 feet above the ground. **1956** *U.S. Air Force Dict.* 513/2 *Target audience*, in psychological warfare, the people at whom propaganda is directed. **1982** *Underground Grammarian* Sept. 2/2 In order to broaden the 'target audience' of your newsletter..I might suggest that such material be written at a lower level of readability. **1934** T. E. LAWRENCE *Let.* 8 June (1938) 805 At the moment we are all up to the teeth in 5 more target boats. [**1938** A. M. BARRETT in *Jrnl. Path. & Bacteriol.* XLVI. 603 They will here be called 'target types of red blood corpuscle', or more briefly, 'target corpuscles'. I have deliberately chosen a name which refers only to their appearance in stained films and not to their three-dimensional form.] *Ibid.* 605 Often the frequency of target cells appeared to be affected by the thickness or thinness of the film. **1940** W. DAMESHEK in *Amer. Jrnl. Med. Sci.* CC. 445 Since an outstanding abnormality was the presence of large numbers of peculiar erythrocytes designated as 'target cells' by Barrett, the name 'target cell anemia' was adopted for this previously undescribed condition. **1969** EDINGTON & GILLES *Path. in Tropics* x. 353 Excluding films obtained from persons homozygous or heterozygous for haemoglobin C, a high percentage of target cells in normal blood films has been observed in Ghana, Nigeria, and from East Africa. **1977** *Time* 17 Oct. 58/3 The firm that eventually acquires the target company. **1945** W. S. CHURCHILL *Victory* (1946) 108 Full hutting..is nearing completion, the target date for which is May. **1977** *Whitaker's Almanack 1978* 595 The Rhodesia conference in Geneva became deadlocked when leaders of White and Black delegations failed to agree on a target date for legal independence. **1972** J. L. DILLARD *Black Eng.* vii. 293 The Network Standard dialect, for which both white and Black speakers have shown marked preferences, is obviously the preferable target dialect. **1978** J. IRVING *World according to Garp* viii. 163 Roberta was a target figure; she had made some people very angry. **1972** *Times* 13 Dec. 4/7 It made no discriminations among target groups. **1979** *Bull. Amer. Acad. Arts & Sci.* Mar. 33 The programs to be undertaken in reaching these target groups were to involve workers in both the public and private sectors of health, agriculture, and education. **1944** *Times* 11 Apr. 4/4 The attack began with the dropping of target-indicators through cloud. [**1974** *Times* 23 Feb. 14/8 Even eight, nine and ten-year-olds these days are taught by games masters in terms of 'striker', 'target player'..and the rest.] **1975** *Times* 14 Oct. 10/2 (*caption*) Stuart Pearson, a target man with Manchester United. **1978** *Sunday Times* (Colour Suppl.) 28 May 34/4 *Target man*, forward, usually a large one, used in central positions where colleagues can find him with long passes, usually to his head. **1955** FRIEDMAN & WEISSKOPF in W. Pauli *Niels Bohr* 134 According to this model the effect of the target nucleus upon an incident particle can be described, at least as a first approximation, by an attractive potential. **1947** H. SELYE *Textbk. Endocrinol.* 17/1 The so-called 'target organs' or 'end organs' do not necessarily react to hormones under all conditions. **1972** *Sci. Amer.* Nov. 24/1 The pituitary secretes several complex hormones that travel through the bloodstream to target organs, notably the thyroid gland, the gonads and the cortex of the adrenal glands. **1944** *Hutchinson's Pict. Hist. War.* 27 Oct. 1943–11 Apr. 1944. 441 Once more the merchantship target output was achieved. **1971** *Computers & Humanities* V. 292 SPIRES is based on a behavioral science analysis of the information needs of a target population. **1949** H. PREECE in B. A. Botkin *Treas. S. Folklore* II. iv. 341 The rumbling underground is Britt Bailey target-practising for a million years of shooting in hell. **1982** *Sunday Sun-Times* (Chicago) 8 Aug. 9 A witness..allegedly saw Hartmann's widow, Debra, target practicing at a suburban gun shop. **1962** Target price [see *off-farm* s.v. *OFF- 4 b]. **1969** P. B. JORDAIN *Condensed Computer Encycl.* 516 The process begins with a source-language program..and ends with a target program. **1979** *Personal Computer World* Nov. 84/1 Any areas of data must be excluded from both and left intact as they are used by both the target program and the trace routine. **1947** *Britannica Bk. of Year* 841/2 *Target-seeking missile*, a missile, equipped with a target-seeking mechanism, which is attracted toward its target when it approaches its vicinity. **1977** *R. Air Force Yearbk.* 4/2 (*caption*) A Harrier GR Mk 3..with laser-ranging and target-seeking equipment in the nose. **1855** GEO. ELIOT in *Fraser's Mag.* LI. 706/2, I will tell you of Weimar fairs and target-shooting. **1966** *Observer* 17 Apr. 10/3 Is there any magic in the figure of 30—the target size for classes? **1936** D. E. LEA et al. in *Proc. R. Soc.* B. CXX. 62 That regions of special sensitivity to radiation do exist..has been demonstrated and the additional postulate of the target theory, namely that there is only one such region, in an individual organism, is not improbable for bacteria. **1979** I. M. LEAHY et al. *Nurse & Radiotherapy* iii. 30 One theory that has proved to be applicable to radiation biology experimentation is known as target theory. Briefly stated, this theory proposes that if alterations are produced within certain critical molecules in the cell, the loss of vital function that would result would lead to the death of the cell. **1960** JENSEN & JACOBSEN in Pincus & Vollmer. *Biol. Activities Steroids* iii. 162 Information concerning the chemical fate—in the specific target tissues—of physiological amounts of steroid sex hormones should prove of value. **1974** M. C. GERALD *Pharmacol.* xxiii. 409 Whereas growth hormone and thyroid hormone are capable of influencing virtually all the cells of the body, most hormones act rather selectively on specific tissues referred to as target tissues. **1975** *Sci. Amer.* July 94/1 Where trees are concerned one of the target tissues for auxin is the cambium. **1965** *New Scientist* 18 Mar. 701/2 The spacecraft will be manoeuvred by the pilots to approach the target vehicle closely, and finally to dock with it in a firm, mechanical manner. **1946** D. E. LEA *Actions of Radiations* iii. 91 That dose..produces an average of one cluster in a volume equal to the target volume.

target, *v.* Add: **4.** To plan or schedule (something) to attain an objective. Chiefly in *Econ.*

1948 *Observer* 14 Mar. 3/6 Even herrings have targets now: 175,000 tons of fish are being 'targeted' to yield 17,000 tons of oil a year. **1959** *Time* (Atlantic ed.) 17 Aug. 53 Exports of heavy goods..are targeted to rise this year some 40%. **1972** *Newsweek* 7 Aug. 43/3 With test flights now targeted for 1976, the Shuttle is expected to be ready for operational missions in 1978. **1973** *Daily Tel.* 8 Dec. 23/2 Investment income..is targeted to reach £1 million in two years.

5. To aim (a nuclear weapon) at a target. Freq. const. *on.*

1964 *Financial Times* 23 Mar. (Defence Suppl.) 17/4 The Soviet presence..comprises..a force of about 100 MRBMs targeted on Japan. **1972** *Sci. Amer.* Nov. 21/1 Each missile launches a 'bus', which has on board a large number of reentry missiles, each of which can be accurately and independently targeted. **1978** *Observer* 25 June 21/3 There were enough warheads to target some on China as well.

transf. **1973** *Times* 2 Nov. 4/2 The scheme is targeted at those wanting to buy an older property. **1974** *Nature* 1 Mar. 1/1 Research money should be targeted on problems whose solution would have the greatest benefit for society. **1983** *New Scientist* 21 July 208/1 Practical conservation can rarely preserve an entire fauna: rather it is targeted at particular species.

6. To mark out or identify (a place, person, etc.) as a target. Chiefly *U.S.*

1966 *Guardian* 30 Dec. 14/8 US policy is to target North Vietnamese military targets only. **1976** *National Observer* (U.S.) 27 Nov. 5/1 He has no worlds left to conquer, for NCEC has captured all the 'marginal' conservative seats it had targeted. **1978** S. BRILL *Teamsters* vii. 297 The airline industry was being targeted for a recruiting drive. **1983** *Listener* 25 Aug. 4/3 They've targeted 22 airlines for special treatment.

7. To direct or aim on a course. Freq. const. *to.*

1974 *Nature* 1 Mar. 16/3 Temperature profiles of the moons of those planets will be helpful in targeting the spacecraft to take a look at the most interesting features. **1976** *Sci. Amer.* June 74/1 The second spacecraft will be targeted to fly past Saturn and on toward Uranus. **1976** *National Observer* (U.S.) 21 Aug. 3/3 Then allocations are made with about one-third going to state governments and two-thirds to local governments, targeted to those jurisdictions with the highest unemployment. **1980** *Sci. Amer.* Aug. 88/2 Highly specialized transport systems that are in effect independent of the tissue through which they convey substances might be exploited as a means of 'targeting' therapeutic drugs for particular organs or tissues. **1981** *New Scientist* 6 Aug. 343/2 Later perhaps it will be possible to target liposomes or red cells ..to whatever part of the body they are needed [*sic*].

Hence **ta·rgeting** *vbl. sb.*

1961 *Guardian* 24 Oct. 8/4 Being forced to rely on so much inspection..that targeting information would be given away to the other side. **1963** *Newsweek* 11 Feb. 23 Planners have recently put forward the notion of city-avoidance, a tacit agreement between potential enemies to arrange their targeting so that missiles are aimed at military objectives rather than civilian populations. **1968** *Economist* 8 June 65/2 A general complaint is that consultants sometimes stick too much to their business precepts, such as 'targeting' and do not bend enough to the particular needs of the company. **1976** *National Observer* (U.S.) 27 Nov. 5/1 NCEC laid out $350,000 for candidates in 1976. That paid for 64 polls in 32 separate congressional districts and for computerized precinct targeting and analysis in more than 40 districts. **1977** *Time* 21 Nov. 24/2 None of these possess as sophisticated a targeting system as the new Soviet model's [*sc.* a T-72 tank]. **1982** *Financial Times* 13 Mar. 14/1 In terms of targeting ability.

targetable (tā·rgėtăb'l), *a.* [f. TARGET *v.* + -ABLE.] **a.** Of nuclear missiles or warheads: capable of being aimed at a target. **b.** Of military installations or equipment, etc.: that may be picked out as a target.

1968 *N.Y. Times* 8 Apr. 46 The United States will in the next few years add to its arsenal missiles capable of putting into space a number of individually targetable warheads. **1968** *Economist* 6 July 10/2 Both in submarine-borne and land-based missiles the Americans have established a lead over the Russians in the development of MIRVs (multiple independently targetable re-entry vehicles). **1972** *Sci. Amer.* June 15/3 Land-based intercontinental ballistic missiles..can readily be located with the aid of surveillance satellites, so that they must be regarded as 'targetable' in the event of an enemy first strike. **1981** *Ibid.* Feb. 20/3 Silos are targetable. **1982** M. DUKE *Flashpoint* xxi. 151 Minuteman-III, with its multiple independently targetable warheads.

targeted, *ppl. a.* [f. TARGET *v.* + -ED[1].]

1. Designated or chosen as a target.

1965 *Economist* 20 Feb. 733 We must..have a short take off and landing (STOL) capability; otherwise the aircraft is tied to targeted concrete and will be destroyed on the ground by the enemy. **1971** *Nature* 22 Oct. 517/3 He labelled sickle cell anaemia a targeted disease for concentrated research. **1974** *Spartanburg* (S. Carolina) *Herald-Jrnl.* 21 Apr. A8/3 Light industry was just meeting a targeted 4 per cent increase. **1979** *Sci. Amer.* Aug. 139/2 In the late 1960's the U.S. Government's 'Operation Shamrock' intercepted international Telex communications to and from 'targeted' invididuals, including antiwar activists. **1983** D. WILLIAMS *Treasure Preserved* i. 8 Anyone..who detected Louella engaged in private ombudsman activity had a duty immediately to alert the targeted department.

2. Aimed, directed; given a target.

1969 *Guardian* 23 June 10/2 MIRV (Multiple Independently Targeted Re-Entry Vehicle). **1974** L. THOMAS *Lives of Cell* 116 We need more targeted research, more mission-oriented science. **1978** *Dædalus* Spring p. xiv, The distinction between basic and applied or targeted knowledge becomes crucial.

target language. [f. TARGET *sb.*[1] + LANGUAGE *sb.*] **a.** The language into which a translation is made.

1953 *Philos. Sci.* XX. 217 Imagine an utterly moronic student without the slightest knowledge of either the source-language or the target-language, i.e., the language into which the given text is to be translated. **1959** [see *LANGUAGE *sb.* 1 d]. **1969** P. B. JORDAIN *Condensed Computer Encycl.* 515 In assembly and compiler operations, a programmer-oriented language is converted to a target language for execution on the computer. **1976** *Canad. Jrnl. Linguistics* Spring 96 A translator needs to have deciphered the ambiguity in a given sentence..in order to be able to translate it, provided of course that this sentence does not have a syntactic homonym in the target language.

b. A foreign language which it is aimed to learn or acquire.

1965 P. STREVENS *Papers in Lang. & Lang. Teaching* viii. 103 The difficulties..vary according to the learner's mother-tongue as well as his target-language. **1973** K. A. SEY *Ghanaian English* ii. 22 Lacking the native speaker's linguistic intuitions, the L_2 speaker has to depend on his limited acquaintance with the target language. **1976** *Word 1971* XXVII. 351 Integratively oriented students are more strongly motivated and more successful in learning the target language than instrumentally oriented students.

tarheel. Add: Also **Tar Heel, Tar-heel, tar-heel.** (Earlier and later examples.) Hence **ta·r-heeled** *a.*

1864 R. E. PARK *Diary* 9 Dec. in *Southern Hist. Soc. Papers* (1876) II. 232 A poor, starving Tar Heel at Elmira. **1869** *Overland Monthly* III. 128 A brigade of North Carolinians..failed to hold a certain hill, and were laughed at by the Mississippians for having forgotten to tar their heels that morning. Hence originated their cant name, 'Tar-heels'. **1878** *Scribner's Monthly* Apr. 833/1 A little fellow from North Carolina..announced to the convention he was from 'the tar-heeled state'. **1942** S. KENNEDY *Palmetto Country* 260 North Carolina became known as the Tar-heel State. **1959** [see *REDNECK 1 a].

tariff, *sb.* Add: **4. a.** attrib., *tariff war*; **c.** objective, *tariff adjustment, -cutting.* **d.** Special comb., **tariff wall,** a national trade barrier in the form of a tariff; hence **tariff-walled** *a.*

1889 *Puck* (U.S.) XXV. 248 (*heading*) High tariff-wall. **1904** J. DENNEY *Let.* 4 Aug. (1920) 50 We..have nothing to offer..like a Free Trade Government dealing with tariff-walled nations. **1909** H. W. V. TEMPERLEY in *Cambr. Mod. Hist.* VI. ii. 49 The tariff-war was often the precursor of the trade-war. **1932** *Sun* (Baltimore) 17 Sept. 8/3 The proposed policy is variously known as a bargaining or trade-building policy of tariff adjustment. **1934** A. HUXLEY *Beyond Mexique Bay* 85 Symptoms, such as tariff-wars and armaments. **1935** E. WINGFIELD-STRATFORD *Harvest of Victory* I. ii. 19 The combined handicaps of tariff-walled markets, ruined customers, slackening demand for..coal, [etc.]. **1962** *Daily Tel.* 16 Jan. 20/4 The agreement nearing completion in Brussels on a tariff-cutting agreement with the Common Market is satisfactory on the whole. **1964** *Ann. Reg. 1963* 70 Feelings were ruffled by..the Secretary of Commerce's denunciation of a Canadian tariff-adjustment scheme. **1973** *Times* 3 Jan. (Forward into Europe Suppl.) p. xi/2 The tariff walls begin to crumble. **1977** *Whitaker's Almanack 1978* 978 The CET is based on the arithmetical average of those national tariffs it replaced, and after two international tariff-cutting rounds now stands at an average of 6 per cent.

tariffite. (In Dict. s.v. TARIFF *sb.*) (Earlier U.S. example.)

1830 *Western Monthly Rev.* III. 376 She is a true tariffite, a hearty and staunch advocate for the genuine American system.

tariff-reform. (Earlier example.)
1859 R. COBDEN *Let.* 8 Nov. in F. A. Wellesley *Paris Embassy during Second Empire* (1928) ix. 193 There is no Imperial road to tariff reform, and if he [*sc.* Napoleon III] goes to work à la Villafranca, he will find himself in a supplement of vexations and troubles.

‖ **tarkashi** (tāɹka·ʃi). Also **tar-kashi.** [Hindi *tār-kaśī*, lit. 'wire-drawing'.] The Indian craft of inlaying wood with brass wire; the artefacts so produced.
1878 G. C. M. BIRDWOOD *Handbk. Brit. Indian Section* (Paris Universal Exhibition) 79 In Mynpuri work,..we find..wood inlaid with brass wire in various geometrical ..patterns... At Mynpuri,..it goes by the name of *tarkashi*, or 'wire work'; a word which suggests the possible etymology of the word *tarsia*. **1910** E. R. NEAVE *Mainpuri: Gazetteer* 73 Mainpuri has long been noted for its beautiful wood work inlaid with brass wire, known as *tarkashi* (lit. wire-drawing). The best dark *shisham* is the only wood employed... There are about twenty artisans in the town engaged in the trade. **1979** *Inside-Outside* (Bombay) June–July 51 That was 1963, which you could say was the year that *tarkashi* arrived—in its new incarnation. *Ibid.* 54 The raw material of *tarkashi* used to be brass sheet.

tarlatan. Add: Freq. *attrib.* Also *absol.*, to designate a dress made of this fabric. (Further examples.)
1844 *Lexington* (Kentucky) *Observer* 25 Sept. 1/6 Tarlatan Muslin..will be sold. **1849** *Trelawny* (Jamaica) 24 Apr. 1/2 Rich colored gingham, and tarleton plaid. **1852** MRS. STOWE *Uncle Tom's Cabin* I. xviii. 309, I was just dying to know whether you would appear in your pink tarletane. **1873** *Young Englishwoman* Jan. 51/3 Does she never go to a ball or dance, and require the extra dress in the shape of a white tarlatan or something of that sort? **1936** M. MITCHELL *Gone with Wind* 175 Maybelle Merriwether went toward the next booth..in an apple-green tarlatan so wide that it reduced her waist to nothingness. **1936** N. STREATFEILD *Ballet Shoes* iv. 50 When you start on Monday you're having rompers, two each, black-patent ankle-strap shoes, and white tarlatan dresses, two each, with white sandal shoes. **1975** *New Yorker* 29 Dec. 23/3 Sleptsov also found..a tarlatan bag on a collapsible hoop (and the muslin still smelled of summer and sun-hot grass).

Tarmac. (In Dict. s.v. TAR MACADAM.) Add: Now freq. with small initial. Also designating a surface made of tar macadam; *the tarmac* (colloq.), the airfield or runway.
1905 *Chambers's Jrnl.* 14 Jan. 110/2 The road surveyor ..appears to have almost solved the problem of finding a dustless, a rainproof, and a cheap material by the employment of an iron-slag mixed with tar. This material he calls tarmac. **1919** C. ROBERTS *Training Airmen* v. 37 An open, wind-swept place... A broad strip of tarmac on which various aeroplanes are receiving the solicitous attention... That is the sight which quickens the cadet's pulse. **1921** *Flight* 11 Aug. 544/2 Aerodrome improvements..are now being carried out on the tarmac. Work has been commenced on the laying of a tarmac road from the sheds to the Customs enclosure. **1931** *Observer* 10 May 5 The lanes that he once used to choose have now been straightened out into fine, noble tarmac highways. **1948** 'N. SHUTE' *No Highway* iv. 109 Samuelson met them on the tarmac. **1970** *Drum* (E. Afr. ed.) Feb. 31/3 One travels on tarmac the whole way to the Kenya border on some of the finest road surfaces on the continent. **1976** *Sunday Telegraph* (Colour Suppl.) 28 Nov. 57/2 A speed established with the car on dry Tarmac. **1979** J. RABAN *Arabia through Looking Glass* iii. 67 People in gold-trimmed robes stepped off aeroplanes and were embraced by similarly robed officials who stood in waiting on the tarmac.

ta·rmac, *v.* [f. the sb.] To cover with tar macadam. Chiefly *pass.* or as *ppl. a.*, with spelling *tarmac(c)ed, tarmacked.* Hence **ta·rmacing** *vbl. sb.* Cf. *TARMACADAM *v.*
1966 C. WILSON *Glass Cage* II. 90 It was a row of small, semi-detached modern houses with front gardens, and the road had not yet been fully tarmacced. **1972** 'R. GORDON' *Doctor on Brain* xiv. 97 All that lies before me is a well-tarmacked dead straight motorway leading to the grave. **1974** *New Society* 14 Mar. 627/3 Ponds which are filled in and reclaimed by farmers, or tarmacked for car parking by the local pub. **1975** *Ibid.* 18 Dec. 663/3 The aesthetic and environmental objections to the tarmacing of 15 odd acres of land. **1977** *Belfast Tel.* 28 Feb. 13/1 (Advt.), Now's the time to have your driveways Bitmaced or Tarmaced. **1981** E. NORTH *Dames* vii. 129 The tarmacked runway.

tar macadam. Add: Now usu. **tarmacadam.**
1959 *Chambers's Encycl.* XI. 724/2 A modification of the tarred macadam road is that known as 'tarmacadam', in which all the pieces of road metal are coated with tar before being spread on the road and rolled. **1965** P. WAYRE *Wind in Reeds* xvi. 229 Concrete or tarmacadam paths..were out as far as we were concerned. **1980** *West Lancs. Even. Gaz.* 6 Mar. 17 (Advt.), Tarmacadam—concrete and flagging.

Hence **tarmaca·dam** *v.* (in quots. as *pa. pple.* and *ppl. a.*). Cf. *TARMAC *v.*
1910 *Times* 23 July 8/6 The tar-macadamed Madeira-road..proved them to have been pioneers in this matter. **1976** *Glasgow Herald* 26 Nov. 2/7 (Advt.), Driveways excavated, slabbed, tarmacadamed, trees pruned and lopped. **1978** *Morecambe Guardian* 14 Mar. 22/1 (Advt.), Partly tarmacadamed playground.

tarmac(c)ed, tarmacked: see *TARMAC *v.*

tarnally, *adv.* (Later examples.)
a **1828** J. BERNARD *Retrospections Amer.* (1887) x. 241 May I be 'tarnally starved down for mutton broth, if [etc.]. **1922** JOYCE *Ulysses* 419 Tarnally dog gone my shins if this beent the bestest puttiest longbreakyet.

tarnation, *sb.* Delete *rare* and add earlier and further examples.
1790 R. TYLER *Contrast* v. i. 68 Tarnation! That's no laughing matter though. **1830** W. CARLETON *Traits Irish Peasantry* I. 49 Tare-nation to the rap itself's in my company. **1922** JOYCE *Ulysses* 183 Wall, tarnation strike me! **1938** M. K. RAWLINGS *Yearling* v. 49 Git away, you blasted bacon-thieves!.. Git to tarnation! **1983** C. MACLEOD *Bilbao Looking-Glass* xix. 175 Tarnation! Here comes another o' them mobile camera units.

tarn-cap. (Later example.)
1863 C. M. YONGE *Hist. Christian Names* II. 312 Siegfried, by means of his tarn cap, invisibly vanquished the Valkyr.

ta·rnhelm. Also **Tarn-helm, tarn-helm.** [Ger.; cf. TARN-CAP and DERN *a.*] In Wagner's opera *Der Ring des Nibelungen*, a magic helmet which either secures the invisibility of the wearer or enables him to change his appearance at will; = TARN-CAP. Also *fig.* Hence **ta·rn-helmed** *a.*
1877 A. FORMAN tr. *Wagner's Nibelung's Ring: Rhinegold* 45 (*stage direction*) He puts the..'Tarn-helm' on his head... His figure disappears; in his place a pillar of cloud is seen. *Ibid.* 57 (*stage direction*) He puts the tarn-helm on again... He disappears; the gods perceive..a toad creeping towards them. **1896** G. B. SHAW in *Star* 22 July 1/7 The magical strangeness of the wishing cap or 'tarnhelm'. *a* **1930** D. H. LAWRENCE *Sex, Literature & Censorship* (1955) 84 It is something in her *will*. It is her tarnhelm. **1971** *Daily Tel.* 4 Oct. 13/3 The fateful ring is grabbed by the tarnhelmed Siegfried.

taro. a. (Earlier example.)
1769 S. PARKINSON *Jrnl.* 1 Oct. in *Jrnl. Voy. South Seas* (1773) II. 97 Adjoining to their houses are plantations of Koomarra and Taro.

tarogato (ta·rǭgato). Also **tárogató.** [a. Hungarian *tárogató*.] A Hungarian wood-wind instrument with a conical bore, orig. a double-reeded instrument resembling a shawm, but in the 1880s reconstructed with a single reed and fitted with keys. (Now obsolescent in Hungary, and treated as a historical national instrument.)
1907 T. S. WOTTON *Dict. Mus. Terms* 195 *Tárogató*, an instrument which has been used in Paris and Brussels etc. to take the *cor anglais* part at the end of Scene 1 Act III *Tristan und Isolde*. **1935** *Swing Music* Mar. 18/2, I had schemes for original instruments—among them the harpsichord..and a Hungarian reed-instrument called a tárogató. **1965** *Listener* 24 June 940/3 The *tárogató*, resembling the clarinet, but essentially an oboe family instrument. **1974** *Encycl. Brit. Micropædia* IX. 828/3 *Tárogató*, single-reed wind instrument, widely played in the folk music of Romania and, especially, Hungary.

tarot. Delete ‖ and add: **a.** (Later *attrib.* examples.)
1928 D. BYRNE *Destiny Bay* vii. 319 An old woman crazed by gambling and tarot cards. **1957** L. DURRELL *Justine* III. 180 Justine..would sit cross-legged on the bed and begin to lay out the little pack of Tarot cards. **1972** *Time* 19 June 26/2 The Center also presents tarot-card readings. **1977** *Jrnl. Playing-Card Soc.* May 3 Some Milan card makers reached a high degree of technical and artistic quality, including specialisation in a particular type of Tarot pack, usually with a narrow format.

tarp (tāɹp). Orig. *U.S.* abbrev. of TARPAULIN *sb.*
1906 *Out West* Apr. 319 The men had unrolled their 'tarps' and spread their beds for the night on the ground in front of the little shack. **1919** W. H. DOWNING *Digger Dial.* 49 *Tarp*, a tarpaulin. **1941** *Times* (Weekly ed.) 15 Oct. 7/3 The gunner had taken the tarp off the seven-pounder forward and was adjusting the sights and oiling the gun. **1964** F. O'ROURKE *Mule for Marquesa* (1967) ii. 33 Saddles, blankets, pack cushions, sweat cloths, tarps, ropes. **1971** C. BONINGTON *Annapurna South Face* 249 Coated nylon tarps..Plastic tarps. **1980** *Christian Sci. Monitor* (Midwestern ed.) 4 Dec. B 32/1 Caked with ice from the violent waves, the tarps were almost unmanageable.

tarpaulin, *sb.* Add: **2. a.** (Later examples.)
1922 JOYCE *Ulysses* 610 Chews coca all day long, the communicative tarpaulin added. **1963** *Australasian Post* 14 Mar. 44/1 All the 'tarpaulins' had abandoned their lives of near slavery at sea and with fine wisdom had scattered inland.

4. tarpaulin muster [MUSTER *sb.*[1]], a collection or pooling of money among seamen; also *transf.* and *fig.*
1889 in *Cent. Dict.* **1904** E. S. EMERSON *Shanty Entertainment* 26 Each one in the room to sing, recite, or shout all round, and..a tarpaulin muster every half-hour for drinks, or smokes. **1907** J. MASEFIELD (*title*) A tarpaulin muster. **1920** P. L. WALDRON *Afloat & Ashore* vii. 83 The crew had a tarpaulin muster to have a last evening ashore. **1945** E. GEORGE *Two at Daly Waters* 102 As she had not brought a town outfit, Daly Waters had what we call in the bush a tarpaulin muster (the loan of everybody's best clothes). **1954** H. W. EDWARDS *Under Four Flags* xxiv. 125 With the generosity proverbial among sailors, they had a 'tarpaulin muster'.

Tarpeian, *a.* Add: Also *Comb.*, as *Tarpeian-fast* adj. *poet.*
1876 G. M. HOPKINS *Wreck of Deutschland* xxix, in *Poems* (1967) 61 The Simon Peter of a soul! to the blast Tarpeïan-fast, but a blown beacon of light.

Tarquinian (tāɹkwi·niăn), *a.* [f. L. *Tarquinius* + -AN: ult. Etruscan.] Of or pertaining to either of two kings of ancient Rome traditionally named Tarquinius, or to the dynasty to which these kings belonged.
1600 Index to *P. Holland's Romane Hist.* sig. 6Dvv, Tarquinien gentlemen beheaded in Rome. **1740** J. DYER *Ruins of Rome* 4 Such the Sewers huge, Whither the great Tarquinian Genius dooms Each wave impure. **1849** D. SPILLAN tr. *Livy's Hist. Rome* I. II. iii. 82 Only with the Tarquinian race will kingly power depart hence. **1977** G. CLARK *World Prehistory* (ed. 3) IV. 198 The Roman republic dates from the expulsion of the Tarquinian (Etruscan) dynasty in 510 B.C.

tarragon. Add: **3. tarragon vinegar** (earlier example).
1845 E. ACTON *Mod. Cookery* v. 163 Tarragon vinegar... Gather the tarragon late in July,..put it into small stone jars..pour in..vinegar to cover.

Tarragona (tæ:răgōu·nă). The name of a town and a province in north-eastern Spain, used *attrib.* and *absol.* to designate any of various wines produced there (see quot. 1958).
1888 *Encycl. Brit.* XXIV. 607/2 In Catalonia there is a much more important wine industry, the district producing what is known in England as Tarragona or Spanish red. **1926** F. H. BUTLER *Wines & Wine Lands of World* v. 50 From the Catalan country, on the same sea-board but much to the north, come the abundant Tarragona wines. **1958** A. L. SIMON *Dict. Wines* 153/2 Tarragona.. is also the name given to the best fortified wines of Catalonia, wines very dark in colour, naturally very sweet, and the fermentation of which is checked by added Brandy—as with Port. Tarragona was for many years the poor man's Port. Its chief merits were its deep colour, its great sweetness, its high alcoholic strength and its low price. **1967** A. LICHINE *Encycl. Wines* 504/2 The wine actually named Tarragona is sweet... The appellation is restricted to the dessert and fortified red and white wines produced within a delimited area and matured or prepared in the cellars of Tarragona, or of Reus close by.

tarra(h), var. *TARA *int.*[2]

tarrer. (Earlier example.)
1784 MRS. R. B. SHERIDAN *Let.* in T. Moore *Mem. Life R. B. Sheridan* (1825) xv. 485 You mistake, if you suppose I am a friend to your tarrers and featherers:—it is such wretches that always ruin a good cause.

tarring, *vbl. sb.* (Earlier examples of phr. *tarring and feathering.*)
1774 T. HUTCHINSON *Diary* 1 July (1883) I. 164 The committee for tarring and feathering blamed the people for doing it. **1784** [see TAR *v.*[1] b]. **1844** DICKENS *Martin Chuzzlewit* xxxiii. 390 He..invariably recommended..the 'tarring and feathering' of any unpopular person who differed from himself.

tarryhooting (tærihū·tiŋ), *vbl. sb.* Chiefly *U.S. dial.* [Prob. var. of *callyhooting* (*Dict. Americanisms*) in same sense.] Going about with much noise and motion; gallivanting. Freq. const. *around.* Also as *v. intr.* (chiefly *pres. pple.*).
1940 *N.Y. Jrnl. & American* (*Amer. Weekly*) 16 June 4/3 Her husband was 'tarryhootin'' around payin' court to gals on both cricks. *Ibid.* 4/4 He took to disappearing & 'tarryhootin' ' during the ninth year of the marriage. **1950** R. MOORE *Candlemas Bay* iv. 219 'Hi,' Grampie said. 'You're quite a feller for tarryhooting around the woods.' 'Apparently,' Mr. Raymond said. 'Was 'you chasing Evelyn?' 'Yes... Yes, by God, I was.' **1959** *Spectator* 27 Nov. 779/2 The pundits in Vigo Street.. turned this new venture [sc. *The Wind in the Willows*] down... After a certain amount of tarry-hooting around, Mr. Mole..was deposited in the amiable bosom of Sir Algernon Methuen.

ta·r-sealed, *a. N.Z.* (and *Austral.*). [f. TAR *sb.* + SEALED *ppl. a.*] Of a road, etc.: surfaced with asphalt. Also as *v. trans.* (chiefly *pa. pple*).
1928 R. G. STAPLEDON *Tour in Austral. & N.Z.* i. 12 Practically every mile of the road so traversed is 'tar sealed'. **1936** 'R. HYDE' *Passport to Hell* iii. 68 The oakum comes in little short rope-lengths, ship-ropes tarsealed, greasy, and hard. **1959** A. H. MCLINTOCK *Descr. Atlas N.Z.* 62, 10,384 miles of roads and highways are tar-sealed or concreted. **1960** I. CROSS *Backward Sex* i. 14 Across a tarsealed yard was the New Wing. **1963** A. LUBBOCK *Austral. Roundabout* 10 The bitumen, or tar-sealed, roads are only made over the most frequented highways, and through towns. **1966** G. W. TURNER *Eng. Lang. in Austral. & N.Z.* viii. 172 Roads are still 'tar-sealed'. **1977** *N.Z. Herald* 8 Jan. 4-1/3 (Advt.), Situated at Ola Point on the Whangaroa Harbour and gently sloping from tarsealed road frontage to the reserve at Harbour edge.

Hence **ta·r-seal** *sb.*, a road surface made with asphalt; a road so surfaced; also **ta·r-sealing.**

1957 *Numbers* Mar. 14 The tar-seal led purposefully to a wall of..stiff pale grasses. **1959** M. Shadbolt *New Zealanders* 88 They descended..into a lonely part of country. Tar-seal gave way to a road of clay and pumice. **1963** N. Hilliard *Piece of Land* 91 They'd brought in a lot of land around here since the new tarseal went through. **1964** *Evening Post* (Wellington, N.Z.) 10 Mar. 9/4 'Tar-sealing originated in Taranaki,' said Mr. Daniell [of Akura, Masterton]. 'Metal for the roads in the New Plymouth area had to be carted all the way from the Patea River and was, of course, expensive. Traffic threw much of the metal off the roads and one day a New Plymouth councillor suggested that they 'seal the metal on the roads' with tar, and so 'tarsealing' was born.' **1972** M. Gee *In my Father's Den* 26 Her sandals made a clacking noise on the tar-seal. **1977** *N.Z. Herald* 8 Jan. IV. 5/1 (Advt.), Situated on corner of 600 acres. This is very private yet adjacent to tarseal.

Tarsian (tā·ɹsiăn), *a.* and *sb.* [f. *Tars(us* (see below) + -ian.] **A.** *adj.* Of or pertaining to Tarsus, a Cilician city in south-eastern Asia Minor, and the birthplace of St. Paul. **B.** *sb.* A native or inhabitant of Tarsus.

1895 W. M. Ramsay *St. Paul Traveller* I. ii. 31 Paul was careful to keep within demonstrable law..when he claimed to be a Tarsian citizen. **1914** W. R. Inge in *Q. Rev.* CCXX. 50 The Emperor showed great favour to the Tarsians. **1920** J. A. Robertson *Hidden Romance N.T.* iv. 69, The Tarsian, a diminutive youth, nervous and awkward in manner. **1928** J. P. Arendzen *Men & Manners in Times of Christ* viii. 128 Did St. Paul, by claiming Tarsian citizenship, mean to imply that..he was a man of means?

tarsioid (tā·ɹsiˌoid), *sb.* and *a.* *Palæont.* [f. Tarsi(er + -oid.] **A.** *sb.* A fossil primate belonging to the suborder Tarsioidea, of which tarsiers are the only living members. **B.** *adj.* Of, pertaining to, or resembling a fossil tarsioid or a tarsier.

1913 G. E. Smith in *Rep. Brit. Assoc. Adv. Sci. 1912* 585 It may have been the case that the original habitat of the Tarsioids ranged from North America to South-eastern Europe. *Ibid.* 590 The factors that..have transformed a Tarsioid Prosimian into an Ape. **1925** *Bull. Geol. Soc. China* IV. 142 Primitive lemuroid and tarsioid fossil remains are widely known from England eastwards to the Carpathians. **1929** F. W. Jones *Man's Place among Mammals* xl. 359 We have further grounds in analogy with the jaws of the known tarsioids. **1968** W. Le Gros Clark *Chant of Pleasant Exploration* iii. 76 A rich assortment of extinct 'tarsioids'..extended their range over considerable areas. **1973** B. J. Williams *Evolution & Human Origins* ix. 124/1 It has been suggested that the higher primates did go through a tarsioid stage of evolution.

tarsonemid (tāɹsǒnī·mid), *a.* (and *sb.*). [f. mod.L. family name *Tarsonemidæ*, f. generic name *Tarsonemus* (Canestrini and Fanzago 1876, in *Atti Soc. Veneto-trentina Sci. Nat.* V. 14), f. Tarso- + Gr. νῆμα thread: see -id³.] Of or pertaining to a mite of the family Tarsonemidæ. Also as *sb.*

1922 *Nature* 20 Mar. 396/1 A Tarsonemid mite..feeds on the blood of the bee. **1951** *Dict. Gardening* (R. Hort. Soc.) IV. 2082/1 Tarsonemid mites..are of great economic importance owing to the injury caused by them to cultivated plants. **1959** T. E. Hughes *Mites* v. 73 Many other tarsonemids are plant parasites.

tart, *sb.* **2.** Substitute for def.: *fig.* **a.** Applied, *gen.* (orig. often endearingly) to a girl or woman; freq. in Australia and N.Z. Also in Liverpool dial. (with def. article or possessive pron.): a wife or girl-friend. *slang.*

1864 Hotten *Slang Dict.* 254 *Tart*, a term of approval applied by the London lower orders to a young woman for whom some affection is felt. The expression is not generally employed by the young men, unless the female is in 'her best'. **1898** [in Dict.]. **1916** [see *dinkum *a.*]. **1918** *N.Z.E.F. Chrons.* 5 July 252/2, I blushes like a 14-year old tart. **1931** 'G. Orwell' *Coll. Essays* (1968) 71 This word [*sc.* tart] now seems absolutely interchangeable with 'girl', with no implication of 'prostitute'. People will speak of their daughter or sister as a tart. *a* **1943** L. Esson in *Penguin Bk. Austral. Ballads* (1964) 233 All the tarts iz waitin'..In their flashest clobber. **1959** I. & P. Opie *Lore & Lang. Schoolch.* xv. 327 In the south of England a girl is often spoken of as a 'tart' (referred to as such by boys aged 11), and..no disrespect is implied by the word. A 'posh tart' is indeed a general term of admiration for a well-dressed, nice-looking girl. **1962** *Guardian* 24 Dec. 4/2 It's the little things at home that start nagging, and the tart's not well. **1966** [see *judy]. **1980** V. S. Pritchett *Tale Bearers* 84 His mother, a decent, now elderly tart found living with her black servant.

b. A female of immoral character; a prostitute. Also *loosely* as a term of abuse. *slang.*

1887, etc. [in Dict.]. **1922** E. O'Neill *Hairy Ape* v. 57 I see yuh, yuh white-faced tart, yuh! **1936** G. Greene *Gun for Sale* ii. 37 A woman policeman kept an eye on the tarts at the corner. **1951** S. Longstreet *Pedlocks* II. v. 93 Real fancy night[-gown], pink drawers, black lace... Nothing cheap for us like the grimy tarts on Mercury Street. **1965** E. J. Howard *After Julius* ix. 133 People don't..call other people tarts because they go to bed with people without marrying them. **1979** J. Cooper *Class* 17, I evolved a new way of dressing: five-inch high-heeled shoes, tight straight skirts, very very tight cheap sweaters, and masses of make-up... I looked just like a tart.

c. The young favourite of an older man; a catamite. Also *loosely*, a male prostitute. *slang.*

1935 I. Miller *School Tie* II. ix. 110 Being a tart. The sort of thing you were getting up to with Black last Easter term. **1943** D. Welch *Jrnl.* 23 Feb. (1952) 43 A week afterwards I had a letter from this old boy—quite elaborately romantic... As Geoffrey approached I held the letter down, against me. 'What are you engrossed in?' he jeered... 'A tart-note I bet. You've had a tart-note.' **1952** A. Wilson *Hemlock & After* I. v. 95, I can usually manage a tart's holiday at Cannes or Ischia. **1976** *Times Lit. Suppl.* 30 Jan. 100/3 He nearly loses the boy to a male tart in the city. **1977** *Ibid.* 1 Apr. 401/4 The boys that Isherwood and his friends picked up were not professional tarts only out for what they could get.

tart, *v.*² *slang.* [f. *tart *sb.* 2.] **1.** *trans.* To treat in the manner of a catamite or tart; to favour. *nonce-use.*

1930 Auden *Poems* 31 For where are Basley who won the Ten, Dickon so tarted by the House, Thomas who kept a sparrow-hawk?

2. To dress *up* or adorn (a person), usu. in a showy or gaudy manner; to titivate; also *refl.* and *intr.* for *refl.* Freq. *trans.* and *fig.*

1938 [implied at *tarted *ppl. a.* a]. **1952** *Archit. Rev.* CXII. 371/2 Unfortunately these devices to prevent the neighbourhood's slip from showing, have been 'tarted-up' with a variety of recessed panels, pipe ends, exposed brick heads and so forth, which seem to have no function. **1959** *Times Lit. Suppl.* 29 May p. xix, There seems nowadays a disposition to tart up Shakespeare as if he cannot be taken straight. **1961** [see *pretty *v.*]. **1967** *Spectator* 1 Dec. 690/3 Peacetime seems to have been passed in seducing the daughters of the local townsfolk..or tarting up one's uniform with more feathers or buttons. **1972** J. Wilson *Hide & Seek* ii. 35 You won't be able to tart yourself up like a teenager much longer, Rose. **1976** J. Cooper *Harriet* II. xiv. 115 They were tarting up in the Ladies. **1978** *Observer* 16 Apr. 38/1 American dealers would tart up the junk and sell it at suburban auctions at three times the English price.

3. *intr.* **a.** To meet or pursue women. **b.** Of a girl or woman: to behave like an immoral woman or a 'tart'; freq. const. *(a)round.*

1948 D. Ballantyne *Cunninghams* 30, I bet he's been tarting. **1949** J. B. Priestley *Home is Tomorrow* II. i. 47, I know I've behaved badly tarting around. **1959** K. Waterhouse *Billy Liar* ii. 33, I would fall to wondering whether she was tarting round the streets with some American airman. **1960** *Spectator* 18 Nov. 784 The boy would now turn soft and the girl start tarting. **1981** P. Vansittart *Death of Robin Hood* IV. v. 206 All had tales of adventure... Some claimed to have been tarting. **1983** J. Wainwright *Their Evil Ways* II. 66 Her mother was tarting around with this other bloke.

tartan, *sb.*¹ Add: **1. a.** Also preceded by a clan-name, etc. denoting a particular traditional or authorized design.

1821 D. Stewart *Sk. Highlanders Scotl.* I. III. i. 229 The pipers wore a red tartan of very bright colours, (of the pattern known by the name of the Stewart tartan). **1897** *Private Life of Queen* xxv. 209 The writing-room is hung entirely with the Balmoral tartan. **1949** 'J. Tey' *Brat Farrar* xiii. 114 A frayed Stewart tartan ribbon off a box of Edinburgh rock. **1981** *Times* 3 Feb. 17/6 Streaming from her helmet were two lengths of Colquhoun tartan from the clan of which her father was chief.

c. Used to denote young people who are members of Protestant gangs in Northern Ireland, from their traditional support of Glasgow Rangers Football Club.

1972 *Guardian* 17 Mar. 1/3 The local Protestant street gangs, mainly known as 'Tartans' because of their traditional association with the Rangers Football club. **1974** *Listener* 14 Mar. 324/2 Until recently these streets were terrorised by Tartan Gangs. Now their place has been taken by these youngsters, acting in the name of the Loyalist cause... Their behaviour is modelled on the Tartans. **1977** P. Carter *Under Goliath* iii. 15 Most of the kids were in tough Prod gangs, like the Tartans.

2. (Earlier examples.)

1837 J. Kirkbride *Northern Angler* 73 What is called the tartan-fly kills well in the Highlands at the clearing of the water. **1847** T. T. Stoddart *Angler's Compan.* xiii. 240 Salmon flies... The Tartan. Mottled black and white tail feather from turkey.

3.* (Properly with capital initial.) The proprietary name of a synthetic resin material used for surfacing running tracks, ramps, etc. Usu. *attrib.*, as *Tartan track.*

1964 *Official Gaz.* (U.S. Patent Office) 14 Jan. TM 60/1 Tartan. For synthetic resin material for application to various surfaces..To provide a resilient surface thereon. First use Aug. 28, 1962. **1968** *Listener* 10 Oct. 485/2 The 100-metre final is also on Day Three. A fast time with thin air, the 'tartan' track and, maybe, the new brush spike, is inevitable. **1969** *Trade Marks Jrnl.* 22 Oct. 1732/1 *Tartan*... Synthetic resins for use as floor and road surfacing materials. **1972** *Radio Times* 1 June 13/3 Britain's sprint hope..says..'I've got a good coach, there's a tartan track two minutes up the road.'

4. c. Used *loosely* in various *transf.* and *fig.* collocations to designate something pertaining to Scotland or which evokes Scottish nationalist fervour.

1954 J. P. Barter (*title*) Ritchie; or, behind the Tartan Curtain. **1975** *Globe & Mail* (Toronto) 27 Sept. 6/6 The British press has taken extreme care to avoid the suggestion that the activities of the 'Tartan Army' are linked to the legitimate national movement embodied in the Scottish National Party. **1976** *Listener* 28 Oct. 555/2 Radio 3's *Scottish Evening*... Overall there was a blessed absence of..Tartan Romanticism. **1982** *Times* 9 Jan. 6/1 Almost all Scottish MPs..are Scots by birth... It is not simply raw xenophobic tartan nationalism.

Tartar, *sb.*² (*a.*) Add: **A.** *sb.*² **5.** (Earlier examples.)

1668 [see Scythian *sb.* 2]. **1862** *Jrnl. Amer. Oriental Soc. 1861* VII. 272 They have by some been designated the 'Tartar', by others the 'Finnish', 'Ural-Altaic', 'Mongolian', and 'Turanian'.

C. tartar (also ‖ **-e**) **sauce** [tr. Fr. *sauce tartare*], a sauce made of mayonnaise and chopped gherkins, capers, etc., usu. served with fish.

1855 E. Acton *Mod. Cookery* (rev. ed.) vi. 143 Tartar sauce. (Sauce à la Tartare.)... Tartar-mustard..is to be preferred to English for this sauce. **1889** C. Owen *Choice Cookery* 48 Tartare sauce is mayonnaise with the addition of mustard, chives, pickles, and tarragon, chopped. **1951** *Good Housek. Home Encycl.* 677/1 *Tartare Sauce*..is served with fish, salads, and such vegetables as globe artichokes. **1959** *Good Food Guide* 292 Seafood pilaf with tartare sauce. **1973** 'D. Jordan' *Nile Green* xxiii. 93 The waiter..nearly tipped the tartare sauce down Mara's neck.

Tartary. Add: **3.** *attrib.* **Tartary oat**, a wild oat, *Avena fatua*, which has a loose inflorescence.

1790 S. Deane *New-England Farmer* 193/2 I have lately met with the Tartary oats, which..differ in their manner of growing. **1891** R. Wallace *Rural Econ. Austral. & N.Z.* xviii. 260 The straw is not so long or of such good quality as the straw of the Tartary Oat.

tarted (tā·ɹtėd), *ppl. a.* [f. *tart *v.*² 2 + -ed¹.] **a.** Of a person: dressed *up* in a showy manner, gaudily adorned. Also without *up*.

1938 E. Bowen *Death of Heart* I. iii. 61 After dark, she [*sc.* London] is like a governess gone to the bad, in a Woolworth tiara, tarted up all wrong. **1952** D. Adams *Murder, Maestro, Please* xvi. 113 These tarted-up hags! **1972** 'R. Crawford' *Whip Hand* I. viii. 49, I know your natures, you tarted-up toffs. **1979** *Even. Standard* 13 Sept. 19/6 Prostitutes..are of the conventional kind, in high heeled shoes and characteristically 'tarted' both cosmetically and sartorially.

b. *transf.* and *fig.*

1958 K. Amis *I like it Here* ii. 21 A collection of tarted-up reviews. **1967** *Spectator* 20 Oct. 455/3 The tarted-up village inn, remodelled with the single aim of attracting motor trade from a distance. **1972** *Where?* Mar. 96/3 ROSLA enthusiasts for tarted-up curricula need to heed the warning. **1981** J. Scott *Distant View of Death* xiv. 182 The tarted panda reversed..and drove in the wake of the quarry. **1983** *Listener* 21 July 33/2 At the other end of the spectrum of the Higher Rubbish—defined for the moment as tarted-up junk..—is Elizabeth Taylor in the vastly enjoyable, utterly brainless *The VIPs*.

tarten, *v.* Add: **2.** To affect with sharpness or acidity. *rare.*⁻¹

1925 W. de la Mare *Broomsticks* 58 Hardly had its juice tartened my tongue.

tartine. a. (Earlier example.)

1804 F. Burney *Jrnl.* 1 Oct. (1975) VI. 477, I have given no more medicine—plenty of tisanes &c, & tartines of Honey & salad are all he has taken.

tartish, *a.*² *colloq.* [f. *tart *sb.* 2 b + -ish.] = *tarty *a.* (and *sb.*)

1929 C. Connolly *Let.* Nov. in *Romantic Friendship* (1975) 327 We both felt that you thought she was tartish. **1944** E. Bowen in *Penguin New Writing* XX. 62 Collie was wearing that tartish house-coat. **1956** E. Grierson *Second Man* xiv. 249 A brocade house-coat and mules of a pink, tartish shade. **1972** *Daily Tel.* 4 Oct. 13/2 His mother is snappish, tartish and neglectful.

tartlet. Add: **1.** (Later examples.)

1889 Stevenson & Osbourne *Wrong Box* v. 79 He returned with a large bag of the choicest and most tempting of cakes and tartlets. **1965** [see *salpicon].

2. A young woman of immoral character, a young 'tart'.

a **1890** in Barrère & Leland *Dict. Slang* (1890) II. 337/1 E'en tartlets are stale, be they ever so tasty—The magic has fled from their langourous looks. **1961** *Spectator* 3 Mar. 304/3 Love for a tartlet in Florence.

Tartuffe, Tartufe. Add: Hence also **Tartu·ffily** *adv.* (*nonce-wd.*).

1915 [see *Pecksniff].

tarty (tā·ɹti), *a.* (and *sb.*) *colloq.* [f. *tart *sb.* 2 b + -y¹.] Resembling or suggestive of a 'tart', or woman of immoral character; cheap, gaudy. Occas. *absol.* as *sb.*

1918 G. Frankau *One of Them* xxi. 163 Of that barred citadel whose mincing misses Persuade the chaste to emulate the tarty. **1929** D. H. Lawrence *Pansies* 123, I suppose most girls are a bit tarty to-day So that's why so many young men have long faces. **1944** M. Laski *Love on Supertax* ix. 85 Some very tarty South American perfume. **1956** L. McIntosh *Oxford Folly* xiv. 231 A fat middle-aged woman with henna'd hair and clothes that managed to be at once tatty and tarty. **1978** M. Dickens *Open Bk.* ix. 78 Frank, who was respectably married, was half afraid of Jean, but half delighted. Her tarty teasing made him feel shockingly male.

Tarvia (tā·ɪviă). Chiefly *N. Amer.* [f. TAR *sb.* + L. *via* road.] The proprietary name of a road-surfacing and binding material made from tar. Also (irregularly) **ta·rviate** *v. trans.*; hence **ta·rviated** *ppl. a.*

1912 *Official Gaz.* (U.S. Patent Office) 23 July 1125/1 Tarvia..Pitch prepared from natural or manufactured bituminous oils and tars for road and pavement construction, roofing, waterproofing, and insulating. Claims use since June 1, 1903. **1926** *Daily Colonist* (Victoria, B.C.) 23 July 18/1 There has been a saving, over contract price, of $12,000, in tarviating the twenty-six miles of Island Highway. **1928** *Trade Marks Jrnl.* 18 Jan. 82 *Tarvia*... Raw or partly prepared mineral substances, for use in the manufacture of road-making materials. **1940** *Chambers's Techn. Dict.* 835/1 *Tarviated*.., a term applied to macadam road surfacings in which the stone is bound together with tar. **1947** *Archit. Rev.* CI. 163 A tarvia floor was chosen because of its cheapness and its acoustical properties. **1952** *Jrnl. Acoustical Soc. Amer.* XXIV. 662/1 It is..necessary to record on the identical stretch of tarvia road. **1966** R. H. RIMMER *Harrad Experiment* (1967) 25 A one lane tarvia road between two stone pillars. **1972** *Islander* (Victoria, B.C.) 23 Jan. 16/2 My feet got so sensitive I could sense the difference between tarvia, gravel, or concrete immediately.

tarwinie, var. of *TAUHINU.

Tarzan (tā·ɪzăn). The name of a character in a series of novels by the American author Edgar Rice Burroughs (1875–1950), and in subsequent films and television series, who is orphaned in West Africa in his infancy and reared in the jungle by a mother-ape, used *transf.* to designate a person distinguished by physical strength or agility.

[**1914** E. R. BURROUGHS (*title*) Tarzan of the apes.] **1921** *Glasgow Herald* 25 Oct. 5/5 At fruit picking time there is a regular colony of Tarzans disporting themselves in the branches. **1938** M. ALLINGHAM *Fashion in Shrouds* vi. 78 Ramillies was ruddy pleased... Saw 'imself a Tarzan. **1946** KOESTLER *Thieves in Night* 150 Their bodies [are] those of a horde of Hebrew Tarzans roaming in the hills of Galilee. **1960** *John o' London's* 14 Apr. 436 The tough 'Tarzan's' relationship with his landlady..is tenderly portrayed. **1974** H. MACINNES *Climb to Lost World* vi. 85 It wasn't a normal four hour walk—more like an obstacle course for budding Tarzans. **1981** R. BARNARD *Mother's Boys* i. 15 Gordon began his morning liturgy of exercises. ..'Bloody Tarzan,' said Brian.

b. Allusively in *attrib.* use.

1932 R. KNOX *Broadcast Minds* vii. 161 Though the Tarzan-stuff may make snappy reading. **1941** A. COTTERELL *What! No Morning Tea?* 103 Not hothouse gymnasium overdevelopment, but sheer Tarzan physical well-being. **1961** M. JONES *Potbank* xxvi. 114 A remarkably handsome young man with a Tarzan physique. **1974** V. CANNING *Painted Tent* ix. 189 Nearly killed myself on the tower ladder today. Saved by a Tarzan act.

Hence **Ta:rzane·sque** [-ESQUE], **Ta·rzan-like** *adjs.*

1933 *Punch* 27 Dec. 712/1 Taken in conjunction with my Tarzanesque agility, They constitute a clue to my athletic versatility. **1943** *Copper Camp* (Writers' Program, Montana) 214 Butt Block gazed pridefull at his partner, smiled and then with brawny fists pounded, Tarzan-like, upon his hairy chest. **1973** C. BONINGTON *Next Horizon* xi. 158 He loved being the centre of attraction, dropped easily into Tarzanesque poses, and enjoyed showing off the odd feat of strength. **1980** T. HOLME *Neapolitan Streak* 160 He had to perform a Tarzan-like operation, lowering himself..and then swinging down.

Tasaday (tasā·dai), *sb.* and *a.* [a. *Tasaday*, prob. f. *tau* person + *sa* (place marker) + *ddya* inland.] **A.** *sb.* **a.** (A member of) a people living on the Philippine island of Mindanao (see note). **b.** The Manobo language of this people.

The Tasaday isolated themselves (most probably in flight from a plague epidemic) some eight hundred years ago, forsaking their skills in rice-agriculture, metallurgy, etc., and taking up a less advanced form of existence (see quots.).

1971 *Guardian* 19 July 3/1 Dark skinned, fruit-eating men, known as Tasadays..near Lake Sebu, in Cotabato Province..south of Manila. The tribesmen..number about sixty... Their isolation was total until 1966. **1971** *Philippine Jrnl. Linguistics* II. 3 A comparison of the lexical items of Tasaday..reveals that the language has most cognates with..B'ht Manobo. **1972** *National Geographic* Aug. 232/2 Igna..translated from T'boli..to Tasaday. *Ibid.* 239 (*caption*) The staple of the Tasaday diet..is a wild yam. **1973** E. HYAMS *Final Agenda* ix. 118 The pacific and gentle manners of the Tasaday people, a Stone Age vestige still living on Mindanao. **1975** *New Society* 4 Dec. 559/2 In the early 1960s, Dafal, a wandering hunter, came across a small and timid band of food-gatherers, calling themselves Tasaday, living deep in the forest reaches of southern Mindanao in the Philippines.

Taser (tē̆i·zəɪ). orig. and chiefly *U.S.* Also **taser.** [f. the initial letters of *Tom Swift's electric rifle* (a fictitious weapon), after *LASER².] A weapon which fires barbs attached by wires to batteries, and causes temporary paralysis. Hence **Ta·sered** *a.*, paralysed by means of a Taser.

Developed by Taser Systems Inc., Los Angeles.

1972 *Science* 12 May 615/2 A taser is an instrument that fires a cluster of electrified barbs which become snagged in the victim's clothing and paralyze him until the current is switched off. **1973** *Guardian* 16 Apr. 11 A pan-lethal weapon called the Taser, developed by a California manufacturer... Two electrical wires lash out... The suspect stiffens from shock. His muscles are paralysed. **1975** *Globe & Mail* (Toronto) 4 Oct. 10/1 The Taser Public Defender, as it's called, can penetrate nearly two inches of clothing and give up to a 50,000-volt charge. Taser Systems Inc. of Los Angeles, the manufacturer, says it is not lethal but is designed to stop attackers in their tracks. **1976** *N.Y. Times Mag.* 4 Jan. 13 A powerful transformer within the Taser generates 50,000 volts when a trigger is pressed. This jolt, sent through the wires into the darts, which have been shot into the skin or clothing of the victim, cause him to become 'Tasered'. **1977** *Observer* 21 Aug. 2/7 There was the taser that fired barbs attached to wires into demonstrators to paralyse them with electric shocks.

tash (tæʃ). Also **'tache.** Colloq. abbrev. of MOUSTACHE, MUSTACHE *sb.* 1 a.

1893–4 R. O. HESLOP *Northumberland Words* II. 719 *Tash*, a moustache. 'Him wi' the *tash*.' **1943** HUNT & PRINGLE *Service Slang* 64 *Tash*, moustache. **1965** R. SIMONS *Dead Reckoning* iv. 56 'E 'ad a little tash, just under 'is nose. **1968** A. DIMENT *Great Spy Race* viii. 123 He was..spluttering through his straggly 'tache. **1973** A. MACVICAR *Painted Doll Affair* vi. 70 A wee runt wi' a Mexican 'tache. **1980** *Home & Country* Nov. 602/1 (Advt.), 12" male dolls..Painted hair and tash.

Tashi Lama (ta·ʃi lā·mă). Also 8–9 **Teshoo Lama, Teshu Lama;** 9 **Tishu Lama,** etc. [f. *Tashi* Lhunpo, the name of the monastery ruled by the Tashi Lama, + LAMA¹.] A title of the Panchen Lama (see *PANCHEN).

1774 G. BOGLE *Mission to Tibet* (1876) p. xlvii, There have been two great incarnations of equal rank: the Dalai Lama at Potala..; and the Teshu Lama at Teshu Lumbo, the incarnation of the Buddhisatwa Amitabha. **1784** S. TURNER *Let.* 2 Mar. in *Acct. of Embassy to Court of Teshoo Lama in Tibet* (1800) III. 366 He will ratify the promises made to the former Teshoo Lama, the moment the present Lama is capable of renewing the application. **1811** W. KIRKPATRICK *Acct. of Kingdom of Nepaul* 341 Some persons of rank on the part of the Teeshoo Lama, and Sankia Lama, came into the Goorkha camp. **1819** F. HAMILTON *Acct. of Kingdom of Nepal* I. i. 57 Still more celebrated is the Tishu Lama, who resides at Degarchi, and is the spiritual guide of the Chinese emperors. **1876** [see LAMA¹]. **1923** *Daily Mail* 18 Apr. 5 The Tashi Lama is of equal rank with the better-known Lama Guru of Lhassa, but he rules over a smaller area, and has not nearly so much temporal power as the latter, though he is regarded as a holier person. **1950** A. DE RIENCOURT *Lost World* viii. 96 His new name was Panchen Rimpoche or Precious Great Sage and his successors became known all over the world as Panchen or Tashi Lamas.

Tasian (tā·siăn, tē̆i·ʃ¹ăn), *a.* and *sb. Archæol.* [f. Deir *Tasa*, the name of a village in Upper Egypt, + -IAN.] **A.** *adj.* Of, pertaining to, or designating the pre-Dynastic Neolithic culture represented by remains found at Deir Tasa. **B.** *sb.* A person of the Tasian culture; the culture itself.

1929 G. BRUNTON in *Antiquity* III. 459 This new cultural phase we have named Tasian from the village of Deir Tasa where the graves were first located. *Ibid.* 466 It may be premature to say definitely that the Tasians preceded the Badarians, but all the evidence points in that direction. **1931** [see *BADARIAN *a.*]. **1934** V. G. CHILDE *New Light on Most Anc. East* iii. 52 Remains found at Deir Tasa and other sites on the east bank of the Nile in Middle Egypt..belong to a people who have been termed Tasians. **1939** —— *Dawn Europ. Civilization* (ed. 3) xii. 218 Beaker-like vases decorated with zones of incision which might be clay translations of such basketry vessels occur in Egypt in the early 'Tasian' phase of culture. **1961** G. CLARK *World Prehist.* v. 103 Although no radiocarbon or absolute dates are available for the Tasian it is generally held on not very impressive evidence to have preceded the Badarian.

task, *sb.* Add: **I. 2. b.** (Further examples.) *spec.* (*Winchester College slang*) an essay or composition to be written.

1900 J. S. FARMER *Public School Word-Bk.* 201 *Task*, (*subs.*) (Winchester), all kinds of composition other than an Essay or Vulgus. **1980** 'T. HINDE' *Sir Henry & Sons* xv. 151 The weekly essay..called a task, is written by every boy in the school.

c. *Psychol.* A piece of work or an exercise given to a subject in a psychological test or experiment. Cf. *AUFGABE.

1913 H. MÜNSTERBERG *Psychol. & Industrial Efficiency* xviii. 237 We know how the consciousness of the task to be performed has an organizing influence on the system of those psychophysical acts which lead to the goal. **1951** G. HUMPHREY *Thinking* 99 The energy [for mental operations] may..conceivably originate in..the task or motive. **1972** *Jrnl. Social Psychol.* LXXXVII. 96 Sixty males received..electric shocks of varying magnitude from a confederate during a 10-trial probability estimation task.

III. 6. (senses 2 and 3) *task assignment, performance, role*; *task-directed, -orientated, -oriented, -related* adjs.; **task force** orig. *U.S.*, an armed force organized for a special operation under a unified command; hence *transf.*, any group of persons organized for a special task, esp. an investigative committee; **task group,** a naval task force, or a subdivision of such a force.

1964 Task assignment [see *ASSIGNMENT 13]. **1971** J. S. BRUNER *Beyond Information Given* (1974) xvii. 302 The picture of development drawn thus far is much too task-directed, too playless to be characteristic of the first year of life. **1941** *Time* 23 June 41/3 A division of Marines and one of infantry..as a potential A.E.F. 'task force'—for action overseas. **1942** *Jrnl. R. Aeronaut. Soc.* XLVI. 340 Low speed battleships are useless as a constituent of so-called 'task' forces. **1949** *Richmond* (Va.) *Times-Dispatch* 1 Mar. 1/1 The work stoppage resulted from an attempt by the city to try out a 'task force' system of collections. Under this plan, workers are assigned a certain route to be covered each day. When they complete their route, they can go home, regardless of how long it has taken. **1954** *Economist* 9 Jan. 97 The task force appointed..to examine the civil service. **1966** [see *PROJECT *sb.* 5 d]. **1971** *Nature* 24 Dec. 435/3 A task force set up under the auspices of the National Heart and Lung Institute. **1980** *Birds* Autumn 13/3 The problem [of bird smuggling] has become so serious in the USA that the Justice Department has been ordered to establish a special task force. Over a period of 12 months, nearly 1,000 birds have been seized by Customs officers. **1982** *Times* 3 June 8/6 The work of getting the components of the task force to sea has often been swift. **1943** *Daily Tel.* 23 Oct. 1/4 Capt. Mackintosh, as the senior commanding officer, commanded a Task Group, which included one of the latest battleships and American destroyers. **1952** [see *KAMIKAZE *sb.* 2]. **1979** *Navy News* Feb. 2/1 Ships in a Royal Navy task group broke off from their work surveying the coast of Iran last month to ferry British and American dependants away from the troubled country. **1953** *Jrnl. Abnormal & Soc. Psychol.* XLVIII. 401 (*heading*) Coding noise in a task-oriented group. **1971** J. Z. YOUNG *Introd. Study Man* xx. 273 Both social and task-orientated behaviours are relatively consistent for both boys and girls from about 4 to 12 years. **1974** tr. *Wertheim's Evolution & Revolution* i. 38 Equally, modernity in political structure is positively related to a task-oriented bureaucracy and a recruitment on the basis of skills. **1970** *Jrnl. Gen. Psychol.* Jan. 91 The findings of this study that the task performance of internals was better. **1956** J. KLEIN *Study of Groups* viii. 112 If a member proposes that the group shall rehearse a play and another says that he hates play-acting, that is a task-related contribution. **1972** *Accountant* 21 Sept. 357/2 A more task-related analysis might be used. **1967** M. ARGYLE *Psychol. Interpersonal Behaviour* iv. 71 The task roles of providing 'fuel', putting the 'threads' of the discussion together, and clarification, were generally performed by the same person; the social roles of making tactful comments to heal hurt feelings, and joking, were performed by others.

task, *v.* Add: **2. b.** (Later examples.) Also const. *with.*

1975 *Sentinel* (Ottawa) III. 11. 3/2 Capt. Ditter was tasked to help prepare this issue. **1980** *Oxf. Star* 20 Nov. (Advt.), A small engineering team tasked with the design, building and commissioning of high volume production lines.

5. Delete † *Obs.* (Later examples.) Now const. *with.*

1965 K. GRAHAM *Eng. Criticism of Novel* iv. 117 Trollope is another offender who is frequently tasked with endangering the wholeness of his novels. **1976** *Times Lit. Suppl.* 20 Feb. 197/1 He tasks Taylor with suggesting that Hegel reappeared in Anglo-Saxon thought at the turn of the century.

Taslan (tæ·slăn). [Invented word.] The proprietary name of a process for bulking or texturing synthetic yarns; also, a yarn which has been subjected to this process.

1954 *Trade Marks Jrnl.* 31 Mar. 328/2 Taslan 726,376. All goods included in Class 23. **1954** *Official Gaz.* (U.S. Patent Office) 13 July 263/2 E.I. du Pont de Nemours and Company, Wilmington, Del... *Taslan* for thread and yarn. Use since Jan. 4, 1954. **1957** *Times* 14 Jan. 11 *Taslan*, a process for 'texturing', or 'bulking' synthetic yarns such as acetate, nylon or Terylene to give softer handle and improve draping qualities. **1959** A. J. HALL *Stand. Handbk. Textiles* (ed. 5) iii. 131 Bulk yarns can be produced in various ways..but much success has attended the method used for the production of Taslan yarns. **1960** *Skinner's Silk & Rayon Rec.* Oct. 994/2 Car upholstery is another field in which *Taslan* has found a good reception in the U.S. **1963** A. J. HALL *Textile Sci.* iii. 130 There are various types of textured yarns which have now become available for weaving and knitting into fabrics under branded names such as Agilon, Banlon, Taslan, etc.

Tasmanian, *a.* Add: (Examples.)

1851 *Illustr. Catal. Gt. Exhib.* IV. I. 998/3 Many Tasmanian plants bloom throughout the winter months. **1874** M. CLARKE *His Natural Life* II. v. 104 'And what books do you read?'..' "Blair's Sermons," and "The Tasmanian Almanack".' **1920** *Glasgow Herald* 23 July 6 He..attended the royal meeting of the Tasmanian Racing Club in the afternoon. **1964** W. L. GOODMAN *Hist. Woodworking Tools* 157 The Sanderson Brothers & Newbould catalogue has a variation of this called the 'Tasmanian' tooth. **1975** *Listener* 7 Aug. 172 The remnants of the four Tasmanian tribes, the last of the 5,000 Tasmanians who were there when the Europeans landed.

B. as *sb.* **a.** A member of the aboriginal people of Tasmania, now extinct.

1842 *Penny Cycl.* XXIV. 90/2 That courage was rewarded by the appointment of Mr. Robinson to the office of 'civilizing' the Tasmanians at Flinders' Island. **1899** J. MILNE *Romance of Pro-Consul* viii. 79 The Tasmanians have now been extinct for years. **1918** L. HUXLEY *Life J. D. Hooker* I. 106 A meagre record of the thousands of native Tasmanians. **1935** HUXLEY & HADDON *We Europeans* iv. 120 Of all existing men the Arctic Eskimo is the most leptorrhine and the equatorial negro one of the most platyrrhine, but the Tasmanians, who lived in a temperate climate, were also platyrrhine. **1978** *Nature* 18 May 185/2 Within a few decades they were nearly exterminated by European settlers, until the scattered survivors were removed in 1834 to Flinders Island, where the last full-blooded Tasmanian died in 1876.

b. A native or inhabitant of Tasmania.

1934 T. Wood *Cobbers* xiii. 163 Tasmanians, I found, grumble. **1974** *Country Life* 7 Nov. 1388/2 Although.. whaling had started in its adjacent waters, the Tasmanians themselves were prohibited from engaging in the industry. **1978** A. Waugh *Best Wine Last* x. 118 One of my two uncles..married a Tasmanian.

Tasmanoid (tæ·zmănoid), *a.* [f. *Tasman(ian *sb.* + -oid.] Resembling or allied to the ethnological type of the aborigines of Tasmania.

1938 *Skr. Norske Videnskaps-Akademi (Mat.-Nat. Kl.)* *1937* 153 It is not inconceivable that an original Tasmanoid population in Australia was driven south. **1943** *Mem. Nat. Mus. Melbourne* XIII. 44 The evidence.. strongly suggests that the earliest migrants belonged to a Tasmanoid (Negrito) race..and that this race..found its way to Tasmania. **1958** F. E. Zeuner *Dating the Past* 281 Wunderly comes to the conclusion that the skull combines Australoid and Tasmanoid characteristics in about equal proportions.

Tass[3] (tæs). Also **TASS.** [a. Russ., acronym f. the initial letters of *T*elegrafnoe *a*gentstvo *S*ovetskogo *S*oyuza.] The official Soviet news agency.

1925 *Times* 27 Aug. 11/7 A decree ratified by the Soviet authorities changes the name of Rosta (Russian Telegraph Agency) to Tass (Telegrafnoye Agenstvo Sovietskovo Soyuza=Telegraph Agency of the Soviet Union), as from August 1 next. **1942** *Nature* 25 Apr. 475/1 It is announced by the Tass Agency that [etc.]. **1950** A. Huxley *Themes & Variations* 52 Not..that he had the faintest premonition of Harmsworth or Hearst,..of Goebbels or Tass. **1958** *Spectator* 27 June 824/1 The new Tass statement on the Lebanon. **1974** T. P. Whitney tr. *Solzhenitsyn's Gulag Archipelago* I. I. i. 9 Several days later TASS will issue an angry statement to all the papers. **1981** *Guardian* 27 Apr. 5/2 Tass, reporting from Warsaw, said..that 'revisionist elements in the party' were trying to paralyse it.

tassel, *sb.*[1] Add: **5. tassel-flower,** (*a*) (earlier and later examples); **tassel hyacinth** (examples).

1836 A. Lincoln *Familiar Lect. Bot.* (ed. 5) 83 Tassel-flower; from the East Indies. **1863** 'G. Hamilton' *Gala-Days* 10 The scarlet tassel-flower utterly refuses to unfold his brave plumes. **1957** C. O. Booth *Encycl. Ann. & Biennial Plants* 261/2 *E[milia] sagittata*..is the popular Tassel Flower, or Flora's Paintbrush, a charming half-hardy annual. **1790** *Curtis's Bot. Mag.* IV. 133 (*heading*) Two Coloured, or Tassel Hyacinth. **1865** M. Eyre *Lady's Walks in S. France* xxiii. 251 The starch, and the tassel-hyacinth,..and many others..are all common flowers about Bagnères. **1961** R. Genders *Miniature Bulbs* ii. 165 The 'Tassel Hyacinth' grows a foot high.

tassel, *v.* Add: **2.** (Earlier and further examples.) Also *tassel out.*

1757 in C. R. Woodward *Ploughs & Politicks* (1941) 278 Just before it Tossles it should be plowed & hoed again. **1774** P. V. Fithian *Jrnl.* (1900) 212 The Corn is beginning pretty generally to tassel. **1843** *Amer. Pioneer* II. 83 Corn, if planted, grows a foot high, tassels out and dies. **1887** M. E. Wilkins *Humble Romance* 29 His corn tasselled out..as soon as anybody's. **1966** R. G. Toepfer *Witness* v. 34 Mr. Davis Miller's corn was starting to tassel out and you could pretty near see it grow.

Tassie[2] (tæ·si). Also ¶ **Tassi, tassie.** The name of James *Tassie* (1735–99), Scottish gem engraver, used *attrib.* and *absol.* of replicas of ancient engraved gems or original portrait reliefs made in glass paste by him or by his nephew William Tassie (1777–1860) who succeeded him.

1819 Keats *Let.* 13 Mar. (1958) II. 45 On looking at your seal I cannot tell whether or not it is done with a Tassi—it seems to me to be paste. **1894** J. M. Gray *James & William Tassie* viii. 65 The Shadford Walker Sale included..over a hundred large Tassie medallions of contemporary personages. **1942** E. Blunden *Romantic Poetry & Fine Arts* 10 His [*sc.* Keats's] own particular Tassie was 'a lyre with the strings broken'. **1972** *Times* 1 Aug. 11/5 (Advt.), A collection of paintings..Tassi medallions. **1979** Mills & Mansfield *Genuine Article* vii. 109 Many people fail, when encountering what might be a 'Tassie', to..see if the alleged diamond is backed by metal. **1981** 'J. Gash' *Vatican Rip* iii. 36 That glimpse of Mrs Culpepper's 'tassie', as we call such incised semi-precious carvings. *Ibid.* v. 46 The silly bitch laughingly refused to sell me her tassie ring.

Tassie[3] (æ·zi). *Austral. slang.* Also **Tassey, Tassy.** [Hypocoristic, f. *Tasmania* or *Tasmanian *sb.* b: see -ie.] **a.** Tasmania. **b.** A Tasmanian.

1894 *Argus* (Melbourne) 26 Jan. 3 Today Tassy—as most Victorian cricketers and footballers familiarly term our neighbour over the straits—will send a team into the field. **1905** in A. B. Paterson *Old Bush Songs* 51 Once more the Maorilander and the Tassey will be seen Cooking johnny cakes and jimmies on the plains of Riverine. **1915** H. Lawson *Coll. Verse* (1969) III. 154 Fighting hard for little Tassy, where the apple orchards grow. **1936** F. Clune *Roaming round Darling* xix. 188 The Poet says that's the area of Tasmania. I'll take his word for it, as I haven't time to go and measure Tassie. **1938** N. Marsh *Artists in Crime* vi. 76 'Aussie', 'Tassie', 'a goodee', 'a badee'. Pray spare me these bloody abbreviations. **1956** S. Hope *Digger's Paradise* 77 The Hobart–Launceston express has the advantage of allowing the customer to see Tassie's beautiful countryside. **1977** *Herald* (Melbourne) 17 Jan. 14/2 (Advt.), Come to 'Tassie' the Casino State.

tasso (tæ·so). [perh. f. Tasajo: cf. Louisiana French *tasseau* jerked beef.] = Tasajo.

1841 *Southern Lit. Messenger* VII. 77/2 The evening banquet of gumbo, tasso, and beef, in every variety of form, was shortly served up by their attendants. **1934** E. Waugh *Handful of Dust* vi. 336 Mr. Todd..gave him farine and *tasso* and sent him on his journey. **1958** J. Carew *Wild Coast* viii. 106 Enough food to last Hector for a week—unleavened bread and bits of jerked pork in it, strips of tasso, cassava bread. **1959** P. Capon *Amongst those Missing* 168 He bought two sacks of farine, two of tasso, one of Brazil nuts and one of cashew nuts.

taste, *sb.*[1] Add: **II. 3. b.** (Further examples.) Also *spec.*, an alcoholic drink; alcohol. *U.S. slang.*

1919 E. O'Neill *Rope* in *Moon of Caribbees* 202 Will ye have a taste? It's real stuff. **1966** *New Yorker* 25 June 33 Why don't you stop up Wednesday, and we'll have a taste. **1973** T. Kochman *Rappin' & Stylin' Out* 162, I view such terms as 'pluck' for wine and 'taste' for liquor as embodying an action element retained from its more conventional use as a verb. **1976** *New Yorker* 1 Mar. 84/2 He said, 'Take me for a taste.' We went into a bar, and I thought he'd settle down for a few, but he only had two shots. **1978** *Maledicta* *1977* I. 224 Had a complete and unabetting weakness for *taste* (liquor).

5. c. In fig. phr. *a bad* (or *nasty*) *taste in the mouth* and varr., a lingering feeling of repugnance or disgust left behind by a distasteful or unpleasant experience.

1857 Mrs. Gaskell *Life C. Brontë* II. viii. 186 They [*sc.* Balzac's novels] leave such a bad taste in my mouth. **1899** R. Whiteing *No. 5 John St.* ii. xxv. 255 Never before have I heard such a speech... 'Sort o' gives yer a nasty taste in the mouth,' says Low Covey. **1904** [in Dict., sense 5 a]. **1943** *Sun* (Baltimore) 22 Apr. 18/1 A decidedly sour taste was left by the opening number. **1969** R. Harper *World of Thriller* ii. 71 When all the characters are corrupt or shoddy, the reader goes away with a bad taste in his mouth. **1979** R. Perry *Bishop's Pawn* iv. 70 It had taken me nearly an hour to go through the dossier and when I'd finished reading I had a nasty taste in my mouth.

IV. 9. *taste-leader, -maker, -organ*; **taste-blindness** *Biol.* (see quot. 1934); so **taste-blind** *a.*; **taste-bud** (examples); also *fig.*; **taste-test** *v. trans.*, to test (something) by tasting it, to test the taste of (something); also *absol.*; so **taste-tested** *a.*; **taste-tester.**

1934 *Jrnl. Heredity* XXV. 189/2 There is less likelihood of finding a group entirely taste blind. *Ibid.* 190/1 Taste blindness is an inherited inability to taste certain thiocarbamides as crystals or in cold diluted solutions as bitter. **1965** M. A. Amerine et al. *Princ. Sensory Evaluation Food* ii. 112 Based on studies of families and twins, 'taste blindness' was first reported to be a simple recessive character. **1975** *Nature* 6 Feb. 442/1 The designation 'tasters' for the more sensitive individual and 'non-tasters' or 'taste blind' for the less sensitive. **1879** J. Fulton *Text Bk. Physiol.* (ed. 2) xiv. 365 Peculiar structures, known as taste buds, or taste goblets, have been discovered in the circumvallate papillæ. **1951** V. Nabokov *Speak, Memory* ii. 30 It is..to the lowly and ugly agarics, that nations with timorous taste-buds limit their knowledge and appetite. **1963** *Listener* 3 Jan. 40/1 Vested interests and pressure-groups work upon everything from our political opinions to our taste-buds. **1970** T. S. & C. R. Leeson *Histology* (ed. 2) xiv. 274/2 A few taste buds are found also in the palate and epiglottis. **1952** D. Riesman *Individualism Reconsidered* (1954) 207 The problem..of becoming a possible taste-leader. **1961** *New Left Rev.* Jan.–Feb. 34/2 These areas of work are excluded, by the tastemakers, from the concept of 'serious' art. **1978** *Jrnl. R. Soc. Arts* CXXVI. 725/2 Federigo's artistic patronage did prove a tastemaker, though of a limited kind. **1927** Haldane & Huxley *Animal Biol.* i. 25 A number of very small taste-organs are scattered over certain parts of the tongue [of the frog]. **1970** G. Ordish tr. *Chauvin's World of Ants* vii. 175 The taste organ is situated in the antennae. **1979** *Wichita* (Kansas) *Eagle* 23 May 1-B/4 If you've never cooked with fresh ginger.. taste-test before adding more. **1980** D. Williams *Murder for Treasure* xx. 198 He found himself staring into the eyes of a gargantuan dog whose giant tongue was taste-testing his chin. **1960** *Time* (Atlantic ed.) 11 Apr. 58 Critically taste-tested piles of free cigarettes. **1969** *Listener* 24 July 127/3 Game would be virtually tasteless if taste-testers succeeded in eliminating all its off-flavours.

taster[1]. Add: **4.** Also *spec.*, a portion of ice cream served in a shallow glass. *colloq.*

1891 [in Dict.]. **1901** *Daily Tel.* 21 May 10 The irate signor..produced—not a half-penny taster for the policeman but a tattered copy of a work called 'Law without Lawyers'. **1927** W. E. Collinson *Contemp. Eng.* 16 The Italian often known as an ice-cream Jack with his ice-cream barrow still follows his calling and no doubt the youngsters still ask for wafers and tasters.

‖ **tastevin** (tastəvæ̃n, tāt-). [An earlier form of mod.Fr. *tâte-vin*, lit. 'wine-taster', revived as in the title of the *Confrérie des Chevaliers du Tastevin* (founded 1933).] **1. a.** = Taster[1] 3 a. **b.** (With capital initial.) In France, a member of an order or guild of wine-tasters.

1952 A. Lichine *Wines of France* viii. 79 Most tasters use the *tastevin* in Burgundy. **1966** P. V. Price *France: Food & Wine Guide* 147 The three top sketches show a Burgundy tastevin, with irregularly patterned indentations and a thumb-rest. **1969** Dorozynski & Bell *Wine Bk.* 280 Wine-tasting orders, associations, fraternities and clubs are born almost every year... The Tastevins de Bourgogne..are among the best known in France. **1971** *Esquire* July 22/4 The enthronement of the Tastevins takes place in nearby Clos de Vougeot. **1979** *Homes & Gardens* June 129/1 We moved on to the splendid Beaune Boucherottes, its dusky red lights twinkling in the tiny silver *tastevin* that Andre always uses to assess colour.

2. *attrib.* (in sense 1 b), signifying approval by a special committee of wine-tasters.

1964 H. Johnson *Encycl. Wine* 290 System of labelling certain Burgundy wines... Upon payment of a certain sum per bottle, these wines may carry a special, rather elaborate Tastevin label. **1968** *Times* 3 Sept. 20/5 An invitation to attend the Tastevin banquet at the Château Clos de Vougeot. **1977** W. M. Spackman *Armful of Warm Girl* 109 This was a Tastevin bottling which he'd never found before outside of France.

tasting, *vbl. sb.* Add: **2. b.** A gathering for the purpose of tasting and comparing various kinds of drink, usu. wine. See also *wine-tasting* s.v. *wine *sb.*[1] 8.

1959 I. Ross *Image Merchants* viii. 128 'Cognac and coffee' tastings which Kaduson persuaded leading hotels ..to hold. **1963** *Harper's Bazaar* Feb. 22/3 The Lebègue tastings usher in the autumn wine season. **1977** T. Heald *Just Desserts* i. 23 It's their annual tasting..for one or two of the better known wine and food writers. **1978** *Times* 4 Mar. 10/7 The Malmaison Wine Club..holds sit-down tastings, which are often attended by wine trade trainees.

3. *tasting party, room.*

1978 *Times* 4 Mar. 10/3 The 'tasting parties' offered by many [wine] firms..are social rather than studious occasions. *a* **1966** 'M. Na Gopaleen' *Best of Myles* (1977) 122 Gallantry and distinguished conduct in the [ice-cream] tasting room. **1970** *Country Life* 1 Oct. 837/3 It is distinctly cool..in the subterranean tasting room where red and white..wines are sampled.

tasto (ta·sto). *Mus.* [It., = touch, key.] **a.** The key of a piano or the finger-board of a stringed instrument. **b.** Phr. *sul tasto* [lit. 'over the finger-board']: a direction in a musical score that the stringed instrument is to be played with the bow over the finger-board; *tasto solo*: a direction that the bass notes are to be played alone without any harmony.

1740 J. Grassineau *Mus. Dict.* 268 *Tasto*, the touch or part of an instrument whereon, or by means of which its notes are made to sound, be it on the neck, as lutes..; or the front of organs. **1772** W. Tans'ur *Elements of Mus.* v. 221 *Tasto*, the Touches or Keys of Organs &c. *Tasto solo*, to strike such Sounds till other Words, or Parts come on. **1876** Stainer & Barrett *Dict. Mus. Terms* 421/2 *Tasto*,..(1) A key of a pianoforte. (2) The touch of a pianoforte or organ. **1889** Grove *Dict. Mus.* IV. 63/2 'Tasto solo', the key alone, is in old music written over those portions of the bass or continuo part in which the mere notes were to be played by the accompanyist, without the chords or harmonies founded on them. **1946** E. Blom *Everyman's Dict. Mus.* 600/1 *Sul tasto* (It.), a direction indicating that a passage of string mus. is to be played with the bow over the finger-board. **1974** *Sci. Amer.* Jan. 93/2 Farthest from the bridge..the timbre has the gentle character that composers seek by designating *sul tasto*: 'bow over the fingerboard'. **1980** *Early Music* Apr. 150/2 In Rameau's day the single harpsichordist either did not play during the purely orchestral music and choruses or at most played the bass line only, either *tasto solo* (at pitch) or *all'unisono* (doubling an octave above or below).

tasty, *a.* Add: Also † **tastey. 1. b.** (Later examples.)

1899 R. Whiteing *No. 5 John St.* vii. 61 'Nice and tastey,' observes my friend..as he points to a leg that seems to fear nothing on earth..not even Lord Campbell's Act. **1976** *Sounds* 11 Dec. 41/5, I couldn't help wishing Can'd..pump out a tasty three minute song like their last single,..'I Want More'.

c. (See quots.). *slang.*

1975 *Observer* 11 May 2/7 'I got the impression that he with a bit tasty' (i.e., had a criminal record). **1980** *Daily Mail* 21 Mar. 7/2 A 'tasty villain' (a known criminal).

2. b. Fastidious. *rare.*

1905 A. Adams *Outlet* 102 The two strangers were rather tasty, but Siringo ate ravenously.

tat, *sb.*[1] Add: **2.** *pl.* **tats, tatts.** Teeth; now usu. with ref. to a set of false teeth. *slang* (chiefly *Austral.*).

1919 W. H. Downing *Digger Dialects* 49 *Tats*, teeth. **1935** A. J. Pollock *Underworld Speaks* 119/2 *Tats*, teeth. **1962** *Coast to Coast 1961–62* 131 He'd lost his 'tatts' in a brawl in Townsville the night before we left Australia. **1976** *Express* (Austral.) 3 Nov. 2/3 Talking of 'tats' a dental standards official said false teeth for animals are nothing new.

tat, *sb.*[2] Add: **b.** In tea-drying: a tray or shelf, freq. of hessian, on which green tea leaves are spread to wither.

1922 H. J. Moppett *Tea Manuf.* 14 Withering tats must present a smooth even surface free from corrugations or pockets. *Ibid.* 15 Insufficient tat space is a bad fault. **1935** W. H. Ukers *All about Tea* II. 515/1 *Tat*, a shelf made of wire or Hessian..on which green tea leaves are spread for withering. **1957** *Encycl. Brit.* XXI. 863/2 After plucking, the leaf is withered by being spread on bamboo trays in the sun, or on withering tats within doors. **1958** T. Eden *Tea* xiii. 150 Some factories have 'mobile tats'. They are slung from pulleys travelling on overhead rails such that each individual bank of tats can be removed from its internal location and brought to a loading and weighing platform at any time.

tat, *sb.*[5] Add: Also **tatt. 1. a.** (Earlier and later examples.) Now usu. only in *sing.* Also, poorly made or tasteless clothes. Hence, a shabby person, a slut.

1839 [see *posh *sb.*[2] 1]. **1882** *Sydney Slang Dict.* 9/2 The paper makers get the tats. **1936** N. Coward *To-Night at 8.30* I. 93 You should have seen the company: a couple of old tats got up as Elizabethan pages. **1947** N. Marsh *Final Curtain* iv. 53 Do they think it's any catch living in a mausoleum with a couple of old tats? **1972** D. Goddard *Blimey!* (1974) iv. 43 King's Road beckons the well-heeled traveller into a cloud-cuckoo land of high-priced tat and gear. **1977** M. Drabble *Ice Age* II. 212 She was dressed..in a horrible collection of tat—a long shiny maroon skirt, a baggy flowered blouse, a grey cardigan, and a green cardigan on top of that.

b. Rubbish, junk, worthless goods. Also *transf.* and *fig.*

1951 W. Sansom *Face of Innocence* iv. 55 He was talking of his business in Georgian and early Victorian objets d'oeil. He called it tat. **1958** A. Wilson *Middle Age of Mrs Eliot* II. 151 It was filled..with a jumble of pleasing, valuable antique furniture and hideous, worthless bric-a-brac... 'I like tatt,' he had said. **1967** N. Marsh *Death at Dolphin* ii. 40 A small shop in Walton Street where they sold what he described as: 'Very superior tatt. Jacobean purses, stomachers and the odd codpiece.' **1970** 'D. Halliday' *Dolly & Cookie Bird* iv. 52 Are they selling tat medals as well? **1971** D. Lees *Rainbow Conspiracy* iii. 38 Oh no! Not that load of old tat. We threw it out at afternoon [news] conference. **1976** *New Musical Express* 12 Feb. 26/3 That long deleted album..sounds like a heap of prissy irrelevant whimsical lysergic tat with Disney lyrics. **1981** *Times Lit. Suppl.* 18 Sept. 1060/1 New ways of getting the johns to spend their money on previously unsellable old tat.

tat, *sb.*[6] Delete *Sc.* and add: Also **tatt.** (Later examples.)

1922 Joyce *Ulysses* 423 A slut combs out the tatts from the hair of a scrofulous child. **1968** *Saturday Night* Mar. 34/3 The hair was full of tats so it was easy to find places to stick the flowers.

Tat (tāt), *sb.*[8] Also **Tât.** [a. Russ., from Turkish.] (A member of) an agricultural people perh. related to the Tajiks and living in Azerbaijan and Dagestan; also, the Iranian language spoken by this people.

1834 A. Burnes *Trav. Bokhara* II. 265 We find as great a variety among the citizens of Toorkistan as in the sub-divisions of the Tartars. The aborigines of the country are the Tajiks or Tats. **1888** *Encycl. Brit.* XXIII. 25/1 The Tajaks are known as Tâts on the west side of the Caspian. **1939** H. Field *Contrib. Anthropol. Iran* iii. 157 While..these elements cannot be considered pure Iranian there remain the Talych (91,000), Tat (74,000) and Persian (50,000), all of which are clearly Iranian dialects. **1951** W. K. Matthews *Lang. U.S.S.R.* vii. 104 The Tat of Azerbaijan, north of Baku, is like Talysh, a divergent variety of Persian. **1981** *Jewish Chron.* 24 Apr. 6/5 A Tat, a mountain Jew from Daghestan in the Caucasus, Mr Irmiya Rabayev, 31, has been a refusenik for seven years.

ta-ta, *int.* Add: Also **tata, ta ta,** etc., and with pronunc. (tæ·ta). **1.** Now in gen. colloq. use. Cf. *tatty-bye *int.* and T.T.F.N. s.v. *T 6. (Earlier and later examples.)

1823 S. Hutchinson *Let.* Sept.–Oct. (1954) 261 Baby I believe has not learnt any new words since Mrs M. wrote last, but she has the old ones very perfect—'Gone'—'Ta ta'—'By bye'. **1901** 'M. Franklin' *My Brilliant Career* xxxii. 272 (*heading*) Ta-Ta to Barney's Gap. **1922** T. S. Eliot *Waste Land* II. 26 Goonight Bill. Goonight Lou. Goonight May. Goonight. Ta ta. Goonight. **1934** —— *Rock* ii. 69 Well, tar tar, boys. **1949** G. B. Shaw *Buoyant Billions* iv. 52, I must go now to see about Father's lunch. Tata. **1951** R. Braddon *Naked Island* II. vi. 153 'All right, Mr. McLeod, fall out.'.. 'Ta-ta, Rod—see you in Australia.' **1960** L. Reid Banks *L-Shaped Room* xxiii. 297 Charlie'll come up in a few minutes and see how you're getting on. Tata for now. **1983** P. Inchbald *Short Break in Venice* vii. 68 Sod off!.. We'll talk later... Tata.

2. *ta-ta theory* (Philol.), the theory that language originated in an attempt to imitate the body's gestures with the vocal organs.

1930 J. R. Firth *Speech* i. 7 According to the *ta-ta* theory of Sir Richard Paget, the tongue makes the same gesture while saying *ta-ta* or *hither* as would be made by the hand with similar intention. **1939** L. H. Gray *Foundations of Lang.* 40 Language has been traced..by others to sounds produced by the vocal organs when half-consciously imitating the movements of the body in performing some activity (the ta-ta theory). **1972** Hartmann & Stork *Dict. Lang. & Linguistics* 160/1 R. Paget (1869–1955) claimed that language comes from the combination of certain gestures and tongue movements (*ta-ta theory*).

B. as *sb.* A nursery or playful term. **a.** A walk or outing. Also *fig.* **b.** A hat, bonnet, etc.

(*a*) **1886** J. Sully *Teacher's Handbk. Psychol.* x. 185 A child of eighteen months will mentally rehearse a series of experiences, as those of a walk: 'Go tata, see geegee.' **1912** D. H. Lawrence *Let.* 28 Mar. (1962) I. 104 In the evening Diddler took me a tat-tar, and of course got lost. **1930** —— *Nettles* 9 Want to go a little tattah? So it shall... If it's good!.. It shall go a tattah with its Auntie In a motor. **1958** 'N. Blake' *Penknife in my Heart* iii. 45 Sharp at 10.45 every night..he takes his dog out for a ta-ta. **1969** J. Wainwright *Take-Over Men* vii. 121 They're a con man's dream. They're taken for a ta-ta every market day. (*b*) *c* **1910** F. W. Leigh in *Francis & Day's Album of Famous Old Songs* (1956) viii, Put on your tat-ta, little girlie. **1912** C. Mackenzie *Carnival* iii. 21 The tying on of her 'ta-ta'—at first a frilled bonnet, later on a rakish Tam o' Shanter. **1920** 'K. Mansfield' *Lett. to J. M. Murry* (1951) 506, I put on my ta-ta. **1949** M. Steen *Twilight on Floods* iv. viii. 644 How about having the ta-tas ready to show her?

‖ **tatami** (tata·mi). Also 7 **tatamee, tattami.** [Jap.] A rush-covered straw mat which is the usual floor-covering in Japan and the size of which (approx. six feet by three feet) functions as a standard unit in room measurement.

1614 R. Wickham in *Trans. Asiatic Soc. Japan* (1898) XXVI. 209, I..made Tatamee of Meaco 15$. *Ibid.*, I sold it per 14 Tatamees at 120 Mas per tatame. **1616** R. Cocks *Diary* 23 Jan. (1883) I. 103, 20 *tattamis* for Matingas howse. **1625** Purchas *Pilgrimes* II. v. 326 Hee caused at Ozaca a Hall to bee erected, with a thousand Tatami (very elegant mats). **1880** I. L. Bird *Unbeaten Tracks in Japan* I. ix. 89 Japanese house-mats, *tatami*, are as neat, refined, and soft a covering for the floor as the finest Axminster carpet. **1886** A. C. Maclay *Budget of Lett. from Japan* 42 *Tatamis* are heavy padded mats about seven feet long, three feet wide, and about two inches thick. They are the only covering that the Japanese ever use for their floors... They are manufactured of soft rushes, and are bordered with silken edges. **1909** *Cent. Dict.* Suppl., *Tatami*..2. A Japanese measure of surface, that of a mat 6 shaku in length by 3 shaku in width, or nearly 6 feet by 3 feet. **1924** *Public Opinion* 28 Nov. 527/2 It is a strict rule that tatamis must be kept clean. **1933** R. V. C. Bodley *Japanese Omelette* xii. 116 The dining room floor, instead of being matted with *tatami* as in Japan, was made of some kind of oilcloth. **1957** *New Yorker* 23 Nov. 120/2 *Tatami* cover the floors of nearly all Japanese houses. **1960** B. Leach *Potter in Japan* iii. 68 In twenty years' time, won't the Japanese room with 'tatami' (the thick compressed straw matting) become a luxury as the foreign style is today? **1974** *Encycl. Brit. Micropædia* IX. 837/3 The standardized size of the mat has created an important modular unit in the development of Japanese architecture; for example the *shōji*..are approximately as high as the tatami are long. **1976** P. Quennell *Marble Foot* v. 182 No less beautiful..were the *tatami* that lined our floors, long greenish slabs, that turn with age a dull gold, of finely woven rush-matting. **1981** G. MacBeth *Kind of Treason* ix. 92 He relaxed on the tatami and spoke with polite approval of the cousin's *tsuba*.

2. Freq. *attrib.*, as *tatami mat, matting, room.* Also *Comb.*, as *tatami-floored, -matted* adjs.

1947 J. Bertram *Shadow of War* vi. 200 Each man had some two and a half feet by six feet of *tatami* mat. **1962** *Times* 25 Jan. 13/4 The man who comes to lay the *tatami* matting in his house. **1979** S. Coe in I. Webb *Compl. Guide to Flower & Foliage Arrangement* xvii. 231/2 The room..is quite small, about 3 × 3 m (10 × 10 ft) or four and a half *tatami* mats. **1979** *Jrnl. R. Soc. Arts* Nov. 749/1 The interior spaces provide everything that the harsh exterior rejects: complex flowing geometries, traditional tatami room, lush furnishing and peaceful, controlled nature. **1980** J. Melville *Chrysanthemum Chain* 127 The tatami-matted floor of Yamamoto's room. **1981** C. Potok *Bk. of Lights* (1982) v. 162 He had a fish dinner in a lovely tatami-floored Japanese restaurant. **1982** *Nature* 20 May 181/1 Thus the popular, but erroneous, Japanese view that they have grown taller by adopting the habit of sitting on Western chairs rather than sitting with legs folded underneath the body on a *tatami* mat.

tater (tēⁱ·təɹ). Also **tator, tatur. 1.** Further dial. variants of Potato *sb.* 2 dγ. Cf. next.

1759 L. Wood *Jrnl.* 27 May in *Essex Inst. Hist. Coll.* (1882) XIX. 65 We travelled..9 miles to Capt Curtises and there we Dined upon codfish and taters. **1911** F. H. Burnett *Secret Garden* xxiv. 252 Anything'll grow for him. His 'taters and cabbages is twice th' size of anyone else's. **1939** F. Thompson *Lark Rise* i. 11 Mother spent hours boiling up the 'little taturs'. **1943** W. Stevens in O. Williams *New Poems 1943* 236 (*title of poem*) No possum, no sop, no taters. **1977** *New Yorker* 27 June 76/3, I et 3lbs. of taters.

2. *attrib.* and *Comb.* **tater-trap** *slang* = *tattie-trap* s.v. *tattie 2.

1845 W. T. Porter *Big Bear Arkansas* 22 Them ar 'Indian mounds' ar tater Rills. **1846** *Swell's Night Guide* 133/2 *Tater trap*, the mummer, mouth. **1847** J. R. Lowell *Biglow Papers* 1st Ser. iii. 34 He draws his furrer ez straight ez he can, An' into nobody's tater-patch pokes. *c* **1869** Taylor & Dubourg in M. R. Booth *Eng. Plays of 19th Cent.* (1973) III. 303 The coal and 'tatur shed where he worked all the week. **1876** I. Banks *Manchester Man* III. i. 12 Shut up his tater-trap fur him! **1890** P. H. Emerson *Wild Life* 38, I adwised them fellers at the pub ter keep their tater-traps shut. **1902** W. N. Harben *Abner Daniel* 198, I got up on the head of a tater-barrel behind the counter. **1917** 'H. H. Richardson' *Fortunes R. Mahony* I. ii. 20 From the back of the hall came the curt request to him to shut his 'tater-trap'. **1930** *Dialect Notes* VI. 89 *Tater jack*, variety of fermented liquor, made in [lumber] camp from potatoes.

tatie, 'tato. 1. These variants are more widespread than is implied in Dict. Other variants recorded, mostly in dialectical works, include **taty, tautie,** and **tauty.** (The examples that follow supplement those given in Dict. s.v. Potato *sb.* 2 dγ.)

1793 R. Brown *Comic Poems* (1817) 118 Sawt herrings, tawties, water kale. **1812** P. Forbes *Poems* 31 A charger's just a muckle pig, For ha'din' kail or 'tatoes. **1870** D. J. Kirwan *Palace & Hovel* xiv. 214 Guv us a taty, Jenny. **1894** J. Menzies *Our Town* 240 We div look at our tauties on Saubbath. **1920** W. de la Mare *Poems 1901–1919* II. 170 There's goose, baked taties and cabbage. **1979** *Bull. Yorks. Dial. Soc.* Summer 15 The wor acres o gowden corn, taties an sugar beet, pearce an quiet.

2. *attrib.* and *Comb.*, as *tatie pot*; **tatie-bogle** = *tattie-bogle* s.v. *tattie 2.

1838 J. M. Wilson *Hist. Tales Borders* IV. 306 Ye look mair like a tauty bogle than a Christian man. **1853** S. R. Whitehead *Nelly Armstrong* I. i. 24 It was fitter for a tatie-bogle's back than a leddy's. **1871** J. Richardson *Cummerland Talk* 1st Ser. 7 A dish consisting of beef or mutton, cut into pieces, and put into a large dish along with potatoes, onions, pepper, salt, etc., and then baked in the oven,..is called in Cumberland *taty-pot.* **1893** *West Cumberland Times* (Holiday No.) 5/4 'Begok, it's tatie pot!' says Ben. **1974** *Times Lit. Suppl.* 1 Mar. 215/1 Mr Wyatt soon made friends among the woodmen and farm workers, enjoyed a tatie-pot supper at the nearest inn. **1976** *Cumberland News* 3 Dec. 24/2 Lazonby Methodist Church raised over £70 with a 'tatie-pot' supper. **1978** R. Hill *Pinch of Snuff* xxiii. 234 Going off home for a tatie-pot supper and an early night. **1982** *Sunday Tel.* 21 Feb. 16/7 There await you, in all their rich goodness, leek pie and Mendip snails, Cumbrian tatie pot and tripe,..Dorset sausage and Somerset apple cake.

‖ **tâtonnement** (tatǫnmaṅ). Also **tatonnement.** [Fr., f. *tâtonner* to feel one's way, proceed cautiously.] Experimentation, tentative procedure; *tâtonnement process*, a process of trial and error.

1847 A. De Morgan *Formal Logic* II. 324 M. Gergonne's complex propositions..requiring a separate *tâtonnement* for many things the analogues of which appear as connected results of my system. **1964** W. S. Vickrey *Metastatics & Macroeconomics* i. 21 The postulate that an equilibrium would be reached by a series of adjustments through recontracting, or 'tâtonnements'. **1975** *Jrnl. Econ. Theory* X. 122 W. Neuefeind, A tatonnement process for *N*-person games, *CORE Discussion Paper* 7136. **1978** S. Weintraub *Capitalism's Inflation & Unemployment Crisis* ix. 176 Unbounded pathological Wicksellian-Hayekian cases can be discounted, though some minor (*tatonnement*) imbalances are inevitable.

‖ **tatpurusha** (tatpu·rŭʃă). *Philol.* Also **tatpuruṣ(h)a** and with capital initial. [Skr., lit. 'his servant'.] A compound in which the first element qualifies or determines the second, while the second retains its grammatical independence as noun, adjective, or participle.

1846 M. Williams *Elem. Gram. Sanscrit* ix. 157 Native grammarians class compound nouns under five heads: the 1st they call *Tatpurusha* or those composed of two nouns. **1872** [see *bahuvrihi]. **1901** A. A. Macdonell *Sanskrit Gram.* vi. 159 The past part...gata, 'gone to', is often used at the end of Tatpuruṣas in the sense of 'relating to', 'existing in'. **1946** *Trans. Philol. Soc. 1945* 86 From this combination we get the tatpuruṣa compounds *śilōñcha-* and *śilōñchana-*. **1957** S. Potter *Mod. Ling.* iv. 91 *Bookcase* consists of substantival attribute + substantive. It belongs to that class of compounds known as *tatpurusha* to Indian grammarians because the first component determines or qualifies the second. **1969** —— *Changing English* ii. 58 It [*sc.* 'year-book'] is a tatpurusha type of compound that has been in use in English for hundreds of years, written solid by Anglo-Saxon scribes.

tattami, obs. var. *tatami.

tattarrattat (tæ:tăræ̆tæ·t). *nonce-wd.* [Echoic.] = Rat-a-tat.

1922 Joyce *Ulysses* 732, I knew his tattarrattat at the door.

tatter, *sb.*[1] Add: **3.** *tatter-eared, -skinned, -tangled* adjs.

1953 R. Graves *Poems* 18 Tatter-eared and slinking alley-toms. **1924** R. Campbell *Flaming Terrapin* ii. 26 And like a leper, faint and tatter-skinned, The wan moon makes a ghost of every tree. **1876** G. M. Hopkins *Poems* (1967) 177 Tatter-tangled and dingle-a-dangled Dandy-hung dainty head.

tatter, *sb.*[3] *slang.* [f. Tat *v.*[3] + -er[1].] A refuse-gatherer, a rag-collector. Cf. Totter (in Dict. s.v. Tot *sb.*[5]). Also **tatterer.**

1890 Barrère & Leland *Dict. Slang, Tatter* (tramps), a rag-gatherer. **1910** *Church Times* 15 July, Their occupations being largely that of 'Tatterers'—*i.e.* rag and bone and bottle-gatherers, and casual labourers. **1921** *Dict. Occup. Terms* (1927) § 970 Tatter,..collects [waste] with a hand-pushed barrow or cart. **1969** *Telegraph & Argus* (Bradford) 16 Oct. 9 He was wearing a dark jacket, and light drill trousers. He is believed to be a rag tatter.

tatter, *v.*[1] **b.** (Example.)

1934 Dylan Thomas in *New Verse* Apr. 12 Our strips of stuff that tatter as we move.

Tattersall (tæ·təɹsăl), *sb.* (and *a.*) [The name of Richard *Tattersall* (1724–95), horse-auctioneer.] **1.** Used chiefly in the possessive (occas. abbrev. **Tatt's, Tatts**) to denote: **a.**

The horse-auction market established by him in 1766 at Hyde Park Corner. Also *transf.* and *fig.*

1795 *Sporting Mag.* VI. 5/1 The gentlemen of the turf assembled every sale day..at Tattersalls. **1825** *Monthly Mag.* I Mar. 129/2 The sale days, at Tattersall's, formerly on Monday and Thursday. **1834** Carlyle *Sartor Resartus* I. iv. 12/1 He burst forth like the neighing of all Tattersall's. **1846** 'Sylvanus' *Pedestrian & Other Remin.* xxv. 241 They've three or four working the oracle at Tatt's. **1880** *Illustr. Sporting & Dramatic News* 4 Dec. 282/1 There has lately been opened at Christchurch, New Zealand a new 'Tattersall's', the want of which has long been felt. **1882** C. M. Yonge *Unknown to History* II. v. 64 'Paul's Walk' was the Bond Street, the Row, the Tattersall's, the Club of London. **1893** *Cassell's Family Mag.* Aug. 646/1 Ponies and donkeys are here too, for the costermongers. Indeed we might call it the costermonger's horse fair, the Tattersall's of the poorer classes. **1973** *Country Life* 15 Nov. 1547/3 Tattersall's..moved from Hyde Park Corner in 1865, to Knightsbridge Green... Tattersall's continued selling bloodstock and hunters.. for some years after the ring of carriage horses' hooves had ceased. **1982** *Daily Tel.* 4 Mar. 18/3 The [Hunters' Improvement and National Horse Breeding] society.. based..for the past 16 years at Tattersalls.

b. The principal betting enclosure on a racecourse. Also *Tattersall's Ring.*

1836 T. Hood *Let.* 12 Jan. (1973) 211 Tattersall style of betting. **1843** *Illustr. London News* 17 June 418/1 The winners have been haunting Tattersall's..in search of a settlement. **1863** *Observer* 18 Jan. 2/4 The lobby of the hall is like the betting-room at Tattershall's in a low way. **1865** *Once a Week* 28 Oct. 523/1 At one time..rarely did the flood of speculation overflow the dykes of 'The Corner'. Now we have an *al fresco* Tattersall's at nearly every open space in London. **1901** *Cassell's Mag.* Sept. 368/2 Tattersall's Ring at race-meetings and the committee of Tattersall's which rules the betting world, have now no connection with the firm..at Albert Gate. **1922** *N. & Q.* 9 Sept. 206/2 *Outside*, all other enclosures on a racecourse save Tattersall's, which is 'inside'. **1951** E. Rickman *Come racing with Me* xvi. 151 The customary reference to the chief betting 'ring' on any racecourse as 'Tattersalls' or 'Tatts' is a relic of the rough-and-ready days when it was an enclosure used principally by bookmakers and backers who were members of Tattersalls' Subscription Room. **1962** [see *rail *sb.*[2] 2 f]. **1973** [see *silver ring* s.v. *silver *sb.* and *a.* 21 a]. **1983** 'F. Parrish' *Bait on Hook* v. 68 He had no real idea what class of man they were looking for—a denizen of the Members' Enclosure] at £6, Tattersalls at £3.50, the Silver Ring for £1, the course for nothing.

c. The name of a lottery which originated in Sydney in 1881, moved to Tasmania in 1896, and since 1954 has operated from Victoria. Freq. abbrev. in *colloq.* use.

1895 N. Gould *On & off Turf in Austral.* vi. 52 (*heading*) 'Tattersalls' and 'Oxenhams'. *Ibid.* 61 Mr. George Adams..runs his consultations, or sweeps, under the name of 'Tattersall', and they are very popular all over the Colonies. **1945** Baker *Austral. Lang.* xv. 264 *To take a ticket in Tatt's* is to buy a ticket in Tattersall's sweepstakes, Tasmania. *Safe as Tatt's* is synonymous with perfect safety. **1951** J. Frame *Lagoon* 57 His fingers search an envelope for the pink sheet that means Tatts results, ten thousand pounds first prize. **1957** —— *Owls do Cry* xvii. 73 The Art Union? There was a theory that if you bought a ticket up north where the population was thickest you were sure to win a prize. The raffle? Tatts? **1965** *Austral. Encycl.* V. 371/2 The oldest continuing public lottery in Australia is 'Tattersall's',..established at Sydney in 1881... It took its name from Richard Tattersall's horse-auction mart in London. **1969** *Australian* 24 May 40/4 My man asked if he would abolish Tatts, seeing gambling was such a reprehensible thing.

2. *attrib.* or as *adj.* (freq. with small initial). Designating (a fabric with) a small and even check pattern or garments made from such a material. Hence *tattersall-checked* adj. Also *absol.*

From the traditional design of horse blankets.

1891 *Cassell's Family Mag.* Dec. 58/1 All those curious checked cloths which rejoice in the name of 'Tattersall' because, I suppose, they resemble horse cloth. **1951** J. D. Salinger *Catcher in Rye* xii. 103 This..guy, in a grey flannel suit and one of those flitty-looking tattersall vests. **1958** *Vogue* Jan. 35 Tattersall checks of black and caramel. **1963** *Guardian* 2 Oct. 8/5 Simpsons have Tattersall check shirts of woollen fabric. **1967** [see *gun club* s.v. *gun *sb.* 15]. **1972** *New Yorker* 7 Oct. 12/1 (Advt.), Snuggle yourself..inside our tattersall-checked robe. **1976** *National Observer* (U.S.) 2 Oct. 3/3 (Advt.), Also available in neat tattersall checks of rust/green on camel ground. **1978** *N.Y. Times* 30 Mar. c 11/1 The collection's subdued neutral colors, sedate tattersalls and similarly classic patterns. **1980** U. Curtiss *Poisoned Orchard* xii. 126 Fawn corduroys and a yellow tattersall shirt. **1981** *Daily Tel.* 14 Sept. 13/2 Viyella Tattersall check shirt.

tattery, *a.* Add: Also *Comb.*, as *tattery-clothed* adj.

1941 S. O'Casey *Let.* Jan. (1975) I. 874 The half-fed, tattery-clothed, lice-lorn children scattered now over England by the falling bombs.

tattie. 1. This variant of Potato *sb.* 2 d*γ* is now more widespread than is implied in Dict. See dialect dicts. for fuller documentation. Cf. *tater; *tatie, 'tato. Also *fig.*, a stupid person.

c **1800** in F. P. Hett *Mem. S. Sibbald* (1926) 203 Then there's champit tatties, after they are boiled, the water is poured off them then they ar' champet wi' the champer in the pot. **1879** *Forfar Poets* 139 Gae hame, ye simple tattie. **1901** G. Douglas *House with Green Shutters* 234 I'll feenish the tatties at ony rate. **1921** A. S. Neill *Carroty Broon* xv. 202 I'm at the tatties wi' achteenpence a day. **1973** *Stornoway Gazette* 27 Jan. 10/4 Tatties and herrings for supper. **1976** *Sunday Mail* (Glasgow) 26 Dec. 18/1 A tractor ran over her leg as she was picking tatties from a field on the outskirts of Monifeith.

2. *attrib.* and *Comb.*, as *tattie-field*; **tattie-bogle** = *potato-bogle* s.v. Potato *sb.* 7; also *fig.*, a simpleton; **tattie-trap** *slang* = *potato-trap* s.v. Potato *sb.* 7.

1865 *Scotsman* 28 June, First then come the trades' unions and strikes,..as a tattie-bogle..to scare the black and croaking denizens of the wood. **1922** J. Buchan *Huntingtower* xii. 240 There's..me..no more use than a tattie-bogle. **1969** M. Pugh *Last Place Left* xii. 73 The gasworks doctor, you tattie bogle. There's only one doctor. **1979** L. Derwent *Border Bairn* xi. 128 Others I dredged up from somewhere in my head, about tattie-bogles, bubblyjocks and real adventures. **1891** Barrie *Little Minister* III. xxxv. 64 The Retery's in flood..; T'now-dunnie's tattie field's out o' sicht. **1983** *Listener* 18 Aug. 23/2 *Another Time, Another Place* includes a vivid background of wet and windy tattie fields. **1894** J. B. Salmond *My Man Sandy* 175 Juist you keep your tattie-trap steekit. **1899** A. L. Salmon *West-Country Ballads* 74 Cureit's tattie-trap an' muzzle, Like a bwoy's be smooth an' bare.

tatting (tæ·tiŋ), *vbl. sb.*[2] [f. Tat *v.*[3] + -ing[1].] Rag- or scrap-collecting (see also quot. 1926). Cf. Totting (in Dict. s.v. Tot *sb.*[5]).

1926 *Glasgow Herald* 14 Dec. 10/7 The word 'tatting'.. appears..to mean the annexation by dustmen..of stray articles of small value found in dustbins. **1969** *Listener* 6 Feb. 169/2 Now,..scrap-collecting and dealing are the biggest stand-by, with 'tatting' (rag-collecting), [etc.]. **1977** Scollins & Titford *Ey up, mi Duck!* III. 52 *Tattin'*, going round collecting scrap, as a scrap-merchant does.

tattle-tale (tæ·t'l,tē[i]l), *sb.* (and *a.*) *colloq.* (orig. and chiefly *U.S.*). [f. Tattle *sb.* (or *v.*), after *tell-tale*.] **1.** = Tell-tale *sb.* (*a.*) 1 a. Occas. *attrib.* or as *adj.* (cf. Tell-tale *sb.* (*a.*) 3 b).

1889 'C. E. Craddock' *Despot of Broomsedge Cove* 429 I'd strangle that tattle-tale with a mighty good will. **1918** J. G. Thompson *Lest we Forget* 230 An American boy was expelled from a German gymnasium in Berlin, because he refused to 'tattle-tale' on the pupils in his class. **1929** W. Faulkner *Sound & Fury* 91 'I already told on her,' Jason said... 'And see what you got by it,' Caddy said. 'Tattletale.' **1946** C. McCullers *Member of Wedding* I. 45 'Frankie ain't no tattle-tale,' said Berenice. **1962** 'K. Orvis' *Damned & Destroyed* xiii. 89 Helen's tattle-tale scars. **1964** D. Macarthur *Reminiscences* I. 26 Come what may, I would be no tattletale. **1977** D. Bagley *Enemy* v. 37 Nellie *is* a tattle-tale, isn't she? Too bloody gossipy.

2. A tachograph; also in oil-well drilling (see quot. 1942).

1942 Berrey & Van den Bark *Amer. Thes. Slang* § 516/5 *Tattletale*, an instrument recording the pressure of the bit on the bottom and the work done during a shift. **1949** *Amer. Speech* XXIV. 35 Another characteristic of oil-field language is the predominance of compound words... Compound nouns coined from a verb and its object are *bore hole*..*swamp pole*, and *tattle tale*. **1962** *Ibid.* XXXVII. 272 *Tattletale*,..a complex device used on trucks, buses, and locomotives which records exact time, distance, and speed on a cylinder, and is used to check on how much speed and how many stops a vehicle made. **1971** M. Tak *Truck Talk* 165 *Tattletale*, a sealed tachograph in a tractor that simultaneously records a truck's speed and the time of day; thus producing a record of driving hours and stops. Installed by large companies to check on driver efficiency and running time, tattletales are, needless to say, unpopular with drivers.

3. *Comb.* **tattle-tale grey**, an off-white colour resulting from inadequate laundering. Also *fig.*

1943 D. W. Brogan *Eng. People* 11 If the victory of the United Nations is a good thing for all..a member of this alliance may be well advised to put up with the fact that the other members' records are not snowy white, but at best tattle-tale grey. **1973** *Houston* (Texas) *Chron. Mag. People, Places, Pleasures* 14 Oct. 11/4 In case all this still leaves the tattle tale grey, one must begin it all over again.

Hence (*rarely*) as *v. intr.*, to tell tales or 'sneak' on (somebody).

1918 J. G. Thompson *Lest we Forget* 230 An American boy was expelled from a German gymnasium in Berlin, because he refused to 'tattle-tale' on the pupils in his class.

tattoo, *sb.*[2] Add: **b.** *tattoo mark* (earlier example).

1892 'Mark Twain' *Amer. Claimant* xvi. 164 His horny hands and wrists were covered with tattoo-marks.

tattooer. (Earlier example.)

1789 *Loiterer* 18 July 7 The most famous Tataower in the Country.

Tatt's: see *Tattersall *sb.* (and *a.*).

tatty (tæ·ti), *a.*[2] *colloq.* [f. Tat *sb.*[5] + -y[1].]
1. Of a person, an animal: untidy, disreputable, 'scruffy'. Cf. Tatty *a.*[1]

1933 N. Coward *Design for Living* II. iii. 67 Going round in a troupe, with all those tatty old girls. **1951** J. Cannan *And All I Learned* x. 165 You mustn't call Brownie a tatty old trout. **1967** N. Freeling *Strike Out* 38 I've seen the painter..rather a tatty chappy by their standards. **1978** *Lancashire Life* Apr. 36/2 A widower living with his one son and a tatty collie dog, he had been a soldier for many years.

2. Of clothes, decoration, etc.: shabby, tawdry, cheap.

1940 N. Mitford *Pigeon Pie* vii. 117 The 'King's' tatty striped wall-papers. **1951** 'A. Garve' *Murder in Moscow* vii. 84 Ivan pushed up his tatty fur hat. **1959** H. R. F. Keating *Death & Visiting Firemen* xv. 195 You're a man, I can see that, in spite of your tatty old clothes. **1963** *Times* 4 June 14/2 Nineteenth-century-style songs, played by a jaunty orchestra before tatty red-plush curtains and even tattier scenery, accompany the high jinks. **1976** *Sunday Post* (Glasgow) 26 Dec. 29/4 It [*sc.* the car] was a tatty green, so a pal and I painted it navy blue.

3. Of a place or a building: badly cared for, neglected, run down.

1956 L. McIntosh *Oxford Folly* iv. 53 This is Oxford's latest coffee-bar... The others are getting so tatty. **1966** *Listener* 12 May 686/1 Some distance from the edge of the Falls a sizeable crack has opened up... Neither the Americans nor the Canadians can afford to have Niagara looking so tatty. **1978** L. Heren *Growing up on The Times* iii. 63 The car drove through the rather tatty outskirts of Tel Aviv.

4. *transf.* In other miscellaneous uses.

1957 *Listener* 19 Dec. 1026/1 Look what we did to that tatty second act. **1959** *Economist* 28 Mar. 1153/2 The Prime Minister's reply looks like a foretaste of the tattier tactics that will be used by the less inhibited Tories in the election. **1965** *New Statesman* 9 Apr. 585/2 The entire vision's too enormous for accommodation within the tatty ingenuities of the stage. **1975** in R. Crossman *Diaries* I. 376 This was a somewhat tatty account of Labour's first year in Government, prepared in Transport House as a diatribe against the Tories.

Hence **ta·ttily** *adv.*; **ta·ttiness.**

1952 A. Wilson *Hemlock & After* I. v. 93 He rejected the 'tattiness' of dead mullion and withered sycamore berries. **1957** *Observer* 29 Sept. 12/1 The keynote of these tattily exotic revues is imitation. **1959** S. Gibbons *Pink Front Door* ix. 118 I've got you the rooms. Four of them, furnished rather tattily. **1973** J. Wainwright *Pride of Pigs* 8 The impression of tarted up tattiness. **1980** *Times Lit. Suppl.* 3 Oct. 1118/5 The novel is firmly set in the very recent past..and rock music, fashion, the death of Elvis, the tattiness of London are described in detail.

tatty-bye (tæti bəi) (stress variable), *int.* [Fanciful formation: cf. Ta-ta *int.* and Good-bye.] A colloquial form of farewell.

1971 A. Morice *Murder in Married Life* vi. 56 'Ta-ta for now, then.' 'Tatty-bye, Sandy darling.' **1974** M. Babson *Stalking Lamb* xv. 113 I'll say tatty-bye for now then... And we'll see you soon. You know the way, don't you?

‖ **ta tzu-pao** (dā dzə bɑu). Also **dazebao, dazibao, tatzepao, ta-tzu-pao.** [Chinese *dàzìbào*, f. *dà* big + *zì* character + *bào* newspaper, poster.] In the People's Republic of China, a wall poster written in large characters that expresses a (political) opinion or other message.

The posting of *ta tzu-pao* is no longer encouraged in China.

1960 *Peking Rev.* 5 Apr. 8/2 Criticism and self-criticism through large-scale airing of views and opinions, big debates and putting up *dazibao* (posters in large characters) are carried out in government and people's organizations. **1962** E. Snow *Other Side of River* (1963) xlviii. 368 Around the basketball court and a stage which prisoners had built were bulletin boards posted with *ta tzu-pao* such as you see before any Chinese factory: essays, rhymes, praise and mutual criticism, lists of model workers and their awards. **1967** S. Knight *Window on Shanghai* lviii. 250 Four foreigners in Peking put up a 'dazebao' criticizing the treatment given us by the Chinese. **1968** *Globe & Mail* (Toronto) 5 Feb. 10/2 A tatzepao (big-character poster) reproduced by the Shanghai newspaper claimed that the handful of party leaders now accused of being capitalist roaders exaggerated the role played by technical knowledge. **1973** T. R. Tregear *Chinese* iii. 58 Walls everywhere were covered with *ta-tzu-pao*, big-character newspapers. **1979** *Globe & Mail* (Toronto) 4 Apr. 1/2 Some students at Peking University told Western journalists that the repression was wrong as far as the poster or dazibao writers at Xidan democracy wall were concerned.

tau. Add: **2. b.** (Earlier examples.)

1785 [see *ansated *ppl. a.*]. **1841** J. G. Wilkinson *Manners & Customs Ancient Egyptians* 2nd Ser. II. xv. 283 The sacred *tau*, or sign of Life, was presented to him.

4*. *Particle Physics.* Freq. written τ. **a.** A meson that decays into three pions, now identified with the kaon. Also *tau meson.*

1949 *Nature* 15 Jan. 86/2 We have considered the possible relations of the present results to the particles.. referred to as τ-mesons, evidence for which has been recently reported by Bradt and Peters. **1955** *Proc. Glasgow Conf. Nucl. & Meson Physics 1954* 347 The striking similarity of the masses of the θ^0 and $\tau^{\pm}$-mesons. **1968** M. S. Livingston *Particle Physics* vii. 138 The θ decayed into two pions while the τ decayed into three pions. **1973** L. J. Tassie *Physics Elem. Particles* vii. 61 The solution to the θ–τ puzzle was that the θ and τ particles were the same, now called the *K*-meson, and the parity was not conserved in the decay of *K*-mesons. **1974** Frauenfelder & Henley *Subatomic Physics* ix. 205 The decays of the tau and the theta were so slow that they were known to be weak.

b. An unstable heavy charged lepton which has a spin of ½ and a mass of approximately 1780 MeV (3490 times that of the electron) and which decays into an electron or muon or into hadrons, in every case with one or more neutrinos. Also *tau lepton, particle.*

1977 M. L. PERL in *Proc. Internat. Symposium Lepton & Photon Interactions at High Energies* 146 All..data ..agree on the following points... c. The behavior of these [leptonic] events is consistent with the hypothesis that a new charged lepton, τ, exists with a mass of 1.9±0.1 GeV/c². **1978** PERL & KIRK in *Sci. Amer.* Mar. 50/3 We shall relate here the story of the discovery of the new heavy lepton and its antiparticle, which we have named the tau and the antitau. **1979** *McGraw-Hill Yearbk. Sci. & Technol.* 240/1 It was first discovered through reaction (1), in which a positron (e^+) and electron (e^-) annihilate and produce a pair of τ-leptons of opposite electrical charge. **1980** *Sci. Amer.* July 60/1 More recently a third neutrino flavor has been added to accompany the newly discovered tau particle, which is a massive sibling of the electron and the muon. **1981** D. H. PERKINS in J. H. Mulvey *Nature of Matter* iv. 79 The neutrino is a muon-type neutrino and in subsequent interactions will always produce a charged μ, not an e or τ.

tau, obs. var. *TAO.

‖ **taua** (tɑu·ă). [Maori.] A Maori army or war party.

1858 J. WHITELEY *Let.* 19 Apr. in *Richmond-Atkinson Papers* (1960) I. 390 The taua seemed to be mustering their forces last night from the south. **1882** W. D. HAY *Brighter Britain!* I. x. 254 Instead of leading a ferocious taua, he finds himself the venerated pastor of a little community. **1921** H. GUTHRIE-SMITH *Tutira* x. 69 Two *tauas* or war-parties. **1959** TINDALE & LINDSAY *Rangatira* viii. 79 A taua of fighting-men, about fifty strong, was advancing towards them. **1978** [see *RANGATIRA].

‖ **taubada** (tɑubā·dă). [Local word.] On the island of New Guinea, used to refer to anyone in a position of authority, esp. as a respectful form of address.

1891 W. D. PITCAIRN *Two Years among Savages of New Guinea* iii. 58 If he be a 'Taubada' that is to say a person of importance. **1924** 'R. DALY' *Outpost* xii. 116 Did the Taubada want to make them the laughing-stock of their enemies? **1945** *Coast to Coast 1944* 101 A native voice said, 'One more come, taubada.' **1963** *Times* 3 Dec. 8/1 Some *taubadas* and *mastas* have forsaken the hotels for clubs to which natives are not yet admitted.

Tauberian (tɑubīᵊ·riăn), *a. Math.* [f. the name of Alfred *Tauber* (1866–?1942), Slovak mathematician + -IAN.] Applied to theorems in which the behaviour in the limit of a series or function is deduced from a weaker limiting property together with some additional condition, esp. theorems in which convergence is deduced from summability.

1913 HARDY & LITTLEWOOD in *Proc. London Math. Soc.* XI. 411 The general character of the theorems which it [*sc.* this paper] contains is 'Tauberian': they are theorems of the type whose first example was the beautiful converse of Abel's theorem originally proved by Tauber. **1962** D. R. COX *Renewal Theory* i. 14 A result of this type, enabling the limiting behaviour of $k(x)$ to be deduced from that of $k^*(s)$, is called a Tauberian theorem. **1979** *Nature* 24 May 358/1 Rau is well known and remembered for his valuable contributions to the theory of Tauberian theorems, function-theory and the theory of Dirichlet series.

Tauchnitz (tɑu·knits, tɑu·χnits). The name of Christian Bernhard, Baron von *Tauchnitz* (1816–95), publisher of Leipzig, used *attrib.* and *absol.* with reference to volumes in the Collection of British and American Authors, a series begun by him in 1841 for sale on the continent.

1856 MRS. GASKELL *Let.* 26 Dec. (1966) 430 For 'North & South' I received 600£..having the Tauchnitz profit... I suppose however you would allow me to retain the profits arising from the American & Tauchnitz edit:. **1863** J. MORREL *Jrnl.* 10 July (1963) iii. 94 In a twinkling all our 'Tauchnitzes' became pocket editions. **1895** *Daily News* 15 Aug. 5/1 The excitement lest the Customs' officer were to find the Tauchnitz in the trunk. **1901** *Ibid.* 5 Jan. 7/4 Desolate dwellings, strewn with a few sixpenny magazines and smuggled Tauchnitzes. **1902** H. JAMES *Wings of Dove* III. v. 102 The uncut but antiquated Tauchnitz volume of which, before going out, she had mechanically possessed herself. **1920** JOYCE *Let.* 12 May (1966) II. 464 The head of the firm would like to have a copy with a view to including it in the Tauchnitz edition. **1936** E. AMBLER *Dark Frontier* vi. 88 A Tauchnitz edition of Butler's *Erewhon* purchased hastily from a station bookstall. **1960** *Times* 7 July 14/7 A library of 'Tauchnitz' books. **1975** T. ALLBEURY *Special Collection* iv. 125 A handful of Tauchnitz pocket editions.

tauhinu (tɑuhī·nu). *N.Z.* Also **tarwinie.** [a. Maori.] A health-life evergreen shrub, *Pomaderris phylicifolia,* of the family Rhamnaceæ, native to New Zealand and south-eastern Australia and bearing downy leaves and clusters of small yellow flowers. Also *attrib.*

1848 R. TAYLOR *Leaf from Nat. Hist. N.Z.* 25/2 *Tauhinu,* a shrub. **1903** B. E. BAUGHAN in Chapman & Bennett *N.Z. Verse* (1956) 54 Briar, tauhinu, an' ruin. **1927** J. DEVANNY *Old Savage* 47 Behind her, tough shrubs, tarwinie and gorse, mantled the terrace leading back to the low hills. **1950** *N.Z. Jrnl. Agric.* Oct. 297 (*caption*) Note the prevalence of tauhinu scrub. **1964** *Weekly News* (Auckland) 15 Apr. 37/3 Tauhinu was the worst scrub to plough, for it grew outward along the ground.

‖ **taula** (tɑu·lă). *Archæol.* [Cat., f. L. *tabula* table.] A Bronze Age stone structure found on Minorca in the Balearic Islands, consisting of two slabs forming a T-shaped column, freq. enclosed by a horseshoe-shaped wall and believed to be a place of worship.

1881 R. L. PLAYFAIR *Handbk. Mediterranean* II. 459/2 A bi-lithon, or altar, composed of two immense monoliths,..carefully dressed, called *Altar* or *Taula,* altar or table. **1911** M. S. BOYD *Fortunate Isles* xvi. 192 Just behind the talayot..stands another relic of prehistoric times in the shape of a *taula.* **1932** *Discovery* July 238/2 Minorca possesses a form of megalithic structure which does not occur elsewhere. This is the *taula,* a table consisting of a slab of stone set upright in a groove in the flat rock-floor. **1950** *Antiquity* XXIV. 154 These excavations might have solved the problems of the date and purpose of the constructions known as 'taulas'. **1979** SERVICE & BRADBERY *Megaliths* vii. 134 The largest taula (the name means 'table' in Catalan..)..is beside the talayot of Trepuco. *Ibid.*, As with all taulas, it is very broad in one dimension, very narrow in the other.

Taung (tɑuŋ). Also **Taungs.** The name of a town in the northern Cape Province, South Africa, used *attrib.* in *Taung child, skull,* etc., to designate the remains of a fossil hominid, *Australopithecus africanus,* found in a limestone cliff there in 1924. Cf. *AUSTRALOPITHECUS.

1931 A. KEITH *New Discoveries Antiquity Man* iii. 61 How does the brain development of the Taungs skull fit into the human scheme of growth? **1962** G. H. R. VON KOENIGSWALD *Evol. Man* iii. 61 (*caption*) Front view of original Taungs skull. **1973** B. J. WILLIAMS *Evol. & Human Origins* ix. 136/1 The Taung child had an endocranial capacity of approximately 405 cc. *Ibid.* 136/2 Judging the Taung specimen from tooth eruption to be around five years of age, the adult individual would have had a cranial capacity of 440 cc. **1978** P. V. TOBIAS in C. J. Jolly *Early Hominids in Africa* 45 The *prima facie* case for the likely taxonomic affinities of the Taung skull rests on the concept that two main hominid lineages.. existed side by side in Africa.

‖ **taungya** (tɑu·ŋyă). Also **taunggya,** † **toungya.** [Burmese, f. *taung* hill + *ya* plot, field.] A temporary hillside clearing. Usu. *attrib.*, designating a method of shifting cultivation practised in Burma, and a system of forest management based on this (see quot. 1938) and employed in tropical countries.

1876 *Encycl. Brit.* IV. 560/2 The system of cultivation known in Bengal as the *júm,* that is clearing virgin soil by burning, cultivating it for one or two years, and then leaving it again to the jungle, is here [*sc.* in Burma] extensively practised under the name of *toungya* cultivation. **1904** [see *KUMRI]. **1921** *Times Lit. Suppl.* 8 Sept. 574/3 The best system of raising teak is in taungya plantations. **1926** TANSLEY & CHIPP *Study of Vegetation* xi. 257 Plant succession in deserted taungyas or cultivated land. **1938** H. G. CHAMPION in Champion & Trevor *Man. Indian Silviculture* I. vi. 182 *Taungya* plantation procedure.. depends on getting the cultivator to plant or sow a new forest crop with his food crop, so that when he moves on, useful trees and not weeds will restock the area. **1946** [see *JHOOM, JHUM]. **1952** [see *shifting cultivation* s.v. *SHIFTING *ppl. a.* 1 b]. **1975** *Daily Tel.* 6 Oct. 9/3 Dr. Earl commends the 'taungya' method of managing eucalyptus plantations in Uganda.

taunt, *sb.*¹ Add: **4.** *Comb.*, as **taunt-song,** used to refer to certain passages in the Old Testament, *spec.* as a rendering of Heb. *māšāl.*

1906 S. R. DRIVER *Habakkuk* (Cent. Bible) 78 'Parable' in these passages [*sc.* Habakkuk 2: 6] suggests a wholly incorrect idea; and the best rendering is probably *taunt-song.* **1928** C. GORE et al. *New Commentary on Holy Scripture* 444/1 In that day of relief from sorrow and fear a taunt-song will be sung against the King of Babylon. **1959** G. W. ANDERSON *Crit. Introd. O.T.* v. 109 The second contains a striking taunt-song over the descent of a tyrant ..to the abode of the dead.

tau·ntless, *a. nonce-wd.* [f. TAUNT *sb.*¹ + -LESS.] Lacking or without a taunt (sense 3).

c **1879** G. M. HOPKINS *Poems* (1967) 82 Tongue true, vaunt- and tauntless.

Taunton turkey (tǭ·ntən tɜ̄·ɹki). *U.S.* The name of *Taunton,* Massachusetts, used *attrib.* to designate the ale-wife, *Pomodorus pseudoharengus,* a fish resembling a herring found in marine or fresh water in eastern North America; = ALE-WIFE².

1851 A. ALLIN *Home Ballads* 18 'Taunton turkeys' are so thick, We sell them by the rod! **1950** *Chicago Tribune* 17 Jan. 14/3 In Massachusetts..the spring herring is known as 'Taunton turkey'.

taupata (tɑu·pătă). *N.Z.* [a. Maori.] An evergreen shrub or small tree, *Coprosma repens,* of the family Rubiaceæ, native to New Zealand, and bearing shiny leaves and clusters of small white flowers followed by orange-red berries.

1864 J. D. HOOKER *Handbk. N.Z. Flora* 268/1 Taupata *Coprosma retusa.* **1906** LAING & BLACKWELL *Plants N.Z.* 392 C[*oprosma*] *Baueri* is much used for hedges in Wellington and Melbourne. In the former place it is generally known as *taupata.* **1946** *Jrnl. Polynesian Soc.* LV. 159 *Taupata,* a tree..with dark green leaves shining as if varnished. **1960** N. HILLIARD *Maori Girl* III. vi. 215 And there's the lights on the leaves of the taupata. **1966** G. DURRELL *Two in Bush* ii. 68 The list of plants used in this nest building reads like something out of Lewis Carroll: taupata twigs, scurvy grass and mesembryanthemum. **1982** F. BREAM *Island of Fear* 6 The graves..under the taupata trees.

taupe (tōp, tǭp). [a. Fr., f. L. *talpa* mole.] A brownish shade of grey resembling the colour of moleskin. Also *Comb.*, as *taupe-coloured* adj.

1911 *Daily Colonist* (Victoria, B.C.) 5 Apr. 24/1 (Advt.), Important silk purchase..in colors of rose, Persian blue.. taupe, purple, mauve. **1921** *Glasgow Herald* 18 June 4 Pearl, smoke, taupe, mouse and other soft becoming shades of grey. **1955** W. GADDIS *Recognitions* II. ix. 714 The hole in the roof had, of course, been repaired; and the interior done over in taupe and white. **1967** *Boston Sunday Herald Mag.* 26 Mar. 21/1 Use taupe powder to create depth. **1976** L. ST. CLAIR *Fortune in Death* xxi. 215 The subdued taupe of her suit. **1982** M. MCMULLEN *Better off Dead* (1983) I. iii. 19 The velvet was taupe-coloured.

Taurean, *a.* Restrict *rare* to sense in Dict. and add: **b.** Of or pertaining to the constellation or zodiacal sign of Taurus. Cf. *TAURIAN *a.* b.

1924 C. E. O. CARTER *Conc. Encycl. Psychol. Astrol.* 105 Obedience is generally regarded as a Taurean virtue. **1928** W. H. SAMPSON *Zodiac* iii. 25 The Pleiades are part of the constellation Taurus..more Taurean in nature. **1974** *Woman* 4 May 56/1 A Taurean mother will help her Piscean children to develop their own talents.

B. as *sb.* = *TAURUS 1 c.

1911 I. M. PAGAN *From Pioneer to Poet* ii. 31 The burlesque Taurean is fat, thick-necked, gross and overfed looking, and often has a great love of low comedy. **1916** K. T. CRAIG *Stars of Destiny* 37 Mental exactness and persistence are attributed to Taureans. **1969** 'V. PACKER' *Don't rely on Gemini* (1970) xiv. 118 Brahms was a Taurus. .. Fred Astaire, Bing Crosby, and Perry Como are all Taureans, too. **1976** *Sunday Mail* (Glasgow) 26 Dec. 27/6, I always believed Taureans were home-lovers.

taureau (tǫ·ro). *Canad. Hist.* Also † **toreau.** Pl. **taureaux.** [a. Canad. Fr., a. Fr. *taureau* bull.] A bag of buffalo-hide for carrying pemmican; also *transf.*, the pemmican itself.

1794 J. MACDONNELL *Jrnl.* 14 Jan. in L. E. R. Masson *Les Bourgeois de la Compagnie du Nord-Ouest* (1889) I. 287, I cut 20 sacks or *taureaux* to put pemican in and gave them to Minie to sew. **1795** —— *Jrnl.* 28 Apr. in *Ibid.* 294 Started them for the Forks with 138 + 137 taureaux of pemican. **1807** W. F. WENTZEL *Let.* 27 Mar. in *Ibid.* 90 This is our staple article of provisions when travelling, it is called *taureau* or *Pimecan.* **1821** G. SIMPSON *Jrnl. Occurrences Athabasca Dept.* (1938) 278 It may be well to have the Toreau in Store. **1890** *Trans. R. Soc. Canada* VIII. II. 104 A sack or 'toreau' of pemmican, as it was called, consisted of nearly equal quantities of tallow and dried meat. **1911** K. HUGHES *Father Lacombe* iii. 32 They pounded dried meat to powder in wooden bowls, mixing hot grease and dried berries with it, packing the whole into large sacks of buffalo-hide, called by the Metis—*taureaux*... This was *pimik-kan,* the manna of the Canadian prairies. **1927** A. P. WOOLLACOTT *Mackenzie & his Voyageurs* 52 It [*sc.* pemmican] was a staple food among the fur-traders on long journeys, when..game could not be had. Also known as 'taureaux'. **1931** G. L. NUTE *Voyageur* 213 The train wound its slow way back to Pembina laden with..228 *taureaux,* or leather bags of pemmican. **1951** W. O'MEARA *Grand Portage* xxiv. 139 The pemmican [had been] mixed and stored in shaggy taureaux.

Taurian, *a.* Delete *rare*⁻¹ and add: **b.** Of or pertaining to the constellation Taurus; characteristic of a person born under the zodiacal sign of Taurus. Cf. *TAUREAN *a.* b. Occas. as *sb.*, = TAURUS 1 c.

1909 WEBSTER, *Taurian*..Of or pert. to Mount Taurus, or the constellation Taurus. **1928** W. WILSON *Astrology* iii. 53 The Taurian life has been spoken of as happier at the end than at the beginning. **1938** D. ANRIAS *Man & Zodiac* vii. 69 Afflicted Taurians rarely trust men or circumstances. **1972** D. LEES *Zodiac* 15 Zodiac..predicted that Julius would make a tremendous coup on the stock market, provided he got off his lazy Taurian arse and acted immediately. **1972** *Vogue* 1 Mar. 144/4 He's a Gemini... I'd be much better off with a Taurian.

taurine, *a.* Add: Also *spec.*, pertaining to bull-fighting.

1932 R. CAMPBELL *Taurine Provence* 28 Every village westward of Martigues has three or four fêtes a year all accompanied by taurine ceremonies. Nearly every village has its small arena. **1977** *Monitor* (McAllen, Texas) 3 July 6B/3 Longinos Mendoza is also slated to appear on the card having shown exceptional taurine skill during his last performance [*sc.* a bullfight].

tauro-. Add: **tau·robole** [cf. TAUROBOLY], a bull-slayer; also **taurobo·lic** *a.*, of the nature of tauroboly. (Both *rare.*)

1934 R. CAMPBELL *Broken Record* viii. 183 These two great horsemen are superior equestrian tauroboles to any of the Portuguese, Spanish or Mexican. *Ibid.* iii. 67 A truly taurobolic and Mithraic sensation.

tauroboly. (Earlier example of form *taurobolium*.)

1845 *Encycl. Metrop.* XVI. 114/1 They offered a sacrifice of a bull or ram, (whence the terms *Taurobolium* and *Ariobolium*,) in the blood of which the hierophant was also sprinkled.

taurodont (tǭ·rodǫnt), *a.* [f. TAURO- + Gr. ὀδούς, ὀδοντ- tooth.] Of mammalian molar teeth: having large broad crowns and short roots.

1915 A. KEITH *Antiquity of Man* viii. 148 Molar teeth [in Neanderthal man] are large in crown and body and extremely short in root... To [*sic*] this peculiar form of molar tooth..I have proposed the name of 'taurodont'. **1927** PEAKE & FLEURE *Hunters & Artists* 18 This condition of the teeth, known as taurodont, has been found among some representatives of Neanderthal man. **1948** *New Biol.* V. 84 The teeth [of Neanderthal man]..are often of that specialised kind called 'taurodont'—they are stumpy with short roots. **1971** *Nature* 5 Feb. 409/2 The frequent lack of incisors and well worn flattened taurodont molars superficially suggest the crateriform decay of Moon's mulberry molars. **1973** B. J. WILLIAMS *Evolution & Human Origins* x. 159/2 The molars and premolars are 'taurodont', meaning that they have an enlarged pulp cavity.

taurodontism (tǭrodǫ·ntiz'm). [f. as prec. + -ISM 3.] In certain mammals, the condition of having taurodont teeth.

1913 A. KEITH in *Proc. R. Soc. Med.* (Odontol. Sect.) VI. 103 For this condition or tendency Professor Keith proposed the name of 'taurodontism'. **1939** *Nature* 23 Dec. 1055/2 In some peculiarities of the teeth he [*sc.* Sinanthropus] approaches the gorilla..and..the female orang in 'taurodontism'. **1959** J. D. EVANS *Malta* i. 36 They are molars, but the roots, instead of being separate, as in normal human teeth, are fused together. This is a phenomenon known technically as *taurodontism*, and it is particularly characteristic of the primitive type of human known as Neanderthal man. **1982** *Times* 27 Nov. 4/1 The molar exhibits marked taurodontism, an enlargement of the pulp cavity extending down into the roots, which..is characteristic of early Neanderthals.

tauromachy. Add: Also sometimes in foreign forms (Gr. and Fr. in quots.). Hence **tauroma·chics** [-IC 2], the business of bullfighting.

[**1910** *Encycl. Brit.* IV. 789/1 *Bull-fighting*, the national Spanish sport. The Spanish name is *tauromaquia*.] **1923** W. J. LOCKE *Moordius & Co.* xi. 147 After public renunciation of *tauromachie*, gracefully made among a circle of Spanish friends. **1934** F. M. FORD *Let.* 14 Sept. (1965) 234, I don't know why I should deluge you with..tauromachics. **1967** MCCORMICK & MASCAREÑAS *Compl. Aficionado* ii. 35 One has only..to read certain of the early manuals of tauromachia..to realize that..a good deal has been gained through modern changes. **1969** C. IRVING *Fake!* (1970) viii. 99 He was to do over two hundred of them [*sc.* drawings], the best of which are probably in the Picasso *Tauromachia* series.

Taurus. Add: **1. c.** A person born under the zodiacal sign of Taurus. Also *attrib.* or as *adj.*

1901 C. A. WALKER *Under a Lucky Star* 84 The headworkers of humanity could accomplish but little without assistance from the practical, executive Taurus. **1927** G. SULLY *First Princ. Astrol.* iii. 24 Taurus and Gemini make good mates when they set out to help one another unselfishly. **1943** D. POWELL *Time to be Born* xi. 272 Her astrologer..failed her by promising a new man, a Taurus with a heart condition. **1964** L. MACNEICE *Astrol.* v. 147 A 19th-century astrologer's idea of a Taurus woman. **1971** V. CANNING *Firecrest* iii. 35 Henry Martin Dilling, born 1927, the same age as himself; though Dilling was a Leo and he Taurus. **1979** S. RIFKIN *McQuaid in August* (1980) ix. 85 I'm Sagittarius. If you're Taurus..we can get a big thing going.

Tau Sug (tɑu sug), *sb.* (and *a.*) Also **Tao Sug, Tausug, Taw Sug.** [Tau Sug, f. *taw* person + *sug, sulúg* current.] One of the Islamic groups inhabiting the Sulu Archipelago in the Philippine Islands, whose ancestors can be traced back to the Butuan area of north-east Mindanao; the Austronesian language spoken by this people. Also *attrib.* or as *adj.* Cf. *SULU[1].

1923 [see *SULU[1]]. **1964** P. G. GOWING *Mosque & Moro* i. 1 Ninety-two percent of all Muslim Filipinos belong to the Tau Sug, Maranao,..and Samal groups. *Ibid.* 2 A vigorous and proud people, the Tau Sug are the backbone of the historic Sultanate of Sulu. **1964** E. A. NIDA *Toward Sci. Transl.* ix. 207 In the expression 'sat and begged' as rendered into Tau Sug, a language of the Philippines, one must specify one of these actions as primary and the other as secondary. **1973** J. A. BRUNO (*title*) The social world of the Tausug. **1977** [see *SULU[1]].

taut, taught, *a.* Add: The only current spelling is *taut*. **2. b.** (Earlier and later examples.) Esp. in phr. *taut ship*, a disciplined or strictly run ship. Also *attrib.* and *fig.* Cf. sense 2 c in Dict.

1829 D. JERROLD *Black-Ey'd Susan* III. ii. 43 The trimmest sailor as ever handled rope..give me taut Bill before any able seaman in his Majesty's fleet. **1941** *Time* 29 Dec. 8/1 The promoted admirals were 'taut ship' commanders (meaning rigid disciplinarians, as opposed to 'happy ship' officers). **1970** H. WAUGH *Finish me Off* (1971) 106 Yesterday she had been haughty and taut-ship, but today..Mrs. Hardell's position had suddenly become tenuous. **1974** *Progress* (Easley, S. Carolina) 24 Apr. 2/2 His language was salty and he ran a taut ship. He demanded discipline, accuracy, integrity and honesty, as well as good writing. **1977** *Navy News* July 20 All the taut-ship zeal for a tip-top navy, which gave Whale Island its fame as one of the best-known of service establishments, has been redirected. **1980** *Globe & Laurel* July/Aug. 250/1, I found the first half of the book, which describes Trevelyan's efforts to create a taut ship, as he takes Icarus through a NATO exercise, a ship's fire, and a funeral at sea, sketchy and unsatisfactory.

d. *fig.* Of music, literature, etc.: concise, controlled; of the human voice: strained.

1966 *Listener* 10 Feb. 219/2 The music..did not seem to have quite the structural control or clarity of texture one discerned in the piano concerto, where..the thought seems more taut and the tension is therefore more easily maintained. **1972** *Observer* 16 Apr. 33/6 A short, taut, yet circumstantially detailed account. **1976** M. MACHLIN *Pipeline* lv. 557 Coutts voice was taut with worry. **1978** *Internat. Herald Tribune* 24 July 14/4 Among reviewers, the favored adjectives of the past—trenchant and ironic for books, taut, pert and luminous for theatrical productions—have been overtaken by sentimental.

3. Used adverbially and parasynthetically in *Comb.*, as *taut-necked, -rigged, -stretched* adjs.

1829 D. JERROLD *Black-Ey'd Susan* I. i. 15 There's not so fine, so noble, so taut-rigged a fellow in His Majesty's navy. **1943** D. GASCOYNE *Poems 1937–42* 42 The sky's a faded blue and taut-stretched flag Tenting the quadrangle. **1948** L. MACNEICE *Holes in Sky* 31 The taut-necked donkey's..lamenting.

tautened, *ppl. a.* Add: Also *fig.*

1929 E. CARFRAE *Guarded Heights* xxiii. 202 Carey's voice had a queer little tautened note when he spoke again.

tauto-. Add: **tautophone** = *SUMMATOR 2; **tau:tosylla·bic** *a.*, belonging to the same syllable.

1940 *Character & Personality* VIII. 216 (*title*) The use of the tautophone ('verbal summator') as an auditory apperceptive test for the study of personality. **1888** J. WRIGHT tr. *Brugmann's Elem. Compar. Gram. Indo-Gmc. Lang.* I. 92 Before the Christian era tautosyllabic *ai* became *ē* in Latin. **1953** *Archivum Linguisticum* V. 22 The lengthening of short vowels before tautosyllabic *s* or [z]. **1978** *Language* LIV. 193 A tautosyllabic consonant.

tautological, *a.* Add: **1. b.** *Mod. Logic.* Characterized by or involving tautology (in sense *f). Hence **tautologica·lity**, the quality of being tautological.

1922 tr. *Wittgenstein's Tractatus* 97 In the one case the proposition is true for all the truth-possibilities of the elementary propositions. We say that the truth-conditions are *tautological*. **1926** F. P. RAMSEY in *Proc. London Math. Soc.* XXV. 341 The idea to be defined is one of the essential sides of mathematical propositions, their content, and their form. Their content must be completely generalized, and their form tautological. **1933** *Mind* XLII. 41 Each postulate functions in limiting the ranges of the variables in such a manner that any change in one postulate..involves a reciprocal change in its other parts, which change causes it to remain analytic or tautological. **1936** J. R. WEINBERG *Exam. Logical Positivism* ii. 80 The formal property of certain combinations of symbols, which is called tautologicality, is solely responsible for the unconditional truth of the truths of logic. **1950** R. CARNAP *Logical Found. Probability* iv. 289 With respect to the tautological evidence '*t*'. **1971** G. HUNTER *Metalogic* III. 171 Suppose that A is an instance of a tautological schema of Q.

tautologically, *adv.* (Later example.)

1979 J. A. ROBINSON *Logic: Form & Function* iii. 43 We can extend this idea to the case when infinitely many sentences together tautologically imply a given sentence.

tautologous, *a.* (Examples in sense of *TAUTOLOGICAL *a.* 1 b.)

1935 *Mind* XLIV. 195 The tautologous '*p* or not *p*'. **1940** W. V. O. QUINE *Mathematical Logic* i. 50 Statements which are true by virtue solely of the truth-functional modes of composition will be called *tautologous*.

tautology. Add: **f.** *Mod. Logic.* A compound proposition which is unconditionally true for all the truth-possibilities of its elementary propositions and by virtue of its logical form.

1919 B. RUSSELL *Introd. Math. Philos.* xviii. 203 The characteristic of logical propositions that we are in search of is the one which was felt..by those who said that it consisted in deducibility from the law of contradiction. This characteristic we may call *tautology*. *Ibid.* 205 The importance of 'tautology' for a definition of mathematics was pointed out to me by..Ludwig Wittgenstein, who was working on the problem. **1922** tr. *Wittgenstein's Tractatus* 97 The tautology..is unconditionally true. **1933** *Mind* XLII. 37 So taken, a postulate is a tautology and cannot be denied. **1959** *Listener* 19 Mar. 510/1 The simplest rigorous proof is tautology. This consists, essentially, of showing that some statement covers all possibilities. **1964** M. BLACK *Compan. Wittgenstein's Tractatus* xliii. 231 Johnson's..'formal truth' and 'formal falsity'..seem to correspond exactly to W.'s 'tautology' and 'contradiction'. **1979** J. A. ROBINSON *Logic: Form & Function* iii. 42 A..general decision procedure for determining whether or not a sentence is a tautology.

tautomerism. Add: *esp.* such a property due to the reversible migration of an atom (esp. of hydrogen) or group within a molecule (see also quots.).

1927 T. M. LOWRY in *Chem. Rev.* IV. 233 The necessity for a new definition of tautomerism arises from the fact that Laar embedded in his original definition a theory which is now universally recognized as being incorrect,..namely, that the various formulae which can be assigned to a tautomerism compound represent 'not isomeric but identical substances'. The new definition [*sc.* that in Dict.] has the advantage that there is no theory behind it, since it is limited to a mere statement of the fact of dual reactivity. **1927, 1936** [see *keto-enol* s.v. *KETO- b]. **1937** H. B. WATSON *Mod. Theories Org. Chem.* ix. 117 Until a relatively recent date..'tautomerism' was used exclusively to denote the migration of hydrogen. The similar migration of anionic atoms or groups is now recognized, however; this..is included under..'tautomerism'. **1964** [see *PROTOTROPY]. **1969** C. K. INGOLD *Structure & Mechanism Org. Chem.* (ed. 2) xi. 795 Laar's interpretation was that two such structures did not represent distinct and potentially separable species, but only the end-phases of an intramolecular oscillatory situation in a single chemical species. *Ibid.* 799 Since 1911 there has been no question but that the concept of tautomerism, in terms of which Conrad Laar had incorporated so many scattered observations into a phenomenon, has to be redefined..as meaning reversible isomeric change. Problems of isolation and proof of identity of tautomers are dependent simply on temperature and the available techniques.

Hence **tauto·merize** *v. intr.*, to change into another tautomeric form; **tauto:meri·zable** *a.*, capable of being changed into a tautomeric form; **tauto:meriza·tion.**

1934 WEBSTER, Tautomerize... Tautomerizable... Tautomerization. **1938** H. ADKINS in H. Gilman *Org. Chem.* I. ix. 820 Unsaturated acids tautomerize in the absence of added reagents at temperatures near their boiling points. *Ibid.*, There is little or no correlation between the rate of tautomerization (mobility) and the extent of the reaction. **1962** Tautomerizable [see *RAMAN]. **1972** R. A. JACKSON *Mechanism* iv. 60 This could plausibly lose carbon dioxide to give the carbanion 82 which would rapidly tautomerize to pyridine 83 by a proton shift. **1978** *Jrnl. Amer. Chem. Soc.* C. 4627/2 Activation of the catalyst by tautomerization to a rhodium (I) complex.

tava(h), var. *TAWA[2].

tavarish, var. *TOVARISH, TOVARICH.

Tavastian (tavæ·stian), *sb.* (and *a.*) [f. *Tavast(ehus*, Sw. name of the Finnish town of Hämeenlinna in the province of Häme + -IAN.] A member of one of the major ethnic groups of the Finnish people. Also *attrib.* or as *adj.* Also **Ta·vastlander.**

[**1891** A. FEATHERMAN *Social Hist. Races Mankind* IV. 417 The Finns call themselves in their own language Suomalainen (swamp men)... From the dialects which they speak they are divided into two tribes: the Tawaster and the Karelian... The Tawasters..inhabit the central part of Finland.] **1898** J. ABERCROMBY *Pre- & Proto-Historic Finns* I. i. 3 The Finns of Finland (*Suomi*) call themselves *Suomalaiset*, and are broadly divided into two branches, the Tavastlanders (Hämäläiset) and the Karelians (*Karjalaiset*). **1911** WEBSTER, *Tavast*,..*Tavastian*.. *n.*, a Finn of a type characterized by broad, thickset figure and blond complexion. **1934** *Ibid.*, Tavastian, *adj.* **1935** HUXLEY & HADDON *We Europeans* vi. 181 These characters are seen among Finns, White Russians and..the Tavastians of Finland. **1957** *Encycl. Brit.* IX. 257/2 The *Finns* proper... There are two principal subdivisions, the Tavastlanders or Hämäläiset in the south and west and the Karelians or Karjalaiset in the east and north. The Tavastlander has a round head, a broad face, concave nose, fair complexion. **1965** E. JUTIKKALA in Glass & Eversley *Pop. in Hist.* xxiii. 569 The growth was by no means proportional to that of the 11 Tavastian parishes mentioned. **1966** L. DEIGHTON *Billion-Dollar Brain* ix. 79, I am a typical Tavastian... We are Tavastian people from the south and centre of Finland. **1974** *Encycl. Brit. Micropædia* IV. 145/3 The Finns proper, the Tavastlanders (or Tavastians), and the Karelians..had their own chiefs.

Tavel (ta·vel). The name of a commune on the Rhône (department of Gard, France), used *attrib.* and *absol.* to designate a rosé wine produced there.

1875 H. VIZETELLY *Wines of World* I. iii. 28 Of the rose-colour wines of the Côtes du Rhône, such as the dry and insidious Tavel,..and the robust Roquemaure,..the majority made default. **1926** P. M. SHAND *Bk. Wine* v. 178 On the opposite bank of the Rhône..is the little village of Tavel, which produces the delicious Tavel Rosé (Ancien Vignoble). **1934** J. I. DAVIS *Beginner's Guide to Wines* 49 Tavel..is a most delicious table wine. **1951** R. POSTGATE *Plain Man's Guide to Wine* iv. 90 Tavel is both dry and fruity... All rosés are a pretty colour; Tavel is perhaps the prettiest. **1963** N. FREELING *Gun before Butter* III. 153 They drank a Tavel wine from near Avignon. **1974** *Guardian* 24 Jan. 13/5 The best rosé in the world is probably Tavel. **1980** 'M. HARRIS' *Treasure of Sainte Foy* xviii. 229 He goes on through the small town of Tavel—this is where Tavel rosé comes from.

tavern, *sb.* Add: **1.** (Earlier example referring to *New Inn Hall*.)

1854 'C. BEDE' *Verdant Green* II. xi. 103 He seemed to feel that the Dons of his college would look shy upon him, and he expressed his opinion that it would be better for him to migrate to the Tavern... A name given to New Inn Hall, not only from its title..but also because the buttery is open all day, and members of the Hall can call for what they please at any hour.

4. a. *tavern-music* (later example), *-restaurant, -song.*

1979 *Listener* 30 Aug. 275/2 The best tavern music in South London is..jazz. **1880** W. D. Hay *Doom of Gt. City* 46 One place I knew slightly, a tavern-restaurant, where I had occasionally dined. **1973** *Washington Post* 13 Jan. A3/6 Mr. and Mrs. Harry Grenwalt..were celebrating their 42nd wedding anniversary at the tavern-restaurant. **1823** Byron *Don Juan* viii. lxiii. 142 Without which Glory's but a tavern song. **1917** J. Masefield *Lollingdon Downs* 90 Within the tavern-song, hid in the wine. **1959** I. & P. Opie *Lore & Lang. Schoolch.* xvi. 346 This jingle may be compared with the tavern song which was printed in *Vinculum Societatis*.

taverna (tăvɔ̄·rnă). [a. mod.Gr. ταβέρνα tavern.] A Greek eating-house.

1914 L. M. J. Garnett *Greece of Hellenes* xii. 151 The typical 'public-house' of Greece is a small tavern... Adjoining many of these humble wayside *tavérnas* are gardens roofed with spreading vines. **1952** [see *bouzouki]. **1963** *Harper's Bazaar* Jan. 59/2 Food in *tavernas* is..not always very good. **1972** *Daily Tel.* (Colour Suppl.) 24 Nov. 20/4 Multitudes of rather second-rate tavernas and pizza-houses [in Australia]. **1977** B. Pym *Quartet in Autumn* xviii. 160 Not Greece of course..—one could hardly imagine Marcia in a taverna, eating octopus. **1978** *Chicago* June 34/2 Penny Evans..is the best taverna singer we've ever heard. **1980** R. Tine *State of Grace* (1982) xix. 169 They won't respect you. In every corner *taverna* [in Sicily] they'll be laughing at you.

Tavgi (tæ·vgi), *sb.* (and *a.*) Also **Tavghi, Tavghy, Tavgy.** [a. Russ.] **a.** (A member of) a Finno-Ugric people (now called Nganasan) living between the Yenisey and Khatanga rivers in north-west Siberia. **b.** The language of this people. Also *attrib.* or as *adj.*, esp. in *Tavgi-Samoyed*.

1886 *Encycl. Brit.* XXI. 251/2 The Tavghi Samoyedes may number about 1000. **1888** *Ibid.* XXIV. 1/1 *Ural-Altaic languages..Tavghi*, between lower Yenisei and Khatanga rivers. **1934** Webster, *Tavgi*, var. of *Tavghi*. **1951** W. K. Matthews *Lang. U.S.S.R.* iii. 17 Tavgi (Nganasan) in Taimyr. **1954, 1967** [see *Nenets]. **1975** G. F. Cushing tr. *Hajdu's Finno-Ugrian Lang. & Peoples* iii. 216 The Nganasans are called Tavgi-Samoyeds. **1977** C. F. & F. M. Voegelin *Classification & Index World's Lang.* 343 Yenisei Samoyed..appears to be transitional between Yurak and Tavgy Samoyed.

taw, *sb.*[2] Add: **c.** (Further examples in *fig.* phrases.)

1840 *Spirit of Times* 7 Mar. 6 We have understood that Boston..will be *en route* for the stable..at Columbia, South Carolina—that is, if Wagner 'comes to taw'. **1868** in *Amer. Speech* (1965) XL. 132 He smiles at all the girls he meets, And you smile at him on the crowded streets, Why don't you make him 'come to taw', I know he wants a mother-in-law. **1904** W. N. Harben *Georgians* xxxii. 292 His wife's a bully woman; she fetched 'im to taw. **1934** D. Runyon in *Collier's* 3 Mar. 41/1 Georges takes a wonderful liking to Princess O'Hara right from taw. **1935** H. Davis *Honey in Horn* ix. 113 The only way Mrs. Yarbro could tell anything was to start from taw. **1956** *Coast to Coast* 183 Starting off from taws with a big load to carry. **1969** *Sunday Truth* (Brisbane) 5 Oct. 14/4 Without a share of overseas star shows, Seven has been battling from taws, but..is..getting stuck into the other networks with a 'super-specials' policy change.

tawa[1]. (Earlier example.)

1839 [see *billy[3]].

tawa[2] (tawā·). Also **tava(h).** [a. Hindi, Punjabi *tavā* frying-pan, griddle.] A circular griddle used in the Indian subcontinent for cooking chupattis and other food.

c **1843** H. Lawrence *Jrnls.* (1980) viii. 134 The *tavah* a convex iron plate on which are [*sic*] baked the thin unleavened bread of the people. **1963** *Guardian* 1 May 6/4 Iron 'tawa' (a baking utensil like the Scots girdle for oatcakes). **1969** *Eve's Weekly* (Bombay) 20 Dec. 65/3 Make a gash in the flat side of each chestnut and dry roast in the oil in a large tava for a few minutes. **1971** *Femina* (Bombay) 16 Apr. 55/1 Roll out into *chappatis* and bake on a *tawa* on a very low fire till it cooks through.

Tawarek, var. *Tuareg *sb.* and *a.*

tawn, *sb.* For † read *rare* and add later examples. Occas. as *adj.*, tan or tawny-coloured.

1851 H. Melville *Moby Dick* I. v. 48 This young fellow's..cheek is like a sun-toasted pear in hue... That man..looks a few shades lighter... In the complexion of a third still lingers a tropic tawn. **1920** E. Pound *H. S. Mauberley* 27 Tawn fore-shores. **1939** Joyce *Finnegans Wake* 540 Redu Negru may be black in tawn.

tawny, *a.* and *sb.* Add: **B.** as *sb.* **6.** = *tawny port*, sense C. c below.

1929 J. B. Priestley *Good Companions* ii. i. 278 'Waiter, I want a bottle of port.'..'Well, we've the Tawny at three-and-nine the bottle.' **1959** W. James *Word-Bk. of Wine* 148 The commonest style of port is tawny, a blend of several vintages between four and ten years old. *Ibid.*, White port is simply port made from white grapes, and is sometimes blended with young red port to make the cheaper sorts of tawny. **1976** *Times* 6 Nov. 13/2 Prices are around £3 for a fine old tawny, about £4 to £5 for a vintage.

C. a. *tawny-eyed, -necked, -stained, -throated.*

1853 M. Arnold *Philomela* in *Poems* (new ed.) 64 Hark! ah, the nightingale! The tawny-throated! **1930** E. Blunden *Poems* 42 And tawny-stained with ruin [the brook] trolls across The tiny village battered into dross. **1940** C. Day Lewis tr. *Virgil's Georgics* iv. 90 A laminated dragon or lioness tawny-necked. **1952** R. Campbell tr. *Baudelaire's Poems* 87 Like angels fierce and tawny-eyed, Back to your chamber I will glide.

c. tawny eagle, *Aquila rapax*, found in Africa and western Asia; **tawny frogmouth** = *podargus; **tawny owl:** see *owl *sb.* 2 b; **tawny port,** a port wine made from a blend of several vintages matured in wood (see quot. 1951).

1859 *Ibis* I. 88 The claim of the Tawny Eagle..to be considered European rests at present solely upon a trophy of the Russian war. **1912** J. Stevenson-Hamilton *Animal Life Afr.* xvii. 286 The tawny eagle is of mottled brown colour above, and tawny chestnut beneath, with yellow legs. **1979** G. & D. Lloyd *Birds of Prey* 82 The Tawny Eagle..of Africa and Asia is 26 to 31 inches in size and is the world's commonest eagle. **1901** A. J. Campbell *Nests & Eggs Austral. Birds* II. 539 (*heading*) Tawny frogmouth. **1933** [see *podargus]. **1968** Breeden & Slater *Birds Austral.* 69 (*caption*) The yawn of this Tawny Frogmouth reveals its enormous gape. **1848** Thackeray *Van. Fair* xliii. 382 The particular tawny port was produced when he dined with Mr. Osborne. **1951** R. Postgate *Plain Man's Guide to Wine* viii. 116 Tawny port is port of various years, blended and matured in cask... Tawny port..soon loses the rich purple colour of vintage port, and is ready to drink much sooner. **1979** *Country Life* 4 Jan. 40/1 (Advt.), Old Tawny Port wines by *Quinta do Noval*..Portugal.

tax, *sb.*[1] Add: **7. a.** *tax bill, bracket, consultant, -defaulter, dodge* (also as *v. intr.*), *fiddle* (colloq.), *return* (earlier example), *year; tax-collector* (earlier example), *-fiddler* (colloq.), *inspector; tax-free* adj. (later examples). **b. tax allowance,** a sum that is to be deducted from gross income in the calculation of taxable income; **tax avoidance,** the arrangement of financial affairs so as to reduce tax liability within the law; so **tax-avoider, -avoiding** *ppl. a.*; **tax bite** *U.S. colloq.*, a deduction in the form of tax; **tax break** *colloq.* (orig. *U.S.*), a tax advantage or concession allowed by government; **tax code,** a code number representing the tax-free part of an employee's income, assigned by tax authorities for use by employers in calculating the amount of tax to deduct under the PAYE system; **tax credit,** a sum that can be offset against a tax liability; *spec.* one that results in a payment to any person whose liability is less than this sum; **tax-deductible** *a.*, allowable as a tax deduction; so **tax-deductibility; tax deduction** chiefly *U.S.*, an expense that can be deducted from gross income in calculating taxable income; **tax disc,** a circular label displayed in the window of a motor vehicle showing the date up to which motor vehicle excise duty has been paid; **tax dollar** *U.S.*, a dollar paid as tax; **tax-eater, -eating** *a.* (later U.S. examples); **tax evasion** orig. *U.S.*, the reduction of tax payments by misstatement of income or other illegal means; so **tax-evader, -evading** *vbl. sb.*; **tax-exempt** *a.*, free from a liability to be taxed; *sb.*, a tax-exempt security; so **tax exemption; tax exile,** one who lives in a country chosen for its lower taxes on personal income; the state of doing this; **tax haven,** a country that attracts companies or individuals by its low taxes; **tax holiday** *colloq.*, a period of tax exemption or tax reduction, esp. one of fixed duration; **tax-loss,** a loss that can be offset against taxable profit earned elsewhere or in a different period; also *transf.* and *attrib.*; **taxman:** also, an inspector of taxes or similar official; (with *the*) the Board of Inland Revenue, personified; (earlier and later examples); **tax point,** the date upon which value added tax becomes chargeable in any particular transaction; **tax relief** = *relief[2] 7; **tax shelter,** an opportunity for incurring expenses so that they can be used to reduce tax liability; so **tax-sheltered** *a.*, providing such an opportunity; **tax threshold,** the level of income at which tax begins to be payable.

[**1935** *Times* 16 Apr. 9/3 The cost of these various amendments in income-tax allowances will amount to £10,000,000.] **1950** *Economist* 22 Apr. 903/2 Statisticians have allowed an increase..to reflect the increase in initial tax allowances on plant purchased from April. *a* **1974** R. Crossman *Diaries* (1976) II. 174 The Chancellor's only votes were gained from those who shared his male views and in particular objected to taking away money from middle-class families by tampering with their children's tax allowances. **1927** *Hansard Commons* 4 July 961, I think that all these devices for tax avoidance ought to be stopped. **1951** L. H. Seltzer *Nature & Tax Treatment Capital Gains & Losses* ii. 43 Wide openings for tax avoidance through so-called reorganization provisions were soon discovered. **1972** *Accountant* 28 Sept. 401/2 This amendment was designed to counteract certain tax avoidance schemes. **1960** *Guardian* 9 July 10/2 Every word of this was fascinating to all tax-payers and tax-avoiders. **1980** *Listener* 1 May 578/3 The tax-avoiding English who have arrived [on the Isle of Man] since the war. **1720** in *Mass. House of Representatives Jrnl.* (1921) II. 284 A Petition..Complaning of the Proceedings of the Court..in their Nulling Three Tax-Bills by them made..[was] Sent up. **1850** R. W. Emerson *Let.* 6 Mar. in R. B. Perry *Thought & Char. W. James* (1935) I. 68 If a good bookseller thinks that such readings in New York will pay my taxbills and bad gardening in Concord, I shall try the experiment. **1978** W. White *W. Whitman's Daybks. & Notebks.* I. p. xii, Tax bills, water bills, subscriptions to daily papers. **1954** *Sun* (Baltimore) 26 Jan. (B ed.) 1/4 The Iowa senator called for..legislation by Congress to put a tax bite on foreign coffee traders operating in this country. **1976** *National Observer* (U.S.) 22 May 2/4 The upshot of the committee's action is a proposal to enlarge the tax bite for some wealthy individuals and contract it for others. **1975** R. Stout *Family Affair* (1976) xviii. 189, I am already in an uncomfortably high tax bracket for the year and would take no jobs anyway. **1968** *Nation* 4 Nov. 463/1 What better way to entice private enterprise than with a tax credit or some other sort of tax break? **1969** *N.Y. Times* 4 Sept. 6/1 Companies will not get the tax breaks they formerly got on amortization of new equipment. **1982** *Economist* 18 Dec. 17/2 Governments should cease to shower capital with tax breaks that artificially lower capital's price. **1961** M. Kelly *Spoilt Kill* iii. 163 Writing paper, annual notice of tax code, medical card. **1976** *Star* (Sheffield) 3 Dec. 6/7 We have reached a ludicrous state of taxation when a man on state aid receives enough to exceed his tax allowance but this does not prove that the social security payments are too high, but rather, that wage rates, and especially tax codes are far too low. **1833** J. S. Mill in *Monthly Repos.* VII. 581 These taxes..throw electioneering influence into the hands of the tax-collectors. **1976** J. R. L. Anderson *Redundancy Pay* i. 10 He had..developed a shrewd ability as a tax consultant, particularly in the property market. **1946** H. M. Groves *Postwar Taxation & Econ. Progress* vii. 227 This could be done readily by permitting the taxpayer [with a fluctuating income] to sum his taxes over a period of years, calculate what his tax bill would have been if his income had been distributed evenly among these years, determine the difference between the two, and claim the difference as a refund or tax credit. **1973** *Guardian* 24 Jan. 14 The Green Paper proposes first that most tax allowances..should be replaced by tax credits... Anyone whose tax liability was less than their tax credits would be paid the difference. **1974** *Nature* 10 May 103/3 A company can obtain 'foreign tax credits' (which can be offset against United States tax) in respect of taxes paid to foreign governments. **1980** *Daily Tel.* 23 Feb. 19/2 A final of 8p a share payable on April 3, makes 14.25p net against 10.15p net or 20.36p including the related tax credit compared with 15.15p. **1972** *Accountant* 5 Oct. 422/1 Many captives are established to take advantage of this tax deductibility of insurance reserves. **1954, 1965** Tax-deductible [see *deductible *a.*]. **1977** D. Anthony *Stud Game* vii. 45 Most of Grant's calls were on business, tax-deductible items. **1942** F. W. Marshall *Legitimate Deductions* vi. 40 In enacting provision for income tax deductions, Congress is only interested in determining what part of a company's [or person's] gross income it believes should be treated as net income for the purpose of income taxation. **1971** 'O. Bleeck' *Thief who painted Sunlight* (1972) xiv. 122 He can contribute fifty percent of his income each year and claim it as a tax deduction. **1979** *Guardian* 5 July 3/4 The tax deduction for having a company car is a tiny fraction of its real value. **1951** Auden *Nones* (1952) 28 Agents of the Fisc pursue Absconding tax-defaulters through The sewers of provincial towns. **1972** *Times* 3 Oct. 2/8 (*heading*) 'Scrap tax discs' call. **1962** J. Braine *Life at Top* xxiii. 254 The usual tax dodge... It makes me sick to the stomach. **1972** *Listener* 21 Dec. 865/1 He hasn't killed himself yet... He's waiting till 5 April... Some sort of tax dodge. **1976** *Morecambe Guardian* 7 Dec. 17/2 With that film is '*The Swiss Conspiracy*' which is all about people who tax dodge, and blackmail, are blackmailed, and murdered, not necessarily in that order. **1976** *Billings* (Montana) *Gaz.* 17 June 2-E/1 The fate of a plan to use tax dollars to improve off-street parking in downtown Bozeman will be decided July 7. **1965** Mrs. L. B. Johnson *White House Diary* 12 Aug. (1970) 310 We hope for fewer dropouts thirteen years from now, for children able to grow up with a prospect of being responsible citizens, taxpayers, not tax-eaters. **1936** *Sun* (Baltimore) 30 Jan. 1/1 The time has come for a direct attack on the attempt at Washington to substitute a tax-eating bureaucracy for a liberal democratic system. **1927** *Hansard Commons* 4 July 955 What is to be done with the tax evader meanwhile? **1960** Tax-evader [see *snobocracy]. **1971** 'G. Black' *Time for Pirates* iv. 78 If this deal went all right..the Hydes could be on their tax-evading boat in a couple of years. **1922** *Hansard Commons* 27 June 1920 That type of company must be perfectly well identifiable when it is seen. You notice the stigmata of tax evasion about it when you see it, not in the mere registration, but in the conduct and carrying on of its business. **1977** Warren & Ponse in Douglas & Johnson *Existential Sociol.* x. 277 It is stigmatized..in the courts of law..and (unlike tax evasion) it is stigmatized morally in the courts of public opinion. **1925** *Contemp. Rev.* June 703 He has a deep resentment against their taking refuge in tax-exempt securities. **1933** *Business Week* 22 Feb. 4/1 Elimination of tax exempts is the object of an amendment to the Constitution offered by Senator Hull of Tennessee. **1966** *Economist* 30 Mar. 78/3 These industrial bonds..have so dogged the market as to increase all borrowing costs for tax-exempts. **1977** *New Yorker* 19 Sept. 27/2 One way to do this is to float a municipal-bond issue, which traditionally pays tax-exempt interest. **1978** G. Vidal *Kalki* v. 117 Any bona fide religion is tax-exempt in the United States. **1927** Bowley & Stamp *Nat. Income 1924* v. 42 Incomes above the tax-exemption limit. **1975** *N.Y. Times* 28 Nov. 37/4 One example of the use of incentives to attract investment is the tax-exemption on municipal bond income. **1969** *Manch. Guardian Weekly* 22 Nov. 11 Has Anthony Grey..joined the ranks of the tax exiles? **1978** J. R. L. Anderson *Death in Greenhouse* ii. 27 Neither of us was attracted by the prospect of living in tax-exile. **1959** 'M. INNES' *Hare sitting Up* I. i. 27 Tax fiddle of some kind? I don't like that sort. **1961** *Times* 31 May 10/4 Inclined to see in every taxpayer a more or less skilful..tax-fiddler. **1917** W. S. CHURCHILL 9 Sept. in M. Gilbert *Winston S. Churchill* (1977) IV. Compan. I. 156, I do not however exclude the possibilities of a special bonus, presumably tax free. **1964** A. WYKES *Gambling* x. 241 Tax-free prizes. **1960** *Business Week* 24 Dec. 32/2 Interest in tax havens is largely due to the fact that U.S. tax law permits a company to accumulate profits abroad tax-free. **1973** *Times* 18 May 29/6 The Briton wanting to minimize his taxes through getting paid in a tax haven. **1950** *Times* 24 Apr. 5/7 The stimulation of enterprise is essentially best organized on a regional footing. At present it is undertaken with varying determination by different colonies. Some grant free import of capital equipment and 'tax holidays' for pioneer industries. **1977** *Time* 10 Oct. 60/1 Haughey's notion of a permanent tax holiday for artists has at least stopped the drain of home-grown talent. **1978** *Jrnl. R. Soc. Arts* CXXVI. 224/2 There was firstly a three-year tax holiday followed by a period allowing accelerated depreciation and gradually increasing rates of tax. **1959** J. WOOD *Simple Guide for Taxpayer* iii. 28 Once the form has been completed it must be sent back to the Tax Inspector who sent it out. **1959** *Times* 24 Dec. 7/4 (*heading*) Tax-loss farming. *Ibid.*, Sir,—The so-called tax-loss farmer is generally speaking a man who carries on two businesses, one profitable and the other unprofitable. As a matter of taxation machinery he pays tax in respect of his profitable business and afterwards claims a refund of tax in respect of his unprofitable farming business. **1965** I. FLEMING *Man with Golden Gun* vii. 100 Others would want to buy in..cheaply, and use it [*sc.* a hotel] as a tax-loss to set against more profitable enterprises elsewhere. **1970** *Money Which?* Mar. 64/3 Don't wait until the very end of the tax-year before selling shares for tax-loss purposes. **1975** *Times* 14 Jan. 12/6 (Advt.), *Wanted.* Large run-down school... High tax losses an inducement to purchase. **1803** G. COLMAN *John Bull* I. i. 3 She had disgraced her family by marrying herself to a tax-man. **1968** *Guardian* 22 June 5/5, I don't know what the taxman would say if you tried to get that as an expense allowance. **1970** *Money Which?* Mar. 43/2 You are allowed free of tax..family allowances, most pensions and some other social security benefits. The taxman views all these as earned income. **1972** *Accountant* 21 Sept. 369/2 It might be of interest..to mention the special rule for the tax point of barristers' services. [**1916** Tax relief: see *INCOME-TAX.] **1931**, etc. [see *RELIEF² 7]. **1980** *Times* 9 Aug. 16/4, I have been offered remortgage, but my accountant says it will not qualify for tax relief. **1870** 'MARK TWAIN' *Sketches New & Old* (1875) 319 A wicked tax-return..calculated to make a man report about four times his actual income to keep from swearing to a falsehood. **1961** *Guardian* 20 Feb. 16/7 If all the tax shelters were eliminated..the income tax yield would be increased by a third. **1982** *Financial Times* 13 Mar. 14/3 Investors will be seeking to use up the effective tax shelter offered by an appreciation of their assets each year in line with inflation. **1959** *Wall Street Jrnl.* 17 Sept. (Eastern ed.) 21 (Advt.), Tax-sheltered investment. **1976** *National Observer* (U.S.) 17 Jan. 9/6 And how to defer income tax on the interest you get. Plans that offer marvelous tax-sheltered advantages. **1976** F. ZWEIG *New Acquisitive Society* II. iv. 108 The tax thresholds in real terms have been substantially lowered over the years. **1971** *Money Which?* Mar. 4/1 These taxes are charged for a particular year of assessment, which always starts on 6 April and ends on 5 April in the following year. This is commonly called a tax year.

tax-cart. (Earlier example.)

1796 J. WOODFORDE *Diary* 31 Oct. (1929) IV. 316 They came in Mrs. Bodhams little Tax-Cart.

taxed, *ppl. a.* Add: **1. b.** Of a motor vehicle: having had excise duty paid for the current period.

1933 *Motor* 2 May (Suppl.) 99/3 (Advt.), Riley... 4-door coachbuilt sunshine saloon.., maroon, taxed. **1976** *Jrnl.* (Newcastle) 26 Nov., (Advt.), Volvo 144 Saloon 1974 N regn, orange, red striped upholstery, taxed Oct. '77.

‖ **taxe de séjour** (taks də seʒur). [Fr., lit. 'tax of visit'.] A tax imposed on visitors to spas or tourist resorts in France and other countries.

1922 *Michelin Guide Gt. Brit.* 764 France... 'Taxe de Séjour.'—The following special taxes are payable. **1979** G. POTTINGER *Secretaries of State for Scotland 1926–76* xiv. 151 Another proposal that emerged from the Fraser exercise was to levy a *kurtax* [sic], or *taxe de séjour*, on the continental model, to find funds for tourist amenities.

taxeme (tæ·ksīm). *Linguistics.* [f. Gr. τάξ-ις arrangement + *-EME.] A unit of syntactic relationship, esp. one that cannot be further analysed or lacks meaning by itself, such as word order or stress. Hence **taxe·mic** *a.*; **taxe·mics** *sb. pl.* (const. as *sing.*), the study and description of language in terms of taxemes.

1933 L. BLOOMFIELD *Lang.* x. 166 A simple feature of grammatical arrangement is a grammatical feature or taxeme. A taxeme is in grammar what a phoneme is in the lexicon—namely, the smallest unit of form. **1943** [see *TAGMEME 2]. **1947** Taxemics [see *TAGMEMICS *sb. pl.*]. **1950** WEBSTER Add., Taxemic. **1967** M. SCHLAUCH *Language* vi. 127 A taxeme, taken by itself, may have no meaning; when one or more taken together do have meaning the combination is called a tagmeme (for instance, *duch+ess*). *Ibid.* 128 It would seem that the terminology of taxemics requires further study. **1970** G. C. LEPSCHY *Survey Structural Linguistics* v. 89 Taxemes occur in conventional grammatical arrangements.

taxi, *sb.* Add: Pl. **taxis,** † **taxies. I. 1.a.** (Examples of *pl.* forms.)

1908 Taxies [in Dict.]. **1911** G. B. SHAW *Getting Married* 285 Me and the beadle have been all over the place in a couple of taxies, maam. **1914** —— *Pygmalion* (1916) III. 128 In future you shall have as many taxis as you want. **1923** A. BENNETT *Riceyman Steps* IV. v. 198 Even in the daytime taxies were few in King's Cross Road. **1925** F. SCOTT FITZGERALD *Great Gatsby* iii. 70 Forms leaned together in the taxis as they waited, and voices sang. **1979** *United States 1980/81* (Penguin Travel Guides) 150 Taxis cannot be hailed in the streets.

b. *colloq.* A (small) passenger aeroplane; also short for *taxiplane* (see sense 4 below).

1911 *Flight* 11 Nov. 986/1 Baldwin, Sabelli and Lieut. Esnie Chinnery were making straight flights on the taxi. **1918** *Atlantic Monthly* Aug. 260 Our hero is..helping his mechanic give the 'taxi' a final looking over. **1919** *N.Y. Times Mag.* 30 Mar. 4 An airplane was..usually [called] a boat, ship, bus, or taxi. **1922** *Daily Mail Year Bk. 1923* 74/2 The 100 miles-an-hour 'aerial taxi'. *Ibid.*, He kept his winged 'taxi' waiting while he transacted urgent business, and then flew on. **1923** *Daily Mail* 7 Aug. 8/2 Companies..which send 'taxis', or aerial tramps, to anywhere between Plymouth and Stockholm. **1943** C. H. WARD-JACKSON *It's Piece of Cake* 60 *Taxi*, an aircraft for the conveyance of a small number of passengers.

2. [f. the vb.] An act or spell of taxiing.

1931 *Daily Mirror* 27 Aug. 2/2 The machine..was lost in clouds of spray as it ploughed its way in a graceful 'taxi'. **1965** 'J. LE CARRÉ' *Looking-Glass War* i. 9 The plane..began the long taxi to the reception point.

II. 3. *U.S. slang.* A prison sentence of between five and fifteen years.

1930 J. LAIT *Big House* i. 1 Five to fifteen years, the judge had decreed—a 'stretch' that the convicts call a 'taxi', because most New York cabs bear conspicuously their rates, and are known as 'fifteen-and-fives'. **1935** A. J. POLLOCK *Underworld Speaks* 119/2 *Taxi*, 5, 10 or 15 years prison sentence. **1962** 'D. SHANNON' *Extra Kill* viii. 127 Whalen had done a five-to-fifteen year stretch—that's a taxi.

III. 4. *attrib.* and *Comb.*, as (sense 1) *taxi fare, fleet, -horn, man, queue, rank* [*RANK *sb.*¹ 1 c], *stand, station*; *taxi-driving* vbl. sb. and ppl. adj.; (sense *2) *taxi apron, clearance, work;* **taxi-boat,** a boat that may be hired like a taxi; **taxi-dance** orig. and chiefly *U.S.*, a dance at which taxi-dancers are available; so *taxi-dance hall*; **taxi-dancer** orig. *U.S.*, a woman (or man) whose services as a dance-partner may be hired; a professional dance-partner; so **taxi-dance** *v. intr.*, **-dancing** *vbl. sb.*; **taxi-driver,** the driver of a taxi-cab; also *transf.*, esp. (*colloq.*) an aeroplane pilot; **taxi-girl,** a young female taxi-dancer; **taxiplane,** a piloted light aeroplane available for public hire; **taxi-ride,** a journey in a taxi; a short distance by car; also *transf.*; **taxi service,** a service providing transport in taxi-cabs (in quot. 1952, a shuttle service of aircraft); **taxi squad** *N. Amer. Football*, a group of players who take part in practices and can serve as reserves for the team; hence **taxi squadder,** a member of such a group; **taxi strip, track** = *taxiway* below; **taxi-truck** *Austral.*, a van, with a driver, for public hire; **taxiway** [after *RUNWAY 2 b], a route along which aircraft can taxi on the way to or from a runway.

1978 T. L. SMITH *Money War* I. 136 Captain Imman eased the 727 forward on the taxi apron. **1949** *Newsweek* 26 Sept. 44/2 A taxiboat pilot told how, 'as soon as I pulled alongside, the passengers began plummeting down'. **1953** R. GODDEN *Kingfishers catch Fire* x. 117 Subhan's *shikara* had not cushions and curtains like a real taxi-boat. **1974** *Islander* (Victoria, B.C.) 8 Sept. 6/4 There was a 24-hour taxiboat service supplied. **1966** D. FRANCIS *Flying Finish* ii. 25, I filed my flight plan, checked with the control tower for taxy clearance. **1932** P. G. CRESSY (*title*) The taxi-dance hall. **1938** W. SMITTER *F.O.B. Detroit* 9 On it there was the name of a taxi-dance place over a store on Woodward Avenue. **1955** N. MARSH *Scales of Justice* ix. 205 [He] cohabited with a so-called Miss Kitty de Vere whom he..met at a taxi-dance. **1972** J. WAMBAUGH *Blue Knight* (1973) i. 26 She was thirty-eight years old now..and taxi dancing part-time down the street at the ballroom. **1976** *New Yorker* 1 Mar. 80/2 He also played in a taxi-dance-hall band. **1930** *Variety* 12 Feb. 49/4 The Filipino is a much better spender than his white brother and a favorite with the gal taxi-dancers. **1979** P. DRISCOLL *Pangolin* iii. 36 He would simply pay Mama-san Julie..to take one of her taxi dancers home for the night. **1982** *Times* 8 Feb. 22/7 The ancient (well, 61-year-old) custom of taxi-dancing has returned in style to New York. **1907** Taxi-driver [in Dict.]. **1924** J. BUCHAN *Three Hostages* vi. 84 It is an outlandish place to get to, but most taxi-drivers know it. **1937** PARTRIDGE *Dict. Slang* 868/1 *Taxi-driver*, an aeroplane pilot. **1955** W. FAULKNER *Fable* 110 Somebody owes something for that poor bloodstained taxi-driver [*sc.* an aeroplane pilot]. **1971** *Daily Tel.* 30 Jan. 3/3 For the first time separate experiments are being performed by the 'taxi driver', the lonely astronaut in the orbiting Command Module. **1975** J. MELDRUM *Semonov Impulse* x. 173 She leaned forward and gave the taxi driver Dörflinger's address. **1909** Taxi-driving [in Dict.]. **1951** KOESTLER *Age of Longing* II. iii. 234 But there were no grand dukes, taxi-driving generals, or princesses at the Kronstadt. **1932** H. CRANE *Let.* Feb. (1965) 401 I'm sure you wouldn't mind advancing the bus and taxi fare, would you? **1965** F. SARGESON *Memoirs of Peon* viii. 264 The taxi fleet was being doubled. **1963** J. KIRKUP *Tropic Temper* xv. 163 The professional dance-girls, or taxi-girls as they are sometimes called in Singapore and Hong Kong, sit in a long row in front of the band. **1974** E. BRAWLEY *Rap* (1975) I. xii. 166 Freddy paid a few piastres and danced with the taxi girls on the bandstand. **1943** G. GREENE *Ministry of Fear* I. iv. 54 Far away a taxi-horn cried through an empty world. **1909** Taxi man [in Dict.]. **1946** E. O'NEILL *Iceman Cometh* II. 111 Sneaking? Why, me and the taxi man made enough noise..to wake the dead. **1982** P. FITZGERALD *At Freddie's* vii. 54 They could all see him..cutting short whatever the taxi-man was saying. **1920** *Daily Tel.* 13 Apr. 1/7 Taxiplanes for any journey. Per mile, 2*s.* 6*d.* **1926** *Bulletin* 6 Aug. 3/1 He made a dash to Constantinople with a taxiplane. **1982** G. HAMMOND *Game* v. 60, I whistled up the taxi-plane. **1969** G. LYALL *Venus with Pistol* xv. 98 Everybody else in the coach.. charged out to get into the taxi queue. **1929** T. S. MOORE in *Yeats & Moore: Corr.* (1953) 155 There is a taxi-rank a few steps above the station. **1943** G. GREENE *Ministry of Fear* IV. i. 222 A taxi-rank with one cab left. **1917** KIPLING *Diversity of Creatures* 333 It demanded Work in the shape of many taxi-rides daily. **1941** B. SCHULBERG *What makes Sammy Run?* iii. 44 It was a five-dollar taxi ride from the Villa España. **1976** E. WARD *Hanged Man* x. 59 He was no good for the tricky stuff. Just taxi-rides. Light planes over flat country. **1952** *Times* 23 Aug. 4/6 British European Airways..are to make eight flights daily, mainly to Hanover, in addition to a new public 'taxi' service..to west Germany. **1962** L. DAVIDSON *Rose of Tibet* 316 The p.c. questioned the local taxi service. **1981** L. DEIGHTON *XPD* xxvi. 214 London... The parking problem was horrendous, the taxi service inadequate. **1966** ROTE & WINTER *Lang. Pro Football* III. 141 *Taxi squad*, group of players under contract who practice with team but are not included on official team roster and do not take part in league games. **1967** *N.Y. Times* 8 Dec. 64 The Atlanta Falcons of the National Football League..activated a cornerback.. from the taxi squad. **1976** *Globe & Mail* (Toronto) 19 July S9/2 This is the first season the CFL has allowed teams an official taxi squad. **1975** B. MEGGS *Matter of Paradise* v. iv. 154 These boys are first string, and a taxi squader like yourself..can get hurt. **1922** M. A. VON ARNIM *Enchanted April* ix. 135 A taxi stand was at the end of the road. **1982** T. ALLBEURY *Shadow of Shadows* xxii. 190 He had to walk almost to the bridge before he found a taxi stand. **1930** J. DOS PASSOS *42nd Parallel* v. 366 Instead she went out to the taxistation. **1943** *Yank* 12 Nov. 6/3 We rode up the taxi strips to our head stand where the crew stood around the ship. **1976** B. JACKSON *Flameout* (1977) xii. 209 The small jet began to lose height, and soon airport buildings, a runway, and taxi strips were in sight. **1945** *Tee Emm* (Air Ministry) V. 42 The unit did not use lighted tar barrels to mark taxi tracks. **1966** D. FRANCIS *Flying Finish* x. 127 Patrick moved down the taxy track and turned on to the apron. **1962** *Southerly* XXIII. 98 Taxi-truck. **1974** P. CAVE *Dirtiest Picture Postcard* ii. 13 He packed all his books and records into two large cardboard boxes and phoned a taxi-truck. **1933** C. K. STEWART *Speech Amer. Airman* (thesis, Univ. of Akron) 96 *Taxi-way*, a route along the field designated for planes to taxi upon. **1939** *Sun* (Baltimore) 17 Apr. 8/1 The remaining $70,000 would be used for roadways, aprons, taxiways and fences. **1982** I. JOHNSTON *Special Drug Squad* ii. 25 The taxiway..allows aircraft to be towed across the perimeter road to British Airways' maintenance hangars. **1945** *Ann. Reg. 1944* 23 A small land plane of 8,000 lb. to seat eight passengers and suitable for taxi work.

taxi (tæ·ksi), *v.* Also **taxy** (now only in pres. pple.). [f. the sb.] **1. a.** *intr.* Of an aeroplane, etc., or its pilot: to travel slowly along the ground or water under the machine's own power. Also *transf. to taxi in,* to taxi from a runway to a terminal or hangar; similarly *to taxi out.*

1911 [see *REMOUS]. **1914** *Aeroplane* 5 Feb. 140/1 He taxied out to leeward,..turned,..opened out his engine. *Ibid.* 1 July 21/2 The de Bolotoff triplane was 'taxying', but showed no signs of lifting. **1915** [see *COME v. 24 d]. **1918** H. BARBER *Aerobatics* I. 37 In a high wind don't taxy unless necessary. **1927** C. A. LINDBERGH *We* ii. 19, I.. taxied back to the hangar. **1932** S. GIBBONS *Cold Comfort Farm* xxiii. 304 The aeroplane..was taxi-ing comfortably to a standstill. **1955** *Times* 24 Aug. 6/4 Crowds waited at London Airport, and the Canberra was greeted with cheers as it taxied in. **1959** D. A. BANNERMAN *Birds Brit. Isles* VIII. 280 When well out from the land both birds became silent and 'taxied' heavily over the water until air-borne. **1961** J. HELLER *Catch 22* (1962) v. 47 The planes lumbered around and nosed forward lamely.. until they taxied into the line at the foot of the landing strip and took off swiftly. **1975** *Daily Tel.* (Colour Suppl.) 4 Apr. 16/2 The ton of fuel..would be burnt while taxiing out to the runway.

b. *trans.* To cause (an aeroplane, etc.) to taxi.

1915 H. ROSHER *In R.N.A.S.* (1916) 67, I was taxying my machine to the far end of the aerodrome, to start off into the wind. **1933** *Discovery* Mar. 79 A Moth fuselage is used to 'taxy' a 25 ft. model of a flying boat hull by means of a force-recording undercarriage. **1946** *Proc. IRE* XXXIV. 380/2 (*caption*) General Motors Bug being taxied by radio control from B-23 airplane at Muroc Lake, California. **1977** *R.A.F. Yearbk.* 29 Taxying the aircraft requires a little practice.

2. a. *intr.* To travel in a taxi.

1918 A. QUILLER-COUCH *Foe-Farrell* xxiv. 397 From Victoria that evening I taxi'd straight to Jermyn Street. **1942** E. PAUL *Narrow St.* iv. 33 Anne's father..used to taxi to the rue de la Huchette from the avenue de la Bourdonnais. **1971** L. BLACKWELL *Blackwell Remembers* xxii. 200 As we taxied down the Mall it was gaily set out with Union Jacks and the Finnish flag.

b. *trans.* To convey in a taxi. Also *transf.*

1973 J. THOMSON *Death Cap* ix. 134 I'll get where I want to on my own feet... I don't want no bloody police taxiing me around. **1977** G. McDonald *Confess, Fletch* xxxviii. 178 He taxies Ms. Fryer to her motel. Allows her time to change.

Hence **ta·xiing** *vbl. sb.* and *ppl. a.*, in sense 1 a above; also *fig.*

1916 N. J. Gill *Flyer's Guide* iii. 32 If, however, the machine is subject to a sudden loss of forward way (i.e., taxying over rough ground) the planes then tend to go on. **1946** R. A. McFarland *Human Factors in Air Transport Design* ix. 390 To permit good ground vision during taxiing. **1958** Castle & 'Hailey' *Flight into Danger* vi. 76 One slowly taxi-ing aircraft came to a stop and cut its engines. **1968** J. Ziman *Public Knowledge* i. 10 Greek Science never finally took off from its brilliant taxying runs. **1972** *Guardian* 22 Dec. 4/1 An airliner ran into a taxi-ing plane while taking off. **1982** L. Cook *Under Etna* I. i. 11 The first jarring bounce of touchdown and..the gentle taxi-ing in.

taxi-cab. Add: (Later examples.)

1916 G. B. Shaw *Pygmalion* I. 116 She gets in and pulls the door to with a slam as the taxicab starts. **1978** M. Gilbert *Empty House* xii. 102 An aged taxi-cab parked in the [station] forecourt. **1981** P. Theroux *Mosquito Coast* xxxi. 392 The world..was glorious even here, in this old taxi-cab, with the radio playing.

Hence **ta·xi-cabby**, a driver of a taxi-cab.

1910 'W. Lawton' *Boy Aviators in Nicaragua* 19 The taxi-cabby, like most of his kind, was not averse to making a tip. **1918** G. Frankau *One of Them* xx. 155 Whether five-bob tip to taxi-cabby Presaged the sorting-bells of Hell Fire Abbey?

taximeter. Add: Now only with stress on first syllable. **a.** Also *ellipt.* for *taximeter cab. rare.*

β. **1908** A. Bennett *Buried Alive* iv. 102 He then hailed a taximeter from the stand opposite the Army and Navy Stores.

b. *taximeter-cabriolet.*

1959 P. Bull *I know the Face, But...* xi. 200 Lambert kindly escorted me in a taximeter-cabriolet.

taxis. Add: Pl. **taxes** (-īz). **6.** (Earlier and later examples.) [Introduced in this sense in Ger. by F. Czapek 1898, in *Jahrb. für wissensch. Bot.* XXXII. 308.]

1899 *Jrnl. R. Microsc. Soc.* 180 The phenomena of this [irritability] reaction may be classed under the following heads:—(1) Taxis or movement ('geo-' or 'photo-taxis') [etc.]. **1940, 1955** [see *kinesis 2]. **1973** *Nature* 17 Aug. 468/1 Behaviourism as a general theory of animal behaviour was woefully inadequate—a fact of which anyone must be convinced who tries today to read Jacques Loeb on tropism, taxes and the like.

-taxis (tæ·ksis), the word Taxis (sense 6) used as a suffix in *Biol.*, as in *geotaxis* s.v. *geo-, Phototaxis, etc.

taxogen (tæ·ksǒdʒěn). *Chem.* [f. Taxo- + -gen.] The monomer in the chain of a telomer.

1948 [see *telomer]. **1974** C. M. Starks *Free Radical Telomerization* i. 2 The term *monomer* is normally employed instead of taxogen, except in the patent literature. **1980** *U.S. Patent 4,183,901* 2 The maleic acid telomers are lower molecular weight polymers formed by reacting a chain transfer agent, or telogen with an olefinic monomer of taxogen.

taxon (tæ·ksǫn). Pl. **taxa.** [a. G. *taxon* (A. Meyer *Logik der Morphologie* (1926) 127), f. *taxonomie* Taxonomy.] A taxonomic group, as a genus or species. Also *fig.*

1929 *Scientific Monthly* Feb. 107/2 Such conceptions as the 'species', or 'taxon' in taxonomy. **1936** *Acta Biotheoretica* II. 180 Meyer's taxa (and phyla) are more valuable concepts in theory than in practice. **1948** *Minutes Utrecht Conf.* 14 June in *Chronica Botanica* (1950) XII. 12 Dr. Lam explained that in order to simplify the wording of the Rules, it is proposed to indicate a taxonomic group of any rank with the term taxon (plural taxa). **1951** [see *endemic *a.* a]. **1953** *Proc. 7th Internat. Bot. Congr. 1950* 465/1 Taxon..was, however, a very convenient word, and after two years [*sc.* by 1950] 60% to 70% of botanists were using it. **1961** *Watsonia* V. 68 Many infraspecific taxa [of *Trifolium repens*] have been described for wild populations. **1971** J. Z. Young *Introd. Study Man* xxviii. 400 There is no fixed typological criterion of an extinct species, genus, family, or other taxon. **1973** *Jrnl. Indo-European Studies* I. 405 A few words should be said about the main taxon in question; namely: Indo-Europeanist. **1976** *Sci. Amer.* Aug. 32/3 His work has revealed a surprisingly wide range of vertebrates: at least a dozen taxa of mammals, 22 of birds, three of fishes and one taxon of reptiles. **1980** *Dædalus* Spring 85 A Renaissance similitude (biblical giants) eventually converted into an Enlightenment taxon (species-giants).

taxonomic, *a.* (In Dict. s.v. Taxonomy.) Add: *spec.* in *Linguistics*, involving or concerned with the identification and classification of the terms into which languages are analysed; esp. as *taxonomic linguistics* (the dominant methodology of the 1940s and 1950s), *phonetics*, etc.

1962 N. Chomsky in *Internat. Preprints Papers 9th Internat. Congr. of Linguists* 556 In the case of perception of language,..the step-by-step analytic models of taxonomic linguistics are not in the least convincing. **1964** —— in *Proc. 9th Internat. Congr. Linguists* 951 Structural linguistics marks a departure from a more traditional point of view... Let us coin the term 'taxonomic phonemics' to refer to this body of doctrine, thus emphasizing its striking reliance..on procedures of segmentation and classification. **1968** P. M. Postal *Aspects Phonol. Theory* p. x, I shall refer..to the dominant conception of phonological structure as 'autonomous phonology' or 'autonomous phonemics', considering this terminology preferable to that of 'taxonomic phonemics' which has been used in the recent past. **1973** *Archivum Linguisticum* IV. 117 He goes on to claim a tacit dependence of transformational grammar on the findings of taxonomic analysis. **1976** *Canad. Jrnl. Linguistics* Spring 128 FBG present excellent discussions of taxonomic structural linguistics, how it is done, what it discovered about language (observing that many of the facts about language structure that taxonomic grammarians set out to capture are real), and the psycholinguistics of taxonomic grammar.

taxonomy. Add: **1.** The systematic classification of living organisms.

2. (With *a* and *pl.*) A classification *of* anything.

1960 *Times Lit. Suppl.* 29 Apr. 277/4 Professor Goldschmidt..has constructed what he calls a 'taxonomy' of human societies. **1971** *Nature* 10 Dec. 319/2 He complained of the taxonomy put forward by Sir Frederick Dainton's committee, with its concepts of basic research, strategic research and technical research. **1972** *Sci. Amer.* Jan. 116/3 His taxonomy of bridge structures before the age of steel and concrete. **1979** *Dictionaries* I. 64 The prefatory notes to the volumes of the *DAE* offer taxonomies of American usages and Americanisms. **1983** *Sci. Amer.* Mar. 102/2 We can outline a taxonomy of chlorite oscillators, and we are beginning to see how they can be related to oscillators of the bromate and iodate families.

taxpayer, tax-payer. Add: **2.** *U.S. colloq.* A building just large enough to provide an income sufficient to meet the expenses it incurs; hence, any small building.

1921 B. Matthews *Ess. on Eng.* vi. 134 A resplendent electric sign on top of a two-story tax-payer. **1950** *N.Y. Times* 28 Dec. (Late city ed.) 39/8 The three-story taxpayer at 288 Jackson Avenue in Jersey City, N.J...has been sold.

taxpaying *sb.* and *a.* (earlier examples).

1832 *Reg. Deb. Congress U.S.* 4 Apr. 2390 As a representative of the tax paying people of the South, I must ask..what becomes of the excessive heavy amount of revenue? **1849** J. S. Mill in *Westm. Rev.* LI. 44 A tax-paying or other property qualification.

Tayacian (tăyẽi·ʃăn), *a. Archæol.* [ad. F. *Tayacien* (H. Breuil 1932, in *Préhistoire* I. 131), f. *Tayac* (see def.): see -ian.] Of, pertaining to, or designating a palæolithic flake industry of which remains were first found at Tayac (Dordogne), SW France. Also *absol.*

1934 *Nature* 7 July 30/1 The Carmel cave series covers from Natufian (Mesolithic) to Tayacian, the recently recognised rough flake industry. **1946** F. E. Zeuner *Dating the Past* ix. 288 The combination of Levalloisian, Acheulian and Tayacian or Clactonian elements which resulted in the Mousterian industry of Europe occurred during the Last Interglacial. **1974** *Encycl. Brit. Macropædia* VIII. 1050/1 The earlier flake tools at this site [*sc.* Fontéchevade] are termed Clactonian tools.., while the later are known as Tayacian tools. **1979** M. Leakey *Olduvai Gorge* ix. 87 The chopper-small-tool complex.. is represented in Europe by the Clactonian..and the Tayacian.

tayberry (tẽi·běri). Also **Tay-.** [f. *Tay*, the name of a river in Scotland + Berry *sb.*[1]] A dark purple soft fruit produced by crossing the blackberry and the raspberry, introduced in Scotland in 1977; also, the plant bearing this fruit.

1977 *Ann. Rep. Scottish Hort. Res. Inst. 1976* 42 The new *Rubus* hybrid has been named 'Tayberry' and is being propagated for release. **1980** *Economist* 9 Aug. 63/2 To the strawberry, gooseberry, raspberry, blackcurrant and blackberry cycle is now added a new fruit—the tayberry. **1980** *Amateur Gardening* 8 Nov. 35 The tayberry is deep purple in colour, roughly $1\frac{1}{2}$ in. long and has a refreshing, not-too-sweet flavour. **1982** *Observer* 7 Feb. 43/4 (Advt.), Delicious soft fruits for autumn planting... The new virus-free Tayberry and all soft fruits.

Taylor (tẽi·lǝɹ). **1.** *Math.* [The name of Brook *Taylor* (1685–1731), English mathematician, who published the theorem in his *Methodus Incrementorum Directa et Inversa* (1715).] *Taylor('s) series*, an infinite series of the form $f(a) + hf'(a) + h^2f''(a)/2! + \ldots + h^{n-1}f^{(n-1)}(a)/(n-1)! + \ldots$, where $f^{(i)}(a)$ is the value of the *i*th derivative of a function $f(x)$ at $x = a$; an analogous series for a function of more than one variable; *Taylor's theorem*, the theorem that a function $f(x)$ can be approximated over any interval throughout which its first n derivatives exist by the first n terms of Taylor's series (with $h = x - a$) plus a remainder dependent on $f^{(n)}(a + \theta h)$ $(0 < \theta < 1)$.

1816 [see Theorem *sb.* a]. **1842** *Penny Cycl.* XXIV. 126/2 Lagrange's paper in the Berlin Memoirs for 1772, in which he proposed to make Taylor's theorem the foundation of the Differential Calculus. *Ibid.*, D'Alembert.. gave for the first time..a method of finding the remnant of Taylor's series after a certain number of terms have been taken. **1908** G. H. Hardy *Pure Math.* vii. 255 This expansion of f(a+h) is known as Taylor's series. *Ibid.* 287 (*heading*) Proof of Taylor's theorem by integration of parts. **1968** C. G. Kuper *Introd. Theory Superconductivity* ii. 24 Near the transition temperature, g may be expanded in a Taylor series: $g = g_0 + \alpha\zeta + \frac{1}{2}\beta\zeta^2 + \ldots$ **1972** A. W. F. Edwards *Likelihood* v. 72 An alternative method, which readily generalizes to the case of many parameters, is to obtain the Taylor's series approximation to the support curve in the region of the maximum. **1972** M. Kline *Math. Thought* xx. 442 Taylor's theorem for $a = 0$ is now called Maclaurin's theorem. **1979** Page & Wilson *Introd. Computational Combinatorics* ii. 10 We write $E = 1 + \Delta$ and expand the polynomial f by Taylor's theorem.

2. The name of F. W. *Taylor* (1856–1915), U.S. engineer, used *attrib.* to designate the system of scientific management and work efficiency that he expounded.

1911 *Assoc. Machinists Circular* in C. B. Thompson *Scientific Managem.* (1914) 783 The latest danger..is the so-called Taylor system of shop management. **1926** Whiteman & McBride *Jazz* vii. 154 At their work, men and women are the victims of efficiency, the Taylor system, so that humanity itself is being made into machines. **1972** [see *scientific management* s.v. *scientific *a.* 6].

3. Port wine shipped by the firm of *Taylor*, Fladgate, and Yeatman.

1940 M. Healy *Stay me with Flagons* 212 We had some Taylor of the same year, and the connoisseurs usually accorded it a higher place. **1952** H. W. Allen *Sherry & Port* II. i. 126, I tasted some of these wines in the Oporto Lodges, notably Sandeman 1942 and 1945 and Taylor of the same years. **1968** 'J. Welcome' *Hell is where you find It* x. 137 Benson brought in the decanter and put it beside me. 'It's the Taylor 47, sir,' he said.

Taylorian (tẽilǭ·riăn), *a.* and *sb.* [f. the name *Taylor* (see def.) + -ian.] The familiar name (used as *adj.* and *sb.*) of the Taylor Institution of the University of Oxford, established for the teaching of modern languages from money left for the purpose by Sir Robert Taylor (1714–88), English architect.

1898 *Dict. Nat. Biogr.* LV. s.v. *Taylor, Sir Robert*, The lecture-rooms and library which compose the Taylorian buildings were built in 1841–5. **1913** H. E. Salter *Oxford Deeds of Balliol College* 212 Ball's house was..on the site of the Taylorian. **1932** L. Magnus *Herbert Warren* v. 147 He took much interest as Vice-Chancellor in the Taylorian Institute. **1937** H. Nicolson *Diary* 26 Nov. (1966) 313 Then to the Taylorian where I address a large and interested audience on the German colonies. **1965** Doughty & Wahl *Lett. D. G. Rossetti* I. 47 There is a copy of this letter at Oxford, in the Taylorian.

Taylorism. Add: **2.** [f. the name of F. W. *Taylor*: see *Taylor 2.] The principles or practice of the Taylor system of management.

1928 *Times Lit. Suppl.* 11 Oct. 724/2 The second [essential] was the substitution of exact scientific investigation and knowledge for the old individual judgment or opinion. Mr. Meakin, who speaks somewhat slightingly of 'Taylorism', seems to be unacquainted with this passage. **1952** E. H. Carr *Bolshevik Rev.* II. xvi. 111 The Menshevik journal declared that the Bolsheviks..'are attempting to abolish the eight-hour day and introduce piece-rates and Taylorism'. **1983** *Futurist* June 25/1 Taylorism reduces work to machine-tending that requires little training and effort and that maximizes productivity.

taylorite (tẽi·lǝrəit). *Min.* [f. the name of its discoverer, W. J. *Taylor* (1833–64), U.S. mineral chemist + -ite[1].] A sulphate of potassium and ammonia found in Peruvian guano beds as yellowish white bitter-tasting orthorhombic crystals.

1868 J. D. Dana *Syst. Min.* (ed. 5) 614 Taylorite... In small compact lumps or concretions. **1968** I. Kostov *Mineralogy* 503 Arcanite and mascagnite are isostructural..and form mixed crystals $(K,NH_4)_2SO_4$ termed taylorite. **1975** *Mineral. Abstr.* XXVI. 353/1 The annual mineral lists for newly recorded Western Australian minerals include..taylorite.

Taylorize (tẽi·lǝrəiz), *v.* Also **taylorize.** [f. *Taylor + -ize.] *trans.* To introduce the Taylor system into (see *Taylor 2); to manage in accordance with this system. Chiefly as **Ta·ylorized, Ta·ylorizing** *ppl. adjs.* Also **Tayloriza·tion**, the action of Taylorizing; Taylorism.

1929 A. Huxley *Holy Face* 64 Machinery, Taylorization..had not yet begun to produce their dehumanizing effects. **1930** *N. & Q.* 26 Apr. 301/2 'Taylorize', then, means 'manage scientifically'. **1939** J. A. Schumpeter *Business Cycles* II. xiv. 783n. A major movement, which however resolves itself into an almost infinite number of small ones, is what may be called Taylorization. Its spread during our period is a typical consequence of the struggle for survival amidst the readjustments of downgrades. **1957** R. Burlingame *Henry Ford* v. 76 In the 'taylorized' industries the pay rise had been more gradual. *Ibid.*, A good many industrialists had repudiated 'taylorization' and called Taylor a crackpot. **1979** *Internat. Jrnl. Sociol. of Law* Feb. 112 Their Taylorizing bureaucracies are only matched by British amateurism..and American razmatazz.

tayn, var. *T'IEN.

Tay–Sachs (tēɪ,sæ·ks). *Path.* The names of Warren *Tay* (1843–1927), British ophthalmologist, and Bernard *Sachs* (1858–1944), American physician and neurologist, used *attrib.* and *absol.* with reference to a fatal inherited metabolic disorder in which an enzyme deficiency causes accumulation of a ganglioside in the brain and elsewhere, resulting in idiocy and death in childhood (described by them in 1881 and 1887 respectively). [Named in Ger. by H. Higier 1901, in *Neurologisches Centralblatt* XX. 851.]

1907 *Index Medicus* V. 841/1 Hereditary infantile cerebellar ataxy and the Tay-Sachs disease. **1937** [see *AMAUROTIC *a.*]. **1974** *Sci. Amer.* Mar. 63/2 (Advt.), A Tay-Sachs child develops normally for his first six months. Then, as excessive fatty deposits accumulate in his brain cells, he regresses... Usually before his fifth birthday, he dies. **1975** *Nature* 8 May 101/3 Israel's best known ethnic malady is Tay-Sachs Disease, a fatal genetic disorder limited almost entirely to infants whose forebears came here from certain parts of East Europe.

taz (tæz). *colloq.* = *TASH.

1951 PARTRIDGE *Dict. Slang* (ed. 4) 1198/1 *Taz.* A beard: Cockneys': C. 20... 2. An immature moustache; youthful down, wherever growing: mostly Cockneys': since ca. 1920. **1969** M. DUFFY *Wounds* i. 19 He was proud of his little toothbrush taz and elegant white raincoat.

tazetta (tæze·tă). Also **Tazetta.** [mod.L., specific epithet (Linnæus *Species Plantarum* (1753) I. 290), ad. It. *tazzetta* little cup, f. *tazza* (see TASS[2]): see -ET.] A fragrant white or yellow polyanthus narcissus, *Narcissus tazetta*, native to the Mediterranean, or any of the numerous varieties developed from it.

1847 *Jrnl. Hort. Soc.* II. 26 Sweet's Hermione Cypri are the produce of poeticus and a white-limbed Hermione, and N[arcissus] bifrons and compressus of Tazetta and jonquil. **1924** L. H. BAILEY *Man. Cultivated Plants* 187 They [*sc.* the Poetaz narcissi] are like large-flowered Tazetta. **1956** C. MACKENZIE *Thin Ice* iii. 36 The rising sun lighted a green plain covered with tazetta narcissus. **1977** *Chicago Tribune* 2 Oct. XI. 13/2 Midseason... Short-cupped daffodils; poeticus narcissus; jonquils; tazetta daffodils.

‖ **tazia** (tăzī·ă). Also **tazieh, taziyah, tazzia,** etc. [ad. Arab. *ta'ziya* consolation, mourning.] **1.** A representation of the tombs of Hasan and Husain (grandsons of Muhammad) carried in the Moharram procession.

1809 T. D. BROUGHTON *Let.* 26 Feb. (1813) 72 There were more than a hundred *Taziyas*, each followed by a long train of *Fuqeers*..beating their breasts. **1862** [see *TABOOT[1]]. **1885** T. P. HUGHES *Dict. Islam* 410/2 Against the side of the Imambarrah, directed towards Mecca, is set the *tabut*—also called *tazia* (*ta'ziyah*), or model of the tombs at Kerbela. **1889** KIPLING *In Black & White* 94 Gilt and painted paper presentations of their tombs are borne with shouting and wailing..which fakements are called *tazias*. **1924** *Glasgow Herald* 26 Sept. 10 The procession was a long one, including a number of tazias, or many-storeyed turrets, and followed by 7000 Mussulmans. **1946** *Times of India* 6 Dec. 10/4 Richly decorated in customary Muslim fashion *tazias* looked resplendent.

2. A play commemorating the 'martyrdom' of Hasan and Husain, performed esp. on the anniversary of the event each year.

1893 E. G. BROWNE *Year amongst Persians* iv. 70 Many people were assembled to witness a *ta'ziya*, or representation of the sufferings of the Imáms Hasan and Huseyn. **1911** D. S. MARGOLIOUTH *Mohammedanism* iv. 127 The Indo-Germanic affinities of the Persians have led to the production of miracle-plays, called *ta'ziyah* (consolation), whereby the atrocities are more vividly brought home. **1951** G. E. VON GRUNEBAUM *Muhammadan Festivals* (1976) v. 89 At a comparatively recent date..the *ta'ziya*, or Passion play..became the real climax of the Shí'ite Tenth of Muharram celebrations. **1972** *Times* 28 Sept. 9/3 In place of the traditional *ta'zieh* and *ruhozi* performances, a pair of new Iranian plays figured on the main bill. **1974** F. ROSENTHAL in Schacht & Bosworth *Legacy of Islam* (ed. 2) vii. 335 Numerous librettos for such *ta'ziya* plays have been preserved.

tazza. (Earlier example.)

1824 LADY BLESSINGTON *Jrnl.* May in E. Clay *Lady Blessington at Naples* (1979) 86 Antique vases and *tazze*, on which are sculptured bacchanalian orgies.

Tazzie, Tazzy, varr. *TASSIE[3]. **T-bone steak:** see *T 3 b.

tch, *int.* Also **tchk, tcht.** A representation of the dental click (freq. reduplicated) used to express vexation (cf. TCHICK *sb.*, TCK *int.*, TUT *int.* (*sb.*[3])). Hence **tch** *v. intr.*, to utter this exclamation; also as *sb.*, an utterance of this exclamation.

1898 G. B. SHAW *Mrs. Warren's Profession* I. 176 (Correcting him quickly in a loud whisper) Tch! Nonsense. **1906** N. MUNRO *Daft Days* ix. 74 'You'll find a curious fearless independence in her.' The twins held up their hands in amazement, 'tcht-tcht-tchting' simultaneously. '*What* a pity!' said Miss Jean, as if it were a physical affliction. **1910** —— in *Blackw. Mag.* Aug. 236/2 Aunt Amelia..tchk-tchked at such preposterous views. **1930** G. B. SHAW *Apple Cart* I. 21 Tch-tch-tch! Gently, Amanda, gently. **1971** *N.Z. Listener* 16 Aug. 50/3 The mind boggles. The dreadful deeds the little monkeys might perpetrate. Tch tch. **1977** *Daily Mirror* 31 Mar. 24 Tch! Of all the times to go down wi' flu! We've got a very important darts match tonight!

Tchaikovskian (tʃaikǭ·fskiăn), *a.* and *sb.* Also **Tchaikovskyan, Tschaikowskian.** [f. the name of Peter Ilyich *Tchaikovsky* (1840–93), Russian composer + -IAN.] **A.** *adj.* Of, pertaining to, or characteristic of Tchaikovsky or his style. **B.** *sb.* One who favours or imitates the style of Tchaikovsky.

1937 *Observer* 15 Aug. 3/3 When the time comes for an appraisal..it will not be the Tschaikowskian.., or the Egdon Heath Sibelius..who seems nearest to being a composer of the very greatest rank. **1945** G. ABRAHAM *Tchaikovsky* VII. 138 The G minor andante portion of the ..penultimate scene stands out as truly Tchaïkovskian. **1967** *Listener* 12 Jan. 73/3 It reminds one of what Tchaikovsky thought about Mozart, and incidentally of what Stravinsky—a Tchaikovskian to the hilt—thought about musical expression in general. **1973** *Gramophone* 29 June 15/3 The violin concerto is the least Finnish of Sibelius's major works, and its combination of Tchaikovskyan elements with a cosmopolitan concerto-style was emphasised by Pinchas Zukerman's suave, uncommitted manner. **1977** *Ibid.* Dec. 1097/2 The reprise of the Symphony's big tune at the end..lacks the expansive richness that can give the Tchaikovskian a real *frisson* of pleasure. **1979** *Guardian* 23 Mar. 12/7 Tchaikovskian delicacy misses fire in this theatre.

tchaush, tchawoosh, varr. CHIAUS.

1819 T. HOPE *Anastasius* (1820) II. 377 A Tchawoosh.. walked in, and summoned me before the Soo-bashee. **1902** *Encycl. Brit.* XXVII. 213/2 The Sultan's guard consists of ..the 'Tufenkdjis'..the 'Tchaush', of whom there are between 50 and 60, and who are messengers as well as guards [etc.]. **1930** *Observer* 26 Jan. 11 In the last war a peasant's wife, Fatma Hanem, served in the Army as a tchaush, i.e. a sergeant.

tche, var. *SE. **Tchehovian,** var. *CHEKHOVIAN *a.* and *sb.* **Tcheka,** var. *CHEKA. **Tcheremiss,** var. *CHEREMIS(S. **tchernozem,** var. *CHERNOZEM. **tchervonetz,** var. *CHERVONETZ.

tchetvert. (Earlier example.)

1814 *The Commercial Secretary—Il Segretario di Commercio* (Leghorn) 290 Wheat. R 10 1/2 Stock expected to increase to nearly 15/m tschetwer, which embarasses the holders greatly.

tchin. (Earlier example.)

1861 R. CECIL in *Sat. Rev.* 2 Mar. 228/2 The Emperor is practically an absentee landlord, knowing nothing of his estate except what the tchin is pleased to tell him.

tchinovnik, var. *CHINOVNIK. **tchornozem,** var. *CHERNOZEM. **tchotchke:** see *TSATSKE. **Tchuktchi,** var. *CHUKCHEE, CHUKCHI.

te[1], ti (tī). Also **tee.** *Mus.* Now the more usual name, in English-speaking countries, of SI. Cf. *Tonic Sol-fa* s.v. TONIC *a.* 3 b.

1839 S. A. GLOVER *Scheme for rendering Psalmody Congregational* (ed. 2) 41 *Te* is the *subsemitone* or leading half tone *below* the tonic. **1889** GROVE *Dict. Mus.* IV. 144/1 Tonic Sol-fa... The ancient sound-names do, re, mi, etc...are put before a class..in the form of a printed picture of the scale, called a 'Modulator'. For simplicity's sake they are spelt English-wise, and *si* is called *te* to avoid having two names with the same initial letter. **1944** W. APFEL *Harvard Dict. Mus.* 690/1 The syllables mostly used today are: *do.., re, mi, fa, sol, la, si* (*ti*). **1969** *Listener* 31 July 162/2 Everything becomes dubious if you suddenly decide to make tee a new doh. **1980** C. HEADINGTON *Illustr. Dict. Mus. Terms* 134/1 Solmisation, a system of designating the notes of a diatonic scale by syllables..*do, re, mi, fa, sol.., la, ti.*

‖ **te[2]** (də). Also **Te, teh, tih.** [Chinese *dé* virtue.] **a.** In Taoism, the essence of Tao inherent in all beings. **b.** In Confucianism and in extended use, moral virtue.

1895 G. G. ALEXANDER *Lâo-Tsze: Great Thinker* 123 It is very puzzling to know when '*tih*' is to be treated as a Divine attribute, and when it is to be taken as a moral virtue. **1904** W. G. OLD tr. *Laotze's Bk. of Simple Way* li. 114 Tao brings forth, and Teh nourishes. **1912** [see *LI[3]]. **1934** A. D. WALEY *Way & its Power* 32 Hence *tê* means a latent power, a 'virtue' inherent in something. **1955** E. HERBERT *Taoist Notebk.* 18 If allowed free play.. these gifts of *Tê* were ample to insure the orderly progression of 'heaven and earth', the disciplined march of 'the ten thousand creatures', all in their ranks and all in step with *Tao.* **1963** D. C. LAU *Lao Tzu* 42 *Te* means 'virtue', and seems to be related to its homophone meaning 'to get'. In its Taoist usage, *te* refers to the virtue of a thing (which is what it 'gets' from the *tao*). In other words, *te* is the nature of a thing, because it is in virtue of its *te* that a thing is what it is. **1975** C.-Y. CHANG *Tao* xxxviii. 107 The real meaning of *Tê* is thus the attainment of the self-cultivation of non-discrimination, non-differentiation, and above all, non-willing.

tea, *sb.* Add: **1. c.** Phrases. *given away with a pound of tea*: see *GIVE *v.* 54 a; *not for all the tea in China* (colloq., orig. Austral.): not at any price.

1937 PARTRIDGE *Dict. Slang* 148/1 *China!, not for all the tea in*, certainly not!; on no account: Australian coll.: from the 1890's. **1943** K. TENNANT *Ride on Stranger* ii. 19 I'm not going to stand in my girl's light for all the tea in China. **1958** J. CANNAN *And be Villain* vi. 137 She wouldn't get into a sidecar or on a pillion for all the tea in China. **1978** *Radio Times* 11–24 Mar. 25/5, I wouldn't change Newcastle for all the tea in China... It's a lovely place to live in.

2. b. *cup of tea* (colloq. phr.): see *CUP *sb.* 12 b.

c. A cupful of tea.

1922 JOYCE *Ulysses* 729 We both ordered 2 teas and plain bread and butter. **1976** B. GIBSON *Birmingham Bombs* xii. 104 Three teas, two coffees, and a large steak and kidney pie.

d. *one's tea*: what interests or suits one. *rare.* Cf. *CUP *sb.* 12 b (ii).

1934 E. WAUGH *Handful of Dust* iii. 135 Are you *certain* Jenny will be Tony's tea?

e. *tea and sympathy*: consolation offered to a distressed person. Also *attrib.*

1956 (*film title*) Tea and sympathy. **1958** *Listener* 2 Oct. 537/1 We leave Mrs. Newby enjoying tea and sympathy. **1970** Y. CARTER *Mr. Campion's Falcon* i. 7 He was a tea-and-sympathy man, full of tactful advice. **1978** J. HIGGINS *Day of Judgment* xii. 168 'There may be something I could do.' 'Tea and sympathy... No more than that.'

4. a. (Later examples.) Now usu. a light meal in the late afternoon, but locally in the U.K. (esp. northern), and in Australia and N.Z., a cooked evening meal; in Jamaica, the first meal of the day.

1914 G. B. SHAW *Misalliance* 80 He calls his lunch his dinner, and has his tea at half-past six. Havnt you, dear? *a* **1925** [see *MARKET *sb.* 1 b]. **1938** N. MARSH *Artists in Crime* vi. 81 'We finished tea at half-past eight, about.' 'The gentleman is talking of the evening meal. They dine at noon in the Antipodes, I understand.' **1952** in Cassidy & Le Page *Dict. Jamaican English* (1967) 439/1 Tea—same as chaklata... Tea at 6:30 A.M. **1957** *N.Z. Listener* 22 Nov. 4/3 More than one New Zealander has been invited to 'tea' in England and arrived hours too late, the meal finished and the guests gone. **1968** *Southerly* XXVIII. 5 'What have you got for tea?' he asked... 'It's a coupla nice little bits of fillet Mr Ballard let me have.'

c. *to go (out) for one's tea* (see quots.). *N. Ir. slang.*

1978 F. BURTON *Politics of Legitimacy* iii. 78 A Provo would scoff at the Officials' merely elocutionary skills while they were 'going out for their tea' (that is, going on military operations which might result in their death). **1979** *Courier-Mail* (Brisbane) 1 Mar. 5/1 'Going for your tea' in Belfast can be a painful experience—being dragged out by a terrorist punishment squad to get a bullet in the legs.

7. c. Marijuana; *spec.* marijuana brewed in hot water to make a drink. orig. *U.S.*

1935 A. J. POLLOCK *Underworld Speaks* 119/2 *Tea*, mariahuana; hashish. **1940** [see *JU-JU[2]]. **1950** *San Francisco Chron.* 22 Feb. 20/1 A couple of years ago she started blowing tea. **1957** [see *CONNEXION 6 c]. **1967** *Boston Sunday Herald* 26 Mar. IV. 1/1 Marijuana..when brewed with hot water,..is called 'tea'. **1979** *High Times* Mar. 18/2 Consider the number of words that served for a time and then passed into embarrassed silence. 'Muggles' and 'tea'—words that sound right only in Raymond Chandler novels now.

8. (Earlier example.)

1869 S. R. HOLE *Bk. Roses* vi. 77 The autumn leaves.., decayed to mould, are very advantageous to the Teas, Noisettes, and Bourbons.

9. a. *tea-jar* (examples), *-merchant* (earlier Amer. example), *-mug, -slop.* **b.** (Objective and obj. gen.) *tea-strainer, tea-swilling* adj.; (instrumental and parasynthetic) *tea-bathed, -coated, -drowned, -dunked* adjs.; also similative, as *tea-brown* adj.

1922 JOYCE *Ulysses* 258 He smiled at bronze's teabathed lips, at listening lips and eyes. *Ibid.* 532 A nymph with hair unbound, lightly clad in tea-brown art colours, descends from her grotto. **1953** DYLAN THOMAS *Under Milk Wood* (1954) 48 Willy Nilly the Postman's dark and sizzling damp tea-coated misty pygmy kitchen. **1882** W. D. HAY *Brighter Britain!* I. 161 What will be the future of these young tea-drowned nations? **1973** M. AMIS *Rachel Papers* 68 A small middle-aged man (with unusually big brown ears, like tea-dunked ginger-biscuits). **1870** C. SCHREIBER *Jrnl.* (1911) I. 74 An old Staffordshire Ware tea-jar. *Ibid.*, Our purchase of the George III tea-jar. **1983** J. SLIGO *Concert Masters* iv. 105 The Chinese tea jar on the mantelpiece. **1781** S. A. PETERS *Hist. Connecticut* 407 [To] exert themselves..in favour of the Bostonian tea-merchants. **1955** T. H. PEAR *English Social Differences* viii. 186 There is said to be a class which considers the tea-mug very *chic.* **1906** JOYCE *Let.* 8 Dec. (1966) II. 201 Your friend..ought to get a running kick in the arse for writing his tea-slop about it. **1967** E. A. GOLLSCHEWSKY in *Coast to Coast 1965–6* 94 Ettie surveyed the tea-table. It was still fairly orderly... No tea-slops in saucers. **1906** *Daily Colonist* (Victoria, B.C.) 26 Jan. 4/6 Kitchen utilities..Tea Strainers. **1970** *Kay's Catal.* 1970/71 Autumn/Winter 895 A stainless steel tea strainer and a decorated ceramic tile are set into a Teak wood base in this contemporary Danish design. **1961** *Times* 2 Oct. 13/4 Arms akimbo, bridling, bristling, and scolding, the tea-swilling Dame would at last be caught in the mangle.

c. tea-bag, (*a*) *Canad.*, a bag for carrying provisions; (*b*) a small permeable bag of paper or cloth containing tea for infusion; **tea ball,** a ball of wire or perforated metal in which tea is placed for infusion; **tea bar,** a bar (BAR *sb.*[1] 28) at which tea is sold as a beverage; **tea basket** (earlier example); **tea-bell** (earlier example); **tea-billy,** also used in New Zealand; **tea-boiler** (example); **tea-bottle,** a bottle containing tea (sense 2 a); also *slang,* an old maid; **tea-box,** (*a*) (earlier example); (*b*) *Canad.*, a box for carrying food and cooking utensils on an expedition; **tea-boy,** (*a*) (later example); also used outside Ireland; (*b*) a youth (occas. a man) employed to serve tea to workers; **tea-break,** an interval, usu. between periods of work, when tea is drunk; **tea-brick,** a brick of compressed tea leaves (cf. *brick-tea* s.v. BRICK *sb.*[1] 10); **tea-caddy** (earlier U.S. example); **tea-cake** (earlier examples); **tea-can,** a metal can used for brewing or carrying tea; **tea-canister** (earlier example); **tea cart** *U.S.*, a tea-trolley; **tea ceremony,** in Japan, the preparation and consumption of green tea, according to strict rules of ceremony, as an expression of Zen Buddhist philosophy; **tea-china** (earlier example); **tea-chop** [CHOP *sb.*[5] 5], in China, a chop-boat or lighter for the transportation of tea; **tea-cloth** (earlier Amer. examples); **tea-cosy,** (*b*) in full *tea-cosy hat,* a round knitted woollen hat resembling a tea-cosy; **tea dance** = *thé dansant* s.v. *DANSANT *a.*; also *Canad.*, 'a social gathering held by Indians, so called because in the early days the Hudson's Bay Company contributed tea, bannock, etc.' (*Dict. Canadianisms,* 1967); hence **tea-dance** *v. intr.*; **tea-dancer; tea-dancing** *vbl. sb.*; **tea-dust,** tea of inferior quality, often made from leaves broken in the course of production; *attrib.* [tr. Chinese *chá yè mò* tea-leaf dust], used to designate a dark green or brownish (often speckled) glaze on Chinese pottery (see quot. 1899), esp. used on decorative ware; **tea-girl,** a girl who serves tea; **tea-glass,** a glass from which tea (esp. without milk) is drunk; **tea-green,** a shade of greyish green resembling the colour of tea; **tea-head** *slang* (orig. *U.S.*), a habitual user of marijuana (cf. sense 7 c above and *HEAD *sb.* 7 e); **tea hostess,** a woman in charge of serving tea at a tea-party or other social occasion; **tea-hound** [*HOUND *sb.*[1] 4 e] *U.S. slang* (now *rare*), a man given to frequenting tea-parties; also in extended use, a lady's man (see quot. 1921); **tea-house** (further examples, in oriental contexts); **tea infuser** = *tea-maker* (*c*); **tea interval,** a break for afternoon tea or light refreshment (esp. during a cricket match); **tea-jacket** (earlier example); † **tea-kitchen,** a tea-urn (cf. KITCHEN *sb.* 2 b); † **tea-ladle,** a ladle for serving tea; **tea-lady,** a woman who serves tea (esp. in an office); **tea machine,** a machine which makes or dispenses tea; **tea-maker,** (*b*) (earlier example); (*d*) an apparatus incorporating a timer and designed to be kept at the bedside which can be pre-set to make tea automatically at any time (typically on awaking); **tea master,** an expert in the proper conduct of the tea ceremony; **tea money,** money paid by employees for drinks of tea at work (in quot. 1906, money paid by an employer to employees to buy their own tea); also *transf.* (see quot. 1979); **tea olive** [from the Chinese use of the flowers to add scent to tea] = *sweet olive* s.v. *SWEET *a.* and *adv.* C. 1 b; **tea pad** *U.S. slang,* a place where one can purchase and smoke marijuana; † **tea-paper,** the ornamental paper used as a wrapper for tea (*obs.*); **tea place** = *TEA-SHOP b; **tea plate,** a small shallow plate for use at tea-time; **tea room,** (*a*) (earlier examples); (*b*) *U.S. slang,* a public lavatory used as a meeting-place by homosexuals; **tea-seed oil** = *tea oil* (*a*); **tea-service** (earlier examples); **tea-set** (earlier example); **tea-ship,** (*a*) (earlier example); **tea-stall,** (*b*) a stall at which tea is sold; **tea-tent,** a tent in which tea is served at an outdoor event; **tea-time,** (*a*) earlier examples); also *transf.*; (*b*) (*rare*), the time occupied by or allowed for taking tea; **tea-towel** = *tea-cloth* (*a*); **tea-treat,** (chiefly in Cornwall) a publicly provided out-door tea-party for children, esp. of a Sunday-school; also *attrib.*; **tea-trolley,** a trolley (sense *3 c) for conveying tea-things; **tea-urn** (later example); **tea-wagon,** † (*a*) an East Indiaman used to carry cargoes of tea (*obs.*); (*b*) = *tea-trolley* above; **tea-ware** (earlier example); **tea-wrap,** a wrap worn by women and girls at tea (*rare*); **tea yellows,** a deficiency disease of the tea-plant, esp. in Africa, caused by a lack of sulphur and indicated by small, chlorotic leaves, and the eventual death of the bush.

1898 F. RUSSELL *Explorations in Far North* 161 If a crooked knife, a tea bag, or anything that is in the heap is needed, everything is tumbled about until it is found. **1936** K. CONIBEAR *Northland Footprints* p. xii, Give him a large piece of bannock from your tea-bag. **1940** R. CHANDLER *Farewell, my Lovely* xiii. 102 They put Dad in charge of the Bureau of Records and Identification, which in Bay City is about the size of a tea-bag. **1958** *Sunday Times* 30 Mar. 12/3 The sale of tea-bags is creeping up. **1977** *Lancashire Life* Feb. 19/1 Those who think that tea is grown in teabags will be pleasantly surprised to find the enormous number of teas blended and packaged in Britain. **1895** *Montgomery Ward Catal.* Spring & Summer 187/1 Pure Aluminium, Tea Ball, total length, 7 in. Ball 1½ in. dia. **1929** *Nation* (N.Y.) 4 Dec. 666 The tea ball enables one to pull the tea out before it has given off its tannin. **1976** *National Observer* (U.S.) 16 Oct. 10/3 Peel and crush six cloves of garlic and tie them in a piece of cheesecloth or put them in a tea ball and add this to the warm liquid. **1952** *Times* 12 Nov. 3/2 Tea bars are increasing. **1976** *Lancs. Evening Post* 7 Dec. 2/2 Mrs. Alice Durdle serves tea to the over 60s at the Lilian Wood Memorial Centre tea bar in Market Street, Preston. **1891** *Queen* 31 Oct. p. xxxvii (Advt.), Drews' Patent En Route 5 o'clock Tea Basket. **1836** *Knickerbocker* VIII. 418 It was nearly time for the tea-bell to ring. **1939** J. MULGAN *Man Alone* 81 viii. 81 Around him were spread his belongings..clothes, boots, two black tea-billies..and a grey blanket. **1839** A. LANGTON *Jrnl.* in *Gentlewoman Upper Canada* (1950) 101 The pie plates, too, are very nice, and also the little tea-boiler. **1909** J. R. WARE *Passing Eng.* 241/2 *Tea-bottle* (*Mid.-class*), an old maid—from the ordinary drink of spinsters. **1975** B. MEYRICK *Behind Light* xv. 198 He unwedged the sought-after tea bottle from its place behind the pipes. **1758** A. PITT *Let.* 10 Nov. in *Lett. Lady Suffolk* (1824) II. 252 So I design to send it [*sc.* a letter] with a tea box my sister left and does not want. **1972** S. BURNFORD *One Woman's Arctic* vii. 154 In no time at all had the team hitched up, and his rifle and teabox aboard. **1852** LD. GRANVILLE *Let.* 19 Jan. in E. Fitzmaurice *Life Ld. Granville* (1905) I. iii. 68 The teaboys of our own and our neighbour's establishments. **1954** *Atlantic Monthly* Aug. 35/1 The auction porters ate their dinners off thick white plates brought over by a cross-eyed teaboy from a café down the road. **1963** *Times* 31 May 12/6 Brutus..said that because of the banning order he was no longer able to work as a teacher and had had to take a job as a 'tea boy' with a research worker at the University of the Witwatersrand, for which he got £10 a month. **1977** *Time Out* 28 Jan.–3 Feb. 3/2 He certainly writes with all the flowing panache of a trainee teaboy. **1948** *Brit. Jrnl. Psychol.* Mar. 113 Many reasons were given for the almost universal appreciation of the tea break. **1958** A. SILLITOE *Saturday Night & Sunday Morning* ii. 35 The light flashed: tea-break over. **1981** *Economist* 18 Nov. 17/2 Strikes during the contract period (like the present tea-break strike at BL) would bring heavy damages on the unions. **1962** L. DAVIDSON *Rose of Tibet* v. 87 He had bought tea bricks..and a large cake of yak butter. **1981** *Times* 7 July 12/7 A food shop in Covent Garden..has introduced..tea-bricks, such as Chinese mandarins once used to pay their taxes. **1790** *Pennsylvania Packet* 7 Dec. 3/3 Joseph Anthony, Junior, ..Has Imported..Tea cadies, cannisters and salts. **1832** L. M. CHILD *Amer. Frugal Housewife* 71 There is a kind of tea cake still cheaper. **1844** DICKENS *Martin Chuzzlewit* xvii. 216 Tea and coffee arrived (with sweet preserves, and cunning tea-cakes in its train). **1890** H. K. DANIELS *Me & Jim* 67 The new plumber he gave him no answer except to drink from his tea-can and go on reading where he'd left off. **1951** J. FLEMING *Man who looked Back* x. 120 He picked up his tea-can. **1978** *Lancashire Life* Nov. 75/2 Erect, at Uncle Dan's immediate righthand, was a large, shining tea-can, its lid back in place. **1726** in *N. & Q.* (1942) 24 Jan. 46/1 Bowl & tea canister. **1934** WEBSTER, Tea cart. **1958** P. DE VRIES *Mackerel Plaza* iv. 56 A teacart hove into view, laden with goodies. **1978** M. DELVING *No Sign of Life* i. 15 His wife came into the room followed by the maid pushing a tea-cart. **1886** E. S. MORSE *Jap. Homes* iii. 149 The party comes about by the host inviting a company of four to attend the tea-ceremony, and in their presence making the tea in a bowl after certain prescribed forms, and offering it to the guests. **1935** *Burlington Mag.* Mar. 147/2 The tea ceremony, a rite so essentially Japanese that it might be said to epitomize Japanese culture. **1980** J. MELVILLE *Chrysanthemum Chain* 16 A classic four-and-a-half mat tea room with a blond foreigner in full formal Japanese dress performing the tea ceremony. **1790** J. WOODFORDE *Diary* 15 Dec. (1927) III. 235 My Maid Betty Dade breaking likewise the only Tea China-Slop-Basin..made me more fretful. **1876** F. W. H. SYMONDSON *Two Yrs. abaft Mast* vii. 136 A large 'tea chop' (a tea barge) came alongside. **1886** R. BROWN *Spunyarn & Spindrift* xxvii. 328 The river was so swollen by the rains that the tea-chops could not get through Foo-chow bridge. **1770** C. CARROLL *Let.* 11 Oct. in *Maryland Hist. Mag.* (1918) XIII. 62 A Hierling.. stole a napkin two Towels & a Tea Cloath wh we Recovered. **1881** C. C. HARRISON *Woman's Handiwork* I. 49 The beautiful tea-cloth linen, with its firm round thread, the warp and woof of equal thickness, so common in England. **1966** Tea-cosy [see *ENSEMBLE *v.*]. **1975** M. RUSSELL *Murder by Mile* x. 101 A scarlet tea-cosy hat perched on top of her hair. **1885** T. GOWANLOCK *Two Months Camp of Big Bear* 119 When the Indians held their tea-dances or pow-wows in times of peace, the squaws and their children joined in and it was a very amusing sight to watch them. **1916** W. STEVENS *Let.* 23 Apr. (1967) 193 People are pretty much dependent on the same things as in New-York: band concerts, tea-dances and..coffee-parties. **1962** A. BUCHWALD *How much is that in Dollars?* 128 Now you can see why the Patterson-Johansson fight didn't mean much to me. Those kids in the U.S. were just tea-dancing. **1964** *Camsell Arrow* (Edmonton, Alberta) Summer 60/4 High point of their four months in the north was the invitation to join the Indians 'tea dancing' Anne said. **1965** *News of North* (Yellowknife, N.W. Territories) 29 July 5/4 The ceremony was marked by a tea dance, in which everyone joined. **1978** *Lancashire Life* Nov. 129/2 For in a brave gesture of defiance in the punk era, the management has resurrected the Sunday Afternoon Tea Dance. It's all very Palm Court, even if the palms are plastic. **1980** *Radio Times* 29 Nov.–5 Dec. 87/4 So keen are the Tea Dancers that they have picked up all these [dances]. **1946** *New Yorker* 2 Feb. 4 A Melba trio plays in the Café Pierre, where there is tea dancing daily. **1977** *Ibid.* 3 Oct. 95/1 Tea dancing at the Kempinski. This goes on every day. **1899** S. W. BUSHELL *Oriental Ceramic Art* xviii. 518 One of the best-known glazes..is the *Ch'a-yeh-mo,* or 'Tea-dust' glaze, produced by the insufflation of green enamel upon a yellowish-brown ground, which owes its color to iron. The combination produces a peculiarly soft tint of greenish tone, which was highly prized in the reign of *Ch'ien-lung.* **1909** *Cent. Dict.* Suppl., Tea-dust. **1922** JOYCE *Ulysses* 57 Through the open doorway the bar squirted out whiffs of ginger, teadust, biscuitmush. **1945** W. B. HONEY *Ceramic Art of China* 145 The 'iron-rust' and greenish 'tea-dust' glazes..are usually of Ch'ien Lung date. **1979** P. NIHALANI et al. *Indian & Brit. English* I. 175 Good quality tea packaged in the form of leaf and known as 'leaf tea', and an inferior variety, comparatively inexpensive, called tea-dust. **1980** *Catal. Fine Chinese Ceramics* (Sotheby, Hong Kong) 84 A massive tea-dust bowl..with a finely speckled deep olive-green glaze,..the base covered in an ochre-yellow glaze. **1889** KIPLING *From Sea to Sea* (1900) I. 444 The tea-girls giggled. **1976** *S. Wales Echo* 23 Nov. 6/9 Every employee.., from senior executives to tea girls, would be interviewed. **1898** A. CAHAN *Imported Bridegroom* xi. 121 Jealousy..of the empty tea-glasses.., of the whole excited crowd. **1979** D. GURR *Troika* xxxiv. 260 Alexey grabbing at the rail, tea glass dropping from his fingers. **1956** W. EDWARDS in D. L. Linton *Sheffield* 16 East of the River Trent it [*sc.* the Rhaetic] overlies the 'Tea-Green Marls' at the top of the Keuper. **1967** *Vogue* 1 Mar. (International Collection) 161/1 She loves the colours. White, pink, blue, butterscotch, tea green, [etc.]. **1953** W. BURROUGHS *Junkie* (1972) ii. 29 Perhaps weed does affect the brain with constant use, or maybe teaheads are naturally silly. **1967** *Guardian* 8 July 6/2 Doctors, commissions, and plain tea-heads have been ready to go on record about the innocence of the weed cannabis sativa. **1970** Tea-head [see *HEAD *sb.* 7 e]. **1976** *Norwich Mercury* 19 Nov. 2/5 Mrs J. Bowhill acted as model for the evening dress... Tea hostesses were Mrs Kedge and Mrs Williams. **1921** *Dialect Notes* V. 111 *Tea-hound,* a lady's man. **1925** *Scribner's Mag.* Oct. 353/2 He was a regular tea-hound, he was seen at so many teas. **1763** J. BELL *Travels from St. Petersburg* II. x. 54 From the temple we went to a publick tea-house, where we saw many people drinking tea [in Peking]. **1959** L.-H. LIANG tr. *Ting Yi's Short Hist. Mod. Chinese Lit.* x. 221 In the rear areas, there were other dramatic forms akin to the 'street play', such as the 'tea-house play', 'demonstration play' and the 'lantern play'. **1972** K. LO *Chinese Food* I. 50 There are no pubs or bars and most of the informal leisurely drinking takes place in tea-houses. **1889** A. JAMES *Diary* 5 Aug. (1965) 52 A note of farewell from Mr. Godkin with a tea-infuser. **1907** *Yesterday's Shopping* (1969) 188/3 Travellers' Companion... For making tea when touring, boating, &c. ..Comprises kettle,..stand, spirit stove,..and muslin tea infuser. **1960** *Guardian* 4 Jan. 3/1 Collapsible tea infusers. **1923** E. P. OPPENHEIM *Inevitable Millionaires* xxix. 288 'I haven't done wrong in making the tea, have I?' she asked timidly... 'Of course not,' George Henry assured her. 'The tea interval is an established custom.' **1976** DEXTER & MAKINS *Testkill* 143 In the tea interval..I slipped into the pavilion. **1887** *Girl's Own Paper* 25 June 618/3 New tea-jacket, or *après midi,* for indoor wear. **1770** J. WEDGWOOD *Let.* 24–26 Dec. (1965) 100 Mr Boulton.. shewed me some bodys and necks made of Porcelaine coloured green to be mounted in Ormoleau for Tea Kitchens. **1808** JANE AUSTEN *Let.* 27 Dec. (1952) 243 A silver tea-ladle is also added [to the list]. **1964** *Listener* 13 Feb. 287/1 'Filthy,' said a friend's tea-lady the next morning. **1980** *Times* 13 Nov. 4/8 The tea trolley is being wheeled back... Two years ago, it seemed the ubiquitous tea lady was vanishing beneath a tide of vending machines. This year..automated services are in decline. **1963** *Punch* 8 May 675/1, I..fetched the tea machine into the house. **1972** J. THOMSON *Not One of Us* xvii. 227, I kept..some paper cups. I used to nick them from the tea machine at the warehouse. **1814** JANE AUSTEN *Mansfield Park* III. vii. 160 There was..found a chair, and with some hasty washing of the young tea-maker's, a cup and saucer. **1961** 'T. HINDE' *For Good of Company* xix. 214 Mary had switched on the bedside tea-maker. **1970** *Sunday Times* 20 Dec. 26/3 When the clock on the tea-maker began to go backwards its owners got their alarm call and a nice pot of tea at three a.m. **1914** Y. NOGUCHI *Through Torii* 2 It is the high art of the tea-master to make you really taste the water beside the taste of the tea. **1974** *Times Lit. Suppl.* 25 Oct. 1190/3 In Kamakura for the first time a tea master did the tea ceremony for me. **1906** E. DYSON *Fact'ry 'Ands* xvii. 225 We're.. puttin' down er mill that'll..never look fer tea money. **1962** L. DEIGHTON *Ipcress File* i. 11 The office tea money. **1979** *Rydge's* (Sydney) Apr. 68/2, I observed a case in Thailand, where payoffs are euphemistically called tea-money. **1952** M. STEEN *Phoenix Rising* vi. 117 An overpowering fragrance of tea-olive rose from under her window. **1975** *Country Life* 2 Jan. 39/3 The grassy glade leading from river to house..heavy with the scent of tea olive..and banana tree. **1938** *New Yorker* 12 Mar. 47/1 All tea pads, or marijuana joints, use the blue lamps and nickel machines to induce and sustain the hashish mood. **1963** *Lancet* 9 Nov. 989/2 For a few years the cult of the 'tea pad'..threatened to be imported from the United States. **1814** F. BURNEY *Let.* 28 Oct. (1978) VII. 488 If you write to me again upon a scrap that can hardly arrive—I shall answer upon a bit of Tea paper. **1884** *Birmingham Daily Post* 23 Feb. 3/4 Lithographic printers. Wanted, a man..well up in Tea-paper and Commercial

Work. **1929** D. H. Lawrence *Let.* 11 Jan. (1932) 780 We were in Toulon yesterday..and went to the same tea-place. **1978** P. Marsh et al. *Rules of Disorder* iii. 72 At the back there you can see down to the tea place underneath. **1862** M. D. Colt *Went to Kansas* iii. 48 Have arranged on them..our five tin plates, two tin cups, one tin tumbler, the nine tea-plates. **1972** *Country Life* 9 Mar. 547/3 These plates were made by the Britannia China Company..between 1895 and 1906. Such plates were known as..tea plates. *c* **1702** C. Fiennes *Journeys* (1947) iv. 359 Another little closet with the tea equipage and under that was such a little tea roome within the drawing roome. *c* **1748** Richardson *Let.* in *Corr.* (1804) III. 317 Miss Chudleigh is gone into the tea-room. **1970** [see *nelly[2] 3]. **1976** *New Society* 29 Jan. 227/2 Sentences for what are known in America as 'tearoom' offences—homosexual sodomy or oral copulation—vary. **1884** *Encycl. Brit.* XVII. 746/2 Tea-seed oil is a commercial product in China, where it is used for food, lighting, and soap-making. **1951** E. David *French Country Cooking* 220 Tea seed oil. Much lighter than olive oil and preferred by many for salads. **1809** A. Burr *Private Jrnl.* (1903) I. 253 A splendid tea service of silver and two cups. **1838** J. Romilly *Diary* 26 Feb. (1967) 140 Treated myself with a new tea Service for the occasion (cost 5½ Gnas). **1786** J. Wedgwood *Let.* 30 June (1965) 297 A single line of colour put on..while it is in the clay state..upon our beer mugs, flower-pots, tea and coffee sets..constitutes *fayence*. **1859** *Harper's Mag.* Sept. 507/2 You might have seen their sign—ay, and their fine stanch tea-ships too—any day you chose to stroll down South. **1889** Kipling *From Sea to Sea* (1900) I. 360 The lower stories were full of tea-stalls and tea-drinkers. **1962** R. Prawer Jhabvala *Get Ready for Battle* ii. 94 A tea-stall under a tree built on upturned kerosene tins. **1890** *Monthly Packet* Christmas 188 She..was not sorry to depart to the tea-tent. **1934** 'E. M. Delafield' *Provincial Lady in Amer.* 6 Go with Robert..to..Agricultural Show... We..repair to tea-tent... I drink strong tea and eat chudleighs. **1977** *Oxf. Diocesan Mag.* Oct. 20/2 A tea-tent..apart from affecting the custom of the catering contractors, would give a false picture of the Church as a tea-making machine. **1741** Richardson *Pamela* II. 223, I hope to join you there by your Tea-time in the Afternoon. **1749** J. Cleland *Mem. Woman Pleasure* I. 47 He sat down..and all tea-time kept ogling me. **1936** *Punch* 19 Feb. 204/1 It's still tea-time, you know. **1963** *Times* 31 Jan. 3/3 In the evening of life—or at any rate the tea-time—it is occasionally pleasant to look back. **1863** S. S. Jones *Northumberland* 116 The guid lady shakes her lap an' rubs an' scrapes at her gown wi' the tea-towel. *c* **1909** D. H. Lawrence *Collier's Friday Night* (1934) ii. 55 *Beatrice*:..You want to wrap it in a damp cloth now. Have you got a cloth? *Ernest*: What?—a clean tea-towel? **1980** *Habitat Catal. 1980/81* 111/1 Honeycomb weave teatowel. Pure cotton. Excellent for easy drying up. *c* **1748** Richardson *Let.* in *Corr.* (1804) III. 317, I thought..you were of the party at the tea-treats. **1898** C. P. Penberthy *Warp & Woof of Cornish Life* 153 Whas our lil tay-trait to a towser? *Ibid.* 168 Go long up tay-trait field. **1977** *West Briton* 25 Aug. 22/6 Mr. Ken Roberts..said 150 traditional tea-treat buns would be distributed free to children on the estate. **1937** A. Thirkell *Summer Half* x. 275 Mrs. Keith had then bought an excellent tea-trolley with rubber wheels and ball bearings. **1958** J. Cannan *To be a Villain* i. 24 A tea-trolley now stood laden with sandwiches, cakes and buttered buns. **1980** *Times* 13 Nov. 4/8 The tea trolley is being wheeled back. *a* **1948** D. Welch *Voice through Cloud* (1950) i. 9 This noble room was spoilt by a counter with sizzling tea-urns. **1840** R. H. Dana *Two Yrs. before Mast* xxxiv. 428 Like a true English 'tea-wagon'. **1878** *Appleton's Jrnl.* Jan. 9/2 The good, heavy-bowed, square-countered 'tea-wagons', as the sailors call them, meant for cumbrous freight, heavy stowage, and long passages. **1921** *Daily Colonist* (Victoria, B.C.) 30 Mar. 18/2 A neat Tea Wagon, in walnut finish, fitted with a moveable glass tray top, and mounted on four rubber tired wheels. **1939** J. B. Priestley *Let People Sing* ii. 23 The magazine boy..called to the tea-wagon girl: 'Come and 'ave a look.' **1978** D. Bloodworth *Crosstalk* xv. 122 Don't tell me the tea wagon's come and gone already? **1766** J. Wedgwood *Let.* 15 Sept. (1965) 42 The Teaware, vases, and all other pretty things I shall let alone until I have the pleasure of seeing you here. **1909** H. G. Wells *Tono-Bungay* ii. ii. 176 My aunt too, looking bright and pretty, in a blue-patterned tea-wrap. **1931** *Ann. Rep. Dept. Agric. Nyasaland 1930* 32 Tea Yellows—Investigations into this disease have been carried out. **1958** T. Eden *Tea* ix. 91 Tea yellows, caused by sulphur deficiency, is less severe under shade trees than in open situations.

tea, *v.* Add: **2.** (Earlier example.)

1810 G. Betts *Diary* in K. F. Doughty *Betts of Wortham* (1912) xxix. 286 Mr. Lee..came and *tea-ed* here.

teaing *vbl. sb.* (earlier example).

1845 *Ainsworth's Mag.* VII. 504 During my 'teaing' I was amused with the conversation of my companions.

tea-berry. (Earlier example.)

1818 W. P. C. Barton *Compendium Floræ Philadelphicæ* I. 194 *Gaultheria..procumbens...* Mountain Tea. Tea-berry. Partridge-berry. Wintergreen.

teach, *v.* Add: **II. 6. d.** Also without direct object.

c **1863** T. Taylor *Ticket-of-Leave Man* ii. 33 Sam! is it? Confound him! I'll teach him.

e. *teach yourself* (a subject): vbl. phr. used *attrib.* to designate a textbook or manual intended for use without the assistance of a teacher.

The phr. is derived from the titles of books in the Teach Yourself series, published from 1938.

1938 M. Thomas (*title*) Teach yourself embroidery. **1960** G. Butler *Death lives Next Door* He was..going through the Catalogue issued with the Teach Yourself Everything Series. **1961** *Guardian* 4 Feb. 14/6 As I was taught in a teach-yourself book. **1978** P. O'Donnell *Dragon's Claw* ii. 29, I usually spend a few hours with the tape recorder and a Teach Yourself Russian course.

teach (tītʃ), *sb.* Colloq. abbrev. of Teacher 2 a.

1958 F. Norman *Bang to Rights* iii. 90 'Now now give him a chance,' said the teach. **1976** A. Hill *Summer's End* i. 6, 'I always suspected it, Hill,' Teach had called across the classroom. *Ibid.* 9 The Teach with the cardboard box stopped in front of each kid and gave him or her a paper bag.

teache, var. Tache *sb.*[3]

teacher, *sb.* Add: **3.** *teacher-factory, -trainee, -trainer, -training* (later examples); appositive, as *teacher-librarian*; *teacher-proof* adj.; also pertaining to each element, as *teacher–pupil* adj. (cf. *pupil-teacher* s.v. *pupil *sb.*[1] 3 b); **teachers' aide,** an assistant employed to help the teaching staff of a school in a variety of duties (see quot. 1967).

1889 'Mark Twain' *Connecticut Yankee* x. 118, I had started a teacher-factory and a lot of Sunday-schools. **1975** *Language for Life* (Dept. Educ. & Sci.) xxi. 304 Except for the Teacher-Librarians' Certificate there have been few opportunities for teachers to acquire help in how to organise and manage a library. **1979** *Jrnl. R. Soc. Arts* July 487/1 A simple handbook for those teacher-librarians in Commonwealth developing countries who are called on to undertake this duty without any previous experience. **1964** P. Strevens *Papers in Lang.* (1965) ii. 32 It is sometimes necessary to prepare 'teacher-proof' materials, if it is known in advance that the proficiency of the teacher is not going to be up to the optimum required. **1965** M. Morse *Unattached* iv. 131 Despite the teacher-pupil relationship the worker could in no way afford to make the girls feel inferior to herself. **1977** *New Yorker* 19 Sept. 44/1 He is a warm, compassionate man, outside the private teacher–pupil relationship in music. **1956** *Sun* (Baltimore) 17 Nov. 6/3 It is another thing when a teacher is also required to be clerk, accountant and nursemaid, as the Parent–Teacher Association of Howard Park Elementary School has recognized in its hiring of two teachers' aides. **1967** *Children & their Primary Schools* (Dept. Educ. & Sci.) I. vi. xxiv. 330 The type of help that is..given by teachers' aides, who ought to have equal status with nursery assistants.., falls into three kinds: (a) Help that amounts to an extra pair of hands for the teacher... (b) help..from those with special skills. This could be available for needlework, art and craft, handicraft... (c) supervising children after school hours while they are waiting for their parents. **1959** *Listener* 12 Mar. 463/1 A graduate teacher-trainee. **1982** *Underground Grammarian* Nov. 6/2 He might actually decide to become a student of something rather than a teacher-trainee. **1964** *Economist* 22 Aug. 709/3 Sending teachers, and teacher-trainers, to the country in question. **1977** P. Strevens *New Orientations Teaching Eng.* vi. 79 Many teacher-trainers regard statements of the kind 'We concentrate on practical teaching—none of this theoretical nonsense!' as if they were robust common sense. **1949** M. Mead *Male & Female* 456 Directed towards particular problems—adolescence, teacher-training, nutrition, housing. **1967** *Listener* 14 Sept. 351/2 You could go to a college of education—they used to be called teacher training colleges. **1975** *Language for Life* (Dept. Educ. & Sci.) xxiii. 331 Our Report emerges at a critical and uncertain time in the development of teacher training.

teacherage (tī·tʃərĕdʒ). *N. Amer.* [f. Teacher *sb.* + -age, after Parsonage (sense 2), Vicarage (sense 3), etc.] A house or lodgings provided for a teacher by a school.

1916 *Boston Evening Transcript* 12 July xi. 3 Educational officials of Monroe County are showing much interest in the new movement for establishing so-called teacherages—cottages for country school teachers—which is spreading rapidly in several Far-Western States. **1959** R. E. Campbell *I would do it Again* vi. 22 There was a teacherage with all the necessaries. **1968** *Globe & Mail* (Toronto) 15 Jan. 26/6 (Advt.), Required immediately, qualified teacher for one-room school... Three-room teacherage available. **1976** T. Walker *Spatsizi* ix. 81 Hungry dogs rushed out to bark, and this brought Lester Dorsey to the door of the teacherage.

teacherly (tī·tʃəɹli), *a.* [f. Teacher *sb.* + -ly[1].] Of, pertaining to, or characteristic of a teacher; schoolmasterly, schoolmistressy; pedagogic.

a **1683** J. Hull in *Archeologia Americana* (Amer. Antiquarian Soc.) (1857) III. 173 Mr. John Norton..who continued with us three years and upward..laboring in God's work, and joined in a teacherly office with us.

1934 Webster, *Teacherly*,..teacherlike. **1979** *Washington Post* 21 Jan. G1/5 Hesse the German who became a Swiss, the teacherly Peter Pan who hankered after things Asian. **1980** E. Blishen *Nest of Teachers* ii. xii. 124 He knew the teacherly value of conspiracy. **1982** *N. & Q.* Feb. 80/2 A symptom of the book's teacherly liveliness is its wit.

tea·ch-in. orig. *U.S.* [f. Teach *v.* + *-in[3] (after *sit-in*, etc.).] An informal debate (often of some length) on a matter of public, usu. political, interest, orig. between the staff and students of a university. Hence, a conference attended by members of a profession on topics of common concern. Also *loosely*, a lecture or meeting held for the purpose of discussion or disseminating information.

1965 *N.Y. Times* 25 Mar. 9/1 Bomb scares marked the start tonight of a 12-hour series of rallies, speeches and seminars sponsored by some 200 University of Michigan faculty members to protest United States policy in Vietnam... Policemen evacuated..the site of the protest gathering which the faculty members have named a 'teach-in'. **1965** *Economist* 24 Apr. 416/1 Universities all over the country [*sc.* USA] have conducted informal 'teach-ins' on Vietnam, running from eight in the evening to eight the following morning. **1965** *Times* 17 June 8/5 This free-for-all debate..was called by the ugly new jargon name of 'teach-in'—a concept recently invented at Harvard, which has crossed the Atlantic. **1967** McLuhan & Fiore *Medium is Massage* 101 The dropout represents a rejection of nineteenth-century technology... The teach-in represents a creative effort. **1969** *New Scientist* 30 Jan. 219/1 The great Edinburgh Teach-in..on chemical and biological warfare. **1971** *Ibid.* 24 June 741/1 Engineers have run a series of 'teach-ins' to show designers how they wish to apply the new rules. **1973** R. Ludlum *Matlock Paper* iii. 21 Six days of riots on campus. Half a semester lost on teach-ins. **1975** D. Lodge *Changing Places* iv. 138 A two day teach-in on the constitution and scope of the proposed commission.

teaching, *vbl. sb.* Add: **4.** *teaching aid, load, material, post, process*; **teaching hospital,** a hospital at which medical students are instructed; **teaching machine,** a mechanical device for giving instruction in the form of a teaching programme which allows a pupil to progress according to his response to questions of choice.

1966 *Rep. Comm. Inquiry Univ. Oxf.* II. 470 They might even be encouraged to use occasionally the odd teaching aid. **1980** *Underground Grammarian* Dec. 1/2 Think of the audio-visual devices and the teaching aids. **1963** in A. Heron *Towards Quaker View of Sex* 51 All the large teaching hospitals have psychiatric out-patient departments. **1980** *Brit. Med. Jrnl.* 29 Mar. 924/2 The London teaching hospitals, which for so long had served their local population, and which had now been set aside to serve the needs of education, began instead to bear the brunt of the specialised services. **1958,** etc. Teaching load [see *load *sb.* 4 c]. **1958** *Science* 24 Oct. 971 (*caption*) Student at work on a teaching machine. **1969** J. Argenti *Managem. Techniques* 215 This method can be used..with a teaching machine. These machines consist of a box like a television set in which there is a film strip. **1972** H. J. Eysenck *Psychol. is about People* iii. 147 Sidney L. Pressey in the mid-1920s designed the precursors of our modern automated teaching machines. **1960** *Tuscaloosa* (Alabama) *News* 20 Nov. 4/4 The student fits teaching material into the box and then uses them [*sic*] at his own speed. **1962** *Sunday Times* (Colour Suppl.) 10 June 4 There have been no sinecures or teaching posts for famous jazzmen. **1975** *Language for Life* (Dept. Educ. & Sci.) xvii. 254 We regard recording as an essential element in the actual teaching process.

teaching, *ppl. a.* Add: **b.** Special collocations, as **teaching elder**: see Elder *sb.*[3] 4; **teaching fellow** *U.S.*, a student at a graduate school who carries out teaching or laboratory duties in return for a stipend, free tuition, or other benefit.

1642 T. Lechford *Plain Dealing* 15 Some Churches have no ruling Elders, some but one, some but one teaching Elder, some have two ruling, and two teaching Elders. **1735** in C. Hazard *Thos. Hazard* (1893) 226 We the Subscribers, Teaching Elders or Pastors of the first gathered..Church in Boston New England. **1936** S. E. Morison *Three Centuries of Harvard* i. 18 There were no funds to maintain more than two teaching fellows. **1979** C. MacLeod *Luck runs Out* (1981) xvii. 169 He'd come there as a teaching fellow... He taught the subject ably.

tea-cup. Add: **a.** (*b*) With reference to fortune-telling by means of interpreting the arrangement of tea-leaves left in a cup. Cf. *tea-leaf 1.

1883 C. S. Burne *Shropshire Folk-Lore* xxi. 277 The apparitions which..nurses used to discover in their tea-cups when they had..emptied the last remains of the tea in such a manner as to leave the dregs scattered well over the bottom and sides of the cup. **1921** C. Kent *Fortune-Telling by Tea-Leaves* ii. 24 A confused looking tea-cup, without any symbols..is useless for the purpose of divination. **1954** M. Sharp *Gipsy in Parlour* xii. 127 Cook..had an eye for tall dark strangers, who frequently appeared in her tea-cup. **1976** A. E. Lindop in *Winter's Crimes 8* 216 She can 'see' what's best for us... She'll look into our teacups.

c. (Earlier example.) Similarly *tea-cup storm*, etc.

1854 W. B. Bernard (*title*) A storm in a teacup. **1932** *Times Lit. Suppl.* 15 Sept. 639/1 Those old disputes were no teacup squalls. **1951** *Sport* 16–22 Mar. 14/3 Earlier this season a slight 'teacup storm' occurred in Yorkshire Rugby Union circles. **1981** W. Safire in *N.Y. Times Mag.* 15 Feb. 11/1 In the midst of this teacup contretemps came a clear message from John Radosta.

tea-drinker. Add: (Earlier example.)

1737 *London Mag.* Apr. 186/1 Considering the Number of Tea Drinkers, it [*sc.* tea-drinking] has done a great deal more Hurt than Dram-Drinking.

tea-drinking *vbl. sb.* (earlier examples in all senses).

1737 *London Mag.* Apr. 183/2 (*heading*) Of Diet in general, and the bad Effects of Tea-drinking. **1781** A. Storer *Let.* 28 June in *15th Rep. R. Comm. Hist. MSS.* App. vi. 508 in *Parl. Papers 1897* (C.8551) LI. 1. Lady Craven gave a tea-drinking last night. **1793** W. B. Stevens *Jrnl.* 8 July (1965) 91 Walked with Mrs Cutts, etc...to Schobley Mill, a Tea-Drinking Place.

teaed (tīd), *a. U.S. slang.* Also **tea-d.** [f. *TEA *sb.* 7 c + -ED[2].] In a state of euphoria induced by alcohol or marijuana. Usu. with *up*.

1928 L. E. LAWES *Life & Death in Sing Sing* iv. 53 'Didn't alcohol have something to do with your coming here?' 'Yes, sah, dey was bofe considerable teaed up.' **1944** *War Med.* VI. 383/2 Just those thoughts will drive me mad—thinking about my 'boys' all 'tea-d up', and here I am, sitting and thinking about it, and I can't get it. **1966** C. HIMES *Heat's On* xvii. 157 The driver was teaed to the gills and on a livewire edge.

Teague. Restrict *Obs.* or *arch.* to sense in Dict. and add: **2.** Usu. in form **Taig** (tēig). In Northern Ireland, a Protestant term of contempt for a Roman Catholic.

1971 *Times* 13 May 2/6 Taig is Protestant slang for a Roman Catholic. **1973** *Spectator* 3 Mar. 263/2 The Prods are only having their shops blown up and suffering a few slight cases of murder; the Teagues are losing their souls. **1978** D. MURPHY *Place Apart* vii. 133 In times of stress Loyalist paramilitaries can easily rouse large mobs and lead them out of the ghettos on Taig-bashing expeditions. **1982** *Observer* 31 Oct. 8/3 This week a new slogan appeared along the Shankill Road, the backbone of Protestant West Belfast. It read: 'All Taigs are targets.'

teak. Add: **1. b.** A fashion shade resembling the colour of teak-wood, a rich reddish brown.

1934 in WEBSTER. **1971** [see *MOLE *sb.*[2] 6*].

3. *teak log, -oil; -built* (earlier lit. example), *-panelled, -veneered* adjs.

1835 J. E. ALEXANDER *Sketches in Portugal* viii. 179 In May, the fleet of her Most Faithful Majesty consisted of the following ships:—..50, Don Pedro,..Very strong, teak-built. **1889** KIPLING *From Sea to Sea* (1899) I. iii. 220, I saw the elephants playing with the teak logs. **1968** A. DIMONT *Bang Bang Birds* vi. 89 We stepped into a small, teak-panelled lift. **1968** J. ARNOLD *Shell Bk. Country Crafts* 198 For such articles as salad-bowls..teak-oil is used. **1970** *Interior Design* Dec. 753/3 Small teak-veneered tables. **1979** P. WAY *Sunrise* xv. 157 Two wrought-iron gates, massively reinforced by teak logs.

tea-kettle. Add: Phr. *ass* (=arse) *over tea-kettle,* head over heels (cf. *arse over tip* s.v. *ARSE *sb.* 1 b). *U.S. slang.*

1963 T. PYNCHON *V.* i. 23 Fast enough..only to send Profane, garbage can and lettuce leaves flying ass over teakettle in a great green shower. **1977** J. CROSBY *Company of Friends* vii. 51 Sascha's horse..stopped short... Sascha went ass over teakettle into the brambles.

teal. Add: **1. c.** A shade of dark greenish blue resembling the patches of this colour on the head and wings of the teal.

1923 *Daily Mail* 14 Feb. 10 (Advt.), Jersey frocks... Colours: Teal, Purple and Champ. **1978** *N.Y. Times* 29 Mar. A 14 (Advt.), Both in a delicious new shade of teal... we call it Prussian blue!

3. teal blue, a shade of dark blue tinged with green (cf. sense 1 c above).

1949 *Dict. Colours Interior Decoration* (Brit. Colour Council) III. 26/2 *Teal blue,* a descriptive colour name from the plumage of the small freshwater duck. **1963** *New Yorker* 1 June 75 Sandwich-board sheaths in teal-blue linen are piped down the sides with double rows of lime. **1980** M. H. CLARK *Cradle will Fall* iv. 24 Her teal-blue uniform.

tea-leaf. Add: **1.** Also with reference to fortune-telling. Cf. *TEA-CUP a (*b*).

1883 C. S. BURNE *Shropshire Folk-Lore* xxi. 277 A stalk or long tea-leaf floating in the tea was called a 'chap'.. was at once taken out and laid on the back of one hand, which was then struck sharply with the palm of the other, in order to see whether the 'chap' would come to the back door or the front. **1931** E. SACKVILLE-WEST *Simpson* I. 66 Tea-leaves, thought Amy, tell fortunes. **1941** [see *RIDDLE *v.*[1] 2 c]. **1981** *Times* 21 Jan. 11/4 They..read marriage prospects in the tea leaves.

2. Rhyming slang for 'thief'. So **tea-leafing,** thieving.

1899 C. ROOK *Hooligan Nights* ii. 23 He could do more than his share at tea-leafing, which denotes the picking up of unconsidered trifles. **1903** C. BOOTH *Life & Labour of People in London* XVII. II. 139 'Tea-leaf' is for some inexplicable reason the name used by the police for pick-pockets. **1930** A. BENNETT *Imperial Palace* v. 20 The badinage..was more picturesque... 'You dirty old tea-leaf.' **1963** J. PRESCOT *Case for Hearing* ii. 36 Proper tea-leaves they looked, the pair of 'em. **1977** D. CLARK *Gimmel Flask* iv. 63 A tea-leaf wouldn't find the key on your person if he broke in.

teallite (tī·ləit). *Min.* [f. the name of Sir J. J. H. *Teall* (1849–1924), English geologist + -ITE[1].] An orthorhombic sulphide of lead and tin, $PbSnS_2$, found as soft, thin, dark grey crystals having a metallic lustre.

1904 G. T. PRIOR in *Mineral. Mag.* XIV. 21 (*heading*) On teallite, a new sulphostannite of lead from Bolivia. **1962** W. A. DEER et al. *Rock-Forming Minerals* V. 8. It [*sc.* cassiterite]..has also been recorded from the weathering of teallite and stannite.

team, *sb.* Add: **II. 4. b.** (Earlier examples in Cricket and Football and later gen. examples.)

1846 W. DENISON *Cricket: Sk. Players* 32 Hayward.. having become a resident at Cambridge, joined the 'team' of that distinguished Club. **1874** *Bell's Life in London* 14 Mar. 5/2 Although the game was won by Scotland.. the English team played splendidly. **1921** G. B. SHAW *Back to Methuselah* II. 53 You will find yourself at the head of a rabble of Socialists and anti-Socialists, of Jingo Imperialists and Little Englanders,..of Syndicalists and Bureaucrats..and the impossibility of keeping such a team together will force you to sell the pass again to the solid Conservative Opposition. **1923** *N.Y. Times* 15 July VI. 1/6 The method of the comedy team remains more or less unvaried. The team is composed, in the first place, of a comedian and a 'straight' man. **1947** *Ann. Reg. 1946* 314 To prevent further clashes General Marshall organised 'teams' composed of an American, a Nationalist, and a Communist member, to visit both parties and to try to create a better spirit [in China]. **1951** *Times* 26 Nov. 2/5 The report..has been compiled by a team from the [metal-finishing] industry which visited the United States last year. **1965** M. SPARK *Mandelbaum Gate* iii. 66 Russeifa's one of the most conscientious men in the medical team. **1972** *N.Y. Law Jrnl.* 24 Oct. 15/9 Team I is assigned to preside on the circuit for the October 1972 Term. **1978** *Nagel's Encycl.-Guide: China* 272 The basic cells of agrarian collectivisation are the brigade and the team for the moment.

c. *spec.* A gang. *slang* (chiefly *Criminals'*).

1950 in Partridge *Dict. Underworld* Add. (1961) 814/1. **1955** D. W. MAURER in *Publ. Amer. Dialect Soc.* XXIV. 83 Sometimes a *team* [of pickpockets] is *two handed,* while a *troupe* is *three handed* or larger. **1959** *Observer* 1 Mar. 10/1 Mainly the older brothers in long-resident..families, they are known and feared by other 'teams' (gangs) in North London as the Punchers. **1970** P. LAURIE *Scotland Yard* viii. 184 We had a whisper about a team going to do a certain pay van. **1973** 'J. PATRICK' *Glasgow Gang Observed* ii. 21 The boys themselves never used the word 'gang', always 'team'.

5. c. *fig.* Usually *a whole team. U.S. colloq.*

1832 *Polit. Examiner* (Shelbyville, Kentucky) 17 Nov. 4/2 'Whoop! Ain't I a horse?' 'A whole team, I should think,' said Rainsford. **1832** [see *HALF *sb.* 7 h]. **1843** 'J. SLICK' *High Life N.Y.* II. 193, I tell you what, he's a hull team, and a horse to let. **1854** *Knickerbocker* XLIV. 416 (Th.), Jump him up when you will, and you'll find him a 'full team' at anything. **1856** G. D. BREWERTON *War in Kansas* 270 Avow yourself ready to declare that..a clear-grit Yankee woman quite equal, upon an emergency, to what, in vulgar parlance, is quaintly styled 'a whole team, and *a dog under the wagon*' to boot. **1922** *Dialect Notes* V. 180 *Whole team an(d) little dog under the waggin',* n. phr. Used facetiously to indicate one's self-importance, energy, etc. Alabama.

V. 11. (sense 4 b) *team-building, leader, manager, player, sport*; (in a team ministry; see below) *team rector, vicar*; **team handball,** a game played by two teams of seven players each on a rectangular court using a ball directed only with the hands; **team honours,** honours awarded to a sporting team; **team-man,** (*a*) (earlier example of *teamsman*); (*b*) with preceding descriptive adj., a member of a sporting team who co-operates (well or badly) with his colleagues; **team-mate,** (*a*) = TEAMSTER (Webster 1934); (*b*) a fellow member of a team; **team ministry,** a group of clergy of incumbent status who minister jointly to several parishes under the leadership of the team rector (contrasted with *group ministry,* in which all members function as equals); the administration of a scheme for such an operation; **team policing,** community policing; **team race,** a race which is won by the team whose members finish on aggregate in higher positions than their opponents; **team spirit,** the spirit of subordination of personal interests to those of the team; **team-talk,** a talk addressed to a team, or a discussion amongst a team; **team-teaching** *vbl. sb.*, the teaching of students by a team of teachers working together; hence (as back-formation) **team-teach** *v. intr.* and *trans.*; **team-work,** (*d*) work done by persons working as a team, i.e. with concerted effort.

1946 *Nature* 12 Oct. 497/1 These are essential conditions for successful team-building and the inherent loyalty it implies. **1970** *Jrnl. Health, Phys. Educ. & Recreation* Mar. 46/1 To the uninformed spectator, the game of team handball would look like a combination of football, basketball, and lacrosse... It is often confused with a popular squash-related sport also dubbed 'handball'. **1978** *Official Associated Press Sports Almanac* 764 The sport spread to gymnasiums throughout Germany and Eastern Europe and full recognition of team handball was achieved when it was included in the 1936 Berlin Olympics. **1928** *Daily Mail* 7 Aug. 15/5 Eagle Road Club secured team honours. **1962** E. SNOW *Other Side of River* (1963) lviii. 440 They chose me as team leader. **1977** *R.A.F. News* 11–24 May 8/4 Deputy team leader Chf Tech Mick Young. **1977** *Times* 9 Sept. 3/5 Team leaders, the preferred name for those formerly known as charge hands. **1954** A. G. MOYES *Austral. Batsmen* x. 151 A fighter who was an excellent team-man and therefore most valuable. **1976** J. SNOW *Cricket Rebel* 138 His brother Eric [Bedser]..was overheard to say that I was not a good team man. **1926** E. HEMINGWAY *Sun also Rises* xix. 247, I had coffee out on the terrasse with the team manager of one of the big bicycle manufacturers. He said it had been a very pleasant race. **1976** *Evening Post* (Nottingham) 15 Dec. 23/1 Team manager John Sherriff believes the side is now on the right track. **1915** M. E. MCLOUGHLIN *Tennis as I play It* xi. 231 Service and the net position go together, the initial stroke giving the server the opportunity to reach the net where his team-mate is already stationed. **1942** BERREY & VAN DEN BARK *Amer. Thes. Slang* § 440/4 *Confederate or partner*..team-mate. **1954** W. K. HANCOCK *Country & Calling* viii. 223 An orderly row of boxes into which to put the facts that he and his team-mates (for 'team work' is very much the fashion) are collecting. **1977** *Times* 15 July (Motor Racing Suppl.) p. vi/1 James Hunt..was put out of the race by a crash... His German team-mate.. had retired three laps earlier. **1964** L. PAUL *Deployment & Payment of Clergy* xv. 142 One much-publicised remedy for manpower shortage is a group or team ministry. Caution is necessary here... Group or team ministries in town may cut down 'the plant', or what a tradesman might call the points of service, but they ought eventually to increase the total urban ministry rather than decrease it. **1968** *Pastoral Measure* II. 13 in *Parl. Papers 1967–68* XVII. 843 A pastoral scheme may provide for the establishment of a team ministry for the area of any benefice, that is to say, for the sharing of the cure of souls in that area by a team of ministers consisting of—(*a*) the incumbent of the benefice which, if it is not or would not otherwise be a rectory, shall be a rectory; (*b*) one or more other ministers who shall have the title of vicar and a status equal to that of an incumbent of a benefice. **1980** *Oxf. Diocesan Mag.* May 15/2 The faint hearts in the Diocese who see team ministry as a threat. **1886** H. CHADWICK *Art of Batting* 7 The practical effect of all this is to destroy a batsman's ambition to excel as a 'team player' in batting. **1980** *Newsweek* 17 Nov. 13/3 Reagan wants 'team players' for his Administration—men and women loyal to him personally and to his philosophy generally, willing to argue over policy, but not fundamental ideology. **1977** J. WAMBAUGH *Black Marble* (1978) iv. 42 Every few years the brass had to come up with some new catchword to justify the budget. 'Team policing.' **1976** *Southern Even. Echo* (Southampton) 10 Nov. 21/7 Southampton were always in control in the team race and were easy team winners from Portsmouth, through Tony Nixon 5th, Bryan Dawkins 8th, and Malcolm Beavis 10th. **1976** *Milton Keynes Express* 11 June 15/1 He will be assisting the Rev Christopher Drummond, team rector from the Christ Church Centre at Stantonbury. **1895** *Wales* Apr. 168/1 He was able to drive a furrow to the delight of even the most envious of surrounding teamsmen. **1928** *Britain's Industrial Future* (Liberal Industrial Inquiry) III. xvi. 195 The 'fellowship-bonus' system..evokes the team-spirit. **1938** R. G. COLLINGWOOD *Princ. Art* iv. 74 These sports, we are told, inculcate a team-spirit. **1976** F. MUIR *Frank Muir Bk.* 96 The schools..were sending forth..superbly fit chaps, light on imagination but strong on team-spirit. **1964** G. MCDONALD *Running Scared* iii. 37 He had never gone out for any team sports. **1947** A. P. GASKELL *Big Game* 12 And then of course, the team-talk on Friday night. The coach would stand on the platform and start on his old game of building us up to fighting pitch. **1960** V. JENKINS *Lions Down Under* viii. 114 The post-mortem at a team-talk in Timaru was a searching one. **1976** *Science News* 28 Feb. 135 Two answers to this problem..are to teach science ethics to college students by presenting them realistic case studies and to bring industrial scientists into the universities to team-teach. **1979** *Maledicta* III. 144 Mary Salawuh Warren, a Yoruba, has team-taught Yoruba and other West African languages with her husband, D. M. Warren, at Iowa State University and in Peace Corps training programs. **1960** *Washington Post* 20 Dec. B2 Principal Harold Wilson..tallied the benefits of team teaching at his school. **1964** *Observer* 13 Sept. 11/8 Team teaching, in which a corps of teachers work with a very large group, already has a long history in the United States. **1976** *Church Times* 8 Oct. 17/5 *Team vicar* required for church of St. Martin, Southdene, to serve large neighbourhood unit and to work as a member of a large established team. **1981** *Ibid.* 10 July 17/4 (Advt.), Applications invited for team vicar to complete established team of three. Priest appointed will have particular pastoral responsibility for four attractively-situated villages. **1909** *World To-day* (U.S.) Sept. 3 (*heading*) Team work in municipal progress. **1954** [see *team-mate* above]. **1977** *Lancet* 23 Apr. 899/2 We need hospitals, hostels, and homes, but we must be sure that by effective communication and teamwork (and these do not cost money), the service we offer is of the highest.

team, *v.* Add: **1. b.** *intr.* Chiefly with *up*: to join together in or as in a team; to ally oneself or get together *with* someone. Occas. *trans.*

1932 W. FAULKNER *Light in August* iv. 86 Like man and wife for three years, until Brown and him teamed up. **1932** J. T. FLYNN *God's Gold* VII. x. 314 Whetmore was not Rockefeller's agent, but a lawyer and independent promoter who teamed up with the Merritts and worked with them. **1950** D. HYDE *I Believed* ii. 14 The war-wounded were everywhere... Blinded, they teamed up into bands. **1965** J. LAWLOR in J. Gibb *Light on C. S. Lewis* 73, I had thought of myself as God's gift to Lindsay's Balliol, with which Magdalen was teamed for scholarship purposes. **1967** M. CHANDLER *Ceramics in Mod. World* v. 157 In practice two or three refractories may have to be teamed up to do one exacting job. **1978** J. R. L. ANDERSON *Sprig of Sea Lavender* vi. 94 He seems to have teamed up with Trudi... He was a little in love with Sandra once.

c. *trans.* To use or wear in conjunction *with.* Also *intr.* for *pass.*

1948 M. LASKI in *New Statesman* 13 Nov. 417/1 *Team,* vb.: to wear one thing with another; e.g., team your palest grey dress with the subtle flattery of a brief scarlet bolero. **1954** C. L. B. HUBBARD *Compl. Dog Breeders' Man.* xx. 203 Well-pressed linen slacks..can look really nice, especially if teamed up with a contrasting blouse, shirt or jumper. **1958** *House & Garden* Feb. 22 (Advt.), [The furniture] will team happily with the pieces you wish to retain. **1960** *Housewife* May 104/2 This sweater teams happily with pants or shorts. **1977** *Jersey Even. Post* 26 July 10/1 A long, tiered empire-line voile dress, made of a yellow and red floral patterned material with a white background. This was teamed with a white floppy hat.

2. For *U.S.* read *N. Amer.* (Later Canad. examples.)

1968 E. Russenholt *Heart of Continent* III. ix. 162 A sudden freeze-up ends the navigation season, catching many vessels in the ice. Freight which cannot, now, be moved by steamboat, must be teamed. **1951** K. M. Wells *Owl Pen Reader* (1969) iii. 253 He took the road, teamin' hay er cordwood to town.

4. *Comb.* **team-up,** an instance of teaming up (sense 1 b above). *colloq.*

1945 *Richmond* (Va.) *Times-Dispatch* 21 Nov. 15 (Advt.), Santa's a 'good Joe' in their language when he delivers these team-ups [*sc.* a dressing-gown, pyjamas, and slippers]. **1960** *Farmer & Stockbreeder* 8 Mar. 74/1 (*heading*) Poor show but the team-up of American and French manufacturers will be a 'shot in the arm'.

teaman, tea-man. Add: **3.** *U.S. Criminals' slang.* (See quot. 1950.)

1938 *Amer. Speech* XIII. 192/1 *Tea-man*, a reefer-man or marijuana addict. **1950** H. E. Goldin *Dict. Amer. Underworld Lingo* 220/2 *Tea-man*, a smoker or purveyor of marijuana. **1959** in J. E. Schmidt *Narcotics Lingo & Lore* 182.

teamer. Add: **1.** (Earlier U.S. example.)

1778 E. Parkman *Diary* 26 Dec. (1899) 81 May God extend pity to ye miserable poor,—to Sailors, to Soldiers, to Teamers abroad.

2. A member of a team; esp. a member of the first (or second, etc.) team in sport.

1934 R. Macaulay *Going Abroad* ii. 32 Loyal teamers, they agreed that..their team leader's should be the only Guidance sought. **1950** *Sport* 24–30 Mar. 10/1 Phil was in and out of the Liverpool senior side the following season, but was an established first-teamer by 1938–39. **1976** *Evening Post* (Nottingham) 15 Dec. 24/7 Nottingham first teamers Ken MacDonald and Graeme Fraser came back after injury to help Corsairs defeat Nottingham University 36–0 at Beeston last night.

teaming, *vbl. sb.* Add: Also with *up* in senses 1 b and c of *team *v.*

1960 *Farmer & Stockbreeder* 8 Mar. 74/1 The teaming-up of some well-known French manufacturers with..American companies is bound to act as a 'shot in the arm' to the French engineering industry. **1966** *Guardian* 25 Apr. 6/4 A Jaeger shop..in Southport..is making a strong feature of 'teaming up'—that is, exactly matching colours can be found in coats, suits, hats, skirts, slacks, blouses, and knitwear.

teamster. Add: **1.** (Earlier U.S. example.)

1777 in *New Hampshire Hist. Soc. Coll.* (1863) VII. 88 The Committee delivered the Several Teamsters.

2. *N. Amer.* A lorry-driver, a truck-driver; one who drives a truck as his occupation.

1907 J. London *Iron Heel* (1908) x. 182 The teamsters' strike had been broken. **1957** *Economist* 28 Sept. 1024/1 The delegates who are packing their bags this week-end for the convention of the teamsters—as lorry drivers are still called—will also take with them the knowledge that this is likely to be the most momentous meeting in the history of organised labour. **1958** *Daily Express* 29 Aug. 4/2 This type of entertainment is as suspect as the Teamsters' Union. **1978** *New York* 3 Apr. 100/3 The 8,000 sanitationmen represented by a local of the teamsters, usually the most truculent of city unions, are still participating in the coalition talks.

Tean, var. *Teian *a.*

tea party. Add: **2. c.** A gathering at which marijuana is smoked. *slang.*

1944 *War Med.* VI. 383/2 Have you ever been on a 'tea' party? No? You've missed a sensation of a lifetime. **1956** J. Symons *Paper Chase* vii. 32 Used to give tea parties—marihuana. **1972** 'J. Quartermain' *Rock of Diamond* i. 7 Jane hadn't taken tea. She..gave no clue ..as to what an inhibited Englishman should do at a midtown Manhattan tea-party.

3. *attrib.* of attitudes, behaviour, etc., held to be typical of a tea-party; bland, insipid, trite, trivial.

1961 M. Beadle *These Ruins are Inhabited* (1963) ii. 28, I think he expected the boys to have..tea-party manners. **1962** [see *penguin 2 c]. **1973** C. Mullard *Black Britain* ix. 105 Liberal do-gooders with a tea-party attitude towards race.

tea-planter. (Earlier example.)

1887 Kipling *Plain Tales* (1888) 112 A Subaltern, or a Tea-Planter's Assistant, or anybody who..has no care for to-morrow.

tea-pot. Add: **1. b.** *tempest in a tea-pot* (later example). Also in similar phrases.

1928 R. Campbell *Wayzgoose* i. 16 Storms in a teapot often have occurred. **1942** T. DuBois *Body goes round & Round* xiii. 172 You have been indulging in your favourite occupation of stirring up a tempest in a teapot. **1973** *Times* 1 Aug. 6/5 Senator Ervin said the issue of whether the subpoenas were continuing was 'a difference in a teapot'.

2. *attrib.* and *Comb.*, as *tea-pot stand.*

1895 *Montgomery Ward Catal.* Spring & Summer 439/1 Tea or Coffee Pot Stands. **1968** *Canad. Antiques Collector* June 12/2 A tea service at this period..normally consisted of twelve saucers, twelve cups, twelve coffee cups, a tea pot and cover (occasionally a tea pot stand), a sucrier, [etc.].

tea-pot, *v.* For *nonce-wd.* read *Obs. rare.* and add earlier and later examples.

1842 J. Paget *Let.* 25 July in *Mem. & Lett.* (1901) 117 My pupils have proposed to make a demonstration in my favour, and have asked me if they may open a subscription to 'tea-pot' or commit some similar dignity upon me. **1881** V. Lush *Jrnl.* 26 Oct. (1975) 247, I reminded him that for some time past I had been mulcted of my stipend and that to be 'tea-potted' under such circumstances seemed to me to be a case parallel to that of allowing a man to starve and when he is dead to give him an expensive funeral.

Teapot Dome (tī·pǫt dōᵘm). The name of a naval oil reserve in Wyoming, irregularly leased by the U.S. Government in 1922, used *attrib.* and *absol.* to designate the resulting political scandal and, allusively, any similar later scandal.

1936 F. D. Roosevelt *Nothing to Fear* (1947) 64 In spite of all the demand for speed, the complexity of the problem and all the vast sums of money involved, we have had no Teapot Dome. **1973** *New Yorker* 28 Apr. 31/2 Senator Barry Goldwater made his statement: 'The Watergate. The Watergate. It's beginning to be like Teapot Dome.' **1977** *Time* 23 May 54/2 In an era of Teapot Dome and bathtub gin, he [*sc.* Lindbergh] seemed to Americans a cleaner, sharper version of themselves.

tear, *sb.*[1] Add: **1. b.** Also in colloq. phr. *without tears*, without difficulty or distress (freq. used to describe a method whereby some discipline is easily mastered). Also *without-tears* attrib. phr.

1857 F. L. Mortimer (*title*) Reading without tears. **1877** —— (*title*) Latin without tears; or, One word a day. **1896** G. B. Shaw in *Sat. Rev.* 12 Dec. 623/2 (*heading*) Ibsen without tears. **1914** W. Owen *Let.* 1 June (1967) 257, I have a design in sending you this, viz. to keep you hungry to learn French I hope it won't be long before you read such works 'without tears'; at least without tears due to grammatical difficulties. **1932** A. Huxley *Brave New World* xvii. 280 Anybody can be virtuous now. You can carry at least half your morality about in a bottle. Christianity without tears—that's what *soma* is. **1937** T. M. Rattigan (*title*) French without tears. **1956** *New Statesman* 11 Feb. 143/1 The late 19th-century concept of progress without tears. **1962** *Times* 7 June 17/3 It is a without-tears book. **1974** J. I. M. Stewart *Gaudy* i. 19 Charles and Mary..were well-mannered young people, and docile at least to the extent of being resigned to Scrabble as a species of Philology without tears.

6. a. (attributive) *tear-dripping, -flood* (later example), *-tap, -track*; **c.** (instrumental) *tear-bound, -dabbled, -filled* (example), *-logged, -streaked, -strewn, -stuffed, -tricked, -washed* (later examples) adjs.; **d.** (miscellaneous) *tear-tight, -trembling* adjs.

1938 E. Bowen *Death of Heart* II. i. 178 Her manner.. had threatened the afternoon like a cloud that covers the sky but is almost certain never to break. Her eyelids looked rigid—tear-bound, you would have said. **1915** *Pearson's Mag.* Jan. 46/2 She raised a tear dabbled countenance. **1944** W. de la Mare *Coll. Rhymes & Verses* 217 Tear-dabbled cheeks, wild eyes I see. **1893** F. Thompson *Hound of Heaven* in *Poems* 53 And now my heart is as a broken fount, Wherein tear-drippings stagnate. **1951** in M. McLuhan *Mech. Bride* (1967) 11/2 Miss Grable, with tear-filled eyes, showed..a letter she'd received from a soldier's buddy. **1916** R. Graves *Over the Brazier* 21 Till it seemed through a swift tear-flood That dead men blossomed in the garden-close. **1931** R. Campbell *Georgiad* ii. 41 Holding our course among the tear-logged wrecks. **1923** Galsworthy *Captures* 181 The girl's face, tear-streaked, confusedly pretty, had come up before him. **1942** S. Smith *Mother, what is Man?* 76 My reverent reveries and fruitful plod Of tear-strewn steps. **1939** Dylan Thomas *Map of Love* 12 After the feast of tear-stuffed time and thistles. **1922** Joyce *Ulysses* 753 That was the last time she turned on the teartap. **1938** S. Beckett *Murphy* iv. 51 The human eyelid is not teartight. **1965** S. Smith in *Listener* 2 Sept. 347/3 Those awful tear-tracks on her cheeks, As if she had cried a lot! **1916** D. H. Lawrence *Amores* 74 Tear-trembling stars of autumn. **1880** G. M. Hopkins *Poems* (1967) 88 In his hands he has flung His tear-tricked cheeks of flame. **1916** H. G. Wells *Mr. Britling sees it Through* III. i. 389 Her tear-washed mind became vaguely friendly. **1922** Joyce *Ulysses* 175 Davy Byrne, sated after his yawn, said with tearwashed eyes:—And is that a fact?

e. tear bomb, a bomb containing tear gas; **tear-drop,** (*a*) (see sense 6 a in Dict.) (*b*) *transf.*, freq. *attrib.*, denoting something resembling a tear-drop in shape as: (i) an air cavity in glassware; (ii) a tear-shaped run in paintwork or ceramic glaze; (iii) a streamlined body or component of a vehicle, boat, etc.; (iv) *Surfing* = *pig board* s.v. *pig *sb.*[1] 13; (v) a bead or jewel of tear-drop shape; **tear-gas,** a lachrymatory gas used in warfare or riot control to disable opponents or make crowds disperse; hence as *v. trans*, to attack with tear gas, to drive *out of* a place with tear gas; **tear-jug** *rare* = Tear-bottle; **tear-shell,** a shell (Shell *sb.*[1] 21 b) containing tear-gas; **tear-smoke** = *tear gas* above.

1929 M. Lief *Hangover* xv. 238 I'm going to have Katie actually taken for a ride..and Rat-Face Walsh's yeggs following..with machine guns and tear bombs. **1953** Wendt & Kogan *Big Bill of Chicago* xxiii. 271 Police squads cruising the city, machine-guns in their laps and tear bombs in their pockets. **1904** *Burlington Mag.* IV. 141/1 Immediately under the bowl at the top of the stem is an air cavity, known as a 'tear-drop'..a frequent form of decoration. **1922** [see *curtain *sb.*[1] 1 e]. **1933** *Burlington Mag.* June 265/1 The presence of 'tear drops' in the glaze [of Chinese porcelain]. **1936** *Times* 29 Dec. 12/6 The new design will allow the manufacturer [of motor vehicles] to indulge in the 'tear-drop' streamlining which has often been discussed in recent years but never achieved. **1948** *Shell Aviation News* No. 115. 6/1 A 25-foot, streamlined, teardrop antenna will project below the fuselage... This will be the main broadcasting antenna. **1962** *Austral. Women's Weekly* Suppl. 24 Oct. 3/4 *Teardrop*, type of surfboard with wide back and pointed front. **1965** *Harper's Bazaar* June 24 Diamond teardrop, £500. **1980** D. Creed *Scarab* i. 9 A large and most marvellous pendant..suspending a teardrop pearl. **1917** W. Owen *Let.* 19 Jan. (1967) 429 It was only tear-gas from a shell, and I got safely back (to the party) in my helmet. **1927** *New Republic* 12 Oct. 202/2 The troopers on the outskirts..hurled tear-gas bombs and charged. **1927** *Daily Express* 16 Dec. 15, I imagine him, first, tear-gassing a river bank and so reducing all the crocodiles to genuinely hopeless grief. **1934** R. Stout *Fer-de-Lance* ii. 25 A gangster had been tear-gassed out of a Brooklyn flat. **1978** R. Ludlum *Holcroft Covenant* xliii. 499 Tear gas and Mace were not unknown in Yakov's line of work. **1869** Tear-jug [see *Pisan *a.*]. **1916** *War Illustr.* 23 Dec. 451/3 Don't you know the scent of tear-shells when you smell it? **1946** F. Burrows *Let.* 22 Aug. in Mansergh & Moon *Transfer of Power* (1979) VIII. 296 He added that the Police had used tear-smoke on crowds frequently. **1949** Koestler *Promise & Fulfilment* I. xii. 136 The boarding party finally gained control of the vessel by using tear-smoke grenades..against them.

tear, *sb.*[2] Add: **4.** Special Comb.: **tear-fault** *Geol.* = *strike-slip fault* s.v. *strike *sb.* 20.

1900 *Proc. Geologists' Assoc.* XVI. 465 It is this ['lag' fault] which gives one a clue as to the nature of some of the most striking 'tear' faults. **1924** J. G. A. Skerl tr. *Wegener's Orig. Continents & Oceans* 58 A lateral displacement of great dimensions, a so-called tear fault. **1957** [see *slice *sb.*[1] 2 b]. **1977** A. Hallam *Planet Earth* 60/1 Another common type of shear—which caused little trouble to miners and so was unrecognised for many years—is variously known as a strike-slip, wrench, tear or transcurrent fault.

tear, *v.*[1] Add: **3. d.** Also with *apart*, *up*: to render distraught, upset (a person). In *pass.* with *up* (dial. *out*): to be distressed, upset. *N. Amer. colloq.*

1898 F. P. Dunne *Mr. Dooley in Peace & War* 47 They say th' Spanyards is all tore up about it. **1950** R. Moore *Candlemas Bay* 240 Jeb, poor lamb, he was so tore out about you that he never said nothing. **1956** B. Holiday *Lady sings Blues* (1973) xiii. 117 The few I did see when they came back tore me apart. One night..a kid came in to see me... His hair had turned completely white. **1972** *Even. Telegram* (St. John's, Newfoundland) 24 June 9/1 Robert A. Power, who said he was tore up from work in his younger days and was 'no good now to trade and no good to sell.' **1974** K. Millett *Flying* (1975) III. 323 Pete is too delicate to pattern. Tears him up just to hear Winnie yell.

e. *to be torn between*: to be distracted by (two equal but conflicting desires, emotions, or loyalties).

1871 L. W. M. Lockhart *Fair to See* I. viii. 148 Torn between her desire to underrate Eila and to preserve her own dignity. **1888** Mrs. H. Ward *Robert Elsmere* III. xxxv. 111 Agnes, torn between her interest in what was going on and her desire to get back to her mother, had at last hurriedly accepted this Mrs. Sherwood's offer. **1922** T. Wolfe *Lett.* (1956) ii. 31 The girl Laura, 'torn between' (as the saying goes) love for her beaten father and the blunt young apple grower. **1948** A. Paton *Cry, Beloved Country* II. viii. 172 Jarvis was torn between compassion and irritation, and he stood and watched uncomfortably. **1971** G. Charles *Destiny Waltz* iii. 104 As usual in such cases he was torn between both sides, angry with Dorn for his patronage of the couple, impatient with them for being what they were.

f. Colloq. phr. (chiefly in *pa. t.* and *perfect*) *to tear it*: to spoil one's chances; to put an end to one's hopes, plans, etc.

1909 'I. Hay' *Man's Man* xvii. 320 'I've fairly torn it, this time!' he reflected morosely. *a* **1918** W. Owen in *Poems* (1920) 22 First wave we are, first ruddy wave; that's tore it. **1924** Kipling *Debits & Credits* (1926) 258, I expect I must 'ave kept carryin' on, till Headquarters give me that wire from Ma... That wire tore it. **1938** G. Greene *Nineteen Stories* (1947) 77 'I *am* English,' Mr. Calloway said. Even that didn't tear it. **1954** M. Procter *Hell is City* VI. iii. 180 He looked at his watch. 'That's torn it,' he said. **1960** D. Lessing *In Pursuit of English* v. 185 Oh, my God, that tears it, if he's going to start. **1972** D. Delman *Sudden Death* (1973) iv. 110 'Ouch,' she said, grinning... 'Well, that tears that, doesn't it?'

g. In phrases with *up* and indefinite obj., descriptive of unrestrained excitement; esp. in Jazz. *U.S. slang.*

1932 J. Dos Passos *1919* 270 Bud had been tearing things up at the University and was on the edge of getting fired. **1955** Shapiro & Hentoff *Hear Me talkin' to Ya* 204 He had the first big colored band that hit the road and tore it up. **1963** *Listener* 14 Mar. 478/3 The trumpeter Wild Bill Davison, who 'tore it up' with admirable primitivity and sensuality. **1968** [see *identify *v.* 1 b].

h. *to tear down*: to punish; to criticize severely. *U.S. colloq.*

1938 M. K. Rawlings *Yearling* xxix. 381 I'll tear down all two of you. Now git down and pick up ever' one o' them peas and wash 'em off. **1978** I. B. Singer *Shosha* vii. 128 The insolence of a writer tearing down a piece before it's been performed!

i. *to tear apart*, (*a*) to subject to criticism; (*b*) to search (a place) thoroughly.

1953 *Manch. Guardian Weekly* 1 Jan. 13/2 Carefully

tear apart your editorial. **1977** 'C. Aird' *Parting Breath* xv. 176 Somebody was ready to tear the place apart. You should have seen Miss Moleyn's house.

5. c. Phrases. *to tear off a strip, tear a strip off*: see *strip *sb.*[2] 1 i; *to tear off a bit, piece* slang (orig. Austral.): to copulate with a woman.

1941 Baker *Dict. Austral. Slang* 76 *Tear off a piece*, to coit with a woman. **1951** S. Longstreet *Pedlocks* iv. v. 222 Look, you come down and tear off a piece anytime. And the wine—*Asti Spumante*—she is ona me. I stand the wine. The girls, that is up to you. **1970** G. Greer *Female Eunuch* 265 The vocabulary of impersonal sex is peculiarly desolating. Who wants to 'tear off a piece of ass?' **1977** *Custom Car* Nov. 67/2 Italian wives must sit and suffer if the men tear off a bit on the sly.

9. b. To make *one's way* violently or impetuously.

1853 C. Kingsley *Hypatia* II. xiv. 328 Furiously..he burst up as if from the ground..tearing his way toward his idol. **1888** Mrs. H. Ward *Robert Elsmere* I. x. 282 A little gully deep in bracken, up which the blast was tearing its tempestuous way.

c. *to tear into*: (*a*) to make a vigorous start on (an activity, performance, or the like); (*b*) to attack vituperatively, reprimand.

(*a*) **1901** M. Franklin *My Brilliant Career* xxxvi. 301 'Syb, I want to speak to you.'..'Very well; "tear into it",' as Horace would say. **1929** W. Smyth *Girl from Mason Creek* xiii. 131 'Three notes a man if we win out!'..'Aw, make it five an' we'll tear into th' job.' **1949** R. Harvey *Curtain Time* 8 Then the lights went down, the baton rapped sharply, and the orchestra tore into the overture. **1961** J. B. Priestley *Saturn over Water* ii. 12, I tore into the business of getting visas.

(*b*) **1934** in Webster. **1946** F. Sargeson *That Summer* 93 You could still hear them tearing into each other. **1954** J. Masters *Bhowani Junction* ii. xi. 94 The sahib tore into me as if I was a little boy he'd caught making a mess on the carpet. **1984** *Miami Herald* 6 Apr. 10A/1 Jackson..tore into both candidates in past debates.

tear, *v.*[2] Add: **1. c.** (Later examples.) Now chiefly *N. Amer.*

1971 E. Shorris *Death of Great Spirit* i. 16 When your eyes teared and your head fell, I was afraid you were dying. **1980** J. Ball *Then came Violence* (1981) vi. 47 When her eyes teared again, he pulled out his own clean handkerchief

tear-. Add: **1. tear-away** *sb.*: now usu. (written *tearaway*), an unruly young person, a hooligan, ruffian, or petty criminal (formerly applied *spec.* to a kind of thief: see quot. 1938); **tear-down,** the complete dismantling of a piece of machinery; **tear-off** *a.* (later examples); *sb.* (example); **tear-out,** the action of pulling out the fitments, décor, etc., of a room; **tear-up** *sb.*: also (*slang*), the action or an instance of tearing up; a spell of wild, destructive behaviour; a mêlée; in *Jazz*, a lively, rousing performance (cf. *tear v.[1] 3 g).

1938 F. D. Sharpe *Sharpe of Flying Squad* i. 15 A type of crime which has almost died out now was that carried out by thieves known as 'Tearaways' who used to hang about outside the theatres after the show and snatch costly brooches from women's dress fronts. **1950** *Observer* 2 Apr. 7/3 He..boasted of being a proper 'tearaway' (one who sticks at nothing). **1958** *Punch* 19 Feb. 263/2 You get some proper tearaways (quarrelsome fellows) at the dogs. **1962** *Observer* 18 Feb. 21/3 My grandfather was a pickpocket, my six uncles were all villains and tearaways, my brothers and friends were thieves. **1978** L. Davidson *Chelsea Murders* xxiii. 140 He had a bit of form..in younger days a tearaway, the odd charge of violence. **1976** *Lebende Sprachen* XXI. 152/2 After engine teardown exercise special care to replace damaged carbon rubbing type seals. **1981** *Pop. Hot Rodding* Feb. 51/1 Installing new pistons means removing the engine, an almost complete tear-down, and then a re-installation job. **1910** Tear-off [see *block *sb.* 10 c]. **1945** J. Rhys-Williams *Stern Daughter* xxx. 207 The little calendar..was the tear-off kind, with quotations. **1961** 'B. Wells' *Day Earth caught Fire* i. 7 An alert..youngish man..was at his desk busily working on tear-offs with swift, practised strokes of his red pencil. **1980** T. Barling *Goodbye Piccadilly* ii. 50 A big tear-off calendar gave today's date. **1976** *Billings* (Montana) *Gaz.* 17 June 3-F/1 (Advt.), Custom Homes. Apartments. Remodeling...'Specializing in Tear-Out.' Every kind of concrete work. **1886** H. Baumann *Londinismen* 206/2 *Tear-up*.., feine(s) Geschäft. **1890** in Barrère & Leland *Dict. Slang* II. 339/2 'What is it this time?'..'Only a tear up.'..Among the readers of the *St. James's Gazette* there may be some who are unacquainted with the accepted method of obtaining a fresh outfit among the casual poor. *Ibid.* 340/1 At his feet, in a heap on the floor, lay some filthy rags,..the remnants of what had recently been his garments... The heap was the result of the tear up. **1958** S. Race in P. Gammond *Decca Bk. Jazz* x. 125 Max Kaminsky..and of course Bunny Berigan all took turns to roughen up that smooth ensemble.., with the historic Berigan tear-ups especially welcome. **1964** E. Parr *Grafters All* xiii. 151 He enters an orgy of crime, more commonly known as 'having a tear-up'. **1974** J. McVicar *McVicar* i. iii. 62, I decided to have a tear-up. **1982** *New Society* 9 Dec. 422/2 We've had a tear-up with the police. **1983** *Listener* 9 June 35/3 The music is not the tear-up associated with jazz at the Phil.

2. tear-arse *slang*, a very active busy person; hence as *v. intr.* (also *U.S.* **tear-ass**), to drive recklessly, rush *around* wildly and rowdily; **tear-sheet** chiefly *U.S.*, a sheet torn from a publication (or, later, separately printed and unbound) to be sent to an advertiser whose advertisement appears on it as proof of insertion; also one containing an article; more generally, a tear-off sheet from a teleprinter or calendar; **tear-thumb** (later examples).

1923 J. Manchon *Le Slang* 308 Tear-arse,..un qui s'échine (à travailler). **1942** Berry & Van den Bark *Amer. Thes. Slang* § 53/8 *Tear-ass* &c. *around*,..to hasten or rush around. **1954** *Amer. Speech* XXIX. 103 *Tear ass*, v. phr., to drive fast or recklessly. **1968** J. Wainwright *Edge of Extinction* 34 We're the..killjoys. The miserable bastards who won't let 'em tear-arse around the town at sixty miles an hour. **1972** A. Draper *Death Penalty* xix. 119 Some lads were picked up after the cup match for tear-arsing around. **1976** J. Fraser *Who steals my Name?* ii. 17 You'll need to settle down. You can't be a teararse all your life. **1930** H. A. Groesbeck *Practical Photo-Engraving* ii. 4 The 'tear-sheet' of the newspaper advertisement, also the drawing from which it was made, have just been received. **1950** R. Chandler *Let.* 15 Feb. (1981) 210 Herewith the tear sheets from a *Pocket Atlantic* with ..the article you desired. **1962** *Listener* 19 Apr. 672/1 One of the President's advisers came in with a tear-sheet from the news ticker. **1972** M. J. Bosse *Incident at Naha* i. 16 He was slowly flipping the tear sheets of the desk calendar. **1926** *W. Virginia Legislature Hand Bk.* 488 Do you see among those [wild flowers] present, any exotics?..Yes..This bit of smart-weed or tear thumb. **1978** C. B. Dugdale *Mod. Amer. Herbal* II. 124 Tear-thumb; Arrow-leaved Tearthumb... The small cluster of flowers varies in color from pinkish to whitish.

tearer. Add: **1. c.** *tearer-downer* (U.S.), one who tears down, a carping critic (cf. *tear *v.*[1] 3 h).

1942 Berrey & Van den Bark *Amer. Thes. Slag*, § 421/1 Critic; opposer..tearer-downer. **1944** [see *builder c]. **1955** J. D. Salinger in *New Yorker* 29 Jan. 28/1 I'm just so sick of pedants and conceited little tearer-downers I could scream.

tearing, *ppl. a.*[1] **5.** (Later examples.)

1867 A. Stock *Evidence against & for Walter Tricker* 4 Mrs Hitchins, at the Inquest, says 'It was not ordinary barking. They [*sc.* the dogs] were barking like tearing mad.' **1886** E. L. Dorsey *Midshipman Bob* ii. xi. 219 'Don't you get mad ever, eh?'..'Yes, I'm sorry to say I do—tearing mad sometimes.' **1906** [see *jim]. **1942** Berrey & Van den Bark *Amer. Thes. Slang* § 284/8 Angry..tearing, tearing angry or mad.

tear-jerker (tīə·ɹ,dʒɜ̄:ɹkəɹ). *colloq.* (orig. *U.S.*). [f. Tear *sb.*[1] + Jerker[1]; for the sense of *jerker*, cf. *soda-jerker* s.v. *soda *sb.*[1] 7.] Something calculated to evoke sadness or sympathy, usu. a sentimental film, play, song, story, etc. Also applied to a person and, *rarely*, to an event.

1921 *Double Dealer* II. 143/2 But no one today, I believe, mistakes his [*sc.* James Whitcomb Riley's] productions for anything but somewhat shallow, fairly easy tear-jerkers. **1935** *Amer. Mercury* Aug. 400/1 A lawyer was imported from California, a magniloquent tear-jerker named Delphin Delmas. **1936** *New Yorker* 7 Mar. 32/2 'Love on the Dole' turns out to be far more than a conventional tear-jerker. **1940** *Manch. Guardian Weekly* 27 Sept. 212 The German description of the torpedoing of the evacuee ship as a 'tear-jerker' recalls Geobbels's clumsy attempt to deny the torpedoing of the Athenia at the beginning of the war. **1948** *Sunday Pictorial* 18 July 11/3 The cameos are linked with a quiet humour and smooth pathos which make the film an A-plus tear-jerker. **1953** 'P. Wentworth' *Watersplash* xix. 109 Three copies of the famous *East Lynne*. A notorious tear-jerker. **1958** B. Nichols *Sweet & Twenties* xiv. 187 This number, as sung by Al Jolson, became one of the most efficient tear-jerkers of all time. **1975** *Islander* (Victoria, B.C.) 9 Feb. 2/3 He concluded [his speech] with a real tear-jerker.

Hence (as back-formations) **tea·r-jerk** *sb.*, a sentimental effusion; also as *v. trans.*; **tea·r-jerking** *vbl. sb.* and *ppl. a.*

1940 S. Lewis *Bethel Merriday* xv. 127 You..made me understand how much that poor gutter pup longed for a chance to parade, and yet you didn't do much tear-jerking. **1941** E. Snow *Battle for Asia* iv. 88, I remember a tear-jerking letter from a correspondent appealing for people to boil their garbage and put it beside their ash cans for the hungry—*dogs*. **1953** *Times Lit. Suppl.* 31 July 490/5 The ex-Governor of Illinois does not disdain the obvious 'tear-jerk'. **1961** D. Holbrook *English for Maturity* i. iv. 55 The vague undefined tear-jerk of popular graveyard and funeral verses. **1962** 'K. Orvis' *Damned & Destroyed* xvi. 123 She tear-jerked it from a drugstore without a prescription. **1962** Auden *Dyer's Hand* (1963) 430 If Homer had tried reading the Iliad to the gods on Olympus, they would..possibly, even, reacting like ourselves to a tear-jerking movie, have poured pleasing tears. **1965** *Spectator* 5 Feb. 157/3 The prize for tear-jerking seemed..destined for..the *Daily Mail*. **1979** D. Meiring *Foreign Body* xii. 126 Even he [*sc.* God] had sometimes needed a hand, and Hussein had provided that brilliantly, in turn cajoling, tear-jerking, and threatening Americans of huge stature in the oil business. **1981** *Times* 14 Feb. 8/7 An idealized Shavian heroine..the armour-plated, tear-jerking martyr.

tearlet. (Later example.)

1964 V. Nabokov *Defence* x. 162 A warm tearlet would roll down her face.

tea-rose, tea rose. Add: **b.** (Earlier example.)

1872 *Young Englishwoman* Nov. 599/1 The rose colours are *rose frais*..; tea-rose, with yellow tints; and faded rose.

c. A perfume made from or named after this rose.

1897 *Sears, Roebuck Catal.* 19/2 Perfumes..Sweet Pea.. Tea Rose..Tuberose. **1926–7** *Army & Navy Stores Catal.* 486/2 Atkinson's Perfumes..Sweet Pea, Tea Rose, Verbena. **1977** *New Yorker* 10 Oct. 35/3 She..ended with a commercial for her new fragrance, Tea Rose, samples of which her assistants passed around.

teart (tīəɹt), *a.* and *sb.* [Dial. var. of Tart *a.*] **A.** *adj.* Sour; used of pastures containing an excess of molybdenum. **B.** *sb.* Teart quality in grass; the diarrhœa suffered by cattle grazing a teart pasture.

1850 [see Tart *a.* 2 a]. **1896** *Jrnl. Bath & West Soc.* VI. 207 The herbage possesses the peculiar purging quality known as 'teart'. **1903** *Lancet* 6 June 1590/1 This disease, known as parasitic enteritis, is found to be persistently associated with certain pastures (called 'teart' lands in the West of England) upon heavy moisture-retaining soils. **1939** *Nature* 23 Sept. 532/2 Teart, to which cattle in certain areas are subject, is found to be associated with an increased molybdenum content in the herbage. **1970** W. H. Parker *Health & Dis. in Farm Animals* xiv. 193 The teart pastures of Somerset are on the blue Lyas clay.

Hence **tea·rtness** *sb.* = *teart *sb.*

1940 *Nature* 15 June 941/2 The cause of teartness is the presence in the herbage of molybdenum. **1979** *Jrnl. Compar. Pathol.* LXXXIX. 495 'Teartness' i.e. the scouring which occurs in cattle but not in horses on 'teart' pastures of high Mo content.

teary, *a.* Add: **1.** Also *transf.*

1941 B. Schulberg *What makes Sammy Run?* iii. 45 Full of teary nostalgia for the glories of his youth. **1976** *Times Lit. Suppl.* 13 Aug. 1010/2 Paul delivers a long, teary monologue about his homosexuality.

Comb. **1949** N. R. Nash *Young & Fair* i. i. 10 But *Patty* is unashamedly teary-eyed. **1960** R. St. John *Foreign Correspondent* iv. 64 We grew teary-eyed trying to fry a fish or a piece of meat over the brazier.

tease, *sb.* Add: **1. b.** *tease number*, a strip-tease act. *U.S.*

1927 *Variety* 13 July 35/5 The four feminine principals alternated in 'tease' numbers with the help of the chorus. **1930** *Ibid.* 3 Dec. 54 With a fair voice, a nice figure and lots of personality, Miss Almond clicked easily in her tease numbers.

2. b. *spec.* = *cock teaser* s.v. *cock *sb.*[1] 23 (but less coarse). Also *transf.*

1976 *New Yorker* 16 Feb. 107/2 It's easy to get laughs by..showing women..as rich teases, like Mariangela Melato's role in 'Swept Away'. **1978** D. Devine *Sunk without Trace* xxii. 202 Sorry, Ken, but..it's not fair to encourage you to try. I will not be a *tease*. **1979** *Arizona Daily Star* 5 Aug. i. 1/2 Lulu is..a cruel tease to the lesbian countess Geschwitz.

tease, *v.*[1] Add: **1. d.** *U.S. Hairdressing.* = *back-comb* vb. trans. s.v. *back- B.

1957 *Amer. Hairdresser* Sept. 66 Pick up one inch of hair and with comb, tease the strand. This creates the lift so necessary to the style. **1962** E. Frank *Best Hairdos* 7 Tease entire head gently for fullness. **1978** J. Updike *Coup* (1979) iv. 171 Her hair bleached platinum and teased to a bouffant mass.

e. *to tease out* (fig.): to extract, get out, obtain, esp. by painstaking effort. Also *to tease on to*.

1959 N. Mailer *Advts. for Myself* (1961) 17 There was a time when Pirandello could tease a comedy of pain out of six characters in search of an author. **1971** *Language* XLVII. 525 It is only by the most careful discrimination that we are able to tease out the critical referential features from the mass of inferential stuff that surrounds them in normal speech. **1974** J. A. Michener *Centennial* x. 580 He was struck with how easy life was in Pennsylvania and how brutally difficult in Colorado, where you had to dig a ditch twenty miles before you could tease a little water onto your land.

2. c. = *strip-tease* vb. intr. s.v. *strip-tease *sb.* *U.S.*

1927 *Variety* 13 July 35/5 Where they cooch in New York they 'tease' here. **1953** Berrey & Van den Bark *Amer. Thes. Slang* (1954) § 593/22 'Do a striptease.'.. Strip, striptease, tease.

teased, *ppl. a.* Add: **1. b.** Of hair: fluffed out by back-combing. *U.S.*

1965 A. Lurie *Nowhere City* xiv. 147 A waitress appeared in the courtyard, shivering in a teased hair-do and a pink uniform. **1983** J. Valin *Natural Causes* xxix. 200 A pretty nurse with teased brown hair.

2. b. With *out*. Worn out, exhausted. *colloq. rare.*

1943 Hunt & Pringle *Service Slang* 65 *Teased out*, worn out or tired after a long spell of flying or other duty. **1961** D. Moore *Highway of Fear* i. 9 What about you? Still with that teased-out shipping company?

teasel, *sb.* **5. teasel-head** (earlier example).

1743 W. Ellis *Mod. Husbandman* Aug. xvi. 55 One of these stalks has produced..an hundred Teasel Heads.

teaser[1]. Add: **1. b.** (Further example.)

1852 Dickens in *Househ. Words* 24 Apr. 118/2 The clay ..is put into mills or teazers, and is sliced, and dug, and cut at.

2. f. A woman who arouses but evades amorous advances; a 'cock-teaser'. *colloq.*

1895 *Cornh. Mag.* Apr. 395 My Joan allus be a teäzer, zur, and when I's wanted to kiss zhe, zhe zes 'Noa, it ain't proper.' **1939** C. R. Cooper *Teen-Age Vice* (1959) iii. 54 The true B-girl is often nothing more than a professional teaser..selling drinks by fraudulent inferences. **1957** J. Braine *Room at Top* vi. 57 She leads young men on and then she turns prim... She's a born teaser. **1980** J. Gardner *Garden of Weapons* I. xi. 111 Martha..sensual in a very obvious way. Herbert always suspected she was a teaser with men.

g. A strip-tease act; a strip-tease artist.

1929 [see *runway 2 a]. **1930** *Variety* 1 Oct. 49 Miss Dix copped the show from the other femmes with her naughty numbers and teasers. **1931** C. Beaton *Diary* 13 Feb. in *Wandering Years* (1961) 217 There were lots of 'teaser' numbers... The leading lady..tantalisingly takes off one piece of clothing at a time.

3. c. In *Cricket*, a ball that is difficult to play. ? *Obs.*

1856 G. L. H. in V. Dayrell *Weeds from Isis* 69 Your cricketing boy, full of teasers and twisters. **1905** H. A. Vachell *Hill* xii. 249 Fluff's brother bowled slows of a good length, with an awkward break from the off to the leg. 'Teasers,' said the caterpillar critically.

d. *Naut. slang.* A knotted rope's end.

1910 [see *blood-knot* s.v. *blood *sb.* 19]. **1953** J. Masefield *Conway* (rev. ed.) iv. 217 The rope's end, or teaser, made one learn very quickly. **1962** W. Granville *Dict. Sailor's Slang* 118/2 *Teaser*, short length of rope with a 'hangman's knot' at the end, used for chastising *Conway* cadets in the 'tough old days'.

e. *U.S. Theatr.* (See quots.)

1916 A. E. Krows *Play Production in Amer.* xii. 87 The first border (all the borders are numbered consecutively from front to back) is called the teaser. **1923** C. J. De Goveia *Community Playhouse* vii. 80 Just inside the proscenium arch stand two strips of scenery, one on each side of the stage, and usually with a third piece, a border, stretched across the top. The two strips are called *Tormentors* and the particular border the *Teaser*. These pieces are movable. **1933** P. Godfrey *Back-Stage* iii. 34 The 'teaser' and the 'tormentor' are the respective names by which an overhead and side masking arrangement prevents the audience from looking into the wings and the flies.

f. A fisherman's device (orig. live bait) for attracting fish. orig. *U.S.*

1919 Z. Grey *Tales of Fishes* xi. 203 We had three of these flying-fish out as teasers, all close to the boat. **1924** —— *Tales Southern Rivers* 14 The use of teasers..was first used by Avalon boatmen in Marlin fishing. I tried it.., and pronounced it a failure because mackerel, barracuda, and other fish snapped off the cut-bait teasers as fast as they could be put out. **1937** E. Hemingway *To have & have Not* I. i. 17 Eddy put the two big teasers out and the nigger had baits on three rods. **1939** H. Major *Salt Water Fishing Tackle* ii. 69 The first artificial teasers of which I've heard were used by Zane Grey, and I believe he originated them. Most of them are made of wood or metal, brightly colored. **1960** A. Upfield *Myst. Swordfish Reef* vi. 56 To these lines were attached brightly painted cylinders of wood which, when tossed overboard..darted beneath and skimmed over the surface..Teasers, Wilton explained..'the bait-fish and the two teasers look to a shark or swordie just like a small shoal of fish.' **1967** [see *plugger d].

g. A kind of toy pipe with a coil (of paper, etc.) at the end which shoots out when one blows down the stem.

1935 A. J. Cronin *Stars look Down* iii. viii. 554 They had teasers, too, which blew out and hit you as you passed. **1977** D. Jones *My Friend Dylan Thomas* i. 6 Some of them were wearing paper hats..some..blew feather 'teasers' at each other.

4. *Electr. Engin.* † **a.** The shunt winding of a compound-wound dynamo or motor. *Obs.* **b.** The winding or transformer that is connected to the middle of the other transformer in a T-connection. Freq. *attrib.*

1878 C. Brush *Brit. Pat. 2003* 9 This device, which I have called a 'teaser', is used in connection with field magnets..for the purpose of..increasing the magnetic field. *Ibid.*, The teaser wire may be coarser than the principal magnet wire. **1884** S. P. Thompson *Dynamo-Electric Machinery* vi. 92 The shunt part of the circuit, originally called the 'teazer', was adopted at first in machines for electro-plating. **1886** *Ibid.* (ed. 2) x. 238 Brush made the important invention of exciting the field magnets with a compound winding; coarse wire coils being connected in series, with the addition of a so-called 'teazer' coil of finer wire to maintain the magnetism when the main circuit was opened. **1900** —— *Polyphase Electric Currents* (ed. 2) v. 143 The teazer winding is connected with one end to the middle of the main winding. **1937** J. B. Gibbs *Transformer Princ. & Pract.* xi. 82 One transformer, called the 'main transformer' is connected between two of the three-phase lines,..and the 'teaser transformer' is connected between the third line and the 50 per cent tap of the main transformer, using the 86.6 per cent tap of the teaser. **1981** G. McPherson *Introd. Electr. Machines* iii. 221 In the T connection, one transformer has its primary connected directly across two lines. This is called the 'main transformer'. The second transformer is called the 'teaser'.

5. An introductory advertisement, *esp.* an excerpt or sample designed to stimulate interest or curiosity. orig. and chiefly *U.S.*

1934 Webster, *Teaser*, an advertisement meant to arouse curiosity, sometimes by withholding part of the material information (*Trade Slang, U.S.*). **1940** *Chambers's Techn. Dict.* 835/2 *Teaser*, colloquialism for a *trailer* which is intended to advertise films for future exhibition in a cinema. **1960** M. T. Williams *Art of Jazz* 86 Old Town..was plastered with 'teaser' posters heralding the coming of the famous..Minstrels. **1962** *Daily Progress* (Charlottesville, Va.) 8 Nov. 38/1 A teaser is..a stimulating bit from the story to follow and opens a show. **1962** S. E. Hyman *Tangled Bank* 378 At the end of a lecture, Freud will sometimes tack on a teaser for the next, such as: 'At the next lecture we shall see whether we can agree with the poets in their conception of the meaning of psychological errors.' **1977** 'J. le Carré' *Hon. Schoolboy* xii. 270 Our agent asked Ricardo for a teaser so's the information could be evaluated back home.

tea-shop. [f. Tea *sb.* + Shop *sb.*] **a.** A shop where tea (sense 1) is sold. **b.** A café where tea (sense 2 or 4) is served.

a **1745** [in Dict. s.v. Tea *sb.* 9 a]. **1856** A. M. Lang *Diary* (Meean Meer, Punjab) 17 Sept. (MS.), Went to Tea Shop and billiards..at Artillery Mess. **1860** J. R. Edkins *Chinese Scenes* (1863) 153 Drinking tea with about forty nondescript Chinamen... I shall try to give you a little picture of the tea-shop. **1915** W. S. Maugham *Of Human Bondage* lvi. 288 He thought of going to lunch at the tea-shop. **1933** Dylan Thomas *Let.* Oct. (1966) 43 Gower is a very beautiful peninsula,..and so far the Tea-Shop philistines have not spoilt the more beautiful of its bays. **1962** L. Davidson *Rose of Tibet* ii. 48 There were a number of small teashops in the town [*sc.* Kalimpong]; ramshackle sheds with trestle tables containing tea urns and trays of sweetmeats.

c. In the affected spelling **tea-shoppe** [cf. *shoppe] applied (freq. disparagingly) to a tea-shop with sham antique decoration.

Second element sometimes pronounced (ʃǫ·pi).

1925 *Amer. Speech* I. 153/1 These names are not intended to be 'quaint' like 'Betty Anne' of Massachusetts and her eternal 'Tea Shoppe'. **1933**, etc. [see *shoppe]. **1959** *Times* 12 May 3/7 As artificial as a Tudor Tea Shoppe. **1973** Wodehouse *Bachelors Anonymous* v. 50 She had been planning a roll and butter and a cup of coffee at some wayside tea shoppe.

Hence **tea-shoppy** *a.*, characteristic of or resembling a tea-shop (sense b or c).

1931 *Time & Tide* 22 Aug. 992 There are other debatable points, too, in this rather tea-shoppy story. **1959** *Good Food Guide* 52 Portions are ample and not tea-shoppy. **1975** *Times* 27 Dec. 7/3 A restaurant..in a tea-shoppy basement.

teasing, *vbl. sb.*[1] Add: **1. b.** *U.S. Hairdressing.* Back-combing; also, a similar treatment given with a small brush.

1923 F. Korf *Art & Fundamentals of Hairdressing* II. ii. 31 The public seems to fear the back-combing, or as it is often called, teasing of the hair, perhaps with some justification. **1964** D. Z. Hanle *Hairdo Handbk.* vii. 71 Properly done, teasing can play an important part in finishing a hairstyle... Use a small..teasing brush. **1975** C. Calasibetta *Fairchild's Dict. Fashion* 260/1 *Bouffant*, hair exaggeratedly puffed out by means of teasing.

3. (Earlier examples.)

1807 H. Tufts in E. Pearson *Autobiogr. of Criminal* (1930) ii. iv. 292 *Teasing*, whipping. **1821** P. Egan *Life in London* i. 11 The innumerable teazings thou hast book'd.

Teasmade (tī·zmē[i]d). [perh. f. phr. *tea's made.*] The proprietary name of a brand of automatic tea-maker (see *tea-maker* (*d*) s.v. *tea *sb.* 9 c).

1938 *Trade Marks Jrnl.* 26 Jan. 93/2 *Goblin Teasmade.* .. Time controlled electric water heating and tea making apparatus. The British Vacuum Cleaner & Engineering Company Limited,..Fulham, London, S.W.6; manufacturers. **1958** *Spectator* 6 June 754/2 The Goblin Vacuum Cleaner, Goblin Washing Machines and the Goblin Teasmades. **1980** A. N. Wilson *Healing Art* 271 The electric clock on the Teasmade in the bedroom. **1983** *Sunday Tel.* 31 July 8/7 He was wearing a watch—one of those that..cannot be used as a calculator and do not double as a Teasmade. It merely gives the time.

tea-spoon. Add: **b.** = Teaspoonful.

1791 J. Woodforde *Diary* 19 Apr. (1927) III. 266, I took half a very small Tea-Spoon of Ether in Water this Evening. **1935** M. Morphy *Recipes of All Nations* 767 A teaspoon of the mixture is wrapped in..a blanched vine leaf. **1963** R. Carrier *Great Dishes of World* ii. 60/2, 1 level teaspoon dried mustard.

teasy, *a.* For *colloq. rare* read *colloq.* and *dial.* and add: **a.** (Earlier and later examples.)

1901 J. H. Harris *Luck of Wheal Veor* 164 A poor woman wethout a man, an' three gert stramming maids to keep, es like a cow wethout a tail when the flies is taisey. **1938** E. Pound *Let.* 8 May (1971) 315, I forget what he and Domenik have to say, but teckon it's teasy.

b. Bad-tempered, irritable, tetchy.

1866 T. R. Higham *Dial. between Two Cornish Miners* 5 My owld 'umman was..so taisy that I cudden live in the house. **1907** A. Quiller-Couch *Major Vigoureux* xvii. 167 He'll be as teasy as fire when he hears about it. **1931** C. C. Rogers *Gwendra Cove* 193 'E was a teasy oald bachelor, I reckon. **1976** J. C. Trewin in D. V. Baker *Cornish Short Stories* 135 'Go 'long, you teasy toad!' shrilled Mrs Bosworthick.

Hence **tea·sily** *adv.*

1928 A. Bennett in *Daily Express* 1 Sept. 5/5 'And what will Mrs. Meadowes say to all this Red politics?' Alan demanded teasily.

tea-table, *v.* [f. the sb.] *trans.* In literature, to treat a dramatic event in a trivial or casual way. Hence **tea-tabling** *vbl. sb.*

1938 C. Isherwood *Lions & Shadows* iv. 175 The accident was to be in the best Forster tradition, 'tea-tabled', slightly absurd. *Ibid.* vi. 258 The murder was cut—'tea-tabled' down to an indecisive, undignified scuffle; and the ending was an apotheosis of the Tea-Table, a decrescendo of anti-climaxes. **1962** *Times Lit. Suppl.* 22 June 460/4 Certain critics have made far too much of Mr. Forster's 'tea-tabling' and of his casual sudden deaths. **1977** *Ibid.* 28 Jan. 97/2 Christina Rossetti's oblique treatment of detail is an early case of what Isherwood, discussing Forster in *Lions and Shadows*, calls 'tea-tabling', the novel's lyrical domestication of disaster.

tea-tree. Add: **2. b.** *tea-tree oil.*

1933 *Bulletin* (Sydney) 12 July 19/2 The distillation of essential oil from *Melaleuca alternifolia* (tea-tree) has become an established N.S.W. industry... Some 40 tea-tree-oil preparations are on the market. **1954** *Econ. Bot.* VIII. 324/1 Tea-Tree Oil... Collection of leaf material differs from that in operation for eucalyptus leaves.

Tebele (tĕbī·li). Also **Tabele.** [Native name.] A Niger-Congo language belonging to the South Eastern Bantu group. Cf. *Ndebele.

1883 R. N. Cust *Mod. Lang. Africa* II. xii. 300 Travellers write about..the Language of the Ma-tabéle, but there is reason to believe that it is Zulu... Syke, of the London Missionary Society, prepared School Books..: this gives the idea that Tabéle is a separate Language. **1897** W. A. Elliott *Dict. Tebele & Shuna Lang.* p. v, The Tebele language is of course only a variety of the Zulu. *Ibid.* p. vi, Different types have been used for the two languages, clarendon for the Tebele, and small capitals for the Shuna. **1919** [see *Matabele 1]. **1977** C. F. & F. M. Voegelin *Classification & Index World's Lang.* 70 Ndebele = Tabele = Tebele.

Tebeth (te·beþ, te·bet). Also **Tebet, Tevet** (te·vet). [Heb. *ṭēbēt*] The fourth month of the Jewish year (though placed tenth in the traditional list of months), corresponding to parts of December and January.

c **1382** Bible (Wycliffe) *Esther* ii. 16 And so she is lad to the priue chaumbre of king Assuer, the tenthe moneth, that is clepid Thebeth, that is, Januer. **1611** *Ibid.* (A.V.), So Esther was taken vnto king Ahasuerus..in the tenth moneth (which is the moneth Tebeth). **1973** *Jewish Chron.* 19 Jan. 22/5 The Fast of Tevet is mentioned in the Talmud and is therefore observed even on Friday.

Tebilized (tī·biləizd), *a.* Also **-ised** and with small initial. [f. the initials of *T*ootal *B*roadhurst *L*ee Company Ltd., the inventors of the process + -ize + -ed[1].] A proprietary name for cotton and other fabrics which have been rendered crease-resistant by impregnation with a synthetic resin.

1937 *Official Gaz.* (U.S. Patent Office) 7 Dec. 36/1 Tootal Broadhurst Lee Company Limited. Manchester, England. Filed Oct. 16, 1937. Tebilized. For Piece Goods of Cotton, Linen, and Artificial Silk. Claims use since May 10, 1934. **1945** *Trade Marks Jrnl.* 28 Mar. 166/2 Tebilized. **1950** *Sun* (Baltimore) 8 May 10/4 This year with all the wonderful 'ized' things (tebilized and sanforized) that have happened to fabrics. **1955** *Times* 4 June 7 Irish linen for dresses or suits. Tebilized for crease-resistance. **1967** H. Thompson *Fibres & Fabrics of Today* 98 The name 'Tebilised' was adopted by Tootal Broadhurst Lee when they introduced this now universal finish.

tec, *sb.* Add: Also † **teck. 1.** (Earlier and later examples.)

1879 *Sessions Papers* 25 July 238 Look out, there is a b— *tec* from Chalk Farm watching. **1909** Galsworthy *Silver Box* ii. i. 47 Drop it, I say, you blooming teck. *a* **1940** [see *fink *sb.*[2]]. **1977** *Daily Mirror* 30 Mar. 13/4 (*heading*) Porn tec admits bribe plot.

attrib. **1928** D. L. Sayers *Unpleasantness at Bellona Club* viii. 90 He complained of being spied on..like the blighters in the 'tec stories. **1976** *Evening Times* (Glasgow) 1 Dec. 2/1 Softly, Softly: Task Force. Plodding 'tec series which has dragged on too long.

2. Ellipt. for *tec story*, a detective story.

1934 E. Pound *ABC of Reading* ii. 29 Only a very good 'tec' will stand re-reading. **1949** R. Chandler *Let.* 28 Dec. (1966) 76 The mystery and 'tec are on the wane. **1978** S. Hodges *Gollancz* ix. 194 Anthony Price, Nicholas Freeling and Helen McCloy are some of the writers whose 'tecs have been published by Gollancz.

tech (tek), *sb.*[1] *colloq.* (orig. *U.S.*). Also **tec.** Abbreviation for *Technical College*, *Technical School* (see Technical *a.* 3 a in Dict. and Suppl.), and *Institute of Technology.*

1906 *Dialect Notes* III. 161 *The Boston Tech.*, *n. phr.* Massachusetts Institute of Technology. 'The best engineering school is Cornell; the next best is Michigan; and the next, Arkansas. *The Boston Tech.* aint in it.' **1911** H. Quick *Yellowstone Nights* iii. 63 The insufferable breed of dubs—..who..called an Institute of Technology a 'Tech'. *Ibid.*, I shall have outlived the disgrace of my Tech. training. **1915** E. Wallace *Man who bought London* viii. 79 'I'm off to the "Tec",' he said. *c* **1921** D. H Lawrence *Mr. Noon* viii, in *Mod. Lover* (1934) 264 He vowed he'd go up to the Tech. with the book. **1947** *Book* (Christchurch, N.Z.) IX. 32, I told him no, I'd have to finish Tech, I wanted to get matric. **1969** D. Collyer in R. Blythe *Akenfield* iv. 94 The young people..go to Ipswich Tec. or even to the university and they learn to talk about anything. **1974** *Sunday* (Charleston, S. Carolina) 7 Apr. 16-c/1 Texas Tech scientists will visit drought-stricken Africa to try to improve its resources and find a cure for famine and poverty. **1980** R. McCrum *In Secret State* x. 86 Rosie's pride would not let her admit that she..had been to the local Tech.

tech (tek), *sb.*[2] Slang abbrev. of *technician c.

1942 *Yank* 21 Oct. 15 They're the same kind of tech chevrons. **1953** *Mag. Fantasy & Sci. Fiction* Nov. 30 Let the techs worry about that. **1976** *Amer. Speech 1973* XLVIII. 194 They used to be called *orderlies*. Today, however, many of these assistants demand the title of *nursing tech* or *emergency room tech*. **1977** *R.A.F. News* 11–24 May 8/4 Chf Tech Mick Young..took part in a cycling expedition...Jnr Tech Rob Patrick..was a schoolboy..cycling champion. **1980** A. Skinner *Mind's Eye* xx. 258 He's got..a thing the other techs made him.

tech (tek), *sb.*[3] [Abbrev. of Technology.] **1.** **high-tech** = *high-technology* attrib. phr. s.v. *technology 1 d; *spec.* with reference to a style of architecture and interior design that imitates the functionalism of industrial technology. Also (unhyphened) as *sb. phr.* Similarly **low-tech** *attrib. phr.*

1972 *Last Whole Earth Catalog* (Portola Inst.) 247/1 It's the only high-tech home I've found at all lovable. **1978** Kron & Slesin *High-Tech* 1 Some people call this phenomenon 'the industrial style', but we call it 'high-tech'. High-tech..is a term currently used in architectural circles to describe buildings incorporating prefabricated ..building components. **1979** *Jrnl. R. Soc. Arts* Nov. 743/2 Late-Modernism takes the ideas and forms of the Modern Movement to an extreme, exaggerating the structure and technological image of the building beyond the point which the Modernists would have found acceptable, sometimes meriting the label 'High-Tech' as a result. **1980** *New Age* (U.S.) Oct. 36/2 A pocket calculator, a very high-tech gadget. **1981** *Farmstead Mag.* Winter 24/2 These solar greenhouses are often hi-tech. *Ibid.* 26/1 The low-tech greenhouse. **1983** *Times* 25 Jan. 26/7 Mrs Williams touched on such subjects as..the need for more 'high-tech'.

2. Chiefly *attrib.* = Technology 1 b. *rare.*

1982 *Times* 6 May 17/6 (*heading*) Whitehall backs new tech firms. **1983** *New Scientist* 16 June 769/3 (Advt.), Signaal, Philips space-tech company, has developed a meteorological ground station.

tech (tek), *a.* Colloq. (orig. *U.S.*) abbrev. of Technical *a.* **techspeak** [*-speak], technical jargon.

1956 [see *latent *a.* j]. **1974** *Some Technical Terms & Slang* (Granada Television), *Tech run*, technical run. A rehearsal by the actors in the rehearsal room to which the technical staff who will be responsible for the programme in the stuido are invited to sort out technical problems. **1974** *Globe & Mail* (Toronto) 20 Feb. 34/9 Will Genge aim at the championship aside from his duties as tech supervisor? **1982** *80 Microcomputing* Feb. 330/1 This is code, jargon, techspeak, whatever.

technetium (teknī·ʃ[i]ŏm). [mod.L., f. Gr. τεχνητ-ός artificial (f. τεχνᾶσθαι to make by art, f. τέχνη art, craft) + -ium.] A dense, refractory, radioactive metallic element, chemically similar to rhenium, which occurs naturally only in trace amounts but is produced in reactors as a fission product of uranium and by neutron irradiation of molybdenum 98 and is used medically as a tracer in scintigraphy. Symbol Tc; atomic number 43. Formerly called *masurium.

1947 Perrier & Segrè in *Nature* 4 Jan. 24/1 We would like to propose the name of 'technetium', from the Greek τεχνητός, artificial, in recognition of the fact that technetium is the first artificially made element. The corresponding chemical symbol should be 'Tc'. **1960** J. Kleinberg et al. *Inorg. Chem.* xxi. 535 The existence of the heptasulfides of technetium and rhenium and their mode of preparation emphasize the high degree of stability of these elements in the +7 state. **1962** [see *masurium]. **1969** *New Scientist* 13 Mar. 564/1 Astrophysicists are puzzled to explain how the element technetium, which must be produced in the hot cores of stars, reaches the surface. **1974** *Encycl. Brit. Micropædia* IX. 859/2 Technetium metal looks like platinum but is usually obtained as a gray powder. **1977** *Lancet* 7 May 1012/1 Individual limbs were scanned 5–6 hr after administration of 10 mCi technetium-99m diphosphonate.

technetronic (te:knĭtrǫ·nik), *a.* [ult. f. Gr. τέχνη art, craft + *elec)tronic *a.*] Conditioned, determined, or shaped by advanced technology and electronic communications.

1967 Z. Brzezinski in *New Republic* 23 Dec. 18/2 Our society..is entering a more self-conscious stage; ceasing to be an industrial society, it is being shaped to an ever-increasing extent by technology and electronics, and thus becoming the first *technetronic society*. **1970** D. Gabor *Innovations* i. 7 The 'modern industrial state' or the '*technetronic* society', as it has been variously called, is indeed above the head of the man in the street. **1977** *Time* 8 Aug. 10/2 The old order, based largely on military power and nationalism, is giving way to 'a technetronic age' in which there will be increasing emphasis on economic development and social justice.

technic, *a.* and *sb.* Add: **B.** *sb.* **4.** *U.S.* = Technique.

1908 *Arch. Internal Med.* II. 107 Cunningham's technic was crude. **1922** [see *encephalography* s.v. *encephalo-]. **1931** [see *plasmodesma]. **1943** H. L. Mencken *Heathen Days* vii. 93 The Fourth..went even worse than the Eroica, though it actually makes much less demand on technic. **1954** [see *immunohæmatology* s.v. *immuno-].

technica. (Earlier example.)

1782 [see *cancrizans *a.*].

technical, *a.* (*sb.*) **A.** *adj.* **1.** Delete *rare* and add later examples. Also *spec.* in the official designations of certain ranks in the armed forces of the U.K. and U.S.

1917 'Contact' *Airman's Outings* i. 6 As regards the mechanics, the quality of their skilled work is tempered by the technical sergeant-major, who knows most things about an aeroplane, and the quality of their behaviour by the disciplinary sergeant-major, usually an ex-regular with a lively talent for blasting. **1920** *Army & Navy Jrnl.* (U.S.) 26 June 1338/2 Enlisted men of the 'second grade' will be designated as Technical Sergeants or First Sergeants. **1926** *Brit. Gaz.* 12 May 3/2 At Basingstoke there is a supply of technical engineers available for work elsewhere. **1937** *Discovery* June 168/2 Behind the barge followed the baggage canoe, with two technical assistants and two polers. **1961** G. Millerson *Technique Television Production* 15 The technical director is in charge of the technical operational staff on the show. **1978** J. Irving *World according to Garp* i. 15 Technical Sergeant Garp.. served with the Eighth Air Force.

3. a. *technical college, technical school* (earlier example), *university*; *technical fix* (U.S.), a solution produced by technological means (sometimes used with an implication of superficiality); *technical hitch*, an interruption or breakdown due to mechanical failure; *loosely*, an unexpected obstacle or snag.

1879 Technical university [see *buff *sb.*[7] 1]. **1886** S. A. Barnett in H. Barnett *Canon Barnett* (1918) II. xlv. 246 Relief must..provide training. It may be in technical schools in town. **1886** *Times* 20 May 5/5 Yesterday afternoon the foundation-stone of the Technical College, an extension of the existing Mechanics' Institute, was laid at Keighley. **1940** P. Fleming *Flying Visit* v. 37 [Hitler] remained an equally great man to-day and (despite a technical hitch) equally capable of fulfilling his mission. **1958** 'R. Crompton' *William's Television Show* v. 148 Couldn't we say there's been a technical hitch? **1962** D. Lessing *Golden Notebk.* 528 It [*sc.* a film] was running slowly, because there was a technical hitch of some kind. **1971** *N.Y. Times* 8 Sept. 44/2 In recent centuries the scientific revolution has provided much warrant for the notion of the 'technical fix', the idea that scientists or technologists can find an appropriate solution for every problem. **1978** *Nagel's Encycl.-Guide: China* 318 The Technical Universities are in fact like polytechnic or engineering schools, and contain as many faculties as they do specialities. **1980** *Directory of Technical & Further Educ.* (ed. 18) p. xvi, *Technical colleges*, so-called, are usually fairly old-established, with a range of courses for full-time and part-time, day release or block release students, traditionally in engineering, at the levels of Ordinary and often Higher National Certificate..or Diploma. **1980** *New Age* (U.S.) Oct. 30/1 It greatly underestimates the energy savings possible through technical fixes alone—that is, through well-known and presently economic technical measures that would have no significant effect on our lifestyles or economic output.

d. (Later examples.) *technical foul* (Basketball), a foul which does not involve contact between opponents; also *ellipt.* as *sb.*; *technical knockout* (Boxing), the termination of a fight by the referee on the grounds of one boxer's inability to continue (though not counted out), his opponent being declared the winner; abbrev. TKO, t.k.o.: see *T 6.

1921 *Daily Colonist* (Victoria, B.C.) 6 Apr. 10/3 Denial of a report from Saskatoon that in a boxing match in that city on March 24 Bill Barton, of Vancouver, had secured a technical knockout over Billy Mackenzie. **1934** Webster s.v. Foul, *Technical foul.* **1958** F. C. Avis *Boxing Ref. Dict.* 112 *Technical Knock Out*, the decision of the referee when stopping a contest in which one of the boxers, though not knocked out, is scarcely capable of proceeding. **1962** *Times* 2 Aug. 3/3 The ball went to hand off his bat on seven occasions. Most were only technical chances [of a catch], although both Taylor and Swallow..would have held their respective catches more often than not. **1974** *Spartanburg* (S. Carolina) *Herald-Jrnl.* 21 Apr. B1/3 Oscar Robertson sank a free throw on the technical, and Jon McGlocklin hit a long jumper after the Bucks put the ball in play. **1977** *Times* 21 June 10/1 Other technical chances escaped McCosker and O'Keeffe, both at slip, as the ball.. moved about off the seam. **1981** *Washington Post* 17 Feb. D2/2 Before they sat down they had been assessed a technical foul... After Davis missed the first shot of the technical Skipper made the second.

e. So regarded according to a strict legal interpretation. Usu. in phr. *technical assault.*

1911 *Encycl. Brit.* XX. 769/1 Finding himself nonsuited in a court of law he commits a technical assault upon..some high legal functionary. **1914** A. Harrison *Kaiser's War* 126 He [*sc.* an officer] may not accept an apology in the event of a technical assault. Thus a man who on leaving a café, for example, brushes against an officer, is technically liable to be cut down. **1920** Wodehouse *Damsel in Distress* vi. 84 'You ought to have had the scoundrel arrested,' he said vehemently. 'It was a technical assault.'

4. *Finance.* Of, pertaining to, or designating a market in which prices are determined chiefly by internal factors (see also quot. 1962).

1909 in Webster. **1946** *Sun* (Baltimore) 17 July 14/1 A certain amount of support was attracted to individual favorites on the idea the list may have been oversold and was due for a technical comeback. **1962** S. Strand *Marketing Dict.* 732 *Technical position*, a term applied to the various internal factors affecting the market; opposed to external forces such as earnings, dividends, political considerations and general economic conditions. Some internal factors considered in appraising the market's technical position include the size of the short interest, whether the market has had a sustained advance or decline without interruption, a sharp advance or decline on a small volume and the amount of credit in use in the market. **1981** *Times* 22 July 22/6 Most sections of the market staged a technical rally. **1983** *Times* 2 Apr. 10/5 The market remained technical, with positions being covered, and a marked reluctance shown to open new positions.

technician. Add: **c.** *spec.* A person qualified in the practical application of one of the sciences or mechanical arts; now esp., a person whose job is to carry out practical work in a laboratory or to give assistance with technical equipment.

1939 W. A. Richardson *Technical College* xxv. 476 There are certain high-grade technicians, e.g. chemists, physicists, mathematical engineers, who will be engaged in the more elaborate design problems, in industrial research and investigation. **1952**, etc. [see *technologist]. **1954** *Rep. Patent Cases* LXX. 150 The Defendants have a most elaborate system for bringing to the attention of their technicians all technical developments relevant to their work. **1968** *Ibid.* LXXXV. 104 Extracts from laboratory notebooks or other specific records pertaining to the particular strains employed by the laboratory technicians. **1972** *Daily Tel.* 9 Feb. 12 Note that word 'technician'. From today there are no more 'mechanics' at Ford Sure dealers. 'We have changed the name because we think it is time that we built up the image of the man in the workshop.' **1983** *N.Y. Times* 11 Aug. A10/6 French technicians scurry around at the military air base assembling machine guns and helicopters.

technicism. Add: **2.** Technical quality or character; a condition in which practical results or methods are stressed.

1932 tr. *Ortega y Gasset's Revolt of Masses* vi. 61 Three principals have made possible this new world: liberal democracy, scientific experiment, and industrialism. The two latter may be summed-up in one word: technicism. **1951** *Archit. Rev.* CX. 203/2 There is also research into aesthetic functions, and it is due only to this latter, if, instead of arriving at a dry technicism or mere utilitarianism, the modern movement has led to a true new style in architecture. **1977** *Times Educ. Suppl.* 21 Oct. 32/3 Even in the Bullock report..one yet senses, ultimately, a dreary technicism of mind... The report is written in the language of death.

technicist. Add: **2.** *attrib.* or as *adj.* Of or pertaining to technicism (sense *2).

1932 tr. *Ortega y Gasset's Revolt of Masses* 151 We are told quite seriously that the essence of America is its practical and technicist conception of life. **1974** *Times* 16 Mar. 16 A technicist society indifferent to location and continuity will undermine itself by wrecking the structures of meaning on which any society must rest.

technicize (te·knisəiz), *v. rare.* [f. Technic *a.* + -ize.] *trans.* To make technical; to subject to a high degree of technicality. Hence **techniciza·tion**; **te·chnicized** *ppl. a.*

1927 A. Huxley *Proper Studies* 137 The world will become even more completely technicized, even more elaborately regimented, than it is at present. **1959** —— *Let.* 6 May (1969) 869 It dealt with..advancing technicization of everything. **1972** *Listener* 31 Aug. 270/3 The predominant effort..to hang on to and 'technicise' the cult of the socialised warrior—ally the socialised warrior with technology, that is. **1975** J. De Bres tr. *Mandel's Late Capitalism* vii. 243 A far more technicized division of labour now replaces the old factory hierarchy.

technico-. Add: **2.** Forming adjs., as *technico-architectonic, -diplomatic, -economic*, etc.

1951 M. Lowry *Let.* Feb. (1967) 233 Is this a technical technico-architechtonic [*sic*] term? **1970** *New Scientist* 30 July 219/1 Prime Minister Vorster..scored a considerable technico-diplomatic success. **1970** E. Snow *Red China Today* (new ed.) 36 The solution of technico-economic problems of social transformation. *Ibid.*, Centrally led priority programs for essential technico-scientific specialists. **1973** D. Osmond-Smith tr. *Bettetini's Lang. & Technique of Film* i. 45 However, a morphological study of the film, even if conducted on a syntactic level, cannot leave out of account considerations of a technico-grammatical nature.

Technicolor (te·knikɒləɹ). Also **-our.** **1.** A proprietary name for various processes of colour cinematography, esp. ones employing dye transfer and separation negatives. Freq. *attrib.*

1917 *U.S. Patent 1,231,710* Daniel F. Comstock... Assignor, by Mesne Assignments, to Technicolor Motion Picture Corporation, of Boston, Massachusetts. **1929** *Official Gaz.* (U.S. Patent Office) 3 Dec. 24/1 *Technicolor* for motion-picture films. **1930** *Punch* 2 Apr. 385 *Show of Shows* at the Tivoli, the latest and greatest of technicolour talkie reviews. **1932** *Discovery* Dec. 382/2 The subtractive process..has been familiar to picture-goers in the many Technicolor films shown in this country. **1948** *Time* 22 Mar. 85/3 Herbert T. Kalmus,..the co-inventor, developer, majority stockholder and president of Technicolor,..is a graduate of Massachusetts Institute of Technology (after which Technicolor was named). **1950** *Trade Marks Jrnl.* 5 Apr. 314/2 *Technicolor*... Photographic apparatus, cinematographic apparatus, television apparatus, apparatus capable of transmitting and receiving pictures in colour, and talking machines. Technicolor Motion Picture Corporation... 4th August 1949. **1976** L.-A. Bawden *Oxf. Compan. Film* 681/1 A special projector with two apertures—one with a red filter, the other with a green filter—was needed to show early Technicolor films. *Ibid.* 682/1 Eastman Color, introduced in 1949, changed the whole nature of colour filming and from 1951 onwards Technicolor prints were made, still by dye transfer, almost exclusively from Eastman Color negative. **1978** *Amer. Poetry Rev.* Sept./Oct. 10/2 'On the Towpath' begins in black-and-white and quickly shifts to technicolor.

2. *transf.* and *fig.* (Also with small initial.) Vivid colour characteristic of colour cinematography. Chiefly *attrib.* and in phr. *in glorious* (*gorgeous*, etc.) *Technicolor.*

a **1940** F. Scott Fitzgerald *Last Tycoon* (1941) v. 95 The theme..would come in some such guise as the auto horns from the Technicolor boulevards below. **1946** J. B. Priestley *Bright Day* v. 130 She looked very beautiful, and in glorious technicolour. **1954** M. Procter *Hell is City* I. vi. 35 A natural blonde of Technicolor brilliance. **1960** M. Stewart *My Brother Michael* ii. 25 The heavy Technicolor prosperity of the plains. **1962** N. Del Mar *Richard Strauss* iii. 85 The glorious technicolour of Strauss's orchestra. **1966** *Listener* 13 Jan. 71/2 Illustrations in black and white and gorgeous Technicolor. **1977** *New Yorker* 12 Sept. 32/3 A Technicolor-red leotard that matched her lips and her spike heels. **1979** *Church Times* 2 Nov. 9/1 Evelyn Waugh has described how some glamorise it [*sc.* death] in glorious technicolour.

Hence **te·chnicolored** *a.*

1947 E. F. Russell in Aldiss & Harrison *Decade 1940s* (1975) 166 'Laura [*sc.* a macaw] loves nuts.' 'I know it, you technicoloured bully.' **1954** *Newsweek* 27 Dec. 60/2 The palpable business of this Technicolored and CinemaScope production lies in its physical trappings, its underwater photography, and its action. **1962** *Movie* Sept. 22/1 Setting the events of the previous summer on the Riviera as technicolored flashbacks from the black-and-white Parisian winter. **1982** *New Scientist* 21 Jan. 179/2 Our face fuzz makes a pretty poor showing when compared with that bird's [*sc.* the peacock's] exuberant sensuality: you'd think evolution would have provided us with something more spectacular and 'Technicolored'.

‖ **technicum** (te·knikŏm). Also **tekhnikum.** Pl. **-s,** ‖ **-y.** [ad. Russ. *tekhnikum,* f. mod.L. *technicum,* neut. sing. of *technicus* technical (see Technic *a.* and *sb.*).] In the U.S.S.R., a technical college.

1932 M. Dobb *Soviet Russia & World* ii. 43 To-day there are 663 middle technical schools, or *technicums.* **1957** H. Bower *Short Guide Soviet Life* xiii. 52 Technical Colleges (tekhnikumy) train specialist technicians for a wide range of industries and take pupils from 14 to 30. **1963** *Higher Educ.: Rep. Comm. under Ld. Robbins 1961–3* v. 43 in *Parl. Papers 1962–3* (Cmnd. 2154) XI. 639 In the Soviet Union, the output of *Technicums* is not included. **1974** T. P. Whitney tr. *Solzhenitsyn's Gulag Archipelago* I. I. ii. 72 In Leningrad..the Latvian Technicum, and the Latvian and Estonian newspapers were all closed down.

technification (te:knifikēⁱ·ʃən). [f. *techn-* as in Technical *a.*, etc. + -ification.] The adoption or imposition of technical methods. Also **te·chnified** *ppl. a.*, **te·chnify** *v. intr.* (both *rare*).

1959 A. Huxley *Let.* 4 Jan. (1969) 859 In time, I suspect, all fully technified societies will adopt the Russian solution. **1959** *Ibid.* 5 Jan., It may be that the only satisfactory solution..is to accept the inevitability of the technification of everything. **1962** *Spectator* 16 Feb. 199/2 The technification of conditioning minds by emotional images. **1970** J. Cotler in I. L. Horowitz *Masses in Lat. Amer.* xii. 429 Those who might have found employment in the exploitation of sugar and have been unable to do so due to technification, have had to remain in their miserable plots. **1972** *Listener* 18 May 640 This method is designed to be effective against other industrial and technified countries, whose organisation can be so disrupted that they simply can no longer function. **1973** *Harper's Mag.* Nov. 82 They internalized their intelligence activities with headlong speed. They technified senselessly—charts, graphs, bugs, concealed cameras.

technique. Add: **a.** (*a*) Now freq. used of the manner of execution or performance in any discipline, profession, or sport, or of skill or ability in any of these; (*b*) in the sense 'technical or artistic skill', freq. used without article or qualifying word; (*c*) *loosely,* a skilful or efficient means of achieving a purpose; a characteristic way of proceeding; a knack.

(*a*) **1900** [in Dict.]. **1903** [see *astrophotography]. **1920** Oswald & Pryce *Terra Sigillata* ii. 3 The technique of the green-glazed ware was also to a great extent similar to that of the red-glazed fabric; *e.g.* in the use of moulds with impressed designs..and both techniques were obviously inspired by prototypes in beaten metal. **1932** A. Huxley *Brave New World* i. 15 If they could discover a technique for shortening the period of maturation what a triumph, what a benefaction to Society! **1940** K. Mannheim *Man & Society* v. i. 244 Any deliberate rebuilding of human groups in terms of more elastic organization represents another chapter in the development of social techniques. **1959** C. Porter *Rowing to Win* ii. 40 The measure by which the appearance and technique of a Russian crew differs from that of an American crew is that of the difference in their styles... By style, then, I mean largely the technique of rowing. **1968** J. D. Watson *Double Helix* (1970) x. 63 The witchcraft-like techniques of the biochemist. **1972** M. Kline *Math. Thought* xiii. 282 The more complicated algebraic techniques.

(*b*) **1905** A. Bennett *Sacred & Profane Love* i. 23 A generation of pianists who had lifted technique to a plane of which neither Liszt nor Rubenstein dreamed. **1935** W. S. Maugham *Don Fernando* x. 185 Technique is only the method by which the artist achieves his aim. **1960** P. Goodman *Growing Up Absurd* iv. 89 'The trainee,' says William H. Whyte, Jr., 'believes managing is an end in itself—technique is more vital than content.'

(*c*) **1936** J. A. Lee *Hunted* ii. 49 When brought back they told the story of their venturings, so that northern runaways knew the technique of stealing a passage. **1941** *Punch* 31 Dec. 583/1 There is quite a technique to washing a blanket. **1944** E. S. Gardner *Case of Black-eyed Blonde* ii. 22 Now then, you little son-of-a-bitch,..that technique of planting the diamond pendant is something you used about three years ago on that maid your mother had. **1955** L. P. Hartley *Perfect Woman* xiii. 126 She'll want to know all about you—that's her technique. **1979** D. Halberstam *Powers that Be* (1980) i. v. 273 In 1953 Barth wrote an editorial attacking the FBI's technique of gathering irrelevant information in its investigations and making the information a part of a person's dossier.

b. *spec.* Manner of performance or skill in sexual relations.

1921 M. Arlen *Romantic Lady* 11 She was very close to me, smiling, intimate. Pure coquetry, of course—but what perfect *technique*! **1930** V. Sackville-West *Edwardians* vi. 296 When he chose, his technique could be faultless... He was very gentle with Teresa. **1964** R. Braddon *Year Angry Rabbit* ix. 80 The American servicemen appeared to retain an atavistic but irresistible technique with girls which outraged the local boys. **1974** V. Gielgud *In Such a Night* viii. 71 Alec looks at every woman..like that... He hasn't altered his technique.

techno-. Add: *techno-comme·rcial, -econo·mic* adjs.; **te·chnocomplex** *Archæol.* (see quot. 1968); **te·chnofear** = *technophobia* below; **te·chnofreak** [*freak *sb.*[1] 4 c], an enthusiast for technology or for the technical complexities of a particular piece of equipment; hence **techno-frea·kish** *a.*; **technographic** *a.* (earlier U.S. example); **techno-ma·nager,** a person who is both a technologist and a manager; hence **te:chno-manage·rial** *a.*; **technoma·nia,** a mania for technology; hence **technoma·niac**; **te·chnophile,** one who favours technology; **technopho·bia,** fear of technology; so **te·chnophobe,** a person who fears technology; **techno·polis** [-polis], a society dominated by technology; hence **technopo·litan** *a.*; **te·chnosphere** [*-sphere], the technological aspect of human activity; **te·chnostructure,** a group of technologists or technical experts that controls the workings of industry or government; **technotro·nic** *a.* = *technetronic *a.*

1937 *Discovery* Aug. 254/1 The history of this material [*sc.* synthetic rubber] from the early 'academic synthesis' period, through the 'techno-commercial' period, up to the present time. **1979** J. E. Rowley *Mechanised In-House Information Syst.* ii. 107 Some units..assign equal importance to scientific and technical information and techno-commercial material. **1968** D. L. Clarke *Analytical Archaeol.* viii. 357 *Technocomplex,* a group of cultures characterized by assemblages sharing a polythetic range but differing specific types of the same general families of artefact-types, shared as a widely diffused and interlinked response to common factors in environment, economy and technology. **1976** *Sci. Amer.* Feb. 94/2 What game animals supported the hunters of the Tanged Point Technocomplex? **1980** *Cambr. Encycl. Archaeol.* 69/1 The long, stable period of the Oldowan technocomplex. **1960** Techno-economic [see *feed *v.* 8 e (ii)]. **1976** *Nature* 5 Feb. 355/2 A team..will be responsible for investigations into the cost-benefit of research done by the BSC and for techno-economic analysis. **1980** *Times* 14 Mar. 20/3 The consumer is still suffering from what many dealers are beginning to call 'technofear'—fear of commitment to purchasing anything in case the technology changes. **1983** *Times* 28 Sept. 3/3 Techno-fear..is defined as 'difficulties in accepting and using high-technology products in the home'. **1973** *Absolute Sound* I. ii. 42 We have always known it [*sc.* the audio industry] was dominated by techno freaks with an unhealthy irreverence for the live sound. *Ibid.* iii. 173 His prose is..so techno-freakish,..so filled with demonstrations that the Great Expert is at work that it is incomprehensible to virtually every informed audiophile we know. **1983** *Austral. Personal Computer* June/July 62/1 A neat piece of technology that..ought to interest any technofreak simply because it's such a good idea. **1891** *Ann. Rep. Smithsonian Inst. 1889–90* i. 611 The Kunstgewerbe Museum contains much that is like the ethnographic collection, but the reigning concept is technographic. **1962** A. Sampson *Anat. Britain* xiii. 211 It was only after France and Germany had founded their *polytechniques* and *hochschule* [sic] for techno-managers that Britain gradually felt the need to adapt their universities to technical education. **1979** *Times of India* 17 Aug. 12 (Advt.), It has set up a full-fledged Consultancy & Promotional Cell with Indian and Foreign experts for providing technomanagerial Consultancy Services for improving the operational and managerial efficiency of consumer cooperatives. **1969** *Daily Tel.* 29 May 28/3 The days when almost any scientific team could wrest enormous sums from the taxpayer to finance big, glamorous and spectacular projects were coming to an end... 'The era of technomania is passing—and high time too,' Mr. Benn said. *Ibid.* 30 May 20/3 Shall I, who have hated technology all my life... Turn technomaniac myself? **1968** H. Weaver tr. *Ellul's Critique of New Commonplaces* 236 This commonplace is really very common among technicians, technologists, technolasters, technophagi, technophiles, technocrats, [etc.]. **1983** *Daily Tel.* 28 Nov. 12/1 Those technophiles disappointed by the absence of innovative features in IBM's newly announced P. C. Junior home computer have overlooked one splendid novelty. **1965** *New Statesman* 27 Aug. 286/1 Instead of leading us to the golden age, science is dragging us down into a servile, stable hell. Shades of Orwell! Technophobia has struck another good man down. *Ibid.*, The incipient technophobe will rage against the motor-murder of 20 people a day in Britain, without once considering that cars also carry 50 million people and their goods. **1965** H. C. Cox *Secular City* 5 We shall make use of a somewhat contrived word, *technopolis.* It will be used here to signify the fusion of technological and political components into the base on which a new cultural style has appeared... it will call to mind the fact that the contemporary secular metropolis was not possible before modern technology. *Ibid.* iii. 63 To say that technopolitan man is pragmatic means that he is a kind of modern ascetic. He disciplines himself to give up certain things... Life for him is a set of problems, not an unfathomable mystery. **1969** Huxley & Nicholson in *Times* 7 Oct. 8/1 The most striking change which it has brought is to create out of a mass of economic, social and technical developments, an entire semi-autonomous new system, which we may call the technosphere, with its own structure and anatomy, its own programmed inputs and outputs, and its accidental or deliberate releases into the biosphere. **1967** J. K. Galbraith *New Industrial State* vi. 71 Management..includes..only a small proportion of those who..contribute information to group decisions. This..group..extends from the most senior officials of the corporation to..blue collar workers... This ..is the guiding intelligence—the brain—of the enterprise... I propose to call this organization the Technostructure. **1978** *Nature* 9 Nov. 147/2 In discussing the origins of the Soviet technical intelligentsia (throughout inelegantly and inaccurately termed the 'technostructure'), Bailes draws on an impressive range of sources, both Soviet and Western. **1969** *Daily Tel.* 23 Apr. 16/3 The 'technotronic society', as the mass technical world is now sometimes labelled, creates its own problems.

technocracy (teknǫ·krăsi). orig. *U.S.* [f. Techno- + -cracy.] The control of society or industry by technical experts; a ruling body of such experts.

Technocracy has been the name of various groups advocating the technical control of society, esp. Technocracy, Inc., established in New York in 1932–3 by Howard Scott.

1919 W. H. Smyth in *Industr. Management* Mar. 211/2 For this unique experiment in rationalized Industrial Democracy I have coined the term 'technocracy'. **1932** *N.Y. Herald-Tribune* 15 Dec. 11/1 Technocracy..the name for a new system and philosophy of government, in which the nation's industrial resources should be organized and managed by technically competent persons for the good of everyone instead of being left to the management of private interests for their own advantage. **1945** C. S. Lewis *That Hideous Strength* xii. 318 The effect of modern war is to eliminate retrogressive types, while sparing the technocracy and increasing its hold upon public affairs. **1947** *Mind* LVI. 164 Such notions as social and economic planning, technocracy,..the denial of natural rights and individual liberties, etc., are due to them [*sc.* French Utopians, St. Simon, etc.] more than to Godwin or the Utilitarians. **1955** *Times* 23 May 3/4 On that unlikely day when England elects a benevolent technocracy to power a Bill will be passed forbidding more than one performance per year per town of such works as *The Messiah,* the *St. Matthew Passion,* [etc.]. **1975** *Political Studies* XXIII. 82 Nevertheless, if technocracy means rule not just by *individuals* who are members of a particular technocratic *élite,* but rule by a technocratic class as such, one has to show that the latter has either a common interest to defend or a common ideology to pursue.

Hence **te·chnocrat,** (*a*) an advocate of technocracy; (*b*) a member of a technocracy, a technologist exercising administrative power; **technocra·tic** *a.*; **techno·cratism.**

1932 *Sun* (Baltimore) 12 Dec. 6/3 The Technocrats, thanks..largely to a peculiarly fetching 'trade label' which embodies in one word two of the most far-reaching of current concepts, technology and democracy, are succeeding in a remarkable degree in breaking down the apathy. **1932** *N.Y. Herald-Tribune* 15 Dec. 11/2 The haunts of technocratic science were situated at numerous places about town, principally in cubbyhole restaurants in Greenwich village. **1933** *Times Lit. Suppl.* 26 Jan. 46/2 An age that was already substituting the technocrat for the monarch. **1945** C. S. Lewis *That Hideous Strength* xii. 318 It was not the great technocrats of Koenigsberg or Moscow who supplied the casualties in the siege of Stalingrad. **1949** *Mind* LVIII. 416 Lersch denies the widely accepted thesis that man's uniqueness consists in his activities (activism, pragmatism, technocratism) since these are characteristic only of the Male's relation to the world. **1957** *London Mag.* Jan. 48 Sprawling in my revolving chair, behind a man-sized desk, I could imagine myself a brisk and efficient technocrat, a kind of highbrow tycoon. **1958** *Times Lit. Suppl.* 26 Dec. 751/1 Either tending towards reliance on a tradition which has been made obsolete..or else attempting a technocratic rule for which no tradition exists. **1965** W. H. G. Armytage *Rise of Technocrats* v. 66 St. Simonians were the first technocrats: apostles of the religion of industry. **1974** J. White tr. *Poulantzas's Fascism & Dictatorship* v. ii. 254 Imperialist ideology in effect represents a displacement of domination within bourgeois ideology itself, from the juridico-political region which was dominant in liberal-bourgeois ideology to economic technocratism. **1980** *Times* 11 Aug. 11/1 Dr Hoss was chosen after the Syrian-imposed end to the civil war in 1976 to head a 'technocratic', ie non-political, government.

technologic, *a.* (Examples.)

1971 *Amer. N. & Q.* Dec. 61/2 The thread of technologic changes is woven throughout the text. **1979** *Bull. Amer. Acad. Arts & Sci.* Mar. 20 The early insights about the 'technologic misfit' and the need for social and technological 'congruence' have given way to more systematic analysis.

technological, *a.* Add: **3.** Pertaining to or characterized by technology; resulting from developments in technology (esp. *technological unemployment*).

1930 *Econ. Jrnl.* XL. 551 (*title*) Rationalisation and Technological Unemployment. **1942** J. H. OLDHAM in *Christian News-Let.* 6 May 5/2 The question of the stability of our modern technological civilization. **1957** *Technology* Mar. 1/1 The Government is spending millions on the scientific and technological departments of universities and on the technical colleges. **1961** P. DRUCKER *Technology & Culture* II. 348 There is only one thing we do not know about the Technological Revolution—but it is essential: What happened to bring about the basic change ..which released it? **1968** *Economist* 6 July 54/2 Technological forecasting is an exercise in logical deduction rather than straight mathematical calculation... The biggest incentive to technological forecasting is commercial: as industry becomes bigger and more capital-intensive, the cost of mistakes rises. **1970** *Nature* 24 Oct. 387/2 The one dimensional 'technological fixes' that society has so far provided to solve its problems. **1983** *Wall St. Jrnl.* (European ed.) 14 Apr. 1 Computer yahoos who electronically invade other people's computers... 'I call it electronic vandalism or technological trespassing,' says.. a computer-security consultant.

technologically (teknolǫ·dʒikăli), *adv.* [TECHNOLOGICAL *a.* + -LY².] In a technological manner; from a technological point of view.

1862 H. MAYHEW *London Labour* Extra vol. 5/2 So that, technologically considered, there is no difference between them. **1951** R. FIRTH *Elements Soc. Organization* ii. 51 Technologically its culture is very undeveloped. **1976** *Gramophone* June 103/3 The inventiveness of the Japanese mind can operate with special freedom in such a technologically biased society.

technolo·gico-Be·nthamite, *a.* *nonce-wd.* [f. TECHNOLOGIC *a.* + -O + BENTHAMITE *a.*] Characterized by the implementation of Benthamite principles through the agency of technology.

1969 F. R. LEAVIS in *Times Lit. Suppl.* 29 May 569/1 The problem..is one of cultural disinheritance and the meaninglessness of the technologico-Benthamite world. **1973** I. ROBINSON *Survival of English* 247 The principal target of our comment will be the disastrous unwisdom of the prevailing climate of our 'technologico-Benthamite' enlightenment which controls all three parties, the daily and weekly press, and all the television channels.

techno·logism. *rare.* [f. TECHNOLOGY + -ISM.] Belief in the governance of society according to technological principles.

1969 B. BREWSTER tr. *Althusser's For Marx* iii. 108 There are names for these temptations in the history of Marxism: *economism* and even *technologism*. **1980** C. E. SCHORSKE *Fin-de-Siècle Vienna* p. xix, The trends in post-Nietzschean culture—irrationalism, subjectivism, abstractionism, anxiety, technologism.

technologist. Add: (Later examples.) Also *U.S.* = *TECHNICIAN c.

1952 *Economist* 21 June 796/1 Technical colleges should be raised in status in order to produce technologists—as opposed to technicians. **1956** *Technical Educ.* 2 in *Parl. Papers 1955–56* (Cmnd. 9703) XXXVI. 987 A technologist has the qualifications and experience required for membership of a professional institution... A technician is qualified by specialist technical education and practical training to work under the general direction of a technologist. **1966** *Amer. Jrnl. Clin. Path.* XLVI. 465/2, 3 tubes of blood were given to each of a technologists who worked in separate rooms; they were instructed to invert 1 tube until it clotted, then the second tube, and finally the third tube. **1977** *Chicago Tribune* 2 Oct. XII. 70/2 (Advt.), Our busy emergency room requires capable technologist to work weekends.

technologize (teknǫ·lŏdʒəiz), *v.* [f. TECHNOLOGY + -IZE.] *trans.* To make technological. Also *intr.*, to use technical methods. So **techno·logized** *ppl. a.*; **techno·logizing** *vbl. sb.*

1960 *Mod. Lang. Rev.* Jan. 113 The tensions between liberty and equality in technologized society. **1960** *Punch* 27 Apr. 574/1 The arts are in self-defence compelled to technologize themselves, inventing new areas of study which require machinery and grants..in order to maintain a foothold in the university premises. **1964** M. MCLUHAN *Understanding Media* (1967) II. xvi. 173 The West had to technologize more intensively than the ancient world. **1965** M. BRADBURY *Stepping Westward* vi. 298 Look at this vast urbanized and technologized mass-society. **1965** K. AMIS *James Bond Dossier* 147 Nothing could be more characteristic of science fiction than this strategy of technologizing the fairy tale. **1966** D. JENKINS *Educated Society* iv. 165 That technologizing of life which we have seen as constituting a major threat to personal freedom today. **1980** D. MORAES *Mrs Gandhi* iii. 40 The construction of an urban, technologised India.

technology. Add: **1. b.** (Later examples.) Also *transf.*

1949 in W. A. Visser t' Hooft *First Assembly World Council of Churches* 75 There is no inescapable necessity for society to succumb to undirected developments of technology. **1958** J. K. GALBRAITH *Affluent Society* ix. 99 Improvements in technology..are the result of investment in highly organized scientific and engineering knowledge and skills. **1971** *Daily Tel.* (Colour Suppl.) 10 Dec. 18/2 In the production of millions of children a year, it is not surprising that occasionally nature's complex technology should break down to produce an imbalance of hormones with masculinisation of the female foetus or feminisation of the mäle. **1975** *Ecologist* V. 120/1 Guiding technological development effectively is not a matter of being for or against technology, which is the form the discussion usually assumes.

c. With *a* and *pl.* A particular practical or industrial art.

1957 *Technology* Apr. 56/1 It [*sc.* Chemical Engineering] is now recognized as one of the four primary technologies, alongside civil, mechanical, and electrical engineering. **1960** *Electronic Engin.* Mar. 148/1 Electronic data-processing for business is a young technology. **1969** *Listener* 5 June 778/1 To compare one technology with another. **1979** *Computers in Shell* (Shell Internat. Petroleum Co.) 2 Highly complex problems involving the many technologies needed within the energy and associated industries.

d. high-technology applied *attrib.* to a firm, industry, etc., that produces or utilizes highly advanced and specialized technology, or to the products of such a firm. Also (unhyphened) as *sb. phr.* Similarly **low-technology.** Cf. *high tech* s.v. *TECH³ 1.

1964 S. M. MILLER in I. L. Horowitz *New Sociology* 292 The youthful poor possess limited or outmoded skills and inadequate credentials in a high-technology, certificate-demanding economy. **1970** *Physics Bull.* Apr. 146/1 'High technology' industries demand huge capital and R and D investments. **1972** *Nature* 28 Jan. 183/2 In high technology..errors in estimates of development cost are more serious in their effects. **1973** *Newsweek* 18 June 92/2 As their old, low-technology industries wilt under the pressure of mounting labor costs. **1981** *Times* 14 May 1/7 Export licences are required for a variety of high technology goods including computers, electronic equipment, chemicals, metals and building equipment.

4. Special Combs.: **technology assessment,** the assessment of the effects on society of new technology; **technology transfer,** the transfer of new technology or advanced technological information from the developed to the less developed countries of the world.

1966 *Inquiries, Legislation, Policy Stud. Subcomm. Sci., Res., & Devel.* (U.S. Congress: House: Comm. Sci. & Astronaut.) 27 We must be cognizant of what technology is doing to us—the bad as well as the good. Toward this end we would consider the exploration of legislation to establish a Technology Assessment Board—with the somewhat appropriate acronym TAB, since this would be its function. **1979** *Bull. Amer. Acad. Arts & Sci.* Mar. 21 Unanswered questions are threatening to leave technology assessment a mere intellectual pastime. **1969** *Listener* 24 July 106/3 This seems to show that Africa can use western techniques to her advantage, but only so long as the different cultural, intellectual and material contexts are kept firmly in mind when the technology-transfer is being planned. **1978** *Internat. Relations Dict.* (U.S. Dept. State Library) 40/2 *Technology transfer* has been defined as 'the transfer of knowledge generated and developed in one place to another, where it is used to achieve some practical end.'

Teck (tek). The title of Francis, Prince of *Teck* (1837–1900), applied *attrib.* and *absol.* to a kind of necktie fashionable in the late nineteenth century; = *FOUR-IN-HAND 1 b.

1895 *Montgomery Ward Catal.* Spring & Summer 95/3 Pique fancy Teck Scarfs... Fine Lawn Flowing End Tecks. **1897** *Sears, Roebuck Catal.* 223/1 Our 35c All Silk Tecks... Men's Handsome Silk and Satin Fancy Teck Scarves.

teckel (te·kĕl). [a. Ger.] = DACHSHUND.

1877 F. E. KINGSLEY *C. Kingsley* II. xvi. 9 'Victor', a favourite Teckel, given to him by the Queen. **1922** [see *DOBERMANN]. **1952** C. L. B. HUBBARD *Pembrokeshire Corgi Handbk.* i. 8 The very short-legged Teckel or Dachshund types of central Europe. **1971** F. HAMILTON *World Encycl. Dogs* 337 The Dachshund, or Teckel as it is known in Germany, has been evolved from the oldest known breeds of dog.

Tecla (te·klă). The proprietary name of a make of artificial pearl.

1908 *Trade Marks Jrnl.* 9 Sept. 1481 *Tecla*... Imitation or reconstructed pearls, imitation or reconstructed rubies, imitation emeralds, and imitation or reconstructed sapphires. Isaac Blumenthal,..Hendon, Middlesex; merchant and manufacturer. **1923** [see *TITIAN]. **1930** E. WAUGH *Vile Bodies* vi. 113 Heirlooms of priceless value..among Tecla pearls.

tecno-. Add: **tecnolater, tek-** (teknǫ·lătəɪ), one who worships or idolizes children; so **tecno·latry** [-LATRY]; **tecnonymy**: now usu. in form *teknonymy* (later examples).

1914 A. H. SIDGWICK *Promenade Ticket* 30 'Those who are called so [*sc.* happy]' (i.e. by Froebel, Wordsworth, and teknolaters generally) 'are simply congratulated on account of their promise.' **1899** M. BEERBOHM *More* 174 A perfect example of our tecnolatry, our delight in the undirected oddities of children. **1937** R. H. LOWIE *Hist. Ethnological Theory* vii. 81 Teknonymy is no longer the inevitable effect of matrilocal residence or of an avoidance rule. **1951** R. FIRTH *Elem. Social Organization* i. 9 A child does not take its name from its parents; on the contrary, in the institution of teknonymy they are known as 'Father and Mother of So-and-so'.

tectal, *a.*: see *TECTUM.

tectiform, *a.* Add: **2.** *Archæol.* **a.** Applied to a roof-shaped design or symbol found in palæolithic cave-paintings and engravings. **b.** *sb.* A design or symbol of this type.

1921 R. A. S. MACALISTER *Text-bk. Europ. Archæol.* I. ix. 491 Tectiform devices are essentially shaped like a more or less isosceles triangle, with a vertical line running from apex to base. *Ibid.* 492 The resemblance between such huts and the tectiform devices is striking, but not wholly convincing...I have another suggestion to offer.. namely, that they are intended to represent traps. **1921** M. C. BURKITT *Prehist.* 382 (*caption*) The painted tectiform from La Mouthe. **1962** S. GIEDION *Eternal Present* I. iii. 254 The tectiforms of Font-de-Gaume also belong to the class of symbols with more or less straight lines.

tecto- (te·kto), comb. form of L. *tectum* roof, as in **te·ctocu:ticle** *Ent.* (see quot. 1951); **te·ctospi:nal** *a. Anat.*, applied to a group of nerve fibres which run from the tectum of the midbrain to the spinal cord.

1951 A. G. RICHARDS *Integument of Insects* xvi. 149 The term tectocuticle..is here proposed for any material poured onto the outer surface of the formed epicuticle and hardening there as a reasonably permanent component. **1974** R. H. HACKMAN in M. Rockstein *Physiol. Insecta* (ed. 2) VI. iii. 216 The cuticle is divided into..an inner relatively thick procuticle and a thin outer epicuticle... A cement layer or 'tectocuticle' may also be present. **1916** *Gray's Anat.* (ed. 19) 744 The tectospinal fasciculus originates in the superior colliculus..of the opposite side. **1974** D. & M. WEBSTER *Compar. Vertebr. Morphol.* xii. 290 Another prominent component of the extrapyramidal system is the tectospinal tract.

tectogenesis (tektǫdʒe·nĕsis). *Geol.* [ad. G. *tektogenese* (E. Haarman 1926, in *Zeitschr. f. Deutsch. Geol. Ges.* LXXVIII. B. 106), f. Gr. τέκτων, -ον- carpenter, builder: see -GENESIS.] The formation of the highly distorted rock structures characteristic of mountain ranges, as distinct from the formation of mountainous topography itself. Hence **tectogene·tic, tectoge·nic** *adjs.*, of, pertaining to, or involving tectogenesis. Also **te·ctogene** [ad. G. *tektogen* (E. Haarman 1926, loc. cit., 107): see *-GEN 3], a long, narrow belt of downwarping in the earth's crust, said to be an underlying feature of mountain ranges and oceanic trenches.

1937 *Bull. Amer. Assoc. Petroleum Geologists* XXI. 1596 Orogenesis means 'mountain-making', but the term refers only to the production of mountain structure, not to that of mountain topography. Hence, it seems desirable to replace it by 'tectogenesis', as Haarman suggested. *Ibid.*, Tectogenic movements..are incongruent, making structures that vary in the different stories of the crust; and the deformation they produce is wholly irreversible. **1937** *Leidsche Geol. Med.* VIII. 204 (*caption*) Tectogene with root. **1965** *Phil. Trans. R. Soc.* A. CCLVIII. 65 The later Palaeozoic..tectogene stretched in a belt from the Appalachians, through southern Britain and central and southern Europe, to Suess's massive Altaids in the heart of Asia. *Ibid.* 68 Throughout the Caledonides (Spitzbergen, Greenland, Scandinavia and Britain) there seems little doubt that the main tectogenic phase was centred in Silurian time. *Ibid.* 74 Undisturbed marine successions do not necessarily rule out synchronous tectogenesis of a neighbouring region. **1975** *Nature* 24 Jan. 257/1 Sicilian data indicate a time span of only 3–4 Myr for a single 'tectogenetic cycle'. *Ibid.* 10 July 116/1 The radial pattern of transverse folds with respect to the arc..has been taken into account in tectogenetic models of the Alps.

tectonic, *a.* Add: **2.** Also with reference to other planets. Cf. also *plate-tectonic* adj. s.v. *PLATE *sb.* 20. (Further examples.)

1962 F. I. ORDWAY et al. *Basic Astronautics* iii. 65 They [*sc.* the rills on the moon] are apparently the result of tectonic activity. **1976** *Science* 24 Dec. 1386/3 By 2·5 billion years ago the volcanic-tectonic circus on Mars had folded. **1982** *Nature* 28 Jan. 293/2 Additional mapping and analysis based on Voyager images should help resolve many remaining questions about the tectonic evolution of Ganymede.

Hence **tecto·nical** *a.*, in the same sense; **tecto·nically** *adv.*, as regards tectonism; by tectonic processes.

1925 J. JOLY *Surface-Hist. Earth* 191 *Laccolith*, an intrusive mass of igneous rock..generally associated tectonically with a mountain range. **1939** *Geogr. Jrnl.* XCIV. 499 There are also discussions of the tectonical.. and general geological problems of Tanganyika Territory. **1972** *Rep. 24th Internat. Geol. Congr.* III. 3 Among the most important geological (tectonical) factors..are the concentrations of heat flow and juvenile matter ascending from the mantle..along steep, deep-seated tectonic zones. **1974** *Nature* 25 Jan. 194/1 Many investigators interpret ophiolites as slices of oceanic crust which have been tectonically emplaced in orogenic belts. **1976** J. KLECZEK *Universe* iv. 155 On the whole, the Moon is tectonically a very quiet body.

tectonician (tektǫni·ʃăn). *Geol.* [f. TECTON(ICS in Dict. and Suppl. + -ICIAN.] = *TECTONIST 2.

1951 *Amer. Jrnl. Sci.* CCXLIX. 594 For the tectonician, the most useful definition of fold-axis is that given by Wegmann. **1965** *Phil. Trans. R. Soc.* A. CCLVIII. 56 Such tremendous crustal movements within the Alpine fold belt are of a much larger size than those required by the most nappist of tectonicians. **1975** *Nature* 6 Feb. 396/2 The Soviet tectonician Belousov has gone so far as to invoke extensive 'oceanisation' of continental crust to account for the ocean basins.

tectonics. (In Dict. s.v. TECTONIC *a.*) Add: **2.** *Geol.* The structural arrangement of rocks in the earth's crust (or on another planet); the branch of geology concerned with the understanding of rock structures, esp. large-scale ones. Cf. *plate tectonics* s.v. *PLATE *sb.* 20.

1899 *Q. Jrnl. Geol. Soc.* LV. 399 (*heading*) The tectonics of the district. **1914** J. PARK *Textbk. Geol.* xxxiv. 489 By a series of pressure experiments in 1888, Cadell obtained instructive imitations of the tectonics of mountain-building. **1935** [see *AUTOCHTHONOUS *a.*]. **1976** *Daily Colonist* (Victoria, B.C.) 15 May 5/5 The science of tectonics—the study of the movement of these plates—shows that Africa and Europe are in collision. **1982** *Nature* 28 Jan. 290 (*heading*) The tectonics of Ganymede.

tectonism (te·ktǫniz'm). *Geol.* [f. TECTON(IC *a.* + ISM.] = DIASTROPHISM.

1949 F. J. PETTIJOHN *Sedimentary Rocks* vi. 193 The feldspar content [in sands] is primarily an index of crystal [*read* crustal] instability or tectonism. **1960** *Bull. Amer. Assoc. Petroleum Geologists* XLIV. 1924/2 The San Joaquín Valley was undergoing tremendous tectonism during the Middle Tertiary. **1972** *Gloss. Geol.* (Amer. Geol. Inst.) 726/2 *Tectonism*, a less preferred syn. of diastrophism. **1975** G. ANDERSON *Coring* i. 10 Two basic types of tectonism affect a rock's acceptability and transmissibility of fluids—shearing and flexure folding. **1982** *Nature* 28 Jan. 292/1 Further evidence for distinguishing the style of tectonism on Gamymede is provided by structural features.

tectonist. (In Dict. s.v. TECTONIC *a.*) Restrict † *obs. nonce-wd.* to sense in Dict. and add: **2.** *Geol.* A specialist in tectonics. *rare.*

1933 *Amer. Jrnl. Sci.* CCXXV. 441 Becker's work has been to a large extent discarded by tectonists as being too highly theoretical to be of practical value in the interpretation of rock structure. **1935** [see *HERCYNIAN *a.* 2 c].

tectonite (te·ktǫnait). *Petrol.* [ad. G. *tektonit* (B. Sander), f. Gr. τέκτων, -ον-, carpenter, builder: see -ITE[1].] A rock whose fabric shows evidence of differential movement during its formation.

1933 *Amer. Jrnl. Sci.* CCXXV. 433 Rocks that owe their present characters to..the integration of differential movements, he [*sc.* Sander] calls tectonites in distinction to non-tectonites, which are formed under conditions involving no differential movement. **1950** *Geol. Mag.* LXXXVII. 331 (*heading*) Note on two lineated tectonites. **1960** TURNER & VERHOOGEN *Igneous & Metamorphic Petrol.* (ed. 2) xxiii. 638, B-tectonites are tectonites in whose fabrics a linear parallelism of elements with reference to the *b* (= B) axis of the fabric is the outstanding structural feature.

tectonization (te:ktǫnaizē·ʃən). *Geol.* [f. TECTON(IC *a.* + -IZATION.] Modification (of rocks, etc.) by tectonic processes.

1959 *Jrnl. Geol.* LXVII. 26/2 The last schistosity produced was also folded and now preserves the impress of the last phase of tectonization. **1971** *Nature* 2 July 21/1 Part of the central gap may be intermediate crust which has been incorporated, after tectonization, into the neocratons of the Greater Antilles. **1979** *Ibid.* 27 Sept. 267/1 Extensive mélange exists near the base of the Trondheim Nappe, indicating tectonisation of syndepositionally deformed chaotic deposits.

Hence (as a back-formation) **te·ctonize** *v. trans.*, to alter by tectonic processes; **te·ctonized** *ppl. a.*

1970 *Nature* 25 July 351/1 Sedimentary layers have been heavily tectonized. **1975** *Ibid.* 13 Feb. 521/2 Future work should also show whether the distribution of tectonised mantle inclusions in kimberlites is related to tectonic lineaments. **1977** A. HALLAM *Planet Earth* 204 In British Columbia the stratigraphy is less clear in the tectonized zone of the Rockies.

tectono- (tektǫno), comb. form of TECTONIC *a.*, TECTONICS, used in *Geol.*, as in **tecto:nophy·sics**, a branch of geophysics concerned with the forces that cause movement and deformation in the Earth's crust; so **tecto:nophy·sical** *a.*; **tecto:nophy·sicist**, a specialist in tectonophysics; **tecto·nosphere** (see quot. 1926); **tecto:nostratigra·phic** *a.*, of or pertaining to the correlation of rock formations with one another in terms of their connection with a tectonic event; **te:ctonothe·rmal** *a.*, involving both tectonism and geothermal activity.

1960 *Bull. Geol. Soc. Amer.* LXXI. 1255 (*heading*) Tectonophysical investigations. **1979** *Nature* 8 Feb. 495/1 Recently I have been involved in tectonophysical research in the Witwatersrand collar sequence of the Vredefort dome. **1957** *Bull. Geol. Soc. Amer.* LXVIII. 642/1 The various tectonophysicists..have sought to explain the mechanism of the deep-focus earthquakes associated with island arcs. **1978** *Nature* 26 Oct. 733/1 The mechanism by which stress is released in intermediate and deep focus earthquakes is of particular interest to seismologists and tectonophysicists. **1959** *Geosci. Abstr.* July 5/1 The author..theoretically proves the possibility of using scale models in tectonophysics. **1960** *Bull. Geol. Soc. Amer.* LXXI. 1255/1 To Soviet specialists, tectonophysics is a scientific trend dealing with investigations into the physical mechanism of tectonic deformations. Investigators in other countries use the term in a broader, less definite sense. **1971** *Nature* 26 Nov. 185/2 Geophysics as a discipline covers everything from cosmic rays to seismology by way of..tectonophysics and geomagnetism. **1926** G. W. TYRRELL *Princ. Petrol.* i. 2 The inaccessible heavy interior [of the earth] is known as the barysphere. This is followed outwardly by the lithosphere, the thin, rocky crust of the earth... Other zones have been distinguished and named for special purposes... The zone in which crustal movements originate has been named the tectonosphere by certain continental geologists. **1949** R. W. VAN BEMMELEN *Geol. of Indonesia* IA. iv. 283/2 The tectonosphere comprises three shells: the sial-, salsima- and sima- layers. **1971** M. H. P. BOTT *Interior of Earth* vii. 220 It is a well-established facet of isostatic theory that the weak asthenosphere is overlain by a relatively strong lithosphere (or tectonosphere) about 50–100 km thick. **1971** *Nature* 24 Sept. 246/2 The geology of the Scotia Arc region can be simplified by emphasizing what seem to us to be the fundamental tectonostratigraphic units. **1976** *Ibid.* 9 Sept. 117/2 Taking..the tectonostratigraphic evidence into consideration..an alternative model [of the origin of the Himalaya], based on plate tectonics, involving microcontinents, is suggested here. **1971** I. G. GASS et al. *Understanding Earth* xxii. 323/2 It seems likely that the relative paucity of major deposits of these ores is due to the modifying and/or dissipating influences of younger tectono-thermal activity. **1976** *Nature* 8 Apr. 516/2 It is significant that there is, as yet, no evidence for pre-Dalradian tectonothermal events affecting the Central Highland Granulites.

tectosilicate (te·ktosilikĕt). *Min.* Also **tekto-**. [ad. G. *tektosilikat* (H. Strunz 1938, in *Zeitschr. f. ges. Naturwiss.* IV. 189), f. Gr. τεκτο-νεῖα workshops (or τεκτο-νία carpentry), taken as = framework + G. *silikat* SILICATE.] Any of the group of silicates in which the four oxygen atoms of each SiO_4 tetrahedron are shared with four neighbouring tetrahedra in a three-dimensional framework, with a ratio of silicon to oxygen of 1:2.

1947 [see *PHYLLOSILICATE]. **1959** BERRY & MASON *Mineralogy* xv. 471 All the tektosilicates are colorless, white, or pale gray when free from inclusions. **1971** I. G. GASS et al. *Understanding Earth* i. 16/2 The feldspars and quartz are examples of tectosilicates (three-dimensional framework structures).

tectosphere (te·ktosfiᵊɹ). *Geol.* [f. Gr. τέκτ-ων, -ον- carpenter, builder + -o + SPHERE *sb.*] That part of the earth which moves in coherent sections during plate-tectonic activity (see quot. 1979[1]). Hence **tectosphe·ric** *a.*, of or pertaining to the tectosphere.

Tectosphere is sometimes confused in dicts. with *TEKTOSPHERE.

1968 *Jrnl. Geophysical Res.* LXXIII. 1980/2 The required strength [to maintain rigidity] cannot be in the crust alone; the oceanic crust is too thin for this. We instead favor a strong tectosphere, perhaps 100 km thick, sliding over a weak asthenosphere. **1969** W. M. ELSASSER in S. K. Runcorn *Applic. Mod. Physics to Earth & Planetary Interiors* 223 Horizontal sliding of the top layer, here called the 'tectosphere', can be more easily achieved than circulation in the material underneath. **1979** *Sci. Amer.* Jan. 76/3 Under the oceans the tectosphere and the lithosphere are..identical in spatial extent... Under the continents, however,..the cratonic tectosphere extends below the lithosphere, perhaps to depths of 400 kilometers or more. *Ibid.*, Tectospheric thickness also correlates with crustal age.

tectum (te·ktŏm). *Anat.* [L., = roof.] **a.** More fully *tectum mesencephali.* The roof of the midbrain, lying dorsal to the cerebral aqueduct.

1907 J. B. JOHNSTON *Nervous Syst. Vertebrates* xvi. 255 It must be remembered alway that the tectum opticum is only a part of the tectum mesencephali. **1921** TILNEY & RILEY *Form & Functions Central Nervous Syst.* xxviii. 487 Like other suprasegmental parts of the nervous system, the tectum is capable of great expansion to meet the demands of adaptation. **1979** *Sci. Amer.* Sept. 82/1 The mesencephalon..in mammals includes two pairs of structures that together form a region of four hills known as the lamina quadrigemina, the tectum mesencephali or simply the tectum.

b. More fully *optic tectum* (or *tectum opticum*). That part of the tectum mesencephali concerned with the functioning of the visual system.

1907 J. B. JOHNSTON *Nervous Syst. Vertebrates* viii. 147 Structure of the tectum opticum.—In the lower fishes the tectum contains a large number of cells of several forms. **1926** *Jrnl. Compar. Neurol.* XL. 217 The optic tectum far surpasses the cortical areas of the reptilian hemispheres. **1982** *Sci. Amer.* Mar. 104/3 The optic tectum, also known in mammals as the superior colliculus, is one of the major visual centers of the brain.

Hence **te·ctal** *a.*, of or pertaining to the tectum mesencephali or the optic tectum.

1926 *Jrnl. Compar. Neurol.* XL. 217 A group of nuclei which serve as way-stations between the tectal areas and other centers. **1974** *Sci. Amer.* Mar. 38/2 Recording from individual tectal neurons..tells one how the individual retinal ganglion cells that excite them are reacting. **1975** *Nature* 30 Oct. 738/1 In the vertebrates below mammals, the tectal and subtectal areas are the main centres of termination of sensory pathways.

Ted (ted), *sb.*[1] *Services' slang.* [Abbrev. of TEDESCO *sb.*] A German soldier. *Disused.*

1947 D. M. DAVIN *Gorse blooms Pale* 193 D'you know what those bloody Teds have been up to? They've been bloody well shelling us.

Ted (ted), *sb.*[2] Also with small initial. Short for *TEDDY BOY. Cf. *TEDDY 4.

1956 in I. & P. OPIE *Lore & Lang. Schoolch.* (1959) vii. 119 Joined the Teds when he was only three, Coshed a cop when he was only four. **1956** *Time* 24 Sept. 28/1 The Ted's notion of sartorial splendor ranges from a caricature of Edwardian elegance to the zoot padding of a Harlem hepcat. **1959** C. MACINNES *Absolute Beginners* 44 Appearing in a telly programme on the Ted question. **1968** *New Scientist* 11 July 64/3 The gangs [of baboons] appeared to carry out his orders, roaming through the troupe like a bunch of leather-jacketed teds. **1977** *Daily Tel.* 19 July 15 A Metropolitan magistrate complained yesterday that he had inadequate power to deal with gangs of 'punk rockers' and 'Teds' who clashed in the King's Road, Chelsea. **1980** *Daily Mirror* 10 Apr. 12/2 The term Ted is a little less popular nowadays, and Rockabilly is Eighties style.

Teddy. Also **teddy. 1.** Add to first sentence of def.: Short for *TEDDY BEAR 1. Freq. as a proper name for a teddy bear.

1907 *New England Mag.* July 629/2 The Teddy-bear.. suggests to the imaginative owner whatever special being his fancy would have 'Teddy' personify. **1910** *Postcard caption* [to picture of a little girl scrubbing a teddy bear.] You dirty Teddy. **1924** A. A. MILNE *When we were very Young* 90 Then said, 'Excuse me,' with an air, 'But is it Mr. Edward Bear?' And Teddy, bending very low, Replied politely, 'Even so!' **1934** E. TIETJENS in *Child Life* May 214/2, I always find things I'd forgotten, An old brown Teddy stuffed with cotton. **1940** D. WHEATLEY *Faked Passports* xxii. 262 It seemed a rotten business to shoot that harmless Bruin which was so reminiscent of a large teddy in a children's toyshop. **1960** *Sunday Times* 3 Jan. 30/3 My aunt..brought two brown teddies from Vienna in 1904, and in 1905 my mother bought me a white one in Ipswich. **1963** *Sunday Express* 10 Mar. 4/3 Look at teddy—he's got new fur. **1979** *Guardian* 14 June 12/3, I would rather fulfil my role as a mother than have a teddy act as a substitute.

2. [Perh. f. the name of *Theodore* Roosevelt.] (See quot. 1925.)

1917 E. POUND *Let.* 25 Aug. (1971) 118 The *Morning Chronicle* assures me my compatriots are called 'Teddies', which is one in the eye for Mr. Woodie Wilson. **1925** FRASER & GIBBONS *Soldier & Sailor Words* 279 *Teddies, the*, one of the names for the U.S. troops on first landing in France; disliked by the Americans equally with 'Sammies', and soon dropped.

3. orig. and chiefly *N. Amer.* [perh. *transf.* use of sense 1.] A woman's undergarment combining chemise and panties. Also in pl. *teddies.*

1924 H. C. WITWER in *Cosmopolitan* May 122/2 She added..she'd personally get enough enjoyment out of standing before her mirror garbed in a sheer silk teddy to warrant any sacrifice. **1929** *Amer. Speech* IV. 422 There is an article of feminine wearing apparel, a sort of overall piece of underwear, I believe, which is known as a *teddy*. I would suppose that this was so-called from its real or fancied resemblance in general shape (or shapelessness) to the teddy-bear. **1934** J. T. FARRELL *Young Manhood* (1936) xi. 298 Slug whispered to a big..blonde Polack in pink teddies. **1949** GILBRETH & CAREY *Cheaper by Dozen* xvii. 206 Anne..bought silk stockings, two short dresses and four flimsy pieces of underwear known as teddies. *Ibid.* 208 She doesn't even wear a teddy. **1977** *Hartford* (Conn.) *Courant* 6 June 24/4 Teddys are no longer synonymous with teddy bears alone. They also represent the sexiest lingerie around... The teddy is a camisole and tap pants set combined. The chemise bodice, often fashioned after a camisole, unbuttons either in the front or back... The all-in-one feature of teddys has made them more popular as sleepwear. **1978** *Chatelaine* Dec. 72/2 (*caption*) Left: A body-smoothing teddy with deep insets of lace by Emilio Pucci/Formfit Rogers, $30. **1983** *Daily Tel.* 17 Dec. 10/4 The silver satin 'teddy' we picture is one of this Christmas's best-sellers.

4. Short for *TEDDY BOY.

[**1955** *Britannica Bk. of Year* 489/2 *Teddy-boy*, *Teddy-gang* and *Edwardian* were terms used half derisively to describe youths who affected an Edwardian style of dress and who sometimes formed themselves into hooligan or criminal gangs.] **1956** *Saturday Bk.* 213 Our modern 'teddies' are named after their Edwardian clothes—dress in the manner of the times of King Edward VII—popularly known as 'King Teddy'. **1958** *People* 4 May 12/3 'He'd treat you real good,' said this Teddy. **1960** N. MITFORD *Don't tell Alfred* i. 8 His clothes had been distinctly on the Teddy side. **1963** J. FOWLES *Collector* ii. 165 We saw a group of teddies standing round two middle-aged Indians... The teddies were shouting, chivvying and bullying them off the pavement on to the road. **1968** [see *chukka boot* s.v. *CHUKKA].

teddy bear. 1. Add to note:

Theodore Roosevelt's bear-hunting expeditions occasioned a celebrated comic poem, accompanied by cartoons, in the *N.Y. Times* of 7 Jan. 1906, concerning the adventures of two bears named 'Teddy B' and 'Teddy G'; these names were transferred to two bears (also known as the 'Roosevelt bears') presented to Bronx Zoo in the same year; finally the fame of these bears was turned to advantage by toy dealers, whose toy 'Roosevelt bears', imported from Germany, became an instant fashion in the U.S.

(Earlier and later examples.) *teddy bears' picnic*, the title of a song (*c* 1932) by Jimmy Kennedy and J. W. Bratton, used allusively to denote an occasion of innocent enjoyment.

1906 *Amer. Stationer* 22 Sept. 18/2 Probably no novelty of recent years has been so popular as the Teddy Bears. **1907** *New England Mag.* July 629/1 The Teddy-bear has come, and one suspects that he has come to stay. **1922**, etc. [see *KEWPIE]. **1927** [see *BONZO]. **1948** *Parents' Mag.* Mar. 8/2 His gently gruff appearance is in best Teddy

Bear tradition. **1959** D. Beaty *Cone of Silence* xvii. 188 'Judd and George in the same cockpit together—' Dallas grunted. 'Must have been a Teddy Bear's picnic!' **1962** A. Lurie *Love & Friendship* I. viii. 160 What do you think I am, a Teddy bear, first you pick me up and then you put me down, whenever you feel like it? **1968** *Listener* 11 July 44/3 Can we go on indefinitely enjoying the fun of a teddy bears' picnic? **1977** R. Barnard *Death on High C's* iv. 41 You stop her and you'll have an industrial dispute on your hands that will make Lord Harewood's troubles look like the Teddy-bears' picnic.

b. *transf.* A person who resembles a teddy bear in appearance or in being lovable.

1957 K. Mann *(song-title)* (Let me be your) teddy bear. **1961** 'J. le Carré' *Call for Dead* i. 15 His débutante secretary..referred to him..as 'My darling teddy-bear'. **1972** *Radio Times* 1 Dec. 9/1 David Mercer..is a round, comfortable-looking man..a Teddy Bear with a..West Riding accent. **1979** P. Levi *Head in Soup* v. 93 He was an enormous teddy-bear of a man.

2. a. *U.S. slang.* A fur-lined high-altitude flying suit. Freq. *attrib.*

1917 *Let.* 24 Dec. in Hall & Nordhoff *Lafayette Flying Corps* (1920) II. 58 He has issued to him a fur-lined teddy-bear suit. **1920** E. Haslett *Luck on Wing* ix. 196, I immediately threw off my flying 'teddy bear' and hastily ran through my pockets. **1937** C. Codman *Contact* ii. 29 We issue forth..clad in fur-lined Teddy Bears and fleece-lined overshoes. **1968** J. J. Hudson *Hostile Skies* vii. 132 Lieutenant Horace Gilbert..received three bullets in his 'Teddy Bear' flying suit.

b. A heavy or furry coat; *spec.* one of natural-coloured alpaca-pile fabric. Usu. *attrib.*

1925 Fraser & Gibbons *Soldier & Sailor Words* 279 *Teddy bear*, the name given to the shaggy goatskin and fur coats issued for winter wear in the trenches in 1915. **1932** *Daily Tel.* 23 Sept. 13/2 [The Prince of Wales] was hatless and wore a heavy fawn 'Teddy Bear' overcoat. **1944** A. Thirkell *Headmistress* xii. 267 Mr. Adams, looking more thickset than ever in a thick Teddy Bear coat of orange-brown hue. **1965** P. Moyes *Johnny Under Ground* xviii. 210 He pulled his Teddy Bear greatcoat more closely round his plump form. **1979** 'P. O'Connor' *Into Strong City* I. xii. 35 A very tall man in a teddy-bear overcoat.

c. A furry fabric resembling plush. Usu. *attrib.*

1930 *Daily Express* 6 Oct. 5/1 (Advt.), Men's overcoats ... Lined with a teddy bear plush, to give extra warmth. **1977** *New Yorker* 11 July 77/1 Others showed full-blown psychedelic-playtime styles: a mini in canary-colored Teddy-bear pile. **1982** *Times* 2 Apr. 10/3 Teddy bear fur over skinny suede skirts.

3. Austral. rhyming slang for *lair *sb.*[4]

1953 S. J. Baker *Australia Speaks* v. 135 *Teddy bear*, a flashily-dressed, exhibitionistic person; by rhyme on *lair*. **1965** W. Grout *My Country's 'Keeper* 55 Umpire Col Egar was so furious at this amateurish attempt at time-wasting that he snapped to the Pakistani bowler: 'Get up you Teddy Bear' (an Australian expression not meant to be complimentary). **1974** K. Stackpole *Not just for Openers* 128 When Parfitt made the catch Greig jumped in the air, and, as he landed, thumped his fist into the pitch... I said to Greig as I walked past, 'You're nothing but a bloody Teddy Bear.' He returned the pleasantries.

4. = *Teddy 3.

1978 *Maledicta 1977* I. 273 Priorly, she had begun to haul out of the hour-glass corset into teddy-bear and slip. **1979** *Amer. Speech 1976* LI. 8 The new underwear was a convenient garment, a hip-length *chemise* with a narrow strap between the thighs which was secured by two small buttons or snaps. It was affectionately known first as a *teddy-bear*, then as a *teddy* or *shimmy*.

Hence **teddy-bearish** *a.*, resembling a teddy bear.

1973 *Guardian* 9 Mar. 17/1 Tall, dark, teddy-bearish, charming and persuasive. *a* **1976** A. Christie *Autobiogr.* (1977) IX. iii. 451 They took on board eight or ten darling little brown bears... Completely teddy-bearish.

Teddy boy (te·di boi). *colloq.* [f. *Teddy*, pet-form of *Edward* (VII), with reference to the style of dress (cf. *Edwardian *sb.* 3) + Boy *sb.*[1]] A youth affecting a style of dress and appearance held to be characteristic of Edward VII's reign, typically a long velvet-collared jacket and 'drain-pipe' trousers (see *drape suit* s.v. *drape *sb.*[1] d) and sideburns; in extended use, any youthful street rowdy. Hence **Te·ddy-boyish** *a.*, characteristic of a Teddy boy; **Te·ddy-boyism**, the state or condition of being a Teddy boy; group behaviour of a kind associated with Teddy boys. Similarly **Teddy girl**, a girl who associates with or behaves like Teddy boys.

1954 A. Heckstall-Smith *Eighteen Months* x. 118 Craig was just such a fellow. Ronald Coleman, the leader of the 'Edwardians' or the 'Teddy Boys', the gang of young hooligans who ran amok on Clapham Common, was another. **1955** in I. & P. Opie *Lore & Lang. Schoolch.* (1959) vii. 106 Slip-on shoes and a rainbow tie, Kissing his Teddy girl goodbye! **1955** *Times* 27 July 5/1 Young soldiers are now forbidden to 'walk out' when off duty in plain clothes of unorthodox pattern, particularly the so-called Edwardian or 'Teddy boy' style... The forbidden style is not specifically defined in the order but is understood to be that of the long, draped-fronted jacket with velvet collar, and tight trousers shortened to show white socks at the ankles. **1957** *Sunday Times* 17 Feb. 4/4 The girls who are an integral part of the gangs—the so-called Teddy-girls—are probably the worst influence of all. **1959** *Times* 9 Oct. 15/7 The growing tide of teddy-boyism, chiefly in the Athens-Piraeus area, forced the authorities to act. **1960** *Guardian* 7 May 6/6 Looking back with teddy-boyish anger. **1960** *News Chron.* 9 June 9/1 We should not consider them as Teddy boys or Teddy girls, but potential customers. **1962** [see *slim jim 3]. **1977** *Daily Tel.* 19 July 15/4 A group of about 40 'punk rockers' being chased by Teddy boys.

Tedesco, var. *Tudesco.

tediosity. For † read *rare* and add later examples.

1790 J. Byng *Diary* 18 July (1935) II. 257 They are sad sluggards: Mrs. B. most idly breakfasts in bed; C[ec]y is tediocity. **1934** *Jrnl. Theol. Stud.* XXXV. 289 In spite of his tediosity, however, his books present some interesting and picturesque features.

tee, *sb.*[1] Add: **I. 1. b.** Phr. *to a tee*: see T i. c.

4. *tee beam, joint* (examples), *section, slot.*

1888 *Lockwood's Dict. Mech. Engin.* 368 *Tee joint*, a welded joint employed for uniting pieces of bar iron standing at right angles with each other. *Ibid.*, *Tee shots*, slots or grooves cast in the tables of planing, shaping, slotting, and drilling machines for carrying the heads of tee-headed bolts. **1930** *Engineering* 9 May 591/1 *(title)* Simplified formulae for the design of reinforced concrete tee beams. **1963** Jones & Schubert *Engin. Encycl.* 1278 *Tee section*, the standard structural section known as a tee has a T shape. **1964** S. Crawford *Basic Engin. Processes* iii. 93 The down-hand fillet or tee joint is shown in Fig. 14 (a). *Ibid.* v. 116 A circular tee-slot machined in the top face of the centre-slide provides movement for the heads of the clamping bolts. **1965** R. Hammond *Dict. Civil Engin.* 228 *Tee-beam*, a rolled steel section..in the shape of the letter T, the flat top being the table.

tee, *sb.*[2] Add: Now usu. a wooden or plastic peg with a concave top; also called *tee-peg* or *peg-tee*. *tee shot* (earlier example).

1921 *Daily Colonist* (Victoria, B.C.) 9 Oct. 11/6 Golf clubs..bags, balls, tees, [etc.]. **1926** *Amer. Speech* I. 631/2 There are also tees of rubber, and recently wooden pegs on which balls may be teed have come into vogue. **1952** L. T. Stanley *Woman Golfer* 53 Many players prefer to play iron shots to a short hole off a peg-tee. **1959** D. Thomas *Instructions to Young Golfers* xix. 106 He takes a ball.., places it on a tee-peg..and..smites it a good fifty yards. **1962** *Times* 3 Jan. 3/6 The only indication of a satisfactory hit is the speed with which the striker bends down to recover his tee. **1975** *Oxf. Compan. Sports & Games* 422/2 It is usual for the first shot at each hole to be played off a wooden or plastic tee-peg... The tee-peg was invented in 1920 by Lowel of New Jersey.

1862 R. Chambers *Rambling Remarks* 14 The tee-shots are usually the furthest, long drivers being able to send a ball upwards of two hundred yards.

tee, *v.*[3] Add: **1. a.** Also with *up*. Hence *intr.* with *up*: to place a ball on a tee; (*transf.*) to prepare to play.

1906 [in Dict.]. **1906** J. Braid *Golf Guide* v. 34 It is not a good thing to tee up very near to the teeing-box. **1960** *Times* 3 Feb. 15/7 [Rugby] As Pennington tee-ed up, the Thomas's touch judge..was leaning against one of the uprights. **1975** *Daily Tel.* (Colour Suppl.) 12 Sept. 9/4 The players are allowed to tee up every shot, since the ball may land in a tree or a pile of rocks.

b. Also *transf.*, to begin a game or performance.

1961 A. Berkman *Singers' Gloss. Show Business Jargon* 86 *Tee off*, to open the show. **1974** *Spartanburg* (S. Carolina) *Herald* 18 Apr. c2/2 Coluccio teed off on a 3–1 offering from the reliever.

2. *fig.* **a.** Chiefly *trans.* with *up*: to make ready, to arrange. *colloq.*

1938 Partridge *World of Words* ix. 269 Modern sports have provided us with..few words but a very fair 'bag' of phrases..*tee up*..from golf. **1941** [see *promote v. 8]. **1943** C. H. Ward-Jackson *It's a Piece of Cake* 60 *Teed up*, all set to start. **1958** N. Culotta *They're a Weird Mob* iii. 34, I gotta go an' see about all that metal an' stuff, an' tee up the mixer. **1961** 'J. le Carré' *Call for Dead* vii. 78, I left the car out in the yard, full of petrol and teed up. **1973** *Times* 22 Jan. 19/1 Initially he will go to the capitals of the member states for talks with central governments and to tee up trips to problem areas.

b. [Prob. *euphem.* alteration of *peed off* (=*pissed off*: see *piss *v.* 3 c).] *trans.* with *off*: to anger, annoy, irritate. Hence **teed off** *ppl. a.*, angry, annoyed, disgruntled, indignant. *N. Amer. slang.*

1955 *Amer. Speech* XXX. 120 *Teed off*.., angry, indignant. **1961** *Lebende Sprachen* VI. 100/1 Don't tee him off,..raise his dander, get his Irish up. **1963** D. Hughes *Expendable Man* i. 22 You're teed off at me, aren't you? **1969** C. F. Burke *God is Beautiful, Man* (1970) 34 Well this makes old Pharaoh really teed off. So he gets his army and he says, 'Get 'em.' **1977** *New Yorker* 27 June 68/2 Frankly, it just tees me off. I consider them to be a god-damned curse. **1981** G. V. Higgins *Rat on Fire* xvii. 119 He is kind of teed off... I mean, this man is *angry*.

c. *intr.* with *off* (const. *on*): to hit out at, attack, reprimand, criticize severely. *U.S. slang.*

1955 H. Kurnitz *Invasion of Privacy* (1956) i. 10, I thought you were about to tee off on Ben... Let's both stop making cracks. **1976** *Billings* (Montana) *Gaz.* 4 July 2-e/1 Our country is not at war. Despite all the sabre rattling.., the nation is not about to tee off on another nation, large or small.

teeack (tī·ək). *Ork. dial.* Also **teaoo, teeock, teeoo.** [Echoic: cf. Tewhit, tewit.] = Lapwing.

1869 D. Gorrie *Summers & Winters in Orkneys* (ed. 2) v. 194 The plaint of teeacks..blended finely with the shrill pipings of shore-birds. **1884** D. W. Yair in D. H. Edwards *Mod. Scot. Poets* VII. 248 Teeocks, bleatin', skimmed alang. **1909** *Old-Lore Misc.* II. i. 29 Like a doo or a teaoo. **1927** H. Campbell *Jean's Garden* 26 The teeoos crying ower the brecks. **1969** G. M. Brown *Orkney Tapestry* 97 That's a plover... There's a teeack.

teebee, var. *tepee.

teem, *v.*[2] Add: **1. d.** To drain the water off (boiled potatoes, etc.).

1890 in *Eng. Dial. Dict.* (1905) VI. s.v., sense 8. **1922** Joyce *Ulysses* 751 Wouldnt even teem the potatoes for you of course shes right not to ruin her hands. **1982** P. McGinley *Goosefoot* xiii. 210 'The potatoes are done.'.. 'When you've teemed them, we'll all guess the number in the pot.'

2. No longer *dial.* when used with reference to rain. (Later examples.)

Perh. associated with Teem *v.*[1] 3.

1979 J. Grimond *Memoirs* vii. 105 The rain which seemed to teem down incessantly. **1981** G. Boycott *In Fast Lane* v. 22 Not just a drop or a shower but three clammy inches in forty-eight hours, teeming out of a slate-grey sky.

teeming, *vbl. sb.*[2] Add: **2.** Phr. *teeming and lading* (lit. 'unloading and loading'): see quot. 1937. *slang.*

1937 Partridge *Dict. Slang* 869/2 *Teeming and lading*, accountants' slang. 'Using cash received to-day to make up cash embezzled yesterday.' **1957** J. Braine *Room at Top* v. 45 He'd made a dreadful mess of his Cash and Deposits book; such a mess that for a moment I suspected him of teeming and lading. **1979** *Financial Times* 18 May 8/5 Mr Jaggard had..covered the theft by 'accelerating the banking of cheques received in a subsequent accounting period' and later falsifying records—a practice known among accountants as 'teeming and lading'.

teeming, *ppl. a.*[2] For 'Now *dial.*' read 'Now *dial.* except with reference to rain', and add later example.

1955 *Times* 14 May 4/1 Teeming rain ushered in the evening session, but stopped before the arrival of the Queen, who drove round the ring on her arrival.

teen, *sb.*[2] Add: **1. b.** For ǀ**1820** in quot. read ǀ**1818**. Now in revived (chiefly *N. Amer.*) use as a *sb.* used in both *sing.* and *pl.* and apprehended as short for *teenager. Freq. *attrib.* and *Comb.*

1951 *Deseret News* (Salt Lake City) 30 July F-1/1 Doing something fun like redecorating your room..is really interesting biz for a teen who loves being busy. **1959** *Charlottesville* (Va.) *Daily Progress* 18 Aug. 11/2 Today's teens spend money carefully. **1971** *Daily Colonist* (Victoria, B.C.) 30 June 20/3 When a teen leaves home it almost never works out well to call the law and have the kid dragged home. **1978** *Chicago* June 179/1 If you're over 21, you can make a significant contribution by taking an abandoned teen, 16–20 years old, into your home.

attrib. and *Comb.* **1945** *Britannica Bk. of Year* 771/2 *Teen can, teen canteen, teen town*, recreation centre for teen-agers (1944). **1948** *Observer* 28 Mar. 1/7 (Advt.), Teen girls' frocks in a lovely crepe. **1957** *Sun* (Baltimore) 15 Feb. 29/3 The Baltimore Highlands School..had been used..for Friday night dances by a local teen-center. **1960** *Vogue Pattern Bk.* Early Autumn 64 Formula for teen chic. **1967** *Crescendo* Oct. 25 Bob Miller, who has successfully promoted his band in the 'teen-beat field. **1969** N. Cohn *AWopBopaLooBop* (1970) xviii. 170 He chronicled teen lives better than anyong since Eddie Cochran. **1972** *Jazz & Blues* Sept. 12/2 The lyrics became more 'teen-orientated'. **1976** *National Observer* (U.S.) 17 Apr. 17/1 The small red mouth of an eager teen princess. **1977** *Sounds* 1 Jan. 2/4 The 32-year-old teen idol. **1977** *Time Out* 17–23 June 9/2 Irresistibly melodic teendream romance. **1979–80** *Verbatim* Winter 7/1 Teen-crammed schoolbuses. **1980** *Daily Tel.* 25 June 17/1 It takes little investigation of British teen magazines to see that there is a big gap in the market.

2. (Later examples.) Also, years, temperatures, pay, etc., measured in quantities which end in *-teen*.

1932 *Times Lit. Suppl.* 7 July 493/1 Books of the 'teens and early twenties of the last century. **1958** *Listener* 4 Dec. 944/1 In the teens and twenties of this century. **1966** E. P. Hamp in Birnbaum & Puhvel *Ancient Indo-Europ. Dial.* 119 The syntax of the 'teens of the numerals. **1977** *Chicago Tribune* 2 Oct. xii. 59/9 (Advt.), This position may be of interest to you if your current salary is in the upper teens. **1981** *Northeast Woods & Waters* Jan. 11/1 With the mercury plunging into the teens for five nights, the entire river valley was iced-in.

teenage (tī·n,ēⁱdʒ), *a.* and *sb.*[2] orig. *N. Amer.* Also **teen-age, teen age.** [f. Teen *sb.*[2] + Age *sb.*] **A.** *adj.* **1.** Designating someone in their teens.

1921 *Daily Colonist* (Victoria, B.C.) 11 Mar. 8/2 All 'teen age' girls of the city are cordially invited to attend the mass meeting to be held this evening. **1935** *Amer. Speech* X. 192/1 The dress is probably slinky and suitable for the teen-age group. **1948** *Evening Standard* 22 Mar. 6/4 The teen-age twins..reject severe masculine fashions. **1957** *Time* 2 Sept. 62/2 Starting as a teen-age bank runner, he had become president of the Bank of Commerce. **1977** *Dædalus* Fall 83 Society may wish to eliminate teenage street corner gangs, but this does not lead sociologists to write articles on the optimal techniques for eliminating such gangs.

2. Pertaining to, suitable for, or characteristic of a young person in his or her teens.

1942 *Amer. Speech* XVII. 41 Teen age hats now on sale. Teenage apparel of all types. **1950** N. Streatfeild *Mothering Sunday* 200 All those sweetly pretty teen-age frocks. **1967** M. Argyle *Psychol. Interpersonal Behaviour* viii. 140 They [*sc.* normal adolescents] too show a tremendous conformity to the group, for example in clothes, and in the use of teenage slang. **1979** L. Meynell *Hooky & Villainous Chauffeur* i. 14 The first time I ever saw Maude..was at some teenage party.

B. *sb.*² (Usu. as two words.) The period of a person's life between the ages of thirteen and nineteen inclusive, the teens; an age falling between these limits.

1934 Webster s.v. *Teen* adj., Boys of teen age. **1941** *Jrnl. Pediatrics* XIX. 392 The pediatrician's almost unrestricted field..begins shortly after the birth of his patient and does not terminate until the 'teen' age is well advanced. **1973** M. Amis *Rachel Papers* 8 Five hours of teenage to go... Then I wander into that noisome Brobdingnagian world the child sees as adulthood. **1973** *Sci. Amer.* Dec. 135/3 Readers of teen age and beyond will find in its plain language and concrete situations a smooth path to an ethical discussion as deepgoing as the dilemmas of life and death.

Hence **tee·naged** *a.*, of teen age; so **tee·naged-ness.**

1952 *Listener* 31 Jan. 183/1, I hope that modern youth enter 'teen-agedness' with a suitably elated conviction of its own self-importance. **1953** Berrey & Van den Bark *Amer. Thes. Slang* (1954) §383/1 The teenaged set;..a teenaged person. **1971** J. Gray *Red Lights on Prairies* i. 10 In one two-roomed house there was a family of seven, including teen-aged boys and girls. **1981** *Times* 4 Mar. 6/5 A teenaged schoolboy ambulance driver.

teenager (tī·nē¹dʒəɹ). orig. *U.S.* Also **teen-ager.** [f. prec. + -er¹.] One who is in his or her teens; *loosely*, an adolescent.

1941 *Pop. Sci. Monthly* Apr. 223/2, I never knew teen-agers could be so serious. **1947** Auden *Age of Anxiety* (1948) i. 26 Tops in tests by teen-agers. **1952** M. Steen *Phoenix Rising* ii. 38 Do we have to behave like a couple of hysterical 'teen-agers? **1960** K. Amis *Take Girl like You* xxii. 260 Jenny thought to herself that here she was nearly twenty-one, and instead of having been a teenager all she had managed to do was spend a certain amount of time getting from the age of twelve to the age of twenty. **1962** *Guardian* 21 Sept. 11/7 He must be constantly new and different to be able to please the younger teenagers. And 'teenagers' start at the age of nine. **1980** *Times Lit. Suppl.* 15 Aug. 908/1 Teenagers, of course, had not been invented in the 1880s.

teener. (In Dict. s.v. Teen *sb.*²) Add: *U.S.* (Later examples.)

1947 *Richmond* (Va.) *Times-Dispatch* 30 Aug. 7/8 (*heading*) Teener told married life is no game. **1956** *Sun* (Baltimore) 27 Oct. 7/6 Attention, teeners! Come meet these Young Jr. Board members. **1979–80** *Verbatim* Winter 7/1 I've heard things from teeners that widened my education considerably.

teensy (tī·nzi), *a. colloq.* (orig. *U.S. dial.*). Also **teenzy.** [prob. f. Teeny *a.*² + -sy.] = Teeny *a.*² Also in Comb. or redupl. form **teensy-weensy, teensie-weensie,** etc. = *teeny-weeny* (see Teeny *a.*²).

1899 in H. Wentworth *Amer. Dial. Dict.* (1944) 626/1 Little teensy bit of a boy. **1902** W. N. Harben *Abner Daniel* 197 Then Jimmy's young wife come with her little teensy baby. **1906** in H. Wentworth *Amer. Dial. Dict.* (1944) 626/1 Teentsy-weentsy. **1933** O. Nash in *Sat. Even. Post* 2 Sept. 58/4 For the word was out, In palace and cot, Of the teensy, weensy, talented tot. **1951** 'J. Tey' *Daughter of Time* i. 12 Didn't you even try a little teensy taste? **1966** [see *off *adv.* 1 g]. **1973** *Times* 21 Aug. 13/7 The statement as it stands is..just a teensie-weensie bit unfair to my own firm. **1973** P. White *Eye of Storm* xii. 592 He ordered himself another teenzy bottle of Scotch. **1981** S. Strutt *On Edge of Love* vi. 116 'Would you like a drink?'..'Darling, that would be lovely. Perhaps just a teensy one!'

teenty, *a. U.S. colloq.* Add: (Earlier examples.) Also **teenty-taunty, teenty-tointy** *adjs.*

1844 'J. Slick' *High Life N.Y.* II. 227 A little teenty tointy handful of wood keeps 'em [*sc.* stoves] warm as blazes. *Ibid.* 230 Then she took up one teenty glove. **1863** A. D. Whitney *Faith Gartney's Girlhood* v. 46 She would open the window a 'teenty little crack'. **1863** *Harper's Mag.* Dec. 112/2 A pretty little teenty-taunty babe as ever you see.

teeny, *a.*² Add: No longer restricted to childish use. Also as *sb.* (Earlier U.S. and later examples.) **teeny-weeny** (later examples); also as *sb.*

1825 J. Neal *Bro. Jonathan* I. 342 A leetle—teeny, mischievous, good for nothin'. **1929** [see *Kerry 2]. **1931** *Daily Express* 1 Sept. 5/1 But never cold ham and tongue for the tiny 'teenies'. **1931** E. V. Lucas *Visibility Good* 18 Model tea-sets, and all the other teeny weenies. **1948** [see *bird-brain* s.v. *bird *sb.* 9]. **1953** [see *fly-whisk* s.v. *fly *sb.*¹ 11]. **1957** [see *itsy-bitsy *a.*]. **1966** [see *brandade]. **1970** *Oxf. Mail* 27 Jan. 1/9 Today at Courreges in Paris we had teenie-weenie nappies knotted loosely on the loins. **1982** *New Yorker* 17 May 34/1 Their [videodisc] system has a teeny laser beam instead of a needle to get the images onto the TV screen.

teeny (tī·ni), *sb. colloq.* Also **teeney.** [f. as, or abbrev. of, *teeny-bopper but infl. by Teeny *a.*²] A young teenager or pre-teenager, esp. one who is a fan of pop music; a teeny-bopper.

1969 *Oz* Apr. 40/1 A good part of that audience was composed of teeneys, nine to twelve year olds. **1976** *N.Y. Times* 29 July 26 He's [*sc.* 16-year-old Prince Andrew] the biggest thing for teenies since Bjorn Borg. **1977** *Daily Mirror* 21 Mar. 13/3 Teenies find hot line to hope... In 1976 at least 8,000 new callers were under fifteen.

teenybop (tī·nibǫp), *a. colloq.* [Back-formation from next.] Of, pertaining to, or consisting of teeny-boppers.

[**1966** *Current Slang* (Univ. S. Dakota) Winter 3 Teeny-bop, teeny-bopper, high school student who carefully adheres to fads.] **1967** *Observer* 1 Oct. 3/3 We hope it will have more than a teeny-bop audience. **1979** *Fortune* 23 Apr. 65/1 The three British-born Bee Gee brothers, whose recent success has overshadowed the considerable fame they achieved as teenybop idols in the mid-Sixties. **1969** N. Cohn *AWopBopaLooBop* (1970) xxi. 201 They grew their hair long and dressed like teenybop tramps.

teeny-bopper (tī·nibǫ:pəɹ). *colloq.* Also as one word. [f. Teen *sb.*² or *teen(ager + -y⁶ + *bopper and infl. by Teeny *a.*²] A girl in her teens or younger, esp. one who is a fan of pop music and follows the latest fashions.

1966 *Telegraph* (Austral.) 12 Oct. 58/3 The teenybopper is aptly named because her two distinguishing features are her teeny size and her cool boppy with-it attitude to life. **1967** *Punch* 6 Dec. 847/1 To protest about long-haired commies or mini-skirted teenyboppers. **1969** Fabian & Byrne *Groupie* (1970) v. 35, I..suffered paranoid fantasies about him pulling lots of teeny-boppers and groupies when he was away on gigs. **1977** *Time* 18 Apr. 39/1 David Cassidy, 26, teeny-bopper heartthrob who sang his way to rock stardom. **1979** *Guardian* 4 Aug. 19/3 'I think we should be paid for going to school.' Thus my teenybopper daughter.

tee-off (tī-ˌǫf). [f. the vbl. phr. *to tee off*: see Tee *v.*³ b.] The start of play in Golf; now also in other sports.

1952 *Sun* (Baltimore) 19 June (B ed.) 19/1 Boros.. dropped his bombshell an hour before his scheduled 1.52 P.M. teeoff. **1978** *Cornish Guardian* 27 Apr. 5/6 Tee-off on Sunday is at 10.30 when the two teams will play nine holes.

Teepol (tī·pǫl). [prob. f. Tee *sb.*¹ + *p* (repr. initial letters of the name of the orig. manufacturer) + -ol 3.] The proprietary name of an alkyl sulphate industrial detergent obtained by reacting olefins with sulphuric acid and neutralizing the products.

1942 *Progress Appl. Chem.* XXVII. 81 A synthetic detergent, Teepol..is being manufactured from a petroleum fraction. **1942** *Trade Marks Jrnl.* 9 Dec. 514/1 *Teepol*... Detergents. Technical Products Limited, 29, Great St. Helens, London, E.C.3. **1945** *Official Gaz.* (U.S. Patent Office) 10 July 171/2 Shell Union Oil Corporation, San Francisco... *Teepol* for detergent preparation for the cleaning of fabrics..and ceramics. **1976** *Nature* 3 June 406/1 The section [of rock] was first cleaned with 'Teepol' to remove all grease or immersion oil.

tee-shirt, tee-shirted: see *T-shirt.

Teeswater (tī·zwǭ:təɹ). [f. the name of the *Teeswater* district in County Durham.] **1.** Used *attrib.* and *absol.* to designate a breed of long-wool sheep, originally developed in the Tees valley and recently revived; also, a sheep of this breed.

1786 G. Culley *Obs. Live Stock* 82 The Tees-water breed..differs from the Lincolnshire, in their wool not being so long and heavy. **1837** W. Youatt *Sheep* viii. 329 The wool of the Teeswater sheep was remarkably long and coarse. **1861** Mrs. Beeton *Bk. Househ. Managem.* 323 The domesticated sheep..embracing..the Old Leicester, and the Teeswater, or New Leicester. **1951** A. Fraser *Sheep Husbandry* (ed. 2) ii. 67 A local breed, the Teeswater Mug, is coming into greater prominence. **1967** *Brit. Sheep Breeds* (Brit. Wool Marketing Board) 69/1 The Teeswater ram has been found to cross extremely well with hill breeds. **1979** *Country Life* 6 Dec. 2228/3 The Longwool breeds being farmed in Britain today—the Teeswater, Romney and Leicesters are among the other best-known names.

2. *attrib.* = Shorthorn.

1810 J. Bailey *Gen. View Agric. Co. Durham* xiv. 226 The short-horned kind..have for a great many years been known by the appellation of the Tees Water Breed. **1873** G. Armatage *Cattle* i. 9 These fine animals appear to have descended from the Teeswater breed. **1919** K. J. J. Mackenzie *Cattle* vii. 74 The bulk of the Teeswater or Holderness herds..were very famous for their milking qualities. **1950** G. T. Burrows *Hist. Dairy Shorthorn Cattle* i. 11 Men..believed in the dual-purpose merits of their 'Teeswater' breed.

teetee¹: see *titi.²

teeter, *sb.* Add: **1.** (Earlier example.) **teeter-board** (earlier example): also *spec.* in circus use.

1855 *Knickerbocker* XLVI. 88 We were having a grand time with our 'teeter'-boards upon the highest fence. **1863** *Harper's Mag.* Aug. 343/2 Teeters to jump on, rings to swing by. **1965** *Sun* 26 Oct. 5/1 The Seven Halasi, a Hungarian family using teeter boards. **1979** *Times* 13 Dec. 7/6 The Kovatchevi troupe..will..bounce a performer from a teeter-board to the shoulders of the top performer.

2. For 'See quot.' read: The spotted sandpiper, *Actitis macularia*, found in eastern North America. (Earlier and later examples.)

1842 J. E. DeKay *Zool. N.Y.* i. 247 The Spotted Sand-Lark..is known..[as] Teeter and Tiltup, from its often repeated grotesque jerking motions. **1895** *Outing* XXXVII. 69/2 The 'teeter' is fat and well flavored.

teeter, *v.* Restrict *dial.* and *U.S.* to senses 1 a and 2 and add: **1. a.** (Example.)

1843 Mrs. Stowe *Mayflower* 47 Then he was tetering [**1855** *ed.*: teetering] with her on a long board.

b. (Earlier and later examples, chiefly of persons.)

1844 'J. Slick' *High Life N.Y.* II. 231, I teetered up tu her a tiptoe. **1943** C. McCullers *Heart is Lonely Hunter* i. 29 They helped Blount to his feet. He teetered weakly. **1950** R. Macaulay *World my Wilderness* vii. 66 The iron spokes swung teetering and creaking in the breeze. **1961** B. Pym *No Fond Return of Love* xii. 111 Marian left the house, teetering down the path to the bus stop on her stiletto heels. **1973** O. Sacks *Awakenings* 35 Miss D. would teeter forward in tiny rapid steps. **1982** T. Berger *Reinhart's Women* ii. 35 'I'll teeter on the curb,' said Reinhart, 'and try not to fall into the gutter.'

c. Also *fig.*, esp. in phr. *to teeter on the brink* and varr.

1902 A. H. Lewis *Wolfville Nights* xvii. 259 A quorum of the committee is away teeterin' about in their own affairs. **1930** *Punch* 26 Feb. 237/1, I really have not time to go into the whole story now... I will quit stalling lest I teeter. **1937** 'G. Orwell' *Road to Wigan Pier* xiii. 261 Every bank clerk dreaming of the sack, every shopkeeper teetering on the brink of bankruptcy, is in essentially the same position. **1949** *Times* 29 Sept. 5/2 The Government ..still tremble and teeter on the verge. **1958** *Daily Sketch* 2 June 13/7 He effectively suggested an officer teetering on the edge of sanity. **1979** C. James *Pillars of Hercules* i. i. 25 He was teetering on the verge of declaring himself outright. **1980** D. Adams *Restaurant at End of Universe* iii. 25 Zaphod felt he was teetering on the edge of madness. **1983** *Brit. Med. Jrnl.* 23 July 279/2 Subsistence farming is widespread with nutrition teetering on the inadequate.

3. teeter-tail (examples).

1917 *Dialect Notes* IV. 424 The spotted sandpiper..also called swee-swee, teeter-tail. **1937** *National Geogr. Mag.* Aug. 201/2 Spotted Sandpiper... Nearly every pond, stream, or lake shore has its 'tip-up' or 'teeter-tail', as it is familiarly called.

teetering *vbl. sb.* and *ppl. a.* (earlier U.S. and later examples).

1845 C. M. Kirkland *Western Clearings* 213, I laid a teterin' board over it, so that if you stepped on it, down you went. **1851** H. Melville *Moby Dick* III. xxxviii. 218 The tetering ship loweringly pitched down her bowsprit. **1855** —— *Israel Potter* xiv. 147 Israel smote him over the taffrail into the sea, as if the man had fallen backwards over a teetering chair. **1936** M. Allingham *Flowers for Judge* xiv. 202 He was lying on his face with a teetering, kicking thing trying to force him through the concrete floor. **1973** 'M. Innes' *Appleby's Answer* iii. xv. 129 The tea-shop was..kept by teetering old ladies in the interest of their health. **1975** in W. Viereck *Lexikalische Ergebnisse des Lowman-Survey* I. iv. 141 Children also like to play on a..teetering pole.

teeter-totter (tī·təɹ,tǫ:təɹ), *sb.* (and *a.*). *dial.* and *N. Amer.* [Reduplication from stem of Teeter *v.* or Totter *v.*; cf. Titter-totter *sb.* (*adv.*) and *teeter-totter* (vb.) s.v. Teeter *v.* 1 b.] A see-saw; formerly also, the game of see-saw. Also *attrib.* or as *adj.*

[**1895** W. Rye *Gloss. Words E. Anglia* 225 *Teeter-cum-tauter*, a see-saw.] **1905** *Dialect Notes* III. 66 *Teeter-totter, n.* or *v.* See-saw. 'We played teeter-totter.' **1933** *Sun* (Baltimore) 19 Aug. 2/6 Wallace explained the teeter-totter economics of hogs and corn made a solution more difficult, and said the Government had waited for the farmers themselves to produce a plan. **1959** *A. Hitchcock's Mystery Mag.* Feb. 70/2 Her body, which had bounced off a section of hedge onto the fulcrum of a teeter-totter. **1962** W. O. Mitchell *Kite* xv. 197 Got to balance exactly..like two boys on a teeter-totter—same weight to the ounce. **1973** *Jrnl. Genetic Psychol.* June 289 A teeter-totter task and water-level apparatus. **1975** in W. Viereck *Lexikalische Ergebnisse des Lowman-Survey* I. iv. 141 Children also like to play on a...teeter-totter.

teetery (tī·təri), *a.* [f. Teeter *v.* + -y¹.] Tottery, insecure; faint, unsteady.

1900 *N.Y. Jrnl.* 25 Nov. 59/2 An attendant was there to help you off if you felt teetery or uncertain. **1905** R. Beach *Pardners* (1912) i. 34 The orchestra spieled some teetery music. **1935** H. Davis *Honey in Horn* ii. 17 Dogged if I didn't feel teetery to look at it. **1936** 'J. Tey' *Shilling for Candles* vii. 86 My shoes..I feel dreadful in them. Teetery. **1979** *Amer. Poetry Rev.* Mar.-Apr. 45/1 Above the stalks—whole islands teetery over the wasting pedestals, natural bulwarks lifting them free from heavy swells and pounding surf.

teether (tī·ðəɹ). [f. Teethe *v.* + -er¹.] A small object for an infant to bite on while teething; a teething ring.

1949 M. Mead *Male & Female* xiii. 272 Mother is there to put things—bottles, spoons, crackers, teethers—into your mouth. **1966** A. Price *Generous Man* (1967) ii. 177

She touched her breasts..and Milo said, 'They must have got a heap of exercise since then.'..'If acting as teethers for a middle-aged man with false teeth anyhow is your idea of exercise, they have.' **1974** *Daily Colonist* (Victoria, B.C.) 28 Sept. 21/5 Two of her bells were originally babies' rattles. They are rattle-shaped with tiny bells surrounding the metal body, a teether of either agate or coral as the handle.

teething, *vbl. sb.* Add: **3.** *teething stage* (fig.); **teething powder** (examples); **teething ring,** a small ring or disc for an infant to bite on while teething; **teething troubles** *fig.*, problems arising in the early stages of an enterprise.

1869 *Bradshaw's Railway Man.* XXI. App. 102 Pritchard's teething and fever powders, for..children cutting their teeth. **1872** 'MARK TWAIN' *Roughing It* xv. 125 Soothing-syrup! Teething-rings! **1937** *Jrnl. R. Aeronaut. Soc.* XLI. 917 The dynamometer had now been in use for eight or nine months. It was not quite free from small 'teething' troubles. **1954** 'N. SHUTE' *Slide Rule* iv. 92 These were the inevitable teething troubles of any very large aircraft. **1959** *Observer* 19 Apr. 5/3 They speculated on whether Britain should jump the 'teething' stage of supersonic airliners and concentrate on producing an adult machine in twenty years' time. **1967** *Guardian* 21 Sept. 3/4 It was highly likely that many 'corner shops' still contained stocks of teething powders containing mercury. **1980** 'J. BELL' *Question of Inheritance* i. 18 His favourite toy, the bone ring..a teething ring, with three little bells on it. **1980** *Bookseller* 21 June 2560/1 TBL Book Service was still involved in teething troubles and costs.

† **teetotaciously** (tītōtēⁱ·ʃəsli), *adv. U.S. dial. Obs.* Also **tetotaciously.** [Fanciful elaboration of TEETOTALLY *adv.*¹: see -ACIOUS and cf. *BODACIOUS *a.*] = TEETOTALLY *adv.*¹

1833 J. K. PAULDING *Lion of West* (1954) II. ii. 54 I'm the best man—if I ain't, I wish I may be tetotaciously exflunctified! **1837** R. M. BIRD *Nick of Woods* I. xvi. 220 If that don't make me eat a niggur, may I be tetotaciously chawed up myself! **1859** T. DE QUINCEY *Coll. Works* X. 247 The slave in Terence, viz., Davus, though otherwise a clever fellow, when puzzled by a secret, or (as in America they say) *teetotaciously exfluncticated*, excuses himself by saying—'Davus sum, non Oedipus.'

teetotalize, *v.* (In Dict. s.v. TEETOTALIST.) Add: Also *intr.*, to practise teetotalism, to abstain.

1898 G. B. SHAW *Let.* 18 Oct. (1972) II. 66 If I began to eat three beefsteaks a day, the ground would..be shifted to the want of stimulants; but as it is,..I am allowed to teetotallize [*sic*] in comparative peace.

teetotally, *adv.*² *rare.* [f. TEETOTAL *a.* 1; see TEETOTALLY *adv.*¹ b.] In a teetotal manner, with total abstinence from alcoholic drinks.

1934 H. G. WELLS *Exper. Autobiogr.* II. viii. 533, I lived through my Bohemian days as sober as Shaw if not nearly so teetotally.

teetotum, *sb.*¹ Add: **1. b.** (*a*) For *Sc.* read *Sc.* and *Ir.* (Later example.)

1922 JOYCE *Ulysses* 759 Comical little teetotum always stuck up in some pub corner and her or her son waiting.

teevee (tī:vī·). Also **Teevee, tee-vee.** [A rendering of the names of the letters *T* and *V.*] = *TV.

1949 *N.Y. Mirror* 18 Apr. 10/2 Warners, unworried about teevee, showed a 1948 profit of 3 million. **1959** G. FREEMAN *Jack would be Gentleman* i. 7 It was wonderful what you learned from the tee-vee. **1963** *Guardian* 10 Jan. 6/6 Often..viewers do not know which channel they have been watching, and..will say 'Oh, it was the Tee-vee.' **1975** *Listener* 11 Sept. 350/3 In California, he achieves success as a low-budget teevee film-maker.

tefillin: see TEPHILLIM, -IN in Dict. and Suppl.

Teflon (te·flǫn). Also **teflon.** [f. TE(TRA- + FL(UOR- + *-on*, arbitrary ending.] **a.** A proprietary name for *POLYTETRAFLUOROETHYLENE.

1945 *Official Gaz.* (U.S. Patent Office) 23 Oct. 531/1 E. I. du Pont de Nemours and Company... *Teflon* for synthetic resinous fluorine-containing polymers. **1951** *Jrnl. Amer. Chem. Soc.* LXXIII. 5195 (*heading*) Tracer studies of oxidation-reduction polymerization and molecular weight of 'Teflon' tetrafluoroethylene resin. **1954** *Trade Marks Jrnl.* 5 May 438/2 *Teflon...* Mouldable plastics in the form of powder, sheets, rods, tubes, tapes, filaments (non-textile) and shaped pieces. **1965** *New Scientist* 11 Mar. 618/2 One end of the blood-carrying teflon tube is joined to a side opening made in the wall of the pulmonary artery. **1970** *Nature* 25 July 382/2 Exudates were..homogenized using a 'Teflon' grinder to rupture any cells present. **1979** A. L. LYDERSEN *Fluid Flow & Heat Transfer* vi. 150 The mesh is available in materials, such as, acid resistant steel, nickel, copper, aluminium, tantalum, hastelloy and Teflon.

b. *Comb.*

1965 *Family Circle* Oct. 92 Won't scratch, scar or mar Teflon coated cookware. **1972** M. CRICHTON *Terminal Man* II. i. 64 The team was now using Briggs stainless-steel Teflon-coated electrode arrays. **1979** A. L. LYDERSEN *Fluid Flow & Heat Transfer* iv. 80 They..have Teflon-covered piston rings.

Tegean (tedʒī·ăn, te·dʒiăn), *sb.* and *a.* [f. Gr. Τεγέα, L. *Tegea* Tegea.] **A.** *sb.* A native or inhabitant of the ancient city of Tegea in Arcadia. **B.** *adj.* Of or pertaining to Tegea or its inhabitants. Also **Tegeate** *sb.* and *a.* [ad. L. *Tegeātēs*].

1584 B. RICH tr. *Herodotus' History* I. fol. 17 The Lacedæmonians, hauing escaped a scowring, were triumphant conquerous ouer ye Tegeates. **1709** I. LITTLEBURY tr. *Herodotus' History* II. IX. 377 Next to themselves, the Lacedemonians plac'd the Tegeans, consisting of fifteen hundred Men. **1767** A. STRAHAN tr. *Virgil's Æneid* I. v. 137 He from Arcarnania came, This from Arcadia of Tegæan blood. **1808** [see *MANTINEAN *sb.* and *a.*]. **1858** G. RAWLINSON tr. *Herodotus' History* I. I. lxvi. 204 These persons..measured the Tegean plain as they executed their labours. **1888** *Encycl. Brit.* XXIII. 110/1 At Plataea (479 B.C.) 3000 Tegeans fought the good fight of freedom. **1919** E. POUND *Quia pauper Amavi* 35 Tegean Pan. **1949** *Oxf. Classical Dict.* 881/1 *C.* 550 B.C. Sparta came to terms with Tegea after a long war; and for two centuries it followed the Spartan lead, though at times unwillingly, for the Tegeans were tough fighters. **1951** [see *MANTINEAN *sb.* and *a.*]. **1952** C. DAY LEWIS tr. *Virgil's Aeneid* v. 101 After him, side by side, Salius and Patron, the one Acarnanian, the other Arcadian, of a Tegaean family.

tegestology (tedʒestǫ·lŏdʒi). [Irreg. f. L. *teges, -etis* covering, mat, f. *teg-ĕre* to cover + *-t* + -OLOGY.] The collecting of beer mats. So **tegesto·logist.**

1960 *Ironmonger* 23 Jan. 123 Tegestologists (beer-mat secreters). **1960** [see *PHILLUMENIST]. **1966** *Punch* 9 Feb. 202/2 'Here let tegestology exact its tribute from a royal embrace' (meaning, pinch a beer-mat from the *Queen's Arms*) is the sort of thing which any rallyist can work out in between emptying the ashtrays and giving the 'V' sign to a fellow competitor. **1977** *Titbits* 20–26 Jan. 17/5 The British tegestologists (a posh name for beermat collectors) are very upset to discover criminals who.. scoop up mats..and decamp.

tegmen. Add: **d.** *tegmen tympani* (examples). Also *ellipt.* as *tegmen.*

1902 D. J. CUNNINGHAM *Text-bk. Anat.* 704 The roof [of the tympanic cavity]..is formed by a thin plate of bone, the tegmen tympani. **1939** JOYCE *Finnegans Wake* 249 There lies her word, you reder!..It vibroverberates upon the tegmen. **1977** *Proc. R. Soc. Med.* LXX. 821/2 In mandibulofacial dysostosis the attic and antrum are typically absent..being replaced..by descent of the tegmen. **1980** *Gray's Anat.* (ed. 36) 312/1 In a young skull the suture between the petrous and the squamous parts of the temporal bone may be visible at the lateral limit of the tegmen tympani.

tegu (te·gu). Abbrev. of TEGUEXIN.

1954 G. DURRELL *Three Singles to Adventure* i. 28 One of the tegus opened his eyes. **1974** D. & M. WEBSTER *Compar. Vertebr. Morphol.* viii. 164 (*caption*) Surface view of a freshly shed skin of a tegu lizard.

teguexin. For *Teius* substitute *Tupinambis* and add: or a similar member of the family Teiidæ.

tegula. Add: **1.** (Later examples.)

1893 A. E. SHIPLEY *Zool. Invertebrata* xix. 376 On the mesothorax [of Hymenoptera] are two small scales known as the tegulae, covering the base of the wings. **1972** M. S. GARDINER *Biol. Invertebrates* xiv. 573/1 Newly hatched wasps..have been made to sting bees near their tegulae.

2. *Archæol.* and *Archit.* A flat roof-tile (see quot. 1964). Cf. IMBREX 1. Also *fig.*

1871 R. BURN *Rome & Campagna* p. lxxv, The Roman tiles were of two kinds, flat tiles and smaller curved tiles. The flat tiles had raised rims at the sides... The small curved tiles were..laid over the joined edges..and formed a complete protection for the joint... Tegulæ and imbrices. **1938** in P. E. Thomas *Mod. Building Practice* III. 229 The Double Roman tile..is a descendant of the Roman *tegula* and *imbrex*.., which the Romans used extensively for their villa roofs. **1956** 'H. MACDIARMID' *Stony Limits & Scots Unbound* 9 The gold edging of a bough at sunset, its pantile way Forming a double curve, tegula and imbrex in one. **1964** J. S. SCOTT *Dict. Building* 178 *Italian tiling*.., single-lap tiles which form a roof covering with two different sorts of tiles, the curved overtile or imbrex and the flat, tray shaped under-tile or tegula. **1977** *Antiquaries Jrnl.* LVII. 264 Bricks and tegulae can frequently be seen in the debris.

tehee, *int.* and *sb.* Add: Now usually in form **tee-hee.** **A.** *int.* (Later example.)

1944 A. HUXLEY *Let.* 24 Feb. (1969) 500 Tee hee, tee hee, oh sweet delight!

C. *attrib.* or as *adj.* **tee-hee farm** (*nonce*), a mental hospital; cf. *funny farm* s.v. *FUNNY *a.* 4.

1955 W. GADDIS *Recognitions* I. v. 172 Everybody knows about Rose, that they've sent her sister Rose back from the tee-hee farm and Esther has to take her in. **1971** *Publishers' Weekly* 1 Nov. 17/2 This accounts for *Newsweek's* rather snide coverage and the tee-hee reports in the press.

tehee *v.* (later example); also as *tee and hee* (nonce); **tehee·ing** *ppl. a.*

1904 J. C. LINCOLN *Cap'n Eri* v. 81 'That's it, laff!' almost sobbed Captain Jerry. 'Set there and tee-hee-like a Bedlamite.' **1928** V. WOOLF *Orlando* iv. 163 He teed and heed intolerably. **1935** 'G. ORWELL' in *New English Weekly* 14 Nov. 96/1 Life is full of misery when you believe that the grave really finishes you... Hence the tee-heeing brightness of *Punch*, hence Barrie and his bluebells, hence H. G. Wells and his Utopiæ infested by nude school-marms.

Tehrani (te(h)rā·ni), *sb.* and *a.* Also **Teherani.** [f. *Tehran*, name of a city in northern Iran + *-I.] **A.** *sb.* A native or inhabitant of Tehran, the capital of Iran. **B.** *adj.* Of, pertaining to, or characteristic of the city of Tehran, or of its inhabitants.

1939 W. V. EMANUEL *Wild Asses* xiii. 145 'Assassin's' appearance belied his name; he was a strikingly handsome young Teherani, with a Greek nose. **1941** L. P. ELWELL-SUTTON *Modern Iran* i. 11 The favourite summer resorts of the Tehranis are all along this coast. **1953** A. SMITH *Blind White Fish in Persia* vii. 130 The Tehranis cast soulful glances towards America. **1973** *Times* 22 May (Teheran Suppl.) p. i/1 Few Teheranis..have ever seen a drop of domestically produced crude oil. **1975** P. SOMERVILLE-LARGE *Couch of Earth* x. 178 The Tehrāni police consider it unlikely that you killed Mr Otway. **1977** H. OSBORNE *White Poppy* xii. 96 He was a Tehrani.

tehsil, var. *TAHSIL.

Tê-hua (tēⁱhwā, ‖ dəhwā). Also (Pinyin) ‖ **Dehua.** The name of a place in the province of Fujian in south-eastern China, used *attrib.* and *absol.* to designate porcelain made there, also known as *BLANC DE CHINE.

1923 R. L. HOBSON *Wares Ming Dynasty* xiii. 173 The term Chien yao was now transferred to a ware..made more than a hundred miles south at Tê-hua (Tehwa)... There are..no lack of actual examples of the Tehwa porcelain. **1945** W. B. HONEY *Ceramic Art of China* II. 133 The whole body of Tê-hua wares, familiarly called Fukien porcelain,..holds together in a remarkable.. manner. **1953** R. S. JENYNS *Ming Pott. & Porc.* x. 146 Decorated pieces of Têhua, whether painted in blue or enamelled..are of poorer quality than the undecorated pieces. **1980** *Catal. Fine Chinese Ceramics* (Sotheby, Hong Kong) 102 A well modelled Dehua (Te Hua) Seal in the form of a *qilin* (*ch'i-lin*).., the fabulous beast with bushy tail and curly mane shown crouching with horned head sharply turned to one side.

Teian (tī·ăn), *a.* Also **Tean.** [f. Gr. Τήϊος of or from Τέως *Teos* + -IAN.] Of or relating to Teos, an ancient Ionian city on the western coast of Asia Minor north of Ephesus.

1646 J. HALL *Poems* 34 Who light'st Love's dying Torch with purer fire, And breath'st new life into the Teian lyre. **1787** J. NOTT *Select Odes from Hafez* p. ix, Whether Anacreon borrowed the gaiety of his Odes from the Persian *Gazel*, or whether Hafez enriched his native language by an imitation of the Teian bard, I will not venture to determine. **1821** BYRON *Don Juan* III. lxxxvi. 47 The Scian and the Teian muse, The hero's harp, the lover's lute, Have found the fame your shores refuse. **1858** [see *ARGIVE *a.*]. **1902** E. R. BEVAN *House of Seleucus* II. xix. 47 Antiochus..backed the envoys of the Teians in other places. **1941** M. ROSTOVTZEFF *Social & Econ. Hist. Hellenistic World* III. 1348 The Tean decree..which may refer to the synoecism of Teos and Lebedos. **1983** R. E. ALLEN *Attalid Kingdom* iii. 50 Teian envoys had been sent to Antiochos.

teichoic (təikōᵘ·ik), *a. Biochem.* [f. Gr. τεῖχο-ς wall + -IC.] *teichoic acid*: any of various polymers of ribitol or glycerol phosphate that are found in the walls of Gram-positive bacteria.

1958 J. J. ARMSTRONG et al. in *Jrnl. Chem. Soc.* 4346 The general name 'teichoic acid'..is suggested for these polymers of ribitol phosphate with or without other substituents. **1973** *Nature* 4 May 43/2 The wall teichoic acid is responsible for the ability of the cell walls of Gram-positive bacteria to bind divalent cations and the membrane teichoic acid mediates an interaction between magnesium ions..and the cytoplasmic membrane.

Teilhardian (tēⁱyā·ɹdiăn), *a.* and *sb.* [f. the name of Pierre *Teilhard* de Chardin (1881–1955), French scientist and theologian + -IAN.] **A.** *adj.* Of or pertaining to Teilhard de Chardin or his writings, which are noted for their attempt to synthesize science and the Christian faith. **B.** *sb.* An adherent or follower of Teilhard de Chardin.

1967 *Sat. Rev.* (U.S.) 15 Apr. 18/3 Teilhard de Chardin ..restores all the dynamic energies and heroism of Milton's Satan to the Teilhardian Christ. **1970** T. P. O'MALLEY in *Studia Patristica* X. 194 Even if Tertullian was not a Teilhardian, he nevertheless held for a very palpable world here and hereafter. **1971** *Time* 19 Apr. 34 From the Teilhardians, the confidence that God, whoever he is, has something to do with the future and may yet meet man there. **1977** P. JOHNSON *Enemies of Society* ix. 125 Teilhardian phenomenology is a system which enables the more leisured class to accommodate scientific knowledge in a religious setting but which makes no intolerable demands on either flesh or intellect. **1983** KING & SALMON *Teilhard & Unity of Knowledge* i. 1 Teilhardians had long known that May 1, 1981—the centennial of the birth of Pierre Teilhard de Chardin—had to be celebrated in a special way. Two Teilhardian Jesuits would be at Georgetown University on that date.

teindable (tī·ndăb'l), *a. Sc.* [f. TEIND *v.* + -ABLE.] Tithable.

1705 W. FORBES *Treatise on Churchlands* 289 All other Teindable Subjects in Scotland. **1832** *Fife Herald* 14 June, The planted park is valued at £2 10s. sterling, but is found not to be Teindable. **1924** *Kelso Chronicle* 25 July 4 The mansion house, cottages, joiner's shop, smithy and yard..were not teindable.

teineite (tēⁱ·nə͵əit). *Min.* [See quot. 1939 and -ITE¹.] A hydrated sulphate and tellurite of copper, $Cu(Te)O_3 \cdot 2H_2O$, found as blue, prismatic orthorhombic crystals and as fine crusts.

1939 T. YOSIMURA in *Jrnl. Faculty Sci. Hokkaido Univ.: Ser. 4* IV. 465 Professor..Harada collected some.. crystals of a blue mineral... The author proposes the name 'Teineite' from the Teine mine where this new mineral has first been found. **1977** *Mineral. Abstr.* XXVIII. 487/1 A copper-bearing quartz vein cutting phyllites shows..rare azure-blue teineite as single crystals (≤ 1 mm) or crystalline patches (≤ 2·5 mm).

teistie. Add: The form *tystie* is now usual. (Later examples.)

1952 U. VENABLES *Tempestuous Eden* iii. 50 This was an ideal nesting-ground for black guillemots or tysties. **1964** A. L. THOMSON *New Dict. Birds* 69/1 The Tystie (or Black Guillemot)..and its congeners constitute the tribe Cepphini. **1980** *Birds* Summer 51/2 There is a small brackish loch near the shore where tysties display in spring.

tej (tedʒ). Also † **tedge, tedje; tedj.** [Amharic.] A kind of mead that is the national drink of Ethiopia.

1853 M. PARKYNS *Life in Abyssinia* I. xvii. 210 Spirits are of an inferior kind, distilled..from the refuse of the wine or from honey... The grape is called 'wainy', the wine 'wain tedge'. **1877** E. A. DE COSSONS *Cradle of Blue Nile* I. vii. 100 As soon as the baskets of bread had been removed, bottles of tedge were served. **1901** A. B. WYLDE *Mod. Abyssinia* viii. 182 The tedj bearer always pouring out a little of the liquid into..his hand. *Ibid.* xvii. 377 The honey taken from the wanza flowers being greatly prized, as being of a white colour makes very clear tedj. **1925** H. C. MAYDON *Simen* ii. 24 Abdulla, the cook, was ..too apt to celebrate with the local tej and marissa (mead and beer). **1936** E. WAUGH *Waugh in Abyssinia* i. 26 A weekly visit to the cinema, a preference for whisky over *tedj*..were the western innovations that these young men relished. *Ibid.* v. 169 They got very drunk in the *tedj* houses. **1952** [see *POMBE]. **1974** *Country Life* 18 Apr. 938/3 *Tej*, a mead of honey, hops and water. **1981** E. NORTH *Dames* i. 12 It is known as *tedj*... A sort of honey-mead... Some call it *mies*.

‖**Tejano** (tĕhā·no). [Amer. Sp., formerly written *Texano*, f. *Texas* TEXAS.] A native or inhabitant of Texas, esp. one of Mexican stock; a Texan.

1925 O. P. WHITE *Them was Days* 75 The fear of God, as represented by the wrath of the *Tejanos* (Texans). **1933** H. ALLEN *Anthony Adverse* III. IX. lxiv. 1175 The convoy, when it did start, consisted of about sixty unfortunate mestizos and Indians bound for the mines at Chihuahua as well as the captured Americans, or 'Tejanos', whose cases were to be disposed of by the Viceroy Calleja at Mexico. **1976** *Monitor* (McAllen, Texas) 26 Sept. 7E/2 *Tejanos* more than any other ethnic group in Texas have provided a bridge to Texas' past.

tek (tek), *v.* Also **teck.** Repr. U.S. Black and regional pronunc. of TAKE *v.*

1905 [see *WE *pron.* 1 g]. **1924** M. W. BECKWITH in *Mem. Amer. Folklore Soc.* XVII. 76 Him couldn't get away from de woman until rain tek him in de yard. **1938** C. HIMES *Pork Chop Paradise* in *Black on Black* (1973) 165 W'en de panic cum an' de Lawd tek yo' food..den laff. **1981** *Westindian World* 2 Oct. 4/1 One of London's better known Radio London presenters tek time off te go compere beauty show.

tekhnikum, var. *TECHNICUM.

tekke¹ (te·ke). Also 7 **teke;** 9 **takia, takiya(h;** 9—**tek(k)i(y)eh** (tekī·ye). [a. Turk. *tekke*, Ottoman *tekye* (whence Arab. *tak(k)īya*), ad. Pers. *takya* pillow, place of repose, abode of a fakir.] A monastery of dervishes, esp. in Ottoman Turkey.

1668 P. RYCAUT *Pres. State Ottoman Empire* II. xx. 150 Their poverty..as I have seen in some of their *Tekes* where I have been. **1842** C. MASSON *Baluchistan* II. 278 Many takías are interspersed amongst all the burial-places. **1855** R. F. BURTON *Personal Narr. Pilgrimage to El-Medinah* I. 124 A Takiya is a place where Dervishes have rooms, and perform their devotions. *Ibid.* II. 29 It is flanked on the left..by the domes and minarets of a pretty Turkish building, a 'takiyah', erected by the late Mohammed Ali for the reception of Dervish travellers. **1856** LADY EASTHOPE tr. *Ubicini's Lett. on Turkey* I. 109 He had finished and issued forth from the precincts of the tekieh. **1868** J. P. BROWN *Derwishes* 103, I may here add that of the two hundred, or more, *Tekkiehs* in Constantinople, some fifty only are possessed of sufficient wealth for their support. **1875** *Encycl. Brit.* III. 233/1 The Tekiyeh, or shrine of the Bektash dervishes, on the western bank of the [Tigris] river. **1900** 'ODYSSEUS' *Turkey in Europe* v. 194 Monograms of his name [Ali] are a conspicuous feature in most dervish Tekkes. **1932** G. KAMPFFMEYER in H. A. R. Gibb *Whither Islam?* 167 The *tekkes* or monasteries of the religious orders and the *turbes* or the tombs of the saints are closed. **1977** H. KAPLAN *Damascus Cover* (1978) x. 90 Damascus is overflowing with exotic sights: the tomb of Saladin,..the Tekkiyeh of Suleiman. **1980** A. ALPERS *Life K. Mansfield* xxi. 376 Gurdjieff['s]..'study-house'..resembled..a Dervish tekke.

Tekke² (te·ke). [Turkic.] The name of a Turkic tribe inhabiting the Turkmen Soviet Socialist Republic, used to designate a short-piled basically red carpet or rug made by members of this tribe. Also *Tekke Bokhara.*

1900 J. K. MUMFORD *Oriental Rugs* iv. 40 From the rest of it [*sc.* angora fleece] Kashmir shawls are made, and carpet-weaving is illustrated in the finer Tartar fabrics—Tekkes, Yomuds, and Bokhara prayer rugs. *Ibid.* xii. 227 Tekke rugs..will continue to be sold as Bokharas. **1911** G. GRIFFIN LEWIS *Practical Bk. Oriental Rugs* I. x. 135 *Tekke Field Design.*—A repetition of a..Y-shaped design. Found only in the Tekke rugs, especially those of the prayer variety. *Ibid.* II. xvi. 276 *Tekke Bokkara.* Why so named.—Because they are made by the Tekke Turkoman tribes of Nomads. **1931** A. U. DILLEY *Oriental Rugs & Carpets* Pl. 57 (*caption*) Bokhara garden rug. Compare garden designs in Tekke and Saryk prayer rugs. **1967** *Times* 21 Feb. 21/4 (Advt.), A number of fine Turkomans: *Tekke Bokhara.* **1974** *Encycl. Brit. Micropædia* IX. 867/1 *Tekke carpets*... Primarily the rugs that were commonly on the market as Royal Bokharas a generation or two ago... The standard field pattern for the large rugs is a repeat in rows of a particoloured, multifoiled lozenge, a basic motif that serves as the symbol, or gul, of this tribe.

tektite (te·ktəit). [ad. G. *tektit* (F. E. Suess 1900, in *Jahrb. d. K.-K. Geol. Reichsanstalt* L. 194), f. Gr. τηκτ-ός molten (f. τήκειν to make molten): see -ITE¹.] One of the small, roundish, glassy bodies of unknown origin that occur scattered over various parts of the earth.

1909 [see *BILLITONITE]. **1935** *Times* 28 Jan. 15/4 'Tektites' from Bohemia and Moravia have for more than 150 years been cut as gem stones under the names 'obsidian', 'water chrysolite' and 'moldavite'. **1936** [see *AUSTRALITE]. **1956** *Antiquity* XXX. 70 These stone implements, together with the fossil remains of the stegodon (an extinct elephant), rhinoceros and other mammals, were often found in association with tektites, a form of glass meteorite. **1963** [see *OBSIDIANITE]. **1969** *Times* 29 Aug. 10/3 Tektites, glassy, button-shaped objects which are probably of extraterrestrial origin, have been found in the Libyan desert and dated by radioactive methods to 35 million years ago. **1971** *Sci. Amer.* Oct. 55/2 Well-preserved Australian tekites show clear evidence of aerodynamic shaping.

b. *attrib.*, as **tektite field** = *STREWN FIELD.

1960 *Listener* 22 Dec. 1141/2 Some of the tektite fields are well away from either active or extinct volcanoes. **1968** R. A. LYTTLETON *Mysteries Solar Syst.* vi. 183 There are eight main areas in the world generally accepted to be genuine tektite-fields.

† **tektosphere** (te·ktosfīᵊɹ). *Geol. Obs.* Also (in dicts.) **tecto-.** [f. as prec. + -O + *-SPHERE.] = *ASTHENOSPHERE.

1900 J. MURRAY in *Rep. Brit. Assoc. Adv. Sci. 1899* 796 Within [the earth] is situated the vast nucleus or centrosphere; surrounding this is what may be called the tektosphere, a shell of materials in a state bordering on fusion. **1913** [see *geosphere* s.v. *GEO-].

telangiectasis. Add: Also † **teleang-, -ectasia** (pl. **-iæ**). (Further examples.)

1876 VAN DUYN & SEGUIN tr. *Wagner's Man. Gen. Path.* III. 390 Cavernous, or venous tumor. It exists rarely at birth,..and proceeds probably in many cases from teleangiectasia. **1887** T. M'C. ANDERSON *Treat. Dis. Skin* 436 (*heading*) Capillary nævus; mother's mark; port wine or strawberry mark; teleangiectasis. **1948** J. MINCKLER in W. A. D. Anderson *Pathology* xlv. 1390 Telangectasia of cerebral vessels is a fairly common occurrence..and represents a malformation rather than a neoplasm. **1974** PASSMORE & ROBSON *Compan. Med. Stud.* III. xxxiv. 77/1 The disease usually presents in infancy with cerebellar ataxia. Telangiectasiae appear some years later and are distributed over the ears, nose and cheeks.

Telanthropus (telæ·nþrŏpŏs). [mod.L., f. Gr. τέλ-ος end, consummation + ἄνθρωπος man.] A type of hominid, *Telanthropus capensis*, represented by the fragmentary fossil remains found at Swartkrans near Johannesburg, S. Africa, in 1949.

More recent investigation has led some scholars to believe that Telanthropus properly belongs to the species *Homo erectus.*

[**1949** BROOM & ROBINSON in *Nature* 20 Aug. 323/2 In the cave at Swartkrans..there was found by Mr. J. T. Robinson, on April 29, 1949, the lower jaw of what is fairly manifestly a new type of man... The new type of man represented by this fossil jaw we propose to call *Telanthropus capensis.* We regard him as somewhat allied to Heidelberg man, and intermediate between one of the ape-men and true man.] **1955** *Ann. Reg. 1954* 466 The artefacts were probably made by *Telanthropus* who was either a very advanced Australopithecine or a very primitive true man. **1959** J. D. CLARK *Prehist. S. Afr.* iii. 63 In addition some rather fragmentary remains, considered to be essentially more human-like though still preserving Australopithecine features, have been described by Robinson under the generic name of *Telanthropus.* **1960** W. HOWELLS *Mankind in Making* xii. 178 *Telanthropus*' teeth are smaller. **1977** A. HALLAM *Planet Earth* 286 In addition to these is a jaw which represents another line, closer to modern Man. It has been named Telanthropus.

Tel Avivian (tel avī·viăn), *sb.* and *a.* [f. *Tel Aviv* (see below) + -IAN.] **A.** *sb.* A native or inhabitant of Tel Aviv, the largest city in the state of Israel. **B.** *adj.* Of or pertaining to Tel Aviv.

1939 *Palestine Post* 14 Aug. 2/2 (*heading*) New park benches for tired Tel Avivians. **1941** G. G. SCHOLEM *Major Trends in Jewish Mysticism* 384 A Tel-Avivian scholar, Reuben Margulies, has begun to publish an annotated edition of the Zohar. **1949** KOESTLER *Promise & Fulfilment* II. v. 263 Most Tel Avivians agree that the black-out is logically unwarranted. **1983** *Economist* 30 July 39/3 No fewer than 10 construction companies are vying to provide land- and air-hungry Tel Avivians with a variety of lodgings.

tele (te·li), *sb.*² Colloq. abbrev. of *TELEVISION. Cf. *TELLY. Also *attrib.* and *Comb.* (not sharply distinguishable from *TELE- 2).

1936 *Billboard* 14 Nov. 3 (*heading*) RCA–NBC tele progress. **1944** R. E. LEE *Television* vi. 88 The motion picture is a novel; tele is a short-story, or a newspaper article. **1946** [see *lip-read* vb. s.v. *LIP *sb.* 7]. **1956** A. WILSON *Anglo-Saxon Att.* I. iii. 47, I see him on the Tele. **1960** A. KIMMINS *Lugs O'Leary* iii. 33 'Where were you?' 'In my room watching the tele.' **1961** A. WILSON *Old Men at Zoo* iii. 128 Oh, it was on the tele news in the pub I was in. **1964** *Punch* 3 June 833/1 Large sections of the tele-watching population. **1973** J. WAINWRIGHT *Devil you Don't* 5 Sprawling in front of a tele, watching one-day cricket. **1977** *Gay News* 7–20 Apr. 37/2 Hardly home-loving types, likely to be content with baked beans on toast and the tele.

tele (te·li), *sb.*³ *Psychics.* [a. Gr. τῆλε afar, far off.] Psychic affinity between two (or more) people separated by time or space. Cf. *telepsychic* sb. s.v. *TELE- 1.

1937 J. L. MORENO in *Sociometry* I. 16 Tele is defined as a feeling process projected into space and time in which one, two, or more persons may participate. It is an experience of some real factor in the other person and not a subjective fiction... The tele process is..the chief factor in determining the position of an individual in the group. **1952** W. SPROTT *Social Psychol.* ii. 34 A 'monistic origin of life from a common unit' out of which existing networks of 'tele' have been differentiated. *Ibid.* 35 In Moreno's own convention a red line from A towards B represents 'positive tele'.

tele (te·li), *a.* Abbrev. of TELEPHOTOGRAPHIC *a.*² Cf. TELEPHOTO *a.* and *tele-lens* s.v. *TELE- 1.

1979 *SLR Camera* Jan. 42/3 We chose the FD 135 mm f2.5 SC and the FD 200 mm f2.8 SC as being representative of the popular tele range. **1981** *What Camera Weekly* 5 Dec. 3/2 (*heading*) Tele tactics: long lenses with focal lengths of 400 and 500 mm need careful handling.

tele-. Add: **1. te·leba:nking,** a method of effecting banking transactions at a distance by electronic means; **te·le-ca:mera,** (*a*) a telephotographic camera; (*b*) a television camera; **telecentric** *a.* (examples); also *absol.* as *sb.*, a telecentric lens; **teleco·balt,** radioactive cobalt used as a radiation source in teletherapy; usu. *attrib.*; **te:lecomma·nd,** the remote control of machines or the like by electronic means; freq. *attrib.*; **telecommu·te** *v. intr.*, to work from home (esp. at a traditionally office job), communicating with one's place of employment, colleagues, etc., by telephone line or data link; **te·leconne·ction** *Geol.* [tr. Sw. *fjärrkonnektion* (G. De Geer 1916, in *Geol. Fören. Förhandl.* XXXVIII. 18)], the correlation over long distances of varves or other deposits that can be used for dating purposes; also *transf.*; **te:lecontro·l** = *telecommand* above; freq. *attrib.*; **teleconve·rter** *Photogr.*, a camera lens designed to be fitted in front of a standard lens to increase its effective focal length; **te:lecuriethe·rapy** *Med.* [*CURIE] = *teletherapy* below; **tele·diphone** [*Ediphone*, name of a recording machine], a machine for recording speech from a telephone line or radio for subsequent transcription or broadcasting; hence **tele·diphoned** *a.*; **te·le-flash** *U.S.*, (equipment for transmitting) telegraphic news of racing results, odds, etc.; **te:lege·nesis,** the technique of artificial insemination; **tele·gnomy, telegno·sis** *Psychics*, psychic perception of events happening at a distant place; clairvoyance; hence **telegno·stic** *a.*; **telekinesis:** delete ‖ and add later examples; **telekinetic** *a.*: also *transf.* and *fig.* (later examples); **te:lekine·ticist,** one who practises or has the power of telekinesis; **te·le-lens** *Photogr.*, a telephoto lens; **te·leme:ssage,** a form of telegram introduced in October 1981 to replace the inland telegram, and abolished one year later; **te·leordering** *vbl. sb.*, the computerized ordering of books by book sellers from publishers; **telepho·togram,** a message in the form of a picture transmitted by radio or television; **te:lephoto·meter,** an instrument for measuring the brightness of a distant light source; **te·leplasm** *Psychics*, a hypothetical substance psychically materialized; ectoplasm; hence **telepla·smic** *a.*; **Te·le-player** [*PLAYER[1]], the proprietary name in the U.S. of a device for recording and playing back videotape; **telepro·cessing** *vbl. sb.*, data processing that involves terminals located at a distance from the processor; **telepsy·chic** *sb.*, a medium whose psychical powers are exerted at a distance; *adj.*, pertaining to or involving the exertion of psychic powers at a distance; **te·lepuppet** *colloq.*, a telechiric device, esp. one used in space; **te:leradio·graphy** *Med.*, radiography in which the X-ray tube is placed some distance from the plate in order to minimize distortion; **telera·dium**, radium used as a radiation source in teletherapy; **tele·rgic** *a.*, pertaining to or involving telergy; **te:leroe:ntgeno·graphy** (also **-röntgen-**) *Med.* (chiefly *U.S.*) = *teleradiography* above; **teleseism** (examples); hence **telesei·smic** *a.*; **telesei·smically** *adv.*; **te·le-sho:pping**, a method of ordering goods from shops by electronic means; **teleso·ftware** *Computers*, software transmitted by wire or broadcast for use by any number of independent receiving terminals; **te·le-talkies**, cinematographic films broadcast by television (*disused*); **telethe·rapy** *Med.*, radiotherapy using a source of radiation at a distance from the patient; **telethermometer**, substitute for def.: a thermometer that indicates the temperature measured elsewhere; (example); **te:letransporta·tion** = *TELEPORTATION (*rare*); hence (as a back-formation) **teletranspo·rt** *v. trans.*

1981 *Amer. Banker* 18 Feb. 12/3 Consider the things you will be able to do—telereservations, telegames, telebanking, teleshopping. **1910** O. WHEELER *Mod. Telephotography* 68 Messrs. Zeiss also make a special telecamera. **1951** I. ASIMOV *Stars like Dust* xvii. 162 The movement of the tele-camera can be so adjusted as to counteract the motion of the ship in its orbit. **1960** *Harper's Bazaar* Oct. 82/2 It is not too late even now to bring in the tele-cameras. **1980** T. HOLME *Neapolitan Streak* 42 There were tele-camera teams from the RAI. **1902** MANN & MILLIKAN tr. *Drude's Theory of Optics* I. iv. 75 Certain positions of the iris can be chosen for which the entrance- or exit-pupils lie at infinity... To attain this it is necessary to place the iris behind S_1 at its principal focus... The system is them called telecentric. **1921** *Glasgow Herald* 15 June 7 It was fitted with..a 12 in. Telecentric, and a variant of my 'Dodo' tele-lens. **1973** D. A. SPENCER *Focal Dict. Photogr. Technol.* 619 (*caption*) Telecentric optical system. **1956** C. W. WILSON *Radium Therapy* (ed. 2) 286/1 (Index), Telecobalt therapy. **1959** [see *teleradium* below]. **1980** *Jrnl. R. Soc. Arts* Jan. 95/1 These telecobalt..machines are now part of the routine equipment of most radiotherapy departments. **1972** *Sunday Tel.* 30 Apr. 34/4 He sees on a television screen the view he would have from the driver's seat of the car he is controlling remotely. These 'telecommand' cars are about to be used for complex..handling tests. **1978** *Times* 3 Nov. 27/4 The Post Office itself has listed the main telecommunications services..envisaged for the years 1985 and 2000... By 1985 there will be..viewdata,..telemetry (the radio transmission of measurements), telecommand (remote control of machines). **1980** *Times* 15 Jan. 16 A low-power microcomputer system has been built..and a telecommand receiver has been completed. **1974** *Economist* 5 Jan. 14/1 As there is no logical reason why the cost of telecommunication should vary with distance, quite a lot of people by the late 1980s will telecommute daily to their London offices while living on a Pacific island if they want to. **1975** *Ibid.* 25 Oct. 39/3 Telecommuting is coming. When production is properly automated even in service industries, probably 60% of American breadwinners will be brainworkers. *Ibid.* 43/3 Telecommuter terminals will stop social interaction at the workplace. **1976** *Ibid.* 25 Dec. 56/1 Small ones, employing various piecework-earning telecommuting housewives in their own homes. **1981** *Ibid.* 5 Sept. 20/1 Telecommuters are workers who do not have to travel to their office... They need only their terminal links of today, enhanced by new gadgetry, to make sure they never have to leave their villages. **1982** *N.Y. Times Mag.* 14 Nov. 133 A situation known as 'telecommuting' or, more cozily, the 'electronic cottage'. **1934** G. DE GEER in *Geografiska Annaler* XVI. 3 The general law that the annual amount of meltwater deposits along the ice-border varied congruently is..definitely fixed. Teleconnections were thus, by a great number of close connections,..acting every year for..the whole of Fennoscandia. **1939** G. CLARK *Archæol. & Society* v. 141 Attempts to extend the sequence across the Baltic have not met with general acceptance any more than have the still more ambitious 'teleconnexions' between the Swedish varve-sequence and those in North and South America. **1970** S. THORARINSSON in R. Berger *Sci. Methods Medieval Archaeol.* 325 A young Swedish scientist..has realized my old dream of establishing tephrochronological teleconnection between Iceland and Scandinavia. **1979** *Harvard Mag.* May–June 14 Meterologists have coined the phrase 'teleconnections' to describe the apparent correlation between El Niño [*sc.* an erratically recurring ocean current in the Pacific] and disruptive weather patterns all around the earth. **1983** *Nature* 18 Aug. 583/3 Teleconnection with the Bristlecone pine absolute scale..has already been achieved for Bronze Age varves in south Russia and for tree-rings in Turkey. **1933** *Sci. Abstr.* B. XXXVI. 225 A general survey of the subject of telemeasuring with a brief account of telecontrol systems. **1959** *Times* 30 July 2/3 The installation and commissioning of telecontrol and telemetering systems [for an oil company]. **1974** *Sci. Amer.* Nov. 41/1 The control tasks described so far, including the gathering and presentation of information about the system..,can be realized in principle by analogue control circuits,..telecontrol devices and the like. **1966** 'A. HALL' *9th Directive* ix. 83 A Pentax X-15 35 mm single reflex with a 135 mm lens that took a × 2 Auto teleconverter. **1979** *SLR Camera* Mar. 36/3 A short cut to getting involved in tele photography, where your budget is tight, is to use a tele-converter. **1939** E. LILJENKRANTZ *Cancer Handbk.* ii. 23 Telecurietherapy with 10 gm of radium (a quarter of a million dollars' worth) means usually treatment distance of 15 cm. **1954** *Arch. Otolaryngol.* LIX. 345 Advanced inoperable carcinoma is best treated by telecurietherapy. **1953** *Brit. Jrnl. Psychol.* XLIV. 117 The telediphone records of the [television] programmes were broken up into what appeared to be the principal points contained in the programme. **1973** *Listener* 7 June 757/1 The BBC started making telediphone transcripts of what people actually did say, unscripted, on the air. **1957** *Oxford Mag.* 31 Oct. 70/2, I have before me the B.B.C.'s telediphoned transcript of the discussion. **1937** *Sun* (Baltimore) 16 June 4/5 A 'teleflash' and racing slips taken by police in the tavern were not sufficient for a conviction. **1951** *Ibid.* 23 Mar. 28/1 Equipment of the 'teleflash' type which..was used for announcements of racing results and odds. **1935** Telegenesis [see *EUTELEGENESIS]. **1958** *News Chron.* 4 Feb. 4/8 (*heading*) Telegenesis. **1911** W. F. BARRETT *Psychical Research* xi. 161 Dr. Heysinger..suggests the term telegnosis, or knowing at a distance, instead of clairvoyance. **1932** J. BUCHAN *Gap in Curtain* i. 44 The instinct which had its seat in this cell specialised in time-perception... I had been reading lately about telegnosis. **1962** C. D. BROAD *Lect. on Psychical Res.* viii. 222 The distinction between explicitly referential and merely unwilling telegnosis. *Ibid.* 223 Experiences which are only unwittingly telegnostic. **1906** *Pall Mall Gaz.* 24 Mar. 4 Mr. Grier possesses the faculty of 'telegnomy', which enables him..to perceive..events which are taking place on the other side of the Atlantic. **1962** *Punch* 5 Dec. 805/3 Dusailly..has made a first step towards telekinesis by using the electrical cavity of the brain to operate a switch. **1983** J. MELVILLE *Hand of Glass* vi. 146, I *had* seen it move... If you didn't believe in telekinesis.. then Merry must have practised some form of hypnotism on me. *a* **1966** 'M. NA GOPALEEN' *Best of Myles* (1968) 94 An œuvre which would show his telekinetic treatment of over-tonality. **1972** *Countryman* Winter 83 Almost all contemporary investment in the countryside is a telekinetic expression of the distracted town. **1977** A. WILSON *Strange Ride R. Kipling* vi. 291 Trix accumulated clairvoyant, time-travelling, telekinetic and exorcistic powers. **1949** *Startling Stories* May 22/1 'Just what are his potentialities?' queried Shey. 'Is he a hypnotist? A telekineticist?' **1965** J. KINGSTON in J. Carnell *New Writings in S-F* III. 68 Telekineticists..are people who can move things without touching them, change physical states at a distance. **1921** Tele-lens [see *telecentric* adj. above]. **1979** *Amat. Photographer* Feb. 74/2 The modern telelens (and a tele can be as short as 100 mm)..is the biggest boon since sliced bread. **1981** *Times* 20 Oct. 28/4 A new, cheaper form of telegram called the telemessage is to be introduced by British Telecom as an inland service next Monday. **1977** *Bookseller* 14 May 2432/2 A teleordering terminal for bookshops... The value of teleordering from the bookseller's point of view is partly to receive books a few days sooner from publishers. **1929** *Telegr. & Telephone Jrnl.* XVI. 49/1 The transmission of pictures by telegraphic means is coming to the front in the U.S.A... An enterprising firm in New York recently sent out 300 telephotograms of the latest feminine fashions to all parts of the States. **1937** *Times* 30 Oct. 14/2 The London television station transmitted last night the first 'telephotogram' to a ship at sea—a visual message of greeting to the master of the Britannic. **1930** *Monthly Weather Rev.* Nov. 440/2 In the measurements over the sea..the telephotometer..and the theodolite were set up on the point of the mole. **1949** *Proc. Inst. Electr. Engineers* XCVI. II. 456/2 It was possible to calibrate the telephotometer in daylight by reference to tungsten-filament standard lamps of 1-, 2- and 5-kW sizes over ranges varying from 1 500 to 5 000 ft. **1927** *Daily Express* 28 Sept. 9 Teleplasm.. was shown issuing from the face of the tranced woman. **1978** SMYTH & STEMMAN *Mysteries of Afterlife* 225 (*caption*) The teleplasm..is compared with a control sample of ordinary paper. **1930** *Times Lit. Suppl.* 28 Aug. 683/1 Teleplasmic masses resembling arms and hands were seen. **1968** *Daily Tel.* 12 Dec. 25/3 The tele-player will cost about £200 and each tele-cartridge..£20. **1971** *Official Gaz.* (U.S. Patent Office) 23 Nov. TM206/1 *Teleplayer.* For television apparatus... First use Mar. 24 1970. [**1961** *Ibid.* 22 Aug. TM124 *Tele-processing*... For services in organizing, planning, developing, installing, maintaining and operating data processing systems [etc.].] **1962** *Engineering* 8 June 758/2 The development of 'remote computing' or 'teleprocessing' as it is sometimes called. **1970** *Computers & Humanities* IV. 323 Classrooms equipped with voice recorders; and with teletypewriters..for creating perforated paper tape for batch teleprocessing. **1980** R. L. DUNCAN *Brimstone* x. 263 'How will the reprogramming take place?' 'Teleprocessing. Over the telephone lines.' **1914** A. L. TEIXEIRA DE MATTOS tr. *Maeterlinck's Unknown Guest* ii. 63 There are seers, so-called 'telepsychics', who are not psychometers. **1926** F. CAZZAMALLI in *Jrnl. Amer. Soc. Psychical Res.* XX. 1 (*title*) Telepsychic phenomena and cerebral radiations. **1960** *Sci. News Let.* 2 Jan. 4/2 The 'telepuppet', as he [*sc.* F. L. Whipple] called it, would have a little feedback on handling pressure to give the human operator a feel of the object the machine is working on. **1963** *Flight Internat.* LXXXIII. 244/2 It is foreseen that the adaptive machine or 'telepuppet', primitive versions of which are already used in handling radio-active materials, have a key role in space missions. **1973** C. SAGAN *Cosmic Connection* I. viii. 62 There may be telepuppets, devices landed on another planet but fully controlled by an individual human being in orbit. **1909** *Arch. Roentgen Ray* XIV. 38 (*heading*) An instantaneous shutter for teleradiography. **1928** *Brit. Jrnl. Radiol.* I. 368 Arising out of these large milliampereages are the screening stands and radiographic appliances for teleradiography. **1974** *Biol. Abstr.* LVII. 6326/1 Teleradiography and tomography were used to investigate 57 able-bodied male patients. **1937** *Nature* 25 Dec. 1109/1 Teleradium has been practised by several centres in Great Britain over a period of years. **1959** R. W. RAVEN *Cancer* V. 157 Usually a single teleradium or telecobalt field is applied to the undersurface of the chin beneath the tumour. **1909** O. LODGE *Survival of Man* IV. xi. 163 This is the hypothesis of actual telepathic or telergic influence from some outside intelligence. **1912** *Index-Catal. Libr. Surg.-General's Office, U.S. Army* XVII. 712 Teleröntgenography. **1923** R. KNOX *Radiogr. & Radio-Therapy* I. 303 When it is possible to obtain full exposures of the thorax at a distance of 2 metres, then teleröntgenography of the thorax is of decided advantage. **1972** J. E. CULLINAN *Illustrated Guide to X-Ray Technics* i. 3/1 (*caption*) A 72 inch focus-film distance is used for teleroentgenography to minimize geometric enlargement and distortion. **1905** *Rep. Brit. Assoc. Adv. Sci. 1904* 47 [In Italy] there are fifteen first-class observatories provided with apparatus to record teleseisms and local shocks. **1972** J. G. DENNIS *Struct. Geol.* xvi. 363 (*caption*) Teleseism (distant earthquake). **1905** *Rep. Brit. Assoc. Adv. Sci. 1904* 47 Japan has at least five stations for teleseismic observations. **1969** *New Scientist* 25 Dec. 627/1 The so-called teleseismic data.. have provided a rich new fund of research material for analysing the Earth's interior. **1974** *Nature* 23 Aug. 622/3 Nakamura and his colleagues have attempted to determine both P and S wave velocities throughout the lunar mantle from..high frequency teleseismic events and deep moonquakes. **1971** I. G. GASS et al. *Understanding Earth* xxiv. 336/2 A relatively narrow cone at the source can be seen teleseismically. **1981** Teleshopping [see *telebanking* above]. **1983** *Times* 17 Aug. 3/6 The channel will also have the facility for shopping from the armchair at the touch of a switch, now termed 'teleshopping'. **1976** W. J. G. OVERINGTON in *Computing Europe* 4 Mar. 8/2, I have..been theoretically developing a computing system based on Ceefax/Oracle which I call Telesoftware (*ie* software at a distance). **1977** *Wireless World* Sept. 50/2 Perhaps the most marketable use for Telesoftware might be in video games. **1979** *Guardian* 24 Sept. 21/5 Experiments are under way to use Prestel for exchanging software programs and 'telesoftware' is also available for teletext services. **1982** *Datalink* 18 Jan. 5/1 The programme forms only part of the project... There's telesoftware, which uses the BBC's Ceefax teletext service to broadcast software. **1930** MOSELEY & CHAPPLE *Television* viii. 95 Since tele-talkies are sent out in a manner very similar to the transmission of television, they can be received on the identical machine which receives television images. **1913** DORLAND *Med. Dict.* (ed. 7) 946/1 *Teletherapy*, absent treatment. **1929** *Brit. Med. Jrnl.* 11 May 845/1 In teletherapy proper the radium is employed at distances as great as 16 cm. **1945** C. W. WILSON *Radium Therapy* vii. 159 As the name implies, radium teletherapy..is the therapeutic use of a quantity of radium at a distance from the patient. **1974** *Nature* 11 Oct. 521/2 Hyperthermia in conjunction with readily available radiation sources (such as cobalt teletherapy units..) might provide some of the same advantages as heavy particle therapy. **1972** *Science* 5 May 532/3 A thermistor probe which recorded rectal temperatures was connected to a telethermometer. **1968** *Punch* 2 Oct. 488/1 A Royal Martian Vole..teletransported herself to your planet in 1964. **1966** *New Scientist* 20 Jan. 169/3 Each contributing a special faculty such as telekinesis, teletransportation, and so on.

2. [f. *TELE(VISION.] Used to form sbs. denoting activities, persons, things, etc., connected with television (not sharply distinguishable from an attrib. use of *TELE *sb.*[2] **a.** In a virtually limitless range of largely colloq., humorous, or journalistic formations, as *telechair, -course, -drama, -studio*, etc.

1940 *Chambers's Techn. Dict.* 837/2 *Telestudio*,..the enclosure, sound-proofed and treated acoustically, which is used for originating television or broadcasting programmes. **1942** O. E. DUNLAP *Future of Television* vi. 80 The excitement of watching an actual event in progress compensated for any blur or foggy effects, caused chiefly by the tele-eyes' lack of depth and focus. **1953** *Sat. Rev. Lit.* (U.S.) 3 Jan. 3/3 Mr. Sherwood's first teledrama will be seen in the spring by an anticipating nation. **1953** *Sun* (Baltimore) 15 Dec. (B ed.) 10/2 Mr. Gould's teleplay was the better of the two, although by no means a masterpiece. **1954** *Ibid.* 5 Feb. (B ed.) 8/1 The television..reflected both the assets and faults of the original. **1955** *House & Garden* Apr. 70/1 Yellow appears again on the back of the black-seated telechair. **1957** *Economist* 19 Oct. 226/1 'Tele-courses' [in the U.S.] have in some cases completely replaced conventional classes. **1957** *Cinema* 4 Sept. 3 (*heading*) Tele-movies start in U.S. **1957** P. WILDEBLOOD *Main Chance* 54 Ginny had..blossomed out into a quite new kind of star: the Telepersonality. **1958** *Spectator* 10 Jan. 37/2 The Duke [of Bedford] is so anxious to please the telemasses that he has taken voice-production lessons. **1962** *Listener* 30 Aug. 327/1 Three of Mr Bowen's teleplays. **1967** *Daily Tel.* (Colour Suppl.) 22 Mar. 27/1 A few swinging teleclerics try vainly to up-date God's image. **1967** *Which?* Oct. 290/1 Telepundits donned ceremonial expressions of awe. **1970** *Times* 25 July 12 The director of telemedicine at the Massachusetts hospital..says that 60 per cent of the patients have found the automated consultations acceptable. **1972** *Observer* 30 Jan. 9/7 They became something that was to be crucial to the development of television—the first tele-journalists. **1978** *Ibid.* 29 Jan. 29/1, I say 'familiar' because teledrama modes are well established. **1983** *Times* 18 Aug. 7/6 We were hanging on the halting lips of all those returning officers..and marvelling at the sharpness and stamina of the telepundits who could divine at the drop of a percentage that the Tories were sweeping the seaside resorts. **1983** *Listener* 22 Sept. 28/3 This was also the week of *The Godfather*, in Coppola's long tele-version, played on BBC1 at 9.25 pm, every week-night but Wednesday.

b. Special Combs.: **te·lefilm,** a cinematographic film shown on television, esp. one made for that purpose; also, the film medium itself; such films collectively; **te:lepo·litics,** political activity conducted through television; **teleroman** (*tele*roman) [Canad. Fr. *téléroman* (also used): see *ROMAN *sb.*[4]], a French Canadian television soap opera; **te·lescreen,** a television screen; **televa·rsity** [VARSITY], a university that teaches its students by means of television, an open university (*disused*); **tele-vérité** (*televerite*) (also in Fr. form **télé-vérité**) [f. as *CINÉMA-VÉRITÉ], television broadcasting that presents real life; documentary television; **televersity** [*uni*)*versity*] = *televarsity* above (disused).

1939 *Los Angeles Extended Area Telephone Directory* 1003/1 Telefilm 16 mm Productions Co... 6039 Hollywood Blvd. **1950** *Electronic Engin.* XXII. 8/1 With the advent of television recording or 'telefilm' as it is called, a new tool has been placed in the hands of the television programme builders. **1958** *Times* 20 Nov. 3/4 Plans were announced for the largest Anglo-American co-production scheme yet envisaged in the field of the tele-film. **1975** *New Yorker* 19 May 88/2 It has been translated into telefilm with a greater concern for the Indian position than has been shown by most filmmakers in the past. **1959** *Observer* 4 Oct. 21/3 Lennox-Boyd looked a bit tense, but was certainly controlled. His exit line, to the effect that he had been doing the most wonderful work in the world, deserves a place for itself in the annals of telepolitics. **1975** *Listener* 9 Oct. 479/1 It is a pity telepolitics are so unlike the real thing. **1973** *Globe & Mail* (Toronto) 13 July 13/3 CBC President Laurent Picard's marked liking for the numerous serials seen on CBC French TV, called teleromans. **1942** O. E. DUNLAP *Future of Television* vi. 80 The clarity of the telescreen could not be compared to the sharpness of a newsreel. **1949** 'G. ORWELL' *Nineteen Eighty-Four* I. 6 The telescreen received and transmitted simultaneously. **1979** *Globe & Mail* (Toronto) 13 July 14/3 This wit pales towards the end, as Smith is systematically reduced through the clever interplay of video playbacks (read telescreen for life in Oceania) with O'Brien's stiff and triumphant martinet's voice. **1961** *Economist* 16 Dec. 1105/2 The daytime hours on this network, when the voluntary 'televarsity' students would be at their ordinary everyday work. **1964** *New Statesman* 14 Feb. 264/3 *Télé-verité* may have reached its apogee.. when a man was tortured to within a few minutes of death in front of the camera. **1976** *Listener* 11 Mar. 310/1 Selected by their daughter's boyfriend, a television producer, as the subject of his *tele-vérité* film. **1950** *Time* 21 Aug. 44/2 *Televersity.* For years, educators have been talking about television as an ideal teaching medium... [The University of] Michigan will start weekly Sunday afternoon telecasts.

3. [f. TELE(PHONE *sb.*] Prefixed to sbs. with reference to a service obtained by means of the telephone, as **te·le-ad,** an advertisement placed in a newspaper by telephone; **te·lebus,** (a service offering) a bus that can be summoned by telephone; **te:lefacsi·mile** (see quot. 1967); **te·lelecture** (see quot. 1969); **te·lesale,** a sale effected by a salesperson who telephones prospective customers.

1976 *Southern Even. Echo* (Southampton) 3 Nov. 3/8 Tele-Ads from telephone subscribers within the 'Southern Evening Echo' circulation area only are accepted. **1977** *Financial Times* 23 Apr. 13/6 Journalists and tele-ad girls should have direct access to the terminals. **1969** Telebus [see *DIAL *v.* 4 b]. **1972** *Daily Colonist* (Victoria, B.C.) 25 Feb. 8/1 The telebus service..uses half-size buses that pick passengers up at their homes and drive them to the nearest regular bus route terminal. **1967** *Britannica Bk. of Year* 804/3 *Telefacsimile,* a system for the transmission and reproduction of fixed graphic matter (as printing) involving the use of signals transmitted over telephone wires (as between libraries). **1968** *Sat. Rev.* (U.S.) 17 Feb. 60 Colleges today are..piping the specialist's voice and face in by telelecture and television. **1969** *Britannica Bk. of Year* 801/1 *Telelecture,* 1. A loudspeaker connected to a telephone line for amplifying voice communication. 2. A lecture delivered to an audience by telelecture. **1981** *Monitor* (McAllen, Texas) 1 Mar. 24/5 A series of telelectures entitled 'Good Health—the key to Happy Living' is continuing at Knapp Memorial Methodist Hospital. **1963** *Spectator* 12 Apr. 478/3 The advantages of 'telesales' over direct mail. **1981** *Event* 16 Oct. 99/3 (Advt.), Dynamic telesales personnel.

tele-ad: see *TELE- 3.

teleangiectasis, -ia, varr. TELANGIECTASIS in Dict. and Suppl.

telebanking, tele-camera: see *TELE-1.

telecast (te·lĭkɑst), *sb.* orig. *U.S.* [f. TELE- + BROAD)CAST *sb.*] The action or an act of broadcasting by television; a television broadcast or programme.

1937 *Atlantic Monthly* CLIX. 531/2 He can be assured that any receiver he buys will give him the telecasts sent out by all the major systems of transmission. **1951** M. EHRLICH *Big Eye* i. 11 The Telecast Building way downtown. **1954** 'J. CHRISTOPHER' *22nd Cent.* 21 Within three hours of the Atomics telecast there were riotous assemblies in Canberra. **1961** G. MILLERSON *Technique Television Production* iii. 32 The forms of perspective-distortion introduced by narrow-angle lenses are a familiar feature in telecasts where the camera has to be positioned some way from the subject. **1978** J. IRVING *World according to Garp* xvi. 349 Except for the fact that there had been no nudity in the telecast, the event was an X-rated soap opera from start to finish. **1980** *Daily Tel.* 12 July 5/1 The Minister also said in a telecast that value-added tax would be applied to more products.

telecast (te·lĭkɑst), *v.* orig. *U.S.* [f. TELE- + *BROAD)CAST *v.* 3: cf. prec.] *trans.* To broadcast by television.

1940 *Topeka* (Kansas) *Daily Capital* 25 Mar. 1/4 Easter Services..were telecast today. **1949** R. GRAVES *Seven Days in New Crete* iv. 44 The garish, raucous, three-dimensioned cartoon-comedies telecast every hour in mid-air over the harbour. **1952** *Economist* 26 July 228/1 Old films..are telecast over 49 stations. **1968** *Globe & Mail* (Toronto) 13 Jan. 26/3 In Saint Joan (telecast last month) I searched through myself for parts I could put into Joan. **1978** G. VIDAL *Kalki* viii. 182 Since the networks refused to telecast the Kalki–Arlene Wagstaff interview, Giles was obliged to buy thirty minutes of prime-time television.

So **te·lecasting** *vbl. sb.* and *attrib.* or as *ppl. a.*; **te·lecaster,** one who broadcasts on television.

1937 *Electronics* Sept. 13/1 (*caption*) 'Telecasting' in Great Britain. **1940** A. H. MORTON in Porterfield & Reynolds *We present Television* i. 47 Television standards in the United States must be uniformly adopted by all telecasters. **1945** F. BROWN *Angels & Spaceships* (1955) 90 Every major broadcasting and telecasting station in the world has gone off the air. *Ibid.* 92 With telecasting suspended there were no pictures on their screens. **1951** M. EHRLICH *Big Eye* i. 26 News of the world!..Here is your telecaster—Arthur Morrow! **1957** *Observer* 25 Aug. 11/1 This was a commendable piece of telecasting, though a military exercise unopposed..is always a bit of an anti-climax. **1974** *Times* 8 Jan. 13/7 The 10.30 shut-down has shortened the telecasting day.

telechiric (telĭkəiᵊ·rik), *a.* and *sb.* [f. TELE- + Gr. χείρ hand + -IC.] **A.** *adj.* Applied to a device which carries out manipulative operations under the control of a person who is not in the immediate vicinity, but who receives feedback from sensors in the device; also applied to a process or system involving such devices. **B.** *sb.* **a.** *pl.* The branch of technology concerned with telechiric devices. **b.** A telechiric device or system.

1963 J. W. CLARK in *Battelle Technical Rev.* Oct. 3/2 Since the system..can be considered as an extension of man's manipulative and sensory capabilities, even to the use of hand tools, it is well described by the term 'telechirics'. The word is formed from two Greek words—'tele'.., meaning distant, and 'kheir or chir'..which means hand. *Ibid.* 4/2 A well-designed telechiric system replaces man's eyes, hands, and feet with somewhat equivalent mechanical devices. **1968** *Sci. Jrnl.* Oct. 65/2 The commercial cost advantages of the telechiric will displace all competition for work duties undersea. **1970** *Physics Bull.* Oct. 450/1 The telechiric machine requires complete sensing devices, but it presents the sense information to a human as if he were receiving it directly. **1977** *Daily Mail* 11 July 24 (*heading*) Send the telechiric down the pits. *Ibid.* Professor Meredith Thring, Professor of Mechanical Engineering at Queen Mary College, London, is pressing for the development of telechiric mining in Britain. **1978** *Jrnl. R. Soc. Arts* CXXVI. 493/2, I am working on telechirics in mining. It means we shall be able to mine coal in the future without miners going underground, because miners can do their job remotely from the surface.

Hence **telechir** (te·lĭkīᵊɪ) = *TELECHIRIC *sb.* b.

1980 *New Scientist* 3 Jan. 5 A telechir is a mobile machine equipped with TV, sensor devices, mechanical arms and hands, and controlled by a skilled human operator situated at the surface.

telecine (telĭsi·nĭ). [f. *TELE- 2 + *CINE, or f. next.] The broadcasting of cinematographic film on television, or its conversion into television signals; also, apparatus or an organization involved in doing this. Freq. *attrib.*

1935 *Illustr. London News* 23 Feb. 306/1 In the Telecinė apparatus, ordinary standard sound-films may be used. **1937** *Electronics* Aug. 34/3 *Telecine transmission,* the process of transmitting motion-picture film subjects by television. **1938** *Ibid.* July 25/1 A succession of stationary images is projected upon the photoelectric cathode of the pick-up tube in the telecine camera. **1949** *Electronic Engin.* XXI. 194 Two sets of telecine equipment..have just been installed at Alexandra Palace, where they are now being used for televising film programmes. **1959** *Viewpoint* July 32 The telecine operator's in now. Didn't you want to see that piece of film? **1960** D. WILSON *Flight of Dove* 223 Superimpose main title. End telecine (1). **1961** G. MILLERSON *Technique Television Production* vii. 124 Film televising equipment (Telecine) ranges in complexity from slightly adapted cinema projection apparatus, to electronic scanners. **1972** I. HAMILTON *Thrill Machine* xxxix. 187 Joe gave his cues to the men in telecine. **1978** *Gramophone* Aug. 391/3 They have even announced a telecine attachment to use the camera for transcribing home films to video tape. **1983** *New Scientist* 26 May 546/3 The film image is converted to video in the usual way with a 'telecine' machine, which combines a film projector with a video camera.

† **telecinema** (telĭsi·nĭmă). *Obs.* exc. *Hist.* Also **telekinema** and with hyphen. [f. *TELE- 2 + *CINEMA, *KINEMA.] **1.** = prec.

1930 MOSELEY & CHAPPLE *Television* viii. 93 An extraordinary situation in the fascinating history of television was the development of what is now called the tele-cinema.

2. (Also with capital initial.) The name of a building in the Festival of Britain of 1951 in which television programmes could be shown on a large screen as in a cinema; the system or process involved in producing this display.

1951 I. COX *South Bank Exhibition* 83 The Telecinema is the first cinema in the world to be specially designed and built for the showing of both films and television. **1952** *Times* 6 Feb. 4/7 The Minister had suggested that, except for the Telekinema and possibly, also, the Waterloo Road administration blocks, none of the festival buildings should be retained unless the council wished to take them over. **1953** A. K. C. OTTAWAY *Educ. & Society* v. 81 Many new means of mechanical amusement have been created. We have the telecinema; shall we even yet have the 'Feelies'. **1976** *Oxf. Compan. Film* 495/2 *National Film Theatre,* a club cinema established and run by the British Film Institute, took over and rebuilt the Telekinema. **1977** M. STRICKLAND *A. Thirkell* x. 157 Angela treated the events [of the Festival of Britain, 1951] with the greatest scorn, but she agreed nevertheless to be interviewed on the 'telecinema'.

telecobalt: see *TELE- 1.

telecom (te·lĭkǫm). Colloq. abbrev. of *TELECOMMUNICATION. Also (chiefly *attrib.*) in *pl.*

British Telecom, name of a public corporation, formerly part of the Post Office, set up on 1 October 1981 to provide telecommunications and data processing services.

1963 *Telecoms Topics* Aug. 1 This new publication, *Telecoms Topics,*..will contain the latest information about..*G.E.C. Telecommunications.* **1964** D. MACARTHUR *Reminiscences* IX. 331 By 'telecom' I was directed to use the Navy and the Air Force to assist South Korean defenses by whatever use I could make of these two arms. **1970** T. LILLEY *Projects Section* v. 45 That patrol..was now accompanied by telecom and explosive experts. **1981** *Economist* 24 Jan. 100/1 Every big telecoms company is evaluating bubbles (or already buying them) for use in private branch exchanges.

telecommand: see *TELE- 1.

telecommunication (te:lĭkǒmiūnikēⁱ·ʃən). [f. TELE- + COMMUNICATION, after F. *télécommunication.*] Communication over long distances, esp. by electrical means such as by telegraphy, telephony, or broadcasting; (usu. in *pl.*) the branch of technology concerned with this. Also *concr.*, a means or channel of such communication. Freq. *attrib.*, esp. in *pl.*

The term *télécommunication* was adopted by the Convention Internationale des Télécommunications at Madrid in 1932 (the official language at the conference was French). The definition then accepted ('toute communication télégraphique ou téléphonique de signes, de signaux, d'écrits, d'images et de sons de toute nature, par fil, radio ou autres systèmes ou procédés de signalisation électriques ou visuels (sémaphore)'), in so far as it includes non-electrical means of communication, is no longer applicable.

1932 *Times* 18 Nov. 13/4 The new convention which is being drawn up by the International Telegraph and Radiotelegraph Conference..will be called International Telecommunications Convention. **1942** *Electronic Engin.* Aug. 128/2 A telecommunication system where intelligence is communicated by means of a radio-frequency carrier. *Ibid.* Dec. 306/1 Rigid frequency control has become a necessity in radio broadcasting and indeed in all forms of telecommunication. **1944** *Times* 21 July 3/4 Resistance groups in Belgium have..been engaged in the systematic destruction of railways, road bridges, telecommunications, [etc.]. **1953** *Science News* XXX. 70 One has only to consider the field of automatic telecommunication to accept the process [*sc.* electrical manipulation of information] as commonplace. **1957** *Technology* July 187/2 The possible applications of solar batteries in telecommunications. **1961** *Engineering* 6 Jan. 33/1 The plan..to put a telecommunications satellite into orbit round the earth. **1971** F. J. M. LAVER in B. de Ferranti *Living with Computer* v. 44 The capture of data at its point of origin, its rapid transmission over telecommunication links, and its filtering and analysis by computers. *a* **1974** R. CROSSMAN *Diaries* (1977) III. 583 It was an impressive telecommunications feat, which is why Kennedy decided to do it. **1979** MILLER & CHYNOWETH (*title*) Optical fiber telecommunications.

telecon (te·lĭkǫn). *U.S. Mil.* [f. *teletype* s.v. TELE- + CON(FERENCE *sb.*: see next.] **1.** A device of the U.S. army which sends teletype messages over long distances by means of radio or underwater cable and which typically displays them on a screen; a conference held by this means.

1950 *N.Y. Times* 2 July 8E/1 This was the 'telecon' room, equipped with machines that enable officers in Washington to confer with headquarters overseas... The telecon, essentially, is just a teletype machine, but it has certain modifications which make it especially useful for military communications. **1951** *Sun* (Baltimore) 31 Oct. (B ed.) 7/2 Gen. Douglas MacArthur participated in four history-making telecons. **1969** D. ACHESON *Present at Creation* (1970) xliv. 412 A telecon is a secure device by which a typewriter operated at one end records both there and through a similar machine at the other end.

2. [orig. *transf.* from sense 1; later re-formed as shortening of next.] A long-distance con-

ference held by means of teletype or telephone.
1951 *Sun* (Baltimore) 31 Oct. (B ed.) 7/2 The generals like to impress each other with 'sorry, can't see you then, have a telecon with Washington at that time'. **1981** *Aviation Week & Space Technol.* 15 June 128/3 Reference our telecon regarding the operation of company flights to Antarctica and return nonstop. **1982** *Legal Times* 10 May 14/2 A client..may yelp about a 'six-minute telecon' on his bill that costs $10.

teleconference (te·lɪ̆kǫ:nfĕrĕns). [f. TELE- + CONFERENCE *sb.*] A conference held by people who, though separated physically, are linked by telecommunication devices (e.g. telephones, television screens, etc.). So **tele·co·nferencing.**
1953 *Language* XXIX. 71 A general at a teleconference writes out a message for transmission. **1973** *Times* 4 Oct. 35/5 The prospect of similar teleconference equipment in every main commercial or industrial building—just like the telephone on the business desk—is no longer a pipe dream. **1975** *Financial Times* 21 July 6/2 The psychological and travel-replacement aspects of teleconferencing were underlined in a paper by Quebec University. **1981** *Times* 9 Feb. 20/1 Teleconferencing brings together a number of people in different locations for a meeting by means of a tele-audio link.

teleconnection to **-converter:** see *TELE- 1.

telecopier (te·lɪ̆kǫ:piəɹ). Also (*U.S.*) **Tele-.** [f. *TELE- 3 + COPIER.] A facsimile device which transmits and reproduces graphic material over telephone lines.
A proprietary term in the U.S.
1967 *Official Gaz.* (U.S. Patent Office) 24 Jan. TM 152/2 Telecopier. For transmitting and receiving equipment for producing facsimile copies of documents. First use June 13, 1966. **1972** M. GILBERT *Body of Girl* xviii. 160 A photograph..was sent by the tele-copier to the Isle of Wight. **1979** *Fortune* 21 May 123/2 He kept a telecopier in his bedroom to take messages and transmit urgent documents.

telecurietherapy: see *TELE- 1.

telediagnosis (te:lɪ̆,daiăgnō͞u·sis). [f. TELE- + DIAGNOSIS.] The long-distance assessment of a patient's condition by a doctor using closed-circuit television.
1961 *New Scientist* 7 Dec. 604/1 The most recent use of television in medicine is in 'telediagnosis' now being used in Paris. **1972** D. V. TANSLEY *Radionics* 6 He then experimented with telediagnosis which utilized the overhead telephone wires to link him with the patient sample.

telediphone: see *TELE- 1.

teledu. Add: Also † **telagu.** For *Mydaus meliceps* substitute *Mydaus javanensis*. (Earlier and later examples.)
1821 T. S. RAFFLES in *Trans. Linnean Soc.* XIII. 251 *Mephitis Javanensis* Desm. Telagu of the Malays. **1906** E. INGERSOLL *Life of Animals: Mammals* 176 Two related animals of the East are the teledu, or stinking badger, a small nocturnal burrower of Java and Sumatra ..and the large, long-snouted, piglike sand badgers. **1965** D. MORRIS *Mammals* 292 The Teledu is well able to defend itself by means of the offensive secretions of its large anal glands.

telefacsimile: see *TELE- 3.

teleferic (telɪ̆fe·rik). Also ‖ **teleferica, telepheric.** [ad. It. *teleferica*, f. Gr. τῆλε TELE- + φέρειν to carry + -ικος -IC: see next.] A cableway.
1916 *Windsor Mag.* Oct. 498 We walk a little way and then go up by the teleferic. **1918** W. HUTCHINSON *Doctor in War* (1919) xviii. 262 The miniature cable-railway, or teleferica. **1931** R. H. BEADON *Royal Army Service Corps* II. xi. 336 It was found necessary..to use what was known as the Teleferica, or wire rope carrying cradles, which was extensively used by the Italians. **1964** *Harper's Bazaar* Nov. 140/3 New teleferic extension of the Grandes Rousses lift at Alpe d'Huez. **1973** *Good Motoring* May 31/2 A telepheric takes visitors up part of the hill.

‖ **téléférique, téléphérique** (teleferīk). [Fr., f. as prec.] = prec.
1956 I. BROMIGE *Enchanted Garden* III. 150 We'll go up on the *téléphérique* after tea. **1958** *Times* 15 Nov. 11/5 At present there are no ski-lifts or téléfériques [in the Loetschental]. **1965** G. McINNES *Road to Gundagai* vi. 97 We..hoped emptily that..a little téléférique would appear to carry us all up high in the clouds. **1977** *New Yorker* 26 Sept. 107/1 The Brévent, to be sure, could be reached in a few minutes by a system of *téléphériques*.

telefilm: see *TELE- 2 b. **teleflash, telegenesis:** see *TELE- 1.

telegenic (telɪ̆dʒe·nik), *a.* orig. *U.S.* [f. *TELE- 2 + *-GENIC b, after *photogenic*.] Of a person or thing: that shows to advantage on television; providing an interesting or attractive subject for a television broadcast.
1939 *Sun* (Baltimore) 16 Oct. 6/8 Judith Barrett, pretty and blonde actress, is the first Telegenic Girl to go on record. In other words she is the perfect type of beauty for television... She is slated for the first television motion picture. **1948** *Daily Tel.* 23 June 6/4 One word that is playing an important part at this gathering is 'telegenic'. With everything that happens..being reproduced on thousands of television screens, the ability of any speaker to look as attractive as he sounds has become an important political asset. **1950** *New Yorker* 26 Aug. 18/3 Korman has spent many hours in the WOR Television studios, experimenting with telegenic properties of various weaves and colors of cloth and styles of suits. **1962** P. FERRIS *Church of England* ii. 35 The letters 'C.R.' after a man's name keep cropping up..in the *TV Times*, television having discovered that the religious communities have some telegenic personalities. **1971** H. WILSON *Labour Govt.* (1974) xvi. 372 We had not yet reached the position where telegenic situations were planned in advance between a television authority and the demonstrators. **1980** *Times* 7 Nov. 12/2 Conscious that jazz by itself is not very telegenic, producers compensate by building shiny sets.

telegnomy: see *TELE- 1.

telegram. Add: (Later *attrib.* example.) Also *transf.* and *fig.*
1908 E. J. BANFIELD *Confessions of Beachcomber* II. i. 244 Telegrams along the line from the sucker [*sc.* a fish] give precise information. **1922** JOYCE *Ulysses* 117 A telegram boy stepped in nimbly, threw an envelope on the counter and stepped off posthaste. **1963** *Listener* 3 Jan. 14/1 A slim, solid brick tower, a kind of telegram about all the best and strongest things in Germany, stands a few feet away.

telegram, *v.* Delete ? *Obs.*, restrict *rare* to *intr.* use, and add: *trans.* (*a*) (later examples); (*b*) to send (news, information, etc.) by telegraph. Hence **te·legrammed** *ppl. a.*, that has been sent by telegraph; **te·legramming** *vbl. sb.*
1952 M. TRIPP *Faith is Windsock* x. 149 In hospital with a broken leg. His mother has just telegrammed the news. **1969** R. MILLAR *Kut* vii. 154 A miserable Aylmer telegrammed Lake with a copy to Townshend. **1970** *Nature* 18 July 225/1 This information was simultaneously telegrammed to doctors. **1972** D. DOUGLASS *Pit Life in Co. Durham* (History Workshop Pamphlets No. 6) 53 The Executive Committee issued telegrammed instructions to the Lodge. **1973** A. BROINOWSKI *Take One Ambassador* ii. 16 The telephoning and telegramming was to begin once more. **1977** C. McCULLOUGH *Thorn Birds* ix. 201 Mrs. Cleary telegrammed me, a..courtesy I appreciated very much. **1981** *Washington Post* 26 May A15/1 Israeli Premier Menachem Begin's suggestion in telegramming his congratulations for Mitterand's election.

telegraph, *sb.* Add: **1. c.** (Further examples.) See also *bush telegraph* s.v. *BUSH *sb.*[1] 11.
1866 *Tumut & Adelong* (N.S.W.) *Times* 1 Jan. 2/3 They approached to within one hundred yards of the camp unobserved, and then it was apparent that the 'telegraph' had done its work. **1891** 'OLD TIME' *Convict Hulk 'Success'* 20 The 'telegraph' was very extensively worked on board these hulks... The 'telegraph' was a system of speaking from one cell to another by means of tapping on the walls. **1964** D. MACARTHUR *Reminiscences* VI. 206 News of the first such shipment spread rapidly by the 'bamboo telegraph' through the Philippines. **1969** *New Yorker* 14 June 76/2 He would look down at his plate and find two steaks there. He knew what was happening. A message had come from the kitchen, on the Afro-American telegraph.
3. (Earlier example.)
1821 G. GLEIG *Campaigns Brit. Army at Washington & New Orleans 1814–15* vii. 89 We had not proceeded many miles from the river's mouth, when a telegraph from the admiral gave orders for the troops to be in readiness to land.
4. (Earlier example.)
1849 *Sussex Agricultural Express* 8 Sept. 6/4 At the close of the first innings the telegraph showed to the people a score of 61 runs.
5. b. *Austral. spec.* One who warns bushrangers about the movements of police and pursuing troopers.
1864 *Goulburn* (N.S.W.) *Herald* 17 Aug. 2/3 These young scoundrels have got their 'telegraphs' in town, and there is not a stir the police can make but it is known. **1867** *Ibid.* 12 Oct. 4/5 It would make me look a gamer man to the police and other people as has got a down on me for being a telegraph to you chaps. **1908** C. WHITE *John Vane, Bushranger* xv. 76 One of our 'telegraphs' rode up and told us that a party of three police had just gone along the road towards Carcoar.
8. *telegraph house* (earlier and later examples), *line* (earlier U.S. example), *signal, station, wire* (earlier examples); **telegraph blank** *U.S.* = *telegraph form*; **telegraph coach** = *telegraph-carriage*; **telegraph code** (see quot. 1971); **telegraph editor** *U.S.*, on the staff of a newspaper, one who edits news received by telegraph; **telegraph pole, post** (earlier examples).
1893 S. MERRILL in M. Philips *Making of Newspaper* 99 He struck out the formal matter in the heading of the telegraph blank. **1904** [see *BLANK *sb.* 6]. **1928** F. N. HART *Bellamy Trial* i. 3 [He] had..a good-sized stack of telegraph blanks clasped to his heart. **1812** A. CONSTABLE *Let.* 22 Nov. in J. Constable *Corr.* (1962) I. 85 To Mr. Farrington by last night's Telegraph Coach, a brace of pheasants were forwarded. **1835** *N.Y. Commercial Advertiser* 23 July 4/2 Two Telegraph Coaches will leave Albany every day at half-past 10, A.M...and arrive at Rochester in 44 hours. **1885** *List of Subscribers, Classified* (United Telephone Co.) (ed. 6) 231 Universal Translations Institute,..Specialities:..patent specifications, telegraph codes. **1971** *Gloss. Electrotechnical, Power Terms* (*B.S.I.*) III. iii. 12 *Telegraph code*, a system of rules and conventions according to which the telegraph signals forming a message, or the data signal forming a block, should be formed, transmitted, received and processed. **1875** C. F. WINGATE *Views & Interviews* 195 Have been continuously employed on the *Missouri Republican* [as] telegraph editor. **1923** G. C. BASTIAN *Editing Day's News* 9 Inside the News Room..[we find the] Managing Editor..City Editor..Telegraph Editor [etc.]. **1981** *N.Y. Times* 15 June A20/3 The telegraph editors of our [*sc.* the Associated Press's] member papers take our word for it and put it in print. **1808** LD. DUNDONALD *Let.* 28 Sept. in *Autobiogr. Seaman* (1860) I. 288 The newly constructed semaphoric telegraphs..have been blown up and completely demolished, together with their telegraph houses. **1923** KIPLING *Land & Sea Tales* 239 My father is at the telegraph-house sending telegrams. **1847** *Michigan Gen. Statutes* (1882) I. 944 The owner of any land through which said telegraph line may pass..having first given consent. **1851** THOREAU *Jrnl.* 12 Sept. in *Writings* (1906) VIII. 497, I instantly sat down on a stone at the foot of the telegraph-pole, and attended to the communication. **1851** —— *Jrnl.* 30 Sept. in *Ibid.* IX. 37 Methinks these telegraph-posts should bear a great price with musical instrument makers. **1821** G. GLEIG *Campaigns Brit. Army at Washington & New Orleans 1814–15* xv. 206 The minds of all were set at ease, as to the place whither we were going, a telegraph signal being made to steer for Jamaica. **1830** M. EDGEWORTH *Let.* 18 Oct. (1971) 419 They use Telegraph signals—flags white—red—and blue —for *all right—moderate speed—stop*. **1971** *Gloss. Electrotechnical, Power Terms* (*B.S.I.*) III. iii. 12 *Telegraph signal*,..the set of conventional elements established by the code to enable the transmission of a written character [etc.]. **1839** *Knickerbocker* XIV. 187 A recent excursion.. from New-Brighton to the telegraph station. **1973** P. BERTON *Drifting Home* vii. 101 We had stopped at one or more of these solitary telegraph stations whose operators were always fanatically overjoyed to see us. **1848** *Knickerbocker* XXXI. 455 The wrecks of hundreds of little urchins' high-soaring 'hopes'..[hang] on all the telegraph-wires. **1869** *Bradshwa's Railway Man.* XXI. App. 114 Telegraph Wire, Plain or Galvanised, of any length.

telegraph, *v.* Add: **1. b.** (Earlier example in *Cricket*.)
1862 F. LILLYWHITE *Guide to Cricketers* 37 A model of a newly-built covered stand on rollers, with figures for telegraphing on each side.
2. a. (Earlier example.)
1818 'T. BROWN' *Brighton* I. 230 They nod and telegraph to their favourites.
† **3.** *trans.* To send (*esp.* information about police movements) by bush telegraph. *Austral. colloq. Obs.*
1863 *Mudgee* (N.S.W.) *Liberal* 15 Oct. 2/4 The police might have scouts if they would; scouts which would be a match for any system of telegraphing among the bushrangers. **1878** *Australasian Sketcher* 23 Nov. 135/2 The object of the expedition leaked out, and, no doubt, was rapidly telegraphed across the bush to Edward Kelly. **1880** *Victorian Rev.* I. 428 News of the movements of the troopers were 'telegraphed' to them by their confederates.
4. a. In Boxing and other sports: to initiate (a punch, throw, etc.) in such an obvious way as to reveal one's intention. Also in fig. contexts.
1925 J. J. CORBETT *Roar of Crowd* v. 77 Before I would start my right I would, as they say in boxing, 'telegraph' the blow, purposely. **1937** *Daily Mirror* 16 Mar. 30/4 Ford was also landing with some heavy left hooks to the body and although he had never telegraphed his right hand punches..he was now finding Farr's face with such regularity [etc.]. **1945** E. NICHOLS *Hunky Johnny* 68 He telegraphs every curve he throws. **1959** *Charlottesville* (Va.) *Daily Progress* 18 Apr. 10/1 (*caption*), I thought you said he telegraphed his punches! All I saw he delivered personally. **1969** *Wall St. Jrnl.* 1 Dec. 14/1 For competitive reasons, the company won't disclose the nature of the new products now, Mr. Arneson said. 'We're not about to telegraph our punches.'
b. *gen.* To give a clumsily obvious hint or premature indication of (something to come).
1952 *N.Y. Times* 13 Aug. (Late City ed.) 29/5 Inevitably the pay-off gag was 'telegraphed' to the audience far in advance. **1959** *Wall St. Jrnl.* (Eastern ed.) 3 Mar. 12/6 One subplot involving Claudell's mother figures in the story but this development is telegraphed early and does nothing to broaden the book. **1968** *Punch* 16 Oct. 558/3 The exasperating way music [in a film] sometimes not only over-emphasises but even telegraphs effects. **1977** *Time* 7 Nov. 14/2 Young was accurately telegraphing the Administration's view.

telegrapher. 1. For 'Now *rare*' read 'Now chiefly U.S.' and add earlier and later examples.
1851 C. CIST *Sk. Cincinnati in 1851* 51 Telegraphers, 7. **1910** J. HART *Vigilante Girl* 376 This was the room of the man who filled the manifold offices of station-master, ticket-agent, express-agent,..and telegrapher. **1932** E. WILSON *Devil take Hindmost* xvii. 177 The telegrapher ..telephoned ahead along the line to have the niggers taken off. **1955** H. KURNITZ *Invasion of Privacy* (1956) xii. 79 He shared Zorn's hatred of the teletype but..he sometimes operated it himself when the telegrapher was off duty. **1974** T. P. WHITNEY tr. *Solzhenitsyn's Gulag Archipelago* I. I. vi. 268 His White Guard father was just a rank-and-file, unpropertied telegrapher.

telegraphese. Add: **1.** Also *attrib.* or as *adj.*
1951 R. HOGGART *Auden* i. 18 Auden's 'telegraphese' style..is distinguished by its omission of articles, relatives, connectives, personal, demonstrative and other pronouns, and auxiliary verbs. **1978** *Radio Times* 18–24 Mar.

15/1 The actor's opinion hardened into the following telegraphese note: 'Willy beyond question toughest director I've ever worked for.'

telegraphic, *a.* Add: **1. b.** (Earlier example.) Also *telegraphic address*, a brief style of address registered with the postal authorities and designed to reduce the number of words in a telegram.

1839 *Ann. Electricity, Magnetism & Chemistry* III. 442 The telegraph as constructed by Chappe has met with a favourable reception, and since 1793, when the first telegraphic line was established in France, been very generally adopted. **1885** *List of Subscribers, Classified* (United Telephone Co.) (ed. 6) 4 Fraser & Fraser,.. Manufacturers of..Steam Boilers. *Telegraphic address*, 'Pressure, London.' **1910** *Nation* 9 Apr. 54/1 The necessity of being on the right side is self-evident; therefore, when in doubt, write or wire to Mr. Shaw. (Telegraphic address: 'Infallibility', London.) **1930** 'Hay' & Wodehouse *Baa, Baa, Black Sheep* I. i. 12 We'll go to the Grotto!..What-ho for the Grott-ho! Telegraphic address —Tighter London! **1963** *B.S.I. News* May 7/2 BSI's telegraphic addresses have been changed. Overseas cables should now be addressed to 'Standards London W 1' and inland telegrams should be addressed to 'Standards Audley London'.

2. d. *spec.* In *Linguistics*, in the context of language acquisition.

1963 Brown & Fraser in C. N. Cofer *Verbal Behavior & Learning* 192 Young children speak a rather uniform telegraphic English. **1970** D. McNeill *Acquisition of Lang.* iii. 20 Telegraphic speech is the outcome of the process of language acquisition. **1973** R. Brown *First Lang.* I. 143 Telegraphic speech is speech entirely composed of contentive words..and entirely lacking functors or function words. **1978** *Sci. Amer.* Nov. 92/2 Early telegraphic speech is characterized by short, simple sentences made up primarily of content words: words that are rich in semantic content, usually nouns and verbs.

telegraphist. a. (Earlier example.)

1847 *Brit. Patent 11,926* 10 Signals are..quickly received by the mind of the telegraphist.

Telegu, var. Telugu, Teloogoo in Dict. and Suppl.

teleguide (te·lĭgəid), *v.* [f. F. *teleguider* (1947), Quemada (1980): see Tele-, Guide *v.*] *trans.* To control (a missile, etc.) at a distance or indirectly. So **te·leguided** *ppl. a.*, **te·leguiding** *vbl. sb.* Also *telegui·dance* [F. *téléguidage*].

[**1954** *John o' London's Weekly* 12 Feb. 154/3 The French have shortened 'long distance radio control' to 'teleguidance'.] **1960** *Export Service Bull., Suppl.* 4 June 41 The Bell Aircraft Corporation announced that it had signed an agreement..for the production..of the two teleguided target missiles..produced by the French company. **1964** N. Freeling *Double-Barrel* IV. v. 128 'And the aeroplane?' 'Oh that. I built it. We've used it for various experiments; teleguiding and so on.' *Ibid.* 129 If these toys were that simple everyone could have teleguided missiles. **1969** *Africa Digest* June 51/2 An attempt at subversion teleguided from abroad. **1972** *Daily Tel.* 6 May 5/1 Among the new weapons is a teleguided anti-tank rocket fired from a helicopter, which has never previously been used in combat. **1977** *Dædalus* Fall 150 Jacquart does not celebrate the triumph of small familial agriculture, but rather its defeat by the offensive of the 'large enterprises' teleguided by the urban nobility and the Parisian *notables* of the classical age. **1977** N. Freeling *Gadget* v. 218 He's been thinking all day about teleguidance systems.

telekineticist, telelecture, tele-lens: see *Tele- 1, 3, 1.

telemark, Telemark (te·lĭmāɹk). *Skiing.* [f. *Telemark*, the name of an administrative district in southern Norway, where this originated.] A swing turn, now little used, with the leading ski considerably advanced and the knee bent, employed to change direction or stop short. Freq. *attrib.* Also as *v. intr.*

1904 E. C. Richardson *Ski-Running* 59 The telemark swing..should be practised constantly. **1905** *Ibid.* (ed. 2) 78 We propose to deal with the 'Telemark' first. **1920** A. Lunn *Cross-Country Ski-ing* 88 In powder snow one can Telemark in various undefined ways. **1934** Webster, Telemark turn. **1979** R. Fiennes *Hell on Ice* i. 13 Bending low, I began a curving telemark, leading with the left knee. **1981** *Nordic Skiing* Jan. 49/3 It specializes in teaching downhill technique and telemark turns on some of the finest powder in the Sierra Nevada.

telematics (telĭmæ·tiks), *sb. pl.* [f. *Tele-(communication + *infor)matics; cf. F. *télématique* adj.] (The science of) the long-distance transmission of computerized information. So **telema·tic** *a.*, of or pertaining to telematics.

1979 *Economist* 13 Oct. 52/3 The EEC commission is to launch a programme to help European telematics, the new vogue word for the high-growth industries of telecommunications, computers, microchips and databanks. *Ibid.*, Studies to set up a telematic network for the community institutions. **1981** *Jrnl. R. Soc. Arts* CXXIX. 401/2 This story illustrates the importance of possessing advanced telematic equipment. **1982** *Times* 1 Sept. 3/3 Advances in telematics will be far more significant than aircraft design over the next two decades.

telemessage: see *Tele- 1.

telemeter, *sb.* Add: Also with pronunc. (te·lĭmīːtəɹ). **2.** In mod. use, an instrument for measuring a quantity at a distance from the place where the result is displayed or recorded. (Examples.)

1929 *Jrnl. Amer. Inst. Electr. Engineers* XLVIII. 183/1 In addition to surveying the field of application of 'telemetering'..the paper presents several innovations in the types of 'telemeters' available. **1941** T. J. Rhodes *Industr. Instruments for Measurem. & Control* viii. 363 One advantage of this telemeter is that the measuring device requires very little power to move the condenser plate. **1947** *Sun* (Baltimore) 10 Nov. 9/2 Electronic gadgets called 'telemeters'..are installed in high-speed missiles and tuned to send back to the ground by radio whatever information the scientists need. **1975** D. G. Fink *Electronics Engineers' Handbk.* xxvi. 43 The passive implant telemeter may contain a resonant circuit in which the resonant frequency, made to vary with the body signal, can be detected with a grid dip meter.

3. (Usu. with capital initial.) A proprietary term for a system of pay-TV involving the use of a coin-box attached to the television set. *U.S.*

1953 *Wall St. Jrnl.* 27 Nov. 18/4 Another pay-as-you-look television set-up makes its debut here... It [*sc.* the International Telemeter Corp.] has installed 'Telemeters' in 78 local homes. **1955** *Amer. Speech* XXX. 232 For *Telemeter*, the subscriber pays for each program by dropping coins into a box which is attached to the receiver. **1961** *Spectator* 24 Mar. 394/3, 5800 telemeter sets were installed [in Canada]. **1961** *Official Gaz.* (U.S. Patent Office) 17 Oct TM87/1 Telemeter. For pay-television systems including a television transmitter.., equipment at a receiver for processing subscription-television signals, and computer equipment for processing records made at each subscription-television subscriber receiver. First use during June 1951.

telemetric *a.* (further examples); hence also **teleme·trically** *adv.*, by means of telemetry.

1957 *Times* 11 Nov. 10/5 The radio transmitters..and the telemetric apparatus on board have..ceased work. **1961** Webster, Telemetrically. **1970** *Sci. Jrnl.* Aug. 7/1 A cosmonaut in the command module working the Vulcan welding equipment telemetrically by cable. **1971** *Nature* 2 July 65/2 The use of telemetric recording of physiological information from free swimming fish in their natural environment. **1974** W. Garner *Big Enough Wreath* viii. 98 It's definitely a satellite. Multitone telemetric signals. **1977** *Offshore Engineer* May 75/2 Telemetrically operated valves are controlled by two systems in the experiment.

telemeter (te·lĭmītəɹ, tĭle·mĭtəɹ), *v.* [f. the sb.] *trans.* To measure (a quantity) and transmit the result to a distant point; to transmit (a measurement or observation). Freq. with *back*.

1929 *Jrnl. Amer. Inst. Electr. Engineers* XLVIII. 185/2 A carrier wave of constant frequency modulated by an audio frequency which varies with the magnitude of the quantity being telemetered. **1941** T. J. Rhodes *Industr. Instruments for Measurem. & Control* viii. 356 The pressure or liquid-level indication is telemetered to the operating floor. **1953** A. C. Clarke *Prelude to Space* xii. 64 'Alpha's' main instrument readings are telemetered back to Earth. **1965** W. L. Donn *Meteorology* i. 4 The radiosonde.. telemeters the most complete information on the vertical distribution of temperature, pressure and humidity to radio receivers in the laboratory. **1969** *Times* 2 May 16/4 Spacecraft designed to telemeter photographs of the moon's surface back to the earth. **1971** G. G. Luce *Body Time* v. 155 His heart rate was telemetered by a small radio capsule in his undershirt.

Hence **te·lemetered** *ppl. a.*, **te·lemetering** *vbl. sb.* and *ppl. a.*

1929 [see *telemeter *sb.* 2]. **1929** *Jrnl. Amer. Inst. Electr. Engineers* XLVIII. 183/1 In the design of a telemetering equipment it is necessary to study the channel limitations. **1953** *Proc. Inst. Electr. Engineers* C. I. 44/2 The rate of change of a telemetered value can be obtained by means of a feedback amplifier. **1955** *Sci. News Let.* 21 May 324/3 Other methods currently used to track missiles are telemetering, in which the missile radios instrument readings to the ground, and radar. **1960** *Brit. Communications & Electronics* VII. 598/1 Telemetering from the digestive tract. **1976** *Offshore Platforms & Pipelining* 211/1 The operator has a complete telemetering system plus sonar and television. **1978** *Broadcast* 5 June 21/2 All the telemetered information is available on..wall mounted key and lamp panels.

telemetry (tĕ-, tele·mĭtri). [f. Tele- + -metry.] **1. a.** The process or practice of obtaining measurements in one place and relaying them for recording or display to a point at a distance; the transmission of measurements by the apparatus making them.

1885 *Electrician* 9 May 525/1 Telemetry has been practically applied in America..the temperature registrations being exceedingly accurate. **1957** *Economist* 12 Oct. 149 (Advt.), Mullard products are used in almost every electronic application—from radar to radio, from telemetry to television. **1967** *Technology Week* 20 Feb. 10/3 Orbital telemetry indicated that the capsule battery should have sufficient charge to operate the radio beacon and flashing light that serve as recovery aids. **1979** *Sunday Mail* (Brisbane) 7 Jan. 46/5 Occasionally pilots do become disorientated and so a system called air-to-ground telemetry was introduced... Data about the spinning aircraft is transmitted to the ground where another pilot can monitor information and advise the pilot flying how to recover.

b. Apparatus used for telemetry (sense a above).

1958 *Engineering* 28 Feb. 263/3 Instrumentation and telemetry in the satellite are designed to gather and transmit four types of information. **1962** S. Carpenter in *Into Orbit* 160 Everyone keeps one eye on the telemetry to see how the capsule responds.

c. Telemetered information.

1962 *Flight Internat.* LXXXII. 239/2 These receiving stations have been set up..for receiving telemetry from future topside-sounder satellites. **1979** F. Pohl *Jem* i. 8 He had made himself one of the..top experts in reading the telemetry from a tachyon-transmitter probe. **1982** *Daily Tel.* 26 Oct. 28/5 An American spy..gave the Russians details of an NSA satellite system 'rhyolite', which monitored the telemetry of Soviet missile tests.

2. *attrib.*

1953 [see *down-range, downrange *adv.*]. **1958** *Times* 10 Oct. 12/7 Telemetry codes provided from the third Russian satellite are expected to permit an analysis of tape recordings made of the sputnik's transmitters. **1962** S. Carpenter in *Into Orbit* 53 Each time the capsule performs an important function it automatically sends a telemetry report to this effect down to earth. **1976** *Offshore Platforms & Pipelining* 214/2 The latest cable has 65 cores plus telemetry circuits. **1978** R. V. Jones *Most Secret War* xxxviii. 347 Dr. Steinhoff, Head of the Telemetry Department..escaped in his air-raid shelter.

telencephalon (teːlense·fălǫn). *Anat.* [f. Tel(e- + Encephalon.] The anterior of the two vesicles into which the prosencephalon or fore-brain divides in the embryo, or the two antero-lateral vesicles that it gives rise to; the corresponding part of the adult brain, comprising the cerebral hemispheres and the anterior parts of the hypothalamus and the third ventricle.

1897 C. L. Dana *Text-bk. Nerv. Dis.* (ed. 4) i. 3 The anterior vesicle develops two secondary vesicles: the anterior portion of these, including the corpora striata, olfactory lobes, and the cerebral hemispheres, forms the telencephalon. **1934** [see *pallium 3 d]. **1946** B. M. Patten *Human Embryol.* v. 111 By the sixth week of development..the prosencephalon has divided to form the telencephalon and diencephalon. **1948** A. Brodal *Neurol. Anat.* x. 323 In fishes and amphibians the telencephalon is dominated by afferent fibres carrying olfactory impulses to its pallial part. **1977** *Lancet* 9 July 64/1 There was no injury to the mesencephalon in 3 cases, while the telencephalon escaped injury in 2 cases.

Hence **te:lencepha·lic** *a.*, of or pertaining to the telencephalon.

1911 *Jrnl. Compar. Neurol.* XXI. 2 The exact limits of the thalamic and telencephalic gray are discussed later. **1974** D. & M. Webster *Compar. Vertebr. Morphol.* xi. 268 It is not definitely established whether..some of the more superficial avian striatal structures, which are actually large telencephalic nuclei, are homologically related to mammalian cortical structures.

teleo-[2]. Add: **teleo·cracy**, an organization designed to fulfil a specific purpose; hence **te·leocrat, teleocra·tic** *a.*

1973 L. L. & J. M. Constantine *Group Marriage* xiii. 141 In a teleocratic system, leadership depends on the task at hand; teleocratic means 'purpose-centered'. **1975** *Times Lit. Suppl.* 12 Sept. 1018/4 Two notions, both derived from the Roman law, 'societas' and 'universitas'... The latter applies to teleocratic organizations which are supposed to produce specified outcomes. *Ibid.* 1018/5 The full character of the modern state is a condition of unresolved tension between 'societas' and 'universitas'. Teleocracy has always been one of its aspects... He has permitted the teleocrats to impose their self-image upon him. **1976** F. A. Hayek *Law, Legislation & Liberty* II. vii. 15, I understand that Professor Michael Oakeshott, in his oral teaching, has long used the terms *teleocratic* (and *teleocracy*) and *nomocratic*..to bring out the same distinction [*sc.* as between an organization and a spontaneous order].

teleological, *a.* Add: (Earlier and later examples.) *teleological ethics* (see quot. 1967).

1798 A. F. M. Willich *Elem. Critical Philos.* ii. 112 (*heading*) Analysis of the teleological faculty of judging. **1930** C. D. Broad *Five Types of Ethical Theory* vi. 206, I would first divide ethical theories into two classes, which I will call respectively *deontological* and *teleological*. **1966** F. Copleston *Hist. Philos.* VIII. ii. 34 Any form of teleological ethics which interprets the moral imperative as..an assertoric hypothetical imperative. **1967** *Encycl. Philos.* VIII. 88/1 Teleological ethics..is the subordination of the concept of duty, right conduct, or moral obligation to the concept of the good or the humanly desirable. **1973** S. F. Cohen *Bukharin* vii. 228 Rykov.. a perennial foe of grandiose economic projects and teleological planning.

teleonomy (teli,ǫ·nŏmi). *Biol.* [f. Teleo-[2] + -nomy.] The property, common to all living systems, of being organized towards the attainment of ends (see quots.). Hence **teleono·mic** *a.*, of or pertaining to teleonomy.

1958 C. S. Pittendrigh in Roe & Simpson *Behavior & Evolution* xviii. 391 (*heading*) Adaptation: teleonomy versus teleology. *Ibid.* 394 It seems unfortunate that the term 'teleology' should be resurrected... The biologist's long-standing confusion would be more fully removed if all end-directed systems were described by some other term, like 'teleonomic', in order to emphasize that..end-directedness does not carry a commitment to Aristotelian teleology. **1961** *Cold Spring Harbor Symp. Quantitative Biol.* XXVI. 1 (*heading*) The teleonomic significance of biosynthetic control mechanisms. **1976** *Ann. Rev. Microbiol.* XXX. 538 The hoped-for aim of this review is to promote more studies on the diverse glycerol systems in a teleonomic context. **1977** P. B. & J. S. MEDAWAR *Life Sci.* i. 11 Biologists prefer to use the genteelism teleonomy with merely descriptive connotations to signify the goal-directed or 'as-if-purposive' character of biological performances. **1978** J. Z. YOUNG *Programs of Brain* iii. 16 The conception of 'teleology' has been associated with that of a final aim of life, implying metaphysical or religious beliefs. To avoid this, recent authors have used the word 'teleonomy' to describe the directional character of living activities... But words of this sort confuse many people and one is enough, let us keep to 'teleology'.

teleordering: see *TELE- 1.

teleost, *sb.* (In Dict. s.v. TELEOSTEAN *a.* and *sb.*) (Further examples.)

1895 B. DEAN *Fishes* vii. 139 'Teleost' must be used in a popular and convenient..sense..to denote..the modern 'bony fish'. **1955** AUDEN *Shield of Achilles* i. 15 Had He picked a teleost Or an arthropod to inspire, Would our death also have come? **1979** C. E. BOND *Biol. Fishes* i. 6 Arranging the teleosts into lower, middle, and higher levels of organization may be a gross oversimplification.

telepathetic, *a.* For *nonce-wd.* read *rare* and add later example.

1949 KOESTLER *Insight & Outlook* ix. 119 The functional interactions of hypnotic and telepathetic rapports.

telepathize, *v.* Add: Also (tele·pǎþəiz). (Examples.) Also (*c*) *trans.*, to discern by means of telepathy. *rare.*

1895 in *Funk's Stand. Dict.* **1919** E. H. JONES *Road to En-dor* xi. 115 He had put me on parole..not to telepathize with the good folk of Yozgad. **1941** *Mind* L. 315 But this just is telepathy except that you have made the provision that it shall be done by having the same sensation as the person one telepathises. **1954** 'J. CHRISTOPHER' *22nd Cent.* 145 Did they telepathize our coming and retreat to some more civilized solar system? **1963** *Jrnl. Soc. for Psychical Res.* XLII. 33, I have examined a subject telepathized in this way and questioned him. **1980** C. FITZGIBBON *Rat Report* ii. 38 If the rat had telepathized once, then perhaps it would again.

telepheric, var. *TELEFERIC.

telephonable (telǐfōᵘ·năb'l), *a.* [f. TELEPHONE *v.* + -ABLE.] Of a place or person: able to be reached or contacted by telephone.

1908 G. B. SHAW *Lett. to Granville Barker* (1956) 126 She is ill and not telephonable. **1932** *New Statesman* 23 Jan. 88/1 The advertising campaign which is so largely increasing the number of telephonable people. **1973** S. ALSOP *Stay of Execution* (1974) I. 20 Katmandu was not easily telephonable.

telephone, *sb.* Add: **2. b.** *on the telephone* (*a*) (earlier example); (*b*) making a telephone call, ringing up; using or by means of the telephone.

(*a*) **1885** *List of Subscribers, Classified* (United Telephone Co.) (ed. 6) 18 Other people have their own tradesmen, who are doubtless also on the telephone.

(*b*) **1900** C. H. CHAMBERS *Tyranny of Tears* I. 36 (*The telephone bell rings.*).. There's some one on the telephone —forgive me. (*Goes to telephone.*) **1925** F. SCOTT FITZGERALD *Great Gatsby* ii. 35 Mrs. Wilson called up several people on the telephone. *Ibid.* vii. 138 That's Tom's girl on the telephone *Ibid.* ix. 214 You threw me over on the telephone. **1934** G. B. SHAW *Village Wooing* 135 Oh, speak English: you're not on the telephone now. **1963** K. AMIS *One Fat Englishman* xi. 126 Hearing her voice on the telephone in the next room brought an unwelcome reminder of the small hours. **1965** J. H. ROBERTS *'Q' Document* iv. 101 Those moments when he was forced to abandon conversation with Cooper to talk on the telephone.

d. *ellipt.* for *telephone call*, sense 3 below, esp. in *Indian English*. Cf. *PHONE *sb.*² 1.

1935 F. W. CROFT *Crime at Guildford* xxi. 298 A telephone to the manager of the hotel produced the needed information. **1979** P. NIHALANI et al. *Indian & Brit. English* I. 176 'Your telephones have not been very clear.' 'He gave me a telephone.'..In BS..the phrase 'telephone call', or simply 'call', would be used.

3. *telephone bell* (earlier example), *call, caller, cord, dial, extension, line, message* (example), *office, operator, receiver* (earlier example), *survey, table, transmitter, wire*; *telephone-answering* adj.; **telephone bill** = *phone bill* s.v. *PHONE *sb.*² 3; **telephone book** = *telephone directory* below; **telephone booth, box** = *phone booth, box* s.v. *PHONE *sb.*² 3; **telephone directory,** a book containing an alphabetical list of the names, addresses, and numbers of telephone subscribers; *spec.* (with def. article) such a list covering a particular locality and printed by a telephone company; **telephone girl** (earlier example); **telephone kiosk** = *phone booth, box* s.v. *PHONE *sb.*² 3; **telephone number** = *phone number* s.v. *PHONE *sb.*² 3; *colloq.*, a large number (esp. with reference to a sum of money or a prison sentence); **telephone pad,** a writing pad for noting telephone messages, etc.; **telephone set,** the assembly of components including a telephone transmitter, receiver, etc., which make up a telephone (sense 2 b); **telephone tapping** *vbl. sb.*, the act of making a connection to a telephone wire so as to listen in on private telephone conversations; cf. *TAPPING *vbl. sb.*¹ a; so **telephone tap,** an instance of telephone tapping; **telephone token,** a small counter designed to operate a public telephone and on sale in certain countries of Europe; cf. *JETON 2.

1963 *Times* 5 Feb. 11/4 This is the telephone-answering machine of the coke department... The machine will record your order or message... Please speak clearly... Please speak now. **1900** Telephone bell [see sense 2 b (*b*) above]. **1935** C. ISHERWOOD *Mr Norris changes Trains* viii. 117 In the present state of Arthur's finances, it was hardly to be expected that he would have settled his telephone bill. **1915** J. BUCHAN *39 Steps* viii. 201, I picked up the telephone book and looked up the number of his house. **1975** D. LODGE *Changing Places* iii. 132, I got out the telephone book and began ringing round. **1895** *Funk's Stand. Dict.*, Telephone-booth. *a* **1910** [see *CALL *v.* 35 h]. **1982** T. HOLME *Devil of Dolce Vita* xxii. 178 There is [in Venice] a plethora of squares, some scarcely bigger than a telephone booth. **1904** *McClure's Mag.* Feb. 405 Golden could snatch only two opportunities to step into the telephone box that morning. **1980** I. MURDOCH *Nuns & Soldiers* i. 44 I'm in a telephone box near Victoria Station. **1885** *List of Subscribers, Classified* (United Telephone Co.) (ed. 6) 9 Telephone Call Rooms have just been opened at Clapham and Kilburn. **1910** 'O. HENRY' *Strictly Business* 13 She pointed out to him clearly how it [*sc.* a play] could be improved by introducing a messenger instead of a telephone call. **1980** I. MURDOCH *Nuns & Soldiers* iv. 243 The Count was sitting ..in torment, waiting for her telephone call. **1948** 'J. TEY' *Franchise Affair* x. 103 Your telephone callers: were they male or female? **1934** WEBSTER, Telephone cord. **1966** 'A. HALL' *9th Directive* xv. 143, I..fiddled with the telephone cord. **1960** COOKE & MARKUS *Electronics & Nucleonics Dict.* 478/2 *Telephone dial*, a switch operated by a finger wheel, used to make and break a pair of contacts the required number of times for setting up a telephone circuit to the party being called. **1972** 'E. MCBAIN' *Sadie when she Died* viii. 81 There is still all day tomorrow to twirl those little holes in the telephone dial and ring up this or that hot number. **1907** *Yesterday's Shopping* (1969) 397/3 Private Telephone Directory..Spanish roan, lettered in gold, 24 leaves, to stand or hang. **1913** W. P. EATON *Barn Doors & Byways* 81 We fail to find this sort of thing any more thrilling or 'literary' than the telephone directory. **1969** B. WEIL *Dossier IX* iii. 20 The *Service* are always up to date with their telephone directories. **1945** C. MILBURN *Diary* 2 Jan. (1979) 261 The telephone handy men had arrived to instal a telephone extension up into Alan's room. **1977** 'J. LE CARRÉ' *Hon. Schoolboy* II. xiv. 322 A telephone extension hung on the wall. **1893** *Chicago Tribune* 2 July 13/3 The telephone girl sits on her high stool..as she produces alternate order and chaos at her switchboard. **1931** G. B. SHAW *Fabian Ess.* p. viii, A couple of pennies to drop into the slot in a telephone kiosk. **1974** M. BABSON *Stalking Lamb* II. xxiv. 178 George had entered the telephone kiosk and could be clearly seen inside the brightly lit box. **1882** T. D. LOCKWOOD *Pract. Information for Telephonists* 163 Now, to consider the possible disturbing influence that electric light wires may exercise upon telephone lines. **1962** A. NISBETT *Technique Sound Studio* 261 *Music line*, broad-band circuit for carrying programme (including speech), as distinct from a telephone line. **1982** A. BROOKNER *Providence* ix. 109 Supposing there is a telephone message waiting for me at the hotel? **1885** *List of Subscribers, Classified* (United Telephone Co.) (ed. 6) 3 Edwin Fox & Compy..Telephone No. 5,110. **1950** T. S. ELIOT *Cocktail Party* I. i. 17 You have the address, and the telephone number? **1963** L. DEIGHTON *Horse under Water* xliv. 171 It looked like he was going up the river for a telephone number. **1878** G. H. LEWES *Jrnl.* 21 Mar. in *Geo. Eliot. Lett.* (1956) VII. 16 We went to the Telephone office to have the Telephone explained and demonstrated. **1894** *Life* 19 Apr. 256/1 One of the young lady telephone operators might be listening to our talk and we don't want our telephone taken out. **1964** M. MCLUHAN *Understanding Media* xxiv. 243 Boors, who inundate defenseless telephone operators. **1923** *Sci. Amer.* Feb. 115/3 When this telephone pad is not in use it rests out of sight beneath..the telephone. **1967** A. WILSON *No Laughing Matter* III. 386 Jack, seeing the telephone pad, did not want to break the mood by asking Marcus if he had rung Gladys. **1884** *List of Subscribers* (London & Globe Telephone Co.) 3 Any form of telephone transmitter or receiver. **1911** *Encycl. Brit.* XXV. 552/1 Each telephone set was equipped with a special key. **1976** P. LOVESEY, *Swing, swing Together* xxx. 146 If anything develops here, you can use the telephone set to leave a message at the Yard. **1976** *National Observer* (U.S.) 13 Mar. 1/6 The Knight-Ridder newspapers asked a similar question in a telephone survey in January and found 81 per cent agreement. **1929** 'E. QUEEN' *Roman Hat Mystery* III. xvii. 251 They..shook out the pages of the telephone-book in the bedside telephone-table. **1977** M. RUSSELL *Dial Death* II. i. 39 The figure slumped across the telephone table. **1958** 'E. MCBAIN' *Killer's Payoff* (1960) xv. 153 There was no intention of maintaining a *telephone tap* in the strictest sense of the word. **1958** *Listener* 12 June 971/1 Some of the evidence had been obtained by telephone tapping. **1978** *Peace News* 25 Aug. 9/1 It is important to note that firstly, the Special Branch 'ambush' was only made possible by some combination of mail interception and telephone tapping. **1963** 'D. CORY' *Hammerhead* x. 127 He..asked for a glass of cognac and a telephone token. **1884** Telephone transmitter [see *telephone receiver* above]. **1937** *Discovery* Jan. 27/2 The use of this material for..telephone transmitter diaphragms, is suggested. **1881** 'MARK TWAIN' *Let.* 31 Jan. in C. Clemens *Mark Twain* (1932) 36 In one place the telephone wire running along six inches above the comb [of the roof] is covered. **1978** 'A. YORK' *Tallant for Disaster* xii. 172, I want a start made on getting the telephone wires back up again.

telephone, *v.* Add: **1. b.** (Earlier example.) Also *fig.*

1878 W. TEGG *Posts & Telegraphs* III. 305 It is said that the results of these experiments were 'telephoned' to the *Boston Guide.* **1908** KIPLING *Lett. to Family* vi. 47, I hear the hard trail telephone a far-off horse's feet. **1923** D. H. LAWRENCE *Birds, Beasts & Flowers* 44 Almond tree... What are you doing in the December rain?.. Do you telephone the roar of the water over the earth?

c. (Earlier example.)

1877 *Telegraphic Jrnl.* 1 Sept. 201/2, I [*sc.* Prof. Graham Bell] telephoned the leader of the band.

telephoner. (Examples.)

1918 A. BENNETT *Pretty Lady* xviii. 116 The telephone-bell rang... The telephoner was Gilbert. **1932** *New Statesman* 23 Jan. 87/1, I have often watched one of these fanatical telephoners sitting opposite the telephone with his hand on the receiver. **1972** *New Yorker* 21 Oct. 31/3 We picked up a mimeographed sheet that tells the telephoners what to say.

telephonically, *adv.* (Earlier example.)

1878 G. B. PRESCOTT *Speaking Telephone* vi. 226 Stations could exchange business telephonically.

telephonist. Add: The pronunc. (tele·fǒnist) is now standard. **a.** (Earlier example.)

1880 *Harper's Mag.* Oct. 723/1 Nor are the Chicago telephonists driven to such an access of rage.

c. = TELEPHONER. *rare.*

1956 [see *CRADLE *v.* 5 b].

telephonitis (te:lǐfōᵘnəi·tǐs). *joc.* [f. TELEPHONE *sb.* or *v.* + *-ITIS.] A compulsive desire to make telephone calls.

1935 *Even. Sun* (Baltimore) 24 Apr. 4/6 Garrison was suffering from 'telephonitis'. She [*sc.* his wife] has an injunction forbidding him from calling her on the telephone and..Garrison had violated the order because he 'couldn't help it'. **1962** *Punch* 3 Jan. 71 One of the tragedies of telephonitis is that sufferers are unable to help one another. **1979** *Washington Post* 14 Dec. B3/5 Ted [*sc.* Edward Kennedy] has telephonitis and he's on the phone every night.

telephoto[1]**.** Add: (Later examples.)

1913 KIPLING *Diversity of Creatures* (1917) 290 J'ever see a bird's eye telephoto-survey of England for military purposes? **1920** H. E. IVES *Airplane Photography* xxxi. 383 The telephoto lenses used for spotting would be of long equivalent focus..but of handy size. **1947** A. RANSOME *Great Northern?* i. 17 He would have..a camera with a telephoto lens to take photographs of birds without having to come near enough to disturb them. **1964** M. MCLUHAN *Understanding Media* (1967) II. xxi. 230 The press is now not only a telephoto mosaic of the human community hour by hour, but its technology is also a mosaic of all the technologies of the community. **1977** J. HEDGECOE *Photographer's Handbk.* 119 Some telephoto converters are designed to fit between lens and camera.

B. *sb.* **1.** A telephoto lens or camera.

1904 L. W. BROWNELL *Photogr. for Sportsman Naturalist* v. 72 It is always well, in work with the telephoto, to presuppose that your negative is under-exposed. **1931** O. G. PIKE *Nature Photogr.* iii. 16 A telephoto lens is..a most important part of the nature photographer's equipment... A modern telephoto is a very great advance on those used thirty years ago. **1975** BYFIELD & TEDESCHI *Solemn High Murder* (1976) v. 86, I used a time exposure..with a 135 mm telephoto. They were long exposures.

2. = TELEPHOTOGRAPH *sb.*² *rare.*

1974 J. IRVING *158-Pound Marriage* i. 11, I see the close-ups of the shelling of Reims. The telephoto is still unclear.

telephoto[2]**.** Also *U.S.* **Tele-.** [Abbrev. of TELEPHOTOGRAPH *sb.*¹ or one of its derivatives.] Name for a system of telephotographic transmission.

A proprietary term in the U.S.

1925 *Official Gaz.* (U.S. Patent Office) 3 Feb. 46/1 Telephoto... Photographs. *Ibid.* 7 Apr. 27/2 Telephoto... Machines and apparatus for distance transmission of photographs electrically. **1931** *Daily Express* 13 Oct. 1/6 Picture by telephoto. **1938** F. D. SHARPE *Sharpe of Flying Squad* xxvi. 264 Photographs of finger-prints are greatly reduced in size and are flashed across the sea by the telephoto process to European countries.

telephotogram: see *TELE- 1.

telephotography[2]**.** (In Dict. s.v. TELEPHOTOGRAPH *sb.*²) (Earlier example.)

1892 *Anthony's Photographic Bull.* XXIII. 168 A great deal of discussion is going on at present on the subject of telephotography.

telephotometer to **Teleplayer**: see *TELE- 1. **telepolitics**: see *TELE- 2 b.

teleportation (te:lǐpɔɹtē¹·ʃən). *Psychics* and *Sci. Fiction.* [f. TELE- + TRANS)PORTATION.] The conveyance of persons (esp. of oneself) or things by psychic power; also in futuristic description, apparently instantaneous transportation of persons, etc., across space by advanced technological means. Cf. *telekinesis* s.v. TELE-, *PSYCHOKINESIS 1.

1931 C. FORT *Lo!* I. iv. 42 Sometimes, in what I call 'teleportations', there seems to be 'agency' and sometimes not... Some other time I may be able more clearly to think out an expression upon flows of pigeons to their homes, and flows of migratory birds, as teleportative, or quasi-teleportative. **1945** N. COLLINS *London belongs to Me* IV. liv. 421 The weekly copy of *The Spirit World* lay on the occasional table... They were wonderful letters—full of glimpses through the veil, and teleportations and proofs of survival. **1951** 'J. WYNDHAM' in *Science-Fantasy* Winter 8 Suppose the Russians..could project things or people here by teleportation. **1960** *Analog Science Fact & Fiction* Nov. 14/1 It took a latent ability to learn teleportation, and some people had it while others didn't. *Ibid.* 36/1 Going from one place to another is teleportation. **1977** 'L. EGAN' *Blind Search* i. 4 Telepathy, telekinesis, teleportation, apports, whatever the hell psychic forces.

Hence (as a back-formation) **te·leport** *v.* (*a*) *intr.*, to convey oneself by teleportation; (*b*) *trans.*, to convey by teleportation; also *absol.*; **te·leporting** *ppl. a.* and *vbl. sb.*; also **te·leport** *sb.*, one who practises teleportation; **telepo·rtage** *rare* = *TELEPORTATION; **telepo·rtative** *a. rare*, pertaining to teleportation.

1931 Teleportative [see *TELEPORTATION]. **1951** 'J. WYNDHAM' in *Science-Fantasy* Winter 5 If there could be teleportation, or teleportage, or whatever it is. *Ibid.* 6 This teleporting guy. **1953** 'T. STURGEON' *More than Human* III. 204 Bonnie and Beanie can't carry so much as a toothpick with them when they teleport, let alone clothes. **1954–5** *Planet Stories* Winter 26 It might teleport him, too, if he attracted its attention. **1955** *Astounding Sci. Fiction* Feb. 11 The Martian was back in the chair again. 'It's not teleportation. We don't teleport.' **1960** *Analog Science Fact & Fiction* Nov. 41/2 After all, he'd found telepaths in insane asylums, and teleports among the juvenile delinquents of New York. **1965** *New Statesman* 5 Nov. 705/2 So we must adjust to instant teleporting from Raspail Métro to the Donnybrook tram by way of Strangeways Gaol. **1967** E. B. NICKERSON *Kayaks to Arctic* ix. 79 It was a steep bushy bank but he [*sc.* a bear] made it as if teleported and did not rustle even a leaf. **1979** B. SHAW *Dagger of Mind* vii. 116 Albert can teleport people... Miss Connie..does it with objects. Psychokinesis.

teleprinter (te·lĭpriːntəɹ). [f. TELE- + PRINTER.] A telegraph instrument for transmitting telegraph messages as they are typed on a keyboard and printing incoming ones.

1929 *Telegr. & Teleph. Jrnl.* Dec. 42/1 The first Teleprinters to be tried in this country were produced by the Morkrum Corporation under the proprietary name of 'The Teletype'. **1932** *Times Educ. Suppl.* 6 Aug. p. i/4 A service of teleprinters will be opened in London on August 15. **1933** *Post Office Guide* 138 This service is afforded by..the teleprinter, which is a special kind of telegraph instrument operated by a keyboard closely resembling that of an ordinary commercial typewriter, working over the telephone exchange system. **1939** *Daily Tel.* 18 Dec. 12/4 (Advt.), Applicants who are not trained teleprinter operators should possess a typing speed of at least 30 words per minute. **1942** *R.A.F. Jrnl.* 27 June 22 One tribe of Grand Gremlins lives behind typewriter and teleprinter keys. **1957** *Technology* Apr. 68/4 Pushing a button then causes the positions of film-holder and lens to be punched on teleprinter tape. **1959** *Times Rev. Industry* Sept. 34/1 The teleprinter is not a substitute for a telephone. **1964** M. MCLUHAN *Understanding Media* (1967) II. xxv. 263 The teleprinter and the wireless made it possible for orders from the highest levels to be given direct to the lowest levels. **1978** R. V. JONES *Most Secret War* xviii. 148 Grant's interpretation was circulated by teleprinter. *Ibid.* xviii. 150 The teleprinter room into which the messages came was immediately across the corridor from my own.

Hence (as a back-formation) **te·leprint** *v. trans.*, to send or print (a message, etc.) by teleprinter; **te·leprinted** *ppl. a.*

1971 H. WILSON *Labour Govt.* xxvi. 519 On Saturday, 30 March, I was told on the telephone that a very long telegram was coming in from Washington and would be teleprinted to me at Chequers. **1973** G. TALBOT *Ten Seconds from Now* iv. 44 Sheets of teleprinted news 'tape' from the clattering machines. **1980** *Daily Tel.* 4 Aug. 3/3 Some piece of international news,..important enough to rate a teleprinted 'flash'. **1981** *Sci. Digest* Aug. 50/2 Blood samples and X-rays are taken, and the lab data is teleprinted to the team.

teleprocessing: see *TELE- 1.

teleprompter (te·lĭprǫmᵖtəɹ). orig. *U.S.* [f. TELE- + PROMPTER.] An electronic device, placed out of range of the television or cinematographic camera, that slowly unrolls the speaker's script, in order to prompt or assist him.

Formerly a proprietary name in the U.S. The equivalent British proprietary name is *AUTOCUE.

1951 *Life* 12 Mar. 131 Set at the eye level of performers, the Teleprompter unrolls a script whose inch-high letters, printed by special typewriter, can be read 25 feet away. **1953** *Official Gaz.* (U.S. Patent Office) 10 Feb. 232/1 *Teleprompter.* For electrically-operated apparatus for the cuing of speakers and actors by means of scripts advanced in conformity with the action and/or dialogue... Claims use since Sept. 1, 1950. **1958** *Daily Mail* 13 Dec. 8/8 Last night he [*sc.* Lord Montgomery] seemed to be using a teleprompter, so rapidly did the words rattle out. **1961** S. PRICE *Just for Record* ii. 18 That's what the boys in the backroom had written, and it was staring at him..from the teleprompter. **1978** G. VIDAL *Kalki* i. 20 Although most of Arlene's professional career depended upon her ability to read Teleprompters and cue cards, she refused to wear glasses in public.

Hence (as a back-formation) **te·leprompt** *v. trans.*, to assist by means of a teleprompter. Also **te·leprompted** *ppl. a.*, assisted by or by means of a teleprompter.

1956 *Sun* (Baltimore) 29 Aug. (B ed.) 14/2 Two weeks of nominations,..commentaries, teleprompted oratory and gavel-thumping. **1958** *Spectator* 18 July 87/1 Does my conscience need tele-prompting? **1960** *Time* 16 Nov. (Extra ed.) 15/1 The 1960 campaign had been televised, teleguided, teleprompted and telephoned as no other had been before.

telepsychic to **teleradium:** see *TELE- 1.

telerecording (te·lĭrĭkǭɹdiŋ), *vbl. sb.* [f. *TELE- 2 + *RECORDING *vbl. sb.*] A recording of a television programme made while it is being transmitted. Also *occas.*, the action of making such a recording.

1953 *Radio Times* 22 May 44/2 A telerecording of the Abbey Ceremonies and a special Coronation edition of Television Newsreel. **1957** *Times* 16 Nov. 8/4 After the Queen's Christmas Day broadcast, which is to be televised this year for the first time, telerecordings will be flown to Canada and Australia. **1959** *P.O. Telecomm. Jrnl.* Winter 10/1 The signals are..used to operate a slow-speed film telerecording equipment. **1970** A. GLYN *Blood of British-man* xvi. 186 A telerecording of a Football Cup semi-final. **1975** *Gramophone* Jan. 1330/1 Next month the BBC will take its cameras to Covent Garden for a tele-recording.

Hence (as a back-formation) **te·lerecord** *v. trans.*, to record (a television programme) during transmission. Also **te·lerecorded** *ppl. a.*

1955 *Radio Times* 22 Apr. 15/2 Monday's telerecorded programme *The Secret Arts.* **1956** *Ann. Reg. 1955* 390 A ..television production of *Romeo and Juliet* was telerecorded and sent to the U.S.S.R. **1960** *News Chron.* 24 June 3/7 The programme was telerecorded this week. **1978** *Times* 4 Sept. 9/4 BBC 2's cameras will..telerecord the new production.

telergic, teleroentgenography: see *TELE- 1. **teleroman, telesale:** see *TELE- 2 b, 3.

telescope, *sb.* Add: **1. a.** Also, an instrument or apparatus that serves the same purpose at other wavelengths of the electromagnetic spectrum.

1948, etc. [see *radio telescope* s.v. *RADIO *sb.* 7]. **1970** [see *light bucket* s.v. *LIGHT *sb.* 16]. **1974** *Physics Bull.* May 208/4 A balloon-borne gamma ray telescope, sensitive to photons with energies greater than 50 MeV, has observed several regions of the sky. **1978** PASACHOFF & KUTNER *University Astron.* xi. 315 Telescopes in orbit that are sensitive to x-rays have detected a number of strong x-ray sources.

2. *telescope-making*; *telescope-bag* (N. Amer. examples), *-table* (earlier U.S. example); **telescope word** chiefly *U.S.*, a portmanteau word.

1885 J. SHORT *Diary* 10 Apr. in *Kingston* (Ontario) *Whig-Standard* (1973) 11 Apr. 29/3 Telescope bags packed, in case we have to start for Calgary in a hurry. **1949** W. FAULKNER *Knight's Gambit* (1951) 110 A tremendous old-fashioned telescope bag, strapped and bulging, sat on a chair. **1881** T. HARDY *Let.* 13 Dec. (1978) I. 97 The telescope-making in the catalogue is also useful. **1937** *Discovery* Nov. 360/1 Amateur telescope-making is a hobby that has found many more enthusiasts in the United States than in the British Isles. **1869** C. L. EASTLAKE *Hints on Househ. Taste* (ed. 2) iii. 67 What is commonly called a 'telescope' table, or one which can be pulled out to twice its usual length, and, by the addition of extra leaves in its middle, accommodates twice the usual number of diners. **1909** *Cent. Dict.* Suppl., Telescope-word. **1933** H. WENTWORTH *Blends in Eng.* 3 *Telescope word* has also been applied to one formed from the first syllables of words. **1977** *Lebende Sprachen* XXII. 9/1 A rather special form of collocation are the so-called blends or telescope words.

telescope, *v.* Add: **1. a.** *fig.* To combine, compress, or condense (a number of things) *into* a more compact or concise form; to combine or conflate (several things, or one thing *with* another); to shorten by compression.

1894, 1909 [in Dict.]. **1911** BEERBOHM *Zuleika Dobson* xvi. 243, I telescoped my toilet and came rushing round to you. **1953** *Essays in Criticism* III. 57 Shelley's mind.. has telescoped the shattered autumn landscape with a stormy Heaven and Ocean. **1958** *Listener* 2 Jan. 13/2 Our own effort at telescoping education is a biological retrogressive step. **1961** *Amer. Speech* XXXVI. 162 Generalizing over all such cases, the linguist can telescope them into one single, economical rule of agreement as a formal requirement for well-formed English sentences. **1965** *Listener* 20 May 756/1 The complex is worked out in the book with poetry and psychological insight... The adaptation had to telescope something of this. **1978** *Jrnl. R. Soc. Arts* Dec. 29/2 And so, telescoping time, I now leap from 1909..to 6th October 1927.

telescopic, *a.* (*sb.*) Add: **1.** (Further examples.) Also *telescopic(-sighted) rifle*, a rifle with a telescopic sight.

1880 W. JAMES in *Atlantic Monthly* Oct. 447/2 An Ajax gets no fame in the day of telescopic-sighted rifles. **1918** E. A. MACKINTOSH *War, the Liberator* 114 With a telescopic rifle he is looking for a Hun. **1936** *Discovery* Aug. 237 His new giant nine-lens aerial camera. On the right is seen the Telescopic viewfinder. **1947** *E. African Ann. 1946–7* 35/2, I use a 12-inch fixed separation telescopic lens for most bird photographs. **1958** *Observer* 10 Aug. 10/2 The use of the Hasselblad long-distance telescopic camera from a concealed position. **1963** 'E. MCBAIN' *Ten plus One* ii. 30 Forrest's murderer must have used a telescopic sight, the distance..being something over a hundred and fifty yards. **1983** J. SLIGO *Concert Masters* v. 109 As Barbarossa pocketed the passports the telescopic lens of a camera focused from among the sand-dunes. *Ibid.* vi. 155 With a telescopic rifle and night sights, he will be a perfect target.

4. (Later examples.)

1931 [see *shock strut* s.v. *SHOCK *sb.*[2] 7 a]. **1962** *Evening Standard* 2 Oct. 7/3 An umbrella, unless you have one of the portable telescopic kind, is best avoided if you have really a long walk ahead of you. **1973** 'A. HALL' *Tango Briefing* x. 124, I..pulled up the telescopic aerial.

telescoping, *vbl. sb.* (In Dict. s.v. TELESCOPE *v.*) (Earlier and later examples.)

1867 *Commercial & Financial Chron.* V. 6/2 There are two principal dangers which have to be guarded against—the 'telescoping' of cars into each other in case of collision [etc.]. **1937** 'M. INNES' *Hamlet, Revenge!* I. ii. 42 Clay's picture of Pepys *as* Hamlet was..something extraordinary... He had..been examined both in Shakespeare's *Hamlet* and Pepys's *Diaries.* But this sudden telescoping was beyond him. **1951** M. MCLUHAN *Mech. Bridge* (1967) 85/2 The very name 'Wurlitzer', with its telescoping of 'waltz' and 'whirl', conveys the idea of vertigo. **1958** *Listener* 20 Feb. 341 The way in which this telescoping of development and recapitulation is achieved represents the greatest single master-stroke in the work. **1979** *Internat. Jrnl. Sociol. of Law* Feb. 123 Then there is the problem of what has curiously become known as 'telescoping'—the uncertainty and inaccuracy of respondents in identifying precisely the date on which a particular incident took place—which will inflate or deflate the researcher's estimates.

telescreen: see *TELE- 2 b. **teleseismic** to **teleshopping:** see *TELE- 1.

telesis. (Earlier example.)

1896 L. F. WARD in *Amer. Jrnl. Sociol.* II. 248 The only serious lack..is a similar antithetical term to be set over against *genesis,* to denote the distinctively social process which results from the application of the indirect, intellectual or telic method [of human evolution]. In order to supply such a term I propose to revive the Greek form *telesis.*

telesoftware: see *TELE- 1.

telestic, *a.* For † *Obs.* read *rare* and add later example.

1981 *Times Lit. Suppl.* 23 Jan. 79/5 Plato's four types of mania (telestic, or ritual; mantic or divinatory; poetic; and erotic).

tele-talkies: see *TELE- 1.

Teletex (te·lĭteks). [prob. blend of *TELEX and TEXT *sb.*[1]] A proprietary name for a data processing and communication system using interconnected computer terminals.

1978 *Washington Post* 16 Dec. C11/2 It [*sc.* a low cost computer time-sharing network] is directly competitive with the British Viewdata and Teletex system. **1979** *Trade Marks Jrnl.* 16 May 820/1 *Teletex...* Apparatus for the input, output and recording of printed data; printed data storing apparatus and instruments, keyboards for data processing apparatus; [etc.]... Siemens Aktiengesellschaft.; Munich, Federal Republic of Germany; manufacturers and merchants. **1981** *Sci. Amer.* Oct. E5/1 (Advt.), Siemens, for example, is pioneering teletex which is a synthesis of the typewriter and teleprinter and is the first step towards full-scale electronic mail. **1982** *Nature* 27 May 257/1 The information technology community is calling the new service 'teletex'. It is, however, a far cry from teletext, the broadcast information service. Teletex is either a sophisticated form of telex or a standard that allows computer terminals to communicate with each other.

teletext (te·lĭtekst). [f. *TELE- 2 + TEXT *sb.*[1]] A system in which a user's television set is adapted so as to be able to show alphanumeric information selected from displays transmitted using the spare capacity of existing television channels. Cf. *ORACLE *sb.*[1] 9*; contrast *VIEWDATA.

1974 *Wireless World* Nov. 441/1 (*heading*) Teletext to go ahead. **1975** *Electronics & Power* 15 May 548/1 In March 1974, the British Radio Equipment Manufacturers' Association, BBC and IBA reached agreement on a unified standard system, known as TELETEXT, based largely on the CEEFAX system. **1975, 1976** [see *ORACLE *sb.*[1] 9*]. **1980** S. MONEY in K. G. Jackson *Bk. of Video* 89/2 By using the same page format and data coding, viewdata and teletext have been made compatible so that a large part of the decoder can be common for both systems.

teletherapy, telethermometer: see *TELE- 1.

telethon (te·lĭþǫn). orig. and chiefly *U.S.* [f. *TELE- 2 + *-THON.] An especially prolonged television programme used to raise money for a charity or cause; also in extended use, a lengthy television programme for some other purpose.

1949 *Examiner* (San Francisco) 10 Apr. 22/5 'Telethon' nets $702,000. **1952** *Sun* (Baltimore) 23 June (B ed.) 1/6 Bing Crosby and Bob Hope, in a 14½-hour coast-to-coast telethon today raised more than $1,000,000 in contributions and pledges for the United States Olympic fund. **1960** *Daily Tel.* 8 Nov. 1/2 As the climax to his campaign, Mr. Nixon, Republican, answered telephoned questions for four hours in a nation-wide 'telethon'. **1968** *Courier-Mail* (Brisbane) 16 Sept. 6/5 The telethon, now a widely-used fund raising mechanism. **1973** G. W. Hart *Right from Start* iv. 303 Metzenbaum proposed a series of state-wide telethons which would provide an opportunity for the Senator to appear on television hook-ups in the key states in a format in which he excels, answering individual citizens' questions. **1982** *Listener* 8 July 3/2 Perhaps we have all been corrupted by the telethons of Vietnam television reporting.

teletransport(ation: see *tele- 1.

Teletype (te·lĭtəip), *sb.* Also **teletype.** [f. Tele- + Type(writer.] **1. a.** A proprietary name for a make of teleprinter. Hence *loosely*, any teleprinter.

1904 *Sci. Amer.* 17 Sept. 193/3 At Brussels it is the telecryptograph of Engineer Malcotti, at Berlin the teletype and the Heljes apparatus. **1922** *Telegr. & Teleph. Jrnl.* VIII. 71/1 The latent innovation in the way of apparatus in the London C.T.O. [*sc.* Central Telegraph Office] is that of the Teletype. **1925** *Official Gaz.* (U.S. Patent Office) 26 May 815/1 Morkrum-Kleinschmidt Corporation, Chicago... *Teletype*... Printing-telegraph apparatus. **1933** *Jrnl. R. Aeronaut. Soc.* XXXVII. 12 America, where the teletype, or electrical distant-controlled typewriter, is such an important part of the weather reporting system. **1952** *Trade Marks Jrnl.* 17 Dec. 1167/2 *Teletype*... Printing telegraph apparatus. **1958** *Times Rev. Industry* July (Suppl.) p. ii/1 The bedrock of the work of most British information posts is the daily Press service sent to them by radio, Morse, Hellschreiber or teletype, from C.O.I.'s telecommunications room. **1968** J. Sangster *Touchfeather* xiv. 161 As security officer, he had no doubt put the details of my visit on the teletype to all branches of the..Corporation. **1976** *Physics Bull.* July 298/2 Teletypes are rapidly being superseded by cathode ray display terminals.

b. A message received and printed by a teleprinter.

1961 in Webster. **1966** 'D. Shannon' *With a Vengeance* xiii. 184 'I'd sent a teletype off.'..He reached into his breast pocket and brought out two folded pages of teletype. **1972** B. F. Conners *Don't embarrass Bureau* (1973) ii. 104 He had read his Bureau mail, received a few teletypes from the Director. **1978** S. Sheldon *Bloodline* iii. 56 The messenger..handed him an envelope. Inside was a teletype from Rhys Williams.

2. *attrib.*, as *Teletype circuit, key, line, machine, message, network, operator, system, terminal.*

1933 *Sun* (Baltimore) 21 July 22/5 At noon..police of all districts were notified on the department's teletype system to pick up Roft. **1934** W. Saroyan *Daring Young Man* 76, I used to sit at a table all day, working a teletype machine, sending and receiving telegrams. **1937** *Sci. Abstr.* B. XL. 302 (*heading*) Teletype network in civil aviation. **1941** C. G. Halpine *Pilot's Meteorol.* iii. 32 Radiosonde observations are made..and the reports transmitted over the teletype circuits. **1950** *Times* 2 Mar. 7/6 The Austrians cannot instal new telephone or even teletype lines to other countries without Allied Council approval. **1962** *New Scientist* 1 Feb. 260/1 A transistorized microwave system for transmitting verbal data and teletype messages. **1971** *Ibid.* 18 Mar. 617/1 Fingers that itch to perform on the teletype keys. **1973** *Physics Bull.* Oct. 632/1 Since January 1973 a 'conversational' reference retrieval system has been available.., providing access to 10 000 references and abstracts through any teletype terminal or visual display unit. **1978** *N.Y. Times* 30 Mar. B-20/1 (Advt.), Shipping co needs expd teletype operator.

teletype (te·lĭtəip), *v.* [f. prec. sb.] **a.** *intr.* To operate a teleprinter; also, to put in a request *for* by means of a teleprinter. **b.** *trans.* To send by means of a teleprinter.

1924 *Daily News* 19 Dec. 5/4 We must teletype as well as teletalk. **1934** Webster, Teletype *v.t.* & *i.* **1971** 'D. Shannon' *Ringer* viii. 130 Palliser had teletyped an inquiry up to Lompoc... That wasn't a very big town. **1977** D. Anthony *Stud Game* xxvi. 175 Seems he has a record in Texas. We've teletyped for a full report.

So **te·letyped** *ppl. a.*, **te·letyping** *vbl. sb.*

1904 *Knowledge* Feb. 18/2 The Berlin Teletyping Central Station. *Ibid.* 19/2 Teletyping service. **1967** *New Scientist* 28 Dec. 766/2 Professor L. Goldberg and his colleagues..control the course of their observations by daily teletyped instructions to NASA's Goddard Space Flight Center. **1971** *Nature* 25 June 482/3 A human telegraph operator reads the address on an incoming teletyped message, then retypes it in full to send it to its destination.

teletyper (te·lĭtəipəɹ). [f. as *Teletype *sb.* + -er¹.] A teleprinter.

1904 *Electr. Mag.* I. 64/2 The operation..may..be acquired by anybody in the shortest possible time, the teletyper being nothing else than a teletypewriter. **1948** A. Baron *From City, from Plough* 81 Somewhere in an office..teletypers were clacking their frantic messages. **1965** *Punch* 20 Jan. 76/2 If you can make room between the telephones, dictating machines, office intercoms and teletypers. **1976** *National Observer* (U.S.) 10 Apr. 9/1 The equipment includes telephone-answering devices, burglar-alarm systems, automatic dialers, teletypers.

Teletypesetter (te:lĭtəi·psetəɹ). Also with small initial. [f. Tele- + *type-setter* s.v. Type *sb.*¹ 10.] The proprietary name of an apparatus for the automatic casting and setting of type in response to telegraphed signals recorded on perforated tape; also used loosely for any such apparatus. Hence **te:lety·pe-setting** *vbl. sb.*, the action of a Teletypesetter.

1928 *N.Y. Times* 7 Dec. 1/2 Frank E. Gannett, head of the Gannett newspapers..threw the switch which set in motion the new device known as the Teletypesetter. **1931** *Official Gaz.* (U.S. Patent Office) 17 Mar. 551/1 Teletypesetter. For electrically-controlled typesetting and typecasting apparatus. **1953** *Trade Marks Jrnl.* 22 Apr. 343/1 *Teletypesetter*... Apparatus using perforated tape for the control of type casting machines, and parts thereof included in Class 9. Teletypesetter Corporation.., Chicago 14, Illinois, United States of America; manufacturers. **1961** *Spectator* 14 Apr. 509 He referred to teletypesetting, the process by which the *Guardian* proposes to print in London as well as Manchester. **1965** *Economist* 22 May p. xii/3 The West Coast edition of the *Wall St. Journal*..is being printed with much use of modern long-distance tele-typesetting. **1967** [see *key-board *v.*].

telety·pewriter. [f. Tele- + Typewriter.] = *teleprinter.

1904 *Knowledge* Feb. 18/2 The apparatus..is..a tele-typewriter, any letters, figures, or signs of punctuation being printed by pressing down a key corresponding with the signal in question. **1922** *Glasgow Herald* 4 Sept. 11 Another great stride in the advance of civilization is demonstrated by the tele-typewriter. **1954** *Electronic Engin.* XXVI. 260 The effect of one form of telegraph distortion on the teleprinter (British) and teletypewriter (American) will be considered. **1968** *Economist* 21 Dec. 32/2 With time-sharing, he can communicate with a computer by means of a special teletypewriter by his desk. **1979** J. E. Rowley *Mechanised In-House Information Syst.* i. 59 Other devices, such as the tele-typewriter, the visual display unit and the graphical display unit may function both in input and output.

teleutosorus (tĕliŭtosō°·rŏs). *Bot.* [f. as Teleutospore + Sorus¹.] A pustule consisting of a group of teliospores (teleutospores) and their supporting hyphæ.

1905 [see *telium]. **1922** H. Gwynne-Vaughan *Fungi* viii. 205 Sooner or later the mycelium of binucleate cells gives rise to teleutospores; these are characteristically grouped together in teleutosori. **1970** J. Webster *Introd. Fungi* ii. iv. 377 *Gymnosporangium* forms teleutosori on *Juniperus*.

televarsity, tele-vérité, televersity: see *tele- 2 b.

televiewer (te·lĭviū:əɹ). [f. *tele- 2 + Viewer.] One who watches television.

1935 *Discovery* Oct. 285/2 An excellent answer to the questions of the..would-be 'televiewer'. **1937** *Daily Herald* 2 Feb. 3/4 Televiewers will not have to change over a switch on their sets each week to suit the alternate systems of transmission. **1950** *Sun* (Baltimore) 4 Jan. 18/2 Thirty-nine per cent of the entire television and radio broadcast audience during this period were Baltimore televiewers. **1957** E. Hyams *Into Dream* i. v. 40 There was *Dentix*: a half-tone of a face well known to televiewers leered out of the page. **1971** L. Koppett *N.Y. Times Guide Spectator Sports* 3 Many televiewers..had no prior intention to watch a football or basketball game. **1982** *Daily Tel.* 20 Sept. 15/7 Millions of televiewers around the world saw the moving spectacle of Prince Rainier's grief.

So **te·leview** *v. intr.*, to watch television (*rare*); **te·leviewing** *vbl. sb.* and *ppl. a.*

1935 *Times* 15 May 13/2 The German Post Office yesterday opened the first public televiewing post outside Berlin..at Potsdam. **1945** Cooke & Markus *Electronics Dict.* 382 *Teleview*, to watch a scene by means of a television system. **1956** *Encycl. Brit. Bk. of Year* 492/2 *Televiewing*, formerly used as a noun, now appearing as an adjective, as in the phrase 'televiewing families', meaning families habituated to watching television. **1959** *New Statesman* 4 July 10/1 People still like and are permitted to laugh, and occasionally break off from televiewing to have a go at the printed word. **1960** *Twentieth Cent.* Dec. 541 A considerable impression was made..upon the televiewing public. **1976** *Listener* 23 Sept. 366/2 My own loss of televiewing had no effect on the number of times I hit anybody. **1982** *Economist* 5 June 25 By overestimating the numbers who would come, instead of teleview, they left sellers of hot dogs and papal souvenirs bankrupt. **1982** *Nature* 9 Dec. 468/2 Channel 4..seems to have won the allegiance of a mere four per cent of the British televiewing audience.

televisable (te·lĭ-, telĭvəi·zăb'l), *a.* [f. *televise *v.* + -able.] Capable of being televised, suitable for presentation on television. Similarly **televisible** (telĭ·vi·zĭb'l) [after *visible*] *nonce-wd.*

1974 *Times* 18 May 14/7 Unfortunately..Mrs Fawcett [was] eminently less televisable than Mrs Pankhurst. **1975** A. Powell *Hearing Secret Harmonies* ii. 38, I resign St John Clarke to the makers of all things televisible. **1979** *Economist* 3 Nov. 48/1 'Land people' who..have been a deeper tragedy than the more televisable 'boat people'.

televise (te·lĭvəiz), *v.* [Back-formation from *television on the model of verbs that end in -(*v*)*ise* and are related to nouns ending in -(*v*)*ision*, such as *revise*.] **1. a.** *trans.* To transmit (pictures, programmes, scenes, etc.) by television; formerly also, to transmit television pictures of (a person). Also *fig.*

1927 *Glasgow Herald* 14 Jan. 9/1 The distance over which pictures can be televised. **1928** *Television* Mar. 40/3 The subject who is being 'televised' had to face a powerful battery of blinding lights. **1931** *Daily Progress* (Charlottesville, Va.) 2 May 3/4 The first marriage ceremony to be 'televised', if that's the word—is a matter of history today. **1939** [see *interviewer]. **1950** *Sport* 7–11 Apr. 22/2 The Final will definitely not be televised. **1975** *Observer* (Colour Suppl.) 6 Apr. 64 (Advt.), It [*sc.* a series of books on history] is a 'programme' which combines lively and informative reading with vivid illustrations, helpful maps and guides, in such a way that it televises the past for you and your children to understand and enjoy as never before. **1979** S. Brett *Comedian Dies* ix. 95 This..Awards lunch... Big do, being televised. **1983** *Economist* 23 July 24/1 The BBC's Panorama programme on blacks and the police, televised on July 18th.

b. *intr.* for *pass.* To be (well, etc.) suited for television presentation.

1930 *Times* 1 Apr. 28/3 Some faces appear to 'televise' better than others. **1961** G. Millerson *Techn. Telev. Production* 129 Where an iconoscope camera-tube is used as the pick-up device, film shots of dark scenes may televise better in negative form.

2. *intr.* To make a television broadcast.

1948 L. Birch *Something Done* (Central Office of Information) 15 Many performers who are under contract to the big music-halls are not allowed to televise. **1957** [implied at *televising *ppl. a.*].

Hence **te·levised** *ppl. a.*; **te·levising** *vbl. sb.* and *ppl. a.*

1932 *Jrnl. Television Soc.* I. 107/1 The televising of 'The Man with the Flower in his Mouth', in July, 1930. **1934** *Jrnl. Inst. Electr. Engineers* LXXV. 86/2 The difference in detail between a good Baird televized picture and the cathode-ray picture. **1935** *Times* 1 Feb. 8/4 No doubt the televising of sporting and other public events will have a wide appeal. **1946** *Astounding Sci. Fiction* July 63/1 A man he had seen many times before in televised addresses. **1951** M. Ehrlich *Big Eye* i. 34 The blonde began to take off her robe in a kind of televised strip tease. **1957** D. J. Enright *Apoth. Shop* 221 True pleasure—our moralizing, politicizing and..televising generation has thrown *that* overboard. **1958** *Times Lit. Suppl.* 21 Nov. p. xxix/2 Miss Edwards opens her story with the televising of Punchbowl Farm and the Thornton family. **1978** S. Brill *Teamsters* iii. 80 Fumbling through televised testimony like this to protect Hoffa was worth it to Fitzsimmons.

television (te·lĭviʒən, telĭvi·ʒən). [f. Tele- + Vision *sb.*] **1. a.** A system for reproducing an actual or recorded scene at a distance on a screen by radio transmission, usu. with appropriate sounds; the vision of distant objects obtained thus.

The term normally refers to a system of general transmission over the air, but it also includes systems of restricted transmission to subscribers by wire, such as *cable television*; see also *closed circuit* s.v. *closed *ppl. a.* 3.

[**1904** *Daily News* 3 June 7 Dr. Low talks very modestly of the 'televista' (the name he has given to his 'seeing by wire' invention).] **1907** *Sci. Amer. Suppl.* 15 June 26292/1 Now that the photo-telegraph invented by Prof. Korn is on the eve of being introduced into general practice, we are informed of some similar inventions in the same field, all of which tend to achieve some step toward the solution of the problem of television. **1909** [in Dict. s.v. Tele-]. **1913** *Wireless World* Sept. 353/2 The tele-vision,..being based upon the same principle as photo-telegraphy, is possible in itself. **1926** *Glasgow Herald* 20 Dec. 11/8 Mr. John L. Baird, a native of Helensburgh,..recently invented an apparatus which makes television possible. **1930** J. Buckingham *Matter & Radiation* 122 We have heard so much about Television lately that we are apt to forget that no portion of the apparatus used is novel to scientists. **1942** T. S. Eliot *Music of Poetry* 18 There are words which are ugly because of foreignness or ill-breeding (e.g. *television*): but I do not believe that any word well-established in its own language is either beautiful or ugly. **1948** N. Wiener *Cybernetics* 10 Television was destined to be more useful to engineering by the introduction of such new techniques than as an independent industry. **1957** *Technology* Mar. 9/2 The solution of the major problems in colour television, the public introduction of which is now more a question of economics than of technical difficulty. **1970** *Toronto Daily Star* 24 Sept. 28/1 (Advt.), You can receive Channel 19 by..cable television. **1972** *Times* 21 Jan. 2/5 Cable television was originally introduced in the area in 1962 to provide better reception because Shooters Hill in the south consistently interfered with Television pictures.

b. Organized television broadcasting; the television broadcasting service as a whole or (with defining word) a particular television service. Phr. *on (the) television.*

1927 [see *heebie-jeebie(s)]. **1930** N. Coward *Private Lives* ii. 49 Aeroplanes..and Cosmic Atoms, and Television. **1938** *Observer* 26 June 12/6, I reviewed this film three weeks ago when I saw it on television. **1951** *N.Y. Herald-Tribune* 12 Dec. 27/3 Buster is an old playmate and I'm glad to see he..crashed television successfully. **1958**, etc. [see *independent *a.* 5 e]. **1962** *Friend* 1 June 665/1, I have sometimes thought how different life might have been at Haworth if only they had had the television, and Tide, and a Morris Minor. **1965** M. Drabble *Millstone* 194 You could get a job on the television. **1968** *Globe & Mail* (Toronto) 17 Feb. 36 (Advt.), Private balconies, cable television, off street parking. **1976** *Jrnl. R. Soc. Arts* June 365/2 Are there any recent figures of the cost to every household in the country of the advertising on independent television? **1980** *Private Eye* 26 Sept. 13/1 That ghastly woman with the teeth who's always on the television. **1982** *Listener* 16 Dec. 17/1, I have mixed feelings about cable television's 'autumn of debate'.

c. Television entertainment; television broadcasting considered as a medium of communication or as an art form. Cf. *GOOD *a.* 1 f.

1931 *Daily Progress* (Charlottesville, Va.) 2 May 3/4 The ceremony is television, but in every other way the wedding is absolutely regular. **1957** *Observer* 27 Oct. 17/4 It proved, as discussions on these emotive imponderabilia always do, highly absorbing television. **1977** *Times* 2 Sept. 7/3 Television, the art..that speaks daily to almost everybody. **1982** *Sunday Tel.* 3 Jan. 16/7 Attenborough's 'Life on Earth' was perfect television.

2. A television set.

1955 *Observer* 28 Aug. 7/4 The South London landlady was seeking 'a nice new television'. **1972** *Daily Express* 8 Jan. 12/4 We have never been able to afford a car but we do have a television. **1973** D. FRANCIS *Slay-Ride* viii. 96 Behind me on a wide shelf stood my portable television. **1982** *Sunday Sun-Times* (Chicago) 3 Oct. 72/1 Industry workers last year averaged $75 a month. They buy televisions and send money home to wives.

3. *attrib.* and *Comb.* **a.** In general uses, as *television aerial, antenna, apparatus, box, channel, coverage, dealer, frequency, lounge, receiver, room, screen, service, set, signal, studio, supper, system, theatre, transmission, transmitter, van.*

1940 *Amateur Radio Handbk.* (ed. 2) 306/1 (Index), Television aerials. **1972** J. PORTER *Meddler & her Murderer* xi. 136 Rows of ugly little houses, their roofs buckling under a forest of television aerials. **1947** *Electronics* May 96/2 (*heading*) Television antennas for apartments. **1951** W. FAULKNER *Requiem for Nun* III. 246 Lonely farmhouses glittering and gleaming with automatic stoves and washing machines and television antennae. **1930** *Aberdeen Press & Jrnl.* 14 Apr. 6, I do not suppose that many Scottish listeners have yet adopted television apparatus. **1932** A. HUXLEY *Brave New World* xiv. 234 At the foot of every bed..was a television box. **1950** K. HENNEY *Radio Engin. Handbk.* (ed. 4) xix. 1024 Allocation of television channels. Figure 40 shows the allocation of twelve 6-Mc channels for television. **1981** *Ann. Reg. 1980* 427 Plans for the setting up of the fourth television channel..went ahead. **1966** *B.B.C. Handbk.* 51 Gaps of the existing BBC radio and television coverage. **1949** *Radio Times* 15 July 42/1 Your nearest Ultra Television dealer. **1955** *Ibid.* 22 Apr. 3/1 The present television frequencies..are in the V.H.F. band. **1970** K. GILES *Death in Church* v. 150 The ladies have arrived... In the television lounge. **1976** W. J. BURLEY *Wycliffe & Schoolgirls* ii. 42 The door of the television lounge was open and he could see several patients sitting round the set. **1927** Television receiver [see *RECEIVER[1] 7 c]. **1980** *Whitaker's Almanack 1981* 816/1 About 3·8 million television receivers are in use [in the Argentine Republic]. **1959** 'O. MILLS' *Stairway to Murder* viii. 95 The Residents' Lounge and Television Room are both at your disposal. **1971** *Country Life* 23 Dec. (Suppl.) 3/2 (Advt.), Mansion. Ideally suitable for institutional purposes...2 television rooms, chapel. **1927** *Pictorial Weekly* 5 Mar. 100/1 These sets will combine a Television screen and loud-speaker. **1973** D. MAY *Laughter in Djakarta* i. 13 Little figures mouthing words that did not reach him, like a television screen with no sound. **1935** *Times* 1 Feb. 7/4 These first steps being taken towards the establishment of a public television service. **1936** *Radio Times* 30 Oct. 5/3 Television programmes. The BBC Television Service from Alexandra Palace will be opened by the Postmaster-General on Monday. **1966** *B.B.C. Handbk.* 15 *The Northern Echo* [said]..'some parts of the television service are falling asleep'. **1931** *N.Y. Times* 31 May IX. 9/2 The Radio Corporation of America..is concentrating its efforts upon the primary technical developments to be completed before undertaking the manufacture and sale of television sets on a commercial basis. **1976** W. TREVOR *Children of Dynmouth* i. 25 Slowly he walked through Dynmouth again, examining the goods in the shop windows, watching golf being played on various television sets. **1927** *Bell System Technical Jrnl.* VI. 560 (*heading*) The production and utilization of television signals. **1935** *Illustr. London News* 23 Feb. 307 (*caption*) The Baird television studios at the Crystal Palace. **1981** S. BRETT *Situation Tragedy* iv. 43 He wished he knew a bit more about television studios and their sound systems. **1973** D. MILLER *Chinese Jade Affair* xi. 108 This was where the old lady had her television suppers. **1983** *Times* 1 Oct. 8/6 The art of conversation, of manners, of social interplay..cannot be acquired at the nursery table or when eating a solitary television supper with the baby-minder. **1931** *Proc. IRE* XXI. 1655 The experimental television system placed in operation by RCA Victor in..1931..was based on the use of a cathode ray tube as the image reproducing element. **1966** *B.B.C. Handbk.* 35 BBC Television..along with other Western television systems. *Ibid.* 33 There are in the London area six..production studios.., a television theatre, two news studios, and two remote control studios. **1929** *Radio Times* 8 Nov. 412/1, 11.00–11.30 (*London only.*) Experimental television transmission by the Baird Process. **1928** *N.Y. Times* 22 Aug. 1/2 Puppets being used because of the limitations of the television transmitter. **1939** *Electronics* Mar. 26 (*heading*) Television transmitters. **1956** R. ROBINSON *Landscape with Dead Dons* xiii. 117 'You refer to the television van?' 'The one you told me the little men come in.'

b. Connected with, participating in, or transmitted as part of organized television broadcasting, as *television announcer, audience, broadcast, broadcasting, commercial, crew, critic, discussion, drama, dramatist, film, interview, journalist, magazine, news, personality, play, producer, programme, public, pundit, reporter, serial, series, show, spot, star, version, viewer.*

1938 *Radio Times* 23 Dec. 36/1 It would be nice to say that the television announcers will hang up their stockings. **1972** J. MOSEDALE *Football* xi. 148 Gifford, then a television announcer, talked briefly with the coach. **1937** *Discovery* Nov. 331/2 Building up a television audience. **1959** *Twentieth Cent.* Nov. 335 Because of its great size, the television audience now closely resembles the population as a whole. **1928** *N.Y. Times* 21 Aug. 26 Hourly television broadcasts over WRNY to aid amateurs and experimenters will begin tomorrow. **1935** *Times* 1 Feb. 8/3 There will be little, if any, scope for television broadcasts unaccompanied by sound. **1928** *Daily Mail* 3 Aug. 9/5 Mr. J. L. Baird, the inventor of television, stated yesterday that television broadcasting would begin in this country in the autumn. **1977** *Rep. Comm. Future of Broadcasting* (Cmnd. 6753) ii. 10 All sound and television broadcasting which uses radio waves for transmission is in the charge of two public Authorities, the British Broadcasting Corporation and the Independent Broadcasting Authority. **1957** Television commercial [see *COMMERCIAL *sb.* 2]. **1975** R. RENDELL *Shake Hands for Ever* x. 95 Those children's toys which he had often seen on television commercials. **1964** J. MITFORD in *Making of Muckraker* (1979) 90 Our house..was transformed..by television crews filming interviews about the book. **1978** W. F. BUCKLEY *Stained Glass* xviii. 172 All Monday the television crews were at work. **1966** *B.B.C. Handbk.* 13 Television critic Peter Black..asked for a definition of this phrase. **1981** *Listener* 22 Oct. 465/3 He was the best partner I ever had in television discussions. **1949** *Radio Times* 15 July 41/2 A variegated week for television drama. **1973** *Listener* 5 July 27/1 Watergate makes television drama, which rests on an illusion of reality, look pretty thin. **1964** *Ibid.* 16 Apr. 624/2 'Television dramatists'..have the cheek to use television techniques in stage plays. **1951** R. CHANDLER *Let.* 5 Jan. (1981) 256, I have seen a number of the television films of your stories. **1967** M. ARGYLE *Psychol. Interpersonal Behaviour* x. 189 A television film is played back to the trainee after his performance. **1964** D. FRANCIS *Nerve* xiv. 192 That was just what I needed... A big race win and a television interview. **1974** *Listener* 29 Oct. 525/1 A bad, sad month for television journalists. **1955** *Radio Times* 22 Apr. 15/2 The fortnightly television magazine *Ulster Mirror*, broadcast since November. **1947** *Billboard* 1 Nov. 16 Television news borrows from the radio, it is related to the newsreel. **1977** D. L. ALTHEIDE in Douglas & Johnson *Existential Sociol.* iv. 147 Research on television news. **1958** *Times Lit. Suppl.* 4 Apr. 179/1 The man of letters is no longer a household figure—unless, by coincidence, he is also a television personality. **1978** *Times* 15 Aug. 13/7 Who does qualify for VIP lounges; presumably some television 'personalities' and some entertainers? **1946** *B.B.C. Year Book* 21 The old hand may in time come to ear-mark his evenings primarily for full-length television plays. **1968** Television play [see *PREVIEW *v.*2 a]. **1951** *Catal. Exhibits, South Bank Exhib., Festival of Britain* 176 *Television Producer* Malcolm Baker Smith. **1982** *Sunday Tel.* 3 Jan. 16/4 Television and film producers..go for their inspiration to the printed word. **1930** *Billboard* 20 Sept. 30/1 Television programs were being broadcast daily from two studios. **1935** *Radio Times* 27 Dec. 3/1 Television programmes from the new station at the Alexandra Palace start next year. **1981** *Ann. Reg. 1980* 428 By far the greatest impact made by a single television programme in 1980 resulted from the screening..of ATV's *Death of a Princess*. **1937** *Discovery* Nov. 332/2 A television public has not been developed at all. **1981** *Listener* 22 Oct. 465/3 Robert McKenzie..was the greatest of all television pundits on politics and elections. **1959** *Housewife* June 32 As a television reporter I've certainly got used to meeting a lot of unhappy people. **1957** M. SUMMERTON *Sunset Hour* x. 133 He hoped to clinch a contract for a part in a television serial. **1965** B. GLANVILLE *Second Home* xii. 301 He had to go up to Birmingham next day for some television series he was directing. **1982** *Sunday Tel.* 3 Jan. 16/7 The most successful television series..are not from books of the very first rank. **1950** R. CHANDLER *Let.* 22 Nov. (1981) 241 I'd like to have a television show. **1976** W. TREVOR *Children of Dynmouth* i. 25 He'd asked Timothy what he found interesting outside the Comprehensive and Timothy had said television shows. **1960** Television spot [see *SPOT *sb.*[1] 8 d]. **1951** A. C. CLARKE *Sands of Mars* xiii. 163 A..caricature of a well-known television star. **1982** *Sunday Tel.* 3 Jan. 16/5 The experience of watching the television version [of *Brideshead Revisited*] differed very little from that of reading Evelyn Waugh's masterpiece. **1952** *Sun* (Baltimore) 17 Mar. 1/6 (*heading*) Television viewers are able to see operation in hospital. **1961** *Times* 11 Dec. 13/6 Here is a population consisting almost wholly of industrial workers..car owners, television-viewers.

c. Special Combs. **television camera**: see *CAMERA 3 c; **television camera tube**, an electron tube of the kind used in television cameras for converting a visual image into an electrical signal; **television engineer**, one who designs and maintains the mechanical and electrical processes involved in the transmission and reception of television signals; a television repairman; **television image** = *television picture* below; **television licence**, a licence to use a television set, renewable annually on payment of a fee; **television mast**, (*a*) a tall mast, usu. set up on high ground, carrying a television transmitting aerial; (*b*) = *television aerial*, sense 3 a above; **television network**, a system of television broadcasting stations; a television broadcasting organization or channel; **television picture**, the visual image received on a television screen; **television region**, a region of the country receiving television broadcasts from a local as well as a national transmitting station; **television satellite**, a satellite put into orbit round the earth to reflect back television signals; **television station**, a television broadcasting station (see *STATION *sb.* 13 f); **television tube**, (*a*) = *picture tube* s.v. *PICTURE *sb.* 6 d; (*b*) = *television camera tube* above.

1940 D. G. FINK *Princ. Television Engin.* i. 17 (*caption*) A typical television camera tube, the type 1849 iconoscope, now widely used in television broadcasting. **1974** *Encycl. Brit. Macropædia* XVIII. 112/1 The image orthicon is the most highly developed of the television camera tubes. **1930** *Billboard* 20 Sept. 15/2 Equipment to be used will come from General Electric, under the supervision of Dr. E. F. W. Alexanderson, television engineer. **1978** F. KING *Action* x. 31 The failure of the television engineer to call to repair the set. **1933** *Proc. IRE* XXI. 1631 (*heading*) A study of television image characteristics. **1949** *Times* 17 Feb. 5/3 The first hundred thousand mark is about to be reached in..television licences..compared with the eleven million for sound. **1972** C. DRUMMOND *Death at Bar* ii. 52 Jarvis..abandoned the cinema the instant he had paid his first television licence fee. **1958** S. HYLAND *Who goes Hang?* I. vii. 39 They could see the enormous, meccano structure of the television mast on top of Sydenham Hill. **1968** M. ALLINGHAM *Cargo of Eagles* iv. 54 They drove..through an area of open planned villas, writhing television masts, mini cars. **1947** *Billboard* 1 Nov. 16/2 Now that the Columbia Broadcasting System (CBS) has joined the routes of companies working toward a television network [etc.]. **1974** *B.B.C. Handbk. 1975* 19/1 One..fairly brief consequence of the energy crisis was the decision to close down all television networks at 10.30 pm. **1937** *Chron. & Echo* (Northampton) 8 May 6/1 (Advt.), Real television... Demonstration in advance of how Television pictures should appear when broadcast. **1977** J. FRASER *Heart's Ease in Death* i. 7 The wind shaking the aerial had distorted the television picture. **1974** Television region [see *REGION 5 d]. **1960** *Aeroplane* XCVIII. 419/2 Nowhere will the successful launching of the U.S. television satellite be noted with more interest than in this country. **1976** I. LEVIN *Boys from Brazil* vi. 180 Speaking to the whole world at once..by television satellite. **1931** *Billboard* 1 Aug. 4/1 As soon as television stations increase in number so that they can't be fitted into low channel, high band will be used for them exclusively. **1980** *Whitaker's Almanack 1981* 816/1 In addition there are 65 television stations, of which 4 are in Buenos Aires. **1943** *Electronic Engin.* XV. 329/2 The modern television tube has many ancestors. We could start its history in 1897. **1975** D. G. FINK *Electronics Engineers' Handbk.* XI. 57 Antimony trisulfide vidicons, lead oxide vidicons, and image orthicons are the work-horse television tubes.

televisionary (te:lĭvi·ʒənări), *sb.* and *a.* *Humorous.* [Blend of *TELEVISION + VISIONARY *a.* and *sb.*; in adj. use treated as compound with -ARY[1].] **A.** *sb.* **a.** An enthusiast for television. **b.** A television personality.

1928 *Observer* 12 Feb. 11/2 Many 'televisionaries' have spent fortunes in the quest. **1961** A. CLARKE *Later Poems* 94 The Pope forbade the clergy..to indulge in daily amusement. He warned them, too, of the danger of becoming televisionaries. **1962** *Listener* 24 May 924/2 With Dylan Thomas and Gilbert Harding gone, Gwyn Thomas has a great future as a televisionary. **1981** Q. CRISP *How to become a Virgin* 156 Impresarios are frequently asked by televisionaries when some scheme or other first occurred to them.

B. *adj.* Of, possessing, or induced by television.

1934 in WEBSTER s.v. *Television.* **1937** E. BLUNDEN *Elegy* 50 The televisionary world to come. **1958** *Times* 5 July 7/2 If, in a televisionary trance, we are induced to buy some commodity for which our waking self has no appetite [etc.]. **1966** *New Statesman* 16 Dec. 917/3 The longish orchestral interludes, which are enough to drive the average televisionary producer to despair. **1980** *Daily Tel.* 5 Sept. 12/1 Televisionary indoctrination in Luanda.

televisioner (telĭvi·ʒənəɹ). *rare.* [f. *TELEVISION + -ER[1].] One who watches television.

1928 *Television* Mar. 12/1 (*caption*) Some new uses for television. For the toilet—enabling the televisioner to see the back of his head when brushing his hair.

televisionless (te·lĭ-, telĭvi·ʒənlės), *a.* [f. *TELEVISION + -LESS.] Without a television set; that does not include watching television.

1962 *Guardian* 8 Jan. 2/3 Parents..should provide a warm and undisturbed televisionless place for homework. **1981** *Times Lit. Suppl.* 8 May 516/3 Our customary, television-less routine.

te·levision-wise, *adv.* [-WISE.] In the manner of television; with regard to television.

1962 *Listener* 19 Apr. 702/1 Television-wise, his performance was more convincing. **1968** [see *SCAN *v.* 6 c].

televisor (te·lĭvəizǫɹ). Also **Televisor.** [f. as *TELEVISE *v.*: see -OR.] **1.** An apparatus for transmitting or receiving television pictures; orig. the name of that designed and patented by John Logie Baird (1888–1946). Now only *Hist.*

1926 *Glasgow Herald* 11 Jan. 7 The Televisor. *Ibid.* 8 Oct. 9/1 The scene in front of the transmitting televisor is turned into electrical impulses. **1927** *Ibid.* 2 Feb. 9 The cost of televisor equipment for practical use. **1930** MOSELEY & CHAPPLE *Television* viii. 95 The audience can see on the screen of their 'televisors', and hear the person who is broadcasting from the studio. **1935** H. G. WELLS *Things to Come* xii. 98 There is a large televisor disk and telephone and other apparatus on the desk before Cabal. *Ibid.* xiii. 119 A man stands up and switches on a televisor and everybody listens. **1946** *Astounding Science Fiction* July 61/2 The televisor muttered at his elbow and he reached out to flip the toggle. **1984** *Financial Times* 13 June 17/6 A rare John Logie Baird televisor of around 1930 sold for £1,760.

2. A television broadcaster. *rare.*

1942 BERREY & VAN DEN BARK *Amer. Thes. Slang* § 618/3 *Televisor*, the television transmitting apparatus; also a television artist or technician. **1966** *New Statesman* 30 Sept. 497/4 (Advt.), Heather Jenner, televisor, broadcaster and writer.

televisual (te:lĭvi·ʒiuăl, -vi·ziuăl), *a.* [f. *TELEVISION, after VISUAL *a.*] Of, pertaining to, characteristic of, or appearing on television; suitable for or effective in the medium of television.

1934 in WEBSTER. **1956** *Observer* 15 Jan. 8/5 All day he lies in bed, while televisual phantoms flit across his ruffled cerebral screen. **1959** *Listener* 12 Feb. 303/1 Here was something that the theatre could not do, something essentially televisual. **1960** K. AMIS *New Maps of Hell* iii. 82 Televisual views of actual historical scenes. **1973** *Church Times* 16 Nov. 9 Filmic or televisual violence breeds or releases violence in the viewer. **1980** *Times Lit. Suppl.* 25 July 842/2 It is because he keeps in practice with televisual mannerisms that he is so successful a natural in a television-dominated world.

Hence **televi·sually** *adv.*, from the point of view of or as regards television, on or for television.

1957 *Observer* 29 Sept. 13/2 Televisually..there was a surprising amount to be said in favour of this experiment so rich in every kind of producer's death-trap. **1967** *Listener* 9 Feb. 207/2 We had on this uncomfortable occasion not Shakespeare re-worked televisually..but a kind of compromise with what had already been worked in an alien medium. **1979** *Ibid.* 3 May 602/2 A generation ago, we still lived in an age of innocence, televisually, and politicians were apt to come on the box as themselves. **1981** *Times* 27 June 6/2 Who better than Russell, with his televisually perfect mane of white hair?

telex, Telex (te·leks). [f. *TELE(PRINTER + *EX(CHANGE *sb.* 10 c.] **1.** A system of telegraphy in which printed messages are transmitted and received by teleprinters using the public telecommunication lines; the apparatus used in this process. Freq. *attrib.*, esp. in *telex service.*

Despite the frequent use of a capital initial, *telex* in the ordinary uses defined here is not a proprietary term. The names of some specific products (radio equipment, hearing aids, etc.) of the Telex Corporation are registered as trade marks, however.

1932 *Telegr. & Teleph. Jrnl.* Oct. 2/1 In August 1932, came the opening in London of 'Telex' service, otherwise 'teleprinter exchange service'. **1939** *Electrical Communication* Jan. 222/2 Strong grounds exist for the belief that..a spontaneous and universal growth of Telex will follow. **1954** *Communications & Electronics* Nov. 40/1 Telex is an internationally agreed name for a subscriber-to-subscriber public teleprinter exchange service; it is for the printed word what the telephone exchange system is for the spoken word. **1958** *Times* 2 Sept. 5/2 Telex subscribers are linked to a system by which they can exchange typed messages by teleprinter. **1964** C. DENT *Quantity Surveying by Computer* vii. 101 Equipment can be obtained enabling these tapes to be input over the Telex system directly to the computer. **1968** R. V. BESTE *Repeat Instructions* xxii. 233 He..was told to ring back at midnight when they should have the answer on the Telex. **1970** *New Scientist* 16 July (Suppl.) 2/1 It is estimated that by 1980 the total of telex and similar machine to machine (including computer) messages in the United States will be just over one billion. **1974** C. HAMPTON *Savages* (1976) xiii. 64 Installing a telex in the interests of business efficiency. **1981** *Sci. Amer.* Oct. E5/1 (Advt.), Transmission is at 2,400 bit/s and a page of 1500 characters can be sent in ten seconds—20–30 times faster than telex—and received on telexes, electronic typewriters, word processors or other compatible terminals.

2. A message so transmitted.

1978 *Globe & Mail* (Toronto) 12 Oct. 4/4 Here was the only apparent flaw in the Telexes. Mr. Lalonde wasn't elected to the House of Commons and appointed to Cabinet until the following year. **1980** *Daily Tel.* 9 July 16 The first I heard of it was when I got a telex of congratulation.

Hence **te·lex** *v.* (*a*) *trans.*, (i) to contact by telex; (ii) to send (a message) by telex; (*b*) *intr.*, to send a telex message; **te·lexed** *ppl. a.*

1960 *Guardian* 13 Dec. 8/6 In a telexed message to 18 cities and towns Mr. Bevins declared that direct dialling.. was planned to start in six months. **1968** *Aramco World Mag.* May–June 25/1 He..waited while the story was telexed—at 60 words a minute—to a communications center in London. **1968** C. BURKE *Elephant across Border* ii. 74, I must telex Allard by eleven. **1972** *Daily Tel.* 8 Mar. 17 (Advt.), Write, telephone or telex for information now. **1979** *Courier-Mail* (Brisbane) 4 Oct. 3/6 The managing director of Hudson Conway Holdings Ltd...said yesterday he had telexed the Queensland Opposition offering to open his company's files to them. **1983** *Listener* 28 Apr. 24/2 One didn't know one's every word was being..telexed direct to the Shah for his comment.

telharmonium (te:lhāɹmōᵘ·niŏm). [f. TEL(E- + HARMONIUM.] An electrophonic instrument, invented by the American scientist Thaddeus Cahill (1867–1934) and designed to produce tones for transmission over telephone wires by means of rotating electro-magnetic generators.

1906 *Chambers's Jrnl.* June 495/1 In the telharmonium the qualifying ripples are ingeniously added to the waves of the fundamental note by a separate contrivance. **1934** *N.Y. Times* 13 Apr. 19/1 Thaddeus Cahill, who invented an electric typewriter and the device for producing music electrically, known as the telharmonium, died suddenly at 10 o'clock yesterday of a heart attack. **1978** P. GRIFFITHS *Conc. Hist. Mod. Music* viii. 111 The pioneer.. was Thaddeus Cahill, a Canadian scientist who demonstrated an extraordinarily bulky 'telharmonium' in 1906.

teliospore (tī·liospōᵊɹ). *Bot.* [f. *TELI(UM + -O + SPORE.] A spore of the rust fungi (Uredinales) which produces a basidium on germination, often after overwintering; a teleutospore.

1905 [see *TELIUM]. **1970** J. WEBSTER *Introd. Fungi* II. iv. 369 The teliospores [of *Puccinia graminis*] represent the overwintering stage and only develop further after a period of maturation corresponding to winter dormancy. **1981** *Trans. Brit. Mycol. Soc.* LXXVII. 439/2 If in autumn a rusted rose leaf is shaken gently above a glass slide, many single teliospores fall on to it.

telium (tī·liŏm). *Bot.* Pl. **telia.** [mod.L., f. Gr. τέλ-ος end.] = *TELEUTOSORUS.

1905 J. C. ARTHUR in *Bot. Gaz.* XXXIX. 222 For the sorus of the third spore-stage, usually..called teleutosorus, I propose *telium*..; derivatives *telial, teliospore*, etc. **1937** *Nature* 8 May 800/2 (*heading*) Production of uredia and telia of *Puccinia graminis* on *Berberis vulgaris*. **1979** *Trans. Brit. Mycol. Soc.* LXXIII. 231/1 Only telia are present on the leaves.., but a few urediniod spores are found in some telia of this specimen.

Hence **te·lial** *a.*

1905 [see above]. **1925** *Jrnl. Agric. Res.* XXXI. 643 [In *Gallowaya pinicola*] there is very little intermingling or intertwining of hyphae as a preliminary to the formation of the telial sorus. **1967** *Trans. Brit. Mycol. Soc.* L. 190 In taxonomic study of *Endophyllum* and *Kunkelia* there are two possibilities. Their sori can either be compared with aecia of other rusts or with telia of other rusts. .. I propose that they should properly be called 'telial aecia'.

tell, *v.* Add: **I. 3. b.** *tell it not in Gath* (earlier *transf.* examples).

1751 S. RICHARDSON *Let.* 11 July (1964) 185 A wise man to be in love! Tell it not in Gath. **1816** M. R. MITFORD *Let.* 20 Oct. (1925) 135 My favourite play ('tell it not in Gath!') is the first part of *King Henry the Fourth*.

5. a. Also in phr. *to tell all*, to reveal the whole truth, esp. in a sensational manner (freq. with ref. to the printed word). Now usu. without indirect obj.

1897 B. STOKER *Dracula* v. 57, I *do so* want to tell you all. **1936** *Mademoiselle* Aug. 16 (*heading*) Mrs Chester tells all. **1971** J. LOFLAND *Analyzing Social Settings* vi. 132 We delude ourselves if we expect very many field workers actually to 'tell all' in print.

7. a. Also with *apart*.

1925 A. LOOS *Gentlemen prefer Blondes* (1982) iv. 86 How are we going to tell you gentlemen apart? **1958** K. AMIS *I like it Here* xiv. 178 Barbara had complained to him..that she couldn't tell people apart (he found as little difficulty here as he found in telling female film-stars apart). **1982** B. CHATWIN *On Black Hill* i. 10 As boys, only their mother could tell them apart.

b. Now freq. in affirmative sentences. (Later examples.)

1920 F. SCOTT FITZGERALD *This Side of Paradise* I. ii. 56 He was.., as Amory could tell from his general appearance, without much conception of social competition. **1924** 'K. MANSFIELD' *Something Childish* 124 They're not respectable women—you can tell at a glance. **1936** 'G. ORWELL' *Diary* 11 Feb. in *Coll. Essays* (1968) I. 176 You can always tell a miner by the blue tattooing of coal dust on the bridge of his nose. **1963** J. FOWLES *Collector* I. 49, I always thought people could tell I lived on my own. **1966** S. HEANEY *Death of Naturalist* 15 You could tell the weather by frogs too.

8. a. Also with direct speech as obj. *I told you so*: see also *I TOLD YOU SO.

1904 [see *BOUQUET 1 b]. **1916** H. S. WALPOLE *Dark Forest* I. v. 135 'I can't marry you,' she told him, 'because I don't love you.' **1936** M. PLOWMAN *Faith called Pacifism* 81 Mr. Lloyd George, as the wild cat of the House of David, said: 'I told you so.' **1943** G. GREENE *Ministry of Fear* II. i. 135 'Mr Digby,' she told him, 'there's a visitor for you.' **1976** H. MACINNES *Agent in Place* xxii. 231 'The police—call the police.' 'It's done,' Tony told her.

c. Const. *on*. To act as informer to (a person) about (another). Cf. sense 16.

1901 M. FRANKLIN *My Brilliant Career* xiii. 107 Now, not a step do you go, my fine young blood, until you pick up every jolly lemon and put them away tidily, or I'll tell the missus on you. **1943** *Crisis* Mar. 78/3 If he told the Big God on them, no telling what would happen.

16. Const. *on* (further examples).

1943 B. SMITH *Tree grows in Brooklyn* III. xxxv. 206 And I didn't tell on you either, the time you made a cigarette out of coffee grounds and when you smoked it the paper caught fire and fell on her blouse and burned a big hole in it. **1955** J. MASTERS *Coromandel!* 41 Do you think she'll tell on us? **1968** J. LOCK *Lady Policeman* xx. 162 They felt they ought not to 'tell on her' unless it was absolutely necessary. **1974** *Age* (Melbourne) 12 Oct. 12/1 Ooh Aah! I'm going to tell on you: I will inform the authorities.

17. a. *to tell the tale*, to relate a false or exaggerated story, esp. in order to evoke a sympathetic response.

1918 W. J. LOCKE *Rough Road* xi. 133 The temptation to 'tell the tale', to the new-comer was too strong. **1928** *Daily Express* 15 Dec. 7/4 Moneylender at Bow County Court. What did you tell me when you borrowed the money? Debtor: Oh, we all tell the tale when we want money. **1943** J. B. PRIESTLEY *Daylight on Saturday* ii. 9 The absentees tell the tale to the National Service Officer, and he tells the tale to Proscot, and nothing's done. **1968** 'J. LE CARRÉ' *Small Town in Germany* xiii. 204 He couldn't half tell the tale... He could tell you *any* bloody tale and you believed it. **1979** R. BLYTHE *View in Winter* iv. 175 I'm not tellin' the tale. We all went to the war.

d. *to tell* (someone) *goodbye, hello*, etc., to say goodbye, hello, etc., (to someone). Chiefly *U.S.*

1859 BARTLETT *Dict. Amer.* (ed. 2) 475 To *tell* one good-bye, is the Southern phrase for to bid one good-bye. **1872** E. EGGLESTON *End of World* xviii. 128 You aren't going without telling me good-by? **1884** [in Dict., sense 4 a]. **1905** B. TARKINGTON *In Arena* 253 She told me to tell you good-bye. **1973** V. CANNING *Flight of Grey Goose* ii. 28 Tell Albert hello and love to you both. **1979** L. MEYNELL *Hooky & Villainous Chauffeur* viii. 111 Mr Furlong asked me to tell you goodbye.

20. *don't tell me* (later examples); also (with dependent clause) expressing dismay; *do tell!* (earlier and later examples); *to tell the world*, to announce openly; to assert emphatically; *I tell* (or *I am telling*) *a lie*, (in trivial use) I am mistaken (cf. *LIAR 1 a); *you're telling me*, there is no need to tell me; I know that only too well; *to tell* (someone) *what to do with* (something) or *where to put* (something), expressing emphatic rejection with impolite implications; *to tell it like it is*, to relate the facts of a matter realistically or honestly, holding nothing back *colloq.* (orig. *U.S. Blacks'*). Also *tell that to the marines*: see *MARINE *sb.* 4 c; *to tell* (someone) *where he gets* (or *to get*) *off*: see *GET *v.* 62 j.

1861 GEO. ELIOT *Silas Marner* I. ix. 143 Not come to live in this house? Don't tell me. **1944** M. LASKI *Love on Supertax* iv. 52 Who's your latest pick-up?..Not Sir Hubert Porkington! Don't tell me you've actually hooked him! **1952** H. GARNER *Yellow Sweater* 15 'Don't tell me you're in trouble [*sc.* pregnant]?' he asked. **1973** *Farm & Country* 10 Apr. 11/4 'Don't tell me we've got to go through that again,' said one executive member in an audible groan.

1842 J. S. BUCKINGHAM *Eastern & Western States Amer.* I. 177 When a person..has concluded his narrative, the hearer will reply, 'Oh! *do* tell.' **1883** C. F. WILDER *Sister Ridnour's Sacrifice* 138 'Come fur?' 'About eighty miles.'.. 'Du tell!' **1979** C. MACLEOD *Luck runs Out* (1981) i. 17 Do tell. Did she leave any children?

1781 COWPER *Table Talk* in *Poems* (1782) I. 38 And tell the world..That he, who died below and reigns above, Inspires the song, and that his name is love. **a 1871** T. CARLYLE in *Coll. Lett. T. & J. W. Carlyle* (1981) IX. 318 This I *cd* tell the world, you have not had, for 100 years, any Book that came more direct and flamingly sincere from the heart of a living man. **1923** [see *JEEZ(E *int.*]. **1933** *Punch* 11 Jan. 29/3 Say, can he act orr can he act? Ah'll tell de woirrld. **1956** 'C. BLACKSTOCK' *Dewey Death* viii. 169 She persistently told the world about her fiancé, her marriage problems, her piano playing.

1925 S. O'CASEY *Shadow of Gunman* II, in *Two Plays* 172 Adolphus..after takin' his tea at six o'clock—no, I'm tellin' a lie—it was before six, for I remember the Angelus was ringin' out. **1956** 'A. BURGESS' *Time for Tiger* i. 7 Those Japanese tattooists... I seen one fellow in Jerusalem, wait, I'm telling a lie, it was in Alex,..one fellow with a complete foxhunt on his back. **1968** L. DEIGHTON *Only when I Larf* vii. 89 Six Centurion Mark Fives on that hillock... No tell a lie, one of them is a Mark Two. **1973** J. MANN *Only Security* xii. 172 Oh, it must have been fifteen years or so—..No, I tell a lie, I'm afraid,..can't have been more than five or six years that she was like that, poor lady.

1932 G. KAHN (*song-title*) You're telling me. **1938** M. ALLINGHAM *Fashion in Shrouds* xix. 338 'Things are bad enough as they are.' 'You're telling me.' **1954** *Times* 16 July 9/4 When he declares that 'overnutrition has its dangers'..the layman is inclined to reply 'You're telling me.' **1977** 'C. AIRD' *Parting Breath* xvii. 194 'Forensic pathologists don't take chances.' 'You're telling me,' said Crosby with audible scorn.

1946 M. SHULMAN *Zebra Derby* (1947) xxi. 133 Green, an upholsterer, said that he was through with upholstering and had told his old boss what to do with his old job. **1958** M. DICKENS *Man Overboard* xii. 176 He had been going to tell Glenn what he could do with his job. **1968** M. BRAGG *Without City Wall* II. xxi. 207 You could tell the people at the hall what to do with that job of theirs. She'd had enough of being a servant. **1977** *Listener* 14 Apr. 483/2 Protestations that if the government did any such thing, the BBC would probably tell it where to stuff such an instruction.

1964 *Down Beat* 19 Nov. 8/2 (*heading*) Mann tells it like it is. **1965** *New Statesman* 1 Oct. 473/1 Although sometimes tardy, all his speeches make their intended points; as they say in Harlem, he tells it like it is. **1969** L. LOKOS *House Divided* i. 58 The crowd responded fervently with 'Amen, amen,' and 'Tell it like it is.' **1973** *Field & Stream* Jan. 8/3 Keep this tell-it-like-it-is kind of article going. **1979** *Guardian* 14 Apr. 8/6 'Tell it like it is,' said Hemingway, but that was..before we all became ethnic-conscious.

II. 23. b. (Earlier example.)

1804 J. WHITEHOUSE in Lewis & Clark *Orig. Jrnls.*

Lewis & Clark Exped. (1905) VII. I. 70 The Captn. formd. his men On the S.W. Side of the river Missourie and told them off in Sections, from the right.

d. fig. *to tell* (someone) *off*, to scold or reprimand (someone). Cf. *tick off* s.v. *TICK *v.*[1] 3.
1919 *Cassell's New Eng. Dict.* s.v. *Tell, to tell off*, (colloq.) to scold. **1927** A. CHRISTIE *Big Four* xiv. 202 They don't like you to notice things—especially if it should seem you were telling them off about it. **1938** G. ARTHUR *Not Worth Reading* xiv. 216 'It required a very great man,' said F.E. when he emerged from his interview, 'to resist the temptation to tell me off.' **1941** G. HOMES *Forty Whacks* ix. 90 The man had just been told off, and told off plenty. **1974** M. BIRMINGHAM *You can help Me* iv. 97 She's..telling off the police good and proper... She blames them for all the dirt.

III. 26. (Earlier example.)
1783 *Public Advertiser* 7 Oct. 2/2 Yet strange to tell it, this Distinction, which as the Players call it, tells most forcibly, Garrick overlooked.

tell-. Add: **tell-all** *a.* and *sb.*, (an account which is) revelatory, tending to disclose private information; cf. *TELL *v.* 5 a.
1959 J. FINGLETON *Four Chukkas to Australia* (1960) i. 2 This position—in cricket and other sports—has been aggravated by the flood of 'tell-all' books. **1974** *Nat. Geogr. Mag.* Dec. 851/2 A tell-all historian of the time reported that the prince loved to drink and was notably fond of women. **1976** *Publishers Weekly* 7 June 68/1 This man's sometimes engrossing, frenetic, first-person tell-all. **1978** in K. Hudson *Jargon of Professions* iii. 64 A totally engrossing tell-all. Few autobiographies convey so intimately what is involved in creativity.

Tell el-Amarna: see *AMARNA.

tellen. Add: Also **tellin.** (Later examples.)
1901 E. STEP *Shell Life* viii. 118 The members of the Tellin family..are distinctly deep burrowers in sand or mud. **1971** S. P. DANCE *Seashells* 77 The right and left valves of many tellins are unequal in shape and size.

teller. Add: **2. c.** Also *attrib.* in *teller vote* (U.S.), a vote taken by tellers as members file past them; *spec.* a category of vote in the House of Representatives, in which the tellers record the votes of members but not (until 1970) their names.
1924 *Congressional Rec.* 11 Apr. 6142/1 Is not the teller vote the highest in the committee? **1935** *Sun* (Baltimore) 1 July 1/8 The House is working under a rule which precludes a direct roll-call vote..but a teller vote..is to be taken. **1974** *Encycl. Brit. Macropædia* XIV. 722/1 Voting procedures range from the formal procedure of the division or teller vote in the British House of Commons to the electric voting methods employed in the California legislature. **1972** W. WEAVER *Both Your Houses* vii. 99 If the outcome of a division is unsatisfactory to at least twenty members of the Committee of the Whole..they can demand a teller vote.

Teller mine (te·lǝɹ mǝin). Also with hyphen and as one word. [Anglicization of G. *tellermine*, f. *teller* plate + *mine* *MINE *sb.* 3.] A disc-shaped German anti-tank mine containing TNT, used in the war of 1939–45.
1943 *Hutchinson's Pict. Hist. War 4 Aug.–26 Oct.* 11 A huge collection of teller-mines, or disc mines, discovered by the allied forces near Roccalumba. **1945** *Finito! Po Valley Campaign* (15th Army Group) 41 The 10th Mountain Division pushed forward..across a valley studded with Teller mines. **1967** *Punch* 11 Jan. 40/1 We were..taking the fuses out of those wretched Tellermines.

tellina (telǝi·nă). Also **Tellina.** [mod.L. (G. E. Rumphius *D'Amboinsche Rariteitkamer* (1705) II. 145), f. Gr. τελλίνη.] = TELLEN. Also *attrib.* Hence **te·llinoid** *a.*, resembling a bivalve of the genus *Tellina.*
1877 C. M. YONGE in C. Coleridge *C. M. Yonge* (1903) ii. 70 Waves from the Atlantic, bringing in..tellinas of a delicate pink. **1884** G. W. TRYON *Struct. & Syst. Conchol.* III. 170 The branchial apparatus..is..a departure from the Tellina type. **1900** *Proc. U.S. Nat. Mus.* XXIII. 287 The Tellinas are mostly inhabitants of moderate depths. *Ibid.* 291 Shell tellinoid, thin. **1936** A. H. VERRILL *Strange Sea Shells* xiv. 132 Why..is the tellina so beautifully colored within its shells.

telling, *vbl. sb.* Add: **1. c.** *that's telling(s* (examples of sing. form); similarly *that would be telling*; *to lose nothing in the telling,* (of a story) to become embellished in the course of frequent narration.
1897 'S. GRAND' *Beth Bk.* xiii. 112 'May I ask..by whom you were informed?..'Ah, that would be telling,' said Beth. **1921** S. KAYE-SMITH *Joanna Godden* III. 136 'What sort of surprise?' 'That's telling.' **1930** A. CHRISTIE *Murder at Vicarage* x. 78 'When was she talking of earning her own living?'..'That would be telling, wouldn't it?' **1973** G. MITCHELL *Murder of Busy Lizzie* xii. 144 'But what could you inform about?' 'That's telling, isn't it?' **1980** A. PRICE *Hour of Donkey* i. 23 'Are the Germans in Peronne, Dickie?'..'That would be telling!'
[**1721** J. KELLY *Scottish Proverbs* 55 A Tale never loses in the telling. The Fame or Report of a matter of Fact..commonly receives an Addition as it goes from Hand to Hand.] **1906** [in Dict., sense I a]. **1914** E. R. BURROUGHS *Tarzan of Apes* vi. 68 The story of the thunder-stick having lost nothing in the telling during these ten years. **1954** L. P. HARTLEY *White Wand* 15 No doubt Antonio was telling the story to his fellow-gondoliers at the traghetto, and it would lose nothing in the telling.

2. c. *telling-off*, a scolding or reprimand. Cf. *TELL *v.* 23 d. *colloq.*
1911 KIPLING *Diversity of Creatures* (1917) 121 The boys..had had a wildish night..that ended with a telling-off from an artist. **1920** A. J. L. SCOTT *Hist. Sixty Squadron R.A.F.* 57 He got..a well-deserved and proper 'telling-off' from the Brigadier and Wing Commander. **1959** *Times* 22 July 7/4 Then there was and to some extent still is 'a telling off', sometimes met with in the degenerate form of 'ticking off'. **1974** W. FOLEY *Child in Forest* II. 231 Still smarting from my 'telling-off'..and in militant mood.

telling, *ppl. a.* (Earlier example.)
1851 H. MELVILLE *Moby Dick* I. xxv. 180 A staid, steadfast man, whose life for the most part was a telling pantomine of action.

tell-tale, *sb.* (*a.*) Add: **1. b.** (Earlier and later examples.) Also *spec.*, a small hidden object placed so as to reveal a secret intrusion by its disturbance (see quots.).
1754 RICHARDSON *Grandison* II. 295, I was very earnest to know, since my eyes had been such tell-tales, if their brother had any suspicion of my regard for him. **1953** *Sun* (Baltimore) 30 Mar. (B ed.) 26/7 A broken 'tell-tale', one of the little devices policemen set in doorways and fire escapes to help them check on burglars. **1968** 'H. HOWARD' *Eye of Hurricane* iii. 33 After I'd searched..I was well satisfied that nobody had planted tell-tales anywhere..no microphones, no built-in radio transmitters. **1975** B. GARFIELD *Death Sentence* (1976) vii. 44 His hands began to sweat: the familiar telltale. **1979** K. FOLLETT *Triple* viii. 184 There were dozens of ways of planting telltales. A hair lightly stuck across the crack of the door..; a lump of sugar under a thick carpet would be silently crushed by a footstep.

2. h. *Building.* A piece of glass or clear plastic, often graduated, fixed over a crack in a building to reveal whether there is further movement in the fabric.
1938 *Times* 16 Feb. 14/1 Of the many tell-tales planted by Mr. Harvey only a few are known to have broken. **1972** *Besselsleigh & Dry Sandford* (Berks.) *Parish Mag.* Oct., The church council has agreed to the architect's suggestion that a few glass tell-tales should be fixed in some of these cracks. **1976** *Daily Tel.* 25 Sept. 21/4 They will hold back on the job while they put up 'telltales' at strategic points.

i. A light on the dashboard of a motor vehicle which shows when the direction indicator or main-beam lights are in use.
1962 *Autocar* Spring 62/2 When any driving lamps are on, a small green warning light appears, and this is supplemented by a blue tell-tale for the main beams. **1966** *Guardian* 17 Oct. 6/3 The winker tell-tale is..self-cancelling. **1970** K. BALL *Fiat 600, 600D Autobook* xi. 138/1 The high beam indicator is on the dashboard behind a blue screen lens, the parking light indicator behind a green and the direction indicator tell-tale behind another green lens.

tellurion. (Example of *tellurium.*)
1905 *Nature* 14 Sept. 493/2 The ordinary wire model or 'tellurium'.

tellurometer (telĭŭrǫ·mĭtǝɹ). [f. L. *tellūr-em* the earth + -O + -METER.] An instrument that accurately measures distances on land by transmitting a microwave signal and timing the arrival of a return signal that it triggers at the distant point.
1957 T. L. WADLEY in *Empire Survey Rev.* July 100 (*heading*) The tellurometer system of distance measurement. **1961** *Aeroplane* C. 63/2 Five of the parties were to do levelling, and the other two distance measuring with tellurometers. **1975** J. B. HARLEY *O.S. Maps* i. 7 The 'Tellurometer'..has been used to measure distances of 135 km between Great Britain and Ireland as part of the process of checking the triangulation.

telly (te·li). *colloq.* [Shortening of *TELEVISION. Cf. *TELE.] **1.** = *TELEVISION I. Phr. *on (the) telly.*
[**1940** *Chambers's Techn. Dict.* 837/2 *Tellies,* colloquialism for cinematograph films with sound; also for television.] **1942** BERREY & VAN DEN BARK *Amer. Thes. Slang* § 618/3 Lookies, tellies, telly. **1957** *Observer* 3 Nov. 4/5 For all practical purposes, if it hasn't been on telly, it doesn't exist. **1957** *Economist* 7 Dec. 842/1 An evening when Sheffield Wednesday were playing Juventus of Milan at football on the telly. **1958** M. SPARK *The Go-Away Bird* 152 He said, 'What do you do in the evenings, Lorna? Do you watch Telly?' I did take this as an insult, because we call it TV, and his remark made me out to be uneducated. **1967** E. WILLIAMS *Beyond Belief* III. xix. 204 Tonight, the eve of Christmas Eve,..they are watching telly, nice thriller. **1968** J. ARNOLD *Shell Bk. Country Crafts* 70 A growing tendency in domestic life of subordinating activities to the 'telly'. **1970** G. F. NEWMAN *Sir, You Bastard* iv. 117 On the news, on the telly this evening. **1977** *New Yorker* 26 Sept. 37/1 His parents lived an isolated life, but now had the telly.

2. = *TELEVISION 2.
1955 M. ALLINGHAM *Beckoning Lady* i. 5 He..walked back to the village and the telly. **1957** F. KING *Man on Rock* i. 7, I can't even afford to pay the never-never on a wireless, let alone a telly. **1969** A. GLYN *Dragon Variation* vi. 176 An occasional bluish light behind chintz curtains betrayed the night-owls, those who were still glued to the telly, watching the news headlines, the weather forecast. **1978** K. AMIS *Jake's Thing* iii. 30 Let's be absolute devils and have the heating on and huddle round the telly.

3. A television performance; a booking or session of filming for this. *Theatr.* and *Broadcasting.*
1963 E. HUMPHREYS *Gift* 8 Every time I did a telly it was a lovely day, while I sweated my guts out under the artificial light. **1979** S. BRETT *Comedian Dies* ii. 23 I've got you a telly... It's an *Alexander Harvey Show.*

4. *attrib.* and *Comb.*, as *telly ad, don, mast, -viewer,* etc.; **telly man,** a man who works professionally for a television service.
1958 *Times Lit. Suppl.* 15 Aug. p. xii/3 Turning their backs upon the 'telly' screen, they will strain their eyes in the semi-darkness of the living-room. **1960** C. MACINNES *Mr Love & Justice* 85 His part-time trade of mending radios and telly sets. **1963** *Spectator* 22 Feb. 230/3 The Third Programme..is becoming more and more a private club or experimental research establishment unwittingly financed by the telly-viewers. **1963** *Punch* 2 Oct. 475/1 Small vociferous pockets trying to attract tellymen. **1966** J. BETJEMAN *High & Low* 4 Slate cottages with sycamore between, Small fields and telly-masts and wires and poles. **1969** FABIAN & BYRNE *Groupie* (1970) i. 9, I even believe telly ads and things like that. **1971** *Author* LXXXII. 111 Many a paper fills its review columns with inoffensive, but basically uninteresting, books butchered to make a well-known telly don's holiday in the dead summer months. **1977** *Irish Democrat* Mar. 5/2 Surrounded by a regiment of security men, aides, advisers, journalists, tellymen and Unionists. **1977** *Irish Times* 8 June 11/5 But there might have been long telly-watching sessions behind locked doors.

telo-[1]. Add: Also with pronunc. (tī·lo). **telode·ndrion, -de·ndron** (pl. **-dendria** is used for both forms) *Anat.* [Gr. δενδρίον, dim. of δένδρον tree], one of the terminal branches into which the axon of a nerve cell divides; **te·lomere** *Cytology* [*-MERE], the compound structure found at the end of a chromosome in eukaryotes, having only one spindle pole; **telomi·tic** *a. Cytology* [Gr. μίτ-ος thread] = *TELOCENTRIC *a.*; **telope·ptide** *Biochem.*, a peptide which is at or near the end of a polypeptide molecule; **telosyna·psis** *Cytology*, a supposed end-to-end pairing of chromosomes during the zygotene stage of meiosis; = *telosyndesis* below; hence **telosyna·ptic** *a.*, **-syna·ptically** *adv.*; † **telosynde·sis** *Cytology* = *telosynapsis* above.
1899 L. F. BARKER *Nervous System* viii. 82 The ultimate terminals (telodendrions) of the axones have been carefully and exactly studied. **1907** I. HARDESTY in Morris & McMurrich *Morris's Treat. Human Anat.* (ed. 4) 751 The axone bearing the impulse on approaching its termination loses its sheath and breaks up into its numerous terminal twigs, the final of which are called telodendria. **1949** *New Gould Med. Dict.* 1030/2 *Telodendrion.* See *telodendron.* **1966** C. R. & T. S. LEESON *Histology* x. 178/2 In some cases, the telodendria are so numerous as to surround the neuron on which they terminate in a basket-like arrangement. **1940** H. J. MULLER in *Jrnl. Genetics* XL. 2 The reconstructed chromosome cannot continue to be transported..unless it happens to be monocentric and—in *Drosophila* at least—ditelic, one centromere and two telomeres being necessary and permanent organelles. **1960** L. PICKEN *Organization of Cells* vii. 261 Within the nucleus the chromosomes present their telomeres—'centromeres' connected to the chromosomes by terminal filaments—to the aspect of the nuclear membrane nearest to the spindle. **1983** *Nature* 13 Jan. 112/1 Telomeres are very stable as free ends, whereas ends of [DNA] molecules broken *in vivo* tend to stick together irreversibly. **1917** E. E. CAROTHERS in *Jrnl. Morphology* XXVIII. 449 The unusual conditions of the chromosomes in this group have made advisable the introduction of..new terms... Telomitic—a term used to indicate terminal fiber attachment. **1934** L. W. SHARP *Introd. Cytol.* (ed. 3) ix. 116 Supposedly telomitic chromosomes have been shown in some instances to have their attachment region slightly back from the end. **1964** F. O. SCHMITT et al. in *Proc. Nat. Acad. Sci.* LI. 494 The term 'end-chains' with its terminal connotation has been replaced by the term 'telopeptides'. **1971** *Nature* 22 Jan. 242/1 Every third residue in the chain is glycine, except in short 'non-collagenous' telopeptides at the N-terminal ends of the chains. **1975** *Ibid.* 10 July 125/1 Rabbit anti-collagen serum is primarily directed to terminal (telopeptide) antigenic sites, and not to helical or central sites. **1909** Telosynapsis [see *parasynapsis* s.v. *PARA-[1] 1]. **1920** W. E. AGAR *Cytology* ii. 43 Parasyndesis and Telosyndesis. [*Note*] Called parasynapsis and telosynapsis by cytologists, who employ the term synapsis in the sense in which syndesis is here used. **1945** M. J. D. WHITE *Animal Cytol. & Evolution* v. 79 The old controversy between adherants of the theory of telosynapsis and those who believed in the alternative viewpoint..is only of historical interest, since 'parasynapsis'..is now known to be universal. **1912** *Jrnl. Exper. Zool.* XIII. 394 Attention may be called to the increasing tendency..to reject, or at least restrict, the theory of parasynapsis.., in favor of a telosynaptic conception. **1929** *Jrnl. Genetics* XXI. 47 Digby's interpretation, so much quoted in support of the telosynaptic view.., is due to a misunderstanding of the essential features of meiosis. **1910** Telosynaptically [see *parasynaptically* adv. s.v. *PARA-[1]]. **1926** *Genetics* XI. 274 The third element is joined telosynaptically to the other two chromosomes. **1920** L. DONCASTER *Introd. Study Cytol.* v. 68 The end-to-end union [of chromosomes] (formerly supposed to be frequent or universal) is telosyndesis (or telosynapsis).

telocentric (telo-, tīlose·ntrik), *a.* (and *sb.*) *Cytology.* [f. TELO-[1] + *-CENTRIC.] Of a chromosome: having the centromere at the end. Hence as *sb.* Cf. *ACROCENTRIC, *METACENTRIC *adjs.*

1939 C. D. DARLINGTON in *Jrnl. Genetics* XXXVII. 349 This does not mean that terminal centromeres or telocentric chromosomes work satisfactorily or survive permanently. *Ibid.* 352 The misdivided chromosomes..will give the functional telocentrics that I have already described at second anaphase. **1949** DARLINGTON & MATHER *Elem. Genetics* v. 103 Misdivision of the centromere and Formation of two telocentric chromosomes. **1964** *Hereditas* LII. 209 Most cytologists agree that the centromere in acrocentric chromosomes is less terminal than in telocentric chromosomes. **1971** [see *METACENTRIC *sb.*]. **1976** *Nature* 12 Aug. 580/1 The X chromosome is telocentric (X^1) in F344 and AC1 strains.

telogen (te·lodʒĕn). [f. TELO-[1] + -GEN.] **1.** *Biol.* The stage in the life of a hair or hair follicle following cessation of growth of the hair.

1926 F. W. DRY in *Jrnl. Genetics* XVI. 297 For the present purpose it is convenient to divide the developmental history into the following three phases: (1) The Anagen phase... (2) The Catagen phase... (3) The Telogen phase, the hair having become a dub-hair and not growing further. **1955** *Proc. Soc. Exper. Biol. & Med.* LXXXVIII. 450/1 Telogen is the resting stage of a follicle and it is reached approximately 19 days after plucking. **1980** *Practitioner* Nov. 1161/1 Hair growth..is..phasic, there being a phase of growth (anagen) lasting approximately three to five years in normal scalp hair and a resting phase (telogen) lasting for around three months.

2. *Chem.* A simple compound that provides chain-terminating radicals in polymerization and limits the degree of polymerization.

1948 [see *TELOMER]. **1974** C. M. STARKS *Free Radical Polymerization* i. 2 Chain transfer agents (telogens) are often added to polymerization recipes as molecular weight regulators. **1980** [see *TAXOGEN].

telomer (te·ləməɹ). *Chem.* [f. TELO-[1] + *-MER.] A low-molecular-weight polymer consisting of a chain of a limited number of units (taxogens) terminated at each end by a radical from a different compound (the telogen).

1948 HANFORD & JOYCE *U.S. Patent 2,440,800* 1 It has been found necessary to coin new terms to describe the reaction and the participants therein... 'Telomerization' is defined as the process of reacting..a molecule YZ which is called a 'telogen' with more than one unit of a polymerizable compound..called a 'taxogen' to form products called 'telomers' having the formula $Y(A)_nZ$. **1951** *Jrnl. Amer. Chem. Soc.* LXXIII. 5197/1 When it [*sc.* the polymerization] is conducted in the presence of any one of a wide variety of organic compounds, telomers containing 1–25 tetrafluoroethylene units combined with one molecule of the chain transfer compound are obtained. **1966** J. A. BRYDSON *Plastics Materials* xv. 295 With an ethylene–carbon tetrachloride ratio of about 4:1 about 60% of the telomers have 7, 9 or 11 carbon atoms in the molecule. **1980** [see *TAXOGEN].

So **te:lomeriza·tion**, polymerization that is limited by the action of a telogen; also **te·lomerized** *ppl. a.*, **te·lomerizing** *vbl. sb.*

1948 Telomerization [see *TELOMER]. **1954** *Jrnl. Res. Nat. Bureau Standards* (U.S.) LIII. 122 $YZ + nCX_2 = CX_2 \rightarrow Y(CX_2CX_2)nZ$... Such a reaction is called telomerization. **1967** *Gloss. Terms Plastics Industry (B.S.I.)* 1. 7 *Telomerized polymer*, a polymer chain-stopped by a telomer. **1968** G. TRAPPE in P. D. Ritchie *Vinyl & Allied Polymers* xii. 265 Low molecular weight oils, greases, and waxes of polychlorotrifluoroethylene are made by polymerisation in the presence of telomerising agents such as carbon tetrachloride. **1974** H. I. BOLKER *Natural & Synthetic Polymers* iii. 136 About 0·5–1·0 mole % of acetic acid is added as a telomerization agent.., which limits the formation of chains of excessively high molecular weight.

telophase. Delete entry s.v. TELO-[1] and substitute:

telophase (te·lofēiz). *Cytology.* [a. G. *telophase* (M. Heidenhain 1894, in *Arch. f. mikr. Anat.* XLIII. 524): see TELO-[1] and PHASE.] The final phase of mitosis and meiosis, following anaphase and preceding interphase, at which the chromatids or chromosomes are at opposite poles of the cell; also, a cell at this stage.

1895 *Jrnl. R. Microsc. Soc.* 35 The fourth chapter discusses the final movements of mitosis (telophases, telokinesis). **1900** [in Dict. s.v. TELO-[1]]. **1934** *Nature* 26 May 800/1 The anaphase and telophase chromosomes thus contain two spiral chromonemata... In late telophase the two threads are found to approximate very closely. **1971** J. Z. YOUNG *Introd. Study Man* xiv. 179 At the end of mitosis (telophase) these enzymes associate with the chromosomes. **1973** *Nature* 6 Apr. 403/2 The DNA determinations were carried out in metaphases and telophases of the original stained lung cultures.

Hence **telopha·sic** *a.*, of or pertaining to telophase.

1907 *Rep. Brit. Assoc. Adv. Sci. 1906* 757 It [*sc.* the nucleolus] lies in the centre of the telophasic figure. **1929** *Bot. Gaz.* LXXXVIII. 360 The foregoing investigators were correct in interpreting some (although not all) of the telophasic aspects they observed as chromosome doubleness. **1976** *Biol. Abstr.* LXII. 693/1 The telophasic plaque in the root meristem of *Triticum vulgare.*

telotaxis (telotæ·ksis). *Biol.* [mod.L., coined in Ger. (A. Kühn *Die Orientierung der Tiere im Raum* (1919) 60): see TELO-[1] and TAXIS 6.] Directional movement made by an animal in order to keep a particular source of stimulation acting on its sense receptor(s).

1934 *Jrnl. Exper. Biol.* XI. 129 Those movements in which the animal is truly orientated Kühn calls topotaxis, and these again fall into two main groups: tropotaxis and telotaxis. **1976** D. J. HORN *Biol. Insects* vi. 229 An example of telotaxis that has fascinated researchers is light-compass orientation.

telotype. (Earlier example.)

1850 F. GALTON *Telotype* 3 In the Telotype (as our instrument may be termed), by merely touching a key on which any letter is marked that letter is to be printed, almost instantaneously, at the opposite end of the line.

‖ **tel quel** (tɛl kɛl), *adj. phr.* Also in Fr. pl., **tels quels** (masc.), **telles quelles** (fem.). [Fr.] Just as it is; without improvement or modification.

1876 GEO. ELIOT *Let.* 3 Feb. (1956) VI. 220 Don't wear glasses *telles quelles* but consult about getting the right ones. **1903** W. JAMES *Let.* 5 June in R. B. Perry *Thought & Char. W. James* (1935) II. VI. lxxvi. 427 You spoke of publishing these lectures, but not, I hope, *tel quels* [*sic*]. **1967** *Listener* 16 Mar. 368/3 The culled facts have been presented *tel quel*, with inconsistencies noted but not resolved.

telson. Add: Hence **telso·nic** *a.*

1934 in WEBSTER. **1946** *Nature* 28 Dec. 935/2 The caudal segment was probably composed of the sixth abdominal segment with which the telson had become fused, and thus these appendages must be telsonic. **1981** *Israel Jrnl. Zool.* XXX. 115 The more primitive Hyssuridae have no telsonic statocysts.

Teltag (te·ltæg). [?f. TELL- + TAG *sb.*[1]] A label attached to goods manufactured in the U.K. giving information about the size, weight, performance, etc., of the goods.

1965 *Observer* 23 May 9/4 A new label will appear on British goods next year. Called the 'teltag', it has been designed by the Government-backed Consumer Council to give shoppers clear information on the hidden characteristics of their purchases. **1967** *Spectator* 1 Dec. 682/1 So far isn't necessarily very far, since manufacturers are under no obligation to use, and pay for, Teltags. **1971** *Reader's Digest Family Guide to Law* 335/1 The Teltag scheme, devised by the now defunct Consumer Council, is still used to give details of composition, size, performance and use of appliances.

Telugu, Teloogoo, *sb., a.* Add: Also **Telegu.**

1. (Later examples of the form *Telegu*).

1937 W. H. SAUMAREZ SMITH *Let.* 31 Jan. in *Young Man's Country* (1977) ii. 54 Kanarese is the vernacular of Mysore, a language allied to Tamil and Telegu. **1957** *Encycl. Brit.* IV. 978/1 Great movements of people: the Telegu- and Tamil-speaking caste groups to the rubber plantations of Burma and Malaya. **1978** 'M. M. KAYE' *Far Pavilions* I. i. 17 He picked up a number of tongues.. Tamil, Gujerati and Telegu from the southerners.

3. (Earlier and later examples.)

1816 A. D. CAMPBELL (*title*) A grammar of the Teloogoo language. **1821** —— *Dict. Teloogoo Language*, Advt., The following Dictionary was commenced soon after the publication of the Author's Teloogoo Grammar. *Ibid.* Many of the most common Teloogoo words are arranged, absurdly enough, in the order of the *French*, and not of the Teloogoo, alphabet. **1891** C. R. DAY *Music of S. India* v. 61 They..were probably composed by some Telegu pandit at the court of Mysore. **1909** E. THURSTON *Castes & Tribes S. India* VII. 13 The Telugu soldiers might come to be regarded as the Telugus..*par excellence.* **1977** *Listener* 7 Apr. 447 Publishing Telegu books largely for Indians in the Midlands.

temazepam (tĕmē[i]·zĭpæm). *Pharm.* [f. *tem-* (of unknown origin) + Az(o- + *-ep*(*ine* (see *OXAZEPAM) + AM(IDE.] A tricyclic compound, $C_{16}H_{13}ClN_2O_2$, used as a tranquillizer and short-acting hypnotic.

1970 *Approved Names* (Brit. Pharmacopœia Comm.) 74 *Temazepam.* 7-Chloro-3-hydroxy-1-methyl-5-phenyl-1*H*-1,4-benzodiazepin-2(3*H*)-one. **1971** *Pharmacol. Res. Communications* III. 166 Besides the three known benzodiazepines.., in the present experiment a fourth one—temazepam, recently introduced in therapeutic use—was also studied. **1980** *Brit. Med. Jrnl.* 29 Mar. 910/1 Pharmacological differences between 'long'-acting benzodiazepines..and the 'short'-acting rapidly cleared compounds, such as..temazepam. **1984** *Daily Tel.* 11 Feb. 10/2 [He] chose temazepam, a hypnotic drug marketed..for transient insomnia under the trade name of Normison.

‖ **tembe** (te·mbe). [Swahili.] In East Africa, a rectangular house with mud walls and a flat roof.

1887 W. H. G. KINGSTON *Trav. Dr. Livingstone* vii. 135 Sheikh Said Ben Salim invited him [*sc.* Stanley] to take up his quarters in his tembe, or house, a comfortable looking place for the Centre of Africa. **1896** B. K. GREGORY *Story of David Livingstone* xiii. 121 Then the two brave men retired into the doctor's *tembe*, and conversation began, but Stanley could not recollect what it was all about. **1947** *E. African Ann. 1946–7* 93/2 David Livingstone lived for some time in a *tembe* house on the outskirts of Tabora and the house is preserved as a memorial to his name. **1955** *Times* 25 July 5/1 A replica of the tembe (hut) occupied by Livingstone and Stanley, erected near Tabora some years ago and badly damaged by fire recently, is to be rebuilt this year. **1978** J. UPDIKE *Coup* (1979) iii. 111 The space between the square earth houses, the *tembes*, widens.

temblor (tɛmblǭ·ɹ) South-western *U.S.* Pl. **temblores.** [a. Amer. Sp.] An earthquake.

1876 B. HARTE *Gabriel Conroy* v. xvii. 288 The temblor has swallowed him. **1896** *Land of Sunshine* July 72 One freshet of one Ohio river a dozen years ago took more lives than all the *temblores* in California in a century and a half have taken. **1932** F. L. WRIGHT *Autobiogr.* II. 147 One of the features of construction that insured the life of that building in the terrific temblor of 1922. **1950** *Los Angeles Times* 3 Jan. 1/6 The temblor was reported from both Ogden and Logan.

‖ **tembo** (te·mbo). Also **tembu.** [Swahili.] An alcoholic drink made in East Africa, usu. from the sap of the coconut palm; palm wine.

1860 J. KRAPF *Travels, Researches & Missionary Labours* I. ix. 149 One of the elders said that it was really true that God loved men, for He gave the Wanika rain, tembo, and clothes. **1937** K. BLIXEN *Out of Africa* III. i. 170, I sometimes asked the D.C.'s permission for my Squatters to make tembu, a deadly drink, fabricated from sugar cane. *Ibid.* v. v. 411 The old women took a keen interest in everything that was going on on the farm..; a joke, on a cup of tembu, would make their wrinkled toothless faces dissolve in laughter. **1964** R. M. GATHERU *Child of Two Worlds* vii. 101 Others would be drinking some stinking municipally brewed drink—'Tembo'—at Pumwani as an outlet for their handicapped life.

Tembu (te·mbu), *sb.* and *a.* Forms: 9 **Tymba,** 9– **Tembu; Thembu.** [Xhosa.] **A.** *sb.* A member of a Xhosa-speaking people of the south-eastern part of South Africa; also, this people collectively. **B.** *adj.* Of, pertaining to, or designating this people. Cf. *TAMBOOKIE *sb.* and *a.*

1827 G. THOMPSON *Trav. & Adv. Southern Afr.* I. I. xvii. 349 A Tambookie Caffer is termed Tymba or Tembu, while the tribe collectively is called Amatymbae. **1874** *Cape Monthly Mag.* IX. 207 He then dilated upon the enormities of Gangelizwe, the Tambookie Chief, and the ability of the present Resident amongst the Tembus. **1912** WHITESIDE & AYLIFF *Hist. Abambo* i. 4 Madikana and his people, at a certain time, were feasting, when they were attacked by a combined force of the Tembus and Xosas. **1927** C. G. BOTHA in *Wreck of Grosvenor* (Van Riebeeck Soc.) p. iv, The expedition was obliged to turn back owing to the hostile attitude of the Tembu tribe of natives. **1941** C. W. DE KIEWIET *Hist. S. Afr.* 73 It was densest in Kafirland, where dwelt the Ama-Xosa, the Tembu, the Pondo, the Xesibe, and the Ama-Baca. **1961** *Guardian* 27 May 6/3 Mr Mandela is..the son of a Tembu chief. **1967** J. A. BROSTER *Red Blanket Valley* 4 Remember, the Thembu, one of the chief tribes of the Transkei, were never conquered: they asked the European traders to settle. **1971** *Daily Dispatch* (East London, Cape Province) 11 May 2 We have to honour and respect our national leaders such as Faku of the Pondos and Ngubengcuka of the Tembus. **1974** J. FLINT *Cecil Rhodes* (1976) ix. 205 The foundations [of peace] were laid by an African..a Tembu man fluent in English and Ndebele. **1976** *Times* 4 Nov. 17/4 Chief Matanzima..is a Thembu leader.

‖ **temenggong** (tĕmĕŋgǭ·ŋ). Forms: 8 **tamongoong,** 9 **tumângong; temenggong.** [Malay.] In traditional Malay states, a high-ranking official, usu. commanding the army and the police. Also, the title of the rulers of Johore, 1824–85.

1783 W. MARSDEN *Hist. Sumatra* 285 The *tamongoong*, or commander in the wars. **1859** L. OLIPHANT *Narr. Lord Elgin's Mission to China & Japan* ii. 23 We ascended to the comfortable bungalow of the Tumângong. **1907** F. SWETTENHAM *Brit. Malaya* iv. 67 A new treaty was made ..between Raffles on the one hand and the Sultan Husein and the Tĕmĕnggong on the other. **1964** M. TURNBULL in W. Gungwu *Malaysia* II. viii. 133 This political vacuum encouraged the bid for independence by the subordinate chiefs, the temenggong of Johore and the bendahara of Pahang. **1972** M. SHEPPARD *Taman Indera* 108 During the reign of Sultan Mahmud of Malacca (1488–1511), Tun Hassan, the Temenggong, who ranked second only to the chief minister, started a new fashion by wearing the sleeves of his tunic long and loose.

temerack, obs. var. TAMARACK in Dict. and Suppl.

Temiar (te·mi,āɹ), *sb.* and *a.* [Native name.] **A.** *sb.* An aboriginal people of the Malay Peninsula, also called Sakai; a member of this people. **B.** *adj.* Of or pertaining to this people or their language.

1933 *Jrnl. R. Asiatic Soc.* (Malayan Branch) XI. 291 The Temiars showed an extraordinary desire to sample European medicines. *Ibid.*, The most interesting feature in the Temiar life..was their obvious happiness. **1958** J. SLIMMING *Temiar Jungle* iv. 54 A Temiar community lives on the centre tongue of land. **1958** *Listener* 13 Nov. 793/3 A Temiar who coveted his wife. **1965** R. MCKIE *Company of Animals* v. 91 The Temiar are animists who, living among jungle-covered mountains, are perfectly attuned to their environment. **1972** *Times* 6 Dec. (Europe & Third World Suppl.) p. vii/4 (*caption*) Temiar aborigines at the Gombak Aborigine Hospital, Malaysia, for treatment.

te-mine, var. *TAMEIN.

temmoku (te·mokū). Also **tenmoku.** [Jap., ad. Chinese *tiān-mù* eye of heaven (see quot.

1923).] The Japanese name for a type of Chinese porcelain with lustrous black or brown glaze; also, the glaze so used.

1880 A. W. FRANKS *Jap. Pottery* 5 A tea bowl of porcelain or earthenware (*cha-wan*, or, when of large size, *temmoku*), simple in form, but remarkable for its antiquity or historical associations. **1915** R. L. HOBSON *Chinese Pott. & Porc.* I. 31 *Temmoku*..glaze is sometimes flecked with tea green as well as with golden brown. *Ibid.* 131 The Japanese..have always prized the Chien Yao bowls to which they gave the name *temmoku*. **1923** —— & HETHERINGTON *Art of Chinese Potter* 15 The name *temmoku* (*t'ien mu*, or Eye of Heaven) was first given to a bowl, probably of Fukien origin, brought to Japan during the Sung period by a Zen priest from the Zen temple of the *T'ien mu shan* (Eye of Heaven mountain) in the north-west of Chekiang. In later times the generic name of *temmoku* came to be applied to the whole category of wares of this type. **1924** *Trans. Oriental Ceramics Soc. 1923–4* 26 (*title*) The chemistry of the Temmoku glazes. **1934** [see *hare's fur* s.v. *HARE *sb.* 6]. **1940** B. LEACH *Potter's Bk.* viii. 231 Into the tenmoku I dipped several large jars and bowls. **1958** W. WILLETTS *Chinese Art* II. vi. 394 *Temmoku* bowls..made to-day at P'êng-ch'êng.., and at T'ai-yüan.., which in many respects can hardly be told apart from their Sung models. **1971** S. JENYNS *Jap. Pottery* iii. 84 The glazes particularly associated with the Toshiros and their successors for tea ceremony wares are of this *tenmoku* variety: 'thick' and semi-transparent but coloured often to opacity by the presence of iron oxide. **1976** *Canadian Collector* Mar.–Apr. 43/1 In Japan this type of black-glazed ware became known as *temmoku*.

Temne (te·mn*i*), *sb.* and *a.* Forms: 8 **Timmany**; 9 **Timan(n)ee, Timmanah, -ee, -eh, -i**; 9– **Temne**; **Temnee, Timini, Timne, Timni.** [Native name; cf. quot. 1861.] **A.** *sb.* **a.** A people of Sierra Leone; also, a member of this people. **b.** A West Atlantic language spoken by this people. **B.** *adj.* Of, pertaining to, or designating this people or their language.

1791 A. M. FALCONBRIDGE *Let.* 8 June in *Narr. Two Voyages to Sierra Leone* (1802) 81 The Burees..were conquered and drove away to other parts of the country by the Timmany's. **1792** —— *Let.* 10 Feb. in *Ibid.* 27 In every house I was accosted by whoever we found at home, in the Timmany language *Currea Yaa*, which signifies—How do you do, mother? **1803** T. WINTERBOTTOM *Acct. of Native Africans of Sierra Leone* I. iv. 65 The largest kind [of pepper] is distinguished..in Timmanee, by kik bengbay pootoo; and in Soosoo, by foorootoo bengbay. *Ibid.* v. 80 Timanee towns..have Ro *in general* prefixed to them, as Ro-mak-baynee, a town where they finish things. **1825** [see *KORANKO]. **1841** *Penny Cycl.* XXI. 503/1 The Timannees occupy a country extending 90 miles from east to west, and 55 from north to south. **1850** T. E. POOLE *Life, Scenery & Customs in Sierra Leone* II. xvii. 274 He gave himself up to the most diligent study of the Timmanah language. **1861** C. F. SCHLENKER *Collect. Temne Traditions* p. iii, The signification of the term: Témne seems to be 'an old man himself'. They derive it.. from *o*-tem, 'an old man, an old gentleman', to which is affixed the reflexive suffix -*ne*, 'self'; because they believe that the Temne nation will ever exist. **1887** *Encycl. Brit.* XXII. 44/2 The following..can be distinctly classified:—Mandingos, 1190; Timmanehs, 7443 [etc.]. **1903** J. J. CROOKS *Hist. Sierra Leone* ix. 121 Many Timini children were carefully brought up according to the Mohammedan creed. **1911** *Encycl. Brit.* XXV. 55/1 Sierra Leone is inhabited by various negro tribes, the chief being the Timni, the Sulima, the Susu and the Mendi. **1916** H. OSMAN NEWLAND *Sierra Leone* iii. 28 The name of the village is essentially a reminder of the old Temne domination when Kwaia..country embraced all this territory. **1916** N. W. THOMAS *Anthropol. Rep. on Sierra Leone* I. i. 7 The remaining languages are Soudanese, and fall into two main groups, prefix and non-prefix tongues. To the former..belong (a) Timne, (b) Limba, [etc.]. **1926** F. W. H. MIGEOD *View of Sierra Leone* I. iii. 18 The Temne influence is so great that practically all the Bullom north of Freetown speak Temne. **1955** [see *MANDE *sb.* and *a.*]. **1957** M. BANTON *W. Afr. City* iii. 54 The Temne, conservative as he is in many matters, has a readiness to copy certain new ways. **1957** LD. HAILEY *African Survey 1956* iii. 104 In the Protectorate Mende is the language generally used in education, but Temne and the Kono dialect of Vai are used in mission schools. **1980** E. G. WILSON *John Clarkson* vi. 81 Alexander Falconbridge.. had been prevailed upon..to return to Sierra Leone where his experience with the Temne people would pave the way for the immigrant fleet. *Ibid.* vi. 82 John Clarkson could soothe Falconbridge and win the confidence of the Temne as well.

temp. (temp), abbrev. of L. *tempore* (also used) = in the time of.

1658 W. DUGDALE *Hist. St. Paul's Cathedral* 127 Of this, the first mention that I finde, is in that Grant of *Richard de Beaumeir* Bishop of London (*temp.* H.1.) concerning the School. **1767** A. C. DUCAREL *Tour through Normandy* 96 Leases of Crown-Lands in Kent, temp. Eliz. **1859** S. A. ALLIBONE *Dict. Eng. Lit.* I. 27 As we have frequently occasion to refer to the reigns of different English sovereigns without specifying dates,—*temp.* Edward II., *temp.* Henry II., &c. **1892** F. W. MAITLAND *Let.* 6 Sept. (1965) 105 Are you likely to write anything about the frequency of eyres temp. Hen. II? **1932** *N. & Q.* 16 Jan. 46/1 Old registers *tempore* mid-seventeenth century. **1955** *Times* 16 July 7/4 A flying machine, *tempore* Blériot, would almost certainly have crashed in the shrubbery. **1983** W. BLUNT *Married to Single Life* i. 2 My great-grandfather, John Blunt of Lindfield in Sussex (*temp.* James I).

temp (temp), *sb.*¹ Colloq. abbrev. of TEMPERATURE 7.

1886 R. ROOSE *Let.* 15 Mar. in R. S. Churchill *Winston S. Churchill* (1967) I. Compan. I. iv. 117 As long as I can fight the temp and keep it under 105 I shall not feel anxious. **1916** G. BELL *Let.* 23 July (1927) I. xv. 383, I shan't be sorry when the temp. drops 20°. **1924** GALSWORTHY *Forest* II. ii. 48 Collie's temp.'s down. **1940** M. DICKENS *Mariana* v. 170, I wish I had a thermometer with me, I'd take your temp. **1972** J. MCCLURE *Caterpillar Cop* ii. 27 The body temp is above normal. **1977** *Hot Car* Oct. 89/3 The original CF radiator, cooled by a second-hand Kenlowe fan keeps the temps down, no sweat, even in that long hot summer of '76.

temp (temp), *sb.*² *colloq.* [f. next or as abbrev. of TEMPORARY *sb.* 4 in Dict. and Suppl.] A temporary employee; esp., a temporary secretary (see *TEMPORARY *sb.* 4).

1932 *Amer. Speech* VII. 278 *A temp*, a part-timer [i.e. a part-time non-civil service employee of the U.S. Post Office]. **1967** *Economist* 22 Apr. 374/1 Overstaffing is not solely the result of the unwillingness to use temps. **1970** R. HILL *Clubbable Woman* viii. 238 One of his women, a temp, only comes in at weekends [at a public house]. **1975** *Sunday Sun* (Brisbane) 23 Nov. 51/1 A year ago she sold cattle. Now she sells Temps.

temp (temp), *a.* Colloq. abbrev. of TEMPORARY *a.* 1 a.

1909 in WEBSTER. **1964** in Hamblett & Deverson *Generation X* 173 Between school and university I had several temp. jobs ranging from accounts clerk to van driver. **1968** D. E. KNUTH *Art of Computer Programming* I. 632 *Temp storage*, part of memory used to hold a value for a comparatively short time while other values occupy the registers. **1972** *Homes & Gardens* Dec. 22/2 'You do realise it's only temp, dear?' said the Lady Supervisor when I arrived to begin my duties as part-time untrained telephonist. **1977** 'D. CORY' *Bennett* iv. 121 Detective-Inspector (temp.) Eric Hunter.

temp (temp), *v. colloq.* [f. *TEMP *sb.*²] *intr.* To work as a temp (see *TEMP *sb.*²). So **te·mping** *vbl. sb.*

1973 *Times* 15 Mar. 30/5 (Advt.), Bored with temping? We specialise in short term assignments..in the artistic and creative fields. **1974** *Harpers & Queen* Sept. 180/1 You meet such civilized people when temping for Bernardette. **1978** *Times* 2 Oct. (Business Efficiency Suppl.) p. iii/3 Most of the students had given as their explanation for deciding to temp: 'To gain office experience before taking up a permanent job.' **1979** A. PRICE *Tomorrow's Ghost* i. 9 I'm a bit cheesed off with this temping—I think it's time to dig in somewhere comfy.

tempeh (te·mpe). Also **tempe.** [ad. Indonesian *tempe*.] An Indonesian foodstuff made by fermenting soya beans with Rhizopus and deep-frying them in fat.

1966 *N.Y. Times* 17 Apr. IV. 11/4 A cake of food material..somewhat comparable to Indonesian fermented food called tempeh. **1977** *Daily Colonist* (Victoria, B.C.) 9 Jan. 28/5 Sixty-nine persons died and 265 others in East Java were in hospital for food poisoning after eating tempe, a local dish made from soy beans. **1980** *San Francisco Bay Guardian* 16–23 Oct. 13 (Advt.), Delicious Natural Foods to Eat: Soy Ice Cream, Sushi, Tofu, Tempeh, Mochi, Fresh Juices, Organic Burritos.

temper, *sb.* Add: **III. 12. d.** (See quot. 1975.)

1925 C. E. GUTHE *Pueblo Pottery Making* 20 The mixing ..consists of the addition of temper. **1936** K. M. CHAPMAN *Pottery of Santo Domingo Pueblo* 11 The clay and temper are moistened and kneaded together. **1955** BUSHNELL & DIGBY *Anc. Amer. Pottery* iv. 32 The temper is normally rather coarse, but in at least one of the three examples..it is very fine. **1975** R. L. BEALS *Peasant Marketing System of Oaxaca, Mexico* ii. 18 Temper used in pottery making is a coarse material such as sand or decomposed rock to make the clay more ductile and prevent cracking of the shaped vessel during drying.

IV. 13. *temper-fit, tantrum.*

1884 W. JAMES in *Mind* IX. 199 In injuries to the brain ..we have tears, laughter, and temper-fits, on the most insignificant provocation. **1930** G. C. MYERS *Mod. Parent* x. 168 There are vague symptoms of temper tantrum at the age of several weeks when [an infant's] accustomed satisfactions are withheld. **1951** AUDEN *Nones* (1952) 11 Unable To conceive a god whose temper-tantrums are moral. **1980** *Jrnl. R. Soc. Med.* LXXIII. 217 The affected children themselves are liable to behavioural problems such as temper tantrums.

14. temper-brittleness *Metallurgy*, notch-brittleness produced in certain types of steel when it is held in or cooled slowly through a certain temperature range; hence **temper-brittle** *a.*

1918 *Proc. Inst. Automobile Engin.* XII. 349 If an absolutely unnotched bar is taken and tested under impact conditions, it is frequently found that even if that bar happens to show the peculiar 'temper brittleness' it will bend over without any sign of brittleness in the unnotched state... There is..no difference..between the microstructure of the 'temper-brittle' steel and the microstructure of the same steel giving the good impact value. **1930** *Engineering* 24 Oct. 525/3 The metal had been rendered 'temper brittle' by being cooled too slowly in the tempering process. **1967** A. H. COTTRELL *Introd. Metallurgy* xx. 384 This temper-brittleness..is associated with fracture along grain boundaries.

temper, *v.* Add: **III. 14. c.** *trans.* To reduce the brittleness in (hardened steel) by reheating it to a certain temperature and allowing it to cool. Cf. ANNEAL *v.* 4.

1925 *Jrnl. Iron & Steel Inst.* CXI. 334 Careful observations made on specimens which had been tempered just below 200°C. **1967** A. H. COTTRELL *Introd. Metallurgy* xx. 384 If plain carbon or low-alloy steels are tempered below about 250°C they usually remain somewhat brittle.

19. To increase the pliability of straw for corn-dolly making by dampening it with water.

1963 M. LAMBETH *Golden Dolly* 11 When plaiting out of season it is necessary to temper the straw. **1976** S. J. REID *Art of Weaving Corn Dollies* 9 After a period of storage.., straw dries out... To restore it to a supple condition it is necessary to temper (or dampen) the straw.

temperamental, *a.* Add: **2.** Of a person: liable to peculiar moods, having or giving way to an erratic or neurotic temperament. Hence, of a thing: behaving erratically or unpredictably.

1907 *Amer. Mag.* LXIII. 355/2 The Celtic race is above all things temperamental. **1923** E. WALLACE *Clue of New Pin* xxix. 255 Tab decided that she was a little temperamental, and loved her for it. **1939** F. THOMPSON *Lark Rise* iii. 42 A temperamental person was said to be 'one o' them as is either up on the roof or down the well'. **1962** *Amer. N. & Q.* I. 31/1 The horse was particularly suitable in northern Europe where the temperamental climate often made rapid ploughing and planting important. **1965** *Wireless World* Sept. 436/1 He [*sc.* Dr. W. H. Eccles] also started a study of the coherer, the only detector of the period, which led to a better understanding of the action of that temperamental device. **1977** M. DRABBLE *Ice Age* I. 79 The central heating worked, and he had boosted it with an electric fire, albeit a temperamental electric fire, which needed the occasional kick.

Hence **te:mperame·ntalist**, a temperamental person. *rare.*

1924 *Blackw. Mag.* June 786/1, I was what you might call a temperamentalist, and very easily hypnotised.

temperance. Add: **I. 2. b.** *temperance address, badge, drink* (example), *lecture* (example), *man* (earlier example), *meeting* (examples), *ship, society* (earlier example); **temperance hall**, a building used for public meetings or entertainments at which no intoxicants are sold or provided; **temperance hotel** (examples); **temperance house** = *temperance hotel.*

1831 (*title*) Report of the American Temperance Society. **1833** E. T. COKE *Subaltern's Furlough* ii, in *Waldie's Sel. Circulating Library* 24 Sept. 380/3 Many hotels have 'temperance house' inscribed in large gilded letters over the door or sign. **1833** C. F. HOFFMAN *Let.* 26 Dec. in *Winter in West* (1835) I. 211 The most devout temperance man could see no harm in that! **1834** J. J. STRANG *Diary* 1 July in M. M. Quaife *Kingdom of St. James* (1930) 219, I shall soon have to make the temperance address. **1837** W. JENKINS *Ohio Gaz.* 69 Barnesville..has..2 taverns, and 1 temperance hotel. **1840** R. H. DANA *Two Years before Mast* (1841) xxxi. 118/2 This was a 'temperance ship'; and like too many such ships, the temperance was all in the forecastle... The captain..can drink as much as he chooses. **1841** *Cultivator* VIII. 163, I witnessed..a very large temperance meeting at which I saw 'female influence' fully exerted in a most glorious cause. **1843** Temperance hall [see *PERAMBULATORY *sb.* a]. **1862** G. BORROW *Wild Wales* II. xiv. 154, I drew nigh..and read: 'tea made here, the draught which cheers but not inebriates.' I was before what is generally termed a temperance house. **1869** J. H. BROWNE *Great Metropolis* 327 A large number remain open, pretending to sell nothing but 'temperance drinks'. **1881** I. M. RITTENHOUSE *Maud* (1939) 17 Went to the Temperance Meeting last night with Emma and Mabel. **1902** O. WISTER *Virginian* 454 Once I had to sleep in a room next a ladies' temperance meetin'. **1922** JOYCE *Ulysses* 476 Bloom's bodyguard distribute.. loaves and fishes, temperance badges, expensive Henry Clay cigars. **1933** E. O'NEILL *Ah, Wilderness!* IV. iii. 153 I'm not going to read you any temperance lecture. **1978** P. BAILEY *Leisure & Class in Victorian Eng.* iv. 82 Bolton... A vast new town hall, opened in 1873, looked down upon the Free Library..a Second Temperance Hall. **1978** *Times* 5 Apr. (Tourism in Britain Suppl.) 4/9 For those seeking an unusual experience Birmingham..has a famous temperance hotel.

c. Used as *predic. adj.* Practising or advocating total abstinence.

1907 J. MASEFIELD *Tarpaulin Muster* xiii. 138 They're temperance down at the Point in these times. **1977** H. FAST *Immigrants* III. 193 You're not temperance, are you?

temperate, *a.* Add: **3. c.** Of food: produced in, or suitable for production in, a moderate climate.

1960 *Economist* 8 Oct. 125/3 The New Zealanders.. have recognised that reconciling their highly competitive exports of temperate farm products with a common European agricultural policy will be an extremely difficult task. **1962** *Listener* 27 Sept. 462/1 The so-called temperate foodstuffs—that's to say corn and meat and dairy produce. **1980** *Nature* 7 Feb. 514/3 In many parts of the Third World people eat temperate vegetables: cauliflower, onions, carrots, potatoes, cucumber, tomatoes.

8. *Microbiology.* Of a phage: not necessarily causing lysis of the host cell, but able to exist as a prophage for a number of generations; giving rise to lysogenic bacteria. [tr. F. *tempéré* (F. Jacob et al. 1953, in *Ann. de l'Inst. Pasteur* LXXXIV. 223).]

1953 *Cold Spring Harbor Symp. Quantitative Biol.* XVIII. 65/1 It has been proposed..to call temperate (as opposed to virulent) those phages which are able to establish the lysogenic condition in their host cells. **1961**

M. HYNES *Med. Bacteriol.* (ed. 7) xxvi. 401 The virulent phages are often termed lytic, since they disrupt the bacteria they infect; the symbiotic phages are usually termed temperate. Cultures infected with a temperate phage are confusingly termed lysogenic. **1979** ARMS & CAMP *Biology* xvi. 244 A virulent, lytic bacteriophage.. can only replicate and cause cell lysis. Other phages, known as temperate phages, may either replicate and lyse the cell they invade, or may instead enter a dormant phase in which the phage DNA is joined to that of the host cell..and replicated with it over many cell generations.

temperature. Add: **10.** *temperature control, -dependence, -dependency, -independence; temperature-controlled, -dependent, -independent, -regulating, -sensitive* adjs.; **temperature coefficient** *Physics*, a coefficient expressing the relation between a change in a physical property and the change in temperature that causes it; **temperature gradient,** a gradient (sense 2 in Dict. and Suppl.) of temperature; **temperature inversion** *Meteorol.*, the phenomenon of an increase of temperature with height above the ground; **temperature-regulation** *Biol.* = *THERMOREGULATION; **temperature-salinity** *adj. phr.*, relating to the temperature and salinity of water; *spec.* applied to a diagram in which both are plotted as a function of depth.

1902 *Encycl. Brit.* XXVIII. 8/1 The quantity *a* is then called the temperature-coefficient, and its reciprocal is the temperature at which the resistivity would become zero. **1962** *Newnes Conc. Encycl. Nucl. Energy* 791/2 For the practical operation of a reactor the temperature coefficient of reactivity should be small so that a steady power can be maintained by moving control rods at a moderate speed. **1923** GLAZEBROOK *Dict. Appl. Physics* III. 582/1 (*heading*) Temperature control. **1959** E. T. HALL *Silent Language* iii. 79 Clothes and houses are extensions of man's biological temperature-control mechanisms. **1935** *Discovery* Nov. 322/1 The centres are passed by an automatic feeding attachment through a curtain of temperature-controlled chocolate. **1970** *Jrnl. General Psychol.* Oct. 163 They were housed in individual cages in a temperature-controlled laboratory. **1946** *Nature* 7 Sept. 333/1 Experiments on the temperature-dependence of the breakdown strength F. **1974** J. W. DRAKE in Carlile & Skehol *Evolution in Microbial World* 53 The temperature-dependencies of the *Neurospora* and T4 rates differed markedly. **1962** SIMPSON & RICHARDS *Physical Princ. Junction Transistors* ix. 200 The most important temperature-dependent property of transistors is the collector cutoff current. **1882, 1962** Temperature gradient [see GRADIENT *sb.* 2]. **1978** *Jrnl. R. Soc. Arts* CXXVI. 683/1 Structures of supersonic aircraft are subject to thermal stresses due to temperature gradients. **1965** *Math. in Biol. & Med.* (Med. Res. Council) VI. 256 The same difficulty arose with the temperature-independence of temporal rhythms. **1946** *Nature* 7 Sept. 333/1 The latter is temperature-independent but increases with the concentration of foreign atoms. **1945** E. BOLLAY in F. A. Berry et al. *Handbk. Meteorol.* x. 758 (*caption*) Characteristic properties of nonfrontal temperature inversions. **1977** I. M. CAMPBELL *Energy & Atmosphere* viii. 252 A further circumstance of temperature inversion occurs where there is an enclosed valley in which cold air..tends to collect. **1911** J. A. THOMSON *Biol. Seasons* IV. 338 It represents an interesting reminiscence of a more primitive physiological state when the temperature-regulating mechanism was not yet well established in the ancestral mammals. **1957** J. S. HUXLEY *Relig. without Revelation* (rev. ed.) ix. 216 The temperature-regulating mechanism of higher mammals. **1927** HALDANE & HUXLEY *Animal Biol.* xi. 240 The mammals..possess proper temperature-regulation. **1930** *Rep. 'Michael Sars' N. Atlantic Deep-Sea Exped. 1910* I. I. 19 The 'normal' temperature-salinity curve is reproduced..in such a way that the corresponding values of temperature and salinity can easily be read off. **1942** H. U. SVERDRUP et al. *Oceans* iv. 141 Water masses can be classified on the basis of their temperature-salinity characteristics. **1959** H. BARNES *Oceanogr. & Marine Biol.* 157 As one passes across the Gulf Stream there is a fairly sharp temperature-salinity boundary between Gulf Stream water and the so-called Slope water lying over the Continental Shelf. **1962** *Science Survey* XX. 308 The surface of the body contains a number of temperature-sensitive patches which produce patterns of nerve impulses related to the ambient temperature.

tempering, *vbl. sb.* Add: **a.** (Examples in sense *14 c of the vb.)

1881 *Encycl. Brit.* XIII. 352/2 The generic phrase 'tempering' is usually applied to mean a combination of the hardening and annealing processes..hardening [the steel] to a red heat and suddenly cooling, and then heating up again to a somewhat lower temperature and allowing to cool slowly. **1941** JONES & SCHUBERT *Engineering Encycl.* II. 1274 The object of tempering, or 'drawing', is to reduce the brittleness in hardened steel.

b. *tempering temperature.*

1910 *Encycl. Brit.* XIV. 808/1 The higher the tempering-temperature, *i.e.* that to which the hardened steel is..reheated, the more is the molecular rigidity relaxed. **1967** A. H. COTTRELL *Introd. Metallurgy* xx. 384 Higher tempering temperatures may be used, thereby improving the toughness of the steel.

temperish (te·mpərɪʃ), *a.* [f. TEMPER *sb.* 11 + -ISH[1].] Inclined to or exhibiting bad temper.

1925 *Chambers's Jrnl.* Nov. 764/1 From these temperish folk arise strange quarrels. **1929** *Times* 16 Jan. 13/5 His [*sc.* Lord Haig's] reply was more than emphatic; it was almost temperish. **1935** [see *riding-blanket* s.v. *RIDING *vbl. sb.* 5 a].

tempersome (te·mpəɹsəm), *a.* orig. *dial.* [f. TEMPER *sb.* + -SOME[1].] Quick-tempered. Also pseudo-*arch.* [after TEMPER *sb.* 6], displaying extreme conditions of weather. Hence **te·mpersomeness.**

1875 W. D. PARISH *Dict. Sussex Dial.* 119 *Tempersome*, hasty-tempered. **1879–81** G. F. JACKSON *Shropshire Word-bk.* 434 *Tempersome*, adj., hot-tempered; passionate. **1906** W. DE MORGAN *Joseph Vance* xliii. 392 He was very tempersome about it. **1909** —— *It never can happen Again* I. xxv. 370 Marianne, for all her tempersomeness and jealousy, loved and reverenced Challis. **1946** M. PEAKE *Titus Groan* 234 And now that it is so tempersome and cold you are always going out into the nastiness and getting wet or frozen.

tempery (te·mpĕri), *a. dial.* [f. TEMPER *sb.* + -Y[1].] Short-tempered.

1905 *Eng. Dial. Dict.* VI. 60/1 Yorks... 'She was a tempery body.' **1951** H. GILES *Harbin's Ridge* xiii. 116 She had tempery ways..and sometimes I felt like I was in a pot of water with it boiling. **1954** *Landfall* VIII. 266, I cursed on like a tempery child deprived Of what he'd loved.

tempest, *sb.* Add: **1. b.** Also *North-eastern N. Amer.*

1877 R. T. COOKE in *Harper's Mag.* Jan. 297/1 Ominous flashes of tempest began to play about the far horizon. **1892** *Dialect Notes* I. 211 *Tempest*, a thunder-shower. [Plymouth, Massachusetts.] **1951** *Amer. Speech* XXVI. 251 Such localized terms as..the southeastern New England tempest (thunderstorm)... Tempest was recorded from a Schuylerville (Saratoga Co.) informant, definitely conscious of his ultimate Nantucket ancestry. **1965** E. RICHARDSON *Living Island* 171 August is also the month of tempests (for here [in Nova Scotia] electrical storms keep the name used by Shakespeare).

5. b. *tempest-charged, -haunted, -shaken, -shattered, -smitten, -throttled, -torn* (later examples), *-troubled* (later example); **c.** *tempest-cleaving, -walking* (example).

1826 J. G. WHITTIER *Vale of Merrimac* in *Free Press* (Newburyport, Mass.) 29 June 4/1 And the tempest-charg'd vapor their tall tops embraces. **1818** SHELLEY *Rosalind & Helen* (1819) 77 That a tempest-cleaving swan Of the songs of Albion..Found a nest in Thee. **1880** LONGFELLOW *Ultima Thule* 7 Are not these The tempest-haunted Hebrides, Where sea-gulls scream? **1817** SHELLEY *Laon* I. 23 The tempest-shaken wood, The waves, the fountains, and the hush of night. **1845** LONGFELLOW *Seaweed* vii, in *Poems* 99 From the wreck of Hopes far-scattered, Tempest-shattered, Floating waste and desolate. **1844** J. G. WHITTIER *Bridal of Pennacook* in *United States Mag.* Sept. 239 Sometimes The tempest-smitten tree receives From one small root the sap which climbs Its topmost spray and crowning leaves. **1930** R. CAMPBELL *Adamastor* 51 Doomed vessels..Reared to the stars their tempest-throttled cry. **1918** W. S. CHURCHILL in M. Gilbert *Winston S. Churchill* (1977) IV. Compan. I. 418 Prompt and clear must be those great decisions which assign definite limits to the increasing confusion and miseries of the vanquished and above the tempest-torn waters light again the beacons of mankind. **1939** R. CAMPBELL *Flowering Rifle* II. 64 The wide-winged and wounded Albatross The tempest-torn that rides (and bears) the strife. **1952** —— tr. *Baudelaire's Poems* 183 She sought, with tempest-troubled gaze, the skies Of her first innocence. **1820** SHELLEY *Prometh. Unb.* I. 35 These are Jove's tempest-walking hounds.

tempest, *v.* **3.** For ? *Obs.* read *dial.* or *arch.*

1875 W. D. PARISH *Dict. Sussex Dial.* 119 It tempestes so as we're troubled to pitch the hay upon to the stack anyhows in the wurreld. *a* **1907** F. THOMPSON *Works* (1913) I. 120 Flew spurned the pebbled stars: those splendours then Had tempested on earth, star upon star.

tempest-tossed, *a.* (Later examples.)

1817 SHELLEY *Prince Athanase* in *Posthumous Poems* (1824) II. ii. 251 Thus had his age, dark, cold and tempest-tost, shone truth upon Zonoras. *a* **1887** E. LAZARUS *New Colossus* in *Poems* (1889) I. 203 Send these, the homeless, tempest-tost to me, I lift my lamp beside the golden door! **1955** E. POUND *Classic Anthol.* I. 8 My heart is no more tempest-toss'd. **1984** *Times* 10 Mar. 17/1 People wrangle and row as though they were part of a tempest-tossed drama by John Cassavetes.

‖ **tempête** (taňpę̄t). [Fr., lit. 'tempest'.] An English country-dance (and tune) of the late-nineteenth century.

1873 L. TROUBRIDGE *Life amongst Troubridges* (1966) viii. 72 We had a *Tempête*, the Boulanger and 'Wiss'. **1879** *Manners & Tone of Good Society* viii. 139 Country dances, such as the 'Tempête', 'Sir Roger de Coverley', etc., are usually danced at private balls when given in the country. **1923** G. ARTHUR *Further Lett. from Man of no Importance* (1932) 155 Yes, the Tempête was the popular dance at children's and semi-grown-up dances of our young days, and even later at country balls; fancy its being danced again in Paris.

‖ **tempietto** (tempie·to). Pl. **tempietti.** [It., lit. 'little temple': cf. TEMPLET[4].] A colonnaded building, freq. of circular form, surmounted by a dome.

1896 W. J. ANDERSON *Archit. Renaissance in Italy* iv. 77 Bramante's *Tempietto* in the Cloisters of San Pietro in Montorio (1502). **1901** M. CARMICHAEL *In Tuscany* 158 Civitali was..a fine and practical architect. He is thought to have built the Palazzo Pretorio, and to him belongs the honour of having built the dome-like chapel (*Tempietto*) in which is preserved the sacrosanct and venerable Volto Santo. **1922** G. GROMORT *Italian Renaissance Archit.* iv. 80 Palladio himself, half a century later, made a drawing of Bramante's Tempietto. **1960** E. BOWEN *Time in Rome* ii. 47 A *tempietto* in a moist northern garden. **1962** *Listener* 1 Feb. 228/1 The ancient Romans had filled their gardens with statuary as well as with *tempietti*, colonnades, covered galleries, apses, and pavilions. **1971** *Country Life* 7 Oct. 887/1 The Hafeziye [in Shiraz, Iran] is much more than the pleasant municipal garden one might expect, the formal approach, open colonnade and delightful tempietto beyond achieving a simple grandeur that is very memorable.

temping, *vbl. sb.*: see *TEMP *v.*

temple, *sb.*[1] Add: **I. 1. e.** A Jewish synagogue; now *spec.* the place of worship of Reform (and some Conservative) Jews. Now chiefly *U.S.*

1598 J. STOW *Survey of London* 277 But that this house hath beene a Temple or Jewish Sinagogue..I allow not. **1830** *Monthly Intelligence* May 75/2 There is at Frankfort ..a considerable body of Jews, belonging to what is called the 'New Temple'... Mr. Moritz mentions having visited their Temple. **1850** G. AGUILAR *Vale of Cedars* v. 27 The little temple was erected..and the solemn rites of their peculiar faith adhered to. **1914** I. COHEN *Jewish Life in Modern Times* xi. 287 So occidentalized has the Reform temple become that a visitor at first sight can hardly distinguish whether he is in a synagogue or a chapel. **1942** C. ROTH in *Menorah Jrnl.* Winter 4 Their place of worship (no longer a homely *Schul* but, with unhappy retrogression, a Temple). **1978** H. KEMELMAN *Thursday the Rabbi walked Out* (1979) ii. 14 It's the place of women in the temple service I want to talk about, Rabbi. *Ibid.* vii. 45 The synagogue, or as we call it, the temple. **1981** G. V. HIGGINS *Rat on Fire* vii. 56 Saturdays everybody dressed up and went to temple.

III. 6. a. (senses 1–3) *temple-court* (examples), *-door* (examples), *-priest* (example); (appositive) *temple-pyramid* (examples). **c. temple block,** a percussion instrument of oriental origin consisting of a hollow block of wood which is struck with a drum-stick; also known as a *WOOD BLOCK; usu. in *pl.*; **temple prostitute,** a woman maintained by a temple, who performs rituals of a sexual nature (cf. *DEVADASI); also *fig.*; hence **temple prostitution; temple-state:** in antiquity, a city-state centred on a temple or similar sacred edifice.

1929 *Melody Maker* Mar. 295/2 The same remark applies to the Temple blocks, and even the tambourine can easily be played too loudly. **1964** J. CARTER in Norton & Spacey *Drums & Drumming Today* 40 How I yearn for the days of temple blocks and saucepan lids. **1820** SHELLEY *Witch of Atlas* in *Posthumous Poems* (1824) 50 And round each temple-court In dormitories ranged..She saw the priests asleep. **1930** R. GRAVES *Ten Poems More* 13 In every temple-court, for all to see Flourishes one example of each tree In tricunx. *c* **1386** CHAUCER *Knight's Tale* (1875, Harl. MS. 7334) 2422 The rynges on þe tempul dore þat hange. **1729** SWIFT *Directions for Birth-day Song* in *Poems* (1958) 462 What tho for fifteen years and more, Janus hath lock'd his Temple-door? **1921** G. B. SHAW *Back to Methuselah* IV. 178 The temple door is in the middle of the portico. **1941** J. MASEFIELD *Gautama* 31 Like a temple-priest intoning. **1890** A. B. ELLIS *Ewe-Speaking Peoples of Slave Coast of W. Afr.* ix. 141 Girls dedicated to a god do not necessarily serve him during the whole of their lives... In Dahomi there seems to be a marked distinction between those who actually minister to the service of the temple, and those who are merely temple prostitutes. **1951** AUDEN *Nones* (1952) 28 Private rites of magic send The temple prostitutes to sleep. **1980** S. T. HAYMON *Death & Pregnant Virgin* xi. 84 Poor old Charlie! Thought he'd recruited a vestal virgin when what he'd got was a temple prostitute! **1912** J. N. FARQUHAR *Primer of Hinduism* xvi. 194 We are now in a position to realise how it has been possible for the Hindu to admit such things as..cruel torture, temple prostitution. **1961** L. MUMFORD *City in History* iv. 106 The custom of temple prostitution has not merely been preserved down to our own day.., but the temples of the goddesses of love..were traditionally the favored places of assignation for lovers. **1948** *Nat. Geogr. Mag.* Jan. 127 (*caption*) High and steep were the temple pyramids of the Maya. **1966** M. D. COE *Maya* v. 94 Towering above all are the mighty temple-pyramids built from limestone blocks over a rubble core. **1920** H. G. WELLS *Outl. Hist.* 150/2 There is no temple-state stage, no stage of priest Kings, in the Greek record. **1931** *Times Lit. Suppl.* 1 Jan. 3/2 The Pope's temporal domain..is not a city-state but a temple-state.

temple, *v.* **1.** (Later *poet.* example.)

1936 A. CLARKE *Coll. Poems* 98 We saw again How Brigid, while her women slept Around her, temple'd by the flame, Sat in a carven chair.

templed, *ppl. a.* Add: **2.** (Later examples.)

1935 T. S. ELIOT *Murder in Cathedral* i. 27 Power obtained grows to glory,..a permanent possession, A templed tomb. **1951** L. MACNEICE tr. *Goethe's Faust* 217 Does not your templed home persist!

3. (Earlier example.)

1822 SHELLEY *Charles the First* in *Posthumous Poems* (1824) ii. 245 Innocent sleep of templed cities and the smiling fields.

templet[1]. Add: The form *template* is now usual, freq. with the spelling-pronunc. (te·mplĕ[i]t). **2. a.** (Later examples.)

1929 D. S. STEWART *Pract. Design Simple Steel Struct.* I. iii. 24 Templates may be either..the bars which are to be used in the structure or..made from some light and easily worked material. **1942** *Sun* (Baltimore) 25 Nov. 6/4 A ship starts being a ship in the mold loft, where skilled hands make wooden patterns, called templates, from the designer's blueprints. **1967** E. Short *Embroidery & Fabric Collage* iii. 71 The main lines of the design can be chalked in or tacked on to the top fabric, details being put in freely or drawn round a template. **1977** *Early Music* July 443/3 (Advt.), Set of three, fully-explanatory A2 drawings, two templates, [etc.].

c. *Oil Industry.* A frame anchored to the sea-floor to which an offshore platform may be attached.

1975 *Petroleum Rev.* XXIX. 142/1 The system is mounted on a tubular steel frame called a template, which is 124 ft wide and 42 ft high. **1976** *Offshore Platforms & Pipelining* 19/1 The riser..is anchored to a template on the sea floor.

3. Chiefly *Biol.* A molecule or molecular pattern that determines the sequence in which other molecules are assembled into a macromolecule; *spec.* a molecule of nucleic acid that acts thus in the synthesis of nucleic acids or proteins.

[**1904** *Proc. R. Soc.* LXXIII. 542 The protoplasmic complex may be regarded as built up of a series of associated templates which serve as patterns to determine change in the various directions necessary for the maintenance of vital processes and of growth.] **1949** *Q. Rev. Biol.* XXIV. 98/1 If we accept the view that the normal cellular proteins are formed as negative replicas of a positive cellular template, we are confronted with a serious dilemma. **1953** Watson & Crick in *Nature* 30 May 966/1 Previous discussions of self-duplication have usually involved the concept of a template, or mould... Our model for deoxyribonucleic acid is, in effect, a *pair* of templates. **1961** *Ann. Reg. 1960* 402 This theory differed from the older 'instructive' theory in which any cell was able to produce antibody to any pattern using the antigen itself as a template. **1964** *Proc. Nat. Acad. Sci.* LI. 801 (*heading*) A complex of enzymatically synthesised RNA and template DNA. **1970** *Nature* 5 Sept. 1012/2 RNA tumour viruses can act as templates for the synthesis of DNA. **1977** *N.Y. Rev. Bks.* 27 Oct. 17/1 Segments of DNA, selected because they are templates for valuable products such as hormones, antigens or antibodies, might be produced in bulk by multiplying them in culture of *E. coli.* **1980** N. K. Mathur et al. *Polymers as Aids in Org. Chem.* iii. 161 The polymer was prepared with functional groups juxtaposed in an exact, predetermined steric relationship by polymerizing monomers around an optically active template—either D-glyceric acid or [etc.].

4. *transf.* and *fig.*

1965 *Science & Psychoanalysis* VIII. 64 What is established is rather a probabilistic system of implicit or 'unconscious' schemas..which serve as some kind of abstract templates for comparison. **1973** *Computers & Humanities* VII. 159 Each English text to be translated goes through a fragmentation and reordering that allows it to match a template form... The translation into French is then made from the template and the original text. **1976** Nichols & Armstrong *Workers Divided* ii. 143 Their usual point of reference is the old/Northern/real working class. This forms the template against which they judge the modern/militant..generation. **1983** *Microcomputer Printout* Sept. 57/1 Some companies market ready-written models, sometimes called templates on a disk, for standard functions such as a Profit and Loss statement.

tempo. Restrict ‖ to the spec. It. phrases and add: Pl. also **tempos. 1. a.** (Later examples of the plural.) **tempo giusto** (dʒu·sto), strict time; the proper speed that a style of music demands; **tempo rubato** (earlier and later examples).

1740 Grassineau *Mus. Dict.* 283 *Tempo,* or *Tempo giusto,* is often met with after Recitatives, and intimates that the Time be beat equal, which during that recitative was managed otherwise. **1773** C. Burney *Present State of Mus. in Germany* II. 175 It was from her that Quantz first heard what professors call *tempo rubato.* **1810** D. Corri *Singers Preceptor* I. 6 Tempo rubato is a detraction of part of the time from one note, and restoring it by increasing the length of another. **1886** G. M. Hopkins *Let.* 11 Dec. (1935) I. 246 This sonnet shd. be almost sung: it is most carefully timed in *tempo rubato.* **1931** M. D. Calvocoressi tr. *Bartok's Hungarian Folk Music* 23 A few tunes in *tempo giusto. Ibid.* 80 In fairly old tunes ..a liking for variable *tempo giusto* rhythm is evinced. **1934** Webster, *Tempo,* n.; pl. *tempi.., tempos.* **1956** R. C. Marsh *Toscanini* ii. 83 The earlier performance being somewhat more relaxed and containing some *tempo rubato* that the version of thirty years later lacks. **1967** A. L. Lloyd *Folk Song in England* iv. 312 The group refrains..were always sung plain and in a strict *tempo giusto.* **1980** *Times* 13 May 15/3 Tempos were excellently chosen, most of all perhaps, for the Minuet.

b. *transf.* and *fig.* The rate of motion or activity (*of* someone or something).

1898 G. B. Shaw *You never can Tell* ii. 249 *Again changing his tempo to say to Valentine..* If youll allow me, sir? **1901** *Cassell's Mag.* Sept. 388/2 His *tempo,* to use the expression of our acrobats, is perfect—that is to say, he yields at the proper time and at the proper rate to the descending ball. **1918** A. Gray tr. *Grelling's Crime* II. 239 He describes their readiness 'to retard the tempo of the construction of our warships'. **1925** C. Fox *Educ. Psychol.* 271 Each person is possessed of a vital tempo. **1930** W. K. Hancock *Australia* vii. 139 The State might not have achieved as much if it had been content..to quicken the *tempo* of the economic harmonies—by taxing, by disseminating knowledge, by mobilising credit. **1940** W. Faulkner *Hamlet* 219 But when he stood in the door again, save for the slightly increased rasp and tempo of his breathing, he might never have left it. **1961** A. Christie *Pale Horse* xviii. 198 It's a changing world, Easterbrook... Now the changes come more rapidly. The tempo has quickened. **1974** I. Murdoch *Sacred & Profane Love Machine* 202 The partner who created the confidence and set the tempo was Luca.

temporale (tempŏrā·l). Also ‖ **temporal.** [ad. Sp. *temporal* storm, spell of rainy weather.] A weather condition of the Pacific coast of Central America consisting of strong south-west winds bringing heavy rain.

1853 tr. *F. Gerstaecker's Narr. Journey round World* I. ix. 145 A temporale, however, might happen at any moment. *Ibid.* ix. 160 All the threatened dangers of the cordilleras, of snow-drifts and temporales, were past. **1923** J. Hergesheimer *Bright Shawl* 141 The April temporale lay in an even heat over the city. **1936** L. J. Halle *Transcaribbean* ii. 32 Twice or more in the season there will be 'temporals', when it will rain interminably for a week. **1982** *N.Y. Times* 4 Apr. x. 18/4 There is scarcely one temporale, that sudden downpour of sheet-rain bringing with it a fine red tufa dust.

temporalis (tempŏrēi·lis). *Anat.* [L.: see Temporal *a.*[2] and *sb.*[2]] Also *temporalis muscle.* A fan-shaped muscle which closes the lower jaw and which arises from the temporal fossa, passes through the gap between the zygomatic arch and the side of the skull, and is attached to the coronoid process and the anterior border of the ramus of the mandible.

1676 W. Molins *Μυοτομια or Anat. Admin. of Muscles Humane Body* 17 If you throw this Muscle either from his origination or insertion, *Temporalis* will appear in his insertion. **1713** W. Cheselden *Anat. Human Body* ii. ii. 55 Temporalis, arises from the Os Frontis, Parietale, Sphænoides, and Temporis, and..is inserted externally into the Processus Corone of the Lower Jaw which it pulls upwards. **1873** G. Fleming tr. *Chauveau's Compar. Anat.* i. § 3. ii. 223 To dissect the temporalis, excise the external pterygoideus from its inferior border. **1910** *Bull. Amer. Museum Nat. Hist.* XXVIII. 302 The *temporalis* is the most powerful jaw muscle in *Carnivora.* **1938** H. L. Wieman *Gen. Zool.* (ed. 3) iv. 78 A portion of the *temporalis* muscle can be seen between the orbit and the tympanum. **1978** *Sci. Amer.* Apr. 64/2 In 1944 a German surgeon..tried attaching a flap of muscle (the temporalis) from the side of the head to the surface of the brain, hoping that the muscle's blood vessels would join the cerebral arteries and supply them.

temporally, *adv.* Add: **3.** With regard to time.

1961 in Webster. **1971** *Nature* 21 May 172/1 Temporally varying deviations between 40° and 60° were found. **1974** *Sci. Amer.* June 31/2 The pulse, which contains only about 10^{-3} joule of laser energy, is shaped spatially (and also temporally, if desired) prior to amplification. **1982** *Ibid.* Feb. 129/2 Temporally coherent light would show at the sampling point a continuous variation between crest and trough.

‖ **tempora mutantur** (te·mpŏră miūtæ·ntɒɹ), *Latin phr.* [L., in full *tempora mutantur nos et* (or *et nos*) *mutamur in illis* (also used), times change and we change with them.] A statement emphasizing the inevitability of change in human affairs and customs.

A similar saying *Omnia mutantur, nos et mutamur in illis* is found in *Delitiæ Poetarum Germanorum* (1612) I. 685, where it is ascribed to the Emperor Lothair I by the author (who may be Matthias Borbonius), but there is no evidence that it has a medieval origin. The phrase *tempora mutantur,* however, occurs earlier in other contexts: see quot. *c* 1440.

[*c* **1440** *Gesta Romanorum* (Harl. MS.) x. 28 And þei founde þis y-wreten, Tempora mutantur; Homines deteriorantur;..this is to sey, 'tymys ben chaungid; and men ben hyndred, or turnyd, or I-made worse.'] **1577** W. Harrison *Descr. Britayne* iii. iii. 99 in Holinshed *Chron.* I, Oft in one age, diuers iudgementes doe passe upon one maner of casse, wherby the saying of the poet *Tempora mutantur, & nos mutamur in illis.* [**1666** G. Torriano *Piazza Universale di Proverbi Italiani* 281 Times change, and we with them... [*Note,* 292] The Latin says the same, *Tempora mutantur, et nos mutamur in illis.*] **1855** W. Chappell *Popular Music* I. 309 However unobjectionable this song may have been in Queen Mary's time, the three remaining stanzas would not be very courteously received in Queen Victoria's. *Tempora mutantur.* **1934** Blunden *Mind's Eye* 154 He could not repress an exclamatory *Tempora mutantur.* **1961** *Times* 7 Apr. 20/7 The Rugby-watching public can in no way afford to be smug. *Tempora mutantur* indeed, and..not so many years ago a boo would have caused apoplexy in older Rugby followers. **1978** J. I. M. Stewart *Full Term* iv. 56 'Giles has my old rooms..on the floor above this.' 'More *tempora mutantur* stuff.' **1980** *Times* 7 May 18/2 Charlie Chan was always successful... This was '*because*' he was Chinese... *Tempora mutantur, nos et mutamur in illis,* particularly the progeny of a nasty modern breed of censors... working up a protest against the revival of Charlie Chan.

temporary, *a.* (*sb.*). Add: **A.** *adj.* **1. b.** *temporary hardness,* hardness of water that can be removed by boiling, because it is due to bicarbonates which are thereby precipitated.

1895 H. Collet *Water Softening & Purification* i. 2 The temporary hardness is that due to the bicarbonates of lime and magnesia. **1969** Temporary hardness [see *permanent hardness* s.v. *Permanent *a.* (*sb.*) 1 d].

d. Designating one who is commissioned for the duration of a war (esp. that of 1914–18), as *temporary captain, officer,* etc. Also *temporary gent(leman)* (in colloq. or pejorative Services' use); abbrev. T.G. s.v. *T 6 a.

1918 Barrie *Echoes of War* 68 Socially he had fallen..; even..in his uniform the hasty might say something clever about 'temporary gentlemen'. **1925** W. Deeping *Sorrell & Son* ii. 21 'My name is Sorrell, Captain Sorrell.' 'You will have to drop the 'captain'. Temporary, I suppose?' **1938** S. Beckett *Murphy* x. 234 He withheld his hand, the little temporary gent and pure in heart. **1958** S. Raven in H. Thomas *Establishment* 72 Temporary Captain C.C. had been in the very first intake at Sandhurst. **1976** *N.Y. Rev. Bks.* 5 Feb. 20/3 The lower-middle-class officer..who in the First World War would have been called a 'temporary gentleman'. **1983** T. Pocock *1945: Dawn came up like Thunder* v. 151 There were two officers' messes—'A' and 'B'; the former primarily for staff officers..the latter, mostly made up of temporary officers.

B. *sb.* **4.** *spec.* a secretary or clerical worker supplied by an agency to cover absences or vacancies for a short period.

1956 C. Blackstock *Dewey Death* vii. 159 Temporaries came, and temporaries went..and the work produced [was] shocking beyond belief. **1957** R. Hart-Davis *Let.* 7 July in *Lyttelton–Hart-Davis Lett.* (1979) II. 123 This might have been possible if my secretary hadn't been on holiday. Instead I was burdened with a pudding-faced 'temporary'. **1970** *New Yorker* 17 Oct. 148/1 (*caption*) But Mr. Clark! I'm just a temporary.

tempore: see *Temp. (abbrev.).

temporo-. Add: *temporomandibular* adj. (examples).

1889 A. Macalister *Text-bk. Human Anat.* 243 The temporo-mandibular joint forms a double condylarthrosis. **1974** *Nature* 8 Mar. 165/2 An asymmetrical functional activity of both temporomandibular joint mechanisms must compensate during chewing and non-chewing activities.

‖ **temps** (taṅ). *Ballet.* [Fr., lit. = time.] A term used in the names of various ballet movements in which there is no transfer of weight from one foot to the other (see quots.).

1890 G. B. Shaw in *Star* 21 Feb. 2/4, I do not know.. which particular *temps* is a *battement* and which a *ronde de jambe.* **1922** Beaumont & Idzikowski *Man. Classical Theatr. Dancing* V. 195 Ballonné à trois temps. *Ibid.* 196 Temps de cuisse..Temps levé. *Ibid.* 200 Temps d' Allegre. **1930** Craske & Beaumont *Theory & Pract. Allegro in Classical Ballet* (1960) 9 In a *pas d'élévation,* such as a *Temps de Poisson,* the arms are raised *en attitude.* **1947** N. Nicolaeva-Legat *Ballet Educ.* iv. 72 *Temps lié* is a set combination of steps and arm movements executed to the count of 4 or ⅜. **1948** *Ballet Ann.* ii. 66, I set to work on recording a number of *temps d' allegro* and enchaînements. **1957** G. B. L. Wilson *Dict. Ballet* 265 *Temps*..is variously used to describe a movement in which there is no transfer of weight (e.g. temps levé) or the division of a step into a number of movements (e.g. ballonné à trois temps). *c* **1973** J. Cholerton *Theory of Acrobatics* (Assoc. Amer. Dancing) (ed. 12) 9 *Q. What is a Temps lévé?* A. A hop.

‖ **temps perdu** (taṅ pęrdü). [Fr., 'time lost'; used with allusion to Proust: see *Recherche du temps perdu.] The past, contemplated with nostalgia and a sense of irretrievability.

1932 S. O'Faoláin *Midsummer Night Madness* 75 Life is too pitiful in these recapturings of the *temps perdu,* these brief intervals of reality. **1942** Partridge *Usage & Abusage* 95/2 One may question whether peace and prosperity will return with or without this word..the 'Sesame' of *le temps perdu.* **1962** *John o' London's* 20 Sept. 287/3 A nostalgic atmosphere, an old-timers' *temps perdu.* **1969** *Listener* 22 May 734/2 The wizened wordsmith..was on the scent of *temps perdu*: in particular those heady years of the early Thirties. **1975** A. Price *Our Man in Camelot* vi. 111 It's a natural human feeling to yearn for the good old days, *le temps perdu.*

temptingness. (Later example.)

1976 *Conc. Oxf. Dict.* (ed. 6) s.v. *Seduce,* Persuade by temptingness or attractiveness.

‖ **tempura** (te·mpurā). [Jap., prob. ad. Pg. *tempêro* seasoning.] A Japanese dish consisting of prawn, shrimp, or white fish, and often vegetables, coated in batter and deep-fried. Also *attrib.,* esp. in *tempura bar, restaurant.*

1920 *Japan Advertiser* 22 Aug. 5 Tempura means a certain way of cooking,—namely, dipping in thin wheat-flour batter and frying in deep oil... The food which forms the base is some kind of fish. **1936** K. Tezuka *Jap. Food* 71 *Tempura* is a characteristic dish of Japan made by dipping fish or shrimps or shell-fish in batter and frying in deep gingelly oil or torreya oil. **1958** *Japan* (Unesco) (1964) 724/1 *Tempura* was adopted from a recipe in Spain and Portugal. **1967** D. & E. T. Riesman *Conversations in Japan* 223 Donald joined us for lunch at a *tempura* restaurant nearby. **1969** *Sat. Rev.* (U.S.) 13 Sept. 62/3 Some of the most popular eateries are *tempura* bars. **1979** *United States 1980/81* (Penguin Travel Guides) 73 This thoughtfully designed Japanese restaurant has separate dining rooms for teppan-yaki, sukiyaki, and tempura.

temura(h (tĕmūrā·). *Jewish Lit.* Also **Themurah.** [Heb. *tĕmūrāh* exchange.] In cabalistic phraseology, a systematic replacement of the letters of a word with other letters in order to find the hidden meaning of events, laws, etc., in the Torah.

1902 A. E. Waite *Doctrine & Lit. of Kabalah* i. iv. 27 Very curious results were sometimes obtained by these solemn follies which appear so childish and ridiculous at the present day. They comprise: *a. Gematria..b. Notaricon..c. Themurah,* that is the transposition of letters in a given word or sentence. 1911 'SEPHARIAL' *Kabala of Numbers* I. iii. 31 The *Temurah,* in which the letters of a word were replaced by others after a definite method. 1974 C. PONCÉ *Kabbalah* ii. 172 Turning now to Jeremiah xxv. 26,..we discover that Sheshak is none other than Babel. How did the writer of this Biblical passage arrive at Sheshak as another name for Babel? Through the method of *temura.*

ten, *a., sb.* (*adv.*). Add: **A.** *adj.* **2. a.** (Earlier examples in sense 'ten shillings'.)

1837 DICKENS *Let.* 10 Feb. (1965) I. 235, I made it five pounds instead of two pounds ten. 1872 RUSKIN *Munera Pulveris* p. ix, Worth as many ten-and-sixpences as the impressions which might be taken from the lithographic stones.

b. Also with ellipsis of 'minutes' in phr. *ten past* or *to* or (*U.S.*) *till,* ten minutes after or before the hour; *to take ten* (U.S.): see *TAKE *v.* 52 c.

1852 [see To *prep.* 6 b]. 1937 'P. WENTWORTH' *Case is Closed* ix. 95 Then it couldn't have been later than ten past eight when you heard that shot? 1960 S. BARSTOW *Kind of Loving* I. ii. 53 Nobody ever arranges to meet somebody at ten to and so she must either be late or not coming. 1963 [see *TILL *prep.* 5 d]. 1979 'J. LE CARRÉ' *Smiley's People* xxiii. 265 The time was ten to eleven.

c. *ten out of ten,* ten marks or points out of ten; hence *transf.* = *full marks* s.v. *MARK *sb.*[1] 11 g; *the Ten,* (*c*) the group of countries comprising the European Economic Community after January 1981 when Greece joined the existing group of nine countries (the expectation expressed in quot. 1971, but not fulfilled, was that Norway would become a member in 1973 together with Denmark, the Republic of Ireland, and the United Kingdom) (cf. *SIX *a.* 2 j); *to count ten*: see COUNT *v.* 1; *spec.,* to do this in order to check oneself from speaking impetuously; also *to count up to ten.*

[The phrase is much older but printed evidence is lacking.] 1981 P. O'DONNELL *Xanadu Talisman* iv. 69, I can't claim ten out of ten... I was a bit indecisive. 1981 *Listener* 22 Oct. 481/2 For beating down Whitehall opposition, Mr Sproat gets ten out of ten.

1971 *Guardian* 20 Dec. 10/2 The objective for the Six (and the prospective Ten) should be to bring down the trade barriers. 1981 *Times* 24 Dec. 1/2 The EEC denounced 'the grave violation of the human and civil rights of the Polish people'..and said these were causing 'growing concern' among the people and governments of the Ten.

1817 T. JEFFERSON *Let.* 12 July in *Writings* (1899) X. 93 When angry count 10. before you speak. 1939 F. THOMPSON *Lark Rise* xi. 205 Copper-plate maxims..; 'Count ten before you speak', and so on. 1953 E. SIMON *Past Masters* II. 122 Don't say anything. Hold it. Count ten. 1976 R. PERRY *One Good Death deserves Another* vii. 116 He counted up to ten before he answered me.

B. *sb.* **1. c.** (Earlier and later examples of '10 A'.) *Number ten,* also *No. 10*: see *NUMBER *sb.* 5 e.

1906 H. MÜLLER *Reminiscences* 43 Giovanni endured the punishment that is the Austrian equivalent for '10 A'. 1927 P. RILEY *Memories* 74 The drastic punishment, known as '10.A' was introduced into the Service at the same time [*sc.* Jan. 1875].

5. (*b*) (earlier example); (*c*) a ten-dollar note; (*d*) a ten-horse-power car.

c 1863 T. TAYLOR *Ticket-of-Leave Man* III. 54 Here are notes—two hundreds—a ten—and two fives.

1829 *Vancouver Herald* (Fredericksburg) 18 Apr. 3/3 The public are cautioned against receiving spurious 5's 10's and 20 dollar bills, purporting to be on the Bank of Virginia. 1907 'O. HENRY' *Trimmed Lamp* 171 He drew out his 'roll' and slapped five tens upon the bar. 1977 J. CROSBY *Company of Friends* xxvi. 161 Roger tipped the waiter a ten.

1931 *Daily Express* 16 Oct. 11/2 Cheap 'Tens'. There was a big demand also for cars just above the 'baby' class, the numerous 10's that are cheap to buy. 1942 *R.A.F. Jrnl.* 3 Oct. 24 He would soon be driving around in a family eight or ten. 1968 *Compl. Encycl. Motorcars* 59/1 In 1910 a 1·6 litre 4-cylinder [Austin] Ten was made for export only. *Ibid.* 399/1 That year [*sc.* 1933] Morris's sv 1·3-litre Ten-Four came out as an answer to Austin's Ten and Hillman's Minx.

D. *Comb.* **1. a.** *ten-cent* (examples), *-day* (earlier example), *dollar* (earlier examples), *-figure, -shilling* (later examples). **b.** *ten-tongued* (example).

1846 D. CORCORAN *Pickings* 26, I gave him a $2 bill, and he only gave me thirteen of these (ten cent pieces) in change. 1873 E. EGGLESTON *Myst. Metrop.* xviii. 158 The joyful keys and the cheerful ten-cent coins lay in his pocket. 1901 H. ROBERTSON *Inlander* 118 The sleepers in the grass-grown churchyard..had been removed elsewhere to make room for the thriving innovation known as the 'Ten Cent Store'. 1962 E. SNOW *Other Side of River* (1963) xxxix. 283 Ten-cent prints are also sold of Italian Renaissance painters and a few French impressionists. 1883 'MARK TWAIN' *Life on Mississippi* lx. 582 A ten-day trip by steamer. 1807 *Deb. Congr. U.S.* 19 Aug. (1852) 429, I got two of the notes changed, and one, a ten dollar note, was returned on my hands. 1825 J. NEAL *Bro. Jonathan* I. 221 For a 'ten-dollar bill'..Peters would have set fire to it. 1842 *Penny Cycl.* XXIII. 498/1 Nathaniel Roe, 'Tabulæ Logarithmicæ', London. Seven-figure numbers to 100 thousand, ten-figure sines, &c. to hundredths of degrees. 1922 *Biometrika* XIV. 160 It was necessary to calculate τ_1 to eight places, which was done with the help of Vega's ten-figure logarithms. 1959 A. CHRISTIE *Cat among Pigeons* iv. 51 She accepted the ten shilling note her mother handed to her. *a* 1974 R. CROSSMAN *Diaries* (1976) II. 279 Then there came fifteen speakers of whom the ten well-informed were all passionately for the ten-shilling unit. 1867 EMERSON *May-Day* 86 Speaking by the tongues of flowers, By the ten-tongued laurel speaking.

2. ten-code, a code of signals (all beginning with the number ten) originally used in radio communication by police in the U.S. and later adopted by Citizens' Band radio operators; **ten-eighty** (more commonly **1080**) [see quot. 1945], a formation of sodium fluoroacetate used as a poison against predatory animals; **ten-foot** *a.*: fig. phr. *ten feet tall* used contextually to convey extreme self-assurance or pride; **ten-four, 10-4** *int.,* in the ten-code (see above), the code phrase for 'message received'; used *loosely* as an expression of affirmation; also as *v. intr.*; **ten-gallon** *a.,* that can contain ten gallons; **ten-gallon hat, sombrero,** a high-crowned, wide-brimmed hat of a kind esp. worn in the south-western U.S. (cf. *STETSON); **ten-gauge** *a.,* having a calibre such that ten balls of matching size weigh one pound; also *ellipt.* for *ten-gauge shotgun*; **ten-inch** *a.,* measuring ten inches; *spec.* designating a 78 r.p.m. coarse-groove gramophone record having this diameter; also *ellipt.* = *seventy-eight* s.v. *SEVENTY *a.* 2 b; **ten-minute rule** (also **ten minutes rule**), a standing order of the House of Commons allowing brief discussion of a motion for leave to introduce a bill, each speech being limited to ten minutes' duration; **ten o'clock** (example of the plant); also, a name for *Portulaca grandiflora,* a subtropical annual herb whose flowers open late in the morning; **ten per center** *U.S. Theatr. slang,* a theatrical agent (so called from the ten per cent commission that an agent takes); **ten signal** *U.S.,* any of the signals that form part of the ten-code (see above); **ten-speed,** a multiple-speed set of gears on a vehicle, esp. a bicycle; freq. *attrib.*; **ten-spot** *sb.* (earlier and later examples of both senses); **ten-strike** (earlier example); also *spec.* in *fig.* use, a success, esp. in phr. *to make a ten-strike,* to score a success (U.S. colloq.); **ten tenth(s)** *attrib.* (orig. *Meteorol.*), complete, one hundred per cent; **ten-to-two,** a position of the hands or feet resembling that of the hands of a clock at ten minutes to two, *esp.* a position of the hands on the steering-wheel of a car; freq. *attrib.*

1969 T. E. DRABNEK *Lab. Simulation Police Communications Syst. under Stress* 135 Above code corresponds to the 'Ten-Code System' used by many police agencies. 1976 *CB Mag.* June 67/2 Well, it really grabbed me, all this 'good buddy' stuff, the ten-code. 1977 *Rolling Stone* 13 Jan. 45/3 Get a CB and take on a persona, use the 10 code and all the language, and be anybody you want to be. 1945 *Science* 31 Aug. 232 (*heading*) 'Ten-eighty', a war-produced rodenticide. *Ibid.,* One, commonly referred to under its laboratory serial number, '1080',..has been subjected to sufficiently adequate field-testing to warrant the assertion that a promising new rodenticide has been discovered. 1961 *New Scientist* 13 Apr. 17/1 About one and a half grains of 'ten-eighty' are dissolved in a little water and injected into 100 lb of meat. 1971 W. HILLEN *Blackwater River* xii. 117 Then Compound 1080 (ten-eighty)..reached British Columbia and created a 'predator control' bureaucracy more difficult to eliminate than wolves. [1955 (*television film title*) The man is 10 feet tall.] 1962 M. HASTINGS *Yes, & After* II. i. 72 You must always be ten feet tall imagining yourself doing this or doing that. 1964 D. FRANCIS *Nerve* xvii. 237 It made me feel warm inside... I felt ten feet tall. 1970 A. DRAPER *Swansong for Rare Bird* i. 11, I must say I felt 10 feet tall and there was a soppy grin on my face. 1962 *Amer. Speech* XXXVII. 272 *Ten-four* (verb), to understand a message. From the radio code *10-4,* meaning 'I receive you clearly'. 1976 *National Observer* (U.S.) 30 Oct. 5/1 Judge Floyd Smith, a CB operator himself, went by the 'handle' of 'Marryin' Sam', the bride was 'Little Lulu', and the groom was 'Stanley Steamer'. They didn't say 'I do'; they said '10-4'. And the judge didn't pronounce them man and wife; he said, 'Put the hammer down.' 1978 *N.Y. Times Mag.* 23 July 23/2 The CB'ers have a language that's 10-4 with them. 1841 C. GRAY *Lays & Lyrics* 241 This song was written on the presentation of a Ten-Gallon China Punch-Bowl...to the Club. 1922 JOYCE *Ulysses* 303 Hard by the block stood the grim figure of the executioner, his visage being concealed in a tengallon pot with two circular perforated apertures. 1928 *Daily Express* 7 Oct. 3/7 She instinctively recognized that he was a cowboy, even though he did not wear a ten-gallon hat and a jacket embroidered with Mexican dollars. 1929 T. WOLFE *Look homeward, Angel* (1930) xxvii. 374 He removed from his head the ten-gallon grey sombrero. 1939 *Amer. Speech* XIV. 201/1 In the nomenclature of the South-western cowboy, *sombrero* is used interchangeably for hat, but the qualifying phrase of 'ten gallon' has been arrived at by a mistaken translation of a Spanish word. The word 'gallon'..served to describe the braid with which a vaquero's hat was trimmed..it should have been 'galloon'. 1977 C. MCCULLOUGH *Thorn Birds* xiv. 331 Only the handful of half-caste aborigines..aped the cowboys of the American West, in high-heeled fancy boots and ten-gallon Stetsons. 1894 Ten-gauge [in Dict., sense D. 1]. 1936 J. STEINBECK *In Dubious Battle* v. 70 'Shot-guns,' he said... 'Soon's somebody sounds off with a ten-gauge, they go for the brush like rabbits.' 1940 W. FAULKNER *Hamlet* III. 194 Looking..into the face which with his own was wedded and twinned forever now by the explosion of that ten-gauge shell. 1908 *Sears, Roebuck Catal.* 201/2 Disc Record Cases... No. 2 holds 50 10-inch disc records. 1959 *Manch. Guardian* 11 Aug. 5/7 Beecham (whose reading has just reappeared on a Fontana ten-inch, KFR 4003). 1979 *Listener* 4 Oct. 461/3 Nearly all the 23 Gillespie tracks..were originally marketed on ten-inch, 78 rpm discs. 1908 A. E. STEINTHAL tr. *J. Redlich's Procedure House of Commons* III. II. x. i. 86 Under a standing order passed in 1888, popularly known as the 'ten minutes rule' (Standing Order 11) an abbreviated mode of procedure is authorised for the introduction of bills. 1971 HINDELL & SIMMS *Abortion Law Reformed* xi. 232 Ten minute rule bills can be brought before the House with a short speech each Tuesday and Wednesday after question time, but if the House agrees to the introduction of such a bill *all* further progress to a second reading and beyond depends, in practice, on the Government..giving it parliamentary time. 1826 W. DARLINGTON *Flora Cestrica* 40 *Ornithogalum..umbellatum...* Ten o'clock. Twelve o'clock. Star of Bethlehem. 1953 *Caribbean Q.* III. I. 10 Ten o'clock is a kind of portulaca which blooms in mid morning. 1926 *Variety* 29 Dec. XI. 5/4 Broadway chatter is full of theatrical cracks such as..'ten per center'. 1962 *Punch* 26 Dec. 920/1 A condition of the licence being granted is that the applicant advertises for two weeks in The Stage, stating his intention of joining the ten-percenters. 1951 *Directory Nat. Police Communications Network* (ed. 6) 19 The '10' signals were developed by A.P.C.O...and the system has been widely adopted. 1970 V. A. LEONARD *Police Communications Syst.* ii. 34 APCO's Project Series Foundation has produced four nationally recognized projects:..the publication of the APCO Ten Signal Cards. 1971 M. TAK *Truck Talk* 165 *Ten-speed,* a ten-speed Roadranger transmission. 1977 C. MCFADDEN *Serial* (1978) i. 8/2 They spent it rapidly on..twin Motobecane ten-speeds. 1977 *New Yorker* 9 May 34/1 The owner of a ten-speed model asked her why. 1844 'J. SLICK' *High Life N.Y.* II. 215 'Jest so,' sez I, a flingin' down the ten-spot o' clubs. 1848 'N. BUNTLINE' *Mysteries & Miseries N.Y.* IV. iii. 27 Be quick, and I'll give you a *ten spot*! 1936 E. CULBERTSON *Contract Bridge Complete* 21 Any six-card suit, even without a ten-spot, is a biddable suit. 1971 B. MALAMUD *Tenants* 153 Hi, sugar, I took a ten-spot out of your loose change. 1840 *Spirit of Times* 11 July 228/1 [This] he says is an extra touch—a ten strike and two spare balls. 1887 *Scribner's Mag.* May 624/1 But I have got the family to consider, and I am in a position now where I can make a ten-strike for it. 1900 G. ADE *Fables in Slang* 72 He could tell by the Scared Look of the People in Front that he had made a Ten-Strike. 1949 E. POUND *Pisan Cantos* lxxxiii. 124 It comes over me that Mr. Walls must be a ten-strike With the signorinas. [1945 *Meteorol. Office Air Obs. Handbk.* 34 In estimating the amount of cloud the observer should aim to give the fraction (in tenths) of sky covered by cloud.] 1948 *Daily Tel.* 23 Apr. 6/6 There was ten-tenth cloud at the time. 1973 'A. HALL' *Tango Briefing* ix. 114 There was a ten-tenths flap on in London so they'd have alerted the whole network. 1977 C. FORBES *Avalanche Express* xviii. 186 One moment he had ten-tenths vision, the next second he was blind. 1979 D. BRIERLEY *Cold War* vii. 57 There was ten-tenths cloud cover, the clouds coming from the north-east..like billowing poison gas. 1961 C. H. D. TODD *Pop. Whippet* iv. 68 It stands with its feet at 'ten to two'. 1962 *Which? Car Suppl.* Apr. 55/2 The steering wheel was..rather high. This made a 'ten-to-two' hand position uncomfortable after a time. 1974 *Drive* Autumn 26/2 We found the square wheel made it difficult for drivers to hold the rim in the ten-to-two position they are taught to adopt.

tenace. Add: Also *Bridge.*

In Bridge, the opponent's card need not be his highest.

1905 'CUT-CAVENDISH' *Compl. Bridge Player* 11 *Tenace,* the best and the third best cards of any suit, ace and queen if the king has not been played. 1936 [see *end-play* s.v. *END *sb.* 25]. 1959 *Listener* 10 Sept. 414/1 The K J 8 will still constitute a tenace over the 10 9 x. 1984 *Guardian* 6 Oct. 17/2 The ten of diamonds now end-played West to return a club into declarer's tenace.

‖ **tena koe** (tenā·kwe, te·na ko·,e), *int. New Zealand.* Also 9 **teneako, tenáqui**; (with dual and pl. forms of the pronoun) **tena korua, tena koutou.** [Maori, lit. = 'there you are'.] A Maori greeting. Also **tenako·eing** *vbl. sb.* (nonce-wd.).

a 1842 H. WEEKES in Rutherford & Skinner *Establishment of New Plymouth Settlement in N.Z.* (1940) I. 92 The period of *teneāko*-ing, handshaking, etc. *a* 1847 —— in *Ibid.* 119 Came towards me with extended hand and a friendly *Tenáqui.* 1901 A. A. GRACE *Tales of Dying Race* 190 'Aaaaah! *tena koutou,*' wailed she, seizing them by the hands. '*Tena koe! tena koe! Katahi te koa!*' she cried, as she rubbed noses with them one by one. 1905 W. BAUCKE *Where White Man Treads* 170 When I neared the fence I cried the old-time greeting, 'Tena koutou'. 1947 A. P. GASKELL *Big Game* 90 They smiled up at her. 'Tenakoe'. 'A lovely day Miss Brown,' said Mrs. Terari. 1949 P. BUCK *Coming of Maori* (rev. ed.) I. vi. 79 The usual Maori greeting of *Tena koe* applies to one person, *Tena korua* applies to two, and *Tena koutou* to more than two. 1960 N. HILLIARD *Maori Girl* II. 92 She could not catch what he said but..she guessed it was 'Tenakoe!'

tenant, *sb.* Add: **4.** *tenant-farmer* (earlier example); *tenant-farming* (earlier U.S. example); hence (as a back-formation) **tenant farm** *v. trans.* (with hyphen) and *sb.*

1949 *Time* 27 June 84/2 The 1,600 acres he tenant-farms. **1979** P. Theroux *Old Patagonian Express* xvii. 263 These are tenant farms..these people own nothing but the clothes on their backs. **1748** Richardson *Clarissa* V. 208 Attended by Susan Morrison, a tenant-farmer's daughter. **1861** *Trans. Illinois Agric. Soc.* IV. 203 On the greater part of this farm are the usual indices of tenant farming.

tenas (te·næs), *a.* (and *sb.*). [Chinook Jargon, ad. Nootka *t'an'as* child.] Small. Also as *sb.*, and in **tenas man** [cf. *KLOOCHMAN], a child.

1870 *Mainland Guardian* (New Westminster, B.C.) 16 Apr. 3/3 There trip about a few Tenass-men, some with the remains of an old coat and beaver hat, and some [in] almost naked savagedom. **1904** *Wide World Mag.* Sept. 541/2 Klootchmen, tenasses, old bucks, and young hunters..were crowded on the schooner's deck. **1935** H. Davis *Honey in Horn* xxii. 371 Nobody but this *tenas* buck [*i.e.* small Indian] here. **1969** *Islander* (Victoria, B.C.) 19 Oct. 3/2 They were very insolent..laughing at the *tenass* warship for wasting her powder and shot.

Tenby (te·nbi). The name of a town on the coast of Wales, used *attrib.* in **Tenby daffodil** to designate *Narcissus obvallaris*, a small yellow daffodil sometimes found as a wild flower in the region.

[**1830** A. H. Haworth in *Phil. Mag.* VIII. 130 Truby [*sic*] 6-lobed Daffodil.] **1884** J. D. Hooker *Student's Flora Brit. Isles* (ed. 3) 399 The Tenby Daffodil..scarcely differs. **1894** W. Robinson *Wild Garden* (ed. 4) ii. 19 The little Tenby Daffodil is very sturdy and pretty. **1966** J. Berrisford *Wild Garden* iii. 35 The early-blooming *Narcissus obvallaris*, the small 'Tenby Daffodil'. **1981** W. Condry *Nat. Hist. Wales* vi. 171 The Tenby daffodil.. has long puzzled the world.

tend, *sb.* For † *Obs. rare* in Dict. read *rare* and add later example.

1937 V. Woolf *Let.* 30 Apr. (1980) VI. 122 I'm very glad you saw that the tend of the book, its slope to one quarter of the compass and not another, was different from the tend in my other books.

tend, *v.*[1] **2. a.** For *Obs.* exc. *dial.* read *Obs.* exc. *dial.* and *U.S.* and add U.S. examples.

1880 'Mark Twain' *Tramp Abroad* 39, I got to 'tend to business. **1917** G. B. McCutcheon *Green Fancy* 68 They..paid their bills regular, 'tended to their own business, and that's all. **1930** W. Faulkner *As I lay Dying* (1935) 155 You got to wait a little while. Then I'll tend to you. **1936** M. Mitchell *Gone with Wind* x. 197 If anybody dares say one little word about you, I'll tend to them. **1975** A. Davis *Autobiogr.* v. 309 The men's linens and jail clothes were sent elsewhere for laundering; the women were expected to tend to their own.

3. b. (Earlier and later U.S. examples.) Also in phr. *to tend bar* (cf. *BARTENDER) and *absol.*

1809 A. Putnam in *Danvers Hist. Soc. Coll.* (1918) VI. 15 My brother has hired Asa Fletcher a young fellow of my age, who has been tending for Mr. Marcy. **1870** 'Mark Twain' in *Galaxy* Nov. 726/2 Tending bar, and reporting for the newspapers. **1959** *Washington Post* 9 Dec. A7/3 Nixon is staying in Washington to help tend the store while the President is away on his 3-week tour. **1978** *Detroit Free Press* 2 Apr. 4C/3, In 1976, he tended bar and sold swimming pools and encyclopedias.

tend, *v.*[2] Add: **3. b.** (*b*) Now usu. in weakened sense: To have a tendency, to be apt or inclined.

1936 J. Cary *African Witch* ii. 38 Obstinacy and stupidity are things that tend to annoy quick-minded and intelligent people. **1956** H. L. Mencken *Minority Report* 251 Unfortunately, the machine thus devised to halt heresy also tends to halt progress. **1976** M. Machlin *Pipeline* xxxiii. 372 After the initial uproar over the Wainwright raid, the papers tended to ignore it. **1981** *Daily Tel.* 26 Aug. 11/2 She went to Oxford to read English. 'I didn't really want to, but I tended to do what my parents advised then.'

Tendai (te·ndai). [a. Jap., ad. Chinese *T'ien-t'ai*, the name of the mountain in S.E. China where the doctrines were formulated.] A Buddhist sect introduced into Japan from China by the monk Saichō (767–822), founded by Zhi Yi (515–97) and characterized by elaborate ritual, moral idealism, and philosophical eclecticism.

1727 J. G. Scheuchzer tr. *Kæmpfer's Hist. Japan* I. i. viii. 106 Not far from this hot Bath is a Monastery of the Sect of *Tendai*. **1833** *Chinese Repository* (1834) Nov. II. 323 There are now in Japan the following sects which are tolerated by government. 1. Zen... 2. Zyoodo... 4. Tendai. **1880** E. J. Reed *Japan* I. iv. 91 The Tendai, founded by the priest Saicho, under Kuwammu. **1894** *Trans. Asiatic Soc. Japan* XXII. 382 This comprehensiveness ensured the success of the Tendai Sect. **1938** D. T. Suzuki *Zen Buddhism & its Influence on Japanese Culture* i. ii. 23 The philosophy of Tendai is too abstract and abstruse to be understood by the masses. **1973** *Times Lit. Suppl.* 2 Mar. 237/4 Something of the awe Tendai ritual inspired can still be felt by the visitor to the Komponchudo on Hiei-san.

tendency. Add: **1.** Also *pl.* in pregnant use, tendencies towards homosexuality. *colloq.*

1938 J. Betjeman *Oxf. Univ. Chest* ii. 42 Someone who has 'tendencies' as an undergraduate, will in ten years time be settled down to married life. **1958** L. Durrell *Balthazar* ii. 32 Now the Egyptians, they don't give a damn about a man if he has Tendencies.

d. *Pol.* [Infl. by F. *tendance.*] A political association within a larger party or movement, esp. a left-wing group within a socialist party.

1974 J. White tr. *Poulantzas's Fascism & Dictatorship* iv. ii. 171 The communists of the Ruhr, a left tendency, went into combat in isolation in April. **1977** *Politics of Militant* 1 The tendency grouped around the weekly paper 'Militant' has grown considerably in recent years. It absolutely dominates the Labour Party Young Socialists. **1980** *Times* 14 Jan. 1/4 The 'Militant Tendency', a clandestine Trotskyist organization, with its own full-time staff, whose aims are to penetrate the Labour Party. **1981** *Daily Tel.* 10 Dec. 32/5 The arguments of the tendency and other Marxist, Leninist, Stalinist and Trotskyist groups.

3. Also *tendency wit* [after G. *tendenzwitz*].

1916 A. A. Brill tr. *Freud's Wit & its Relation to Unconscious* iii. 138 By virtue of its purpose, the tendency-wit has at its disposal sources of pleasure to which harmless wit has no access. **1954** D. Riesman *Individualism Reconsidered* (1955) xxii. 349 The id expresses its criticism by what Freud called tendency-wit, but then turns to its masters with a smile, saying, 'After all,..it's only a joke.' **1964** M. Wohlgelernter *Israel Zangwill* vi. 87 A determination to self-criticism that Freud called 'tendency-wit'.

tendential, *a.* (Earlier example.)

1847 J. D. Morell *Hist. Philos.* (ed. 2) II. vii. 396 He [*sc.* Buchez] has brought to his aid the notion of progress, the logical development of ideas, and the tendential movements of society.

tendentiously (tende·nʃəsli), *adv.* [f. Tendentious *a.* + -ly[2].] In a tendentious manner; with a purposed tendency or aim. So **tende·ntiousness.**

1920 *Glasgow Herald* 9 Apr. 8 This was not due to any tendenciousness on the part of official reports. **1924** *History* Oct. 215 If we could..speak with our enemies in the gate, we should doubtless teach geography..tendenciously. **1946** *Law. Rep.* 2 Mar. 265 One may perhaps describe the two sides, as little tendentiously as possible, [etc.]. **1966** *Listener* 17 Nov. 745/1 Confessions on the telephone,..and witnesses complaining they were not allowed to say what they wanted to say at the trial. As an exercise in tendentiousness it would be hard to beat. **1983** *Washington Post* 2 Oct. C1/4 The result is a book of findings, tendentiously presented. *Ibid.* 11 Oct. C3/3 The tendentiousness of 'The Final Option' may come as a perversely amusing shock.

‖**tendenz** (tende·nts). [Ger., ad. Eng. Tendence or F. *tendance.*] = Tendency 1 c.

1896 A. W. Small *Let.* 22 May in *Social Forces* (1935) Mar. 337/2 Its connotations are to my mind necessarily with some 'Tendenz' which is exploited. **1951** A. L. Rowse *England of Eliz.* ix. 379 One sees the *tendenz* of this... Coke's view was extremely tendencious, but the *tendenz* was good: it was all in favour of the supremacy of law in the State and of the liberty of the subject. **1967** G. Steiner *Lang. & Silence* 336 He argues that the type of *Tendenz*..which Engels would find acceptable is..'identical with that "Party element" which materialism..encloses in itself'.

Also **tende·nzroma:n** [G. *roman* novel] = *tendency novel* s.v. Tendency 3, *roman à thèse* s.v. *ROMAN *sb.*[4]; similarly, with partial translation, **tendenz novel.**

1855 Geo. Eliot in *Westm. Rev.* July 294 'Constance Herbert' is a *Tendenz-roman*; the characters and incidents are selected with a view to the enforcement of a principle. **1896** J. Jacobs *Jewish Ideals & Other Essays* p. xii, George Eliot's novels..were to us *Tendenz-Romane*, and we studied them as much for the *Tendenz* as for the *Roman*. *a* **1896** G. du Maurier *Martian* (1897) ix. 396 The elderly..virgins who knew nothing of life but what they had read..in 'Tendenz' novels. **1917** A. Waugh *Loom of Youth* 11, I was surprised to find that my young friend..had harnessed his views..to the philosophic poem and the *tendenz* novel of the latest phase of fictional evolution. **1975** *Listener* 18 Dec. 819/2 *Oliver Twist*..has suffered more than some of the others... Humphrey House, the eminent Dickens critic, said that it was the closest thing to a *tendenzroman* that Dickens ever wrote, and yet..very little of that political quality survives.

tender, *sb.*[2] Add: **3. b.** *tender offer* (U.S.) (see quot. 1979), usu. for the purpose of obtaining effective control.

1964 J. Low *Investor's Dict.* 198 In general when an outside interest makes a tender offer the market price rises close to the tender price. **1979** *Yale Law Jrnl.* LXXXVIII. 510 A tender offer is conventionally defined as a public solicitation of the shareholders of a corporation to tender their shares to the offeror at a specified price.

tender, *a.* (*adv.*) and *sb.*[3] Add: **A.** *adj.* **I. 1. b.** (Earlier example.)

1727 D. Eaton *Let.* 25 Mar. (1971) 105 He has carted at a very unseasonable time when the ground was tender.

II. 3. b. *tender annual*, an annual plant needing the protection of a greenhouse all through its life; cf. *hardy annual* s.v. Hardy *a.* 4 b; *tender plant* (fig.), something needing careful nurture if it is to survive and develop.

1769 Rutter & Carter *Mod. Eden* ii. iv. 218 (*heading*) Of raising tender annuals on hot-beds. **1822** J. C. Loudon *Encycl. Gardening* 1070 The green-house is now filled with tender annuals. **1867** T. Bridgeman *Amer. Gardener's Assistant* iii. 21 Varieties from warm climates ..may with great propriety be treated as tender annuals, by sowing the seed every spring. **1933** *Discovery* Mar. 76/2 The runner bean..of Mexican parentage or origin is here grown as a tender annual. **1969** *Times* 10 Mar. 10/7 These capital sources are conditioned by..the confidence felt in the future profitability of agriculture. That confidence is, at present, rather a tender plant. **1974** J. Warren *Macself's Amat. Greenhouse* (ed. 5) viii. 238 The tender annuals of all kinds should be sown in spring rather than autumn. **1978** *U.S. News & World Rep.* 12 June 56/1 Academic and cultural freedom is a very tender plant, which this country has nurtured very effectively.

III. 8. a. *tender loving care* (colloq.), especially solicitous care such as is given by nurses; also *transf.*; *tender mercies* (occas. *tender mercy*) a Biblical phrase usu. used *ironically* (perh. with spec. allusion to quot. 1611) of attention, care, or treatment thought unlikely to be in the best interests of its object.

1611 Bible *Prov.* xii. 10 A righteous man regardeth the life of his beast: but the tender mercies of the wicked are cruell. **1893** [see Mercy *sb.* 5 c]. **1906** Conrad *Mirror of Sea* xxxiii. 182 A ship anchored..is not abandoned by her own men to the tender mercies of shore people. **1925** Galsworthy *Caravan* 575 His feelings revolted against handing 'that poor little beggar' over to the tender mercy of his country's law. **1960**, etc. [see *TLC* s.v. *T 6 a]. **1965** *Listener* 17 June 892/2 Smaller..traders and manufacturers..left to the tender mercies of the open property market. **1973** *Computers & Humanities* VII. 166 The Bernard Quemada *Concordance* to *Les Fleurs du Mal*, which was perhaps prepared with more tender loving care, corrected such mechanical deficiencies. **1977** *Listener* 12 May 605/3 It is in a nurse's nature and in her tradition to give the sick what is well called 'TLC', 'tender loving care', some constant little service to the sick.

C. *tender-handed, -slanted, -spirited*; **tender-eared** *a.* (later lit. example); **tenderpad** [f. after *TENDERFOOT 2: see Pad *sb.*[3] 7], a recruit to the Cub Scout movement who has passed the tenderpad test.

1911 J. Masefield *Everlasting Mercy* (1912) 88 Two hares..Wide-eyed and tender-eared. *a* **1750** A. Hill *Wks.* (1753) IV. 120 Tender-handed stroke a nettle, And it stings you for your pains. **1916** R. Baden-Powell *Wolf Cub's Handbk.* i. ii. 25 A boy Wolf Cub is called a 'Recruit' till he has learnt the Cub laws and secret signs, and then he is admitted to be a 'Tender-pad', and to wear the uniform of the Wolf Cubs. **1965** G. McInnes *Road to Gundagai* x. 158, I received a cap, but no badge ('Not till you pass yer tenderpad test.'). *a* **1868** G. M. Hopkins *Poems* (1967) 175 Crisp lips, straight nose, and tender-slanted cheek. **1853** Mrs. Gaskell *Cranford* xv. 230 Martha was so tearful and tender-spirited, and unlike her usual self, that I said as little as possible about myself.

tenderable, *a.* (Earlier example.)

1868 *Harper's Mag.* Dec. 89/1 The view of Judge Denio that the word 'money' implies the creation of what is tenderable for debts is a much more reasonable..interpretation of the Constitution.

tenderfoot. Add: **2.** In the Scout and Guide movements, a recruit who has passed the enrolment tests (the *tenderfoot tests*); also *tenderfoot badge*, and *ellipt.* = tenderfoot badge, tests.

1908 R. S. S. Baden-Powell *Scouting for Boys* iii. 36 *A Tenderfoot* is a boy who is not yet a scout. **1911** *Boy Scout Tests* (Boy Scouts Assoc.) 1 It should be noted that a tenderfoot may not wear the button-hole badge until he has passed the Tenderfoot Tests. **1918** R. S. S. Baden-Powell *Girl Guiding* ii. i. 64 At first you rank as a Recruit until you pass your Tenderfoot tests. Then you can go on and rise to the following ranks:— Recruit. Tenderfoot. Second-Class Guide. **1920** *Girl Guide Badges* (Girl Guide Assoc.) 6 No Guider or Guide is entitled to wear the Tenderfoot Badge unless she has been enrolled, and has passed the following tests. **1965** G. McInnes *Road to Gundagai* x. 160 He..saw that loads were properly distributed..between..strong scouts and not so strong tenderfeet. **1982** *Times* 19 Jan. 18/5 Mr Bass, who is 6ft 3ins., resigned after passing his Tenderfoot because he did not like wearing short trousers.

tendering, *vbl. sb.*[1] (In Dict. s.v. Tender *v.*[1]) (Later examples.)

1955 *Times* 17 June 9/3 The President of the Board of Trade..proposed to send to the Commission a second general reference covering 'common prices and level tendering'. **1972** G. L. Rees *Britain's Commodity Markets* vii. 165 For this purpose granaries ('tendering points') have been nominated by the Association.

tenderish, *a.* (Later example.)

1922 Joyce *Ulysses* 436 With a sour tenderish smile.

tenderize, *v.* Add: *spec.* to make (food, esp. meat) tender. Also *absol.* orig. *U.S.* Hence **te·nderized** *ppl. a.*; **te·nderizing** *vbl. sb.* and *ppl. a.*

1934 Webster, Tenderize, v.t. **1935** A. P. Herbert in *Punch* 8 May 548/1 He has seen some prunes commended as being 'tenderized by a special process.'..If enough prune-purveyors go on saying 'tenderize' it will be in the next edition of all the dictionaries! **1936** *Amer. Speech* XI. 374/2 Sunsweet Tenderized Prunes, refreshed and pasteurized. **1939** *Sun* (Baltimore) 22 Mar. 3/1 A process of 'tenderizing' meat through the use of ultra violet rays. **1950** [see *PRESSURE COOKER a]. **1958** *House & Garden* Feb. 77/2 Wine has a slightly tenderizing effect, so when it is used the meat will cook a little more quickly. **1960** *Times* 24 Sept. 6/6 The new method..ensures that tenderizing liquid gets into the innermost tissues. **1961** *Harper's Bazaar* June 84/2 Diced cubes [of avocado] which have been 'tenderized' and flavoured by the marinade. **1968** L. DURRELL *Tunc* v. 235 She's as sweet as a tenderised steak. **1977** *Time* 19 Sept. 61/2 (Advt.), Touchmatic Control Panel—enables you to slow cook, simmer, tenderize and blend flavours.

tenderizer (te·ndəraiːzəɹ). [f. TENDERIZE *v.* + -ER¹.] Something used to make meat tender, either (*a*) the enzyme papain, or (*b*) a steak hammer.

1958 *Catal. County Stores, Taunton* June 12 Papaya Juice (meat tenderiser)—a bot. 2/-. **1959** *Housewife* June 75 Steak tenderisers in sycamore. **1969, 1970** [see *meat tenderizer* s.v. *MEAT *sb.* 5 b]. **1975** A. AYCKBOURN *Round & Round the Garden* in *Norman Conquests* 18, I line up the dishes and smash them—slowly—with the steak tenderizer.

tenderloin. Add: **1.** (Further examples.) Also *tenderloin steak*.

1864 *Daily Tel.* 27 Sept. 5/2 The 'tenderloin', the 'porterhouse' steak of America, are infinitely superior to our much-vaunted rump steak. **1875** *Scribner's Monthly* July 274/2 A tenderloin steak,..potatoes, bread and butter, and a cup of coffee will cost fifty cents. **1954** [see *ALASKA b]. **1975** *Times* 19 Mar. 16/3 A tenderloin steak made from textured soy protein..sells for 89 cents a pound—as against two dollars for the real thing.

2. (Earlier example.)

1887 *Harper's Mag.* Mar. 500/2 His precinct is known as the 'Tenderloin', because of its social characteristics.

tender-minded, *a.* (and *sb.*). [Parasynthetic, f. *tender mind* (TENDER *a.* 8): see -ED².] Having a tender mind; sensitive and idealistic (in W. James opp. *TOUGH-MINDED *a.*). Also *absol.* as *sb.* Hence **teːnder-mi·ndedness.**

1605 [in Dict. s.v. TENDER *a.* (*adv.*) and *sb.*³ C]. **1907** W. JAMES *Pragmatism* i. 12 You will..recognize the two types of mental make-up that I mean if I head the columns..*The Tender-Minded*: Rationalistic, Intellectualistic, Idealistic, Optimistic, Religious, Free-Willist, Monistic, Dogmatic. *Ibid.* viii. 295 May not the claims of tender-mindedness go too far? May not the notion of a world already saved *in toto* anyhow, be too saccharine to stand? **1924** T. S. ELIOT *Homage to Dryden* iii. 45 It is not cynicism, though it has a kind of toughness which may be confused with cynicism by the tender-minded. **1952** H. J. EYSENCK in Mace & Vernon *Current Trends Brit. Psychol.* xvii. 210 Idealistic..tender-minded attitudes, such as those approving of church-going and religion, pacifism. **1965** *Listener* 28 Jan. 153/1 According to James, the tender-minded were those who could not endure the violation of a general law... Mathematics, he said, was the typical study of the tender-minded. **1972** H. J. EYSENCK *Psychol. is about People* v. 202, I did in fact discover some evidence in favour of the notion that tender-mindedness and tough-mindedness were correlated with personality as hypothesized.

tenderometer (tendərǫ·mĭtəɹ). [f. TENDER *a.* + -O + -METER.] An instrument for testing the tenderness of raw peas for picking, processing, etc.

1938 *Encycl. Brit. Bk. of Year* 137/2 The 'Tenderometer' intended to determine the tenderness of raw peas used for canning. **1947** *N.Y. Herald Tribune* 18 May II. 10 The tenderometer shows when green peas reach their scientific peak of ripeness by registering the amount of pressure it takes for the gadget to shear through a sample pod. **1960** *Farmer & Stockbreeder* 16 Feb. 97/1 The tenderometer readings of the placement peas were 10 better than the broadcast averages. **1971** *Power Farming* Mar. 12/4 Peas can be valued on a tenderometer reading. **1981** *Southern Horticulture* (N.Z.) Spring 36/1 As soon as the tenderometer reading is at its optimum the whole paddock must be cleared within hours.

‖ **tendido** (tenðī·ðo). [Sp., pa. pple. of *tender* to stretch.] An open tier of seats above the barrera at a bull-fight.

1838 *Q. Rev.* LXII. 407 Those whose poverty..consents, sit in the 'tendido', and brave the sun's perpendicular height. **1967** MCCORMICK & MASCAREÑAS *Compl. Aficionado* ii. 59 The toro lopes off from the horse to the sunny side, where it seems to have spotted a man in a blue shirt in the lower *tendido*.

tendinitis (tendĭnai·tis). *Path.* Also **tendonitis.** [f. med.L. *tendin-em, tendōn-em* TENDON + -ITIS.] Inflammation of a tendon.

1900 in DORLAND *Med. Dict.* **1940** B. I. COMROE *Arthritis* xxx. 368 Classified according to location, fibrositis is known as:..Tendinitis—involvement of the fibrous tissue of tendons. **1948** *Nomencl. Disease* (R. Coll. Physicians) (ed. 7) v. 99/1 Calcareous tendonitis. **1972** *Time* 18 Sept. 35/1 Tendinitis of the knees. **1975** *Daily Colonist* (Victoria, B.C.) 9 Jan. 2/2 Tendonitis is a fairly common occurence, especially in the shoulder or elbow or heel. In tendonitis (tennis elbow is an example of it) the joint has been injured or irritated in some way.

tendo. Add: *tendo calcaneus* (also as one word) [L. *calcāneus, -um* heel] = *tendon of Achilles* s.v. TENDON a.

1900 DORLAND *Med. Dict.* 674 Tendo calcaneus. **1909** *Gray's Anat.* (ed. 17) 582 The tendo Achillis (tendo calcaneus)..is the thickest and strongest tendon in the body. **1937** J. C. B. GRANT *Method Anat.* iv. 302/2 The bellies end at the middle of the leg in a broad aponeurosis that blends with the aponeurosis of the Soleus to form the tendo calcaneus or tendo Achillis. **1967** G. M. WYBURN et al. *Conc. Anat.* vi. 171/1 The muscle groups of the leg are the extensors in front.., the peroneal muscles on the lateral side..and posteriorly the muscles of the calf forming the tendocalcaneus and more deeply the flexors. **1977** *Bone & Joint Diseases* (B.M.A.) 118 At this stage it is essential to elongate the tendocalcaneus through a transverse incision over the heel.

tendon. Add: **b*.** *Engin.* A steel rod or wire that is stretched while in liquid concrete so as to prestress it as it sets.

1958 F. S. MERRITT *Building Construction Handbk.* v. 56 After the concrete has attained sufficient strength, the steel is secured to the anchor plates and the jacks are removed. The tendons will tend to shorten and therefore will put compression in the concrete. **1974** [see *PRE-STRESSING *vbl. sb.*]. **1975** [see *PRE-TENSIONING *vbl. sb.*]. **1981** *Sci. Amer.* June 45/3 The prestressed-concrete reactor vessel..is kept in compression at all times by a network of redundant, tensioned steel tendons that can be monitored and retensioned or even replaced if necessary.

c. tendon organ, spindle = *SPINDLE *sb.* 4 e.

1923 V. H. MOTTRAM *Man. Histol.* vii. 225 Similar apparatus is seen in the Golgi tendon organ. **1974** D. & M. WEBSTER *Compar. Vertebr. Morphol.* x. 202 Both the tendon organ and the muscle spindle fire in response to stretch. **1896** Tendon-spindle [see *SPINDLE *sb.* 4 e]. **1930** MAXIMOW & BLOOM *Text-bk. Histol.* xiv. 276 Not infrequently, of two branches of the same sensory fiber one supplies a muscle spindle, the other a tendon spindle. **1977** D. P. WINSTANLEY tr. *Leonhardt's Human Histol.* 249 Tendon spindles are situated in the tendon close to its junction with the muscle.

tendonitis, var. *TENDINITIS.

tendre. Delete Now *rare* and add later examples.

1887 E. SIMCOX in K. A. McKenzie *Edith Simcox & George Eliot* (1961) 7 Having towards..Garibaldi..perhaps the same sort of *tendre* as that professed by Charlotte Bronte for the Duke of Wellington. **1921** D. H. LAWRENCE *Sea & Sardinia* vii. 298 She..was relieved to escape the new attachment, though she had a great *tendre* for him. **1980** G. M. FRASER *Mr American* xxii. 439 The cunning old gentleman's reading of her character, and of her supposed *tendre* for Mr Franklin.

tendril, *sb.* Add: **3. a.** *tendril career, finger, hand, -hold.*

1957 C. DAY LEWIS *Pegasus* 45 Or too much reason chill the air For your tendril career. **1929** *Oxford Poetry* 5 The tendril fingers groping for the bright Eternal beauty. **1939** DYLAN THOMAS *Map of Love* 14 Shall she receive a bellyful of weeds And bear those tendril hands I touch across The agonized, two seas. **1967** J. STALLWORTHY *Almond Tree* 11, I am called to the cot to see your focus shift, take tendril-hold on a shaft of sun.

‖ **tendu** (tãndü), *a. Ballet.* [Fr., pa. pple. of *tendre* to stretch.] Stretched out or held tautly, esp. in *battement tendu* (see *BATTEMENT).

1922 BEAUMONT & IDZIKOWSKI *Man. Classical Theatr. Dancing* I. 34 *Battements Tendus* serve to stretch and strengthen the muscles. **1950** *Ballet Ann.* IV. 129/2 The return, with the Russian masters of 1925–30, of the traditional French style, strictly *tendu*. **1952** [see *BATTEMENT].

-tene (tīn), f. Gr. ταινία band, ribbon, used in *Cytology* as a formative element of terms denoting stages of the first meiotic division (in nomenclature due to H. von Winiwarter 1900, in *Arch. de Biol.* XVII).

tenebrescence (tenėbre·sěns). *Physics.* [ad. L. *tenebrescens*, pr. pple. of *tenebrescere* to grow dark, f. *tenebræ* darkness.] The property of reversibly darkening and bleaching in response to radiation of different wavelengths (orig. restricted to the property of darkening only). Hence **tenebre·scent** *a.*; **tenebre·sce** *v. intr.*, to darken or bleach thus.

1946 H. W. LEVERENZ in *RCA Rev.* VII. 199 (heading) Luminescence and tenebrescence as applied in radar. [*Note*] The terms 'tenebrescence' and 'scotophor' are derived..to correspond to the terms 'luminescence' and 'phosphor'... Tenebrescence is any absorption of light not intrinsic to the materials involved;..a scotophor is a tenebrescent material..which may be made to tenebresce reversibly, i.e., visibly darken and bleach (irrespective of chromaticity), under suitable irradiations. **1953** *Amer. Mineralogist* XXXVIII. 919 (*heading*) Composition, tenebrescence and luminescence of spodumene minerals. *Ibid.*, Only non-chromian spodumene is luminescent and tenebrescent. **1970** DORION & WEIBE *Photochromism* i. 9 Tenebrescent and scotophoric materials are crystals that may be colored by radiation such as electron bombardment, X-rays, or light, and that are bleached by other radiation

tenebrionid (tėneːbriǫ·nid), *sb.* (and *a.*) [a. mod.L. family name *Tenebrionidæ*, f. TENEBRIO 2, adopted as a generic name by Linnæus (*Fauna suecica* (1746) 189): see -ID³.] A dark-coloured beetle of the family Tenebrionidæ, which is widely distributed, esp. in dry regions. Also as *adj.*, of or designating a beetle of this kind. Cf. *meal-worm* s.v. MEAL *sb.*¹ 3 b.

1921 C. A. EALAND *Insect Life* vi. 204 One of the commonest of our sand-loving Tenebrionids is *Heliopathes gibbus*. **1925** A. D. IMMS *Gen. Textbk. Ent.* III. 498 For a bibliography of Tenebrionid larvae vide Graveley. **1942** C. BARRETT *On Wallaby* v. 96 Many kinds of Desert beetles are black, notably the large and active Tenebrionids. **1966** [see *CARABID *a.*]. **1979** *Jrnl. Arid Environments* II. 265 Such an aposematic function is admirably demonstrated..in a Müllerian complex of American desert tenebrionids.

tenebrity. (Later example.)

1973 E. P. MATEN tr. *Budhasvāmin's Bṛhatkathāślokasaṃgraha* i. 32 Light..soiled..by a dense tenebrity.

tenebrosity. (Later examples.)

1815 J. GILCHRIST *Labyrinth Demolished* 19 But sure it must be the very essence of tenebrosity to suppose that the hand changes its nature or the name of it its meaning with change of purpose, and application or use. **1922** JOYCE *Ulysses* 387 This tenebrosity of the interior..hath not been illumined by the wit of the septuagint. **1924** *Times* 8 Apr. 14/1 Mr. Baldwin was joined by Mr. Asquith in his condemnation of the tenebrosity of the Government statements.

‖ **tenebroso** (tenebrō·so), *sb.* and *a.* Also *pl.* (as *sb.*) **tenebrosi.** [It. *tenebroso* dark: see TENEBROUS *a.* (*sb.*).] **A.** *sb.* One of a group of early seventeenth-century Italian painters influenced by Caravaggio, whose work is characterized by dramatic contrasts of light and shade. **B.** *adj.* Designating the style of this group of painters.

1886 W. M. ROSSETTI in *Encycl. Brit.* XX. 532/1 The naturalist school, called also the school of the Tenebrosi, or shadow painters. *Ibid.*, Ribera..had by this time acquired so much mastery over the tenebroso style that his performances were barely distinguishable from Caravaggio's own. **1938** *Burlington Mag.* Feb. 63/1 *The Last Supper*..introduces us to a *tenebroso* effect. **1982** C. WHITFIELD in Whitfield & Martineau *Painting in Naples* (Catal. of R. Acad. Exhibition) 165/2 Artemisia Gentileschi trained with her father Orazio in the early Seicento, when his style was at its most *tenebroso*.

Hence **te·nebrist** = *TENEBROSO *sb.*; **te·nebrism,** the style of the *tenebrosi*.

1923 F. J. MATHER *Hist. Italian Painting* ix. 454 Both at Rome and Naples swaggering Caravaggio had enormous success... He boasted himself the greatest painter of all time, and he was often believed. From his swarthy tones his entire school took the name, the Tenebrists. **1958** *Archit. Rev.* CXXIV. 56/3 As a belated tenebrist, he [*sc.* Wright of Derby] handles artificial light intelligently without making any visual discoveries of his own. **1959** *Penguin Dict. Art* 313 Tenebrism..is the name given to painting in a very low key, specifically to the works of those early 17th c. painters who were much influenced by Caravaggio. **1978** *Times Lit. Suppl.* 17 Feb. 213/3 Elsheimer's..tenebrism sprang from the same source.

tenement. Add: **5. tenement house** (earlier U.S. example).

1858 W. A. BUTLER *Two Millions* 47 The Tenement House, o'er which no friendly movement Has waved the Enchanter's wand of 'Modern Improvement'.

‖ **tenente** (tenę·nte). [It., Pg.] A lieutenant.

1929 E. HEMINGWAY *Farewell to Arms* iv. 15 'Do they ever shell that battery?'.. 'No, Signor Tenente.' **1969** M. GILBERT *Etruscan Net* III. i. 215 He sat down, and motioned the Tenente to be seated also. **1970** F. C. WEFFORT in I. L. Horowitz *Masses in Lat. Amer.* xi. 388 Their [*sc.* the Brazilian middle class's] most radical acts, generally undertaken by young military men—the *tenentes*.

teneral, *a.* (Examples of *lit.* use.)

1900 W. J. LUCAS *Brit. Dragonflies* vi. 66 (*heading*) Immature colour. [*Note*] Also called 'teneral'. **1921** G. H. CARPENTER *Insect Transformation* ii. 52 For some time after it has acquired the power of flying the dragon-fly has not yet assumed the deep colours and developed pattern that characterize its species; such a relatively newly-emerged insect is defined as teneral. **1957** *Jrnl. Exper. Biol.* XXXIV. 189 The word 'teneral' has been used to describe alate insects at about this time [between emergence and the first flight], although its usage varies between different orders. **1975** *Nature* 15 May 226/1 This [*sc.* a reduction in probing behaviour] was easier to demonstrate in teneral flies (newly emerged flies before their first meal) than in post-teneral flies.

Teneriffe (tenĕrī·f). [The name of one of the Canary Islands.] **1.** A white wine produced on Teneriffe.

1791 J. WOODFORDE *Diary* 11 Nov. (1927) III. 312 Claret, Teneriffe, and Port Wines to drink. **1833** C. REDDING *Mod. Wines* vi. 194 What is called Vidonia is properly the dry Canary wine, best known as Teneriffe. **1855** E. ACTON *Mod. Cookery* (rev. ed.) xxxii. 611 A couple of wineglassesful of Madeira (Sherry or Teneriffe will do).

2. Used *attrib.* to designate a kind of lace made in the Canary Islands.

1907 *Yesterday's Shopping* (1969) 3520/2 Teneriffe D'Oyley. **1920** 'K. MANSFIELD' *Bliss* 137 Now my best little Teneriffe-work teacloth is simply in ribbons. **1969** R. T. WILCOX *Dict. Costume* 342/2 *Teneriffe lace*, a lace of circles and wheels similar to Paraguay lace, made chiefly in the Canary islands.

tenger, var. *TANGER. **tengku,** var. *TUNKU.

‖ **teniente** (tenʸi,ę·nte). [Sp.] A lieutenant.
1798 in *Lett. from Paraguay* (1805) 248 Every thing..is known to the tenientes. **1906** *Soldier Slang* in C. McGovern *Sarjint Larry an' Frinds, Teniente*, Spanish for 'Lieutenant'. **1938** *New Statesman* 1 Oct. 488 Aren't we going to eat to-day, teniente? **1979** A. Melville-Ross *Two Faces of Nemesis* xxii. 157 *Teniente* Descola had done his job well enough to be *Capitan* Descola by evening.

tenii-, var. Taenii- in Dict. and Suppl.

‖ **tenko** (te·ŋko). [Jap.] In Japanese prison camps in the war of 1939–45: a muster parade or roll-call of prisoners.
1947 J. Bertram *Shadow of a War* vi. iii. 190 They drilled us by the hour..and firmly broke us in to the sacred mysteries of '*tenko*'—the morning and evening muster parade..that was routine in all prison camps in Japan... In time even *tenko* lost its terrors. **1961** R. Braddon *Naked Island* in *Plays of Year, 1960* I. iii. 153, I got him a bashing on tenko tonight.

tenmoku, var. *TEMMOKU.

tenné, tenny, *a.* and *sb.* (Later example of *tenney*).
1922 Joyce *Ulysses* 47 On a field tenney a buck, trippant, proper unattired.

tenner. a. (Earlier examples.)
1845 *Ainsworth's Mag.* VIII. 121 The races..he went to as a matter of course, though..he never betted at them beyond a 'tenner'. **1848** *Sessions Papers* 7 Mar. 847 'I was concerned in that affair of Covill's, for which I had a *tenner* out.'.. 'Oh, did they give you 10*l*?'.. I understood by a *tenner*, a 10*l*.-note.

Tennessean (tenĕsī·ăn), *sb.* and *a.* Also **Tennesseean.** [f. next + -AN.] **A.** *sb.* A native or inhabitant of Tennessee. **B.** *adj.* Of, pertaining to, or characteristic of Tennessee.
1815 *Niles' Reg.* VII. 373/1 Glory to..the hardy and gallant Tennesseeans, Kentuckians and Louisianians. **1834** [see *HUNT *v.* 3 b]. **1853** J. L. McConnel *Western Characters* 269 Its dye a favorite 'Tennessean' brownish-yellow. **1872** 'Mark Twain' *Sketches* 135 The fervent spirit of Tennesseean journalism. **1945** H. F. Woods *Amer. Sayings* 274 A Tennesseean-born pioneer, he was in the tradition of Daniel Boone and other border heroes of his time. **1959** C. Ogburn *Marauders* (1960) ii. 49 Lieutenant Caldwell..was an angular young Tennessean. **1978** *Times* 24 Oct. 8/6 Her own campaign slogan.. [claims] that she 'has not lost touch' with Tennesseans.

Tennessee (tenĕsī·). The name of one of the United States of America, used *attrib.* in **Tennessee Marble,** a kind of marble found in Tennessee and freq. used in building and sculpture; **Tennessee walker, walking horse,** a lightly built horse belonging to a breed developed in the region and distinguished by an easy natural gait.
1875 T. Yelverton *Teresina in Amer.* II. xiv. 177 It is a lofty, domed structure, the dome supported upon pillars of the red Tennessee marble. **1947** J. C. Rich *Materials & Methods of Sculpture* viii. 226 *Tennessee* is the largest producer of marble in the United States... Many sculptors compare Tennessee marble to granite... Tennessee marble is an excellent sculptural stone. **1968** *N.Y. City* (Michelin Tire Corp.) 74 Pierpont Morgan Library..in pink Tennessee marble. **1960** J. W. Patten *Light Horse Breeds* 147 The breed is variously referred to as Tennessee Walkers, Tennessee Plantation Horses, Tennessee Walking Horses. **1979** *Arizona Daily Star* 1 Apr. (Advt. Section) 10/10 Tennessee walker 7 years old, well trained. **1938** *Reg. Tennessee Walking Horse Breeders' Assoc.* I. 5 The Tennessee Walking Horse Breeders' Association of America held its first meeting at Lewisburg, Tenn., April 27, 1935. **1950** *Congress. Rec.* XCVI. App. A 740/3, I [*sc.* Pat Sutton] am delighted today to advise the House that the United States Department of Agriculture in a letter to me dated February 1, 1950, has recognized the Tennessee walking horse as a distinct and standard breed. **1952** J. Sherman *Real Bk. about Horses* iii. 69 The Tennessee walking horse is noted for his three natural gaits—the flat-footed walk, the running walk and the canter. **1976** *Billings* (Montana) *Gaz.* 2 July 11-c/6 (Advt.), Registered Tennessee Walking horse mares, yearlings, and colts.

tennies (te·niz), *sb. pl. U.S. colloq.* [f. *tenn(is shoe* + *ies* (repr. -Y[6] + *pl. suff.*).] Tennis shoes.
1969 *Rolling Stone* 28 June 19/3 Electric guitarist James Burton, replete in white turtleneck and matching 'tennies', puts together a lead. **1976** T. Gifford *Cavanaugh Quest* (1977) i. 17 Margaret, one of the cleaning ladies, got out in her green smock and blue shorts... Her costume was completed with blue tennies. **1980** *Outdoor Life* (U.S.) (Northeast ed.) Oct. 63/3 This is good-boot country, so leave your tennies home.

tennis, *sb.* Add: **2. a.** This is now the usual sense. (Earlier example.)
Tennis has replaced *lawn tennis* as the official international name of the sport. Sense 1 is now usually distinguished as *real tennis* (see *REAL *a.*[2] 4 e).
1878 Geo. Eliot *Let.* 8 Aug. (1956) VII. 54 My little man..fights resolutely against these ills..having mild games of tennis.

b. *anyone for tennis?, who's for tennis,* etc., a typical entrance or exit line given to a young man in a superficial drawing-room comedy, used *attrib.* of (someone or something reminiscent of) this kind of comedy. Also in extended uses.
1953 J. van Druten *Playwright at Work* viii. 99 There is no average Mr. and Mrs. Blank at all. An attempt to draw one..will lead you into the pit of emptiness, and you will emerge with something as unreal as the juveniles in plays who come in impertinently swinging tennis rackets, and when the time for their exit arrives, make it with the remark: 'Tennis, anyone?' **1965** *Listener* 17 June 911/3 One of the panel spoke of 'Who's-for-tennis' comedy,..now a too-familiar pejorative. **1973** *Times* 16 Jan. 11/1 The most unlikely men around London are now dressing as though they might say 'Anyone for tennis?' at any moment. **1974** N. Freeling *Dressing of Diamond* 34 She had seen him..spring up to answer the telephone with an Anyone-for-tennis voice that filled her with pity. **1978** H. MacInnes *Prelude to Terror* ii. 20 He walked over to the small group of staff members... 'Who's for tennis?' he asked, and raised a smile.

c. See *table-tennis* s.v. Table *sb.* 22.

3. b. *tennis apron, dress, frock, -lawn* (earlier U.S. and later examples), *match* (also *fig.*), *netting, partner, party, shirt, shorts, sock, tournament*; **tennis arm** (example); **tennis club:** see Club *sb.* 14; **tennis flannels** (see Flannel *sb.* 2 b); **tennis net,** a net stretched across the centre of a tennis-court, over which the players strike the ball; **tennis pro(fessional,** a tennis player who is paid to act as an instructor and a player at a tennis club, holiday resort, etc.; **tennis shoe,** a light canvas soft-soled shoe suitable for tennis or general casual wear; **tennis stringer** *U.S.*, a person who strings tennis rackets; **tennis whites** (see White *sb.* 9 b).
1880 L. Higgin *Handbk. Needlework* ii. 11 *Kirriemuir Twill*..is good for tennis aprons, dresses, curtains, &c. **1977** *New Yorker* 10 Oct. 123/3 It now sells not only tennis balls, racquets, and apparel but all sorts of knick-knacks—..telephone books, tennis aprons, [etc.]. **1887** *Epoch* 19 Aug. 26/2 The 'base-ball pitcher's arm' as well as the 'tennis arm' are recognized in the medical profession as special diseases. **1894** *Harper's Mag.* June 156/1 The champion player in our tennis club. **1914** L. S. Woolf *Wise Virgins* ii. 41 May was describing the tennis club dance. **1979** K. Conlon *Move in Game* i. i. 14 Why don't you take her with you to the tennis club? **1885** C. M. Yonge *Nuttie's Father* I. xi. 123 Nuttie was very much pleased with her own pretty tennis dress. **1977** J. Didion *Bk. Common Prayer* v. xvii. 258, I never saw her in a tennis dress. **1899** Kipling *From Sea to Sea* I. xx. 404 Member of the Clapham Athletic Club in tennis flannels. **1934** Tennis flannels [see *gravel court* s.v. *GRAVEL *sb.* 9]. **1981** J. Johnston *Christmas Tree* 33 There was a green stain on his tennis flannels, just below the knee. **1934** A. Thirkell *Wild Strawberries* ix. 191 Ursule, in a short silk tennis frock, looked quite presentable. **1882** *Wheelman* (Boston) I. 55 A tennis-lawn..is seldom far removed from the smoke of the town. **1981** T. Thompson *Edwardian Childhoods* v. 130 My grandparents had a big house with a tennis lawn. **1895** E. F. Benson *Dodo* II. xv. 314 A series of tennis matches which he had taken part in a few years ago. **1961** *Listener* 28 Sept. 483/2 A brilliant 'tennis match' between God and Satan. **1979** Reese & Flint *Trick 13* 134, I had a date to play in a tennis match. **1900** C. M. Yonge *Modern Broods* x. 94 Placing tennis nets, arranging croquet hoops. **1977** *Listener* 7 Apr. 450/1 Table tennis..smashing or retrieving a small celluloid sphere over a miniature tennis net. **1915** Kipling *Let.* 22 Aug. in C. Carrington *Rudyard Kipling* (1955) xvii. 436 Don't forget the beauty of rabbit netting overhead against hand-grenades. Even tennis netting is better than nothing. **1934** P. Bottome *Private Worlds* iii. 26 The girl was going to be married to her tennis partner. **1974** E. Ambler *Dr Frigo* ii. 133 My tennis partner at the army communication centre must have been busy. **1887** Kipling *Plain Tales from Hills* (1888) 256 There are garden-parties, and tennis-parties and picnics. **1981** *Times* 24 Mar. 4/4 Sir Roger Hollis.. met an MI5 officer at a tennis party and was finally recommended for recruitment. **1942** A. Christie *Body in Library* iii. 31, I do a couple of exhibition dances every evening with Raymond..he's the tennis and dancing pro. **1977** I. Shaw *Beggarman, Thief* III. vi. 257 A Belgian businessman..had offered him a contract for a year as a tennis pro. **1938** D. du Maurier *Rebecca* v. 52 The tennis professional had complained, the manager has sent a note. **1979** K. Conlon *Move in Game* i. iii. 32 The bronzed tennis professional, who had all the ladies of the club in a lather of longing. **1889** Tennis shirt [see *CELLULAR *a.* (and *sb.*) 2 b]. **1978** *Country Life* 22 June 1841/1 Cotton tennis dress..navy and white tennis shirt..tennis shoes. **1887** Kipling *Plain Tales* (1888) 222 Miss Hollis ..was..five foot seven in her tennis-shoes. **1928** E. Wallace *Flying Squad* xiii. 122 They walked noiselessly, for Mr. Tiser had obligingly supplied them with..tennis shoes. **1975** *Time* (Canada ed.) 22 Dec. 12/3 [He] once flew out to settle a strike at the Vancouver *Sun* wearing tennis shoes and carrying clothes in a Loblaws shopping bag. **1963** D. B. Hughes *Expendable Man* (1964) iv. 122 She was in tennis shorts and a white blouse. **1932** D. C. Minter *Modern Needlecraft* 253/1 Tennis Socks... 3-ply fingering. **1976** *Washington Post* 19 Apr. C15/4 (Advt.), Tennis stringer. Experience preferred but not necessary. **1892** C. M. Yonge *Cross Roads* xii. 127 Miss Clara caught a chill while driving home after a tennis tournament. **1976** *Wymondham & Attleborough Express* 10 Dec. 21/6 Sue Rich..has made great progress in tennis tournaments in several parts of England this year. **1974** M. Ehrlich *Reincarnation* (1975) xxiii. 203 She was in tennis whites now and volleying with the pro.

tennis, *v.* Restrict † *Obs.* to senses in Dict. and add: **2. b.** To play lawn-tennis. Also with quasi-*obj. rare.*
1895 Kipling in *Cent. Mag.* Dec. 276/1 They picnicked and they tennised. **1979** *United States 1980/81* (Penguin Travel Guides) 493 Whether you tennis-it at a camp or a clinic, you're guaranteed a certain number of hours of court time every day. **1983** *Washington Post* 15 Aug. c8/6 They'd rather be golfing, or snorkeling, or tennising.

tennis-court. Add: **1.** *Comb.* Also *esp.* in *tennis-court oath,* the pledge given on June 20, 1789, by members of the States General of France that they would not separate before a constitution was granted (see quot. 1911). Also *fig.*
1893 L. Creighton *First Hist. France* xxvi. 231 The Tennis-Court Oath.—Under his [*sc.* Mirabeau's] guidance the Third estate now declared themselves the National Assembly. **1911** H. A. Guerber *Story Mod. France* x. 55 The Third Estate met tumultuously in the Versailles Tennis Court, where..they bound themselves, by the famous 'Tennis Court Oath'. **1959** *Listener* 31 Dec. 1151/1 The integrity of Anatolia was the tennis-court oath of the Kemalist revolution. **1977** *Socialist Press* 2 Mar. 6/3 Faced with procedural fencing on the part of the King's ministers and the Court, they declare themselves a 'National Assembly' and vow (the 'tennis-court oath', June 20th) not to depart until a constitution is drawn up.

tennis-play. 1. (Later example.)
1918 G. Frankau *One of Them* in *Poet. Wks.* (1923) II. xxiv. 143 Who in all Albion on that fateful day..Left not his office-work, his tennis-play, To read black Montmorency's slander-red lines?

tennis-playing, *ppl. a.* [f. as Tennis-player.] That plays (lawn-)tennis.
1956 H. Gold *Man who was not with It* (1965) vi. 58 The long, tennis-playing, suburban legs. **1965** M. Spark *Mandelbaum Gate* ii. 27 Her energetic tennis-playing grandmother..sat on the arm of a chair. **1979** D. Eden *Storrington Papers* iv. 47 'The new governess..arrived this afternoon.' 'Promising?'.. 'No more tennis-playing amazons.'

Tennysonian, *a.* and *sb.* Add: **A.** *adj.* (Earlier example.)
1846 Lytton *New Timon* ii. 51 Where all the airs of patchwork-pastoral chime To drowsy ears in Tennysonian rhyme!
B. *sb.* (Earlier and later examples.)
1850 J. Brown *Let.* Dec. (1912) 116, I am not a Tennysonian, as many are. **1864** H. Sidgwick *Let.* May in A. & E. M. Sidgwick *Henry Sidgwick* (1906) ii. 108 The compressed *inhaltsvoll* classic style of Tennyson and Tennysonians. **1970** T. Hilton *Pre-Raphaelites* vi. 161 William Morris..like all reading men, was a Tennysonian.
Tennysonia·na [*-IANA], matters connected with Tennyson; **Tennyso·nianized** *ppl. a.*, rendered in the manner of Tennyson; **Tennyso·nianly** *adv.*; **Tennyso·nianness** = Tennysonianism, Tennysonism; **Tennyso·nize** *v. trans.*, to render in the style of Tennyson.
1866 R. H. Shepherd (*title*) Tennysoniana. **1910** A. D. Godley *Lectures Eng. Lit.* ii, in *Reliquiae* (1926) II. 288 Tennyson is full of reminiscences of the great classics, thoughts and phrases not slavishly copied but Tennysonised—passed through the medium of an art which added beauty to everything it touched. **1915** E. Pound *Let.* Jan. (1971) 49 [In poetry] there must be..no straddled adjectives (as 'addled mosses dank'), no Tennysonianness of speech. **1916** *Ibid.* ? 20 July (1971) 87 Virgil is a second-rater, a Tennysonianized version of Homer. **1932** L. Magnus *Herbert Warren* viii. 215 His own annotated copy of the one-volume edition of the *Memoir* is a veritable treasure of Tennysoniana. **1964** *English Studies* XLV. 73 'Lycidas' once read 'under the glimmering eyelids of the morne', most Tennysonianly. **1975** *Listener* 20 Nov. 685/1 Superintendent Dalziel, on unwanted holiday in sodden fens, meets a Tennysonianly aqueous funeral cortège.

tenon, *sb.* Add: **2. tenon-saw** (later examples).
1898 *Monthly South Dakotan* I. 57 This operation was successfully performed by Dr. Phillips with no further implements at hand than a large butcher's knife and a small tenon-saw. **1979** A. B. Emary *Woodworking* xxix. 125 Saws (a hand saw and a tenon saw) can be stored in the lid.

tenon, *v.* Add: **1. a.** (Later examples.)
1949 H. M. Cautley *Norfolk Churches* 37 A massive sill, frequently unbroken at the entrance to chancel, into which the muntins are tenoned. **1980** *Early Music* Jan. 62/2 At the other end, the neck is tenoned into the post and pegged.
2. b. (Later examples.) Also *fig.*
1935 'E. Queen' *Spanish Cape Mystery* iv. 103 There are a few facts floating about which don't precisely tenon with the psychopathic theory. **1981** *Rescue News* Mar. 8/1 The oak timbers..tenoned and pegged into sole-plates lying on the bottom of the moat.
tenoner (examples).
1944 J. C. Jones in N. W. Kay *Practical Carpenter & Joiner* x. 227/1 The rails are first fed into the tenoner edgeways up for the machining of the haunchings. **1971** *Cabinet Maker & Retail Furnisher* 24 Sept. 532 Mr Taylor has retained in use with the new line a Schwabedissen double end tenoner with overhead beam.

Tenonian, *a.* Add: *Tenon's capsule* (examples); *Tenon's space,* the episcleral space between Tenon's capsule and the sclera.

1868 HACKLEY & ROOSA tr. *C. Stellwag von Carion's Treat. Dis. Eye* I. xi. 434 This anterior part of the sheath of the eye-ball..is also described as Tenon's capsule. **1892** A. DUANE tr. *Fuchs's Text-bk. Ophthalm.* II. xv. 285 Exudation into Tenon's space also occurs after it has been laid open by injuries. **1950** *Sci. News* XV. 25 The eye does not form part of a ball-and-socket joint, like the hip joint, but resembles a ball in a sling, the latter..being composed of a thin sheet of fibrous and smooth muscle tissue, called Tenon's Capsule. **1979** G. W. CIBIS tr. *Hollwich's Ophthalm.* xvi. 238 The inflammation involves Tenon's capsule in either a serous or a purulent form. As a rule it remains restricted to Tenon's space.

tenor, *sb.*[1] (*a.*) Add: **I. 1. d.** The underlying idea or subject to which a metaphor refers, as distinct from the literal meaning of the words used. Cf. *VEHICLE *sb.* 3 d.

1936 I. A. RICHARDS *Philos. Rhet.* v. 96 A first step is to introduce two technical terms to assist us in distinguishing..what Dr. Johnson called the two ideas that any metaphor, at its simplest, gives us. Let me call them the tenor and the vehicle. The tenor, as I am calling it—[is] the underlying idea or principal subject which the vehicle or figure means. *Ibid.* 100 The tenor may become almost a mere excuse for the introduction of the vehicle, and so no longer be 'the principal subject'. **1949** *Poetry* (Chicago) Feb. 304 The tenor is the *new* meaning, the vehicle the *old* meaning on which the new meaning is conveyed. **1962** S. ULLMANN *Semantics* viii. 213 An important factor in the effectiveness of a metaphor is the distance between tenor and vehicle. **1973** A. RODWAY in R. Fowler *Dict. Mod. Crit. Terms* 112 In the phrase 'Now is the winter of our discontent'..discontentedness is the tenor, and an aspect of winter..the vehicle. **1980** G. B. CAIRD *Lang. & Imagery of Bible* viii. 152 In a living metaphor, although both speaker and hearer are aware that vehicle and tenor are distinct entities, they are not grasped as two but as one.

II. 4. d. (Earlier examples.)

1785 *Daily Universal Register* 1 Jan. 3/2 (Advt.), Mr. Giardini's capital old Violins, Tenors, and Violoncellos for sale. **1833** [see ALTO *sb.*[2] 5].

e. *ellipt.* for *tenor saxophone*, sense B. 1 below.

1876 [see *ALTO *sb.*[2] 6]. **1927** *Melody Maker* Aug. 738 (Advt.), The manufacturers..have been hailed as the saviours of Tenor Saxophonists through their innovation of the astounding B♭ tenor with the extra automatic octave note. **1952** [see *BARITONE]. **1975** [see *SAXIST].

B. *attrib.* or *adj.*, and *Comb.* **1.** *attrib.* or *adj. tenor banjo*: see *BANJO 1; *tenor clarinet*, an alto clarinet pitched in F; also, one who plays this instrument; *tenor cor*: see *COR[3]; *tenor drum*: see DRUM *sb.*[1] 1 b; *tenor horn* = *ALTHORN; *tenor sax, saxophone*, a member of the saxophone family intermediate between the alto and the baritone, usu. pitched in B flat; also, one who plays this instrument; hence *tenor saxist, sax-man, saxophonist*; *tenor violin* (examples).

1802 Tenor violin [see ALTO- 1]. **1859**, etc. Tenor horn [see *ALTHORN]. **1865** C. MANDEL *Mandel's Syst. Mus.* xvi. 68 There are various kinds of Saxophones. The smallest, or Soprano Saxophone, is in B flat... The.. Tenor Saxophone is an octave lower than the Soprano Saxophone. **1879** GROVE *Dict. Mus.* I. 362/2 In F we have the tenor clarinet. **1926** WHITEMAN & MCBRIDE *Jazz* ix. 193 We have computed..that one tenor saxophone equals eight violas. **1927** Tenor saxophonist [see sense *4 e]. **1934** S. R. NELSON *All about Jazz* vi. 127 A brilliant tenor sax was unmistakable. **1938** D. BAKER *Young Man with Horn* I. iv. 28 There were five men in Jeff's band—a tenor clarinet, a trombone, a trumpet, traps, and a piano. **1954** *Grove's Dict. Mus.* (ed. 5) II. 326/2 The higher-pitched of the two [alto clarinets] was long known as the 'tenor clarinet' in England. *Ibid.* VIII. 809/1 The true Tenor Violin was the alto of the *viola da braccio* family... The gradual suppression of this instrument in the 18th century was a disaster: neither the lower register of the viola nor the upper register of the violoncello can give its effect. **1954**, etc. Tenor saxophone [see *SAXOPHONE sb. 1]. **1955** KEEPNEWS & GRAUER *Pict. Hist. Jazz* x. 110 Key members included tenor sax Andy Brown. **1955** Tenor saxist [see *BASSIST 2]. **1955** Tenor sax-man [see *sax-man* s.v. *SAX *sb.*[2] 3]. **1958** T. HALL in P. Gammond *Decca Bk. Jazz* xix. 229 He was mainly featured on an E-flat tenor-horn, which produced a mellophone-like sound. **1963** *Listener* 7 Feb. 264/1 Two virtuoso tenor sax players. **1972** *Guardian* 4 Feb. 10/5 No one strove harder than the tenor saxist John Coltrane. **1979** *Country Life* 12 July 95/2 A..solo by tenor saxophonist Steve Marcus. **1979** *Listener* 4 Oct. 461/3 Charlie Parker..plays tenor-sax on the Miles Davis set.

2. *Comb.* in sense 4 e, as *tenor-man, player, solo, soloist, style.*

1928 *Melody Maker* Feb. 201/2 Quite a few successful tenor players. **1935** *Vanity Fair* (N.Y.) Nov. 38/2 Tenor-men like Hawkins or Fletcher Henderson, are stars in the hot sky. **1943** P. E. MILLER *Yearbk. Popular Music* 8/2 He borrowed a tenor from a fellow musician, sat in on a jam session, and from that point forward became a hot tenorman. **1958** R. HORRICKS in P. Gammond *Decca Bk. Jazz* ix. 118 The prominent tenor soloists outshone even those of the New York scene. **1959** F. NEWTON *Jazz Scene* ii. 35 A fine tenor player in the Parker tradition. **1962** *Melody Maker* 21 July 7/3 The perfect tenor style for Dixieland jazz. **1966** *Crescendo* Dec. 9/2 Good clarinet, trumpet and tenor solos. **1977** J. WAINWRIGHT *Do Nothin'* viii. 125 Tenor men are not *that* hard to find.

te·noring *ppl. a.*

1905 H. G. WELLS *Mod. Utopia* iv. 127 It is not only such gross and palpable cases as our blond and tenoring friend. **1930** —— *Autocr. Mr. Parham* II. iii. 119 'But,' said Mr. Mountain in tenoring remonstrance to Sir Bussy, 'doesn't this evening satisfy you, sir?' **1934** —— *Exper. Autobiogr.* II. viii. 602 Bland was a thick-set, broad-faced aggressive man..with a tenoring voice.

‖ **tenore** (tenō·re). [It.; cf. TENOR *sb.*[1] (*a.*).] = TENOR *sb.*[1] 4 a and b. Usu. with qualifying adj. or phrase, as *tenore di grazia*, a light or lyric tenor; *tenore robusto* (see quot. 1876), a dramatic tenor.

1740 GRASSINEAU *Mus. Dict.* 272 *Tenore*, the first mean or middle part: or that which is the ordinary pitch of the voice, when neither raised to a treble, or lowered to a bass. **1876** STAINER & BARRETT *Dict. Mus. Terms* 432/1 *Tenore robusto*, a tenor singer with a full, strong, sonorous voice. **1889** GROVE *Dict. Mus.* IV. 87/1 Hence we have *tenore robusto* (which used to be of about the compass of a modern high baritone), *tenore di forza, tenore di mezzo carattere, tenore di grazia*, and *tenore leggiero*, one type of which is sometimes called *tenore contraltino*. **1894** G. DU MAURIER *Trilby* I. i. 25 A voice so rich and deep and full as almost to suggest an incipient *tenore robusto*. **1925** *New Yorker* 19 Sept. 20/2 He is the first *tenore robusto* to emerge since Caruso. **1938** J. JOYCE *Let.* 8 Sept. (1966) III. 427 It needs a deep strong voice, not my *tenore di grazia*. **1960** *Times* 4 Mar. 4/1 Mr. Kenneth Macdonald, who has an enviable affinity for *tenore di grazie* singing. **1979** *Times* 19 Nov. 7/5 The..refinements of phrasing and nuance which are hall-marks of a *tenore di grazia*.

tenorino (tenǒrī·no). Pl. **-ini.** [a. It., dim. of *tenore* tenor.] A high tenor; *spec.* a castrato alto.

1867 *Cornh. Mag.* Jan. 32 At present the signor is the pearl of tenorini, and no other artist can match his delivery of the embroidered melodies of the *Cenerentola*, or the *Italiana in Algieri*. **1898** *Harper's Mag.* XCVI. 512, I was..to be the tenor, or rather the *tenorino*. **1980** *New Grove Dict. Mus.* XVIII. 690/2 Another type of light tenor voice was known in the 19th century as the 'tenorino'; such singers were often amateurs who made a speciality of performing love-songs to salon audiences.

tenorist. Add: (Later examples.) Also, one who plays the tenor saxophone.

1958 K. GOODWIN in P. Gammond *Decca Bk. Jazz* xiii. 154 Vinegar was also featured..when the tenorist opened a short season at Zardi's. **1962** *Melody Maker* 7 July 9 It is quite remarkable..that so popular a tenorist..has not had a broadcast or TV appearance for more than three years. **1972** *Blues & Jazz* Sept. 11/2 The backing on 'The Fat Man' was provided by the Bartholomew band, including tenorists Herb Hardesty and Red Tyler. **1977** *Listener* 1 Dec. 729/4 Roy Plomley has marooned tenorist Ronnie Scott..on his desert island.

tenoroon. Add: **a.** (Later example.) The use of this instrument has recently been revived in performances of baroque music.

1980 *Early Music Gaz.* Jan. 9/2 William Waterhouse.. performed music by Selma, Böddecker..on racket, two original 18th-century bassoons (Handel period 4-key and Mozart period 7-key, tenoroon and modern Heckel).

tenpence. Add: (Earlier and later examples of *ten pence in the shilling* and varr.) Since 1971, a coin worth ten (new) pence superseding the earlier two-shilling piece or florin; often as two words with pronunc. (ten pens). Also *attrib.* as *tenpence coin, piece.*

1860 HOTTEN *Dict. Slang* (ed. 2) 235 *Tenpence to the shilling*, a vulgar phrase denoting a deficiency in intellect. **1922** J. BUCHAN *Huntingtower* vii. 142 There's a certain old lady, an aunt of Mr. Quentin and his sisters, who has always been about tenpence in the shilling. **1936** W. HOLTBY *South Riding* 9 'Mental?' 'Tenpence halfpenny in the shilling.' **1971** P. PURSER *Holy Father's Navy* xxiv. 114, I gave her a ten pence piece and hurried away. **1974** A. FOWLES *Pastime* xii. 98 Awkward, that had been, in a phone box. He'd used up two ten pences. **1976** G. SEYMOUR *Glory Boys* xi. 144 He put down two tenpence coins.

Hence **te·npenceworth**, the amount of anything to be bought for tenpence; used contemptuously.

1896 G. B. SHAW *Let.* 16 Nov. in *Ellen Terry & Bernard Shaw* (1931) 124, I have been to Paris, and seen Peer Gynt done in the sentimentallest French style with te npenceworth of scenery.

tenpenny, *a.* (*sb.*) Add: **A.** *adj.* **1. a.** *tenpenny piece* (later examples); also, a coin worth ten (new) pence.

1968 *Guardian* 24 Apr. 3/3, I handed the woman a new tenpenny piece worth 2s. **1971** I. MURDOCH *Accidental Man* 305 The room was unheated except for a weak one-bar electric fire which had to be continually fed with tenpenny pieces. **1973** J. PORTER *It's Murder with Dover* xiii. 130 MacGregor watched his tenpenny pieces disappearing down the greedy slot of the one-armed bandit.

b. *tenpenny nail* (later examples); in U.S. *spec.* a three-inch nail.

1890 WEBSTER, *Penny*.., denoting pound weight for one thousand;—used in combination, with respect to nails; as, tenpenny nails, nails of which one thousand weigh ten pounds. **1906** *Dialect Notes* III. 146 *Mad enough to bite a tenpenny nail in two, adj. phr.*, very angry. **1909** WEBSTER, *Penny* is used in combination with prefixed numerals..to form adjectives denoting price or value. As applied to nails these adjectives now denote certain arbitrary sizes, though originally, in the 15th century, they designated the price per hundred; as, a *tenpenny* nail, one then costing tenpence per hundred. **1967** *Countryman* Autumn 29 My American companion said: 'I guess we should get some tenpenny nails.' Then he looked at me: 'I suppose you don't know what they are.' I did not. Next day, when we asked for them by that name at the hardware store, we got what we wanted —three-inch nails.

B. *sb.* **1. a.** (Earlier example.)

1822 D. O'CONNELL *Let.* 13 Apr. (1972) II. 379, I will hug every tenpenny as a link in the chain that is to draw back my Mary to me.

ten-pins. Add: **b.** *ten-pin alley* (earlier examples), *ball* (earlier example), *bowling.*

1835 P. H. NICKLIN *Lett. Descr. Va. Springs* 23 The means of amusement at the Warm Springs, consist of a bagatelle table..a ten-pin alley [etc.]. **1842** [see *bowling saloon* s.v. *BOWLING *vbl. sb.* 3]. **1852** C. A. BRISTED *Upper Ten Thousand* v. 117 Perhaps we shall find him at the ten-pin alley. **1870** O. LOGAN *Before Footlights* 120 Finely cut bits of paper, for fatal snowstorms; ten-pin balls, for the distant muttering of the storm. **1934** *A.B.C. Bulletin* 25 Oct. 11/1 (*heading*) Tenpin Bowling—'The Sport of Kings'. **1960** *Observer* 17 Jan. 3/3 Ten-pin bowling, as its sponsors call it, went to America with the planters and the pilgrims... The game that is being reimported is hedged about with expensive equipment and social ballyhoo, but is simple enough in itself. **1975** *Oxf. Compan. Sports & Games* 90/1 Tenpin bowling has reached a stage where it can claim to be the largest participant sport in the world.

ten-pounder. Add: **2. a.** (Later examples.)

1844 *Ainsworth's Mag.* VI. 354, I feared I should very soon be obliged to change..my ten-pounder. **1888** C. M. YONGE *Our New Mistress* xii. 109 He took it from me as if I were paying him his wages, and..said..a crisp ten-pounder was a handier thing to drag about than a puling woman.

b. (Earlier example.)

1833 R. SOUTHEY *Let.* 13 Jan. in J. Aitken *Eng. Lett. of XIX Century* (1946) 147 The ten-pounders have sent just such members as might have been expected to *Parldemonium* from the great manufacturing towns.

tense, *sb.* Add: **1. a.** (Later example.)

1922 JOYCE *Ulysses* 604 To fast and abstain on the days commanded, it being quarter tense or, if not, ember days or something like that.

3. *attrib.* and *Comb.*, as (in sense 2) *tense-aspect, marker, stem, system*; *tense-marking, -modal* adjs.

1892 H. SWEET *New Eng. Gram.* I. 101 By tense-aspect we understand distinctions of time independent of any reference to past, present, or future. **1980** *English World-Wide* I. I. 113 It seems as though the tense-aspect system of English has been restructured. **1971** E. JONES in J. Spencer *Eng. Lang. W. Afr.* 83 Krio is equipped with a range of tense markers, as may be seen from the following set. **1978** *Language* LIV. 84 The advocates of abstract remote structures posit auxiliaries including negative and tense markers as main verbs. **1962** C. L. BARBER in F. Behre *Contrib. Eng. Syntax* 27 Any combination of four tense-markings. **1921** E. SAPIR *Language* v. 96 Had the statement been made on another's authority, a totally different 'tense-modal' suffix would have had to be used. **1965** *Language* XLI. 173, 1200 adverbial suffixes, partly tense-modal. **1935** T. HUDSON-WILLIAMS *Short Introd. Study Compar. Gram.* xiii. 72 The endings were added to each tense-stem. **1971** *Archivum Linguisticum* II. 100 The subjunctive is originally independent from the so-called tense stems, as is evident in Celtic and Tocharian and also in Latin. **1951** W. K. MATTHEWS *Lang. U.S.S.R.* iv. 75 The tense system is complicated by being carried into the non-finite grammatical categories, including the gerund. **1963** J. LYONS *Structural Semantics* vi. 112 The 'tense-system' may be set out in terms of the two dimensions of time and aspect.

tense, *a.* Add: **1. a.** Also *spec.* in *Phonetics*, applied to (the articulation of) a speech-sound pronounced with enhanced tension in the muscles of the speech organs. Cf. *LAX *a.* 5 c, *SLACK *a.* 7 e.

1909, etc. [see *LAX *a.* 5 c]. **1909** [see *SLACK *a.* 7 e]. **1918** D. JONES *Outl. Eng. Phonetics* 21 When pronouncing the..tense vowel..the throat feels considerably tenser and is somewhat pushed forward. **1933** L. BLOOMFIELD *Language* vii. 109 In German the tense vowels are longer than the loose; this difference of length is more striking than that of tenseness. **1968** W. S. ALLEN *Vox Graeca* v. 103 The usually tenser articulation of voiceless plosives might also tend to emphasize the crescendo. **1978** *Canad. Jrnl. Linguistics* 1977 XXII. 211 *Rêve* and *âge* have inherited, underlying tense vowels.

tense, *v.* **a.** Delete *rare* and add: Also *refl.* and with *up*. (Later examples). Also *spec.* of vowel sounds (cf. *TENSE *a.* 1 a).

1929 P. GIBBS *Hidden City* I Rage causes an increase of adrenal secretion, tensing up the nerve cells. **1942** G. CASEY *It's Harder for Girls* 130 When his turn came he tensed himself to go through with it. **1951** C. S. FORESTER *Randall & River of Time* xviii. 263 The constable was tensing himself, ready to restrain him if he should do anything violent. **1978** *Canad. Jrnl. Linguistics* 1977 XXII. 211 Historically, /v/ and /ž/, although lengthening preceding vowels, did not automatically tense them.

b. *intr.* To become tense. Also const. *up.*

1946 *Sunday Express* 31 Mar. 8/2 The court tensed as Ribbentrop gave inside glimpses of events which shaped the war. **1959** *Encounter* Feb. 31, I was tensing for the death-blow. **1973** *Houston* (Texas) *Chron. Texas Mag.* 14 Oct. 2/3 They..feared the kids would tense up if they knew a reporter was in their midst. **1975** I. MCEWAN *First Love, Last Rites* 42 There was such a sudden ferocity in her silence that I found myself tensing like a sprinter on the starting line.

Hence **te·nsing** *vbl. sb.* (also with *up*).
1921 L. R. FREEMAN *In Tracks of Trades* 85 There was a sharp tensing of the powerful frame. **1977** *Washington Post* 23 Nov. B2/3 It is the isometric tensing of muscles opposite ones that have been over-developed. **1983** *N.Y. Times* 9 Oct. VI. 56/2 More like a tensing-up that begged for relief.

tensed, *ppl. a.* Add: (Later examples.) Also *fig.* (cf. TENSE *a.* 2). Freq. const. *up* and now rarely used *attrib.*
1911 J. LONDON *Adventure* i. 11 The tensed body relaxed. **1934** E. O'NEILL *Days without End* I. 29 His eyes fixed before him.., his body tensed defensively. **1952** G. THOMAS *Now lead us Home* 191 All tensed up in wait for the hand that will draw some heavenly melody out of them. **1971** S. HILL *Strange Meeting* i. 41 There would be no more anxieties..about how he could bear to sit in the sour-smelling room with the Major, tensed with dread of the night to come. **1980** 'R. B. DOMINIC' *Attending Physician* xxii. 198 Ben sounds pretty tensed-up to me.

tensed (tenst), *a.* [f. TENSE *sb.* + -ED[2].] Having a grammatical tense or tenses.
1972 *Language* XLVIII. 314 The situation of [examples] 34 and 35 is particularly interesting: we do not, in general, find this type of stress in tensed (i.e. non-infinitival) relative clauses. **1978** *Ibid.* LIV. 289 It is also common to most of these proposals to assume that deverbatives are derived from clauses which contain tensed verb forms or their equivalents. **1982** BAKER & HACKER in *Language & Communication* II. III. 240 Animals have immediate purposes and intentions, but long term goals, projects and intentions are available only to creatures who have forms of expression for such things, viz. a tensed language.

tensegrity (tense·grĭti). [f. *tens(ional int)egrity.*] A stable three-dimensional structure consisting of members under tension that are contiguous and members under compression that are not; the characteristic property of such a structure; also *fig.* Freq. *attrib.*
1959 *Art News* Oct. 29 Of all the ways out of the blind alley in which so much of modern architecture luxuriously relaxes, R. Buckminster Fuller's 'tensegrity' structures seem the most inventive and promising. **1963** R. B. FULLER *Ideas & Integrities* viii. 170 We have in the Geodesic Tensegrity (my name for the discontinuous-compression, continuous-tension structures) the ability to assemble unprecedentedly large, clear-span structures. **1972** *Last Whole Earth Catalog* (Portola Inst.) 4/3 The Universe is a tensegrity. **1976** A. PUGH *Introd. Tensegrity* ii. 11 One of the most impressive Tensegrity figures has six struts which do not touch one another and twenty-four tendons. **1976** H. KENNER *Geodesic Math* p. viii, No useful structures exploiting pure Tensegrity—tension wholly separated from compression—have been built. **1976** *Sci. Amer.* Dec. 144/1 The Kenner book..derives the very nature of a geodesic dome..as the limiting case of a more complex skin of simple tensegrities.

tenseness. Add: Also *spec.* of vowel sounds (cf. *TENSE *a.* 1 a).
1918 D. JONES *Outl. Eng. Phonetics* 20 The 'tenseness' or 'laxness' of a vowel may be observed mechanically in the case of some vowels by placing the finger on the throat. **1933** [see *TENSE *a.* 1 a]. **1958** A. S. C. ROSS *Etym.* ii. 125 OE *e o* became opened to *ę ǫ* soon after 1200... This loss of tenseness is of great consequence in the development of new diphthongs. **1978** *Canad. Jrnl. Linguistics* 1977 XXII. 211 There appears to have been a recent tendency to attribute tenseness to all lengthened vowels.

tensify, *v.* (Later example.)
1932 V. WOOLF *Common Reader* 2nd Ser. 145 That strain of..passion did..not tensify the quiet of the country morning.

tensile, *a.* Add: **2.** *tensile test* (Engin.), a test for determining the tensile strength of a sample of material (usu. metal); so *tensile testing* (also *attrib.*).
a **1877** KNIGHT *Dict. Mech.* III. 2539/1 In the hydraulic tensile testing-machine..the specimen is held by the two clips. **1883** *Jrnl. Iron & Steel Inst.* 98 (*heading*) Results of tensile tests made at University College, London. **1923** GLAZEBROOK *Dict. Appl. Physics* V. 53/1 Two types of testing machine are in use for the tensile testing of fabric specimens. **1953** D. J. O. BRANDT *Manuf. Iron & Steel* 362 Fig. 203 shows a tensile testing machine and the method of setting up the test piece. **1973** J. G. TWEEDDALE *Materials Technol.* I. iv. 78 (*caption*) A tensile test piece.

tensimeter (tensi·mĭtəɹ). [f. TENSI(ON *sb.* + -METER.] An instrument for measuring vapour pressure.
1907 *Jrnl. Amer. Chem. Soc.* XXIX. 1055 The hygrometer used above may conveniently serve the purpose of a tensimeter. **1946** J. R. PARTINGTON *Gen. & Inorg. Chem.* iii. 54 The dissociation pressure of a salt hydrate is measured in a tensimeter.

tensiometer (tensi,ǫ·mĭtəɹ). [f. TENSI(ON *sb.* + -OMETER.] **1. a.** An instrument for measuring the surface tension of a liquid. **b.** One for measuring the tension of soil water.
1922 *Jrnl. Exper. Med.* XXXV. 576 The tensiometer was used with an accurately calibrated platinum-iridium ring..and is reliable to ±0·1 dyne. **1936** RICHARDS & GARDNER in *Jrnl. Amer. Soc. Agronomy* XXVIII. 352 Rogers.., lacking a more suitable name, has called the combination a soil moisture meter. In the interest of brevity and unambiguity, the name tensiometer is here used. **1973** *McGraw-Hill Yearbk. Sci. & Technol.* 382/1 Tensiometers placed in the active root zone and near the bottom of the root zone..provide information that permits control of deep percolation [in irrigated soil]. **1975** YONG & WARKENTIN *Soil Properties & Behaviour* iv. 129 Tensiometers are widely used to indicate when irrigation is required.

2. An instrument for measuring the tension in yarn, a rope, etc.
1947 *Textile Research Jrnl.* Jan. 27/1 The thread then passes to a tensiometer,..which instrument feeds voltage proportional to the thread tension into a..chart recorder. **1952** *Electronic Engin.* XXIV. 531 The most common instrument for measuring yarn tension is the pocket-size dial tensiometer. **1978** A. WELCH *Bk. of Airsports* vi. 98/2 The tensiometer is important, so that the canopy will never be overloaded by the car being driven too fast in strong winds.

Hence **tensiome·tric** *a.*, **tensio·metry.**
1965 *New Scientist* 18 Nov. 497/1 The rocks are simulated by microscopic glass balls and polymers... They claim that these models enable reliable forecasts of what will happen to the springs if this or that method of mining is adopted. Tensiometry..and ultrasound measurements play an important role in this work. **1968** *McGraw-Hill Yearbk. Sci. & Technol.* 351/1 A tensiometric method utilizes a porous cup filled with water connected by a tube to a vacuum indicator. This approach measures the capillary potential or suction of soil water. **1979** *Acta Protozoologica* XVIII. 64 Two radial measurements by tensiometry.

tension, *sb.* Add: **2. c.** esp. *Psychol.* A condition of strain produced by anxiety, need, or by a sense of mental, emotional, or physical disequilibrium; also *attrib.* or as *adj.*
1884 W. JAMES in *Mind* IX. 12 The states of tension.. have as positive an influence as the discharges in determining the total condition, and consequently in deciding what the *psychosis* shall be to which the complex *neurosis* corresponds. **1925** H. M. & E. R. GUTHRIE tr. *Janet's Princ. Psychotherapy* iv. 234 Psychic tension [is] characterized by the degree of activation and the hierarchical degree of acts. **1930** J. RIVIERE tr. *Freud's Civilization & its Discontents* 127 The sense of guilt..is..the ego's appreciation of the tension between its strivings and the standards of the super-ego; and the anxiety that lies behind. **1935** ADAMS & ZENER tr. *Lewin's Dynamic Theory of Personality* ii. 59 A tendency may readily be observed toward immediate discharge of tension (to a state of equilibrium at the lowest possible state of tension). **1958** H. A. MURRAY in G. Lindzey *Assessment of Human Motives* vii. 194 The concept of human nature..is a concept of perpetually recurrent drives, or tensions.

d. The conflict created by interplay of the constituent elements of a work of art. Used esp. of poetry. (See also quot. 1941.)
1941 A. TATE *Reason in Madness* 72, I proposed..the term *tension*..using the term not as a general metaphor, but as a special one, derived from lopping the prefixes off the logical terms *ex*tension and *in*tension... The meaning of poetry is its 'tension', the full organized body of all the extension and intension that we can find in it. **1949** *Poetry* Feb. 305 *Tension*,..the resultant effectual unity of the poem derived from the operation of such conflict-structures as wit, paradox and irony, slackness being the result of a failure in tension. **1957** N. FRYE *Anat. Crit.* 256 It is more likely to be the harsh, rugged, dissonant poem.. that will show in poetry the tension and the driving accented impetus of music. **1975** *Language* LI. 583 Metrical tension can be construed as the degree of difference between underlying and derived metrical patterns.

3. b. Substitute for def.: = PRESSURE 2 a; now chiefly *Biol.* and *Med.* (Later examples.)
1906 W. MARRIOTT *Hints to Meteorol. Observers* (ed. 6) 69/1 Tension of vapour. **1907** J. H. PARSONS *Dis. Eye* ii. 18 The pressure inside the eye is called the intraocular pressure, or the tension, of the eye. **1940** *Jrnl. Bacteriol.* XXXIX. 307 (*heading*) The effect of oxygen tension on the oxygen uptake of lake bacteria. **1971** *Brit. Med. Bull.* XXVII. 55/2 The oxygen tension in the arterial blood may be somewhat lowered. **1972** A. H. HALASA *Basic Aspects of Glaucomas* xi. 97 Low tension glaucoma refers to a condition characterized by a normal intraocular pressure associated with..glaucomatous visual field defects.

c. (Later example.) Also, the degree of tightness or looseness of the stitches in machine sewing or in knitting.
1932 D. C. MINTER *Mod. Needlecraft* 199/2 Learn how to regulate machine stitch and tension. **1933** TILLOTSON & MINTER *Compl. Knitting Bk.* ii. 21 The knitted loops, for a correct tension, should just cling lightly and closely to the reader. **1950** J. NORBURY *Knitter's Craft* i. 10 A loose tension will produce a flabby, ill-fitting garment. **1973** *Tucson* (Arizona) *Daily Citizen* 22 Aug. 3 (Advt.), Brother sewing machine Lightweight zig zag..fingertip touch tension. **1980** C. FREMLIN *With no Crying* x. 61 Alison was concentrating on those first vital rows of her knitting, making sure that she was getting the tension right.

4. (Earlier example.)
1785 G. ADAMS *Essay on Electricity* (ed. 2) x. 208 The whole energy of electricity depends on its tension, or the force with which it endeavours to fly off from the electrified body.

5. a. *high tension* (earlier examples).
1833 FARADAY in *Phil. Trans. R. Soc.* CXXIII. 516, I was anxious..to obtain some idea of the conducting power of ice and solid salts by electricity of high tension. **1877** *Telegr. Jrnl.* V. 289/2 (*heading*) On the effects produced by electric currents of high tension.

c. *transf.* and *fig.*
1898 G. B. SHAW *Candida* III. 148 Eugene, strung to the highest tension, does not move a muscle. **1906** J. M. SYNGE *Let.* ?6 Nov. (1971) 47, I am working now at very high tension. **1959** D. COOKE *Lang. Music* iv. 183 The high-tension 'current' of Beethoven's emotion, we may say, had to be converted into a high-tension rhythmic energy.

6. (in sense 2) *tension state, system*; *tension-relieving* adj.; **tension bar,** (*a*) (example); (*b*) a metal bar used to apply pressure or exert tension; **tension spring,** (*b*) a spring used to maintain a required degree of tautness; **tension wood** = *reaction wood* s.v. *REACTION 5.
1879 *Car-Builder's Dict.* 163/1 *Tension bar*, a bar which is subjected to a strain of tension. **1963** R. A. HIGHAM *Handbk. Papermaking* viii. 212 Tension bars are usually found on calendars, especially when treating light-weight papers, and in action these serve to keep the sheet flat and taut across the working width. **1977** 'E. MCBAIN' *Long Time no See* xiii. 215 The telephone was as vital a tool to policemen as was a tension bar to a burglar. **1949** KOESTLER *Insight & Outlook* 421 Neglect of the emotional dynamics of laughter, of its tension-relieving aspect. **1974** M. C. GERALD *Pharmacol.* xi. 201 *Quiet World* contains 'special calming and tension-relieving ingredients'. **1966** J. S. COX *Illustr. Dict. Hairdressing & Wigmaking* 148/1 *Tension spring*, a spirally wound and flattened wire spring which, when stretched returns to its original length... The tension spring is sometimes replaced by elastic. **1970** *Which?* Aug. 238/2 A faulty tension spring on the bobbin case stopped the tensioning adjustment from working properly. **1946** *Mind* LV. 149 We have, therefore, to discover these responses that are the most successful in resolving the personal tension state of which political argument is the expression. **1977** J. D. DOUGLAS in Douglas & Johnson *Existential Sociol.* i. 43 Anomie appears to be a tension state that is produced in the individual by an inability to achieve success by legitimate means. **1936** *Mind* XLV. 248 The technique which seeks to make an undesired goal palatable or a desired goal unpalatable, by linking them up somehow with the 'natural' tension-systems of the child. **1953** M. HORWITZ in Cartwright & Zander *Group Dynamics* xx. 371 Individuals develop tension systems coordinated to reaching their own goals. **1924** W. S. JONES *Timbers* iv. 27 'Tension' or 'white' wood differs from 'red' wood in that the cell walls of the tracheids show a well-developed, strongly-lignified, tertiary layer. **1951** MCLEAN & IVIMEY-COOK *Textbk. Theoret. Bot.* I. xxi. 907 In conifers the lower wood is reddish, the upper white..the upper wood being called tension-wood. **1972** *Gloss. Terms Timber* (*B.S.I.*) 15 Tension wood. Abnormal wood.. formed typically on the upper sides of branches and of leaning or crooked trunks of hardwood trees.

Hence **te·nsionally** *adv.*, by means of tension, as a result of tension.
1960 R. W. MARKS *Dymaxion World of B. Fuller* 195 Magnesium ball-jointed tripods..were tensionally opened by piston-elevated masts. **1975** *New Yorker* 12 May 41/1 Tensionally cohered universe here today and gone tomorrow.

tension, *v.* (Examples.)
1891 *Engineer* LXXI. 120/2 [List of patents.] Tensioning saddles of velocipedes, F. A. Matthews, London. **1950** *Jrnl. R. Aeronaut. Soc.* LIV. 631/1 The 'floating stud'..is a slotted template stud contained in a metal ring, and tensioned by three or four springs. **1975** KONG & EVANS *Reinforced & Prestressed Concrete* ix. 196 When the concrete has hardened sufficiently, the tendons are tensioned by jacking against one or both ends of the member.

tensioner (te·nʃənəɹ). *Mech.* [f. TENSION *sb.* + -ER[1].] A device for applying tension to cables, pipelines, etc.
1950 *Engineering* 5 May 489/3 Heavy spring tensioners are fitted to the front sprockets. **1972** L. M. HARRIS *Introd. Deepwater Floating Drilling Operations* xiii. 140 Marine-riser tensioning can be provided either by a dead-weight system or by the use of pneumatic tensioner cylinders. **1977** *Austral. Sailing* Jan. 54/1 The luff tensioner..is the most subtle control.

tensometer (tenso·mĭtəɹ). [f. TENS(ION *sb.* + -OMETER.] **1.** An apparatus for measuring the tensile strength of a material.
1937 *Nature* 1 May 765/2 The Griffin Gale testing machine enables tensile..tests to be carried out on small samples of metals... In the same class is the Hounsfield tensometer. **1950** *Chem. Abstr.* XLIV. 7 (*heading*) Mechanical tensometer for measurements of deformations on temperature change. **1971** *Nature* 2 Apr. 323/1 The specimens were strained at a rate of 1mm min^{-1}; the tensometer and electrometer head amplifier were enclosed in an earthed brass gauze to screen out extraneous electrical fields.

2. = *TENSIOMETER 1 a.
1941 *Abstr. Sci. & Technical Press* No. 91. 178 The author has designed an interfacial tensometer... In this instrument the force exerted by the interfacial layer on a platinum ring is measured by means of a torsion balance.

3. = *TENSIOMETER 2.
1953 K. H. INDERFURTH *Nylon Technol.* vii. 159 It is essential that the yarn tension be frequently checked with a tensometer.

tensor. Add: **2. a.** (Earlier example.)
1846 W. R. HAMILTON in *Phil. Mag.* XXIX. 27 Since the square of a scalar is always positive, while the square of a vector is always negative, the algebraical excess of the former over the latter square is always a positive number; if then we make $(TQ)^2 = (SQ)^2 - (VQ)^2$, and if we suppose TQ to be always a real and positive or absolute number, which we may call the tensor of the quater-

nion Q, we shall not thereby diminish the generality of that quaternion. This tensor is what was called in former articles the modulus.

c. An abstract entity represented by an array of components that are functions of co-ordinates such that, under a transformation of co-ordinates, the new components are related to the transformation and to the original components in a definite way. [This sense is due to W. Voigt (*Die Fund. Physik. Eigenschaften der Krystalle* (1898) p. vi).]

1916 *Monthly Notices R. Astron. Soc.* LXXVI. 701 In the four-dimensional time-space we consider tensors of different orders. The tensor of order zero is a pure number (scalar), the tensor of the first order is a vector, which has 4 components, the tensor of the second order has 16 components, and so on. *Ibid.* 702 If once we have expressed the laws of nature in the form of linear relations between tensors, they will be invariant for all transformations. Thus with the aid of the calculus of tensors Einstein has succeeded in satisfying the postulate of general relativity. **1934** *Nature* 20 Oct. 612 The theory of tensors, so important in physics and geometry on account of their property of vanishing in every co-ordinate system if they vanish in one, was created by Ricci (1887) and his pupil Levi-Civita, although the name *tensor* was not introduced by them. **1943** *Jrnl. London Math. Soc.* XVIII. 109 The study of the particular class of invariants known as tensors goes back to the work of Riemann and Christoffel on quadratic differential forms. **1953** C.-T. Wang *Applied Elasticity* i. 1 Stress is called a tensor, because in addition to its magnitude, direction, and sense, which define a vector, it depends on another vector, which represents the surface upon which it acts. **1970** G. K. Woodgate *Elem. Atomic Struct.* iii. 50 The operator in eqn. (3.95) is a component of a second-rank tensor, the atomic electric quadrupole moment. **1974** G. Reece tr. *Hund's Hist. Quantum Theory* xv. 211 ψ and χ were scalars, spinors, vectors or tensors.

d. *attrib.* and *Comb.*, as *tensor algebra, analysis, calculus, product*; **tensor field,** a field for which a tensor is defined at each point; **tensor force,** a force between two bodies that has to be expressed as a tensor rather than a vector, *esp.* a non-central force between subatomic particles.

1922 Tensor algebra [see *tensor analysis* below]. **1936** *Electr. Engin.* LV. 1214/1 The object of this paper is to apply tensor algebra to the solution of the circuits of multi-winding transformers. **1971** C. W. Curtis in Powell & Higman *Finite Simple Groups* iii. 142 Form a vector space *M* with basis *X*, and let $\mathscr{F}_X$ be the tensor algebra over *M*. **1922** H. L. Brose tr. *Weyl's Space–Time–Matter* i. 58 Tensor analysis tells us how, by differentiating with respect to the space co-ordinates, a new tensor can be derived from the old one in a manner entirely independent of the co-ordinate system. This method, like tensor algebra, is of extreme simplicity. **1939** G. Kron *Tensor Analysis of Networks* p. xvi, Tensor analysis may be considered as an extension and generalization of vector analysis from three- to n-dimensional spaces and from Euclidean to non-Euclidean spaces. **1976** *Sci. Amer.* Aug. 98/2 Einstein's ideas were cast in a language very different from even non-Euclidean geometry, called the absolute differential calculus... Einstein used it and changed its name to tensor analysis. **1977** D. Bagley *Enemy* xxxiii. 266 This joker is using Hamiltonian quaternions!.. No one..has used Hamiltonian quaternions since 1915 when tensor analysis was invented. **1922** H. L. Brose tr. *Weyl's Space–Time–Matter* i. 53 The study of tensor-calculus is, without doubt, attended by conceptual difficulties—over and above the apprehension inspired by indices. **1944** G. B. Shaw *Everybody's Political What's What?* ii. 22 Experts in the tensor calculus. **1981** *Sci. Amer.* July 95/1 Tensor calculus..was essential to Einstein's formulation of his general theory of relativity. **1922** H. L. Brose tr. *Weyl's Space–Time–Matter* i. 61 An important example of a tensor field is offered by the stresses occurring in an elastic body. **1934** R. C. Tolman *Relativity, Thermodynamics, & Cosmol.* 36 Tensor fields may..be constructed, in which a value of the field tensor is associated with each point in the continuum. **1948** *Physical Rev.* LXXII. 987/1 The result of the present calculation and that of the proton–neutron scattering, which includes the tensor forces, show that the difference among the three potentials is quite pronounced at these high energies. **1972** *Physics Bull.* June 349/2 The noncentral force causing the anomalies mentioned above is called the tensor force, and it results from a neutron–protonspin–spin interaction. **1964** A. P. & W. Robertson *Topological Vector Spaces* vii. 141 It is essential to form the completion of the tensor product under the correct topology. **1971** E. C. Dade in Powell & Higman *Finite Simple Groups* viii. 252 The tensor product ..is again a finite-dimensional vector space over *F*.

Hence **tenso·rial** *a.*

1934 [see *anti-¹ 2 d]. **1968** C. G. Kuper *Introd. Theory Superconductivity* iv. 58 Since..Pippard's experimental data..do not support the idea of a tensorial anisotropy, these equations have not proved useful.

tent, *sb.*¹ Add: **2. a.** (Later examples.)

1923 T. S. Eliot *Waste Land* iii. 14 The river's tent is broken: the last fingers of leaf Clutch and sink into the wet bank. **1929** *Oxford Poetry* 13 Here in this harbour where straw glows..and overhead The unbroken tent of heaven covers.

f. A plastic or fabric enclosure that can be placed round a patient in bed so that the air he or she breathes can be modified and controlled. Cf. *oxygen tent* s.v. *oxygen 3 b.

1892 J. Carmichael *Dis. Children* xvii. 235 The room should be well ventilated, and the temperature of the tent kept between 65°and 70°. **1941** M. Davidson *Pract. Man. Dis. Chest* (ed. 2) xxxv. 559 Many varieties of tent have been constructed, all of which..demand considerable supervision. **1971** S. M. Bates *Pract. Pediatric Nursing* xii. 237 Both tents are designed to achieve cool supersaturation of the contained air with minimal wetting. **1979** Whaley & Wong *Nursing Care Infants & Children* xxxii. 1201/1 For continuous aerosol therapy a misting device is attached to or incorporated in the mist tent.

5. a. *tent curtain* (examples), *-flap, -frame* (example), *-hand, -mate* (later example), *-picket, -pole* (later example; also *fig.*), *-talk, wagon* (earlier example); *tent-pitching* (examples); (in sense 4) *tent-meeting, -preacher, -preaching* (earlier example).

1835 N. P. Willis *Pencillings by Way* II. xviii. 199 Most of the officers lay asleep on low ottomans, with their tent curtains undrawn. **1926** T. E. Lawrence *Seven Pillars* (1935) viii. xcvi. 532 He crawled back through the tent-curtain. **1920** *Blackw. Mag.* Sept. 319/2 He paused with his shaking hand on the tent-flap. **1980** D. Hart-Davis *Heights of Rimring* vii. 67 He unrolled the tent-flaps and let them hang down. *Ibid.* vi. 65 The porters.. began to fit tent-frames together. **1938** N. Streatfeild *Circus is Coming* v. 57 The man finished fixing a seat. 'I'm a tent hand.' **1965** H. Gold *Man who was not with It* xiv. 115 A couple of tenthands are taking their flannel shirts off a line. **1972** J. Minifie *Homesteader* xviii. 158, I used the Army-issue straight blade [razor] myself, to the intense admiration of my tent-mates. **1950** *Reader's Digest* Jan. 85/2 Frakes joined the Methodist Church at an evangelistic tent meeting. **1913** S. O'Casey *Let.* 7 June (1975) I. 28 There will be exhibitions of drill, tent-pitching, [etc.]. **1925** G. Bell *Let.* 28 Jan. (1927) II. xxv. 721 The ordinary Scout exercises and tent pitchings—which they did extremely well. **1864** G. M. Hopkins *Poems* (1967) 14 Your hands have borne the tent-poles. **1974** R. Adams *Shardik* xviii. 134 His ugly, unmarriageable tent-pole of a daughter. **1979** *Guardian* 12 June 2/4 These..facts..were..'the fixed and rigid tentpoles' of the whole edifice of the prosecution case. **1966** *Punch* 9 Mar. 362/2 A tent-preacher and healer tells a diabetic woman she is cured. **1977** *Time* 26 Dec. 41/1 The latter include everything from Episcopalians to nearly a million Roman Catholics, to oddball healers and assorted tent preachers. *c* **1795** *Stat. Acct. Scotland 1791–9* XV. 537 At the celebration of..the Sacrament of the Supper, there is no field or tent preaching..so derogatory from the solemnity of this institution. **1932** Auden *Orators* iii. 108 The tent-talk pauses a little till a veteran answers 'Go to sleep, Sonny!' **1819** *Acct. Colony Cape of Good Hope* iii. 118 A light tent waggon, drawn by six or eight horses, constitutes the carriage of the wine boor.

b. tent caterpillar: for 'bombycid moth, *Clisiocampa*' read 'moth of the genus *Malacosoma* of the family Lasiocampidæ'; (earlier and later examples); **tent city,** a very large collection of tents; **tent club**: in India, a club organized for the sport of pig-sticking; **tent coat,** a coat resembling a tent in shape, being narrow at the shoulders and very wide at the hem; **tent-fly** (earlier example); **tent-man,** (*a*) (later example); (*b*) (examples); **tent-master** (later examples); **tent-pin** (earlier example); **tent ring** *Canad.*, a ring of stones used to hold down a tent, teepee, etc.; **tent-sack** (see quot. 1940); **tent show,** a show (such as a circus) given in a tent; **tent-stake** *U.S.* = Tent-peg; also in fig. phr. to *pull up tent-stakes*: to close down a business etc.; cf. Stake *sb.*¹ 1 e; **tent town,** a temporary settlement (as of gold-miners or the like); **tent-trailer** orig. and chiefly *U.S.*, a kind of trailer consisting of a wheeled frame with a collapsible tent cover attached; **tent village,** a small encampment; *spec.* = Douar, dowar.

1854 E. Emmons *Agric. N.Y.* V. 236 To eradicate completely the tent caterpillar, it will be necessary to give attention to the wild cherry trees. **1977** Richards & Davies *Imms's Gen. Textbk. Entomol.* (ed. 10) II. iii. 1135 The larvae of *M. americana*..are commonly known as 'tent-caterpillars', their webs measuring 2 feet or more in length. **1934** M. F. K. Fisher in *As they Were* (1983) 64 A tent city, many umbrella and hot-dog concessions. **1980** J. Domatilla *Last Crime* 5 A tent city of tourists on a similar pilgrimage. **1889** R. S. S. Baden-Powell *Pig-sticking or Hoghunting* xvii. 152 Every station near which pig are to be found has its Tent Club. This is an association of the sportsmen of the place for carrying out the preservation of the pig, and successful hunting. **1895** Kipling in *Cent. Mag.* Dec. 271/1 He became a member of the local Tent Club, and chased the mighty boar on horseback. **1920** *Blackw. Mag.* Jan. 105/1 A Tent Club corresponds to a Hunt; the Hon. Secretary to the Master. **1961** *Guardian* 1 Feb. 7/5 A vast tent coat..over an elegant little sheath dress. **1971** *Vogue* 15 Sept. 51 Short tent coat with cape yoke. **1849** T. T. Johnson *Sights Gold Region* 169 The tent-fly is a second roof usually erected over the tent. **1945** *Sun* (Baltimore) 22 Feb. 7/2 Circus men sentenced... Chief tentman, two to seven years in State prison. **1961** *Times* 28 Mar. 12/6 The sweating 'tentman'..will be clown, drummer, lion-tamer rolled into one. **1978** *Illustr. London News* Nov. 32/3 As a kid..I used to take my waddie bottle..full of tea to the tentmen, they were travelling labourers, really. **1864** Tent master [see *tenter *sb.*² 2]. **1938** N. Streatfeild *Circus is Coming* v. 57 You'll have the tent master after me. **1763** J. Bell *Trav. from St. Petersburg* I. 323 Our European tents are of little use, as there is no earth in which the tent-pins can be fastened. **1945** *Beaver* Mar. 39/2 When a tent is struck.., the ring of stones which held it down lies there for years to come, and these tent rings are found today scattered even more widely..than the old igloos. **1958** *Even. Telegram* (St. John's, Newfoundland) 29 Apr. 13/3 My large tent needed more rocks to hold it down firmly than the usual tent ring supplied. **1940** F. Smythe *Adventures of Mountaineer* vii. 89 There was little else we could do save..unpack our tent-sack... It was simply a large sack of jaconet waterproof and windproof material intended to shelter climbers in an emergency. **1972** D. Haston *In High Places* iv. 52 As we were sitting comfortably in our tent sacks there was suddenly a loud explosion and a great hissing all around. **1878** M. Long *Life Mason Long* iv. 60, I made the acquaintance of a man named McCoole, who was travelling with a small tent show. **1935** [see *shill *sb.*]. **1973** *Times Lit. Suppl.* 28 Dec. 1593/4 Her life of the tent show, the Black touring company, race labels and buffet flats. **1862** *Rebellion Record* V. ii. 156 The desolated, hard-trodden ground, and a few tent-stakes, remain to tell the story. **1923** H. Crane *Let.* 15 Feb. (1965) 123 *Broom*..has busted; N.Y. office closed last Saturday; March issue, the last, to be distributed from Berlin while the tent-stakes are being pulled up. **1956** H. Gold *Man who was not with It* (1965) i. 7 The Popcorn Man was throwing canvas over his machine and had it almost covered when a rube heaved a tent-stake. **1878** J. H. Beadle *Western Wilds* 103 Along the track west of it had sprung up five tent-towns. **1923** H. Steele *Spirit of Iron* 108 He came in touch with all the vice, wretchedness and stark tragedy abounding in the tent-towns and construction camps. **1965** *Globe & Mail* (Toronto) 26 May 3/2 Near this town..there is a tent-town of marginal people and transients. **1963** *Better Camping* Mar.–Apr. 32/2 It is only in the last six years or so that the tent trailer has grown from modest beginnings—little more than a bed on a trailer and just canvas cover enough to turn around in—to fold-out apartment-size dwellings. **1970** *Daily Tel.* 14 Nov. 9 Midway between tent and caravan..come the tent-trailers. **1899** A. E. W. Mason *Miranda of Balcony* x. 139 The Arab..belonged to a douar, a tent village. **1977** *N.Z. Herald* 8 Jan. 1–3/6 They also called for reinforcements for their tent village.

tent, *v.*⁶ Add: **1. a.** *spec.* of travelling circus folk.

1875 T. Frost *Circus Life* xvii. 292 During the summer months they 'tented', and in the winter erected temporary wooden buildings in populous towns. **1931** S. McKechnie *Pop. Entertainments* viii. 209 The circus..was purchased by Frederick and Edward, who tented in the summer and spent the winter in..towns. **1952** N. Streatfeild *Aunt Clara* 111 They had been tenting with their mother.

5. To arrange in a shape suggesting a tent; *esp.*, with the fingers as obj., = *steeple *v.* 4.

1966 D. Bagley *Wyatt's Hurricane* ii. 60 He tented his fingers and regarded Wyatt closely. **1977** 'E. McBain' *Long Time no See* xi. 182 She herself sat on the sofa.. pulling her legs up under her Indian-fashion, the caftan tented over her knees. **1980** *TWA Ambassador* Oct. 57/2 Gatmun tented the fat sausages of his fingers.

tentacle. Add: **d. tentacle-feeder,** an invertebrate animal possessing tentacles to trap its food.

1953 J. S. Huxley *Evolution in Action* iii. 73 Tentacle-feeders may either float free in the water or be attached to the bottom. **1963** R. P. Dales *Annelids* 15 The more familiar tentacle-feeders include the terebellids, which have a mass of extensile tentacles.

tentage. (Later examples.)

1905 'L. Hope' *Indian Love* 20 No more the rugged road of Khorasan, The scanty food and tentage of the past! **1948** *Sporting Mirror* 21 May 13/3 (Advt.), Every type of Marquee, tentage and camping equipment. **1978** *B.S.I. News* July 6/1 It is considered unreasonable to deal with the flammability of tentage in isolation from other important features such as resistance to water penetration.

tented, *a.* Add: **1. b.** Of an encampment: consisting of tents.

1872 *Rep. Indian Affairs 1871* (U.S.) 261 Urah..had collected some of the chiefs and headmen of the tribe to receive me in their tented camp. **1955** *Times* 25 May 13/5 The cost of their fares..and their five months' stay in a tented camp in Cyprus will be about £300 each. **1982** *Listener* 23 and 30 Dec. 4/1 On a gentle rise..there is the tented city for the RAF Phantom and Harrier squadrons.

3. b. Of activities, etc.: held in or taking place in a tent or tents.

1898 N. E. Jones *Squirrel Hunters of Ohio* 131 Protracted, tented, or camp-meetings increased,..becoming very popular with preachers and people. **1971** *Morning Star* 22 June 2/5 The percentage of people taking tented holidays in Britain has gone up by 50 per cent since 1965. **1976** J. Wainwright *Bastard* iii. 48 A circus was visiting a neighbouring town. One of the hand-to-mouth, tented circuses. **1976** *Time* 20 Dec. 31/1 Circus Vargas, billed as the world's largest tented show.

tenter, *sb.*² Add: **1.** (Earlier U.S. example.)

1846 *Indiana Hist. Mag.* XXIII. 409 The eating hours were the same as those of the tenters.

2. One whose job is to erect and strike tents.

1864 'P. Paterson' *Glimpses of Real Life* xiii. 123 There must be a tent-master and tenters, besides the agent in advance, the members of the brass band, [etc.]. **1979** *Daily Tel.* 23 Apr. 14/8 The slow building and dismantling of the marquee on stage was..a documentary about tenters and their jobs.

tenterhook. 3. (Later example.)

1980 P. Van Greenaway *Dissident* ii. 41 Alex had listened with tenterhook attention.

tenth, *a.* and *sb.* Add: **B.** *absol.* and *sb.* **4.** The tenth day of the month.

1580 in H. Foley *Jesuits in Conflict* (1873) 105 The tenth of September, 1580. **1868** E. S. P. Ward in *Atlantic Monthly* Mar. 345 (*heading*) The tenth of January. **1951** W. Faulkner *Requiem for a Nun* I. 36 It was barely the tenth of July. *Ibid.* III. 250 On the morning after June tenth.

C. tenth-value *a.*, designating a thickness of material that reduces the intensity of radiation passing through it by a factor of 10.

1955 *Gloss. Terms Radiology* (*B.S.I.*) 17 Tenth-value thickness. **1957** *Effects Nucl. Weapons* (U.S. Defense Atomic Support Agency) viii. 378 For concrete, the tenth-value thickness is..about 48 cm.

tenthredinid, *a.* and *sb.* (Examples.)

1890 *Insect Life* III. 157 Tenthredinid larva on black birch. **1913** *Oxf. Univ. Gaz.* 4 June 954/1 The Tenthredinid *Allantus arcuatus* together with a ♂ humble bee.., a much larger insect. **1970** G. Ordish tr. *Chauvin's World of Ants* i. 61 The biologist Lange put some Tenthredinid larvae..near an ant track.

tenting. Add: **1.** *vbl. sb.*[1] Also (with reference to a touring circus or the like) camping and performing in a tent.

1861 *All Year Round* 16 Nov. 186/1 The tenting system is now so well organised, that everything connected with it is conducted with effect and punctuality. **1878** L. M. Alcott *Under Lilacs* iv. 40 Father..went off sudden.. just before the tentin' season was over. **1931** S. McKechnie *Pop. Entertainments* viii. 222 Bertram W. Mills' Circus and Menagerie..only in its second tenting season..has already revolutionised the status of the circus. **1952** N. Streatfeild *Aunt Clara* 114 We have a little time when tenting is finished. **1971** *Esquire* July 88/2 The Hartford Circus fire of 1944..caused the big show to forswear tenting in 1956 and resolve to play only arena engagements indoors.

2. *sb.* (Later non-attrib. example.)

1936 *Discovery* Dec. 381/1 The second assistant had been carried down the rapids on the tenting.

tenting, *ppl. a.* Add: **1.** (Later example.)

1932 S. O'Faoláin *Midsummer Night Madness* 26 The tenting chestnuts filled the lanes with darkness.

2. Of a circus: that tents (Tent *v.*[6] 1 a in Dict. and Suppl.).

1875 T. Frost *Circus Life* iii. 67 The tenting circuses of those days were on a more limited scale than those of the present time, and were met with chiefly at fairs. **1931** S. McKechnie *Popular Entertainments* viii. 206 The early tenting circuses were unpretentious concerns. **1981** P. O'Donnell *Xanadu Talisman* i. 18 He..owned half a small tenting circus.

tention[3] (**'tention**). Add: Also **ten-shun** (cf. *'shun).

1908 M. Beerbohm in *Sat. Rev.* 26 Sept. 390/1 He.. stood at 'tention to be tapped on the chest by the hero. **1922** Joyce *Ulysses* 417 Get a spurt on. Tention. **1978** J. Blackburn *Dead Man's Handle* viii. 91 He..bellowed an order. 'Ten-shun, Sarn't-Major.'

tenue. Add: (Earlier and later examples.) Also *transf.*

1828 Lady Granville *Let.* 30 Aug. in B. Askwith *Piety & Wit* (1982) x. 154 The tenue, the neatness, the training up of flowers and fruit trees..are what in no other country is dreamt of. **1865** Crown Princess of Prussia *Let.* 12 Dec. in R. Fulford *Your Dear Letter* (1971) 46 She went through it all [*sc.* the marriage].. with the most perfect *tenue.* **1929** R. Fry *Let.* 4 Sept. (1972) II. 641 The building has a certain Florentine *tenue,* very refreshing after the rather sloppy magnificence..of the Venetians. **1956** S. Bedford *Legacy* I. i. 17 A tall, cool..woman,..who had complete *tenu* [sic] and a great deal of character. **1971** A. Fremantle *Three-Cornered Heart* vi. 97 We had quite as many 'love affairs' as girls have now, though we were more reticent about them and carried on our flirtations with a certain amount of *tenue.*

tenurable (te·niŭrăb'l), *a.* Chiefly *U.S.* [f. next + -able.] Of an academic post: subject to tenure (sense *1 c). Of an applicant for such a post: fit to be granted tenure.

1977 *Science* 4 Feb. 440/3 What is their effect on the bright..young scholar-teacher who has not, unfortunately, been productive enough to be undebatably tenurable? **1977** *Nature* 10 Nov. p. xlvi/2 (Advt.), Applications are invited for a full-time, tenurable appointment in the Division of Pharmacy and Pharmaceutics.

tenure. Add: **1. c.** *spec.* (orig. and chiefly *U.S.*) Guaranteed tenure of office, as a right granted to the holder of a position (usu. in a university or school) after a probationary period and protecting him against dismissal under most circumstances.

1957 V. Nabokov *Pnin* vi. 139 Pnin, who had no life tenure at Waindell, would be forced to leave—unless some other literature-and-language Department agreed to adopt him. *Ibid.* 167 'Naturally, I am expecting that I will get tenure at last,' said Pnin rather slyly. 'I am now Assistant Professor nine years.' **1976** *National Observer* (U.S.) 31 July 8/2 Idaho tried to abolish tenure a year ago, but the teachers' lobby was so strong the bill was defeated. **1981** *Listener* 5 Feb. 166/3 Can universities in a time of declining resources still preserve tenure in all its old form?

4. b. In sense 1 c above, as *tenure decision, member, system*; *tenure-heavy* adj.; **tenure track** *U.S.*, an employment structure whereby the holder of a post is guaranteed consideration for eventual tenure, usu. within a stated number of years.

1978 *Chron. Higher Educ.* 2 Oct. 8/3 Some 1,000 complaints of unfair tenure decisions his organization handles each year. **1979** *Yale Alumni Mag.* Apr. 13/1 Faculties are becoming increasingly tenure-heavy. **1960** J. J. Corson *Governance of Colleges & Universities* v. 101 In some institutions only the tenure members of the faculty will be privileged to participate in the school faculty. **1971** *Nature* 31 Dec. 502/2 The tenure system simply allows dead wood to remain in the university. **1979** *Ibid.* 4 Oct. p. xix/1 (Advt.), Two-year appointment with the possibility of tenure track. **1981** *Washington Post* 2 Jan. B16/4 People get into the feeling that they are on a tenure track and that they are unshakeable.

tenured (te·niŭɹd), *a.* Chiefly *U.S.* [f. prec. + -ed[2].] Of an official position, usu. one in a university or school: carrying a guarantee of permanent employment until retirement. Of a teacher, lecturer, etc.: having guaranteed tenure of office.

1969 *Guardian* 24 May 1/6 Left-wing professors, whose only protection is tenured appointment. **1970** 'A. Cross' *Poetic Justice* I. iv. 62 What does she look like?.. I thought I knew all the tenured English faculty. **1975** *Nature* 25 Dec. 653/2 A growing number of French scientists have found themselves having to work on short-term contracts, as tenured posts have dried up. **1976** *Maclean's Mag.* 27 Dec. 46/1 A board's right to fire any teacher, probationary or tenured, who violates the moral principles [etc.].

Hence (as a back-formation) **te·nure** *v. trans.*, to provide (someone) with a tenured post.

1975 *Times Lit. Suppl.* 13 June 639/1 How you propose to recruit, train, tenure and retire faculty [*sc.* in an American university]. **1983** *N.Y. Times* 23 Oct. I. 35/1 We have 22 women who were tenured by this department as a result of evaluations that said they could do the job.

tenuto, *a.* and *adv.* Add: (Examples.) Also *transf.*

1762 Sterne *Tr. Shandy* VI. xi. 50 What *Yorick* could mean by the words *lentamente,—tenutè* [sic],—*grave,*—and sometimes *adagio,*—as applied to theological compositions..I dare not venture to guess. **1801** Busby *Dict. Mus., Tenuto,* or *Ten.* (Ital.), a word signifying that the notes are to be sustained, or held on. **1931** D. F. Tovey in Tovey & Craxton *Beethoven Pianoforte Sonatas* (Associated Board of Royal Schools of Music) III. 69/2 *Bars* 1–4.—The *forte* is a matter of string-tone and cantabile... Express the *tenuto* marks without hard accent, and see that in bar 3 the *piano* does not come too soon. **1975** *Gramophone* Nov. 839/1 In the *Meistersinger* piece I..like lots of notes played more *tenuto.*

B. *sb.* Pl. *tenutos.* A note or chord played *tenuto.*

1966 in *Random House Dict.* **1976** *Gramophone* Feb. 1349/3, I should have preferred him not to linger with so pronounced a tenuto on each bar in the bassoon solo. **1977** *Ibid.* Feb. 1279/2 He allows himself few of the momentary tenutos which have become a natural part of phrasing Franck melodies. **1982** *Guardian Weekly* 25 Apr. 20 Variations (with many tenutos Elgar never dreamed of).

Teochew, Teo-chew (tī:o tʃiū·). Also **Teo-chieu, Teochiu, Tiuchiu.** [A place-name in Swatow Chinese, = Putonghua *Cháozhōu.*] (A member of) a people of the Swatow district of Kwangtung in southern China; the dialect spoken by this people. Also *attrib.*

1893 J. D. Ball *Things Chinese* (ed. 2) 229 By..1891 there were 43,791 Teo Chews in the Straits Settlements: Teo Chews is the term applied generally to them in that part of the country, while Hoklo is the name by which they are generally known by the Cantonese speakers in China; the former name being derived from the Departmental city Ch'ao Chao fú (in the local dialect Tíú Chíú fú, or Teo Chew fu). **1927** in R. J. H. Sidney *In Brit. Malaya To-Day* xii. 144 Trouble had been brewing between Hok-kiens and the Teo-chews for some time. **1962** *B.B.C. Handbk.* 109 Adaptations..in the following languages: Chibemba,..Teochew. **1966** M. Freedman *Chinese Lineage & Society* iii. 95 People will assume for all Hakka or Hokkien or Cantonese or Tiuchiu that [etc.]. **1970** M. Pereira *Pigeon's Blood* xv. 164 He was speaking in the Teo-chieu dialect. **1979** *China Now* Jan.–Feb. 10/2 The Teochiu group from one district in Guangdong (Kwangtung) province.

teonanacatl (tī:ŏnanaka·t'l). [a. Nahuatl, f. *teotl* god + *nancatl* mushroom.] Any of several hallucinogenic fungi, esp. *Psilocybe mexicana,* found in Central America. Also *attrib.*

1875 H. H. Bancroft *Native Races Pacific States* II. 360 Among the ingredients used to make their drinks more intoxicating the most powerful was the *teonanacatl,* 'flesh of God', a kind of mushroom which excited the passions. **1915** *Jrnl. Heredity* VII. 294/2 The writer has sought diligently for a fungus having the properties attributed to the *teonanacatl.* **1940** *Amer. Anthropologist* XLII. 439 The identity of teonanacatl was unknown for three centuries. **1953** J. Ramsbottom *Mushrooms & Toadstools* vi. 49 The Aztecs and Chichimecas were the earliest recorders of this teonanacatl. **1966** *Listener* 14 July 47/1 Another Mexican fantasy-producing drug that is used in religious ceremonial comes from the teonanacatl mushroom. **1975** [see *psilocin].

tepa (tī·pă). *Chem.* Also **TEPA.** [f. *t*ri*e*thylene *p*hosphor*a*mide.] An organophosphorus compound, $PO(N(CH_2)_2)_3$, used as an insect sterilant and formerly in the treatment of cancer.

1953 *Cancer* VI. 140/2 These observations justify the continuation of studies of the action of tepa in advanced cancer. **1963** *New Scientist* 13 June 603/2 More than 3½ million flies..had been sexually sterilised by dipping their pupae in a 5 per cent solution of tepa. **1973** J. J. McKelvey *Man against Tsetse* iii. 196 [Experimenters] tried to eradicate tsetse from an area in Rhodesia by sterilizing male flies with..tepa.

‖ **tepache** (tepæ·tʃe). [Mexican Sp., ad. Nahuatl *tepiatl.*] Any of several Mexican drinks of varying degrees of fermentation, typically made with pineapple, water, and brown sugar.

1926 D. H. Lawrence *Mornings in Mexico* (1927) 42 *Tepache* is a fermented drink of pineapple rinds and brown sugar. **1930** R. Macaulay *Staying with Relations* xix. 273, I tried for a drink of Mexicali and only got tepache. **1983** M. Gorman *Cooking with Fruit* III. 188 Tepache..is an old Mexican household fruit drink... It is a simple mixture that uses 1 pineapple.

tepal. Delete *rare*[−0] and add: [ad. F. *tépale* (A. P. de Candolle *Organographie Végétale* (1827) I. III. ii. 503).] A segment of a perianth which is not divided into a corolla and a calyx.

1840 B. Kingdon tr. *A. P. de Candolle's Veget. Organogr.* II. ii. 90 It is well to retain for these doubtful cases of a single envelope a particular name... Following the analogy of the terms sepals and petals, I propose..the name of Tepals. **1939** *Rep. Bot. Soc. Brit. Isles* XII. 120 It is proposed to refer to them [*sc.* the perianth segments of *Rumex*] as Inner and Outer Perianth Segments, or Tepals. **1951** G. H. M. Lawrence *Taxon. Vascular Plants* II. 413 Perianth..generally undifferentiated into corolla and calyx, and when so the segments termed tepals. **1968** A. Cronquist *Evol. & Classification Flowering Plants* iii. 87 The tepals of the more primitive angiosperm families are modified leaves. **1972** *Jrnl. R. Hort. Soc.* XCVII. 336 Because magnolia flowers usually have no distinction between petals and sepals the term tepal has been generally accepted for these floral parts.

tepary (te·pări). Also **tepari.** [Origin unknown.] In full, *tepary bean.* An annual legume, *Phaseolus acutifolius,* native to southwestern North America, or a cultivated plant belonging to a variety developed from it and resistant to drought; also, the seed of a plant of this kind.

1912 G. F. Freeman *Southwestern Beans* 582 The name tepary or tepari (Spanish) originated from the Papago. **1912** K. S. Lumholtz *New Trails in Mexico* 318 He had cooked bones of mountain-sheep with tépari beans for us. **1925** K. Bryan *Papago Country* 354 The beans known as tépari..are said to be so resistant to drought that the plants may wither three successive times and then, if enough rain comes, mature a crop. **1942** Castetter & Bell *Pima & Papago Indian Agric.* 92 The cultivated tepary bean antedates the coming of the white man in the southwest. *Ibid.* 191 The Papago made only one planting of teparies. **1972** Y. Lovelock *Vegetable Bk.* I. 56 The Texas or tepary bean..grows wild and is much cultivated in Mexico and the adjoining states of the U.S.

tepee. Add: Also † **teebee, tepe, ti pee; tipi** (sometimes preferred). **1.** (Earlier and later examples.) In extended uses, applied to a similar structure used by peoples of other parts of the world, as a child's toy, or for camping.

1743 J. Isham in *Publ. Hudson's Bay Record Soc.* (1949) XII. 45 A tent Build ti pee. **1847** G. W. Featherstonhaugh *Canoe Voyage* I. xxx. 338 Here, also, were their spring teebees, which they inhabit at that season. **1849** M. H. Eastman *Dahcotah* p. xxii, The messenger enters the wigwam (or *teepee,* as the houses of the Sioux are called) of the juggler. **1910** *Encycl. Brit.* XIV. 469/1 The skin tents or tipis of many of the Plains peoples. **1959** A. Moorehead *No Room in Ark* ix. 211 I liked the Dinka villages... They looked like Red Indian encampments of a century or two ago: tall teepees made of grass and arranged in a rough circle on the bank. **1960** D. Jenness *Indians of Canada* (ed. 5) vii. 90 The Plains' area was the home of the tipi, a tent of buffalo hide stretched around a conical framework formed by fourteen to eighteen long poles, whose points radiated like a funnel above the peak. **1970** *New Yorker* 12 Dec. 138/2 A six-and-a-half-foot tepee costs $25 [in a toy-shop]. **1974** N. Gordimer *Conservationist* 42 The newly-ploughed field, where the mealie stalks are piled into tepees. **1976** *Billings* (Montana) *Gaz.* 2 July 8-A/1 (Advt.), You'll love the weekend activities in store for you at four nearby KOA Kampgrounds. All you need to take is your family or friends, sleeping bags and food. The Tepee or Tent will be waiting for you to move right in and there's a grill for cooking.

2. *attrib.* and *Comb.*, as *tepee cloth, cover, pole, trail*; *tepee-like* adj.; **tepee ring** (see quot.).

1877 *Rep. Indian Affairs* (U.S.) 50 Tepee cloth should be discontinued, and..log or frame houses should be substituted. **1890** E. Custer *Following Guidon* 6 The hides were dressed for robes or tepee covers. **1925** *Blackw. Mag.* May 658/1 There were three large tepee-like tents. **1897** J. W. Tyrrell *Across Sub-Arctics of Canada* 68 Instead of Indians, [we] found only old forsaken 'tepee' poles and blackened fire-places. **1899** Tepee pole [in Dict.]. **1956** D. Leechman *Native Tribes of Canada* 10 We find.. on the prairies, tipi rings, circles of stones that once were used to hold down the edges of the skin tents. **1869** *Amer. Naturalist* II. 648 [We] follow upon the dim road or the tepe trail over the broad prairie.

tephigram (te·figræm). *Meteorol.* [f. TE(E *sb.*[1] (*T* being a symbol for temperature) + *PHI (ϕ being a symbol for entropy) + -GRAM.] A diagram in which one axis represents temperature and another potential temperature (as a measure of entropy), used to represent the thermodynamic state of the atmosphere at different heights.

[*c* **1925** N. SHAW *Sel. Meteorol. Papers* (1955) 226/2, I have found the representation known to engineers as a θ, ϕ (temperature-entropy) diagram (or, as I shall call it here, a tϕ diagram) has the advantage of being..more expressive than the direct pressure-temperature diagram.] **1929** W. J. HUMPHREYS *Physics of Air* (ed. 2) xv. 259 Tephigram... It is convenient, as developed by Sir Napier Shaw and his colleagues, to plot values on a temperature-entropy diagram. *Ibid.* 261 Figure 77 is a tephigram..of a balloon sounding. **1938** *Nature* 29 Oct. 804/1 Daily tephigrams based on aeroplane soundings constitute the most valuable items in forecasting..clearing or persistence of cloud. **1969** *Ibid.* 11 Oct. 170/1 The uniformity of weather conditions over the region in question justified our taking these tephigrams as representative of the state of the atmosphere over the area.

tephillim, -in, *sb. pl.* Add: Now usu. in form **tefillin.** (Later examples.)

1865 *Chambers's Encycl.* VII. 519/2 Certain strips of parchment, inscribed with certain passages from the Scripture.., enclosed in small cases, and fastened to the forehead and the left arm (*Tefillin*)..in use with the Jews..are..called in the New Testament phylacteries. **1967** C. POTOK *Chosen* I. iii. 61, I got the tefillin and prayer book out of the drawer of the night table and began to put on the tefillin. *Ibid.*, When I finished praying, I took off the tefillin and put them and the prayer book back in the drawer. **1978** J. SACKS in P. Moore *Man, Woman, & Priesthood* iii. 33 They [*sc.* women] are not obliged, as men are, to put on the phylacteries (*tefillin*) or the fringed garment (*tzitzit*).

tephra (te·frǎ). *Geol.* [ad. Sw. *tefra* (S. Thórarinsson 1944, in *Geografiska Annaler* XXVI. 114), f. Gr. τέφρα ash.] Dust and rock fragments that have been ejected into the air by a volcanic eruption. Freq. *attrib.*

1944 *Geografiska Annaler* XXVI. 210 The author suggests (*volcanic*) *ash* or (better) *tephra* as a collective term for all clastic ejectamenta. **1970** *Nature* 25 July 335/1 The maximum thickness of the tephra layer was 7 cm at 15 km from the volcano. **1972** *Nat. Geographic* CXLI. 718/2 Commercial interests are removing this layer—known as tephra—since it makes a highly cohesive and waterproof mortar, serves as an insulating material, and constitutes an important component of cement. **1973** *Nature* 9 Feb. 372/2 Because of its close vicinity to the eruption the town was threatened by tephra fall. **1979** *Sci. Amer.* Dec. 134/2 The cloud of tephra and gas rises high above the volcano, and particles in it are carried downwind, producing a rain of tephra that forms a deposit called a tephra mantle.

tephrochronology (te:frokronǫ·lǒdʒi). Also **tephra-**. [ad. Sw. *tefrokronologi* (S. Thórarinsson 1944, in *Geografiska Annaler* XXVI. 6), f. as prec.: see CHRONOLOGY.] The dating of volcanic eruptions and other events by studying layers of tephra. Hence **te:phrochronolo·gical** *a.*

1944 S. THÓRARINSSON in *Geografiska Annaler* XXVI. 204 As an international term to designate a geological chronology based on the measuring, interconnecting, and dating of volcanic ash layers in soil profiles the author suggests the term *Tephrochronology*. *Ibid.* (*heading*) Tephrochronological studies in Iceland. **1976** P. FRANCIS *Volcanoes* v. 178 The use of successive pumice or ash deposits in building up a history of the eruptive activity in an area is known as tephrachronology. **1979** *Nature* 25 Oct. 642/1 The tephrochronology of these ashes is well documented, but volcanological interpretations have seldom been attempted. **1979** *Sci. Amer.* Dec. 132/1 A volcano produces successive showers of tephra that fall throughout the surrounding countryside, forming layers that constitute a tephrochronological record of the volcano's activity.

tepid, *a.* **b.** (Later examples of the word applied to persons.)

1926 *Scribner's Mag.* Sept. 259/2 Her smile said that pastels were thin things for tepid people. **1941** A. CHRISTIE *Evil under Sun* x. 197 Some tepid little man, vain and sensitive—the kind of man who broods.

tepidarium. Add: Also applied to a similar room in a Turkish bath.

1969 J. WAINWRIGHT *Take-Over Men* ii. 27, I followed him..into the warm room (the *Tepidarium*)..into the hot room (the *Calidarium*); and finally..into the *Laconicum.* **1975** *Daily Colonist* (Victoria, B.C.) 5 Oct. 4/3 When you are gleaming horribly [with sweat], you go into the tepidarium.

teporingo (tepori·ŋgo). [a. Amer. Sp.] = *volcano rabbit* s.v. *VOLCANO *sb.* 3.

1969 J. FISHER et al. *Red Bk.* 54/2 The *teporingo*.. exists only on the middle slopes of Popocatépetl and Ixtacihuatl and some of the nearby ridges. **1972** [see *park ranger* s.v. *PARK *sb.* 7]. **1980** *Listener* 17 July 90/3 The teporingo appears to be a kind of Mexican rabbit. There aren't many left.

‖ **teppan-yaki** (te:panyā·ki). [Jap.] A Japanese dish consisting of meat, fish, (or both) fried with vegetables on a hot steel plate which forms the centre of the table at which the diners are seated.

1970 P. & J. MARTIN *Japanese Cooking* 80 (*heading*) Teppan-yaki steak. *Ibid.*, Teppan-yaki means literally 'iron plate grilling'. This type of cooking, too, is usually done in front of guests on a large, rectangular griddle. *Ibid.* 81 Teppan-yaki duck. **1972** *Mainichi Daily News* (Japan) 6 Nov. 11/6 (Advt.), A variety of foods including Teppan-yaki (meats roasted before your eyes on hot steel plates). **1979** *United States 1980/81* (Penguin Travel Guides) 73 This thoughtfully designed Japanese restaurant has separate dining rooms for teppan-yaki, sukiyaki, and tempura.

tequila (tekī·lǎ). Also **tequela, tequilla.** [a. Mexican Sp., f. the name of a town which is one of the centres of its production.] **a.** A gin-like Mexican spirit made by distilling the fermented sap of a maguey, *Agave tequilana*; cf. MESCAL.

1849 J. GREGG *Diary & Lett.* (1944) II. 317 So celebrated has this place become, for the manufacture of superior *mezcal*, that that taken from here is known by the name of *Tequila*. **1894** *Harper's Mag.* Feb. 351/2 Between various cigarettes, the last drink of tequela, and the drying of our clothes, we passed the time. **1926** [see *MESCAL 1]. **1941** B. SCHULBERG *What makes Sammy Run?* vii. 110 Burning my stomach with *enchillada* and my brain with more *tequilla*. **1953** W. BURROUGHS *Junkie* (1972) xiii. 129 Every morning when I woke up, I washed down benzedrine, sanicin, and a piece of hop with black coffee and a shot of tequila. **1958** P. HIGHSMITH *Game for Living* (1959) ii. 22 Theodore heard..liquor being poured into a glass, and he knew it would be Lelia's yellowish tequila. **1969** J. MANDER *Static Society* vii. 196 Fuentes had been initiating me into the art of drinking Mexican *tequila* (with salt and lemon). **1977** *Playgirl* May 124/1 For the woman whose liquor larder extends beyond beer and wine, tequila is now a necessity.

b. *attrib.* and *Comb.*, as *tequila sour*; *tequila-based* adj.; **tequila plant,** the maguey from the sap of which tequila is made; **tequila sunrise,** a name given to cocktails containing tequila and grenadine.

1977 T. HEALD *Just Desserts* vii. 156 He was drinking a tequila-based cocktail. **1979** P. THEROUX *Old Patagonian Express* iii. 52, I saw a field of upright swords. It might have been sisal, but more likely was the tequila plant. **1966** T. PYNCHON *Crying of Lot 49* iii. 59 'Who's your client?' asked Metzger, holding out a tequila sour. **1965** O. A. MENDELSOHN *Dict. Drink & Drinking* 336 *Tequila Sunrise*, mixed drink of tequila, lemon juice, grenadine and cinnamon liqueur. **1976** *Daily Tel.* (Colour Suppl.) 11 June 42/3 A Tequila Sunrise has become the 'in' drink at many ski resorts and single bars. It is tequila and orange juice, with half an ounce of grenadine poured on top to filter dramatically down through the drink.

Tequistlatec (teki·stlǎtek). Also **Tequistlate·ca, Tequistlate·co.** [Native name.] (A member of) an Indian people of south-east Oaxaca, Mexico; also, the language of this people. Hence **Tequistlate·can,** the Tequistlatec language or (later) the linguistic family of which it is the principal member; also *attrib.*

1891 D. G. BRINTON *American Race* 112 Quite to the south, in the mountains of Oaxaco and Guerrero, the Tequistlatecas, usually known by the meaningless term, Chontales, belong to this stem. *Ibid.* 148 The only specimen of their idiom which I have obtained is a vocabulary of 23 words... Provisionally, however, I give it the name of *Tequistlatecan*, from the principal village of the tribe. **1902** *Encycl. Brit.* XXV. 374/1 [Linguistic families of Middle America] Tehuantepecan, Isthmus; Tequistlatecan, Oax. **1915** A. L. KROEBER in *Univ. Calif. Publ. Amer. Archaeol. & Ethnol.* XI. 279 (*title*) Serian, Tequistlatecan, and Hokan. **1929** E. SAPIR in *Encycl. Brit.* V. 140/2 *Hokan* proper, which includes Seri (coast of Sonora), Yuman (in Lower California) and Tequistlateco or Chontal (coast of Oaxaca). **1965** *Language* XLI. 305 Seri and Tequistlatec, both separate branches of Hokan. *Ibid.*, The Tequistlatecan form seems at least as similar to the Proto-Palaihnihan as the Proto-Shastan. **1974** *Encycl. Brit. Micropædia* IX. 894/1 Tequistlatec, Hokan-speaking Middle American Indians of the Sierra Madre del Sur of Oaxaca, Mex.

ter (teɹ), repr. vulg. and dial. pronunc. of To *prep.*, *conj.*, *adv.* Cf. *ORTER; *OUGHTA, OUGHTER; *USETA, USETER.

1867 *Harper's New Monthly Mag.* Feb. 274/2 This yere is Colonel N—., who wants ter know yer. **1895** W. J. LOCKE *At Gate of Samaria* v. 49 She's bloomin' well got ter. **1926** J. K. STRECKER in J. F. Dobie *Rainbow in Morning* (1965) 61 Ef he sting yo, yo sho gwine ter die. **1934** [see *quarter-turn* s.v. *QUARTER *sb.* 30]. **1944** E. THOMPSON *Robert Bridges* i. 7 One he used in print..that of the cockney who saw on his medicine chart the words *ter die*, and fled in terror to escape his scheduled destruction. **1952** [see *KIN var. CAN *v.*[1]]. **1976** *Southern Even. Echo* (Southampton) 13 Nov. 2/7 You gence wan' anyfing ter drink?

ter-. Add: **2. b. termole·cular** *a.*, involving three molecules; **terpo·lymer,** a polymer whose molecule is composed of three different monomers; hence **terpo:lymeriza·tion,** polymerization in which three different monomers go to form a terpolymer.

1901 *Jrnl. Chem. Soc.* LXXIX. I. 229 Even in darkness the action is termolecular. **1931** MAASS & STEACIE *Introd. Princ. Physical Chem.* xii. 199 The reaction between nitric oxide and chlorine is an example of a termolecular reaction. **1974** *Nature* 19 Apr. 666/2 The dimer must be formed by a termolecular collision. **1961** WEBSTER, Terpolymer. **1967** *New Scientist* 18 May 423/3 Terpolymers (e.g. ABS plastics) are in use already. **1975** *Sci. Amer.* Oct. 54/3 The three products that proved to be most broadly successful are generically classified as a urethane, a dimethyl silicone and a styrene acrylonitrile terpolymer. **1964** *Jrnl. Polymer Sci.* A. II. 2740 Penultimate effects in copolymerization can be determined more precisely from composition studies in terpolymerization experiments than in binary polymerizations. **1976** H. SAWADA *Thermodynamics of Polymerization* ix. 262 (*caption*) Heat of terpolymerization for the acrylonitrile-methyl methacrylate-styrene system.

tera- (te·rǎ). *prefix.* [f. Gr. τέρας monster.] Prefixed to the names of units to form the names of units 10^{12} (one million million) times larger (symbol T), as *terabit* [*BIT *sb.*[4]], *-electron-volt*, *-hertz*, *-pascal*, *-second*, *-volt*, *-watt* (hence *-watt-hour*, *-year*).

[**1947** *Compt. Rend. de la 14ème Conf.* (Union Internat. de Chimie) 115 The following prefixes to abbreviations for the names of units should be used to indicate the specified multiples or sub-multiples of these units: T tira- 10^{12} ×.] **1951** *Symbols, Signs & Abbreviations* (R. Soc.) 15 Tera (× 10^{12}) T. **1971** *New Scientist* 8 July 80/2 A bigger machine..which will be available next year, will have a 50-terabit memory with only slightly slower cycle time of 100 nanoseconds. **1974** *Sci. Amer.* Feb. 82/2 An energy of 1,000 GeV (one teraelectron-volt, or TeV) does not seem an impossible goal. **1970** *McGraw-Hill Yearbk. Sci. & Technol.* 233/1 M. A. Duguay and coworkers..tuned a mode-locked He-Ne laser..from −45 to +45 GHz, about the central optical frequency of 473·61 terahertz. **1980** *Nature* 21 Feb. 715/1 In relatively simple experiments laser-driven shock waves can be used to study the propagation of shocks in solids for shock pressures up to terapascals (1 TPa = 10^7 bar = 10^{13} dyne cm^{-2}). **1969** *Proc. Geol. Soc.* Aug. 142 Alternatively the second of time may prove to be a more convenient unit as recommended by S.I., thus 1 million years (m.y.) = 31·557 tera seconds (Ts). **1975** *Sci. Amer.* Feb. 40/2 A development program looking toward the creation of a proton beam of about 1,000 GeV, or one teravolt (TeV). **1970** *Britannica Bk. of Year* 322/2 It had an output of 4 trillion watts (4 terawatts). **1972** *Physics Bull.* Mar. 175/2 The terawatt carbon dioxide laser may not be far away. **1979** *Internat. Atomic Energy Agency Bull.* Jan. 7 Let us consider two scenarios which would lead to a total primary energy consumption rate of 50 terawatts (50 000 000 MW) at the end of the next century. **1979** *Times* 11 Dec. 18 The American Department of Energy, Dr Musgrove says,.. could economically produce 500 tera-watt-hours (500 million mega-watt-hours) of electricity. **1980** *Sci. Amer.* Sept. 111/1 From the base year of the IIASA study (1975) to 2030 the total primary-energy consumption rate is projected to rise from 8.2 terawatt-years per year to 36 terawatt-years per year in the high-growth scenario and to 22 terawatt-years per year in the low-growth one.

terai. Add: Also **tarai.** (Examples in the lit. sense (see etym.) and earlier examples of sense in Dict.)

1852 T. SMITH *Narr. Five Years' Residence Nepaul* I. ii. 56 The Terai, or Turay, or Turyanee, is a long strip or belt of low level-land. **1860** W. H. RUSSELL *My Diary in India* II. ii. 31 This gentleman was one of the unhappy refugees who was sheltered in the terai..and, although he saved his life, he was struck down by terai fever. **1911** *Encycl. Brit.* XIX. 379/1 The low alluvial land of the tarai is well adapted for cultivation, and is, so to speak, the granary of Nepal. **1918** W. BEEBE *Jungle Peace* (1919) xi. 268 The *terai* jungles of Garhwal, the tree-ferns of Pahang, and the mighty *moras*..will stand in silvery silence. **1954** O. H. K. SPATE *India & Pakistan* xviii. 496 Originally the terai covered a zone perhaps 50–60 miles wide... Much of this has been so altered by settlement that the true terai is now confined to a relatively narrow strip. **1981** V. POWELL *Flora Annie Steel* xii. 104 To soothe her fever—terai fever as it was then called—she was given hashish.

1888 KIPLING *Under Deodars* 43 Mrs. Boulte put on a big terai hat. *Ibid.* 73 She was wearing an unclean Terai with the elastic under her chin. **1894** *County Gentlemen's Catal.* 155/2 Soft drab terai double felt hats.

terakihi, var. *TARAKIHI.

‖ **terakoya** (terakō·ya). *Japanese Hist.* [Jap., = temple school, f. *tera* temple + *ko* child(ren) + *ya* place.] In the Japanese feudal period, a private elementary school of a kind established orig. in the Buddhist temples.

1909 D. KIKUCHI *Japanese Education* ii. 33 The name *Terakoya*, or 'House for the Children of the Temple', given to elementary schools up to the beginning of the present era. **1911** *Encycl. Brit.* XV. 220/1 They [*sc.* Buddhist priests] organized schools at the temples.., and at these *tera-koya*..lessons in ethics, calligraphy, reading and etiquette were given to the sons of samurai and even to youths of the mercantile and manufacturing classes. **1938** D. T. SUZUKI *Zen Buddhism & its Influence on Japanese Culture* I. v. 106 The *Terakoya* system was the only popular educational institution during the feudal ages of Japan. **1965** W. SWAAN *Jap. Lantern* xii. 143 The *terakoya*, or 'temple schools' attached to the monasteries, provide the only institution of popular education. **1974** *Encycl. Brit. Macropædia* VI. 342/2 As time passed, some *terakoya* used parts of the houses of commoners as classrooms.

terap (tĕra·p). Also **tarap.** [a. Malay.] An evergreen tree, *Artocarpus elasticus*, of the family Moraceæ, native to Malaysia and closely related to the bread-fruit tree, also, the large edible fruit of this tree or its fibrous bark, which is used to make string or cloth. Also *attrib.*

1839 T. J. NEWBOLD *Straits of Malacca* II. ix. 119 The cloth that encircles their loins is made from the fibrous bark of the Terap tree. **1900** W. W. SKEAT *Malay Magic* v. 225 A string of *tĕrap* bark to tie up the rice that is cut first. **1913** L. W. W. GUDGEON *Brit. N. Borneo* x. 69 The fruit falls in all directions. If it is 'durian' or 'tarap', the size and weight of which are considerable, the Dusuns stand clear. **1935** I. H. BURKILL *Dict. Econ. Products Malay Penin.* I. 248 Every one knows the name 'tĕrap' which is applied to *A[rtocarpus] elastica* by Malays and Sakai. **1940** E. J. H. CORNER *Wayside Trees of Malaya* I. 654 The *Terap* is, undoubtedly, the commonest and best known of our wild species of Artocarpus. **1964** M. E. D. POORE in Wang Gungwu *Malaysia* I. ii. 48 Such occur in..many species of terap or breadfruit (*Artocarpus*).

terato-, comb. form repr. Gr. τέρας, τερατ- monster: **te:ratocarcino·ma** *Path.*, a malignant teratoma containing carcinomatous elements, occurring chiefly in the testis.

1946 FRIEDMAN & MOORE in *Military Surgeon* XCIX. 573 A new term, 'teratocarcinoma', is proposed for the large group of pleomorphic tumours in which both differentiated teratoid structures and histologically malignant elements were present. **1958** *Jrnl. Amer. Med. Assoc.* 28 June 1066/2 A testicular teratocarcinoma occurring in a 35-year-old man was treated initially by surgery. **1975** [see *TERATOMA]. **1979** *Sci. Amer.* Apr. 87/1 As long as the tumors contain embryonal carcinoma cells they continue to grow; such tumors are malignant and are referred to as teratocarcinomas.

teratogen (teræ·tŏdʒĕn, te·rătodʒĕn). *Med.* [f. *TERATO- + -GEN.] An agent or factor which causes malformation of the developing embryo.

1959 *Jrnl. Chronic Dis.* X. 125 Present knowledge of the mechanisms of teratogenic action is meager... The ultimate action of all teratogens seems to be to produce either cell death or an alteration in the rate of cell growth. **1970** G. LEACH *Biocrats* vi. 141 Animals are rarely good models for men when it comes to testing the effects of drugs and other teratogens on the foetus. **1978** *Jrnl. R. Soc. Med.* LXXI. 668 The patient should be seen earlier in pregnancy to help her avoid potential teratogens.

teratogenesis. Add: Also **te:ratogeni·city**, teratogenic property.

1959 *Jrnl. Chronic Dis.* X. 117 More than 20 closely related azo dyes have been tested for teratogenicity in my laboratory. **1964** *Listener* 20 Feb. 311/1 It is apparent that many of the tests that can, in our present state of knowledge, be applied to new drugs to attempt to produce teratogenicity, are neither meaningful nor justifiable. **1981** *Internat. Jrnl. Environmental Stud.* XVII. 10/2 The weak teratogenicity and growth retardative propensity of such a ubiquitous drug as aspirin.

teratologist. b. (Examples.)

1844 *London & Edin. Monthly Jrnl. Med. Sci.* IV. 484 Teratologists are now agreed in referring a considerable number of malformations by defect to the occurrence of an interruption..of natural fœtal development. **1908** *Jrnl. Morphol.* XIX. 51 Teratologists are inclined to read these facts in favor of the germinal origin of monsters, which may even be hereditary. **1973** *Daily Tel.* 13 Jan. 16 Many distinguished obstetricians, pathologists, paediatricians, teratologists and editors were reluctant to accept my hypothesis that thalidomide did cause abnormalities.

teratoma. Substitute for def.: A tumour, esp. of the gonads, characteristically formed of numerous distinct tissues and believed usually to arise from germ cells or their precursors. (Earlier and later examples.)

1879 *Amer. Jrnl. Med. Sci.* LXXVII. 91 (*heading*) Extirpation of teratoma; or, teratoid tumor. *Ibid.* 93 To such tumors Virchow has applied the term teratoma. **1906** [see *LANGHANS]. **1948** R. A. WILLIS *Path. of Tumours* lxi. 940 A teratoma is a true tumour or neoplasm composed of multiple tissues of kinds foreign to the part in which it arises. **1975** *Nature* 6 Nov. 12/1 Teratomas and teratocarcinomas are rare tumours which arise in the gonads, and contain a whole variety of differentiated tissues of ectodermal, mesodermal and endodermal origin (such as skin, nerve, muscle, cartilage, gut and lung), mixed together in a disorganised mass. **1979** *Sci. Amer.* Apr. 87/1 When all the embryonal cells differentiate into various kinds of normal tissue, the tumors stop growing: they are benign and are usually referred to simply as teratomas.

teratomatous *a.* (examples).

1893 *Index-Catal. Library Surgeon-General's Office, U.S. Army* XIV. 896/1 (*heading*) Tumors (teratomatous). **1948** MARTIN & HYNES *Clinical Endocrinol.* ix. 193 A few arrhenoblastomata have been teratomatous, containing cartilage and other tissues. **1962** *Punch* 7 Nov. 658/2 A teratomatous growth of mixed tissues, probably of only low malignancy.

tercio, tertio. Delete 'Now only *Hist.*' and add: **1.** (Later example.) Also used of Spanish units in mod. times.

1938 C. S. FORESTER *Ship of Line* xvii. 236, I am Colonel Juan Claros, of the third tercio of Catalan migueletes... That is to say a thousand men. **1957** P. KEMP *Mine were of Trouble* ii. 19 A Tercio in the sixteenth century was a Regiment of Spanish infantry. The Spanish Foreign Legion is also called *El Tercio*... But the Requetés in the Civil War also organized their fighting units into *tercios*, each approximately of battalion strength. **1965** C. D. EBY *Siege of Alcázar* i. 14 The crack Tercios of the Foreign Legion.

2. *Bull-fighting.* **a.** One of the three parts of a bullfight. **b.** Each of the three concentric circles into which a bullring is technically divided.

1932 E. HEMINGWAY *Death in Afternoon* 331 The bullfight is divided into three parts, the *tercio de varas*, that of the pic, *tercio de banderillas*, and *tercio del muerte* or third of death. **1932** R. CAMPBELL *Taurine Provence* iii. 68 The arena is divided into three areas—tablas, tercios, and medios. It is in the tercios, which extend from a third of the way to the centre until quite near the central area, that the bull is the best to deal with. **1962** J. STEWART tr. *J. Cousseau's Death of Miss Cunningham* 136 The final *tercio* was about to be sounded. **1967** MCCORMICK & MASCAREÑAS *Compl. Aficionado* i. 20 The luring of the bull,..and the ritual staining of the garments of the bridegroom with the bull's blood..aid us in comprehending both the origin of the tercio of the banderillas, and our response to that tercio.

Tercom (tɜ·ɪkɒm). [Abbrev. f. initial letters of ter*rain* con*tour* m*atching*.] A computerized system for controlling the flight path of a cruise missile which enables it to stay close to the ground.

1975 *Bull. Atomic Sci.* Apr. 13/2 Tercom—Terrain matching device—a system which enables a missile to hug the ground and follow a programmed path. **1980** R. L. DUNCAN *Brimstone* x. 261 The cruise missile would be guided by TERCOM—terrain contour matching.

Terek. For *Terekia cinerea* substitute *Xenus cinereus* and add: Also *Terek sandpiper*. (Later examples.)

1879 *Ibis* XXI. 152 The Terek Sandpiper arrived at our quarters [in Siberia] on the 8th of June. **1915** *Brit. Birds* IX. 69 Three Terek Sandpipers..were shot at Rye in the month of May, 1915. **1956** *Ibis* XCVIII. 161 The Terek Sandpiper thus becomes *Tringa terek* (Latham), the name *Tringa cinerea* being pre-occupied. **1982** *Times* 23 Mar. 10/5 Leicester Museum spent..£400 on a family of [stuffed] Terek sandpipers.

‖ **terem** (te·rĕm). *Russ. Hist.* [Russ., lit. 'tower'.] Secluded separate quarters for women.

1898 G. B. SHAW in *Sat. Rev.* 8 Jan. 42/2 The seclusion of Russian women in the Terem was one of the sacred institutions of his [*sc.* Peter the Great's] country. **1908** *Cambr. Mod. Hist.* V. xvii. 519 The boy soon felt cramped and stifled in the dim and close semi-religious atmosphere of Natalia's *terem*. **1929** S. RUNCIMAN *Emperor Romanus Lecapenus* i. 28 It has been customary to regard the gynaecum as a prison from which Byzantine women never emerged—an exact equivalent of the Russian terem, which most historians say derived from it, forgetting Russia's two and a half centuries of Mongol rule. **1943** E. M. ALMEDINGEN *Frossia* iv. 169 The maiden lived in her *terem*, its windows strictly latticed.

Terena (terē̆·nă). Also **Ter(r)eno.** (A member of) an Arawak group of South American Indians of the southern Mato Grosso in Brazil; the language of this group. Also *attrib.*

1891 D. G. BRINTON *American Race* 244 The Terenos.. are members of the Guaycuru stock of the Chaco. **1928** A. R. HAY *Indians of S. Amer. & Gospel* vi. 101 In the Terena tribe we have a typical group of forest Indians who are fast adopting civilized ways. **1932** P. RADIN *Indians of S. Amer.* xi. 204 No evidence exists for its presence [*sc.* class division] in any other of the continental Arawak tribes except the *Terreno*. **1946** *Internat. Jrnl. Amer. Linguistics* XII. 60/1 The basic unit of structure in Terena phonology is the syllable. **1952** E. FISCHER-JØRGENSEN in E. Hamp et al. *Readings in Linguistics II* (1966) 315 It is not at all rare to find particularly nasals entering into the category of phonemes never adjoining the vowel in clusters..; this is the case e.g. in Terena. **1960** *Word* XVI. 349 A phonemic analysis of Tereno establishes as full phonemes a bilabial nasal and an alveolar nasal. **1974** *Encycl. Brit. Macropædia* XVII. 125/1 The Terena..work on cattle breeding farms.

terephthalic, *a.* (Further examples.)

1964 N. G. CLARK *Mod. Org. Chem.* xxiii. 491 Terephthalic acid, after conversion to the dimethyl ester, is an important intermediate in the manufacture of 'Terylene'. **1971** D. POTTER *Brit. Eliz. Stamps* ii. 27 Lettalite B.3 or tere-phthalic acid became known as violet phosphor. **1973** *Materials & Technol.* VI. iv. 326 The starting materials for the manufacture of polyethylene terephthalate are ethylene glycol and terephthalic acid, both obtained from petroleum sources.

terephthalate (also stressed *terephtha·late*) (further examples).

1946, etc. [see *polyethylene terephthalate* s.v. *POLYETHYLENE a]. **1958** *Times Rev. Industry* Aug. 57/3 Mylar polyester film..is a polyester terephthalate film. **1973** *Materials & Technol.* VI. iv. 280 While other fibre-forming polyesters were prepared, none proved to be as satisfactory as the polyethylene terephthalate developed by Whinfield, and this has continued to dominate the commercial fibre-forming polyester field.

teres (te·rīz), *a.* and *sb.* *Anat.* [L.: see TERETE *a.*] **A.** *adj.* In *pronator teres*: a pronating muscle of the forearm that arises from the humerus and ulna, near the elbow, and is inserted into the radius. **B.** *sb.* [sc. *musculus*.] Either of two muscles arising from the shoulder blade and inserted into the upper part of the humerus: the *teres major* draws the humerus towards the body and rotates it inwards; the *teres minor* rotates it outwards and helps steady its head.

1713 W. CHESELDEN *Anat. Human Body* (ed. 3) II. iii. 59 Teres minor, is a small Muscle arising below the former [*sc.* infraspinatus] from the inferior Costa Scapulæ. *Ibid.*, Teres major, arises from the lower Angle of the Scapula. *Ibid.* 66 Pronator Teres, arises from the inner Apophysis of the Os Humeri, and upper and forepart of the Ulna. **1889** J. LEIDY *Elem. Treat. Human Anat.* (ed. 2) v. 295 The greater teres..contributes with the latissimus to form the posterior border of the axilla. **1979** *Sci. Amer.* Dec. 99/3 This feature seems to reflect the strong development in Neanderthals of the teres minor muscle. **1980** *Gray's Anat.* (ed. 36) v. 574/1 The pronator teres rotates the radius upon the ulna, turning the palm of the hand backwards.

tereu. (Later examples.)

1923 T. S. ELIOT *Waste Land* iii. 15 Twit twit twit Jug jug jug jug jug So rudely forc'd. Tereu. **1936** R. CAMPBELL *Mithraic Emblems* 125 Hear how it whistles 'jug, puff-puff, tereu' Better than any nightingale could do.

Tergal (tɜ·ɪgăl), *a.*[2] and *sb.* Also **tergal.** [a. F. *Tergal*, f. *tér-éphtalique* TEREPHTHALIC *a.* + *gal-lique* GALLIC *a.*[1]] A proprietary name for polyester fibre and fabrics. Cf. *TERITAL.

1954 *Trade Marks Jrnl.* 22 Dec. 1301/2 *Tergal*... Textile piece goods; bed and table covers, curtains; and household textile articles... Societe Rhodiaceta.., Paris VIIIe, France; manufacturers. **1955** *Official Gaz.* (U.S. Patent Office) 26 Apr. TM 192/1 *Tergal*... For..textile fabrics..of synthetic fibers, table cloths and napkins, bed sheets, blankets, and quilts. **1959** *Guardian* 16 Oct. 7/3 Loden or tergal or plaid lined. **1967** *Jane's Surface Skimmer Systems 1967–68* 7/1 The airflow is ducted to ten individual neoprene-coated tergal skirts. **1968** *Economist* 15 June 72/2 Rhone Poulenc had a French monopoly of nylon and terylene (tergal). **1973** 'D. RUTHERFORD' *Kick Start* i. 12 My dark blue Tergal trousers.

-teria (tīᵊ·riă), *suffix.* orig. and chiefly *U.S.* Also **-eteria.** [Derived from *CAFETERIA by analysis of its components as *café* + *-teria*.] A suffix used commercially to form the names of self-service retail or catering establishments.

1923 *Mod. Lang. Notes* XXXVIII. 188 Every one knows by this time that a cafeteria is a 'help-yourself' restaurant. Apparently in the popular mind the ending *-teria* or *-eteria* has come to indicate just such a process. **1929** *Amer. Speech* IV. 334 To the vast and growing progeny of 'cafeteria' may be added the name given to 'Maxwell's Vegetarian Healthateria', 35 West Van Buren Street, Chicago. **1941** [see *BURGER]. **1959** *Times* 27 Oct. 13/5 To the collection of *-teria* and *-toria* add 'Valeteria' and 'Washeteria'—in Cambridge, Massachusetts. **1965** *Listener* 2 Sept. 339/1 An Italian café-owner..has.. switched his sign from Pizzeria to Pie-teria.

Terital (te·rităl). Also **terital.** [a. It. *Terital*, f. *ter-eftalico* TEREPHTHALIC *a.* + *ital-iano* ITALIAN *a.*] A trade name for natural and synthetic (chiefly polyester) fibre, fabrics, and floor-coverings. Cf. *TERGAL.

A proprietary name in the U.S.

1960 *Guardian* 28 Sept. 8/6 Lilion, helion, terital and viscose are blended with wool in textiles by the high fashion houses. **1963** *Official Gaz.* (U.S. Patent Office) 4 June TM 31/2 Società Rhodiatoce S.p.A., Milan... *Terital*... For fabrics (obtained from natural or synthetic fibers). **1963** *Times* 11 June 19/1 Output of 'Rhodia' and 'Albene' yarns was maintained at the 1961 level, while production of 'Nailon' and 'Terital' increased considerably. **1972** *Guardian* 22 Aug. 9/1 See-through blouse.. made in terital which is non-crushable and drip-dry.

‖ **teriyaki** (teriyā·ki). [Jap., f. *teri* gloss, lustre + *yaki* roast.] A Japanese dish consisting of fish or meat marinated in soy sauce and broiled.

1962 M. DOI *Art of Japanese Cookery* 72 In *Teri-yaki*, rich sauce which gives a sheen to ingredients is used as seasoning. **1963** H. TANAKA *Pleasures of Japanese Cooking* iv. 76 Almost as popular as *yakitori* is *teriyaki*, usually fish marinated in a *shoyu* sauce, arranged on long skewers, and then broiled over charcoal. *Teriyaki* means 'glaze broiled'. **1972** A. FOWLES *Double Feature* i. 20 The predictable teriyaki dinner, more edible..than its infra-red mini-grilled BOAC counterpart. **1978** *Amer. Speech 1975* L. 304 The recipe, one of a number for Japanese dishes, calls for chicken livers marinated in teriyaki sauce, wrapped in bacon, and broiled.

terlinguaite (tɜ̄ɹli·ŋgwă,ɔit). *Min.* [f. *Terlingua*, name of the village in Texas where it was found + -ITE[1].] An oxychloride of mercury, Hg_2OCl, found as transparent or translucent yellow or greenish yellow monoclinic crystals (see also quot. 1900).

1900 H. W. TURNER in *Mining & Sci. Press* (San Francisco) 21 July 64/1 In addition to cinnabar, mercury occurs in the native form..and as yellow-green crystals. Prof. S. L. Penfield has identified the white coating as calomel or mercury chloride (Hg_2Cl_2), and the greenish crystals as an oxychloride of mercury, forming a new mineral species, for which I have suggested the name terlinguaite. **1903** A. J. MOSES in *Amer. Jrnl. Sci.* CLXVI. 259 Of the three possibly different substances to which the name terlinguaite has hitherto been applied we have.. 1st. The mineral here described. 2d. The undetermined rough yellow crystals mentioned in No. 5. 3d. The pulverulent yellow masses. *Ibid.*, Terlinguaite.—This name should be limited to the yellow monoclinic oxychloride of mercury here described. **1932** [see *MONTROYDITE]. **1964** *Mineral. Abstr.* XVI. 619/1 The ore deposit is in Upper Cretaceous liparites and tuffs [in Kamchatka, U.S.S.R.]. Brief descriptions..are given for native mercury, calomel, eglestonite, terlinguaite, and mosesite.

term, *sb.* Add: **II. 4. c.** *long-term, short-term* adjs.: see as main entries.

5. c. In *pl.* in phrases (esp. *to keep terms*) indicating that a person has attended the required number of lectures at a university, has been in residence for the period of time laid down in the statutes, and has satisfied the authorities in other statutory respects. *N.Z. colloq.*

1959 G. SLATTER *Gun in my Hand* 37 The Old Prof.. gave me 'terms' out of the kindness of his heart, but it was no use. **1962** M. K. JOSEPH *Pound of Saffron* ii. 38 You know the way he barks at you like a sergeant-major and then sees you don't miss terms.

III. 8. b. 3) *to come to terms*: also *fig.* (const. *with*), to reconcile oneself to, to become reconciled with; 7) *terms of reference*: the points referred to an individual or body of persons for decision or report; that which defines the scope of an inquiry.

3) **1923** J. B. PRIESTLEY *I for One* 235 The few [pictures] that it has do not seem so bright, so ideal, but seem to have come to terms with sad reality, showing us the pudding as it is and not as it ought to be. **1934** R. MACAULAY *Milton* vii. 109 He had here come to terms with life, or bravely pretended to have done so. **1965** *Listener* 30 Dec. 1067/1 Kipling, I think characteristically, came to terms with his tormentor. **1970** L. DEIGHTON *Bomber* i. 12 Each of the airmen guests was already coming to terms with the return to duty.
7) **1892** *Daily Graphic* (Suppl.) 30 Dec. 3/1 On the 14th October the constitution of the Commission and the exact terms of reference were made known. **1913** *Rep. Brit. Assoc. Adv. Sci. 1912* 549 The nature of the Inquiry of the Industrial Council is explained in the following 'terms of reference'. **1927** [see *REFER *v.* 8 a]. **1967** G. F. FIENNES *I tried to run Railway* vii. 88 We wrote ourselves new terms of reference in that sense. *a* **1974** R. CROSSMAN *Diaries* (1976) II. 661, I had to point out this was not excluded by the Committee's terms of reference, which had been drafted after consultation with the Foreign Office.

c. *terms of trade*, the ratio between the prices paid for imports and those received for exports.

1923 A. MARSHALL *Money, Credit, & Commerce* III. vi. 161 Illustration of the demands of each of two countries which trade together, for the goods of the other: and the general dependence of the terms of trade on the relative volumes and intensities of those demands. **1942** J. R. HICKS *Social Framework* xvi. 174 *Terms of Trade*, the amount of other countries' products which the nation gets in exchange for a unit of its own products. **1957** A. C. L. DAY *Outl. Monetary Econ.* xxxi. 399 Home terms of trade. [*Note*] An index of the home price of exports divided by the home price of imports. **1976** *Economist* 16 Oct. 22/3 Until exports expand enough, and/or imports fall enough, to offset the terms of trade deterioration, a devaluation makes the balance of payments worse before better.

IV. 11. b. Also, *in* (..) *terms*: in terms of what is designated by (..); *to think in terms of* (colloq.): to make (a particular consideration) the basis of one's attention, enquiries, plans, etc.

1947 MULGAN & DAVIN *Introd. Eng. Lit.* xiii. 164 The impact of Ibsen..did much to revitalize the degenerate English theatre and force it to think in terms of living ideas and contemporary realities. **1959** D. W. BROGAN in F. M. Joseph *As Others see Us* 4, I was predisposed to see American problems in European terms. **1973** 'E. McBAIN' *Hail to Chief* iii. 39 Carella..had suspected the ditch murders were related to organized crime... As it turned out, the cops had been thinking correctly in terms of gang warfare. **1978** *Listener* 26 Jan. 119/1 The hour's delay—a mere hiccup in cricketing terms—was caused by politics.

d. *Physics.* Each of a set of numbers such that lines in the spectrum of an atom have wave numbers given by the differences between two numbers in the set; an atomic state corresponding to one of these numbers, the number being proportional to the binding energy of a valence electron; a symbol representing such a state. Freq. as *spectral term*.

1909 *Sci. Abstr.* A. XII. 20 In any combination formula each of the terms represents the influence of one pole. **1915** *Astrophysical Jrnl.* XLI. 324 The difference in 'wave-number'..between the limit of the series and each member is called the 'term'... The limit itself is commonly a 'term' of some other series. **1922** A. D. UDDEN tr. *Bohr's Theory of Spectra* II. ii. 30 The arrangement of the states in horizontal rows corresponds to the ordinary arrangement of the 'spectral terms' in the spectroscopic tables. **1925** [see *LEVEL *sb.* 3 e]. **1935** [see *STATE *sb.* 4 b]. **1935** W. M. HICKS *Structure of Spectral Terms* i. 1 Any given term in a neutral spectrum is expressible in the form $R/(m+\phi)^2$, where R is a constant..*m* is an ordinal integer and ϕ a fraction which depends on *m*. **1938** *Nature* 22 Oct. 735/1 Dr. Dobbie has extended the number of classified lines to some 1,700 and has identified 73 terms involving 218 levels. **1967** [see *LYMAN]. **1970** G. K. WOODGATE *Elem. Atomic Struct.* vii. 110 For calcium.. the ^3P and ^1P terms of the configuration $4s4p$ are separated by about 8,000 cm^{-1}.

VI. 17. term paper *U.S. Educ.*, an essay or dissertation representative of the work done during a single term; **term symbol** *Physics*, a symbol of the type ^3P, denoting the values of *L* and *S* for a spectral term; **termwise** *adv.* and *a. Math.*, (carried out) term by term, treating each term separately.

1931 *High School Jrnl.* Jan. 17 A long term paper that will incorporate the results of a semester's reading. **1962** A. LURIE *Love & Friendship* xiv. 281 Students plagiarizing their term papers. **1975** M. BRADBURY *History Man* x. 164 Students..discuss..term-papers, union politics, theses. **1932** BACHER & GOUDSMIT *Atomic Energy States* i. 9 Each of the doublets occurs twice, and it is necessary to distinguish them in the term symbols. **1977** I. M. CAMPBELL *Energy & Atmosphere* viii. 220 The first electronically excited state of the oxygen atom would have in principle the two unpaired electrons of the ground state with opposite spins, producing a singlet state. In fact more detailed quantum mechanical treatment shows that there are two such states, designated by term symbols ^1D and ^1S, with the former the lower in energy of the two. **1912** J. PIERPONT *Lect. Theory of Functions Real Variable* II. v. 180 In this case we can obviously integrate termwise, although the convergence is not uniform. **1930** T. FORT *Infinite Series* vii. 74 Termwise multiplication of series. **1979** *Proc. London Math. Soc.* XXXVIII. 390 We then integrate termwise.

terminable, *a.* (*sb.*) Add: **2.** *minimum terminable unit* (see quot. 1975). Abbrev. *T-unit* s.v. *T 6*.

1965 [see *T-unit* s.v. *T 6*]. **1975** *Language for Life* (Dept. Educ. & Sci.) iii. 39 The minimum terminable unit, or T-unit, is 'roughly any sentence or part of a sentence that is an independent clause, possibly containing, however, one or more dependent clauses'.

terminal, *a.* and *sb.* Add: **A.** *adj.* **3. b.** (Earlier example.)

1869 *Bradshaw's Railway Manual* XXI. 87 This line.. terminates in the city, at a great terminal station in Liverpool Street.

4. b. (*a*) (further examples); (*b*) applied to a patient suffering from such a disease; (*c*) applied to an institution or ward in which such patients are nursed.

(*a*) **1958** A. HUXLEY *Let.* 2 Feb. (1969) 845 The administration of LSD to terminal cancer cases, in the hope that it would make dying a more spiritual, less strictly physiological process. **1961** *Lancet* 2 Sept. 549/1 It is they who have the closest contact with people who are going through 'terminal illnesses'. **1976** *Church Times* 23 July 11/1, I now have several progressive illnesses; one is terminal. **1980** D. LODGE *How Far can you Go?* vi. 160 What would it be like to be told you had a terminal illness, he wondered.
(*b*) **1961** *Amer. Speech* XXXVI. 145 *Terminal* adj., approaching death, moribund. 'The patient looks terminal to me.' **1965** E. M. K. PILLERS in J. S. Mitchell *Treatment of Cancer* 91 Response to this has been disappointing and the patient is now terminal. **1969** *Guardian* 19 Aug. 2/2 We started off with patients who were going to die anyway—terminal patients.
(*c*) **1961** *Lancet* 2 Sept. 548/2 Excellent care of these patients has been carried out not only at St. Joseph's but also in other terminal homes and hospitals. **1974** F. WARNER *Meeting Ends* I. ii. 13 The old lady was taken into the terminal ward, inarticulate, jabbering away.

c. *colloq.* In various *transf.* and *fig.* uses of sense 4 b above (freq. *joc.* or *trivial*).

1973 *Black Panther* 11 Aug. 8/2 The country was plunged into shock and the President faced a terminal crisis. **1975** D. LODGE *Changing Places* iii. 112, I continue to hope that our marital problems are not terminal. **1981** *Daily Tel.* 21 Dec. 2/1 Another contest for Labour's deputy leadership next year could prove 'terminal' for the party, Mr Neil Kinnock..said. **1983** *Times* 23 Sept. 6/4 One commentator said yesterday that his insensitivity was terminal. *Ibid.* 26 Sept. 9/5 A bad case of terminal tiredness had lowered my resistance to every loitering bug.

7. Special collocations: **terminal ballistics,** that branch of ballistics which deals with the impact of the projectile on the target; **terminal guidance** *Aeronaut.* (see quot. 1955); **terminal juncture** *Linguistics*, a juncture (sense *2 c) that occurs at the end of a syntactic unit; **terminal market** *Comm.*, a market that deals in futures; **terminal nose-dive** *Aeronaut.*, a nose-dive during which an aircraft reaches its terminal velocity; **terminal string** *Transformational Gram.*, a string consisting wholly of terminal symbols; **terminal symbol** *Transformational Gram.*, a symbol that denotes a lexical class and cannot be further rewritten; **terminal velocity,** the constant speed of fall that any particular object, given time, will eventually attain, at which the air resistance is equal to its weight.

1947 L. E. SIMON *German Research World War II* vii. 109 Terminal ballistics is concerned with the motion of the projectile, its fragments, and gases in the neighbourhood of the target. **1974** *Encycl. Brit. Macropædia* II. 659/2 A theoretical structure for terminal ballistics is a relatively current development. **1955** A. S. LOCKE *Guidance* i. 19 Terminal guidance is the guidance applied to the missile between the end of the midcourse guidance and contact with or detonation in close proximity to the target. **1979** *Jrnl. R. Soc. Arts* CXXVII. 555/1 Long-range, sea-skimming missiles with terminal guidance. **1956** *Language* XXXII. 653 This set of phonetic phenomena we assign to the terminal juncture. **1975** *Ibid.* LI. 57 The final element, *hacer*, accompanied by terminal juncture, is associated with zero following elements, signals absolute completion, and receives maximum contrast. **1895** Terminal market [in Dict., sense 4]. **1952** *Economist* 22 Nov. 567/1 There is little hope of restoration of a terminal market until the domestic allocation of sugar is freed from rationing. **1962** H. O. BEECHENO *Introd. Business Stud.* xi. 94 Future or terminal markets where goods can be bought and sold in advance. **1933** *Gloss. Aeronaut. Terms (B.S.I.)* 9 *Terminal nose-dive*, a dive at terminal velocity. **1956** N. CHOMSKY *Logical Struct. Linguistic Theory* (1975) vii. 174 The mapping in question may rearrange the order of elements of terminal strings and may specify their morphemic shape in various ways. **1967** D. G. HAYS *Introd. Computational Linguistics* vi. 118 A terminal string is composed of a certain number, say n, of terminal symbols. **1964** E. BACH *Introd. Transformational Gram.* ii. 14 Among the symbols of the grammar..there are some which never appear to the left of the arrow in a rule as symbols to be replaced. These are called *terminal symbols*. **1967** D. G. HAYS *Introd. Computational Linguistics* vi. 119 In terms of dependency theory, let the level of a structure be one greater than the number of links from its origin to the terminal symbol furthest removed. **1832** Terminal velocity [in Dict., sense 4 a]. **1910** [see *STOKES[1] c]. **1914** *Aeronaut. Jrnl.* XVIII. 50 He had dived, and had reached a speed so high that he thought it wise to straighten out without waiting to reach the terminal velocity. **1946** T. C. OHART *Elements Ammunition* IV. viii. 199 This theoretical maximum velocity for a given size and shape of bomb is called the terminal velocity; it is really a function of a given design, depending upon the aerodynamic characteristics of a bomb.

B. *sb.* **2. a.** (Earlier example.)

1838 W. STURGEON in *Ann. Electr., Magn., & Chem.* II. 11 That [part] which is connected with the positive pole of the exciting apparatus..may very conveniently be called the 'salient terminal metal', or occasionally the 'salient terminal' only.

d. A device for feeding data into a computer or receiving its output; *esp.* one that can be used by a person as a means of two-way communication with a computer.

1954 *Trans. IRE Prof. Group Electronic Computers* Mar. 2/1 Since the two machines employ the same digital language, this attachment can easily be made through their regular input-output terminals. **1958** *Oxf. Mag.* 29 May 470/1 The 'terminal' equipment, consisting of punched paper tape and a teleprinter, is relatively slow. **1965** *Jrnl. Assoc. Computing Machinery* XII. 350 (*heading*) On a problem concerning a central storage device served by multiple terminals. **1970** O. DOPPING *Computers & Data Processing* ix. 131 An 'impersonal' terminal with card reader, line printer, etc. can be started automatically at the end of the waiting time, but in case of a 'personal' terminal, the computer may send a message to the terminal indicating that the conversation may begin. **1971** *Daily Tel.* (Colour Suppl.) 19 Feb. 5/3 The national police computer with 700 terminals throughout the country opens this year. **1973** *Nature* 12 Oct. p. xxviii/3 (Advt.), There are good in-house computing facilities and a terminal to an IBM 360/195. **1977** *Hongkong Standard* 12 Apr. (Business Suppl.) 5/1 Terminal operators have been responding actively to the encouraging scene. **1979** *Computers in Shell* (Shell Internat. Petroleum Co.) (*recto rear cover*), Types of terminals include card readers, printers, video screens and teletypes. **1981** *Sci. Amer.* Dec. 112/3 The computer executes the operation, simplifies the resulting expression and prints it or displays it on a video terminal.

5. a. For *U.S.* read orig. and chiefly *U.S.* (Later examples.) Hence, in extended use, applied to the terminal point of an airline (= *air terminal* (a) s.v. *AIR *sb.*[1] III. 1), a bus service (= *bus terminal* s.v. *BUS *sb.*[2] 3), or occas. some other transportation service.

1921 *Flight* 16 June 401 (*caption*) Two London–Paris terminals.—The lower photograph shows Cricklewood aerodrome..the upper picture shows the Paris air port. **1922** JOYCE *Ulysses* 699 When citybound frequent connection by train or tram from their respective intermediate station or terminal. **1924** *London Guide No. 3* 152 At all the principal traffic centres and at the route terminals are uniformed 'General' Inspectors [of buses]. **1937** *New Statesman* 25 Dec. 1094/1 A rail-cum-steamer terminal on the Firth of Clyde. **1958** 'N. SHUTE' *Rainbow & Rose* vi. 270 Walking from the hostel to the terminal [of an airline]. **1958** *Times* 1 Mar. 7/4 Each city or town would adopt the type of terminal [for helicopters] best suited to its own locality. **1969** *Jane's Freight Containers 1968–69* 113/3 Scheduled national services: door-to-door and terminal-to-terminal. **1975** N. LUARD *Robespierre Serial* xvii. 153 All he could do was head for the bus terminal... The terminal was only twenty minutes by taxi from the hotel. **1980** R. McCRUM *In Secret State* xiii. 122 Quitman took the Piccadilly line to Heathrow... Soon he was standing on the travolator, riding up towards Terminal Three. **1981** M. MOORCOCK *Byzantium Endures* ii. 50 We eventually arrived at Glavnaya Station, the main terminal of Odessa situated in the heart of the city.

b. An installation where oil is stored, situated at the end of a pipeline or at a port of call for oil tankers.

[**1940** *Petroleum Press Service* 19 Apr. 182 This has included laying down a 100-mile 16 inch pipe-line to the coast and constructing ocean terminal facilities at Puerto

La Cruz.] **1947** L. M. Fanning *Amer. Oil Operations Abroad* xi. (*caption*) Oil-loading dock, Puerto La Cruz Terminal. **1948** *Economist* 14 Aug. 259/2 It is obviously difficult to pump oil from an Arab source in Iraq to a terminal in a Jewish-held town. **1976** M. Machlin *Pipeline* vi. 70 The 707 could then descend to a relatively low level and follow the route of the pipeline to its terminal.

7. One suffering from a terminal illness.

1960 J. G. Ballard in *New Worlds* Oct. 95 The terminals sleeping in the adjacent dormitory block attracted hordes of would-be sightseers. **1976** *Church Times* 23 July 11/2 Mr. Rice recently paid a third visit to the nun—who is bedridden and a terminal—and questioned her again, mainly about prayer and intercession. **1982** P. Van Greenaway *Lazarus Lie* vi. 61 'You have maybe a couple of thousand patients.'.. 'How many terminals?' 'Terminals?' 'Inoperables, end of the liners.'

8. Special Combs.: **terminal building,** a building housing the main facilities for air passengers; **terminal screw** *Electr.*, a screw for fastening an electric wire to the object with the screw hole.

1933 *Jrnl. R. Aeronaut. Soc.* XXXVII. 10 A terminal building will house traffic control and airport administration. **1977** G. Scott *Hot Pursuit* iv. 38 At the airport.. I got out of the terminal building and on to the bus. **1931** S. R. Roget *Dict. Electr. Terms* (ed. 2) 349/2 Terminal screw. **1978** *N.Y. Times* 30 Mar. c-4/1 Aluminum wire is stiffer than copper wire and does not bend as easily when wrapped around small terminal screws on switches and outlets.

terminalia (tɜːmineɪ·liă). [mod.L. (Linnæus *Mantissa Plantarum* (1767) I. 21), f. L. *terminăl-is* Terminal *a.* + -ia².] An evergreen tree of the large genus of this name, belonging to the family Combretaceæ, native to tropical or sub-tropical regions, having leaves clustered at the end of branches, and often producing a valuable timber. Also *attrib.*

1830 *Curtis's Bot. Mag.* LVII. 3004 (*heading*) Broad Downy-leaved Terminalia. **1926** *Chambers's Jrnl.* June 411/2 He halted the elephant under one of the Terminalia trees. **1964** C. Willock *Enormous Zoo* iii. 39 The elephants had taken a liking to *terminalia* bark. **1973** *Times* 20 Sept. 8/3 David Dibnah,..convicted of wilfully destroying a flowering terminalia tree, has been ordered by a magistrate to plant another.

terminalization (tɜːminăləizeɪ·ʃən). *Cytology.* [f. Terminal *a.* and *sb.* + -ization.] The movement of a chiasma or chiasmata towards the end of a separating bivalent.

1929 C. D. Darlington in *Jrnl. Genetics* XXI. 266 The post-diplotene stages in this species are characterised by a regular movement of chiasmata towards the attachment constriction. The opposite movement, which I will call 'terminalisation', affords a sufficient and indeed the only explanation of the exceptional metaphase configurations found in *Tradescantia*. **1932** *Amer. Naturalist* LXVI. 32 Related species differ in the degree of terminalization of chiasmata. **1979** *Nature* 22 Mar. 349/2 The issue of terminalisation is relevant both theoretically (assessment of chiasma and crossover frequency) and practically (alleged factor in maternal-age-dependent non-disjunction in mammals).

Hence **te·rminalized** *ppl. a.*, (of a chiasma) having moved to, or situated at, the end of a separating bivalent.

1932 C. D. Darlington *Rec. Adv. Cytol.* iv. 103 However many chiasmata are terminalised, the chromosomes remain associated by terminal chiasmata. *Ibid.* 104 (*caption*) Completely terminalised chiasmata. **1959** *Genetics* XLIV. 711 Incompletely terminalized chiasmata were observed in these configurations. **1979** *Nature* 22 Mar. 349/2 Our data do not indicate whether or not chiasmata are terminalised in the mouse.

terminally, *adv.* Add: **2. b.** *Comb.* with an adj. in sense 4 b of Terminal *a.*

1973 *Sci. Amer.* Sept. 56/1 One of the terminally sick patients has been given a change of scene by moving his bed to the garden. **1976** M. Millar *Ask for me Tomorrow* (1977) iv. 37 This was Aragon's first time in the presence of a terminally ill person.

terminate, *ppl. a.* Add: **1. c.** *Gram.* = *terminative *a.* 4 b. Also as *sb.*

Restricted to the writings of G. O. Curme and a few others.

1931 G. O. Curme *Syntax* xix. 385 A large number of simple and compound verbs indicate an action *as a whole*. Such verbs are called terminates. *Ibid.* 386 The terminate aspect has relations also to the durative aspect. **1935** —— *Gram. Eng. Lang.* II. 206 The expanded form often represents the act as a whole, hence it has terminate force: 'I am sorry you doubt my statement. I *am telling* you the truth.' *Ibid.* 237 In terminates it [*sc.* the present participle] represents the act as a whole, as a fact. **1946** [see *progressive *a.* 3 h]. **1972** M. L. Samuels *Linguistic Evol.* 161 If a terminate or point-action meaning was required for a majority of its occurrences in the preterite, the short vowel was preferred.

terminate, *v.* Add: **I. 4. c.** In pregnant use: (*a*) to dismiss from employment; (*b*) to assassinate; *to terminate with extreme prejudice*: see *prejudice *sb.* 1 c. *N. Amer. colloq.*

(*a*) **1973** *N.Y. Law Jrnl.* 25 July 13/1 The complainant had been discharged because of an unauthorized absence..and..there was no probable cause to believe that he had been terminated in retaliation for having filed previous complaints against petitioners. **1976** M. Machlin *Pipeline* xviii. 228 If the boss didn't care for you very much in the first place, you could be terminated without having any appeal to the union. **1980** R. L. Duncan *Brimstone* ii. 36 Adamson's putting pressure on me to terminate you.

(*b*) **1975** N. Luard *Robespierre Serial* iv. 27 A free-lance agent who'd been given a contract to terminate an individual the Service had declared hostile. **1981** T. Barling *Bikini Red North* ii. 51 Haddad was terminated by persons unknown.

11. (Earlier example.)

1789 J. Woodforde *Diary* 24 Mar. (1927) III. 91 His case is a violent Stranguary and if some remedy or other does not soon, very soon do good, it will terminate fatally to him.

termination. Add: **I. 3. c.** *Chem.* and *Biochem.* The cessation of the building up of a polymer molecule. Freq. *attrib.*

1951 *Jrnl. Amer. Chem. Soc.* LXXIII. 5197/1 It is assumed in the case of tetrafluoroethylene polymerization initiated by inorganic free radicals that chain termination occurs by combination of a polymer radical with either another polymer radical or an initiator radical. **1967** Margerison & East *Introd. Polymer Chem.* v. 246 Termination may be brought about by many types of reagent. **1968** A. White et al. *Princ. Biochem.* (ed. 4) xxix. 678 The mechanism by which these three codons accomplish chain termination and polypeptide release is not understood. **1978** Hayes & George in C. E. Carraher et al. *Organometallic Polymers* 16 In vinylferrocene polymerizations, the termination step is monomolecular. **1981** *Sci. Amer.* Aug. 63/2 Two proteins called termination factors are involved, and it appears that UAG, UAA and UGA all serve as termination codons: triplets on the mRNA that cause the ribosome to release the messenger and the newly synthesized protein.

d. The ending of a person's employment; dismissal. Chiefly *N. Amer.*

1961 *Wall St. Jrnl.* 23 Jan. 2/3 They qualify for termination payments and most are eligible for deferred pensions. **1982** *Chicago Sun-Times* 3 Dec. 89 He and fellow workers were informed of the terminations at 10:30 a.m. Wednesday and told to 'pack up and leave immediately'. **1983** M. Edwardes *Back from Brink* iv. 56 In most cases we allowed the manager to 'resign' but in truth most of these people were dismissed, and were paid termination payments.

e. The ending of a pregnancy before term by artificial means; an induced abortion.

1969 *Times* 3 July 7/6 Women denied a legal abortion commonly seek termination elsewhere. **1973** *Times* 26 Nov. 6/1 The pregnant women walking about the hospital ward were all in for abortions. Or terminations, as they called them—a much nicer word. **1978** F. Weldon *Praxis* xxiv. 256 You can't possibly go through with the pregnancy... If you don't have a termination, you're finished.

f. Assassination (*spec.* of an intelligence agent).

1975 N. Luard *Robespierre Serial* v. 28 The escort role..was one Carswell had carried out..before, although this was the first occasion where it involved a termination mission. **1980** [see *prejudice *sb.* 1 c]. **1983** G. Markstein *Ferret* 164 Terminations are no longer as fashionable as they were. Unless the top says so.

terminative, *a.* Add: **4. a.** (Earlier example.)

1860 *Trans. Philol. Soc. 1857* 34 The declension of the personal pronouns [in the Tushi language] is as follows.. Nominative..Genitive..Comitative..Terminative.

b. Applied to an aspect of a verb which denotes a completed action, or its completion.

1911 Kruisinga & Erades *Eng. Gram.* (1953) I. ii. vii. 257 Verbs of a terminative character, that is such as express the final stage of an activity. **1924** O. Jespersen *Philos. Gram.* xx. 273 Lindroth for the first class uses the term 'successive' (with the subdivisions 'terminative' and 'resultative'.) **1930** B. Trnka *Syntax Eng. Verb* 32 A differentiation between two series of aspects, the *ingressive, continuative* and *terminative* (resultative) on the one hand, and the *imperfective* and *perfective*, on the other... The former, common to both Slavonic and Germanic languages, express the ingressive, continuative and terminative stages of the verbal action. **1963** F. T. Visser *Hist. Syntax Eng. Lang.* III. ii. 1372 There are three kinds [of verbs of aspect]: (1) of egressive or terminative aspect. **1984** *Eng. World-Wide* IV. 208 The *terminative* markers *gaan* and *kom*, which occur only with motion verbs in this *perfective* function, follow the main verb.

terminator. Add: **3.** *Biochem.* A sequence of polynucleotides that causes transcription to end and results in the release of the newly synthesized nucleic acid from the template molecule. Freq. *attrib.*

1969 *Biochemistry* VIII. 4897/1 Would chains bearing such a chain-growth terminator be susceptible to the hydrolytic and pyrophosphorolytic reactions? **1977** *World Bk. Sci. Ann. 1978* 249 To get the gene to work.. certain controlling base sequences had to be added at each end. One end had to have a 'promoter' sequence so transcription could start; the other end had to have a 'terminator' sequence to stop transcription. **1978** *Nature* 30 Mar. 398/1 Analysis of several ρ-independent terminators has revealed that in every case termination occurs distal to a GC-rich region within a run of uridine residues.

terminism. a. (Earlier example.)

1878 S. H. Hodgson *Philos. Reflection* I. i. 66 Nominalism..in its later shape, in which it is opposed to Conceptualism and is then more properly to be called *Terminism*.

terminological, *a.* (In Dict. s.v. Terminology.) Add: *terminological inexactitude* (later examples); freq. as a humorous expression for a falsehood.

1926 Fowler *Mod. Eng. Usage* 444/1 *Polysyllabic humour*... Of the long as distinguished from the abstruse, *terminological inexactitude* for lie or falsehood is a favourable example, but much less amusing at the hundredth than at the first time of hearing. **1940** C. Milburn *Diary* 19 July (1979) 49, I can't think..why he [*sc.* Hitler] does not choke himself with his 'terminological inexactitudes'! **1976** A. Price *War Game* i. viii. 159 It all adds up to a little terminological inexactitude——he was lying through his goddamn teeth.

terminus. Add: **4. b.** *terminus a quo*: also used *spec.* in dating to indicate the starting-point of a period; similarly *terminus ante quem, terminus post quem* (='term before which', 'term after which') used to indicate the finishing- or starting-point of a period; also *ellipt.*, as *terminus ante, terminus post.*

1930 A. H. Krappe *Sci. Folklore* i. 14 Generally speaking..a *terminus ante quem* is furnished by the oldest European historical variant. **1936** *Burlington Mag.* Aug. 75/1 The dress the king is wearing did not become fashionable before 1796, a fact which indicates a *terminus post quem*. **1939** *Ibid.* May 218/1 The *termini post* and *ante* of the glass, thus given by the birth of Charles (1500) and the death of Philip (1506). **1953** R. J. C. Atkinson *Field Archæol.* vi. 166 It must be clearly understood that these *termini post* and *ante quem* are the closest that the archæologist can get (at least with present methods of research) to an absolute date. **1968** *English Studies* XLIX. 455 The chapter..provides a good survey of the evidence..that seems to point to a date around 1200 as the most probable date of composition. However, the *terminus a quo* (1193) that is suggested..on p. 19, seems quite unwarranted. **1973** *Nature* 9 Nov. 77/1 These dates..merely provide, however, a *terminus post quem* for the valley deepening and widening during which cavern opening occurred. **1974** *Bodleian Library Rec.* Dec. 174 Such evidence clearly establishes for the annotations a *terminus a quo* of 1602. **1978** *Maledicta* II. 243, I must now propose 1888 as a conservative *terminus ante quem* for that species, and the evidence at that date points back considerably farther.

6. (Examples of the place at which a tram-line or bus route ends.)

1877 *Tramways Intelligence* 17 The lines of the company have their London termini at Westminster Bridge-road, Blackfriars-road. **1936** J. B. Priestley *They walk in City* iii. 39 The tram was full, but they pushed their way in... By the time they had arrived at the terminus in Gladstone Lane..a few drops [of rain] were falling. *Ibid.* iv. 85 Taking a bus as far as the edge of the moors, walking over to some place where he could get tea, then walking back to the terminus again. **1975** R. L. Beals *Peasant Marketing System of Oaxaca* i. 9. Around the peripheries of the district are the termini of most of the bus lines.

termitarium. (In Dict. s.v. Termite.) (Later examples.)

1934 *Discovery* Nov. 308/2 A big termitarium..must contain a population of seven million, or even more. **1971** *World Archaeology* III. 124 The large refuse filled pit near the adult burials is at the site of a termitarium dug out for building material. **1981** *Atlantic Monthly* July 49 The nearest thing to a termitarium that I can think of in human behavior is the making of a language, which we do by keeping *at* each other all our lives,..changing the structure by some sort of instinct.

termitary. (In Dict. s.v. Termite.) Add: Also *fig.* (Later examples.)

1901 *Jrnl. R. Microsc. Soc.* 32 The Cicindelids select the termitaries as sunny places well suited for play and for hunting. **1935** *Times* 11 Feb. 14/2 Man as a personality is destined to be a free citizen in a free world, not an ant in some human termitary. **1937** *Discovery* Sept. 292/2 One must consider a termitary as a single animal. **1955** J. B. Priestley in Priestley & Hawkes *Journey down Rainbow* xii. 177 I'd rather stand on the pavement and eat a sandwich than lunch in that underground termitary. **1961** L. Mumford *City in History* i. 6 The social functions of the beehive, the termitary, and the ant-hill..have indeed.. many resemblances to those of the city. **1977** *Time* 10 Oct. 51/2 But they linger on paper as the dream architecture of the 20th century. Because these termitaries were never built, they could not be destroyed.

termite. Add: **1. b.** Also *Comb.*, as *termite-proof* adj.; **termite heap, mound** = *termite hill.*

1910 *Dundee Advertiser* 25 Nov. 6 The athletes had to.. jump from a small termite heap. **1920** *Blackw. Mag.* Feb. 205/1 Several enormous termite heaps. **1977** 'J. McVean' *Bloodspoor* x. 96 Haston was lying by a termite mound. **1934** Webster, Termite-proof. **1937** *Discovery* Feb. 63/1 Care must be taken to ensure that the timber work is termite-proof. **1971** *Guardian* 18 Nov. 15/1 The immediate problem is to make sure such a building is termite proof.

2. *transf.* (with reference to the destructiveness of the insect).

1943 in S. J. Baker *Austral. Lang.* (1945) 245 The secretary of the party said 'We can't say too much; there are termites about.' **1949** Koestler *Promise & Fulfilment* ii. v. 282 One delegation would immediately settle down to silent termite work. **1951** *Economist* 8 Dec. 1402/2 'Any man who betrays the people's trust in a public office is a public enemy..' declared the new chairman..calling on his fellow members to punish the 'termites' relentlessly. **1961** A. Maund *Worthy Termites* ii. 22 'So you want me to police Great Port for woodpiles which might have somebody besides nigras under them,' Ed said. 'Yes. Look for the *termites*.'

termitologist (tɜːmaitɒ·lŏdʒist). [f. TERMITE + -OLOGIST.] One who studies termites.
1936 *Times* 9 June 10/3 Dr. Noyes, of California—a celebrated termitologist—writes doubtfully of *Zootermopsis*. **1971** E. O. WILSON *Insect Societies* vi. 106/2 Termitologists had long looked to the Mesozoic or beyond for traces of a truly archaic termite fauna.

termitophile. (Examples.)
1922 [see *PHYSOGASTRISM]. **1971** E. O. WILSON *Insect Societies* vi. 111/2 Termitophiles, often species-specific and highly modified.

termly, *a.* Delete *rare* and add later examples. Now freq. in the sense: occurring every academic term.
1969 T. FAWTHROP in Cockburn & Blackburn *Student Power* 101 There should be a variety of means by which assessment is arrived at: from termly work standards to dissertations. **1970** M. JONES *Ducal Brittany* vi. 166 The termly sums demanded from individual parishes were always the same. **1983** *Bull. Univ. Coll. London* May 8/2 A termly whole-day inter-disciplinary seminar is proposed.

termorrer (təɪmɒ·rəɪ), repr. vulgar or dial. pronunc. of TO-MORROW *adv.* and *sb.* Cf. *TER.
1898 J. D. BRAYSHAW *Slum Silhouettes* 118 That's ninepence I owes Newsy: must pay that or there won't be no papers to start wiv ter-morrer. **1932** S. GIBBONS *Cold Comfort Farm* xii. 178 Ter-day's dinner... Ter-morrer's too, for all I know. **1974** P. CAVE *Mama* (new ed.) iv. 28 Adolph slipped the merchandise into his pocket. 'I'll do it termorrer,' he vowed.

terna. (Earlier example.)
1885 W. J. WALSH *Let.* 7 Mar. in P. J. Walsh *William J. Walsh* (1928) vii. 163 Then I would, as a matter of course, vote for your Grace, which would put you on the *terna*.

ternary, *a.* Add: **1. b.** Mus. *ternary form.* Substitute for def: The form of a movement which consists of three main divisions, *spec.* one in which the first subject recurs after a contrasting subject. Also *absol.* as *ternary.* (Earlier and further examples.)
1875 F. A. G. OUSELEY *Treat. Mus. Form & Gen. Composition* vi. 41 (*heading*) Of the ternary form. *Ibid.* vii. 44 If the minuet form is adopted for a complete and isolated composition, it should be lengthened considerably, and then both the minuet and trio may be written in the ternary form. **1896** W. H. HADOW *Sonata Form* iv. 29 In its use for purposes of the Folk-song the most primitive Ternary form consists of a melody in three clauses: one of assertion..one of contrast..one of re-assertion. **1931** D. F. TOVEY *Compan. Beethoven's Pianoforte Sonatas* 2 The vital distinction between 'binary' and 'ternary' is that between an aggregate whose members are inseparable and an aggregate containing one or more things already complete. **1938** *Oxf. Compan. Mus.* 334/2 Properly, any composition in which the ear seizes two clear divisions is binary, and any in which it seizes three is ternary... 'Sonata Form'..is often called 'Compound Binary'... Certain text-books..speak of it as 'Ternary'. *Ibid.* 335/1 *Rondo Form.* This may be looked upon as an extension of simple ternary form. **1944** W. APEL *Harvard Dict. Mus.* 88/1 The principle of ternary structure appeared first in the French chansons of the 16th century... The idea of a contrasting middle section is quite clearly expressed in the shepherd's solo of Monteverdi's *Orfeo*... Ternary form became clearly established in the da-capo aria, *c.* 1700. **1980** *New Grove Dict. Mus.* XVIII. 694/1 Tripartite musical form designated symbolically as *ABA*. The two elements *A* and *B* are often thematically independent and each is generally a 'closed' structure tonally, so that the interdependence of the two sections characteristic of binary form is not necessarily evident in ternary.
c. Also (of an alloy), composed of three principal metals; (of a mixture) containing three independent components; of or pertaining to such an alloy or mixture.
1889 *Proc. R. Soc.* XLV. 481 Ternary alloys obtained by adding tin to the immiscible pairs of metals, zinc and bismuth, aluminium and lead. **1897** W. D. BANCROFT *Phase Rule* xi. 156 The change of isotherms with the temperature for a ternary system which permits of no compounds and no second solution phase. **1923** GLAZEBROOK *Dict. Appl. Physics* V. 251/2 (*heading*) Methods of representing ternary equilibria. **1969** BENNISON & WRIGHT *Geol. Hist. Brit. Isles* xi. 261 The theoretical succession of deposition of minerals produced by the evaporation of sea-water is supported to a large extent by experimental work... However, the detailed course of crystallization, which varies considerably with different temperatures, can only be adequately represented by ternary diagrams. **1978** P. W. ATKINS *Physical Chem.* x. 305 Consider a ternary solution of composition a_1. This is unsaturated, and is a single phase. **1979** *Sci. Amer.* Nov. 73/3 The new ternary alloys consist of between 68 and 80 percent copper.
g. Nucl. Physics. *ternary fission*, fission of an atomic nucleus into three parts.
1955 *Physical Rev.* XCVII. 748/2 There is some uncertainty regarding the occurrence in ternary fission of a light fragment having a mass and charge greater than an alpha particle. **1979** *Nature* 12 Apr. 615/2 Uranium and plutonium decay by ternary fission with only very low probability.

ternery. Delete *rare* and add examples.
1905 E. SELOUS *Bird Watcher in Shetlands* xxiii. 180, I have mentioned the case of a dog making regular daily expeditions to a ternery, in order to feast upon the eggs. **1932** *Times Lit. Suppl.* 15 Sept. 637/2 The sanctuary at Dungeness, established presumably for the protection of the interesting ternery. **1943** HAGGARD & WILLIAMSON *Norfolk Life* i. 12 There is the azure tide inflowing past the Ternery on the point. **1979** *Woman & Home* June 154/3 The ternery, no longer out of bounds, was uncannily silent.

terotechnology (tiᵊːro-, teːroteknɒ·lŏdʒi). [f. Gr. τηρεῖν to watch over, take care of + -O + TECHNOLOGY.] The branch of technology and engineering concerned with the installation, maintenance, and replacement of industrial plant and equipment and with related subjects and practices.
1970 H. P. JOST *Let.* 2 Feb. (in files of *Suppl. to O.E.D.*), Last Saturday a Mintech Steering Committee, which I chaired, took some decisions on a proposed 'Committee on Terotechnology'. We felt that Terotechnology was preferable to Teromechanics, particularly as a good deal of electronics were involved. **1970** *Hansard Commons: Written Answers* 29 Apr. 338 The scope of the subject..includes.. installation, commissioning and replacement of plant, machinery and equipment, feedback to designers, and management techniques... It was considered advisable to utilise a name reflecting the wider concept now envisaged. The word Terotechnology has therefore been adopted. **1975** *Daily Tel.* 9 Dec. 11/6 British Leyland has won the award of 'Conservationist of the Year' for its work in saving materials, plant and manpower. The firm estimated that it saved £321,182 on terotechnology—economy in materials, plant and manpower. **1977** *Engin. Synopses* Jan.–Feb. 20 (Advt.), With the continual increase in size and complexity of industrial undertakings terotechnology has emerged as a discipline in its own right. **1980** *Sunday Times* 9 Nov. 19/4 The science of maintenance, or terotechnology if you want to sound knowledgeable about it, is beginning to attract serious interest in industry and universities.
Hence **teːrotechnolo·gical** *a.*, **teːrotechno·logist.**
1970 *Chartered Mech. Engineer* June 243/1 According to Mintech, this new high-status role will be filled by none other than the Terotechnologist. *Ibid.*, A Committee of Terotechnology..will advise..on how to introduce appropriate measures to effect terotechnological progress. **1973** *New Scientist* 12 Apr. 95 Terotechnologists quote the case of breakdowns of waste heat boilers for 300 tonne oxygen steelmaking vessels. **1977** *Engin. Synopses* Jan.–Feb. 20 (Advt.), The terotechnologist must be able to call upon a wide variety of other skills and specialisms.

terp[1]. Delete ‖ and add: Also applied to similar mounds outside Friesland itself. Now with anglicized pl. *terps* in *Archæol.* contexts. (Later examples.)
1939 G. CLARK *Archæol. & Society* iv. 105 '*Terps*.' Settlement mounds or tells are a commonplace feature of Greek and Middle Danubian prehistory. **1969** G. C. DICKINSON *Maps & Air Photographs* xiv. 217 (*caption*) The villages are built on or (now) around man-made mounds (*terps*) erected as a defence against flooding by the sea.

terp[2] (tɜrp). *Theatr. slang.* [Abbrev. of TERPSICHORE(AN *a.*).] A stage dancer, esp. a chorus-girl; also, a ballroom dancer. Also *attrib.* and *pl.*, dancing. Hence **terp** *v. intr.*, to dance; **te·rping** *vbl. sb.*
1937 *Amer. Speech* XII. 317/2 *Terp*, a dancer. **1937** *Variety* 10 Nov. 58/3 Philly Orch on Thursday (11) night will preem composition of 23-year-old Omaha college soph. Cleffer, titled 'Mystic Pool'... 'Pool' originally composed for his terp. orch. **1942** BERREY & VAN DEN BARK *Amer. Thes. Slang* § 594/1 *Stage dancing*,..terping, terp stuff, toesmithing. **1945** MENCKEN *Amer. Lang.* Suppl. I. v. 338 It [sc. *Variety*] makes verbs of nouns, *e.g.* ..*to preem* and *to terp.* **1951** GREEN & LAURIE *Show Biz* 571/2 *Terps*, dancing. *Ibid.* 572/1 *Terp team*, ballroom dance team. **1952** GRANVILLE *Dict. Theatr. Terms* 183 *Terp*, a stage dancer. **1974** *Spartanburg* (S. Carolina) *Herald* 18 Apr. A6/1 Donna McKechnie is the best dancer in the musical comedy theater (one dance critic tripped over his typewriter when he suggested Donna can't terp).

terpane (tɜ·ɹpēɪn). *Chem.* [ad. G. *terpan* (A. Baeyer 1894, in *Ber. d. Deut. Chem. Ges.* XXVII. 436), f. *terpen* TERPENE: see -ANE.] Any of a class of saturated hydrocarbons related to the terpenes and possessing their carbon skeleton; *spec.* 4-methylprop-2-ylcyclohexane, $CH_3C_6H_{10}CH(CH_3)_2$, a monocyclic liquid.
1902 F. J. POND tr. *Heusler's Chem. Terpenes* 23 Baeyer has..advanced the proposition to designate hexahydrocymene as *terpane.* **1965** *Proc. Nat. Acad. Sci.* LIV. 1412 Peaks [in the mass spectrum] at m/e 191, 203, and 231 probably arise from small amounts of terpane impurities. **1981** *Jrnl. Chromatogr. Sci.* XIX. 156/1 Terpanes and steranes are well-known biological marker hydrocarbons.

terpene. Add: Hence **te·rpeneless** *a.*, rendered free of terpenes.
1921 *Jrnl. R. Naval Med. Service* VII. 89 Terpeneless and sesquiterpeneless oils. **1972** *Materials & Technol.* V. i. 17 'Terpeneless bergamot oil' is used in high-class perfumes.

terpenoid (tɜ·ɹpĕnoid), *sb.* (and *a.*) *Chem.* [a. G. *terpenoid* (Vogel & Stohl 1933, in *Ber. d. Deut. Chem. Ges.* LXVI. B. 1066): see TERPENE and -OID.] A terpene in the broadest sense: used when *terpene* itself is restricted to compounds with the formula $C_{10}H_{16}$. Also *attrib.* and as *adj.*
1933 *Chem. Abstr.* XXVII. 4807 The name *terpenoids* is suggested for the resin alcs., resin acids, sterols and xanthophylls, including carotene. **1956** I. L. FINAR *Organic Chem.* II. viii. 250 There is..a tendency to call the whole group terpenoids instead of terpenes, and to restrict the name terpene to the compounds $C_{10}H_{16}$. **1972** *Science* 5 May 512/2 Some species of caterpillars..possess oxidases in their gut that are capable of metabolizing the repellent terpenoids such as pyrethrin from chrysanthemums. **1975** *Nature* 31 Jan. 365/2 Both substances are terpenoid, derived from the essential oils absinthol and cannabinol.

terr (tɜɹ). *Rhodesian slang.* [abbrev. of TERRORIST.] In Rhodesia (now Zimbabwe) prior to independence, a guerrilla fighting to overthrow the White minority government. Usu. in *pl.*
1976 *Verbatim* Sept. 14/2 Rhodesians, according to a recent news dispatch, now have one [*sc.* a 'clipping'] they could do without, namely *the Terrs* (general for 'the terrorists'). **1976** *Listener* 23/30 Dec. 835/3 It may help ..to know the kind of slang that they [*sc.* Rhodesian Whites] are going to be using. 'Terrs' is short for 'terrorists'... To 'rev' is to shoot somebody. **1980** *Times* 18 Jan. 19/2 Infiltration over the Zambesi River by 'terrs'—or terrorists/freedom fighters, depending on your politics.

terra. Add: **terra alba,** (*b*) pulverized gypsum used industrially. Also used, with qualifying adjectives, in some general expressions, as **terra cognita** [as opp. to TERRA INCOGNITA], *fig.*, familiar territory; **terra ignota** = TERRA INCOGNITA; **terra irredenta** = *IRREDENTA.
1905 H. RIES *Econ. Geol.* vii. 143 Gypsum is also used.. under the name of 'Terra Alba', as an adulterant of foods and medicinal preparations. **1917** J. SHELTON in G. Martin *Industr. & Manuf. Chem.* I. XXXI. 545 Under trade names, such as 'terra alba'.., a certain amount of the purer forms of gypsum is employed by paint manufacturers for admixture with pigments. **1947** J. C. RICH *Materials & Methods of Sculpture* iv. 65 Terra Alba, a finely pulverized raw gypsum powder may be used [as an accelerator in casting plaster of Paris.] **1963** R. R. A. HIGHAM *Handbk. Papermaking* iv. 93 The form containing no water of crystallization..is prepared by calcining the natural gypsum ($CaSO_4,2H_2O$), often referred to as terra alba. **1962** E. SNOW *Other Side of River* (1963) xxxiii. 253 My last remark had put them back on terra cognita and it would have been an appropriate moment to leave. **1975** *Publishers Weekly* 21 July 66/3 But it's all the same old *terra cognita* to those who have read Gerold Frank, Anne Edwards et al. *a* **1925** LD. CURZON *Leaves from Viceroy's Notebook* (1926) vi. 231 The whole country of Annam seems to be almost a *terra ignota* to our countrymen. **1977** *Times* 12 Oct. 9/5 These records [at Greenwich Museum] are largely terra ignota to the outside world. **1934** WEBSTER, Terra irredenta. **1936** *International Affairs* XV. 39 *A terra irredenta*—that is to say, a territory, at present under foreign sovereignty, which, in the claimants' views, ought to be transferred to the sovereignty of his own State and to be incorporated (or re-incorporated) into his own national domain. **1965** *Listener* 20 May 735/1 French Somaliland,..Ethiopian Somaliland, and..a strip of northern Kenya. These represent the Somalis' '*terra irredenta*'.
2. *Science Fiction.* (With capital initial.) The Earth.
1947 E. F. RUSSELL in Aldiss & Harrison *Decade 1940s* (1975) 157 This world..was ten times the size of Terra. But his weight didn't seem abnormal. **1952** P. J. FARMER in —— *Decade 1950s* (1976) 215 It follows the moon around Terra..a much smaller and unseen satellite.

terra a terra. **2.** Transfer entry to *TERRE-À-TERRE, q.v.

terrace, *sb.* Add: **1. d.** *Archæol.* = *cultivation terrace* s.v. *CULTIVATION 1 a.
1796, etc. [see *LYNCHET b]. *a* **1964** G. UNDERWOOD *Pattern of Past* (1968) viii. 82 *Terraces*..are found on steep hillsides, and..mark places where a number of geodetic lines run parallel, with wide spaces between them... It seems reasonable to assume that they formed processional ways.
e. At an Association Football or other sports ground, a row for the accommodation of standing spectators; usually in *pl.* Cf. *TERRACING *vbl. sb.* 1 b. Also *attrib.* in *sing.*
1950 *Sport* 7–11 Apr. 2/1 The terrace regulars are..the backbone of many present day clubs. **1959** *Listener* 19 Feb. 332/2 As I saw them from the terraces, I learnt that on top of everything else..they often had to play against their own supporters. **1971** [see *FRIENDLY *a.* 3 c]. **1977** *Times* 6 May 2/5 [The] Minister of State for Sport..imposed his ban on the sale of terrace tickets to Chelsea supporters at away games. **1980** *Observer* 7 Sept. 11/6 It was more like a football terrace than Lord's.
3. Revived in the sense 'balcony in a theatre' or other auditorium (see quot. 1961).
1961 *Ann. Rep. Lincoln Center for Performing Arts* (N.Y.) 10/1 The auditorium's shallow terraces—only six rows deep at the back and two to four seats wide at the sides—surround the orchestra level and flow towards the orchestra platform [in the Philharmonic Hall at the Lincoln Center, N.Y.]. **1963** *Guardian* 5 Mar. 7/3 The music sounds better in the top terrace..than in the lower terraces and orchestra.
7. *terrace cottage, -garden* (later and *attrib.*

examples), *-parapet*, *-walk* (later examples); *terrace-like* adj.; **terrace house,** one of a row of usu. similar houses joined by party-walls.

1973 A. Hunter *Gently French* iv. 34 Adjacent to the Barge-House were three sad terrace cottages. **1978** *Spectator* 13 May 12/2 Neat little freshly painted two-storey terrace cottages with gardens nearby—already a century old. **1861** Queen Victoria *Jrnl.* 20 Sept. (1980) 99 The Castle of Auch Mill, which..has traces of a terrace garden remaining. **1931** A. U. Dilley *Oriental Rugs & Carpets* iii. 58 Many 'tree' and 'landscape' rugs are terrace-garden rugs. **1817** Jane Austen *Sanditon* (1954) x. 413 They were in one of the Terrace Houses. **1922** Joyce *Ulysses* 697 A terracehouse or semidetached villa. **1958** *Listener* 5 June 947/1 Look at the new hospital-block in Guildford Street, Bloomsbury, and see how well it goes with the old terrace-houses. **1972** *Guardian* 6 Nov. 15/3 The rank and file knew that the real Ulster crisis was happening inside the terrace houses. **1880** 'Mark Twain' *Tramp Abr.* xxxv. 397 This pile of stone..comes down out of the clouds in a succession of rounded, colossal, terrace-like projections. **1963** *Times* 18 May 5/2 One of the finest things was his terrace-like build-up of the beginning of the allegretto from the Seventh Symphony. **1974** C. Taylor *Fieldwork in Medieval Archaeol.* iii. 28 These terrace-like features [*sc.* strip lynchets] on hillsides are the remains of medieval strip cultivation. **1854** Dickens *Hard Times* ii. vii. 207 Tom sat down on a terrace-parapet, plucking buds. **1707** Terrace walk [see *side-wing* s.v. *Side *sb.*[1] 27]. **1775** J. Woodforde *Diary* 14 Apr. (1924) I. 151 Round it is a fine Terrass Walk which commands the whole City. **1858** M. Tuckett *Diary* 16 Sept. (*c* 1975) 5 A broad terrace walk goes along the front of the new part of the house.

b. Used to designate a style of women's and girls' clothing suitable for wearing at an informal party.

1963 *Guardian* 2 Feb. 5/2 A series of terrace (ex-casino) dresses. **1965** *Sunday Mail* (Brisbane) 24 Oct. 24 (*caption*) Terrace skirt combines bright red, white, and blue in a lively outfit for girls who want to look graceful at casual parties. **1971** *Rand Daily Mail* (Johannesburg) 4 Dec. 3/8 (Advt.), A fabulous collection of the popular terrace gowns. **1972** *Times* 19 Dec. 11/3, I do not like the idea of little girls in low-cut evening dresses..but I do think that the pale blue terrace two-piece..is a delight.

terraced, *ppl. a.* Add: (Later examples.) Of a house: cf. *terrace house* s.v. *Terrace *sb.* 7.

1958 *Daily Express* 3 Apr. 7/7 Their tiny terraced home in the back streets of Horden, Durham. **1976** *Milton Keynes Express* 28 May 1/3 She has no intention of leaving her terraced home. **1979** *Guardian* 19 June 4/2 The old-fashioned terraced house..is on the way back.

terrace·ntric, *a. nonce-wd.* [f. Terra + Centric *a.*] Having, or taking, the earth as centre; = Geocentric *a.* 2.

1932 G. B. Shaw *Adventures Black Girl* 66 As to Bible science..its astronomy is terracentric.

terracette (teræse·t). *Geomorphol.* [f. Terrace *sb.* + -ette.] A small (natural) terrace; *spec.* one of a parallel series on a steep hillside.

1922 H. Odum in *Dan. Geol. Undersøg.* IV. i. 27 The phenomenon..occurs on hill-slopes with a steep inclination, and consists in the surface being covered with a number of small terracettes or low ledges, all running parallel, horizontal and at about an equal distance from each other. **1959** G. H. Dury *Face of Earth* ii. 13 On very many steep slopes a kind of ribbed pattern appears on the surface of the creeping waste, with little steps a foot or two in height running horizontally. These steps are called terracettes. An alternative name is sheep-tracks, but this title is grossly misleading. Terracettes can be found where no sheep have ever been. **1971** I. G. Gass et al. *Understanding Earth* xiii. 182/2 Tiny terracettes can be cut into the sides of the ripples [on a beach]. **1974** C. Taylor *Fieldwork in Medieval Archaeol.* iv. 85 Terracettes are another form of natural feature likely to be misinterpreted.

terracing, *vbl. sb.* Add: **1. b.** *spec.* = *Terrace *sb.* 1 e.

1902 [in Dict.]. **1942** *R.A.F. Jrnl.* 30 May 33 It was like the empty terracings of Wembley or Hampden Park after an international. **1976** J. Snow *Cricket Rebel* 68 The occasional fires on the terracing which are part and parcel of cricket matches in Pakistan. **1978** P. Marsh et al. *Rules of Disorder* iii. 58 Young supporters at every football league ground..have defined sections of the terracing as their own territory.

Terra da (de, di) Sienna, varr. Terra Sienna in Dict. and Suppl.

terraglia (terā·lyă). *Ceramics.* [a. It., = earthenware, china, f. L. *terra* earth.] An (Italian) cream-coloured earthenware, esp. that manufactured from 1728 at Nove, near Bassano, Italy, by G. B. Antonibon and his descendants.

1850 J. Marryat *Coll. Hist. Pott. & Porc.* 290 *Terraglia*, the Italian term for fine pottery of hard paste. **1870** W. Chaffers *Marks & Monogr. Pott. & Porc.* (ed. 3) 118 Pasqual [Antonibon]..carried on..the manufacture of *maioliche fine* or fayence, and *terraglia* or terre de pipe. **1877** C. Schreiber *Jrnl.* 20 June (1911) II. 28 A very fine Terraglia dish (red ground with figures in white..)..of old Paduan manufacture. **1960** R. G. Haggar *Conc. Encycl. Continental Pott. & Porc.* 471/1 *Terraglia*, cream-coloured earthenware.

terrain, *sb.* (*a.*) Add: **A.** *sb.* **2. b.** *fig.*

1860 Princess Royal *Let.* 3 Dec. in R. Fulford *Dearest Child* (1964) 288 She will..not [have] such a difficult 'terrain' to work upon as God knows I have here. **1979** *Amer. Poetry Rev.* Mar./Apr. 19/4 He found authors in that terrain of brotherhood and contact the reader calls for and which they, the writers I've named and so many others, gave and go on giving by the courses and the conduct which touch their responsibility as Latin Americans.

4. *attrib.* and *Comb.*, as **terrain-following radar** *Aeronaut.*, a radar system which enables an aircraft or missile to fly at high speed close to the ground by automatically adjusting its altitude in relation to the surface over which it is flying; so **terrain follower.**

1961 *Daily Tel.* 4 Oct. 17/1 A device known as the 'terrain follower', which keeps the plane automatically at a predetermined height above the ground. **1970** *Times* 4 Sept. (Aviation Suppl.) p. ix/8 Advanced avionics technology for the European multirole combat aircraft will be shown, with strike and terrain-following radar. **1980** *Guardian Weekly* 13 July 1/2 Terrain-following radar for low-level penetration of enemy defences.

‖ **terrain vague** (teræ̃ vāg). [Fr. colloq., lit. 'waste ground'.] Wasteland, no man's land (*transf.* and *fig.*).

1920 R. Fry *Let.* 12 Oct. (1972) II. 493 I'm..painting up on Montmartre in a *terrain vague* with the hideous white tower of the Sacré Coeur dominating a jumble of modern houses. **1934** C. Lambert *Music Ho!* iii. 207 The same rapprochement between highbrow and lowbrow—both meeting in an emotional *terrain vague*—can be seen in literature. **1957** L. Durrell *Bitter Lemons* 48 His desk was in the far corner against the wall, and to reach it one traversed a *terrain vague* which resembled the basement of Maple's, so crowded was it with armchairs, desks, prams..and all the impedimenta of gracious living. **1984** *Sunday Times* 26 Aug. 38/8 Alastair Reid occupies a *terrain vague* between reportage and *belles lettres*.

terral. Add to def.: Off the coast of Spain or South America. (Earlier and later examples.)

1863 H. W. Bates *Naturalist on River Amazons* II. ii. 144 Canoes, in descending, only travel at night, when the terral, or light land-breeze, blows off the eastern shore. **1928** *Bryologist* XXXI. 125 The weather was very cold. We had been feeling the intense icy blasts of the *Terral* wind from the North [of Spain]. **1953** W. G. Kendrew *Climates of Continents* (ed. 4) xxxix. 481 The sea-breeze (virazon) and land-breeze (terral) are regular and prominent; the sea-breeze is often so strong on summer afternoons at Valparaiso..that boat-work is stopped. **1961** L. D. Stamp *Gloss. Geogr. Terms* 448/2 *Terral*, the land breeze along the coasts of western Peru.

terramare. (Later examples of *β*: *terremare* is sometimes used as an invariable form.)

1928 C. Dawson *Age of Gods* xiv. 330 With the Bronze Age there appears in North Italy the new and highly distinctive type of culture known as the Terremare. It receives its name from the peculiar pile settlements which form its characteristic feature. Unlike the lake villages the Terremare were built on dry land and surrounded by an artificial moat and rampart. **1939** *Antiquity* XIII. 490 A terramara is defined by Säflund as 'a station containing the typical bronze-age culture of central and western Emilia'. **1961** L. Mumford *City in Hist.* viii. 206 It is doubtful if there is any direct connexion between the *terremare* settlements and the Roman towns.

Terramycin (terămai·sin). *Pharm.* Also **terramycin.** [f. L. *terra* earth + *-mycin.] A proprietary name for *oxytetracycline.

1950 A. C. Finlay et al. in *Science* 27 Jan. 85/1 From both cultures of this organism, a crystalline antibiotic was isolated; the name Terramycin has been assigned to this compound. **1953** *Official Gaz.* (U.S. Patent Office) 5 May 22/1 Chas. Pfizer & Co., Inc...*Terramycin* for antibiotic preparation containing oxytetracycline or a derivative thereof. **1954** *Trade Marks Jrnl.* 11 May 479/1 *Terramycin*... Oxytetracycline and derivatives thereof, and substances containing oxytetracycline or derivatives thereof, all prepared for use as antibiotics. Chas. Pfizer & Co., Inc. **1956** A. Huxley *Let.* 25 Dec. (1969) 814, I was put on to acromycin, after terramycin had failed to do much good. **1960** *Spectator* 2 Sept. 353 As compensation for the loss of his farmyard freedom he gets a dose of aureomycin, terramycin or penicillin. **1976** *Daily Times* (Lagos) 5 Aug. 14/1 (Advt.), Terramycin eye ointment.

Terran (te·răn), *a.* and *sb.* *Science Fiction.* [f. L. *terra* earth + -an.] **A.** *adj.* Of or pertaining to the planet Earth or its inhabitants. **B.** *sb.* An inhabitant of the planet Earth.

[**1881** W. D. Hay *Three Hundred Years Hence* xi. 267 I am speaking of the Terrane Exodus and the Cities of the Sea.] **1953** *Cosmos Sci. Fiction & Fantasy Mag.* Nov. 83 A chant rose to assail his ears, and the steady beat of a drum thundered in the Terran night. *Ibid.* 78 They set about the tremendous task of educating Martians and Terrans. **1960** K. Amis *New Maps of Hell* (1961) ii. 63 Any Martian survey team would be well advised to read a sample of the stuff before reporting on Terran civilisation. **1962** E. F. Russell *Great Explosion* i. 13 We shall face them and defeat them as Terrans always have done. **1969** *New Scientist* 23 Jan. 191/3 Like our planet, we Terrans tend to be fat and slow or thin and quick.

terranean, *a.* Add: (Later example.)

1939 Joyce *Finnegans Wake* 120 Of an early muddy terranean origin.

B. *sb.* Also **terranian.** An inhabitant of the planet Earth. *Science Fiction. rare.*

1913 'Sepharial' *Kabala of Numbers* II. xi. 175 Red is an irritant to all but Martians, and to them green probably means the same thing as does red to us Terranians. **1965** *Punch* 27 Jan. 141/3 When one of the anemone-harnessers..tells a couple of captive 'terraneans', i.e., grown-ups, 'You must be destroyed!' I could sense a tremble of joy in children everywhere.

terrapin. Add: **c. Terrapin State,** a colloquial name for the State of Maryland.

1937 G. E. Shankle *Amer. Nicknames* 338/1 Maryland is nicknamed *The Terrapin State* because of the extensive diamondback terrapin farms. **1949** B. A. Botkin *Treas. S. Folklore* i. ii. 35 Maryland has had half a dozen or more nicknames since colonial times, but only *Old Line State* and *Terrapin State* have any remaining vitality today.

Terrapin[2] (te·răpin). Also **terrapin.** The proprietary name of a make of prefabricated building, usu. having one storey and designed for temporary use.

1949 *Trade Marks Jrnl.* 21 Sept. 841/2 *Terrapin*... Portable buildings. Harry Collett Bolt, 21, Kings Gardens, West End Lane, Hampstead, London, N.W... Manufacturer and Merchant. **1962** *Ibid.* 25 July 958/2 Terrapin Minihouses... All goods included in Class 19. Terrapin Limited, Haddon House, 2–4, Fitzroy Street, London, W.1; Manufacturers. **1972** *Guardian* 5 Dec. 17/6 The main concerns of [school] governors tend to be.. asking the Works Department for an extra radiator in an exposed 'terrapin'. **1976** T. Sharpe *Wilt* vi. 56 He looked round the car park at the terrapin huts and the main building.

terrarium. Add: Pl. now usu. **terrariums. 1.** (Later examples.)

1952 M. K. Wilson tr. *Lorenz's King Solomon's Ring* vii. 67 On the table..stands the nucleus of my golden hamster stud, a simple little terrarium. **1976** N. Coleman *Shell Collecting in Australia* ix. 149 The larger the terrarium and the smaller the number of snails, the less work will be involved in keeping it sanitary. **1977** *Sci. Amer.* Dec. 36/1 Spiders and scorpions in neat terrariums.

2. A sealed transparent globe or similar container in which plants are grown, usu. for decoration. Cf. *Wardian case. orig. *U.S.*

1931 *St. Nicholas* Oct. 846/1 Have you ever tried making a terrarium?.. It means a little garden under glass—not a conservatory or a cold frame, but a real little landscape. **1942** *Amer. Speech* XVII. 284/1 He also saw on his rambles a *Terrarium*—a covered glass globe or fish-tank containing flowers and plants to be grown indoors during the winter. **1974** *Evening Herald* (Rock Hill, S. Carolina) 19 Apr. 6/5 (Advt.), Globe shaped terrarium kit... A unique way to display foliage. **1979** *Sunday Mail* (Brisbane) 6 May 5/1 (Advt.), Terrariums add life to any room. In long lasting plastic; each containing an African violet plus three other selected plants. **1982** *N.Y. Times* 11 Apr. ii. 33/4 Partridgeberry..is often used in terrariums for its evergreen foliage and red berries.

terra rosa (te·ră rōu·ză). *Painting.* [a. It., lit. = rose-coloured earth.] A light red colour of paint similar to Venetian red.

1897 *Sears, Roebuck Catal.* 360/3 Colors for Artists.. Gold Ochre,..Terra Rosa, Terre Verte. **1935** *Winsor & Newton's Sales Man.* 56 Colours which may be regarded.. inflexible under all conditions of Oil Painting..Terra Rosa. **1973** F. Taubes *Painter's Dict. Materials & Methods* 224 *Terra rosa* is a very light Iron Oxide Red of relatively slight Tinting Strength. For all practical purposes, this color is interchangeable with *Terra di Pozzuoli*.

terra rossa (te·ră rǫ·să). [a. It., = red earth.] A reddish soil occurring on limestone in Mediterranean climates (see also quot. 1938).

1882 A. Geikie *Text-bk. Geol.* 458 Fuchs believes that the 'terra rossa' is only present in dry climates where the amount of humus is small. **1938** *U.S. Dept. Agric. Yearbk.* 991 Many writers have preferred to limit Terra Rossa to soils developed on limestones, while some would have it include any red soil in a Mediterranean climate... At present its only distinction lies in its color. **1956** *Proc. Prehist. Soc.* XXI. 53 Most brown-earths are characteristic of deciduous forests, chernozems of steppe, and terra rossas of Mediterranean forests on limestone. **1975** *Nature* 14 Aug. 566/1 Further evidence for the role of climate is provided by the fact that the limestone soils from Apulia, the Orbetello region and the southern Apennines, which are mainly of the red Mediterranean type (that is, terra rossa) exhibit higher percentage conversions than those from the Central Apennines which are mainly rendzinas.

‖ **terra roxa** (te·ră rǫ·ʃă). [Pg., = reddish-purple soil.] A deep, humus-rich soil of a dark reddish-purple colour on the Paraná Plateau in southern Brazil.

1870 C. F. Hartt *Thayer Exped: Sci. Results Journey Brazil: Geol. & Physical Geogr.* xvii. 514 The terra roxa of Campinas Paulo is..the continuation of the drift-paste of the higher lands and seaward slope of the serra. **1977** *Econ. Geogr.* LIII. 78/2 Areas with larger concentrations of *terra roxas*, the soil of exceptional fertility for coffee, are usually associated with higher levels of production.

Terra Sienna. (Earlier and later examples of *Terra de Sienna* and var.)

1794 A. Thomas *Newfoundland Jrnl.* (1968) ii. 29 The shores of the Scilly Islands abound with rare and very curious Shells. Some are highly polish'd, of the colour of Terra de Sina [*sic*].., others are striped. **1869** *Bradshaw's Railway Manual* XXI. 460/3 (Advt.), Browns. Vandyke Brown..Terra de Sienna. **1885** *Encycl. Brit.* XIX. 87/1 The well-known ochre Terra da Sienna which in its raw state is a dull-coloured ochre, becomes when burnt a fine warm mahogany brown hue highly valued for artistic purposes.

terra sigillata. Add: **3.** *Archæol.* [Cf. W. Dorow *Opferstätte und Grabhügel der Germanen und Römer am Rhein* (1821) II. 32, etc.] A type of fine Roman pottery made from the first century B.C. to the third century A.D. in Gaul (also Italy and Germany), usu. red in colour and sometimes decorated with stamped figures or patterns. Not the preferred term in English: see *ARRETINE *a.*, SAMIAN *a.* and *sb.* in Dict. and Suppl.

H. Brunsting, in *Overdruk uit Westerheem* (1972) XXI. 252–68, provides a detailed glossary of references to the ware in English and Continental sources. Quot. 1845 below is often mistaken for the first English use of the term: it relates in fact to the medicinal tablet or pastille (sense 1).

[**1845** E. B. PRICE in *Gentl. Mag.* Feb. 142/1 It is termed 'Terra Samia sigillata', of circular form, about ⅞ of an inch diameter... It is of a pale dull red colour, and has apparently been made into a paste and dried in a mould.] **1903** *Amer. Jrnl. Archaeol.* VII. 485 J. Déchelette publishes the results of a study of the *terra sigillata* ..in the territory of the Ruteni near Millau. **1920** OSWALD & PRYCE *Introd. Stud. Terra Sigillata* i. 1 Next to datable inscriptions, there is, perhaps, no relic of Roman occupation which yields such valuable chronological evidence as *Terra Sigillata.* **1936** *Oxoniensia* I. 50 In and immediately below this layer much pottery was found including Terra Sigillata of the second century. **1959** *Chambers's Encycl.* XI. 761/2 Italian *terra sigillata*, or Arretine ware, was chiefly manufactured at Arretium. **1978** M. GILBERT *Empty House* xi. 94 The stuff we call Samian, or Terra Sigillata, which was manufactured in Central Gaul.

‖ **terrasse** (tęras). [Fr.: see TERRACE *sb.*] In France, etc.: a flat, paved area outside a building, esp. a café, where people sit to take refreshments.

1918 A. BENNETT *Roll-Call* I. ix. 197 They sat down on the *terrasse* of a large café near the Place des Ternes. **1930** —— *Imperial Palace* II. lvii. 433 Evelyn, in his big overcoat, was sitting on the *terrasse* of a large café. **1967** R. PETRIE *Foreign Bodies* i. 8 On the *terrasse* Nassim Yussif was turning between his hands a small white envelope. **1979** P. WAY *Sunrise* II. xii. 127 On the hotel *terrasse*, Olsen tipped his chair back and regarded Marriott.

‖ **terra verde,** etc., varr. TERRE VERTE in Dict. and Suppl.

terrazzo (tĕrā·tso). [a. It., = terrace, balcony.] A flooring material made of chips of marble or granite set in concrete and polished to give a smooth surface.

1902 *Encycl. Brit.* XXIX. 340/1 Wood has been superseded by terrazzo... Cracks may be seen in terrazzo floors introduced into several of the recently erected modern hospitals. **1925** *Glasgow Herald* 27 Feb. 7 Terazzo-faced concrete blocks. *Ibid.*, The outer walls being of the terrazzo block. **1958** *House & Garden* Mar. 69/1 The Esse-Dura stove sits on a terrazzo hearth in the living room **1973** [see *RAILED *ppl. a.* 1]. **1983** *Listener* 19 May 16/1 Italians were brought from Italy to lay terrazzo in a new building in West Africa.

‖ **terre-à-terre** (tęr a tęr), *adj.* (and *adv.*) *phr.* The usual form of TERRA A TERRA 2. Substitute for def.: In *Ballet*, applied to a step or manner of dancing in which the feet remain on or close to the ground. In *transf.* use: down-to-earth, realistic, matter-of-fact; pedestrian, unimaginative. Also as *adv. phr.* (Further examples.)

1830 [see *ELEVATION 1 e]. **1884** W. JAMES *Ess. Radical Empiricism* (1912) xii. 266 No seeker of truth can fail to rejoice at the terre-à-terre sort of discussion of the issues between Empiricism and Transcendentalism..that seems to have begun in *Mind.* **1907** —— *Pragmatism* vii. 268 Shutting out all wider metaphysical views and condemning us to the most *terre-à-terre* naturalism. **1915** M. E. PERUGINI *Art of Ballet* iii. 33 To dance, '*terre-à-terre*', that is, with the feet, or one foot at least, on or close to the ground. **1920** *Athenæum* 5 Nov. 617/2 The author of 'Les Baisers' always elegantly *terre-à-terre*, formulates his more concrete desires. **1930** *Time & Tide* 18 Apr. 500/2 He was too frank not to admit that his friend and chief was, intellectually, very *terre-à-terre.* **1941** *Burlington Mag.* Aug. 37/2 The romanticism of this portrait is not the sophisticated, rarefied one..: it is definitely more terre-à-terre. **1961** *Times* 27 May 6/2 He regrets that the Bolshoi ballet seemed to pay so little attention to *terre à terre* dancing. **1981** *Listener* 26 Feb. 284/3 She..was 'a credible girl who suffered from menstrual cramps'... You can't get more *terre à terre* than that. **1983** M. KEYNES *Lydia Lopokova* 59 During the next year, 1912, Lydia.. danced an extremely difficult terre-à-terre 'toe dance'.

‖ **terre cuite** (tęr kwit). [Fr., lit. 'baked (cooked) earth'.] = TERRA-COTTA 1.

1869 C. SCHREIBER *Jrnl.* 14 Oct. (1911) I. 53 We were charmed with four ancient costume pictures of fêtes.. and five terre cuites portraits by J. R. Nini. **1870** *Ibid.* 26 Feb. 76 One of the dealers..took us to her private house to show us some terre cuites. **1882** 'OUIDA' *Bimbi* 55 The *terres cuites* of Blasius date from 1560. **1926** R. FIRBANK *Concerning Eccentricities of Cardinal Pirelli* v. 57 A voluptuous small *terre cuite*, depicting a pair of hermaphrodites amusing themselves. **1951** N. MITFORD *Blessing* I. xi. 113 Once you fall into Louis XV you are immediately in the domain of restored terre cuite and broken china.

terrella. Restrict † *Obs.* to sense 2 in Dict. and add: **1.** (Later example.) *rare.*

1959 *Daily Tel.* 23 Feb. 11/8 Col. Steinkamp used the word 'terrella'—a little world or earth—in the context of space flight.

terrenity. For † *Obs.* read *rare* and add later example.

1973 T. PYNCHON *Gravity's Rainbow* IV. 733 Trees creak in sorrow for the engineered wound through their terrain, their terrenity or earthhood.

‖ **terre pisée** (tęr pize). [Fr., lit. 'beaten earth'.] = PISÉ a in Dict. and Suppl. Cf. COB *sb.*^{2} a.

1936 V. G. CHILDE *Man makes Himself* vi. 124 Soon houses built of mud or *terre pisée* were being erected. **1949** W. F. ALBRIGHT *Archaeol. of Palestine* v. 86 A concomitant of the introduction of chariotry into warfare was the spread of the art of building great fortifications of beaten earth (*terre pisée*), usually rectangular in plan. **1972** Y. YADIN *Hazor* 203 As for the claim that the earthen ramparts and *terre pisée* defences were first built in the MB IIA, only little has to be added here.

terrestrial, *a.* and *sb.* Add: **A.** *adj.* **2. e.** *Astr.* Designating planets which are similar in size or composition to the Earth.

1888 C. A. YOUNG *Textbk. Gen. Astron.* xiv. 322 The terrestrial planets are Mercury, Venus, the earth, and Mars. They are bodies of the same order of magnitude.., not very different in density.., and are probably roughly alike in physical constitution. **1926** E. A. FATH *Elem. Astron.* xi. 135 The eight planets fall into two groups, the first usually being termed the terrestrial planets. **1973** *Nature* 17 Aug. 424/2 The terrestrial planets..are solid bodies. **1980** *Sci. Amer.* Jan. 68/2 Io..and Callisto belong to the family of objects designated terrestrial.

terre-verte. (Later examples of variant forms.)

1897 *Sears, Roebuck Catal.* 361/1 Colors for Artists... King's Yellow, Lamp Black, Terra Verta. **1907** *Yesterday's Shopping* (1969) 471/2 Water Colours... Sunny green..Terra vert..Turner brown. **1919** R. FRY *Let.* 27 Oct. (1972) II. 463, I use..burnt umber, indian red and terra verte. Terra verte pure is too bright for the sky. **1944** *Burlington Mag.* Apr. 92/2 According to the literary tradition this fresco was painted in *terra verde.* **1973** *Times Lit. Suppl.* 8 June 634/5 Florence,..where Uccello's fresco of him, in terra-verde, adorns a wall of the Duomo.

‖ **terribilità** (teribilita·). Also **terribiltà.** [It.] **a.** In an artist or work of art: awesomeness of conception and execution, orig. as a quality attributed to Michelangelo by his contemporaries (e.g. by S. del Piombo in a letter of 9 Nov. 1520: see G. Milanesi *Les Correspondants de Michel-Ange* (1890) 24).

1883 *Encycl. Brit.* XVI. 230/2 In it the qualities afterwards proverbially associated with Michelangelo—his *furia*, his *terribilità*, the tempest and hurricane of the spirit which accompanied his unequalled technical mastery and knowledge—first found expression. **1923** A. HUXLEY *Antic Hay* xviii. 253 All this *folie de grandeur*, all this hankering after *terribiltà*..it's led so many people astray. **1948** *Penguin New Writing* XXXIV. 47 The Edwardian Mannerist arcade..with its stork and swiss-roll terribiltà. **1961** *Daily Tel.* 5 Dec. 13/4 In these [*sc.* Piranesi's engravings of prisons] he conveys a degree of terribilità no one else has conferred upon architecture. **1970** *Oxf. Compan. Art* 720/1 That emotional intensity which Michelangelo's contemporaries recognized as his *terribilità* and which earned him the veneration of his juniors.

b. In general use: terrifying or awesome quality.

1957 J. RAYMOND in *New Statesman* 28 Sept. 386/2 Half the horror of Rolfe's life—and its accompanying virtue, his pathetic and gallant attempt to live up to a self-taught conception of honour, *terribilità*, and esteem.. —sprang from the fact that he was a *déraciné* and a homosexual. **1959** *Times* 1 Apr. 11/4 The terribilità has long been drained from air travel. **1975** *New Yorker* 12 May 42/2 Fathers have voices, and each voice has a *terribilità* of its own.

terribility. (Later example.)

1922 JOYCE *Ulysses* 686 The terribility of her.. propinquity.

terrible, *a.* Add: **2. a.** (Later examples.)

1884 QUEEN VICTORIA *Let.* 27 Feb. in R. Fulford *Beloved Mama* (1981) 161 The amount of writing is as they say at Balmoral 'just terrible'. **1924** 'K. MANSFIELD' in *Collier's* 5 Jan. 37/2 She leaned against him and looked into his eyes. 'Hasn't it been terrible, all to-day?' said Edna. 'I knew what was the matter.' **1939** G. B. SHAW *In Good King Charles's Golden Days* I. 7 Just as I have my terrible weakness for figures Mr. Rowley has a very similar weakness for women. **1945** [see *SHOW *v.* 25 d]. **1965** E. J. HOWARD *After Julius* vii. 100 Her mother had made his life so terrible—not worth living.

b. Applied to a person who behaves in a shocking or outrageous manner; *terrible child* or *infant* = *ENFANT TERRIBLE; *terrible twins*, applied *joc.* to a pair of associates whose behaviour is troublesome or outrageous.

1859 C. READE *Love me Little, love me Long* I. i. 6 Poor Reginald was not analytical,..like certain pedanticules, who figure in story as children. He was a terrible infant, not a horrible one. **1926** A. HUXLEY *Two or Three Graces* 25 Peddley was not the man to be put out by even the most terrible of terrible infants. **1958** B. BEHAN *Borstal Boy* I. 77 When I was a child, my father used to get the *News of the World*... I used to wonder..why my mother said, half-laughing in spite of herself, that he was a terrible man, because it was banned at home. **1964** in Hamblett & Deverson *Generation X* 47, I used to be terrible. I couldn't stand my girls looking at other men, but I'm different now. **1965** M. SPARK *Mandelbaum Gate* vii. 207 An English female voice..said, 'Oh, look at that terrible man—,' obviously referring to Freddy. **1970** C. HAMPTON *Philanthropist* v. 69 All the men I fall in love with turn out to be such terrible people. **1976** *Evening Advertiser* (Swindon) 31 Dec. 8/1 The 'Terrible Twins' of yesteryear, Mr Jack Jones, general secretary of the Transport and General Workers, and Mr Hugh Scanlon, president of the Engineering Workers, have mellowed. **1978** CADOGAN & CRAIG *Women & Children First* x. 222 Violet Elizabeth, the terrible child of the William books. **1982** *Financial Times* 10 May 10/3 Since the 'terrible twins', as they were dubbed, were both powerful figures, and did not always see eye-to-eye on matters, this rivalry was reflected down the line.

c. As a hyperbolic term of depreciation: of shockingly poor performance or quality; incompetent; defective.

1925 F. SCOTT FITZGERALD *Great Gatsby* ii. 35, I..read a chapter of 'Simon Called Peter'—either it was terrible stuff or the whiskey distorted things, because it didn't make any sense to me. **1946** 'E. CRISPIN' *Moving Toyshop* i. 8 Three books..about me (all terrible, but never mind that). **1948** C. FRY *Thor with Angels* 20 As far as he can remember, Though he has a terrible memory for names, His name is Merlin. **1964** in Hamblett & Deverson *Generation X* 88 He was hopeless—you follow me?—terrible in bed. That's why his missus left him..to himself. **1972** [see *LINE *sb.*^{2} 1.e]. **1979** 'J. LE CARRÉ' *Smiley's People* (1980) xxi. 257 Grigorieva got herself a driving license two months ago... She's a terrible driver, George. And I mean terrible. **1983** R. RENDELL *Speaker of Mandarin* xvi. 190, I got this Hollywood offer and I went to Hollywood and made that terrible *Mind over Matter.*

3. quasi-*adv.* Now chiefly *dial.* and *U.S.* (Later examples.)

1901 M. FRANKLIN *My Brilliant Career* (1966) xxxi. 197 The old yeos [ewes] looks terrible skinny. **1926** E. O'NEILL *Great God Brown* Prol. 16 My mother used to believe the full of the moon was the time to sow. She was terrible old-fashioned. **1959** L. HUGHES *Sel. Poems* 144 He mistreated her terrible.

terribly, *adv.* Add: **2. a.** (Earlier example as a general intensive.)

1833 DICKENS *Let.* ?Oct. (1965) I. 31, I am terribly out of spirits this morning.

b. Extraordinarily badly; incompetently, feebly. Cf. sense *2 c of the adj. *colloq.*

1930 *Publishers' Weekly* 29 Mar. 1741 (Advt.), About 1,000,000 [bridge players] now play Contract, almost all of them terribly. **1964** J. MITCHELL *White Father* iii. 54 You can sing terribly and get away with it if only you have the right backing.

terricolous, *a.* Add: **2.** = TERRICOLE *a.* 1.

1921 A. L. SMITH *Handbk. Brit. Lichens* 142/1 Terricolous, living on soil. **1959** U. K. DUNCAN *Guide to Study of Lichens* p. xiv, Sand-dunes and heaths are usually rich in terricolous species.

terrier^2. Add: **3.** (Later examples.)

1915 [see *DO *sb.*^{1} 2 b]. **1935** *Economist* 7 Sept. 464/1 This change-over of responsibilities inside the War Office places the 'Terriers' within the same organisation as the 'Regulars'. **1980** *Times* 12 Mar. 12/4 More Terriers. The strength of the Territorial Army on December 31 last year was just under 62,000.

4. terrier-man *Hunting*, a man employed to head the terriers.

1930 C. FREDERICK et al. *Foxhunting* x. 130 If the bag is suspended..by strong pieces of india-rubber..it is more comfortable for the terrier and the terrier man. **1983** *Times* 19 Sept. 4/6 The terrierman..had slashed a fox's paw with a knife before releasing it for young hounds to chase.

terrier (te·riəɹ), *v. rare.* [f. prec.] *intr.* To burrow in the manner of a terrier; to make *one's way* like a terrier.

1959 R. COLLIER *City that wouldn't Die* ix. 155 Working with hand-shovels and even bare hands, Marotta and his crew began to terrier away. **1965** 'J. CHRISTOPHER' *Wrinkle in Skin* iii. 26 He began to terrier his way into the mound.

terrific, *a.* (*sb.*) Add: **A.** *adj.* **2. b.** As an enthusiastic term of commendation: superlatively good, 'marvellous', 'great'. Also *Comb. colloq.*

1930 D. MACKAIL *Young Livingstones* xi. 271 'Thanks awfully,' said Rex. 'That'll be ripping.' 'Fine!' said Derek Yardley. 'Great! Terrific!' **1940** *Chatelaine* Dec. 10/3 But think what it means that they want to come to you. Your bedside manner must be terrific. **1944** *Sun* (Baltimore) 20 Dec. 1/7 Lee McCardell [a reporter] is terrific—first into Metz, first into St. Avold, first into Saarlautern. **1951** 'A. GARVE' *Murder in Moscow* iii. 47 Perdita..looked terrific in midnight-blue velvet. **1951** J. D. SALINGER *Catcher in Rye* xii. 103 This..guy had a terrific-looking girl with him. Boy, she was good-looking. **1971** *Farmer & Stockbreeder* 23 Feb. 39/1 He believes the soil is 'terrific' for potatoes and wheat. **1981** *Daily Mail* 14 Oct. 15/1, 'I feel great, really terrific,' said the former Wings guitarist.

terrifyingly, *adv.* (Later examples.)

1908 H. G. WELLS *War in Air* vi. 194 It had crept in upon his mind, chillingly terrifyingly, that these illuminated black masses were great offices afire. **1944** D.

WELCH *In Youth is Pleasure* v. 89 He grinned, and then began to make the flesh round his eyes terrifyingly inflamed.

terrifyingness (te·rifəi,iŋnès). *rare.* [f. TERRIFYING *ppl. a.* + -NESS.] Frightening quality.
1940 *Scrutiny* IX. 294 It is not the terrifyingness of great poetry because it is too exclusively personal.

terrigenous, *a.* Restrict *rare* to senses 1 and 2. **3.** Add *esp.* after 'applied'. (Further examples.)
1884, etc. [see *PELAGIC *a.* c]. **1957** G. E. HUTCHINSON *Treat. Limnol.* I. viii. 550 Most of the calcium in atmospheric precipitation is of terrigenous origin. **1973** *Nature* 27 July 202/1 Deformed early Cainozoic, terrigenous and carbonate sediments form the highest parts of the island.

terrine. Add: **1.** Now, an earthenware or similar fireproof cooking vessel, esp. one in which a terrine (sense *2) is cooked.
1905 A. KENNEY-HERBERT *Common-Sense Cookery* (ed. 2) xxii. 358 Uncooked meats with forcemeat lining.. arranged as within a paste-lined mould, can be baked and finished in a *terrine*. **1914** F. B. JACKS *Cookery for Every Household* 304/2 Compote of Game... Put the joints [of roasted birds] into a fireproof terrine or casserole with the mushrooms and cherries..and leave these until the sauce is prepared. **1960** E. DAVID *French Provincial Cooking* 69 A pâté *en terrine* indicates that the pâté concerned has been cooked and is served in the terrine rather than in a crust. **1979** *Homes & Gardens* June 135/2 The sheets of fat removed from the roast should be thinly sliced and used for lining terrines when making pâté.

2. Delete ‖. In modern use, a kind of pâté cooked in a terrine (sense *1).
1906 A. FILIPPINI *Internat. Cook Bk.* 631 (*heading*) Terrine of duckling. **1914** F. B. JACKS *Cookery for Every Household* 297/2 A terrine like this will keep good for two or three months in cold weather. **1968** D. BRIGGS *Entertaining Single-Handed* iv. 81 *Terrine Andrew.* A terrine is made from he same kind of bits and pieces as a pâté, but..the texture is rougher and it is cooked in a pie-dish or, indeed, a terrine. **1979** REESE & FLINT *Trick 13* 159, I bought an appetizing selection of rough terrine.

territorial, *a.* (*sb.*) Add: **1. d.** *territorial water(s)*, *territorial sea*: the area of sea adjoining the shores of a state and under its jurisdiction (traditionally reckoned as three miles from low water mark, but recently extended by many states). Cf. WATER *sb.* 6 d. Also *territorial limits*, the limits of such water.
1841 J. DODSON in Ld. McNair *Internat. Law Opinions* (1956) I. x. 334 A free permission to Foreign Fishing Vessels so to use the Ports and Territorial waters of our Coasts, would seem likely to lead to constant evasions and violations of the stipulation which prohibits them from fishing within the Limits. **1870** *Act* 33 & 34 *Vict.* c. 90 §2 This Act shall extend to all the dominions of Her Majesty, including the adjacent territorial waters. **1875** [in Dict., sense 1]. **1939** *Daily Tel.* 18 Dec. 1/1 Just beyond the three-mile limit of Uruguayan territorial waters, an unidentified British warship and an Argentine patrol boat had earlier been seen. **1955** *Times* 2 July 6/4 Passage is innocent as long as the vessel does not use the territorial sea for committing acts prejudicial to the security of the coastal State. **1962** *Britannia Bk. of Year* 207/2 Many states had declared, unilaterally, the right to exclusive fishing beyond the territorial limits claimed; *e.g.* Argentina, 3 mi. territorial limits (1869) and 10 mi. exclusive fisheries rights (1907); Thailand, 6 mi. (1958) and 12 mi. (1958). **1976** in R. Crossman *Diaries* II. 71 Since March 1964 pirate radio stations had been transmitting pop music and advertisements, usually from ships anchored outside territorial waters.

e. *Zool.* Of or pertaining to an area defended by an animal or a group of animals against others of the same species; also designating an animal or species that defends its territory in this way; *territorial imperative*, the need to claim and defend a territory.
1920 E. HOWARD *Territory in Bird Life* vi. 228 Do these battles..contribute towards the attainment of the end for which the whole territorial system has been evolved? **1940** *Misc. Publ. Mus. Zool. Univ. Michigan* XLV (*title*) Territorial behavior and populations of some small mammals in southern Michigan. **1961** *Science* 10 Mar. 698/1 The well-defined pattern of year-around territorial behavior of the Uganda kob was discovered in March 1957. **1966** R. ARDREY (*title*) The territorial imperative. *Ibid.* iii. 101 That man is a territorial species has been the conclusion of many a scientist. **1968** K. LORENZ in *Harper's Mag.* May 74 The 'territorial imperative' does much to explain the causes of war, such as the Arab-Israeli dispute, which I consider almost purely territorial. **1971** *Nature* 4 June 295/2 A territorial bull establishes himself as supremely dominant within the confines of his territory. **1980** C. AIRD *Passing Strange* iv. 47 If any one single instinct came to the fore in Superintendent Leeyes it was the territorial imperative. **1981** *Oxf. Compan. Animal Behaviour* 551/1 One benefit of territorial defence is food acquisition.

3. (Earlier example.) Also, of or belonging to one of the 'territories' of Canada (see *TERRITORY¹ 4).
1802 A. GALLATIN *Let.* 13 Feb. in *Deb. Congr. U.S.* 30 Mar. (1851) 1101 If..it is..the interest of the United States to obtain some further security against an injurious sale, under the Territorial or State laws, of lands sold by them to individuals. **1935** *Chambers's Encycl.* II. 703/1 Yukon has a 'Gold Commissioner' and an elected territorial council. **1953** R. MOON *This is Saskatchewan* 18 That day [*sc.* 18 Dec. 1901] the Territorial Grain Growers' Association was formed.

4. b. (Later examples of *Territorial Army.*) In other collocations: of or pertaining to the Territorial Army. *Territorial* as *sb.*: esp. in *pl.* = *Territorial Army.*
The Territorial and Army Volunteer Reserve was a civilian defence force created in 1967 by merging the Territorial Army and the Army Emergency Reserve and was itself renamed the Territorial Army in 1979.
1910 KIPLING *Divers. Creatures* (1917) 315 That was when we found the Territorial battalion undressin' in slow time. It lay on the left flank o' the Blue Army. **1914** G. B. SHAW *Misalliance* 65 *Tarleton*: Why not join the Territorials? *The man*: Because I shouldnt be let. **1938** W. S. CHURCHILL *Into Battle* (1941) 31 Why..are the Guards drilling with flags instead of machine-guns? Why is it that our small Territorial Army is in such a rudimentary condition? **1940** GRAVES & HODGE *Long Week-end* xxvi. 441 Hore-Belisha..called in the Attorney-General, asking him to warn Sandys, who was a Territorial officer,..that he had rendered himself liable to a court martial..for being in possession of confidential data. **1940** J. F. KENNEDY *Why England Slept* vii. 158 From this time on, it was also established that the Territorial Army, which corresponded somewhat to our National Guard, had 'a claim on the same sources and standards of instruction as the Regular Army'. **1962** M. & M. HARDWICK *Sherlock Holmes Companion* 231 He [*sc.* Conan Doyle] campaigned incessantly for the better training of Territorial reservists. **1970** *Daily Tel.* 14 Jan. 16 Trying to get a snappy recruiting message home to the public is a testing business for the TAVR Council now that they have been saddled with the ponderous legal name 'Territorial Army Volunteer Reserve'. *a* **1974** R. CROSSMAN *Diaries* (1976) II. 664 The proposal to disband the Territorials would now naturally be discussed with the Territorial Association.

territorialism. Add: **5.** *Zool.* = *TERRITORIALITY 2.
1933 M. M. NICE in *Fifty Years' Progress Amer. Ornithol.* (Amer. Ornithologists' Union) 89 (*title*) The theory of territorialism and its development. **1969** A. WHEELER *Fishes Brit. Isles & N.-W. Europe* 410 Strong territorialism is shown [in gobies], the males defending a suitable nesting site.

territoriality. Add: **2.** *Zool.* A pattern of behaviour in which an animal or a group of animals defends an area against others of the same species. Cf. prec.
1941 M. M. NICE in *Amer. Midland Naturalist* XXVI. 441 (*title*) The role of territoriality in bird life. **1943** *Jrnl. Mammalogy* XXIV. 346 The more we study the detailed behavior of animals, the larger is the list of kinds known to display some sort of territoriality. **1955** *Sci. Amer.* Oct. 92/3 No room was left for doubting..the territoriality of the owls. **1979** *Nature* 20–27 Dec. 885/1 Territoriality seems to be rare in bees and wasps, with the exception perhaps of males and their mate search behaviour.

Territorian. Substitute for def.: An inhabitant of the Northern Territory of Australia. (Later examples.)
1941 C. BARRETT *Coast of Adventure* 121 Old Territorians, over..a pannikin of tea by the campfire, will tell yarns as long as you'll listen. **1961** J. DANVERS *Living come First* vii. 121 All the people mixed up in the case are far more Territorians than South Australians. **1971** *Southerly* XXXI. 137 I'm a Territorian, Kenny Buckman's my name, n you gohher be good t'survive out there in the desert, I tell you.

‖ **territorium** (teritōᵊ·riŭm). *Rom. Hist.* Pl. **territoria.** [L.] The area of land surrounding and within the boundaries of a Roman city, *municipium*, etc., and under its jurisdiction. Also *transf.* of States having dealings with Rome.
1918 [see *CENTURIATE *v.* 2]. **1926** ABBOTT & JOHNSON *Municipal Admin. Roman Empire* ix. 134 The chief revenues of cities in other parts of the empire came from their *territoria*. **1949** *Oxf. Classical Dict.* 623/2 In Roman territory before 89 B.C. the chief *oppida* were those of the ex-Latin incorporated States. In them was centred the local administration of their former *territorium*. **1962** D. HARDEN *Phoenicians* v. 74 Carthage's fleet was burnt, her domain was henceforth to be confined to her *territorium* in eastern Tunisia.

territory¹. Add: **1. e.** *Zool.* An area chosen by an animal or a group of animals and defended against others of the same species.
1774 O. GOLDSMITH *Hist. Earth* V. 301 All these small birds mark out a territory to themselves, which they will permit none of their own species to remain in. **1914** J. S. HUXLEY in *Proc. Zool. Soc.* 521 There may be hostility between members of one pair and members of another... The only reason I can discover for it is the trespassing of one or both birds of a strange pair upon the 'territory' of another. **1920** E. HOWARD *Territory in Bird Life* i. 3 Securing a territory is then part of a process which has for its goal the successful rearing of offspring. **1933** *Brit. Birds* XXVII. 20 A certain area of land or territory.. extends around the nesting site. **1949** W. C. ALLEE et al. *Princ. Animal Ecol.* xxiii. 412/2 Territories tend to be larger when population pressure is low. **1953** N. TINBERGEN *Herring Gull's World* ix. 82 A Herring Gull returns to the same colony, and often even to the same territory. **1981** *Oxf. Compan. Animal Behaviour* 550/2 Territories range in size from the few millimetres that separate barnacles..on a rock to the distances of several kilometres that separate neighbouring herds of African buffalo.

f. The geographical area within which a firm or salesman operates. orig. *U.S.*
1900 *Cent. Mag.* Feb. 644/1 We've got to begin small. Our territory is Ohio. **1907** F. H. BURNETT *Shuttle* xxxviii. 379 Nick Baumgarten, who having for some time 'beaten' certain streets as assistant salesman.., had recently been elevated to a 'territory' of his own. **1925** *Daily Tel.* 13 May 20/7 Traveller Wanted... Live men can earn £10 a week. Territory given. **1931** *Economist* 26 Dec. 1235/2 A convenient pocket tabulation of the financial results of oil companies, which shows also the area of their territory, the number of wells. **1977** *Evening Gaz.* (Middlesbrough) 11 Jan. 9/1 (Advt.), A career in sales... Local territories available.

3. a. Also in various vague figurative contexts.
1927 *Daily Express* 30 Nov. 3/1, I think it is a fine plan to refuse, if possible, to be affected by an opponent's play... But I am sure I took in entirely too much territory when I said that his work should be ignored. **1971** N. CHOMSKY *Probl. Knowledge & Freedom* (1972) i. 34 To illustrate further, I would like to turn to some still unexplored territory. **1977** J. I. M. STEWART *Madonna of Astrolabe* v. 93 She was frowning now, aware of having got on territory she hadn't designed to tread.

4. Also applied, outside the U.S., to a region administered by a federal or external government, esp. a part of Canada (now only Northwest Territories and Yukon Territory) or Australia (Northern Territory) not yet organized as a province or state.
1897 C. R. TUTTLE *Golden North* 119 Two new provisional districts or territories have been erected in the far northwest by the Canadian government. The first is that called Mackenzie, lying to the north of Athabasca... The second is called Yukon. **1935** *Chambers's Encycl.* II. 699/1 In 1871, after confederation, the population of Canada (including seven provinces and the territories) was 3,689,257. **1936** I. L. IDRIESS *Cattle King* xii. 106 It dribbles south close to the Territory border all in the sand-hill country, until here it crosses the South Australian border. **1957** *Encycl. Brit.* XVII. 12/1 The Territory of Papua in the south-east [of New Guinea], formerly a British protectorate, is administered by Australia under a governor. *Ibid.*, It [*sc.* Norfolk Island] is a dependency of the Commonwealth of Australia, known officially as the Territory of Norfolk Island. **1969** *Northern Territory News* (Darwin) 11 July 3/2 It also has mining interests in the Territory and Queensland. **1979** G. WOODCOCK *Canadians* ii. x. 222 Even in Yellowknife, the capital of the [Northwest] Territories, I encountered an astonishing collection of people.

5. *territory-holder, -holding.*
1929 E. M. NICHOLSON *How Birds Live* iii. 31 The solitary territory-holder can only deal with single intruders. **1953** N. TINBERGEN *Herring Gull's World* vi. 55 A territory-holder stretches its neck as soon as a stranger alights in its neighbourhood. *Ibid.* 58 This [fight] happens.. when a territory-holding bird makes a surprise attack **1962** *Science Survey* XV. 238 A 'territory-holding' male robin will attack a bundle of red feathers.

terror, *sb.* Add: **2. a.** Also, this action or quality in fiction, esp. in *novel* (or *tale*) *of terror.*
a **1832** G. CRABBE *Posthumous Tales* xv, in *Poet. Wks.* (1834) VIII. 205 Yet tales of terror are her dear delight, All in the wintry storm to read at night. **1917** D. SCARBOROUGH *Supernatural in Mod. Eng. Fiction* i. 6 And so the Gothic novel came into being. *Gothic* is here used to designate the eighteenth-century novel of terror dealing with mediaeval materials. **1921** E. BIRKHEAD (*title*) The tale of terror: a study of the Gothic romance. **1977** M. ASHLEY *Who's who in Horror & Fantasy Fiction* 103 His masterpiece of terror was *The Castle of Ehrenstein* (1854), a superb portrayal of a ghost-ridden castle.

b. *Trivially.* A person (occas., a thing) fancied to excite terror; esp. a troublesome child; *holy terror*: see *HOLY *a.* 4 c.
1883, etc. [see *HOLY *a.* 4 c]. **1889** *Harper's Mag.* May 933/1 That bright boy..who was a terror six months ago. **1892** LADY R. CHURCHILL *Let.* 10 Jan. in R. S. Churchill *Winston S. Churchill* (1967) I. Compan. i. v. 305 Papa is very well & in good spirits but his beard is a 'terror'. **1900** [in Dict., sense 2]. **1908** G. SANGER *70 Yrs. a Showman* xvii. 58 Brumley..was a bit of a terror in his way, being a drunken bully. **1925** S. LEWIS *Martin Arrowsmith* vi. 63 She's an old terror. If she found a child like you wandering around here she'd drag you out by the ear. **1953** K. TENNANT *Joyful Condemned* xxxii. 311 It wasn't your fault. René was always a terror. You did what you could. **1979** A. MCCOWEN *Young Gemini* 25 At school I was known as a terror and went looking for fights.

4. *Reign of Terror* (earlier transf. examples); *the terror* (later examples applied to any period of remorseless repression). Hence, without article or pl., the use of organized intimidation, terrorism.
Red Terror, White Terror: see also under the adjs. in Suppl.
1831 *Wexford Herald* 11 June 2/3 The reign of terror—of Terryaltism. **1848** GEO. ELIOT *Let.* 8 Mar. (1954) I. 255 The Glasgow riots are more serious, but one cannot believe in a Scotch Reign of Terror in these days. **1920** *Glasgow Herald* 7 May 9 It was admitted that outrages were committed against the Socialists [in Hungary], but it was denied that a 'terror' existed. **1937** KOESTLER *Spanish Testament* vi. 132 They had neither the inclination nor the need to terrorise the population, to make warning examples, to safeguard the territory behind the lines by the application of methods of Terror. **1951** H. ARENDT *Burden of Our Time* I. i. 6 Terror as we know it today strikes without any preliminary provocation. **1966** G. GREENE *Comedians* iii. 100 The Trianon soufflé au Grand Marnier was famous for a time, until the terror started [in

Haiti] and the American Mission left. **1970** G. Jackson *Let.* 4 Apr. in *Soledad Brother* (1971) 212 All times of the day or night our cells were being invaded by the goon squad: you wake up, take your licks, get skin-searched... This treatment, fear therapy, was not accorded to all however... Mostly it came down on us. Rehabilitational terror. **1977** P. Johnson *Enemies of Society* xviii. 241 Thanks to their use of terror, they [*sc.* the Assassins] often controlled local authorities, and forced governments into compliance or impotence. **1978** *Encounter* July 15/1 Anyone who cannot see and appreciate the true difference between Russia today and Russia at the height of the Stalinist terror has a very poor idea of one or other of these phenomena.

5. a. *terror-novel, -romance*; (in sense 4) *terror act, group, organization, régime, tactics.* **b.** *terror-causing, -inspiring* (earlier example). **c.** *terror-stiffened, -stricken* (earlier example). **d.** Special Combs. **terror-bombing,** intensive and indiscriminate bombing designed to frighten a country into surrender; **terror raid,** a bombing raid of this nature.

1946 Koestler *Thieves in Night* 243 While the usual terror acts continued, the Jewish representative bodies issued their usual protests. **1941** *Reader's Digest* June 58/2 It must be remembered that this government today is Hitler, Göring, Goebbels, Himmler and a few others—men who..ordered the terror bombing of Rotterdam last summer and of London last winter. **1945** *Time* 26 Feb. 32/1 Terror bombing of German cities was deliberate military policy. **1959** R. Collier *City that wouldn't Die* ii. 27 To Sperrle the primary consideration was always that the pilot should see his target;..a Nuremberg tribunal absolved him of terror bombing. **1922** Joyce *Ulysses* 384 The terrorcausing shrieking of shrill women in their labour. **1977** P. Johnson *Enemies of Society* xviii. 242 The diabolism of Stavrogin, who preaches the doctrine that the terror-group can only be united by fear and moral depravity. **1839** Poe *William Wilson* in *Gift* 235 In a remote and terror-inspiring angle was a square enclosure. **1917** D. Scarborough *Supernatural in Mod. Eng. Fiction* i. 6 The terror novel proper is generally conceded to begin with his [*sc.* Horace Walpole's] Romantic curiosity, *The Castle of Otranto.* **1972** P. Haining *Gt. Brit. Tales of Terror* I. 117 William Beckford, author of the great Oriental terror-novel, *Vathek.* **1977** *Belfast Tel.* 22 Feb. 5/7 Growing police and Army success against the terror organisations. **1945** *Ann. Reg. 1944* 3 Lord Cranborne..pointed out that the Royal Air Force had never indulged in purely terror raids like those perpetrated by the Luftwaffe. **1977** J. Wainwright *Pool of Tears* 208 Dresden..That was a terror raid... A town turned into a blow-torch. **1952** Koestler *Arrow in Blue* viii. 68 Admiral Horthy established the first semi-Fascist terror régime in post-war Europe. **1931** R. L. Mégroz *Conrad's Mind & Method* x. 237 The 'Gothic' terror-romance of the eighteenth century. **1972** P. Haining *Gt. Brit. Tales of Terror* I. 477 From the later work comes the following grim story which contains much of that chilling atmosphere which made the Gothic terror-romance so widely popular in its time. **1887** Kipling *Departmental Ditties* (1888) 21 Felt the brute's proboscis fingering my terror-stiffened hair. **1831** Poe *Poems* (ed. 2) 75 There the.. clouds do fly..Through the terror-stricken sky. **1974** *Encycl. Brit. Micropædia* V. 427/2 A 'provisional' wing [of the IRA]..comprising the younger, militant majority committed to the use of terror tactics.

terrorism. Add: **2.** (Later examples; cf. *terrorist 1 b). Also *transf.*

1936 W. H. S. Smith *Let.* 27 July in *Young Man's Country* (1977) ii. 19 The Constitutional League [of India], whose main purpose is to rouse public opinion against terrorism. **1957** L. Durrell *Bitter Lemons* 243 Though his complicity in EOKA was obvious, nevertheless he [*sc.* Makarios] was the only brake to terrorism and the only person who could curb it. **1958** B. Behan *Borstal Boy* III. 271 He said it was the fault of the British boss class that the Irish were forced always into terrorism to get their demands. **1963** *Ann. Reg. 1962* 236 The first half of the year was dominated by the difficulties of obtaining an Algerian settlement and, in particular, by the challenge to the authority of State presented by O.A.S. terrorism. **1973** *Cape Times* 27 Oct. 12 The Minister cannot expect journalists to do violence to the English language..by describing guerilla warfare as terrorism at all times and in all circumstances. **1977** *New Yorker* 24 Oct. 35/1 Last week's manifestations of political terrorism were crowded off the front pages..by more upbeat occurrences.

terrorist. 1. b. (Later examples in general use.)

In modern use the term usually refers to a member of a clandestine or expatriate organization aiming to coerce an established government by acts of violence against it or its subjects.

1947 *Ann. Reg. 1946* 60 The latest and worst of the outrages committed by the Jewish terrorists in Palestine—the blowing up of the King David Hotel in Jerusalem. **1956** H. Nicolson *Diary* 29 Oct. (1968) 311 When people rise against foreign oppression, they are hailed as patriots and heroes; but the Greeks whom we are shooting and hanging in Cyprus are dismissed as terrorists. What cant! **1969** E. J. Hobsbawm *Bandits* viii. 101 The war between police and terrorists is one of nerves as well as of guns. Whoever is more frightened has lost the initiative. **1977** P. Johnson *Enemies of Society* xviii. 240 The Baader-Meinhof gang of ultra-Left terrorists. **1979** *Spectator* 20 Oct. 20/1 (Advt.), In this enthralling autobiography the author of *Maquis*..retravels the course of his life from his childhood to his war-time exploits as a terrorist in the Resistance.

3. (Later examples.)

1937 Koestler *Spanish Testament* vi. 132 The civilian population...whose sympathies they could but alienate by terrorist acts. **1955** *Britannia Bk. of Year* 263/2, 756 Africans executed..incl. 219 for Mau Mau murders and 508 for other terrorist crimes. **1979** R. Perry *Bishop's Pawn* viii. 130 We weren't dealing with ordinary kidnappers. We were faced by a relatively sophisticated terrorist organization. **1983** *Listener* 19 May 8/1 Terrorist theory..says that the brigades should be subdivided into tight terrorist cells.

terroristic, *a.* Add: (Later examples.) Also **terrori·stically.**

1919 M. Beer *Hist. Brit. Socialism* I. II. ii. 103 The terroristic acts and wars into which that social earthquake had degenerated. **1945** R. Hargreaves *Enemy at Gate* 308 The terroristic procedure associated in these days with Nazism, Fascism and Bolshevism. **1951** McWhiney & Simkins in A. Dundes *Mother Wit* (1973) 590/2 The klansmen used the methods of violence as extensively as any of the other white terroristic organizations. **1972** *Econ. & Polit. Weekly* 1 Apr. 692/1 Consisting almost exclusively of guerilla squads, they [*sc.* the Naxals] moved secretively and acted terroristically. **1977** *Time* 26 Sept. 9/1 The background of terroristic acts is connected with a deep hatred of bourgeois society.

terry, *sb.*[1] and *a.* Add: **A.** *sb.* **1.** In later use = *terry cloth, terry towelling* (see B below).

1895 *Montgomery Ward Catal.* Spring & Summer 24/1 White Turkish Towelling or Terry. The following Terry or Turkish Towelling is for children's cloaking, roller towels, etc. **1972** *New Yorker* 22 July 74/1 Our new multicolor stripe combines red, navy, gold and sky-blue on white terry. **1981** *Guardian* 19 Oct. 14/5 Having immersed the terries in a steriliser, I give them a short cold water rinse... This regime means that washing terry nappies is no longer a great chore.

B. *adj.* (Later examples.) Now esp. of or pertaining to *terry towelling,* an absorbent cotton or linen cloth used for making towels, beachwear, babies' napkins, etc.; in the U.S. called *terry cloth* (freq. *attrib.*).

1897 H. Neville *Students' Handbk. Pract. Fabric Structure* xii. 136 Beginning with terry-towelling, as the simplest form of looped pile work. **1906** H. Nisbet *Gram. Textile Design* viii. 163 Terry fabrics produced by means of terry motions are exemplified in so-called Turkish towels... The majority of these goods are produced entirely from cotton, although terry towels are sometimes produced either entirely or in part from linen. **1917** *Harrods Catal.* 1440/1 Terry Dusters or Paint Cloths. **1921** *Daily Colonist* (Victoria, B.C.) 15 Mar. 4/5 (Advt.), 36-Inch New Terry Cloth $1.69 a Yard. **1937** *Night & Day* 8 July 22/1 Terry towelling is responsible for a great many irresistible beach affairs. **1944** R. Chandler *Lady in Lake* iii. 18 A big guy in bathing trunks..and a white terrycloth bathrobe. **1959** *Harrods News* Summer 9 Terry towel for bath or beach. **1961** A. Miller *Misfits* iv. 44 He turns and sees Roslyn in a terry-cloth robe emerging from the bedroom doorway. **1961** *Listener* 12 Oct. 558/1 An artificial mother constructed of wire and terry towelling. **1975** *Guardian* 27 Jan. 15/2 A completely new type of tufting machine which is directed specifically at the terry trade...[It] makes a cloth with one face of terry material. **1980** L. Birnbach et al. *Official Preppy Handbk.* 155/1 Need a pair of frog-print slacks or a terry cloth halter jumpsuit? **1981** [see sense A. 1 above].

Terry Alt, Terryalt (te·ri ǭlt). *Irish Hist.* Also *ellipt.* **Terry.** [According to a MS. diary of 1831 quoted in *Times Lit. Suppl.* (1932) 29 Sept. 691/4, *Terry Alts* was the name of an innocent bystander suspected of an outrage on a man.] A member of a secret agrarian association active in western Ireland in the 1830s. Also *attrib.*

1831 D. O'Connell *Let.* 15 May (1888) I. 263 It is probable that, without the aid of the 'Terry Alt' system, he could not poll one hundred votes by all his other exertions. **1931** *Dublin Even. Post* 31 May 3/3 Michael Connelly, a chief leader of the Terry Alts. **1832** *Courier* 17 Feb. 2/5 The Terries in the County of Galway are levying contributions. **1861** W. J. FitzPatrick *Life Dr. Doyle* II. xxxix. 334 He urged the 'Shanavests', the 'Caravats', the 'Terryalts', and the 'Rockites', to abandon their deeds of blood; he implored of the Ribbonmen to cast their evil combinations to the winds. **1898** *Westm. Gaz.* 14 Nov. 4/2 The man was suspected of being a 'Terry Alt', or a member of a local agrarian conspiracy.

tertiary, *a.* and *sb.* Add: **A.** *adj.* **1. b.** Substitute for entry: (i) Applied to compounds regarded as being derived from ammonia by replacement of three hydrogen atoms by organic radicals, and to derivatives of such compounds; also extended to analogous derivatives of other elements, esp. phosphorus. [The sense is due to Gerhardt & Chiozza, who used F. *tertiaire* (*Compt. Rend.* (1853) XXXVII. 88).]

1854 *Q. Jrnl. Chem. Soc.* VI. 195 With regard to the tertiary amides,..their preparation is generally easier than that of the secondary amides. **1888,** etc. [see *primary *a.* 6 f (i)]. **1964** N. G. Clark *Mod. Org. Chem.* xii. 232 The tertiary amines,..with no available hydrogen, are the nitrogen counterparts of the ethers.

(ii) Applied to organic compounds other than amines, etc. (see prec. sense) in which the characteristic functional group is located on a saturated carbon atom which is itself bonded to three other carbon atoms. [Applied orig. to alcohols by H. Kolbe, who used G. *tertiär* (*Ann. der Chem. und Pharm.* (1864) CXXXII. 104).]

1872 *Jrnl. Chem. Soc.* XXV. 295 The oxidation of tertiary alcohols takes place according to a law similar to that which rules the oxidation of ketones. **1932** I. D. Garard *Introd. Org. Chem.* iii. 34 This formation of a ketone having fewer carbon atoms than the alcohol is characteristic of the oxidation of tertiary alcohols. **1964** N. G. Clark *Mod. Org. Chem.* xi. 222 The use of acyl chlorides in the above manner produces hydrogen chloride, which may have a deleterious effect on the compound undergoing acylation, e.g. tertiary alcohols readily give the alkyl chlorides. **1981** Wingrove & Caret *Org. Chem.* x. 435 Under basic conditions, tertiary alcohols do not undergo oxidation.

(iii) Applied to a saturated carbon atom which is bonded to three other carbon atoms; also, bonded to or involving a tertiary carbon atom. Of an ion or a free radical: having (respectively) the electric charge or the unpaired electron located on a tertiary carbon atom.

1903, etc. [see *secondary *a.* 3 i (iii)]. **1972** [see *primary *a.* 6 f (iii)].

c. *Surveying.* Designating triangulation derived by subdivision from secondary triangulation (which in turn results from subdivision of primary triangulation) or points, bench-marks, etc., established by this.

1851 C. Davies *Elementary Surveying* (rev. ed.) iv. i. 181 When the *secondary* and *tertiary* triangles have been considerably multiplied, the compass is taken in hand. **1883** J. R. Oliver *Pract. Astron. for Surveyors* II. ii. 121 The sides of the secondary triangles are from about 5 to 20 miles, and those of the tertiary triangles five or less. **1920** W. N. Thomas *Surveying* xiii. 382 A further subdivision resulted in the 'Tertiary' triangulation. **1965** Bannister & Raymond *Surveying* (ed. 2) ix. 293 The fourth order points give closer spacing in towns—tertiary and higher order points cover almost the whole country at a density of 0·05 trig point per km^2, with a density of about 0·1 per km^2 in towns. **1975** [see *secondary *a.* 3 a].

d. *Physics.* Produced by the impact of secondary particles with matter.

1938 R. W. Lawson tr. *Hevesy & Paneth's Man. Radioactivity* (ed. 2) v. 61 On the average 2 or 3 tertiary electrons result from each secondary electron, when the primary β-radiation has a velocity 33 per cent. that of light. **1961** G. R. Choppin *Exper. Nuclear Chem.* iii. 35 Tertiary electrons may be produced by photoemission resulting from the photons of the secondary ionization process.

e. Designating the part of the economy or work-force concerned with services of all kinds, rather than with the production of foodstuffs or raw materials, or with manufacturing.

1940 *Economist* 21 Sept. 363/1 There is a steady tendency for labour to move out of primary production into secondary production (manufacture) and from secondary to tertiary production (all forms of services). **1961,** etc. [see *quaternary *a.* 3 a]. **1974** B. Pearce tr. *Amin's Accumulation on World Scale* I. 16 The sectors of the tertiary part of the economy—transport, trade, financial services—..are grafted upon the foreign economy. **1975** *Guardian* 20 Jan. 16/4 Tertiary industries are also being introduced..plants for the preparation of prefabricated houses and timber for construction.

f. *tertiary structure* (Biochem.): the way the helix of a polynucleotide or polypeptide molecule is folded in three dimensions and bound to other helices.

1952, etc. [see *primary *a.* 6 v]. **1964** G. H. Haggis et al. *Introd. Molecular Biol.* iii. 59 The run of the peptide chain through the molecule..is known as the tertiary structure of a protein. **1978** *Nature* 5 Jan. 15/2 Studies on pancreatic trypsin inhibitor and hen egg white lysozyme suggest that at most there are only a limited number of folding pathways to the tertiary structure.

g. *tertiary road* (orig. *U.S.*), a Class III road.

1960 Baker & Stebbins *Dict. Highway Traffic* 114 *Land-service road,* a road which is used primarily to give access to land. Sometimes called: tertiary road. **1971** J. Drummond *Farewell Party* xxx. 149 We were out on a tertiary road, and more or less alone. **1975** M. Kenyon *Mr. Big* xxii. 224 The secondary road became a tertiary road of muddy craters.

h. *tertiary education,* that which follows secondary education and precedes, includes, or replaces university or professional training; so *tertiary level*; *tertiary college,* one at which such education is provided.

1961 *Mind* LXX. 105 The spread of secondary and latterly of tertiary education has created a large population of people..educated far beyond their capacity to undertake analytical thought. **1969** *Guardian* 26 Aug. 16/4 A 'tertiary college'..in Exeter where sixth forms are to be merged in the College of Further Education. **1971** *New Scientist* 27 May 513/1 Whenever Britons wrote or talked about tertiary education, they generally meant university education. **1974** *Bookseller* 18 May 2402/1 (Advt.), Can you sell our tertiary-level academic titles to booksellers in Scotland and North-East England? **1981** *New Society* 29 Jan. 192/1 Tertiary colleges—providing everything from A level Russian to pre-nursing courses and apprenticeship courses in motor engineering—are the colleges of the future..A *sixth form college* is for the more traditional sixth form intake. A *tertiary college* provides for all over-16s whatever their needs.

i. *tertiary recovery,* the recovery of oil by

advanced methods after conventional artificial means have ceased to be productive. Cf. *secondary recovery* s.v. *SECONDARY *a.* 5 k.

1975 *Petroleum Economist* Aug. 292/2 Oil produced by tertiary recovery methods, from above the Arctic circle,.. could sell at US $8·50 a barrel. **1976** *National Observer* (U.S.) 10 July 13/3 Given that profits hold, what is next for the oilmen? They answer, almost in unison: 'tertiary recovery'.

3. (Later example.)

1967 E. SHORT *Embroidery & Fabric Collage* i. 11 A mixture of all three primary colours results in tertiary colours. These are the subtle colours such as khaki, various browns, etc.

B. *sb.* **6.** *Gram.* In Jespersen's terminology, a word or group of words of tertiary rank or importance in a phrase or sentence; = *SUBJUNCT. Cf. quote 1871, sense A. 1 a in Dict.

1924, 1940 [see *SECONDARY *sb.* 12]. **1959** M. SCHLAUCH *Eng. Lang. in Mod. Times* viii. 221 In this system [of Otto Jespersen's]..the modifier of a modifier (e.g., an adverb) is a tertiary.

‖ **tertium comparationis** (tɜ·ɹʃiŏm kɒmpærēⁱʃiōᵘ·nis, kɒmpærātiōᵘ·nis). [L., = the third element in comparison.] The factor which links or is the common ground between two elements in comparison.

1922 J. RIVIERE tr. *Freud's Introd. Lectures Psycho-Anal.* x. 128 In one set of symbols the underlying comparison may be easily apparent, but there are others in which we have to look about for the common factor, the *tertium comparationis* contained in the supposed comparison. **1945** *Mind* LIV. 209 A comparison without a *tertium comparationis.* **1956** J. H. GREENBERG in Saporta & Bastian *Psycholinguistics* (1961) 470/1 With what cultural or other facts would one connect a contrast between aspirated and nonaspirated consonants in a given language? Where is the *tertium comparationis?*

‖ **tertium non datur** (tɜ·ɹʃiŏm nɒn dēⁱ·tŏɹ), *Lat. phr.* No third possibility exists. Also as *sb. phr.* Cf. *excluded middle, third* s.v. EXCLUDED *ppl. a.* b.

1887 S. H. HODGSON *Let.* 8 Apr. in R. B. Perry *Tht. & Char. of W. James* (1935) I. 642 You are neither empiricist nor transcendentalist; and *tertium non datur.* **1932** tr. *Ortega y Gasset's Revolt of Masses* xiv. 190 The nation is always either in the making, or in the unmaking. *Tertium non datur.* **1948** H. REICHENBACH *Elem. Symb. Logic* vi. 227 An example of such a substitution is given by the various forms of the *tertium non datur* for higher functions. **1977** *Language* LIII. 319 After all, a pronoun must be either prefixed or infixed; tertium non datur.

tertius. Add: (Earlier *Sc.* example, appended to the name of an adult.)

1818 *Blackw. Mag.* II. 424/2 Nicol Jarvie, tertius, M.D.

‖ **tertius gaudens** (tɜ·ɹʃiŏs gau·denz). [L., f. *tertius* third + *gaudens*, pres. ppl. of *gaudere* to rejoice.] A third party that benefits by the conflict or estrangement of two others.

1892 tr. Bismarck in *Ann. Reg. 1891* 284, I should like to interfere in such cases, like a parish beadle bringing peace, and prove that the *tertius gaudens* is the worst enemy. **1933** G. ARTHUR *Septuagenarian's Scrap Bk.* 39 Having ascertained from M. Bompard..that France would flatly refuse..to be a *tertius gaudens* with Germany and Russia. **1957** R. K. MERTON *Social Theory* (rev. ed.) II. ix. 376 The occupant of the status..can become cast in the role of the *tertius gaudens.* **1974** 'M. INNES' *Mysterious Commission* xix. 170 He saw himself as a kind of third force—or even as what the learned would call a *tertius gaudens*, meaning a chap who nips in and does both contending sides down. **1980** D. NEWSOME *On Edge of Paradise* v. 160 It would be better for them both to withdraw to allow the election of a *tertius gaudens.*

tertschite (tɜ·ɹtʃəit). *Min.* [ad. G. *tertschit* (H. Meixner 1953, in *Fortschritte der Mineral.*, etc. XXXI. 41), f. the name of H. *Tertsch* (1880–1962), Austrian mineralogist: see -ITE¹.] A hydrated calcium borate found as white, fibrous, probably monoclinic crystals.

1953 *Chem. Abstr.* XLVII. 10413 New borate deposits were discovered in 1951... The following types were distinguished:..tertschite, about $Ca_4B_{10}O_{19}.20H_2O$. **1978** *Mercian Geol.* VI. 261 Tertschite is found only in one locality in the Bigadiç deposits... It is white, contains very fine fibres, shines like silk... Its rare occurrence makes this mineral unique among the other borate minerals.

teruggite (tĕrū·dʒəit). *Min.* [f. the name of M. E. *Teruggi*, 20th-c. Argentinian geologist + -ITE¹.] A hydrated arsenate and borate of calcium and magnesium, $Ca_4MgB_{12}O_{20}(AsO_4)_2.18H_2O$, found as colourless or white monoclinic crystals.

1968 ARISTARAIN & HURLBUT in *Amer. Mineralogist* LIII. 1815 Teruggite, a new borate mineral, was collected in June, 1967, during a field study of Argentine borates. **1973** *Amer. Mineralogist* LVIII. 1034/2 No chemical analysis was made for the teruggite sample used in the present study. The crystal structure determination confirms the chemical composition reported by Aristarain and Hurlbut (1968) except for the water content which consists of twenty molecules instead of eighteen. **1978** *Mercian Geol.* VI. 264 Teruggite is rare, occurring sporadically at one horizon in the southern basin of the Emet deposits [in Turkey], as very pure white, powdery potato-shaped nodules containing countless minute white euhedral crystals.

Tervueren (tɜɹvū̆ə·rən). Also **Tervuren.** [a. Flemish *Tervueren*, Fr. *Tervuren*, the name of a small town in Belgium, some ten miles east of Brussels.] A fawn, rough-coated, Belgian sheepdog, with dark pricked ears and a black muzzle. Also *attrib.*

1947 C. L. B. HUBBARD *Working Dogs of World* II. 138 The Tervueren is the third main type among the sheepdogs of Belgium. **1964** [see *GROENENDAEL]. **1978** *Detroit Free Press* 2 Apr. 16F/3 Belgian Tervuren Pups, ex show-obedience-guard.

Terylene (te·rilīn). Also **terylene.** [f. *poly-eth)ylene ter(ephthalate* s.v. *POLYETHYLENE a, by inversion.] **a.** A proprietary name for polyethylene terephthalate used as a textile fibre.

1946 [see *fibre-forming* adj. s.v. *FIBRE *sb.* 8]. **1946** [see *polyethylene terephthalate* s.v. *POLYETHYLENE a]. **1947** *Trade Marks Jrnl.* 23 Apr. 233/1 *Terylene*... All goods in Class 23. Imperial Chemical Industries Limited. **1949** *Official Gaz.* (U.S. Patent Office) 27 Sept. 951/2 Imperial Chemical Industries, Limited... *Terylene*... For synthetic yarns and thread. **1951** *Economist* 22 Sept. 686/1 Dacron, ..known in Britain as Terylene and made under licence in the United States, replaces light-weight worsted for summer suits. **1958** *Sunday Times* 27 Apr. 7/5 New materials, nylon, Terylene and so on bring a certain spick-and-spanness within the reach of all. **1961** *Times* 30 May (I.C.I. Suppl.) p. vi, A conveyor belt made with 'Terylene' will out-work, out-last, out-wear any other belt. **1976** P. CAVE *High Flying Birds* i. 9 The sails are usually made of terylene.

b. *attrib.*

1951 *Catal. of Exhibits, South Bank Exhib., Festival of Britain* 109/1 Terylene lace, rope, silk, blanket, etc. **1958** *New Statesman* 28 June 831/1 The men who had nylon shirts and terylene suits before those fabrics got into Marks and Spencer's where the rest of us buy our clothes. **1967** E. SHORT *Embroidery & Fabric Collage* iii. 70 A synthetic interlining such as terylene wadding makes the quilt easy to launder. **1977** B. PYM *Quartet in Autumn* xi. 97 A crisp-looking terylene surplice was suspended from a hook.

'tes, var. 'TIS in Dict. and Suppl.

teschemacherite (teʃĕmæ·kĕrəit). *Min.* [f. the name of E. F. *Teschemacher* (1791–1863), English chemist, who first described it: see -ITE¹.] Ammonium bicarbonate, $(NH_4)HCO_3$, occurring as transparent white to yellowish orthorhombic crystals.

1868 J. D. DANA *Syst. Min.* (ed. 5) 705 (*heading*) Teschemacherite. **1968** [see *KALICINE]. **1972** *Amer. Mineralogist* LVII. 1305 Teschemacherite, ammonium bicarbonate, was deposited inside the wellhead of the Broadlands [New Zealand] geothermal drillhole BR9 after the bore had been shut for several weeks... Teschemacherite has not been reported from other geothermal fields but occurs in some guano deposits.

Teshoo Lama, Teshu Lama, varr. *TASHI LAMA.

Tesla (te·zlă). [The name of Nicola *Tesla* (1856–1943), Croatian-born American electrical physicist.] **1.** *Tesla coil*, a type of induction coil invented by Tesla, employing a spark gap in place of an interruptor and capable of producing an intense high-frequency discharge.

1896 *Amer. Jrnl. Sci.* CLI. 245 By changing the size of the spark gap in the primary circuit of the Tesla coil one has a great range of electrical energy at command. **1930** *Proc. R. Soc.* A. CXXIX. 479 If it is desired simply to obtain the highest possible potentials with the minimum of trouble then the Tesla coil is obviously the ideal solution. **1975** *Bio Systems* VII. 6/2 Thus far, energy has only been fed in by sparking electrodes kept at roughly controlled voltage level with Tesla coils.

2. *Physics.* (Usu. with small initial.) Pl. **tesla, teslas.** The SI unit of magnetic flux density, equal to one weber (*WEBER) per square metre; 10,000 gauss. Symbol T.

1960 in COOKE & MARKUS *Electronics & Nucleonics Dict.* 482/2. **1961** *Symbols, Units & Nomencl. Physics* (Internat. Union Pure & Appl. Physics) 18 The following units of the MKSA system have special names and symbols, which have been approved by the General Conference on Weights and Measures:... tesla (Wb/m^2). **1969** *Sci. Jrnl.* June 36/3 The oscillating magnetic field in the radio pulse itself as it leaves the pulsar is probably greater than 10 teslas (10^5 gauss). **1971** *New Scientist* 24 June 737/2 Superconductors cannot yet sustain fields greater than 12 Tesla. **1980** J. F. O'HANLON *User's Guide Vacuum Technol.* ix. 216 Modern [sputter-ion] pumps are constructed..with external permanent magnets of 0·1 to 0·2 Tesla strength.

Teso (te·so). [Native name.] **a.** (Also *Iteso.*) A Nilo-Hamitic people of central Uganda and western Kenya; a member of this people. **b.** (Also *Ateso.*) The Nilo-Hamitic language of this people. Also *attrib.*

1910 *Bible in World* Nov. 323/2 Teso is the speech of one of the Nilotic tribes who are found in the north of the Uganda Protectorate. *Ibid.* 324/1 The Teso language belongs to a group which also includes the dialects spoken by the famous Masai..and the Karamojo tribes. *Ibid.*, Kitching..gave a most encouraging account of his successful work among the Teso. **1915** A. L. KITCHING *Handbk. Ateso Lang.* p. v, The Teso are a cheerful, industrious people, amenable to control..yet the name of this tribe does not appear..in any of the works on the peoples of the Uganda Protectorate... The Ateso dialect is spoken by a tribe of some 300,000 people living between Lake Kioga and Mt. Ehgon in..the Ugandan Protectorate. **1935**, etc. [see *SEBEI]. **1966** [see *KARAMOJO]. **1973** *Sunday Tel.* 4 Mar. 8/2 The taller and more gaunt appearance of the Nilotic tribes—the Lango, the Acholi and the Iteso.

tesseract (te·sĕrækt). *Math.* Also **tessaract.** [f. TESSARA- + Gr. ἀκτ-ίς ray.] A four-dimensional hypercube. Also *fig.* Hence **tessera·ctic** *a.*

1888 C. H. HINTON *New Era of Thought* II. iii. 118 We call the figure it [*sc.* a cube] traces a Tessaract. *Ibid.* vii. 161 The whole of the 81 cubes make one single tessaractic set extending three inches in each of the four directions. **1919** R. T. BROWNE *Mystery of Space* v. 134 The hypercube or tesseract is described by moving the generating cube in the direction in which the fourth dimension extends. **1960** *Electronic Engin.* XXXII. 347/1 Fig. 8.. shows a four-dimensional 'tessaract' (the four-dimensional analogue of a cube). **1968** *Listener* 15 Feb. 201 He likes to see A gulping of tesseracts and Gondals in Our crazed search. **1974** S. SHELDON *Other Side of Midnight* xviii. 332 For Catherine time had lost its circadian rhythm; she had fallen into a tesseract of time, and day and night blended into one.

tessitura. Add: (Examples.) Also *transf.*

1884 GROVE *Dict. Mus.* IV. 94/1 A term..used by the Italians to indicate how the music of a piece 'lies';..what is the prevailing or average position of its notes in relation to the compass of the voice or instrument for which it is written... 'Range' does not at all give the idea, as the range may be extended, and the general *tessitura* limited; while the range may be high and the *tessitura* low or medium. **1948** *Penguin Music Mag.* Feb. 76 One can hardly blame him, for the *tessitura* is sometimes cruelly high—so many Italian baritone parts seem to have been written for tenors in reduced circumstances. **1956** AUDEN & KALLMAN *Magic Flute* (1957) 116 You won't hear a word in Our high tessitura. **1978** *Early Music* Apr. 197/2 He chose singers for whom the resulting tessituras did not mean any strain. **1982** *English World-Wide* II. 136 Tessitura (or the characteristic range of notes, or compass, within which the pitch fluctuation falls) was felt to be generally wider in Br[itish] E[nglish] than in S[ingapore] E[nglish].

test, *sb.*¹ Add: **2. a.** *spec.* (*Austral.* and *N.Z.*) a test for the proportion of butter fat in milk.

1928 *Bulletin* (Sydney) 14 Mar. 32/1 'You should be proud of her,' said I... 'My oath I am!' he made reply—'She gives an eight-five test!' **1950** *N.Z. Jrnl. Agric.* Mar. 270/2 Several [milk] cans can be filled at the same time so that the tests of all cans are, as far as practicable, identical. **1966** G. W. TURNER *Eng. Lang. Austral. & N.Z.* iii. 45 A cow with 'a good test', that is, milk rich in butter-fat, may be more valuable than another cow that gives more milk.

c. (Later examples.) Also in *Rugby Football* (cf. *test match*, sense 7 b below); *S. Afr.*, an international match in any of a wide range of games and sports, including Rugby.

1933 M. NICHOLLS in I. D. Difford *Hist. S. Afr. Rugby Football* xxiv. 336 In the first Test we won 16 scrums to their 36. **1934** [see *BUCKLEY'S]. **1954** R. T. GABE in Wooller & Owen *Fifty Years of All Blacks* i. 14 We travelled over land and a rough sea..to play a Test in Wellington..to lose by 9 points to 3. **1955** [see *DEPUTIZE *v.* 2]. **1971** *Rand Daily Mail* 4 Sept. 24/7 A series of diving Tests have been arranged against Rhodesia. **1972** *Daily Tel.* 14 Dec. 35/5 A week off before an international, or Test as we call them, is preferable to a mid-week match [New Zealander *loq.*].

4. b. (Later examples.) Also applied to the process or an instance of testing the academic, mental, physiological, or other qualities and conditions of a human subject; in academic and similar contexts usu. implying a simpler, less formal procedure than an examination; freq. as the second element in a collocation or combination denoting a particular kind of test, or used contextually to imply one of these.

A number of other collocations and combinations will be found under the first element in Suppl., as *aptitude, blood, breath, intelligence, means, mental, performance, pregnancy, screen, skin, spot test*; also *ROAD TEST.

1910, etc. [see *BINET-SIMON]. **1918** [see *proficiency test* s.v. *PROFICIENCY 3]. **1927** [see *personality test* s.v. *PERSONALITY 7]. **1928** *Sunday Dispatch* 22 July 4/2 He had had a film test, at the conclusion of which he was told that he filmed remarkably well. **1933** [see *DRIVING *vbl. sb.* 3 a]. **a 1935** [see *FITNESS]. **1941** B. SCHULBERG *What makes Sammy Run?* xi. 198 I'm getting fed up with these floosies you're always promising..a day's work or a test [i.e. a screen test]. **1955** E. H. CLEMENTS *Discord in Air* xi. 149 Mummy always drives. I haven't taken my test yet. **1956** [see *NUCLEAR *a.* 3 c]. **1958** *Economist* 8 Nov. 481/2 Russia is trying to make the West agree to a ban on tests. **1959** [see *PASS-FAIL *a.*]. **1960** [see *BREATHALYSER]. **1968** [see *I.Q.* s.v. I. III]. **1968** [see *M.O.T.* s.v. M 5]. **1976** *Star* (Sheffield) 30 Nov. 12/6 Up to £50 paid for scrap and test failure cars and vans.

7. a. (in sense 2 a) *test-sentence, -tree*; (in sense 2 c) *test batsman, captain, cricket, cricketer, team, trial*; (in sense 4 b) *test anxiety, certificate, performance.*

1972 *Jrnl. Social Psychol.* LXXXVII. 155 Few studies have examined the relationship of birth order to test anxiety. **1976** DEXTER & MAKINS *Testkill* 139 The Test batsman, even after net practice, is still forced to use the first few overs in the middle as a warm-up. **1975** *Cricketer* May 8/1 Ian Michael Chappell, the activist of Test captains, has led Australia in 26 Tests in four countries. **1976** *Alyn & Deeside Observer* 10 Dec. 10/2 He did not have an excise licence, a driving licence or a test certificate. **1931** J. HOBBS (*title*) Playing for England! My test-cricket story. **1959** M. GILBERT *Blood & Judgement* iii. 36 In September a test cricketer was still news. **1942** *Mind* LI. 175 A factor which improves certain test-performances when it is not merely absent, but actually negative. **1901** KIPLING *Kim* x. 262 Kim repeated the test-sentence. **1977** *Word 1972* XXVIII. 104 There were 15 test sentences in the battery in which the English strongly suggested the use of a diminutive ending in Gaelic. **1955** *Radio Times* 22 Apr. 31/2 The Test Team arrived in this country at the beginning of the week. **1883** G. M. HOPKINS *Let.* 25 Oct. (1956) 323 This was the sin of Adam and Eve, who, both in different ways, eat of the 'Test-tree'. **1977** Test trial [see *PENCIL *v.* 2 c].

b. test ban, a ban on the testing of nuclear weapons; **test bed,** a piece of equipment for testing machines, esp. aircraft engines, before their acceptance for general use; also *attrib.* and *fig.*; **test-body** *Physics,* the imaginary object on which a thought-experiment is carried out; **test card,** (*a*) *Ophthalm.*, a large card printed with rows of letters of decreasing size for use in testing visual acuity (cf. *SNELLEN); (*b*) *Television,* a diagrammatic still picture transmitted outside normal programme hours and designed for use in judging the quality and position of the image on any particular screen; **test-case** (earlier example); also *transf.* and *attrib.*; **test chart** *Ophthalm.* = *test card* (a) above; **test-drive** *v. trans.* (orig. *U.S.*), to drive (a motor vehicle) in order to determine its qualities with a view to its regular use; **test-fire** orig. *U.S.*, to fire (a gun or missile) experimentally; **test flight,** a flight during which the performance of an aircraft is tested; **test-fly** *v. trans.*, to test the performance of (an aircraft) in flight; hence **test-flying** *vbl. sb.*; **test-hole,** (*b*) = *test well* below; **test letter,** (*b*) (examples); **test-market** *v. trans.* (and *intr.*) (orig. *U.S.*), to put (a new product) on to the market, usu. in a limited area, in order to determine consumers' response to it; also *transf.*; also as *sb.*, an area in which a product is test-marketed; hence **test-marketing** *vbl. sb.*; **test match** (earlier and further examples); also in *Rugby Football* (orig. *S. Afr.*), one of a series of matches between a touring team and teams representing the country of the tour; an international; **test-paper,** (*c*) (example); **test-piece,** (*b*) (see sense 7 a in Dict.); (*c*) a piece performed by each of the competitors in a musical contest to determine which is the best; **test pilot,** one who test-flies an aircraft; also (with hyphen) as *v. trans*; hence **test-piloting** *vbl. sb.*; **test-pit,** (*a*) (see sense 7 a in Dict.); (*b*) *Archæol.*, a pit dug to gain an idea of the contents of a site; **test range,** a range (*RANGE *sb.*[1] 11 c) where missiles are tested; **test-retest** *a. Psychol.*, of or designating a method by which a test is given to a subject on two occasions separated by a lapse of time; **test rig** *Engin.*, an apparatus used for assessing the performance of a piece of mechanical or electrical equipment; **test signal,** a sequence of electrical impulses used for testing purposes in television broadcasting; **test strip,** (*a*) *Cinemat.* (see quot. 1940); (*b*) *Photogr.* (see quot. 1973); **test-type** (examples); **test well** *Oil Industry,* a well made in testing a site for oil; **test-word,** (*a*) *Psychol.*, a word used in a test; (*b*) *Onomastics,* a word used to determine the presence of a particular linguistic form or influence.

1958 *New Statesman* 27 Dec. 898/1 More progress was registered at Geneva last week, when the test-ban conference approved a British draft of Article Four of the treaty. **1971** H. TREVELYAN *Worlds Apart* xvi. 177 As we saw it, there were two elements in Soviet thinking about a test-ban. **1979** G. F. NEWMAN *List* vi. 55 Kennedy sees the test ban treaty as a step toward peace. **1914** *Flight* 21 Mar. 312/1 The 120 h.p. engine entered by the Green Engine Co. for the Military Aeroplane Engine Competition is mounted on a tilting test bed. **1924** S. R. ROGET *Dict. Electr. Terms* 260 *Test bed,* a base plate or foundation upon which machines may readily be mounted for testing purposes. **1937** *Times* 13 Apr. (Brit. Motor Number) p. xv/4 The car engines undergo a long and thorough trial on the test-bed. **1961** *Aeroplane* CI. 791/1 Two VTOL test-bed aircraft using the G.E. J85-5 fan-lift engine. **1963** *Listener* 28 Mar. 542/2 The Russian leaders ..have spent the last fifteen years on the test-bed of world strategy, feeling the fearful and complex stresses and strains that that involves. **1978** *Sci. Amer.* July 30/1 On test beds turbine-inlet temperatures of well over 1,650 degrees C. have been achieved for at least a decade. **1920** A. S. EDDINGTON *Space, Time & Gravitation* iv. 64 A massive body, such as the earth, seems to be surrounded by a field of latent force, ready, if another body enters the field, to become active, and transmit motion. One usually thinks of this influence as existing in the space round the earth even when there is no test-body to be affected. **1955** L. ROSENFELD in W. Pauli *Niels Bohr* 71 This meant that in studying the measurability of field components we must use as test-bodies finite distributions of charge and current, and not point charges. **1892** A. DUANE tr. *Fuchs's Text-bk. Opthalm.* III. ii. 609 When the visual acuity has become so reduced that the largest letters of Snellen's test-card can no longer be recognized at 6 metres, the patient must go up nearer it. **1935** *Popular Wireless* 16 Mar. 14/2 The 'test cards' radiated recently by the B.B.C. have..been the cause of a lot of correspondence. **1949** H. C. WESTON *Sight, Light & Efficiency* vii. 245 External light sources must be relied upon for illuminating the test-cards. **1962** *Which?* Mar. 70/2 To measure the resolution, we used the BS test-slide which has blocks of parallel lines of various thicknesses and spacings, similar to the test card shown to television viewers so that they can adjust their sets for a clear, sharp picture. **1978** S. WILSON *Dealer's Move* III. vi. 103 A buzzing in my head to match the buzzing of the test card on the screen. **1894** W. ARCHER in *World* 31 Jan. 25/2 Mr. Gattie is of opinion that the insanity of one of the parties to a marriage should be..a compulsory ground for divorce... He indicts the law by making his hero break it, and showing..that his crime is a law-made crime... He is ..bent upon getting up a good 'test case'. **1911** M. CORELLI *Life Everlasting* ix. 205 Because he had seen in me the possibility of a 'test case', Santoris had tried his power upon me. **1959** B. & R. NORTH tr. *M. Duverger's Pol. Parties* (ed. 2) I. ii. 112 Such counts.. presuppose that the leaders of a number of test-case branches..would make a very careful check of attendances over a period of time. **1910** H. C. PARKER *Handbk. Dis. Eye* v. 62 (*caption*) Test chart for illiterates. **1978** J. PARR *Introd. Ophthalm.* II. 64 If a subject's visual acuity is less than 6/60 the distance from the test chart can be progressively reduced down to 1m. **1954** *Sun* (Baltimore) 1 Nov. (B ed.) 9/1 Shaw and his companions were returning from Detroit, where he had test driven a 1955 Chrysler. **1971** *Guardian* 30 Oct. 20/1 Mrs Joy Johnson.. demolished a 'No Entry' sign while test-driving a double-deck bus. **1947** *Birmingham* (Alabama) *News* 27 Oct. 1/2 He stole the automatic pistol from an automobile and test-fired it twice before calling for the cab. **1952** *N.Y. Times* 27 Apr. IV. E5/2 The atomic gun-fired shell..will probably be test-fired in the course of the next year or so. **1960** *Daily Tel.* 8 Jan. 1/3 Russia is to test-fire new heavy rockets, intended for use on inter-planetary flights. **1980** N. FREELING *Castang's City* xxix. 202 We'll have it test-fired tomorrow and the cartridge marks compared. **1912** *Flight* 3 Feb. 106/2 No flying on Friday beyond a test flight by Pizey on the Bristol. **1927** C. A. LINDBERGH *We* iv. 59, I took off for a test flight before taking the lady over Pensacola. **1976** *Derbyshire Times* (Peak ed.) 3 Sept. 28/1 The twin-engined Beechcraft monoplane.. was on a test flight at the time. **1936** *Meccano Mag.* Aug. 433/2, I hope it will fall to my lot to test fly these great super-clippers. **1942** W. SIMPSON *One of our Pilots is Safe* ii. 40 During the day each aircraft received a special check-up and was test-flown by its pilot and crew. **1978** J. A. MICHENER *Chesapeake* 739 When the time came to test-fly the contraption,..an aviator from Washington.. studied the seaplane. **1928** N. MACMILLAN *Art of Flying* 7 Immediately after the War, he took up test-flying with considerable success. **1961** Test-flying [see *flight-testing vbl. sb.* s.v. *FLIGHT *sb.*[1] 15]. **1909** *Chambers's Jrnl.* Mar. 160/1 He [*sc.* the prospector] digs here and there, making test-holes. **1971** *Sunday Australian* 8 Aug. 17/2 The new test hole is sited about 100 miles south-west of Fitzroy Crossing, W.A. **1869** *Trans. 4th & 5th Ann. Meeting Amer. Ophthalm. Soc.* 68 (*heading*) On a new series of test-letters for determining the acuteness of vision. **1970** A. H. KEENEY *Ocular Examination* ii. 18/2 Snellen's real contribution was to standardize the size and form of test letters with relation to the distance from the observer. **1958** *Wall St. Jrnl.* 6 Nov. 23/5 A new line of cookingware which is now being test-marketed in three cities of the United States. **1964** *Listener* 12 Mar. 422/1 Many products are produced and tried out in test-markets (usually medium-sized cities or commercial-television areas) for a year or more. *Ibid.*, Decisions about test-marketing..are the cause of severe anxiety. **1972** 'J. MELVILLE' *Ironwood* ix. 154 She had come to me seeking recipes for a new sort of cooking chocolate she was helping test-market in this area. **1862** W. J. HAMMERSLEY *Victorian Cricketer's Guide 1861–2* 159 Of the thirteen matches, five only can be termed 'test matches'; the three played at Melbourne, and the two played at Sydney. **1889** *Wisden's Cricketers' Almanack* 162 There was a considerable amount of anxiety as to the result of the first of the three great test matches. **1905** *Westm. Gaz.* 19 Aug. 2/3 Until the year 1894 no one had ever heard of a 'Test' match, but..since that time we have been accustomed thus to speak of an England v. Australia match. **1924** *Times* 15 Aug. 5/4 The British team for the first Rugby Football Test Match on Saturday will be selected [in S. Africa]. **1933** M. NICHOLLS in I. D. Difford *Hist. S. Afr. Rugby Football* xxiv. 335 We won this fourth Test match by 13 points to 5, and squared the rubber. **1974** *Encycl. Brit. Micropædia* IX. 458/2 Rugby League football... The three principal Test-match series stand as follows. **1926** KIPLING *Debits & Credits* 273 To prepare for the Form a General Knowledge test-paper. **1927** *Melody Maker* Aug. 792/1 Some bandsmen tell you that after playing a test-piece for perhaps a hundred times they feel they are only just beginning to appreciate it. **1960** *Times* 23 May 16/6 It would make a good test-piece for an international Eisteddfod. **1917** W. L. WADE *Flying Bk.* 193/1 Now with Parnell and Sons, of Bristol, as chief test pilot. **1927** C. A. LINDBERGH *We* iv. 61 The service parachute... gave the test pilot a safe means of escape in most cases when all else had failed. **1947** *Sat. Even. Post* 6 Dec. 78/2 They reminded him of the fiery trail left by the high-altitude jet plane he had test-piloted in the last week of the war. **1978** J. A. MICHENER *Chesapeake* 740 The trial run was without incident, the test pilot pronouncing the craft airworthy. **1958** *Times Lit. Suppl.* 16 May 274/3 The beauty and immensity of the skies have always been a spiritual bonus added to the satisfactions of test-piloting work well done. **1905** D. MACKENZIE *Let.* Sept. in *Observer* (1962) 11 Feb. 11/4 The examination of the later test-pits was reserved for a future time at your own express desire. **1952** V. G. CHILDE *New Light Most Anc. East* vii. 123 How far other innovations ..coincide with the change in pottery cannot be decided from the limited material furnished by a narrow test pit. **1973** *Lebende Sprachen* XVIII. 72/2 On 5th May..Ariel 3 was successfully launched by a scout rocket from the western test range..at Vandenburg Air Force base, California. **1945** L. GUTTMAN in *Psychometrika* X. 255 (*heading*) A basis for analyzing test-retest reliability. *Ibid.* 266 That the universe of trials be indefinitely large seems part of the *definition* of the problem of test-retest reliability. **1960** F. LAND *Lang. Math.* xiv. 253 The 'test re-test' method..involves giving the test and then, after some lapse of time, giving it again to the same group of people. .. A correlation less than 0·9 between the two performances of the same test would indicate that its reliability was below the acceptable level. **1957** *Technology* Sept. 244/3 The..mechanical engineering research laboratory ..developed a new test rig for..fittings for oil hydraulic circuits. **1978** R. V. JONES *Most Secret War* xlv. 435 If only we had complete photographic cover of the Blizna area we could have found the launching site or test rig. **1945** *Daily Herald* 31 Aug. 4/4 The B.B.C. is already sending out test signals on the sound channel. **1975** D. G. FINK *Electronics Engineers' Handbk.* XXI. 29 The use of test signals must not result in significant degradation of the program transmissions. **1940** *Chambers's Techn. Dict.*, *Test strip* (*Cinema.*), the specially exposed unmodulated sound-track which is made to ascertain the current in the exciter lamp of a recording machine which gives the requisite density on the negative, after normal development. **1958** T. L. J. BENTLEY in *Newnes Compl. Amat. Photogr.* iv. 78 By giving a series of test strips different periods of development and measuring the resulting gammas and plotting them against development times, a curve is produced. **1973** D. A. SPENCER *Focal Dict. Photogr. Technol.* 623 *Test strip,* a piece of the sensitised material on which exposure is to be made which is exposed in sections, each receiving a different exposure to enable the correct exposure to be judged by the appearance of the developed strip. Each successive section typically receives twice the exposure of the previous section. **1864** W. D. MOORE tr. *Donders' Anomalies of Accommodation & Refraction* ii. 99 We give him small print—I to IV of Snellen's test-types to read. **1907, 1962** Test-type [see *JAEGER[2]]. **1877** *Sci. Amer.* 22 Dec. 387/3 A large number of 'wildcats', or test wells, have gone down off the eastern edge of the defined line, but with very few exceptions they have proved dusters. **1925** A. B. THOMPSON *Oil-Field Explor.* I. v. 208 The selection of sites for test wells is one of the most responsible duties that devolves on pioneers. **1975** *Offshore* Sept. 91/1 A total of 12 deep onshore test wells have been drilled, all of which have been dry holes. **1905** A. MEYER in *Psychol. Bull.* 15 July 242 The time was measured with a stop-watch from the chief syllable of the test-word to the reaction. **1924** E. EKWALL in Mawer & Stenton *Introd. Survey Eng. Place-Names* iv. 60 Norwegian test-words are *breck, buth* (ON *búð*), *gill, scale, slack.* **1965** G. KRISTENSSON in *English Studies* Apr. 142 This surname [*sc.* Ladyman] is..too unreliable to be used as a test-word for the appearance of OE (*ge*)*lǣd.*

test, *v.*[2] Add: **2.** Also, to subject (a person) to a test of a particular kind; *to test out,* to put (a theory, etc.) to a practical test. Phrases: *to test* (something) *to failure* or *destruction*; *to test the water* (fig.: cf. quot. 1888 in Dict.).

1926 *Publishers' Weekly* 29 May 1794/2 To test out the value of radio publicity. **1939** *Brit. Jrnl. Psychol.* July 1 The range of chronological age of persons tested was so wide that a special enquiry had to be undertaken. **1957** C. N. PARKINSON *Parkinson's Law* (1958) 23 So much time has been spent in studying the art of being tested that the candidate has rarely had time for anything else. **1962** F. I. ORDWAY et al. *Basic Astronautics* vii. 325 We first select 100 units and test them to failure. **1972** D. RAMSAY *Little Murder Music* 62 'If you're attempting to establish a motive—' 'I'm just testing the water,' Meredith said. **1974** *Howard Jrnl.* XIV. 104 Legal philosophers could back up these efforts by testing out some of their theories with research projects. **1978** *Washington Post* 20 Jan. D1 Hepburn had played bit or supporting roles in several European movies..before William Wyler tested her and cast her as the runaway princess in 'Roman Holiday'. **1978** A. PRICE *'44 Vintage* xviii. 203 Sergeant Winston tested the statement to destruction. **1980** J. KRANTZ *Princess Daisy* xxv. 443 'I guess it's just..lucky..that Supracorp's such a big business,' Kiki said, testing the waters.

5. *intr.* **a.** To undergo a test. *U.S.*

1934 in WEBSTER. **1961** in WEBSTER, Actors..best suited to the roles for which they tested. *Ibid.*, The great turboprop..was still testing. **1981** *Times* 29 Apr. 12/3, I tested with Jack Nicholson for his own film *Goin' South.* It came down to a choice between myself and Mary Steenburger and she got the part.

b. With phrasal compl. To achieve a rating of (so much) as the result of a test. *U.S.*

1934 WEBSTER, s.v. A compound that tests ten per cent. *a* **1961** R. BENEDICT in Webster, The eyesight of different peoples may test the same. **1971** 'L. EGAN' *Malicious Mischief* viii. 135 They could guess that he might test dull-normal. He was seventeen, not very big and not very bright. **1976** M. MACHLIN *Pipeline* ii. 32 It tests over two thousand barrels a day.

6. *absol.* or *intr.* To apply or carry out a test.

1961 WEBSTER, s.v., Use the scratch technique in

testing for allergies. **1978** T. Sharpe *Throwback* ix. 87 Then say 'Testing. Testing. Testing' into that little transmitter.

testability (testăbi·lĭti). [f. Testable *a.*[2] + -ity.] The quality or state of being testable (see next).

1936 R. Carnap in *Philos. of Sci.* III. 421 An attempt will be made to formulate the principle of empiricism in a more exact way, by stating a requirement of confirmability or testability as a criterion of meaning. **1945** [see *confirmability]. **1952** C. G. Hempel *Fund. of Concept Formation in Empirical Sci.* 43 Just another formulation of the empiricist requirements of testability. **1968** K. R. Popper *Conjectures & Refutations* (ed. 3) i. 37 The criterion of the scientific status of a theory is its falsifiability, or refutability, or testability. **1981** *Word 1980* XXXI. 151 It is only in this way that the model can attain a high degree of testability.

testable, *a.*[2] Delete *rare* and add later examples; *spec.* in *Philos. of Science*, of a theory: capable of being empirically tested.

1922 *Glasgow Herald* 14 Apr. 8 Japanese history does not become a record of testable facts until the fifth or sixth century A.D. **1945** [see *disconfirm *v.*]. **1959** K. R. Popper *Logic of Sci. Discovery* vi. 112 Theories may be more, or less, severely testable; that is to say, more, or less, easily falsifiable. The degree of their testability is of significance for the selection of theories. **1968** P. A. P. Moran *Introd. Probability Theory* i. 57 The two laws differ in their empirical nature in that the first is empirically testable whilst the second is not. **1973** B. Magee *Popper* ii. 22 Scientific laws are testable in spite of being unprovable: they can be tested by systematic tests to refute them.

testate (te·stēⁱt), *a.*[2] [f. as Testacean *a.*: see -ate[2].] = Testacean *a.*, Testaceous *a.* 2.

1947 *Ann. Rev. Microbiol.* I. 4 In the testate *Pontigulasia vas*, a hypothecal layer of endosomal granules or plaques disappears during the anaphase and reappears during the telophase. **1978** *Bio Systems* X. 79/2 The Foraminifera appear to have had an origin in organisms similar to the testate amoebae.

te·st-cross, *sb.* and *v. Genetics.* [f. Test *sb.*[1] + Cross *sb.*] **A.** *sb.* A cross between an individual whose genotype for a certain trait is unknown and one that is homozygous recessive for that trait, so that the unknown genotype may be determined from that of the offspring.

1934 C. B. Bridges in *Jrnl. Heredity* XXV. 18 The type of cross designated..as the 'backcross' is here to stay... Because of this characteristic we may employ the term 'testcross' wherever 'backcross' has been used in the special meaning. **1979** Arms & Camp *Biology* xiii. 198 If the red-flowered plant of unknown genotype were actually heterozygous (Rr), half the offspring of the test cross would be expected to be white-flowered and half red-flowered.

B. *v. trans.* To make the subject of such a cross.

1950 E. W. Sinnott et al. *Princ. Genetics* (ed. 4) iii. 68 The trihybrid with round and yellow seeds and colored flowers.., when test-crossed to plants with wrinkled, green seeds and white flowers..will produce 8 combinations. **1978** *Nature* 27 July 317/1 A proportion of the males from a wild population in Texas showed low levels of recombination when heterozygous males were test-crossed to homozygous marked females.

teste[2]. **1.** (Later examples.)

1916 G. Saintsbury *Peace of Augustans* iii. 130 Lamb (*teste* Hazlitt..) was inclined to agree with Scott. **1968** *Listener* 6 June 737/2 He tells us, *teste* Evelyn Waugh, of a Sitwellian habit of leaving Sitwell press cuttings (surely not *all* their press cuttings?) in bowls on the drawing-room table.

testee[2] (testī·). [f. Test *v.*[2] + -ee[1].] One who is subjected to a test of his or her health, intelligence, knowledge, etc.

1932 W. S. Duke-Elder *Text-bk. Ophthalm.* I. xxv. 986 The fact that picking skeins of wool does not appeal to the average workman, while the reading of pseudo-chromatic diagrams requires a considerable amount of intelligence, has popularized the adoption of lantern tests wherein coloured glasses are illuminated and the testee is asked to name the colour and (sometimes) to match it with wools or some other coloured material. **1947** *Sci. News* IV. 19 The main difficulty with such tests was that the tester was usually as intoxicated as the testee, and often forgot to press the spindle of his stopwatch, or to take proper notes. **1952** C. P. Blacker *Eugenics: Galton & After* 190 These gaps..make it all the more surprising that so little account was taken of the testee's subsequent services and achievements. **1964** M. Critchley *Developmental Dyslexia* vii. 50 The testee is required to detect which of the simple figures lies concealed or incorporated within the complex design. **1976** K. S. Bowers *Hypnosis for Seriously Curious* iii. 43 Even on the subset of questions for which the testee subjectively feels he is simply guessing, the likelihood is high that he will get more than 25% correct answers. **1983** *Daily Tel.* 22 Sept. 18 Gascoigne..said of his testees [on a quiz programme]: 'They were far more argumentative in the 60s and 70s.'

tester[1]. Add: **3.** *tester cloth.*

1776 in J. S. Moore *Goods & Chattels of our Forefathers* (1976) 270 Bedstead, Green Curtains, Vallens and Head and Tester Cloths etc. **1853** *Heal & Sons Catal.: Bedsteads* 59 Half-Tester Bedstead..Chintz Furniture..fringed and fluted head and tester cloth.

tester[4]. Add: **b.** *Biol.* A stock or strain of organism used to investigate some genetic characteristic of another strain.

1925 *Genetics* X. 421 Two other stocks were needed as 'testers'. **1969** A. M. Campbell *Episomes* iii. 37 Operationally, a bacterial culture is termed F+ if it will mate with an F− tester strain.

testibiopalladite (testi:biopæ·lădəit). *Min.* [f. Te(llurium + Stibi(um (or Sti(bium + Bi(smuth) + -o + Pallad)ium[2] + -ite[1].] A mineral, Pd(Sb,Bi)Te, found as minute whitish or grey cubic crystals having a metallic lustre.

1974 *Ti Ch'iu Hua Hsueh (Geochimica)* III. 181 Sixteen new minerals..were found from two nickelsulfide deposits in China. The three well studied are: Testibiopalladite, Pd(Sb,Bi)Te. **1978** *Canad. Mineralogist* XVI. 126/1 The first occurrence of testibiopalladite outside China is reported from Kambalda, Western Australia, where it occurs as cores to zoned inclusions of michenerite–testibiopalladite in altaite.

testicular, *a.* Add: **1. b.** *testicular feminization* (or *feminizing*): a familial condition produced in genetically male persons by the failure of tissue to respond to male sex hormones, resulting in a normal female appearance (including external genitalia) but with testes in place of ovaries; usu. *attrib.*

1953 J. M. Morris in *Amer. Jrnl. Obstetr. & Gynecol.* LXV. 1192 Actually these patients present a fairly typical clinical picture. For this reason they have been singled out from the other forms of intersexuality, and we have called the clinical syndrome 'testicular feminization'. **1959, 1970** [see *feminization 2]. **1974** Passmore & Robson *Compan. Med. Stud.* III. xxix. 2/2 One other specific condition is the testicular feminizing syndrome in which XY individuals with testes nevertheless develop female external genitalia and female secondary development at puberty. **1978** *Price's Textbk. Practice of Med.* (ed. 12) v. 550/2 In the testicular feminization syndrome a different approach is indicated because..'she' may already be married and having satisfactory sexual intercourse.

testimonial, *a.* and *sb.* Add: **B.** *sb.* **6.** (sense 5) = serving as a testimonial or token of esteem, esp. in *testimonial dinner, game, match.*

1851 'Bat' *Cricketer's Man.* (ed. 5) 94 On the 26th July, 1847, the Committee at Lord's got up a testimonial match between Kent and England [for Mynn's benefit]. **1895** *Funk's Stand. Dict.* s.v., A testomonial certificate, benefit, or banquet. **1931** *Daily Express* 21 Sept. 11/5 A testimonial dinner was given to..the millionaire American capitalist. **1972** G. Green *Great Moments in Sport: Soccer* iii. 46 The Russians went to the unusual lengths of giving him [Yashin] a testimonial match at Lenin Stadium. **1977** in *Fremdsprachen* XXIII. (1979) 209/1 The long-serving defender, who collected £35,000 from a testimonial game on Friday, was due to retire. **1979** *Tucson (Arizona) Citizen* (Weekender Mag.) 28 Apr. 18/1 Sol Stein..was decorating a dais with his presence at a testimonial dinner for a minor television personality.

testimony, *sb.* **5.** Add: except in Evangelical circles. Phr. *to give one's testimony* = Testify *v.* 3 b.

1877 *Independent* 29 Mar. 12/1 A fine-looking young man gave a clear, decided testimony for Christ. **1885** C. T. Studd *Let.* in N. P. Grubb *C. T. Studd* (1933) vi. 53 Now he is just as active for the Lord Jesus as he was formerly for the devil. He has three times publicly given his testimony. **1935** N. L. McClung *Clearing in West* iii. 21 So when an old man who stuttered, was giving his testimony and holding back the meeting with everyone getting impatient, I kept my one eye on the minister and the other one shut. **1966** H. Roseveare *Give me this Mountain* ii. 31 Our leader opened the meeting for testimonies. I didn't know what she meant by a 'testimony' so I waited... She made another attempt to get us talking by pointing out what a blessing it could be to testify to others... 'Well, hasn't anyone anything to tell of what God has done for her during the week?'

testing, *vbl. sb.*[2] Add: **b. testing-ground,** an area used for demonstration and experiment; also *fig.*

1872 *Gentl. Mag.* Jan. 71 Since the battle field is the only thorough testing ground for weapons and military schemes. **1919** H. S. Walpole *Secret City* ii. vii. 213, I turned and devoted myself to Uncle Ivan, who was always delighted to make me a testing-ground for his English. **1943** in R. V. Jones *Most Secret War* (1978) xxxvii. 322 The new weapon is in the form of a rocket which has been seen fired from the testing ground.

testo. Add: **c.** The narrator in an oratorio or similar piece of music.

1947 A. Einstein *Music in Romantic Era* xiii. 177 Through the gradual elimination of the *testo* or narrator, oratorio had approached opera to such a degree as to be confused with it. **1980** *New Grove Dict. Mus.* XVIII. 706/2 The *testo* part was normally set as recitative with continuo accompaniment and sung either by one or more soloists... In secular music the term was occasionally used for the narrator in dramatic dialogues and similar works.

testosterone (testǫ·stĕrōᵘn). *Biol.* [a. G. *testosteron* (K. David et al. 1935, in *Zeitschr. f. physiol. Chem.* CCXXXIII. 281): see Testis[2] and *-sterone.] **a.** A steroid hormone that stimulates the development of male secondary sexual characteristics and which is produced in the testes, and, in very much smaller quantities, in the ovaries and adrenal cortex.

1935 *Chem. Abstr.* XXIX. 5165 (*heading*) Crystalline male hormone from testes (testosterone), more active than androsterone prepared from urine or cholesterol. **1939** A. Huxley *After Many a Summer* ii. vi. 234 With a course of thiamin chloride and some testosterone I could have made him as happy as a sand-boy. **1947** *Nature* 4 Jan. 15/1 Many mammary cancers would regress when the influence of the female sex hormone was lessened by removal of the ovaries or by injections of testosterone. **1961** *New Scientist* 9 Nov. 340/1 Naturally occurring steroid sex hormones can inhibit ovulation... Testosterone, progesterone and the oestrogens fall into this group. **1969** *Nature* 6 Dec. 945/1 Celibacy apparently has no effect on the androgens, for most of the monks excreted as much testosterone—the most potent naturally occurring androgen—as normal sexually active males. **1976** *Maclean's Mag.* 3 May 60/3 Among women virilized in the womb from an excess of testosterone (the male sex hormone), 60% registered IQs over 110.

b. testosterone propionate, the propionic acid ester of testosterone, given parenterally as a longer-lasting alternative to testosterone.

1937 *Proc. R. Soc.* B. CXXIV. 363 Six normally cyclic rats..were injected daily for 10 days with 0·2 mg. of testosterone propionate. **1941** [see *premenopause]. **1970** Passmore & Robson *Compan. Med. Stud.* II. xii. 11/2 Testosterone propionate, given intramuscularly in oily solution, is active over a period of 1–3 days.

test-tube. Add: **b. test-tube baby,** (*a*) a baby conceived by artificial insemination; (*b*) a baby that has developed from an ovum fertilized outside the mother's body; also *fig.* and in similar Combs., as *test-tube child, pregnancy.*

1935 E. Novak *Woman asks Doctor* xii. 155 There has been..a good deal of unfortunate newspaper discussion on the subject of artificial insemination and 'test-tube babies'. **1945** *Daily Herald* 20 Apr. 3/8 Warning on test tube babies. Artificial insemination of women is being performed on a small scale in this country. **1958** *Times* 18 Jan. 7/2 A 'test-tube' child cannot grow up knowing about his true origin. **1965** *New Scientist* 11 Nov. 392/3 The idea of 'test-tube babies' is no longer something to be woven into the plot of a science fiction novel. Serious-minded scientists are not only thinking about cultivating human embryos on the laboratory bench—they are developing the techniques which will make this a practical possibility. **1978** *Times* 26 July 1/1 The world's first test-tube baby, a girl, was born by caesarian section just before midnight at Oldham and District General Hospital, Greater Manchester... The embryo was implanted in Mrs Brown's womb after being fertilized in Mr Steptoe's laboratories. **1982** *New Scientist* 4 Feb. 290 Since the birth of the first 'test-tube baby' three and a half years ago it has become increasingly obvious that fertilising human eggs in the laboratory is not simply a clinical technique for relieving infertility.

‖ **Tet** (tet). [Vietnamese.] **a.** The Vietnamese lunar New Year. Also *attrib.*

1885 J. G. Scott *France & Tongking* v. 104 The especial great season for every one, rich and poor, is the new year, the Têt, the Annamese new year..which corresponds with the Chinese and falls about the beginning of February. *Ibid.* 105 At a season such as the Têt, the evil spirits are particularly active and spiteful on account of the general rejoicing. **1931** H. Norden *Wanderer in Indo-China* iii. 55 Tet is the month-long New Year's festival which begins a month later than the Occidental new year. During Tet all work is suspended. **1968** *Times* 30 Jan. 4/1 The United States and South Vietnam authorities announced today that they would not observe the 36-hour Tet (Lunar New Year) truce. **1973** *Times* 28 Dec. 5/1 More than 4,000 civilian and military prisoners still held by the South Vietnamese and the communists are to be released before the Tet (Buddhist new year) celebrations on January 23. **1974** P. Gore-Booth *With Great Truth & Respect* 359 The truce agreed on for the traditional *Tet* (New Year) holiday in Vietnam would start on Wednesday 8 February, and finish on Sunday afternoon, 12 February.

b. Tet offensive, in the war in Vietnam, an offensive launched by North Vietnamese and Viet Cong forces on 30 January 1968.

1968 *Times* 17 Feb. 4/4 The Vietcong Tet new year offensive was evidence of the correctness of the United States analysis. *Ibid.* 19 Feb. 1/5 The Vietcong are expected to follow up their Tet offensive. **1977** J. Crosby *Company of Friends* xiv. 95 The CIA had missed the Tet offensive.

‖ **tetampan** (tĕta·mpan). [Malay.] In Western Malaysia, an ornate shoulder cloth worn by those serving royalty.

1821 J. Leyden tr. *Malay Annals* 342 Tun Sura di Raja..brought the creese from the raja..and covered it with a tetampan. **1909** R. O. Winstedt *Life & Customs* (Papers on Malay Subjects) ii. 90 *Kain tĕtampan*, a shoulder-cloth of yellow silk, embroidered, and with gold or silver fringe, worn by court attendants when waiting on Rajas. **1972** M. Sheppard *Taman Indera* 26 Shoulder cloths of the first grade are called *Tetampan*. They are made of velvet and are usually embroidered with the royal emblem or cypher in gold thread. *Ibid.* 84 A short shoulder cloth of yellow velvet, embroidered with silver thread, called *Tetampan*.

tetarteron (tĭtā·ɹtĕrǫn). *Numism.* [a. Gr. τεταρτηρόν, lit. 'measure of capacity', f. τέταρτος fourth.] A Byzantine gold coin of the 10th–11th cent., a copper coin replacing the old follis from the late 11th cent. (see quot. 1969).

1908 W. Wroth *Catal. Imperial Byzantine Coins in Brit. Mus.* [I. p.l, This..coin is stated to have been called..τεταρτερόν. This was probably..its popular nickname.] *Ibid.* II. 659/1 'Tetarteron', l. **1959** E. Pound *Thrones* xcvi. 12 Here, surely, is a refinement of language. ἢ καὶ νομίσματα ξέει Wd/ appear to be tetarteron tokens not affecting the aureus. **1969** M. S. Hendy *Coinage & Money in Byzantine Empire 1081–1261* vi. 28 The tetarteron nomisma..originally a gold coin,..was first struck by Nicephorus II, and continued until early in the reign of Alexius I. At some point after this, the name was appropriated to describe a copper coin of similar small, thick fabric, first struck by Alexius as an element of his reformed coinage. This change had taken place by 1097. **1973** P. D. Whitting *Byzantine Coins* iii. 40 A *new* gold coin lighter than the solidus was introduced... The new and lighter coin was called the nomisma tetarteron. These tetartera cannot be distinguished by eye until the later part of Basil II's reign... The name means 'a fourth part', *i.e.* a piece of standard weight diminished by a quarter of a tremissis equivalent to ½ of the whole.

tetched (tetʃt), *pa. pple.* and *ppl. a.* U.S. dial. and colloq. var. of *touched* (see Touch *v.* 23 b); mentally deranged to a slight degree; somewhat mad, crazy, or 'cracked'.

1930–41 in H. Wentworth *Amer. Dial. Dict.* (1944) 657/1. **1983** C. McCarry *Last Supper* III. vi. 333 These people are tetched in the head. **1984** S. Bellow *Him with his Foot in his Mouth* 39 If she had been a little tetched before, melodramatic, in her fifties she seemed to become crazed.

tetchous (te·tʃəs), *a. U.S. dial.* Also **tetchious, tetchus.** [f. Tetchy *a.*: see -ous.] = Tetchy, techy *a.* 1.

1890 *Dialect Notes* I. 66 *Tetchus*,..tetchy. **1893** H. A. Shands *Some Peculiarities of Speech in Mississippi* 62 *Tetchous*.., common among negroes and illiterate whites for *tetchy*. Used also in Kentucky. **1913** H. Kephart *Our Southern Highlanders* xiii. 294 A choleric or fretful person is tetchious. **1948** A. Lomax in A. Dundes *Mother Wit* (1973) 484/1 That's what makes the Negro so *tetchious* till today. **1959** W. Faulkner *Mansion* iii. 58 A respectability that delicate and tetchous that wouldn't nothing else suit.

tête-à-tête, *adv.*, *sb.*, and *a.* Add: **C.** *adj.* *tête-à-tête set* (example).

1870 L. M. Alcott *Old-Fashioned Girl* viii. 163 Such a cunning teakettle and saucepan, and a tête-à-tête set.

Hence as *v. intr.*, to engage in private conversation (together or *with* another).

1861 Mrs. Gaskell *Let.* 10 June (1966) 657 The reason why she & I were tête à têteing in this way was that Mr Gaskell was gone to Liverpool. **1943** *Two Masques* Nov. 4/2 Maureen O'Hara, Patricia Morison and Martha O'Driscoll are the ladies with whom Garfield goes 'tete-a-tete'ing. **1979** G. Swarthout *Skeletons* 48 I'll tête-à-tête with him, too.

tête-bêche (tɛ̄tˌbɛ̄ʃ), *sb.* (*a*). *Philately.* [a. Fr., lit. '(sleeping) head to foot', f. *tête* head + *bêche*, reduced from *béchevet*, lit. 'double bed-head'.] (A stamp) printed upside down relative to the next stamp in the same row or column (see quot. 1913). Freq. *attrib.* in phr. *tête-bêche pair*. Also as *adv.*

1874 *Stamp-Collector's Mag.* XII. 10 The Marquis de L—— has kindly forwarded for notice a reversed 4 centime laureated French empire stamp; technically termed a *tête-bêche*. **1882** E. B. Evans *Catal. Collectors Postage Stamps* 56 One or more stamps upside down,.. forming the varieties termed *têtes-bêches*. *Ibid.*, Varieties 2 and 3 are the result of stamps placed *tête-bêche*. **1891** *S. Gibbons' Monthly Jrnl.* 30 Jan. 153/2 The sheets are composed of four horizontal rows of five stamps,..each row is placed *tête-bêche* to the one below it. **1913** E. B. Evans *Stamps & Stamp Collecting* (ed. 4) 103 *Tête-bêche*. A term applied in French to stamps printed upside down in reference to one another. One such stamp may appear in a sheet, through one of the dies forming the plate being accidentally set the wrong way; this stamp will be *tête-bêche* as regards those surrounding it. Some of the stamps of Grenada were printed with alternate rows reversed, so that the stamps in one row were *tête-bêche* with reference to those in the next. Such varieties must of course be shown in pairs, as the stamps when separated exhibit no peculiarity. **1921** F. A. Bellamy *Oxf. & Cambr. Coll. Messenger Postage Stamps* 14 Balliol, a number of impressions were made one way, then the paper strip was turned round; so a tête bêche pair can be found on each strip. **1971** *Daily Tel.* 16 July 7/6 The 2 annas is known in a tête bêche pair (one stamp upside down in relation to the other).

‖ **tête de bœuf** (tɛ̄t də böf). *Embroidery.* [Fr., lit. 'ox's head'.] Used *attrib.* to designate an embroidery stitch (see quots.).

1882 Caulfeild & Saward *Dict. Needlework* 195/1 *Tête de Bœuf Stitch*. The name of this stitch is derived from its shape, the two upper stitches having the appearance of horns, and the lower ones of an animal's head... The needle is inserted and brought out for the two slanting stitches that commence the next Tête de Bœuf. **1923** *Daily Mail* 19 Jan. 15 *Tete de bœuf stitch*... Two slanting stitches which meet in the form of a V are made, and from the inside of this, at the bottom, is taken a chain-stitch which is caught down with a short over-stitch. **1934** M. Thomas *Dict. Embroidery Stitches* 198 Tête-de-bœuf filling stitch. Single daisy stitches set between two right-angled straight stitches make up this pretty filling.

‖ **tête de cuvée** (tɛ̄t də küve). [Fr., lit. 'head of the vatful'.] A vineyard producing the best wine in a village area; wine from such a vineyard.

[**1833** C. Redding *Hist. & Descr. Mod. Wines* v. 100 The best Burgundies, called *les têtes de cuves*, are from the choicest vines..grown on the best spots in the vineyard, having the finest aspect.] **1908** E. & A. Vizetelly *Wines of France* 122 The finer Volnay, what is called the *tête-de-cuvée* wine, has a most refreshing flavour. **1952** W. Stevens *Let.* 29 Sept. (1967) 761, I sat at lunch with a little Corton (1929, tete de cuvée). **1965** A. Sichel *Penguin Bk. Wines* III. 147 The above listed vineyards are all *têtes de cuvées*, that is the highest class in their village area... It must not be assumed that the *têtes de cuvées* of different villages are equal in quality. Many names of the next category—the *premier cru* or *cuvée*.. may be better.

‖ **tête de nègre** (tɛ̄t də nɛ̄gr'). [Fr., lit. 'Negro's head'.] A dark brown colour approaching black. Usu. *attrib.* Cf. *nigger brown* s.v. *nigger *sb.* 2 d.

1916 in G. Howell *In Vogue* (1975) 20/1 (Advt.), Tête de Negre..Hat, gold embroidery. **1923** *Daily Mail* 5 Mar. 15/3 A striking gown..is worn over a slip of tete de negre silk. **1973** *Country Life* 22 Feb. 455/1 Design of baskets of spring flowers..on a *tete de nègre* (that is a not dead black) ground.

tête de pont. (Later examples.)

1853 J. H. Stocqueler *Milit. Encycl.* 283/2 In order to add to the defence of *Têtes de Pont*, reduits have been constructed within them. **1918** E. S. Farrow *Dict. Milit. Terms* 613 *Tête-de-pont*, a work thrown up at the end of a bridge to cover communication across a river; a bridgehead. **1926** Fowler *Mod. Eng. Usage* 329/1 The strong tête-de-pont fortifications were rushed by our troops, & a battalion crossed the bridge.

‖ **tête exaltée** (tɛ̄t egzalte), *adv. phr.* [Fr., lit. 'with head elated'.] In an elated or euphoric manner. Also as *sb.*, someone behaving thus.

1841 C. Fox *Jrnl.* 6 June in *Memories of Old Friends* (1882) vii. 128 Carlyle..said, 'Give my love to your dear interesting nephew and nieces!'.. I walked *tête-exaltée* the rest of the day. **1856** C. M. Yonge *Daisy Chain* I. xxii. 232 Flora thought of the words *'tête exaltée'*, and considered herself alone to have sober sense enough to see things in a true light. **1873** —— *Pillars of House* III. xxviii. 128 A pious utterance that only a *tête exaltée* takes literally.

tetel (tē^i·təl, te·təl). Also **tetl.** [Local name.] = *tora.

1867 S. W. Baker *Nile Trib.* 308 We had hardly ridden half a mile, when I perceived a fine bull tétel..standing near a bush. **1894** Sclater & Thomas *Bk. Antelopes* I. 16 The Tora or Tétel was confounded by von Heaglin and Sir Samuel Baker, its first discoverers, with the Bubal. **1920** *Blackw. Mag.* Nov. 672/2 A great herd of tetl—big animals the size of a mule—sprang up.

‖ **tête montée** (tɛ̄t moṅte), *adj. phr.* Also *erron.* **tête monté.** [Fr., lit. 'excited head'.] Over-excited, agitated, worked up. Also as *sb.*, this state of mind.

1825 H. Wilson *Memoirs* I. 12, I had suffered severely from wounded pride, and, in fact, I was very much tête monté. **1836** E. Grosvenor *Let.* in G. Huxley *Lady Elizabeth & Grosvenors* (1965) vii. 160 The tête montée state of the young *Brutus's* and patriots..in France. **1859** Trollope *Bertrams* I. viii. 155 But in truth George was somewhat afflicted by a *tête montée* in this matter. **1882** E. W. Hamilton *Diary* 29 Aug. (1972) I. 328 She regards Davitt as the incarnation of vanity and Dillon as a *tête montée*. **1936** J. M. Keynes *Gen. Theory Employment* vi. 64 It might be, of course, that individuals were so *tête montée* in their decisions as to how much they themselves would save and invest respectively, that there would be no point of price equilibrium at which transactions could take place. **1960** L. Cooper *Certain Compass* 118 Adrian was *tête monté* .., in that slightly exalted state.

tether, *sb.* Add: **5.** *tether-length* (example); **tether-ball** (examples).

1900 *Queen* 29 Sept. (Advt.), Parlour tether ball... This..game consists of a perpendicular pole, to the top of which an india-rubber ball is attached by a cord... Each player is provided with a bat, with which to strike the ball. **1925** T. Dreiser *Amer. Tragedy* I. II. xxxviii. 425 His own mental tether-length having been strained to the breaking point. **1937** J. Bancroft *Games* 632 Tetherball... This is one of the most delightful and vigorous games that is adapted to small playing space. **1973** E. S. Shneidman *Deaths of Man* ix. 95 A..bachelor was found hanging from a tetherball pole.

Tethys (te·þis). *Geol.* [L. *Tēthys*, Gr. Τηθύς, a sea-goddess: see quot. 1893.] The name of a large sea that formerly lay between Eurasia and Africa. Hence **Te·thyan** *a.*

1893 E. Suess in *Nat. Sci.* II. 183 Modern geology permits us to follow the first outlines of the history of a great ocean which once stretched across part of Eurasia. The folded and crumpled deposits of this ocean stand forth to heaven in Thibet, Himalaya, and the Alps. This ocean we designate by the name 'Tethys', after the sister and consort of Oceanus. *Ibid.* 184 The later Tethyan history.. forms certainly one of the most attractive chapters of historical geography. **1931** [see *Laurasia]. **1947** Auden *Age of Anxiety* vi. 133 The Laurentian Landshield was ruthlessly gerrymandered, And there was a terrible tussle over the Tethys Ocean. **1970** R. M. Black *Elements Palaeont.* vi. 52 The rudists occur mainly in the deposits of Tethys. **1971** *Nature* 29 Jan. 311/1 Old ocean floor was subducted into the Tethyan trench. **1972** *Sci. Amer.* June 61/3 In late Paleozoic times a wide tropical seaway, the Tethys, almost circled the globe. The only barrier to the Tethys Sea was formed by the combined land masses of North America and western Europe, which were then connected.

Teton (tī·tǫn). *U.S.* [ad. Dakota *tʰí* + *ʰuwą*, dwellers on the prairie.] **a.** (A member of) a Western division of the Dakota or Sioux Indian tribe. Also *attrib.*

1806 *Message from President of U.S., communicating Discoveries made in exploring the Missouri by Captains Lewis & Clark* 32 This trade, as small as it may appear, has been sufficient to render the Tetones independent of the trade of the Missouri. **1840** *N.Y. Mirror* 4 July 12/3 His household was the whole tribe of the Teton Dahcotas. **1873** *Forest & Stream* 9 Oct. 133/1 For several hours we followed on the trail of the Tetons. **1937** R. H. Lowie *Hist. Ethnol. Theory* ix. 133 Boas has trained Miss Ella Delovia to take down Teton stories among her people. **1975** J. A. Hanson *Metal Weapons, Tools, & Ornaments of Teton Dakota Indians* i. 3 The Tetons, who spoke Lakota, took their name from the term *Titonwan*, 'Dwellers of the Prairie'.

b. The dialect spoken by this people.

1911 F. Boas *Handbk. Amer. Indian Lang.* (U.S. Bureau Amer. Ethnol. Bull. No. 40) 880 We give here the description of the Teton as obtained by Dr. Swanton. **1933** [see *Dakota *sb.* 2]. **1976** W. L. Chafe in T. A. Sebeok *Native Lang. Americas* I. 542 There are usually said to be four major Dakota dialects: Santee (Dakota proper), Teton (Lakota), and Yankton and Assiniboine.

tetotaciously, var. *teetotaciously *adv.*

tetra-. Add: **1. tetra·bolo** [f. *di)abolo by deliberately false analogy (see quot. 1961)], a polyabolo composed of four triangles; **tetraco·ccus** (pl. **-cocci**) *Biol.* [Coccus] (see quot. 1968); **tetragamy:** also, marriage with four women simultaneously; **tetralemma** (earlier example); **tetrapare·ntal** *a. Biol.*, (of an organism) produced by the fusion of two embryos; also as *sb.*, a tetraparental individual; **tetrapare·sis** *Path.* [Paresis], muscular weakness of all four limbs; hence **tetrapare·tic** *a.*; **tetrape·ptide** *Biochem.* [ad. G. *tetrapeptid* (see *peptide)], an oligopeptide in which there are four amino-acid residues in the molecule; **tetrapho·nic** [Gr. φωνή voice, sound], applied to certain forms of quadraphonic recording and reproduction (see quots.); **tetratonon** (earlier example); **tetrawi·ckmanite** *Min.*, a tetragonal polymorph of wickmanite, $MnSn(OH)_6$, found as yellow crystals.

1961 *New Scientist* 21 Dec. 752/3 Mr. S. J. Collins..has experimented with the various plane shapes that can be formed by edgewise joins of four isosceles right-angled triangles; for these he most ingeniously suggests the name 'tetraboloes'. His excuse is that a 'diabolo' has two such triangles in its cross-section (joined pointwise, not edgewise: but no matter!). **1967** Tetrabolo [see *polyabolo* s.v. *poly- 1]. **1893** W. R. Dawson tr. *Schenk's Man. Bacteriol.* i. 2 Cocci are..found either singly or united in groups... If the elements are joined in pairs and fours we distinguish respectively, according to the number, diplococci and tetracocci. **1907** *Practitioner* Apr. 488 Two diplococci are frequently seen together, giving a tetracoccus form. **1968** M. Hynes *Med. Bacteriol.* (ed. 9) i. 1 Cocci which divide regularly in two planes at right angles to one another result in collections of four organisms, and are known as tetrads or tetracocci. **1907** W. De Morgan *Alice-for-Short* xviii. 203 Charles had said to his friend, jokingly, that if he had fifty sisters, single ones, Johnson was welcome to make offers to them all round.—'But then, my dear Paracelsus, that was to be *if* I *had* fifty. That would leave me forty-nine—or in case of bigamy, forty-eight; or quadrogamy—tetragamy—whatever it ought to be—forty-six. **1918** R. A. Knox *Spiritual Aeneid* x. 166 We could always split the difference between monogamy and tetragamy by having two wives all round. *a* **1856** W. Hamilton *Lect. Metaphysics & Logic* (1860) III. xviii. 352 If it [*sc.* the syllogism] has three, four, or five members, it is called *trilemma* (*tricornis*), *tetralemma* (*quadricornis*), *pentalemma* (*quinquecornis*). **1970** *Nature* 31 Jan. 462/2 Tetraparental mice are produced by fusing two eight-cell stage embryos. *Ibid.*, Allelic differences between the strains produce mosaic patterns in the adult tetraparental which make possible inferences about development. **1971** *New Scientist* 8 Apr. 72/1 One of the most fascinating tools employed in studying these processes [of tissue differentiation]..is provided by 'tetraparental' mice. **1979** *Nature* 11 Oct. 429/1 B. Mintz (Institute for Cancer Research, Philadelphia)..pioneered the use of allophenic mice (formed by aggregating cells from two 8-cell embryos from two different pregnant mice, hence tetraparental). **1972** *New Gould Med. Dict.* (ed. 3), *Tetraparesis*, weakness of all four extremities. **1980** *Brit. Med. Jrnl.* 29 Mar. 902/2 She was anarthric and bedridden with spastic tetraparesis and twitching tremors. **1978** *Jrnl. R. Soc. Med.* LXXI. 449 A woman.. who was tetraparetic following operation for a cerebral tumour. **1906** *Jrnl. Chem. Soc.* XC. I. 810 Triglycylglycine methyl ester, prepared by esterifying the tetrapeptide with methyl alcohol and hydrogen chloride, crystallises in microscopic, glistening needles. **1927** P. A. LEVENE *Chem. Relationships of Sugars* 2 in *Contemp. Devel. in Chem.*, A tetrapeptide composed of naturally occurring amino acids is hydrolyzed by trypsin. **1970** R. W. MCGILVERY *Biochem.* iv. 51 Peptide subunits join to make the tetrapeptide because of interactions between side chains of residues exposed at the meshing surfaces. **1969** *db Mag.* Dec. 23/2 Microphones are placed so channels 1 and 3, and 2 and 4 will operate as pairs to give three walls of sound... In addition, channels 3 and 4 operate as a stereo pair to sharpen the directionality of the reflected sound... When we discovered this..we called it Tetraphonic Sound. **1974** *Wireless World* July 236/2 Gerzon's assertion that 'the optimum characteristic is not known' in regard to a particular tetraphonic technique could be equally well applied to any quadraphonic system. **1977** *Daily Tel.* 4 May 18 'Tetraphonic' has already been given the technical meaning of a set of signals giving complete first-order directional information including height. **1740** J. GRASSINEAU *Mus. Dict.* 276 Tetratonon; the superfluous fifth may be thus called, as containing four tones. **1973** WHITE & NELEN in *Mineral. Rec.* IV. 24/1 The mineral..was not wickmanite, but its tetragonal dimorph! To emphasize this dimorphic relationship the mineral has been named tetrawickmanite. **1978** *Ibid.* IX. 41/2 The Langban tetrawickmanite occurs as bright yellow euhedra implanted on magnetite.

2. a. te:traalkyllea·d [*ALKYL], any compound in which the molecule consists of four alkyl radicals bonded to an atom of lead; **tetrabe·nazine** *Pharm.* [f. *benz*o(*a*)quinol*izin*-2-on*e*, f. BENZ(ENE + *-izine*, denoting two fused rings with a nitrogen atom common to both], a tricyclic compound, $C_{19}H_{27}NO_3$, used in the treatment of chorea; **tetrachloride:** *carbon tetrachloride*, a dense, colourless liquid, CCl_4, used chiefly in the manufacture of refrigerants and aerosols and in fire extinguishers, and also as a solvent; **tetrachlo:rodibe:nzo(-p-)dioxin,** a polychlorinated tricyclic hydrocarbon, $C_{12}H_4O_2Cl_4$, that is carcinogenic and teratogenic in animals and is formed in the manufacture of chlorinated phenols; also called *dioxin*; abbrev. TCDD (see *T 6 a); **tetrachlo:rodibe:nzoparadio·xin** = prec.; **te:trachlor(o)e·thane,** either of two isomeric compounds, $C_2H_2Cl_4$, that are dense colourless liquids; *spec.* the symmetrical isomer, which is used chiefly in the manufacture of solvents and is toxic; **te:tradecape·ptide,** a polypeptide having fourteen amino-acid residues in the molecule; **te:tra,e:thylammo·nium** *Chem.* (also † **tetre:thyl-**), the quaternary ion $(C_2H_5)_4N^+$, which is a ganglion-blocking agent and has been used (in the form of its chloride or bromide salt) in the treatment of hypertension; **tetraethyl lead,** a poisonous oily liquid, $Pb(C_2H_5)_4$, which is added to petrol as an anti-knock agent making possible higher compression ratios; = *lead tetraethyl* s.v. *LEAD *sb.*[1] 12 b; **tetrae:thylpyropho·sphate,** a colourless, hygroscopic liquid, $(C_2H_5)_4P_2O_7$, that is a cholinesterase inhibitor and is used as a garden insecticide and formerly to relieve the symptoms of myasthenia gravis; **tetrahy·drate,** a hydrate containing four molecules of water; **te:trahy:droca·nnabinol,** a hydrogenated derivative of cannabinol that is the active principle in cannabis and hashish; **te:trahydrofu·ran,** a colourless liquid, C_4H_8O, used as a solvent for plastics and other polymers and as an intermediate in the manufacture of organic chemicals; **te:trahy:drofu·rfuryl,** the monovalent radical $C_4H_7O.CH_2$—; **te:trahy:drona·phthalene,** any compound derived from naphthalene by the addition of four hydrogen atoms; *spec.* 1,2,3,4-tetrahydronaphthalene, a colourless liquid used as a solvent for hydrocarbons, esp. varnishes, lacquers, etc.; = *TETRALIN; **te:tra,iodothy·ronine** *Biochem.* [*THYRONINE] = *THYROXINE; **tetrame·thylene,** the gaseous alicyclic compound $(CH_2)_4$; also, (a compound containing) the bivalent straight-chain radical $—CH_2(CH_2)_2CH_2—$; **tetra·misole** *Pharm.* [f. I)MI(DE + *thia*)*zole* s.v. THIO- 1, with alteration of *z*], an anthelminthic drug used in man and animals, usu. as the hydrochloride; 2,3,5,6-tetrahydro-6-phenylimidazo[2,1-*b*]thiazole, $C_{11}H_{12}N_2S$; **tetrapy·rrole** [PYRROL in Dict. and Suppl.], any compound containing four pyrrole nuclei, esp. when in the form of a ring (cf. *PORPHIN); hence **tetrapyrro·lic** *a.*

1923 *Jrnl. Amer. Chem. Soc.* July 1821 The method used by Krause..always yields a tetra-alkyl lead compound when an alkyl halide is used. **1978** *Nature* 26 Oct. 738/1 Particulate lead and tetraalkyllead in the atmosphere are due principally to emissions from vehicles fuelled by leaded petrol. **1958** *Federation Proc.* XVII. 404/1 (*heading*) Inhibition of reserpine tranquilizing effects by tetrabenazine, a synthetic tranquilizing agent. **1974** *Lancet* 26 Jan. 107/1 Tetrabenazine is the drug of first choice for the suppression of chorea in patients with Huntington's chorea. **1866** Carbon tetrachloride [in Dict.]. **1930** *Engineering* 26 Dec. 814/2 The use of chemical cleaners, such as..carbon tetrachloride,..is more effective. **1947** J. C. RICH *Materials & Methods of Sculpture* v. 94 The wax is placed in the carbon tetrachloride and set aside for about two days to dissolve, after which it can be used. **1972** *Materials & Technol.* IV. vi. 201 Carbon tetrachloride was originally made from coke and chlorine, carbon disulphide being used as an intermediate, but is now mainly produced by the chlorination of methane, or the chlorinolysis of higher hydrocarbons. **1959** *Jrnl. Pharm. Soc. Japan* LXXIX. 188 (*caption*) 2,3,7,8-Tetrachlorodibenzo-*p*-dioxin. **1970** *Kirk-Othmer Encycl. Chem. Technol.* (ed. 2) XXII. 180 Dioxins, including 2,3,7,8-tetrachlorodibenzo-*p*-dioxin, have been detected as contaminants in samples of 2,4,5-T. **1976** *Daily Tel.* 2 Aug. 11/8 He is to attempt to clean an experimental patch of land 100 yards square by the introduction of healthy micro-organisms of yeast and mould, which he hopes will 'seed' upon the poisonous substance, breaking down the molecules of TCDD (Tetrachlorodibenzo-dioxine). **1977** *New Yorker* 25 July 30/1 The samples of the chemical used in the experiments had contained uncharacteristically high levels of a toxic contaminant, 2,3,7,8 tetrachlorodibenzo-*p*-dioxin—commonly referred to as TCDD, or, by chemists familiar with the subject, either as tetra dioxin or simply as dioxin. **1978** *Price's Textbk. Pract. Med.* (ed. 12) III. 284/2 Under conditions of high reaction temperatures in the manufacture of 2,4,5-T there has been formed tetrachlorodibenzoparadioxine (dioxine) which has produced chloracne in laboratory workers. **1980** *National Geographic* Aug. 181 TCDD—shorthand for 2,3,7,8-tetrachlorodibenzoparadioxin, frequently simply called dioxin —is the inevitable by-product of the manufacture of the herbicides 2,4,5-T and silvex. **1871** *Jrnl. Chem. Soc.* XXIV. 1191 The former has the composition of tetrachlorethane, $C_2H_2Cl_4$, and is formed, according to the usual reaction of phosphorus pentachloride on aldehydes, by the substitution of 2 at. Cl. for 1 at. O in dichloraldehyde. **1922** *Encycl. Brit.* XXX. 35/1 Tetrachlorethane was tried with success, but it proved dangerous to the operatives applying it in enclosed places. Moreover, sunlight decomposed tetrachlorethane. **1933** *Jrnl. R. Hort. Soc.* LVIII. 282 Tetrachlorethane as a Greenhouse Fumigant. **1934** H. HILER *Notes on Technique of Painting* iii. 235 Dissolve hard copal resin in tetra-chlor-ethan [*sic*]. **1963** A. J. HALL *Textile Sci.* vii. 307 Dry cleaning involves the extraction of dirt, and grease, oil, fat and wax stains from all kinds of textile materials by treatment with a hot organic solvent such as..tetrachloroethane. **1974** *Encycl. Brit. Micropædia* IX. 910/3 The other isomer, 1,1,1,2-tetrachloroethane,..has no commercial application. **1973** *Science* 5 Jan. 79/1 The linear tetradecapeptide was synthesized by solid-phase methodology. **1979** *Nature* 8 Nov. 208/2 A tetradecapeptide originally isolated from amphibian skin. **1852** A. W. HOFMANN in *Q. Jrnl. Chem. Soc.* IV. 306 For this [organic] metal I propose..the name Tetrethylammonium..which implies that it is built up by the intimate union of nitrogen with four equivalents of the hypothetical hydrocarbon called ethyl. **1940** *Thorpe's Dict. Appl. Chem.* (ed. 4) IV. 355/2 Tetraethylammonium hydroxide, $NEt_4·OH$, known only in solution or as solid hydrates. **1962** J. H. BURN *Drugs, Med. & Man* vi. 65 Two American workers attempted to use..tetraethylammonium to reduce blood pressure in patients in 1946, and then two workers in England introduced hexamethonium which was much more powerful and acted for a much longer time. **1923** *Jrnl. Amer. Chem. Soc.* July 1821 Tetra-ethyl lead was prepared by P. Pfeiffer by the action of lead chloride on ethyl-magnesium iodide. **1940** *Economist* 30 Mar. 586/2 The 87-octane spirit is generally obtained by the addition of small quantities of tetra-ethyl lead to good-quality 'straight-run' petrol. **1970** *Nature* 14 Mar. 990/1 Lead, in the form which it is added to petrols—tetraethyl lead, $Pb(C_2H_5)_4$—is undoubtedly poisonous. **1947** *Ibid.* 29 Nov. 760/1 During the War, the Germans introduced as insecticides a series of phosphate esters, including tetraethylpyrophosphate and hexaethyltetraphosphate. **1952** H. BECKMAN *Pharmacol. in Clin. Pract.* 568 Prostigmin may usually be discontinued at this point and tetraethylpyrophosphate cautiously increased..until there is maximal relief of symptoms without toxic effects. **1974** *Encycl. Brit. Micropædia* IX. 911/3 Tetraethyl pyrophosphate is extremely poisonous to humans, the toxic effects being similar to those of parathion. **1886** *Jrnl. Chem. Soc.* XLIX. 418 The thermal reaction..is made up of two distinct quantities—(1) the decomposition of the trihydrate, (2) the formation of the tetrahydrate. **1951** [see *hexahydrate* s.v. *HEXA-]. **1963** *Acta Crystallogr.* XVI. 376 (*heading*) Refinement of the structure of potassium pentaborate tetrahydrate. **1940** *Jrnl. Chem. Soc.* 1121 The compounds prepared include 6″-hydroxy-2:2:5′-trimethyl-4″-*n*-amyl-3′:4′:5′:6′-tetrahydrodibenzopyran.., which may be a tetrahydrocannabinol. **1967** *New Scientist* 31 Aug. 436/1 The classical analysis of hashish..yielded three types of related compound as the characteristic components of the drug. These were cannabidiol, cannabinol and tetrahydrocannabinol. **1980** *Daily Tel.* 19 Sept. 11/2 If the female is pollinated, it uses some of its resinous tetrahydrocannabinol]*printed* -cannibol]—the stimulant in marijuana—to produce seeds. **1908** *Jrnl. Chem. Soc.* XCIV. I. 280 When furan is hydrogenated at 170° by Sabatier and Senderens' method, the principal product consists of tetrahydrofuran. **1956** *Nature* 21 Jan. 128/2 Both the nylon 6:6-cyclic monomer..and the cyclic dimer from caprolactam..were reduced by lithium aluminium hydride in boiling tetrahydrofuran without difficulty. **1978** *Further Perspectives Organic Chem.* (CIBA) 23 Why should the gas phase be a better model for enzymic reactions than a solvent which is more protein-like than, say, water..or tetrahydrofuran? **1928** *Jrnl. Amer. Chem. Soc.* L. 1821 α-Tetrahydrofurfuryl alcohol will shortly be available on a commercial scale from the catalytic reduction of furfural. **1951** KIRK & OTHMER *Encycl. Chem. Technol.* VI. 1004 In the United Kingdom, tetrahydrofurfuryl acetate has been used as a lipstick ingredient, based on the high solubility of eosin in it. *Ibid.*, Tetrahydrofurfuryl alcohol is used in the preparation of esters, especially tetrahydrofurfuryl oleate, which is almost colourless and has excellent light and heat stability. **1887** *Abstr. Proc. Chem. Soc.* III. 88 At the next meeting..the following Papers will be read... 'Derivatives of Hydrindonaphthene and Tetrahydronaphthalene'. By W. H. Perkin, jun. **1904** [see *DECAHYDRONAPHTHALENE]. **1935** *Industr. & Engin. Chem.* (*News Ed.*) 20 Aug. 332/1 The merit of tetrahydronaphthalene for town gas mains lies in the fact that, being a close chemical relative of naphthalene it has the power of absorbing larger quantities of naphthalene than any of the other solvents in present use. **1964** N. G. CLARK *Mod. Organic Chem.* xix. 391 Naphthalene quite readily undergoes addition reactions. For example at 200° catalytic hydrogenation over nickel yields tetrahydronaphthalene ('tetralin'). **1969** N. A. J. ROGERS in S. Coffey *Rodd's Chem. Carbon Compounds* (ed. 2) IIc. x. 71, 1,4,5,8-Tetrahydronaphthalene, 'isotetralin'.., m.p. 58°, may be prepared by the reduction of 1,4-dihydronaphthalene by the 'metal in ammonia' method. **1928** Tetraiodothyronine [see *THYRONINE]. **1974** D. & M. WEBSTER *Compar. Vertebr. Morphol.* xiii. 310 The two hormones, triiodothyronine and tetraiodothyronine (thyroxine), are iodinated amino acids. **1885** W. H. PERKIN in *Jrnl. Chem. Soc.* XLVII. 806 It was thought that the simplest method would be to regard the saturated hydrocarbons themselves as multiples of methylene, CH_2, and thus name them di-, tri-, tetra-, penta-, &c., methylene, as is easiest seen from the following table:—..Tetra-methylene. **1898** J. WADE *Introd. Study Org. Chem.* xxxv. 219 The tetramethylene compound..is formed by the reduction of ethylene cyanide with sodium amalgam in alcoholic solution. **1909** [see *pentamethylene* s.v. *PENTA-]. **1944** S. J. SMITH *Princ. Org. Chem.* x. 197 Both their methods of preparation and their parachors..show them to be cyclic compounds containing no unsaturated linkage:.. Cyclobutane tetramethylene. **1966** [see *ETHYLENE 2]. **1971** N. L. ALLINGER et al. *Org. Chem.* iv. 63 Frequently occurring hydrocarbon groupings that have more than one site for the attachment of substituents are also given common or trivial names..$ICH_2CH_2CH_2CH_2I$ 1,4-Diiodobutane (Tetramethylene iodide). **1966** D. THIENPONT et al. in *Nature* 12 Mar. 1084/1 This article reports the discovery of tetramisole.., a new, potent broad spectrum anthelmintic. **1978** *Ibid.* 22 June 629/1 Tetramisole and/or its levorotatory isomer levamisole is used in many countries against a broad range of nematodal infections in birds, pigs, ruminants and man. **1917** *Chem. Abstr.* XI. 452 Baeyer's method..gives the cryst[alline] substance $C_{28}H_{36}N_4$.. which may be named tetrapyrroletetracetone. **1968** [see *PRODIGIOSIN]. **1976** *Ann. Rev. Microbiol.* XXX. 410 Relatively general metabolic criteria, such as..tetrapyrrole biosynthesis..have proven useful in defining taxonomic relationships. **1944** *Ann. Reg. 1943* 358 Vitamins operate as coenzymes in plant respiration, which is catalysed by the same types of tetrapyrrolic compounds as are present in animal tissues. **1975** *Nature* 22 May 357/2 The Hans Fischer school which then dominated tetrapyrrolic chemistry.

tetraalkyllead, tetrabenazine: see *TETRA- 2 a. **tetrabolo:** see *TETRA- 1.

tetracaine (te·trăkēⁱn). *U.S. Pharm.* [f. TETRA- + CO)CAINE.] A compound related to procaine that is used, as a solution of the hydrochloride, as a local anæsthetic, esp. for surface application; amethocaine, $C_4H_9NHC_6H_4COOCH_2CH_2N(CH_3)_2$.

1943 *Dispensatory U.S.A.* (ed. 23) 1121/1 Tetracaine Hydrochloride occurs as a fine, white, crystalline, odorless powder. **1974** [see *spinal anæsthesia* s.v. *SPINAL *a.* 6*]. **1979** SHNIDER & LEVINSON *Anesthesia for Obstetrics* ix. 110/2 Although tetracaine remains one of the most effective and popular drugs for subarachnoid block, it is a poor choice in epidural analgesia.

tetrachloro-: see *TETRA- 2 a.

tetrachloroethylene (te:traklōᵊro,e·þilīn). *Chem.* Also **-chlorethylene.** [f. TETRA- + CHLORO-[2] + ETHYL + -ENE.] = *PERCHLOROETHYLENE. Also called **te:trachloroe·thene.**

1911 *Chem. Abstr.* V. 2815 In this way the author has obtained..tetrachloroethylene. **1930** A. F. HOLLEMAN *Text-bk. Org. Chem.* (ed. 7) I. 197 In contact with water tetrachloroethene reacts with chlorine under the influence of sunlight to form trichloroacetic acid. **1948** J. H. BURN *Lect. Notes Pharmacol.* 99 Hook worms..live in the duodenum. The infestation is treated by carbon tetrachloride and tetrachlorethylene. **1968** A. A. BAKER *Unsaturation in Org. Chem.* iii. 27 Faraday..heated the perchloride of carbon to dull redness, finding that chlorine was liberated, and a new compound, which he called protochloride of carbon was formed..known today as tetrachloroethene (C_2Cl_4). **1969** *Times* 20 Feb. 17/5 Some 100,000 gallons of the cleaning fluid tetrachloroethylene were buried in a gold mine, so as to avoid contamination with cosmic rays, and left in place for nearly four months.

tetrachordon. (In Dict. s.v. TETRACHORD.) (Earlier example.)

1740 J. GRASSINEAU *Mus. Dict.* 274 Tetrachordon. See Tetrachord.

tetrachoric (tetrăkōᵊ·rik), *a. Statistics.* [f. Gr. τετράχωρ-ος divided into four (f. χῶρος place: see TETRA-) + -IC 1.] Applied to a table in which data are divided into two according to each of two criteria, and so having four subdivisions; of or pertaining to such a table; applied *esp.* to an estimate of the product-moment coefficient derived from such a table, and to concepts used in obtaining such an estimate.

1910 P. F. EVERITT in *Biometrika* VII. 438 In the present tables the values of the first six τ functions, henceforth to be termed tetrachoric functions, have been computed for values of ½ (1 − α) from ·001 to ·500 by successive increments of ·001. **1918** *Ibid.* XII. 95 In the ordinary scheme for a tetrachoric table, the quadrants are denoted by *a, b, c, d.* **1943** M. G. KENDALL *Adv. Theory Statistics* I. xiv. 354 Tetrachoric *r* and biserial *η*. Both these coefficients are, in effect, estimates of a putative product-moment correlation for data which are not specified with the detail of an ordinary bivariate table. **1956** J. WHATMOUGH *Language* 241 The statistical method of the so-called 'tetrachoric R'..is valuable in revealing the degree of correlation..between languages which may be suspected of being historically akin. **1964** [see *POLYCHORIC *a.*].

tetrachotomy. (In Dict. s.v. TETRACHOTOMOUS *a.*) Restrict *Zool.* and *Bot.* to sense in Dict. and add: (*b*) *Logic*, a division having four members.

a **1856** W. HAMILTON *Lect. Metaphysics & Logic* (1860) IV. xxv. 23 If a division has only two members, it is called a dichotomy;..if four, a tetrachotomy.

tetracoccus: see *TETRA- 1.

tetracosactrin (teːtrăkǫsæ·ktrin). *Pharm.* [f. TETRA- + I)COS- + *A(DRENO)C(ORTICO)-TR(OPH)IN.] A synthetic polypeptide (see quot. 1967) which resembles corticotrophin in its action and uses but lacks its antigenic property, and is given (as the acetate) by injection in the long-term treatment of inflammatory and degenerative disorders.

1967 *Brit. Med. Jrnl.* 18 Nov. 391/1 Tetracosactrin (β^{1-24} corticotrophin, Synacthen) is a synthetic polypeptide containing the first 24 amino-acids found in naturally occurring corticotrophin (A.C.T.H.). **1972** *Ibid.* 11 Mar. 680/1 The pathognomic finding is their failure [*sc.* that of urinary and plasma corticosteroids] to show a rise after the administration of ACTH or tetracosactrin. **1979** *Jrnl. R. Soc. Med.* LXXII. 530 A tetracosactrin (Synacthen) stimulation test.

tetracyclic (tetrăsəi·klik, -si·klik), *a.* [f. TETRA- + CYCLIC *a.*] **1.** (In Dict. s.v. TETRA- 1.)

2. *Chem.* Of a compound: containing four fused hydrocarbon rings in the molecule.

1928 *Chem. Abstr.* XXII. 2748 (*heading*) Synthesis of tetracyclic compounds and of pyrene. **1977** J. L. HARPER *Population Biol. of Plants* xiii. 414 Plants that are only lightly predated contain three or four isomers of lupanine and closely related tetracyclic compounds.

tetracycline (tetrăsəi·klīn). *Pharm.* [f. *TETRACYCL(IC *a.* + -INE⁵.] **a.** A tetracyclic compound, $C_{22}H_{24}N_2O_8$, which is a broad-spectrum antibiotic (usu. administered as the hydrochloride). **b.** Any of a number of antibiotics structurally related to this compound.

1952 C. R. STEPHENS et al. in *Jrnl. Amer. Chem. Soc.* LXXIV. 4977/1 Common to both Terramycin and aureomycin is the structure A for which we propose the name tetracycline. **1956** *Nature* 3 Mar. 433/2 (*heading*) Avidity of the tetracyclines for the cations of metals. *Ibid.*, This investigation is now extended to the parent substance, tetracycline,..[and] also includes some new values for the substituted tetracyclines. **1966** I. JEFFERIES *House-Surgeon* vi. 115 Start her on one of the tetracyclines. **1974** M. C. GERALD *Pharmacol.* xxvi. 457 Tetracyclines are believed to inhibit protein synthesis by blocking the binding of the amino acid-transfer RNA complex to ribosomes. **1978** *Time* 3 July 43/2 Like almost all U.S. farmers, the cattleman is aggrieved... The costs of everything he buys —gasoline, fertilizer, tetracycline for ailing heifers..—have climbed like corn in August.

tetrad. Add: **2. f.** *Ecol.* (See quot. 1976.)

1963 HAWKES & READETT in P. J. Wanstall *Local Floras* 37 We soon realized that it would be impossible to record from every basic square in the county and we modified the method by considering the squares in blocks of four ('tetrads') and selecting one square at random from each tetrad for surveying. **1968** *Watsonia* VI. 351 This involved the detailed survey of 1 km squares as the unit of recording, one square at random being selected from each block of four or 'tetrad'. **1976** J. G. DONY *Bedfordshire Plant Atlas* 10/1 It has become usual in the survey of areas as small as Bedfordshire to divide the ten-kilometre grid squares into 25 smaller squares each 2 km. × 2 km. known as tetrads. Each tetrad has an area of four square kilometres. **1983** *Natural World* Spring 18 Distributional maps based on 2 × 2 kilometre squares, or tetrads.

tetradecapeptide: see *TETRA- 2 a.

tetradic, *a.* **a.** (Later examples.)

a **1914** C. S. PEIRCE *Coll. Papers* (1935) VI. 222 A tetradic, pentadic, etc. relationship is of no higher nature than a triadic relationship. **1921** [see *MONADIC *a.* 1 b].

tetraethyl(-): see *TETRA- 2 a.

teːtrafluːoroe·thylene (-flŭ·ŏro͵e·þ-). *Chem.* Also **-fluorethylene.** [f. TETRA- + *FLUORO- + ETHYLENE.] A dense, colourless gas, $F_2C{:}CF_2$, which is polymerized to make plastics. Cf. *POLYTETRAFLUOROETHYLENE.

1933 *Jrnl. Amer. Chem. Soc.* LV. 3177 There is good evidence that tetrafluoroethylene is produced in small quantities. **1946** *Sci. News* IV. 63 Polymerisation of tetrafluorethylene..yields heat-resistant, chemically inert solids, which can be moulded into any desired shape. **1958** *Times Rev. Industry* Feb. 81/2 A rather typical example of what can be achieved with fluorocarbons is the polymerization of tetrafluorethylene to yield a commercial plastic. **1973** *Materials & Technol.* VI. 544 The monomer tetrafluoroethylene is obtained by pyrolysis from $CHFCl_2$ (..that is, the refrigerants Freon-22 and Genetron-141).

tetragamy: see TETRA- 1 in Dict. and Suppl.

tetragonal, *a.* (*sb.*) Add: **5.** Also applied to (the structure and symmetry of) substances crystallizing in this system. (Further examples.)

1878 Tetragonal symmetry [in Dict.]. **1886** [see *grey tin* s.v. *GREY, GRAY *a.* 8 c]. **1912** *Dana's Man. Mineral.* (ed. 13) 36 The cross section of a crystal when viewed in the direction of the axis of tetragonal symmetry consists usually of a square or a truncated square. **1937** A. F. ROGERS *Introd. Study Minerals* (ed. 3) I. 67 Interfacial angles in the prism zone are the same for corresponding faces of all tetragonal crystals. **1973** H. D. MEGAW *Crystal Structures* xii. 307 Several other modifications of the spinel structure have been reported. Cr_2CuO_4 has a different tetragonal structure, with approximately the same unit cell as Cr_2NiO_4.

tetragonally *adv.* (examples).

1963 *Q. Jrnl. Geol. Soc.* CXIX. 326 Tetragonally symmetrical flattened pumice lapilli. **1966** PHILLIPS & WILLIAMS *Inorg. Chem.* II. xxv. 248 CuF_2 has a tetragonally-distorted rutile structure.

tetrahedral, *a.* Add: **3.** Math. *tetrahedral numbers*, the series of integers 1, 4, 10, 20,..., the *n*th member of which is the sum of the first *n* triangular numbers.

1939 W. W. R. BALL *Math. Recreations & Ess.* (ed. 11) ii. 59 The sums of consecutive triangular numbers are the tetrahedral numbers. **1983** *Austral. Personal Computer* IV. v. 103/1 The Tetrahedral Numbers..represent the number of identical spheres that can be stacked in a complete triangular pyramid, or tetrahedron.

tetrahedrane (tetrăhī·drēⁱn). *Chem.* [f. TETRAHEDR(ON + -ANE.] A compound whose molecule consists of four CH groups forming the corners of a tetrahedron.

1964 *Tetrahedron Lett.* No. 22. 1418 Tetrahedrane (C_4H_4), which has local C_{3v} symmetry, should have a $J_{C\text{-}H}$ of about 225 c.p.s. **1976** *Sci. Amer.* Feb. 106/1 If this carbene were to undergo internal addition, the product would be the hypothetical tetrahedral molecule tetrahedrane (C_4H_4). Although the reaction has been tried many times, tetrahedrane has so far eluded isolation.

tetrahydrate to **-iodothyronine:** see *TETRA- 2 a.

tetrakis- (te·trăkis), formative element [f. Gr. τετράκις four times] used in *Chem.* in the names of compounds to signify four identical groups all substituted in the same way; formerly = TETRA- 2.

1850 [see TRI- 5 a]. **1912** *Jrnl. Chem. Soc.* CI. 2003 The product obtained was tetrakisazobenzene, a deep red substance. **1951** KIRK & OTHMER *Encycl. Chem. Technol.* VII. 580 Tetrakis(*p*-dimethylaminophenyl)hydrazine is dissociated to the extent of 10% in benzene solution and 21% in nitrobenzene. **1963** A. J. HALL *Student's Handbk. Textile Sci.* v. 259 The Proban flameproofing process is essentially based on the use of tetrakis-hydroxymethyl-phosphonium chloride. **1979** G. C. BARRETT in D. N. Jones *Comprehensive Organic Chem.* III. XI. iv. 77 Tetrakis(methylthio)methane, $(MeS)_4C$, undergoes exchange with dithiols.

tetralemma: see TETRA- 1 in Dict. and Suppl.

Tetralin (te·trălin). Also **tetralin.** [f. TETRA- + NAPHTHA)LIN(E.] = *tetrahydronaphthalene* s.v. *TETRA- 2 a. (A proprietary name in the U.S.)

1920, etc. [see *DECALIN]. **1924** *Nature* 14 June 866/2 Excluding benzol..alternative fuels of greatest promise include 'tetralin' (tetrahydronaphthalene), which, mixed with benzol and alcohol, was used considerably by the Germans during the war. **1944** *Official Gaz.* (U.S. Patent Office) 18 Jan. 350/1 E. I. du Pont de Nemours and Company... *Tetralin* for tetrahydronaphthalene. **1980** *Sci. Amer.* May 89/1 Certain trialkyl tin compounds,.. and acetyl-ethyl-tetramethyl tetralin, a synthetic fragrance at one time used in certain cosmetics, have also been shown to damage myelin preferentially.

tetralogy. Add: **3.** *Med.* A set of four symptoms jointly characteristic of a disorder; chiefly with reference to Fallot's tetralogy (see *FALLOT).

1927 [see *FALLOT]. **1966** WRIGHT & SUMMERS *Systemic Path.* I. ii. 75/2 The tetralogy..consists of pulmonary stenosis.., ventricular septal defect, displacement of the aorta to the right,..and right ventricular hypertrophy. **1970** [see *FALLOT].

tetramer (te·trămər). *Chem.* [f. TETRA- + *-MER.] A compound whose molecule is composed of four molecules of monomer.

1929 *Chem. Abstr.* XXIII. 3213 The dimer and tetramer have also been obtained in cryst. form. **1939** *Jrnl. Amer. Chem. Soc.* LXI. 2320/1 With the aid of a molecular still we isolated the trimer and tetramer of hexatriene. **1966** *New Scientist* 16 June 724/2 The structures of the trimer and tetramer have been determined, and it is known that the trimer is virtually flat, whereas the tetramer is puckered. **1978** *Nature* 6 Apr. 496/2 The haemoglobin molecule is a tetramer of two pairs of identical polypeptide chains, the α and β chains.

Hence **tetrame·ric** *a.*; **tetraːmeriza·tion**, the formation of a tetramer from smaller molecules.

1938 *Jrnl. Chem. Soc.* 290 The study of the trimeric and the tetrameric products of acid-catalysed polymerisation. **1962** [see *DEPOLYMERIZE *v.*]. **1971** *Chem. Abstr.* LXXIII. Subject Index 3626S/3 Tetramerization catalysts. **1974** GILL & WILLIS *Pericyclic Reactions* iii. 69 In certain circumstances it might then be possible to arrange for a concerted cyclic trimerization or tetramerization to occur. **1976** *Ann. Rev. Microbiol.* XXX. 96 Each tetrameric isozyme is thought to contain the three gene products in the ratio of 2:1:1. **1979** *Nature* 29 Feb. 625/1 Stacked A_4 groups in between the cloverleaf branches are supposed to aid in lining up the protein-complexed individual cloverleaf elements for tetramerisation.

tetramethylene, tetramisole: see *TETRA- 2 a.

tetranu·cleotide. *Biochem.* Also † **-nucleotid.** [f. TETRA- + *NUCLEOTIDE.] An oligonucleotide composed of four (unspecified) nucleotides; orig., one composed of one each of four different bases and formerly thought to constitute the nucleic acid molecule (so *tetranucleotide hypothesis, theory*).

1912 W. JONES in *Jrnl. Biol. Chem.* XII. 34 The writer will be permitted to suggest that the nomenclature be made conformable to that which Levene and his coworkers have adopted for the nucleic acids. The term 'tetranuclease' indicates clearly a ferment which exerts its activity upon a tetranucleotide. **1912** A. E. TAYLOR *Digestion & Metabolism* vii. 429 Mononucleotids and tetranucleotids are definitely known; the most common of the tissue nucleic acids are tetranucleotids. **1914** *Jrnl. Biol. Chem.* XVII. 73 Yeast nucleic acid is a *tetra*-nucleotide and is composed of four mono-nucleotide groups. **1931** LEVENE & BASS *Nucleic Acids* II. ix. 289 The tetranucleotide theory is the minimum molecular weight and the nucleic acid may as well be a multiple of it. **1952** *Biochem. Jrnl.* LII. 566/1 The core is composed of the tetra- and penta-nucleotides and possibly some of the trinucleotides. **1960** L. PICKIN *Organization of Cells* iv. 108 Simultaneously in 1948, several groups of workers independently put forward evidence throwing doubt on the old tetranucleotide hypothesis, according to which the four nitrogenous bases present: adenine, guanine, cytosine, and thymine, were combined in equimolecular proportions in a tetranucleotide. This itself was supposed to consist of four nucleotides, each bearing a molecule of one of the four bases. **1974** *Nature* 26 Apr. 783/1 The tetranucleotide hypothesis..asserted that DNA and RNA had a molecular weight of about 1,300, and contained one of each of the four bases (adenine, guanine, cytosine and thymine in DNA; adenine, guanine, cytosine and uracil in RNA). Because these bases were found to be present in the form of nucleotides (sugar-phosphate + base) the molecule was called a tetranucleotide.

Tetra Pak (te·tră͵pæk). Also **Tetra pack** and as one word. [f. TETRA- + PACK *sb.*¹] A proprietary term in the U.S. for a tetrahedral carton used for packing milk and other drinks. Hence as *v. trans.* (nonce-wd.), to sell in such a pack.

1953 *Official Gaz.* (U.S. Patent Office) 16 June 616/2 Ser. No. 623,384. Aktiebolaget Tetra Pak, Lund, Sweden. Filed Jan. 10, 1952. *Tetra Pak.* **1958** *Mod. Packaging Encycl.* 1959 in *Mod. Packaging* Nov. 232 (*caption*) Triangular milk packs are formed, filled from a single roll of paper by this machine. ('Tetra Pak' machine.) **1963** *Economist* 10 Aug. 535/2 Express Dairies only 'tetra-packs' its milk for vending machines and half-pints. **1973** *Times* 29 Oct. 15/8 Just take a look at the Channel Islands, they don't use *any* bottles, not one, they use Tetrapacks; so why can't we. They are cheap, there is no disposal problems [*sic*] as with plastic.

tetraparental to **tetraphonic:** see *TETRA- 1.

tetraplegia (tetrăplī·dʒăi). *Path.* [f. TETRA- + PARA)PLEGIA.] = *QUADRIPLEGIA.

1911 F. S. ARNOLD tr. *Bing's Compendium of Regional Diagnosis* IIA. ii. 105 The pyramids are in such close apposition to each other in the medulla, that minimal lesions may cause a condition of tetraplegia. **1964** J. J. WALSH *Understanding Paraplegia* ii. 6 When the arms are involved it is more correct..to use the term 'tetraplegia' or 'quadriplegia', and throughout this book the former word will be adopted. **1974** A. HENRY in R. M. Kirk et al. *Surgery* xvi. 349 The incidence of tetraplegia is high in this injury as the spine may have angled acutely ..and thus severely pinched the spinal cord.

Hence **tetraple·gic** *a.* and *sb.* = *QUADRIPLEGIC *a.* and *sb.*

1911 F. S. ARNOLD tr. *Bing's Compendium of Regional Diagnosis* IA. iii. 36 In a complete transverse lesion of the [spinal] cord in the upper cervical region the simultaneous paralysis and anæsthesia affect the four extremities and trunk (tetraplegic type). **1939** W. HAYMAKER *Bing's Textbk. Nervous Dis.* xix. 523 The contractures give way to flaccid paralyses. The latter may be monoplegic, hemiplegic, paraplegic, even tetraplegic. **1964** J. J. WALSH *Understanding Paraplegia* xvi. 110 Many tetraplegics..are capable of driving a properly converted car with automatic gear box. **1977** *Lancet* 7 May 1013/2 A strain *Ps[eudomonas] æruginosa* was isolated from a catheter specimen of urine from a tetraplegic patient. **1979** *Daily Tel.* 27 Jan. 18 As a tetraplegic may I thank your Health Services Correspondent..for continued interest in what he describes as the 'shambles' at Stoke Mandeville.

tetraploid (te·trăploid), *a.* (and *sb.*) *Biol.* [f. TETRA- + *-PLOID.] (Made up of somatic cells) containing the diploid chromosome complement twice over. Also as *sb.*, a tetraploid organism.

1914 *Proc. R. Soc.* B. LXXXVII. 484 In the tetraploid giants the chromosomes are $2x(24)$ in the gametic and.. $4x(48)$ in the somatic cells. **1921** *Amer. Naturalist* LV. 261 Few-noded tetraploids, however, are less easily distinguished. **1932** [see *QUADRUPLEX *a.* 3]. **1952** *New Biol.* XIII. 38 It is necessary, before tetraploid rye can be introduced for general cultivation, to see that no normal rye is grown in the locality where the tetraploid is to be grown. **1974** E. STACEY *Peace Country Heritage* ii. 90 Clover..breeders also have concentrated some of the better features, such as leaf retention and plant vigor, into 'tetraploids' by doubling the usual number of chromosomes. **1982** *Sci. Amer.* May 118/3 Potato plants are tetraploid.

Hence **te·traploidy**, the state of being tetraploid.

1918 BABCOCK & CLAUSEN *Genetics* xiv. 263 The doubling of the number of chromosomes typical of the species is known as tetraploidy. **1941** *Amer. Naturalist* LXXV. 321 In many ornamental plants there is a definite need for new types with larger flowers, later blooming habit, and other characteristics usually associated with tetraploidy. **1970** *Sci. Jrnl.* June 78/3 In lower animal forms both triploidy and tetraploidy are compatible with normal development.

tetrapod, *a.* and *sb.* For **a, b** read **A, B** and add: **B.** *sb.* **2.** (See quot. 1962.)

1962 *Newsletter Brit. Petroleum Co. Ltd.* No. 314. 1 An ingenious type of concrete block will next year be helping to protect the harbour at Das Island off the Arabian coast against storms. Known as Tetrapods, these blocks..may be visualised as a central sphere around which are equally spaced four truncated cone-shaped legs. When a number of Tetrapods are placed in position these legs interlock. **1980** *Citizen* (Ottawa) 3 Dec. 43/1 The tetrapods, which look like children's playing jacks, are designed to break up heavy waves in the event of a hurricane.

tetrapyrrole, -ic: see *TETRA- 2 a.

tetrasome (te·trăsōᵘm). *Cytology.* [f. TETRA- + *-SOME⁴.] A chromosome which is represented four times in a chromosomal complement; also, a tetrasomic individual.

1921 [see *hexasome* s.v. *HEXA-]. **1944** *Genetics* XXIX. 232 Through selfing of plants possessing these aberrations, the corresponding nullisomes and tetrasomes have been obtained. **1958** C. P. SWANSON *Cytol. & Cytogenetics* vi. 192 Trisomes $(6n+1)$ and tetrasomes $(6n+2)$ have also been found..in *T[riticum] vulgare.* **1973** [see *NULLISOME].

tetrasomic (tetrăsōᵘ·mik), *a.* (*sb.*) *Cytology.* [f. as prec. + -IC.] Of or pertaining to a tetrasome. Also as *sb.*, a tetrasomic chromosome, cell, or individual.

1922 A. F. BLAKESLEE in *Amer. Naturalist* LVI. 19, I have suggested..the terms disome [etc.]..with the adjectives disomic, trisomic, tetrasomic. **1923** *Bot. Gaz.* LXXVI. 345 Since in the somatic cells of a tetraploid *Datura* each of the 12 chromosomal sets consists of 4 homologous chromosomes instead of only 2 as in diploids, it is obvious that in dealing with the transmission of Mendelian characters we have to do with tetrasomic rather than with the disomic inheritance more familiar to students of heredity. **1937** C. D. DARLINGTON *Rec. Adv. Cytol.* 325 Tetrasomics (whether of fragments or whole chromosomes) are more markedly abnormal..than the corresponding trisomics. **1946** *Nature* 21 Sept. 418/1 Lucerne.., having also given segregation ratios which can best be interpreted as tetrasomic, may be regarded as an autotetraploid. **1961** *Lancet* 7 Oct. 789/1 His father was in effect tetrasomic for that chromosome. **1974** *Nature* 19 Apr. 714/3 The book is then divided into two main parts, the first dealing with trisomics, with some mention of tetrasomics, and the second dealing mainly with monosomics but also mentioning nullisomics.

So **te·trasomy**, tetrasomic state.

1961 *Lancet* 23 Sept. 724/1 Monosomy, trisomy, or even tetrasomy have very little functional effect. **1977** ZELLWEGER & SIMPSON *Chromosomes of Man* p. xii, Trisomy = 46 + 1 chromosome. Tetrasomy = 46 + 2 chromosomes of the same type.

tetrathlon (tetræ·þlǫn). [f. TETRA- + Gk. ἄθλον contest, after PENTATHLON.] An athletic contest comprising a series of four events, esp. one (for juveniles) comprising riding, shooting, swimming, and running.

1959 in *Chambers's 20th Cent. Dict.* Add. **1961** *Times* 29 May 4/4 The 1961 Schools tetrathlon competition, organized by the Modern Pentathlon Association of Great Britain and the R.M.A. Sandhurst, was won by Whitgift. **1973** *Daily Mail* 4 Sept. 33/5 Recently winning the British Horse Society's Pony Club tetrathlon in Warwickshire. **1979** *Daily Tel.* 2 Oct. 19/4 In the recent Pony Club Tetrathlon championships (pentathlon minus fencing) more than 100 girls..competed.

tetratonon: see *TETRA- 1 in Dict. and Suppl.

tetravalent, *a.* Add: = *QUADRIVALENT *a.* 1; (further example); **tetravalence** (example); also **tetrava·lency.**

1887 *Trans. R. Soc. Edin.* XXXII. 456 The tetravalence of Carbon unsatiated by the bivalence of Oxygen. **1913** *Phil. Mag.* XXVI. 495 The observed trivalency and tetravalency respectively of these elements. **1976** *Sci. Amer.* Dec. 33/1 In the solvents that were used..tetravalent plutonium ions, Pu^{4+} (plutonium atoms from which four electrons have been removed), are soluble. **1982** *Nature* 25 Nov. 386/1 Organic chemistry, thanks to the tetravalency of carbon and the stability of its incestuous bonds, is responsible for most of the compounds.

tetrawickmannite: see *TETRA- 1.

tetrazolium (tetrăzōᵘ·liŏm). *Chem.* [f. TETRAZOL(E + *-IUM b.] **a.** The ion or radical $N_4CH_3^{(+)}$ derived from tetrazole. **b.** Any of various derivatives of this, esp. triphenyl tetrazolium chloride, a reagent used as a test for viability in biological material. Usu. *attrib.*

1895 *Jrnl. Chem. Soc.* LXVIII. I. 574 (*heading*) Constitution of tetrazolium bases. *Ibid.*, When tetrazolium derivatives are oxidised, the phenyl radicle is not eliminated. **1947** *Nature* 31 May 748/1 (*heading*) Tetrazolium salt as a seed germination indicator. **1969** J. LEVITT *Introd. Plant Physiol.* ii. 13/1 Tetrazolium dyes..are converted from the colorless to the colored (e.g., red) form by freshly cut surfaces of living cells. **1980** *Nature* 8 May 80/1 The resulting recombinants are Mal⁻ when scored on maltose tetrazolium agar.

tetrazotize (tetræ·zŏtəiz), *v. Chem.* [f. TETRA- + AZOTE + -IZE: cf. DIAZOTIZE *v.* in Dict. and Suppl.] *trans.* To convert (a compound) into one that contains two diazo groups. Hence **tetra:zoti·zable** *a.*, **tetra·zotized** *ppl. a.*; **tetra:zotiza·tion**, the process of tetrazotizing.

1908 J. C. CAIN *Chem. of Diazo-Compounds* 165 Benzidine, when tetrazotized, becomes [etc.]. *Ibid.* 166 This explains why the tetrazotization does not proceed normally. **1933** *Jrnl. Amer. Chem. Soc.* LV. 4540 The technical importance of a method of tetrazotizing *p*-phenylenediamine..in a quantitative way has been shown. *Ibid.* 4541 It appears that *o*-phenylenediamine is tetrazotizable. **1940** [see *CONGO 3]. **1972** *Science* 9 June 1132/2 Tetrazotized benzidine spray..aided in the identification of the four major components.

tetrode. Add: **2.** *Electronics.* A thermionic valve with four electrodes.

1919, 1932 [see *PENTODE]. **1941** *Electronic Engin.* XIV. 385 The valves in this section are push-pull beam tetrodes. **1943**, etc. [see *KINKLESS *a.*]. **1962** D. F. SHAW *Introd. Electronics* xi. 234 The defect in the tetrode characteristics ..is eliminated by the insertion of a third grid, called the suppressor grid, between the anode and the screen. **1976** *Physics Bull.* Aug. 359/3 (*caption*) This component is a new tetrode from Thomson-CSF.

† **B.** *adj. Telegr.* Applied to a mode of multiplex telegraphy by which four messages can be transmitted along a wire simultaneously. *Obs.*

1886 [see *HEXODE *a.*].

tetrodotoxin (te:trŏdotǫ·ksin). [a. G. *tetrodotoxin* (Y. Tahara 1911, in *Biochem. Zeitschr.* XXX. 263), f. TETRODO(N + TOXIN.] A poisonous substance found in the ovaries of certain fish of the family Tetraodontidæ.

1911 *Jrnl. Chem. Soc.* C. II. 133 Tetrodotoxin is neither acid nor base, and yields on hydrolysis a base and a crystalline substance. **1938** *Chem. Abstr.* XXXII. 8582 The toxic action of tetrodotoxin is decreased by vitacamphor, coramine,..and cardiazol. **1965** *New Scientist* 18 Feb. 442/3 As deadly as tetrodotoxin from the Japanese globe or 'puffer' fish. **1977** *Lancet* 24/31 Dec. 1331/1 The electrical and mechanical consequences of stimulation are prevented by tetrodotoxin.

tetromino (tetrǫ·mino). [f. TETR(A- + D)OMINO by deliberately false analogy: see quot. 1961.] Any of the five distinct planar shapes that can be formed by joining four identical squares by their edges.

1954 S. W. GOLOMB in *Amer. Math. Monthly* LXI. 678 The checker board cannot be covered with 15 L-tetrominoes and one square tetromino. **1961** [see *PENTOMINO]. **1979** *Sci. Amer.* Apr. 19/1 It is when we turn to the 4-cell animals (the tetrominoes) that the project really becomes interesting.

tetrose. Delete 'the class of' and add examples.

1904 [see *DIOSE]. **1916** [see *BIOSE]. **1963** [see *ERYTHROSE]. **1970** A. L. LEHNINGER *Biochemistry* xi. 218 If the carbon chains of the trioses are extended by the addition of carbon atoms, we have, successively, tetroses, pentoses, hexoses, heptoses, and octoses.

tetryl. Add: **2.** Also **Tetryl.** [ad. G. *tetril.*] A yellow crystalline nitro-amino explosive, tetranitromethylaniline, $(NO_2)_3C_6H_2N(CH_3)NO_2$, used esp. as a detonator and priming agent.

1909 O. GUTTMANN *Manuf. Explosives* iii. 47 The Rheinisch-Westfälische Gesellschaft of Troisdorf make now detonators of Tetranitromethylaniline (called Tetryl). **1977** D. MACKENZIE *Raven & Ratcatcher* v. 75 A box of detonating-caps, the type with tetryl booster-charges.

tetter, *v.* Restrict † *Obs.* to sense in Dict. and add: **2.** *intr.* To crack, to disintegrate.

1911 J. MASEFIELD *Everlasting Mercy* 30 My mind began to carp and tetter. **1967** T. KENEALLY *Bring Larks & Heroes* ii. 16 In dutiful vegetable gardens, the leaves of carrots and turnips had tettered and split, shot full of holes by antipodean summer.

tettered (te·təɹd), *a.* [f. TETTER *sb.*, *v.* + -ED²,¹.] Afflicted with tetter (usu. *fig.*).

1906 W. DE LA MARE *Poems* 84, I marvelled at..this poor creature..tettered with worms of fear. **1908** G. BOTTOMLEY *Chambers of Imagery* 2nd Ser. (1912) 19 Iron misused must turn to blight And dwindle to a tettered crust. **1975** J. I. M. STEWART *Gaudy* xvi. 281 The great façade with its massive columns was crumbling, flaked and tettered.

tetterous, *a.* (Later example.)

1977 J. I. M. STEWART *Madonna of Astrolabe* xii. 181 The lizards, darting from crevice to crevice on a crumbling wall, were in process of shedding tetterous skins to reveal a summer green.

tettigonian (tetigōᵘ·niăn). [f. mod.L. *Tettigonia* (see next) + -AN.] = next.

1842 T. W. HARRIS *Treat. Insects Injurious to Vegetation* 183 The Tettigonians, or leaf-hoppers, have the head and thorax somewhat like those of frog-hoppers.

tettigoniid (tetigōᵘ·ni,id). Also **tettigonid.** [a. mod.L. family name *Tettigoniidæ*, f. generic name *Tettigonia* (Linnæus *Systema Naturæ* (ed. 10, 1758) I. 429), f. TETTIX + *-onia*: see -ID³.] = *long-horn(ed) grasshopper* s.v. *LONGHORN 4. Also *attrib.*, of or pertaining to an insect of this kind or the family in which it is included.

1921 H. T. FERNALD *Appl. Entomol.* xvi. 86 Some of the Tettigoniids are wingless and come out only at night. **1935** *Discovery* Nov. 317/2 Certain long-horned grasshoppers or Tettigonids..are representatives of extensive groups. **1939** M. BARR *Insect Legion* ii. 12 The big Tettigonids..are capable of biting a piece of flesh out of a finger. **1946** F. E. ZEUNER *Dating Past* xii. 365 *Platycleis occidentalis jerseyana*.., a tettigoniid grasshopper, is well distinguished in size. **1957** *New Biol.* XXIII. 31 This wing mechanism is also found in the Tettigoniids. **1972** [see *long-horn(ed) grasshopper* s.v. *LONG-HORN 4].

teuchter (tiu·χtəɹ). *Sc.* Also **teuchtar.** [Origin unknown.] A Highlander (see also quots. 1962 and 1977).

1940 R. GARIOCH *17 Poems for 6d.* 13 Thir a glaikit pair o Teuchters, as an Heilant as a peat. **1962** *Scotsman* 26 Jan. 11 There is ample evidence that she referred to him as a 'teuchter', a word which I understand to mean a country bumpkin. **1977** *Times Lit. Suppl.* 9 Sept. 1084/2 For the inhabitants of Harris are mainly what most Scots call 'teuchtars'—a word which I had never heard till I had it applied to me by a teacher in a Glasgow school. What is a teuchtar? It is a Lowland Scots imitation of a Gaelic noise, a term of now genial contempt for a crofter or, more generally, for anyone from beyond the Highland line. **1979** R. LAIDLAW *Lion is Rampant* xviii. 137, I look like the archetypal teuchter, right down to the fur-bearing cheeks.

teucrium (tiū·kriŏm). [mod.L., a. Gr. τεύκριον, a name used by Dioscorides.] A herb or shrub of the genus of this name, belonging to the family Labiatæ; = GERMANDER.

1673 J. RAY *Obs. Journey Low-Countries* 257 On the sides of the Mountains..*Teucrium*. **1917** L. H. BAILEY *Stand. Cycl. Hort.* VI. 3324/2 The teucriums are little known in cultivation. **1962** R. PAGE *Educ. of Gardener* v. 151, I would plant grey-leaved shrubs to grow wild and make a thicket: rosemary, cistus, the grey-leaved teucrium so much used in the South of France. **1974** *Country Life* 25 Apr. 997/2 The terraced paths..take you across the hillside..between hedges of rosemary and lavender and teucrium, always aromatic in the sunshine.

teuf-teuf (tö̆f,töf). [a. Fr.: echoic.] An imitation of the repeated sound of gases escaping from the exhaust of a petrol engine. Hence as *v. intr.*, (of a motor) to make such a sound; (of a person) to ride in a chugging motor vehicle. Now usually anglicized as *TUFF-TUFF.

1902 *Daily Chron.* 22 Aug. 3/4 The 'teuf-teuf' of the rapid motor is everywhere on the splendid roads. **1904** H. G. WELLS *Food of Gods* I. iv. 125 People..used to see him almost daily teufteufing slowly about Hyde Park. **1905** *Westm. Gaz.* 9 Sept. 11/3 The teuf-teufing of the motor is drowned by the tinkle of marriage bells. **1907** G. B. SHAW *John Bull's Other Island* III. 77 His ear catches an approaching teuf-teuf. **1914** T. A. BAGGS *Back from Front* xxiv. 121 Suddenly, piercing the night stillness, came the harsh teuf-teuf of a motor-car.

teuthologist. (Later example.)
1982 *Sci. Amer.* Apr. 82/1 Teuthologists, the specialists who study cephalopods (the group of marine animals that includes the squid, the cuttlefish and the octopus).

teuto-. Add: **1.** (Earlier examples.)
1866 *Anthrop. Rev.* IV. 62 The Teuto-Celts, under Charlemagne, vanquished the pure Saxons of the fatherland. *Ibid.* 66 A Teuto-Celtic race extends from the northern shores of the Shetland Isles to the Gulf of Lyons.
2. Teutophobia (earlier example).
1876 H. JAMES *Let.* 1 Apr. in *Parisian Sketches* (1958) x. 102 [M. Tissot's] Teutophobia, as an exhibition of vivacity and energy, is really very fine.

Teutonic, *a.* and *sb.* Add: **A.** *adj.* **1.** (Later examples.) Esp., displaying the characteristics attributed to Germans. Cf. TEUTONICALLY *adv.*
1925 F. SCOTT FITZGERALD *Great Gatsby* i. 3 A little later I participated in that delayed Teutonic migration known as the Great War. **1955** *Times* 5 July 14/3 The arresting self-portrait of 1914 has a teutonic assurance of manner. **1976** *Broadcast* Dec. 18/2 He was Teutonic in appearance, and wearing what appeared to be an Army type of tunic, slate grey in colour. **1983** *Financial Times* 11 Oct. 34/5 Research has shown that Hertz has a rather Teutonic, super-efficient but cold image.
C. *Comb.*, as *Teutonic-Edwardian* adj.
1976 J. WHEELER-BENNETT *Friends, Enemies & Sovereigns* iii. 73 It was hideous, since neither of its previous owners seemed to have had any decorative taste at all, but comfortable in a sort of Teutonic-Edwardian way.

Teu·tonized, *ppl. a.* [f. TEUTON + -IZE + -ED[1].] Made Teutonic; Germanized.
1866 *Anthrop. Rev.* IV. 131 The Teutonized Celts of Britain. **1918** *Hist. Amer. Lit.* I. 357 The Teutonized rhapsodies of Coleridge. **1924** *Blackw. Mag.* Aug. 280/2 All Germans kept their eyes firmly fixed on a Teutonised Europe.

Tevet, var. *TEBETH. **tevish,** var. *THIVISH.

tew, *v.*[1] Add: **I. 4. c.** Also *pass.*, to be involved or mixed *up with.*
1890 KIPLING *Life's Handicap* (1981) 67 Happen there was a lass tewed up wi' it. **1904** S. R. CROCKETT *Strong Mac* xxxix. 323 Ye were somedeal tewed up wi' a lass, were ye no?

Tewa (tē̆ⁱ·wä), *sb.* and *a.* Also † **Tegua.** [a. Tewa *téwa.*] **A.** *sb.* **a.** An Indian people of the south-western U.S.; a member of this people. **b.** The Tanoan language of this people. **B.** *adj.* Of or pertaining to the Tewa or their language.
1865 *Rep. U.S. Bureau Indian Affairs 1864* 191 The only reliable, genuine name ascertained is that of the dialect spoken by San Juan, Santa Clara, and others included in that class, which is the *Tegua*, pronounced Té-wa. **1896** *Amer. Anthropologist* IX. 345 The Pueblo tribes..embody four linguistic stocks... The Tanoan stock is..composed of five dialectical divisions—Tano, Tewa, Jemez, and Piro. **1910** F. W. HODGE *Handbk. Amer. Indians* II. 737/2 *Tewa* ('moccasins', their Keresan name). A group of Pueblo tribes belonging to the Tanoan linguistic family. *Ibid.*, In 1598 Juan de Oñate named 11 of the Tewa pueblos. **1910** *Amer. Anthropologist* XII. 503 Tewa is rich in sentence-words. **1912** *Ibid.* XIV. 472 The Tewa-speaking Indians occupy..five villages northwest of Santa Fé. **1914** W. H. RIVERS *Kinship & Social Organization* 53 The Tewa of Hano, a Pueblo tribe, call the father's sister's son *tada.* **1937** R. H. LOWIE *Hist. Ethnological Theory* ix. 135 In the same category..belongs the Tewa Indian's diary kept at Dr. Elsie Clews Parsons' suggestion. **1959** E. TUNIS *Indians* 115/1 The Hopi still occupy three high mesas in Arizona where they have six towns, plus a seventh occupied by a band of Tewa who have lived with the Hopi for two hundred years. **1980** *Smithsonian* Oct. 87 Tesuque, a smallish pueblo of some 200 souls, was considered one of the most restive of the six Tewa pueblos north and northwest of Santa Fe.

TEWT (tiūt). *Army slang.* Also **Tewt**, etc. An acronym formed on the initial letters of *t*actical *e*xercise *w*ithout *t*roops, an exercise used in the training of junior officers.
1942 PARTRIDGE *Dict. Abbrev.* 95/2 *T.E.W.T.*, slangily, a *tewt* or *tute.* A tactical exercise without troops. **1948** PARTRIDGE *Dict. Forces' Slang* 191 *Tewt*,..on which junior officers learnt how to be generals. Invaluable according to some authorities (those who set the Tewts), a complete waste of time according to others (those who carried them out). **1952** E. WAUGH *Men at Arms* II. iii. 194 Leonard improvised 'No more TEWTS and no more drill, No night ops to cause a chill.' **1956** J. MASTERS *Bugles & Tiger* viii. 117 Above all, individual training was the time for TEWTs. **1980** *Globe & Laurel* July/Aug. 206/1 Two TEWTs were laid on for the officers and NCOs.

Tex (teks), *sb.*[1] *U.S. colloq.* [Abbrev. of TEXAN *a.* and *sb.*] (A nickname for) a Texan.
1909 *Cent. Dict.* Suppl., *Tex*, an abbreviation (a) of Texas; (b) of Texan. **1943** R. VANCE *They made me Leatherneck* vii. 29 Call the aborigines 'Tex' and they seem to think that at least you acknowledge Texas to be in the Union and its name well circulated. **1979** P. THEROUX *Old Patagonian Express* x. 140, I could tell you were interested in poetry, Tex. *Ibid.*, That Tex is a real fun guy.

tex (teks), *sb.*[2] [Abbrev. of TEXTILE *a.* and *sb.*] A unit of weight used to estimate the fineness of fibres and yarns.
1953 *Textile Research Jrnl.* XXIII. 947/1 The Textile Institute recommends the tex and the British Rayon and Synthetic Fibers Federation prefers the grex. **1956** *Rev. Textile Progress* VIII. 258 A universal system for yarn count in all fibres has been adopted... The system, based on units of grammes per kilometre, is applicable to all types of yarn and is known as the Tex System. **1963** A. J. HALL *Textile Sci.* iii. 135 This is known as the Tex system and by this the count of a yarn or any other length of fibres in bundle form..is the number of grams which 1,000 metres of the yarn weigh. **1973** *Materials & Technol.* VI. 263 Silk is a relatively strong fibre, having a tenacity which lies between 3·5 and 4·5 g/denier (31·5 and 40·5 g/tex).

Texan, *a.* and *sb.* Add: **A.** *adj.* (Earlier example.)
1832 W. B. DEWEES *Lett. from Early Settler Texas* (1852) 142 On arriving at that place the Texan troops put to flight seven hundred Mexicans.
B. *sb.* A person or animal native to or inhabiting Texas.
1837 H. MARTINEAU *Society in America* II. II. i. 81 If the government wished all possible success to the Texans, it could hardly do better than be quiet. **1868** *Trans. Illinois Agric. Soc.* (1870) VII. 138 We also put five cows and a buffalo with some Texans about the 20th of June. **1940** W. FAULKNER *Hamlet* IV. i. 246 The Texan..managed to saw the mules about and so lock the wheels. **1974** 'R. B. DOMINIC' *Epitaph for Lobbyist* ii. 14 He combined formidable intelligence with a Texan's charm.

Texas. 1. Also **texas.** Delete 'pilot-house and' from def. (Earlier simple and attrib. examples.)
1853 *Pen & Pencil* I. 789/2 The roof of the cabin which offered a splendid promenade, and the spectacle of a second edifice of state-rooms, surrounded by a broad promenade and curiously denominated 'Texas'. **1857** F. L. OLMSTED *Journey Texas* 27 To this Texas, inveterate card-players retire on Sundays. **1875** 'MARK TWAIN' in *Atlantic Monthly* Feb. 220/2 A tidy, white-aproned, black 'texas-tender', to bring up tarts and ices and coffee.
2. Texas fever, substitute for def.: a North American form of bovine piroplasmosis (redwater) first identified in Texas, indicated by a high fever, reddish urine, and an enlarged spleen, and caused by a protozoan parasite, *Babesia bigemina*, which is transmitted by the cattle tick; (earlier example); **Texas leaguer** *Baseball* (now *rare*), a fly ball that falls to the ground between the infield and the outfield and results in a base hit; **Texas longhorn,** a bull or cow belonging to a breed once common in Texas, distinguished by long horns and able to thrive in dry regions; also *transf.* (see quot. 1908); **Texas Ranger** [RANGER *sb.*[1] 3 a in Dict. and Suppl.], a member of the state constabulary of Texas (formerly, of certain locally mustered regiments in the federal service during the Mexican War); **Texas Tower** [so called from its resemblance to a Texas oil rig], one of a chain of radar towers built along the eastern coast of the U.S.
1866 *2nd Ann. Rep. Missouri State Board of Agric.* (1867) 16 Another pest..is the Texas fever',..or 'Texas murrain', as it is variously known. **1905** *Sporting Life* (Philad.) 7 Oct. 9/4 A bit of bad coaching euchered him out of one bingle the other afternoon, when a Texas Leaguer from his bat had to be chalked down a force out instead of a hit. **1935** J. T. FARRELL *Judgement Day* viii. 185 A dumpy texas-leaguer over third base placed runners on first and second. **1977** *Verbatim* May 5/2 We are no longer besieged with such terms as 'hot corner', 'keystone', 'Texas Leaguer', 'flyhawk', 'maskman', and 'grasscutter'. **1908** *Pacific Monthly* July 19/1 Pink got here about the same time but he come of old Texas-longhorn stock. *a* **1918** G. STUART *Forty Years on Frontier* (1925) II. 178 None of our cattle were Texas longhorns. **1946** *Nat. Geogr. Mag.* Jan. 17/1 Cattle then were the rangy Texas longhorns—more head, horns, and tail than thick, juicy steaks. **1972** K. BONFIGLIOLI *Don't point that Thing at Me* xiii. 101 The bleached skeleton of a Texas Longhorn..beside a faint track. **1846** *Whig Almanac 1847* 19/1 Capt. Samuel Walker, at the head of a small company of Texas Rangers, left Point Isabel. **1911** *Everybody's Mag.* Sept. 354/1 Two Texas rangers faced Antonio Carrasco and his seventeen thieves sometime in December of 1910. **1943** B. HOUSE *I give you Texas* 31 A city was threatened by mob violence, so a telegram was sent to the governor to rush a force of Texas Rangers to the scene. **1980** E. BEHR *Getting Even* x. 114 The Chairman was wearing a Texas Ranger hat the American President had given him. **1954** *Tuscaloosa* (Albama) *News* 13 Aug. 3 (*caption*) Here is a closeup of a section of one of the 'Texas Towers'..being built offshore along the Atlantic coast. Towers, named for oil rigs in the Gulf of Mexico, will be built along the continental shelf. **1971** S. E. MORISON *European Discovery Amer.: Northern Voy.* xix. 653 The Gulf Stream flows within twelve miles of Cape Hatteras, and the counter-currents, strong winds, and shifting sands are a menace to navigation even today. A Texas Tower was established off Diamond Shoals, the most dangerous, in 1966.
3. Used in various depreciatory collocations.
1905, etc. [see *Texas Leaguer*, sense 2 above]. **1942** BERREY & VAN DEN BARK *Amer. Thes. Slang* § 926/1 Texas butter, a gravy made with flour and water in meat grease. **1944** R. F. ADAMS *Western Words* 164/2 *Texas cakewalk*, a hanging. *Ibid.*, *Texas gate*, a makeshift gate made of barbed wire fastened to a pole. **1962** *Amer. Speech* XXXVII. 266 *Arizona stop*; *Texas stop*, *n.* Slowing down, but not making a full stop at a stop sign. **1968–70** *Current Slang* (Univ. S. Dakota) III–IV. 125 *Texas strawberries*, *n.* Red beans.—New Mexico State. **1969** *Britannica Bk. of Year* (U.S.) 801/1 *Texas toast*, a thick slice of bread warmed and covered with butter. **1975** D. BAGLEY *Snow Tiger* xi. 97 A Texas nightingale isn't a bird... It's a donkey. This is a similar New Zealand joke. **1976** BOOT & THOMAS *Jamaica* 76/2 It certainly had more flair than old LBJ taking a table of journalists and staffers into the men's room, there to reduce them to awe and wonderment at the size of his whopping great Texas trouser snake. **1979** G. SWARTHOUT *Skeletons* 172 They call it a 'Texas horserace'. Blaise and his deputies sneaked the Mexicans..to the edge of town and told them to hot-foot it for the line. They'd give them an hour's head start. Then they'd come after them, mounted... If Blaise and his boys caught up with them on this side, it was their bad luck... The Mexs didn't make it.

Texel (te·ksəl). The name of an island in the West Frisian group off the northern coast of the Netherlands, used *absol.* or *attrib.* to designate a hardy, hornless sheep belonging to a breed originally developed there; also, the breed itself.
1949 A. FRASER *Sheep Husbandry* ii. 118 Milch breeds—East Friesian Milch sheep and their strains, the Texel and the West Friesian. **1957** *Encycl. Brit.* XX. 475/2 The Texel is a medium-wool, white-face, hornless sheep of the Netherlands, well adapted to range conditions and very prolific. **1978** *Times* 2 Sept. 2/4 (*caption*) Record prices were paid..at the first sale in Britain of the British Texel Sheep Society.

Texian (te·ksiăn), *a.* and *sb.* Now *rare.* [f. TEX(AS + -IAN.] = TEXAN *a.* and *sb.* (See also quot. 1943.)
1835 *Franklin Repository* (Chambersburg, Pennsylvania) 8 Dec. 1/6 Volunteers are moving from almost every section of the west to the assistance of the Texians. **1836** D. B. EDWARD *Hist. Texas* 45 The Texian farmer of the Gulf coast. *Ibid.* 74 [It] adds to the variety of a Texian landscape. **1943** *Sat. Even. Post* 11 Sept. 61 Texians are the old rock; Texans, a term which came into use only after the Civil War, are those out of the old rock; the people who live in Texas are those who are wearing the old rock away. **1955** W. FOSTER-HARRIS *Look of Old West* v. 125 The value of the Texian dollar was then descending rapidly and reached an ultimate low of around 2 cents. **1973** R. SYMONS *Where Wagon Led* I. vii. 114 All cow people like the Hesters and other Texas folk (or as they said, 'Texians').

Texican (te·ksikăn). [Blend of TEXAN *a.* and *sb.* and MEXICAN *a.* and *sb.*] = *TEXAN *sb.* (sometimes used more narrowly).
1863 *Lawrence* (Kansas) *Republican* 16 Apr. 2/4 (*heading*) 'Texicans' and 'Injuns' again. **1937** D. COOLIDGE *Texas Cowboys* x. 149 That's one thing you'll never find around a Mormon town..you'll never find no Texicans. **1969** in *Current Trends in Linguistics* (1972) X. 596 *Texican*, a Texan of Mexican background. (Wis.). **1978** *Maledicta* II. 172 While Texas remained a part of Mexico, Anglo settlers there called themselves *Texicans* to distinguish themselves from Spanish-speaking Mexicans.

Tex-Mex (te·ks,meks), *a.* and *sb.* [f. TEX(AN *a.* and *sb.* + MEX(ICAN *a.* and *sb.*: cf. *TEX *sb.*[1] and *MEX *a.* and *sb.*] **A.** *adj.* Designating the Texan variety of something Mexican; also *occas.*, of or pertaining to both Texas and Mexico.
1949 *Time* 14 Feb. 38/1 Fluent in Texmex Spanish, he had been one of the most promising rodeo riders around Tucson, Ariz... The half English, half Spanish patois of the U.S.–Mexican border region. **1973** *News* (Mexico City) (*Vistas Suppl.*) 22 July 7 It is a mistake to come to Mexico and not try the local cuisine. It is not the Tex-Mex cooking that one is used to getting in the United States. **1976** M. MACHLIN *Pipeline* xx. 246 The voice of Miss Martinez, one of Wilbur's gestures toward Tex-Mex integration, came softly over the intercom. **1977** *Time Out* 28 Jan.–3 Feb. 8/2 Cooder's current concern is the music of Southern Texas, the 'Tex-Mex' style.
B. *sb.* The Texan variety of Mexican Spanish.
1955 W. FOSTER-HARRIS *Look of Old West* vii. 211 Northern cowboys had their chance to mess up Spanish even more than had the Texas cowhands, with their Tex-Mex, which, incidentally, is a language in itself. **1969** J. MANDER *Static Society* i. 32 A hybrid, like the 'Tex-Mex' spoken in the south-west of the United States. **1981** *Verbatim* Spring 24/1 The only foreign language she knows is Tex-Mex.

text, *sb.*[1] Add: **7.** *text-editing* vbl. sb., *-figure, -frequency, -processing* ppl. adj. and vbl. sb., *processor, -source, tape*; **text editor**, a machine that permits the user to alter text using a keyboard; also, a program or component for modifying text held in a computer or processor, in accordance with a user's instructions; **text linguistics** [G. *textlinguistik*] (see quot. 1977); hence **text linguist**; **text paper**, a newspaper containing serious articles.
1972 H. S. STONE *Introd. Computer Organization & Structures* ix. 208 Another important application of the linked list is text editing. **1975** *Business Week* 30 June 80 Vydec Corp...soon will add communications to its display text editor. Xerox Corp. will announce the same capability for its automatic typewriter. **1983** I. FLORES *Word Processing Handbk.* vi. 170 If the last word entered

does not fit on this line, then the text editor removes that word from the line and puts it at the left of the next line. **1983** *Your Computer* Sept. 21/1 The M100 runs a full Microsoft BASIC interpreter, appointment scheduler, address filer, text editor and communications utility. **1938** *British Birds* XXXI. 359 The book is illustrated.. by good, if rather infrequent text figures and a coloured plate. **1963** T. G. E. Powell in Foster & Alcock *Culture & Environment* vi. 169 My thanks are also due to Miss Frances Lynch for preparing the text-figure drawings. **1942** M. Joos in *Language* XVIII. 33 The Dewey count gives us a statistical picture of *text* frequencies; the Twaddell count of *list* frequencies. **1962** P. S. Ray in F. A. Rice *Study of Role of Second Languages in Asia, Africa & Latin Amer.* (Center for Applied Linguistics) 92 'Text frequency' compares two lexical forms in their repetitions within a body of discourse. **1973** W. O. Hendricks *Essays on Semiolinguistics & Verbal Art* ii. 53 See Fries..for a discussion of the theme-rheme distinction in text linguistics. **1977** *Language* LIII. 247 The rapidly growing school of 'text-linguistics'... The general belief shared by these scholars is that the 'natural domain' of linguistic theory consists of discourses, or texts, rather than sentences. However,..this belief is not what distinguishes text-linguistics from other discourse-oriented.. trends in linguistics. *Ibid.* 248 Text-linguistics differs from these approaches in its interpretation of the claim that texts are the natural domain of linguistics. For generative text-linguists, this means that the grammar must actually generate (all and only) possible well-formed texts of the language. **1961** *Guardian* 30 Jan. 18/2 All possible steps will be taken to make the future of the 'Daily Herald' as a text paper more secure. **1977** *Times* 5 Sept. 12/6 Tabloid papers sell better than serious text papers. **1968** *Jrnl. Assoc. Computing Machinery* XV. 8 (*heading*) Computer evaluation of indexing and text processing. **1980** *Lebende Sprachen* XXV. 10/2 Other texts..can probably be dealt with more efficiently by an extended text-processing system, than by machine translation as such. **1983** G. Leech et al. in *Trans. Philol. Soc.* 28 We may..proceed now to consider the kinds of text-processing that can be performed, using a computer corpus as a database. **1970** *Technical Disclosure Bull.* XIII. iv. 9 A flow chart for a text collection program which operates to collect lines of text for a text processor is described. **1980** *Daily Tel.* 23 Apr. 3 (Advt.), If you have bought or are about to buy a small computer or text processor, you need Cave Tab to ensure you make the most of it. **1947** A. Einstein *Music in Romantic Era* xvi. 265 Shakespeare..was no more novel as a text-source for Italian opera than was Sir Walter Scott..or Victor Hugo. **1978** *Early Music* Oct. 609/1 What is described as a 'text source', the 1545 *King's Primer*, is also used. **1970** A. Cameron et al. *Computers & O.E. Concordances* 18 The first thing of course is the production of text tapes and the printing thereof.

text-book. Add: **5.** *attrib.* passing into *adj.* Derived from, dependent upon, or typical of a text-book (sense 2); orig. and still occas. in a derogatory sense, implying mechanical adherence to a stereotype; now freq. used in an approbatory sense of an exemplary or classic instance of something. Cf. Copy-book 2 b in Dict. and Suppl.

1916 [see *Middle Western* adj. s.v. *middle *a.* 6]. **1927** M. Sadleir *Trollope* iv. 183 The presentation of Gresh-amsbury House..is perfunctory... Trollope..was content to parrot text-book phrases of appreciation. **1939** G. Household *Rogue Male* 230 To deny..I was uncomfortable, but to produce hypothetical justification for getting more comfort. It was a text-book illustration good enough to take in the foreigner. **1949** 'G. Orwell' *Nineteen Eighty-Four* iii. 260 It was a perfect conversion, a textbook case. **1954** W. Faulkner *Fable* 33 An authority..among textbook soldiers on how to keep troops fit. **1957** [see *real *a.*² 2 a]. **1963** *Times* 4 May 3/6 Smith tertius (Edwin, of Derbyshire) hit a swinging six into the Mound stand and followed this with two text-book fours. **1970** *Times* 13 Feb. 25/7 The..strike..was a textbook example of response to loss of 'our management'. **1979** N. Hynd *False Flags* xix. 173 He followed an evasive path, a textbook lesson in how to move without leaving a trace.

Hence **te·xt-bookish** *a.*

1914 H. G. Wells *Englishman looks at World* 84 An educational system..has to be grown; and in the beginning it is bound to be thin, ragged, forced, crammy, text-bookish, superficial. **1951** *Sport* 27 Apr.–3 May 3/1 Newcastle can be the more brilliant, the more dazzling, the more text-bookish on their day. **1974** *Publishers Weekly* 4 Feb. 68/2 A textbookish survey of Arab history, religion and culture since the days of Mohammed.

textile, *a.* and *sb.* Add: **A.** *adj.* **1.** Also, of or pertaining to a man-made fibre or filament, not necessarily woven.

1910 Mitchell & Prideaux *Fibres used in Textile & Allied Industries* i. 8 Textile papers. (a) Spinning fibres in raw state... (b) Cotton or flax fibre previously spun. **1931** K. P. Hess *Textile Fibers & their Use* v. 232 The fourth method of dissolving cellulose and forming it into fine filaments was worked out... Textile fibres were not developed to any great extent by this method until the close of the World War. **1961** *Wall St. Jrnl.* 23 Jan. 2/3 DuPont Co. announced it will close its textile rayon operation..by August. **1972** *Daily Tel.* 20 Nov. 11/4 One single step is..required to convert the chemical raw material of the synthetic fibres into a finished textile cloth, no weaving or knitting being required. **1981** M. L. Joseph *Essentials of Textiles* ii. 9 Textile fibres..can be manufactured from natural fibrous materials such as wood pulp (rayon) or synthesized from chemicals with no resemblance to fibrous forms (nylon, polyester).

3. *Naturism.* Non-naturist; *spec.* applied to places, etc., prohibited to nudists. Cf. sense *3 of the sb.

1970 *Newsweek* 25 May 55/2 Its guests follow a daily routine little different from that of the 'textile tourists'—or non-nudists—in nearby hotels. **1979** P. Vallack *Free Sun* xi. 125 The peninsula that separates textile camping from Funtona Bay designated for nudism.

B. *sb.* **1.** Also, a synthetic material suitable for weaving; any of various materials, as a bonded fabric, which do not require weaving.

1908 A. E. Garrett *Fibres for Fabrics* iv. 100 Since the Chardonnet silk [*sc.* artificial silk] is so much more deteriorated by pure water..it matters little, so far as its extended use in textiles is concerned. **1927** M. H. Avram *Rayon Industry* i. 1 'Rayon'—the first synthetic textile... We shall briefly trace the steps from its conception; through..its struggle to gain a place as a commercially possible textile fibre. **1961** *Wall St. Jrnl.* 1 Dec. 14/2 Mead,..in cooperation with M. Lowenstein & Sons, Inc... is working on paper 'textiles'. **1962** Z. Travníček tr. *Krčma's Nonwoven Textiles* i. 11 Nonwoven textiles and, particularly, adhesively bonded textiles can be manufactured by many processes. **1970** *Cabinet Maker & Retail Furnisher* 23 Oct. 173/2 The original term 'non-woven textiles' used for adhesively-bonded fabrics has grown more and more obscure as novel manufacturing technologies based on mechanical bonding processes have been introduced. *Ibid.*, As a first simplification we can say that 'non-woven' textiles do not comprise traditional textile structures made by processes other than weaving (ie knitting, braiding, lace manufacture, etc). The present meaning of 'non-woven textiles' refers to pliable and porous products from textile materials that are reinforced by mechanical or chemical means.

b. (Later examples.) Also, of non-woven fabric.

1971 *N.Y. Law Jrnl.* 23 Nov. 1/8 Suskin was a principal in Derby Fabrics, Inc..., a textile converting and jobbing concern. *Ibid.*, Suskin entered a business relationship with Jerry Kassel, Inc..., also a textile converter. **1974** *Times* 12 Feb. 11 Louis van Praag has a theory that textiles should not be designed by textile designers. **1976** *Jrnl. R. Soc. Arts* CXXV. 21/1 Most textile conservation begins with cleaning to remove the harmful effects of atmospheric pollution, dust, dirt and undesirable or damaging stains or soiling. *Ibid.* 24/2 The Textile Conservation Centre came into being primarily to provide the foundation for new textile conservators to base their studies.

3. *Naturism.* A non-naturist; *spec.* one who wears a swimming costume on the beach.

1979 *Listener* 4 Jan. 20/1 The world's first naturist community..is up for sale and will probably become a holiday resort for 'textiles'—the word naturists use for people who keep their clothes on when they could take them off. **1979** P. Vallack *Free Sun* vii. 85 What would the sign have to do? Alert non-naturists (textiles) that they will see nude bathers if they continue in that direction. **1983** *Times* 6 July 32/2 The topless generally inhabit the more remote ends of the beach well away from the 'textiles'.

textless (te·kstlės), *a.* [-less.] Having no text.

1926 *United Free Church Missionary Record* May 225/1 What a windy textless sermon we got. **1957** J. Hollander in N. Frye *Sound & Poetry* i. 65 Plato had disapproved of textless music. **1980** *Christian Sci. Monitor* 12 May B12/4 Another textless wonder, 'Truck' [*sc.* a book] is a bold and bouncy salute to the open road.

textuality. Add: **2.** (See quot. 1970.)

1970 *Babel* XVI. 76/1 By textuality, we mean the result of the transformation of the common language of a given type of civilization into the language of a work of literature belonging to that type of civilization. **1976** G. C. Spivak in J. Derrida *Of Grammatology* p. lxv, Exploiting a false etymological kinship between semantics and semen, Derrida offers this version of textuality: A sowing that does not produce plants, but is simply infinitely repeated. **1979** *N. & Q.* June 285/2 *Glyph* is a 'new serial publication' concerned with 'the problems of representation and textuality'.

textura (tekstiū·ra). *Typogr.* [a. G. *textura* (also *textur*), f. L. *textūra*: see Texture *sb.*] One of a group of typefaces first used in the earliest printed books, distinguished by narrow, angular letters and a strong vertical emphasis; also, the manuscript hand on which these typefaces were based. Also *attrib.*

[**1922** D. B. Updike *Printing Types* II. 323/1 (Index), Textur type.] **1929** A. F. Johnson in *Library* IX. 359 The term which the Germans usually employ is Textur, or Textura, meaning 'woven', from the resemblance of a page in this letter to a woven pattern. **1955** *Archit. Rev.* CXVIII. 399/3 It [*sc.* the Gothic letter] is a magnificent letter, both formal textura and Gothic cursive. **1962** [see *lettre b]. **1969** M. B. Parkes *Eng. Cursive Book Hands 1250–1500* p. xvii, In the fourteenth century Textura became increasingly more artificial and more difficult to write. **1970** *Times Lit. Suppl.* 7 Aug. 884/5 The textura types survived in England into the eighteenth century. **1976** [see *rotunda 2*]. **1977** *Studies in Eng. Lit.: Eng. Number* (Tokyo) 7 Ad is written in a very neat *textura* hand, which differs from that which copied the rest of the MS.

textural, *a.* Add: **c.** *Mus.* and *Literary Criticism.* See *texture *sb.* 5.

1962 *Listener* 1 Nov. 735/3 Outward clarity of form, of rhythmic definition, and of textural contrasts, are the most striking features. **1963** *Ibid.* 3 Jan. 23/1 Joyce's *Portrait of the Artist* is characterized by organic form, both textural and structural. **1983** *Ibid.* 10 Feb. 35/4 There are no more than one and a half piano quartets whose great music does not produce textural insuperabilities for the players.

texturally *adv.* (later examples in sense *c of the adj.).

1962 *Listener* 22 Nov. 885/1 The structurally and texturally elaborate *String Quartet*. **1976** *Gramophone* Mar. 1442/3 *Missa Salisburgensis*..is texturally complex, with its seven 'choirs' of voices and instruments spread over 54 staves.

texture, *sb.* Add: **5.** Also, in Literary Criticism: the constitution or quality of a piece of writing; esp. such perceptible qualities as the imagery, alliteration, assonance, rhythm, etc. (freq. opp. *structure*). In Music: the quality of sound formed by the combination of the different (orchestral, vocal, etc.) parts.

1812 J. Mackintosh in *Mem. Life Sir J. Mackintosh* (1835) II. iii. 215 This is increased when a few bolder and higher words are happily wrought into the texture of this familiar eloquence. **1895** W. D. Howells *My Literary Passions* xxxi. 223 All that Mr. De Forest has written is of a texture and color distinctly his own. **1931** *Week-End Rev.* 3 Jan. 24/2 The texture of the book is much more satisfactory than its theme. **1934** M. Bodkin *Archetypal Patterns in Poetry* 320 This duality in unity, and harmonized clash, of cosmic and personal that Blake has woven into the texture of his verses. **1941** J. C. Ransom *New Criticism* iv. 280 The texture, likewise, seems to be of any real content that may be come upon, provided it is so free, unrestricted, and large that it cannot properly get into the structure. One guesses that it is an *order* of content, rather than a *kind* of content, that distinguishes texture from structure, and poetry from prose. **1956** M. Krieger *New Apologists for Poetry* v. 83 The indeterminacies of meaning, into which the poet is forced by his devotion to the determinate sound, constitute the poem's texture [according to J. C. Ransom]. **1956–7** *Modern Fiction Studies* Winter 209 The birth of Lena's child means more in the texture of the story than a simple event.

1934 C. Lambert *Music Ho!* iii. 165 The first symphony [of Borodin]..achieves an admirable symphonic texture. **1959** *Listener* 10 Dec. 1034/1 For a long time now it has been fashionable to cry after new 'textures' in sound. **1963** *Ibid.* 21 Feb. 354/1 In his last decade as an opera composer Handel..made less use of wind instruments and tended to favour sparser textures. **1980** *Dædalus* Spring 194 The thinning of texture, and the descending succession of pitches in measures 100 to 103 of Berlioz's melody all seem to foster and presage closure.

6. (Earlier example.)

1845 [see *pearly *a.* 4].

7. texture brick, a roughened or rough-hewn brick.

1940 *Chambers's Techn. Dict.* 843/1 *Texture brick*, a rustic brick. **1961** [see *septic *sb.* 2].

textured, *a.* Add: Now freq. without specific adj.: Provided with a texture, esp. as opposed to smooth or plain.

1923 *Times Lit. Suppl.* 28 Jan. 64/1 The method of colour woodcut, with its bold lines and textured tones, suits very well an artist whose painting is apt to be a little thin. **1938** *Burlington Mag.* Apr. 200/2 Plain or 'textured' weaves. **1943** J. S. Huxley *TVA* 100 The textured concrete wall finish. **1959** *Times* 12 Jan. 11/5 Textured: a term frequently met with indicating a process has been used that fluffs up surface or fabric giving greater density, softness of handle and appearance, extra warmth and some degree of absorbency. **1962** *Listener* 29 Mar. 566/3 They [*sc.* the collages and picture reliefs] appear to have both an ambivalent scale, a tiny world of textured pleasure inside the larger images they set out to establish, and a somewhat suave finish. **1969** *Amateur Photographer* 21 May 56/1 These units..have black cases of plastic with simulated textured panelling. **1977** *Time* 7 Feb. 54/1 Her far-flung locations are not textured settings but flimsy sets where the author vainly attempts to stage her quiet drama of rootlessness and disaffection.

b. *textured yarn*, a yarn which has been modified so as to give a special texture to the fabric.

1960 *Which?* Jan. 17/2 In recent years..methods of treating continuous filament synthetic yarns have been introduced that modify their properties remarkably. These modified yarns are described as 'textured'. **1964** *Ibid.* Sept. 285/1 Textured yarns are mainly of two kinds—bulked yarns and stretch yarns. **1975** C. Calasibetta *Fairchild's Dict. Fashion* 543/2 *Textured y[arn].* 1. Man-made continuous-filament yarns permanently heat-set in crimped manner or otherwise modified to give more elasticity, used to make stretch fabrics. 2. Man-made filament yarns processed to change their appearance; e.g., abraded.

c. Designating protein foods derived from vegetables but given a texture that resembles meat, esp. in *textured vegetable protein* (cf. TVP s.v. *T 6 a).

1968 *Manch. Guardian Weekly* 11 July 12/3 The second exciting stage was launched this May by a Minneapolis manufacturer... TVP (textured vegetable protein) 'could hardly look or taste better..', the makers claim. **1970** *New Scientist* 24 Dec. 561/2 There is already a big sale for..textured meat analogies. **1977** *Times* 23 Feb. 4/8 Mincemeat will sometimes be mixed with textured vegetable protein in 800 schools in Kent. **1983** *Listener* 21 July 23/3 Let us..settle down to textured soya sandwiches for tea.

texturing. Add: Also in other contexts (esp. corresponding to the senses of *textured *a.*).

1958 *Listener* 18 Dec. 1055/3 Some texturing material such as sawdust, ordinary sand, or silver sand. **1960**

Times 4 Jan. 14/1 The two Moores..both avoid the mannered type of texturing of so many of his drawings. **1960** *Wall St. Jrnl.* (Eastern ed.) 13 Jan. 1/4 This 'texturing' alters the surface of the long, continuous strands of nylon, giving them new properties such as elasticity and bulk without adding weight. **1961** G. Millerson *Technique Television Production* viii. 151 (*caption*) The arrangement, distribution and texturing of scenery. **1978** *Gramophone* June 85/2 It is clear that Lill's stylish performance, with its crystalline texturing and finely pulsing inner voices, is one very much to be reckoned with.

texturize (te·kstiŭrəiz), *v.* [f. Textur(e *sb.* + -ize.] *trans.* To impart a particular texture to (fabrics or food). Also *fig.* Chiefly in *ppl. a.* So **te·xturizing** *vbl. sb.*

1958 *Times* 26 June 15/3 We have..entered the texturized yarn field with 'Ban-Lon'. **1959** *Wall St. Jrnl.* 20 Nov. 17/2 Allied Chemical Corp's 'Caprolan' filament nylon is offered to the carpet industry, too. But to achieve the bulkiness of spun yarns, carpet mills have to have 'Caprolan' filament yarn 'texturized', or bulked. **1969** *Daily Tel.* 24 July 3/2 This involves the design and manufacture of machinery for yarn texturising and the production of texturised yarns, hosiery and knitwear. **1976** *Jrnl. R. Soc. Arts* CXXIV. 579/1 A great deal of work has been done on converting soyabeans and other high-energy substrates (even oil feedstock) into proteinaceous material that can be spun, like nylon, and given a texture like that of lean meat. This 'Texturized Vegetable Protein' (TVP) has been successfully promoted and seems likely to have a growing impact on the food market. **1976** *Times Lit. Suppl.* 13 Feb. 166/1 This selfconsciousness distinguishes the whole show from the chunks of fictionalized, texturized social history (which are to drama as TVP to steak) the BBC now seems so casually expert with.

te:xturo·logy. [ad. F. *texturologie*: see -ology.] A term coined by Jean-Philippe-Arthur Dubuffet (b. 1901) for a kind of painting created by him, composed of minute drops of paint entirely covering a flat surface.

1959 J. A. Thwaites in *Arts Yearbk.* III. 134/2 In the *Texturologies*..he [*sc.* Jean Dubuffet] has pulverized the form and color as never before. **1964** *New Statesman* 1 May 695/2 Dubuffet's finely granulated texturologies. **1973** *Art Internat.* Mar. 30/2, I don't want to comment here on the nature of Dubuffet's 'texturologies'.

-th, *suffix*². Add: **2.** Used in works of fiction with preceding dash or hyphen to denote an unspecified ordinal number presented as the name of an unspecified or fictitious regiment.

1847 Thackeray *Van. Fair* (1848) xxxvi. 324 Colonel O'Dowd, of the —th regiment. **1867** 'Ouida' *Under Two Flags* I. v. 101 The —th came back to Brighton and to barracks. **1931** S. Jameson *Richer Dust* x. 297 Someone asked him if it were true that the —th had run like hell in front of Festubert. **1949** G. Heyer *Arabella* ii. 33 Algernon..held a commission in the -th Regiment.

thaccy (ðæ·ki), a dial. form of *that.*

Examples of related variants, *thac(k, thact, thackey,* etc., from 1814 onward, are listed in *Eng. Dial. Dict.* (Devon, Cornwall, Glos., Wilts.) s.v. *Thac(k.* See note at Thilk *dem. adj.* and *pron.*

1929 H. Williamson *Beautiful Years* (rev. ed.) i. 21 He produced it [*sc.* a knife] from his pocket, and opened an enormous blade. 'Not bad, eh?' 'A gude 'un, thaccy!' **1940** J. Cary *Charley is my Darling* lxi. 332 Tis only booys badness in you and you'll grow out of thaccy.

Thackerayan, *a.* and *sb.* Add: Also with pronunc. (þækərē¹·ăn). **a.** *adj.* (Earlier and later examples.) **b.** *sb.* (Examples.)

1857 J. Blackwood *Let.* 8 June in *Geo. Eliot Lett.* (1954) II. 344 The harsher Thackerayan view of human nature. **1909** G. K. Chesterton *Thackeray* p. xxiii, Any Thackerayan must recognize my meaning. **1917** J. B. Cabell *Cream of Jest* vi. iv. 264, I am thus digressing, in obsolete Thackerayan fashion, to twaddle about love matches alone. **1958** G. N. Ray *Thackeray* II. vi. 175 Devoted Thackerayans persist in putting it at the top of their favourite's work. **1978** *Encounter* Feb. 71/1 They have trouble with the inevitable Thackerayan mother-in-law.

Also **Thackeraya·na** [Ana *suff.*], items associated with Thackeray.

1905 *Spectator* 18 Feb. 256/2 The voracious collector of Thackerayana cannot have too much of a good thing. **1979** *Times* 27 Dec. 8/1 The cupboard was packed with Thackerayana, early and special editions of his works, bound volumes of the journals he wrote for and a pile of his pictures.

Thai (tai), *sb.* and *a.* Also 9 **T'hai, Thay, T'hay.** [Native name, meaning 'free': the same word as *Tai *sb.*² and *a.*] (Occasionally used where *Tai *sb.*² and *a.* might be expected.) **A.** *sb.* **a.** The language of the Thai people, a member of the Tai group of languages; Siamese.

1808 *Asiatick Res.* X. 173 The more ancient eastern languages, are Jawa, Búgís, T'hay, and Barma. **1880** A. H. Sayce *Introd. Sci. Lang.* II. viii. 224 In Siamese or T'hai every word which defines another must follow it. **1963** *Time & Tide* 2 May 23/2 HRH Prince Chula-Chakrabongse of Thailand..has written more than 30 books in Thai and English. **1972** E. A. Nida *Bk. Thousand Tongues* (ed. 2) 427/1 Thai and related languages are linguistically grouped in a class known as the Tai languages, a class that comprises tongues spoken by at least 40 million people, from Burma to south-eastern China. **1977** *Times* 15 June 16/6 McGonagall..had just had his prolific collection of bizarre poems translated into Russian, Chinese, Japanese and..Thai.

b. A native or inhabitant of Thailand (called Siam before 1939 and again briefly between 1945 and 1948); a member of the racial group that constitutes the bulk of the population of Thailand. Also, the Thais collectively.

1841 *Penny Cycl.* XXI. 452/1 The Siamese call themselves Thay. **1939** *Times* 30 May 11/3 Muang-Thai is the name by which the dominant element in the country, the Thai, call their land... The newcomers amalgamated with their Lao and Thai kinsmen. **1941** *Engineer* 15 Aug. 99/1 The Thais have always been agriculturists. **1957** *Encycl. Brit.* XX. 593B/1 Of the total population [of Siam] the great majority (about 75%–80%) belongs to the Thai group of peoples. These may be divided into the southern Thai or Siamese and the northern Thai or Lao. **1962** E. Snow *Other Side of River* (1963) lxxxv. 681 Cambodians, like the people of Thailand and Upper Burma, are mixed descendants of the same stock as the Thai and other minority peoples of China. **1978** T. Williamson *Technicians of Death* xi. 90 He was operating his own ship ..with a mixed crew of Thais and Filipinos.

B. *adj.* Of or pertaining to Thailand, its people, or its language; *Thai silk,* wild silk woven in Thailand according to traditional designs, often with bright colours; *Thai stick* [cf. *stick *sb.*¹ 11 h], a marijuana cigarette.

1808 [see Siamese *sb.* 2]. **1939** *Times* 5 July 15/7 The Siamese Legation, now officially renamed the Thai Legation, issued the following announcement yesterday:– ..The word 'Thailand' for 'Siam' and the word 'Thai' for 'Siamese' will be used from now on by the Ministries and Departments of the Thai Government. **1948** D. Diringer *Alphabet* ii. vii. 413 The thirteenth century witnessed a general advance of the Thai or Shan race, facilitated by the fall of Pagan dynasty. **1955** *Times* 9 May 8/4 The many millions of people of Thai race considered linguistically and ethnologically now scattered across south-west China, north Viet Nam, and Burma are split into different groups, and in many cases the split dates back for hundreds of years. **1958** A. Toynbee *East to West* xxviii. 85 A skiff will carry the Thai housewife to a shop-front that could not be reached on foot. **1976** *National Observer* (U.S.) 25 Sept. 22/2 Cannabis connoisseurs rank Colombian marijuana alongside such Asian types as so-called Thai-sticks from Thailand. **1977** *Times* 17 May 8/1 (Advt.), Our beautiful slim-bodied hostesses in their glamorous Thai silk outfits. **1978** *Chicago* June 245/1 Tom yum gung soup..is almost a meal in itself as is Thai fried rice, a combination of green peppers, chicken, and tiny bits of bacon, garnished with cucumber and tomato slices. **1978** [see *stick *sb.*¹ 11 h]. **1981** *Times* 22 Apr. 4/3 He had made..money through smuggling Thai sticks.

Thailander (tai·lændəɹ). [f. *Thailand* + -er¹.] A native or inhabitant of Thailand.

1961 in Webster. **1973** P. O'Donnell *Silver Mistress* v. 81 His personal bodyguard, the silent Thailander who stood two paces away.

Thakali (tăkā·lī). [Native name.] **a.** A member of one of the tribes or castes of Nepal, of Mongol origin. **b.** The language or dialect spoken by this tribe. Also *attrib.* or as *adj.*

1928 Northey & Morris *Gurkhas* xiii. 202 Prosperous, and great traders..the Thakales are of mixed religion and are closely allied to Tibetans. **1961** L. Bajracharya *Nepal 1960–61* 10/2 Of the trading tribes those next to the Newars are the Thakalis, residents of Thak in Central Nepal. **1974** M. Peissel *Gt. Himalayan Passage* xvii. 246 Prosperous businessmen..are attempting to obtain for the Thakali people a high rank in the Hindu caste system. **1974** *Encycl. Brit. Macropædia* XII. 954/1 The languages of the north and east belong predominantly to the Tibeto-Burman family. These include Magar, Gurung,..and a number of Bhote dialects, including Sherpa and Thakali.

Thakin (þā·kin), *sb.* [Burmese.] **a.** A term of respectful address used by the Burmese, formerly in addressing white people. **b.** A member of a militant nationalist movement that arose in Burma during the 1930s; also *attrib.*

1920 *Blackw. Mag.* June 835/1, I do not know about the deer, *thakin.* **1934** 'G. Orwell' *Burmese Days* iv. 74 God go with you, *thakin.* **1942** J. L. Christian *Mod. Burma* xiii. 238 A current expression of nationalism in Burma is the 'Thakin' movement. *Ibid.,* The Thakins..have done their country little good. **1957** 'F. Clifford' *Ten Minutes on June Morning* (1977) 39 'Who is it?' I asked. ..'A Sikh, *thakin.*' **1971** W. Laqueur *Dict. Politics* 66 During the 1930s popular pressure for independence led to anti-British riots, militant student strikes and the formation of political private armies, e.g. the Thakin Army which was trained in Japan. **1974** *Encycl. Brit. Macropædia* III. 515/1 The young Thakins won the trust of the villagers and emerged as leaders. *Ibid.* IX. 923/1 Thant was educated at the University of Rangoon, where he met Thakin Nu (afterward U Nu, who became prime minister of Burma in 1948).

thalamo-. Add: **thalamoco·rtical** *a.,* applied to nerves running from the thalamus to the cerebral cortex; **thalamostri·ate** *a.,* connecting or serving the thalamus and the corpus striatum; **thalamo·tomy** *Surg.* [-tomy], an operation to destroy specific groups of cells in the thalamus, used for the relief of pain or for treatment of Parkinson's disease or mental disorders.

1902 D. J. Cunningham *Text-bk. Anat.* 504 Flechsig divides the thalamo-cortical fibres of ordinary sensation into three sensory systems. **1954** *Gray's Anat.* (ed. 31) 994 The wealth of thalamo-cortical and cortico-thalamic connexions indicate a very close functional relationship between the two. **1970** *Jrnl. Physiol.* CCX. 15p The afferent thalamo-cortical pathways to the visual cortex of the cat and monkey have been studied. **1902** D. J. Cunningham *Text-bk. Anat.* 540 Numerous fibres from the optic thalamus pass into the anterior limb of the internal capsule and enter both the caudate and the lenticular nuclei. These may be termed the thalamo-striate fibres. **1968** Passmore & Robson *Compan. Med. Stud.* I. xxiv. 73/1 The thalamostriate vein passes forwards between the caudate nucleus and thalamus draining both. **1948** *Time* 21 June 76/2 Last week they announced first results of their new operation, called thalamotomy. **1955** *Sci. News Let.* 11 June 381/1 The studies were made on 30 patients who underwent a special brain operation called thalamotomy. In this operation the cutting is done on part of the thalamus, the structure in the brain that serves as the main relay center for feelings of heat, cold, pain and the like to the thinking part of the brain. **1973** *Brit. Med. Jrnl.* 15 Dec. 666/1 The movements can be abolished only with thalamotomy. **1977** J. N. Walton *Brain's Diseases Nervous System* (ed. 8) xi. 595 The operations of pallidectomy and ventrolateral thalamotomy.

thalamus. Add: **1.** Now *Obs.* exc. in *spec.* sense, and used without *optic.* (Further examples.)

1902 D. J. Cunningham *Text-bk. Anat.* 501 The two optic thalami, in their anterior two-thirds, lie close together on either side of a deep mesial cleft, which receives the name of the third ventricle of the brain. **1947** *Sci. News* IV. 112 There is an anatomically distinct region, the thalamus, deep in the brain-stem which has something to do with the perception of pain and other sensations and the judgment of their quality. **1948** A. Brodal *Neurol. Anat.* vi. 157 It appears..that the thalamus is not only an important relay station in the large afferent sensory fibre systems and the optic and acoustic systems, but in addition extensive parts of it..also discharge their impulses to the cerebral cortex. **1979** *Sci. Amer.* Sept. 85/2 The rest of the forebrain is the diencephalon: the upper two-thirds comprises the thalamus (which has numerous subdivisions) and the lower third the hypothalamus.

thalassæmia (þælăsī·miă). *Path.* Also (chiefly *U.S.*) **-emia.** [f. Thalass(o- + Gr. αἷμα blood + -ia¹.] A hereditary hæmolytic anæmia common in malarious (or formerly malarious) areas and caused by the faulty synthesis of part of the hæmoglobin molecule, with symptoms that depend on the part of the molecule affected and on whether the individual is homozygous or heterozygous for the gene concerned; so *thalassæmia major, intermedia, minor.*

1932 Whipple & Bradford in *Amer. Jrnl. Dis. Children* XLIV. 364 We do not like the term 'erythroblastic anemia'... The disease is limited almost wholly to Italians, Greeks and Syrians, i. e., to the people originating about the Mediterranean Sea. For this reason the term 'thalassemia'..may have an appeal. **1936,** etc. [see *Mediterranean *sb.* 1 b]. **1944** Valentine & Neel in *Arch. Internal Med.* LXXIV. 196/2 It is suggested, on the basis of the pathologic and genetic evidence, that the full-blown disease be designated 'thalassemia major' and the milder carrier state 'thalassemia minor'. **1954** K. Singer et al. in *Blood* IX. 1039 We have found the following simple classification very useful; it is based on the alterations of the red cell and hemoglobin levels: 1. Thalassemia major (Cooley's anemia): very severe microcytic hemolytic anemia. 2. Thalassemia intermedia, characterized by a less severe, but still marked anemia. 3. Thalassemia minor: mild anemia. **1962** [see *haemoglobinopathy]. **1972** D. E. Comings in W. J. Williams et al. *Hematology* xxxi. 332/2 Although the total number of individuals with thalassemia intermedia is relatively small .., it constitutes a clinically important group, since its relatively benign course (compared to thalassemia major) allows affected individuals to live to adulthood. **1973** B. J. Williams *Evolution & Human Origins* iv. 61/2 Osteoporosis occurs even with thalassemia minor. **1978** *Jrnl. R. Soc. Med.* LXXI. 465/1 The hepatic cirrhosis of thalassaemia major. **1979** *Brit. Med. Jrnl.* 17 Nov. 1298/2 The 26-year-old Chinese with beta-thalassaemia who had been transfused with 404 units of blood in his lifetime. His total body iron was so high that it triggered the alarm at an airport security checkpoint. **1982** *New Scientist* 21 Jan. 164/1 Red blood cells in people with thalassæmia cannot carry oxygen well enough, and patients survive only with regular blood transfusions.

Hence **thalassæ·mic,** a person with thalassæmia.

1974 *Nature* 8 Feb. 380/1 The δβ-thalassaemics were Sicilian and have been previously reported. **1979** *Ibid.* 15 Nov. 317/2 In one study, the incidence of HbF Sardinia in β-thalassaemics in Italy was 90%, compared with only 40% in normal Italians.

thalass(o-. Add: **thalassotherapy** (examples).

1910 *Index-Catal. Libr. Surgeon-General's Office, U.S. Army* 2nd Ser. XV. 362/1 Nyström (O. E.) Några ord om hafskuren eller thalassotherapien. (A few words on sea-baths and thalassotherapy.) 8°. Göteborg, 1907. **1966** *Punch* 5 Oct. 531 Thalassotherapy is sea-bathing in a warm, enclosed and controlled area... Pure sea water is pumped in from several hundred metres out. **1983** Inglis & West *Alternative Health Guide* 25 Establishments which provide thalassotherapy have been springing up around the continent of Europe..to provide a holiday in which the usual seaside ingredients..are supplemented..by a regime of salt-water treatments.

thalenite (þā·lĕn-, þălī·nəit). *Min.* [ad. Sw. *thalénit* (C. Benedicks 1898, in *Geol. För. Förh.* XX. 308), f. the name of T. R. *Thalén* (1827–1905), Swedish physicist: see -ITE[1].] An yttrium silicate, $Y_3Si_3O_{10}OH$, found as translucent monoclinic crystals.

1899 *Jrnl. Chem. Soc.* LXXVI. II. 766 Minerals allied to thalénite are yttrialite, rowlandite, and kainosite. **1972** *Prof. Papers U.S. Geol. Survey* No. 800-c. 63/1 The rarity of thalenite in pegmatites, in which other rare-earth minerals may be abundant, suggests that it can form only under very unusual conditions.

‖ **thali**[1] (tā·li). Also **tali.** [Tamil *tāli.*] A gold pendant that is hung round the bride's neck as part of a Hindu wedding ceremony.

1875 *Indian Antiquary* IV. 173/1, I am surprised that the opponents of the Kuḍumî have not yet commenced to put down the use of the tâli. This is the Hindu sign of marriage, answering to the ring of European Christendom. .. It is always tied round the Hindu bride's neck. **1957** L. DUMONT *Hierarchy & Marriage Alliance in S. Indian Kinship* (Occasional Papers R. Anthrop. Inst. No. 12) iii. 29 The tying of a string, with or without the well-known marriage badge or *tāli*, round the bride's neck has certainly a sacramental value. **1963** *Guardian* 11 Apr. 11/4 At marriage in the wealthier, and even in the not-so-wealthy, families a good deal of gold is passed over from the bride's family to the bridegroom's. And the tokens of marriage are not the miserable rings of the Christian West but gold pendants called thalis which are then hung on solid gold necklaces. **1981** *Times* 24 Jan. 11/1 The thali is a phallic symbol worn by brides in the Dravidian South.

‖ **thali**[2] (tā·li). [Hind. *thālī.*] In India, a metal platter or flat dish on which food is served.

1969 *Times* 13 Oct. (Indian Suppl.) p. xx/4 The Apollo room in Bombay's Taj Hotel where a 'thali' platter of assorted spoonfuls of curries and sauces is a good introduction. **1978** F. OLBRICH *Desouza pays Price* xxii. 137 The little serving-boy..brought..a 'thali', a gleaming round metal tray with an assortment of cooked vegetables and pulses arranged in small helpings.

thalidomide (þăli·dŏməid). Also **Thalidomide.** [f. ph*thal*im*ido*glutar*imide*, f. PHTHALIMID(E + -O + *glutaric* adj. s.v. GLUT- + IMIDE.] **a.** A non-barbiturate sedative and hypnotic, $C_{13}H_{10}N_2O_4$, which was found to be teratogenic when taken early in pregnancy, sometimes causing malformation or absence of limbs in the fœtus.

1958 *Lancet* 1 Feb. 271 The British Pharmacopœia Commission has issued the following new supplementary list of approved names:..Thalidomide..α-Phthalimido-glutarimide. **1961** *Ibid.* 2 Dec. 1262/1 We have just received reports from two overseas sources possibly associating thalidomide ('Distaval') with harmful effects on the fœtus in early pregnancy. **1962** *New Scientist* 28 June 717/1 The tragic cost of the use of thalidomide. **1969** N. W. PIRIE *Food Resources* vii. 167 Thalidomide is the classic example of a substance that passed orthodox tests that were, as it turned out, not relevant. **1978** *Dædalus* Spring 136 Passage of the 1962 drug law might not have occurred without the public demand for stricter controls over the testing of new drugs following disclosure of deformities caused by Thalidomide. **1979** *Nature* 29 Nov. 509/1 Other agents, notably Thalidomide, are believed to be teratogenic by virtue of metabolic products rather than the parent compound.

b. *attrib.* and *Comb.*: **thalidomide baby, child,** etc., one born deformed through the effects of thalidomide.

1962 *Guardian* 31 July 14/2 There is still no information about the number of 'thalidomide babies' in the country. **1962** *Lancet* 1 Dec. 1155/2 Attempts have been made to lengthen stunted thalidomide arms by grafts from fibula and scapula. **1971** *New Scientist* 18 Mar. 613/1 The construction of a body harness for armless thalidomide children. **1973** *Daily Tel.* 9 Jan. 2/2 A Pharmaceutical Society spokesman said..that the scale of the thalidomide compensation would undoubtedly have a 'profound effect' on the manufacture of new drugs in Britain. **1977** J. D. DOUGLAS in Douglas & Johnson *Existential Sociol.* i. 26 Her highly publicized abortion in Sweden for a thalidomide-damaged fetus. **1979** T. BENN *Arguments for Socialism* ii. 49 There was also the initial refusal by Distillers to compensate the thalidomide children properly. **1980** *Nature* 1 May 54/1 The thalidomide tragedy, for example, could have been averted if this synthetic racemate had been separated into its optical isomers, for only the left-handed (s)-(—)-isomer has teratogenic properties. **1981** *Daily Tel.* 3 Feb. 2/2 This is the first known case of a thalidomide victim becoming a father, although a couple of incidences of thalidomide mothers are known.

thallium. Add: **b. thallium-activated** *a.*, containing a small amount of added thallium so as to make the substance active as a phosphor.

1956 *Nature* 3 Mar. 413/1 A single-crystal spectrometer (thallium-activated sodium iodide crystal). **1974** *Encycl. Brit. Macropædia* XV. 397/2 The phosphor in greatest use in scintillation counters is thallium activated sodium iodide.

thalweg. Add: Also **talweg** [after the reformed Ger. spelling]. (Earlier and later examples.)

1831 W. WHEWELL *Let.* 22 Feb. in I. Todhunter *William Whewell* (1876) II. 113 For *thalweg* and *riggin'* I do not think you can do better than take *daleway* and *ridgeway.* **1937** *Geogr. Jrnl.* LXXXIX. 260 The development of a terrace..involves two clearly distinguishable phases—firstly, the formation of a continuous flood plain, and secondly, the incision of the talweg below it. **1946** L. D. STAMP *Britain's Struct. & Scenery* v. 49 Soundings show that the floor of a ria, the old river talweg, slopes steadily seawards and there is no 'lip'. **1966** J. S. HARDMAN tr. *R. Boulanger's Middle East* 608 Whilst conducting excavations towards the thalweg of the Kidron valley the Franco-British expedition discovered the remains of a rampart belonging to the Canaanaean (or Jebusite) Jerusalem. **1968** R. W. FAIRBRIDGE *Encycl. Geomorphol.* 1149/1 The opposite of the talweg itself is a divide, i.e., the lines joining all high points in topography.

Thames. Add: **a.** *Thames barge, valley.*

1883 *Boats of World* 4 Who can mistake the world-renowned Thames Barge, with her long, flat side, picturesque rig, and bright-coloured sails? **1961** F. H. BURGESS *Dict. Sailing* 207 *Thames barge*, a ketch or yawl-rigged sailing barge with a large spritsail, common on the Thames estuary. **1979** D. MAY *Revenger's Comedy* viii. 105 Out on the estuary, a big, red-sailed Thames barge was moving. **1902** *Encycl. Brit.* XXVIII. 533/2 In the London district the country in the Thames valley..is as largely occupied by flower farms as it is by fruit farms. **1977** D. JAMES *Spy at Evening* xiv. 113 He..let himself out into the early-morning Thames valley mist.

Thamudic (þămū·dik), *a.* and *sb.* [f. *Thamūd* (Arab. *ṯamūd*) + -IC.] **A.** *adj.* **a.** Of, pertaining to, or designating a class of inscriptions in northern and central Arabia dating from the 5th to the 1st centuries B.C., or the ancient Semitic language of which they are the only evidence. **b.** Of or pertaining to the Thamūd, a tribe that lived in northern Arabia between the 4th century B.C. and the 7th century A.D.

1909 WEBSTER, Thamudic, *a.* **1937** P. K. HITTI *Hist. Arabs* vi. 72 The Lihyānites seem also to have held..al-Hijr..once a Thamūdic town. **1951** [see *SAFAITIC *a.*]. **1974** *Encycl. Brit. Micropædia* IX. 921/2 Recent archaeological work has revealed numerous Thamūdic rock writings and pictures not only on Mt. Athlith but also throughout central Arabia.

B. *sb.* The Thamudic language.

1937 F. V. WINNETT *Study Lihyanite & Thamudic Inscr.* 27 In view of the fact that it has the value *zāi* in both Lihyanite and Ethiopic, there is little likelihood of its having a different value in Thamudic. **1952** HARDING & LITTMANN *Some Thamudic Inscr.* 47 In Thamudic and Safaïtic the verb..often means 'he acquired, he bought'.

Also **Thamudæ·an, Thamu·dene, Thamude·nic** *adjs.*, **Thamudian** *a.* and *sb.*

1909 WEBSTER, Thamudene *adj.* **1911** *Encycl. Brit.* XXIII. 956/2 The Thamudaean inscriptions are locally nearer to Phoenicia, and the letters are more like the Phoenician. **1934** J. A. MONTGOMERY *Arabia & Bible* v. 91 A peculiar and much discussed special type of Arabic inscriptions, the Thamudene, has been discovered. **1936**, etc. [see *LIHYANIC *sb.*]. **1948** D. DIRINGER *Alphabet* II. ii. 227 The North Arabian inscriptions..can be separated into three groups: (1) Thamudene or Thamudic... (2) The Dedanite inscriptions... (3) The Safaitic or Safahitic inscriptions. **1981** *Word 1980* XXXI. 222 We have here an important isogloss for the chronological division of the Semitic languages into languages with *š*.., languages with *h* (Amorite, Hebrew,.. and Thamudian), languages with '.., and languages with *y.*

Thamudite (þæ·miūdəit), *sb.* and *a.* [f. *Thamūd* (see *THAMUDIC *a.* b) + -ITE[1].] **A.** *sb.* One of the Thamūd. **B.** *adj.* = *THAMUDIC *a.* b.

1833 A. CRICHTON *Hist. Arabia* I. iii. 92 The circumstance of dwelling in caves..was common to other tribes besides the Thamudites. **1881** *Encycl. Brit.* XIII. 117/2 [The graffiti] are mostly the productions of Thamudite soldiers in the Roman army.

than, *conj.* Add: **2. b.** *different(ly) than* is not uncommon, esp. in the U.S., but continues to be regarded by many as incorrect. (Further examples.)

1857 TROLLOPE *Barchester Towers* III. xiv. 248 Things were conducted very differently now than in former times. **1912** J. WEBSTER *Daddy-Long-Legs* (1913) 146 It's different with me than with other girls. **1962** D. LESSING *Golden Notebk.* 59 Both come from a different world than the housing estate outside London. **1970** *Amer. N. & Q.* Nov. 39/1 Geoffrey and Erasmus are concerned with classifying metaphors along quite different lines than is Quintilian. **1980** *Outdoor Life* (U.S.) (Northeast ed.) Oct. 101/1 Mule deer bucks behave differently than whitetails in a few other ways.

thanato-. Add: **tha:natocœno·sis, -cœ·nose** (also *U.S.* **-cen-**) *Ecol.* [a. G. *thanatocoenose* (E. Wasmund 1926, in *Arch. f. Hydrobiol.* XVII. 6), f. Gr. κοίνωσις sharing, as in *BIOCŒNOSIS], a group of fossils occurring in the same location but not necessarily representing a former biocœnosis; **thanatophi·lia** [*-PHILIA], an undue fascination with death; **thanatopho·ric** *a. Path.* [ad. F. *thanatophore* (P. Maroteaux et al. 1967, in *Presse Méd.* LXXV. 2519), ad. Gr. θανατηφόρος death-bringing] applied to a form of dwarfism that results in death (see quot. 1977).

1953 *Amer. Jrnl. Sci.* CCLI. 25 The term 'thanatocoenosis' implies a community of death; as used by Wasmund, however, it has come to mean the aggregated remains of organisms that in many cases never constituted a biocoenosis. **1957** *Sci. News* XLIII. 71 A fossil 'community' (a thanatocoenose or death assemblage) is seldom if ever identical with the original biocoenose. **1967** *Oceanogr. & Marine Biol.* V. 452 The following (and last) regression..left a very rich fauna which forms most of the thanatocoenoses lying under the present sea level. **1975** *Nature* 23 Oct. 667/2 It is well known that factors such as habitat preference of the animals in question,..and the environmental setting influence the likelihood of the preservation of thanatocoenoses. **1977** *Biotropica* IX. 131 (*heading*) A small-vertebrate thanatocenosis from northern Peru. **1974** *Time* 28 Jan. 77/2 Romantic cults seem to spring up rapidly round poets who die young. An element of thanatophilia enters into the worship of such poets. **1979** *N.Y. Rev. Bks.* 25 Oct. 18/4 Many of Sciascia's tales have, at their heart, thanatophilia. **1971** *Lancet* 12 June 1234/1 An achondroplastic shows some cartilage formation (in fact quite a lot, even in the thanatophoric form). **1977** *Ibid.* 16 Apr. 854/1 Thanatophoric dwarfism is a congenital chondrodystrophy characterised by short extremities, narrow thorax, a trunk of normal length, and a relatively large head... Affected infants usually die soon after birth.

thanatologist. Add: **a.** (Further examples.)

1972 *New Scientist* 2 Mar. 497 Thanatologists ask doctors..to help the terminal patient and his family to meet his own death. **1975** *Times Lit. Suppl.* 31 Oct. 1305/4 Their real subject, as is customary with Signor Manganelli, is death. He has always been proud of introducing himself as the supreme thanatologist. **1983** *Oxf. Bk. Death* p. xiii, While to 'deny' death would sound as foolish as the lady who told Carlyle she had decided to accept the universe, I cannot say that I share the thanatologists' missionary urge to bring death out into the open.

b. An undertaker.

1972 *Daily Colonist* (Victoria, B.C.) 1 Mar. 1/8 Quebec's 450 undertakers want to be called thanatologists. **1980** *Times* 25 Apr. 6/4 He was one of 300 thanatologists, better known as undertakers, gathered in the principality [of Monaco] to discuss death in all its aspects.

thanatology. Delete *rare* and add: (Later examples.) Also (orig. *U.S.*), the study of the effects of approaching death and of the needs of the terminally ill and their families; **thanatological** *a.* (further example).

1912 *Jrnl. Amer. Med. Assoc.* 27 Apr. 1246/1 There is something more than mere transcendentalism in the Science of Thanatology. **1968** *Jrnl. Indiana Med. Assoc.* LXI. 1159/1 (*heading*) Thanatology resurrected. **1969** *Courier-Mail* (Brisbane) 13 Sept. 12/7 A Foundation of Thanatology is being formed in New York. **1972** *New Scientist* 2 Mar. 497/2 The most disturbing issue that has arisen anew with thanatology is the problem of what to tell the terminal patient about his illness. *Ibid.*, Another area of thanatological controversy concerns the administration of drugs to relieve the pain of the terminally ill. **1976** *Billings* (Montana) *Gaz.* 11 July 3-F/4 Workers in the new field of thanatology are encouraging parents to take their children, even small ones, to funerals. **1977** *New York Rev. Bks.* 12 May 10/1 There is now a special branch of learning called 'Thanatology', and historians of death, like Philippe Ariès or Michel Vovelle, have suddenly appeared on the scene. **1979** *Brit. Med. Jrnl.* 15 Dec. 1530/2 The near-dead are not dead; and the dead, whether surviving in some form or not, can be left to thanatology and eschatology.

thanatorium (þænătōə·riŏm). *nonce-wd.* Pl. **-oria.** [Alteration of *sanatorium*, after THANATO-.] An establishment where people are received in order to be killed.

1970 *Times* 1 May 11/4 We should need public thanatoria, just as we have public crematoria and abattoirs. **1970** *New Scientist* 24 Sept. 626/2 The Thanatoria, the most negative of all the departments. **1976** *Times Lit. Suppl.* 13 Feb. 166/1 The violent jerks from excess to excess of the patients at Dr Sacks's pseudonymous New York hospital—'not a sanatorium but a thanatorium', as one of the inmates remarked.

Thanatos (þæ·nătǫs). [a. Gr. θάνατος death.] = *death-instinct* s.v. *DEATH *sb.* 19.

1935 *Brit. Jrnl. Psychol.* XXVI. 283 Freud's final duality was the division of the mind into two sets of instincts which he termed life instincts and death instincts respectively—or, if one prefers the Greek names, Eros and Thanatos. *Ibid.* 284 He was inclined..to regard the voice of Thanatos as mute. **1955** [see *DEFUSION]. **1967** [see *EROS 1 b]. **1970** G. GREER *Female Eunuch* 148 Our life-style contains more *thanatos* than *eros.* **1979** H. SEGAL *Klein* i. 20 The fundamental conflict, between Eros—life, including sexuality—and Thanatos—self-destruction and destruction—is the deepest source of ambivalence, anxiety and guilt.

thang (þæŋ). Repr. a Southern U.S. pronunc. of THING *sb.*[1]

1937 *Frontier & Midland* Autumn 14/2 He done one thang he ought never done. **1941** W. A. PERCY *Lanterns on Levee* xx. 259 Negroes..insisted on going to their [flooded] cabins..to see about their 'thangs'. **1971** in A. Dundes *Mother Wit* (1973) 319/2 You ain' so bad yourself, girl... I want to help a sweet thang like you all I can. **1973** *Black World* Sept. 84 Ourselves illusionize About doin our thang.

Thanga, obs. var. *SANGHA.

thank, *sb.* Add: **II. 5. b.** With intensifying advbs. and phrases, as *thanks awfully, ever so, a lot, a million* (orig. *U.S.*), *very much*, etc. Also used ironically.

1890 A. TUER *Thenks Awf'lly!* i. 11 He at once burst into conversation: 'Thenks awf'lly! I nurly missed the trine.' **1911** D. H. LAWRENCE *Let.* 7 Nov. (1962) I. 84 Dear Garnett: Just got your letter—I am very glad with the *Nation*—thanks very much. **1914** 'SAKI' *Beasts & Super-Beasts* 217 If you lend me three pounds that ought to see me through comfortably. Thanks ever so. **1916** E. F. BENSON *David Blaize* vii. 134, I couldn't possibly. But thanks, most awfully. **1936** *Sat. Even. Post* 12 Sept. 10/1 That was a swell lunch. Thanks a million. **1942** N. BALCHIN *Darkness falls from Air* xiv. 237, I gave him a pound and said, 'Thanks a lot.' **1965** WODEHOUSE *Galahad at Blandings* i. 8 The 'Oh, thanks awfully' which betrayed the other's English origin. **1966** H. NICHOLSON *Duckling in Capri* xv. 194 'Spend it on Pam.' 'Shall I? Thanks a million.' **1967** *Plays & Players* Apr. 41/1 *Trebor*: Couldn't we go on an aeroplane, somewhere? *Webster*: No, we couldn't go on an aeroplane. *Trebor*: Thanks very much. **1972** J. MANN *Mrs Knox's Profession* ii. 15 'Thanks ever so,' he said, his voice an octave higher than usual. **1982** 'J. BELL' *Innocent* ii. 16 'You'll want a tray, love.'..'Of course, thanks a lot.'

c. *thanks be*: ellipt. for 'thanks be to God', as an expression of relief or satisfaction. *colloq.*

1924 D. MOORE *Fen's First Term* ix. 97 Me 'arf dye, thanks be. **1942** C. MILBURN *Diary* 7 Oct. (1979) 154 Hats are to be fewer—I seem to have many, thanks be! **1963** *Times* 4 Feb. 13/2 And thanks be, that aging design, the longer fitted jacket has not reappeared.

11. (Earlier example of sense 'to say grace'.)

1803 D. WORDSWORTH *Jrnl.* 27 Aug. (1941) I. 269 When breakfast was ended the mistress desired..her husband to 'return thanks'. He said a short grace.

thank, *v.* Add: **3. e.** (Earlier and later examples.) Now usu. ironic, implying a rebuke or command.

1813 I. POCOCK *Miller & his Men* I. iii. 9 Cockatrice!—I'll thank you for that portmanteau. **1907** G. C. WHITWORTH *Indian English* xii. 248 The offence is much mitigated if..the word is followed by 'if' instead of the usual infinitive, as 'I'll thank you to be quiet.' **1930** J. B. PRIESTLEY *Angel Pavement* i. 12 Just say to 'er: 'Mrs. Cross 'as seen the note left..., and..Mrs. Cross'll thank her to keep 'er notes to 'erself in future till they're asked for.' Just you tell 'er that, boy. **1940** H. G. WELLS *Babes in Darkling Wood* II. ii. 160 No decent people are going to bother about it, Mother. And they will thank you not to be bothered about it. **1975** 'D. JORDAN' *Black Account* II. xx. 110 I'm here to sell tractors and I'll thank you to remember it.

f. (Later examples.)

1908 A. BENNETT *Old Wives' Tale* IV. v. 559 'Thank you for nothing!' said Dick. 'I don't want it.' **1940** W. S. CHURCHILL *Second World War* (1949) I. II. xxxiv. 548 Sweden will say 'Thank you for nothing' about any offers on our part to defend the Gällivare ironfield. **1975** 'R. PLAYER' *Let's talk of Graves* v. 202 I'm not respectable. The Judge has just told everybody that—thank ye' for nothing, my Lord.

g. See also GOD 9 e. Also *thank God for that* (now freq. in weakened use); *thank God hold* (Mountaineering): an easy hold at the top of a difficult climb.

1918 A. P. MCKISHNIE *Willow, the Wisp* xxi. 303 His world was at rest, once more. Thank God for that! **1949** G. DAVENPORT *Family Fortunes* III. ii. 222 'Thank God for that,' he said. **1955** S. STYLES *Introd. Mountaineering* xi. 127 The term *thank-god hold*, which has become part of British climbing jargon, originated on the third ascent of the slab on Route II, Lliwedd East Buttress, when as each climber got his hand over the good knob at the top he expressed his heartfelt gratitude in the same two words. **1978** P. GILLMAN *Fitness on Foot* v. 67 A sense of relief on reaching the top of a difficult climb to discover enormous holds to finish on. These are known as 'thank God' holds. **1978** I. B. SINGER *Shosha* i. 16 Thank God, I found friends among members of the Writers' Club.

h. In negative conditional sentences as an ironical understatement, as *he would not thank you for doing it*, he would be displeased if you did it. Cf. *THANK YOU B. 3.

[**1739–40** RICHARDSON *Pamela* (1740) I. xxiv. 65 Now I did not thank her for this, as I told her afterwards (for it brought a great deal of Trouble upon me).] **1873** TROLLOPE *Phineas Redux* (1874) I. iv. 32 His party would not thank him for ventilating a measure which..might well be postponed. **1896** KIPLING *Seven Seas* 148 The things I knew was proper you wouldn't thank me to give. And the things I knew was rotten you said was the way to live. **1970** 'A. GILBERT' *Death wears Mask* i. 19 Miss Alice wouldn't thank you for tying her into a chair. **1983** M. HINXMAN *Corpse now Arriving* ii. 14 He was probably in the middle of some world-shattering story and wouldn't thank her for the interruption.

thanka, var. *TANKA^3.

thankful, *a.* Add: **1. a.** Phr. *thankful for small mercies.*

1818 SCOTT *Heart Midl.* in *Tales my Landlord* 2nd Ser. II. xii. 295 'Ye are thankfu' for sma' mercies, then,' said Mrs Howden, with a toss of her head. **1844** EMERSON *Ess.* 2nd Ser. 41, I am thankful for small mercies. **1874** GEO. ELIOT *Let.* 3 Aug. (1956) VI. 72 One has learned to be thankful for sma' mercies in this world of dreadful possibilities. **1947** A. HUXLEY *Let.* 14 Nov. (1969) 576 It is raining harder and harder and Little Rock feels.. remote. However, the Blue Bird is clean and comfortable; so let us be thankful for small mercies. **1950** C. S. FORESTER *Mr. Midshipman Hornblower* viii. 207 Then be thankful for small mercies. And even more thankful for big ones.

thankfully, *adv.* Add: **II. 4.** Let us be thankful (that); one is thankful to say. orig. *U.S.*

This use as a sentence adverb, like *HOPEFULLY *adv.* 2, is deprecated by some writers.

1966 in W. Follett *Mod. Amer. Usage* 170/1 The 'suicide needle' which—thankfully—he didn't see fit to use. **1969** *Chatelaine* July 1/1 Thankfully there are fewer movies to endure in which the men have all the lines. **1976** *Shooting Mag.* Dec. 41/2 An alarming safety situation.. caused many a raised eyebrow but thankfully nothing worse. **1980** *New Society* 3 Jan. 33/2 But thankfully social workers will plod on, hopefully with small regard for new fashions. **1982** *Daily Tel.* 30 Aug. 8/4 Thankfully, however, the old style has not entirely disappeared. **1983** *Times* 11 Nov. 2/4 Aldabra Island in the Indian Ocean, where man 'has thankfully failed to establish himself'.

thank-offering. Add: Also **thanks-offering.**

1921 G. O'DONOVAN *Vocations* xi. 171 The united prayers of the nuns were a thanks-offering to God for her. **1952** C. DAY LEWIS tr. *Virgil's Aeneid* VI. 118 A thanks-offering to Phoebus. **1978** *Washington Post* 7 Mar. A13/2 Obermammergau..has performed the Passion play every 10 years for centuries as a thanks offering for the end of the plague.

thanksgive, *v.* For *Obs. rare^{-1}* read *rare* and add later examples.

1908 HARDY *Dynasts* III. 353 You almost charm my long philosophy Out of my strong-built thought, and bear me back To when I thanksgave thus. **1938** O. NASH *I'm a Stranger here Myself* 227 And each Thanksgiving I Thanksgive.

thanksgiving. Add: **1. b.** (Later examples of U.S. use in sense *Thanksgiving Day.*)

1930 J. DOS PASSOS *42nd Parallel* I. 87 By Thanksgiving Mac had beaten his way to Sacramento. **1981** *Nordic Skiing* Jan. 50/1 The resort is situated at 7,000 feet..with a ski season extending from Thanksgiving to mid-May.

3. a. *thanksgiving service.*

1902 I. HAMILTON *Let.* 8 June in R. S. Churchill *Winston S. Churchill* (1969) II. Compan. I. 145 We have just had our Thanksgiving Service. **1923** KIPLING *Irish Guards in Gt. War* I. 338 On the 14th a great thanksgiving-service was held in the Cathedral.

b. Thanksgiving day: in the United States, celebrated since 1941 on the fourth Thursday in November; also in Canada, celebrated on the second Monday in October; **Thanksgiving dinner** *U.S.*, a dinner, usu. consisting of traditional dishes, served on Thanksgiving Day; **Thanksgiving turkey** *U.S.*, a turkey served as a traditional part of a Thanksgiving dinner.

1830 *Workingman's Gaz.* (Woodstock, Vermont) 1 Dec. 78/2 They have added to the comfort and happiness of those, whose scanty pittance would hardly allow them to enjoy the luxuries of Thanksgiving dinner. *a* **1892** W. WHITMAN *Daybks. & Notebks.* (1978) I. 89 Took Thanksgiving dinner there Nov 26 '80. **1981** *Washington Post* 22 Nov. K-1/3 Thanksgiving dinner starts with an enormous glut of oysters. **1829** *Virginia Herald* (Fredericksburg) 25 Apr. 4/1 (*heading*) A Thanksgiving Turkey. **1960** *American Home* Nov. 50 Who should know better how to roast a Thanksgiving turkey or bake a mince pie than the women of early America. **1981** *Washington Post* 26 Nov. B1/1 Such a small Thanksgiving turkey.

thank you. For **b** read **B** and add: **A.** *phr.*

1. Occas. with intensifying advbs. and phrases: cf. *THANK *sb.* 5 b.

1885 A. EDWARDES *Girton Girl* III. x. 182 Oscar Jones looked radiant. 'Thank you, awfully, Miss Bartrand.' **1967** K. GILES *Death in Diamonds* ix. 155 Thank you a million.

2. a. Used to add emphasis to a preceding expression of wish or opinion (usu. one implying a denial or refusal).

1904 E. NESBIT *Phoenix & Carpet* xi. 212 He didn't mean stay and be roasted... No boys on burning decks for me, thank you. **1928** E. O'NEILL *Strange Interlude* IV. 148 No, I've enough guilt in my memory now, thank you! **1940** *Punch* 5 June 624/1, I still have some remnants of self-respect, thank you. **1959** *Times* 27 Apr. 11/3 It was there..that the emissaries of Noah came to give warning of the impending flood, only to be told that the Macneils had a boat of their own, thank you. **1963** N. MARSH *Dead Water* (1964) vii. 170 'Do you mean that you confronted her?' 'Me! No, thank you!' **1974** M. FORSTER *Seduction of Mrs. Pendlebury* x. 105, I don't want to do her good, I just want to keep her out of sight and mind, thank you very much. **1983** *Listener* 27 Jan. 25/3 Those of us who felt that nuclear weapons were quite enough to be worrying about, thank you very much, were given a nasty jolt by the documentary *Overcast, with Outbreaks of Yellow Rain.*

b. Used in imitation of direct speech to imply self-satisfaction or complacency on the part of a person just referred to; chiefly in phr. *to do very well, thank you* and varr.

1931 S. JAMESON *Richer Dust* xix. 524 He himself was doing very well, thank you. **1969** *Guardian* 4 July 7/1 One of them was Louise Purnell, and you know she's doing very nicely, thank you. **1971** S. JEPSON *Let. to Dead Girl* viii. 85 Merchant bankers..encouraged people like John Kinnon and..did very well out of it thank you. **1972** *National Observer* (U.S.) 27 May 8/4 Pat dresses stylishly, favoring white boots, and gets around just fine, thank you.

B. *sb.* **1.** (Earlier examples.) Also, an unspoken expression of thanks.

1792 F. BURNEY *Jrnl.* May (1972) I. 174 He looked even extremely gratified..& Bowed expressively a *thank you*. **1824** J. KEBLE *Let.* in G. Battiscombe *John Keble* (1963) I. iv. 80 And so with as hearty a thank-you and farewell as ever you received I am your obliged and very faithful John Keble.

3. In negative contexts, used like *THANK *v.* 3 h.

1935 D. L. SAYERS *Gaudy Night* xvii. 365 That's what the man wants. *He* wouldn't say thank you for a critic on the hearth. **1969** W. J. BURLEY *Death in Willow Pattern* v. 56, I wouldn't say thank you for it! **1970** D. BAGLEY *Running Blind* ix. 199 Nordlinger's Chevrolet was too long... I wouldn't have given a thank you for it.

C. *attrib.*, designating something written or done to convey thanks (in quot. 1922, that merits thanks); esp. *thank-you letter, note.*

1912 J. WEBSTER *Daddy-Long-Legs* 57, I meant this to be just a short little thank-you note. **1915** —— *Dear Enemy* 111, I spend my entire time composing thank-you letters that aren't exact copies of the ones I've sent before. **1922** JOYCE *Ulysses* 131 Saving princes is a thank you job. **1939** F. SCOTT FITZGERALD *Let.* 5 Apr. (1964) 55 Got a nice thank-you letter from Frances Turnbull for the check I sent her. **1948** 'P. QUENTIN' *Run to Death* x. 83 Vera and I said 'thank-you' speeches to Mrs. Snood and left. **1979** R. JAFFE *Class Reunion* (1980) II. i. 183 After she saw his play she wrote him a thank-you note. **1981** P. DICKINSON *Seventh Raven* xiii. 189 The thank-you party ..for the children—ice-cream and sausage rolls and lemonade.

thanx (þæŋks), commercial and informal spelling of *thanks* (see THANK *sb.* 5). orig. *U.S.*

1936 H. L. MENCKEN *Amer. Lang.* (ed. 4) viii. 406 Such forms as *burlesk..thanx* and *kreem..*are used freely by the advertising writers. **1977** *Zigzag* Apr. 24/1 Thanx for writing.

thar (var. THERE): revived to repr. U.S. pronunc. See *THERE *adv.* (*a.*, *sb.*) A. γ.

thass (ðæs). Also **thas, thash, thazz.** Repr. *that's* in dial. pronunc. or in speech slurred through intoxication.

1919 G. B. SHAW *Great Catherine* II. 138 Thas true. Drungn ruffian... Thas whas he said. **1932** S. GIBBONS *Cold Comfort Farm* xvii. 237 Lessee, thass twenty years ago. **1951** 'J. WYNDHAM' *Day of Triffids* i. 25 'S that bloody comet... Thash what done it. **1959** E. POUND *Thrones* xcix. 52 Thazz all there is to it. **1973** C. HIMES *Black on Black* 196 Thass 'cause you's a fool. **1981** M. C. SMITH *Gorky Park* III. iii. 341 Wasn't no mink, it was differ'nt. Thass why I took it to town, to fine [*sic*] out what it was.

that, *dem. pron., adj.*, and *adv.* Add: **B. I.** Demonstrative Pronoun. **1. b.** (Further examples of *that's a —, that's my —*, used as expressions of commendation or encouragement.) Cf. THERE *adv.* 3 b.

1849 T. ARNOLD *Let.* 10 Aug. (1966) 128 Do you, my dear K, have them sent to me, that's a darling. **1936** [see *BOY *sb.*^{1} 2 c]. **1956** M. DICKENS *Angel in Corner* x. 198 'Good girl.' He lay back on the pillow. 'That's my girl,' he murmured. **1964** J. P. CLARK *Three Plays* 32 *Zifa*: He must not see my tears. *Orukorere*: That's my boy. The strong weep only at dead of night. **1973** W. H. CANAWAY *Harry doing Good* II. ii. 139 'Never mind, then,' he said, and kissed her cheek. 'That's my girl.'

4. a. (Further examples, freq. contrasted with *what.*)

1890 W. JAMES *Princ. Psychol.* I. xii. 466 The conception of some object as a whole..points to and identifies for future thought a certain *that.* **1899** F. W. MAITLAND *Let.* 4 Dec. (1965) 205, I wander in a maze of *whiches* and *thats.* **1909** W. JAMES *Pluralistic Universe* 342 All the *whats* as well as the *thats* of reality, relational as well as terminal, are in the end contents of immediate concrete perception. **1933** *Mind* XLII. 27 A fundamental tenet rather insistently taught us..; namely, that things and events, as real, are *thats*, as well as *whats.* **1975** *New Yorker* 5 May 139/1 We wish not to guess but to know more than thises and thats, to know universal truths.

5. a. *that is*: (*b*) accompanying (usu. following) an explanatory limitation or condition of a preceding statement.

1945 N. MITFORD *Pursuit of Love* xiii. 101 I bet the Scotsboro' boys will be electrocuted in the end, if they don't die of old age first, that is. **1965** W. GOLDING *Pincher Martin* x. 155 'I think finally, I shall go into the Navy.' 'You!'..'If they'd have me, that is.' **1958** *Argosy* Sept. 30 The Buttafava household was happy as could be. All, that is, except Fiorella. **1969** R. HUTCHINGS *Lucky in Jeopardy* iii. 99 You'll be tasting it for yourself up at the House this very evening—if you don't go missing another meal there, that is.

b. *all that* (further examples); *and all that* (further examples); freq. implying a diffident or dismissive attitude on the part of the speaker; *and all that jazz*: see *JAZZ *sb.* 3 b; *and that* (further examples); now chiefly in substandard speech or representations of it.

1925 E. P. OPPENHEIM *Wrath to Come* II. xvi. 271 'Glad to see you and all that, Slattery,' he said. **1929** R. GRAVES (*title*) Good bye to all that. **1930** SELLAR & YEATMAN (*title*) 1066 and all that. **1934** J. HILTON *Good-Bye, Mr. Chips* xi. 80 We don't like the fellow a great deal. Very clever and all that, but a bit *too* clever. **1965** *Listener* 2 Dec. 914/1 Having a fag and talking about sex and that just like she was, you know, ordinary. **1968** *Ibid.* 20 June 801/2 Boy: What do you do then? Girl: Well, you know, typing and filing and that. **1971** D. POTTER *Brit. Eliz. Stamps* iii. 43 The Battle of Hastings, 1066 and all that, was given special treatment. **1974** *Economist* 21 Dec. 26/3 Chairman Mao has formally ordered his revolutionary genie back into the bottle... It sounds like goodbye to all that. **1977** *Listener* 19 May 644/1 They wait outside the pubs for them, and that.

c. (Earlier example.)

1830 *Massachusetts Spy* 28 July 2/3 The march was now hurried on, yet slow at that, for I..could not walk fast.

d. *that's what*: used to add emphasis to a preceding statement: = 'and that is the truth'; *that's that*: indicating that a discussion is closed, a matter settled, a job finished, etc.; similarly *that was that*; *that's so*: that is as you say; that statement is correct; also interrog., (*is*) *that so? that's right*: see *RIGHT *a.* 7 e; *that's it* = *that's that* above. All *colloq.*

1790 F. GROSE *Provincial Gloss.* Suppl., *That's what*, just so; you are right. North. **1813** E. S. BARRETT *Heroine* I. ix. 95 Not a step shall she stir in our cloathes... So that's that. **1857** *Knickerbocker* Jan. 86 The new and popular phrase of '*That's so*', which is working its way into common parlance. **1872** S. BUTLER *Erewhon* vi. 45 'So that's that,' said I to myself, as I watched them scampering. **1891** M. E. RYAN *Pagan of Alleghanies* vi. 93 'That so?' she said. **1914** *Sat. Even. Post* 4 Apr. 10/2 He's a valyable road-kid, that's what, and he ain't for sale. **1924** P. MARKS *Plastic Age* 24 'Well,' he exclaimed, 'that's that. At last I know where I'm going.' **1930** *Times* 26 Mar. 7/2 Martin-Smith and Bond..raced away with 4's, 5's, and 2's; so that was that. **1937** R. MACAULAY *I would be Private* II. v. 196 I'll not be putting up with it. And, that's that. **1967** *Listener* 14 Sept. 326/1, Well, that's it. I don't want to know. **1973** *Ibid.* 15 Nov. 662/3 When I get to bed I absolutely hit the pillow and that's it, I don't know anything until the next morning. **1974** A. FOWLES *Pastime* ii. 14 When she'd gone after the job..and got it, he'd sort of thought that was that and he wouldn't be seeing any more of her. **1976** J. LEE *Ninth Man* I. 79 Ulysses S. Grant..was a war hero, that's what. **1978** B. PARVIN *Deadly Dyke* (1979) v. 25 Alright..that's it Sergeant. Now, where's Alan Tucker's place?

e. *that is* or *was*: added to give emphasis to a statement beginning with those words or the equivalent. *colloq.*

1911 C. E. W. BEAN *'Dreadnought' of Darling* ix. 78 That's exac'ly how it used to be. It's all right, that is. **1911** A. BENNETT *Card* xi. 278 Well, that was a bit of a lark, that was. **1963** *B.B.C. Handbk. 1964* 25 The political world of..'Panorama', or the eventful world of 'That Was the Week That Was'. **1977** *Film & Television Technician* Apr. 4/2 That was the boom that was—and is. **1977** N. MARSH *Last Ditch* ii. 37 He..suddenly ran off down the street. 'That's Master Ferrant, that was,' said Ricky.

II. Demonstrative Adjective. **1. b.** Also *that one*, used disparagingly of a woman.

1848 THACKERAY *Vanity Fair* liv. 486 You don't know how fond I was of that one...Damme, I followed her like a footman. **1922** F. H. BURNETT *Head of House of Coombe* vii. 75 That one in the drawing-room isn't going to interfere with the Nursery. Not her! **1980** J. DRUMMOND *Such a Nice Family* v. 22, I tell you, it's her!..I wouldn't forget that one, not if I lived to be a thousand.

III. Demonstrative Adverb. **a.** For Now only *dial.* and *Sc.* read Now common in *colloq.* use, esp. with a negative: *not* (*all*) *that*, not very. (Later examples.)

1932 R. LEHMANN *Invit. Waltz* I. iii. 39 This weather's that treacherous, you never know. **1937** D. L. SAYERS *Busman's Honeymoon* iv. 85, I was that ashamed I didden know w'ere to look. **1962** *Harper's Bazaar* Aug. 60/3 The Spanish gypsies..hired to do the sweeping were not all that handy with a broom. **1969** J. LEASOR *They don't make Them like That any More* i. 7, I..looked around the stock. It wasn't all that brilliant, I must admit. **1977** *Spare Rib* May 16/1 It's not that easy in a place like Sheffield. **1980** S. BRETT *Dead Side of Mike* xvii. 173 Charles Paris found it difficult to get that excited. **1981** *Listener* 22 Oct. 462/1 The forgiveness of sin isn't just an easygoing matter, as if to say: 'Well, you sinned, but it doesn't matter all that much—I forgive you.'

that, *relative pron.* Add: **I. 1. c.** *that was*: added when a married woman is referred to by her maiden name; occas. also added following the name of a deceased person.

1785 A. SEWARD *Let.* 31 Dec. (1811) I. 97 Miss Jenny Harry that was, for she afterwards married. **1872** GEO. ELIOT *Middlemarch* IV. VIII. lxxiv. 201, I am not so sorry for Rosamond Vincy that was, as I am for her aunt. **1937** D. L. SAYERS *Busman's Honeymoon* 21 Her new ladyship, Miss Vane that was, went down to Oxford the day before. **1970** S. J. PERELMAN *Baby, it's Cold Inside* 178 You remember her, don't you—Luba Pneumatiç that was? **1977** N. MARSH *Last Ditch* v. 135 A..photograph displayed a truculent young woman... 'That's Dulce [*sic*],' said Sergeant Plank. 'That was,' he added.

that, *conj.* Add: **III. 11.** *'that'-clause*: a clause introduced by the word 'that' (as conjunction or, less commonly, as relative pronoun).

1955 J. L. AUSTIN *How to do Things with Words* (1962) vi. 70 Although we have in this type of utterance a 'that' clause following a verb..we must not allude to this as 'indirect speech'. **1964** E. BACH *Introd. Transformational Gram.* v. 102 The rules for *that* clauses..must be made less general. **1978** *Language* LIV. 67 None of the (a) sentences would be appropriate if the proposition expressed in the *that*-clause were part of the undisputed background of already-held belief common to all the participants in the conversation.

thataboy (ðæ·tăboi), *int. slang* (chiefly U.S.). Also **that a boy, thatta boy,** etc. [Corruption of *that's the boy* (cf. *THAT *dem. pron.* B. 1 b), or alteration of *ATTABOY *int.*] An exclamation of encouragement or admiration; = *ATTABOY *int.*

1936 J. DOS PASSOS *Big Money* 287 'All right, let's go,' he said. 'Thataboy,' roared Farrell. **1975** M. BOSSE *Man who loved Zoos* iv. 96 'What should I tell Hopkins?' 'Tell him..I'm not up a blind alley yet.' 'Thatta boy.' **1978** M. PUZO *Fools Die* xi. 114 Frank patted me on the shoulder. 'That a boy,' he said.

that-a-way (ðæ·tăwēⁱ), *adv.* Chiefly *dial.* and *U.S.* Also **thataway, that a way,** etc. [f. THAT *dem. adj.* + AWAY *adv.*] **1.** In that direction.

1839 *Southern Lit. Messenger* V. 378/2, I expect, Tommy, you're *a* sparking that *a* way. **1847** *Paddiana* I. 139 It's very careless I hear they are that aways. **1866** H. JACKSON *Gilbert Rugge* II. xii. 174 Down in the marsh lands, that-a-way. **1901** J. PRIOR *Forest Folk* iv. 41 It's out o' my road or I'd show yer; that-away. **1920** M. WEBB *House in Dormer Forest* vii. 89 'I canna see as it's to be found out,' he nodded sideways towards the murmur, 'that-a-way.' **1973** *Washington Post* 13 Jan. B8/7 'Bonanza', the Western series that went thataway a couple of weeks ago after a 14-year ride on the NBC network. **1978** G. MCDONALD *Fletch's Fortune* (1979) xviii. 127 He went thet-away.

2. In that manner; like that.

1887 *Scribner's Mag.* Sept. 366/1, I hadn' 'a' thought ye'd 'a' evidenced agin me that-a-way. **1889** *Spectator* 26 Oct. 549/2 Whin I sees him that a way the second time, your Reverence. **1938** M. K. RAWLINGS *Yearling* v. 46 'You want to tote lunch?' she called after him. 'I'd not insult my neighbors that-a-way. We'll noon with them.' **1959** *Times Lit. Suppl.* 9 Jan. 15/3, I didn't mean to treat her that-a-way. **1973** K. GILES *File on Death* iii. 72 You bloody well don't do it thataway.

thatch, *sb.* Add: **2. b.** orig. and chiefly *U.S.* A matted layer of plant debris, moss, etc., on a lawn; the material of this layer.

1955 *How to install & care for Your Lawn* 59/1 Opening up a thatch of interwoven stolons and stems can be difficult. **1964** *Book of Lawn Care* (N.Y. Times) iii. 15 Because of its rapid growth, this grass has a tendency to form a heavy mat or thatch. **1977** *Western Living* (Vancouver) Apr. 61/1 Power raking for the removal of moss 'thatch' in spring often does harm to the turf. **1980** *Amat. Gardening* 4 Oct. 16/3 Another cause of moss is 'thatch', a layer of dead, moisture retentive grass and debris that builds up on the lawn's surface.

3. b. *U.S.* Tall, coarse grass.

1622 *Relation Eng. Plantation Plimoth, New England* 25 Some of our people being abroad, to get and gather thatch, they saw great fires. **1695** in *Early Rec. Providence, Rhode Island* (1894) VI. 156 That Parcell of Meadow marsh & thatch..belongeth to me. **1797** B. TRUMBULL *Compl. Hist. Connecticut* I. iii. 24 There grew bent grass, or as some called it, thatch, two, three and four feet high. **1863** D. G. MITCHELL *My Farm of Edgewood* 49, I gave them [*sc.* bees] a warm shelter of thatch. **1951** E. GRAHAM *My Window looks down East* iv. 34 Salt hay and thatch, or evergreens, are piled around the houses to insulate against the cold.

4. *thatch-roofed* adj. (earlier example).

1774 J. TRUMBULL *Poet. Wks.* (1820) II. 210 The thatch-roof'd hamlet and defenceless shed..are their fate.

Thatcherite (þæ·tʃərəit), *sb.* and *a. Pol.* [f. the name *Thatcher* (see def.) + -ITE¹.] **A.** *sb.* One who supports the views or policies of Mrs. Margaret Thatcher (b. 1925), British (Conservative) politician, who became Leader of the Opposition in 1975 and Prime Minister in 1979. **B.** *adj.* Of, pertaining to, or characteristic of Mrs. Thatcher or Thatcherism.

1976 *Economist* 17 Apr. 13/2 Tory constituency rooms were by 1974 fuller of anti-Butler Thatcherites than Mr Heath dreamed. **1977** *Times* 16 May 11/7 The Thatcherite philosophy can be summed-up in two words, 'non-interference'. **1980** J. BOYD-CARPENTER *Way of Life* xxiv. 265 The Thatcherite view accepts the..thesis that 'equality of opportunity means equal opportunity to be unequal'. **1982** *Daily Tel.* 3 Apr. 18/4 The Thatcherites..are genuinely trying to restore the private sphere, to bring back a world fit for gentlemen. *Ibid.* 11 Aug. 8/1 With the exception of that large part of the Labour party which is now authentically Bennite, we are all, to a greater or lesser extent, Thatcherites now.

So **Tha·tcherism,** the political and economic policies advocated by Mrs. Thatcher, esp. as contrasted with those of earlier Conservative leaders.

1979 *Times* 24 Nov. 2/2 The party was fighting off the shrill divisiveness of Thatcherism, with its simple monetarist policies. **1981** GLYN & HARRISON *Brit. Econ. Disaster* v. 138 Many workers..see Thatcherism as an outmoded nineteenth century ideology with little relevance to contemporary economic reality. **1982** *Daily Tel.* 11 Aug. 8 At heart, Thatcherism is a liberal economic reaction to the collectivism and corporatism of the past 40 years.

thatching, *vbl. sb.* Add: **3. thatching-beetle,** a thatcher's mallet.

1874 HARDY *Far from Madding Crowd* II. vi. 77 Where's your thatching-beetle and rick-stick and spars?

thatchy, *a.* Delete *rare* and add: Also, like thatch. Also *Comb.* (Further examples.)

1944 E. BLUNDEN *Cricket Country* v. 61 The sweetest of hamlets and thatchiest of little old inns. **1952** L. MACNEICE *Ten Burnt Offerings* 30 Like a sick bird..Its thatchy feathers moulting. **1973** T. PYNCHON *Gravity's Rainbow* I. 28 The flooded quarries and logged-off hillsides they'd left..across all that thatchy-brown, moldering witch-country.

Thathanabaing (þaþā:năbai·ŋ). [a. Burmese, f. *thathana* teaching, instruction (f. Pali *sassana*) + *baing* to possess.] The chief Buddhist dignitary in Burma.

1839 H. MALCOM *Trav. S.-E. Asia* I. II. vi. 315 The highest functionary is the *Tha-thena-byng*, or archbishop. **1858** P. BIGANDET *Life Gaudama* 252 In our days, the power of the Thathana-paing is merely nominal. **1912** *Rangoon Gaz.* 31 Oct. 19/1 A rectangular pandal, the central position of which was assigned to the Thathanabaing (Buddhist Archbishop) and his learned sadaws. **1934** 'G. ORWELL' *Burmese Days* xv. 234 A big heathen idol..fell down on top of the thathanabaing, that is Buddhist bishop. **1972** A. T. Q. STEWART *Pagoda War* xiii. 151 The *Thaihanabaing*, the hierarch whom the English generally referred to as 'the Buddhist Archbishop', had formerly been recognized throughout Burma as the Head of the Buddhist Church.

thattaboy, thatta boy, varr. *THATABOY *int.*

thaumatin (þǭ·mătin). *Biochem.* [f. *Thaumat*(*ococcus*, mod.L. generic name (f. THAUMATO- + COCCUS) + -IN¹.] Either or both of two related sweet-tasting proteins isolated from the fruit of the African plant *Thaumatococcus daniellii.*

1972 VAN DER WEL & LOEVE in *European Jrnl. Biochem.* XXXI. 221/1 This paper deals with the isolation and characterization of the sweet principles we call thaumatin I and II. *Ibid.* 225/2 The thaumatins are the first sweet-tasting proteins that have been found in nature **1973** [see *MONELLIN]. **1980** *Nature* 24 Apr. 653/2 Tate and Lyle..are to apply recombinant DNA techniques to improve production of the protein thaumatin—a substance 2,500 times sweeter than a 10% sugar solution.

thaw, *sb.* Add: **2. b.** (Earlier example.)

1840 M. EDGEWORTH *Let.* 30 Dec. (1971) 575 Lord Monteagle seated himself..beside Miss Edgeworth who had..made him rather a drawback stand-off curtsey... He seemed determined there should be a thaw.

c. *Pol.* A relaxation of control or restriction; a lessening of harshness, hostility, etc.; *spec.* that which occurred in the U.S.S.R. after the death of Stalin in 1953.

1950 *Times* 13 June 5/3 The statement on foreign policy is the latest symptom of a thaw in Labour doctrine. **1956** R. MACAULAY *Towers of Trebizond* ii. 19 She had started..working away at Russian visas..some time before the Great Thaw. **1957** *Economist* 30 Nov. 787/2 When the Polish thaw made emigration again possible, some of these 'autochthons' joined the queue. **1969** A. G. FRANK *Latin Amer.* xxi. 338 In the countries that took the Marxist road there was an increase in freedom or a noticeable thaw after a relatively short period of time. **1971** *Guardian* 13 Sept. 10/1 Krushchev inaugurated the thaw that mitigated some of the harsh intolerance of Stalinist communism. **1981** *Times* 2 Nov. 8/7 Andrei Voznesensky, arguably Russia's greatest living poet..mirrored the hopes and naivety of the post-Stalin thaw.

3. *thaw-water*; *thaw-cold* adj.

1917 D. H. LAWRENCE *Look! We have come Through!* 156 They are the flowers of ice-vivid mortification, thaw-cold, ice-corrupt blossoms. **1947** K. M. WELLS *Owl Pen Reader* (1969) i. 38 He bumped and slithered over the ice the thaw had laid bare. He splashed through thaw water. **1976** *Times Lit. Suppl.* 23 July 926/3 Lush new green and blue sky reflected in the thaw-waters.

thaw, *v.* Add: **2. a.** (Earlier U.S. example with *out.*)

1835 J. H. INGRAHAM *South-West* I. 33 When vessels in their winter voyages..become coated with ice,..they seek the genial warmth of this region to 'thaw out'.

thawed, thawing *ppl. adjs.* (later examples).

1942 W. FAULKNER *Go down, Moses* 238 Out of the wet and thawing woods. *Ibid.* 240 They plunged down the bank, slipping and sliding in the thawed earth.

thawing, *vbl. sb.* Add: Also *attrib.*, and with *out* (or *up*).

1905 *Kynoch Jrnl.* Oct.–Dec. 200 Many consumers..put frozen cartridges in thawing pans several hours before they are required. **1946** KOESTLER *Thieves in Night* 150 Ellen was engaged in a serious and measured conversation... Dina took no part in the thawing-up proceedings. **1973** 'R. MACLEOD' *Nest of Vultures* v. 97 A large whisky gently completing the thawing-out process.

the, *dem. adj.* ('*def. article*') and *pron.* Add: **B. I. 3. b.** (Further examples.) Also forming part of the present and former names of certain countries, as *the Argentine, the Congo, The Gambia, the Lebanon, the Sudan, the Yemen*; with the names of streets, *locally* with ellipsis of the word *Street.*

1853, etc. [see *HIGH *sb.* 1 c]. **1920** G. BELL *Let.* 14 Mar. (1927) II. xviii. 484 On my way home I went to see Frank Balfour..and heard from him the afternoon's news which was that Faisal had been crowned King of Syria and Abdullah King of the Iraq. **1951** DUKE OF WINDSOR *King's Story* xii. 209 Britain had an investment of £400,000,000 in the Argentine. **1959** *Chambers's Encycl.* VIII. 431/2 In internal affairs the Lebanon had to face considerable economic and financial difficulties after the end of the 1939–45 war. *Ibid.* XIV. 796/1 In March 1958 a federal link was established between the Yemen and the United Arab Republic. **1959** *Even. Standard* 31 Dec. 8/6, I am home from the Argentine and would like to link up with some of my old friends. **1975** J. I. M. STEWART

Gaudy xii. 225 The industrious little whirr of his camera was for a moment the only sound in the Broad. *Ibid.* 228, I had crossed Broad Street and was walking down the Turl. **1981** *Church Times* 6 Nov. 14/5 The Hoopoe had nested in his walls when he was in the Yemen. **1984** *Times* 18 Feb. 1/2 Princess Anne's four-day visit to The Gambia brings an extra air of festivity and importance to a tiny African country.

6. Also with names of paintings and sculptures.

1705 ADDISON *Remarks on Several Parts of Italy* 349, I have seen on coins..the Hercules Farnese, the Venus of Medicis, the Apollo in the Belvidere, and the famous Marcus Aurelius on Horseback. *a* **1706** EVELYN *Diary* an. 1693 (1955) V. 147, I..saw & indeede admired the Venus of Coreggio. **1845** *Encycl. Metropolitana* IX. 408 The Apollo Belvidere, the Venus de Medicis, and the Laocoon, have for ages been regarded as the highest possible models of excellence. **1984** *Times* 13 Sept. 13/4 Difficult to think of an art theft with greater sex appeal than that of the Mona Lisa.

7. (Further examples.)

The degree of ellipsis is not easy to determine.

1823 COBBETT *Gram. Eng. Lang.* XIX. 131 It is the same word, you see, in both instances; but you will see it different in the French. **1922** CHESTERTON *Eugenics & Other Evils* I. i. 11, I am content to answer that 'chivalrous' is not the French for 'horsy'. **1934** WEBSTER p. lxxxii/1, The modern descendants of the Latin are called the Romance languages. They include the Italian, the Spanish, the Portuguese [etc.]. *a* **1965** B. HIGGINS *Northern Fiddler* (1966) 34 'I'm corrupt' he said to me in the French, 'I think I live in corruption's stench.'

8. a. (Further examples.)

Still in common use side by side with forms without the definite article.

1961 I. FLEMING *Thunderball* i. 10 His secretary had gone down with the flu. **1972** *Time* 17 Apr. 41/2 Shortly before he was scheduled to make his first space flight aboard Apollo 13 two years ago, the longtime bachelor.. was accidentlly exposed to the German measles.

b. With colloq. or humorous names of afflictions, as *the blues, collywobbles, creeps, D.T.'s, habdabs, heebie-jeebies, jitters,* etc., q.v. in Dict. and Suppl. Hence in analogous nonce-expressions.

1976 *Publishers Weekly* 11 Oct. 90/3 The case of the 'cutes' infecting text and pictures. **1976** *Listener* 11 Nov. 626/2 The whole story, like the chateau, has an unmistakable touch of the Enid Blytons.

10. a. (Later examples of formal use with titles of rank. In informal use *the* is usu. omitted.)

1935 C. HAMILTON *Pillion* 25 He was the third son of Colonel the Hon. Almeric Sounds Sharnal Piers Clement Piers, late of the Rifle Brigade. **1939** E. BAX *Miss Bax of Embassy* xviii. 238 Someone is always dashing in to ask me questions like...is Lady V. *The* Lady or only Lady? **1943** H. SAUNDERS *Combined Operations* vii. 52 Admiral of the Fleet Sir Roger Keyes was succeeded as Director of Combined Operations by Captain the Lord Louis Mountbatten. **1981** *Daily Tel.* 5 Nov. 16/2 Her Majesty's Body Guard of the Honourable Corps of Gentlemen-at-Arms under the command of the Lord Denham.

d. (Earlier example.) Also *slang* and sometimes *derogatory,* with a woman's surname or nickname. Cf. *LA, LA.

1730 O. SWINY *Let.* 29 July in R. B. Peake *Mem. Colman Family* (1841) I. 18 If he does not, then we must provide a soprano man, and a contr'alto woman (though the Merighi stays). **1922** *Dialect Notes* V. 143 [At] Somerville..'The Pen' is the Lady Principal, Miss Penrose, 'The Darb', Miss Derbyshire, etc. **1930** WODEHOUSE *Very Good, Jeeves!* iv. 96 The Bellinger..had sung us a few songs before digging in at the trough. **1973** —— *Bachelors Anonymous* xii. 155 The Fitch was at the hair stylist's having a permanent.

15. b. (Further examples.)

1780 COWPER *Progress of Error* in *Wks.* (1905) 29 The creature is so sure to kick and bite, A muleteer's the man to set him right. **1813** JANE AUSTEN *Pride & Prej.* I. xiii. 142, I shall not be the person to discourage him.

16. c. With a sb. characterizing the trade or profession of the person whose name precedes. *local* (esp. in Wales).

1894 SOMERVILLE & 'ROSS' *Real Charlotte* I. iv. 40 Norry the Boat, daughter of Shaunapickeen, the ferryman (whence her title). **1951** W. MORUM *Gabriel* II. vii. 230 He thought Larry the Groan far worse. The effeminate singer..was positively embarrassing. **1974** *Times* 27 Apr. 15/8 The Welsh tradition of referring to people by the names of their jobs, as Jones the Post or Davis the Bread. **1980** R. H. LEWIS *Cracking of Spines* vii. 113 'The prospective client,'..I assumed a Welsh accent. 'Matt the Book.'

II. 21. Also forming phrases with the preposition *on,* as *on the cheap, quiet, sly,* etc., q.v. in Dict. and Suppl.

D. as *sb.* with pl. *thes.*

1882 'MARK TWAIN' *Stolen White Elephant* 269 You [English] say 'out of window'; we always put in a *the.* **1907** —— *Chr. Sci.* II. viii. 239, I uncover to that imperial word... The rare and..exclusive company of the THE's of deathless glory..*the* Saviour..*the* Bible. **1959** *Amer. Speech* XXXIV. 111 The Syrian student tends to put in *the*'s where they are not needed. **1977** *Guardian Weekly* 4 Dec. 4/1 If you are really serious about something and want to be taken seriously yourself, never, ever, under any circumstances, sully its name by putting a 'the' in front of it.

‖ **thé** (te). [Fr., = tea.] † **1.** A tea-party. *Obs.*

1788 H. MORE *Let.* 22 May (1925) 123 A *Thé* is among the stupid new follies of the winter. You are to invite fifty or a hundred people to come at eight o'clock..tea and coffee are made by the company,..and what constitutes the very essence of a *Thé,* an immense load of hot buttered rolls and muffins. **1802** C. WILMOT *Let.* 3 Jan. in T. U. Sadleir *Irish Peer* (1920) 22 We have had.. Plays, Balls, Soirees, Thés, &c.; the first Thé was at Monsieur Amoulin's. **1827** E. GROSVENOR in G. Huxley *Lady Elizabeth & Grosvenors* (1965) vii. 136 On Friday we are to have a thé at the Viceroy's.

2. Phrases. **thé complet** [Fr., lit. 'complete tea'], a light meal including tea and usu. bread and cake; cf. *café complet* s.v. *CAFÉ 3; **thé dansant**: see *DANSANT, DANSANTE *a.*

1951 E. COXHEAD *One Green Bottle* v. 113 She darted away with another *thé complet.* **1967** N. FREELING *Strike out where not Applicable* 113 The Dutch 'thé complet' accessories..sandwiches. Glacé fours. Dry petits fours. Fan wafers.

theatre, theater, *sb.* Add: **2. a.** *saloon theatre* (earlier example) (*obs.* exc. *Hist.*).

1864 G. A. SALA *Robson* 14 Early in 1844 he accepted an engagement at the Grecian Saloon Theatre, in the City Road.

b. *N. Amer.* and *N.Z.* A picture theatre, cinema.

1923 H. CRANE *Let.* 5 Oct. (1965) 149 [Chaplin] is here in New York..to see that the first film he has produced in it [*sc.* a new studio] gets over profitably... It's running now..at the 'Lyric' theatre. **1956** H. KURNITZ *Invasion of Privacy* ii. 20 Do I want to book that man's pictures in my theatres? **1966** G. W. TURNER *Eng. Lang. in Austral. & N.Z.* viii. 176 'Theatre' nearly always a 'picture theatre' or cinema in New Zealand. **1977** *Chicago Tribune* 2 Oct. (TV Week Suppl.) 2/1, I went to the theater and saw George Segal and Goldie Hawn in 'The Duchess and the Dirtwater Fox'.

3. c. (Later examples.) Also, the drama of a particular time or place; dramatic art as a craft, the theatrical profession. Phrases: *theatre-in-the-round*: see *ROUND *sb.*[1] 5 d; *Theatre of Cruelty* [tr. F. *théâtre de la cruauté* (A. Artaud (1932) *Manifeste du théâtre de la cruauté*)], a collective term for plays in which the dramatist seeks to communicate a sense of pain, suffering, and evil through the portrayal of extreme physical violence; *Theatre of the Absurd,* a collective term for plays (chiefly French) portraying the futility and anguish of man's struggle in a senseless and inexplicable world (cf. *ABSURD *sb.*); also *fig.*; *Theatre of Fact,* documentary drama.

1908 E. TERRY *Story of my Life* xiv. 332 The life of an actress belongs to the theatre. *Ibid.* 333, I have had many friends outside the theatre, but I have had very little time to see them. **1938** R. G. COLLINGWOOD *Princ. of Art* xiv. 323 In the Renaissance theatre collaboration between author and actors on the one hand, and audience on the other, was a lively reality. **1955** G. GORER *Exploring English Character* ii. 14 Of the theatre I know of, only the Burmese drama of the second half of the nineteenth century approaches the Elizabethan in its search for horror. **1976** J. ARCHER *Not a Penny More, Not a Penny Less* xvi. 174 Harvey recognized Dame Flora Robson, the actress, who was being honoured for a distinguished lifetime in the theatre. **1977** S. BRETT *Star Trap* IV. xiii. 143 He is a hard-working performer with a great belief in the live theatre.

1954 E. BENTLEY *In Search of Theater* II. vii. 198 Antonin Artaud's 'theatre of cruelty', that theater of Dionysian energy and visionary power. **1958** M. C. RICHARDS tr. *Artaud's Theater & its Double* vi. 79 '*Theater of cruelty*' means a theatre difficult and cruel..on the level of performance, it is not the cruelty we can exercise upon each other..but the much more terrible and necessary cruelty which things can exercise against us. **1964** *Punch* 21 Oct. 627/3 To watch the 'Theatre of Cruelty' season safely on the audience side. **1973** J. ELSOM *Erotic Theatre* x. 190 The one adjective which cannot be used to describe the Theatre of Cruelty evening is, however, *unexpected.*

1961 M. ESSLIN *Theatre of the Absurd* 17 The Theatre of the Absurd strives to express its sense of the senselessness of the human condition and the inadequacy of the rational approach by the open abandonment of rational devices and discursive thought. **1962** [see *ABSURD *sb.*]. **1963** *Sunday Times* 24 Feb. 24/5 They deserved to win, but two of the goals they scored came straight from the theatre of the absurd. **1977** P. JOHNSON *Enemies of Society* xix. 253 We must not be surprised to find that the United Nations..should have become the World Theatre of the Absurd, a global madhouse where lunatic falsehood reigns.

1966 *Punch* 7 Dec. 864/1 Together they make up the most successful example so far of the Theatre of Fact, a gripping story, the clash of widely different personalities and many sharp remarks on the relationship between Science and Government. **1970** *Times* 9 Feb. 5 *Murderous Angels* is another example of the Theatre of Fact... The two main characters are Dag Hammarskjold and Patrice Lumumba. **1974** *Encycl. Brit. Macropædia* XVIII. 232/2 The Brecht approach to stage presentation has something in common with the Theatre of Fact.

e. Without article or pl. (chiefly predicatively). With a descriptive adjective: theatrical or dramatic entertainment (of a specified quality); esp. in *good theatre* (see *GOOD *a.* 1 f); also used *transf.* of an action or work of art that has the quality of (good, etc.) drama or theatrical technique; hence *fig.,* dramatic effect or sensation, spectacle, outward show without serious inward intent.

1926, etc. [see *GOOD *a.* 1 f]. **1927** *Sunday Times* 27 Feb. 6/4 'The Letter' is superb theatre throughout. **1934** *Sun* (Baltimore) 1 June 12/1 Superb tennis and 'goop theater' have never been so generously mixed in the performance of any other player. **1939** A. THIRKELL *Before Lunch* iv. 96 It would have been rather too much theatre to awaken heroine with soft music, don't you think? **1948** A. J. P. TAYLOR *Habsburg Monarchy* i. 12 Austrian Baroque civilisation..was grandiose, full of superficial life, yet sterile within: it was theatre, not reality. **1951** in M. McLuhan *Mech. Bride* (1967) 89 They bring real 'theater' to a sales presentation. **1955** W. W. DENLINGER *Compl. Boston* II. 9 Some of the competition exercises are almost useless; some I consider pure 'theatre' and others are practical. **1958** *Listener* 2 Oct. 499/2 You have to admit that the Old City is good theatre. **1965** *Ibid.* 21 Oct. 630/2 Standing spotlit at the end of a great black-draped room all by itself, it [*sc.* a piece of sculpture]..was above all dramatic. It was, in its way, even great theatre. **1975** J. O'FAOLAIN *Women in Wall* xii. 211 She encourages zeal and all she gets is theatre... This sort of thing was new to the convent.

5. b. A room in a hospital specially designed for surgical operations (orig. one resembling a theatre, for the performance of such operations before observers); = *operating-theatre* s.v. OPERATING *vbl. sb.* b.

1641, 1766 [in Dict., sense 5]. **1823** *Lancet* 5 Oct. 3/1 At half-past Seven this Theatre was crowded in every part, by upwards of four hundred Students, of the most respectable description; in fact we never before witnessed so genteel a Surgical class. **1935** MARSH & JELLETT *Nursing-Home Murder* iii. 38 In the anteroom of the theatre two nurses and a sister prepared for the operation. **1976** J. ARCHER *Not a Penny More, Not a Penny Less* xii. 129 Although the hospital had only some 200 beds, the theatre was of the highest standard.

6. c. A particular region or one of the separate regions of the world in which a war is being fought. Also *theatre of war.*

1914 W. S. CHURCHILL *Let.* 15 Oct. in M. Gilbert *Winston S. Churchill* (1972) III. Compan. I. 193 The hand of war will I expect be heavy upon us in the Western Theatre during the next four weeks. **1928** BLUNDEN *Undertones of War* xv. 160 (*heading*) Theatre of War. **1940** W. S. CHURCHILL *Into Battle* (1941) 261 Far larger operations no doubt impend in the Middle East theatre. **1958** E. BIRNEY *Turvey* vii. 76 Turvey straightened his helmet and marched down the gangplank into the European Theatre of War. **1961** G. F. KENNAN *Russia & West* viii. 118 Real fighting took place between Allied and Bolshevik forces only in one theater, in the Russian north. **1977** C. MCCULLOUGH *Thorn Birds* xv. 352 The biggest and most decisive battle of the North African theater had been fought.

9. a. *theatre audience, bill* (example), *hat* (example), *house* (later example), *man, people, stall, ticket* (examples); *theatre-loving* adj.

1936 *Vogue* 18 Mar. 101/2 The London theatre audience is still all dressed in black and white. **1977** S. BRETT *Star Trap* xiii. 143 It doesn't bear comparison with the contact you can get with a live theatre audience. That's electrifying. **1895** G. B. SHAW *Our Theatres in Nineties* (1932) I. 1 It is not a work of art at all: it is a mere contrivance for filling a theatre bill. **1930** Theatre hat [see *JULIET]. **1977** *N.Y. Rev. Bks.* 29 Sept. 12/4 On the rickety stages of a thousand provincial theater houses, alternative worlds blazed like magic by limelight. **1846** GEO. ELIOT *Let.* 1 June (1954) I. 219 Please to come in a very mischievous, unconscientious, theatre-loving humour. **1933** P. GODFREY *Back-Stage* viii. 112 Every experienced theatre-man knows that there is ample room for criticism inside the theatre. **1961** *Guardian* 6 Mar. 9/4 Some knowing theatre-men say it would have flopped.. even a few years ago. **1952** E. WILSON *Shores of Light* 382, I did not want to see the theater people again; I could not face another evening. **1907** G. B. SHAW *Let.* Dec. (1972) II. 739 With..society out of town during the parliamentary recess, theatre stalls have been empty. **1902** A. C. HEGAN *Mrs. Wiggs of Cabbage Patch* vi. 73 Couldn't you use a whole load [of kindling], if I was to take it out in..theayter tickets? **1980** P. G. WINSLOW *Counsellor Heart* v. 94 Up for a day in town, to get theatre tickets.. and then go shopping.

b. theatre club, a theatre for which tickets are sold only to members (esp. in order to circumvent the censorship of public performances); **theatre-goer** (earlier example); **theatre-going** *sb.* and *adj.* (earlier examples); **theatre-list** *Med.,* a list of patients about to undergo surgical operations; **theatre nurse** *Med.,* a hospital nurse qualified to assist in the operating theatre; **theatre organ** = *cinema organ* s.v. *CINEMA c; hence **theatre organist; theatre party**: for *U.S.* read orig. *U.S.* and add earlier and later examples; **theatre-restaurant,** a restaurant where theatrical entertainment is provided for customers; **theatre seat,** (*b*) a seat that may be booked for a performance at a theatre; **theatre sister** *Med.,* in a hospital, nursing-home, etc., a sister qualified to assist in the operating theatre; **theatre suit** *Fashion* (see quot. 1969); **theatre workshop,** a non-commercial theatre company concerned esp. with experimental and unconventional theatrical productions; orig. and *spec.* a company founded by Joan Littlewood and others in 1945 and based in the East End of London from 1953 to 1973.

1961 R. WILLIAMS *Long Revolution* II. vi. 267 The growth of 'free theatres' and theatre-clubs. **1978** R. HOLLES *Spawn* iv. 31 Marianne had met him..at a theatre club in Notting Hill Gate. **1870** *Boston Transcript* 1 Nov. 2/4 If the theatre is not crowded.., we shall be much disappointed in our estimation of the taste of Boston theatre-goers. **1846** B. I. LANE *Mysteries of Tobacco* 11 The classical theological, feat-haunting, theatre-going, card-playing Reverend Gentleman. **1852** GEO. ELIOT *Let.* 15 June (1954) II. 36 Between theatre-going and proof-reading, my spiritual eyes are burning as dim and bleared as gas-lights. **1964** G. L. COHEN *What's Wrong with Hospitals?* i. 17 A student will undertake the pre-medication of patients on theatre-list. **1934** P. BOTTOME *Private Worlds* xxxi. 302 Matron..is a first-rate surgical nurse... The theatre nurse is about too, in case we want her. **1959** T. S. ELIOT *Elder Statesman* II. 45, I feel in love with him During an appendicitis operation! I was a theatre nurse. **1930** R. WHITWORTH *Electric Organ* xvi. 156 The building of theatre organs has..helped to bring electric..actions to their present state of efficiency. **1977** *Lancashire Life* Nov. 101/1 The story of Ronald Curtis and theatre organs is in effect the chronicle of a love affair which began in his childhood. **1932** R. WHITWORTH *Cinema & Theatre Organ* ix. 105 The cinema or theatre organist fills a very important rôle. **1883** *Cent. Mag.* Sept. 787/1 A report.. of Mrs. Dash's theater party. **1884** L. TROUBRIDGE *Life amongst Troubridges* (1966) 170 To a theatre party on the 15th and supper after. **1962** J. F. POWERS *Morte d'Urban* viii. 164 The Cathedral curates..wangled an invitation to the Saturday-morning theatre-parties. **1958** *Hotel & Catering Rev.* Oct. 35/1 The only theatre restaurant of its size and type in the world. *a* **1911** D. G. PHILLIPS *Susan Lenox* (1917) II. xviii. 421 A clever play that'll draw the damn fools who buy theater seats. **1982** C. CASTLE *Folies Bergère* vii. 254 As a student..the only theatre seat he could afford was in the gallery. **1935** MARSH & JELLETT *Nursing-Home Murder* iii. 37 Tell the theatre sister I'll operate as soon as they are ready. **1976** C. STORR *Unnatural Fathers* i. 10 The staff nurse on the surgical side who deputised for the theatre sister. **1964** MRS. L. B. JOHNSON *White House Diary* (1970) 202, I changed into my black theater suit en route. **1969** R. T. WILCOX *Dict. Costume* 107/2 *Dinner* or *theater suit*, the feminine 'covered-up' look for evening of the 1930's and '40's, consisting generally of a long black skirt, a delicate blouse, a cummerbund and short jacket. **1945** *Westmorland Gaz.* 4 Aug. 4/9 Addresses were given by Miss Joan Littlewood ..now in Westmorland with the Theatre Workshop, a new venture aimed at furthering the arts in local towns. **1962** *Guardian* 7 Nov. 7/6 A theatre workshop is about to be started in Dublin. **1973** E. BULLINS *Theme is Blackness* 10 Some of the Black Arts approaches and techniques that Marvin X and I had developed in revolutionary theater and literature workshops on the Coast. **1981** *Sunday Tel.* 20 Dec. 16/5 The Arts Council refuses it [*sc.* the D'Oyly Carte Company] a grant—preferring its own East End revolutionary theatre workshops.

c. *attrib.* Designating nuclear weapons for use within a 'theatre' (at present thought of as Europe) as opp. to intercontinental or strategic weapons (cf. *STRATEGIC *a.* 2), or their targets.

1977 *Observer* 3 Apr. 12/4 In a tactical role, Backfire.. is ideally suited to attacking local or 'theatre' targets in Western Europe. **1978** *Orbis* XXII. 309 The United States has deployed a varied array of theater-nuclear weapons and delivery systems in Europe. **1980** *Daily Tel.* 18 June 1/2 Theatre nuclear missiles..have a longer range than battlefield weapons but cannot be fired as far as intercontinental missiles. **1983** *Chicago Sun-Times* 26 Nov. 5/2 'What worries us is the buildup of theater nuclear forces in Europe,' Defense Undersecretary Fred C. Ikle said.

theatrette (þī·ătəre·t). [f. THEATR(E *sb.* + -ETTE.] A small theatre.

1927 *Melody Maker* Sept. 849/3 Things soon went wrong at his Leicester Square Theatrette. **1972** *Malay Mail* 27 May 1/7 The building..will house a theatrette for 200.

theatric, *a.* (*sb.*) Add: **B.** *sb. pl.* **2.** orig. *U.S.* Doings of a theatrical character; theatrical behaviour, effects, or mannerisms; theatricality.

1929 W. FAULKNER *Sartoris* i. 3 With his race's fine feeling for potential theatrics he drew himself up. **1958** A. MILLER *Coll. Plays* iii. 18 Plays..had been written for a theatrical performance, when they should have been written as a kind of testimony whose relevance far surpassed theatrics. **1964** L. HANSBERRY in J. H. Clarke *Harlem* 136 The..little committees..have dragged on their particular obscene theatrics for all these years. **1972** *Time* 2 Oct. 52/2 A desperate device intended to lend a little spine to the sponge-cake theatrics [in a film]. **1977** *Daily Tel.* 12 July 17/6 The 'theatrics' of the Church are important to many Catholics and, in a way, this is what Lefebvre offers. **1983** *Times* 24 Aug. 5/2 Today's so-called peace movement—for all its modern hype and theatrics—makes the same old mistake.

theatrical, *a.* Add: **A.** *adj.* **4.** Special collocations, as *theatrical agency, agent*, an agency, agent whose business is to act as an intermediary between actors and actresses seeking parts and producers offering them.

1825 P. EGAN *Life of Actor* ii. 62 We are engaged at the Harp to meet Mr. Schemer, the theatrical agent, to-morrow night. **1828** J. EBERS *Seven Yrs. King's Theatre* vii. 196 Been actively engaged in theatrical concerns, and the business of theatrical agency. *a* **1911** D. G. PHILLIPS *Susan Lenox* (1917) II. v. 126 She read an advertisement of a theatrical agency. **1973** D. RAMSAY *Deadly Discretion* 111 Why not go to Actors' Equity and theatrical agencies and dance studios? **1978** *Detroit Free Press* 2 Apr. 13c/5 Marco talks Mrs. Hopkins into letting him stay on as boarder by becoming her theatrical agent.

B. *sb.* **1.** *pl.* Now usu. *amateur theatricals.*

1873, etc. [see *AMATEUR 3 a]. **1892** G. & W. GROSSMITH *Diary of Nobody* viii. 118, I..totally disapproved of amateur theatricals. **1965** *Listener* 23 Sept. 462/3 He proved..fond of..amateur theatricals.

2. (Earlier example.) Also *transf.*, the theatrical column of a newspaper.

1763 D. GARRICK *Let.* 8 Oct. in R. B. Peake *Mem. Colman Family* (1841) I. iii. 84 God bless you! my dear Colman, and have a corner of your eye upon my theatricals. **1819** KEATS *Let.* 22 Sept. (1958) II. 176, I purpose living in town in a cheap lodging, and endeavouring, for a beginning, to get the theatricals of some paper.

theatrified (þi,æ·trifəid), *a. nonce-wd.* [f. THEATR(E *sb.* + -IFY + -ED[1].] Deluded by the conventions of popular drama.

1902 G. B. SHAW *Mrs. Warren's Profession* p. xxiv, People with completely theatrified imaginations tell me that no girl would treat her mother as Vivie Warren does.

theatrist (þī·ătrist). *rare.* [f. THEATRE *sb.* + -IST.] A lover or frequenter of the theatre; an expert in theatrical matters.

1889 E. DOWSON *Let.* 24 Dec. (1967) 120 Last night—lo what a theatrist I am becoming—I went to Benson's 'Midsummer Night's Dream'. **1905** M. BEERBOHM in *Sat. Rev.* 13 May 623/1, I do not mean that 'Salomé' has less dramatic than literary fibre. Mr. Wilde was a born dramatist—a born theatrist, too.

theatro-. Add: **theatrophone** (earlier example).

1889 *Telephone* I. 406/1 A 'theatrophone'..is an adaptation of the telephone, by which any one can be put into communication with a certain theatre.

‖ **theatrum** (te,ā·trŏm). [L.: see THEATRE, THEATER.] Theatre, playhouse.

1786 [see *ORCHESTRA 1 c]. **1890** E. DOWSON *Let.* 23 Feb. (1967) 139 We must try & work a theatrum this week. **1967** *Oxf. Compan. Theatre* (ed. 3) 36/1 The line of general development followed the 'Theatrum' of the Lyon Terence, absorbing on the way the lessons learned in the temporary spectacle-theatres.

‖ **theatrum mundi** (te,ā·trŏm mu·ndi). [L., = theatre of the world.] The theatre thought of as a presentation of all aspects of human life; *spec.* (see quot. 1932).

1566 J. ALDAY tr. P. Boaistuau (*title*) Theatrum Mundi, the Theatre or rule of the world, wherein may be sene the running race and course of everye mans life, as touching miserie and felicity, wherein is contained wonderfull examples, learned devices, to the overthrow of vice, and exalting of vertue. **1932** J. NICOLL tr. *von Boehn's Dolls & Puppets* II. i. 261 Gottfried Hautsch, who died in 1703,..constructed in Nürnberg a mechanical automaton with many figures, which was nicknamed his 'little world'. This is a kind of automaton which, to distinguish it from the others, is technically indicated by the term *theatrum mundi*. The *theatrum mundi* for centuries provided the traditional afterpiece of the wandering marionette theatres; by means of small movable figures running on rails it showed a diversity of scenes. **1953** W. R. TRASK tr. *Curtius's European Lit. & Lat. Middle Ages* vii. 140 A *theatrum mundi*, then, with men as actors, Fortune as the stage director, and Heaven as spectator. **1966** H. B. HAWKINS in *Shakespeare Q.* XVII. 174 The idea of the *theatrum mundi* was widely known in the Renaissance, and a number of themes..came to be associated with this concept. The idea that the world itself was God's theater gave cosmic significance to the contemporary stage. **1967** *Listener* 8 June 744/1 Television offers an almost Elizabethan comprehension of the world; it is the new *theatrum mundi*. **1979** C. E. SCHORSKE *Fin-de-Siècle Vienna* v. 227 Klimt..presents the world to us as if we were viewing it from the pit, a *theatrum mundi* in the Baroque tradition... The Baroque *theatrum mundi* was clearly stratified into Heaven, Earth, and Hell.

Theban, *a.* and *sb.* Add: **A.** *adj.* **2.** (Later example.)

1962 E. COLLEDGE *Mediæval Mystics of England* 15 The hermit settlements of the Theban desert.

B. *sb.* **2.** The variety of Greek spoken in Bœotian Thebes. *poet. rare.*

1820 SHELLEY *Oedipus Tyrannus* (1904) II. ii. 451 In plain Theban, that is to say, My name's John Bull.

thebe (þē·be). Pl. **thebe.** [a. Setswana, lit. 'shield'.] A currency unit in Botswana, equal to $\frac{1}{100}$ of a *PULA (sense 2). Also, a coin of this value.

1976 *Botswana: Ten Years of Progress 1966–76* 17 The Bank of Botswana will ultimately perform all of the functions of a modern central bank. Its first task has been to conduct the issuance of the new notes (Pula) and coins (Thebe) in 1976. **1976** *N.Y. Times* 15 Aug. 6/1 The new unit—the pula, which will be divided into 100 thebe—will have the same value, however, as the rand, which ceases to become legal tender in this country as of Aug. 23.

theca. Add: **3. b.** In full *theca folliculi.* A layer of hormonally active cells enclosing a tertiary (vesicular) or a mature (Graafian) ovarian follicle, consisting of an inner, vascular layer (*theca interna*) and an outer, fibrous layer (*theca externa*). [So named in Ger. by C. E. von Baer (*Über Entwickelungsgeschichte der Thiere* (1837) II. III. xv. 23).]

1857 DUNGLISON *Dict. Med. Sci.* (rev. ed.) 400/1 *Folliculi Graafiani*, small spherical vesicles in the stroma of the ovary, which have at least two coats; the outer termed ovicapsule..and theca folliculi. **1859** R. B. TODD *Cycl. Anat. & Physiol.* V. 551/1 The external or vascular coat [of the Graafian follicle]..constitutes the tunic of the ovisac of Barry, the tunica fibrosa, S. theca folliculi of Baer. **1929** [see *LUTEINIZED *ppl. a.*]. **1930** MAXIMOW & BLOOM *Text-bk. Histol.* xxxii. 640 There is no sharp limit between the two layers of the theca or between the theca externa and the stroma. **1966** *McGraw-Hill Encycl. Sci. & Technol.* XI. 474/1 A growing follicle has several layers of follicular cells, or granulosa cells.., and a surrounding capsule of connective tissue, the theca folliculi. **1978** D. B. & W. J. WILSON *Human Anat.* xvi. 388/2 The inner layer is the theca interna, which secretes the hormone estrogen into the vascular system.

4. Special Comb.: **theca cell tumour** *Path.*, an œstrogen-secreting ovarian tumour that consists of cells resembling those of the theca folliculi and is sometimes malignant; = *THECOMA.

1937 *Amer. Jrnl. Obstetr. & Gynecol.* XXXIV. 988 It was not until 1932 that the last member of this interesting group of tumors was reported by Loeffler and Priesel, to which they gave the name of 'fibroma theca cellulare xanthomatodes ovarii', more commonly known as the theca cell tumor. **1974** PASSMORE & ROBSON *Compan. Med. Stud.* III. xxviii. 50/1 Luteinization of the cells of granulosa cell and theca cell tumours may occur.

thecodont, *a.* and *sb.* For '*Thecodontes*, an extinct family of saurians' substitute 'Thecodontia, an extinct order of primitive reptiles'. (Later examples.)

1933 A. S. ROMER *Vertebr. Paleontol.* viii. 170 An overgrown offshoot from the early thecodont stock was.. a large South African Lower Triassic form. *Ibid.*, Confined exclusively to the Triassic, the history of the thecodonts was a brief one. **1980** N. ORRISS tr. *Babin's Elem. Palaeontol.* xviii. 327 In the classical conception, birds originated directly from the Triassic thecodonts.

thecodontian (þīkŏdǫ·ntiăn), *sb.* and *a.* [f. mod.L. order name *Thecodontia* (R. Owen 1859, in *Rep. Brit. Assoc. Adv. Sci.* 163) + -AN: cf. THECODONT.] = prec.

1974 *Nature* 8 Mar. 168/2 The Saurischia and Ornithischia, are usually interpreted as independent derivatives of primitive thecondontian reptiles of the Triassic, but all known Triassic dinosaurs can be distinguished from typical thecodontians. **1979** *Ibid.* 17 May 234/2 Dinosaurs apparently lacked a fenestra pseudorotunda, as did the early thecodontians, eosuchians and captorhinomorphs.

thecoma (þīkōᵘ·mă). *Path.* [f. THEC(A + *-OMA.] = *theca cell tumour* s.v. *THECA 4.

1937 *Amer. Jrnl. Obstetr. & Gynecol.* XXXIV. 988 The luteoma, like the thecoma, is also a rare tumor. **1966** WRIGHT & SYMMERS *Systemic Path.* I. xxvi. 869/1 Although they may occur at any age, thecomas are most frequent in women between 50 and 60. **1981** A. D. T. GOVAN et al. *Path. Illustrated* xiii. 685 It has been suggested that fibromas found in ovaries are thecomas which have undergone fibrous degeneration.

thee, *pers. pron.* Add: **3.** (Later examples of use by Quakers or their relatives.) Now *rare.*

1926 *Amer. Speech* I. 638/1 Even in my boyhood in New England I heard very few Quakers who habitually said *thee.* **1950** B. RUSSELL *Let.* 6 Mar. in B. Strachey *Remarkable Relations* (1980) xxi. 312 What thee says about our marriage is very generous. **1964** *Friend* 10 Apr. 453/1 Perhaps thee has noticed the comment on this point in our *Friends Journal* on February 15. **1980** B. STRACHEY *Remarkable Relations* xxi. 314 Alys [Russell (1867–1951)] had been the last of the older ones; the last to say Thee and Thy.

theelin (þī·lin). *Biochem.* [f. Gr. θῆλυς female + -IN[1].] = *ŒSTRONE.

1930 C. D. VELER et al. in *Jrnl. Biol. Chem.* LXXXVII. 357 The isolation of the crystalline hormone seems to justify the selection of a new name... Accordingly, we suggest the term 'theelin'. **1935** [see *OESTRIN]. **1936** *Jrnl. Amer. Med. Assoc.* 10 Oct. 1222/2 The term theelin has not been widely accepted. *Ibid.* 1223/1 The Council [on Pharmacy and Chemistry of the American Medical Association]..decided (1) to adopt the system of nomenclature based on the root *estr-*; (2) to retain *theelin, theelol*..as synonyms for..*estrone, estriol.* **1947** *Sci. News* IV. 137 Among the substances administered to plants..are: the juice of leaves subjected to the 'right' length of day; yeast extract;..theelin.

So **thee·lol** [-OL] = *ŒSTRIOL.

1931 DOISY & THAYER in *Jrnl. Biol. Chem.* XCI. 642 We propose now, in view of the facts that the new substance is a trihydroxy compound and that it shows physiological and possibly chemical similarities to theelin, to name it theelol. **1936** [see above]. **1977** *Martindale's Extra Pharmacopoeia* (ed. 27) 1419/1 Oestriol. Estriol; theelol.

theeward, in phr. *to theeward*: see -WARD 6 c.

thegosis (þęgōᵘ·sis). *Zool.* [f. Gr θηγός sharp + -OSIS.] Tooth-grinding in animals as a means of sharpening the teeth.

1971 EVERY & KÜHNE in D. M. & K. A. Kermack *Early Mammals* 25 While shear edges are used in mastication, they lose their feature which they develop during a powerful and short action of sharpening. This action we call active wear or thegosis. **1974** *Nature* 30 Aug. 730/1 In mammals thegosis wear is accompanied by a second type of tooth wear, dental abrasion, which occurs at food/tooth interfaces during mastication.

theileria (þailīᵊ·riă). Also **Theileria.** [mod.L. (A. Bettencourt et al. 1907, in *Archives R. Inst. Bacteriol. Camara Pestana* I. 343), f. the name of Sir Arnold *Theiler* (1867–1936), South African zoologist + -IA[1].] A tiny, tick-borne protozoan parasite of the genus of this name, which includes those causing theileriasis.

1910 *Parasitology* III. 127 Observations on *Theileria* are fraught with considerable difficulty owing to the minuteness of the parasite. **1927** HALDANE & HUXLEY *Animal Biol.* xii. 279 Smallest parasitic Protozoa (Theileria in ox blood-corpuscle). **1979** *Nature* 5 July p. xiii (Advt.), The research will include the infection and transformation of bovine lymphocytes and other cell types by theileria parasites.

theileriasis (þailĕrəi·ăsis). Also **theilerio·sis** [f. *THEILERIA + *-IASIS, -OSIS.] An acute, usually fatal, feverish disease of cattle, sheep, and certain other vertebrates caused by a protozoan of the genus *Theileria* or a closely related genus and transmitted by ticks; cf. *East Coast fever* s.v. *EAST D. 1 b.

1944 *Indian Jrnl. Vet. Sci.* XV. 149 (*title*) Control of cattle theileriasis in calves in the Punjab. **1959** *Adv. Vet. Sci.* V. 241 The name theileriosis has come to designate any member of a group of diseases of vertebrates produced by several species of protozoan parasites belonging to the genera *Theileria, Gonderia,* and *Crytauxzoon.* **1962** J. A. SMYTH *Introd. Animal Parasitol.* ix. 109 This organism [sc. *Theileria parva*] is the cause of the deadly 'theileriasis' or East-Coast Fever in cattle. **1979** *Protozool. Abstracts* III. 38/1 A good review is given of theileriasis of cattle in India. **1979** *Nature* 5 July p. xiii (Advt.), There are in the laboratory of the Director of ILRAD two vacancies for immunologists to work on theileriosis.

theirn. Add: Also *U.S. dial.*

1836 T. C. HALIBURTON *Clockmaker* 1st Ser. x. 50 When other folks lost theirn from the boys, hisn always hung there like bait to a hook. **1896** 'MARK TWAIN' in *Harper's Mag.* Sept. 532/1, I hain't ever seen eyes bug out..the way theirn did. **1930** *Amer. Speech* V. 267 Such possessive forms as *ourn, yourn, hisn, hern* and *theirn* are almost universal in the Ozarks.

theistical, *a.* Add: **theistically** *adv.* (example).

1881 MAX MÜLLER tr. *Kant's Critique Pure Reason* II. 635 On one side, theistically, that there is a Supreme Being.

thelemic (þelī·mik), *a.* [f. Gr. θέλημα will + -IC, with reference to the abbey of Thelème in Rabelais; see THELEMITE.] That permits people to do as they wish; *spec.* designating the Satanist activities of Aleister Crowley (1875–1947).

1926 T. E. LAWRENCE *Seven Pillars* (1935) V. lix. 335 The Catholic Christians would counter them by demanding European protection of a thelemic order, conferring privileges without obligation. **1951** J. SYMONDS *Great Beast* III. xvi. 151 The intention of these two founders [*sc.* Sir Francis Dashwood and Aleister Crowley] of Thelemic Abbeys was different. *Ibid.* 152 Five rooms were planned around a central hall, the Sanctum Sanctorum, or the temple, of the Thelemic mysteries. **1956** —— *Ibid.* (rev. ed.) 155 Those *Orgia* which so shocked the readers of the *Sunday Express* and *John Bull*; although through ignorance of magic..these two papers could only hint at the nature of the Thelemic ceremonies. **1973** K. GRANT *Aleister Crowley & Hidden God* v. 73 Elaborate ceremonial and the establishment of fixed Lodges in specific localities would be superseded by a fluid and far-flung web comprised of Thelemic power-zones.

thelemite. (Later example.)

1973 K. GRANT *Aleister Crowley & Hidden God* v. 77 Thelema represents a necessary stage in the spiritual development of the individual. Paradoxically, no one can create or contribute anything original, or bring more to life than he takes from it, unless he is already a Thelemite. The term 'Thelemite' has a wider connotation than its hitherto exclusive use in Crowleian literature might suggest. The artist, the scientist,..the poet, is such only to the degree that he expresses his true will.

them, *pers. pron.* Add: **I. 1. e.** As objective case of *THEY 3 b. Hence phr. *them and us* used *attrib.*

1924 W. HOLTBY *Crowded Street* iii. 27 The magic circle of 'Them', the great ones. 'They' were the élite, the prefects and the games captains. **1945** H. NICOLSON *Let.* 27 May (1967) 465 People feel, in a vague and muddled way, that all the sacrifices to which they have been exposed.. are all the fault of 'them'—namely the authority or the Government. **1957** R. HOGGART *Uses of Literacy* iii. 62 To the very poor, especially, they compose a shadowy but numerous and powerful group affecting their lives at almost every point: the world is divided into 'Them' and 'Us'. **1962** *Listener* 8 Mar. 439/1 It is this feeling of being in a world that belongs to 'them' and not to 'us' that puts a strain on working-class children. **1966** *Guardian* 11 Oct. 3/1 The 'ordinary people' who looked on, who made..the Them and Us division [between cripples and other people]. **1980** A. CORNELISEN *Flight from Torregreca* x. 230 The vicious estrangements of a two-class, a Them-and-us society.

3. a. Also in phr. *them's my sentiments* (now freq. used humorously).

1847 THACKERAY *Van. Fair* (1848) xxi. 179 The sooner it is done the better, Mr. Osborne; them's my sentiments. *c* **1864** BROUGH & 'HALLIDAY' *Area Belle* 8 Cold mutton to begin with... Cut near the knuckle, with a little currant jelly if you've got it. Them's my sentiments. **1900** F. NIGHTINGALE *Let.* in C. Woodham-Smith *Florence Nightingale* (1951) xxiv. 590 'Drat' hockey and long live the horse! Them's my sentiments. **1924** E. M. FORSTER *Passage to India* v. 48 We're out here to do justice and keep the peace. Them's my sentiments. **1972** 'J. & E. BONETT' *No Time to Kill* viii. 100 'Them's my sentiments too,' he said. 'As Thackeray wrote,' she exclaimed in delight.

c. As nominative case of sense 1 e above.

1957 R. HOGGART *Uses of Literacy* iii. 62 'Them' is a composite dramatic figure, the chief character in modern urban forms of the rural peasant-big-house relationships. **1962** *Listener* 14 June 1044/2 With their use of Christian names in accusing one another of wilful misrepresentation they impressed me most with being collectively Them trying to get power from Us. **1970** *Guardian* 19 Nov. 1/4 In..the Talk of the Town restaurant, 'them' and 'us' dined last night to earn money for the world's wildlife.

thematic, *a.* (*sb.*) **A.** *adj.* **1. a.** Delete *rare* and add later examples.

1957 N. FRYE *Anatomy of Criticism* 367 Thematic; Relating to works of literature in which no characters are involved except the author and his audience, as in most lyrics and essays, or to works of literature in which internal characters are subordinated to an argument maintained by the author..opposed to fictional. **1974** R. QUIRK *Linguist & Eng. Lang.* iv. 75 There is formulaic and thematic structure..yielding striking if controversial theories about the composition of early English poetry. **1979** *N. & Q.* Feb. 63/2 The orientation of this anthology is essentially thematic.

c. Psychol. *Thematic Apperception Test*: a projective test designed to reveal a person's actual social drives or needs by means of the theme common to the interpretations which he gives to each of a standard series of pictures.

1935 MORGAN & MURRAY in *Arch. Neurol. & Psychiatry* XXXIV. 289 (*title*) Method for investigating fantasies. The Thematic Apperception Test. **1938** H. A. MURRAY et al. *Explorations in Personality* vi. 531 As the subjects who took this test were asked to interpret each picture—that is, to apperceive the plot or dramatic structure exhibited by each picture—we named it the 'Thematic Apperception Test'. **1957** P. LAFITTE *Person in Psychol.* 120 The Thematic Apperception Test is more abstract because of the deliberate vagueness of its pictures as well as the fantastic nature of some. **1981** L. KRISTAL et al. *ABC Psychol.* 189 Two of the best known projective tests are the Thematic Apperception Test..and the Rorschach Inkblot Test.

d. *Philately.* Applied to the collecting of stamps with designs which relate to the same subject, or to such a collection.

1951 R. J. SUTTON *Stamp Collector's Encycl.* 231 Thematic Collecting: Collecting to a theme or subject. **1965** E. H. SPIRE *Adventures in Stamp Collecting* ix. 111 It was ..only a logical development from selected collecting that brought about the advent of Thematic Philately. *Ibid.*, Collections of stamps depicting animals, flowers, ships, railways..and so on, are described as 'thematic'. **1972** *Police Rev.* 1 Dec. 1558 The American Topical Society has recorded more than one thousand subjects for thematic stamp collecting.

e. *Linguistics.* Of, pertaining to, or designating the theme of a sentence: see *THEME *sb.* 1 d.

1959, etc. [see *RHEMATIC *a.* 2]. **1969** K. H. WAGNER *Generative Grammatical Studies in Old Eng. Lang.* i. 52 In interrogative clauses..the initial constituent must be regarded as rhematic rather than thematic. **1977** J. LYONS *Semantics* II. xii. 506 *John Smith I haven't seen for ages.* Here the grammatical subject is 'I', but the thematic subject is 'John Smith'.

3. (Later examples.) Hence, of verb-forms: having a connecting vowel between the verb-stem and the suffixes or inflections.

1894 [see *ATHEMATIC *a.* 1]. **1933** *Language* IX. 82 The athematic verbs were primarily durative in aspect, while the thematic were momentary. **1933, 1955** [see *NON-THEMATIC *a.* 1 a]. **1972** *Language* XLVIII. 389 Except for certain 'thematic verbs', which are exceptional, the presence of a post-position is mutually implicative with the presence of an ind. obj. morpheme.

4. Of or pertaining to the division of the Byzantine Empire into 'themes' or provinces.

1911 E. FOORD *Byzantine Empire* xi. 203 The army—The thematic system and its development—Organization, arms, equipment, and tactics. **1933** S. RUNCIMAN *Byzantine Civilisation* iv. 90 The thematic tax-gatherers took orders directly from the central government. **1980** C. MANGO *Byzantium* I. ii. 46 The accepted view is that the 'thematic' reform was accompanied by a general fragmentation of the large estates.

B. *sb.* **2.** *Gram.* A thematic verb-form.

1968 *Language* XLIV. 717 The conventional view of the distribution of athematics and thematics seems to be that both types existed even in quite early Proto-Indo-European.

3. *Philately.* A collection of stamps with designs which relate to the same subject.

1972 *Police Rev.* 1 Dec. 1572/3 It was known as United Kingdom Thematics 1972, open to thematic entries from anywhere. **1979** *West Lancs. Even. Gaz.* 6 Apr. 18 (Advt.), Stamp collectors world-wide approvals and thematics.

4. *pl.* const. as *sing.* A body of subjects or topics of discussion or study.

1975 *Amer. Speech 1973* XLVIII. 125 Conklin's unique credentials..allow him to be catholic in his approach, both in terms of thematics and in his world-wide coverage. **1977** A. SHERIDAN tr. *J. Lacan's Écrits* v. 149 The thematics of this science is henceforth suspended, in effect at the primordial position of the signifier and the signified. **1980** *Encounter* May 34/2 Even if Dr Henry Kissinger's picture of a world of 'multi-polarity' is more a neo-Bismarckian fiction than a reality, the confrontation of two Super-powers describes neither the thematics nor the structure of world politics today.

thematization (þī:mătəizēⁱ·ʃən). [f. *THEMATIZE *v.* + -ATION.] **1.** The action of *THEMATIZE *v.* 2.

1955 T. BURROW *Sanskrit Lang.* iv. 153 This tendency to thematisation had already been operating in the prehistoric period. **1972** *Language* XLVIII. 399 The thematization process..is triggered by violations of canons of permissible plus and minus values of pronominal features for non-ergator and indirect object. **1977** *Ibid.* LIII. 50 Thus the form **somos* can be regarded as a partial thematization of the copula.

2. The action of *THEMATIZE *v.* 1.

1959 J. FIRBAS in *Brno Studies in English* I. 52 Whereas only two elements ([*the*] *girl* and *broke*) of the three in *The girl broke a vase* allow of thematization, any of the three elements occurring in *The girl broke the vase* can be thematized. **1969** K. H. WAGNER *Generative Grammatical Studies in Old Eng. Lang.* i. 50 In the abstract structure *Th* and *Rh* are empty places, i.e. they will not be expanded by subsequent rules. These places will be filled with constituents from the nucleus by transformation rules which may be termed rules of *thematization* and *rhematization*, respectively. **1977** J. LYONS *Semantics* II. xii. 507 It is certainly true that the processes that different languages make available for the thematization of one expression rather than another frequently involve putting the expression earlier rather than later in the utterance.

thematize (þī·mătəiz), *v. Linguistics.* [f. Gr. θεματ-, stem of θέμα THEME *sb.* + -IZE.] **1.** *trans.* To convert (part of a sentence) into a theme: see *THEME *sb.* 1 d.

1959 J. FIRBAS in *Brno Studies in English* I. 43 When thematic elements..occur in basically transitional or basically thematic positions, they communicatively weaken them, or so to speak, 'dedynamize', 'thematize' them. **1969** [see *RHEMATIZE *v.*]. **1976** *Archivum Linguisticum* VII. 145 The following functional constituents (derived from the mood system) may be thematized by fronting them.

2. To modify (a verb-form) by the addition of a thematic vowel: see THEMATIC *a.* 3 in Dict. and Suppl.

1966 E. P. HAMP in Birnbaum & Puhvel *Anc. Indo-Europ. Dial.* 115 **ĝhē(s)r-om*, thematized from **ĝhēsr.* **1977** *Language* LIII. 50 In addition, Isg. **esmi* was thematized.

Hence **the·matized** *ppl. a.*

1972 *Language* XLVIII. 402 We would expect **n-mi-* at the beginning of the relationship terms; instead we get the thematized form, a transitive construction. **1976** *Ibid.* LII. 68 Kuno proposes..that the deep structure of every relative clause in Japanese contains a thematized sentence.

Thembu *sb.* and *a.*, var. *TEMBU *sb.* and *a.*

theme, *sb.* Add: **1. d.** *Linguistics.* That part of a sentence which indicates what is being talked about. Cf. *RHEME.

1959, etc. [see *RHEME]. **1966** J. VACHEK *Linguistic School of Prague* ii. 18 'Functional' elements, the most important of which appear to be the *theme* and the *rheme* (the first being the basis of the statement, known from the context or situation). *Ibid.* v. 89 The *theme*, is that part of the utterance which refers to a fact or facts already known from the preceding context. **1969** K. H. WAGNER *Generative Grammatical Studies in Old Eng. Lang.* i. 48 There is evidence supporting the hypothesis that O.E. is a *theme-rheme* language. That is to say that unless certain factors intervene the most natural order of the elements of a sentence is that progressing from what is known to what is unknown, or rather from what has already been mentioned to what is newly introduced into discourse. **1977** *Language* LIII. 444 Like the article by Cinque, this one gets into the theme/rheme distinction.

3. (Later examples.) For 'now *rare*' read 'now *U.S.*'.

1924 [see *DRIP *sb.* 3 b]. **1955** E. B. WHITE *Let.* 1 Apr. (1976) 406 If you are engaged in writing a theme about my works, I think your best bet is to read them. **1976** *National Observer* (U.S.) 14 Feb. 17/3 In my spare time I go to college and the real reason is that it is here that this small flutter comes alive... Late at night when an English theme, which an hour ago had seemed impossible, starts to jell, I feel it.

8. *themebook*; **theme music,** music which recurs in a film, television programme, or the like; also = *signature tune* s.v. *SIGNATURE *sb.* 9; cf. *theme song, tune* below; **theme park** chiefly *U.S.*, an amusement park organized round a unifying idea or group of ideas; similarly **theme pub, restaurant; theme song, tune,** a song or tune which recurs in a musical play, film, or the like; also = *signature tune* s.v. *SIGNATURE *sb.* 9; also *fig.*; cf. *theme music* above.

1916 JOYCE *Portrait of Artist* (1969) i. 47 Father Arnall gave out the themebooks and he said that they were scandalous. **1957** MANVELL & HUNTLEY *Technique Film Music* 226 Martin and Gaston (1954). 'Theme Music'... Sound-track recording of the music from the English version of the French film on children's drawings. **1967** *Listener* 17 Aug. 222/3 Electronic music..is certainly not restricted to the novel presentation of sounds in familiar patterns, like the theme music of *Dr Who*. **1976** A. Davis *Television: First Forty Years* 136 The commercial was a favourite with viewers and with advertising men. It won awards and its theme music was issued on record. **1960** *Amer. Peoples Encycl. Year Bk.* 881 While most established parks and kiddielands were profitable, the theme parks, seeking to duplicate Disneyland's success, were often in trouble. **1967** *Encycl. Brit. Bk. of Year* 335/2 American-type theme parks around the world included Edenlandia Fun Park, Naples, Italy; Prater Fun Park, Vienna; and a new park, Centro de Diversion, opened at Puerto Rico's Isla Verde. **1983** *Times* 16 Aug. 15/3 The acquisition of a tourist attraction in London and a theme park outside the capital. *Ibid.* 19 July 17 A growth segment of the pub trade is emerging..theme pubs. Their hall mark is a design concept to create a particularly individual atmosphere (the theme) with varying combinations of restaurant, cocktail bar and normal bar service. Various theme restaurants have emerged in the past five years. *Ibid.* 4 Nov. 17/3 Grand Metropolitan's Host Group..is to spend well over £100m over the next three years on converting its outlets to a wide range of theme pubs. **1983** *9,000 Words* 196/2 Theme restaurants that look like railroad cars or Polynesian villages. **1929** Theme song [see *release *sb.*[1] 7 b]. **1946** Koestler *Thieves in Night* 348 The theme-song of all evolution is the trend towards greater articulateness. **1949** 'G. Orwell' *Nineteen Eighty-Four* II. 149 The new tune which was to be the theme-song of Hate Week..had already been composed. **1977** J. Fleming *Every Inch a Lady* III. vi. 141 Nathaniel returned to his theme-song..murder must have a plan, a blue-print. **1950** *Sport* 24–30 Mar. 15/4 'This couldn't happen again!' should be the theme-tune of Doncaster Rovers' fans. **1983** *Listener* 21 Apr. 30/3 The furore over the *Today* theme-tune..perfectly illustrates the BBC attitude.

theme *v.* (later example); also **themed** *a.*, having a theme.

1963 *Observer* 29 Sept. 7/4 A themed sequence on summer holidays. **1977** *Broadcast* 28 Nov. 12/2 There are.. possibilities for ethnic themed radio services. *Ibid.* 12/3 He continued the themed service subject. **1979** S. Brett *Comedian Dies* iii. 32 Great Expectations..was a concept restaurant, themed wittily around the works of Dickens.

themselves, *pron. pl.* **III.** (Later examples.)

a. *c* **1926** 'Mixer' *Transport Workers' Song Bk.* 92 Their ambition is theirself. **1969** in Halpert & Story *Christmas Mumming in Newfoundland* 159 They used to work theirself from all shapes. They have a couple of pillows up their back and another one on their stomach. **1979** N. Mailer *Executioner's Song* I. xxvii. 422 All they want to do is leave theirself a case for appeal.

γ. **1901** M. Franklin *My Brilliant Career* xxxiii. 277 A new fowl-house which 'Horace and Stanley built all by theirselves'. **1907** G. B. Shaw *Major Barbara* II. 241 Arf the street prayed; an the tother arf larfed fit to split theirselves. **1955** F. O'Connor *Wise Blood* x. 167 The unredeemed are redeeming theirselves and the new jesus is at hand! **1965** C. Brown *Manchild in Promised Land* xiii. 314 Them damn junkies take care of theirselves twice as good as you can.

then, *adv.* (*conj.*, *adj.*, *sb.*) Add: **B. 3. b.** Phr. *and then some*: see *some *indef. pron.* 4 f.

4. (Later examples of emphatic use in an apodosis.)

1925 L. Abercrombie *Idea of Great Poetry* i. 8 We have busied ourselves, if not on our own account, then vicariously in the newspapers, with the appreciation of these poets in their several qualities. **1956** A. J. Ayer *Probl. Knowledge* i. 7 Can it reasonably be held that knowledge is always knowledge that something is the case? If knowing that something is the case is taken to involve the making of a conscious judgment, then plainly it cannot. **1972** M. Kline *Math. Thought* li. 1194 This is the principle of *reductio ad absurdum*. In words, if the assumption of *p* implies that *p* is false, then *p* is false.

10. a. *then-current*, *-known*; **b. then-clause,** the apodosis in a conditional sentence.

1750 S. Richardson *Let.* 4 June (1964) 161 From robbery to robbery they proceeded, till they had enlarged their den so as to take in the greatest part of the then-known world. **1905** G. B. Shaw *Let.* 28 Sept. (1972) II. 563 She subscribed to the philosophy of a then-current song, 'I Want What I Want When I Want It'. **1927** G. A. Grierson *Ling. Survey India* I. I. 376 If the conditional sentence is such a one as we would require the use of 'would' or 'would have' in English, the word *sik* is appended to the apodosis, or then-clause. **1962** *John o' London's* 22 Feb. 188/3 *Would* is often used to express a wish..as in..the *then*-clause of a conditional sentence, as in 'You would enjoy it if you went'. **1976** *Scotsman* 24 Dec. (Weekend Suppl.) 3/2 The military republic of Julius Caesar that ruled the then-known world. **1978** *Detroit Free Press* 5 Mar. c 24/5 (Advt.), The interest..will be recalculated..at the then-current regular passbook interest rate.

thenabouts. Delete *rare* and add further examples. Also (rarely) **thenabout.**

1843 Dickens *Martin Chuzzlewit* (1844) xiii. 164 Five year ago, or thenabout. **1922** *Times Lit. Suppl.* 19 Oct. 664/2 If Archdeacon Brandon..must go down, it is then or thenabouts that go down he will. *a* **1967** A. Ransome *Autobiogr.* (1976) i. 18 When I first came to fish the Beela ..in 1930 or thenabouts.

Thénard's blue (te·nāɪz blū). The name of a bright blue pigment of considerable stability invented by the French chemist Louis-Jacques *Thénard* (1777–1857), consisting essentially of cobalt aluminate; cobalt blue.

1837 *Penny Cycl.* VII. 301/1 Phosphate of Cobalt..is used in making a pigment known by the name of Thenard's or Cobalt Blue. **1911** *Encycl. Brit.* XXI. 599/1 Several mixed cobalt compounds..represented by cobalt violet and Thénard's blue. **1958** *Listener* 2 Oct. 514/2 With their vivid Thénard's blue, the gleaming black of some of the boots and of Dick Turpin's horse..they have a place with the painted fair-ground horses and roundabouts. **1974** *Encycl. Brit. Micropædia* IX. 930/3 In 1799 he [*sc.* Thénard] made a discovery that assured him prosperity—Thenard's blue, a pigment used in the colouring of porcelain.

thence-after. (Later examples.)

1921 B. Jarrett *English Dominicans* ix. 180 The boy finished what remained of his noviciate..and thenceafter was no longer interfered with. **1932** Belloc *Napoleon* iii. 182 Thenceafter, for a week or more, it was intrigue upon intrigue.

theo-. Add: **theoce·ntrism,** theocentric doctrine or belief, also (occas.) **theoce·ntricism;** **theomaniac** (earlier example).

1925 E. Underhill *Mystics of Church* x. 205 The best traditions of French spirituality, its lofty theocentricism. **1930** *Monument to St. Augustine* viii. 272 The apparent theocentrism of the Calvinist 'glory of God'. **1941** Theocentrism [see *anthropocentricism, anthropocentrism]. **1863** C. Reade *Hard Cash* III. ii. 53 Dr. Wycherley..put down any man a lunatic, whose intellect was manifestly superior to his own... Nor did the dead escape him entirely. Pascal, according to Wycherley, was a madman with an illusion about a precipice... Joan of Arc a theomaniac.

theocrasia (þīokrēⁱ·ziă). Also **-krasia.** [a. Gr. θεοκρᾱσία, a mingling with God.] = Theocrasy 1.

1913 *Encycl. Relig. & Ethics* VI. 422/1 The working of the *theokrasia* in the domain of religion and religious art. **1920** H. G. Wells *Outline Hist.* 496/2 A sort of theocrasia went on between Christianity and Judaism..and other competing cults. **1971** R. E. Witt *Isis* xi. 146 Bast was the intermediary when the process of theocrasia began.

Theocritean (þīǫkritī·ăn), *a.* [f. L. *Theocritus*, a. Gr. Θεόκριτος Theocritus, a Greek poet of Sicily, of the 3rd c. B.C.: cf. Sophoclean *a.*] Of, pertaining to, or characteristic of Theocritus or his writings, esp. his pastoral poetry; of the style of Theocritus; hence pastoral, idyllic. Also **Theo·critan** *a.*

1846 T. Keightley *Notes Bucolics Virgil* 73 He [*sc.* Virgil] was thoroughly imbued with the Theocritean poetry. **1879** [see *bucolicism]. **1896** *McClure's Mag.* VI. 467/2 With his [*sc.* Corot's] Theocritan spirit, he could see the fountain of Jouvence in the woods of Sèvres. **1910** *Daily News* 17 Oct. 3 All this is more real and more grim than Arcadia, but even Arcadia had its reality, and there is something of Theocritean sweetness penetrating the intimate truth of this book. **1935** L. MacNeice *Eclogue by Five-Barred Gate* in *Poems* 24, I am a shepherd of the Theocritean breed. **1969** V. de S. Pinto *City that Shone* xii. 293 A Theocritean flavour was given to our courtship by the fact that Irène had two white goats.

theodicaea (þīǫdisī·ă). *rare.* [App. an erron. Latinization of Fr. *théodicée* in the title of a work by Leibniz: see Theodicy.] = Theodicy.

1845 *Encycl. Metrop.* II. 659/1 Leibnitz fancied that.. he could construct a *Theodicæa*, in which the doctrines of theology should be reconciled with philosophy. **1883** J. Sibree tr. *Hegel's Lect. on Philos. of Hist.* 16 Our mode of treating the subject is, in this aspect, a Theodicæa [rendering G. *Theodicee*],—a justification of the ways of God..in indefinite abstract categories. **1974** *Times Lit. Suppl.* 18 Oct. 1161/2 The mysterious 'Spirit' which presides over, or constitutes, reality in the Hegelian scheme of things is supposed..to be pursuing in history a plan of which historical agents are largely or wholly unaware: that is why Hegel can claim to be offering a theodicaea.

theogonical, *a.* (Earlier example.)

1702 *Lives of Anc. Philosophers* p. xxvi, A Magus..was imploy'd to sing a theogonical hymn, as a powerful enchantment.

theologate. 2. (Earlier example.)

1879 H. Foley *Records Eng. Province Soc. of Jesus* V. 944 *The College of St. Beuno*... This extensive pile of building was erected in 1848–9 for a Theologate, or House of Divinity, by the late Father Randal Lythgoe, then Provincial.

theologian. Add: **d.** In sense 1 d of *theology.

1968 *Listener* 10 Oct. 469/2 To speak well of the past was a mortal sin and got you into trouble with the party theologians and eventually with the police. **1982** 'I. I. Magdalen' *Search for Anderson* II. ii. 147 We had the ideologists and the purists and the theologians.

theological, *a.* (*sb.*) Add: **3.** *transf.* In trivial or disparaging use: of, pertaining to, or characterized by dogma or abstract principles (as opposed to practical considerations); doctrinaire, academic.

1959 *Times Lit. Suppl.* 5 June 329/4 The 'theological' approach to Soviet Marxism..proves in the long run unsatisfactory. **1964** S. Brittan *Treasury Under Tories* II. vi. 196 The three Treasury ministers played straight into the Prime Minister's hands, by their theological stress on permitting no increase at all on government expenditure for the coming financial year in money terms (which meant cutting it in real terms). **1964** *Listener* 30 July 148/2 Mr Walt Rostow..referred to 'the whole insoluble theological issue' of control... 'Theological' has two senses... He was clearly using the second or vernacular meaning, which is 'as impractical and as irrelevant to the matter in hand as the study of the nature of God'. **1968** *Observer* 28 Apr. 8/3 The doctrinal arguments which used to involve Labour in theological warfare. **1979** H. Kissinger *White House Years* xviii. 719 It was a reflection on the theological nature of our China debate that many experts still regarded the 'solution' of the UN issue, liturgically, as the absolute precondition of any improvement in our relations with Peking. **1980** *Spectator* 2 Feb. 5/3 The dispute..nominally involves theological distinctions between 'News' and 'Current Events'.

theologically, *adv.* Add: Also in sense 3 of prec.

1973 *Times* 13 Oct. 14 There is a fundamental fascism of the left which is the real problem in the universities: they are theologically right, as they believe, and you are so wrong that you should even be denied the freedom to speak. **1978** *Guardian Weekly* 5 Feb. 5/5 The Government is no longer theologically wedded to it [*sc.* free trade].

theologico-. Add: *theologico-metaphysical* (earlier example).

1855 H. Martineau *Autobiogr.* (1877) I. 120 Trying my hand at a sort of theologico-metaphysical novel.

theology. Add: **1. a.** *Biblical theology*: orig. theology as a non-dogmatic description of the religious doctrines contained in the Bible, following J. P. Gabler's distinction, in 1787, between biblical and dogmatic theology; now usu. the exposition of biblical texts (both O.T. and N.T.), based on the presupposition that there is a common biblical way of thinking which informs the Bible as a whole.

[**1787** J. P. Gabler *Kleinere Theologische Schriften* (1831) II. 179 (*title*) De iusto discrimine theologiae biblicae et dogmaticae regundisque recte utriusque finibus.] **1846** C. W. Buch tr. *Hagenbach's Compendium Hist. of Doctrines* I. 5 In our opinion biblical theology is only to be regarded as the *foundation-stone* of the edifice..and dogmatic theology as the builder. **1888** *Encycl. Brit.* XXIII. 264/2 Biblical theology is the delineation of a section of religious ideas,—that section of which the traces and records remain in the Bible. **1904** A. B. Davidson *Theology of O.T.* i. 1 In Biblical Theology the Bible is the source of the knowledge, and also supplies the form in which the knowledge is presented. **1951** H. H. Rowley *Old Testament & Modern Study* xi. 312 Since the publication of Gabler's famous address in 1787, the correctness of the distinction which he drew between biblical and dogmatic theology has been accepted as axiomatic by the majority of scholars. **1958** *Listener* 14 Aug. 241/1 A new subject has appeared called Biblical Theology. This means that the Bible, or rather the New Testament, is now subjected to analysis in order to see what is the total message or picture that it contains. **1969** A. Richardson *Dict. Christian Theol.* 36/2 The question ..remains whether there can be a completely presuppositionless interpretation of any historical documents (as tended to be assumed by those who regarded biblical theology as a purely descriptive science).

b. Also *fig.*

1956 P. A. Larkin *Less Deceived* 36 Our garden, first: where I did not invent Blinding theologies of flowers and fruit, And wasn't spoken to by an old hat.

d. In trivial or disparaging use: a system of theoretical principles; an (impractical or rigid) ideology. Cf. *theological *a.* (*sb.*) 3.

1962 *Listener* 29 Mar. 551/2, I would also like to see a couple of first-class philosophers, who would..check the new brand of strategists, who have produced a complete theology, not only about the deterrent but about conventional weapons, and about morale and everything else. I think the spectacle of Whitehall trying to keep up with American theologies is too sad for words. **1973** *Times* 3 Oct. 14/4 There were also a few rival interpretations of Marxist theology. *a* **1974** R. Crossman *Diaries* (1976) II. 391 At S.E.P., this morning, we were discussing Paper 105, a brilliant demolition of the theology of PESC. **1980** *Times Lit. Suppl.* 8 Feb. 134/2 Like the farmers of Iowa in relation to China in a later period, they were impatient with the theology of diplomatic recognition.

theomorphism. (Earlier example.)

1822 tr. *Malte-Brun's Universal Geogr.* I. 576 *Theomorphism*, the religion of the Hindoos, is the best supported of all the ancient systems of worship; it still exists.

Theopaschite. Add: Also *attrib.*

1914 W. E. Beet *Medieval Papacy* 15 Uncompromising was the attitude of Hormisdas with reference to the so-called Theopaschite formula. **1971** R. Browning *Justinian & Theodora* iii. 102 His [*sc.* Justinian's] new 'Theopaschite' doctrine in the end contributed nothing to the religious unity of the empire.

theophagous, *a.* Add: (Later example in sense (*b*) of *theophagy*). **theophagy,** (*a*) (earlier example); (*b*) *Anthrop.*, the eating of meals at which the participants believe that they ingest a deity with the consecrated food. (Restrict nonce-wd. to *theophagite* and 'dyslogistic' to definitions in Dict.)

1875 Swinburne *Lett.* (1960) III. 49 Would the exalted privilege of theophagy be conceded to a believer in the identity of those two Beings? **1903** G. B. Shaw *Revolutionist's Handbk.* viii, in *Man & Superman* 209 We have relapsed into disputes about transubstantiation at the very moment when the discovery of the wide prevalence of theophagy as a tribal custom has deprived us of the last excuse for believing that our official religious rites differ in essentials from those of barbarians. **1912** *Encycl. Relig. & Ethics* V. 136/1 The chief among the reasons given for the correlated rite of theophagy. *Ibid.* 137/1 A more detailed account supplies a valuable type of such theophagous ceremonies. **1937** *Jrnl. Theol. Stud.* XXXVIII. 97 Notable also is the demonstration how slight evidence we have, not only that any one ever associated theophagy with the Dionysiac omophagy, but even that any one in the centuries with which we are concerned ever celebrated an omophagy at all. **1956** C. Winick *Dict. Anthropol.* (1957) 533/2 *Theophagy*, the practice of ingesting the god. It probably stemmed from the ancient habit of eating the sacred animal to secure blessing, grace, and identity with the deity.

theophany. Add: Also *transf.*

1962 Auden *Dyer's Hand* (1963) 256 The practical joker desires to make others obey him without being aware of his existence until the moment of his theophany.

theophanism: also, belief in theophanies.

1938 S. Beckett *Murphy* v. 81 An adherent (on and off) of the extreme theophanism of William of Champeaux. **1970** R. Manheim tr. *Corbin's Creative Imagination Ṣūfism* 52 Not to understand..Ibn 'Arabī's conscious intention..of expressing a divine love, would be..to close one's eyes to the theophanism on which this book insists.

theophilanthropist. Add: **theophilanthrope** (earlier example); **theophilanthropical** *a.* (example).

1801 W. Dupré *Lexicographia Neologica Gallica* 275 *Théophilantrope*,..a theophilanthrope. *Ibid.* 276 *Théophilantropique*.., theophilanthropical.

Theophrastian (þīofræ·stiăn), *a.* Also **-an, -ean.** [f. L. *Theophrastus*, a. Gr. Θεόφραστος, a Greek philosopher of Eresus in Lesbos (4th c. B.C.) + -IAN.] Of, pertaining to, or characteristic of Theophrastus or his writings, esp. his *Characters*, a set of thirty sketches on disagreeable aspects of human behaviour. So **Theophra·stic**, † **Theophra·stical** *adjs.*

1662 J. Sparrow tr. J. Boehme in *Remainder of Bks.: Apol. conc. Perfection* 132 Not Tinctured, according to the Cabalisticall, Theophrasticall, Roso-Crucian kind. **1924** *Public Opinion* 18 Jan. 53/2 Some charming little essay or Theophrastan Study. **1926** *Glasgow Herald* 8 Apr. 4 One of the earliest [Characters] which has the true Theophrastian ring. **1928** *Observer* 12 Feb. 4 Some of these Theophrastic 'characters' are very charming. **1962** W. & M. Kneale *Devel. Logic* iv. 190 Any account of modal syllogisms, either Aristotelian or Theophrastean.

theophylline. (Examples.)

1957 [see *ORAL *a.* 4 b]. **1976** *Lancet* 20 Nov. 1115/2 Theophylline..and caffeine have been shown to be strong prostaglandin antagonists and weak agonists. **1983** *Daily Tel.* 18 Aug. 8/6 The council found that tea has three bracing ingredients—caffeine which stimulates the nervous system, and theophylline and theobromine which relax muscles and stimulate the heart.

theoplasm (þī·,oplæz'm). *rare.* [f. THEO- + PLASM.] (See quot. 1901.)

1901 E. S. Hartland in *Folk-Lore* XII. 27 *Tilo*,..like the Siouan *Wakanda*, is found to be theoplasm, god-stuff, not a god fully formed and finally evolved. **1941** R. R. Marett *Jerseyman at Oxford* xi. 161 My conception of the process whereby both magic and religion had evolved out of the same 'theoplasm or god-stuff', as Hartland was for calling it.

theopolitics, *sb. pl.* (Later example.)

1945 in J. H. Whyte *Church & State in Mod. Ireland* (1980) iii. 71 The Catholic press. A study in theopolitics.

theorbist. (Later examples.)

1976 *Early Music* Oct. 414/2 Quantz wrote that the theorbist should sit behind the second harpsichord, between two cellists. **1980** *Early Music* Jan. 50/1 A lutenist and theorbist are shown in the orchestra in two contemporary drawings of the performance of *Teofane.*

theorem, *sb.* Add: **2.** A stencil. Also *transf.*, a design executed by means of a stencil. *Obs.* exc. *Hist.*

1824 *Federal Gaz.* 29 Apr. 1/5 Theorem painting on velvet..varnished theorems or theorems cut from any design..may be had. **1832** L. M. Child *Girl's Own Book* (ed. 4) 137 After all the parts are in readiness, lay your theorem upon your drawing paper, take a stiff brush of bristles..fill it with the colour you want. **1968** *Canad. Antiques Collector* June 21/1 Theorem Painting, designs painted on white cotton velvet, was an art introduced to America from England. Also known as Formula or, if on silk, Poonah painting. **1973** *New Yorker* 3 Feb. 40/3 Old theorems (stencilled paintings or watercolors done on velvet or paper by genteel housebound girls in the nineteenth century).

theoretic, *a.* Add: **5.** As the second element of parasynthetic adjs. formed from compound sbs. of the type *quantum theory.*

1930 *Acta Math.* LIV. 81 (*heading*) A maximal theorem with function-theoretic applications. **1971** E. C. Dade in Powell & Higman *Finite Simple Groups* viii. 249 To use the minimum of ring-theoretic machinery. **1973** *Times Lit. Suppl.* 9 Mar. 267/5 (Advt.), The systems are approached from two directions—proof-theoretic and model-theoretic.

theoretical, *a.* Add: **3. b.** (Further examples.)

1922 *Glasgow Herald* 30 Oct. 10 He was a brilliant theoretical chemist. **1936** *Proc. IRE* XXIV. 353 In our search for good emitters, very little aid can be obtained from the theoretical physicist. **1951** C. P. Snow *Masters* I. v. 48 One of the earliest theoretical chemists. **1958** J. Cleugh tr. *Jungk's Brighter than Thousand Suns* i. 17 Rutherford for his part did not hesitate to declare that it was the theoretical, not the experimental, physicists who were to blame for the confusion. **1968** J. J. C. Smart *Betw. Sci. & Philos.* 13 Theoretical physicists have far outstripped philosophers in their imaginativeness. **1980** *English World-Wide* I. 251 The importance of this book is that it is by a scholar who is generally considered to be a 'theoretical' linguist, but who is sympathetic to sociolinguistics and its implications for theory.

5. Used as *THEORETIC *a.* 5.

1920, etc. [see *QUANTUM-THEORETICAL *a.*]. **1934** [see *FIELD-THEORETICAL *a.*].

theoretician. (Later examples.)

1931 *Times Lit. Suppl.* 26 Mar. 255/2 The most articulate theoretician among the Russian film producers. **1954** [see *ACTIVIST]. **1959** K. R. Popper *Logic of Sci. Discovery* v. 107 The theoretician..shows the experimenter the way. **1970** *Physics Bull.* Apr. 150/2 These results..provide an incentive for theoreticians to tackle the much more complex problem posed by real finite nuclei. **1980** 'M. Fonteyn' *Magic of Dance* 288 He was by no means a dry, boring theoretician even though he wrote extraordinarily advanced books on dance.

theoreticism (þīore·tisiz'm). [f. THEORETIC *a.* (*sb.*) + -ISM.] (See quot. 1974.) So **theore·ticist** *a.*

1970 B. Brewster tr. L. Althusser in *Althusser & Balibar's Reading Capital* 8 One of the theses I advanced as to the nature of philosophy did express a certain 'theoreticist' tendency. More precisely, the definition of philosophy as a theory of theoretical practice..is unilateral and therefore inaccurate. **1974** *Science & Society* XXXVIII. 404 After 1965..Althusser responded to 'theoreticist' and 'positivist' readings of his texts by reformulating in particular his concept of 'philosophy' and its relationship to 'science'. *Ibid.* 421 This dialectical understanding..preserves method against three forms of reductionism and their corresponding ideologies: historical empiricism (historicism)..; structural idealism/empiricism..; and speculative idealism (theoreticism), which radically separates historical and structural analysis. **1981** *Times Lit. Suppl.* 6 Feb. 136/4 They were ..saturated in what would have been called—had the word not borne the double taint of 'jargon' and 'theory'—theoreticism.

theoretico-. Add: **theore:tico-histo·rical** *a.*, pertaining to both the theoretical and the historical sides of a subject.

1922 D. Ainslie tr. *Croce's Aesthetic* (ed. 2) II. vi. 241 Cesarotti purposed (1762) bringing out a great theoretico-historical book. **1970** B. Brewster tr. *Althusser & Balibar's Reading Capital* II. i. 73, I intended to interrogate Marx himself, to see where and how he had theoretically reflected the relationship between his work and the theoretico-historical conditions of its production.

theorism. (Earlier example.)

1820 T. Campbell *Let.* 14 July in W. Beattie *Life Thomas Campbell* (1849) II. 370 At times, perhaps, there is a little German theorism in it [*sc.* Arndt's conversation].

theorizing, *vbl. sb.* (Earlier example.) Also **the·orized** *ppl. a.*

1817 Coleridge *Biog. Lit.* I. xii. 258 The necessity of theorising. **1975** *Amer. Economic Rev.* LXV. 416/1 It is not obvious whether the net effect of all these shortcomings necessarily exaggerates the regression results in favor of the theorized results. **1979** *Internat. Jrnl. Sociol. of Law* VII. 319 The material that is reproduced here would undoubtedly be of considerable use in some more theorized or general analysis.

theory.[1] Add: **4. b.** *theory of knowledge, of logic, of naming.*

1828 J. S. Mill in *Westm. Rev.* IX. 155 A prodigious step in the theory of naming. *a* **1854** —— *Early Draft Autobiogr.* (1961) 135, I pushed on..to try whether I could do anything further to clear up the theory of Logic generally. **1885** *Encycl. Brit.* XVIII. 793/2 Epistemology (theory of knowledge, Erkenntnisstheorie). **1927** B. Russell *Outl. Philos.* xxiii. 248 Descartes..inaugurated two movements, one in metaphysics, one in theory of knowledge. **1966** R. M. Chisholm (*title*) Theory of Knowledge.

7. *theory-building* (later example), *-mad* adjs., *-making* adj. and sb., *-ridden* adj.; **theory-laden** *a.*, applied to a term, statement, etc., the use of which implies the acceptance of some theory; contrasted with *theory-free, -neutral* adjs.

1964 *Language* XL. 225 Spelling out..how its results have been incorporated into other experiments and theory-building. **1977** A. Giddens *Stud. in Social & Polit. Theory* i. 49 As Feigl says, most positivistically inclined authors today..recognize that observation statements cannot be entirely 'theory-free'. **1958** N. R. Hanson *Patterns of Discovery* i. 19 There is a sense..in which seeing is a 'theory-laden' undertaking. Observation of *x* is shaped by prior knowledge of *x*. **1977** A. Giddens *Stud. in Social & Polit. Theory* 12 The theory-laden character of observation-statements in natural sciences entails that the meaning of scientific contexts is tied-in to the meaning of other terms in a theoretical network. **1850** E. A. Poe in *Sartain's Union Mag.* Oct. 233/1 He must be theory-mad beyond redemption who, in spite of these differences, shall still persist in attempting to reconcile the obstinate oils and waters of Poetry and Truth. **1931** A. Huxley *Music at Night* 77 The theory-making mind. **1964** I. L. Horowitz *New Sociology* 31 Problems of this kind can be multiplied..in every sphere of sociology from poll-taking to theory-making. **1968** J. J. C. Smart *Betw. Sci. & Philos.* iii. 80 Observation reports can not be couched in theory-neutral language. **1977** A. Giddens *Stud. in Social & Polit. Theory* iii. 150 The 'orthodox view' has an answer which Habermas has apparently (although..not finally) rejected: correspondence to sensorily apprehended reality, grounded in the descriptions of a theory-neutral observation language. **1922** R. Fry *Let.* 6 Mar. (1972) II. 522, I don't take it to heart when you say that my pictures are the utterly dismal performances of a theory-ridden painter.

theosis (þi,ōu·sis). *Theol. rare.* [a. med.L. *theōsis*, ad. Patristic Gr. θέωσις deification.] Deification.

1875 J. W. Draper *Hist. Conflict between Relig. & Sci.* v. 126 The return of the soul to the universal Intellect is designated by Erigena as Theosis, or Deification. **1934** *Theology* XXVIII. 24 Both natures, therefore, can be correlated positively through the communion of qualities, *communicatio idiomatum*, in the theosis of the created by the Divine. **1967** *Eastern Churches Rev.* I. 246 This is a kind of *theosis* whereby the symbols become life-giving.

Theotiscan (þīoti·skăn). *rare.* [f. med.L. (8th–9th cent.) (*lingua*) *theotisca* (the) German (language), reflecting early forms of OHG. *diutisc*, G. *deutsch* (see DUTCH) + -AN.] (See quot.)

1817 Coleridge *Biog. Lit.* I. x. 203, I read through..the most important remains of the Theotiscan, or the transitional state of the Teutonic language from the Gothic to the old German of the Swabian period.

‖ **theotokion** (þīŏtǫ·kiǫn). *Eastern Church.* [eccl. Gr., f. θεοτόκος: see THEOTOKOS.] A *sticheron* or *troparion* addressed to the Mother of God; usu. the last in a series of stanzas.

1850 J. M. Neale *Hist. Holy Eastern Church* I. 832 The theotokion is simply a sticheron or troparion addressed to the Mother of God. **1880** *Encycl. Brit.* XII. 580/1 A 'theotokion', or ascription of praise to the mother of our Lord. **1961** D. Attwater *Christian Churches of East* I. 225 *Theotokos* (*Gk.*, *tokos*, childbirth), the Mother of God. *Theotokion*, a hymn in her honour.

theralite (þīᵊ·rălǝit). *Petrogr.* [ad. G. *theralith* (H. Rosenbusch *Mikrosk. Physiogr.* (ed. 2, 1887) II. 248), f. Gr. θηρᾶν to hunt, pursue: see -LITE, -LITH.] Any of a group of mafic, intrusive, igneous rocks that contain nepheline and calcic plagioclase.

1898 *Bull. U.S. Geol. Survey* No. 150. 197 This feldspar was determined as in part ordinary sanidine, in part a soda-lime feldspar, and the rocks were therefore made the types of a plutonic rock characterized by the mineral combination nephelite, soda-lime feldspar, and named theralite by Professor Rosenbusch. **1938** A. Johannsen *Descr. Petrogr. Igneous Rocks* IV. 222 Among rocks difficult to place are the shonkinites, theralites, and teschenites. On the basis of their limited extent and mode of occurrence as sills, small intruded masses, and border facies, the rocks are hypabyssal; on the character of their usual textures, they are plutonic. **1978** S. R. Nockolds in S. R. Nockolds et al. *Petrol. for Students* xvi. 177 Theralites appear to be rather rare but occur, for instance, as dykes cutting nepheline syenite in the Khibina complex, Kola Peninsula, U.S.S.R... Theralites are found also in the Lugar sill, Ayrshire.

therapeutic, *a.* Add: **1.** Also *loosely* in weakened use.

1970 *Daily Tel.* 11 Feb. 15 She doesn't get bad-tempered; she merely picks up the piece of patchwork she is working on. 'It is so peaceful and relaxing, quite therapeutic.' **1982** L. Chamberlain *Food & Cooking of Russia* 253 Bread-making in the last century was a continuous process rather than a therapeutic exercise on a wet afternoon.

3. Special collocations: *therapeutic community*, a residential unit comprising staff and certain classes of mentally or behaviourally disturbed patients run in a deliberately informal manner to encourage social reintegration and rehabilitation; *therapeutic index*, the ratio of the lethal or toxic dose of a drug to the therapeutically effective dose.

1964 G. L. Cohen *What's Wrong with Hospitals?* viii. 167 In the past decade, reformers have gone a step further, attempting to put inmate and authority on the same level: partners in a 'therapeutic community'. This endearing phrase originated at Belmont. **1977** *Lancet* 24/31 Dec. 1344/2 Common-milieu therapy, used by most therapeutic communities, is probably best regarded as re-educative psychotherapy. **1942** H. R. Rosenberg *Chem. & Physiol. Vitamins* 150 The therapeutic index [of vitamin B_1]..is extremely high. **1973** J. J. McKelvey *Man against Tsetse* iii. 200 It had a narrow therapeutic index, that is, a small difference between the 'curative' dose that would kill trypanosomes in human blood and the 'tolerated' dose beyond which the host would suffer damage.

therapeutical, *a.* (*sb.*) **a.** (Later examples.)

1950 G. B. Shaw *Farfetched Fables* Pref. 90 Such a public department should be manned not by chemists analyzing the advertized wares and determining their therapeutical value, but by mathematicians criticizing their statistical pretentions. **1952** E. Hobsbawm in *Granta* 15 Nov. 12/1 We did not take to politics for therapeutical or aesthetic reasons.

therapist. Delete *rare* and add later examples.

1917 G. B. Shaw in *Eng. Rev.* Dec. 490 A homœopath, or a bonesetter, or a serum therapist. **1937** *Brit. Jrnl. Psychol.* XXVIII. 109 He describes how the therapist.. is able through unconscious observation to conjecture the nature of the patient's unconscious processes. **1978** *Listener* 5 Oct. 430/3, I would describe psychotherapy.. as a treatment in which the doctor or therapist uses talking: first, to establish a relationship with the patient; secondly, to help him understand what is happening to him.

therapsid (þeræ·psid) *sb.* (and *a.*) [*a.* the name of the order *Therapsida* (R. Broom 1905, in *Rec. Albany Museum* I. 269), f. Thero- + Apsis: see -id[3].] A mammal-like fossil reptile of the order Therapsida; also as *adj.*, of or pertaining to an animal of this kind.

1912 *Rep. Brit. Assoc. Adv. Sci.* 581 The humble Therapsid-like mammal felt the impetus of its new-found power of adaptation. **1933** A. S. Romer *Vertebr. Paleontol.* xi. 229 The limbs in advanced therapsids are greatly changed from the primitive sprawling position. **1966** E. Palmer *Plains of Camdeboo* vi. 95 The first of the mammal-like reptiles, or Therapsids as these famous fossil reptiles of the Karoo are known, had been discovered in 1838. **1971** J. Z. Young *Introd. Study Man* xxix. 408 Probably we shall never know whether the therapsid reptiles possessed the features of the soft parts that are so characteristic of mammals. **1973** B. J. Williams *Evolution & Human Origins* vii. 103/1 The therapsids had developed mammal-like features in locomotion and in their dentition. **1979** C. Kilian *Icequake* i. 14 His sermons on President Wood..had been as boring as his lectures on therapsid endothermy.

therapy. Add: **1.** See also *group therapy* s.v. *group *sb.* 6 b.

2. As the final element in words denoting treatment by means expressed in the first element, as *actinotherapy, *chemotherapy, Psycho-therapy in Dict. and Suppl., *radiotherapy, *roentgenotherapy* s.v. *roentgen-, roentgeno-, etc.

Theravada (þerăvā·dă). [a. Pali, lit. 'doctrine of the elders'.] = *Hinayana.

[**1875** R. C. Childers *Dict. Pali Lang.* 545/1 The adj. *theravâdî (theravâda..)* means holding the orthodox doctrine.] **1882** W. Hoey tr. *Oldenberg's Buddha* i. i. 75 The Church of Ceylon remained true to the simple, homely, 'Word of the Ancients' (Theravâda). **1923** Ld. Ronaldshay *Lands of Thunderbolt* vii. 48, I shall refer to it as the Thera Vada—'the way of the Elders'—because this is the title which its adherents themselves prefer, the term Hinayāna being objectionable to them. **1959** *Encounter* Jan. 19 Theravada Buddhism stems directly from the Indian tradition. **1978** C. Humphreys *Both Sides of Circle* xii. 132 My own list, however, was far wider than Olcott's 'Fourteen Fundamental Principles', which were largely confined to the Canon of the Southern or Theravada school.

therblig (þə̄·ɹblig). [Anagrammatic formation by partial reversal of the name of its inventor, F. B. *Gilbreth* (1868–1924), American engineer and pioneer of time-and-motion studies.] In time-and-motion study, a unit of work or absence of work into which an industrial operation may be divided (see quot. 1921); a symbol representing such a unit.

1921 F. B. Gilbreth in *Bull. Taylor Soc.* June 128/2 We believe that there are but sixteen sub-divisions of a cycle of motions. They are called therbligs. They are as follows: 1. Search, 2. Find,..13. Transport, empty, 14. Rest for overcoming fatigue [etc.]. **1930** *Movie Makers* Nov. 687/1 The motions of the operator are broken down into fundamental motions known as 'therbligs' (Gilbreth spelled backwards). **1947** [see *micromotion]. **1948** Ghiselli & Brown *Personnel & Industrial Psychol.* xi. 279 The therblig type of classification of movements is important principally in such problems as changing the sequence of movements and in the elimination of unnecessary movements. **1963** *Engineering* 27 Dec. 826/3 Maynard intended to allocate time values to Gilbreth's therbligs. **1964** A. Battersby *Network Analysis* ii. 13 Two main sets of symbols are used: Gilbreth's 'therbligs' for motion study and the standard ASME (American Society of Mechanical Engineers) symbols for method study. **1975** *Daily Tel.* 11 Dec. 14/5 There are 18 therbligs altogether. Each has its own symbol and colour (e.g. 'search' is black, 'grasp' is red, 'use' is purple) and these can be used to construct simultaneous motion charts. **1976** W. H. Canaway *Willow-Pattern War* vii. 82 She was skilled..in lovemaking, and only now and then did you get the feeling that..in her mind there was a stopwatch and a work-study chart covered with therbligs.

there, *adv.* (*a.*, *sb.*) Add: **A.** *γ.* **thar** (now U.S. *dial.* and *colloq.*: see also sense B. 2 c (*c*) below).

1859 Bartlett *Dict. Amer.* (ed. 2) 477 A person wishing to imply that he is perfectly at home in any thing, says he is *thar*; a good hunter or fisher is also *thar*. **1885** *Weekly New Mexican Rev.* 29 Jan. 4/5 The Santa Rifles had their first drill at Alhambra hall last night... Nearly all the boys have 'been thar' before, and as a consequence, catch up the command very readily. **1887** [see Tchick *sb.*]. **1937** W. Blair in B. A. Botkin *Treas. S. Folklore* (1949) iv. iii. 645 Hello, thar, gin us 'Forked Deer', old fiddle-teazer. **1980** 'D. Shannon' *Felony File* i. 27 Thar's a big store, with a lot of different departments.

B. I. 2. b. Now also appended casually to exclamations of greeting, etc., as *hi* (or *hello*) *there!*, with varying purpose: freq. to attract attention or to express cordiality.

1589 [see Hollo, hollow *int.*]. **1840** [see Hallo, halloa *int.*]. **1885** [see *hi *int.* 2]. **1924** *Dialect Notes* V. 270 *Hi there*, (call or warning). **1945** T. Williams *Battle of Angels* ii. i. 33 *A girl*: Hello! *Val*: (amiably) Hello there. **1962** J. Braine *Life at Top* xv. 188 'Hello there,' I said, 'What's new?'

c. (*b*) *that there.* Used adjectivally and absolutely, often in *euphem.* reference to sexual activity, esp. in catch-phrase *you can't do that there 'ere* (see quot. 1933).

1819 Byron *Let.* 26 Oct. (1976) VI. 232 As to 'Don Juan' confess—confess—you dog—and be candid—that it is the sublime of *that there* sort of writing—it may be bawdy—but is it not good English? **1933** Squiers & Wark *You can't do that there 'Ere* in *Feldman's 41st Song & Dance Album* 37 As they took a kiss, The keeper shouted this: You can't do that there 'ere, so there! You can't do that there 'ere. You'd ought to know you 'ad, I'm sure, That that there 'ere's agin the law. **1937** *Even. News* 13 Apr. 8/3 The British Government gives vent to a 'John-Bullism', and says, after the abduction of a Hindu girl from within the border, 'You can't do that there 'ere!' **1962** Auden *Dyer's Hand* (1963) 406 How suitable, too, for a that-there poet that the room in which his 'Memoirs' were burned should now be called the Byron Room. **1974** P. Wright *Lang. Brit. Industry* xi. 96 Long before the song 'You can't do that there here', Northerners used *that there* as a euphemism for the sexual act. It is a standard phrase in the north when youngsters of both sexes are 'educating' themselves by discussing sex matters.

(*c*) Phr. *there's gold in them there* (freq. *thar*) *hills*, with reference to a potentially profitable enterprise or activity. Also allusively. orig. *U.S.*

1941 C. B. Kelland *House of Cards* xiv. 159 She heard him chuckle. 'Thar's gold in them thar hills.' **1961** J. L. Austin *Philos. Papers* vi. 129 There is gold in them thar hills. **1965** E. Gundrey *Foot in Door* xxxiii. 189 There's money in them thar pills—but very little else. **1976** *New Society* 16 Sept. 607/1 There's gold in them there sand-dunes, about 10 million people enjoyed a naturist holiday last year.

3. c. *there is*, usu. contracted to *there's* (with succeeding adj.): used in statements or exclamations in place of standard English *that is* or How *adv.* 7. *Welsh dial.*

1939 R. Llewellyn *How Green was my Valley* ii. 23 'Go on, boy,' Cedric whispered, 'there is soft you are to eat old cake.' **1951** E. Coxhead *One Green Bottle* v. 113 There's tantalising! Plenty of company and no time for a word. **1968** A. Laski *Keeper* vi. 68 There's sad, about Japhet; that was a good man. **1971** 'H. Calvin' *Poison Chasers* ix. 123 There's selfish you are, I had him saved up for myself.

7. (Further examples.) Hence *there-there* vb. trans., to soothe or comfort by saying these words.

1798 Jane Austen *Lett.* (1952) 42 There! I may now finish my letter and go and hang myself. **1840** T. C. Haliburton *Clockmaker* 3rd Ser. xx. 284 It's no such thing, says mother, quite snappishly; Sam is only twenty-one last Thanksgiving-day, and he was born just nine months and one day arter we was married, so there now. **1875** L. Troubridge *Life amongst Troubridges* (1966) 101 There now, if I haven't entirely forgotten to say anything about the boys. **1924** R. Macaulay *Orphan Island* xxi. 280, I suppose you think I'm in love with you. Well, I'm not, so there. **1938** D. Runyon *Furthermore* viii. 159 He.. starts whispering, 'There, there, there, my itty oddleums.' **1948** 'J. Tey' *Franchise Affair* iv. 39 Only one thing your Aunt Lin makes better than me..hot cross buns, and that's only once a year. So there! **1968** J. Sangster *Touchfeather* xv. 180, I was sobbing my heart out on his chest and he was there there-ing me all over the place. **1969** *Listener* 15 May 698/1 But Gwen was going to marry her lecherous tutor, so there. **1977** 'E. Crispin' *Glimpses of Moon* xii. 240 There, There, sir. **1977** C. Dexter *Silent World N. Quinn* 254 Joyce took the baby..and lovingly there-thered his raucous cries.

8. *there and back* (earlier examples); also as a catch-phrase reply (see quot. 1937).

1772 in S. Rosenfeld *Temples of Thespis* (1978) v. 78 Pd Mr. Richards..at 2 Guineas pr Day & expenses there & Back £62.5.0. **1803** G. Colman *John Bull* iii. ii. 32 Aye, he might have been there and back, over and over again; but my husband is slow enough in his motions. **1830** M. Edgeworth *Let.* 18 Oct. (1971) 419 This 'Trip to the Viaduct'..five shillings apiece there and *back*. **1937** Partridge *Dict. Slang.* 874/2 *There and back*, a c.p. reply to an impertinent or unwelcome inquiry 'where are you going (to)?': late C. 19–20. **1977** *Transatlantic Rev.* lx. 191 'Where are we going?' 'Oh, there and back,' said the cabbie, giggling.

IV. 12. c. *to have been there* (*before*) (colloq.): to have had previous experience of the activity or thing under review; to be fully conversant with or know something at first hand. orig. *U.S.*

1877 *Sat. Even. Post* in J. R. Ware *Passing Eng.* (1909) 24/1 Some reasons why I left off drinking whiskey, by one who has been there. **1913** A. Bennett *Great Adv.* i. ii. 46 But I'm not a young girl. If it's a question of the male sex, I may say that I've been there before. **1977** J. Wambaugh *Black Marble* (1978) viii. 106 Philo Skinner's been in this racket thirty years. Philo Skinner's *been* there, baby!

d. *in there* (U.S. slang): excellent, superlative (esp. of a jazz musician's performance); well-informed, *au fait.*

1944 D. Burley *Orig. Handbk. Harlem Jive* 104 Now, this skull was in there, Jack. **1945** L. Shelley *Jive Talk Dict.* 26 *In there*, superlative performance. **1955** Shapiro & Hentoff *Hear me talkin' to Ya* vii. 101 The Lincoln Gardens, of course, was still in there. **1958** J. Kerouac *On Road* i. i. 6 It took him just a few months..to become completely *in there* with all the terms and jargon. **1962** *Down Beat* 13 Sept. 37 A guy playing a horn has..gotta get in there.

16. a. (*b*) (earlier example); (*c*) = What did I tell you? (*d*) expressing resignation to an unpleasant fact.

1857 Dickens *Dorrit* ii. xxv. 536 All the people who had tried to make money and had not been able to do it, said, There you were! [**1863** H. E. P. Spofford *Amber Gods* 133 She couldn't hire him a nurse, and there he was.] **1883** 'Mark Twain' *Life on Mississippi* xlii. 431 The immortelle requires no attention: you just hang it up, and there you are. **1894** A. Conan Doyle *Mem. Sherlock Holmes* 142 'There you are!' said Holmes smiling. **1915** Conrad *Victory* iv. x. 373 'There you are!' Ricardo shrugged his shoulders philosophically. 'Can't be helped.' **1937** M. Sharp *Nutmeg Tree* xix. 250 '*We've* no business to talk about him. But there you are,' said Julia harshly, 'I'm the sort of woman any one talks to about anything. **1926** S. Jameson *Three Kingdoms* i. 49 I'm sure that's a revolting sentiment, and revoltingly sentimental, but there you are. **1953** L. P. Hartley *Go-Between* xiv. 173 It's a pity we have to shoot so many of them but there you are.

b. *there it is* = sense 16 a (*d*) above. Also with past tense.

1857 Trollope *Barchester T.* III. i. 10 There it is. If they haven't the spirit to enjoy it, the fault shan't be mine. **1884** 'Mark Twain' *Huck. Finn* xxxiii. 345 So there it was!—but I couldn't help it. **1904** H. James *Golden Bowl* I. xviii. 311 'It's not, at any rate,' she went on, 'my fault. There it is.' **1932** 'A. Bridge' *Peking Picnic* xxiii. 296 He had been hurt hideously, and it made her cry; she was nearly as much surprised as he, but there it was. **1954** R. Macaulay *Last Lett. to Friend* (1962) 196, I feel a little mean about the dear Chapel, but there it is. **1973** C. Sagan *Cosmic Connection* xxii. 150 We would not ordinarily consider the flatulence of cattle as a dominant manifestation of life on Earth, but there it is.

V. 17. b. thereamid (later example).

1901 G. Gissing in *Literature* 21 Dec. 572/1 Thereamid stood a girl, her eyes fixed upon the prospect of city roofs.

theremin (þe·rĕmin). Also **thérémin**, and with capital initial. [f. the name of its inventor, L. *Thérémin* (b. 1896), Russian engineer.] An electronic musical instrument in which the tone is generated by two high-frequency oscillators and the pitch controlled by the movement of the performer's hand towards and away from the circuit (see quot. 1971).

1927 *Times* 12 Dec. 11/1 Professor Theremin and his collaborator play duets for two 'theremins' and piano. **1934** S. Robertson *Devel. Mod. Eng.* x. 418 Miscellaneous examples..of the taking over of a surname..and using it as a common noun are *boycott*,..*theremin*, and *zeppelin*. **1950** Blesh & Janis *They all played Ragtime* x. 199 And then those long metal cylinders, different lengths. The players wore gloves and would pull on them and make weird sounds like a Theremin. **1971** *Daily Colonist* (Victoria, B.C.) 13 Feb. 25/5 Greenway, of Vancouver, will play a theremin. The instrument was developed and introduced to the public in 1920 by Leo Theremin, a Russian scientist. A box-like apparatus, it produced musical tones from two electric circuits running through vibrating radio tubes. The player stands in front of the theremin and moves his hands through the air... The left hand controls volume or tone, and the right hand raises pitch as it nears the instrument and lowers pitch as it moves away. **1974** *Times* 5 Feb. 11 Most illuminating of all were the live performances of Varèse's *Ecuatorial*,.. its original thérémin part now played by two..*ondes Martenot.* **1982** *New Scientist* 16 Dec. 753 Moog recently recorded her playing the theremin.

thereness. Delete *rare* and add later examples.

1929 D. H. Lawrence *Paintings D. H. L.* (Introd.) fo. 7 *verso*, All the host of other defiant..cats that have come back..to form and substance and *thereness*, instead of delicious nowhereness. **1958** *Listener* 20 Nov. 822/2 The immense Thereness of someone else. **1976** I. Murdoch *Henry & Cato* i. 196 All those would-be deep explanations are so abstract and so simple when confronted with the awful complex thereness of a relationship which has gone wrong. **1983** J. Jones *Dostoevsky* i. 7 Its absurd yet maddening thereness like that of the pea under the mattress of the princess.

the·reward, *adv. rare*$^{-1}$. [f. There *adv.* + -ward.] = Theretoward *adv.*

1922 Joyce *Ulysses* 378 Thereward carrying desire immense among all one another.

therian (þī^{ə}·riăn), *a.* (*sb.*) *Zool.* [a. mod.L. *Theria* (Parker & Haswell *Textbk. Zool.* (1897) II. 448), f. Gr. θήρ, θηρίον wild beast.] Of or pertaining to the subclass Theria, one of the four subclasses into which the class Mammalia is commonly divided. Also as *sb.*, a placental or marsupial mammal belonging to this subclass.

1960 *McGraw-Hill Encycl. Sci. & Technol.* XIII. 549/2 Therian mammals are characterized by the distinctive structural history of the molar teeth. **1971** *Nature* 23 Apr. 506/1 The 'cochlea' in birds and reptiles is only slightly curved, in contrast to the tightly coiled cochlea of therian mammals. **1974** D. & M. Webster *Compar. Vertebr. Morphol.* v. 99 The more generalized therians have a clavicle, extending ventromedially and articulating with the anterior portion of the sternum. **1977** *Sci. Amer.* Aug. 79/3 The marsupials have retained the basic ancestral therian reproductive pattern.

theriomorph (þɪ͡ᵊ·riomǭɹf), *sb.* and *a.* [f. Therio- + *-morph; cf. Theriomorphic *a.*]

A. *sb.* **a.** A representation of an animal form in art.

1913 [see *anthropomorph]. **1928** V. G. Childe *Most Anc. East* iv. 84 Some theriomorphs are made of just those variegated stones.

b. = Theromorph. Also *fig.*

1920 H. G. Wells *Outl. Hist.* i. vi. 24/1 These little Theriomorphs, these ancestral mammals, developed hair. **1934** A. J. Toynbee *Study of Hist.* III. 194 But he [*sc.* Wells] comes to grief in the recent annals of our own Western history when he has to size up that singularly etherialized theriomorph William Ewart Gladstone.

B. *adj.* Having the form or characteristics of a beast.

1969 H. Arendt *On Violence* (1970) 60 Why should we, after having 'eliminated' all anthropomorphisms from animal psychology (whether we actually succeeded is another matter), now try to discover 'how "theriomorph" man is'?

theriomorphism (þɪ͡ᵊ:riomǭ·ɪfiz'm). [f. Therio- + *-morphism; cf. Theriomorphic *a.*] The ascription to God or to a god of the form or characteristics of a beast.

1908 *Encycl. Relig. & Ethics* I. 538/1 The Annamese believes in..beings who can pass from one genus or species to another under certain conditions of space and time. Hence theriomorphism and totemism. **1912** H. M. Chadwick *Heroic Age* vi. 125 It may be remarked in passing that theriomorphism plays a very prominent part in the religious practices and conceptions of primitive peoples, and..we hear not unfrequently of a struggle between a god or national hero and some theriomorphic being whose sanctuary or attributes he appears to have taken over. **1930** A. S. Pringle-Pattison *Stud. Philos. of Relig.* vi. 75 Theriomorphism seems..to precede anthropomorphism, and it is only gradually that the gods are humanized. **1969** *Times Lit. Suppl.* 11 Dec. 1431 The Charollais becomes the focal-point for a manic, if short-lived, cult of theriomorphism. **1982** *Jrnl. Indo-European Stud.* X. 159 Volos is subsumed by theriomorphism.. heavenly bodies..fertility..and the realm of life.

therm, *sb.*[2] Add: = *calorie b. Now *Obs.*

2. A quantity of heat equal to 100,000 British thermal units, used in Britain as the statutory unit in expressing the quantity of gas supplied.

1920 *Act* 10 & 11 *Geo. V* c. 28 § 1 (2) A standard or maximum price for each hundred thousand British thermal units (in this Act referred to as 'a therm'). **1922** *Westm. Gaz.* 18 Oct. 8/5 The new method of charging by therm. **1955** *Times* 20 July 8/3 A 'substantial increase' was forecast by the chairman of the South Eastern Gas Board when he announced recently an increase of 2d, a therm in the price of gas. **1982** *Daily Tel.* 26 Apr. 2/8 The average price being paid by British Gas for existing and new supplies is 10p–12p a therm.

therm, *sb.*[3] Add: **2.** In 18th.-c. cabinet-making, a rectangular, tapering leg or foot of a chair, table, or the like. Also *attrib.* or as *adj.*

1788 *Cabinet-Makers' London Bk. Prices* (1803) No. 7, If the plinth of the Therms is work'd hollow [price, extra, 1½d]. **1925** Penderel-Brodhurst & Layton *Gloss. Eng. Furnit.* 173 *Therm foot*, a rectangular tapering foot to the legs of chairs and tables, also called a spade or taper foot, often used by the brothers Adam and Hepplewhite, and to a lesser degree by Sheraton. *Therm leg*, the taper or therm leg was a favourite feature of Hepplewhite and later designers. **1952** J. Gloag *Short Dict. Furnit.* 475 (*caption*) Ten designs for therms for claws.

† **therm** (þɜɹm), *sb.*[4] Colloq. abbrev. of Thermometer. *Obs.*

1791 J. Woodforde *Diary* 11 Dec. (1927) III. 318 It froze all day long even within doors very quick Therm at 52. **1799** Malthus *Diary* 21 July (1966) 173 Yesterday his therm was 18, & mine in a deep shade was 71. **1877** W. Whitman *Daybks. & Notebks.* (1978) I. 58 *Very hot*—therm 90–96.

therm (þɜɹm), *v.* [f. Therm *sb.*[3]] *trans.* In 18th.-c. cabinet-making, to turn (a leg or foot of a chair, table, or the like) to a rectangular, tapering form; also *absol.* Hence **thermed** *ppl. a.*, **the·rming** *vbl. sb.*

1788 *Cabinet-Makers' London Bk. Prices* (1803) No. 12, The Price of Therming Legs... The Price of Therming in the Neck... When the legs are therm'd at the top only, the tapering to be paid for extra. **1907** G. O. Wheeler *Old Eng. Furnit.* 461 *Therming*, a process of conferring a delicate taper, especially applied to the feet of chairs, sideboards, and tables of the Sheraton order. **1925** Penderel-Brodhurst & Layton *Gloss. Eng. Furnit.* 173 *Therming*, a process in use towards the end of the eighteenth century, before circular and band saws were invented, by which the legs of chairs and tables were thermed or tapered, by means of a lathe provided with a cylinder about six feet in diameter, on which the legs were placed and turned down one side at a time. **1952** J. Gloag *Short Dict. Furnit.* 470 *Taper leg*, a leg of square section, sometimes called a thermed leg, gradually diminishing towards the foot, introduced in the second half of the 18th century for chairs, tables and sideboards.

thermal, *a.* Add: **2. a.** (Further examples.) Also, caused by heat; *thermal agitation*, the motion of atoms or the like due to their thermal energy; *thermal analysis*, analysis of a substance by examination of the way its temperature falls on cooling or rises on heating; *thermal barrier* (Aeronaut.) = *heat barrier* s.v. *heat *sb.* 14 d; *thermal bremsstrahlung*, electromagnetic radiation produced by the thermal motion of charged particles in a plasma; *thermal capacity* (earlier example); *thermal column* (Nucl. Physics), a body of moderator inside or projecting from a reactor such that it serves as a source of thermal neutrons for experimental purposes; *thermal cycle*, a cycle in which the temperature of a substance rises or falls and then returns to its initial value; *thermal cycling*, the periodic heating and cooling of a substance; *thermal death point*, the lowest temperature at which a micro-organism is killed under specified conditions; *thermal diffusion*, diffusion occurring as a result of the thermal motion of atoms or molecules, esp. as a technique for separating gaseous compounds of different isotopes of an element (which diffuse at different rates in a temperature gradient); *thermal diffusivity*, the thermal conductivity of a substance divided by the product of its density and its specific heat capacity; *thermal imaging*, the technique of using the heat given off by objects or substances to produce an image of them; so *thermal imager*; *thermal lance* = *thermic lance* s.v. *thermic *a.*; *thermal noise* (Electronics), noise arising from the random thermal motion of electrons; *thermal pollution*, the production of heat, or the discharge of warm water, esp. into a river or lake, on a scale that is potentially harmful ecologically; *thermal printer*, a printer having a matrix of fine pins as the print-head, which are selectively heated to form a character on heat-sensitive paper; *thermal runaway* (Electronics), a dramatic or destructive rise in the temperature of a transistor as a result of an increase in its temperature causing an increase in the current through it, and vice versa; *thermal shock* (cf. *shock *sb.*[3] 2); *thermal storage* (later examples); also used *attrib.* to designate appliances which store heat in other ways; *thermal unit* (earlier and further examples); *British thermal unit* is also abbreviated B.T.U., B.t.u.

1853 *Trans. R. Soc. Edin.* XX. 170 The mechanical equivalent of the ordinary thermal unit. **1880** W. Thomson in *Encycl. Brit.* XI. 558/2 Regnault's measurements of the thermal capacity of water at different temperatures. *Ibid.* 578/1 The thermal conductivity of the substance is not generally the same at different temperatures. *Ibid.* 581/2 It is *k*/*c*, not merely *k*, that expresses the quantity of the substance on which the phenomenon chiefly depends. We therefore propose to give to *k*/*c* the name of thermal diffusivity. **1898** *Public Health Papers & Rep.* (Amer. Public Health Assoc.) XXIII. 86 In determining the thermal death point cultures should always be moist. **1916** S. Chapman in *Proc. R. Soc.* A. XCIII. 10 We may call D_{12}, D_{12}', D_p, and D_T respectively the coefficients of diffusion, forced diffusion, pressure diffusion, and thermal diffusion. The definition of D_{12} agrees with that usually given for the coefficient of diffusion. The other coefficients seem to be defined here for the first time. **1925** *Jrnl. Iron & Steel Inst.* CXII. 489 Thermal analysis was followed by determination of the hardness and a study of the microstructure of the test-pieces. **1925** Thermal shock [see *pulpal *a.*]. **1927** *Physical Rev.* XXIX. 367 Ordinary electric conductors are sources of random voltage fluctuations, as a result of thermal agitation of the electric charges of the conductor. **1930** F. B. Llewellyn in *Proc. IRE* XVIII. 244 The importance of this noise, which will be termed 'thermal noise', in high-frequency radio receiving circuit design will be discussed. **1932** Hardy & Perrin *Princ. Optics* 142 Thermal radiation is characteristic of the temperature of the radiating body rather than the material of which it is composed. **1933** *Archit. Rev.* Oct. p. xl/1 During the last two or three years an entirely new kind of cooking appliance has made its appearance in England. It is known as the thermal storage or stored heat cooker. **1935** *Discovery* July 214/2 Barometric depressions are discussed..in their modern guise as interacting air masses, the forced ascent necessary to give rain being related to dynamical instability instead of to thermal instability as in the older theories. **1936** W. L. Nelson *Petroleum Refinery Engin.* xvii. 304 The thermal decomposition or cracking of oil was called to our attention by Silliman in 1871. **1943** *Gloss. Terms Electr. Engin.* (*B.S.I.*) 14 A B.t.u. is equivalent to 1054 joules. **1945** H. D. Smyth *Gen. Acct. Devel. Atomic Energy Mil. Purposes* viii. 79 We now introduce a factor f, called the thermal utilization factor, which is defined as the probability that a given thermal neutron will be absorbed in the uranium. **1950** *Sci. News* XV. Plate 16 (*caption*) Sliplines in pure zinc after exposure to 50 thermal cycles between 30°C and 150°C (×500). **1950** *Canad. Jrnl. Res.* A. XXVIII. 434 The thermal column of the Chalk River pile was used as a large block of scattering material with a high flux of thermal neutrons. **1951** *Jrnl. R. Aeronaut. Soc.* LV. 757/2 A new barrier is faced after 'climbing' the sonic barrier, namely the Thermal Barrier. **1954** R. Stephenson *Introd. Nucl. Engin.* vi. 249 The X-pile has no thermal shield... After 10 years operation there is no material damage of the concrete, which would indicate that the possibility of failure of concrete due to thermal stress may be much less severe than is generally assumed. *Ibid.*, A thermal shield is an inner wall..which is placed between the reactor and the biological shield. Its function is to remove most of the heat energy of the gammas and thermal neutrons..and thereby protect the biological shield from damage. **1955** *Sci. Amer.* July 58/1 Coal supplied only 34 per cent of the nation's total B.T.U.'s (British thermal units). **1957** *Times* 12 Nov. (Canada Suppl.) p. iii/2 A 1,200,000 h.p. thermal power station is to be built near Vancouver, using natural gas. *Ibid.* 11 Dec. 16/4 It has been necessary to increase the capacity of the distillation unit and provide a thermal cracker. **1958** C. C. Adams *Space Flight* 265 The MA-2 is a special suit that is ventilated for travel through the thermal barrier, and the MA-1 is a new ARDC helmet. **1960** Chalmers & Quarrell *Physical Examination of Metals* (ed. 2) iii. 183 The simplest method of carrying out a thermal analysis is to place the specimen in a furnace which is arranged to have a negligible temperature gradient over a zone somewhat greater than the length of the specimen. **1961** *Guardian* 12 June 6/6 A domestic thermal storage heater is now available. **1962** *Research* XV. 80/1 Uranium polycarbide..is much more resistant to thermal shock and thermal cycling. **1962** Simpson & Richards *Physical Princ. Junction Transistors* ix. 210 In extreme cases this positive feedback may lead to a catastrophic increase in temperature—a phenomenon commonly called 'thermal runaway'. **1962** *Newnes Conc. Encycl. Nucl. Energy* 357/2 The separations achieved in a convection-free system are small, and are only used to determine the magnitude of the thermal diffusion effect and to provide information on intermolecular force fields. **1963** B. Fozard *Instrumentation Nucl. Reactors* xiii. 166 A count rate from the fission chamber of 10^6 c/s..is produced by a neutron flux, in the thermal column, of about 5×10^6 neutrons cm^{-2} sec^{-1}. *Ibid.* 170 Thus the reactor can be operated under virtually isothermal conditions over a wide range of load, with consequent constancy of steam conditions and absence of thermal cycling. **1964** H. S. Hvistendahl *Engin. Units* vii. 110 The legal definition of the Btu is the amount of heat required to raise 1lb of water from 60 to 61°F at standard atmospheric pressure. **1965** R. G. Kazmann *Mod. Hydrol.* iv. 109 The so-called thermal pollution of streams has resulted primarily from the installation of steam-electric generating plants along our rivers. **1966** C. R. Tottle *Sci. Engin. Materials* v. 117 The mean free path *l* depends on the thermal agitation of the lattice. *Ibid.*, In less regular lattices, such as those of amorphous materials, there is a reduced probability of attenuation of the thermal wave, by virtue of the variable distances between the atoms. **1968** R. R. Ernst in Lawrence & Block *Disinfection, Sterilization & Preservation* vii. xliii. 707/2 The thermal death point is the lowest temperature at which a suspension of bacteria is killed in 10 minutes. This standard has been almost abandoned. **1969** Thermal pollution [see *pollution 1 a]. **1970** *Nature* 19 Sept. 1182/1 The technique of thermal imaging—picking up infrared radiation from the human body and displaying the resulting thermal image on an oscilloscope—..has been used to map the flow of warm arterial blood into, for example, tumours and varicose veins. **1971** *Gloss. Soil Sci. Terms* (Soil Sci. Soc. Amer.) 21/1 *Thermal analysis* (*differential thermal analysis*), a method of analyzing a soil sample for constituents, based on a differential rate of heating of the unknown and standard samples when a uniform source of heat is applied. **1972** *Sci. Amer.* July 33/3 This combination of conditions is all that is needed to produce the X rays, since accelerated charges are a source of electromagnetic radiation. A compact name for the process is 'thermal bremsstrahlung'. **1972** *Oxf. Univ. Gaz.* CII. Suppl. No. 8. 3 Work has begun on the installation of a second thermal storage boiler. **1973** 'K. Royce' *Spider Underground* viii. 119 Someone must be on tap to answer awkward questions if Old Bill [*sc.* the police] arrives. The thermal lance men will be below. **1973** J. G. Tweeddale *Materials Technol.* I. iv. 95 Thermal diffusivity (*a*) is important when it is necessary to consider the effects of temperature differences set up in a material during transfer of heat. *Ibid.*, Both thermal conductivity and diffusivity cease to have much meaning for the liquid state since in that state the principal mechanism of transfer becomes convective mixing. **1974** *Sci. Amer.* Dec. 95/2 They are not die-cast in significant quantity now because the thermal shock to the metal components, including the mold, is so severe that the life of the components is short. **1975** *McGraw-Hill Yearbk. Sci. & Technol.* 44/2 Some kind of thermal shield had to be designed, fabricated, and deployed quickly if Skylab was to be saved. **1975** G. J. King *Audio Handbk.* iv. 106 Since f.e.t.s are less temperature sensitive than bipolar transistors, temperature compensation is not necessary, neither can thermal runaway occur, for I_0 tends to fall with increasing temperature. **1975** D. G. Fink *Electronics Engineers' Handbk.* xxii. 60 Thermal noise for the most part originates in the first stages of the radio receiver and sets the minimum signal amplitude acceptable for a given signal-to-noise ratio. **1977** F. Webb *Go for Out* vii. 125 A modern peterman needs explosives—else thermal lances. **1977** I. M. Campbell *Energy & Atmosphere* v. 86 There is unlikely to be a thermal pollution problem of any importance on a global basis within the forseeable future. **1978** *Jrnl. R. Soc. Arts* CXXVI. 683/1 Structures of supersonic aircraft are subject to thermal stresses due to temperature gradients. **1980** *Times* 4 Aug. 17/2 Thermal imaging..involves the visualization of objects and scenes by detecting and processing the infra-red energy they emit. **1982** *Daily Tel.* 20 Aug. 5/2 Their passive infra-red viewers, image intensifiers, and thermal imagers were excellent. **1982** *Sci. Amer.* Dec. 93/1 Thermal printers, which cost less than $500, burn an image into a special paper at a rate of some 50 characters per second.

b. Nucl. Physics. *thermal neutron*, a neutron which is in thermal equilibrium with its environment (see quot. 1966); so *thermal speed*, *velocity*, the speed characteristic of such a neutron; *thermal reactor*, a nuclear reactor in which the fission process relies upon thermal neutrons. Cf. *slow neutron, slow reactor* s.v. *SLOW *a.* 13 c.

1936 *Physical Rev.* XLIX. 520/1 It is therefore not necessary to ascribe all large cross sections to neutrons of thermal velocities. **1938** *Ibid.* LIV. 235/1 (*heading*) Collimated, variable energy beam of pure thermal neutrons. **1949** H. ETHERINGTON in S. C. Rothmann *Constructive Uses of Atomic Energy* v. 76 In a thermal reactor fission is produced by neutrons that have been slowed approximately to thermal velocities. **1959** *Listener* 19 Nov. 872/1 At slow or 'thermal' speeds neutron capture by nuclei of Uranium 238 is less important. **1966** C. R. TOTTLE *Sci. Engin. Materials* x. 236 Fast neutrons may be moving at speeds of the order of 10^{10} cm sec^{-1} with an energy of 1 to 10 MeV. When slowed down to a similar order of energy to that of the thermal vibration of atoms (hence called thermal neutrons) the speed is about 10^5 cm sec^{-1} at an energy of 1 eV. **1971** *Nature* 23 July 211/1 The companies say that they have between them a good deal of experience in building thermal reactors of several types.

c. Promoting the retention of heat. Usu. of clothes, esp. underwear. *thermal pane* = *Thermopane* s.v. *THERMO-.

1970 *Toronto Daily Star* 24 Sept. 16/2 (Advt.), Quilted thermal suits. **1973** *Times* 9 Aug. 5/6 He has thermal underwear for use at high altitudes. **1974** H. MACINNES *Climb to Lost World* viii. 122, I had taken the precaution of carrying my pair of calf-length thermal boots with me. .. They proved very useful in this swampy ground. **1978** *Detroit Free Press* 16 Apr. E 5/1 In addition to long johns, thermal socks and two caps, Harwell wore a tee shirt. **1978** T. GIFFORD *Glendower Legacy* 39 He..glanced out the wide thermal-pane window. **1982** *Oxford Star* 4–5 Feb. 10/7 Tartan Cottage, Oxfordshire's crashed mail order clothing firm, has been rescued by a thermal underwear company.

thermal (þɔ̄·ɹmăl), *sb.* [f. prec. adj.] A rising current of relatively warm air, used by gliders and birds to gain height.

1933 *Jrnl. R. Aeronaut. Soc.* XXXVII. 678 Herr Hirth had gained a great deal of experience regarding 'thermals', that is to say, ascending currents of warm air which can be used for soaring as distinct from soaring in the currents beneath clouds. **1950** 'N. SHUTE' *Town like Alice* 229 She rolled over on her back and watched a seagull soaring in the thermals from the island. **1962** *Amer. Scientist* L. 180 Thermal soaring is the method most commonly used by soaring birds. **1974** 'G. BLACK' *Golden Cockatrice* iii. 60 He had been using that moving water belt beyond the harbour as a bird uses a thermal.

Hence **the·rmalling** *vbl. sb.*, soaring in thermals.

1936 *Archit. Rev.* LXXIX. 255/3 For greater heights the second and more interesting method is employed; what is known as 'thermalling.' This is the utilization of the columns of rising air that are always in existence under certain weather conditions. **1974** *Reader's Digest* Feb. 89 With a Rogallo you can also do another type of soaring, called thermaling, where you circle in chimney-like updrafts of warm air that rise from sun-heated ground.

Thermalite (þɔ̄·ɹmăləit). Also with small initial. [f. THERMAL *a.* + -ITE[1].] The proprietary name of a type of cellular concrete building block with good insulating qualities.

1949 *Trade Marks Jrnl.* 3 Aug. 690/1 *Thermalite*... Concrete products included in Class 19. **1955** *Archit. Rev.* CXVII. 117/2 The construction is cavity brick walls with inner skin of thermalite blocks, with a roof of ⅜ inch asphalt on rafters at 5° pitch, and 2 inch cork insulation. **1960** *Times* 3 Oct. (Suppl.) p. iii/2 External walls are of cavity construction with brick facing and Thermalite inner leaf. **1977** *Reader's Digest Bk. of Do-It-Yourself Skills & Techniques* 201/1 Aerated blocks, e.g. Celcon or Thermalite, are also easy to work and have better insulation qualities [than lightweight aggregate blocks] but are more expensive and are unsuitable for exposed garden walls.

thermalize (þɔ̄·ɹmăləiz), *v. Physics.* [f. THERMAL *a.* + -IZE.] **a.** *trans.* To bring into thermal equilibrium with the environment.

1956 *Ann. Rev. Nucl. Sci.* VI. 317 The coolant..slows down the neutrons, acting as a 'moderator' and tending to thermalize the assembly. **1961** G. R. CHOPPIN *Exper. Nuclear Chem.* viii. 116 It is necessary to surround the source with paraffin or water to thermalize the neutrons. **1979** *Nature* 29 Nov. 456/1 The hypothetical Oort cloud should be thermalised by weak stellar encounters on a time scale ~1 Myr.

b. *intr.* Of sub-atomic particles, etc.: to attain thermal equilibrium with their environment.

1966 *New Scientist* 17 Mar. 707/1 It has been predicted that a positron in a metal should 'thermalize'—that is, reach the kinetic energy characteristic of the temperature of the metal—in about 10^{-12} s. **1973** *Physics Bull.* Nov. 652/3 The density was so high that any radiation generated would have readily thermalized. **1978** *Nature* 11 May 133/2 If the infalling protons thermalise just at the surface of the compact object, the radiation will be in the form of γ rays.

Hence **the·rmalized, the·rmalizing** *ppl. adj.*; also **rheamaliza·tion**, the process of thermalizing.

1950 GLASSTONE *Sourcebk. Atomic Energy* xi. 294/1 The process of reducing the energy of a neutron to the thermal region by elastic scattering is sometimes called thermalization or, more commonly, slowing down. **1971** *Nature* 16 Apr. 450/1 A more likely possibility..is that electron thermalization during trapping produces local heating of the matrix. **1971** *Engineering* Apr. 34/2 Moderating materials are often an integral part of the structure of nuclear reactors so that thermalized beams can be obtained directly. **1979** *Nature* 30 Aug. 749/2 The major issue remaining is whether sputtered atoms escape Io or are merely supplied to a thermalising atmosphere for later escape.

thermic, *a.* Add: (Earlier example.) *thermic lance*, a steel pipe packed with steel wool through which a jet of suitable gas may be passed in order to burn away metal, concrete, or the like using heat generated by the burning of the pipe; cf. *LANCE *sb.*[1] 6** a, *thermal lance* s.v. *THERMAL *a.* 2 a.

1842 J. F. W. HERSCHEL *Let.* Nov. in *Phil. Trans. R. Soc.* (1843) CXXXIII. 5 If the restriction to these rays of the term *thermic* as distinct from *calorific* be not..a sufficient distinction, I would propose the term *parathermic rays* to designate them. **1970** P. LAURIE *Scotland Yard* x. 251 The thieves..penetrate the wall of the vault with a thermic lance. **1982** *Daily Tel.* 7 Sept. 3/3 He planned to break into the bank with a thermic lance.

Hence **the·rmics** *sb. pl.*, the study of heat, thermotics. *rare.*

1854 [see *palæometeorology* s.v. *PALÆO-, PALEO-]. **1953** *Archit. Rev.* CXIV. 195/2 (*heading*) Kitchen thermics.

Thermidor. Add: **1.** (Earlier examples.)

1801 W. DUPRÉ *Neological French Dict.* 276 *Thermidor*,..hot month... The 9th Thermidor answers to the 27th of July. **1802** C. WILMOT *Let.* 30 July in *Irish Peer* (1920) 75 Paris, 30th July, 1802. 9 Thermidor.

2. *lobster thermidor:* see *LOBSTER[1] 5.

3. A moderate reaction following a revolution. Cf. quot. 1842, sense 1 in Dict.

1938 C. BRINTON *Anatomy of Revolution* viii. 244 We shall have to call Thermidor a convalescence from the fever of revolution. **1960** *Commentary* June 508/1 The retreat from 'war communism'..did not lead to the revolutionary regime's overthrow by a new Thermidor. **1974** tr. *Wertheim's Evolution & Revolution* 341 Should all such symptoms be taken as evidence that the Cultural Revolution..got stuck in a kind of Thermidor, and that consequently the fight of Mao and his allies against a Thermidor was a last stand, a losing battle? **1981** *Times* 30 June 15/1 Iran is about to enter its Thermidor.

Thermidorian, *sb.* and *a.* Add: **A.** *sb.* **a.** (Earlier example.)

1801 W. DUPRÉ *Neological French Dict.* 276 Un thermidorien, spéculateur révolutionnaire—A thermidorian, and speculator in revolutions.

b. A moderate opponent of a revolutionary movement; a counter-revolutionary.

1981 *Encounter* Dec. 34/1 The Thermidorians..are themselves not easy to define..and the Thermidorian régime..is so fragmented as to defy any simple analysis.

B. *adj.* **c.** Of, pertaining to, or designating a moderate reaction following a revolution.

1938 C. BRINTON *Anatomy of Revolution* viii. 244 The ensuing slow and uneven return to quieter, less heroic times has long been known to French historians as the Thermidorean reaction. **1974** tr. *Wertheim's Evolution & Revolution* 333 It is against the background of these Thermidorian tendencies in the Soviet Union that we have to view the so-called 'Great Proletarian Cultural Revolution' in China. **1978** *Pacific Affairs* LI. 474 For them the Thermidorian effects of the bureaucratic restoration were much mitigated by the emergence at the helm of the enlightened Chou En-lai. **1981** [see sense b of the *sb.* above].

thermion (þɔ̄·ɹmiǫn). *Physics.* [f. THERM(O- + ION.] An electron or ion emitted from an incandescent surface.

1909 O. W. RICHARDSON in *Phil. Mag.* XVII. 814 The substantive Thermionics furnishes naturally the further substantive Thermion. **1922** J. MILLS *Within Atom* vii. 73 An electron which is emitted in this way is sometimes called a 'thermion'. **1973** H. A. ENGE *Introd. Atomic Physics* iii. 81 In 1899, J. J. Thomson showed that the thermions in this effect are electrons.

thermionic (þɔ̄ɹmiǫ·nik), *a. Physics.* [f. prec. + -IC.] Of, pertaining to, or employing electrons emitted from an incandescent surface; *thermionic valve*, an electronic device consisting of an evacuated envelope containing two or more electrodes, such that a current can flow only in one direction as a result of thermionic emission from one electrode.

1909 O. W. RICHARDSON in *Phil. Mag.* XVII. 814 Here we have two currents: the current used to heat the wire and the thermionic current away from the surface of the latter. **1915** *Electrician* 21 May 241/1 The thermionic current..increased at first. **1917** *Wireless World* June 152 The invention by the writer [*sc.* J. A. Fleming] of this article of the thermionic detector. *Ibid.* 158 Known by various titles, such as Fleming valve, vacuum valve,.. thermionic valve, and audion valve, it is the result of experiments extending over a large number of years. **1920** *Glasgow Herald* 9 July 10 What with the high-frequency alternator, and..the thermionic valve, wireless practice has been very much revolutionised. **1933** *Jrnl. Exper. Biol.* X. 293 (*heading*) A thermionic potentiometer for measuring light intensity with photo-electric cells. **1956** G. A. MONTGOMERIE *Digital Calculating Machines* xi. 216 By using thermionic valves and similar devices, the speed of automatic computors can be made very much higher. **1957** *Times* 26 Nov. 10/6 A new 'thermionic converter'.. takes advantage of the fact that electrons can be 'boiled out' of a hot metal surface and used to produce an electric current directly. **1975** D. G. FINK *Electronics Engineers' Handbk.* XXVII. 18 In a thermionic generator..electrons are emitted from the heated cathode..and collected by a cooler anode.

So **thermio·nically** *adv.*; **thermio·nics** *sb. pl.*, the branch of science and technology concerned with thermionic emission.

1909 O. W. RICHARDSON in *Phil. Mag.* XVII. 814 The author ventures to suggest that the word 'Thermionics'.. is very suitable for the purpose. **1922** J. MILLS *Within Atom* vii. 74 When electrons are being thermionically emitted from a heated wire. **1933** E. L. CHAFFEE *Theory of Thermionic Vacuum Tubes* i. 8 Early experimenters in the field of thermionics believed that the emission of electricity from hot bodies..was the result of some sort of chemical reaction. **1940** *Times* 31 Aug. 7/4 New branches of knowledge like..photo-electricity, and thermionics sprang up out of the fertile soil. **1947** *Jrnl. Optical Soc. Amer.* XXXVII. 424/2 Associated with this component of the dark current is a shot noise resulting from random thermionically emitted electrons. **1966** *McGraw-Hill Encycl. Sci. & Technol.* XII. 542a/1 In thermionics, power densities of 25 watt/cm^2 at emitter temperatures of 1700°C have been obtained with hardware which is suitable for [space] flight.

thermistor (þɔ̄ɹmi·stəɹ). [Contraction of *therm(al res)istor.*] A small piece of semiconducting material the resistance of which falls with increasing temperature, enabling it to be used for the sensitive measurement and control of the latter.

1940 G. L. PEARSON in *Physical Rev.* LVII. 1065/2 Thermistor is a contraction of the words 'thermal resistor' and designates an electrical resistance whose value is markedly dependent on its temperature. **1955** *Sci. Amer.* Oct. 50/3 The heart of the instrument is a flake of metallic oxides called a thermistor, whose conduction of electric current is increased when it is heated. An amplifying and recording system translates this conductivity into a temperature reading. **1962** *New Scientist* 15 Mar. 638/3 The usual method of measuring the temperature in a borehole from the surface involves the use of thermistor probes. **1973** *Sci. Amer.* Feb. 42/3 The thermistor that sensed the muscle temperature was in the tip of the harpoon and the one that sensed the water temperature was attached to the transmitter, outside the fish's body on the harpoon shaft. **1979** *Guardian* 8 Sept. 20/2 When the water in the panels becomes warm enough, a thermistor produces a signal which is interpreted by the control unit, so that a standard central heating pump takes the hot water from the panel to the bulk storage tank, and from there to the radiators.

thermite. Add **1.** (Later examples.)

1918 *Nature* 14 Nov. 217/2 Thermit, now an important munition of war, is in a class by itself. It is used for charging incendiary bombs and sometimes in a kind of shrapnel. **1971** B. SCHARF *Engin. & its Lang.* xi. 115 The thermite is ignited and the hot metal allowed to flow into the mould, where it fills the gap between the two parts and forms a collar around them. **1973** R. DENTRY *Encounter at Kharmel* xi. 198 The third explosion..set off thermite positioned under the big transceiver.

2. *attrib.* and *Comb.*, as *thermite method, reaction, shell, weld*; **thermite process**, the reduction of finely divided oxides of iron or other metals by means of an exothermic reaction with finely divided aluminium; also, thermite welding; **thermite welding**, fusion welding in which the heat and the weld metal are produced by the thermite process.

1929 *Times* 16 Jan. 12/4 The thermit method of welding has proved its worth in long-continued use. **1905** *Chambers's Jrnl.* Dec. 78/2 A perfectly successful joint..has been made by utilising the thermite process. **1910** C. H. DESCH *Metallography* vi. 109 The great reducing power of aluminium at high temperatures has been utilized in what is known as the Thermit process to produce metals and alloys free from carbon. **1930** *Engineering* 14 Mar. 349/2 The Thermit process, the oxy-acetylene and similar blowpipes,..have all attained to a usefulness and convenience applicable..to single jobs. **1958** [see *ALUMINO-THERMIC *a.*]. **1980** *Daily Tel.* 19 Feb. 6/8 British Rail uses two main welding techniques. One, the thermit process used along the Bushey track, involves welding long stretches of rail together at the site. **1915** *Chambers's Jrnl.* July 558/1 The thermit reaction is used largely in the preparation of metals from their oxides. **1923** KIPLING *Irish Guards in Gt. War* I. 219 Oil-drums, gas and thermit shells were added to the regular allowances sent over. **1980** *Times* 19 Feb. 3/3 There are at least 700 track welds, called thermit welds, similar to the one that failed. **1906** *Jrnl. Iron & Steel Inst.* I. 452 Experiments with electric and thermite welding for tramway rails. **1927** [see *METALLIC *a.* 1 h]. **1952** FUCHS & BRADLEY *Welding Practice* II. ii. 39 It must be remembered that Thermit welding can only be carried out successfully by specially trained and experienced personnel.

thermo-. Add: **thermocline** (further examples); also, a layer of water marked by such a gradient, the water above and below being at different temperatures; **the:rmocoagula·tion** *Surg.*, the coagulation of tissue, esp. in the brain, by means of heat; so **thermo-coa·gulated** *ppl. a.*, **-coa·gulative** *a.*; **thermo-compre·ssion**, the simultaneous application of heat and pressure; usu. *attrib.*; **thermodu·ric** *a. Biol.* [L. *dūr-āre* to hold out, last] (of bacteria, etc.) capable of surviving high temperatures, esp. those of pasteurization; **the·rmoforming** *vbl. sb.*, the process of heating a thermoplastic material and shaping it in a mould; so **the·rmoform** *v. trans.*; **the·rmo-former,** a person who carries out thermo-forming; **thermoha·line** *a. Oceanogr.* [Gr. ἅλς, ἁλι- salt + -INE[1]], of or pertaining to the temperature and salinity of seawater; **thermo-ha·locline** *Oceanogr.* [after *thermocline*], a narrow layer of water separating layers of differing temperature and salinity; **thermo-ha·rden** *v. trans.*, to harden permanently by subjection to heat; **thermo-ha·rdening** *ppl. a.*, rendered permanently hard by heat; **the·rmo-karst** [a. Russ. *termokárst* (M. M. Ermolaev 1932, in *Trudy̆ Soveta po Izuch. proizv. Sil: Ser. yakutsk.* 211)], topography in which the melting of permafrost has produced hollows, hummocks, and the like reminiscent of karst; **thermoly·sin** *Biochem.* [Gr. λύσις a parting], a heat-stable proteolytic enzyme found in some thermophilic bacteria; **thermo-magnetic** *a.* (later example); **thermo-magnetism** (example); **thermona·sty** *Bot.* [*NASTY *sb.*[2]], a nastic movement caused by a change in temperature; so **thermona·stic** *a.*; **The·rmopane** *N. Amer.*, a proprietary name for an openable double-glazed window unit; **thermophy·sics,** the branch of physics dealing with the physical properties of substances at high temperatures; so **thermophy·sical** *a.*; **the·rmo-power** *Electr.* [f. *thermo(electric power)*], the thermoelectric e.m.f. developed by a substance per degree difference in temperature; **thermore·manent** *a.*, pertaining to or being magnetism acquired, esp. by rock, as a result of cooling or solidifying in a magnetic field; so **thermore·manence; thermose·nsitive** *a.*, possessing or relating to sensitivity to heat; so **the:rmosensiti·vity;** † **thermo-tank,** a tank containing pipes through which water, air, or the like circulates for heating or cooling, esp. as a heating or ventilating system (*obs.*); **thermoto·lerant** *a.* (see quot. 1940).

1955 *Sci. News Let.* 2 Apr. 217/1 Investigations off the coast of California showed that skin divers can spot thermoclines, the layers of water which mark the sharp change in water temperature, in three different ways. **1973** *Sci. Amer.* Feb. 42/3 The coastal waters of Nova Scotia are characterized by a marked thermocline (a sharp drop in temperature as the depth increases), so that a free-swimming fish might encounter a wide range of water temperature. **1973** P. A. COLINVAUX *Introd. Ecol.* xxxiii. 470 The animals have to feed in the warm surface waters..but they go down to cold water below the thermocline in daytime. **1938** *Yale Jrnl. Biol. & Med.* X. 575 The thermocoagulated layers are completely 'resorbed' within four months. **1933** J. G. DUSSER DE BARENNE in *Science* 2 June 547/1 This method of laminar thermo-coagulation of the cerebral cortex, as it might be called, results..in a sharply localized, selective destruction of the nervous elements. **1974** *Nature* 4 Jan. 58/2 The destruction of the area postrema was perfomed by sight through the occipital foramen by thermocoagulation. **1976** *Ibid.* 22 Apr. 660/2 The thermocoagulative lesions were aimed at various limbic tracts, and each estimated at 6 mm in diameter. **1965** *Wireless World* July 337/2 Typically this is done by thermo-compression bonding of extremely thin gold or aluminium wires to the electrodes and terminal posts. **1972** *Physics Bull.* Mar. 154/1 Circuits can now be made with..active components subsequently soldered or thermocompression bonded to the microstrip. **1979** A. L. LYDERSEN *Fluid Flow & Heat Transfer* xi. 323 The waste heat is often available at a temperature which is too low for direct use in the process. However, it may be utilized in conjunction with thermocompression. **1927** *Techn. Bull. N.Y. State Agric. Exper. Station* No. 130. 6 Thermoduric spore-forming bacteria are common types in pasteurized, sterilized, and boiled milk. **1946** *Nature* 23 Nov. 755/1 Working with suspensions of *Staph. aureus*, thermoduric micrococci, and spores of *B. subtilis*, we found that..solutions [of hypochlorite] of low *p*H were more germicidal than at higher *p*H. **1975** CAMPBELL & MARSHALL *Sci. of providing Milk for Man* xxiii. 501 Bacteria that survive specific heat treatments are usually said to be thermoduric (heat-tolerant). **1958** *Times Rev. Industry* Aug. 57/2 Machine..for thermoforming.. industrial parts. **1972** *Sci. Amer.* Aug. 9 (Advt.), By helping the thermoformer with mold modifications and adjustments to equipment and operating conditions which enabled him to produce high quality parts economically. **1978** *Detroit Free Press* 5 Mar. C-14/7 (Advt.), Machinist assembler, parts and stock man, and a thermo-former. **1963** SIMONDS & CHURCH *Conc. Guide to Plastics* (ed. 2) vii. 182 There are seven basic techniques for the thermo-forming of plastics sheet. **1972** *Sci. Amer.* Aug. 9 (Advt.), By supplying the sheet extruder with a high molecular weight Marlex thermoforming resin ideally suited for the production of large thick sheet. **1978** *N.Y. Times* 30 Mar. B-19/1 (Advt.), We are seeking manager for our model-making dept. in thermoforming. **1942** H. U. SVERDRUP et al. *Oceans* xiii. 509 When examining the circulation [of the waters of the oceans] that arises because of the external factors influencing the density of the surface waters, one must take changes of both temperature and salinity into account, and must consider not the thermal but the thermohaline circulation. **1963** G. L. PICKARD *Descriptive Physical Oceanogr.* vii. 107 The ocean circulation can be divided into two parts, the thermohaline and the wind-driven components. **1978** *Nature* 13 July 151/1 The observed distribution patterns of late Quaternary sapropels favour the hypothesis of periodically altered basin-wide thermohaline circulation entrained by regionally important climatic and eustatic changes. **1964** *Oceanogr. & Marine Biol.* II. 135 When a basin is permanently stagnant, the redox discontinuity may rise to the level of the thermo-halocline, as is well known in the Black Sea. **1976** *Nature* 2 Sept. 23/1 Mechanism and rate of molecular exchange across a well developed thermo-halocline have been studied thoroughly. **1949** R. J. W. REYNOLDS in J. M. Preston *Fibre Science* xvii. 318 The final products may be thermo-hardened by a suitable cross-linking treatment. **1933** *Archit. Rev.* LXXIII. 266/1 The elaborate laboratory researches into the nature of thermo-plastic and thermo-hardening materials. **1961** J. N. ANDERSON *Appl. Dental Materials* (ed. 2) xxi. 220 The Bakelite type of resin is called thermohardening or thermoset as..heat is applied to cure the resin. **1943** S. W. MULLER *Permafrost or Permanently Frozen Ground* 84 Phenomena of thermokarst. a. Cave-in lakes. b. Settling lakes. c. Cave-in and settling funnels. **1970** *Globe Mag.* 17 Jan. 4/3 Even south of the Alaska Range there is much permafrost within the forested areas which will create further problems of heat loss, permafrost melt and thermokarst development. **1965** H. MATSUBARA et al. in *Biochem. & Biophysical Res. Communications* XXI. 242 A proteolytic enzyme with the commercial name 'Thermoase' was isolated by Endo..from cultures of *Bac. thermoproteolyticus* Rokko... It was recently reported that the enzyme had a strong elastase-like activity... We propose the trivial name *thermolysin* for this enzyme. **1979** *Nature* 29 Feb. 667/1 The determination of the three-dimensional structure of the thermostable protease thermolysin showed that heat-stable proteins do not contain unusual structural features absent from less stable proteins. **1954** *Jrnl. Geomagnetism & Geoelectricity* VI. 6 This simple apparatus could be used for the study of the thermomagnetic analysis of ferromagnetic mineral with a fair accuracy. **1828** F. WATKINS *Electro-Magnetism* 22 Experiments in thermo-magnetism teach us that magnetical phænomena will arise from a disturbance in the equilibrium of temperature of metals. **1936** L. J. F. BRIMBLE *Intermediate Bot.* xx. 294 Examples of thermonastic movements are seen in the flowers of the crocus and tulip. **1936** J. B. HILL et al. *Bot.* ix. 228 The rapid opening of certain flowers when brought into a warm room from a cold place is a thermonasty. **1951** Thermonasty [see *NASTIC *a.*]. **1976** BELL & COOMBE tr. *Strasburger's Textbk. Bot.* (rev. ed.) 365 Many flowers.. open or close according to the temperature. Such a phenomenon is referred to as thermonasty. *Ibid.*, Repeated thermonastic curvatures may cause an increase in length. **1941** *Official Gaz.* (U.S. Patent Office) 14/2 *Thermopane.* For multiple glass sheet glazing units.. Claims use since May 1, 1931. **1968** *Globe & Mail* (Toronto) 13 Jan. 42/8 (Advt.), Large brick and cut stone bungalow..2 fireplaces, drapes, thermopane windows etc. **1974** *Whig-Standard* (Kingston, Ontario) 9 Feb. 15/1 Modernisation of the whole interior of the present building, including modern heating, thermopane, air-conditioning and elevator service. **1978** *N.Y. Times* 29 Mar. B8/1 (Advt.), Builder's custom built 72′ hi ranch, 2 acs, circ driveway, thermopane windows. **1957** *Ibid.* 25 Aug. IV. 9/3 Purdue University has established a thermophysical properties research center. **1976** *Physics Bull.* Dec. 561/3 The symposium is concerned with both theoretical and experimental aspects of thermophysical properties of all matter in solid, liquid, gaseous and plasma states. **1962** A. L. KING (*title*) Thermophysics. **1966** G. B. HELLER *Thermophysics & Temperature Control of Spacecraft* p. xi, The modern field of thermophysics rests on some of the oldest branches of physics, namely, thermodynamics, heat transfer, and electromagnetic radiation. **1963** *Canad. Jrnl. Physics* XLI. 1080 The thermopower of the special copper was measured carefully at the low-temperature end. **1976** *Physics Bull.* June 248/2 In figure 4 are plotted the conductivity and thermopower of the magnesium-bismuth alloy as a function of composition. **1938** J. G. KOENIGSBERGER in *Terrestr. Magnetism & Atmospheric Electr.* XLIII. 120 The full apparent remanence acquired by cooling in a given field from *Tc*..may be denoted the thermoremanence. **1967** *Nature* 28 Oct. 359/2 The mean directions [of magnetization]..are..fairly well grouped, and are believed to represent the direction of thermo-remanence acquired when the rocks cooled. **1951** *Proc. Jap. Acad.* XXVII. 643 The remanent magnetism thus produced has been called the thermo-remanent magnetism. **1958** *Antiquity* XXXII. 124 Measurement of the thermoremanent magnetism in the clay. **1971** *Physics Bull.* Aug. 476/3 Half the papers..were concerned with the analysis of contact printing processes, both the anhysteretic transfer method with $\gamma\ Fe_2O_3$ slave tapes and the thermoremanent method with chromium dioxide tapes. **1975** *Nature* 27 Feb. 701/2 Stable remanent magnetisation discovered in lava samples collected during the Apollo 11 mission has been interpreted as thermoremanent magnetisation acquired when the lava flows cooled through the Curie point 3·6 Gyr ago. **1918** *Jrnl. Exper. Zool.* XXV. 279 The animal is thermosensitive. **1952** *Archit. Rev.* CXI. 278/3 Suitable safety devices operated by a thermosensitive bi-metal strip are fitted. **1978** *Nature* 2 Feb. 470/1 Our results indicate that temperature control of reproduction in an ectothermic thermosensitive species may also be mediated in part by circadian systems. **1918** *Jrnl. Exper. Zool.* XXV. 281 This method.. demonstrated the thermosensitivity of the species, because the animals gave an ejection reflex when brought into a region of higher temperature. **1981** *Pflügers Archiv: European Jrnl. Physiol.* CCCXCI. 66/2 It turns out that in the goose a minor fraction only of total body thermosensitivity can be attributed to the spinal cord. **1909** WEBSTER, Thermo-tank. **1920** *Lancet* 25 Sept. 666/2 Eight thermo-tanks. **1928** *Observer* 15 July 9/4 A new Thermo-Tank heating system. **1940** *Chambers's Techn. Dict.* 846/1 *Thermotolerant*, able to endure high temperatures, but not growing well under such conditions. **1964** COONEY & EMERSON *Thermophilic Fungi* 161 [Fungi] which may grow at or near 50°C but which also grow well at temperatures below 20°C, are considered thermotolerant and are excluded from the true thermophilic fungi. **1973** *Nature* 16 Mar. 203/2 Many species of thermophilic and thermotolerant fungi isolated from natural thermal habitats similarly occur in man-made heated habitats.

thermochromism (þɜɪmokrōᵘ·miz'm). [ad. G. *thermochromie* (H. Stobbe 1904, in *Ber. d. Deut. Chem. Ges.* XXXVII. 2239), f. Gr. χρῶμα colour: see THERMO- and -ISM.] The phenomenon whereby certain substances undergo a reversible change of colour or shade when heated or cooled. Also **the·rmochromy,** in the same sense.

1911 *Chem. Abstr.* V. 2087 Characteristics of 'thermochromy'. **1914** *Ibid.* VIII. 2387 The corresponding salts of the thiourethans..are colorless and do not exhibit thermochromism. **1960** *New Scientist* 2 June 1424/1 In all cases where the substance was both thermochromic and photochromic the colour formed either by heat (thermochromism) or by ultra-violet irradiation at low temperature (photochromism) was spectroscopically identical. **1963** [see *PHOTOCHROMY c]. **1965** *New Scientist* 14 Jan. 102/1 Thermochromy..may well be a quite general property of solids containing trivalent chromium ions. **1974** *Inorg. Chem.* XIII. 2512/2 The thermochromism of these compounds involves a gradual change in color from gold to yellow to light green as the temperatures are lowered from 100° down to liquid nitrogen temperature.

So **thermochro·mic** *a.*, of, pertaining to, or displaying thermochromism.

1904 *Jrnl. Chem. Soc.* LXXXVI. I. 672 (*heading*) Thermochromic properties of dibenzylidensuccinic anhydride. **1953** [see *PHOTOCHROMIC *a.*]. **1965** *New Scientist* 14 Jan. 102/1 Heating has the same effect and the higher the chromium content, the lower the temperature required for the 'thermochromic' transition. **1974** *Inorg. Chem.* XIII. 2106/1 This salt is thermochromic: green at 25° and yellow at 80°.

thermocline to **thermocompression:** see *THERMO-.

the·rmocouple. Formerly also **thermo-couple** (with hyphen). [f. THERMO- + COUPLE *sb.*] A thermoelectric device for measuring temperature, consisting of two different metals joined at a point so that the junction develops a voltage dependent on the amount by which its temperature differs from that of the other end of each metal.

1890, 1901 [in Dict. s.v. THERMO-]. **1934** *Jrnl. R. Aeronaut. Soc.* XXXVIII. 618 Twenty-two thermocouples were installed on the heads and bases of all rear-bank cylinders..for temperature tests. **1953** *Brit. Jrnl. Psychol.* XLIV. 41 A thermocouple was used [for recording respiration] It converted temperature variations in front of the nostrils into electrical variations. **1966** *McGraw-Hill Encycl. Sci. & Technol.* XIII. 562/2 Two dissimilar wires welded together at one end form the basic thermocouple. **1977** J. L. HARPER *Population Biol. Plants* v. 145 Emerged seedlings were recorded and marked every week. Surface temperatures were measured with thermo-couples.

thermode (þɜ·ɹmōᵘd). [f. THERMO-, after *electrode*.] An object that is introduced into a medium, esp. living tissue, as a means by which heat may enter or leave it.

1938 *Yale Jrnl. Biol. & Med.* X. 573 A simple coagulator was used, the one inconvenience of which was that only the heating surface, the 'thermode' proper, could be sterilized. **1951** *Jrnl. Neurophysiol.* XIV. 424 A metal thermode..was applied on the tongue and kept there at constant pressure during the total experiment. **1967** *New Scientist* 16 Mar. 553/1 About 10 cu. cm of clean mercury is placed in a Perspex boat with mild steel 'thermodes' at either end, one electrically heated, the other water-cooled. **1975** *Nature* 1 May 72/1 Unilateral water-perfused thermodes with thermistors fixed to the tips were placed stereotaxically into the POA [*sc.* preoptic area]. **1978** *Sci. Amer.* Aug. 91/1 In classic experiments conducted by Henry G. Barbour in 1912 silver thermodes were implanted in the hypothalamus.

thermoduric: see *THERMO-.

thermoelectrically, *adv.* (Examples.)

1895 *Electrician* 13 Sept. 637/1 He also considered the possibility of the back E.M.F. being produced thermo-electrically. **1979** *Nature* 11 Oct. 498/1 (*caption*) Photo-multiplier in..thermoelectrically cooled housing.

Thermo-Fax (þɜ·ɹmofæks). Also **Thermofax.** [f. THERMO- + FACS(IMILE *sb.*] The proprietary name of a process for copying documents by means of infra-red radiation, and of a type of overhead projector employing copies made by this process.

1953 *Official Gaz.* (U.S. Patent Office) 17 Mar. 574/1 *Thermo-Fax.* For electrically operated machine employing infrared light source for producing copies of printed or pictorial matter by means of heat-sensitive paper. Claims use since November 1949. **1956** *Trade Marks Jrnl.* 18 Apr. 236/2 *Thermo-fax*... Reproducing (copying) apparatus for office use. Minnesota Mining and Manufacturing Company.., manufacturers. **1962** A. GÜNTHER *Microphotogr. in Library* (Unesco) 16 Some microfilm readers have special accessories for the occasional production of enlarged prints. Either a dry process such as 'Thermofax' is used or a semi-dry process such as diffusion printing (e.g. 'Copy-rapid') or stabilization techniques. **1964** *Times* 7 Feb. (Advt. Suppl.) p. ii/5 This is the situation the Thermo-Fax overhead projector is designed to overcome... It uses large transparencies which are inexpensive and simple to make—a Thermo-Fax infra-red copying machine takes just 4 seconds to produce one.

thermoform, -er, -ing: see *THERMO-.

Thermogene (þɔ̄·ɹmodʒīn). Also **thermo-, † -gène.** [ad. F. *thermogène* THERMOGENIC *a.*] A proprietary name for medicated cotton wool.

1902 *Official Gaz.* (U.S. Patent Office) 18 Mar. 2357/2 Absorbent wadding. Vandenbroeck & Cie., Brussels, Belgium... *Thermogène.* **1905** *Trade Marks Jrnl.* 22 Nov. 1449 Thermogène absorbent wadding... Medicated wadding for human use. Thomas Other Windsor, trading as the Thermogène Co., Invermay, Lucastes Avenue, Hayward's Heath, Sussex; manufacturer. **1907** *Yesterday's shopping* (1969) 520/1 Thermogene..pkt. 1/o. **1928** A. HUXLEY *Point Counter Point* xviii. 327 What you need..is a good rubbing with camphorated oil and a wad of Thermogene. **1939** M. SPRING RICE *Working-Class Wives* iv. 75 The doctor told her to keep the parts warm, so she used thermogene wool. **1958** W. SANSOM *Cautious Heart* 157 Pinkish brown clouds flew across the cold iron sky like tufts of thermogene loose in the night. **1962** C. WATSON *Hopjoy was Here* xv. 173 I'd been downstairs for some Thermogene.

thermogram. Add: **2.** A photograph or image produced by infra-red radiation emanating naturally from the subject under study.

1957 *Canad. Services Med. Jrnl.* 523 (*caption*) Thermogram lower left showed an area of increased heat. **1964** *Amer. Jrnl. Roentgenol.* XCI. 919/2 The normal breast in the thermogram can be recognized by its size, shape and the heat pattern of the overlying skin. **1967** *Idle Moments* (Austral.) Oct. 5/2 Thermograms..are taken in total darkness, since they are photographic reproductions of infra-red radiations of longer wavelength emitted by the object itself. **1968** *New Scientist* 1 Feb. 263/3 A pair of 'thermograms' of the crater Tycho.

thermograph. Add: **4. a.** = *THERMOGRAM 2. **b.** An apparatus for obtaining thermograms.

1964 *New Scientist* 16 July 163/1 Personal thermographs can sometimes with practice be recognised individually. **1964** *Amer. Jrnl. Roentgenol.* XCI. 919/2 This thermograph has been in daily use in this institution for over a year and has quite recently been replaced by a new model. **1970** *New Scientist* 5 Feb. 260/3 Thermographs of a person's finger before and after smoking show significant changes in the heat pattern.

thermographic, *a.* Add: (Examples corresponding to sense *2 of THERMOGRAPHY.)

1964 *Amer. Jrnl. Roentgenol.* XCI. 925/2 Their experience with thermographic scanning using electrochemical paper was limited, but suggested a promising future. **1975** J. TAYLOR *Superminds* vii. 116 The general features of the aura seem very comparable to pictures obtained by the thermographic camera.

Hence **thermogra·phically** *adv.*, in a thermographic manner; by means of thermography.

1840 *Phil. Trans. R. Soc.* CXXX. 59 The focal image.. had acquired the power of imprinting itself thermographically on the paper. **1964** *New Scientist* 16 July 163/2 It now seems clear that most cancers of the breast raise the skin temperature and can be demonstrated thermographically.

thermography. Add: **2.** The taking or use of infra-red thermograms, esp. to detect tumours.

1957 R. LAWSON in *Canad. Services Med. Jrnl.* XIII. 519 It was apparent that 'thermography' or heat imaging by suitable equipment might have a very important place in the early diagnosis of breast lesions. **1963** *Science* 24 May 873/2 The human body is an ideal subject for thermography. **1969** *New Scientist* 8 May 276/1 Thermography is a completely harmless method in which the patient is 'photographed' by her own body heat. **1971** *Daily Tel.* (Colour Suppl.) 22 Jan. 22/2 Aerial thermography has been used to locate old mineshafts, and coal seams burning underground. **1977** *Time* 20 June 48/1 Thermography, or heat scanning, concentrates on looking for infra-red radiation to find tumors.

thermogravimetry (þɔ̄ɹmogrǎvi·mètri). *Physical Chem.* [f. THERMO- + GRAVIMETRY.] The technique of chemically analysing substances by measuring changes in weight as a function of increasing temperature.

1951 *Chem. Abstr.* XLV. 2274 (*heading*) Thermogravimetry and automatic gravimetry. **1953** *Nature* 22 Aug. 365/1 The advantage of the differential thermogravimetry over differential thermal analysis is that it is quantitative. **1975** H. L. FRIEDMAN in I. M. Kolthoff et al. *Treat. Analytical Chem.* III. III. D-1. 401 In thermogravimetry (TG), one generally records the weight of a sample continually as it is heated through a preselected rate of temperature rise.

Hence **the:rmogravime·tric** *a.*

1953 C. DUVAL *Inorg. Thermogravimetric Analysis* i. 3 The investigations of Honda.., and the construction by Chevenard of automatic recording instruments, have all combined to give birth to a new science which we may perhaps call thermogravimetric analysis. **1972** *Nature* 15 Dec. 418/1 According to our thermogravimetric analyses compounds (III)–(V) contain one molecule of lattice water per formula unit. **1977** *Proc. R. Soc. Med.* LXX. 518/2 If the stone has been passed or removed it should be analysed. This may be by wet chemistry..or by physical methods such as infra-red spectroscopy..X-ray crystallography..or thermogravimetric analysis.

thermohaline to **thermokarst:** see *THERMO-.

thermology. (Earlier example.) **thermological** *a.* (earlier example).

1838 tr. A. Comte in *Edin. Rev.* July 282 The most important and precise laws of thermological phenomena are developed without the slightest enquiry into the intimate nature of heat. *Ibid.* 284 It remained only [for Comte]..to tack to Hydrodynamics the sciences of Magnetism, Electricity, Galvanism and Thermology.

thermolumine·scence. (In Dict. s.v. THERMO-.) Add: (Further examples.) Also, *spec.* used as a means of dating ancient pottery and other material.

1967 *New Scientist* 26 Oct. 206/3 Proposals for thermoluminescence on the Moon are not new. **1968** *New Scientist* 21 Mar. 644/1 Methods of using the natural thermoluminescence of minerals in fired ceramics to find out when they were made have been investigated.. for several years. **1968** *Times* 14 Oct. 8/1 Archaeological fakes, some so convincing that they have deceived experts, are being exposed by a new scientific technique developed for dating ancient pottery. The results of one test, known as thermoluminescence dating, are to be used in a court case in America. **1977** G. CLARK *World Prehistory* (ed. 3) p. xx, The degree of thermoluminescence given out by a sample of pottery or stone under heat is proportional to the amount of radiation accumulated since the sample was last fired.

thermolumine·scent, *a.* (In Dict. s.v. THERMO-.) Add: (Further examples.) Also used *spec.* in sense of prec.; abbrev. TL s.v. *T 6 a.

1962 *Oxf. Univ. Gaz.* 9 Mar. 788/2 *Thermoluminescent Dating.* The principle of this technique is that radiation damage accumulates in all clay due to the natural radioactivity of uranium and thorium impurities [etc.]. **1968** *New Scientist* 21 Mar. 644/2 The initial thermoluminescent measurements are capable of good accuracy and reproducibility. **1970** *Daily Tel.* 25 Apr. 11/6 The thermoluminescent method is based on the fact that many minerals when heated to temperatures around 500°C. emit light, additional to the ordinary red-hot glow. **1971** *Physics Bull.* Oct. 579/1 Nearly all acidic rocks and sedimentary carbonates are thermoluminescent.

thermolysin, thermo-magnetic, -ism: see THERMO- in Dict. and Suppl.

thermomecha·nical, *a.* [f. THERMO- + MECHANICAL *a.* and *sb.*] **a.** *Physics.* Designating or referring to an effect observed in helium II in which the liquid tends to flow from a region of lower to one of higher temperature.

1939 H. LONDON in *Proc. R. Soc.* A. CLXXI. 484 By maintaining a temperature gradient along the capillary, it is thus possible to produce a flow of helium against a pressure gradient... The phenomenon which we shall call the 'thermomechanical effect' reveals a new mechanism by which heat can be transformed into mechanical work. **1959** K. R. ATKINS *Liquid Helium* i. 11 The thermomechanical pressure difference Δp arising from a temperature difference ΔT is given by $\Delta p/\Delta T = Q^*/TV$, where Q^* is the heat transfer associated with the transfer of unit mass..and V is the volume of unit mass. **1964** [see *mechanocaloric* adj. s.v. *MECHANO-]. **1974** D. R. & J. TILLEY *Superfluidity & Superconductivity* i. 9 These manifestations of the thermomechanical effect show clearly that heat transfer and mass transfer in the II are inseparable.

b. *gen.* Both thermal and mechanical; *spec.* in *Metallurgy*, involving simultaneous thermal and mechanical treatment to achieve results not obtained when they are applied separately.

1974 *Sci. Amer.* June 34/3 The less energetic ions (thermal deuterons and tritons)..are capable of producing sharp thermomechanical stresses in a thin skin of the first wall. **1975** *Nature* 7 Aug. 455/3 The uncertainty in geochemical characteristics, especially of the radiogenic isotopes, leaves many degrees of freedom in predicting the present thermo-mechanical state of the interior [of Mercury]. **1976** *Ibid.* 22 July p. iii (Advt.), The journal will welcome papers concerned with the relevant areas of materials technology and metallurgy, e.g. thermomechanical treatments.

thermonastic, -nasty: see *THERMO-.

thermoneu·tral, *a.* [f. THERMO- + NEUTRAL *a.* and *sb.*] **1.** *Biol.* Of an environment or its temperature: such that an organism is in thermal equilibrium without thermoregulation.

1961 in WEBSTER. **1966** *Respiration Physiol.* I. 30 The thermoneutral skin temperature zone for fasting adult sheep has been found to be 33–35°C as determined by immersion in a water bath. **1976** *Nature* 13 May 134/1 Neonates and infants were tested using a tight-fitting face mask with minimal dead space while the subjects were asleep in a thermoneutral condition. **1977** *Lancet* 7 May 988/1 The incubator should if possible be kept at the lower end of the thermoneutral range.

2. *Chem.* Of a reaction: accompanied by neither the absorption nor the emission of heat.

1970 *Nature* 12 Sept. 1097/1 Because the translational energies of the reactant ions are approximately thermal, these two reactions must be thermoneutral or exothermic. **1971** *Sci. Amer.* Dec. 57/3 The first and second reactions are strongly endothermic; the third is exothermic; the fourth is essentially thermoneutral. **1977** I. M. CAMPBELL *Energy & Atmosphere* v. 106 It appears probable that this depends upon the attack of radicals like CH upon N_2 in a near thermoneutral elementary reaction.

So **the:rmoneutra·lity,** the condition of being thermoneutral.

1881 [in Dict. s.v. THERMO-]. **1960** K. SCHMIDT-NIELSEN *Animal Physiol.* iii. 43 Thus, man has a narrow range of thermoneutrality between 27°C and 31°C. **1979** *Nature* 24 May 322/1 The abnormal thermoregulatory thermogenesis quantitatively accounts for most of the metabolic efficiency of the obese animals as pair feeding at thermoneutrality rather than at 23°C reduces the excess fat deposited by 65%.

thermonuclear (þɔ̄ɹmoniū·kliǎɹ). Also **thermo-nuclear.** [f. THERMO- + NUCLEAR *a.*]

a. Derived from, utilizing, or being a nuclear reaction that occurs only at very high temperatures (such as those inside stars), viz. fusion of hydrogen or other light nuclei.

[**1937** G. GAMOW *Struct. Atomic Nuclei* 232 The first calculations concerning thermal nuclear reactions were carried out by Atkinson and Houtermans] **1938** *Physical Rev.* LIII. 595/1 The behavior of a star with a thermonuclear energy source..is studied. **1942** B. BLIVEN *Men who make Future* xi. 202 This perhaps represents a struggle between two almost unbelievably powerful forces within each star—what is called the 'thermo-nuclear reaction' and gravitation. **1954** *Ann. Reg. 1953* 377 *Pravda* described the results of a 'thermo-nuclear' explosion. **1958** *New Statesman* 1 Feb. 123/2 Thermonuclear energy depends on building up atoms of hydrogen into atoms of helium. **1962** F. I. ORDWAY et al. *Basic Astronautics* vi. 284 A new star not yet hot enough to initiate thermonuclear reactions obtains its luminosity from gravitational contraction. **1964** M. GOWING *Britain & Atomic Energy 1939–1945* ix. 260 Thermonuclear fusion of light elements would provide infinitely more powerful reactions than fission of heavy elements. **1969** *Times* 20 Feb. 17/5 It implied that their calculations of the sun's thermonuclear fuel budget were considerably in error. **1976** *McGraw-Hill Yearbk. Sci. & Technol.* 342/1 In controlled thermonuclear reactors the nuclear reaction $D + T \rightarrow {}^4He + n + 17{\cdot}6$ MeV occurs in a plasma at temperatures of 100–500 × 10^6 kelvins.

b. Pertaining to, characterized by, or possessing weapons that utilize thermonuclear reactions.

1953 *Time* 19 Oct. 25/3 Secretary of Defense Wilson, at his press conference, cast doubt on a suggestion that the Russians had a thermonuclear bomb 'in droppable form'. **1955** *Ann. Reg. 1954* 169 Mr. Adlai Stevenson.. inquired whether the 'New Look' meant leaving the country with 'the choice of inaction or a thermo-nuclear holocaust'. **1955** *Times* 13 July 9/5 They draw attention to the possibility that a thermo-nuclear war might put an end to the human race. **1958** *Listener* 7 Aug. 207/3 So long as Britain makes her own nuclear weapons, and particularly the thermo-nuclear weapon, there is no possibility of dissuading France or Germany or Sweden from developing theirs. **1959** *Times Lit. Suppl.* 16 Jan. 27/3 In the thermo-nuclear age, if civilization is not to disintegrate.., the premises of Gandhi have an immediate relevance. **1959** *Daily Tel.* 4 Mar. 8 With the thermonuclear cloud overshadowing the world no statesman, not even a Soviet Prime Minister, can afford to disregard mankind's longing for peace. **1965** H. KAHN *On Escalation* ii. 42 In a thermonuclear balance of terror, both nations will be reluctant to start a crisis. **1966** J. W. BURTON in de Reuck & Knight *Conflict in Society* xxiii. 380 In the relations of the two thermo-nuclear States, tensions arise from unacceptable enactments of their respective roles. **1972** M. H. HALPERIN *Contemporary Mil. Strategy* i. 7 One has only to recall Mr. Khruschev's statements during the Cuban missile crisis about the world being close to thermonuclear war.

Thermopane: see *THERMO-.

thermophil, -phile, *sb.* Add: (Examples.) **thermophilic** *a.* (earlier and further examples); **thermophilous** *a.* (further examples).

1894 MACFADYEN & BLAXALL in *Jrnl. Path. & Bacteriol.* III. 88 To those organisms that grow best at very high temperatures we have applied the name of thermophilic bacteria. **1909** H. W. CONN *Agric. Bacteriol.* (ed. 2) i. 16 A few species..grow best at unexpectedly high temperatures, some having been found flourishing at 140° or even higher. These peculiar bacteria are called thermophiles. **1964** COONEY & EMERSON *Thermophilic Fungi* i. 6 To the algologist a thermophile may have a maximum between 60° and 80°C..to the bacteriologist..55° to 80°C, and the acarologist 35° to 45°C. **1965** BELL & COOMBE tr. *Strasburger's Textbk. Bot.* III. 774 The wood and fruits of thermophilous trees and shrubs have been repeatedly found some hundreds of metres above their present altitudinal limits. **1975** J. G. EVANS *Environment Early Man Brit. Isles* ii. 49 The Allerød Interstadial..was the first zone to see the appearance of thermophilous land snails. **1977** *Time* 26 Dec. 20/3 Their droppings will be placed into fermenter tanks filled with thermophilic (heat-loving) bacteria. **1981** *New Scientist* 10 Sept. 667/2 The plasmid may be of value..for transferring genes into thermophiles (bacteria that like high temperatures).

thermophysical, -physics: see *THERMO-.

thermoplastic, *a.* Delete entry s.v. THERMO- in Dict. and substitute:

thermoplastic (þɔ̄ɹmoplæ·stik), *a.* and *sb.* [f. THERMO- + PLASTIC *a.*] **A.** *adj.* Becoming soft when heated and rigid when allowed to cool, and capable of being repeatedly reheated and reshaped without loss of properties; made of such a substance.

1883 [in Dict. s.v. THERMO-]. **1909** *Chem. Abstr.* III. 2063 Thermo-plastic composition containing keratin. Keratin is mixed with β-naphthol and the compn. subjected to heat and pressure, to form a subst. for rubber, celluloid, etc. **1937** *Jrnl. R. Aeronaut. Soc.* XLI. 525 Some kinds of synthetic resins and to a limited extent one natural resin (shellac) have the valuable characteristic of being 'thermosetting', i.e., when once moulded they set to permanently infusible products. Most resins are 'thermoplastic', i.e., they become soft whenever the temperature exceeds a certain value. **1951** [see *benzyl* s.v. *BENZO-]. **1958** *Listener* 4 Dec. 967/1 Thermoplastic tiles and rubber floors. **1976** J. FLEMING *To make an Underworld* xi. 128 These small thermo-plastic boats..were safer than houses, kids could play with them.

B. *sb.* A thermoplastic substance.

1929 *Brit. Plastics & Moulded Products Trader* June 25/1 Thermoplastics are divided into pheno-plastics..and amino-plastics. **1945** *Electronic Engin.* XVII. 516 It is frequently used in association with polythene and other thermoplastics. **1967** *Times Rev. Industry* May 75/3 Other thermoplastics, including polyvinyl chloride (PVC), polypropylene and polyvinylidene chloride comprise about 10 per cent..of the total weight of plastics used in packaging. **1976** *Shooting Mag.* Dec. 33/2 (Advt.), Lightweight muff-type ear protector... Earcups are manufactured from thermoplastic with soft sponge-filled ear cushions.

Hence **the:rmoplasti·city**, the quality of being thermoplastic.

1935 C. ELLIS *Chem. Synthetic Resins* II. lvi. 1150 The thermoplasticity of the resins is a disadvantage. **1962** J. T. MARSH *Self-Smoothing Fabrics* x. 141 Some of these mixed products can be used to reduce the solubility and swelling of the linear polymer but the thermoplasticity will be reduced. **1980** *Nuclear Engin. & Design* LVII. 323 (*heading*) Coupling phenomena in thermoplasticity.

thermopower: see *THERMO-.

Thermopylae (þɜɪmǫ·pılī, -pilai). The name of a narrow pass on the north-east coast of Greece between Thessaly and Locris, the scene of a battle in 480 B.C. in which a small Greek force temporarily withheld a Persian invasion; used *transf.* and *fig.* with reference to heroic resistance against strong opposition.

1928 A. HUXLEY *Point Counter Point* xxix. 471 E. talked a lot about Thermophylae and the Spartans. But my resistance was even more heroic. Leonidas had three hundred companions. I defended my spiritual Thermopylae single-handed against E. and his Freemen. **1929** J. BUCHAN *Courts of Morning* III. iii. 335 I'm going to try the Themopylae stunt... Our Thermopylae is going to be a more cunning affair than the old one. **1955** in R. Megarry *Second Miscellany-at-Law* (1973) 157 It courageously held the line of reason at the Thermopylae of logic and did not give way at the Gettysburg of fact. **1967** C. SETON-WATSON *Italy from Liberalism to Fascism* iii. 125 A column of 500 Italian troops had been wiped out by several thousand Ethiopians at Dogali, after fighting almost to the last man and the last round. This 'Italian Thermopylae' caught the public imagination. **1972** V. G. KIERNAN *Lords of Human Kind* (ed. 2) p. xxiv, The consequence has been Vietnam's Thermopylae of twenty years.

thermoreceptor (þɜ·ɪmorīse:ptǫɪ). *Physiol.* [f. THERMO- + RECEPTOR.] A nerve ending that is sensitive to stimulation by heat and cold.

1937 L. V. HERBRUNN *Outl. Gen. Physiol.* xli. 506 Animals in general are sensitive to heat and cold but, except in higher animals, thermoreceptors are rare, or at any rate not well known. **1951** *Jrnl. Neurophysiol.* XIV. 423 Knowledge of the intracutaneous depth of the thermoreceptors is of very great importance. **1961** *Lancet* 9 Sept. 610/1 Professor Hensel will lecture..on the electrophysiology of thermoreceptors. **1971** D. J. AIDLEY *Physiol. of Excitable Cells* xv. 307 The sense organs themselves can be classified according to the type of stimulus which normally excites them. Thus mechanoreceptors are excited by mechanical stimuli, photoreceptors are sensitive to light, thermoreceptors are temperature sensitive.

thermoregulation (þɜɪmoregiŭlē·ʃən). [f. THERMO- + REGULATION.] Regulation of temperature, esp. body temperature in an animal or human.

1927 *Jrnl. Exper. Zool.* XLVII. 156 We deal in nest-building with a behavior pattern definitely adapted to the thermoregulation of the organism. **1932** *Jrnl. Gen. Physiol.* XVI. 9 The machine described above is kept in a thermoregulated room. The thermoregulation of a room for such purposes has been regarded..as a difficult and expensive undertaking. **1962** *Lancet* 8 Dec. 1207/1 Most of the research into human problems of thermoregulation in hot surroundings has been sponsored by the Government and the Services. **1972** *Sci. Amer.* June 74/2 Understanding of the physiology of the sphinx moth's thermoregulation requires..an examination of the levels of body temperature maintained during flight.

So **thermore·gulate** *v. intr.*, to regulate temperature, esp. body temperature; **thermore·gulated, -re·gulating** *ppl. adjs.*; **thermore·gulative** (*rare*), **the:rmoregula·tory** *adjs.*, of, pertaining to, or effecting thermoregulation.

1917 T. SOLLMAN *Man. Pharmacol.* 449 (*heading*) The hypothetical thermoregulating centres. **1927** *Jrnl. Exper. Zool.* XLVII. 152 Nest-building may be considered a thermoregulative activity. **1932** Thermoregulated [see above]. **1949** KOESTLER *Insight & Outlook* xi. 168 Animals..develop techniques such as nest building..and, in the case of the termites, even contriving thermo-regulatory devices. **1972** *Science* 12 May 601/3 Bumblebees, which can also thermoregulate, occur on the neotropical and Asian mountains. **1973** *Brit. Med. Jrnl.* 22 Dec. 727/2 Some degree of thermoregulatory failure is common in old age. **1974** M. C. GERALD *Pharmacology* xiv. 265 Aspirin..does increase heat loss from the body by its action on the thermoregulatory centers in the hypothalamus. **1978** *Nature* 19 Oct. 646/2 Reptiles which thermoregulate behaviourally..are subject to considerable daily fluctuations in body temperature.

thermoremanence, -remanent: see *THERMO-.

Thermos. Add: (Further examples.) Hence (freq. with small initial) applied loosely to any vacuum flask. Also *absol.*, and designating a liquid which has been kept in a Thermos flask.

Still (1984) a proprietary term in Great Britain.

1922 S. LEWIS *Babbitt* xx. 255 Say, could I borrow your thermos—just dropped in to see if I could borrow your thermos bottle. **1923** R. FRY *Let.* 21 June (1972) II. 541 I'd got my thermos filled the day before. **1938** C. G. NORRIS *Bricks without Straw* 350 He poured a glass of water from his thermos jug. **1950** *Time* 3 Apr. 24/3 Simon began to pack blankets and Thermoses for a fishing trip. **1960** E. L. WALLANT *Human Season* (1965) v. 55 'Let me pour you some coffee.' He poured a cupful from the big Thermos. **1977** *New Yorker* 27 June 53/1 Stoical munching forms in mackintoshes taking a swig of something hot out of thermoses. **1978** P. GRACE *Mutuwhenua* vii. 40 The others had home-made biscuits in their parcels or fruit. Oranges, apples, and reeking bananas. Chocolates, a thermos of soup. **1979** *Church Times* 14 Sept. 12/4 No registration is necessary, but please bring sandwiches and a thermos. **1979** *Nature* 15 Nov. 227/1 Sipping green tea poured out of a large thermos flask, we discussed differences between Chinese and UK science. **1979** *Beautiful Brit. Columbia* Winter 6 Relaxing with a hot cup of thermos coffee. **1980** P. FITZGERALD *Human Voices* ii. 47 Workers off work, each with their own thermos.

thermosensitive, -sensitivity: see *THERMO-.

thermoset (þɜ·ɪmoset), *a.* and *sb.* [f. THERMO- + SET *ppl. a.*] **A.** *adj.* Incapable of being softened or melted by heat like a thermoplastic; also = *THERMOSETTING *ppl. a.*

1947 [see *CURE *v.*[1] 10]. **1972** *Physics Bull.* Nov. 663/2 Epoxy resins are polymers with one or more epoxide groups..which can be converted to a thermoset stage by reaction with appropriate curing agents. **1973** *Sci. Amer.* July 42/3 Today the matrix in glass-reinforced composites may be either a thermoset plastic, such as polyester, phenolic or epoxy, or any of a number of thermoplastic resins, such as nylon, polyethylene or polystyrene. **1973** J. M. G. COWIE *Polymers* i. 19 The thermoset plastics generally have superior abrasion and dimensional stability characteristics compared with the thermoplastics which have better flexural and impact properties. In contrast to the thermoplastics, thermosetting polymers..are changed irreversibly from fusible, soluble products into highly intractable crosslinked resins which cannot be moulded by flow.

B. *sb.* A thermoset substance.

1955 in M. Reifer *Dict. New Words.* **1958** *Times Rev. Industry* Aug. 57/1 Thermoplastics have gained a.. market at the expense of thermosets. **1970** *New Scientist* 19 Mar. Suppl. 9/1 Reinforced thermosets are used in many high-strength applications from boat hulls to aircraft radomes. **1975** *Sci. Amer.* July 63/1 Nonmetals such as thermoplastics, thermosets, polytetrafluoroethylene and carbon-graphites are successful bearing materials because of their excellent resistance to scoring and erosion.

thermose·tting, *ppl. a.* [f. THERMO- + SETTING *ppl. a.*] Of a plastic: solidifying and becoming thermoset when heated; also, = *THERMOSET *a.*

[**1929** *Brit. Plastics & Moulded Products Trader* June 24/2 Thermoplastic mouldings..comprise substances which go through a process of thermo-setting on the application of heat and pressure.] **1931** *British Plastics Yearbk.* 74 *Thermo-setting plastics*, those compositions that though thermo-plastic in the first instance, harden off rapidly under the influence of heat. **1937** [see *THERMOPLASTIC *a.*]. **1951** *Archit. Rev.* CIX. 166/2 Hardness and resistance to scratching and heat..is one of the main advantages of the thermo-setting plastics. **1973** [see *THERMOSET *a.*]. **1982** M. DUKE *Flashpoint* xviii. 134 The thermosetting polyurethane plastic floor. **1983** *Daily Tel.* 12 Dec. 19/3 The inclusion of fillers, particularly metallic ones, in thermosetting plastics is a known and recognised practice for reducing and dissipating exotherm.

thermo-siphon. Add: (Further examples, esp. with reference to internal-combustion engines.) So **thermo-sipho·nic** *a.*

1904 A. B. F. YOUNG *Compl. Motorist* iii. 55 Circulation is maintained either by a centrifugal pump driven by a chain off the engine shaft, or, automatically, by means of what is known as the 'Thermo-Syphon' system, in which advantage is taken of the fact that hot water rises to the top of a tank and cold water sinks to the bottom. **1920** *Autocar* 7 Feb. 251/1 Water is circulated by thermo-syphonic action. **1963** R. F. WEBB *Motorists' Dict.* 210 *Thermo syphon cooling*, a type of liquid cooling for an automobile engine where there is no mechanical assistance for the flow of the liquid through the system. **1968** G. N. GEORGANO *Compl. Encycl. Motorcars* 473 Cooling was by thermo-syphon, the hallmark of the Renault being the huge dashboard radiator. **1982** *Solar Energy* (Shell Internat. Petroleum Co.) 3/2 (*caption*) Typical solar water heater thermo-syphon system.

thermosphere (þɜ·ɪmosfīᵊɪ). [f. THERMO- + SPHERE *sb.*] **1.** † **a.** (See quot. 1924.) *Obs. rare*⁻¹. **b.** The part of the atmosphere between the mesopause and the height at which it ceases to have the properties of a continuous medium, characterized throughout by an increase of temperature with height.

1924 S. N. SEN in *Q. Jrnl. R. Meteorol. Soc.* L. 29 Up to an approximate height of 8 km. above the ground the air density is chiefly controlled by the temperature. The name 'thermosphere' is proposed to denote this layer of the atmosphere. **1950** S. CHAPMAN in *Jrnl. Geophysical Res.* LV. 396, I propose the name..thermosphere for the layer of upward increasing temperature above that level [i.e. of the mesosphere]. **1967** R. W. FAIRBRIDGE *Encycl. Atmospheric Sci.* 731/2 At the top of the thermosphere, the temperature approaches a constant value of ~ 1500°K. **1981** *Sci. Amer.* July 46/3 On the earth the thermosphere is present day and night; the large-scale rotation of the atmosphere with the planet carries the heated day-side upper atmosphere to the night side of the planet. On the night side of Venus, however, the thermosphere disappears.

2. The warmer, upper part of the oceans.

1956 *Nature* 16 June 1106 (*in figure*) Thermosphere. **1957** [see *psychrosphere* s.v. *PSYCHRO-].

Hence **thermosphe·ric** *a.*

1971 *Nature* 29 Jan. 333/2 Calculations suggest that the thermospheric winds may produce some net rotation [of the atmosphere] at low latitudes. **1979** *Ibid.* 8 Feb. 458/2 Rocket measurements of mesospheric and thermospheric nitric oxide concentrations revealed strong enhancements during auroral particle precipitation events.

thermostabile (þɜɪmostēi·bəil). *a. Biol.* [f. THERMO- + L. *stabilis* STABLE *a.*] = THERMOSTABLE *a.*

1908 *Practitioner* Feb. 249 In the proglottides of tapeworms..there exists a lipoid substance..which..is thermo-stabile and is similar to proteolytic ferment. **1947** *Ann. Rev. Microbiol.* I. 92 Mottling type strains are more thermostabile than the ringspot type strains.

thermostat. Add: Hence as *v. trans.*, to regulate the temperature of (a substance or a piece of apparatus) by means of a thermostat. Also **the·rmostat(t)ed** *ppl. a.*

1940 *Brit. Jrnl. Psychol.* July 63 The tests were done in a roughly thermostated water-bath. **1950** W. J. MOORE *Physical Chem.* xv. 424 The cell must be well thermostated since the conductivity increases with the temperature. **1962** *Plant & Cell Physiol.* III. 212 The temperature of the algal suspension was controlled by flowing thermostated water on the surface of the vessel. **1963** G. L. PICKARD *Descriptive Physical Oceanogr.* vi. 86 This necessitates thermostating the samples to ±0·001C° during measurement. **1967** MARGERISON & EAST *Introd. Polymer Chem.* ii. 94 The data..were obtained using solutions of polystyrene in benzene illuminated by light of 5461Å and thermostatted at 25°C. **1979** *Nature* 25 Jan. 291/2 The complete reaction chamber was heated in a thermostatted oven.

thermo-tank: see *THERMO-.

thermotic, *a.* Add: **thermotics** *sb. pl.* (earlier example).

1831 W. WHEWELL *Let.* 18 Sept. in I. Todhunter *William Whewell* (1876) II. 132 It is very true that we very much want a name for the part of science which treats of *light*..also..that which treats of *Heat*...[In my MSS.] I have called one *Photistics* and the other *Thermotics*.

thermotolerant: see *THERMO-.

thermotropic, *a.* Add: Also with pronunc. (-trǭᵘ·pik). **2.** *Physical Chem.* Brought about or effected by a change in temperature: used esp. with reference to mesophases and their phase transitions.

1909 SENIER & SHEPHEARD in *Jrnl. Chem. Soc.* XCV. II. 1945 Phototropic and thermotropic reactions are more probably due to isomeric changes affecting the aggregation of molecules in solids than to intramolecular change. **1962** G. W. GRAY *Molecular Structure & Properties of Liquid Crystals* i. 5 Mesophases are most commonly observed when a suitable compound is heated to a temperature above that at which the crystal lattice is stable. This type of mesomorphism is called thermotropic. **1966,** etc. [see *LYOTROPIC *a.* 2]. **1972** *Physics Bull.* May 279/3 This article will be concerned only with those liquid crystals, known as thermotropic, where the phase transitions are induced by a change in temperature. **1978** *Nature* 13 Apr. 646/1 The membrane lipids of cells cultured in these conditions show a greatly sharpened thermotropic gel-to-liquid crystalline phase transition.

therophyte (thīᵊ·rofəit). *Bot.* [ad. Da. *therofyte* (C. Raunkiaer 1904, in *Bot. Tidsskrift* XXVI. p. xiv) f. Gr. θέρο(ς summer + -PHYTE.] (See quot. 1960.)

1913 *Jrnl. Ecol.* I. 18 Therophytes, or plants of the favourable season, live through the unfavourable season as seeds; hence they are annual plants. **1932** FULLER & CONARD tr. *Braun-Blanquet's Plant Sociol.* i. 13 Many communities of the subtropics begin their annual development with a therophyte aspect. **1952** P. W. RICHARDS *Trop. Rain Forest* i. 10 Therophytes are entirely absent, except in clearings. **1960** N. POLUNIN *Introd.*

Plant Geogr. iii. 93 Therophytes (annuals)..complete their life-cycle, from germination to ripe seed, within a single limited vegetative period, surviving the unfavourable times as seeds, spores, or other special (usually resistant) reproductive bodies. They are especially abundant in deserts.

theropod, *a.*, *sb.* (Examples.)

1933 A. S. ROMER *Vertebr. Paleontol.* ix. 181 The theropods (using this term in a broad sense) include all the characteristic terrestrial reptilian carnivores of the late Triassic, Jurassic, and Cretaceous. **1970** *Nature* 11 Apr. 109/1 Theropod dinosaurs normally walked on three toes on each hind foot, leaving birdlike tracks. **1981** *Sci. Digest* Aug. 36 (*caption*) The most complete theropod found in China, *Yangchuanosaurus shangyouensis* (discovered 1977, described in 1978).

theropodous, *a.* Add after *Thēropoda* in etym. (O. C. Marsh 1881, in *Amer. Jrnl. Sci.* CXXI. 423). For Cope's substitute Marsh's in def.

thesaurosis (þisǭrōu·sis). *Path.* [f. Gr. θησαυρ-ός store + -OSIS.] A disorder of the lungs caused by the accumulation in them of inhaled material.

1958 *New England Jrnl. Med.* 6 Mar. 475/1 Evidence concerning the etiology of the pulmonary lesion of Case 2 is..less compelling, but we believe that..this, too, was a case of thesaurosis due to hair-spray constituents. **1975** *New Yorker* 7 Apr. 56/3 For at least fifteen years, it has been suspected that the plastic resins in hair sprays cause a restrictive-lung-storage disease called thesaurosis, as well as abnormal lung cells that may be the precursors of lung cancer.

thesaurus. Delete ‖ and add: **2. b.** A collection of concepts or words arranged according to sense; also (*U.S.*) a dictionary of synonyms and antonyms.

1852 [in Dict., sense 2.] **1898** 'MARK TWAIN' *Autobiogr.* (1924) I. 172 The fact that the writer's balance at the vocabulary bank has run short and that he is too lazy to replenish it from the thesaurus. **1942** BERREY & VAN DEN BARK (*title*) The American thesaurus of slang. **1960** W. NAYLOR *Silver Birch Anthol.* 8, I know how you have to polish and repolish, alter words, delete others, change sentences, consult the dictionary and the thesaurus, before you are satisfied. **1962** U. WEINREICH in Householder & Saporta *Probl. Lexicogr.* 30 The grouping of synonyms along a continuum yields a thesaurus, like Roget's. **1975** (*title*) Family word finder: a new thesaurus of synonyms and antonyms in dictionary form.

c. A classified list of terms, esp. key-words, in a particular field, for use in indexing and information retrieval.

1957 H. BROWNSON in *Proc. Internat. Study Conference on Classification for Information Retrieval* 100 The best answer..may be the application of a mechanized thesaurus based on networks of related meanings. **1961** *Aslib Proc.* XIII. 265 We decided to..designate the analytical compilation a 'thesaurus'. **1965** *Revue Internat. de Documentation* XXXII. 21/1 It has become commonplace to hear of retrieval systems embodying a thesaurus. In this context a thesarus usually means an arrangement of a vocabulary of terms in each group being connected in some defined way. **1974** *Encycl. Brit. Macropædia* IX. 572/2 The second stage should be a fully automatic selection and matching process, preferably using a thesaurus.

these, *dem. adj.* Add: **1. f.** *these days* advb. phr., nowadays, at present.

1936 R. LEHMANN *Weather in Streets* I. v. 97 An estate like this must be a terrible problem these days. **1948** M. DICKENS *Joy & Josephine* I. iv. 132 'Play golf?' Mr. Gray asked George, who answered: 'Not these days,' as if he ever had. **1960** S. BARSTOW *Kind of Loving* II. iii. 181 He looks as though he's walked out of an American picture. It's all Yankeeland these days. **1981** *Woman* 5 Dec. 5/1 These days women are educated to expect some choice in how they spend their lives.

Thesean, *a.* Add: Also †**Theseian.** (Earlier example.)

1815 B. R. HAYDON *Jrnl.* 6 Nov. in T. Taylor *Life Haydon* (1853) I. xv. 294 Lord Elgin's steward..thus entirely ruined the moulds of the Theseian bas-reliefs, which had cost Lord Elgin so much.

thesis. Add: **2.** *spec.* in Old English prosody and in the prosody of other Germanic languages.

1870 F. A. MARCH *Introd. Anglo-Saxon* 147 The regular Germanic epic line has four..arses in each section, each of which may have a thesis or not. **1888** A. H. TOLMAN in *Trans. Mod. Lang. Assoc. Amer.* III. 20 Only one accented syllable, out of the first sixteen in this poem [sc. *Beowulf*], has a syllable expressed as its thesis or senkung. **1910** J. SCHIPPER *Hist. Eng. Versification* 28 Syllables with this secondary accent are necessary in certain cases as links between the arsis and the thesis. **1938** A. CAMPBELL *Battle of Brunanburh* 18 A dissyllabic second thesis seems not to be found in lines of type A. **1942** J. C. POPE *Rhythm of Beowulf* 49 We fill the down-beat or thesis of this measure with a rest.

6. *thesis-monger* (see MONGER[1] 2); **thesis-novel** = *roman à thèse* s.v. *ROMAN *sb.*[4]

1932 *Essays & Stud.* XVII. 75 The aimless burrowings of a thesis-monger. **1959** *Listener* 13 Aug. 255/1 Subjects like the Henrician Reformation..have been far too much in the hands of thesis-mongers. **1934** WEBSTER, Thesis novel. **1954** K. TILLOTSON *Novels of Eighteen-Forties* I. 117 Novelists who..avoided the thesis-novel. **1979** S. WEINTRAUB *London Yankees* vii. 233 Elizabeth Robins..continued writing thesis-novels on euthanasia, prostitution, women's rights.

Thesmophoric, *a.* Add: Also **Thesmophoria** (see Dict.).

1788 J. LEMPRIERE *Bibliotheca Classica* s.v. *Thesmophora*, The Thesmophoria were instituted by Triptolemus, or according to some by Orpheus, or the daughters of Danaus. *Ibid.*, Such as were initiated at the festivals of Eleusis assisted at the Thesmophoria. **1890** J. G. FRAZER *Golden Bough* II. iii. 46 The casting of the pigs into the vaults at the Thesmophoria formed part of the dramatic representation of Proserpine's descent into the lower world. **1940** M. P. NILSSON *Gr. Folk Relig.* 24 Best known is the festival of the autumn sowing, the Thesmophoria. **1978** *Times Lit. Suppl.* 18 Aug. 922/4 The regular female festival of fertility, the Thesmophoria, was entirely confined to women.

thesp (þesp), colloq. abbrev. of THESPIAN *sb.*

1962 *New Statesman* 23 Feb. 274/3 Like all tales about thesps, [it] seems to involve us just that much less in their fate. **1976** *Times Lit. Suppl.* 5 Mar. 262/2 More commonly than not, Shakespeare productions by Eng Lit dons involving undergraduate actors come with terrific programme notes but scrawny thesps. **1978** *Guardian Weekly* 15 Jan. 21/4 Hero and heroine—actors both..a famous pair of Budapest thesps.

Thespianism (þe·spiăniz'm). [f. THESPIAN *sb.* + -ISM.] The art of acting, dramatic art.

1914 C. MACKENZIE *Sinister Street* II. III. viii. 664 Scarcely ever did the Academic Muse enter the O.U.D.S. ..She must greatly dislike Thespianism with all that it connoted of mildewed statuary in an English garden. **1928** *Daily Express* 79 Oct. 9 He still wraps round him..the rags of a tattered toga of Thespianism.

Thessalian (þesē^i·liăn), *a.* and *sb. Gr. Antiq.* [f. L. *Thessalius, Thessalus* (Gr. Θεσσάλειος, Θεσσαλός) adjs. f. *Thessalia* (Θεσσαλία) Thessaly: see -AN, -IAN.] **A.** *adj.* Of or pertaining to Thessaly, a region in northern Greece.

1590 SHAKES. *Mids. N.* IV. i. 127 Crooke kneed, and dew-lapt, like Thessalian Buls. **1667** MILTON *P.L.* II. 544 As when Alcides..tore Through pain up by the roots Thessalian Pines. **1757** J. DYER *Fleece* II. 56 When, o'er the deep by flying Phryxus brought, The fam'd Thessalian ram enrich'd her plains. **1842** TENNYSON *Talking Oak* 292 Or that Thessalian growth, In which the swarthy ringdove sat, And mystic sentence spoke. **1888** *Encycl. Brit.* XXIII. 299/1 These Thessalian passes were of the utmost importance to southern Greece. **1973** R. LANE-FOX *Alexander* I. iii. 47 Demeratus the Corinthian..had bought the horse from his Thessalian breeder.

B. *sb.* An inhabitant of Thessaly; the dialect of Greek spoken there.

1608 E. TOPSELL *Serpents* 5 One Aleua a Thessalian, who feeding his Oxen in Thessaly..there fell in loue with him a Serpent. **1704** S. PARKER tr. *Tully's Old Age* 34 When Cineas the Thessalian told him of it. **1888** *Encycl. Brit.* XXIII. 299/2 In race, as in geographical position, the Thessalians held an intermediate place between the non-Hellenic Macedonians and the Greeks of pure blood. **1910** C. D. BUCK *Gr. Dial.* I. 3 Thessalian is of all dialects the most closely related to Lesbian, and at the same time shares in some of the characteristics of the West Greek dialects. **1973** R. LANE-FOX *Alexander* I. iii. 60 Philip's heir was ruler of the Thessalians, a people essential for his army. **1978** *Language* LIV. 179 Thereafter Thessalian underwent some influence from Northwest Greek.

theta. Add: **1. b. theta-function**: in def., after 'integral' read '$\int \exp(-t^2)\,dt$'.

2. *Biol.* Used to designate rhythmic activity of the brain recorded by an electroencephalograph and having a frequency of between four and seven cycles per second.

1944 WALTER & DOVEY in *Jrnl. Neurol., Neurosurg., & Psychiatry* VII. 64/1 In the case of the 4–7 c/s. waves the term we suggest is 'theta'. *Ibid.* 65/1 It is suggested that rhythms at about 6 c/s. should be termed 'theta' rhythms and that such rhythms are characteristic of the resting, immature or isolated parieto-temporal complex. **1953** *Brit. Jrnl. Psychol.* XLIV. 320 The excessive theta rhythm ..found in some aggressive psychopaths. **1961** *Lancet* 26 Aug. 465/1 An E.E.G. recorded when fasting showed some abnormality, with rhythmic 6 c.p.s. theta activity in the resting tracing. **1972** *Sci. Amer.* Feb. 85/3 Subjects with a great deal of experience in meditation showed other changes: the alpha waves slowed..and rhythmical theta waves at six to seven cycles per second appeared. **1975** J. TAYLOR *Superminds* vii. 121 In states of extreme emotion, theta waves of four to seven cycles and up to thirty microvolts occur.

3. In Scientology: creative energy or spirit. Also **the·tan,** the embodiment of this spirit in the individual. (See quots. 1965.)

1951 L. R. HUBBARD *Handbk. for Preclears* 77/1 *Theta.* The mathematical symbol for the static of thought. By *theta* is meant the static itself. **1952** —— *Scientology: 8–80*, 83 The thetan, or theta being, takes over a body only a few days or a week before birth. **1957** J. F. HORNER *Summary of Scientol.* iv. 56 In Scientology, the specialized term, 'theta', is used to refer to thought and spirit. The term, 'Thetan', refers to the single unit of beingness which each person is. **1965** L. R. HUBBARD *Scientol. Abridged Dict.* 33 *Theta*, energy peculiar to life or a thetan which acts upon material in the physical universe. *Ibid.*, *Thetan*, the person himself..; that which is aware of being aware; the identity that is the individual. **1971** [see *SCIENTOLOGY]. **1977** C. MCFADDEN *Serial* (1978) xxvii. 60/2 Marlene said Theta taught you how to overcome Specific Negatives. **1977** *Times Lit. Suppl.* 13 May 582/5 The gnosis centres on the 'thetan', the true self... The core task of the cult ought to be to cleanse and return the thetan to its immortal, pristine, form.

4. Chem. *theta* (or θ, Θ) *temperature*, the temperature of a polymer solution at which it behaves ideally as regards its osmotic pressure; so *theta condition, solvent*, etc.

1953 P. J. FLORY *Princ. Polymer Chem.* xii. 523 Frequently it is preferred to use as a parameter the 'ideal' temperature Θ... At the temperature $T=\Theta$, the chemical potential due to segment-solvent interactions is zero... Hence the temperature Θ is that at which the excess chemical potential is zero and deviations from ideality vanish. *Ibid.* xiv. 612 An ideal solvent, or Θ-solvent. *Ibid.*, The intrinsic viscosity usually changes rapidly with temperature in the vicinity of the Θ-point. **1966** BRANDRUP & IMMERGUT *Polymer Handbk.* IV. 163 Theta-solvents (θ-solvents) are solvents in which, at a given temperature, a polymer molecule is in the so-called theta-state, where it behaves like an ideal statistical coil. **1973** J. M. G. COWIE *Polymers* vii. 138 Above the theta temperature expansion of the coil takes place, caused by interactions with the solvent, whereas below Θ the polymer segments attract one another, the excluded volume is negative, and eventual phase separation occurs. **1974** *Sci. Amer.* Dec. 60/2 At that temperature, which varies for different polymers and solvents, the measured properties of the polymer can be usefully compared with those of other polymers at their theta temperature.

5. *Particle Physics.* Freq. written θ. A meson that decays into two pions, now identified with the kaon. Also *theta meson.*

1954 *Physical Rev.* XCIV. 1732/1 A large fraction of these V^0 decays are consistent with the decay scheme $\theta^0 \to \pi^{\pm} + \pi^{\pm}$ (or $\mu^{\mp}$). **1955**, etc. [see *TAU].

6. *theta pinch* (Nucl. Physics): a toroidal pinch (*PINCH *sb.* 10**) in which the magnetic field follows the axis of the plasma and the current-carrying coils encircle it. [θ, the symbol of the angle of the radius vector of the circular path of the current.]

1959 *Nucleonics* Oct. 82/2 The conference topic that aroused greatest interest was the theta pinch. **1967** *New Scientist* 9 Nov. 369/1 The simplicity of the theta pinch as a means of achieving that sought after goal of power from thermonuclear reactions had led to considerable studies of its real effectiveness in confining and heating up a plasma. **1974** *Nature* 20 Sept. 193/2 In the theta-pinch design, the compression coils are not superconducting and no special measures are taken to reduce neutron heating.

thetatron (þī·tătrǫn). *Nucl. Physics.* Also **Thetatron.** [f. THETA + *-TRON.] A fusion reactor employing a theta pinch in which the plasma is compressed axially by causing the current in the coils, and hence the axial magnetic field, to increase suddenly.

1959 *Nucl. Instruments & Methods* IV. 323/1 At A.W.R.E. both straight and toroidal magnetic compression devices ('Thetatron') have been examined. **1962** W. B. THOMPSON *Introd. Plasma Physics* iv. 63 Much interest has been shown in the axial compression devices, or thetatron, in which a cyclindrical plasma is compressed by a rapidly rising axial field. **1964** *Times Sci. Rev.* Autumn 14/1 Thetatrons produce hot dense plasmas for..a few microseconds. **1980** W. M. GIBSON *Physics Nucl. Reactors* x. 200 At the Culham laboratory..magnetic mirror and bottle systems have received thorough investigation in experiments with Thetatron and Phoenix devices.

Thetford (þe·tfǭɹd). The name of a town in Norfolk, England, used *attrib.* to designate Saxo-Norman pottery of a type made there and in other parts of East Anglia. Usu. as *Thetford ware.*

1949 *Archaeological News Let.* Feb. 3/1 Until quite recently the origin and affinities of St. Neots (or Thetford) pottery have been misunderstood. **1956** *Proc. Cambridge Antiquarian Soc.* XLIX. 46 There is also evidence that Thetford ware was made at Norwich and Ipswich. **1966** *Daily Tel.* 31 Oct. 14/5 The kilns themselves and the finds of pottery may shed new light on Thetford ware which is known all over East Anglia... This is the first time that a good specimen of a Thetford ware kiln has been available for examination. **1971** *Canad. Antiques Collector* Apr. 17/2 Thetford Ware which is very frequently found at North Elmham is well made, fired hard and has a very characteristic 'feel' which is sandy, but not as friable as the shell-gritted St. Neots Ware also found in this region.

thew, *sb.*[1] Add: **3. b.** Also in *sing.* Also *fig.*

c **1863** E. DICKINSON *Poems* (1955) II. 512 Thigh of Granite—and thew—of Steel. **1873** G. M. HOPKINS *Jrnls. & Papers* (1959) 233 A floating flag is like wind visible and what weeds are in a current; it gives it thew and fires it and bloods it in. **1876** —— *Wr. Deutschland* xvi, in *Poems* (1967) 56 He was pitched to his death at a blow, For all his dreadnought breast and braids of thew. **1887** [in Dict.]. **1930** R. CAMPBELL *Adamastor* 77 A Hercules of matchless thew Whose body is the breath of flowers. **1977** *N.Y. Rev. Bks.* 15 Sept. 40/3 By 'language' he means not the whole body of speech, the thew and sinew of the language..but a precursor's language.

they, *pers. pron.* Add: **I. 1. b.** Also as *theyselves* (var. *theysel(l)s*) for *themselves.*

1882 *Century Mag.* Apr. 892 They're pretty peart at the game theyselves. **1893** P. H. EMERSON *On English Lagoons* xlii. 256 Those gents expect you to keep as clean as theysels. **1901** C. HARE *Dinah Kellow* 255 Passon didn' like for they to be locked in by theysells. **1974** *Black World* Apr. 8 He was presenting the street nigguhs in all they glory without no overt exhortation to them to git theyselves togetha.

c. For † read 'Now *rare*'. (Later examples.)

1889 A. LANG in *Scribner's Mag.* Sept. 265/2 They are small-minded and small-hearted people who are most shocked by what they call 'vanity' in the great. **1899** L. C. CORNFORD *R. L. Stevenson* vi. 140 Alan Breck Stewart is the central figure, and they are his sayings and deeds of arms that go to make the chief interest.

3. b. *colloq.* Used to refer collectively to people in authority, regarded as impersonal and oppressive.

1886 KIPLING *Delilah* in *Definitive Verse* (1940) 7 One day, *they* [*sc.* people in power] brewed a secret... It related to Appointments. **1939** AUDEN in *Times Lit. Suppl.* 25 Mar. (Spring Books Suppl.) p. i, The legions of cruel inquisitive 'They' Were so solid and strong, like dogs. **1945** H. NICOLSON *Let.* 27 May (1967) 465 People.. believe that 'they' mean the upper classes, or the Conservatives. **1947** 'G. ORWELL' *Eng. People* 24 English political thinking is much governed by the word 'They'. 'They' are the higher-ups, the mysterious powers. **1967** G. F. FIENNES *I tried to run a Railway* iii. 25 'They' shifted me to York. **1976** *Leicester Chron.* 26 Nov., 'They' are always doing you down. **1981** I. BOLAND tr. *Ginzberg's Within Whirlwind* II. v. 228 How could I go and work in a children's establishment, where 'they' would be able to keep tabs on me?

II. 6. As possessive pronoun: = THEIR *poss. pron.* I. *U.S. dial.*

1928 J. PETERKIN *Scarlet Sister Mary* 162 When dey is worried in dey mind. **1929** W. FAULKNER *Sartoris* i. 23 They was a-settin' behind a table with they pistols layin' on the table. **1935** in Z. N. Hurston *Mules & Men* I. ii. 45 They all brought they rocks and Christ turned 'em into bread. **1974** *Black World* Nov. 58 Just because all the pussy they can snatch is what they can lick off they goddam fingers.

III. 7. As advb.: = THERE *adv.* 4 d. *U.S. dial.*

1874 'MARK TWAIN' in *Atlantic Monthly* Nov. 592/2 Dey was de biggest dey *is*. **1889** J. W. RILEY *Pipes o' Pan at Zekesbury* 41 They's music in the twitter of the bluebird and the jay. **1920** [see *monkey suit* s.v. *MONKEY *sb.* 17 a]. **1949** H. HORNSBY *Lonesome Valley* 185 They's more ways than one to skin a cat. **1973** *Black World* Aug. 61/2 They was ten packets looked like Horse.

thiabendazole (þəi,ăbe·ndăzōul). *Vet. Med.* and *Pharm.* [f. *thia*(*zole* s.v. THIO- 1 in Dict. and Suppl. + *ben*(*zimi*)*dazole* f. BENZ(ENE, BENZINE + IMID(E + AZO- + *-OLE.] An anthelmintic used in veterinary and human medicine, esp. against intestinal nematodes.

1961 H. D. BROWN et al. in *Jrnl. Amer. Chem. Soc.* LXXXIII. 1765/1, 2-(4'-Thiazolyl)-benzimidazole (I, generic name: thiabendazole) was outstanding in anthelmintic activity. **1970** W. H. PARKER *Health & Dis. in Farm Animals* xx. 265 New worm medicines are appearing frequently. At the present time the choice is likely to be either thiabendazole or tetramisole. **1978** R. B. SCOTT *Price's Textbk. Pract. Med.* (ed. 12) II. 236/2 Thiabendazole has been shown to destroy adult female worms [*sc. Trichinella spiralis*] and larvae but must be used with extreme caution because it may precipitate serious reactions with anorexia, nausea, headache, giddiness, and drowsiness, possibly as a result of allergy to dead larvae.

thiamine (þəi·ămīn). [f. THI(O- + AMINE.] †**1.** *Chem.* (See quot.) *Obs. rare.*

1886 C. A. BENNERT *Brit. Pat. 13,466* 3 This invention has for its object the manufacture or production of a new class of organic coloring compounds or materials by reactions between certain amines of the aromatic series and the dioxide of sulphur group, which organic colouring compounds or materials so obtained I designate 'Thiamines'.

†**2.** *Chem.* (In Dict. s.v. THIO- 1.) *Obs. rare.*

3. *Biochem.* Also **thiamin. a.** Vitamin B_1; a water-soluble, heat-labile, sulphur-containing compound that is present in many foods (esp. whole cereal grains, pork, and liver) but absent from fats and is necessary for carbohydrate metabolism, its dietary deficiency resulting in disturbances of the nervous system.

1937 *Jrnl. Amer. Med. Assoc.* 18 Sept. 952/1 Dr. Jansen has been very cooperative in discussing the matter of nomenclature for vitamin B1 and suggested..that Dr. R. R. Williams..propose a name based on the chemical structure. Dr. Williams..proposed the term Thiamin Chloride. **1939** A. HUXLEY *After Many a Summer* II. vi. 234 With a course of thiamin chloride and some testosterone I could have made him as happy as a sand-boy. **1951** A. GROLLMAN *Pharmacol. & Therapeutics* xxvii. 597 Thiamine contains thiazole and pyrimidine rings. **1952** *New Biol.* XIII. 111 The role of thiamin in cell metabolism is to provide a portion of certain enzyme systems. **1972** *Materials & Technol.* V. xix. 674 In Great Britain, all bread except wholemeal must be fortified with thiamin.. to compensate for the losses of the natural vitamin consequent on milling. **1980** D. MADDEN *Food & Nutrition* i. 23/2 After vitamin C, thiamine is probably the most unstable vitamin.

b. thiamine pyrophosphate, the active form of thiamine in which it acts as a co-enzyme: = *COCARBOXYLASE.

1949 *New Biol.* VII. 108 These include thiamine pyrophosphate, nicotinamide nucleoside and riboflavine, all of which are involved in systems through which carbohydrates are oxidised. **1960** [see *DIPHOSPHOTHIAMINE]. **1973** YUDKIN & OFFORD *Comprehensive Biochem.* (1980) xvii. 297 Transketolase needs as co-factor the vitamin derivative thiamine pyrophosphate, which..is also involved in the transfer of a two-carbon fragment from pyruvate to lipoic acid.

Hence **thia·minase** [*-ASE], an enzyme that destroys thiamine, splitting the thiazole and the pyrimidine rings.

1938 BONNER & BUCHMAN in *Proc. Nat. Acad. Sci.* XXIV. 437 It has been shown..that the pea root synthesizes vitamin B_1..from a mixture of the pyrimidine and thiazole components of the vitamin molecule... This must..be a synthesis in which a specific enzyme, a 'thiaminase'.., takes part. **1972** L. HANCOCK *There's a Seal in my Sleeping Bag* ii. 23 Herring is a fish that contains an enzyme called thiaminase, which breaks down thiamin in the body.

thiazide (þəi·ăzəid). *Pharm.* [f. THI(O- + *AZ(INE + OX)IDE, elements in the systematic name of the parent compound.] Any of a class of drugs derived from 1,2,4-benzothiadiazine-1,1-dioxide that increase the excretion of sodium and chloride and are used as diuretics and as auxiliary hypotensive agents.

1959 *Jrnl. Amer. Med. Assoc.* 22 Aug. 2052/2 When the thiazide derivatives are first administered to hypertensive patients being treated with other drugs, it is advisable to continue giving Rauwolfia derivatives. **1961** *Lancet* 12 Aug. 334/1 The use of guanethidine in combination with one of the thiazide group of diuretics extends the application of these drugs in the management of patients with high blood-pressure. **1974** M. C. GERALD *Pharmacol.* xxii. 399 When used alone, the thiazides have only weak antihypertensive effects. **1980** *Brit. Med. Jrnl.* 18 Oct. 1053 Vasodilators are used mainly as additional treatment in patients who are not controlled by thiazides and beta-blockers.

thiazolidine (þəi,ăzǫ·lidīn). *Chem.* and *Pharm.* [f. *thiazole* s.v. THIO- 1 in Dict. and Suppl. + *-IDINE.] **a.** A liquid, C_3H_7NS, whose molecular structure is that of thiazole with an additional hydrogen atom attached to the nitrogen and each carbon atom. **b.** Any compound containing this ring structure in its molecule.

1916 *Chem. Abstr.* X. 3647/2 (Index), Thiazolidine (tetrahydrothiazole). **1945** *Science* 21 Dec. 628/2 Penicilloic acids are undoubtedly thiazolidines. **1949** E. CHAIN in H. W. Florey et al. *Antibiotics* II. xxii. 823 Penicillamine and its esters react readily with aldehydes or ketones to form thiazolidines. **1951** A. GROLLMAN *Pharmacol. & Therapeutics* xxii. 443 Penicillin is a monocarboxylic acid with β-lactam and thiazolidine rings attached through a CONH linkage to a prosthetic group. **1979** *Nature* 25 Oct. 716/2 The chemical assay based on the behaviour of the fused thiazolidine-β-lactam ring consistently gave higher results than the bioassay which required the full penicillin molecule for biological activity.

thick, *a.* (*sb.*) Add: **I. 3. a.** *a bit thick* (earlier example).

1902 G. W. E. RUSSELL *Londoner's Log-bk.* iii. 46 These manifold exercises of culture are characterized by our curate as 'a bit thick', and he owns himself 'fairly out of it'.

b. *the thick end of the stick* = *the dirty end* (*of the stick*) s.v. *DIRTY *a.* 1 e.

1957 *Times* 22 Nov. 8/3 Sir Ralph Richardson has the thick end of the stick... He has to represent an ordinary city insurance clerk. **1960** *Woman's Own* 13 Feb. 17/2 I'm the one to get what Father used to call 'the thick end of the stick'.

II. 5. a. Also in colloq. phr. *thick on the ground*: (chiefly of persons) numerous, abundant; closely concentrated or crowded. Cf. *THIN *a.* 2 e.

1893 J. SALISBURY *Gloss. Words S.E. Worcestershire* 42 *Thick on the ground* = crowded. **1919** J. BUCHAN *Mr Standfast* xii. 218, I see you're some kind of general. They're pretty thick on the ground here. **1964** C. WILLOCK *Enormous Zoo* viii. 133 Where animals are thick on the ground as with the herds, often three hundred strong, of topi [etc.]. **1978** 'E. PETERS' *Rainbow's End* i. 24 Willing workers are not so thick on the ground these days.

7. a. Also *dial.* or *colloq.* in phr. (*to be*) *thick o' fog*.

1935 L. LUARD *Conquering Seas* ii. 19 Thick o' fog—can't see whaleback. **1972** E. STAEBLER *Cape Breton Harbour* xvii. 148 We wanted to go back next day but thought we better wait till it was thick-a-fog and nobody'd see us.

III. 9. b. For 'Now *dial.*' read 'Now chiefly *colloq.* of persons' and add later examples. Also emphatically, *as thick as two planks*, etc. Cf. THICK-HEADED *a.* b.

1865 *Harper's Mag.* Dec. 133/2 [He] is nevertheless slow to see the point—in fact, 'thick' otherwise than crosswise. **1961** S. CHAPLIN *Day of Sardine* ii. 53 Free rides on trains and trolleys were routine stuff; and the thickest character in the school could find a buckshee road into a cinema. **1974** G. HONEYCOMBE *Adam's Tale* I. ii. 27 'He must be as thick as two planks,' said Nick. **1976** J. I. M. STEWART *Memorial Service* iii. 40 You might expect to become P.M. if you hadn't been so thick as to accept your idiotic life peerage. **1980** 'J. GASH' *Spend Game* xiii. 130 Rough-mannered and a bit greedy... Corporal's thick as a plank.

V. 12. a. (A further selection of collocations.) *thick-billed* (earlier and later examples), *-fingered*, *-fleeced* (examples), *-legged* (example), *-lensed*, *-lugged*, *-piled*, *-rimmed*, *-shouldered*, *-stemmed* (example), *-walled* (earlier example), *-wooled*.

1770 G. WHITE *Let.* 21 May in *Nat. Hist. Selborne* (1789) II. vi. 131 The bird you kept..abides all the year, and is a thick-billed bird. **1939** F. C. LINCOLN *Migration Amer. Birds* 103 As an exemplar of vagrant migration from south to north, the Thick-billed Parrot may be cited. **1980** CYRUS & ROBSON *Bird Atlas of Natal* 274 Thick-billed Weaver..inhabits coastal bush. **1874** 'MARK TWAIN' *Let.* 9 Dec. (1917) I. xiv. 238, I am so thick-fingered that I miss the keys. **1864** G. M. HOPKINS *Poems* (1967) 136 Thick-fleeced bushes like a heifer's ear. **1924** E. SITWELL *Sleeping Beauty* xxvi. 95 As lovely as the thick-fleeced waters. **1873** J. BROWN *Let.* 23 June (1912) 280 Uig is a pretty snug little bay, with its tidy Inn and its thick-legged, humorous landlord, John Urquhart. **1946** E. O'NEILL *Iceman Cometh* I. 4 He has black eyes which peer near-sightedly from behind thick-lensed spectacles. **1973** J. GOODFIELD *Courier to Peking* ii. 23 A short, squat person with thick-lensed glasses. **1922** JOYCE *Ulysses* 319 The curse of a goodfornothing God light sideways on the bloody thicklugged sons of whores' gets! **1853** M. ARNOLD *Sohrab & Rustum* in *Poems* 6 Upon the thick-pil'd carpets in the tent. **1976** *Sounds* 11 Dec., His hair, short at the sides and thickpiled high on top, makes him look faintly ridiculous. **1976** 'R. GORDON' *Doctor on Job* iii. 18 A small, round, well-scrubbed looking man in a grey business suit and thick-rimmed glasses. **1965** J. A. MICHENER *Source* (1966) 564 And he knelt in the boat, a thick-shouldered, heavy-necked, sandy-haired German seeking God. **1840** EMERSON *Woodnotes* in *Dial* (Boston) Oct. 244 You ask..what guide Me through trackless thickets led, Through thick-stemmed woodlands. **1820** M. EDGEWORTH *Let.* 26 Dec. (1971) 231 Old thick-walled mansions. **1913** W. DE LA MARE *Peacock Pie* 85 Roasting a thick-wooled mountain sheep Upon an iron spit.

b. thick-back, substitute for def.: in full, *thickback sole*; a flat-fish, *Microchirus variegatus*, found in the Mediterranean and off western European coasts; (examples); **thick ear,** an ear swollen or numbed by a sharp blow; usu. in phrases, as *to give* (someone) *a thick ear*; also *spec.* used *attrib.* to designate literature, etc., marked by rough violence and horseplay, or the writers of such material; **thick end:** now also *colloq.*; **thick-knit** *a.*, designating a garment knitted from wool of greater thickness than double knitting; also *absol.* as *sb.*, a thick-knit sweater; **thick sandwich (course),** a sandwich course (see *SANDWICH $sb.^2$ 1 b) with an extended theoretical component between two periods of practical instruction (see quot. 1978); **thick space** *Typog.*, a third of an em space used in separating words; cf. *thin space* s.v. *THIN *a.* D b; hence **thick-spaced** *a.*; **thick tea** (earlier U.S. example); **thick woods** *Canad.* = *strong wood*(*s* s.v. *STRONG *a.* 12 b.

1864 J. COUCH *Hist. Fishes Brit. Isles* III. 203 The Thickback seldom exceeds the length of eight or nine inches. **1896** J. T. CUNNINGHAM *Nat. Hist. Marketable Marine Fishes Brit. Isles* 259 The Thickback... Pectoral fins very small. **1925** J. T. JENKINS *Fishes Brit. Isles* 198 The Thickback Sole..is brownish-red, with six or seven dark bands running across the body. **1969** A. WHEELER *Fishes Brit. Isles & N.-W. Europe* 557/1 The thickback sole is found rather more offshore. *Ibid.* 557/2 The thickback makes a very minor contribution to fishery landings of 'soles', but its flesh is of high quality. **1909** J. R. WARE *Passing Eng.* 243/2 Thick ear. **1916** 'TAFFRAIL' *Pincher Martin* ii. 28, I sed I'd give yer a thick ear if yer went on worryin' me. **1922** A. HADDON *Green Room Gossip* ix. 248 'A thick-ear play' was Sir Gerald du Maurier's description of 'Bull-dog Drummond'. **1943** *Gen* 2 Jan. 28/1 A member of the thick-ear fraternity. **1978** *Lancashire Life* Oct. 83/2 Ah geet a reyt thick ear yon time Ah tarned sheets in a tangle! **1981** N. TUCKER *Child & Book* v. 133 One particular favourite type of comic—referred to in the trade as the 'thick-ear market'—is chiefly concerned with crude, knockabout humour. **1938** 'N. SHUTE' *Ruined City* x. 195 It would be the thick end of that sum before we're cracking as a proper yard again. **1965** P. O'DONNELL *Modesty Blaise* xviii. 196 Willie.. tested the weight. 'It's the thick end of a hundredweight .. But I could manage one on me own all right.' **1971** D. LEES *Rainbow Conspiracy* i. 13 It will take them the thick end of half an hour to get to the Travellers from here. **1961** Thickknit [see *COVER-UP]. **1976** J. FLEMING *To make Underworld* xii. 138 The three Irishmen, ill-disguised as sailors or fishermen in their thick-knits. **1962** *Engineering* 13 July 57/2 The 1-3-1 type of 'thick sandwich' course (one year in industry, three years at university, and one year in industry again). *Ibid.* 26 Oct. 555 A pre-university year in industry (as in 1:3:1 thick sandwiches). **1978** *Jrnl. R. Soc. Arts* CXXVI. 549/1 A sandwich course such as the 'thick' sandwich, where you do one year in industry, three years at university and then one year back in industry. **1683** MOXON *Mech. Exerc.* II. 99 Some [letters] are Space thick; that is, one quarter so thick as the Body is high; though Spaces are seldom Cast so,..and therefore..we shall call these Spaces, Thick Spaces. **1808** C. STOWER *Printer's Gram.* iii. 90 Of Spaces... They are cast to various thicknesses... Three to an m—or three thick spaces. **1967** E. CHAMBERS *Photolitho-Offset* ii. 12 The *thick space* and *middle space* are a third and a quarter respectively of the width of the *em quad*. **1824** J. JOHNSON *Typographia* II. 132 A *d* and an *h*..will admit an addition, but not more than a middle and thin space to a thick spaced line. **1893** HART *Rules for Compositors* 22 When the last line but one of a paragraph is widely spaced and the first line of the following paragraph is also more than thick-spaced. **1886** S.

COOLIDGE *What Katy did Next* xi. 305 The month's house-keeping wound up that night with a 'thick tea'. **1754** A. HENDRY *Jrnl.* 2 Dec. in *Trans. R. Soc. Canada* (1907) I. II. 343 Strong gale with Snow & Sleet. Obliged to remove into thick woods. **1865** MILTON & CHEADLE *N.W. Passage by Land* xii. 223 We had thirteen horses to pack and drive through the thick woods. **1957** C. HARRIS *Cariboo Trail* 137 The gold-seekers had arrived at the fort after making their way through the thickwoods.

B. *absol.* passing into *sb.* **I. 2. b.** A beverage of thick or heavy consistency, as cocoa, porter, etc. *slang.*

1887 J. W. HORSLEY *Jottings from Jail* i. 26 A somewhat..despairing view of prison life is indicated by 'Lads, your only friend here is your brown lofe [*sic*] and pint of thick'. **1903** FARMER & HENLEY *Slang* VII. 99/1 *Thick*, (common).—porter: ironically said to be 'a decoction of brewers' aprons'. **1923** J. MANCHON *Le Slang* 309 *Thick*, le café, le *jus*. **1947** W. DE LA MARE *Coll. Stories for Children* 222 The mugs of thick proved to be cocoa.

II. *sb.* with *pl.* **6.** For *School slang* read *colloq.* and *slang* (orig. *Schoolboys'*) and add later examples.

1925 S. O'CASEY *Juno & Paycock* III, in *Two Plays* 97 The thick made out the Will wrong. **1960** B. MOORE *Luck of Ginger Coffey* vii. 123 Ha, Ha! cried all the countrified young thicks he had gone to school with. **1970** G. LORD *Marshmallow Pie* iii. 28 Some of those thicks in Earls Court would do it just for the kicks.

7. A thick fog. Cf. sense 7 a of the adj. in Dict. and Suppl. *slang.*

1936 J. BUCHAN *Island of Sheep* ii. 35 Out of the marshes a fog crept which the gunners call a 'thick'. **1961** PARTRIDGE *Slang* Suppl. 1463/1 *Thick, in the*, in, esp. caught in, a thick fog: R.A.F. (operational 'types'): since ca. 1930.

thick, *adv.* Add: **1. c.** (Earlier and later examples.) Also, *to put* (*spread*, etc.) *it on thick.*

1740 *Champion* 29 Jan. (1741) I. 225 You may lay on Honour and Beauty, and all Manner of Virtues as thick as you please. **1865** 'MARK TWAIN' in *Californian* 6 May 9/3 Don't you think he is spreading it on rather thick? **1929** A. CHRISTIE *Seven Dials Mystery* xviii. 148, I thought Bundle was laying it on a bit thick myself... But Codders is such an ass he'd swallow anything. **1955** W. C. GAULT *Ring around Rosa* xiv. 165 Now she was putting it on as thick as a starlet at a producer's party. **1976** *Times* 24 Mar. 3/2 (Advt.), If we are laying it on a bit thick it's only because we want you to volunteer out of a mature realisation of what the Army can be like.

7. Further examples: **a.** *thick-mined, -tangled*; **d.** *thick-plotting, -scarred.*

1957 C. DAY LEWIS *Pegasus* 35 The rescuer plunging through some thick-mined region Who cannot rescue and is not to die. **1922** JOYCE *Ulysses* 35 They swarmed loud ..their heads thickplotting under maladroit silk hats. **1969** G. MACBETH *War Quartet* 59 Its enormous back, thick-scarred From under-water struggles. **1956** D. GASCOYNE *Night Thoughts* 15 The shadows drift in tattered velvet bunches, Thick-tangled rags of shadow are set swaying.

thick and thin, thick-and-thin, *phr.* **A. 2. b.** *attrib.* or *adj.* (Earlier example.)

1822 M. EDGEWORTH *Let.* 1 Feb. (1971) 339 Mr. Ellice is a *thick and thin* friend of Lord Byron's and defends him..against his wife and all the world.

thickety, *a.* (Earlier Amer. examples.)

1640 in *Maryland Hist. Mag.* (1910) V. 374 The Neck of land..lyeing between thicketty Creek on the North, hog pen Creek on the South. **1740** J. E. OGLETHORPE *Jrnl.* 14 May in *Coll. S. Carolina Hist. Soc.* (1887) IV. 152 They got into such thickety ground that they could not overtake them.

thick-head. 1. (Earlier example.)

1824 H. WILSON *Mem.* I. ii. 41 'Don't you know,' said thickhead, '..that I am blind as well as deaf?'

thickie (þi·ki). *colloq.* [f. THICK *a.* (*sb.*) + -IE.] = THICK-HEAD 1 a. Cf. THICK *sb.* 6 in Dict. and Suppl.

1968 B. EARNSHAW *At St. David's a Year* 52 When I hear that one of our Sixth Form boys Has been kicked-up by a Haverfordwest thickie For stealing his girl friend, I think 'Good'. **1976** J. I. M. STEWART *Memorial Service* v. 74 Just one more grouse-slaughtering thickie like my father. **1983** *Times* 5 Sept. 3/1 Teachers still think that engineering is a subject for 'thickies'.

thicknesser (þi·knĕsəɹ). [-ER[1].] A thicknessing machine.

1920 F. T. HILL *Pract. Aeroplane Constr.* 103 Another machine is the surfacer and thicknesser, in which one set of cutters is used for both operations, the top table for the truing-up process..and the bottom table for thicknessing. **1930** *Times Educ. Suppl.* 20 Sept. 400/1 Panel planer and thicknesser. **1959** *Times* 29 Oct. 13/4 A planing machine, which reduces sawn timber to specified dimensions, or sometimes merely smoothes the surface, is frequently referred to as a thicknesser. **1977** *West Briton* 25 Aug. 8/6 (Advt.), Carpenter's universal planer, thicknesser.

thicknessing *vbl. sb.* (In Dict. s.v. THICKNESS.) Hence **thi·ckness** *v. trans.*, **thi·cknessed** *ppl. a.* (back-formations).

1915 Thicknessed [see *spindle machine* s.v. *SPINDLE *sb.* 17]. **1978** *Early Music* Oct. 506 The marks on the inside of the belly..have contributed to the theory that the central strip was first thicknessed and then bent to the long arch, the outer strip being glued to this solid and then carved in the usual way.

thicko (þi·ko). *colloq.* [f. THICK *a.* (*sb.*) + *-O[2].] = THICK-HEAD 1 a.

1976 *Oxford Diocesan Mag.* Nov. 8/2 You have mixed ability teaching throughout, which means..having the thickos in with the brainy and the in-betweens. **1981** P. THEROUX *Mosquito Coast* xiv. 176 Where's the camp store, thicko?

thick-set, *a.* Add: **4.** (Later examples.) (This is now the commonest use.)

1893 H. VIZETELLY *Glances back through Seventy Years* I. viii. 165 Captain Marryat was tall,..but broad shouldered and thick set. **1977** N. ADAM *Triplehip Cracksman* xiv. 143 A thickset..guy in a thick woollen polo-neck sweater.

thick 'un (þi·kˌŏn). *slang.* Also **thick one.** [f. THICK *a.* + UN, 'UN[2] (= ONE *pron.*).] Formerly, a gold sovereign (*half a thick 'un*, ten shillings); *to smash a thick 'un* (see SMASH *v.*[2] 2). Also, a crown or five-shilling piece, and rarely in mod. use applied *loosely* to a pound.

1848 *Sessions Papers Cent. Criminal Court* (Kent cases) 7 Mar. 847 Would not a *thick* one or two be very serviceable this cold weather? **1862** *Cornh. Mag.* Nov. 648 If you like..I will send a few thickuns. **1888** J. PAYN *Eavesdropper* II. ii. 79 'Can you smash a thick un for me?' inquired one, handing his friend a sovereign. **1897** HALL CAINE *Christian* IV. iv. 376 A 'thick 'un'? Oh, that was a sovereign, half a thick'un half a sovereign. **1926** 'SAPPER' *Final Count* iii. 66 Done with you, your Graces; a thick 'un it is. **1968** *Gloss. Brit. Argot* (Paramount Pictures), Quid, nicker, thick 'un, one pound.

thicky, *a.* (Later nonce *poet.* example.)

c **1868** G. M. HOPKINS *Poems* (1967) 211 And light us, Lord, with Thy day-break. Beat from our brains the thicky night And fill the world up with delight.

thief. Add: **5.** *thief-den*; *thief-resistant* adj.; **thief-ant**, a small ant of the genus *Solenopsis* which raids the nests of other ants to steal food; **thief-catcher,** (*b*) (earlier example, applied *loosely* to a lantern); **thieves' kitchen:** see *KITCHEN *sb.* 1 b; **thieves' market,** a street market of a type found in many Eastern cities and elsewhere, at which cheap (sometimes, stolen) goods are offered for sale; cf. *flea market* s.v. *FLEA *sb.* 6.

1904 W. M. WHEELER in *Amer. Naturalist* XXXVI. 952 The walls of the galleries in some of the formicaries were tenanted by teeming colonies of the..thief ant. **1971** E. O. WILSON *Insect Societies* xix. 357/1 Colonies of the 'thief ants'..often nest next to larger ant species. **1851** H. MELVILLE *Moby Dick* III. xxii. 150 What art thou thrusting that thief-catcher into my face for, man? Thrusted light is worse than presented pistols. **1844** POE *Marginalia* in *Wks.* (1902) XVI. 20 A race of dolts.. whose clumsily stolen bulls never fail of leaving behind them ample evidence of having been dragged into the thief-den by the tail. **1963** *B.S.I. News* June 9/1 It was the insurance companies and police who first asked the British Standards Institution to lay down a standard for locks for outside doors which really would be thief-resistant. **1968** *Observer* 22 Dec. 22/2 Locks should be built in and made to British Standard 3621, which ensures that they are thief-resistant, although not thief-proof. **1873** TROLLOPE *Eustace Diamonds* II. xlvii. 278 If such a lot of diamonds had been through the thieves' market in London, they would have left some track behind them. [**1927** B. DIQUI *Visit to Bombay* 62 Null Bazaar is..a big market... An interesting section..is the Chor Bazaar. Chor really means 'thieves.' Chor Bazaar, then, means the bazaar of thieves. Probably in the past thieves disposed of their stolen property here. In this bazaar—the Petticoat Lane of Bombay—you can buy secondhand articles of any description.] **1953** S. BEDFORD *Sudden View* I. xi. 103 The Thieves' Market at Mexico City..where thieves offer goods for sale during a limited time to give the owners a chance. **1979** P. DRISCOLL *Pangolin* xiv. 114 Upper Lascar Row, better known as Cat Street, the thieves' market of Hong Kong.

Hence **thie·fwise** *adv. rare* = THIEF-LIKE *adv.*

1898 W. J. LOCKE *Idols* vi. 75 Creeping thiefwise up the stairs. **1904** HARDY *Dynasts* I. IV. iii. 114 Stealing up to us Thiefwise, by our back door.

Thiersch (tīəɹʃ). *Surg.* The name of Karl *Thiersch* (1822–95), German surgeon, used *attrib.* and formerly in the possessive with reference to a split-skin graft including only superficial layers, so that regeneration of the donor area can occur (described by him in *Verhandl. d. Deutsch. Ges. f. Chir.* (1874) III. 69).

1890 W. J. WALSHAM *Surgery* (ed. 3) I. 35 New method of skin-grafting (Thiersch's). **1892** KEEN & WHITE *Amer. Text-bk. Surg.* IV. iii. 1095 (*heading*) Thiersch's method of skin-grafting. **1911** F. S. KOUE *Plastic & Cosmetic Surg.* xi. 180 The remaining raw surface is either allowed to heal by granulation or is covered immediately with Thiersch grafts. **1977** *Brit. Med. Jrnl.* 29 Jan. 278/1 Simple division with a Thiersch graft to the raw areas suffices.

thigh, *sb.* Add: **4.** *thigh-slapping*; **thigh-length** *a.*, (of a garment, boot, etc.) extending down or up to the thigh; **thigh lift**, a dance movement or gymnastic exercise in which the thigh is raised; the lifting of the thigh in this; **thigh roll,** a roll of padding on a saddle, designed to prevent the girths from slipping backwards and to support the rider's legs in jumping and dressage; **thigh-slapper** *colloq.*, an exceptionally funny joke, description, or the like.

1895 Thigh-length [see *knee-length* s.v. *KNEE *sb.* 13]. **1979** S. SMITH *Survivor* xvii. 177, I wore a thigh-length Indian-print chemise. **1949** SHURR & YOCOM *Mod. Dance* v. 113 Do not allow body to tip forward on thigh lift. *c* **1973** J. CHOLERTON *Acrobatic Section Syllabus* (Assoc. Amer. Dancing) (ed. 6) 2 Thigh Lifts.—sit: legs straight in front—hands on the floor behind, lean slightly back. **1963** E. H. EDWARDS *Saddlery* xiv. 101 The Continental panel is similar, but with..the addition of a thigh roll at the rear... The thigh roll is rarely evident to the rider unless it is very heavily stuffed, and its real use is to prevent the girth straps moving back off the flap. **1976** *Horse & Hound* 3 Dec. 31 (Advt.), Colombo the unique jumping saddle... The exterior thigh roll is an unusual but effective feature. **1965** *Wall St. Jrnl.* 13 Sept. 14/4 The thigh-slapper..the President got off to reporters when Lynda Bird showed up in a billowy muu-muu dress. **1932** V. WOOLF *Common Reader* 2nd Ser. 216 [Meredith] overdoes the pith and the sap; the fist-shaking and the thigh-slapping. **1979** *Dance Mag.* Feb. 32/3 'Lovesick Blues' unexpectedly serves as the up-beat, thigh-slapping finale.

thigmokinesis (þigmokəⁱnī·sis, -kĭn-). *Zool.* [f. Gr. θίγμ-α touch + *o* + *KINESIS.] A kinesis in which the stimulus is absence of touch or body contact.

1940 FRAENKEL & GUNN *Orientation of Animals* ii. 23 It seems probable, therefore, that the contact is the positive stimulus involved and that its action is inhibitory. In that case, *thigmo-kinesis* (θίγμα, touch) is the appropriate name for the reaction. **1954** *New Biol.* XVII. 49 There is..a low thigmokinesis, causing the animals to assume positions in which as much as possible of their surface is in contact with another surface. **1961** *Listener* 21 Sept. 439/3 The earwig..displays marked thigmokinesis. **1976** *Acta Neurobiol. Exper.* XXXVI. 579 Crickets attain their ethological praeferendum of resting site owing to their innate photo- and thigmo-kinesis, which are supplemented by hygrophilia and thermophilia.

thill.[1] **a.** (*a*) For (*obs.*) read 'Now only U.S.' and add later examples.

c **1873** E. DICKINSON *Poems* (1955) III. 869 Elijah's wagon has no thill—Was innocent of wheel. **1901** *Century Mag.* Jan. 452/1 I'm like a bronco in a buggy. I want to bust a thill every time I feel the rein. **1944** *Sun* (Baltimore) 16 May 10/3 An old slave cabin and an old ox thill.

thimble, *sb.* Add: **9. a. thimble-berry:** also, any of several other North American raspberries having thimble-shaped fruit; (earlier and later examples); **thimble-screwer** *Criminals' slang*, one who steals watches or 'thimbles' (sense 7); cf. *SCREWER 2.

1789 R. HASWELL *Jrnl.* 16 Mar. in F. W. Howay *Voy. Columbia to Northwest Coast* (1941) 60 We frequently met with gooseberrys rousberrys currants blackberries strawberries and thimble berries. **1847, 1886** [see *BLACK-CAP 5]. **1946** T. M. STANWELL-FLETCHER *Driftwood Valley* 219 Here the devil's-club gave way..to a dense growth of alders, azaleas, and thimbleberry. **1862** H. MAYHEW *London Labour* Extra vol. 25 'Thimble-screwers', those who wrench watches from their guards. **1932** Thimble-screwer [see *RAMPSMAN].

b. More generally applied *attrib.* or as *adj.* to various objects considered to resemble a thimble in size or shape, esp. as *thimble cup, glass.* Also *fig.*

1843 *Ainsworth's Mag.* III 470 Having now taken a lump of sugar..and thrown the same into a thimble glass. **1899** H. B. CUSHMAN *Hist. Indians* 501 The monotonous tinkling and rattling of the thimble bells..could be heard. **1907** G. O. WHEELER *Old Eng. Furnit.* xv. 390 The feet [in Sheraton's chairs] were of the thimble-toe or thermed variety. **1933** N. WALN *House of Exile* i. 24 Warm rice-wine, served in thimble cups. **1955** M. ALLINGHAM *Beckoning Lady* xi. 157 The comfortable landlady brought two thimble-glasses, frighteningly overfilled. **1962** *Flight International* LXXXII. 354/1 The new thimble blower is believed to be the world's smallest pressure blower. **1971** *Daily Colonist* (Victoria, B.C.) 24 Nov. 2/1 The thimble-brains who perpetrate the law-breaking know the police are so manacled. **1983** *Times* 16 Dec. 6/4 The thimble measure should be filled to the top.

thimble-eyed, *a.* (Example.)

1815 *Trans. Lit. & Philos. Soc. N.Y.* I. 422 Thimble eyed, bull eyed, or chub mackerel..comes occasionally in prodigious numbers to the coast of New-York in autumn.

thin, *a.* (*sb.*) and *adv.* Add: **A.** *adj.* **I. 1. e.** Phr. *the thin end of the wedge*: see WEDGE *sb.* 2 b.

II. 2. a. Also *thin on top*: of a man, having little hair on the (top of the) scalp, balding. Also, of the hair itself.

1868 TROLLOPE *He knew He was Right* (1869) I. xxxi. 243 'You are not bald at all.'..'I am beginning to be thin enough at the top.' **1921** G. B. SHAW *Back to Methuselah* v. 217 Getting a little hard set and flat-chested and thin on the top, wasn't she? **1933** W. S. MAUGHAM *Sheppey* I. 2 'Air's very dry, sir..getting a bit thin on top. **1950** J. CANNAN *Murder Included* vi. 124 There 'e goes—thin on top, ain't 'e? **1978** L. MEYNELL *Papersnake* vi. 77 At forty-one his hair was definitely receding and getting thin on top.

e. *thin on the ground*: (chiefly of persons) few in number, widely scattered; scarce, and therefore difficult to find. Also of a group, having few members. Cf. *THICK *a.* 5 a.

1951 W. S. CHURCHILL *2nd World War* IV. I. vi. 86 There was very heavy fighting and many craft were sunk, but the Australians were thin on the ground and enemy parties got ashore at many points. *a* **1957** A. BROOKE in A. Bryant *Turn of Tide 1939–43* (1957) ii. 115, I got up early..and started with the 3rd Division, which I found well established but infernally thin on the ground. **1964** 'A. GILBERT' *Knock, knock, who's There?* i. 14 The customers were still pretty thin on the ground. **1976** A. HILL *Summer's End* ii. 22 Work was a bit thin on the ground everywhere, wi' long dole queues. **1980** *Times Lit. Suppl.* 25 July 850/1 Even now, when the Anglo-Irish are precariously thin on the ground, people among them who don't like horses can be miserable in certain counties.

f. *Mountaineering.* Of or pertaining to a rock face on which good climbing holds are hard to find.

1955 S. STYLES *Introd. Mountaineering* 144 *Thin*, generally used of steep rock, meaning 'smooth; having few or very small holds'. **1963** A. GREENBANK *Instructions in Rock Climbing* vi. 73 When a guidebook says '*strenuous*', it usually means steep, fierce-looking rock; '*delicate*' or '*thin*', the footholds and/or handholds are tiny. **1970** R. JAMES *Rock Climbing in Wales* 161 Climb this buttress up the L. side, centre and R. side respectively, each giving a thin lower pitch followed by a short artificial section. **1981** *Fell & Rock Jrnl.* XXIII. II. 199 To its left Wafer Thin gives some very thin climbing up flaky pockets to a final smooth slab.

g. *thin red line*: see *RED LINE *sb. phr.* Similarly *thin blue line*: a line of policemen, esp. one which holds back a surging crowd; also *transf.*, the defensive barrier of the law.

1962 *Sunday Times* 16 Dec. 17/2 (*caption*) The 'thin blue line' at an anti-nuclear demonstration. **1970** G. JACKSON *Let.* 17 Apr. in *Soledad Brother* (1971) 222 You've heard the patronizing shit about the thin blue line that protects property and the owners of property. **1979** 'M. UNDERWOOD' *Smooth Justice* ii. 45 The sort of protection we can give..isn't even a thin blue line.

3. b. Also in phr. *to vanish* (*melt*, etc.) *into thin air*: to disappear completely from sight or existence (formerly only of spirits). More rarely *to come* (etc.) *out of thin air*. Now chiefly *colloq.*

1610 [in Dict.]. **1671** MILTON *P.R.* I. 499 Satan bowing low His gray dissimulation, disappear'd Into thin air diffus'd. *c* **1800** BLAKE *Vala* v, in *Compl. Writings* (1966) 305 As plants wither'd by winter..Melt into thin air. **1904** CONRAD *Nostromo* I. i. 4 Vapours that..vanish into thin air. **1918** L. STRACHEY *Eminent Victorians* 223 The Ever Victorious Army..was an ill-disciplined, ill-organised body..constantly on the verge of mutiny..and, at the slightest provocation, melting into thin air. **1932** W. FAULKNER *Light in August* ix. 204 Having apparently materialised out of thin air. **1951** *Sport* 7–13 Jan. 16/2 Speed, confidence, shooting ability, all seemed to have vanished into thin air. **1977** 'E. MCBAIN' *Long Time no See* xi. 181 The recurring nightmares hadn't come out of thin air.

4. d. Phr. *a thin time*: a wretched period of experience. *colloq.*

1924 A. J. SMALL *Frozen Gold* iv. 108 Yes, sure, you go ..If you don't, she will give me such a thin time. **1935** *Economist* 17 Aug. 326/1 Dairy farming and lumbering and doing poorly; while the mountain peasantry especially are having a thin time. **1955** *Times* 22 Aug. 3/3 The London sides in the Championship had a thin time. Not one of them won.

e. *Econ.* Of or pertaining to a stock market (or to stocks, shares) in which trading is light.

1931 *Economist* 28 Feb. 441/2 Prices were marked up to 10 cents a pound in the hope of attracting buyers who had refused to take metal at 9½ cents, but the market remains thin. **1946** *Sun* (Baltimore) 17 Jan. 12-0/1 Some of the 'thin' shares tacked on around six points. **1964** *Financial Times* 3 Mar. 19/2 Further speculative buying in a thin market led to a fresh rise. **1981** *Times* 30 June 20/1 Dealers described turnover as thin.

D. I. a. *thin-blooded, -flanked* (example).

1934 WEBSTER Thin-blooded. **1959** *Times* 10 June 7/3 The rest of the programme, though it sometimes achieved a sort of thin-blooded distinction, was really rather disappointing. **1894** KIPLING *Seven Seas* (1896) 148 Till you married that thin-flanked woman.

b. thin-film *a.*, applied to processes and devices that employ or involve a very thin solid or liquid film; **thin-layer chromatography** *Chem.* [tr. G. *dünnschicht-chromatographie* (E. Stahl 1956, in *Pharmazie* XI. 633)], chromatography in which compounds are separated on a thin layer of adsorbent material such as charcoal or silica gel; **thin-minded** *a. rare*$^{-1}$, narrow-minded, prejudiced; **thin section**, a thin, flat piece of rock or tissue prepared with a thickness of about 0·03 mm. for examination with an optical microscope; also, a piece of tissue of the order of 30 nm. thick prepared for electron microscopy; hence **thin-sectioning** *vbl. sb.*, the making of thin sections; **thin space** *Typogr.*, a piece of metal used for separating words, cast five to an em of its own body; cf. *thick space* s.v. *THICK *a.* 12 b.

1956 *Nature* 24 Mar. 571/2 Thin-film lubrication. **1963** *New Scientist* 21 Mar. 632/3 Thin-film memories and logic devices. **1966** D. G. BRANDON *Mod. Techniques Metallogr.* ii. 90 Variations in absorption with crystalline perfection contribute significantly to the contrast in thin-film transmission microscopy. **1970** *Brit. Printer* July 69/2 The advent of thin-film inks gave the screen printer a choice which had not previously existed. **1957** *Chem. Abstr.* LI. 6948 (*heading*) Thin-layer chromatography (the method, affecting factors, and a few examples of application). **1961** *Jrnl. Amer. Oil Chemists' Soc.* XXXVIII. 313/1 Two procedures for the analysis of mixtures of mono-, di-, and triglycerides. One employs.. thin-layer chromatography. **1967** *Oceanogr. & Marine Biol.* V. 267 Thin layer chromatography can pinpoint some inaccuracies in the interpretation of spectra and give a more adequate image of the variety of pigments. **1978** H. H. BAUER et al. *Instrumental Analysis* xxi. 626 Appreciation of the full advantages of planar chromatography then led to thin-layer chromatography (TLC). **1864** TROLLOPE *Small House at Allington* I. ii. 11 Such thin-minded men can hardly go to the proof of any matter without some pre-judgment in their minds. **1858** *Q. Jrnl. Geol. Soc.* XIV. 469 For some purposes, however, thin sections are quite indispensable. **1872** F. DELAFIELD *Handbk. Post-Mortem Examinations* I. 21 The proportion of alcohol is to be afterward increased until the mucous membrane is hard enough to be cut into thin sections. **1916** JORDAN & FERGUSON *Text-bk. Histol.* xx. 734 Thick sections may be obtained from the firmer tissues by free-hand sectioning with a razor, but for the satisfactory preparation of thin sections a microtome is a necessity. **1956** *Nature* 14 Jan. 98/1 Although electron microscope contrast may be increased by the use of objective apertures, accurate focusing in thin-section work is still difficult. **1970** *Ibid.* 17 Oct. 251/2 Petrological analysis by thin section has enabled the locality of origin of axes made from hard rock to be identified. **1964** G. H. HAGGIS et al. *Introd. Molecular Biol.* v. 135 The pellet which contains them [*sc.* mitochondria] can be identified, and its purity assessed, by thin-sectioning of the osmium-fixed embedded pellet. **1978** *Sci. Amer.* May 141/2 There are two principal specimen-preparation methods for rendering cells suitable for examination in the electron microscope: thin-sectioning and freeze-fracturing. **1683** Thin space [see SPACE *sb.*[1] 15 b]. **1808** C. STOWER *Printer's Gram.* iii. 90 Of Spaces... Five to an m—or five thin spaces. **1968** J. R. BIGGS *Basic Typogr.* 76/2 Space between words is achieved by means of tiny bricks of metal... They are..thin space..thick space..hair space.

II. thin-clad *a.*: also (*U.S. colloq.*) *absol.* as *sb.*, an athlete.

1947 *Sun* (Baltimore) 30 Oct. 19/2 (*heading*) Maryland thinclads beat navy. **1974** *Anderson* (S. Carolina) *Independent* 24 Apr. 5B/1 Cliff Satterwhite..has been coaching the few Trojan thinclads.

thing, *sb.*[1] Add: **I. 3. b.** With possessive adj. One's particular interest, speciality, or talent. *spec.* in colloq. phr. *to do one's* (*own*) *thing*: to do what one wants, to follow one's interest or inclination.

Evidence for this sense is patchy into the early-twentieth cent. The phrase had become a cliché (often associated with the 'hippie' culture) by the late nineteen-sixties.

1841 EMERSON *Essays* ii. 54 But do your thing and I shall know you. Do your work, and you shall reinforce yourself. **1861** R. W. DIXON *Christ's Company* 98 Go thy way, all things say, Thou hast thy way to go..Do thy thing. **1909** H. G. WELLS *Ann Veronica* xvi. 328 Every human being..exists to do new things... Well, this is *our* thing. **1914** *Egoist* 1 June 216/1, I cannot picture the spring of the editor's actions as being a..desire to do the decent thing. I think, rather, she insists on doing her own thing—what it pleases or suits her to do. **1951** 'M. INNES' *Operation Pax* VI. vi. 285 Roof-climbing used to be one of my things, rather. **1962** I. MURDOCH *Unofficial Rose* xxii. 214 Mummy won't be happy, it's not her thing. **1968** [see *FREAK *v.* 3]. **1968** *Melody Maker* 23 Nov. 23/6 No one is right and no one is wrong as long as they say what they feel—as long as they do their thing. **1970** E. BULLINS *Theme is Blackness* (1973) 165 Anything that anybody wants to do is groovy with me... Go ahead and do your thing, champ. **1971** M. SPARK *Not to Disturb* ii. 49 'What are they doing here, anyway in this world?' Heloise, pink and white of skin, fresh from her little sleep, says, 'Doing their own thing.' **1974** K. MILLETT *Flying* (1975) II. 207 She knows her thing. And I am doing mine. **1981** R. BARNARD *Sheer Torture* x. 109 A ghastly warning against..aiming at total self-fulfilment, doing your own thing regardless.

c. *Loosely*, with qualifying adj. or noun (phrase): matter, business; preoccupation (influenced by next sense).

1906 'H. MCHUGH' *Skiddoo!* vii. 94 When it comes to that poetry thing he thinks he can make Hank Longfellow beat it up a tree. **1909** ST. J. LUCAS *First Round* III. xxxiii. 320, I shall have to stay there I suppose; they spoke of giving me a fellowship at Balliol, and of course there is the All Souls thing later on.

1968 T. WOLFE *Electric Kool-Aid Acid Test* i. 11 Thousands of kids were moving into San Francisco for a life based on LSD and the psychedelic thing. **1969** *Listener* 27 Mar. 434/1 The male fashion thing. **1976** *National Observer* (U.S.) 7 Aug. 13/1 You can write the nostalgia thing, but it's been done a thousand times before. It's so easy. **1977** A. SHERIDAN tr. *J. Lacan's Écrits* iv. 131 The psychoanalytic thing has become an accepted thing.

d. A preoccupation or obsession. *spec.* (*a*) *to make a thing about* or *of* (something), to preoccupy oneself greatly with (a matter); to make an issue out of (something), or to (over)-exaggerate its importance; (*b*) *to have a thing about* (occas. *for*) (a person or thing), to be obsessed by (something); to harbour a prejudice or fear about. *colloq.*

1934 E. WAUGH *Handful of Dust* ii. 32, I know we aren't going. I'm not making a thing about it. I just thought it might be fun. **1936** 'J. TEY' *Shilling for Candles* xix. 201 You got a 'thing' about astrology? **1938** D. SMITH *Dear Octopus* II. i. 59 It's one of my things like turning bath-taps off. **1940** N. MITFORD *Pigeon Pie* ii. 25, I nearly fainted. I can't bear knees, I've got a thing about them. **1952** E. GRIERSON *Reputation for Song* (1955) 22 Steady on, Laura... Don't let's make a thing of it. **1955** 'E. C. R. LORAC' *Ask Policeman* ii. 19 Connie's got a 'thing' about police. 'Never trust a policeman' is her motto. **1958** E. H. CLEMENTS *Uncommon Cold* viii. 185 Remin was her 'thing' at the moment. **1967** T. WOLFE in *N.Y. Mag.* 29 Jan. 6/1 The plainclothes men are beginning to pick up on all that, but they still fog up on the shoes. The heads have a thing about the shoes straight people wear. **1971** 'A. BURGESS' *MF* ii. 22 There was an American thing against knives. **1973** R. PARKES *Guardians* ii. 49 He's made a thing of championing cultural minorities.

e. *spec.* a love affair, a romance; esp. in phr. *to have a thing* (*with* someone). *colloq.*

1967 M. SHARMAN *Face of Danger* viii. 77 'Are you—er —sort of having a—thing—with Madalena?'..'I'm interested in her,' he said. 'But not sexually.' **1970** 'D. HALLIDAY' *Dolly & Cookie Bird* v. 61 Janey..had obviously just finished a thing with Guppy Collins-Smith and was looking for new material. **1978** R. LEWIS *Uncertain Sound* v. 128, I know Sandy Kyle, had a thing going with her.

4. (*the*) *last thing* (earlier example); also *last thing at night*.

1848 TROLLOPE *Kellys & O'Kellys* II. xii. 281, I must see her the last thing,—about nine. **1935** *Discovery* Apr. 95/2 It [*sc.* the pump] is run last thing at night. **1966** 'C. AIRD' *Religious Body* viii. 74, I do a round of doors and windows last thing at night.

II. 7. c. Also (often with initial capital) applied to some particular supernatural or other dreadful monster (i.e. *the Thing*). Hence *transf.* (sometimes *humorously*) of persons.

1888 KIPLING *Smith Administration* (1891) 64 The burning-*ghât*, where a man was piling logs on some Thing that lay wrapped in white cloth. **1917** CONRAD *Shadow-Line* vi. 197 The hair of my head stirred... I could see It—that Thing! **1954** L. M. BOSTON *Children of Green Knowe* 126 The Thing..gave a silent yell... Then it went fumbling round the room. **1973** 'B. MATHER' *Snowline* i. 7, I find The Thing hard to take. He's blind,..he can only make mewing noises, and he has no legs and only one arm.

10. a. Also in phrases: *dear old thing*, an expression of affection applied esp. to an elderly person; *old thing*, a jocular or affectionate form of address (not necessarily to an elder). *colloq.*

1852 *Punch* 31 July 55/2 Aunt Ratchet and I had quietly sat down, I to read and she to listen to a new novel—the greatest pleasure the dear old thing can experience. **1864** C. M. YONGE *Trial* II. xiv. 273 I'll do anything for you..you know that, you old thing! **1865** 'L. CARROLL' *Alice's Adventures in Wonderland* ix. 130 'You can't think how glad I am to see you again, you dear old thing!' said the Duchess, as she tucked her arm affectionately into Alice's, and they walked off together. **1905** KIPLING *Actions & Reactions* (1909) 18 No, thanks, old thing! Isn't that quite English? **1921** [see *CLEVER-CLEVER *a.*]. **1975** J. DRUMMOND *Slowly the Poison* 13 Don't worry, old thing. It may not be as bad as it sounds.

11. c. (Later examples.) Usu. preceded by possessive pron.

1955 J. P. DONLEAVY *Ginger Man* (1957) vi. 38 Men wagging their things at you from doorways. Disgusting. **1969** L. HELLMAN *Unfinished Woman* ii. 23 One..had opened his pants and was shaking what my circle called 'his thing'. **1981** P. TURNBULL *Deep & Crisp & Even* vi. 110 'His coat was open and his thing...' 'Thing?' 'You know, between his legs... Penis.'

d. With capital initial. Substituted (esp. after a title, as *Miss Thing*, etc.) for the proper name of a person which the speaker cannot recall. Cf. THINGUMMY, WHAT'S-HIS-NAME. *colloq.*

1920 J. M. BARRIE *Kiss for Cinderella* I. 12 She was called something else when she came—Miss Thing, or some such name. **1954** M. RIDDELL *M for Mother* x. 44 Mrs. Thing had absolutely washed her hands of him and my mother was never going to speak to her again. **1977** M. KENYON *Rapist* vi. 70 Keane could not remember the name of..the colonel. Too many names. Colonel Thing.

III. 14. e. (Earlier examples.)

1798 A. F. M. WILLICH *Elem. Crit. Philos.* 21 The position of the sufficient ground, in general, depends.. upon *things in themselves*. **1817** COLERIDGE *Biog. Lit.* I. x. 195 Of this sheet of paper..as a thing in itself, separate from the phænomenon or image in my perception.

f. Also *to tell* (or *teach*) (someone) *a thing or two*; similarly, *to be up to a thing or two*, to be knowing or shrewd.

1816 *Sporting Mag.* XLVIII. 173 The training-groom was up to a thing or two. **1859** HOTTEN *Dict. Slang* 113. **1930** WODEHOUSE *Very Good, Jeeves!* vi. 143 'Listen, Bertie,' said Aunt Dahlia earnestly, 'I'm an older woman than you are—well, you know what I mean—and I can tell you a thing or two.' **1932** L. GOLDING *Magnolia St.* III. ix. 592 It's taught us both a thing or two. **1973** M. BENCE-JONES *Palaces of Raj* xi. 191 Simla could teach Naini Tal a thing or two as regards dances.

g. *one thing..another* (*thing*): see *ONE *numeral a.* 17 c.

h. (*the*) *things of the mind*, matters of a specifically intellectual character. Cf. *life of the mind* s.v. *LIFE *sb.* 12 e.

[**1902** H. JAMES *Wings of Dove* II. iii. 44 All the high, dim things she lumped together as of the mind.] **1903** G. K. CHESTERTON *Robert Browning* iii. 61 She..lived her second and real life in literature and the things of the mind. **1965** *New Society* 15 July 10/3 The superiority of the things of the mind over the externals of bodily appearance and success in competitive enterprises. **1980** T. MORGAN *Somerset Maugham* III. 222 Syrie..had no interest in things of the mind. She was the sort who says 'how extraordinary' when a book is being discussed.

i. *of all things*: of all conceivable possibilities (often parenthetically implying that the eventuality is surprising or unexpected).

1925 T. DREISER *Amer. Tragedy* II. II. xii. 170 Well, well, of all things! Well, I'll be damned! **1958** A. HUXLEY *Let.* 22 June (1969) 851 There have been endless contretemps, including, as a last straw, the collapse of the publicity woman with, of all things, chickenpox. **1977** McKNIGHT & TOBLER *Bob Marley* ix. 110 Keyboard instrument effects..which sound like a harmonium of all things.

j. (*just*) *one of those things*: see *ONE *pron.* **29**f.**

k. *like one thing*, 'like anything'. *Austral. colloq.* and *U.S. dial.*

1946 B. JAMES in Murdoch & Drake-Brockman *Austral. Short Stories* (1951) 249 No good for crops,..but it would 'grow cherries like one thing'. **1948** D. BALLANTYNE *Cunninghams* xiv. 75 He saw Phil..and some other..jokers skiting like one thing. **1972** J. S. HALL *Sayings from Old Smoky* 136 *Like one thing*, said of something very well done or in large quantity. 'He can mimic Windy Bill just like one thing.'

l. With reference to a previous statement: *to do that* (*small*, etc.) *thing*, to act in the manner indicated (esp. when taking up a suggestion). *colloq.*

1958 I. MURDOCH *Bell* xiv. 186 'I'm going to have a bath.' 'Darling, you do that small thing!' **1960** K. AMIS *Take Girl like You* vi. 83 'Grab one with us.'..'I'll do that small thing if I may.' **1963** N. FREELING *Because of Cats* i. 23 'I'll plan that.' 'You do that thing.' **1967** N. MARSH *Death at Dolphin* iii. 57 'Will you bear me in mind, then?' 'I'll do that thing,' said Peregrine. **1977** J. TARRANT *Rommel Plot* ix. 89 'I'll be there in twenty minutes.' 'You do that small thing.'

15. a. (Earlier examples of a person's physical condition.)

1832 J. ROMILLY *Diary* 20 Sept. (1967) 19 Better today: tho not quite the thing: dined at home. **1854** C. M. YONGE *Heartsease* I. II. i. 115 And how are you? You don't look quite the thing.

b. Also *colloq.* in weakened use (*the thing is*..), the truth or the fact of the matter.

1971 C. BONINGTON *Annapurna South Face* xiv. 175, I think the thing is that we want to start pushing out the route as fast as possible because the faster we can push the route out the less oxygen we need to use. **1976** 'A. HALL' *Kobra Manifesto* xv. 208 They've struck some kind of problem... The thing is they've seized a TWA Boeing.

f. *any old thing*: any thing whatever. *slang* (orig. *U.S.*).

1900 ADE *More Fables in Slang* 205 An Author was sitting at his Desk trying to..grind out Any Old Thing that could be converted into Breakfast Food. **1911**, etc. [see *any old*.. s.v. *ANY *a.* I e].

18. thing-word, a substantive referring to some material object; after Jespersen, *spec.* a countable noun.

1877 H. SWEET in *Trans. Philol. Soc.* 1875–6 487 'Snow'..is both a thing-word and a noun, 'white' is a quality-word and an adjective, 'whiteness' a quality-word and a noun. **1914** O. JESPERSEN *Mod. Eng. Gram.* II. v. 115 Another difference in the adjuncts of mass-words and thing-words: the former have *what*, the latter *what a* in exclamatory quasi-questions. **1937** A. SMEATON tr. *R. Carnap's Logical Syntax Lang.* v. lxxvii. 297 'Thing' is a universal word (provided that the designation of things constitutes a genus)... 'Moon' is a thing-word..; 'five' is not a thing-word, but a number-word.

For 'all' read 'chiefly' in 'all *rare* or *nonce-wds.*' **thinghood** (later examples); **thingification** = REIFICATION; hence **thi·ngify** *v. trans.*, **thi·ngifying** *vbl. sb.*; **thinginess**, (*a*) (examples); (*b*) (example); **thi·ngism** *Fr. Lit.* [tr. Fr. *chosisme*] (see quot. 1966); **thingling** (later humorous example); **thingly** *a.* (earlier example); **thingness** (later examples).

1919 A. N. WHITEHEAD *Princ. Natural Knowledge* II. vi. 73 Events appear as indefinite entities without clear demarcations and with mutual relations of baffling complexity. They seem..deficient in thinghood. **1950** A. HUXLEY *Themes & Variations* 55 A completer deification of the State, accompanied by a completer reification, or reduction to thing-hood, of individual persons. **1972** L. HUDSON *Cult of Fact* 76 To know about nature, and especially about people, in a way that reduces them to thing-hood, is to pursue knowledge in a way that is inimical to the proper growth of human self-awareness. **1947** *Partisan Rev.* XIV. 456 Everything in this icy landscape must be adapted to the *things* of cold steel. The organic must fuse with the mechanical, the *thingification* of man be pushed to its extreme, and the world of the workers become functional and naked. **1979** E. P. THOMPSON in *PN Rev.* No. 9 (Suppl.) p. xxvi, He had fallen on the 1844 MSS, was high on alienation and reification (which he insisted upon rendering as 'thingification'), and he had put Marx and Freud together in the bed of a single book. **1931** Thingify [see *REIFY *v.*]. **1972** *Guardian* 7 Feb. 12/8 The thingifying of anything else on the road—whether it's another competitor or..a stray pedestrian. **1914** *Morning Post* 26 Feb. 2/2 Let us hear the second-hand eloquence of one of those second-rate authorities in his vain attempt to get at the thinginess of such things. **1962** W. NOWOTTNY *Lang. Poets Use* v. 107 The 'thinginess' even of what we call 'concrete objects' is so inaccessible to the probe of our common language. **1976** *New Yorker* 15 Mar. 118/2 The very thinginess of the contemporary city life in the film shows—the fast cars, the unobtrusive chic, the small cafes—seems to deprive us of any illumination. **1982** T. GUNN *Occasions of Poetry* I. 22 He was in love with the bare fact of the external world, its thinginess. **1961** *Guardian* 7 Feb. 9/6 M. Robbe-Grillet..hears his method described as 'thingism' because he concentrates on..things. **1966** H. T. MOORE *Twentieth Cent. French Lit.* II. v. 116 They often produce the antiroman (antinovel) or indulge in chosisme (which might be literally translated as thingism)... In their novels and manifestoes, the antinovelists emphasize their escape from the conventional novel's preoccupation with straight-line plot, psychological analysis, and moral involvements. The group of chosistes concentrate on material objects because, in the words of one of their practitioners and spokesmen, Alain Robbe-Grillet, 'things *are there*'. **1950** O. NASH *Family Reunion* 45 I'd rather shake hands with Mr. Ringling And tell him his circus is a beautiful thingling. **1860** J. W. PALMER tr. *Michelet's Love* II. iv. 101 Things have cast off their *thingly* qualities. **1930** 'WYNDHAM LEWIS' *Apes of God* IX. 288 Health as intended by Kalman is '*thingness*' right enough! It is vegetable bulk, it is unconsciousness. **1967** S. BECKETT *No's Knife* 34 Into what nightmare thingness am I fallen? **1975** *New Yorker* 2 June 90/1 Clouseau finds himself forced into unkind collision with the thingness of things.

thingum. Add: **thingumajig** (earlier example).

1824 *Casket* June 76 I'd a lot of cousins, that 'com'd all the way down from Varmount to larn the fashions, and to hear and see all the cute and curious thingumajigs of the Old Colony'.

thingummy. Add: Also in extended form **thingummytight** (**-tite**, etc.).

1937 G. FRANKAU *More of Us* xvii. 177 Quick. The small green phial. It's in my bathroom. In the thingummytight—The corner cupboard. **1939** J. CARY *Mister Johnson* 23 What's the trouble? Why, it's thingummytite, aren't you? **1977** D. CLARK *Gimmel Flask* viii. 147 We've got a thingumitite with us...a sort of visionary. Young cops with fantouche ideas! **1980** D. BOGARDE *Gentle Occupation* i. 21 Nothing in the taps of course because the terrorists had buggered up the hydroelectric thingummytites.

thingy, *sb.* (In Dict. s.v. THING *sb.*[1]). Add: **2.** Also **thingie,** (occas. **-ee**). = THING *sb.*[1] (in various senses); cf. THINGUMMY. *colloq.*

1933 GREEN & STEPT (*song-title*) Swingy little thingy. **1968** M. RICHLER *Cocksure* v. 32 It was going to be the rage. A thingee . Like TW3. **1977** *Spare Rib* June 26/3 Then there are those women who make men wear things on their thingies. **1981** J. BARNETT *Firing Squad* xiii. 184 We don't do crime here... Contracts, copyright, companies floated, that's our thingie.

think, *v.*[2] Add: **I. 2. c.** Also, with adj. as quasi-obj. or used quasi-advb., to think in terms of, prefer, have in view (things that are —), esp. *to think big*, to be ambitious.

1960 J. CARSWELL *South Sea Bubble* vi. 100 Even Blunt, though his maxim was certainly to 'think big', would hardly have suggested anything so obviously unacceptable. **1962** A. LURIE *Love & Friendship* xv. 300 Living in a small town had subtly affected my mind, and I had begun to Think Small. **1970** in M. PEI *Words in Sheep's Clothing* ii. 14 For those who think old! **1972** D. HASTON *In High Places* xii. 139 With people pulling off tricks like the West Ridge, Dhynenfurth was not day-dreaming in thinking tall. **1978** *National Geographic* Nov. 615/2 When people think apple,..they usually think red. **1979** *Now!* 21–27 Sept. 134/3 Simple, uncluttered and tubular they illustrate fashion's new mood of 'think thin'. **1981** *Daily Tel.* 21 Dec. 2/3 (*heading*) 'Think British' call to CBI firms.

3. a. *to think for oneself*: to form independent judgements, not to be overinfluenced by preconceptions or received opinions; *to think out loud* = *to think aloud*; *to think straight*: see *STRAIGHT *adv.* 1 g.

1735 BERKELEY *Defence of Free-Thinking in Math.* xix. 19 The only advantage I pretend to, is that I have always thought and judged for myself. **1853** DICKENS *Let.* 28 Nov. (1938) II. 522 One of the great uses of travelling is to encourage a man to think for himself. **1870** J. P. SMITH *Widow Goldsmith's Daughter* vi. 90 The merry mischief in his eyes..made her feel her absurdity in thinking out loud. **1974** *Times* 1 May 6/6 Those matters were thoroughly probed..the President often taking the role of devil's advocate; sometimes merely thinking out loud. **1974** D. L. EDWARDS *What Anglicans Believe* xii. 100 Anglican laymen have been encouraged to think for themselves.

b. *to give* (one) *furiously to think*: see *GIVE *v.* 38.

II. 5. a. *to think that—!* (int.): introducing a statement of a fact thought of as remarkable or surprising.

1906 BELLOC *Hills & Sea* 30 To think that you can get to a place like that for less than a pound! **1919** G. B. SHAW *Heartbreak House* II. 60 And to think that I actually condescended to fascinate that creature there to save you from him! **1946** M. PEAKE *Titus Groan* 337 To think that an hour earlier she had been helping to plait those locks.

b. (Examples of (*it*) *makes you think*.)

1879 J. BLACKWOOD *Let.* 14 Jan. in *Geo. Eliot Lett.* (1956) VII. 94, I have been reading it all with great interest, and it does make one think. **1933** M. LOWRY *Ultramarine* i. 41, I wonder why it [*sc.* a carrier pigeon] had a message from Swansea... Makes you think, that, doesn't it? **1968** G. MITCHELL *Three Quick & Five Dead* ii. 67 'But young Otto is a psychopath!' said Laura. 'Makes you think a bit, that does,' agreed the Superintendent. **1976** 'D. HALLIDAY' *Dolly & Nanny Bird* x. 127 Remember how Comer came bursting in one evening?.. It makes you think, doesn't it?

c. Also, *to think back* (*on* or *to*), to recall, reflect on; (*when one*) *come*(*s*) *to think of it*: see *COME *v.* 23 b.

1960 *Times Lit. Suppl.* 17 June 387/1, I think back to the sixth forms of the twenties. **1965** H. GOLD *Man who was not with It* iii. 29 Goombye, I thought back to him. **1976** *Times Lit. Suppl.* 22 Oct. 1327/2 When I think back on it now, that was the best thing I could have done.

g. *to think twice* (const. *about* or *absol.*): to hesitate, change one's mind (about), decide against (something); also, in a negative context: (not) to take any notice of or worry about.

1898 G. B. SHAW *Philanderer* III. 119 He thinks twice before he commits himself. **1910** [in Dict., sense 5 b]. **1936** W. H. SAUMAREZ SMITH *Let.* 21 Nov. in *Young Man's Country* (1977) ii. 43 When they find that I am neither a Blue..nor a bridge-player, they may think twice about offering the appointment to me. **1955** M. HASTINGS *Cork & Serpent* v. 67 Don't worry. Nobody here thinks twice about me. **1956** A. HUXLEY *Let.* 13 Aug. (1969) 805 He thought I had been wise to think twice about talking on TV about mescalin. **1979** R. RENDELL *Make Death love Me* i. 8 The rule was made to be broken and no one ever thought twice about breaking it. **1981** P. SALWAY *Roman Britain* 705 This must make us think twice before attributing reasons to *any* funerary or religious practice from the ancient world for which we have no written evidence.

h. *to think again*: to realize that one is mistaken, to change one's mind, to have second thoughts. Cf. THOUGHT[1] 2 c.

1911 G. B. SHAW *Getting Married* 291 So youre not coming home with me. *Hotchkiss*..: Yes I am. *Mrs George*: No. *Hotchkiss*: Yes. Think again. **1935** C. S. FORESTER *African Queen* ii. 35 It would blow this ole launch..to Kingdom Come. You think again, miss. **1958** P. SHORE in N. Mackenzie *Conviction* 37 Those who imagine that the problem of the public schools will disappear..will have to think again. **1974** M. GILBERT *Flash Point* xiii. 109 It *was* a put-up job. If they think I'm going to sit down under it, they can think again.

7. c. *to think on one's feet*: to react to events, etc., quickly and effectively.

1935 WODEHOUSE *Luck of Bodkins* xvi. 202 PS. Think on your feet, boy! **1960** *Analog Science Fact/Fiction* Oct. 73/2 Your records show that you can think on your feet. **1976** J. ARCHER *Not a Penny More* x. 116 'James,' said Jean-Pierre, thinking on his feet for not the first time in his life. 'You take a taxi immediately.' **1981** T. WRIGHT in *Believing in Church* v. 112 Reports approved by Synod (the Church thinking on its feet).

III. 9. b. *that's what you think* (cliché, with stress on *you*): an expression of emphatic, sometimes scornful, disagreement.

1934 J. O'HARA *Appointment in Samarra* ii. 31 'I can handle that.' 'That's what you think.' **1973** P. MOYES *Curious Affair of Third Dog* xi. 148 'We're going to have the pleasure of your company for several days at least.' 'That's what you think.'

d. *I thought as much*: see AS C. 1 in Dict. and Suppl.

e. *I should think*—, introducing emphatic assent: certainly, assuredly, indeed. Also *ellipt.* in neg., *I should think not*.

1894 A. JESSOPP *Random Roaming* iv. 160 Fish? I should think there was fish! There was fish enough to come to at least £15 of our money. **1903** G. B. SHAW *Man & Superman* IV. 167 Promise me that you wont. *Violet* (very decidedly) I should think not indeed. **1944** L. P. HARTLEY *Shrimp & Anemone* iv. 41 'Do you know.. Nancy Steptoe?' 'I should think I did.'

11. a. For '† *on*, † *at*, dial. *to*' read '† *at*, dial. *to*, *on*', and add later examples with *on*.

1974 *Amer. Speech* 1971 XLVI. 117 We should think on each student as unique. **1978** R. HILL *Pinch of Snuff* ix. 85 I've known Charlie for years. I asked what he thought on it.

b. (*c*) *imp.* phr. deprecating proffered thanks or apology.

1948 M. ALLINGHAM *More Work for Undertaker* vii. 87 'We did not disturb you, I hope?' 'Think nothing of it,' murmured the torchbearer magnanimously. **1950** [see *PLEASURE *sb.* 2]. **1980** F. OLBRICH *Desouza in Stardust* iv. 41 'Thank you for giving up so much of your time, Mr Chiknis.' 'Think nothing of it, Chief Inspector.' **1982** W. J. BURLEY *Wycliffe's Wild-Goose Chase* i. 17 'Sorry to bother you on a Sunday morning.' ..'Think nothing of it.'

IV. 16*. *think through* = *think out* (sense 15) (*b*) or (*c*).

1922 HARDY *Late Lyrics* 150 I've been thinking it through, as I play here to-night. **1934** T. N. WILDER *Heaven's my Destination* iii. 42 During the journey he.. 'thought through' the matter of capital punishment. **1961** *Observer* 8 Oct. 10/3 It is doubtful if Mr. Gaitskell himself had thought through the problem of inner-party democracy. **1979** B. HEBBLETHWAITE in M. Goulder *Incarnation & Myth* iv. 97 A remarkable attempt to think through what it means for our concept of God to say that Christ's cross is God's cross in our world.

17. For ? *U.S. colloq.* read orig. *U.S.* and add: to devise, invent, contrive, or produce by thought or cogitation. (Earlier and later examples.)

1855 MRS. STOWE *Tales & Sk. New Eng. Life* 79 Christmas is coming..and I have got to think up presents for everybody. **1872** S. HALE *Lett.* (1918) iv. 83 He asked our plans at once, took right hold and thought up what we had better do. **1901** MERWIN & WEBSTER *Calumet 'K'* vii. 108, I had him pretty busy there for a while thinking up lies. **1930** *G.K.'s Weekly* 15 Nov. 146/1 If Mr. Lloyd George can think up a good ticket. **1956** *People* 13 May 8/6 In America the magic new process—it was thought up over there—is being developed in all sorts of wonderful ways. **1977** J. WAINWRIGHT *Nest of Rats* I. xii. 103 There's a way round it... There *has* to be. Some brainy type thought it up.

V. *Comb.* **18.** (It is not clear in every case whether the verbal or the nominal sense of *think* is dominant.) **think(s) balloon, bubble,** in a comic-strip cartoon, a circle resembling a balloon or bubble floating above a character's head and containing (the word 'thinks' followed by) the character's thought in direct speech; **think book,** a book containing the writer's thoughts, opinions, observations, etc.; one that makes the reader think; **think box** *colloq.* or *joc.*, the brain; **think factory** *U.S. colloq.*, a research institution; **think-fest** [*FEST], an intellectual treat; **think group,** a group of people that meets to thrash out a subject or problem; **think-man** = *idea(s) man* s.v. *IDEA *sb.* 12; **think-piece** chiefly *Journalism*, a general article containing discussion, analysis, opinion, etc., as opp. to fact or news; **think tank:** see as main entry.

1959 *Spectator* 31 July 133/3 In a 'thinks' balloon are the words: 'Rock Hanson..looks an awful wolf'. **1977** *Times* 31 May 7/6 Roy Lichtenstein's *Girl at the Piano* has a nice verbal irony in the 'thinks balloon' as she muses. **1962** *Listener* 25 Oct. 694/2 People who want a short, quick holiday from newspapers, problems, and 'think' books. **1917** *Dialect Notes* IV. 330 Brain. Also *think tank, think box.* **1937** *Daily Express* 5 Feb. 10/6 I do not believe that their brains, or think-boxes, are of sufficient calibre to understand what they are preaching. **1964** C. HODDER-WILLIAMS *Main Experiment* I. viii. 95 A drawing of a computer with a think-bubble coming out of it with the caption, 'Computers'. **1981** N. TUCKER *Child & Book* v. 141 The self-proclaiming speech styles of the main characters [in comics], and their periodic 'thinks' bubbles. **1959** *Nation* 24 Jan. 62/2 Other think-factories are Johns Hopkins University Operations Research Office... Johns Hopkins thinks for the Army. Stanford Research Institute..does the bulk of its thinking for a variety of government agencies. **1947** AUDEN *Age of Anxiety* (1948) i. 28 Assembled again For a Think-Fest. **1958** *Sunday Times* 21 Dec. 12/3 The most stimulating think-fest in my week was Sir Kenneth Clark's lucid lecture on the revolting subject, 'Can Art Be Democratic?'. **1967** *Guardian* 26 Sept. 8/1 Think groups, in which scientists frighten one another with visions of a not too distant future. **1967** *Economist* 15 July 187/1 Nor is Mr Brezhnev the think-man who throws up bright new ideas to keep his colleagues on the ball. **1947** *Partisan Rev.* XIV. 478 Rapid withering of talent, as shown in slick formula novels or plays or 'think-pieces' for periodicals, has more often than not been the fate of the intellectual. **1966** E. WEST *Night is Time for Listening* iv. 120 I'm not reporting stories... I'm in the think piece business these days. *a* **1974** R. CROSSMAN *Diaries* (1977) III. 546 They are producing various think-pieces, including one on industrial relations, one on social services and one on poverty, discussion papers out of which will be boiled one policy paper to be presented at Conference.

think, *sb.* Add: **2. b.** *to have another think coming*: to be greatly mistaken.

1937 *Amer. Speech* XII. 317/1 Several different statements used for the same idea—that of *some one's making a mistake*...[e.g.] you have another think coming. **1942** T. BAILEY *Pink Camellia* xxvii. 199 If you think you can get me out of Gaywood, you have another think coming. **1979** *Jrnl. R. Soc. Arts* CXXVII. 221/2 Any design consultant who thinks he is going to get British Leyland right by himself on his own has got another think coming.

thinkable, *a.* Add: Also (*rare*) as *sb.*, a thing that can be thought of, a thinkable thing.

1890 W. JAMES *Princ. Psychol.* I. xiii. 529 As 'thinkables' or 'existents' even the smoke of a cigarette and the worth of a dollar-bill are comparable. **1907** —— *Pragmatism* iv. 140 *Absolute* generic unity would obtain if there were one *summum genus* under which all things without exception could be eventually subsumed. 'Beings', 'thinkables', 'experiences', would be candidates for this position.

Hence **thi·nkably** *adv.*, in thought, according to thought; conceivably.

1935 *Mind* XLIV. 325 For finitists, 'to exist' means 'to be thinkably constructible'. **1966** *Listener* 9 June 840/3 Death is thinkably of two sorts—(i) the physical breakup of animate entities,..and (ii) our own projected death.

thinkful, *a.* (Earlier example.)

1864 'MARK TWAIN' in *Californian* 1 Oct. 9/3 There is a handsome portrait in the Art Gallery of a pensive young girl... Says she, 'I like it—it is so sad and thinkful.'

think-in. [f. THINK *v.*[2] + *-IN[3] (after *SIT-IN *a.* and *sb.*, *TEACH-IN, etc.).] A meeting, conference, etc., for thoughtful discussion.

1966 *Newsweek* 19 Sept. 30/3 The think-ins..produced only a few flickers of..anti-war sentiment. **1973** *Belfast Tel.* 23 Feb. 4 The Social Democratic and Labour Party is to have a major 'think-in' this weekend to prepare the party and its supporters for the White Paper.

thinking, *vbl. sb.* Add: **1. a.** *high thinking*, idealistic opinions on or attitudes to social, moral, or religious questions; *good* (or *nice*) *thinking*: an expression of approval of a neat, ingenious, or well-thought-out plan, explanation, observation, etc.

1802 High thinking [in Dict.]. **1910** J. LONDON *Let.* 5 June (1966) 307 Bourgeois circles where he expected to find refinement, culture, high-living and high-thinking. **1959** *Manch. Guardian* 11 Aug. 5/2 For all the high thinking that goes with a branch of the United Nations Association and with folk dancing..there is not much sign of hard living. **1968** *Listener* 26 Dec. 848/2 Marc's *Trendy Ape* saw the final disappearance of high thinking in our new Bloomsbury before the onslaught of the Colonel's cry: 'Good thinking!' **1974** L. DEIGHTON *Spy Story* xx. 214 'They might be security police holding your friend Remoziva in custody.' 'Nice thinking, Pat,' said Schlegel. **1977** D. BAGLEY *Enemy* ix. 65 'We need to keep in his good books.' 'Very good thinking,' said Ogilvie.

3. *thinking-material*; **thinking-box,** *colloq.* (*a*) = *think box* s.v. *THINK *v.*[2] 18; (*b*) a study; **Thinking Day,** 22 February, the joint birthday of the first Chief Scout and Chief Guide, kept by members of the Girl Guides Association for thinking of other Guides all over the world; **thinking distance,** the distance travelled by a motor vehicle from the time when the driver first decides to stop until the time when he begins to apply the brake; cf. *stopping-distance* s.v. *STOPPING *vbl. sb.* 7; **thinking-machine,** (*a*) a person whose thinking consists (merely) in mechanical response to symbols; (*b*) *colloq.*, an electronic computer; **thinking-out** [f. vbl. phr. *to think out* s.v. THINK *v.*[2] 15], the activity of reaching an understanding or a solution of (some problem) by a process of thought; **thinking part** (earlier example); **thinking-through** [f. vbl. phr. *to think through* s.v. THINK *v.*[2] 16*] = *thinking-out* above.

1911 'SEPHARIAL' *Kabala of Numbers* I. vii. 75 The thinking-box of a scientific man [*sc.* Newton]. **1915** GALSWORTHY *Bit o' Love* I. 10 He'm in his thinkin' box. **1951** N. G. ANNAN *Leslie Stephen* i. 29 Stephen wanted to appear..as an athlete who incidentally owned a competent thinking-box. **1927** *Girl Guide Gaz.* Feb. 33/1 At the World Conference in America it was suggested by one of the French delegates that there should be an international 'Thinking Day', on which the Guides of all our different countries should remember each other. **1977** *Guider* July 327/2 The colours of the Retford Unit of Ranger Guides were dedicated on Thinking Day this year. **1947** *Highway Code* (*recto rear cover*), Think in terms of overall stopping distance... Thinking distance = Distance travelled before driver reacts. **1980** J. W. HILL *Intermediate Physics* iii. 20 The Highway Code shows that for a car travelling at 70 m.p.h...the 'thinking distance' travelled is 70ft.. before the brakes are applied. **1943** H. READ *Politics of Unpolitical* iii. 46 We teach them [*sc.* children]..to master abstract symbols and the processes of conceptual thought, and by the age of eleven or twelve we have produced a thinking-machine of sorts. **1948** BLUNDEN *Shakespeare to Hardy* ii. 47 His [*sc.* Francis Bacon's] danger was to turn himself into a thinking-machine. **1950** *Mind* LIX. 436 The present interest in 'thinking machines' has been aroused by a particular kind of machine, usually called an 'electronic computer' or 'digital computer'. **1842** POE in *Graham's Mag.* Jan. 68/2 With the increase of the thinking-material comes the desire..of abandoning particulars for masses. **1971** B. Z. DE FERRANTI *Living with Computer* ix. 80 The amount of 'thinking material' in the brains of a number of fishes was doubled by transplantation from other fishes. **1934** H. G. WELLS *Exper. Autobiogr.* II. ix. 654, I was using my prestige and possibilities as an imaginative writer, to do the thinking-out of this problem of human will and government, under fantastic forms. **1946** R. G. COLLINGWOOD *Idea of Hist.* 196 This thinking-out of the meaning of a concept is philosophy. **1890** 'B. HALL' *Turnover Club* i. 17 Then he uses this man to play thinking parts, like the *Bleeding Officer* and the two armies. **1971** *Listener* 16 Dec. 838/2 An inadequate thinking-through of what those fine phrases will mean in practice.

thi·nk-tank. orig. *U.S.* [f. THINK *v.*[2] + TANK *sb.*[1]] **1.** *colloq.* The brain. *U.S.*

1905 A. L. STILLMAN in A. H. Shearer *Little Bk. Rutgers Tales* 51 There's too much scrapping in the Joint... Your Think-tanks are getting to be Air-tight Compartments. **1910** [see *MAVERICK *v.* b]. **1964** *St. Louis Post-Dispatch* 8 May 2A/3 Truman..said he hoped to live to be 90 but only 'if the old think-tank is working'.

2. A research institute or other organization providing advice and ideas on national or commercial problems; an interdisciplinary group of specialist consultants. Also in extended (usu. facetious) use.

1959 *Times Lit. Suppl.* 6 Nov. p. xix/2 Even the Institute of Advanced Studies at Princeton does not quite meet the bill, nor does the 'think tank', the Center for Behavioral Sciences at Palo Alto. **1963** *Business Week* 13 July 61 There are many others..in the special groups—or 'think tanks'—that do analytical work for the armed forces, such as the Air Force's RAND Corp., the Navy's Operations Evaluation Group, the Army's Research Analysis Group, the Defense Dept.'s Institute for Defense Analysis. **1967** MRS. L. B. JOHNSON *White House Diary* 8 Oct. (1970) 577 Mt. Hope Farm..will be the site for the environmental planning center—a sort of a 'think tank' for city-planning experts. **1968** *Sunday Times* 25 Feb. 10 The private research corporations, or 'think tanks' (in the current American terminology) which are paid, mostly by departments of Government, to think about problems. **1968** *Economist* 13 Apr. 29/3 'Think tank' work is usually secret. **1969** *Sunday Mail Mag.* (Brisbane) 4 May 2/7 He's pretty busy as a 'Business Doctor' there—runs a 'think-tank'. **1970** *Daily Tel.* 22 Jan. 3/5 P & O, the world's largest shipping group, have formed a special company to exploit the inventions of their technical staff. A 'think tank' of 40 graduate engineers and naval architects will work on ideas and suggestions sent in by the sea-going and shore staffs. **1971** *Ann. Reg. 1970* 36 Lord Rothschild..described the task of the new organization (or, as it was nicknamed, the 'think-tank') as being to 'weigh up the pros and cons and consequences' of a proposed policy and to advise the Cabinet on it. **1973** *Listener* 26 Apr. 534/3 It has become the fashion among heads of governments and chiefs of state in the parliamentary democracies to equip themselves with a special staff of personal advisers—a think-tank, an entourage..—whose views supplement and sometimes run counter to the processed findings of civil servants. **1976** H. WILSON *Governance of Britain* iv. 95 In addition to establishing the Central Policy Review Staff (the Think Tank),..he [*sc.* Edward Heath] initiated the practice of the Cabinet Office Units, which has been developed since. **1978** R. HILL *Pinch of Snuff* xiv. 146 He leaves the service, possibly under a cloud... The inference in the rugby club think-tank was that the cloud was sexual. **1981** *Daily Tel.* 15 Dec. 13/2 The Rand Corporation, a 'think tank' which undertakes various studies for the Pentagon, completed an analysis of all the Communist-bloc armies. *Ibid.* 29 Dec. 10/4 Lean times are looming for the private consulting firms, 'think tanks' and universities.

3. A meeting or conference of experts, scholars, specialists, etc.

1976 T. SHARPE *Wilt* iv. 39 She had been accepted by people who flew to California or Tokyo to conferences and Think Tanks as casually as she took the bus to town. **1978** *Washington Post* 8 May A14/2 The meeting here, which one official called the NAACP's first 'think tank', was an effort to develop new positions for the association.

Hence **think-tanker,** a member of a think-tank.

1971 *New Scientist* 2 Sept. 536/2 Throughout this century think-tankers have been confidently predicting the imminent exploitation..of the seas. **1975** 'J. LYMINGTON' *Spider in Bath* vii. 124 A brief report from our Think Tankers on hypnotising the village people.

thinner. Add: **1.** Also a machine for thinning plants, seeds, etc.

1943 [see *PELLETED *ppl. a.* 2]. **1962** *Times* 21 May 18/4 More use of mechanical beet thinners.

2. (Also in colloq. pl. form.) A liquid used to dilute paint, printing-ink, etc., to a suitable consistency.

1904 *Jrnl. Franklin Inst.* July 17 The painter then adds thinners until the paint will work under his brush. **1958** B. BEHAN *Borstal Boy* III. 338 He..told me where I'd find an extra can of turps, if I wanted thinners. **1967** *Gloss. Paper/Ink Terms for Letterpress Printing* (*B.S.I.*) 9 *Thinner*, a fluid for addition to a printing ink to reduce its consistency. **1973** J. G. TWEEDDALE *Materials Technol.* II. ii. 33 A viscous liquid constituent may present particular problems, perhaps requiring..thinning by solution with a volatile thinner, to make it fluid enough for mixing and pouring. **1980** *New Scientist* 23 Oct. 244/1 This bottle of correction fluid..would be all right if I..added thinners.

thinness. 1. b. (Later example.)

1932 G. GREENE *Stamboul Train* I. i. 5 Her mackintosh showed the thinness of her body.

thinning, *vbl. sb.* Add: spec. in *Forestry*, removal of some of the trees in an immature stand, or removal of part of the crown of an individual tree. Also *attrib.*

1800 W. PONTEY *Profitable Planter* 33 It is not to be wondered at, if, even before thinning, the soil should be nearly exhausted, and the trees checked in their growth. **1822** J. C. LOUDON *Encycl. Gardening* III. iii. 1108 Autumn, or very early in spring, are the proper seasons for thinning where the trees are to be taken up by the root and replanted elsewhere. **1880, 1922** [see *COPPICING *vbl. sb.* b]. **1970** H. L. EDLIN *Collins Guide to Tree Planting & Cultivation* xi. 170 The thinning cycle, or interval of years between thinnings, can be short..or long. *Ibid.*, In regular thinnings a definite proportion of the growing stock of trees is taken out.

thio-. Add: **1. thi·azine** [*AZINE], any of a class of dyes that contain a ring of one nitrogen, one sulphur, and four carbon atoms in the molecule, such as thionine and methylene blue; **thiazole,** also, any of the substituted derivatives of this compound; (further examples); [ad. G. *thiazol* (Hantzsch & Weber 1887, in *Ber. d. Deut. Chem. Ges.* XX. 3118)]; **thiocho·line,** the sulphur analogue of choline, $HS{\cdot}CH_2CH_2N(CH_3)_3OH$, or a derivative in which the hydroxyl group is replaced by an organic radical; **thioe·ster,** the sulphur analogue of an ester, containing the group

—CO·S—; **thio-e·ther,** any compound in which an atom of sulphur is bonded to two organic radicals; **thioglyco·llic** (also **-glycolic) acid** [tr. G. *thioglycolsäure* (P. Claesson 1877, in *Ann. d. Chem.* CLXXXVII. 113): see GLYCOLLIC, GLYCOLIC *a.*], a colourless liquid, $CH_2(SH)\cdot COOH$, that is a strong reducing agent used as a reagent for detecting ferric iron; so **thioglyco·l(l)ate,** a salt or ester of this acid, esp. the sodium salt, used in culture media to produce anaerobic conditions; **thioke·tone,** a sulphur analogue of a ketone, containing the group $>CS$; **thi·onate,** a salt of a thionic acid; **thionine** (examples); **thionyl** (earlier example); **thiophene**: also **thiophen**; (further examples); **thi:osemica·rbazide** [*SEMICARBAZIDE], a colourless crystalline compound, $H_2N\cdot CS\cdot NH\cdot NH_2$, used esp. as a rodenticide and as a stabilizer in organic liquids; **thi:osemica·rbazone,** any of a class of compounds analogous to the semicarbazones, the oxygen being replaced by a sulphur atom; **thiote·pa, -TEPA** [*TEPA], the thio analogue, $PS(N(CH_2)_2)_3$, of tepa, used in the treatment of cancer; **thiou·racil,** a mercapto derivative of uracil that has been used to depress the activity of the thyroid gland; 4-hydroxy-2-mercaptopyrimidine, $C_4H_4N_2OS$; **thioxa·nthene,** † **-en,** a tricyclic crystalline compound, $C_{13}H_{10}S$, that is the sulphur analogue of xanthene; also, any of a class of derivatives of this that includes several anti-psychotic tranquillizers similar to the pheno-thiazines.

1893 *Jrnl. Soc. Chem. Industry* 31 Jan. 4 The original colour quickly reappears on exposure to air: Azine-, Oxazine-, Thiazine-, and Acridine-Colours. **1971** R. L. M. ALLEN *Colour Chem.* viii. 130 Thiazine dyes are used on cellulosic fibres, silk, bast fibres, leather and paper. **1888** *Jrnl. Chem. Soc.* LIV. 574 Thioamides condense with α-halogen-substituted ketones to form thiazoles. **1956** I. L. FINAR *Org. Chem.* II. xii. 451 A general method for preparing thiazoles is the condensation between α-halo-genocarbonyl compounds..and thioamides. **1929** *Bull. Chem. Soc. Japan* IV. 176 Thio-choline bromide was prepared by heating bromocholine bromide with 2-thio-uracil or 4-methyl-2-thio-uracil with water. **1980** *Sci. Amer.* Apr. 37/3 Nerve gas in the sampled air inhibits the enzyme, just as it would in the human body, resulting in a drop in the thiocholine level, which triggers the alarm. **1952** *Jrnl. Biol. Chem.* CXCVI. 545 These results thus confirm the conclusions of Lynen and Reichert that the acetyl group of acetyl CoA is attached, in thioester link-age, to the thioethanolamine portion of the CoA molecule. **1979** *Nature* 1 Mar. 86/1 The role of ATP and other energy-rich phosphates is considered in detail and this is followed by a study of thioesters including coenzyme A derivatives. **1889** G. M'GOWAN tr. *Bernthsen's Text-bk. Org. Chem.* iv. 94 The Thio-ethers, also termed alkyl sulphides, *e.g.* ethyl sulphide, $(C_2H_5)_2S$, are..neutral volatile liquids. **1979** *Nature* 20–27 Dec. 808/2 Each haem is linked, as in cytochrome *c*, to the apoprotein by two thioether bonds. **1877** *Jrnl. Chem. Soc.* XXXII. 595 Carius obtained an acid of the formula $H.C_2H_2(HS)O_2$, which he called mono-sulphoglycollic acid. Some uncertainty was attached, however, to the constitution of the product of this reac-tion, and the author now shows that both thioglycollic acid, $H.C_2H_2(HS)O_2$, and thiodiglycollic acid..are pro-duced. **1980** A. L. SMITH *Microbiol. & Path.* (ed. 12) v. 64/1 Thioglycollate broth, a special medium containing thioglycollic acid, supports the growth of anaerobes.. without special seal. **1877** *Jrnl. Chem. Soc.* XXXII. 595 Potassium thioglycollate..crystallises in masses of small needles, and is readily soluble in water and alcohol. **1976** *Nature* 24 June 652/1 Much early work was concerned with the evaluation of different methods for breaking disulphide bonds, and procedures were developed using.. sodium thioglycollate. **1889** G. M'GOWAN tr. *Bernthsen's Text-bk. Org. Chem.* 542/1 (Index), Thio-ketones. **1965** *New Scientist* 30 Dec. 921/2 The thioketones (compounds containing the $>C=S$ group) are in general red oils with intense nauseating smells. **1878** *Chem. News* 20 Dec. 294/2 (*heading*) Notes on certain thionates. **1938** *Thorpe's Dict. Appl. Chem.* (ed. 4) II. 574/2 All thionates are de-composed by heat, yielding generally sulphates, sulphur dioxide, and, except with dithionates, sulphur. **1886** *Jrnl. Chem. Soc.* L. 53 The addition of strong hydrochloric acid does not turn the solution blue, as is the case with thionine. **1956** *Thorpe's Dict. Appl. Chem.* (ed. 4) XI. 590/1 Lauth had already indicated that bright blue dyes could be obtained by methylating thionine but such a process was not economic. **1976** *Nature* 1–8 Jan. 60/2 Feulgen reaction carried out on the specimens treated with..thionin and exposed to light gave differential staining. **1866** *Chem. News* 9 Mar. 117/1 M. Wurtz presented a note 'On the Synthesis of Chloride of Thio-nyle'. **1903** A. J. WALKER tr. *Holleman's Textbk. Org. Chem.* 500 Thiophen can be synthesized by various meth-ods, the most important being the interaction of succinic acid and pentasulphide of phosphorus. **1932** I. D. GARARD *Introd. Org. Chem.* xiii. 183 Coal tar benzene always con-tains thiophene, C_4H_4S, which boils at 85° and is therefore not readily removed by distillation. **1951** *Engineering* 23 Nov. 667/3 Thiophen cannot be removed from [town] gas by any practical chemical method. **1967** M. J. JANSSEN *Organosulfur Chem.* i. 10 Benzene derivatives are much less readily hydrogenated than thiophene. **1894** *Jrnl. Chem. Soc.* LXVI. I. 76 (*heading*) Derivatives of thiosemicarbazide. **1971** *Chem. Abstr.* LXXIV. 74835 Thiosemicarbazide .. given i.p. to mice did not affect the incorporation of intraventricularly administered..putres-cine-2HCl..into γ-aminobutyric acid in the brain. **1902** *Jrnl. Chem. Soc.* LXXXII. 572 The thiosemicarbazones of aldehydes and ketones readily yield insoluble copper, silver and mercury derivatives, which can be used for the purpose of isolating these compounds. **1979** *Cancer Res.* XXXIX. 4601/1 The isoquinoline thiosemicarbazone derivatives have been shown to be potent inhibitors of ribonucleotide reductase. **1953** *Arch. Internal Med.* XCII. 629 The purpose of this communication is to present our preliminary experience in the treatment of..human leu-kemias..with triethylene thiophosphoramide (Thio-TEPA). **1976** *Nature* 13 May 135/1 Criticism of the use of the alkylating agent thiotepa (triethylene thiophosphora-mide) to sterilise mosquitoes, as part of an eradication programme in India, focused on its toxicity and the possi-bility that it or its breakdown products would harm other animal components of the food chain. **1905** WHEELER & BRISTOL in *Amer. Chem. Jrnl.* XXXIII. 458, 2-Thio-uracil... This compound was first obtained..when pseudoethylthiourea, containing some thiourea, was con-densed with ethyl sodium formylacetate. **1977** *Martin-dale's Extra Pharmacopœia* (ed. 27) 304/1 Thiouracil was formerly used in the control and treatment of thyrotoxi-cosis and in the preparation of patients for thyroidec-tomy. **1911** *Jrnl. Chem. Soc.* XCIX. 145 In order to obtain this sulphoxide [*sc.* diphenylmethane *o*-sulphoxide], thio-xanthen was oxidised with hydrogen dioxide in acetic anhydride solution. **1924** '*Chem. Age' Chem. Dict.* 148/2 *Thioxanthenes*, derivatives of thioxanthene. **1945** *Jrnl. Chem. Soc.* 659 (*heading*) Action of oxygen in sunlight on thioxanthen.

2. thiace·tazone [ACET(YL + *SEMICARB)-AZONE], a semicarbazone used as a bacterio-static drug in the treatment of tuberculosis and leprosy; 4-acetamidobenzaldehyde thio-semicarbazone, $C_{10}H_{12}N_4OS$; **thi·obacillus** *Biol.* [mod.L., coined in Ger. (M. W. Beijerinck 1904, in *Centralbl. f. Bakteriol.* II Abt. 597)], a rod-shaped Gram-negative autotrophic bacterium deriving energy from the oxidation of sulphur and certain sulphur compounds, and belonging to the genus *Thiobacillus*; **thi·ochrome** *Biochem.* [ad. G. *thiocrom* (R. Kuhn et al. 1935, in *Zeitschr. f. physiol. Chem.* CCXXXIV. 196), f. Gr. χρῶμα colour], a yellow basic solid, $C_{12}H_{14}N_4OS$, that has a strong blue fluorescence in solution and is formed when thiamine is oxidized in a pro-cedure for the estimation of the latter; **Thiokol,** a proprietary name for various poly-sulphide rubbers and liquids; **thiome·rsal** 'MER(CURY *sb.* + SAL(ICYLATE *sb.*], a bacterio-static and fungistatic organomercury com-pound used as a disinfectant for the skin and internally and as a preservative for biological products; sodium ethylmercurithiosalicylate, $H_5C_2\cdot Hg\cdot S\cdot C_6H_4COONa$; cf. *MERTHIOLATE; **thiona·zin** [*pyr*)*azin*(*yl* in the systemic name, f. PYR(O- + AZ(O- + -IN[1] + -YL], an insecti-cide and nematocide, $(C_2H_5O)_2\cdot PS\cdot O\cdot C_4N_2H_3$; **thioridazine** (-ridē[1]·zīn) [f. PIPE)RID(INE + *AZINE], a phenothiazine derivative, $C_{21}H_{26}$-N_2S_2, that is a white or yellow powder and is given orally as a tranquillizer, esp. in cases of schizophrenia and mania; **thiothi·xene** [f. *thi*(*o*)*x*(*anth*)*ene*], a derivative, $C_{23}H_{29}N_3O_2S_2$, of thioxanthene given orally as an anti-psychotic drug.

1952 *Lancet* 1 Mar. 436/2 Para-acetamidobenzaldehyde Thiosemicarbazone. [*Note*] This substance..is marketed under various names;..thiacetazone, &c. **1976** MAC-GILLIVRAY & HALL in G. S. Avery *Drug Treatment* xiv. 382/2 Massive breast enlargement has been seen with isoniazid regimens containing thiacetazone. **1951** *Biol. Abstr.* XXV. 811/2 It was possible to isolate thiobacilli capable of changing hyposulfides into sulfates. **1973** *Nature* 11 May 99/2 Thiobacilli, iron bacteria and algae can survive in acidic water of about pH 2. **1935** *Chem. Abstr.* XXIX. 6242 When crude lactoflavin is made alk., the fluorescence changes from yellowish green to blue. This phenomenon is due to the presence of a S-contg. pigment for which the name thiochrome is proposed. **1963** STEYN-PARVÉ & MONFOORT in Florkin & Stotz *Com-prehensive Biochem.* XI. i. 16 The thiochrome method is based on the observation..that oxidation with alkaline ferricyanide converts thiamine into a compound with intense blue fluorescence: thiochrome... The thiochrome is extracted..and the fluorescence of the extract mea-sured. **1930** *Official Gaz.* (U.S. Patent Office) 20 May 555/2 *Thiokol* for sulfur-containing plastic material used in the manufacture of gaskets,..protective coatings, and like products. **1936** *Industr. & Engin. Chem.* Mar. 275/1 Various olefin-polysulfide reaction products.., under the trade name of Thiokols, have been presented to the in-dustry. **1943** *Trade Marks Jrnl.* 8 Dec. 525/1 *Thiokol*... Thermo-setting or thermo-plastic condensation products of the nature of rubber, being compounds of or containing sulphur, and articles (not included in other Classes) made therefrom. Thiokol Corporation.., Trenton, New Jersey. **1972** *Materials & Technol.* V. xiv. 491 All thiokols are originally obtained in latex form, and as such they have found some industrial applications as an impregnant for textiles and leather. **1958** *Brit. Pharmacopœia* 675 Thiomersal should be protected from light. **1968** WILSON & SCHILD *Appl. Pharmacol.* (ed. 10) xxxvi. 671 Phenyl-mercuric nitrate, thiomersal (merthiolate), and other organic mercurials, have a better therapeutic index than mercuric chloride. **1964** *B.S.I. News* Mar. 23 Thionazin. **1974** MARTIN & WORTHING *Pesticide Man.* (Brit. Crop Protection Council) (ed. 4) 488 Thionazin is a soil in-secticide and nematicide effective against..nematodes,.. root maggots and..aphids. **1959** *Jrnl. Pharmacol. & Exper. Therapeutics* CXXVI. 312 (*heading*) Some neuro-pharmacological properties of thioridazine hydrochloride (Mellaril). **1965** SIMPSON & IQBAL in *Current Therapeutic Res.* VII. 697 (*heading*) A preliminary study of thio-thixene in chronic schizophrenics. **1976** SMYTHIES & CORBETT *Psychiatry* x. 194 Thiothixene is a potent and effective antipsychotic agent in acute and chronic schizophrenia.

3. Used *attrib.* as an independent word (without hyphen), denoting the presence of a sulphur atom, usu. in place of one of oxygen.

1879 *Chem. News* 24 Oct. 204/2 (*heading*) Organic thio compounds. **1926** *Chem. Abstr.* XX. 364 An investigation of the chemistry of the thio ketones as compared with that of the ordinary O ketones. **1955** KIRK & OTHMER *Encycl. Chem. Technol.* XIV. 61 Thio amides may react in either the thiono form, $RC(:S)NH_2$, or the tautomeric thiol form, RC(:NH)SH. **1980** J. W. COOPER *Spectro-scopic Techniques Organic Chemists* vi. 186 Amino, cyano, and thio groups.

thioctic (þəiˌǫ·ktik), *a. Chem.* [f. THIO- + OCT(A- + -IC.] *thioctic acid*: any of the sulphur-containing acids with the formula

$$\underbrace{S\text{—}S\text{—}CH_2(CH_2)_x}CH(CH_2)_{5-x}COOH,$$

where x = 1, 2, 3, 4, or 5; *spec.* 6,8-dithio-*n*-octanoic acid (x = 1), = *α-lipoic acid* s.v. *LIPO-.

1952 J. A. BROCKMAN et al. in *Jrnl. Amer. Chem. Soc.* LXXIV. 1868/2 The name 'thioctic acid' is proposed for this structure (x = 2), a sulfur-containing organic acid with 8 carbon atoms. **1953** FRUTON & SIMMONDS *Gen. Biochem.* xxxviii. 900 Recent work has assigned to α-lipoic acid.. the structure of 6,8-dithio-*n*-octanoic acid ('6-thioctic acid'). Isomers of this compound such as the 4,8-dithio acid ('4-thioctic acid') or the 5,8-dithio acid ('5-thioctic acid') have less POF [*sc.* pyruvate oxidation factor] activity. **1975** *Sci. Amer.* Mar. 98/2 In the 1950's thioctic acid had been proposed as a remedy for liver damage caused by heavy-metal poisoning.

thioindigo (þəiˌoˌi·ndigo). [f. THIO- + INDIGO *sb.* (*a.*).] A red vat dye in which the two imino groups of indigotin are replaced by sulphur atoms; also, any of various derivatives of this also used as dyes.

1906 *Textile Colorist* XXVIII. 321/1 Messrs. Kalle & Co., Aktiengesellschaft, have placed upon the market, under the name of Thio Indigo Red B, a new coloring matter, which like Indigo is admirably suited for dyeing the various textile fibres and for calico printing. **1923** THORPE & INGOLD *Vat Colours* vi. 131 The following aromatic bases have been converted..into the corres-ponding aromatic thioglycollic acids, which have been transformed..into thioindigos. **1951** KIRK & OTHMER *Encycl. Chem. Technol.* VII. 823 Thioindigo..forms brownish-red metallic crystals when recrystallized from xylene or other organic solvents... On reduction with sodium hyposulfite in the presence of alkali, it forms a pale yellow leuco compound, Thioindigo White. **1961** COCKETT & HILTON *Dyeing Cellulosic Fibres* v. 185 Thio-indigo is an important basic structure for a number of useful vat dyes.

So **thioi·ndigoid,** any of a class of vat dyes that are substituted derivatives of thioindigo and are used esp. in textile printing; also *attrib.* or as *adj.*

1943 *Thorpe's Dict. Appl. Chem.* (ed. 4) VI. 454/1 This process has been applied..for preparing the orange thio-indigoid dye from *p*-phenetioline. **1951** KIRK & OTHMER *Encycl. Chem. Technol.* VII. 824 Although the fastness of thioindigoids does not in general approach that of the anthraquinone vat dyes, the brightness and clarity of shade are in many cases considerably superior. **1952** [see *INDIGOID *a.* (*sb.*)]. **1970** K. VENKATARAMAN *Chem. Synthetic Dyes* III. i. 36 With the exception of halogenated indigo and a few thioindigoids..the indigoid group is steadily declining in commercial importance. **1972** *Materials & Technol.* V. xi. 358 Thioindigoid reds and maroons are vat dyestuff pigments with good light-fastness in full colours and reduced shades and excellent acid and alkali resistance.

thiol (þəi·ǫl). *Chem.* [f. next.] **a.** = MER-CAPTAN.

1900 *Jrnl. Chem. Soc.* LXXVIII. I. 163 Methods used for the preparation of aromatic thiols. **1971** *Nature* 31 Dec. 507/1 This interpretation is supported by the res-toration of the equilibrium..when an extraneous thiol, mercaptoethanol, is added.

b. = *MERCAPTO(-) b, SULPHYDRYL in Dict. and Suppl.

1951 C. R. NOLLER *Chem. Organic Compounds* xiv. 265 The —SH group is known as the thiol or sulfhydryl group, or more commonly as the mercapto group. **1973** *Sci. Amer.* Apr. 60/3 All the simplest organic molecules have been found in interstellar space, whereas many of the even simpler nonorganic species such as nitric oxide (NO), sulfur monoxide (SO) and the thiol radical (SH) have not been detected in spite of sensitive searches.

thiol-. Substitute for etym.: [f. THIO- + -OL.]

thiopental (þəiˌope·ntăl). *Pharm.* Chiefly *U.S.* [f. next + -AL (cf. PENTAL).] = next. Also called *thiopental sodium.*

1947 *U.S. Pharmacopœia* 572 Thiopental Sodium occurs as a yellowish white, hygroscopic powder. **1955** GOODMAN

& Gilman *Pharmacol. Basis Therapeutics* (ed. 2) v. 60/2 Ether (as well as cyclopropane and thiopental) causes renal vasoconstriction.

thiopentone (þaiˌope·ntōᵘn). *Pharm.* [f. Thio- + *pento(barbit)one.] A sulphur analogue of pentobarbital sodium that is given intravenously as a short-acting general anæsthetic; sodium 5-ethyl-5-(1-methylbutyl)-2-thiobarbiturate, $C_{11}H_{17}N_2O_2SNa$. Also called *thiopentone sodium.* Cf. *Pentothal.

1945 *Brit. Pharmacopœia 1932* Add. vii. 65 (*heading*) Soluble thiopentone. **1952** [see *hexobarbitone]. **1965** J. Pollitt *Depression & its Treatm.* iv. 50 It [*sc.* electro-convulsive treatment] is usually administered after the patient has been anæsthetised with thiopentone sodium. **1977** *Proc. R. Soc. Med.* LXX. 782/1 Generalized reactions were not seen for the first twenty years after the introduction of thiopentone.

thiram (þai·ræm). *Chem.* [f. *thi(u)ram* in the systematic name (see def.), f. *thi(o)-ur(ea* s.v. Thio 1 + Carb)am(ic *a.*] Tetramethylthiuram disulphide, $[(CH_3)_2N{\cdot}CS{\cdot}S—]_2$, used as a fungicide and a seed protectant.

1950 *Phytopathology* XL. 118 The Subcommittee on Fungicide Nomenclature of The American Phytopathological Society, cooperating with the Interdepartmental Committee on Pest Control, has selected common names for five commercially-available fungicidal chemicals... The coined common names and designations are:.. *Thiram* for the fungicidal chemical tetramethylthiuram disulfide. **1962** *Amateur Gardening* 10 Feb. 10 The chemical known as thiram..remarkably increases the percentage of germination of most garden seeds. **1975** *Daily Tel.* 15 Nov. 8/2 A refinement would be to dust them over with antiseptic thiram powder before putting them in a box of peat..to await another spring for replanting.

third, *a.* (*adv.*), *sb.* Add: **I.** *adj.* **1. e.** In proverbial phr. (*the*) *third time*('*s*) *lucky.*

[*c* **1840** Browning *Lett.* (1933) 5 'The luck of the third adventure' is proverbial.] **1862** A. Hislop *Proverbs Scotl.* 194 The third time's lucky. **1882** R. L. Stevenson *New Arabian Nights* II. 59 'The next time we come to blows—' 'Will make the third,' I interrupted... 'Ay, true... Well, the third time's lucky.' **1942** N. Marsh *Death & Dancing Footman* vii. 123 It was a glancing blow..but..it might have been my head... One of them's saying to himself: 'Third time lucky'. **1979** J. Tate tr. *Blom's Limits of Pain* ix. 82 Lars Westerberg discovered that the expression third time lucky had something in it.

4*. With following superlative: having two superior in the specified attribute; third in point of quality, position, etc.

1375, 1859 Third best [in Dict., sense 5]. **1938** [see *last *a.* 1 b]. **1962** E. Snow *Other Side of River* (1963) lxvii. 508 In 1960 it was the world's third-greatest reservoir. *Ibid.* lxxv. 577 The most significant additions to China's third-largest educational center are the T'ung Chi Medical College and hospitals. **1979** *Dædalus* Winter 62 Pursuing policies that would be optimal in a first-class world when one actually lives in a..third-best world can be highly inefficient.

5. *third base* (examples), *baseman, cousin* (examples), *-level, realm, -stage, story* (later example); **third dimension,** the dimension of thickness or depth (see Dimension *sb.* 3 a); hence **third-dimensional** *a.*; **third ear** esp. in *Psychoanal.*, a figurative ear which listens intuitively for what lies behind the words heard by the actual ears; **third eye** *Hinduism* and *Buddhism,* the eye of insight or destruction located in the middle of the forehead of the god Siva; hence *transf.*, the power of inward or intuitive sight occasionally gained by humans; **third eyelid,** the nictitating membrane of many animals; **third flute** *Mus.*, a flute pitched a minor third above the ordinary flute (see quots.); **third force, Third Force** [after Fr. *Troisième Force*], a political party or parties standing between two extreme or opposing parties (formerly, esp. between the French Gaullists and Communists); also *loosely*, any neutral power or third body; **third-generation** *attrib.*: see *generation 4 b; **third-grader** *N. Amer.*, a pupil in the third grade (*grade *sb.* 4 c) at school; **third house** (earlier and later examples); **Third International:** see *international *sb.* b; **third man,** (*a*) *Cricket* (earlier example); (*b*) *Lacrosse*, a defence player placed behind the centre; the position occupied by him; (*c*) *Philos.* [Gr. τρίτος ἄνθρωπος], a term from Aristotle (*Metaphysics* Bk. A 990b 17) for a third element (or man) which, in the paradox stated in Plato's *Parmenides,* seems to be needed in arguments from the particular instance (of a man) to the ideal form (of Man); hence *attrib.*, as *third-man argument;* (*d*) *Boxing slang,* the referee; (*e*) an unidentified third participant in a crime; **third market** *U.S.*, trade in stock undertaken outside the stock exchange; cf. *off-board *a.*; **third point:** hence **third-pointed** *a.*; **Third Position,** a name applied to the political stance of Juan Domingo Perón (1895–1974), President of Argentina (1944–55 and 1973–4), being neither capitalist nor communist, but a combination of Fascism and socialism; cf. *Justicialism, *Peronism; **Third Programme,** (from 1946 to 1967, when its name was changed to 'Radio 3': see *radio *sb.* 2 d) one of the three national radio networks of the BBC, broadcasting programmes of a predominantly cultural nature; often used allusively to qualify what is considered intellectually superior or 'highbrow'; **third rail,** (*a*) (i) (earlier example); cf. *conductor rail* s.v. *conductor 12 d; (ii) an additional rail for the accommodation of trains with a wider gauge; (*b*) *U.S. slang,* used *attrib.* to designate highly intoxicating liquor; **third reading, Third Reading,** the third and final presentation of a parliamentary bill after amendments have been made, sometimes allowing for a final debate before it is voted on; cf. Reading *vbl. sb.* 2 c; **third sex,** homosexuals (in quot. 1821, eunuchs) regarded as a separate sexual group; **third slip:** see *slip *sb.*³ 14 c; **third stream** (also hyphenated and with capital initials), a style of music which combines elements of jazz and classical music (see quots.); **third wave** [in allusion to Plato's metaphor (*Republic* 472 a) τὸ μέγιστον τῆς τρικυμίας 'the greatest of the three waves'], the last and most forceful of three successive arguments or propositions; **third way, Third Way,** used in a variety of contexts to designate a third possible ideology or solution to a problem (see quots.); **Third World War,** a hypothetical third war involving the majority of the world's nations (cf. *First World War* s.v. *first *a.* C. 2; *Second World War* s.v. *second *a.* 7 a); **third year:** see also Year 3 b.

1845 in *Appleton's Ann. Cycl. 1885* (1886) XXV. 77/2 A ball knocked outside the range of the first or third base is foul. **1946** *Chicago Sun* 2 July 25/3 He can start a club that would have a Red Sox star at every position except third base and right field. **1857** *Spirit of Times* 7 Feb. 373/1 Mr. Scott, their third base man is always at his post. **1936** O. Nash *Primrose Path* 38 Long have I wondered why a locomotive engineer should be so much nicer than an ambassador or a novelist or a banker or a third-baseman or a quartermaster or a lancer. **1978** *Detroit Free Press* 16 Apr. (Detroit Suppl.) 23/3 Phil spent all of 1977 with Tigers and figures to be the club's 3rd baseman of the future. **1840** Lytton *Money* i. ii. 7 You are very, very, very distantly connected with the deceased—a third cousin, I think? **1921** G. B. Shaw *Back to Methuselah* ii. 65 They are all third cousins of somebody with a title or a park. **1858** Third dimension [see Dimension 3 a]. **1923** H. Crane *Let.* 20 Jan. (1965) 116, I prefer Egyptian sculpture to the Greek, and this book makes me feel that the Greeks had more to express in line and design than they had in the third dimension. **1964** M. McLuhan *Understanding Media* (1967) i. i. 28 He acquires the illusion of the third dimension. **1934** H. C. Warren *Dict. Psychol.* 277/1 Third-dimensional. **1937** *Univ. Calif. Publ. Mod. Philol.* XX. 188 Only with such a spray [*sc.* lipiodol] can the third-dimensional aspect be brought out, giving vivid pictures of the epiglottis and tongue. **1954** *Ann. Reg. 1953* 365 Third dimensional (3-D) or stereoscopic films viewed through polaroid spectacles were no novelty in London. **1907** H. Zimmern tr. *Nietzsche's Beyond Good & Evil* viii. 202 What a torture are books written in German to a reader who has a *third* ear... These were my thoughts when I noticed how..unintuitively two masters in the art of prose-writing have been confounded. **1948** T. Reik *Listening with Third Ear* ii. xv. 144 The psychoanalyst has to learn how one mind speaks to another beyond words and silence. He must learn to listen 'with the third ear'. **1979** F. Kermode *Genesis of Secrecy* i. 5 The best psychoanalysts are admired ..for their powers of divination, for the acuteness of their third ear. **1810** E. Moor *Hindu Pantheon* 36 He [*sc.* Siva] has a third eye in his forehead, pointing up and down. **1921** [see *satori]. **1936** Dylan Thomas *Twenty-Five Poems* 38 No third eye probe into a rainbow's sex That bridged the human halves. **1978** S. Gooch *Paranormal* v. 202 It is the pineal gland to which the Hindu mystics of 3000 years ago gave the name of 'the third eye'—the 'eye' of clairvoyance and second sight. **1822–34** Third eyelid [see Nictitating *ppl. a.*]. **1892** C. S. Minot *Human Embryol.* (1897) xxviii. 727 The third eyelid is well developed in birds, etc., but is rudimentary in man. **1983** *Sci. Amer.* Apr. 86/2 When a cat falls asleep..its eyes close, and the nictitating membrane (the 'third eyelid') covers part of the eye under the outer eyelids. **1876** Stainer & Barrett *Dict. Mus. Terms* 433/2 Third flute. [Terzflöte]. **1906** Goodchild & Tweney *Technol. & Sci. Dict.* 434/2 There is also a flute in E♭ (often spoken of as the third flute in F, but tuned to E♭), which transposes a minor third higher. **1954** *Grove's Dict. Mus.* (ed. 5) III. 168/1 In the 18th century this [*sc.* the Flute in F] was known as the 'third' flute or 'tierce', since it stood in pitch a minor third above the ordinary flute, whose lowest note at that time was most usually d′. [**1933** *Esprit* 1 Sept. 718 Le projet qui suit a été établi par le Comité économique du mouvement de la Troisième Force et adopté par son Congrès National, à Tours, les 28 et 29 juillet.] **1936** E. Burns tr. *Thorez's France To-day & People's Front* iv. xxv. 228 The 'new economic régime' proposed in the 'Third Force' plan is dressed up in anti-Capitalist garb to make it capable of attracting and winning over the masses. **1951** N. Mitford *Blessing* ii. xi. 256 Mr Clarkley, more interested in French politics than English elegance, began asking a few questions about the Third Force. **1955** G. Greene *Quiet American* ii. iii. 160 There was always a Third Force to be found free from Communism and the taint of colonialism—national democracy he called it. **1956** *Foreign Affairs* XXXV. 60 An armed 'third force'. **1963** *Listener* 31 Jan. 194/2 Some Europeans have a vision of a great power arising to take its place alongside the Soviet Union and the United States—a third force, possibly armed with a separate European deterrent free of American control. **1971** *Irish News* 31 Aug. 1 What was needed was an immediate increase in the strength of the UDR—or if necessary the formation of a 'third force'. **1974** *Times* 27 Feb. 6/2 A doubling of the vote for the third-force candidates would still leave the relative positions of the Conservative and Labour parties unaffected on current evidence from the polls. **1981** *Daily Tel.* 24 Nov. 1/4 The 'third force' which Loyalist hardliners have formed as their own anti-IRA vigilante group made its first significant appearance on the streets during a commemoration service for terrorist victims. **1962** A. Lurie *Love & Friendship* i. 19 You make me sound like a third-grader. 'I learned simple division, Mummy, and drew a picture of an Eskimo.' **1849** *Alta California* (San Francisco) 31 Dec. 1 The solicitude manifested by the members of the legislature to ascertain where they are to get their mileage and per diem, is a subject of much jocularity among the *third house.* **1950** *Look* 31 Jan. 24/1 In a state where the Third House, the lobbyists,..spend millions every year.., a legislator going on a payroll for 75 bucks a week is looked upon as just a precedent-setting price-cutter, undermining the foundations of a fine profession. **1959** M. Schlauch *Eng. Lang. in Mod. Times* iv. 121 These deviations from strictly completed structure, occurring in formal discourse, are obviously very different from the rambling repetitions, the loose pleonasms and unfinished statements of third-level speech as exemplified in Juliet's nurse. **1975** *Cork Examiner* 30 May 10/4 About 55,200 students were expected to leave the primary, post-primary and third-level education this year. **1801** T. Taylor tr. *Aristotle's Metaphysics* i. vii. 26 Some make ideas of things relative, of which we do not say there is an essential genus, and some assert that there is a third man. **1851** F. Lillywhite *Guide to Cricketers* 23 If Long-slip is required, take the Third man away. **1897** E. T. Sachs in S. Christopherson et al. *Hockey & Lacrosse* 104 In third man I like a powerful player, and a tall. **1916** A. E. Taylor in *Proc. Aristotelian Soc.* XVI. 255 What I propose to show is that the appeal to the regress..is certainly not what Aristotle usually has in mind when he speaks of a certain type of argument as the 'third man'. **1920** S. Alexander *Space, Time, & Deity* I. ii. iii. 218 This objection..is analogous to one of the kinds of objection taken in ancient Greece to the Forms under the name of the argument of the 'third man'. **1924** W. D. Ross *Aristotle's Metaphysics* I. 195 Other forms of the 'third man' argument. **1927** J. Palmer *Recoll. Boxing Referee* i. 2, I have acted as third man in the ring on at least three thousand occasions. **1949** G. Greene in *Amer. Mag.* Mar. 142 (*title*) The 3rd Man. *Ibid.* 149/2 And the third man? Who was he? **1954** *Philos. Rev.* LXIII. 342 Plato could neither convince himself that the Third Man Argument was valid, nor refute it convincingly. **1960** M. Golesworthy *Encycl. Boxing* 171/2 Corri..was the third man in the ring for the middleweight bout. **1964** *Lacrosse* ('Know the Game' Ser.) 34/2 Third Man should mark Third Home closely. **1977** M. Green *Children of Sun* (rev. ed.) ix. 434 Kim Philby was finally identified as the 'Third Man', in 1963, when he too fled to Moscow. **1964** *Wall Street Jrnl.* 15 Jan. 1/6 A 10-man Big Board committee..is..studying the expanding role of off-board trading, or the 'third market' as it has come to be known. (The other two are the exchange markets and the over-the-counter market in unlisted securities.) **1868** G. M. Hopkins *Jrnls. & Papers* (1959) 186 The nave is very long, the roof, Third-Pointed, very low... The Third-Pointed altar-screen..and the choir screen..were beautiful in design and proportion. **1953** Third Position [see *Peronism]. **1971** Third Position [see *Justicialism]. **1946** *Times* 1 July 8/3 The future of broadcasting and television was outlined by Sir William Haley... He said that a third programme was planned and awaited only the completion of the Brookman's Park high mast. **1946** *Whitaker's Almanack 1947* 349/2 The *Third Programme,* introduced on Sept. 29, 1946, is broadcast on 203·5 metres and 514·6 metres. **1946** *Lancet* 21 Dec. 921/1 Oh yes, I've met *him*, of course—awfully decent fellow and all that, but frightfully Third Programme! **1951** J. B. Priestley *Festival at Farbridge* ii. i. 145 She had fine eyes but a rather ugly despairing sort of mouth, as if she came out of one of those Greek tragedies on the Third Programme. **1960** *Guardian* 22 July 6/3 The lectures—one of the 'Third Programme' ventures that Radio Eireann manages to squeeze in to its narrow broadcasting hours. **1966** H. Ogdon in 'H. MacDiarmid' *Company I've Kept* ii. 56 In England, of course, it [*sc.* an Indian *naga*] is esoteric, 'Third Programme'; a thesis could be written on it. **1980** *Daily Tel.* 29 May 14/6 MacNeice's most famous two plays..had an impact on a mass Home Service audience before he and his work disappeared into the Third Programme. **1867** *Commercial & Financial Chron.* 29 June 808 It is throughout a double track road, and a third rail is laid..for the accommodation of the wide cars of that line. **1890** *Jrnl. Franklin Inst.* CXXIX. 268 In 1879, Dr. Werner Siemens constructed and operated an exhibition railway... A third rail centrally placed between the other two was used as the outgoing conductor. **1916** *Gazette-News* (Asheville, N. Carolina) 7 Jan. 1/2 This recipe is for fourteen and one-half gallons of the 'third-rail' liquor. **1929** J. Callahan *Man's Grim Justice* i. 4 A shot of the third-rail booze that the Silver Alley joints peddled. **1972** *Modern Railways* Sept. 331/3 Invalides is the terminus of the Western Region 750V third-rail service to Versailles Rive Gauche. *Ibid.* 332/3 From October 1, the third-rail electric trains from Paris St Lazare to St Germain will be replaced by 1500V dc RER trains. ?**1571** *House of Commons Orig. Jrnls.* 14 Apr. II. 16 The Bill for Seweres the thirde readinge. **1878** W. STUBBS *Constitutional Hist. England* III. xx. 466 It [*sc.* a bill] is brought up for a third reading, debated again if necessary, read a third time and passed. *a* **1974** R. CROSSMAN *Diaries* (1976) II. 407 Though we had 116 to start with there were only ninety-nine left when the Third Reading vote came. **1908** W. JAMES *Let.* 9 Jan. in R. B. Perry *Tht. & Char. W. James* (1935) II. 485 Surely truth can't inhabit a third realm between realities and statements or beliefs. **1957** G. RYLE in M. Black *Importance of Lang.* (1962) 167 It is..positively misleading to speak as if there existed a Third Realm whose denizens are Meanings. **1821** BYRON *Don Juan* v. xxvi. 148 A black old neutral personage Of the third sex stept up. **1896** J. A. SYMONDS *Probl. Mod. Ethics* vi. 78 Burton..was led to surmise a crasis of the two sexes in persons subject to sexual inversion. Thus he came to speak of 'the third sex'. **1924** J. RIVIERE et al. tr. *Freud's Coll. Papers* II. xviii. 230 A very considerable measure of latent or unconscious homosexuality can be detected in all normal people. If these findings are taken into account, then, to be sure, the supposition that nature in a freakish mood created a 'third sex' falls to the ground. **1977** C. ISHERWOOD *Christopher & his Kind* ii. 20 Hirschfield.. was..notorious all over western Europe as a leading expert on homosexuality. Thousands of members of The Third Sex, as he called it, looked up to him as their champion. **1961** *Lancet* 5 Aug. 321/1 We had a total of 236 calls, of which 177 were for third-stage complications. **1967** J. H. SUDD *Introd. Behaviour Ants* vi. 125 Large third-stage larvae are fed more often than small ones of the same stage. **1930** W. B. YEATS *Wild Apples* 16 The third-story skylarks are singing again. **1960** *N.Y. Times* 17 May 44 Gunther Schuller..has been heralding the arrival of what he calls a 'third stream' of music—a music that is neither jazz nor 'classical' but that draws on the techniques of both. **1962** W. BALLIETT *Dinosaurs in Morning* 214 'What about the third stream?' I asked. 'I [*sc.* Gunther Schuller] coined the term as an *adjective*, not a noun... This music is only *beginning*. I conceive of it as the result of two tributaries—one from the stream of classical music and one from the other stream, jazz—that have recently flowed out toward each other. **1977** *Times Lit. Suppl.* 11 Feb. 144/5 The heady days of the 'Third Stream' of the late 1950s, when it seemed possible that string quartets and free-form saxophonists might sit down and make common cause together. **1866** SWINBURNE *Poems & Ballads* 43 Who swims in sight of the great third wave That never a swimmer shall cross or climb. **1933** *Mind* XLII. 175 We come now to the 'third wave' of the discussion. **1965** *Observer* 4 Apr. 31/3 The third wave in the tide of emancipation. **1949** Third way [see *PHENOMENOLOGY b]. **1956** *Sun* (Baltimore) 11 Oct. (B ed.) 16/2 People 'in the know' in Holland have been talking about the influence over the Queen held by a faith-healer... The healer..professes to be uninterested in politics, but she is closely connected with a movement called 'The Third Way', something like the 'Third Force' which swept Europe after the war. The movement is strongly neutralist and pacifist..and is opposed to Holland's commitments to NATO. **1972** *Times* 13 Aug. 16/2 At present, the only possible alternative route for the big tanker lies some 1,200 miles to the south... The idea of a 'third way', as it is often called here, could be attractive to the Japanese. **1947** *Civil & Mil. Gaz.* 27 May 16/3 Sir John Boyd Orr..said in an interview..that a Third World War would be in the making unless some sort of world food plan was established. **1976** *Glasgow Herald* 26 Nov. 6/4 He is correct when he says that 'dreaming of a world free from conflict will get nowhere', but working for such a world is a different proposition, and unless people are prepared to devote time and energy to that end there can only be a third world war.

II. *sb.* **8.** (Earlier example.)

1768 J. WEDGWOOD *Let.* June (1965) 66 All our thirds shall be saved for you.

9. e. (Further examples.)

1902 J. E. FLECKER *Let.* in J. Sherwood *No Golden Journey* (1973) iii. 37, I have got a third in Mods! **1908** *Westm. Gaz.* 25 Apr. 2/3 Off they went into the stokehole, where the Third put two of them to mind the feed-checks. **1909** J. S. V. BICKFORD *Faults & how to find Them* § 1173 Let us now consider a change from a lower gear to a higher (neutral to first, first to second, second to third, etc.). **1924** C. CONNOLLY *Let.* 21 Sept. in *Romantic Friendship* (1975) 13, I have run out of money and have to spend three nights Third in the train. **1942** *Horizon* Nov. 297 For the polished word of an Oxford Third Has left them cheerfully chastened. **1952** *Radio Times* 4 Jan. 7/3 The 'Third' is continuing a series of programmes on Dvořák. **1970** N. FLEMING *Czech Point* viii. 107 Melanie flipped the car deftly into third and tramped on the accelerator. **1972** P. BLACK *Biggest Aspidistra in World* III. iv. 173 The job of the Home was to reflect..the life of the whole community... The Third's was to broadcast only those things that had artistic value and serious purpose. **1979** 'G. BLACK' *Night Run from Java* i. 9 'I've my Second Mate's papers,' 'And you sail as third?' 'No. A Third.'

10. a. *pl.* Esp. in phr. *on thirds.* An agreement whereby an owner of sheep has them grazed and cared for by another person who in return receives one third of the profits (see quots.). *Austral.* and *N.Z.*

1824 E. CURR *Account Van Diemen's Land* 78 It is a common practice for persons who have not sufficient land, or who cannot attend personally to their flocks, to give them in charge to another party, who receives one third of the increase for his trouble..and if the party taking them [*sc.* the flocks] for 'the thirds' be careful and trustworthy, it is beneficial to both parties. **1852** G. C. MUNDY *Our Antipodes* I. viii. 282 One may buy stock,..or take stock on the system of 'thirds', in which the working partner gets one third of the wool and of the increase, while the proprietary partner..follows some other profession. **1878** E. JOLLIE *Reminisc.* 18 [Watts]..agreed to take my sheep on 'thirds' for three years. On 'thirds' meant that he was to have one third of the wool each year and I had to have two thirds. **1930** L. G. D. ACLAND *Early Canterbury Runs* 1st Ser. viii. 206 For five years part of the run and sheep were let on thirds to a man named Thomas.

b. *third(s)-and-fourth(s)*: in cotton and corn farming, a system whereby the tenant contributes towards the cost of seed and fertilizer and the landowner receives a proportion of the crops (see quots. 1964, 1967, 1976). *U.S.*

1940 W. FAULKNER *Hamlet* I. i. 8 'What rent were you aiming to pay?' 'What do you rent for?' 'Third and fourths,' Varner said. **1964** *Amer. Folk Music Occasional* I. 62 He could take advantage of the new system of farming rented land. 'You call that third-and-fourths, now. I do my own furnishing and then the man that owned the land would get [e]very third bale of cotton, every fourth load of corn.' **1967** G. W. WALTON in *Publ. Amer. Dial. Soc.* XLVII. 29 *Thirds and fourths*,..a method of tenant farming whereby the following practices are common: the landowner furnishes the land and a house for the tenant; the tenant furnishes his own plow animals and tools and does all the work; the tenant then pays for one-fourth of the seed and fertilizer for growing the cotton and receives one-fourth of the cotton grown; the tenant pays for one-third of the seed and fertilizer for growing corn and receives one-third of the corn. **1976** C. S. BROWN *Gloss. Faulkner's South* 198 *Third and fourth*,.. One who pays at this rate is a 'share tenant'... He supplies his own equipment... Then he pays one third of the seed and fertilizer for cotton, and pays one fourth of his crop as rent.

third class, third-class, *phr.* (*sb.* and *a.*) **1.** (Earlier example.)

1844 *Punch* VII. 258/2 *Third class.* Make up your mind for unmitigated hail, rain, sleet, snow and lightning... Do not expect the luxury of a seat.

third degree, third-degree, *phr.* (*sb.* and *a.*) **A.** *sb. phr.* **1.** *gen.* The third step or stage in succession, intensity, or amount.

1578 [see DEGREE *sb.* 6 c]. **1601** SHAKS. *Twel. N.* I. v. 145 For he s in the third degree of drinke: hee's drown'd: go looke after him. **1716** POPE tr. *Homer's Iliad* II. v. 48 He got *Orsilochus*, *Diöcleus* He, And these descended in the third Degree. **1966** TACHERON & UDALL *Job of Congressman* ix. 250 House Rule XIX prohibits amendments in the third degree. An amendment to an amendment is permitted, but not an amendment to an amendment to an amendment.

2. *Freemasonry.* The highest grade in freemasonry, that of master-mason. Cf. DEGREE *sb.* 7 b.

1772 W. PRESTON *Illustrations of Masonry* 205 (*heading*) A charge, to be delivered at Initiation in the Third Degree. **1865** J. HOW *Freemason's Man.* (ed. 2) 138 The Third Degree, or the Master Mason. *Ibid.*, The Fellow-Craft who is duly qualified by time, on presenting himself as candidate for the Third Degree, has to submit himself to an examination of his qualifications as a Craftsman. **1901** [in Dict. s.v. THIRD *a.* 5].

3. *U.S. Law.* In defining the extent of criminality, the least serious grade of a particular crime. Cf. DEGREE *sb.* 6 d.

1865 *Penal Code State of New York* xv. i. 192 Maliciously burning in the day time a building, the burning of which in the night time would be arson in the second degree, is arson in the third degree. *Ibid.* ii. 195 Every person who breaks into any dwelling house in the night time, with intent to commit a crime, but under such circumstances as do not constitute the offense of burglary in the first degree, is guilty of burglary in the third degree. **1949** BRANHAM & KUTASH *Encycl. Criminology* 20/2 Assault in the third degree.

4. In many classifications of burns, the deepest variety, resulting in the death of all layers of skin.

Today a twofold classification tends to be used (see quot. 1961).

[**1832** G. DUPUYTREN *Leçons Orales* I. xvi. 209 Nous avons divisé les brûlures en six degrés ainsi caractérisés: ..3° destruction d'une partie de l'épaisseur du corps papillaire.] **1866** C. H. FAGGE tr. *Hebra's On Diseases of Skin* I. xiii. 317 For all practical purposes, the three grades which I have described are sufficient... We may include under burns of the third degree those forms which Dupuytren and others have spoken of as burns of the fourth, fifth and sixth degrees. **1930** J. J. MORTON in E. A. Graham *Surgical Diagnosis* II. 136 Injuries of the first and second degree will leave practically no scarring but serious deformities may result from the third degree burns. **1961** *Brit. Med. Dict.* 231/2 Classification of burns. Dupuytren's classification: 1st degree..3rd degree..6th degree... Modern classification: superficial burn or partial thickness skin destruction; deep burn or whole thickness skin destruction.

5. An interrogation of a prisoner by the police involving the infliction of mental or physical suffering in order to bring about a confession or to secure information. orig. *U.S.*

[**1880** *Harvard Lampoon* 6 Feb. 166/1 He met the large and celebrated brother of one of his houries. He stopped to greet him, and was surprised at receiving a clip over the head from the brother's cane. This was followed by a personal chastisement in the third degree.] **1900** *Everybody's Mag.* Nov. 406 From time to time a prisoner.. claims to have had the Third Degree administered to him. **1930** G. B. SHAW *Apple Cart* I. 15 *Boanerges.* What do you mean? put me through it? Is this a police office? *Pliny.* The third degree is not unknown in this palace, my boy. **1976** T. SHARPE *Wilt* xiii. 136 'You don't think they're giving him third degree or anything of that sort?' 'My dear fellow, third degree? You've been watching too many old movies on the TV. The police don't use strong-arm methods in this country.'

B. *attrib.* or *adj.* Of or belonging to the third step or stage (in the senses above).

1926 *Scribner's Mag.* Aug. 193/1 Everybody at Police Headquarters agreed that it was ominously dull that night. There was scarcely a third-degree assault to disturb the city. **1930** J. J. MORTON in E. A. Graham *Surgical Diagnosis* II. 136 Serious deformities may result from the third degree burns. **1972** MILLER & KEANE *Encycl. & Dict. Med. & Nursing* 155/1 Third-degree burns damage the epidermis, dermis and subcutaneous tissue. **1976** 'E. MCBAIN' *Guns* (1977) iv. 86 They'd charged Colley with..second-degree assault... Even better than that, Colley's lawyer thought, would be for him to plead guilty to the lesser charge of *third*-degree assault.

Hence **third-degree** *v. trans.*, to subject to an intensive or violent interrogation; **third-degreeing** *vbl. sb.*

1928 W. GILLETTE *Astounding Crime Torrington Rd.* v. 260 They third-degreed Jimmy Dreek good and plenty. *Ibid.* 269 The fools in Boston had third-degreed an innocent man to his death. **1944** 'G. ORWELL' in *Horizon* Oct. 237 The third-degreeing of the gangster. **1979** C. WATSON *Blue Murder* xiii. 111 He third-degreed me about Birdie... The man just goes on and on.

thirdness. *Philos.* [f. THIRD *a.* + -NESS.] The quality or state of belonging to a third category or of being a third element, *spec.* in the philosophy of C. S. Peirce (1839–1914), that which connects, mediates between, etc., the ontological categories that he designated as firstness and secondness (cf. *SECONDNESS).

c **1875** C. S. PEIRCE *Coll. Papers* (1931) I. § 337. 170 (*heading*) Examples of thirdness. *Ibid.* 171 Continuity represents Thirdness almost to perfection. **1914** W. DE MORGAN *When Ghost meets Ghost* I. xx. 219 The first person plural pronoun, used as a dual by a lady to a gentleman, sometimes makes hay of the thirdness of their respective persons singular. **1934** *Mind* XLIII. 490 Thirdness includes the meaning of signs, the conception of general laws, 'infinity, continuity, diffusion, growth, and intelligence'... It is the category that is concerned with connecting, and it is involved in all reflective thought. **1978** *Sci. Amer.* July 19/3 Thirdness concerns two things 'mediated' by a third, for example an apple falling from a tree. The tree and the apple are linked by the relation 'falling from'.

third party. Add: **2.** *spec.* **a.** Used *attrib.* to designate insurance arranged against injury to persons other than the insured.

1901 C. H. GREEN in A. W. Tarn *Insurance Guide & Handbk.* (ed. 3) 254 Indemnity or Third Party Insurance, dealing with the Common Law Liability of the individual with regard to the general public and their property. **1910** E. M. FORSTER *Howards End* x. 84 As we've insured against third-party risks, it won't so much matter. **1931** *Daily Express* 5 Sept. 9/1 Each man was fined £5 with an additional £2 for Dougson for driving without a third party insurance. **1978** *Dumfries Courier* 13 Oct. 15/4 Clark was fined £5 and licence endorsed in two other charges—using the car without a third party risks insurance and using it while the handbrake was defective.

b. *third party adoption*, an adoption of a child arranged by a third party who is a private individual rather than an adoption agency.

1965 HALL & HOWES *Church in Social Work* iii. 57 That social worker's bane, the 'third party' adoption.

third-rate, *a.* Add: **2.** Also *absol.* (Earlier examples.)

1814 *Theatrical Inquisitor* IV. 357 Allusions, which have long constituted the commonplaces of poetry among third-rate makers of verse. **1816** JANE AUSTEN *Emma* II. i. 2 In danger of falling in with the second rate and third rate of Highbury.

Third Reich (þɜːd raɪχʸ, raɪk). [Partial tr. of (med.) G. *drittes Reich*: see *REICH.] The German state under the rule of Hitler and the Nazi party, 1933–45; the regime of Hitler.

Of the sequence *First, Second* (etc.) *Reich*, only *Third Reich* forms part of recognized English historical terminology.

[**1923** A. MOELLER VAN DEN BRUCK (*title*) Das dritte Reich.] **1930** *Times* 26 Sept. 12/2 Asked to give some idea of the 'Third Reich', Herr Hitler said the old Germany was a State of great honour and of glorious events, but the conception of 'the people' was not the central pillar of its structure. The second State had placed democracy and pacificism in the centre. They hoped for the Third Reich, which would have as its keystone the conception of the people and the national idea. **1933** L. STOWE *Nazi Germany means War* i. 9 On October 18th, four days after he had led the Third Reich out of the League of Nations ..Adolf Hitler made the following peace declaration before eight hundred of his party leaders in Berlin. **1946** J. FLANNER *Janet Flanner's World* (1980) I. 105 It was odd to..hear young Dr. Horn..state that it might well have been the international London Naval Conference of 1935 that drove Hitler's hypersensitive Third Reich into rearmament. **1966** *Listener* 3 Nov. 659/2 In the early years of the Third Reich, certain ideological ambiguities in Mann's attitude aroused Lukacs's apprehension. **1981** S. DUNMORE *Ace* 6 The good old days when the flyers of the Third Reich could do no wrong.

Third World, third world, *sb.* (and *a.*) [tr. Fr. *tiers monde.*] The countries of the world, esp. those of Africa and Asia, which are aligned with neither the Communist nor the non-Communist bloc; hence, the under-developed or poorer countries of the world, usu. those of Africa, Asia, and Latin America. Cf. *Second World* s.v. *SECOND *a.* 7a. Also *attrib.* or as *adj.*, and in extended use.

[**1956** G. BALANDIER *Tiers Monde* 369 La conférence tenue à Bandoeng en avril 1955, par les délégués de vingt-neuf nations asiatiques et africaines..manifeste l'accès, au premier plan de la scène politique internationale, de ces peuples qui constituent un 'Tiers Monde' entre les deux 'blocs', selon l'expression d'A. Sauvy.] **1963** *Economist* 26 Oct. 353/1 Relations between Europe and the third world nowadays. **1964** *Ibid.* 18 Jan. 178/2 The ingredients common to most 'third world' countries (poverty, ignorance, love-hate of the former colonial powers). **1967** A. A. MAZRUI in *Jrnl. of Politics* XXIX. 792 The concept of the Third World in the sense of the economically underprivileged sector of mankind must include Latin America, as well as the Asian-African countries. But in this paper we use the word, 'the Third World' in a more restrictive sense, meaning the world of the new states. **1969** *Wall St. Jrnl.* 15 May 14/2 By 'Third World' students Jerry means Orientals, Latins and American Indians. **1970** D. CAUTE *Fanon* v. 65 The 'Third World'..means 'positive neutralism' and 'non-alignment' between the Western and Soviet camps. **1974** *Globe & Mail* (Toronto) 29 Jan. 13/1 The First World Development was Capitalist... The Second World was Communism, in particular Russian Communism. The Third World takes in all the other countries that are not developed. Everyone counts China in the Third World... It includes the whole of Africa, Asia, Latin America. It has to do with income and low standard of living and so this takes in such countries as Greece, Yugoslavia, and some include Spain and Portugal. **1978** *Poland* May 1/2 You will find statements and articles written by Poles, people from other socialist and from capitalist countries as well as from the countries of the Third World. **1978** *Listener* 14 Sept. 322/1 The long ride into town underlines just how Third World, poor and underdeveloped Vietnam still is. **1980** *Times* 6 May 12/8 Andalusia, often described as Spain's 'third world', with its high crime rate and unemployment.

Hence **Third Wo·rlder**, an inhabitant of the Third World; **Third Wo·rldism**, an ideology or policy of support for the Third World.

1970 *New Scientist* 29 Oct. 227/2 Skills which the average 16-year-old western youth would have little difficulty in mastering apparently pose almost insoluble problems for the average Third Worlder. **1970** *New Yorker* 26 Dec. 46 The revolutionary Third Worldism of large sections of Sweden's politically active youth and intellectuals. **1975** *New Left Rev.* Nov.–Dec. 13 It comes down to little more than a more sophisticated justification of romantic nationalism, now transformed in 'Third Worldism'. **1978** G. VIDAL *Kalki* v. 119 We have a superb military machine second to none, not to mention a standard of living that is the envy of every commie and the despair of every Third Worlder. **1980** *Encounter* Nov. 40/1 Third-Worldism will not continue to be a one-sided problem for the West..but will also..be embarrassing..the East.

thirst, *sb.* Add: **3.** *thirst-mad, -making* adjs.; **thirstland** (earlier examples).

1878 P. GILLMORE (*title*) The great thirstland: a trek through Natal, Transvaal, Orange Free State and the Kalahari Desert. **1889** FARMER *Americanisms* 532/1 The region of extinct lakes and inland seas of Southern Nevada and South-eastern California is the great thirstland of the continent. **1969** G. MACBETH *War Quartet* 68 They.. lived As beasts, thirst-mad. **1952** J. CANNAN *Body in Beck* ii. 41 Will you excuse me if I beetle through for another pint?..That's a thirst-making rock if ever there was one.

thirsty, *a.* Add: **2. b.** Of a motor vehicle, engine, etc.: that has a high fuel-consumption rate.

1977 *Jrnl. R. Soc. Arts* CXXV. 364/1 Larger and quieter aeroplanes and less thirsty engines. **1980** *Daily Tel.* 9 July 12/5 It should..appeal to motorists wishing to move up from the normal run of mass-produced saloons without ..running a bigger and thirstier model.

thirteen. Add: **A. 1, 2.** (Examples referring to the original thirteen states (previously, colonies) of the U.S.A.)

1776 *Declaration of Independence*, The unanimous Declaration of the thirteen united States of America. **1776** in *Huntington* (N.Y.) *Town Rec.* (1889) III. 6 Yesterday the Freedom and Independence of the Thirteen United Colonies was..proclaimed. **1834** H. M. BRACKENRIDGE *Recollections* vii. 69 Fort Fayette, surmounted by the stripes and stars of the old thirteen. **1904** *Hartford* (Conn.) *Courant* 30 Aug. 10 We want to see the Old Thirteen draw closer and closer together. **1941** S. V. BENÉT *Listen to People* (1942) 471 There are the pretty girls with their hair curled Who represent the Thirteen Colonies. **1950** *Chicago Tribune* 23 Feb. 4/4 Our 13 original states found that survival and progress depend on closer association and common effort.

4. a. thirteen-year cicada, locust, a periodical cicada that reappears every 13 years rather than every 17.

1846 *Dollar Newspaper* (Philad.) 17 June 2/3 The locusts are said to be thirteen years' locusts, having made their appearance before this time in 1833. **1964** BORROR & DELONG *Introd. Study Insects* (ed. 2) xx. 204 There are at least 13 broods of 17-year cicadas and 5 of 13-year cicadas.

thirteener. Add: **2. b.** Also in the game of bridge.

1914 M. C. WORK *Auction Developments* 611 *Thirteener*, the last card of any suit. **1964** FREY & TRUSCOTT *Official Encycl. Bridge* 614/2 *Thirteener*, the card remaining in a suit when all other cards in that suit have been played on the first three tricks of the suit.

thirty, *a.* and *sb.* Add: **A.** *adj.* **1. c.** *like thirty cents* and varr., cheap, worthless. *U.S. slang.*

1896 [see *REUB, RUBE]. **1906** J. LONDON *Let.* 24 Nov. (1966) 225 You made my exposition look like thirty cents. **1944** *Chicago Daily News* 31 July 3/6 (*heading*) Sues to make Uncle Sam feel like a 30-cent refund. **1973** T. TOBIN *Lett. G. Ade* 2 Feeling 'like thirty cents' and 'the cold gray dawn of the morning after' became part of the American idiom.

B. *sb.* **2. b.** *attrib. spec.* Of, pertaining to, or characteristic of the 1930s.

1967 *Observer* 10 Sept. 24/3 Heaven knows, you can peg people by their opinions—'thirties communist' or '*New Statesman* type' seems as hard a definition as 'whisky priest' or 'teacher's pet'. **1969** 'J. MUNRO' *Innocent Bystanders* xiv. 205 The whole thing was as English as a Thirties farce: sandwiches and tinkling spoons. **1971** G. CHARLES *Destiny Waltz* v. 149 It was...furnished in a heavy, thirties style. **1976** S. HYNES *Auden Generation* iii. 82 *New Signatures*..was the first anthology of 'thirties poets. **1981** C. LEOPOLD *Night Fishers of Antibes* ii. 15 His Thirties forehead with the thin black hair brushed back from a parting precisely dead centre.

3. *U.S.* Also in journalism, broadcasting, and wider slang use. (Examples.)

1929 *Amer. Speech* IV. 290 '30' or 'Thirty' indicates the end of a shift or of the day's work, and has come to mean, also, death. **1938** *Sun* (Baltimore) 20 Jan. 2/8 Newsmen.. mourned today at the bier of Edward J. Neil,..who was killed by shrapnel while covering the civil war..in Spain. Prominent..was a shield of white carnations with a red-flowered figure '30'—the traditional 'good night' in the lore of the fourth estate. **1941** J. SMILEY *Hash House Lingo* 58 *30*, end of anything. **1945** J. O'HARA in *New Yorker* 27 Jan. 22/3 'I say thank you and thirty.' This last, the word 'thirty', is the traditional signing-off signal of the newspaper business. **1973** R. LUDLUM *Matlock Paper* xxix. 251 The number 30 at the bottom of any news copy meant the story was finished. **1978** G. VIDAL *Kalki* IV. i. 88 'When we know those two things, it's fat thirty time.' Bruce had obviously been impressed by journalism school.

4. *thirty-eight,* a revolver of ·38 calibre; ammunition for such a revolver; *thirty-three (and a third), 33(⅓),* 33⅓ revolutions per minute; a gramophone record to be played at this speed; *thirty-two,* also a revolver of ·32 calibre.

1942 L. HUGHES *Shakespeare in Harlem* 3 Gonna go get my pistol, I mean thirty-two. **1951** SACKVILLE-WEST & SHAWE-TAYLOR *Record Guide* 716 While we in England cannot say how bad were the worst of the early Columbia 33s, or how good the best of the Victor 45s, the difference would have to be great to justify..the Victor system. **1953** W. BURROUGHS *Junkie* i. 20 Jack's voice..went on and on... 'Give me a thirty-eight every time. Just flick back the hammer and let her go. I'll drop anyone at five hundred feet.' **1959** I. JEFFERIES *Thirteen Days* iv. 46 Mostly I filled up with nine-milli..but I threw in some thirty-eights and three-oh-three. **1968** *Melody Maker* 22 June 2 This is the EP which is recorded at 33⅓ and plays for 18 minutes. **1974** R. B. PARKER *Godwulf Manuscript* iii. 17 The girl's voice..was thick and very slow, almost like a 45 record played at 33. **1978** R. THOMAS *Chinaman's Chance* III. xxix. 291 We need a couple of pieces... Revolvers. No smaller than a thirty-two, no larger than a thirty-eight.

C. *Comb.* **a.** *thirty-foot* (examples); *thirty-five millimetre, mm., mil(l).* (photographic film, camera).

1880 J. F. CARLL *Geol. of Oil Regions* III. 197 Sand shells and slate, '30' Rock'. **1938** R. M. FANSTONE *Colour Photogr.* i. 17 Agfacolor... 35 mm. film for miniature cameras. **1969** 'H. PENTECOST' *Girl Watcher's Funeral* (1970) III. i. 123 'What kind of a camera was it, Morrie?' I asked. 'Leica—thirty-five millimeter,' he said. **1971** O. NORTON *Corpse-Bird Cries* vi. 116 'He couldn't have—well, turned the film back, or anything?' 'On a thirty-five mil Paxette? No, he couldn't.' **1972** I. HAMILTON *Thrill Machine* xxii. 102 It's a low-quality blow-up from thirty-five mill. movie film. **1978** F. MACLEAN *Take Nine Spies* vi. 196 His visitor brought out two rolls of 35 mm film. **1978** S. SHELDON *Bloodline* xxxviii. 341 The thirty-foot police boat..had been built for service, not comfort.

b. Thirty-nine Articles: clauses of a doctrinal statement drawn up by the Church of England in the sixteenth century, to which those taking orders in that Church have to assent; **thirty-year rule,** a rule that public records should normally be open to inspection after a lapse of thirty years from their compilation.

1607 T. ROGERS *Faith, Doctrine, & Relig. in Realme of Eng. expressed in 39 Articles* 3 The purpose of our church is best knowne by the doctrine which shee doth professe; the Doctrine by the 39. Articles established by Act of Parliament. **1739** (*title*) Thirty nine articles of constitutions & canons of Church of England. **1903** G. B. SHAW *Man & Superman* viii. 211 Straightforward public lying has reached gigantic developments, there being nothing to choose..between..the clergyman subscribing the thirty-nine articles, and the vivisector who pledges his knightly honor that no animal operated on in the physiological laboratory suffers the slightest pain. **1969** A. RICHARDSON *Dict. Christian Theol.* 336/1 In their revised form the Thirty-nine Articles were passed by Convocation in 1571 and the text finally determined in 1604... Subscription is still required from clergymen on their ordination. **1966** *Times* 11 Aug. 13/2 In two years' time the 30-year rule will be operating. **1979** *N.Y. Rev. Bks.* 25 Oct. 52/2 British Foreign Office papers recently opened under the thirty-year rule verify Butterfield's point.

thirtyish (þɜ·ɹti,ɪʃ), *a. colloq.* [f. THIRTY *a.* + *-ISH[1] 4.] **1.** Of about thirty years of age.

1925 F. M. FORD *No More Parades* I. i. 20 A very thin man; thirtyish. **1926** A. BENNETT *Lord Raingo* II. lxxi. 320 The..little thirtyish nurse. **1979** 'J. ROSS' *Rattling of Old Bones* vii. 63 'How old was he?' 'Thirty-ish. Perhaps less, perhaps more.'

2. Characteristic of or reminiscent of the 1930s; = *THIRTY *sb.* 2 b.

1962 *Times* 8 Mar. 16/7 Stuart Davis's hard, bright, 'Thirtyish' cubism. **1976** S. HYNES *Auden Generation* x. 355 The Berlin that their lives express..belongs to the 'thirties... And what makes it 'thirty-ish is that it can define its hell in political terms. **1978** *Broadcast* 20 Nov. 8/1 The decor is full of thirty-ish touches.

this, *dem. pron.* and *adj.* Add: **B. I.** Demonstrative pronoun. **1. b.** Now also indicating a person speaking or (interrog.) being spoken to on a telephone, etc.

1947 *Sun* (Baltimore) 8 Jan. 17 (*caption*) Very well, we'll expect you at nine this evening. Who did you say this was?

c. (Further examples.)

1954 G. KERSH in D. Knight *100 Yrs. Sci. Fiction* (1969) 223 So you came back to life—more than four hundred years ago! Is this right? **1965** *Times* 16 Mar. 13/4, I cannot refrain from a violent protest against the ever increasing use of 'this' instead of 'that': e.g., 'Will you come to supper tomorrow?' Answer: '*This* would be very nice.' **1970** *Nature* 4 Apr. 47/2 The reader..may come to think that this new approach to mathematics is not worth while. This would be a shame.

e. (Later examples.)

1922 YEATS *Player Queen* i. 20 The basket-makers and the sieve-makers will be out by this. **1971** in *Sc. Nat. Dict.* (1974) IX. 283/2 I'll hae plenty adee atween this and Whitsunday.

3. *this, that, and* (or *or*) *the other,* every sort (of), every possible or imaginable.

1824 SCOTT *St. Ronan's* II. i. 24, I am sure I aye took your part when folk miscaa'd ye, and said ye were this, that, and the other thing. **1918** *Nation* (N.Y.) 7 Feb. 161/1 They..offered us a contract in this, that, or the other company, whose dividend-paying record had been thus and so. **1938** N. MARSH *Artists in Crime* xvii. 255 It's a bit awkward what with this and that and the other thing.

II. Demonstrative adjective. **1. d.** Also, the present or existing. *colloq.*

1785 BOSWELL *Jrnl. Tour Hebrides* 86 We were told this Mr. Waller was a plain country gentleman. **1788** H. WALPOLE *Let.* 26 July (1918) Suppl. II. 24 Do you know the medals of gold belonged to this Lord Pembroke's grandfather? **1933** *O.E.D. Suppl.* s.v., [*Mod.*] I knew the last doctor very well. I don't get on with this one.

k. In unliterary narrative: referring to a person, place, etc., not previously mentioned or implied. orig. *U.S.*

1922 S. LEWIS *Babbitt* viii. 116 Did you read about this fellow that went and paid a thousand dollars for ten cases of red-eye that proved to be nothing but water? **1946** K. TENNANT *Lost Haven* (1947) ii. 41 They dug this great big trench with bull-dozers. **1969** FABIAN & BYRNE *Groupie* (1970) xvi. 111 The rest of the letters were all written on small sheets of blue notepaper in this really childish handwriting. **1976** *Drive* Nov.–Dec. 24/1 It was on the Chester road, in Birmingham. I saw this car with the keys in the ignition.

2. (Further examples, in attrib. phr.)

1930 R. GRAVES *Ten Poems More* 11 Neat this-way-that-way and without mistake. **1937** C. DAY LEWIS *Starting Point* I. iii. 51 The field was scored..with streaking,..incessant this-way that-way movement.

III. this child: see CHILD *sb.* 7 b.

this, *adv.* Add: **2. b.** Now also qualifying adjs. and advs. other than those of quantity, and no longer chiefly in *this much.* (Grading into an intensive.)

1932 J. LEATHAM *Fisherfolk* 13 A'm this aul', an' I never had a sy-ystem! **1967** *Boston Sunday Herald* 30 Apr. (Mag.) 34/2, I have a stack of telegrams this thick. **1971** *Where* Dec. 376/3 Yet the picture is usually not even this good. Most teachers..talk much more than half the time in their classes, and the time that is left is not all used for children talking. **1972** *Real Estate Rev.* Winter 8/2 Keep in mind, however, that no existing property is this typical. **1976** *Woman's Day* (U.S.) Nov. 154/2, I haven't felt this well in years.

this-a-way (ðɪ·săwēɪ), *adv. dial.* and *U.S.* Also **thisaway, this a-way, this-away, thisser-way.** [Repr. pronunc. of THIS *dem. adj.* + intrusive *-a-* + WAY *sb.*[1]: cf. *THAT-A-WAY ADV.] **1.** In this manner or respect.

1834 S. LOVER *Legends & Stories of Ireland* 2nd Ser. 54 Don't ruinate me this-a-way. **1901** A. C. HEGAN *Mrs Wiggs* v. 58 Did I ever tell you 'bout how Jim brought our other hoss to town?..It was this a-way. **1938** M. K. RAWLINGS *Yearling* xxxiv. 310 He's mean, at best. He's been this-a-way ever since Oliver takened his gal away from him. **1939** *Best Short Stories* 53 Why can't it last? We're sitting pretty, thisserway. **1956** H. GOLD *Man who was not with It* (1965) xix. 166 Boy, if I wanted to tell you that, I would say it this-away: Git! My dotter's too good for screwing! **1978** J. A. MICHENER *Chesapeake* xii. 728 'I jes' cain't believe it,' he said... 'Goddamnit, he's my own brother-in-law and he hadn't oughta behave thisaway.'

2. In this direction.

1903 *Dialect Notes* II. 333 Was he coming this-a-way when you seed him? **1955** F. O'CONNOR *Wise Blood* iii. 57 I'm going thisaway too. **1959** *Observer* 11 Oct. 6/4 Politically, Chataway can run thisaway or thataway.

thistle, *sb.* Add: **1. c.** Hence, *Knight of the Thistle*, a member of this order.

1732 *Gentl. Mag.* June 827/1 The E. of Portmore, made a Kt of the Thistle in the Room of the E. of Loudoun, dec. **1828** N. H. NICOLAS *Statutes of Order of Thistle* 21 After its [*sc.* Order of the Thistle's] Revival by King James, the Knights of the Thistle were Installed in the Chapel of Holyrood House. **1911** J. WARRACK *Knights of Most Noble Order of Thistle* 29 The King, after consulting the Chapter of the Knights of the Thistle, ordered a letter to be sent. **1963** *Times* 30 Apr. 10/7 Sir Robert Menzies, the Prime Minister, is expected to visit Britain and the United States in June,..later going to Edinburgh to be installed as a Knight of the Thistle.

3. Californian thistle *N.Z.* = *Canada thistle*.

1891 R. WALLACE *Rural Econ. Austral. & N.Z.* xxii. 310 One of the most recent importations..is that of the 'Canadian' or 'Californian' thistle. **1948** D. W. BALLANTYNE *Cunninghams* I. ii. 10 It's been awful with Californian thistle up there.

4. *thistle-clock* [CLOCK *sb.*[1] 8]; **thistle cup,** a silver cup with an outward-turning rim, of a type formerly manufactured in Scotland; **thistle glass,** a drinking glass with a round bowl and an outward-turning rim.

1948 C. DAY LEWIS *Poems 1943–47* 63 Thistle-clocks fly. **1947** W. C. WALLIS *Silver, Glass & Pott.* 4 Another type of vessel, unique in Scotland, which made its appearance during the last twenty years of the seventeenth century, is the little mug known, from its supposed resemblance to a thistle, as a 'thistle' cup. **1968** *Canadian Antiques Collector* July 17/1 Late in the seventeenth century appear two forms of secular silver unique to Scotland. One is a drinking cup of a type often called a 'thistle' cup, though it has little resemblance to a thistle. **1935** M. MITCHISON *We have been Warned* II. 138 Alex.. got a bottle of hock and poured it out into thistle glasses. **1973** *Times* 20 Oct. 14/3 The 'thistle' glass, with its outward-angled rim.

this world. Add: **this-worldliness** (further examples); **thi·s-worldly** *a.*, concerned with the things of this world or the present state of existence; **thi·s-worldness** = THIS-WORLDLINESS.

1883 'MARK TWAIN' *Life on Mississippi* xlviii. 480 The guests were always this-worldly, and often profane. **1928** C. H. DODD *Authority of Bible* IV. xii. 268 Hard experience revealed the insufficiency of the robust 'this-worldliness' of the classical Hebrew religion. **1930** G. GREENE *Two Witnesses* 92 His sensitively spiritual soul could make no truce with any thisworldness. **1944** J. S. HUXLEY *On Living in Revol.* xv. 187 The Churches..feel themselves threatened by the rise of an outlook more concerned with social planning for this-worldly improvement than with individual concern for other-worldly salvation. **1957** *Times Lit. Suppl.* 20 Dec. 776/1 Our civilization acquired its secular, scientific, anti-theological character, its 'this-worldliness'. **1978** J. SKORUPSKI in Hookway & Pettit *Action & Interpretation* 83 It treats the magical and, by and large, the religious practices as 'instrumental': as attempts to control the course of events in such a way as to bring about this-worldly ends which the actors seek.

thivish (þəi·viʃ). *Anglo-Ir.* Also **tevish.** Pl. **-es**; also **tevishies, thevshi.** [ad. Ir. *taibhse*, pl. *taibhsí*.] A ghost, apparition, or spectre.

1852 W. WILDE *Irish Pop. Superstitions* i. 14 Thivishes or thoushas (shadowy apparitions) are literally ghosts. *Ibid.* iii. 71 (*heading*) Reminiscences of the West.—The Welshes.—The Thivish or Fetch. *Ibid.* 111 'Mother,' said he, gazing steadily upon the pale anxious face that was bent upon him, 'I've seen the *thivish*.' **1888** W. B. YEATS *Fairy & Folk Tales of Irish Peasantry* 128 Ghosts, or as they are called in Irish, *Thevshi* or *Tash* (*taidhbhse, tais*), live in a state intermediary between this life and the rest. They are held there by some earthly longing or affection. **1892, 1963** [see *SOWLTH].

thixotropy (þiksǫ̆·trǫ·pi). [ad. G. *tixotropie* (T. Péterfi 1927, in *Arch. f. Entwicklungsmech.* CXII. 689), f. Gr. θίξ-ις touching + -O + Gr. τροπ-ή turning: see -Y[3].] The property of certain gels of becoming fluid when agitated and of reverting back to a gel when left to stand.

1927 *Chem. Abstr.* XXI. 1391 Thixotropy is the phenomenon that a coagulated sol can be liquefied by merely shaking and always again coagulated to a gel by stopping agitation. **1949** P. C. CARMAN *Chem. Constitution & Properties Engin. Materials* xiii. 379 This type of reversible gelation is known as thixotropy and is particularly strongly marked in montmorillonite clays. **1971** *New Scientist* 19 Aug. 435/2 How to demonstrate thixotropy with custard.

Hence **thixotro·pic** *a.*, exhibiting or pertaining to thixotropy; **thixotro·pically** *adv.*

1927 *Chem. Abstr.* XXI. 1391 (*heading*) Thixotropic behavior of aluminum hydroxide gels. **1947** *Nature* 11 Jan. 70/2 The range of thixotropic materials extends from the hardest solids, through doughs and pastes to liquids such as blood or milk. **1958** *Woman* 22 Feb. 11/2 Thixotropic paint is the non-spill type. **1963** *Geol. Mag.* C. 209 Nodules..produced by allowing a thin layer of sand to sink into thixotropically mobilized mud. **1971** *Nature* 30 July 328/1 A thin layer of grey silt covered a 20 cm layer of black thixotropic mud.

tholeiite (þōu·lĭəit). *Petrogr.* Also 9 **tholeite.** [ad. G. *tholeiit* (J. Steininger *Geognostische Beschreibung des Landes zwischen der unteren Saar und dem Rheine: Nachträge* (1841) 26), f. *Tholei* (now *Tholey*), name of a village in N.E. Saar, W. Germany: see -ITE[1].] Formerly, a basaltic rock containing plagioclase feldspar, pyroxene, and glass, with little or no olivine, and having an intersertal texture; in recent use, any basaltic rock typically containing augite and a calcium-poor pyroxene (pigeonite or hypersthene), and distinguished from alkali basalts by a higher silica and lower alkali content.

1866 P. H. LAWRENCE tr. *von Cotta's Rocks Classified & Described* II. i. 138 Steininger has given the name of Tholeite to a rock found at the Schaumberg near Tholei, which he took for a compound of albite and titanite. But according to Bergemann's analysis this rock consists of 70 labradorite, 5 augite... It must therefore from its composition be considered a dolerite or basalt unless indeed it be considered as plutonic and classed with melaphyre. **1893** [see *INTERSERTAL *a.*]. **1922** *Q. Jrnl. Geol. Soc.* LXXVIII. 229 The rocks were described as being.. of one type: namely, olivine-free dolerites or tholeiites. **1924** THOMAS & BAILEY in E. B. Bailey et al. *Tertiary & Post-Tertiary Geol. Mull* xxv. 280 Olivine-free and olivine-poor plagioclase-augite rocks with intersertal structure are classed by Rosenbusch as tholeiites. **1962** *Jrnl. Petrol.* III. 352 The two planes identified in Fig. 1.. divide the basalts into five unique groups..: 1. Tholeiite (oversaturated): normative quartz and hypersthene. 2. Tholeiite (saturated; hypersthene basalt): normative hypersthene. 3. Olivine tholeiite (undersaturated): normative hypersthene and olivine. 4. Olivine basalt: normative olivine. 5. Alkali basalt: normative olivine and nepheline. **1967** *Geol. Mag.* CIV. 337 Significant use of the term tholeiite dates from 1887 when Rosenbusch redefined Steininger's Schaumberg, Saar tholeiite (1840) from Tholey as a melaphyre with intersertal texture... Bailey and Thomas (1924) in setting up their non-porphyritic central magma type of Mull recognized its 'tholeiitic' character using..Rosenbusch's definition of 1887... A more precise petrographic and chemical definition was to follow in Kennedy's important papers of 1931 and 1933 in which the non-porphyritic central magma type was redefined as the Tholeiitic Magma Type... Paramount in this definition was the recognition of the presence of an enstatite-augite or pigeonite series pyroxene in the ground-mass of tholeiitic lavas. **1978** *Nature* 13 July 128/1 The two principal Icelandic basalt types are evolved tholeiites, mostly quartz-normative, with $Mg/Mg+Fe^{2+}$ atomic ratio of 0·40 to 0·50, associated with fissure swarms and central volcanoes; and second, olivine tholeiites with $Mg/Mg+Fe^{2+}$ in the 0·60–0·70 range and predominantly associated with monogenetic shield volcanoes.

Hence **tholeii·tic** *a.*

1922 *Q. Jrnl. Geol. Soc.* LXXVIII. 237 The tholeiitic intrusions have produced little thermal alteration of the rocks into which they have been ultimately injected. **1933** [see *plateau basalt* s.v. *PLATEAU 4]. **1933** *Amer. Jrnl. Sci.* CCXXV. 247 The general thesis is..advanced that the olivine-basalt magma-type is the parent of the alkaline line of descent while the tholeiitic magma-type occupies a similar position with respect to the calc-alkaline rock suite. **1967** [see THOLEIITE above]. **1970** *Nature* 12 Dec. 1030/2 Geochemists have known for some time that [ocean] ridge basalts tend to be tholeiitic whereas alkali basalts are more likely to be found away from ridges. **1972** F. H. HATCH et al. *Petrol. Igneous Rocks* (ed. 13) vii. 364 Alkali olivine-basalt magmas can differentiate towards alkali-enrichment; but tholeiitic magmas differentiate towards silica-enrichment.

tholoid (þōu·loid). *Geol.* [f. Gr. θόλος (see THOLUS) + -OID.] A dome-shaped, steep-sided extrusion of hardened lava plugging the vent of a volcano.

In quot. 1912 repr. a Ger. form.

1912 *Jrnl. Geol.* XX. 85 'Tholoides' have slopes of over 35° and are convex upward. **1939** *Nature* 25 Nov. 913/2 Of the latter [*sc.* new volcanoes] there were two:.. (*b*) Iōzima-Sintō, south of Kyūsyū.., which was of the tholoid type. **1976** P. FRANCIS *Volcanoes* iv. 151 Even when the tholoid is shrouded in mist and invisible, as it often is in the afternoon, the dry clattering continues, with every now and then a much larger collapse taking place.

tholos, var. THOLUS in Dict. and Suppl.

tholus. Add: **b.** *tholos* is the usual form. (Later examples.) Also *tholos-tomb.*

1921 *Discovery* Feb. 33/1 The principle of the tholos-tomb was most in use in Mycenæan times. **1957** [see *beehive tomb* s.v. *BEEHIVE 3]. **1975** *Times Lit. Suppl.* 14 Mar. 282/1 The megalithic architecture of Britain.. had no conceivable ancestry in the Mycenaean *tholoi*. **1983** *Times* 10 Feb. 1/3 The underground *tholos* tomb, shaped like a giant beehive, lies in a fifteenth-century BC cemetery..three miles south of Argos.

Thomas. Add: **3.** (Earlier *absol.* example.)

1888 KIPLING *From Sea to Sea* (1899) I. 185 Every Thomas is interesting, except when he is too drunk to speak.

5. *Surg.* The name of H. O. *Thomas* (1834–91), English surgeon, used *attrib.* and in the possessive to designate a splint that he invented for immobilizing the hip, consisting of a rigid bar that extends from the back to the calf and is bandaged to the leg, and with rings attached that partly encircle the chest and leg; also (now the usual sense), a splint consisting of a soft ring encircling the thigh from which two rigid rods extend on each side of the leg and meet beyond the foot, allowing traction to be applied to the leg via the cross-piece or the knee to be immobilized.

1884 W. PYE *Surg. Handicraft* xxiii. 291 There are many other ways of treating acute hip disease... By Thomas' splint. **1940** N. MITFORD *Pigeon Pie* vi. 102 If.. real casualties were brought in and found all the personnel tied up in Thomas's splints. **1961** *Countryman* LVIII. III. 600 The M.O...fixed my fractured leg in a Thomas splint. **1974** PASSMORE & ROBSON *Compan. Med. Stud.* III. iv. 11/2 The Thomas' splint is designed so that when the traction tapes are tightened over the end of the splint, a counter thrust is exerted through the padded ring against the bony prominence of the ischium.

6. The name of S. G. *Thomas* (1850–85), English metallurgist and inventor, used *attrib.* to designate a steel-making process like the Bessemer process but using a converter with a basic instead of an acid lining, so that phosphorus is removed (invented by Thomas in 1878). Also *Thomas–Gilchrist* [P. *Gilchrist* (1851–1935), cousin and collaborator of Thomas].

1881 *Encycl. Brit.* XIII. 346/1 Owing to the success of these operations, the 'basic' process has been more frequently spoken of as the 'Thomas-Gilchrist process'. **1925** *Jrnl. Iron & Steel Inst.* CXII. 523 Notwithstanding prognostications as to the supersession..of the Bessemer acid and basic (Thomas) process by the open-hearth process, it is certain that..the Bessemer process will long continue to hold its own. **1948** H. W. BAKER *Mod. Workshop Technol.* I. 22 In the Thomas process the necessary amount of lime..is charged into the converter..before the iron.. is poured in. **1973** [see *SIEMENS a].

Thomas–Fermi (tǫmăs,fɜ̄·ɹmi). *Physics.* The names of L. H. *Thomas* (b. 1903), English physicist, and E. *FERMI, used *attrib.* with reference to a model of the electronic charge distribution in an atom in which the electrons are treated as a gas of independent particles obeying Fermi–Dirac statistics and the exclusion principle is taken into account, proposed by them in 1927 and 1928 respectively.

1931 *Phil. Mag.* XII. 111 The Thomas–Fermi method of approximating to the atomic charge distribution. **1955** J. LINDHARD in W. Pauli *Niels Bohr* 190 If we ask for the behaviour for heavier atoms,..a Thomas–Fermi treatment should again be preferable. **1970** G. K. WOODGATE *Elem. Atomic Struct.* vi. 101 The Thomas–Fermi potential does serve as a trial potential for self-consistent field methods.

Thompson (tǫ·msən). *Mil.* (orig. *U.S.*). The name of John T. *Thompson* (1860–1940), U.S. general, used *attrib.* and *absol.* to designate a type of sub-machine-gun which was conceived by him and financed by his company, and named after him in 1919 at the insistence of its designer, O. V. Payne. Cf. *TOMMY GUN.

1920 *Army & Navy Jrnl.* 2 Oct. 120/1 Colonel Thompson is now connected with the Auto-Ordnance Corporation of New York City, which has put the Thompson sub-machine gun on the market. **1921** M. THOMPSON *Let.* 26 Apr. in W. J. Helmer *Gun that made Twenties Roar* (1969) iv. 69 We came back with a tentative agreement on their part to purchase 50,000 Thompsons. **1933** 'J. SPENSER' *Limey* ii. 27 There was a Thompson sub-machine gun, universally known in gangland as a 'Tommy gun'. **1946** D. M. WARD *Other Battle* xxi. 140 An order was placed in America for Thompsons, but by the time the first few were delivered it was realized that not enough ·45 ammunition could be made. **1970** E. K. WALKER in W. King *Black Short Story Anthol.* (1972) 54 Captain Bull..carried a Thompson submachine gun at high port. **1978** D. MURPHY *Place Apart* ii. 22 Kerins had a Thompson under the bed but he never had a chance to use it.

Thompsonian (tǫmsōu·niăn), *sb.* and *a.* [f. the name *Thompson* (see below) + -IAN.] **A.** *sb.* An admirer of the work of Francis Thompson (1859–1907), English poet and writer. **B.** *adj.* Of, belonging to, or characteristic of Thompson or his work.

1913 T. HARDY in V. Meynell *Francis Thompson & Wilfrid Meynell* (1952) xiii. 198 You may be sure I am a Thompsonian. ?**1921** J. THOMSON *Remarks on Francis Thompson's Hound of Heaven* 9 Nearer than either to the Thompsonian *Hound of Heaven*..comes the *heaven's wingèd hound* of Shelley. **1927** *Observer* 19 June 8 The next in the series is a choice from Francis Thompson's prose... This Thompsonian addition to the 'handy Harraps' is no end of a shillingsworth. **1948** *Tablet* 30 Oct. 282/2 Answering the letters of the growing army of Thompsonians all over the world. **1962** J. BRODRICK in F. Thompson *St Ignatius Loyola* p. xii, He made one precious contribution to Thompsonian psychology.

Thomson (tǫ·msən). Also (*erron.*) **Thompson.**

1. *Physics.* [The name of Sir William *Thomson*: see *KELVIN, KELVIN.] *Thomson effect*: the effect an electric current has, when flowing in the direction of a temperature gradient, of absorbing or giving out heat independently of the Joule heating; so *Thomson coefficient*, a numerical measure of this effect for a material.

1878 *Encycl. Brit.* VIII. 98/1 This anomaly led Tait to the discovery..that the Thomson effect in iron changes its sign..at a temperature near low red heat. **1906**, etc. [see *SEEBECK]. **1930** *Engineering* 9 May 596/2 The Thomson and Peltier coefficients were given values of the right general order of magnitude. **1966** C. R. TOTTLE *Sci. Engin. Materials* vi. 130 By choosing appropriate values of the Peltier and Thomson coefficients, two dissimilar materials can be arranged to produce a substantial e.m.f. if one junction is maintained at a high temperature and the other at a lower one. **1975** D. G. FINK *Electronics Engineers' Handbk.* XXVII. 3 At large values of dT/dx the Thompson effect may be comparable with the Seebeck effect and must be taken into account in the design of generators and refrigerators.

2. *Zool.* The name of Joseph *Thomson* (1858–94), Scottish explorer, used in the possessive (rarely *attrib.*) to designate an East African gazelle with a broad black lateral stripe, *Gazella thomsoni*, first collected by him and named in his honour by A. Günther in 1884 (*Ann. & Mag. Nat. Hist.* XIV. 428).

1897 *Proc. Zool. Soc.* 454 Thomson's Gazelle does not.. extend beyond a few miles north of Lake Nakuru. **1906** [see TOMMY 3 c]. **1915** ROOSEVELT & HELLER *Life-Hist. Afr. Game Animals* II. xviii. 600 The Thomson gazelle is essentially a highland antelope. **1969** *Daily Tel.* 13 Aug. 17/3 A Thomson's gazelle, born at Whipsnade Zoo, brings the number in the herd..to 20. **1980** R. W. HAYMAN tr. *Haltenorth & Diller's Field Guide Mammals Afr.* 94 Thomson's Gazelle..horns lyre-shaped and weakly S-formed.

3. *Physics.* [The name of Sir J. J. *Thomson* (1856–1940), British physicist.] *Thomson scattering*: scattering of light by free charged particles, *spec.* electrons, in accordance with classical mechanics.

1935 COMPTON & ALLISON *X-Rays in Theory & Exper.* (ed. 2) iv. 298 This classical scattering from a free electron is often called 'J. J. Thomson scattering'. *Ibid.* 827/2 (Index), Thomson scattering. **1962** *Sci. Survey* III. 123 Knowing the brightness of the corona and, from the theory of Thomson scattering, the proportion of sunlight scattered towards the observer by each electron, we can calculate the number of electrons per cubic centimetre. **1978** *Nature* 19 Jan. 220/1 One..expects that up to a certain radial distance from the accretion column the neutron star surface is covered by a dense atmosphere and represents a 'tarnished mirror', reflecting quasi-isotropically by Thomson scattering.

-thon, *suffix.* Var. *-ATHON used in some words, as *TELETHON.

1954 *Amer. Speech* XXIX. 229 The word *moviethon* is merely the most recent in what promises to be a long list of words created arbitrarily by means of the *-thon* suffix. **1963** R. I. McDAVID *Mencken's Amer. Lang.* 228 *Rockerthon, poolathon* and *pianothon* appeared in Canada in 1955.

thong, *sb.* Add: **1. d.** *spec.* A root or root-cutting of horse-radish or sea-kale.

1927 *Smallholder* 26 Mar. 105 Plant [horseradish] each year..fresh pieces..made from the side roots or thongs. *Ibid.*, It is now time to plant out thongs of seakale. **1951** *Dict. Gardening* (R. Hort. Soc.) IV. 1916/2 Cuttings [of seakale], or thongs as they are frequently called, are clean straight pieces of the side roots. **1961** *Amat. Gardening* 21 Oct. 9/3 The thick roots [of seakale] or 'thongs'..are not needed for forcing.

f. *Austral.* and *U.S.* = *FLIP-FLOP f. Cf. *thong-sandal*, sense 2 below.

1967 *Coast to Coast 1965–6* 87 Her feet, in scuffed leather thongs, were none too clean. **1976** *New Yorker* 17 May 35/2 Please, no clogs, Earth Shoes, or thongs. **1981** H. ENGEL *Ransom Game* (1982) xxx. 197 She..handed me a pair of Japanese thongs. I slipped them on and felt the skin between my first two toes protest.

2. thong sandal *Austral.* and *U.S.* = sense 1 f above; **thong weed** = *sea thong* s.v. SEA *sb.* 23 e.

1965 *Times Lit. Suppl.* 25 Nov. 1057/2 Supporting activities, like teaching and editing and selling thong-sandals. **1972** J. AIKEN *Butterfly Picnic* iii. 59 He wore a magenta tussore shirt..burnt-orange shorts, and local-made thong sandals. **1958** *Listener* 31 July 179/2 With *I-Spy at the Seaside* I shall look for..some thong weed. **1966** *Oxf. Bk. Flowerless Plants* 4/2 *Himanthalia elongata* ('Thong Weed') is to be found attached to rock surfaces.

Thonga, var. *TSONGA[4].

thonged, *ppl. a.* (In Dict. s.v. THONG *v.*) Add: esp. *thonged sandal*.

1958 N. MARSH *Singing in Shrouds* (1959) ix. 189 She had high-heeled thonged sandals on her feet. **1972** D. BLOODWORTH *Any Number can Play* xv. 135 Fashionable accessories, including thonged sandals. **1982** J. ELLIOTT *Country of her Dreams* ii. 15 Rosa Treadwell, in thonged sandals and sweat-stained smock, flumped herself down.

thora·cically, *adv.* [f. THORACIC *a.*: see -ICALLY.] In the thorax.

1901 W. JAMES *Let.* 13 Apr. (1920) II. 143, I find myself much more comfortable thoracically already than when I came. **1977** *Archivum Linguisticum* VIII. 87 Syllables with long vowels are 'thoracically arrested'.

thoraco-. Add: **thoracolu·mbar** *a.*, pertaining to the thoracic and lumbar parts of the spine; *spec.* an epithet of the sympathetic nervous system (see quot. 1948); **thoracotomy** (examples).

1918 STEDMAN *Med. Dict.* (ed. 5) 999/1 Thoracolumbar. **1935** J. C. WHITE *Autonomic Nervous System* iv. 52 The tendency to asphyxia, acidosis, dehydration, and loss of body heat which follow general anæsthesia and prolonged operations are all combated by the thoracolumbar division of the autonomic nervous system. **1948** A. BRODAL *Neurol. Anat.* xi. 340 The preganglionic efferent neurons of the sympathetic nervous system in man have their perikarya in the spinal cord, more precisely in all the thoracic and the uppermost two lumbar segments... Synonymous designations for the sympathetic and parasympathetic system therefore are the thoraco-lumbar and cranio-sacral systems. **1957** *Jrnl. Nervous & Mental Disease* CXXV. 462/2 Cannon's distinction between the thoraco-lumbar and the cranio-sacral division of the autonomic nervous system deals with the same sort of temporal division. **1967** G. M. WYBURN et al. *Conc. Anat.* i. 2/2 Latissimus dors; arises from the spines of the lower six thoracic vertebrae, the thoracolumbar fascia, [etc.]. **1974** PASSMORE & ROBSON *Compan. Med. Stud.* III. ix. 3/2 The thoracic spine is relatively immobile... The most mobile part..is the thoracolumbar junction and this is damaged most commonly. **1944** *Lancet* 26 Aug. 265/1 A right anterior thoracotomy exposed the bleeding-point. **1976** *Proc. R. Soc. Med.* LXIX. 851/1 Subcutaneous midline sternotomy is a method whereby an upper abdominal vertical incision may be extended into the chest without performing a formal thoracotomy and without opening the pleura.

Thorazine (þōə·răzīn). *Pharm.* Also **thorazine.** [f. parts of the systematic name, 2-chl*oro*-N,N-dimethyl-10-H-phenot*hiazine*-10-propanamine, rearranged: see CHLORO-[2], THIO-, *AZINE.] A proprietary name for *CHLORPROMAZINE.

1954 *Official Gaz.* (U.S. Patent Office) 9 Mar. 299/1 Smith, Kline & French Laboratories... *Thorazine* for central nervous system depressant. **1968** J. HUDSON *Case of Need* II. x. 164 Thorazine is a tranquilizer universally used as an antidote to LSD and employed to end bad trips. **1972** *Trade Marks Jrnl.* 20 Sept. 1873/2 *Thorazine* ... Pharmaceutical and veterinary preparations and substances, all consisting of or containing azine compounds. Smith Kline & French Laboratories Limited. **1979** *Time* 2 Apr. 46/2 The stronger antipsychotic drugs like Thorazine are useful for handling schizophrenics, whose behavior is characterized by hallucinations and severely disordered thinking.

thoreaulite (þǫ·roləit). *Min.* [a. F. *thoreaulite* (H. Buttgenbach 1933, in *Bull. Soc. géol. Belgique* LVI. 328), f. the name of J. *Thoreau*, 20th-c. Belgian geologist: see -ITE[1].] A monoclinic oxide of tin and tantalum, $SnTa_2O_6$, found as rough brown prismatic crystals that are transparent in thin splinters.

1934 *Chem. Abstr.* XXVIII. 6658 Thoreaulite (new) is monoclinic with high *n* and birefringence. **1959** *Mineral. Abstr.* XIV. 107/1 Two flat veins break off from the north of the dyke of pegmatite at Manono (Katanga)... The heavy minerals are: cassiterite, tantalo-columbite, thoreaulite, löllingite, pyrite, galena. **1974** *Amer. Mineralogist* LIX. 1036/1 It is necessary to justify the choice of $SnTa_2O_6$ as the ideal composition of thoreaulite, since the ideal formula is usually given as $SnTa_2O_7$.

Thoreauvian (þǫ̆rōu·viăn), *sb.* and *a.* [f. *Thoreauv-ius*, Latinized form of *Thoreau* (see below) + -IAN.] **A.** *sb.* One who admires the writings or shares the philosophy of Henry David Thoreau (1817–62), U.S. naturalist and writer. **B.** *adj.* Resembling or characteristic of Thoreau's writing or philosophy.

1927 *Observer* 14 Aug. 8 There was a fair sprinkling of conscious or sub-conscious Thoreauvians among bygone seamen. **1964** *Sat. Rev.* (U.S.) 10 Oct. 70/2 Thoreauvians favor solitude. **1971** D. CONOVER *One Man's Island* 142, I am a Thoreauvian by thought and by deed. **1975** *Yankee* Oct. 113/2 In case any reader wishes to test his own ability to distinguish the true Thoreauvian style from the 'ghost-written'. **1977** *Time* 21 Feb. 59/1 It is a relaxed Thoreauvian journal of a year spent dismantling and rebuilding a 1950 Dodge pickup.

thorian (þōə·riăn), *a.* *Min.* [f. THOR(IUM + *-IAN 2.] Of a mineral: having a (small) proportion of a constituent element replaced by thorium.

1930 *Amer. Mineralogist* XV. 572 Thorian. **1974** A. R. PHILPOTTS in H. Sørensen *Alkaline Rocks* IV. vi. 303/1 Hydrothermal activity along fractures, producing biotite and enrichment of the carbonatite in thorian pyrochlore.

thoriated (þōə·riēɪtėd), *a.* [f. THORI(UM + -ATE[3] + -ED[1].] Of tungsten, or a valve filament made of tungsten: containing a proportion of thorium, e.g. to enhance electron emission in a valve.

1922 *Encycl. Brit.* XXXII. 1025/1 A thermionic valve of the latter type comprises a highly exhausted glass bulb having in it a filament of tungsten, or thoriated tungsten. **1951** *Engineering* 12 Oct. 459/1 The final..output stage consists of two water-cooled thoriated-filament triodes. **1973** J. G. TWEEDDALE *Materials Technol.* II. v. 118 Commonly, a non consumable electrode is made of tungsten or a tungsten alloy (notably thoriated tungsten).

thorium. Add: **2.** Special Combs.: **thorium lead,** (*a*) the isotope lead 208, which is the final decay product of the series of radioactive transformations beginning with the common isotope of thorium; (*b*) used *attrib.* (with hyphen) to designate a method of isotopic dating, and results obtained with it, based upon measurement of the relative amounts in rock of thorium 232 and its ultimate decay product, lead 208; **thorium series,** the series of isotopes produced by the radioactive decay of thorium 232 (the major natural isotope), each member resulting from the decay of the previous one.

1914 *Phil. Mag.* XXVIII. 827 It may be concluded with reasonable certainty [*though erroneously*] that thorium lead is unstable. **1946** F. E. ZEUNER *Dating Past* x. 319 The thorium-family begins with the element thorium (atomic weight 232). In the course of its disintegration, 6 atoms of helium are given off, and thorium-lead remains. **1955** *Bull. Amer. Geol. Soc.* LXVI. 1141/2 The low thorium-lead age for the zircon could have been the result of addition of thorium to the mineral. *Ibid.*, The analysis..demonstrates that small amounts of uranium lead and major amounts of thorium and thorium lead are very loosely bound, chemically. **1971** I. G. GASS et al. *Understanding Earth* ii. 46/1 (*heading*) Uranium-lead.., lead-lead..and thorium-lead..methods. **1913** *Chem. News* 28 Feb. 97/2 The parent of ionium, the product in the uranium series corresponding with radio-thorium in the thorium series, is still experimentally unknown. **1955** I. KAPLAN *Nucl. Physics* x. 207 In the actinium and thorium series, the mass numbers are given by the expressions $4n+3$ and $4n$, respectively. **1973** J. YARWOOD *Atomic & Nucl. Physics* viii. 246 There are three main series of radioactive elements: the uranium, thorium, and actinium series, leaving out, for the present, the comparatively recently discovered neptunium series.

thorn, *sb.* Add: **I. 2.** (Earlier example of *thorn in the side* and later examples of *to be on thorns* (also *a thorn*) and *thorn in the flesh*.)

1611 BIBLE *Numbers* xxxiii. 55 Those which ye let remaine of them, shall be..thornes in your sides. **1853** MRS. GASKELL *Cranford* vii. 100 Peggy wanted now to make several little confidences to her, which Miss Barker was on thorns to hear. **1913** D. H. LAWRENCE *Sons & Lovers* xiii. 379 He was on thorns to be gone from so trying a situation. **1923** —— *Stud. in Classic Amer. Lit.* ii. 21 Probably I haven't got over those Poor Richard tags yet. I rankle still with them. They are thorns in young flesh. **1924** E. M. FORSTER *Passage to India* iv. 34, I can be a thorn in Mr. Turton's flesh, and if he asks me I accept the invitation. **1929** J. BUCHAN *Courts of Morning* II. iii. 187 You've given me a thorn to lie on, just when I was feeling comfortable. **1946** W. S. MAUGHAM *Then & Now* xxxi. 187 The family that had been for so long a thorn in the flesh of the Vicars of Christ. **1977** E. QUINN tr. *Kung & Lapide's Brother or Lord* 36 Jesus was undoubtedly a thorn in the flesh for many Saducees.

3. d. *thorn needle* = *fibre needle* s.v. *FIBRE *sb.* 8. (*Disused.*)

1950 *Vogue* Aug. 98/2 Intellectuals often have an E.M.G gramophone..and they play with thorns, not steels. **1973** *Amateur Photographer* 3 Jan. 33/2 A 'thorn' needle was composed of some soft woody or fibrous substance, which was ground to a point in a special machine.

IV. 8. a. *thorn fence* (examples), *forest* (examples), *jungle* (examples), *scrub* (examples), *-twig, woodland*; *thornproof* adj. (also as sb., *sc.* 'material'). **b. thornberry,** (the fruit of) the hawthorn; **thorn-bill,** (*b*) any of several small warblers of the genus *Acanthiza* or a closely related genus, found in Australia, New Guinea, and New Zealand; **thornveld** *S. Afr.*, veld in which Acacias predominate.

1766 LD. FIFE *Let.* 30 Nov. in A. & H. Tayler *Lord Fife & his Factor* (1925) ii. 36 Tell Thos. Reid that his Information as to there being no Thornberrys this season is wrong. **1886** BRITTEN & HOLLAND *Dict. Eng. Plant-Names* 467 Thornberries. Fruit of *Cratægus Oxyacantha*. **1934** E. REYNARD *Narrow Land* v. 248 The Dover cliff was a thornberry scratch compared with what befell Cape Cod. **1911** J. A. LEACH *Austral. Bird Bk.* 141 These birds..have been called Thornbills by Mr. A. J. North. **1933** *Bulletin* (Sydney) 5 Apr. 27/1 The yellow-tailed thornbill constructs a double nest, the lower cavity.. containing the eggs. **1964** *Courier-Mail* (Brisbane) 17 Oct. 2/1 There is a species or more of Thornbill in every mainland State. **1975** I. ROWLEY *Bird Life* iii. 40 The real diminutives forage..by rapid and nearly continuous searching of ground or shrub layer as by wrens and thornbills. **1843** *Farmers' Cabinet* 15 Jan. 184/1 Our fences are either the worm, post-and-rail, or thorn. **1946** L. G. GREEN *So Few are Free* 226 Deep in the mountains they discovered a high thorn fence, obviously a man-made obstruction. **1903** W. R. FISHER tr. *Schimper's Plant-Geogr.* I. iii. 260 The Thorn-forest..is very rich in underwood. **1960** N. POLUNIN *Introd. Plant Geogr.* xiv. 442 Tropical thorn-forests..are usually still more xerophilous. **1913** 'SAKI' *When William Came* vi. 102 We have somewhere to go to..better than the scrub and the veldt and the thorn-jungles. **1936** *Discovery* Nov. 337/1 The City of the Lake, buried deep in thorn jungle, through which we cut a path. **1955** W. GADDIS *Recognitions* III. iv. 846 Engulfed in the flow of a tartan lap robe and folds of Irish thorn-proof, he stared fixedly at an open book. **1978** *Birds* Spring 3/2 (Advt.), *Gamefair Jacket*... In natural olive Beacon Thornproof. **1903** KIPLING *Five Nations* 54 The thickets dwined to thorn-scrub, and the water drained to shallows. **1974** R. ADAMS *Shardik* lviii. 496 This is a country of thorn-scrub and fine, blowing sand.

1895 G. B. SHAW *Let.* 31 Aug. (1965) I. 556, I lay there looking up peacefully at the moon through..the laced thorntwigs of the briar. **1878** A. AYLWARD *Transvaal of To-Day* xii. 246 Four young men, all Africanders, nearly lost their lives in the Speckboom thornveld. **1936** L. HERRMAN in N. Isaacs *Trav. & Adventures Eastern Afr.* I. ii. 19 His 'panthers' are the small dark-skinned leopards of the thornveld. **1972** PALMER & PITMAN *Trees S. Afr.* I. iii. 81 In the thornveld of Zululand, *Acacia karoo, Acacia nilotica, Acacia caffra*,..and *Acacia tortilis* subsp. *heteracantha* are frequent. **1903** W. R. FISHER tr. *Schimper's Plant-Geogr.* III. iv. 492 Thorn-woodland appears..on very permeable, dry, sandy soil. **1960** N. POLUNIN *Introd. Plant Geogr.* xiv. 442 Grasses are often lacking in the drier thorn-woodlands.

thornless, *a.* (Later examples.)

1900 L. H. BAILEY *Cycl. Amer. Hort.* I. 164/2 The Thornless or Mountain Blackberry..is not in cultivation. **1980** M. SPILLER *Growing Fruit* vii. 159 The thornless form of the parsley-leaved blackberry..can be planted a little closer than other varieties.

thorn-tree. Add: (Earlier mod. and later examples.) In southern Africa, usually an acacia.

1785 G. FORSTER tr. *Sparrman's Voy. Cape of Good Hope* I. ix. 324 Being once upon a plain under the shelter of a few scambling thorn-trees, (*mimosa Nilotica*) he thought he should steal upon an elephant that was near the spot. **1798** LADY A. BARNARD *Jrnl.* 13 May in *Lives of Lindsays* (1849) III. 440, I plucked from the great thorn-trees some of their prickles. **1970** *Stand. Encycl. S. Afr.* I. 10/2 In South Africa the indigenous members of the genus [*Acacia*] as a whole are generally referred to as 'thorn-trees' or 'acacias'.

thorny, *a.* Add: **5. b.** **thorny devil** = MOLOCH 2.

1899 *Strand Mag.* June 653 The Western Australians.. describe it [*sc.* the moloch lizard] familiarly as the 'thorny devil'. **1932** *Discovery* Nov. 364/2 The Thorny Devil,..a sturdy creature about a foot long, covered with horny spikes and knobs, killed a puff adder with its tail. **1975** H. G. COGGER *Reptiles & Amphibians Austral.* 226/1 Thorny devil or Moloch... An unmistakable lizard, unique in scalation and form.

thoron (þō^ə·rǫn). *Chem.* and *Physics.* [a. G. *thoron* (C. Schmidt 1918, in *Zeitschr. f. anorg. Chem.* CIII. 114), f. THOR(IUM + *-ON[2].
Quot. 1920 represents an independent coinage.]
A radioactive isotope of radon, atomic weight 220, that is a gaseous decay product of thorium, being formed by the decay of radium 224; thorium emanation.

1918 *Jrnl. Chem. Soc.* CXIV. II. 306 A rational system of nomenclature for the radioactive elements and their degradation products is suggested. Radium emanation is given the name Radon, Ro... The other emanations become Thoron, To, and Acton, Ao. **1920** E. Q. ADAMS in *Jrnl. Amer. Chem. Soc.* XLII. 2206 The names 'radium emanation', 'actinium emanation' and 'thorium emanation' have been shortened, respectively, to 'radon', 'actinon' and 'thoron', names which suggest that the element in question is an inert gas. **1938** R. W. LAWSON tr. *Hevesy & Paneth's Man. Radioactivity* (ed. 2) xi. 132 The emanation of thorium (thoron) decays with a half-value period of 55 seconds. **1961** *New Scientist* 2 Nov. 290/3 The filter is placed in a lead cask and, after allowing four days for the decay of the 'daughter' products of natural radon and thoron, the total beta-activity of the sample is recorded. **1981** *Indian Jrnl. Earth Sci.* VIII. 1 (*heading*) On the behaviour and measurement of thoron (Rn^{220}) in soil. **1983** *Canad. Mining Jrnl.* Mar. 34/1 Measurements were carried out to estimate the radon and thoron daughter levels.

Thorotrast (þō^ə·rotrɑst). *Med.* Also **thorotrast.** [a. G. *thorotrast* (A. Weiser 1930, in *Wiener med. Wochenschr.* 25 Oct. 1428/2), f. *thoro-* THORO- + *kon)trast* CONTRAST *sb.*] A colloidal solution of thorium dioxide formerly used as a contrast medium in radiography.
A proprietary name in the U.S.

1932 *Official Gaz.* (U.S. Patent Office) 5 Apr. 14/2 Heyden Chemical Corporation, New York... *Thorotrast* for medicinal preparation finding its application in the photography by X-rays for medicinal and similar purposes. **1933** [see *ANGIOGRAM]. **1947** *Radiology* XLIX. 362/2 The fact that 'thorotrast' (a colloidal suspension of thorium dioxide) is frequently used in human diagnostic work. **1976** P. COLLARD *Devel. of Microbiol.* x. 136 Animals were injected intravenously with particulate materials, indian ink, colloidal iron or thorotrast. **1977** *Lancet* 18 June 1297/1 The main long-term sequelæ of thorotrast are local effects and tumours at the site of injection and/or deposit..and fatal blood dyscrasias, including leukæmia and aplastic anæmias.

thorough, *adj.* **2. b.** (Earlier example with reference to servants.)

1822 M. EDGEWORTH *Let.* 26 Feb. (1971) 359, I have engaged a ladys maid..and a *thorough* maid for cooking and brooming.

thorough-. Add: **2. thorough-draught** (earlier example); **thorough-souled** *a.*, to one's inmost soul, downright.

1853 C. M. YONGE *Heir of Redclyffe* II. ix. 141 Three rooms..opening into each other..so that it was possible to produce a thorough draught. **1842** POE *Lett.* (1948) I. 193, I cannot bring myself to like that man... He is too thorough-souled a time-server.

thoroughbrace. Add: †**b.** A vehicle whose body is supported on thoroughbraces. *Obs.* **thoroughbraced** *a.* (earlier example).

1865 *Harper's Mag.* Nov. 700/1 Preference to be given to a thorough-braced ambulance of Concord manufacture. **1886** *Leslie's Pop. Monthly* Dec. 722/1 The mustangs looked worse than the thorough-brace itself. **1930** A. W. GROOM *Merry Christmas* xv. 111 The heavily laden thoroughbrace was hitched behind seven lively horses.

thoroughfare, *sb.* (*a.*) **1. a.** (Earlier example of *no thoroughfare*.)

a **1817** JANE AUSTEN *Persuasion* (1818) III. xi. 235 The 'no-thoroughfare of Lyme'.

thoroughgoing, *a.* Add: (Earlier example.)

1800 M. EDGEWORTH *Parent's Assistant* (ed. 3) VI. 168, I am a *thorough-going* friend at any rate.

thoroughgoingness (earlier example).

1838 C. GILMAN *Recoll. Southern Matron* xxviii. 194 The gentleman had even the thoroughgoingness to request that my brother's large, stout new slate might be exchanged for a recently-invented tablet.

thoroughwax. (Later examples.)

1925 E. MELLOR tr. *Bonnier's Brit. Flora* 76 *Bupleurum* ..Leaves oval, perfoliate..Throw-wax. **1971** *Country Life* 4 Nov. 1192/1 Our cornfield weed thorow wax..is virtually extinct in Britain.

thoroughwort. Add: Also used as a name for other species of *Eupatorium.* (Earlier and further examples.)

1814 J. BIGELOW *Florula Bostoniensis* 190 Thoroughwort..has acquired great medicinal reputation. **1842** [see *number six* s.v. *NUMBER *sb.* 19]. **1906** *Harper's Mag.* Oct. 712 The boggy place where she came..for..the wild marsh-marigold, good for greens, thoroughwort, and the root of the sweet-flag. **1968** PETERSON & MCKENNY *Field Guide to Wildflowers* 46 The thoroughworts..are composites of late summer and fall with numerous small fuzzy heads in rounded or flat-topped clusters.

thortveitite (þǭ·ɹtvəɪtəɪt, -vē[i]təɪt, tǭ·ɹt-). *Min.* [ad. G. *thortveitit* (J. Schetelig 1911, in *Centralbl. f. Min.* 721), f. the name of O. *Thortveit* of Norway, its discoverer: see -ITE[1].] A silicate of scandium, $(Sc,Y)_2Si_2O_7$, found as colourless or greyish monoclinic crystals.

1912 *Jrnl. Chem. Soc.* CII. II. 56 (*heading*) Thortveitite, a new mineral. **1963** *Prof. Papers U.S. Geol. Survey* No. 475-B. 11/1 The association of thortveitite with fluorite in the deposit at Crystal Mountain represents a new type of occurrence, which contrasts strongly with the occurrences in granitic pegmatites of Norway and Madagascar.

tho't, thot, repr. a U.S. pronunc. of *thought.*

1879 W. WHITMAN *Daybks. & Notebks.* (1978) I. 161 *Very bad spells*, unable sometimes to walk a block (sometimes tho't it all nearing the end). *a* **1886** E. DICKINSON *Poems* (1955) III. 1148 The right to perish might be tho't An undisputed right. **1888** W. WHITMAN *Daybks. & Notebks.* (1978) II. 453 The Calming Tho't of all. **1971** *Black World* Mar. 53/1 She wuzn't sure but she thot it had. **1975** *Budget* (Sugarcreek, Ohio) 20 Mar. 12/2 Thot: Troubled waters cleanse the garments best.

thou, *sb.* Add: Also **thou.** (with point), **thou'.** (Earlier and later examples.) Also *spec.* a thousandth of an inch; (*U.S.*) a thousand dollars.

1867 'OUIDA' *Under Two Flags* I. vi. 113 Losing "long odds in thou' " over the Oaks. **1924** GALSWORTHY *White Monkey* III. ix. 276 If he did take a few thou. under the rose, he took 'em off the Huns. **1934** *Practical Motorist* 19 May 94/2 The width of the gap..should not be more than 3 to 5 'thous'. **1952** M. TRIPP *Faith is Windsock* xi. 173 We're below ten thou..; you can take off your oxygen masks. **1965** *New Yorker* 20 Feb. 34/3 The gesture cost me a cool ten thou, but I didn't begrudge it. **1975** *Hi-Fi Answers* Feb. 36/1 The AT21X carries an elliptical stylus of 0·3 × 0·7 thou. dimensions.

though, *adv.* and *conj.* Add: **A.** *γ.* The form *tho* has been used in the U.S. as a reformed spelling, and (like *tho'*) is used informally as an abbreviation of the word.

1796 R. BARRIE *Let.* 12 Oct. in N. Tolstoy *Half-Mad Lord* (1978) ii. 35 Tho: he sometimes might act imprudently his conduct never merited the ignominious punishment he receiv'd. **1818** M. EDGEWORTH *Let.* 8 Sept. (1971) 84 The library *tho* magnificent is a most comfortable.. room. **1842** TENNYSON *Poems* II. 91 Tho' much is taken, much abides. **1849** G. GRAY *Let.* 22 June in M. Lutyens *Ruskins & Grays* (1972) xxiii. 217, I have now taken the opportunity..tho' without alluding to your Letter, of asking her how it was. **1879** *Proc. Amer. Philol. Assoc.* 6 The committee now present the following words as the beginning of such [a] list [of reformed spellings], and recommend them for immediate use:..Tho. Thru. Wisht. **1906** *Simplified Spelling Board Circular* (U.S.) No. 2. 12 Tho... Thru. **1973** *Black World* June 66 Sister Habiba's party was still smokin. Tho all the good food and wine and reefer was gone now. **1982** *N.Y. Times* 22 Sept. C-2/3 Tho' the trip's less than a mile it's still a dreary, cheerless bore.

B. I. *adv.* **b.** *colloq.* Used as an intensive after a question or emphatic statement: indeed, truly.

1905 *Eng. Dial. Dict.* VI. 102/1 'How it do rain!' indicates a heavy shower; but, 'How it do rain though!' marks a much heavier. **1906** [see *GEEWHILLIKINS *int.*]. **1912** B. HARRADEN *Out of Wreck I Rise* viii. 153 'I didn't know that persons who wrote plays made thousands.' 'Don't they, though,' Hailsham answered, laughing. **1929** E. M. BRENT-DYER *Rivals of Chalet School* vi. 83 'We've got more than an hour yet!' 'Have you, though?' said Mrs Maynard's voice just behind her. 'You've nothing of the kind.' **1948** G. VIDAL *City & Pillar* I. v. 147 'What a sad story!' said Maria. 'Isn't it, though?' **1974** J. AIKEN *Midnight is Place* iv. 128 'I get enough money..for Papa and me.' 'Did you though?' said Lucas..with surprise.

II. *conj.* **1. a.** Proverbial phr. *though I say it that should not* and varr.: see SAY *v.*[1] B. 2 b in Dict. and Suppl.

4. b. Also with verb in present indicative.

1963 D. STOREY *Radcliffe* xxxvi. 367 It's the sense of imitation that's so forbidding... As though it's all a deception, and the only person it doesn't deceive is me.

thought[1]. Add: **1. c.** *train of thought*: see *TRAIN *sb.*[1] 12 b.

d. Also (without defining adj.), that of a named person [cf. G. *denken*].

1903 P. SHOREY (*title*) The unity of Plato's thought. **1935** R. B. PERRY (*title*) The thought and character of William James as revealed in unpublished correspondence and notes, together with his published writings. **1960** G. HARLAND *Thought of Reinhold Niebuhr* i. 13 The centrality of Christology in Niebuhr's thought is clear and unmistakable. **1964** S. J. WILSON (*title*) The thought of Cicero. **1968** in Gray & Cavendish *Chinese Communism in Crisis* 222 A force of revolutionised workers, armed with the thought of Mao Tse-tung, has been trained and tempered. **1971** D. MCLELLAN *Thought of Karl Marx* p. ix, An exposition of certain themes central to Marx's thought. **1974** *Encycl. Brit. Macropædia* IV. 395/2 Socialist education at first had a rather abstract quality, because people had to measure their lives against the 'thought of Mao Tse-tung', a slogan that was to grow in popularity.

2. a. (Further examples.)

1967 tr. Mao Tse-Tung (*title*) The thoughts of Chairman Mao Tse-Tung. **1971** [see *RED BOOK, RED-BOOK 4]. **1977** 'S. LEYS' *Chinese Shadows* (1978) i. 11 'We have friends all over the world.' This Thought of Chairman Mao can be seen on many walls. **1982** *Sunday Tel.* 7 Mar. 10/2 Between 1928 and 1941 there were less than 5,000 prosecutions [in Japan] for 'dangerous thoughts'.

b. *thought for the day* (*week*, etc.): a pregnant or gnomic thought (esp. one published or broadcast) to be pondered in the course of the day.

1932 R. LEHMANN *Invit. Waltz* I. ii. 6 'Remember what Mother said yesterday.' 'What?' 'She'd have to start calling you herself.' Olivia gave a hoarse chuckle. 'Thought for the day...' **1972** *B.B.C. Handbk. 1973* 82 *Thought for The Day* is broadcast as part of the morning *Today* sequence at 7.45 a.m. **1973** J. LEASOR *Host of Extras* iii. 41 Gratitude is sufficiently rare to cause surprise in those who find it, which is my thought for today. **1976** *Listener* 2 Dec. 716/3 So there, for the programme-makers' suggestion box, is a thought for the week. **1978** R. THOMAS *Chinaman's Chance* xv. 152 They pay a lot to live here and then they never get up in time to watch the sun rise... Just my thought for the day.

3. c. Phr. *it is the thought that counts* and varr.: the value (to the recipient of a gift) lies in the goodwill, affection, etc., with which it is given.

1934 D. L. SAYERS *Nine Tailors* II. iv. 148 Not that I minded..where my poor little remembrance was placed, for..it is the thought that counts. **1961** C. MCCULLERS *Clock without Hands* iv. 78 A house-warming present..not too modern or attractive, but it's the thought that counts. **1976** L. THOMAS *Dangerous Davies* ix. 105 'He's eaten your Smarties.'..'Thanks for bringing them anyway... It's the thought, really.' **1982** *Preview Shopper* (London ed.) Spring 7 It's the thought that matters. When someone you care for has a special occasion to celebrate you want to choose exactly the right gift.

4. b. *lost in thought*: abstracted; absorbed in reverie or contemplation.

1806 J. PORTER *Thaddeus of Warsaw* (ed. 4) III. x. 251 Miss Beaufort..was standing by one of the windows, evidently lost in thought. **1863** W. COLLINS *No Name* I. x. 44/1 He..sat at the table, drawing lines on the blotting-paper with his pen, lost in thought. **1926** B. A. MCKELVIE *Huldowget* iii. 35 He seemed lost in thought. **1955** L. P. HARTLEY *Perfect Woman* xxvii. 240 Jeremy stood lost in thought. 'She hasn't been away very long,' he said.

g. Phr. *perish the thought*: see *PERISH *v.* 1 e; *it's a thought* (colloq. phr.): it is an idea worth considering.

1967 'S. MITCHELL' *Come, Sweet Death* vii. 63 'Possibly he'd had a key cut.' 'It's a thought.' But I gathered from his tone that he didn't think much of it. **1974** M. HASTINGS *Dragon Island* xiii. 113 'Did they..kill him?' 'Quite a thought. It hadn't occurred to me, but it's a logical explanation.' **1980** J. DITTON *Copley's Hunch* II. iii. 154 'It's a thought, sir.'.. 'If so, it doesn't help us.'

h. In negative contexts: *not to give* (something or someone) *a* (or *another*) *thought*, not to think at all (or any more) about, to dismiss from one's mind.

[**1864** [in Dict., sense 2 a].] **1925** F. SCOTT FITZGERALD *Great Gatsby* iii. 64, I wanted..to apologize for not having known him in the garden. 'Don't mention it,' he enjoined me eagerly. 'Don't give it another thought, old sport.' **1952** M. ALLINGHAM *Tiger in Smoke* ii. 50 If it was Martin that was on the tiles I wouldn't give it another thought. **1953** H. CLEVELY *Public Enemy* xxvii. 214 'After your wife's death, didn't you miss this bag?' 'I didn't even give it a thought.' **1956** M. DICKENS *Angel in Corner* viii. 116 There will be plenty of young men in America... You won't give this Joe creature another thought. **1973** W. H. CANAWAY *Harry doing Good* I. iii. 35 I'll do that. Don't you give it another thought.

6. b. *U.S.* A very short length of time, a moment; usu. in advb. phr.

1912 L. J. VANCE *Destroying Angel* xi. 142 Suddenly she turned her head and intercepted his whole-hearted stare. For a thought wonder glimmered in the violet eyes. **1937** in J. S. Hall *Sayings from Old Smoky* (1972) 122 A panther was attracted by the frying venison. In just a thought or two it came out and screamed. **1949** H. HORNSBY *Lonesome Valley* 59 Johnny loved to hear the screech owl, except that when the scream came unexpectedly it was enough to scare anybody, for a thought.

7. a. *thought-action, -barrier, -centre, -construction, -content, -entity, -habit, -mode, -object, -picture, -process, -product, -relation, -scheme, -structure, -stuff.* **b.** *thought-destroying, -engendering, -saving; thought block.* **c.** *thought-woven*; limitative, as *thought-tight* [after *airtight*]. **d. thought control,** the control of a person's thoughts; *esp.* the attempt by a government to restrict ideas and impose opinions by such means as censorship and the control of curricula; **thoughtcrime, thought-crime,** in George Orwell's novel *Nineteen Eighty-Four*, the offence of failing in absolute loyalty to the ruling power; hence in any totalitarian system, unorthodox thinking considered as a criminal offence; **thought-experiment** = *GEDANKENEXPERIMENT; **thought-forms** *pl.*, chiefly *Theol.*, the combination of presuppositions, imagery, vocabulary, etc., current at a particular time or place and in terms of which thinking on a subject takes place; **thought model,** a system of related ideas or images; **thought-pattern,** a set of assumptions and concepts underlying thought; an habitual way of thinking; in *pl.*, thought-forms; **thought police,** in a totalitarian state, a police force established to suppress freedom of thought; *spec.* in pre-war Japan, the Special Higher Police (*Tokubetsu Kōtō Keisatsu* or *Tokkō*); hence **thought-policing** *vbl. sb.*; **thought-provoking** *a.*, prompting serious thought; **thought reform,** a process of individual political indoctrination used in Communist China; also in extended sense; **thought-saver,** a trite expression used to save one the trouble of thinking, a cliché; **thought-stream,** the continuous succession of a person's thoughts, *spec.* as represented in fiction of a certain kind (cf. *STREAM OF CONSCIOUSNESS 2); **thought-wave,** (*b*) (further example); **thoughtway,** a customary way of thinking; an unconscious assumption or idea; **thought-word** (earlier example); **thought-world** [cf. G. *gedankenwelt*], the amalgam of mental attitudes, beliefs, presuppositions, and concepts about the world characteristic of any particular people, time, place, etc.

1909 *Encycl. Relig. & Ethics* II. 85/2 Purely mental exercise consists in those 'thought-actions' (*Denkhandlungen* as Eucken calls them) which determine both our mental attitude and our conduct. **1935** Thought-action [see *brain-wave* s.v. *BRAIN *sb.* 6]. **1958** *New Statesman* 15 Mar. 338/3 This thought-barrier, the difficulty of re-thinking the problems of defence in nuclear terms, is a very real thing. **1969** *Listener* 24 July 98/2 It seems we are again about to ram what C. H. Rolph calls 'a thought-barrier at least as old as the Great Rebellion'. This is the instant assumption of many Englishmen that whatever they dislike ought to be put a stop to. **1965** J. POLLITT *Depression & its Treatment* i. 5 Definite features of schizophrenic illness, e.g. thought block. **1846** E. A. POE in *U.S. Mag. & Democratic Rev.* Apr. 268/1 We think in cycles, and may, from the frequency or infrequency of our revolutions about the various thought-centres, form an accurate estimate of the advance of our thought toward maturity. **1890** W. JAMES *Princ. Psychol.* I. iv. 115 But our higher thought-centres knew hardly anything about the matter. Few men can tell off-hand which sock, shoe, or trousers-leg they put on first. **1904** Thought-centre [see *ASSOCIATION 9]. **1920** S. ALEXANDER *Space, Time, & Deity* I. 161 In these thought constructions we are dealing all the time with ideas belonging to the empirical world. **1962** *Listener* 15 Mar. 470/2 In science, no thought-construction about the real world can be taken as more than provisionally true. **1916** L. BLOOMFIELD in C. Hockett *Bloomfield Anthol.* (1970) 73 The type of sentence we have so far examined is..often used as the expression of a logical thought-content. **1972** *Jrnl. Social Psychol.* LXXXVI. 258 A 'thought-content' unit refers to all of a subject's utterance which..seems to express a single moral idea. **1935** U. CLOSE *Behind Face of Japan* xxviii. 332 'Thought control' in Japan is strictly constitutional. **1939** R. LEHMANN *No More Music* 87 Have you ever tried this healing by thought control?..It seems that if you think right you'll never have an ache or pain. **1945** *Ann. Reg. 1944* 295 Mr. Chen Li-fu, who as Minister of Education had attempted to institute 'thought control' for Chinese students abroad. **1954** T. S. ELIOT *Confidential Clerk* I. 33 No, Claude, he only teaches *thought* control. Mind control is a different matter. **1980** 'J. MELVILLE' *Chrysanthemum Chain* 10 A scientist of high intellectual integrity opposed to any form of thought control. **1949** 'G. ORWELL' *Nineteen Eighty-Four* I. 22 He had committed..the essential crime that contained all others in itself. Thoughtcrime, they called it. **1954** *Encounter* May 28/1 [The Revolution] first created the 'People's Democracy' of the Terror and of compulsory unanimity, of thought-crimes, and of denunciation as the supreme duty of the citizen. **1968** *Economist* 22 June 19/1 If it were not the habit of Herr Ulbricht's government to put so many people in prison for thought-crime [etc.]. **1909** G. K. CHESTERTON *Orthodoxy* iii. 62 This..summary of the thought-destroying forces of our time would not be complete without some reference to pragmatism. **1851** H. MELVILLE *Moby Dick* I. xxxiv. 253 How could I—being left completely to myself at such a thought-engendering altitude,—how could I but lightly hold my obligations to observe all whale-ships' standing orders, 'keep your weather eye open, and sing out every time'. **1892** Thought-entity [see TRANSCENDENTALISTIC *a.*]. **1949** *Mind* LVIII. 340 There is present, in addition to the imagery, an entity of another kind, a thought-entity. **1945** M. WERTHEIMER *Productive Thinking* vii. 180 (*heading*) On movement, on space, a thought experiment. **1965** P. CAWS *Philos. of Sci.* xxix. 218 The situation may be illustrated by means of the following thought experiment. **1982** *New Scientist* 14 Jan. 75/2 Bekenstein considered a 'thought experiment' in which a box full of heat radiation was slowly lowered on a rope towards the surface (the horizon) of a black hole. **1890** W. JAMES *Princ. Psychol.* II. xxviii. 664 Kant..insisted on thought-forms with which experience largely *agrees*. **1892** [in Dict.]. **1958** E. L. MASCALL *Recovery of Unity* iv. 91 The deadlock between Catholics and Protestants..has been mainly due to their common inheritance of uncriticised..assumptions and thought-forms from the theologically decadent late Middle Ages. **1976** *Times* 2 Aug. 14/8 Bultmann insisted on the task of re-interpreting the substance of the mythological [biblical] materials in terms of thought-forms intelligible and acceptable in the twentieth century. **1939** P. CHRISTOPHERSEN *Articles* i. 18 The rise of new grammatical categories must be supposed to result from thought-habits that have become so common and urgent that they demand linguistic expression. **1954** *Essays & Stud.* VII. 66 The common and ancient thought-habit that sight is the chief and most powerful of the senses. **1939** V. A. DEMANT *Religious Prospect* vi. 145 Dialectical thought has..a kinship with traditional religious thought-modes. **1936** WIRTH & SHILS tr. *Mannheim's Ideology & Utopia* v. 247 The next factor which may serve to characterize the perspective of thought is the so-called thought-model; i.e. the model that is implicitly in the mind of a person when he proceeds to reflect about an object. **1942** *Mind* LI. 137 It is the perception of spatio-temporal objects, and not the conception of real entities, that is providing the thought-model. **1958** W. STARK *Sociol. of Knowl.* iv. 193 Pareto devalues, and indeed abolishes, the relative in reality; but that means..that he operates with a thought-model which is unrealistic. **1890** W. JAMES *Princ. Psychol.* I. ix. 283 It will show the relative intensities..of the several nerve-processes to which the various parts of the thought-object correspond. **1957** G. RYLE in M. Black *Importance of Lang.* (1962) 166 It is left to philosophy to be the science of this third domain which consists largely..of thought objects or Meanings. **1937** Thought-pattern [see *PATTERN *sb.* 8 c]. **1943** *Mind* LII. 123 Those elements in the nineteenth-century thought-pattern, which are frequently referred to as Darwinism. **1962** *N. & Q.* Jan. 33/1 This strenuous attempt to convey the archaic thought-patterns of the New Testament into 'the natural vocabulary, constructions, and rhythms of contemporary speech'. **1977** T. ALLBEURY *Man with President's Mind* iii. 23 The rigid education..that surrounded all Soviet citizens..led to a thought pattern that automatically rejected anything but the Soviet official position. **1919** W. DEEPING *Second Youth* xxix. 243 The arched vestibule..and the figure of the man standing there..reminded Laverach of the picture of the Roman sentinel..at his post in doomed Pompeii, and the..crashing of successive bombs made the thought-picture more vivid. **1963** *Times Lit. Suppl.* 10 May 344/4 Wesley's slowly evolving thought-picture of the nature of sin. **1945** *Sun* (Baltimore) 6 Oct. 4/1 It is an order imposing freedom of speech, thought, religion and assembly on the Japanese people, and requiring the immediate liberation of those imprisoned for political offenses by the so-called 'thought police'. **1949** 'G. ORWELL' *Nineteen Eighty-Four* I. 49 He had denounced his uncle to the Thought Police after overhearing a conversation which appeared to him to have criminal tendencies. **1969** *Guardian* 5 Feb. 3/1 The Kremlin's thought-police are moving in slowly, circumspectly, on the Soviet scientific community. **1982** *Sunday Tel.* 7 Mar. 10/2 It may be that the reviewer has confused the latter with the Special Higher Police, or 'Thought Police' as they are sometimes called. **1968** *Listener* 26 Sept. 412/3 To submit to censorship..is to submit to thought-policing, censorship being the prevention of certain thoughts and images from entering your mind. **1973** *Howard Jrnl.* XIII. 268 The attitude develops into official self-protectiveness—restricting law books in case prisoners become litigious, for example—and downright thought-policing. **1889** J. M. BALDWIN *Handbk. Psychol.* I. xiv. 271 We are concerned merely with the nature of the thought process—though a full treatment would include also its logic,—its value and bearing in the mental life. **1907** J. LONDON *Iron Heel* i. 18 Each and every thought-process of the scientific reasoner is metaphysical. **1981** 'M. INNES' *Lord Mullion's Secret* ii. 22 This was a well-trodden little path in Honeybath's thought-processes. **1906** J. N. KEYNES *Formal Logic* (ed. 4) 6 We may..say that psychology is concerned with thought-processes, logic with thought-products. **1933** *Mind* XLII. 111 The..view..that there must be radical discontinuity between the antecedents of a valid thought and a valid thought-product. **1916** J. DEWEY *Ess. Exper. Logic* ii. 84 It..endeavours to define *what* in the various occasions renders them thought-provoking. **1936** *Discovery* Oct. 332/2 Mr Berenson..contributes a thought-provoking foreword. **1983** I. MURDOCH *Philosopher's Pupil* 323 This was the most thought-provoking observation John Robert had ever elicited from her. **1959** *Atlantic Monthly* Dec. 75/1 xlviii. 371 In serious cases where criminality is involved..thought reform and punishment are combined. **1964** M. ARGYLE *Psychol. & Social Probl.* x. 134 Great interest has been aroused by Chinese thought reform, because it has been used on a very wide scale with considerable success and because the methods used are novel. **1966** F. SCHURMANN *Ideology & Organization in Communist China* i. 47 One of the most important questions..is whether 'thought reform' (*szuhsiang kaitsao*) can produce 'correct' behavior in the individual. **1981** J. BANCROFT in Bloch & Chodoff *Psychiatric Ethics* ix. 174 'Thought reform' techniques and aversion therapy. **1887** A. SETH *Hegelianism* i. 36 It does not..follow that the whole external world is nothing more than a complex of thought-relations. **1931** L. STEFFENS *Autobiogr.* III. i. 632 They were thoughtless conservatives..whose thought-saver was: 'My father was a Republican, and what was good enough for him is good enough for me.' **1948** E. GOWERS *Plain Words* vii. 55 It [*sc.* the word *involve*] is used as a thought-saver because it is so faded. **1963** *Times Lit. Suppl.* 10 May 342/3 Those old thought-savers 'the imagination of England' and 'the American mind'. **1927** A. HUXLEY *Proper Stud.* 298 There are plenty of people..who feel as much enthusiasm for thought-saving devices as for automatic dishwashers and sewing-machines. **1948** *Mind* LVII. 259 Treating existential intuitions as the perceived convergencies of complementary thought-schemes—the sort of structures that Wittgenstein used to call 'hypotheses'. **1962** *Listener* 15 Mar. 470/2 By purely logical processes of combination, inference, and construction, [mathematics] builds up the most elaborate thought-schemes. **1930** WYNDHAM LEWIS *Let.* 30 July (1963) 191 The Ulyssean 'thought-stream' method is only appropriate to the depiction of children, morons, and the extremely infirm. **1948** E. BOWEN *Who do I Write?* 23 But, of course, your monologue isn't simply a thought-stream. **1960** R. ST. JOHN *Foreign Correspondent* xi. 225 Could I make it a vital memory for them and part of their thought stream for ever after? **1980** D. LODGE *How Far can You Go?* i. 5 American psychologists have..established..that the thought stream of the normal healthy male turns to sex every other minute between the ages of sixteen and twenty-six. **1931** O. JESPERSEN in H. N. Shenton et al. *Internat. Communication* iii. 112 Collinson..has been..driven to the view that 'it is precisely through our individual use of and reaction to our mother tongue that we can approach these general and fundamental problems of thought-structures and realize to the full their complexity and subtlety'. **1965** *Eng. Stud.* XLVI. 371 He envisages an extremely..complicated Coleridgean thought-structure which is realized or clothed in a number of images. **1890** W. JAMES *Princ. Psychol.* II. xviii. 58 In some individuals the habitual 'thought-stuff', if one may so call it, is visual. **1915** *New Statesman* 23 Jan. 386/1 Hampered by so much ready-made reach-me-down thoughtstuff. **1913** L. JERROLD *French & English* viii. 153 One is often amazed by..thought-tight compartments in a walled-up mind. **1937** L. HART *Europe in Arms* xv. 190 Departmentalism tends to thought-tight compartments. *a* **1930** D. H. LAWRENCE *Last Poems* (1932) 24 A tremendous body of silence Enveloping even the edges of the thought-waves. **1954** L. J. COHEN *Princ. World Citizenship* 4 The middle-class southern English have many thoughtways, like their conception of liberty, which they do not share with Cato. **1976** NICHOLS & ARMSTRONG *Workers Divided* 19 They provide..ready-made and well trodden thoughtways (so straightaway it appears 'natural' that 'militants' will be 'mindless' [etc.]). **1980** *Times* 13 May 16/4 Their Civil service advisers—whose thoughtways and corporate interest impel them in certain directions. *a* **1866** J. GROTE in *Jrnl. Philol.* (1872) IV. 66 Looking at language as it naturally presents itself, its apparently most simple units are what we call words, and therefore I describe a noem as a thought-word. **1947** N. H. BAYNES (*title*) The thought-world of East Rome. **1958** *Spectator* 20 June 812/2 The thought-world of the laity, high and low, was in many ways pagan and magical. **1979** J. HICK in M. Goulder *Incarnation & Myth* iv. 78 No Christian who has ever lived within the evangelical thought-world can read without emotion such lines as Cowper's, There is a fountain filled with Blood [etc.]. **1892** W. B. YEATS *Countess Kathleen* 132 The tall thought-woven sails that flap unfurled Above the tide of hours, rise on the air.

thoughtography (þǭtǫ·grăfi). [f. THOUGHT[1] + PHOT)OGRAPHY.] The production of a visible, usu. photographic, image (supposedly) by purely mental means. Hence **thou·ghtograph,** the image produced; **thoughto·grapher,** one who is said to practise thoughtography; **thoughtogra·phic** *a.*

1931 T. FUKURAI (*title*) Clairvoyance and thoughtography. *Ibid.* x. 245 The medium can make the thoughtograph of the object presented by the sitter. **1967** *Psychic News* 20 May 4/2 Thus thoughtographic research spans more than half a century. **1968** J. EISENBUD *World of Ted Serios* xiii. 299 These [nightmares] kept up until he began his 'thoughtography'. **1976** C. WILSON *Geller Phenomenon* 33 (caption) Serios producing a thoughtograph. **1978** *Sunday Sun* (Brisbane) 5 Feb. 66/3 Professor Eisenbud..subjected thoughtographer Serios to scientific scrutiny. *Ibid.* 66/5 Ted randomly imprinted on film a thoughtograph.

thousand, *sb.* and *a.* Add: **2. a.** Also *thousand and one.*

1832 F. TROLLOPE *Dom. Manners Amer.* II. xxxiii. 239 Of all the thousand and one towns I saw in America, I think Buffalo is the queerest looking. **1839** E. W. LANE (*title*) The thousand and one nights, commonly called, in England, The Arabian Nights' Entertainments. A new translation from the Arabic, with copious notes. **1842** [in Dict.]. **1910** W. L. PHELPS *Essays Mod. Novelists* iii. 63 All the thousand and one details that make up the daily routine of the average person. **1962** J. WAIN *Strike Father Dead* IV. 206 Would I be likely to suggest coming along as your manager if I didn't know a thousand and one ways of making myself useful?

b. Phrases: *a thousand times, no*: certainly not; similarly *a thousand times, yes* (rare); *I believe you, thousands wouldn't* (and similar expressions): ambiguous responses to remarks received with scepticism; *death of* (or *by*) *a thousand cuts*: a succession of minor hurts that are cumulatively very serious or annoying; *a thousand of bricks*: see *BRICK *sb.*[1] 5 a.

1896 'M. Rutherford' *Clara Hopgood* v. 57 'No,' said Madge, 'a thousand times no.' **1897** H. James *Spoils of Poynton* xxii. 279 A thousand times yes—her choice should know no scruple. **1926** R. H. Mottram *Crime at Vanderlynden's* 46 'I did twelve months in the line, as a platoon commander. How long did you do that?' 'Twelve months about!' 'I believe you where thousands wouldn't.' **1932** A. Christie *Peril at End House* xvii. 199 Am I sure, myself, about anything at all? No, no—a thousand times, no. **1966** tr. *Quotations from Chairman Mao Tse-Tung* xxvii. 258 'He who is not afraid of death by a thousand cuts dares to unhorse the emperor'—this is the indomitable spirit needed in our struggle to build socialism and communism. **1968** C. Aird *Henrietta Who?* x. 97 'I don't even know..what I don't know.' Bill Thorpe nodded comprehendingly. 'I follow you—though thousands wouldn't.' **1974** D. Seaman *Bomb that could Lip-Read* ix. 73 The head of the rocket..chips off tiny fragments of steel... The poor buggers who get in the way die the death of a thousand cuts. **1980** G. Greene *Doctor Fischer* vii. 39 It had to be the death of a thousand cuts. He told her he forgave her..but he told her also that he could never forget her betrayal. **1980** P. Moyes *Angel Death* xx. 255 I can believe it. Thousands wouldn't. **1981** P. Turnbull *Deep & Crisp & Even* vii. 116 'Don't you think I'm too old?' 'No, a thousand times, no!' **1982** P. Inchbald *Sweet Short Grass* xx. 172 Oh, Franco! *Yes!* A thousand times yes!

3. a. (Further examples.)

1873 Trollope *Phineas Redux* II. xxi. 172 Mere words, supplied at so much the thousand. **1896** G. B. Shaw *Let.* 15 Feb. (1965) I. 597 Men who rattle off their copy at anything from 20/- to 40/- a thousand. **1919** W. S. Maugham *Moon & Sixpence* iii. 14 We would talk..of editors and the sort of contributions they welcomed, how much they paid a thousand, and whether they paid promptly or otherwise.

b. Also (*U.S.*), a thousand dollars.

1919 E. O'Neill *Moon of Carib.* 163 Smith said he would give two thousand cash if I would sell the place to him. **1942** *Amer. Mercury* July 85 He might confidence Sweet Back out of a thousand on a plate.

5. *thousand-mile* (example); *thousand-petalled* adj.; **thousand-head(ed) kale**, a branching variety of cabbage, *Brassica oleracea* var. *fruticosa*, cultivated as fodder for sheep or cattle; **thousand island** [f. *Thousand Islands*, name of a large group of islands in the St. Lawrence River], used *attrib.* and *absol.* to designate Russian salad-dressing containing added pieces of garnishing; also **thousand isle**; **thousand-jacket** *N.Z.* = *HOUHERE; **thousand-legs** (later example); **thousand-miler** *slang*, a dark shirt that does not show the dirt; **thousand-year(-old) egg**, a Chinese delicacy consisting of a pickled egg that has been kept in earth, lime, and chopped straw for some weeks; **Thousand-Year Reich** [G. *tausendjähriges Reich*], the German Third Reich (1933–45), as a regime envisaged by the Nazis as established for an indefinite period.

1887 *Times* 22 Oct. 8/1 This practice of making thousand-headed kale stand down..on poor land..is likely to come rapidly into favour. **1925** Thousandhead kale [see *marrow-stem* (*kale*) s.v. *MARROW *sb.*[1] 5]. **1929** Oldershaw & Porter *Brit. Farm Crops* v. 235 Thousand-headed kale is a very useful crop to grow both for sheep- and cattle-feed. **1975** Park & Eddowes *Crop Husbandry* (ed. 2) xiii. 294 Marrow stem kale should be used before the new year followed by the hardier thousand head kale. **1916** *Daily Colonist* (Victoria, B.C.) 19 July 6/1 (Advt.), Mrs. Porter's Thousand Island Salad Dressing, bottle 35¢. **1945** J. L. Marshall *Santa Fe* 106 For years, Bill Gardner, steward on the Kansas City–Chicago run, handed out a special '1001 Dressing', an improvement on the usual Thousand Island mixture. **1962** Thousand-isle [see *ROQUEFORT b]. **1981** *Times* 2 Mar. 12/5 In a year or two she will be specifying that the thousand island dressing (a pinkish salad cream with bits of vegetables in it) should be low-calorie. **1888** *Cassell's Picturesque Austral.* III. 210 Toi-toi, supplejack, thousand-jacket, are names of things known well enough to the inhabitants of Napier and Taranaki. **1946** Thousand-jacket [see *HOUHERE]. **1962** Gordon & Lavoipierre *Entomol. for Students of Med.* vii. 41 The class Diplopoda contains all the millipedes or 'thousand legs'. **1875** 'Mark Twain' in *Atlantic Monthly* Apr. 450/1 The thousand-mile wall of dense forest. **1929** F. C. Bowen *Sea Slang* 139 *Thousand milers*, black twill shirts. **1959** *Washington Post* 8 Oct. C3/3 A thousand-miler is a navy blue shirt which doesn't show the gravy stains and may be worn for days at a time without washing. Slim must have a wardrobe of thousand-milers. **1978** K. Bonfiglioli *All Tea in China* vii. 86 A 'thousand-miler' turned out to be a sort of durable shirt made of black twill; so-called..because it should be washed.. after every thousand miles of the voyage. **1951** L. MacNeice tr. *Goethe's Faust* ii. ii. 204 But here at Pharsalus was fought a master model To prove how might opposes greater might and tears To shreds the lovely thousand-petalled wreath of freedom. **1970** *Times* 10 Mar. 17/2 (Advt.), A hitherto unrecorded Baccarat 'thousand-petalled' rose weight. **1961** E.-M. Wong *Chinese Cookery* v. 36 Everyone has heard of 'thousand-year-old' eggs, but in reality these eggs are only a few months old. **1972** K. Lo *Chinese Food* i. 47 Thousand-Year-Old Egg (which, to be more precise, should be called Pickled Eggs)..can be incorporated into a Chinese breakfast. **1980** E. Behr *Getting Even* xviii. 208 Seaslugs, jellyfish and thousand-year eggs appeared on the table. [**1934** *Times* 6 Sept. 12/4 Herr Hitler's proclamation to the rally was read... Herr Hitler declares that 'there will be no further revolution in Germany for a thousand years.'] **1946** A. Huxley *Let.* 27 Oct. (1969) 553 When people think of far-off communist Utopias or Thousand-Year Reichs, they are so much dazzled by the beauty of what they see..in the unknowable future, that they are ready to commit any atrocity in the present. **1970** A. Price *Labyrinth Makers* vi. 89 The Wagnerian last hours of the Thousand Year Reich. **1979** J. Crosby *Party of Year* xviii. 109 Now that the 1,000-year Reich had crumbled, what else was there?

'thout. (Examples.)

1893 H. A. Shands *Some Peculiarities of Speech in Mississippi* 63 *Thout*, Negro for *without.* **1897** Kipling *Capt. Cour.* iv. 91 Don't let's hev another [sad song] 'thout somethin' between. **1917** —— *Divers. Creatures* 341 I'm the only farmer you've got. Nothin' goes off my place 'thout it walks on its own feet. **1935** Z. N. Hurston *Mules & Men* i. x. 205 Nobody can't mention fat 'thout you makin' out they talkin' bout you. **1979** 'E. McBain' *Calypso* iv. 37 *You* ain't gettin *nothin* 'thout the forty dollars.

Thracian (þrēⁱ·ʃiăn), *sb.* and *a.* [f. L. *Thrăcius, Thrācus*, a. Gr. θρᾴκιος, f. θρᾴκη Thrace: see -AN, -IAN.] **A.** *sb.* **a.** A native or inhabitant of Thrace, in antiquity a region to the N.E. of Macedonia, and now comprising European Turkey, southern Bulgaria, and the region of Thrace in N.E. Greece.

1569 T. Stocker tr. *Diodorus Siculus' Hist. Successors Alexander* 105 Aboute two thousand Mercenarie Grekes, and so many Thracians. **1618** E. Bolton tr. *Lucius Julius Florus' Roman Hist.* (1636) 176 The Sordiscans were of all the Thracians the most savage. **1875** *Encycl. Brit.* III. 854/1 In the earliest times of history Bœotia was inhabited by various tribes, such as the Aonians, Temmicians, Thracians, [etc.]. **1949** *Oxf. Classical Dict.* 901/2 The Thracians were not without a native culture. **1976** *Daily Tel.* 31 Aug. 6 A major archaeological discovery..has been made in Bulgaria. Knowledge of the Thracians is advanced substantially. **1982** K. Follett *Man from St. Petersburg* ix. 178 'I wonder how the Thracians would feel about all this.' 'They would rather belong to Russia than Turkey.'

b. The language of the ancient Thracians, an Indo-European language thought to be related to Phrygian or Illyrian.

1879 *Academy* XV. 99/1 It is still doubted by..philologists whether Albanian should be classed as an Aryan language... However.., I am quite willing to allow that it is..a descendant of the ancient Illyrian or Thracian, and I will not quarrel with anyone who wishes to call the latter Pelasgian. **1933** C. D. Buck *Compar. Gram. Gk. & Lat.* 14 Thracian is known from proper names and glosses, and there is one obscure inscription believed to be Thracian. **1962** A. J. Beattie in Wace & Stubbings *Compan. to Homer* x. 312 From the Hellespont to Chalcidice most of the inhabitants spoke Thracian. **1972** W. B. Lockwood *Panorama Indo-Europ. Lang.* 172 At the time of its greatest known extent, in antiquity, Thracian was spoken throughout the eastern half of the Balkan Peninsula and stretched northwards into the Central European Plain.

B. *adj.* Of or pertaining to Thrace.

1588 Shakes. *Tit. A.* i. i. 138 The selfe same Gods that arm'd the Queene of Troy With opportunitie of sharpe reuenge Vpon the Thracian Tyrant in his Tent. **1594** Kyd *Cornelia* iii. ii. 49 Stoute Thracian Mars. **1667** Milton *P.L.* vii. 34 The Race Of that wilde Rout that tore the Thracian Bard In Rhodope. **1697** Dryden *Æneis* vi. 877 The Thracian bard..There stands conspicuous in his flowing vest. **1781** Gibbon *Decl. & F.* II. xxvi. 593 Orders were immediately dispatched to the civil and military governors of the Thracian diocese. *a* **1822** Shelley *Cyclops* in *Posthumous Poems* (1824) 343 And when the Thracian wind pours down the snow, I wrap my body in the skins of beasts. **1848** *Rep. Brit. Assoc. Adv. Sci. 1847* 266 The second family is the Thracian or Illyrian, once spread on the Dnieper, the Hellespont, and in Asia Minor. **1920** *Glasgow Herald* 12 May 9 Several of the Thracian harbours now under Greek sovereignty.. are to be free. *Ibid.* 27 July 7 To-day at dawn the Thracian Army launched its offensive. **1949** *Oxf. Classical Dict.* 901/2 Greek recruiting officers (especially in the fourth century) enlisted Thracian 'peltasto' or light-armed fighters. **1977** *Jrnl. R. Soc. Arts* CXXV. 485/1 The nearest parallels which we can refer to are two helmets of the so-called 'Thracian' type.

Thraco- (þrēⁱ·ko), (*rare*) **Thrako-**, used as comb. form of *THRACIAN *sb.* and *a.*, as in *Thraco-Illyrian* adj., *Thraco-Phrygian* adj. and sb.

1902 *Encycl. Brit.* XXV. 249/2 Albanian is peculiarly interesting as the only surviving representative of the so-called Thraco-Illyrian group of languages which formed the primitive speech of the peninsula. **1924** G. Murray *Rise Gk. Epic* (ed. 3) ii. 40 A great movement of Thraco-Phrygian tribes with eastern linguistic affinities. **1931** *Times Lit. Suppl.* 12 Feb. 116/4 The Thrako-Illyrian stratum which underlies all the races of the Peninsular. **1946** Priebsch & Collinson *German Lang.* (ed. 2) i. 19 He places the prehistoric connexions of the Tokharians with the progenitors of Balts, Slavs, Armenians and Thraco-Phrygians in the steppes of South-East Russia between the Dniepr and the Urals. **1968** D. L. Clarke *Analytical Archaeol.* ix. 391 An older, outer ring of non-Urnfield Indo-European areas—Teutonic and Baltic on one hand and Thraco-Phrygian, Greek, and Hittite on another. **1972** W. B. Lockwood *Panorama Indo-Europ. Lang.* 172 Thraco-Phrygian is the term used to denote a group of languages whose earliest known homeland was South-East Europe. Three languages are distinguished: Thracian, Phrygian and Armenian.

thrash, thresh, *v.* Add: **III. 7. a.** Also *refl.* and *fig.*

1939 T. S. Eliot *Family Reunion* i. ii. 60 The fish Thrashing itself upstream.

8. (Earlier and further examples.) Esp. with *about* or *around*. Also *fig.*

1846 *Boston Courier* 17 June 2/4 Arter I'd gone to bed & heern Him a thrashin round like a short tailed Bull in fli time. **1884** 'Mark Twain' *Huck. Finn* vi. 45 He didn't go sound asleep, but was uneasy. He groaned, and moaned, and thrashed around this way and that. **1962** K. A. Porter *Ship of Fools* 178 He groans and yells and thrashes about at night. **1962** K. Kesey *One Flew over Cuckoo's Nest* iv. 309 It fought a long time against having it taken away, flailing and thrashing around. **1973** *Times* 12 Nov. 11/8 His is in many ways a sad life to watch, as he thrashes around for the opening that will bring him fame. **1978** R. Barnard *Unruly Son* xvii. 190 This little detail panicked you..and then you started thrashing around... You did silly things.

thrash, thresh, *sb.*[1] Add: **3.** A party, esp. one that is lavish or unrestrained. *slang.*

1957 G. Smith *Friends* 120, I think he stole away to London for an occasional thrash when it got too much for him, but in general he was a model pupil. **1968** K. Amis *I want it Now* ii. 68 No quiet family party at all, it had turned out, but a twenty-cover thrash. **1976** *Times Lit. Suppl.* 6 Feb. 131/3 Staggering..from his sick-bed to play host at an enormous black-tie thrash at a Belgravia mansion borrowed for the night. **1980** C. Matthew *Loosely Engaged* 17 Occasionally someone throws a thrash, but most of the time we just bomb round to Wedgies..and have a bit of a giggle.

thrasher[1]**. 4. thrasher-whale**: for *Orca gladiator* substitute *Orcinus orca*; (earlier example).

1782 'J. H. St. J. de Crèvecœur' *Lett. from Amer. Farmer* vi. 169 The following are..the various species of whales known to these people... The killer, or thrasher about thirty feet; they often kill the other whales.

thrawnly, *adv.* (Later examples.)

1899 J. Buchan *Grey Weather* 250 'What bird are ye?' he asked thrawnly. **1980** *Times Lit. Suppl.* 28 Mar. 373/1 The Kilbrandon Commission found the stage army of the Scottish good solidly pro-devolution... Only the Labour Party remained thrawnly hostile to the whole idea.

thread, *sb.* Add: **I. 2. f.** *pl.* Clothes. *slang* (orig. and chiefly *U.S.*).

1926 Maines & Grant *Wise-Crack Dict.* 11/2 *New set of threads*, new suit of clothes. **1959** R. Bloch *Blood Runs Cold* (1963) 163 Mitch got into some decent threads—he had this one blue suit and he wore a white shirt and a tie too. **1972** M. J. Bosse *Incident at Naha* ii. 64 *My friends*, who grooved the way I did... I mean, love beads, wild threads, granny glasses..and a bit of grass. **1978** J. Gardner *Dancing Dodo* xxiii. 175 Load it and get in on under that set of executive threads.

5. Also, a similar ridge round the inside of a cylindrical hole, as in a nut or a screwhole.

1677, 1875 [see Tap *sb.*[1] 4]. **1938** [see *SELF-TAPPING *ppl. a.*]. **1972** *How Things Work* III. 168 For the majority of screwed work a tap is used for internal threading (Fig. 3, showing the thread being cut in a nut) and a die head is used for external threading. **1977** *Reader's Digest Bk. Do-It-Yourself Skills & Techniques* vi. 175/2 As soon as the tap starts to cut, stop pressing down, and let the tap screw itself into the hole, cutting a thread as it goes.

II. 8. Esp. in phr. *to pick* (or *take*) *up the thread*(*s*) (*of*), to continue (with) after an interruption or separation; *spec.* to resume an interrupted friendship; *to lose the thread*, to cease to follow the sense of what is being said.

1881 R. L. Stevenson *Virginibus Puerisque* 137 We shall..take up again the thread of our enjoyment in the same spirit as we let it fall. **1907** G. B. Shaw *John Bull's Other Island* iv. 95 Eighteen years is a devilish long time, Nora. Now if it had been eighteen minutes, or even eighteen months, we should be able to pick up the interrupted thread, and chatter like two magpies. **1924** A. Christie *Poirot Investigates* v. 125 Philip Ridgeway narrated the circumstances leading to the disappearance of the bonds... When he had finished, Poirot took up the thread with a question. **1929** H. J. Laski in *Holmes-Laski Lett.* (1953) II. 1169, I don't, I suppose, see him more than once in two years; but I always find that we can take up the threads and plunge *in medias res* without any difficulty. **1944** E. S. Gardner *D.A. calls Turn* (1947) xi. 101 If it were true, he'd make some sort of a financial adjustment, but could hardly be expected to pick up the thread of a life where it had been broken ten years ago. **1956** A. Wilson *Anglo-Saxon Attitudes* ii. i. 215 He stopped and, for a moment, he appeared to have lost the thread of his remarks. **1980** D. Lodge *How Far can you Go?* vi. 226 Dennis and Angela picked up the threads of their lives together,.. a little chastened, but both hugely relieved. **1981** A. Schlee *Rhine Journey* xi. 143 He chose..to appear to have lost the thread of the discussion and looked from one to another with a kind of cautious bewilderment.

14. a. (*a*) *threadball.* (*c*) *thread-spinner*; *thread-forming* adj.; *thread-wise* adv.

1896 G. B. Shaw *Our Theatres in Nineties* (1932) II. 252 Peer's wild run through the night over the charred heath, stumbling over the threadballs and broken straws. **1918** G. Frankau *One of Them* xvi. 123 How the three crones must laugh as they entwine Cat's-cradle-wise our mortal threadball's tangle. **1927** T. Woodhouse *Artif. Silk* 34 The tanks which supply the solution to the thread-forming apparatus. **1892** 'Mark Twain' *Amer. Claimant* x. 102 Today, the work of..the 2,000,000 thread-spinners [women] is done by 1,000 girls. **1918** MRS. BELLOC LOWNDES *Out of the War?* xx. 255 The narrow, winding road which ran thread-wise on the cliffs.

b. thread bag *Jamaica*, a small cloth bag, tied or drawn closed with a thread or string; **thread belay** *Mountaineering*, a belay in which the rope or sling is passed through a hole in the rock before being secured again to the climber; **thread clips** (see quot. 1964); also *attrib.* in *sing.*; **thread-fin** (examples); **thread-guide** (examples).

1924 M. W. BECKWITH *Jamaica Anansi Stories* 35 An' Goat cut her up an' put her in his tread-bag. **1953** R. MAIS *Hills were Joyful Together* II. xii. 226 Her money gone! Somebody had robbed her while she was asleep. She carried it in a threadbag tied with a string around her neck. **1935** *Jrnl. Fell & Rock Climbing Club* X. 236 (*caption*) Thread belay. **1941** C. F. KIRKUS *Let's go Climbing* iv. 54 Here you use a thread belay, passing a loop of your rope through a muddy hole behind a chockstone.. and tying it round the stone or on to your waist line. **1965** A. BLACKSHAW *Mountaineering* viii. 225 Because a thread belay with the main climbing rope is usually very awkward and complicated..slings are normally used. **1958** *Times* 27 Dec. 4/1 Threadclip scissors..are employed in the weaving trade for snipping loose ends during the weaving process. **1964** *McCall's Sewing* v. 62/2 *Thread clips*, a real time-saving little clipper that can be used effectively for snipping threads and making the small clips needed for marking or for curved seams. It has one ring which fits over the little finger, and is operated by squeezing with the palm of the hand. **1896** JORDAN & EVERMANN *Check-List Fishes* 335 Polynemidæ. The Threadfins. **1933** *Bulletin* (Sydney) 5 Apr. 27/3 Threadfins..rarely extend southward to the coast of N.S. Wales. **1979** *Arizona Daily Star* 5 Aug. c-5/1 He was credited with introducing threadfin shad as a forage fish for bass. **1924** LD. RONALDSHAY *India* xiii. 159 The supply from abroad of such things as bobbins, plane tree-rollers..and porcelain thread-guides was cut off. **1964** *McCall's Sewing* v. 69/2 On most machines, the last thread guide will indicate the direction in which the thread must enter the needle.

thread, *v.* Add: **1. d.** Of a man: to have sexual intercourse with (a woman). *slang.*

[**1903** FARMER & HENLEY *Slang* VII. 109/1 *To thread the needle*, to possess a woman.] **1958** B. BEHAN *Borstal Boy* I. 15 Sheila would be sorry she did not let me thread her, the night we walked the canal.

10. a. To place the thread, film, or tape in its proper course in (a sewing machine, projector, etc.). Usu. with *up*. Also *absol.*

1873 *Young Englishwoman* Mar. 150/1 Thread up the machine with the same coloured silk. **1913** F. A. TALBOT *Pract. Cinematogr.* vii. 85 In threading up the camera it is only necessary to make sure that the image on the negative comes squarely and truly before the window in the gate. **1923** —— *Moving Pictures* 81 Threading the camera, as it is called, completed, the door of the exposed magazine is closed. **1932** SIMPSON & WEIR *Weaver's Craft* x. 92 Threading the Loom.—It is still an advantage for two people to work together for this. **1962** L. DEIGHTON *Ipcress File* xxiv. 155 He threaded up the 16mm projector. **1964** *McCall's Sewing* v. 69/1 Your machine simply won't work if it isn't threaded exactly according to plan. **1970** A. FOWLES *Dupe Negative* i. 8 It's [*sc.* the film's] just back from the lab. Take a couple of minutes to thread up.

b. To pass (film, etc.) *through* a projector, recorder, etc., so that it occupies the correct path; = *LACE *v.* 4 f.

1915 J. B. RATHBUN *Motion Picture Making & Exhibiting* ii. 33 The loading of a motion picture camera is usually no more difficult than threading the film through a projector. **1932** SIMPSON & WEIR *Weaver's Craft* xi. 115 Thread the new piece through the correct heddle and dent of the reed, then wrap the loose end round a pin in the woven fabric. **1959** N. MAILER *Advts. for Myself* (1961) 168 Sam attempts to talk while he is threading the film. **1961** *N.Y. Times* 10 Sept. x. 15/3 The user has to thread the tape through the machine before starting, and rewind the tape after playing or recording. **1972** W. P. BLATTY *Exorcist* (1974) III. i. 279 The priest quickly set up the tape recorder; looked for an outlet; plugged it in; threaded tape.

threaded, *ppl. a.* Add: **1. b.** *Computers.* Of a list or tree: in which items contain a pointer to a preceding node as well as one to the following node.

1960 PERLIS & THORNTON in *Commun. Assoc. Computing Machinery* III. 196/1 This paper presents an addition to the list structure languages which is expected to add to the above advantages while simplifying machine processing of lists. This is done by the use of threaded lists. A threaded list is a structure in which the last element of each list specifies the location of the head of the list of which it is the terminal member. **1979** TREMBLAY & BUNT *Introd. Computer Sci.* xi. 583 Given the threaded representation of a binary tree with respect to inorder traversal, it is a simple matter to formulate algorithms for obtaining the inorder predecessor and successor of a designated node.

threading, *vbl. sb.* (Examples corresponding to *THREAD *v.* 10.)

1913 F. H. RICHARDSON *Motion Picture Handbk.* (ed. 2) 219 It is aggravating for the operator who has to do rapid work in threading up, to be obliged to work with reels in bad condition. **1932** SIMPSON & WEIR *Weaver's Craft* x. 92 For the threading up one person should sit at the back of the loom in such a position that the 'shed' sticks and warp threads can be easily seen. **1933** *Sight & Sound* Spring 34/2 Accessibility of the gates and sprockets for threading up. **1964** *McCall's Sewing* v. 69/1 Always check your instruction manual for proper threading. **1970** *Which?* Jan. 8/1 Threading can be a tedious and sometimes tricky business, especially if the thread has to go *through* other openings as well as the eye of the needle.

Threa·dnee:dle Street. The name of the street in the City of London where the Bank of England is located, used allusively to mean the Bank or its directors. Cf. *the Old Lady of Threadneedle Street* s.v. *LADY *sb.* 4 e.

1924 LD. BIRKENHEAD *Amer. Revisited* i. 10 They [*sc.* U.S. economists and financiers] lack something of the sophistication and age-long sagacity of Threadneedle Street. **1974** G. VAIZEY *Tangled Web* ii. 25 It's only a question of time..before it gets to 'the ferret's' ears in Threadneedle Street. Then, heaven help you.

threat, *sb.* Add: **II. 4.** *Zool.* Animal behaviour that keeps other animals at a distance or strengthens social dominance without physical conflict. Freq. *attrib.*

1933 R. W. G. HINGSTON *Meaning of Animal Colour* v. 119 Whenever a bird has threat-colours on the crown, it either lowers its head so that the colours can be seen, or erects the feathers..to make them visible above the level of the beak. *Ibid.* x. 291 Song is an exhibition of threat. **1943** D. LACK *Life of Robin* iii. 26 It is..a threat display, serving to intimidate a trespassing robin. **1949** *Brit. Birds* XLII. 234 One female called a peculiar, low, harsh, single note..similar to a harsh growling threat-note. **1966** N. TINBERGEN *Animal Behaviour* viii. 177 The signalling movements of higher animals, particularly those used in threat and courtship. **1978** P. MARSH et al. *Rules of Disorder* v. 127 Certain threat signals are evolved such that intra-specific conflicts became ceremonial in character. **1981** *Oxf. Compan. Animal Behaviour* 563/2 The opening of the mouth that precedes biting has evolved into a ritualized baring of the teeth that is characteristic of threat in many mammals.

threaten, *v.* Add: **7.** In weakened use: to express an intention *to do* something, not necessarily evil.

1925 *Dialect Notes* V. 344 *Threaten, v.i.*, promise; as, he threatened to give me money. **1928** A. HUXLEY *Let.* 1 May (1969) 296 [He] was lunching here today and broached a notion about a preliminary limited edition. ..He threatens to come and talk to you about it.

threatened, *ppl. a.* Add: **1. b.** Of a wild animal or plant: in danger of becoming rare or extinct.

1960 *Oryx* V. 381 (*heading*) Australia's threatened mammals. **1966** *Red Data Bk.* II. 2 The object of these lists and sheets of threatened species is not only to draw universal attention to the dangers facing some unique creatures,..but also to provide the factual information necessary for action. **1972** *Ibid.* (new ed.) I. Preamble 1 The threatened species include those that are in immediate danger of extinction (endangered species), those that are likely to enter this category (vulnerable species), and those that are rare and at risk (rare species). **1976** *New Yorker* 12 Jan. 58 Seven hundred and sixty-one plants were designated as 'endangered', meaning their survival was in serious doubt, twelve hundred and thirty-eight were listed as 'threatened' and an even one hundred were declared extinct. **1979** *Birds* Summer 56/1 The most authoritative and comprehensive reference book published on the world's rare, endangered and threatened birds. **1979** *Red Data Bk.* (ed. 2) II. Preamble 3 *Endangered* (E)..Taxa in danger of extinction and whose survival is unlikely if the causal factors continue operating... *Vulnerable* (V)..Taxa believed likely to move into the endangered category in the near future if the causal factors continue operating... *Rare* (R)..Taxa with small world populations that are not at present endangered or vulnerable, but are at risk... A taxon at subspecific level which might qualify for the V..category has not been included if no other subspecies of the species concerned is in a threatened (E, V, R or I) category.

threatful, *a.* Delete *rare* and add further examples.

1895 G. MACDONALD *Lilith* viii. 53 The eagle, perched with outstretched wings on the top, appeared threatful. **1922** E. R. EDDISON *Worm Ouroboros* xxxi. 391, I have read signs in heaven: nought clear, but threatful unto both you and me. **1923** M. SADLEIR *Desolate Splendour* 199 He felt a desire still further to ingratiate himself with this threatful lord. **1932** W. FAULKNER *Light in August* ii. 42 It still lingers about her..something dark and outlandish and threatful.

three, *a.* and *sb.* Add: **B. I. 1. g.** (*the three B's*, etc.: examples preceding initial letters other than those of uses referred to in Dict.) *three acres and a cow*: regarded as the requirement for self-sufficiency; *three ages* (Archæol.), the Stone, Bronze, and Iron Ages (see also *three-age*, sense III. 1 a below); *the Three Bishoprics* (Hist.), Metz, Toul, and Verdun; *three cheers*, three successive cheers in unison, freq. *for* someone or something; *three musketeers*, [tr. Fr. *les trois mousquetaires* (title of a novel (1844) by Alexandre Dumas père] three close associates; *the three wise men* = *the three Kings* s.v. KING *sb.* 1 c; *transf.*, three men who act as advisers or arbitrators.

1909 J. R. WARE *Passing Eng.* 244/2 *Three B's, the* (*Clerical*), bright, brief, and brotherly—the modern protest against the sleepy nature of a majority of the 19th century church services. **1934** WEBSTER s.v., *Three B's, Music*, the three great composers, Bach, Beethoven, and Brahms. **1969** Three B's [see *OFF *adj.* 4]. **1885** Three C's [see C I. 1]. **1976** *Casper* (Wyoming) *Star-Tribune* 29 June 3/3 Q. In money matters, what's meant by 'The Three Cs'? A. That's a term used by the credit experts. Capital, capacity to pay and collectibility. Of the three, capacity to pay is generally thought to be the most important, capital the least. **1955** D. W. MAURER in *Publ. Amer. Dialect Soc.* XXIV. 187 Excuses for *missing meets* are sometimes delicately referred to as the *three esses*: *shit, shave*, and *shine*. **1974** P. WRIGHT *Lang. Brit. Industry* xii. 105 Alliteration, slang and a desire to hide the meaning all contribute to the *three Hs*, standing for 'high, hot, and a hell of a lot', and used when a soft soap and water enema has to be applied. **1976** *Guardian Weekly* 10 Oct. 12/4 Women's groups rebelling against the old commandment of the 'Three Ks'—Kinder, Kirche, Küche (children, church and kitchen). **1938** J. DANIELS *Southerner* 136 It was impressive how directly the town's merchants made their appeal to poverty with the heavy necessities of living—the three M's, meat, meal and molasses. **1929** F. C. BOWEN *Sea Slang* 140 Three Ss, The. The old naval rule to promotion, to mind your three Ss. That is to say, to be Sober, Silly and Civil.

1885 J. CHAMBERLAIN in *Times* 17 Nov. 10/2 This man ..reported..that wherever the labourer had land and kept a cow—'three acres and a cow' (loud laughter)..the poor rates were reduced. **1889** G. N. CURZON *Russia in Central Asia* vii. 239 The majority of residents would seem to have attained the ideal of Arcadian bliss expressed elsewhere in the historical phrase, 'Three acres and a cow'. **1964** *English Studies* XLV. (Suppl.) 214 Chesterton the Distributist and advocate of 'three acres and a cow'. **1866** J. CRAWFURD in *Trans Ethnol. Soc. London* IV. 1 The theory which supposes three different ages of civilisation, marked respectively by the use of arms and implements of stone, of bronze, and of iron, seems to have originated in the discoveries recently made by the examination of the refuse heaps of Denmark and the pile buildings of the Swiss lakes... There can be little doubt but that the three ages above indicated did really exist. **1944** V. G. CHILDE *Progress & Archæol.* i. 5 Of course Thomsen's three 'Ages' are just periods of this relative kind and would be better designated *Stages*. **1794** A. YOUNG *Trav. France* II. xix. 420 The provinces of Loraine, Alsace, the three Bishoprics, and the West Indies, not included. **1910** H. N. WILLIAMS *Henri II* xxi. 271 The princes..authorised him to take possession of the towns of Toul, Metz and Verdun—the 'Three Bishoprics'. **1964** C. DUFFY *Wild Goose & Eagle* viii. 111 Conti..might be tempted to harry the Three Bishoprics and the Austrian-garrisoned Duchy of Luxemburg. **1751** Three chears [see CHEER *sb.* 8]. **1840** *Brother Jonathan* 10 Oct. 4/6 They gave him three cheers. **1907** G. B. SHAW *John Bull's Other Island* II. 30 Three cheers for ould Ireland, is it? **1970** G. F. NEWMAN *Sir, You Bastard* vi. 174 Three cheers for any good publicity we can get. **1887** KIPLING in *Civil & Mil. Gaz.* 11 Mar. (*title*) The three musketeers. **1903** G. B. SHAW *Man & Superman* p. xxviii, He and I and Mr Sidney Webb were sowing our political wild oats as a sort of Fabian Three Musketeers. **1923** Three musketeers [see *BLOW *v.*[1] 1 b]. **1979** *Nature* 8 Nov. 136/2 Those were the three musketeers who soon agreed that in publishing their joint work they would always share the credit for all ideas, whoever had thought them up. **1867** *Chambers's Encycl.* IX. 419/2 The visit of the three magi or wise men of the East. **1904** Three wise men [used s.v. MAGUS 2]. **1961** *Ann. Reg. 1960* 467 The conference decided that three wise men (who later became four) should recommend the best means of co-ordinating Western economic policies. **1976** *Hansard Commons* 9 June 578 The three wise men ..who make up the Programme Complaints Commission. **1979** G. ST. AUBYN *Edward VII* iv. 185 The Prince of Wales decided..to submit the negotiations to the Prime Minister, the Lord Chancellor and Lord Hartington... These three wise men produced a memorandum.

3. (Examples short for *three farthings* (now *Hist.*); further examples short for *three inches*.)

1913 J. VAIZEY *College Girl* II. xxvi. 360, I paid eleven-three for it. **1947** *Vogue* Apr. 73/1 Three-and-eleven-three is much less than four shillings. **1962** M. DUFFY *That's how it Was* iii. 33 The girls would buy a few yard of stuff at two-and-eleven, three, a yard. **1965** *Canad. Jrnl. Linguistics* Spring 121 A three-by-five card was made out for each address. **1978** W. STOVALL *Presidential Emergency* v. 119 Solving his problems on three-by-five index cards.

II. 1. b. Add to def.: Also, a figure resembling that denoting the number three, *esp.* in *Skating*. (Further examples.)

1903 [see *GRAPE-VINE 2 c]. **1938** J. CARY *Castle Corner* 378 He cut a three. **1975** *Oxf. Compan. Sports & Games* 522/1 The three, a two-lobed figure, so named because the turn involved at the extreme end of each circle leaves a tracing on the ice resembling the numeral '3'.

2. (Further examples of *in threes*.)

1889 W. B. YEATS *Wanderings of Oisin* 130 Children sing in twos and threes. **1953** R. CHANDLER *Long Goodbye* xix. 117 Three shots, three misses. I hate it when they come in threes. **1977** 'M. YORKE' *Cost of Silence* xvi. 130 'First Pedro—then Emma Widnes—now Jamie Renshaw. Who'll be next?'..'Things do go in threes, don't they?'

3. c. *Three in One*, (*b*) *attrib.* as *three-in-one*, combining three items, functions, etc., in one whole; (*c*) *Three in One* (attrib. also *Three-in-One*), the proprietary name of a lubricating oil; *three-o(h)-three* (usually printed ·303), a rifle of ·303 calibre; also, ammunition manufactured for use in such a rifle; *three times three* (earlier example).

1909 *Grocery Catal.* (T. Eaton & Co.) 26/2 Three-in-One Hand Saw..combining in one tool a saw, 2 ft. rule and square. **1928** *Trade Marks Jrnl.* 22 Aug. 1354/1 '*Three in One*'... Lubricating oil. Three in One Oil Co..., 130, William Street, City, County, and State of New York,

United States of America; manufacturers. **1931** *Advertiser* (Adelaide) 7 Oct. 10 (Advt.), A three-in-one garment, comprising vest, bloomers, and underskirt. **1962** E. Snow *Other Side of River* (1963) xxxii. 245 We call it a three-in-one technique. It combines, in all grades, teaching, practical research work, and actual production. **1967** N. Marsh *Death at Dolphin* i. 14 The key..refused to turn... 'You want a touch of the old free-in-one... Oil, mate. Loobrication.' **1970** W. Klatt in D. J. Dwyer *China Now* (1974) xviii. 341 Lin Piao gave high priority to the task of 'struggle—criticism—transformation' which is apparently being carried out by the chief organ of the new order, i.e. the 'three-in-one combination' of the Revolutionary Committees, embracing representatives of the revolutionary cadres, of the People's Liberation Army and of the revolutionary masses. **1977** O. Schell *China* (1978) I. 104 And those old factories with pollution problems must form three-in-one groups to solve their problems. **1979** T. Gifford *Hollywood Gothic* (1980) xxiv. 240 The lock had gotten rusty, but..Three-in-One oil did the job. **1903** *Kynock Jrnl.* Aug.–Sept. 128/1 The ·303 Sporting Rifle. The ·303 is used a great deal as a sporting rifle, and being the Government arm is quoted in comparison with Express rifles. **1928** E. Blunden *Undertones of War* xix. 202, I was at least more skilful with the shots of epigram than with the three-o-three of the small-arms factory. **1959** [see *thirty-eight* s.v. *Thirty *sb.* 4]. **1981** J. Barnett *Firing Squad* viii. 79 Firearm certificate holders on ·303 Lee Enfields..were mostly rifle clubs. **1789** *Loiterer* 19 Sept. 4 My health has been drank in a bumper, with three times three, by every Club of Tradesmen in the City.

III. 1. a. *three-act* (earlier example), *-age*, *-alarm*, *-bean*, *-blade*, *-car*, *-cent*, *-class* (examples), *-core*, *-dollar*, *-electrode*, *-island*, *-judge*, *-lane* [*Lane *sb.* 2 d], *-level*, *-member*, *-mile* (earlier and later examples), *-month(s)* (examples), *-party*, *-person*, *-phase* (later examples), *-pin*, *-place*, *-ply* (later and *ellipt.* examples), *-position*, *-shilling* (example); *-speed* (earlier and *ellipt.* examples), *-stage*, *-syllable*, *-term*, *-tier* (examples), *-wheel* (examples), *-word*. **b.** *three-dimensioned*, *-engined*, *-fanged*, *-handed* (later examples), *-heeled*, *-numbered*, *-pronged* (later examples), *-storied* (later examples), *-tailed* (earlier example), *-tiered* (later example), *-wheeled* (later examples). **c.** *three-acter*, *-alarmer*, *-hitter*, *-mover* (earlier example), *-tonner* (motor vehicle), *-volumer* (examples), *-wheeler* (later examples).

1825 H. Wilson *Memoirs* II. 76, I..fixed, upon Moliere's comedy of the Malade Imaginaire, which I hastily transformed into an English three-act piece! **1948** C. McCullers in *Mademoiselle* Sept. 257/1 By autumn I was writing a three-acter about revenge and incest. **1957** G. Bibby *Testimony of Spade* 31 He [*sc.* Christian Thomsen] was constrained to write a short account of his arrangement of the Copenhagen museum and of his Three Age system. **1970** Bray & Trump *Dict. Archaeol.* 231/2 *Three Age System*, the scheme for dividing prehistory into a stone age, bronze age and iron age. It was first formulated by C. Thomsen 1816–19. **1932** *Amer. Speech* VII. 337 Three alarm fire, used with negative to indicate mediocrity. *a* **1975** Wodehouse *Sunset at Blandings* (1977) xii. 80 Lord Emsworth entered looking like a refugee from a three-alarm fire. **1950** O. Nash *Family Reunion* 80 The author's attention has been called to a type of conflagration known as a three-alarmer. **1976** *Billings* (Montana) *Gaz.* 17 June 7-B/1 Create a picnic-like atmosphere with such favorites as potato salad and three bean salad. **1931** D. Rose *J. de la Cierva's Wings of Tomorrow* vi. 92 For certain purposes the three-blade rotor may prove the most efficient. **1967** *Jane's Surface Skimmer Systems 1967–68* 9 (*caption*) A. Turboméca Artouste IIC drives..two three-blade variable-pitch propellers for thrust. **1944** R. Chandler *Lady in Lake* iv. 23 Outside the wall to the left was the three-car garage. **1980** J. McNeil *Spy Game* ix. 93 There was..a three-car garage. **1851** *Statutes at Large U.S.A.* IX. 587 No ingots shall be used for the coinage of the three-cent pieces herein authorized, of which the quality differs more than five-thousandths from the legal standard. **1898** P. L. Ford *Hon. Peter Stirling* 281 The three-cent papers..abuse me. **1946** *Publ. Amer. Dial. Soc.* vi. 37 To feel like a three-cent piece with a hole in it. (To feel worthless and do-less.) **1910** *Westm. Gaz.* 14 Feb. 6/4 [Germany] The detested three-class system..and..the system of promotion of certain classes of electors from one class to another on other than property qualifications. **1980** *Jrnl. R. Soc. Arts* June 411/1 Gone are..the limitations on political rights of a 'three-class franchise'. **1922** *B.I. Hand-bk.* (Brit. Insulated & Helsby Cables Ltd.) (ed. 3) 106 Three-core cables. **1958** *Spectator* 8 Aug. 190/2, 3-core electric wiring. **1904** Kipling *Traffics & Discoveries* 212 'Heaven is beautiful, Earth is ugly,' The three-dimensioned preacher saith. **1858** J. H. Hickcox *Hist. Acct. Amer. Coinage* 56 Three Dollar gold coins were coined..under an act passed in 1853. **1918** *Wireless World* VI. 144 De Forest was experimenting with a three-electrode valve. **1932** *Discovery* July 216/1 The starting point of modern wireless is what is known as the three-electrode thermionic valve. **1931** *Nineteenth Cent.* Feb. 159 The three-engined types. **1967** *Economist* 16 Sept. 1022/1 What might happen to passenger traffic if one's competitor should advertise 'three engined safety'. **1915** D. H. Lawrence *Let.* 15 July in *Lett. to B. Russell* (1948) 53 Liberty, Equality & Fraternity is the three-fanged serpent. **1792** J. Woodforde *Diary* 10 Feb. (1927) III. 335 After Coffee and Tea we got to Cards to three-handed Cribbage. **1907** W. M. Cockrum *Pioneer Hist. Indiana* xiv. 344 Dancing was the principal amusement..three- and four-handed reels and jigs. **1937** G. Greene *19 Stories* (1947) 57 They had played their usual rubber of three-handed bridge. **1976** 'Trevanian' *Main* (1977) ii. 23 They were playing three-handed cut-throat. *a* **1889** G. M. Hopkins *Poems* (1967) 180 Yet Arthur is a Bowman: his three-heeled timber'll hit The bald..gold. **1976** *Billings* (Montana) *Gaz.* 30 June 3-E/1 John Candelaria fired a three-hitter and tripled in two runs during an eight-run first inning. **1920** *Blackw. Mag.* July 1/1 The *Ulidia* was a typical 'three-island' tramp steamer. **1962** A. G. Course *Dict. Naut. Terms* 198 *Three island ship*, a vessel with a raised forecastle forward, a raised bridge deck amidships, and a raised poop aft. **1944** *Mod. Lang. Notes* Dec. 515, 3-judge court. **1981** *Times of India* 30 Aug. 4/5 A three-judge bench. **1929** *Sat. Even. Post* 16 Nov. 41/2 On a three-lane boulevard a local driver generally keeps well toward the center. **1972** M. Jones *Life on Dole* xii. 88 This road..was eventually completed not as a dual carriageway but as a three-lane road. **1956** J. Lotz in L. White *Frontiers of Knowledge* xiv. 221 This multistage, three-level construction involving phonemes, morphemes, and sentences characterizes natural language. **1979** *Guardian Weekly* 28 Oct. 18/4 A three-level promenade. **1944** *Mod. Lang. Notes* Dec. 515 The three-member compound is peculiarly modern. **1957** Ld. Hailey *African Survey 1956* vi. 303 Such elections..might be tried as an experiment in two three-member constituencies. **1889** *Cent. Dict.*, Three-mile limit. **1911** *Daily Colonist* (Victoria, B.C.) 14 Apr. 15/4 The schooners were well within the three-mile limit, poaching on the British Columbia fisheries grounds. **1977** G. V. Higgins *Dreamland* xii. 151 Small freighters. Plying..between Scotland and the three-mile limits, until Repeal, they easily returned their cost of purchase. **1838** E. B. Browning *Seraphim & Other Poems* 160 In the eyes all undefiled Of a little three months' child. **1861** *Chicago Tribune* 26 May 1/3 So shameful has been the treatment of many of the three month volunteers, that most of them will certainly return home as soon as their terms expire. **1977** J. M. Johnson in Douglas & Johnson *Existential Sociol.* viii. 251 The three-month period when the events occurred. **1881** *Brentano's Chess Monthly* June 86 The sacrifice of Queen is very much the same as in the 'Welcome' three-mover. **1876** G. M. Hopkins *Wr. Deutschland* ix, in *Poems* (1967) 54 Be adored among men, God, three-numberèd form. **1925** J. A. Spender *Public Life* II. xix. 27 The difficulties of the three-party system. **1978** A. Gilchrist *Cod Wars* viii. 66 As a result of the 1956 election [in Iceland], the conservative-dominated coalition of the Independence and Progressive parties gave way to a three-party coalition from which the Independence Party was excluded. **1964** I. L. Horowitz *New Sociol.* 33 Models devised to deal with two- or three-person groups need not lead to the trivialization of sociology. **1922** Three-phase system [see *Bias *v.* 5]. **1926** *Jrnl. Iron & Steel Inst.* CXIV. 77 These solutions of the important problem gave a simple and comparatively cheap installation, without transforming the three-phase current to direct current or ..regulating the speed of the generator. **1961** *Listener* 9 Nov. 767/2 The normal three-phase alternating current system. **1868** J. C. Atkinson *Gloss. Cleveland Dial.* 335 *Merls*, sb... Other names are..Five-pin, Nine-pin, Three-pin, Morris or Merels. **1940** *Chambers's Techn. Dict.* 848/1 *Three-pin plug*, a plug with three contact pins, two for the main circuit and one for the earth connexion. **1974** A. Ross *Bradford Business* 75 A length of insulated cable ..snaked across the floor to a three-pin socket. **1947** H. Reichenbach *Elem. Symbolic Logic* § 17. 83 A three-place function is given by the verb 'gives' in the sentence 'Peter gives Paul a book'. **1964** R. H. Robins *Gen. Linguistics* viii. 330 English plosive and nasal consonants fall into a three-place..system, bilabial, alveolar, velar. **1905** *Timber Trades Jrnl.* 21 Jan. 72/1 Date cases, made entirely of three-ply wood. **1910**, etc. Three ply [see *Ply *sb.* 1]. **1921** *Daily Mail Year Bk.* 112/2 The new..railway is..equipped with three-position signals. **1971** *Gloss. Electrotechnical, Power Terms* (*B.S.I.*) I. iii. 16 *Three-position relay*, a relay which has one unenergized and two energized conditions. **1944** T. H. Wisdom *Triumph over Tunisia* vi. 54 Jerry..dropped a load of three-pronged spikes on the runway. **1968** N. Mitchell *Sir George Cunningham* vii. 138 A Punjabi called Khurshid Anwar..was on the Hazara border organising a three-pronged drive into Kashmir. *a* **1817** Jane Austen *Persuasion* (1818) IV. vi. 116 She has a blister on one of her heels, as large as a three shilling piece. **1895** *People* 6 Jan. 4/5 The three-speed gear bicycle invented by Messrs. Lindley and Biggs. **1977** *New Yorker* 9 May 34/1 A.. young woman..had just bought a three-speed Raleigh. *Ibid.* 34/2 Why did I buy a three-speed? **1977** *Lancs. Life* Nov. 138/2 Her bike had broken down—something to do with the three-speed. **1980** J. L. Carr *Month in Country* 69 You can have Dad's bike... It's a three-speed and the chain has an oil bath. **1936** *Discovery* Sept. 299/2 The proposed three-stage rocket-ship. **1965** *Language* XLI. 117 A three-stage process of increasing deprovincialization in Russian linguistics. **1939** *Oxoniensia* IV. 127 No. 2 is part of a 'three-storeyed' pitcher, showing a combination of various decorative ideas. **1963** J. Robinson *Honest to God* i. 13 The traditional language of a three-storeyed universe. **1886** *Amer. Jrnl. Philol.* VII. 246 In early Latin this energetic stress-accent was not bound by the three-syllable limit. **1964** W. S. Allen in D. Abercrombie et al. *Daniel Jones* 4 It [*sc.* stress] falls..on a light antepenultimate only because of the overriding three-syllable rule, which will not permit it to recede further. **1718** M. W. Montagu *Let.* 19 May (1965) I. 413 'Tis common for the Heirs of a great three-tail'd Bassa not to be rich enough to keep in repair the House he built. **1957** E. B. Jones *Instrument Technol.* III. ii. 72 (*caption*) Response of a three-term controller to an artificial disturbance. **1977** *Time* 21 Nov. 28/2 In Cleveland, scrappy Dennis Kucinich, 31, a former three-term city councilman, edged out Edward Feighan, 30, the candidate of the regular Democratic organization. **1883** *Heal & Son Catal.: Dining Rm., Libr., & Drawing Rm. Furnit.* 215 Three-tier Whatnot, in Walnut or Ebonised. **1957** Ld. Hailey *African Survey 1956* viii. 467 In form this constituted a 'three-tier' system of Councils, but it was the District Council which was to form the focal point in it. **1977** *Guardian Weekly* 23 Oct. 8/3 The three-tier agreement is to be made up of a treaty limiting the numbers of certain strategic weapons for a period of eight years, a protocol imposing certain limits on other weapons for three years, and a statement of principles looking toward major arms reductions in the future. **1973** 'M. Innes' *Appleby's Answer* xv. 129 A three-tiered contraption loaded with pastries and éclairs. *a* **1944** K. Douglas *Alamein to Zem Zem* (1946) 38 This necessitated sweating about to find a three-tonner or a tank to tow us out. **1971** B. W. Aldiss *Soldier Erect* 39 We marched off the platform in good order..and transferred our kit to a line of three-tonners standing waiting for us outside the station. **1864** G. Meredith *Let.* Oct. (1912) I. 162 My 'plain story' is first to right me and then the 3 volumer will play trumpets. **1927** *Daily Tel.* 27 Sept. 5/1 When the 'three-volumer' went out it was thought we had ceased to ask for literary quantity. **1936** *Discovery* Nov. 351/1 An 1888 Benz three-wheel motor car. **1973** *Times* 30 Oct. 4/1 A new three-wheel car, the Robin, for which an average fuel consumption of 50 miles to the gallon is claimed. **1900** W. S. Churchill in *Morning Post* 1 Jan. 5/7 Suddenly three-wheeled things appeared on the crest. **1981** *London Mag.* July 69/1 We were rattled and rocked in our three-wheeled *samlor*. **1958** C. Fremlin *Hours before Dawn* iv. 41 She saw Mrs Henderson's miniature three-wheeler drawn up in front of the house. **1975** *Times* 22 Dec. 3/1 Their three-wheeler disintegrated in collision with another car. **1880** 'Mark Twain' *Tramp Abroad* xxx. 321 They know a *word* here and there, of a foreign language, or a few little beggarly three-word phrases, filched from the back of the Dictionary. **1978** R. Ludlum *Holcroft Covenant* xiii. 154 He had sent Sam a three-word cablegram from the airport in Lisbon.

2. three-address *a. Computers*, (employing instructions) having three addresses, two that specify the location of the two operands and one that specifies where the result is to be stored; **three-anti** *China* = *Sanfan; **three-axis** *a.*, having or involving an ability to be rotated about each of three mutually perpendicular axes; **three-ball** *a.*, of a golf match: involving three players, each playing his own ball; **three-ball(s)**, a three-ball golf match; **three-banded** (later examples); **three-bar** *a.*, (*b*) of an electric fire: having three heating elements; **three-body** *a. Math.* and *Physics*, involving or pertaining to three objects or particles; *three-body problem* = *problem of three bodies* (see sense I. 1 g); **three-card** *a.* (later examples); **three-centre** *a. Chem.*, applied to a bond in which the orbital of the two electrons forming it is spread over three contributing atoms; **three-circle diagram,** a Venn diagram in which there are three circles; **three-crop** *a.*, of a ewe: that has borne lambs in three successive years; **three-cushion** *a.*, designating a type of billiards in which the cushion must be struck at least three times by a ball at each play (see quot. 1957); **three-D, 3-D, 3 D** *a.*, three-dimensional, used *esp.* of a stereoptic process of filming; also *ellipt.* as *sb.*, a three-dimensional realization or state; **three-day** *a.*, extending over three days, that takes three days to complete or come to an end, as *three-day event*, a tripartite equestrian competition, usu. with the first day given over to dressage, the second to cross-country riding, and the third to show-jumping in a ring (hence *three-day eventer*, a horse that participates in such competitions), *three-day week*, a reduced working week of only three days; **three-dimensional** *a.*, having, or appearing to have, the three dimensions of length, breadth, and depth (cf. Dimension *sb.* 3 a); = Tri-dimensional *a.*; also *fig.*; hence **three-dimensionality; three-dimensionally** *adv.*; **three-figure** *a.*, consisting of three digits; one hundred or more (pounds, runs, miles per hour, etc.); calculated to three decimal places; **three-halves power,** the square root of the cube of a number; in *Electronics* used *attrib.* to designate a law that the anode current of a valve is proportional to the three-halves power of the anode voltage; **Three Hours** (or **Hours'**) **Service,** a devotional service lasting from 12 to 3 o'clock in the afternoon of Good Friday, designed to cover the hours of the crucifixion of Jesus Christ; also *ellipt.*; **three-letter man,** (*a*) *U.S.*, a person awarded a mark of distinction (cf. *Letter *sb.*[1] 1 e) in three different sports; (*b*) *colloq.*, an obnoxious person; **three-light,** (*a*) (later examples); also *ellipt.*; **three-line, -lined** *a.*, also, *three-line* (occas. *-lined*) *whip*, a written notice, underlined three times to indicate great urgency, requesting the attendance of members of Parliament at a particular parliamentary session; the discipline of such a notice; (further examples); **three-martini lunch** *U.S.*, a lavish lunch, esp. one charged to a business expense account; **three-minute** *a.*, that occupies, or completes or is completed within, three minutes (in quot. 1833, that completes a mile in three minutes); that indicates the passage of three minutes; **three-nines** *a.*, (*a*) (see quot. 1927); (*b*) of a telephone call: made to an emergency service, for which in the U.K. 999 is dialled; **three-out**: see *OUT *sb.* 1 b; **three-pipe problem,** a problem which requires considerable thought (for the duration of the smoking of three pipes of tobacco); **three-putt** *v. intr.* (Golf), to take three putts to hole the ball on a particular green; *trans.* to play (a green or hole) taking three putts; **three-ring, -ringed, circus,** a circus having three rings; hence *fig.*, a showy or extravagant spectacle; a scene of confusion or disorder; cf. *one-ring circus* s.v. *ONE *numeral a.* 33; **three-sixty,** in various sports, aerobatics, etc.: a turn through three-hundred-and-sixty degrees; **three-space,** three-dimensional space; **three-spined stickleback:** *Gasterosteus aculeatus*; (examples); **three-star** *a.*, having, displaying, bearing as insignia, or being designated by three stars as a mark of quality, rank, etc., usu. in a four- or five-star grading system (see *STAR *sb.*[1] 10 c, d); *spec.* used to designate: (*a*) a good quality French brandy; (*b*) a highly-rated hotel or restaurant; (*c*) *U.S.*, a lieutenant general (in rank below a general, above a major general); (*d*) a grade of petrol; (*e*) *transf.*, anything of high quality or in a high degree characteristic; also *ellipt.* as *sb.*, three-star brandy, petrol, etc.; **three-striper:** see *STRIPER 1; **three-horned acacia:** = *honey locust* s.v. HONEY *sb.* 7 b in Dict. and Suppl.; (earlier example); **three-time** *a.*, that has occurred or been done three times; of a person, to whom something has happened, or who has achieved something, three times; spec. *three-time loser*, a person who has served three prison sentences; **three-valued** *a.*, having three values; *spec.* in *Philos.*, designating a logical system or technique which incorporates a third value such as indeterminacy, uncertainty, half-truth, etc., in addition to the values of truth and falsehood customary in two-valued systems; **three-wire** *a.*, (*b*) applied to a system of mooring used to keep an airship or balloon at a constant height from the ground; **three-wood,** (*a*) *Archery*, a bow made of three pieces of wood; also *attrib.*; (*b*) *Golf*, a wooden club providing medium loft, formerly called a spoon (SPOON *sb.* 4 c).

1948 *Math. Tables & other Aids to Computation* III. 69 The control of this machine is accomplished, for the most part, by means of three-address orders. In contrast, the 'Mark I' at Harvard uses a two-address system. **1970** O. DOPPING *Computers & Data Processing* vi. 103 A three-address machine. **1976** BANKS & DOUPNIK *Introd. Computer Sci.* vii. 242 The principal disadvantage of three address instructions is their great length and consequent excessive use of memory space. **1966,** etc. Three-anti [see *SANFAN]. **1975** A. WATSON *Living in China* iv. 90 The 'three anti' campaign which opposed the three evils of corruption, waste and excessive red tape in the Party and government. **1962** V. GRISSOM in *Into Orbit* 78 We had to learn from scratch..how to manipulate the new three-axis control stick and make the precise adjustments in yaw, pitch and roll. **1977** *Dædalus* Fall 52 Some [satellites] are provided..with three-axis stabilization, so that their instruments can be pointed steadily, for long periods of time, to a chosen target. **1839** *Rules of Hon. Co. Edin. Golfers* in C. B. Clapcott *Rules of Ten Oldest Golf Clubs* (1935) 69 In a Three-ball match, the Ball nearest the hole, and within the prescribed distance, must be lifted, if the third party require it, where the Player does so or not. **1890** H. G. HUTCHINSON *Golf* ix. 241 The three-ball match;..these matches are of two kinds, that wherin each plays against each, and that wherin two are in combination against a third, though each play his individual ball. **1901** *Rules of Golf* 5 Three players may play against each other, each playing his own ball, when the match is called 'a three-ball match'. **1952** *Chambers's Jrnl.* May 299/1 The Major introduced them without enthusiasm and Basil promptly attached himself to the party, much to the Major's annoyance, for he hated three-balls. **1976** *Webster's Sports Dict.* 450/1 *Three-ball,* a golf match in which 3 players compete against each other with each playing his own ball. **1956** G. DURRELL *Drunken Forest* iv. 75 Inside the hat, curled into a tight ball, lay..a three-banded armadillo. **1966** E. PALMER *Plains of Camdeboo* xii. 196 A three-banded plover was paddling in the furrow. **1973** 'H. CARMICHAEL' *Too Late for Tears* vi. 81 In the hearth stood a 3-bar electric fire. **1979** T. WISEMAN *Game of Secrets* iv. 49 A three-bar electric heater. **1936** *Physical Rev.* L. 638/2 The procedure for the three-body problem. **1968** M. S. LIVINGSTON *Particle Physics* iv. 74 Evidence that this is a three-body decay is that the electrons have a wide distribution in energy. **1972** *Sci. Amer.* Jan. 85/1 The Herzberg bands of O_2 and the atmospheric infrared bands probably both owe their origin to three-body association: $O + O + X \rightarrow O_2^* + X$, where X, the third atom..is unchanged in the process. **1920** C. SANDBURG *Smoke & Steel* 175 Pickpockets, yeggs, three card men. **1938** [see *BROAD *sb.* 6]. **1973** *Times* 19 Jan. 3/8 Three-card tricksters are a nuisance. They have someone posted to watch for the police, then they invite people to lay down money on which of three cards..is the 'lady'. **1979** W. H. CANAWAY *Solid Gold Buddha* xxii. 145 Sam was as confused as a yokel watching a three-card artist. **1954** W. H. EBERHARDT et al. in *Jrnl. Chem. Physics* XXII. 989/1 In our approach, the only new, or rather, unfamiliar concept is that which we call the 'three-center bond'. **1978** *Further Perspectives Organic Chem.* (CIBA Symp.) 61 The short S—O bonds in the thioimine may reflect a three-centre bond. **1883** J. VENN in *Proc. Cambr. Philos. Soc.* IV. 51 Both Drobisch and Schröder have used what I have called..the three-circle diagram. **1952** W. V. QUINE *Methods of Logic* I. 79 We set up a three circle diagram as usual. **1946** J. CARY *Moonlight* viii. 53 One heard first a single 'aw-aw' from some old three-crop mother, followed at once by a hearty 'mey' from her stout lamb. **1960** *Farmer & Stockbreeder* 1 Mar. 77/3 Mr. McIlwraith also paid..£180 for a three-crop ewe. **1910** *Encycl. Brit.* III. 939/2 There is also Three-Cushion Carom..and the Bank-Shot game. **1957** *Ibid.* III. 569/1 A count is validly made in three-cushion billiards in any one of four ways: (1) when the cue ball strikes an object ball and then strikes three or more cushions before striking the second object ball; (2) when the cue ball strikes three or more cushions before contacting the two object balls; (3) when the one ball strikes a cushion, then the first object ball, then two or more cushions and then the second object ball; (4) when the cue ball strikes two or more cushions, then the first object ball, then one or more cushions and finally the second object ball. **1974** *Mark Twain Jrnl.* Summer 3/1 Cure and Cutler played a game of three cushion billiards, a novelty at the time [*sc.* 1906]. **1952** *Jrnl. Soc. Motion Picture & Television Engineers* Oct. 249/1 Up to now the production of three-dimensional (3-D) films has been sporadic. **1953** *Sun* (Baltimore) 5 Feb. 14/1 We receive with mixed reaction the news that three-dimensional motion pictures, coyly called '3-D', will shortly come into general distribution. **1953,** etc. 3-D, 3D [see D., dimensional, s.v. *D III. 3]. **1955** W. GADDIS *Recognitions* III. v. 914 She's terrific, even in 3-D she'd be terrific. **1966** *T.V. Times* (Austral.) 7 Dec. 10/2 Three-D Television is now the subject of experiment in several overseas countries, particularly Russia. **1971** 'D. HALLIDAY' *Dolly & Doctor Bird* x. 130 Monopoly would maybe do. Or three-D noughts and crosses? **1983** *U.S.A. Today* 20 May 5D/4 But in a 3-D comic, futility flattens the actors even as the visual gimmick pops them out. **1890** Three-day [in Dict., sense III. 1 a]. **1937** S. CLOETE *Turning Wheels* ix. 143 Three day sickness, which as a rule animals recovered from if left alone, meant abandoning beasts since there was no time to wait for them to recover. **1952** *Rules & Reg. governing One-Day Events* (Brit. Horse Soc.) 5 One Day combined Tests.. lead up to the Olympic Three Day Event. **1963** E. H. EDWARDS *Saddlery* vii. 69 This is not of importance by the time one's horse is sufficiently advanced to perform Three Day Event tests. **1965** *N.Y. Herald Tribune* 18 Apr. 3 An annual three-day..walk. **1974** *Times* 16 Feb. 1/1 The three-day week will carry unemployment to a very high level. **1976** *Times* 21 May 2/5 The committee's three-day conference on negotiated independence..has been postponed. **1976** *Horse & Hound* 10 Dec. 57/1 (Advt.), An ideal type to sire top quality point-to-pointers and three-day-eventers. **1977** M. WALKER *National Front* vi. 147 The state of national emergency and the three-day week. **1982** BARR & YORK *Official Sloane Ranger Handbk.* 152/1 The easiest house parties are for a sport—racing, three-day event, shooting. **1878** Three-dimensional [see DIMENSION *sb.* 3 a]. **1882** [see DIMENSIONAL *a.* 2]. **1920** W. W. STRONG *New Philos. of Mod. Sci.* xvi. 142 In gravitational phenomena a small disturbance leaves a circular trajectory finite in a three dimensional space. **1923** H. CRANE *Let.* 2 Mar. (1965) 129 O yes, the 'background of life'—and all that is still there, but that is only three-dimensional. **1925** B. DOBRÉE in W. Congreve *Comedies* p. xvii, Congreve..made his people three-dimensional. **1953** *N.Y. Times* 19 Feb. 20 This much touted picture..is advertised as the first feature made in the three-dimensional Natural Vision process. **1971** A. DRUMMOND *Auckland Jrnls. Vicesimus Lush* 22 His children..emerge from the pages of his journals as sufficiently three-dimensional figures to be of interest to readers a century later. **1926** H. READ *Eng. Stained Glass* I. 11/2 Three-dimensionality. Perspective and shading give the proper spatial relations of the various details represented. **1956** E. H. HUTTEN *Lang. Mod. Physics* vi. 208 This..suggests that causal action exemplified by the inverse-square law is connected with the three-dimensionality of space. **1977** *Jrnl. Playing-Card Soc.* Nov. 69 The three-dimensionality of 19th- and 20th-century German cards is one of their distinguishing features. **1958** C. SMITH in 'E. Crispin' *Best SF Three* 210 Light..allowed the ships to reform three-dimensionally.. as they moved from star to star. **1979** *Nature* 29 Mar. 439/2 The method for producing these three-dimensionally interconnected fibrous structures is described here. **1855** J. LANG *Forger's Wife* xv. 44 'There is not a really good placard on the walls—tens, and fifteens, and twenties; but not a single three-figure gentleman' (he meant £100) 'among 'em.' **1861** C. KNIGHT *Eng. Cycl.: Arts & Sci.* VII. 1007 A. De Morgan. Three-figure logarithms: three figures of numbers to three of logarithm, complete, on a sheet of 7½ by 6 inches. **1929** *Star* 21 Aug. 12/1 A three-figure stand. **1973** J. WAINWRIGHT *Devil you Don't* 5 It was a great car—a Jag. Mark II—well capable of three-figure speeds. **1978** R. V. JONES *Most Secret War* xxi. 174 Assuming..that the three-figure entries were bearings. **1920** *Proc. Inst. Radio Engineers* VIII. 70 At low plate voltages..the measured values of the amplification constant are lower and the three-halves power law does not appear to hold. **1963** B. FOZARD *Instrumentation Nucl. Reactors* xi. 138 As the anode voltage is raised the equation to the anode characteristic takes the commonly assumed three-halves power law. [**1864** *Guardian* 30 Mar. 299/2 The English Church is indebted to Mr. Mackonochie for the revival of..the admirable ancient Office in Commemoration of the Three Hours.] **1898** (*title*) The three hours' service for Good Friday. **1923** *Spectator* 5 May 753/2 Two hours afterwards I went to the Three Hours at a church in a residential southern suburb. **1976** *Oxford Mission Q. Paper* July/Sept. 5 The little church was packed from beginning to end of the Three Hours. **1929** R. H. BARBOUR *Tod Hale on Nine* xxiv. 264 He wanted to be a 'three-letter man', and until a few days ago his chance had looked very bright. **1941** *Amer. Speech* XVI. 190 Three-letter man, F-A-G. **1946** J. IRVING *Royal Navalese* 81 A three-letter man is a 'cad'. **1972** *Sci. Amer.* Feb. 114/2 A boxer of almost professional caliber; a three-letter man in college, a Rhodes scholar, he passed the bar examination but after only a year of practice decided 'to chuck the law for astronomy'. **1853** in *Notes on Cheshire Churches* (Chetham Soc.) (1894) 10 Each side of the porch having open three-light windows. **1908–9** H. R. BARKER *E. Suffolk Illustr.* 330 The east window is a Transitional three-light, and in the side walls are very good two-lights in square heads. **1937** *Burlington Mag.* Mar. 149/1 The three-light Peter de Dene window of the Minster. **1939** W. I. JENNINGS *Parliament* iii. 78 A 'three-line whip' indicates that all other engagements should be put aside. **1958** *Spectator* 27 June 826/3 A debate sufficiently important to warrant a three-line whip. **1975** J. P. MORGAN *House of Lords & Labour Govt.* iv. 127 Labour Peers took their own vote on the question of the vote in the Lords, choosing a free vote, unlike M.P.s who agreed to submit to a three-line whip. **1972** G. MCGOVERN in W. Safire *Polit. Dict.* (1978) 727/1 The rich businessman can deduct his three-martini lunch, but you can't take off the price of a baloney sandwich. **1977** *Time* 26 Sept. 49/2 Carter has railed so vehemently against the 'three-martini lunch' that his staff has to come up with something. **1833** *Knickerbocker* I. 160 The present Mrs. S. admired his three minute roan. **1857** *Uncle Jack the Fault Killer* ix. 131 My three-minute glass lets the sand run through just in three minutes, which is time to boil an egg. **1958** Three minute [see *LONG-PLAYING *a.*]. **1927** W. COLLINSON *Contemp. Eng.* 89 The house-agent's repulsive terminology e.g...a three nines agreement (i.e. 999 years). **1982** P. TURNBULL *Dead Knock* i. 11 Tango Delta Foxtrot..responded to a three-nines call for a fire appliance. **1891** A. CONAN DOYLE in *Strand Mag.* Aug. 197/2 It is quite a three-pipe problem, and I beg that you won't speak to me for fifty minutes. **1976** *Lancet* 20 Nov. 1131/2 Appraising and comparing the effectiveness of what we do has certainly up to now proved to be what Sherlock Holmes would have called 'a 3-pipe problem'. **1946** *Sun* (Baltimore) 2 July 17/6 Joe Kirkwood..scored a 74,.. three-putting the last green. *Ibid.*, Lawson Little overshot the greens and three-putted frequently. **1978** *Detroit Free Press* 16 Apr. E7/3 McLendon..three-putted the 18th about the same time. **1904** *Everybody's Mag.* Aug. 161/2 A Barnum three-ring circus compared to Henry H. Rogers's exhibitions. **1914** KIPLING *Divers. Creatures* (1917) 394, I can see lots of things from here. It's like a three-ring circus! **1951, 1955** [see *CIRCUS 2 c]. **1981** D. CLARK *Roast Eggs* viii. 159 Don't m'lud me... You turned my court into a damned three-ring circus. **1898** B. MATTHEWS *Outlines in Local Color* 145 What good is a three-ringed circus to anybody, except the boss of it? **1904** 'O. HENRY' in *McClure's Mag.* Apr. 613/2 They commenced to scramble down, and for awhile we had a three-ringed circus. **1927** C. A. LINDBERGH *We* v. 82 One of the first lessons was the 'three sixty'—so named because its completion required a total change in direction of three hundred and sixty degrees. **1977** *Skateboard Special* Sept. 7/1 The first really difficult stunt I learned then was a three-sixty. That..is a stunt where you spin the board through a full circle on its back wheels. **1972** *Sci. Amer.* Dec. 102/2 A Möbius strip, for example, has a handedness in 3-space that cannot be altered by twisting and stretching. **1977** *New York Rev. Bks.* 12 May 29/1 A plane is infinite and unbounded. Bend it through 'three-space' (i.e., three-dimensional space) and it can be the closed surface of a sphere. **1769** T. PENNANT *Brit. Zool.* III. 217 The three spined s[tickle] back... These are common in many of our rivers. **1836** W. YARRELL *Hist. Brit. Fishes* I. 77 The Three-spined Stickleback was first described by Belon. **1971** *Nature* 23 Apr. 536/2 The three-spined stickleback..found sanctuary in the Atlantic. [**1871** G. H. LEWES *Let.* 27 Aug. in *Geo. Eliot Lett.* (1955) V. 180 Will you meanwhile order for me from the Stores.. 3 bottles of Martorell's three stars Brandy at 5/-.] **1879** R. J. ATCHERLEY *Trip to Boërland* ii. 32 In the up-country towns of the Transvaal..common brandy is retailed at 1*s.*, and 'Three Star' at 1*s.* 6*d.* per glass. **1929** *Amer. Speech* IV. 387 A little *three-star Hennessey* brought overland from Detroit. **1931** S. COOKE *This Motoring* xvii. 172 The..Lion at Guildford..is a typical three-star A.A. hotel. **1939** [see S.A.E., s.a.e. s.v. *S 4 a]. **1944** *Mod. Lang. Notes* Dec. 526 Whereas once a sword, a ship, was given an epithet fit for a hero or a goddess, today a warrior is labelled in the manner of a manufactured product:..*3-star general.* **1960** *Harper's Bazaar* July 19/1 The number of three-star restaurants in France has just dropped from 11 to 10. This reduction has been effected by the *Guide Michelin.* **1968** *Listener* 28 Mar. 405/3 Courvoisier V.S.O.P., he croaked, none of your rotten Three Star. *Ibid.* 1 Aug. 159/3 To ask for..two gallons of three-star. **1973** J. BURROWS *Like an Evening Gone* xvii. 220 'I'd respect any decent woman.' 'What about Tamara Tayne?' 'That three star whore? That's a different category.' **1973** H. GILBERT *Hotels with Empty Rooms* xiii. 114 He..poured himself a glass of three-star cognac. **1977** *Air Mail* Spring 45/2 (Advt.), Six-berth luxury caravan for hire on three-star site with all amenities. **1977** A. SAMPSON *Arms Bazaar* xvii. 288 He is a stocky three-star general from Alabama..on his tie was a three-star tie pin. **1979** *Country Life* 13 Sept. 807/2 The typical three-star menu..of foie gras and truffles with everything... And still, in too many three-stars, foie gras with every. thing. **1982** S. WILSON *Dealer's Wheels* ix. 85 We filled up with three-star..and I went to check the oil and tyres. **1818** *Mass Agric. Repository & Jrnl.* V. 56 Gleditsia Triacanthos. It is also called Three-Thorned Acacia in the catalogues of nurserymen. **1908** J. KELLEY *Thirteen Yrs. Oregon Penitentiary* vii. 81 Pat came back again; he was a three-time loser. **1914,** etc. Three-time [see *LOSER 4]. **1943** P. CHEYNEY *You can always Duck* vi. 96 He's a three-time killer. **1979** *Tucson* (Arizona) *Citizen* 20 Sept. 6D/1 The Cats..will be led into tomorrow's meet by three-time All-America selection Thom Hunt and 1978 All-America choice Dirk Lakeman. **1932** LEWIS & LANGFORD *Symbolic Logic* vii. 213 One such alternative is the Three-valued Calculus, developed by Lukasiewicz and Tarski. *Ibid.*, If, in addition, the number ½ is taken, then we have the matrix of the three-valued system. **1934**

Mind XLIII. 104 Professor Lukasiewicz is sole author of these systems, having originated the three-valued system in 1920, and *n*-valued systems in 1922. **1946** *Nature* 14 Sept. 356/2 This decisive step opens the way for the construction of a new non-Aristotelian logic, a 'three-valued logic' as it is called. **1965** N. CHOMSKY *Aspects of Theory of Syntax* 232 Thus we can regard..gender as a three-valued..dimension. **1967** *Encycl. Philos.* VII. 118/1 With this way of reconstructing quantum mechanics, use must be made of a three-valued logic. **1974** tr. *Wertheim's Evol. & Revol.* i. 100 Three-valued prestige models were used by people who placed themselves in the middle class. **1933** Three wire mooring [in *OED Suppl.*]. **1934** J. A. SINCLAIR *Airships in Peace & War* ix. 186 Then came the three-wire system, which was first employed on the rigid airship No. 9 in 1917... To steady the bow, three wires were taken from the mooring point and attached to three bollards set in a triangle... A three-wire mooring was prepared at Pulham. **1875** *Encycl. Brit.* II. 376/1 Bows..made of three pieces..are called three-woods... Three-wood bows being made a little reflex, should retain their shape. [**1938** R. A. WHITCOMBE *Golf's no Mystery* xiii. 80 The spoon—or as it is called the No. 3 wood—is one of the golfer's greatest friends.] **1949** B. HOGAN *Power Golf* ii. 15 Three wood.. 235 [yards]. **1960** *Times* 24 June 19/2 Second shots with a three-wood and a one-iron at these two holes brought him just short of the green in each case.

three-colour (stress variable), *a.* [THREE *a.*] **1.** Utilizing or involving three distinct colours or wavelengths of light, usu. as a means of reproducing any desired colour by a combination of three primary colours in appropriate proportions. Cf. TRICHROMATIC *a.*

1893 *Jrnl. Soc. Arts* 19 May 669/1 This three-colour print, a reproduction of a chromo-lithograph. **1898, 1902** [in Dict. s.v. THREE *a.* and *sb.* III. 1 a]. **1906** [see *ADDITIVE *a.* c]. **1932** R. C. BAYLEY *Compl. Photographer* xxiv. 291 The amateur who makes his own three-colour prints. **1972** [see *PSYCHO-PHYSICAL *a.*]. **1978** PASACHOFF & KUTNER *University Astron.* iii. 55 Thousands of stars have had their colors measured with this UBV set of filters; we call the process three-color photometry... A four-color system, uvby, has ultraviolet, violet, blue and yellow filters.

2. Designating *san ts'ai* ware; also *ellipt.* as *sb.*

1933 *Burlington Mag.* Nov. 211/1 The early Ming three-colour ware. **1959, 1972** [see *SAN TS'AI].

three-corner, *a.* Add: **three-corner jack** *Austral.* = *three-cornered jack* s.v. *THREE-CORNERED *a.* 3; **three-corner-ways** (earlier example replacing quot. 1796).

1919 G. E. A. RUSSELL *Wild Life in Bushland* 32 Springing from the centre or core of each burr are three long spikes or prongs, often half an inch in length—an uninviting thing to sit upon. Most bushmen will recognise the seed—it is the Centralian-famed 'three-corner jack'. **1748** H. GLASSE *Art of Cookery* (ed. 3) ix. 199 Toast some thin Slices of Bread cut three-corner ways.

three-cornered, *a.* Add: **3. three-cornered jack** *Austral.*, the spiny burr of the annual weed, *Emex australis.*

1953 A. UPFIELD *Murder must Wait* xxv. 223 'You lie there.'..'But not on the three-cornered jacks.'.. Her husband..swept the place clean of the skin-piercing burrs.

three-decker. Add: **1.** (Earlier example.)

1792 A. YOUNG *Trav. France* 181 The bason of Toulon, with ranges of three deckers, and other large men of war.

2. a. (Earlier example.) **c.** (Earlier example.) **d.** A three-storey building. *U.S. local.*

1852 A. MOZLEY in *Christian Remembrancer* July 92 In the midst of the church stands, elaborately carved, the offensive structure of pulpit, reading-desk, and clerk's desk; in fact, a regular old three-decker in full sail westward. **1894** KIPLING in *Sat. Rev.* 14 July 44/1 The old three-decker. And the three-volume novel is doomed. **1942** BERREY & VAN DEN BARK *Amer. Thes. Slang* § 83/1 *Three-* (or more) *decker*, a building of three, or more, stories. **1961** L. MUMFORD *City in History* xv. 465 Vast wooden firetraps called three-deckers in New England, happily blessed with open-air porches. **1978** J. CARROLL *Mortal Friends* II. iii. 151 The flat, the top floor of a Southie three-decker, was large enough.

3. (Further examples, in sense 2 c.)

1926 G. ADE *Let.* 8 Sept. (1973) 110 While some of us have been building chicken coops.., Mr. Dreiser has been creating sky-scrapers. He makes the old three-decker novel look like a pamphlet. **1981** *N. & Q.* June 271/1 The widespread circulation of Evangelical tracts and sermons helped to create a sympathetic readership for the voluminous three-decker novel.

three-double, *a.* (Later examples.)

1728 E. SMITH *Compleat Housewife* (ed. 2) 128 Butter Papers three double, one white, and two brown. **1874** HARDY *Far from Madding Crowd* I. viii. 105 'And he's growed terrible crooked, too, lately,' Jacob continued, surveying his father's figure, which was rather more bowed than his own. 'Really, one may say that father there is three-double.'

three-legged, *a.* (Earlier example of *three-legged race.*)

1876 *N.Y. Times* 21 May 2/5 The three-legged race of 100 yards was won by the Brown–Hammond team.

three-masted, *a.* (In Dict. s.v. THREE-MAST *a.*) (Earlier and later examples.)

1798 *Connecticut Jrnl.* 23 May 3/1 New York... May 14. Loss of the armed three masted schooner Harmony, captain Price, who sailed on Saturday the 5th inst. from this port for Surinam. **1861** *Mitchell's Maritime Register* 28 Sept. 1241/1 On the 21st inst. was launched from the yard of Messrs. Thomas Harvey & Sons, Wivenhoe, a three-masted brigantine. **1970** E. J. MARCH *Inshore Craft* II. iii. 144 Mention should also be made of the big three-masted lugger *New Moon.*

three-master. (In Dict. s.v. THREE-MAST *a.*) (Earlier example.)

1827 F. WITTS *Diary* 26 Apr. (1978) 70 One of these ships was a three-master.

threepenny, *a.* (*sb.*) Add: **3.** *sb.* A length of rod used in basket-making.

1912 [see *long-small* s.v. *LONG *a.*[1] A. 18]. **1953** A. G. KNOCK *Willow Basket-Work* (ed. 5) 9 Three feet, Tacks;.. six feet, Threepenny.

three-piece, *a.* and *sb.* **A.** *adj.* **1.** Of a suite of furniture: comprising three separate items; freq. of a lounge suite: (usu.) comprising two armchairs and a sofa.

1908 *Sears, Roebuck Catal.* 455 Five-piece parlor suite... Three-piece parlor suite. **1952** *New Statesman* 5 July 10/1 Thankfully home, not to sink onto the centre couch of a three-piece suite. **1976** G. MOFFAT *Short Time to Live* ix. 82 The bathroom held..the usual three-piece suite. **1978** E. MALPASS *Wind brings up Rain* xi. 109 A three-piece suite in blue moquette for the front room.

2. Of a suit of clothes: comprising three separate garments; freq. of a man's suit: comprising trousers, jacket, and waistcoat.

1909 in C. W. Cunnington *Eng. Women's Clothing in Present Cent.* (1952) iii. 91 New Three Piece Suit. **1923** *Queen* 26 July p. viii, The three-piece coat-frock. **1965** F. SARGESON *Memoirs of Peon* vi. 134 Three-piece suits were the rule. **1980** *TWA Ambassador* Oct. 84/2 We try to be a little lively, just to get out of that staid, gray, three-piece-suit mold.

3. *Mus.* Of a band: comprising three instruments or players.

1939 C. R. COOPER *Designs in Scarlet* ii. 13 A three-piece string band or a full orchestra. **1959** WALLIS & BLAIR *Thunder Above* xii. 125 The band struck up again. The three-piece combination..played German dance music. **1978** M. RUSSELL *Daylight Robbery* i. 20 The assortment of dance-floor routines that were accompanying the pulsation of a three-piece Latin-American group.

B. *sb.* **1.** A three-piece suit.

1931 W. HOLTBY *Poor Caroline* 18 Oh, Mums, I *must* show you my new blue three-piece. **1982** BARR & YORK *Official Sloane Ranger Handbk.* 42/1 There are a few basic lines that continue practically for ever, like..the basic City three-piece.

2. A three-piece suite.

1966 G. BURNETT *Dead Account* iv. 27 The room looked more expensive..a grey/red three-piece that wouldn't show much change out of two hundred guineas. **1977** *Times* 24 Dec. 16/6 What suburban child is going to believe that..Santa would be allowed..to put his great sooty footmarks all over the Dralon three piece and the wall to wall?

Hence **three-piecer** *U.S.*, a three-piece suit.

1964 *N.Y. Post* 9 Nov. 13 Orlon® cardigan three-piecer a-glitter with trim. **1976** *Billings* (Montana) *Gaz.* 20 June 5-E (Advt.), Our all polyester knit shirt is great for leisure suits, a three piecer, even tucked into a pair of casual pants.

three-point, *a.* **1.** Marked with three points; *spec.* designating a grade of point blanket (see *POINT *sb.*[1] B. 14).

1855 [see *point blanket* s.v. *POINT *sb.*[1] B. 14]. **1921** [see *POINT *sb.*[1] A. 32]. **1948** *Beaver* June 21/2 The simple voyageur Leger lost only a three-point blanket..a portage strap, a pair of French shoes.

2. At three points; with contact or support at three points; *spec.* of an aircraft landing: in which all three wheels, or two wheels and the tail skid, touch the ground simultaneously.

1909 *Westm. Gaz.* 9 Nov. 5/1 What is actually achieved by the Rolls-Royce plan is to make a three-point suspension without complication. **1918** R. FROST *Let.* 24 Oct. (1972) 39 You have to learn to make a 'three-point landing' that is on your two wheels and skid simultaneously. **1953** C. A. LINDBERGH *Spirit of St. Louis* II. vi. 266 Boy, *he* always makes 'em three-point! **1960** *Farmer & Stockbreeder* 15 Mar. 103 It connects to any modern tractor by the three-point hitch..and the category shaft. **1969** *Gloss. Terms Dentistry* (*B.S.I.*) 78 *Three-point contact*, a term used to indicate that when the jaws are in eccentric position there is a minimum of three points of occlusal contact, as widely spaced as possible. **1971** *Power Farming* Mar. 15/4 Hitching up an implement to the three-point-linkage could be both difficult and dangerous. **1977** *New Yorker* 4 July 42/1 He came in on final, flared, and made a three-point full-stall landing.

3. In surveying, navigation, etc.: involving the measurement of three known points to determine one's position.

1900 H. M. WILSON *Topographic Surveying* ix. 185 The three-point problem calls for the finding of distances from an unknown and occupied point to three others whose relative positions and distances are known. **1960** E. L. DELMAR-MORGAN *Cruising Yacht Equipment & Navigation* 18 The best..fix obtainable in coastal navigation is the Three-Point Fix... Here three identified objects are required, and either the sextant is used to measure the angles or, less accurately, by [*sic*] compass bearings.

4. *three-point turn*, a method of turning a vehicle round in a narrow space, whereby the vehicle moves in three arcs, forwards, backwards, then forwards again.

1957 C. SMITH *Case of Torches* xiii. 152, I switched on the motor..and did a three-point turn. **1976** 'Z. STONE' *Modigliani Scandal* III. i. 114 He did a three-point turn on the narrow road.

Hence **three-pointer,** (*a*) a three-point landing; (*b*) a three-point turn.

1932 D. GARNETT *Rabbit in Air* III. 106 This time the wind took off the extra height just as planned and with an almost dead machine made a perfect three-pointer. **1965** P. M. HUBBARD *Hive of Glass* i. 12, I did a copy-book three-pointer, drove back to the main street. **1976** B. LECOMBER *Dead Weight* i. 21 The Gemini rumbles on to the ground in a neat three-pointer.

three-quarter, -quarters, *sb.*, *a.*, and *advb. phr.* Add: **B.** as *adj.* **b.** (*b*) For '(Also to a lady's coat of similar length.)' read 'Also of a coat, sleeve, etc.: (having) three-fourths of the normal length.' (Further examples.)

1919 in C. W. Cunnington *Eng. Women's Clothing in Present Cent.* (1952) 156 The three-quarter coat is the latest rage. **1940** GRAVES & HODGE *Long Week-End* xvi. 280 Swagger coats..were of three-quarter length. **1943** P. CHEYNEY *You can always Duck* v. 85 She is wearin'.. a loose three-quarter length coat. **1960** *Woman's Own* 19 Mar. 42/3 Three-quarter sleeve overblouse. **1960** *News Chron.* 4 Apr. 6/1 The collar sits well away from the face; the sleeves are definitely three-quarter. **1960** *Harper's Bazaar* Aug. 8/2 A brief tartan jacket..which has..three-quarter length sleeves. *Ibid.* Oct. 119 A three-quarter coat in oatmeal tweed. **1972** A. PRICE *Col. Butler's Wolf* xi. 119 A reversible three-quarter length overcoat.

D. three-quarter bed, a bed intermediate in width between a single and a double bed; **three-quarter line** *Rugby Football*, the row of three-quarter backs aligned (and usu. angled back) across the field, esp. at a set-piece; **three-quarter veneer** *Dentistry* = *partial veneer* s.v. *PARTIAL *a.* 3 i.

1919 L. R. BALDERSTON *Housewifery* vii. 196 *Size of Bedspreads*..80 in. × 100 in.—three-quarter bed. **1978** *Lancashire Life* Oct. 141/2 The old four foot wide 'three-quarter' bed—known in the trade as a 'landlady's double' because seaside landladies used it to get two people into what should have been a single room—is rarely seen nowadays. **1960** E. S. & W. J. HIGHAM *High Speed Rugby* vii. 58 The scrum-half's first and foremost duty is to feed the three-quarter-line. **1976** *Eastern Even. News* (Norwich) 9 Dec. 19/8 Norfolk took an early lead when the ball was quickly fed along the three-quarter line to put Hopkins over for a try. **1924** J. F. HOVESTAD *Pract. Dental Porcelains* xii. 110 (*heading*) The partial coping or the all porcelain three-quarter veneer crown. **1963** J. OSBORNE *Dental Mechanics* (ed. 5) xxiii. 415 Three-quarter or partial veneer crowns. Such crowns are usually employed as bridge retainers.

threescore, *a.* (*sb.*) (Further examples, esp. in phr. *threescore* (*years*) *and ten.*)

1850 N. HAWTHORNE *Scarlet Letter* 22 The brave soldier had already numbered, nearly or quite, his threescore years and ten. **1896** A. E. HOUSMAN *Shropshire Lad* 3 Now of my threescore years and ten, Twenty will not come again. **1922** JOYCE *Ulysses* 683 Evermoving from immeasurably remote eons to infinitely remote futures in comparison with which the years, threescore and ten, of allotted human life formed a parenthesis of infinitesimal brevity. **1977** *Drive* Mar.–Apr. 44/3 Cyril shed..more than threescore pounds of weight from his celebrated 28-stone frame. **1977** *Chicago Tribune Mag.* 2 Oct. 49/1 Those of us who have attained 'three score years and ten' more often now look backward with nostalgia, remembering the years when we were younger.

threesome, *sb.* and *a.* (*adv.*) Restrict 'Chiefly *Sc.*' to sense B and add: **A.** *sb.* **a.** (Further examples.)

1926 [see *FOURSOME *sb.* 2]. **1951** [see *GAY *a.* 2 c]. **1959** *Times Lit. Suppl.* 5 June 333/2 The stresses and strains of this uneasy threesome are subtly conveyed. **1972** *Screw* 12 June 33/1 (Advt.), Especially well endowed & very fond of threesomes (with couples or 2 women). **1977** *Gay News* 24 Mar. 14/4 These may include threesomes in which one or both partners bring home a person who is shared in bed. **1977** *New Yorker* 8 Aug. 57/1 A number of them were looking down from the Turnberry Hotel at the Ailsa course, on which the last threesomes were finishing their rounds. **1980** *TWA Ambassador* Oct. 92/1 Robbins's first and better novel, *Another Roadside Attraction* (praised by an odd threesome: Lawrence Ferlinghetti, Graham Greene and Thomas Pynchon). **1981** M. MCMULLEN *Other Shoe* (1982) ii. 22 Justin, why don't you squire Meg?..Threesomes are awkward.

b. A game of golf in which one person plays against two opponents.

1901 *Rules of Golf* 5 A single player may play against two, when the match is called 'a threesome'. **1931** W. MARTYN *Scarlett Murder* iv. 48, I was playing a threesome against Sir Griffith Wadham and Lord Berrington.

three-way, *a.* Add: Also, involving three participants; *three-way mirror*, one with three panels to provide a view from three different angles, and often forming part of a dressing-table suite.

1961 WEBSTER s.v., A three-way profit split, a three-way play-off. **1964** *McCall's Sewing* v. 60/2 If you can arrange a three-way mirror it will be even better. **1967**

Economist 29 Apr. 459/1 The slogan of 'three-way alliances' was coined [in China] three months ago. **1978** *Lancashire Life* Oct. 143/2 (*caption*) With a threeway mirror, concealed lighting and a matching stool it is about £154. **1979** *Tucson* (Arizona) *Citizen* 20 Sept. 9D/1 Billie Harper won the second flight with 38, followed by a three-way tie at 41 between Ann Pearsall, Lori Emery and Mary Stewart. **1983** *Daily Tel.* 27 Oct. 21/2 A three-way merger among property groups could result in a new company with combined assets of around £700 million.

b. Of a loudspeaker: having three separate drive units for different frequency ranges.

1960 C. BROWN *Introd. Hi-Fi* iv. 91 Small horn-loaded diaphragm loudspeakers are used in some two- and three-way systems of the direct radiator type (*i.e.* all units facing the listener). **1972** *N.Y. Times* 3 Nov. 10/4 (Advt.), One of the finest 3-way speaker systems available. ..Contains a 10″ woofer, 5″ direct radiating mid-range element and Sonodome ultra-tweeter.

threitol (þrī·itǫl). *Chem.* [f. *THRE(OSE + *-ITOL.] A crystalline tetrahydroxy alcohol, $HOCH_2(CHOH)_2CH_2OH$, formed by the reduction of threose.

1935 *Jrnl. Amer. Chem. Soc.* LVII. 2262/2 Consistency also strongly urges limiting the term 'erythritol' to the natural inactive alcohol.., and using the terms '*d*-threitol' (rotating +4·33° in water) and '*l*-threitol' (rotating −4·4° in water) for the active tetritols derived, respectively, from the two threoses. **1948** *Biochem. Jrnl.* XLII. 330/1 The new product is apparently identical with the substance synthesized by Maquenne from natural xylose and described under the name of '*l*-erythritol'. The name was later changed to '*d*-erythritol' in accordance with the Rosanoff convention for sugars, but recently it has been thought advisable to change the name to D-threitol to relate it more closely to the tetrose threose. **1960** *Ibid.* LXXVII. 272/1 Preparations are given for L-threitol and *meso*erythritol. **1975** *Nature* 11 Dec. 519/1 In adult tenebrionid beetles..an unusual combination of two polyhydric alcohols, sorbitol and threitol, is associated with the ability to tolerate prolonged freezing to at least −50°C. The occurrence of threitol is of particular interest, since this compound has not previously been found in nature.

threne. (Later example.)

1960 R. EBERHART *Coll. Poems 1930–60* 14 The perfect lament, and threne of sorrow's throat.

threonine (þrī·onīn). *Biochem.* [f. *THREO(SE + *-n-* + -INE[5].] A natural amino-acid, α-amino-β-hydroxy-butyric acid, $C_4H_9NO_3$, considered essential for growth and for maintenance of the nitrogen equilibrium in adults.

1936 MEYER & ROSE in *Jrnl. Biol. Chem.* CXV. 727 It is proposed that henceforth natural α-amino-β-hydroxy-*n*-butyric acid be known as d(−)-threonine, inasmuch as it possesses a spatial configuration analogous to that of *d*(−)-threose. **1956** [see *PLASMA 6 b]. **1974** *Nature* 19 Apr. 643/2 Eight essential amino acids—[including]..valine, threonine, phenylalanine and tryptophan—are required by human adults.

threose (þrī·ōᵘz). *Chem.* [a. G. *threose* (O. Ruff 1901, in *Ber. d. Deut. Chem. Ges.* XXXIV. 1364), f. *erythrose* *ERYTHROSE by omission and transposition of letters.] A tetrose sugar, $CHO{\cdot}[CH(OH)]_2{\cdot}CH_2OH$, isolated as a hygroscopic solid and existing in two molecular configurations; it differs from erythrose in having the hydroxyl groups on the second and third carbon atoms on opposite sides of the carbon chain.

1901 *Jrnl. Chem. Soc.* LXXX. I. 449 The calcium salt [of *l*-xylonic acid]..was then oxidised with hydrogen peroxide and ferric acetate to *l*-threose. **1963** [see *ERYTHROSE]. **1982** T. W. G. SOLOMONS *Fund. of Org. Chem.* xix. 709 One cyanohydrin ultimately yields D-(−)-erythrose and the other yields D-(−)-threose.

threshold, *sb.* Add: Now also with pronunc. (þre·ʃhōᵘld). **2. a.** Also, in an airfield: the beginning of the landing area on a runway. Also *attrib.*

1937 *Jrnl. R. Aeronaut. Soc.* XLI. 295 Sites..for threshold lighting and other signal apparatus required to assist the pilot. **1960** *Guide Civil Land Aerodrome Lighting* (*B.S.I.*) 15 A pilot needs to be given a clear indication of the runway threshold and the addition of wingbars, composed of green lights, is recommended to make the threshold more conspicuous in poor visibility.

c. (i) Also in *Physiol.* and more widely: the limit below which a stimulus is not perceptible; the magnitude or intensity of a stimulus which has to be exceeded for it to produce a certain response. (ii) The magnitude or intensity that must be exceeded for a certain reaction or phenomenon to occur.

1902 J. M. BALDWIN *Dict. Philos. & Psychol.* II. 696/2 The least noticeable difference in sensation is called the threshold of discrimination or difference. **1919** W. D. HALLIBURTON *Handbk. Physiol.* (ed. 14) lii. 767 That strength of stimulus which just suffices to evoke a sensation is called..its absolute threshold. **1922** *Electr. Communication* I. I. 45/1 Articulation tests were made upon the..telephone system..when it was set to deliver various intensities from the threshold of audibility to very large values. **1930** *City Noise* (N.Y. Noise Abatement Commission) 34 This means decibels above the threshold of hearing. **1931** *Brit. Jrnl. Psychol.* Jan. 285 There is a definite 'colourless interval' between the 'general threshold', or the intensity which just suffices to produce a sensation of light, and the 'specific threshold', or the intensity at which colour is just noticeable. **1936** G. K. ZIPF *Psycho-Biol. of Lang.* 113 Every phoneme must also have a lower threshold below which it cannot pass without strengthening. **1938** *Ann. Reg. 1937* 346 The view [was] advanced that spontaneous mutations are mono-molecular reactions produced by thermal agitation when this oversteps the energy threshold of the chemical bonds. **1941** in M. Gowing *Britain & Atomic Energy 1939–1945* (1964) 403 From..the fact that [uranium] 238 does not give fission with slow neutrons, it is clear that the jump at 1 MeV represents the threshold of 238. The fission which takes place with neutrons of energy less than 1 MeV must therefore be ascribed to 235. **1948** P. M. MORSE *Vibration & Sound* (ed. 2) vi. 227 The upper contour is the threshold of pain, above which the sensation is more of pain than of sound (and the result is more or less damaging to the ear). **1949** KOESTLER *Insight & Outlook* xv. 207 Heightening the threshold of some sensory receptors and lowering the threshold of others. **1949** S. C. ROTHMANN *Constructive Uses Atomic Energy* 205 The Geiger threshold of a radiation counter tube is the lowest operating voltage at which the charge transferred per isolated count is substantially independent of the nature of the initial ionizing event. **1950** *Gloss. Aeronaut. Terms* (*B.S.I.*) I. 25 *Cruising threshold*, the equivalent air speed giving the lowest comfortable continuous cruising speed. **1955** J. A. WHEELER in W. Pauli *Niels Bohr* 166 A photofission threshold of 5·15 MeV..goes with a half life against spontaneous fission of the order of $10^{15.8}$ years. **1958** *Oxford Univ. Gaz.* 27 Jan. 524/2 (*heading*) Non-random sequences in visual threshold experiments. **1959** *Sunday Times* 5 July 8/6 The absence of a lower threshold for the production of mutations by radiation. **1962** A. NISBETT *Technique Sound Studio* v. 98 At 1,000 c/s the threshold of pain is 110 dB or more above the threshold of hearing. **1963** B. FOZARD *Instrumentation Nucl. Reactors* v. 46 The scaling circuit which is used to count the pulses from the G.M. tube has some more or less well defined 'threshold', *i.e.* it accepts only those pulses which exceed a certain amplitude. **1965** *Proc. R. Soc.* B. CLXI. 338 While a climatic change in one area may have produced conditions very favourable for a new species, in another area the same climatic change may have produced conditions only just above the critical physiological thresholds for the existence of that species. **1965** W. LAMB *Posture & Gesture* iii. 44 There has been a lot of investigation of the threshold of fatigue in athletics and the type of training required to push this threshold back is well understood. **1972** J. MOSEDALE *Football* ix. 124 Performances like Nevers' demonstrates [*sic*] the high threshold of pain common to many athletes. **1973** *Times* 19 Oct. 7/8 A GP who might only see one case of child abuse a year might not have as low a threshold of suspicion as I have. **1983** *Sci. Amer.* Jan. 98/2 Above a certain threshold, known as the critical density, the expansion [of the universe] will eventually cease and contraction will begin.

(iii) In contexts of wages and taxation, in which wage or tax increases become due or obligatory when some predetermined conditions are fulfilled (esp. above a specified point on a graduated scale). Also in more general use in contexts of work. Freq. *attrib.*

1967 L. B. ARCHER in Wills & Yearsley *Handbk. Managem. Technol.* 131 Usually there is a threshold between 'good enough' and 'not good enough' in respect of each objective, below which a design proposal would not be acceptable. **1971** *Guardian* 7 Sept. 11/2 Mr [Tom] Jackson..argued in favour of a single threshold claim on behalf of all public employees. **1972** *Observer* 13 Aug. 10/8 Threshold cost of living agreements could make things much happier so long as the threshold is put fairly high and/or there is a big reduction in the effective basic level of wage settlements. **1974** *Ann. Reg. 1973* 14 The main features of the incomes plan [of Mr. Edward Heath] were..threshold payments of a maximum of 40p. a week if the retail price index were to rise by 7 per cent [etc.]. **1976** [see *tax threshold* s.v. *TAX *sb.*[1] 7 b]. **1979** H. WILSON *Final Term* ii. 42 Viewed with hindsight the thresholds were a disastrous mistake. That does not in fact mean that Mr Heath had been wrong to introduce them in October 1973. **1980** J. BOYD-CARPENTER *Way of Life* xiii. 169 The alternative relief was to make a big increase in the level of the 'Thresholds', that is to say the point on the income scale at which people became liable to tax.

3. b. (Having a value or intensity) equal to that of a threshold (sense 2 c in Dict. and Suppl.).

1906 J. R. MURLIN tr. *Tigerstedt's Text-bk. Human Physiol.* xvi. 455 In order that an external stimulus may produce a sensation, it must exceed a certain lower limit of strength, which is called, after Herbart, the threshold value of the stimulus. **1921** J. MILLS *Within Atom* 215 *Threshold frequency*, the minimum frequency of radiation which will produce photo-electric effects. **1926** J. S. HUXLEY *Ess. Pop. Sci.* 199 It is needful, not merely that some thyroid secretion should be circulating in the body, but that it should reach a certain definite concentration, a certain 'threshold value'. **1941** in M. Gowing *Britain & Atomic Energy 1939–45* (1964) 400 Neutrons of less than a certain threshold energy..do not cause fission of ^{238}U. **1959** *Listener* 26 Nov. 929/1 It is possible that the radiation level has to exceed a critical or threshold value before any genetical effects arise. **1964** W. G. SMITH *Allergy & Tissue Metabolism* ii. 23 The tissue response would depend upon the number of susceptible cells..reached by a threshold concentration of histamine. **1971** J. H. SMITH *Digital Logic* iv. 69 The device is actuated when the input signal crosses a certain 'threshold' voltage. **1978** J. PAXTON *Dict. European Econ. Community* (rev. ed.) 46 Imports were kept up to minimum, or threshold, prices by means of variable import levies.

c. Electronics. *threshold device, element,* etc.: a circuit element having one output and a number of inputs, each of which accepts a binary signal and multiplies it by some factor; the output is 0 or 1 depending on whether or not the sum of the resulting quantities is less than a certain threshold value; *threshold function*, a Boolean function that can be realized by such an element; *threshold logic, switching* (based on such elements).

1960 *IRE Trans. Electronic Computers* IX. 122/1 Another useful logical two-state device is a threshold element. **1960** *Proc. IRE* XLVIII. 1335/3 The increasing use of threshold devices such as magnetic cores and parametrons. **1961** *IRE Trans. Electronic Computers* X. 6/1 Linearly separable switching functions..have been studied under different names, such as..linear-input logic, threshold logic, majority logic, and voting logic. *Ibid.* 798/2 Elementary threshold functions, *i.e.*, functions that can be implemented by a single threshold circuit, are first characterized for the cases of 2, 3, and 4 variables. **1962** *Proc. Internat. Federation Information Processing Congr.* 757/1 A threshold gate determines its output in two steps: a linear summation followed by a discrimination. **1964** H. C. TORNG *Introd. Logical Design of Switching Systems* viii. 133 Threshold switching devices are..extensively used in pattern recognition systems and perception-like automata. **1970** Z. KOHAVI *Switching & Finite Automata Theory* vii. 183 One of the limitations of threshold logic is its sensitivity to variations in circuit parameters. **1975** N. N. BISWAS *Introd. Logic & Switching Theory* vii. 183 In many cases where the NAND or NOR realizations may require a number of gates, the threshold logic may realize the function by only one gate. **1978** S. C. LEE *Mod. Switching Theory* iv. 117 As another simple example of a threshold function, consider $f(x_1, x_2, x_3) = x_1x_2 + x_3$.

threshold (þre·ʃhōᵘld), *v.* [f. the sb.] *trans.* To alter (an image) by reproducing it in two tones only, each part being dark or light according as the original is darker or lighter than some chosen threshold shade. Hence **thre·sholding** *vbl. sb.*

1968 *Brit. Med. Bull.* XXIV. 262/2 One..comes across objects which have obviously been thresholded at too low or too high a level, resulting in incorrect segmentation. *Ibid.*, Simple thresholding (setting a limit above which everything is considered to be picture and below which everything is considered to be background) seems to work out quite well in coarse density-resolution scanners. **1976** *Physics Bull.* Sept. 381/3 Figure 2 shows the result of magnifying and electronically thresholding a small portion of a LANDSAT infrared image of the UK. **1983** *What's New in Computing* Jan. 16/2 The software modules comprise such algorithms as image thresholding, edge enhancement, [etc.].

thribble, thrible (þri·b'l), dial. var. of TREBLE *sb., a.* and *adv., v.* Also *spec.* in oil drilling (see quots. 1932, 1975).

1829 J. HUNTER *Hallamshire Gloss.* 90 *Thribble*, treble. **1877** *Wide Awake* IV. 348/2 O, let the corn swell till it's three times as bulky as it was in the beginning; that's that's [*sic*] we call 'thribbling'. **1904** E. NESBIT *Phoenix & Carpet* i. 1 The man at the shop said they were worth thribble the money. **1932** *Amer. Speech* VII. 271 *Thrible* .., a *stand* of three joints of pipe. *Thrible-board*.., a platform in the derrick at the height of a *thrible*. **1975** J. BLACK *Oil* II. ii. 158 Drill pipe came in thirty-foot lengths. These were screwed into sixty- or ninety-foot segments, known to oil field workers as 'doubles' or 'thribbles'.

thrice-cock (þrəi·skǫk). *dial.* [f. var. THRUSH[1] + COCK *sb.*[1] 9 b.] = MISSEL-THRUSH; cf. *storm-cock* s.v. STORM *sb.* 6 e.

1819 M. EDGEWORTH *Let.* 26 Jan. (1971) 160 The Thrice-Cock..is the largest kind of thrush. **1913** H. K. SWANN *Dict. Eng. & Folk-Names Brit. Birds* 236 Thrice Cock. A Midland and North of England name for the Mistle-thrush. **1965** *Jrnl. Lancs. Dial. Soc.* XIV. 9 Mistle Thrush... Thricecock: Oldham. Cf. Fieldfare.

thrift, *sb.*[1] Add: **3. b.** *U.S.* A savings and loan association.

1981 *Economist* 24 Jan. 28/1 This new charter for the thrifts, as they are called, has not been welcomed by all of them. **1982** *Sunday Sun-Times* (Chicago) 12 Sept. 65 In an effort to keep the funds, banks and thrifts will fire a fusillade of advertising.

5. thrift industry *U.S.*, savings and loan associations as a whole; **thrift institution** *U.S.*, a savings and loan association; **thrift shop** chiefly *U.S.*, **thrift store** *U.S.*, a shop at which second-hand goods (esp. clothes) are sold, usu. in aid of charity.

1981 *Financial Rev.* (Australia) 1 May 18 When higher interest rates were paid, the thrift industry—building societies, savings banks, credit unions—tended to lose funds to competing institutions. **1982** *Times* 22 May 13/3 The United States House of Representatives..voted to shore up ailing thrift institutions. **1947** S. J. PERELMAN *Westward Ha!* (1949) xii. 153 A mound of shawls, brocades, bracelets, necklaces, purses, fans, and bric-a-brac resembling the contents of a thrift shop. **1976** *Eastern Even. News* (Norwich) 9 Dec. 2/5 Mums and toddlers and thrift shop, 76, Cadge Road, Community House, 2–4. **1972** T. ARDIES *This Suitcase* ix. 85 Someone had probably gone to thrift stores to put together his wardrobe... Even his socks were the wrong size.

thrift, *sb.*[2] (Later example.)

1969 G. E. EVANS *Farm & Village* xiv. 150 The *mill-bill*—it's a kind of steel pick or bill mounted in a *thrift* or handle, made of wych-elm or some other suitable wood.

thriftful (þri·ftfŭl), *a. rare.* [f. THRIFT *sb.*[1] + -FUL.] Marked by frugality or careful expenditure, thrifty.

1933 V. McNABB *Nazareth or Social Chaos* 75 If..only a country organization is naturally thriftful, it would seem that a town-organization will..end with a famine of real wealth. **1968** P. FALVURY *Poems Old & New* 130 No thriftful scrutiny was drawn When, ere creation's mighty dawn, Thou plannedst man's abode.

thrill, *sb.*[3] Add: **1. b.** Also, a thrilling experience or incident.

1936 G. B. SHAW *Simpleton Unexpected Isles* I. 48 *The Clergyman*: Yes: I know I should have explained that. But she let me kiss her. *Mrs Hyering*: That must have been a thrill, Mr Hammingtap. Life came to you that time, didn't it? **1947** *Sporting Mirror* 7 Nov. 8/1, I must add that in actual fact there was not much scientific football. But the dizzy paced thrills made up for that. **1951** R. CAMPBELL *Light on Dark Horse* ii. 37 To be driven round in these new horse-less machines was a thrill of which we never tired in those days. **1964** in Hamblett & Deverson *Generation X* 32 Going to a party and being rowdy, dancing to very loud music,..being driven in a very fast car, are all great thrills.

3. a. *Comb.*, as *thrill-seeker*. **b.** *attrib.* passing into *adj.*, of a crime: committed purely for the sake of the excitement experienced in carrying it out, as *thrill hold-up, killing, murder*.

1928 *Daily Tel.* 30 Oct. 11/5 A long series of 'thrill' hold-ups [at Atlanta, Georgia]..is cleared up here with the arrest of two Oglethorpe University students. The youthful thrill-seekers are George Harsh and James Galogly, both members of good families. **1978** LAROSA & TANENBAUM *Random Factor* (1979) xi. 172 Billy Krieg died because he was part in a series of thrill killings. **1973** R. C. DENNIS *Sweat of Fear* xiii. 98 The police think it was a thrill murder. Do you feel such a person can be wholly sane? **1928** Thrill-seeker [see *thrill hold-up* above]. **1967** W. & J. BREEDLOVE *Swinging Set* xii. 146 A variety of sexual thrill-seekers.

thrill, *v.*[1] Add: **II. 5.** Also as *pa. pple.*, extremely pleased or delighted (*colloq.*).

1908 E. F. BENSON *Climber* vii. 98 Though she would not have dreamed of doing what Elizabeth had done and looked over the letter, she could not but be thrilled with the fact that there were four pages. **1964** in Hamblett & Deverson *Generation X* 153, I adore Nureyev. When he danced on the Palladium show on telly I was thrilled to bits. **1976** A. MILLER *Inside Outside* iv. 40 Naturally I was thrilled to bits and accepted with alacrity.

c. Now often const. *to*.

1935 *Motion Picture* Nov. 29/2 If you live within range of a national radio network, you've thrilled to their voices. **1940** J. BUCHAN *Memory Hold-the-Door* ii. 42 Stevenson..thrilled as we did to those antecedents—the lights and glooms of Scottish history. **1952** T. PYLES *Words & Ways Amer. Eng.* ii. 34 Generations of European children have thrilled to the novels of J. F. Cooper.

thriller. Add: (Examples in general use.) Also *spec.* applied to a film.

1934 C. LAMBERT *Music Ho!* v. 301 The opera *Wozzek* is on paper a soberly planned symphony, but in performance a 'thriller' of the most theatrical order. **1950** *Sport* 24–30 Mar. 3/2 That was in 1946 when the 'Bishops' were beaten 3–2 by Barnet in a Stamford Bridge thriller. **1968** M. RICHLER in R. Weaver *Canad. Short Stories* 2nd Ser. 186 'My mother made me promise that one day I would make a picture in Israel.' 'Did she specify a sexy thriller?' **1976** *New Yorker* 16 Feb. 54/3 The thriller of the afternoon occurred when Redundancy came up in the last stride to beat Summertime Promise by a nose in the Columbiana Handicap.

b. *Comb.*, as *thriller-writer, -writing*.

1925 J. M. ROBERTSON *Mr. Shaw & 'The Maid'* ix. 85 Villains there are in plenty, though those shaped by the thriller-writers are apt to be improbable. **1983** *Listener* 20 Jan. 23/3 The pseudonymous A. J. Quinnell belongs to the generation of good thriller-writers who specialised in South-East Asia. **1958** *Times Lit. Suppl.* 17 Jan. 33/2 It is a fair guess that thriller-writing led to his first interest in the precious stones which are the lure for so many crimes of real life.

Hence **thri·llerdom** [-DOM], the world of thrillers or exciting, sensational novels; **thri·llerish** *a.* [-ISH[1]], suggestive of such a novel.

1922 *John o' London's* 4 Jan. 18/2 The first three-quarters of the play were so good anyway, simply on the level of off-beat thrillerdom. **1957** *Times Lit. Suppl.* 28 June 395/1 When, in the 1930s, one of his best novels, *La Condition Humaine*, was translated under the thrillerish title of *Storm in Shanghai*, many young people must have opened it in the hope that they were going to read a thriller.

thrillingly, *adv.* (Earlier example.)

a **1822** SHELLEY *Posthum. Poems* (1824) 320 The liquid voice Of pipes, that fills the clear air thrillingly.

thrilly, *a.* Delete *rare* and add further examples.

1924 R. FROST *New Hampshire* 68 A likeness to surprise the thrilly tourist. **1947** *Sun* (Baltimore) 2 Jan. 13/7 The thrilly spot was at Pasadena where the Rose Bowl job was unfolded for the fans. **1967** *Listener* 16 Feb. 239/2 It [*sc.* a story by Conan Doyle] was a chilly, thrilly piece not at all in the Holmes tradition.

thrin, *sb.* (Earlier example.)

1838 THOREAU *Jrnl.* 14 June (1949) I. 51 Truth, Goodness, Beauty,—those celestial thrins.

thrip, *sb.* (Earlier U.S. example.)

1834 W. G. SIMMS *Guy Rivers* II. 108 Whom he rewarded with a *thrip* (the smallest silver coin known in the southern currency—the five cent issue excepted).

thrive, *v.* Add: **1, 2.** Freq. const. *on*.

c **1862** E. DICKINSON *Poems* (1955) II. 403 The Hemlock's nature thrives—on cold. **1907** [see sense 1 b in Dict.]. **1930** G. B. SHAW *Apple Cart* p. xxv, The armament firms thrive on war; the glaziers gain by broken windows. **1940** J. BUCHAN *Memory Hold-the-Door* iii. 84, I throve on a diet of oatmeal, mutton and strong tea. **1961** J. HELLER *Catch-22* (1962) ix. 83 He thrived on good wit and stimulating intellectual conversation. **1972** *Sci. Amer.* Aug. 73/1 Patient rapport and cooperation thrived on specific instructions.

throat, *sb.* Add: **I. 2. b.** A sore throat. *colloq.*

1885 A. EDWARDES *Girton Girl* I. iii. 68 That reasonless creature..has one of her throats again, and I did so want her to take some of my globules. **1915** LD. FISHER *Let.* 2 Apr. in M. Gilbert *Winston S. Churchill* (1972) III. Compan. I. 764, I thought I had a throat coming on but drastic measures have relieved it. **1979** M. SOAMES *Clementine Churchill* xiii. 201 In the last year she had been subject to 'throats' and coughs.

3. a. *to jump down one's throat*, substitute for def.: † (*a*) to be excessively attentive to one; also, to accept one with alacrity as prospective husband (*obs.*); (*b*) to reprimand or contradict one fiercely; (earlier and later examples).

1871 *Monthly Packet* Sept. 287 The small boat held only three... 'Just as well,' Hugh said... 'We don't want *all* to jump down her throat in a moment.' **1879** TROLLOPE *Cousin Henry* I. iii. 52 Was she to jump down your throat when you asked her? **1916** E. F. BENSON *David Blaize* xi. 215 He simply jumped down my throat the other day in your defence. **1940** 'N. BLAKE' *Malice in Wonderland* I. vii. 88 There's no need to jump down my throat. I was only trying to be helpful.

d. *to be at each other's throats*, to quarrel violently; *to have* (*got*) *the game* or *it by the throat* (Austral. slang), to have the situation under control.

1947 J. MORRISON *Sailors belong Ships* 15 We're sailors, see? Two sailors. We got the game by the throat. **1949** D. M. DAVIN *Roads from Home* I. i. 21 'The old fellow's gone at last.' 'You don't say.' 'Yes, and a hard fight he made of it, they say, with the sons hardly waiting for him to go before they were at one another's throats over who was to have his leavings.' **1960** R. TULLIPAN *Follow the Sun* 105 'Think we'll get it done to-day?' 'Can't miss... We have it by the throat now all right.' **1978** I. B. SINGER *Shosha* 265 The women are at each other's throats.

8. c. *throat-clearing* sb. (later examples); *throat-catching* adj. **d. throat-mane,** a growth of hair on the front of an animal's neck; **throat microphone,** (*colloq.*) **mike,** a microphone attached to a speaker's throat and actuated directly by his larynx.

1958 *Times Lit. Suppl.* 1 Aug. 438/4 Everything about Happy Knoll that inspires such back-slapping, throat-catching loyalty in its members. **1958** B. HAMILTON *Too Much of Water* iv. 80 Tremendous expectorations and shattering throat-clearings. **1973** T. PYNCHON *Gravity's Rainbow* I. 31 Relaxation, chairs squeaking, sighs and throatclearings. **1908** H. JOHNSTON *George Grenfell & Congo* II. xxiv. 618 The larger, taller domestic sheep of East and South Africa..changes its throat-mane into a dewlap. **1948** A. L. RAND *Mammals Eastern Rockies* 213 Mountain caribou... Neck greyish brown with a small white throat mane. **1945** N. M. COOKE *Electronics Dict.* 391 Throat microphone. **1972** K. BENTON *Spy in Chancery* i. 13 He began to talk quietly through his throat microphone, which connected with a transmitter in his pocket. **1965** P. O'DONNELL *Modesty Blaise* xvi. 170 The sensitive throat-mike would pick up the vibration of his vocal chords and relay them.

throat, *v.* **1.** Delete † *Obs.* and add later examples.

1908 A. S. M. HUTCHINSON *Once aboard Lugger* v. iii. 304 'Barley water!' Mr. Marrapit throated. 'Barley water!' **1929** S. LESLIE *Anglo-Catholic* ix. 116 Music was being throated from a reed organ.

throat-cutting, *vbl. sb.* Add: Also *fig.*, mutually destructive competition in trade. Cf. *to cut one another's throats* s.v. THROAT *sb.* 3 d.

1888 E. BELLAMY *Looking Backward* xxii. 323 Your contemporaries, with their mutual throat-cutting, knew very well what they were at. **1931** L. STEFFENS *Autobiogr.* II. III. xxxv. 609 It was not exactly a pool, but there had been a lot of throat-cutting in the trade; the competitive bidding had cut prices down till no man could make any profit.

throater. (Earlier example.)

1846 *Knickerbocker* XXVII. 511 The 'throater', the 'header', the 'splitter' take stations at the speedily-erected table.

throa·tful. [f. THROAT *sb.* + -FUL.] As much as the throat can hold at once.

1920 D. H. LAWRENCE *Lost Girl* vii. 139 Geoffrey gulped beer in large throatfuls.

throb, *v.* **3.** (Further example.)

1939 T. S. ELIOT *Family Reunion* I. ii. 59 The cold spring now is the time For the ache in the moving root.. The slow flow throbbing the trunk.

throbber (þrǫ·bəɹ). *rare.* [f. THROB *v.* + -ER[1].] A person or thing that throbs.

1890 G. MEREDITH *Let.* 10 Jan. (1970) II. 988 How glad is your poet that he secured his forgiveness before the Voice was..sharpened to hush the Thousands, and whip or curb their hearts. Else—but this poor throbber would have broken. **1934** WEBSTER, *Throbber*,..one who or that which throbs; esp., *Colloq.*, one whose emotions are easily moved. **1983** *Maledicta 1982* VI. 23 *Erection*,..throbber.

Thro:gmo·rton Street. The name of the street in the City of London where the Stock Exchange is located, used allusively for the Stock Exchange or its members.

1900 A. CONAN DOYLE *Green Flag* 243 What could Worlington Dodds know at Dunsloe which was not known in Throgmorton Street? **1952** *Economist* 13 Sept. 658/2 If prosperity is to return to Throgmorton Street the Stock Exchange Council will have to attract more investors.

thrombo-. Add: **thrombasthe·nia** (also **thrombo-**) [ad. G. *thrombasthenie* (E. Glanzmann 1918, in *Jahrb. f. Kinderheilkunde* LXXXVIII. 28), f. Gr. ἀσθένεια (see ASTHENIA)], a condition in which the number of platelets is normal but their clotting power is defective; so **thromb(o)asthe·nic** *a.*; **thrombe·ctomy** *Surg.* [*-ECTOMY], surgical removal of a thrombus from a blood vessel; **thro:mbo-angiitis obli·terans** (-ændʒiˌəi·tis) [L. *obliterans* OBLITERATING *ppl. a.*: see ANGIO-] = *Buerger's disease* s.v. *BUERGER; **thrombocythæmia,** (U.S. **-hemia**) (-səithī·mia) [ad. G. *thrombozythämie* (E. Epstein 1929, in *Zeitschr. f. Stomatologie* XXVII. 377): see HÆMO-, HEMO-], thrombocytosis, esp. when it is a persistent or primary condition; **thro:mbocytope·nia** [ad. G. *thrombocytopenie* (H. Eppinger in L. Langstein et al. *Enzykl. der klin. Med.* (1920) V. 295): see *-PENIA], a reduced number of platelets in the blood; hence **thro:mbocytope·nic** *a.*; **thrombocyto·sis** [-OSIS], a significantly increased number of platelets in the blood; **thromboe·mbolism,** embolism of a blood vessel caused by the dislodgement of a thrombus from its site of origin; hence **thromboembo·lic** *a.*; **thrombo-e·mbolus,** an embolus consisting of a thrombus which has become dislodged from its site; **thro:mboendarter(i)e·ctomy** *Surg.* [f. END(O- + ARTER(Y *sb.* + *-ECTOMY], an operation to remove a thrombus and part of the inner lining of an obstructed artery; **thrombope·nia** *-PENIA] = *thrombocytopenia* above; hence **thrombope·nic** *a.*; **thrombopla·stic** *a. Med.*, causing or promoting the clotting of blood; **thrombopla·stin** *Med.* [-IN[1]], a natural thromboplastic substance; now *spec.* an enzyme converting prothrombin to thrombin during the early stages of blood coagulation; **thrombosthe·nin** *Biochem.* [Gr. σθένος strength], a contractile protein or mixture of proteins in blood platelets; **thrombo·xane** *Biochem.* [f. OX- + -ANE], any of several compounds formed from prostaglandin endoperoxides which, when released from blood platelets, induce platelet aggregation and constriction of arterial muscle.

1935 L. E. H. WHITBY *Disorders of Blood* xiv. 276 (*heading*) Hereditary hæmorrhagic thrombasthenia. **1962** *Lancet* 22 Dec. 1316/2 This thromboasthenia is a familial hæmorrhagic disease in which the platelet-count is normal but the bleeding-time prolonged and clot retraction defective. **1974** PASSMORE & ROBSON *Compan. Med. Stud.* III. xxi. 45/1 Hereditary thrombasthenia or Glanzmann's disease is characterized by abnormal platelet aggregation and clot retraction. **1928** *Jrnl. Laboratory & Clin. Med.* XIII. 319 Chronic hereditary thrombasthenic purpura.. still requires further study before it can be definitely said that the blood platelets are wholly responsible for the condition. **1979** *Nature* 6 Dec. 622/1 T-transferase activity was measured in lysates obtained from platelets isolated from a thrombasthenic and a Bernard-Soulier patient, respectively. **1910** *Lippincott's New Med. Dict.* 998/1 Thrombectomy. **1945** *Urologic & Cutaneous Rev.* XL. 672/2 Thrombectomy is an extremely difficult and daring operation..but..in thrombosis of the renal vein prompt surgical intervention offers the only hope for a cure. **1972** D. A. K. BLACK *Renal Dis.* (ed. 3) vi. 165/1 Clinical improvement has been documented..with thrombectomy. **1908** L. BUERGER in *Amer. Jrnl. Med. Sci.* CXXXVI. 567 (*heading*) Thrombo-angiitis obliterans: a study of the vascular lesions leading to presenile spontaneous gangrene. *Ibid.* 580 Taking the true nature of the lesion into consideration, I would suggest that the names 'endarteritis obliterans' and 'arteriosclerotic gangrene' be discarded in this connection, and that we adopt the terms 'obliterating thrombo-angiitis' of the lower extremities when we wish to speak of the disease under discussion. **1914** [see *BUERGER]. **1955** *Sci. News Let.* 11 May 377/2 The relation of cigarette smoking to thromboangiitis obliterans..is well established. **1974** PASSMORE & ROBSON *Compan. Med. Stud.* III. xvii. 18/2 In thromboangiitis obliterans the upper limbs are more frequently affected.

1966, 1972 Thrombocythæmia [see *thrombocytosis* below]. **1977** *Lancet* 9 Apr. 775/1 Thrombocythæmia predisposes patients to thrombosis. **1923** *Arch. Internal Med.* XXXII. 939 This constant diminution of the platelets without any known cause..has given rise to the modern name of essential thrombopenia..or better still, thrombocytopenia. **1977** Thrombocytopenia [see *thrombocytosis* below]. **1925** *Jrnl. Amer. Med. Assoc.* 20 June 1888 (*caption*) Blood platelet variations following splenectomy in the thrombocytopenic group of Banti's disease. **1978** *Detroit Free Press* 14 Apr. 4B/1 Andra had a rare blood disease called thrombocytopenic purpura, in which a deficiency of platelets causes bleeding. **1936** *Jrnl. Amer. Med. Assoc.* 21 Mar. 1005/2 (*heading*) Leukemia with thrombocytosis. **1966** Wright & Symmers *Systemic Path.* I. iv. 187/2 In disease, the number of circulating platelets may be greatly raised (thrombocytosis, or thrombocythaemia). **1972** W. J. Williams et al. *Hematology* lxxxiii. 704/1 Whereas the symptomatic rise in the platelet count termed thrombocytosis may be substantial, it is temporary and self-limited. In thrombocythemia the platelet counts are higher..and persistently elevated: the condition is self-perpetuating and must be regarded as neoplastic. **1977** *Lancet* 9 Apr. 774/1 Thrombocytopenia caused by alcohol is reversible after alcohol withdrawal, and is followed by rebound thrombocytosis. **1940** *Acta Chir. Scand.* Suppl. LXI. 37 The first signs of the thrombo-embolic disease itself..can be venographically determined. **1981** *Brit. Med. Jrnl.* 7 Feb. 466/2 The best approach to the prophylaxis of thromboembolic disease is through low-dose heparin. **1907** *Jrnl. Amer. Med. Assoc.* 27 July 360/1 (*heading*) Postoperative thrombo-embolism. **1941** *Archives Surg.* XLIII. 462 In heparin there is available an almost infallible prophylactic against thromboembolism. **1970** *Daily Tel.* 17 July 2/8 Investigations showed that the increased risk of thrombo-embolism declined rapidly after the patient stopped taking the pill. **1955** *Sci. News Let.* 17 Sept. 183/3 The primary reaction is the formation of plugs in arteries and veins. The plugs, or thromboemboli as they are known technically, are made up of blood platelets stuck together. **1977** *Lancet* 29 Jan. 251/2 Fulton and Duckett report a significant correlation between high plasma-fibrogen levels..and thromboemboli. **1948** *Index Medicus* XLIV. 1204/2 Aneurysmal development after dos Santos thromboendarteriectomy. **1974** J. D. Maynard in R. M. Kirk et al. *Surgery* xi. 235/1 Thrombo-endarterectomy is successful in over 90 per cent of patients with disease above the inguinal ligaments. **1915** *Index Medicus* XIII. (Subject Index) 166/1 Thrombopenia. **1922** *Nature* 20 May 666/1 The absence of the fat-soluble vitamin from the diet leads, in the rat,..to a progressive diminution in the number of blood-platelets known as thrombopenia. **1981** *Cancer* XLVIII. 198/2 All staging systems isolate a high-risk group of patients defined by anemia and/or thrombopenia. **1934** *Lancet* 21 Apr. 845/1 This thrombopenic hæmorrhagic diathesis occurs regularly when the bone-marrow with its megacaryocytes has been extensively damaged by proliferating lymphadenoid..or neoplastic tissue. **1981** *Cancer* XLVIII. 202/1 The evidence was strong enough to justify putting anemic and thrombopenic patients aside. **1911** W. H. Howell in *Amer. Jrnl. Physiol.* XXIX. 189 They [*sc.* tissue extracts] furnish a substance, which may be designated as a thromboplastic substance or thromboplastin. **1981** *Obstetrics & Gynecol.* LVII. 490/2 Acceleration of the rate of clotting of whole blood is due to the thromboplastic activity of amniotic fluid. **1911** Thromboplastin [see *thromboplastic* adj. above]. **1979** R. Hawkey *Side-Effect* xi. 86 We used a thromboplastin preparation. .. They're hardly likely to test for..thromboplastins. **1961** Bettex-Galland & Lüscher in *Biochim. & Biophysica Acta* XLIX. 537 We have named this protein 'thrombosthenin', firstly because of its role in thrombocyte function, and secondly because of its properties, which in many respects let it appear distinct from muscle actomyosin. **1974** *Encycl. Brit. Macropædia* II. 1107/2 There are about 250,000 platelets per cubic millimetre of blood... They..contain..a contractile protein (thrombosthenin) that allows platelets to extend and retract long footlike projections called pseudopodia. **1975** *Nature* 3 July 14/1 This new intermediate does not have a classical prostaglandin structure and has been named 'Thromboxane'.., because it is a very potent platelet aggregating agent. Since it is the first member of a new series of compounds and contains two double bonds it was further designated 'Thromboxane A_2': its metabolite..becomes 'Thromboxane B_2.' **1979** *Ibid.* 6 Sept. 14/3 Because of their fish diet, Greenland Eskimos have high plasma levels of eicosapentenoic acid which is the precursor of the three series of endoperoxides—prostaglandins, thromboxane and prostacyclin.

thrombocyte (þrǫ·mbosəit). *Biol.* [ad. G. *thrombocyt* (M. C. Dekhuyzen 1892, in *Verh. d. Anat. Ges.* 94): see Thrombo- and -cyte.] **a.** A spindle-cell of the lower vertebrates, responsible for the clotting of blood.

1893 *Jrnl. R. Microsc. Soc.* 25 In analogy with Löwit's nomenclature he uses the ending 'blast' for young forms, and 'cyt' for those which are adult. He distinguishes.. thromboblasts and thrombocytes, as the 'spindles' of Eberth and Schimmelbusch may be called. **1910** *Jrnl. Morphol.* XXI. 273 The spindle cells or thrombocytes of certain amphibian blood have a cytoplasm which stains in the same way as does that of the megakaryocyte. **1979** *Nature* 1 Mar. 13/1 The rapid adhesion of platelets (or of their non-mammalian counterpart, the thrombocytes) to the vascular wall when the endothelial lining is breached has been a subject of interest since Wharton-Jones showed in 1851 that thrombocytes accumulated at points of local damage in blood vessels of the frog's foot.

b. A blood platelet.

1907 E. A. Schäfer *Essent. Histol.* (ed. 7) 35 These often seem to radiate from minute round colourless discoid particles less than one-third the diameter of a red corpuscle... These are the..blood-platelets, or thrombocytes. **1938** W. Magner *Textbk. Hematol.* i. 1 The cellular elements of the blood are of three types: red corpuscles or erythrocytes, white corpuscles or leukocytes, and platelets or thrombocytes. **1977** J. Raynor *Anat. & Physiol.* x. 245 There are about 150,000–300,000 thrombocytes per cubic millimeter of blood.

thrombolytic (þrǫmboli·tik), *a.* and *sb. Med.* [f. Thrombo- + *-lytic *a.*] **A.** *adj.* Pertaining to or causing the dissolving and breaking down of a thrombus. **B.** *sb.* A thrombolytic agent.

1962 A. P. Fletcher et al. in *Amer. Jrnl. Med.* XXXIII. 738/1 The adjective 'thrombolytic' will be used to designate biochemical moieties capable of inducing thrombolysis. **1965** *Zeitschr. f. d. Ges. Innere Med.* XX. 720/2 The thrombolytics really have enriched the palette of antithrombotics. **1971** *Times* 6 Aug. 4/1 Deaths among patients admitted to hospital with coronary thrombosis have been cut by a third in a trial of a compound, streptokinase... The thrombolytic treatment was assessed in 700 patients in eight hospital centres. **1974** R. M. Kirk in R. M. Kirk et al. *Surgery* ii. 14/1 The thrombus may be removed surgically; at present this is less expensive than giving thrombolytics.

thrombose (þrǫmbōᵘ·z), *v. Path.* [Back-formation from Thrombosis.] **a.** *trans.* To cause thrombosis in (a blood vessel). Cf. Thrombosed *a.*

1910 *Practitioner* June 779 Acute endometritis... When sufficiently severe..to thrombose the endometrial capillaries.

b. *intr.* To become occupied by a thrombus.

1938 *Arch. Path.* XXV. 486 When the hemorrhage occurs into the deeper intimal layers, the capillaries adjacent to the point of rupture may thrombose. **1977** *Proc. R. Soc. Med.* LXX. 401/1 Small blood vessels thrombose but larger vessels appear to be undamaged.

Hence **thrombo·sing** *ppl. a.*, undergoing or causing thrombosis.

1923 *Surg., Gynecol. & Obstetr.* XXXVI. 313/1 The thrombosing part can sometimes be palpated. **1965** *Revue Roumaine d'Inframicrobiol.* II. 71 Caudal thrombosing vasculopathies can be considered as manifestations of a latent pararickettsial infection.

thrombosis. Delete ‖ and add: Also *fig.* with reference to traffic congestion.

1959 *Times* 27 Nov. 8/4 It was clear that the heart of London had traffic thrombosis, said Mr. Ernest Marples.. at a Press conference yesterday. **1975** *Times* 9 June 12/4 In the big cities expansion of car ownership has brought inevitable thrombosis.

thrombus. **b.** Substitute for def.: A clot which forms on the wall of a blood vessel or a chamber of the heart, often impeding or obstructing the flow. (Further examples.)

1961 R. D. Baker *Essent. Path.* v. 82 There is danger of a portion of the thrombus breaking loose and passing as an embolus to the pulmonary artery and lungs. **1970** Passmore & Robson *Compan. Med. Stud.* II. xxvi. 3/1 In large vessels, the thrombus usually remains plastered as a plaque against the wall of the vessel, whereas in small arteries continuation of the process may lead to an occlusive thrombus which blocks completely the direct blood flow.

throne. Add: **1. d.** *fig.* A lavatory bowl and pedestal or other supporting structure. *colloq.*

1922 Joyce *Ulysses* 39 In a Greek watercloset he breathed his last... With beaded mitre and with crozier, stalled upon his throne. **1941** F. Thompson *Over to Candleford* vi. 95 The commode turned out to be a kind of throne with carpeted steps and a lid which opened. **1960** J. J. Rowlands *Spindrift* 52 Our plumber..revealed that the water level in the 'throne' works just like the old glass water barometer. **1981** S. Rushdie *Midnight's Children* i. 62 A wooden 'thunderbox'—a 'throne'—lay on one side, empty enamel pot rolling on coir matting.

2. b. Phr. *the Great White Throne*, used of the throne of God with allusion to Revelation xx. 11. Also *fig.*

1850 Browning *Christmas-Eve & Easter-Day* 116 Is Judgment past for me alone?—And where had place the Great White Throne? **1873** C. M. Yonge *Pillars of House* III. xxxii. 212 It was his first mountain... He raised his hat with an instinct of reverence..then murmured, 'One seems nearer the Great White Throne!' **1922** E. E. Cummings *Enormous Room* vii. 155 The Mecca of respectability, the Great White Throne of purity.

8. *throne-room* (further example, in sense *1 d); **Throne Speech** *Canad.* = *Speech from the Throne* s.v. *speech *sb.*[1] 8 d.

1941 W. Fortescue *Trampled Lilies* xxv. 247 Could I bear to walk through the kitchen to reach the only bath and throne-room? **1955** *Toronto Daily Star* 2 Feb. 6/2 An experimental program for the treatment of drug addicts was announced in this year's Throne speech at the opening of the British Columbia legislature. **1972** *Farm & Country* 19 Dec. 1/3 Informants..say they will be 'very surprised' if the Throne Speech does not contain new provisions to help farmers transfer their properties to following generations.

throng, *sb.* Add: **II. 3.** (Later examples.) Also *transf.*, of impersonal objects.

1912 'Saki' *Unbearable Bassington* x. 170 The Rutland Galleries were crowded..by a fashionable throng of art-patrons. **1955** S. Wilson *Man in Grey Flannel Suit* xxxiv. 256 He joined a throng of men pushing to get aboard the train. **1971** H. Wouk *Winds of War* iv. 53 Was Nazi Germany as strong as the ever-marching columns in the streets, and the throngs of uniforms in cafés, suggested? **1977** P. L. Fermor *Time of Gifts* ii. 35 A throng of villagers had assembled round an enormous bonfire. **1980** D. Adams *Restaurant at End of Universe* xvi. 83 'The End of the Universe is very popular,' said Zaphod threading his way unsteadily through the throng of tables.

throng, *v.* **3.** (Later examples.)

1947 P. Larkin *Girl in Winter* II. vi. 150 Besides—the impossibilities thronged upon her—she was sixteen, while Jane was twenty-five, middle-aged, and foreign, too. **1969** M. Puzo *Godfather* II. xii. 163 The young beautiful girls thronged through the city like lemmings, lasting one year, some two. **1979** A. Fraser *King Charles II* I. ii. 25 This maddened mob was thronging round the palace of Whitehall. **1981** A. N. Wilson *Who was Oswald Fish?* xi. 121 A hundred half-memories of childhood thronged back: the smell of baking from the house next door—the Trenimans.

thronged, *ppl. a.* **2. b.** (Later non-*dial.* example.)

1943 *R.A.F. Jrnl.* Aug. 15 Members of the R.A.F. who in the midst of their thronged days find time to encourage and assist the Air Training Corps squadrons.

throttle, *sb.* Add: **4. a.** (Further examples.) Also, the throttle-pedal.

1957 A. C. Clarke *Deep Range* I. iv. 44 Franklin pressed down the throttle and felt the surge of power as the torpedo leaped forward. **1966** T. Wisdom *High-Performance Driving* viii. 74 You brake with the ball of your foot and blip the throttle with your heel or the side of your foot. **1983** *Listener* 28 July 13/1 Mine was no longer with a functioning throttle, gear change or front-brake on arrival.

b. Phrs.: *to cut* or *chop the throttle*, to close the throttle in order to slow down or stop; (*at*) *full, half, part*, etc., *throttle*, (at) maximum, etc., power or speed (also *fig.*).

1936 *Motor Man.* (ed. 29) ii. 26 When the throttle is lying flat in the direction of the gas flow, the engine is running 'full bore', the term generally used for this being 'full throttle'. **1948** *N.Y. World-Telegram* 30 Dec. 11/8 The pilot, coming in, doesn't chop the throttle. The jet pilot 'turns down the wick'. **1958** [see *cut *v.* 21 f]. **1969** J. Argenti *Managem. Techniques* viii. 50 Once one has grasped the principle behind Cost-Benefit..one can use the technique at quarter throttle, so to speak. *Ibid.* 51 The results will be less impressive than when an expert uses it at full throttle. **1973** *Daily Tel.* 9 Jan. 1/5 The gunboat, believed to be the Odinn, avoided the ramming by sailing away at full throttle. **1977** J. F. Fixx *Compl. Bk. Running* iii. 42 Even in a race there's no need to run at full throttle if you don't want to.

5. throttle ice (see quots.); **throttle jockey** *slang* (see quot. 1946), **throttleman,** one who controls the throttle(s) of an engine.

1942 *S.A.E. Jrnl.* Jan. 22/1 Ice which collects in the induction system was divided into three classes: impact ice, throttle ice, and fuel evaporation ice... 'Throttle ice' is that which is formed at or near the throttle when the throttle is in a part-closed position due to the cooling effect of the increase in kinetic energy of the air in the restricted flow region. **1972** *Gloss. Aeronaut. & Astronaut. Terms* (*B.S.I.*) xv. 12 *Throttle ice*, ice formed in or near the engine throttle by the cooling due to isentropic expansion of the inspired air in the temperature range of 0°C to 5°C. **1946** *Amer. Speech* XXI. 310/2 *Throttle jockey*, a pilot. **1947** *Seafarers' Log* 25 Apr. 13/2 How could you crush a seamen's strike without captains and throttle-jockeys? **1904** *Everybody's Mag.* X. 663/1 When the officials came out and stood around the engine, there were throttle-men on waiting locals. **1973** H. Gruppe *Truxton Cipher* (1974) xiv. 140 The throttleman nervously wiped his sweating hands on a hank of oily cotton waste. **1982** *Fortune* 22 Mar. 172/2 The throttleman then has to reduce power because the boat's propellers are out of the water and meeting no resistance.

throttle, *v.* Add: **4. a.** Also const. *down.*

1914 Hamel & Turner *Flying* 134 Nearer and nearer we approach and now our pilot throttles down the engine.

b. *absol.* in phrs. *to throttle back, down*, to close the throttle in order to slow down or stop.

1932 D. Garnett *Rabbit in Air* III. 82 The altimeter was at 3000. I throttled back. *Ibid.* 91, I turned over the cement works, flew her level, and turned again by the river, throttled down and made my approach. **1953** C. A. Lindbergh *Spirit of St. Louis* II. vi. 188 The air speed's still over 100 miles an hour... I throttle down to 1750. **1973** R. Rosenblum *Mushroom Cave* (1974) 101 The pilot throttled back to float the helicopter over a large network of paths. **1979** 'K. M. Peyton' *Marion's Angels* viii. 130 He throttled down sharply for the turning to the church.

throttleable (þrǫ·t'lăb'l) *a.* (of an engine) that can be controlled by means of a throttle.

1960 *Aeroplane* XCVIII. 261/2 The Thiokol XLR-99 'throttleable' rocket engine..has completed preliminary static tests and will shortly be installed in an X-15. **1969** *New Scientist* 1 May 243/2 The rotors could be fitted with small, throttleable rockets on their tips.

through, *a.* Add: **1. a.** *spec.* in *Carpentry*, of a housing: running through the whole thickness of the member, not stopped.

1934 [see *stopped *ppl. a.* 9]. **1979** A. B. Emary *Woodworking* iii. 18 (*caption*) Through housing.

b. *through booking* (earlier example), *carriage, passenger* (example); **through traffic:** also, traffic which passes through a particular town, etc., rather than stopping there.

1848 *Amer. Railroad Jrnl.* 29 July 482/1 A *through* passenger in the 9 and 4½ o'clock lines, pays more than $1 25, for each of those parts of the line. **1869** *Bradshaw's*

Railway Man. XXI. 43 Through-booking arrangements with the Scottish North Eastern. **1891** S. J. Weyman *New Rector* I. iii. 28 Oh, dear, they are in a through carriage... I would rather go in another carriage and change. **1944** *Sun* (Baltimore) 16 Feb. 9/1 A mid-town express highway as a through-traffic route. **1961** Through-traffic [see *route *v.*]. **1976** *Alyn & Deeside Observer* 10 Dec. 1/6 The new by-pass will provide an additional crossing of the River Dee that will enable much through traffic to avoid the city. **1978** O. S. Nock *Great Western* 110 In such conditions the through carriage was an inestimable boon.

through, *prep.* and *adv.* Add: **A.** **β.** **thro** (later examples); **thru:** now used informally as a reformed spelling and abbreviation (chiefly) in *N. Amer.*

1878 W. Whitman *Daybks. & Notebks.* (1978) I. 122 Sent piece 'Three Young Men's Deaths' $12 to Mr John Frazer, Tobacco Plant, Liverpool—thro Josiah Child. **1879,** etc. [see *though *adv.* and *conj.* A. γ]. **1904** R. Garnett *Let.* in A. Mizener *Ford Madox Ford* (1971) ix. 96 If Conrad..paid £3 a week thro Pinker it would be a very considerable help. **1917** E. E. Cummings *Let. c* Nov. (1969) 40, I see the thing thru, alone. **1921** *Jrnl. Nat. Dental Assoc.* VIII. 609/1 As we look thru our daily papers and our magazines. **1971** *Black World* Mar. 57/1 When she wuz little and she had stuttered thru a sentence. **1977** *Hot Car* Oct. 11/1 Available for S types right thru to Mk 10s it retails for 26 notes.

B. I. *prep.* **1. b.** *through-the-lens* adj., used with reference to light measurement in which it is the light passing through the lens of the camera that is measured (the same light that would form the image).

1965 *Focal Encycl. Photogr.* (rev. ed.) I. 554/1 Through-the-lens exposure measurement has the advantage..that the meter cell receives light from exactly the same subject field as is taken in by the lens. **1977** J. Hedgecoe *Photographer's Handbk.* 14/3 Solid state through-the-lens metering, zoom lenses, motor-drive, are all part of an ever-widening 'system' built around the single lens reflex body. **1984** *What Video?* Aug. 59/2 Fair picture, basic colour temperature controls, through-the-lens viewfinder.

h. (Later example.)

1932 H. S. Walpole *Fortress* iii. 562 The mist immediately surrounding him was..so wetting that he was already soaked through and through his clothes.

5. b. Also used in sequences or lists, without necessarily denoting consecutive development.

1938 M. K. Rawlings *Yearling* xi. 110 His wares included the necessities and scanty luxuries of the whole country-side, from plows, wagons, buggies and implements, through food staples to whiskey and hardware, dry goods and notions and medicines. **1962** *Listener* 26 July 130/2 Rents range from just over £3 a month for a small flat, through about £14 for a two-bedroom house, to £23 for the most elegant apartments. **1975** *Nature* 10 Apr. 501/2 Nine recognised glaze types, ranging in colour from pale blue, through green, to yellow, brown and red.

d. *U.S.* Up to (a date, a number, a specified item, etc.) inclusively, up to the end of, up to and including, to, until; often correlative to *from.*

1798 T. Holcroft *Jrnl.* 4 Aug. in *Mem.* (1816) III. 51 Continued the opera through scene 9, Act 3. **1930** H. Brown (*title*) Rabelais in English literature through Sterne. **1932** *Atlantic Monthly* May 538 Mr. Heffernan was mayor for four years, from 1927 through 1931. **1942** M. Kraitchik *Math. Recreations* vi. 130 Poisson calculated this probability, taking into account the cards dealt in the first hand. His result does not differ through the third decimal place. **1950** H. Craig *Hist. Eng. Lit.* 250 Spenser treats of England from the Reformation through the reign of Queen Elizabeth. **1967** *N.Y. Times* (Internat. ed.) 11 Feb. 1/6 At a background briefing early in November, the American command made available infiltration figures covering the year through Sept. 30 and a rough estimate for October. **1971** *Physics Bull.* Dec. 738/1 In the review copy pages 1469 through 1472 are already loose which does not say too much for the quality of the binding. **1977** *Time* 8 Aug. 19/3 We will continue to govern through the end of our term. **1981** L. Deighton *XPD* xliii. 342 A..notice stating that deliveries were only accepted between eight and eleven Monday through Friday.

II. *adv.* **3. b.** (Earlier example of passing an examination and further examples of gen. sense, esp. of persons.) Also, defeated, having no further prospects, no longer friends or associates, outmoded, 'done for'; *to be through with*: also, to be tired of, to have had enough of; (further examples).

1849 Thackeray *Pendennis* I. xxi. 196 'This man has passed,' he thought, 'and I have failed!'..'Good bye, Spavin,' said he. 'I'm very glad you are through.' **1887** *Scribner's Mag.* May 622/2 He..then..scrawled a dash underneath. 'There! I'm through!' he said. **1897** J. L. Allen *Choir Invisible* ii. 22, I was through with the lessons. **1902** W. N. Harben *Abner Daniel* vii. 55, 'I don't understand you.' 'Well, you will before I'm through with you.' **1930** J. B. Priestley *Angel Pavement* x. 508 'You're through then, eh?' 'All I can do to-night, Mr Smeeth. One or two things I've had to leave till tomorrow morning.' **1931** H. F. Pringle *Theodore Roosevelt* I. iii. 37 He..was through with breakfast by 8.30. **1934** G. B. Shaw *On Rocks* II. 271 We were born into good society; and we are through with it: we have no illusions about it, even if we are fit for nothing better. **1939** I. Baird *Waste Heritage* ii. 23 Now when we get down to the hall we're through, see? I don't want nothin' more to do with you, I don't even know your name. **1942** E. Paul *Narrow St.* xxxi. 281 An outsider not familiar with French politics might have thought that Daladier was through. Not at all. He got himself elected by the Popular Front..in April, 1938. **1956** B. Holiday *Lady sings Blues* (1973) xix. 154 It was only a few weeks before, people had been telling me I was through in the United States, that the public would never accept me. **1969** A. Lurie *Real People* 108, I hope you don't think anyone who doesn't paint soda-pop bottles and stripes is through artistically. **1970** *Wall St. Jrnl.* 30 Mar. 1/1 An executive with two dependent children earning the equivalent of $24,000 a year is left with $14,300..after the Board of the Inland Revenue is through.

c. Of a telephone call or caller: connected.

1929 *Telegr. & Teleph. Jrnl.* XVI. 47/2 'You are through' (which is the English way of saying 'here is your party'). **1932** D. L. Sayers *Have his Carcase* iii. 33 The grocer announced that Harriet's call was through... 'Hullo!' she said. **1954** F. P. Keyes *Royal Box* i. 14 Won't you ever learn that when an English operator asks you if you're 'through', she doesn't mean have you *finished*, she means have you got your connection all right? **1977** *Rolling Stone* 30 June 80/3 Directly getting Honolulu information, I got a number for Wiley Hampson and presently was through to him at his home in Hawaii Kai.

5. c. *through-and-through sawing, sawn* = *plain sawing* vbl. sb., *plain-sawn* ppl. adj. s.v. *plain *a.*[1] and *adv.* C. c. Also *through-and-through method.*

1966 [see *plain-sawn* ppl. adj. s.v. *plain *a.*[1] and *adv.* C. c]. **1963** *Gloss. Terms Timber* (*B.S.I.*) 14 *Through-and-through sawing*, a method of converting..logs by parallel cuts in the general direction of the grain. **1979** A. B. Emary *Woodworking* i. 9 Most of the timber at a merchant's will be from logs cut by the through and through method.

through-, in combination. Add: **1.** **through-compo·sed** *pa. pple.* and *ppl. a.* = *durchkomponiert *a.*

1884 F. Niecks *Conc. Dict. Mus. Terms* 122 A durchcomponiertes Lied, 'a through-composed song', is a song of which each verse has a setting of its own. **1947** A. Einstein *Music in Romantic Era* x. 117 In this prologue there is no longer any spoken dialogue; the scene is 'through-composed'. **1962** *Listener* 11 Jan. 105/2 The opera opens with a Prologue of the spirits..which is the only 'through-composed' portion. **1981** *Times Lit. Suppl.* 20 Feb. 203/2 The first 'Razumovsky' [Quartet]..abandoned the normal first-movement repeat, had the rarity of a through-composed scherzo (without trio or 'da capo'), and only repeated the exposition of the finale.

2. (Some could equally well be placed s.v. *through *a.*) **throu·gh-ball** *Assoc. Football*, etc., a forward pass which goes through the other team's defensive formation; **through deck,** a flight deck which runs the full length of a ship; **throu·gh-deck crui·ser,** a type of lightly-armed aircraft-carrier (see quots.); **throu·gh-draught:** see *thorough-draught* s.v. Thorough- 2; **throu·gh-feed,** in centreless grinding, movement of the work-piece right through the space between the two wheels (cf. *in-feed); also *attrib.*; **throu·ghflow,** the flowing of a fluid, air, etc., through something; also *attrib.*; **through-lounge** (stress variable): in a private house, a lounge that extends from the front to the back of the house; **throu·gh-pass** = *through-ball* above; **throu·gh-valley** (see quot. 1972).

1969 *Punch* 12 Feb. 248/4, I wish I could recall the lingo—the through-balls, high crosses, work-rates and searching diagonals. **1977** *Times* 28 Feb. 8/5 Another through ball and Souness was racing away to make a cross which Armstrong converted. **1969** *Times* 30 Oct. 2/7 Such an aircraft..would be operated from a cruiser-type ship with a newly designed 'through deck'. **1971** *Guardian* 22 Nov. 12/4 The Royal Navy is now considering the operation of Harriers from a new class of flat topped 19,000-ton ships euphemistically known as 'Through-deck cruisers'. **1980** A. Preston *Warships of World* 29/2 The troubled political background accounts for the ludicrous nomenclature applied to the class. First of all *Invincible* was a 'through-deck' cruiser to disguise the flight deck, then a command cruiser, and only now..an aircraft carrier. *Ibid.* 221/2 *Through-deck cruiser*, cumbersome term concocted by the Royal Navy to obtain political and Treasury approval for a ship designed to operate helicopters and V/Stol aircraft. The 'through deck' was a euphemism for a full-length flight deck. **1905** Through-draught [see *thorough-draught* s.v. Thorough- 2]. **1976** B. Lecomber *Dead Weight* vi. 73, I..opened the pilots' side-windows in the pious hope of creating a through-draught of fresh air. **1937** Colvin & Stanley *Grinding Pract.* v. 73 There are two primary methods of grinding the work. One is the through-feed method in which the work passes axially from one side of the machine to the other. **1963** Jones & Schubert *Engin. Encycl.* 215 There are three general methods of centerless grinding which may be described as through-feed, in-feed, and end-feed methods. **1967** M. E. Hale *Biol. Lichens* vii. 96 Stemflow on trees..has been shown to be enriched, relative to throughflow, with potassium and calcium. **1974** *Country Life* 17 Jan. 103/1, 2 litre family saloon..throughflow heating and ventilation. **1962** Jackson & Marsden *Educ. & Working Class* v. 157 The interview took place in the through-lounge. **1976** *Evening Post* (Nottingham) 15 Dec. 15/5 (Advt.), Modern well situated detached house consisting of through lounge, fully fitted kitchen, [etc.]. **1937** F. N. S. Creek *Association Football* iii. 58 Short passing should always consist of 'through' passes so that the ball is sent behind an opponent and never..across his front. **1967** J. Potter *Foul Play* (1968) ii. 29 If you're playing on the left wing I'll feed you with through-passes to the corner flag. **1976** *Denbighshire Free Press* 8 Dec. 24/7 Ian McCarter..got to a splendid through pass from Wildermuth. **1905** *Bull. Geol. Soc. Amer.* XVI. 233 In discussing this paper at the Geological Society meeting in Philadelphia, Professor Davis applied the very descriptive name of 'through valleys' to this condition of valleys connected across lowered divides. **1969** G. C. Dickinson *Maps & Air Photographs* xiii. 208 A valley from one system may meet one from another system 'back-to-back' so that together they form a through valley with scarcely any feature separating the headwaters of the two systems. **1972** *Gloss. Geol.* (Amer. Geol. Inst.) 739/1 *Through valley*, a flat-floored depression or channel eroded across a divide by glacier ice or meltwater streams.

through other, through-other, *adv. phr.* and *adj.* Add: Also 9 **throughther.**

a **1889** G. M. Hopkins *Poems* (1967) 97 For earth her being has unbound; her dapple is at an end, astray or aswarm, all throughther, in throngs.

throughout, *prep.*, *adv.* Add: Also (chiefly *N. Amer.*) **thruout, thru-out** (see *thru* s.v. *through *prep.* and *adv.* A. β).

1922 *Proc. IRE* X. 260 During the past winter an amateur spark station located at Cleveland, Ohio..was received nightly at Yonkers, New York..with sufficient intensity to enable the signals to be read thruout the room. **1968** *Globe & Mail* (Toronto) 17 Feb. 46/6 (Advt.), 6 room brick bungalow with 3 finished rooms in basement, new broadloom thruout. **1976–7** *Sea Spray* (N.Z.) Dec./Jan. 119/1 (Advt.), All kauri ply and timber used exclusively thru-out.

throughput (þrū·put). [f. Through-: cf. Input *sb.*, Output *sb.*] **1.** *Sc.* 'Energy, activity, capacity for or progress at work' (S.N.D.).

1808 Jamieson *Etym. Dict. Sc. Lang.* I. s.v. *ithand*, He has nae great throw-pit, but he's very eident. **1845** *Chambers's Jrnl.* 28 June 412 They'd hang as long as I like at the plough-tail, but I want through-put; and so commend me to my own men and reasonable hours. **1923** G. Watson *Roxburghshire Word-bk.* 309 *Throw-pit*, capacity for accomplishing work.

2. The amount of oil or other raw materials, etc., processed by an industrial plant; *transf.*, the amount or number of units passing through a system, the amount of data processed by a computer (over a stated time period). Also, processing, production, or handling capacity. Also *attrib.*

1915 J. Wilson *Lowland Scotch Lower Strathearn* 273/1 *Throo-put, n.* out-turn. **1922** *Daily Mail* 15 Nov. 3 Throughput of oil will necessarily be interfered with temporarily. **1930** *Daily Express* 22 May 15/2 The larger throughput was sufficient to..yield the handsome margin of £89 per ton of ore. **1945** H. D. Smyth *Gen. Acct. Devel. Atomic Energy Mil. Purposes* xi. 113 By the middle of January 1942, a run had been made with a reasonable beam strength and an aggregate flow or through-put of appreciable amount which showed a much improved separation factor. **1950** *Engineering* 20 Jan. 69/1 Plant and machinery made ready to handle maximum throughputs. **1958** *Spectator* 1 Aug. 178/2 The Magheralin Creamery, N. Ireland, had a considerably higher throughput of milk. **1959** *Times Rev. Industry* Mar. 24/1 Coal throughput rates. **1961** B. Fergusson *Watery Maze* ii. 59 The drains..were unable to cope with the 'through-put', as industrialists say, of more than eighteen lavatories. **1962** *Economist* 20 Oct. 215/1 With Stonehenge and the Tower already showing maximum throughput. **1965** *New Scientist* 24 June 883 Time sharing (or multi-programming) is already well established as a means of increasing the throughput and utilization of a computer. **1967** *Listener* 31 Aug. 263/3 Russian economists now discover that prepackaging..not only makes for better hygiene, but trebles a shop assistant's throughput. **1968** P. Dickinson *Skin Deep* i. 6 Estate agents must be doing nicely down this way, with a constant through-put of moneyed youngsters moving in with one kid and moving out with three. **1969** J. Argenti *Managem. Techniques* 168 By re-siting the factory entrance gates at a cost of a few hundred pounds it was possible for one company to increase the throughput of customers' lorries by 50 per cent. **1970** D. Kut *Warm Air Heating* xx. 338 The grade of oil fuel best suited for a particular installation depends on the type of oil burner and on the hourly through-put of oil. **1972** *Daily Tel.* 11 May 2/4 Prince Philip said..that the criterion for a university was the quality and standard of its life and work, not the total through-put of students. **1974** *Information Handbk.* 1974–5 (Shell Internat. Petroleum Co.) 105 The graphs show that costs increase as throughputs exceed or fall below the 'optimum', that is the throughput at which the total unit cost reaches the lowest point. **1976** P. R. White *Planning for Public Transport* iv. 76 An alternative means of maximizing station throughput is to build a station in which a single track carrying a one-way flow bifurcates to form a loop around an island platform. **1978** *Jrnl. R. Soc. Arts* CXXVI. 425/1 Increasing the throughput of vehicles on an existing highway.

throughway (þrū·wē[i]). Also (*N. Amer.*) **thruway,** and with hyphen. [f. Through- + Way *sb.*[1]] **1.** *N. Amer.* An expressway; a large toll road.

1934 in Webster. **1946** *Sun* (Baltimore) 25 Mar. 24/9 The proposal..for a throughway across a filled-in inner harbor. **1951** *Economist* 22 Sept. 685/3 Plans for a 'Thruway' from New York City..to Buffalo on Lake Erie, are well advanced. **1969** A. Lurie *Real People* 42 Down below the rose garden I can hear cars whirring past on the thruway. **1976** T. Heald *Let Sleeping Dogs Die* ix. 176 The Dog Centre..was no more than three and a half hours' fast driving on the thru-way from Kennedy Airport.

2. *gen.* A way through; a means of passage through or between.

1935 C. Day Lewis *Time to Dance* 22 Speak up, speak up, you skyward man, Speak up and tell us true; To east or west—which is the best, The through-way of the two? **1977** 'E. Crispin' *Glimpses of Moon* xii. 233 The cradle jolts and jerks under their combined assault, but remains obstinately blocking the throughway.

throw, *sb.*[2] Add: **I. 2. a.** Also, the extent through which a switch or lever may be moved.

1975 *Gramophone* Sept. 533/3 These are toggle type switches,..and protrude quite appreciably from the facia. They therefore have quite a long throw. **1979** *SLR Camera* Jan. 41/2 The wind-on lever has a short throw of around 120 degrees.

b. (Examples.)

1890 E. Atkinson tr. *Ganot's Elem. Treat. Physics* (ed. 13) x. ii. 794 When a current of very small duration is passed through a galvanometer, a momentary deflection or swing or throw of the needle will be produced. **1931** L. B. Loeb *Fund. Electr. & Magnetism* xxiii. 272 Even the first throw of the galvanometer has not the true value which it would have had in the absence of damping.

9. A decorative piece of fabric used as a casual covering for furniture, as a rug, counterpane, etc. Also, a shawl or stole. *N. Amer.* (chiefly *U.S.*).

1895 [see *drape *sb.*[1] c]. **1913** F. H. Burnett *T. Tembarom* xl. 524 They..transformed the cot into a 'couch' by covering it with what Tracy's knew as a 'throw'. **1936** W. Greene *Death in Deep South* ii. 142 Her last summer's scarf made a throw over the pine table. **1952** E. Ferber *Giant* ii. 14 I'm only going to buy a little white mink cape throw. **1963** G. S. Maxwell *Navajo Rugs* iii. 30 Continuing south we come to the city of Gallup, a center for the inexpensive rug known as a 'Throw'. **1980** M. McMullen *My Cousin Death* (1981) xvii. 195 She..brought a plaid throw and tenderly tucked it in around him.

10. *colloq.* (orig. *U.S.*). A 'go' at anything; freq. in phr. — *a throw*, preceded by a specified sum of money to denote 'so much a go' or 'so much apiece'.

1898 F. P. Dunne *Mr. Dooley in Peace & War* 101 Smaller thin New York, but th' livin' was cheaper, with Mon'gahela rye at five a throw, put ye'er hand around th' glass. **1931** 'D. Stiff' *Milk & Honey Route* 177 Beer or wine at a jitney a throw. **1948** [see *dope *sb.* 3 a]. **1958** B. Malamud *Magic Barrel* 30 A column..inviting contributions in the form of stories at five bucks the thousand-word throw. **1966** N. Freeling *Dresden Green* i. 38 Coffee-table books..at a hundred and forty francs the throw. **1975** *Author* Winter 153 The cost of research... The BBC Archives charge £2 a throw.

throw, *v.*[1] Add: **II. 10. c.** (Earlier example.)

1768 W. Musgrave *Let.* 12 Feb. in *15th Rep. R. Comm. Hist. Manuscripts* App. vi. 241 *in Parl. Papers 1897* (C. 8551) LI. i. 1 But if they will be artful enough to throw their votes so as to choose one of your candidates, it is my opinion we ought to remain contented for the present.

12. (Earlier example.)

1777 J. Woodforde *Diary* 8 May (1924) I. 203 Bill caught only one little Miney but he did not throw above four times.

15. a. Also, to project (the voice); also, *spec.* as in ventriloquism. Cf. sense 44 c below.

1962 A. Nisbett *Technique Sound Studio* 263 In dead acoustics the ratio of direct to indirect sound cannot be varied, as indirect sound must be kept to a minimum. In this case it may help if an actor 'throws' his voice, simulating raising it to talk or shout from a distance. **1972** A. Price *Col. Butler's Wolf* xx. 222 He threw his voice past Ryleiev into the mist. **1976** *Listener* 23/30 Dec. 830/1, I can throw my voice. I could make a fortune as a medium.

17. a. Delete † *Obs. rare.* Now usu. in phr. *to throw a punch*, to deliver a blow with the clenched first; occas. with fist as obj.

1923 H. C. Witwer *Fighting Blood* xi. 348, I set myself, took careful aim and threw my right at his chin. **1950** J. Dempsey *Championship Fighting* xvi. 92 You're throwing perfect punches. **1976** J. Lewis *Shadows of Death* iv. 54 Maybe the kid had a hammer in his glove; surely he couldn't have thrown a punch hard enough to hurt him like that one had. **1983** *Daily Tel.* 3 Feb. 3/3 Mr Oatway.. threw punches at the second bandit.

18. a. *to throw a fit.* For *U.S. slang* read *slang* (orig. *U.S.*). (Earlier and later examples.) Chiefly *fig.*

1896 S. Crane *Maggie* (rev. ed.) iii. 22 Deh ol' woman 'ill be trowin' fits. **1926** *S.P.E. Tract* xxiv. 126 Father threw a fit when I came home drunk. **1930** *Observer* 4 May 15 Caesar throws his fit, off stage. **1954** Koestler *Invis. Writing* 172 One day this was discovered by Zsuzsa, who threw a fit. **1973** 'R. Macleod' *Burial in Portugal* v. 97 'Please, Jonathan. If I am late—.' 'The management will throw a fit,' he completed for her.

b. To give or hold (a party), esp. one of an informal or impromptu nature. *colloq.* (orig. *U.S.*).

1922 S. Lewis *Babbitt* xxxix. 339 Saturday night, when they would..'throw a party'. **1937** *Even. News* 6 Mar. 11/5 Anona Winn threw a party a few nights ago at her flat in Maida Vale. **1960** *Sunday Express* 13 Mar. 12/7 She..threw a champagne and scampi party at a nearby pub. **1978** *Detroit Free Press* 5 Mar. B 2/2 When all else fails, throw a party.

III. 19. c. To lose (a contest, race, etc.) deliberately or by corrupt prearrangement. *colloq.* (orig. *U.S.*).

1868 H. Woodruff *Trotting Horse Amer.* xxxi. 263 It was..very unjust to charge Mr. Nodine with throwing the race. **1940** 'E. Queen' in *Blue Bk.* Oct. 27/1 'Brown threw the fight?' asked..a member of the Boxing Commission. **1951** *Manch. Guardian Weekly* 1 Mar. 15/1 Baseball games had been 'thrown' by bribed players. **1959** *News Chron.* 19 Aug. 6/3 He was accused of..fixing the World Series of 1919. This was the equivalent of arranging that one side in the Cup Final should throw the game. **1978** *Times* 9 Jan. 8/5 During the Chancellorship of Mr Roy Jenkins, Lord Allen had to 'throw' their occasional [tennis] matches for fear of puncturing the considerable vanity of his political master.

25. (Later examples of *transf.* sense.) *U.S.*

1907 [see *poke-out* s.v. *poke *sb.*[3] 1 b]. **1934** *Amer. Ballads & Folk Songs* 24 They had mooched the stem and threw their feet.

V. 30. b. *to throw oneself at* (earlier example).

1789 H. More *Lett.* (1925) 127 The women all threw themselves at his head.

e. *colloq.* To engage (the clutch or gears) of a motor vehicle. Also *transf.* with the vehicle as obj. Usu. with *in, into.*

1904 A. B. F. Young *Compl. Motorist* vii. 176 The mighty engine is fretting and heating itself with impatience, and the clutch is continually being thrown in and out. **1969** J. T. Story *Dishonourable Member* ii. 16, I was forced to rev my engine and throw the gears into reverse. **1979** N. Slater *Falcon* x. 177 He threw the cruising Alfa into third gear and powered away.

f. *trans.* = *throw down*, sense 40 d in Dict. Also *absol.*

1923 A. L. Simon *Supply, Care & Sale of Wine* xvi. 111 If red wines be shipped and bottled too early, they will throw a heavy sediment in the bottle instead of lees in casks. **1930** Field & Weill *Electro-Plating* iv. 64 With copper and zinc sulphate solutions..there is little tendency to 'throw'. **1956** S. M. Tritton *Amateur Wine Making* iii. 89 The wine..should not throw a deposit nor form bubbles round the perimeter of the liquid. **1970** *Daily Tel.* 7 July 13/1 Wines throw their deposit or sediment differently.

g. To operate (a switch), esp. by moving a lever. *colloq.* (orig. *U.S.*).

1930 E. B. White *Let.* July (1976) 94 One of the men ran and threw the switch in the foundry, cutting off the current. **1940** 'N. Shute' *Landfall* 152 If it goes higher you must throw this switch. **1959** *Listener* 29 Jan. 211/1 If the trespasser's clothes are caught in moving machinery, is not the owner of the premises under a duty to throw the switch in order to stop the machine? **1978** *Times* 20 Nov. 2/3 More than 14,000 civil servants are engaged on government computer work. Those with the direct power to throw the switches..number 1,728.

32. d. To disconcert or confuse (someone), to disturb, upset. Cf. sense 44 l in Dict. *colloq.* (orig. *U.S.*).

1844 E. B. Browning *Lett. to M. R. Mitford* (1983) II. 431 He appeared to me far more *thrown* by this last adversity than he ever was by the death of his Katy. **1941** B. Schulberg *What makes Sammy Run?* vi. 104 Don't let Julian's worries throw you. **1950** L. Kaufman *Jubel's Children* xxiii. 247, I knew my way around in a restaurant and a bill of fare. Sometimes, even those French dishes didn't throw me. **1961** C. Willock *Death in Covert* ix. 172 Miche refused to be thrown. 'I rather like enthusiasms,' she said gallantly. **1964** Mrs. L. B. Johnson *White House Diary* 16 June (1970) 169 Although I was a bit thrown by the mix-up over the two Mrs. Does, I felt this was one of those times that shows whether or not you've got poise and inner calm. **1978** *Browning Inst. Studies* VI. 72 One might almost suspect that Browning was trying to 'throw' his reader. **1981** P. Dickinson *Seventh Raven* iv. 47 It'll throw those kids if they have to make the change at the last moment.

e. To break or render inoperable (something mechanical). *colloq.* (orig. and chiefly *U.S.*).

1954 *Amer. Speech* XXIX. 103 *Throw a clutch,*..to break a clutch, usually in speed-shifting. 'On the fourth run we threw a clutch, so that was the end.' **1976** *Billings* (Montana) *Gaz.* 1 July 4-E/1 A truck for Springfield, Va., threw its transmission near Towson. **1980** *Dirt Bike* Oct. 43/2 Suzuki teammate Barnett threw a chain while running fourth early in the race.

34. a. (Earlier example.)

1847 C. Brontë *Jane Eyre* III. viii. 184 And try to restrain the disproportionate fervour with which you throw yourself into common-place home pleasures.

35. *throw about.* **a.** (Examples with reference to aircraft and motor vehicles.)

1942 *Tee Emm* (Air Ministry) II. 85 The operational fighter pilot..wants an aircraft..easily manœuvreable so that he can throw it about when necessary. **1959** *Motor* 11 Nov. 524/1 On the confined test ground it seemed easier to 'throw about' than the big B.M.W., but neither car could show its paces in the space available.

37. throw away. c. Also *spec.* in *Cricket*, to lose (a wicket) through careless play.

1898 K. S. Ranjitsinhji *With Stoddart's Team* (ed. 4) xii. 237 Many wickets were thrown away by the batsmen at critical periods by careless and hasty strokes. **1904** P. F. Warner *How we recovered Ashes* ix. 185 Braund, Bosanquet, and Rhodes literally threw their wickets away. **1977** *World of Cricket Monthly* June 42/3 Once in Lahore, Pakistan, he threw away his wicket so that Australia could win.

e. *Theatr.* To deliver (lines) in a casual manner; to underemphasize or play down (usu. for increased dramatic effect). Also *absol.* and *transf.* Cf. *throw-away B. 3.

1934 J. Agate in *Sunday Times* 18 Nov. 4/1 The spectator becomes aware of a fixed determination on the actor's part to make as little as possible of anything that can be called the orthodox 'acting' of the part, to throw away—in the actor's sense—everything except the highest of its poetry and the most sensitive of its philosophy. **1957** *Times Lit. Suppl.* 11 Oct. 611/3 Mr Fleming can be exuberant; but he prefers, in the stage term, to 'throw away', something he does just as neatly and wittily as du Maurier used to do it in the theatre. **1959** *Times* 26 May 13/4 In this part he again covered up for his author by charmingly throwing away as many lines as possible. **1959** *Listener* 14 May 861/1 The acting was deliberately played down for microphone purposes... This no doubt necessary business of 'throwing it away' must involve some losses as well as some odd reading of parts.

40. throw down. i. *Cricket.* To knock down (a wicket) with a throw-in from the field, with the intention of dismissing the batsman.

1860 *Baily's Mag.* Sept. 429 John Lillywhite..from long leg..threw down the wicket, and Mr. Davidson was thus run out. **1912** P. F. Warner *England v. Australia* v. 44 Hobbs throwing down Kortlang's wicket from cover-point. **1962** E. W. Swanton in Altham & Swanton *Hist. Cricket* (new ed.) II. xii. 244 All seemed over when Solomon from 25 yards range and square with the wicket on the leg-side threw down the stumps to run out Davidson.

41. throw in. d. (*d*) (Examples in *Cricket.*)

1816 W. Lambert *Cricketer's Guide* (ed. 6) iii. 43 Long Stop. This man..should be one who is not afraid of the Ball,..and who can throw in well. **1938** *Times* 16 Apr. 8/1 Those 'girls' at the Oval..threw in from the boundary with an accuracy which would have done credit to a University side. **1976** J. Snow *Cricket Rebel* 118 My back troubled me from the strain of bowling on the harder Australian wickets for four months and my right shoulder had 'gone' when it came to throwing the ball in.

e. Also *intr.* (chiefly *U.S.*), *to throw in* (*with*).

1923 *Century Mag.* Oct. 829/1 Lead me to them humans, and I'll throw in with them. **1954** W. Faulkner *Fable* 359 When we threw in together that day..he didn't know how long he had been on the road. **1978** J. Carroll *Mortal Friends* i. 15 The important thing was that Jim Brady's best boy—a strong and not unwise lad—had thrown in for good with his own people. **1981** M. Moorcock *Byzantium Endures* xi. 262 We should have stayed with the peasants and not thrown in with Russians and Jews.

g. *to throw in one's hand*: (*a*) to retire from a card game, esp. poker; (*b*) *fig.*, to give up a contest or struggle. *colloq.*

[**1904** R. F. Foster *Pract. Poker* 49 Players should be careful never to throw their hands into the deadwood until they have seen openers.] **1923** *Daily Mail* 3 July 8 Our plucky farmers are not 'throwing in their hands'. **1926** *Auction Bridge Mag.* July 119/1 People get so tired of throwing in hand after hand that they come in, regardless of their position... It needs great self-control to throw in hand after hand. **1938** G. March-Phillipps *Ace High* ii. ii. 141 She turned it up and saw the six of Hearts... 'Bitched again!' Bobby said, and threw in his hand. **1957** *Economist* 5 Oct. 59/2 An international understanding outside Egypt is needed before the board can throw in its hand. **1962** D. Francis *Dead Cert* ii. 20, I threw in my hand. I pushed the four chips across to him. **1973** J. Ashford *Double Run* ii. 9 Nina Ryan had thrown in her hand without bothering to buy cards. She wasn't really fond of poker. **1978** 'S. Woods' *Exit Murderer* 145 Sykes looked at him for a long moment.. and then suddenly threw in his hand. 'She knew,' he said positively.

42. throw off. e. (Earlier *intr.* examples.)

1789 *Loiterer* 14 Feb. 8 No sooner had the hounds thrown off than my horse grew..hot. *Ibid.* 11 Apr. 5, I have been assured by very experienced Hunters of Tufts, that they never threw off earlier than twelve.

44. throw out. c. Also, to project (the voice), esp. in singing. Cf. sense 15 a above.

1792 H. Newdigate *Let.* Feb. in A. E. Newdigate-Newdegate *Cheverels* (1898) ix. 123 Mortellari..is giving her an Artful Manner of throwing out her Voice to be heard in public.

g. (Earlier example of sense 'to put forward tentatively'.)

1824 M. Wilmot *Let.* 26 May (1935) 214, I only throw out this idea to shew I am ready to act on it.

h. (Earlier *trans.* example.)

1798 Jane Austen *Let.* 1 Dec. (1952) 34 He wants my mother to look yellow and to throw out a rash, but she will do neither.

l. (Earlier example.) Also *transf.*, of a plan, calculation, etc.

1824 H. Davy *Diary* July (1836) II. v. 211 My *senza cura* servant, threw me out by not putting powder enough in my horn. **1892** A. W. Pinero *Magistrate* i. 24, I took five years from my total... It has thrown everything out. As I am now thirty-one, instead of thirty-six as I ought to be, it stands to reason that I couldn't have been married twenty years ago.

45. throw over. b. (Earlier and later examples.) Also, to cancel (an appointment) with someone, to put (someone) off.

1835 Dickens *Let.* 5 Nov. (1965) I. 88, I will throw Bell's life over, altogether. **1891** O. Wilde *Pict. Dorian Gray* iii. 62 'Are you disengaged Tuesday?' 'For you I would throw over anybody, Duchess.' **1903** G. B. Shaw *Man & Superman* i. 40 Tavy will kiss; and you will only turn the cheek. And you will throw him over if anybody better turns up. **1908** E. F. Benson *Climber* x. 146 He had another engagement, and though I urged him not to throw it over when I heard that, he really insisted on coming.

47. throw together. a. (Later examples.)

1878 I. L. Bird *Lady's Life Rocky Mountains* (1879) iii. 37, I threw a few things together and came here. **1967** E. Short *Embroidery & Fabric Collage* i. 18 A bundle of threads or fabrics accidentally thrown together may suggest an exciting scheme.

c. (Earlier example.)

1818 SCOTT *Heart Midl.* I. viii. 226 The circumstances of their families threw the young people constantly together.

d. To prepare (a snack, meal, etc.) hastily or in an improvised manner.

1962 'E. FERRARS' *Busy Body* i. 13 If we haven't eaten she'll throw something together. **1980** P. G. WINSLOW *Counsellor Heart* iv. 64 She hadn't been listening much, throwing a quick supper together.

48. throw up. b. (Further examples.) Also *intr.* (now the usual use). Now chiefly *colloq.* or *slang.*

1793 *Morning Chron.* 20 Feb. 3/1 In what odd ways we taste misfortune's cup—While France throws *down* the gauntlet—Pitt throws *up.* **1887** V. MARTIN *Let.* in M. Collis *Somerville & Ross* (1968) iii. 44 To show that he was quite unembarrassed he began to play with the favourite pug, finally dancing it round on its hind legs. It immediately threw up and that I think ends the story. **1895** HERRON & BACON in A. Dundes *Mother Wit* (1973) 367/2 He made a tea which acted as an emetic and the patient threw up a variety of reptiles. **1934** T. N. WILDER *Heaven's my Destination* 6 He thought he was going to throw up. **1956** [see *SHOWBUSINESS 1 b]. **1970** G. F. NEWMAN *Sir, You Bastard* i. 24 What if the scene was a man with the front wheel of a bus on his chest? Wasn't the calm, inspiring copper entitled to throw up? **1977** *New Yorker* 19 Sept. 49/3 I'm not sure anyone else even noticed, but it upset me so much I threw up. **1980** A. E. FISHER *Midnight Men* viii. 102 Ogy got drunk and threw up in the backyard.

h. Also without *it* and with personal object: to hold (someone) up as an example, object of reproach, etc. (Earlier and later examples.)

1815 R. FINDLEY *Let.* 6 Dec. in N. E. Eliason *Tarheel Talk* (1956) 300 Betsey..throwed up to me that I made a better bed for Sally then her little Betsey. **1870** 'MARK TWAIN' in *Galaxy* July 139/1 He [*sc.* Benjamin Franklin] would work all day and then sit up nights..so that all other boys might have to do that also or else have Benjamin Franklin thrown up to them. **1957** R. LAWLER *Summer of Seventeenth Doll* I. i. 22 Every time he's away and we have a row, Emma throws him up at me like a dirty dish-cloth.

i. (Earlier example.)

1832 *Q. Rev.* XLVII. 237 For heaven's sake, take care of my hounds in case they may throw up in the lane.

k. *trans.* To produce or provide. *colloq.*

1963 *Guardian* 23 Sept. 3/5 Their memories of this year's fortnight may last even longer than anything Uncle Ted can throw up from his family joke repertoire on Christmas Day. **1981** M. MOORCOCK *Byzantium Endures* xii. 287 Russia was throwing up better women than men at that time. All the worthwhile men had been killed.

VII. 49. *throw the* *BOOK *at, a* *MONKEY-*wrench into the machinery, a* *SPANNER *in the works, one's* *WEIGHT *about.*

throw-. Add: **1. b. throw cushion** *N. Amer.* = *scatter cushion* s.v. *SCATTER *v.* 7 b; **throw-net,** a fishing net cast out by hand; **throw pillow** = *throw cushion* above; **throw weight** (see quot. 1982[1]). **c.** (sense 9 of *THROW $sb.^2$) *throw rug*; *throw-style, type* adjs. Cf. *throw cushion, pillow* above. *N. Amer.* (chiefly *U.S.*).

1970 *Toronto Daily Star* 24 Sept. 28/6 (Advt.), Throw cushions, chests, dressers. **1931** *Times Educ. Suppl.* 21 Mar. (Home & Classroom Suppl.) p. ii (*caption*), The photograph shows the different kinds of 'nets' used. On the left is the throw-net. **1979** *Field* 9 May 975/4 For smaller fish the locals used circular throw-nets some eight feet in diameter. **1974** *Progress* (Easley, S. Carolina) 24 Apr. III. 5/2 (Advt.), Decorator throw pillows. **1952** *Better Homes & Gardens* Feb. 173/1 How to vacuum your throw rugs. **1978** R. LUDLUM *Holcroft Covenant* xi. 132 She leaned forward on the hassock, picking at an imaginary piece of lint on the throw rug beneath his feet. **1974** *Spartanburg* (S. Carolina) *Herald* 18 Apr. (Kmart Advts. Suppl.) 8 Tailored, throw-style bedspread, elegantly puff-quilted to the floor. **1970** *Toronto Daily Star* 24 Sept. 37/4 (Advt.), Quilted throw type bedspreads. **1969** *Sci. Amer.* Aug. 19/2 Parity..is clearly not numerical equality in the number of warheads or in the number of megatons or in the total 'throw weight'. **1982** *Times* 10 May 22/1 The second stage would seek to achieve equal ceilings on ballistic missile 'throw weight' at less than current American levels. 'Throw weight' is the term used to describe the weight of the warheads which missiles can carry onto a target. **1982** H. KISSINGER *Years of Upheaval* vii. 264 The Soviets were ahead in numbers of land-based missiles and throwweight.

2. throw-down, (*b*) *Austral.* and *N.Z.*, a type of small firework, a squib; **throw-in,** (*a*) (earlier examples); (*b*) in Bridge, an end play in which the declarer throws the lead to an opponent who has to play into a tenace combination; (*c*) in Polo, the act of throwing the ball (by the umpire) between opposing ranks of players, each team being on its own side of the line of the throw, in order to (re)start the game; (*d*) in Baseball, a throw made by an outfielder to an infielder; **throw-out,** (*b*) in Cricket, the act of throwing out a batsman (see THROW $v.^1$ 44 n); (*c*) *Bookbinding* (see quot. 1976); (*d*) the mechanism by which the driven and driving plates of a clutch in a motor vehicle are separated; usu. *attrib.*

1896 E. TURNER *Little Larrikin* xxvi. 321 Lol was.. projecting jumping Jacks and throwdowns on the floor, and keeping the cook..on the table. **1948** D. W. BALLANTYNE *Cunninghams* xiv. 75 Kids were exploding throw-downs on the footpaths. **1864** *Baily's Mag.* July 173 What a recreation!—wherein..the hands, dropping for a while the pen.., can..deliver a 'throw-in' decisive of all argument. **1891** [see *goal-kick* s.v. *GOAL *sb.* 6]. **1898** T. B. DRYBROUGH *Polo* xi. 245 Players should leave room for the ball to pass between them. In case of overlapping, the umpire may delay throwing-in or recall the throw, and he may recall a faulty throw-in. **1935** [see *EXIT *sb.* 2 b]. **1937** *Times* 12 July 5/2 Captain Robinson got away from the throw-in but broke his stick. **1940** *Sun* (Baltimore) 13 May 13 (*caption*) Dolph Camilli..slides safely into third..after a throw-in from outfielder Chuck Klein. **1952** *Ibid.* 2 Oct. 20/1 The Yankees might have had a big inning on the way since Martin had taken second on the throw-in. **1959** M. GILBERT *Blood & Judgement* x. 108 He settled down with *Reese on Play*, to study the tactics of the Throw-in. **1964** *Official Encycl. Bridge* 619/1 In a throw-in play, an opponent gains the lead, but it costs him a trick (or more) to do so. **1977** *Navy News* Sept. 38/4 (*caption*) All eyes on the ball at a throw-in during the Rundle Cup polo match between the Navy and Army at Tidworth. **1928** *Weekly Dispatch* 24 June 20/5 That 'throw-out' which has to be executed so quickly at cover-point. **1953** *Vocab. Bibliothec.* (Unesco) 190/1 Throw out (for maps, illus., etc.). **1966** *New Statesman* 18 Mar. 393/1 (Advt.), Illustrated and with 4 coloured throwout maps. **1969** *Catal. Austral., N.Z., & Pacific* (O.U.P., Melbourne) 16, 20 half-tone plates, 2 maps, end-paper map, 1 coloured throw out. **1970** K. BALL *Fiat 600, 600D Autobook* v. 46/2 (*caption*) Diagrammatic view of clutch throwout mechanism. **1976** *Gloss. Documentation Terms* (*B.S.I.*) 68 *Throw-out*, a leaf, usually bearing illustrative material, bound in at one edge and designed to fit the book when folded. **1979** P. WALLAGE *Restoration of Post-War Cars* 6 Clutch release bearing, throwout bearing.

throwable (þrōu·ăb'l), *a.* [f. THROW $v.^1$ + -ABLE.] Capable of being thrown.

1888 LEES & CLUTTERBUCK *Ramble in Brit. Columbia* xxiii. 264 We had thrown every throwable article at him. **1966** J. DERRICK *Teaching English to Immigrants* iv. 172 If it is difficult to find throwable objects, balls can be used instead..to represent them. **1977** G. V. HIGGINS *Dreamland* iii. 27, I reached for a throwable life preserver cushion.

throw-away. (In Dict. s.v. THROW-.) Add: **A.** *sb.* **1. a.** Now usu. with reference to ephemeral material distributed free of charge, as pamphlets, advertising leaflets, certain newspapers, etc. (Later examples.)

1922 JOYCE *Ulysses* 149 A sombre Y.M.C.A. young man..placed a throwaway in a hand of Mr Bloom. **1944** *Sun* (Baltimore) 1 June 16-0/3 The small throw-aways contain the latest authentic reports of the progress of the war. **1954** [see *junk mail* s.v. *JUNK $sb.^2$ 5]. **1965** *Newsweek* 21 June 70/2 The advertisements in the two editions of the weekly shopper's throwaway. **1973** D. RAMSAY *Deadly Discretion* 102 Here's our throwaway. It's also the ad we run in the papers.

b. More generally, anything designed to be thrown away after use; *spec.* a disposable container. Cf. sense 2 a of the adj. below. *colloq.*

1953 *Sun* (Baltimore) 17 Feb. (B ed.) 30/7 The group of county delegates submitted a bill..which would ban the dispensing of alcoholic beverages in throw-aways. **1976** *Monitor* (McAllen, Texas) 29 Oct. 3A/3 Consumers could save millions of dollars a year in lower prices if soft drinks and beer were sold in returnable containers instead of throwaways.

2. An act of throwing away, or that which is thrown away, in various senses. Also *fig.* Cf. THROW $v.^1$ 37 in Dict. and Suppl.

1911 G. B. SHAW *Lett. to Granville Barker* (1956) 178 If the attempt proves a throw away, it is only a throw-away of the chance I promised him, not of the play. **1922** JOYCE *Ulysses* 223 A skiff, a crumpled throwaway..rode lightly down the Liffey. **1955** *N.Y. Times* 29 May VI. 15/1 Generally, the program opens with a line of girls in two or three minutes of fast-stepping, high-kicking precision dancing. This is a throwaway, designed to get late-comers settled into their seats before the real show starts. **1960** *Twentieth Cent.* Aug. 137 Each is a finely polished stylist: let no one be deceived by the easy, laconic throw-away of Ada Leverson. **1976** B. JACKSON *Flameout* vi. 115 It was a pity that the best question was a throwaway to the other reporters: they didn't deserve it. **1983** *Listener* 13 Oct. 21/1 Even in films they hiss 'What did he say?' at a throwaway of dialogue, thus ensuring that the next few minutes are lost to all around.

B. as *adj.* **1.** Of prices: so low as to represent virtually no return for the goods sold; 'give-away'.

1924 A. J. SMALL *Frozen Gold* xiii. 288 With a modicum of luck they might even be able to record every claim they had pegged—and then get rid of them at throw-away prices. **1967** *Spectator* 14 July 53/3 At throwaway prices everyone can afford the latest Camp, and there will be something new coming along next month. **1976** [see *SATURATE *v.* 2 d].

2. a. Designating something designed to be thrown away after use; disposable.

1928 *Weekly Dispatch* 13 May 17 You can..clean your face at intervals with those throwaway hankies you buy from any chemist. **1945** *Forbes* (N.Y.) 15 Oct. 16/1 'Throw-away' towels will arrive soon. **1958** *Engineering* 7 Feb. 192/3 The butane comes from a throwaway cartridge. **1970** *Worship* Jan. 41 Already one hears of loose-leaf prayer books and throw-away hymn books. **1982** J. HANSEN *Gravedigger* iv. 33 Two plastic-handled throwaway razors.

b. Pertaining to or characterized by the use of disposable goods or those with a short life-span.

1969 *New Scientist* 25 Sept. 648/1 We will undoubtedly have a formidable litter problem in our 'throw away' world..from..household equipment with built-in obsolescence. **1977** M. DRABBLE *Ice Age* II. 114 She thanked God that she lived in a consumer throw-away flush-away advertising society. **1980** *Jrnl. R. Soc. Arts* Mar. 188/1 At the same time the 'throw away' attitude developed in society.

3. Underemphatic or casual in style or technique; understated (usu. for increased effect). Cf. *THROW $v.^1$ 37 e.

1955 *Time* 4 Apr. 77/2 It takes a certain nerve for a comedian to try a throwaway line. **1958** M. DICKENS *Man Overboard* vii. 102 He was more cunning than he seemed with that throw-away sixth-form voice. **1961** *John o' London's* 25 May 591/4, I remember his beautiful throw-away performance in *Mr. Deeds goes to Town.* **1969** *N.Y. Rev. Bks.* 30 Jan. 27/1 He will..carry us with him, a little breathless perhaps, and dizzy with his throw-away allusions and polyglot versatility. **1972** *Daily Tel.* 29 June 7/7 You can carry your enthusiasm..into casual slouchy nonchalance, and the outstanding collection of Stephen Adnitt had plenty of this throwaway chic. **1980** *Times Lit. Suppl.* 11 July 786/3 The style of the narrative is measured but evocative; a little throw-away, a little affected by the insidious influence of Peter Fleming.

throw-back. Add: **3.** (Earlier example.) Also, a reversion to the technique or methods of an earlier period. Also applied to a person using such techniques.

1888 KIPLING *Plain Tales from Hills* 209 The queer, savage feeling..must be a 'throw back' to times when men and women were rather worse than they are now. **1930** E. BLUNDEN in *Nation & Athenaeum* 6 Dec. 327/1 The Canterbury Poets were a throw-back to Cooke's little volumes. **1938** *Sun* (Baltimore) 19 July 8/3 His flight was harebrained and foolhardy... It was an unnecessary throwback to the romantic era of long-distance aviation. **1949** *Ibid.* 14 July 23/1 On the whole it was wartime baseball, a throwback to the hilarious 1945 World Series between the Tigers and the Cubs. **1976** *UCT Stud. in Eng.* (Univ. of Cape Town) Oct. 13 If..modern literature is distinctive in its claim on our moral attention, Stevens is distinctly un-modern, a transcendental throwback.

throwed, pa. t. and pa. pple. of THROW $v.^1$ (Later U.S. dial. examples.)

1914 *Sat. Even. Post* 3 Oct. 20/3 This should ought to of gave me a record of 16 wins and 0 defeats because the only games I lost was throwed away behind me. **1930** [see *HONKY-TONK 1]. **1949** [see *GRAIN $v.^1$ 8]. **1968** E. J. GAINES in A. Chapman *New Black Voices* (1972) 91 He wiped his mouth and throwed his cup on his bunk.

thrower. Add: **II. 3. a.** (Earlier example in *Cricket.*)

1832 P. EGAN *Bk. Sports* 344/1 Mr. K–ngsc—e comes next.. An excellent thrower—a hundred yards clear.

b. *thrower-out* (later example).

1963 N. STREATFEILD *Vicarage Family* vi. 75 Some of the members of his men's society..are coming by train as throwers-out. If there is a rumpus it will be all over almost before it begins.

throwing, *vbl. sb.*[1] Add: **III. 5. b.** *throwing arm* (properly *ppl. a.*). **c. throwing power,** the ability of an electrodepositing solution to produce an even coating on an irregularly shaped object.

1972 J. MOSEDALE *Football* ii. 19 Thanks to his accurate throwing arm, New Orleans was..one of the darkest cities in America. **1977** *World of Cricket Monthly* June 47/2 He had one of the strongest throwing arms ever seen in Australian cricket. **1922** *Trans. Amer. Electrochem. Soc.* XLI. 363 The object of this study was the development of a zinc plating bath of high 'throwing power'. **1932** *Metal Industry* XL. 501/2 He had to undertake the task of determining the throwing power of several selected plating baths. **1966** D. G. BRANDON *Mod. Techniques Metallogr.* 5 Electropolishing..may even give a poor macropolish as a result of..poor throwing power in the electrolyte.

thrown, *ppl. a.* Add: **II. 4.** *thrown-away, -back* (earlier example), *-together.*

1778 'J. H. ST. JOHN DE CRÈVECŒUR' *Sk. 18th-Cent. Amer.* (1925) 323 Your neighbours won't thank you for this thrownaway humanity. **1890** W. JAMES *Princ. Psychol.* II. xxv. 484 The frowning brow, the thrown-back shoulders, and clenched fists of rage. **1934** Thrown-together [see *RED-HOT *a.* (and *sb.*) 4]. **1973** J. LEASOR *Host of Extras* v. 69 The beach was littered with..thrown-away cigarette packets.

throw-off. a. (Earlier example.)

1843 *Ainsworth's Mag.* III. 144 The throw-off will be unusually great to-morrow.

throw-over. Add: **throw-over switch** *Electr. Engin.* (see quot. 1943).

1902 [in Dict.]. **1919** *Wireless World* VII. 40/1 A simple differential indicator operated by a throw-over switch. **1943** *Gloss. Terms Electr. Engin.* (*B.S.I.*) 52 *Throw-over switch*, a switch for changing over from one set of connections to another set of connections.

thrum, $sb.^2$ Add: **7. a.** *thrum mat* (later examples). **b. thrum cap,** (*b*) *Canad.* (*obs.* exc. in place-names), a small island with a conical shape suggestive of a thrum cap.

1832 T. BAILLIE *Acct. New Brunswick* 120 Opposite to this point an islet or thrum-cap..was once considered available for the purpose of drawing fish. **1903** G. S. WASSON *Cap'n Simeon's Store* xi. 248 They had..taken to their boat and pulled for Thrumcap Island Light. **1966** T. H. RADDALL *Hangman's Beach* II. xiv. 217 'Why is this called the Thrum Cap?' 'Thrumb's a coarse kind of wool. ..Sailors used to wear knitted caps of red thrum... You notice the red bank of the knoll standing up like a thrum cap.' **1883** *Man. Seamanship Boys' Training Ships* (Admiralty) (1886) 184 A thrum mat is made by cutting a certain number of yarns of equal length and reeving them through holes made in the mat, both ends to come through on one side. **1961** F. H. BURGESS *Dict. Sailing* 208 *Thrum mat*, a piece of canvas or other coarse material into which thrums are inserted, either roughly for chafing purposes and collision mats, or in decorative pattern with materials suitable for homes.

thrumming, *vbl. sb.* Add: (Examples in sense 2 of THRUM *v.*³)

1941 D. C. PEATTIE *Road of Naturalist* (1946) i. 9 Unleashed for the long stretch, the motor took up a loyal thrumming. **1969** *Daily Tel.* 14 Apr. 19/6 The arrival of a hovercraft..brings a thrumming which rattles the window. **1977** *Islander* (Victoria, B.C.) 21 Aug. 10/1 Switch on, and the Yanmar diesel barked into life, warming up slowly to a soft thrumming.

thrump (þrʊ̆mp). [Echoic.] The sound of a blow, heavy fall or beat, etc. Freq. redupl.

1871 *Daily News* 25 Jan., The heavy thrump, thrump of the mitrailleuse. **1886** *Century Mag.* Feb. 520/1 The banjo's thrump and strum. **1903** *Westm. Gaz.* 5 Oct. 2/1, I awoke with the music of marching men's feet in my ears—thrump, thrump, thrump, thrump.

† **thrums** (þrʊ̆ms). *Obs. slang.* Also quasi-*sing.* thrum (7 **thrumm**). [Repr. colloq. or dial. pronunc. of *THRUP(P)ENCE.] = THREEPENCE.

1699 B. E. *New Dict. Canting Crew, Thrumms*, threepence. **1846** *Swell's Night Guide* 78 There is a hanger on here who teaches the art of self defence—thrums (three pence) a lesson. **1865** *Leaves from Diary of Celebrated Burglar & Pickpocket* 108/2 His first putting-up place was at a low padding ken in St. Giles's, where he paid a 'thrum' per night for share of a 'doss'. **1880** W. H. PATTERSON *Gloss. Words Antrim & Down* 106 *Thrum*,..a threepence. A commission of three pence per stone of flax, paid by a flax-buyer to a person who brings the buyer and seller together in open market. **1933** *Bulletin* (Sydney) 23 Aug. 10/2, I haven't encountered a crook thrum yet.

thrup(p)ence, thrup(p)enny (þrʊ̆·pĕns, þrʊ̆·pĕni; þru·-). Repr. colloq. or dial. pronunc. of THREEPENCE, THREEPENNY *a.* (*sb.*).

1895 H. NEVINSON *Neighbours of Ours* v. 142 They paid 'er fivepence for doin' each large flag... So she sublets to Ginger at thruppence a flag. **1962** *Spectator* 27 July 117 A letter with a thrupenny stamp.

thrush¹. Add: **2*.** *fig.* A female singer. *U.S.*

1940 *Amer. Speech* XV. 205/1 *Thrush*, a songstress. **1966** *Crescendo* Oct. 31/2 She has established herself as one of the best female thrushes in this area. **1982** B. FANTONI *Stickman* iv. 38 The band's thrush and Moons argued so long over the tempo to play 'Lover Man' we ditched it.

thrush². Add: **1.** Also, an infection of any other part with the same fungus (now called *Candida albicans*), esp. of a woman's vagina. (Further examples.)

1967 *Current Medicine & Drugs* Dec. 4/1 The occurrence of Thrush Bowel Infection after antibiotics is..argued by the makers of Nystatin. **1970** PASSMORE & ROBSON *Compan. Med. Stud.* II. xviii. 19/2 Vaginal thrush is fairly commonly associated with pregnancy. **1977** *Spare Rib* Jan. 36/1 Thrush is very irritating and can make you extremely sore if it's allowed to continue.

thrust, *sb.* Add: **I. 3. a.** (*b*) (Further examples.) (*e*) The propulsive force developed by a jet or rocket engine.

1870 *4th Ann. Rep. Aëronaut. Soc. 1869* 9 The thrust of aërial screw propellers. **1933** *Aircraft Engin.* Jan. 22/2 This series of tests were undertaken to determine how much the reaction thrust of a jet could be increased by the use of thrust augmentors. **1950** *Sci. News* XV. 72 Since news of Whittle's jet engine was released there has been a popular misconception that if there is no atmosphere for the exhaust gases to push against there will be no thrust. **1977** *R.A.F. Yearbk.* 31/1 Recovery..involves unstalling the wing and re-establishing lift rather than blasting the aircraft out with thrust. **1982** *Daily Tel.* 14 Jan. 16/5 The engine was a Russian-built Nene of higher thrust (6,000 lb) than the original models. **1983** D. STINTON *Design of Aeroplane* vii. 297 A propeller consists of a number of wing-like aerofoils designed to convert torque into thrust.

II. 6. e. The principal theme or gist (*of* remarks, an argument, etc.); a point, aim, or purpose. orig. and chiefly *U.S.*

1968 MRS. L. B. JOHNSON *White House Diary* 17 Apr. (1970) 667 He spoke well... His thrust was that we.. 'make open spaces and recreation facilities a part of the daily..environment of people'. **1972** A. CHAPMAN *New Black Voices* 575 The Institute of the Black World in Atlanta... Its central thrust is towards the creation of an international center for Black Studies. **1973** *Globe & Mail* (Toronto) 1 Aug. 6/3 The thrust of your editorial..is premised on the discredited 'compact theory'. **1977** *Guardian Weekly* 28 Aug. 18/4 That was the thrust of the exclusive story in the New York Times on March 10. *Ibid.* 6 Nov. 16/1 The postwar thrust of U.S. policy..has been to enlist Thailand in an anti-Communist alliance. **1982** *Church Times* 15 Jan. 12/4 A major part of the thrust of my article was to dissuade others from proposing such a cutback.

6*. *Geol.* = *thrust-fault* s.v. THRUST *sb.* 7 in Dict. and Suppl.

1888 *Q. Jrnl. Geol. Soc.* XLIV. 420 Outliers of the 'Fucoid-beds' and Serpulite-grit are found,..separated from each other by major thrusts. **1910** *Ibid.* LXVI. 593 Thrust is here employed in the sense of a fold-fault replacing the lower limb of an overturned anticline. Lag..is employed in the sense of a fold-fault replacing the upper limb of an overturned anticline. **1926** *Ibid.* LXXXII. 315 The Creag-an-Lochan Thrust. [*Note*] Equivalent to the 'lag' of E. B. Bailey [*preceding quot.*]; but the term 'thrust' is preferred and used throughout this paper for all structures indicating differential resistance to folding forces at a comparatively early stage. **1934** B. & R. WILLIS *Geologic Structures* (ed. 3) vii. 153 The term 'thrust' too often connotes the idea of an overthrust, whereas the structure may be an underthrust. **1942** E. M. ANDERSON *Dynamics of Faulting* i. 1 Overthrusts, or more simply thrusts, are faults which are inclined, in theory, at well under 45° to the horizon, and in field experience it is found that they are sometimes nearly horizontal. **1942** [see *OVERTHRUST *ppl. a.*]. **1971** C. R. TWIDALE *Structural Landforms* iv. 98 In a normal thrust the upper block rides over the lower.. but in a lag thrust the lower block is thrust forward and upwards beneath the upper.

7. thrust augmentor *Aeronaut.*, a procedure or modification used with a jet engine to increase its thrust; so **thrust augmentation; thrust-bearing** (earlier example); **thrust-box** (example); **thrust chamber** *Astronautics* (see quot.); **thrust-fault**: in mod. use, a low-angle reverse fault; also, any low-angle fault; = sense 6* above; (further examples); hence **thrust-faulted** *a.*, **-faulting** *vbl. sb.*; **thrust reverser** *Aeronaut.*, a device for reversing the flow of gas from a jet engine so as to produce a retarding backward thrust; **thrust spoiler** *Aeronaut.*, a device for deflecting the flow of gas from a jet engine so as to reduce the thrust quickly without reducing the engine power; **thrust vector**, a vector representing the direction (and magnitude) of the thrust produced by a jet engine, propeller, etc.; **thrust washer,** a washer (WASHER *sb.*²) against which a thrust-bearing rests.

1956 W. A. HEFLIN *U.S. Air Force Dict.* 524/2 Thrust augmentation for jet engines is accomplished by afterburning, reheating, water injection, etc. **1967** N. E. BORDEN *Jet-Engine Fundamentals* 126 On some jet engines, it is advantageous to provide a means of thrust augmentation during take-off on warm or hot days. **1933** Thrust augmentor [see sense 3 a (*e*) above]. **1947** *Jrnl. R. Aeronaut. Soc.* LI. 79/1 The pumping could be directly produced by a ducted fan, when again a thrust augmentor effect would result. **1858** *Mechanichs' Mag.* 6 Mar. 230/2 (*heading*) Thrust bearing for screw propeller. **1918** *Blackw. Mag.* Mar. 291 Pretty drawings in colour of such things as thrust-boxes and oil-pumps. **1962** F. I. ORDWAY et al. *Basic Astronautics* x. 413 The rocket thrust chamber is a device into which propellants are injected and burned to form gases. The basic components of the thrust chamber are the injector, the combustion chamber, and the exhaust nozzle. **1889** *Rep. Brit. Assoc. Adv. Sci. 1888* 659 He suggested a thrust-fault through the Mendip axis carrying its upper portion northward. **1915** C. SCHUCHERT in Pirsson & Schuchert *Text-bk. Geol.* I. xiv. 344 Reverse faults..having a gently inclined fault-surface are known as thrust-faults or simply thrusts. **1944** [see *OVERTHRUST *sb.*]. **1972** J. G. DENNIS *Structural Geol.* xii. 271 Since thrust faults were originally considered a class of reverse faults, they should bring older rocks over younger. So many low-dip normal faults have been called thrusts, however, that we must include all low-dip faults in this class. **1980** *Sci. Amer.* Oct. 127/2 The thrust faults and folds indicate that the rocks were much compressed in the horizontal direction. *Ibid.*, The Valley and Ridge province is characterized by folded and thrust-faulted strata of mostly unmetamorphosed sedimentary rocks formed between 600 million and 300 million years ago. **1912** *Q. Jrnl. Geol. Soc.* LXVIII. 59 The occurrence of these inliers is due to thrust-faulting. **1936** *Geogr. Jrnl.* LXXXVII. 224 The Purari Plateau is characterized by.. extensive uplifting with the accompanying development of block-faulting, probably more normal faulting than thrust-faulting. **1954** *Flight Handbk.* (ed. 5) xi. 164 (*caption*) A turbojet thrust-reverser developed by the American Boeing company. The jet is deflected by a W-shaped pair of clamshell doors. **1976** B. JACKSON *Flame-out* (1977) x. 182 At his low altitude there was simply no way he could correct the thrust reverser before he hit the deck. **1947** *Jrnl. R. Aeronaut. Soc.* LI. 679/2 The thrust spoiler could be operated in one second. So that if a pilot came in with the thrust spoiled, failed to land, and wished to make another circuit, the full thrust was available in one second. **1962** *Flight Internat.* LXXXII. 395/1 In the pioneer SC.1 the lift units are arranged in two pairs both mounted on lateral trunnions to pivot some 25° fore and aft, in order to provide longitudinal thrust components to assist transition to and from wing-supported flight. This idea has now given way to a fixed installation with thrust-vector control. **1975** *Offshore Engineer* Dec. 54/2 (Advt.), The whole unit, and thus the thrust vector, can be directed through 360°, which means that it has been possible to optimise the nozzle and propeller for one main flow direction. **1954** Thrust washer [see *SPACER 1 a]. **1962** [see *oil-retaining* s.v. *OIL *sb.*¹ 6 b]. **1970** K. BALL *Fiat 600, 600D Autobook* ix. 106/2 If the line is out of centre, vary the number of shims beneath the thrust washer.

thrust, *v.* Add: **IV. 8.** *Comb.*, as **thrust stage** *Theatr.*, an open stage that projects into the auditorium so that the audience is seated around three sides.

1968 *Sat. Rev.* (U.S.) 1 June 22 The Fine Arts Theatre.. is a compact, multipurpose amphitheater seating 600, which can be utilized for conventional theatricals, as a thrust stage, or even—with the built-in pit—for musicals and intimate opera. **1969** *Guardian* 28 Oct. 7/3 Knighted actors argue the merits of a 'thrust' stage for the costly new Sheffield Theatre. **1977** *Times* 25 Aug. 15/4 Kate went to the University of Toronto where they had just built a superb thrust-stage theatre.

thrust, *ppl. a.* [See the vb.] With adverbs, as *thrust-out* adj. = OUT-THRUST *ppl. a.*

1872 R. W. BUCHANAN *St. Abe & his Seven Wives* 153 And with thrust-out jaw and set Teeth, the Yankee threatens yet. **1976** [see *snake-hipped* s.v. *SNAKE *sb.* 10].

thruster. Add: **2. b.** *fig.* One who pushes his way; an aggressive or go-ahead person. Also *spec.* with reference to driving.

1925 FRASER & GIBBONS *Soldier & Sailor Words & Phr.* 280 *Thruster, a*, an obnoxious, pushing person. A 'bounder'. **1927** *Observer* 6 Nov. 13/1 Those who described their more successful fellows as 'thrusters' and 'climbers'. **1927** *Morning Post* 28 Nov. 10/4 The 'road thruster', or the man with the 'passing' mania, is usually a nuisance. **1960** *Times* 7 June 13/7 The ordinary lorry or van driver.. is often the worst thruster of all. **1964** C. WILLOCK *Enormous Zoo* ii. 21 Bere..was known as a thruster when it came to administration. **1974** R. HARRIS *Double Snare* xxvi. 197 Robert's car has fallen back, displaced by an Italian thruster's enormous red tourer. **1982** BARR & YORK *Official Sloane Ranger Handbk.* 106/1 She will not lend her support to any ambitious young thruster or leak the firm's secrets to a rival.

3. a. *Astronaut.* A small rocket engine on a spacecraft for providing the thrust needed to alter or correct its flight path or its attitude.

1962 J. GLENN in *Into Orbit* 146 This would include warming up the hydrogen peroxide thrusters so that they would go to work without delay when I activated the controls. **1965** *Newsweek* 13 Dec. 60 In past missions, excitement, the thump of the thruster rockets and a busy schedule all conspired to deprive the astronauts of sleep. **1969** *Guardian* 22 July 18/3 A 46-second firing of the reaction control thrusters altered Eagle's orbit. **1973** *Times* 28 Nov. 8/2 Small thrusters were fired yesterday which put the 570lb craft on course so that it will fly to within 81,000 miles of Jupiter on December 3. **1977** *Sci. Amer.* Feb. 61/1 The satellite is carefully tracked by ground stations, the propulsion vector needed to compensate for drift is computed and the appropriate thrusters are fired by radio command.

b. *Oil Industry.* Each of several jets or propellers on a drill ship or offshore rig, used for accurate manœuvring and maintenance of position.

1972 L. M. HARRIS *Introd. Deepwater Floating Drilling Operations* i. 3 Several vessels have been built, or are in the design and construction stage, that depend entirely upon thrusters, or powered units, to position the vessel dynamically. **1975** *Gen. Electric Investor* Winter 18/2 In the newest technique called 'dynamic positioning', gimbaled motors driving thruster propellers keep the rigs positioned over the drilling hole despite wind, waves and currents. **1983** *New Scientist* 2 June 627/2 When it is semi-submerged, a 'dynamic positioning' system, thrusters controlled by computers, keeps the ship within two metres of a programmed position in a force seven gale.

thrustful, thrustfulness. (Later examples.)

1963 *Economist* 22 June 1236/1 A Butler government might be a force for..greater economic thrustfulness. **1978** *Church Times* 1 Sept. 1/4 Few men have a good word for the Curial cardinals... They are the automatic targets ..of the frustrations of thrustful priests.

thruway, var. *THROUGHWAY.

thucholite (þiū·tʃoləit). *Min.* Also **thucolite.** [f. Th, U, C, H, O, symbols of the constituent elements + -LITE.] A naturally occurring brittle, highly lustrous, black mixture or complex of carbon and hydrocarbons with uraninite.

1928 H. V. ELLSWORTH in *Amer. Mineralogist* XIII. 66 A remarkable carbon mineral, which will be described in another paper under the name of thucholite, is sometimes very intimately associated with both uraninite and samarskite. **1938** R. W. LAWSON tr. *Hevesy & Paneth's Man. Radioactivity* (ed. 2) v. 62 Fig. 22..shows the *L*-spectrum of the mineral thucolite. **1965** G. J. WILLIAMS *Econ. Geol. N.Z.* xiii. 207/2 'The radioactivity in the carbonaceous matter is due to myriads of minute uraninites, 1 to 5 microns in size, distributed at random or as strings of granules.' Mr Whittle identified this uraniferous mineral as thucolite. **1980** *Mineral. Abstr.* XXXI. 487/2 Assemblages of thucholite in sandstone, dolomite, and shale of Polish Zechstein rocks are described. The thucholite..forms disseminated spheroidal or irregular bodies.

thuck (þʊk). [Echoic.] The sound of a missile, as an arrow, bullet, etc., hitting a target.

1948 F. BLAKE *Johnny Christmas* I. 46 Knifings, headblows muffled by sand, the *thuck* of arrows striking home. **1979** P. COSGRAVE *Three Colonels* 202 The whine of the rifle bullet and the *thuck* of its striking home.

Thucydidean (þiūːsididī·ăn), *a.* Also † -æan, -ian. [f. L. *Thūcȳdidēs* (Gr. Θουκυδίδης), name of a Greek historian of the fifth century B.C. +

-ean; cf. *Thūcȳdidēus* adj. (Cicero).] Of, pertaining to, or characteristic of Thucydides or his work.

1752 *Phil. Trans. R. Soc.* XLVII. 385 The European plagues are much more violent than the eastern; those being really the Thucydidian, which sweep all away. **1826** K. H. DIGBY *Morus* 125 Having no character of solemn reserve or Thucydidean dignity of style to support. **1834** —— *Mores Cath.* v. vi. 183 The Thucydidæan expression. **1888** *Encycl. Brit.* XXIII. 326/2 The best clue to Thucydidean bibliography is in Engelmann's *Scriptores Graeci.* **1911** *19th Cent.* Apr. 697 He even heightens the pathos of the Thucydidean original. **1945** E. K. CHAMBERS *Eng. Lit. at Close of Middle Ages* iii. 130 It was not long before, in Thucydidean phrase, he had won his way to the mythical. **1977** *Trans. Philol. Soc. 1975* 128 The Hellenizing and specifically Thucydidean tradition of Sallust and Tacitus.

thuddingly, *adv.* Add: Also *fig.*

1976 *Daily Tel.* 16 Dec. 10/5 The man who shot her, incidentally, is called Lord Lichfield—just one of the names dropped thuddingly at every opportunity. **1979** *Ibid.* 18 July 16/3 'Human stories'..even more thuddingly boring than the well-boiled cabbage-slabs of opinion.

thug, *sb.* **b.** Delete Now *U.S.* and add further examples.

1881 R. L. STEVENSON *Virginibus Puerisque* 164 Sometimes it [*sc.* death] leaps suddenly upon its victims, like a Thug. **1958** P. GIBBS *Curtains of Yesterday* xxvii. 216 'Isn't he a madman?' he asked. 'Isn't he raising an army of young thugs, his brutish young Brownshirts? Haven't they been fighting and brawling in Bavaria?' **1967** S. FAESSLER in *Atlantic Monthly* Apr. 103/2 The old man ducked for cover.., but not my father. Unarmed he stood up to the thugs, and was cracked over the head for it. **1982** *Daily Tel.* 7 Jan. 16/6 A plea..that it [*sc.* corporal punishment] should be retained as the final deterrent for school 'thugs'.

thug, *v.* Add: **2.** *intr.* To be a thug (sense b). *U.S.*

1937 *Sun* (Baltimore) 6 May 7/2 When I was thugging in Harlan county,..Merle Middleton was the chief of the gang. **1965** W. SOYINKA *Road* 22 *Chief*: ..Are you..one of the boys? *Samson*: I won't thug for you if that is what you mean.

thuggee. (Earlier *attrib.* example.)

1858 J. S. MILL *Memo. of Improvements in Admin. of India during Last Thirty Years* 46 The work of the Thuggee Suppression Department was nearly completed.

thuggery. (Later *transf.* examples.)

1930 E. D. SULLIVAN *Chicago Surrenders* xiv. 239 Thuggery..has met no serious rebuff on any front. **1959** *Economist* 29 June 1154/2 The police are having an extremely difficult task combating thuggery. **1973** *Nation Rev.* (Melbourne) 31 Aug. III. 1445/2 Envoys confronted with unfamiliar thuggery can be as naive as Birmingham businessmen who have become top politicians.

thuggish (þʊ·giʃ), *a.* [f. THUG *sb.* + -ISH[1].] Resembling a thug. Also *Comb.*, as *thuggish-looking* adj.

1953 W. BURROUGHS *Junkie* viii. 75, I..got in conversation with a thuggish-looking young Italian. **1976** *Daily Tel.* 25 Oct. 2/4 Thuggish youths streaming from the rival demonstration. **1977** *N.Y. Rev. Bks.* 24 Nov. 41/1 The Nationalists..had allowed some of their thuggish supporters to make [a mistake].

‖ **thugyi** (þə·dʒi). Also 9 **thoogyee.** [Burmese.] The headman of a village.

1863 C. WILLIAMS *Jrnl.* 3 Feb. in *Through Burmah* (1868) 57 On the Thoogyee sending for some pieces, I found the characters to be Nagiri. **1887** *Rangoon Gaz. Weekly Budget* 7 Jan. 8/4 On 18th a thugyi successfully attacked dacoits and recovered dacoited cattle. **1934** 'G. ORWELL' *Burmese Days* xxv. 369 Old thugyis with their grey hair knotted behind their heads. **1957** *Encycl. Brit.* IV. 430/2 In the villages, the *thugyis* or headmen, chosen by the villagers and approved by the government, have limited magisterial powers and collect the revenue. **1980** J. SILVERSTEIN *Burmese Politics* ii. 26 The *thugyi* was directly responsible to the deputy commissioner.

thuja. Add: Hence **thujaplicin** (-pləi·sin) [L. *plic-ātus*, pa. pple. of *plicāre* to fold], any of three isomers of isopropyltropolone, $C_3H_7{\cdot}C_7H_5O_2$, that have fungicidal properties and occur in the conifer *Thuja plicata.*

1948 ERDTMAN & GRIPENBERG in *Nature* 8 May 719/2 The compound, m.p. 82°, is termed γ-thujaplicin because the isopropyl group occupies the γ-position in the cycloheptatrieneolone. **1964** *New Scientist* 4 June 613/1 The tropolones beta thujaplicin and gamma thujaplicin were highly toxic to the four test basidiomycetes. **1978** *Further Perspectives Org. Chem.* 29 He did visualize the formation of simpler natural tropolones—the thujaplicins—by ring expansion in some unknown way from a benzene ring and an attached carbon.

thula (þu·lă). [*a.* ON *þula.*] A metrical list of names or poetic synonyms assembled in categories (orig. for oral recitation) to preserve traditional knowledge.

1936 K. MALONE *Widsith* 1 Three name-lists (and one fragment of such a list), to which I will refer by the technical term *thula*, taken from the Icelandic. **1937** —— in *Angl. Beibl.* XLVIII. 221 In an old thula-fragment quoted in the Icelandic *Hervararsaga* we are told that a certain Kíarr ruled the Valir. **1963** BROWN & FOOTE *Early Eng. & Norse Stud.* 113 It is undoubtedly because of these lists of names that the poem is called a *þula.* **1974** *Eng. Stud.* LV. 507 The first and third thulas are..parallel in introducing kings uninterruptedly.

Thule. Add: **1. b.** *ultima Thule*: in *fig.* use, also the lowest limit, the nadir.

1954 M. LOWRY *Let.* 22 May (1967) 370 Before you write off that behaviour as being the ultima thule of ingratitude..try to understand the effect your news..had on me. **1976** L. DAVIDOFF et al. in Mitchell & Oakley *Rights & Wrongs of Women* iv. 157 The one who had 'fallen' out of the respectable society..to the *ultima Thule* of prostitution.

2. *Archæol.* (with pronunc. þūl, þiūl). Used chiefly *attrib.* to designate a prehistoric Eskimo culture widely distributed from Alaska to Greenland *c* 500–1400 A.D. [From the name *Thule* (now Dundas), a settlement in N.W. Greenland.]

1927 T. MATHIASSEN *Archæol. of Central Eskimos* II. i. 2 We have..found remnants of an older culture which, after a locality outside the Central Eskimo territory, in North Greenland, we have called the Thule culture. **1935** *Nature* 3 Aug. 188/1 He [*sc.* Mathiassen] regards the Thule culture as originating in Asia. **1956** G. FREEMAN tr. *Malaurie's Last Kings of Thule* I. vii. 87 The Thule Culture—neo-Eskimo—would be derived from an anterior continental culture—palaeo-Eskimo. **1962** *Times* 4 Aug. 7/7 Within recent historical times Greenland has known three Eskimo cultures. The most recent is that of the Thule people who moved across Canada from Alaska. **1972** *Country Life* 12 Oct. 880 About AD 1100 a second Eskimo culture, known to archaeologists as the Thule period because it was first identified at Thule in Greenland, spread eastward from Alaska. *Ibid.* 881 The Thule Eskimos lived in stone houses. **1974** *Encycl. Brit. Macropædia* I. 1130/2 The spread of Thule..has been traced eastward from Alaska, arriving in Greenland about 1200. .. Later there was a resurge of Thule back toward the west, reaching all the way to Bering Strait. **1977** G. CLARK *World Prehist.* (ed. 3) IX. 411 The Neo-Eskimo bearers of the Thule culture, immediate forebears of the existing population.

Thulean (þiū·liăn), *a. Geol.* [f. THULE + -AN.] Of, pertaining to, or designating a region of Tertiary volcanic activity including Iceland and parts of Britain and Greenland.

1925 *Glasgow Herald* 10 Nov. 11/5 Jan Mayen, he said, formed a part of the Thulean or Brito-Arctic petrographical province. **1938** A. K. WELLS *Outl. Hist. Geol.* xvii. 206 Evidently Britain lay on the fringe of a vast North Atlantic (or Thulean) volcanic province. **1976** P. FRANCIS *Volcanoes* vii. 219 The Giant's Causeway in Antrim, and Fingal's Cave on the island of Staffa both originated when the Thulean plateau was being formed.

thulia (þiū·liă). *Chem.* [mod.L., f. next after THORIA, YTTRIA, etc.] The sesquioxide of thulium, Tm_2O_3, a dense white powder.

1886 [see *FRACTIONAL *a.* b]. **1924** J. W. MELLOR *Comprehensive Treat. Inorg. & Theoret. Chem.* V. xxxviii. 698 C. James has described processes for the extraction of thulia from ytterspar (Norwegian xenotime), euxenite, and a Norwegian columbate. **1968** C. A. HAMPEL *Encycl. Chem. Elements* 718/2 Should the demand arise, thulia, Tm_2O_3, could be isolated readily, as one of a number of individual rare earth by-products from the current (1967) commercial production of yttria by ion exchange, at a rate exceeding 1000 pounds per annum.

thulium (þiū·liŏm). *Chem.* [mod.L., coined in Fr. (P. T. Cleve 1879, in *Compt. Rend.* LXXXIX. 480), f. THULE + -IUM.] A rare metallic element of the lanthanide series that forms pale green salts in which it is trivalent. Atomic number 69; symbol Tm.

1879 P. T. CLEVE in *Chem. News* 12 Sept. 126/2 For the radical of the oxide placed between ytterbia and erbia..I propose the name of Thullium [*sic*], derived from Thulé, the ancient name of Scandinavia. **1923** U. R. EVANS *Metals & Metallic Compounds* II. 236 Thulium can be separated in a fairly pure state by oft-repeated recrystallization as bromate. **1924** [see *HOLMIUM]. **1956** *Nature* 17 Mar. 494/2 Iridium-192 continues to be the source most commonly used in industry for gamma-radiography... Thulium-170 has only gained slightly in popularity. **1968** *Punch* 24 Apr. 604/3 Gold, silver and platinum are starting to look pretty square as well as pricey these days. More sophisticated speculators have already shifted into antimony and zinc: while an *avant garde* group is believed to have plunged heavily on thulium.

thumb, *sb.* Add: **5. h.** Also in mod. use (with significance the reverse of that in the ancient amphitheatre): *thumbs down, up*, gestures made with the fingers closed and the thumb pointing vertically downwards (indicating disapproval or rejection) or upwards (as a sign of approval, acceptance, encouragement, etc.); also *attrib.* and *fig.*

1906 KIPLING *Puck of Pook's Hill* 180 We're finished men—thumbs down against both of us. **1917** A. G. EMPEY *Over Top* 311 *Thumbs up*, Tommy's expression which means 'everything is fine with me'. **1929** A. C. & C. EDINGTON *Studio Murder Myst.* iii. 26 The irrevocable 'thumbs down' on a lovely female actor, because certain shady pages in her past had been turned to the light. **1939** *War Illustr.* 4 Nov. p. iii/1 French peasants now return the 'thumbs up' gesture with which they are greeted by British troops on their way to the front. **1946** *Sunday Dispatch* 8 Sept. 1/2 He ran from his machine giving the thumbs-up sign. **1951** *Sport* 7–13 Jan. 16/3 The London team has been given the thumbs down sign by a meeting of 1st division promoters. **1951** S. SPENDER *World within World* v. 275 Our chief comedian was Buckfast... Everything about him suggested a 'thumbs up' attitude. **1954** R. SUTCLIFF *Eagle of Ninth* iii. 27 He laughed, and made the 'thumbs up' to his troops, calling 'Well done, lads!' **1961** *Guardian* 25 Mar. 6/7 The Chancellor of the Exchequer's thumbs-down to a National Theatre. **1967** *Technology Week* XX. 95/2 Giving a final 'thumbs up' on the rocket's readiness. **1971** *Sunday Times* (Johannesburg) 28 Mar. 5/1 She said the thumbs-down vote was not unanimous. **1976** *Scotsman* 25 Nov. 3/7 The market yesterday gave Sir Hugh the thumbs-up. The Fraser shares went up 3p to 58p on the report, which was apparently better than expected. **1979** R. FIENNES *Hell on Ice* i. 14 Both drivers gave a 'thumbs up'. **1982** *Daily Tel.* 5 Mar. 17/1 (*heading*) Baldwin statue gets thumbs down from Foot.

i. *to have a green thumb*: see *GREEN *a.* 1 k; *to stick out like a sore thumb*: see *SORE *a.* 9 f.

6. c. *thumb-latch* (earlier example), *-wheel* (examples). **d.** *thumb-sucking* (earlier example) *-twiddling* (cf. TWIDDLE *v.*[1] 2 c); *thumb -stained, -worn* (earlier example). **e. thumb-pad** (later example); **thumb paper** *U.S.*, a paper or card inserted in a book at the bottom of a page to protect it from thumb-marks; **thumb piano** *Mus.* = *SANSA; **thumb pick** *Mus.*, a kind of plectrum; **thumb print:** also *fig.*; **thumb-stick,** a tall walking-stick with a forked thumb-rest at the top; **thumb-sucker,** (*a*) a child who habitually sucks his thumb; (*b*) *Journalists' slang* (see quots. 1974, 1980); **thumb-tack,** add to def.: *N. Amer.* = *drawing-pin* s.v. DRAWING *vbl. sb.* 6 b; (earlier example); also as *v. trans.*; hence **thumb-tacked** *ppl. a.*

1761 *Essex Inst. Hist. Coll.* (1912) XLVIII. 96 Hinges, thumb latches, hammers. **1965** LEE & KNOWLES *Animal Hormones* iii. 53 At sexual maturity in male frogs (for example *Rana temporaria*) there is hypertrophy of the muscles of the forearms and thickening of the thumb-pads. **1843** B. R. HALL *New Purchase* I. xxx. 286 To have used..any other than the thumb-paper just named would have been considerably worse than ridiculous. **1888** E. EGGLESTON *Graysons* viii. 79 Fervid little love-notes.. were folded like the 'thumb-papers' that served to protect their books. **1942** F. WARNICK *Dial. Garrett County, Maryland* 15 *Thumb-paper*,..a small piece of paper used to protect the pages. **1952** R. A. WATERMAN in *Proc. 29th Internat. Congress Americanists 1949* II. 212 Melodic instruments..are utilized for their percussive value, as in the case of 'thumb pianos', [etc.]. **1974** *Encycl. Brit. Macropædia* I. 250/1 The *mbira* is also known as..thumb piano, and by other regional names. The common term *sansa* is not correct; it is not found in Africa. **1969** *John Edwards Mem. Foundation Q.* V. I. 13 Riley used a thumb pick to achieve the heavy bass runs. **1973** Thumb pick [see *PICK *sb.*[1] 5 c]. **1967** G. STEINER *Lang. & Silence* 66 Rimbaud left his thumb-print on language, on the name and nature of the modern poet. **1979** *Time* 30 July 12 Caddell's thumb-prints also were on the energy speech that Carter delivered to the nation Sunday after returning to Washington. **1934** DYLAN THOMAS in *New Verse* XII. 11 The halves that pierce the pin's point in the air, And prick the thumb-stained heaven through the thimble. **1945** *Sun* (Baltimore) 25 Oct. 4/3 Believing the thumbstick to be mightier than the sword, the Boy Scouts are going to lend a hand in the formidable task of re-educating German youth. **1974** R. ADAMS *Shardik* xi. 79 Bel-ka-Trazet walked with the help of a long thumb-stick which Kelderek remembered to have seen him trimming the evening before. **1982** *Church Times* 2 Apr. (Advt. Feature) p. iv/4 Whether it is..a military swagger cane, a stick you have whittled, a Shepherd's crook or a thumb stick from Scouting days. **1891** 'MARK TWAIN' tr. *Hoffman-Donner's Slovenly Peter* (1935, Ltd. Ed.) 25 Story of the thumb-sucker. **1964** M. ARGYLE *Psychol. & Social Probl.* ix. 121 There is also some evidence that children who have little opportunity for sucking, either at the breast or at a dummy, are more likely to become thumb-suckers. **1974** S. ALSOP *Stay of Execution* I. 103 Walter Lippmann wrote the best straight think-pieces, or thumb-suckers as they are called in the trade, of any journalist of our time. **1980** *N.Y. Times Mag.* 11 May 12/4 Slurs like 'paper pusher' for bureaucrat, or 'thumbsucker' for columnist. **1858** GEO. ELIOT *Scenes Clerical Life* I. 36 Baby is given to the infantine peccadillo of thumb-sucking. **1884** I. M. RITTENHOUSE *Maud* (1939) 278 [He] coolly left me to put the thumb-tacks in my picture by myself. **1951** R. MAYER *Artist's Handbk. Materials & Techniques* v. 187 A much better way to preserve unstretched pictures..is to thumb-tack them face down to sheets of wallboard. **1975** *N.Y. Times* 14 Sept. x. 1/2 Thumbtacked to the bulletin board was a color snapshot. **1966** D. FRANCIS *Flying Finish* ii. 24 Round the walls hung framed charts.., a thumb-tacked weather report. **1930** *Times* 26 Mar. 14/1 Conversation about the weather and sport..often degenerates into dreary thumb-twiddling. **1964** in M. McLuhan *Understanding Media* viii. 78 More aesthetic than thumb-twiddling, less expensive than smoking. **1967** *Electronics* 6 Mar. 129/1 High and low limits can be set separately on the comparator by: Dialing thumbwheel switches on the front panel during routine testing [etc.]. **1976** *Sci. Amer.* Jan. 130/3 There are even correcting thumbwheels for feeding in ambient air conditions in order to get standardized results on the digital display; they affect only the fourth digit and beyond. **1980** *Nature* 1 May p. xxii/2 A continuous rheostat thumbwheel control provides a full range of illumination. **1851** H. MELVILLE *Moby Dick* II. xi. 72 She will..let her have some papers..and thumb-worn files.

thumb, *v.* Add: **3. b.** = *thumb-read* vb. s.v. THUMB *sb.* 6 e; freq. const. *through.* Also, to turn (pages) with or as with the thumb in glancing through a book, etc.

1930 D. HAMMETT *Maltese Falcon* xvi. 186 He took a battered memorandum-book from a vest-pocket, licked his thumb, thumbed pages, and held the book out open to Spade. **1934** WEBSTER, *thumb..v.,*..to run over the pages of, (a book, periodical, newspaper, pamphlet, or the like), as by turning them rapidly with the thumb. **1966** G. GREENE *Comedians* I. v. 140 He sat on the sofa and thumbed through *Paris-Match.* **1966** S. SMITH *Frog Prince* 37, I dare say he had thumbed a book about it. **1976** J. ARCHER *Not Penny More* v. 62 Stephen left his study for the Senior Common Room where he thumbed through the latest copy of *Who's Who* and found the noble lord.

4. c. *to thumb one's nose*: see *NOSE *sb.* 8 f.

5. To seek or get (a ride or lift) in a passing vehicle by signalling with one's thumb the direction in which one hopes to travel (also *fig.*); to signal to (a driver or vehicle) with the thumb. Also *intr.*, to make *one's way* by thumbing lifts, to hitch-hike. orig. *U.S.*

1932 *Sun* (Baltimore) 4 Oct. 15/8 He was 'thumbed' into picking up two lads. **1933** *Ibid.* 26 Aug. 6/7 New England..is filled with young men and young women who are continually thumbing their way from one camp to another. **1934** *Amer. Speech* IX. 111/1 Those not fortunate enough to possess a car of their own stand by the side of the road and attempt to thumb a ride. **1939** N. MONSARRAT *This is Schoolroom* xii. 250, I thumbed my way across England..spending..four-and-sixpence and walking about thirty miles out of the hundred and fifty. **1944** H. NICOLSON *Diary* 1 May (1967) 369 Eventually an American lorry came along. We thumbed them. They stopped, and jumped off and with many jokes mended the tyre for us. **1952** J. CANNAN *Body in Beck* vii. 135 He had been thumbed for a lift by a desperate man. **1958** *Landfall* XII. 32 When a likely lift came by, Pat would..thumb it with a slow impressive sweep of his arm. **1958** *Oxford Mail* 15 Feb. 1/5 Photographed thumbing a lift near Wolverhampton are two..boys..who hitch-hiked to see the Wolves cup-tie with Darlington at Molineux. **1959** *News Chron.* 14 Aug. 7/5 The only Government-sponsored effort has been a plan to 'thumb a lift' in American rockets for British-made instruments. **1960** O. MANNING *Great Fortune* II. 146 He..had been 'thumbing' his way through Galicia when war broke out. **1975** D. NOBBS *Death of R. Perrin* 184 Reggie stood at the entrance to the lay-by and tried to thumb a lift. **1979** *Listener* 1 Mar. 314/2 Like many students..I had thumbed my way through France.

6. *intr.* To gesture with the thumb; *esp.* to signal with the thumb in the hope of getting a lift in a passing vehicle.

1935 G. STEIN *Let.* Dec. in R. L. White *S. Anderson/G. Stein* (1972) 99 Yesterday an American described thumbing on the roads. **1951** E. PAUL *Springtime in Paris* xvi. 309 Gilles thumbed over toward the Abbot. 'His Nibs should have given us the list in advance.' **1955** *Times* 18 Aug. 10/7, I thumbed for four hours without stopping a single vehicle. **1966** R. PRICE *Generous Man* (1967) ii. 142 He turned to Yancey.., thumbing to the house—'Is that all the house old Rooster can afford?' **1976** N. THORNBURG *Cutter & Bone* viii. 191 He was on the freeway entrance ramp, thumbing with his usual touch of calculated restraint.

thumber (þʌ·məɹ). *N. Amer. colloq.* [f. *THUMB *v.* 5, 6 + -ER[1].] One who 'thumbs' a lift, a hitch-hiker.

1935 *Even. Sun* (Baltimore) 8 Feb. 39/8 Chief of Police.. has turned 'thumbs down' on the 'thumbers'. **1973** *Daily Colonist* (Victoria, B.C.) 29 June 31/5 For the hitch-hiker, Canada's roads hold little but terror and horrors, say many thumbers from Toronto.

thumbful (þʌ·mful). [f. THUMB *sb.* + -FUL.] As much as a thumb can hold.

1930 E. POUND *XXX Cantos* xxii. 109 He..pulled out his snuff-box, And sniffed up a thumb-full. **1957** [see *RIFFLE *v.* 3 b].

thumb-mark, *v.* (Earlier example.)

1891 J. L. KIPLING *Beast & Man in India* xviii. 400 St. Peter thumb-marked the haddock when he took from its gills the providential tribute money.

thumb-nail. Add: **2.** (Earlier and later examples.)

1852 E. E. HALE in *Sartain's Mag.* Jan. 39 (*heading*) The old and the new, face to face. A thumb-nail sketch. **1911** R. D. SAUNDERS *Col. Todhunter* 125 A full-length 'character-cartoon' of the Colonel surrounded by 'thumb-nail' impressions of his face and bodily pose. **1968** R. GITTINGS *John Keats* xi. 148 He wrote a brilliant thumb-nail sketch of Oxford.

3. *thumb-nail scraper* (Archæol.), a kind of microlith made for scraping.

1937 GARROD & BATE *Stone Age of Mt. Carmel* I. I. iii. 31 *Thumb-nail scraper*..a very well-made minute round scraper. **1977** G. CLARK *World Prehist.* (ed. 3) v. 226 Late Stone Age assemblages including..microliths and thumb-nail scrapers, which in this part of Africa [*sc.* Nigeria] were usually made of quartz.

thumby (þʌ·mi), *a. colloq.* [f. THUMB *sb.* + -Y[1].] **1.** Soiled by thumb-marks.

1900 *Daily News* 11 Jan. 7/2 The report books look as prosaic as any ordinary account books, only very black and 'thumby'.

2. Clumsy, 'all thumbs'. Cf. THUMB *sb.* 5 c.

1909 R. A. WASON *Happy Hawkins* 103 One day we was kiddin' him about bein' so thumby. **1915** *Pearson's Mag.* XXXIX. 28 You have no idea how thumby your fingers are when fixing a bike under shrapnel fire. **1939** X. HERBERT *Capricornia* ix. 122 The box was set down, the stiff buckles of its mildewed straps tackled by a dozen thumby hands. **1974** P. WRIGHT *Lang. Brit. Industry* vi. 59 Their efficiency is affected when..they are known to be ..awkward,..numb-pawed, or thumby.

thump, *sb.* **3.** In Yorkshire (esp. Halifax): a local festival; a feast, wake, etc. **Thump Sunday**, the Sunday of the annual fair or festival week.

1884 *Folk-Lore Jrnl.* II. 25 Last Halifax Thump, a teetotaller..was punished, according to custom, by the company laying him face downwards and beating him on the back of the body with a heated fire-shovel. **1916** J. HARTLEY *Seets i' Yorks. & Lancs.* ii. 19 It'll be five year sin come Halifax thump Sunday. **1930** *Brit. Weekly* 4 Sept. 448/4 A correspondent sends us a description of 'Deanhead Thump Sunday', the..annual musical festival. **1976** H. WILSON *Governance of Britain* ii. 40 A prime minister must, and if he is a northerner usually does, understand the complex of Wakes Weeks and Feast Weeks, to say nothing of Longwood Thump.

thump, *v.* Add: **1.** (Earlier and later examples with a person as obj.)

1746 *Exmoor Scolding* 6 Chell vump tha. **1803** G. COLMAN *John Bull* III. ii. 35 If he don't behave himself, I'll come in and thump him blue. **1848** THACKERAY *Vanity Fair* viii. 67 Don't you remember..how she was always thumping Louisa? **1960** J. RAE *Custard Boys* II. xii. 145 If you interrupt me again, Felix, I'll bloody well thump you. **1978** D. DEVINE *Sunk without Trace* xxi. 194, I saw red. If I didn't get out, I would thump him.

b. Also, with *out*: to produce (a tune, beat, etc.) by thumping.

1929 T. WOLFE *Look Homeward, Angel* xxiii. 315 She.. thumped out popular tunes on a battered piano. **1974** C. RYAN *Bridge Too Far* III. i. 134 The bass drummer.. thumped out a symbolic beat in Morse code: three dots and a dash—V for victory.

e. To express by thumps.

1928 *Manch. Guardian Weekly* 26 Oct. 335/3 His [*sc.* a dog's] tail..thumped a welcome.

thumper. Add: **1. b.** *Geol.* A device for creating artificial seismic waves in the earth.

1962 *Times* 18 Apr. 4/7 Another device carried is a hydroprod, more familiarly known as a 'thumper'... It transmits a powerful sound impulse which penetrates the sub-surface strata of the sea bed, the return echo recording the depths of the different layers of sea bed material. **1977** *Sci. Amer.* July 65/2 (Advt.), Seismic excitation—a shock wave from an explosive charge or a mechanical 'thumper' —is applied to the earth.

thumpingly, *adv.* Add: **a.** (Later examples); **b.** *colloq.*, very, exceedingly.

1923 *Chambers's Jrnl.* Apr. 211/1 [He] gripped my hand —Shook it thumpingly. **1948** *Manch. Guardian Weekly* 11 Nov. 3 There was a thumpingly false assumption made about the American farmer. **1977** *Times* 17 Feb. 8/5 A book of thumpingly high entertainment value. **1983** *N. & Q.* Feb. 85/2 Even the thumpingly main statement of the last couplet of Spenser's 'tradefull Merchants' sonnet can be regarded as a mere gesture.

thu·mp-up. *slang.* [f. THUMP *v.* + UP *adv.*[1]] = *PUNCH-UP.

1967 H. W. SUTHERLAND *Magnie* vi. 80 There'd be a killing... But need it get as far as that?.. Just a thump up, maybe. **1978** *Maledicta* 1977 I. 130 Teacher: 'What would you have if you had 10 apples, and the boy next to you took 6 apples from you?' Boy: 'A thump-up (fight), Miss.'

thumri (tʰu·mrī, þ-). [a. Hindi *ṭhumrī.*] A light classical form of North Indian vocal or instrumental music; a piece in this form. Also *attrib.*, designating this style of music.

1834 N. A. WILLARD *Treat. on Mus. Hindoostan* 89 *Thoomree.* This is an impure dialect of the Vrujbhasha. The measure is lively, and so peculiar, that it is not mistaken by one who has heard a few songs of this class. **1914** A. H. F. STRANGWAYS *Music of Hindostan* vi. 165 'Hādi e illah' is a *Thumri* from Benares. **1964** AHMED ALI *Ocean of Night* II. v. 71 The poets were writing songs, sonnets, free verse, and no one cared for the *ghazal*, *thumri* or *mustezad*. **1972** P. HOLROYDE *Indian Music* iii. 97 Thumri style of singing evolved from the more austere forms of dhrupad and khayal. **1981** LD. HAREWOOD *Tongs & Bones* xvii. 257 The sarangi player..finished with a gentle and rather sentimental thumri.

thunbergia. Add to etym. after mod.L.: (A. J. Retzius 1776, in *Handl. K. Physiografiska Sällsk. Lund* I. 163). Also, a plant of this genus. (Earlier and further examples.)

1797 H. ANDREWS *Botanist's Repository* I. 123 Twining Thunbergia... The Thunbergia, here figured, is a native of the East Indies. **1867** H. KINGSLEY *Silcote of Silcotes* I. xi. 110 Thunbergias, when clumsily gathered, are apt to come up by the root. **1935** H. NICOLSON *Let.* 22 Feb. (1966) 198 On the wall..is a vast *Thunbergia* with blue morning-glory flowers. **1977** M. ALLAN *Darwin & his Flowers* xii. 215 The woody shoots of the wisteria move faster than those of the flexible Morning Glory and thunbergia.

thunder, *sb.* Add: **3. d.** Fig. phr. *to steal* (someone's) *thunder*: to use the ideas, policies, etc., devised by another person, political party, etc., for one's own advantage or to anticipate their use by the originator.

Derived from the utterance of John Dennis (1657–1734), 'Damn them!..they will not let my play run, but they steal my thunder,' on hearing the stage thunder produced by a method designed for his own play of *Appius & Virginia* being used for a performance of *Macbeth.* (Spence quoted in W. S. Walsh *Lit. Curios.* (1893) 1052; cf. Pope's note on *Dunciad* II. 223.)

1900 E. E. PEAKE *Darlingtons* iii. 23 You must all remember that papa had stolen my thunder. **1911** M. BEERBOHM *Zuleika Dobson* ix. 144 'Happy maid!' he murmured. Zuleika replied that he was stealing her thunder: hadn't she envied the girl at his lodgings? **1931** *Time & Tide* 12 Sept. 1049 Sir Oswald Mosley's exploit was to steal a little of the protectionist thunder temporarily abandoned by the Conservatives. **1937** 'G. ORWELL' *Road to Wigan Pier* xii. 222 It is important..to disregard the jealousy of the modern literary gent who hates science because science has stolen literature's thunder. **1973** A. BROINOWSKI *Take One Ambassador* ii. 19 He would have been watching the returns in the Senate elections I guess. This'll steal a bit of their thunder, that's for sure.

4. (Further examples, including earlier and later examples of *in thunder*.)

1826 *Massachusetts Spy* 23 Aug. (Th.), The bull roared like thunder! I split like lightning! **1834** C. A. DAVIS *Lett. J. Downing* xxxiii. 274 He turned..and giv me a look as black as thunder. **1841** H. GREELEY in R. W. Griswold *Passages from Corr.* (1898) 94 Why in thunder did you go off on Saturday without seeing me? **1852** MRS. STOWE *Uncle Tom's Cabin* I. vii. 95 Go to thunder, gal! **1854** M. J. HOLMES *Tempest & Sunshine* xv. 204 Don't none on you tread on my corns for thunder's sake. **1867** H. J. DANIEL *Muse in Motley* 25 He'll screech like thoonder, iss he will. **1876** E. W. HEAP *Diary* 24 Nov. in *Publ. Amer. Dial. Soc.* (1969) LII. 55 Every paper around is giving the road Thunder. **1916** G. B. SHAW *Pygmalion* v. 188 Of course they do. Then what in thunder are we quarrelling about? **1920** E. O'NEILL *Beyond Horizon* I. ii. 48 You kin go to thunder, Jim Mayo! **1927** —— *Marco Millions* II. i. 102 War is a waste of money which eats into the profits of life like thunder! **1940** W. FAULKNER *Hamlet* I. iii. 77 What in thunder are you fellows up to over at Varner's?

5. a. *thunder-burst, -colour, -crackle, -quake, -rain* (later example), *-sound, -throne.* **b.** *thunder-throning* adj. **c.** *thunder-cloven, -scathed* (earlier example) adjs.; *thunder-heavy, -stormy* adjs. **d.** *thunder-browed, -coloured* adjs.; *thunder-purple, -red* adjs.

1913 J. MASEFIELD *Daffodil Fields* 44 Full of wrath and thunder-browed. **1882** *Imperial Dict.*, Thunder-burst. *a* **1910** 'MARK TWAIN' *Autobiogr.* (1924) II. 176, I can remember those awful thunder-bursts and the white glare of the lightning yet. **1939** JOYCE *Finnegans Wake* 362 Thunderburst, ravishment, dissolution and providentiality. **1851** H. MELVILLE *Moby Dick* I. xxvii. 197 The barest..most thunder-cloven old oak. **1873** G. M. HOPKINS *Jrnls. & Papers* (1959) 232 The others [*sc.* pigeons] are dull thundercolour or black-grape-colour. **1907** R. BROOKE *Let.* Sept. (1968) 106 We have been sitting at an evil café sipping thunder-coloured coffee from glasses. **1941** L. MACNEICE *Plant & Phantom* 20 Thunder-crackle and the bounce of hail. **1922** BLUNDEN *Bonadventure* xii. 68 After the storm, the air was thunder-heavy all that day. **1879** G. M. HOPKINS *Poems* (1967) 80 The thunder-purple seabeach plumèd purple-of-thunder. **1940** J. BETJEMAN *Coll. Poems* (1958) 58 Not Satan's thunder-quake Can cause the mighty walls of Heaven to shake. **1926** D. H. LAWRENCE *David* xi. 78 Till they drop in drops of blood, like thunder-rain, and the land is red. **1949** BLUNDEN *After Bombing* 15 And foam, pearl-pink and thunder-red. **1826** J. G. WHITTIER *Writings* (1888) IV. App. 303 Where the thunder-scath'd peaks of Helvetia are frowning. **1886** W. B. YEATS *Mosada* 7 The faint far thunder-sound. **1930** J. DOS PASSOS *42nd Parallel* II. 149 Hot thunderstormy Washington summers. *a* **1974** R. CROSSMAN *Diaries* (1975) I. 197 A fairly restful Easter weekend of mixed, blowy, brilliant, shiny, thunder-stormy weather. **1876** G. M. HOPKINS *Wreck of Deutschland* xxxiv, in *Poems* (1967) 62 Mid-numberèd he [*sc.* Christ] in three of the thunder-throne! *a* **1918** W. OWEN *Poems* (1963) 135 That columnar, thunder-throning cloud.

6. *thunder-ball*, (*b*) (later examples); **thunderboat** *U.S.*, an unlimited hydroplane; **thunder-box** *slang*, a portable commode; by extension, any lavatory; **thunderbug** *dial.*, (*a*) *U.S.*, a horse-fly; (*b*) a midge; **thunder-drum,** (*a*) (later example); **thunder egg** *N. Amer.* and *Austral.*, a geode, esp. of chalcedony; **thunder-flash**: in military use, a harmless, very noisy, form of explosive; a firework imitating this; **thunder-head,** (*b*) *nonce-use*, a large head, as a whale's head; **thunder-mug** *slang* = CHAMBER-POT; **thunder-pumper,** (*a*) (earlier example); **thunder-rod** (earlier example); **thunder run** *Theatr.*, two wooden troughs down which iron balls were rolled to imitate thunder; **thunder-sheet** *Theatr.*, a piece of sheet metal shaken to imitate thunder; **thunder-shower,** now chiefly *U.S.* (later examples); **thunder stick,** a name said to have been given to a rifle or cannon by peoples who did not possess firearms; **thunder-trunk** *Theatr.*, a trunk in which iron balls were rolled to imitate thunder.

1889 W. B. YEATS *Wanderings of Oisin* II. 30 Trembling, on the flags we fall, Fearful of the thunder-ball. **1942** L. BENNETT *Jamaica Dial. Verses* 41 Wen..Him tun roun..Him se de sinting two yeye dem A roll like tunder-ball... It was a rollin' keaolf. **1967** *Compton Yearbk.* 153/2 Through the previous 20 years, only three 'thunderboat' drivers had died in races. **1976** *Popular Mechanics* June 61/1 Officially, they are..hydroplane racing boats... To their hundreds of thousands of fans, they are unlimited hydros, thunderboats, gold cuppers, or just unlimiteds—the fastest racing machines afloat. **1939** Auden & Isherwood *Journey to War* vii. 182 We should wash the dishes and clean the thunder-boxes. **1952** E. Waugh *Men at Arms* II. ii. 178 'If you *must* know, it's my thunderbox.'.. He..dragged out the treasure, a brass-bound, oak cube... On the inside of the lid was a plaque bearing the embossed title *Connolly's Chemical Closet.* **1955** N. Fitzgerald *House is Falling* xi. 188 When the plumber called for instructions, Hapleigh chose the ground floor for the new thunder-box. **1980** *Daily Tel.* 18 Oct. 18 Life in India was ..coping with the indignities of the 'thunder box' (a portable earth commode) and searching sponges for stealthy scorpions. **1837** J. L. Williams *Territory of Florida* 71 Horse Fly.—..Of these there are five kinds. —1st. the large black, called thunder bug, an inch long. **1875** W. D. Parish *Dict. Sussex Dial.* 66 Those thunderbugs did kiddle [*sc.* tickle] me so. **1974** P. Haines *Tea at Gunter's* xx. 214 Outside the air was still heavy; there were thunderbugs everywhere... I felt them settle on my skin, my hair. **1967** *Stage* 2 Mar. 4/2 (Advt.), Thunder drums, bells, chimes, gongs and effects of every description. **1951** W. F. Heald *Scenic Guide to Oregon* 25 Agate- and opal-filled nodules called 'Thunder Eggs' can be found near Madras. **1962** E. Lucia *Klondike Kate* ix. 187 She never returned empty-handed, hauling back..petrified woods, agates..thundereggs, [etc.]. **1973** *Sunday Mail Mag.* (Brisbane) 25 Feb. 14/5 The individual bays of the caravan park are marked off by 'thunder eggs' (round stones a foot and more in diameter, many of which contain fossilised fish). **1977** *Trailer Life* July 16/3 'Thunder eggs', the agate-colored nodules familiar to many rockhounds, are a variety of spherulite. **1943** C. C. Knights *What H.G. needs to know about Explosives* 10 The only 'fireworks' issued to the typical H.G. unit are crackers and thunder-flashes used to give 'an air of verisimilitude to an otherwise bald and unconvincing' exercise. **1959** G. Adamson *Let.* 19 Mar. in J. Adamson *Born Free* (1960) 139, I went to visit Elsa... I let off three thunder flashes..and..she suddenly appeared. **1977** 'E. Crispin' *Glimpses of Moon* xi. 210 And we did ought to have..used firecrackers and thunderflashes and horns and whistles. **1851** H. Melville *Moby Dick* II. lxxiii. 59 Throw all these thunder-heads overboard, and then you will float light and right. **1890** Barrère & Leland *Dict. Slang* II. 347/2 *Thunder-mug* (American low), a chamber utensil. **1942** D. Gilbert *Lost Chords* 6 His room furnishings were meager—a rag carpet,..a bowl and pitcher on a washstand whose closet concealed a chamber, or 'thunder mug'. **1966** 'L. Lane' *ABZ of Scouse* II. 108 *Thundermug*, a chamber-pot. **1877** *Scribner's Monthly* July 285/2 The natives call these bitterns by the very appropriate if not euphonious name of 'thunder-pumper'. **1784** G. Adams *Ess. Electricity* ix. 154 When lightning strikes a tree..or a thunder-rod, it is not because these objects are high..but because they communicate with..the surface of the ground. **1944** *Archit. Rev.* XCV. 135/2 Archaic devices like the 'thunder run', the 'sloat' system of raising scenery, the 'drum and shaft' method of hanging it, still survive at Bristol. **1976** *Early Music* Oct. 401/1 The thunder simulated at the beginning and end of the Cave scene must be..baroque-artificial—for preference made by cannon-balls in a thunder run. **1913** 'V. D. Browne' *Secrets Scene Painting & Stage Effects* 66 Hung from flies. A thunder Sheet. **1939** Joyce *Finnegans Wake* 503 Raindrum, windmachine, snowbox. But thundersheet? **1967** *Oxf. Compan. Theatre* (ed. 3) 947/2 The noise of thunder is usually produced off-stage by the shaking of a suspended iron sheet known as the Thunder Sheet. **1856** E. B. Browning *Aurora Leigh* IV. 174 Softly, as the last repenting drops Of a thunder-shower. **1947** S. Bellow *Victim* i. 5 A thundershower began when he approached the outside door. **1980** *News & Observer* (Raleigh, N. Carolina) 28 Oct. 2/3 Clouds will prevail across much of North Carolina today, with some showers or thundershowers possible through Wednesday. **1918** E. R. Burroughs *Tarzan & Jewels of Opar* (1919) xvii. 157 The ape folk fear the thunder-sticks of the Tarmangani. **1947** I. L. Idriess *Isles of Despair* xxxiv. 229 A puff of smoke belched from the brig... They had expected resistance, but had hoped the vessel was too small to carry the 'big thunder sticks'. **1965** *Canad. Geogr. Jrnl.* Apr. 115/1 The white man came to shatter the silence of the wilderness with his thunder stick. **1767** D. Garrick *Peep Behind Curtain* I. 22 Ladies, you can't possibly have any thunder and lightning this morning; one of the planks of the thunder-trunk started the other night. **1830** G. Colman *Random Rec.* I. vii. 229 For then did my Evil Genius enthrone himself upon a thunder-trunk, with a roll of play-bills in his hand.

thunder, *v.* **2.** (Further examples connoting movement.)

1934 J. B. Priestley *Eng. Journey* i. 4 The children of these fist-shakers now go thundering by in their own huge coaches and loll in velvet as they go. **1946** *R.A.F. Jrnl.* May 169 Lancasters..thundered through the night to pinpoint their objectives. **1951** 'J. Wyndham' *Day of Triffids* i. 9 The westbound buses thundered along trying to beat the lights. **1960** C. Day Lewis *Buried Day* ii. 38 We thundered down the steep hill into the centre of the town, the squawking hens bouncing up and down on the flat cart, straw and feathers flying.

thunder and lightning. Add: **6.** *Angling.* A variety of artificial fly.

1910 *Encycl. Brit.* II. 26/1 In most fly-books great variety of patterns will be discoverable, while certain old standard favourites such as the Jock Scott, Durham Ranger, Silver Doctor, and Thunder and Lightning will be prominent. **1972** *Country Life* 23 Mar. 697/3 Three large salmon were clearly visible... I changed to a tiny low water Thunder and Lightning.

7. *attrib.* Melodramatic, startling, violent.

1892 'Mark Twain' *Amer. Claimant* ix. 71 Take What's-her-name, that plays those sensational thunder-and-lightning parts. **1981** J. Wainwright *All on Summer's Day* 12 Some thunder-and-lightning speed merchant on the opposing side bowled a yorker and chipped a bone in the batsman's ankle.

thunderation. For *U.S. slang* read *slang* (orig. and chiefly *U.S.*) and add earlier and later examples.

1836 *Crockett's Yaller Flower Almanac* 21, I don't know as I can say he was so all darned thunderation fat. **1939** Joyce *Finnegans Wake* 245 Bing. Bong. Bangbong. Thunderation! **1949** *Sat. Even. Post* 9 July 86/2 Why in thunderation does he have to play such a hay-in-the-hair?

thunderbolt, *sb.* Add: **2. c.** In *Sport*, a fast hard-struck shot or stroke.

1959 *Times* 29 May 4/7 [Lawn Tennis] Maloney, with his 'thunderbolts' made no mistake in the next for the match. **1977** *Times* 7 Feb. 7/2 Heighway, at full steam, lashed a thunderbolt past Latchford from the edge of the box.

3. d. (Further examples.)

1884 A. Lang *Custom & Myth* i. 10 Village wisdom determines that the wedge-shaped piece of metal is a 'thunderbolt'. **1949** 'J. Nelson' *Backwoods Teacher* vi. 57 We spoke of lightning and 'thunderbolts'. Of these latter, Fritz Baily said his uncle used to 'gather them up—and we still get lots kickin' 'round the barn.'.. He promised to bring me one. (Next morning he did—a meteorite the size of his fist.)

5. thunderbolt attack, raid, a short-lived but heavy air-raid.

1943 *Hutchinson's Pictorial Hist. War* 25 Nov. 1942–16 Feb. 1943 240/1 At night Lancasters and Halifaxes carry out a large-scale 'thunderbolt' raid on Duesseldorf, dropping several hundred tons of bombs in a 20-minutes attack. **1944** H. Hawton *Night Bombing* v. 66 There is no necessary connection between concentrated and precision bombing, but it would be quite wrong to think that the 'thunderbolt attack', as it is sometimes called, lacks exactness. The Renault factory was almost completely demolished in an attack of short duration.

thunder-clap. b. (Later example.)

1924 R. Campbell *Flaming Terrapin* iv. 65 And steepled cities stun the hollow sky With thunderclaps of bells as they go by.

thunderer. 2. (Earlier example applied to *The Times.*)

1830 *Morning Herald* 15 Feb. 3/1 Any person or persons..may receive further particulars..by application.. at the office of *The Thunderer*, Printing House-square.

thundering, *ppl. a.* (*adv.*) **4. b.** Delete quot. 1839 and add earlier examples.

1809 *Salmagundi* 7 Mar. 95 He..prefers..telling his story among cronies of his own gender..and thundering long stories they are. **1839** *Havana* (N.Y.) *Republican* 25 Dec. (Th.), He is thundering shy of me.

thunk (þʌŋk), *sb.*[1] Joc. var. Think *sb.*

1922 Joyce *Ulysses* 503 Have a good old thunk.

thunk (þʌŋk), *sb.*[2] (*int.* or *adv.*) [Onomatopœic.] A sound of an impact, either dull or plangent. Also *int.* or as *adv.*

1952 B. Harwin *Home is Upriver* xviii. 178 He heard the dull thunk of wood against wood and felt the planking jar over his head. **1958** 'W. Henry' *Seven Men at Mimbres Springs* vi. 70 Presently the sodden 'thunk!' of an ax blade caving in barrel staves echoed wetly. **1968** W. Garner *Deep, Deep Freeze* ix. 109 The door said *thunk* in a well-bred whisper. **1970** M. Chisholm *McAllister says No* x. 93 The bullet tore through the canvas of the cover and went *thunk* into a barrel. **1971** A. Ross *Huddersfield Job* 57, I heard the triple *thunk* of the undercarriage locks. **1979** *Herald* (Melbourne) 23 Apr. 2 The familiar 'thunk, zing, ding' of a pinball machine.

thunk (þʌŋk), *v.* [f. *thunk *sb.*[2]] *intr.* To make a thunk; to fall or land with a thunk.

a **1963** S. Plath *Johnny Panic & Bible of Dreams* (1977) I. 133 With shovels and picks they crawled through the attic trapdoor and soon great masses of snow were thunking from the roof into the yard. **1972** *Daily Tel.* (Colour Suppl.) 14 Jan. 21/4 A quoit which thunks into the clay just to the left of the hob, leaning towards it, bevel downwards, is called a pot. **1976** *New Yorker* 3 May 44/3 Last night, I slept nine hours, rain thunking on the tent.

thunk (þʌŋk), dial. and joc. pa. t. and pa. pple. of Think *v.*[2] Cf. *thunk *sb.*[1]

1876 C. C. Robinson *Dial. Mid-Yorks.* p. xlii, Think.. (Thuongk) The last form is less employed participially than in the past, in which tense it is of constant occurrence. **1887** *Lantern* (New Orleans) 15 Oct. 3/2 Who'd a thunk it? **1908** N. Duncan *Every Man for Himself* ii. 60 Leastwise, he *thunk* so, admittin' 'twas open t' argument. **1939** Joyce *Finnegans Wake* 504, I then tuk my taken-place lying down, I thunk I told you. **1967** T. Savage *Power of Dog* xiii. 240 Phil had most excellent use of the hides after all. Who'd a thunk it!

Thurberesque (þɜ̄ːɹbəre·sk), *a.* [-esque.] Of or pertaining to the American cartoonist and writer James *Thurber* (1894–1961), the characters in his work, or his style of writing or drawing.

1954 *Encounter* June 88/1 The essentially sexual (we might almost say Thurberesque) nature of true comedy, its concern with the war of men and women. **1958** *Times Lit. Suppl.* 31 Oct. 626/4 A very amusing Thurberesque anecdote by Miss Rebecca West about meeting Pirandello, without knowing it, on a wild night out in New York in the 1920s. **1972** *Listener* 6 Apr. 458/1 A Thurberesque doodle. **1980** *Washington Star* 23 Oct. D6 Nabokov is in it as kind of a Thurberesque stage manager character.

thuringer (þiūᵊ·riŋəɹ). Also **thüringer.** [ad. G. *thüringer*, lit. = next.] Summer sausage.

1933 *Sausage Man. & Text Bk.* (Oppenheimer Casing Co.) 70 (*heading*) Thueringer (fresh Summer sausage) 120 lbs. regular beef trimmings, 40 lbs. beef heart, 60 lbs. chuck, 80 lbs. regular pork trimmings, [etc.]. **1938** *Packer's Encycl.* III. vii. 123 Hang thuringer on clean sticks and place in cooler. **1965** [see *summer sausage* s.v. *summer *sb.*[1] 6 a]. **1978** *Chicago* June 241/2 The restaurant serves a variety of sandwiches..thuringer, and delicious homemade soups.

Thuringian (þiuri·ndʒiăn), *a.* and *sb.* [f. the name *Thuringia* (see below) + -an.] **A.** *adj.* Of or pertaining to (the inhabitants of) Thuringia, a region of central Germany, in mediæval times a principality. **B.** *sb.* A native or inhabitant of Thuringia.

1607 E. Topsell *Foure-footed Beasts* 293 The Thuringean horsses are neighbors to Hessis. **1618** Selden *Hist. Tithes* vi. 90 As in the examples which wee anon have of the Turingians, and those of Holtz. **1812** C. Butler *Hist. Revolutions of Empire of Germany* App. 35 The electorate was successively enjoyed by Frederick the warlike, and Frederick the wise, of the *Thuringian* branch of the Wittikindian stem. **1839** J. F. Stanford *Jrnl.* 21 Sept. in *Rambles & Researches in Thuringian Saxony* (1842) 2 Old Palace of Friedenstein..commanding the finest view of the Thuringian Forest. **1839** —— *Let.* Aug. in *Ibid.* 158 In physical development the Thuringians..are..fine powerful men. **1881** C. C. Harrison *Woman's Handiwork* III. 232 Small plates for tea or dessert, in Thuringian ware, imitating old Dresden. **1974** P. Gore-Booth *With Great Truth & Respect* 41 The Münchs had living with them..a brother of Frau Münch's, a general who..spoke such total Thuringian dialect that I never learned to understand a word he said. **1975** F. Heer *Charlemagne & his World* ix. 121 Hessians and Franconians were divisions of the Austrasian sub-kingdom... The Thuringians were a distinct group, but fairly well assimilated into France.

Thurstone (þɜ̄·ɹstən). *Psychol.* The name of the American psychologist, Louis Leon *Thurstone* (1887–1955), used *attrib.* to denote tests or methods devised by him, esp. for the measurement of mental abilities and attitudes, for factor analysis, and the study of personality.

1935 R. R. Willoughby in C. Murchison *Handbk. Soc. Psychol.* xii. 502 Perhaps the most definite evidence is that secured..with personality inventories of the Thurstone type. **1954** A. Anastasi *Psychol. Testing* ix. 229 Another abbreviated adaptation..is to be found in the Thurstone Test of Mental Alertness. *Ibid.* xx. 538 The resulting inventory is known as the Thurstone Temperament Schedule. **1958** M. Argyle *Relig. Behaviour* viii. 97 A group of eighty-three delinquent girls scored higher on Thurstone scales measuring attitudes towards Sunday observance. **1972** *Jrnl. Soc. Psychol.* Dec. 243 Attitude toward reclaimed water for noningestive, close-contact use was assessed by a Thurstone-type scale.

thus, *adv.* **1. e.** *thus and thus*: delete † *Obs.* and add later examples.

1892 Kipling & Balestier *Naulahka* xviii. 211 Now we are come to our Kingdom, And the State is thus and thus. **1909** H. G. Wells *Tono-Bungay* II. iv. 200 Nobody, no book, ever came and said to me, thus and thus is the world made and so and so is necessary. *Ibid.* 225 Thus and thus it was the Will in things had its way with me. **1942** R. Chandler *Let.* 15 Mar. (1981) 20 The reader expects thus and thus of Chandler because he did it before.

g. *thus and so* = So-and-so *a., adv.* 2. *dial.* and *U.S.*

1824 W. Carr *Craven Dial.* i. 6 Hees lang been vara indifferent, and hees now nobbud thus an seea. **1901** F. E. Taylor *Folk-Speech S. Lancashire* s.v. *Thus an'-so*, 'Heawsto bin gerrin' on?' 'Well, nobbo thus an' so.' **1904** *N.Y. Even. Post* 23 Apr., The statement that matters will result thus and so 'if the crops turn out all right'. **1924** R. M. Ogden tr. *Koffka's Growth of Mind* iii. 100 The present situation appears..not as one that is constituted thus-and-so. **1932** *Atlantic Monthly* Apr. 407/1 We know why we stand thus and so in the sample of conflicting faiths.

thusly, *adv.* (Earlier examples.)

1865 *Harper's Mag.* Dec. 133/2 It happened, as J. Billings would say, 'thusly'. **1876** [see *dingus].

thwack, *sb.* Add: Also as *int.*

1908 L. M. Montgomery *Anne of Green Gables* xv. 156 And then—Thwack! Anne had brought her slate down on Gilbert's head. **1976** *National Observer* (U.S.) 14 Aug. 6/3 Thwack! Boston's Jim Rice sends the first pitch sailing over the left-field wall.

thwartly, *adv.* **2.** (Later example.)

1914 Hardy *Satires of Circumstance* 192 Then grinned the Ancient Briton from the tumulus treed with pine: 'So, hearts are thwartly smitted In these days as in mine!'

thwartness. (Later example.)

a **1907** F. Thompson *Works* (1913) III. 66 It is full of thwartness and eating and drinking, and selffulness.

thylakoid (þəi·lăkoid) *Bot.* [a. G. *thylakoid* (W. Menke 1961, in *Zeitschr. f. Naturforsch.* B. XVI. 335/1), f. Gr. θυλακοειδ-ής pouch-like, f. θύλακ-ος pouch: see -oid.] Each of the flattened, fluid-filled, membranous sacs inside a chloroplast in which photochemical reactions take place.

1962 *Ann. Rev. Plant Physiol.* XIII. 35 These are designated discs by Gibbs, flattened vesicles by Mühlethaler, and thylakoids by Menke. **1967** [see *GRANUM]. **1974** R. Y. STANIER in Carlile & Skehel *Evolution in Microbial World* 231 The enclosing thylakoid membrane provides an external constraint to prevent disaggregation.

thymallus. Add: = GRAYLING 1 a. (Later example.)

1921 *Chambers's Jrnl.* Jan. 114/2 We have fished that river again, and succeeded in capturing good baskets of thymallus.

thyme, *sb.* **3. thyme-leaved** *a.* (later examples).

1859 D. BUNCE *Trav. Dr. Leichhardt* iv. 27 *Decaspora disticha* and *Thymifolia*, the first two-leaved, and the latter the thyme-leaved *Decaspora.* **1972** Y. LOVELOCK *Veg. Bk.* III. 336 Small or thyme-leaved mint..is only found in Tasmania.

thymectomy, thymectomize. (Later examples.)

1963 *Lancet* 5 Jan. 43/1 In the adult animal, thymectomy is associated with little or no significant depression of the immune response. **1970** *Nature* 26 Sept. 1353/1 This preliminary observation on the long term persistence of T cells has been extended by thymectomizing CBA/Lac mice. **1974** R. M. KIRK et al. *Surgery* ii. 33 Neonatal thymectomy suppresses the immune response in experimental animals. **1976** *Ann. Rev. Microbiol.* XXX. 584 Some adjuvants fail to work in thymectomized mice treated with antilymphocyte (anti-T) serum.

thymidine (þəi·midīn). *Biochem.* [f. THYM(INE + *-IDINE.] A pyrimidine nucleoside, $C_5H_9O_3{\cdot}C_5H_4N_2O_2$, in which the base is thymine and the sugar deoxyribose, and which is obtained by the partial hydrolysis of DNA.

1912 *Jrnl. Biol. Chem.* XII. 414 Barium salts of a hexocytidine diphosphoric acid and a hexo-thymidine diphosphoric acid were obtained. **1931** LEVENE & BASS *Nucleic Acids* 335/1 (Index), Thymidine. *See* Thymine desoxyribonucleoside. **1963** *New Scientist* 21 Mar. 616/2 Before a cell can divide, it has to duplicate its own normal complement of DNA and this it synthesises from many different starting products, one of the most important being thymidine. **1978** *Bull. Amer. Acad. Arts & Sci.* Feb. 17 If, during the culturing process which forms an essential feature of the preparation of cells for examination of their karyotype, tritiated thymidine (a radioactive precursor of DNA) is added, the resultant metaphase chromosomes become radioactively labeled to a degree that is a function of their recent activity in synthesizing DNA.

thymidylic (þəimidi·lik), *a.* *Biochem.* [f. prec. + -YL + -IC.] *thymidylic acid*: any phosphoric acid ester of thymidine, $C_5H_8O_2$-$(PH_2O_4).C_5H_4N_2O_2$, one or other of which is one of the four nucleotides present in most DNA.

1951 *Jrnl. Bacteriol.* LXI. 41 Samples of thymidylic acid, desoxyadenylic acid..and desoxyguanylic acid.. were made available. **1968** A. WHITE et al. *Princ. Biochem.* (ed. 4) ix. 186 Deoxyguanylic, thymidylic, and deoxycytidylic acids esterified at positions 3′ and 5′ are also found in hydrolysates of DNA. **1972** *Sci. Amer.* Dec. 85/1 Until well into the 1930's DNA was generally thought to be merely a tetranucleotide composed of one unit each of adenylic, guanylic, thymidylic and cytidylic acids.

Hence **thymi·dylate,** the anion derived from thymidylic acid by the loss of a hydrogen atom from the phosphate group.

1959 FLAKS & COHEN in *Jrnl. Biol. Chem.* CCXXXIV. 2981/1 We are designating the latter catalytic activity.. as 'thymidylate synthetase'. **1974** J. W. DRAKE in Carlile & Skehel *Evolution in Microbial World* 51 The *td* gene encodes the viral thymidylate synthetase.

thymin. Add: **1.** Now always **thymine.** (Further examples.)

1954 *New Biol.* XVI. 15 In desoxyribose nucleic acid the purine is either adenine or guanine, the pyrimidine either cytosine or thymine. **1976** *Sci. Amer.* Jan. 64/3 The DNA molecule consists of two long chains of nucleotides wound in a double helix... Each nucleotide consists of a deoxyribose sugar, a phosphate group and one of four nitrogenous bases: adenine, guanine, thymine or cytosine.

2. *Biochem.* = *THYMOPOIETIN.

1968 G. GOLDSTEIN in *Lancet* 20 July 122/1 'Thymin'.. seems an appropriate name for this substance, which not only is present in normal thymus but also appears to be secreted normally and to have an effect in physiological concentrations on neuromuscular transmission. **1974** [see *THYMOPOIETIN].

thymocyte (þəi·mosəit). *Histology.* [f. THYM(US + -O + -CYTE.] A lymphocyte-like cell derived from the thymus gland; a T-lymphocyte.

1929 E. S. SCHAFER *Essent. Histol.* (ed. 12) xxii. 265 Besides lymphocyte-like cells (thymocytes) it [*sc.* the thymus] contains peculiar granular cells. **1976** *Nature* 13 May 139/1 Differentiation of T cells is generally depicted as involving transformation of prethymic cells to immunoincompetent thymocytes, which themselves are precursors of functionally mature, immunocompetent T cells.

thymoleptic (þeimole·ptik), *a.* (*sb.*) *Pharm.* [f. Gr. θυμός soul, spirit + λῆψις seizing: see -IC.] (Of or pertaining to) a psychic energizer (see *PSYCHIC *a.* (*sb.*) 1 a).

1959 *New Scientist* 31 Dec. 1351/2 So novel are these [psychotherapeutic] drugs that even the scientific terms used to describe their action—ataractic, thymoleptic—have been coined within the past few years. *Ibid.* 1353/1 The psychotherapeutic drugs fall at present into two classes:..the major tranquillizers..and those that relieve psychotic depression—the psychic energizers or thymoleptics. **1967** W. L. L. REES *Short Textbk. Psychiatry* xxxii. 281 The tricyclic (thymoleptic) group of anti-depressants are quite dissimilar in chemical structure to the monoamine oxidase inhibitors. **1971** H. B. MURPHREE in J. R. DiPalma *Drill's Pharmacol. in Med.* (ed. 4) xxiii. 437/2 A term used in Europe, thymoleptic..has not gained currency in North America.

thymoma (þəi·mǭᵘmă). *Path.* [ad. G. *thymome* (F. Grandhomme *Ueber Tumoren des Vorderen Mediastinums* (1900) 43): see THYMUS, *-OMA.] A rare, usually benign tumour arising from tissue of the thymus gland and often associated with myasthenia gravis.

1919 J. EWING *Neoplastic Dis.* xlvi. 894 Lymphosarcoma or thymoma is the most frequent form of thymus tumor. **1961** R. D. BAKER *Essent. Path.* xviii. 510 Thymomas may at times be lymphomas, and be associated with myasthenia gravis. **1974** J. D. MAYNARD in R. M. Kirk et al. *Surgery* x. 219 Thymoma is a soft lobulated tumour situated in the thymus or close to it.

thymo-nucleic, *a.* Add: *thymo-nucleic acid* (examples); now identified with DNA.

1904 *Jrnl. Chem. Soc.* LXXXVI. I. 127 (*heading*) Oxidation of thymonucleic acid with calcium permanganate. **1942** *Nature* 17 Jan. 66/1 To these fibres..are attached desoxyribose-, or thymo-, nucleic acid which is responsible for the specific aldehyde reaction given by the chromosomes in Feulgen's test. **1951** *New Biol.* X. 48 Phosphorus-32 uptake is found to be intimately related to the process of synthesis of thymonucleic acid.

thymopoietin (þəimopoi,e·tin). *Biochem.* [f. THYM(US + -O + Gr. ποιητικ-ός (see POIETIC *a.*) + -IN[1].] A polypeptide hormone secreted by the thymus which stimulates the development of thymocytes.

1974 BASCH & GOLDSTEIN in *Proc. Nat. Acad. Sci.* LXXI. 1477/2 It has been brought to our attention that our term thymin for this polypeptide hormone is being confused with the base thymine... We therefore intend to change our terminology in the future and use the term thymopoietin. **1980** H. N. EISEN *Immunology* (ed. 2) xviii. 416/2 Thymopoietin, a small protein (49 amino acid residues), has been sequenced and synthesized. It causes pre-T cells..to become somewhat sensitive to mitogens, but not to become immunologically competent.

thymosin (þəi·mǒsin). *Biochem.* [f. Gr. θύμος THYMUS + -IN[1].] An extract of the thymus gland which has a stimulating effect on the immune system (see quots.).

1966 A. L. GOLDSTEIN et al. in *Proc. Nat. Acad. Sci.* LVI. 1010 We wish to report the preparation..from calf thymic tissue of a product which stimulates incorporation of H^3-thymidine into mesenteric lymph node cells. The lymphocytopoietic factor, which we term thymosin, is active..*in vivo*, as well as..*in vitro.* **1980** H. N. EISEN *Immunology* (ed. 2) xviii. 416/2 Thymosin, a mixture of many active low-molecular-weight polypeptides.., probably comes closer than many others to behaving like a natural hormone... It restores immune function to neonatally thymectomized mice.

thymus. Add: **1. c.** *thymus nucleic acid* = *thymonucleic acid* s.v. THYMONUCLEIC *a.* in Dict. and Suppl. Now *Hist.*

1904 *Jrnl. Chem. Soc.* LXXXVI. I. 837 (*heading*) Thymus nucleic acid. **1938** [see *DEOXYRIBONUCLEIC ACID].

3. *Comb.*, as *thymus-dependent, -derived, -independent* adjs.

1963 *Jrnl. Nat. Cancer Inst.* XXXI. 1466 In the thymectomized newborn mouse..re-establishment of immunologic competence..is also known to be thymus-dependent. **1977** *Proc. R. Soc. Med.* LXX. 524/2 This change may be responsible for the diminished response to thymus-dependent antigens that is seen in subjects with chronic liver disease. **1970** *New Scientist* 7 May 271/2 The thymus-derived T cells apparently move through the body more actively than the B cells. **1974** *Ciba Symposium* XX. 114 They suggest that, by one means or another, trypanosome infections break the control link between thymus-dependent lymphocytes (T cells) and thymus-independent lymphocytes (B cells).

thyratron (þəi·rătrǫn). *Electronics.* [f. Gr. θύρα door + *-TRON.] A thermionic valve utilizing an arc discharge in mercury vapour or low-pressure gas and having a heated cathode and at least one grid.

1929 *General Electr. Rev.* Apr. 213/1 The thyratron is an electrically controlled arc rectifier. **1948** *Jrnl. R. Aeronaut. Soc.* LII. 216/1 An automatic speed control has been provided in which the voltage from a tachometer generator driven by the fan shaft is composed with a preset standard voltage, and the difference amplified by thyratrons is fed back to an auxiliary field in the generator. **1981** [see *THYRISTOR].

thyristor (þəiri·stəɹ). *Electronics.* [f. *THYR(ATRON + *TRANS)ISTOR.] A three-terminal semiconductor rectifier made up of four layers, *p-n-p-n*, so that when the fourth is positive with respect to the first, a voltage pulse applied to the third layer initiates a flow of current through the device which continues as long as it is greater than some minimum value.

1958 MUELLER & HILIBRAND in *IRE Trans. Electron Devices* V. 2/2 Because of its thyratron-like properties, the device has been named a Thyristor. **1965** *New Scientist* 19 Aug. 446/2 Its transmission system eliminates the commutator by employing thyristors (silicon-controlled rectifiers) as inverters under electronic control. **1981** J. SEYMOUR *Electronic Devices & Components* iv. 185 Industrial process control, the control of electrical machines and high voltage d.c. transmission are among the many areas in which thyristors are applied. They have superseded the thyratron..in all but the highest voltage applications.

thyro-. Add: **2. thy:rocalcitonin** (-kælsitǭᵘ·nin [*calcitonin* f. L. *calx, calc(i)-* lime + TON(IC *a.* and *sb.* + -IN[1]], a polypeptide hormone secreted by the thyroid gland which reduces the levels of calcium in the blood; also called *calcitonin*; **thy:roparathyroide·ctomy,** excision of both the thyroid and the parathyroids; so **thy:roparathyroide·ctomize** *v. trans.*, **-e·ctomized** *ppl. a.*; **thy·rotoxico:sis,** a disorder in which there is an excessive amount of thyroid hormones in the blood; **thyrotro·p(h)ic** *a.* (also † **thyreo-**) [*-TROPHIC, *-TROPIC], applied to a hormone secreted by the pituitary which regulates the activity of the thyroid gland; hence **thyrotro·p(h)in,** thyrotropic hormone; *thyrotrop(h)in-releasing factor, hormone*, a hormone secreted by the hypothalamus which stimulates the release of thyrotropin from the pituitary.

1963 P. F. HIRSCH et al. in *Endocrinology* LXXIII. 252/2 Whether or not the thyroid hypocalcemic agent that we have demonstrated is the same as..calcitonin..it is of considerable pharmacological interest. As a tentative name for the substance we propose 'thyrocalcitonin'. **1974** D. & M. WEBSTER *Compar. Vertebr. Morphol.* xiii. 311 The parafollicular cells of the thyroid gland produce quite a different hormone, called calcitonin or thyrocalcitonin. **1956** *Nature* 21 Jan. 138/1 Six animals were adrenalectomized..: the remaining six were thyroparathyroidectomized. **1932** *Amer. Jrnl. Physiol.* C. 262 (*heading*) Heterotopic bone formation in thyroparathyroidectomized dogs. **1976** H. CAMPION et al. in B.E.C. Nordin *Calcium, Phosphate & Mineral Metabolism* xii. 466 Thyroparathyroidectomized (TPTX) rats had their serum phosphate levels manipulated by dietary means. **1920** *Nature* 9 Dec. 488/2 The effect of thyroid-feeding and of thyroparathyroidectomy upon the pituitrin content of the posterior lobe of the pituitary. **1956** *Ibid.* 21 Jan. 138/1 The effect of thyro-parathyroidectomy on the blood changes induced by injected cortisone..has been studied. **1911** STEDMAN *Med. Dict.* 887/1 *Thyrotoxicosis*, exophthalmic goiter. **1912** *Jrnl. Amer. Med. Assoc.* 3 Aug. 328/1 A patient 23 years of age having an adenoma has a definite fixed chance of developing thyrotoxicosis during her thirty-seventh year. **1977** *Lancet* 27 Aug. 438/2 Simpson hypothesised an autoimmune basis for myasthenia gravis on account of its association with disorders thought to have an autoimmune ætiology—such as..thyrotoxicosis. **1930** CREW & WIESNER in *Brit. Med. Jrnl.* 26 Apr. 777/1 (*heading*) On the existence of a fourth hormone, thyreotropic in nature, of the anterior pituitary. **1957** *New Biol.* XXIII. 117 The pituitary gland exerts some control over the thyroid gland, as it secretes a 'thyrotropic' hormone. **1965** LEE & KNOWLES *Animal Hormones* ii. 21 Adrenocorticotrophic hormone..and thyrotrophic hormone..are also secreted by the adenohypophysis. **1944** *Hackh's Chem. Dict.* (ed. 3) 856/2 Thyrotrophin. **1952** *New Biol.* XIII. 65 Activity of the thyroid is maintained by the stimulus of a hormone, thyrotropin. **1959** [see *TRF* s.v. *T 6]. **1968** [see *TRH* s.v. *T 6]. **1976** *Nature* 8 Apr. 480/2 The α subunit of HCG..is nearly identical to the α subunits of thyroid-stimulating hormone (thyrotropin) ..and luteinising hormone. **1980** *Brit. Med. Jrnl.* 29 Mar. 895/1 Two patients..had impaired responses of serum thyroid stimulating hormone to thyrotrophin releasing hormone.

thyroid, *sb.* Add: **2. b. thyroid-stimulating** *a.* = *thyrotrop(h)ic* adj. s.v. *THYRO-.

1941 *Trans. Amer. Assoc. Study Goiter* 159 Attempts have been made to demonstrate the thyroid stimulating hormone in the urine of patients with thyroid disease. **1974** D. & M. WEBSTER *Compar. Vertebr. Morphol.* xiii. 307 The thyroid-stimulating hormone, TSH, is produced by basophilic cells [within the pituitary].

thyroidectomize *v.* (examples); **thyroide·ctomized** *ppl. a.*, deprived of the thyroid; **thyroi·dic** *a.* and *sb.*, (designating) a person with a disordered thyroid gland; **thyroidless** *a.* (examples).

1932 J. S. HUXLEY *Probl. Relative Growth* VI. iv. 183 Groups of these [albino rats] were thyroidectomized. **1974** *Nature* 5 Apr. 525/1 All rats were ovariectomised and thyroidectomised on day 1 of the experiment. **1899** Thyroidectomized [in Dict.]. **1946** *Nature* 19 Oct. 557/2 Another series of experiments was carried out with thyroidectomized mice. **1922** G. B. SHAW in S. & B. Webb *English Local Govt.* VI. p. lxiii, By all means let the endocrinists go on dividing abnormal people, in prison and out, into hyper and sub pituitaries and thyroidics and adrenals. **1965** M. BRADBURY *Stepping Westward* i. 31 This was James Walker, a stout, slightly thyroidic, very shambling person. **1908** Thyroidless [see *anti-thyroid* s.v. *ANTI-[1] 3 b and c]. **1946** *Nature* 26 Oct. 590/1 During the third month, mortality was as high as 75 per cent in thyroidless animals, 60 per cent in the controls, and only 15 per cent of the hyperthyroid animals.

thyronine (þəiᵊ·rǒnīn). *Chem.* [f. THYRO- + -*n*- + -INE[5].] The amino-acid $HOC_6H_4OC_6H_4CH_2CH(NH_2)COOH$, of which thyroxine can be regarded as a formal derivative (see quots.).

1928 C. R. HARINGTON in *Biochem. Jrnl.* XXII. 1430 In order to lessen the clumsiness of the systematic nomenclature of thyroxine derivatives it is proposed to call the amino-acid, desiodothyroxine, 'thyronine'..so that thyroxine would be '3:5:3':5'-tetraiodothyronine'. **1970** R. W. MCGILVERY *Biochemistry* xxiii. 562 (*caption*) The active thyroid hormone, thyroxine, is in a formal sense the tetraiodo derivative of an amino acid called thyronine.

thyroxine (þəiᵊrǫ·ksīn). *Biochem.* Also **-in.** [f. THYR(O- + OX(Y- + IN(DOLE *sb.*, after the original (erroneous) description of its chemical composition: see quot. 1918.] A hormone secreted by the thyroid gland which increases the metabolic rate and regulates growth and development in animals; tetraiodothyronine, $HO{\cdot}C_6H_2I_2{\cdot}O{\cdot}C_6H_2I_2{\cdot}CH_2CH(NH_2)COOH$.

1918 E. C. KENDALL in *Endocrinology* II. 90 It appeared desirable to emphasize the presence of the oxy-indol nucleus and it appeared equally desirable not to emphasize the presence of iodin. The substance was therefore named 'Thyro-oxy-indol', which has been shortened to 'thyroxin' for every-day reference to the substance. **1926** C. R. HARINGTON in *Biochem. Jrnl.* XX. 294 It is impossible to accept the formula proposed by Kendall, and..the constitution of thyroxine must be regarded as not proven. **1969** *Daily Tel.* 19 Dec. 11/7 Thyroxine, given to thyroid-deficient babies and adults, saves them from cretinism and myxoedema. **1979** ARMS & CAMP *Biology* xxx. 501 If the tail is removed from a tadpole and placed in a bath containing thyroxin, the white blood cells in the tail will digest it.

ti. Add: (Earlier example.)

1832 G. BENNETT in *London Med. Gaz.* 22 Sept. 795/2 *Dracæna indivisa. Ti* of the natives. This species of Dracæna..attains an elevation of ten or twelve feet,.. The leaves form an excellent food as sea stock for cattle, &c.

b. *ti-palm* (earlier example), *-tree* (earlier example). Cf. TEA-TREE 2.

1851 V. LUSH *Jrnl.* 25 Sept. (1971) 86 Planted 14 Ti-palms in various parts of my grounds. **1864** R. ANDERSON *Hawaiian Islands* 134 Then came..an extensive tract covered with the *ti* trees.

ti: see *TE[1], TI.

Tiahuanaco (tīːäwänä·co). *Hist.* The name of a ruined ceremonial site south of Lake Titicaca in Bolivia, used *attrib.* and as *adj.* with reference to a pre-Incan culture, esp. notable for its stonemasonry and distinctive pottery, which flourished in South America in the first millennium A.D. Hence **Tiːahuana·coid** *a.* [-OID].

1892 C. R. MARKHAM *Hist. Peru* i. 19 The work of the builders of the Tiahuanaco period is met with in other parts of Peru. **1926** *Brief Guide to Peruvian Textiles* (Victoria & Albert Museum, Dept. Textiles) 6 The culture of the highlands has been termed 'Tiahuanaco' after the place..where stands the ruined archway. **1957** *Encycl. Brit.* II. 259 V/2 Nazca ceramics and textiles and Tiahuanaco stone carving. *Ibid.*, concomitant with this change is the Peruvian-wide diffusion of an art style referred to as 'Tiahuanacoid'. **1973** D. MENZEL in D. R. Gross *Peoples & Cultures Native S. Amer.* I. ii. 20 The Inca-period vogue of antiquarianism which revives post-Tiahuanacoid styles first appears at a time just preceding the Inca conquest of the area. **1976** *Times* 16 Nov. 19/2 The Tiahuanaco culture..flourished from about AD 130 to 1170.

Tia Maria (tī·ä mări·ä). Also **tia maria.** [Sp., lit. 'Aunt Mary'.] The proprietary name of a coffee-flavoured liqueur based on rum, made originally in the West Indies. Also, a drink or glassful of this.

1948 *Trade Marks Jrnl.* 29 Sept. 794/2 *Tia-Maria*... Liqueurs (alcoholic). **1951** E. DAVID *French Country Cooking* 190 A tablespoon of rum liqueur such as Courantin or Tia Maria. **1954** *Official Gaz.* (U.S. Patent Office) 31 Aug. 968 Tia Maria. For liqueurs. **1957** J. FRAME *Owls do Cry* 127 Tim has said something about drinks, a liqueur, benedictine, or tia maria. **1967** C. DRUMMOND *Death at Furlong Post* vi. 80 'Justifies a taxi back..,' said Hart eventually, after a Tia Maria. **1981** 'D. KAVANAGH' *Fiddle City* vii. 133 Soft, package-tour airports where bandits swirl through the green channel in a bustle of tired perms and duty-free Tia Maria.

tiang (ti͵æ·ŋ). [Dinka.] A small dark brown antelope belonging to a race of the korrigum, *Damaliscus lunatus*, found in the Sudan and neighbouring parts of Ethiopia.

1894 SCLATER & THOMAS *Bk. Antelopes* I. 63 The Tiang, as the well-known German traveller and naturalist Theodor von Heuglin proposed to call this Antelope, after its native name, is a representative form of the Korrigum in the upper valley of the Nile. **1920** *Blackw. Mag.* Nov. 668/2 Herds of hartebeeste and tiang. **1969** *Times* 30 Jan. (Ethiopia Suppl.) p. iii/3 The south-west corner of Ethiopia is an area inhabited by Sudanese lowland fauna, including..tiang.

‖ **tiare** (ti͵ā·re). Also **tiara, tiaré, tiari.** [a. Fr. *tiare* tiara.] In Tahiti, one of several species of *Gardenia* bearing fragrant white flowers. Also *attrib.*

[*a* **1771** S. PARKINSON *Jrnl. Voy. S. Seas* (1773) 37 Plants of Use for Food, Medicine, &c., in Otaheite..E teea-ree Gardenia-florida.] **1888** W. HILLEBRAND *Flora Hawaiian Islands* 171 Cultivated species: *G*[*ardenia*] *Tahitensis*—Tiara [etc.]. **1891** D. HORT *Tahiti* ii. 25 The houses are..surrounded by umbrageous trees, and.. gardenias—called there *tiari*. **1914** R. BROOKE in *New Numbers* Aug. 110 With the starred *tiare's* white.. Mamua, your lovelier head! **1919** W. S. MAUGHAM *Moon & Sixpence* xlix. 214 Tiaré..the white, scented flower which..will always draw you back to Tahiti in the end. **1931** A. WAUGH *Most Women* iv. 71 On her face was a look of serene contentment, and behind her left ear was the white tiare flower. **1960** H. E. BATES *Aspidistra in Babylon* 222 She was wearing in her hair not the big customary hibiscus flower but a little cluster of *tiare*, not more than six or seven blooms of small wax-white stars. **1980** *Daily Tel.* 26 Jan. 16 The local *tiaré* flower..is similar to a tiny gardenia.

tiarella (tiăre·lă). [mod.L. (Linnæus *Dissertatio Botanica qua Nova Plantarum Genera* (1751) 29), f. L. *tiara* turban + dim. suffix *-ella*.] A small perennial herb of the genus of this name, belonging to the family Saxifragaceæ, native to North America and Asia, and bearing basal, lobed leaves and clusters of small white or reddish flowers. Also *attrib.* Cf. *foam flower* s.v. *FOAM *sb.* 5 b.

1759 P. MILLER *Gardener's Dict.* (ed. 7) s.v. Tiarella, Tiarella with Heart-shaped leaves. This is the Mitella Americana. **1871** *Scribner's Monthly* II. 470 Tiarella leaves just tipped with claret colour. **1887** *Harper's Mag.* July 303/1 The tiarella sent up feathery spikes of white. **1944** T. C. MANSFIELD *Border in Colour* 224 Tiarellas.. are, fortunately, indifferent as to soil. **1976** J. BERRISFORD *Backyards & Tiny Gardens* vi. 47 Solomon's seal, epimediums and tiarella will also do well in shady places.

‖ **tibbin** (ti·bin). Also **tibben, tibn.** [Arab. *tibn*.] Hay or chopped straw.

1900 A. CONAN DOYLE *Green Flag* 271 Each camel provided with his own little heap of tibbin laid in the centre of the tablecloth. **1909** T. E. LAWRENCE *Let.* 29 Aug. (1938) 77 A bed for the night in a threshing floor, on a pile of tibn, chopped straw. **1923** *Blackw. Mag.* Nov. 692/2 Their sister-craft in the Ægean..filling up with stores for the Army—tibben (or Egyptian hay), barley, firewood, eggs,..and pigs. **1958** L. DURRELL *Balthazar* iv. 73 River-craft moved about their task of loading *tibbin* (corn).

Tibet. Add: The spelling *Thibet* is now obs. **Tibet dog, mastiff** = *Tibetan mastiff* s.v. *TIBETAN *a.* 2.

1845 W. YOUATT *Dog* ii. 18 The colour of the Thibet dog is of a deep black slightly clouded on the sides... He has the broad short truncated muzzle of the mastiff. **1884** G. STABLES *Our Friend the Dog* xxv. 245 He was called a Thibet Mastiff.

Tibetan, *a.* Substitute for entry:

Tibetan (tibe·tăn), *sb.* and *a.* Also † **Thibetan. A.** *sb.* A native or inhabitant of Tibet; also, the language of Tibet, a member of the Tibeto-Burmese sub-family of the Sino-Tibetan language group.

1822 tr. *Malte-Brun's Universal Geogr.* I. 571 The stock or family of the languages of Eastern Asia..differs entirely from that of the Indo-Germanic languages. It comprehends the *Thibetan*, the *Chinese*, the *Burman*, [etc.]. **1842** *Penny Cycl.* XXIV. 429/1 The Tibetans belong to the Mongol race. **1891** W. W. ROCKHILL *Land of Lamas* 97 It was with him..that I commenced studying Tibetan. **1962** L. DAVIDSON *Rose of Tibet* ii. 48 Caravan teamsters strolled everywhere; but..he noticed no Tibetans. **1979** A. HENNING tr. *Myrdal's Silk Road* (1980) ix. 71 Large steles..inscribed in Han, Manchu, Oirat, and Tibetan.

B. *adj.* **1.** Of or pertaining to Tibet, its inhabitants, or their language.

1828 *Asiatick Res.* XVI. 410, I have added a few words from the Tibetan vocabularies of the *Asia Polyglotta*. **1888** *Encycl. Brit.* XXIII. 343/1 The centres for *Tibetan* trade. *Ibid.* 843/2 The Tibetan race is not thoroughly homogeneous. **1942** M. CABLE *Gobi Desert* 32 Flowing beards made from the soft white tail of the Tibetan yak. **1960** [see *BHUTANESE *sb.* and *a.*]. **1974** *China Reconstructs* July 35/3 It used to be thought that the Tibetan plateau had no coal... For generations the Tibetan serfs used butter lamps and pine knots for lighting.

2. Special collocations: **Tibetan cherry,** a white-flowered cherry tree, *Prunus serrula*, native to western China; **Tibetan mastiff,** a large black-and-tan dog with a thick coat and drop ears, belonging to the breed of this name; **Tibetan spaniel,** a small white, brown, or black dog with a silky coat of medium length, belonging to the breed of this name; **Tibetan terrier,** a grey, black, cream, or parti-coloured terrier with a thick, shaggy coat, belonging to the breed of this name.

1948 C. INGRAM *Ornamental Cherries* II. 138 In cultivation the Tibetan Cherry tends to lose its squat, compact habit of growth. **1982** *Times* 20 Nov. (Saturday Suppl.) 3/3 A tree which likes to be stroked is the Tibetan cherry. .. The bark has probably the richest shade of all the coloured-bark trees—a striking mahogany is discovered when the outer bark peels away. **1852** T. SMITH *Narr. Five Years' Residence at Nepaul* II. 295 Young Porcupine. Tibetan Mastiff. Common Hare of central region. **1905** P. LANDON *Lhasa* I. xi. 403 The so-called Tibetan mastiff.. is a great shaggy creature, with a very massive head. **1976** T. HEALD *Let Sleeping Dogs Die* ix. 186 A more than generous helping of Tibetan mastiff, so fierce a dog that Aristotle thought it half tiger. **1930** *Observer* 9 Feb. 13/2 The foreign classes..will contain such rarities as Lhasa terriers, Thibetan spaniels, [etc.]. **1970** *Times* 5 Feb. (Pedigree Dog Suppl.) p. ii/2 Recently there was a market tip for Tibetan spaniels, golden-coated, lion-like dogs of pleasing temperament. **1905** P. LANDON *Lhasa* I. xi. 387 The typical Tibetan terrier, a long-coated little fellow with a sharp nose, prick ears, and..black from muzzle to tail. **1976** T. HEALD *Let Sleeping Dogs Die* i. 12 The latest is a Tibetan terrier in Tokyo.

Tibetian (tibe·tiăn, -ʃiăn), *sb.* and *a.* Now *rare.* Also † **Thibetian.** [f. TIBET, THIBET + -IAN.] = *TIBETAN *sb.* and *a.*

1747 *Astley's New Gen. Coll. Voyages* IV. II. iv. 451/2 The Mogul's Empire; called by the Tibetians, Anonkek, or Anonjen. **1790** *Asiatick Res.* II. 32 We know, that rolls of Tibetian writing have been brought even from the borders of the Caspian. **1841** G. BORROW *Zincali* II. III. 108 Many of the principal languages of Asia are..of the great Tartar family, at the head of which there is good reason for placing the Chinese and the Tibetian. **1889** J. J. REIN *Industries Japan* IV. iii. 517 Thibetian cats. **1973** *Times* 12 Apr. 8/6 [The Chogyal's] American wife.. is also said to be a devotee of Tibetian culture.

Tibeto- (tibe·to), combining form of TIBET, = 'pertaining to Tibet and —', as **Tibeto-Burman:** see below as main entry; **Tibeto-Burme·se** *sb.* and *a.* = *TIBETO-BURMAN; **Tibeto-Chine·se** *a.* = *Sino-Tibetan* adj. s.v. *SINO- 2; also as *sb.*; **Tibeto-Himala·yan** *a.* and *sb.*, (*a*) *adj.*, pertaining to Tibet and the Himalayas; (*b*) *sb.*, a branch of the Tibeto-Burmese sub-family of the Sino-Tibetan language group.

1954 PEI & GAYNOR *Dict. Linguistics* 217 Tibeto-Burmese (Tibeto-Burman). **1974** M. PEISSEL *Great Himalayan Passage* xv. 230 Tibetan is the root of the Tibeto-Burmese languages. **1910** *Encycl. Brit.* XIV. 384/1 Of the Tibeto-Chinese family, the Tibeto-Burman sub-family..is spoken from Tibet to Burma. **1960** C. WINICK *Dict. Anthropol.* 537/2 *Tibeto-Chinese*, a language family that is both agglutinative..and isolating... It has two sub-families: Tibeto-Burmese and Siamese-Chinese. **1961** L. F. BROSNAHAN *Sounds of Language* viii. 179 The Tibeto-Chinese languages..have neither palatalisation nor simple accentuation. **1875** *Encycl. Brit.* II. 684/1 Tibeto-Himalayan mountains. **1939** Tibeto-Himalayan [see *TIBETO-BURMAN *a.* and *sb.*].

Tibeto-Bu·rman, *a.* and *sb.* [f. *TIBETO- + *BURMAN *a.* and *sb.*] **A.** *adj.* Pertaining to Tibet and Burma; *spec.* designating or belonging to a group of languages spoken in Asia, belonging to the Sino-Tibetan family, or the peoples speaking any of these languages. **B.** *sb.* The Tibeto-Burman group of languages.

1878 R. N. CUST *Sk. Mod. Lang. E. Indies* 4 The great Tibeto-Burman sea. *Ibid.* 93 The Bhramu speak a purely Tibeto-Burman language. **1880** *Encycl. Brit.* XII. 777/2 The early peoples of India belonged to three great stocks, known as the Tibeto-Burman, the Kolarian, and the Dravidian. **1895** E. W. HOPKINS *Relig. India* (1896) xviii. 525 The native wild tribes of India (excluding the extreme Northern Tibeto-Burman group) fall into two great classes. **1939** L. H. GRAY *Foundations of Lang.* 389 *Tibeto-Burman* is divided into *Tibeto-Himalayan*, consisting of Tibetan..; and of Himalayan, [etc.]. **1976** W. H. CANAWAY *Willow-Pattern War* xv. 156 Thupten's own language was some impenetrable offshoot of Tibeto-Burman. **1982** *Whitaker's Almanack 1983* 803/2 The indigenous inhabitants who entered Burma from the north and east are of similar racial types and speak languages of the Tibeto-Burman, Mon-Khmer and Thai groups.

Tibetology (tibetǫ·lŏdʒi). [f. TIBET + -OLOGY.] The study of Tibetan culture. Also **Tibeto·logist,** one who specializes or is expert in this branch of study.

1964 *Bull. Tibetology* I. 5 Tibetology, that is, study of culture or cultures expressed through the medium of Po Key (Bod Sked=Tibetan language), is not confined to the geographical boundaries of Tibet. *Ibid.* 6 The very first difficulty which a Tibetologist faces is that of non-availability of literary data. **1974** M. PEISSEL *Great Himalayan Passage* iv. 84 Professor Tucci, the noted Italian Tibetologist, wrote of Nepal. **1982** *Bodl. Libr. Record* X. 371 The modern discipline of Tibetology.

tibicinist. For *rare*[−1] read *rare* and add earlier example.

1776 J. HAWKINS *Hist. Music* I. p. xlvi, A scene in an ancient comedy, in which a tibicinist is delineated standing on the stage.

tic. 3. For 'see' read '=' and add examples.

1896 [see TICK *sb.*[5] 2]. **1927** F. M. FORD *Let.* 28 Mar. (1935) 172, I have such a tic against writing letters that I cannot do it. **1960** *Twentieth Cent.* Apr. 361 This is an irritating tic of the British Left, this substitution of moral gestures for practical policies. **1978** C. P. SNOW *Realists* vi. 176 He had the tic, common to many writers, of insisting that the table be kept pernicketily tidy.

ticarcillin (tikāɹsi·lin). *Pharm.* [f. *ti-* (of unknown origin) + *CAR(BOXY- + *-cillin*, after *PENICILLIN.] A semisynthetic penicillin antibiotic, (6R)-6-[2-carboxy-2-(3-thienyl)-acetamido]penicillanic acid, usu. administered as the disodium salt, $C_{15}H_{14}N_2Na_2O_6S_2$.

1972 in *Approved Names* (Brit. Pharmacopœia Comm.) Suppl. v. 4. **1974** *Jrnl. Clin. Pharmacol.* XIV. 172/1 Ticarcillin..is a new semisynthetic penicillin, with a wide spectrum of activity against gram-positive and gram-negative bacteria. **1980** *Brit. Med. Jrnl.* 24 May 1240/2 Bacteriological monitoring of seriously ill patients may be rewarding if combined with early and energetic use of suitable antibiotics such as tobramycin, plus ticarcillin.., when septicaemia is clinically suspected.

tice, *sb.* **a.** (Earlier examples in *Cricket.*)

1843 'WYKEHAMIST' *Pract. Hints Cricket* 15 The 'Tice', which may be described as a short pitched full-pitch..is one of the most destructive Balls that can be bowled. **1869** L. M. ALCOTT *Little Women* II. ix. 128 The phrases, 'caught off a tice', 'stumped off his ground',..were as intelligible to her as Sanscrit.

tich (titʃ). *slang.* Also **Tich, titch.** The stage name Little *Tich* of the dwarfish music-hall comedian Harry Relph (1868–1928), who was given the nickname as a child because of a resemblance to the Tichborne claimant (see below), used as a name for any small person. Cf. *TITCHY *a.*

Arthur Orton (1834–98), the Tichborne claimant, claimed in 1866 to be Roger Charles Tichborne (1829–54), the heir to an English baronetcy, who was lost at sea. Orton was finally discredited and imprisoned in 1874.

1934 W. POLLOCK *Cream of Cricket* xi. 66 'Tich' Freeman would toss up his slows with that maddening lure to come and commit cricket suicide which so many misguided batsmen cannot resist. **1959** I. & P. OPIE *Lore & Lang. Schoolch.* ix. 169 A chap who has got duck's disease is most often labelled 'Tich' in a friendly manner, or 'squirt'. **1960** D. ABSE in J. C. Trewin *Plays of Year 1960–61* XXIII. 147, I vowed to work harder. To make more money. For you and the titch. **1962** *Daily Mail* 7 Mar. 12/5 *(caption)* This will prove we're not 'tiches' in space communications.

Ticinese (titʃinī·z), *sb.* and *a.* Pl. **Ticinese,** ‖ **-esi.** [a. It. *Ticinese*: see -ESE.] **A.** *sb. collect.* The natives or inhabitants of Ticino, an Italian-speaking canton in southern Switzerland. **B.** *adj.* Of or pertaining to Ticino or its inhabitants.

1961 'W. HAGGARD' *Arena* x. 84 Walter didn't much care for Ticinesi, but it was certain they weren't Swiss-Germans. **1964** *Language* XL. 287 The article gives a detailed description of Ticinese customs. **1974** *Sat. Rev. World* (U.S.) 19 Oct. 43/2 The Ticinese can manage most of the other tongues in current employ in Switzerland. **1978** [see *SCHWEIZERDEUTSCH, SCHWYZERTÜTSCH].

tick, *sb.*[1] **1. b.** Delete † and add later *colloq.* examples. Freq. as *little tick.*

1909 WODEHOUSE *Mike* xl. 231 Can't you see that.. we've got a chance of getting a jolly good bit of our own back against those Downing's ticks? **1928** J. VAN DRUTEN *Young Woodley* i. 17 Milner: 'Cope, your presence is urgently desired... Scrimshanking, the little tic.' **1952** E. O'NEILL *Moon for Misbegotten* I. 17 Everyone says you're a wicked old tick, as crooked as a corkscrew. **1973** R. FULFORD in D. Pryce-Jones *Evelyn Waugh & his World* ii. 17 How often in those early days did I hear those ominous words 'that awful little tick Waugh'.

c. Phr. *as full* (or *tight*) *as a tick*: full to repletion, esp. with alcoholic drink.

1678 J. RAY *Coll. Eng. Proverbs* (ed. 2) 284 As full as a pipers bag; as a tick. **1822** *Yankee Phrases* in *New Jersey Alm. 1823* (Elizabethtown, N.J.) 31 Though of love I'm as full as a tick. **1911** L. STONE *Jonah* 226 'Ard luck, to grudge a man a pint, with 'is own missis inside there gittin' as full as a tick. **1933** M. LOWRY *Ultramarine* iv. 177 He was tight as a tick so couldn't tell the difference. **1952** E. O'NEILL *Moon for Misbegotten* IV. 168 'You must have seen how blotto I was.'..'I did. You were as full as a tick.' **1981** A. PRICE *Soldier no More* v. 59 He was drunk as a lord..tight as a tick.

3. *tick-infested* adj.; **tick-bean** (earlier and later examples); **tick-bird** (earlier example); **tick-borne** *a.*, transmitted by ticks; *tick-borne fever*, a mild, transient, rickettsial, febrile disease of sheep, cattle, and goats; **tick paralysis,** paralysis caused by neurotoxin in the saliva of certain biting ticks; **tick pyæmia,** a type of blood-poisoning in sheep, esp. lambs, caused by *Staphylococcus aureus* and leading to lameness or death; **tick-trefoil** (earlier example); **tick typhus** = *Rocky Mountain fever* s.v. *ROCKY *a.*[1] 1 b.

1744 W. ELLIS *Mod. Husbandman* Feb. ii. 17 Chilturn Farmers can get a full Crop of Horse or Tick-beans. **1969** *Oxf. Bk. Food Plants* 40/1 Prehistoric specimens are all small-seeded forms—even smaller than the 'Horse bean' or 'Tick bean' varieties grown as food for livestock in modern times. **1850** T. E. POOLE *Life, Scenery, & Customs in Sierra Leone & Gambia* II. xiv. 220 Perched upon these animals [*sc.* cattle], which did not seem in the least to mind them, were a species of birds called 'Tick-birds', from the circumstances of their feeding upon certain insects of that name, which they find in great numbers on these beasts. **1921** *Indian Med. Gaz.* LVI. 368/1 It [*sc.* Brill's disease] has no epidemiological relationship whatever with the Rocky Mountain fever which is tick-borne. **1932** W. S. GORDON et al. in *Jrnl. Compar. Path. & Therapeutics* XLV. 122 A disease characterised by a low mortality, with an incubation period of about four days, followed by a sharp rise in temperature and a period of fever... We have..shown..that this reaction is a 'tick-borne fever'. *Ibid.* 301 This condition we have..named 'tick-borne fever'. **1970** W. H. PARKER *Health & Dis. in Farm Animals* xviii. 241 In areas of late lambing, abortions in ewes are sometimes attributable to tick-borne fever. **1973** J. J. MCKELVEY *Man Against Tsetse* i. 42 Dutton died at Kasongo in February 1905 of tick-borne relapsing fever. **1932** C. FULLER *Louis Trigardt's Trek* 128 Our small stock were so tick-infested that we despaired of saving them. **1960** *Times* 1 Oct. 7/7 Tick-infested hinterland. **1914** P. MANSON *Trop. Dis.* (ed. 5) xvii. 307 *(heading)* Tick paralysis. **1962** GORDON & LAVOIPIERRE *Entomol. for Students of Med.* xliii. 260 In Australia, North America, South Africa and South Eastern Europe several species of ticks..produce a type of ascending motor paralysis known as 'tick paralysis'. **1946** *Nature* 27 July 132/2 The sheep tick, *Ixodes ricinus,* is involved in the transmission of..tick-pyæmia. **1970** W. H. PARKER *Health & Dis. in Farm Animals* xviii. 241 Tick pyaemia is caused by the ubiquitous bacterium *Staphylococcus.* **1853** THOREAU *Jrnl.* 31 July in *Writings* (1906) XI. 350 *Desmodium nudiflorum,* naked-flowered tick trefoil, some already with loments round-angled. **1921** *Indian Med. Gaz.* LVI. 370/2 *(heading)* Possible human origin of tick typhus. **1981** D. R. BELL *Lect. Notes Trop. Med.* vii. 68 American tick typhus caused by *R[ickettsia] rickettsi* occurs in Colombia and Brazil.

tick, *sb.*[2] (Further examples.)

1853 *Heal & Son Catal.: Bedsteads* 3 Best Grey Goose.. in Fine Linen Ticks. **1908** L. M. MONTGOMERY *Anne of Green Gables* iv. 49 She made her bed less successfully, for she had never learned the art of wrestling with a feather tick. **1951** *People* 3 June 6/8 (Advt.), Pillow ticks black white striped. **1980** J. C. OATES *Bellefleur* (1981) IV. 329 A plain four-poster with white ruffled skirts, a cornhusk tick and feather bed on top.

tick, *sb.*[3] Add: **3. c.** A ticked item on a list, esp. a list of birds to be observed. Also *Comb.*, as *tick-hunter, -hunting.*

1975 W. CONDRY *Pathway to Wild* vi. 93 R. S. Thomas.. saw it [*sc.* foreign travel] as an opportunity of adding to his life-list of birds. 'Tick-hunting' is what bird-watchers call it. You carry a card with a list of all the birds on it and you..tick them off as you spot them. *Ibid.* 94 We saw a signpost on our right, 'La Route des Lacs', and what tick-hunter short of waterbirds could resist a lake-side road? **1981** *Birds* Autumn 60/3 Their [*sc.* the *Country Life* team's] ticks..included glossy ibis, spoonbill, Savi's warbler, [etc.].

4. (Further examples.) *on* or *to the tick,* exactly at the appointed time, punctually; cf. *on the dot* s.v. *DOT *sb.*[1] 4 d.

1902 [see *COMMUTER]. **1907** To the tick [in Dict.]. **1913** A. BENNETT *Regent* ix. 262 If you don't clear out on the tick I'll chuck this cup and saucer down into the stalls. **1927** *Daily Express* 6 July 3/5, I am always here on the tick myself, and I do not see why jurors should not do the same. **1963** T. PARKER *Unknown Citizen* i. 38 Won't be a tick, don't go away. **1972** J. WILSON *Hide & Seek* i. 18 Just wait till I get these grotty old school things off, Mary. I won't be a tick. **1973** P. WHITE *Eye of Storm* ii. 83 Shan't be a couple of ticks, love. **1983** E. REVELEY *In Good Faith* vi. 104 Just wait a tick while I tell George where we'll be, and then we can go down together.

tick, *sb.*[5] Delete 'Rarely tic.'

tick, *v.*[1] Add: **1. c.** *trans.* = TIG *v.* 2.

1913 A. G. CATON *Romance of Wirral* viii. 69 One out of the one township would tick one out of the other. Then a chase over the country began between these two. **1969** I. & P. OPIE *Children's Games* ii. 64 In the west midlands they 'tick' him, and he is then said to have been 'took', 'tuck', or sometimes 'tucked'. **1981** T. THOMPSON *Edwardian Childhoods* iii. 83 We used to play..tick... You had to..tick your neighbour.

2. d. *intr.* with *over.* Of an internal combustion engine: to run or work with the propeller or gears disengaged, or at a low rate of revolutions; to idle. Also *transf.* and *fig.*, to function (merely); to work or operate continuously, esp. at a low capacity. Chiefly in *pres. pple.*

1916 H. BARBER *Aeroplane Speaks* 50 The engine is awake again and slowly ticking over. **1934** *Humorist* 28 July 38/2 How shall I know when the influence is ticking over? **1950** *Sport* 7–11 Apr. 22/4 It is the money in the pocket of the man-in-the-street which keeps sport, the cinemas and the B.B.C. ticking over. **1952** A. BEVAN *In Place of Fear* iv. 70 Old out-of-date steel plants were kept ticking over by means of bank overdrafts. **1953** C. A. LINDBERGH *Spirit of St. Louis* I. i. 9, I..pull back my throttle until the propeller is just ticking over. **1960** 'M. CRONIN' *Begin with Gun* vii. 81 Just the way you said, chief. All ticking over nicely. **1977** F. WEBB *Go for Out* v. 97 The car engine fired. He let it tick-over for a moment, then switched it off.

e. *intr.* Of a taximeter (cab): to make a ticking sound while recording the fare due for a period of hire, esp. while waiting; also quasi-*trans.* with complement. With *up*, to record an increasing fare.

1926 W. S. MAUGHAM *Constant Wife* III. 208, I don't want to hurry you, but the taxi is just ticking its head off. **1930** E. P. OPPENHEIM *Million Pound Deposit* xi. 104 'Got a car?' she enquired. 'No, a taxi, ticking up like blazes.' **1938** E. BOWEN *Death of Heart* III. vi. 438 A taxi ticked outside. **1940** DYLAN THOMAS *Portrait of Artist as Young Dog* 155 The taxi was ticking away, and that worried Beatrice and Betti, and at last the sisters and the cousin and Mary drove together to the church. **1954** T. RATTIGAN *Sleeping Prince* I. 44 *Mary.* The taxi isn't ticking up, is it? *Regent.* No. They will tell us when it arrives. **1966** A. L. COBURN *Autobiogr.* vi. 72 He..whisked away in the cab which he had kept ticking at the door. **1979** J. GRIMOND *Memoirs* vi. 93 The General was alarmed to find a taxi waiting, the clock on it ticking up from £15.8.6 to £15.8.9.

f. *intr. fig.* To work, function, operate; *what makes* (someone) *tick,* what motivates (a person). *colloq.*

1931 E. F. BENSON *Mapp & Lucia* i. 26, I want to get roused up again and shaken and made to tick. **1947** AUDEN *Age of Anxiety* (1948) I. 13 They watch others with a covert but passionate curiosity. What makes them tick? **1957** *Listener* 3 Oct. 541/1 Television could show the minds ticking; no need here for those stage directions. **1964** MRS. L. B. JOHNSON *White House Diary* 6 Jan. (1970) 31 Then came the big event of the day—the White House staff reception... We would be meeting..everybody who makes the house tick. **1971** A. PRICE *Alamut Ambush* xii. 151, I still don't quite know what makes Razzak tick. You were going to find out about him. **1980** *Nature* 24 Apr. 695/2 The first step to correct this source of insecurity and fear is to learn what makes it 'tick'.

g. *intr.* with *by* or *away*: (of time, events, etc.) to pass, come to an end. Cf. sense 2 b in Dict.

1937 C. ODETS *Golden Boy* 42 You don't know what it means to sit around here and watch the months go ticking by! **1974** *Publishers Weekly* 30 Sept. 15 (Advt.), Their father, his own life ticking away after a freak accident, must prepare his children for the grueling battle ahead. **1981** G. BOYCOTT *In Fast Lane* xii. 92 A statement was expected by the hour but each hour ticked away without any news.

3. a. (Earlier and later *fig.* examples.)

1854 DICKENS *Hard Times* I. xiv. 108 He was not sure that if he had been required..to tick her off into columns in a parliamentary return, he would have quite known how to divide her. **1932** A. HUXLEY *Let.* 1 Oct. (1969) 363 All that stupid unreal rhetoric of fascism... It's beautifully ticked off, in its earlier and different manifestation, by Tolstoy. **1966** N. MAILER *Cannibals & Christians* (1967) I. 38 Could you tick off just a few of the major issues you think will be in the campaign against the Democrats?

c. To reprimand or scold. Cf. *to tell off* s.v. *TELL *v.* 23 d. *colloq.* (orig. *Mil. slang*).

1915 W. OWEN *Let.* 2 Nov. (1967) 365 He has been 'ticked-off' four or five times for it; but is not yet shot at dawn. **1936** [see *ESSENCE *sb.* 8]. **1957** *Listener* 29 Aug. 297/1 'Ticked off' by one of the boys for leaving his car unlocked and complete with ignition key. **1978** K. AMIS *Jake's Thing* xvii. 182 He'd ticked Ed off without being told to.

d. To annoy, anger; to dispirit. Cf. *TICKED *ppl. a.* c. *U.S. slang.*

1975 *Washington Post* 19 Feb. C 12/7 We got hit somethin' fierce. It really ticked me off! We lost everything! **1979** R. L. SIMON *Peking Duck* xvi. 117 Shit, it ticks me off I spent all the money on this tour and look what happens.

tick, *v.*[2] Add: **1. b.** (Later Austral. and N.Z. examples.) Also const. *up.*

c **1926** 'MIXER' *Transport Workers' Song Bk.* 42 You've never 'ticked' a penny Whilst you worked. **1947** M. MORRIS in 'B. James' *Austral. Short Stories* (1963) 355 Best be off soon. No use ticking things up. **1966** 'J. HACKSTON' *Father clears Out* 114 Going on the slate and ticking up a few rounds of drinks.

ticked, *ppl. a.* Add: **c.** *ticked off*: angry, annoyed, 'fed up'. Cf. *TICK *v.*[1] 3 d. *U.S. slang.*

1959 *Amer. Speech* XXXIV. 156 When one is angry, he's *ticked* or *teed off.* **1972** 'T. COE' *Don't lie to Me* (1974) v. 54 Now you can see why Grazko is so ticked off. **1977** C. MCFADDEN *Serial* (1978) xxxiii. 72/1 Joan was beginning to get ticked off.

ticker[3]. Add: **1. a.** (Earlier example, in sense 'a watch'.)

1821 P. EGAN *Boxiana* III. 622 To nail the ticker..or to mill the cly.

c. *slang* (orig. *U.S.*). The heart; also *U.S.* and *Austral.*, courage, spirit, 'guts'. Cf. HEART *sb.* 11.

1930 J. TAIT *Big House* 7 Because the heart is a 'ticker'. **1935** D. RUNYON *Money from Home* 87, I never see a guy with more ticker than Shamus. **1950** *Chambers's Jrnl.* Mar. 149/1 Then I leapt to my feet, and the sight that met my eyes made the old ticker miss more beats than it had done when Martin clamped his gun on the back of my neck. **1979** *Sunday Sun* (Brisbane) 4 Nov. 54/1 The lady has ticker... She didn't opt for the soft life. **1980** J. CARTWRIGHT *Horse of Darius* viii. 106 Put something at the bottom about your heart. Say, 'The ticker seems to be a little dodgy at the moment.'

2. Someone who ticks off items in a list, etc.; *spec.* = *TWITCHER 4.

1980 *Guardian* 25 June 12/5 'Twitchers' or 'tickers'—

the serious ornithologists' somewhat disparaging term for those bird watchers whose main interest in their hobby is adding new species to their lists. **1982** *Birds* Spring 70/2 Bird tickers contribute little to the well being of the environment and often do little but disturb it.

3. Special Comb.: **ticker tape,** the paper strip on which telegraphic messages are recorded in a tape-machine; this or similar paper material thrown from windows as a form of greeting for a celebrity; also *attrib.*

1902 H. L. WILSON *Spenders* 407 For two days he clung to the ticker tape as to a life line. **1957** *Listener* 10 Oct. 556/1 A traditional ticker-tape reception is to be accorded. **1972** D. E. WESTLAKE *Cops & Robbers* (1973) x. 135 The Wall Street ticker-tape parade is a tradition. **1976** H. WILSON *Governance of Britain* iii. 51 On the afternoon of the second day, the ticker-tape carried a story that President Truman had said that General MacArthur, supreme commnder in Korea, had the authority to use the nuclear weapon there, without reference to the President. **1980** L. ST. CLAIR *Obsessions* ii. 48 Tomorrow's ticker-tape welcome to Commander Richard E. Byrd.

ticket, *sb.*^{1} Add: **2. b.** An official documentary notification of an offence, esp. in connection with traffic regulations. Cf. *parking ticket* s.v. *PARKING *vbl. sb.* 3 b. orig. *U.S.*

1930 *Outlook* 12 Feb. 249/1 He wrote the young professor a ticket for speeding. **1935** J. O'HARA *Appointment in Samarra* vii. 201 It was two blocks from the hotel, and he might get a ticket for parking, but if he couldn't get the ticket fixed it was worth the two-dollar fine to have things straightened out with Harry. **1956** S. BELLOW *Seize the Day* (1957) ii. 46 Some fool puts advertising leaflets under your windshield wiper and you have heart failure a block away because you think you've got a ticket. **1964** M. BANTON *Policeman in Community* iii. 62 A driver who made an illegal turn against a red light was 'given a ticket' (i.e. a citation was issued against him). **1981** C. DEXTER *Dead of Jericho* xxxii. 176 Cheque for £6, being the penalty fixed for the traffic offence detailed on the ticket.

c. *big* (or *large*) *ticket item,* something expensive. Cf. *price ticket* s.v. *PRICE *sb.* 14. *N. Amer. colloq.*

1970 *Globe & Mail* (Toronto) 25 Sept. B2/2 Buying plans for big ticket items are up since the previous survey in May and June. **1972** *Mod. Law Rev.* XXXV. 20 Legal aid does not seem to have made much difference, except with regard to large ticket items in middle class communities. **1975** *Washington Post* 28 Jan. A19/3 His proposed tax rebate obviously is designed to stimulate consumption of what is known in this week's argot as 'big ticket items' like cars.

4. b. *spec.* an airman's or seaman's certificate of qualification (further examples).

1907 M. ROBERTS *Flying Cloud* 7 Seventeen years before he got his 'ticket', his second greaser's, second mate's ticket, he served in the foc'sle before the mast. **1910** *Flight* 26 Nov. 970/1 He did rolling practice in the morning, straight flights before luncheon, circuits in the afternoon, and qualified for his 'ticket' before dark. **1947** M. LOWRY *Under Volcano* iv. 111 If all goes well I'll be sailing from Vera Cruz in about a week. As quartermaster, you knew I had an A.B.'s ticket, didn't you? **1977** 'E. CRISPIN' *Glimpses of Moon* xiii. 268 George..had eventually got his Mate's ticket.

† **c.** A certificate given to children at Sunday school recording their progress in religious instruction, esp. their readiness for confirmation. *Obs.*

1838 J. ROMILLY *Diary* 18 July (1967) 153 George went..to St Mary's vestry to be exam^d by Mr Carus:—he only asked him..'the meaning of "Sacrament"', & gave him his ticket. **1879** C. M. YONGE *Burnt Out* i. 11 Mother! mother! where's my ticket bag? Oh! my tickets! my tickets and my Bible and all my prize books!

5. a. *meal ticket*: see *MEAL *sb.*^{2} 4.

c. *to have tickets on* (a person or thing), to have a strong liking for; esp. *to have tickets on oneself* and varr., to be vain, to be conceited. *Austral. slang.*

1908 W. H. KOEBEL *Anchorage* viii. 140, I don't know whether she's got any tickets on me. **1938** 'R. HYDE' *Nor Years Condemn* ix. 179 You must have tickets on her, Starkie. **1941** K. TENNANT *Battlers* 20 'Arr,' the busker said disgustedly, 'you've got tickets all over yourself.' **1951** CUSACK & JAMES *Come in Spinner* iv. 32 If people have got any tickets on themselves, Blue don't get nowhere with them. **1970** J. HIBBERD *Plays* 227 You're the bastard that's always been smug and had tickets on himself.

d. *to write one's own ticket*: to be able to stipulate one's own conditions, to be in an advantageous position. *colloq.*

1928 WODEHOUSE *Money for Nothing* v. 94 'But Oil's the stuff, and if you want to part with any of that Silver River of yours, Tom,' he said, 'pass it across this desk and write your own ticket.' **1961** C. COCKBURN *View from West* vii. 75 A prelate in the Archbishop's position can..write his own ticket as to what is in the mind of God. **1981** A. PRICE *Soldier no More* xvii. 246 He could make his own terms, and write his own ticket.

e. A (counterfeit) pass or passport. *slang.*

1969 R. AIRTH *Snatch!* ii. 23 A small but select stock of tickets—Ziggy sold only the best, no London-issued Lithuanians for him. **1973** G. M. FRASER *Flashman at Charge* 164 Russia—where everyone has to show his damned ticket every few miles.

f. A piece of paper impregnated with lysergic acid diethylamide (see quot. 1969). *slang* (chiefly *Austral.*).

1969 *Pix* 19 Apr. 11/1 It [*sc.* LSD] is sold usually in absorbent paper in a portion of 120 micrograms known as a ticket. When you take a ticket you are on a trip.

6. a. Also, any certificate of discharge from service, prison, etc.; freq. in phr. *to work one's ticket,* to obtain (by scheming) one's discharge.

1869 *Temple Bar* XXV. 217 'Coiners'..as a rule returned to their profession as soon as they got their 'ticket'. Prison is..a great punishment to such men. **1899** H. WYNDHAM *Queen's Service* xxxiii. 231 It is a comparatively easy matter for a discontented man to 'work his ticket'. **1952** M. ALLINGHAM *Tiger in Smoke* iv. 77 He ..attempted to work his ticket to one of these new-style open prisons. **1970** W. SMITH *Gold Mine* xxiv. 56 My boss boy has worked his ticket... Can you see that I get a good man to replace him?

b. (Earlier example.)

1843 in *Occasional Papers Univ. Sydney Lang. Res. Centre* (1981) No. 19. 61, I have this day given the prisoner named in the margin a pass to proceed to Bathurst as he wished to have his Ticket issued for that District.

7. b. = *pawn-ticket* s.v. PAWN *sb.*^{2} 4.

1835 DICKENS *Sk. Boz.* (1836) 1st Ser. II. 152 You leave your ticket here till you're sober, and send your wife for them two planes. **1863** E. BARLEE in N. Longmate *Hungry Mills* (1978) viii. 112 [He] coomed straight home, made up the fire and burnt every blessed ticket. **1899** KIPLING *Stalky & Co.* 45 Why, last month you and Beetle sold mine [*sc.* a watch]! 'Never got a sniff of any ticket.

8. For 'In U.S. politics' read 'In politics (orig. U.S.)' and add further examples. Also, the subject or theme of an election campaign; the principles of a political party as presented for an election.

1863 *Clare Jrnl.* 18 May 2/4 We venture to tell Mr Vereker and Captain Knox that they need not..attempt to go into Parliament on the Conservative 'ticket'. **1899** G. B. SHAW *Let.* 30 Dec. (1972) II. 127 Suppose we do run a ticket, how is it to be done? The [Fabian] Society would not vote a ticket except as between two rival tails to the Exec. **1927** A. HUXLEY *Let.* 24 Mar. (1969) 286 How are you going to make a strong working government from a body of people elected on a great variety of different tickets? **1962** *Listener* 22 Mar. 505/2 Lloyd George had actually fought the election of 1929 on the ticket 'We can conquer unemployment'. **1968** *Globe & Mail* (Toronto) 3 Feb. 3/8 Mr. Woodcock..is running on a youth ticket. **1974** *Argus* (Cape Town) 2 Aug. 8/7 In 1966, the then Mayor..had to contest an election... He won by topping the poll on a ticket of two. **1977** *Grimsby Even. Tel.* 14 May 7/4, I did not ask Mr. Muggeridge for permission to put his name on the 'ticket'. **1979** H. KISSINGER *White House Years* ii. 24 Dwight Eisenhower had been elected on the Republican ticket, but he owed little to the Republican Party.

10. a. *ticket-pocket* (later examples), *stub*; **b.** *ticket agency, agent* (examples), *booth, counter, hall, machine, money* (examples), *office* (examples), *wagon, wicket, window*; **d.** *ticket-collector* (examples), *-dispenser, -examiner* (examples), *-holder, punch, -seller, -writer*; *ticket-collecting* (earlier example), *-issuing* (examples), *writing* (examples).

1923 *Variety* 1 Nov. 14/3 The ticket agencies took the attraction on the basis of an eight week buy. **1975** R. HOBAN *Turtle Diary* li. 206 A lady from the ticket agency where Miss Neap had worked. **1861** *Richmond* (Va.) *Examiner* 6 Dec. 3/3 Mr. John M. Parker, for several years the efficient General Freight and Ticket Agent of the Richmond and Petersburg railroad. **1976** SCOTT & KOSKI *Walk-In* (1977) I. iii. 20 The ticket agent was..the wrong side of middle age. **1926** E. HEMINGWAY *Sun also Rises* II. xvii. 196 The ticket-booths out in the square. **1981** P. FOX *Satan's Messenger* II. xiv. 108 A ticket booth where he paid 20p to proceed. **1889** KIPLING *From Sea to Sea* (1899) I. xx. 397 The crush of a ticket-collecting. **1850** F. B. HEAD in E. R. Pike *Human Doc. Victorian Golden Age* 97 The ticket collector at Camden station. **1977** R. BARNARD *Blood Brotherhood* ii. 18 The Bishop..bestowed his ticket on the ticket-collector. **1862** *Railway Traveller's Handy Bk.* 68 An elderly lady presents herself at the ticket counter. **1962** A. LURIE *Love & Friendship* xv. 293 Will..leaning on the ticket counter below the boarded window. **1977** G. SCOTT *Hot Pursuit* iii. 34 When I got to the airport I..walked over to the ticket counter for my airline. **1976** P. CAVE *High Flying Birds* ii. 17 He turned the handle on his little ticket dispenser and delivered my receipt. **1943** K. TENNANT *Ride on Stranger* v. 48 He dived under the seat as they drew in at a station. The ranks drew together and out-stared the ticket-examiner. **1971** *Sunday Times* (Johannesburg) 28 Mar. 1/4 Mr. Manaka reported this to the ticket examiner. **1969** *Listener* 6 Mar. 295/3 The miners set about the job of unearthing a new ticket hall, designed to become the busiest in London. **1978** H. R. F. KEATING *Long Walk to Wimbledon* x. 165 She made her way..to the station entrance... There were yet more people inside the old ticket hall. **1859** J. ROBERT-HOUDIN *Memoirs* I. viii. 154 Suppose the ticket-holder declined, he was not admitted, and when matters came to that pass, people always paid. **1979** D. HURD *End to Promises* i. 15 To avert violence these rallies were to be for ticket-holders only. **1952** *Evening News* (Port of Spain, Trinidad) 11 Jan. 2/1 Recently 'Tim', a ticket-issuing machine, was introduced to save time and money. **1964** A. WYKES *Gambling* x. 237 Mechanical ticket-issuing machines. **1963** *Times* 24 May (Suppl.) p. vii/4 Another relic of postwar contempt for the passenger is the refusal to install at Underground stations that have automatic ticket machines a single machine that will enable the passenger without small change to obtain it so that he can operate the ticket machine. **1979** *Listener* 18 Oct. 520/1 Ten-pence pieces have to be hoarded for..the ticket machine at St James's Park tube station. **1827** L. T. REDE *Road to Stage* 56, I remember Miss S—, at Drury, from neglecting this precaution, having to pay one hundred and ninety-eight pounds, out of her ticket money alone, to her co-partner in the benefit. **1902** 'MARK TWAIN' in *Harper's Weekly* 6 Dec. 4/2 The man could not get back the ticket-money. **1667** PEPYS *Diary* 4 Jan. (1974) VIII. 4 My lord Brouncker went away after dinner to the Ticket Office. **1835** J. H. INGRAHAM *South-West* I. 221 A noisy crowd was gathering around the ticket-office. **1980** J. O'FAOLAIN *No Country for Young Men* iii. 56 'No point travelling First', the man at the Euston ticket office had advised. **1934** L. A. G. STRONG *Corporal Tune* 80 He..then felt in the ticket pocket. **1978** F. MACLEAN *Take Nine Spies* vii. 266 Kim Philby..was ..carrying a Soviet Secret Service Cipher in the ticket pocket of his trousers. **1866** *Outing* 7 Feb. 588/1 Conductor..H. is unlocking his little corner cupboard and taking therefrom his punch (I mean ticket-punch, of course). **1978** E. MALPASS *Wind brings up Rain* iv. 39 The girl sat down, fiddling with her ticket punch. **1844** J. COWELL *Thirty Years passed among Players* iv. 65 John Blake I appointed secretary of the treasury and principal ticket-seller. **1929** 'E. QUEEN' *Roman Hat Mystery* I. iii. 46 You'll be looking for ticket-stubs... Anything resembling half a ticket. **1979** 'M. HEBDEN' *Death set to Music* v. 50 'But I was in Paris!' 'We have only your word and two ticket stubs to confirm that.' **1895** *McClure's Mag.* June 55/1 The band-wagons and the chariots, the calliope, the chimes, the oil-tank, the sprinklers, the ticket-wagon..have arrived. **1946** E. O'NEILL *Iceman Cometh* I. 60 Thinking of the old ticket wagon brings those days back. **1892** KIPLING & BALESTIER *Naulahka* v. 49 Tarvin..stepped out through the ticket wicket into Rajputana. **1964** M. LAURENCE *Stone Angel* v. 124 The ticket wicket's straight ahead. You can't miss it. **1865** *Harper's Mag.* May 816/1 [He] asked me to await his return while he crowded to the ticket-window and procured tickets for both. **1979** P. THEROUX *Old Patagonian Express* xiii. 201 Ticket windows were only opened a few hours before the train was to go. **1922** JOYCE *Ulysses* 471 Export bottlers, fellmongers, ticket-writers, heraldic seal engravers. **1962** E. GODFREY *Retail Selling & Organization* vii. 57 A ticket-writing department, where price tickets for displays and sales placards are written or printed. **1979** *Arizona Daily Star* 8 Apr. D1/1 Tucson travel agents and the University of Arizona are at loggerheads over the proposed creation of a taxpayer-financed ticket-writing service that would handle at least some of the $2 million the school expects to spend on air travel this year.

11. ticket barrier, the point at a railway station beyond which one cannot proceed without a ticket; **ticket chopper,** (*a*) also, a similar device used in cinemas; (*b*) (earlier and later examples); **ticket fine,** a fine imposed on a motorist for violation of traffic regulations by the issuing of a ticket (sense *2 b) rather than by prosecution in court; **ticket-scalper** (example); **ticket-splitting** *vbl. sb.* and *ppl. a. U.S.*, the practice of voting for candidates of different political parties in the same election; hence **ticket-splitter; ticket tout,** one who obtains tickets for sporting, theatrical, or other events and attempts to resell them at more than the published price.

1939 AUDEN in *New Writing* Spring 2 Crowds round the ticket barrier. **1981** J. B. HILTON *Surrender Value* iii. 29 The man who stood beyond the ticket barrier, scanning the boat-train. **1898** C. B. DAVIS *Borderland of Society* 90 She took up with ticket-chopper on the elevated road. **1915** J. B. RATHBUN *Motion Picture Making* 119 To prevent the tickets from being used a second time a 'ticket chopper' may be used that mutilates the ticket in such a way that it is impossible to present it without detection. **1932** Ticket-chopper [see **movie house*]. **1959** *Daily Tel.* 18 Dec. 1 (*heading*) Ticket-fine system for drivers opposed. **1979** T. SKYRME *Changing Image of Magistracy* vii. 80 Further relief came in 1960 with the introduction of 'ticket fines' for illegal parking and some other minor offences. **1875** W. N. BRYANT *Railroad Guide* 12 It would prevent the deception daily practiced upon this class by ticket scalpers. **1972** DE VRIES & TARRANCE *Ticket-Splitter* i. 22 We will examine the way the ticket splitter makes up his mind about politics and government. **1980** *Washington Star* 10 Oct. A-6 The area also has been very strong for Republican Gov. William Milliken, a moderate who has been elected three times by ticket splitters. **1957** *Amer. Pol. Sci. Rev.* LI. 308 (*heading*) Other motives and ticket splitting. **1972** *Times* 13 Oct. 9/3 Mr Nixon..is obviously complacent at the prospect of ticket-splitting, under which Democrats are being invited to salve their consciences by voting for their local party candidates while giving their presidential vote to Mr Nixon. **1976** *National Observer* (U.S.) 22 May 5/1 This is the damndest crossover, ticket-splitting state in the nation. **1950** *Sport* 24–30 Mar. 20/4 A final word about the ticket touts. **1982** *Times* 17 Mar. 11/2 *Cats*..is still giving the ticket touts an excellent living.

ticket, *v.* Add: **4.** *trans.* To attach a parking ticket, etc. to (a vehicle); to serve with a ticket for a traffic or other offence. *U.S.*

1955 V. NABOKOV *Lolita* (1959) I. xxiii. 97, I should explain that the prompt appearance of the patrolmen ..was due to their having been ticketing the illegally parked cars in a cross lane two blocks down the grade. **1966** *Cavalier Daily* (Charlottesville, Va.) 8 Feb. 2/1 If you don't park next to the curb, you're still liable to be ticketed. **1976** *Billings* (Montana) *Gaz.* 30 June 1-B/3 Two dog owners who were ticketed by animal wardens because their animals were allegedly involved in a wading pool melee are planning to fight back. **1979** R. BALLANTINE *Richard's Bicycle Bk.* (rev. ed.) I. vii. 122 Cyclists have been ticketed for causing an obstruction by riding too far to the right.

ticketing, *vbl. sb.* Add: **1. c.** The buying and selling of (airline) tickets. Freq. *attrib.*

1962 *Flight International* LXXXII. 382/2 If after expiry of a 'ticketing time limit' a provisional reservation is cancelled by a passenger, his booking deposit..must be forfeited. **1972** *Accountant* 28 Sept. 386/2 An International airline employing very many highly-qualified people—engineers, cabin-crew, pilots, ticketing and reservation clerks. **1977** 'O. JACKS' *Autumn Heroes* iii. 48 'Get the ticketing under way. Sixty-two.'..'Can you get me sixty-two air tickets?' **1983** *Jetaway* (Air New Zealand) Sept.–Oct. 26 (*caption*) Artist's impression of the completed 'ticketing street' in the West Terminal at Los Angeles International Airport.

ticketless, *a.* (Later examples.)

1946 F. WYLIE *Let.* 31 Aug. in Mansergh & Moon *Transfer of Power* (1979) VIII. 369 Simultaneously a regular campaign of ticketless travel on the railways will be started. **1979** P. NIHALANI et al. *Indian & Brit. English* I. 179, 2500 cases of ticketless travel and unbooked luggage were reported last month by the railway authorities.

ticket of leave. Add: **a.** (Earlier *Austral.* and further *gen.* or *transf.* examples.)

1801 *Hist. Rec. New S. Wales* (1896) IV. 300 All prisoners whose terms of transportation is [*sic*] not expired and are off the stores, or those with settlers, are to attend at the Secretary's office at Sydney..to receive their tickets of leave. **1876** *Yale Rev.* XXV. 769 Those [slaves] who went visiting, came for a 'ticket of leave'.. stating in a line or two the name of the person, and where he was going. **1917** 'CONTACT' *Airman's Outings* v. 111 On the last occasion when I was let loose from the front on ticket-of-leave, I added twenty-four hours to my Blighty period. **1918** [see *COUPON 4].

b. *ticket-of-leave man* (earlier example).

1807 *Hist. Rec. New S. Wales* (1898) VI. 292 A considerable injury to the colony had crept in: that of ticket-of leave [hyphenation *sic*] men—men that were taken off the stores, and permitted to work for themselves.

tickety-boo (tiːkĕtibūˑ), *a. colloq.* Also **ticketty-boo, tiggity-boo,** etc. [Etym. obscure: perh. f. Hindi *ṭhīk hai* all right; cf. also TICKET *sb.*[1] 9.] In order, correct, satisfactory.

1939 N. STREATFEILD *Luke* 186 Things ought to have shaped right... Couldn't have looked more tickety-boo. **1947** *Amer. N. & Q.* Sept. 94/1 Lord Mountbatten, now Governor General of India, is credited in the *New York Times Magazine* (June 22, 1947, p. 45) with 'giving currency' to the phrase 'tickety-boo' (or 'tiggerty-boo'). This Royal Navy term for 'okay' is derived from the Hindustani. **1954** 'G. CARR' *Death under Snowdon* xi. 143 'All tiggity-boo.' 'Tiggity—? Never mind, Sergeant. Go on.' 'Everything's jake, sir.' **1957** J. BRAINE *Room at Top* xxi. 179 Everything was tickety-boo again. **1960** D. FEARON *Murder-on-Thames* xviii. 168 'I never killed Mr. Evans either'. 'Then that's all ticketty-boo.' **1977** *Listener* 7 Apr. 450/3 Attempting vainly to get everything tickety-boo for the Big Day. **1981** S. RUSHDIE *Midnight's Children* I. 97 Everything's in fine fettle, don't you agree? Tickety-boo, we used to say.

ticking, *vbl. sb.*[1] Add: **4.** *ticking-off*, a scolding or reprimand: see *TICK *v.*[1] 3 c. Cf. *telling-off* s.v. *TELLING *vbl. sb.* 2 c.

1950 J. CANNAN *Murder Included* ii. 16 Iona's a little beast, but she knows how to take a ticking off—she's learned that at St. Olaf's. **1960** *News Chron.* 23 July 5/5 The machine shop inspector..expects a 'ticking-off' when he goes back to work. **1977** E. AMBLER *Send no More Roses* ii. 36, I gave him a ticking-off. Not that he cared. Too clever by half.

5. *ticking-over*: the idling of an engine; also *transf.* See *TICK *v.*[1] 2 d.

1972 J. WAINWRIGHT *Requiem for Loser* i. 9 Originally the talk..had been meant as the first of a quartet of 'stop gap' lectures.., a ticking-over of the association's activities until the end of the holiday season. **1973** —— *Pride of Pigs* 88 The youth..revved the engine, then quietened it down to the soft ticking-over.

ticking, *ppl. a.*[1] Add: **2.** *ticking-over*: (merely) working or functioning; unproductive. See *TICK *v.*[1] 2 d.

1960 *Guardian* 31 Dec. 6/3 It seemed to be rather a ticking-over year so far as new buildings..were concerned. **1963** *Times* 13 June 8/6 As long as we have a 'ticking over' laity who are still living in the Victorian era and don't want to be shaken out of their complacency, so long will the ministry remain a reflection of the body of laity from which they came. **1974** 'J. ROSS' *Burning of Billy Toober* xvi. 149 Waiting like a ticking-over computer to be programmed.

3. Special collocation: **ticking bomb** = *time bomb* s.v. TIME *sb.* 51 a.

1960 WODEHOUSE *Jeeves in Offing* i. 13 But while equipped with eyes like twin stars..B. Wickham had also the disposition and general outlook on life of a ticking bomb. **1980** G. M. FRASER *Mr American* II. xvii. 322 Mr Asquith..would find himself out of office, and the ticking bomb of Ireland could be hastily passed to his successor.

ticklace, var. *TICKLE-ACE.

tickle, *sb.*[2] Add: **2.** *Criminals' slang.* A successful deal or crime. Cf. *TICKLE *v.* 6 e.

1938 F. D. SHARPE *Sharpe of Flying Squad* 333 *Tickle*, a successful deal. **1955** D. WEBB *Deadline for Crime* i. 13 If there is a good tickle, say for as much as £10,000, which is as much as anyone got from any job, it soon goes to the birds,..the bookmakers, the hangers-on. **1960** [see *GRAFT *v.*[4]]. **1979** 'P. O'CONNOR' *Into Strong City* I. xiv. 48 Keeps me going till the big tickle comes along.

tickle, *v.* Add: **II. 3.** (Examples of *to tickle to death.*) Also in colloq. phr. *to tickle pink*, to delight; to overcome with pleasure or amusement. Cf. sense 5 in Dict.

1834 C. A. DAVIS *Lett. J. Downing* xxv. 188 It has tickled me eny most to death. **1907** *St. Nicholas* May 607/1 I'm tickled to death to find some one with what they call human emotions. **1922** 'G. EMERY' in A. H. Quinn *Contemporary Amer. Plays* 238 He'll be tickled pink. **1939** W. FORTESCUE *There's Rosemary* xlvi. 268 Knowing the great artist, he had hopes that my rather cheeky suggestion might 'tickle him to death'. **1948** F. A. IREMONGER *William Temple* xxiv. 416 An American delegate who sat opposite Temple at the table—'Archbishop, you tickle me pink!' **1950** WODEHOUSE *Nothing Serious* 29 Your view, then, is that he is tickled pink to be freed from his obligations? **1976** *Scottish Daily Express* 23 Dec. 8/7 We are tickled pink that we were able to come home to do the concert at Liverpool Philharmonic Hall. **1977** E. LEONARD *Unknown Man No. 89* xvi. 141 'I'm tickled to death I'm talking to you,' Mr. Perez said..smiling into the telephone.

6. a. Also, to play or operate (the keys of a keyboard instrument or machine); esp. in phr. *to tickle the ivories* (*IVORY 5 d). *colloq.*

1926 H. CRANE *Let.* 5 Dec. (1965) 278 Tickling the typewriter keys is a stiff proposition. **1930** S. SASSOON *Mem. Infantry Officer* VIII. ii. 194 He now told us that he had discovered a place where we could 'buy some bubbly and tickle the ivories'. **1940** M. SADLEIR *Fanny by Gaslight* II. 371 Chunks..shouted to the pianist to tickle the ivories. **1980** *Times* 1 Oct. 12/6 The 24-year-old virtuoso who tickles the very keys once played by Reginald Dixon.

c. (Earlier example.)

1833 C. MATHEWS *Let.* 11 Oct. in A. Mathews *Mem. Charles Mathews* (1839) IV. x. 208 If you do not tickle up my matter for me after I have put it down, I will not contrive my 'Life'.

d. (See quot. 1967.)

1919 C. P. THOMPSON *Cocktails* 257 We had got out to his cycle, and he bent to tickle the carburettor. **1967** D. M. DESOUTTER *Your Bk. of Engines & Turbines* viii. 33 Often the float chamber has a little plunger on top, and by pushing it you can sink the float a little and allow petrol to run through into the carburettor. People call this 'tickling the carburettor'.

e. *Criminals' slang.* To rob or burgle. Esp. in phr. *to tickle the peter,* to rob the till or cash box; also in extended use. Chiefly *Austral.* and *N.Z.* Cf. *TICKLE *sb.*[2] 2.

1945, etc. [see *PETER *sb.*[1] 6 b]. **1950** *Austral. Police Jrnl.* Apr. 119 *Tickle the peter*, to embezzle or steal funds, usually by the servant of an employer. **1973** *Courier-Mail* (Brisbane) 14 Mar. 14/9 Senator Georges..was accused in State Parliament last night of having 'tickled the peter' when he was 18. **1976** F. GREENLAND *Misericordia Drop* I. vi. 44 Get a Portuguese villain to tickle the place.

f. *Cricket.* Of a batsman: to deflect (a delivery) with a light stroke or glance. (In quots., with bowler as obj.)

1963 *Times* 5 Mar. 4/1 Dowling, who..is probably New Zealand's finest batsman..today tickled Trueman round the corner. **1977** *Sunday Times* 3 July 28/6 At last, however, Brearley tickled Doshi away behind the wicket for three.

tickle-ace (tiˑk'lēⁱs). *Newfoundland* and *Labrador.* Also **ticklace, tickle-ass, tickle-else,** etc. [perh. imit. of the bird's cry.] The kittiwake.

1819 in H. J. Paddock *Languages in Newfoundland & Labrador* (1977) 16 Titlass-Gotheyet. **1889** J. P. HOWLEY in G. M. Story et al. *Dict. Newfoundland Eng.* (1982) 565/2 They were chiefly Murres, Turres, Pigeons and Ticklaces. **1909** P. W. BROWNE *Where Fishers Go* 207 The Kittiwake..is known to fishermen as 'Tickelelse ('Ticklers'). **1932** J. BARBOUR *Forty-Eight Days Adrift* 53 The only thing alive, to be seen, was a tickalass, and we tried with poles to kill it, to eat. **1951** PETERS & BURLEIGH *Birds of Newfoundland* 235 Atlantic Black-legged Kittiwake... Local names: Tickle-lace, Tickle-ace, Tickle-ass. **1966** A. R. SCAMMELL *My Newfoundland* 36 Jim Parsons was out shooting tickle-aces yesterday. **1974** F. MOWAT *Boat who wouldn't Float* xviii. 219 She [*sc.* a boat] lay lightly on the harbour looking as pretty as a tickle-ass. **1975** T. RUSSELL *Chron. Uncle Mose* 23 There'd been a few ticklaces around that morning.., and being as how I liked ticklace soup as well as the next man, I wished I'd had my breech-loader and a few cartridges.

tickler. Add: **1. b.** A pianist. Cf. *TICKLE *v.* 6 a. *slang.*

[**1948** *N.Y. Age* 9 Oct. 2/7 The Round Mr. Fletcher Butler, the distinguished Chicago piano tickler.] **1962** *Down Beat* 16 Aug. 26/3 He had a magnificent attack.. combined with the gaiety and shy humor that one looks for in a true 'tickler'. **1975** J. MCCLURE *Snake* vi. 86 Me? I'm the tickler. Pianist. Y'know.

2. j. Also *transf.*, anything intended to serve as a reminder.

1905 CALKINS & HOLDEN *Art Mod. Advertising* 351 A tickler is any small piece of printed matter sent out to keep open a prospective sale on the part of the inquirer. **1970** *New Yorker* 3 Oct. 34/3 The new lineup of teams can be easily remembered with the aid of a handy mental 'tickler'.

k. A stern or severe letter. Cf. TICKLE *v.* 6 b. *rare.*

1846 LD. PALMERSTON *Let.* 27 Sept. in H. L. E. Bulwer *Life Palmerston* (1874) III. viii. 299 Do not mention it to anyone; but the Queen has written the King of the French a tickler in answer to a letter he sent her. **1902** G. W. E. RUSSELL *Onlooker's Notebook* xiv. 102 An Illustrious Personage wrote to the Dean [of Windsor] suggesting that, as Mr. Gladstone was engaged in violent attacks upon the Government, it might be better if his visits to the Deanery were discontinued. 'Whereupon,' said the stout old Dean.. 'I wrote her a tickler'.

l. An inductance coil in the anode circuit of a valve, giving positive feedback through another coil in the grid circuit.

1922 [see *REACTION 3 e]. **1931** MOYER & WOSTREL *Radio Handbk.* VII. 335 A tickler..usually more than makes up for this decrease in detection coefficient by increasing the strength of the impressed radio signal. **1948** [see *RADIO *sb.* 2 a].

m. A hand-rolled cigarette or the tobacco from which it is made. *Naut. slang.*

1929 F. BOWEN *Sea Slang* 141 *Ticklers*,..is also a name for cigarettes made from the monthly issue of naval tobacco. **1964** J. HALE *Grudge Fight* I. ii. 29 Brooks rolls and lights a tickler. **1977** G. MELLY *Rum, Bum & Concertina* iv. 54 'Tickler' is naval slang for duty-free tobacco.

4. *attrib.* and *Comb.*, as (sense *2 j) *tickler card, file, system, telegram*; **tickler coil** = sense 2 l above.

1931 *New Yorker* 10 Oct. 21/1 He ran the tickler cards in their credit department. **1940** *Chambers's Techn. Dict.* 850/2 *Tickler coil*.., an inductance coil included in the anode circuit of a thermionic valve and magnetically coupled to the grid circuit to obtain reaction. **1975** R. L. SHRADER *Electronic Communication* (ed. 3) xviii. 433/1 To increase the sensitivity and selectivity of the grid-leak detector, a plate-circuit tickler coil can be used. **1939** C. MORLEY *Kitty Foyle* (1940) xix. 174 You might remind me of that sometimes. Put it in the tickler file. **1972** D. BAGLEY *Enemy* xiii. 105 Authority had lost interest in him and he would exist only in a tickler file to remind someone to give an annual check. **1962** 'A. A. FAIR' *Stop at Red Light* iii. 56 Real estate, subdivisions..figuring interest, keeping a tickler system for time payments. **1938** *Sun* (Baltimore) 21 June 6/7 One father..remembered last year to send admonitioning letters to each member of his family and follow them up with 'tickler' telegrams.

tickling, *vbl. sb.* Add: **4. tickling stick** *joc.*, a feather duster or similar device used as a comedian's prop.

1969 *Listener* 6 Mar. 299/2 Beneath your tickling stick and candy floss came Heath and Wilson and Woodcock. **1980** *Times Lit. Suppl.* 24 Oct. 1198/5 Hints of the tickling-stick [in a performance of *Peer Gynt*] vulgarized the first meeting with Solveig. **1983** *Sun* 8 June 4/4 Ken Dodd painted his famous tickling stick blue yesterday for a Liverpool walkabout in support of Mrs Thatcher.

ti·ck-off. *slang.* [f. vbl. phr. *to tick off*: see TICK *v.*[1] 3.] Fortune-telling; a fortune-teller. *to work the tick-off,* to practise fortune-telling.

1934 P. ALLINGHAM *Cheapjack* ii. 18 Several showpeople were in the bar. 'You're working the tick-off, aren't you?' said one of them. *Ibid.*, I discovered that 'tick-off' was the fair-ground slang for fortune-teller. **1966** *Punch* 3 Aug. 193/1 No palmists, tick-offs, character readers, mock auctions, pick-a-straw.

ti·ck-over. [f. vbl. phr. *to tick over*: see *TICK *v.*[1] 2 d.] **1.** The running of an internal combustion engine while out of gear or at a low rate of revolutions. Cf. *ticking over* s.v. *TICKING *vbl. sb.*[1] 5.

1931 *Flight* 2 Oct. 990/2 All engines were tested on a hangar with a propeller fitted before going away, for opening and for tick-over. **1960** *Times* 27 Sept. 5/3 The tick-over is inevitably 'lumpy' and uneven. **1981** P. O'DONNELL *Xanadu Talisman* iii. 60 The tick-over became a roar as a motor was revved.

2. *attrib.*, as *tick-over speed.*

1965 [see *IDLE *v.* 4 a]. **1978** *Country Life* 10 Aug. 393/1 A Mercedez-Benz dieselcar..at tickover speeds..almost runs on pure air.

tick-tack, *sb.* Add: **1. c.** Chiefly *N. Amer.* A contrivance, such as a button on a piece of thread, spun to make a clattering sound against a window or door as a practical joke, esp. at Hallowe'en.

1884 I. M. RITTENHOUSE *Jrnl.* in *Maud* (1939) 288, I formed plan after plan to frighten them. Finally a 'tick-tack' was decided on. **1947** *Sun* (Baltimore) 7 Oct. 16/3 The Park has decided to have an old-time Hallowe'en, with the old boys puttin' tick-tacks on windows.

d. *transf.*

1927 D. H. LAWRENCE *Mornings in Mexico* 63 Seeing the white monkeys for ever mechanically bossing, with their incessant tick-tack of work. **1934** S. BECKETT *More Pricks than Kicks* 133 'God' he exclaimed, executing a kind of passionate tick-tack through his pockets.

2*. = TICK-TACKER.

1918 G. FRANKAU *One of Them* xxi. 159 Silent the tic-tac's tell-tale Semaphore: On thousand tracks, unridden, ..Hay waves.

tick-tack, *v.* Also tic tac, tic-tac. [f. the sb.] **1.** *intr.* = *TICK-TOCK *v.*

1842, *a* **1847** [implied at TICK-TACKING *ppl. a.*]. **1859** MRS. STOWE *Minister's Wooing* ii. 17 The solemn old clock that tick-tacked in the corner.

2. *intr.* and *trans.* To produce a whirring, clattering sound by spinning a tick-tack (sense 1 c) against a window, etc., as a practical joke. *dial.* and *N. Amer.*

1901 F. E. TAYLOR *Folk-Speech S. Lancs.* s.v. *Ticktackin'*, a boys' practical joke. See Window-tackin'. **1970**

J. H. GRAY *Boy from Winnipeg* 188 We got tired of the project and abandoned it in favour of ringing doorbells and tick-tacking windows.

3. *trans.* and *intr.* To signal (information) by means of tick-tack telegraphy.

1907 *Favourite* 30 Nov. 9/3 Kilbeg was 'tick-tacked' out at 4 to 1 by the private clerk of one particular firm. **1908** *Tatler* 3 June 247 The above system of signalling, which is known as tick-tacking, may be seen on any racecourse. **1927** *Observer* 27 Mar. 18/6 A man in the body of the hall was detected tictacing to Labour supporters and guiding the uproar. **1937** L. MANN *Murder in Sydney* xxv. 273, I also noticed Leon Caspar ticktacking to the girl in response to which the girl challenged two of those called on the panel. **1972** *Guardian* 11 Aug. 8/6 The policeman tic-taced to the judge what the punishment should be.

tick-tack-toe. Add: (*b*) *U.S.* = *noughts and crosses* (see NOUGHT *sb.* 7 c; OUGHT *sb.*[3]); also the cross-shaped frame in which this game is played; also *fig.*

1960 S. PLATH in *Sewanee Review* LXVIII. 604 The jacket is patterned with brown squares the size of cigarette packs, each square boldly outlined in black. You could play tick-tack-toe on it. **1975** *Nat. Geographic* Apr. 500 (*caption*) Tick-tack-toe of a new apartment complex rises amid mud-and-wattle houses in Zanzibar town. **1976** N. THORNBURG *Cutter & Bone* xi. 266 A tick-tack-toe form filled with zeros. **1978** G. VIDAL *Kalki* i. 8 Just past the tall sick palms at the edge of the pool, the exhaust of a half-dozen jets was making a kind of tick-tack-toe in the dusty brown sky over Los Angeles. **1980** *Dædalus* Spring 46 A computer designed only to issue the company's pay-checks might stalemate me perpetually in tic-tac-toe.

tick-tock (ti·kˌtǫ·k), *v.* [f. the sb.] *intr.* Of a clock, etc.: to make a rhythmic alternating ticking sound. Hence **tick-tocking** *vbl. sb.*

1921 H. S. WALPOLE *Young Enchanted* III. iii. 274 The gaudy clock..now tick-tocked along in amiable approval of them both. *a* **1947** F. THOMPSON *Country Calendar* (1979) 201 The loud tick-tocking of the clock in the hall. **1950** G. BARKER *Dead Seagull* ii. 89, I heard the murmur in the distance and then the rumbled tick-tocking and then the appalling cacophony all around as the approaching train swept up and past us. **1962** L. DEIGHTON *Ipcress File* ix. 55 The clock tick-tocked on, adding a second or so to its seventy years of tick.

ticky-tacky (ti·kitæ:ki), *sb.* and *a.* orig. *U.S.* Prob. redupl. f. TACKY *sb.* and *a.*[1]]

A. *sb.* Inferior or cheap material, esp. that used in uniform suburban building.

1962 M. REYNOLDS *Little Boxes* (1964) (*song*) 3 And they're all made out of ticky tacky, And they all look just the same. **1973** *Newsweek* 30 July 71 The real point is, will..Watchung Pharmaceutical get those 250 unspoiled acres around Howard's tree farm which have been zoned for a park, there to produce more poppable pills and sprinkle company ticky-tacky over the landscape? **1978** M. BUTTERWORTH *X marks Spot* iii. 26 A large and gloomy Victorian pub, heavily overlaid with up-to-date ticky-tacky.

B. *adj.* Made of ticky-tacky; cheap, in poor taste.

1969 *Sat. Rev.* (U.S.) 10 May 19/1 Men who desecrate the landscape with hundreds of ticky-tacky houses and.. call themselves developers. **1970** O. NORTON *Dead on Prediction* iii. 46 The house was one of those ticky-tacky semi-bungalows, which are given a false air of expensiveness. **1977** *Jrnl. R. Soc. Arts* CXXV. 119/1 Critics of the private sector complain of ticky tacky little boxes spread all over the country.

tidal, *a.* Add: **1. b.** (*b*) (Earlier examples.)

1870 'MARK TWAIN' *Lett. to Publishers* (1967) 45 'We'll have somebody standing ready to launch a book right on our big tidal wave and swim it into a success. **1875** —— *Sketches New & Old* 213 A great tidal wave of grief swept over us all.

2. b. *spec.* Of (esp. rush-hour) road traffic, its flow, or a road carrying it: that uses the same lane(s) for travel in opposite directions, depending on time and conditions.

1954 *Highway Engin. Terms* (*B.S.I.*) 55 *Tidal traffic*, traffic on a two-way road proceeding predominantly in one direction or the other according to time or recurrent circumstances. **1955** *Times* 25 Oct. 9 The reversible lane on tidal highways. **1960** *News Chron.* 26 Feb. 5/1 Tidal-flow traffic was introduced on Chelsea Bridge last year. **1960** *Guardian* 7 June 1/2 The 'tidal flow scheme'..has already been tried out in London. **1969** *Soviet Weekly* 13 Sept. 2 All the flyovers, underpasses, tidal flows and one-way streets the authorities organized only eased the problem without curing it.

3. a. tidal train (earlier example).

1855 DICKENS in *Househ. Words* 29 Sept. 194/1 The South Eastern Company..with their tidal trains and splendid steam-packets.

b. (Earlier example.)

1866 DICKENS in *All Year Round* Christmas No. 18/1 A return pass by South-Eastern Tidal, to go right through ..to Marseilles.

tiddle, *v.* Add: **2. b.** To move potteringly.

1881 W. D. HOWELLS *Modern Instance* (1882) I. x. 173 Mr. Macallister, a slight little straight man..tiddled farcically forward on his toes. **1970** *Times* 6 July 6/8 You can't just tiddle up to the town hall to see the man.

tiddled (ti·dl'd), *a. slang.* [f. *TIDDLY *sb.* + -ED[2].] Drunk, tipsy; = *TIDDLY *a.*[1]

1956 G. DURRELL *My Family & Other Animals* xii. 163 'I've got the most splitting headache.' 'I'm not surprised; you were as tiddled as an owl last night.'

tiddler[1]. Add: Also applied to other small fish, as a minnow. Hence, a child; any small person or thing.

1927 R. LEHMANN *Dusty Answer* IV. 294, I remember you hated lightning when you were a tiddler. **1937** G. FRANKAU *More of Us* vi. 69 When father's under par, Mother suggests a tiddler at the bar. **1966** F. SHAW et al. *Lern yerself Scouse* 33 *Tiddler*, silver threepenny piece. **1971** *Daily Mail* 18 Feb. 5/6 They will scrap the ½p coin—the 'tiddler'—when they change to decimals. **1976** *Courier-Mail* (Brisbane) 26 Aug. 9/6 Pastime anglers would not be allowed to keep 'tiddlers'. **1980** E. BLISHEN *Nest of Teachers* I. viii. 43 A couple of days with Class 1A and.. he will know a deuce of a lot..about the little tiddlers.

ti·ddler[3]. *U.S. colloq.* [f. TIDDL(YWINK + -ER[1].] A tiddlywinks player.

1958 *N.Y. Times* 9 May 28 An Oxford University tiddler..says there's a 100-year-old controversy over proper spelling of the sport. **1962** *Boston Globe* 14 Oct. 81 The Crimson tiddlers winked their way to a 23 to 12 victory over a green Purple team.

tiddly (ti·dli), *sb.* and *a.*[1] *slang.* Also 9 **titley**, 9-**tiddley.** [Origin uncertain: cf. TIDDLYWINK 1 in Dict. and Suppl.] **A.** *sb.* Drink; an alcoholic drink, esp. a 'short'.

1859 HOTTEN *Dict. Slang* 109 *Titley*, drink. **1864** *Ibid.* 258 *Tiddley*, drink, generally applied to intoxicating beverages. **1895** *Punch* 18 May 230/2 It took two 'ot tiddleys to warm 'er. *Ibid.* 12 Oct. 180/1 A helderly humorous gent, on the tiddley. **1923** E. P. OPPENHEIM *Inevitable Millionaires* xxiv. 259 Just a tiddley to drink success to the club. **1930** E. V. LUCAS *Down Sky* 222 It wasn't oysters that she really wanted, but..tiddley.

B. *adj.* Drunk, tipsy.

1905 *To-day* XLVI. 182/2 If ever you was tiddly in crossing the old 'un [*sc.* a bridge], it was as easy as anything to fall into that blarsted river. **1909** *Chambers's Jrnl.* 17 Apr. 316/1 Mind you don't get tiddley and blow the gaff. **1930** W. S. MAUGHAM *Cakes & Ale* xxiii. 232, I don't say he ever got tiddly, but he used to like to sit in the bar and talk. **1958** B. NICHOLS *Sweet & Twenties* xvi. 208 No more wine, George, thank you. I shall be quite tiddly. **1979** 'J. SCOTT' *Angels in your Beer* xxv. 254 Yvonne giggled. 'I do believe I'm tiddly,' she said.

tiddly (ti·dli), *a.*[2] *colloq.* Also 9 **tidly; tiddley.** [var. *TIDDY *a.*] Very little, tiny. Freq. in phr. *tiddly bit.*

1868 TROLLOPE *He knew he was Right* (1869) I. xxiii. 183 The smallest little 'tiddly' things do so often turn up trumps. **1885** E. C. SHARLAND *Ways & Means in Devonshire Village* 42 I'd only got but a tiddly bit o' that mutton left. **1888** B. LOWSLEY *Gloss. Berks. Words* s.v. *Tidly*, I had un in my arms when a was a tidly little chap. **1937** *John o' London's Weekly* 5 Feb. 762/2 When there was a bad harvest he hung the little tiddley sheaves o' corn on his garden railing to let God Almighty know how badly he'd been treated! **1950** WODEHOUSE *Nothing Serious* 106 A mere tiddly seaside competition. **1956** 'N. SHUTE' *Beyond Black Stump* viii. 237 If I have one will you have just a little bit, in your coke? **1978** J. GOODMAN *Last Sentence* iii. 114 The whole bally case for the prosecution is built on tiddly bits of non-evidence.

tiddly (ti·dli), *a.*[3] *slang* (orig. and chiefly *Naut.*). Also **tiddley.** [perh. f. TIDY *a.*] **1.** Smart, shipshape, spruce.

1925 FRASER & GIBBONS *Soldier & Sailor Words* 281 *Tiddly*, smartly dressed... Also applied to a ship of smart appearance. **1942** G. HACKFORTH-JONES *One-One-One* i. 7 Like all sailors he took great pleasure in keeping his surroundings what he described as 'tiddley'. **1960** 'N. SHUTE' *Trustee from Toolroom* ii. 25 We'll have to get everything all tiddley.' **1973** R. DOUGALL *In & out of Box* 119 The aim was to achieve as pale a blue on the collar as possible—this was considered 'tiddley', which in Naval parlance means smart or *comme il faut*. It was also tiddley to have smart horizontal creases in the bell-bottom trousers like a concertina.

2. Special collocation: **tiddly suit**, one's best suit of clothes.

1943 'TAFFRAIL' *White Ensigns* 33 'Tiddley' suits with light jumpers and bell-bottomed trousers cut far wider than the regulation permitted. **1951** C. CAUSLEY *Farewell, Aggie Weston* 9 Farewell, Aggie Weston, the barracks at Guz, Hang my tiddley suit on the door.

tiddly-om-pom-pom (tidliˌǫ·mpǫ·mpǫ·m). [Imit.: cf. *POM-POM 2.] Representing the sound or regular beat of brass-band or similar music. Also **tiddy-pom** *a.*, with a simple beat or tune, trite.

1909 J. A. GLOVER-KIND *I do like to be beside the Seaside* (1970) (*song*) 4 The brass bands play tiddely-om-pom-pom. **1937** *Scrutiny* VI. 333 The tiddy-pom guitar accompaniment. **1958** *Times* 30 Dec. 7/4 The brass band certainly plays tiddly-om-pom-pom with any amount of spirit at Association football matches. **1973** T. HEALD *Unbecoming Habits* iii. 76 The piano had a tiddly pom, tin pan alley, sort of complacency.

tiddlypush (stress variable). *colloq.* A meaningless word substituted for the name of a person or thing which the speaker has forgotten, does not know, or is unwilling to mention. Cf. THINGUMMY.

1923 J. MANCHON *Le Slang* 342 And tidderly push, et patati et patata. **1934** S. BECKETT *More Pricks than Kicks* 168 He wore a belt Whenever he felt A pain in his tiddly-push. **1939** WODEHOUSE *Uncle Fred in Springtime* ii. 27 It simply says 'The marriage arranged between George Tiddlypush and Amelia Stick-in-the-mud will not take place.' **1962** *Guardian* 17 July 16/4 Mr Randolph Churchill..said..he had shown that if he wanted to 'get rid of anyone—from Lord Salisbury down to Mr Tiddlypush —he does so'.

tiddlywink, *sb.* Add: **1. b.** *Rhyming slang.* A drink.

1880 [see *pig's ear* s.v. *PIG *sb.*[1] 13 c]. **1960** J. FRANKLYN *Dict. Rhyming Slang* 129/1 *Tiddly wink*..is applied more frequently to 'shorts'..than to beer.

2. a. (Earlier example.)

1857 'DUCANGE ANGLICUS' *Vulgar Tongue* 43 At *knock'emsdown* and tiddlywink, To be a sharp you must not shrink.

b. orig. **Tiddledy-Winks.** (Earlier examples.) Also *attrib.* Also used *fig.* of a useless or frivolous activity; *esp.* in phr. *to play tiddlywinks*, to waste time on trivia.

1889 *Trade Marks Jrnl.* 15 May 476 Tiddledy-Winks... Toys or games. Joseph Assheton Fincher. **1890** *Amer. Stationer* 18 Sept. 691 In 'Tiddledy Wink Tennis' E. I. Horsman..has brought out a very pretty and lively parlor game. **1892** E. LYTTON *Let.* 24 Apr. in E. Lutyens *Blessed Girl* (1953) vii. 97 We all played the most exciting game that ever was invented, called Tiddleywinks. It consists in flipping counters in a bowl. **1895** *Montgomery Ward Catal.* Spring & Summer 236/2 Tiddledy Winks may be played by any number... Each player is provided with four to six counters..and one larger one..to press to the edge of the smaller one and..cause it to jump into the cup..in the centre of the table. **1919** *Collier's* 8 Feb. 7 There's trouble down there and I've been playing tiddledy-winks on Broadway! **1947** *Economist* 18 Oct. 626/1 The storm was long predicted..yet when its first icy gust blew in the windows of the Cabinet room.., it found the Ministers playing tiddleywinks. **1964** *New Yorker* 4 Apr. 147 Others seem to take little interest in the organized activities, describing them as 'make-work' or 'tiddlywinks'. **1975** *Way to Play* 135/1 Tiddlywinks golf sets, with tiddlywinks, greens, obstacles, and holes, are produced by various toy manufacturers. **1980** *Disarmament Times* 6 Oct. 4/4 This is not a game of diplomatic tiddleywinks. It is, rather, the game of human survival.

c. Any of the counters used in the game of tiddlywinks (sense 2 b); hence, a similar counter used in other games.

1891 J. K. BANGS *Tiddledewinks Tales* 35 Jimmieboy thought a great deal of his Tiddledewinks and had been playing with them nearly all that day. **1939** J. STEINBECK *Grapes of Wrath* iii. 22 His front wheel struck the edge of the shell, flipped the turtle like a tiddly-wink,..and rolled it off the highway. **1949** 'G. ORWELL' *Nineteen Eighty-Four* III. 296 Soon he was wildly excited and shouting with laughter as the tiddleywinks climbed hopefully up the ladders and then came slithering down the snakes again. **1977** B. JEWELL *Sports & Games* 109 The object was to flip the tiddlywink into one of the window openings and so ring the bell.

Hence **ti·ddlywink** *v. intr.*, (*a*) to flip like a counter in tiddlywinks; (*b*) to play tiddlywinks; **tiddlywinker,** (*b*) a tiddlywinks player; **tiddlywinking** *vbl. sb.*, (*b*) the activity of playing tiddlywinks.

1958 *Sports Illustrated* 7 Apr. M5 Each tiddlywinker plays with two large and four medium-size winks. **1965** *Northeastern Reporter* 2nd Ser. CCVI. 847/2 We have raised a lot of manhole covers, and you never walk across them to see if they are going to tiddlywink. **1971** *Ottawa Citizen* 6 Feb. (Canad. Mag.) 24 He loves the game so much that in 1967 he played in a 67-hour tiddlywinking marathon. **1975** *Milwaukee Jrnl.* 25 May IV. 2/2 Dean, a high school mathematics teacher, is certainly Britain's top Tiddlywinker. **1977** P. DICKSON *Mature Person's Guide* 162 The general consensus in tiddlywinking circles is that all of this might change if the game was given a new name. **1980** *Milwaukee Sentinel* 11 Feb. 1. 6/4 (*heading*) Fame opens the eyes of those who tiddlywink.

tiddy (ti·di), *a. dial.* or *nursery.* [Origin obscure. (The spelling *tidy* in quot. 1781 is not recorded elsewhere and may be an error.)] Small, very small, tiny. Also (*redupl.*) **tiddy iddy** *a.*

1781 J. HUTTON *Tour to Caves* (ed. 2) 98 *Tidy*, small. **1869** W. S. GILBERT *Bab Ballads* x. 171 A tiddy iddy daughter, and a tiddy iddy son! **1896** KIPLING *Seven Seas* 191, I got me a tiddy live 'eathen... Doll in a teacup she were. **1907** *Daily News* 4 Feb. 2/5 It was only a 'tiddy' pup. **1958** M. KELLY *Christmas Egg* III. 99 Do you know this Richborough?.. There's a tiddy railway, power cables, and the castle. **1960** 'N. SHUTE' *Trustee from Toolroom* vi. 133, I filled out the buttocks a tiddy bit on this one.

tide, *sb.* Add: **I. 6.** (Later examples in the names of saints' days.) *St. Andrew's tide*: delete †.

1957 *Oxf. Dict. Chr. Ch.* 49/2 In the Anglican Communion, St. Andrewstide is widely observed by intercessions for foreign missions. **1975** *Church Times* 15 Aug. 2/3 Last week—St Laurence-tide—all the churches supported a flower festival in the chapel. **1976** *Ibid.* 15 Oct. 5/1 It has become the custom at St. Luke's-tide for the Church to pray for doctors.

II. 9. (Earlier and later examples with reference to the 'turning' of the tide.)

1593 [see TURN *v.* 20]. **1781** C. WESLEY *Protestant Association* in *Poet. Wks.* (1870) VIII. 464 His faithful troops from every side Are brought to turn the rapid tide.

1843 LYTTON *Last of Barons* I. I. vii. 117 This speech turned the tide. **1915** MRS. BELLOC LOWNDES *Let.* 10 Mar. (1971) 57 There is an invasion scare but I don't believe in that... I do think the tide has now turned. **1935** E. WAUGH *Edmund Campion* i. 24 That generation was inured to change; sooner or later the tide would turn in their favour again. **1941** P. CARR *English are like That* i. 18 He must have patience—patience..in the face of misrepresentation, patience to wait for the turn of the tide. **1982** *Church Times* 5 Feb. 8/3 After that [donation] who will be surprised to hear that the tide shows signs of turning at St. Christopher's? **1982** D. FRASER *Alanbrooke* iv. 79 In the autumn of 1918 the tide finally turned.

V. 16. a. (*a*) *tide-edge, -print, -stream* (earlier example); (*b*) *tide-flat*; (*c*) *tide-master, -turner*; (*d*) *tide-beat* (example), *-borne, -carved, -hoisted, -looped, -tongued, -traced* adjs.

1807 J. BARLOW *Columbiad* VII. 272 Two British forts the growing siege outflank, Rake its wide works and awe the tide-beat bank. **1957** R. CAMPBELL *Coll. Poems* II. 99 The swirl, the spray, the nimbus, and the wave Of tide-borne lust and beauty. **1897** Tide-carved [see *PEDIMENT[1] 1 b]. **1976** *National Observer* (U.S.) 4 Sept. 7/3 We clambered down to tide-carved caverns. **1931** W. FAULKNER *Sanctuary* xxiii. 221 A world left stark and dying above the tide-edge of the fluid in which it lived. **1859** C. KINGSLEY *Glaucus* (ed. 4) 146 The tide-flats below are still unfinished, dry land in the process of creation. **1929** W. FAULKNER *Sound & Fury* 211, I saw the last light supine and tranquil upon tideflats. **1936** DYLAN THOMAS *Twenty-Five Poems* 41 The winder of the clockwise scene..threw on that tide-hoisted screen Love's image. **1939** —— *Map of Love* 4 Or like the tide-looped breastknot reefed again. *Ibid.*, The silent tide Lapping the still canals, the dry tide-master Ribbed between desert and water storm. *Ibid.* 9 Moonfall and sailing emperor, pale as their tide-print. **1795** *Essex Inst. Hist. Coll.* (1918) LIV. 101 To compensate for any supposed inconveniences that may attend a tide stream. **1934** DYLAN THOMAS *New Verse* XII. 11 Among the rabble Of tide-tongued heads and bladders in the deep. **1936** —— *Twenty-Five Poems* 44 Cartoon of slashes on the tide-traced crater. **1922** D. H. LAWRENCE *Fantasia of Unconscious* XV. 272 The moon is the tide-turner.

b. tide-land(s) *N. Amer.*, land(s) covered by the tide; *tide-land spruce* = *Sitka spruce* s.v. *SITKA; **tide-lock** (earlier example).

1787 W. H. SIEBERT *Loyalists in E. Florida, 1851–94* (1929) II. 239, 200 acres of rich tide land well dam'd. **1884** C. S. SARGENT *Rep. Forests N. Amer.* 206 Tide-Land Spruce... A large tree of great economic value. **1891, 1895** [in Dict., sense 16 a]. **1969** R. C. HOSIE *Native Trees Canada* (ed.7) 68 Sitka Spruce. Tideland Spruce... Produces a long, branch-free, cylindrical trunk. **1975** *N.Y. Times* 25 Feb. 16/3 Gas resources did not become a controversial issue until the mid-nineteenthirties when oil companies began drilling wells in the tidelands. **1808** B. H. LATROBE *Let.* 16 Mar. in *Niles' Reg.* (1818) XV. 54/2 It would be necessary to place the tide lock as far out as possible.

tide-mark. Add: *fig..* (examples); *spec.* a line of dirt left on a surface, esp. at the limit to which water has reached (cf. *HIGH-WATER MARK c).

1865 GEO. ELIOT *Ess.* (1884) 203 A particular class of facts..in their relation to certain grand tide-marks of opinion. **1907** N. MUNRO *Daft Days* xxii. 190 With a smut on your nose and tide-marks on your eyebrows. **1928** *Daily Express* 20 Dec. 5/3 Your fur collar leaves a horrid tide-mark after it has been worn for a time. **1934** A. HUXLEY *Beyond Mexique Bay* 197 A tide-mark of grit ..running round the bath. **1957** J. M. MACKINTOSH in 'C. H. Rolph' *Human Sum* ix. 177 The succession of tide-marks round the necks of my young patients. **1973** C. EGLETON *Seven Days to Killing* ii. 27 She..casually lit a cigarette; pink lipstick formed a tide-mark around the filter tip. **1976** T. HEALD *Let Sleeping Dogs Die* i. 21 From the hooks..she took three cups, chipped..and with tidemarks of tea clearly visible an inch below the rim. **1977** A. CARTER *Passion of New Eve* ix. 113 Dead peonies in enormous glass jars streaked with tide marks where the water had evaporated long ago.

tide-mill. 1. (Earlier examples.)

1640 *Essex Inst. Hist. Coll.* (1863) V. 169/2 Captane Traske hath leave to sett up a tyde myll upon the North River. **1755** *Mass. Prov. Acts* (1878) III. 810 Tide-mills that have or shall be set up on across the mouth of rivers.

tide-water. Add: Also **tidewater**. **2.** (Earlier examples.)

1772 *Va. Statutes at Large* (1821) VIII. 564 The extension of the navigation of James river..will be greatly promoted by cutting a canal..from the Westham to the tide water. **1832** J. F. WATSON *Hist. Tales N.Y.* 38 [Hudson City] is deemed at the head of tide water and ship navigation.

b. *attrib.* Designating or pertaining to regions situated on tide-water or affected by tides, *esp.* (also with capital initial) eastern Virginia. Also *ellipt.*, a tide-water region, esp. that of eastern Virginia.

1832 J. P. KENNEDY *Swallow Barn* I. xviii. 179 The tide-water country of Virginia. **1835** *Southern Lit. Messenger* I. 662 The tranquil and affectionate hearths of tide-water Virginia. **1868** [in Dict.]. **1884** *Century Mag.* Apr. 825/2 Mr. Jones..[has] one of those thin, mournful faces common to tide-water Maryland. **1936** W. FAULKNER *Absalom, Absalom!* vii. 222 He didn't listen to the vague and cloudy tales of Tidewater splendor that penetrated even his mountains. **1943** *Sun* (Baltimore) 14 June 10/1 A comprehensive program to increase the annual harvest of the oyster industry has been submitted to conservation authorities in the various tidewater States. **1944** L. MUMFORD *Condition of Man* vi. 216 The stately tide-water mansions of Virginia. **1949** B. A. BOTKIN *Treas. S. Folklore* I. ii. 32 Within his state the Southerner thinks in terms of Eastern Shore or Tobacco Country, Tidewater or Valley, [etc.]. **1976** *Amer. Speech 1974* XLIX. 45 The Delmarva area..comprises southern Delaware, portions of the eastern shore of Maryland, and the peninsula and islands of tidewater Virginia. **1979** D. ANTHONY *Long Hard Cure* xxi. 166 A hardnosed captain of industry who wanted a pretty mannequin from tidewater aristocracy. **1980** *Amer. Speech* LV. 285 It is common in the Virginia piedmont and tidewater.

c. *attrib.* Designating bodies of water affected by tides.

1835 J. MARTIN *Descr. Virginia* 40 A tide water river, or more correctly a bay, the Chowan. **1888** [in Dict.]. **1939** *WPA Guide to Florida* (1984) II. 177 Daytona Beach ..is a city with a triple waterfront, one on the Atlantic Ocean and one on each side of a tidewater lagoon.

tidied (təi·did), *ppl. a.* [f. TIDY *v.* + -ED[1].] That has been made tidy; esp. with *up*.

1922 E. O'NEILL *Hairy Ape* v. 49 A general atmosphere of clean, well-tidied, wide street. **1959** *Daily Tel.* 28 July 5/3 (*heading*) Russians get 'tidied-up' version of Nixon clash.

tidier (təi·diəɪ). [f. TIDY *v.* + -ER[1].] One who makes (something) tidy. Also **tidier-up**, (*colloq.*) **tidier-upper.**

1923 *Public Opinion* 15 June 565/3 He became a champion tidier from that moment on. **1961** J. WILSON *Reason & Morals* i. 8 The philosopher seems to be not so much a universal aunt as a sort of universal tidier-up. **1963** *Times Lit. Suppl.* 25 Oct. 849/3 Among scientists there are collectors, classifiers, and compulsive tidiers up. **1976** CULROSS & ROBB *Leaving Home* iv. 32 Nancy was the neat sort..and..an habitual tidier-upper.

tidingman, U.S. var. TITHINGMAN[1] c.

1703 *Early Rec. Groton, Mass.* (1880) 123 For tiding men [for the year 1703] Joseph gilson Benjmen farnworth. **1878** MRS. STOWE *Poganuc People* vi. 63 They're goin' clean agin everything—Sunday laws and tiding man and all.

tidy, *a.* Add: **5.** *tidy-mindedness*; (in sense 3) *tidy-sized* adj.; **tidy bin**, a bin into which things may be discarded or tidied away, a waste-bin.

1972 *House & Garden* Dec. 84/3 Colourful bathroom accessories, including shelf units, tidy bins, mirrors. **1978** *People's Friend* 13 May 3/3 Lifting some toffee papers and preparing to transfer them to the tidy bin, she spotted the torn photograph. **1951** *Essays & Studies* IV. 21 Too much tidy-mindedness and love of classification. **1975** J. P. MORGAN *House of Lords & Labour Govt.* vi. 163 Even if administrative tidy-mindedness..was the motive behind the Seats Bill.., its consequences would still transcend any administrative convenience. **1922** JOYCE *Ulysses* 628, I want to see everyone..having a comfortable tidysized income. **1945** W. DE LA MARE *Scarecrow* 128 'Lor bless me,' said Alice. 'The questions he asks!'..'And that's a tidy-sized one too!' said Alice, smiling at him again.

B. *sb.* **2.** An act of making tidy; a period of time devoted to tidying. Freq. with *-up*.

1909 E. NESBIT *Daphne in Fitzroy St.* ix. 122 The dreadful neatness that follows a 'good tidy-up'. **1915** KIPLING *Diversity of Creatures* (1917) 428 We'll pull up the blinds and we'll have a general tidy. **1949** N. STREATFEILD *Painted Garden* xiii. 140 Rachel was going on to tell Jane to give her hair a tidy. **1970** C. WHITMAN *Death out of Focus* ix. 141, I bustled around..giving my flat a rough tidy-up. **1971** H. WILSON *Labour Govt.* xxxvi. 756, I went for a quick wash and tidy-up. **1980** 'T. HINDE' *Daymate* I. vi. 53 [She] is coming to give his house its Saturday morning tidy.

tidying, *vbl. sb.* Add: Also with *-up*.

1959 N. MARSH *False Scent* (1960) iv. 102 When they arrived..the tidying-up process had considerably advanced. **1964** M. MCLUHAN *Understanding Media* II. xx. 197 This immense tidying-up of our inner lives..has had its obvious parallels in our attempts to rearrange our homes and gardens. **1975** S. BRETT *Cast, in Order of Disappearance* vi. 47 He'd..even done a token tidying-up of his room.

tie, *sb.* Add: **4. a.** In mod. use the tie or neck-tie is usu. distinguished from the cravat; also, a bow-tie.

b. A lady's ornamental necklet or scarf.

1860 C. M. YONGE *Hopes & Fears* I. II. iii. 204 Ladies affected coats and waistcoats..both cousins..wearing.. black ties round the neck. **1895** *Montgomery Ward Catal.* Spring & Summer 79/2 White Hemstitch Lawn Ties, embroidered ends. (Size 4½ × 44 inch.) **1919** *Queen* 4 Oct. 5 A..Mink Tie beautifully worked in three strands. **1930** *Daily Tel.* 8 Apr. 9/5 Wherever fashionable women may meet this Easter most assuredly will you mark the popularity of the Fur Tie. **1973** *Country Life* 22 Nov. (Suppl.) 721 Important auction sale... Mink & Astrakhan fur coats and ties.

6. c. The locking together of dog and bitch during copulation.

1951 E. F. DAGLISH *Dog Breeder's Man.* xi. 102 Penetration by the dog is usually followed by the 'tie'.. usually considered evidence of a successful union. **1969** M. ROSLIN-WILLIAMS *Dual-Purpose Labrador* iv. 52 When the mating is effective and normal, the 'tie' will be so strong that the dog can be turned carefully round.

8. d. Delete '?*dial.* or *colloq.*' (Examples.)

1868 J. C. ATKINSON *Gloss. Cleveland Dial.* 534 T' au'd lady's a fer age. She'll be a desper't *tie* on em. **1928** A. HUXLEY *Point Counter Point* xix. 343 Free, without ties, unpossessed by any possessions, free to do as one will, to go at a moment's notice wherever the fancy may suggest —it is good. **1960** R. COLLIER *House called Memory* iii. 45 We'd love to do an evening show sometimes but the children are *such* a tie.

¶ *to ride in tie* (earlier example).

1870 G. T. CURTIS *Life D. Webster* I. 37 As Mr Webster once humorously expressed their frequent interchange of study and labour for their joint support, as they had but one horse between them, they 'rode in tie'.

e. *Logic.* Something that unites the elements of a linguistic construct, e.g. the verb 'to be'.

1918 W. E. JOHNSON in *Mind* XXVII. 14 In order to understand the verbal juxtaposition of substantive and adjective, we must recognise a latent element of form in this construct... This element of form constitutes what I shall call the characterising tie. **1921** —— *Logic* I. i. 10 The general term 'tie' is used to denote what..is involved in understanding the specific form of unity that gives significance to the construct. **1923** C. D. BROAD *Sci. Thought* ii. 75 Take first a very simple characterising judgment, like '3 is a prime.'..We might say that the first judgment is about the number 3 and the characteristic of primeness, and asserts that they are connected by the characterising tie. **1959** P. F. STRAWSON *Individuals* v. 168 To the characterizing tie between Socrates and the universal, *dying*, there corresponds the attributive tie between Socrates and the particular, his death.

tie, *v.* Add: **1. f.** *intr.* for *pass.*

1842 *Amer. Pioneer* I. 274 A pair of buckskin leggins,.. made to fit the leg and tie in at the ankle with the moccasins. **1924** A. D. SEDGWICK *Little French Girl* II. iii. 114 Straightly falling dress,..tying at the breast with tassels and at the waist with a loosely knotted sash.

2. *to tie to the stake*: delete † *obs.* and add later examples; *tie that bull outside* or *to another ashcan* (U.S. slang): I do not believe you; 'tell me another'; *to tie a can to* (or *on*) (slang): to reject or dismiss (a person); to stop (an activity); *to tie one on* [cf. *to tie a bun on* s.v. *BUN *sb.*[5]] *slang* (chiefly *U.S.*): to get drunk.

1605 SHAKS. *Lear* III. vii. 54, I am tyed to' th' Stake, And I must stand the Course. **1921** J. DOS PASSOS *Three Soldiers* IV. i. 212 'Fellers, the war's over!'..'Tie that bull outside,' came from every side of the ward. **1922** H. CRANE *Let.* 10 Dec. (1965) 108 Life is meagre with me. I am unsatisfied and left always begging for beauty. I am tied to the stake—a little more wastefully burnt every day of my life. **1926** WODEHOUSE *Heart of Goof* viii. 265 What caused the definite rift was Jane's refusal to tie a can to Rodney Spelvin. **1928** C. SANDBURG *Good Morning, America* 16 They got a fat nerve to try to tie a can on you. **1932** J. T. FARRELL *Young Lonigan* ii. 60 Three-Star told Vinc to tie his bull to another ash can. **1933** E. O'NEILL *Ah, Wilderness!* I. 27 Aw say, you fresh kid, tie that bull outside! **1942** WODEHOUSE *Money in Bank* (1946) xix. 163 Tie a can to the funny stuff, see? If I want to laugh, I'll read the comic strip. **1951** *Western Folklore* X. 82 The Act of Drinking:..to swill one down; to tie one on. **1959** *Listener* 4 June 971/1 That was what lost Mr. Acheson votes when he was tied to the Senatorial stake. **1962** J. ONSLOW *Bowler-Hatted Cowboy* xix. 186 You used to tie one on with the boys. **1972** WODEHOUSE *Pearls, Girls, & Monty Bodkin* v. 65 I'm warning you to kiss her goodbye and tie a can to her. Never marry anyone who makes conditions. **1982** A. MATHER *Impetuous Masquerade* vii. 107 He had..tied one on, if you know what I mean.

3. a. Also with *into*, = *to tie in to* (see sense 10* a below).

1913 in *O.E.D.* s.v. *Tie* vb. 3 e. **1969** D. ACHESON *Present at Creation* xliv. 402 The white telephone tied into the White House switchboard was used sparingly by considerate associates. **1974** *Sci. Amer.* Oct. 113/1 We began work at the complex by establishing over the target area a submerged grid of 10-meter squares that was tied into the Greek ordnance survey grid ashore.

f. *intr.* and *trans.* Of a dog or bitch: to remain linked (with) for a period during copulation.

1910 J. S. TURNER *Kennel Encycl.* III. 919 Occasionally a dog does not tie in the normal fashion... A dog that regularly ties is preferable. **1934** F. W. COUSENS *Dogs & their Managem.* v. 83 When the stud dog is unable to 'tie' a bitch, he is unable to remain sufficiently long in position to impregnate the bitch properly. **1952** C. L. B. HUBBARD *Pembrokeshire Corgi Handbk.* v. 60 Not all breeds tie. **1968** J. F. GORDON *Pet Library's Beagle Guide* x. 149 Once the pair have tied, they can be steadied, and..left to complete their task.

5. f. To impose conditions on (foreign aid), esp. by restricting its use *to* purchases from the source country. Cf. *TIED *ppl. a.* 2 c.

1965 *McGraw-Hill Dict. Mod. Econ.* 515 A considerable part of U.S. foreign aid has been tied. **1965** *New Statesman* 18 June 945/3 This strain [on the balance of payments] can be reduced by 'tying' aid—insisting that it be spent on British exports. **1976** *New Internationalist* Jan. 7/2 Virtually all aid from the USSR is tied to the purchase of Russian goods or expertise. **1980** *North–South* (Rep. Independent Comm. Internat. Devel. Issues) xii. 198 When they tie aid to their own sources the donor countries greatly limit choices and discourage local initiatives.

7. d. (Further examples.) Now chiefly *N. Amer.*

1966 *N.Y. Times* (Internat. ed.) 22 Apr. 12/5 Real Madrid tied Internazionale of Milan, 1–1, last night. **1968** *Globe & Mail* (Toronto) 17 Feb. 39 If Canada ties Russians, Swedes beat Czechs—Russia wins gold on goal spread, Canada takes silver. **1977** *Arab Times* 13 Dec. 9/1 The American Embassy is currently in second place and needs a victory to tie Dresser and force a play-off for the League Championship.

e. *N. Amer.* To match or equal (an existing record or score); colloq. phrases *can you tie that?, tie that!*, expressions of surprise or amazement. Cf. *BEAT *v.*[1] 10 g.

1918 *Collier's* 11 May 46/3 The French won't even admit he's dead yet—they call this joint the Invalides, which is only concedin' that he's *sick!* Can you tie that? **1930** *Sat. Even. Post* 28 June 162 'Can you beat that?' he muttered. 'Can you even tie it?' **1932** W. FAULKNER *Light in August* viii. 172 Well, say. Can you tie that. **1946** *Sat. Even. Post* 30 Mar. 46/2 Mr. Carter got hold of Blily Rose and offered him $1000 a day for 100 days if he would come to Fort Worth and put on a show that not only couldn't be beat but couldn't be tied. **1948** WODEHOUSE *Uncle Dynamite* vi. 83 Tie that for a disaster, Uncle Fred. **1968** *Globe & Mail* (Toronto) 15 Jan. 21/3 Willie Turner, a young sprinter who has yet to reach his peak, tied a world indoor standard Saturday. **1974** *State* (Columbia, S. Carolina) 3 Mar. 6-D/1 Cincinnati tied a school record by hitting 16 of 17 free throws. **1978** *Detroit Free Press* 5 Mar. C2/1 Connors, a 25-year-old lefthander from Belleville, Ill., quickly served a love game to tie the score.

9. Also, to get to work vigorously on; to tuck into (food). (Further examples.) *U.S.*

1912 R. A. WASON *Friar Tuck* xiv. 99 They girded up their loins, an' tied into him a little harder. **1948** 'J. EVANS' *Halo for Satan* ix. 130 She put her head back and tied into her drink with the easy grace of a practiced drinker. **1965** M. BRADBURY *Stepping Westward* v. 238 I'm going to take a peanut-butter sandwich..but I want to see these important men tie into something really good.

II. 10*. tie in. a. *trans.* To connect or join *to* an existing structure or network.

1793 [in Dict., sense 3 a]. **1914** *Dialect Notes* IV. 164 *Tie in*, in surveying, to join or connect up. 'We'll run over to the monument and *tie in* this survey.' **1943** J. S. HUXLEY *TVA* xi. 95 The framing to the exit..neatly ties in the air exhaust trough at the bottom of the walls. **1975** *North Sea Background Notes* (Brit. Petroleum Co.) 30 It is not impossible that a branch line from another nearby oilfield may be tied in to the Forties line in the future. **1978** *Lancashire Life* July 37/3 Instead of being tied-in to the building next-door this 19th century addition was simply slapped-up alongside it.

b. *intr.* To accord or be consonant (*with*); to be connected or associated (*with*).

1938 S. CHASE *Tyranny of Words* viii. 91 This ties in with Korzybski's central idea of knowledge as structural. **1954** 'A. GARVE' *Riddle of Samson* x. 97 There's another thing that ties in rather neatly, too. **1959** H. NIELSEN *Fifth Caller* xiv. 216 A stranger? That didn't tie in with the words Dr. Whitehall was quoted as having used in greeting. **1967** *Sci. Amer.* Sept. 276 The problem ties in with the discussion of Pascal's triangle. **1972** D. LODGE *20th Cent. Lit. Crit.* 174 Jung's theory of the Collective Unconscious tied in neatly with the anthropological study of primitive myth and ritual, initiated..by Sir James Frazer in *The Golden Bough.*

c. *trans.* To associate or connect (*with*).

1958 'A. BRIDGE' *Portuguese Escape* ix. 146 How can they have tied the Monsignor in with the Duke's house? **1959** *Listener* 26 Feb. 364/1 Nowadays, more emphasis is placed on teaching foreign languages phonetically and on trying to tie lessons in with exchange visits of pupils abroad. **1972** 'T. COE' *Don't lie to Me* (1974) xi. 102 The detectives on the case think the two things are tied in. The killing and the acid. **1972** J. L. DILLARD *Black English* iv. 140 Pidgin has been tied in historically with a lot of regrettable racial and economic policies. **1982** R. LEIGH *Girl with Bright Head* xix. 131 'Just tell me what Mrs Storm wanted with you.' 'Not unless you can tie her in with the murder.'

10. tie off. a.** *trans.* To close (a tubular vessel) by tying something round it. Also *transf.*

1903 J. J. MCGRATH *Surg. Anat. & Operative Surg.* I. 13 In resecting portions of the alimentary canal the mesentery or omentum that carries the blood-supply to the parts must be tied off. **1973** 'D. HALLIDAY' *Dolly & Starry Bird* ii. 27 You must have Digham tied off... I won't have you become preggy.

b. *trans.* To secure or make fast (a rope or line); also *fig.* Also *absol.*

1928 *Amer. Speech* IV. 69 [Stage-hand language.] The lines pass..down to a fly-floor,..where they are tied-off, or belayed. **1933** P. GODFREY *Back-Stage* vii. 88 Stage-hands are shouting strangely cryptic phrases to people overhead... 'Up on yer long—dead it—tie off at that—mark yer new set.' **1952** R. BISSELL *Monongahela* xix. 217 While the deckhand is tying off you jump down out of the brain box and knock the face wires loose. **1973** J. THOMSON *Death Cap* x. 143, I like all the ends tied off and *Finis* written on the file. **1974** H. MACINNES *Climb to Lost World* xi. 193, I..asked him to tie-off the bottom end of Joe's rope.

11. tie up. a. Also *intr.* for *pass.*

1865 'L. CARROLL' *Alice's Adv. Wonderland* xi. 172 A large canvass bag, which tied up at the mouth with strings.

c. Also, to hold up; to keep busy or occupied. Chiefly *pass.* orig. *U.S.*

1887 C. B. GEORGE *40 Years on Rail* vii. 140, I ran into a snow-storm that tied us up until we were six days making the run. **1907** *Springfield* (Mass.) *Weekly Republican* 10 Oct. 16 Traffic west of Springfield was tied up until about midnight. **1935** D. L. SAYERS *Gaudy Night* xiv. 295, I meant to come round yesterday evening, but I got tied up with people. **1941** B. SCHULBERG *What makes Sammy Run?* iii. 53 He was tied up in a story conference. **1959** W. D. PEREIRA *North Flight* ii. 29 Sir Arthur's terribly tied up at the moment and regrets he cannot speak to you. **1973** *New Yorker* 24 Feb. 36/1 The *World Almanac and Book of Facts* is a small buoy indeed but one that, whenever we stop to read it, ties us up for several hours. **1978** *Nature* 21 Sept. p. xii/2 The computer or scope is tied up only a fraction of a second while the exposure is made. **1980** D. LODGE *How far can you Go?* iv. 125 She sent her apologies, but she's tied up organizing some bazaar.

i. *to tie* (a person) *up in(to) knots* (or *a knot*): see *KNOT *sb.*[1] 10 a.

j. *intr.* To associate or unite oneself or one's interests *with* (or *to*). Also *trans.*, to associate (one thing) *with* another. orig. *U.S.* Cf. *TIE-UP *sb.* 7 b.

1888 *Texas Siftings* 3 Mar. 3/1 He's all O.K. There is no subterfuge about him... He is a man who will do to tie up to. **1903** *N.Y. Even. Post* 5 Dec. 1 It becomes his first interest to make business for that yard. He can best do this by tying up with the other navy yard representatives on the committee. **1904** *Indianapolis News* 21 June 6 The assurance that Captain New is to have a good post may be the reason that so many fellows want to tie up to him. **1925** *Round Table* June 593 It is clearly to South Africa's interest to tie up definitely either with sterling.. or with gold. **1928** *Daily Express* 13 June 3/4 Registered readers..have..'tied up' with the newspaper which.. offers the best..insurance benefits. **1943** [see *GENERATION 2 b]. **1958** *Times Lit. Suppl.* 19 Sept. 526/2 [He] does not rest solely on his spade but takes every opportunity of tying up archaeological discoveries with references obtainable from written authorities.

k. To bring to a satisfactory conclusion.

1954 'R. CROMPTON' *William & Moon Rocket* i. 25 Taking that lorry's number and giving a description of where the shed was on the Minster road. Tied things up a treat, that did. **1959** *Listener* 12 Feb. 305/1 When the play ends..one is left intentionally with the feeling that not everything has been tied up. **1973** A. BROINOWSKI *Take One Ambassador* vii. 90 The trade mark of the few in the know. That ties it all up. **1980** S. BRETT *Dead Side of Mike* xiii. 147 It all fits in... It just ties up the whole package.

l. *intr.* = sense 10* b above.

1959 M. GILBERT *Blood & Judgement* xiii. 138 'That would make him..in his late fifties now.' 'Which ties up all right with our man.' **1968** *Listener* 20 June 799/2 This may well tie up with the fact that he was an intensely religious person who believed in people going to hell and being saved. **1974** J. AIKEN *Midnight is Place* iv. 130 'He had had two men sent to jail for protesting.' 'Yes, that seems to tie oop with what we had heard.'

tie-. Add: **1.** *tie fabric*; **tie-break, -breaker,** a means of deciding a winner out of two or more contestants who have tied; also *fig.*; so **tie-breaking** *ppl. a.* and *vbl. sb.*; **tie-clasp, clip,** a small ornamental clasp for securing the ends of a tie to one's shirt; **tie press,** an instrument for pressing ties; **tie rack,** a rack on which to hang neckties; **tie silk,** a strong silk fabric used esp. for ties and clothing; cf. FOULARD 1; **tie tack,** a two-part ornamental fastener for a necktie, one part of which is worn under the shirt to receive the point of the part worn on the tie.

1970 *Times* 5 Mar. 13 In principle, the tie-break is an undesirable expedient, but there is a case for it in indoor tournaments confined to one court. **1974** *Observer* 1 Sept. 18/6 In the tie break Miss Mappin led 4–1. **1979** *Daily Tel.* 10 Dec. 19/1 Nigel..failed in a tie-break to win the British Chess championship in August. **1961** WEBSTER, Tie-breaker. **1970** *New Yorker* 10 Oct. 179/1 There are several species of tie-breakers, but the one that Bill Talbert, the tournament director, selected..was the nine-point sudden-death variety. **1971** *Computers & Humanities* VI. 68 The identifiers will be indexed and will serve as ultimate tie-breakers in all sorting operations. **1979** G. HAMMOND *Dead Game* xiv. 188 At the end of the quiz, honours were even..and the chairman asked for a tie-breaker from the audience. **1982** *Daily Tel.* 21 Sept. 16/4 [Rifle-shooting.] Belither..beat Paul Kent..by a single point on a tiebreaker. **1970** *Times* 1 Oct. 10/6 Okker, of the Netherlands, had to battle through two tie-breaking sets to beat El Shafei..7–6, 7–6. **1971** *Jrnl. Gen. Psychol.* LXXXV. 265 The stratification procedure entails a large number of random assignments and tie-breakings. **1978** R. NIXON *Memoirs* 85 His only important functions were to cast occasional tie-breaking votes in the Senate. **1955** W. GADDIS *Recognitions* II. i. 285 They..fastened monogrammed tie-clasps the more firmly. **1971** 'D. SHANNON' *Murder with Love* (1972) ix. 153 His dapper tailoring, gold cuff links and tie-clasp. **1898–9** *T. Eaton & Co. Catal.* Fall & Winter 16/1 Tie clips... For holding the tie in place on shirt or blouse fronts, 2 for 5c. **1913** [see *INNOVATION 6]. **1976** 'R. BOYLE' *Cry Rape* xii. 62 It wasn't an elegant tie-clip. Not the kind with a diamond or emerald in it. **1931** *Fairchild's Fabrics Buyers' Guide* I. 143 (*heading*) Tie and muffler fabrics. **1977** *Man-Made Textiles in India* XX. 92/3 The attributes which make a tie fabric satisfactory in use are similar to those in a dress fabric. **1926–7** *Army & Navy Stores Catal.* 757/3 *'Watts' tie press*..9¼ in. by 3½ in. *a* **1974** T. R. DENNIS in J. Burnett *Useful Toil* (1974) III. 354 A very cheap watch from my parents..a tie-press from a friend. **1916** *Daily Colonist* (Victoria, B.C.) 1 July 9/3 (Advt.), Pipe Racks, Tie Racks and Collar Bags, regular to 75c. **1974** L. DEIGHTON *Spy Story* ii. 22 Rummaging through the wardrobe I..noticed the tie rack had been moved. **1920** M. S. WOOLMAN *Clothing* iv. 53 Ribbons, velvets, tie silks..and knitting silks are made of this fiber. **1934** *Vogue* 30 May 96 (*caption*) Jenny makes a tailored suit of checked tie silk. **1961** *Guardian* 30 Mar. 9/4 Charming and practical tie-silk shirtwaisters. **1961** WEBSTER, Tie tack. **1962** 'D. SHANNON' *Extra Kill* xi. 171 He'd always wear a tie clasp, or one of those new tie tacks. **1970** *New Yorker* 10 Jan. 56/3 (Advt.), Peace Tie Tac. **1980** *Outdoor Life* (U.S.) (Northeast ed.) Oct. 154/3 (Advt.), Detective profession. Easy home study; free tie tack or lapel pin.

2. tie-back: also, a device for holding a drawn curtain back from the window; **tie-down,** the state (of an aircraft, etc.) of being tied down or otherwise kept on the ground; also, a device to or with which something may be tied down; freq. *attrib.*; **tie-on** *a.* (later examples.) See also *TIE-IN, *TIE-OFF.

1927 *Ladies' Home Jrnl.* Dec. 35/3 Flat festoons of green used for tie-backs on the curtains. **1961** *Times* 14 Jan. 9/7 Brass tie-backs in various shapes for holding the drawn but voluminous folds of the mid-Victorian drawing room curtains became a period 'must'. **1982** BARR & YORK *Official Sloane Ranger Handbk.* 148/1 Sloane windows need curtains with a capital C: with pelmets, twiddly bits, bands, tassels, tie-backs, edging. **1952** *Sun* (Baltimore) 4 Aug. 1/5 $1 tiedown fees for [flying] saucers less than 1,000 feet in diameter. **1955** *Ibid.* 11 Feb. 2/4 Exhaustive 'tie-down' ground tests are scheduled for the XV-3..before actual flight tests begin. **1956** W. A. HEFLIN *U.S. Air Force Dict.* 525/1 *Tie-down*, a ring, hook, stake, or the like to which something is secured; a tie-down fitting. **1969** *Jane's Freight Containers 1968–69* 418/1 Forklift entries and tie-down inserts are provided. **1971** *Flying* Apr. 13/1 Big tie-down areas for smaller airplanes. **1974** *Union* (S. Carolina) *Daily Times* 22 Apr. 7/7 (Advt.), Mobile homes anchored: Storm tie-downs to guard you against wind damage. **1978** F. MULLALLY *Deadly Payoff* xii. 171 He let the loosened end of the tie-down rope fall to the ground and kicked the chocks away from the front wheels. **1982** *Chicago Sun-Times* 31 Oct. 8 Another 30 residences..have planes with tie-downs instead of hangars. **1949** Tie-on [see *OCCLUDER]. **1967** E. SHORT *Embroidery & Fabric Collage* iii. 80 Tie-on cushions for dining chairs. **1971** 'D. HALLIDAY' *Dolly & Doctor Bird* xii. 161 My skin became brown..between my tie-on tops and my hipsters.

3. tie belt, a belt which is fastened by tying; hence **tie-belted** *a.*; **tie-dye** *sb.* = *tie-and-dye*, sense 4 below; freq. *attrib.*; also as *v. trans.*, to dye by this process; also *absol.*; hence **tie-dyed** *ppl. a.*, **-dying** *vbl. sb.*; **tie game,** a game in which the result is a tie; **tie-neck,** a collar attached at the back of the neck but left loose in front so that the ends can be tied; hence **tie-necked** *a.*; **tie-post** (earlier example); **tie rail** orig. *U.S.*, a rail or railing to which horses may be hitched; **tie rod,** (*a*) (further examples); (*b*) a track rod, or one of the rods of which it is composed, in the steering gear of a motor vehicle; **tie-teeth** *W. Indian colloq.*, any sticky foodstuff which is difficult to chew; **tie-tie** (earlier and later examples).

1964 *McCall's Sewing* xii. 227/1 A tie belt, without stiffening, becomes a string in no time. **1977** *Daily Mirror* 16 Mar. 16/2 (Advt.), The tie-belt style is 12–18. **1976** *Woman's Weekly* 6 Nov. 4/2 Tunic top is hip-length, tie-belted and tie-necked. **1904** G. WATT *Indian Art at Delhi* VII. xxxi. 255 From Chamba State has been received..a most remarkable..cotton fabric woven in alternate bands of cotton and gold thread, the cotton being tie-dyed so as to show large wavy formations. **1926** *Daily Colonist* (Victoria, B.C.) 22 July 8/7 (Advt.), Marvelous tie-dye patterns, glorious color-blendings are amazingly simple to make. **1951** A. N. GULATI *Patolu of Gujarat* 18 The first essential step, therefore, is to tie-dye both warp and weft in conformity with the proposed design in the fabric. **1956** J. IRWIN in *Textiles & Ornaments India* 29 The so-called *ikat*-technique is another kind of tie-dye. **1970** *Time* 20 Apr. 72 The stars fussed with their see-through dresses, tie-dyes and black ties and then paraded up a red-carpeted walkway. **1971** *New Yorker* 4 Sept. 61 What the boys who tie-dye and the grandmothers who rug-hook are doing is, in effect, as mechanical as anything done by a machine. **1975** *Advocate-News* (Barbados) 28 June 1/7 Organza flowers, soft toys, tie-dye and other craft work will be displayed by the YWCA craft group. **1977** *Guardian* 10 Jan. 8/1 The pallid youth in the tie-die shirt with a sewn-on picture of Marx. **1904** G. WATT *Indian Art at Delhi* VII. xxxi. 257 The beauty of these warp and weft tie-dyed textiles. **1978** J. UPDIKE *Coup* (1979) vi. 236 Their countrymen wearing cowboy hats, blue jeans, tie-dyed T-shirts. **1904** G. WATT *Indian Art at Delhi* VII. xxxi. 252 The once famous Bandana handkerchiefs may be given as the best known example of tie-dyeing. **1939** G. CLARK *Archæol. & Society* iii. 63 The tunics of the notables, which were.. coloured by the tie-dying method. **1970** *Time* 26 Jan. 40 The art is almost as old as India—where it is called *bandhnu.* It is as new as the boutiques that blossom along Sunset Strip and Madison Avenue—where it is called tie-dying. **1742** in H. T. Waghorn *Dawn of Cricket* (1906) 12 That played the tie game the beginning of the season. **1832** P. EGAN *Bk. of Sports* xxii. 347/2 In the first innings Woking gained 71 runs, Shiere then went in and got 71. Second innings, Woking 71; ditto, Shiere 71; it was consequently a *tye*-game, under circumstances unprecedented in the annals of cricket-playing. **1928** *Collier's* 29 Dec. 17/4 A tie game in football is certainly more thrilling..than a one-sided game. **1960** *Washington Post* 18 Oct. A18/1 It was Eddie Erdelatz, the Navy football coach, who once described a tie game as an unsatisfactory experience that permitted no enthusiasm. 'A tie game is like kissing your sister,' he said. **1968** J. IRONSIDE *Fashion Alphabet* 54 Tie neck. **1983** *Daily Tel.* 28 Feb. 24/5 The Queen's outfit was a navy-and-white jacket and dress with ..a tie neck. **1973** *Country Life* 22 Feb. 490/3 A tie-necked silk shirt. **1977** *Harpers & Queen* Sept. 44/1 A tie-necked champagne blouse in washable crepe. **1861** *Harper's Mag.* Feb. 424/2 He alighted,..throwing the reins over a tie-post. **1920** C. E. MULFORD *Johnny Nelson* 238 He'll never forget my kickin' him off'n th' tie-rail. **1970** *Sunday Mail Mag.* (Brisbane) 9 Aug. 14/2 The stranger dismounted and hitched his horse to the tierails in front of the pub. **1910** J. GUNN *Practical Design Motor Cars* ix. 230 The rod which transmits the motion of the steering gear to the front wheels should be connected at the front end..to the tie-rod. **1922** JOYCE *Ulysses* 698 Water closet..provided with opaque singlepane oblong window, tipup seat, bracket lamp, brass tierod brace. **1966** *McGraw-Hill Encycl. Sci. & Technol.* XIII. 640/1 In pressure piping, large forces are produced between connected parts. The pipes or parts are constrained by tie rods. **1976** *Jrnl.* (Newcastle) 26 Nov. (Advt.), Viva, 1969, white, taxed 11 months,..new balls and tie rods. c **1915** in Cassidy & Le Page *Dict. Jamaican Eng.* (1967) 444 Tie-teeth. **1953** *Caribbean Q.* III. I. 9 *Tie-teeth* (candy, sweets, or other very sticky food). **1975** E. L. ORTIZ *Caribbean Cookery* (1977) 266 If it is overcooked the mango paste turns into what Jamaicans graphically call tie-teeth. **1774** E. LONG *Hist. Jamaica* II. 427 The Negroes seem very fond of reduplications..as..*tie-tie, lilly-lilly, fum-fum.* **1827** *Hamel, Obeah Man* II. 257 Stretching what they called a *tie-tie* of tent-ropes, hempen cordage, mahoe bark, and bush ropes, all spliced together, to form..a guide for those who could be induced to cross the bridge. **1931** *Discovery* May 153/1 The whole of the frame-work [of a Nigerian house] is secured with what is known in pidgin English as *tie-tie* which is fibre from certain plants. **1958** C. ACHEBE *Things fall Apart* I. vii. 47 There were little holes..in the upper levels of the wall, and through these Okonkwo passed the rope, or *tie-tie*, to the boys and they passed it round the wooden stays and then back to him; and in this way the cover was strengthened on the wall.

4. Phrasal Comb.: **tie-and-dye,** a technique for producing a mottled appearance in dyed cloth by folding it and tying it before it is put in the dye bath; a garment or piece of cloth so dyed; freq. *attrib.* and unhyphened.

1886 *Jrnl. Indian Art* I. 117 The wonderfully constructed patterns of Patolo weaving with 'tie and die [*sic*]' warp and woof..testify..to the skill achieved by Indian dyers and weavers. **1928** *Daily Express* 21 May 5/2 The 'tie and dye' process—an old craft which gives a charming hazed effect. **1937** M. COVARRUBIAS *Island of Bali* I. vii. 196 The Balinese often decorate pieces of silk by the tie-and-dye process. **1976** *Billings* (Montana) *Gaz.* 7 July 9-B/7 Demonstrations in the hotel courtyard will include ..silver casting, tie and dye, silk screening and oil painting.

tied, *ppl. a.* Add: **2. c.** Of an international loan, etc.: given subject to conditions as to its use (see *TIE *v.* 5 f).

1958 C. N. HENNING *Internat. Finance* IV. xxi. 441/1 The so-called 'tied loan' principle. **1961** *Ann. Reg. 1960* 470 The issue of tied grants and credits was the subject of some dispute at international meetings. **1965** *McGraw-Hill Dict. Mod. Econ.* 515 The advantages of tied loans are that they stimulate employment and income in the creditor nation and do not affect the balance of payments of that country adversely. **1976** *New Internationalist* Jan. 5 For the Third World, 'tied' aid generally means having to pay between 20% and 50% more for goods than the competitive world market level.

d. Of a retail garage: of which the tenant is bound to receive fuel from a particular supplier.

1957 *Economist* 7 Dec. 885/1 About a third of these 'tied garages' have been signed up for periods of five years or less; the other two-thirds, which sell over half the petrol sold through dealers, are tied to their suppliers for longer periods of up to 20 years. **1965** [see *SOLUS *a.* 3 b].

3. b. *tied-back*: held back by tying.

1895 M. BEERBOHM in *Yellow Book* IV. 280 The women wore jerseys and tied-back skirts. **1979** A. BUCK *Dress in Eighteenth-Century England* 32/1 (*caption*) The tied-back hair in a bag.

tied (təid), *a.* [f. TIE *sb.* + -ED².] Wearing a tie.

1911 G. K. CHESTERTON *Innocence of Father Brown* iv. 105 The red-tied youth. **1976** SCOTT & KOSKI *Walk-In* (1977) ii. 17 One clean-shaven, suited and tied, scrubbed Asian.

tie-in (təi·in). orig. and chiefly *U.S.* [f. vbl. phr. *to tie in*: see *TIE *v.* 10*.] **1. a.** A connection or association *with*; a link-up.

1934 in WEBSTER. **1941** W. KOZLENKO *100 Non-Royalty Radio Plays* 535/2 That's the tie in. He killed Tom and after that decided to really cripple the Dominion team so that we wouldn't have a chance at winning. **1949** M. MEAD *Male & Female* vii. 152 The tie-in with birth can be close. **1965** *Listener* 10 June 875/1 The London studio tie-in with the pictures from America was also very successful, with John Tidmarsh getting lucid technical comments out of Geoffrey Pardoe at each stage of the operation. **1972** 'T. COE' *Don't lie to Me* (1974) vii. 66, I didn't know the museum had a tie-in with City College. **1973** *Black Panther* 21 July 2/3 Could you say something about the tie-in of David Hilliard's case with Watergate?

b. Used *attrib.* with reference to sales that are made conditional upon the purchase of some additional item or items from the same supplier.

1943 *Amer. N. & Q.* July 54/2 The phrase 'tie-in sales' (referring to those whereby tradesmen are obliged to buy unwanted stock in order to get even a small amount of a scarce item) appears to have established itself..about the first week of June (1943). **1946** *Sun* (Baltimore) 8 Feb. 12/6 This [liquor] industry can put an immediate stop to tie-in selling. **1980** *Times* 13 Sept. 18/7 It was information from an individual 'mole', working temporarily in a discount store, that first alerted the National Consumer Council to..'tie-in sales' (a stipulation that a buyer must purchase part or all of his requirements of a second (tied) product from the supplier of a first (tying) product).

c. An association between two publicity campaigns in the form of a theme common to both, or an advertisement that appears in two different media.

1949 *Newsweek* 28 Nov. 70/1 By next May, Paramount expects to have spent $1,000,000 calling attention to the show by way of..tie-ins with fashion designers and department stores who will make and sell women's clothes influenced by the 'Minoan period' costumes [in a film about Samson and Delilah]. **1959** I. ROSS *Image Merchants* ix. 149 Ryland [of NBC] also spends a good deal of time working up promotional tie-ins with manufacturers, department stores..and publications. It is a major coup when a national magazine can be persuaded to incorporate a TV plug in its own vast promotional outlay. **1962** *Economist* 10 Feb. 521/1 'Calories Don't Count' has been offered to the public as a promotional tie-in to encourage the purchase of safflower oil.

d. A book, film, or the like published to take advantage of the appearance of the same work in another medium.

1962 *Publishers' Weekly* 23 Apr. 43/1 Students show an interest in books which have been made into successful movies. Watch for these tie-ins. **1976** *Ibid.* 29 Mar. 42/1 The paper edition of Ibsen's 'Hedda Gabler and Other Plays' even has a movie tie-in cover with a still from the recent Glenda Jackson film. **1981** *Times Lit. Suppl.* 17 Apr. 425/2 The 1970s was the decade of the 'tie-in'—the almost simultaneous film of the novel, novel of the film, TV series of the novel.

2. (The making of) a connection between two pipelines or sections of pipeline. Freq. *attrib.*

1975 *North Sea Background Notes* (Brit. Petroleum Co.) 32 The line was welded, trenched and buried as quickly as possible, with only tie-in ends being left temporarily exposed. **1975** *Offshore Engineer* Nov. 18/2 The towing method..could be developed for installing a pipeline across the Norwegian trench in section, with tie-ins between them. **1976** *Ibid.* July 5/3 The 406mm line from SPAR to Brent B is being completed by Serra-Comex tie-in barge *Sandokan.* **1977** *Ibid.* Apr. 9/2 Three wells have been completed on the field and await tie-in when the production decision is made.

tie-·line. [f. TIE- + LINE *sb.*²] **1.** (In Dict. s.v. TIE- 3.)

2. *Teleph.* A line connecting two private branch exchanges. Also *transf.*

1923 T. E. HERBERT *Telephony* xvii. 437 Should an answering plug be inserted into a jack of the tie line, and the corresponding calling plug be placed into an exchange jack, [etc.]. **1955** E. F. RUSSELL *Somewhere a Voice* (1965) 107 Man is born of Earth and needs a tieline to Earth. **1969** J. MARTIN *Telecommunications & Computer* v. 91 Many companies have a leased system of telecommunications lines with switching facilities. To telephone a person in a distant company location, an employee must first obtain the appropriate tie line to that person's private branch exchange. **1978** *Broadcast* 29 May 9/2 Dring got a phone call out [of Zaire] via the BBC's New York office on tie line to the TV Centre just three minutes before the nine o'clock bulletin went out.

3. A line in a phase diagram joining two points that each represent the composition of two phases in equilibrium with one another.

1924 A. E. HILL in H. S. Taylor *Treat. Physical Chem.* I. ix. 400 No solution therefore can exist having composition indicated by points within the area *A–B–C–B′–A′*, but such compositions can lead only to two conjugate solutions of composition lying upon the curves at the intersections with the isothermal tie-lines. **1935** *Amer. Jrnl. Sci.* CCXXIX. 174 All liquids *a–b* are in equilibrium with olivine, each with an olivine of different composition as indicated by the tie-lines. **1961** *Geol. Mag.* XCVIII. 336 (*caption*) Tie-lines joining co-existing, chemically analysed pyroxenes from igneous rocks. **1979** *Nature* 3 May 53/2 (*caption*) Miscibility gap between carbonate and silicate melts... Conjugate liquids at 0·7 kbar and 7·6 kbar are joined by tie-lines.

4. A pipeline or transmission line connecting two distribution systems or two parts of a single system.

1949 *Sun* (Baltimore) 5 July 10/4 With the completion of a 48-inch tie-line..the city Bureau of Water Supply believes it could supply 4,000,000 gallons daily. **1962** *Newnes Conc. Encycl. Electr. Engin.* 348/1 If two machines [*sc.* a.c. generators] are to be coupled together by a tie-line perhaps 50 or 60 miles in length, there may be an appreciable impedance presented to the flow of the synchronizing current. **1974** *Sci. Amer.* Nov. 40/3 Its objective is to maintain the frequency within an area served by several generating stations and to maintain the sum of all active tie-line power exchanges between the area and its neighbors.

‖ **t'ien** (tiʸe·n). Also 7 tayn, 8 **tyen,** 8– **tien.** [Chinese *tiān*.] In Chinese thought: Heaven; the Deity.

1613 PURCHAS *Pilgrimage* IV. xvi. 373 All being a rude and vnformed Chaos, *Tayn* (say they) framed and setled the Heaven and Earth. **1710** *Memoires for Rome concerning State Christian Relig. China* iii. 71 He would not retract, nor acknowledge that *Tien*, that is to say, the visible Heavens was the God of the Christians. **1747** *Astley's New Gen. Coll. Voy.* IV. I. v. 202/1 It appears.. that this *Tyen*, or first Being, is the Creator of all Things. **1788** tr. *Grosier's Gen. Descr. China* II. VI. i. 186 Between the *Tien* and man there is a relation. **1878** *Jrnl. North-China Branch R. Asiatic Soc.* XII. 122 Even in the time of Confucius the change from the personality of T'ien-tsze to the abstract idea of the modern T'ien does not seem to have been complete. **1904** *Athenæum* 17 Sept. 373/2 The Chinese Emperor is not regarded as other than the regent of the empire appointed by *t'ien* or heaven. **1940** E. POUND *Cantos* liv. 39 The rites of *Tien*, that is Heaven Were ploughing and the raising of silk worms. **1958** W. WILLETTS *Chinese Art* I. ii. 92 After the Chou displaced the Shang-Yin, they apparently came to equate the old Shang Ti with their own chief deity T'ien.

tienda (tie·nda). orig. and chiefly *U.S.* [a. Sp., = tent, awning, shop: see TENT *sb.*¹] In the south-western U.S.: a shop or stall, esp. a draper's or general store.

1844 G. W. KENDALL *Santa Fé Exped.* II. ii. 38 Standing in front of a small tienda, or store. **1870** J. C. DUVAL *Adv. Big-Foot Wallace* xxxviii. 235, I searched in vain every shop and 'tienda' in the city for even a pair of No. 11's, though 12's fit me best. **1912** C. F. SAUNDERS *Indians of Terraced Houses* 71 Our proximity to the pueblo was indicated by our meeting Indians..on their way to the trader's *tienda* beneath the shady cottonwoods at Algodones. **1927** *Blackw. Mag.* Nov. 658/2 Its *tienda* with long counter, handsome shelves, and fabulous profits. **1948** F. BLAKE *Johnny Christmas* I. 10 Across the plaza, too, in the sprawling Martinez tienda, were articles that would trade or sell high in northeastern Texas.

‖ **tiens** (tiæṅ), *int.* [Fr., imp. sing. of *tenir* to hold.] An expression of surprise.

1932 G. HEYER *Devil's Cub* xi. 169 '*Tiens!*' said the Duchess with polite interest. 'My son is then a house-breaker.' **1958** L. DURRELL *Mountolive* viii. 179 *Tiens!* I forgot. Here is the thousand I promised you. **1975** A. CHRISTIE *Curtain* xiii. 133 Did he take it by accident or intention. *Tiens*, his fingerprints are not on the bottle.

‖ **tienta** (tie·nta). [Sp., lit. 'probe'.] In Spain, an occasion at which young bulls in the field are tested for spirit as prospective stud and fighting bulls.

1909 J. VILLIERS-WARDELL *Spain of Spanish* vi. 110 It is necessary for the *ganadero*—an owner of cattle—to test his young bulls while they are still running wild... This testing of the young bulls is called a *tienta.* **1932** E. HEMINGWAY *Death in Afternoon* xii. 124 The strain of fighting blood..can only be kept pure by conscientious testing in the tientas. **1957** R. CAMPBELL *Portugal* 109 His name..is given him along with his branded number and noted down on the day of the *tienta.* **1967** MCCORMICK & MASCAREÑAS *Compl. Aficionado* ii. 55 Memory of the *tienta* stirs and fires him to a prompt charge, his weariness forgotten.

‖ **tiento** (tie·nto). *Mus.* [Sp., lit. 'touch, feel'.] In sixteenth- and seventeenth-cent. Spanish music: a contrapuntal piece resembling a *ricercar*, orig. for strings and, later, organ.

1905 C. F. A. WILLIAMS *Story of Organ Music* xi. 163 The compositions of Cabezon's collection consist of nine practice pieces,..short preludes called Versos or Versillos, ..[and] longer preludes called Tientos. **1947** A. EINSTEIN *Music in Romantic Era* xvii. 294 The 'schools' of the ricercar, whether called fugue as in Germany, *tiento* as in Spain, or fancy as in England, were different; but the spirit and form were the same. **1976** D. MUNROW *Instruments Middle Ages & Renaissance* ix. 74/4 The solo *tiento* for harp or organ by Alonso Mudarra, published in his *Tres Libros* (1546). **1980** *Early Music* Apr. 248/1 Some polyphonic works of the period in the tradition of the *tiento* offer most remarkable variety within their stylistic limitations.

Tientsin (tyen(t)si·n, tin(t)si·n). The name of a city and port on the East coast of north China, used *attrib.* and *absol.* to designate carpets made or shipped from there.

1904, 1913 [see *PEKIN 1 b]. **1922** KENDRICK & TATTERSALL *Hand-Woven Carpets* I. I. vi. 66 Many carpets find their way to Tientsin for export, and on that account the term 'Tientsin Carpet' has come into use. **1980** D. CREED *Scarab* II. xiv. 132 Deep-piled Tientsin carpets covered the tiled floor.

tie-off (təi·ǫf). [TIE- 2.] **1.** *Show-jumping.* = *JUMP-OFF 3.

1958 *Listener* 2 Oct. 536/3 We could see the tie-off for the Grand Prix between the Italian and German champions.

2. *Mountaineering.* (See quot. 1968.)

1968 P. CREW *Encyclopædic Dict. Mountaineering* 117/2 *Tie-off*, a method of reducing the leverage on a piton which has not been fully inserted, by tying a short loop of rope to the piton blade, close against the rock face. **1971** C. BONINGTON *Annapurna South Face* 247 We used huge quantities of tape for everything from tie-offs on pitons to belts for trousers. **1974** H. MACINNES *Climb to Lost World* x. 162 It took him most of the day to put a couple of bolts in, with some weird tie-off pegging to do.

Tiepolesque (tie:pole·sk), *a.* [f. *Tiepolo* (see below) + -ESQUE.] Characteristic of or resembling the work of Giovanni Battista Tiepolo (1696–1770), or of his son Domenico (1727–1804), Italian painters famous esp. for (ceiling) frescos. Often used somewhat *loosely.*

1895 G. B. SHAW *Our Theatres in Nineties* (1932) I. 159 Goddesses in a Tiepolesque ceiling. **1934** *Burlington Mag.* Feb. 91/1 The purely Tiepolesque conception of the war-horse. **1958** *Times* 17 Oct. 17/6 The dash of Murillo in 'The Guerilla taking leave of his Confessor', or the much less happy Tiepolesque pose of the figure straining at the wheel of the gun in 'The Defence of Saragossa'. **1974** *Times Lit. Suppl.* 20 Dec. 1449/5 Her inability to understand Visconti's Tiepolesque conception of *Iphigénie en Tauride* is significant: she wanted to look Greek, primeval and savage whereas Visconti wished upon her the bejewelled artificiality of a Venetian fresco.

tier, *sb.*[1] Add: **1. e.** A range or line *of* contiguous lots, townships, counties, or states. *U.S.*

1693 in *Connecticut Hist. Soc. Coll.* (1912) XIV. 212 One lyeing in the Same Teere of lotts abutting on a Highway. **1720, 1722** [in Dict., sense 1 a]. **1824** in S. C. Cox *Recoll. Early Settlem. Wabash Valley* (1860) iii. 18 The land is sold in tiers of townships. **1856** *Spirit of Times* 18 Oct. 113/1 The great varying hare..is no longer to be found in our state,..until we reach the northern tier of counties, on the Canada line. **1949** *Ward County* (North Dakota) *Independent* 21 July 1/3 Each of the big wheat states in the tier from Texas up through North Dakota appears to be coming up with a crop just under that state's all-time record.

f. A mountainous scarp; a mountain. *Tasmania.*

1850 T. ARNOLD *Let.* 29 Sept. (1966) 55 The next day.. we all walked up a 'tier' (Tasmanian for hill) near the house. **1902** *Encycl. Brit.* XXXIII. 185/2 The marginal crests of this mountain table-land, together with its upper surface,..are known locally as 'Tiers'. **1965** *Austral. Encycl.* VIII. 425/2 Along the north-western coast [of Tasmania] there is a strip of rich, undulating land, climbing steadily to the base of steep escarpments called 'tiers'.

g. Each of a number of successively overlapping ruffles or flounces on a garment.

1934 in WEBSTER. **1938** F. P. WALKUP *Dressing Part* xv. 354 Tiers of ruffles, side pleats, and diagonal layers were introduced, for variety. **1978** *Detroit Free Press* 5 Mar. D12/1 Tiers will fall from little squared yokes, freely.

3. tiersman *Tasmanian colloq.* (see quot.); cf. sense 1 f above.

1941 BAKER *Dict. Austral. Slang* 76 'Tiersman': one who lives in the mountains. Tasmanian slang.

tier, *sb.*[2] Add: **3.** *spec.* one for tying a sail.

1860 G. S. NARES *Naval Cadet's Guide* 81 The sail is then secured to the yard with tyers. **1873** 'VANDERDECKEN' *Yachts & Yachting* 265 Let the gaskets, or as they are sometimes called, the tyers, which confine the mainsail in its furl, be taken off. **1939** A. RANSOME *Secret Water* iii. 44 In a minute or two, he had bundled the sail along the boom and put a couple of tiers to hold it there. **1947** —— *Great Northern?* viii. 101 The next few minutes were full of the regular drill of getting under way. Tyers were cast off the sails.

tierce, *sb.* **8.** *tierce de Picardie* (examples).

1849 J. A. HAMILTON *Celebr. Dict.* 117 *Tierce de Picardie* (French), a term applied to the concluding chord of a piece of music in a minor key, when its third is made major by an accidental sharp or natural. **1889** GROVE *Dict. Mus.* IV. 114/2 The Third, thus made major by an accidental sharp or natural, is called the 'tierce de Picardie'. **1940** *Scrutiny* IX. 128 Beneath the suspended F sharp of the concluding tierce de picardie, trombones, violas, and horns emphatically sing. **1959** D. COOKE *Language of Music* ii. 57 For centuries, pieces in a minor key had to have a 'happy ending'—a final major chord (the 'tierce de Picardie') or a bare fifth. **1978** *New Universities Q.* XXXII. 288 The final cadence achieves, and deserves, the bliss of a tierce de Picardie.

tiercé, *a.* Restrict *Her.* to sense in Dict. and add: **B.** *sb.* Also **tierce. a.** A method of betting in which the first three horses in a race have to be named in the correct order. **b.** A French horse-race at which this method prevails. **c.** *fig.*

1964 A. WYKES *Gambling* viii. 195 The French have developed a special way of betting... It is called 'Tiercé' and involves the selection of three horses to finish first, second, and third in specified races held on Sundays and holidays. **1966** *Economist* 24 Dec. 1336/4 The French happily bet vast sums on the *tierce*. **1974** *Times Lit. Suppl.* 6 Sept. 941/4 She had achieved a far more considerable success, having managed both to break up her sister Eliza's marriage..and, better still, indirectly to cause the death of her infant niece... This was not a *tiercé*, but it was a considerable double triumph. **1981** *Times* 30 June 6/5 Frenchmen had to do without the 'Tiercé'..yesterday. *Ibid.* 6/6 It was the third time since ..May, 1968 that the Tiercé fixtures had not taken place.

tiered, *a.* Add: Now freq. not in Combs.

1930 *Antiquity* IV. 422 He regards the tomb of Cyrus as a reproduction in stone of such a tiered temple. **1939** M. B. PICKEN *Lang. of Fashion* 155/1 Tiered skirt. **1951** *Good Housek. Home Encycl.* 276/1 The tiered steamers have..three separate pans which fit on top of each other over a base pan. **1952** C. P. BLACKER *Eugenics* 294 Certain professions—the Church, the law, the fighting Services—have a hierarchical structure, and success can be gauged by the level attained by an individual in such a tiered system. **1955** V. CRONIN *Wise Man from West* 92 Among the limitless paddy-fields and tiered hills. **1971** *Daily Tel.* 28 July 11 The skirt tiered all the way down. **1978** *Morecambe Guardian* 14 Mar. 16/3 She was attended by her sister..who wore a pale blue chiffon tiered dress.

tiering (tīə·riŋ), *vbl. sb.* [f. TIER *sb.*[1] + -ING[1].] Arrangement in tiers; the formation of tiers.

1969 T. E. B. HOWARTH *Culture, Anarchy & Public Schools* v. 78 Local authorities are required under circular 10/65 to plan a complete system of comprehensive education for their areas either by the erection of all-through comprehensive schools or by various devices of amalgamation or tiering ('middle schools', sixth form colleges and so on). **1971** *Daily Tel.* 28 July 11 Cardin has run amok.. with the tucking and tiering attachments on his sewing machine. **1978** *Detroit Free Press* 5 Mar. D12/1 Tiering [of dresses] is a continuation of the peasant theme that has been with us for what seems like a long, long time. **1980** *Amer. Film* Oct. 25/1 Viewers are willing to pay generously..for more programming. There is a term for this program proliferation: 'tiering'. When a cable system adds another channel of programs for an extra fee, there is a new tier of service to offer subscribers.

‖ **tiers monde** (tyęr mǫnd). Also **Tiers Monde.** [Fr.: see *THIRD WORLD.] = *THIRD WORLD.

1963 *Listener* 28 Feb. 386/1 The book exemplifies the need for utter empiricism in our approach to the *tiers monde*. **1964** *Financial Times* 11 Feb. 7/6 France is strongly placed to make a success of her championship of the 'Tiers Monde'. **1966** *Listener* 18 Aug. 229/1 What has commonly come to be called the *tiers monde*, the uncommitted nations, Africa and Asia, have a position in the world.

Tietze (tī·tsə). *Path.* [The name of A. *Tietze* (1864–1927), Polish surgeon, who described the condition in 1921 (*Berlin. klin. Wochenschr.* LVIII. 829).] *Tietze's disease, syndrome*: a condition in which there is painful swelling of one or more costal cartilages without evident cause.

1932 *Index Medicus* XII. 1146/2 Tietze's disease; dystrophy of costal cartilage. **1942** *Brit. Med. Jrnl.* 19 Sept. 352/1 Among the many manifestations of subnutrition recently seen by us have been two cases of swelling of the costal cartilages, associated with weakness and lethargy, which conform to the description of Tietze's disease. **1945** *Canad. Med. Assoc. Jrnl.* LIII. 572/2 It is not suggested that these rib changes are necessarily due to Tietze's syndrome. **1977** *Daily Colonist* (Victoria, B.C.) 20 July 2/1 Tietze's disease can be mistaken for angina.

tie-up, *sb.* (*a.*) Add: **I. 2. b.** A (makeshift) garter.

1970 R. HILL *Clubbable Woman* i. 5 One stocking was down. His tie-up hung loose round his ankle. **1976** E. DUNPHY *Only a Game?* v. 139 Laying the shirts out before the game, making sure the lads have chewing gum, tie-ups, tea at half-time.

3. b. A building or stall in which cattle are tied up for the night. orig. and chiefly *U.S.*

1851 J. S. SPRINGER *Forest Life* 82 At the further end of the 'tie-up' he thinks he hears a little clattering noise. **1883** *Rep. Maine Board Agric. 1882* 49 Those who have not the convenience for a barn cellar can save the manure very well by a tight floor in the tie-up. **1930** W. FAULKNER *As I lay Dying* 117 The cows were still in the tie-up. **1952** E. CALDWELL *Lamp for Nightfall* iii. 32 They constructed a chicken house..and installed six tie-ups in the dairy barn. **1960** *Farmer & Stockbreeder* 2 Feb. 17/1 The property..includes a farmhouse, two cottages and farm buildings in good condition with tie-up accommodation for 80 cows.

II. 6. (Later examples.) Also a stoppage of transport, a traffic hold-up. orig. and chiefly *U.S.*

1904 *N.Y. Tribune* 29 Oct. 1 An accident to one of the motor cars caused a tie-up of the southbound trains. **1923** C. R. COOPER *Under Big Top* xi. 227 Add to all this the handicaps of weather, of railroad tie-ups [etc.]. **1943** *Coast to Coast 1942* 181 Old McAlister had made a reference to some trouble on the Brisbane waterfront that threatened a temporary tie-up in the shipping of produce. **1962** E. SNOW *Other Side of River* (1963) xxiv. 183, I myself saw new motors and parts piled up unprotected in the weather and damaged or ruined because of transport tie-ups or lack of storage facilities. **1977** *Time* 18 July 14/2 Tie-ups extending for 30 miles are almost normal.

7. b. A connection or association. Cf. *TIE *v.* 11 j.

1927 *Daily Express* 7 Mar. 11/5 There is a tie-up, too, over this firm with the gramophone records. Every record of the 'Happiness Boys' is an advertisement for Happiness Chocolates. **1938** F. SCOTT FITZGERALD *Let.* 18 Apr. (1964) 28, I had made the mental tie-up that work equals something unpleasant. **1945** E. DALY *House without Door* xi. 118 It's quite an interesting tie-up... The Locke case and the Gregson murder case. **1960** *Guardian* 27 Sept. 8/4 The Labour Party..has..an out-of-date tie-up with the trades unions. *a* **1963** L. MACNEICE *Astrol.* (1964) vii. 220 The modern astrological tendency..to seek tie-ups between astrology and psychological knowledge. **1974** S. GULLIVER *Vulcan Bulletins* 32 'How the hell did he get in with the Libyans in the first place?' I asked. 'Old school tie-ups,' said Selby.

c. A telecommunication link or network. *U.S.*

1927 *Sci. Amer.* July 37/2, 27 stations..were connected to the battery of microphones in front of the Capitol. This record tie-up of transmitters was surpassed..when President Coolidge addressed a joint session of Congress.. through a network of 42 broadcasters. **1939** *Sun* (Baltimore) 24 Aug. 3/5 (*heading*) Western Union speeds deliveries with tieup. **1940** *Nature* 20 July 91/2 It is reported from Pittsburgh, Pa., that the Bell Telephone Co. has applied for a permit to install transmitters and receivers on what is called a 'tie-up' with existing telephone facilities.

Tiffany[2] (ti·fǎni). The name of Charles L. *Tiffany* (1812–1902), goldsmith and founder of a fashionable New York firm of jewellers *Tiffany and Co.*, and of his son Louis C. *Tiffany* (1848–1933), Art Nouveau decorator noted for his iridescent glassware, used: **a.** *attrib.* (sometimes with small initial) to designate objects made or designed by either of these (but esp. the son) or imitating his style, esp. as *Tiffany glass, lamp.* **b.** Allusively to denote organizations, etc., considered equal to Tiffany and Co. in high-quality craftsmanship or exclusiveness. Also *Comb.*, as *Tiffany-style, -type* adjs.

1895 *Montgomery Ward Catal.* Spring & Summer 153/1, 1K Diamond. Tiffany Setting. **1907** KIPLING *Let.* 10 Dec. (1983) 56 A slippery slidy red leather box—like a huge Tiffany jewel case. **1930** E. WAUGH *Labels* vii. 175 Gaudi alone was able to use it [*sc.* a mosaic of broken china and pebbles embedded in cement] with precision.. and make of it the craft which, in New York, is reverently known as 'Tiffany bathroom'. **1936** J. DOS PASSOS *Big Money* 307 Gladys kept..tiffanyglass bowls full of freezias. [**1964** M. J. SIMON *New York This Way* iii. 31 Tiffany & Co., celebrated American jewellers whose name often is used colloquially to signify highest quality of product or service in any field.] **1969** A. LURIE *Real People* 89 The Tiffany lanterns [had been] lit beside the front door. **1971** P. A. WHITNEY *Listen for Whisperer* v. 95, I switched on the Tiffany lamp. **1973** *Synagogue Light* Sept. 4/2 By maintaining a small, specialized firm, we have been able to attain a consistently high calibre level of financial performance... It is the quality we are noted for, a Tiffany type organization. **1977** *Lancashire Life* Mar. 56/3 (*caption*) His policy is to supplement 'the world's finest exhibition' of Tiffany glass with a monthly change of exhibitions. **1977** *Texas Highways* Dec. 33/1 Tiffany-style lampshades. **1978** M. PUZO *Fools Die* xiii. 144, I had become the Tiffany's of bribe takers, with rich, trusting customers. **1979** *United States 1980/81* (Penguin Travel Guides) 425 This one..has Tiffany lamps, antique tables, and a very friendly atmosphere. **1980** 'E. MCBAIN' *Ghosts* iv. 75 The Tiffany-style lamp on the end table.

tiffin, *sb.* Add: **b. tiffin-carrier,** a tiered container for transporting meals.

1960 R. P. JHABVALA *Householder* i. 13 He always brought his breakfast with him in a tin tiffin-carrier.

tig, *sb.*[1] Add: **3.** *colloq.* (orig. *Sc.*). A fit of bad temper.

1773 R. FERGUSSON in *Weekly Mag.* XXII. 209/1 What tig then takes the fates, that they can thole, Thrawart to fix me i' this weary hole? **1895** R. FORD *Tayside Songs* 71 She left me in a tig. **1934** N. MARSH *A Man lay Dead* xii. 206 'You shall have every opportunity,' soothed Alleyn. 'What a tig you are in, to be sure!' **1943** —— *Colour Scheme* xii. 217, I must say..that I can't see why you're getting into such a tig over it. **1962** *Punch* 24 Oct. 587/1 The spectacle of a man in a tig, even of two men in a tig, is not as a rule wholly entertaining.

tiger, *sb.* Add: **2. a.** (Earlier and later S. Afr. examples.)

1708 tr. F. Leguat in R. Raven-Hart *Cape of Good Hope 1652–1702* (1971) II. 431 The Company gives twenty Crowns to anyone that kills a Lion, and ten to him that kills a Tigre. **1907** P. FITZPATRICK *Jock of Bushveld* (1909) 252 Tigers—as they are almost invariably called, but properly, leopards—were plentiful enough.

c. (*a*) (Earlier example.)

1829 H. WIDOWSON *Present State Van Dieman's Land* xviii. 179 The hyena, or as it is sometimes called, the tiger, is about the size of a large terrier; it frequents the wilds of Tasmania.

4. a. Also *spec.*, a native of the Fens. In full, *fen tiger. colloq.*

1893 [in Dict.]. **1963** 'C. MARCHANT' *Fen Tiger* ii. 40 The term 'fen tiger'... Andrew explained it was the name given to a type of fen man, now almost extinct but not quite, for here and there a descendant of the type of man who had lived deep in the trackless, treacherous fenland, and who fought against the land being drained with cunning, craftiness, and even murder, was still to be found. **1971** *Country Life* 28 Oct. 1128/3 A scattered crowd of rough 'Fen Tigers' in corduroy trousers. **1981** S. MARSHALL *Everyman's Bk. Eng. Folk Tales* 13, I was.. not accorded the welcome I would have expected to be given to a fen-tiger returning home from choice.

d. *colloq.* (chiefly *Austral.* and *N.Z.*). One who has an insatiable appetite *for* something. Cf. GLUTTON *sb.*

1896 *Bulletin* (Sydney) 24 Oct. (Red Page), His father thought a lot of Henry; he used to call him a tiger for work. **1927** R. LEHMANN *Dusty Answer* II. 98 Martin.. was still..a tiger for raw vegetables. *Ibid.* IV. 259 You're a tiger for conversation, aren't you? **1935** W. HATFIELD *Black Waterlily* 15 'Tiger for work, aren't you?' he smiled. 'A good fault, of course, if you don't carry it to extremes.' **1972** P. NEWTON *Sheep Thief* xx. 170 Don't tell me you're up to your capers again... You're a tiger for punishment.

e. A sportsman or climber of outstanding skill and confidence. Cf. *RABBIT *sb.*[1] 2 a. *colloq.*

1929 E. BOWEN *Joining Charles* 166 They may be tigers at ping-pong. **1935** D. PILLEY *Climbing Days* ii. 27 Wet ground, where most climbers—bar the latest 'tigers'—find that they slip. **1941** R. R. MARETT *Jerseyman at Oxford* ix. 138, I was never really worth more than bare scratch, and clean outside the 'tiger' class [in golf]. **1957** CLARK & PYATT *Mountaineering in Britain* x. 178 'Tiger' is the word used to describe the climber whose abilities are outstandingly in advance of his generation. **1974** *Times* 23 Feb. 13/3 There is a third [golf] course strictly for tigers; rabbits should try the excellent par three to seawards of the big course. **1979** *Country Life* 24 May 1674/2 Odon has less of a reputation as a tiger on difficult climbs than his father.

6. b. *Naut. slang.* A captain's personal steward.

1929 F. C. BOWEN *Sea Slang* 141 *Tiger, the*, the steward who acts as personal servant to the captain of a liner. **1936** E. T. BRITTEN *Million Ocean Miles* iii. 30 Croughan is my 'Tiger', as the Captain's steward is called at sea. **1961** 'R. GORDON' *Doctor on Toast* x. 87 In the old days, you could have swapped the Captain's tiger for the butler in any stately home in the kingdom, and no one would have been the wiser. **1982** *Times* 11 May 6/6 Captain Jackson's 'tiger'—the merchant navy equivalent of a batman.. was married after the weekend.

8. (Earlier example.)

1845 *Florence de Lacey* 28/1 Nine cheers for old Tip—one, two, three, four, five, six, seven, eight, nine, and a tiger.

11*. a. In proverbial phrases: *to ride a tiger* and varr. [after the Chinese proverb 'He who rides a tiger is afraid to dismount' (W. Scarborough *Coll. Chinese Proverbs* (1875) xvi. 388)]: to take on a responsibility or embark on a course of action which subsequently cannot safely be abandoned; *to have a tiger by the tail* and varr.: to catch a Tartar (see TARTAR *sb.*² 4).

1902 A. R. COLQUHOUN *Mastery of Pacific* xvi. 388 These colonies are..for her [*sc.* France] the tiger which she has mounted (to use the Chinese phrase), and which she can neither manage nor get rid of. **1940** *Daily Progress* (Charlottesville, Va.) 27 Nov. 1/7, I believe that Hitler is riding a tiger in trying to keep all Europe under control by sheer force. **1969** *Guardian* 7 July 9/5 All African politics to-day is concerned with the art of riding this terrible tiger [*sc.* tribalism]. **1972** 'E. LATHEN' *Murder without Icing* (1973) iii. 30 Convulsions..could be expected... The Sloan Guaranty Trust..might well have a tiger by the tail. **1979** P. DRISCOLL *Pangolin* xii. 101 You're taking on an organization with..reserves you know nothing about. How do you know you won't be catching a tiger by the tail? **1981** W. H. HALLAHAN *Trade* iii. 79 It was done. They were all riding the tiger now.

b. *to put a tiger in one's tank* [after an Esso Petroleum Co. advertising campaign of 1965]: to invest one with energy or 'go'; also in similar allusive phrases.

1965 *Guardian* 31 May 4/7 Esso's tiger has pounced on to the national consciousness within two months. The phrase 'Put a tiger in your tank' has become part of everyday conversation. **1967** *Listener* 22 June 835/2 Westin and Friedman are young men with ideas of their own... They are the tigers in the Ford [Foundation] tank. **1973** P. GEDDES *Ottawa Allegation* iii. 32 Lorimount..began pouring tea... The movements were brisk and purposeful. No safety belts worn here, they said, there's a tiger in the tank. **1981** *N.Z. Tablet* 10 June 10/4 Young girls must be made to realise that boys of the same age have a 'tiger in their tank' as far as sexual desire goes.

c. *paper tiger*: see *PAPER *sb.* 12.

12. a. *tiger cage, country, -pit* (examples), *-skin* (earlier example), *trap*.

1970 *Guardian* 8 July 1 (*caption*) Political prisoners peering up out of a 'tiger cage' in Con Son prison in South Vietnam. **1982** *Times* 28 Sept. 3/4 (*caption*) An apprentice animal trainer, in the tiger cage with six Bengal tigers. **1931** E. A. ROBERTSON *Four Frightened People* v. 178 This was tiger country, she knew, but she had never yet seen one of those animals. **1978** 'M. M. KAYE' *Far Pavilions* xxv. 369 Biju Ram would only have had to wait until they were in tiger country—preferably..where there was known to be a man-eater. **1936** T. S. ELIOT *Coll. Poems 1909–35* 153 The tiger in the tiger-pit Is not more irritable than I. **1970** *Daily Progress* (Charlottesville, Va.) 8 July 5A/3 Harkin said more than 200 men, crammed three to five in 86 5-by-8-foot tiger pits in one building, were unable to stand because they had been there so long. **1763** J. BELL *Trav. from St. Petersburg* xi. 162 There appeared two troops of Tartars, clothed in coats of tiger-skins. **1934** M. MITCHELL *Warning to Wantons* x. 324 They were like two big game-hunters whose elaborate tiger-trap has netted..a domestic cat! **1980** N. FREELING *Castang's City* viii. 47 She was extremely sharp. One kept falling..into tiger traps full of pointed bamboo stakes. One got little out of her.

13. a. tiger barb, any of several brightly coloured freshwater fishes of the genus *Barbus*, esp. *B. tetrazona*; **tiger maple** *N. Amer.*, a kind of maple-wood with strongly contrasting light and dark lines in the grain; **Tiger Milk,** a name given to Yugoslavian dessert wine made from over-ripe grapes; **tiger-nut:** also eaten locally as a sweetmeat by children; (later examples); **tiger prawn** *Austral.*, a large prawn marked with dark bands, *Penæus esculentus*; **tiger salamander:** delete *l* from *Amblystoma*; (examples); **tiger-snake,** (*a*) for *Hoplocephalus curtus* substitute: of the elapid genus *Notechis*, esp. *N. scutatus*; (earlier and later examples); (*b*) a slightly venomous southern African colubrid snake of the genus *Telescopus*, esp. *T. semiannulatus*; **tiger-stripe(d)** = *TIGER CAT d; **tiger suit,** a striped combat uniform worn as camouflage in jungle warfare; **tiger-ware,** substitute for def.: sixteenth- or seventeenth-century German stoneware with a mottled brown glaze, or English stoneware made in imitation of this; (examples).

1951 R. DUTTA *Right Way to keep Pet Fish* xviii. 155/2 Tiger barbs. **1962** *Listener* 22 Nov. 852/2, I brought home a tiger barb, round and flat with bold orange and black stripes. **1976** *Norwich Mercury* 19 Nov. 4/8 (Advt.), This week's Fish Centre offers: Neons..Silvertips..Tiger-barbs. [**1952** J. DOWNS *Amer. Furnit.* p. xxxii, [In] Queen Anne maple furniture..the curly figure is produced by fibers which develop spirally, without any known reason, giving a tiger-stripe pattern much prized by collectors.] **1961** WEBSTER, Tiger maple. **1967** *Canad. Antiques Collector* Apr. 4/1 (Advt.), Canadian Tiger maple desk,..circa 1830. **1978** *Times* 13 Mar. 20/4 Another American Chippendale piece was a tiger maple desk and bookcase. **1961** *Guardian* 21 Nov. 16/5 Yugoslavia is now exporting..'Tiger Milk',..an excellent dessert wine. **1977** T. HEALD *Just Desserts* vii. 172 Not just claret..but ..Tigermilk (or Ranina Radgona Spatlese). **1927** W. E. COLLINSON *Contemp. Eng.* 18 Bull's eyes.., acid drops, fondants..are still in demand, though the popularity of monkey-nuts and tiger-nuts has somewhat waned. **1957** J. KIRKUP *Only Child* ix. 122 We knew..the illicit joy of spending our Sunday school collection money on 'tiger-nuts' and coconut ice. **1972** *Country Life* 30 Nov. 1481/3 The sort of boy who would..find such delight in munching tiger nuts. **1893** J. D. OGILBY *Edible Fishes & Crustaceans N.S.W.* 203 This is the 'Tiger Prawn' of the Sydney fishermen. **1952** W. J. DAKIN *Austral. Seashores* xv. 176 The tiger-prawn is a large northern species that.. has dark vertical bands on its body. **1978** O. WHITE *Silent Reach* vi. 72 It could be arranged..for a marine biologist..to complete his thesis on the breeding habits of..the tiger prawn. **1926** J. K. STRECKER in J. F. Dobie *Rainbow in Morning* (1965) 63 In the plains region of Western Texas, the large tiger salamander is a common animal. **1966** R. C. STEBBINS *Field Guide Western Reptiles & Amphibians* 33 Tiger salamander... A large stocky salamander with small eyes. **1869** Tiger-snake [see *brown-banded snake* s.v. *BROWN *a.* 7]. **1910** F. W. FITZSIMONS *Snakes S. Afr.* iii. 54 Tiger Snake... Average length 2 feet to 2 feet 6 inches. **1941** K. TENNANT *Battlers* xviii. 193 The driver of the car..very efficiently despatched a large tiger snake. **1947** J. STEVENSON-HAMILTON *Wild Life S. Afr.* xxxvi. 330 The tiger snake..is a yellowish snake spotted with brown. **1966** *Southerly* XXVI. 109 A fisherman had been bitten by a tigersnake there and had died. **1974** *Stand. Encycl. S. Afr.* X. 504/1 Tiger-snake..is conspicuously marked throughout its length with alternate black and yellow to reddish brown cross-bands. **1977** *Time* 31 Oct. 49/1 His tabby—a tiger-stripe he calls Dr. Carleton P. Forbes—has amassed $3,000 worth of 'cat toys' by filching checks from Steve's mailbox. **1981** P. MALLORY *Killing Matter* ii. 23 The cat.. was a big grey tiger-stripe. **1965** F. MANOLSON *C is for Cat* 187 A striped cat (even if it's the result of the mating of a Tiger striped with a Tabby striped) is either one or the other. **1970** A. MARIN *Rise with Wind* xx. 241 The soldier was dressed in a tiger suit. **1977** M. HERR *Dispatches* (1978) 5 [He] took his pills by the fistful, downs from the left pocket of his tiger suit and ups from the right. **1874** C. SCHREIBER *Jrnl.* (1911) I. 325 A grand old cruche of Tiger Ware, with Royal Arms of England, and date 1604. **1928** *Daily Express* 5 June 4 There are few [objects] which exercise a stronger fascination over collectors than old stone wine jugs known as tiger-ware. High prices—up to £1,500—have been paid for these 'stone pottes garnished with sylver'. **1983** *Country Life* 1 Dec. (Suppl.) 85/1 A rare Elizabeth I Norwich Tigerware jug.

b. Tiger's Milk = *Tiger Milk*, sense 13 a above.

1959 W. JAMES *Word-bk. Wine* 155 *Ranina*, the 'Tiger's Milk' wine of Radgona, in Yugoslavia, a sweet and strong dessert wine made from late-gathered grapes. **1965** O. A. MENDELSOHN *Dict. Drink & Drinking* 277 *Ranina*, Yugoslavian (Radgona) dessert wine. Syn. 'Tiger's Milk'.

tiger, *v.* Restrict *nonce-wd.* to sense in Dict. and add: **2.** *trans.* To mark like a tiger with lines or streaks of contrasting colour.

1930 R. CAMPBELL *Adamastor* 50 Striped with the fiery colours of the sky, Tigered with war-paint..The green waves charged the sunrise. **1934** —— *Broken Record* iii. 74 She [*sc.* a dog] was tigered with wounds from head to tail. **1960** T. HUGHES *Lupercal* 56 Pike, three inches long, perfect Pike in all parts, green tigering the gold.

Hence **ti·gered** *ppl. a.*, striped or broken into stripes; **ti·gering** *vbl. sb.*, a striated condition (see quot. 1961).

1961 R. D. BAKER *Essent. Path.* xiv. 344 The yellowness of the heart muscle may be diffuse or concentrated in narrow stripes forming a peculiar and distinctive pattern especially along the papillary muscles and the inside of the ventricles... This striated appearance has suggested the descriptive designation of 'tigering' or 'thrush breast'. **1969** *Burpee Catal.* 50/2 *Calceolaria*... Many [flowers] are attractively tigered, blotched, spotted and laced in most unique patterns. **1980** J. O'FAOLAIN *No Country for Young Men* ix. 197 Tigered light which fell slantwise through a Venetian blind.

tiger-cat. Add: **a.** Also *fig.*

1863 M. BRADDON *Aurora Floyd* II. v. 112, I should get nothing—but my revenge upon a tiger-cat. **1959** *Times* 7 Jan. 13/5 Whether as a tiger-cat, a hard-headed business woman..her command of the character was superb. **1979** P. ALEXANDER *Show me a Hero* xx. 208 If she's a trained resistance girl she'll be a tiger-cat.

d. = *tabby cat* s.v. TABBY *a.* 2, esp. a tabby cat with vertical stripes in its markings.

1903 F. SIMPSON *Bk. of Cat* xix. 216/1 The term 'tiger cat' is, I believe, often used in America, and it well describes the true type of a brown tabby. **1915** *Century Mag.* Sept. 673/2 She has..a nice purry tiger cat asleep on a braided rug. **1939** I. M. MELLEN *Pract. Cat Bk.* i. 4 The striped tabby or tiger cat..is the most ancient type of cat known to science. **1969** R. LOWELL *Notebk. 1967–68* 52 A first tiger cat stationed on the record-player spies on a second.

tiggy (ti·gi). [Perh. rel. to dial. *tig* little pig (*Eng. Dial. Dict.*)] = HEDGEHOG 1.

[**1905** B. POTTER *Tale Mrs. Tiggy-winkle* 85 Mrs. Tiggy-winkle was nothing but a Hedgehog!] **1938** T. H. WHITE *Sword in Stone* xxi. 303 Us be'nt no common tiggy Mëaster, for to be munched and mumbled.

tight, *a.* (*adv.*) Add: **A.** *adj.* **2. d.** *spec.* Uncommunicative; secret; *Oil Industry*, applied to a well about which little information is released.

[**1661**: in Dict.] **1949** *Amer. Speech* XXIV. 34 If information about the *venture* is withheld from the public, then it becomes a *tight well*. **1966** *Natural Resources Jrnl.* (Univ. New Mexico) VI. 55 If the draining well is what is commonly known in the industry as a 'tight hole', the information concerning its performance is probably more closely guarded than most national defense secrets. **1976** M. MACHLIN *Pipeline* ii. 32 'Who knows about this [*sc.* an oil-strike]?' 'Nobody but me and a couple of guys here on the platform know for sure... Communication is lousy here, but rumor travels faster than radio waves.' 'Okay. Shut it off..and see if you can keep it as tight a hole as possible.' **1977** B. FREEMANTLE *Charlie Muffin* v. 59 The British..[have] gone completely silent... The British Embassy is tighter than the Kremlin itself.

5. Also in U.S. fig. use, on terms of close friendship, intimate. Cf. THICK *a.* (*sb.*) 10. *slang.*

1956 B. HOLIDAY *Lady sings Blues* (1973) ii. 23 Blue.. had me busted... He and Bub were real tight with the cops. **1971** *Current Slang* (Univ. S. Dakota) VI. 10 *Tight*, very much in love; very friendly. 'John and Mary were really tight for awhile but they seem to have drifted apart.' **1977** *Rolling Stone* 5 May 55/1, I was very tight with him for a long time.

6. c. Of an organization or group: strict, disciplined, well co-ordinated; *spec.* of a pop group or an individual member of it.

1968 L. DEIGHTON *Only when I Larf* vi. 80, I ran a tight unit, and if that meant repeating my lecture every week, then I'd do that. **1971** *Melody Maker* 9 Oct. 21/3 Keef can be proud of his [jazz-rock] band... It's well rehearsed, tight and above all fun. **1977** *Ibid.* 26 Mar. 46/6 (Advt.), Wanted. Good tight drummer for funky group. **1980** MOTSON & ROWLINSON *European Cup 1955–80* ix. 190 This tight triumvirate, Smith in the boardroom, Robinson at the administrative helm, and Paisley on the training ground, headed an Anfield staff which worked as efficiently..as the team.

7. (Earlier examples.)

1830 [implied at *TIGHTISH *a.* 3]. **1840** in *Amer. Speech* (1951) XXVI. 184 After supper I got tight, sick with oysters, and slept.

8. b. Of ground: allowing (vehicles) little room for manœuvre. Of a turn, curve, etc.: having a short radius.

1937 *Sun* (Baltimore) 20 Apr. 4/2 He expressed a hope the airport work would be completed as rapidly as possible, pointing out that Logan Field was 'rather tight' for large transports. **1947** A. C. DOUGLAS *Gliding & Advanced Soaring* i. 24 He based this opinion on the belief..that they [*sc.* contemporary airplanes] could not be turned in tight circles like the birds. **1958** *Times* 19 Feb. 5/4 She [*sc.* an aircraft] started to turn to starboard, and it seemed clear that the turn became tighter and tighter. **1969** *Times* 23 May 1/3 The L.M. was due to spend about an hour in a tight orbit approaching within eight nautical miles of the surface. **1979** *Beautiful Brit. Columbia* Fall 19/1 The highway narrows down to one lane which clings in tight curves around a sheer mountainside.

c. Applied to persons: tough, hard, unyielding; also, aggressive, 'stroppy'. *U.S. dial.* or *slang.*

1928 R. FISHER *Walls of Jericho* 306 *Tight*, tough; redoubtable; hard. **1950** PATTERSON & CONRAD *Scottsboro Boy* I. iii. 30 'You'll get it [*sc.* a bath] Saturday,' he said. Saturday came and he put me off... I got tight with him. 'I got to have a bath!' *Ibid.* 31, I was a tight guy who would not show people tears, but I felt the water behind my lids. *Ibid.* II. vii. 129 There were guys there [*sc.* in a prison], they made reputations for themselves as tight guys and killers just from defending themselves against the insane. **1960** L. BUCKLEY *Hiporama of Classics* 16 He was a hard, tight, tough Cat.

10. b. (Earlier example.)

1805 LEWIS & CLARK *Orig. Jrnls. Lewis & Clark Exped.* (1904) III. 278 They are tite Deelers, value Blu and white beeds very highly, and sell their roots also highly.

c. Also of a person: in financial straits, hard up. *dial.* or *slang.*

1859 HOTTEN *Dict. Slang* 109 *Tight*,..hard up, short of cash. **1864** J. S. LE FANU *Uncle Silas* II. xvi. 247 It is a hard case, Miss, a lad o' spirit should be kep so tight. I havn't a shilling. **1892** 'T. COBBLEIGH' *Gentleman Upcott's Daughter* ix. 173 Any man might find himself tight—temporarily.

d. *Journalism.* (See quot. 1970.) Hence also of (a day of) restricted newspaper space.

1927 *Amer. Speech* II. 241/2 If advertising crowds out news, the paper is said to be 'tight'; if advertising is scant, the paper is 'wide open'. **1927** *New Republic* 12 Oct. 202/1 Possibly space was 'tight' that day, and the newspapers didn't have room for this minor angle of the story. **1928** *Amer. Speech* IV. 135 The 'desk' must know whether 'room' is 'tight', 'fair', 'good' or 'wide open'. If news is 'heavy' on a 'tight day' and is permitted to 'run' in length practically as written, 'oversets'..may result. **1970** R. K. KENT *Lang. Journalism* 133 *Tight*. 1. designating a newspaper that has little room for news because there is a great deal of advertising: opposite of *open*. 2. designating a newspaper on a day when there are a great many newsworthy events to record, and hardly enough space to cover them all.

11. a. Also, of a group or formation: having the individual members positioned close together. Freq. in *Sport*; also *transf.* (esp. in *Cricket*), that allows the opposition little chance to score, etc.: *tight bowling, fielding*, etc.

1942 *R.A.F. Jrnl.* 13 June 22 They lived in dread of our fighters, and normally kept a tight formation. **1961**

F. C. Avis *Sportsman's Gloss.* 138/2 *Tight field*, the fieldsmen when drawn closely round the wicket, so preventing the easy scoring of runs. **1961** *Times* 12 May 4/1 Surrey's bid for quick runs..was foiled by tight bowling. **1965** *Daily Express* 13 Aug. 15/5 *Tight position*, an area of the field in which there are a large number of players, both attacking and defending. **1968** I. Ure *Ure's Truly* xvii. 116 Let's have expressions such as 'a steady defence' rather than a side being described as 'tight at the back'. **1976** *Milton Keynes Express* 11 June 41/5 Farnham Royal found it difficult to score against the tight Wolverton bowling. **1977** *Arab Times* 13 Dec. 9/6 Tight fielding by the Airlines prevented easy scoring and the FSC batsmen had to rely on quick singles and doubles.

b. Also in general, of literary, artistic, or intellectual work: kept within strict limits; pared to essentials; disciplined, taut, not loose or diffuse.

1958 C. A. Larson *Who: Sixty Yrs. Amer. Eminence* 75 Quaint little items and details were often inserted in these early biographical sketches which would scarcely survive the tight editing of a modern Marquis editor. **1962** [see *pilot *sb.* 1 f]. **1979** *Sci. Amer.* Aug. 24/1 The author..seeks the answer in this small book of tight argument.

e. Of a schedule or timetable: packed with engagements, leaving little free time. Also applied to a space of time which is limited or restricted.

1959 J. Pope-Hennessy *Queen Mary* III. ii. 386 Princess May concentrated on seeing as many of the wonders and beauties of the spacious old Imperial city as she could crowd into four days and a tight social schedule. **1968** P. G. Hollowell *Lorry Driver* ii. 31 The older drivers are constantly aware that schedules are getting tighter. **1971** J. Sangster *Your Friendly Neighbourhood Death Pedlar* vii. 187 It was unlikely that anything would happen that night, and the following morning was going to be awfully tight for time. **1972** M. Crichton *Terminal Man* I. v. 42 'I can't see her to-day,' Morris said, 'and to-morrow is tight.' **1976** *New Yorker* 1 Mar. 30/3 'How about seven at O'Hoolihan's? I'm going there with Pat and Betsy.' 'Seven's a little tight.' **1981** P. Harcourt *Turn of Traitors* ix. 82 Time's going to be tight, so take my car.

13. a. Delete *rare* and add later examples.

1939 *Daily Tel.* 18 Dec. 11/1 They were better served by their forwards in the tight. **1979** *Times* 12 Dec. 9/1 They outscrummaged their opponents in the tight.

b. An awkward situation, predicament, 'tight corner' (Tight *a.* 9). Usu. in phr. *in a tight*; occas. const. *for*. *U.S. dial.* or *colloq.*

1896 in *Dialect Notes* (1916) IV. 348 *Tight*, n. (From *tight place.*) A difficult or precarious position. **1902** W. N. Harben *Abner Daniel* xxi. 182 It would tempt five men out of ten if they were inclined to go wrong, and were in a tight. **1930** W. Faulkner *As I lay Dying* 29, I tell him again I will help him out if he gets into a tight, with her sick and all. **1938** M. K. Rawlings *Yearling* xv. 177 Jody's in a tight for a name for the new Baxter. **1950** Patterson & Conrad *Scottsboro Boy* II. xi. 175 'You scared that man almost to death.' 'I was in a tight jam then, Warden. I was trying to get out of a tight.' **1979** G. Swarthout *Skeletons* 18 Pat Garrett..had said of him in public: 'I would rather have Wood with me in a tight than any man I know.'

B. *adv.* **1.** Delete 'Now *dial.* and *U.S.*' Now chiefly in colloq. phr. (*good night*) *sleep tight*, a conventional (rhyming) formula used when parting for the night or at bedtime. Also in slang phr. *blow me tight*: see *Blow *v.*[1] 29.

1933 E. O'Neill *Ah, Wilderness!* III. ii. 101 Good night, Son. Sleep tight. **1957** [see *nighty-night *int.*]. **1960** D. Lessing *In Pursuit of English* iii. 99 When we left him, she patted his shoulder with triumphant patronage, and said: 'Sleep tight. And keep your dreams clean.' **1976** 'R. Boyle' *Cry Rape* xxi. 94 Goodnight, Anne. Sleep tight.

2. b. (Earlier example of sense 'to maintain one's position'.)

1890 G. B. Shaw in *Star* 27 Nov. 2/7 I, therefore, again urge Mr Parnell to 'sit tight'.

4. *as tight as* ( ): as quickly or rapidly as ( ). Cf. Tite *adv.* *U.S. dial.*

1833 S. Smith *Life & Writings J. Downing* lix. 200 The President shook hands with all his might an hour or two until he couldn't hardly stand it... I..stood behind him and reached my arm round under his, and shook for him for about a half an hour as tight as I could spring. **1867** W. L. Goss *Soldier's Story of his Captivity* 185 Captain Sherman..was making for Macon as 'tight as he can come'. **1884** 'Mark Twain' *Huck. Finn* xix. 180 A couple of men were tearen up the path as tight as they could foot it.

5. Close *up to, after*, or *on*. *dial.* or *colloq.*

1886 F. T. Elworthy *W. Somerset Word-bk.* 756 The bitch was tight arter'n. **1901** *Century Mag.* May 123/1 They was tight up t'me all the way. **1919** J. C. Snaith *Love Lane* xxx. 160 He lived to be tight on ninety.

C. 2. *tight-fitting* (earlier example), *-packed* (examples).

1846 E. A. Poe in *Godey's Lady's Bk.* Nov. 216/1 He had on a tight-fitting parti-striped dress. **1918** G. Frankau *One of Them* xxix. 223 Tight-packed as, face to tail and tail to face, Bristle in Watson's tins the silvery 'Skippers'. **1950** Partridge *Slang To-day & Yesterday* (ed. 3) III. iii. 257 The ten-page, tight-packed chapter entitled 'War Words' in Collinson's Contemporary English.

3. tight back *Bookbinding*, a book cover which is stuck directly on to the spine; cf. *fast back, fastback* s.v. *Fast *a.* 11; **tight end** *N. Amer. Football*, an offensive end (*End *sb.* 3 g) who lines up close to the tackle; the position occupied by this player; **tight-fisted** *a.*: hence **tight-fistedness; tight head** *Rugby Football*, (the position of) the prop forward supporting the hooker on the opposite side of the scrum from the loose head; *to win a tight head* = *to win the ball against the head* (see *Head *sb.* 26 c); **tight junction** *Cytology*, a specialized connection of two adjacent animal cell membranes such that the space usually lying between them is absent.

1913 *Funk's Stand. Dict.* II. 2518/1 *Tight back* (Bookbinding), a back that clings to the signatures or to the paster attached to them: distinguished from *loose back* or *spring back*. **1929** A. J. Vaughan *Mod. Bookbinding* I. 2 (*caption*) A limp paper book bound with a tight back. Effect of a tight back binding upon stiff paper. **1957** E. A. Clough *Bookbinding for Librarians* vi. 60 Because the tight back bends with the spine of the book, there is a tendency for the tooling on the spine to crack. **1963** Huff & Smith *Defensive Football* vi. 72 When playing the tight end head to head, the linebacker must be aware [etc.]. **1972** J. Mosedale *Football* ii. 29 With Fears spread out on one side and Shaw in close, the 'three end offense' was born. Today the positions are called split end, tight end and flanker. **1978** J. Irving *World according to Garp* viii. 162 A standout tight end for the Philadelphia Eagles. **1975** *Church Times* 25 Apr. 2/3 Let it be seen..that we have asked the very necessary questions about the liberality or tight-fistedness of the [European] Community's policy on trade with the under-developed countries. **1959** *N.Z. Listener* 28 Aug. 7 You can't afford to give tight heads in your own 25 when you've got fast backs like that against you. **1960** V. Jenkins *Lions down Under* xiii. 170 Dawson won six tight-heads to three in the scrums. **1969** *Advanced Coaching* (Rugby Football Union) 73 On the tight head it may still be preferable to hook with the nearside foot, *but* with the body facing the *loose* head side so as to hook the ball with the *inside*.. part of the foot. **1978** *Rugby World* Apr. 17/1 There seems nothing to stop Graham Price reigning for many years to come as the world's outstanding tight-head prop. **1961** *Jrnl. Exper. Med.* CXIV. 706 The normal slits as well as the tight junctions have structural features reminiscent of usual epithelial desmosomes. **1982** *Nature* 1 Apr. 464/1 Our evidence, which is based on direct rapid freezing of newly formed tight junctions between rat prostate epithelial cells, indicates that individual tight junction strands are pairs of inverted cylindrical micelles sandwiched between linear fusions of the external membrane leaflets of adjacent cells.

ti·ght-ass, *sb.* (and *a*). *slang* (orig. and chiefly *U.S.*). Also **tight-arse.** [Back-formation from next.] An inhibited or strait-laced person; occas. a stingy person, a skinflint. Freq. *attrib.* passing into *adj.* = next; occas. applied (*lit.*) to clothes: fitting tightly around the buttocks.

1969 P. Roth *Portnoy's Complaint* 79 A really constrained and tight-ass human being. **1970** J. G. Vermandel *Dine with Devil* iii. 11 A well-muscled, virile-looking type with a neat little beard, who favors tight-ass pants and rather beautiful, flowing shirts. **1972** 'E. McBain' *Sadie when she Died* x. 105 'Don't be such a tight-ass,' the girl said. 'I'm thirsty as hell here.' **1972** *Southerly* XXXII. 103 Jenny was very friendly but very tightarse inhibited headinnaness. **1981** M. Gordon *Company of Women* II. iv. 190 My three o'clock class was an incredible bummer. Bunch of tight asses. Tight-ass kids. **1982** J. Sherwood *Shot in Arm* x. 96 As though any policeman in his senses would pocket cash..with a virgin-faced tight-arse like Verney looking on.

ti·ght-assed, *a. slang.* Also **tight-arsed.** [f. Tight *a.* + Ass, vulg. and dial. spelling of Arse *sb.* + -ed[2]: see prec.] **a.** Of a woman: (see quot. 1903). **b.** Unwilling to relax or enjoy oneself, full of inhibitions or constraints; occas. stingy, mean.

1903 Farmer & Henley *Slang* VII. 126/1 *Tight-arsed*, chaste; close-legged. **1961** Partridge *Dict. Slang* 885/2 *Tight-arsed*, stingy. **1967** J. Orton *Diary* 28 July in J. Lahr *Prick up your Ears* (1978) 16, I hate this tight-assed civilization. **1974** D. Sears *Lark in Clear Air* iv. 50 Rough quarterings of pine that even the tight-assed mill owners considered too lean to..ship to Toronto. **1976** *Listener* 15 July 54/4 Me and Gambaccini would like tight-assed British radio to relax a bit. **1981** T. Heald *Murder at Moose Jaw* ix. 112 I'd sooner have an entertaining shit than a tight-arsed saint.

tighten, *v.* Add: **2.** Also *intr.* for *pass.* Freq. const. *up*, esp. in *fig.* use.

1933 P. Godfrey *Back-Stage* vi. 86 As the day of the dress rehearsal draws near the acting tightens up. **1947** *Milwaukee Jrnl.* 25 Apr. 2 His stomach tightened up on him. **1959** *Listener* 2 July 24/3 We should alter the tax laws to tighten up on tax-dodging. **1973** *Daily Tel.* 9 Feb. 2/8 Yellow line no-waiting regulations are to tighten up in London.

tightish, *a.* Add: **3.** Somewhat drunk. Cf. Tight *a.* 7. *colloq.*

1830 H. Lee *Mem. of Manager* I. iii. 110 'I think they be getting on pretty tightish!' 'What do you mean, getting drunk!'

ti·ght-li:pped, *a.* [f. Tight *a.* + Lipped *ppl. a.*] Having the lips firmly closed, esp. as a sign of determined suppression of emotion; also *transf.* and *fig.* Also, determinedly reticent or uncommunicative.

1876 [in Dict. s.v. Tight *a.* C.1]. **1918** H. G. Wells *Joan & Peter* iii. 62 Her pride was white and tight-lipped. **1936** P. Fleming *News from Tartary* v. ii. 194 This, I know, is my cue for tight-lipped heroics. **1952** [see *instalment[2] 3]. **1958** *Observer* 15 June 15/2 Joan Mitchell's rather beautiful painting 'Hudson River Day Line' (which has a sensitive, tight-lipped, almost Slade School quality). **1970** J. Sangster *Touchfeather, Too* ii. 32 The Russians, notoriously tight-lipped normally, had been approached through tortuous channels. **1979** A. Price *Tomorrow's Ghost* iii. 37 She smiled her careful tight-lipped smile. **1981** D. Hopkinson *Edward Penrose Arnold* iv. 40 Here is that melancholy resignation which Matthew Arnold so often..conveys... But his finest poetry..is stoically tight-lipped. **1983** *Times* 2 Apr. 10/2 All parties are keeping tight-lipped. A spokesman for DTR issued a firm 'no comment'.

tightness. Add: **3.** (Earlier example.)

1861 E. Cowell *Diary* 1 Jan. in *Cowells in Amer.* (1934) 234, I congratulated him on his remaining free from 'tightness' after so many calls.

4. (Earlier example.)

1847 *Punch* XIII. 77/1 There is a tightness at present in the Omnibus Market.

5. As an artistic quality: (*a*) crampedness, lack of freedom, constraint; (*b*) sense of control, rigorousness.

1933 *Burlington Mag.* Jan. 22/1 The effort to achieve a difficult and unfamiliar piece of modelling gives the penwork a certain tightness. **1959** *Listener* 26 Mar. 542/1 Lack of balance between voice and accompaniment, acoustic 'tightness', restricted and uneven frequency-range. **1973** *Art Internat.* Mar. 73/2 Erlebacher's tightness makes her poetic allegories more like kitsch.

tight rope, tight-rope. Add: Now freq. as one word. **1.** Also *fig.*

1934 *Essays & Stud.* XIX. 123 He moves with complete security on the tight-rope of serio-comic wit. **1959** *Daily Tel.* 30 Nov. 1 For 35 minutes the Deputy Leader balanced himself on a verbal tightrope which purported to bridge the awesome gap within the party. **1979** *Sci. Amer.* Nov. 126/3 The nocturnal *S. laevistriatus* beetles are on an energy tightrope.

2. *Comb.*, as *tight-rope dancer, dancing, walk, walker, -walking* vbl. sb. and ppl. adj.

1824 *Advt.* (Theatre-Royal, Worcester) in *Henry Bristow Ltd. Catal.* (1973) No. 205, The celebrated Mr. Wilson, the tight rope dancer. **1890** Tight-rope dancer [in Dict.]. **1800** W. Dyott *Diary* July (1907) I. 138 Besides rural sports in the gardens, such as gipsies guying, lofty tumbling and tight-rope dancing. **1890** Tight-rope-dancing [see *billiard-playing* s.v. *billiards 2]. **1952** R. Knox *Hidden Stream* vi. 55 We, in this tight-rope-walk business of trying to live our lives..want more than a metaphysical conviction that God exists. **1869** *Atlantic Monthly* July 83/2 This tight-rope walker was one of the most exemplary domestic little bodies imaginable. **1910** *Encycl. Brit.* IV. 77/1 *Blondin* (1824–1897), French tight-rope walker and acrobat. **1979** R. Jaffe *Class Reunion* (1980) II. xi. 287 When he was drunk he had a slow and precise quality, like a tightrope walker. **1982** C. Castle *Folies Bergère* i. 24 Tightrope walkers, magicians and sleight-of-hand artists..attracted Parisians and tourists. **1958** *Spectator* 30 May 675/1 Admiral Auboyneau, who had been doing some tightrope-walking of his own in the previous weeks, finally came out for the rebels. **1981** *Times Lit. Suppl.* 3 Apr. 368/2 Ours is the age of heartless efficiency and tight-rope-walking virtuosity in music.

tights, *sb. pl.* Add: **a.** (Earlier example.)

1827 M. Wilmot *Let.* 24 May (1935) 260 His [*sc.* a jockey's] shirt-collar was open, so were the knees of his 'tights'.

c. A woman's or girl's one-piece stretchable garment covering the legs and body up to the waist, worn in place of stockings; formerly, an undergarment taking the place of knickers and stockings.

1897 *Sears, Roebuck Catal.* 241/2 Ladies' summer drawers and tights..Ladies' fine jersey ribbed fast black open summer tights,..knee length. **1908** *Ibid.* 962 Wool and fleece lined underwear for children..Union suits, tights and sleeping garments. **1929** R. S. & H. M. Lynd *Middletown* xii. 159 Today flannel underwear is almost as obsolete as the long black equestrian tights, high-necked, long-sleeved nightgowns for women, and the heavily-lined trousers of the working men of a generation ago. **1965** P. O'Donnell *Modesty Blaise* ix. 105 Modesty wore ..a full black skirt, with black stretch tights. **1967, 1970** [see *panty-hose* s.v. *panties 3]. **1977** C. McCullough *Thorn Birds* xviii. 469 A five-guinea pair of tights.

tightwad (təi·t,wǫd), *sb.* (and *a.*). *slang* (orig. and chiefly *U.S.*). Also **tight-wad.** [f. Tight *a.* + Wad *sb.*[1] 2 b.] A miserly person; one who keeps his wad of paper money tightly rolled. Also *attrib.* and (*rarely*) as *adj.* Also *fig.*

[**1900** Ade *More Fables* 30 Henry was undoubtedly the Tightest Wad in the Township.] **1906** S. Ford *Shorty McCabe* ii. 32 Keep these, and found a home for Incurable Tight-Wads. *a* **1911** D. G. Phillips *Susan Lenox* (1917) I. xv. 255 You've forgotten what a lot of tightwads and petty swindlers they are. **1914** *Wells Fargo Messenger* III. 9 (*caption*) Tight-wad Tim. **1934** *Punch* 26 Dec. 715/3 'A spendthrift', countered Chloe, 'makes a much more satisfactory husband than a tight-wad.' **1945** S. Lewis *Cass Timberlane* xviii. 107 Hey, don't be so tight-wad with that hootch. *Ibid.* xxxii. 228 The man said to his wife, 'Our friend here has made a pretty good joke?' She said, 'Come on now—don't be a tightwad—what's his pretty good joke?' **1959** 'A. Gilbert' *Death takes*

Wife xv. 188 He may be a bit of a tightwad. **1971** *Sunday Express* (Johannesburg) 28 Mar. (Comic Suppl.) 1/2 Blondie, I have a great idea to get a raise out of old tightwad Mr. Dithers. **1976** *National Observer* (U.S.) 26 June 10/2 When hard times hit..salesmen put the blame for their dwindling commissions on everybody else: the manufacturers, tightwad consumers [etc.]. **1977** *Sunday Tel.* (Colour Suppl.) 31 July 19/4 Bleeding tightwad! You'd think with all that cash he'd take a taxi.

‖ **tignon** (tī·yɒn). [Louisiana Fr., f. F. *tigne*, dial. var. of standard F. *teigne* moth.] A handkerchief worn as a turban head-dress by Creole women.

1884 *Daily Inter-Ocean* (Chicago) 2 July 1/5 [The women's heads were] adorned with the traditional head handkerchief of the tignon. **1935** M. Morphy *Recipes of All Nations* 664 The old Creole women..with their brightly coloured bandana *tignons* or head-dress. **1961** M. G. Eberhart *Cup, Blade or Gun* i. 3 A..Negro woman, in a dark dress and snowy white apron and *tignon*. **1979** —— *Bayou Road* xix. 187 Liss's tightly wrapped tignon, her dark face.

tigon (tai·gɒn). Also **tiglon, tigron.** [f. Tig(er *sb.* + Li)on *sb.*, etc.: cf. *liger.] The offspring of a tiger and a lioness.

1927 G. Jennison *Nat. Hist. Animals* 57 It should be noted particularly that the markings of the Tigon are not stripes, but rhomboids, almost like the markings on the Clouded Leopard. **1932** *Times Educ. Suppl.* 16 Jan. p. iv/2 The male parent of the 'tigon' was a tiger, the female an Indian lioness. **1938** *Times* 28 May 7/7 The name liger is given to the offspring of a male lion and tigress, the opposite cross being called a tigron. **1947** *Partisan Rev.* XIV. 395 Mr. Gielgud's gravity, his sensitive, melancholy profile, here becomes exquisitely comic—he looks like a tiglon with a heart. **1964** *Sunday Mail Mag.* (Brisbane) 8 Nov. 4/6 For many years the London Zoo possessed a magnificent 'Tigon'—a tiger-lion hybrid. **1972** *Times* 15 Feb. 6/5 A 'tigon' has been born in a Calcutta zoo from cross-breeding a tiger with a lioness. **1976** *Observer* (Colour Suppl.) 5 Sept. 42/1 (*caption*) This animal, one of the world's rarest cats, is a tiglon, a cross between a tiger and a lion. **1981** M. Duffy *Gor Saga* v. 214 'Can you combine the sexual elements from two different species?' 'Like tigers and lions making tigrons you mean?'

Tigray (tigrəi·). Also † **Teegray.** An alternative name for *Tigrinya.

a **1860** W. C. Plowden *Trav. Abyssinia* (1868) i. 10 They call their language Teegray. **1939** [see *Tigrinya]. **1954** Pei & Gaynor *Dict. Linguistics* 217 *Tigray*, an alternative name for *Tigriña*.

Tigre (tigre·), *sb.* and *a.* Also **Tigré.** [Native name.] **A.** *sb.* A Semitic language spoken in northern Ethiopia and adjoining parts of Sudan (distinguished from *Tigrinya, spoken in Tigre itself). **B.** *adj.* Of or pertaining to the province of Tigre in northern Ethiopia. Cf. *Tigrean *sb.* (*a.*).

1878 *Encycl. Brit.* VIII. 612/2 There are at least two modern languages which have sprung from the ancient Geez, distinguished in modern philology by the conventional names of Tigriña and Tigré. **1908** [see *Tigrinya]. **1933** L. Bloomfield *Language* iv. 66 Ethiopian... The present-day languages of this group are Tigre, Tigriña, and Amharic. **1972** *Bk. Thousand Tongues* (rev. ed.) 429/1 Tigré is spoken by about 175,000 Muslims living in northern Eritrea and spreading into Sudan. **1978** *Observer* 29 Jan. 10/7 Tigre nationalism: The Tigre people, who inhabit Northern Ethiopia want to redress the balance of power lost with the defeat of the ancient kingdom of Gondar towards the end of the last century.

Tigrean (tigrē·ăn, -ī·ăn), *sb.* (*a.*). Also † **Tigrian.** [f. *Tigre* (see prec.) + -an; cf. -ian.] A native of the Tigre province in northern Ethiopia. Also *attrib.* or as *adj.* Cf. *Tigre *a.*

1842 Isenberg & Krapf *Jrnl.* 22 Apr. (1843) 500, I must confess that I had conceived a more favourable idea of the hospitality of the Tigrians. **1901** [see Stew *v.*[2] 2 c]. **1960** E. Ullendorff *Ethiopians* iii. 37 A greater measure of non-Semitic ingredients in the Amharic language may accurately reflect a lesser degree of ethnic Semitization among the Amharas than is the case with the Tigreans. **1977** *Daily Tel.* 4 May 1/6 The secessionist Eritreans and Tigreans in the North. **1980** *Observer* 21 Sept. 7/5 Guerrillas of the Tigrean People's Liberation Front.

Tigrinya (tigrī·nya). Also **Tigriña, Tigrine.** [Native name.] A Semitic language spoken in the Tigre province of Ethiopia. Cf. *Tigray.

1878 [see *Tigre]. **1908** T. G. Tucker *Introd. Nat. Hist. Lang.* 172 Along with Amharic (of South-West Abyssinia) go the contaminated dialects Tigre (of the north), Tigrine (of the centre), and Harari (of Harai, east of Gallaland). **1939** L. H. Gray *Foundations of Lang.* 364 Ethiopic..still serves as a learned language, though its true linguistic successor is Tigriña or Tigray, which is written by few except officials of the Italian colony of Eritrea. **1955** F. R. Palmer in E. P. Hamp et al. *Readings in Linguistics II* (1966) 341 The paradigms that may be set up for the nominals in Tigrinya..consist of two members. **1976** D. Topolski *Muzungu* iii. 35 She smacked my hand sharply and said something loudly in Tigrinya.

tigron, var. *tigon.

‖ **tika** (tī·kă). Also **tikka.** [Hindi *ṭikā, ṭikkā*: cf. *tilak.] Among Hindus, a mark on the forehead indicating caste, status, sectarian affiliation, etc., or worn simply as an ornament. Also *attrib.*, as *tika mark*, etc.

1884 in J. Stormonth *Dict. Eng. Lang.* 1053/2. **1960** Z. Eglar *Punjabi Village in Pakistan* xi. 114 A *tika* is a gold ornament worn on the forehead. **1963** S. S. Ikramullah *Purdah to Parliament* xvi. 137 The use of *tikka* (a red spot on the forehead, originally a caste-mark among Hindus but now used more or less for its decorative effect). **1965** P. Robinson *Pakistani Agent* iii. 46 On her forehead was the red *tika* dot of marriage. **1973** *Australian Women's Weekly* 27 June 75/4 This colorful tika adds to the Indian woman's adornment. **1979** P. Matthiessen *Snow Leopard* i. 22 The vermilion tikka dot on the women's foreheads. **1980** *Old Lady* June 76/3 We were invited to witness the *tika* ceremony... Granny.. had given the first *tika* mark to her eldest son, Naina Singh.

tiki (ti·ki). Also 8 **tigi.** Pl. **tiki, tikis.** [a. Eastern Polynesian *tiki* image; cf. *hei-tiki.] A large wooden image of Tiki, the creator and first created being of the Maoris and Polynesians, or of an ancestor; also, a small, usu. greenstone, image of the same, worn as a charm or ornament. Also *attrib.*

1777 D. Samwell *Jrnl.* 24 Feb. in Cook *Jrnls.* (1967) III. ii. 1001 They [*sc.* the Maoris] had brought many Articles of Trade such as Ahoos, green Images called Tigis, Stone Adzes &c. **1840** J. S. Polack *Manners & Customs New Zealanders* II. xxi. 178 Around the neck, similar kinds of ornaments are worn, but the principal favourite is the *Tiki*. **1889** Hocken *Catal. N.Z. Exhib.* 81 (Morris), Wooden Tikis, some of immense size, usually represented the ancestors. **1921** *Outward Bound* June 46/2 The beautiful and valuable greenstone from which the Maoris fashion all their..tikis. **1955** W. J. Phillipps *Maori Carving Illustrated* 12 The body is U shaped, humanised below after the manner of a Maori tiki. **1963** *Times* 26 Feb. 8/5 Gas-flared tiki torches. **1974** T. Heyerdahl *Fatu-Hiva* iii. 123 Some large wooden images, *tiki*, barred the entrances. **1975** *Times* 17 Mar. 1/6 (Advt.), By the flickering light of a Tiki lamp, you'll delight in sampling exotic dishes. **1977** *Chicago Tribune* 2 Oct. iv. 13/2 Papeete, the main town of Tahiti, generally isn't considered much of a shopping port, but it can bring surprises. Carved wooden, bone, and shell tikis and other jewelry; [etc.].

tikka[1], var. Ticca.

1888 Kipling *Soldiers Three* (1889) 10 That *tikka*..has been *owin'* an' *fere-owin'* all over the bloomin' *maidan*. **1911** R. E. Vernede *An Ignorant in India* i. 5 He had collected enough porters to get it into a tikka ghari. **1928** *Blackw. Mag.* Apr. 498/1 Tikka-gharris, bullock-carts, hand-trucks, and coolies combined to raise..an excruciating din. **1978** 'M. M. Kaye' *Far Pavilions* ix. 151 The drivers of phaetons and *tikka-gharis*, tongas and *ekkas*.

tikka[2] (ti·kă). [a. Hindi *ṭikkā*.] In Indian and Pakistani cookery, (a dish of) small pieces of meat or vegetable marinaded in spices and cooked on a skewer. Freq. with qualifying word indicating the type of meat, etc. used. Also *attrib.*

1955 *Times* 28 May 5/1 Enormous dishes of *tikka kabab*—pieces of lamb deliciously roasted on skewers. **1960** *Dawn* 17 Apr. 12/5 President Nasser relished 'kabab' and 'tikka' dishes. **1961** *Guardian* 16 Feb. 12/4 You will hear all the gossip..over chicken tikka at Farooq's. **1980** J. Passmore *Indian Cookery* 110 A whole, smallish bird will take a maximum of 30 minutes, while smaller 'Tikkas' (pieces) only a few minutes. **1982** L. Cody *Bad Company* xxx. 200 She set out to find a chicken tikka and some live music.

tikka, var. *tika.

Tikopian (tikōu·piăn), *sb.* and *a.* Also 9 **Tucopean.** [f. *Tikopia* (see below) + -an.] **A.** *sb.* A native or inhabitant of Tikopia, one of the Solomon Islands. **B.** *adj.* Of or pertaining to Tikopia.

1832 A. Earle *Narr. Res. N.Z.* 207 Savages are not much affected by music; but these two Tucopeans were excited to a most extraordinary degree. **1874** C. M. Yonge *Life J. C. Patteson* II. xii. 456 Three Tikopian giants had made a visit at Mota. **1951** W. J. Goode *Relig. among Primitives* 234 The Tikopian emphasis is clearly on the culture-hero.

'til (til), var. of Till *prep.*, *conj.* or short for Until *prep.* and *conj.*

1939 P. G. Perrin *Index to Eng.* 606 Till, until, (*'til*), these three words are not distinguishable in meaning. Since *'til* in speech sounds the same as *till* and looks slightly odd on paper, it may well be abandoned. **1956** H. Kurnitz *Invasion of Privacy* iii. 27 You sit on your tail 'til they come up with another story. **1978** M. Duffy *Housespy* v. 126, I shall have to tell the P.M. but not 'til I'm sure.

tilak (ti·læk). Also **tilaka, tilka.** [a. Hindi *tilak*, Skr. *tilaka*, f. Skr. *tila* sesamum.] = *tika.

1879 E. Arnold *Light of Asia* ii. 72 Slender hands and feet new-stained With crimson, and the tilka-spots stamped bright. **1895** *Funk's Stand. Dict.*, Tilak. **1961** *Spectator* 3 Mar. 281 The traditional welcome with music and *tilak* (a red mark placed in blessing on the honoured guest's forehead). **1969** 'R. Farre' *Beckoning Land* xiii. 151 On his forehead was a tilak mark showing that he was a follower of Shiva. **1974** *Encycl. Brit. Micropædia* IX. 1009/1 Among Śaivas (followers of Lord Śiva), the *tilaka* usually takes the form of three horizontal parallel lines across the forehead, with or without a red dot.

tilapia (tilē·piă). [mod.L. (A. Smith: see quot. 1849), perh. f. Gr. τίλων, a fish name used by Aristotle + ἄπιος distant.] A freshwater fish of the genus of this name, belonging to the family Cichlidæ, native to Africa but introduced elsewhere as a food fish or an aquarium species.

1849 A. Smith *Illustr. Zool. S. Afr.: Pisces* 5 The *fossæ* or caverns connected with the gills are very indistinct, yet such traces of them exist as appears to warrant our regarding *Tilapia* as a fish of an aberrant form. **1901** *Trans. Zool. Soc.* XV. 18 In these *Tilapiæ*..the function of protecting the eggs devolves on the male sex. **1932** *Discovery* Feb. 43 (*caption*) The photograph shows a cat-fish with a *Tilapia* from its stomach. **1954** V. Bartlett *Rep. from Malaya* iii. 56 A fish imported from Egypt, the tilapia,..hatches its eggs in its mouth and provides a refuge there for its young in moments of danger. **1965** A. J. McClane *Standard Fishing Encycl.* 947/2 Tilapias have been experimentally bred in the southern United States (Alabama and Florida) where they have been stocked and caught in public waters. **1971** *Daily Tel.* 13 May 13/5 Families [in Uganda] are widely encouraged to cultivate their own stocks of tilapia, a fat, flat-bodied fish common throughout Africa.

tilasite (tī·lăsəit). *Min.* [ad. Sw. *tilasit* (H. Sjögren 1895, in *Geol. Föreningens i Stockholm Förhandlingar* XVII. 291), f. the name of D. *Tilas* (1712–72), Swedish mining engineer: see -ite[1].] A fluor-arsenate of calcium and magnesium, $CaMg(AsO_4)F$, that is isostructural with sphene and occurs as translucent monoclinic crystals that are colourless, green, or greyish.

1897 *Jrnl. Chem. Soc.* LXXII. ii. 325 Tilasite or fluor-adelite from Långban... Irregular grains of this new mineral are found with hausmannite, berzeliite and calcite in a grey limestone. **1968** [see *isokite]. **1979** *Mineral. Abstr.* XXX. 293/1 Tilasite crystals $< 2{\cdot}5$ mm across have been found with friedelite and baryte at the Sterling Hill mine, Ogdensburg, Sussex County, New Jersey.

tilde. Add: **1. a.** Also, the mark placed in Portuguese above the letters *a* and *o* to indicate nasalization. Used simularly in systems of phonetic transcription.

1915 G. Noël-Armfield *General Phonetics* xvi. 88 The phonetic symbol for nasalised vowels is [˜] (the Spanish *tilde*) placed over the vowel symbol. **1958** J. L. Taylor *Portuguese-Eng. Dict.* (1959) p. x/2 If a word bears a tilde..stress the syllable so marked. **1974** *Encycl. Brit. Micropædia* VIII. 147/2 Typical of the Portuguese sound system is the use of nasal vowels, indicated in the orthography by *m* or *n* following the vowel..or by the use of a tilde..over the vowel.

b. *Palæography* and *Early Printing.* The diacritic mark ~ placed above a letter to indicate contraction of a following *n* or *m*.

1959 *N. & Q.* Feb. 77/2 From c. 1560 the tilde was used in printed English dramatic texts only over the vowels *a*, *e*, *o*, and *u*. **1975** J. Butcher *Copy-Editing* xi. 205 Superscript letters and tildes (nunnation marks) in contractions are normalized to modern usage unless there are good reasons to the contrary.

2. Used as a symbol in *Math.* and *Logic*, chiefly to indicate negation.

1958 *New Scientist* 10 July 364/2 If A is a matrix it is usual to denote the transpose of A by A′ or A*, and the trace of A by tr A. However, the author plays the part of 'the odd man out' by placing a tilde (~) over A to denote the transpose of A. **1971** [see *hook *sb*[1] 10 d]. **1979** D. R. Hofstadter *Gödel, Escher, Bach* viii. 212 With the tilde in front, the whole statement is denied. **1982** *S. Afr. Jrnl. Philos.* I. 117/1 The standard interpretation of the propositional calculus identifies the tilde with the English word *not*.

tile, *sb.*[1] Add: **1. a.** Now freq. made of concrete.

c. (*b*) *transf.* Regularly-shaped pieces (often squares) of floor- or wall-covering made of some other material, as *carpet* (*cork*, etc.) *tile*.

1960 *Mrs. Beeton's Cookery & Househ. Managem.* 44 (*heading*) Cork tiles. **1975** *N.Y. Times* 6 Apr. ii. 40/4 Carpet tiles are installed by starting at the center of the room. **1976** *Evening Post* (Nottingham) 15 Dec. 20/1 (Advt.), Super savings on all branded Axminsters, Wiltons, Foambacks, Cords and Carpet tiles. **1982** *Habitat Catal.* 1982/83 140 Wipe clean natural cork tiles, pre-sealed with polyurethane varnish for protection.

h. *on the tiles*: [after the nocturnal activities of cats] on a spree, on a debauch. *slang.*

1887 H. Baumann *Londinismen* 125/2 *On the tiles*, auf dem Nachtbummel. *c* **1906** Galsworthy *Silver Box* (1910) 7 Been on the tiles and brought 'ome some of yer cat's fur. **1948** 'J. Tey' *Franchise Affair* xi. 119 I'd say she was what is known as 'out on the tiles', sir. A very cool customer she was. **1977** C. McCullough *Thorn Birds* xviii. 458 They all went out on the tiles... It was some night.

3. (Earlier example.)

1813 M. Edgeworth *Let.* 1 May (1971) 33 A number of *Fellows* and scholars with black tiles on their heads.

4. b. A thin flat piece used in a game, esp. in mah-jong or Scrabble.

1923 [see *Mah Jong *v.*]. **1973** *Times* 17 Nov. 2 A mah-jong set with ivory tiles. **1976** 'M. Albrand' *Taste of Terror* ix. 56 The original..was..printed in red block letters. They seemed to think that tiles from a scrabble set had been used.

6. *tile-hat, -top; tile-hatted, -roofed, -topped* adjs.; **tile-and-a-half tile,** a tile one and a half times the width of the tiles used with it; **tile-drainage,** drainage constructed of tiles; **tile game,** a game played with flat pieces; **tile-hanging,** tiling fixed vertically to an outside wall, for its weather-resisting and decorative properties; hence **tile-hung** *a.*

1940 *Chambers's Techn. Dict.* 850/2 *Tile-and-a-half tile*.., a purpose-made tile of extra width, used to form the bond at a laced valley. **1866** Mrs. Gaskell *Wives & Daughters* II. i. 4 He had taken the lead among the neighbouring landowners, when he first began tile-drainage. **1971** *Power Farming* Mar. 36/4 First-time sub-soiling over an existing satisfactory tile drainage system. **1950** E. Culbertson *Culbertson's Hoyle* p. xiii, Tile Games: Mah Jongg..Dominoes. **1974** *Encycl. Brit. Macropædia* II. 1149/2 Board and tile games are games played with a number of pieces on a specially constructed or marked board or with marked pieces (tiles) on a tabletop or other flat surface. **1932** *Times Lit. Suppl.* 7 July 494/3 Suffolk, Essex and Norfolk, counties remarkable for their brick-work, tile-hanging and weather-boarding. **1977** M. Girouard *Sweetness & Light* viii. 202 Stucco was replaced by red brick and tile-hanging. **1937** Partridge *Dict. Slang* 886/1 *Tile*,..extant as *tile-hat*, esp. in Glasgow. **1976** C. Bermant *Coming Home* I. iii. 40 The topper, or a tile-hat as it was known in Scotland..was virtually the badge of office of the Rabbi. **1924** *Glasgow Herald* 24 Dec. 6 There is something as Christmas-like as snow in the sight of a tile-hatted gentleman purchasing a sausage-balloon. **1948** J. Betjeman *Coll. Poems* (1958) 140 Gabled lodges, tile-hung churches, catch the lights of our Lagonda. **1977** Fedden & Joekes *National Trust Guide* (ed. 2) v. 375 Filled with brick nogging and tile-hung. **1962** E. Snow *Other Side of River* (1963) xxxi. 239 On the Sungari River at Harbin I saw a tile-roofed structure really elaborate enough to be called a palace. **1977** H. Fast *Immigrants* II. 86 Seven thousand dollars for the tile-roofed, tile-floored house..was a tremendous bargain. **1907** *Yesterday's Shopping* (1969) 129/1 Bamboo tile top table ..12/4. **1931** 'G. Trevor' *Murder at School* xiii. 253 A sort of lounge, fitted up with tile-topped tables and deep armchairs. **1979** J. Leasor *Love & Land Beyond* iii. 52 He sat down at a tile-topped table.

tilekum, tilicum, varr. *tillicum.

tiling, *vbl. sb.* Add: **2. b.** = *tile-draining* vbl. sb. s.v. Tile *sb.*[1] 6.

1943 J. W. Day *Farming Adventure* xii. 138 The land was drained by tiling and moling, given three ploughings, and by the end of July sown with wheat. **1960** *Times* 5 July (Agric. Suppl.) p. v/3 More tiling has been undertaken.

tilka, var. *tilak.

till, *sb.* Add: **4. till-roll,** a roll of paper recording an account of the transactions made at the till to which it is attached.

1972 *Times* 18 Oct. 4/4 The butcher..examined his till roll, and there was no record of anyone having paid that amount.

till, *prep., conj., adv.* Add: **A.** *prep.* **II. 5. d.** = To *prep.* 6 b, in stating the time of day. *U.S.*

1949 [see *quarter *sb.* 8 c]. **1962** M. & G. Gordon *Journey with Stranger* (1963) iv. 36 'Ten till,' he said... 'I'll go in first.'

B. *conj.* **1. g.** Indicating purpose: in order that (one) may, (*loosely*) 'and let me'. *Sc.* and *Ir.*

1881 A. Mackie *Scotticisms* 18 Give me a match till I light the gas. **1904** W. B. Yeats *Pot of Broth* 78 Give me some vessel, till I give this sky-woman a taste of it. **1931** A. J. Cronin *Hatter's Castle* III. iv. 525 Come till I give ye a grand, big hug. *a* **1966** 'M. na Gopaleen' *Best of Myles* (1977) 57 Will yez all come in here..till I show yez me new picture.

tillage. Add: **1. d.** *fig.* Sexual intercourse (with a woman). *poet.*

c **1600** Shakes. *Sonnets* (1609) sig. B1v, For where is she so faire whose vn-eard wombe Disdaines the tillage of thy husbandry? **1918** E. Pound *Pavannes & Divisions* 41 Some men will live as prudes in their own village And make the tour abroad for their wild tillage.

tiller, *sb.*[2] Add: **4. tillerman** *U.S.*, a fireman who controls the rear portion of a fire-engine; **tiller soup,** the minatory wielding of a tiller by the coxswain to encourage his boat's crew.

1968 L. Lokos *House Divided* vii. 226 A hook and ladder truck went to answer the alarm without the tillerman aboard to control the rear portion. **1929** F. C. Bowen *Sea Slang* 141 *Tiller soup*, the man-handling with the tiller by threat of which a coxswain encourages his boat's crew. **1947** *Sea Breezes* III. 151 We boys got a few gentle taps with the boat's tiller, too. We called it 'tiller soup'.

tilleyite (ti·li,əit). *Min.* [f. the name of C. E. *Tilley* (1894–1973), Australian-born English petrologist + -ite[1].] A silicate and carbonate of calcium, $Ca_5Si_2O_7(CO_3)_2$, found as white monoclinic crystals.

1933 Larsen & Dunham in *Amer. Mineralogist* XVIII. 469 An examination of blocks of the material from the Wet Weather quarry..has revealed the presence of a new lime silicate-carbonate mineral, with distinctive optical and chemical properties. For the new mineral the name tilleyite is proposed in honor of Professor C. E. Tilley of Cambridge University.., in recognition of the contributions he has made to the study of metamorphism. **1977** *Mineral. Abstr.* XXVIII. 71/1 At Kushiro, Tojo-cho, Hiroshima Prefecture, various rare skarn minerals occur in the contact zone between dioritic rock and limestone. These include..tilleyite.

Tilley lamp (ti·li læmp). Also (*erron.*) **Tilly lamp,** and with small initial. [f. the name of the manufacturing company.] The proprietary name of a type of portable oil or paraffin lamp in which air pressure is used to supply the burner with fuel. Also *ellipt.* as *Tilley*.

1932 R. F. Fortune *Sorcerers of Dobu* iv. 181 My great shadow cast..by my Tilley lamp. **1948** *Trade Marks Jrnl.* 17 Mar. 201/2 *Tilley*... Lighting and heating lamps employing liquid fuel. The Tilley Lamp Company Limited,.. Brent Works, Brent Street, Hendon, London, N.W.4; manufacturers. **1953** G. M. Durrell *Overloaded Ark* vi. 115, I left the Tilly lamp in the middle of the swaying hypnotised circle. **1960** A. Wesker *I'm talking about Jerusalem* I. 23 Light the tilly lamp for me. **1966** *Guardian* 22 Dec. 5 Get that 'Tilley' goin', Gary. **1981** J. B. Hilton *Surrender Value* v. 42 Men filed out with Tilley-lamps, wicker baskets and rod-bags.

tillicum (ti·likɒ̆m). *N.W. Amer.* Chiefly in *pl.* Also **tilicum, tilekum.** [a. Chinook Jargon *tilikum* people, ad. Chinook *tilxam*, f. *t-* pl. prefix + ilxam village.] **1.** A member of one's own tribe or people; also *pl.*, the people, common people.

1847 J. Palmer *Jrnl. Trav. Rocky Mts.* 105 A long time ago the Great Spirit became angry with them, set the mountain on fire, destroyed their towns, turned the *tiye* (chief) and *tilicums* (people) into stone, and cast them in the ocean outside of Cape Lookout. **1859** *Brit. Colonist* (Victoria, B.C.) 30 Apr. 2/2 Four Haidah Indians..came to the house of Mr. Oxner, Colquitz Farm, and after agreeing to work for him, one left, when the rest said they preferred to go with tilekum. **1922** E. P. Johnson *Legends of Vancouver* 35, I saw her graceful, high-bowed canoe heading for the beach that is the favourite landing-place of the 'tillicums' from the Mission.

2. A friend.

1869 *Mainland Guardian* (New Westminster, B.C.) 9 Oct. 3/2 The rescue from the courthouse at Kootenay, by his tillicums, of the Indian taken there by the Prices when caught in the act of robbing their sluices. **1906** *Daily Colonist* (Victoria, B.C.) 5 Jan. 2/4 Mr. French expects to resume his citizenship of Princeton after about four years' absence, his present hurried trip precluding a visit with many old tillicums here about. **1969** *Islander* (Victoria, B.C.) 30 Nov. 3/2 Thiepval was in Hakodate when we were there and during our stay in that port we had all become good tillicums.

tillite (ti·ləit). *Geol.* [ad. G. *tillit* (A. Pencke 1906, in *Geogr. Zeitschr.* XII. 608): see Till *sb.*[2], -ite[1].] A sedimentary rock composed of glacial till compacted into hard rock.

1907 E. Blackwelder in B. Willis et al. *Res. in China* (Carnegie Inst. Publ. No. 54) I. I. xii. 267 (*heading*) Basal quartzite and glacial tillite. [*Note*] Tillite, a term recently proposed for consolidated till. **1944** A. Holmes *Princ. Physical Geol.* xxi. 500 Tillites of the same age have been found in the north of Angola, in the eastern Congo, in Uganda, and in Madagascar. **1977** A. Hallam *Planet Earth* 87 (*caption*) Striations on smaller rock bodies may be used to identify those as tillites (glacial till converted to rock) rather than tilloids, which are superficially similar.

tilloid (ti·loid). *Geol.* [f. Till *sb.*[2] + -oid.] A sedimentary rock which is similar in appearance to a tillite but is not known to be of glacial origin; a sedimentary rock composed of non-glacial deposits.

1931 E. Blackwelder in *Bull. Geol. Soc. Amer.* XLII. 903 For these reasons the scarcity of striated stones in the McGee tilloid* need not be given undue weight. [*Note*] *Meaning a till-like deposit of doubtful origin. **1957** F. J. Pettijohn *Sedimentary Rocks* (ed. 2) vi. 265 The non-glacial conglomeratic mudstones or tilloids vary from a chaotic unassorted assemblage of coarse materials set in a mudstone matrix to a mudstone with sparsely distributed cobbles. **1966** *Earth-Sci. Rev.* II. 251 When there is any doubt about the origin of a till-like deposit, we encourage the use of tilloid, as a non-genetic term. **1977** [see *tillite].

tilly (ti·li), *sb.*[2] [f. Ir. *tuilleadh* an additional quantity, a supplement.] In Ireland and places of Irish settlement, an additional article or amount unpaid for by the purchaser, as a gift from the vendor.

1922 Joyce *Ulysses* 15 She poured again a measureful and a tilly. **1958** M. & P. Colum *Our Friend James Joyce* II. ii. 120 As the price of the little volume [*sc.* *Pomes Penyeach*] was a shilling, one expected to find twelve poems in it, one for each penny. Actually there were thirteen, the additional one being named 'Tilly'. In this Joyce was being obscurely local: the extra half-cup of milk that the milkman left in the Dublin householder's jug in the morning was a 'tilly'—something unpaid for. **1975** *Canadian Antiques Collector* Mar.–Apr. 22/2 [In Newfoundland] we have still in common use such Anglo-Irish terms as:..tilly (a small amount over and above what is purchased).

Tilly, tilly: see *Tilley lamp.

tilorone (ti·lŏrō^{u}n). *Biochem.* [f. *tilor-*, of unkn. origin + -one.] An aromatic amine which induces the production of interferon and acts as an anti-viral agent.

1970 *Science* 18 Sept. 1213/1 Tilorone hydrochloride, the orange, water-soluble dihydrochloride salt of 2,7-bis[2-(diethylamino)ethoxy]fluoren-9-one, is a broad spectrum, orally active antiviral agent. **1978** *Nature* 29 June 760/1 Tilorone, statolon and Newcastle disease virus (NDV), all potent inducers of interferon in mice, induced a marked increase in spleen cell cytotoxicity.

Tilsit (ti·lsit). Also **Tilsiter, tilsit(er).** [The name of a town in East Prussia (now Sovetsk, U.S.S.R.); *Tilsiter* f. Ger. (= of Tilsit.).] In full *Tilsit cheese*. A semi-hard cheese orig. made at Tilsit.

1936 *N.Y. Herald-Tribune* 8 Aug. 12/7 First on his list is tilsit, a sharp cheese from Denmark. **1950** J. G. Davis *Dict. Dairying* 130 *Tilsit cheese*,..an East Prussian hard-pressed cheese made from cow's whole milk. **1961** Webster, Tilsiter. **1965** *Harrods Food News* May, Tilsiter (German—per lb. 6/6). **1971** J. Aiken *Nightly Deadshade* iv. 46 They go at once to the larder and eat two pounds of Tilsit cheese.

tilt, *sb.*[1] Add: **3.** Also for a motor vehicle.

1976 *Milton Keynes Express* 16 July 31/3 (Advt.), 1975 Mini Pick-up, green, one owner, fitted tilt. **1977** 'D. Rutherford' *Return Load* iv. 77 One of his employees was fastening the blue canvas cover to the hooks on the side of one of the big, steel-framed tilts that were in such great demand for Continental journeys.

4. Also, a lean-to shelter. (Earlier examples.)

1612 in G. M. Story et al. *Dict. Newfoundland Eng.* (1982) 567/2 They had made a tilte with a sayle, that they got from some Christian. **1819** L. A. Anspach *Hist. Island of Newfoundland* 468 They call *tilts* temporary log houses, which they erect in the woods to pursue there their winter occupations.

tilt, *sb.*[2] Add: **II. 4. d.** *Television* and *Cinematogr.* (See quot. 1959.)

1959 Halas & Manvell *Technique Film Animation* 342 *Tilt*, the upward or downward pivoting movement of the camera across the screen. **1963** D. Botting in A. Smith *Throw out Two Hands* App. I. 266 A Miller tripod with a fully fluid head..giving smooth, controlled pans and tilts even with extreme long-focus lenses.

e. *fig.* An inclination; a bias.

1975 *N.Y. Times Bk. Rev.* 11 May 14 The contribution to the American language of other cultures has long been acknowledged..but it is unscholarly to insist on a 'tilt' toward minority contribution to satisfy resentment over past neglect. **1978** *Time* 18 Dec. 40 The pro-Soviet tilt of the new rulers in Kabul, the Afghan capital, is already stirring some recriminations in Washington.

10. tilt cab, a cab of a lorry, etc., which can tilt forwards; **tilt-cart** (earlier example); **tiltmeter** *Geol.*, an instrument for measuring changes in the steepness of a slope; **tilt-top** *a.*, having a top that tilts; **tilt-wheel,** (*b*) *U.S.*, a steering wheel that tilts; **tilt-wing** *a.* and *sb.*, (designating) an aircraft with wings that tilt.

1963 *Lebende Sprachen* VIII. 166/1 Tilt cab. **1977** *Horse & Hound* 10 June 42/1 (Advt.), Container 21ft Williams with Luton for tilt cab, metal framed and in sound order. **1834** J. B. Buckstone *Wreck Ashore* II. iii. 40, I ha' just brought him home from the Physickiners in a tilt cart. **1937** *Nature* 10 Apr. 616/1 In both the Tango and Ito districts, tiltmeters..were erected. **1980** *New Scientist* 26 June 388/2 Everything that is happening to Mount St Helens is a 'classroom' experience for geologists and scientists scrambling to gather as much data as they can with seismic recording instruments, tiltmeters, and water level gauges. **1940** I. Crump *Our Airliners* vii. 138 For this disassembling operation, the engine is bolted on a portable tilttop table. **1973** *Canadian Antiques Collector* Jan.–Feb. 12/1 A birch tilt-top candlestand with an oval top. **1974** *State* (Columbia, S. Carolina) 15 Feb. 19-B/7 (Advt.), Power steering, power brakes, tilt wheel, vinyl roof, rally wheels. **1953** W. A. Shrader *Fifty Years of Flight* 124/2 Spratt Aircraft Co...test-flies another in a series of tilt-wing flying boats designed by George Spratt. **1963** *Times* 2 Dec. 9/7 Two prototypes of a twin-engined 'tilt-wing' short and vertical take-off and landing transport aircraft. **1970** *New Scientist* 23 Apr. 173/1 Several tilt-wings have flown satisfactorily.

tilt, *v.*[1] Add: **II. 4. a.** Also *fig.*

1976 *Globe & Mail* (Toronto) 12 Nov. 1/3 The UN [*sc.* Union Nationale] will have taken seats from the Liberals and acted as spoiler in many other ridings, tilting the victory toward the Parti Quebecois. **1979** *N.Y. Post* 8 Aug. 2/5 Yesterday Israeli Foreign Minister Moshe Dayan charged that the U.S. was tilting its policy toward the PLO to appease Saudi Arabia and insure a steady flow of oil at reasonable prices.

b. Also *fig.*

1967 *Globe & Mail* (Toronto) 10 Nov. 2/9 During the India-Pakistan war, President Nixon ordered assistance to one side... Press reports at the time said Mr. Nixon wanted to 'tilt' in favour of Pakistan. **1978** *Guardian Weekly* 22 Jan. 17/3 Officials tend to tilt toward secrecy from a parochial view of their responsibilities.

d. *Television* and *Cinematogr.* To move (a camera) in a vertical plane.

1915 A. Lockett in B. E. Jones *Cinematograph Bk.* iv. 26 Tilting the camera causes convergence of upright lines.

tiltable (ti·ltăb'l), *a.* [f. Tilt *v.*[1] + -able.] Able to be tilted.

1934 in Webster. **1955** *Sci. Amer.* Mar. 42/3 Their tiltable antenna has four such units, each 320 feet long and 40 feet wide. **1979** *Observer* (Colour Suppl.) 22 Apr. 94 (Advt.), The steering column is tiltable.

tilting, *vbl. sb.*[1] Add: **2. c.** *Television* and *Cinematogr.* Movement of a camera in a vertical plane.

1938 G. H. Sewell *Amateur Film-Making* ix. 80 Movement [of the camera] in the up and down direction is known as 'tilting'.

TIM (tim). Also **Tim**, etc. Repr. pronunc. of *TIM* (the first three letters of Time *sb.*), the dialling code formerly used to obtain the telephone service giving the correct time in words; hence, this telephone service itself.

1936 [see *talking clock* s.v. *talking *ppl. a.* 2]. **1939** *Times* 23 Mar. 13/5 Public appreciation of the service was shown by the 18,000,000 or so calls a year that were made on 'Tim'. **1951** W. de la Mare *Winged Chariot* 7 Though every minute of your life's your own,..you ring up TIM; consult the telephone. **1978** E. St. Johnston *One Policeman's Story* ii. 41 Always receptive to innovations and new ideas, he [*sc.* Sir Donald Banks] introduced TIM, 999, Greetings Telegrams and the neo-Georgian style of post office buildings.

Tima(n)nee, var. *Temne.

timar. For *Obs.* read *Hist.* and add later examples.

1877 J. Baker *Turkey in Europe* 157 A Timar contained from three to five hundred acres of land. **1974** *Encycl. Brit. Macropædia* XIII. 776/2 The newly conquered lands were assigned to their commanders in the form of *timars.*

timariot. For *Obs.* read *Hist.* and add later examples.

1913 A. H. Lybyer *Government of Ottoman Empire* 101 The *Zaims* and Timariotes..were a class of country gentlemen. **1981** A. Toynbee *Greeks & their Heritage* 183 Ottoman Muslim timariots.

timbal, tymbal. Restrict 'Now *Hist.* or *arch.*' to sense in Dict. and add: **2.** = Timbale 1.

1929 J. G. Myers *Insect Singers* vi. 77 The essential elements of the [sound-producing] apparatus are the tymbals and the tymbal-muscles. **1969** R. F. Chapman *Insects* xxviii. 585 In the dorso-lateral region of the first segment of *Platypleura* (Cicadidae) there is on each side an area of very thin cuticle supported by a thick cuticular rim... This area of cuticle forms the tymbal.

timbale. 2. (Earlier examples.)

1824 Byron *Don Juan* xv. lxvi. 38 Then there was God knows what 'à l'Allemande',..'timballe', and 'Salpicon'. **1866** Mrs. Gaskell *Wives & Daughters* I. xv. 178 Mr. Gibson had to satisfy his healthy English appetite on badly-made omelettes, rissoles, vol-au-vents, croquets, and timbales.

timbales (timbā·lėz), *pl.* [a. F. *timbales*, pl. of *timbale* (or a. Sp., Pg., pl. of *timbal*): see Timbal, tymbal.] Two single-headed drums played as a pair with drumsticks (a percussion instrument of Caribbean or African origin). Also *attrib.*

1928 [see *maraca]. **1955** [see *conga 2]. **1966** *Crescendo* Dec. 27/1 L/A bands heavily feature bongoes, timbales and conga drums. **1974** *Nation* (Barbados) 3 Mar. 5/1 The BRC were doing a calypso and cut for drummer 'Boo' and stand-in timbales player L.O.D. to go into a lengthy drumming session.

timber, *sb.*[1] Add: **4. a.** *tall timber*: see *tall *a.* 7 e.

c. *int.* The warning call of the feller when a tree is about to fall.

1912 J. Sandilands *Western Canad. Dict.* (ed. 2) 47 *Timber-r-r!* the long-drawn melodious warning call of the sawyers in a lumber camp when a tree is about to fall. **1935** 'L. Ford' *Burn Forever* 56 There was a stentorian shout: '*Timber!!*' **1968** *Islander* (Victoria, B.C.) 15 Dec. 2/1 The sharp ring of Father's axe echoed in the icy air, and we cried 'timber' as our tree fell.

5. (Earlier example in sense 'a wicket'.) Also (*rare*), an arrow.

1840 [see *screw *sb.*[1] 11 c]. *c* **1879** G. M. Hopkins *Poems* (1967) 180 Yet Arthur is a Bowman: his three-heeled timber'll hit The bald and bóld blinking gold when áll's dóne.

7. Preceded by a qualifying word: suitable quality or character for the specified office, etc. Cf. material *sb.* 6*. Chiefly *U.S.*

1892 *Chicago Tribune* 4 Apr. 4/5 Senator Cullom of Illinois is better Presidential timber than was generally supposed. **1914** *Emporia Gaz.* 13 Jan. 2/1 He is everlastingly..N.G. as gubernatorial timber. **1954** *Sat. Even. Post* 6 Nov. 64/4 CIA recruits many employees from our colleges and universities through a process beginning even before individual students realize that they are being singled out as possible CIA timber. **1967** R. S. Churchill *Winston S. Churchill* II. vi. 193 His parliamentary stature had grown and he had proved that he was of Cabinet timber. **1975** *Times Lit. Suppl.* 13 June 661/2 My contention that he [*sc.* J. F. Kennedy] was potential Presidential timber.

9. a. *timber-claim* (earlier example), *growth, harvest, jinker* (Austral.) (Jinker[2]), *-land* (examples), *management, -market* (later example), *-merchant* (later example), *preservation, production, -raft* (earlier example), *-slide* (earlier example), *-trade* (earlier example), *truck, value.* **b.** *timber feller* (later example), *-harvester; timber-harvesting.* **c.** *timber-lined* (earlier example) adj.

1857 *Lawrence* (Kansas) *Republican* 4 June, Timber claims..may be purchased on better terms than in any place of equal distance from Lawrence. **1922** E. M. Forster *Life to Come* (1972) 74 There was a tolerable road, made by the timber-fellers. **1968** *Ceiba* XIV. 29 (*heading*) Forecasting timber growth by the point center extension modification of the Bitterlich system. **1969** *U.S. Forest Service Resource Bull.* No. PNW30 (*title*) 1968 Washington timber harvest. **1965** *Canad. Geogr. Jrnl.* Sept. 86/2 The..economic arguments of timber-harvesters. *Ibid.* 86/1 It may also be that top park administrators..apply the terminology and techniques of timber harvesting to areas in which the primary use is recreational. **1916** J. B. Cooper *Coo-oo-ee* i. 1 Along the tracks heavy timber-jinkers groaned on their way to the Ironbark Sawmill. **1977** *Weekly Times* (Melbourne) 19 Jan. 57/2 (Advt.), Quality trucks at lowest prices..also semi trailers, semi tippers, low-loaders, timber jinkers, tippers. **1654** *Suffolk Deeds* (Boston, Mass.) (1883) II. 55 Howses fence or gardens, Tymber Lands broaken & vnbroaken. **1804** P. Gass *Jrnl.* 26 Aug. (1807) ii. 31 We..passed some timber land on the south side. **1981** *Bull. Yale Univ. School Forestry* No. 92. 15 Ownership of timberlands by the forest products industry..grew by almost 10 million acres in the past twenty-five years. **1856** W. Whitman *Leaves of Grass* (ed. 2) xii. 225 You timber-lined sides! You distant ships. **1969** *U.S. Forest Service Research Paper* No. so 40. 1 (*title*) 29 years of selection timber management on the Crossett Experimental Forest. **1981** *Bull. Yale Univ. School Forestry* No. 92. 39 This model could be implemented empirically on a data set for which information on both the land and timber markets were available. **1946** A. R. M. Lower *Colony to Nation* 209 The timber merchants..bought square timber and deals..to ship them to England. **1966** *Encycl. N.Z.* I. 724/1 As building authorities have rightly been unwilling to accept this non-durable sap-timber, a sizable timber preservation industry has grown up. **1968** *Wisconsin Agric. Exper. Sta. Research Bull.* No. 272. 1 (*heading*) Mycorrhizae: their role in tree nutrition and timber production. **1818** F. Hall *Trav. Canada & U.S.* xiii. 118 The frequent sail, or heavy timber-raft, 'floating many a rood'. **1836** *Bytown* (Ottawa) *Gaz.* 21 July 2/5 This improvement with many others (amongst the rest a timber slide at the Chats) the country owes to..George Buchannan. **1732** in *Calendar of State Papers Colonial Series, Amer. & W. Indies 1732* (1939) XXXIX. 243 Abundance of saw-mills are erecting for the timber trade. **1859** D. Bunce *Travels with Dr. Leichhardt* iii. 23 These pipes..afforded excellent substitutes for bridges, wherever it was necessary for a road to be made for the timber-trucks. **1976** M. Birmingham *Heat of Sun* vi. 75 The timber trucks—great articulated monsters each carrying thirty-odd tons of timber, usually in the form of three huge logs. **1917** *Chambers's Jrnl.* Jan. 9/2 What bearing has the presence, or the increase, of woodpeckers upon the problem of timber-values? **1981** *Bull. Yale Univ. School Forestry* No. 92. 33 Some timber values must be foregone to obtain additional nontimber values.

10. timber beast *N. Amer.*, a logger; **timber berth** *Canad.*, a tract of forested land the bounds of which have been established by the government, which leases or sells the rights to fell and remove timber; **timber carriage** = *timber-cart;* **timber cruise** *N. Amer.* = *cruise *sb.* 2; **timber-cruiser** *N. Amer.* [*cruiser 3], a timber prospector; hence **timber cruising; timber-doodle** (examples of *U.S. local* sense and earlier example of *slang* sense); **timber drive** *N. Amer.*, an organized floating of loose timber down a waterway; a quantity of timber so floated; **timber due** *Canad.*, a tax paid to the government on each tree taken out of a timber berth; **timber-frame,** (*c*) *attrib.* = *timber-framed* adj.; **timber-framing,** the construction of buildings having frames of timber; **timber-getter** *Austral.*, a lumberman or logger; **timber-head,** (*b*) *slang* (*rare*) = Block-head 2; **timberjack** *N. Amer.*, a lumberman or logger; **timber jam** = *log-jam 1; **timber-jumper** (earlier example); **timber licence** *Canad.*, a licence to cut timber on a timber berth on payment of dues to the government; **timber-limit** *Canad.*, (*a*) (earlier example); (*b*) any tract of forested land suitable for lumbering; (*c*) = *timberline; **timber-line:** delete and see as main entry; **timber rattler, rattlesnake,** a venomous snake, *Crotalus horridus horridus*, found in the northeastern United States and marked with dark bands or blotches; **timber-tug** (later example); **timber-wolf,** for *Western U.S.* read *N. Amer.* and add earlier and later examples.

1919 *Camp Worker* 26 Apr. 5/2 A large number of our city folk imagine that a 'timber beast' has just about as much need for brain as a Canadian soldier in Siberia has for refrigeration machinery. **1975** J. Gores *Hammett* (1976) xiii. 93 They thought he was a timber beast out of Seattle. **1837** *Times* (Halifax, Nova Scotia) 17 Jan. 22/1 The selling of Crown lands by auction—and the disposal of the timber berths. **1957** *Camsell Arrow* (Edmonton, Alberta) Christmas 68/3 The mission bought a sawmill and set it up on a timber berth just north of the Sunchild reserve buildings. **1747** E. Purefoy *Let.* 12 May in *Purefoy Lett.* (1931) i. 41 This day I ordered the Timber Carriage to be set up by Simon Hobcroft the Carpenter. **1901** 'L. Malet' *Hist. Sir R. Calmady* ii. iii. 110 A miller's tented waggon,..a timber-carriage, and a couple of spring-carts. **1933** E. Merrick *True North* 319 The people in Mud Lake remember the lumbermen by..their timber cruises. **1949** *Boston Globe* 17 July (Fiction Mag.) 8/1 Hard years in mine and timber cruise had given Flood a certain steadiness and maturity. **1956** T. Raddall *Wings of Night* (1957) iii. 33 Someone offered me a job on a timber cruise up in the north Ontario bush. **1894** *Century Mag.* Mar. 671/2 The timber-cruiser is a hero... The location of a choice tract of timber is a secret to be guarded with his life. **1981** *Publ. Amer. Dial. Soc.* LXVII. 5 In 1890 the area was inhabited only by a few transient timber cruisers and mineral prospectors. **1933** *Meccano Mag.* Mar. 195/1 Another activity confined largely to the Eastern Lines is 'timber cruising', which consists of the surveying and mapping out of various forest areas. **1956** T. Raddall *Wings of Night* (1957) xviii. 143 Winter was a good time for timber cruising. A pair of snow-shoes would carry you anywhere. **1842** Dickens *Amer. Notes* I. iii. 141 Mint Julep, Sherry-cobbler, Timber Doodle, and other rare drinks. **1856** *Spirit of Times* 25 Oct. 129/1 While we have been dosing timberdoodles with infinitesimal blue pills, they shall have..been doctoring bruins. **1979** *Globe & Mail* (Toronto) 24 Oct. 41/1 Any hunter who has ever overheated his shotgun barrel trying to down the elusive timberdoodle knows..of the erratic flight of the woodcock. *a* **1861** T. Winthrop *Life in Open Air* (1863) 23 The head-driver of a timber-drive leads a disorderly army. **1920** *Blackw. Mag.* Nov. 616/1, I caught sight..of a second log, followed by a third and yet others in an apparently endless procession. I had never encountered a timber drive before. **1957** B. Hutchison *Canada* 101 He had heard only vague rumors of the old timber drives in the days of Peter Emberley. **1883** J. Fraser *Shanty Life Backwoods of Canada* 87 How easily this could be balanced in the treasury accounts by the smallest additional fraction upon timber dues. **1936** A. R. M. Lower *Settlement & Forest Frontier in Eastern Canada* 77 To Crown timber dues was added 'timber licence', 'timber-limit', or 'timber-berth' arrangement. **1967** *Times Rev. Industry* Apr. 32/2 Timber-frame houses are composed of lightweight sections and therefore are easy to erect. *Ibid.*, Timber-framing has completely overcome the postwar 'pre-fab' image of industrialized building. **1912** *Contemp. Rev.* Aug. 248 The professional timber-getter is a Southern miscreant. **1970** M. Kelly *Spinifex* vi. 103 The word's Timber Getter, not lumberjack. **1849** H. Melville *Redburn* 37 You timber-head..take this bucket here, and go up the rigging. **1916** A. Bridle *Sons of Canada* 5 He was a timberjack in the hardwood bush of western Ontario. **1953** D. Cushman *Timberjack* 127 You boys hired out to be timberjacks. **1888** Lees & Clutterbuck *B.C. 1887* 186 On one of the huge timber jams which so often occurred we passed close to a wolverene. **1937** Kipling *Something of Myself* iv. 101 The removal of the key-log in a timber-jam starts the whole pile. **1832** *Q. Rev.* XLVII. 237 'Now for the timber-jumper,' cries Osbaldeston, pleased to find himself upon Clasher. **1910** J. London *Lost Face* 133 Crossing a timber jam on the frozen bed of the Teelee, the sled suffered a wrenching capsize. **1921** *Daily Colonist* (Victoria, B.C.) 16 Mar. 5/2 It was a wide open invitation to the speculator to buy up large numbers of timber licences in arrears. **1966** *Canad. Forest Industries* Nov. 55/1 Amendments made to the Forest Act in 1965 now permit: Application of the cost of timber sales to the timber licence as a whole, or to cutting permits issued pursuant to the licence. **1854** T. C. Keeper *Ottawa* 56 No timber limits are without water—for it is by water alone that the timber can reach its market. **1890** *Grip* (Toronto) 8 Feb. 83/2 A Journal..is..agitated lest, by disputing our timber-limits.., the Ontario Government shall bring the province to direct taxation. **1898** W. T. Jennings *Rep. Routes to Yukon* 9 The whole valley and slopes to the timber limit are clothed with cotton-wood, spruce and alder trees. **1914** H. Bindloss *Intriguers* 108 We want to get as far north as the timber limit. **1960** *Ottawa Citizen* 18 June 38/5 A Blackfoot Indian band in 1892 surrendered a timber limit in Alberta. **1936** E. G. Barnard *Rider of Cherokee Strip* 51 Some called it the timber rattler or the black diamond rattler. **1974** A. Dillard *Pilgrim at Tinker Creek* xiii. 223 The only other poisonous snake around here is the timber rattler. **1950** *Chicago Tribune* 16 Mar. ii. 12/2 With him to the zoo went five timber rattlesnakes. **1982** J. S. Borthwick *Case of Hook-Billed Kites* (1983) xlviii. 171 He swept from the timber rattlesnake..to the western diamondback. **1977** N. Freeling *Gadget* iii. 142 Sturdy horses could haul carts, timber-tugs, sleds in winter. **1860** *Nor' Wester* (Red River Settlement) 28 Feb. 4/2 We also saw a large timber wolf (not a wolf made of wood, but a gentleman who inhabits prairies and wooded country). **1936, 1964** [see *grey wolf* s.v. *grey, gray *a.* 8 b]. **1980** *Beautiful Brit. Columbia* Spring 19 In the warehouse, red and silver fox furs hang beside the sleek pelts of lynx, timber wolf and beaver.

ti·mberline. Chiefly *N. Amer.* Also **timber line, timber-line.** [Timber *sb.*[1]] **1.** On a mountain, the line or level above which no trees grow. Freq. with omission of *the.* Also *attrib.*

1867 *Harper's Mag.* June 17/2 A high mountain ridge divided into innumerable peaks, all of which tower above the timber-line. **1874** [in Dict. s.v. Timber *sb.*[1] 10]. **1904** *Bull. Geol. Soc. Amer.* XIV. 557 On the mountains of central Idaho, the cold timberline is sharply drawn at an elevation of about 10,000 feet, while the dry timberline, equally well defined, has an elevation of about 7,000 feet. **1936** *Scrutiny* IV. 443 Timber-line settlers. **1961** R. M.

PATTERSON *Buffalo Head* ii. 40 'The timberline country I would learn to call it in the years to come. **1966** *Encycl. N.Z.* I. 730/1 Upper timber-line belts are largely composed of broadleaf shrubs. **1980** *Outdoor Life* (U.S.) (Northeast ed.) Oct. 100/2 Hunters working from 8,000-feet to timberline.

2. In the northern hemisphere, the line north of which no trees grow.

1896 C. WHITNEY *On Snow-Shoes to Barren Grounds* 287 How well I remember that birch-tree! And how delighted I was, for I knew by that sign the timber-line was very close. **1934** P. H. GODSELL *Arctic Trader* 288 We had a warm camp that night, as we were still within the timber line. **1977** A. HALLAM *Planet Earth* 88 In practice we find that the zone of continuous permafrost is limited to those areas where the mean annual temperature is −15°C..and this also roughly coincides with the timber-line, the northernmost point where trees exist.

timberman. Add: **1. c.** *Canad.* An owner or manager of a company engaged in lumbering.

1889 W. H. WITHROW *Our Own Country—Canada* 527 The trees, where the timbermen have not culled out the finest, are most picturesque. **1963** F. W. LINDSAY *B.C. Outlaws* 7 Among them is..a prominent timberman who recently became interested in timber limits at Quatsino.

timbo (ti·mbo·). Also **timbó**. [a. Tupi.] **1.** Any of various South American woody vines cultivated as a source of fish poison and the insecticide rotenone, esp. those of the genus *Lonchocarpus* (family Leguminosæ); also, the poison itself.

1725 H. SLOANE *Voy. to Islands of Madera, ..Jamaica* II. 40 Timbo, a sort of With, intoxicates Fishes. **1930** *Jrnl. Econ. Entomol.* XXIII. 868 Rotenone also occurs in 'cube' roots (*Lonchocarpus nicou*) and in timbo, haiari, and other members of the genus Lonchocarpus. **1949** *Thorpe's Dict. Appl. Chem.* (ed. 4) IX. 306/2 South American sources of rotenone..have been developed recently, chiefly the cubé of Peru, and the timbo of Brazil. **1971** *Nat. Geographic* Sept. 435 Like most Brazilian Indians, they usually fish with the sap of a vine called timbo.

2. A South American timber tree of the genus *Enterolobium* (family Leguminosæ) from which a soft red wood is obtained and used for making furniture.

1924 RECORD & MELL *Timbers Trop. Amer.* 205 'Timbó' is well known to the trade in Argentina..in the form of squared logs and because of its softness and ease of working is used as a cheap substitute for cedar. **1969** T. H. EVERETT *Living Trees of World* 196/2 *Enterolobium*. Ten New World species comprise this genus. The best known are the timbó..(*E. contortisiliquum*) and the guanacaste or elephant's ear (*E. cyclocarpum*).

timbre, *sb.*³ Delete ‖ and add: Now also with pronunc. (tæ·mbəɹ).

timbred (te̥·nbr'd, tæ·mbəɹd) *a.* [f. TIMBRE *sb.*³ + -ED².] Having a timbre of a specified kind.

1942 C. HIMES *Black on Black* (1973) 183 His voice, timbred with a quality of raw intensity, encompassed them both. **1969** 'E. LATHEN' *When in Greece* xvii. 182 Her splendidly timbred voice.

timbrous (te̥·nbrəs, tæ·mbrəs), *a.* [f. TIMBRE *sb.*³ + -OUS.] Sonorous, resonant.

1929 W. FAULKNER *Sartoris* IV. 283 The other one bayed her single timbrous note. **1973** T. WICKER *Facing Lions* 67 The low, timbrous voice was as hesitant and its words as rambling and loosely collected as those of the farmers who preceded him.

Timbuctoo (ti:mbɒktū·). The name of a town (now officially spelt *Timbuktu*) on the edge of the Sahara in West Africa, used as the type of the most distant place imaginable.

1863 L. DUFF-GORDON *Lett. from Egypt* (1969) 104 It is growing dreadfully Cockney here [*sc.* Cairo]. I must go to Timbuctoo. **1935** A. CHRISTIE *Death in Clouds* xiv. 148 'She's sorry—' '—but she may be going to Timbuctoo' finished Norman. **1974** V. CANNING *Painted Tent* ix. 182 Trevor Green wished Smiler in Timbuctoo, but since that couldn't be arranged, he just wished him ill. **1981** *Times* 19 Feb. 2/4 Electors promising to follow their 'Shirl' [*sc.* Shirley Williams] to Timbuctoo if she should choose to go there.

Hence **Ti:mbuctoo·t** *a.* (fanciful *nonce-wd.*), of or pertaining to Timbuctoo, foreign, outlandish.

1930 D. H. LAWRENCE *Nettles* 16 And the world it didn't give a hoot If his blood was British or Timbuctoot.

time, *sb.* Add: **I. 1. a.** *in no time*, etc. (earlier example).

1832 [see *NO *a.* 3 b].

2. (*for the*) *time being* (later examples).

1883 'MARK TWAIN' *Life on Mississippi* xliii. 440 It's human nature—human nature in grief. It don't reason, you see. 'Time being, it don't care a dam. **1913** *Granta* 22 Feb. 225/1 When listening to a singer of such extraordinary natural gifts as Madame Melba, one loses the faculty of criticism for the time being. **1948** V. MASSEY *On being Canadian* xi. 176 It is perhaps natural that there should be a period of pause; that we should not for the time-being be 'on the march'. **1977** J. CROSBY *Company of Friends* xx. 127 The pilot's one of ours—for the time being.

3. e. (*there's*) *a good time coming.*

1817 SCOTT *Rob Roy* III. v. 149 'There's a guid time coming.' 'No time like the time present, Mr Campbell.' **1846** C. MACKAY *Voices from Crowd* (1851) 9 There's a good time coming, boys, A good time coming: We may not live to see the day. **1873** TROLLOPE *Lady Anna* (1874) I. iii. 35 She did not believe in the good time coming as did her mother.

5. a. *behind the time(s)* (examples); *to move with the times*: see *MOVE *v.* 19 c.

1846 DICKENS *Dombey & Son* (1848) ix. 87 I'm old-fashioned, and behind the time. **1921** E. O'NEILL *Diff'rent* II, in *Emperor Jones* 244 You needn't think we're *all* so behind the times..here just because you've been to France and all over. **1937** 'G. ORWELL' *Road to Wigan Pier* viii. 163 Here I shall be accused of being behind the times, for I was a child before and during the war and it may be claimed that children nowadays are brought up with more enlightened notions.

b. Also used *attrib.* to designate typefaces designed for *The Times*.

1932 S. MORISON in *Monotype Recorder* XXXI. 12 (*heading*) The Times New Roman. *Ibid.* 13/1 A set of drawings was completed some two years ago, and the first size of what is now '*The Times* New Roman' was cut in 9 point at the Monotype Works, Redhill, in April, 1931. **1963** *Times* 4 June 8/4 *Time*, the weekly news magazine, appears this week with a changed type face—Times Roman instead of the former old style. **1972** *Times* 9 Oct. 1/4 After 40 years *The Times* today appears in a new body type, Times-Europa. This has been designed for *The Times* to suit changing printing methods and largely replaces Times Roman.

c. *big time*: see *BIG *a.* B. 2. See also *SMALL TIME, SMALL-TIME *sb.* and *a.* (*phr.*).

6. *to make a time* (examples); *to have the time of one's life* (examples); *to have one more time* (U.S. colloq.), to have a very good time; *a good*, etc., *time was had by all*. Also, (without specification, depending on context) a good or bad experience lasting some time; *N. Amer.* a social occasion, a party.

1860 H. J. HAWLEY in *Wisconsin Mag. Hist.* (1936) Mar. 323, I had a time biding them good by. **1878** in G. M. Story et al. *Dict. Newfoundland Eng.* (1982) 568/2 But..while on a visit to Bett's Cove [he] got on a time and 'let the cat out of the bag'. **1882** I. M. RITTENHOUSE *Maud* (1939) 149 I've had a 'time' with Mr. Blauvelt. **1883** A. PINKERTON *Spy of Rebellion* xxi. 328 While there I met some of the boys, and we had a little 'time'. **1887** [see *LIFE *sb.* 8 a]. **1888** *Boston Jrnl.* 31 July 2/5 She doesn't weep at the parting or make any time over it. **1898** E. N. WESTCOTT *David Harum* 14 Mis' Perkins don't hev much of a time herself. **1901** *N. Amer. Rev.* Feb. 228 No other troops made such a time about water as the Americans. **1913** H. KEPHART *Our Southern Highlanders* xiii. 286 'We had one more *time*' means a rousing good time. **1921** R. HICHENS *Spirit of Time* 186 Arab chieftains ..having the time of their lives in the redecorated hotels. **1921** E. O'NEILL *Diff'rent* II, in *Emperor Jones* 251, I told her to cut the rough work and behave—and a nice time was had by all. **1933** GREENLEAF & MANSFIELD *Ballads & Sea Songs Newfoundland* p. xxii, To raise money for the schoolhouse and the church, the Sally's Cove people held a 'toime' on Orangemen's Day, which took the form of an all-day fair and was held in the school-house. **1949** F. MACLEAN *Eastern Approaches* III. ix. 406 After that we mixed a delicious drink in the bath tub, and a good time, as the saying goes, was had by all. **1956** B. HOLIDAY *Lady sings Blues* (1973) ii. 18 So I..decided I'd get off the train in New York, take the subway to Harlem, have myself a time. **1963** L. DIACK *Labrador Nurse* IV. xxxiii. 155 A 'Time' was an evening Social, with Sale of Work, supper and dance, and all the food served at the 'Time' was supplied and cooked and served by those same women. **1964** *Amer. Folk Music Occasional* I. 15 Ah yes, they used to have some times... That was in the old days. **1967** *Boston Sunday Herald* 7 May VI. 8/8 The state stages such exciting and colorful events as the annual Clam, Broiler, Potato,..and Blueberry Festivals.., not to mention..scores of other 'times'. **1969** in Halpert & Story *Christmas Mumming in Newfoundland* 82 A 'time' is any function given in the school, or local Orangemen's Lodge: a card party, a dance, or a dance combined with a 'soup supper'. **1976** 'W. TREVOR' *Children of Dynmouth* i. 13 He hoped..that Lavinia wasn't having a time with the twins, cooped inside on a damp afternoon.

7. b. (*a*) (Later example.) (*d*) (Earlier example.) (*f*) (Further examples.) (*h*) The prescribed duration of opening-hours at a public house; the moment at which this ends; also *ellipt.* as the signal for closing-time.

(*a*) **1965** P. WRIGHTSON *Thirteen paint Portrait* I. 59 Marion looks rather ghastly. Poor girl, she is nearly at the end of her 'time'.

(*d*) **1837** DICKENS *O. Twist* (1838) I. xviii. 306 His 'time' was only out an hour before.

(*f*) **1829** P. EGAN *Boxiana* 2nd Ser. II. 519 The Gas was *defeated*, nay, *hit* out of time..to the great loss and chagrin of his friends. **1833** *Sporting Mag.* Aug. 354/2 On time being called, Pilch went in again. **1892** J. HIGSON *Hist. Salford Football Club* 52 A fight began, and the game was brought to an abrupt termination about five minutes before 'Time'. **1926** [see *END *sb.* 22 f]. **1976** *Sunday Mail* (Glasgow) 28 Nov. 44/6 Scorers were Martin, in the first half, and Johnston just before time.

(*h*) **1912** G. FRANKAU *One of Us* xi. 104 Lingered a remnant; querulous to these, one spake unceasing: 'Gentlemen! Time, Please!!' **1922** T. S. ELIOT *Waste Land* II. 23 Hurry up please its time. **1932** L. GOLDING *Magnolia St.* I. iii. 47 Collecting empty glasses and shouting, 'Time, gentlemen, please!' **1953** J. MORTIMER *Like Men Betrayed* v. 87 It's not very comfortable in our pub... They're always shouting 'time' and turning the lights on and off. **1979** 'C. BRAND' *Rose in Darkness* ii. 20 Soon he must turn her out..five minutes to Time. **1984** *Daily Tel.* 4 Jan. 15/7 A car crashed into the Mermaid public house..and ended up in the bar just as the landlord..was calling time.

8. b. (Earlier example.)

1842 *Congress. Globe* 2 Mar. App. 188/2 A single horse in a sulky would..be able to make..even better time, with the letter mail alone.

c. *pressed for time*, short of time, in a hurry.

1817 [see PRESS *v.*¹ 6 e]. **1833** [in Dict., sense 8 a]. **1942** W. FAULKNER *Go down, Moses* 274 Not impatient but just pressed for time.

d. *it takes* (a person) *all his time*, it presents great difficulties to, it requires great effort from. *colloq.*

1900 R. GUTHRIE *Kitty Fagan* 208 We've a ticklish job on hand, an I'm boond to say, it's taken us all our time. **1905** in *Eng. Dialect Dict.* VI. 151/2 It'll tak him all his time to mak that theäre public paay it waay. **1941** E. CARR *Klee Wyck* 89 It took Jimmie all his time in the shallows to keep us in the channel.

e. Imp. phr. *give* (a person) *time*, be patient with (another), in expectation of some future change of attitude, competence, etc.

1902 [see *SMILE *v.* 8 b]. **1940** W. FAULKNER *Hamlet* I. iii. 60 He'll pick it up though... Just give him time. **1962** J. F. POWERS *Morte d'Urban* vii. 151, I don't say the present population wants it, but give 'em time.

f. With a quantifier: *to have no* (*a lot of*, etc.) *time for*, to have no, etc., respect or admiration for. *colloq.*

1911 E. M. CLOWES *On Wallaby* vi. 166 The merely fictitious value of age they [*sc.* Australian youth] 'have no time for'. **1922** C. WILSON *Rambles in Bookland* 3, I never had much time, to use an effective colloquialism, for the list of 'the best hundred books'. **1938** N. MARSH *Artists in Crime* xi. 156 The only one they seemed to have much time for was the Honourable Basil Pilgrim. **1952** A. GRIMBLE *Pattern of Islands* ix. 177 He never had much time for pen-pushers, as he called them. **1966** J. CLEARY *High Commissioner* xi. 247, I don't think he'd harm her... I think he had a lot of time for my wife. **1979** M. ALLEN *Spence at Blue Bazaar* xix. 121 'Yes, I've got a lot of time for Lester,' the Vicar continued... 'He'll always lend a hand at a fête or whatever.'

g. Time available for a certain purpose, *spec.* for an advertising broadcast.

1930 *Daily Express* 6 Sept. 4/6 To the big advertiser the broadcasting stations came with an offer to 'sell time' to pay the cost of broadcasting programmes. **1935** S. LEWIS *It can't happen Here* iv. 42 Father Charles Coughlin, of Detroit..first thought out the device of freeing himself from any censorship of his political sermons..by 'buying his own time on the air'. **1967** *Boston Sunday Herald* 26 Mar. I. 11/1 CBS-TV explained..that its policy 'prohibits ..the sale of time for the expression of views on current issues other than in connection with elections'. **1970** *Daily Tel.* (Colour Suppl.) 18 Sept. 30 The world's 1300 or so professional astronomers who obtain 'time' on the big telescopes all have different programmes in different parts of the sky. **1977** *Zigzag* June 10/3 A friend of mine who was an engineer rang up to see if I had any songs I wanted to cut, because he could get me some time.

h. *to take* (*one's*) *time*: see TAKE *v.* 28 a; *lost time*: see LOST *ppl. a.* 3.

9. (Earlier and further examples of sense 'pay', esp. at the termination of a period of employment.)

1887 *Courier-Journal* (Louisville, Kentucky) 12 Jan. 6/3 All that remained for the brakemen and switchmen to do was to go to the office..and call for what is known in railroad parlance as their 'time'. **1902** S. E. WHITE *Blazed Trail* viii. 56 So Pat and Henrys were not discharged—were not instructed to 'get their time'. **1926** J. BLACK *You can't Win* xx. 317 He threw down his shovel, walked over to the boss, and demanded his 'time'. I heard the foreman say: 'All right, you're no good anyway. I was going to fire you to-night.' **1935** A. J. CRONIN *Stars look Down* III. xiv. 608 It broke his heart to give these fifty their time, to send them to join the six hundred men from the Neptune already on the dole.

b. *time and a half* and varr., one and a half (or one and a quarter, etc.) times the usual rate of pay.

1888 [in Dict.]. **1921** *Daily Colonist* (Victoria, B.C.) 16 Mar. 3/4 The extra payment was due to the time and a half allowance for overtime. **1931** *Economist* 14 Mar. 552/2 Extra pay for night duty is to be reduced from 'time and a quarter' to 'time and an eighth', and for duty on Sunday, Christmas Day and Good Friday from 'time and a half' to 'time and a third'. **1970** *Daily Tel.* 9 Jan. 9 The claim..is for payment of time-and-a-quarter for the first six hours' overtime, time-and-a-half for the next six, and double time payments thereafter. **1976** *Ibid.* 12 Nov. 2/1 They want holiday pay, at present single time, increased to time and a third. **1978** M. KENYON *Deep Pocket* ii. 28 Tell the men I'm paying time and a half for every forty yards dug by the weekend.

11. *to mark time*: see MARK *v.* 10 b.

II. 13. d. *Stock Exch.* The account.

1901 W. G. CORDINGLEY *Dict. Stock Exch. Terms* 89 Time Bargains refer to those speculative transactions which are made for settlement on the next Account. They are made 'for time', and are 'Bought for the Account' or 'Sold for the Account'. **1928** *Daily Mail* 13 Aug. 18/2 Dealing for 'new time',..the new Stock Exchange account.

15. b. (Later examples in the sense 'time of childbirth'.)

1841 THACKERAY *Gt. Hoggarty Diamond* xii, in *Miscellanies* (1857) IV. 428 My poor wife, then very near her time, insisted upon accompanying me. **1931** H. S. WALPOLE *Judith Paris* III. 582 Judith was very near her time, and, in consideration..that this was her first child, it had been wiser of her perhaps not to have come. **1980** R.

BUTLER *Blood-Red Sun at Noon* (1981) I. i. 19 She..became pregnant... What she called 'her time' approached.

16. (Earlier example of *now's your time.*)

c 1810 W. HICKEY *Mem.* (1960) xix. 309 Now's your time, Hickey. That beast Mordaunt was called away..so that you will have a couple of days' enjoyment together.

17. a. With a price: (so much) *a time*, on each occasion, (*colloq.*) for each item.

1718 R. GROSVENOR in C. T. Gatty *Mary Davies* (1921) II. 205 One that is grown pretty rich by his attendance upon Patients in Garrets at Half-a-Crown a time. **1976** *West Lancs. Evening Gaz.* 13 Dec. 7/5 Buying..cashmere scarves at £15 a time.

c. *every time*: see *EVERY *a.* 1 e.

18. *many a time and oft* (later example); *times* (later examples) also, sometimes, at times; *many's the time.*

1920 E. O'NEILL *Beyond Horizon* II. i. 67 Many's the time I've said to her [etc.]. **1936** WODEHOUSE *Laughing Gas* xxiii. 247 You have many a time and oft referred to her as a piece of cheese. **1938** M. K. RAWLINGS *Yearling* xvii. 213 Seems to me, times, hit ain't done nothin' to you but sharpen your tongue. **1956** A. WILSON *Anglo-Saxon Attitudes* I. iii. 48 Many's the time Sir Beerbohm Tree's stood outside the theatre. **1968** C. AIRD *Henrietta Who?* xiv. 130 Times, it's a bit quiet at Holly Tree. **1980** P. G. WINSLOW *Counsellor Heart* iii. 52 There's one that likes a joke. Times I've had her in fits. **1982** S. JOHNSON *Of Wilful Intent* i. 13 'And you say this has all been reported before?' the sergeant asked him. 'Times,' came the despondent reply.

19. Also *attrib.* with *table* or *ellipt.*, designating the multiplication table of the preceding cardinal number. Cf. *times table*, sense 52 below.

1906 KIPLING *Puck of Pook's Hill* 38, I don't know my Nine Times—not to say it dodging. **1973** J. WAINWRIGHT *Touch of Malice* 124 A long-suffering father explaining the two-times-table to his dull-witted son. **1976** D. STOREY *Saville* xi. 133, I want you to recite the two times, the three times, right through to your twelve times. **1982** *Sunday Tel.* 2 May 11/1 (*heading*) Know your 6-times table.

III. 24. b. *time will tell* (and varr.); *borrowed time*: see *BORROWED *ppl. a.* 1; *the (very) nick of time*: see NICK *sb.*[1] 9.

[**1539** R. TAVERNER tr. *Erasmus's Proverbes* f. 37 *Tempus omnia reuelat.* Tyme discloseth all thynges. **1616** T. DRAXE *Bibliotheca Scholastica* 205/2 Time reuealeth all things.] **1771** C. STUART *Let.* 15 Apr. in *Publ. Miss. Hist. Soc.* (1925) V. 50 Time only will shew how far those Informations have been well founded. **1863** C. READE *Hard Cash* I. v. 164/2 She shall speak as distinctly to music as you do in conversation. *Sampson*... Time will show, madam. **1913** E. H. PORTER *Pollyanna* xxiii. 234 The doctor had looked very grave..and had said that time alone could tell. **1957** A. HUXLEY *Lett.* (1969) 839 It may turn out, of course, that the experts are right and that their play is better... Time will show. **1971** D. EDEN *Afternoon Walk* vii. 94 Time will tell, Mrs. Simpson. **1980** J. GARDNER *Garden of Weapons* III. xi. 332 'Big Herbie gone over, has he?' Fincher said that time would tell. **1983** *Sunday Tel.* 20 Feb. 16/4 Whether this general mania for physical purification extends also to schoolgirls we are not told. Time alone will tell.

c. *it's* (*only*, etc.) *a question* (or *matter*) *of time*: said of an event that is thought certain to happen sooner or later.

1867 E. A. FREEMAN *Hist. Norman Conquest of England* I. iv. 251 The definitive alliance of Rouen and Paris fixed the extinction..of the royalty of Laôn. It was a question of time. **1928** E. O'NEILL *Strange Interlude* III. 94 I'm making good, all right..since I got married—and it's only a question of time. **1960** S. BARSTOW *Kind of Loving* II. viii. 273 It's just a question of time now, apparently. Making all the arrangements and all that. **1960** D. STOREY *This Sporting Life* II. v. 236 Mrs. Hammond was in a coma. It seemed only a matter of time before she died. **1963** 'J. LE CARRÉ' *Spy who came in from Cold* viii. 81 It was only a matter of time before it packed up. **1982** *N.Y. Times* 30 Sept. c 18/4 It's only a matter of time before something terrible happens.

d. *to kill time*: see KILL *v.* 5; *time hangs heav(il)y*: see HANG *v.* 15 b; *to redeem the time*: see REDEEM *v.* 8.

27. (Further examples.) *standard time*, a standard system of reckoning time adopted throughout a country or region, now based on the time zone in which it is situated; cf. *zone time* s.v. *ZONE *sb.* 9 a. With preceding place-name or possessive pronoun, the time as reckoned at the place referred to (normally differing from one's own). Cf. *Greenwich time* s.v. GREENWICH, SUMMER TIME 2, *RAILWAY TIME.

1840 *Minutes Board of G.W.R.* in *Railway Gaz.* (1935) 30 Aug. (G.W.R. Suppl.) 7/2 Outside clock to be provided for each station so as to be seen by passing trains, in order to ensure punctuality. London time to be adopted at all stations. **1841** *G.W.R. Timetable* in *Ibid.*, London time is about 4 min. earlier than Reading time. **1847** H. BOOTH *Uniformity of Time* 4 The managers [of the Post Office]..are quite aware of the advantages of one uniform system of time..; accordingly all their movements are regulated by 'London Time'. **1847** *Minutes Railway Clearing House Committee* 22 Sept. in *Vistas in Astron.* (1976) XX. 221 That it be recommended to each company to adopt Greenwich Time as soon as the Post Office permits them to do so. **1847**, etc. [see *RAILWAY TIME]. **1863** DICKENS in *All Year Round* 2 May 232/1 They don't keep 'London time' on a French railway. **1879** S. FLEMING *Papers on Time-Reckoning* 13 On a journey from Paris to Vienna..the standard time employed by the railways changes frequently. **1883** *N.Y. Times* 19 Nov. 5/2 Standard time clocks were set to correspond to the new signals. **1917** *Whitaker's Almanack* 90/1 Since the year 1883 the system of Standard Time by Zones has been gradually accepted, and now the majority of the countries of the world use as Standard Time the time of some meridian which differs from that of Greenwich by a multiple of 15°. **1924** J. C. W. REITH in *Radio Times* 4 Jan. 42/3 We broadcast standard time. **1935** *Cook's Continental Time Table* Mar. 102 Moscow time is two hours later than that of Greenwich. **1941** *Ann. Reg. 1940* 126 A state of war existed..as from 9 a.m. (Eastern standard time). **1948** A. N. KEITH *Three came Home* xviii. 295 He telephones me from Australia... We speak at twelve midnight, my time. **1958** 'N. SHUTE' *Rainbow & Rose* vi. 229, I would hand over to him at two in the morning, Honolulu time. **1974** *Encycl. Brit. Macropædia* XVIII. 415/1 All clocks in the United States were kept one hour ahead of standard time for the interval February 9, 1942–September 30, 1945... Since then, the time in a large part of Europe has been kept one hour ahead of standard zone time without any change during the summer. **1979** P. HILL *Washermen* xxxiv. 81 [He] arrives at Kai Tak Airport, Hong Kong, 3 p.m. tomorrow afternoon our time.

IV. Phrases.

*With another sb.

28. time of day. a. *not to give* (a person) *the time of day* (colloq.), not to help or cooperate with (a person) at all, to be surly or mean towards. Cf. salutations at sense 28 b.

1951 N. MAILER *Advts. for Myself* (1961) 146 You don't even give me the time of day. You're the coldest man I've ever known. **1979** A. MALING *Koberg Link* (1980) xxiii. 123 You've come to the wrong place. Paul Carmichael won't give me the time of day. **1982** A. PRICE *Old 'Vengeful'* vii. 112 Lippy wouldn't have given Danny the time of day on a wet Sunday afternoon, not if he'd have come to him on bended knees.

b. *to pass the time of day*: see also PASS *v.* 52 c.

28*. time of life, the age of a person, *esp.* middle age, the menopause.

1764 [in Dict., sense 13]. **1838** MRS. GASKELL *Let.* 17 Aug. (1966) 25 We agreed..that when people are come to *yr time of life*, there is no use having long engagements. **1971** 'E. FERRARS' *Stranger & Afraid* vi. 100 Whatever's wrong with a woman over forty, it seems to me, people say it's her Time of Life. **1981** J. MANN *Funeral Sites* xxii. 132 Aidan has already threatened me with psychiatrists. He says it is 'my time of life'.

30. time and tide. (Further examples.)

1639 J. CLARKE *Parœmiologia Anglo-Latina* 233 Time and tide tary on no man. **1796** 'A. BARTON' *Disappointment* II. iv. 50 Let's step into the state-room, you know the old saying, 'Time and tide waits for no one'. **1935** J. MASEFIELD *Box of Delights* i. 21 Time and Tide and Buttered eggs wait for no man. **1979** 'C. AIRD' *Some die Eloquent* x. 112 Time and tide and newspapers wait for no man. **1983** *Out of Town* Dec. 19/2 Only two years ago it [*sc.* The National Trust] completed a major repair to the tiny and beautiful Mullion Harbour on the Lizard Peninsula. Time and tide wait for no man.

**With a following adv.

33. a. Also, **time and time again.**

1887 J. HARTLEY *Halifax Orig. Illuminated Clock Almanack* 48 He's browt us in a bit o' dinner time an' time again. **1957** E. WAUGH *Ordeal of Gilbert Pinfold* i. 2 He would dearly have liked to revise it, envying painters, who are allowed to return to the same theme time and time again. **1977** *It* May 29/2 Time and time again we have been told of the desperate need to coordinate squatting activities.

35*. time off, a break from one's occupation, absence from work, school, service, etc. (cf. *OFF *adv.* 4 d); also, remission of part of a prison sentence.

1930 H. CRANE *Let.* 30 Sept. (1965) 356 I'm taking 'time off' to answer in the hope that you'll write me more news. **1951** 'J. TEY' *Daughter of Time* i. 9 Benny would get time off for good behaviour. **1954** *Spectator* 10 Dec. 736/2 Theorists who indulge the undemocratic vice of taking time off to think. **1977** *Whitaker's Almanack 1978* 580/2 The *Financial Times* was not published because of a dispute between management and N.G.A. compositors over time-off.

35. time out, time-out, timeout** (orig. and chiefly *U.S.*). **a.** (Usu. as one word.) In various games: a deduction of playing time for a stoppage; a (usu. brief) break in play called by a coach, referee, or player.

1896 CAMP & DELAND *Football* vi. 61 *Time out*, time taken out by the referee when play is not actually in progress. **1930** *Sun* (Baltimore) 26 Dec. 11/7 The game..takes up about two and a quarter hours, when one allows for the intermission between halves and the innumerable 'times out'. **1946** [see *DOLLY VARDEN]. **1972** J. MOSEDALE *Football* v. 61 We'd just stopped them on our one-yard line and called time-out. **1979** *Arizona Daily Star* 5 Aug. c 1/2 Clark's directive created a difference of opinion during a Tucson timeout in the opening game. **1981** *Times* 11 Nov. 8/8 Experts said Korchnoi might postpone the fifteenth game, which is due on Thursday. Each man has used up two of the three timeouts allowed each player under the championship rules.

b. A break from one's occupation.

1939 I. BAIRD *Waste Heritage* vi. 76 An' I took time out to tell you why we got to have those rules. **1962** J. D. MACDONALD *Girl, Gold Watch, & Everything* ix. 115 Everybody in such a damn hurry, sugar, it's good for them to take a little time out. **1978** *Chicago* June 131/2 Sandwiching Sunday-morning Mass between an appearance on *Meet the Press* and a press conference back at the Ramada Inn was the only time-out Schtafly took in Houston.

***With a governing preposition or adverb.

35*. about time**, approximately the right time; usu. *iron.*, long past the right time; (also with *too*) this should have happened much earlier, this is long overdue.

1920 E. O'NEILL *Beyond Horizon* II. i. 67 It's about time you put a stop to his nonsense. **1931** [see *CURVE *sb.* 2]. **1940** W. FAULKNER *Hamlet* IV. i. 285, I reckon it's about time to get dinner started. **1952** M. R. RINEHART *Swimming Pool* xxvii. 240 'It's about time,' he said, pushing aside the junket Jennie had served him. **1977** A. CLARKE *Letter from Dead* ix. 103 'Now you're talking,' said Jill, 'and about time too.'

36. against time. (Earlier and later examples.)

1835 DICKENS *Sk. Boz* (1836) 1st Ser. II. 178 The kennels seem to be doing matches against time. **1933** D. L. SAYERS *Hangman's Holiday* 37 It must have been put in the wrong way round... You know, sir, we often have to work against time, and I suppose—but it's very careless. **1935** 'E. QUEEN' *Adventures* 86 What would you gentlemen expect a thief, working against time, to do under these circumstances? **1975** *Economist* 1 Feb. 16 Sheikh Mujib's 'second revolution' last weekend was his personal answer to this race against time. **1982** *Washington Post* 11 Nov. D 11 Whether it realizes it or not, the government of Japan is in a race against time.

42. in time. d. *what* (*why*, etc.) *in time..*, 'what (etc.) in the world..' or 'on earth..'. *U.S. colloq.*

1849 J. T. FIELDS *Let.* 28 Feb. in R. W. Griswold *Passages from Corr.* (1898) 250 Why in Time don't you come our way and see the boys? **1883** *Harper's Mag.* Jan. 212/1 He wondered what In time made 'em keep the cars so hot. **1904** J. C. LINCOLN *Cap'n Eri* vii. 125 What in time did you tell the Doctor that she was a relation of mine for?

42*. not before (*dial.* **afore**) **time**, not soon enough, almost too late, long overdue.

1905 in *Eng. Dialect Dict.* VI. 15/1 Ah see they're beginnin' ti mend rooad, an nat afoor time. **1955** 'N. SHUTE' *Requiem for Wren* v. 144 She got her clothes brush from her quarters and gave him a grooming with it, not before time. **1967** *Listener* 26 Oct. 553/3 The Minister..is right: 'the licensed victualler must now recognise that he has to provide a different kind of social life in his pub.' It is not before time. **1972** *Observer* 16 July 13/6 It all points to a wind of change blowing in the direction of the Ordinary shares..: and not before time either. **1974** *New Statesman* 29 Nov. 766/1 It's..goodbye to cheap sugar—and perhaps not before time so far as the developing countries are concerned.

43. on time. a. For 'Chiefly' read 'Formerly chiefly'. (Earlier example.) Also (with hyphen) *attrib.* (see *ON-[1] 4 b).

1821 R. CADELL *Let.* 28 Nov. in *Times Lit. Suppl.* (1933) 7 Sept. 592/2 In order to effect this *and on time* we have resolved [etc.]. **1965** *Economist* 13 Feb. 675/1 Exact scheduling..and perfect coordination to assure on-time completion of the project. **1967** R. J. SERLING *President's Plane is Missing* (1968) i. 13 As my airline friends would say, I prefer on-time departures.

c. On credit. *N. Amer.*

1840 *Spirit of Times* 15 Aug. 277/1 *On time*, the prices would at once be enhanced. **1873** W. MATHEWS *Getting on in World* xix. 316 We need not expect that the practice of selling goods on time will ever be abandoned. **1925** *Sat. Even. Post* 10 Oct. 133/1 It's like peddling lots on time, instead of selling and developing acreage. **1972** J. M. MINIFIE *Homesteader* vi. 44 Everything was bought 'on time', hardly any transactions involved cash. **1979** R. L. SIMON *Peking Duck* xx. 144 On the table with Harvey's Sony tape recorder was a Nikon FT... I wondered if he had bought it all on time.

44. out of time. c. *out of one's time*, in an era unsympathetic to one's attitudes, aspirations, etc.; at the wrong season.

1950 'D. DIVINE' *King of Fassarai* xvi. 125 Kellie was born out of his time. Last piece of history he could have flourished in was the Alaska rushes. **1958** B. BEHAN *Borstal Boy* III. 334 It was a little undersized goat born out of its time, and it was so small now that it wouldn't be any bigger than a lamb at Christmas when we put on the play. **1973** R. LEWIS *Of Singular Purpose* vi. 130 'Major Cornelius Van Rijk.' He laughed shortly. 'A man out of his time.' **1976** L. HENDERSON *Major Enquiry* xii. 78 You know, Mildred, you were born out of your time, you really belong to the naughty nineties.

44*. over time, gradually, during a period of (past or future) time.

1966 *Rep. Comm. Inquiry Univ. Oxf.* II. 46 The proportion from independent schools has fallen over time. **1973** *New Society* 1 Nov. 258/3 Like the Foot-Steel proposals, these would be introduced over time.

****With a verb.

50*. *to make time* (*with*): see *MAKE *v.*[1] 66.

IV*. Ellipt.

50.** as *conj.* At or by the time that; as soon as; when. *U.S. dial.* and *colloq.*

1919 E. O'NEILL *Moon of Caribbees* 6 It *was* in New Guinea, time I was shipwrecked there. **1938** M. K. RAWLINGS *Yearling* iv. 30 You'll likely not be so merry, time the day be done. *Ibid.* ix. 78 You git on to the sink-hole, son, and I'll foller time I've skinned out your 'coon hide. **1950** R. MOORE *Candlemas Bay* 13 Time Joel Walls had his net, one night he caught seven hogsids.

V. Combinations.

51. a. (*a*) *time-behaviour*, *-consciousness*, *-co-ordinate*, *-cycle*, *-depth*, *-dimension*, *-direction*, *-displacement*, *-evolution*, *-factor*, *-flow*,

-foot, -gap, -horizon, -integral (earlier example), *-interval, -measure, -order, -pattern, -period, -perspective* (earlier example), *-plane, -process, -ratio, -relation, -rhythm, -scheme, -sense* (earlier example), *-sequence, -shift, -slip, -span, -sphere, -stream, -succession, -unit, -word*; (*b*) *time-budget, -chart*; (*c*) *time-bomb* (*fig.* and *attrib.* examples).

a **1974** R. Crossman *Diaries* (1975) I. 259 A mere day and a half was a crazy time-allocation if only because the eight new clauses and fifty amendments..would take all the time available. **1955** Friedman & Weisskopf in W. Pauli *Niels Bohr* 153 We can then examine the time behaviour of the outgoing parts of the wave packet as they pass a given radius. **1977** *Jrnl. R. Soc. Arts* CXXV. 765/2 Other types of lasers..can be controlled in either frequency or time-behaviour with the limits set only by the Uncertainty Principle. **1939** Dylan Thomas *Map of Love* 21 Strike in the time-bomb town. **1941** B. Schulberg *What makes Sammy Run?* vi. 128 Sammy Glick is a time bomb in my brain and it's going to go off. **1966** N. Nicolson *Diaries & Lett. H. Nicolson* 275 Harold Nicolson had long been aware that a constitutional time-bomb was ticking beneath the throne. **1981** 'M. Underwood' *Double Jeopardy* xxiii. 181 His official diary could become a time bomb. **1948** Time-budget [see *participant *sb.* 1]. **1976** P. R. White *Planning for Public Transport* ii. 46 Within a fixed time-budget, as work trips become longer, less time is available for shopping and recreational trips on weekdays. **1934** *Burlington Mag.* Jan. 50/1 The author establishes his time-chart, proving conclusively that the wide early influence..has no foundation in fact. **1958** *Times Lit. Suppl.* 17 Jan. 33/2 Mr Sullivan..gives a much more orderly unfolding of the time-chart of discovery because he sticks to a straight-forward chronology. **1890** W. James *Princ. Psychol.* I. xv. 632 Th. Waitz is guilty of similar question-begging when he explains our time-consciousness. **1963** H. Lindenberger *On Wordsworth's 'Prelude'* vi. 199 The dissolution of the traditional literary genres and the increasing eccentricity of structure..have proved co-incidental with..the development of time-consciousness among writers. *a* **1942** B. Malinowski *Sci. Theory of Culture* (1944) iii. 20 In order..to make an historical process ..significant in terms of explanation or analysis, it is.. necessary to prove that we are, along the time coördinate, linking up phenomena that are strictly comparable. **1903** A. W. Patterson *Schumann* 7 That the mind should work in a regular time-cycle, passing from one phase of sentiment to another with almost mechanical exactness. **1968** *Brit. Med. Bull.* XXIV. 197/2 All disease, whether it be physical or emotional, appears to have its time-cycles. **1957** P. Worsley *Trumpet shall Sound* 266 There is time-depth to all social action. **1978** *Archivum Linguisticum* IX. 76 The ultimate sources of the verbal root **es-* can never be definitively known because of the huge time-depth involved here. **1937** *Mind* XLVI. 162 It is rather unfortunate that philosophers..should have paid little attention to the problem suggested by Minkowski's imaginary time-dimensions. **1982** M. Duke *Flashpoint* vii. 46 Shmuel let his mind slip into a new time-dimension. The near future looked good. **1890** W. James *Princ. Psychol.* I. ix. 283 With each prolongation of the scheme in the time-direction, the summit of the curve of section would come further towards the end of the sentence. **1937** *Mind* XLVI. 177 We may agree..to regard as the time-direction that in which the number of beats registered by the clock is increasing. **1890** W. James *Princ. Psychol.* I. xi. 411 The cases he [*sc.* Wundt] describes are really cases of anachronistic perception, of subjective time-displacement, to use his own term. **1901** Time-displacement [see *attentional *a.*]. **1937** R. A. Wilson *Birth of Language* II. ii. 79 To one..who tries to work out a concrete philosophical view of the world..on the basis of a time-evolution of all its forms from matter to man, the mechanistic hypothesis appears..to obscure the real problem of the beginnings of life. **1911** *Aeronaut. Jrnl.* XV. 66 This switch has a 'time-factor' approximating to that of the motor. **1976** M. & G. Gordon *Ordeal* (1977) xxix. 198 He worked fast, conscious of the time factor. **1936** J. Kantor *Objective Psychol. Gram.* xvii. 240 Grammarians mean by time the abstract points in a field-spread or an equally abstract time-flow. **1956** E. L. Mascall *Christian Theol. & Natural Sci.* iv. 134 This continuous activity of God is not to be thought of as if it were the insertion of the creatures into a time-flow which existed antecedently to them. **1883** Time-foot [see *rhythm-foot* s.v. *rhythm *sb.* 9 a]. **1890** W. James *Princ. Psychol.* I. ix. 237 Interruptions, time-gaps during which the consciousness went out altogether to come into existence again at a later moment. **1978** *Early Music Gaz.* Oct. 15/2 Leonhardt emphasises the large time-gap between the two books of the so-called '48'. **1965** H. I. Ansoff *Corporate Strategy* iii. 40 To make this concept meaningful, we need the idea of the *time horizon* of a firm—the period over which the firm seeks to optimize its resource conversion efficiency. **1983** *Listener* 8 Dec. 23/3 The time-horizon over which policy is formulated would become markedly biased towards the short-term. **1873** J. C. Maxwell *Electr. & Magn.* II. 186 The time-integral of a force is called the Impulse of the force. **1871** *Cornh. Mag.* July 58 The imagination is wholly unable either to conceive the duration of the time-intervals..occupied by these wonderful processes. **1975** *Language for Life* (Dept. Educ. & Sci.) xxv. 503 We had to ask whether the width of the time intervals had forced the pattern of responses and rendered suspect our method of calculating average times. **1911** W. James *Some Probl. Philos.* xi. 179 Mr. Bertrand Russell..treats the Achilles-puzzle as if the difficulty lay only in seeing how the paths traversed by the two runners.. should have the same time-measure if they be not themselves of the same length. **1943** *Mind* LII. 61 From no sort of correlation between space-measures and time-measures can the obliteration of the ontological distinction between space and time be validly inferred. **1890** W. James *Princ. Psychol.* I. iii. 88 The whole succession is so rapid that perception seems to be retrospective, and the time-order of events to be read off in memory rather than known at the moment. **1960** *Colston Research Soc. Symposium* XII. 90 These paranormal cognitive powers, it seems, are indifferent in some degree to a physical time order, which of course raises frightful difficulties. **1946** R. Blesh *Shining Trumpets* ii. 42 The..sequential time-patterns of human or divine speech. **1968** D. L. Clarke *Analytical Archaeol.* vi. 254 The time pattern regularities ..in the trajectories and traditions of many quite different cultures. **1894** *Jrnl. Inst. Electrical Engineers* XXIII. III. 295 It was due to synchronism between the changes of load *on the engines* and the time-period of the governor. **1953** *Scottish Jrnl. Theol.* VI. 162 We believe that patterns and expanding purposes have been established through such time-periods. **1965** *Canad. Jrnl. Linguistics* Spring 125 Seven languages..died out during the twenty-three year period ending in 1964... In this same time-period Coos was reduced to a single informant. **1890** W. James *Princ. Psychol.* I. xv. 639 In hashish-intoxication there is a curious increase in the apparent time-perspective. **1969** Bennison & Wright *Geol. Hist. Brit. Isles* ii. 26 Lines indicating contemporaneity, so-called 'time-planes', are normally presented diagrammatically as horizontal. **1977** G. Clark *World Prehist.* (ed. 3) I. 24 Among the factors that caused peoples living on the same time-plane to retain or discard old forms while adopting new ones were ..variations in the environment to which they had to adapt. **1887** A. Seth *Hegelianism* v. 170 The time-process of the finite world is..the reality with which we are immediately acquainted. **1938** E. Bevan *Symbolism & Belief* iv. 114 The time-process goes on throughout a universe of which our planet is, spatially, only an infinitesimal part. **1964** W. S. Allen in D. Abercombie et al. *Daniel Jones* 3 Whereas in modern verse the rhythms are marked by 'stress', the classical rhythms were expressed solely in terms of time-ratios. **1965** *Wireless World* July 336/2 The same idea of time-ratio control can be used in regulated power supplies. **1924** R. M. Ogden tr. *Koffka's Growth of Mind* iii. 118 When a pianist..articulates a series of muscular innervations..fixed time-relations are determined in the series of sound-waves. **1962** D. Nichols *Echinoderms* v. 71 There is no clear-cut evidence as to the origin of the echinoids. Time-relations do not allow their derivation from the Ophiocistioidea of the Silurian. *c* **1873–4** Time-rhythm [see *beat *sb.*[1] 5]. **1934** J. J. Hogan *Outl. Eng. Philol.* iv. 29 Quantity or time-rhythm, consisting of the alternation of longer and shorter, not of stronger and weaker beats, is the rhythm of music. **1904** *Mind* Oct. 468 The distribution of terms in our inner time-scheme and space-scheme must be an exact copy of the distribution in real time and space of the real terms. **1978** *N. & Q.* Feb. 55/1 Given Sterne's complicated time-scheme..such inconsistencies are surprisingly rare. **1890** W. James *Princ. Psychol.* I. xv. 611 The units of duration ..which the time-sense is able to take in at a single stroke, are groups of a few seconds. *Ibid.* II. xxviii. 671 The principle [of causality] expresses a demand for *some* deeper sort of inward connection between phenomena than their merely habitual time-sequence seems to us to be. **1974** G. Jenkins *Bridge of Magpies* viii. 135 What the time sequence of events was in regard to the two killings I'd never know. **1933** F. M. Ford *Let.* 24 Aug. (1965) 222 To them, on account of the 'time-shift'..they [*sc.* novels] must be quite incomprehensible. **1958** *Times Lit. Suppl.* 18 July 414/2 This device, moreover, involves Mr. Young in irritating time-shifts and flash-backs and rather strained symbolism. **1978** Cadogan & Craig *Women & Children First* xi. 268 The technical problems involved in the time-shift structure have simply failed to interest the author. **1983** *Listener* 24 Nov. 37/2 The whole business of recording broadcasts and watching them later is known to the trade as 'time-shift'. **1952** P. Wentworth *Brading Collection* xii. 72 It brought a horrid feeling that there had been a kind of time-slip—that they had been caught back again, she and Charles, to where they were three years ago. **1974** *Bookseller* 10 Aug. 999/2 (Advt.), Four children, a disused railway line, a time-slip to an Edwardian scene—this enchanting fantasy [etc.]. **1981** V. Glendinning *Edith Sitwell* xv. 195 Old Beau Nash, in her *Bath*, sees the past float by... This conceit, or technique of the time slip was not unique. **1933** A. N. Whitehead *Adventures of Ideas* vi. 98 The recent shortening of the time-span between notable changes in social customs is very obvious, if we examine history. **1979** A. Storr *Art of Psychotherapy* ii. 11 Attention is difficult to sustain without a break beyond a time-span of forty-five to fifty minutes. **1928** H. Poutsma *Gram. Late Mod. Eng.* (ed. 2) I. I. i. 43 *Should*, as a modal verb, is a preterite conditional, used irrespective of the time-sphere of the predication. **1957** R. W. Zandvoort *Handbk. Eng. Gram.* iv. 61 The perfect tense usually denotes an action that falls within the time-sphere of the present. **1937** R. A. Wilson *Birth of Lang.* II. i. 69 In his emergence to consciousness man rose above the time-stream of sense. **1978** P. G. Winslow *Coppergold* 125 At some point a man begins to feel out of place in the time stream. **1890** W. James *Princ. Psychol.* II. xx. 147 There enters thus an element of time-succession into our perception of ourselves which transforms the latter from an act of intuition to one of construction. **1922** A. S. Eddington *Theory of Relativity* 18 It [*sc.* the relativity theory] fully recognizes that the chain of events in such a time-succession is a series of an entirely distinctive character from the succession of points along a line in space. **1925** J. Joly *Surface-Hist. Earth* v. 79 Our time-units have become millions of years. **1968** R. A. Lyttleton *Mysteries Solar Syst.* iv. 133 The time-unit of the abscissa i. 50,000 years. **1933** W. A. Russell *Devel. Art of Lang.* viii. 57 The thought of an action is intimately associated with the thought of time; so much so that some grammarians have called the verb the *Time-word.* **1973** *Archivum Linguisticum* IV. 5 The distinction between /bin/ and /dɔŋ/ is clear when we consider..the time words with which they collocate.

b. *time-waster* (later examples); *time-allocation, -consuming, -measuring, -reckoning, -saving, -wasting* (examples) adjs. and sbs.

1951 Parsons & Shils *Toward General Theory of Action* II. iii. 143 A compulsive fixation on time-allocation is a familiar phenomenon. **1890** *Proc. Soc. for Psychical Research* Dec. 654, I dropped my inquiries..for a period of about two years,..being over-freighted with time-consuming duties. **1978** R. Mitchison *Life in Scotland* viii. 161 There were a great many strenuous, unpleasant and time-consuming tasks to be done in any house. **1890** W. James *Princ. Psychol.* I. xiv. 557 The time-measuring psychologists of recent days have tried their hand at this problem. **1959** *Publ. Mod. Lang. Assoc. Amer.* LXXIV. 589/2 Music—or at least music with bar-lines—is precisely a time-measuring notation; it divides the time into equal intervals. **1974** tr. *Wertheim's Evolution & Revolution* 363 The relatively rapid and consistent process of evolution—slow as it was in terms of time-measuring as applied by mankind. **1920** A. S. Eddington *Space, Time & Gravit.* ii. 31 Observers with different motions use different space- and time-reckoning. **1964** L. MacNeice *Astrol.* iv. 112 The skies were observed..for the old time-reckoning reasons. **1891** A. James *Diary* 24 June (1965) 216 A restricted nature, not admirable or generous in its impulses, but highly practical and time saving. **1960** *Farmer & Stockbreeder* 15 Mar. 140/2 The light tractor with all the features for time-saving. **1977** *Listener* 10 Nov. 607/2 The amounts that air travellers would be willing to pay for the time-savings that it [*sc.* Concorde] made possible. **1982** R. Ludlum *Parsifal Mosaic* xiv. 215 It's basically an economic, time-saving decision. **1930** J. Bailey *Let.* 5 Apr. (1935) 311 All these new inventions are time wasters for people like you and me. **1980** M. Drabble *Middle Ground* 118 Sally was a moaner and a timewaster. **1845** Geo. Eliot *Let.* *c* 16 Apr. (1954) I. 187, I am..full of hope that..I shall be able to ward off these time-wasting visitations. **1853** C. M. Yonge *Heir of Redclyffe* I. xv. 258 Abstaining from the time-wasting that might have tempted him if he had had plenty of money to spend. **1976** S. R. Simpson *Land Law & Registration* viii. 144 Sporadic survey is expensive and time-wasting. **1981** 'J. Ross' *Dark Blue & Dangerous* x. 58 The time-wasting had gone on long enough.

c. *time-blurred, -bound* (later examples), *-conditioned, -constrained, -controlled, -dulled, -eaten* (for *a* 1849 in Dict. read 1831), *-hallowed, -limited, -obsessed* (also *absol.*), *-ridden, -sanctioned, -shaken, -stained, -tested, -tormented* adjs.

1916 A. Huxley *Burning Wheel* 24 Some lover of an older day Has carved in time-blurred lettering One word only:– 'Alas'. **1924** R. Graves *Mock Beggar Hall* 79 Neither eternal nor time-bound, Not certain, nor in change. **1978** *Dædalus* Summer 168 Our ideas about childhood..are very much time-bound and culture-bound. **1951** R. A. Knox *Stimuli* i. 3 We force our time-conditioned minds, once a year, into an artificial mood of expectancy. **1967** A. Battersby *Network Analysis* (ed. 2) ix. 146 If we simply say that the project must be completed as quickly as possible, we have what is called a 'time constrained' network. **1979** *Jrnl. R. Soc. Arts* Dec. 9/1 Colleges will be asked..to specify the learning objectives which they wish to assess by time-constrained examination. **1954** *Gloss. Highway Engin. Terms* (*B.S.I.*) 58 *Time controlled traffic signals*, signals in which the aspects are displayed for fixed periods which are determined by manual or time-clock adjustment of the controller. **1960** *Farmer & Stockbreeder* 23 Feb. 100/2 Light for time-controlled poultry-house lighting. **1971** P. C. Sylvester-Bradley in I. G. Gass et al. *Understanding Earth* ix. 124/1 Evolution is a time-controlled process. **1922** Joyce *Ulysses* 238 Stephen Dedalus watched..the lapidary's fingers prove a timedulled chain. **1749** W. Collins in R. Dodsley *Collection of Poems* IV. 65 Where..some time-hallow'd pile, Or up-land fallows grey Reflect it's last cool gleam. **1959** J. L. Austin *Sense & Sensibilia* (1962) vi. 61 His wholesale acceptance of the traditional, time-hallowed, and disastrous manner of expounding them [*sc.* arguments]. **1974** Dawa Norbu *Red Star over Tibet* i. 30 The nomads were given a time-hallowed concoction. **1947** Partridge *Usage & Abusage* 51/1 Turn those sentences into *to be* equivalents: 'To receive wounds is no fun'; 'To become a casualty is no fun'; 'To be wounded is no fun': crisp, clear-cut, single-action, time-limited connotations. **1977** *Jrnl. R. Soc. Arts* CXXV. 462/2 The price he pays for that time-limited monopoly is to give up any other advantages which the usual rights of exclusive ownership..might otherwise confer on him. **1945** Auden *Coll. Poetry* 12 These only feared another kind of Death To which the time-obsessed are all condemned. **1951** S. Spender *World within World* 137 No wonder that the literature of this period is time-obsessed, time-tormented, as though beaten with rods of restless days. **1936** T. S. Eliot *Burnt Norton* in *Coll. Poems 1909–35* 188 A flicker Over the strained time-ridden faces. **1838** J. S. Mill in *London & Westm. Rev.* Aug. 469 The inconsistencies and absurdities of time-sanctioned opinions and institutions. **1949** Dylan Thomas in *Botteghe Oscure* IV. 399, I who hear..the notes on this time-shaken Stone. **1835** W. C. Bryant in *N.Y. Mirror* 19 Sept. 92/1 How the time-stained walls That earthquakes shook not from their poise, appear To shiver. **1904** W. S. Kennedy *Walt Whitman's Diary in Canada* p. v, The transcribing of these out-door notes from the worn and time-stained fragments of paper. **1930** *Times Lit. Suppl.* 10 July 566/3 The kind of faith which cheerfully believes things about the East which time-tested experience has proved to be untrue. **1977** *Daily Express* 29 Jan. 7/1, I will defend.. the right of the ingenious and time-tested Mr. [Peter] Hall to spend my taxes any way his fancy takes him. **1947** Auden *Age of Anxiety* v. 125 Transpose our plight like a poignant theme Into twenty tongues, time-tormented But His People still. **1951** Time-tormented [see *time-obsessed* adj. above].

d. *time-based, -centred, -conscious, -dead, -dependent, -faced, -independent, -kept, -lost, -old, -pressed, -served* (later examples), *-varying* adjs.

1976 P. R. White *Planning for Public Transport* vi. 123 The classification of time-based, mileage-based and peak-vehicle-based costs..was adopted. **1964** I. L. Horowitz *New Sociol.* i. 25 We can draw..upon the information available from the historian and the journalist to forge a time-centered sociology. **1977** P. Johnson *Enemies of Society* iii. 33 Against this background of a time-centred religion, there were also solid economic reasons why the fulcrum of progress would shift northwards across the Alps. **1934** A. Huxley *Beyond Mexique Bay* 218 What causes a people..to become as acutely time-conscious as the priestly mathematicians of the Maya Old Empire? **1962** J. GLENN in *Into Orbit* 43 All of us wear very exact watches... As you can see, we are extremely time-conscious during a mission. **1923** L. HUGHES in *Crisis* (N.Y.) Feb. 174/2 When Susanna Jones wears red, A queen from some time-dead Egyptian night Walks once again. **1955** O. KLEIN in W. Pauli *Niels Bohr* 113 We need a time-dependent operator. **1974** J. W. DRAKE in Carlile & Skehel *Evolution in Microbial World* 53 When *E. coli* is maintained in the chemostat, mutant accumulation is generation-dependent when growth is limited by glucose, but becomes time-dependent when growth is limited by amino acids. **1936** DYLAN THOMAS *Twenty-five Poems* 38 Now Jack my fathers let the time-faced crook..Sneak down the stallion grave. **1953** *Physical Rev.* XCI. 740/1 Initial and final currents that are time-independent with respect to different reference systems. **1970** G. K. WOODGATE *Elem. Atomic Struct.* ii. 14 The value of *E'* has to be found from eq. (2.22)..which is a time-independent eigenvalue equation. **1934** T. S. ELIOT *Rock* i. 7, I journeyed to London, to the timekept City. **1930** L. HUGHES in *Crisis* (N.Y.) July 235/1 Subdued and time lost are the drums. **1861** J. R. LOWELL *Washers of Shroud* in *Poems* (1912) 476 The time-old web of the implacable Three. **1922** D. H. LAWRENCE *England, my England* 8 The wide, black, time-old chimney. **1886** HARDY *Mayor of Casterbridge* I. ix. 110 The bow-windows protruded like bastions, necessitating a pleasing *chassez-déchassez* movement to the time-pressed pedestrian at every few yards. **1960** *Times* 18 Feb. 3/3 Only time-served engineers..will be considered. **1979** *Navy News* Feb. 9/1 To say that every seaman is a good seaman by virtue of being a time-served man would be very much open to question. **1962** W. B. THOMPSON *Introd. Plasma Physics* vii. 151 A particle going past a point target at a distance *l* produces a time-varying field at the target. **1981** *Word 1980* XXXI. 172 The time-varying spectral pattern of the processed stimuli differed radically from that of the natural speech.

52. time-and-motion, used *attrib.* to designate a study, person, etc., concerned with the measurement of the efficiency of an industrial or other operation; **time-average** *Physics* and *Math.*, an average evaluated over a period of time; hence **time-averaged** *a.*; **time-barred** *a.*, disqualified or invalid by reasons of arriving or being presented after the expiry of a statutory time-limit; **time capsule,** a container used to store for posterity a selection of objects thought to be representative of life at a particular time; also *fig.*; **time-change,** (*a*) change that takes place with the passage of time; (*b*) the difference in standard time between widely separated localities, as experienced by travellers; **time-charter** *v. trans.*, to hire (a vessel) under a time-charter agreement; **time check,** (*a*) *Canad.* a chit from a foreman stating the number of hours for which a man is due to be paid; (*b*) the act of ascertaining or stating the exact time; **time clock,** (*a*) a clock with a mechanism for recording the time on time-cards pressed into it; (*b*) a clock which can be set to switch an appliance on or off at specified times; **time-constant,** substitute for def.: the time taken by an exponentially varying quantity to change by a factor $1-1/e$ (approximately 0.6321), regarded as a parameter of the system in which the variation occurs; more widely, a time taken as representative of the speed of response of a system; (examples); **time-course,** (*b*) the period of time in which something happens, the length of time taken; **time-delay** = *time-lag*; used chiefly *attrib.* of a mechanism, system, etc., into the operation of which a time-lag has been deliberately introduced; **time deposit** (orig. *U.S.*), a sum placed in a bank at interest and not to be drawn before a set maturity date; **time derivative** *Physics* and *Math.*, a derivative of a variable with respect to time; **time difference,** (*a*) the difference between the lengths of time taken by different operations or processes; (*b*) the difference in standard time between widely separated localities; **time differential,** (*a*) = *time difference* (b) above; (*b*) the difference in the length of time taken by a process in different places or at different stages; **time dilatation** or **dilation** *Physics*, the apparent slowing down of the passage of time in a frame of reference moving relative to the observer, a relativistic effect analogous to the increase in mass and the Lorentz contraction of length; **time–distance,** used *attrib.* of the relation (*esp.* as expressed in graphs) between time and distance; **time division** *Telecommunication*, allocation of transmission time to each of a number of signals in quick rotation, so that all can be transmitted over the same channel if the sampling rate is sufficiently high; usu. *attrib.*; **time-element,** (*a*) time conceived as the natural element of temporal beings; (*b*) time as a factor to be taken into consideration; **time-expired** *a.*, (*a*) also of convicts: whose term of sentence has expired; (*b*) of perishable goods: of which the term of safe storage (before sale or use) has expired; **time-frame,** a limited and established period of time during which an event, etc., took place or is planned to take place; a schedule; **time-lag** (examples); **time lapse,** lapse of time; *spec.* (usu. with hyphen) *attrib.*, designating or pertaining to a technique of taking a sequence of photographs at set intervals to record changes that take place slowly over time; **time-line,** (*b*) (earlier example); (*c*) a schedule, a deadline; **time-lock** (earlier example); **time machine,** an imaginary machine capable of transporting a person backwards or forwards in time; **time-of-flight** *a. Physics*, designating techniques and apparatus that depend on the time taken by particles to traverse a set distance, e.g. in the separation of ions according to their mass; **time-payment** (later examples); **time pencil,** a type of delayed-action firing-switch or detonator for setting off explosive devices; **time-release** *a.* = *slow-release* adj. (b) s.v. *SLOW *a.* 16 d; **time-resolved** *a. Chem.* and *Physics*, produced by or pertaining to a spectroscopic technique in which the spectrum is obtained at known times after excitation; **time reversal** *Physics*, a transformation in which the passage of time (and so all velocities) is imagined to be reversed; *time reversal invariance*, invariance of laws of nature under this transformation, so that all processes allowed by them are also allowable when all motions in them are reversed; so **time-reverse** *v. trans.*, to subject to time reversal; **time-reversed** *a.*; **time-sampling,** the collection of data or observation of events at given times or intervals or within given periods of time; **time-scale,** (the relative length of) the period of time in which a sequence of events takes place, the successive stages of a process, operation, etc.; a representation or exposition of the stages of such a sequence, etc.; **time-series,** (*a*) the sequence of events which constitutes or is measured by time; (*b*) a series of values of some quantity obtained at successive times (often with equal intervals between them); *time-series analysis*, the statistical analysis of such series; **time-signal,** (*b*) a signal transmitted to indicate the exact time of day, *esp.* that broadcast by the BBC at certain hours; **time slice,** (*a*) a short period in the continuum of time; (*b*) *Computers*, each of the short intervals of time during which a computer or its central processor deals uninterruptedly with one user or program, before switching to another; so **time-slicing** *vbl. sb.*, the division of processor running time into a succession of short intervals that are allocated in turn to different users or programs; **time slot,** (*a*) a portion of time allocated to a purpose or person, *esp.* to an individual broadcast programme; (*b*) *Computers*, = *time slice* (b) above; **times table,** a multiplication table; cf. sense 19 above; **time-stamp,** a mechanical device for stamping letters, tickets, etc., with the date and time of receipt; hence as *v. trans.*; **time-stamped** *ppl. a.*; **time step,** an even-timed basic tap-dancing step; **time study,** a time-and-motion study; the close observation of an industrial or other process with a view to time-saving alterations in procedure; also *attrib.*; **time switch,** a switch that acts automatically at a set time; **time term,** a term of an equation in which time is the main variable; **time train** = *going train* s.v. TRAIN *sb.*[1] 15; **time travel** = *time-travelling* vbl. sb. below; also (hyphened) as *v. intr.*, **time-traveller,** one who practises time-travelling; **time-travelling** *vbl. sb.*, the imagined activity of travelling into the past or future, hypothetical movement through time; also *fig.* and as *ppl. a.* (also = 'extending through time'); **time trial,** a test of individual speed over a set distance, a race in which competitors are separately timed; **time wage** (see quot. 1892); **time warp** *Science fiction*, a distortion of space-time that is conceived as causing or enabling a person to remain stationary in time or to travel backwards or forwards in time; also (with hyphen) as *v. trans.*, to transport in a time warp; **timewise** *adv.*, with regard to time; **time-worker** (examples); **time-zone** (earlier and later examples).

1932 C. REYNOLDS *Production Planning* ix. 87 (*heading*) Time and motion studies. **1959** *Listener* 5 Nov. 762/2 That sinister figure, the man with the stop-watch, the time-and-motion expert, disliked by union men the world over. **1966** *Punch* 20 July 127/1 Time-and-motion study techniques, applied to American office workers, enable employers to reorganise office procedures and streamline routine chores. **1973** M. WOODHOUSE *Blue Bone* vi. 61 We have decided to divide the job according to the best work-study, time-and-motion principles. **1980** *Daily Tel.* 11 Sept. 29 (Advt.), Knowledge of..time and motion studies is very advantageous. **1875** *Encycl. Brit.* III. 39/1 In a material system in a state of stationary motion the time-average of the kinetic energy is equal to the time-average of the virial. **1914** *Phil. Mag.* XXVIII. 826 The ratios have been calculated using the time-average values. **1965** PHILLIPS & WILLIAMS *Inorg. Chem.* I. i. 11 Time-average potential and kinetic energies. **1946** Time-averaged [see *space-averaged* adj. s.v. *SPACE *sb.*[1] 19]. **1957** *Financial Times* 23 Mar. 4/3, I would appreciate advice..whether such a claim is now time-barred or not. **1971** *E. Afr. Standard* (Nairobi) 10 Apr. 1/3 The fourth car in the Datsun 240Z team..was time-barred at Korogwe. **1978** *Observer* 4 June 16/6 Employees must make their claim.. within six months of ceasing work. Failure to do this results in employees being 'time-barred'. **1938** *N.Y. Times* 19 Aug. 21 A record of the world of the present era ..will be buried on the site of the World's Fair in the hope that it will give to historians 5,000 years hence a picture of the middle twentieth century... The record will be contained in a 'time capsule', a specially devised container of metallic alloy of high corrosion resistance. **1947** CAMPBELL & ROBINSON *Skeleton Key to 'Finnegans Wake'* 8 The *Wake*..is a huge time-capsule, a complete and permanent record of our age. **1965** *Christian Century* 27 Oct. 1313/1 With the cooperation of a hospital physician, the hospital administrator, a funeral director and a local commercial firm which happened to be building 'time capsules' or cryogenic (low temperature) storage units.. preparations were made for this pioneering effort. **1973** *Art Internat.* Mar. 56/1 This image of Venice, as a water-logged time capsule, is very much the creation of outsiders. **1982** *Daily Tel.* 6 July 12/4 George Howard, the BBC chairman, is..asking around for corporation 'artefacts' to be sealed into an age-proof time capsule, so future generations may be able to discover the wonder of our broadcasting services. **1937** BLUNDEN *Elegy* 31 To haunt and cling To this one ground, whatever closed Of strange power, or time-change. **1941** *Mind* L. 182 A person as a 'self' exhibits beside its individuality and its identity in time-change the peculiar character of self-assertion through vicissitudes. **1969** N. DENNY tr. *Veraldi's Spies of Good Intent* xi. 177 I'm suffering from the time-change. With me it's three in the morning. **1976** 'M. DELVING' *China Expert* i. 9 I'd been in Honolulu two days before, and when I got back to New York I'd forgotten about the time change. I lost eight hours. **1963** *Times* 10 June 21/5 The companion for our new ship will be time-chartered.. until we decide about building another. **1974** *Information Handbk. 1974–5* (Shell Internat. Petroleum Co.) 100 Ships time-chartered by Shell companies total 235 of 20·6 million dwt. **1911** *Daily Colonist* (Victoria, B.C.) 26 Apr. 2/4 He cashed a time check after working a short time on a log drive. **1937** *Printer's Ink Monthly* May 45/1 *Time check*, synchronizing the time pieces of all concerned in a broadcast. **1968** M. WOODHOUSE *Rock Baby* xv. 149, I.. got a time-check to correct my watch. **1887** C. B. GEORGE *40 Yrs. on Rail* 56 [He] pulled a wire leading to a time-clock. **1930** *Engineering* 1 Aug. 130/1 Special terms for night service has encouraged the use of heat-storage ovens... In France, on weekdays, the luncheon interval lasts two hours, and that gives a pause in the factory power consumption which, with the aid of time-clocks, allows of a valuable heat storage period. **1943** Time-clock [see *PUNCH *v.*[1] 3 c]. **1961** *Listener* 19 Oct. 629/3 Running costs also tend to be higher but a judicious use of time clocks can keep these in check. **1976** *Billings* (Montana) *Gaz.* 4 July 6-c/4, I am not the nine-to-five cat—couldn't punch a time clock if my life depended on it. **1869** LD. RAYLEIGH in *Phil. Mag.* XXXVIII. 4 There is for every conducting circuit a certain time-constant which determines the rapidity of the rise or fall of currents, and which is proportional to the self-induction and conductivity of the circuit. Thus, to use Maxwell's notation,.. the time-constant is $L/R = \tau$. **1892** O. LODGE *Lightning Conductors* xxvi. 297 A column shows the time taken for the current amplitude to decay to one-millionth of its initial value, *i.e.*, 14 times what is ordinarily called the 'time constant'. **1943** *Electronic Engin.* XV. 346 The amplifier..is a standard three-stage..circuit. The time constant of the stages is 6 seconds. **1962** A. NISBETT *Technique Sound Studio* v. 94 The PPM is a special type of voltmeter... It has a rapid rise characteristic (the BBC version has a time constant of 2·5 milliseconds; this gives 80% of full deflection in 4 milliseconds). **1977** *Nature* 1 Sept. 11/1 The radiative time constant is the time taken for a mass of air to warm up or cool by radiating in the infrared portion of the spectrum. **1971** *Jrnl. Gen. Psychol.* Jan. 38 The time course for recovery from these effects was found to be slower for the subfusional stimulation effect than the suprafusional stimulation effect. **1977** J. L. HARPER *Population Biol. Plants* 678 The way in which the time course of the risk of death is related to the time course of producing offspring. **1959** H. BARNES *Oceanography & Marine Biol.* 183 Instead of using a bottom release to start the camera, a time-delay mechanism, set for the depth to which it is intended to work, is used. **1963** *Times* 15 Feb. 7/6 The levels from which different frequencies are reflected are thus obtained from the time-delay between outgoing pulse and received echo. **1978** *Tucson Mag.* Dec. 30/1 A digital time-delay system ..that brings 'concert hall sound' into the living room.

By delaying the impulse coming out of the back speakers ..by something under one one-thousandth of a second, this tiny wonder simulates the spatial quality of sound present in large auditoriums. **1851** C. Cist *Sk. Cincinnati in 1851* 90 Their policy of taking *time* deposits and allowing eight and ten per cent interest..[has] attracted public attention. **1930** J. M. Keynes *Treatise on Money* II. xxiii. 7 In the United States the law requires that the amounts of Time Deposits and Demand Deposits respectively shall be separately published. **1982** *Bank of England Q. Bull.* Dec. 519/1 Sight deposits grew by 28% and time deposits by 30%. **1956** *Nature* 11 Feb. 267/1 The passage of electrolytic current through the first coil induces its time-derivative in the second one. **1909** E. B. Titchener *Text-Bk. Psychol.* I. 134 In ordinary life, these time-differences escape notice, so that we may regard two tastes as occurring together when really they occur in succession. **1953** [see *capitalize *v.* 1 c]. **1981** 'W. Haggard' *Money Men* iii. 38 Seven-thirty from Schiphol and an hour for the flight. Time difference at the moment one hour. **1968** J. Sangster *Touchfeather* xi. 112 With the time differential on my side, I was back in Los Angeles by three-thirty p.m. local time. **1974** tr. *Wertheim's Evolution & Revolution* i. 33 The differential in space-time between more or less parallel processes in the past..might..imply time differentials in future developments. **1980** L. St. Clair *Obsessions* xvii. 291 Due to the time differential between New York and Paris, which he had left at sundown, he arrived at La Guardia shortly after 10 p.m. **1973** Time dilatation [see *relativity 2]. **1934** R. C. Tolman *Relativity, Thermodynamics & Cosmology* ii. 24 This time dilation and the conclusions as to the setting of clocks..are to be regarded except for experimental difficulties as an entirely verifiable mutual property of systems of clocks in relative motion. **1968** *Guardian* 28 Dec. 9 After two years the spacecraft's velocity would be such for 'time dilation' to have an effect. In other words time would be slowing down on board the craft and, to those on board, a single lifetime would be longer than for those on earth. **1981** *Sci. Amer.* Feb. 108/1 The relativistic effect of time dilation prolongs the life of pions and kaons that are particularly energetic. **1936** Time–distance [see *P III 3]. **1965** *Math. in Biol. & Med.* (Med. Res. Council) v. 230 The question whether short distances are correlated with short times is represented by the third degree of freedom, the interaction of the table, and for this reason this component can be referred to as a space-time, or time-distance, interaction. **1905** Time-division [see *Skiddavian *a.*]. **1938** *Proc. IRE* XXVI. 56 Many proposals have been offered for multiplexing. These divide naturally into two major categories; (1) frequency division and (2) time division. *Ibid.* 57 The major disadvantage of time-division multiplex..is that provision must always be made to insure accurate timing of the channel assignments. **1947** [see *quantization b]. **1975** D. G. Fink *Electronics Engineers' Handbk.* xxii. 35 In time-division multiplexing message information from many channels is sampled briefly in time sequence. **1831** Time element [in Dict., sense 51 a]. **1936** J. M. Keynes *Gen. Theory Employment* xxii. 317 The explanation of the *time-element* in the trade cycle. **1979** D. Anthony *Long Hard Cure* ix. 77 The time element fits... You heard the shot about nine forty-five. That gave him half an hour. **1931** *Times Lit. Suppl.* 21 May 402/4 The kindly Egyptian prince who..helped time-expired convicts to find honest employment. **1972** *Times* 17 Oct. 14/7 Return of time-expired stock like sausages and yoghurt. **1973** [see *hot-house, hothouse *sb.* 3 b]. **1974** *Ciba Symposium* XX. 253 Those of us who have used 'time-expired' human blood from blood banks in culture media have frequently found that some batches are highly toxic to trypanosomes. **1964** *Sunday Times* 5 July 14/4 All three considerations argue for abandoning the artificial time-frame which the Johnson Administration has now set. **1969** *Ottawa Commons Debates* 24 July 11573/1 In a timeframe of less than seven decades in length,..man has ceased to remain earthbound. **1976** 'R. B. Dominic' *Murder out of Commission* xx. 179 Somebody had..shot him. The time frame was pretty well established: between twelve o'clock, when he had phoned the desk, and twelve fifteen, when Ben and Tony arrived. **1980** D. Bloodworth *Trapdoor* xii. 71 It's right outside our brief, and our time-frame would not allow it. **1983** *Listener* 16 June 37/2 The time-frame is one intense, meandering weekend. **1892** O. J. Lodge *Lightning Conductors* vii. 48 Lord Rayleigh.. thinks these induced peripheral currents competent to explain magnetic time-lag in every case. **1939** *John o' London's* 7 Apr. 46/2 There is often a necessary time-lag between discovery and application. **1979** *Bull. Amer. Acad. Arts & Sci.* Mar. 40 Even if it were granted that a given intervention would..produce a given result..there would inevitably be time lags..which would diminish the efficacy of the remedy. **1937** *Mind* XLVI. 169 The duration which will be indicated as a 'time-lapse' in the standard clock which S carries. **1937** *Discovery* June 192/1 Experimenters in time-lapse photography and nature photography in general. **1956** *Kenyon Rev.* XVIII. 418 The time-lapse between any two primary stresses tends to be the same irrespective of the number of syllables and the junctures between them. **1957** [see *high-speed *a.*]. **1957** *New Scientist* 19 Sept. 14/1 The study of living cells by time-lapse cinematography... Special ciné-cameras are used to take microphotographs..at the rate of about eight photographs per minute. **1974** *Sci. Amer.* Apr. 123/2 In that industrial valley, the time-lapse photographs show, exposure from A.D. 1702 up to 1908 induced only light damage. **1983** *Listener* 3 Nov. 35/3 Time-lapse, slow-motion, stop frame, microscopic, infra-red and underwater techniques are part of the stock-in-trade of the TV wildlife producer. **1890** W. James *Princ. Psychol.* I. iii. 86 Another electric pen..traces alongside the former line a 'time-line' of which each undulation or link stands for a certain fraction of a second. **1967** *Sci. Year* 51 The *time line* (sequence of the mission) and trajectory of the specific mission are analyzed. **1976** *New Yorker* 30 Aug. 59 They were well behind the timeline, for the ground had allotted only ten minutes to move from one experiment to the next. **1871** *Rep. Comm. Patents 1869* (U.S.) II. 224/2 *Time-Lock*... The combination of the shaft [etc.]. **1895** H. G. Wells (*title*) The time machine. **1944** C. Day Lewis *Poetry for You* ii. 12 *How Poetry Began.* To find this out, we'll have to jump into a Time Machine, put its gear-lever into reverse, and race backwards through many thousands of years into prehistoric time. **1960** *Guardian* 7 Oct. 16/4 Nigel and Wendy arrive by time-machine in the Garden of Eden. **1978** I. Watson in C. Priest *Anticipations* 22 The assumption that a time machine should proceed to its destination *instanter* instead of at a snail's pace. **1945** H. D. Smyth *Gen. Acct. Devel. Atomic Energy Mil. Purposes* xii. 131 One elegant scheme for studying the effects of neutrons of a single, arbitrarily-selected velocity is the 'time of flight' method. **1948** S. A. Goudsmit in *Physical Rev.* LXXIV. 622/2 (*heading*) A time-of-flight mass spectrometer. **1969** Egelstaff & Poole *Exper. Neutron Thermalisation* iv. 74 Measuring the velocity of the scattered neutrons by the time-of-flight technique. **1975** *McGraw-Hill Yearbk. Sci. & Technol.* 189/2 Both types exceed a mass resolution $M/\Delta M$ of 1000,..and in addition the time-of-flight version is completely free of artifacts. **1927** *Ladies' Home Jrnl.* Dec. 45/2 Chrysler dealers are in a position to extend the convenience of time-payments. **1955** *Times* 25 Aug. 6/6 The Government had been greatly concerned at the rapid expansion of time payment and hire purchase and its effects upon the economy. **1955** J. Thomas *No Banners* xix. 171 Two sticks of plastic, a primer bound with a length of instantaneous fuse, and a ten-minute time pencil. **1977** J. Hutchison *That Drug Danger* xi. 88/1 Having pressed the time pencil which set off the explosive a quarter of an hour or one or two hours later. **1977** H. J. Eysenck *You & Neurosis* iv. 135 They were told that this was a peripheral-acting time-release muscle-relaxant known to be effective. **1980** *Holistic Health News* Sept./Oct. 2/1 This treatment is called 'Magnetroph' and was developed by Dr. Ernest Pescetti, renowned as 'the father of the time-release principle'. **1956** *Nature* 4 Feb. 222 (*caption*) Optical arrangement for spectrochemical analyses with time-resolved spectra. **1977** *Ibid.* 17 Feb. 659/2 (*heading*) Time-resolved resonance Raman spectroscopy of bacteriorhodopsin. [**1922** I. Fisher *Making of Index Numbers* iv. 64 The time reversal test... The index number reckoned forward should be the reciprocal of that reckoned backward.] **1955** *Proc. Glasgow Conf. Nucl. & Meson Physics 1954* viii. 341 The superselection rule on the parity of spinor-particle number is derived from a consideration which does not depend on double time-reversal. **1958** *Physical Rev.* CX. 783/2 We see that at least one prediction of time reversal invariance is very well fulfilled. **1979** *Sci. Amer.* June 116/3 The discovery of an electric dipole moment of the neutron would reveal a violation of the physical principle known as time-reversal symmetry. **1971** *Ibid.* Dec. 97/1 Time-reverse all motions and the three will return at the same instant to the starting point. **1962** M. A. Preston *Physics of Nucleus* xvi. 475 The wave function of a time-reversed state is obtained by taking the complex conjugate of the wave function of the original state and reversing all spin directions. **1981** T. D. Lee *Particle Physics & Introd. Field Theory* xiii. 283 If the T-invariant classical system consists of a large number of particles, although the time-reversed sequence is always possible, it is in general improbable. **1960** J. B. Carroll in *Encycl. Educ. Research* (ed. 3) 746/1 Careful time-sampling and situation-sampling designs seem to be in order if one wants purely normative or 'typical' data. **1973** *Jrnl. Genetic Psychol.* Sept. 99 Time sampling has been demonstrated to be an effective observational technique. **1979** J. Jaffe et al. in Aaronson & Rieber *Psycholinguistic Research* 404 Assume the two states are digitized as 'one' or 'two' by discrete time sampling at intervals that must be shorter than the expected minimum time the system spends in any state. **1890** W. James *Princ. Psychol.* I. ix. 283 We make a solid wooden frame with the sentence written on its front, and the time-scale on one of its sides. **1923** N. Shaw *Air & its Ways* v. 46 The time-scale of the operations which tend to cause deviation is so large that the course of the operations escapes observation. **1934** *Discovery* Aug. 227/1 The constructing of a geological and meteorological time-scale for the Southern Hemisphere. **1958** F. E. Zeuner *Dating Past* 5 All these studies aiming at the establishment of absolute time-scales for the past are comprised by the term *Geochronology*. **1972** *Country Life* 23 Mar. 672/2 The timescale of planning is a long one. **1979** *Jrnl. R. Soc. Arts* CXXVII. 409/1 We must also bear in mind the timescale involved in exploitation of oil and gas discoveries. **1892** J. Royce *Spirit Mod. Philos.* 431 This transcending of a time-series..is in fact what one might call the soul of the natural order. **1919** *Rev. Econ. Statistics* Apr. 123/2, *x* and *y* represent the deviations of the items of two time series from their respective linear secular trends. **1928** *Jrnl. Amer. Statistical Assoc.* XXIII. 407 The inferential possibilities of time series analysis are contingent upon segregating from the specific historical the repeatable, recurrent element. **1978** *Nature* 19 Oct. 630/2 The resulting time series is then smoothed by using a 13-month running mean average to remove seasonal variations. **1979** *Daily Tel.* 6 July 16 He has confirmed his original time series analysis with a more recent cross-sectional study. **1979** J. Hicks *Causality in Economics* v. 64 There are two kinds of time-series, with different kinds of time reference. In one of them each item relates to a point of time, in the other to a period. **1853** *Rep. Brit. Assoc. Adv. Sci. 1852* ii. 131 On the 5th of August 1852, the first time-signal passed;..the clock at Greenwich..originates the signals. **1862** *Monthly Notices R. Astron. Soc.* XXII. 119 At any time, day or night, when the wire is not wanted for ordinary work, London can receive time-signals from Liverpool every minute. **1923** [see *news *sb.*(*pl.*) 5c]. **1972** P. Lively *Driftway* v. 59 Through the atmospherics there came the time-signal, and then a man reading the news. **1965** *Language* XLI. 193 To the comparativists of the 1870's..a 'synchronic' view could be nothing more than taking a relatively thin time-slice and doing the best one can with it. **1973** Murrill & Smith *Introd. Computer Sci.* i. 31 A user receives the processor's undivided attention for one time slice but then receives no attention over the next three time slices. **1981** *Kilobaud Microcomputing* June 35/2 At the end of the current user's time slice, he is put on hold by the scheduler, and the next user gets to run his program. **1967** J. Martin *Design of Real-Time Computer Systems* 628/2 (Index), Time-slicing. **1978** W. S. Davies *Information Processing Systems* xv. 328 The whole purpose of the time-slicing approach..is to prevent any single user from dominating the system at the expense of everyone else. **1962** Time slot [see *programme planning* s.v. *program, programme *sb.* 4]. **1967** J. Martin *Design of Real-Time Computer Systems* ix. 130 When the time-slot..for one user ends, it may be necessary to bring in a completely new set of data and programs for the next user. **1979** *Arizona Daily Star* 5 Aug. 1. 7/5 It..will be interesting to learn what the viewer response is to a program concept of this dimension when aired at an odd afternoon time slot. **1980** Pužman & Pořízek *Communication Control in Computer Networks* iii. 168 Time division multiplexing means that a certain time slot is to be assigned for a station for the time during which it can exchange data with another station. **1982** 'W. R. Duncan' *Queen's Messenger* vi. 49 People were units to be fitted into Sir John's available time slots. **1960** N. Hilliard *Maori Girl* i. ii. 14 Netta was supposed to learn her words and the older ones their times-tables. **1983** *Cotswold Life* Nov. 19/1 Here the infants practised wobbly letters, began to chant the Times Tables, and spilt paint water all over the floor. **1984** *Reader's Digest* Jan. 81/2 Children..slipping from ignorance to knowledge.., until one day finally they know their times tables. **1892** *Work* IV. 75/3 The time-stamp is altered every minute. **1963** L. Meynell *Virgin Luck* viii. 181 Each slip is time-stamped as it comes from the telephonist who takes the bet. **1973** *Times* 6 Dec. 9/8 Waiter's [*sic*] checks are time-stamped on receipt... This way, the clerk knows exactly when each item was ordered. **1962** *Times* 16 Apr. 11/3 The 'limpet' meter for issuing time-stamped tickets. **1929** Time-step [see *stooge *sb.* 1]. **1956** B. Holiday *Lady sings Blues* (1973) iii. 32, I knew exactly two steps, the time step and the crossover. **1975** Time step [see *pull-back 1 d]. **1911** F. W. Taylor *Princ. Scientific Managem.* 75 A careful time study of men working under these conditions will disclose facts which are ludicrous as well as pitiable. **1928** *Britain's Industrial Future* (Liberal Industr. Inquiry) III. xvi. 194 There should be means of revising rates..in consultation, with all the facts and time-study figures on the table. **1944** *Jrnl. R. Aeronaut. Soc.* XLVIII. 257 Mr. Westbrook asked whether time study was used sufficiently to convince shop superintendents of the amount of labour necessary for any job. **1970** T. Lupton *Managem. & Social Sci.* (ed. 2) i. 14 The organization as a whole, or at least those members of it with whom they have close contact, the supervisor, the time study man, and so on. **1979** J. Harvey *Plate Shop* iii. 15 He was the best plater in the shop, and the Time Study would never believe he was working as fast as he could; and it was true, he always did work slow when studied, out of loyalty to his mates. **1902** *Specifications of Patents* (U.S. Patent Office) 14 Oct. 1560/1, I, William B. Coulter,..have invented certain new and useful Improvements in Time-Switches for Electric Lights. **1963** *Listener* 3 Jan. 47/1 Portable time-switches vary in elaborateness and price. *a* **1977** *Harrison Mayer Ltd. Catal.* 64/2 A time switch can be installed on any kiln. **1920** A. S. Eddington *Space, Time & Gravit.* vi. 103 Leaving aside now the time-term as sufficiently discussed, we consider the space-terms alone. **1974** *Nature* 15 Mar. 204/1 If..the true P_n velocity is 8·0 km s^{-1}, then the average time terms are slightly reduced and the resulting crustal thickness estimates are about 5–10% lower. **1965** E. Tunis *Colonial Craftsmen* vi. 146 Both the time train and the striking train of a Terry clock are driven by weights wound up by a key. **1977** *Lancashire Life* Jan. 39/2 One of the chief technical advances in the making of watches..was the improved design of the escapement, the device which secures uniformity in the rate of movement of the time-train. **1953** A. C. Clarke *Prelude to Space* xxvi. 137 That lurid magazine..that goes in for hyperspace time-travel. **1969** *Punch* 1 Jan. 35/2 This intelligent and ingenious story..has a fascinating climax where people from both sides time-travel back to see the Passion and Crucifixion. **1975** G. Ewart *Be my Guest!* 1. 23 Belief in Time Travel and supernatural facilities. **1930** *Wonder Stories* Nov. 489 We have purposely allowed our time travellers to become known to the people of the eras that they visit, for in this way the great drama of the story becomes apparent. **1934** C. Lambert *Music Ho!* ii. 69 The most successful time traveller of our days was undoubtedly Serge Diaghileff. **1972** M. Crichton *Terminal Man* iii. i. 106 Slowly..he seemed to emerge like a time-traveler advancing through the years. **1871** Swinburne *Songs before Sunrise* 171 Mother of man's time-travelling generations,..The temples and the towers of time thou breakest. **1895** H. G. Wells *Time Machine* iv. 28, I am afraid I cannot convey the peculiar sensations of time travelling. They are excessively unpleasant. **1934** C. Lambert *Music Ho!* ii. 73 By his adoption or even invention of the particular type of present-day pastiche that can conveniently be described as time travelling Diaghileff immediately established a position of mastery again. **1961** *Guardian* 16 June 9/5 This musical time-travelling is presumably deliberate. **1981** Craig & Cadogan *Lady Investigates* viii. 152 In children's fiction in general..magic and time-travelling were acceptable forms of the supernatural; ghosts were not. **1954** *Amer. Speech* XXIX. 103 *Time trial*,..a competitive event..in which cars are separately timed for top speed over set distances. **1976** *Scottish Daily Express* 24 Dec. 13/6 Ten days ago an unknown sprinter ran an impressive time-trial against local man Jim Smith. **1977** *Wandsworth Borough News* 16 Sept. 10/4 The Wandsworth and District Cycling Club Open 10 miles' Time-trial..resulted in a win for Eddie Adkins.. in the fine time of 22 mins, 4 secs. **1887** Moore & Aveling tr. *Marx's Capital* II. vi. xx. 553 The converted form under which the daily, weekly, &c., value of labour-power presents itself, is hence that of time-wages, therefore day-wages, &c. **1892** D. F. Schloss *Methods Industrial Remuneration* i. 11 The two leading forms of Industrial Remuneration under the wage-system are time-wages and piece-wages... The employee engaged on time-wages sells to his employer the labour which he shall perform within a given period, irrespective of the amount of labour performed within that period. **1954** W. M. Miller in *Fantastic* Jan.–Feb. 34/1 They showed me a dozen pictures of moppets with LTR-guns, moppets in time-warp suits, moppets wearing Captain Chronos costumes, [etc.]. **1954** *Sociological Rev.* Dec. 242 Instead of the 'dream' to move us out of lived time, it [*sc.* science and fantasy fiction] uses some machine to 'move across the "time-warp" ', 'to cut across the 4th dimension'. **1971** *Guardian* 17 June 10/5 The time warp effect was..intensified by having David Frost—essentially an early sixties figure. **1974** *Times* 22 Aug. 6 He pauses in his narrative and time-warps it back to South Staffs. **1976** N. THORNBURG *Cutter & Bone* i. 13 A sensation that always made him feel as if he had been time-warped back into wet diapers. **1983** *Listener* 3 Nov. 32/3 Molly Kean's images are of psychic rather than physical decay, of families able to live beyond their means because they are trapped in a peculiar time-warp. **1953** *Sun* (Baltimore) 27 Aug. 21/3 Of course, we [*sc.* railroads] can't meet the planes timewise. **1981** J. D. MACDONALD *Free Fall in Crimson* xx. 229 'How far are you from a pay phone, timewise?' 'Ten minutes.' **1917** W. S. CHURCHILL in M. Gilbert *Winston S. Churchill* (1975) IV. iv. 63 These advances arose out of an intention to remedy the contrast between the wages of skilled time workers in certain munitions industries which had grown up during the war. **1971** *Daily Tel.* 15 Sept. 7/1 Representatives of nearly 3,000 'timeworkers' at the Austin-Morris car body plant..have said that [their] pay offers..are not acceptable. **1892** E. NOEL *Internat. Time* 4 The country [*sc.* United States of America]..is divided into time-zones, each stretching over fifteen degrees of longitude, and differing one hour in time from the zone on either side of it. **1929** [see *DIACHRONOUS *a.* 1]. **1976** M. MACHLIN *Pipeline* lv. 553 Due to the time zone differences, they would have plenty of time to make the six o'clock news coast to coast. **1982** *Daily Tel.* 24 Apr. 9/1 They conclude..that rapid travel through time zones precipitates psychiatric illness in people already predisposed to it.

b. Comb. with *time's*: **time's arrow,** the temporal asymmetry whereby many macroscopic phenomena do not occur in reverse even though such an event would not conflict with the laws of nature.

1928 A. S. EDDINGTON *Nature of Physical World* iv. 69, I shall use the phrase 'time's arrow' to express this one-way property of time which has no analogue in space. **1937** *Nature* 27 Feb. 356/2 Eddington's statement..that the second law of thermodynamics holds 'the supreme position among the laws of nature'. His reason is that this law alone reveals 'time's arrow'. **1972** S. WEINBERG *Gravitation & Cosmol.* xv. 597 It is the expansion of the universe that, by providing a heat sink, sets the direction of time's arrow in thermodynamic processes.

time base. *Electronics.* [f. TIME *sb.* + BASE *sb.*[1]] **a.** A line on a cathode-ray tube display representing the time axis, usu. horizontally. **b.** A signal for uniformly and repeatedly deflecting the electron beam so as to produce such a line, usu. consisting of a saw-tooth waveform. **c.** Also *time-base generator.* A circuit for generating such a signal; a sweep generator.

1925 *Proc. Physical Soc.* XXXVII. 167 Circular and elliptical time-bases were not nearly so useful as a linear and unidirectional base obtainable from a special type of triode oscillator circuit. **1933** R. A. W. WATT et al. *Applications Cathode Ray Oscillograph* ii. 44 The general nature of the e.m.f. desirable as a linear time-base for use with a cathode-ray oscillograph. **1942** *Electronic Engin.* XV. 102/2 An outstanding case where stroboscopic viewing is a necessity is in conjunction with a spiral timebase. *Ibid.* 664 The mechanism of the time-base circuit. **1959** DAVIES & PALMER *Radio Studies of Universe* iii. 43 As the speed of radio waves is 3×10^5 km/s, the horizontal trace of the tube, called the time base, can be calibrated in range directly. **1960** *Practical Wireless* XXXVI. 408/2 A lead from the timebase is brought out to the front panel of the oscilloscope. **1962** SIMPSON & RICHARDS *Physical Princ. Junction Transistors* xiii. 309 This form of operational amplifier..has been used extensively as a time-base generator. **1977** *Broadcast* 7 Feb. 5 (Advt.), VPR-1 systems, with..timebase correction..for installation in studio.

Time-ese, Timese (təimīˑz), *sb.* and *a.* [-ESE.] (Characteristic of) the prose style of *Time* magazine.

1958 C. LOGUE in *Times Lit. Suppl.* 15 Aug. p. xxiii/1 They can model their syntax on the new 'international-English' style—a compound of Hemingway and *Time*-ese. **1967** *Time* 17 Mar. 7 The humor of a *Playboy* cartoon is often more sophisticated than the cleverness of Timese. **1973** *N.Y. Times Mag.* 8 July 4/2 Mr. Kanfer's prose: part showbiz, part Time-ese, and all posturing absurdity. **1977** *Globe & Mail* (Toronto) 15 Mar. 6/3 Elaine Dewar's review..is..bad book reviewing with a Timese style.

timeist (təiˑmist). Now *Obs.* or *rare.* [f. TIME *sb.* + -IST.] = TIME-KEEPER, TIMEKEEPER 3.

1830 W. T. PARKE *Musical Mem.* II. 320 This habit [of playing in concert] made him a good timeist. *a* **1837** E. C. KNIGHT *Autobiogr.* (1861) I. i. 7 The dancing-master was ..graceful without affection, a good time-ist, and..a good domestic character.

time-keeper, timekeeper. 2. c. (Later examples.)

1829 P. EGAN *Boxiana* 2nd Ser. II. 128 *Maurice*.. repeated the signal for fighting. *Randall* was the time-keeper. **1896** [see *CORNER *sb.*[1] 13 d]. **1950** *Sport* 7–11 Apr. 7/1 Did the timekeeper and second ..want to catch the early train home?

timeless, *a.* Add: **2. a.** Esp. in phr. *timeless moment.*

1942 T. S. ELIOT *Little Gidding* i. 9 Here, the intersection of the timeless moment Is England and nowhere. Never and always. *Ibid.* v. 15 History is a pattern Of timeless moments. **1957** L. MACNEICE *Visitations* 22 A timeless moment where the nether blue meets the upper blue. **1981** J. BRABAZON *Dorothy L. Sayers* xix. 238 The timeless moment after death, when choices made while living are seen in the light of eternal reality.

tiˑme-like, *a. Physics.* [f. TIME *sb.* + -LIKE.] Being or related to an interval between two points in space-time that lie inside one another's light cones (so that a signal or an observer can pass from one to another).

1914 [see *four-vector* s.v. *FOUR C. 2]. **1920** [see *SPACE-LIKE *a.*]. **1955** O. KLEIN in W. Pauli *Niels Bohr* 112 We divide the *k*-states into those belonging to time-like *k*-vectors..and those belonging to space-like *k*-vectors.., a division which is relativistically invariant. **1959** [see *NULL *a.* 4 d]. **1978** PASACHOFF & KUTNER *University Astron.* xxvii. 694 The world lines of light divide space-time into spacelike and timelike regions.

timenoguy (tiˑmĕnǫgi). Delete † *Obs.* and add: Also **timm(e)y-nog(gy). 1.** (Further examples.) In extended sense, a gadget.

1880 W. BOTTRELL *Traditions W. Cornwall* 3rd Ser. 198/2 *Timmy-noggy*, a notched square piece of wood, used to support the lower end of the Vargord. **1886** [see *GADGET]. **1925** FRASER & GIBBONS *Soldier & Sailor Words* 282 *Timmynoggy*,..a name given to various strop and toggle gadgets on board ship... A device more or less makeshift, to enable something to be done more expeditiously than would be possible in the ordinary way. **1963** R. M. NANCE *Gloss. Cornish Sea-Words* 160 *Timmy-noggy*,..may be a nautical substitute word like 'thingum-a-bob'. **1976** *Oxf. Compan. Ships & Sea* 870/2 *Timenoguy*, ..more recently it was a rope made fast in the mizen rigging with a thimble in the end through which passed the hauling part of the mainbrace.

timer. Add: **3. d.** An instrument for automatically timing a process or activating a device at a set time or set times; a time-switch; *egg-timer*: see *EGG *sb.* 7; *oven timer*: see *OVEN *sb.* 4.

1908 *Sears, Roebuck Catal.* 266/1 Stem wind, jeweled horse timer. This timer is operated from the crown by merely pressing down the..mechanism. **1939** C. MORLEY *Kitty Foyle* i. 9 They worked right round the clock..making some kind of timers for shells. **1953** R. CHANDLER *Long Good-Bye* ii. 25, I stirred the coffee and covered it. I set my timer for three minutes... The bell of the timer went just as I got back. **1961** *Which?* Dec. 335/1 Two.. were clockwork dial timers, similar to kitchen timers, which have to be wound up by rotating the dial. **1972** *Jrnl. Social Psychol.* Dec. 225 The timer was preset so that the signals for all shock options were of three seconds duration, with a 15-second intertrial interval. **1977** *New Yorker* 27 June 89/1 Attached to the timer of the bomb was a note. **1982** *Listener* 15 July 34/3 These timers are perfectly adequate for some domestic tasks, like..switching lights on and off in a house to fool..burglars.

4. See also *TWO-TIMER.

tiˑme-sharing, *vbl. sb.* [f. TIME *sb.* + SHARING *vbl. sb.*[2]] **1.** *Computers.* The automatic sharing of (central) processor time so that a computer can serve two or more users or devices concurrently, switching between them rapidly and automatically so that each user has the impression of continuous exclusive use. Also *attrib.*

1953 *Digital & Analog Computers* (Amer. Soc. Mech. Engineers) 41 'Time-sharing' can be relatively simple. Nearly all the machines have convenient features for changing the problems easily. **1958** *Computer Jrnl.* Apr. 4/1 If time-sharing is being employed it can be arranged that the control unit proceeds to another branch of the program which is not held up in the same way. **1960** *Information Processing* 336 Time sharing, in the sense of causing the main computer to interrupt its program to perform the arithmetic and control operations required by external or peripheral equipment, has been used on a limited scale for a long time. This paper explores the possibility of applying time sharing to a large fast computer on a very extensive scale. **1964** *Discovery* Oct. 56/2 The advent of time-sharing machines. **1965** *Math. in Biol. & Med.* (Med. Res. Council) 295 Without time-sharing, the 'on-line' use of a fast modern machine would be unthinkably costly. **1969** *New Scientist* 2 Jan. 16/1 With a time-sharing system, the user can now call the system over the ordinary GPO network using an adapted telephone. **1980** P. WAY *Icarus* iii. 20 'Where is this computer?' 'Texas... You dial a telephone number. Ring it up. Bounces off a satellite. It's called time-sharing.'

2. The ownership or right to use of a property (esp. as a holiday home) for a fixed limited time each year. Also *attrib.* orig. *U.S.*

1976 *Time* 30 Aug. 67 In exchange for guaranteed occupancy over an extended period time-sharing resorts offer low prices, [etc.]. **1977** *Detroit Free Press* 11 Dec. 17-C/1 Time-sharing..is proving to be a popular concept for vacations. **1980** *Country Life* 27 Nov. 2038/3 The concept of time-sharing (that is, buying an annual choice of weeks in a holiday home instead of buying the home outright).

Hence **tiˑme-share** *sb.*, (*a*) = *TIME-SHARING *vbl. sb.* 2 (freq. *attrib.*); (*b*) a share in a property under a time-sharing scheme; **tiˑme-share** *v. trans.*, to use concurrently with others on a time-sharing basis; **tiˑme-shared** *ppl. a.*; **tiˑme-sharer** *sb.*, a participant in a time-sharing scheme.

1954 *Jrnl. Assoc. Computing Machinery* I. 136/1 It seems reasonable to investigate the possibility of time-sharing one or more integrators in such circuits. **1962** *Spring Joint Computer Conf.* 307/1 By having these programs time share areas of memory, the program may be executed. **1973** *Lebende Sprachen* XVIII. 72/2 Subsequent data processing can then be carried out with a small and cheap dedicated computer, by a time-shared processor or off-line on a large computer. **1977** *Sci. Amer.* Sept. 135 (*caption*) One head can serve for both reading and writing on a time-shared basis. *Ibid.* 177/1 At a terminal an operator is connected to the computer and time-shares the computer with other operators. **1978** *Detroit Free Press* 2 Apr. 6F/1 The Minnesota resort is among more than 150 time share facilities in 26 states. **1980** R. REJNIS *Her Home* 73 A time-share can be very inexpensive.. compared to hotel costs. **1980** *Times* 13 Oct. 24/4 (Advt.), Time-share ownership of luxury 8-berth yacht in Mediterranean. **1981** *Times* 31 Jan. 17/5 An organization.. which offers an exchange service with other timesharers elsewhere. **1981** *Sunday Express Mag.* 14 June 33/2 It is important for the public to be aware that time-share is a property-based purchase.

time-spaˑce, *sb.* and *adj. phr.* [f. TIME *sb.* + SPACE *sb.*[1]] **A.** *sb.* = *SPACE–TIME *sb.*

1916 [see *METRIC *a.*[1] 2]. **1942** E. WAUGH *Put out More Flags* i. 86 Metaphysical war, war in time-space, war eternal..all war is nonsense. **1978** *Church Times* 15 Dec. 6/5 Using the discoveries of Einstein concerning the nature of time-space, Professor Macquarrie sketches in a theory of both individual and cosmic hope which depends upon the idea that God occupies every point in space-time.

B. *adj. phr.* = *SPACE–TIME *adj. phr.*

1951 N. M. GUNN *Well at World's End* xxviii. 264 Giving and receiving are aspects of the same thing; as time and space are aspects of the one time-space continuum, according to the latest mode of scientific utterance. **1961** G. CLARK *World Prehistory* 4 It is important to avoid European or other regional bias, yet it would be pointless to try and achieve a kind of time-space parity for its own sake. **1968** D. L. CLARKE *Analytical Archaeol.* viii. 327 Strongly localized and smaller time-space entities..by contrast suggest culture group transforms in time depth. **1977** *Brit. Med. Bull.* XXVII. 20/1 One of the most interesting features has been the recognition in some areas of time–space clusters.

timetable, *sb.* Add: **1. e.** (Earlier example.)

1820 *Edin. Monthly Rev.* Jan. 15 One of the most striking epochs in music, as we conceive, was that of the invention of the time-table.

2. *timetable motion* = *guillotine motion* s.v. *GUILLOTINE 4 a.

1976 S. LLOYD *Mr Speaker, Sir* iii. 76 Peyton protested about the timetable motion, and asked why aid to Norton-Villiers had suddenly become so urgent. **1977** *Whitaker's Almanack 1978* 349/2 A third timetable motion to limit debate on Lords' amendments to the Bills..was carried by 312–296.

tiˑmetaːble, time-table, *v.* [f. the sb.] *trans.* To schedule, to plan or arrange according to a time-table, to include in a time-table.

1917 'CONTACT' *Airman's Outings* v. 111 The leave train at Arrière was time-tabled for midnight. **1939** G. GREENE *Confidential Agent* I. i. 29 'My employers..wouldn't understand the delay.' They would have time-tabled his movements. **1970** *Times* 20 Oct. 4 Next year the school will admit 15 musically talented children who will be separately timetabled to give full scope for their abilities. **1974** *Times* 3 June 7/5 Headmistresses..were adamant that non-examinable, creative subjects must be time-tabled in girls' schools.

Hence **tiˑmetaːbled** *ppl. a.*; **tiˑmetaːbling** *vbl. sb.*

1960 *Farmer & Stockbreeder* 22 Mar. 47/1 Apart from complex timetabling, his work included liaison with police ..and dovetailing turn-rounds. **1963** *Times* 24 May p. xii/5 Regular timetabled lorry services between the depots and Acton. **1969** *Guardian* 24 Oct. 9/2 Some will protest that the division of school time into 40-minute periods is essential for time-tabling. **1975** *Language for Life* (Dept. Educ. & Sci.) xxv. 403, 93 per cent of classes..were taught English as a separately time-tabled subject. **1977** *Modern Railways* Dec. 481/3 The obsolete layout at Liverpool Street is a major timetabling handicap particularly in that there has to be a comfortable margin at Platform 9 between the 00.30 Norwich departures and the 00.39 arrivals. **1978** P. BAILEY *Leisure & Class in Victorian England* vii. 167 Cutting down ad libs and encores..helped ensure the predictable time-tabling of acts. **1982** *Daily Tel.* 12 Feb. 2/5 While many timetabled [rail] services will be axed, staff shortages mean there will be few cuts in services operated.

timing, *vbl. sb.* Add: **2. a.** (Earlier example in *Cricket.*)

1863 *Boys' Jrnl.* I. 264/1 He..showed us all the power and velocity resulting from hitting the balls at the right time. He called this the art of *timing.*

3. In an internal-combustion engine, the times when the valves open and close, and the time of the ignition spark, in relation to the movement of the piston in the cylinder. Freq. *attrib.*, as *timing diagram*; **timing chain,** the chain that drives the camshaft of an engine from the crankshaft, part of the timing gear; **timing gear,** the mechanism by which the valves of an internal-combustion engine are made to open and close at the right moment; **timing mark,** each of the marks on an engine that are used as guides when assembling the timing gear or altering the valve timing.

1915 V. W. PAGÉ *Automobile Repairing made Easy* iii. 304 In these diagrams the timing used is: Inlet opens at 8 degrees past the upper center; [etc.] *Ibid.* 306 Two typical valve timing diagrams, one for a four cyclinder engine having a flywheel diameter of 15⅝ inches, the other of a six cylinder engine are given. **1929** —— *Ford Model A Car* vii. 270 (*caption*) Diagram showing timing marks on crankshaft and camshaft timing gears of Ford model A engines. **1935** F. J. CAMM *Practical Motorist's Encycl.* 319/1 Timing chain. **1970** K. BALL *Fiat 600D Autobook* i. 20/1 Replace and secure timing gear gasket, cover and crankshaft oilseal. *Ibid.*, Install camshaft, crankshaft sprockets with timing chain so that timing marks are adjacent. **1977** *Hot Car* Oct. 81/1 When setting the timing on a Mini engine with a stroboscopic light, it is often difficult to see the timing marks. **1977** 'J. FRASER' *Hearts Ease* ix. 107 That lorry..needed the tappets adjusting. And I don't think the timing was right.

Timini, Timmanah, Timni, obs. varr. *TEMNE *sb.* and *a.*

timolol (ti·mŏlǫl). *Pharm.* [f. *tim-* (of unknown origin) + *-olol*, after *PROPRANOLOL.] A *β*-adrenergic blocking agent used in the treatment of hypertension; (−)-1-*tert*-butylamino-3-(4-morpholino-1,2,5-thiadiazol-3-yloxy)-propan-2-ol, $C_{13}H_{24}N_4O_3S$.

1973 *Arch. Internat. de Pharmacodyn. et de Thérapie* CCV. 92 As a *β*-adrenergic blocking agent, timolol was found to be more potent than propranolol. **1976** *Nature* 22 July 307/2 Neither phentolamine..nor timolol, a specific blocker of beta-receptors..had any effect.

Timor (tī·mǭɹ). The name of an Indonesian island off the north-west coast of Australia, part of which was before 1976 a Portuguese colony, used *attrib.* in **Timor pony,** a small, stocky horse belonging to a variety first found there. Also *absol.*

[**1841** G. GREY *Jrnls. Two Exped. N.-W. & W. Austral.* I. iv. 68 The vessel could then proceed..to the Island of Timor, to procure the requisite number of ponies for our expedition.] **1895** A. B. PATERSON *Man from Snowy River* (1896) 4 He was something like a racehorse undersized, With a touch of Timor pony. **1928** 'BRENT OF BIN BIN' *Up Country* xv. 253 He rode a yellow bay with a dash of Timor, hardy and sure-footed as a goat. **1933** *Bulletin* (Sydney) 27 Sept. 21/2 Those Timor ponies..date back to 1840. **1965** *Austral. Encycl.* IV. 552/1 The Timor pony possesses remarkable hardiness and stamina.

Timorese (tīmorī·z), *sb.* and *a.* [f. *Timor* (see prec.) + -ESE.] **A.** *sb.* (A member of) the indigenous people of Timor, of Indonesian-Malay stock. **B.** *adj.* Of, pertaining to, or characteristic of Timor or its inhabitants.

1869 A. R. WALLACE *Malay Archipelago* I. xiii. 290 The native Timorese predominate. **1875** [see *PAPUAN *a.* 1]. **1964** M. DICKSON *World Elsewhere* iii. 122 The standard of the game was mainly due to the exemplary keenness.. of the Timorese and Dusan opponents. **1979** *Times* 28 Dec. 16/2 Left-wing Timorese students..began to return to the island. *Ibid.*, Not a few Timorese are in somewhat uneasy cooperation with the Indonesians.

timothy. 1. b. *timothy hay* (examples).

1772 *Pennsylvania Gaz.* 16 Apr. 4/3 (Advt.), Timothy and blue grass hay to be sold. **1911** *Daily Colonist* (Victoria, B.C.) 25 Apr. 6/1 (Advt.), *Horses.* Try some of our Washington Timothy Hay—big load just in.

timpani (ti·mpăni), *sb. pl.* [a. It., pl. of *timpano* kettledrum (also used), f. L. *tympanum* drum: cf. TYMPANUM, TYMPANY 3.] **a.** The kettledrums. (The preferred spelling: see also *TYMPANI.) **b.** Timpani-players, timpanists.

[**1557**: see TYMPANY 3.] **1740** J. GRASSINEAU *Mus. Dict.* 283 *Timpano.* See *Tympanum.* **1876** STAINER & BARRETT *Dict. Mus. Terms* 435/1 Timpani, (*It.*) kettle-drums. **1906** [see TYMPANIST]. **1947** A. EINSTEIN *Mus. in Romantic Era* ii. 14 One of them, that in G minor, renounces trumpets and timpani. **1962** N. DEL MAR *R. Strauss* v. 161 It takes the form of a powerful pedal-point reinforced by regular strokes on the timpani. **1970** J. BLADES *Percussion Instruments* xii. 270 The soft pulsation of the C timpano. **1977** *Listener* 27 Jan. 128/3 BBC Northern Orchestra..requires: Timpani and Percussion... Salary £3,876 per annum.

Hence **ti·mpanist,** one who plays the kettledrums.

1939 J. HARRISON *Brahms & his Four Symphonies* vi. 79 The Timpanist reiterates those challenging Cs. **1948** *Penguin Music Mag.* June 40 The timpanist's job is extremely responsible. **1978** *Washington Post* 28 Mar. c2/3 The kid snuck down to the front and got a wink from the timpanist in the orchestra.

timps (timps), *sb. pl.* Colloq. abbrev. of prec.

1934 S. R. NELSON *All about Jazz* ii. 50 There were drummers who could already read and play timps, etc. **1948** *Penguin Music Mag.* June 40 He himself was a 'timps' player as well as conductor. **1978** R. DONINGTON in J. M. Thomson *Future of Early Music in Britain* 15 The baroque orchestra..should have a basic need for.. trumpets and timps as required.

Timurid (ti·miurid), *a.* and *sb.* [f. the personal name *Timur* (see below) + patronymic suff. *-id.*] **A.** *adj.* Descended from Timur Lenk (see TAMERLANE, TAMBURLAINE); of or pertaining to the Turkic dynasty which ruled in Central Asia after the death of Timur in 1405 until 1506. **B.** *sb.* A descendant of Timur Lenk; a member of the Timurid dynasty.

1889 G. N. CURZON *Russia in Central Asia* vii. 216 The *Koktash*, or coronation-stone, of the Timurid sovereigns. **1908** C. ELIOT *Turkey in Europe* (ed. 2) iii. 87 Shah Shaitan..and his descendants struggled with the Timurids for the supreme power in Transoxiana. **1934** A. TOYNBEE *Study of Hist.* I. II. 369 The Timurid Empire had held together..for half a century longer. **1947** AUDEN *Age of Anxiety* v. 110 The Timurids and Torguts. **1958** O. CAROE *Pathans* x. 138 His claim to the Delhi throne was based on his Timurid ancestry. **1975** [see *SAFAVID *a.* and *sb.*].

tin, *sb.* **1. b.** **block tin,** substitute for def.: tin of second quality cast into blocks; solid tin as distinct from tin plate; a receptacle made from this; (further examples).

1836 DICKENS in *Bell's Life in London* 17 Jan. 1/1 The little block-tin temple sacred to 'baked 'taturs'. **1852** —— *Bleak Ho.* (1853) xxvi. 259 He could play 'em a tune on any sort of pot you please, so as it was iron or block tin. **1879** M. E. BRADDON *Vixen* I. xiii. 255 The silver kettle..was conducting itself as spitfireishly as any blackened block-tin on a kitchen hob. **1910** G. B. SHAW *Let.* 21 Mar. (1972) II. 915 You inherited from your father a sense of the importance of block-tin piping.

2. a. (Earlier examples in first two senses.)

1795 S. MARTIN *New Experienced Eng.-Housekeeper* v. 73 Butter the tins, and bake them in a pretty quick oven. **1861** MRS. BEETON *Bk. Househ. Managem.* 100 Many cooks use the tinned turtle..preserved in hermetically-sealed canisters... The cost of a tin..is about £2.

c. Cricket colloq. *the tins*, rectangular metal pieces each with a single white number painted on a black ground, set on the score-board or 'telegraph' to show the score, etc., during a match. Phr. *on the tins*, on the score-board.

1903 D. L. A. JEPHSON in H. G. Hutchinson *Cricket* iv. 97 Poor old Surrey in the soup again!.. The mouldy eight runs on the tins were only hoisted there by a mighty effort. **1944** E. BLUNDEN *Cricket Country* i. 19 The call from the pavilion..sent the tins hustling up on the score-board.

d. *Squash Rackets.* A strip of metal or other material fitted along the bottom of the front wall of the court, which resounds when struck by the ball, showing it to have dropped out of play. With *the*.

[**1926** C. ARNOLD *Game of Squash Rackets* i. 1 On the front wall is fixed the playboard or tell tale. This consists of a piece of boarding backed with tin extending to a height of 19 inches from the ground. A ball striking this surface would not count, hence the name and the tin backing which sends forth a metallic clang when struck.] **1933** *Times* 18 Nov. 5/7 Time after time he got his opponent out of position and then, in too great a hurry to finish off the rally, put the ball on to the tin. **1960** *Times* 29 Nov. 17/4 Gordon..cast away his chances into the tin. **1973** M. RUSSELL *Double Hit* xxv. 187 The boy aimed a stroke which missed. The fourth he returned into the tin.

3. b. *the Tins*: a nickname of the Household Cavalry (from their cuirasses).

1918 G. FRANKAU *Poet. Works* (1923) 181 Why ride the Tins in full review-array? 'Tis Hazeline Tredither's wedding-day! **1947** *Times* 16 Sept. 5/4 The Household Cavalry are the 'Tins', in allusion to their cuirasses; the shrapnel helmet of our day is a 'tinhat'. **1982** BARR & YORK *Official Sloane Ranger Handbk.* 90/1 Household Cavalry (the Tins: the Life Guards, and the Blues & Royals).

c. The badge or shield of a policeman. *U.S.*

1949 PARTRIDGE *Dict. Underworld* 725/2 *Tin*,..as 'a sheriff's badge', it is American s[lang]. **1956** 'E. MCBAIN' *Cop Hater* (1958) xiii. 109 They reached for the leather cases to which their shields were pinned... They pinned the tin to their collars. **1975** 'S. MARLOWE' *Cawthorn Jrnls.* (1976) II. xix. 170 Mason Reed flashed the tin. 'Police officer. March right out of here.'

4. a. *tin box* (earlier example), *roof, trunk, ware* (earlier example); *tin-shop* (examples).

1723 J. NOTT *Cook's & Confectioner's Dict.* sig. I i 8, You may boil it [*sc.* spinach] in a Tin-box, which shuts so close, that no Liquor can get in. **1912** E. LUTYENS *Let.* May in M. Lutyens *Edwin Lutyens* (1980) vii. 105 It is.. very English!—to have a capital as Simla is entirely of tin roofs. **1982** M. DUKE *Flashpoint* x. 69 Untidy shanties with tin roofs. **1851** H. MAYHEW *London Labour* I. 336/1 The street-sellers of that order are supplied at the 'tin-shops'. **1979** *United States 1980/81* (Penguin Travel Guides) 546 The bakery, tin shop and garden house look ..as if they were still open for business. **1922** E. H. YOUNG *Bridge Dividing* II. i. 79 Henrietta went to her room to unpack the brown tin trunk which contained all her possessions. **1981** R. GRAYSON *Death of Abbé Didier* xiv. 125 He could see in the bedroom two large tin trunks. **1812** 'H. BULL-US' *Diverting Hist. John Bull & Brother Jonathan* xiii. 91 These people are also very ingenious in making tin ware, brooms, cider-brandy, wooden bowls, and tallow candles.

b. Freq. in phr. (*little*) *tin god* (later examples). Also *tin Jesus* (only in the work of G. B. Shaw).

1909 *Our German Cousins* xv. 89 In Prussia alone there are 492 Landräte—a sort of district commissioner—all Government officials or directly in touch with the central government, and all little tin gods in their own district. **1917** S. LEWIS *Job* xiii. 193 If they'd work like sixty they might get to be little tin gods on wheels like himself? **1928** R. CAMPBELL *Wayzgoose* ii. 55 Of Tin Gods you may oft have heard or read But this one was entirely made of lead. **1930** G. B. SHAW *What I really wrote about War* xii. 368 The victorious Chauvinists..derided him [*sc.* Woodrow Wilson] as 'a tin Jesus'. **1951** E. COXHEAD *One Green Bottle* v. 115 We economists are going to be the little tin gods of this generation. **1978** 'M. M. KAYE' *Far Pavilions* VI. xxxvi. 534 With luck the 'Tin Gods' who had banished him to Gujerat..would leave him alone.

c. *tin-pedlar* (earlier example), *smelter, -smelting* (example), *-stamping* (example); *tin-roofed* (earlier example).

1812 J. K. PAULDING *Beauties Bro. Bull-Us* 53 Feather-merchants, rag-men, tin-pedlars, and horse-jockies. **1882** J. G. WHITTIER in *Atlantic Monthly* Feb. 145 Its tin-roofed chapel stood Half hid in the dwarf spruce wood. **1885** *List of Subscribers, Classified* (United Telephone Co.) (ed. 6) 211 Tin Smelters... Redruth Tin Smelting Co. **1977** *Whitaker's Almanack 1978* 757 Some of the country's more important industrial installations include..a tin smelter. **1885** *List of Subscribers, Classified* (United Telephone Co.) (ed. 6) 151 Anglo-American Tin Stamping Co., Limited.

d. Applied disparagingly to buildings (esp. Nonconformist churches) made partly of corrugated iron: *tin chapel, tabernacle* (cf. TABERNACLE *sb.* 6 b), etc. Also, *tin town.*

1884 *Lichfield Diocesan Mag.* Jan. 11/2 It was decided to build 'a little bit of a tin tabernacle'. **1886** MARQUESS OF BUTE *Let.* 17 Apr. in D. H. Blair *John Patrick 3rd Marquess of Bute* (1921) ix. 154 The persistent wish of my Lord of Argyll to have what he calls an 'opening' of the tin temple in August. **1897** E. EDWARDS *Journey through S. Afr.* viii. 48 It would not be out of place to refer to Kimberley as a 'tin town'. **1919** A. T. BASSETT *S. Barnabas' Oxford* iv. 36 This was before the 'tin' church at Cowley S. John existed. **1929** J. B. PRIESTLEY *Good Companions* I. vi. 242 That's the Station Refreshment Rooms, a tin place, just opposite. **1934** DYLAN THOMAS *Let.* Oct. (1966) 143 We made a tour of the pubs..drinking to the..destruction of the Tin Bethels. **1937** *New Statesman* 13 Nov. 802/2 The several designs of late-Victorian tin-chapel in the slums of a northern industrial town. **1962** 'J. LE CARRÉ' *Murder of Quality* x. 108 That parson man from the tin tabernacle. **1979** 'P. O'CONNOR' *Into Strong City* II. xxix. 103 *Being born again* had become no longer a derisive tin chapel slogan but a phrase to describe what was happening to me.

5. tin-arsed *a. Austral.* and *N.Z. slang*, very lucky; **tin-back** *Austral. slang*, a very lucky man; **tin can,** (*a*) (see sense 4 a in Dict.) (earlier example); (*b*) *slang* (chiefly *U.S.*), a warship, esp. a destroyer (often, one of an older design); also applied to a submarine; **tin-canning** *N.Z.*, a greeting or serenading on a special occasion by beating tin cans; hence **tin-can** *v. trans.* (cf. TIN-KETTLE *v.*); **tin disease** = *tin pest* below; **tin ear,** (*a*) *slang* = *cauliflower ear* s.v. *CAULIFLOWER 2; (*b*) *colloq.* (usu. with indefinite art.), tone-deafness, aural insensitivity, esp. in phr. *to have a tin ear*; also *fig.*; hence **tin-eared** *a.*; **tin-enamel,** white tin-glaze decorated in enamel colours; hence **tin-enamelled** *a.*; **tin fish**: see *FISH *sb.*[1] 1 h; **tin-glaze** (examples); **tin hare** *slang* (chiefly *Austral.*) = *electric hare* s.v. *ELECTRIC *a.* 2 b; also fig. (in quot. 1941 a nickname for a train); **tin helmet** = *TIN HAT 1 a; hence **tin-helmeted** *a.*; **Tin Lizzie**: see *LIZZIE 2; **tin-mouth** (earlier example); **tin pest,** the crumbling of pure tin that occurs at low temperatures as the ordinary white allotrope changes to grey tin; cf. *grey modification* s.v. *GREY, GRAY *a.* 8 c; **tin printing** (see quot. 1957); **tin wedding** orig. *U.S.*, the tenth anniversary of a wedding (cf. WEDDING *vbl. sb.* 2 b).

1937 PARTRIDGE *Dict. Slang* 888/1 *Tinny*, adj...Occ. tin-arsed. **1971** R. F. BRISSENDEN *Winter Matins* 25 This tin-arsed character Hasn't been there six months before he starts To fidget, gets to grizzling in his beer. **1897** W. T. GOODGE *Hits! Skits! & Jingles!* (1899) 150 And a 'tin-back.' is a party Who's remarkable for luck. **1770** G. WASHINGTON *Diary* 18 Nov. (1925) I. 442, I was to pay 6 Dollars and give them a Quart Tinn Can. **1937** *Sun* (Baltimore) 20 Apr. 15/3 Of the forty-seven destroyers out with the United States fleet..thirty-nine are the 'tin cans' of the World War days. **1957** J. FRAME *Owls do Cry* II. xix. 84 We tin-canned them and threw rice at them. **1959** *N.Z. Listener* 10 July 5/3 With us were the first warships I had seen in the heavy seas, and some of the American tin cans they gave us under Lease Lend. **1974** H. GRUPPE *Truxton Cipher* iii. 31 He had noticed the Admiral's wince at Pozo's use of the archaic phrase 'tin cans' to denote destroyers. **1981** G. MARKSTEIN *Ultimate Issue* 27 'Boy, you must have been cramped in that sub.'..'Plenty of space. You'd be surprised how roomy those tin cans are.' **1926** A. F. WEBB *Miss Peters' Special* vii. 62 A promoter of most of the tin-canning parties when anyone got married. **1953** M. SCOTT *Breakfast at Six* (1960) ii. 19 The chaps are coming up tonight. Tin-canning. The usual thing. Thought I'd better warn you. **1908** H. C. COOPER tr. *Holleman's Text-bk. Inorg. Chem.* (ed. 3) 275 It [*sc.* white tin] turns very slowly into gray tin, falling to powder, probably because of the increase in volume (this phenomenon is called the 'tin disease'). **1965** PHILLIPS & WILLIAMS *Inorg. Chem.* I. vii. 246 In cold countries the disintegration of organ pipes and other tin objects has..been observed, and the phenomenon was known as tin disease. **1923** *Dialect Notes* V.

239 *Tin ear on, to put a*, v. phr. To strike or beat, especially, about the head. **1935** *Peabody Bull.* (Baltimore) Dec. 42/2 A player has a 'tin ear' when his intonation is poor and his playing is mechanical. **1958** *Times Lit. Suppl.* 24 Jan. 39/2 He gives the, possibly false, impression, that he has a 'tin ear', as his countrymen put it, for many of the popular art-forms he discusses. **1962** YOUNG & WILLMOTT *Family & Kinship in E. London* (rev. ed.) I. vi. 101 A man with skill as a boxer, and a 'tin ear' (cauliflower ear) to prove it, had..prestige. **1975** *Times* 17 Apr. 14/4 Manson had a tin ear but..the Beach Boys recorded at least one of his songs. **1981** L. DEIGHTON *XPD* xviii. 159 'Do you play the piano?'..'My wife insisted I get it for Billy, but that kid's got a tin ear.' **1975** *New Yorker* 28 Apr. 130/1 Who but a tin-eared organ fancier..can bear to listen to elaborate contrapuntal textures sounded in consecutive fifths? **1900** F. LITCHFIELD *Pottery & Porcelain* ii. 14 Stanniferous or tin-enamel. **1964** H. HODGES *Artifacts* ii. 51 Today the terms faience, majolica and tin-enamel glaze are all variously applied to mean wares with a red body covered with a tin-opacified lead glaze which has been coloured with over-glaze designs. **1981** 'J. GASH' *Vatican Rip* x. 86 Forged nineteenth-century tin-enamel porcelain maiolicas. **1933** *Burlington Mag.* July 16/1 The tin-enamelled ware, façon de Pise, especially for the shelves of pharmacies and still-rooms. **1974** *Country Life* 5 Dec. 1728/1 Faience is tin-enamelled earthenware, not porcelain. **1897** C. F. BINNS *Ceramic Technol.* ii. 17 These wares were uniformly coated with opaque tin glazes. **1975** *Times* 18 Feb. 13/1 Tin glaze earthenware chalice. **1934** WEBSTER, Tin hare. **1941** K. TENNANT *Battlers* 159 The 'Tin Hare's' whistle was heard in the distance. **1969** *Northern Territory News* (Darwin) *Focus '69* 109/1 Many top notch tin hare chasers tried at open coursing are 'left for dead' by very ordinary live hare chasers. **1934** WEBSTER, Tin helmet. **1942** E. WAUGH *Put out More Flags* i. 40 A man in a tin helmet shouted.., 'Take cover, there.' **1980** 'T. HINDE' *Sir Henry & Sons* i. 10 He mounted a tin helmet on the top of a rifle. **1939** 'N. BLAKE' *Smiler with Knife* xi. 156 The black-faced miners, tin-helmeted. **1983** C. DEXTER *Riddle of Third Mile* i. 10 The tin-helmeted head spattered with blood. **1878** C. HALLOCK *Sportsman's Gaz.* 378 Sand Perch, or Bachelor Perch; called also 'Tin-Mouth'. **1902** H. C. COOPER tr. *Holleman's Text-bk. Inorg. Chem.* 261 It [*sc.* white tin] turns very slowly into gray tin, falling to powder (this phenomenon is called the tin-pest). **1933** *Jrnl. R. Aeronaut. Soc.* XXXVII. 540 This change does not proceed with disintegrating effects until considerably lower temperatures, when the 'Tin-Pest', experienced in organ-pipes, during cold winters on the Continent, occurs. **1960** E. S. HEDGES *Tin & its Alloys* i. 2 There seems to be a paucity of very ancient objects made entirely of tin—a lack which is sometimes laid at the door of the disintegration of tin through 'tin pest'. **1887** *Amer. Lithographer & Printer* 2 Apr. 192/3 Could you give me something practical on tin printing? **1957** *Encycl. Brit.* XIV. 214/1 Tin Printing, which was introduced about 1875, is the application of the lithographic process to the decoration of metal plate. A substantial percentage of can-label work formerly done by the paper lithographer has in recent years gone to the tin lithographers... Sheets of prepared tin..are fed into the press and are then oven dried at high temperature, this procedure being repeated for each additional colour. **1968** *Gloss. Terms Offset Lithogr. Printing* (*B.S.I.*) 33 *Tin printing machine*, (deprecated) a machine for printing on sheet metal. **1863** *Harper's Mag.* Nov. 856/2 Mr Jones's people made him a tin-wedding visit on the tenth anniversary of his marriage. **1981** *N.Y. Times* 19 July II. 25/4 A tin wedding bouquet and a brooch of jewelled flowers sit side by side.

‖ **tinaja** (tina·χa). [Sp.: see TINAGE.] **1.** In Spain: a large earthenware jar used to hold wine, oil, olives, or salted fish or meat; in parts of Spanish America, such a jar used for storing water.

1676, 1845 [see TINAGE]. **1885** *Encycl. Brit.* XIX. 629/1 The earliest kinds now existing of Spanish pottery without either enamel or glaze are chiefly large wine-jars, 'tinajas', about 3 or 4 feet high, of graceful amphora-like shape, stamped with simple patterns in relief. **1924** GORGAS & HENDRICK *William Crawford Gorgas* v. 179 An assault on the water barrels, cisterns, tinajas, and dish pans of the cities of Colon and Panama involved greater difficulties. **1949** *Jrnl. N.Y. Bot. Garden* Mar. 59 The women look like animated tea cozies..loaded down..with *tinajas* (jars) or rolls of mats made of reeds. **1971** L. BOGER *Dict. World Pott. & Porc.* 343/1 Tinajas were produced in all parts of Moslem Spain with..little variety in design.

2. *South-west U.S.* A rock hollow where water is retained; hence, any temporary or intermittent pool.

1835 T. COULTER *Notes on Upper California* 65 The only water to be had is found..in excavations called Tinajas, made by the Indians. **1857** A. SCHOTT *Obs. on Country along Mexican Boundary* 69 Permanent water is found under a cleft of igneous rocks, and does not properly deserve the name of a spring, but is rather a tinaja supplied by water trickling through the rocks from water-holes above. **1896** *Science* 3 Apr. 494/1 Knowledge of the few widely separated tinajas and springs was bought at the price of many lives. **1958** 'W. HENRY' *Seven Men at Mimbres Springs* v. 55 The wells were pothole water tanks, rock *tinajas*.

tincalconite (tinkæ·lkŏnəit). *Min.* [f. TINCAL + Gr. κον-ία powder + -ITE[1].] A hydrated basic borate of sodium, $Na_2B_4O_5(OH)_4.3H_2O$, occurring as a fine white powder with rhombohedral symmetry and formed by the dehydration of borax.

[**1878** C. U. SHEPARD in *Bull. Soc. Franç. de Minéral.* I. 144 Tincalconite (Shepard). Borax pulvérulent et efflorescent, de Californie.] **1892** E. S. DANA *Dana's Syst. Min.* (ed. 6) 887 Tincalconite. **1930** *Prof. Papers U.S. Geol. Survey* No. 158. 164/2 Tincalconite can readily be made by boiling a solution of borax until crystallization ensues. **1977** *Mineral. Abstr.* XXVIII. 280/2 Tincalconite and meyerhofferite are thought to be metastable, and unsuccessful attempts to bring about their dehydration to kernite and colemanite are reported.

tinctorially, *adv.* (Earlier example.)

1895 *Sci. Progress* II. 418 In 'acid' solutions the staining principle is the acid although the dye may be a chemically neutral salt; tinctorially it reacts as a free acid.

tincture, *sb.* Add: **7. c.** An alcoholic drink, a 'snifter'. *colloq.*

1914 JOYCE *Dubliners* 115 Weathers made them all have just one little tincture at his expense. **1980** INGRAMS & WELLS *Dear Bill* 36 Rough diamond, especially after a tincture or two.

tinder, *sb.* Add: **d.** *tinder-lighter.*

1915 V. ASQUITH *Let.* 16 Nov. in M. Gilbert *Winston S. Churchill* (1972) III. Compan. II. 1272 Is there anything you *haven't* got for the Front? Compass? Luminous wristwatch? Muffler? Tinderlighter? **1977** 'J. GASH' *Judas Pair* ii. 25 Flintlocks..the standard tinder-lighter of history.

tinderish *a.* (earlier Canad. example).

1837 A. LANGTON *Jrnl.* 8 July in *Gentlewoman in Upper Canada* (1950) 15 From her gingham never having been washed I suppose it was more tinderish than my sister's and mine.

tine, *sb.*[1] **1.** (Later examples.)

1968 J. ARNOLD *Shell Bk. Country Crafts* 92 The larger, called a drag rake, carrying about thirty tines compared with fifteen for the garden rake. **1978** *Cornish Guardian* 27 Apr. 10/4 (Advt.), 60in rotavator with new tines. **1979** P. THEROUX *Old Patagonian Express* (1980) xiv. 289 The man jerked the tines of his fork into a slab of ham.

tinea. Add: **tinean** *sb.* (example), **tineid** *a.* and *sb.* (examples).

1842 T. W. HARRIS *Insects Injurious to Vegetation* 361 The Tineans..have four short and slender feelers. **1888** *Insect Life* I. 191 These insects..are cloth-feeding Tineids. **1890** *Ibid.* II. 330 The Tineid Leaf-miner..affects the younger leaves only. **1924** J. A. THOMSON *Science Old & New* x. 55 There is a very interesting Tineid caterpillar, found in the tree-nest of one of the Termites. **1964** EDWARDS & HEATH *Princ. Agric. Entom.* xiii. 285 Corn moth..is one of the most common Tineid moths which attacks grain.

tined, *a.* **a.** (Later examples.)

1886 R. E. G. COLE *Gloss. S.-W. Lincs.* 154 He was charged with stealing a steel-tined fork. **1971** *Farmers Weekly* 19 Mar. 84 There was plenty to interest traditionalists, particularly among tined implements.

ting, *sb.*[1] Add: **b.** Also *ting a ling ling* and (*rarely*) *tingating.* Cf. *tink-a-tink* s.v. TINK *int.* and *sb.*

1922 JOYCE *Ulysses* 734 And he so quiet and mild with his tingating zither. **1932** T. S. ELIOT *Sweeney Agonistes* 12 *Telephone*: Ting a ling ling. Ting a ling ling.

‖ **t'ing** (tiŋ), *sb.*[2] Also **ting.** [Chinese *tíng.*] In China: a small open pavilion, esp. in which one may rest or enjoy the landscape.

1853 *North-China Herald* 7 May 159/2 Another accommodation for travellers, called *ting*, are of more frequent occurrence. **1947** *Archit. Rev.* CII. 12/2 An island in a lake will have its t'ing, a bridge spanning the water is crowned by a t'ing, and a t'ing will invariably mark any particularly charming viewpoint. **1958** W. WILLETTS *Chinese Art* II. viii. 701 A small Chinese open pavilion (*t'ing*) of traditional form at Fuchow in Fukien, dating from the nineteenth century.

Ting (diŋ, tiŋ), *sb.*[3] Also **Ding. a.** The name of a county in Hebei province, China, used *attrib.* to designate a type of white porcelain first made there during the Tang dynasty and perfected during the Song dynasty. **b.** **Ting-yao,** the name of a kiln in this county, used *attrib.* and *absol.* to denote the porcelain made there.

1904 E. DILLON *Porcelain* v. 67 In the Ting yao of the Sung dynasty..we have the oldest type of an important class of porcelain. **1915** R. L. HOBSON *Chinese Pott. & Porc.* I. iv. 51 Many of the white Ting wares are thin enough to be translucent. **1933** *Burlington Mag.* June 265/1 The standard Ting ware was white..porcelain, which was either perfectly plain or decorated with free-hand carved designs. **1953** B. GRAY *Early Chinese Pott. & Porc.* v. 31 To return to the Ting wares. The most characteristic Ting shape is a conical bowl on a small foot. **1958** W. WILLETTS *Chinese Art* II. vi. 446 North is Ting Chou and the district where Ting wares are supposed to have originated. **1971** L. A. BOGER *Dict. World Pott. & Porc.* 343/2 As a rule the Ting bowls had a raw edge, as though placed in the furnace in an inverted position. **1972** *Times* 30 May 11/2 (Advt.), A carved ting yao plate. **1980** *Catal. Fine Chinese Ceramics* (Sotheby, Hong Kong) 32 A small Ding (Ting) Ware bowl with curved sides, freely carved with a lotus blossom in the interior.

‖ **ting** (diŋ, tiŋ), *sb.*[4] [Chinese *dǐng.*] An ancient Chinese vessel, usu. bronze, having two looped handles and three or four legs (see quots.).

1904 S. W. BUSHELL *Chinese Art* I. iv. 80 The word *ting* is occasionally rendered 'tripod', but this is hardly applicable to a second not uncommon form which has a rectangular body of oblong section supported by four legs. **1958** W. WILLETTS *Chinese Art* I. iii. 138 The Han dictionary *Êrh ya* defines the *ting* as a *li* with solid legs. **1959** G. SAVAGE *Antique Collector's Handbk.* 40 The *ting* is a bowl of hemispherical shape with three legs and two upstanding handles. **1973** *Genius of China* 12/1 In 219 BC the Ch'in emperor tried to recover from a river the nine *ting* tripods on which the power of the Chou king over his feudal subordinates was said to depend.

ting, *v.* Add: **1. c.** To announce (a person) by 'ringing in' (see RING *v.*[2] 7 c). *rare.*

1880 HARDY *Trumpet-Major* II. xxiii. 157 'There, they be tinging in the passon!' exclaimed David,..as the bells changed from chiming all three together to a quick beating of one.

tingle, *sb.*[1] Add: **2. b.** A sheet of metal, usu. copper, used for making temporary repairs on a small wooden boat when it has been holed.

1909 in WEBSTER. **1932** F. B. COOKE *Cruising Chats* xxv. 228 The best material for a tingle is a piece of thin sheet lead. **1961** B. FERGUSSON *Watery Maze* ix. 222 Plans should never be regarded as immutable. If they leak when first floated, it is no good patching them up until they are all tingles and no hull; scrap and start again. **1969** *Beaver* Spring 30/2 It has been suggested that these pieces [of sheet copper] may be nothing more than a tingle or patch on a ship's boat.

tingle, *sb.*[3] [Abbrev. of *whelk-tingle* s.v. WHELK[1] d.] Any of several marine molluscs, esp. the rough tingle, *Ocenebra erinacea*, the smooth tingle, *Nucella lapillus*, or the American tingle, *Urosalpinx cinerea*, all of which bore holes in the shells of oysters and other molluscs.

1930 *Essex Naturalist* XXII. 299 In the autumn of 1928 samples of living tingles dredged in the River Blackwater were forwarded to me. **1959** *Times* 25 Aug. 5/6 The investigation was designed to control the tingles. **1974** P. R. WALNE *Culture of Bivalve Molluscs* vi. 125 The introduction of the American slipper limpet..and the American tingle..on to the south-east coast of England.. are well-documented examples.

tingler. (Earlier example.)

1829 P. EGAN *Boxiana* 2nd Ser. II. 703 Johnson fell from a tingler on the left lug.

ti·ngle-ta·ngle[2]. Also **tingel-tangel.** [ad. G. *tingeltangel* (with orig. reference to Berlin café chantant music); cf. TINGLE-TANGLE[1].] A cheap or disreputable music-hall or night-club, esp. in Germany; cabaret.

1911 *Mariner's Mirror* I. 190/1 Those sing-song houses of ill repute, which in German and Scandinavian ports are called 'tingle-tangles'. **1939** ADELER & WEST *Remember Fred Karno?* 71 The music halls in Glasgow in those days were pretty rough houses. There was one called The White Bait, where the artistes were all girls, as in the Continental Tingel-Tangels. **1948** [see *PECK HORN]. **1972** *Sat. Rev.* (U.S.) 25 Mar. 68/2 Cabaret in Germany never managed to be counted as a major or serious artistic venture... People came to refer to cabaret by a term whose unimportance needs no translation: *Tingel-tangel.*

tingly, *a.* Delete *rare* and add later examples.

1945 B. MACDONALD *Egg & I* (1946) 185 There was already beginning to be a tingly feel of autumn in the air. **1975** R. H. RIMMER *Premar Experiments* (1976) iii. 219 Arguing with Bren is like standing under a cool needle shower spray. He forces you into an alive, tingly state.

tinguaite (ti·ŋgwă,əit). *Petrogr.* [ad. G. *tinguait* (H. Rosenbusch *Mikrosk. Physiogr. der massigen Gesteine* (ed. 2, 1887) II. 628), f. Serra de *Tinguá*, name of a spur of the Serra do Mar, W. of Rio de Janeiro: see -ITE[1].] A hypabyssal rock similar to phonolite and nepheline-syenite, composed essentially of alkali feldspar, nepheline, and ægirine (acmite), the last occurring usu. as acicular crystals and conferring a greenish colour.

1893 *Mineral. Mag.* X. 173 More markedly porphyritic types are a rock with porphyritic elæolite, an 'elæolite tinguaite' with porphyritic orthoclase. **1965** G. J. WILLIAMS *Econ. Geol. N.Z.* xi. 167/2 Among these rocks is a tinguaite consisting of a network of aegirine crystals with phenocrysts of anorthoclase in a groundmass of anorthoclase, cancrinite and nepheline. **1978** S. R. NOCKOLDS in S. R. Nockolds et al. *Petrol. for Students* xv. 173 Some tinguaites have small amounts of a sodalite mineral, of analcite.., or of cancrinite. More rarely, one or other of these becomes an important constituent.

tin hat. *slang.* **1. a.** A metal hat or helmet; *spec.* a steel helmet worn for protection against shrapnel. Chiefly *Mil.*

1903 A. M. BINSTEAD *Pitcher in Paradise* viii. 194 A Tommy in a tin hat as I squared with a couple o'blow. **1917** W. E. MOLESWORTH *Let.* Mar. in A. J. L. Scott *Sixty Squadron R.A.F.* (1920) iii. 38 We managed to collect some tin hats bombs,..and a few other odds and ends. **1923** *Sci. Amer.* Nov. 360/2 The trench hat, 'the old tin hat', is coming into quite extensive use as a means of head protection against small falls of rock in mines. **1932** G. CAMPBELL *Number Thirteen* vii. 107, I happened to be dressed in a rather extraordinary rig, consisting of a tin hat, a naval monkey-jacket, grey flannel trousers, and puttees. **1940** *War Illustr.* 5 Jan. 563 'Tin Hats' for the Heads of Britain's Defenders. **1961** JOSWICK & KEATING *Combat Cameraman* xiv. 124 An upside-down tin hat lay nearby. **1976** 'A. HALL' *Kobra Manifesto* vi. 86 We haven't got a single tin hat in the place... Not even a blinking first aid kit!

† **b.** A general officer. Cf. *brass-hat* s.v. *BRASS *sb.* 7. *Mil. Obs.*

1919 *Athenæum* 18 July 632/2 May I add one or two more army slang terms? 'Tin hat' or 'brass hat' for general officer.

2. Used predicatively, usu. in *pl.*: drunk.

1909 J. R. WARE *Passing Eng.* 246/2 *Tin hat* (Anglo-Port Said), drunk—two tin hats very drunk—three, incapable, and to be carried on board. **1916** 'TAFFRAIL' *Pincher Martin* ii. 24 'No, sir, not drunk, only a bit shaky like,' I sez, though I knowed orl the time I'd bin properly tin 'ats. **1919** W. LANG *Sea-Lawyer's Log* 69 If you do come off tin 'ats (i.e. inebriated), go quietly below to the Mess Deck.

3. Phr. *to put the tin hat on (it, things,* etc.): to bring something to a (usu. unwelcome) close or climax. Cf. *to put the lid on* s.v. *LID *sb.* 1 e.

1919 *Athenæum* 8 Aug. 727/2 The shrapnel helmet was invariably a 'tin hat', and 'to put the tin hat on it' is.. 'to ki-bosh it'. **1927** 'SAPPER' *Saving Clause* i. 22 This second exhibition of cowardice had put the tin-hat on. **1933** WODEHOUSE *Mulliner Nights* vii. 225 It was the limit, he felt, the extreme edge. It put the tin hat on things. **1943** 'C. DICKSON' *She died a Lady* xx. 177 Next.. came the point that put the tin hat on it. **1977** J. M. JOHNSON in Douglas & Johnson *Existential Sociol.* viii. 244 He reflected that, at the time, he thought his efforts had 'put the tin hat on it'.

Hence **tin-hatted** *a.*, wearing a metal helmet or helmets.

1926 *British Worker* 10 May 2/3 At the Iron Bridge, at Canning Town, I met a half company of soldiers, tin-hatted, and with rifles and packs, marching into the docks. **1940** HARRISSON & MADGE *War begins at Home* iii. 46 A tin-hatted policeman began to push the crowd back. **1978** E. MALPASS *Wind brings up Rain* xxvi. 232 A tin-hatted Air Raid Warden.

tinhorn (ti·nhǫɹn), *a.* and *sb. slang* (orig. and chiefly *U.S.*) Also **tin-horn.** [f. TIN *sb.* + HORN *sb.*; cf. quot. 1931, sense A 1 below.]

A. *adj.* **1.** *tinhorn gambler*: a cheap gambler, esp. one who acts showily.

1885 *Weekly New Mexican Rev.* 26 Feb. 4/2 We have been greatly annoyed of late by a lot of tin horn gamblers and prostitutes. **1912** *Maclean's Mag.* Mar. 478/1 He says he aint no piker, and he is a game loser, and nobody can walk around his collar, and he begins to put on airs like a tin horn gambler. **1931** G. F. WILLISON *Here they dug Gold* 216 Chuck-a-luck operators shake their dice in a 'small churn-like affair of metal'—hence the expression, 'tinhorn gambler', for the game is rather looked down upon as one for 'chubbers' and chuck-a-luck gamblers are never admitted within the aristocratic circle of faro-dealers. **1958** P. BERTON *Klondike Fever* 6 A circus parade of camp-followers crowded in upon them, saloon-keepers,..tinhorn gamblers and three-card monte men. **1963** *Punch* 17 July 102/2 A Western..with..tinhorn gamblers, fisticuffs, guns and so on.

2. Inferior, contemptible; pretentious, flashy. Cf. TIN-POT 4.

1886 *San Juan* (Colorado) *Prospector* 4 Sept. 3/7 The Silverton vigilantes have notified the tin-horn element to meander. **1903** A. ADAMS *Log of Cowboy* xii. 80 A tin horn lawyer. **1935** E. POUND *Let.* 25 Sept. (1971) 276 All American Communists are, as far as I can discover, absolute boneheads, tinhorn repeaters. **1959** R. STOUT *Crime & Again* vii. 104 'You tin-horn Casanova,' she said... 'Hinting to me that you had her, and I knew all the time you didn't.' **1977** C. WESTON *Rouse Demon* xxiii. 111 This godforsaken tinhorn paradise.

3. *tinhorn sport*: a contemptible person.

1906 S. FORD *Shorty McCabe* ii. 34 He wasn't no Johnnie, and he wasn't no tinhorn sport. **1925** S. LEWIS *Arrowsmith* v. 47 I'm a—I'm a—Martin, I'm a tin-horn sport! **1958** 'W. HENRY' *Seven Men at Mimbres Springs* x. 120 The stage roads of this whole plateau are littered with the bones of tinhorn sports who didn't have the brains to fort up before morning. **1975** R. DAVIES *World of Wonders* (1977) I. vi. 57 Swifty Dealer, the village tin-horn sport.

B. *sb.* A poor or contemptible person, esp. one who is pretentious or flashy; *spec.* one who gambles for low stakes.

1887 F. FRANCIS *Saddle & Moccasin* 225 The tin-horns were there in a body, with a few stacks of chips, playing light. **1908** S. E. WHITE *Riverman* vi. 55 You ain't a tin-horn yourself? **1922** S. LEWIS *Babbitt* ii. 22 I'll bet I make a whole lot more money than some of those tin-horns that spend all they got on dress-suits. **1949** *Penguin New Writing* XXXVI. 91 A guy got off at the next stop and came back for the change. A tin-horn. **1962** E. LUCIA *Klondike Kate* iii. 65 Conditions produced the greatest opportunity for the tinhorns in the history of nineteenth-century gold strikes. **1977** D. ANTHONY *Stud Game* xix. 118 Tony Hunter called me... 'Greetings, Tinhorn,' he said.

tink (tiŋk), *sb.*[2] Chiefly *Sc.* Colloq. abbrev. of TINKER *sb.* 1 b; hence, a foul-mouthed, brawling, or disreputable person.

1857 J. STEWART *Sketches Sc. Character* 74 Nae swearing tink', nor beggar body That tak's a glass. **1894** J. B. SALMOND *B. Bowden* (1922) iv. 36 To sleep on the Common amon' the tinks. **1914** R. B. CUNNINGHAME GRAHAM *Sc. Stories* 19 Ca' ye yon man a gentleman? I just ca' him naething better than a tink. **1939** J. M. CAIE *'Twixt Hills & Sea* 58 There's kindly, honest ,eident fowk There's kyaards an' tinks forbye. **1968** A. MACLEOD *Dam* i. 15 How disgusting it was to..back up a drunken tink like Sorley. **1980** D. K. CAMERON *Willie Gavin* viii. 73 A fear that had driven her..in the hope that she might spot.. another human soul (a tink on the road, some shepherd walking the hill fields).

tink, *v.*[1] Restrict ? *Obs.* to senses 1 and 2 and add: **3.** (Modern example.) Now *rare.*

1968 B. HINES *Kestrel for Knave* 168 The glass shone. He tinked it with his nails, tapped it with a knuckle, then rapped it with his knuckles.

tink (tiŋk), *v.*[3] Repr. dial. or foreign pronunc. of THINK *v.*[2]

1767 'A. BARTON' *Disappointment* I. ii. 53, I put too much confidence in dose I tought my friends, and dey deceib'd me. **1801** T. TENNEY *Female Quixotism* II. xi. 117 How cou'd I tink, ma'am, it was John, in massa chamber? **1821** J. F. COOPER *Spy* II. xii. 186 'I don't tink he look a bit like me,' said Caesar. **1916** E. O'NEILL *Bound East for Cardiff* in *Provincetown Plays* 1st Ser. 7 Yust tink of it! **1933** M. LOWRY *Ultramarine* i. 20, I tink you are very much English all the same. **1944** in H. Wentworth *Amer. Dial. Dict.* 637 'I never t'ought it would happen... I have to keep t'inkin' about de dough I'm gettin',' mumbled Bill in his best Brooklynese. **1973** *Nation* (Barbados) 25 Nov. 1/1 Yuh tink it easy?

tinker, *sb.* Add: **1. d.** *not to be worth a tinker's damn* (earlier example); also *not to be worth* (etc.) *a tinker's cuss* and (ellipt.) *a tinker's.*

1839 THOREAU *Jrnl.* 25 Apr. in *Writings* (1906) VII. 78 'Tis true they are not worth a 'tinker's damn'. **1865** [see CUSS *sb.* 1]. **1891** KIPLING *Light that Failed* vii. 137 The real world doesn't care a tinker's—doesn't care a bit. **1947** [see *HOOT *sb.*[2]]. **1973** *Jewish Chron.* 2 Feb. 19/3 It doesn't matter a tinker's cuss whether you amend the constitution to call the chairman president. **1983** J. SYMONS *Name of Annabel Lee* II. viii. 139, I don't give a tinker's, if you'll forgive the old fashioned way of putting it, who killed Ira Wolfdale.

e. A rascal, a persistently naughty child. As a term of mild contempt, usu. familiarly or playfully. Cf. BEGGAR *sb.* 6.

1925 R. REES *Lake of Enchantment* 50 I'll soon settle the young tinker if he's up to them tricks. **1953** K. TENNANT *Joyful Condemned* xiv. 124 She's a little tinker. ..Even *you* couldn't do anything with her. **1960** J. STROUD *Shorn Lamb* xxiii. 247 I'm not so sure about Clement, he's a bit of a tinker at the moment. **1971** G. SIMS *Deadhand* II. viii. 141 Did the boys scare you? I expect they did. The tinkers!

3. e. (Earlier example.)

1771 G. CARTWRIGHT *Jrnl.* 1 June (1792) I. 128 They killed a duck and a tinker.

5. tinker-bird, any of several African birds having a call like repetitive hammering, esp. a barbet of the genus *Pogoniulus*; **Tinkertoy** orig. and chiefly *U.S.*, the proprietary name of a type of child's construction set; a toy made of this; also *fig.*

a **1884** T. AYRES in R. B. Sharpe *Layard's Birds S. Afr.* (1884) 175 The note of this curious little bird so much resembles the tapping of a hammer on an anvil (having that peculiar metallic ring) that it is called in Natal the tinker bird. **1960** G. DURRELL *Zoo in my Luggage* 12 A tinker-bird was giving its monotonous cry, toink..toink.. toink.., like someone beating forever on a tiny anvil. **1914** *Official Gaz.* (U.S. Patent Office) 3 Feb. 283/2 Charles H. Pajeau, Chicago, Ill. Filed June 27, 1913. *Tinkertoy.* Particular description of goods.—Games, Toys, and Children's Building-Blocks. Claims use since June 12, 1913. **1915** *Trade Marks Jrnl.* 22 Dec. 1279 *Tinkertoy...* Toys. Charles Hamilton Pajeau, McCormick Building, 332, South Michigan Avenue, Chicago, County of Cook, State of Illinois, United States of America; manufacturers. **1918** *Sears, Roebuck Catal.* Fall 829/1 Tinker Toy is the Wonder Builder. **1938** *Harper's Mag.* Dec. 72 At the Tinkertoy factory in Evanston, Illinois, I was shown a Japanese imitation of the construction sets faithful even to the trademark drawing and two typographical errors in the instruction sheet. **1972** *Newsweek* 19 June 23/3 McGovern will go into the campaign against Nixon with those Tinkertoy proposals of his.

tinker, *v.* Add: **1. b.** (Later examples const. *with.*)

1903 G. B. SHAW *Man & Superman* 193 Parliaments and synods may tinker as much as they please with their codes and creeds. **1936** *Discovery* Sept. 273/2 When the harbour is reached he will be at liberty to tinker with it [*sc.* a boat] to his heart's content. **1955** *Times* 2 May 13/7 Nobody is prepared to tinker with a social structure that has withstood every kind of outside pressure. **1977** J. L. HOULDEN *Patterns of Faith* iii. 39 Matthew often 'tinkers' with Mark's work as he received it.

2. a. (Earlier example.)

1769 J. WEDGWOOD *Let.* 23 Feb. (1965) 71, I have settled a plan..to Tinker all the black Vases that are crooked.

tin-kettle, *sb.* Add: **tin-kettle** *v.* (earlier example); **tin-kettling** *vbl. sb.* (earlier example).

1881 A. BATHGATE *Waitaruna* xvii. 234, I was wakened by the din caused by a lot of the diggers tin-kettling the newly-married pair. **1892** B. BOAKE *Where Dead Men Lie* (1897) 103 What cheering and tin-kettling Had they after at the 'settling'.

tinkle, *sb.* Add: **d.** *colloq.* A telephone call. Usu. in phr. *to give* (someone) *a tinkle.* Cf. *RING *sb.*[2] 3 c.

1938 F. D. SHARPE *Sharpe of Flying Squad* xxiii. 241 As soon as we find 'em I'll give you a tinkle on the blower. **1939** N. MONSARRAT *This is Schoolroom* ix. 207 Shall I give you a tinkle later? **1949** S. GIBBONS *Matchmaker* 51 And then not another word for three weeks! Not even a tinkle to ask if my cold was better! **1959** 'D. BUCKINGHAM' *Wind Tunnel* xix. 153 Shall we give Robin a tinkle and tell him that you're home? **1960** H. E. BATES *Aspidistra in Babylon* 143 Give us a tinkle. **1980** B. BAINBRIDGE *Winter Garden* xii. 89 'Next time you're in London,' advised Ashburner, 'give me a tinkle and I'll take you to my Oxfam shop.'

e. *colloq.* An act of urination. Cf. *TINKLE *v.* 6.

1965 J. R. HETHERINGTON *Selina's Aunt* 54 *Tinkle* (have a).., No. 1. **1974** E. BRAWLEY *Rap* (1975) II. xiv. 239 And went over and had a tinkle. **1978** C. MACLEOD *Rest you Merry* (1979) vi. 57, I was making my tinkle.

tinkle, *v.* Add: **6.** *intr.* To urinate. Cf. *TINKLE *sb.* e. *colloq.*

1960 WENTWORTH & FLEXNER *Dict. Amer. Slang* 547/1 *Tinkle..v.i.*, to urinate. Common usage by small children; humorously used by adults. **1972** *Sat. Rev.* (U.S.) 17 June 77/2 The handy man..picked the wrong moment to urinate on the roses. 'He's been tinkling on the roses for twenty-five years.' **1976** 'E. MCBAIN' *Guns* (1977) vii. 198 I'm looking for the loo... I really have to tinkle.

tinktinkie (tiŋkti·ŋki). *S. Afr.* [Afrikaans.] = *tinker-bird* s.v. *TINKER *sb.* 5.

1874 [see *BUSHMAN, BUSHMAN 3]. **1908** F. C. SLATER *Sunburnt South* 186 The little mouse-coloured tinktinkie ..is a most mischievous little creature. **1956** A. G. MCRAE *Hill called Grazing* iii. 24 Big birds and small birds, from huge vultures..to the tiniest tink-tinkies piping their thin little reeds of song.

tinman. Add: **2.** Comb. **tinman's solder,** a common low-melting solder composed of tin and lead in similar proportions, suitable for joining either of those metals; **tinmen's snips** = *TINSNIPS.

1937 *Archit. Rev.* LXXXI. 272/1 Solders vary in their proportions, fine solder or 'tinman's' consisting of equal parts of lead and tin and 'wiping' solder two of lead to one of tin. **1976** *Pract. Householder* Nov. 46/1 With a soft flamed blow lamp..tin the tube end with tinmans solder. **1950** *N.Z. Jrnl. Agric.* June 563/2 Tinmen's snips are used by almost every beekeeper, as they are necessary for cutting sheet metal or wire gauze. **1974** G. STOKES *Jewelry Making* v. 76 A small pair of tinmen's snips for shaping sheet metal.

tinned, *ppl. a.* Add: **2. a.** (Earlier example.) *tinned dog* (Austral. slang), canned meat.

1861 MRS. BEETON *Bk. Househ. Managem.* 100 When live turtle is dear, many cooks use the tinned turtle. **1895** *Bulletin* (Sydney) 17 Aug. 27 We gave him some 'tinned dorg' and a drink. **1950** G. CASEY *City of Men* 326 We'll be living in a tent and eating tinned dog. It's no place for a woman.

b. *tinned air,* air supplied by an artificial ventilation system (*Naut. slang*); also (chiefly *oc.*) air sealed in a tin for sale.

1913 *Rep. Brit. Assoc. Adv. Sci. 1912* 635 The fresh air driven in by fans through the metal conduits..is spoken of by the officers [in the battleship]..as 'tinned' or 'potted' air. **1929** F. BOWEN *Sea Slang* 142 *Tinned air,* artificial ventilation. **1962** *Daily Tel.* 12 Dec. 13/3, I shouldn't think even the American who bought Brooklyn Bridge would fall for tinned air as a serious buy.

c. Of music: = *CANNED *ppl. a.* b. Cf. *POTTED *ppl. a.* 3 b.

1924 J. REITH in *Radio Times* 23 May 1/3 The sound is metallic and unsatisfying, and..we do not like our music inned. *a* **1976** A. CHRISTIE *Autobiogr.* (1977) IV. v. 196 There was..no 'tinned' music in those days: no broadcasting, no tape-recorders, no stereophonic gramophones.

tinny, tinnie, *sb.* Restrict *Sc.* to sense in Dict. and add: **2.** *Austral. colloq.* A can of beer.

1974 *Telegraph* (Brisbane) 2 Mar. 6/5 In olden days audiences took the equivalent of a cut lunch and a few tinnies to the theatre and expected to be entertained for hour after hour. **1978** *Sydney Morning Herald* 20 Feb. 1 Next time you feel inclined to toss that scrap of paper or tinnie carelessly to the ground, give a thought. **1980** *Truck & Bus Transportation* Feb. 34/3 We doubt if the driver would have enough room on board to stow his lunch box or a couple of tinnies.

tinny, *a.* Add: **2. a.** (Earlier example of a sound.) Also applied dismissively to (a device which produces) sound of poor quality from which the lower frequencies are largely missing; cheaply contrived.

1884 *Encycl. Brit.* XVII. 831/1 The tone tends towards a certain quality which may be described as 'tinny' or metallic. **1926** *Encycl. Brit.* III. 281/2 When the low notes are dropped out, the result is 'tinny'—high-pitched, shrill, mechanical, lacking in body. **1933** A. HUXLEY *Lett.* (1969) 377 The particular nature of the device gives to the brevity something rather tinny, something (in an undesirable sense) artificial. **1980** G. LANCASTER *Seward's Folly* vi. 66 A tinny radio was playing pop music.

b. (Earlier example.)

1873 'S. COOLIDGE' *What Katy did at School* ii. 30 The cans gave the oysters a curious taste,—tinny, or was it more like solder?

4. *Austral.* and *N.Z. slang.* Lucky. †*on*

the tinny luck: by a lucky chance. Cf. *tinarsed* adj., *-back* s.v. *TIN *sb.* 5.

1918 *Chrons. N.Z.E.F.* 7 June 205/1 Remarks are heard on the 'tinny' luck. **1919** W. H. DOWNING *Digger Dialects* 50 *Tinny*, lucky. **1947** I. DOUGLAS *Opportunity in Australia* 90 *Tinny*—lucky. **1951** D. W. BALLANTYNE in *Landfall* V. 168 And this one's yours, Edith. Hey, you're tinny, aren't you? **1959** G. SLATTER *Gun in Hand* xvii. 229 He'll score because some people are tinny and always win. **1978** O. WHITE *Silent Reach* xvii. 173 You'll have to be pretty tinny to pin down those blokes.

Hence **ti·nnily** *adv.*, with a tinny sound.

1927 J. MASEFIELD *Midnight Folk* 298 He had no sooner wished, than invisible someones came silently, blocked up the approach to Otter's lair, tinnily reported, 'Entrance blocked securely', and disappeared. **1954** M. SHARP *Gipsy in Parlour* III. xiii. 133 A bell above my head rang tinnily. **1980** A. DESAI *Clear Light of Day* iv. 171 Teacups clinked on the saucers, tinnily.

tin pan. (In Dict. s.v. TIN *sb.* 5.) Add: **1.** (Earlier examples.)

1806 *Austin Papers* (1924) I. 102, 1 doz. Tin pans. **1843** *Knickerbocker* XXII. 50 With discordant fife and old tin-pans for drums.

2. A cheap, 'tinny' piano. Cf. *TIN-PANNY *a. U.S. slang.*

1882 C. FARRAR *Amat. & Prof. Stage Life* viii. 156 It was now Linwood's turn, and with a wail, that sounded like 'Oh, if I only had a decent piano!' he went out and tackled the old 'tin-pan' again.

3. Special Comb. **Tin Pan Alley** *colloq.* (orig. *U.S.*), the world of the composers and publishers of popular music; also applied *loosely* to a district where song publishing houses abound, *spec.* (formerly) in New York in 28th Street and in London around Denmark Street (see *DENMARK).

1908 *Hampton's Broadway Mag.* Oct. 456/2 Oh it's a world in itself, is Tin Pan Alley. It has its laughter and its tears. **1909** *Busy Man's Mag.* Jan. 48/1 Down Twenty-eighth Street, which is known as 'Tin Pan Alley', a dozen music publishing houses grind out new song 'hits' daily. **1926** WHITEMAN & MCBRIDE *Jazz* viii. 161 Like everybody else, I think of the Alley as a street. As a matter of fact, Tin Pan Alley exists now only as a tradition. **1934** [see *Denmark Street* s.v. *DENMARK]. **1944** S. BELLOW *Dangling Man* 132, I guess she sees herself in Tin-Pan Alley, her face streaked with tears. **1950** BLESH & JANIS *They all played Ragtime* (1958) xi. 220 While Tin Pan Alley was squeezing ragtime dry, a few people made a lot of money and a great number of people made a little. **1979** P. O'CONNOR *Into Strong City* I. xvii. 61, I found Seven Dials... Then Denmark Street. O this is Tin Pan Alley it belongs in the pages of the Melody Maker.

tin-panny *a. U.S.*, of a piano: tinny-sounding. Cf. *TIN PAN 2.

1904 J. C. LINCOLN *Cap'n Eri* ii. 30 On the platform of one [shop] a small crowd was gathered, and from the interior came shouts of laughter and the sound of a tin-panny piano. **1931** G. O. RUSSELL *Speech & Voice* III. xv. 158 The high partials become 'metallic' like the tin-panny piano.

tin-pot. 4. (Earlier example.)

1838 *Remarks G. F. Taylor's Factory Strike* 5 in *Pattie's Mod. Stage* II, Mr. Taylor, is a patriot in his little tin pot way.

tinsel, *sb.*³ and *a.* Add: **5.** Also similative, as *tinsel-pink, -violet.*

1920 E. SITWELL *Wooden Pegasus* 49 As I, a puppet tinsel-pink, Leap on my springs. **1956** D. BARNHAM *One Man's Window* vi. 67 The hills are tinsel-violet with distance, encrusted with the Valetta buildings and almost encircled by the blue waters of Grand Harbour.

6. b. Special Comb.: **Tinseltown**, a nickname for Hollywood; also *transf.*, the supposedly glittering world of Hollywood cinema; the Hollywood 'myth'.

1975 *Bookseller* 16 Aug. 1305/1 The tinseltown stuff when Wodehouse won the applause of the theatre-going fans. **1984** *Times* 5 Mar. 8/7 When a filmmaker starts cherishing the natural roar of traffic on the soundtrack.. you know she believes in Tinseltown.

tinsnips, *sb. pl.* Also **tin snips.** [f. TIN *sb.* + SNIP *sb.* 8 (*pl.*).] A pair of hand-held clippers used for cutting (sheet) metal. Cf. *tinmen's snips* s.v. *TINMAN 2.

1944 *Living off Land* vii. 131 Materials required are: four sound kerosene tins, tin snips, soldering-iron and flux. **1947** J. CONROY *Midland Humor* 182 Ain't you got no tinsmiths in this town?.. Get a pair of tinsnips, extra large. **1964** C. WILLOCK *Enormous Zoo* v. 85 Our work..consisted of cutting off lengths of heavy gauge wire with tin snips. **1976** *Conservation News* Sept./Oct. 24/1 As a parent I am very wary of allowing a child not considered competent at fixing an electric plug to be playing about with tin snips.

tint, *sb.*¹ Add: **1. c.** *Hairdressing.* An artificial colouring, less permanent than a dye, applied to enhance the colour of the hair; an application of this.

1921 [see *TINTER d]. **1957** *Encycl. Brit.* VI. 496A/2 The tint..is only temporary and is not a dye in the true sense. **1979** 'M. HEBDEN' *Pel & Faceless Corpse* x. 109 What is it you wanted? Tint? Shampoo? Or a cut?

tint, *v.* Add: **d.** *trans. Hairdressing.* To colour (the hair) with a tint. See *TINT *sb.*¹ 1 c.

1921 [implied at *TINTER d]. **1966** J. S. COX *Illustr. Dict. Hairdressing* 149/2 *Tint*, to dye. The word tint, used for dye, is one of the many euphemisms employed in the hairdressing craft. **1977** A. MORICE *Scared to Death* xvii. 119 I'm going a bit grey... So I have it tinted three or four times a year.

ti·ntable *a.* [-ABLE], capable of being tinted.

1974 *Spartanburg* (S. Carolina) *Herald* 18 Apr. (K mart Advts. Suppl.) 10 Washable latex acrylic is tintable to hundreds of colors! **1979** *Chatelaine* (Canada) Jan. 95/2 (Advt.), The bifocals with no lines. They're featherweight and tintable.

tin-tack. Add: **a.** (Earlier example.)

1839 DICKENS *Nicholas Nickleby* xxxv. 346 A..parcel of tin tacks and a very large hammer.

b. Colloq. phr. *to come* (or *get*) *down to tin tacks* = *to come* (or *get*) *down to brass tacks* s.v. *BRASS *sb.* 5 b. (Found only in the work of G. B. Shaw.)

1921 G. B. SHAW *Pen Portraits* (1932) 183 Keats..had he lived, would no doubt have come down from Hyperions and Endymions to tin tacks as a very full-blooded modern revolutionist. **1949** —— *Buoyant Billions* (1950) III. 45 Do let us get back to tin tacks. Is Clemmy going to marry him or is she not?

tinted, *ppl. a.* (In Dict. s.v. TINT *v.*) Add: **a.** (Earlier *fig.* example.) Also, coloured in a manner specified by defining word in Comb. **b.** Coloured, as for reducing the strength of light, e.g. *tinted glass.*

1756 *Crit. Rev.* II. 340 The French author is not much oblig'd..to his English translator. We meet with.. *tinted* ideas, *propell'd*, ..*devastated*, *bilious*, and many others of this kind. To what language these most properly belong the translator best knows, most certainly not to our own. **1816** SOUTHEY *Poet's Pilgr.* I. iv. 92 The autumnal-tinted groves. **1905** *Proc. R. Soc.* LXXIV. 528 A similar experiment was tried on a sample of the purple-tinted glass. **1905** *Westm. Gaz.* 1 July 14/1 Frowning heights the outline of which stood out dark and desolate against the orange-tinted sky. **1911** *Index Catal. Libr. Surg.-Genl.'s Office, U.S. Army* XVI. 222 (*heading*) Spectacles (tinted). **1973** E. LEMARCHAND *Let or Hindrance* xiii. 160 A small brisk woman with auburn-tinted hair. **1978** *Morecambe Guardian* 14 Mar. 32/6 (Advt.), 1974 Ford Capri..black vinyl roof, tinted glass.

tinter. Add: **d.** *Hairdressing.* One employed to tint hair. Cf. *TINT *v.* d.

1921 *Dict. Occup. Terms* (1927) § 920 *Tinter*,.. washes and applies tint or colour to human hair on the head or in the manufacture of wigs. **1966** J. S. COX *Illustr. Dict. Hairdressing* p. ix, Words denoting a person engaged in some aspect of the Hairdressing or Wigmaking crafts.. *tinter.*

tinticite (ti·ntikəit). *Min.* [f. *Tintic* (see quot. 1946) + -ITE¹.] A hydrated basic ferric phosphate, $Fe_6(PO_4)_4(OH)_6.7H_2O$, found as whitish masses of submicroscopic crystals.

1946 B. STRINGHAM in *Amer. Mineralogist* XXXI. 395 A creamy white clay-like substance with unusual optical and chemical properties was found as a wall coating in a limestone cave near the Tintic Standard Mine in the Tintic Mining District, Utah. The chemical analysis and x-ray comparative data shows the mineral to be new and is here named tinticite. **1967** *Virginia Jrnl. Sci.* XVIII. 189/2 Secondary minerals, formed primarily by weathering processes, include aragonite..rozenite..and tinticite.

tintinnid (tinti·nid). [a. mod.L. family name *Tintinnidæ*, f. generic name *Tintinnus* (F. von P. von Schrank *Fauna Boica* (1803) III. 302): see TINTINNABULUM and -ID³.] A ciliated protozoan of the family Tintinnidæ or the order Tintinnina, often distinguished by a bell-shaped test. Also *attrib.*

1945 M. F. GLAESSNER *Princ. Micropalaeont.* ii. 12 The structural analogy between *Calpionella* and the chitinous tintinnid tests suggestive of taxonomic relations. **1953** SHROCK & TWENHOFEL *Princ. Invertebr. Paleontol.* (ed. 2) ii. 67 Fossil tintinnids have been found in Pleistocene peat bogs. **1970** *Nature* 25 July 381/1 Microzooplankton.. consisting mostly of copepod nauplii, with some veligers, polychaete larvae and tintinnids. **1979** *Jrnl. Protozool.* XXVI. 415/1 The process of lorica building by tintinnids is poorly understood.

tinto, *sb.*¹ Delete † *Obs.* In recent use, short for *vino tinto* s.v. *VINO 3 or [Pg.] *vinho tinto* s.v. *VINHO (= red wine); a glass or drink of this.

1958 K. AMIS *I like it Here* x. 128 What about some wine? Will you have the *branco* or the *tinto*? **1978** M. WALKER *Infiltrator* iii. 35 We got to one of the Galician bars..and I ordered two *tintos.*

Tintometer. Add: This is a proprietary term. (Further examples.)

1893 J. W. LOVIBOND *Measurement of Light & Colour Sensations* 3 This work is a record of some investigations on light and colour carried out whilst the author was perfecting a colorimeter, which he terms 'The Tintometer'. **1957** G. E. HUTCHINSON *Treat. Limnol.* I. vi. 416 Kalle (1938), in his studies of the color of the sea, has introduced a tintometer which permits the color to be expressed as a single equivalent wave length. **1966** *Trade Marks Jrnl.* 17 Aug. 1188/1 Tintometer. B856,033. Colorimeters. The Tintometer Limited...1st November, 1963.

tintype. Add: **a.** (Earlier example.)

1864 E. W. PEARSON *Lett. from Port Royal* (1906) 243 You will probably in due course..see the tin-types of Rose and Demus.

b. Colloq. phr. (orig. *U.S.*) *not on your tintype*, certainly not. Cf. *not on your Nelly* s.v. *NELLY².

1900 ADE *Fables in Slang* 78 Oh, rats! Not on your Tintype. **1918** E. E. CUMMINGS *Let.* 11 Sept. (1969) 52 Not on your tintype; as Uncle George ecstatically would remark. **1934** C. STEAD *Seven Poor Men of Sydney* iii. 100 Does the Pope keep beggars, or the Vatican police hand out alms? Not on your tintype! But you do, Jo. **1963** P. H. JOHNSON *Night & Silence* xvii. 109 No,..she couldn't make a breakfast for three gentlemen... 'I got standards... Two gents, just about. Three, not on your tintype.' **1970** S. J. PERELMAN *Baby, It's Cold Inside* 118 Let's eschew all pious cant to the effect that it turned to ashes in my mouth. Not on your tintype—it was nectar.

tiny, *a.* (*sb.*) Add: **A.** *adj.* **b.** *tiny garment*, an article of clothing made for an expected baby.

1965 'E. QUEEN' *Fourth Side of Triangle* i. 12 Her 'needlework'..consisted of 'tiny garments', prepared for a lay sisterhood which aided 'unfortunate' young women. **1978** N. FREELING *Night Lords* i. 9 She..had managed to get herself pregnant..but there was no display of tiny garments.

c. *tiny mind*: exc. when used self-deprecatingly, a term of abuse suggesting an absence of common sense. Chiefly in colloq. phr. *out of one's tiny mind*, an emphatic form of *out of one's mind* s.v. MIND *sb.*¹ 19 a.

1965 'W. HAGGARD' *Hard Sell* vi. 68 Why don't you use your tiny mind? **1970** K. BENTON *Sole Agent* vi. 71 We'd had a row... I was nearly out of my tiny mind. **1977** D. BEATY *Excellency* xix. 215 Everyone with the possible exception of H.E. was scared out of their tiny British minds.

B. as *sb.* **2. a.** (Earlier example.)

1797 F. BURNEY *Jrnls. & Lett.* July (1973) III. 326 He ..hesitated before he could persuade himself to give at all to any bigger Children, if they came accompanied by tinies.

b. A nickname for a very large or tall man. Cf. *TICH.

1931 *Literary Digest* 18 Apr. 40 A big fat guy will be called 'Babe' or 'Tiny'. **1976** *Burnham-on-Sea Gaz.* 20 Apr. 12/8 He is 6ft 7in tall and not unnaturally, is known as 'Tiny'.

tinzenite (ti·nzĕnəit). *Min.* [ad. G. *tinzenit* (J. Jakob 1923, in *Schweiz. mineral. und petrogr. Mitteil.* III. 234), f. *Tinzen*, name of a mountain in Graubünden, Switzerland: see -ITE¹.] A basic silicate of calcium, manganese, aluminium, boron, and iron that occurs as triclinic yellow crystals and is now regarded as a member of the axinite group.

1924 *Chem. Abstr.* XVIII. 3337 Tinzenite: yellow; radial platy masses in quartz. **1968** *Amer. Mineralogist* LIII. 1409 The name 'tinzenite' must be used for those axinites with Ca < 1·5 and Mn > Fe (but usually Mn ≫ Fe). At this stage it is impossible to say whether tinzenite is an independent mineralogical species or only a variety.

Tio Pepe (ti·o pe·pe). [a. Sp., lit. 'Uncle Joe'; cf. *TIA MARIA.] The proprietary name of a dry Spanish fino sherry. A glass or drink of this.

1886 *Trade Marks Jrnl.* 15 Sept. 953 *Tio Pepe*... Gonzalez, Byass, & Co.,..London, E.C.; Wine and Spirit Merchants. **1907** *Yesterday's Shopping* (1969) 95/1 'Tio Pepe', very dry, delicate—per doz. botts...48/6. **1920** G. SAINTSBURY *Notes on Cellar-Bk.* ii. 18 Some of the finer kinds are really supernacular—the best 'Tio Pepe', for instance. **1943** G. GREENE *Ministry of Fear* II. i. 115 He..took out a glass and a bottle of sherry... 'Tio Pepe,' Digby said. **1955** N. FITZGERALD *House is Falling* xi. 177 They had brought in a bottle of Tio Pepe to keep them company. **1968** *Official Gaz.* (U.S. Patent Office) 16 Apr. 141/2 Gonzalez Byass & Co. Limited..*Tio Pepe*.. For Wines..First use 1905. **1976** H. MACINNES *Agent in Place* xvii. 182 Tony ordered a Tio Pepe.

tip, *sb.*¹ Add: **2. a.** (Earlier example with reference to shoes.)

1840 H. MOZLEY *Let.* 11 Feb. in D. Mozley *Newman Family Lett.* (1962) III. 86 They danced very prettily, though he had 'tips'.

e. Used in *pl.* to denote the leaf-buds used in tea-making, preceded by an adj. or trade-name to designate a particular brand of tea.

1897 *Sears, Roebuck Catal.* 8/1 Golden tips. **1952** 'W. COOPER' *Struggles of Albert Woods* II. iv. 98 He said: 'I hope you'll like my tea.'.. 'What sort is it?'.. 'Ty-phoo tips.' **1978** *Listener* 16 Nov. 642/3 (*caption*) Come back to my pad, man, I've got some amazing PG tips.

f. Formerly, a band of (gold, etc.) paper round a cigarette at the end held by the lips; now, = *FILTER *sb.* 3 c. Cf. *gold-tipped* adj. s.v. *GOLD¹ 10 a.

1897 KIPLING *Captains Courageous* v. 107 Cigarettes with gold-leaf tips. **1981** *Times* 25 July 3/8 Filter cigarettes were..assumed to be safer than those without tips.

5. e. *arse over tip*: see ***ARSE** *sb.* 1 b.

6. Also spec. in *Aeronaut.* with reference to the extremity of an aerofoil, as *tip loss, speed, stall, stalling, tank*; **tip-touch** *v. trans.*, to touch with the tips of one's fingers.

1938 *Jrnl. R. Aeronaut. Soc.* XLII. 380 The engine r.p.m. can with advantage be increased until the tip speed of the airscrew approaches the speed of sound, at which speed there are serious tip losses which reduce the thrust. Thin bladed metal airscrews show less tip loss due to high speed than the thicker sections. **1969** *Gloss. Aeronaut. & Astronaut. Terms* (*B.S.I.*) IV. 15 *Tip loss*, loss of lift at the tip of an aerofoil associated with the formation of tip vortices. **1911** R. M. PIERCE *Dict. Aviation* 231 *Tip speed*, the oscillatory speed of the tip of a reciprocating wing; the up-and-down velocity of a wing-tip in flapping flight. **1925** *Flight* 22 Oct. 686/2 (*caption*) The 'Autogiro'... Note how the high tip speed of the windmill beat our photographer. **1969** *Gloss. Aeronaut. & Astronaut. Terms* (*B.S.I.*) V. 20 *Tip speed*, the mean angular velocity of the rotor multiplied by the rotor radius. **1946** *Jrnl. Brit. Interplanetary Soc.* VI. 95 The phenomenon of tip stall is brought about by spanwise drift in the boundary layer over a swept wing. **1937** *Jrnl. R. Aeronaut. Soc.* XLI. 205, I consider wing tip slots as the most efficient means known at present to prevent tip stalling of highly tapered wings. **1952** *Wall St. Jrnl.* 15 Apr. 5 First conceived in 1938, tiptanks became standard as auxiliary fuel containers for the early-day F-80 jet fighters. **1977** *R.A.F. Yearbk.* 11/1 Max range with tip tanks, 900 mls..at 35,000 ft. **1922** JOYCE *Ulysses* 523 Must I tiptouch it with my nails? **1956** H. GOLD *Man who was not with It* (1965) i. 6 Tricksie with her pretty little hand tip-touching the black-and-blue spot.

tip, *sb.*[3] Add: **a.** Also, a present of money given to a schoolboy by an older person.

c **1810** W. HICKEY *Mem.* (1960) ii. 38, I secured a handsome tip, the Westminster phrase for a present of cash. **1855** [in Dict.]

tip, *sb.*[4] Add: **d.** (Earlier example.)

1847 *Punch* 9 Oct. 138/1 You attack him for making himself conspicuous at the sale of Shakspeare's house. You seem to think he has missed his tip.

e. *tip-sheet* (orig. *U.S.*), *-slinger* (*Austral. slang*).

1945 *Sun* (Baltimore) 21 Feb. 12 (*caption*) Tip sheet. **1955** *Sci. News Let.* 20 Aug. 126/3 Tip sheets may feature an electrocardiogram of the long-shot horse's heart before long. **1972** *Daily Tel.* 14 Nov. 18 A tip sheet on ways of fitting in smoothly in America has been handed to the 1,000 Asian refugees accepted by the United States. **1983** *Times* 11 Nov. 16/6 A and C Black..enjoyed the day's most spectacular gain—up 58p to 321p on a tip-sheet comment. **1926** 'J. DOONE' *Timely Tips for New Australians* 24 *Tipslinger*, the slang term for race-course tipster. **1934** *Bulletin* (Sydney) 15 Aug. 49/1 By their conversation most of them were tipslingers or urgers.

tip, *v.*[1] Add: **1. b.** Also *spec.*, to glance or touch with the edge of the bat. *tip-and-run*: (earlier examples); also *transf.* in *attrib.* use, esp. to designate short, sudden attacks in war; also as *v. intr.*

1816 W. LAMBERT *Cricketer's Guide* (ed. 3) iii. 43 It is.. to such [balls] as are just tipped with the edge of the Bat.. that he [*sc.* long-stop] will have to attend. **1851** J. PYCROFT *Cricket Field* x. 185 Put in two batsmen..to tip and run. **1858** 'G. FORREST' *Playground* ix. 132 If you only tip the [fast] ball, it will go far enough without giving you the trouble of striking it. **1918** *Chambers's Jrnl.* June 477/2 Any dark night might see one of the enemy's favourite 'tip-and-run' dashes to sea. **1927** *Rep. Commissioner Police Metropolis 1926* 16 Stolen cars are used in..'tip and run' raids on jewellers' shops. **1942** *R.A.F. Jrnl.* 13 June 26 The Italians, with their half-hearted enthusiasm and their 'tip-and-run' type of bombing. **1946** J. W. DAY *Harvest Adventure* xvi. 273 At Mersea Island..we exposed the Committee's folly in placing a machinery dump within a hundred yards of the sea and tip-and-run raiders.

c. *U.S. Sport.* To hit (a ball, puck, etc.) into the net or goal with a light touch or push. Freq. const. *in*(*to*).

1958 G. F. PINHOLSTER *Encycl. Basketball* ix. 111 The player with the best position tries to tip in the goal as the other two players block for him. **1963** F. A. LINDEBORG *How to play and teach Basketball* vi. 131 The tip-in shot is used when a player has the opportunity to tip an offensive rebound up into the air again and into the basket... The shooter times his jump so that he is able to tip the ball with the fingers of his right hand. **1968** [see ***RAP** *v.*[1] 2 a].

tip, *v.*[2] Add: **I. 2. b.** Similarly *to tip the balance, the beam.*

1895 FUNK *Stand. Dict.*, To tip the beam. **1927** *Observer* 11 Dec. 13/3 The view which will tip the beam is that of a member who said [etc.]. **1956** *People* 13 May 8/8 In an effort to tip the balance, New Zealand began to take British shopgirls and hairdressers. **1972** *Times* 20 Oct. 8/7 This might be the beginning of a process where the balance might be 'tipped' from predominantly white to predominantly black.

c. *to tip one's hand*(*s*) (or *mitt*): to disclose one's intentions inadvertently. *slang* (orig. and chiefly *U.S.*).

1917 G. ADE *Let.* 8 July (1973) 67 For a time in the play it should appear that the plans of the smooth citizen are working out perfectly. He becomes confident and over reaches himself, 'tips his hands', so to speak. **1930** *Sat. Even. Post* 28 June 162/2 They've tipped their mitt. That guy's probably got a rod under his coat. **1938** *New Republic* 26 Oct. 331/1 That would be tipping her mitt too much. **1966** M. WOODHOUSE *Tree Frog* xviii. 133 We couldn't very well oppose it without tipping our hand. **1979** *Economist* 17 Nov. 122/2 Mr Hunt will not tip his hand on the price at which he will buy more bullion.

d. *Bookbinding. to tip in*, to attach a single leaf, often an illustration, to the neighbouring leaf of a book by a thin line of paste down its inner margin.

1926 S. UNWIN *Truth about Publishing* v. 131 Should an extra page..be needed, it may have to be separately printed and specially 'tipped' or 'pasted in' as a frontispiece often is. **1949** MELCHER & LARRICK *Printing & Promotion Handbk.* 289/2 The leaf to be tipped in is first given a narrow coating of paste along its inner edge. **1966** H. WILLIAMSON *Methods Bk. Design* (ed. 2) xix. 322 So far as placing the plates appropriately in the text is concerned, the best method is to tip them into the section. **1978** W. WHITE in W. Whitman *Daybks. & Notebks.* III. 724 Tipped in here is a clipping from a magazine, with a notation in the margin in WW's hand.

5*. To dispose of or kill (a person). Also *fig.* Cf. sense 9 and *to bump off s.v.* ***BUMP** *v.*[1] 1 c. *slang.*

1920 W. CAMP *Football without Coach* vii. 129 Time after time methods such as these have 'tipped off' keen football players and have spelled the failure of good plays. **1928** *Evening News* 18 Aug. 11/5 Jake's sort o' done me a good turn, getting himself tipped off.

tip, *v.*[4] Add: **1. b.** (Earlier example with *up*, and later *absol.* example.)

1829 P. EGAN *Boxiana* 2nd Ser. II. 13, I shall expect, before we part, that you will tip up my half of the prize. **1965** *Sunday Times* (Colour Suppl.) 7 Nov. 41/2 For t'first two year she tipped up, she give me her wage packet and I give her her spending money.

2. (Earlier and later examples of presenting a schoolboy with money.)

c **1810** W. HICKEY *Mem.* (1960) x. 164 Joseph Polt.. whom I had frequently called upon, and tipped at Eton School. **1939** G. B. SHAW *Geneva* II. 38, I havnt exchanged twenty words with the boy since I tipped him when he was going from Eton to Oxford.

tip, *v.*[5] Add: **1.** (Earlier example of the simple vb.)

1889 E. DOWSON *Let.* 16 Nov. (1967) 117 Ye gods what of the Manchester Nov. I have been tipped (i) Lady Roseberry (ii) Goldseeker (iii) Phil—(by you).

2. Also, to warn, alert, or inform (a person); to make known or give away (someone or something). Freq. const. *off. slang* (orig. *U.S.*).

1893 L. W. MOORE *His Own Story* xxi. 292 This was 'tipped off' to me on Thursday, and also that the arrest of the whole party was to be made. *Ibid.* xxxiv. 445 When I saw he had 'tipped me off' to her, I said, 'Look at me, for I am the man he told you to identify.' **1896** *Chicago Tribune* 28 June 4/2 The fact that the telegram to her had 'tipped off' the situation made Mrs. Jones particularly downhearted. **1899** S. CRANE *Monster* xix. 76, I told him to keep his trap shut... You know how he'll go all over town yapping about the thing. I thought I'd better tip you. **1932** E. WALLACE *When Gangs came to London* xv. 136 He was doing badly and was tipped off there was good money in England. **1950** *Harper's Mag.* Feb. 70/2 Marks that have been tipped off are those that have been pointed out by others. **1955** M. GILBERT *Sky High* xiii. 184 That one [crime] we got tipped off about and put out a dragnet. **1960** M. SPARK *Bachelors* x. 163 'Someone has tipped the police,' said Mike Garland. **1964** MCLUHAN *Understanding Media* (1967) II. xxxi. 359 There could be no more telling touch to tip us off to the character of TV. **1975** T. ALLBEURY *Special Collection* xiv. 96 Was there any mileage in tipping them off? Experience said that tippers-off always got their hands caught in the machinery. **1978** G. MCDONALD *Fletch's Fortune* xix. 130 Who tipped you?.. Who told you about the editorial, and the campaign?

tip-. Add: **tip-horse** (example).

1912 A. BENNETT *Matador of Five Towns* 207 The old horse-car..climbing hills with the aid of a tip-horse and a boy perched on the back thereof.

tip-in. [f. vbl. phr. *to tip in*: see ***TIP** *v.*[1] 1 c and *v.*[2] 2 d.] **1.** *Bookbinding.* = ***PASTE-IN** *sb.*

1949 MELCHER & LARRICK *Printing & Promotion Handbk.* 359/2 Illustrations on coated paper are often inserted as wraps or tip-ins. **1969** C. IRVING *Fake!* (1970) xii. 149 Large color reproductions in many fine art books and portfolios, so that they can be removed and individually framed by the buyer, are often only lightly glued to the center of the page... Such detachable reproductions [are] sometimes called tip-ins.

2. *U.S. Sport* (esp. *Basketball*). A score made by tipping a rebound into the basket or net.

1958 G. F. PINHOLSTER *Encycl. Basketball* ix. 110 Tipping a basketball into the basket is a spectacular feat of timing, coordination, and jumping ability... Several tip-ins in a game can mean the difference between victory and defeat. **1963** [see ***TIP** *v.*[1] 1 c]. **1969** [see ***LAY-UP** 3]. **1980** *Washington Star* 17 Dec. E3 Theus..led all scorers with 23 points, including a tip-in with 1:51 [left] that put the Bulls in front.

tipiti (tipitī·). [a. Tupi.] A strainer used by Amazonian Indians for expressing the poisonous juice of the cassava.

1860 MAYNE REID *Odd People* 52 A long elastic cylinder-shaped basket or net, of the bark of the 'jacitara' palm (*Desmoncus macrocanthus*). This is the tipiti. **1866** LINDLEY & MOORE *Treas. Bot.* I. 396/1 Indians use strips of the stem [of the Jacitara palm] for platting the tipitis or strainers used for squeezing out the poisonous juice of the mandioc root. **1952** G. SARTON *Hist. Sci.* I. i. 5 The South American tipiti is an elastic plaited cylinder of jacitara-palm bark which is used to express the juice of the cassava.

tiple (ti·ple). [a. Sp., lit. 'treble'.] Any of various high-pitched stringed instruments played in Spain and the Spanish-speaking parts of the Americas, each resembling a small guitar.

1942 N. MACDONALD *Orchid Hunters* xi. 125 He strummed lightly on the tiple, changed to one of the quick-tempoed, popular Colombian airs. **1964** S. MARCUSE *Mus. Instruments* 525/2 *Tiple*... 1. syn. of guitarillo ..; 2. in Cuba a small bandurria with 5 pairs of strings. **1976** *New Yorker* 12 Apr. 111/1 He played the tiple (a stringed instrument between the guitar and the ukulele).

ti·p-off. Also **tip off, tipoff. 1.** [f. vbl. phr. *to tip off*: see ***TIP** *v.*[5] 2.] **a.** Information, a 'tip', esp. about criminal activity; a hint or 'give-away'. *slang* (orig. *U.S.*).

1901 J. F. WILLARD *World of Graft* 164 'So much down now,' he said, 'and so much when the show's over. Otherwise it's a tip-off and pinch.' **1918** H. C. WITWER *From Baseball to Boches* IV. i. 142 Nobody knew we was comin' up to the front... The first real tip off was when they served out the identification tags. **1938** E. WAUGH *Scoop* II. xii. 138 Now *he* had something under his hat; a tip-off straight from headquarters, news of high international importance. **1945** *Richmond* (Va.) *Times-Dispatch* 23 May 8 One of the first tipoffs on this romance came when La Bacall followed 'The Leer' to New York some months ago. **1955** W. TUCKER *Wild Talent* xi. 151 Karen was driving the tip-off car. **1960** *Observer* 24 Jan. 5/2 There was a tip-off available about when it [*sc.* a bank] was going to be stacked up with cash. **1977** *Birds* Winter 15/2 There was a tip-off about the robbery and RSPB staff lay in wait near the nest.

b. A person supplying information, esp. in connection with criminal activity. *slang.*

1941 M. ALLINGHAM *Traitor's Purse* xiv. 163 The other little syndicate..must have a tip-off in the police somewhere. **1961** J. WELCOME *Beware of Midnight* xiii. 166, I don't know which of the servants here is a tip-off to the Secret Police, but one of them is. **1973** R. BUSBY *Pattern of Violence* vi. 90 They've got a good tip-off man on the inside.

2. [f. TIP *v.*[1] 1 a, after *kick-off*, etc.] *Basketball.* A method of (re)starting play, in which two opposing players contest a jump-ball; an instance of this.

1924 [see **jump-ball, jump ball* s.v. ***JUMP-**]. **1937** F. C. ALLEN *Better Basketball* 181 On the tip-off, a player should tap the ball up and over his opponent. **1977** *Evening Gaz.* (Middlesbrough) 11 Jan. 13/9 Loughborough are the visitors to Newton Aycliffe on Sunday for a 3 p.m. tip-off.

tippable (ti·păb'l), *a.* [f. TIP *v.*[2] and *v.*[4] + -ABLE.] **1.** [TIP v.[4]] Designating one who may be tipped, or who is open to tips or *douceurs*. Occas. *absol.* as *sb.*

1907 *Sat. Rev.* 21 Dec. 752/1 The great aim of the tippable is to squeeze. **1921** S. GRAHAM *Europe—Whither Bound?* 27 A tippable man was keeping a queue of all the rabble of the East.

2. [TIP *v.*[2]] Of seats, etc.: that can be tilted or tipped up.

1936 *Times* 15 Oct. 8/4 The Austin Seven seems fresher than ever... In its latest form the front tippable seats have a longer range of adjustment.

tipped, tipt, *ppl. a.*[1] Add: **4.** = *filter-tipped* adj. s.v. ***FILTER** *sb.* 5. Also *absol.*, filter-tipped cigarettes.

1964 M. DRABBLE *Garrick Year* ii. 27 'I don't smoke tipped,' I said. *Ibid.* 28 He let me have the other Gauloise, and smoked the tipped cigarettes himself. **1972** *Guardian* 24 June 9/6 Have you got any cigarettes?.. Anything tipped. **1978** C. A. BERRY *Gentleman of Road* ix. 81 The gamut of grades of the cigarette-ends, ranging from..the complete cigarette left in a thrown-away packet..to the abhorred tipped variety and the trodden-out stub.

5. *Bookbinding.* Of a leaf, plate, etc.: inserted in a book by attaching to another leaf with a narrow strip of paste at the inner edge. Usu. with *in.* Cf. ***TIP** *v.*[2] 2 d; ***TIP-IN** 1.

1912 A. J. PHILIP *Business of Bookbinding* 217/2 *Tipped-in*, when a leaf, illustration, map, etc., is pasted in without guarding it is said to be tipped in. **1952** J. CARTER *ABC for Book-Collectors* 175 *Tipped in*, lightly attached, by gum or paste, usually at the inner edge. **1960** J. BETJEMAN *Summoned by Bells* v. 47, I bought a book with tipped-in colour plates. **1966** H. WILLIAMSON *Methods Bk. Design* (ed. 2) xix. 322 Unless the tipping is very accurate.., the tipped plate will raise the text page to which it is attached when it is turned. **1977** W. MATHESON in *Q. Jrnl. Libr. Congr.* July 233/2 The collector's difficulties are further complicated by the fact that the tipped-in plates by Augustus Peck are sometimes lacking.

tippee. Add: Also **tipee. 2.** [f. TIP *v.*[5]] One who receives inside information about a company or business enterprise and uses it to trade profitably in stocks and shares. orig. and chiefly *U.S.*

1961 L. LOSS *Securities Regulation* (ed. 2) III. ix. 1451 To hold 'tippees' liable under Rule 10b–5 when they had no reason to suspect that their informant was an insider might result in an unreasonable entrapment of innocent persons. **1967** *Federal Suppl.* CCLVIII. 284/2 This is strong circumstantial evidence that Darke must have passed the word to one or more of his 'tippees' that drilling on the Kidd 55 segment was about to be resumed. **1973** *N.Y. Law Jrnl.* 23 July 5/5 New rules for tippors [*sic*] and tippees. **1978** *Times* 12 Oct. 29/1 What about so called 'tipees'—people who come by price sensitive information often because of a breakdown in security by a professional adviser or within the company? **1980** *U.S. Reports* CCCCXLV. 242 It [*sc.* the SEC] did not hesitate to extend *Cady, Roberts* to reach a 'tippee' of a Government insider.

tipper^{1}. Add: **2. a.** (Earlier example.)
1861 *MacMillan's Mag.* Dec. 143/2, I got some work in Sussex, as a 'tipper'.

c. (Examples without comb. element.) Freq. *attrib.*
1920 *Glasgow Herald* 18 Apr. 10 The farmer can get on with his work, and the waggon which, in preference to being a 'tipper' would have a moving lattice floor and a removable drum..would spread the manure direct on the fields. **1950** *Engineering* 3 Feb. 140/1 Specialised vehicles, such as tippers. **1955** *Times* 14 June 4/5 There had been a shortage of tipper vehicles for emergency purposes. **1977** *Jersey Even. Post* 26 July 25/7 (Advt.), Tipper lorry (high sided), immediately available for contract work, etc. **1979** *West Lancs. Even. Gaz.* 10 Sept. 12 (Advt.), Tipper driver required. **1983** *Truckin' Life* Aug. 70/3 I've watched some poor little tipper struggling up a 5 per cent grade in second gear with two or three tonnes of topsoil.

tippet (ti·pėt), *v.*^{2} [perh. alteration of TIPTOE *v.*] To move on tiptoe. Also *transf.* and *fig.* Hence **ti·ppeting** *vbl. sb.*
1916 W. DE LA MARE *Songs of Childhood* (new ed.) 3 See they're tippeting at the door; Their wee feet in measure falling. **1932** E. BOWEN *To North* vii. 72 Then someone's wife opened a cold piano: she tinkled, she tippetted, she struck false chords and tried them again. **1934** —— *Cat Jumps* 84 Her affronted, muddled and rather tippeting manner. **1944** R. LEHMANN *Ballad & Source* 258 Their wives tippet about on the bank in high heels.

tipping, *vbl. sb.*^{1} Add: Also **tippen. 2. b.** = TIPPET *sb.* 4 a.
1881 W. GREGOR *Folk-Lore N.E. Scotl.* 52 Lines, hair for tippens, hooks. **1924** *Chambers's Jrnl.* Oct. 710/1 Many of the hooks have been torn from their tippings.

4. *Bookbinding.* (See quot. 1931.) Usu. with *in*. Cf. *TIP *v.*^{2} 2 d; *TIP-IN 1.
1931 A. ESDAILE *Man. Bibliogr.* 183 *Tipping-in*; pasting the edge of a single leaf to the next leaf. **1963** W. CLOWES *Guide to Printing* i. 8 Sometimes..tipping-in might not give sufficient strength. **1966** [see *TIPPED, TIPT *ppl.a.*^{1} 5].

tipping, *vbl. sb.*^{2} Add: **1.** (Earlier example.)
1853 DICKENS in *Househ. Words* 7 May 218/2 'Tippings' ..denotes the spiritual movements of the tables and chairs.

3. d. *tipping machine.*
1877 *Scotsman* 1 Sept. 4/7 Tipping machine.

tipple, *v.*^{1} Add: **5.** *intr.* To rain heavily; to gush, to pour. Freq. const. *down*.
a **1930** D. H. LAWRENCE *Last Poems* (1932) 204 Now it is almost night, from the bronzey soft sky Jugfull after jugfull of pure white liquid fire, bright white Tipples over and spills down. **1968** J. PORTER *Dover goes to Pott* xiv. 177, I saw her from the office window. No hat, no coat, nothing... It was tippling down too, absolutely tippling. **1971** *Country Life* 27 May 1283/1 After getting out of bed on the wrong side because the day is overcast or rain is tippling down.

tippy, *a.*^{1} (*sb.*) Add: **1. b.** (Earlier example.)
1790 A. M. WOODFORDE *Let.* 3 Sept. in *Parson Woodforde Soc. Jrnl.* (1972) V. III. 55 Your Bonnets are quite the *Tippy*.

† **c.** as *sb.* A dandy. *Obs.*
1798 *Monthly Mag. & Brit. Reg.* VI. 173/1 His dress.. will be, elegant; exhibiting no articles of apparel but such as are 'All the rage', he is 'Quite the tippy'. **1844** 'J. SLICK' *High Life N.Y.* II. 92 You wouldn't ketch one of our York tippies at that, let alone a ginuine Lord.

tippy, *a.*^{2} Add: (Later example.) *U.S.*
1923 E. F. WYATT *Invisible Gods* III. i. 93 A tippy, wire-legged table.

tippy-toe (ti·pi,tōᵘ), *sb.* (*adv.*, *a.*). Also **tippi-toe.** [Alteration of TIPTOE, TIP-TOE *sb.* (*adv.*, *a.*): cf. -Y^{6}.] **A.** *sb. pl.* The tips of the toes. Usu. in phr. *on* (one's) *tippy-toes*. Occas. also as collect. *sing.*
1899 *Century Mag.* Nov. 47/2 The whole court now stood on its tippy-toes. **1965** *New Statesman* 3 Dec. 897/2 Illustrations..show the dear little mite standing on tippy-toe to fecd famished and deserted nestlings. **1980** *Dirt Bike* Oct. 68/1, I stood on tippi-toes to watch.

B. *adv.* Short for *on tippy-toes* (see sense A above).
1901 'ZACK' *Dunstable Weir* 216 The rocking stone stud tippy-toe above his girt shadder. **1975** R. HELMS *Tolkien's World* iv. 126 A rather vulgar sugar-iced concoction, with a doll tippy-toe on its pinnacle as the Fairy Queen.

C. *adj.* Standing or walking on tiptoe. Also *fig.*
1951 J. STEINBECK *Log from 'Sea of Cortez'* p. xli, Ed would be smiling and doing his tippy-toe mouse dance. **1968** *Courier-Mail* (Brisbane) 8 Nov. 1/5 He [*sc.* Richard Nixon] is not as cautious and tippy-toe as he appeared to many voters. **1980** S. T. HAYMON *Death & Pregnant Virgin* ix. 71 When Jack Ellers was excited he rose up on the balls of his feet... Now he came into the dreary room..all tippy-toe.

ti·ppy-toe, *v.* Also **tippie-toe.** [f. prec.] *intr.* To go on tiptoe, to move lightly. Also *fig.* Cf. TIPTOE *v.* 2.
1901 'ZACK' *Dunstable Weir* 232, I tippy-toed back to the fire. **1942** C. MORLEY *Thorofare* xxxvi. 169, I tippy-toed down one side to join the Confed'racy while my old man was pretending to look up the other. **1974** *Globe & Mail* (Toronto) 29 Oct. 6/6 Did he tippy-toe across the press? **1980** *Daily Tel.* 2 Sept. 11/2 The roly-poly little girl who tippy-toed through Sandy Wilson's enchanting 'Big Best Shoes' number in 'Valmouth' all those years ago.

Hence **ti·ppy-toed** *ppl. a.* (in quot. as quasi-*adv.*).
1938 M. K. RAWLINGS *Yearling* iv. 31 A deer track'll prove the same. A deer or bear that's fat and heavy'll sink in that-a-way [at the heel]. A lettle ol' light doe or yearlin' 'll walk tippy-toed, and you'll not see more than the front of their hooves.

tipster. Add: **1. a.** Also *attrib.*, as *tipster sheet* (U.S.). Cf. *tip-sheet* s.v. *TIP *sb.*^{4} e.
1933 *Sun* (Baltimore) 17 July 1/2 Warning against the use of 'tipster sheets' and 'market service' by stock market and other investment patrons was issued today.

tip-tap *sb.* (*a.*, *v.*). Add: **d.** as *adv.* With a tapping sound.
1911 H. S. WALPOLE *Mr. Perrin & Mr. Traill* vi. 104 He came tip-tap across the floor to him.

tip-top, *sb.* Add: Also **tiptop. 3.** *Angling.* A line guide on a fishing-rod. *N. Amer.*
1961 *Washington Post* 5 Feb. c 6/6 A tiptop for flyrod and casting rod. **1971** *Islander* (Victoria, B.C.) 5 Sept. 5/3 Many cases of broken lines can be traced to cracks or nicks on a fishing rod's guides or tiptop.

Hence **ti:p-to·pmost** *a. colloq.*, (*a*) highest; (*b*) best; **tip-topper** (earlier example of a person).
1937 G. FRANKAU *More of Us* ii. 26 Clashed home the gates. Slow to tip-topmost storey Groaned lift. **1960** *Guardian* 22 Apr. 8/5 All their tip-topmost British merchandise. **1829** P. EGAN *Boxiana* 2nd Ser. II. 239 Some *tip-toppers* on the *Corinthian list* were witnessed getting over the ground as 'gaily as larks'.

tipulid, *sb.* (Examples.)
1951 C. N. COLYER *Flies Brit. Isles* xxv. 317 It will seem a far cry from the large, long-winged, long-legged Tipulids. **1976** *Nature* 22 Jan. 251/2 There is no evidence that hen grouse do eat tipulids during incubation.

tip-up, *sb.* and *a.* Add: **3.** (Examples.)
1850 S. F. COOPER *Rural Hours* 42 The boys call these contrivances 'tip-ups', from the bit of stick to which the line is attached, falling over when the fish bite. **1880** *Harper's Mag.* Mar. 517 With baited lines and tip-ups set, we waited. **1923** H. E. WILLIAMS *Spinning Wheels & Homespun* 247 Fishing through the ice... With the aid of what they call 'tip-upses' several lines can be used simultaneously. **1978** *Globe & Mail* (Toronto) 1 Feb. 34/1 Anglers using jigs were more successful than those waiting by a tipup.

4. A tip-up seat (see sense B in Dict. and Suppl.).
1966 'A. HALL' *9th Directive* xxvi. 234 The other sat on the tip-up behind the front seat.

B. *adj.* Esp. as *tip-up seat* (later examples); also with reference to a method of opening, as *tip-up door*.
1936 N. STREATFEILD *Ballet Shoes* xiii. 203 Mr. French pulled down the tip-up seat next to him. **1959** *News Chron.* 7 July 6/5 A local vicar, whose garage had tip-up doors. **1973** J. DRUMMOND *Bang! Bang! You're Dead* xxxvii. 127 Garages with tip-up doors. **1980** *Oxf. Diocesan Mag.* May 8/1 They are halls with tip-up seats designed for secular entertainment..as well as worship.

tirade, *sb.* **2.** (Earlier example.)
1806 SCOTT *Let.* Sept. (1932) I. 321 Tales they had heard in infancy with here & there a tirade really taken from an old poem.

tire, *sb.*^{2} Add: In the twentieth cent. the revived spelling *tyre* has become standard in the British Isles, whilst American English retains the traditional *tire*. **3.** *tire pressure, repair, track*; **tire chain,** a metal chain designed to be attached to the tyre of a motor vehicle to prevent skidding on snow or ice; **tire-iron:** also (*N. Amer.*), a length of steel flattened at one end, used as a lever for removing tyres from wheel-rims.
1917 *T. Eaton & Co. Catal.* Spring & Summer 282 Every car owner should carry a pair of tire chains. **1980** 'E. MCBAIN' *Ghosts* ii. 20 Carella could hear the sounds of tire chains jangling. **1952** R. ELLISON *Invisible Man* xxv. 426 You could hear that gun striking that ole shield like somebody dropping tire irons out a twelve-story window. **1976** *Globe & Mail* (Toronto) 16 Feb. 10/1 Two 19-year old brothers have been arrested after a man, his wife and son were assaulted with tire irons in a Towers Department Store parking lot. **1920** *T. Eaton & Co. Catal.* Spring & Summer 224 Tire pressure gauge. Accurate and reliable for correct air pressure. **1895** *Montgomery Ward Catal.* Spring & Summer 556/3 Pneumatic tire repair outfit. **1975** J. GRADY *Shadow of Condor* viii. 128 The man..stowed the tire-repair items..in the trunk. **1947** E. S. GARDNER in *Amer. Mag.* Aug. 150/3 Mason, studying the tire tracks, said, 'It was an automobile and a horse trailer.' **1973** T. PYNCHON *Gravity's Rainbow* I. 113 The Dutch resistance will then 'raid' this site, making a lot of commotion, faking in tire-tracks and detailing the litter of hasty departure.

tired, *ppl. a.*^{1} Add: **1. a.** Also in phr. *to make* (someone) *tired*: to get on the nerves of, irritate. *slang* (orig. *U.S.*).
c **1883** C. H. HOYT *Bunch of Keys* 1, in *America's Lost Plays* (1941) IX. 13 That makes me tired! **1904** S. E. WHITE *Blazed Trail Stories* iv. 65 Such talk made Daly tired, and he said so. **1925** W. J. LOCKE *Great Pandolfo* xiii. 172 'Women like you,' said Myrtilla a trifle sourly, 'make me tired.' **1950** P. WOODRUFF *Island of Chamba* viii. 124 They make me tired... Things are bound to get worse.

c. *tired Tim* (or *Timothy*), usu. associated with *weary Willie*: the names of two tramps, characters in the comic magazine *Illustrated Chips*; hence both used as nicknames for tramps or other work-shy people. Also *attrib.*
1906 *Daily Chron.* 15 Feb. 3/5 Heroes of the Tired Timothy stamp. **1927** W. E. COLLINSON *Contemp. Eng.* 27 Comic papers..brought home to us the picturesque language of Weary Willy and Tired Tim (the genial tramps—whence these words are frequently used as appellatives for 'tramps' in general). **1930** H. HERD *Diagnosis of Mental Deficiency* 10 Mental defectives are the 'weary Willies and tired Tims' *par excellence*. **1932** W. S. CHURCHILL *Let.* 6 Feb. in Ld. Boothby *Recoll. Rebel* (1978) vi. 86 These two old tired Tims of the Commons have ceased to command my allegiance. **1972** J. PORTER *Meddler & her Murder* xii. 157 With Miss Jones in..her Tired-Tim-and-Weary-Willie mood, there was no temptation to linger.

d. *the tired business man*: a cliché, often used with satirical allusion to the short working hours and pleasure-loving habits popularly ascribed to business men.

The phrase is said to have been used by Mark Twain in 1896.

1913 *Vanity Fair* Nov. 37/2 'I mean simply this, my dear,' replied the Tired Business Man. **1927** A. HUXLEY *Proper Studies* 186 From the fetish-worshipper to the metaphysician, from the tired business man to the mystic ..every type of human being can find in Catholicism the spiritual nourishment which he or she requires. **1940** I. BROWN in *Best One-Act Plays of 1939* 141 Oh, how I've longed to be a Tired Business Man once more—office at ten, out at twelve-thirty, back at three, sign the letters, off home! **1969** *Listener* 20 Mar. 399/1 We often use the cliché of the tired businessman to define the low response ..that sustains leg-shows.

2. a. Also, of language, literature, etc.: hackneyed, trite.
1951 *Chambers's Jrnl.* Sept. 521/1 The start of the paper was promising enough, for Greenwood collected a group of writers around him equal to deserving that tired word 'brilliant'. **1956** *Sat. Rev.* (U.S.) 30 June 34/1 It [*sc.* a book] is (to use a tired phrase) history made interesting. **1966** *Listener* 28 Apr. 630/3 *The Pipeline*..turned out to be as tired and cliché-ridden a spy story as any I have heard.

b. Of food, flowers, etc.: limp with long exposure, no longer fresh. Of clothes: crumpled, shapeless, or baggy with long wear.
1897, 1909 [in Dict.]. **1933** *N. & Q.* 26 Aug. 130/1 To-day people speak of stale vegetables or fruits as 'tired'. **1934** E. BOWEN *Cat Jumps* 252 Tired dance dresses. **1947** H. NICOLSON *Diary* 9 May (1968) 97 The spring-garden has lost its early bloom... The primroses are looking a trifle tired. **1958** *Spectator* 15 Aug. 222/1 The last batch of eggs I got from the local grocer turned out to be very tired. **1963** *Times* 11 June 10/6 In the present heat, merchants are reluctant to pay high prices for 'tired' fish. **1974** A. LURIE *War between Tates* (1977) v. 117 He is ill-dressed in a tired grey turtleneck sweater and sagging work pants. **1977** G. MARTON *Alarum* 16 Chris read.. occasionally munching on a very tired cheese sandwich.

tiringly (təiᵊ·riŋli), *adv.* [f. TIRING *ppl. a.*^{1} + -LY^{2}.] In a tiring manner, to a wearisome degree.
1894 E. FAWCETT *New Nero* xx. 219 'It's a trifle tyrannical, is it not?' 'Yes; amusingly so.' 'Never tiringly so.'

Tir-na-nog (tīᵊ·ɹnanōᵘg). *Irish Mythol.* Also **Tir-nan-og, Tir-n-an-oge,** etc. [a. Ir. *Tír na nÓg* land of the young.] A fabled land of perpetual youth, an Irish version of Elysium. Also *transf.*
1889 W. B. YEATS *Let.* 29 July (1954) 132 The Irish peasant's notion that Tir-n-an-oge (the Country of the Young) is made up of three phantom islands. **1898** E. C. BREWER *Reader's Handbk. Allusions* (new ed.) 590/2 The ancient inhabitants of Erin had..the vague belief that there somewhere existed a land where people were always youthful..and lived for ever. This country went by various names, as *Tir-na-nóg*, etc. **1906** P. E. MORE *Shelburne Ess.* 4th Ser. 245 It is the Tir-nan-og of the Celts, the country of the young. **1938** L. MACNEICE *I crossed Minch* II. x. 155 Don't talk to me about the Isles of Youth. These are the Isles of Senescence, of Inactivity. ..I do not want to sleep or dream of Tir n'an Og. **1955** *Bull. Atomic Sci.* Mar. 82/3 Without a better balance, the science-created *Tir na nog*, the legendary Irish land of youth on earth, must result in the rigid Malthusian principle which population experts sternly predicted.

1980 *London Mag.* Mar. 23 The old Irish myth of Tir nan-Og, the land of everlasting youthfulness.

tirodite (tirōu·dəit). *Min.* [f. *Tirodi*, name of a village in Madhya Pradesh, India + -ITE[1].] A monoclinic mineral, $Mn_2Mg_5Si_8O_{22}(OH)_2$, of the amphibole group which forms a series with dannemorite ($Mn_2Fe_5Si_8O_{22}(OH)_2$); also, any member of this series having more magnesium than iron.

1938 DUNN & ROY in *Rec. Geol. Survey India* LXXIII. 295 (*heading*) Tirodite, a manganese amphibole from Tirodi, Central Provinces. **1973** *Indian Jrnl. Earth Sci.* I. 38/2 The colour of tirodite is distinctive as opposed to the vivid colours shown by other manganese-bearing amphiboles occurring in the area.

tirra-lirra. Add: Hence also as *v. intr.*, to sing tirra-lirra.

1879 G. MEREDITH in *New Q. Mag.* July 83 Duchess Susan was distinguished coming across a broad, uncut meadow, tirra-lirraing beneath a lark.

‖ **Tirthankara** (tīᵊɹpa·ŋkară). Also **Tirthankar, tirthankara, Tirthanker.** [Skr., lit. 'maker of a ford', f. *tīrthá* ford, passage + *kará* maker.] In the Jain region, one of the twenty-four founding prophets or Jinas, venerated as having successfully crossed the stream of time and having made a path for others to follow.

1835 J. WILSON *Let.* 13 Mar. in G. Smith *Life of John Wilson* (1878) vi. 205 In the inferior parts there are the images of all the twenty-four Tirthankars. **1881** *Encycl. Brit.* XIII. 543/2 The Jains count twenty-four such prophets, whom they call Jinas, or Tīrthankaras, that is, conquerors or leaders of schools of thought. **1901** KIPLING *Kim* vi. 159, I'd give a month's pay to hear how he explained it all at the Tirthankers' Temple at Benares. **1961** A. J. TOYNBEE *Between Oxus & Jumna* xii. 37 At Ludra..there is a Jain temple containing a hallowed image of the last Jain tirthankara but one. **1971** *Illustr. Weekly of India* 11 Apr. 8/1 (*caption*) Rishabha and Vardhamana are the most honoured among the twenty-four Tirthankaras.

'tis. Add: Also in dial. and colloq. use. (Later examples.) Also **'tes.**

1896 I. T. THURSTON *Well Won* iv. 39 'Henderson, is that true?' demanded Gordon sternly... For once, Henderson absolutely looked ashamed of himself..as he said sulkily, 'Yes, 'tis.' **1922** JOYCE *Ulysses* 58 'Lovely weather, sir.' ''Tis all that.' **1922** E. O'NEILL *Anna Christie* III. 177 'Tis quare, rough talk, that—for a dacent girl the like of you! **1932** S. GIBBONS *Cold Comfort Farm* iv. 53 'Tes the cowshed! 'Tes our Feckless openin' the door fer me! **1977** P. HILL *Liars* (1978) xii. 154 'Tis your business if'n you want to waste your time.

tisane (tiza·n). [Mod. re-adoption of Fr. *tisane*: see PTISAN, which it has largely supplanted.] A medicinal tea or infusion made from herbs.

1931 W. CATHER *Shadows on Rock* I. iv. 29 He kept them away from doctors,—gave them tisanes and herb-teas and poultices. **1941** W. FORTESCUE *Trampled Lilies* v. 52 A communicating room could be used as a kitchen.. where hot chocolate, coffee, and *tisanes* could be prepared for the men. **1959** *News Chron.* 6 July 6/5 Old ladies.. drink herb teas in France, where they are called tisanes. **1965** *Punch* 7 July p. xii/2 The health food shop with.. lime flower tisanes and heather honey. **1981** M. GEE *Dying, in Other Words* xlix. 114 And the tea, the lime-flower *tisane* which was good for her chest and smelled citrous and fresh, singing to her when she drank it of blue summer skies over yellow-green lime trees.

Tiselius (tisē·liŏs, tiz-). *Biochem.* [The name of A. W. K. *Tiselius* (1902–71), Swedish biochemist.] *Tiselius* (*electrophoresis*) *apparatus*: an apparatus in which electrophoresis is carried out in free solution in a U-tube (see quot. 1964).

1939 *Jrnl. Franklin Inst.* CCXXVIII. 798 (*heading*) U-tube portion of the Tiselius electrophoresis apparatus. **1946** *Nature* 13 July 41/2 The Tiselius electrophoresis apparatus is now established as an essential part of the equipment of protein chemists... Its first appearance.., in 1937, was the result of a careful technical study. **1964** G. H. HAGGIS et al. *Introd. Molecular Biol.* ii. 23 In the Tiselius apparatus a potential is applied across a boundary between the solution containing the proteins and a protein-free buffer solution (moving boundary electrophoresis).

‖ **Tisha b'Av** (ti·ʃă bɒv). Also **Tisha be-Ab, Tisha Bov,** etc. [Heb. *tiš'āh bə'āḇ*.] The ninth day of the month Av, on which both the First and the Second Temples are said to have been destroyed: observed by Jews as a day of mourning.

1938 *Vallentine's Jewish Encycl.* 2/1 The 9th of Ab (*Tisha be-Ab*..) is a fast day commemorating the destruction of the 1st and 2nd Temples. **1958** A. L. EISENBERG *Story Jewish Calendar* 19 Later on, the three months in which Hannukah, Purim, and the fast day of Tisha B'Av occur were also included. **1970** *New Yorker* 19 Sept. 32/2 My grandfather always fasted on Tisha b'Av and slept with his head on a stone. **1973** *Synagogue Light* Sept. 12/1 On Tish B'Av [*sic*], the traditional day of mourning, we take off our shoes. **1978** I. B. SINGER *Shosha* I. ii. 10 The day that Zelig and Bashele moved.. was like Tisha Bov for me.

tisicky (ti·ziki), *a.* Also **tissicky, tizzicky.** [dial. var. of PHTHISICKY *a.*] Wheezy, asthmatic; also *transf.*, delicate, squeamish.

1905 E. PHILPOTTS *Secret Woman* II. x. 193 Once a labourer have gone in the back an' thighs, an' growed tisicky in the breathing parts—then [etc.]. **1924** *Western Daily Press* (Bristol) 18 Mar. 8/3 A person troubled with a slight but frequent and annoying cough is said to be Tissicky. **1961** 'K. NORWAY' *Waterfront Hospital* iii. 44 Men are more tissicky than women when it comes to telling people the worst. They're kinder by nature. **1969** J. CLARKE *Foxon's Hole* iii. 23, I can see you've a good appetite. None of Frances's tizzicky ways.

'tisn't (ti·zěnt), dial. or colloq. shortening of *it isn't* (= it is not); see IT *pron.* A. γ; NOT *adv.* 2, 3. Cf. 'TIS.

1803 G. COLMAN *John Bull* IV. i. 42, I be but the guide, and 'tisn't for I to go first. **1888** KIPLING *Under Deodars* 93 Remember, Bobby, 't isn't the best drill..it's the man who knows how to handle men. **1924** M. KENNEDY *Constant Nymph* II. viii. 117 ''Tisn't yours,' cried Antonia... 'It ought to be mine.' **1972** P. CLEIFE *Slick & Dead* I. i. 14 Oh, come now—'tisn't always like that.

tissue, *sb.* Add: **6. a.** (Later examples.)

1880 J. DUNBAR *Pract. Papermaker* 32 (*heading*) Lilac tissue, deep shade. **1937** E. J. LABARRE *Dict. Paper & Paper-Making Terms* 244/1 *Tissue* or tissue-papers are fine, thin, soft papers made of strong materials such as rag and hemp fibres... They are usually unsized, nearly transparent, chiefly used for wrapping and protective purposes. **1977** J. HEDGECOE *Photographer's Handbk.* 309 Carefully trim the print, with its attached tissue.

b. *Racing.* A sheet of paper showing the 'form' of the horses competing in a race (see also quot. 1866).

1866 *Daily Tel.* 24 Feb. 3/4 A 'tissue' is a slip of paper written for a telegraph company, showing results of betting transactions and accounts. **1914** JOYCE *Dubliners* 59 No one knew how he achieved the stern task of living, but his name was vaguely associated with racing tissues. **1972** G. F. NEWMAN *You Nice Bastard* ii. 83 Manso quickly got a bet on the fifth and sixth, and studied the tissue for the previous races.

c. A piece of soft absorbent paper used as a handkerchief, for drying or cleaning the skin, etc. Hence as *v. trans.*, to wipe with a tissue.

1929 *Punch* 10 Apr. p. xv (Advt.), Two or three times every day you should massage the hands with Ponds' Cold Cream, removing the cream after a minute or so with a Ponds' Cleansing Tissue. **1938** [see *COMPLEXION *sb.*]. **1958** M. DICKENS *Man Overboard* x. 162 Ben grabbed a make-up stick and scrawled it [*sc.* an address] on the side of a box of tissues. **1960** *Woman* 25 Apr. 2/1 Pond's Cold Cream..goes on moisturising long after you tissue it off. **1976** M. & G. GORDON *Ordeal* (1977) 142 Sniffling, he asked Penny for a tissue. **1981** *Economist* 8 Aug. 79/1 The battle against the common cold may not be over... So do not throw away your tissues yet. **1983** *Harrods Mag.* Spring/Summer 72 Yellow Herbal Astringent is sprayed on..then tissued dry.

d. A cigarette paper. *Austral.* and *N.Z. slang.*

1952 *Here & Now* (N.Z.) Jan. 32/2 Better go and see if the parole-jumper in Number 8 has got any tissues left. **1966** G. W. TURNER *Eng. Lang. Austral. & N.Z.* viii. 164 In Hobart the [expression]..'Got a tissue, mate?' [is commoner than elsewhere]. A *tissue* is a cigarette paper.

9. b. *tissue-specificity*; *tissue-dwelling*, *-specific* adjs.; **tissue-bank** [*BANK *sb.*[3] 7 f], a place where a supply of human or animal tissue for grafting is stored; **tissue culture,** a culture [*CULTURE *sb.* 3 c] of cells derived from tissue; the practice of culturing such cells; **tissue fluid,** extracellular fluid which bathes the cells of most tissues, arriving via blood capillaries and being removed via the lymphatic vessels; **tissue type** *Med.*, a class of tissues all of which are immunologically compatible with each other; **tissue-type** *v. trans.*, to determine the tissue type of; **tissue typing** *Med.*, the assessment of tissue in order to predict its immunological compatibility with other tissue, esp. prior to transplantation.

1968 *Punch* 14 Feb. 239 Donald Pleasence plays the night attendant at a central tissue-bank in Montreal... A stupid, illiterate man with inexplicable operatic aspirations, he thinks that if he can only get the right larynx he will be able to sing. **1971** *New Scientist* 8 Apr. 101/2 Tissue Banks where human and animal tissues could be readily obtained. **1912** *Anat. Rec.* VI. 91 The character of the growth in tissue cultures varies primarily with the kind of tissue used. **1926** J. S. HUXLEY *Ess. Pop. Sci.* 283 A fundamental experiment from which sprang the whole sub-science of tissue-culture. **1955** *Sci. News* XXXVI. 8 It is interesting to compare the events in regeneration with what happens in tissue culture. **1975** *Daily Tel.* 8 Sept. 8/4 At present, if a dog or other animal is sick or dies it takes several days to grow the virus in tissue culture to be sure rabies is to blame. **1964** M. HYNES *Med. Bacteriol.* (ed. 8) xxviii. 443 The tissue-dwelling parasites which cause relapses [in malaria] are not affected. **1974** *Ciba Symposium* XX. 309 Few drugs have any significant action against its tissue-dwelling amastigotes. **1900** E. H. STARLING *Elem. Human Physiol.* (ed. 4) vii. 292 This absorption depends on the small proportion of proteid contained in the tissue-fluid as compared with the blood-plasma. **1954** S. DUKE-ELDER *Parsons' Dis. Eye* (ed. 12) i. 4 It [*sc.* the cornea] has no blood vessels with the exception of minute arcades, about 1 mm. broad, at the limbus so that it is dependent for its nourishment upon the diffusion of tissue-fluid from the vessels at its periphery and materials from the aqueous humour. **1976** D. JENSEN *Princ. Physiol.* ix. 524/1 The interstitial (or tissue) fluid forms the actual internal environment of the body. **1962** *Sci. Survey* III. 224 This type of change may be associated with the changes in tissue-specific antigens. **1932** J. S. HUXLEY *Probl. Relative Growth* VI. iv. 177 The tissue-specificity is apparently the same..in both sexes. **1967** *Science* 25 Aug. 942/1 The first two explanations should be tested more critically if applied to a single tissue type. **1968** *Times* 7 Nov. 3/2 In a year or two it might be possible to store human hearts for a period of hours; this would enable donors and recipients to be tissue-typed on an international basis. **1969** *Private Eye* 6 June 3/2 Experts from Guys Hospital came to tissue type her to see if she was a 'suitable donor'. **1971** H. FESTENSTEIN et al. in R. Y. Calne *Clin. Organ Transplantation* vi. 158 It may be possible to tissue type potential recipients from several hospitals in one central laboratory. **1973** *Daily Tel.* 27 Feb. 2/7 Simon has a tissue type shared by only one in 50,000 of the population. **1965** *Israel Jrnl. Med. Sci.* I. 498/2 This seems..a hopeful avenue toward the goal of tissue typing. **1967** *Observer* 26 Nov. 1/5 Research on tissue-typing has reached the stage where tissues from different people can be matched (just as blood can be matched) so that grafts will 'take' without resort to drugs to suppress the immune mechanism. **1971** *New Scientist* 8 July 63/2 One or two of these cases, particularly when recipient and donor have been well 'matched' by tissue typing, have been spectacularly successful.

tissuey (ti·siui, ti·ʃⁱui), *a.* [TISSUE *sb.* + -Y[1].] Having the quality or texture of tissue.

1867 G. MEREDITH *Vittoria* III. xiii. 196 Letting her.. crumble the black tissuey fragments to smut in her hands. **1965** P. WYLIE *They both were Naked* I. i. 4, I could see that overcast less than a hundred feet above..its tissuey substance was rolling and boiling. **1974** J. HELLER *Something Happened* 210 The..silken feel of the tissuey things between her legs the first time she let me touch her there.

tiswas (ti·zwɒz). *slang.* Also **tis-was, tizz-wozz,** etc. [Perh. a fanciful enlargement of *TIZZ, TIZ.] A state of nervous agitation or confusion; occas. a state of physical disorder or chaos.

1960 M. CECIL *Something in Common* xvii. 195 Gets you all of a tiswas, when he's up the wall. **1974** *Observer* 27 Oct. 5/5 A young man rang up in quite a 'tis-was. **1980** *Encounter* May 7 She doesn't clean, but circumvents the dirt. Chairs stand on tables—'All of a tizz-wozz.' Has that been spelt before?

tiswin. (Earlier example.)

1877 *Rep. Indian Affairs* (U.S.) 162 Addicted..to the use of intoxicating liquors, 'tiswin', which they manufacture from corn, and whiskey obtained from strangers.

tit, *sb.*[2] Add: **1. tit for tat.** Also used as rhyming slang for 'hat'. Cf. *TITFER.

1925 FRASER & GIBBONS *Soldier & Sailor Words & Phrases* 285 *Tit for tat*, hat. (Rhyming slang). **1930, 1937** [see *TITFER].

3. tit-tat-toe, (*b*) *dial.* or *U.S.* = *noughts and crosses* (see NOUGHT *sb.* 7 c); cf. *TICK-TACK-TOE (b).

The precise nature of the activity referred to in quot. 1865 is uncertain and cannot be determined from the context.

1865 TROLLOPE *Can you forgive Her?* II. xxi. 164 The signing-clerk's clerk..playing tit-tat-to by himself upon official blotting-paper. **1888** B. LOWSLEY *Gloss. Berks. Words & Phrases* 164 *Tit-tat-toe*, the first game taught to children when they can use a slate pencil, the words 'Tit-tat-toe, My first go', being said by the one who first makes three crosses, or noughts in a row. **1898** A. T. SLOSSON *Dumb Foxglove* 11 Checkers, and tit-tat-toe, and fox-and-geese, and set down games like those. **1961** *New Scientist* 9 Nov. 367 Noughts and Crosses (known in America as Tit-Tat-To). **1973** J. SCARNE *Encycl. Games* 583 Tit-tat-toe. This simple game, also called Noughts and Crosses in Great Britain, is played on diagrams consisting of intersecting parallel lines.

tit, *sb.*[3] Add: **2.** Also applied indiscriminately to women of any age. ?*dial.*

1922 E. R. EDDISON *Worm Ouroboros* xxxi. 397 The Demons,..since they had a strong loathing for such ugly tits and stale old trots, would no doubt hang her up or disembowel her. **1932** S. O'FAOLAIN *Midsummer Night Madness* 62 I'm sorry for his two tits of sisters, though. **1969** H. E. BATES *Vanished World* ix. 87 'The old tit' doddered forth... I see her as a kind of..diminutive nun, untouched and unprotected.

3. c. tit-bell, a bell-shaped container filled with seeds, fat, etc., and suspended out of doors to supply food to tits and other birds of similar habits.

1934 J. M. CROSTHWAITE in H. M. Batten *Our Garden Birds* 184 Mr. Mortimer Batten has..invented and developed many ingenious and artistic feeding devices... The tit bell is filled with melted fat, which is allowed to set, after which the bell is hung. **1976** *Southern Even. Echo* (Southampton) 3 Nov. 12/3 Another useful device for feeding tits and woodpeckers is to make a 'tit bell'.

tit, *sb.*[6] [Var. of TEAT.] **1. a.** See TEAT 1 a for dial. uses.

b. *pl.* A woman's breasts. Also in *sing. slang* (orig. *U.S.*).

1928 in A. W. Read *Classical Amer. Graffiti* (1935) 80 A girl may sit & finger her tits and play with her cunt all day. **1947** C. WILLINGHAM *End as Man* 93 'Well,' said Munro.

'That girl ought to go to Hollywood.' 'She wouldn't make it out there,' blushed Wilson. 'No tits.' **1962** J. HELLER *Catch-22* xviii. 181 How do you expect anyone to believe you have a liver condition if you keep squeezing the nurses tits every time you get a chance. **1969** *Oz* May 40/2 Mary Anne Shelley, with the best tits off-off-Broadway. **1980** J. BARNES *Metroland* I. xi. 63 Tits? I asked myself in furtive panic. Well, you couldn't really see, not with that dress.

c. *to get on one's tits* or (occas.) *tit*: to irritate intensely, get on the nerves of. *slang.*

1945 BAKER *Austral. Lang.* vi. 121 Someone or something disagreeable is said *to get on one's..tit.* **1966** 'L. LANE' *ABZ of Scouse* 40 *Gets on me tits*, annoys me very much. **1967** N. FREELING *Strike out where not Applicable* 114 Those women, who even wear a corset under riding breeches..they're the ones who get on my tits. **1973** P. WHITE *Eye of Storm* vii. 304 Much as she disliked men, Sister Manhood began to think women got on her tits as badly. **1977** J. WILSON *Making Hate* xiii. 153 This Sherlock Holmes act of yours gets right on my tits.

d. *tits and ass* or *arse*: slang phr. used to denote crude sexuality. Similarly *tits and bums*. Also *transf.*, a magazine containing photographs of nude women; also called *tit mag(azine)*.

1972 R. A. WILSON *Playboy's Bk. Forbidden Words* 288 The late Lenny Bruce once suggested that 'Tits and Ass' would be the most accurate advertisement for most night-club acts. **1975** *New Society* 3 July 26/3 His lascivious sisters in the tit mags who part their legs and leer. **1975** *Wentworth & Flexner's Dict. Amer. Slang* Suppl. 750/1 *Tits and ass* [taboo] adj., of, being, or pertaining to commercial photographs of nude young women. **1976** N. THORNBURG *Cutter & Bone* i. 24 A tits-and-ass independent, you might call him. **1977** D. FRANCIS *Risk* xii. 150 On Wednesday, paragraphs in all the dailies... 'Fun Jock Twice Removed?' from a tits and bums. **1977** *Zigzag* Apr. 34/1 Not unless you look at some jerk-off magazine, a tit-and-ass magazine disguised as some junior hippy kind of thing. **1978** K. AMIS *Jake's Thing* (1979) v. 49 A keen buyer of tit-magazines. **1978** *Globe & Mail* (Toronto) 4 Nov. 13/2 Victor Matthews, chairman of Express Newspapers..put his people to work on plans for a new tabloid 'with plenty of tits and bums'. **1980** in S. Terkel *Amer. Dreams* 1 There are certain images that come to mind when people talk about beauty queens. It's mostly what's known as t and a, tits and arse. No talent. **1982** *Sunday Times* 2 Sept. 29/1 Ugly George, America's prime TV porn artist (who invites women to undress for his video camera), with his 'tit n' ass' cable channel.

2. = TEAT 2; *spec.* a push-button, esp. one used to fire a gun or release a bomb. orig. *Forces' slang.*

1942 J. GLEED *Arise to Conquer* iv. 30 Pull the tit. [*Note*] This is the emergency control which, by driving the supercharger at its very maximum pace, gives the aeroplane considerable extra speed. **1943** 'T. DUDLEY-GORDON' *Coastal Command at War* xvii. 165 It was time to release the depth-charges... I pressed the tit and that was the last I saw of it [*sc.* the bomb] for a bit. **1972** A. PRICE *Colonel Butler's Wolf* xii. 135 They've built this mock-up in the Museum... You press the tit, and the lights go out. **1976** 'J. ROSS' *I know what it's like to Die* xxi. 136 He pressed the tit of the bell push and she opened the door.

tit, *sb.*[7] *slang.* [Of uncertain origin: perh. f. *TIT *sb.*[6]; cf. TIT *sb.*[3], *TWIT *sb.*[1] 2 b.] A foolish or ineffectual person, a nincompoop.

1947 *Landfall* (N.Z.) Dec. 290 Why didn't Lachlan go, the silly tit? **1965** M. FRAYN *Tin Men* (1966) xv. 69 'Who are all these people?' they shouted at one another. 'All which people?' 'All these tits in tweed sports jackets.' *Ibid.* 70 'Peculiar friends he has.' 'Tits, a lot of them.' **1968** *Listener* 19 Sept. 370/2, I don't think much of this little tit Hitler, do you, ducky? **1978** S. WILSON *Dealer's Move* vii. 122 We always took a gun, and it kept me quite alert, not wishing to make a tit of myself in front of the laird.

titania (təitēⁱ·niă). *Chem.* [f. TITAN(IUM + -IA[1], after YTTRIA, etc.] = *titanium dioxide* s.v. *TITANIUM b.

1922 *Jrnl. Amer. Chem. Soc.* XLIV. 387 Titania was prepared by dissolving the oxide in hot conc. sulfuric acid, diluting with 10 volumes of water and precipitating as with alumina. **1971** *Materials & Technol.* II. v. 326 Titania and its compounds..are important for high-capacity condensers, and have considerably displaced the natural product mica.

titanian, *a.*[2] Restrict † *Obs.* to sense in Dict. and add: **b.** *Min.* [*-IAN 2.] Of a mineral: having a (small) proportion of a constituent element replaced by titanium.

1930 *Amer. Mineralogist* XV. 572 Titanium—titanian. **1944** [see *PLUMBIAN *a.*]. **1967** *Amer. Mineralogist* LII. 780 Zr also has been reported in amounts up to a few weight percent in titanian andradite (melanite).

Titanic, *sb.* [f. TITANIC *a.*[1]] The name of a giant British liner which sank on its maiden voyage in 1912 after collision with an iceberg; used allusively or as a metaphor for a vast and supposedly indestructible organization fated to disaster. Also *Titanic clause* (see quot. 1915).

1915 *N.Y. World* 3 Aug. 5/4 When he executed his will on March 16, 1914, Joseph E. Greenfield inserted what is known as a 'Titanic' clause, which anticipated the possibility of the testator and his wife meeting death together in a catastrophe. **1975** S. LAUDER *Killing Time on Corvo* x. 91 It was some horrifying *Titanic* disaster. **1975** *Times* 3 Sept. 10/6 The implications of the final song, that England is a Titanic with a crew composed only of vagabonds and privileged yachtsmen. **1976** *Times* 13 May 1/3 The hapless President's campaign manager..sounded..fatalistic... 'I'm not going to do anything to re-arrange the furniture on the deck of the Titanic,' he said. **1980** K. HAGENBACH *Fox Potential* vi. 57, I wanted to leave England... I did not intend to be aboard when that particular Titanic finally foundered in a sea of bureaucracy.

Titanism. b. (Earlier example.)

1851 H. MELVILLE *Moby Dick* II. xliv. 297 Where infantileness of ease undulates through a Titanism of power.

titanium. Add: **b. titanium dioxide,** the oxide TiO_2, occurring naturally as the minerals rutile, anatase, and brookite, and used esp. as a white pigment and opacifying agent; **titanium oxide,** any oxide of titanium, esp. the dioxide; **titanium sponge,** titanium in a porous form; **titanium white,** a white pigment consisting chiefly or wholly of titanium dioxide.

1877 *Jrnl. Chem. Soc.* I. 688 Sulphate of titanium dioxide, $TiS_2O_8 + 3H_2O$, is a yellow resinous mass. **1963** R. R. A. HIGHAM *Handbk. Papermaking* iv. 94 Titanium dioxide has the property of extreme chemical inertness, i.e., it is not affected by acids, alkalis, or the common solvents at standard temperature and pressure and is insoluble in water. **1982** *Sci. Amer.* Oct. 58 (Advt.), Titanium dioxide makes the plastic of your coffee cup opaque and the color of your telephone deep and bright. **1885** *Jrnl. Chem. Soc.* XLVIII. 1. 640 The author describes the hydrated titanium oxide with phosphoric acid and various earths from the diamond diggings of Diamantina, in Brazil. **1955** *Sci. News Let.* 9 Apr. 233/1 A liquid at ordinary temperatures, titanium tetrachloride changes to smoky fumes of titanium oxide when air touches it. **1977** *Whitaker's Almanack 1978* 152/2 The M stars, like Betelgeuse, show very complex molecular spectra, chiefly of titanium oxide. **1950** *Metal Industry Handbk. & Directory* (ed. 39) I. 39/1 The resultant mixture of molten magnesium chloride, unused magnesium and titanium sponge is allowed to cool..and the product is bored out as chips. **1978** *Jrnl. R. Soc. Arts* CXXVI. 679/1 The extraction method normally used now is to chlorinate rutile (TiO_2), turning it into titanium tetrachloride ($TiCl_4$) liquid, which is then reduced with magnesium or sodium to produce titanium sponge which can subsequently be melted and cast into ingots. **1920** *Chem. Abstr.* XIV. 355 (*heading*) Titanium and titanium white. **1934** H. HILER *Notes on Technique of Painting* ii. 101 Titanium white is the oxide of a metal which until lately was considered as a curiosity in the laboratory.

titano-[2]. Add: **titanau·gite** *Min.* [ad. G. *titan-augit* (A. Knop *Der Kaiserstuhl im Breisgau* (1892) ii. 72)], a variety of augite containing titanium; **titan(o)hæ·matite** (also **-hem-**) *Min.*, a variety of hæmatite containing titanium dioxide in solid solution; **ti:tano-maghe·mite** [*MAGHEMITE] *Min.*, a titanian variety of maghemite; **titanoma·gnetite** *Min.* [ad. G. *titanomagnetit* (P. Groth *Tabellarische Übersicht der Min.* (ed. 4, 1898) 79)], a variety of magnetite containing titanium.

1933 *Zeitschr. für Kristallogr.* LXXXVI. 112 The titanaugite in question forms a small patch or segregation within a sphene-rich, plagioclase-diopside-hornfels xenolith in the Haddo norite. **1963** W. A. DEER et al. *Rock-Forming Minerals* II. 109 Titanaugites are the typical pyroxenes of basic alkaline rocks, *e.g.* teschenite, essexite and nepheline dolerite. **1970** *Nature* 28 Nov. 850/2 The principal minerals in the rock are zoned plagioclase..; nepheline; and titanaugite, grading at the edges of the crystals into aegirine. **1938** A. B. EDWARDS in *Proc. Australasian Inst. Mining & Metallurgy* No. 110. 42 This 'white ilmenite' is quite distinct from ordinary hematite... The name 'titanhematite' is here suggested to indicate its difference from pure hematite. **1945** *N.Z. Jrnl. Sci. & Technol.* B. XXVI. 299 A range from pure titanomagnetite to pure titanhæmatite is..present in a small percentage of the iron-ore grains. **1971** I. G. GASS et al. *Understanding Earth* xvii. 255/1 Ultimately, in the highest state of oxidation.., the original titanomagnetite has been converted mainly to pseudobrookite (Fe_2TiO_5) and titanohaematite (Fe_2O_3) containing a little titanium. **1953** E. Z. BASTA *Mineral. Aspects of System FeO–Fe_2O_3–TiO_2* (Ph.D. Thesis, Univ. of Bristol) vi. 71 For those minerals with composition approaching (Fe, Ti)$_2O_3$ (e.g. the Bushveld maghemites) I propose the new name 'titanomaghemite'. **1971** *Nature* 5 Mar. 28/1 Under conditions of low temperature and high oxygen fugacity..titanomagnetite tends to oxidize to an equilibrium mineral assemblage of rutile and haematite, with intermediate formation of titanomaghemite, ilmenite and iron-rich titanomagnetite. **1900** *Mineral. Mag.* XII. 393 Titanomagnetite... Titaniferous magnetite. [(Fe,Ti)O_2]$_2$Fe. **1945** [see *titanohæmatite* above]. **1962** W. A. DEER et al. *Rock-Forming Minerals* V. 68 A considerable amount of Ti can enter the magnetite structure, there being a continuous relationship between magnetite and the ulvöspinel molecule, Fe_2TiO_4... The term titanomagnetite is best restricted to those specimens where the presence of an ulvöspinel phase can be demonstrated. **1971** I. G. GASS et al. *Understanding Earth* xvii. 255/1 The mineral which accounts for the magnetic properties of most rocks, and especially basalts, is titanomagnetite.

tit-bit, tid-bit. Add: **tid-bit** is now chiefly *N. Amer.* **a, b.** (Later N. Amer. examples.)

1906 U. SINCLAIR *Jungle* xiv. 162 Things..went into the sausages in comparison with which a poisoned rat was a tidbit. **1941** AUDEN *New Year Let.* I. 26 Add his small tid-bit to the rest. **1968** *Globe & Mail* (Toronto) 17 Feb. 28 An unusually good selection of hot and cold tid bits. **1976** *Time* 27 Dec. 49/3 There were enough tidbits of good news last week to soothe the fears of some Ford Administration economists.

titch, var. *TICH.

titchy (ti·tʃi), *a. colloq.* [f. *titch*, var. of *TICH + -Y[1].] Insignificantly small, diminutive, tiny.

1950 A. BUCKERIDGE *Jennings goes to School* vii. 139 Well, anyway,..there'll be a titchy hunk all round, so no one'll have any reason to grumble. **1958** *Spectator* 13 June 768/2 Towering six foot three inches over a titchy Laertes. **1967** J. PORTER *Chinks in Curtain* ii. 20 Titchy little automatics. **1978** *Lancashire Life* Sept. 96/1 'E 'olds a titchy rod an' line An' angles in a pond.

titfer (ti·tfəɹ). *slang.* Also **titfa, titfor.** [Shortened from *tit for tat* used as rhyming slang: see *TIT *sb.*[2] 1.] A hat.

1930 BROPHY & PARTRIDGE *Songs & Slang Brit. Soldier* 171 *Tit-for*, tit-for-tat, i.e. hat. **1937** N. GAY *Me & my Girl* I. i, in J. Franklyn *Dict. Rhyming Slang* (1960) 172 *Duchess*: I hope you enjoyed your drive. *Bill*: Not 'arf—but I nearly lost my titfa! *All*: Titfa? *Bill*: Me tit for tat. *All*: Tit for tat? *Bill*: My Hat! **1939** J. B. PRIESTLEY *Let People Sing* x. 257 I'll see Billy Fitt, with me titfer in me 'and. **1943** HUNT & PRINGLE *Service Slang* 67 *Tin titfor*, steel helmet. **1952** M. TRIPP *Faith is Windsock* x. 151 I've got a lucky scarf too, so's Jake. Dig always takes his titfer, and Arthur's got a brassiere. **1960** *Observer* 20 Mar. 10/3 Last week I told you about the time I popped my titfa. **1976** U. HOLDEN *String Horses* viii. 102 The old lady made a show... Lil Pratt forgot to fill her mouth... She'd not seen a titfer like that since the film of mountain people in the Dardanelles, made after World War one.

tithe, *a.* and *sb.*[1] Add: **B.** *sb.* **1. a.** Also, in recent use, in certain religious sects: a tenth part of an individual's income which is pledged to the church. Cf. *TITHE *v.*[2] 1 b, 2.

1965 M. J. C. CALLEY *God's People* ix. 106 The 1960–1 income of a London congregation of the New Testament Church of God which claimed fifty-nine members in 1961 consisted of £900 from tithes and £200 from free-will offerings.

4. b. *tithe-accounts, -audit, -campaign, -dinner, -map* (earlier example), *-payer* (later example), *-war*; *tithe-free* adj. (later example).

1781 J. WOODFORDE *Diary* 6 Nov. (1924) I. 329 Being obliged to go to Lenewade Bridge to settle Dr. Bathurst's Tithe accounts. *Ibid.* 4 Dec. 333, I asked them to dine with us..this day being my Tithe Audit. **1878** F. KILVERT *Jrnl.* 5 Feb. (1977) 302 Today was the Tithe audit and tithe dinner to the farmers, both held at the Vicarage. About 50 tithe payers came. **1832** COBBETT *Weekly Reg.* 21 Apr. 134 Look at the tithe-campaign preparing for Ireland; the tithe-war, indeed. **1878** Tithe dinner [see *tithe-audit* above]. **1960** *Farmer & Stockbreeder* 29 Mar. 31/3 Gentleman's tithe-free residential farm. **1895** *Law Jrnl. Rep., Queen's Bench* LXIV. 159/2 The late Master of the Rolls held that a tithe-map was not evidence of boundaries between two adjoining owners. **1878** Tithe-payer [see *tithe-audit* above]. **1832** Tithe-war [see *tithe-campaign* above]. **1979** V. BOGDANOR *Devolution* v. 123 The 'tithe war', under which tithes were withheld.

tithe, *v.*[2] **1. b.** Delete † *Obs.* and add: (Later examples.) Also *gen.*, to pledge or contribute as a levy.

1967 *Observer* 6 Aug. 4/5 A reply sent to a young member by the sect's letter-answering department was more precise: 'A person working for wages is to tithe one-tenth of the total amount of his wages before income tax, national health, or other deductions are removed.' **1976** *Billings* (Montana) *Gaz.* 20 June 6-c/1 Former Southern officers prospered and tithed up to 50 percent for Civil War II, which never came.

2. Delete † *Obs.* Revived in recent use in connection with voluntary church giving. Cf. *TITHE *sb.*[1] 1 a.

1942 *Esquire* Sept. 174/2 They went to the Six Hickories church—tithed—and behaved themselves. **1968** N. GIOVANNI in W. King *Black Short Story Anthol.* (1972) 23 He quit church after a couple of months, but he continued to tithe every month faithfully and never drank again.

Hence **ti·thing** *ppl. a.*

1965 M. J. C. CALLEY *God's People* ix. 111 Everybody [in the congregation]..gives generously, probably more than the tenth required by tithing sects.

tither (ti·ðəɹ), *sb.*[2] [Of obscure origin; cf. Hampshire dial. *to be on tither-thorns* 'to be tremulously anxious' (*Eng. Dial. Dict.*) and DITHER *sb.*] A state of feverish excitement.

1960 V. JENKINS *Lions Down Under* vi. 91 His amazing side-stepping and running had the crowd in a tither. *a* **1974** R. CROSSMAN *Diaries* (1977) III. 640 He adored discussing the Health Service, he was all of a tither and quiver of excitement at having the Secretary of State there.

tithing, *vbl. sb.* Add: **a.** (Later U.S. example: cf. *TITHE *v.*[2] 2.)

1929 R. S. & H. M. LYND *Middletown* xxii. 356 Traditionally every Christian 'returns a tenth of his substance to the Lord'. A few families in Middletown continue this practice of tithing, but..the great majority contribute far less than a tenth.

d. *tithing-system.*
1904 F. W. MAITLAND *Let.* 19 May (1965) 305 We still want a little more light on the tithing system. **1978** *Daily Mirror* 12 Jan. 6/6 Much of their wealth comes from the use of the 'tithe-ing' system—members of the religion are required (like the Mormons) to donate one-tenth of their income to the funds.

Tithonian (təipōu·niăn), *a. Geol.* [ad. G. *tithonisch* (A. Oppel 1865, in *Zeitschr. der deutsch. geol. Ges.* XVII. 535), f. L. *Tīthōnus*, Gr. Τιθωνός: see -IAN.] Designating a stage of the European Upper Jurassic, thought to correspond to the Portlandian, or the Portlandian and part of the Kimmeridgian, in Britain; also *ellipt.*
1871 *Q. Jrnl. Geol. Soc.* XXVII. 208 The deposition of the Wealden strata..commenced before the close of the Oolitic period; it continued during the whole of the Tithonian. **1882** A. GEIKIE *Text-bk. Geol.* 800 At the top of the Alpine Jurassic series an important group of deposits occurs to which the name of Tithonian stage was given by Oppel. **1975** *Nature* 13 Mar. 108/1 Two different directions have been obtained from sediments in the lower and upper parts of the Morrison formation (Kimmeridgian–Tithonian respectively).

titi[2]. Add: Now the usual spelling of TEETEE[1]. Substitute for def.: A small long-coated monkey of the genus *Callicebus*, native to the tropical forests of S. America. (Later examples.)
1927 *Ann. Mag. Nat. Hist.* 9th Ser. XIX. 509 (*title*) On the Titi Monkeys. *Ibid.*, The British Museum has received ..some further specimens of..the Yellow-handed Titis. **1963** *Mammalia* XXVII. 3 Other names..have been applied to the titis of eastern Brazil. **1976** *Nature* 23 Sept. 321/1 Titi monkeys..remain paired throughout the year. **1978** *Ibid.* 18 May 193/2 Titis and siamangs carry the infant(s) for much of the day.

Titian. Add: (Later example in sense 'a picture by Titian'.) Also, a person with Titian or bright auburn hair. As *adj.*, also 'painted by or in the style of Titian'; (earlier examples); freq. in *Comb.*, as *Titian-haired* (occas. with small initial).
1841 M. E. LUCY *Diary* 10 Mar. (1983) 66 Lord Byron's favourite, Countess Guiccioli was there; she had..reddish auburn hair..looking very much like a Titian Magdalene. **1892** S. WATERLOO *Man & Woman* xiii. 97 A setter, with Titian hair and big eyes, which slept on the clover beside him. **1903** H. JAMES *Ambassadors* III. vii. 86 Standing with his fellow-visitor before one of the splendid Titians. **1923** *Times* 3 May 14/6 (Advt.), Tecla pearls..are equally becoming whether worn by blondes, brunettes or Titians. **1934** *Times Lit. Suppl.* 25 Oct. 732/2 His Titian-haired wife. **1959** W. BURROUGHS *Naked Lunch* 77 Titian-haired Venetian lads. **1982** 'D. SERAFIN' *Madrid Underground* 103 The tall, titian-haired girl.

Titius (ti·ʃɒs). *Astr.* [The name of J. D. *Titius* (1729–96), German astronomer, who published the law in 1766, six years before Bode.] *Titius–Bode law*: = *Bode's law* s.v. LAW *sb.*[1] 17 c.
1954 H. ALFVÉN *Origin of Solar System* viii. 128 The so-called Titius-Bode's law gives an empirical formula for the distance of the planets from the sun. **1972** *Nature* 21 Apr. 374/2 The chief facts which have to be explained are..the peculiar regularities in the planetary and satellite spacings, summed up by the Titius–Bode law.

titivate, tittivate, *v.* Add: ¶ **2.** Used by confusion for TITILLATE *v.* 1.
1915 [see *EROTICIZE *v.*]. **1933** DYLAN THOMAS *Let.* Sept. (1966) 23 Even now twelve heartfelt pages are titivating the senses of a Dead Letter superintendent. **1976** *Telegraph-Journal* (Saint John, New Brunswick) 27 Aug. 2/4 What would the exhibition be without the midway, with its sounds, sights and smells to titivate the senses?

titivating *ppl. a.*, **titivator**: also in similar erron. use; hence **ti·tivatory** *a.* ¶ = TITILLATORY *a.*
1928 GALSWORTHY *Swan Song* I. iv. 29 The papers were like cocktails—titivators mostly of the appetite and the nerves. **1964** E. HUXLEY *Back Street New Worlds* ix. 95 Displaying a shapely but naked midriff, eyelids kohl-ed, hands henna'd, perfumed with eastern essences as titivating to the senses as they were no doubt unsettling to the aldermen. **1975** *Time Out* 24 Jan. 5/2 All the magazine lacks is a titivatory piece on 'what they do in bed'.

title, *sb.* **1.** Restrict † *Obs.* to sense in Dict. and add: **c.** A piece of written material introduced into a film or television programme to explain action or represent dialogue; a caption; cf. *SUB-TITLE *sb.* 3. Also, a credit title (see *CREDIT *sb.* 13 f).
1905 *Billboard* 21 Oct. 42 All our films come with red titles, and show our trade mark. **1909** *Moving Picture World* 10 July 57 We make film titles, 5 feet for 50 cents in any color desired. **1922** [see *CREDIT *sb.* 13 f]. **1929** I. MONTAGU tr. *Pudovkin's On Film Technique* III. 45 *Scene I*... A passer-by, coming towards the waggon, pauses... The driver turns to him. Title: *'Is it far to Nakhabin?'* The pedestrian answers, pointing with his hand. **1958** *Punch* 27 Aug. 285/3, I shall remember [this film] as the first exception I have noticed to the rule that amusingly well-designed titles..mean a good film. **1961** G. MILLERSON *Technique Television Production* xix. 358 Roll titles give us a continuous, unbroken stream of information. **1964** T. RATTIGAN *Heart to Heart* in *Coll. Plays* III. 498 Cut, sound. Start titles... Cue grams.

3. c. (*a*) Chiefly in *Publishing*, a book, a magazine, a newspaper; (*b*) a gramophone record.
1895 *Montgomery Ward Catal.* Spring & Summer 62/1 Burt's Library of the World's Best Books... This series comprises titles selected from the standard works of the world's literature. **1908** *Sears, Roebuck Catal.* 200 Columbia P Records. Your own selection of subjects, any of the titles shown on the list. **1935** A. C. BAUGH *Hist. Eng. Lang.* viii. 246 In England over 20,000 titles in English appeared by 1640, ranging all the way from mere pamphlets to massive folios. **1953** J. MORTIMER *Like Men Betrayed* v. 83 I'd never read any titles by Dickens, but we're thinking of bringing out a Victorian Omnibus so I read one. **1958** G. BOATFIELD in P. Gammond *Decca Bk. Jazz* xxiv. 313 A 1938 session with Pete Brown on alto and flamboyant trumpeter Charlie Shavers produced eight titles. **1977** *Times* 10 Sept. 2/5 The *Daily Express*.. Mr Matthews thought 'had lost its way'... Mr Matthews is..fairly satisfied with Beaverbrook's other titles, the *Sunday Express* and *Evening Standard*. **1979** P. THEROUX *Old Patagonian Express* xix. 301, I..introduced myself as the author of the three titles I had seen in the bookstores in Tucuman. **1982** *Times* 4 May 15/2 The latest casualty is the IPC romantic weekly for teenage girls, Love Affair... The title is no longer profitable.

5. b. *Sport.* The championship or supremacy in a contest or competition; the game or contest in which this is decided.
1922 *Encycl. Brit.* XXXII. 566/1 J. J. McDermott won the [golf] open tournament both in 1911 and 1912. Travers defeated Anderson for the amateur title in 1913. **1930** *Amer. Speech* VI. 121 *Title*, championship: Al Brown Signed For Title Battle. **1939** *Encycl. Brit. Bk. of Year* 117/1 Joe Louis reigned as world heavyweight champion and defended his title three times. **1955** R. BANNISTER *First Four Minutes* vi. 59 To win the 100 and 200 metre titles in the World Student Games. **1971** *Rand Daily Mail* 4 Sept. 3/6 The visit of South African squash players to Hobart to compete in the Australian squash titles. **1973** P. EVANS *Bodyguard Man* iv. 33 He goes straight into the Fiorentina first team, in his first year helps to win the League title for his new club.

11. *title-leaf* (later example), *-registration, -search, -searching*; **title catalogue** *Librarianship* (see quots.); **title entry** *Librarianship*, an entry for a book in a library catalogue made under the title (as opp. under the author); **title fight** *Boxing*, a match held to decide the championship; **title-holder,** (*a*) one who holds title-deeds; (*b*) *Sport*, the reigning champion in a particular field; **title insurance** *U.S.*, insurance protecting the owner or mortgagee of real estate against lawsuits arising from defective title; **title-music,** music played during the credits at the beginning of a film or television programme; **title-part** (examples); **title-piece,** an essay, piece of music, etc., giving its name to the collection of which it forms part; **title song, -track,** the song or track giving its name to a long-playing record.
1876 C. A. CUTTER in *Public Libraries in U.S.A.* xxvii. 528 *Title-catalogue*, one in which the entries are arranged alphabetically according to some word of the title, especially the first, (a dictionary of titles). **1910** A. E. BOSTWICK *Amer. Public Library* 175 If they [*sc.* entries] are arranged alphabetically by the chief word in the title, it is a title catalogue. **1968** P. QUIGG *Theory of Cataloguing* vi. 63 The *author catalogue* is a catalogue with, in the main, authors' names... The entries will, however, usually include..for certain works..title entries. Added entries for significant titles are usually included..so that..the form of the catalogue should be designated as an *author/title catalogue*. **1875** C. A. CUTTER in *Nation* 4 Mar. 151/1 especially impressed with the usefulness of title-entries. **1935** *Library Q.* V. 459 He..had obtained permission to change entries in the university library catalog for publications of corporate bodies from title entry to entry under their names. **1969** P. S. DUNKIN *Cataloging U.S.A.* iii. 46 So much for author entry, title entry, and arbitrary entry and the heading which introduces each. **1951** *Sport* 7 Jan. 14 The forthcoming feather-weight title fight between champion Ronnie Clayton and veteran Al Phillips. **1973** 'S. HARVESTER' *Corner of Playground* I. viii. 71 She went away, walking on her heels like a boxer after thirteen rounds of a title fight. **1904** Title-holder [in Dict.]. **1938** *Encycl. Brit. Bk. of Year* 113/1 Three of the title-holders, Louis (heavy), Lewis (light-heavy), and Armstrong (bantam), are negroes. **1978** H. COOPER *Great Heavyweights* 86 Willie Pastrano, the then world light-heavy titleholder and a boxer of beautiful science. **1902** C. J. PIDGIN *Stephen Holton* 260 That was a mighty good idea of yours, Mr. Lethbridge—telling me to go to a title insurance company. **1942** *Federal Reporter* (U.S.) CXXXII. 44 The contention of the appellant is that premiums paid for title insurance are earned when received. **1979** *Arizona Daily Star* 5 Aug. D 2/4 The firm has been a division of First American Title for 20 years, offering title insurance and escrow services nationally. **1936** *Discovery* Dec. 384/2 The booksellers also displayed the title-leaves of new works as advertisements. **1977** *Gramophone* Apr. 1555/3 The opening and closing are of great impact (like the title-music for one of the more dramatic of those films). **1898** G. B. SHAW in *Sat. Review* 5 Feb. 171/2 Miss Irene Vanbrugh, in the title part..vanquishes it easily and successfully. **1927** F. HARRIS *My Life* III. xix. 334 'Poil de Carotte', (Carrots!) I think it was, with Madame Nau in the title part. **1927** *New Republic* 12 Oct. 211/1 He has possibly scored some moderate hits: in 'Manhattan Mary', 'Broadway', 'The Five Step'.., a curiously constructed sob-song called 'Memories', and the title-piece. **1936** in A. Huxley *Olive Tree* (dust-jacket), This is one of the best collections of essays that Mr. Huxley has ever made. The title-piece is a completely new departure in technique. **1968** ROBERTS & MOORE in D. H. Lawrence *Phoenix II* p. xii, 'The Gentleman from San Francisco' appeared as the title-piece of a collection of Bunin's stories. **1971** A. AXELROD et al. *Land Transfer & Finance* 693 Patton has been a strong proponent of title registration. **1965** *Amer. Bar Assoc. Jrnl.* LI. 1071/1 In the second step the contract is drawn up by the lawyer and he handles the closing, but the title search is conducted by full-time, salaried employees of the title company. **1980** *Daily Tel.* 16 Jan. 23/3 They will ask you to complete a 'title search' on the new property to make sure that all deeds and papers are in order. **1899** G. B. SHAW *Let.* 1 Aug. (1972) II. 95 After much title-searching, I have resolved to give that play..the ugly but arresting name 'Captain Brassbound's Conversion'. **1971** A. AXELROD et al. *Land Transfer & Finance* 499 This loss of title searching and examination illustrates the vulnerability of lawyers in private practice to competition from specialized high volume businesses and professions. **1961** *New Musical Express* 6 Jan. 4/2 *Am I that easy to forget*..is the title song of a soft-sung album by Debbie Reynolds. **1970** *Melody Maker* 21 Feb. 21/3 It's hard to believe that the same man who could write and play the extraordinary title track could also be responsible for 'Spirits' and 'Search'.

titling, *vbl. sb.* Add: **c.** The action of providing a film, television programme, or photograph with captions or titles (sense *1 c).
1913 *Moving Picture World* 4 Oct. 25 The perfect picture tells its story without any titles, but as there are very few perfect pictures good titling becomes a necessity. **1958** *Punch* 1 Jan. 80/2 This horrible cliché of TV drama presentation, known to the trade as delayed titling. **1966** *Ibid.* 22 June 922/1 We may have seen an unsuccessful copy [of the Yugoslavian film *Covek Nija Tica*], and certainly the titling wasn't very efficient. **1970** *Amateur Photographer* 11 Mar. 61/1 Positive in the camera comes into its own for titling.

titlist (təi·tlist). *U.S. Sport.* [f. TITLE *sb.* + -IST.] A title-holder or champion.
1924 [see *STRING *sb.* 12 c]. **1955** M. REIFER *Dict. New Words* 209/2 *Titlist*, one who has won a title, usually in a sport or game contest. **1973** *Internat. Herald Tribune* 15 June 15/2 Defending titlist Manuel Orantes of Spain joined other top seeds on the sidelines of the German tennis championships. **1976** *Billings* (Montana) *Gaz.* 11 July 7-G/1 Carner, the 1971 titlist, a winner three times on the LPGA tour this year.

Titoism (tī·toiz'm). [f. *Tito*, name adopted by Josip Broz (?1892–1980) premier of Yugoslavia from 1945 + -ISM.] The ideas or policies associated with Marshal Tito; *spec.* a form of communism which concentrates on the national interest without reference to the Soviet Union.
1949 *Economist* 2 July 5/1 During the year which has followed the famous resolution of the Cominform expelling Jugoslavia from its membership, Titoism has become an international phenomenon. **1949** [see *TITOIST *sb.* and *a.*]. **1958** F. W. NEAL (*title*) Titoism in action. **1962** [see *MAOISM]. **1965** *Listener* 30 Sept. 480/1 Where communism cannot be avoided the best hope is to steer it towards affluence and Titoism. **1973** R. J. ALEXANDER *Latin Amer. Polit. Parties* xx. 397 Titoism was more attractive to some of the Latin American Socialist parties than to the Communists of the area. **1978** *Time* 3 July 7/2 Exactly 30 years after fiercely independent Yugoslavia was expelled from Joseph Stalin's Cominform for what became known as 'Titoism'.

Titoist (tī·toist), *sb.* and *a.* [f. as prec. + -IST.] **A.** *sb.* A follower or adherent of Titoism. **B.** *adj.* Of, pertaining to, or resembling Titoism.
1949 *Newsweek* 15 Aug. 9 Titoism has now infected the Communist Party in the Middle East, a split is developing between Stalinists and Titoists in Beirut. **1949** *N.Y. Times* 30 Oct. I. 17/1 The delegation denied any intention of starting a Titoist 'movement' in Italy. **1951** *Round Table* CLXIII. 247 (*heading*) The Titoist schism. **1954** KOESTLER *Invisible Writing* ii. 21 These [*sc.* communist cells] are living, pulsating units..susceptible to various diseases—to the Titoist virus, to bourgeois infection or Trotskyist cancer. *Ibid.* xiv. 155 Every Communist who had lived in the Soviet Union for some length of time, returned to his country as a Titoist at heart. **1961** *Listener* 9 Nov. 754/1 This aspect of Titoist reforms looms large in official literature. **1971** 'P. KAVANAGH' *Triumph of Evil* iii. 25 Dorn, a Croat, had spent the war years with Ante Pavelic, killing Serbs and Titoist partisans. **1977** *Time* 27 June 12/3 My son recently wrote to me that he is a liberal conservative. I replied, 'In Yugoslavia, that means a Titoist.'

Titoite (tī·toəit), *sb.* (and *a.*) [f. as prec. + -ITE[1].] = *TITOIST *sb.* Also *attrib.* or as *adj.* Usu. with derog. implication.
1955 H. HODGKINSON *Doubletalk* 129 Soviet writers have not thought fit to elevate Tito's heresy to the rank of an 'ism'... He and his colleagues were..referred to abusively as Titoites. **1961** *Spectator* 9 June 829 He was.. not even a Titoite or fellow-traveller. **1973** R. J. ALEXANDER *Latin Amer. Political Parties* xx. 396 (*heading*) The Titoite heresy. *Ibid.*, In the Communist-controlled countries of Eastern Europe, the Titoite dissidence had considerable support.

titrate, *v.* Add: Also with pronunc. (təi-). Hence **titra·table** *a.*, capable of being titrated.

1919 *Jrnl. Physiol.* LIII. 189 Duplicate estimations were made..of titratable acidity and ammonia by the method of Folin. **1929** *Amer. Jrnl. Physiol.* LXXXVII. 538 During the experiments no marked change occurred in the titratable acid concentration of the urine. **1963** [see *END-POINT 1]. **1973** *Nature* 14 Dec. 425/1 Calculation of the total titratable acid in the collected effluent.

titrator (tai-, titrē̆ɪ·təɪ). *Chem.* [f. TITRATE *v.* + -OR.] An apparatus for automatically performing a titration.

1948 *Analytical Chem.* XX. 288/1 The recorder switch should be set so that when the titrator stops finally the potential of the indicator electrode will coincide with the equivalence point potential of the particular titration. **1964** *Oceanogr. & Marine Biol.* II. 103 Many commercially produced titrators would doubtless prove suitable for routine work of moderate accuracy. **1979** *Nature* 25 Jan. p. xx/3 The range, consisting of Karl Fischer, endpoint, *p*h stat and recording titrators, all incorporate a unique photoelectric counting device.

titre, titer. Add: Also with pronunc. (təi·təɹ). (Further examples.) In *Med.*, the concentration of an antibody, as measured by the extent to which it can be diluted before ceasing to give a positive reaction with antigen.

1868 *Chem. News* 13 Mar. 132/1 Provided the 'tinctorial' power, and consequently 'titre' of the ammonia standard be correctly ascertained in terms of the iodine solution, the former may be dispensed with. **1918** [see *PEPTIDASE]. **1947** *Ann. Rev. Microbiol.* I. 337 If soluble antigen has been released it may be detected in relatively high titer in the supernatant fluid. **1958** *Spectator* 19 Sept. 379/1 The shot I'm going to give you..ought to moderate the symptoms until you've developed a high anti-body titer of your own. **1979** *Jrnl. R. Soc. Arts* CXXVII. 421/1 As the anti-body titres waned they would go through a succession of mid-gestation abortions.

2. (See quots.)

1895 J. LEWKOWITSCH *Chem. Analysis Oils, Fats, Waxes* iv. 100 The temperature will continue to fall, but then it will rise suddenly..and reach a maximum, remaining thereat stationary for some little time before it falls again. This point is called the titer or solidifying point. **1951** KIRK & OTHMER *Encycl. Chem. Technol.* VI. 153 (*heading of table*) Fat or oil... Titer range, °C. **1972** *Materials & Technol.* V. viii. 193 Fats containing fatty acids with a titre above 40°C are known as tallows. (The titre of an oil is the highest temperature reached when the liberated water-insoluble fatty acids are crystallizing under controlled conditions. It is generally taken to be the solidification point of the fatty acids.)

ti-tree. (Earlier and later examples.)

1864 R. ANDERSON *Hawaiian Islands* vii. 134 Then came gigantic ferns, and an extensive tract covered with the *ti* trees. **1881** [in Dict. s.v. TI b]. **1981** M. GEE *Meg* xiii. 116 A ti-tree prop.

tit-tat-toe: see *TIT *sb.*^{2} 3 in Dict. and Suppl.

titter, *sb.*^{3} *slang.* [Of uncertain origin: cf. TIT *sb.*^{3}, *TIT *sb.*^{6}] A young woman or girl.

1812 J. H. VAUX *Vocab. Flash Lang.* in *Mem.* (1964) 274 *Titter*, a young woman or girl. **1845** E. J. WAKEFIELD *Adventure in N.Z.* I. xi. 319 A chief was called [by whalers] a 'nob'; a slave, a 'doctor'; a woman, a 'heifer'; a girl, a 'titter'. **1882** *Sydney Slang Dict.* 6/2 Nark, to watch, to look after; 'Nark the *titter*', watch the girl. *a* **1890** in Barrère & Leland *Dict. Slang* (1890) II. 356/2 Only a glass of bitter! Only a sandwich mild! Only a stupid titter! Only she's not a child! **1953** *Landfall* (N.Z.) Sept. 179 Boys, she's a larky little titter.

tittery (ti·təri), *a.* [f. TITTER *v.*^{1} or *sb.*^{2} + -Y^{1}.] Of laughter, remarks, etc.: having a nervous, tittering quality.

1936 M. MITCHELL *Gone with Wind* xxxv. 591 The tittery cackling laugh which she always found so annoying. **1962** E. O'BRIEN *Lonely Girls* ii. 23 He would have seen me..saying foolish tittery things to amuse the others. **1983** *Financial Times* 15 Sept. 13 After a richly funny beginning the characters and story fracture into a series of fluttery, tittery vignettes.

tittup, *v.* Add: (Later examples with reference to a person's gait.) Also *fig.*

1910 E. M. FORSTER *Howard's End* xiv. 121 No one felt uneasy as he titupped along the pavements. **1968** B. HEALEY *Murder without Crime* vii. 126 Like benevolent Mr. Pickwick he tittuped along beside us. **1972** N. FREELING *Long Silence* I. 51 'We're not very happy about art,' Van der Valk tittupped on.

titty, *sb.*^{3} Add: Also **tittie.** Now *colloq.* or *slang* and also as dim. of *TIT *sb.*^{6} **1.** (Later examples.) Chiefly *pl.* Applied both to a nipple (sometimes of a boy) and to a woman's breast including the nipple; *tough titty*: see *TOUGH *a.* 6 d.

1922 JOYCE *Ulysses* 738 Yes I think he made them a bit firmer sucking them like that so long he made me thirsty titties he calls them. **1940** C. MCCULLERS *Heart is Lonely Hunter* I. iii. 39 His little titties were like blue raisins on his chest. **1957** J. FRAME *Owls do Cry* vii. 33 She had pink bulges where Daphne had mere tittie dots. **1972** *Screw* 12 June 10/2 Man, those firm nice buttocks and titties filled that bikini to overflowing. **1976** M. MACHLIN *Pipeline* iv. 46 Man, that *is* cold. My titties feel like a pair of Pecos strawberries.

2. *Comb.*, as **titty-bag,** a sweetened object given to a baby to suck; **titty-bottle,** a baby's feeding bottle with teat.

1923 J. MANCHON *Le Slang* 314 *Titty-bag*, un suçon. **1976** A. HILL *Summer's End* x. 147 A titty-bag was a piece of rag with sugar poured inside, then the rag was tied up with string and the sugar-lump stuck into the blarting mouth. **1871** B. BRIERLEY *Cotters of Mossburn* iv. 46 He's suckin' th' sofy bowster i' th' bar an' doesno' know but it's a titty-bottle. **1920** D. H. LAWRENCE *Lost Girl* xi. 280 'Eh, tha can ta'e th' titty-bottle wi' thee,' said the labourer.

titty (ti·ti), *a. dial.* and *colloq.* [f. TIT *sb.*^{3} + -Y^{1}.] Diminutive, insignificant.

1884 *Rep. & Trans. Devonshire Assoc.* XVI. 118 A titty piece of cake. **1943** J. W. DAY *Farming Adventure* iii. 41 War Agricultural Committee officials, whom he described as 'titty little bits on motor-bikes—never got their feet wet yet'. **1967** K. GILES *Death & Mr. Prettyman* viii. 156 One of those titty little bikes with a one-horse engine. **1969** E. MCGIRR *Entry of Death* iii. 38 It was a sliver of card... 'This titty little bit of card could be anything.'

Hence in reduplicated form **titty-totty** *a.* (*sb.*) (*dial.*).

1893 H. COZENS-HARDY *Broad Norfolk* 56 *Titty totty*, extremely tiny. **1943** J. W. DAY *Farming Adventure* v. 62 He hed a little owd titty-totty boy from Tollesbury as a hand—a furriner! **1970** *Morning Star* 28 Mar. 2/8 It is a titty-totty of a tree, a crab apple, a tree nonetheless.

titular, *a.* and *sb.* Add: **A.** *adj.* **1.** *titular abbot*, one holding the title of abbot from a monastery that no longer exists as a religious community; *titular bishop* (earlier example).

1767 A. BUTLER *Short Acct. Life & Virtues of Mary of Holy Cross* p. xviii, He repeated this Charge..to his Coadjutor and Successor the Right Reverend Benjamin Petre, titular Bishop of Prusa. **1934** WEBSTER, Titular abbot. **1977** *Church Times* 1 July 14/2 Coventry. Benedictine anniversary... The Titular Abbot of Westminster will preach.

titulature (ti·tiŭlătiŭɹ). *Anc. Hist.* [f. late L. *titulātum*, pa. pple. of *titulāre* to give title to: see -URE.] The set of titles borne by an official; the form of title by which an official is known.

1893 E. G. HARDY in *Classical Rev.* VII. 49/1 It is well known how carefully the proconsulare imperium was omitted in the imperial titulature. **1971** R. BROWNING *Justinian & Theodora* iii. 97 The memory of it [*sc.* the city Justiniana Prima] remained, and its name appeared in the titulature of certain Serbian archbishops down to 1718. **1973** J. BRISCOE *Commentary on Livy Books XXXI–XXXIII* 5 The titulature of the governors of the Spanish provinces is a more complex problem. L[ivy] describes them variously as praetors, propraetors and proconsuls.

‖ **titulus** (ti·tiŭlŭs). [L.: see TITLE *sb.*] An inscription on or over something; esp. the inscription on the Cross.

1918 *By an Unknown Disciple* xx. 238 He ordered the centurion to have it so inscribed on the Titulus. **1927** A. H. MCNEILE *Introd. N.T.* 10 There was a deep irony in the mockery by the soldiers, and in the *titulus* on the Cross. **1963** *N. & Q.* May 166/2 The best-known type [of 'illustrated' poem] is the inscription-poem used as a *titulus*, carved or painted on tombs or the walls of buildings.

‖ **ti-tzu** (di·dzə). *Mus.* Also **Ti tzu.** [Chinese *dízi.*] A type of Chinese bamboo flute (see quots.).

1874 *Jrnl. N. China Branch R. Asiatic Soc.* VIII. 109 The modern *Ti-tzu*..has seven holes besides the embouchure. **1917** *Encycl. Sinica* 389/1 The *Ti tzŭ* is a very popular flute, about 26 inches long, formerly with 11 finger-holes, one of which was covered with membrane, but now having 6 finger-holes and a 7th covered with membrane. **1954** *Grove's Dict. Mus.* (ed. 5) II. 235/2 *Ti* (to-day usually *ti-tzu*), a transverse flute, the common or popular flute of China... A bamboo tube..pierced with 8 holes (6 fingerholes, 1 blown across and 1 covered with a paper membrane). **1975** C. P. MACKERRAS *Chinese Theatre in Mod. Times* 16 The *K'un-ch'ü*..found most of its admirers among the gentry, officials and scholars. Its music was softer and more melodious than that of the popular drama and it was accompanied principally by the *ti-tzu*, or Chinese transverse flute.

Tiuchiu, var. *TEOCHEW.

Tiv (tiv), *a.* and *sb.* [Native name.] **A.** *adj.* Of, pertaining to, or designating a people of central Nigeria, who live on either side of the Benue River, or the language spoken by them. **B.** *sb.* **a.** A member of this people; also *collect.* **b.** The Bantu language of this people.

1939 R. M. EAST tr. B. Abiga (*title*) Abiga's story: the Tiv tribe as seen by one of its members. **1957** W. M. HAILEY *Afr. Survey* (rev. ed.) iii. 101 The languages of the Tiv group are largely used in mass literacy schemes in the Benue Province. **1960** *Guardian* 15 July 14/4 The important smaller peoples like the Tivs, Kanauris, Binis and Ibibias. **1962** *Listener* 25 Jan. 187/3 Artists and critics among the Tiv of Nigeria. **1973** T. KOCHMAN *Rappin' & Stylin' Out* 83 [Charles Keil] studied Tiv language, culture, music, and aesthetics, and Yoruba urban music. **1976** *Nigeria Herald* 21 May 2/2 News in Kanuri, Tiv and Yoruba. **1977** *Language* LIII. 290 Loanwords are not all lumped into one class (as they tend to be in Tiv). **1982** B. EMECHETA *Destination Biafra* i. 8 In Nigeria..there are smaller groups..surrounding each major tribe... Around the Hausas you have the Tivs, the Fulanis.

tizz, tiz (tiz), shortened form of *TIZZY^{2}.

1954 B. BOLAND *Return* II. iii, in *Plays of Year* IX. 326 *Peter*: Nothing matters. *Angela*: Practically nothing. All the things people get in such a tizz about—. **1958** 'N. BLAKE' *Penknife in my Heart* iv. 52 Miriam was as usual in a tiz. **1967** R. RENDELL *New Lease of Death* vi. 54 When Burden looked murderous, he added, 'Don't get in a tiz with me.' **1978** *Illustr. London News* Nov. 97/1 The people of Morecambe were thrown into a tizz by this idea of a barrage [across Morecambe Bay].

tizz-wozz, var. *TISWAS.

tizzy^{1}. Add: Also *Comb.*, as **tizzy-snatcher** *Naut. slang*, an assistant paymaster.

1914 'BARTIMEUS' *Naval Occasions* xiii. 107 'Bloomin' tizzy-snatcher' he muttered slipping the coins into his trousers pocket. He referred to the A.P. (Assistant Paymaster, who had mulched him of sixpence). **1916** 'TAFFRAIL' *Pincher Martin* v. 74, I cursed them for a couple of tizzy-snatchers. **1946** J. IRVING *Royal Navalese* 176 *Tizzysnatcher*, a disillusioned Nor' Easter's name for the Paymaster. The derivation is the Cockney 'tizzy' meaning sixpence.

tizzy^{2}. *colloq.* (orig. *U.S.*). [Of uncertain origin.] A state of nervous excitement, agitation or worry, a 'flap'; esp. in phr. *in a tizzy.*

1935 *Amer. Speech* X. 192/1 The *tizzy* in which a huge wedding kept society columnists for weeks. **1938** *Ladies' Home Jrnl.* Oct. 14/2 Maybe it's better for the future of the race to live from daze to daze in a perpetual tizzy like Alix. **1952** A. WILSON *Hemlock & After* II. iii. 170 Politics and the sun together always put me into a mad tizzy. **1958** N. MARSH *Singing in Shrouds* (1959) v. 83 Gets in a tizzy over details. **1967** *Spectator* 10 Nov. 582/3 John Whiting's play..about the tizzies of English gentlefolk involved in the Napoleonic invasion scare. **1974** *Courier-Mail* (Brisbane) 14 Sept. 10/6 A small band of private fliers has had the RAAF base at Amberley in a tizzy. **1983** *Daily Tel.* 8 June 20/3 He hopes this mass production of original art may throw 'into a state of total tizzy' an art world where 'more and more money is being made by less and less people'.

tjaele (‖ʃē·lə, tʃē̆ɪ·lə). *Geol.* Also **taele, tjäle.** [a. Sw. *tjäle* ice in frozen ground.] Frozen ground; also, permafrost. Freq. *attrib.*

1924 *Geogr. Jrnl.* LXIII. 210 The arrangement of materials can usually be traced right down to the tjaele. *Ibid.* 211 The tjaele ice was still very close to the surface. **1937** *Nature* 4 Sept. 410/1 The Third Glaciation is represented in the north-west by the Irish Sea Drifts,..and by taele-gravels and melt-water flood-gravels. **1939** *Geogr. Jrnl.* XCIV. 451 Near the edge of the snow the *tjäle* approaches the surface and underneath the snow the soil is completely frozen. **1960** B. W. SPARKS *Geomorphol.* xiv. 314 Solifluxion gravels of various sorts have long been recognised and mapped in Great Britain, where they are known by a variety of names, e.g. head, coombe rock, taele gravel..warp and trail. **1970** R. J. SMALL *Study of Landforms* iv. 124 A climatic refrigeration, allied to the onset of periglacial conditions and the formation of permafrost or annual taele.., is capable of rendering permeable rocks impermeable.

tjalk. (Earlier example.)

1861 *Mitchell's Maritime Reg.* 1417/1 Eja, Dutch tjalk, Bronuma, from London for Amsterdam, was totally lost Nov. 1 at West Kapelle.

tjurunga, var. *CHURINGA.

‖ **tlachtli** (tlæ·tʃtli). Also **tlaxtli.** [Nahuatl.] The ceremonial ball-game of the Aztecs; = *POK-TA-POK. Also *attrib.*, as *tlachtli-court, -field.*

1875 H. H. BANCROFT *Native Races Pacific States N. Amer.* II. viii. 297 The national game of the Nahuas was the *tlachtli*, which strongly resembled in many points our game of football. **1914** T. A. JOYCE *Mexican Archaeol.* vi. 165 But the national game, tlaxtli, was closely connected with the worship of the gods, and the tlaxtli-courts..were generally associated with temples. **1959** *Times* 27 Apr. (Rubber Industry Suppl.) p. v/1 The sacramental Tlachtli played by Aztecs in the temple courts of Mexico. **1963** [see *POK-TA-POK]. **1968** H. HELFRITZ *Mexican Cities of Gods* xv. 157 The playing area, or *tlachtli*-field,..is 199 ft. wide.

Tlapanec (tlæ·pănek), *sb.* (and *a.*) Also **Tlapaneco, Tlappanec.** [ad. Sp. *tlapaneca, tlapaneco*, ad. Nahuatl (Aztec) *tlapanecatl.*] **a.** An Indian people of south-west Guerrero, Mexico. **b.** The language of this people, formerly classified as Hokan but now regarded as Otomanguean. Also *attrib.* or as *adj.* Also in *Comb.*, as *Subtiaba-Tlapanec* (see *SUBTIABA).

1875 H. H. BANCROFT *Native Races Pacific States N. Amer.* I. vi. 677 The Tlapanecs, Coviscas, Yopes, Yopis.., Chochos,..or Popolucas are one and the same people, who by different writers are described under one or other of these names. *Ibid.* III. x. 752 Several tongues, of which.. I find nothing mentioned but the names;..further there are mentioned the Chatino, Tlapanec, and Popoluca. **1900** F. STARR *Notes Ethnography S. Mexico* 71 The name Chocho is said by Orozco to be applied to a language in Oaxaca, while to the same language in Puebla is given the name *popoloco*; it is also the *tlapaneco* of Guerrero..and the ancient *Yope.* **1911** THOMAS & SWANTON *Indian Languages Mexico & Central Amer.* 53 Sahagun..says the

Tlapaneco language is precisely the same as those called Tenime, Pinome..in the singular Pinotl.. This brings Tlapaneco into the same relation as that given by Orozco y Berra. *Ibid.* 54 The Tlapanec group is illustrated in Orozco y Berra in Guerrero. **1925**, etc. [see *SUBTIABA]. **1940** J. A. MASON in *Maya & Their Neighbors* v. 61 According to Sapir..Subtiaba in Nicaragua differs hardly more than dialectically from Tlapanec in Guerrero. **1972** *Bk. Thousand Tongues* (Amer. Bible Soc.) (rev. ed.) 430/2 The Tlapaneco Indians..live in Guerrero, Mexico. Tlapaneco, spoken with numerous dialectal variations, is a Hokan language, related in Mexico to Seri and Chontal of Oaxaca. **1974** *Encycl. Brit. Macropædia* XI. 960/1 The Tlapanec complex was first correctly identified by Walter Lehmann..in 1920. *Ibid.*, He [*sc.* Sapir] believed Tlapanec to be Oto-Manguean.

Tlingit (kli·ŋkit, kli·ŋgit; also, incorrectly, tl-), *sb.* and *a.* Also **Thlinget, Thlinkeet, Tlinget, Tlinkit,** etc. [a. Tlingit *łingit, łi·ngit* person, Tlingit.] **A.** *sb.* **a.** (A member of) an Indian people of the coasts and islands of south-eastern Alaska. **b.** The language spoken by this people.

1865 M. MACFIE *Vancouver Island & British Columbia* xvi. 452 The 'Clingats', which name is applied to all the northern tribes, relate the following tradition. **1876** *Encycl. Brit.* V. 187/2 This [*sc.* exogamy] is illustrated in the case of the Thlinkeets, or Kolosches, who inhabit the coasts and islands from Mt. St Elias to the River Nass. **1901** G. W. JAMES *Indian Basketry* 50 In Alaska the chief basket-makers are the Thlinkets and Haidas. **1908** *26th Ann. Rep. Bureau Amer. Ethnol.* 472 In Tlingit..*p* and *b* do not occur in words of native origin. *Ibid.* 407 The Tlingit..trace the origin of nearly all their clans..to the neighbourhood of the mouth of the Skeena river. **1921** E. SAPIR *Language* iv. 84 A good example of such a pitch language is Tlingit, spoken by the Indians of the southern coast of Alaska. **1951** R. FIRTH *Elem. Social Organiz.* iv. 145 The *potlach* of the Haida, Tlinkit and other Indians of the American North-West coast. **1965** *Canad. Jrnl. Linguistics* X. 97 To this Athapaskan-Eyak unit, Tlingit seems related definitely but remotely. **1970** *Language* XLVI. 401 Similar problems are presented by the so-called 'third modals' of Tlingit. **1978** *Amer. Poetry Rev.* Sept./Oct. 18/4 The Tlingit of Alaska prescribe the wearing of broad-brimmed hats.

B. *adj.* Of, pertaining to, or designating these Indians.

1881 [see *ALEUT]. **1908** *26th Ann. Rep. Bureau Amer. Ethnol.* 463 Each Tlingit shaman was guarded by a number of helpers and possessed a number of masks. *Ibid.* 472 The Tlingit language tends to shorten its vowels. **1932** D. JENNESS *Indians of Canada* xxi. 331 Feasts and ceremonies occurred constantly in all the Tlinkit villages. **1963** *Times* 29 Apr. 5/5 A Thlinget Indian from Alaska. **1966** [see *CHILKAT]. **1976** *Times* 25 Sept. 12/8 The Tlingit screen..was used as a partition in the house of Chief Shakes of the Tlingit tribe in Wrangell, Alaska.

to, *prep., conj., adv.* Add: **A.** *prep.* **I. 4. a.** (Earlier and later U.S. examples.) Cf. *HOME *sb.*[1] 13*.

1795, etc. [see *HOME *sb.*[1] 13*]. **1801** J. QUINCY in *Proc. Mass. Hist. Soc.* (1888) 2nd Ser. IV. 130 Mr. William Hammatt and Mr. Josiah Barker..called and invited us to a party they had made for us to the East end of the Island. **1818** L. D. CLARK *Jrnl.* 10 Sept. in *Firelands Pioneer* (1920) XXI. 2321 Stayed to Canfields all night. **1977** *New Yorker* 15 Aug. 37/2 Suzanne said, 'What about Sunday? We could do something in the afternoon. Were you ever to the Botanic Gardens?'

b. *to work*: at work, working. *U.S. colloq.*

1776 *Proc. Mass. Hist. Soc.* (1886) 2nd. Ser. II. 304 [We] met some people to work on the High: way. **1827** S. S. ARNOLD *Proc. Vermont Hist. Soc.* (1940) VIII. 111 Her husband..had died instantly in the barn, where he was to work. **1834** C. A. DAVIS *Lett. J. Downing* 116, I have been to work on it ever since we was at the Rip-Raps. **1858** *Rome* (N.Y.) *Sentinel* Sept., The boiler.. passed through the main building..without injuring the workmen there, although men were to work on each side of where the boiler passed. **1949** *N.Y. Herald Tribune* 6 Dec. 1 Some 450,000 miners were back to work today. **1978** M. Z. LEWIN *Silent Salesman* xxvii. 146 He's to work... Don't rightly know what time he'll be back.

II. 6. b. (Earlier and later examples of use with ellipsis of the hour.)

1842 TENNYSON *Walking to the Mail* in *Poems* II. 47 *James.* The mail? At one o'clock. *John.* What is it now? *James.* A quarter to. **1968** 'R. PETRIE' *MacLurg goes West* II. vii. 60 'I thought we might just catch you before dinner,' said Mrs. Robbins to them quickly. 'It's twelve minutes to.'

III. 8. d. Indicating the crop with which ground is planted. Chiefly *U.S.*

1799, etc. [see *PLANT *v.* 6 a]. **1833** S. SMITH *Life & Writings Major J. Downing* 22 [He]..planted the ground all over to corn, and potatoes. **1848** F. A. DURIVAGE *Stray Subjects* 21 Having laid down a few acres to oats. **1902** [in Dict., sense 8 a]. **1945** B. MACDONALD *Egg & I* (1946) I. iii. 45 The garden..was planted to peas, beets, beans, corn, Swiss chard, lettuce, cabbage, onions, turnips, celery, cucumbers, tomatoes and squash. **1980** *Daily Tel.* 17 Sept. 8/3 The area sown to winter barley was greatly increased.

V. 15. a. (Further examples.) Now only indicating food taken in addition to a dish or meal, and in this use *dial.*

1792 W. COWPER *Let.* 30 Nov. in J. A. Roy *Cowper & his Poetry* (1914) viii. 166 It is impossible any longer to find a pound of butter or cream to our tea in all the country. **1916** 'TAFFRAIL' *Pincher Martin* vii. 107 My poor John was fond of a hegg to 'is tea. **1925** V. WOOLF *Let.* 20 Sept. (1977) III. 213, I am growing old, and want more mustard to my meat.

b. Also indicating the tune to which words are set.

1591 [see TUNE *sb.* 2 a]. **1611, 1702** [see GO *v.* 17]. **1825** C. WATERTON *Wanderings S. Amer.* iv. 279 There is an old song, to the tune of La Belle Catharine. **1906** BELLOC *Hills & Sea* 116 The two trumpets of the battery sounding the call which is known among French gunners as 'the eighty hunters', because the words to it are '*Quatre-vingt, quatre-vingt..chasseurs*'.

17. c. In colloq. phrases with *there is* and a quantitative or pronominal expression: belonging as a quality, attribute, or capacity to (someone or something, freq. *it*); *that is all there is to it*: it is that and nothing more; *there's nothing to it*: see *NOTHING *sb.* 10 c. orig. *U.S.*

1880 'MARK TWAIN' *Tramp Abroad* ii. 36 There's more *to* a blue-jay than any other creature. **1883** —— *Life on Mississippi* xlv. 459 The steamboat shoved out up the creek. That was all there was 'to it'. **1895** KIPLING *Day's Work* (1898) 83 'That's all there is to it,' seethed the white water roaring through the scuppers. **1903** A. H. LEWIS *Boss* 14 Tell me what there is to this shindy. **1914** V. CASTLE *Mod. Dancing* 44 Simply *walk* as softly and smoothly as possible... This is the One Step, and this is all there is to it. **1936** L. C. DOUGLAS *White Banners* xvi. 343 He's a wonderful person, you know. There's a lot to him that doesn't show up on the surface. **1974** J. THOMSON *Long Revenge* iii. 40 He had the feeling that there was a great deal more to it [*sc.* a case] than he had so far discovered. **1976** *New Yorker* 26 Apr. 38/1, I thought she had a lot to her, a lot to offer.

VI. 19. a. (Earlier example with reference to votes.)

1836 J. ROMILLY *Diary* 30 Nov. (1967) 109 The grace.. was thrown out in the White hood house by 30 to 21; it past in the black by 23 to 20.

VIII. 34. *Book-keeping.* Placed before debit entries, and followed by particulars of the goods or services for which money has been paid, or by the name of the account containing the corresponding credit entry. Cf. BY *prep.* 37.

1772 in *Country Life* (1973) 7 June (Suppl.) 104 To mending a Waiter & Candlestick & a Sauceboat 5s. **1803** G. COLMAN *John Bull* III. i. 31 These charges are brought in like a bill!—To attending your ladyship at such a time —to dancing down twenty couple at another. **1876** *Encycl. Brit.* IV. 46 To J. Bevan and Co., for Bales, *ex* 'Mary Jane' £2349 0*s.* 0*d.* **1901** *Jrnl. R. Microsc. Soc.* 109 The Treasurer's Account for 1900... To Balance from 1899..£195 11*s.* 3*d.* **1968** G. M. WHITEHEAD *Book-Keeping made Simple* v. 79 Whenever a debit entry is made on an account we begin with the word 'To' and follow with the name of the account where the other half of the double entry is to be found. **1978** J. KELLOCK *Elements of Accounting* i. 11 In many accounting text books the words 'To' and 'By' are used to preface debit and credit entries respectively in the ledger... These prefixes are now being discontinued in modern accounting systems.

35. Preceding the name of persons or groups who use a specified name or expression: in the language or usage of.

1922 P. S. O'HEGARTY *Terence MacSwiney* ii. 3 Terence James MacSwiney on the baptismal register, but Terry always to his friends and to Cork generally, was born in Cork City on March 28th, 1879. **1941** *Poor Souls' Friend* June 111 Her father, Edmund William Roe (Ted to his friends) was a man of character and great individuality. **1956** J. BRODRICK *St Ignatius Loyola* i. 12 In the Basque countries (to the Basques Euskalerria). **1970** *Outlook* Mar. 34 Owen Glyn Dwr—Glendower to the Anglo-Saxon—was the Welsh prince who made most of the mischief. **1977** *Transatlantic Rev.* LX. 118 Lindy (Miss Hoffmann to the kids) had to glide it back down to them.

B. To before an infinitive.

11. a. (*c*) *to let* used *absol.* as *sb.* Freq. applied *attrib.* to a board, sign, etc., indicating that premises are offered for rent.

1886 F. H. BURNETT *Little Lord Fauntleroy* xi. 174 He stopped opposite the empty house..staring at the 'To Let', and smoking his pipe. **1894** A. MORRISON *Martin Hewitt, Investigator* ii. 80 The three shops..appeared not yet to have been occupied. A dusty 'To Let' bill hung in each window. **1903** A. BENNETT *Truth about an Author* xv. 206 A To-let notice flourished suddenly in my front-garden. **1936** A. CHRISTIE *ABC Murders* vi. 46 A 'To Let' sign appeared in the windows. **1938** G. GREENE *Brighton Rock* III. iii. 122 A vista of To Let boards. **1976** J. BINGHAM *God's Defector* v. 54 One day they have hope, a basement, a letter-head, and the next their place is occupied by a 'To let' sign.

‖ **to** (tǫ), *sb.* Now *rare.* Pl. **to.** [Jap.] A Japanese unit of capacity equal to ten *sho*, equivalent to approximately 3·97 gallons (18·0 litres) or 0·496 bushel.

1871 A. B. MITFORD *Tales of Old Japan* II. 2 Each of these bags holds four tô (a tô is rather less than half an imperial bushel). **1884** *Murray's Handbk. Japan* (ed. 2) 18, 10 *shō* = 1 *to.* **1901** F. BRINKLEY *Japan* II. iii. 118 At the close of the sixteenth century,..the measure of capacity was exactly fixed, and its volume was called *tō*; ten *tō* (i.e. a sheaf of grain) being called a *koku.* **1956** R. J. SMITH in Cornell & Smith *Two Japanese Villages* 90 The most expensive *hōji*..costs a minimum of 4,000 *yen* (one *koku* of rice). The least expensive costs 1,000 *yen* (1 *tō* of rice). **1959** R. K. BEARDSLEY et al. *Village Japan* 488/2 *Tō*, measure of volume; about 4 gallons.

toa. (Earlier example.)

1792 W. BLIGH *Voy. South Sea* xii. 148 A wooden spear ..pointed with the toa wood. *Ibid.* xvi. 213 The soil is little other than sand, yet it produced small toa-trees.

‖ **toa**[2] (tōᵘ·ă). *N.Z.* [Maori.] A brave warrior.

1860 A. S. ATKINSON *Jrnl.* 25 Dec. in *Richmond-Atkinson Papers* (1960) I. 671 A remark of Manuka's was rather good—Maori chiefs (leaders) were toas & went out at the head of their men, Pakeha chiefs stayed in Town & ate biscuit. **1881** C. W. HURSTHOUSE *Let.* 12 June in *Ibid.* (1960) II. 486 Tuninia was a celebrated toa, and knew it. **1901** A. H. GRACE in D. M. Davin *N.Z. Short Stories* (1953) 19 You can imagine what joy it is to become the wife of such a brave *toa.* **1949** P. H. BUCK *Coming of Maori* (1950) III. i. 338 Those who had distinguished themselves in battle were termed *toa* and were usually of the *rangatira* class, for ruling chiefs had to lead in war as well as in peace.

toad, *sb.* Add: **3. b.** Applied to children. Cf. *TAD 2.

1836 T. C. HALIBURTON *Clockmaker* 1st Ser. xxvii. 178 Two little orphan children, the prettiest little toads I ever beheld. **1897** *Private Life of Queen* xi. 93 Jonathan Mace..had been a day labourer at Frogmore... He always spoke of the Queen's spirited sons as 'rare young toads'. **1954** M. SHARP *Gipsy in Parlour* IV. xxiv. 234 Why shouldn't 'ee wed the poor toad? **1958** 'MISS READ' *Storm in Village* iii. 38 If our Billy has the nightmares, I shan't wonder! Poor little toad, and him so high strung! **1981** V. CANNING *Boy on Platform One* vii. 108 I'll show you. Never seen a salmon! You poor little toad.

4. (Later example.)

1959 I. & P. OPIE *Lore & Lang. Schoolch.* x. 191 One who makes up to a teacher is recognized as being in a slightly different category from an outright sneak, although almost as nauseous. The usual epithets are 'toad' or 'toady', 'worms', 'crawler', or, in Camberwell, 'grease boy' or 'grease rat'.

6. a. For '*toad in a hole*: see quots.' read *toad in the* († *a*) *hole*: meat, now usu. sausages, baked in batter. (Later examples.)

1927 [see *SCHOONER *sb.*[1] 1 b]. **1934** *Cassell's Mod. Practical Cookery* 145/1 Put in the sausages. Season the batter,..and pour it over them. Put the toad-in-the-hole into a good, moderately hot oven. **1934** T. S. ELIOT *Rock* i. 40 Restaurants where you can get..sausage and mashed or toad-in-the-'ole for twopence. **1943** L. CHATTERTON *Mod. Cookery* 167/1 Toad in the hole without eggs... Milk,..flour,..bicarbonate of soda,..vinegar,..salt,.. sausages,..dripping... Small sausages are best.., or.. steak cut in two-inch pieces may be used. **1959** B. NILSON *Penguin Cookery Bk.* 330 Toad-in-the-hole is made like Yorkshire pudding, but 1lb. skinned sausages is heated in the fat for 5 minutes before adding the batter. **1971** *Guardian* 18 June 11/6 Although 'toad-in-the-hole' is an unprepossessing name it must be one of the few dishes which sounds even worse in French. I am sure no one would eat 'Le crapaud au trou'.

b. *toad in the hole*: a name applied to various games, esp. a form of hide-and-seek and a game in which lead discs are thrown at holes in a wooden structure.

1930 J. DOS PASSOS *42nd Parallel* 381 They got tired playing toad in the hole in the deep weeds. **1969** I. & P. OPIE *Children's Games* iv. 154 When played after dark, as is not unusual, it [*sc.* Hide-and-Seek] may have a special name, such as ..'Toad in the Hole' (Forfar). **1969** E. H. PINTO *Treen* 229 Toad-in-the-hole..probably originated in England in Tudor times. Since then, it has been played in many parts of the world, including Argentina, where it is known as *Sapo.* **1970** *Daily Tel.* 18 Mar. 15/6 Mr. P. N. Barnard's letter..about the 'charity game' known as toad in the hole..has provided me with a translation into English of this very old game which used to be played a great deal in France, where it is known as *tonneau.* **1975** *Country Life* 11 Dec. 1677/4, I am..looking for examples of the following regional inn sports:..twister (Suffolk), and toad in the hole (Sussex)... Every one of the games I have mentioned is actually played in English pubs today.

7. a. *toad-bellied* (later example), *-spotted* (later example).

1922 JOYCE *Ulysses* 465 Beside him stands Father Coffey, chaplain, toadbellied, wrynecked. **1915** W. OWEN *Let.* Apr. (1967) 331 It's Measles!... Bloody eyes—toad-spotted, raw-meat-coloured skin.

b. toad-cheese: (earlier example of form *toad's cheese*); **toad-frog,** (*b*) *U.S. dial.* = sense 1 a in Dict.; † **toadskin** *N. Amer. slang* (*obs.*), (*a*) a five-cent stamp; (*b*) a banknote; **toad-stabber** *slang* (chiefly *U.S.*), a large pocket-knife or jack-knife; **toad-sticker** *U.S. slang,* a large knife; formerly also, a sword; **toad-strangler** *U.S. dial.*, a heavy downpour of rain.

1853 J. LOUSLEY *Let.* 9 Jan. in *N. & Q.* (1962) Mar. 84/1 Toads cheeses are the poisenous Fungusses which grow in our hedgerows and woods. **1861** *Harper's Mag.* Aug. 421/1 Every body is a pitching into this matter like toad-frogs into a willow swamp. **1913** H. KEPHART *Our Southern Highlanders* xiii. 295 In the Smokies a toad is called a frog or a toad-frog. **1964** J. H. CLARKE *Harlem* 276 She just stood..swellin' up like a big toad frog. **1981** *Amer. Speech* LVI. 45 Toad-frog is Southern and Midland. **1867** F.-H. LUDLOW *Little Brother* 251 'Why, ma, don't you know what a toadskin is?' said Billy, drawing a dingy five-cent stamp from his pocket. 'Here's one... And don't I wish I had lots of 'em!' **1912** J. SANDILANDS *Western Canad. Dict. & Phrase-Bk.*, *Toadskin*, a dollar bill. Originally, in the States, a toadskin meant a five-cent stamp, and of a mean, grasping person it was said 'His purse is made of toad's skin.' **1926** Toadskin [see *IRON-MAN 1 c]. **1885** G. SWEETMAN *Gloss. Wincanton, Toad-stabber*,..a bad knife. **1915** S. LEWIS *Trail of Hawk* x. 102

Carl..pried open a class-room window with his large jack-knife..known as a 'toad-stabber'. **1938** W. SMITTER *F.O.B. Detroit* 48 'There you are,' said Russ, snapping the blade open. 'A regular toad-stabber of a thing.' **1858** *Calif. Spirit of Times* 7 Aug. 1/8 The Judge put his toad sticker atween his teeth, tuk a pistol in won hand, and a slung shot in the other, an sez thru his nose, 'cum on'. **1944** J. S. PENNELL *Hist. Rome Hanks* 293, I must have picked up this old toadsticker. **1938** M. K. RAWLINGS *Yearling* xix. 228 Hit's a toad-strangler of a rain. **1980** *Knoxville* (Tennessee) *News-Sentinel* 6 Apr. c4/5 'We say toad-strangler for a hard rain around here,' Farley said.

toad-fish. a. Substitute for second part of def.: also, a fish belonging to any of numerous other species of the family Tetraodontidæ, many of which are poisonous. (Further Austral. examples.)

1871 G. BENNETT in *N.S.W. Med. Gaz.* I. 176 (*title*) On the 'toad fish'..of New South Wales. **1923** *Med. Jrnl. Austral.* 1 Dec. 572/1 The toad fish belongs to the genus Tetraodon of which a number of species are known to be poisonous. **1974** [see *TOADO].

toadless (tō^u·dˌlės), *a.* [f. TOAD *sb.* + -LESS.] Devoid of toads.

1911 *Chambers's Jrnl.* July 435/2 When the garden was dug..it was toadless. **1922** M. TEMPLE *Shallowdale* iii. 39 No dog can be thoroughly happy in a toadless garden.

toado (tō^u·do). *Austral.* [f. TOAD(-FISH + *-O^2.] A poisonous puffer-fish of the family Tetraodontidæ.

1943 G. P. WHITLEY in *Bull. Council Sci. & Industrial Res.* (Australia) CLIX. 8 Australia alone has more than 30 different species of Toadoes. **1953** *Copeia* I. 32/2 The terms 'tetrodon', fugu, globefish, toad-fish, toado, and puffer poisoning are synonymous. **1965** *Courier-Mail* (Brisbane) 11 Sept. 2/1 Few fish in the sea..pack such deadly poison as the Toadoes. **1974** J. M. THOMSON *Fish of Ocean & Shore* xv. 162 The common toadfish or toado.. has a splotchy brown or green coat. *Ibid.*, The silver-cheeked toadfish or giant toado..attains a metre in length.

toa·dstool, *v. rare.* [f. the sb.] *intr.* To grow up like a toadstool; to expand or increase rapidly and objectionably. Cf. *MUSHROOM *v.* 4.

1939 R. CAMPBELL *Flowering Rifle* I. 14 As limply fungoid in the idle rich As when it grimly toadstools from a ditch. **1971** M. McCARTHY *Birds of America* 60 New little houses had toadstooled; they passed a trailer camp.

toa·dstooled, *a. rare.* [f. as prec. + -ED^2.] Overgrown with toadstools.

1910 KIPLING *Rewards & Fairies* 282 They hit an old toadstooled stump.

toadyish (tō^u·diˌiʃ), *a.* [f. TOADY *sb.* + -ISH^1.] Characteristic of or resembling a toady; meanly servile.

1909 in WEBSTER. **1955** M. COOPER in H. Van Thal *Fanfare for E. Newman* 50 A particularly toadyish begging letter. **1977** B. PYM *Quartet in Autumn* vi. 57 Only Marya, toadyish with her murmurs of 'such delicious coffee', accepted the offer.

toa grass, var. of *TWA(A-GRAS(S.

to and fro, *phr.* **D.** *adj.* (Earlier example.)

1749 J. CLELAND *Mem. Woman of Pleasure* I. 212 The sweet urgency of this to-and-fro friction.

toast, *sb.*^{1} Add: **1. a.** For 'Now *rare* or *Obs.* except as in b' read 'Now *rare* or *Obs.* except in India' and add later examples.

1838 DICKENS *Let.* 1 Feb. (1965) I. 366 We have had for breakfast, toasts, cakes, a yorkshire pie [etc.]. **1978** *Vishveshvaranand Indological Jrnl.* XVI. 218 He had stopped taking cereals after the age of sixty but after 85 he had to re-start on medical advice taking two toasts or some cornflakes.

b. (Earlier example of phr. *as warm as toast.*)

1855 A. S. STEPHENS *Old Homestead* i. 16 Every thing nice and warm as toast.

2. a. *French toast*: see *FRENCH *a.* 3.

c. Add to def.: *to have* (one) *on toast* (colloq.), to have (a person) at one's mercy or 'where one wants him'; to subject to anxiety (later examples). Also with other verbs.

1896 B. L. FARJEON *Betrayal of John Fordham* III. 288 'It's my night,' I sed. 'Didn't I tell yer? I've got 'im on toast.' **1916** E. F. BENSON *David Blaize* xiv. 285 To think that half an hour ago that little squirt thought he had us on toast. **1929** D. H. LAWRENCE *Pansies* 127 But Tolstoi was a traitor To the Russia that needed him most... He shifted his job on to the peasants And landed them all on toast. **1942** 'R. CROMPTON' *William Carries On* v. 119 Well, let's have 'em on toast for a bit wonderin' what's happened to him. **1964** J. CREASEY *Guilt of Innocence* xvii. 151, I think the time has come to tell the Press we want to interview him... That will get 'em both on toast. **1981** 'J. ASHFORD' *Loss of Culion* xix. 151 'You've been positively identified by Mr Barnard.'..'Then he's having you on toast.' 'He has no reason for lying.'

4. *toast-crumb* (example); **toast Melba**: see *MELBA.

1872 G. M. HOPKINS *Let.* 22 Mar. (1956) 55 If you say the Mahâbhârata is your toast-crumb ordinary breakfast book I am jaundiced all marigold under the eyes.

toast, *sb.*^{2} Add: **3. toast-master('s) glass,** a drinking-glass having a thick bowl on a tall stem and thus giving the impression of having greater capacity than it really has; **toast-mistress,** a female toast-master.

1916 J. H. YOXALL *Collecting Old Glass* ix. 63 (*heading*) Toastmaster glasses. **1919** M. PERCIVAL *Glass Collector* 162 Toast-masters' [*sic*] glasses are found in many varieties. **1969** *Canad. Antiques Collector* Oct. 25/1 The tiny, clear toastmaster glass was usually solid except for a narrow v-shaped depression at the top capable of holding a bare half-ounce of liquor. **1921** *Daily Colonist* (Victoria, B.C.) 7 Apr. 7/5 The toast mistress, Mrs. Sutton, referred in very complimentary terms to the naval lads and their splendid services during the war. **1979** *Arizona Daily Star* 5 Aug. J 6/1 She..has been picked as 'Toastmistress of the Year'.

toast (tō^{u}st), *sb.*^{3} Chiefly *U.S.* (and *W. Indies*). [Perh. f. TOAST *sb.*^{2}] **1.** A type of long narrative poem recited extempore by American and Caribbean Blacks.

1962 R. D. ABRAHAMS in A. Dundes *Mother Wit* (1973) 300/1 Many of them [*sc.* insults] take the form of rhymes or puns, signaling the beginning of the bloom of verbal dexterity which comes to fruition later in the long narrative poem called the 'toast'. **1972** T. KOCHMAN *Rappin' & Stylin' Out* 261 The best talkers from this group often become the successful streetcorner, barber shop, and pool hall storytellers who deliver the long, rhymed, witty narrative stories called 'toasts'. **1978** *Maledicta* II. 290 An extraordinary collection of black American folk poetry (*toasts*) collected by the author from lower-class black males (inmates of county jails, streetcorner gangs).

2. In reggae, a performance by a disc-jockey who speaks or shouts while playing a record.

1980 N. KIMBERLEY in J. Collis *Rock Primer* 249 The wedding of John Holt's sentimental singing and Roy's effervescent toast..show [*sic*] us the new musical idiom in full flower. **1983** *Listener* 19 May 22/3 Loud and bass-heavy 'dub' music with a patois talkover 'toast' booms into the bus.

toast, *v.*^{1} Add: **toasting-fork** (earlier example).

1807 SOUTHEY *Lett. from Eng.* I. xvii. 185 Pocket-toasting-forks have been invented, as if it were possible to want a toasting-fork in the pocket.

toast (tō^{u}st), *v.*^{3} [See *TOAST *sb.*^{3}] *trans.* and *intr.* In reggae, to accompany (music) by speaking or shouting. Freq. **toa·sting** *vbl. sb.*^{3}

1976 *New Musical Express* 17 Apr. 17/5 Another bass riff that cracks foundations, knocks down walls, and brushes aside nine stone weaklings, but this and all the dubwise trickery in Trenchtown can't hide the absolute ordinariness of Woosh's toasting. **1980** N. KIMBERLEY in J. Collis *Rock Primer* 249 Much of the strength of 'Your Ace From Space', 'Version Galore', etc, lies in the original rhythm which Roy toasts. **1980** *Times* 19 May 9/4 A group of young London blacks whose lives centre on their reggae music—the technology of sound systems, the virtuoso techniques of improvisational 'toasting'.

toaster^1. Add: **3.** An electric appliance for toasting bread; = *electric toaster* s.v. *ELECTRIC *a.* 2 b. See also *pop-up toaster* s.v. *POP-UP *a.* b.

1913 *Maclean's Mag.* Feb. 163/1 Electric cooking appliances—the shining nickel-plated or aluminum utensils, including coffee percolators, toasters, chafing dishes, each with its long connecting cord and plug for attachment to the electric light socket. **1948** *Clarke County Democrat* (Grove Hill, Alabama) 2 Dec. 4/4 Frigidaire Ranges, Water Heaters, Sunbeam Mixmasters, Toasters..are here. **1962** A. LURIE *Love & Friendship* x. 187 He has to have it quiet so he can fix our toaster for us. **1975** C. FREMLIN *Long Shadow* xi. 82 The second lot of crumpets were out of the toaster.

4. Special Comb.: **toaster-oven,** a small oven suitable for toasting, broiling, and baking.

1961 *Better Homes & Gardens* Sept. 74/2 Toasters come in family-fitting styles... New dual purpose styles: a toaster-oven and a toaster-broiler. **1976** *Woman's Day* (U.S.) Nov. 124 The island's taller side..houses a microwave oven, toaster-oven and..a waffle grill. **1980** *Redbook* Oct. 54/1 In the kitchen, use a small toaster-oven whenever possible rather than the main oven, particularly if the latter is electric.

toaster^3 (tō^u·stəɹ). [f. *TOAST *v.*^{3} + -ER^1.] In reggae, one who accompanies music by speaking or shouting.

1976 in Cassidy & Le Page *Dict. Jamaican Eng.* (1980) 507/2 The toaster has the microphone; he introduces the performers, comments, beats time and talks with the music—keeps things lively. **1977** *Melody Maker* 5 Feb. 16/2 New albums by two of Jamaica's most popular toasters. **1980** *Guardian* 6 Nov. 9/1 Blue..is a garage mechanic by day and a 'toaster' for a reggae group by night.

toast-rack. For '(quot. 1905)' read: a vehicle, esp. a tram, having full-width seats and (usu.) open sides; also *attrib.* (Later examples.)

1941 BAKER *Dict. Austral. Slang* 77 *Toastrack*, one of the old-style footboard trams still used in Sydney. **1957** *Railway Mag.* June 427/2 There are now 24 bogie motor cars and 25 bogie trailers. Toastrack and saloon types exist in both categories; the former, as befits a holiday line, are in the majority. **1966** P. MATHERS *Trap* 190 A tram now, it would be a toast-rack with ten or so compartments with the only physical intercommunication along the outside footboards, and the concertina doors. **1970** *Railway Mag.* Oct. 587/2 Only horse traction was used, and there were two four-wheel cars, a closed one for winter service, and an open 'toast-rack', used in the summer. **1976** *Country Life* 22 Jan. 191/4 Single-deck 'toast-rack' trams, so named because they closely resembled that table implement on wheels.

toasty, *a.* Add: (Earlier and later examples.) Now usu. *spec.*, warm and comfortable.

1890 BARRÈRE & LELAND *Dict. Slang* II. 357/1 *Toasty* (studios) is said of a picture painted in very warm tints. French painters call this *rôti.* **1961** WEBSTER, *Toasty*, pleasantly or comfortably warmed. **1970** *New Yorker* 19 Sept. 14/1 (Advt.), A smart, double-breasted coat... In soft wool melton with..a toasty wool interlining for cold weather. **1977** *Time* 14 Feb. 32/2 His toasty (75°) office on Kutuzovsky Prospekt. **1978** *Nieman-Marcus Xmas Bk.* 80/2 Natural shearling ear muffs keep ears toasty in the bitterest weather.

toatoa (tō^u·ătō^u:ă). *N.Z.* [a. Maori.] = *celery pine* s.v. *CELERY 2.

1831 G. BENNETT in *London Med. Gaz.* 12 Nov. 184/1 Toatoa, of the natives of New Zealand, is an unpublished species of Phyllocladus. **1845** E. J. WAKEFIELD *Adv. N.Z.* II. 120 The *toa toa*..is much prized by the natives for walking-sticks. **1910** L. COCKAYNE *N.Z. Plants* iii. 46 Confined to the north are..the toatoa (*Phyllocladus glaucus*) and some other trees. **1966** *Encycl. N.Z.* I. 730/1 In the same forests are rimu, tanekaha..and, in places, toatoa.

tobacco. Add: **1. b.** A fashion shade; cf. *TABAC *a.* Cf. sense 3 c below.

1923 *Daily Mail* 10 Jan. 1 Becoming Hat in good quality Petersham Ribbon... Colours: Grey, Cherry, Nigger, Tobacco, Peacock. *Ibid.* 5 June 6 In Pale and Mid Fawn,..Sky, Tobacco, Lemon. **1954** [see *ALIZARIN]. **1972** *Country Life* 7 Dec. (Suppl.) 24/2 Haroun Keshan [rug] with rich tobacco field. **1980** G. M. FRASER *Mr American* I. iii. 41 Socks, in the fashionable shades of tobacco, Leander, Wedgwood and crushed strawberry.

3. a. *tobacco bag, barn, field, -jar* (examples), *tin.* **b.** *tobacco-chewing* (earlier examples), *-growing* (example); *tobacco-chewer, -planter, trader* (example). **c.** *tobacco-brown* sb. and adj. (cf. sense 1 b above); *tobacco-coloured* adj. **d. tobacco baron** [*BARON 2 b, c], (*a*) *colloq.*, a powerful tobacco merchant or manufacturer; (*b*) *slang*, a prisoner who dominates his companions because he is able to sell tobacco to them (cf. quot. 1950 s.v. *BARON 2 c); **tobacco beetle** (examples); **tobacco dove,** substitute for def.: a small light brown ground-dove, *Columbina passerina,* native to central America; (example); **tobacco fly,** a hawk moth of the genus *Protoparce,* either *P. quinquemaculata* or *P. sexta,* the larva of which feeds on tobacco leaves; **tobacco-grater** (example); **tobacco housing** (see quot. 1965); **tobacco-leaf,** (*a*) see sense 3 a in Dict.; (*b*) used *attrib.* to designate eighteenth-century Chinese porcelain decorated with a floral pattern including tobacco-leaves; **tobacco lord** (now *Sc. Hist.*), a wealthy tobacco merchant of Glasgow; **tobacco mosaic virus,** the virus that causes mosaic disease in tobacco and similar effects in other plants, much used as an experimental subject; **Tobacco Road,** the title of a novel (1932) and play by Erskine Caldwell, used allusively with reference to conditions of extreme poverty, esp. in rural districts of the Southern U.S.; **tobacco-root,** also = VALERIAN 1; (earlier and later examples); **tobacco-shop** (later example); **tobacco streak,** a streak disease of tobacco (*STREAK *sb.*^{1} 6*); **tobacco worm,** substitute for def.: the larva of the tobacco fly; (earlier and later examples).

1643 R. WILLIAMS *Key into Lang. of America* vi. 44 Generally all the men throughout the countrey have a Tobacco-bag, with a pipe in it, hanging at their back. **1864** K. CUMMING *Jrnl. Hospital Life* (1866) 120/2, I hinted to some of the ladies about having tobacco bags made. **1961** L. VAN DER POST *Heart of Hunter* vii. 115 He poured the capsules into an empty canvas tobacco bag. **1877** G. W. BAGBY *Old Virginia Gentleman* (1910) 3 Where is your plank to come from, and your logs for new cabins and tobacco barns? **1971** *Country Life* 22 July 214/2 (*caption*) The tobacco barns are a characteristic feature of the landscape. **1961** *Spectator* 7 July 5/1 The brewers and the 'tobacco barons', who had recently raised their prices. **1964** *Daily Tel.* 15 Jan. 15/1 Powers to limit the activities of prison 'tobacco barons' are provided in modernised prison and Borstal rules. **1896, 1959** Tobacco beetle [see *cigarette beetle* s.v. *CIGARETTE 2]. **1908** *Sears, Roebuck Catal.* 437/1 We can furnish plain brocaded velour in solid color of myrtle green, deep red or tobacco brown. **1940** R. CHANDLER *Farewell, my Lovely* xiii. 99 She was wearing a tobacco-brown suit. **1977** Tobacco-brown [see *SMOKING *vbl. sb.* 2 c]. *a* **1832** F. TROLLOPE *Notebk.* in *Dom. Manners Amer.* (1949) 421 Doom to worse than death the spitter and tobacco chewer. *Ibid.*, Whether a tobacco-chewing age preceded that of Anacreon, my books do not say. **1972** D. BLOODWORTH *Any Number can Play* xiii. 113 A tobacco-coloured dress of coarse linen. **1954** SMILEY & WHITE *Hurricane Road* xi. 97 Blackbirds, tobacco doves, and a roseate tern fluttered about in bewilderment. **1852** J. B. Jones *Adventures Col. Vanderbomb* 46 They rode by a large tobacco field. **1981** B. Healey *Week of Scorpion* vi. 112 They turned aside along a quieter lane between tobacco fields. [**1688** *Phil. Trans. R. Soc.* XVII. 947 There be various Accidents and Distempers, whereunto Tobacco is liable, as the Worm, the Flie,..and the like.] **1807** Tobacco fly [in Dict.]. **1904** E. Glasgow *Deliverance* 126 It was..mid-August—the time of the harvest moon and the dreaded tobacco fly. **1962** Metcalf & Flint *Destructive & Useful Insects* (ed. 4) xiii. 594 The parent 'tobacco flies', or hawk moths,..lay the eggs of the hornworm. *a* **1877** Knight *Dict. Mech.* III. 2583/1 *Tobacco-grater*, a machine for grinding tobacco into small pieces suitable for smoking in pipes. **1824** *Deb. Congress U.S.* 13 Apr. (1856) 2324 The effect of this measure on the cotton, rice, and tobacco-growing States will be pernicious in the extreme. **1960** *Encounter* Feb. 31/1 Those [G.I.s] who live in the semi-luxury of on-base 'tobacco' housing. **1965** *New Society* 22 Apr. 5/3 'Tobacco housing' constructed with sterling funds from sales of American tobacco in England. **1775** J. Lovell *Let.* 26 June in *Essex Inst. Hist. Coll.* (1875) XIII. 186, 1 Tobacco Jar; 1 Large Lead.ⁿ d.° **1857** T. B. Gunn *N.Y. Boarding-Houses* 26 Hair-brush and tobacco-jar jumbled among your shirt-collars. **1967** M. Kenyon *Whole Hog* xxv. 252 A tobacco jar bounced..to the floor, where it exploded into fragments. **1969** *Times* 25 Feb. 12/5 A magnificent tobacco leaf dinner service of 96 pieces. **1976** *Times* 27 July 14/5 A famille rose tobacco leaf part service, painted with a lady punting a lotus leaf of flowers. **1832** J. Cleland *Enumeration Inhabitants of Glasgow* 258 When any of the most respectable master tradesmen of the city had occasion to speak to a tobacco lord, he required to walk on the other side of the street till he was fortunate enough to meet his eye. **1975** T. M. Devine (*title*) The tobacco lords. **1914** *Bull. U.S. Dept. Agric.* No. 40. 15, 15 healthy tobacco plants..were inoculated with tobacco mosaic virus. **1947** *Ann. Rev. Microbiol.* I. 87 Ordinary tobacco mosaic virus consists of submicroscopic, rod-shaped particles..composed chiefly of nucleoprotein and possessing a high degree of resistance to heat, desiccation and deleterious chemicals. **1970** Passmore & Robson *Compan. Med. Stud.* II. xviii. 93/2 Plant viruses, such as tobacco mosaic virus (TMV), are more easily studied than animal viruses. **1775** *Amer. Husbandry* I. 66 Those who have dealings with London.. are the tobacco and rice planters. **1838** *Southern Lit. Messenger* IV. 197 A fine old specimen of the real Virginia tobacco planter, a half domesticated son of France. **1937** *Harper's Mag.* Nov. 566/1 Nobody in his senses wants slums, Tobacco Roads, and undernourished, ragged schoolchildren in a land of potential economic plenty. **1961** Tobacco Road [see *over-exploit *v.*]. **1845** J. C. Frémont *Rep. Exploring Exped.* 135, I ate here, for the first time, the *kooyah*, or tobacco root, (*valeriana edulis*). **1919** E. L. Sturtevant *Notes Edible Plants* 589 Tobacco Root. Valerian. Ohio to Wisconsin and westward. **1974** J. Aiken *Midnight is Place* v. 145, I have sold some [cigar] ends..to a man in a tobacco-shop. **1936** Tobacco streak [see *streak *sb.*[1] 6*]. **1968** *Times* 3 Oct. 13/5 Tobacco streak virus, so called because of the symptoms it produces in tobacco plants, infects a wide variety of plants, including French beans, peas and clover. **1930** J. S. Huxley *Bird-Watching & Bird Behaviour* v. Plate VII, A Black-headed gull contentedly brooding a tobacco-tin which has been substituted for its eggs. **1975** M. Bradbury *History Man* ix. 153 Ashtrays have been stolen, and replaced by..tobacco tins. **1840** *Picayune* (New Orleans) 13 Sept. 3/1 The same Mac..[is] well known to the Western country Tobacco Traders. [**1688** Tobacco worm: see *tobacco fly* above.] **1737** J. Brickell *Nat. Hist. N. Carolina* 168 The Tobacco-worm..has two sharp horns on its Head. **1872** *Rep. Vermont Board Agric.* I. 319 The large night-flying moths..produce the large larvæ, as the potato-worm and the tobacco-worm. **1962** Metcalf & Flint *Destructive & Useful Insects* (ed. 4) xiii. 594 The best known of tobacco insects..are the large green tobacco worms with white bars on the sides and a slender horn at the end of the body.

tobacco-box. **2.** For *Pomotis* read *Lepomis*. (Examples.)

1877 C. Hallock *Sportsman's Gazetteer* I. 379 Black Perch, sometimes called 'tobacco-box'; found in ponds. **1903** *Outing* Apr. 134/1 He is content to lure to the surface..the 'sunny', 'tobacco box', or 'pumpkin seed'. **1913** A. Douglas *Fast Nine* 150 The commonest and smallest skate of the Eastern coast of the United States is the 'Tobacco Box'.

tobacconalian, *a.* (Earlier example.)

1835 J. H. Ingraham *South-West by Yankee* I. viii. 89 Every other gentleman we met was enveloped in a cloud, not of bacchanalian, but tobacconalian incense.

Tobagonian (tŏbēⁱgōᵘ·niăn), *sb.* and *a.* [f. *Tobago* (see below and etym. of Tobacco) + -*n*- + -ian.] **A.** *sb.* A native or inhabitant of Tobago, an island in the West Indies, part of the nation of Trinidad and Tobago. **B.** *adj.* Of or pertaining to Tobago.

1955 *Caribbean Q.* IV. ii. 158 The Tobagonian says *is go ah goin'* (it's go I'm going). **1957** C. MacInnes *City of Spades* ii. xiii. 189 Word will reach the ear of this Tobagonian owner and I lose my good job. **1962** *Times* 31 Aug. (Trinidad Suppl.) p. iv/5 There are more Tobagonians living in Trinidad than in Tobago. **1972** [see *ring-play* s.v. *ring *sb.*[1] 18 a]. **1974** *Trinidad Guardian* (Port-of-Spain) 16 Oct. 24/9 Trinidadians and Tobagonians have an outstanding record in bodybuilding.

to-be. Add: **B.** (Later examples.) Esp. following sbs. of kinship, as *grandfather-*, *wife-to-be*; see also *mother-to-be* s.v. *mother *sb.*[1] 16 a.

1930 A. Bennett *Imperial Palace* lxix. 581 The excited grandfather-to-be. **1969** L. Hellman *Unfinished Woman* xii. 174 The so-called good life for us is the to-be-good life for them. **1973** H. Nielsen *Severed Key* iii. 33 My wife-to-be is going to be fabulously successful.

tober (tōᵘ·bəɹ). *Showmen's slang.* Also **tobur.** [a. Shelta; see Toby *sb.*[2]] The site occupied by a circus, fair, or market.

1890 Barrère & Leland *Dict. Slang* II. 357/2 *Tobur, toba* (showmen, &c.), the ground or field at fairs, hired to put the waggons on for show or circuses, or other *al fresco* entertainments, which does not amount to much, so that a man or manager is considered very hard up if he has not enough to pay the *tobur*. Gypsy *tober*, the road, hence ground. **1933** E. Seago *Circus Company* vi. 85 How can I walk about the tober without me trousers, I'd be askin' ye? **1939** J. B. Priestley *Let the People Sing* x. 256 'It's not a bad tober—but what's 'is bunce?'..'It's all fair-ground slang... Micky..said this wasn't a bad market here, but what had Knocker made?' **1957** *Times Lit. Suppl.* 6 Dec. 742/1 She lived with it [*sc.* a circus] for some time as a privileged outsider, parking her caravan on the tober, as the site is called. **1968** [see *joint *sb.* 14 b].

tobermorite (tōᵘbəɹmōᵊ·rəit). *Min.* [f. *Tobermory*, name of a village on the Isle of Mull, Scotland + -ite[1].] A hydrated, basic calcium silicate occurring as masses of pale pinkish white translucent orthorhombic crystals.

1880 M. F. Heddle in *Mineral. Mag.* IV. 119 Tobermorite. This is a zeolite which I first found filling small druses in the cliffs of the shore immediately to the north of the pier of Tobermory in the Island of Mull. **1962** *Engineering* 3 Aug. 137 All tobermorites, natural or synthetic, are layer crystals having some similarity to vermiculite. **1978** *Mineral. Mag.* XLII. 229/1 Tobermorite minerals vary in some properties, most notably in whether loss of molecular water is accompanied by unidimensional lattice shrinkage... Tobermorites that show this lattice shrinkage have come to be called 'normal' and ones that do not, 'anomalous'.

Tobias night (tobəi·ăs nəit). [tr. G. *Tobiasnacht*, which alludes to Tobit viii. 1–3.] (See quots.) Cf. *Toby-night* s.v. *toby *sb.*[1] 6.

1960 C. Winick *Dict. Anthropol.* 539/1 *Tobias nights*, in the Catholic church, postponing the consummation of a marriage for several nights. **1975** *Amer. Speech 1973* XLVIII. 73 One need not go all the way back to Semitic antiquity..nor to the derivative nineteenth-century Swiss and German custom of the 'Tobiasnächte', the 'Tobias nights', in which the next of kin slept between the newlyweds for the first three nights of marriage to protect them at a time when their resistance to evil would be at its lowest ebb.

toboggan, *sb.* Add: **2. c.** *U.S. slang.* A rapid decline, a progression towards disaster. Usu. in phr. *on the toboggan*.

1910 E. A. Walcott *Open Door* xii. 153 Do you remember the time I got Conny Mulnix off, when the police had him on the toboggan for the Kinsley affair? **1947** *Christian Cent.* 20 Aug. 999/1 The United States is sliding down the toboggan with 75 per cent of the south a negroid population. **1950** J. Dempsey *Championship Fighting* 197 A veteran of thirty or thirty-one who is on the 'toboggan'. **1978** J. A. Michener *Chesapeake* 853 My daughter Clara's a little younger than you. For three years she's been on one hell of a toboggan.

2*. *U.S.* A long woollen cap. Cf. *toboggan-cap*, in Dict. and Suppl.

1929 *Amer. Speech* V. 152 *Toboggan*, a woolen cap. 'Take off your toboggan.' **1948** *Pacific Spectator* Winter 83 He had on faded overalls with new blue patches on the knees, and a sweater under the overalls, and a knitted blue toboggan on his head, against the cold. **1975** *Raleigh* (N. Carolina) *News & Observer* 6 Jan. 24/4 He [*sc.* a burglar] was wearing a red toboggan and tight pants, police said.

3. *toboggan-cap* (examples), *club* (earlier example), *-sleigh* (example); **toboggan-chute** (examples); **toboggan-slide** (earlier example).

1884 *Brandon* (Manitoba) *Blade* 21 Feb. 9/2 The several Toboggan Slides were illuminated every evening. **1890** *Silverton* (Colorado) *Miner* 1 Mar. 3/2 During the storm, the big tree on Anvil, which was generally known as the starting point for snow shoers and the toboggan club, was blown down. **1902** *Sears, Roebuck Catal.* 1159/3 Toboggan Caps or Toques. **1902** A. C. Laut *Story of Trapper* xiv. 196 Wrapping her husband in robes on the long toboggan sleigh, the squaw placed her younger child beside him and with the other began tramping through the forest drawing the sleigh behind. **1913** W. P. Eaton *Barn Doors & Byways* 223 One road runs along the ridge, the other plunges over it and crosses the intervale like the smooth, straight drop of a great toboggan chute. **1928** *Chicago Tribune* 11 June 10/5 Women and children in winter wore toboggan caps which wrapped two or three times around the neck and hung about a yard down the back. **1936** J. H. Street *Look Away!* xiii. 91 Tiller wore a faded green coat, woolen stockings, and a toboggan cap. **1964** *Globe & Mail* (Toronto) 15 Dec. 32/3 Winter fun-seekers will take to..two new toboggan chutes.

toboggan, *v.* Add: (Earlier example.) **tobogganing** *vbl. sb.* (earlier example).

1846 E. Warburton *Hochelaga* I. v. 68 They tarbogginned, slid, and trudged about merrily in the deep dry snow. **1849** J. E. Alexander *L'Acadie* I. 186 An amusement of which Canadian boys, and sometimes ladies too, are passionately fond..is called 'toboggoning'.

tobogganer. (Earlier example.)

1878 *Canad. Gentleman's Jrnl.* 8 Mar. 1/5 In fact, there has been so little snow this winter that the tobogganers have not had a good time.

Tobralco (tobræ·lko). [f. the name of *To*otal *Br*oadhurst *L*ee *Co*mpany, Limited, the manufacturers.] The proprietary name of a type of cotton fabric.

1910 *Westm. Gaz.* 25 Jan. 9/3 (Advt.), 'Tobralco', a new material, made in White, Ecru, and Black. **1917** *Trade Marks Jrnl.* 26 Sept. 942 *Tobralco*... Textile fabrics (not included in other Classes) made from substances covered by Class 50, but not including Incandescent Gas Mantles and not including any goods of a like kind... Tootal Broadhurst Lee Company, Limited, 56, Oxford Street, Manchester, manufacturers and merchants. **1932** D. C. Minter *Modern Needlecraft* 250 *Kimono Pinafore*... Gingham, zephyr, tobralco. **1961** D. Stuart *Driven* xx. 200 The agent was a middle-aged man, sharp and alert, clean-shaven, in gaberdines and Tobralco shirt.

tobramycin (tǫbrăməi·sin). *Pharm.* [f. *to-* (of unkn. origin) + L. *tene*)*brā*(*rius* belonging to darkness (see def.), f. *tenebræ* darkness: see *-mycin.] An antibiotic related to streptomycin that is produced by the fungus *Streptomyces tenebrarius* and is active mainly against Gram-negative bacteria, being used esp. to treat *Pseudomonas* infections.

1971 *Appl. Microbiol.* XXII. 1147/2 Factor 6 of the nebramycin complex was originally given the generic name of ebbramycin in 1970. Subsequently, its official generic designation was changed to tobramycin. **1977** *Lancet* 19 Mar. 655/2 She had a *Pseudomonas æruginosa* skin infection which responded rapidly to tobramycin and carbenicillin. **1980** [see *ticarcillin].

toby, *sb.*[1] Add: **4.** In full *toby tub*. (Earlier and later examples.)

1842 *London Jrnl. Arts & Sci.* XIX. 35 The printing [of the fabric] is to be done in an ordinary machine or press, the colours being furnished from what is called the 'toby tub'. **1881** *Instructions to Census Clerks* (1885) 43 Toby and Rainbow Tub Maker.

5. (Earlier example.)

1894 T. B. Searight *Old Pike* 144 They [*sc.* cheap cigars] became very popular with the drivers, and were at first called Conestoga cigars; since, by usage, corrupted into 'stogies' and 'tobies'.

6. *Toby-night* = *Tobias night.

1910 T. M. Parrott *Chapman's Plays & Poems* I. 699 The custom..is the well-known 'Toby-night', or 'nights', ordained as a rule of the Church by the Council at Carthage, A.D. 398. The rule was authorized by the example of Tobith (Toby), who spent the first three nights of his marriage in prayer.

7. *Austral. slang.* A stick of ochre used for marking sheep which have not been shorn to the owner's satisfaction.

1912 in Stewart & Keesing *Old Bush Songs* (1957) 273 I've been shearing on the Goulburn side and down at Douglas Park, Where every day 'twas 'Wool away!' and toby did his work. **1964** H. P. Tritton *Time means Tucker* 41 Raddle was a stick of blue or yellow ochre, also called 'Toby'. **1965** J. S. Gunn *Terminol. Shearing Indust.* ii. 11 The raddle stick was also called 'Toby', and its improper use was one of the main reasons for the formation of the first Shearers' Union.

8. (With capital initial.) The name of a stock character of American comedy (see quot. 1961), used *attrib.*, esp. in *Toby show*.

1946 *Theatre Arts* Nov. 652/1 Young actors who have played juveniles or ingenues with a Toby show seldom succumb to first-night nerves in later years. **1961** Bowman & Ball *Theatre Language* 393 *Toby*,..a comic character type, a boisterous, blundering yokel as the protagonist. Hence *Toby play* (or *show*), a repertory favorite. **1964** *Tennessee Folklore Soc. Bull.* June 49 Bisbee's Comedians..is one of the two surviving Toby Shows left in the entire country. **1967** *Oxf. Compan. Theatre* (ed. 3) 949/1 Most travelling dramatic tent-shows, playing one-week stands in rural communities, feature a Toby-comedian. *Ibid.*, Frederick R. Wilson, member of a touring tent-show company known as Horace Murphy's Comedians, was the first of a long line of actors to specialize in Toby roles. *Ibid.*, Toby-comedy includes generous use of the topical 'ad-lib'. **1978** *Chicago* June 56/2 We thought this [*sc.* donkey baseball] had gone the way of the Toby shows.

9. *Angling.* (With capital initial.) A type of lure used in spinning.

1969 V. Canning *Queen's Pawn* i. 2 The river would be high... No use for a fly. He wanted..a few small Tobies for spinning. *Ibid.* 3 He bought some..four-gram golden Tobies, and the rod. **1973** A. Ross *Dunfermline Affair* 139 Bayne's biggest lure—a six-inch metal Toby with a big triple hook.

toby, *sb.*[2] Add: *toby concern* (example); *low toby* (earlier example); *toby-gill* (earlier example).

1807 *Sessions' Papers* Feb. 133/1 He..asked me if I had any objection of being in a good thing... I asked him when and..he replied it was *low* toby, meaning a fotpad [*sic*] robbery. **1811** *Lexicon Balatronicum* s.v. *galloper*, The toby gill clapped his bleeders to his galloper. **1830** Lytton *Paul Clifford* I. iv. 76, I heered as ow Long Ned started for Hampshire this werry morning on a toby consarn!

toc (tǫk). Also **tock.** Used for *t* in telecommunication codes and in the oral transliteration of coded messages. Cf. *toc emma, *Toc H.

1898 [see *ack]. **1913** [see *pip *sb.* 4]. **1944** K. Douglas *Alamein to Zem Zem* (1946) xvii. 100 This means they are hopelessly broken down and want the technical adjutant, known officially over the wireless as 'Tock Ack', to arrange their recovery.

toccatina (tǫkătī·nă). *Mus.* [a. It., dim. of TOCCATA.] A short toccata. Also **toccatella** (-e·lă).

1740 J. GRASSINEAU *Mus. Dict.* 284 Toccatina, a small research when we have not time to perform it in all its parts. **1889** GROVE *Dict. Mus.* IV. 130/1 Dupont has published a little pf. piece entitled Toccatella. *Ibid.*, The same composer [*sc.* Rheinberger] has used the diminutive term Toccatina for one of a set of short pieces. **1938** *Oxf. Compan. Mus.* 937/1 Widor in his seventh Organ Symphony has a toccatina—a sort of *Perpetuum Mobile.*

toc emma (tǫk e·mă). *Mil. slang.* Also **tock** (and **toch**) **emma** and with capital initials. [Representing T.M. (see *T 6); see *TOC, *EMMA.] A trench mortar. Also *transf.*

1916 *B.E.F. Times* 1 Dec. f. 3/1 Completely oblivious of the dangers I encountered from our own artillery and Tock Emmas! **1918** J. H. DOUGLAS *Captured* ii. 25 He turned out to be Bombardier 'Chuck' Gibson who was with the sixty-pound 'Tock Emma' (Trench Mortar) Battery located on our frontage. **1928** R. C. SHERRIFF *Journey's End* (1929) II. ii. 57 Can't have men out there while the toch-emmas are blowing holes in the Boche wire. **1931** [see *EMMA].

Toc H (tǫk ēitʃ). [Representing T.H., initials of *T*albot *H*ouse (see sense 1 below), which was so called in memory of Gilbert W. L. Talbot (d. 1915); see *TOC.] **1.** Colloq. abbrev. of the name of *Talbot House*, a rest-house and club for soldiers opened at Poperinghe, 15 Dec. 1915.

1918 in P. B. Clayton *Tales Talbot House* (1919) 138 Owing to the inconsiderate retirement of our old neighbours, the Boche, Toc. H. is in a pretty fix. **1925** FRASER & GIBBONS *Soldier & Sailor Words* 286 Poperinghe..was visited by thousands of officers and men, for practically every one of whom 'Toc H', with its unique atmosphere and surroundings, proved alike a club and a home from home.

2. An association, orig. of ex-servicemen, founded by the Rev. P. T. B. Clayton after the war of 1914–18 to embody Christian fellowship and service.

1920 *Christmas Spirit 'Toc. H.' Ann.* 77 (*heading*) Toc. H. *Late* Talbot House. *Ibid.*, To open the club houses, Toc. H. asks for sympathy and help in many practical forms... H.R.H. The Prince of Wales has consented to open the H.Q. Club in London in 1921. **1930** *Toc H Jrnl.* Jan. 3 Toc H will indeed begin..to be..a power making for righteousness. **1954** P. TOYNBEE *Friends Apart* i. 17, I intended to work in a Toc H settlement. **1981** J. BRABAZON *Dorothy L. Sayers* xix. 241 An Anglican priest, chaplain to the Toc H hostel where I was staying.

3. *Toc H lamp*: an oil lamp, an emblem of Toc H, used *iron.* as a type of dimness.

1977 *New Statesman* 9 Sept. 341/1 'He is as dim as a Toc H Lamp'..is not yet rare as a phrase though members of the Toc H organisation may well be thin on the ground. **1977** J. PORTER *Who the Heck is Sylvia?* v. 46 Sometimes you can be dimmer than a Toc H lamp.

Tocharian (tǫkēə·riăn, -āriăn), *a.* and *sb.* Also **Tokharian.** [ad. F. *tocharien* (or next), f. Gr. Τοχάροι (Strabo) a Central Asiatic people formerly thought to speak Tocharian; see -IAN.] **A.** *adj.* Of, pertaining to, or designating an extinct Indo-European language spoken in the latter half of the first millennium A.D., of which remains have been discovered in Chinese Turkestan. **B.** *sb.* This language; also, a member of the people or peoples speaking the language.

Two dialects of Tocharian are recognized: an eastern, *Tocharian A* (= *TURFANIAN), and a western, *Tocharian B* (= *KUCHAEAN, KUCHEAN).

1927 PEAKE & FLEURE *Peasants & Potters* 134 The Tocharian language of parts of Turkestan. **1934** A. TOYNBEE *Study of Hist.* I. i. iii. 113 One isolated language in the far north-east (the now extinct 'Tokharian', which has become known to Western scholars through the discovery..of documents in this language.) **1950** *Trans. Philol. Soc. 1949* 9 The system of *r*-endings found in the verbal paradigms of various I[ndo-] E[uropean] languages ..is clearly attested in Hittite, Indo-Iranian, Tocharian, Phrygian and Armenian, Italic, Celtic. **1960** PARTRIDGE *Charm of Words* 170 The *-k-* variation attested by Lett *aka*, a water-spring, and Hittite *eku-*, to drink, and dubiously Tokharian *yoko*, (a) thirst, should perhaps be aligned with certain OE and ON *-g-* words. **1966** G. S. LANE in Birnbaum & Puhvel *Anc. Indo-European Dial.* 218 If we could ever find out what non-Indo-European influence brought about the distinction in gender in A, we might know considerably more about the wanderings and contacts of the 'Tocharians'. **1975** *Language* LI. 141 Tocharian *-tsi*..is regularly added to a verbal stem, the present stem in East Tocharian and the subjunctive stem in West Tocharian. **1977** *Word 1972* XXVIII. 1 We have on one side Latin and Keltic, on the other Indo-Aryan, Iranian ..and Tocharian.

Tocharish (tǫkā·riʃ, -ēəriʃ). Also **Tokharish.** [ad. G. *tocharisch*; see *TOCHARIAN *a.* and *sb.*, -ISH¹.] The Tocharian language.

1910 *Encycl. Brit.* II. 712/2 Up to 1909 only a preliminary account had been given of Tocharish, a hitherto unknown Indo-European language. **1926** J. R. R. TOLKIEN in *Year's Work in Eng. Stud. 1924* 27 The traditional Indo-European philology has suffered shocks in recent years, shocks from Tokharish and Hittite that begin at last to be felt even by the inexpert. **1939** [see *KUCHAEAN, KUCHEAN]. **1956** J. WHATMOUGH *Language* ix. 179 Irish and Welsh have a middle or passive voice in *-r*, analogies to which are known in Hittite, Phrygian, Tocharish, Latin, [etc.].

tochilinite (tǫ̈tʃi·linəit). *Min.* [ad. Russ. *tochilinit* (N. I. Organova et al. 1971, in *Zap. Vsesoyuznogo Min. Obshch.* C. 477), f. the name of M. S. *Tochilin* (1910–55), Russian geologist: see -ITE¹.] A mineral that is a complex of iron sulphide and magnesium and iron hydroxides, found as bronze-black grains and fibrous aggregates.

1973 *Mineral. Abstr.* XXIV. 186/2 A new mineral tochilinite..occurs in two habit modifications. **1976** *Papers Geol. Survey Canada* No. 76-1B. 66/1 Tochilinite is associated with clear and white calcites, some of which are coarse euhedral crystals.

tochus (tōu·χəs, tǫ·χəs). *slang* (chiefly *Jewish* and *N. Amer.*). Also **tochas** (-ess, etc.), **tuchus** (tu·χəs), **-as**; *Anglicized* **tokus** (tōu·kəs), **tocus**, etc. [ad. Yiddish *tokhes*, ad. Heb. *taḥaṯ* beneath.] The backside, buttocks; the anus.

1914 *Dialect Notes* IV. 114 *Tookis, n.*, the anus:—said to be of Jewish origin. Also *tukis.* **1930** M. GOLD *Jews without Money* 250 I'll spit in his face..and tell him to kiss my *tochess* for his rent. **1934** J. T. FARRELL *Young Manhood of Studs Lonigan* i. 11 He was hurtled forwards by three swift kicks in the tocus. **1938** J. CURTIS *They drive by Night* xxiv. 269, I could do three months on me tochas. **1951** B. SCHULBERG *Disenchanted* xvii. 308, I don't go for all these fancy conferences and I don't kiss anybody's tochis. **1952** W. R. BURNETT *Vanity Row* v. 43, I was.. getting my tokus pinched all over the place. **1963** 'R. L. PIKE' *Mute Witness* (1965) iv. 59 They call this stuff Sun-Bay Tinge... I'd call it Tuchus Pink myself. **1973** *Kingston* (Ontario) *Whig-Standard* 22 Dec. 7/3 Now get your tokus off my beat. You want to get killed go over on the next beat. **1975** R. H. RIMMER *Premar Experiments* (1976) i. 99 Your tuchas is smiling sideways at me.

tock (tǫk), *v.* [Echoic; cf. TICK-TOCK.] *intr.* To make a sound similar to TICK *sb.*³ 2, but slightly lower and therefore more resonant. Esp. of a clock, and in phr. *to tick and tock.*

1913 J. MASEFIELD *Daffodil Fields* 72 A stately timepiece ticked and tocked. **1917** S. GRAHAM *Priest of Ideal* xxxi. 306 The comfortable grandfather clock ticked and tocked temperamentally. **1961** H. R. F. KEATING *Rush on Ultimate* iv. 69 There were tears in her eyes as Sebastian's second ball tocked against the peg. **1967** T. KENEALLY *Bring Larks & Heroes* iv. 24 Their ears, drenched by the south wind, tocked like clocks, thumped like sails. **1970** W. BROWN in Ramchand & Gray *West Indian Poetry* (1972) 14 The clock tocked and the stable dried.

toco². Substitute for etym.: [ad. Hindi *ṭhōko*, imp. of *ṭhoknā* beat, thrash.] Replace quot. 1823 and add: Also *fig.* and in phr. *to get toco for yam.*

1823 'J. BEE' *Slang* s.v., Yams are food for negroes in the West-Indies,..and if, instead of receiving his proper ration of these, Blackee gets a whip (*toco*) about his back, why 'he has caught *toco*' instead of yam. **1848** J. R. PLANCHÉ *Theseus & Ariadne* (1859) I. ii. 14 Toco from my father I instead of yam shall get. **1885** W. S. GILBERT *Mikado* i. 16 To embrace you thus, *con fuoco*, Would distinctly be no gioco, And for yam I should get toco. **1910** KIPLING *Let.* in Ld. Birkenhead *R. Kipling* (1978) xvi. 252 The Teuton..prepares to give us toko when he feels good and ready. **1921** [see *BOLSHY, BOLSHIE]. **1941** J. CARY *Herself Surprised* lviii. 143 You'd better tell people how I took your trousers down last time and gave you toko.

tocopherol (tǫkǫ·fĕrǫl). *Biochem.* [f. Toco- + Gr. φέρ-ειν to bear + -OL.] Vitamin E: any or all of a group of closely related fat-soluble compounds that occur esp. in plant oils and are anti-oxidants essential in the diets of many animals and probably of man.

1936 H. M. EVANS in *Jrnl. Biol. Chem.* CXIII. 321 For this alcohol we propose the name 'α-tocopherol'. **1956** *Nature* 14 Jan. 86/2 (*heading*), η-Tocopherol (7-methyltocol): a new tocopherol in rice. **1968** PASSMORE & ROBSON *Compan. Med. Stud.* I. x. 9/1 Vitamin E is a mixture of tocopherols, which are yellow oily liquids remarkably stable to heat. **1972** *Daily Colonist* (Victoria, B.C.) 13 Feb. 27/4 Glib armchair vitamin experts discuss tocopherol, the chemical name of Vitamin E, as easily as they talked of ascorbic acid and riboflavin two years ago. **1979** *Nature* 19 Apr. 737/2 Vitamin E (α-tocopherol) and vitamin C (ascorbic acid) react rapidly with organic free radicals, and it is widely accepted that the antioxidant properties of these compounds are responsible in part for their biological activity.

tocusso (toku·so). Also **tocussa.** [a. Amharic.] A name used in Ethiopia for finger millet, *Eleusine coracana*, the ear of which is composed of several spikes resembling the fingers of a hand.

1790 J. BRUCE *Trav. Source of Nile* V. 79 In place of Teff..there grows a black grain called Tocusso. **1866** LINDLEY & MOORE *Treas. Bot.* II. 1154/2 Tocusso. An Abyssinian corn-plant or millet. **1875** *Encycl. Brit.* I. 63/1 The low grounds produce also a kind of corn known as *tocussa*, of which a black bread is made.

tod (tǫd), *sb.*⁴ *slang.* [Short for *Tod* Sloan (occas. used in full), name of a U.S. jockey (1874–1933), used as rhyming slang for 'own' in the phr. *on one's own.*] *on one's tod*: alone, on one's own. Cf. *PAT MALONE.

1934 P. ALLINGHAM *Cheapjack* vi. 56 'Are you on your tod?' I gathered that she was asking me if I was on my own. **1956** L. GODFREY in *Pick of Today's Short Stories* 91, I was in a small ward, and one evening some clot turned on the bloomin' wireless, and then went out, leaving me on my tod. **1959** J. WAIN *Travelling Woman* 7 Frequent visits to town on your Tod Sloan—no need to account for your doings. Leave her to keep the home fires burning. **1966** T. E. B. CLARKE *Wide Open Door* xi. 156 I'm on me Tod 'cept for the baby. **1972** J. BROWN *Chancer* v. 64 That left Sonny and me on our tod in the public. **1981** 'G. GAUNT' *Incomer* xiii. 71 Maybe they don't want your company... Never seen you on your tod before.

Toda (tōu·dă), *sb.* and *a.* **A.** *sb.* **a.** (A member of) a people of southern India. **b.** The language of this people, a Dravidian language closely related to Tamil. **B.** *adj.* Of or pertaining to this people.

1864 F. METZ *Tribes inhabiting Neilgherry Hills* 19 The Todas justify their belief in intermediate spiritual agencies by a reference to analogy. *Ibid.* 20 Great sanctity attaches to the person of the Pa'laul in the eyes of his Toda brethren. **1873** W. E. MARSHALL *Travels amongst Todas* xxiv. 208 Everything with the Toda is taken *au sérieux.* **1900** *Knowledge* 1 Mar. 67/1 On the clearances amid the dense and luxuriant primeval forest, or on the open grass-lands of the hill-tops, dwell a number of interesting aboriginal wild tribes, among whom the Todas and the Kotas are perhaps those whose names are the least unfamiliar to European ears. **1921** *Blackw. Mag.* July 28/1 The Toda puzzles and interests the Occidental because the Toda's origin is undiscoverable. **1938** [see *MOIETY 4]. **1939** L. H. GRAY *Foundations of Language* 386 [Dravidian] falls into four great divisions, the first of which is *Tamil-Kurukh*, comprising Tamil..; Malayāḷam..; Ṭulu..; Koḍagu..; Kanarese, including Toda, Kōta, and Baḍaga ..; and Kurukh. **1955** T. BURROW *Sanskrit Language* viii. 376 Besides the major languages there are numerous minor non-literary Dravidian languages spoken in various parts of India, namely: (i) Southern: Tulu, Coorg, Toda, Kota. **1976** *Language* LII. 259 This latest monograph..is most easily understood when studied in conjunction with his massive earlier tome on Toda songs. **1980** H. TREVELYAN *Public & Private* 7 The bee-hive huts of the Todas, the earliest known inhabitants of the [Nilgiri] hills who still lived there.

to-day, *adv.* and *sb.* Add: **A.** *adv.* Freq. in phr. *here today and gone tomorrow*: see *HERE *adv.* 1 e.

C. *adj. colloq.* Modern, characteristic of or suitable for the present day.

1969 *Harper's Mag.* Oct. 65/2 I'm a today writer. **1976** A. CROSS *Question of Max* III. xiii. 154 It's old-fashioned and sentimental and altogether not 'today' to talk of restitution. **1980** J. WAINWRIGHT *Eye of Beholder* 24 The today song-smiths..wrote boy-girl-and-bed words.

Todd-AO (tǫd,ēi,ōu). *Cinemat.* [f. the name of Mike *Todd* (1907–58), U.S. stage and film producer, + the initials of *A*merican *O*ptical Co.] The proprietary name (in the U.S.) of a cinematic process producing a wide-screen image. Freq. *attrib.*

1955 *Times* 6 Aug. 3/5 The Todd-AO process uses 70mm. film instead of the standard 35mm. It has six sound tracks running at 30 frames a second as against the usual 24. The image is projected on to a huge curved screen presenting a picture about 25 ft. high and 65 ft. wide. **1955** *Official Gaz.* (U.S. Patent Office) 29 Nov. TM 239/2 *Todd-AO.* For motion picture equipment. Use since August 1953 on motion picture camera equipment... The Todd-AO Corporation, New York. **1958** *New Statesman* 26 Apr. 530/3 There can be no question about it; Todd-AO wipes the floor with Cinerama. **1958** *Observer* 27 Apr. 15/6 The Todd-AO screen is a huge, incurved affair, rather like the other side of a monstrous broken cup. **1976** *Oxf. Compan. Film* 692/2 His [*sc.* Todd's] main contribution to films..was his promotion of a new 70mm wide screen process, called Todd-AO, in the mid-fifties.

toddle, *sb.* Add: **toddlekins** (earlier example).

1852 C. J. MATHEWS (*title*) Little Toddlekins.

to·ddlerhood. [f. TODDLER + -HOOD.] The condition of being a toddler.

1966 'L. LANE' *ABZ of Scouse* Foreword, In his very toddlerhood his mother *lerned* him. **1967** *Punch* 15 Mar. 377/2 A normal childhood needs a good decade to run its full noisy course from toddlerhood to puberty. **1976** *Word 1971* XXVII. 37 The physical transition from infancy to early toddlerhood is marked by a qualitative transition in the nature of mother-child communication.

toddy, *sb.* Add: **3. a.** *toddy-wine* (later example); **toddy-maker** = *toddy-man* (see also sense 3 b in Dict.); **toddy-tapper** = *toddy-man*; **toddy-tapping,** the collection of toddy from palms.

1821 J. Leyden tr. *Malay Annals* 151 There was a toddy-maker, who went to amuse himself on the sea. **1937** *Discovery* May 143/2 It [*sc.* coconut shell] is an indispensable part of the toddy-tapper's outfit, for it is in a coconut shell that he carries his cinnamon leaf paste and his lime for the purpose of stimulating the reluctant flowers to give up their sweet nectar. **1971** *National Geographic* Mar. 355/2 Ko Than Shwe, like many men around Pagan, is a toddy tapper. **1946** *Nature* 5 Oct. 493/2 Toddy-tapping is a popular occupation as it only occupies a small portion of the day. **1958** *Contributions to Indian Sociology* II. 54 Toddy-tapping and the taking of animal life are associated with low status. **1971** *National Geographic* Mar. 358/1 Juice collected at 8 a.m. ferments to toddy wine by 5 that evening.

b. toddy-lifter, a device used in the manner of a pipette to transfer hot toddy from a bowl to a glass; **toddy-stick** (earlier example).

1840 *Picayune* (New Orleans) 4 Oct. 2/5 A 'toddy stick' is as spirit-stirring an article as any poet can boast. **1923** *Classical Q.* July–Oct. 173 The 'Toddy-lifter', known in Scotch and Irish households during the eighteenth and early nineteenth centuries, a bulbous glass cylinder, is exactly the instrument [*sc.* the clepsydra] described here. **1954** E. M. Elville *Paperweights* x. 107 A toddy-lifter was something like a miniature decanter in shape, with a body large enough to hold a glassful of liquid. **1970** G. Savage *Dict. Antiques* 430/1 The toddy-lifter was dipped into the bowl and allowed to fill through the hole in the bottom. The thumb was then placed over the upper orifice, air-pressure keeping the contents from flowing out.

todorokite (todǭ·rǒkəit). *Min.* [f. the name of the *Todoroki* mine, Hokkaidô, Japan + -ite[1].] A hydrated oxide of manganese, calcium, and other elements occurring as soft black aggregates of minute, probably monoclinic laths having a metallic lustre; also, any of a group of minerals structurally related to this.

1934 T. Yoshimura in *Jrnl. Faculty Sci. Hokkaidô Univ.* Ser. IV. II. 297 The new mineral belonged to the purest species of crystalline manganomelane. As such a mineral had not yet been reported, this mineral was named 'todorokite' after the name of the mine where it had been first noticed. **1981** *Science* 29 May 1024/1 Todorokites are calcium-bearing manganese oxides found in terrestrial manganese ore deposits, in weathering products of manganese-bearing rocks, and in some manganese nodules.

toe, *sb.* Add: **1. e.** *fig.* Speed, energy. *Austral.* and *N.Z. slang.*

1963 *Truth* (Wellington) 8 Oct., Happy Song has a fair share of toe in spite of her nine years and she was flying in fifth place after losing ground at the start. **1969** *Sun* (Melbourne) 12 July 58/1 The North half-forward line.. has a ton of toe and could give Richmond's novice half-back line a torrid afternoon.

4. f. In full *the toe of Italy.* The south-western extremity of that country. Cf. Heel *sb.*[1] 6.

1894 [in Dict., sense 4 a]. **1941** C. Milburn *Diary* 15 Feb. (1979) 83 We have dropped parachutists..on Italy's toe..near Brindisi. **1974** *Times* 7 Jan. 3 The boy had been kept in various hideouts in the southwestern 'toe' of Italy. **1979** R. Perry *Bishop's Pawn* iv. 68 The advancing Allied armies..forced themselves northwards from the toe of Italy.

g. A flattish portion at the foot of an otherwise steep curve.

1940 *Wall's Dict. Photogr.* (ed. 15) 573 The method of speed-measurement used must..depend on the position, not of the extreme under-exposed 'toe' of the curve, but of its straight-line portion. **1948** *Rep. Progress Physics* XI. 284 A pronounced toe can be obtained on a density-development-time curve by adding bromide ions to a hydroquinone developer. **1982** *Sci. Amer.* Apr. 41/2 The design of tension-leg platforms, like the design of guyed towers, is still at the toe of the learning curve and will undoubtedly go through several generations of improvement.

h. *Hort.* A section of a fleshy root.

1952 A. G. L. Hellyer *Sanders' Encycl. Gardening* (ed. 22) 169 Dracaena... Propagation: by cuttings or 'toes' of fleshy roots in sandy peat in spring. **1976** *Billings* (Montana) *Gaz.* 27 June 4-G/6 Rhizomes branching from the old toe will bear flowers next year. **1984** *Gardening from 'Which'?* (Consumers' Assoc.) Mar. 64/1 Remove the offsets..known as yucca toes... Remove the 'toes' if new plants are needed.

5. i. *to tread on the toes of* (earlier example).

1866 Trollope *Belton Est.* (ed. 3) I. iii. 71 'But you mustn't offend my father.'..'I won't tread on his toes.'

l. *on one's toes*: alert, eager.

1921 J. Dos Passos *Three Soldiers* II. i. 56 If he just watched out and kept on his toes, he'd be sure to get it. **1958** B. Nichols *Sweet & Twenties* 94 You have to be on your toes to make the right sort of riposte on such an occasion. **1972** P. Marks *Collector's Choice* ii. 123 Anavi was convinced that he had the right to delude even the most experienced connoisseurs; he was doing them a service because it kept them on their toes.

m. *toe-to-toe*: (carried on) in close combat, at close quarters; also, neck and neck. Cf. *foot to foot* s.v. Foot *sb.* 26 b.

1942 Berrey & Van den Bark *Amer. Thes. Slang.* § 701/14 *Toe-to-toe,* evenly matched. **1950** J. Dempsey *Championship Fighting* 199 Has each enough confidence in his own punching ability..to engage the other in toe-to-toe exchanges? **1952** *Newsweek* 23 June 21/1 In the toe-to-toe fight for the Republican Presidential nomination, last week's round went to Sen. Robert A. Taft of Ohio. **1958** *Oxf. Mag.* 15 May 429/2 The sense of toe-to-toe negotiation with financial giants. **1971** *Flying* Apr. 42/1 My wife and I landed..to top up the tanks and have a toe-to-toe talk with the weather guys. **1977** *Sounds* 9 July 23/3, I love real eccentric people, getting toe to toe with them.

n. *to have it on one's toes*: to run away. *slang.*

1958 F. Norman *Bang to Rights* 53 They hold us responsable for anyone haveing it on their toes [*sic*]. **1976** 'P. B. Yuill' *Hazell & Menacing Jester* vi. 67, I had it across the road on my toes.

o. *toes over* (Surfing) (see quots.).

1962 T. Masters *Surfing made Easy* 65 *Toes over,* walking to the very front of the board during a ride on a steep hollow wave. **1965** J. Pollard *Surfrider* ii. 19 Walking the board when you don't wish to put all your toes over you can still put a few over the edge—do a 'toes over'.

p. *a toe in the door*: a position from which progress can be made.

1977 *Times* 7 Oct. 17/2 Gail Sheehy stopped her sample at 50... She says she now has a toe in the door of the 50's and 60's. **1978** *Dumfries Courier* 20 Oct. 6/5 He was only using the application for boating as a 'toe in the door' to sell something else. **1979** D. Sanders *Queen sends for Mrs Chadwick* 11 He'd be thirty-five at the next election. Just the right age to get a toe in the door.

q. *to dig in one's toes*: see *Dig *v.* 11 c.

6. toe-board (earlier example); **toe brake** *Aeronaut.*, in an aircraft, a brake that is operated with the foot; so **toe braking** *vbl. sb.*; **toe-clip,** (*a*) (earlier example); **toe-cover** *slang,* an inexpensive and useless present; **toe-dancing,** dancing on points; **toe-end** *v. trans.*, to kick with the point of one's foot; **toe-hold,** (*b*) a place of support for the toe (of a boot) in climbing; hence *fig.*, a position of little significance or influence, esp. one seen as providing a base from which they may be increased; **toe-hole** *rare,* a place of support for the toe (of a boot) in climbing; **toe-jam** *slang,* dirt which accumulates between the toes; **toe jump** *Skating,* a jump initiated with the help of the toe of the non-skating foot; **toe loop,** (*a*) *Skating,* a loop jump that is also a toe jump (see quot. 1979); more fully *toe loop jump*; (*b*) a loop on a sandal through which a toe is placed; **toe-nail** *sb.*, (*a*) (earlier example); also *fig.*; (*b*) an iron nail employed for the toe in shoeing; **toe-puff,** a stiffener for the toe of the upper of a shoe; **toe rake** *Skating,* a set of teeth at the front of the blade of a skate; **toe-ring** (earlier example); **toe-rubber** *N. Amer.*, a rubber overshoe that covers only the front part of a shoe; **toe shoe** *N. Amer. Ballet,* a shoe with a reinforced toe, worn for toe-dancing; a point shoe; **toe-spin** *Skating,* a spin performed on the toe; **toe-strap,** (*a*) (earlier example); (*b*) a strap on a bicycle pedal to keep the foot from slipping off it; (*c*) a band fixed to a boat and serving to hold the foot of someone leaning out; **toe-tapping** *vbl. sb.*, the tapping of feet in time to music; (in quot. 1929, a derogatory term for 'dancing'); *ppl. a.*, that makes one want to tap one's feet; **toe-thong sandal** = *thong sandal* s.v. *Thong *sb.* 2; **toe wall** a low wall built at the foot of an embankment to help keep the earth in place.

1892 *Harper's Mag.* Jan. 271/1 The..bag..to put under his feet on the toe-board. **1944** *Jrnl. R. Aeronaut. Soc.* XLVIII. 297 The toe brakes are awkward to operate, and heavy pressure is needed on them to get the desired braking effect. **1976** B. Lecomber *Dead Weight* ii. 32, I stood on the toe-brakes and opened the throttle. **1977** *R.A.F. Yearbk.* 29 Direction is maintained or altered by holding the rudder central and applying differential toe-braking as required. **1895** *Army & Navy Co-op. Soc. Price List* 1379/2 The Courier Toe Clips... For Rat Trap Pedals (adjustable), price 2/0. **1948** B. MacDonald *Plague & I* xvi. 193 Toecover is a family name for a useless gift. A crocheted napkin ring is a toecover. **1983** *Listener* 3 Feb. 21/2 Gifts are given, not only the completely useless trivia or 'toe-covers' which litter the surgery, but more substantial gifts, such as briefcases. **1924** Sharp & Oppé *Dance* 47 Toe-dancing is perhaps the most extreme instance of the virtuosity achieved by the ballet-dancers of the last century. **1976** F. Muir *Frank Muir Bk.* 42 About 1820 the ballerina Taglioni popularized toe-dancing, which called for special built-up shoes. **1968** B. Hines *Kestrel for Knave* 98 He pivoted on his left foot and toe-ended a lump of coke back across the asphalt. **1976** *Sunday Mail* (Glasgow) 21 Nov., Jonquin took a free-kick and the inside-right toe-ended the ball into the net. **1880** 'Mark Twain' *Tramp Abroad* xxxiv. 379 One man's toe-hold broke and he fell! **1918** *Observer* 10 Nov. 8/6 The enemy retains a toehold in the Rimeuse Valley. **1945** Mencken *Amer. Lang.* Suppl. I. 324 So many novelties swarm in... A large number come and go without the lexicographers so much as hearing of them... At least four-fifths of those which get any sort of toe-hold in the language originate in the United States. **1963** M. I. Finley *Ancient Greeks* ii. 12 Small groups of men began to migrate eastward across the Aegean to find toeholds on the Asia Minor coast. **1965** *Listener* 10 June 869/3 By Carletti's time Europe..retained only a toe-hold on the China trade. **1980** 'M. Fonteyn' *Magic of Dance* 155 A model rock about twelve inches high was dragged onto the stage by the corps de ballet. It had a special toehold into which I had to place my foot and balance for a moment on pointe. **1876** H. Melville *Clarel* I. ii. xix. 224 A ladder of steep stone With toe-holes cut. **1934** R. Campbell *Broken Record* 165 The stale smell of the toe-jam of the shuffling pedestrian Charlot. **1973** *Black World* June 21 If you miss nose Picking time Then you collect Three and one half milograms Of toejam And give it to barbara's cat. **1938** M. Y. Vinson *Primer Figure Skating* ix. 150 Another nice toe jump is the 'ballet hop'. **1975** *Oxf. Compan. Sports & Games* 523/1 The split jump, a toe jump in which the skater takes off from a back inside edge, assisted by the toe-point of the free foot, half-turning in mid-air [etc.]. **1964** J. Noel *Figure Skating for Beginners* ix. 92 The toe loop and double toe loop jumps are the ordinary loop and double loop jumps with the addition of toe-strikes. **1973** K. Markandaya *Nowhere Man* iii. 18 Sandals on her smooth-skinned feet, with thongs and a toe-loop. **1976** *Times* 19 Jan. 9/6 Miss de Leeuw fell on her triple jump, a toe loop. **1979** M. Heller *Illustr. Encycl. Ice Skating* 209 The toe loop is the simplest skating jump from the backward outside edge with the assistance of the free toe, a 360° turn to backward inside edge of the same foot. **1841** *Knickerbocker* XVII. 407 All the young ladies were on the very toe-nail of curiosity. **1908** *Animal Managem.* (War Office) 238 The smith begins with the toenails first. **1929** *Footwear Organiser* July 81/2 (Advt.), For unvarying high quality and thoroughly reliable service use Walker prepared toe-puffs. **1958** *Observer* 21 Sept. 10/5 The modern toe-puff makes feeling the position of the toes impossible. **1963** T. D. Richardson *Your Bk. of Skating* iii. 20 The strike must be from the edge of the blade—*and not from the point or toe* rakes of the skate. **1973** *Times* 3 Mar. 18/1 Towards the end of the programme..Miss Buck tripped over the toe rake of her skate. **1980** *Radio Times* 16 Feb. 33 The front of the blade has teeth (the toe-rake) to assist with spins, pivots and jumps. **1896** 'Mark Twain' *Diary* 30 Jan. in *Following Equator* (1897) xliv. 403 All the females among them [*sc.* Hindoos]..bejeweled with cheap and showy nose-rings, toe-rings, leglets, and armlets. **1948** *Sun* (Baltimore) 16 Jan. 7 (Advt.), Handy, dual-purpose umbrella that protects you top to toe! Its smart plastic handle holds a pair of excellent quality toe-rubbers that fit any size foot. **1975** *Toronto Star* 25 Oct. H7/1 Who wouldn't develop a sense of humor in a country where some men have to wear toe rubbers half the year. **1949** Chujoy & Manchester *Dance Encycl.* 480/2 Toe-shoes are usually, but not always, made of silk and the toe of the shoe is re-enforced with a box made of several layers of strong glue between layers of material. **1979** T. Gifford *Hollywood Gothic* (1980) vi. 71, I played so much tennis that my sneakers actually got bloody, like toe shoes—like ballet. **1921** B. Meyer *Skating with Bror Meyer* 117 All the toe-spins are beautiful if well executed. **1928** [see *Counter *sb.*[4] 6]. **1960** M. V. Owen *Fun Figure Skating* vii. 130 Back toe spins (with the free leg closing in in front) and back sit spins should be learned by all those expecting to go on to advanced free skating. **1884** *Queen* 29 Nov. (Advt.), Superior polished wood skates with broad toe-straps. **1910** *Cycling* 26 Jan. 66/1 The first time I ever essayed to climb Westerham I had no toe-straps, and I failed. **1948** I. Proctor *Racing Dinghy Handling* vi. 56 At least one foot should be tucked under the canvas toe strap. **1966** [see *Cross-bar *sb.* 1 a]. **1968** *Daily Tel.* 29 Jan. 7/8 Dean hit the buoy, and Hinton fell in when his toestrap broke. **1981** B. Webb tr. *Schult's Sailing Dict.* 257/2 A crew can only sit out effectively if the boat has toe-straps or some other device to enable weight to be placed well outboard. **1929** 'Seamark' *Down River* iii. 46 You didn't think *I* wanted to come toe-tapping in a shanty like this, did you? **1935** *Motion Picture* Nov. 4 (Advt.), Roaring comedy, warm romance, sensational song hits, toe-tapping dances. **1966** C. Keil in T. Kochman *Rappin' & Stylin' Out* (1972) 87 The jazz audience now remains immobile save for some head-bobbing, toe-tapping, and finger-popping. **1975** *Broadcast* 3 Nov. 14/1 A charming presentation of ..music in a toe-tapping reminiscent mood. **1966** M. Laurence *Jest of God* viii. 130 Her feet..slap with the rubbery sound of her royal-blue toe-thong sandals. **1934** Webster, Toe wall. **1947** *Sun* (Baltimore) 5 May 16/6 Concrete toe walls have been installed on both sides of the river. **1975** Winterkorn & Fang *Foundation Engin. Handbk.* xi. 398/2 In England wide dry-stone toe walls have been used successfully to stabilize cuts in over-consolidated clay.

toe, *v.* Add: **1.** Also with *off,* to complete (a sock, etc.) by knitting the toe and then casting off. Also *fig.*

1856 M. J. Holmes *Homestead* 126 She..was toeing off the stocking only that morning commenced. **1870** G. M. Hopkins *Jrnls. & Papers* (1959) 196 The next morning a heavy fall of snow. It tufted and toed the firs and yews.

2. *to toe the line,* etc. (earlier examples); also *to toe the trig* (Trig *sb.*[2]).

1813 'H. Bull-Us' *Diverting Hist. John Bull & Bro. Jonathan* (ed. 2) xii. 62 He began to think it was high time to toe the mark. **1817** *Deb. Congress U.S.* 30 Jan. (1854) 792 The necessity appeared..of toeing the trig, and standing there at all hazards. **1826** W. N. Glascock *Naval Sketch-Bk.* (ed. 2) I. 271 The brigades of seamen embodied to act with our troops in America, as well as in the north coast of Spain, contrived to '*ship a bagnet*' on a pinch, and to '*toe*' (for that was the phrase) 'a tolerable line'. **1905** *Eng. Dial. Dict.* VI. 235/2 The player may 'toe the trig', but may not overstep it.

6. orig. *U.S.* **a.** *intr.* To turn the toes *in* or *out.* Also *fig.*

1877 Bartlett *Dict. Amer.* (ed. 4) 710 *To toe in,* to turn in the toes. **1894** *Vermont Agric. Rep.* XIV. 120 Avoid a horse which toes in or toes out. **1945** B. MacDonald *Egg & I* (1946) i. 16 She toed out and had trouble with her arches. **1950** J. Dempsey *Championship Fighting* 70 If you toe-in slightly with the left foot, you'll get greater freedom in the whirl.

b. Of a pair of wheels: to have a slight forward convergence (*toe in*) or divergence (*toe out*). Also *trans.* (causatively).

1926 J. A. MOYER *Gasoline Automobiles* (ed. 2) i. 25 To facilitate steering, the front wheels of the conventional rear-wheel drive 'toe in' about ¼ to ⅜ inch. **1929** NEWTON & STEEDS *Motor Vehicle* xxvii. 324 The alignment of the wheels should be checked occasionally since if the wheels should get to 'toe-out' the wear on the tyres will be excessive. **1939** *Automobile Engineer* XXIX. 40/1 In addition to a camber change, the wheel is 'toed-in' as it rises or falls in relation to the car. **1962** *Which? Car Suppl.* Oct. 139/1 Front wheel alignment [was] toeing out ⅛ in. instead of toeing in ⅛ in. **1976** CROUSE & ANGLIN *Pocket Automotive Dict.* 101 On a turn, the inner wheel turns, or toes out, more.

toeing *vbl. sb.* (examples in senses 1 and *6 of the vb.).

1876 A. D. WHITNEY *Sights & Insights* I. 21 It is the 'toeing off' that is the satisfaction, after all, even whilst you knit the stocking. **1891** S. M. WELCH *Home Hist.* 116 That peculiar turn of the foot called 'toeing in' which in the white girl would be called 'pigeon toed'. **1904** M. E. WALLER *Wood-Carver of 'Lympus* 36 Ther ain't nothin' more ter learn but 'toein' off'. **1928** *Bureau of Standards Jrnl. Res.* (U.S.) I. 24 The common practice of cambering and toeing in of the front wheels of an automobile doubtless influences the tread wear. **1962** R. H. SMYTHE *Anat. Dog Breeding* 77 Such a dog might show no sign of toeing-in. **1970** K. BALL *Fiat 600, 600D Autobook* vii. 78/1 The final torque loading of the short arm mounting pin nut is determined after the toeing-in procedure.

toeding, var. *TOERING.

toe-in (tōᵘ·,in). [f. vbl. phr. *to toe in*: see *TOE *v.* 6 b.] The inclination of a pair of wheels so that they are closer together in front than behind.

1929 NEWTON & STEEDS *Motor Vehicle* xxvii. 324 The distances between the marks at the front and at the rear should then be measured and the amount of toe-in determined. **1979** *Arizona Daily Star* 5 Aug. c 9/2 (Advt.), We'll set caster, camber and toe-in to manufacturer's original specifications.

toeless, *a.* (Examples referring to footwear.)

1942 D. POWELL *Time to be Born* viii. 187 Her feet in toeless, heelless sandals. **1952** C. W. CUNNINGTON *Eng. Women's Clothing* vii. 248 (*caption*) Toeless sandal with low square heel.

‖ **toenadering** (tu·nadərīŋ). *S. Afr.* [Du., f. *toe* To *prep., conj., adv.* + *nadering* approach (f. *na* NEAR *adv.*²).] Rapprochement, esp. between political parties or factions.

1920 S. BLACK *Dorp* 187 All Oakley saw in any toenadering (coming together) of the bickering factions, was a trick to deprive King George and his heirs of their legitimate ownership of the country. **1947** *Forum* (Johannesburg) 3 May 3/2 The whole question of toenadering with the English-speaking section has..been..an apple of discord in Nationalist-Afrikaner Party circles. **1957** *Cape Times* 18 June 8/7 He must draw a large Nationalist vote if he is to win those English-speaking people who want White *toenadering*. **1971** *Financial Mail* (Johannesburg) 26 Feb. 669/1 Michael Botha..revealed to shareholders.. details of a deal with the Afrikaanse Pers... It certainly is a fairly ingenious bit of *toenadering*. **1973** *Star* (Johannesburg) 16 June 13, I have a feeling there is a good deal of public support for 'toenadering', particularly on the part of the unthinking and the wishful thinkers.

toe-out (tōᵘ·,aut). [f. vbl. phr. *to toe out*: see *TOE *v.* 6 b.] The inclination of a pair of wheels so that they are closer together behind than in front.

1930 *Flight* 25 Apr. 460 Toe in or toe out of wheels should be carefully avoided. **1970** K. BALL *Fiat 600, 600D Autobook* ix. 112/2 With toe-in or toe-out correctly set, securely tighten the track rod clamps.

Toepler, var. *TÖPLER.

toe-·rag. [f. TOE *sb.* + RAG *sb.*¹] **1.** A rag wrapped round the foot and worn inside a shoe, in place of a sock.

1864 J. F. MORTLOCK *Experiences of Convict* II. ix. 80 Stockings being unknown, some luxurious men wrapped round their feet a piece of old shirting, called, in language more expressive than elegant, a 'toe-rag'. **1932** F. JENNINGS *Tramping with Tramps* vi. 98 Socks are very seldom worn. Instead you get a winding of cotton rag round the ball and toes of the foot as a safeguard against blisters. Toe-rags, the tramp calls them. **1933** 'G. ORWELL' *Down & Out in Paris & London* xxvii. 197 Less than half the tramps actually bathed.., but they all washed their faces and feet, and the horrid greasy little clouts known as toe-rags which they bind round their toes.

2. A tramp or vagrant; a despicable or worthless person. Also *attrib.*

1875 T. FROST *Circus Life & Circus Celebrities* xvi. 278 *Toe rags* is another expression of contempt..used.. chiefly by the lower grades of circus men, and the acrobats who stroll about the country, performing at fairs. **1903** 'T. COLLINS' *Such is Life* (1937) v. 229 'Come over to the wagon, and have a drink of tea,' says I. 'No, no,' says he, 'none of your toe-rag business.' **1912** D. H. LAWRENCE *Let.* (1962) I. 154 Remember, whatever toe-rag I may be personally, I am the person she livanted with. So you be careful. **1960** H. PINTER *Caretaker* I. 9 All them toe-rags, mate, got the manners of pigs. **1971** 'H. CALVIN' *Poison Chasers* xii. 168 Move, ya useless big toerag! **1978** M. KENYON *Deep Pocket* xiii. 165 Could she have loved this toe-rag sheikh out of the desert? **1980** J. WAINWRIGHT *Tainted Man* 171 The Law doesn't differentiate between you and the most miserable towrag [*sic*] on the face of the earth.

Hence **toe-ragger** *Austral. slang* = sense 2 above.

1896 *Truth* (Sydney) 12 Jan. (Morris), The bushie's favourite term of opprobrium 'a toe-ragger' is also probably from the Maori. Amongst whom the nastiest term of contempt was that of *tau rika rika*, or slave. **1919** V. MARSHALL *World of Living Dead* (1969) 82 Over the way a 'trial' man had tossed a 'chew' to a 'toeragger'. **1953** E. PARTRIDGE in I. Bevan *Sunburnt Country* 217 Some of the gold-diggers were tramps,..and several terms connected with them are worth recording—..*toe-ragger*, a dead-beat wanderer. **1966** G. W. TURNER *Eng. Lang. Austral. & N.Z.* vii. 144 The battler seems to have been the poorest itinerant. The toeragger was not much wealthier than the battler.

‖ **toering** (tū·rīŋ). *S. Afr.* Also **toeding, toudang, tudong.** [Afrikaans, ad. Malay *tudong* (now *tudung*) cover, lid, sun-hat.] A wide-brimmed conical hat of straw, formerly worn by Cape Malays.

1855 J. S. MAYSON *Malays of Capetown* 10 The coloured cap, the *tudong* or hat, and the sandals of wood, formerly formed a part of the national dress; but being adopted by Mahometan converts of every class, are now regarded as badges of a common faith. **1909** *Cape* 25 June 9 There was..the 'toeding' (sometimes spelt 'toering'), a conical, wide-brimmed hat of plaited straw. **1913** D. FAIRBRIDGE *That which hath Been* 52 The *toudang* of the old Malay coachmen is still to be seen at the Cape, but it is fast disappearing. **1944** I. D. DU PLESSIS *Cape Malays* iii. 48 The *toering* is still worn by Malay coachmen when driving the wedding group. **1965** A. GORDON-BROWN *C. W. Smith, Artist at Cape of Good Hope* iv. 18 Very small figures appear in some of the drawings... They are usually Malays in which the 'toering', or conical straw hat worn by the men, is prominent.

toey (tōᵘ·i), *a. slang* (chiefly *Austral.*). [f. TOE *sb.* + -Y¹.] Restive, anxious, touchy.

1930 *Bulletin* (Sydney) 8 Oct. 35/2 Wise Force [*sc.* a horse] was 'toey' before the race, and behaved in alarming fashion on his way to and at the post. **1961** *Coast to Coast 1959–60* 47 And the other umpire a bit toey out there at square leg. **1968** K. WEATHERLY *Roo Shooter* 91 He knew that the roos were toey, and, as they were drinking on the opposite side, they would be gone as soon as he moved a muscle. **1969** C. DRUMMOND *Odds on Death* viii. 175 The horse seemed to him a bit on the toey side. He looked down to see if saliva was dripping. **1974** *Sydney Morning Herald* 1 Jan. 2 He's that toey he's got us all nervous, too. **1981** *National Times* (Austral.) 25–31 Jan. 24/3 Dallas Jongs..had a hotel bouncer friend who could get as toey as a Roman sandal.

toff, *sb.* Add: **toffish** *a.* (earlier example); hence **to·ffishness,** behaviour characteristic of a 'toff'.

1873 J. GREENWOOD *In Strange Company* 43 Thick slices, bear in mind: anything under an inch thick would be regarded with contempt by the bony young barrowman, and perhaps with an uncomfortable suspicion that you have designs to inveigle him into the detestable ways of gentility. He calls it 'toffishness'. *Ibid.*, To affect thin bread and butter is undoubtedly 'toffish'. *c* **1876** J. ALBERY *Dramatic Wks.* (1939) II. 105 But only because his toffishness wexes me.

toff (tǫf), *v. slang.* [f. TOFF *sb.*] *trans.* and *refl.* To dress *up* like a 'toff'.

1914 D. H. LAWRENCE *Widowing of Mrs. Holroyd* I. i. 5 He'd got a game on somewhere—toffed himself up to the nines, and skedaddled off as brisk as a turkey-cock. **1928** *East End Star* Dec. 2/2 Notice the perfect stillness when the 'lovely lidy all toffed up' sings. **1932** L. GOLDING *Magnolia Street* II. ii. 298 The fellows come in [to a hair-dressing saloon] when they're on leave. They want to get toffed up for their girls.

toffee, toffy, *sb.* and *a.* Add: **A.** *sb.* **1. c.** A small, shaped piece of toffee, usu. sold wrapped.

1938 G. GREENE *Brighton Rock* I. iii. 52 'Have a toffee.' 'It's bad for the figure.' **1984** W. GARNER *Rats' Alley* x. 195 He..bought..a box of her favourite toffees from the shop next door.

2. Phr. *not to be able* (to do a thing) *for toffee*: to be incompetent at it. *colloq.*

1914 *Illustr. London News* 12 Sept. 380/1 Their opponents cannot 'shoot for nuts' (or 'for toffee', as one Tommy more expressly put it). **1932** D. L. SAYERS *Have his Carcase* xii. 145 The Morgan wouldn't start, not for toffee. **1951** M. KENNEDY *Lucy Carmichael* II. 76 Those dreary girls you get in every Drama School who can't act for toffee. **1977** C. MCCULLOUGH *Thorn Birds* xiii. 325 You can't kiss for toffee. You open your mouth too wide.

3. Nonsense, rubbish.

a **1930** D. H. LAWRENCE *Phoenix* (1936) 588 The eternal flame of the high ideal is all my-eye. It's all toffee, my dear sirs. **1957** P. WILDEBLOOD *Main Chance* 220 Working-class to the backbone, just like us... And if he's been filling you up with a lot of toffee to the contrary, more fool you. **1970** M. TRIPP *Man without Friends* vii. 77 'It was all a lot of toffee,' I said, 'as Hardacre very well knows.'

4. A medium shade of brown. Cf. sense B below.

1960 *Woman's Own* 19 Mar. 42/2 In stone, toffee, scarlet, green. **1976** *Honolulu Star-Bull.* 21 Dec. A-12 (Advt.), In toffee, green or blue... Jacket with stitched back-belt.

5. *toffee-coloured, -like* adjs.; **toffee apple,** (*a*) an apple coated with toffee and mounted on a stick; (*b*) *slang*, a bomb of similar shape that is fired from a trench mortar; **toffee-brown** = sense A. 4 above; **toffee hammer,** a miniature hammer such as may be used to break pieces of toffee; **toffee-nose** *slang*, a snob or supercilious person; also *attrib.*; **toffee-nosed** *a. slang*, snobbish, supercilious; **toffee paper,** a small piece of paper in which a toffee is wrapped.

1917 *B.E.F. Times* 25 Dec. f. 3/2 The planting of Toffee-apples on the border of your neighbour's allotment will seriously interfere with the ripening of his gooseberries. **1930** BROPHY & PARTRIDGE *Songs & Slang 1914–18* 171 Toffee Apples.—Trench mortar bombs, so called from the haft, like the skewer in a toffee-apple. **1937** 'R. CROMPTON' *William—the Showman* vi. 127 A little girl was leaning against the wall, eating a toffee-apple on a stick. **1957** *Times* 5 Sept. 11/4 We must kill the idea that Weymouth is just a candy-floss, toffee-apple resort. **1975** P. FUSSELL *Gt. War & Mod. Memory* (1977) ix. 313 Everything from shovels,..and rolls of barbed wire, to.. the perverse toffee-apple. **1976** *Milton Keynes Express* 16 July 8/2 Toffee apples and ice-cream, sweets and raffles, pony rides and competitions—these were all part of the scene. **1961** M. KELLY *Spoilt Kill* I. 30 Creased forehead, receding toffee-brown hair. **1978** R. RENDELL *Sleeping Life* xvi. 129 Malina..wore jeans, of toffee-brown silk. **1948** M. ALLINGHAM *More Work for Undertaker* xiii. 167 The clear toffee-coloured pavements. **1979** D. MACKENZIE *Raven settles Score* 5 His long toffee-coloured hair. **1958** B. BEHAN *Borstal Boy* III. 230, I sometimes saw a fellow wearing overalls and walking round..carrying brushes and paint and sometimes glazing tools; hacking knife, glazing knife, toffee hammer,..and rule. **1978** D. BLOODWORTH *Crosstalk* vii. 54 Toby jugs and toffee hammers. **1919** Toffee-like [see *RAFT *v.*¹ 5]. **1944** K. DOUGLAS *Alamein to Zem Zem* (1946) 78 A tin of treacle, which had been well heated, contained a delicious black toffee-like substance. **1943** HUNT & PRINGLE *Service Slang* 67 *Toffee-nose*, another of the expressions chiefly heard amongst the W.A.A.F. This refers to a snob or someone who considers herself 'superior'. It is very apt since it implies that the nose is kept high to prevent it coming into contact with the mouth. **1958** *Woman* 12 Apr. 69/4 People thought I was a bit of a toffee-nose for the first few months because I didn't speak to them. **1962** *John o' London's* 29 Nov. 506/3 Christian was a gentleman, hence Mr. Brando's toffee-nose accent. **1974** Toffee-nose [see *Jew boy* s.v. *JEW *sb.* 3 a]. **1925** FRASER & GIBBONS *Soldier & Sailor Words* 287 *Toffee-nosed*, stuck up. **1928** T. E. LAWRENCE *Let.* 20 Jan. (1938) 568 A premature 'life' will do more to disgust the select and superior people (the R.A.F. call them the 'toffee-nosed') than anything. **1960** K. AMIS *Take a Girl like You* iv. 60 She did not want any more chat, but could not think how to say so without running the risk of sounding both stagey and toffee-nosed. **1978** *Radio Times* 28 Jan.–3 Feb. 17/2 Let Elkan Allan and the rest of the toffee-nosed critics sneer; I shall be watching *Big Jim McLain* this Sunday and so, I am sure, will a lot of other people. **1958** G. BELLAIRS *Corpse at Carnival* i. 9 A little Manx cat..chasing a piece of toffee-paper. **1983** R. SUTCLIFF *Blue Remembered Hills* xii. 91 They..flipped screwed-up toffee papers onto the heads of the orchestra.

B. *adj.* Toffee-coloured; medium brown. Cf. sense A. 4 above.

1962 J. D. MACDONALD *Key to Suite* (1968) vii. 116 A very pretty slender girl with toffee hair and dark-blue eyes. **1971** *Homes & Gardens* Aug. 57/1 The dining chairs are covered in a toffee and black houndstooth check. **1975** G. HOWELL *In Vogue* 259/2 (*caption*) A toffee and gold mesh sweater.

Tofranil (tǫ·frănil). *Pharm.* [Of unknown origin.] A proprietary name for the drug imipramine.

1958 *Trade Marks Jrnl.* 4 June 564/2 *Tofranil*... Pharmaceutical preparations for human and veterinary use... J. R. Geigy..Basle, Switzerland. **1958** *Official Gaz.* (U.S. Patent Office) 16 Sept. TM 91/2 Geigy Chemical Corporation, Ardsley, N.Y... *Tofranil* for antidepressants. **1963, 1965** [see *IMIPRAMINE]. **1979** *Daily Tel.* 27 Nov. 12/7 Prescriptions for the brand leaders Tofranil and Tryptizol accounted for an estimated £5 million.

to-fro (tū·,frōᵘ·), *adj., adv.,* and *sb. poet.* [f. TO AND FRO *phr.*] **A.** *adj.* = TO AND FRO *adj. phr.*

1879 G. M. HOPKINS *Poems* (1967) 81 To-fro tender trambeams truckle at the eye. **1936** R. CAMPBELL *Mithraic Emblems* 83 How shrill the long hosannahs of despair With which those to-fro scolopendras bear, Statesmen to conferences, troops to war. **1952** C. DAY LEWIS tr. *Virgil's Aeneid* XI. 253 It was like the to-fro rhythm of the sea, when a wave runs forward..then rapidly draws away. **1983** T. HUGHES in *Listener* 13 Jan. 21/1 The silent to-fro hurrying of nurses, The bowed stillness of surgeons.

B. *adv.* = TO AND FRO *adv. phr.* 1. *rare.*

1920 BLUNDEN *Waggoner* 44 A sharp snatch, swirling to-fro of the line.

C. *sb.* = TO AND FRO *sb. phr.* 1. *rare.*

1937 C. DAY LEWIS *Starting Point* 200 The rhythmic tap and to-fro of the white ball. **1960** —— *Buried Day* viii. 157 Almost from the start I seem to have been aware of a fidgetiness, and a constant to-fro made up of many individual, desultory movements.

toft¹. **1.** (Later examples.)

1870 LADY VERNEY *Lettice Lisle* xiii. 146, I might ha' been a comfortable man by this; and now I'm like to have neither toft nor croft. **1955** *Times* 19 Aug. 8/5 Even a layman, with guidance, can recognize the signs pointing to medieval occupation: the hollow said to be the main street; the adjoining humps of the house enclosures, each with its 'toft' (garden) and croft, or small holding. **1965**

AUDEN *About House* (1966) 17 A toft-and-croft Where I needn't, ever, be at home *to* Those I am not at home *with*.

Toft[2] (tǫft). The surname of a Staffordshire family used *attrib.* to designate (a style of) lead-glazed slipware made there in the late-seventeenth cent., some of the best examples of which bear the name of Thomas Toft (d. 1689) or another Toft, usu. regarded as the maker of the piece.

1878 L. JEWITT *Ceramic Art of Gt. Brit.* I. iv. 103 Another Toft dish..bears a female figure..and the name Ralphoft, or Ralph Toft, the h and t being apparently conjoined. **1900** F. LITCHFIELD *Pottery & Porcelain* ii. 26 Those buff-coloured dishes which we now recognise as 'Toft ware'. **1957** MANKOWITZ & HAGGAR *Conc. Encycl. Eng. Pottery & Porcelain* 222/2 The name [of Ralph Toft] occurs on many typical large Toft-style dishes. **1961** L. G. G. RAMSEY *Connoisseur New Guide Antique Eng. Pottery* 20 Signed Toft pieces are known dated 1671 and 1674. **1975** *Country Life* 26 June (Suppl.) 56/1 Christie's. .. Fine English Porcelain and Pottery... Toft dated slipware bragget-pot.

tofu (tō͡u·fū). [a. Jap. *tōfu*, ad. Chinese *dòufu*, f. *dòu* beans + *fŭ* rotten.] A curd made in Japan and China from mashed soya beans; bean curd.

1880 *Trans. Asiatic Soc. Japan* VIII. 399 *Tôfu* is made by pounding the soy beans after soaking in water. **1905** *Bull. U.S. Dept. Agric.* CLIX. 46 The larger part of the leguminous food in the Japanese diet consists of the preparations of soy beans, such as miso, shoyu and tofu. **1934** BLUNDEN *Mind's Eye* 109 Two hawks have raided the *tofu*. **1936** K. TEZUKA *Jap. Food* 28 Tōfu (bean-curd) is made by soaking soy beans in water, mashing them, straining the mass through cloth and solidifying with the addition of magnesium chloride. **1979** *Sunset* Apr. 214/2 Arrange all tofu strips in the casserole and cover with ½ of the cheese. **1981** *Guardian* 14 Aug. 7/1 In the United States,..tofu has become an 'in' food.

tog, *sb.*[1] Add: **1.** (Earlier examples.)

1708 *Memoirs Right Villanous John Hall* (ed. 4) 10/2 *Togge*, a Coat. **1718** C. HITCHING *Regulator* 20 The names of the flash words now in vogue among thieves... Togge, *alias* Coat. **1755** J. POTTS *Jrnl.* in R. Price *Howling Arctic* (1970) i. 16 Having no beaver coats in the factory to make their togs, mittens nor caps.

2. a. (Earlier examples.)

1779 J. WEDGWOOD *Let.* 9 May (1965) 233 He determined to strip off his waistcoat, and put on the togs at once. *a* **1790** H. T. POTTER *New Dict. Cant & Flash* (1795) 59 *Toges* or *toggs*, cloaths for both sexes.

c. *Austral.* and *N.Z. colloq.* A swimming-costume.

1930 V. PALMER *Passage* I. x. 83 'You nip in and get my togs.'.. He was much more at ease in his bathing-trunks than in his..suit and slippery shoes. **1935** J. GUTHRIE *Little Country* xiii. 216 We..tore down to a quiet beach, stripped off our clothes, and plunged in... We didn't bother about togs. **1944** G. TEXIDOR in D. M. Davin *N.Z. Short Stories* (1953) 313 Mum came over and said.. they could put on their togs. But they mustn't stay in for long, it was getting chilly. **1959** M. SHADBOLT *New Zealanders* 96 'I forgot my togs. I left them at the other place.' 'Never mind, you can swim in your shorts, can't you?' **1971** *N.Z. Listener* 15 Feb. 14/5 'I haven't got a costume.'..'Go back and get your togs.'

2*. A unit of thermal resistance used to express the insulating properties of clothes and quilts (see quots. 1945, 1978); so *tog rating, value*. [Modelled on the earlier U.S. term *clo*.]

1945 PEIRCE & REES in *Shirley Inst. Mem.* XIX. 343 So that practical clothing may be described conveniently by a range of small integers, the unit of thermal resistance, to be called the 'tog', is the resistance that will maintain a temperature difference of 0·1°C. with a flux of 1 watt per square metre, or in more practical terms, 10°C. with a flux of 1 watt per square decimetre. This is the resistance of a light summer suit, and 10 togs represents about the thickest clothing..practicable to wear. **1975** *Daily Tel.* 9 Dec. 13/4 White goose down: 10·5 togs (which means that it is extra-warm and light)... Terylene P.3: 8·5 to 9 togs (normal warmth). The heaviest quilt, I am told, gives the same tog warmth as five blankets at less than half the weight. **1977** *Observer* (Colour Suppl.) 25 Sept. 60/1 (Advt.), Genuine continental quilt luxury at bargain prices: Tog rating (warmth factor) 9·5+. **1978** *Textiles* VII. II. 50/2 The tog value of a textile is equal to ten times the temperature difference between its two faces when the flow of heat is equal to one watt per square metre. One tog is the thermal resistance of a fabric for a conventional man's suiting or of a blanket of medium quality.

togavirus (tō͡u·găvəiᵊrŏs). *Min.* [f. L. *toga* TOGA + VIRUS.] Any of a group of RNA animal viruses with enveloped icosahedral capsids, many of which are arthropod-borne and including the viruses of rubella, yellow fever, dengue, and several forms of encephalitis.

1970 C. H. ANDREWES et al. in *Virology* XL. 1070/1 Togavirus (from the Latin toga = a cloak) is the name now proposed to cover what is likely to prove the great majority of arboviruses having taxonomic characters like those of the A and B groups. **1974** *Nature* 27 Sept. 343/1 We have examined only one virus outside the picornavirus family, the togavirus, Semliki Forest virus. **1980** R. W. SCHLESINGER *Togaviruses* i. 10 The rubiviruses, pestiviruses and other 'non-arbo' togaviruses are also of enormous medical or veterinary importance.

together, *adv.* Add: **2. f.** Colloq. phr. (*all*) *girls together*: see *GIRL *sb.* 2 f.

D. *adj.* **a.** Fashionable, up-to-date; hence used as a general term of commendation. *slang.*

1968 *Daily Mirror* 27 Aug. 7/5 No finer honour can be bestowed on a man down the King's Road than to be called a together cat. **1970** E. BULLINS *Theme is Blackness* (1973) 176 Honey, with the right clothes and a together front I'd be a knockout. **1971** *Jamaican Weekly Gleaner* 3 Nov. 5/1, I read in the Miami Herald that conditions in the women's jails [are] not so together.

b. Composed, self-assured; free of emotional difficulties or inhibitions. *colloq.*

1969 FABIAN & BYRNE *Groupie* ii. 19, I reckoned it was no good putting on a together image if you were all screwed up inside. **1971** *New Yorker* 18 Dec. 31 A young lady of twenty-two who's been through what Twiggy has been through has got to be a very together person to survive. **1974** A. LURIE *War between Tates* (1977) iii. 67, I forgot you, and me, and where I was—I felt very calm, very together. **1977** *O.D.* No. 3. 13/3 All free festivals dream of a together stage manager—try your best to get one, as on the day it's all up to him. **1978** I. M. GASKIN *Spiritual Midwifery* (rev. ed.) 1. 41, I knew William was together enough to be there through the whole birthing and I was really excited that he was going to get to see such a heavy thing as a birth. **1979** *Amat. Photographer* 10 Jan. 67 (*caption*) Biddy and Eve—a very together cabaret act. **1983** *Times* 25 Mar. 13/3 An amateur flute player, well groomed and articulate, she looks a very together young woman.

togetherness. Delete *nonce-wd.* and add: **a.** (Later examples.)

1909 F. BARCLAY *Rosary* xv. 156 Having been apart for a little while seemed to make this curious feeling of 'togetherness' deeper and sweeter than ever. **1912** [see *COMPRESENCE]. **1920** A. S. PRINGLE-PATTISON *Idea of God* 354 Our primitive and basal experience of time is thus characterized by a togetherness of parts or elements. **1953** E. L. MASCALL *Corpus Christi* iii. 57 Assuming that the corporateness of the liturgy is produced by a merely geographical togetherness of the worshippers. **1966** J. PORTER *Sour Cream* ix. 123 'I thought I'd take Katia out somewhere.' 'How about making up a foursome?' This blasted Russian passion for togetherness! **1971** *Sci. Amer.* May 105/3 Bullheads often form a dense community, composed of hundreds of individuals, that is based not on a hierarchy or a collection of territories but on close togetherness, with the members swimming freely and peacefully throughout the pond.

b. The fact of getting on well together or being well suited to one another; a sense of belonging together, fellowship.

1930 D. H. LAWRENCE *A Propos of Lady Chatterley's Lover* 58 Class-hate and class-consciousness are only a sign that the old togetherness, the old blood-warmth has collapsed. **1930** *Times Lit. Suppl.* 13 Nov. 925/3 Characters..must also be real in relation to each other... The personages of Tourneur have this togetherness. **1941** AUDEN *New Year Let.* 34 O cruel intellect that chills His natural warmth until it kills The roots of all togetherness! **1952** C. BARDSLEY *Bishop's Move* vi. 74, I wish I saw more of this 'togetherness' in church congregations. **1963** *Economist* 9 Mar. 876/2 The new togetherness [in the Ministry of Defence] is unlikely to mean that..controversies..will disappear. **1972** M. WILLIAMS *Inside Number 10* xiv. 352 So there we had social class divisions within the organization itself, so one can imagine how much 'togetherness' that encouraged. **1981** G. CLARE *Last Waltz in Vienna* II. 126 What mattered to me was the ideal of scouting, one for all and all for one, the togetherness in a good and just cause.

Toggenburg (tǫ·gənbɒ̈ɹg). Also **Toggenburgh.** The name of a valley in the canton of St. Gall, N.E. Switzerland, used *attrib.* and *absol.* to designate a hornless light brown goat belonging to a breed first developed in the region.

1886 H. S. H. PEGLER *Bk. Goat* (ed. 3) iii. 27 The Toggenburgh goat is generally hornless, and of a rather unusual colour, being a pale drab. **1891** *Goat-Keeper* Sept. 7/2 Champion Zampa, Swiss Toggenburg Goat, 5 years old, short-haired, hornless. **1921** *Blackw. Mag.* June 764/2 The white Nanny and her kid are Alpino goats, and the brown lot are Toggenburgs. **1937** E. B. WHITE *Let.* 9 Sept. (1976) 162 He lives there, with a wife, three children, and a Toggenburg goat. **1979** B. MALAMUD *Dubin's Lives* ix. 356 One of the Toggenburgs was killed in the goat pasture by a dog.

Togger. (Earlier example.)

1891 P. S. ALLEN *Let.* Oct. (1939) 10, I hope to combine reading and rowing, for both I hugely desire to get into the Eight next summer and also they are rather hard up for men for the Togger.

toggle, *sb.* Add: **2. a.** Also, a short rod attached to one side of a garment to fasten it by being passed through a loop attached to the other side.

1903 W. F. PETRIE *Abydos* II. ii. 26/2, 141–3 appear to be toggles for fastening dress through a loop, like the frogs on a modern military cloak. **1916** *Chambers's Jrnl.* Sept. 617/1 He undid the toggles of his thick lammy coat. **1968** [see *duffle coat* s.v. *DUFFEL, DUFFLE 3]. **1982** B. ALDISS *Helliconia Spring* ix. 231 She was buttoning up her tunic, looking down at the toggles.

f. A kind of wall fastener for use on open-backed plasterboarding, etc., having a part that springs open or turns through 90 degrees after it is inserted, so as to prevent withdrawal and aid gripping.

1934 in WEBSTER. **1964** *Practical Householder* Nov. 1369/1, I had an occasion to use Rawlplug ⅛ in. 3/16 in. gravity toggles... If you decide to remove the toggle at a later date, when the burr on the screw comes up against the swivel nut, the whole device will turn. **1977** *Reader's Digest Bk. Do-It-Yourself Skills & Techniques* v. 154 Gravity toggles have a swivel toggle that drops vertically when pushed through a hole bored in the wall... Spring toggles have two spring-loaded gripping arms which expand after the toggle is pushed through a hole.

g. *Electronics.* = *LATCH *sb.*[1] 3 b. Also *toggle circuit.*

1953 *Proc. IRE* XLI. 1429/1 The toggles or other storage elements hold the accumulated count. **1955** *Sci. Amer.* June 93/2 In the logical circuits of a modern computer the memory units commonly consist of pairs of vacuum tubes connected in a circuit which is called a 'toggle' because of its analogy with a toggle switch. **1962** [see *BISTABLE *a.*]. **1971** J. H. SMITH *Digital Logic* iv. 54 The latch or toggle circuit is used to hold signals fed momentarily into a system.

h. *Computers.* A key or command that is always operated the same way but has the opposite effect on successive occasions.

1982 *Personal Computer World* Dec. 138/1, I find that the 'Install' program is unable to make the best of configuring for my printer as Wordstar expects toggles where the Epson has separate control codes for turning on and off certain modes.

3. *toggle fastening*; **toggle-bolt,** (*b*) = sense 2 f above; **toggle switch,** an electric switch operated by means of a projecting lever that is moved with a snap action, usu. up and down.

1934 WEBSTER, *Toggle bolt*, a bolt having a nut with pivoted flanged wings that close against a spring when passed through a constricted passage and open after emerging. **1968** *Trade Marks Jrnl.* 8 May 736/2 *Rawlplug*. .. Bolt anchoring devices, expansion bolts; toggle bolts, wall plugs and sockets. **1976** *Country Life* 29 Apr. 1143/1 Suit with toggle fastenings. **1976** *Woman's Weekly* 6 Nov. 49/2 Plus a zingy crochet jacket in bold bright stripes with toggle fastenings. **1938** *Rev. Sci. Instruments* IX. 86/1 A toggle switch allows application of the input pulses either..to the scaling circuit or to a thyratron pulse sharpener. **1962** *Times* 8 May 16/5 A steering column lever would be handier than the headlight toggle switch. **1976** *Gramophone* Apr. 1687/3 Neat toggle switches are provided for loudness, tape monitor, low and high filters and tone cancel.

toggle, *v.*[1] Add: **1.** (Earlier example.) Also *fig.*

1836 *Knickerbocker* VIII. 207 What,..has the devil toggled you at last, Jacky?

togidashi (tǫgida·ʃi). Also **togi-dashi.** [a. Jap. f. *togu* to whet, grind + *dasu* to produce, let appear.] A kind of Japanese lacquering in which several coats of lacquer, applied over gold or silver designs, are rubbed and ground down to let the underlying picture appear as if floating below the lacquer surface.

1881 *Trans. Asiatic Soc. Japan* IX. 26 For making *Togi-dashi*, gold dust of a slightly coarser quality is used than for ordinary *Hira-makiye*. **1911** *Encycl. Brit.* XV. 189/1 The togi-dashi design, when finely executed, seems to hang suspended in the velvety lacquer. **1911** [see *NASHIJI]. **1972** *Times* 15 June 21/3 A two-case togidashi inro by Moei at £1,000.

Togolese (togolī·z), *a.* and *sb.* [f. *Togo* + -ESE, after F. *togolais*.] **A.** *adj.* Of or pertaining to the state of Togo (formerly Togoland) in W. Africa. **B.** *sb.* The people of Togo.

1957 *Keesing's Contemp. Archives* 27 Apr.–4 May 15511/1 Continued Togolese representation in the French National Assembly. **1962** A. LEJEUNE *Duel in Shadows* II. x. 142 The Togolese..are not too fond of Dr. Nkrumah. **1972** *Times* 9 Oct. (Nigeria Suppl.) p. ii/2 General Gowon visited Lome for the twelfth anniversary of Togolese independence. **1983** *Times* 25 Jan. 6/1 Thousands of Togolese and Beninese have already left Lagos.

togt (toχt). *S. Afr.* [a. Afrikaans, a. Du. *tocht* expedition, journey.] †**1.** A trading expedition or venture. *Obs.*

[**1816** C. I. LATROBE *Jrnl.* 6 May (1818) 265 The master ..was about to set off..on a trip..to dispose of it [*sc.* arrack] in barter... They call this, going *op de tocht*.] **1860** *Queenstown Free Press* 8 Feb., Horses have been discovered amongst those of 'smouses' who were returning..after a somewhat successful *togt*. **1862** LADY DUFF-GORDON *Lett.* (1921) 105 He has made a fortune by 'going on *Togt*'.

2. Casual labour, hired for a specific job.

1901 A. R. R. TURNBULL *Tales from Natal* 120 The black devils..so often put us about by deserting—without even the possibility of our being able to obtain togt even. **1948** *Rep. Native Laws Comm. 1946–8* (Dept. Native Affairs, S. Afr.) 37/1 Migrant labour tends to be casual and to produce less and earn less than stable labour. The supply of such labour is often badly adjusted to the demand... In Durban it is..a characteristic of so-called togt or daily labour.

3. *attrib.* and *Comb.*, as *togt labour, labourer, work*; **togt boy,** a casual labourer; **togt-ganger** [ad. Afrikans *togganger* (also used)], a travelling trader; **togt licence,** a licence authorizing the holder to undertake casual labour.

1898 *Port Elizabeth Tel.* (Weekly ed.) 2 Sept., A Chinaman refused to supply a small quantity of bread and sugar to a togt boy on Saturday. **1972** J. McClure *Caterpillar Cop* ix. 139 He had slunk up to the door..and informed the maid he was a *togt* boy. She..said there were no odd jobs going. **1879** *Cape Monthly Mag.* Feb. 88 For a long time he used to accompany the togtgangers (hawkers or traders). **1896** R. Wallace *Farming Industr. Cape Colony* 91 The plant [*sc.* prickly pear] was first spread in the Colony by transport riders or 'togt-gangers'. **1957** L. G. Green *Beyond City Lights* 31 In slack times the clever speculators known as *toggangers* would drive out of Paarl with cavalcades of carts and wagons. **1951** *Cape Argus* 5 Jan. 5/7 Durban harbour had been crippled by a shortage of rail trucks and togt (casual) labour. *Ibid.*, A compound capable of housing up to 1,000 togt labourers should be set aside for this purpose. **1960** J. L. L. Sisson *S. Afr. Judicial Dict.* 121 Casual Labourer, in terms of Native Pass Laws, is synonymous with the term togt labourer. **1948** O. Walker *Kaffirs are Lively* 172 A Native is required to carry on his person..one or more of the following documents... 7. A receipt for *togt* (casual labour) licence. **1968** K. L. McMagh *Dinner of Herbs* xiv. 101 Is there work, togt work nearby?

toheroa (tōu:ərōu·ă). Also 9 **tairoa.** [a. Maori.] A large edible bivalve mollusc, *Amphidesma ventricosum*, native to New Zealand.

1873 J. E. Tinne *Wonderland of Antipodes* 66 She sent us a present of a basket of tairoas, a large white shell-fish from the coast, which is considered a delicacy... When roasted, or, better still, made into soup, they are not unlike the clams of New England. **1908** A. Hamilton *Fishing & Sea-Foods Anc. Maori* 13 An enterprising firm in Auckland has recently started a factory for canning toheroa. **1934** *Bulletin* (Sydney) 18 Apr. 20/4 It is only quite recently that toheroa soup has had any standing in culinary circles. **1967** K. Giles *Death & Mr. Prettyman* i. 37 The number one has special black caviar, but the two has smoked Spanish swordfish and New Zealand toheroa patties. **1976** *Daily Colonist* (Victoria, B.C.) 1 Oct. 25/5 The toheroa has a distinctive flavor.

tohoro, var. *Taharah.

tohunga. Delete 'of the second rank' in def. and add earlier and further examples.

1831 G. Bennett in *London Med. Gaz.* 12 Nov. 182/1 This species of Asplenium is a sacred plant among the New Zealanders..; it is used by the Tohunga, or Priest, when praying over a sick person. **1843** E. Dieffenbach *Trav. N.Z.* II. I. iv. 60 If a chief or his wife falls sick, the most influential tohunga..attends. **1928** [see *Atua]. **1938** R. D. Finlayson *Brown Man's Burden* 42 She was a witch all right—like her father the tohunga. **1943** [see *Rangatira]. **1955** W. J. Phillipps *Maori Carving Illustrated* 4 Some [carvings] were carried out under the instruction of the old tohunga. **1976–7** *Art N.Z.* Dec./Jan. 34/1 The art of kite making and flying played an important role in the lifestyles of the ancient Maoris. Their manufacture was a sacred and time-consuming affair, for, according to tradition, only a tohunga (priest) of some standing in the tribe could prepare them.

toich (toiχ). *Geogr.* [a. Dinka.] In Southern Sudan, a stretch of flat land near a river that is subject to annual flooding.

1948 J. D. Tothill *Agric. in Sudan* vii. 136 The 'toich' lands..are primarily used as grazing lands. *Ibid.* 954 Toiches are a feature of Equatoria Province. **1955** P. A. Buxton *Nat. Hist. Tsetse Flies* ix. 271 The same sharp edge may generally be observed in the southern Anglo-Egyptian Sudan, at the boundary of the 'toich' or grassy flood-plain on cotton soil, with deciduous woodland on ironstone. **1974** *Nature* 10 May 121/2 The site may have been subject to the type of annual flooding and partial drying which now occurs in 'toich' soils which adjoin rivers or 'khors' in the permanent swamps of the Sudd region in the southern Sudan.

Toidey (toi·di). Also **toid(e)y.** The proprietary name (in the U.S.) for a toilet-training apparatus that can be clipped or strapped on to an ordinary lavatory seat. Also *attrib.*

1924 *Official Gaz.* (U.S. Patent Office) 9 Dec. 300/2 Little Toidey... Water-Closet Seats for Infants, Attachable to Ordinary Water-Closet Seats. **1956** *Ibid.* 6 Mar. 42/2 Toidey. The Toidey Company, Gertrude A. Muller. **1963** M. McCarthy *Group* xiv. 323 She had set him on the new toidey-seat strapped to the regular toilet. *Ibid.*, She tried leaving him on the toidey. **1981** D. Uhnak *False Witness* xxiv. 164 It is the current day-by-day life we have to deal with, not mama and the toidy potty and papa and the primal scene.

toil, *sb.*[1] Add: **4.** *toil-bowed* adj.

1890 Kipling *Poems 1886–1929* (1929) III. 289 They strove to stand to attention, to straighten the toil-bowed back.

toil, *sb.*[2] Add: **3.** (Further *pl.* examples.)

1897 B. Stoker *Dracula* iv. 41, I am surely in the toils. .. In the present state of things it would be madness to quarrel openly with the Count whilst I am so absolutely in his power. **1931** V. Sackville-West *All Passion Spent* I. 69 Their mother quietly disentangling herself from their toils. **1958** E. Birney *Turvey* v. 46 Soldiers in the toils of civilian law for thefts, burglaries, assaults, rapes and the odd murder. **1973** J. G. Farrell *Siege of Krishnapur* vi. 91 How hopelessly Prejudice, on the point of throwing a net over Truth, had become enmeshed in its own toils.

toile. Add: Also 8 **toille. 1. b.** A painting on canvas.

1919 R. Fry *Let.* 6 Oct. (1972) II. 458 Her old studio.. was stacked with her husband's immense *toiles* of Majorca. **1949** N. Mitford *Love in Cold Climate* II. v. 237 The dozens of *toiles* by him..are worthy of the Douanier himself.

2. Also with Fr. defining addition; esp. *toile de Jouy*, a fabric for upholstery or drapery with a characteristic floral, figure, or landscape design, usu. in one colour on a light background, orig. made at Jouy-en-Josas near Paris.

1794 A. Young *Trav. France* (ed. 2) I. xix. 552 The linens..are *toille de menage*; that exported to Spain is.. called *toille de leon*. **1873** *Young Englishwoman* Oct. 506/1 Paletot of grey-coloured toile de laine. **1923** *Weekly Dispatch* 11 Feb. 14, 5,000 Yards of Toile de Chine. Made of finest Spun Silk. **1934** E. Waugh *Handful of Dust* i. 16 She hasn't paid for the toile-de-jouy chaircovers we made her last April. **1958** I. Murdoch *Bell* ix. 135 She saw the flat in Knightsbridge..glowing with stripy wallpaper and *toile de Jouy*. **1983** *Harrods Mag.* Spring & Summer 143 'Toile de Jouy', a French pastoral scene in Deep Pink on Plain Pink.

3. A pattern for a garment made up in muslin, cotton, or the like, for fitting or for use in making copies.

1959 *Guardian* 18 Nov. 6/4 An excellent little collection of models made from toiles bought in Paris. **1982** *Times* 29 June 13/4, I spent seven months of a two-year couture course *just* making toiles for skirts.

‖ **toilé** (twale). [Fr. *toilé*, f. *toile* Toile.] In lace-making, an area with a closely-worked inwrought pattern.

1865 F. B. Palliser *Hist. Lace* iii. 27 The flower or ornament..is called 'toilé', from the flat, close texture resembling linen, and also from its being often made of that material, or of muslin. **1902** [see *Binche]. **1953** M. Powys *Lace & Lace-Making* v. 41 The linen part or Toilé should show the effect of the raised work.

toilet, *sb.* Add: With spelling **toilette** now usu. pronounced (twāle·t).

5. a. (Further examples, with emphasis on washing and grooming.)

1811 B. Wynne *Diary* 18 Sept. in *Wynne Diaries* (1940) III. x. 340 We began our toilette which refreshed us much after the fatigue of having sat up the whole night. **1890** G. Gissing *Emancipated* I. I. iii. 83 But when at length he appeared at the dinner-table, once more fresh from his toilet, then did a gleam of animation transform his countenance. **1939** T. S. Eliot *Old Possum's Bk. Pract. Cats* 20 They make their toilette and take their repose.

6. (Earlier example.)

1752 A. Hervey *Let.* 27 Nov. in *11th Rep. Hist. MSS. Comm.* App. IV. 380 in *Parl. Papers 1887* (C. 5060–111) XLVII. 309 'Tis so long (tell Lady Caroline) since I have seen so spruce a Toylet as hers.

7. The restricted sense 'a lavatory' is now in widespread use. (Further examples.) Also (contextually), a lavatory bowl or pedestal; a room or cubicle containing a lavatory.

1917 C. R. Wadhams *Simple Directions for Chambermaid* 50 The toilet should be kept absolutely clean. Hot water with washing soda or cleanser is often needed to clean it thoroughly, using the chamber-cloth or toilet brush for that purpose. **1930** F. J. Eble tr. *Grisar's Martin Luther* v. 108 In the second story of this tower there was a so-called hypocaust, i.e., a furnace-room, and beneath it the toilet (*cloaca*) of the monks. **1955** A. Huxley *Genius & Goddess* 109 She..poured the perfume into the toilet and pulled the plug. **1957** J. Braine *Room at Top* xxiv. 196 You could watch me on the toilet. **1959** S. Gibbons *Pink Front Door* xviii. 222 Such a *gentleman*.. always pretended not to see you if he met you coming out of the toilet. **1968** B. Hines *Kestrel for Knave* 193 He struck a match. A moment while it flared, then two urinals, a toilet in a doorless cubicle, and the sink without a tap. **1979** L. & J. Brown *Our Miracle called Louise* i. 16 A harsh voice beat against the door of a toilet at the home. I had bolted myself inside.

9. a. (mainly sense *7) *toilet article, bucket, jug, kit, -service* (earlier example), *-set* (further examples), *-tidy, ware*; *toilet block, bowl, lid, seat, stall, tank.*

1868 *Mich. Agric. Rep.* VII. 351 Perfumery toilet articles. **1981** 'J. Ross' *Dark Blue & Dangerous* iv. 23 He checked the essentially male shaver and toilet articles. **1976** *Star* (Sheffield) 26 Nov. 26/5 A two-classroom mobile unit and toilet block. **1947** E. Hodgins *Mr. Blandings builds his Dream House* II. xii. 164 One bathroom seemed all but finished... A toilet bowl was in place. **1983** *Out of Town* Dec. 16/3 We could at least instal the odd alligator in the toilet-bowl. **1957** H. Roosenburg *Walls came tumbling Down* 11 A guard would..open one cell, and allow two prisoners to come out, one with the toilet bucket, the other with the water jug. **1873** J. H. Ewing *Flat Iron for Farthing* iv. 37, I fancied that I heard the familiar sound of Rubens lapping water from the toilette jug in my room at home. **1913** C. Mackenzie *Sinister Street* I. II. iv. 198 After trying to soak a shadowy tomcat down below with water from the toilet-jug Michael and Alan would undress. **1922** S. Lewis *Babbitt* xiii. 163 The leather seat piled with dingy toilet-kits, and the air nauseating with the smell of soap and toothpaste. **1982** D. Bagley *Windfall* xxii. 221 Stafford took his toilet kit and went into the bathroom. **1971** J. D. Macdonald *Seven* (1974) vi. 143 Turned toilet lid down. Sat on it. **1941** N. Last *Diary* 4 Aug. in *Nella Last's War* (1983) 165, I remember washing the floor and toilet seat. **1982** J. Aiken *Whisper in Night* 114 A small round lavatory, with a mahogany Victorian toilet seat. **1855** Geo. Eliot in *Fraser's Mag.* June 706/1 A decanter and a sugar-basin or pie-dish, are an ample toilette service for them. **1890** O. Wilde *Picture of Dorian Gray* (1891) viii. 138 A chased silver Louis-Quinze toilet-set. **1977** G. Marton *Alarum* 6 The *New Yorkers* on top of Claire's toilet set. **1978** R. Ludlum *Holcroft Covenant* xxiii. 265 If they let the weapon through, he was to reassemble it immediately, in the toilet stall of a men's room. **1974** R. B. Parker *Godwulf Manuscript* xvi. 126 There was nothing in the toilet tank. **1912** Toilet-tidy [used s.v. Tidy *sb.* c]. **1921** D. H. Lawrence *Let.* 10 Nov. (1962) 674, I haven't heard from him, so I can't send him..a set of toilet-tidies until I do. **1928** A. M. Davies *Bk. with Seven Seals* xvii. 380 Mary Anne was not inspired with any admiration for the antimacassars and toilet-tidies that she made. **1864** *Hist. North-Western Soldiers' Fair* (Chicago) 168, 1 set fancy toilet ware. **1977** *Western Morning News* 30 Aug. 2/3 Woolland, Son & Manico have received instructions from private vendors to sell by auction..toilet ware.

b. toilet box, a box containing toilet articles; **toilet brush,** (*a*) a brush used in washing and grooming; (*b*) a lavatory brush; **toilet-case** (earlier example); **toilet club** (see quot. 1966); **toilet-cover** (earlier example); **toilet-glass** (earlier example); **toilet humour** = *lavatory humour* s.v. *Lavatory *sb.* 8; **toilet-paper** (examples of use in lavatories); also *attrib.*; **toilet powder,** a form of dusting powder employed in the toilet, talcum powder; **toilet roll,** a roll of toilet paper; also *attrib.*; **toilet tent,** a tent serving as a lavatory; **toilet tissue,** tissue for use as toilet paper; **toilet-training** *vbl. sb.*, the training of a child to adopt acceptable habits of urination and defecation; hence **toilet-train** *v. trans.*, **toilet-trained** *ppl. a.*

1774 J. Wedgwood *Let.* 2 Mar. (1965) 158 We shall send you some Toilet boxes. **1869** Lady C. Schreiber *Jrnl.* (1950) I. 10 A fan-shaped toilet box made of Chelsea china. **1936** *Burlington Mag.* July 26/1 The tall rectangular toilet-box bears the old standard hall-marks of 1723–24. **1897** *Sears, Roebuck Catal.* 33/2 Rubber Toilet Brush. For the nails and hands. **1917** Toilet brush [see sense 7 above]. **1976** *Sunday Mail* (Glasgow) 26 Dec. 5/7 We went into a bar and found a toilet brush in the gents which still had a price label on it. ?**1879** S. F. P. *Stepping Westward* 8 My toilet case for my brush and comb. **1884** W. S. Gilbert *Princess Ida* ii. 69 He grew moustachios, and he took his tub, And he paid a gui-nea to a toi-let club—And he paid a gui-nea to a toi-let club. **1966** J. S. Cox *Illustr. Dict. Hairdressing & Wigmaking* 150/2 *Toilet club*, a barber's shop which, in the 19th cent., offered reduced charges to clients who paid a regular quarterly or yearly subscription. **1838** C. Gilman *Recoll. Southern Matron* xxix. 207 The bride's chamber..neatly set off with white curtains and toilet cover. **1818** M. Edgeworth *Let.* 29 Oct. (1971) 132 Long rolling toilette glass and every piece of furniture belonging to better times. **1956** Auden & Kallman *Magic Flute* (1957) 60 Indulged in toilet-humour with his cousin. **1907** *Yesterday's Shopping* (1969) 340/1 Automatic toilet paper rack... Only one sheet of paper can be drawn at a time. **1956** [see *lavatory paper* s.v. *Lavatory *sb.* 8]. **1976** M. H. Kingston *Woman Warrior* (1977) 181 Her sister went into one of the stalls and got handfuls of toilet paper and wiped her off. **1840** *Picayune* (New Orleans) 28 July 4/1 [Merchandise includes]..perfumed toilet and pearl powders. **1898** W. J. Locke *Idols* viii. 107 A delicate odour of toilette-washes and powder hung on the warmth of the room. **1934** A. P. Herbert *Holy Deadlock* 172 Mr. Rigby..propped the door open with a toilet roll. **1961** *Guardian* 20 Jan. 2/7, 17 toilet roll holders..have been broken or stolen. **1982** *Times* 1 June 18/6 There would seem to be very little difference between one soft toilet roll and another. **1969** *Guardian* 2 Sept. 6/7 A crushed marquee, two burnt-out toilet tents, and a partly demolished fence. **1968** N. Giovanni in W. King *Black Short Story Anthol.* (1972) 30 We'd get slightly used toilet tissue with an article on it or brown paper bags with short sayings or just a note to say they dig us. **1982** *Verbatim* Summer 5/1 Take lavatory paper, or, in the genteel euphemism of Adspeak, toilet tissue. **1951** *Med. Jrnl. Austral.* XXXVIII. II. 111/2 Of our 73 children, 43 were toilet trained with impatience. **1961** *Guardian* 8 May 6/1 When a baby shows signs of being 'toilet trained' a mother can look forward to the end of nappy washing. **1980** A. Cornelisen *Flight from Torregreca* x. 202 The long process of toilet training her children. **1940** *Time* 15 Apr. 48/1 Toilet Training. **1955** B. Spock *Baby & Child Care* 177 Sometimes parents make a great fuss about toilet training. **1964** M. Argyle *Psychol. & Social Probl.* i. 19 An example of a Freudian hypothesis which has been definitely refuted is the hypothesis that early or traumatic toilet training should lead to an anal personality. **1973** E.-J. Bahr *Nice Neighbourhood* ii. 19, I hope Women's Lib never gets to hear about it, but..it was like fun to sit and talk about toilet training.

toilet, *v.* Add: **c.** To assist or supervise in using a toilet (sense 7); *refl.* to use a toilet unaided.

1954 F. G. Blake *Child, his Parents & Nurse* v. 150 Some children stay awake after they have been toileted. **1973** *Lancet* 9 June 1301/1 The same type of elderly patient..may be..wheeled to the toilet in sanitary chairs, or toileted on these within the ward. **1976** *Listener* 19 Feb. 206/1 He is 100 per cent physically and mentally handicapped... He cannot walk, talk, feed or toilet himself.

toileted *ppl. a.* (earlier example); **toi·leting** *vbl. sb.*

1864 'P. Paterson' *Glimpses of Real Life* xxx. 289 There is a gay cavalcade of exquisitely-'toileted' ladies. **1954** F. G. Blake *Child, his Parents & Nurse* v. 157 Until the child has thoroughly mastered his impulses to soil and has incorporated his mother's standards into his conscience, successful achievement in toileting is dependent upon his reward (mother's pride and acceptance). **1977** *Lancet* 17 Dec. 1294/2 She was found to be depressed, occasionally aggressive, and totally dependent on others in all self-care activities, including feeding, toileting, and grooming.

toiletry. (In Dict. s.v. TOILET *sb.*) Restrict *nonce* to senses in Dict. and add: **c.** A preparation for use in washing or grooming. Chiefly in *pl.*

1927 *Glasgow Herald* 5 May 8 One really up-to-date shop coins a new and compact name for these indispensable odds and ends and calls them 'toiletteries'. **1927** *Hollis St. Theatre Programme* (U.S.) 19 Sept. (Advt.), Her keen individuality finds in the inimitable Djer-Kiss *odeur* a refreshing complement; she fastidiously insists upon it in *all* her toiletries! **1957** *Observer* 10 Nov. 11/2 'Men's toiletries' are now accepted here as they have been in America for years past. **1981** M. KENYON *Zigzag* iv. 23 The hold-all..held clothing and toiletries.

to-·infi·nitive. [f. To *prep.* + INFINITIVE *sb.*] The infinitive form of the verb immediately preceded by *to.*

1946 O. JESPERSEN *Mod. Eng. Gram.* V. 154 There is no reason to have a separate name for the to-infinitive. **1964** C. BARBER *Linguistic Change in Present-Day Eng.* vi. 135 Another auxiliary which is becoming extremely important is *be going* followed by a *to*-infinitive.

toi-toi. Now the usual spelling of TOE-TOE.

1843 [see TOE-TOE]. **1907** 'K. MANSFIELD' *Jrnl.* Nov.–Dec. (1954) 23 A clump of *toi-toi* waving in the wind, and looking for all the world like a family of little girls drying their hair. **1957** J. FRAME *Owls do Cry* 13 The place was like a shell with gold tickle of toi-toi around its edges. **1981** M. GEE *Meg* xxi. 244 Hedges of toi-toi and fields of fat spring grass.

tokamak (tōᵘ·kămæk). *Physics.* [a. Russ. *tokamák*, f. *to*roidálnaya *ká*mera s *ma*gnítnym pólem, toroidal chamber with magnetic field.] One kind of toroidal apparatus for producing controlled fusion reactions in a hot plasma, distinguished by the fact that the controlling magnetic field is the sum of a toroidal field due to external windings and a poloidal field due to an induced longitudinal current in the plasma.

1969 *Nature* 1 Nov. 488/1 Measurements have been made of the electron temperature and density of the plasma in the toroidal discharge apparatus Tokamak T3..at the Kurchatov Institute. **1972** *Sci. Amer.* July 73/3 The first large Tokamak machine put into operation in the U.S. resulted from a conversion of the Model *C* stellarator in the Princeton University Plasma Physics Laboratory. **1980** *Ann. Rep. 1979/80* (U.K. Atomic Energy Authority) 31/1 In tokamaks, plasma is heated and confined by an electric current induced by transformer action, while a strong external field stabilizes the plasma. **1981** [see *STELLARATOR]. **1984** *N.Y. Times Bk. Rev.* 1 Apr. 23/2 In the race to achieve commercial success, Princeton's tokamak (the original Russian acronym for a toroidal magnetic chamber) is pitted against..laser technology.

Tokarev (tǫ·kärʸef). The name of the Russian designer of firearms F. V. *Tokarev* (1871–1968), used *attrib.* and *absol.* to designate any of a range of automatic and semi-automatic firearms designed or developed by him.

1953 W. G. B. ALLEN *Pistols, Rifles & Machine Guns* iii. 33 Hotchkiss machine guns and the Russian Tokarev rifles provide examples of the cupped piston. *Ibid.* xi. 138 Modern manufacturing techniques permit the weight to be no greater than that of an orthodox rifle; the Russian Tokarev weighs 8¾ pounds. **1956** 'E. MCBAIN' *Cop Hater* (1958) xiv. 123, I keep a few guns... There's a Luger, and a Mauser, and I even got a Tokarev. **1981** S. DUNMORE *Ace* II. i. 150 The Russian was dead..a Tokarev pistol in his right hand.

Tokay[1]. Add: Also, in Alsace (more fully *Tokay d'Alsace*) the Pinot Gris vine, grape, or white wine made from this. Also, an Australian vine, grape, and white wine.

1959 W. JAMES *Word-bk. Wine* 190 The tokay of Alsace bears no resemblance to the Hungarian wine; light and fruity, with sometimes a pink tinge, it is made from the pinot gris,..Australia, too, has a vine called the tokay, which yields a good sweet white dessert wine. **1967** A. LICHINE *Encycl. Wines & Spirits* 67/2 Wines from the Pinot Gris (which, in this region, has for centuries been called the Tokay d'Alsace) and Gewürztraminer varieties. *Ibid.* 107/1 The versatility of Australian soil has been amply demonstrated..by its ability to produce..from Tokay either a dry white or a luscious dessert wine. **1976** [see *PINOT]. **1983** *Wine Soc. 1982/1983* (Ann. Rep., Internat. Exhib. Co-operative Wine Soc.) 21 These '82s..are good by any standard, the Gewürztraminer and Tokay particularly so.

toke (tōᵘk), *sb.*[1] *slang.* [Origin uncertain.] (A piece of) bread; also *fig.* (see quot. 1967).

1843 DICKENS *Let.* 7 June (1974) III. 503 Now, we don't want none of your sarse—and if you bung any of them tokes of yours in this direction, you'll find your shuttlecock sent back as heavy as it came. **1874** M. CLARKE *His Natural Life* I. vii. 53 Sarah was standing on the poop throwing bits o' toke to the gulls... She..throwed crumbs and such like up in the air over the side. **1905** [see *GROUND *ppl. a.* 1 a]. **1963** M. KENDON *Ladies College, Goudhurst* 8 Dripping..spread on 'tokes', was eaten for eleven o'clock lunch by schoolgirls for well nigh forty years. **1967** K. GILES *Death in Diamonds* v. 90 'If you fall foul of Tiny Holdsworth he gives you toke.'..'In the local dialect..toke used to be poor quality bread, hence toke and water equals punishment.'

toke (tōᵘk), *sb.*[2] *U.S. slang.* [Origin uncertain: cf. *TOKE *v.*] An inhalation of smoke from a cigarette or pipe containing marijuana or other narcotic substance.

1968 *Harper's Mag.* Mar. 48 If he still took a toke of marijuana from time to time..still! Mailer was not in approval of any drug. **1973** R. L. SIMON *Big Fix* xii. 87, I packed my pipe with..hashish... I took a good heavy toke and held it in as long as I could. **1976** *New Yorker* 17 May 34/3 The host shall light up and take the first toke. He will then offer the joint to the first woman on his left. **1980** *London Mag.* Aug.–Sept. 106/1 He takes huge tokes from a home-made hookah.

toke (tōᵘk), *sb.*[3] *N. Amer. slang.* [Origin uncertain: perh. an abbrev. of TOKEN *sb.*] A gratuity or tip.

1971 *Daily Colonist* (Victoria, B.C.) 22 June 18/4 The prime advantage [of being a waitress] is instant money—tips or 'tokes' as they are known in the profession. **1981** *Miami Herald* 26 Mar. 30A/2 They have just gone in and hassled people on tips and tokes.

toke (tōᵘk), *v.* *U.S. slang.* [Origin uncertain: cf. *TOKE *sb.*[2]] *intr.* and *trans.* To smoke (a marijuana cigarette). Also const. *up.* Hence **to·ker.**

1952 *Amer. Speech* XXVII. 30 *Toke v.*, to smoke a cigarette; to take a puff of a cigarette. **1973** *Newsweek* 1 Jan. 4 Bill Buckley says he went 'outside the 3-mile limit —I'm a law-and-order advocate, you know'—to toke up, but neglects to mention where he got the stuff. **1975** *High Times* Dec. 6/2 Thousands of tokers. *Ibid.* 13/2 This hash oil joint is one of the most satisfying ways of toking oil. **1979** N. MAILER *Executioner's Song* (1980) I. xxi. 339 He had been over at a friend of his selling drugs, a little crystal, some speed, toked a couple, got blasted.

token, *sb.* Add: **1. f.** *Semiotics*, etc. A particular and individual sign, as opposed to the type of which it is an instance. Cf. *TYPE *sb.*[1] 8 e.

1908 C. S. PEIRCE in *Coll. Papers* (1958) VIII. 240, I devoted much study to my ten trichotomies of signs... I ..called..an Actisign a Token, a Famisign a Type. **1955** N. CHOMSKY *Logical Struct. Linguistic Theory* (microfilm, Mass. Inst. Technol.) i. 31 The assumption..that it is possible to assign a meaning to each utterance token to be compared with other meanings. **1971** J. B. CARROLL et al. *Word Freq. Bk.* p. xix, A *type* is a particular word, counted just once, regardless of how many times it occurs; a *token* is any of the individual occurrences of the type. **1979** *Computers & Humanities* X. 135/1 Without further intervention concordances remain concordances of word tokens and not of headwords.

7. b. *Railways.* (See quot. 1936.)

1936 *Gloss. Terms Railway Signalling* (*B.S.I.*) 51 *Token*, the authority which must be carried by trainmen to permit a train to travel over a prescribed section of a single line. **1968** O. S. NOCK *Railway Enthusiast's Encycl.* 273 The tokens are engraved with the stations at each end of the sections to which they apply. **1971** D. J. SMITH *Discovering Railwayana* iv. 20 Tokens for single-line working were frequently fitted with a looped end and attached to a vertical post near a junction with the main line.

11. b. A voucher exchangeable for goods or services; *book token*: see *BOOK *sb.* 18; *gift-token*: see *GIFT *sb.* 9 b; *record token*: see *RECORD *sb.* 14. Also, a small disc or other piece representing or resembling a coin, esp. one used to operate a machine or in exchange for goods or services. Freq. with defining word.

1908 R. BROOKE *Let.* Mar. (1968) 123 Dear Mother, I am so sorry about the Boots token. I quite failed to realize..that it was wanted at once. **1934** WEBSTER, *Token*, ..the metal fare or ticket issued by a transportation company. **1942** BERREY & VAN DEN BARK *Amer. Thes. Slang* § 560/4 Scrip; tokens; coupons; etc. **1954** *Daily Progress* (Charlottesville, Va.) 26 July 16/2 If the Department of Urbiculture will hand out free bus tokens, I'm not too much against the ideas. **1961** WEBSTER, *Token*,..a game counter. **1965** AYLLON & AZRIN in *Jrnl. Exper. Anal. Behav.* VIII. 358/2 Special metal tokens were used as conditioned reinforcers. **1966** G. W. TURNER *Eng. Lang. Austral. & N.Z.* viii. 174 The *milk tokens*..are put out for milk last thing at night. **1968** *Listener* 29 Aug. 266/3 The patients are paid with tokens resembling money for acting normally, and..behaving inappropriately or psychotically results in a loss of tokens. **1973** *People's Jrnl.* (Inverness) 4 Aug. 16/4 A little boy who joined in the scramble collected, in addition to money, nine milk tokens, at that time each valid for 'a pinta'. **1976** *Southern Even. Echo* (Southampton) 18 Nov. 18/5 Those who come to watch the show and contribute nothing (or only fruit machine tokens!) if the show is to be held again. **1977** *Washington Post* 16 June DC3 The subway will no longer accept the 10-cent student bus tokens. **1978** *Times Lit. Suppl.* 1 Dec. 1400/3 Boards range in style from Cruikshank's 'Comic Game of the Great Exhibition of 1851' to the Mondrian simplicity of 'Quartette' and counters or tokens are provided. **1980** J. BARNES *Metroland* II. iv. 113 Orange ten-shilling notes at Christmas and Boots tokens. **1980** *Washington Post Mag.* 29 June 20 The valet reminds you to present your parking token to your waiter 15 minutes before you plan to leave so that your car will be waiting. **1981** M. GEE *Dying, in Other Words* 111 The milkman, who was dishonest, and sometimes stole Clothilde's token, leaving no milk. **1982** *Christian Sci. Monitor* 15 Nov. 1 A collector of transportation tokens. **1983** *N.Y. Times* 9 Oct. I. 1/1 The price of bus and subway tokens..must be increased.

15. a. Restrict *'arch.* or *dial.'* to *by this* (or *that*) *token* and sense (b) and add: (*a*) (later examples of *by the same token*).

1875 'MARK TWAIN' in *Atlantic Monthly* Aug. 193/2 By the same token any person can see that seven hundred and forty-two years from now the Lower Mississippi will be only a mile and three quarters long. **1945** B. MACDONALD *Egg & I* (1946) I. i. 11 If you marry a doctor, don't whine because he doesn't keep the hours of a shoe clerk, and by the same token if you marry a shoe clerk, don't complain because he doesn't make as much money as a doctor. **1970** 'D. HALLIDAY' *Dolly & Cookie Bird* v. 66 I've dined out on a few stories about her. But not ones that matter. By the same token, she could have made quite a good thing about telling how she saw you..that night. **1978** *Jrnl. R. Soc. Arts* CXXVI. 701/1 By the same token, among the most interesting and valuable sections of this book are those which deal with technique.

16. a. token booth *U.S.*, a booth from which tokens are sold, esp. those for obtaining tickets for a subway; **token economy,** in the treatment of behavioural disorders, the principle or practice of rewarding desirable behaviour with tokens which can be exchanged for goods or privileges and punishing undesirable behaviour by withholding or forfeiting such tokens; **token-reflexive** *a.* (*Logic*), denoting words the referent or temporal or spatial orientation of which is contextually determined, e.g. 'I', 'now', 'here', 'today'; also as *sb.*

1970 *New Yorker* 31 Oct. 123/1 Their reptile-papered basement..is a bit bigger than a token booth. **1968** AYLLON & AZRIN *Token Economy* ii. 16 We first conceived of the token economy and its use as a motivational system for therapy during the early part of 1961. **1981** W. REICH in Bloch & Chodoff *Psychiatr. Ethics* iv. 59 The development of aversive techniques of control, 'token economies' and other forms of behaviour modification. **1947** H. REICHENBACH *Elem. Symbolic Logic* vii. 284 Words which refer to the corresponding token used in an individual act of speech, or writing..may therefore be called *token-reflexive* words. **1949** *Mind* LVIII. 356 Personal pronouns are to be distinguished from personal proper names such as 'Jones', or 'Fleur',..by their different use, the former 'token reflexive', the latter 'proper name'. **1962** W. & M. KNEALE *Devel. Logic* ii. 53 A sentence containing a token-reflexive taken out of context expresses no proposition at all. **1968** A. J. AYER *Origins of Pragmatism* 156 With the exception of quantifiers and relative pronouns,..designations are token-reflexive. That is to say, their use is determined by the context.

b. passing into *adj.* Serving as a token; pro forma; (purely) symbolic; constituting a gesture (only); minimal, nominal, perfunctory; cf. *STATUTORY *a.* 3 b; **token estimate,** a provisional statement of a sum of money, placed before Parliament to allow discussion to proceed; **token payment,** (*a*) the payment of a small proportion of a sum due, as an indication that the debt has not been repudiated; (*b*) a nominal payment; **token stoppage, strike,** a brief strike to demonstrate strength of feeling only; **token vote,** a vote of money on the basis of a token estimate.

1915 *Political Q.* May 147 For form's sake 'token' estimates were presented, on the basis of £1,000 for each vote and £100 for each appropriation in aid. **1923** *Times* 27 Feb. 18/3 On the Supplementary Vote of £10 for Diplomatic and Consular Services..the anticipated savings under various subheads were rather larger than £155,198, and would..be sufficient to cover the whole amount now asked for; but inasmuch as all but one of the subheads referred to new services, it had been thought right that a token vote of £10 should be put down in order to provide the opportunity for discussing these new services. **1933** *Sun* (Baltimore) 15 June 1/7 The British Government..tendered a partial or 'token' payment of $10,000,000 to the United States 'as an acknowledgment of the (war) debts pending a final settlement'. **1937** *Ibid.* 19 Oct. 6/1 British and French authorities have expressed belief that there are at least 100,000 Italians serving under Generalissimo Francisco Franco and have urged a 'token' withdrawal on that basis as a guarantee of good faith. **1941** *Ibid.* 28 June 6/3 Less than a week after launching its aggression, Berlin has requested other European states to dispatch 'token forces' to the battlefield. *Ibid.* 29 Aug. 12/3 They [sc. the Persians] have insured themselves against this..by making a token resistance and yielding to demonstrated superior force. **1947** *Daily Mail* 22 May 1 Civil Servants in some sections are considering 'token' strikes if their wages claims continue to drag on without result. **1954** *Times* 20 Jan. 6/7 Twenty-six workers employed by a Manchester contractor have been dismissed for participating in Monday's token stoppage. **1958** *Listener* 12 June 978/1 Some London railway workers vote in favour of an unofficial 'token' strike in support of busmen. **1960** *Time* 12 Dec. 56 The schools took in token Negroes. **1962** *N.Y. Times Mag.* 5 Aug. 11 The current notion that token integration will satisfy his people, says Dr. King, is an illusion. **1968** C. BROOKE-ROSE *Between* 7 More often the bathroom..has a token window on the hotel corridor or no window at all, merely a ventilation shaft. **1970** J. G. FARRELL *Troubles* I. 10 For some reason —the poor quality of the soil or the proximity of the sea—vegetation has only made a token attempt to possess them. **1971** H. MACMILLAN *Riding Storm* xiv. 442, I..only agreed to a very small, almost a token, delivery of arms to Tunisia. **1972** D. E. WESTLAKE *Bank Shot* ix. 64 He and his wife Linda were the token whites at this dinner party..the three other couples all being black. **1974** *Times* 21 May 7/8 No tightly run business will have 'token' women on the board. Each director must be able to offer some exceptional contribution. **1976** *New Society* 7 Oct.

28/3 The resistance is little more than token. **1979** J. COOPER *Class* iv. 82 'We've even got two Punk Rockers' (rather like token blacks).

tokenism (tōᵘ·kĕniz'm). orig. *U.S.* [f. *TOKEN *sb.* 16 b + -ISM.] The practice or policy of making merely a token effort or granting only minimal concessions, esp. to minority or suppressed groups.

1962 *N.Y. Times Mag.* 5 Aug. 11 (*heading*) The case against tokenism. **1963** *Times* 28 May 10/1 Tactics such as 'tokenism', which have been adopted in some southern states seeking to delay the process of desegregation without opposing the original court order. **1972** [see *JOUAL]. **1976** R. BAXANDALL in Mitchell & Oakley *Rights & Wrongs of Women* viii. 265 Women are not encouraged to become leaders in unions. Tokenism is a standard practice. **1980** *Jewish Chron.* 12 Sept. 27/3 Philip Rosenthal.. waffled on about 'tokenism' in his factory, where two workers sit on the board, as if real democracy had been achieved.

Hence **tokeni·stic** *a.*, of the nature of tokenism.

1976 in *6,000 Words.* **1977** M. EDELMAN *Political Lang.* vii. 125 Disorder..invites a response that is only tokenistic or symbolic when the protest is narrow in scope and expressed through conventional tactics. **1983** *Daily Tel.* 14 Sept. 32/5 That was just a tokenistic load of knackers about gay rights.

tokenless, *a.* (Later example.)

1969 *Railway Mag.* Feb. 88 (*caption*) Introduction of tokenless-block working over this route will make these [*sc.* tablet-catchers], and associated lineside equipment, redundant.

‖ **toki** (tǫ·ki). *N.Z.* [Maori.] A Maori war adze or axe, usu. of stone. Freq. with defining addition.

1860 A. S. ATKINSON *Let.* 9 Apr. in *Richmond–Atkinson Papers* (1960) I. 559 It was perfectly innocuous, I believe, in the ordinary way of guns and was probably intended not to hit us but to frighten us into a fit state for nobbling with the toki. **1905** W. B. *Where White Man Treads* 93 The Maori was..provided with no more efficient tool.. than the 'toki panehe' (stone axe). **1949** P. BUCK *Coming of Maori* II. vi. 188 The ceremonial adze termed *toki pou tangata* was formed of a nephrite adze lashed to a carved haft.

‖ **tokoloshe** (tǫ:kǭlǫ·ʃi). *S. Afr.* Also **thikoloshe, tikolosh(e), tokolosh,** etc. [Sotho *thokolosi, t(h)ikoloshi,* Xhosa *uThikoloshe,* Zulu *utokoloshe.*] In African folklore, a mischievous and lascivious hairy dwarf.

1833 S. KAY *Trav. in Caffraria* xiii. 339 *Tikaloshi* also is much more frequently and familiarly talked about than amongst the more southern tribes. **1894** E. GLANVILLE *Fair Colonist* 82 Tikoloshe is supposed to be an evil spirit which takes the shape of a small man. **1911** *Daily Dispatch* (E. London, S. Afr.) 24 Nov. 7 One might be dragged into the watery den of the *tikolosh.* **1927** W. PLOMER *Notes for Poems* 30 The water spirits laughed at her, my friends the tokoloshes. **1949** *Handbk. Race Relations in S. Afr.* 561 The most widely believed in amongst many Nguni tribes is *thikoloshe.* **1959** L. G. GREEN *These Wonders to Behold* 22 Witchcraft has never lost its grip on the African native. Wherever you go, from Algiers to Cape Town..you will find black millions who are still ruled by the fear of djinns and demons,..ngogwe and tokoloshe. **1972** *Country Life* 10 Feb. 348/2, I was looking at a modern bronze..of a Tokoloshe, a Bantu evil spirit. **1974** *Stand. Encycl. S. Afr.* X. 504/2 The tikolosh (or tokolosh) is believed to be a dwarfish being, pitch-black, with a hairy body and baboon-like face..half-human and half-animal, having only one buttock, while the male has an enormous sexual organ.

‖ **tokonoma** (tōᵘ:kǫ̆nōᵘ·mă). Also 8–9 **toko, tokko.** [Jap.] In a Japanese house, a recess or alcove, usu. a few inches above floor-level, in which pictures, ornaments, etc., are displayed. Also *attrib.*

1727 J. G. SCHEUCHZER tr. *Kæmpfer's Hist. Japan* II. iv. 421 In the solid wall of the room there is allways a *Tokko*..or a sort of a cupboard, raised about a foot.. above the floor, and very near two feet deep. **1822** F. SHOBERL tr. *Titsingh's Illustrations of Japan* II. 202 Two cakes..which are placed as an ornament within the *toko.* **1871** A. B. MITFORD *Tales of Old Japan* II. 127 The *tokonoma*—that portion of the Japanese room which is raised a few inches above the rest of the floor, and which is regarded as the place of honour. **1929** *Periodical* Feb. 25 The whole set [of the *O.E.D.*] of mine is now sitting stately on the 'tokonoma' of my study in my residence by the side of a Japanese 'Oxford Dictionary'. **1957** C. BROOKE-ROSE *Languages of Love* 45 The recess on the left of the chimney-breast, which Georgina had turned into a *tokonoma.* **1980** J. MELVILLE *Chrysanthemum Chain* 14 In the *tokonoma* alcove a modest flower arrangement stood in a simple bowl.

Tok Pisin (tǫk pi·zin). Also **talk Pidgin.** [Pidgin, = talk pidgin.] A Melanesian pidgin English spoken in Papua New Guinea.

1943 R. A. HALL *Melanesian Pidgin Phrase-Bk. & Vocab.* 52 *Pidgin,*..talk Pidgin. **1976** *Language* LII. 631 We first began working on the problem of relativization in New Guinea Tok Pisin (Melanesian Pidgin English, Neo-Melanesian) in 1972. **1982** *Trans. Philol. Soc.* 103 Unfortunately, data about the use of Tok Pisin by the indigenous population is very scarce.

tola² (tōᵘ·lă). [a. *ntola,* name used in Zaïre.] = *AGBA.

1897 M. KINGSLEY *Trav. W. Afr.* iii. 58 The Bubi... His idea of decoration goes in the direction of a plaster of 'tola' pomatum over his body. **1959** *Archit. Rev.* CXXVI. 313 The table top and chair seats are covered with black imitation leather; the chair backs are of tola. **1962** *House & Garden* Jan. 45/2 (*caption*) 3-drawer desk in tola wood.

tolazamide (tǫlēⁱ·zămǝid). *Pharm.* [f. *tol(uene* s.v. TOLU- + AZ(O- + AMIDE.] A hypoglycæmic sulphonylurea drug given orally in the treatment of diabetes; 1-perhydroazepin-1-yl-3-*p*-tolylsulphonylurea, $C_{14}H_{21}N_3O_3S$.

1963 *Canad. Med. Assoc. Jrnl.* LXXXIX. 669/1 Tolazamide is a new sulfonylurea compound which has hypoglycemic properties said to be six to eight times as potent as tolbutamide. **1974** M. C. GERALD *Pharmacology* xxv. 441 Several oral hypoglycemic sulfonylurea agents are currently used in the United States, including..tolazamide.

tolazoline (tǫlēⁱ·zǫ̆līn). *Pharm.* [f. TOL(YL + *imid)azoline,* f. *IMIDAZOL(E + -INE⁵.] An adrenergic blocking agent and vasodilator, used esp. in the treatment of spasm of the peripheral arteries; 2-benzyl-2-imidazoline, $C_{10}H_{12}N_2$.

1952 *Martindale's Extra Pharmacopœia* (ed. 23) I. 605 Tolazoline hydrochloride is a sympatholytic and adrenolytic compound which also exerts a vasodilator effect. **1959** S. DUKE-ELDER *Parsons' Dis. Eye* (ed. 13) 582/1 (*heading*) Tolazoline ('Priscol') injection. **1972** [see *PHENTOLAMINE].

tolbooth, toll-booth. 1. Delete † and add: *spec.* a booth at which the toll for the right of passage across a bridge, along a road, etc., is collected. (Later examples.)

The spelling *tolbooth* is now *arch.* or *Sc.*

1973 *Times* 8 May (Hong Kong Suppl.) p. iii/9 Fourteen toll booths can be seen from the control room. **1978** D. DEVINE *Sunk without Trace* xxvi. 243 The car halted at the toll. He jumped out..to question the man in the toll-booth.

tolbutamide (tǫlbiū·tămǝid). *Pharm.* [f. *tol(uene* s.v. TOLU- + BUT(YL + AMIDE.] A hypoglycæmic sulphonylurea drug given orally in the treatment of diabetes; 1-butyl-3-tosylurea, $C_{12}H_{18}N_2O_3S$.

1956 *Metabolism* V. 801 (*heading*) Hypoglycemic actions of tolbutamide and carbutamide. **1974** M. C. GERALD *Pharmacol.* xxv. 436 Tolbutamide (Orinase) and related sulfonylurea compounds used for the oral treatment of diabetes act by enhancing the release of insulin from the pancreas.

tole (tōᵘl), *sb.*² Also ‖ **tôle.** [a. F. *tôle* sheet-iron, f. dial. *taule* table, f. L. *tabula* a flat board.] **a.** Tin-plated sheet-iron which is first varnished and then ornamented by decorative painting. Also in phr. *tôle peinte,* painted sheet-iron.

1946 *National Button Bull.* (U.S.) Oct. 290 Let's consider these buttons of japanned or lacquered metals. First we have those of Tôle, which are really of tin... Tôle is composed of thinly rolled sheets of iron, tinned. **1958** *Times* 29 Nov. 8/6 A Regency library table decorated in *tôle peinte*..made £540. **1973** *Canadian Antiques Collector* Jan.–Feb. 28/2 The French-Canadian workers in 'tole' or sheet iron.

b. *attrib.* and *Comb.*

1948 E. O. CHRISTENSEN *Popular Art in U.S.* 19 *Toleware Coffee-pot...* Though called Pennsylvania Dutch, it was of English production... The term 'japanned' tinware, or toleware, is applied to..household utensils.. made of sheet iron, covered with a coating of tin. **1960** *Washington Post* 12 Mar. A-6 (Advt.), All metal tole lamps with brass accents. **1973** *New Yorker* 3 Feb. 40/3 Toleware—exquisite hand-painted tinware produced in the nineteenth century in Pennsylvania, New York State, Ohio, and New England. **1975** *Country Life* 11 Dec. (Suppl.) 22/1 Pair of Austrian tôle peinte figures of red Indians..sold at Christie's..for £4,200. **1976** *National Observer* (U.S.) 17 Jan. 10/2 The city's community-education system offers hundreds of classes that vary from appliance repair to tole painting.

tole (tōᵘl), repr. a U.S. dial. and Black English pronunc. of *told* pa.t. and pa. pple.

1797 J. BARTON *Let.* in *Amer. Speech 1969* (1973) XLIV. 304 If I had a tole any such a story. *a* **1911** D. G. PHILLIPS *Susan Lenox* (1917) I. ix. 152 So you ain't tole her? Well, Keziah, I've been and gone and got married. **1935** Z. N. HURSTON *Mules & Men* (1970) I. i. 26 John tole him, 'Massa, he had two great big eyes lak balls of fire.' **1955** F. O'CONNOR *Wise Blood* iv. 72, I done tole you them tires won't bust. **1979** 'E. MCBAIN' *Calypso* ix. 122 She tole me what she'd been doin.

Toledan (tolēⁱ·dăn, tolī·dăn), *a.* and *sb.* [f. *Toledo* (see TOLEDO) + -AN.] **A.** *adj.* Of or pertaining to Toledo. Cf. TOLETAN *a.* **B.** *sb.* A native or inhabitant of Toiedo.

1846 R. FORD *Gatherings from Spain* iii. 28 The Toledan chroniclers derive the name from Tagus, fifth king of Iberia. *Ibid.* 29 The performance has been contemplated by many *foreigners,* the Toledans looking lazily on. **1914** J. MASEFIELD *Philip the King* 47 Till their Toledan armour was burnt black. **1965** C. D. EBY *Siege of Alcazar* (1966) viii. 156 Once and for all the Toledan nightmare must be ended.

tolerable, *a.* (*adv.*) Add: **5. a.** As *adv.* (Later U.S. example.)

1884 'MARK TWAIN' *Huck. Finn* i. 3 Her sister, Miss Watson, a tolerable slim old maid, with goggles on.

b. (Earlier example.)

1812 J. CONSTABLE *Let.* 16 Feb. (1962) I. 77 Your Father looks well & is very tolerable as to his cough & breathing.

tolerance, *sb.* Add: **1. b.** Also, diminution in the response to a drug after continued use. Also const. *to.* (Further examples.)

1951 A. GROLLMAN *Pharmacol. & Therapeutics* xviii. 362 A certain degree of tolerance to the nitrites is gained by man from their repeated administration. Especially is this true as regards the headache which they often produce. **1974** M. C. GERALD *Pharmacol.* iii. 62 For the heroin addict, tolerance represents a very real problem, for he is obliged to take larger and larger doses to get the same psychological response. **1982** *Sci. Amer.* Mar. 112/3 The body may accumulate the drug or develop a tolerance to it.

c. For *U.S.* read orig. *U.S.* More widely in *Biol.*, the ability of any organism to withstand some particular environmental condition. Const. *to.* (Further examples.)

1932 FULLER & CONARD tr. *Braun-Blanquet's Plant Sociol.* vi. 169 The higher plants have a more or less wide pH tolerance. **1939** *Ecology* XX. 71 (*heading*) A study of the tolerance of trees to breakage by ice accumulation. **1953** E. P. ODUM *Fund. Ecol.* iii. 29 Trees give way to grassland as the amount of available water drops below the limits of tolerance for forests. **1960** N. POLUNIN *Introd. Plant Geogr.* xiv. 428 The arborescent species..fall into groups having a particular height-limit and degree of tolerance to shading. **1961** *Biol. Abstr.* XXXVI. 6632/1 Restraint may affect altitude tolerance in the rat by hastening the body temperature fall. **1979** *Environmental Biol. Fishes* IV. 253/1 Cox..found differences in thermal tolerance of large and small 26°C acclimated bluegill sunfish warmed at 0·1 and 1·0° C min⁻¹.

d. *Biol.* The ability of an organism to survive or to flourish despite infection with a parasite or an otherwise pathogenic organism.

1904 *Q. Rev.* July 137 It is probable that the sleeping-sickness parasite flourished innocently in a state of adjustment due to tolerance on the part of the aboriginal men and animals of West Africa. **1951** R. H. PAINTER *Insect Resistance in Plant Crops* ii. 59 Corn strains that are tolerant to chinch bug infestation under the moisture conditions of Illinois may not show as much tolerance under drier conditions in Kansas. **1976** GIBBS & HARRISON *Plant Virology* xv. 226/1 The use of tomato plants containing a single gene for tolerance to TMV resulted in the selection and rapid spread of virus strains virulent for the plants.

e. *Immunol.* The ability to accept without an immunological reaction an antigen that normally produces one.

1951 *Heredity* V. 396 It may seem surprising that the interchange of red cell precursors should confer tolerance upon homografts of, effectively, skin epithelium. **1968** PASSMORE & ROBSON *Compan. Med. Stud.* I. xxvii. 21/2 Experimentally tolerance can be induced by exposure to antigens either in utero or..in the neonatal period. **1979** *Nature* 15 Mar. 257/2 It is pertinent to ask whether the induction and maintenance of specific immunological unresponsiveness (tolerance) to foreign antigens is also under genetic control.

4. a, b. More widely, the allowable amount of variation in any specified quantity.

1916 *Yorkshire Post* 28 Mar. 8/1 Permissible margins of error in workmanship are known as tolerances. **1937** *Times* 13 Apr. (Suppl.) p. xii/4 Visitors may see..how the metal cools and can be withdrawn a minute or two later, finally to be machined to within a tolerance of 0·001 in. on the inside and 0·0005 in. on the outside. **1957** R. W. G. HUNT *Reproduction of Colour* xii. 174 With this system, discrepancies..will result only in errors in chrominance and not in errors of luminance. The tolerances thus become slightly larger. **1965** *Economist* 28 Aug. 812/2 The Ministry will be able to tighten up on tolerances in the road building specifications which it is now rewriting. **1973** A. PARRISH *Mech. Engineer's Ref. Bk.* III. 17 A geometrical tolerance is applied to a feature when there is a requirement to control its variation of form or position. **1975** D. G. FINK *Electronics Engineers' Handbk.* I. 48 Stations must operate on an assigned carrier frequency.. which must be maintained within specified limits of frequency tolerances.

5. *attrib.* and *Comb.*: **tolerance dose** *Med.*, a dose, esp. of radiation, believed to be received or taken without harm; **tolerance level,** the level that can be tolerated or is acceptable; *spec.* in *Med.* = *tolerance dose* above; **tolerance limit,** a limit laid down for the permitted variation of a parameter of a product.

1925 *Amer. Jrnl. Röntgenol.* XIII. 66/2 We will have then to decide upon a tolerance dose which can be considered harmless for the operator within a certain assumed period of time. **1958** W. D. CLAUS *Radiation Biol. & Med.* xvi. 390 The concept of 'tolerance dose' has changed somewhat to the thought that there is no such thing as a literally harmless dose of radiation. **1972** H. C. RAE *Shooting Gallery* III. 202 You know what controlled tolerance doses [of drugs] are?..I had it under control. **1947** *Radiology* XLIX. 364/2 What are the first changes produced by exposures just above the tolerance level? **1964** F. G. W. & M. G. JONES *Pests of Field Crops* xvi. 361 The U.S.A. and Canada have laws determining the tolerance levels for those pesticides that leave residues on or in the crops. **1977** *New Yorker* 19 Sept. 82/2 It's very important to gauge your audience's tolerance level—decide what it's receptive to, what it can take. **1931** W. A. SHEWHART *Econ. Control of Quality of Manufactured Product* xvii. 249 The tolerance range for a given quality X is defined as the range between the maximum and minimum tolerance limits specified for this quality. **1963** BEGEMAN & AMSTEAD *Manuf. Processes* (ed. 5) xv. 356 The tolerance limits for a part are placed outside of the control limits.

tolerance (tǫ·lĕrăns), *v. Engin.* [f. the sb.] *trans.* To specify a tolerance for (a machine part, etc.). So **to·leranced** *ppl. a.*, **to·lerancing** *vbl. sb.*

1950 W. STANIAR *Plant Engin. Handbk.* ii. 45 (*caption*) Quality-control chart—correct tolerancing of operations. **1953** F. ZOZZORA *Engin. Drawing* viii. 126/2 As a general rule, nonmating members are toleranced bilaterally, while mating surfaces are toleranced unilaterally. **1959** *B.S.I. News* Aug. 13 British proposals on dimensioning and tolerancing of tapers were generally approved. **1971** J. H. SMITH *Digital Logic* ii. 19 The designs are well toleranced and the reader will find that almost any small-signal transistor will function quite satisfactorily. **1973** A. PARRISH *Mech. Engineer's Ref. Bk.* III. 18 The concept of geometrical tolerancing is complex. *Ibid.* 19 The feature toleranced is indicated by a leader line.

tolerant, *a.* (*sb.*) Add: **d.** For *U.S.* read orig. *U.S.* More widely in *Biol.*, capable of withstanding any particular environmental condition. (Further examples.)

1929 WEAVER & CLEMENTS *Plant Ecol.* xiii. 321 Tolerant species..retain their branches. **1943** D. V. BAXTER *Path. Forest Practice* viii. 478 Certain woody species tolerant of wet soil. **1979** *Austral. Jrnl. Bot.* XXVII. 531 *Coleochloa setifera* is a desiccation-tolerant sedge which becomes yellow during drying. **1980** SPURR & BARNES *Forest Ecol.* (ed. 3) xiv. 380 A forest tree that can survive and prosper under a forest canopy is said to be tolerant.

e. *Biol.* Of an organism: exhibiting tolerance (sense *1 d) to infection.

1904 E. R. LANKESTER in *Q. Rev.* July 128 A more precise nomenclature would describe the attacked organism..as 'tolerant', for it tolerates the presence and multiplication of the parasite without suffering by it. **1951** [see *TOLERANCE *sb.* 1 d]. **1976** GIBBS & HARRISON *Plant Virology* xv. 225/2 In the western U.S.A., where beet curly top virus is widespread, the sugar-beet industry has been saved by introducing tolerant cultivars.

f. *Immunol.* Exhibiting immunological tolerance (sense *1 e). Const. *of*, *to*.

1951 *Heredity* V. 396 Not all dizygotic twins are completely tolerant to grafts of each other's skin. **1969** R. S. WEISER et al. *Fund. Immunol.* xviii. 227 The F_1 hybrid is an example of an allogeneic recipient which for genetic reasons is immunologically tolerant of parental grafts.

toleration. 2. b. (Earlier examples.)

1796 *Rec. Smithtown, N.Y.* (1898) 129 Any person not an inhabitant..taking Soft shelled clams within the limits of said Town shall pay six pence for every bushel as toleration for taking the same. **1881** E. INGERSOLL *Oyster-Industry* III. 249 Toleration.—License to gather oysters or operate beds... The money paid is called a Toleration fee.

tolerize (tǫ·lĕrəiz), *v. Immunol.* [f. TOLER(ANT *a.* (*sb.*) + -IZE.] *trans.* To render immunologically tolerant. So **to·lerizing** *ppl. a.*; also **toleriza·tion**, the action of tolerizing.

1967 *Immunology* XIII. 156 Immunocompetent cells might not have been exposed to the tolerizing antigen. **1973** *Nature* 16 Mar. 161/3 Free IgT complexes are present and these effectively tolerize B cells. **1974** I. M. ROITT *Essent. Immunol.* (ed. 2) viii. 202 It may be that the tolerance-inducing regimen does truly tolerize T cells.. but not all B-cells. **1978** *Jrnl. R. Soc. Med.* LXXI. 161/1 The interaction of bacteria with the adjuvant and tolerizing agents in plaque may induce immune responses which could enhance or inhibit the development of caries. **1979** *Nature* 15 Mar. 258/2 One day after tolerisation the recipient mice plus appropriate controls were sensitised by two paintings with DNFB.

tolerogen (tǫ·lĕrŏdʒĕn). *Immunol.* [f. TOLER(ANCE + -O + -GEN.] A substance inducing immunological tolerance.

1967 *Immunochemistry* IV. 180 The multi-chain polymer was a very efficient tolerogen. **1980** *Nature* 28 Aug. 837/2 Both generations, neither of which had been intentionally exposed to the tolerogen, showed a wide range of response, from normal down to undetectable.

Hence **toleroge·nic** *a.*, **to:lerogeni·city**.

1967 *Immunochemistry* IV. 180 The protein carrier is not necessary to endow a molecule with tolerogenic capacity. **1970** *Nature* 11 July 176/1 There is much evidence for a reciprocal relationship between immunogenicity and tolerogenicity. **1979** *Jrnl. Immunol.* CXXII. 1886/2 Polyethylene glycol has been shown to serve as an effective tolerogenic carrier.

tolidine (tǫ·lidīn). *Chem.* [f. TOL(YL + BENZ)IDINE.] A benzidine derivative, $(NH_2-(CH_3)C_6H_3—)_2$, which is the parent compound of a group of azo dyes and is used (in the *ortho* form) as a reagent in chemical analysis.

1879 *Jrnl. Chem. Soc.* XXXVI. 235 (*heading*) The three isomeric tolidines (diamido-ditolyls). **1935** *Discovery* July 208/1 A minute sample of the bath water is taken and 'doped' by the mixture of few drops of 'O.T.' (Ortho-Tolidine), a chemical which turns chlorinated water yellow. **1964** *Kirk-Othmer Encycl. Chem. Technol.* (ed. 2) III. 414 *o*-Tolidine is used to a rather large extent in qualitative and quantitative analysis. It is employed for the detection..of such substances as chlorine..gold.. and tungsten. *Ibid.* 415 Azo dyes prepared from *m*-tolidine..have little affinity for cotton, but are interesting dyes for wool.

tolite (tǫ·ləit). Also **Tolite.** [f. TOL(U- + -ITE[1].] Trinitrotoluene used as an explosive.

1909 O. GUTTMANN *Manuf. Explosives* i. 14 Trinitrotoluene has been introduced into the French Service under the name of Tolite. **1924** *Chem. Abstr.* XVIII. 2604 During the war..use was made of a cold, dil. soln. of Na_2SO_3 for the purification of crude trinitrotoluene (tolite) to produce TNT. **1953** J. Y. COUSTEAU *Silent World* 39 With one-pound tablets of German tolite explosive the effect was different. **1968** *New Scientist* 7 Nov. 304/3 Molène favours the use of classic explosives such as TNT, Tolite, Melinite or Trinitrophenylamine.

‖ **tolkach** (tǫ·lkatʃ). Pl. **tolkachi.** [Russ., f. *tolkat'* to push or jostle.] In the U.S.S.R., a person who negotiates difficulties or arranges things, a 'fixer'.

1955 H. HODGKINSON *Doubletalk* 129 *Tolkach* (from *tolkat*, to push or jostle), a 'fixer'; the man who knows a man; the man who can get it for you wholesale; who has *blat*. **1957** J. S. BERLINER *Factory & Manager in U.S.S.R.* xii. 215 The key figure in financing all these operations of the tolkachi is the accountant. **1963** *Economist* 29 June 1390/2 Plant directors..buy..supplies illegally from each other, through *tolkachi* or spivs. **1977** *Western Political Q.* XXX. 217 The premier practitioner of *blat* is the *tolkach*. He is the plant's representative who travels the country searching for needed supplies or unsnarling bureaucratic bottlenecks.

Tolkienian (tǫlkī·niăn), *a.* Also **Tolkinian** (tǫlki·niăn). [f. the name *Tolkien* (see below) + -IAN.] Of or pertaining to the philologist and author of fantasy literature John Ronald Reuel Tolkien (1892–1973) or his writings.

1954 C. S. LEWIS in *Time & Tide* 14 Aug. 1083/1 In the Tolkinian world you can hardly put your foot down.. without stirring the dust of history. **1975** C. N. MANLOVE *Mod. Fantasy* v. 160 Escape merges into another Tolkinian criterion of the higher fairy-tale—Consolation. **1979** J. C. NITZSCHE *Tolkien's Art* 4 A pattern emerges upon an examination of the titles of other Tolkienian works. **1980** *Times Lit. Suppl.* 7 Nov. 1258/3 If nursery puddings, Tolkienian fantasy and public school cuddles are anything to do with politics at all, they are slightly more identifiable with the Right.

So **To:lkiene·sque** *a.* [-ESQUE], characteristic of or resembling Tolkien or his writings.

1970 *Nature* 18 July 215/2 Earlier this month it was announced that Loch Morar, too, would be screened for a monster, already christened with suitably Tolkienesque undertones, as Morag. **1977** *Sounds* 9 July 28/3 Tyrannosaurus Rex, a duo small in sound but big in Tolkienesque fantastical imagery.

toll, *sb.*[1] Add: **2. g.** (Further examples, esp. of death, loss, or injury.)

1870 J. C. DUVAL *Adv. Big-Foot Wallace* p. xv, Wallace joined Colonel Hays's regiment..and was with it at the storming of Monterey, where he says he took 'full toll' out of the Mexicans for killing his brother and cousin.. in 1836. **1927** W. E. COLLINSON *Contemp. Eng.* 34 The 'toll of the road' (often used by the Daily Mail in 1925–6) has been so heavy that some of the local authorities have adopted the expedient of the white line. **1929** *Daily Express* 7 Nov. 2/3 Miners' members were artists in presenting the toll of the mines in its most impressive form. **1959** *Listener* 6 Aug. 222/1 A thoroughly well-intentioned programme aimed at reducing the toll on the roads. **1962** E. ROOSEVELT *Autobiogr.* II. xv. 123 The war had taken from France a heavy toll of her young men from 1914 to 1918. **1972** N. FREELING *Long Silence* II. 189 In fact it had been very hardbought, some of the winnings, taking fearful tolls of nerve, straining every atom of him. **1974** F. FORSYTH *Dogs of War* xiv. 264 He felt tired and flat; the strain of the past thirty days was taking its toll. **1974** C. RYAN *Bridge too Far* III. ii. 147 Forty-five patients were dead (the toll would increase to over eighty), and countless more were wounded. **1981** *Times* 9 June 6/3 The death toll in the train disaster..could be more than 1,000. **1982** S. BRETT *Murder Unprompted* xii. 113 The obscurity of the play, and the..lack of star names—all the elements which pessimists had predicted would work against the show—were now beginning to take their toll.

i. A charge for a telephone call. Usu. *attrib.* (see also *toll call*, sense 3 below, *TOLL-FREE *a.*). *N. Amer.*

1886 *Jrnl. Soc. Telegr. Engineers* XV. 275 Another term also very largely used in America is 'toll line working'; i.e., communication between town and town.. which is paid for by tolls per message, and not by annual subscription such as usually occurs in local exchanges. **1912** THIESS & JOY *Toll Telephone Pract.* i. 3 In Bell practice the terms 'suburban' and 'toll' are often used synonymously, but suburban business is always short haul..while toll business may be long haul but not exceeding 100 miles. The term 'long distance' in Bell practice implies any haul exceeding 100 miles and in many cases the toll and the long distance business are handled at different switchboards... The terms 'toll' and 'long distance' do not have this distinction in independent practice and are commonly synonymous. *Ibid.* iv. 43 When a toll subscriber desires to call central, he will operate his generator. *Ibid.* 44 If the jack of the subscriber wanted terminates in the toll position.., the toll operator will simply insert her calling plug and ring. **1921** *Telegraph & Telephone Jrnl.* VII. 180/2 It was eventually decided to remove all the short trunk lines (i.e. up to 25 miles in length) from the Trunk Exchange and to connect them to one or more Toll Exchanges. **1926** *Daily Colonist* (Victoria, B.C.) 11 July 16/1 The British Columbia Telephone Co...built the first toll line to Nanaimo. **1933** K. B. MILLER *Telephone Theory & Pract.* III. xi. 466 Telephone traffic between subscribers whose lines are connected to different local exchanges is ordinarily called 'toll traffic'... Toll traffic is generally classified as 'short haul' or 'suburban' for distances up to the neighborhood of about 50 miles, and 'long haul' or 'long distance' for connections between more widely separated points. **1970** N. ARMSTRONG et al. *First on Moon* xiv. 363, I had a telephone call yesterday. The toll wasn't..as great as the one I made to you fellows..on the moon. **1978** *Sci. Amer.* June 90/2 It may also provide paths between trunks, but this task is usually performed by special exchanges called toll exchanges.

3. toll call, orig., † a telephone call which was not a local call and for which an individual charge was therefore made; in later (not British) use, a long-distance call, or a call between different telephone areas; **toll plaza** *U.S.*, a row of toll booths on a toll road; **toll television, TV** = *pay television*, *-TV* s.v. *PAY- 4; **tollway** *U.S.*, a highway for the use of which a charge is made.

1912 THIESS & JOY *Toll Telephone Pract.* i. 3 Common usage among telephone men has led to the general classification of telephone service under four headings, as follows: local, suburban, toll and long distance... Any telephone call which is not local bears a special or toll charge and broadly may be termed a toll call; hence it seems proper to use the term 'toll' to embrace all service of this class, whether it be suburban, toll, or long distance in the narrow sense. **1928** E. WALLACE *Again Three Just Men* x. 223 The telephone-bell rang. The voice of the porter informed him that a toll call had come through. **1965** S. T. OLLIVIER *Petticoat Farm* vi. 88 This ring was a toll call and would be costing a fortune. **1977** D. ANTHONY *Stud Game* vii. 45 Grant must have called the Bishop girl from here. She lives in Santa Monica, which makes it a toll call. **1948** *Sun* (Baltimore) 20 Nov. 14/2 All tolls for travel across the Chesapeake Bay Bridge will be paid at booths on the 1,000-foot toll plaza on the Western Shore approach to the bridge. **1983** *N.Y. Times* 16 July 26/6 Connecticut state police have been stopping northbound trucks at the Greenwich toll plaza on the Connecticut Turnpike. **1956** *Britannica Bk. of Year* 492/2 *Pay T.V.*, *Toll T.V.*,..these phrases having been coined in America during a discussion of the possibilities of providing additional television programmes to viewers willing to pay for them on a subscription basis. **1960** *News Chron.* 13 Oct. 14/2 The pioneer Toll-TV service working in a suburb of Toronto. **1960** *Spectator* 30 Dec. 1039 The principle of toll television is that the viewer should pay only for films..he wants to see. **1955** *Britannica Bk. of Year* 490/1 Modern automobile transport continued to produce new words. Among these were *Tollway*, a modern version of the old toll road. **1958** *Times* 22 Nov. 7/6 To the other points of the compass the expressways—and even newer, faster, tollways—throw out rippling tentacles. **1969** 'E. LATHEN' *When in Greece* vi. 61 The new tollway along the coast..was..the only high speed road in Greece. **1982** S. PARETSKY *Indemnity Only* xvi. 214, I headed back to the tollway and Chicago.

toll, *v.*[3] Add: **2. d.** To charge a toll for the use of (a bridge, crossing, etc.). Chiefly as *ppl. a.*

1978 *Financial Times* 24 Oct. 11/3 The tolled Humber bridge. **1978** in H. Wilson *Final Term* (1979) 247 Concessions to 'Orange Badge' holders at most tolled crossings.

toll-bait. (Earlier example.)

1870 *Amer. Naturalist* IV. 516 The 'tole-bait' consists chiefly of Menhaden (*Alausa menhaden*) ground very fine.

Tollens (tǫ·lĕnz). *Chem.* [The name of B. C. G. *Tollens* (1841–1918), German chemist.] *Tollens'(s) reagent*: a solution of ammoniacal silver nitrate and sodium hydroxide, used as a test for aldehydes with which it reacts to give a silver precipitate; so *Tollens' test* (described by Tollens in *Ber. d. deut. Chem. Ges.* (1882) XV. 1828).

1904 S. P. MULLIKEN *Method for Identification Pure Organic Compounds* I. 22 (*heading*) Compounds reducing silver from Tollen's [*sic*] reagent. **1946** F. SCHNEIDER *Qualitative Organic Microanalysis* vii. 198 A blank experiment should be run with the Tollens' reagent and the original substance. **1964** N. G. CLARK *Mod. Organic Chem.* x. 187 Tollens's reagent..gives a precipitate of silver, often in the form of a silver mirror. **1981** WINGROVE & CARET *Organic Chem.* xxi. 867 A simple chemical test to distinguish between aldehydes and ketones is based on aldehydes being readily oxidized to carboxylic acids whereas ketones are not. Tollens' test..is used most frequently.

tollent, *a.* (Earlier example.)

1770 tr. *C. F. von Wolff's Logic* 87 The Tollent mode.

toller[2]**, toler. 2.** Delete second quot. and add earlier example.

1831 I. T. SHARPLESS in *Cabinet of Nat. Hist.* I. 43/2 Most persons on these waters, have a race of small, white or liver coloured dogs, which are familiarly called the *toler* breed.

tolley (tǫ·li). [Var. of *taw-alley* (Eng. Dial. Dict. s.v. TAW *sb.*[1]): see ALLY, ALLEY, ALAY *sb.*[2]] = TAW *sb.*[2] a.

1970 *Times* 18 Feb. 2 Playing marbles requires a player to bend double to flick the tolley. **1972** *Daily Tel.* (Colour Suppl.) 14 Jan. 25/1 You flick the tolley with your thumb.

toll-free, *a.* (Later N. Amer. examples, of telephone calls, lines, etc.)
1970 *Globe & Mail* (Toronto) 26 Sept. 31/1 (Advt), For reservations, call toll-free 368-7474. **1971** *Sci. Amer.* Oct. 7/2 (Advt.), When you buy a '72, you get the name and toll-free number of a person in Detroit. **1976** *National Observer* (U.S.) 13 Mar. 3/6 (Advt.), Write or call now. Our toll-free lines are open 24 hours daily, 7 days a week. **1979** *Arizona Daily Star* 5 Aug. (Advt. Section) 4/3 Make a toll-free call to Bill Jackson. **1984** *Gainesville* (Florida) *Sun* 28 Mar. 2A/3, I have called the same toll-free number I ordered from several times but these people will not return my call.

toll-house. Add: **3.** *attrib.* and *Comb.*: **toll-house cookie** *U.S.*, a biscuit containing chocolate chips.
1973 *Publishers Weekly* 22 Jan. 71/2 Henry begins suffering from dark spots that pop out all over his body; he soon looks like a toll-house cookie. **1978** R. Nixon *Memoirs* 316 After our meeting we had a delicious lunch of steak and fresh corn on the cob, followed by Lady Bird's homemade toll-house cookies.

tolling, toling, *vbl. sb.*[1] **b.** (Earlier example.)
1838 J. J. Audubon *Ornith. Biogr.* IV. 6 The usual mode of taking these birds has been..by *toling*, as it is strangely termed, an operation by which the ducks are sometimes induced to approach within a few feet of the shore.

tol-lol-ish, *a.* (Earlier example.)
1840 H. Cockton *Valentine Vox* xxvii. 210 'And the ladies, how are they?' 'Why, they're only tollolish. You know what women are.'

tolly (tǫ·li). *School slang.* Now *arch.* or *Hist.* [app. f. Tallow *sb.*] A (tallow) candle.
1890 Barrère & Leland *Dict. Slang.* II. 360/2 *Tolly* (public schools), a candle. **1905** *Daily News* 2 Aug. 4 Who does not recognise a living experience in Hugh working after prohibited hours for a scholarship, caught by the master and 'jawed for having a tolly alight'. **1924** E. Marsh tr. *La Fontaine's Fables* 77 The luckless tolly.. Ended as a pool of grease.

Also as *v. intr.* (*Harrow*), to work by candle-light after the lights have been extinguished; to 'burn the midnight oil'; usu. with *up*.
1890 Barrère & Leland *Dict. Slang.* II. 360/2 *Tolly up, to* (Harrow School), to keep a candle alight after the gas has been turned off. **1894** Wilkins & Vivian *Green Bay Tree* I. 73 The process known as 'tollying up', or working by candle-light after the legal hours.

Tolman (tǫ·lmăn). Also **Tallman.** The surname *Tolman* used *ellipt.*, *attrib.*, or in the possessive in **Tolman('s) sweet(ing),** to designate a yellow-skinned apple belonging to a variety originally developed in Rhode Island; also, the variety itself, or the tree bearing this fruit.
1822 J. Thacher *Amer. Orchardist* 139 Tolman sweeting..is held in much estimation for family use during the autumn. **1838** *Genesee Farmer* 17 Mar. 81/1 Winter Fruit..Tallman Sweeting. **1845** A. J. Downing *Fruits & Fruit Trees Amer.* viii. 137 The Tolman's Sweeting..is one of the most popular orchard sorts. **1867** J. A. Warder *Amer. Pomology—Apples* 557 Tallman's Sweet..has traveled from Rhode Island wherever her hardy sons have gone westward. **1875** J. Burroughs *Winter Sunshine* 155 Now you have got a Tolman sweet. **1878** [see *McIntosh]. **1893** A. M. Diaz *William Henry Lett.* 7 He..set out Baldwins and Tallmans and Porters. **1909** S. B. Green *Pop. Fruit Growing* ix. 169 Some varieties..are adapted to a wide range as..Tolman Sweet. **1928** W. H. Chandler *N. Amer. Orchards* iv. 105 Tolman, the leading sweet apple to reach the market,..but few trees now being planted. **1949** *Boston Globe* 14 Aug. (Fiction Mag.) 11/4 We could look squarely at the tolman sweet standing all alone with the moonlight making its blossoms burn like candles. **1970** [see *russet *a.* 1 b].

toloache (tǫlwæ·tʃi). Also **toloachi.** [a. Mexican Sp. *toloache*, a. Nahuatl *toloatzin*, f. *toloa* to bow the head + *tzin* reverential.] A preparation of a plant of the genus *Datura* used as an intoxicating and hallucinogenic drug.
1894 [see *marijuana, marihuana 1 a]. **1948** A. L. Kroeber *Anthropol.* (rev. ed.) xiv. 567 Southern and south-central California: Initiation of youths with *toloache* or jimson-weed drug (*Datura* species). The narcosis is accompanied by visions, which were considered sacred. **1964** I. Fleming *You only live Twice* vii. 93 Addiction to toloachi, a drink made from *D. tatula*, causes chronic imbecility.

Toltec (tǫ·ltek), *sb.* and *a.* Also 8 **Tolteca,** 9 **Tolteck, Tultec.** [ad. Sp. *tolteca*, ad. Nahuatl *toltecatl*, pl. *tolteca*.] **A.** *sb.* (A member of) a Nahuatl people who dominated the valley of Mexico *c* 900–1150 A.D., before the arrival of the Aztecs. **B.** *adj.* Of or pertaining to this people.
1787, etc. [see *Olmec 1]. **1814** [see *Aztec *sb.* and *a.*]. **1843** W. H. Prescott *Conquest of Mexico* I. i. 12 The Toltecs were well instructed in agriculture. **1875** *Encycl. Brit.* I. 696/1 The Toltec and Aztec races. **1939** G. Greene *Lawless Roads* iii. 104 Quetzalcoatl..was the white Toltec god of culture. **1955** *Sci. Amer.* May 82 To be a Toltec in Mexico was to be an exponent of civilization. **1977** *Time* 21 Feb. 19/1 He wrote his mystical novelette about the god Quetzalcoatl, who figures so largely in the Toltec legends of the Mexican people. **1979** P. Theroux *Old Patagonian Express* iii. 52 Towards Tula, a treeless desert ..rose into peaks like pyramids. This was the capital of the Toltecs.

Hence **To·ltecan** *sb.* and *a.*
1839 *Penny Cycl.* XV. 165/1 The older..monuments of Mexico are..the productions..of the Toltecans. *Ibid.* 165/2 The extraordinary vastness of..these..Toltecan constructions.

tolu-. Add: **toluqui·none** [Quinone], the aromatic compound $CH_3C_6H_3O_2$; also, any of the derivatives of this compound.
[**1870** *Jrnl. Chem. Soc.* XXXIII. 135 (*caption*) Trichlorotoluquinone.] **1874** *Index Jrnl. Chem. Soc. 1848–72* 254/1 Toluquinones. **1975** *Nature* 20 Nov. 194/1 The chemicals present in the glandular secretions of insects are often exceedingly diverse... They comprise..a great number of phenolic substances and quinones (such as phenol.. and toluquinone).

toluidine. (In Dict. s.v. Tolu-.) Add: Also **toluidene, -in. toluidine blue,** a thiazine dye, $C_{15}H_{16}ClN_3S$, now used chiefly as a biological stain.
1898 *Philadelphia Med. Jrnl.* II. 343 Toluidin-blue is a member of the aniline group closely related chemically to methylene-blue. **1908** Toluidene blue [see *metachromatically *adv.*]. **1947** *Ann. Rev. Microbiol.* I. 346 Both methylene blue..and toluidin blue..have shown therapeutic activity in experimental rickettsial infections in animals. **1981** J. A. Kiernan *Histol. & Histochem. Methods* xviii. 258/1 The procedure..for demonstrating metachromasia with toluidine blue gives excellent results when used as a Nissl stain.

tom, *sb.*[1] Add: **1. a.** *Tom, Dick, and Harry* (earlier example). Also with *or*.
1734 *Vocal Miscellany* (ed. 2) I. 332 Farewell, Tom, Dick, and Harry, Farewell, Moll, Nell, and Sue. **1762** J. Otis *Vindication House Representatives Massachusetts-Bay* 21 That I should die very soon after my head should be cut off..whether chopped off to gratify a tyrant by the christian name of Tom, Dick or Harry is evident. **1864** Trollope *Can you forgive Her?* I. xxxii. 254 Didn't he want to squander every shilling of the property,..property which I could give to Tom, Dick, or Harry tomorrow, if I liked? **1906** I. Zangwill *Let.* 29 Oct. in K. Gregory *First Cuckoo* (1978) 64 And have these wise and witty ladies less right than Tom, Dick or 'Arry to a direct influence on the government of their country? **1974** *New Statesman* 22 Nov. 740/3 There is no legislation for giving them a licence, so that any Tom, Dick or Harry can work as a guide and give..wrong information.

d. A girl or woman. *Austral. slang.*
[**1882** *Sydney Slang Dict.* 8 Tom-tart, Sydney, phrase for a girl or sweetheart.] **1906** E. Dyson *Fact'ry 'Ands* i. 8, I may be wrong in thinkin' your tom was tryin' t' mash ther man shootin' off ther camera. **1951** D. Stivens *Jimmy Brockett* 102 'You did, darling,' one of the little social toms said. She was a nuggety little sheila.

e. A prostitute. *slang.*
[**1914** Jackson & Hellyer *Vocab. Criminal Slang* 84 *Tommy*... A prostitute.] **1941** V. Davis *Phenomena in Crime* xix. 255 *Tom*, old prostitute. **1955** M. Hastings *Cork & Serpent* i. 12 I'll bet she's holding out on us. We know these toms, sir. **1957** H. Williamson *Golden Virgin* ix. 134 'Is Lily a tom?'..'Not within the meaning of the act. She works in Nett's Laundry, on the lower side of Randiswell Bridge. Of course, I don't say she doesn't have a bit of fun at times, but that's her business.' **1977** *Time Out* 17–23 June 18/1 What doesn't appear in the film but is very revealing about police mentality, is the filing room on prostitutes (or Toms as they are called).

f. Short for *Uncle Tom*: a Black regarded, esp. by other Blacks, as behaving in a servile, ingratiating, or complaisant manner towards white people. *slang.*
1959 *Esquire* Nov. 122/1 *Tom*.., a Negro who does not try to maintain his complete dignity before whites. **1968** N. Giovanni in W. King *Black Short Story Anthol.* (1972) 26 Toms, I told him, only have power if we let them have power. I mean, if a tom says get off the streets and you get off the streets, then that's your fault, not his. **1973** R. Ludlum *Matlock Paper* ii. 14 The African studies may be in trouble. That 'Tom' I recruited from Howard turned out to be..a little to the right of Louis XIV. **1975** *Publishers Weekly* 3 Feb. 72/1 By installing 'American Nigger Toms' as the Third World élite, the U.S. has controlled the angry hunger of the poor populace.

7. b. Tom Collins orig. *U.S.*, a cocktail made of gin, lime or lemon juice, sugar, and soda water (cf. sense 5 in Dict. and *Collins[2]); **Tom Walker** *U.S. dial.*, the Devil; also *the Devil and Tom Walker.*
1888 H. Johnson *New Improved Bartenders Man.* (rev. ed.) 227 Tom Collins. **1906** L. Muckensturm *Louis' Mixed Drinks* 99 (*heading*) Tom Collins. **1959** 'M. Ainsworth' *Murder is Catching* xvi. 178 She made us both long cool Tom Collinses, the tumblers frosted with ice-chips. **1979** S. Rifkin *McQuaid in August* (1980) ii. 7 The bartender would make me a tall tom collins without any cherry. **1833** S. Smith *Life & Writings J. Downing* 139 They always would have their way in spite of every body and Tom Walker besides. **1914** *Dial. Notes* IV. 71 He wukked like the Devil an' Tom Walker. **1949** 'T. Nelson' *Backwoods Teacher* xiii. 136, I don't know nary charm, but they's an' old sayin' that some folks says but all it is is, 'Ol' Tom Walker [the devil] under yore hat, God the Father, God the Son, an' God the Holy Ghost.' **1958** *Virginia Q. Rev.* Spring 261 He whispered: 'Old Tom Walker under your hat. Father, son and holy ghost,' the way blue-eyed Dulcie would have done.

c. Tom Pudding *slang*, one of the box-like iron boats that are connected together and towed by a tug to carry coal on canals. (See also sense 8 b in Dict.)
1906 *Westm. Gaz.* ?8 Mar. 8/2 Trains of iron compartment boats, known locally as 'Tom Puddings', are towed all the way to Goole. **1949** *Archit. Rev.* CVI. 8/3 On the Aire and Calder, compartment boats, or Tom Puddings, are used. These are oblong iron boxes towed in trains up to 32 in number by steam tugs. **1970** *New Society* 19 Nov. 898/2 If you haven't seen a chain of tom puddings then you've missed one of the sights of England.

tom (tǫm), *sb.*[2] Colloq. abbrev. of Tomato.
1920 *Chambers's Jrnl.* 15 May 384/1 The acreage of 'outside toms' is increasing annually. **1935** [see *cue *sb.* 4]. **1976** *Coventry Evening Tel.* 27 Oct. 9/3 (*heading*) Summer of the giant toms.

tom (tǫm), *sb.*[3] Slang abbrev. of Tomfoolery (sense *2, = jewellery).
1955 P. Wildeblood *Against the Law* 119 Two grand's worth of tom. **1970** G. F. Newman *Sir, You Bastard* ii. 68 What d'you do with the tom and money you had out of Manor Gardens this afternoon? **1980** *Times* 23 Feb. 3/3 One of thieves..told police: 'When we found the tom (Cockney slang: tomfoolery jewellery) in the car we were amazed.'

tom (tǫm), *sb.*[4] Slang abbrev. of *tom-tom *sb.* 1 d.
1970 J. Wainwright *Freeze thy Blood* 11 Fatso grinned and notched the buckle of a tom case. **1975** J. Pidgeon *Flame* v. 65 Around the drum kit he arranged four mikes, one for the bass drum, one for the floor tom, one for the snare, and one overhead.

tom, *v.* Restrict *nonce-wd.* to sense in Dict. (s.v. Tom *sb.*) and add: **2.** *intr.* [f. *tom *sb.*[1] 1 f.] To behave in an ingratiating and servile way to someone of another (esp. white) race. Also *to tom it* (*up*). *U.S. slang.*
1963 L. Bennett in W. King *Black Short Story Anthol.* (1972) 161 They say you are going to chicken out, Papa... They're betting you'll 'Tom'. **1972** M. J. Bosse *Incident at Naha* ii. 94 Virgil just smiled, Tomming it up. **1976** *Public Opinion Q.* XXXIX. 527 The respondent 'accommodates', or to use the colloquial term, 'toms', in order to get through the racial interaction with minimal tension.

3. *intr.* To practise prostitution, to behave promiscuously; also, to have sexual intercourse in such a context. Also *to tom* (*it*) *around. slang.*
1964 Z. Progl *Woman of Underworld* iii. 35 They were perfectly willing to go 'tomming' on the streets to earn a few quid, but I never could. **1968** 'J. Ross' *Diminished by Death* i. 14 She's just tomming around. **1973** J. Rossiter *Manipulators* ix. 102 This woman... Is she tomming it around with the local villains? **1981** A. Sewart *Close your Eyes & Sleep* xviii. 181 What was she doing? Tomming, to put it bluntly. She was having it off with a bloke.

Hence **to·mming** *vbl. sb.*
1968 J. Lock *Lady Policeman* ii. 12 A prostitute was a 'tom'..and to practise prostitution was 'tomming'. **1973** *Black World* May 44 Afrikan People all over the world Conscious, unconscious, struggling, sleeping, Resisting, tomming, killing the enemy. **1981** J. Ross *Dark Blue & Dangerous* ix. 55 His own tomming around had given him a charitable view of casual sex.

tomahawk, *sb.* Add: **1. d.** (Earlier example.)
c **1825** J. Clare in M. Grainger *Nat. Hist. Prose Writings J. Clare* (1982) 88 The hookd bill usd by hedgers & calld by them a tomahawk.

2. *to bury the tomahawk* (earlier and *lit.* examples).
1705 R. Beverley *Hist. Virginia* iii. 27 They use.. very ceremonious ways in concluding of Peace..such as burying a tomahawk. **1775** in *Virginia Hist. Coll.* (1887) VI. 80, I..resolve never to bury the Tomahawk untill liberty shall be fixed on an immovable basis thro' the whole Continent.

tomalley. (Later examples.)
1950 R. Moore *Candlemas Bay* 289 The lobsters boiled to a fine, even red. Grampie ate five. Then he wiped the tomalley off his jacknife. **1981** *Times* 13 June 12/7 The [lobster's] red coral and the creamy green liver, known as tomalley, are delicious.

tomatin (tǫ·mătin). *Biochem.* Also **-ine.** [f. Tomat(o + -in[1].] A steroidal alkaloid present as a glycoside in the stems and leaves of the tomato plant and some other members of the family Solanaceæ.

The distinction made in quot. 1948 was not generally adopted.
1946 [see *lycopersicin b]. **1948** *Arch. Biochem.* XVI. 399 The crystalline compound has very low antibacterial activity..and is designated tomatine to distinguish it from the crude or partially purified tomatin. **1959** H. Martin *Sci. Princ. Crop Protection* (ed. 4) ii. 19 Although tomatine effectively inhibits the growth of *F*[*usarium*] *lycopersici* in pure culture.., no direct evidence has been obtained that it is responsible for wilt resistance. **1973** L. P. Miller *Phytochemistry* I. vi. 160 Lycobiose (4-*O*-β-D-glucopyranosyl-D-galactose) and the trisaccharide lycotriose were obtained from the tetrasaccharide tomatin in tomato leaf. **1980** *Phytochemistry* XIX. 1322/1 Tomatin in neutral or alkaline pH is highly membranolytic..and forms a complex with cholesterol.

tomato. Add: **1. b.** = *tomato-red* sense 3 in Dict.

1920 *Queen* 22 May (front cover), Colours:..Apricot, Ivory, Mastic, Tomato, Suede, and Saxe. **1923** *Daily Mail* 29 Jan. 1 (Advt.), Striped suitings... On grounds of mole, grey, fawn, black and tomato. **1977** M. Kenyon *Rapist* v. 56 Her rosy cheeks turned tomato with indignation. **1978** P. McCutchan *Blackmail North* viii. 93 She got into the tomato Mini and drove away.

c. An attractive girl. *slang* (orig. *U.S.*).

1929 D. Runyon in *Hearst's Internat.* Nov. 74/1 Different guys have different names for dolls, such as broads,..and tomatoes, which I claim are not respectful. **1962** J. Heller *Catch-22* xvi. 153, I can rush back to that night club before Aarfy leaves with that wonderful tomato he's got without giving me a chance to ask about an aunt or friend she must have who's just like her. **1977** H. Fast *Immigrants* v. 303 This tomato is twenty-three years old and she's a virgin.

2. b. tree tomato (later examples).

1944 *Living off Land* ii. 40 Tree-tomatoes will be found as garden-escapees. **1959** *N.Z. Listener* 8 May 22/3 Tree Tomato Sauce. Eight pounds tree tomatoes, 2 large onions, [etc.]. **1966** G. W. Turner *Eng. Lang. Austral. & N.Z.* viii. 172 Tree tomato and Chinese gooseberry seem to be commoner in New Zealand than in other English-speaking countries. **1976** K. Thackeray *Crownbird* v. 91 A separate table bore..tree tomatoes, portions of yellow jackfruit and chilled mountain paw-paw.

3. *tomato can* (examples), *chutney, ketchup* (earlier example), *purée, salad, sandwich, soup*; *tomato-coloured* adj. (earlier example); **tomato hornworm** = *tomato worm* in Dict.; **tomato juice,** the juice from tomatoes; also, a drink of this; **tomato paste,** thick, concentrated tomato purée; **tomato pinworm,** the larva of a small moth, *Keiferia lycopersicella,* which bores holes in the buds or fruit of the tomato plant; **tomato vine** *U.S.*, a tomato plant.

1868 'O. C. Kerr' *Smoked Glass* xviii. 216 What mean these letters which I find imprinted upon..the tomato can? **1914** *Sat. Even. Post* 4 Apr. 11/1 A gay-cat..will turn against a friend when that friend is down to tomato cans. **1855** E. Acton *Mod. Cookery* (rev. ed.) xxxii. 609 Tomata and other chatnies. **1963** A. L. Simon *Guide Good Food & Wines* 133/1 (*heading*) Green tomato chutney. **1869** L. M. Alcott *Little Women* ii. iii. 31 Brown rain, and purple clouds, with a tomato-coloured splash in the middle. **1928** Metcalf & Flint *Destructive & Useful Insects* xvi. 488 The southern or tomato hornworm ranges from the northern states southward far into South America. **1972** Swan & Papp *Common Insects N. Amer.* xix. 263 Tomato hornworm...sometimes called the five-spotted hawk moth. **1935** M. Morphy *Recipes of All Nations* 595 Tomato juice cocktail. **1936** 'R. West' *Thinking Reed* ii. 56 She ordered some tomato juice, for she would never again need a cocktail. **1981** P. Van Greenaway *'Cassandra' Bell* iv. 47, I ordered another tomato juice to calm his nerves. **1845** E. Acton *Mod. Cookery* v. 136 Tomata catsup. *c* **1938** *Fortnum & Mason Price List* 59/1 Tomato Paste. **1979** *Guardian* 25 Aug. 10/4 Pepsi's had been selling cola in Budapest..but all the company had been able to get out of the country was tomato paste. **1931** *Monthly Bull. Calif. Dept. Agric.* XX. 458 (*heading*) Damage to tomatoes in Southern California by the tomato pin worm. **1972** Swan & Papp *Common Insects N. Amer.* xix. 323 The closely related Tomato Pinworm ..bores pinholes in the developing buds, green and ripening fruits of tomatoes. **1877** E. S. Dallas *Kettner's Bk. of Table* 122 Add to the sauce a tablespoonful of tomato purée. **1977** B. Pym *Quartet in Autumn* vii. 64 Tomato purée, stuffed vine leaves..and tapioca pudding. **1877** E. S. Dallas *Kettner's Bk. of Table* 460 For the tomato salad a dash of mustard is not a bad addition. **1980** I. Murdoch *Nuns & Soldiers* 176 Supper consisted of onion soup, black sausage with tomato salad, and a local cheese with herbs. **1911** W. J. Locke *Glory of Clementina Wing* ii. 17 Tomato sandwiches and plum-cake set out for a visitor's tea. **1978** F. Olbrich *Desouza pays Price* xxv. 161 Delicate tomato sandwiches and fragrant Darjeeling tea. **1846** *Jewish Manual, or Pract. Information Jewish & Mod. Cookery* v. 97 Dry tomato soup. **1974** 'E. Lathen' *Sweet & Low* xvi. 154 The problem we have with tomato soup in my cannery. **1876** 'Mark Twain' *Adventures Tom Sawyer* i. 18 [She] looked out among the tomato vines and jimpson weeds that constituted the garden. **1981** G. V. Higgins *Rat on Fire* xii. 92 You..tromp all over the old people's tomato vines.

Hence **toma·toey** *a.*, having the taste or flavour of tomatoes.

1972 *Homes & Gardens* Aug. 101 (Advt.), The result is a tomato juice that's thicker, smoother and more tomatoey than any you've ever tasted. **1982** D. Wiltse *Wedding Guest* xv. 205 The shared appreciation of the wine, the spicy sausage, the tomatoey beans.

tomb, *sb.* Add: **4*.** *The Tombs*: New York City prison. *U.S. slang.*

1840 *Daily Picayune* (New Orleans) 27 Aug. 2/3 Poor Chapman..is in the 'Tombs', charged with false swearing at an election. **1842** Dickens *Amer. Notes* I. vi. 199 What is this dismal-fronted pile of bastard Egyptian?.. A famous prison, called the Tombs. **1935** A. G. Macdonell *Visit to Amer.* iii. 53 A criminal had been brought from the Tombs..to be examined in the 'Line-Up'. **1981** M. C. Smith *Gorky Park* iii. iii. 330 It's the Tombs... Night Court's open now.

5. a. *tomb chest, figure, figurine, furniture, house* (later example), *monument.* **b.** *tomb-haunter.*

1955 M. D. Anderson *Imagery Brit. Churches* ii. ii. 44 The late medieval tomb chests often have small figures arranged in niches all round them. **1925** B. Rackham in R. Fry et al. *Chinese Art* 13 In his wonderful tomb figures.. we come to the very border-line of sculpture. **1970** Tomb figure [see *haniwa]. **1933** *Burlington Mag.* Nov. 233/2 There are several tomb figurines which show vivacity and able characterization. **1976** 'M. Delving' *China Expert* v. 56 Tashjian..had..unloaded an extremely dubious Han tomb figurine on an unsuspecting German dealer. **1908** *Chambers's Jrnl.* July 527/2 We were in the midst of such a medley of tomb-furniture. **1977** *Times* 23 Apr. 13/3 The increasing vogue for tomb 'furniture' among the lower echelons of T'ang society. **1939** W. B. Yeats *Last Poems* 20 What great tomb-haunter sweeps the distant sky. **1975** G. Ewart *Be My Guest!* 1. 15 But stay! who is this totally melodramatic opium-smoking tomb-haunter? **1963** E. M. Jope in Foster & Alcock *Culture & Environment* xiii. 338 It is an area where hog-backed tomb-houses are to be found. **1948** D. Diringer *Alphabet* ii. iv. 261 Tomb-monuments in various countries.

tombac. Add: In *Archæol.* usu. **tumbaga, -bago.**

1931 E. Nordenskiöld *Compar. Ethnogr. Stud.* IX. 104 The awl..has been analyzed by Dr. K. G. Almström, and found to contain 33% Au, 12% Ag and 55% Cu. This is the composition generally known in archaeological literature as tumbaga. **1936** *Nature* 4 Jan. 29/1 In Antioquia, in Colombia,..objects are found made particularly of the gold alloy..which is known as 'tumbago'. **1974** S. E. Morison *European Discovery of America: Southern Voy.* vii. 152 As ornaments they [*sc.* Venezuelan Indians] displayed great polished disks made of an alloy of copper and gold that they called *guanin,* and which modern archaeologists have named *tumbaga.*

‖ **tombarolo** (tǫmbărǭ·lo). Pl. **tombaroli.** [It.] A grave-robber.

1973 *New Yorker* 7 Apr. 98/2 A skilled *tombarolo* knows the surface indications of a tomb and pilfers the treasure inside after using an ingenious probing device known as an *asta* ('lance') or *chiave* ('key'). **1975** *Listener* 11 Dec. 793/2 The ware..had been illegally excavated from an Etruscan tomb..by a gang of grave robbers, the notorious *tombaroli.*

tombola. Add: Now usu. with pronunc. (tǫmbōᵘ·lă).

tombolo (tǫ·mbŏlo). *Physical Geogr.* [a. It. *tombolo* sand dune, tombolo.] A bar joining an island to the mainland.

1899 F. P. Gulliver in *Proc. Amer. Acad. Arts & Sci.* XXXIV. 189 Upon the coast of Italy where island-tying ..is beautifully shown, such a bar is called a tombolo. For convenience in distinguishing island-tying bars from those of other kinds, the writer proposes to call every bar of this kind a tombolo, giving an English plural tombolos. **1937** *Geogr. Jrnl.* XC. 190 The writer goes on to discuss bars, spits, and tombolos along the more sheltered shores of the Firth of Clyde. **1960** B. W. Sparks *Geomorphol.* viii. 201 In the British Isles a fine example of a tombolo is provided by Chesil Beach, an eighteen-mile-long ridge connecting the Isle of Portland to the mainland. **1977** A. Hallam *Planet Earth* 94/3 In high-latitude, previously glaciated areas, tombolos are often formed of shingle, the commonest beach material in such regions.

tombstone. Add: **2*.** *Comm.* An advertisement displaying the names of the underwriters or firms associated with a new issue or the like. Also *tombstone ad(vertisement.*

1968 *Times* 27 Feb. 22/3 'Tombstones'..are getting bigger. I am referring, of course, to the new issue advertisements. **1972** *Times* 24 Oct. 2 The Times is now able to offer financial advertisers an exclusive service for the placing of Tombstone advertising (public announcements and notices of redemption) in Europe. **1977** *National Times* (Austral.) 17 Jan. 40/2 The advertising of trusts is limited to 'tombstone' advertising. **1981** *U.S. Banker* Dec. 56/1 The old tombstone ad, promoting a service and basing the appeal largely on price,..is long gone, according to advertising men. **1983** *Marketing* 24 Mar. 39/1 Financial advertising columnage, i.e. tombstones, company meetings, prospectuses, takeovers, etc.

3. (Earlier example.)

1751 B. Lynde *Diary* 16 Oct. (1880) 176 Yesterday Cox and Stacy ½ day abo. Tombstone monument.

tom-cat, tomcat, *v. U.S. slang.* [f. the sb.] *intr.* To pursue women promiscuously for sexual gratification. Freq. const. *around.* Hence **to·mcatting** *vbl. sb.*

1927 *Dial. Notes* V. 478 *Tom catting,* v., to seek illicit sexual adventure. 'Jeff he's out a-tomcattin' roun' some 'ers.' **1932** W. Faulkner *Light in August* xii. 259 So this is where you tomcat to every night. **1939** J. Steinbeck *Grapes of Wrath* xvi. 239, I was goin' out an' dance, an' I was gonna go tom-cattin'. **1953** W. P. McGivern *Big Heat* ii. 23 A guy tom-catting around while his wife's away. **1962** H. Green *Time to pass Over* iii. 42 Don't drink, don't chew, don't tomcat with the women so far as I know. **1975** *New Review* May 20/1 'He had a very strong tendency to be doing a lot of tomcatting.'..Would go out looking for women. **1980** G. Thompson *Murder Mystery* (1981) xxii. 172 A man who's been tom-catting around with three women all day long.

-tome (tōᵘm), terminal element: (*a*) f. Gr. -τόμον, neut. of -τόμος that cuts (see -tomy), used in names of instruments for cutting, esp. ones used in surgical operations denoted by the corresponding word in *-tomy,* as in *cystotome* s.v. Cysto-, Hysterotome, Microtome; (*b*) f. Gr. τομή a cutting, used in words denoting a distinct section or segment of a body or part, as in Myotome 1, *gonotome* s.v. *gono-.

tom-fool, *sb.* **d.** (Earlier example.)

1762 Sterne *Tr. Shandy* V. xxx. 107 'Twas a Tom-fool-battle.

tomfoolery. Add: **2.** *Rhyming slang.* Jewellery. Cf. *tom *sb.*[3].

1931 C. Rimington *Bon Voyage Bk.* xv. 88 *Tomfoolery,* jewelry. **1943** M. Harrison *Reported Safe Arrival* 52, I wouldn' be surprised if you both done a stretch fer knockin' orf some ole bloke's tom-foolery. **1975** *Sunday Times* 30 Mar. 49/2 He will have contacts in 'tomfoolery', or jewellery outlets.

Tom Jones. The name of the hero of Fielding's novel *History of Tom Jones* (1749), used *attrib.* to designate dress and hair styles represented in the film version of 1963 and considered suggestive of eighteenth-century styles.

1964 *Glamour* May 186 Wonderful way to wear hair that's fit and silky: Brush it back from the brow, catch it at the nape, tie in a Tom Jones queue. **1967** *Observer* 14 May 28/6 A chiffon scarf in a Tom Jones bow. **1971** *Jamaican Weekly Gleaner* 10 Nov. 15/2 Looking..beautiful in belted tan tailored pants with chocolate Tom Jones blouse.

‖ **tomme** (tǫm). Also (erron.) **tome.** [Fr.] The name given to a variety of cheeses made in Savoy, a region of S.E. France.

1946 A. L. Simon *Conc. Encycl. Gastron.* IX. 24/2 [One of] the best known *Tommes* of Savoy [is]..*Tomme au Fenouil.* **1958** *Catal. County Stores, Taunton* June 9 Cheese... Tome de Savoie—each 7/6. **1966** P. V. Price *France* ii. 310 There are several *tommes* in the region and this is the most famous. **1972** *Sat. Rev.* (U.S.) 24 June 77/3 In Savoy I sampled..*reblochon*..and the famous *tomme aux raisins,* a blander cheese coated on the outside with dried grape pips.

tommelaitje, var. *tameletjie.

Tommy. Add: **1. c.** (Earlier example.)

1884 Kipling in L. L. Cornell *Kipling in India* (1966) iii. 83 (*title*) The story of Tommy.

3. b. Substitute for def.: = *tommy bar,* sense 6 below. (Earlier example.)

1843 J. J. Greer *Brit. Patent 9811* (1856) 2 My invention..consists..first, in working a double screw..from a central axis into two separate boxes or cases, either by a lever commonly called a tommy, or by a spanner.

6. tommy-bag (example); **tommy bar** *Mech.*, a short bar that can be inserted into a hole in a box-spanner or screw to assist in turning it; **Tommy('s) cooker** *Mil. slang,* a small portable spirit stove; also, a piece of rolled-up canvas soaked in grease used in place of this; **Tommy Dodd** (earlier example); **Tommy talker** *colloq.* = Kazoo in Dict. and Suppl.

1983 P. Nash *Coup de Grass* ii. 23 He was wearing overalls and carrying a canvas tommy-bag. **1920** Webster, Tommy bar. **1930** *Engineering* 25 Apr. 538/1 The cylinder is removed bodily from its supporting bracket, by unscrewing a hinged fixing pillar by means of a tommy bar. **1953** E. Hyams *Vineyards in England* 226 Pass a tommy-bar through the hole at the top of the screw and spin the screw to bring the piston down on to the grapes. **1973** D. Lees *Rape of Quiet Town* vii. 121 He fixed each jack separately..then gave the tommy bars a few..twists until they were tight. **1917** W. Owen *Let.* 4 Feb. (1963) 430 We had 5 Tommy's cookers between the Platoon, but they did not suffice to melt the ice in the water-cans. **1919** *N.Y. Times* 23 Feb. iv. 12/2 When 4 o'clock came around every manjack of us would take out his Tommy-cooker and begin making his tea. **1948** A. Baron *From City, from Plough* xviii. 165 On the little tommy-cookers that they sheltered between their feet they brewed..tea in their mess-tins. **1870** A. Steinmetz *Gaming-Table* II. 221 Not long ago a returned tradesman ..allowed himself to be induced to play at Tommy Dodd with two low sharpers. **1938** Tommy Talker [see *kazoo]. **1976** S. Barstow *Right True End* i. iii. 38 Learn the piano... Well, the french horn, clarinet, fiddle, trombone; mouth-organ, jew's harp, tommy-talker.

to·mmy[2]. *Austral.* and *N.Z. colloq.* [Shortened f. Tomahawk *sb.*] A hatchet. Also **tommy-axe.**

1873 M. A. Barker *Station Amusements N.Z.* ix. 148, I had to get the tommy (*anglicé*—tomahawk) and *chop* his boots off. **1898** Morris *Austral Eng.* 474/2 *Tommy-axe,* a popular corruption of the word *Tomahawk.* **1939** X. Herbert *Capricornia* xxii. 328 Cutting a strip of bark from the tree with the tommy-axe.

to·mmy-gun. *colloq.* (orig. *U.S.*). Also **Tommy-** and as two words. [f. Tommy, repr. the name of J. T. *Thompson*: see *Thompson.] A Thompson or other sub-machine-gun.

1929 *Sat. Even. Post* 13 Apr. 54/3 There are three types of machine gun used—Tommy guns, Browny guns and Louie guns. **1934** E. Hemingway in *Cosmopolitan* Apr. 23/2 The nigger shot him in the belly with the Tommy gun. **1941** *Times* 21 Nov. 3/4 Twelve of the enemy were killed with bayonets and tommy-guns. **1955** M. Banks *Commando Climber* iii. 40 He survived the war by a combination of good fortune and adroitness with a tommy-gun. **1973** D. Lees *Rape of Quiet Town* vii. 111 A wild assortment of weapons, including a couple of tommy guns and a cavalry sabre.

Hence as *v. trans.*; also **to·mmy-gunner.**

1942 *Times* 3 Oct. 4/1 A party of our tommy-gunners penetrated enemy barbed wire entanglements. *Ibid.* 24 Nov. 4/1 When one Soviet tank was engaged in pursuing the retreating Germans its crew leapt out and tommy-gunned them. **1973** A. MANN *Tiara* iii. 22 Thirty years ago he was the best tommy-gunner in the Appennines. **1978** T. GIFFORD *Glendower Legacy* (1979) 144 Maybe they're waiting for me to leave so they can come in and tommy-gun you.

tomo (tōᵘ·mo). *N.Z.* [a. Maori.] A depression or hole in limestone terrain.

1952 *Arena* (N.Z.) xxxi. 3 See him drag a gully full of tomos and patches of scrub. **1961** R. PARK *Hole in Hill* (1962) x. 76, I fell down a big hole... Not just a hole, but a *tomo*, a limestone shaft. **1975** *N.Z. Jrnl. Agric.* Sept. 24/2 It may be located in a tomo or natural depression down the back, or in a corner, of a paddock.

tomography (tǒmǫ·grăfi). *Med.* [f. Gr. τόμος slice, section + -GRAPHY.] Radiography in which an image of a predetermined plane in the body or other object is obtained by rotating the detector and the source of radiation in such a way that points outside the plane give a blurred image. Also in extended use, any analogous technique using other forms of radiation.

1935 *Brit. Jrnl. Radiol.* VIII. 750 The most significant field of application for the method of reproducing body layers (tomography) will, in practice, be lung diagnosis. **1949** *Ibid.* XXII. 627/1 Today, sectional röntgenography, commonly called tomography has indeed, in many places, found recognition as a method of radiological diagnosis. **1968** *Brit. Med. Bull.* XXIV. 242/1 With the advent of transverse tomography, it is now possible to get much more accurate estimations of the various volumes and areas of tissues of differing density, in any cross-section of the body. **1977** 'E. TREVOR' *Theta Syndrome* iii. 40 The axial tomography revealed bilateral subdural hematomas. **1982** *New Scientist* 21 Jan. 155/1 Paul Carson and others ..have been comparing the new-developed technique of ultrasonic computed tomography (UCT) with pulse echo imaging. **1983** *Ibid.* 17 Mar. 725/3 Tree physiology and dendrochronology are just two of the possible applications for portable computer tomography. **1984** *McGraw-Hill Yearbk. Sci. & Technol. 1985* 335/1 Positron emission tomography (PET scan) now allows scientists to measure noninvasively the functional activity of the living human brain.

So **to·mogram**, an X-ray picture taken by tomography; **to·mograph,** (*a*) a tomogram; (*b*) an apparatus for carrying out tomography; **tomogra·phic** *a.*, **tomogra·phically** *adv.*

1935 *Brit. Jrnl. Radiol.* VIII. 736 The new tomographic method is also based upon the principle of the method already mentioned. *Ibid.* 750 Three tomographs are generally sufficient for lung diagnosis. *Ibid.*, A new device, the tomograph, is described, which permits the radiography of body layers of any size and variable thickness. **1936** *Lancet* 25 July 185/2 For all practical purposes three tomograms are ample for accurate diagnosis. **1949** *Radiography* XV. 242/1 (*caption*) Aneurysm demonstrated by lesion of dorsal vertebræ tomographically. **1950** *Times* 22 Nov. 6/6 The infection was discovered, thanks to the use of a tomograph, a new X-ray apparatus, apparently during Sir Stafford Cripps's last stay at Zurich. **1955** D. B. FRY in B. I. Evans *Stud. in Communication* 156 The internal action of the larynx was for a long time inaccessible to X-ray photography but the development of the tomogram technique has enabled Ardram and Kemp to obtain remarkable pictures of the larynx in action. **1968** Tomographic [see *LAMINAGRAPHIC *a.*]. **1975** *Radio Times* 1–7 Nov. 7/1 The EMI ('Emmy')-scanner is a machine for taking axial X-ray tomograms. **1975** *Sci. Amer.* Oct. 56/3 In most tomographic instruments the X-ray source moves in one direction and the photographic film simultaneously moves in the opposite direction. The patient lies in between. **1976** *Physics Bull.* Oct. 436/3 X-ray tomography has become a popular method of medical imaging over the past few years... A M Cormack and A M Koehler have come up with an alternative idea for improving the density resolution of tomographs. **1982** *Times* 26 July 2/3 Using the tomograms, the interior of the helmet has now been excavated.

tomorrer (tŭmǫ·rəɪ), *adv.* Also **to-morrer.** Repr. a dial. and slang pronunc. of TOMORROW *adv.*

1901 M. FRANKLIN *My Brilliant Career* iii. 16 Only I promised to stick to the missus a while, I'd scoot to-morrer. **1921** H. WILLIAMSON *Beautiful Yrs.* 81 Go when you like, miboy. Only I shall be a-mowing to-morrer. **1959** [see *SICKIE 1]. **1970** T. HUGHES *Crow* 63 O do not chop his winkle off His Mammy cried with horrer Think of the joy will come of it Tomorrer and tomorrer.

to-morrow, *adv.* and *sb.* Add: Now usu. written **tomorrow. A.** *adv.* **1. c.** *fig.* In the (near) future.

1871, etc. [see *jam tomorrow* s.v. *JAM *sb.*² b]. **1957** *Listener* 15 Aug. 223/1 An accelerated movement towards independence: Ghana yesterday; Nigeria, French West Africa, the Cameroons, tomorrow.

B. *sb.* **1*.** *fig.* The (near) future. Freq. in the possessive.

1943 J. B. PRIESTLEY *Daylight on Saturday* ii. 5 He belonged to tomorrow's new ruling class. **1959** *Brno Studies in English* I. 73 Progressive poets preferred to look forward into distant future and dreamed..of a better to-morrow. **1979** *Guardian* 30 Oct. 32/8 The Prime Minister..told the Wales TUC that British industry was not going to get tomorrow's jobs 'unless we move into tomorrow's world'.

4. *as if there were no tomorrow* and varr., recklessly, with no regard for the future.

1862 WHYTE-MELVILLE *Queen's Maries* II. xxii. 10 Why should you thus risk your life as if there was no to-morrow? **1980** *Guardian Weekly* 3 Feb. 1/3 Oil supplies that Americans at home continue to consume as though there were no tomorrow.

5. Proverb. *tomorrow is another* (or † *a new*) *day.*

c **1527** J. RASTELL *Calisto & Melebea* sig. C 1ᵛ, Well mother to morrow is a new day. **1603** FLORIO tr. *Montaigne's Ess.* II. iv. 57 A letter..beeing delivered him..at supper, he deferred the opening of it, pronouncing this byword, *To morrow is a new day.* **1824** SCOTT *St. Ronan's* III. vii. 192 We will say no more of it at present... Tomorrow is a new day. **1927** P. GREEN *Field God* I. 148 Go to it, you Mag and Lonie! To-morrow's another day, and you'll need all you can hold. **1956** M. DICKENS *Angel in Corner* vi. 90 'You can run along now... Those few letters will keep until the morning.'..'But there will be a whole heap of new ones by the morning.'..'I know, dear... If the letters didn't come, that would be the time to start worrying. But tomorrow is another day.' **1980** B. PYM *Few Green Leaves* xiii. 107 He would probably have said nothing and so missed his opportunity. Still, tomorrow was another day.

tom-tit, tomtit. Add: **1. a.** Also, the great tit, *Parus major.*

1965 *Jrnl. Lancs. Dial. Soc.* Jan. 19 Great Tit... Tom Tit. Accrington. **1972** *Guardian* 23 Feb. 12/2 An octogenarian farm worker..pointed out that, just as one's largest toe is the 'tom toe', so it followed naturally that the largest tit was the tom-tit.

2. A small sailing boat.

1857 A. W. HABERSHAM *My Last Cruise* xvii. 333 Some of us also took the tomtit, (a boat smaller even than the dingy). **1925** A. B. ARMITAGE *Cadet to Commodore* xx. 278 Out with the 'Tom-tits' in the harbour on a breezy Saturday afternoon was another delightful sport.

3. Rhyming slang for 'shit'. Freq. with *the* in *fig.* use: 'the willies'; also, nonsense.

1943 'R. LLEWELLYN' *None but Lonely Heart* xx. 116 'You're always doing it, you shower of tom tit, you.' **1944** L. GLASSOP *We were Rats* 67 'Break it down,' said the corporal. 'You'll give these blokes the tomtits before they get their first lot of C.B.' **1967** J. GARDNER *Madrigal* I. iii. 54 You can cut the Tom Tit, sergeant. **1970** C. WOOD *'Terrible Hard,' says Alice* vii. 91 Perhaps 'e stopped for a tomtit. **1973** P. A. SMITH *Barcoo Salute* 14 What's the matter, got the tom tits? **1982** L. CODY *Bad Company* xii. 80, I was just sitting there, trousers round me ankles. .. If I hadn't been doing it already, he'd 've given me the tom-tits.

tom-tom, *sb.* **1. b.** Delete entry and see *TAM-TAM.

d. A low-toned drum (without snares), used in Western music.

1934 E. LITTLE *Mod. Rhythmic Drumming* (rev. ed.) 26 No outfit is complete without at least one tomtom. **1977** *Rolling Stone* 30 June 97/2 Ringo slams away on his tom-toms.

ton¹. Add: **4. b.** (Earlier and later examples, in *sing.*)

1770 P. FRENEAU in Brackenridge & Freneau *Father Bombo* (1975) I. iii. 13 My head stuck a considerable time in a ton of mud. **1899** H. SWEET *Pract. Study Languages* x. 115, I am told that the great English lexicographers of the present day look down with contempt on anything less than a ton of such materials. **1971** *Scope* (S. Afr.) 19 Mar. 38/1 Fine, thanks a ton, Len. I won't be a sec. **1977** *Belfast Tel.* 28 Feb. 20/8 This has brought the lass on a ton.

c. *pl.* As *adv.* qualifying comparative or (*U.S.*) positive adjs.: much; very. *colloq.*

1908 S. WILSON *Let.* 17 Aug. in R. S. Churchill *Winston S. Churchill* (1969) II. Compan. II. 804. I feel tons better for being in the wonderful air. **1970** 'D. HALLIDAY' *Dolly & Cookie Bird* viii. 127 He was looking tons better, with his ribs done up in crêpe. **1977** *Amer. Speech 1975* L. 68 *Tons adv*, very, extremely. 'Her outfit is tons neat.'

d. Phr. *to come down* (*on* or *upon*) (a person) *like a ton of bricks*: see *COME *v.* 56 g.

4*. *transf.* **a.** *colloq.* A score of one hundred in a game, *spec.* in *Cricket* (= *CENTURY 3 b) and *Darts.*

1936 R. CROFT-COOKE *Darts* vi. 42 *Ton,* the word means simply 100. While in more gentlemanly games they speak of Centuries, in Darts we curtly say 'One Ton'. **1946** J. MOORE *Brensham Village* III. 95 Darts has its own esoteric terminology... A hundred is a 'ton', of course, all over England. **1958** *Punch* 9 July 40/2, I owe everything to Cambridge. I got a ton in the Freshman's Match of 1941. **1973** *Atlantic Monthly* Aug. 73 Now he's averaging 60 or more, frequently throws a 'ton'—a round of 100 or more points—and can put a dart into a fifty-cent piece area every time. **1978** *Lancashire Life* Apr. 41/3 Scoring a century didn't mean a hoot to me then... Now, as an experienced pro, I know I must make a 'ton' and then keep going to get another.

b. *slang.* A hundred pounds.

1946 *People* 7 Apr. 2/6 A red-faced punter..whose conversational powers were limited to..jargon, which translated fivers as 'flims'..; £100 as a 'ton' [etc.]. **1960** 'A. BURGESS' *Doctor is Sick* 164 'And what's the first prize?' asked Edwin. 'A ton,' screamed Harry Stone. ''Undred nicker an' a film test.' **1981** P. TURNBULL *Deep & Crisp & Even* vii. 131 The old man would charge three ton for this but me and the boys will do it for half-price.

c. *colloq.* A speed of one hundred miles per hour (esp. with reference to motor cycles). Freq. in phr. *to do the* (or *a*) *ton.* Cf. *TON-UP *sb.* and *a.*

1954 G. SMITH *Flaw in Crystal* iv. 36 At eighty I felt a wild sense of elation... I watched to see if Several would triumphantly lead Teddy onwards at a majestic full ton. **1959** *News Chron.* 17 Dec. 3/1 The dangerous noddles who boast about doing the ton on the public roads. **1964** *New Statesman* 21 Feb. 288/3 We do the ton sometimes, but not where any one's goin' to get 'urt. **1973** *Hansard Lords* 5 Dec. 684 In that case, you must have been doing a 'ton', if very few cars passed you.

d. In other miscellaneous colloq. uses to denote one hundred.

1962 *Electronics Weekly* 21 Nov. 3/1 Elliott reach a ton. The 100th National Elliott 803 computer has been installed. **1970** *Sunday Tel.* 22 Mar. 13/3 Blissful summer breezes..ease the discomfort of temperatures which occasionally threaten to make the ton. **1980** *Financial Rev.* (Sydney) 29 Aug. 29/1 Australians staying at the best capital city hotels..will have reached 'the ton' in their room rates—accommodation will be costing $100 a night.

6. ton-force (pl. *tons-force*), a unit of force equal to the weight of a mass of one ton, esp. under standard gravity; **ton weight,** the weight of one ton; usu. *fig.*

1961 *B.S.I. News* Oct. 26/2 A similar distinction is made between..ton (no abbreviation) and ton-force (tonf). **1972** *Physics Bull.* May 285/1 The 50 tonf deadweight standard was originally designed to give forces only in units of tons-force. *a* **1855** C. BRONTË *Professor* (1857) I. vi. 87 This liability is a ton weight at least. **1893** H. FREDERIC *Return of O'Mahony* I. x. 83 Then would come..the fierce buffeting of ton-weight blows as the boat staggered blindly at the bottom of the abyss. **1936** *Discovery* Feb. 37/2 The power developed per ton-weight of the engine. **1960** H. PINTER *Caretaker* I. 18 I'll give you a hand. (*They lift it.*) It's a ton weight, en't? **1981** J. WAINWRIGHT *All on Summer's Day* 198 She'd been like a ton weight across his shoulders. Her and her infernal daughters.

ton³. Delete 'Now *rare*' and add: **a.** (Later examples.)

1939 D. CECIL *Young Melbourne* viii. 220 Some humble country acquaintances and a few persons of ton. **1978** J. KRANTZ *Scruples* ii. 39 And these Bostonians..did own a gratifying number of mills and plants and banks and brokerage firms. Also they had *ton.*

b. (Earlier and later examples.)

c **1770** in de Vries & Fryer *Venus Unmasked* (1967) 33 Miss P... D... will only..take engagements from billiard table gentlemen, gentlemen of the ton, and young shopmen. **1969** H. ELSNA *Abbot's House* 99 A waste, when all the *ton* will flock here for this event. *Ibid.* 103 The *ton* are here in force.

‖ **tonadilla** (tonadī·lyă). [Sp., dim. of *tonada* tune, song.] A light operatic interlude of the mid-eighteenth to early-nineteenth cent., orig. forming an intermezzo between the acts of a serious play or opera, but later performed independently.

1830 W. C. STAFFORD *Hist. Music* xviii. 263 The Tonadilla, originally a simple and popular song, sung in the *Zarguela* and *Saynette*, now frequently represents an entire action, consisting of a whole scene, or even of an act. **1876** STAINER & BARRETT *Dict. Mus. Terms* 435/2 *Tonadilla* (*Sp.*), a short tune, an interlude, ritornello, symphony to a song. **1920** C. VAN VECHTEN *Mus. Spain* v. 82 The *tonadilla*..accompanied by a guitar or violin and interspersed with dances, was very popular for a number of years. **1947** A. EINSTEIN *Mus. Romantic Era* xvii. 329 The works decisive in bringing out this national style were..*zarzuelas* in the realistic manner of the *tonadilla.* **1973** *Oxford Times* 30 Mar. 14/4 The scenic tonadilla in the 18th century can be described as miniature comic opera.

tonal *a.* Add: **1. c.** Of tonality; pertaining to music written in keys. Opp. *ATONAL *a.*

1884 G. OAKEY *Text Bk. Harmony* viii. 51 A sequence.. in which the intervals belong to one scale, is termed..a Tonal Sequence. **1922** [see *ATONAL *a.*] **1957** *Encycl. Brit.* XI. 205/1 With the development of polyphony, tonality becomes as important as the concord-discord system itself; and, indeed, that system could not have existed without tonal guidance at every point. **1978** P. GRIFFITHS *Conc. Hist. Mod. Music* ii. 23 Sibelius's long silence..may suggest the difficulty of maintaining tonal composition in the twentieth century.

3. Pertaining to or characterized by shades of colour or effects of light and shade. Cf. TONE *sb.* 10 a, b.

1910 S. J. SOLOMON *Practice of Oil Painting* vi. 62 The same method is applicable in arriving at a similar decision with regard to the relation of shadows, all intervening tones, and the general tonal aspect of the whole figure. **1931** J. H. BROWN *Water-Colour Guidance* x. 192 Present-day colour work..has tended to divert the colourist's attention from the *tonal* aspect of painting. **1967** E. SHORT *Embroidery & Fabric Collage* i. 4 (*caption*) As one fabric is used throughout, there are no contrasts of colour or texture, and the design relies for interest on the tonal pattern made by the shadows. **1980** *Economist* 20 Aug. 62/1 Plain and tonal designs—mingled colours, but no pattern—are the fashion. *Ibid.* 62/2 Tonal carpets are what the customer wants.

tonalite. Add: [ad. G. *tonalit* (G. vom Rath 1864, in *Zeitschr. der deutsch. geol. Ges.* XVI. 249).] Later used for any quartz-diorite; now *spec.* a rock in which quartz represents 20–60 per cent of quartz plus feldspars (a higher proportion than in quartz-diorite) and alkali feldspar is less than 10 per cent of total feldspars. (Further examples.)

1913 *Jrnl. Geol.* XXI. 213 Lindgren has defined tonalite (or quartz diorite), as containing less than 8 per cent of alkali feldspar, granodiorite as containing 8–20 per cent of alkali feldspar. **1932** A. JOHANNSEN *Descr. Petrogr. Igneous Rocks* II. 379 Diorites with less than 5 per cent of quartz may be called quartz-bearing-diorites. With more than 5 per cent, they become quartz-diorites (tonalites). **1962** W. T. HUANG *Petrology* iv. 91 From granite, granodiorite, tonalite to diorite, the proportional amounts of quartz and alkalic feldspar decrease, while that of sodic plagioclase increases. **1976** *Earth-Sci. Rev.* XII. 14 For field 5 the term *tonalite* is recommended, whether hornblende is present or not, in agreement with Johannsen..; whereas quartz diorite, frequently used for this field, is restricted to field 10*. *Ibid.* 27, 20–60% of light-colored minerals... Plag 90–100% of total feldspar: (5) tonalite. **1977** *Sci. Amer.* Mar. 94/1 The average chemical composition [of gneisses] resembles that of the common igneous rocks diorite and tonalite.

Hence **tonali·tic** *a.*

1963 *Revista de la Asociación Geológica Argentina* XVIII. 97 In the Pampean Ranges, tungsten ore deposits are related to tonalitic-granitic intrusives of the pre-Cambrian tectomagmatic cycle. **1978** *Nature* 16 Mar. 241/1 Although the gneiss belts show great structural complexity..granodioritic and tonalitic compositions greatly predominate.

tonalitive (tonæ·litiv), *a. Mus. Obs.* or *rare.* [f. TONALIT(Y + -IVE.] Of or pertaining to tonality.

1907 M. H. GLYN *Rhythmic Conception of Music* iii. 64 Nothing would seem more natural than that tonality should suggest 'tonalitive', but the word has not hitherto appeared. **1918** *Mus. Assoc. Proc. 1917–18* 162, I should expect the new tonalitive schemes of such composers as Debussy and Ravel to bring about great changes in composition. **1924** T. H. Y. TROTTER *Music & Mind* 237 The old major and minor tonalitive schemes are giving way.

tonality. Add: **1. b.** The principle or practice of organizing musical composition around a key note or tonic.

1932 J. YASSER *Theory Evolving Tonality* 375 *Tonality*, a principle which organically and tonocentrically unites the function of a certain number of systematically arranged sounds..in their melodic and harmonic aspects. **1957** *Encycl. Brit.* XI. 205/2 Palestrina's tonality is one of the most mature and subtle things in music. **1978** P. GRIFFITHS *Conc. Hist. Mod. Music* iii. 39 Berg's opera differs from Schoenberg's monodrama in its direct references back to tonality.

3. *Linguistics.* The differentiation of words, phrases, or syllables by a change in the pitch of the voice.

1948 R. A. D. FORREST *Chinese Lang.* i. 26 All the languages which we group under the term Sinitic have..a tendency to develop significant tonality. **1956** JAKOBSON & HALLE *Fundamentals of Lang.* iii. 29 All the inherent features are divided into two classes that might be termed sonority features and tonality features,..the latter [akin] to the prosodic pitch features. **1973** *Archivum Linguisticum* IV. 23 The 'paratonality system' determines the relationship between sentences and paratone groups in the same way as the tonality system relates clauses and tone-groups.

‖ **tonari gumi** (tonā·ri gū·mi). Also **tonari-gumi, tonarigumi.** [Jap.] A neighbourhood association in Japan, formed of groups of families who assume responsibility for their own community affairs.

1947 R. BENEDICT *Chrysanthemum & Sword* iv. 82 Japan had, like China, tiny units of five to ten families, called in recent times the *tonari gumi*, which were the smallest responsible units of the population. **1958** W. J. H. SPROTT *Human Groups* 93 In Japanese cities they have associations called *tonari-gumi*, made up of from ten to twenty households. **1980** J. MELVILLE *Chrysanthemum Chain* 119 People who lived nearby..members of Murrow's *tonari-gumi* or neighbourhood association.

tondino. Restrict *Arch.* to sense in Dict. and add: **2.** *Ceramics.* Pl. **tondini.** A plate with a wide flat rim and deep centre made of majolica.

1885 [see *FAENZA]. **1900** F. LITCHFIELD *Pott. & Porc.* ii. 16 A set of round plates or *tondini*. **1958** M. WYKES-JOYCE *7000 Years Pottery* vi. 76 What we may term useless wares, a particular kind of *piatto con fondo*, the *tondino*, which would be sent by a gallant to his current inamorata, filled with candied flower petals... A flirtatious signorina would have some dozen or score of the *tondini* on display. **1971** *Times* 30 Nov. 24/3 (Advt.), A Faenza tondino by the 'Green Man'.

tondo. (Earlier example.)

1877 GEO. ELIOT *Let.* 29 Mar. (1956) VI. 359 The little *tondi* on the covers of the 3/6 edition are charming.

tone, *sb.* Add: **I. 2. a.** Also, such a sound produced electrically; cf. *pure tone* s.v. *PURE *a.* 1 e; in *Teleph.*, a pure tone or a more complex sound generated automatically to convey to a calling subscriber information about the line or the number required (see *busy, dial, dialling, engaged,* etc., *tone* under the first elements in Suppl.).

1919 J. POOLE *Pract. Telephone Handbk.* (ed. 6) xxi. 364 The tones and interruptions required are as follows:— (1) A 'tone' of 24 interruptions per revolution of the armature or 400 interruptions per second, [etc.]. **1958** G. HIGGS in E. Molloy *High Fidelity Sound Reproduction* i. 10 The specification of a definite acoustical or electrical level necessarily involves reference to a steady-value test-tone of the stipulated frequency. **1962** A. NISBETT *Technique Sound Studio* v. 103 To calibrate for this, the most accurate method is to replay a reference tone (or some other steady sound). **1973** T. J. GLATTKE in F. D. Minifie et al. *Normal Aspects of Speech* viii. 329 A series of three tones at 800 Hz..followed by a series at 800, 1,000, and 800 Hz..was differentiated by cats following cortical ablation. **1976** T. H. FLOWERS *Introd. Exchange Syst.* iii. 67 Each tone is generated by a tone generator common to the whole exchange.

5. d. Also *spec.* in literary criticism, an author's attitude to his subject matter or audience; the distinctive mood created by this.

1929 I. A. RICHARDS *Pract. Crit.* III. i. 183 A man writing a scientific treatise, for example, will put the *Sense* of what he has to say first... His *Tone* will be settled for him by academic convention. **1950** F. B. MILLETT *Reading Fiction* 11 This tone, the general feeling which suffuses and surrounds the work, arises ultimately out of the writer's attitude toward his subject. **1959** H. GARDNER *Business of Crit.* 40 The tone of the close of the play. **1973** G. W. TURNER *Stylistics* vi. 186, I shall use..*tone* for the range of variation reflecting adjustments to an audience. **1977** *N.Y. Rev. Bks.* 15 Sept. 40/2 His practical criticism is not much concerned with the structure of an individual poem except as an embodiment of crisis; it has little to say of diction, the metres, rhythm, syntax, or tone.

6. a. (Earlier example.)

1679 R. HOOKE *Diary* 14 May (1935) 412 At Garways, Chinese Language Tones.

III. 11. (sense 2) *tone-quality*; (sense 6) *tone-curve, -group, -mark, -pattern, -sequence, -unit*; *tone-bearing* adj.; (sense 9) *tone-setter*; *tone-setting* adj.; (sense 10) *tone relation, value*; **tone-arm,** †(*a*) the tubular arm connecting the sound-box of a gramophone to the horn (*obs.*); (*b*) = *pick-up arm* s.v. *PICK-UP *a.* a; **tone burst,** an audio signal used in testing the transient response of audio components; **tone cluster** *Mus.*, a group of adjacent notes on a piano played simultaneously by placing the forearm or flat of the hand on the keys; cf. *note-cluster* s.v. *NOTE *sb.*[2] 21; **tone control,** the adjustment of the proportion of high and low frequencies in reproduced sound; a device or manual control for achieving this; **tone-deaf** *a.*: also *transf.* and *fig.*, insensitive, lacking in perception; hence **tone-deafness; tone-full** *a.*: now usu. *toneful*; cf. TUNEFUL *a.*; **tone generator,** an apparatus for electronically producing tones of a desired frequency; **tone language** *Linguistics*, a language which uses variations in pitch, in addition to different consonants and vowels, to distinguish words, e.g. Chinese; **tone-on-tone** *a.*, applied to designs, textiles, etc., composed of toning rather than contrasting shades of colour; **tone-painting** (earlier example); hence **tone-painter; tone poem** *Mus.* = *symphonic poem* s.v. SYMPHONIC *a.* (*sb.*) 3; **tone poet,** (*b*) *spec.* one who composes tone poems; hence **tone poetry; tone-row** *Mus.*, the twelve notes of the chromatic scale arranged in a fixed order to form the basis of a composition; **tone sandhi** *Linguistics* [*SANDHI], in tone languages: the differences between the tones of words through the influence of contiguous tonal patterns; **tone separation** *Photogr.* = *POSTERIZATION.

1907 *T. Eaton & Co. Catal.* Spring & Summer 249/1 Columbia Graphophone..patent aluminium tone-arm. **1923** *Gramophone* Apr. p. vii/2 (Advt.), 18 models of Tonearms with and without Goosenecks. **1946** [see *record groove* s.v. *RECORD *sb.* 13 b]. **1981** *Popular Hi-Fi* Mar. 85/3 This is a direct drive, quartz locked, fully automatic turntable with integrated tonearm. **1971** B. MAFENI in J. Spencer *Eng. Lang. W. Afr.* 107 There is a syllabic nasal /N/ [in Nigerian Pidgin] which is tone-bearing and is always homorganic with the succeeding consonant. **1981** *Word 1980* XXXI. 186 Other syllables..may be higher, lower, or on the same level relative to the onset of the tone-bearing syllable. **1967** *Electronics* 6 Mar. 82/1 (Advt.), See the little boxes. See what they can do... Tone burst..trigger..sweep. **1978** *Gramophone* Jan. 1336/1 The toneburst oscillogram..shows that the output across an 8-ohm dummy load is virtually identical with the input signal. **1921** *Freeman* 13 Apr. 112/2 The significance of the tone cluster, like that of the single tone, is to be found in its possibility of combinations with other tone clusters. **1937** N. SLONIMSKY *Music since 1900* 122 [12 March 1912.] At the San Francisco Music Club Henry Cowell performs for the first time in public, on the day after his fifteenth birthday, piano tone-clusters on white or black keys, struck with the forearm. **1973** *Daily Tel.* 24 Nov. 11/2 He watched the Sinfonietta's resident pianist..elbowing his way through the tone clusters of an early Roberto Gerhard. **1983** *Listener* 28 July 30/3 The music abounds in such special effects as tone-clusters like smudged chords, microtones, fragmentation of the text, whistling, whispers, shouts. **1930** *Electronics* July 195/1 Tone control was the most evident technical idea at the Trade Show of the Radio Manufacturers Association in June. **1934** *Discovery* Nov. 324/2 The models..have effective tone and volume controls fitted. **1974** *Harrods Christmas Catal.* 70/3 Electric Guitar..with volume and tone controls. **1922** H. E. PALMER *Eng. Intonation* i. 3 That part which is concerned chiefly with the tone-curves irrespective of their meanings has been called *Tonetics*. **1953** C. E. BAZELL *Linguistic Form* 99 'Questioning intonation' (a special tone-curve) in English. **1932** R. KNOX *Broadcast Minds* iv. 85 When we ask him precisely what it is which 'religion' can give us that is inaccessible to a nature..tone-deaf to religion, he has nothing to point to except those moments themselves. **1972** F. WARNER *Lying Figures* III. 35 We are spiritually tone-deaf. Mum's the word! **1884** T. BARR *Man. Dis. Ear* IV. ii. 459 If this partial tone-deafness is not connected with disease of the conducting apparatus, the anomaly is probably due to cochlear disturbance. **1941** F. MATTHIESSEN *Amer. Renaissance* I. iv. 34 The honesty of Whittier's effort was somewhat vitiated by the tone-deafness that robbed his verse of any full variety of cadences. **1973** *Listener* 14 June 786/3 Mr Nixon..has persistently shown ..a disturbing tone-deafness to the legal restraints which ..are built into the American system. **1977** *Proc. R. Soc. Med.* LXX. 134/1 Tone deafness is a defect of pitch discrimination in which the relationship of one musical tone to others cannot be accurately assessed or imitated. **1925** T. DREISER *Amer. Trag.* I. I. xi. 77 The none too toneful piano. **1927** *Observer* 10 Apr. 24 The short, quick flutter of the wing and the most toneful croak of satisfaction. **1942** *Brit. Jrnl. Psychol.* XXXII. 292 We now have in the laboratory a tone generator capable of sounding tones of any desired harmonic structure. **1980** *Sci. Amer.* Oct. 74/1 Each phoneme is generated by a particular setting of various tone generators, noise generators and acoustic filters. **1922** H. E. PALMER *Eng. Intonation* i. 6 The more serious difficulty is the teaching of the semantic values of the tone-groups. **1977** *Bull. School Oriental & African Stud.* XL. 654/2 The structure of the basic intonational unit, the *tone-group*, consists of an obligatory *tonic*, i.e. the syllable where the pitch movement identifying the *tonic type* begins, and an optional *pretonic* element. **1930** R. PAGET *Human Speech* 188 In the Tone-languages, the melody of phonation is tied to the articulation. **1971** G. ANSRE in J. Spencer *Eng. Lang. W. Afr.* 157 Most of the languages of the region [*sc.* West Africa] use pitch in their phonological patterning in a way which has earned them the term 'tone languages'. **1978** *Sci. Amer.* Nov. 96/1 Many African and Asian languages are tone languages. **1924** H. E. PALMER *Gram. Spoken Eng.* 6 When tone-marks are provided, the use of the sign ['] may therefore be entirely dispensed with. **1964** M. SCHUBIGER in D. Abercrombie et al. *Daniel Jones* 265 The tone-marks are mine. **1939** *Country Life* 11 Feb. p. xxxviii/2 This Matita two-piece redingote and dress is in a tone-on-tone effect in light and dark grey. **1965** 'L. EGAN' *Detective's Due* i. 10 Beige tone-on-tone carpet. **1979** *Arizona Daily Star* 5 Aug. A-12/3 (Advt.), From the tip of its tone-on-tone toe to its sleek, stacked heel, it's everything you'd expect from Evan Picone. **1903** A. W. PATTERSON *Schumann* 49 How first the pianoforte, next the orchestra, and lastly the string quartet suggested sound pictures to the tone-painter. **1897** *Daily Tel.* 31 Mar. 10/4 Even great musicians do not appear at their best in tone-painting. **1931** T. H. PEAR *Voice & Personality* 74 The tone-pattern of the Welsh sentence. **1961** *Amer. Speech* XXXVI. 221 Tone patterns illustrated by Kingdon's tonetic stress marks. **1889** G. B. SHAW *London Music 1888–89* (1937) 68 A long, scrappy movement which is neither bravura nor tone poem. **1942** E. PAUL *Narrow St.* xviii. 142 Jacques Benoit-Mechin, who wrote tone poems about South America. **1977** *Gramophone* Apr. 1561/3 Nor does the performance..really project the work as the blazing tone poem that it self-evidently is. **1983** *Listener* 3 Nov. 36/4 At seven and a half minutes it is perhaps a little short-winded for a full-blown tone poem. **1892** *Review of Reviews* Sept. 289/1 A most original tone-poet. **1903** A. W. PATTERSON *Schumann* p. viii, The writer.. has endeavoured..to let the great tone poet speak to the readers through his own thoughts. **1890** Tone poetry [see *absolute music* s.v. *ABSOLUTE *a.* 16]. **1934** WEBSTER, Tone quality. **1936** *Discovery* July 224/1 The tone-quality [can] be very considerably altered. **1961** *Times* 10 Mar. 22/2 No conductor in my experience has shaped a melody with more tenderness and lustre of tone-quality. **1903** R. FRY *Let.* 6 Mar. (1972) I. 204 The tone relations are nearer to Moretto's in breadth. **1955** *Times* 9 May 3/5 He was before everything a colourist, and all the machinery of his art—composition, drawing, tone relation, and touch—was organised in the interests of his ruling passion. **1936** *Musical Q.* XXII. 14 (*title*) Schoenberg's tone-rows and the tonal system of the future. **1958** *Times* 6 June 4/3 Composition in tone-rows of 12 notes. **1967** A. L. LLOYD *Folk Song in England* i. 38 The scale of a folk tune is the series of notes used, the tone-row and no more. **1925** E. SAPIR in *Language* I. 45 In Sarcee, an Athabaskan language..there is a true middle tone and a pseudo-middle tone which results from the lowering of a high tone to the middle position because of certain mechanical rules of tone sandhi. **1968** P. KRATOCHVÍL *Chinese Lang. Today* ii. 38 One of the factors which cause modifications of these general tendencies of tones in continuous speech is the influence of the tone environment of the given syllable. This is what is known as tone sandhi. **1943** Tone separation [see *POSTERIZE *v.*]. **1977** Tone separation [see *POSTERIZATION]. **1924** H. E. PALMER *Gram. Spoken Eng.* 21 Any pair or more of tone-groups in one sentence constitutes a tone-sequence. **1973** *Archivum Linguisticum* IV. 17 Halliday..though he describes certain tone sequences ..implies that these are no more than chance associations of tones. **1973** *Publishers Weekly* 9 July 44/2 A tone-setter on the field, he contributed to five Packer championships and two Super Bowl wins. **1979** C. E. SCHORSKE *Fin-de-Siècle Vienna* p. xxiii, The intellectual tone-setters among college students. **1962** Y. MALKIEL in Householder & Saporta *Probl. Lexicogr.* 11 Many tone-setting Academy dictionaries. **1978** *Language* LIV. 430 Condillac and other tone-setting figures were concerned solely with generalities. **1964** CRYSTAL & QUIRK *Prosodic & Paralinguistic Features in Eng.* iv. 50 We come now to the system which has the tone-unit..as its actual matrix. **1981** *Word 1980*

XXXI. 154 The vertical bar marks the 'onset' of the tone unit. **1927** R. H. WILENSKI *Mod. Movement in Art* 35 Taught successfully to draw 'by the shadows' and paint 'by the tone values'. **1967** E. SHORT *Embroidery & Fabric Collage* i. 9 It is easy to assess the relative tone values of strong contrasts, such as black and white.

tone, *v.* Add: **II. 5. a.** (Earlier example, const. *down.*) Cf. sense 6 b in Dict.

1831 J. CONSTABLE *Let.* 13 Oct. (1966) IV. 357, I think the *large sail*..much too light. I shall like it toned down very considerably.

c. Also without const.

1976 W. J. BURLEY *Wycliffe & Schoolgirls* i. 31 The colour scheme was old gold from the carpet to the wall-paper, cushions and curtains. Everything was 'to tone' as Mrs Clarke would..have said.

III. 6. b. (Earlier example.)

1847 DICKENS *Dombey* (1848) xx. 197 The Native.. handed him..his hat; which..the Mayor wore with a rakish air on one side of his head, by way of toning down his remarkable visage.

d. The vb.-stem in Comb. **to·ne-up,** an act or means of raising to a higher tone; a strengthening or improvement.

1943 W. S. CHURCHILL *Second World War* (1951) IV. 852 It is time to have another tone-up of security arrangements. **1950** *Times* 2 Feb. 2/7 He was a man of 37, and if I had known he was going on this course I should have advised a period of drill training as a tone-up.

toned, *ppl. a.* and *adj.* Add: **I.** *ppl. a.* **3.** *toned-down,* modified, reduced in intensity.

1974 *Listener* 24 Jan. 122/2 The dances are in effect toned-down Bartok. **1981** V. GLENDINNING *Edith Sitwell* v. 83 Edith published two very similar accounts of Wyndham Lewis..both toned-down versions of a provocative essay she wrote.

toneless, *a.* **2.** (*a*) (Earlier example.)

1833 *Philol. Museum* II. 386 The Old English..the Middle English, and the New, inflect all these verbs in a plain and toneless -*ed.*

toneme (tōᵘ·nīm). *Linguistics.* [f. TONE *sb.* + *-EME.] A tone or set of tones functioning as a distinctive unit in a tone language (cf. *PHONEME 1 b). Hence **tone·mic** *a.*; **tone·-mically** *adv.*

1923 D. M. BEACH *Phonetics of Pekingese* (London Univ. thesis) ii. 9 Corresponding to the phoneme is the *toneme*, which is a group of tones no one of which may be used in the same position as any other. **1924** —— in *Bantu Stud.* Dec. 90 The key to all tonetic transcription is the principle of the *toneme*,..a group of tones within a given language. **1926** C. M. DOKE in *Ibid.* July 218 Words tonemically different and differing in meaning may under certain morphological circumstances become tonemically alike. **1930** J. R. FIRTH *Speech* iii. 27 A proper understanding and use of the tonemes of these languages would appear to be a *sine qua non.* **1944** *Internat. Jrnl. Amer. Linguistics* X. 123/2 The tonemic changes are by no means always substitution of a high for a mid toneme. **1957** D. JONES *Hist. & Meaning of Term 'Phoneme'* 12 One day—..about February 1921—he [*sc.* D. M. Beach] gave a lecture in the Department of Phonetics at University College, London,..in the course of which he demonstrated that each of the four so-called 'tones' of that language [*sc.* Pekingese] had 'variants' conditioned by the tones of syllables adjoining them in connected speech, and sometimes by other factors. The word 'toneme' was coined at my suggestion: it was readily accepted by Beach and the..staff of the Department. **1965** [see *INTONEME]. **1976** *Word 1971* XXVII. 379 The toneme distinction in Swedish (accent 1 and accent 2), differentiating words like *stegen* [ste:gen] with accent 1 'the ladder' and *stegen* [*ste:gen] with accent 2 'the steps', however, is not mastered at an early stage. **1978** *Language* LIV. 245/2 R. W. Wilkinson..argues that mid tone is tonemic.

toner. Add: **2.** *Photogr.* A chemical bath used to change the tone or colour of a (black-and-white) photographic print.

1920 E. J. WALL *Dict. Photogr.* (ed. 10) 661 There are many alternative toners for different colours which may be used alone or in combination on the same print. **1950** O. R CROY *Compl. Art Printing & Enlarging* IV. 201 Immerse the print in the toner until the desired tone is reached. **1977** J. HEDGECOE *Photographer's Handbk.* 275 (*caption*) The already stark appearance of the print..was further accentuated by processing in a blue toner.

3. Particles of pigment used in xerographic processes to render an electrostatic image visible.

1954 *RCA Rev.* XV. 471 Developing consists in bringing fine positively charged particles of developer powder, or toner, close to the surface, so that they will be attracted to those areas which are still charged. **1977** *Sci. Amer.* Nov. 69/1 (Advt.), Develop in a second or two by a dip through any of at least three makes of commercial electrographic liquid developers that carry positive-charging toner particles.

4. *Hairdressing.* (See quot. 1966.)

1966 J. S. COX *Illustr. Dict. Hairdressing* 151/1 *Toner,* a substance which when applied to the hair effects a change of tone or an accentuation of an existing tone. **1969** E. TASHO *Hair Styling for Women* x. 182 Temporary rinses can be used as toners on bleached hair. **1976** *Wymondham & Attleborough Express* 10 Dec. 6/3 Brassiness in blondes can be cured by an application of one of the latest ash blonde toners—or by a visit to your hairdresser.

5. = *toning lotion* s.v. *TONING *vbl. sb.* and *ppl. a.*

1970 *Vogue* Jan. 5/2 (Advt.), Toners that polish, purify, pep up circulation. **1983** *Harrods Mag.* Spring–Summer 74 Skin care products..Refresher Toner..£15·75.

tonetic (tone·tik), *a. Linguistics.* [f. TONE *sb.*, after *phonetic.*] Of or pertaining to the use of tones in languages. So **tone·tics,** the study of tones; **tone·tically** *adv.*

1921 in *Trans. Philol. Soc. 1921–4* (1932) 11 A paper on Tonetics by Mr. D. H. Beach. **1921** H. E. PALMER *Princ. Lang.-Study* i. 37 Learned specialist in 'tonetics' (or whatever the science of tones will come to be called). **1922** —— *Eng. Intonation* i. 6 The teacher articulates one or more syllables and calls upon the students to write down in tonetic symbols what they think they have heard. **1924** [see *TONEME.] **1926** *Bantu Stud.* July 198 Phonetics treats of phones, phone-groups, and phonemes: tonetics treats of tones, tone-groups, and tonemes. **1934** WEBSTER Tonetically. **1938** D. M. BEACH *Phonetics Hottentot Lang.* ix. 125 In Hottentot, as in Chinese, two roots which are identical *phonetically* may differ *tonetically* when pronounced in isolation. **1958** R. KINGDON *Groundwork Eng. Intonation* p. xxix, The tonetic stress-mark system used in this book was developed..in an endeavour to find the most practical system of marking intonation. **1964** M. SCHUBIGER in D. Abercrombie et al. *Daniel Jones* 256 Even without extra tonetic prominence, it [*sc.* the self-pronoun] increases the weight of the head. **1975** *Language* LI. 561 A considerable residue of cases still remains which must be analysed in terms of underlying homonyms yielding tonetically distinct forms in many environments. **1981** *Word 1980* XXXI. 151 (*heading*) Intonation: tonetic stress marks *versus* levels *versus* configurations.

tonette (tōᵘne·t). [f. TONE *sb.* + -ETTE.] A simple end-blown wind-instrument resembling a small flute.

1958 E. BIRNEY *Turvey* i. 10 'Plays tonette.' Some kind of a whistle, wasn't it? **1963** *Guardian* 29 Oct. 7/1 [He] is able to produce notes from a small flute, called a Tonette, by sticking the mouthpiece in his nostrils. **1979** *Arizona Daily Star* 1 Apr. K10/1 Tonettes, recorders, triangles and tambourines are the types of instruments needed.

tone-up, *sb.*: see *TONE *v.* 6 d. **toney,** var. TONY *a.* in Dict. and Suppl.

tong (tǫŋ), *sb.*² Also **Tong.** [ad. Cantonese *tohng* hall, meeting place.] **a.** An association or secret society of Chinese in the U.S., orig. formed as a benevolent or protective society but freq. associated with underworld criminal activity.

1883 *Harper's Mag.* May 831/1 This burial-place..is parcelled off by white fences into enclosures for a large number of separate burial guilds, or *tongs*, as the Fook Yam Tong [etc.]. **1913** [see *HATCHET-MAN 2]. **1924** *Glasgow Herald* 29 Oct. 8 Rival Tongs, whose principal object seems to be mutual extermination. **1948** P. JOHNSTON *Lost & Living Cities of California Gold Rush* 15/2 Chinese who were members of two tongs, the Sam-yap and the Yan-wo, were working side by side at Two-mile Bar, on the Stanislaus River. **1968** *New York City* (Michelin Tire Corp.) 83 Chinatown was then an area rife with debauchery and vice, the scene of 'tong wars' fought by rival 'tongs' to win control over opium dens, gambling haunts and houses of ill fame. **1972** K. BONFIGLIOLI *Don't point that Thing at Me* xv. 128 The Chinese Tongs used to favour a six-inch nail, the Japanese use a sharpened umbrella-rib. **1977** *Time* 12 Dec. 28/2 The famous Tongs were something else, more mysterious—secret societies similar to Mafia families. They ran gambling, prostitution, drugs, and offered merchants 'protection'.

b. *attrib.*, esp. in *tong war.*

1927 *Daily Express* 25 Mar. 2/1 Chinese Tong (secret society) warfare broke out at midnight throughout the United States. **1928** H. ASBURY *Gangs of N.Y.* 301 The tong wars appeared to have begun about 1899, and..were all caused by conflicting gambling interests. **1950** *Los Angeles Times Home Mag.* 26 Mar. 5/2 The servants of 70 years ago were mostly Chinese whose favorite outdoor sports were tong wars. **1962** 'K. ORVIS' *Damned & Destroyed* ii. 20, I was called in by a tong leader. **1966** 'G. BLACK' *You want to die, Johnny?* iii. 51 The police are not neutrals in the little wars. Our interests are not entirely focussed on Tong feuds. **1972** J. BALL *Five Pieces of Jade* xvi. 220 He had the idea that he could get rid of the two Chinese by..making it look like a ritual killing or a tong murder. **1976** J. O'CONNOR *Eleventh Commandment* viii. 101 The screws weren't standing for Tong warfare. **1980** G. V. HIGGINS *Kennedy for Defence* xvii. 149 We are liable to have a nice little tong war on our hands.

tong, *v.*² Add: **d.** To style (hair, etc.) with curling tongs.

1932 'E. M. DELAFIELD' *Thank Heaven Fasting* I. ii. 35 Monica's hair had been tonged into waves. **1953** P. L. FERMOR *Violins of Saint-Jacques* 48 His moustache was crisply tonged. **1976** 'D. HALLIDAY' *Dolly & Nanny Bird* iii. 37 She had her hair waved to her ears, and then tonged out sideways.

tonga¹. Add: **b. tonga wallah,** the driver of a tonga.

1942 M. R. ANAND *Sword & Sickle* i. 27 A tonga wallah called rudely. **1955** R. P. JHABVALA *To whom she Will* xiv. 98 The tonga-walla in his stained turban cursed and muttered and whipped his horse. **1978** 'M. M. KAYE' *Far Pavilions* II. x. 155 Tell the tonga-wallah to wait.

Tonga (tǫ·ŋă), *sb.*⁴ and *a.* [Native name: cf. Zulu *i(li) Thonga* member of the Tonga tribe, perh. f. *-thonga* member of a subject race.] **A.** *sb.* The name of several African peoples living chiefly in southern Mozambique, Malawi, and Zambia; a member of these peoples. Also, the Bantu language spoken by them. Cf. *TSONGA. **B.** *adj.* Of, pertaining to, or designating these peoples or their language.

1866 in A. Mackenzie *Memorials Henrietta Robertson* 247 He might make beginnings both in the Amaswazi and Amatonga countries. **1872** *Cape Monthly Mag.* Feb. 117 The Tonga does not own a single head of cattle. **1875** *Jrnl. R. Geogr. Soc.* XLV. 53 The Portuguese..must have found conquest south of the Zambesi an easy matter when the country was entirely peopled by these industrious natives, called generally by the Zulus by the contemptuous title of Tongas. *Ibid.* 93 We found..the poor Tonga Chief at his wit's end. **1910** *Jrnl. Afr. Soc.* IX. 305 The Tonga of the Zambezi is..a different language from the one just mentioned [*sc.* Thonga], and also distinct from the Tonga of Lake Nyasa. **1910** *Encycl. Brit.* III. 360/1 The *Ronga* (*Tonga*) languages of Portuguese South-East Africa..are almost equally related to the *Nyanja* group ..and to *Zulu.* **1929** [see *NGUNI *sb.* and *a.*]. **1951** COLSON & GLUCKMAN *Seven Tribes Brit. Central Africa* II. i. 94 The Plateau Tonga, a matrilineal people, occupy a large portion of the Southern Province of Northern Rhodesia. *Ibid.* 95 Within the Tonga group itself slight changes accumulate. **1968** C. BURKE *Elephant across Border* iii. 79 Roger broke the silence, translating his discussion in Tonga dialect to Gomez. **1968** *Guardian* 15 Apr. 9/4 In Zambia..there are four strong tribal vernaculars —Bemba, Tonga, Lozi and Nyanja. **1970** [see *ILA *sb.* and *a.*]. **1977** *Times Lit. Suppl.* 30 Sept. 1109/3, I am a chi-Tonga speaker from the lakeside Tonga of Malawi, and I should say that the so-called Tongas of Zambia, Mozambique, Malawi, etc., are one people.

Tongan (tǫ·ŋan), *a.* and *sb.* [f. *Tonga* (see def.) + -AN.] **A.** *adj.* Of or pertaining to the island kingdom of Tonga in the south-west Pacific Ocean. **B.** *sb.* A native of Tonga. Also, the Polynesian language spoken in Tonga.

[**1818** J. MARTIN in Mariner & Martin *Acct. Natives Tonga Islands* p. iii, Having written down sundry examples in English,..I gave them to Mr. Mariner to translate into Tonga.] **1853** J. E. ERSKINE *Jrnl. Cruise Western Pacific* iv. 119 The group has from time immemorial formed part of the Tongan dominions. *Ibid.* iv. 157 In imitation of the Feejeeans, the Tongans have occasionally practised cannibalism. **1897** S. W. BAKER *Eng. & Tongan Vocab.* II. iii. 35 The present tense in the Tongan language ..for which we have two forms in English... In Tongan.. there is but one form. **1901,** etc. [see *NIUEAN *sb.* and *a.*]. **1927** J. S. HUXLEY *Relig. without Revelation* vi. 183 The Tongans became..the most virulent Sabbatarians. **1939** G. BLAMIRES *Little Island Kingdom of South* 13 We had at least five anthems that evening, some of Tongan composition, others European, in the latter case the words being translated into Tongan. **1951** R. FIRTH *Elem. Social Organization* iii. 105 Every male Tongan is entitled by law when he becomes a taxpayer to receive a residential plot of land in a village or town. **1966** *Listener* 13 Jan. 62/1, I wrote it out in Tongan. **1972** *Vogue* June (Special no.) 135/1 Rate of exchange: 2·14 Tongan dollars to £1. **1976** S. R. ANDERSON in *Symposium on Subject & Topic* 3 A language in which ergativity is indicated by case marking alone is Tongan. **1978** *Times* 17 Jan. 17/4 Captain Cook..noted that Tongans boxed in much the same way as the English.

tongkang (tǫŋkæ·ŋ). Also **tongkan, tonkang.** [a. Malay.] A sea-going barge used as a cargo boat in the Malay archipelago.

1834 *Singapore Chron.* 2 Jan. 3/2 The fourth [race] was a sailing match, between several tonkangs or cargo-boats. **1858** P. L. SIMMONDS *Dict. Trade Products* 383/2 *Tongkang*, a kind of boat or junk used in the seas of the Eastern archipelago. **1892** *Nautical Mag.* Dec. 1155 *Hydra*, s.s. and a tongkang, in collision in Singapore Harbour. **1922** *Chambers's Jrnl.* 8 July 503/1 A string of big, heavy *tongkangs*, towed by a puffing launch. **1950** *People* (Austral.) 11 Oct. 16/2 It was a hazardous adventure but they brought it off in spectacular fashion, first by sampan and then by tongkan. **1972** *Straits Times* (Malaysian ed.) 25 Nov. 87/2 Liew Kim..later became a trishaw puller and a tongkang builder.

Tongkinese, var. *TONKINESE *sb.* and *a.*

tongs, *sb. pl.* Add: **3. h.** *Oil Industry.* A large pipe wrench used for making up or breaking out lengths of pipe or casing.

1922 F. M. TOWL in D. T. Day *Handbk. Petroleum Industry* I. 411 When the friction becomes so great that this method cannot be used, the tongs are placed on the line. **1972** L. M. HARRIS *Introd. Deepwater Floating Drilling Operations* v. 46 The normal rig-floor tools, such as, tongs, slips, and small hand tools.

4. tongsman, (*b*) *Oil Industry,* one who handles the large pipe wrench used for making up or breaking out lengths of pipe.

1974 *China Reconstructs* July 47/1 Before long he became a skilled tongsman.

tongue, *sb.* Add: **II. 4. b.** (Further examples.)

1911 H. H. HARPER *Bob Hardwick* 88, I was so angry at her that I..made no answer... Presently she said, 'Has the cat got your tongue?' **1940** 'J. FALSTAFF' *Jacoby's Corners* vi. 69 The cat has got his tongue. **1981** I. ST. JAMES *Balfour Conspiracy* vi. 229 Shaughnessy shook his head. 'Cat got your tongue?'

d. Also in phr. *to stick* (or *thrust*) *one's tongue in one's cheek,* as a gesture of sly or † contemptuous humour. Hence *with* (one's) *tongue in* (one's) *cheek,* with sly irony or humorous insincerity. Cf. *tongue-in-cheek *a.* and *adv.*

1748 [see Cheek *sb.* 2]. **1828** Scott *Fair Maid of Perth* in *Chron. Canongate* 2nd Ser. I. viii. 153 The fellow who gave this all-hail thrust his tongue in his cheek to some scapegraces like himself. **1849** *Blackw. Edin. Mag.* Oct. 450/2 Hows'ever, I just sticks my tongue in my cheek,.. watches my chance, an' off by a track-boat..to New Orleens. **1887** R. H. Roberts *In Shires* i. 10 [He] sticks his tongue in his cheek, and whispers to his neighbour. **1928** *Observer* 19 Feb. 5/1, I must confess my utter inability to grasp what Mr. B. Nicholson is after, though I am loath to believe that he painted his apparently flippant still life arrangements with his tongue in his cheek. **1951** *Sport* 30 Mar.–5 Apr. 9/3 Walsall fans will tell you, with tongue in cheek, that the Fellows Park club is always on the alert where transfer of players is concerned.

e. *with* (one's) *tongue hanging out* and varr., with great thirst or (*fig.*) eager expectation. *colloq.*

1897 Kipling *Day's Work* (1898) 102 They've been waiting for this youth with their tongues hanging out. **1928** Wodehouse *Money for Nothing* x. 222, I should hurry. His tongue was hanging out when I left him. **1967** E. Lemarchand *Death of Old Girl* xii. 141 My tongue was hanging out, so I thought I'd..see if there was any sherry going. **1974** L. Lamb *Man in Mist* ii. 16, I don't have to run round to them with my tongue hanging out the moment I am promised something.

8. c. (Later examples of sense *glossolalia.*) Also *pl.* in *collect.* sense.

1965 *Sunday Mail* (Brisbane) 5 Dec. 31/5 Some parishioners have complained to the Diocesan authorities.. about Mr. Schofield's interest in speaking with tongues. **1972** S. Tugwell *Did you receive Spirit?* v. 40 Some manifestation, usually tongues, is generally expected; indeed, strict Pentecostals demand it. **1976** *Church Times* 5 Mar. 14/2 Tongues is a personal and devotional gift as opposed to the others, which are intended to help people.

III. 13. d. *Geol.* A part of a formation that projects laterally into the material of an adjacent formation, becoming thinner in the direction of its length.

1917 L. W. Stephenson in *Jrnl. Washington Acad. Sci.* VII. 245 It is..proposed that such features as *x* and *y* in figure 1 be designated 'tongues'... A tongue is not a member nor a lentil, either one of which differs lithologically from the typical material composing the formation of which it forms part. **1953, 1970** [see *lentil 4*].

e. *gen.*

1881 E. A. Freeman *Sk. Subject & Neighbour Lands Venice* 207 Columns with richly carved capitals, and..with tongues of foliage at their bases. **1954** F. T. Prince *Soldiers Bathing* 7 Letting the sea-waves coil Their frothy tongues about his feet. **1965** E. L. Myles *Emperor of Peace River* ii. iv. 226 The frantic bawling of a calf in the edge of a tongue of brush near the river's bank. **1966** D. Bagley *Wyatt's Hurricane* v. 129 They emerged on to an open place, an incursive tongue of the countryside licking into the suburbs.

14. o. *Mus.* = *plaque 1 d.

1953, 1957[see *plaque 1 d]. **1977** Goossens & Roxburgh *Oboe* iii. 34 The scraping tongue (or plaque). A flat oval plate of steel... Some players prefer a narrower plate to prevent the knife from coming into contact at the edges.

IV. 15. a. *tongue-position.* **b.** *tongue-wagger.* **c.** *tongue-lashing* vbl. sb.

1881 'Mark Twain' *Prince & Pauper* xix. 222 She promptly brought the King out of his dreams with a brisk and cordial tongue-lashing. **1918** D. Jones *Outl. Eng. Phonetics* vi. 16 We examine the tongue positions of these five classes [of vowels]. **1977** *Word 1972* XXVIII. 321 The most important feature for the correct perception of this phoneme from the viewpoint of the listener is high tongue position. **1913** D. H. Lawrence *Sons & Lovers* i. 16 He was blab-mouthed, a tongue-wagger.

16. tongue-and-groove, applied (chiefly *attrib.*) to boards in which a tongue along one edge fits into a groove along the edge of its neighbour, and to joints, etc., so made; also *fig.*; **tongue-slip,** a slip of the tongue; **tongue-speaker,** one who speaks with tongues (see sense 8 c in Dict. and Suppl.); **tongue-twisting** *a.*, difficult to articulate.

1882 W. J. Christy *Practical Treat. Joints* iii. 52 Joggle Joint.—This term is applied to a square, semicircular,..or otherwise shaped tongue and groove joint generally of equal depth the full way through. **1929** W. Faulkner *Sound & Fury* 353 He emerged carrying a sawn section of tongue-and-groove planking. **1939** —— *Wild Palms* 19 The flimsy walls (they were not even tongue-and-groove..but were of ship-lap). **1976** *Southern Even. Echo* (Southampton) 11 Nov. (Advt. Suppl.) 4/2 End terr. house, built 1972,..d. glazing, tongue and groove floors, etc. **1977** *Time* 3 Oct. 53/1 Despite its style and tongue-and-groove plotting, *The Honourable Schoolboy* sometimes displays a Balzacian tendency to turn urges into passions. **1913** Tongue-slip [listed in Dict. in sense 15 a]. **1948** *Sunday Pictorial* 18 July 5/2 Freud took up this pioneer work and showed how the half-forgotten world of dreams and tongue-slips could be explored. **1978** *Canadian Jrnl. Linguistics 1977* XXII. 179 The penultimate chapter of AM whips through pauses, tongue slips, and other topics in the science of word-botching. **1910** *Encycl. Relig. & Ethics* III. 370/2 The 'tongue-speaker' needed as his complement the 'interpreter'. **1978** *Amer. Speech* LIII. 59 They..associate these utterances with the inspiration of the Holy Spirit, although tongue-speakers differ in their beliefs about the significance of the gift of tongues. **1949** Koestler *Insight & Outlook* vii. 109 Its name, too, is funny—foreign and tongue-twisting. **1961** E. S. Turner *Phoney War* viii. 109 Each new campaign brought them a crop of tongue-twisting place names.

tongue, *v.* Add: **2. c.** *Mus.* To move the tongue when playing a woodwind instrument so as to interrupt the air flow briefly. Also *trans.*, to produce (a note) repeatedly interrupted in this way. Cf. Tonguing *vbl. sb.* a.

1936 F. B. Chapman *Flute Technique* iv. 18 The student must..ultimately aim at producing notes by multiple tonguing..: he should..be able to tongue them continuously and quite clearly at the rate of nine or ten to the second. **1953** E. Rothwell *Oboe Technique* iii. 30 To 'tongue' a note pronounce the consonant 'T' with your tongue on the reed. **1977** *Early Music* July 343/1 Do not tongue too much or you may dislodge the reed from its staple.

5. Delete '(of ice)'.

1942 *Bull. U.S. Geol. Survey* No. 936. 374 In places a thick shale lens lies within, or tongues into, an ore-bearing sandstone lens. **1973** *Nature* 2 Mar. 41/2 The patch reef, 13 m long and over 2 m high, tongues out to the west. **1980** D. Creed *Scarab* iii. xix. 183 A low spit of land tongued out into the shallow water.

tongued, *a.* (*ppl. a.*) Add: *tongued and grooved,* furnished with a tongue and groove joint (see *tongue *sb.* 16).

1773 *Bristol* (Va.) *Vestry Bk.* (1898) 238 A Dwelling House [shall] be built..[with] Good flouring Plank, well Tong'd & Groved. **1897** F. C. Moore *How to build Home* 15 The sheathing should be tongued and grooved and planed on one side. **1955** J. S. Chappell *Woodworking* x. 136 A..stronger form of tongued and grooved joint is made by ploughing a groove in both edges to be joined.

tongue-in-cheek, *a.* and *adv.* [See Tongue *sb.* 4 d in Dict. and Suppl.] **A.** *adj.* Ironic, slyly humorous; not meant to be taken seriously. Also **tongue-in-the-cheek.**

1933 *Times Lit. Suppl.* 30 Mar. 223/4 *Shooting the Bull* ..is a tongue-in-the-cheek march through newspaperdom. **1937** M. Covarrubias *Island of Bali* xi. 375 A typical tongue-in-cheek Balinese answer to dodge a complicated explanation for outsiders. **1953** *Spectator* 13 Mar. 320/2 This..novel..seems too facile, too tongue-in-cheek. **1959** *Times* 4 Sept. 5/1 Though the piece was energetic and often exuberant it was certainly not tongue-in-the-cheek or humorous in style. **1976** *National Observer* (U.S.) 27 Mar. 10/1, I enjoyed Wesley Pruden's tongue-in-cheek suggestion..that every man, woman, and child in the United States be given a college degree so they 'become equal'. **1982** *Listener* 16 Dec. 28/1 Angela Carter translated Perrault's fairy tales..with absolute fidelity to the understatement, the tongue-in-cheek charm of the originals.

B. *adv.* = *with tongue in cheek* s.v. *tongue *sb.* 4 d.

1934 in Webster. **1976** *Listener* 18 Mar. 334/3 Someone told Muhammad Ali, tongue-in-cheek, that his book made him come over as a 'deep thinker'. **1979** H. McLeave *Borderline Case* xi. 113 'You mean you're a spy.' 'Only for those people who have something sinister to hide,' he said, tongue-in-cheek.

tonguer. (In Dict. s.v. Tongue *v.*) Add: † **2.** *N.Z.* (See quots.) *Obs.* exc. *hist.*

1836 in R. McNab *Old Whaling Days* (1913) 436 Some mention of what are called tonguers... When the whale is cut in they are entitled to the carcass and the tongue. **1843** [see *cutter *sb.*^{1} 1 b]. **1845** E. J. Wakefield *Adventure N.Z.* I. xi. 323 The proper officers have been selected—such as cooper, carpenter, cooks, painter, and 'tonguer'..[who] takes his name from having an exclusive right to the oil obtained from the tongue..in payment of his duty of 'cutting-in', or dissecting, the whale. **1941** Baker *N.Z. Slang* ii. 13 A tonguer was a native or white living in New Zealand who assisted a whaling crew to cut up whales... These men earned their name..from the fact that they were given the whale's carcass and tongue to dispose of as they wished.

toni (tōᵘ·ni). *India.* Also **tonee, tony.** [a. Tamil: see Dhoney, doney.] **a.** See Tony *sb.*^{2} **b.** A dug-out boat. **c.** A ferry boat.

1881 *Naval Encycl.* 811/2 *Tonee,* a canoe formerly used on the coast of Malabar. **1914** *Yachting Monthly* June 83/2 Inshore the flood tide had already turned the tony and bunder boats, the former a canoe-like craft hollowed straight out from the tree. **1917** *Ibid.* Sept. 268/2 The large Tonis are between 25 and 30 feet long. **1946** *Mariner's Mirror* XXXII. 209 The ordinary Malabar dug-out, called *toni* in Bombay. **1978** *Times of India* 15 Jan. 3/5 Contraband radios and cassettes..were seized from a toni, Laxmi, on Thursday at the Ferry Wharf.

-tonia (tōᵘ·niă), also anglicized as **-tony,** terminal element [f. Gr. τόν-ος Tone *sb.* + -ia^1] with the sense 'tone, condition' in terms in *Med.*, as *hypotonia, *sympathicotonia.

tonic, *a.* and *sb.* Add: **A.** *adj.* **2.** *tonic water,* a non-alcoholic carbonated drink containing quinine or another bitter as a stimulant of appetite and digestion; a drink or glass of this; *tonic wine,* weak, flavoured wine sold as a medicinal tonic.

1899 *Graphic* 11 Mar. 320/1 (Advt.), His Holiness the Pope writes that he has fully appreciated the beneficent effects of this Tonic Wine. **1926** *Daily Colonist* (Victoria, B.C.) 6 July 9/6 (Advt.), Schweppes famous British table waters. Soda water,..ginger beer, tonic water. **1958** S. Hyland *Who goes Hang?* xi. 53 'What will there be to draft?' asked Mrs. Kimmis..over the top of a tonic water. **1970** G. Greer *Female Eunuch* 276 Perhaps she can try a glass or two of tonic wine? More likely her G.P. will.. prescribe a happiness pill. **1982** G. F. Newman *Men with Guns* x. 74 He drank gin swamped with Indian tonic water.

4. b. (Earlier example.)

1849 *Jrnl. Indian Archipelago* III. 668 The influence of this habit of the tonic languages is still largely impressed on their Malay-Polynesian and Turonian descendants and congeners.

B. *sb.* **1. c.** Tonic water.

1935, 1949 [see *gin and tonic* s.v. *gin *sb.*^{2} 2 a]. **1972** M. J. Bosse *Incident at Naha* ii. 108 We all had vodka and tonics.

2. b. The principal key of a musical composition or passage; the home key.

1896 G. Grove *Beethoven & his Nine Symphonies* 8 The *Coda* which closes the first movement, after repeating in the tonic the phrase already quoted as No. 5, combines the wind instrument passage with the first subject. **1923** E. Evans *Beethoven's Nine Symphonies* I. 177 At the third portion we have a new treatment of the first part of the same subject..leading to a triumphant cadence in C as tonic. **1961** A. Hopkins *Talking about Symphonies* i. 20 The key you start in is called the 'Tonic'. **1979** D. R. Hofstadter *Gödel, Escher, Bach* v. 130 With the inversion of the theme for our melody, we begin in D as if that had always been the tonic—but we modulate back to G after all, which means that we pop back into the tonic, and the *B*-section ends properly.

Tonica, var. *Tunica^2.

toning, *vbl. sb.* and *ppl. a.* (In Dict. s.v. Tone *v.*) Add: *spec.* Having or being a colour that certain place in an intonation pattern.

1963 M. A. K. Halliday in *Archivum Linguisticum* XV. 13 Second [is]..the placing of the tonic syllable..—the location, in each tone group, of the pretonic and tonic sections... I propose to call these three systems 'tonality', 'tonicity' and 'tone'. **1966** G. N. Leech *Eng. in Advertising* ix. 88 Devices of graphic emphasis such as underlining and italics can be used to represent special tonicity in speech. **1973** [see *nucleus *sb.* 12 a].

Tonikan, var. *Tunica(n.

toning, *vbl. sb.* and *ppl. a.* (In Dict. s.v. Tone *v.*) Add: *spec.* Having or being a colour that tones in (with something previously mentioned). *toning lotion,* a lotion, usu. slightly astringent, used for cosmetic purposes to refine the texture of the skin.

1960 *Harper's Bazaar* (U.K. ed.) Aug. 22/2 An easy seven-eighths suit, that wraps around a simple toning dress. **1965** *Ibid.* (U.K. ed.) June 40 A toning lotion beneath base provides a protective film beneath make-up. **1970** *Cabinet Maker & Retail Furnisher* 30 Oct. 204/1 It is available in toning shades of browns, blues, red and greens. **1977** *Sunday Times* 6 June 43/1 The attack on the Cooper pores was maintained with Fresh Toning Lotion. **1982** Barr & York *Official Sloane Ranger Handbk.* 31/1 She has, naturally, a kilt, which she wears with toning tights.

tonite (tənai·t). Simplified spelling of Tonight *adv.* and *sb.*, after *nite *sb.*^{2}, used chiefly in advertisements.

1968 R. Clapperton *No News on Monday* iv. 35 Another placard announced..'Tonite, for one nite only, the fabulous Lisa Mundt.' **1971** *Black World* Mar. 55/1 They wud be up all nite tonite if they didn't wake up soon. **1976** *Leicester Mercury* 16 July (Advt.), Riverside disco. Tonite. All welcome.

tonk (tɒŋk), *sb.*^{1} *slang* (chiefly *Austral.*). [Etym. unknown.] **a.** A term of abuse: a fool, an idiot.

1941 Baker *Dict. Austral. Slang* 77 *Tonk,* a simpleton or fool. (2) A dude or fop. (3) A general term of contempt. **1963** *New Society* 22 Aug. 5/1 'Bleg', 'thick boot', 'tonk', and 'greb' are all of uncertain origin, but probably have euphemistic backgrounds. **1965** [see *nana^2].

b. A homosexual man.

1943 *Penguin New Writing* XVII. 83 The cook got my goat when he started trying to do the same thing. He was a tonk all right, just a real old auntie. **1965** H. Porter *Stars Austral. Stage & Screen* 280 During the last ten years or more, there have been imported a coterie of *untalented* English homosexuals, English tonks unheard of outside their home country. **1970** *TV Times* (Austral.) 15 July 41/3 There was also a homosexual (who was referred to as a 'tonk'—thereby dating Mr Porter rather badly).

tonk (tɒŋk), *sb.*^{2} Colloq. abbrev. of *honky-tonk.

1937 [see *smoke-shop* s.v. *smoke *sb.* 11]. **1948** *Common Ground* VIII. 38 The man who owned the little country Tonk was named Hamp... It was a one-room shanty store that doubled as a country bar room at night. **1960** C. Hamblett in J. Pudney *Pick of Today's Short Stories* XI. 138 None of the other rundown bars and tonks had anyone remotely like Lia.

tonk (tɒŋk), *v.* *colloq.* (chiefly *Sport*). [Echoic.] *trans.* **a.** To strike. **b.** To beat or defeat. Freq. *pass.*

1910 A. A. Milne *Day's Play* 114 Wanting four to win, I fairly tried to tonk the leather. **1926** Galsworthy *Silver Spoon* iii. i. 224 'He seems to enjoy the prospect of getting tonked,' murmured Michael. **1945** Baker *Austral. Lang.* 207 Here are a few general expressions concerned with school life:..*to get tonked,* to receive corporal punishment. **1963** A. Ross *Australia 63* ii. 55 Our spinners have been tonked about yet again by uncouth country batsmen.

Tonkawa (tǫ·ŋkăwă), *sb.* (*a.*) [ad. Sp. *tancagueis, tancahues*, etc., prob. ad. Wichita (Waco dial.) *tonkawéya*, said to mean 'they all stay together'.] **a.** (A member of) an Indian people of Texas. **b.** The language of this people. Also *attrib.* or as *adj.*

1806 J. Sibley in *Message from President of U.S., communicating Discoveries made in exploring the Missouri by Captains Lewis & Clark* 74 Tankaways..have no land, ..but are always moving. **1870** J. C. Duval *Adventures Big-Foot Wallace* xxv. 148, I got it from 'Puppy's Foot', the Tonkawa chief. *Ibid.* xl. 245 My old friend 'Bah-pish-na-ba-hoo-tee' (which means 'Little blue whistling thunder' in the Tonkawa language). **1933** H. Hoijer *Tonkawa* (thesis, Columbia Univ.) p. ix, The Tonkawa appear to have been an important and warlike tribe living in central Texas during most of the 18th and 19th centuries. *Ibid.* p. x, Tonkawa is now spoken by only six persons—all of them past middle age. **1974** *Encycl. Brit. Micropædia* X. 43/3 By the 1970s the Tonkawa reservation in Oklahoma was reported to have a total population of about 60.

Tonkinese (tǫŋkinī·z), *sb.* and *a.* Also 8–9 **Tonquinese**, 9 **Tong-, Tungkin(g)ese.** [f. *Ton-kin* (*Tongking*) + -ese.] **A.** *sb.* **a.** The people of Tongking, a region of northern Vietnam on the border with China; also, a member of this people. **b.** The language of the Tonkinese. **B.** *adj.* Of or pertaining to the Tonkinese.

1726 Swift *Gulliver* II. iii. i. 4 Several sorts of Goods, wherewith the Tonquinese usually trade to the Neighbouring Islands. **1806** J. Barrow *Voy. Cochinchina* ix. 251 The *Tung-quinese*, being in fact of the same character and disposition as the Chinese, were little able to cope with the hardy and disciplined troops. **1845** *Encycl. Metrop.* XXV. 673/1 In self-sufficiency and jealousy of strangers, the Tonkinese do not yield to their neighbours in China. **1884** W. Mesny *Tungking* xviii. 115 The protracted struggle that has been going on for long months is quite as much due to the action of China as to the Tungkingese themselves. **1885** J. G. Scott *France & Tongking* i. 11 Garnier and his lieutenants..enrolled many thousand Tongkinese auxiliaries. **1890** J. Frazer *Golden Bough* I. i. 36 Many other peoples (Tonquinese, Hindoos, Chuwash, etc.) have adopted the same test of a suitable victim. **1926** H. A. Franck *East of Siam* xii. 220 In the mess that followed the Manchu conquest of China, a Tonkinese fisherman founded a new dynasty. **1934** Webster, *Tonkinese*, the Annamese dialect of Tonkin. **1951** M. B. Emeneau *Stud. Vietnamese (Annamese) Gram.* p. v, Tonkinese and Chochin Chinese are slightly differentiated from one another by differences of pronunciation and of vocabulary. **1983** C. McCarry *Last Supper* 172 Christopher met a fellow poet, a Tonkinese who had studied at the Sorbonne... The Tonkinese poet was a female.

tonlet (tʊ·nlėt). [ad. MF. *tonnel(l)et* short, full skirt, (also) *tonlet*, dim. of *tonneau* cask (see Tonnel, -ell).] A short skirt of armour; also, each of the overlapping horizontal bands of which this was sometimes made.

[*a* **1480** *Traictié de la Forme et Devis d'ung Tournoy* in *Œuvres Complètes du Roi René* (1844) II. 11 Le harnoys de corps est come une cuirasse ou comme ung harnoys à pié qu'on appelle tonnellet.] *a* **1486** in *Archaeologia* LVII (2nd Ser. VII. 1900) 43 *To arme a man*... Firste ye muste sette on Sabatones.. & þe the breche of mayle And thē tonletis And thē brest And þe vambras [etc.]. **1894** *Antiquary* Jan. 26/2 Another suit, or rather part of one, of Henry VIII..is that which has been called the tonlet, or, as in the Tower inventories it is written, the trundlet suit. **1910** *Encycl. Brit.* II. 587/2 The surcoat being gone we see him armed in breast and back plate, his loins covered by a skirt of 'tonlets', as the defence of overlapping horizontal bands comes to be named. **1934** G. C. Stone *Gloss. Construction, Decoration & Use of Arms & Armor* 622/2 The tonlet suit was used mainly for fighting on foot, but was sometimes used in place of other leg armor when jousting at the barrier. It had wide, bell-shaped skirts of plate which were often solid and elaborately fluted with deep vertical folds... Sometimes it was made of horizontal plates. **1975** *Country Life* 3 July 45/3 The superb 'tonlet' or skirted armour made for King Henry VIII for foot combat in about 1512. **1983** *Daily Tel.* 18 Oct. 10 (*caption*) Henry VIII's tonlet armour ready to go on view at the Burlington House Fair.

tonne (obs. form of Ton, Tun). Add: Reintroduced from Fr. in mod. use to denote a metric ton of 1000 kilogrammes (Ton[1] 4).

1877 *Rep. Brit. Assoc. Adv. Sci. 1876* ii. 32 The Tonne is the mass or quantity of matter contained in a cubic metre of water, and is very nearly the same as the British Ton. **1930** *Engineering* 25 July 119/3 Each of the two high-pressure turbines takes some 224 tonnes of steam per hour. **1953** *Economist* 28 Mar. 902/1 The country's refining capacity, in terms of crude oil throughput, was about 23 million tonnes a year. **1972** *Which?* May 130/3 The British Steel Corporation, going metric but realising the possible confusion between a ton and a tonne (1,000 kilograms) has directed its staff to pronounce 'tonne' 'tunnie'. **1975** *B.S.I. News* Apr. 5/1 Our units committee has been asked to advise how, in speech, confusion between 'tonne' and 'ton' can best be avoided. Their advice is simply this: when saying the word 'tonne' never say it alone; always say 'metric tonne'. **1977** A. Hallam *Planet Earth* 24/2 Meteorites vary in weight from a few tens of grammes to several tonnes. **1981** *Southern Horticulture* (N.Z.) Spring 3 It should be possible to achieve yields of 5 tonne/ha or more from mature roots.

tonneau. Add: **1.** Also, the rear part of a car with front and rear compartments or of an open car; a car having a tonneau; **tonneau cover**, a removable, flexible cover for protecting the rear or passenger seats in an open car when they are not in use; also *transf.*

1905 A. M. Binstead *Mop Fair* 118 With the entrancing little green *tonneau* which a railway rustic delivered.. next morning, it was entirely different. So winsome was the diminutive car [etc.]. **1931** Garrard & Geddes *Practical Motoring* 643/1 *Tonneau*. The rear part of an open four or five seater motor car body was at one time commonly referred to as the tonneau but this term is now rarely used by itself. When the front seats only are used, a special cover known as the tonneau cover is sometimes stretched across the whole of the rear part. **1976** *Glasgow Herald* 26 Nov. 21/6 (Advt.), 16ft cabin cruiser... Complete with tonneau cover and canopy, £3000. **1978** *Sat. Rev.* (U.S.) 1 Apr. 45 That leaves London [taxis]. Ah, how civilized... There is room in the tonneau for five, with two on jump seats. **1979** J. Leasor *Love & Land Beyond* vi. 88 Victoria brought the plane down... Love helped her batten down tonneau covers over the two cockpits. **1980** *Times* 1 Nov. 14/3 (*caption*) During the 1975 run, an 1898 Daimler wagonette..overtakes a 1903 de Dietrich tonneau. **1981** *West Lancs. Evening Gaz.* 25 Feb. 15 (Advt.), Sports boat.., complete with trailer, tonneau cover, etc.

2. (A gallicism.) A barrel or cask; a measure of capacity for wine, equal to one tun (198 gallons).

1794 A. Young *Trav. France* (ed. 2) I. xviii. 535 Wine has increased in its export to England..; before the treaty it was 8000 tonneaux a year. **1851** [see *queue *sb.* 6]. **1978** S. Sheldon *Bloodline* iv. 69 We should get three hundred thousand francs a *tonneau* for the first pressings.

‖ **tonnelle** (tonẹl). [Fr., = Tunnel *sb.*] An arbour. Also *fig.*

1861 Thackeray *Roundabout Papers* (1863) 219 Those who sit down under my *tonnelle*, and have a half-hour's drink and gossip. *a* **1922** H. Jones *Old Memories* (1923) 160, I can even yet see him sitting peaceably, sheltering from the heat in our vine *tonnelle*. **1947** *Horizon* Feb. 106 The Queen is looking back along the flowery *tonnelle* of her day.

tonner. Add: (Earlier example.) Also, a lorry of (so many) tons weight.

1851 A. O. Hall *Manhattaner in New Orleans* 177 A seven hundred tonner,..full of Dutch emigrants. **1959** I. Jefferies *Thirteen Days* iv. 43 The Arab six-tonner driver. **1978** R. Mark *Office of Constable* iii. 38 Came the great day when the survivors were packed with their kit into a three-tonner en route for Sandhurst.

tono-. Add: **tonofi·bril** *Histology* [ad. G. *tonofibrille* (M. Heidenhain 1899, in *Arch. f. mikrosk. Anat.* LIV. 212)], a bundle of tonofilaments; **tonofibri·lla**, (*a*) *Histology* = prec.; (*b*) *Ent.*, a non-contractile fibril in an insect that passes from a myofibril through the epidermis into the cuticle; **to·nofilament** *Histology*, one of the minute supportive or non-contractile filaments that occur aggregated into networks in the cytoplasm of many epithelial cells, esp. in the epidermis; **tono·logy**, the study of tones or of intonation in speech; hence **tonolo·gical** *a.*; **tonoto·pic, -topical** *adjs. Anat.* [Gr. τόπος place], exhibiting a spatial correspondence with the frequency of heard sound; hence **tonoto·pically** *adv.*

1901 *Jrnl. R. Microsc. Soc.* 512 (*table*) Tonofibrils or resistance fibrils, e.g. in intestinal epithelial cells, epidermis cells. **1964** G. H. Haggis et al. *Introd. Molecular Biol.* v. 120 In the stratified squamous epithelium of the skin, tonofibrils arch through all the cells like scaffolding and they are attached to numerous desmosomes over the entire surface of the cells. **1976** *Path. Ann.* XI. 220 At a fine structural level, the cells of thymoma contain tonofibrils and complex desmosomes, but no neurosecretory granules. **1925** E. B. Wilson *Cell* (ed. 3) i. 41 The greater number of writers have..accepted the conclusion..that they are of the nature of supporting or skeletal structures, hence the term tonofibrillæ (Heidenhain). **1935** R. E. Snodgrass *Princ. Insect Morphol.* iii. 63 It frequently appears not only that the tonofibrillae traverse the epidermal layer, but that they penetrate a varying distance into the cuticula. **1969** R. F. Chapman *Insects* xii. 211 In *Musca* each myofibril is attached to the cuticle by about twelve tonofibrillae. **1964** *Jrnl. Investigative Dermatol.* XLIII. 278/1 In pemphigus vulgaris, a severe necrotizing injury of unknown etiology leads to complete destruction of the tonofilaments with ensuing loss of desmosomes. **1978** *Sci. Amer.* May 145/1 The tonofilaments are not contractile but seem to form a tensile, structural framework for the cell cytoplasm. **1980** *Nature* 17 Jan. 249/1 Electron microscopy shows that bundles of keratin tonofilaments often terminate in membrane-bound desmosomes. **1934** Webster, Tonological. **1975** *Language* LI. 565 The nouns in the two classes with L final vowels show tonological behavior parallel to that of the nouns in the two classes with Ø final vowels. **1983** *Word 1982* XXXIII. 230 With regard to other tonological features in the area, one can mention a number of languages with four-tone systems. **1874** H. Sweet in *Trans. Philol. Soc. 1873–4* 98 What is wanted, then, is a comparative 'tonology' of the Danish dialects. **1924** D. M. Beach in *Bantu Studies* Dec. 77 An entirely new field..is lying open before us—the comparative and historical study of tones. This study.. will be called tonology. **1970** *Stud. Afr. Linguistics* I. 100 (*heading*) Nupe tonology. **1978** *Language* LIV. 245/2 There are ten papers on phonology, seven of which deal specifically with tonology. **1942** *Anat. Rec.* LXXXII. 430 In the monkey and chimpanzee..surface positive potentials evoked by various pitches indicate tonotopic localization within the primary auditory cortex. **1983** *Nature* 10 Feb. 463/1 This 'tonotopic' organization is preserved in all levels of the central auditory pathway. **1948** A. Brodal *Neurol. Anat.* ix. 314 Pfeifer (1936)..was led to conclude that if there exists any tonotopical localization in the primary acoustic cortex, tones of the highest pitch must be represented medially, those of lowest pitch laterally. **1963** *Jrnl. Neurophysiol.* XXVI. 294 (*heading*) Tonotopical organization, relation of spike counts to tone intensity, and firing patterns of single elements. **1971** *Brain Res.* XXVI. 402 There is good evidence that cells in the cochlear nucleus, superior olivary nuclei, nuclei of the lateral lemniscus, and inferior colliculus are organized according to their best frequencies, or tonotopically. **1978** *Nature* 9 Mar. 139/2 Spatial analyses of the evoked potentials indicate that the auditory centre in the midbrain is organised tonotopically.

Tonquinese, obs. var. *Tonkinese *sb.* and *a.*

tonsillectomy (tǫnsil,e·ktŏmi). *Surg.* Also **tonsilectomy.** [f. Tonsil + *-ectomy.] Removal of the tonsils.

1899 *Jrnl. Amer. Med. Assoc.* 23 Sept. 768/2 What then are the general results of tonsillectomy, as compared with those obtained by the usual operation of tonsillotomy? **1932** *Oxford Times* 23 Sept. 22/7 It would be a mistake to suppose that tonsilectomy..is indicated only where there is throat trouble. **1961** J. Heller *Catch-22* (1962) xvii. 164 He could come through other people's tonsilectomies without suffering any postoperative distress. **1977** *Rolling Stone* 16 June 43/2 They told him he was going to the circus but instead took him for a tonsillectomy.

tonsillotomy. Add: Usu. applied to partial removal of the tonsils, in contrast to *tonsillectomy. Now *rare*. (Earlier and further examples.)

1876 *Louisville Med. News* I. 280 (*heading*) Dangerous hemorrhage after tonsillotomy. **1899** [see *tonsillectomy]. **1902** C. Joyes (*title*) Tonsillotomy or tonsillectomy, which? **1924** W. D. Harmer in H. W. Carson *Mod. Operative Surg.* II. 272 The question whether it is better to cut away part of the tonsils (tonsillotomy) or to remove them entirely with their capsules (tonsillectomy) has been hotly discussed.

tonsorial, *a.* Add: Hence **tonso·rialist** *humorous*, a 'tonsorial artist', a barber.

1869 *New North West* (Deer Lodge, Montana) 6 Aug. 3/1 Mr. Plummer, the colored tonsorialist..has the misfortune to be a 'bloody Hinglishman'. **1898** A. M. Binstead *Pink 'Un & Pelican* xi. 253 One of them [*sc.* constables]..gazed..at the abstracted sign of the tonsorialist.

tonstein (tǫ·nstəin). *Geol.* [a. Ger., lit. 'clay stone'.] A rock composed mainly of kaolinite which is commonly found in association with certain coal seams, or a thin band of such a rock (see quots.).

1961 I. A. Williamson in *Mining Mag.* CIV. 9 Tonsteins are essentially argillaceous rocks containing kaolinite in a variety of forms together with occasional detrital and carbonaceous material. **1971** *Nature* 6 Aug. 371/2 The thin, curious, kaolinitic bands called tonsteins discovered more recently in the coalfields of Western Europe have provided welcome additional markers for coalfield correlation.

tontine, *a.* (Earlier example.)

1790 J. Woodforde *Diary* 3 Sept. (1927) III. 211 Mr. Custance brought some Papers for me to sign respecting all his Children being put into the new Tontine Annuities.

Tonton Macoute (toṅtoṅ makū·t). Also **Ton Ton Macoute** and with small initials. [a. Haitian French, of uncertain origin.] **a.** A militia which was formed by President Duvalier in Haiti and became notorious for its brutal and arbitrary behaviour; also, a member of this. Also *ellipt.* as **Tonton.**

1962 S. E. Finer *Man on Horseback* ix. 133 Duvalier took office in October 1957... Instead of relying upon the *Garde Nationale*, he has built himself up a 5,000 strong counterforce of palace guards, civilian militia, and civilian hoodlums called '*tonton macoute*'. **1965** J. E. Fagg *Cuba, Haiti & Dominican Republic* 136 A gang of ruffians known as *Tonton Macoute* murdered or beat citizens who complained. **1966** G. Greene *Comedians* i. i. 16 The Tontons Macoute... The President's bogey men. They wear dark glasses and they call on their victims after dark. *Ibid.* ii. 47 He was believed by some to have connections with the Tontons. *Ibid.*, He exchanged some words with a Tonton Macoute at the door. **1972** *Times* 23 Nov. 10/8 Mr Luckner Cambronne, former Haitian Minister of Defence and of the Interior, who organized the dreaded Ton Ton Macoutes, has sought asylum in the Colombian Embassy in Port-au-Prince. **1976** *Globe & Mail* (Toronto) 5 Nov. 7/2 Rather than fire his father's tontons, (and risk sending a bunch of disgruntled triggermen underground) the young President found them jobs in public institutions such as hospitals. **1981** Plate & Darvi *Secret Police* ii. 47 There is no agreement among scholars of Haiti about what 'Tonton Macoutes' means. Some claim the name refers to a primitive bad figure in Haitian voodoo culture who takes you away when you misbehave.

b. *fig.*

1970 'D. Craig' *Young Men may Die* xi. 83 Our two people..have on Tonton Macoute sunglasses. **1973** *Publishers' Weekly* 8 Jan. 34/1 'Veronica Ganz', the one-girl *ton ton macoute*.

to·n-up, *sb.* and *a. slang.* [f. Ton[1] + Up *adv.*[2] 12 c.] **A.** *sb.* A speed of 100 m.p.h.; a motor-cyclist who achieves this. Also in the sense of *TON¹ 4*a. Also *fig.*

1961 *Daily Tel.* 11 Feb. 1/2 The term 'Ton Up' is used by young motor-cyclists to indicate doing 100 m.p.h. **1964** *New Statesman* 21 Feb. 288/3 Many made a point of.. assuring me that the ton-ups weren't as black as they thought I'd painted them. **1964** in Hamblett & Deverson *Generation X* 146 Of course, there were the Tonups (now Rockers) who mustn't be forgotten, but then they have always been an untouchable group on their own, kinkily keen on their bikes. **1972** J. BLACKBURN *For Fear of Little Men* xiv. 147 Eighty miles an hour, ninety, a ton-up —as the motorcycle maniacs call a hundred. **1976** J. SNOW *Cricket Rebel* 44 My return read nought for 117. I got a ton-up in my next Test at Headingley as well. **1978** *Gramophone* Aug. 329/3 The sleeve photograph shows Perényi in action, head, hands and cello blurred as if moving at too great a rate for even the fastest stop on the camera. There is indeed an element of the 'ton-up' about his performance.

B. *attrib.* **1. a.** Applied to young motor-cyclists who enjoy travelling at high speed.

1961 *Harper's Bazaar* May 104/2 Gangs, rebels without a cause and ton-up kids. **1961** *Times* 1 Sept. 11/1 A reasoned defence, of the 'throttle-potties 'or 'ton up boys' was submitted to the psychology section. **1965** G. McINNES *Road to Gundagai* xiii. 225 Dad wore leather hip boots and jacket, goggles and a cap with its peak at the rear... The Ton-Up kids on the M1 had nothing on him. **1982** 'C. AIRD' *Last Respects* iii. 31 I'm not stupid enough to want that boy Crosby behind the wheel of one of Traffic Division's vehicles... He'd be after a ton-up kid.

b. *fig.* Applied to a person who incongruously imitates the dress or behaviour of such people.

1964 *Economist* 13 June 1246/2 The ton-up type of vicar who is trying to be 'with it'.

2. Achieving a speed or score of 100 in other contexts.

1967 *Daily Tel.* 17 Feb. 1/4 Plans are being made to cut BEA's Manchester-to-London air service..as a result of big passenger losses to British Railways 'ton-up' trains. **1976** *Southern Even. Echo* (Southampton) 6 Nov. 13/4 After his two records for the number of winners trained in a season on the flat, it is the North Country that has the ton-up trainers of the jumping game. **1977** *News of World* 17 Apr. 19/1 'Ton-up' Taylor—he landed 100 winners last season for the first time.

Tony, *sb.*¹ Restrict † *Obs. slang* to sense in Dict. and add: **2.** [The nickname of Antoinette Perry (1888–1946), U.S. actress, manager, and producer, arbitrarily used.] One of the medallions that have been awarded annually since 1947 by the American Theatre Wing (New York) for excellence in some aspect of the theatre. Freq. in *Tony award.*

1947 *N.Y. Times* 7 Apr. 40/1 The award already has been dubbed a 'Tony', as her associates called Miss Perry. **1948** *Ibid.* 29 Mar. 23/6 John Garfield represented the Experimental Theatre in accepting a 'Tony' for 'experiment in theatre'. **1975** *Times* 10 May 9/3 The Tonys have been awarded, and the 1974/75 New York theatre season is over. **1976** *Time* 27 Dec. 5/3 He later starred in several musicals, including his 1963 Tony Award-winning performance in *She Loves Me.*

tony, *sb.*²: see also *TONI.

tony, *a.* For '*U.S.* and *Colon. colloq.*' read '*colloq.* (orig. *U.S.*)' and add: Also **toney. 1.** (Earlier and later examples.)

1877 R. J. BURDETTE *Rise & Fall of Mustache* 177 He's a toney old cyclopedia on the patter. **1880** *Harper's Mag.* Jan. 209/2 He just put on heaps of style..you know—regular tony. **1920** D. H. LAWRENCE *Lost Girl* xii. 299 The really toney women of the place came to take tea. **1922** JOYCE *Ulysses* 158 Theodore's cousin in Dublin Castle. One tony relative in every family. **1959** D. BARTON *Loving Cup* I. iii. 60 Have you got your dinner-jacket with you, old man?.. I'm afraid we're very toney these days. We seem to get tonier. **1966** 'J. HACKSTON' *Father clears Out* 84 Father, dignified and collected,.. entered the calm, cool tony atmosphere of the Commercial Hotel. **1982** A. H. GARNET *Maze* (1983) iii. 14 He was charming..what Cyrus's mother used to call a 'toney fella'.

2. A fashion colour between red and brown; also as *sb. temporary.*

1921 *Punch* 4 May 357/1 Ladies' artificial silk stockings. In black, white, nigger, grey and toney. **1927** W. E. COLLINSON *Contemp. Eng.* 61 Brogues..sometimes of ox-blood or tony red colour. **1965** *Guardian* 31 Mar. 15/1 Toney was a colour of the twenties which died with the twenties.

-tony [-Y³], anglicized f. *-TONIA.

Tony Curtis (tōᵘ·ni kɒ̄·ɹtis). The film-name of Bernard Schwarz (b. 1925), U.S. actor, used *attrib.* and *absol.* to designate a style of haircut in which the hair at the sides of the head is combed back and that on the forehead is combed forward.

1956 *People* 13 May 10/2 The blokes with crew cuts or Tony Curtises. **1961** J. I. M. STEWART *Man who won Pools* iv. 48 His girl had..made him quit that Duck's Behind for a straight sleeking back with oil. George Pratley had his Tony Curtis still. **1969** *It* 13–28 June, She had seen him..with a well slicked back Tony Curtis style complete with DA at the back.

too, *adv.* Add: **I. 1. a.** The use at the beginning of a clause has been revived, at first in the U.S.

1930 *Publishers' Weekly* 17 May 2514/2 Too, chain store merchandising tactics are the result..of the keenest.. retailing brains in this country. **1956** GARDNER & SMITH *Geneal. Res. Eng. & Wales* I. iv. 46 Many births and deaths were not recorded in the parish registers of England and Wales. Too, some of the other denominations kept poor records. **1969** *Daily Tel.* (Colour Suppl.) 17 Oct. 59/1 And, too, is there any future for the Dunebuggy in Britain? **1976** *National Observer* (U.S.) 7 Mar. 13/2 Too, supermarket officials note, the projected 10 to 20 per cent saving ..covers only part of the..bill. **1978** R. LUDLUM *Holcroft Covenant* vii. 89 Too, the windows were not that close to one another.

b. Used after a vb. to emphasize a reassertion of a denied statement. orig. and chiefly *U.S.*

1914 B. TARKINGTON *Penrod* xiv. 122 'No, I didn't.'.. 'He did, too! Didn't he, Sam?' **1936** M. MITCHELL *Gone with Wind* xlvii. 843 'Surely you can't be thinking of marrying a man who wasn't in the army..?' 'He was, too, in the army.' **1937** WODEHOUSE *Summer Moonshine* (1938) v. 59 'Do you know the Princess?' 'My stepmother.' 'She isn't!' 'She is, too. I have documents to prove it.' **1939** *Reader's Digest* Dec. 25 'She hasn't got appendicitis.' The husband became even wilder, insisting that she did too have appendicitis. **1963** L. DEIGHTON *Horse under Water* xxi. 92 'How do you think she guessed?' 'No idea,' I said. 'You have too. Please tell me,' said Jean. **1969** tr. *Godard's Masculine Feminine* 60 *Madeleine*: You don't care, but for me my first record is very important. *Paul*: I do too care. **1978** A. MALING *Lucky Devil* xxxiii. 181 'Well, you can't really believe in both,' she said. 'You can too!' Frances said hotly.

2. c. (Examples of *too true.*) *just too bad*: see *JUST *adv.* 6 c.

1568 [in Dict.]. **1849** [in Dict., sense 5 c]. **1900** C. M. YONGE *Modern Broods* i. 5 'I am considered quite passée—' 'My dear! With your art, and music, and all!' 'Too true!' **1930** 'E. QUEEN' *French Powder Mystery* xxxi. 261 'The presumption is that he slept home all night and therefore couldn't have committed the crime. Yet physically it was possible.'..' Too true, too true,' murmured Ellery. **1976** N. FREELING *Lake Isle* x. 67 'Rare, that sort of saint.' 'Too true.'

4. c. (Earlier example.)

1881 *Punch* 26 Mar. 138 (*caption*) 'Have you seen the Old Masters at Burlington House?'..'Are they not really quite *too* TOO!!'

5. b. (Earlier example of *too much for.*) *too much*: also (orig. *U.S.*), excellent, first-rate.

1794 A. RADCLIFFE *Myst. Udolpho* I. ix. 251 The sight of this poor old woman would have been too much for Emily. **1937** *Metronome* Mar. 55/1 Man, if you didn't you really missed something. That man's too much! What great bass drum work he shows. **1958** G. LEA *Somewhere there's Music* xviii. 155, I want to make it to the City... Man, like the City is too much—and that's where I want to be. **1966** *Melody Maker* 15 Oct. 19, I just can't wait for his Spring return with Earl Hines, Budd Johnson and the rest. This could be too much. **1967** [see *LEAN *v.*¹ 6 d]. **1968** *Scottish Daily Mail* 3 Jan. 6 They got 'Absolutely divine'; we get 'Too much'... One day 'Too much' will sound as old fashioned as 'ripping'.

e. Also, rather less than; only moderately; not very. Also in other negative contexts, esp. *not too*— (cf. *NOT *adv.* 15 d).

1842 E. A. POE in *Graham's Mag.* Feb. 126/2 The mind of the not-too-acute reader. **1866** GEO. ELIOT *Felix Holt* I. iii. 86 They were not too hopeful about Protestants who adhered to a bloated and worldly Prelacy. **1866,** etc. [see *NOT *adv.* 15 d]. **1892** E. G. WHITE *Steps to Christ* (1908) 108 We do not pray any too much, but we are too sparing of giving thanks. **1909** GALSWORTHY *Fraternity* xxxvii. 313 There were not too many people in London who.. would have behaved with such seemliness—not too many so civilised as they! **1912** J. SANDILANDS *Western Canad. Dict. & Phrase-Bk.*, *Not too bad*, a characteristic Canadian reply to an inquiry regarding one's health or circumstances. **1947** *Sun* (Baltimore) 5 Nov. 2/7 There is little incentive for him to do more than seek a mere existence for himself and family, without too keen a regard for the plight of others. **1956** *English* Summer 45 The English Association..having survived half a century and two world wars..has not done too badly. **1967** L. DEIGHTON *Expensive Place to Die* iii. 19 'Can I have a shower?' she asked. 'The water's not too warm I'm afraid,' said Byrd. **1984** A. BROOKNER *Hotel du Lac* i. 10 My intervention did not seem to be too welcome.

h. *too right*: expressing emphatic agreement or assertion. orig. *Austral.*

1926 'J. DOONE' *Timely Tips to New Australians*, Too right!—A slang term expressing agreement or corroboration. **1934** T. WOOD *Cobbers* v. 76 What I says is, give 'em an axe and send 'em into the bush. Then they'd work, or starve. Too right they would. **1951** J. FLEMING *Man who looked Back* xi. 145 'We should have thought of that before we started out.' 'Too right,' Joe agreed. **1961** *Lancet* 5 Aug. 311/2 The chairman agreed it was thumbs down for Dr. Y., too right it was. **1978** P. McCUTCHAN *Blackmail North* viii. 95 'He'll see you now sir.' 'Too right he will.'

toodle-oo (tū̆d'l,ū·), *int. colloq.* [Origin unknown; perh. f. TOOT *sb.*²] Goodbye. Cf. *PIP-PIP.

1907 *Punch* 26 June 465 'Toodle-oo, old sport.' Mr. Punch turned round at the amazing words and gazed at his companion. **1908** T. E. LAWRENCE *Let.* 16 Aug. (1938) 62 Tootle 'oo. E.L. **1931** D. L. SAYERS *Five Red Herrings* vi. 64 Well, toodle-oo! **1960** [see *BLOT *sb.*¹ 1 c]. **1981** R. BARNARD *Sheer Torture* xi. 121 I'll be downstairs. Toodle-oo.

Also **toodle-, tootle-pip.**

1977 A. C. H. SMITH *Jericho Gun* v. 67 Well, tootle-pip for now. **1983** *Standard* 26 Oct. 23 (*heading*) Toodlepip to the poor British Exec.

toofer, var. *TWOFER.

tool, *sb.* **1. b.** Restrict *arch.* to def. in Dict. and add: In *Criminals' slang*, any weapon.

1938 F. D. SHARPE *Sharpe of Flying Squad* xix. 209 'Here they are, boys; get your tools ready.'..As they ran they pulled weapons from under their coats, hatchets, knuckle-dusters, hammers, and bars of iron. **1971** J. MANDELKAU *Buttons* i. 28 We grabbed our tools and by then the Mods were at the bottom of the street.

2. b. (Further examples of the sense 'penis'.)

1922 JOYCE *Ulysses* 299 The poor bugger's tool that's being hanged. **1966** L. COHEN *Beautiful Losers* (1970) I. 114 You uncovered his nakedness!—You peeked at his tool! **1971** J. STEWART tr. *Simenon's Rich Man* iii. 64 A little slut of a girl..who had not protested when he had put his tool in her hand.

3. c. A pickpocket; the member of a pair or team of pickpockets who actually picks pockets; = WIRE *sb.* 13.

1865 *Leaves from Diary Celebr. Burglar* xviii. 62/1 They were getting uneasy about the absence of their 'tool'. **1886** A. PINKERTON *Thirty Yrs. a Detective* 38 The man who is to do the actual stealing is called the 'tool' or 'hook' and the others are known as 'stalls'. **1936** *Evening News* 9 Dec. 8/5 Modern pickpockets are either 'tools' or 'stalls.'..Really clever tools work alone, disdaining the assistance of a stall. **1955** *Publ. Amer. Dial. Soc.* xxiv. 60 The tool selects the mark to be robbed, and actually takes the score.

5. *tool bag* (also *fig.*), *box* (earlier example), *-kit*, *-maker* (earlier example), *-roll*, *-room* (*attrib.* examples); **tool-bar,** a frame fitted to a tractor on which interchangeable implements may be mounted; **tool-crib,** a place from which tools or other stores are issued to workmen; **tool-dresser** *Oil Industry* = *ROUST-ABOUT 3; **tool head,** a part of a machine that carries the tool or tool-holder and can be moved to bring the tool to bear on the work; **tool-man,** (*a*) a worker with tools; a toolroom worker; (*b*) *Criminals' slang*, a lock-picker or (*U.S.*) safe-breaker; **tool-pusher** *Oil Industry*, someone in charge of a drilling rig; **tool slide,** a sliding machine part which carries a tool; **tool subject** *Educ.*, a subject taught or studied as a help to a main subject.

1892–3 *T. Eaton & Co. Catal.* Fall & Winter 95/1 Bicycle Accessories... Tool Bags—Flat pouch with fastener. **1970** *New York* 16 Nov. 42/2 Talk is the most unreliable and over-reacted-to weapon in the black revolutionary toolbag. **1960** *Farmer & Stockbreeder* 8 Mar. 74/3 In a great many cases they are designed as units to be carried on an ordinary toolbar. **1832** *Chambers's Edin. Jrnl.* I. 236/2 Lifting his tool-box, and going through all the operations of horse-shoeing. **1936** J. DOS PASSOS *Big Money* 19 In six years he rose from machinist's helper to keeper of toolcribs. **1973** T. PYNCHON *Gravity's Rainbow* I. 160 It must have been the wind that was carrying him down a dirt road..among the shacks and tool cribs to a wire fence with a gate. **1896** B. REDWOOD *Petroleum* I. v. 258 The drilling 'crew' consists of two drillers and two tool-dressers. **1976** M. MACHLIN *Pipeline* iv. 53 His Daddy started him as a tool dresser—same way I started. **1950** W. COOPER in A. W. Judge *Centre, Capstan & Automatic Lathes* I. iv. 212 Independent feed for the tool heads is provided at each [work] station. **1977** *Sci. Amer.* Sept. 188/1 The appropriate toolhead was selected automatically by a punched-paper-tape program that was read by an electronic computer-controller. **1963** A. LUBBOCK *Austral. Roundabout* 108, I took..a tool-kit, a box of spare parts, two spare wheels, [etc.]. **1977** C. McFADDEN *Serial* (1978) iv. 14/2 Did she have enough cash in her Swedish carpenter's tool kit? **1844** MILL *Ess. Pol. Econ.* iv. 98 The producer..must set aside a portion of the produce to replace not only the wages paid both by himself and by the tool-maker, but also the profits of the tool-maker. **1909** WEBSTER, *Toolman*, one who works with or makes tools. **1949** W. R. BURNETT *Asphalt Jungle* vii. 47 We need an expert toolman. **1970** R. BUSBY *Frighteners* xvi. 157 The toolman..got his nickname and reputation by proving there wasn't a lock made that he couldn't tickle. **1977** *Whitaker's Almanack 1978* 577 British Leyland was given 28 days to get the striking toolmen back to work. **1979** K. BONFIGLIOLI *After you with Pistol* xxiv. 149 Every sound, professional team of thieves has..a 'toolman' who knows how to neutralize burglar-alarm systems and to open locks. **1932** *Amer. Speech* VII. 271 *Tool pusher*, a foreman in charge of drilling operations—distinct from driller. **1976** M. MACHLIN *Pipeline* xlii. 460 Around day-light a tool-pusher comes out and he tells us we better shut down our rig and put out the fire because the crew on the next well's going to change their control head. **1917** *Harrods Gen. Catal.* 1059/4 Motor car tool roll.. containing 19 best quality tools. **1979** W. H. CANAWAY *Solid Gold Buddha* xxii. 146 Pete spread a toolroll on the spillway. **1937** *Times* 13 Apr. p. xv/2 This checking is the function of the tool room staff in which are to be found the finest craftsmen in the factory. **1963** *Times* 28 May 5/2 More than 1,400 toolroom workers in 10 Birmingham factories of the Joseph Lucas group took part in a 24-hour token strike today. **1976** *Milton Keynes Express* 16 July 13/4 (Advt.), Toolmaker and toolroom miller required. **1919** G. W. BURLEY *Lathes* vii. 108 In some special forms of vertical turning and boring mills the tool-slide is of the non-swivelling variety,..and only vertical and horizontal movements are possible. **1936** COLVIN & STANLEY *Turning & Boring Practice* vii. 101 When the cut is completed the spindle stops, the flow of coolant is shut off, and the tool slides return..to the starting point. **1963** Tool slide [see *SEMI-AUTOMATIC *sb.* 1]. **1934** WEBSTER, Tool subject. **1966** *Rep. Comm. Inquiry Univ. Oxf.* II. 456 Teaching in any 'ancillary' or 'tool' subject (e.g. languages for historians or mathematics for economists).

tool, *v.* Add: **1. d.** *trans.* To equip (a factory) with the machine tools needed for a particular product; to provide the tools needed for (a new product); also *intr.* Usu. with *up.* Also *fig.*

1927 *Observer* 25 Sept. 4 The work of tooling up the Manchester and Cork factories may result in production within the next two months. **1939** *Times* 4 Nov. 6/3 The United States National Defence Council is taking steps to see that American plants shall not be tooled to fit European needs at the expense..of the United States' own later military needs. **1933** *Flight* 27 Apr. 392 It is standard practice to 'tool up' for a certain type as soon as the size of the order warrants the expenditure on jigs and dies. **1940** E. J. H. JONES *Production Engin.* i. 6 The expression to 'tool up' a component means to design and supply all jigs, fixtures, cutting tools, and gauges required for the manufacture and inspection of the piece. **1957** *Observer* 3 Nov. 11/4 Makers must be given a chance to sell models already tooled-up. **1959** *Times Rev. Industry* Apr. 57/3 Much expenditure had to be faced for tooling new models. **1962** *Listener* 13 Sept. 375/1 The automobile factories have tooled up for their new models. **1972** M. KAYE *Lively Game* v. 23, I saw all of the specs..and I helped to tool it up.

e. intr. *to tool up* (fig.): to arm oneself. *slang.*

1959 *Times* 7 Apr. 6/3 There seemed a general agreement that the fashion of carrying dangerous weapons was more widespread to-day than formerly. One read all too often about groups of young men 'tooling up' before setting off for a showdown with a rival gang. **1971** J. MANDELKAU *Buttons* xiii. 142 We tooled up with pieces of wood and iron bars and hiked over towards their main camp. **1978** H. WOUK *War & Remembrance* xxi. 213 We might have closed the Mediterranean and forced England to her knees even while..we tooled up for our summer Caucasus thrust.

2. *slang.* **b.** (Earlier example.) In mod. use, to travel in any kind of vehicle.

1835 DICKENS *Let.* 11 Jan. (1965) I. 53, I wish..you could have seen me tooling in and out of the banners, drums,..and go-carts. **1923** WODEHOUSE *Inimitable Jeeves* xiii. 155, I borrowed a bicycle from one of the grooms and tooled off. **1964** *Manhunt* May 134/1, I was tooling home from the Mexican border in a light blue convertible. **1977** D. ANTHONY *Skid Game* xix. 114, I tooled down the Coast Highway to Sunset.

c. Of a person: to go (or come) in an easy manner; to go *off* quickly.

1862 A. J. MUNBY *Diary* 23 Feb. (1972) 116 Near S. Martin's Lane, I met W. M. Thackeray; 'tooling' along quietly, alone, with hands in pockets. **1881** *Punch* 17 Dec. 285/2 Now we'll just tool off to some quiet sort of a place where we can divide this 'ere shining swag without fireworks. **1936** WODEHOUSE *Laughing Gas* xxviii. 293 Well, I know when I'm licked. I tooled straight round to the Temple of the New Dawn and asked for an entrance form. **1937** D. L. SAYERS *Busman's Honeymoon* 25 The Dowager saw them and was quite nice to them, so they tooled off, fairly happy. **1940** WODEHOUSE *Eggs, Beans & Crumpets* 58 Bingo was tooling along the road with the Peke in his arms. **1945** 'A. GILBERT' *Don't open Door!* xix. 176 Citizens come tooling up to the Police Station..to give information. **1955** E. WAUGH *Officers & Gentlemen* 8 Tool off to Headquarters and get the gen about tonight's do. **1977** 'E. CRISPIN' *Glimpses of Moon* vi. 90 Then along comes the boy-friend..and tools off without the least idea that anything's seriously wrong.

d. To play *around*; to behave in an aimless or irresponsible manner.

1932 F. ILES *Before the Fact* I. v. 77 'Well, anyhow, what are you doing with yourself.'..'Oh, tooling around, you know. Nothing much.' **1957** *New Yorker* 21 Sept. 37/3 Let him stay parched or get a head cold tooling around in ferryboats. **1973** 'A. HALL' *Tango Briefing* ii. 22 We were tooling around in Malta on a friendly visit. **1981** J. WAINWRIGHT *All on Summer's Day* 8 Tool around long enough with the paper work and..half the night has slipped by.

tooled, *a.* (Later example.)

1935 [see *middle leg* s.v. *MIDDLE *a.* 6].

tooled, *ppl. a.* Add: **2.** *tooled up*: equipped with an offensive weapon. *slang.*

1959 *Observer* 1 Mar. 10/1 They sit in all-night cafés, 'tooled up' sometimes with knives and 'choppers' and crank handles. **1973** *Time Out* 2–8 Mar. 13/2 They had knives, chains, house-bricks, iron bars, and everything. We weren't tooled up, because we were coming out of school, and so couldn't get ready properly. **1982** J. BARNETT *Marked for Destruction* v. 58 Smith brandished the shotgun..to let the minder know he was tooled up.

toolie (tū·li). *Oil Industry. slang.* [f. TOOL *sb.* + -IE.] = *tool-dresser* s.v. *TOOL *sb.* 5.

1932 *Amer. Speech* VII. 271 *Toolie*.., a tool-dresser—i.e., the assistant of a cable-tool driller, who dresses bits, fires the boilers, and maintains the rig in order. **1976** L. ST. CLAIR *Fortune in Death* i. 13 He wouldn't be the first wildcatter to end up a toolie, a roustabout.

toolies (tū·liz), *sb. pl. Canad.* [Respelling of *tules*, pl. of TULE.] Backwoods; remote or thinly populated regions.

1961 R. P. HOBSON *Rancher takes Wife* i. 22 We're plenty far back in the toolies at Batnuni. **1976** M. MACHLIN *Pipeline* xii. 141 This here's a program they got for people out in the toolies.

tooling, *vbl. sb.* Add: **2. c.** The process of designing and supplying the machine tools needed for a product or model; also *concr.*, these tools collectively.

1939 *Daily Tel.* 18 Dec. 12/3 (Advt.), Experience should include the setting up and tooling of automatic and turret lathes. **1940** *Sun* (Baltimore) 9 Dec. 14/8 War plants emerge from the 'tooling up' phase into production. **1958** *Times Rev. Industry* June 57/2 A minimum of three-year development time is necessary..through all stages of design, prototypes, testing and tooling. **1963** *Wall St. Jrnl.* 1 Oct., Dayton Reliable Tool & Manufacturing Co... has switched 90% of its manufacturing to making tooling for turning out pull-open devices. **1967** L. B. ARCHER in Wills & Yearsley *Handbk. Management Technol.* 125 Should we begin to sell at a high price to recover our tooling costs quickly? **1977** G. V. HIGGINS *Dreamland* xii. 150, I had earned commissions in hand, from cleaning out Vulcan's obsolete tooling.

toon[2] (tūn), repr. a dial. pronunc. of TUNE *sb.*

1901 M. FRANKLIN *My Brilliant Career* iii. 16 Some of us wuz always good for a toon on the concertina. **1977** *New Musical Express* 12 Feb. 17/1 How the mighty are fallen. Shel Talony..is reduced to dealing with a non-voice churning out four mock country toons for a 99p line.

toonie (tū·ni). [f. *toon*, repr. Sc. pronunc. of TOWN *sb.* (in Shetland, *spec.* = the arable land on a croft) + -IE.] In full *toonie dog*: = *Shetland sheepdog* s.v. *SHETLAND 1 d.

1910 J. A. LOGGIE in J. S. Turner *Kennel Encycl.* III. 1249 The 'Shetland Sheep-dog'..was originally known as the 'Shetland Collie' or 'Toonie Dog'..from the fact of its being used to drive the sheep off the township, croft, or what is known in Shetland as the 'Toon'. **1958** O. GWYNNE-JONES *Shetland Sheepdog Handbk.* i. 4 The 'Toonie' dogs ('Toonies' or Shetland Sheepdogs) are of great service to the farmer. **1971** [see *PEERIE *sb.*].

tooraloo (tūrălū·), *int. colloq.* [Var. *TOODLE-OO *int.*] 'Goodbye.'

c **1921** D. H. LAWRENCE *Phoenix II* (1968) 121 So long! See you soon! Too-ra-loo! **1922** JOYCE *Ulysses* 229 Tooraloo, Lenehan said, see you later. **1974** J. JOHNSTON *How Many Miles to Babylon?* 22 I'll have to be off... Tooraloo.

toot, *sb.*[3] Add: **3.** Cocaine; a 'snort' of cocaine. *U.S. slang.*

1977 *Maclean's Mag.* 2 May 24 They slink into some of the finer furnished bathrooms of the city for a quick toot. **1978** *Detroit Free Press* 16 Apr. (Parade Suppl.) 21/1 Cocaine—also called 'coke', 'C', 'snow' and 'toot'. **1979** *Daily News* (N.Y.) 23 Sept. 5 Each man dipped a spoon into the white powder and got his toot. **1981** W. SAFIRE in *N.Y. Times Mag.* 15 Mar. 1981 The familiar 'to go on a toot', or to drink heavily and thereby lose a weekend, has been replaced by 'to blow a toot', or to inhale a 'line' of cocaine.

toot, *sb.*[5] **a.** For *ruscifolia* substitute *arborea*. See also TUTU.[1] (Earlier and later examples.)

1851 E. WARD *Jrnl.* 18 Feb. (1951) 131 Found poor Novice had taken the 'toot' and had been very ill. **1949** F. SARGESON *I saw in my Dream* 126 There wasn't even any fern, only a few pieces of the tutu which everybody called toot.

b. *to eat* (one's) *toot*: see *TUTU[1] b. *N.Z. slang* (now *Obs.* exc. *Hist.*).

Hence **too·ted** (*ppl.*) *a.* = *TUTUED *a.*; also as *pa. pple.*

1879 in H. Guthrie-Smith *Tutira* (1921) xvi. 123 Two bullocks dead at Troutbeck's. One 'tuted', the other bogged.. **1930** L. G. D. ACLAND *Early Canterbury Runs* 1st Ser. vii. 169 A travelling showman had the bad luck to get his elephant tooted near the Waitaki.

toot, *v.*[3] Add: **4.** *trans.* To inhale (cocaine).

1975 *High Times* Dec. 110/2 Counterculture advocates of cocaine sniffing now have public confirmation of what they've known for a long time: the chief drawbacks to tooting coke are high costs and the law. **1979** *Ibid.* Jan. 52 You'll feel better knowing that what you toot is cut with the original Italian Mannite Conoscenti.

tooter[2]. Add: **3.** One who proclaims loudly; *spec.* = TOUTER 1. *U.S.*

1863 *Rio Abajo Weekly Press* (Albuquerque, New Mexico) 19 May 2 The nameless party's tooter speaks confidently of the success of its nominee. **1886** *Harper's Mag.* Aug. 417/2 The wharf..was alive with vehicles and tooters for the hotels. **1897** R. E. ROBINSON *Uncle Lisha's Outing* 297 Noisiest of all were the tooters, vociferously proclaiming the wonders of the side shows.

tooth, *sb.* Add: **I. 2. b.** (*b*) *pl.* Denoting the ability to compel or enforce, esp. by the exaction of penalties, etc.

1925 *Country Gentleman* 25 July 15/1 How many teeth can you put in a grower's contract of membership with a cooperative marketing association? **1931** *Week-End Rev.* 14 Mar. 380/1 It is even more urgent to take steps which will lead to the success of the Disarmamemt Conference next February than to 'give teeth' to the Paris Peace Pact. **1935** *Evening Sun* (Baltimore) 27 May 13/3 (*heading*) Coal control bill with teeth studied. **1949** *Economist* 16 Apr. 694/2 It is well that President Truman should have made quite clear, not only that the Atlantic Pact is meant to have teeth in it, but also what sort of teeth. **1963** *Listener* 7 Mar. 432/3 It needed guts to fight a battle against an Establishment with teeth. **1964** *Daily Tel.* 20 Mar. 24 (*heading*) 'Teeth' put in scheme for fair coal sales. **1976** *Howard Jrnl.* XV. I. 29 The Magistrates' Association..asked for an order stronger than a care order to show that 'in the last resort the law has teeth'.

(*c*) *spec.*, denoting the combatant personnel of an armed service or military unit. Cf. *TAIL *sb.*[1] 4 c.

1946, 1961 [see *TAIL *sb.*[1] 4 c]. **1962** *Daily Tel.* 26 Sept. 12/2 There is, indeed, room for a 'teeth' rôle for certain units [of the Territorial Army]. **1967** M. AYUB KHAN *Friends, not Masters* iv. 45 These changes gave the infantry more teeth and less tail. **1968** *Listener* 25 July 99/3 As for recruiting, the 'teeth arms' of the three Services are likely to go on attracting young men of high quality. **1977** J. HAINES *Politics of Power* ii. 24 He knew..that the Labour Government's great 'defence review' had left a vast area of spending—administrative 'tail' as opposed to front-line 'teeth'—almost untouched and unharmed.

II. 3. a. (Later example.)

1966 B. MALAMUD *Fixer* VII. iii. 239 He combed his hair and beard until the teeth of the comb fell out.

f. (Earlier example.)

1806 J. DAVIS *Post-Captain* iv. 19 'She looks, sir, like a whacking frigate.' 'Can you see her teeth?' 'Yes, sir; she has a very heavy tire of teeth.'

6. c. So as to be utterly committed; *up to the teeth*: heavily involved or absorbed.

1934 T. E. LAWRENCE *Let.* 8 June (1938) 805 At the moment we are all up to the teeth in 5 more target boats. **1974** *Spartanburg* (S. Carolina) *Herald* 25 Apr. A11/6 A young farmer who is starting out and he's mortgaged to the teeth at the bank would not look at it the same way.

d. *fed* (*up*) *to the* (*back*) *teeth*: see *FED *pa. pple.*

7. a. (Earlier *attrib.* example.)

1872 B. JERROLD *London* xiv. 116 Honourable instinct making a tooth-and-nail fight against adverse circumstances.

8. h. *to get one's teeth into*, to become engrossed in; to come to grips with, to begin serious work on. **i.** *long in the tooth*: see *LONG *a.*[1] 1 c.

h. 1935 D. L. SAYERS *Gaudy Night* i. 23 If one could work here steadily..getting one's teeth into something dull and durable. **1961** B. FERGUSSON *Watery Maze* vi. 140 American eagerness to get their teeth into the enemy. **1983** G. MITCHELL *Cold, Lone, & Still* x. 111 He's not the man to let go while he's got his teeth into a suspect.

9. a. tooth-comb, (*a*) usu. in *fig.* use (later examples); also *attrib.* and as *v. trans.*, to investigate minutely; cf. *FINE-TOOTH *a.*; (*b*) *Zool.*, a group of procumbent lower front teeth found in tree shrews and lemurs; **tooth fairy,** a fairy believed by children to take away milk teeth and leave a small sum of money; also *transf.*; **tooth-glass,** (*a*) (see quot. 1858); (*b*) a glass used to hold false teeth; **tooth-mug** = prec. (*b*); **tooth-paste** (earlier and later examples); freq. *attrib.* in *tooth-paste tube*; also in fig. phr. *to put the toothpaste back in the tube*, illustrating the futility of trying to restore a stable state of affairs in the light of subsequent events; **tooth-root**: for 1 substitute 3; (example); **tooth wash,** a liquid dentifrice.

1918 *Daily Chron.* 25 Jan. 3/7 The Army behind the front is being tooth-combed of all men fit for the fighting line. **1924** *Glasgow Herald* 28 Aug. 4/2 She was a strong woman, well accustomed to 'toothcomb' her husband's MS. **1931** *Times Lit. Suppl.* 1 Oct. 749/3 Whatever the 'tooth-combs' of Dr. Hotson's fellow-scholars may leave of it, he must be congratulated on his discovery. **1958** *N.Y. Times Mag.* 6 Apr. 68/4 The three officers start their own toothcomb check of their huge ship. **1962** *Amer. Jrnl. Physical Anthropol.* XX. 128/1 The closely spaced incisors [of lemurs] seem to scrape the fur rather than comb it. The use of the term 'tooth comb' may be, therefore, objectionable. **1972** *Times Lit. Suppl.* 11 Aug. 946/1 A novel which has been picked over with toothcombs, in search of clues to 'The Mystery'. **1977** *Listener* 7 Apr. 442/1 Decides whether the bid is contentious enough to be toothcombed by the mergers panel. **1980** J. GARDNER *Garden of Weapons* I. xi. 110 The four men and one woman trained after a toothcomb selection. **1981** *Times* 16 Feb. 14/4 Tooth combs are found today in tree shrews..as well as in the lemurs and lorises. **1977** *Age* (Melbourne) 18 Jan. 15/5 Who do you suppose pays for the $50 billion difference? The tooth fairy? Hardly. You do. **1977** *Rolling Stone* 7 Apr. 45/4 Anyone who thinks they acted alone must also believe in Santa Claus, the Easter Bunny and the Tooth Fairy. **1978** J. HYAMS *Pool* xi. 163 Alan had ceased to believe in miracles at about the same age he stopped believing in the Tooth Fairy. **1858** P. L. SIMMONDS *Dict. Trade Products* 384/2 *Tooth-glass*, a toilet water-glass for washing the mouth. **1915** KIPLING *Diversity of Creatures* (1917) 411 That plate of the four lower ones in the blue tooth-glass. **1978** G. GREENE *Human Factor* v. iii. 286 The toothglasses were swathed in plastic. **1891** *Outing* (U.S.) Dec. 244/2 Some drank their champagne out of tooth mugs. **1935** *Discovery* Apr. 114/1 To this communal tooth-mug débris and food particles get transferred. **1979** A. MORICE *Murder in Outline* ix. 77 Why not repair to..our room, where tooth mugs abound, and push the boat out? **1832** *Amer. Railroad Jrnl.* I. 607/3 (Advt.), Seidlitz powders, chloride of soda, chlorine tooth paste. **1966** A. SACHS *Jail Diary* vi. 62, I get up off the floor, fetch my toothpaste-tube. **1975** *Listener* 9 Jan. 44/3 Haldeman says to him: 'John, you ought to think about that, because once the toothpaste is out of the tube, it is awfully hard to put it back again.' **1978** F. KING *Action* xxxi. 105 Pinching at an exhausted toothpaste tube. **1818** Tooth-root [see *DENTARIA]. **1871** 'MARK TWAIN' in *Galaxy* Aug. 284/2 He tendered me a tooth-wash atrocity of his own invention. **1895** *Army & Navy Co-op. Soc. Price List* 716/2 Tooth-wash. **1949** E. POUND *Pisan Cantos* lxxx. 104 Pepitone was wasting toothwash.

b. *teeth-grinding* adj. (later example), *-ridge*.

1969 FABIAN & BYRNE *Groupie* (1970) xxvi. 173 Teeth-grinding teenagers from Muswell Hill picking you up in Cortinas. **1928** I. C. WARD *Phonetics of Eng.* xiii. 117 *T* and *d* before *r* are articulated on the teeth, not on the teeth-ridge. **1966** J. DERRICK *Teaching Eng. to Immigrants* iii. 127 The tip or blade (i.e. the very front part) of the tongue is just behind the upper gums ('the teeth ridge'), i.e. towards the front of the mouth.

tooth-brush. Add: **b.** *tooth-brush glass, holder, rack.*

1931 H. E. L. MELLERSH *Salt of Earth* vii. 159 Put them [*sc.* flowers] in the toothbrush glass or something till May can see to them. **1979** R. JAFFE *Class Reunion* (1980) I. i. 30 Go get your toothbrush glasses and we'll lock the door. **1911** *T. Eaton & Co. Catal.* Spring & Summer 199/2 Combination tumbler and tooth brush holder, nickel-plated. **1979** M. MILLAR *Murder of Miranda* II. 85 The chrome toothbrush holder was empty. **1926–7** *Army & Navy Stores Catal.* 121/2 Bath bracket outfit consisting of..tumbler ring, tooth brush rack. **1969** HURD & OSMOND *Smile on Face of Tiger* v. 184 [He] stood leaning against the toothbrush rack, cup in hand.

Hence **too·thbrushing** *vbl. sb.*

1920 A. HUXLEY *Limbo* 168 A foam of tooth-brushing. **1976** J. PHILIPS *Backlash* (1977) II. ii. 93 Go into the bathrooms... Time for tooth brushing.

toothily (tū·þili), *adv.* [f. TOOTHY *a.* + -LY².] In a toothy manner; so as to display the teeth.

1930 R. MACAULAY *Staying with Relations* xiii. 193 She stared at her master tied up in his chair,..and sunnily and toothily grinned. **1939** A. HUXLEY *After Many a Summer* i. 4 The chauffeur.., slightly over-acting the part of an old-world negro retainer, bowed, smiled toothily. **1977** P. D. JAMES *Death of Expert Witness* IV. 190 A studio photograph of Miss Willard herself, young, toothily coy.

toothless, *a.* Add: **3. c.** Lacking the means of compulsion or enforcement; ineffectual. Cf. *TOOTH *sb.* 2 b (*b*).

1961 in WEBSTER. **1966** *Federal Suppl.* (U.S.) CCXLIV. 823/2 Congress might as well have legalized the closed shop as have enacted such a cynical and toothless provision. **1971** *Nature* 23 Apr. 486/1 Reasons for the failure include unenforceable and toothless laws,..foot dragging by local and state authorities, [etc.]. **1973** *Guardian* 16 Feb. 13 The EEC's social and economic committee..is a toothless organisation... Its views are not seriously taken into account. **1984** *N.Y. Times Mag.* 22 Jan. 46/4 If we do not do what we propose to do, we shall be reviled as toothless and irrelevant.

toothsomely, *adv.* (Earlier example.)

1871 'MARK TWAIN' *Let.* 25 Dec. in C. Clemens *My Father Mark Twain* (1931) 53 Gossip of any kind, and about anybody is one of the most toothsomely Christian dishes I know of.

toothy-peg. Add: Also **toospeg.** (Later examples.) Also used *joc.* in other contexts.

1921 'K. MANSFIELD' *Let.* 3 Feb. (1928) II. 91 When the time comes just put your toospeg brush, pyjamas and a collar..into a handkerchief. **1931** A. CHRISTIE *Sittaford Mystery* xxi. 171 [He] took his elephant's trotters and his hippopotamus's toothy pegs and all the sporting rifles and what nots. **1977** J. WILSON *Making Hate* vi. 71 It's those toothypegs, isn't it, my lovey, those naughty old toothypegs.

tooting, *ppl. a.* (In Dict. s.v. TOOT *v.*²) **1.** See also *rootin' tootin'* s.v. *ROOTING *ppl. a.*² 2.

2. *U.S. slang.* Used, usu. with preceding adv. or adj. (as *damn* or var.), as a strong affirmative or intensive.

1932 *Amer. Speech* VII. 338 You're damn tootin', emphatic affirmative. **1933** E. CALDWELL *God's Little Acre* i. 12 'After the albino, Pa?' Buck asked. 'You're durn tooting, son,' he said. **1952** B. MALAMUD *Natural* 36 You're plumb tootin' crazy. **1970** E. BERCKMAN *She asked for It* xi. 134 You're goddam' tootin' I'm on that again. Y'say I've been prying, you admit there's something to pry into. **1981** G. MCDONALD *Fletch & Widow Bradley* xviii. 72, I got pregnant, when you said I wouldn't... You tol' me a tootin' lie.

tootle, *v.* Add: **2.** *trans.* To play music on (a wind instrument). Also *transf.* and with music as direct obj. *colloq.*

1890 J. SERVICE *Thir Notandums* xiv. 99 Heralds clad in green tootled glorious musick frae their siller horns. **1895** G. MORTIMER *Like Stars that Fall* iii. 28 'There's no need for the cornet in this piece,' said Jenny. 'No, only Abrahams is so fond of tootling his bloomin' instrument,' said Larpenti. **1939** [see *SMOKER 4 b]. **1978** J. GALWAY *Autobiogr.* xiv. 164, I had tootled my flute to some purpose with Herbert von Karajan.

3. *intr.* To walk, to wander casually or aimlessly; usu. const. *along, around,* etc. Also *transf.* with reference to motor transport; *to tootle off,* to go, to depart. *colloq.*

1902 *Cornh. Mag.* July 102, I tootled down to Cooney's a half-hour before time. **1914** M. & J. FINDLATER *Crossriggs* xx. 149 Take that beast and stop all his work, feed him fat and let him sleep on the rug and tootle around the garden. **1918** *Punch* 3 Apr. 222 Well, I must tootle off now. **1951** J. B. PRIESTLEY *Festival at Farbridge* II. ii. 272 You're going to be tootling round to a lot of big houses. **1956** N. COWARD *South Sea Bubble* II. i. 52 It's getting late. ..It is time for me to tootle off home. *a* **1974** R. CROSSMAN *Diaries* (1975) I. 532 We had a real honeymoon holiday..tootling round in a Volkswagen which Helga Greene's villainous friend Johnnie in Heraklion had rented to us. **1978** E. O'BRIEN *Mrs. Reinhardt* 55 He would work for an hour or so and then tootle off. **1983** *Listener* 20 Oct. 31/3 Veteran cars tootle down country lanes.

toots (tuts). *slang* (orig. and chiefly *U.S.*). Also **Toots.** [Prob. abbrev. of *TOOTSY 2.] A woman, a girl; freq. used as a familiar form of address, esp. to a female.

1936 *Amer. Speech* XI. 375/2 *Toots* used to be used in families here and there as a nickname, or a term of endearment, the vowel sounded as in 'boots'... Is this term the ancestor of the present mode of address in 'O.K., toots!', 'Hello, toots!' etc., the vowel shortened into that of 'full'? **1936** *Mademoiselle* Jan. 63 Out here everyone who isn't 'Toots' or 'Cookie' is 'Darling'. **1941** H. A. SMITH *Low Man* iii. 30, I..raised my hand in a clumsy wave and cried out: 'Hiya, toots!'... I had called J. P. Morgan 'toots' to his face. **1946** E. LINKLATER *Private Angelo* xii. 143 'Hiya, toots,' repeated the Count. 'I like that. It is the felicitous expression of a young people who are making their own language.' **1951** J. B. PRIESTLEY *Festival at Farbridge* III. 565 'Wasting it on you, Toots,' said Smith reproachfully. **1975** *New Yorker* 29 Dec. 33/2 'Hi, toots,' Ducky said in Donald's voice a few minutes later to a tiny girl. **1981** G. HAMMOND *Revenge Game* xv. 161 Maybe it's in his mind to come back for you and dig a quiet grave... How does that grab you, Toots?

Tootsie Roll (tu·tsi rōᵘl). *U.S.* The proprietary name of a type of sweet or candy bar.

1925 *Official Gaz.* (U.S. Patent Office) 7 Apr. 19/1 The Sweets Company of America, Incorporated, New York, N.Y. Filed Oct. 24, 1924. Tootsie Rolls... Claims use since September, 1908. **1955** W. GADDIS *Recognitions* I. v. 177 And so brown. Like a tootsie roll. **1969** L. HELLMAN *Unfinished Woman* ii. 22, I bought a few Tootsie Rolls and a half loaf of bread. **1980** J. KRANTZ *Princess Daisy* xxiv. 421 Her Tootsie Roll brown eyes sparkling.

toot sweet (tūt swīt), *adv.* Also **toot and sweat, toots sweet;** *compar.* **the tooter the sweeter.** [Repr. colloq. anglicization of F. *tout de suite.*] Straightaway; promptly, quickly; freq. used as *imp.*

1917 A. G. EMPEY *Over Top* 311 '*Toots Sweet.*' Tommy's French for 'hurry up', 'look smart'. **1917** *Punch* 5 Dec. 389 (*caption*) Tommy (to inquisitive French children): 'Nah, then, alley toot sweet, an' the tooter the sweeter.' **1929** [see *FUCK *v.* 3]. **1942** 'N. SHUTE' *Pied Piper* v. 109 Get them kids dressed toot and sweet—I ain't going to wait all night. **1959** R. POSTGATE *Every Man is God* xxiii. 216 'The tooter the sweeter' was an adjuration to do something, usually bringing a drink, more *tout de suite,* more promptly. **1967** *Guardian* 16 May 2/8 Your two brace of crocodiles[' eggs] have arrived—Yes. I'll get 'em incubated toot sweet. **1978** D. WILLIAMS *Treasure up in Smoke* xiii. 118 The Governor wanted him toot sweet this morning but he hasn't shown up.

tootsy, tootsy-wootsy. Add: **2.** Also **tootsie, tootsey-wootsey, tootsie-wootsie,** etc. A woman, a girl; a sweetheart; occas. applied to a male lover. Freq. as a familiar form of address. *slang* (chiefly *U.S.*).

1895 W. STEVENS *Let.* 23 July (1967) 6, I can be your own dearest tootsey wootsey. **1901** 'H. MCHUGH' *John Henry* 88 One of the kind that's anxious to lead you away from your own tootsie-wootsie, in the hope that you may have a spare bunch of sweet talk you can hand her on the quiet. **1905** E. M. FORSTER *Purple Envelope* in *Life to Come* (1972) 48 'Well, she's not my idea of a tootsy!' said Howard, and clenched his criticism by a coarse and vapid jest. **1920** D. H. LAWRENCE *Lost Girl* vi. 114 Underneath the oak-tree nice and shady Calling me your tootsey-wootsey lady? **1930** *Sat. Even. Post* 5 Apr. 72/4 'Hello, tootsie,' Rusty Charley says. **1938** 'E. QUEEN' *Four of Hearts* ii. 23 The future Mrs. Butcher wouldn't throw her tootsie, would she? **1952** B. WOLFE *Limbo* xvi. 239 'What's the matter, tootsie?' she whispered. **1952** *Sat. Even. Post* 1 Mar. 21/2 What about one of those tootsy-wootsies? **1968** G. DE FRAGA *Murder at Cookout* xv. 71 Don't bother to kiss me. Save that for the little tootsies who think you're as marvellous as you do yourself. **1979** 'P. O'CONNOR' *Into Strong City* xx. 74 Two chicks. One for me... One of the hot-time tootsies.

top, *sb.*¹ Add: **II. 3. a.** Also *pl.,* mountain tops, high moorland, etc.

1930 L. G. D. ACLAND *Early Canterbury Runs* 1st Ser. viii. 190 A wedge-shaped block of ninety thousand acres of high tops, mostly bush-bound. **1948** A. PATON *Cry, Beloved Country* I. x. 65 He would tell him of..the mist that shrouded the tops above Ndotsheni. **1951** E. COXHEAD *One Green Bottle* ii. 45 Cathy saw the great Welsh tops at last..four great blue mountains grouped at its farther end. **1976** *Lancs. Evening Post* 7 Dec. 8/3 There's no collective name for these tops but I've always known them as the Troutbeck Fells. **1980** J. WAINWRIGHT *Kill of Small Consequence* xiv. 109 Up on The Tops the first snows of winter had already etched the dry-stone walls.

c. (Examples in *Billiards.*)

1896 W. BROADFOOT *Billiards* i. 51 McNeil..certainly played the 'top of the table' game better than any of his contemporaries. **1927** *Observer* 20 Mar. 29 Prior..is essentially an all-round player with a tendency to make the top of the table game his chief scoring medium.

d. In the war of 1914–18, with reference to the parapet of a trench; esp. in phr. (*to go*) *over the top* (at the start of an attack). Also *fig.*

1916 *War Illustr.* 9 Sept. 80/1 Some fellows asked our captain when we were going over the top. **1917** 'CONTACT' *Airman's Outings* 184 When, at a scheduled time, the infantry emerge over the top behind a curtain of shells, the contact patrol buses follow their doings. **1923** *Publishers' Circular* 24 Nov. 703/2 If Canada, metaphorically speaking, 'goes over the top', it will be against the wishes of the rest of the Empire and against the wishes of her own authors and publishers. **1933** J. BUCHAN *Prince of Captivity* II. i. 154 Life's a perpetual affair of going over the top. **1962** [see *AUNTIE, AUNTY b]. **1971** S. HILL *Strange Meeting* 120 Armstrong went over the top with the first wave and was hit almost at once. **1978** T. WILLIS *Buckingham Palace Connection* ix. 179 'This is it, then.' 'Yep... Over the top and the best of luck.'

4. a. Also in slang phrases, as *to blow one's top*: see *BLOW *v.*¹ 24 i; *to be off one's top* (chiefly *Austral.*) = *to be off one's nut* s.v. NUT *sb.*¹ 7 b; *to do one's top* = *to do one's nut* s.v. *NUT *sb.*¹ 7 d. Also *up top,* with reference to brains, intelligence.

1916 C. J. DENNIS *Songs Sentimental Bloke* vi. 48 'E's fair orf 'is top wiv love. **1945** BAKER *Austral. Lang.* vi. 130 The state of being stupid is described variously as being *off one's..tile, top* or *saucer.* **1961** *She* Oct. 28/3 Peg, you've got enough up top for both of us. **1972** F. WARNER *Lying Figures* III. 32 Mousey little creature, bless her, not much up top if y'know what I mean. **1977** *Shoot* 18 June 22 (*caption*) Always does his top when he scores, you know.

8. f. A circus tent. Cf. *big top* s.v. *BIG *a.* B. 2. orig. *U.S.*

1931 *Amer. Mercury* Nov. 354/2 *Top,* a tent. **1942** D. POWELL *Time to be Born* xii. 291 A perpetual rain cloud spread like a circus top. **1959** *Manch. Guardian* 16 July 5/1 He supervises the erection of the 'top'.

III. 11. g. Also, the lid of other kinds of container, esp. the metal-foil cover of a milk bottle, the colour of which may indicate the kind or quality of the milk, as *gold top, silver top,* etc. **h.** Also of a motor-car (chiefly *U.S.*); see *hard top* s.v. *HARD *a.* 22 a, *soft top* s.v. *SOFT *a.* 27. **j.** Now usu. a blouse or similar upper garment for wearing with a skirt, trousers, etc.; cf. *sun-top* s.v. *SUN *sb.*11 d, *tank top* s.v. *TANK *sb.*¹ 4, etc.

g. 1958 A. SILLITOE *Saturday Night & Sunday Morning* ii. 35 Screwing the top back on the flask. **1959, 1972** [see *milk bottle* s.v. *MILK *sb.* 9 a]. **1979** *Dairy Mirror* Nov. 8/3 (*caption*) Lisa Faulkner..displays the 10,000th Gold Top Milk Gymnastics Award Scheme double gold certificate. **1980** *Ibid.* Feb. 1/1 The retail price of a pint of ordinary silver top milk goes up from 15p to 16½p. **1981** J. BARNETT *Firing Squad* v. 48 What do you think this is, laddie? The top off a Fry's cocoa-tin? **h. 1910** *Sears, Roebuck Catal.* 1143/2 Three-bow skeleton automobile top of heavy moroccoline. **1942** D. POWELL *Time to be Born* ii. 51 Ted would never put the top down when he drove. **1977** H. FAST *Immigrants* III. 199 They argued about putting up the top. **j. 1922** JOYCE *Ulysses* 341 His little man-o'-war top and unmentionables were full of sand. **1949** N. MITFORD *Love in Cold Climate* II. i. 186 A jersey top, however Parisian, was obviously unacceptable for evening wear in high Oxford society. **1968** *Daily Mirror* 20 Aug. 9/2 And I got a couple of bright flowery roll-neck tops..and some super things for the beach, stretch bikini bottoms and loose towelling tops in hectic colours.

IV. 14. a. Also in Journalism, Broadcasting, etc., the leading position in a news bulletin, or the top of a column in a newspaper.

1973 L. HEREN *Growing up Poor in London* vi. 163 The first flashes were coming through on the attempt to get an abandoned ship in tow somewhere in the Atlantic... The story rated a top. **1979** 'A. HAILEY' *Overload* I. iv. 23 On the radio,..a news bulletin. The item Nim had been waiting for was at the top.

b. Also *spec.* in Journalism. Cf. sense 14 a above.

1960 R. ST. JOHN *Foreign Correspondent* x. 195, I.. dictated a new 'top' for Sunday papers.

c. *ellipt.* for *top sergeant,* sense 32 below. *U.S. Mil. slang.*

1898 E. H. BLATCHFORD *Let.* 30 July (1920) 53 The 'top' said he wanted us to sign the pay-roll and be back at ten to-night. **1930** T. FREDENBURGH *Soldiers March!* ii. 12 The Top says he'll pass the word along. **1970** W. JUST *Military Men* iii. 95 Don't worry, Top.

15. a. Also, *at the top of one's form* (FORM *sb.* 16 a).

1933 A. POWELL *From View to Death* iii. 89 It had come at a time when he was not feeling at the top of his form. **1947** L. P. HARTLEY *Eustace & Hilda* vii. 138, I can't pretend that she was at the top of her form.

c. Now in various constructions, esp. *in(to) top.*

1925 *Morris Owner's Man.* 10 When changing gear up from first to second, or second to top, the clutch pedal should be pressed down. **1932** S. GIBBONS *Cold Comfort Farm* xvi. 217 They heard him change into top. **1953** [see *CHANGE *v.* 6 d]. **1958** [see *GEAR *sb.* 7 b]. **1970** N. FLEMING *Czech Point* (1971) viii. 107 Melanie rammed the car into top and kept up the acceleration.

d. *Bridge.* (*a*) Either of the two highest cards of a suit; (*b*) the best score made in the play of a particular hand.

1929 M. C. WORK *Compl. Contract Bridge* Gloss. 246 *Tops,* Aces and Kings. **1945** 'S. J. SIMON' *Why you lose at Bridge* ix. 103 As the Clubs didn't break, and he took the Heart finesse to try and save something from the wreck, he went six down. A cold top for us. **1958** *Listener* 23 Oct. 669/2 To ask whether, at match points, East-West should try for Seven Hearts is like asking whether a golfer should play for a birdie or a bogey: it all depends on the state of the game. If they need a 'top' they take the chance. **1977** *Hongkong Standard* 12 Apr. 10/3 Romik was able to claim all 13 tricks for an outright 'top' on the hand.

16. Also in fig. phr. *on top of the world*, at the peak of well-being, prosperity, or elation; hence *top of the world* attrib. phr. (also with hyphens).

c **1920** D. HAMMETT in W. F. Nolan *Dashiell Hammett* (1969) ii. 19 A Samuels diamond puts you on top of the world! **1930** WODEHOUSE *Very Good, Jeeves!* ix. 226 If ever a bird was sitting on top of the world, that bird was Bingo. **1946** E. S. GARDNER *Case of Borrowed Brunette* xi. 132 This time Gulling, with this new evidence making him feel he's sitting on top of the world, slapped my proposition right back in my face. **1962** D. FRANCIS *Dead Cert* vii. 79 His eyes were alight with that fantastic, top-of-the-world elation. **1978** D. DEVINE *Sunk without Trace* v. 51 Last time I spoke to Liz she was on top of the world. **1979** *Guardian* 12 Jan. 9/8 As Colt's say in their publicity handout: 'This top of the world feeling can now be reproduced in a factory, office or shop.'

17. b. (*d*) In gen. colloq. use (predicatively): the best. Freq. with *the*. orig. *U.S.*

1935 *Motion Picture* Nov. 41/1 *Top Hat* is tops—it has everything! **1937** R. STOUT *Red Box* xv. 249 Your conversation is an intellectual and esthetic delight. It's the tops. **1942** N. STREATFEILD *I ordered Table for Six* 243 He didn't go near your mother until he was the tops, so to speak. **1948** C. DAY LEWIS *Otterbury Incident* 94 Toppy is tops at spur-of-the-moment tactics. **1958** *Punch* 9 July 44/3 Cooney's Cassocks stand the test, Choosy Churchmen say they're best. Sure-fire sermons, never flops; Cooney's Cassocks are the tops. **1976** 'W. TREVOR' *Children of Dynmouth* i. 36 'You're easily tops, lad,' Hughie Green was enthusing, putting an arm round his shoulder. **1979** L. MEYNELL *Hooky & Villainous Chauffeur* i. 14, I always looked up to him... I just thought he was the tops.

17*. *Particle Physics.* [An arbitrary choice of name.] The name of (a quark carrying) a possible sixth flavour, with a charge of $+\frac{2}{3}$. Freq. *attrib.*

1977 *Sci. Amer.* Oct. 74/2 The new quarks will apparently be called 'top' and 'bottom', the names being meant to suggest properties surpassing those of the up and down quarks found in ordinary matter. **1978** *Nature* 2 Feb. 407/2 Similarly if top quarks exist then 'naked top' —or 'topless' states will eventually be found. The prudish may care to note that t and b are said to stand for truth and beauty, rather than top and bottom, by some physicists. It is predicted that..top decays to bottom. **1980** J. S. TREFIL *From Atoms to Quarks* xii. 184 As I write (spring 1979), there is no evidence to indicate that particles made from a top quark have been seen. **1982** *Sci. Amer.* Mar. 64/2 The member of the top family that should be easiest to identify would be made up of a top quark bound to a top antiquark. **1984** *Nature* 12 July 97/1 Last week, the 80-strong collaboration..announced the discovery of the missing sixth quark, called *top*. *Ibid.* 97/3 The discovery of the *top* quark. *Ibid.*, The discovery of *top*.

VI. Phrases. **21. a. on (the) top of,** (*a*) also, in addition to (further examples); (*b*) too close to; esp. *on top of one another*, in crowded conditions; (*c*) burdensome to, too much for; *to get on top of*: to overwhelm, harass, depress; (*d*) in control of.

1824 M. WILMOT *Let.* 5 Feb. (1935) 207, I came home hungry, took some hot tea on the top of a cold ice which I got there, got an indigestion. **1947** A. L. ROWSE *Tudor Cornwall* xvi. 434 There was little privacy, for they lived on top of one another. **1952** *Chambers's Jrnl.* May 267/1 Our work consisted, mainly, in safeguarding road convoys from attack by hostile tribesmen. By no stretch of the imagination could it have been termed exhausting, but it was always on top of you. **1952** M. ALLINGHAM *Tiger in Smoke* x. 167 This time there was..no faltering. He was on top of himself and them. **1955** —— *Beckoning Lady* iv. 55 None of us saw her until she was right on top of us. **1962** B. COBB *Murder: Men Only* ix. 109 Oh, Kitty, it's Thursday and I know we agreed, but how? With everything on top of me. **1965** *New Society* 11 Nov. 7/1 People..do not necessarily want to live 'on top of each other'. **1968** *Listener* 4 July 5/1 On top of all this there are the continuing constitutional negotiations. **1974** A. MORICE *Killing with Kindness* ii. 21, I didn't mean to be rude. It's all got so much on top of me that I don't know what I'm saying half the time. **1977** M. ALLEN *Spence in Petal Park* xxxiii. 158 He still lives in Downsea. Near enough for me to babysit but not so close that we're on top of him. **1977** 'A. YORK' *Tallant for Trouble* vi. 87 He really felt he was getting on top of the situation. **1981** *Sunday Express Mag.* 2 Aug./33 Lord Mackan has had a busy programme of special ceremonial events on top of his normal Household chores.

b. at the top: in a position of power or authority. Cf. sense 14 in Dict. and *room at the top* s.v. *ROOM *sb.*[1] 2 a.

1936 G. B. SHAW *Millionairess* I. 145 That's what keeps him at the top in the city. **1962** J. BRAINE (*title*) Life at the top. **1979** A. FOX *Threat Warning Red* iii. 41 The machines..hadn't made life easier at the top.

c. over the top, beyond reasonable limits, too far, into exaggeration.

1968 C. WATSON *Charity ends at Home* x. 129 For instance, you said at our first interview that your wife got so worked up about some things that she was in danger of going 'over the top', as you put it. **1974** *Times* 6 Mar. 2/8 We agreed to give every possible support to the Labour Government, including not going over the top with wage claims. **1981** 'D. JORDAN' *Double Red* i. 11, I could summon less and less response to Magnus's more rhetorical flights: so here we are, going over the top again, I was thinking.

22. b. off the top of one's head and varr., impromptu, without consideration, superficially; hence *top-of-the-head* attrib. phr.

1939 H. L. ICKES *Secret Diary* (1954) II. 718 He was impetuous and inclined to think off the top of his head at times. **1959** 'E. MCBAIN' *'Til Death* xiii. 169 The jokes.. took on an ad lib quality, each prankster..coming up with top-of-the-head advice on the proper hotel-room behaviour. **1967** *Listener* 20 Apr. 518/2 His [*sc.* Bertrand Russell's] political activities..are not something that is coming out of the top of his head, they are coming from his nature. **1972** J. RIPLEY *My Word you should have seen Us* 159 You're talking out of the top of your head, mac. **1977** W. J. BATE *Samuel Johnson* (1978) xi. 173 London.. seems breezy, as if written off the top of the head..; it lacks the sublime moral elevation of the *Vanity*. **1981** C. DEXTER *Dead of Jericho* xxviii. 160 A bit of bread-and-butter investigation was worth a good deal more than some of that top-of-the-head stuff.

VII. 26. *top buggy* (earlier examples), *-wagon* (earlier examples).

1849 *Knickerbocker* XXXIV. 266 An ordinary 'top-buggy' wagon. **1866** 'MARK TWAIN' *Lett. from Hawaii* (1967) 45 His 'turnout', as he calls a top buggy that Captain Cook brought here in 1778. **1852** C. A. BRISTED *Upper Ten Thousand* 208, I have a top-wagon. **1880** W. WHITMAN *Daybks. & Notebks.* (1978) III. 639 Many queer old one-horse top-wagons.

29. (Later examples.) Also, of high standing. See also *TOP PEOPLE *sb. pl.*

c **1926** [see *RUNNING *vbl. sb.* 2 e (*b*)]. **1936** *Publishers' Weekly* 21 Nov. 1965/2 Publishers involved in recent top-seller crises. **1938** E. AMBLER *Cause for Alarm* xiii. 213 The prisons would be overflowing..and most of the top men would be with them. **1939** *Supervision* Feb. 1/1 The whole related circle which reaches from top management down to the worker. **1945** *Richmond* (Va.) *Times-Dispatch* 25 Oct. 12/1 The A-bomb has aroused so much interest a complex technical tome on that subject is now a top-seller. **1958** *Observer* 3 Aug. 5/1 Grouse-shooting, it must be conceded, is the top sport. **1965** *Mod. Law Rev.* XXVIII. v. 587 Corporations, seemingly, will be liable for the acts and omissions of 'top management'. **1972** L. DEIGHTON *Close-Up* viii. 166 They are going to spend a hundred thousand dollars just on this one story. They'll get a top outside photographer to do it. **1981** R. SAMUEL *East End Underworld* xi. 133 Cockney Cohen was the favourite; he was regarded as the top man of the two [boxers]. **1982** *Lakeland Echo* 18 Mar. 6/7 Peter Frankl was going to play there..on May 1, and other top performers were lined up for the future.

31. a. *top lacing; top-feeding, -opening* adjs.

1925 F. SCOTT FITZGERALD *Great Gatsby* i. 8 He seemed to fill those glistening boots until he strained the top lacing. **1926–7** *Army & Navy Stores Catal.* 409/2 Top-opening handbag. **1933** *Sun* (Baltimore) 20 Apr. 5/6 Some 200,000 of the American top-feeding minnow species Gambusia were dumped into some of the ponds. **1963** *Which?* 6 Feb. 36/1 The chest top-opening freezer.

31*. In sense 'highest or first'. **a.** With nouns forming attrib. phr., as *top class, quality, rank*, etc. See also *top drawer, flight*, sense 32 below.

1948 J. TOWSTER *Political Power in U.S.S.R.* III. xiii. 318 'Stakhanovites', that is, top-efficiency workers. **1950** *N.Y. Times* 20 Apr. 1/3 Virtually every top bracket job.. could be filled from the proposed register. **1950** *Times* 23 May 5/6 Time and again one reads..of top grade British films which will never be shown here at all. **1953** *Newsweek* 30 Mar. 81/2 Higgins-built mine sweepers..became the top-priority ships on the Navy's program. **1959** *Times* 29 Oct. 2/2 Position calls for top-calibre executive with experience of marketing. **1960** *Farmer & Stockbreeder* 9 Feb. 74/3 These..would only be interested in top-quality products tailor-made to suit their demand. **1960** *Times* 12 July 13/4 It isn't only the field events that are a poor show at top-class athletics meetings. **1961** *Lancet* 9 Sept. 598/1 We have very few top-rate managers. **1962** L. DEIGHTON *Ipcress File* i. 15 It makes eight top rank Disappearances in..six and a half weeks. **1972** J. AIKEN *Butterfly Picnic* x. 190 [He] is doing forty years in a top-security prison for handing over state secrets. **1973** *Country Life* 29 Nov. 1773/1 No champagne is made exclusively from top-price grapes. **1975** G. ST. GEORGE *Proteus Pact* i. 36 An urgent matter, a top-priority project. **1977** *National Observer* (U.S.) 8 Jan. 7/1 They conclude that there are no significant differences in intellectual and social development between young children reared at home and those placed in a top-quality day-care center. **1978** K. HUDSON *Jargon of Professions* v. 122 X is a top-class product manager because his father and mother were top-class product managers. **1979** *Jrnl. R. Soc. Arts* July 504/2 Something should be done to encourage a really efficient and top-grade display of arts and crafts. **1982** *Lakeland Echo* 18 Mar. 6/4 Special attention has been paid to acoustics and lighting so that really top-rank artistes can be persuaded to play there.

b. Adverbially with adjs. or ppl. adjs., as *top-ranking, -rated, -secret*, etc.

1936 *Time* 19 Oct. 67/1 Adapting a story which is to be played by four top-ranking film personalities. **1944** Top secret [see *CLASSIFIED *ppl. a.* c]. **1946** KOESTLER *Thieves in Night* 194 Turning to the urgent blue and so to the top-urgent red tray. **1958** *People* 4 May 19/7 Top-rated American Davey Moore said yes. **1960** *Farmer & Stockbreeder* 22 Mar. 83/3 Top-priced bull at Hereford last week was Haven Possible. **1962** *Guardian* 13 July 8/1 Drambuie..ranks with Benedictine and Cointreau among the world's five top-selling digestifs. **1975** *Listener* 17 July 69/1 Top-paid people should agree to limit their incomes. **1976** *Billings* (Montana) *Gaz.* 16 June 3-c/2 The victory by the third-rated Hurons left top-rated Arizona State one defeat from elimination. **1976** *Scotsman* 25 Nov. 14/5 A commercial paper nowadays would have to be less 'Left-of-centre'..to be read by the top-earning businessmen and stockbrokers who justify expensive advertising. **1976** H. WILSON *Governance of Britain* iv. 92 The Churchill and Macmillan appointees inevitably had the same access to secret and top-secret documents as any civil service appointee. **1978** *N.Y. Times* 30 Mar. D22/1 In a postponed first-round match, top seeded Vitas Gerulaitis.. defeated Ray Moore. **1978** *Observer* (Colour Suppl.) 9 Apr. 30 These two were 'top rankin'' gunmen in the ghetto for Jamaica's two main political parties. **1980** *Washington Star* 17 Dec. E2/6 Mississippi State jumped into national prominence with its big win over top-ranked Alabama.

32. top banana *Theatr. slang* (chiefly *U.S.*), the leading comic in a burlesque entertainment; also *fig.*; **top board** *Chess*, the principal player of a team in a tournament; **top box,** on a motor-cycle, a carrier box for baggage, etc., placed on top of the cycle behind the saddle (as opp. to panniers at the sides); **top brass:** see *BRASS *sb.* 2 e; **top-coat,** (*a*) (earlier example); (*b*) any of the finishing layers of paint applied after undercoat; **top copy,** the original typescript of a document, of which the under-sheets are carbon copies; also *ellipt.*; **top-cut,** reduction of the strength of the higher-frequency components of a signal; **top cutter** *U.S. Mil. slang* = *top sergeant* below; **top cymbal** *Mus.* = *ride cymbal* s.v. *RIDE *sb.*[1] 7; **top dead centre** (see quot. 1978); **top deck:** see *DECK *sb.*[1] 3 d; **top dollar** *N. Amer. colloq.*, a high price; **top-down** *a.*, (*a*) *Computers*, working from the top or root of a tree towards the branches (with or without backtracking); (*b*) that proceeds from the top downwards; authoritarian, hierarchical; occas. as *adv.*; (*c*) (of planning or design) starting with the overall structure and going on to successively more detailed parts of it; **top drawer:** in *fig.* use freq. with reference to social standing (later example); also *attrib.* or as *adj.*, first-class, of the highest level; **Top End** *Austral. colloq.*, the Northern Territory of Australia; hence **Top-Ender; top fermentation** *Brewing*, a process in which the yeast rises to the surface during fermentation; **top flight,** the highest rank or peak of excellence; also *attrib.* or as *adj.*; hence **top-flighter; top gear,** (*b*) also *fig.*, a fast pace, full speed; **top-graft** *v.*, substitute for def.: = *top-work* vb. s.v. *TOP *sb.*[1] 32; hence **top-grafting** *vbl. sb.*; **top hand** *N. Amer. colloq.*, a cowboy who is an experienced or first-rate ranch-worker; also *fig.*; **top kick** *U.S. Mil. slang* = *top sergeant* below; also **top kicker; top light,** a pane of glass affording illumination from overhead; a skylight; hence **top-lighted, top-lit** *adjs.*; **top loader,** a machine or device designed to be loaded from the top; opp. *front-loader* s.v. *FRONT *sb.* (and *a.*) 14; hence **top-loading** *vbl. sb.*; **top minnow,** a small, often brightly coloured, fish belonging to the family Cyprinodontidæ or Poeciliidæ; **top notch** (*attrib.* examples); **top of the bill** *Theatr.*, the chief place on a bill of entertainment; also (with hyphens) *attrib.* and *fig.* (cf. *to top the bill* s.v. *TOP *v.*[1] 16 a); **top-of-the-line** *a.* (chiefly *U.S.*), designating a commercially produced commodity that is the best, most expensive or luxurious, etc., of its kind; **top of the milk,** the cream that rises to the top of milk when left undisturbed; **top of the pops:** see *POP *a.* (*sb.*[8]) 1 b; **top-score** *v. intr. Cricket*, to make the greatest number of runs of an innings; hence **top scorer; top sergeant** *U.S. Mil. slang*, first sergeant; **top-slicing** *vbl. sb.*, (*a*) *Mining*, a method of working in which successive slices up to 12 feet thick are mined from the top of an ore body, working downwards, the material overlying each slice being made to cave after its completion; so **top-slice** *v. trans.*, to work in this way; (*b*) a method of assessing income- or surtax chargeable on a lump sum by averaging it out over the years for which it has accrued and charging tax accordingly; **top-soil,** the cultivatable) surface layer of the soil, as distinct from the subsoil; in *Archæol.*, the soil covering a site being investigated; **top soldier** *U.S. Mil. slang* = *top sergeant* above; **top-spin** = *OVERSPIN *sb.*; see also sense 19 in Dict.; also *fig.*; **top-spinner** = *overspinner* s.v. *OVERSPIN *sb.*; also **top-spun** *a.*; **top-stitch** *v. trans.*, to make a row of stitches on (the right side of a garment or other piece of sewn work), usu. as a form of decoration; so **top-stitched** *ppl. a.*; **top-stitching** *vbl. sb.*; **top table,** at a formal dinner, the table at which the chief guests are placed; also *fig.*, esp. in *Pol.*; **top-tail** *v.*

(example); **top ten** *Popular Music*, the first ten tunes or gramophone records in the popularity charts (*CHART *sb.* 3 c) at a particular time; also *transf.*; similarly **top twenty,** etc.; **top view** = *plan view* s.v. *PLAN *sb.* 6; **top-water,** (*b*) as *adj.* (of a lure) that floats on top of the water; **top-work** *v. trans. Horticulture*, to replace part or all of the top of (a fruit tree) by grafts of another variety; so **top-worked** *ppl. a.*, **-working** *vbl. sb.*

1953 BERREY & VAN DEN BARK *Amer. Thes. Slang* (1954) § 583/12 *Top banana*, the burlesque comedian who gets top billing. **1956** *Picturegoer* 21 July 29/3 'Top banana' is the comic-in-chief of a burlesque show. **1974** *Time* 21 Jan. 53/3 Dentsu Advertising Ltd...has become the new top banana of world-wide advertising. **1978** *N.Y. Times* 29 Mar. c 27/1 Miss Burnett is a..very, very funny woman. She is a superb top banana. **1910** *British Chess Mag.* XXX. 463 A top-board winning seven times successively might find himself temporarily or unjustly displaced in the ninth match. **1976** *Milton Keynes Express* 28 May 55/7 The competition was won..by county top board Norman Stephenson. **1976** *Eastern Daily Press* (Norwich) 19 Nov. 5/6 (Advt.), 1975 Yamaha FS1E, excellent condition, low mileage, winkers, topbox. **1804** F. ASBURY *Jrnl.* 18 Apr. (1821) III. 136, I had heedlessly thrown off my top-coat for a few hours, and caught cold. **1959** *Sears, Roebuck Catal.* Spring & Summer 1182/3 House paint undercoat... Insures longer wear..and a smoother appearance of top coat. **1977** *Custom Car* Nov. 26/3 After three undercoats and four topcoats of Dulux Golden Yellow Coach Paint,..Chris describes the finish as 'not bad'. **1919** H. ETHERIDGE *Dict. Typewriting* 68 If an error is made whilst taking carbon copies, it is a lengthy process to make the correction, as, in erasing the original or top copy, the pressure of the eraser will make a bad smudge on the copies. **1967** L. MEYNELL *Mauve Front Door* vii. 89 If you could possibly do a top and two carbons of these notes. **1979** G. MITCHELL *Mudflats of Dead* II. xvi. 162 The bill is for typing a top copy and two carbons of a book. **1957** *Practical Wireless* XXXIII. 706/1 Simple switched bass-boost and top-cut compensation is provided by S1 and S2 respectively. **1962** A. NISBETT *Technique Sound Studio* ii. 35 There is no worse microphone defect..for emphasizing any slight sibilance which may be present (and you cannot get rid of it by top cut if the emphasis lies in upper middle peaks). **1917** *Editor* 13 Jan. 33 *Top cutter*, first sergeant. **1930** T. FREDENBURGH *Soldiers March!* 279 It's a damn good book. Lots of swell dope for Top Cutters in it. **1948** *Record Changer* July 12/1 The top cymbal has become the main tool of the bebop drummer. **1956** M. STEARNS *Story of Jazz* (1957) xviii. 234 Clarke made the single right-hand 'ride' or 'top' or 'front' cymbal the rhythmic center... The top cymbal was the only regular and continuous sound made by the drummer. **1924** E. C. M. SHEPHERD *Motor Car* ii. 23 When a piston is at the top of its stroke..on the point of changing from an upward motion to a downward motion, it is said to have reached top dead centre. **1978** *Vocab. Reciprocating Int. Combust. Engines* (*B.S.I.*) (1979) 7 *Top dead centre*, dead centre when the piston is farthest from the crankshaft. **1970** *Toronto Daily Star* 24 Sept. 15/9 He said Sault residents 'are paying top dollar for a second-rate flight'. **1978** M. PUZO *Fools Die* xvi. 170 A lot of those guys..had paid him top dollar to buy their enlistment in the six months' program. **1964** *Communications Assoc. Computing Machinery* VII. 80 [What are your general views regarding the merits of doing the syntax analysis from the 'top down' as against the 'bottom up'?] *Ibid.*, My analyzer is bottom-up and Warshall's is top-down. **1969** R. BLACKBURN in Cockburn & Blackburn *Student Power* 178 Its officials are robbed of all real initiative by the requirements of rule obedience, top-down control and hierarchy. **1972** O. J. DAHL et al. *Structured Programming* p. v, Structured programming principles can be equally applied in 'bottom-up' as in 'top-down' program design. **1975** *Nature* 16 Oct. 548/1 Many somewhat different algorithms are properly classified as top-down parsing algorithms. **1976** *Eastern Daily Press* (Norwich) 16 Dec. 8/6 You take the familiar top-down view, pointing out the various problems which always beset constitutional changes. **1977** *N.Y. Rev. Bks.* 13 Oct. 28/1 The students were intent on showing that..'every decision was made top-down by the power structure'. **1979** *Personal Computer World* Nov. 74/2 The approach we shall take in programming this problem is known as 'Top-Down Design'. **1980** *Times* 9 Feb. 17/2 The emphasis in the latest public spending round has shifted from 'bottom up' planning, where spending totals are built up from the individual elements in the programmes, to 'top down' planning. **1920** R. MACAULAY *Potterism* I. i. 10 The Potter family, however respectable now, wasn't really 'top-drawer'. **1946** *Sun* (Baltimore) 10 Oct. 12/2 The National Bureau of Economic Research, a top-drawer group of research economists. **1958** 'A. BRIDGE' *Portuguese Escape* iii. 42 The composed decision that somehow had so much distinction. 'She *is* out of the top drawer, isn't she?' **1959** *Vogue* Dec. 61 Vedonis also make ladies' underwear, sweaters, nightwear and bed jackets. They're top-drawer because everything about Vedonis is so good. **1960** *Guardian* 25 June 4/4 The word 'Hampstead' with all its associations of top-drawer socialism. **1976** *Time* 20 Dec. 10/3 Tanaka and four other Diet members linked to Lockheed's scheme to buy top-drawer influence and stimulate sales with more than $2 million in bribes were re-elected by loyal rural constituencies. **1977** C. MCCULLOUGH *Thorn Birds* vii. 149 Quite respectable, socially admissible, but not top drawer. Never top drawer. **1933** F. E. BAUME *Tragedy Track* 93 She..left again for the more human..regions of the Top End, where at least one could drink fresh water occasionally. **1969** *Northern Territory News* (Darwin) *Focus '69* 81/1 Beef roads..will criss-cross the Top End with 665 miles of good bitumen. **1941** C. BARRETT *Coast of Adventure* 14 The old Top-ender drank beer, which, to the men up there, is more desirable than iced nectar is to gods. **1961** T. RONAN *Only a Short Walk* 52 Any 'Top-Ender' who wanted..a tip for the races..went to Billy. **1902** *Encycl. Brit.* XXVI. 367/1 The system is called *top-fermentation*, because the type of yeast employed develops on the surface of the liquid, forming the 'head'. **1905** [see *bottom fermentation* s.v. *BOTTOM *sb.* 19]. **1974** *Encycl. Brit. Macropædia* III. 161/2 Top fermentations are usually carried out using selected strains of *Saccharomyces cerevisiae*, botanically identical with bakers' yeast. **1939** R. CHANDLER *Big Sleep* xx. 150 Top-flight racketeers have business brains. **1958** *Times* 19 July 3/4 Lifting himself into the top flight of English batsmen. **1959** J. THURBER *Years with Ross* viii. 138 Reporters.. joined the staff, all of them top flight. **1967** *Punch* 20 Dec. 951/3 Good though it is, it isn't top-flight. **1979** E. NEWMAN *Sunday Punch* xv. 123 Every successful fighter when he reaches a point just below the top flight. **1981** *Beautiful Brit. Columbia* Fall 37 The University of Victoria, with its new, acoustically exuberant auditorium, is the scene now for many top-flight performances. **1950** 'M. INNES' *Hare sitting Up* II. ii. 52 He lives on his nerves, as so many top-flighters do. **1959** J. DEMPSEY *Championship Fighting* v. 21 If you boast only nine professional fights, there's little danger of your being tossed in with a top-flighter or a champion. **1932** E. BOWEN *To North* xxii. 235, I can't live at top gear. **1973** *Nature* 13 Apr. 440/1 The coal industry must now put its research and development programmes into top gear. **1912** F. A. WAUGH *Beginners' Guide Fruit Growing* i. 13 Trees for top-grafting may be of almost any age. **1975** W. E. SHEWELL-COOPER *Compost Fruit Grower* viii. 118 Many of the trees consist of quite unsuitable varieties... It is, therefore, worth realising that top-grafting methods may be adopted which will convert one variety into another. **1912** 'B. M. BOWER' *Flying U Ranch* 201 We can both safely consider ourselves top-hands when it comes to lying. **1955** R. P. HOBSON *Nothing too Good for Cowboy* i. 12 It will be impossible to line up enough top hands to carry on. **1972** T. A. BULMAN *Kamloops Cattlemen* iii. 19 They were all top hands with either saddle or work horses. **1918** J. E. RENDINELL *Diary* 28 Mar. in *One Man's War* (1928) viii. 63 The old top-kick would make a running dive for the dugout. **1976** L. DEIGHTON *Twinkle, twinkle, Little Spy* vii. 70, I was a gunner, nineteen—youngest top-kick in the group. **1979** *Arizona Daily Star* 22 July A8/1 The president's appointment of Hamilton Jordan as the White House topkick. **1919** L. L. LINCOLN *Company C, Eleventh Engineers* 8 Veeder was our first top-kicker. **1843** J. BALLANTINE *Gaberlunzie's Wallet* ix. 199 The speck of sky overhead looked not larger than a common top-light or cupola. **1873** *Young Englishwoman* July 342/2 The top-lights were..removed..and whitewashing and painting were done. **1924** GALSWORTHY *White Monkey* II. ii. 131 A high room with rafters and a top light, and lots of pictures. **1972** P. DIAMAND in D. Sutton *Lett. R. Fry* I. 60 On the top floor was Roger's studio... It had a top light. **1911** W. J. LOCKE *Glory of Clementina Wing* xxiv. 374 The room, spacious and top-lighted, was converted into a studio. **1932** F. L. WRIGHT *Autobiogr.* II. 152 The top-lighted interior created the effect of a great official family at work in day-lit, clean airy quarters. **1962** *Times* 16 May 5/5 The great, top-lit room of the Whitechapel Gallery. **1979** *Jrnl. R. Soc. Arts* CXXVII. 655/1 The new galleries should be on the same level as the old and top-lit by natural light. **1968** *Which?* May 149/1 This machine is a top loader, but has a horizontal stainless steel drum—you have to lift the top lid before being able to open the doors of the wash drum. **1976** *Gramophone* Dec. 1084/3 Included in the 1977 Tandy catalogue..are..two new stereo cassette decks with Dolby—a front-loader.. and a top-loader. **1978** *Nature* 18 May p. xviii/3 The Sartorius 3802MP electronic balance is a toploader of large capacity and high readability. **1976** *CB Mag.* June 59/1 (Advt.), And top loading eliminates vehicle body obstructions, a common problem for base loaded antennas. **1884** *Bull. U.S. Nat. Museum* No. 27. 471 *Gambusia patruelis*..Top Minnow..Southern United States, from Virginia to Texas. **1962** K. F. LAGLER et al. *Ichthyology* vi. 180 The mouths are superior in most of the topminnows. **1900** *Billboard* 29 Dec. 8/1 The last is a top-notch figure, and it is reached no oftener than can be helped. **1928** *Amer. Speech* IV. 244 Some successful criminals escape getting a monicker, for they, especially top-notch con men and syndicate members, think it adds 'class' to be without one. **1912** *Music Hall & Theatre Rev.* 7 Mar. 157/1 The divided 'top' of the bill happens with these two artistes. **1933** P. GODFREY *Back-Stage* xviii. 222 The London theatre queues provide a great variety of performances. At the top of the bill are a few well-organized teams of strolling players. **1965** *Times Lit. Suppl.* 25 Nov. 1047/4 The..top-of-the-bill entertainer. **1963** *Economist* 19 Oct. 301/1 The top-of-the-line sporty version [of a car]. **1981** *Sci. Amer.* Feb. 4/1 (Advt.), The new, top-of-the-line HP 3000 Series 44 computer has up to double the throughput power and memory size of its predecessor. **1942** C. SPRY *Come into Garden, Cook* v. 51 Make a mixture of tomato sauce..and a little 'top of the milk' cream. **1958** *Listener* 21 Aug. 287/2 Serve hot or cold, with cream or top of the milk. **1979** A. PARKER *Country Recipe Notebk.* viii. 103 The milk..pasteurized..has no 'top of the milk'. **1960** J. FINGLETON *Four Chukkas to Australia* 29 Huntington..top-scored with 73. **1977** *World of Cricket Monthly* June 26/3 Mohsin Khan batted well to top-score with 55. **1860** *Baily's Mag.* Aug. 367 The top scorer for the Midland was Mr. J. H. Marshall. **1976** *Milton Keynes Express* 30 July 41/1 Arnold Mann was top scorer with a patient knock of 24. **1898** J. BOWE *Diary* 2 June in *With 13th Minnesota in Philippines* (1905) 12 The top sergeant went around with a lantern. **1969** I. KEMP *Brit. G.I. in Vietnam* vii. 150 My immediate superior was First (or Top) Sergeant Rutledge, a dour and somewhat autocratic professional soldier in his early forties. **1905** IHLSENG & WILSON *Man. Mining* (ed. 4) I. iii. 79 (*heading*) Top-slicing and caving. *Ibid.* (*caption*) A system of top-slicing the ore. **1963** *Economist* 23 Mar. 1141/2 Other taxpayers..deserve some form of relief by 'top-slicing'. **1973** L. J. THOMAS *Introd. Mining* vi. 209 Top slicing is more suitable for large horizontal deposits. *Ibid.*, Small pillars that could be top sliced are more likely to be recovered by cut and fill methods or to be abandoned. **1983** *Sunday Tel.* 5 June 28/7 If the recipient pays tax above the basic, 'top slicing' relief is provided to mitigate the effect of taxing the whole gain in one year. **1836, 1850** Top-soil [see *ENCALLOW *sb.*]. **1868, 1904** [in Dict. s.v. TOP *sb.*[1] 28]. **1967** *Antiquaries Jrnl.* XLVII. 188 In 1965 the stripping of the turf and topsoil from the rampart defences..exposed the top of the wall and an internal tower. **1975** J. G. EVANS *Environment Early Man Brit. Isles* vi. 128 Chalk waste bringing about the burial of topsoil and the destruction of what may have been valuable pasture or arable land. **1926** ANDERSON & STALLINGS *What Price Glory?* in *Three Amer. Plays* I. 10 I'm the new top soldier here. **1935** *Our Army* Nov. 39 Top Soldier Rawhide was sitting in the NCO club. **1913** *Daily Mail* 7 July 9/2 A good straight ball, with top spin, that comes off the ground very quickly. **1934** *Punch* 7 Feb. 141/1 She has thrown her husband out of the house sixty-one times, but he always returned. It looks as if she put too much top-spin on him. **1977** *Time* 4 July 10/3 Guillermo Vilas,..winner of the French Open last month, never could get his big topspin game going on grass. **1980** *Times Lit. Suppl.* 12 Sept. 983/5 Such existentialist propositions..sound pedestrian when summarized. The kind of intellectual top-spin required to give them philosophic solemnity is supplied. **1921** P. F. WARNER *My Cricketing Life* x. 194 A. R. Littlejohn..bowled an occasional top spinner which came very quickly off the ground. **1975** *Times* 13 Aug. 6/8 Intikhab..beat him with a top-spinner and hit his middle stump. **1969** *New Yorker* 14 June 44/3 He just can't hit a heavily top-spun backhand. **1977** *Sunday Times* (Perth, Austral.) 16 Jan. 11/4 The large crowd..reserved their warmest applause for some Wilkinson top-spun forehand lobs. **1960** *Lebende Sprachen* V. 35/3 *Top stitch*, Steppstich, steppen. **1964** *McCall's Sewing* vii. 100/2 Faced edges should be top-stitched to keep them flat. **1976** N. C. ANDERS *Appliqué Old & New* v. 104 Bind edge of each potholder with double fold bias tape. Cut two 2½" strips for loops. Topstitch edges. Attach to potholder. **1934** A. L. HIRD *Needlework & Dressmaking* v. 100 List of seams..plain lapped = top stitched. **1975** *New Yorker* 17 Nov. 138/2 Bottega Veneta has some splendid wrist-length styles..in topstitched pigskin. **1947** C. TALBOT *Compl. Bk. Sewing* xxi. 145/1 Top-stitching is the frank use of stitching on the outside of a dress, suit or coat to emphasize lines that are important in the design. **1979** *Tucson* (Arizona) *Citizen* 20 Sept. 2B/1 Remove any top-stitching to 4 inches above the 'new' hemline. **1964** *Guardian* 7 Oct. 10/1 (*heading*) At the top table in Washington. *a* **1974** R. CROSSMAN *Diaries* (1976) II. 125 We found ourselves at the top table. I was sitting opposite the Bishop of London and next to the wife of a City alderman. **1977** 'J. LE CARRÉ' *Hon. Schoolboy* I. viii. 191, I have a standing instruction..to repair our American liaison... 'To get us back at the top table.' **1983** *Daily Tel.* 1 Mar. 16/4 A late guest [at the St. David's Day banquet] will be Simon Hughes, Liberal victor of Bermondsey—too late to get a place on the top table. **1839** *Knickerbocker* XIII. 385 'There she top-tails! there she blows!' added he,..after taking a long look at the sporting shoal. **1958** J. ASMAN in P. Gammond *Decca Bk. Jazz* xiv. 174 Traditional jazz records vie with the accepted 'pop' Top Ten in selling power. **1960** *News Chron.* 7 May 3/5 Buxton will have to change..to make the tourist top ten. **1979** E. H. GOMBRICH *Ideas & Idols* 157 It [*sc.* a Beethoven Quartet] will never belong to the top ten. But it does belong to the canon. **1981** R. D. EDWARDS *Corridors of Death* v. 22 One of the country's top ten management whizz-kids. **1959** 'F. NEWTON' *Jazz Scene* (1960) xiii. 236 Jazz has until recently simply not been big business in Britain, in the terms in which those who prepare records for the 'hit parade' of the 'top ten' or 'top twenty' think of it. **1962** *Listener* 20 Sept. 451/3 TAM puts the repeats of *Steptoe and Son* in the top twenty week after week. **1982** *Daily Tel.* 15 Apr. 16/6 All we need now is a royal baby named George.., and the name may be back in the top 20 once more! **1895** T. S. LAWLEY *Lessons in Woodwork Drawing* 10 The top view of a penny..placed on a table will.be a circle. **1912** V. C. GETTY *How to Read a Drawing* i. 8 As we were..looking at the top of the object, this view would be known as the top view, or plan view. **1953** A. C. PARKINSON *Pictorial Drawing for Engineers* vi. 44/1 We commence by drawing a true-shape top view or plan view of the object. **1945** *Richmond* (Va.) *Times-Dispatch* 21 Sept. 18/2 It is well to try your top-water lures first, and if they fail, then try the under-water varieties. **1980** *Hunting Ann. 1981* 36/2 Rather than look for a long stick or get clothing and boots wet and muddy, the hunter can use a multihooked topwater lure and cast for his bird. **1883** *Maine Agric. Rep.* XXVI. 342 The Bourassa..does well top-worked on a strong stock, and then produces bountifully of apples. **1910** PADDOCK & WHIPPLE *Fruit-Growing in Arid Regions* ix. 150 It seldom pays to top-work any crab. **1968** *Punch* 27 Mar. 466/2 Though apples can be 'top worked' by grafting another kind on the sawn off branch ends, no peach will stand this treatment. **1934** WEBSTER, Top-worked. **1974** *Country Life* 28 Nov. 1660/1 Topworked trees, that is those which are grafted at the top of a standard stem and trunk. **1897** L. H. BAILEY *Princ. Fruit-Growing* v. 235 Some persons have proposed to sow seeds in the very spot where the trees are to stand, and thereby to raise stocks for top-working without transplanting them. **1946** *Nature* 28 Dec. 941/2 There is a particularly good chapter on top-working and frame-working, but that on pruning might have been improved.

top, *sb.*[2] Add: **4.** *top-spinning* sb. (examples), *-string* (example).

1964 *Catal. National Mus. Kuala Lumpur* 3/1 Dioramas present aspects of Malay dances, Kelantan top spinning, [etc.]. **1979** *Arizona Daily Star* 5 Aug. B 5/3 For relaxation, the brothers have taken up juggling, motocross bike-riding and top-spinning. **1855** MRS. GASKELL *Lizzie Leigh & Other Tales* 247 He had been the..Robin Goodfellow of the neighbourhood..whose top-strings were always hanging in nooses to catch the unwary.

top, *v.*[1] Add: **II. 3. b.** *to top and tail*, to wash the face and bottom of (a baby or small child); also *absol.*; hence *top-and-tail* attrib. phr. *colloq.*

1924 H. DE SÉLINCOURT *Cricket Match* ii. 22 She topped and tailed each small boy with the same rubber sponge. **1931** P. W. YEOMANS *Happy Motherhood* vii. 61, 5.50 to 6.20 p.m.—Top-and-tail wash, and feed baby. **1964** *Guardian* 24 June 6/2 Freda showed me how to top and tail (which is done on the lap because these babies do not get enough cuddling). **1983** *Woman's Weekly* 8 Jan. 53/3 There is no need to bath your new baby more than twice a week, 'topping and tailing' on the other days.

6. (Earlier example.) Also simply, to kill (someone); chiefly *refl.*, to commit suicide.

1718 C. HITCHIN *Regulator* in F. J. Lyons *Jonathan Wild* (1936) 238 He, being known to be an old practitioner, will certainly be *cast* and *top'd, alias* hang'd for the same. **1958** F. NORMAN *Bang to Rights* 30 He also took my tie and belt so that I could not top myself. **1961** [see *SLAG *sb.*[1] 4* (*b*)]. **1983** *Listener* 3 Feb. 18/3, I have to try and get a key to it all, otherwise I'll just top myself. **1984** M. LITCHFIELD *See how they Run* xvii. 157 That shooter..wasn't used to top Frost.

III. 11. For *Obs. rare* read *Obs.* exc. *U.S.* (Later example.)

1959 W. FAULKNER *Mansion* i. 14 My young bull topped her last week.

IV. 16. a. Freq. in phr. *to top the bill*: to be at the top of a bill of entertainment (*BILL *sb.*[3] 8 c); to be the star of a show. Also *fig.* and with the entertainment as object.

1910 WODEHOUSE *Psmith in City* 3 He is a man of hobbies... When I left the house this morning he was all for cricket... Cricket seems still to be topping the bill. **1933** P. GODFREY *Back-Stage* xiv. 179 The old favourites, when they still topped the bill, had to revise the material they had formerly worked. **1959** [see *BILL *sb.*[3] 8 c]. **1977** *Sounds* 9 July 4/4 Led Zeppelin remain favourites to top a one-day festival at Wrotham Park.

b. (Later examples in *U.S. Sport.*)

1951 *Amer. Speech* XXVI. 230/2 Dartmouth tops Harvard. **1974** *State* (Columbia, S. Carolina) 27 Feb. 3-B/1 The Panthers demolished both, topping Duquesne, 82–65, and trouncing Davidson in Charlotte, 90–63. **1979** *Tucson* (Arizona) *Citizen* 20 Sept. 8D/3 Boston topped Toronto, 8–0.

VI. Idiomatically combined with adverbs. (See also sense 9 in Dict. and Suppl.)

19. top off. a. *intr.* Of a ship, aircraft, etc.: to fill up or complete a cargo. Cf. sense 20 b below. *colloq.* (chiefly *U.S.*).

1937 G. S. DOORLY *In Wake* 22 A tramp steamer.. called in to the Gulf to top-off with sugar. **1950** *Sun* (Baltimore) 3 July 14/2 Ships go to other ports to 'top off'. **1961** *Aeroplane* C. 761/2 Since the passenger carriers ..'top-off' with cargo, it..seems fair and reasonable to permit the all-cargo carriers to carry cargo and to 'top-off' with passengers. **1978** H. WOUK *War & Remembrance* v. 46 We top off, take on provisions and torpedoes, and go.

b. *trans.* To fill up to the top (a tank already partly full) with fuel. *U.S. colloq.*

1943 F. J. BELL *Condition Red* 16 There'll be a fuel barge alongside some time tonight to top us off. **1953** C. A. LINDBERGH *Spirit of St. Louis* II. vi. 182 The fuel tanks would need topping off again. **1970** N. ARMSTRONG et al. *First on Moon* iii. 65 White streaks of vapor were emitted by the fuel tanks—which were constantly being 'topped off'. **1979** *Farmington* (New Mexico) *Daily Times* 27 May 3C/6 If everyone in New Mexico topped off their tank, that would use about 10 million gallons of gasoline.

c. *intr.* = *top out*, sense 20 c below.

1970 *Toronto Daily Star* 24 Sept. 4/2 If wage rates show signs of topping off, the Cabinet can face Parliament. **1976** *Survey* Spring 60 The progressive character of the scale tops off at 3 per cent of earnings for any income over 300 R/mo.

20. top out. a. *trans.* To put the finishing touch to (the roof of a building, etc.), freq. (in modern times) accompanied by some form of ceremony. *colloq.*

1834 W. SEWALL *Diary* 22 Dec. (1930) 160 Topped out house chimney, and went to saw mill. **1962** *Engineering* 16 Nov. 640 The dome was 'topped out' on 2 November. **1969** *Daily Tel.* 18 Apr. 27 (*caption*) Ald. Walter C. Dennis, Mayor of Lambeth, toasting the workmen..when the G.L.C.'s..Lambeth Walk development was 'topped out' yesterday. **1979** *Guardian* 25 July 3/2 Britain's most expensive new homes in Knightsbridge, London, were 'topped out' at a champagne reception yesterday.

b. Of a ship: to fill up or complete (its cargo). Also *absol.* Cf. sense 19 a above. *U.S. colloq.*

1940 *Sun* (Baltimore) 16 Apr. 24/6 Preparations were being made to tow her into the stream to 'top out' a 12,500-ton cargo. **1941** *Ibid.* 24 June 22/4 Every ship.. 'topped out' with scrap, if there was any room left.

c. *intr.* To reach a peak, to cease rising. Cf. sense 19 c above and *BOTTOM *v.* 4 c.

1972 *Sunday Tel.* 26 Mar. 30/4 Gilts now look as though they have topped out, and this is another sign that we are in the late stages of this bull market. **1972** *Guardian* 24 June 10/6 World population, he says, will probably top out at 10,000 millions sometime in the twenty-first century. **1979** *Sci. Amer.* Feb. 28/1 From the 10th century to the Mongol Wars, numbers rose, topping out in A.D. 1200.

21. top up. *trans.* **a.** To bring (something) up to its full capacity; to fill to the top (a partly full container, *spec.* (the cells of) a motor vehicle's battery). Used esp. with reference to a drinker's glass, freq. with the person as object. Occas. *absol.* and *transf.*

1937 *Times* 13 Apr. p. xxii/2 In order to help the owner-driver to look after his battery, a combined acid-level indicator, vent plug and filler cup has been introduced, thus enabling the cells to be 'topped up' accurately and visibly, without removing the vent plugs. **1946** *Happy Landings* July 12/1 Failure to..top-up brake pressure.. and to check the voltage readings of batteries, are common examples. **1958** *Times* 1 Mar. 6/3 Liquid oxygen..to top up its [*sc.* a missile's] fuel tanks. **1960** 'N. SHUTE' *Trustee from Toolroom* ix. 237 We'll need water, and top up with diesel fuel. **1965** *Listener* 18 Nov. 800/3 Tea is expensive.. so you economize by topping up your mug with hot water. **1969** 'R. PETRIE' in *E. Queen's Mystery Mag.* Mar. 33/1 Jim Morris tiptoed over to the sideboard for the bottle of brandy... Top him up, he told himself. **1971** 'E. FERRARS' *Stranger & Afraid* iii. 40 She..picked up the glass of sherry that she had started earlier. He said at once, 'Shall I top that up?' and..filled the glass to the brim. **1976** J. I. M. STEWART *Memorial Service* i. 14, I tried to teach him how to translate Tacitus, but had more success in topping him up with madeira. **1981** G. BOYCOTT *In Fast Lane* xi. 79 There was at least three feet of water in the main channel, constantly topped up by torrential showers.

b. *fig.*

1968 *Listener* 27 June 835/3 They..topped up the Welfare State with plenty of money for its more exquisite and bizarre excrescences. **1973** *Times* 20 Oct. 20/3 (*heading*) Topping up a mortgage with a loan from a life office. **1976** *Scotsman* 27 Dec. 1/2 It proposes a Scottish Assembly of 100 members... An Assembly member elected for each of the 71 parliamentary constituencies, 'topped up' by 29 additional members.

topaz. Add: **1. b.** The dark yellow colour of topaz.

1908 *Sears, Roebuck Catal.* 360/2 These colors are.. sapphire blue, emerald green, topaz, etc. **1942** W. FAULKNER *Go down, Moses* 237 A horse stands, blinking his sleepy topaz eyes at nothing. **1974** *Times* 2 Dec. (Wines & Spirits Suppl.) p. iii/5 Pale topaz with a gentle grapey aroma..it [*sc.* a wine] costs less than £12 a dozen.

top-boot. 1. (Earlier U.S. example.)

1768 J. R. PEYTON *Let.* 10 Apr. in J. L. Peyton *Adventures of my Grandfather* (1867) ii. 17, I found my heavy top-boots of immense service.

top-booted, *a.* (Earlier example.)

1829 G. GRIFFIN *Collegians* I. viii. 169 A stout top-booted elderly gentleman.

‖ **topchee** (tōu·ptʃī). Also 7 **topagee, toptchi,** 9 **topechee, topdji, topgi; topgey.** [Hind. *topcī*, Pers. *topchī*, Turk. *topçu* artilleryman, f. Pers., Turk. *top* gun, cannon.] A term used in the former Ottoman Empire for a gunner or artilleryman.

1623 in W. Foster *Eng. Factories India* (1908) 234 They delivered mee..into the hands of the Topagee. **1668** P. RYCAUT *Present State Ottoman Empire* III. x. 200 The Toptchi. These are Gunners, called so from the word *Tope*, which in Turkish signifies a Cannon. **1828** J. B. FRASER *Kuzzilbash* I. 337 The men..bore down like lightning on the topechees. **1854** R. CURZON *Armenia* 73 He brought four guns with him, and a number of topgis, or gunners, to work these instruments of destruction. **1892** P. L. SIMMONDS *Dict. Trade Products* (new ed.) Suppl. 502/1 *Topdjis*, militia artillerymen in Turkey. **1918** E. S. FARROW *Dict. Mil. Terms* 620 *Topgeys*, the term for Turkish artillerymen or gunners. Also written *topgis.*

top-dressing, *vbl. sb.* **a.** (Earlier example.)

1744 W. ELLIS *Mod. Husbandman* Mar. i. 7 The Top-dressing of a powdered Manure is far more preferable on this Account to the Top-dressing of Dung.

topectomy (tǫpe·ktŏmi). *Surg.* [f. TOP(O- + *-ECTOMY.] An operation in which specific areas are removed from the frontal lobe of the cerebral cortex as a treatment for mental illness.

1948 *Newsweek* 29 Mar. 47/3 In the new operation, called a topectomy, the brain fibers are not cut. **1967** [see *GYRECTOMY].

topgallant, *sb.* and *a.* Add: **B. 2.** *topgallant breeze* (earlier example).

1798 *Authentic Narrative Battle of Nile* 21 The wind was at this time N.N.W. and blew what Seamen call a Topgallant breeze.

top hat. Add: **1. b.** *transf.* A person of the kind or class that wears a top hat; an important or senior person (see also quot. 1938).

1936 *Amer. Speech* XI. 221 The ermines and top-hats, the carriage trade of the early part of the century. **1938** F. D. SHARPE *Sharpe of Flying Squad* xix. 209 It's no good here, boys, there are too many top-hats (detectives). **1974** *Globe & Mail* (Toronto) 4 Oct. 7/1 Mr. White brought Mr. Benoit along to the Albany Club, and the Tory party tophats liked what they saw.

2. *attrib.* **a.** With reference to the wearing of top hats. **b.** Shaped like a top hat.

1902 [in Dict.]. **1958** *Engineering* 14 Mar. 344/2 Shallow 'top-hat' sections are used for the horizontal rails. **1966** MRS. L. B. JOHNSON *White House Diary* 13 Dec. (1970) 461 Lyndon made a splendid toast. He said he wanted American art to be enjoyed at the grass-roots level, just as it is by the top-hat crowd. **1967** M. CHANDLER *Ceramics in Mod. World* ii. 83 (*caption*) A 'top-hat' kiln loaded for firing.

3. Passing into *adj.* Designating insurance or pension schemes devised as a means of deferred payment for senior executives.

1952 *Economist* 8 Nov. 417/1 'Top-hat' contracts for higher executives. **1964** *Daily Tel.* 16 Apr. 23/1 The annual check on senior executives under the 'top-hat scheme', because of the neurosis it created, was a pernicious plan. **1979** *Guardian* 18 June 10/4 It would be good to know that the company car, the top hat pension,.. will not survive the axe next spring.

top-heavy, *a.* Add: **c.** *fig.* Of a business, organization, etc.: (*a*) overcapitalized; (*b*) having a disproportionately large number of people in senior administrative positions.

1934 in WEBSTER. **1945** A. HUXLEY *Let.* 8 Aug. (1969) 531 A country with a decentralized..economy could not compete as a military power with countries having a top-heavy capital goods industry. **1962** *Rep. Comm. Broadcasting 1960* in *Parl. Papers 1961–2* (Cmnd. 1753) IX. 259 Some witnesses alleged..that the BBC was 'top-heavy': that is, it spent too much on administration at the expense of programme production. **1963** *Listener* 7 Mar. 417/1 Petty officials multiplied till the administration became top-heavy. **1976** M. MACHLIN *Pipeline* vi. 71 Even now his firm was top-heavy on distribution and transportation.

Hence **to·p-hea·vily** *adv.*; **top-heaviness** (earlier *fig.* example).

1843 H. JAMES *Let.* 11 May in R. B. Perry *Tht. & Char. W. James* (1935) I. 46 Thought heaped up to top-heaviness and inevitable lopsidedness. **1926** FOWLER *Mod Eng. Usage* 504/2 What reads well & what reads..jerkily, lopsidedly, topheavily, or otherwise badly. **1947** *Penguin New Writing* XXXI. 172 In the cottage gardens the crumpled, bunchy flowers of double daffodils waved top-heavily in the wind.

topi[2] (to·pi). [a. Mende.] A glossy dark brown antelope belonging to a race of the korrigum, *Damaliscus lunatus*, found in the coastal region of East Africa.

1894 SCLATER & THOMAS *Bk. Antelopes* I. 68 The 'Topi', as we propose to designate another local representative of the Korrigum, from the name given to it by the Swahili, has been known for some years. **1910** R. E. DRAKE-BROCKMAN *Mammals Somaliland* 59 The Topi Hartebeest ..is purplish brown. *Ibid.*, The Topi I have never seen in large herds. **1959** A. MOOREHEAD *No Room in Ark* iv. 91 The topi is a fairly mad animal.., a large brown gleaming antelope with gun-metal blazes on its legs and an air of continual stage-fright. **1976** K. THACKERAY *Crownbird* i. 9 They were now doing fifty..and overhauling the topi fast.

topic, *a.* and *sb.* Add: **B.** *sb.* **I. 3. b.** *Gram.* The part of a sentence which is marked as that on which the rest of the sentence makes a statement (comment), asks a question, etc.

Topic sometimes corresponds to *subject*, but the *topic/comment* contrast is not necessarily the same as that of *subject/predicate.*

1958 C. F. HOCKETT *Course in Mod. Linguistics* xxiii. 201 In English and the familiar languages of Europe, topics are usually also subjects, and comments are predicates. **1972** HARTMANN & STORK *Dict. Lang. & Linguistics* 239/1 Some languages, e.g. Japanese, have special particles to mark the topic of the sentence, and for such languages the topic/comment is a more satisfactory analysis than the subject/predicate division. **1976** *Archivum Linguisticum* VII. 123 'Topicalization'..will here be used to denote a process of both foregrounding of information..and selection of the 'topic' of information, that is a process which singles out certain elements in a sentence and makes them the 'topic' on which some 'comment' is made. **1979** *Canad. Jrnl. Linguistics* XXIV. I. 42 Topics are created by a rule of Topic Formation, and preposed by a rule of Topic Preposing.

III. *Comb.*, as (sense 3 b) *topic-neutral* adj.; **topic-(and-)comment,** (based on) the dichotomy in grammar of topic and comment.

1964 E. A. NIDA *Toward Sci. Transl.* iv. 66 It has been found that all languages seem to have something equivalent to subject-predicate constructions. These may in some instances be more aptly termed topic-comment, but essentially they are very similar from one language to another. **1978** *Language* LIV. 231 He [*sc.* R. Scollon] then suggests that topic-comment structures themselves may arise from discourse. **1979** *Amer. Speech 1978* LIII. 279, I think the basic type of openness in human language behavior is that of the topic-and-comment pattern. **1951** *Mind* LX. 541 There are..some forms of inference which can occur only in a restricted field of discourse... There are others, depending on the meaning of what Professor Ryle has called 'topic-neutral words', which can occur in the handling of any kind of subject matter. **1961** D. S. SHWAYDER *Modes of Referring* iii. 81 A distinguishing use may be more or less topic-neutral.

topical, *a.* (*sb.*) **B.** *sb.* Restrict † *Obs. rare*$^{-1}$ to sense in Dict. and add: **2.** A film dealing with topical events. (Now *disused.*)

1912 F. A. TALBOT *Moving Pictures* 123 This point of view is responsible for the apathetic American attitude toward the 'topical', as it is called in Great Britain. **1915** B. E. JONES *Cinematograph Bk.* 33 Something may here be said about topicals or 'newsy' films. **1917** C. N. BENNETT *Guide to Kinematogr.* 123 Fourpence or fivepence a foot will be the most a country showman will pay for a local topical. **1976** *Oxf. Compan. Film* 500/2 The early 'topicals' were very short, often less than a minute long, each dealing with a single event. The regular issue of newsreels in the conventional sense—several short items grouped under no general heading other than topicality—was begun by Pathé in 1908.

to·picalize, *v.* [f. TOPICAL *a.* + -IZE.] *trans.* To make into a grammatical topic. Usu. *pass.*

1970 *Language* XLVI. 375 In 47, *le tama* is topicalized out of the objective case. **1976** *Archivum Linguisticum* VII. 132 It must be some other quality inherent in *pay*, the 'abstract predication'.., or more precisely, the act, action, or activity, which is topicalized and appears on the surface as *-ment.* **1977** *Amer. Speech 1975* L. 71 One important aspect of this argument is that those proposing it..question the underlying verbal status of *have* and regard it instead as a surface form that serves to topicalize the possessor, which in other languages would be a locative or dative.

Hence **topicaliza·tion**; **to·picalized** *ppl. a.*

1967 *Foundations of Lang.* III. 47 Topicalization.. means that some major constituent of a sentence, such as a noun phrase, which is identical with (or has the same referent as) a constituent in the given sentence, may be generated before or after this sentence. **1970** *Language* XLVI. 375 Reversing the order of the two topicalized noun phrases is not possible; the sentence cannot be interpreted 'the girl loves the boy'. **1978** [see *preposing* vbl. sb. s.v. *PREPOSE *v.* 2 a]. **1980** *English World-Wide* I. 249 In the structure, only the plural marker, the locative copula, and the topicalized predicator were found to be of African origin. **1983** *Studies in Eng. Lit.: Eng. Number* (Tokyo) 158 Topicalization is a stylistic rule.

Topkhana (tōᵘ·pkā:nă). Also 7 **Tophana,** 8 **Tope Khonnah**; 9 **Tope Khâna**; **top-khana.** [a. Pers. and Hind., ad. Turk. *tophane* (also used), f. *top* (see *TOPCHEE) + Pers. *khāna* house.] **a.** In Turkey, a gun-factory or arsenal, *spec.* the gun-factories in Galata, Constantinople, during the Ottoman Empire; hence (the current sense) the district of Istanbul adjoining them. **b.** In India, artillery; ordnance department.

1656 W. JESSON *Let.* 4 Dec. in W. Foster *Eng. Factories in India 1618–69* (1921) X. 73 The King, being resolved to renue the warr against Candahor, dispeeded Cossom Ckawn..with the tobeconah [*tōp-khāna*, artillery] for Lahore. **1668** P. RYCAUT *Pres. State Ottoman Empire* 200 Their quarters are at Tophana, or the place of Guns in the Suburbs of Constantinople. **1765** J. Z. HOLWELL *Hist. Events* (1766) I. 96 By the treachery of the *Tope Khonnah Droger*, the cannon were loaded with powder only. **1842** C. MASSON *Baluchistan, Afghanistan & Panjab* II. 256 From the court of the Dafta Khâna the Tope Khâna, or artillery ground, is entered. **1901** KIPLING *Kim* iii. 67, I have known Him since he was a lieutenant in the *top-khana* (the Artillery). **1969** D. WALDER *Chanak Affair* xix. 350 An enormous Turkish flag floated over the Tophana naval depot. **1972** D. K. PALIT *Hist. Regiment of Artillery* i. 8 Although Shivaji had a regular department of *Topkhana*..he never had a foundry of his own. He managed to obtain some guns from the foundries at Surat..but by and large his *Topkhana* was described as a collection of 'old and defective' guns. **1974** J. F. GUILMARTIN *Gunpowder & Galleys* i. 44 The cannon foundries of the *Tophane* were directly dependent upon English tin which they could get only through Genoese entrepreneurs.

topknot. Add: **1. b.** Also *Austral.* and *N.Z.*, wool shorn from the top of the head of a sheep.

1950 *N.Z. Jrnl. Agric.* Oct. 313 (*caption*) Pick over lambs' wool. Pick out stained wool, face pieces, leggings, and top-knots. **1972** J. S. GUNN in G. W. Turner *Good Austral. Eng.* iii. 61 One thing I did notice about shearing was that two terms for the one idea sometimes shared popularity, for example *rouseabout/shedhand*,.. *topknot/wig*, [etc.].

Töpler (tə̄plǝɹ). *Physics.* Also **Toepler.** [The name of A. J. I. *Töpler* (1836–1912), German physicist, who invented the pump in 1862.] *Töpler* (or † *Töpler's*) *pump*: a pump in which the reservoir to be evacuated is connected by a glass tube containing a valve to a second reservoir, which in turn is connected by a flexible U-tube to a reservoir of mercury, so that lowering the last draws gas out of the first reservoir into the second and raising it expels gas from the second reservoir into the atmosphere. Also *absol.*

1883 *Encycl. Brit.* XVI. 31/1 In Töpler's pump this is attained by using..for the inlet and the outlet vertical capillary glass tubes. **1922** GLAZEBROOK *Dict. Appl. Physics* I. 8/1 The working of a Töpler by hand is extremely tedious, for several hours may be required to reach the limit of pressure. **1932** [see *SPRENGEL]. **1976** A. ROTH *Vacuum Technol.* v. 201 With the Toepler pump, pressures down to 10^{-6} Torr can be obtained, except the mercury vapour pressure which is about 10^{-3} Torr.

topless, *a.* Add: **3. a.** Designating or pertaining to a garment, esp. a (woman's) bathing-suit or dress, having little or no material above the waist; that does not cover the breasts and upper body.

1937 *Time* 21 June 53/1 With another bathing-suit season at hand, local lawmakers are aiming their ordinances at males on the score of topless suits rather than at underclad females. **1964** *San Francisco Chron.* 16 June 4/1 Saigis introduced San Francisco's first topless bathing suit for women. **1964** *Punch* 1 July 20/2 The topless look. **1964** *New Statesman* 24 July 116/1 A girl who wears a topless dress in the streets of Coventry or Nottingham could be doing as much for her sex as any Mrs Pankhurst. **1966** C. MACKENZIE *Paper Lives* xii. 166 And those topless dresses they're going in for now aren't nearly as topless as those dresses they were wearing about 1500 B.C. **1971** S. JEPSON *Let. to Dead Girl* xvii. 195 Her jeans were covered with dirt, and her shirt torn into topless decolleté. **1978** P. GLYNN *In Fashion* iv. 97 Rudi Gernreich's topless bathing suit had appeared in 1964.

b. Of a person (esp. a woman): naked or almost naked above the waist; bare-breasted.

1966 *Observer* 13 Nov. 2/8 The appearance of topless waitresses. **1968** 'R. RAINE' *Night of Hawk* xxvi. 125 Various acts, the main one being African girl dancers who perform topless. **1969** *Observer* 7 Dec. 25/3 Topless boys with shoulder-length hair pause as they cycle past you: 'Wanna buy some acid?' **1970** *Daily Progress* (Charlottesville, Va.) 29 May 19/5 (*heading*) Topless girl is acquitted. **1981** *Birds* Summer 55/2 New reserve records included nude female bathers on Loch Garten, a 'topless' woman picking blackberries, [etc.].

c. Applied to a place or area in which women are permitted to appear naked above the waist; esp. of bars, etc., employing bare-breasted waitresses or dancers, and of beaches at which women sunbathe topless. Hence also of entertainments, sunbathing, etc., so conducted.

1967 F. WARNER *Madrigals* 30 Draining down screwdrivers in topless Broadway. **1970** G. R. TAYLOR *Doomsday Bk.* x. 246 Fairbanks has become a boom-town with topless entertainment in the bars and saloons. **1972** G. BAXT *Burning Sappho* ii. 41 For Chrissakes not one of them topless joints. Who wants flabby tits hanging over my shrimp cocktail. **1976** P. CAVE *High Flying Birds* iii. 36 This section of the beach was strictly topless. **1978** *N.Y. Times* 30 Mar. B 2/4 He has campaigned against marijuana decriminalization, 'topless' bars, [etc.]. **1979** *Globe & Mail* (Toronto) 26 Jan. 5 Toronto City Council probably will move on Feb. 5 to restrict new bars offering topless or nude entertainment. **1983** *Times* 6 July 32/1 Topless sunbathing is a well-established practice on a great many British beaches.

Hence **to·plessness,** the condition of being topless (sense 3).

1964 *Punch* 22 July 117/3 His pronouncement on toplessness. **1982** C. CASTLE *Folies Bergère* iii. 127 Today, the question of toplessness..evokes little excitement in an age of naked beaches.

top level. orig. *U.S.* [f. TOP *sb.*[1] + LEVEL *sb.*] The highest degree of importance, prestige, or ability; usu. (with hyphen) *attrib.*, designating that which belongs to or takes place at such a level.

1951 *Sci. Amer.* Sept. 43/2 The story is even less favorable when we examine what proportion of able people obtain the Ph.D. degree—today a requirement for many of our top-level intellectual occupations. **1952** *Times* 29 Jan. 3/2 It is estimated by the assistant director of public relations at American University that 'there must be more than 150 ghost writers at the top level in Washington alone'. **1955** *Times* 16 May 4/1 No one can say for certain that the results of a top-level meeting will fulfil our hopes. **1956** WALLIS & BLAIR *Thunder Above* (1959) xii. 116 They'll probably engage you..as a top-level consultant. **1957** *Ann. Reg. 1956* 23 It was announced that a meeting 'at top level' between union officials and the management of Standard Motors had been arranged for 13 May. **1967** C. BERNERS-LEE in Wills & Yearsley *Handbk. Management Technol.* 15 In due course [a really good technical salesman] will find himself inundated with as much top-level work as he can cope with. **1969** *Daily Tel.* 17 Dec. 2/6 Top-level talks to discuss the threatened unofficial strike at 63 power stations..are being held..between employers and unions. *a* **1974** R. CROSSMAN *Diaries* (1976) II. 125 This Lord Mayor's dinner was the first top-level invitation which Anne and I have accepted since I was a Minister. **1979** *Yale Alumni Mag.* Apr. 8/2 The desire to watch top-level squash competition has also increased.

top line. [f. TOP *sb.*[1] + LINE *sb.*[2]] **1.** (In Dict. s.v. TOP *sb.*[1] 32.)

2. The head item on a bill of entertainment; the headline of a newspaper; freq. (with hyphen) *attrib.*; also *fig.*

1906 *N.Y. Times* 6 May IV. 2/1 The rumor of a new $30,000,000 vaudeville act—a regular 'top-line' combination—has been giving Broadway a good deal to talk about. **1922** A. HADDON *Green Room Gossip* vi. 138 His..duets with Miss Muriel George have reached a top-line position on the halls. **1928** *Boston Even. Transcript* 30 Mar. 15/6 This big 'top line' caught my eye: 'The Pocasset filicide.' **1928** *Daily Express* 31 July 13/7 The top-line contest on Saturday next is that between Jack Stanley of Deptford and Gipsey Daniels. **1947** [see *CARE *v.* 4 a]. **1958** *New Statesman* 23 Aug. 211/3 The *Daily Mail* has recently been the most persistent in putting news first in its public appeal and in tying its 'top line' features much more closely to it than most. **1981** B. HEALEY *Last Ferry from Lido* i. 17 A real, top-line Venetian socialite.

3. *on the top line*: in the highest state of perfection, readiness, etc. *slang* (orig. Naval). Phr. *to sweat on the top line*: see *SWEAT *v.* 9* c.

1916 'TAFFRAIL' *Pincher Martin* ix. 155 I've 'eard tell, too, that that there Kayser bloke o' theirs 'as gingered 'em up somethin' cruel, an' a navy wot's been gingered up must be on th' top line same as us, mustn't it? **1942** *Tee Emm* (Air Ministry) II. 81 There are a lot of ways of navigating these days; you ought to be on the top line in them all. **1958** *Punch* 9 July 57/3 The famous scene in which he has to serve both his masters with dinner at the same moment becomes a juggling turn on the top line. **1972** *Times* 30 Nov. 17/4 It cannot be but harmful to the patient to be attended by a doctor who through sheer exhaustion is not on the top line.

4. *Mus.* In music divided into four parts for singing, the highest (usu. soprano) line.

1965 *Listener* 1 July 33/3 The top line could be sung by sopranos and altos in unison, while the baritones..could dodge from the bass line to the tenor line. **1968** E. R. BUCKLER *Ox Bells & Fireflies* iv. 73 We sang—with the teacher always taking what was known as 'top line'.

Hence **top-li·ner,** one who or that which appears in the top line, or in the first or principal place.

1901 *Munsey's Mag.* Nov. 247/1 Grand opera in this and other countries sadly needs a new bright particular star, a 'top liner', as they say in the music halls. **1901** *Daily Colonist* (Victoria, B.C.) 1 Nov. 3/1 One of the four schooners which returned to port yesterday morning was the top-liner of the fleet, the Otto. **1928** *Daily Express* 19 June 16/1 Every Ascot race is a top-liner. **1950** *Sport* 7–11 Apr. 9/1 For months past people have been trying to grab tickets for this match, which is always a top-liner. **1970** *Daily Tel.* 29 Apr. 13/1 On the club circuit there are top-liners..making up to £400 a week. **1982** R. HILL *Who guards a Prince* IV. vi. 227 A journalist..a top-liner as well as an old friend.

topman[1]. Add: **4. c.** (See quot. 1964.)

1961 *Evening Standard* 3 Aug. 21/4 (Advt.), Topmen reqd. for demolition trade. **1962** PARKER & ALLERTON *Courage of his Convictions* i. 22 He's a top man, and don't you forget it... When derelict buildings were being knocked down he was one of those on the roof. **1964** J. S. SCOTT *Dict. Building* 94 *Demolisher* or *mattock man* or *topman* or *housebreaker*, a skilled man who pulls down a wall by standing on top of it and breaking pieces off below him, or by pulling a loose wall with a winch and rope, or by means of a concrete breaker. **1973** *Daily Tel.* 7 Mar. 13/2 Pulling down the YMCA dome, 120ft. or about 15 storeys high, had to begin with a topman..picking away with mattock.

topo, U.S. colloq. abbrev. of TOPOGRAPHIC *a.* Also *ellipt.* for 'topographic map'.

1970 N. ARMSTRONG et al. *First on Moon* xi. 256 The best we can do on topo features is to advise you to look to the west of the irregularly shaped crater. **1977** *Chicago Tribune* 2 Oct. III. 10/3 'Topos' show land contours, elevations, marshes, lakes, streams. **1979** *Amer. Alpine Jrnl.* XXII. I. 35 Japan's foremost mountain magazine.. contains..valuable maps, diagrams and topos with English captions. **1981** *Northeast Woods & Waters* Jan. 16/2 You can buy topos most anywhere in Maine, but they are dated and won't show all the logging roads built in the past 25 years.

topo-. Add: **topoce·ntric** *Astronautics*, (of a parameter of a spacecraft or an orbit) measured relative to a point on the earth's surface (rather than its centre); **to·pocline** [*CLINE *sb.*], a cline associated with variations in the locality of the species concerned; **topo·genous** *a.*, formed as the result of a combination of geographical features; **to:po,inhibi·tion** *Biol.*, the inhibition of cell multiplication by contact with other cells; **topo,iso·merase** *Biochem.*, any enzyme that alters the supercoiled form of a DNA molecule.

1965 P. R. ESCOBAL *Methods Orbit Determination* vii. 241 The topocentric right ascension-declination of the unknown orbit at the three times..can be obtained as follows. **1976** *Sci. Amer.* June 70/2 Since the tracking stations are on the earth's surface, the direct measurements they provide of the spacecraft's radial parameters (range, velocity and acceleration) are topocentric rather than geocentric. **1939** J. W. GREGOR in *New Phytologist* XXXVIII. 317 Prefixes can be used to denote clines of different types, for example topocline. **1953** J. HESLOP-HARRISON *New Concepts Flowering-Plant Taxon.* v. 68 Independent topoclines exist for different morphological features. **1970** *Watsonia* VIII. 140 The two subspecies may be regarded as the relatively extreme end-points of a topocline. **1939** A. G. TANSLEY *Brit. Islands & their Vegetation* xxxv. 719 Valley bog—topogenous, formed in valleys and depressions where water..stagnates, and bog plants establish themselves. **1975** J. G. EVANS *Environment Early Man Brit. Isles* iv. 76 Essentially there are two types of peat, topogenous and ombrogenous. Topogenous peat forms in places of impeded drainage. **1970** *Nature* 22 Aug. 806/1 Topoinhibition is probably an important mechanism regulating cell multiplication in organisms in normal conditions. **1975** *Ibid.* 29 May 371/3 The loss of topoinhibition at wound edges in culture is apparently not due to loss of junctional communication. **1978** *Devel. Biol.* LXIV. 273/2 The enzyme has been referred to as ω-protein.., swivelase.., untwisting enzyme.., relaxing activity.., relaxing protein.., nicking-closing activity.., and DNA topoisomerase. **1979** WANG & LIU in J. H. Taylor *Molecular Genetics* III. ii. 66 We propose that they be called DNA topoisomerases. **1980** *Sci. Amer.* July 109/2 These nicking-closing enzymes, which are also called topoisomerases, generally require no energy source to function.

topochemical (tǫpoke·mikăl), *a.* [f. TOPO- + CHEMICAL *a.*] **1.** *Ent.* Of, pertaining to, or denoting an insect's capacity to perceive spatial relationships through the sense of smell (see quots.).

1908 M. YEARSLEY tr. *A. Forel's Senses of Insects* x. 237 It is..a question of a chemical sense which gives the exact relations between the different parts of space... The faculty of smell-by-contact could be called chemaphesthesia and relational smell topochemical sense. **1967** J. H. SUDD *Introd. Behaviour Ants* ii. 17 Because the antennae are moveable and have sense organs all over the surface it has been suggested that ants can perceive spatial arrangements of chemical stimuli, rather as we can perceive patterns of colour or texture. This is the so-called topochemical sense.

2. *Chem.* [ad. G. *topochemisch* (Kohlschütter & Tüscher 1920, in *Zeitschr. f. anorg. u. allgemeine Chem.* CXI. 193).] Of or pertaining to topochemistry.

1920 *Chem. Abstr.* XIV. 3202 The term topochemical is proposed as a designation of 'locally confined' reactions. **1945** *Electronic Engin.* XVII. 425 Not only pressure and quality of the gas play an important part in vacuum measurement but also its quantity... It may be altered by 'topophysical' or 'topochemical' effects. **1948** *Research* I. 262/2 The topochemical significance is that corrosion is almost always an electrochemical process, in which the anodic localities of corrosion are small surface elements. **1967** [see *BIOGENESIS 3].

Hence **topoche·mically** *adv.*

1962 *Jrnl. Physical Chem.* LXVI. 2442/1 Photochromy in this series is a topochemically determined phenomenon, *i.e.*,..the packing arrangement in the crystal is of importance. **1967** *Science* 26 May 1123/2 When the construction [of the termites] reaches a certain critical density it attracts other termites topochemically.

topochemistry (tǫpoke·mistri). [f. TOPO- + CHEMISTRY.] The chemistry of reactions as affected by local variations in the structure of the medium on or in which they occur.

1948 *Research* I. 260/2 Topochemistry, derived from the Greek τόπος meaning 'location',..and topochemical processes are localized reactions in every sense. **1971** *Nature* 16 July 194/1 We have demonstrated a new method for the study of the topochemistry of membrane surfaces. **1975** *Ibid.* 31 Jan. 310/3 Topochemistry is concerned with the nature and kinetics of chemical reactions, including polymerisation reactions, between adjacent molecules in crystals.

to·p-off, *sb. Austral. slang.* [Of obscure origin: cf. TOP *v.*[1] 6 and *TIP *v.*[5] 2.] An informer. Also *top-off merchant* (*MERCHANT *sb.* 3).

1941 BAKER *Dict. Austral. Slang* 77 *Top-off*, a police informer. **1944** L. GLASSOP *We were Rats* 133 He pooled me with the Q.M. Just a top-off merchant, that's all he is. **1966** B. COLLINS *Copper Crucible* 14 About four o'clock in the morning some top-off rings the cops. **1973** *Sunday Mail* (Brisbane) 4 Mar. 4/2 He believed him to be a prison 'top-off'.

to·p-off, *a.* [f. the vbl. phr. *to top off*: see *TOP *v.*[1] 19 a.] Of a passenger: carried in a freight aircraft that would not otherwise be full.

1961 *Flight* CXXX. 864/2 Seaboard World Airlines is continuing to press hard its proposal to carry 'top-off' passengers on its..cargo flights across the Atlantic. *Ibid.*, 'Top-off' passengers would..afford the necessary extra revenues without interfering with the basic objective of profitable transatlantic freight services. **1962** *Aeroplane* CIII. 5/3 Application to carry 'top-off' passengers on scheduled cargo flights to be rejected.

topograph. Restrict *rare* to senses in Dict. and add: **2.** *Cryst.* A photograph taken in such a way, usu. with X-rays, as to exhibit the variation over the surface of a crystal of some physical or structural characteristic.

1944 G. N. RAMACHANDRAN in *Proc. Indian Acad. Sci.* A. XIX. 292 Eighteen such 'topographs' of cleavage plates of diamond..are reproduced. **1963** G. L. CLARK *Encycl. X-Rays & Gamma Rays* 1053/2 Topographs may be taken that show, for example, the distribution of optical absorption or optical fluorescence in a specimen. **1971** *Physics Bull.* Sept. 553/2 X ray topographs..were used by many authors to assess accurately the quality of their crystals.

topographize, *v.* **b.** (Earlier example.)

1792 W. B. STEVENS *Jrnl.* 30 May (1965) 25 Shaw was topographising around Shenstone Church.

topoi: see *TOPOS.

topological, *a.* (In Dict. s.v. TOPOLOGY.) Add: **2.** *Math.* Of or pertaining to topology; such as is dealt with by topology; *topological invariant*, something invariant under a topological mapping; *topological mapping* or *transformation* = *HOMŒOMORPHISM 2; *topological space* [tr. G. *topologisch raum* (F. Hausdorff *Grundzüge der Mengenlehre* (1914) vii. 213); the sense is due to M. Fréchet (*Compt. Rend.* (1925) CLXXX. 421)], an abstract space together with a topology (sense *3 c) on it.

1913 *Amer. Jrnl. Math.* XXXV. 189 (*heading*) On some topological properties of plane curves and a theorem of Möbius. **1926** *Proc. Sect. Sci. K. Akad. van Wetenschappen te Amsterdam* XXIX. 462 Any normal, not absolutely closed topological space $\mathscr{R}$ can be extended to a normal topological space $R = \mathscr{R} + \xi$ by adjunction of a non isolated point ξ. **1939** M. H. A. NEWMAN *Elem. Topol. Plane Sets of Points* iii. 51 The correlation is called a homoeomorphism between the spaces, or a topological mapping of the one space on the other. **1946** E. LEHMER tr. *Pontryagin's Topological Groups* iii. 53 For any two elements p and q of the group G there exists a topological transformation $f(x)$ of the space G into itself which transforms p into q. **1956** [see *HOMŒOMORPHISM 2]. **1961** A. E. FARLEY tr. *Alexandroff's Elem. Concepts Topology* 16 A simple closed curve (i.e., the topological image of a circle). **1968** E. T. COPSON *Metric Spaces* vii. 92 Properties of a metric space which depend only on its open sets..are called topological properties. **1975** I. STEWART *Concepts Mod. Math.* x. 144 Straightness is not a topological property.

topologize (tǒpǫ·lǒdʒəiz), *v. Math.* [f. TOPOLOG(ICAL *a.* + -IZE.] *trans.* To make into a topological space. So **topo·logized** *ppl. a.*; **topo:logiza·tion,** the process of topologizing.

1946 E. LEHMER tr. *Pontryagin's Topological Groups* iii. 56 The abstract group G admits one and only one topologization under which the system Σ^* is a complete system of neighborhoods of the identity. *Ibid.*, If the group G can be topologized in such a way that [etc.]. **1963** D. BUSHAW *Elem. Gen. Topol.* ii. 29 It is no great step to convert each of these methods of topologization into an alternative definition of the concept of a topological space. **1964** A. P. & W. ROBERTSON *Topological Vector Spaces* i. 8 The real numbers and the complex numbers can both be topologised by taking $d(x, y) = |x-y|$. **1979** *Proc. London Math. Soc.* XXXVIII. 231 For any closed subspace S of ER^n; we topologize the space of continuous maps of S into ER^n with the compact open topology.

topology. For **1. c.** read **3. a.** and add: **3. a.** The branch of mathematics concerned with those properties of figures and surface which are independent of size and shape and are unchanged by any deformation that is continuous, neither creating new points nor fusing existing ones; hence, with those of abstract spaces that are invariant under homœomorphic transformations. (Further examples.) [ad. G. *topologie* (J. B. Listing 1847, in *Göttinger Studien* I. 814).]

1929 *Trans. Amer. Math. Soc.* XXXI. 290 Analysis situs or topology is primarily concerned with invariants under homeomorphic transformations of a space into itself. **1952** F. BAGEMIHL et al. tr. *Pontryagin's Found. Combinatorial Topol.* i. 1 Combinatorial topology studies geometric forms by decomposing them into the simplest geometric figures, simplexes, which adjoin one another in a regular fashion. **1959** E. M. PATTERSON *Topology* i. 1 Nowadays mathematicians are in fairly general agreement that topology is a study of continuity. **1970** *Observer* (Colour Suppl.) 15 Feb. 19/2 Topology is one of the most recent and rapidly advancing branches of mathematics, and is a kind of universal geometry of surfaces. **1972** M. KLINE *Math. Thought* l. 1158 Topology, as it is understood in this century, breaks down into two somewhat separate divisions: point set topology, which is concerned with geometrical figures regarded as collections of points ..; and combinatorial or algebraic topology, which treats geometrical figures as aggregates of smaller building blocks. **1975** I. STEWART *Concepts Mod. Math.* x. 146 The basic objects studied in topology are called topological spaces.

b. (The study of) the topological properties of something. Also *transf.*

1913 *Amer. Jrnl. Math.* XXXV. 189 An application.. of the transformation by inversion to the topology of plane curves. **1930** *Proc. Nat. Acad. Sci.* XVI. 240 (*heading*) Combinatory topology of convex regions. **1959** *Ibid.* XLV. 1607 (*heading*) On the topology of the genetic fine structure. **1972** *Sci. Amer.* Jan. 65/1 With careful dissection techniques one can expose deep-lying sections of bulk specimens so that their topology can be studied by scanning electron microscopy. **1980** D. L. COHN *Measure Theory* p. vii, Chapters 1 through 5..presuppose only the familiarity with the topology of Euclidean spaces that a student should acquire in an advanced calculus course.

c. A family of open subsets of an abstract space such that the union of any of the subsets and the intersection of any two of them are members of the family, together with the space itself and the null set.

1946 E. LEHMER tr. *Pontryagin's Topological Groups* iii. 55 A topology can be introduced into any abstract group G whatsoever in such a way that G becomes a discrete group. **1963** M. J. MANSFIELD *Introd. Topol.* ii. 21 The topologies $\mathscr{S}$ and $\mathscr{U}$ for R..were defined, in effect by specifying neighborhoods for each point and then declaring a set to be a member of the topology if and only if the set contains a neighborhood of each of its points. **1976** *Physics Bull.* Sept. 388/2 A useful way to think of a topology for a space is as a specification of which functions on it are to be continuous.

d. *gen.* The way in which constituent parts are interrelated or arranged.

1967 *Electronics* 6 Mar. 149/1 If consideration is restricted to bipolar gate topologies..there are just three basic forms of IC logic schemes. **1970** *Nature* 7 Nov. 553/1 These data have been used to construct a topology based on the minimal mutation distance method... This topology places castor..closest to sesame.., then mung bean .., then sunflower. **1971** *Physics Bull.* Dec. 717/3 Having an axisymmetric topology permits an easier study [of tokamaks] than, say, stellarators. **1972** *Computer Jrnl.* XV. 204/1 The resulting list structure has the same topology as the old, so that re-entrancy and sharing of common substructure are preserved.

topologically *adv.*, **topologist** (examples in *Math.*).

1915 *Trans. Amer. Math. Soc.* XVI. 153 A manifold.. topologically equivalent to the boundary of an n-dimensional complex. **1938** *Mind* XLVII. 126 Tests are gauged 'topologically' by the extent to which they succeed in grouping together men who are also grouped together in respect of their performances in life. **1954** *Sci. News* XXXIII. 56 If you cross the curve..you must go from one part to another—you cannot stay inside or stay outside. I think that anyone who is not a topologist will accept this as a self-evident fact. **1967** G. STEINER *Lang. & Silence* 33, I have watched topologists, knowing no syllable of each other's language, working effectively together at a blackboard. **1969** R. B. FULLER *Operating Man. Spaceship Earth* v. 67 All the system's paths must be topologically and circularly interrelated. **1971** I. G. GASS et al. *Understanding Earth* iv. 77/1 It is not what the topologists call a simply connected body; it is like a Henry Moore statue: it has a hole in it. **1975** I. STEWART *Concepts Mod. Math.* x. 146 The oft-quoted assertion that to a topologist a doughnut is the same as a coffee-cup provides an example. *Ibid.* 156 Now topologically a dog is a sphere (assuming it keeps its mouth shut and neglecting internal organs) because all we have to do is shrink its legs and fatten it up a bit.

toponium (tǫpō͞u·niŏm). *Particle Physics.* [f. TOP *sb.*[1] + *-ONIUM, after *POSITRONIUM.] A bound state of a top quark and a top antiquark.

1978 *Nature* 28 Sept. 268/2 This gives the prospect of detailed investigation of quark dynamics by studying transitions among these levels of 'toponium' analogous to transitions among levels of positronium and hydrogen in atomic physics. **1984** *New Scientist* 17 May 15/1 Theory suggests that if there is an electrically neutral Higgs boson whose mass is less than that of toponium, then we should be able to observe toponium decaying into a photon and a Higgs.

toponomastic (tǫpǫnomæ·stik), *sb.* and *a.* [f. TOPO- + ONOMASTIC *a.* and *sb.*] **A.** *sb.* (also *pl.*) = TOPONYMY. **B.** *adj.* Of or pertaining to place-names.

1916 T. TAYLOR *Celtic Christianity of Cornwall* iv. 54 Professor Loth, as the result of a careful study of Breton toponomastic, has arrived at the conclusion that the Armorican parishes were placed as early as the sixth and seventh century under the invocation of the saints.. whose names they still bear. **1922** JOYCE *Ulysses* 673 Their..toponomastic, historical and religious literatures. **1971** W. F. H. NICOLAISEN in A. J. Aitken et al. *Edin. Stud. Eng. & Scots* 211 There is no basic difference in the proper handling of the Scottish toponomastic material in this respect. **1977** *Maledicta* I. 41 (*heading*) Macedonian toponomastics.

toponym. (in Dict. s.v. TOPONYMY.) Add: **2. a.** A place-name; a name given to a person or thing marking its place of origin. **b.** = *TOPONYMIC *sb.* 2.

1939 *Antiquity* Sept. 311 Important also are certain long lists of personal names followed by those of the cities from which these persons came... The toponyms include Byblus (*G-b-'l*, the *Gebal* of the Old Testament). **1958** [see *ANTHROPONYMY]. **1973** *Times Lit. Suppl.* 5 Jan. 3/3 *The Manchester Guardian* (before it dropped the toponym). **1978** *Regional Lang. Stud.—Newfoundland* VIII. 3 The surname of the original author of this list, Jeddore, occurs as a toponym in Nova Scotia, and.. Jeddore's Harbour is about 40 miles east of Halifax. **1980** *Sci. Amer.* Feb. 48/1 The Zapotec people also used toponyms, glyphic 'place signs' for important places or landmarks, mountains in particular.

toponymic, *sb.* (In Dict. s.v. TOPONYMY.) Add: **2.** A descriptive place-name, usu. derived from some topographical feature of the place.

1933 *Times Lit. Suppl.* 20 Apr. 280/2 With a few.. exceptions..all Sussex place-names..ought to be explained as toponymics, i.e., as containing descriptive words. **1956** A. H. SMITH *Eng. Place-Name Elements* I. 6 Village names which were originally toponymics. **1957** H. H. JENKINS *Diction of 'Yank'* (Univ. Florida thesis) v. 45 Some of the GI's toponymics are banal and unimaginative; others are witty and colorful. **1977** *Word* 1972 XXVIII. 117 (*heading*) Celtic toponymics in Scotland.

topos (tǫ·pǫs). Pl. **topoi.** [a. Gr. τόπος place: cf. etym. note s.v. TOPIC *a.* and *sb.*] A traditional motif or theme (in a literary composition); a rhetorical commonplace, a literary convention or formula.

1948 L. SPITZER *Linguistics & Lit. Hist.* v. 201 In a proem there is generally present a second topos. **1957** N. FRYE *Anatomy of Criticism* 103 The *topoi* or rhetorical commonplaces..are so dull when stated as propositions, and so rich and variegated when they are used as structural principles in literature. **1957** *Medium Ævum* XXVI. 148 We have identified the *topos* of the sixth age of the world (and its approaching end) in our two OE poems. **1962** D. A. PEARSALL *Floure & Leafe* 68 The submission formula is a *topos* of classical rhetoric. **1966** *Eng. Stud.* XLVII. 150 There must be few literary historians who have traced with such thoroughness the development of a single *topos* through two centuries. **1976** *Classical Q.* XXVI. 246 Kinds of anecdotes which Herodotus loved to include: raiding parties, espionage.., tales of bravery and cowardice, and other such *topoi*. **1981** *Times Lit. Suppl.* 16 Jan. 60/4 It is a common *topos* to remark that thanks are due to the editor or author for raising weighty questions.

toposcope (tǫ·poskō͞up). [f. TOPO- + -SCOPE.] **1.** A device (as a horizontal circular dial) showing the direction of designated features of the landscape and usu. erected on a hilltop.

1907 [see *INDICATOR 1 a]. **1968** V. WAITE *Malvern Country* vi. 77 The direction indicator—or toposcope, to give it the technical name—was set up on the Beacon summit to commemorate the reign of Queen Victoria. **1974** *Victorian* (Victoria, B.C.) 22 Mar. 45/3 Nearby is a panoramic viewing area with a toposcope, giving details of all the islands dotted around in the sparkling blue China Sea 1,800 feet below.

2. *Med.* An instrument used for toposcopy.

1951 WALTER & SHIPTON in *Electroencephalogr. & Clin. Neurophysiol.* III. 282/2 Because it provided a visual display of topographic detail this device was called a Toposcope. **1965** *Math. in Biol. & Med.* (Med. Res. Council) IV. 159 The 'toposcope'..depicts each EEG electrode as a spot on a cathode ray tube. **1977** *Lancet* 21 May 1114/1 He devised the first on-line frequency analyser, which with subsequent modifications led to the 'toposcope'.

toposcopy (tǒpǫ·skǒpi). *Med.* [f. as prec. + -Y³.] Examination of the electrical activity at different points in the brain simultaneously by means of a number of electrodes each connected to a separate oscilloscope or the like. Hence **toposco·pic** *a.*

1950 *Electroencephalogr. & Clin. Neurophysiol.* II. 97/2 The split disc neon lamp method of toposcopy is particularly attractive. **1951** *Ibid.* III. 283/1 The mark I Toposcope was too limited in its resolution, but the results obtained with it were sufficiently encouraging to warrant the initiation of a development programme with the aim of investigating the general problem of toposcopic display. **1974** *Ibid.* XXXVI. 566/2 (*heading*) Current thoughts on toposcopy. *Ibid.*, Many of the toposcopic display devices used in EEG are products of the age of analog computers and devices.

topotaxy (tǫ·potæksi). *Cryst.* [f. TOPO- + *-taxy*, after *EPITAXY.] (See quot. 1959³.) So **topota·ctic, -ical** *adjs.*; **topota·ctically** *adv.*

1959 F. K. LOTGERING in *Jrnl. Inorganic & Nucl. Chem.* IX. 115 For these reactions the name 'topotactical reactions'..is proposed. *Ibid.* Plate facing p. 120 Photomicrographs of topotactically oriented $Co_{0\cdot5}Zn_{0\cdot1}Z$. *Ibid.* 123 We propose the term 'topotaxy' for all chemical solid state reactions that lead to a material with crystal orientations which are correlated with crystal orientations in the initial product [*read* substance]. **1969** *Nature* 9 Aug. 609/1 Studies of the topotaxy of solid state precipitation from spinel crystalline solutions. **1976** *Ibid.* 19 Aug. 721/1 Dislocations in molecular crystals..have been studied on the microscale chiefly with a view to establishing their role in..topotactic transformations. **1982** *Ibid.* 22 Apr. 730/1 (*caption*) Electron micrograph of a fault-free β-phase grain, topotactically replacing faulted ringwoodite.

top people, *sb. pl.* Also with capital initials. [TOP *sb.*¹ 29.] The aristocracy; leaders and people of rank and influence in the arts, politics, the professions, etc. Occas. *sing.* as *top person.*

The expression gained wide currency from the advertising slogan used by *The Times* in 1957.

1752 in M. M. Verney *Verney Lett.* (1930) II. xxxiv. 250 When they get in liquor they are very troublesome and noisy. They kept it up all night, several of the top people. **1957** *Economist* 21 Sept. 929/3 Like the *Times*, it [sc. *Punch*] has been read by top people for a long time. **1959** C. MACINNES *Absolute Beginners* 103 He had a very sharp top-person suit on. **1960** *Sunday Times* 21 Feb. 9/5 (Advt.), The man who gets on is he who makes himself bigger than his job... Top People take *The Times.* **1963** *Punch* 4 Sept. 356/2 Southerners, satiated with Top People prissiness. **1977** *News of World* 17 Apr. 2/3 The top people's directory, Who's Who. **1981** R. D. EDWARDS *Corridors of Death* vi. 29 The need for tact and sensitivity in handling the Top People involved.

topper, *sb.*¹ Add: **3.** An action, remark, etc., that puts a finishing touch to what has gone before, *esp.* an outrageous one or one that cannot be capped. Cf. TOP *v.*¹ 12 b.

1939 J. O'HARA *Pal Joey* (1940) 98 It was a famous historical topper when Josephine was informed that the poor people did not have any bread and she said 'Why don't they eat some cake'. **1973** *Black Panther* 6 Oct. 6/3 The topper is that Foster completes this vicious cycle with a cold beg..to get his money under the..Law Enforcement Assistance Act. **1977** *Amer. Film* July–Aug. 18/1 The shot was part of a gag..a 'topper' that Keaton used to finish off a duel between two Civil War locomotives. **1977** *New Yorker* 12 Sept. 92/3 'Will you do me a favor and take me over to the Carnegie Deli..?' The driver said sure, swung off his bus route, and deposited Henny at the door. Henny's topper? He got off the bus and said, 'Pick me up in twenty minutes.'

topper, *sb.*² Add: **1. b.** *U.S. Mil. slang.* A first sergeant. Cf. *top sergeant* s.v. *TOP *sb.*¹ 32.

1918 *Radiator* 22 Aug. 2 Sergeant Hulbert, the 'topper' of 95. **1937** *Our Army* (U.S.) Jan. 19 'I'm sure there's no Lieutenant McGonigle here,' replies the Topper.

2. b. A kind of loose-fitting jacket or short coat worn by women or children. orig. and chiefly *U.S.*

1937 *Los Angeles Times* 2 Sept. 5/1 (Advt.), Soft, fluffy casual toppers tailored in the best British way. **1938** *Sears, Roebuck Catal.* Spring/Summer 20/2 The absolutely perfect topper coat. **1948** *N.Y. Times Mag.* 8 Feb. 38 (Advt.), A boxy topper with cardigan neckline. **1960** *News Chron.* 22 July 6/4 Attractive little top jackets ('toppers'). **1972** *Country Life* 30 Nov. 1533 Printed dress ..worn with a topper jacket in orange wool. **1978** *Detroit Free Press* 5 Mar. D 10/4 (Advt.), There are girls' topper sets and perky dresses.

3. (Earlier examples.)

1785 *Sessions Papers* 6 Apr. 571/2 One of them said, damn his eyes, *give him a topper at once.* **1803** in *Occasional Papers Univ. Sydney Austral. Lang. Res. Centre* (1980) No. 18. 44 He..had 'knocked him down and given him a topper for luck!'

6. (Earlier example.)

1874 HOTTEN *Slang Dict.* 327 *Topper*, the tobacco which is left in the bottom of a pipe-bowl..; or the stump of a smoked cigar.

Hence **to·ppering** *vbl. sb.*

1829 P. EGAN *Boxiana* 2nd Ser. II. 671 The *topper*-ing system was in full practice, till *poor* Cock Robin went down quite exhausted!

toppie (tǫ·pi). [perh. f. TOPKNOT.] A small brown bulbul of the genus *Pycnonotus*, found in southern Africa, either the Cape bulbul, *P. capensis*, or the red-eyed bulbul, *P. nigricans.*

1899 G. RUSSELL *Hist. Old Durban* viii. 176 Doves cooed and 'Toppies' answered each other obtrusively. **1940** A. ROBERTS *Birds S. Afr.* 225 Cape Bulbul, or Toppie ..is not such a common bird as the Layard's Bulbul found further east. **1951** R. CAMPBELL *Light on Dark Horse* x. 142 The commonest bird in Africa, the Toppie as we call him.., is a great character. **1964** D. VARADAY *Gara-Yaka* xv. 126 His best friends became the Toppies, the conical-helmeted small dark birds that disclose the presence of snakes. **1971** J. DRUMMOND *Farewell Party* vi. 35 There were birds..finches and toppies and a collared sunbird.

topping, *vbl. sb.*¹ Add: **1. e.** Also, filling up or bringing to capacity.

1919 *Gloss. Aeronaut. Terms* (R. Aeronaut. Soc.) 54 *Topping up*, the operation of replenishing the balloon with fresh gas. **1935** *Motor Commerce* Jan. 8 (Advt.), Acid-level indicator..shows when the maximum level is reached on 'topping-up', and so safeguards against over-filling. **1941** *Illustr. London News* CXCIX. 308 (*caption*) Interior contents of the rubber dinghy: bailer, 'topping-up' pump, chocolate, paddles, stoppers or plugs, and sea-drogue. **1959** *Engineering* 6 Feb. 192/3 An infra-red heater provides a focal point for 'topping-up' if required. **1963** *Motor* 17 July 3/1 The automatic gearbox of my 3.4 Jaguar was in need of topping up. **1972** HILLIER & PITTUCK *Fund. Motor Vehicle Technol.* 534 A further check is the need for topping up.

g. *slang.* Execution by hanging.

1699 B. E. *New Dict. Canting Crew*, *Topping cheat*, the gallows. *Topping cove*, the hangman. **1846** *Swell's Night Guide* 134/2 *Topping*, hanging. **1968** *Daily Tel.* 15 Nov. 24/7, I wish they still had topping..because if I get bird.. for this I will get 30 years and I will top myself anyway. **1971** *Times* 6 Oct. 3/8, I deserve topping for shooting a copper.

h. *topping and tailing*, the action or practice of washing a baby's face and bottom; a sketchy wash. Also *top-and-tailing.* Cf. *TOP *v.*¹ 3 b.

1931 P. W. YEOMANS *Happy Motherhood* vii. 69 A.. recommendation of the evening tub comes when the baby crawls and gets really grubby. Topping-and-tailing is not then sufficient. **1941** U. ORANGE *Tom Tiddler's Ground* xi. 205 The next hour was a busy one, what with Norman's 'topping and tailing', Norman's bottle and Marguerite's bath. **1960** C. DAY LEWIS *Buried Day* ii. 31 We did not go in for a desperate amount of washing—top-and-tailing twice a day, and a hip-bath once a week. **1972** *Times* 9 Aug. 7/7 Washing and changing a baby..can be a problem... Topping and tailing is all that is required.

i. *topping out* (*ceremony*), (the ceremony accompanying) the finishing of the roof of a building. Cf. *TOP *v.*¹ 20 a.

1961 *Times* 9 Sept. 16/5 Mr. H. R. Lake, New Zealand Minister of Finance,..performed the topping-out ceremony. **1962** *Guardian* 3 Nov. 6/6 The mystical ceremony of 'topping out' was performed this morning on the domed roof of the new Smithfield Market. A green bough was nailed to the roof..as a means..of warding off evil spirits and protecting the future inhabitants. **1973** *Times* 19 Mar. 11/4 A topping-out ceremony of a new shopping centre being built for Ravenstone Securities..took place in Glasgow. **1977** P. VAN GREENAWAY *Destiny Man* i. 9 For any building, there must be some sort of topping out. **1984** *Daily Tel.* 26 Jan. 6/4 Some concrete words of advice from Mr Gow..as he performed the 'topping-out' ceremony for the International Conference Centre in Westminster yesterday.

4. d. A top layer or garnish put on food, esp. dessert (see also quots. 1926, 1927). Chiefly *U.S.*

1926 *Amer. Speech* I. 653/2 *Toppings*, pastry or cakes. **1927** *Ibid.* II. 389/2 *Toppings* refers to pastry, because it is used to top off a meal. **1950** *Manch. Guardian Weekly* 31 Aug. 5 Sundae 'toppings'. **1978** *Chicago* June 248/2 Toppings—including sausage, pepperoni, green peppers, anchovies, and fresh mushrooms are generously applied [to pizzas]. **1981** *Living Trends* (U.S.) Summer 6 Ice cream plus one or two toppings, such as crushed peanuts, toasted coconut, maple syrup, cherries.

topping, *ppl. a.* **4.** (Earlier examples.)

1815 D. HUMPHREYS *Yankey in Eng.* 30 She's lofty—topping—has her highs—sometimes. **1852** MRS. STOWE *Uncle Tom's Cabin* II. xxix. 147 She'd..have me know.. that I wasn't going to be so topping as I had been.

topple, *v.* Add: **3. a.** (Later *fig.* examples.)

1951 *Amer. Speech* XXVI. 230/2 California topples Washington. **1970** A. TOFFLER *Future Shock* (1971) viii. 177 Research topples older conceptions of man and nature. **1976** *Evening Post* (Nottingham) 15 Dec. 23 They beat Scotland 6-3 (one drawn) in the semi-finals and went on to topple England 'A' 6-1 (three drawn) in the final. **1979** *Daily Tel.* 26 May 14/4 A painting by Burne-Jones..made £48,000, toppling the artist's previous best price of £33,000. **1983** *Times* 15 Feb. 7/1 The revolution that toppled the regime of Emperor Haile Selassie eight years ago.

topply (tǫ·pli), *a.* [f. TOPPLE *v.* + -Y¹.] Liable to topple over.

1913 J. VAIZEY *College Girl* xvii. 236 The screen's..a topply one. **1950** G. GREENE *Third Man* ix. 67 The inadequate too-fancy topply table.

toppy, *a.* Restrict 'Now *low*' to senses in Dict. and add: **d.** *U.S.* Of animals: of superior quality.

1893 [in Dict.]. **1927** J. LOMAX *Cowboy Songs* 303 I've cut your toppy mounts, boys. **1938** *Sun* (Baltimore) 24 Oct. 13/1 Firm rates were paid for vealers..and indications at times suggested that more of the 'toppy' offerings would have met with good reception. **1960** A. WEST *Trend is Up* (1961) v. 145 He turned to his favorite page in the book which showed a nice toppy lot of young lambs.

e. *Mus.* Containing too much treble. *colloq.*

1956 B. EDWARDS in S. Traill *Play that Music* vi. 63, I should want from a side-drum plenty of response and life —without being too 'toppy' so that the drum has a certain amount of 'guts' when it comes to playing in large places. **1969** W. RUTHERFORD *Gallows Set* vi. 85 'What the hell's "toppy sound"?' 'Sound with too much treble in it. It's caused by the camera running slow when the film was taken so when its projected the sound is speeded up.' **1976** *Gramophone* Aug. 360/2 It could be argued that some modern discs are too toppy.

f. *Stock Exchange.* Of a market currency, etc.: high and unstable. *colloq.*

1961 *Spectator* 26 May 774 When markets became 'toppy' he should be busy switching from vulnerable to stronger positions. **1968** *Economist* 5 Oct. 81/2 What could be developing in London is a 'toppy' situation for a few months as the market consolidates the laurels it has earned. **1979** *Daily Tel.* 2 Aug. 17 Sterling suddenly looked toppy. **1983** *Times* 28 Apr. 16/2 If, however, the market looks 'toppy', it is the highest-rated sectors which are likely to suffer most.

TOPS (tǫps). [Acronym f. the initial letters of *T*raining *Op*portunities *S*cheme.] A system of vocational training programmes established in 1972, and organized by the Training Services Agency within the Manpower Services Commission. Also *attrib.*

1975 *Ann. Rep. Manpower Services Comm. 1974–75* 8/3 The government's vocational training programmes, which were to be developed into the Training Opportunities Scheme (TOPS) to meet the needs of individuals. *Ibid.*, The initial target for the TOPS scheme was to increase the number of people trained each year. **1979** *Jrnl. R. Soc. Arts* Dec. 10/1 The Board arranged for TOPS candidates to be provided with special examinations in a limited range of subjects.

topside, *sb.* (*adv.*) Add: **A.** *sb.* **a.** (Later example.)

1980 *Family Handyman* Sept. 85/1 Did you just smear caulk over the topside crack and hope for the best?

c. (Earlier example.)

1896 *Girl's Own Paper* 8 Feb. 295/1 Braised beef.—A piece of 'top-side' is best for the purpose.

f. *Oil Industry.* (See quot. 1948.) Now usu. with reference to the equipment and installations above water in offshore drilling. Freq. *attrib.*

1948 *Dialect Notes* IX. 60 *Top side*, any place above ground or ground level... Borrowed from nautical usage. **1975** *Offshore* Aug. 136/3 The system consists of a neutrally buoyant helmet mounted camera assembly and topside controls. **1977** *Offshore Engineer* Aug. 38/2 The manufacture of topside equipment. **1981** *Daily Tel.* 2 June 2/7 He [*sc.* a diver] complained of 'poor topside management'. **1982** *Sci. Amer.* Apr. 35/1 In designing platforms for North American conditions one can assume extended periods of calm for fastening the platform to the sea floor and erecting the topsides.

g. (With capital initial.) The upper or ruling classes, the Establishment. Freq. *attrib.* passing into *adj.*

1958 J. B. PRIESTLEY *Topside* 5 Topside people. *Ibid.* 8 Topside..takes and uses power, controls all patronage, imposes whatever pattern it prefers on the life of the nation. **1959** *New Statesman* 10 Jan. 47/2, I make this criticism as one who, in general, agrees with Priestley. What he calls Topside, what others call the Establishment, and what others, including myself, still call the capitalist ruling-class, does indeed..behave very much as Jordan asserts. **1962** *Guardian* 6 Oct. 5/2 J. B. Priestley, quite an attraction even in Topside Cheltenham. **1973** *Listener* 7 June 742/3 Jazz in the thirties in Topside circles was synonymous with vulgarity.

h. *Meteorol.* The part of the ionosphere above the height at which the concentration of free electrons is greatest, viz. about 300 km. Freq. *attrib.*

1962 *Canad. Jrnl. Physics* XL. 1692 The sounder is part of the 'Alouette' satellite.., which was launched at 0605 GMT on September 29, 1962... Several unfamiliar phenomena appear on the top-side ionograms... The top-side sounder project is an international one. **1965** HEIKKILA & AXFORD in C. O. Hines et al. *Physics of Earth's Upper Atmosphere* v. 114 Most recently, the technique of 'topside sounding' from a satellite has been accomplished. *Ibid.*, Better geographical coverage can be obtained now for the topside than for the bottom. **1976** *Nature* 19 Aug. 675/1 It may be possible to consider this process as a means of modifying the topside ionosphere by using a high power, low frequency transmitter at high latitudes. **1979** J. K. HARGREAVES *Upper Atmosphere* iii. 39 To study the 'topside', an ionosonde may be carried on a satellite.

B. *adv.* Freq. with reference to the upper deck of a ship. Also, to the top, and in form *topsides.*

1946 P. CARTER in Aldiss & Harrison *Decade 40s* (1975) 115 Chief [Navigator] Schmidt..relayed data topside. **1971** H. T. WALDEN *Anchorage Northeast* i. 27 While the ferry awaited its capacity load of eight vehicles a band topsides serenaded the passengers with martial airs. **1976** L. SANDERS *Hamlet Warning* (1977) II. xix. 164 On the third level below the main deck, they met four men..fleeing topside in panic. **1977** *New Yorker* 15 Aug. 54/3, I bring two of the sandwiches topside. **1978** *Guardian Weekly* 2 Apr. 24/5 A carrion crow..who, though damaged, can get top-sides of the noisy pack of gulls who winter near here.

To·p-sider. Also **topsider.** [f. TOPSIDE *sb.* + -ER[2].] A kind of casual shoe, freq. of canvas with a rubber sole.

A proprietary term in the U.S.

1937 *Official Gaz.* (U.S. Patent Office) 13 Apr. 261/1 Top-sider. For boots and shoes made of a combination of rubber or rubber substitute in combination with either fabric or leather or both. **1958** S. A. GRAU *Hard Blue Sky* (1959) 17 He waited perched on the railing picking the shells from the soles of his topsiders. **1968** [see *SPANDY *a.*]. **1977** *New Yorker* 10 Oct. 121/1 Standing in Topsiders and white ducks.

Topsy (tǫ·psi). The name of a character in Mrs. H. B. Stowe's novel *Uncle Tom's Cabin*; used allusively as the type of something that seems to have grown of itself without anyone's intention or direction (see quot. 1851).

[**1851** MRS. STOWE *Uncle Tom's Cabin* in *Nat. Era* 6 Nov. 1/5 Have you ever heard anything about God, Topsy?.. Do you know who made you?' 'Nobody, as I knows on,' said the child... 'I spect I grow'd. Don't think nobody never made me.'] **1885** KIPLING *Let.* in Ld. Birkenhead *Rudyard Kipling* (1978) vi. 81, I have really embarked..on my novel *Mother Maturin*—Like Topsy 'it growed' while I wrote. **1936** C. ROUSE *Old Towns* i. 17 The planning of towns in medieval England can be said to have followed no given rule—they were like Topsy who 'just growed'. **1955** *Times* 30 Aug. 9/7 It may be that political parties must emulate Topsy and just grow. **1967** *Boston Sunday Herald* 9 Apr. 27/4 This practice [*sc.* bugging] has grown like Topsy. **1973** 'J. RYDER' *Trevayne* (1974) xxv. 201 Are you implying that it [*sc.* a business] just grew—a Topsy? **1982** *Oxford Times* 30 Apr. 31/1 The garden, like Topsy, 'just growed'.

topsy-turvy, *adv.* (*a.*, *sb.*, and *v.*) Add: **topsy-turvydom** (earlier example); **topsy-turvying** *vbl. sb.* (later example).

1870 W. S. GILBERT in *Fun* 19 Mar. 15/1, I dreamt that somehow I had come To dwell in Topsy-Turveydom! **1967** [see *SKOOB].

to·psy ve·rsy, colloq. alteration of TOPSY-TURVY *adv.*, after ARSY-VERSY.

1767 D. GARRICK *Peep behind Curtain* (1772) 9 Damn all these new vagaries, that put us all upon our heads topsy versy. **1911** J. MASEFIELD *Everlasting Mercy* 46 Joe, and Si, and Nick, and Percy I rolled together topsy versy.

to·p-up. [f. the vbl. phr. *to top up* s.v. *TOP *v.*[1] 21.] An addition; that which serves to complete an amount or a number; a filling up to the top of something already partly full (esp. a glass of alcoholic drink). Freq. *attrib.*

1967 N. FREELING *Strike Out* 55 Fifty children that already had their top-up shots [against polio] in February. **1968** J. LOCK *Lady Policeman* xvi. 138 Cypriots..predominated, then a fair sprinkling of Italians, with a top-up of every nationality under the sun. **1971** A. MORICE *Death of Gay Dog* vii. 85 'Time for a top-up.' 'No more, thank you.' **1977** *Proc. R. Soc. Med.* LXX. 160/2 Post-operative analgesia occurs for a few hours after short operations, but is otherwise much as after other methods, unless 'top-up' doses are given through a catheter. **1978** A. BAINES in J. M. Thomson *Future of Early Music in Britain* 23 The next stage should be..to..get the Associated Board to accept this instrument—but excluding the crumhorns etc. save perhaps as optional top-ups. **1983** *Truckin' Life* Aug. 66/1 We..were looking for some improvement in consumption at the top-up point, the Ampol station. **1984** *Times* 13 July 2/5 Moneylenders..offer 'top-up' loans..before the original debt has been settled.

toque. Add: **1. c.** *Canad.* = TUQUE.

1890 S. M. ST. MAUR *Impressions Tenderfoot* 265 [He] was..made picturesque by a red cap 'toque', sash and red duffel overall stockings. **1906** G. LAWRENCE *Let.* 20 Jan. in R. E. Watters *Brit. Columbia* (1958) 7 With his toque pulled down..he looked for all the world like one of the small gnomes we children used to see pictures of. **1945** K. M. HAIG *Brave Harvest* 170 They were matched by toques and mittens, and tied in with gay voyageur sashes streaming like banners against the snow. **1972** *Daily Tel.* (Colour Suppl.) 8 Dec. 10/4 He wore a woollen ski toque on his head. **1977** *Westworld* (Vancouver, B.C.) Jan.–Feb. 44/2 A few other clothing essentials to remember are an extra pair of wool socks, some wool mitts, with a waterproof outer mitt, and a woolen toque.

d. A kind of tall white hat worn by chefs. In full *toque blanche.* orig. *U.S.*

[**1965** C. KLEIN *Professional Cook* ii. 28 The origin of the high white hat (*la toque blanche*) that has been the cook's trademark for centuries is in the monastery.] **1966** *McCall's* June 168/4 The symposium ended with a discussion about the shape of the chef's hat, the *toque blanche.* **1975** *N.Y. Times* 1 Nov. 18/1 The wearer of the toque blanche..is among a handful of women now presiding over restaurant kitchens here. **1977** *Guardian Weekly* 9 Oct. 19/1 France's two super-gourmets..found only 21 restaurants worth a chef's toque, their mark of at least qualified approval. **1978** R. CONDON *Bandicoot* i. 2 His cook..was a man of great height, made taller still by the two-foot-high, fluted *toque blanche* he wore to ventilate his head. **1981** *Listener* 17 & 24 Dec. 772/1 When the celebrated Swiss *chef de cuisine*..retired..he handed his toque to another Swiss.

toquilla (tǫkī·lya). [a. Amer. Sp.] = *JIPIJAPA *a.*

1877 *Encycl. Brit.* VII. 647/2 The leaves of the toquilla ..furnish material for the well-known hats. **1924** *Countries of World* III. 1713/1 The toquilla palm yields the leaf-fibre for the famous 'Panama' hats of Ecuador.

tor, *sb.* **3.** Add: **tor grass,** a perennial grass, *Brachypodium pinnatum*; cf. TORE *sb.*[3]

1954 C. E. HUBBARD *Grasses* 71 Tor grass..A worthless grass of neglected open grassland on chalk and limestone. **1976** *Times* 28 June 14/8 Coarse Tor and Erect Brome grasses have supplanted the grazed pastures.

tora (tōᵊ·ra). [a. Amharic.] In full, *tora hartebeest.* A light brown hartebeest, *Alcelaphus buselaphus tora,* found in parts of north-eastern Africa.

1873 J. E. GRAY in *Nature* 4 Sept. 364 The British Museum has just received a series of skins of a new Bubale from Abyssinia called Tora... I propose to call it *Alcephalus tora.* **1873** —— in *Ann. Mag. Nat. Hist.* XII. 341 The male of the Tora..has a large, round, convex tuft..of darker hair in front of each eye. **1894** [see *TETEL]. **1912** J. STEVENSON-HAMILTON *Animal Life Afr.* vii. 102 The Tora Hartebeest..is found in Abyssinia and the Blue Nile Valley. **1970** DORST & DANDELOT *Field Guide Large Mammals Afr.* 220 The Tora Hartebeest..is pale tawny.

Toradja (tora·dʒă). Also **Toraja.** [Native name.] **a.** An Austronesian people living in central Sulawesi (formerly Celebes); a member of this people. **b.** The language of the Toradja.

1911 J. FRAZER *Golden Bough: Magic Art* (ed. 3) I. iii. 109 The Toradjas of Central Celebes believe that things of the same sort attract each other by means of their indwelling spirits. **1937** M. COVARRUBIAS *Island of Bali* ii. 16 The ancient inhabitants of the Malay Archipelago were 'Indonesians', also called Malayo-Polynesians,..and so forth. Of these, pure branches are to be found today in the Dyak of Borneo, the Batak of Sumatra, the Toradja of Celebes. **1957** *Encycl. Brit.* V. 89/2 The Toraja are a collection of tribes, living in central, southeast and east Celebes. **1964** E. A. NIDA *Toward Sci. Transl.* ix. 208 In east Toradja, spoken in Indonesia, 'they mentioned his-he-ness' is a way of rendering 'they spoke about him'. **1979** *Radio Times* 5–11 May 61/1 It's in the mountains of central Sulawesi that you find the land of the Torajas.

Torah. Add: **b.** *attrib.* and *Comb.*, as *Torah scroll*; esp. denoting ornaments or accoutrements of the parchment scrolls of the Torah, as *Torah breastplate, crown, curtain, finial, mantle, pointer, wrapper.*

1901 *Ann. Rep. Board of Regents Smithsonian Inst. 1899* 545 *Torah scroll,* parchment scroll of the Pentateuch in Hebrew mounted on wooden rollers. **1941** F. LANDSBERGER in *Hebrew Union College Ann.* XVI. 374 The ritual implements used in the synagogues, above all the Torah crowns..must have been made by Jews. *Ibid.* 398 The desire of German Jews for costly..ceremonial objects was strong, and there were..a few wealthy benefactors who could donate rich Torah curtains, Torah mantles, Torah finials, Torah breastplates, pointers..and the like. **1950** S. S. KAYSER in *Ibid.* XXIII. II. vii. 498 The final benediction of the Brith Milah ceremony and therefore.. the text on Torah wrappers. **1968** *N.Y. City* (Michelin Tire Corp.) 112 Jewish Museum..admirable examples of Torah Scrolls, the sacred texts of the Pentateuch... You can also admire..Torah wrappers, in finely engraved silver, and Torah mantles with silk and gold embroidery, ..and Torah pointers, used by rabbis to follow the text. **1976** Y. L. BIALER *Jewish Life* 100 (*caption*) Torah crown, hammered, gilded silver with precious stones..Poland, 18th century. *Ibid.* 120 (*caption*) Torah breastplate, pierced and engraved silver, Turkey, 19th century.

Toraja, var. *TORADJA.

‖**torba** (tǭ·ɹbă). [ad. Arab. *turba* dust, earth, soil.] A primitive kind of cement made with broken pottery, traditionally used in Malta for the floors of buildings. Freq. *attrib.*

1910 *Ann. Rep. Valetta Mus. 1909–10* 4 The original 'torba' floor existed at a depth of about 15 cms. **1923** M. A. MURRAY *Excavations in Malta* I. v. 33 The beaten-earth floor, known as *torba,* is made as follows: the pots are broken..or..pounded; [etc.]. **1953** *Proc. Prehistoric Soc.* XIX. 43 They were found only on the lowest torba floor at Santa Verna and Kordin III. **1968** J. D. EVANS in S. Rossiter *Malta* 13 Remains of huts..were found at Skorba... The floors were of beaten earth or *torba* (a plaster made of crushed limestone).

torch, *sb.* Add: **1. a.** Now also = *electric torch* (*b*) s.v. *ELECTRIC *a.* 2 b.

1901 E. W. HORNUNG *Black Mask* xii. 253, I saw Raffles on my right striking with his torch; a face flew out of the darkness to meet the thick glass bulb with the glowing wire enclosed. **1936** W. FAULKNER *Absalom, Absalom!* ix. 370 He..saw the light of the torch approaching along the upper hall. **1967** P. SHAFFER *Black Comedy* 48 The Colonel takes the torch from Harold and shines it pitilessly in Schuppanzigh's face.

b. Also in phrs.: *to hand* (*pass*, etc.) *on the torch* (and varr.), to pass on a tradition, etc., esp. one of enlightenment (after L. *lampada tradere,* Gk. *λαμπάδα παραδιδόναι*, a metaphor from the ancient Greek torch-race; cf. LAMP *sb.*[1] 1 c); *to carry* (etc.) *a torch for* (someone), to feel (esp. unrequited) love for, to feel lingering affection for.

1887 *Q. Rev.* Oct. 276 Her [*sc.* Italy's] work has been done among the nations, and in their turn France, England and Germany hand on the torch. **1912** E. GOSSE *Portr. & Sk.* p. viii, They were all..engaged in keeping bright, and in handing on unquenched, the torch of literary tradition. **1927** *Vanity Fair* (N.Y.) Nov. 132/3 When a fellow 'carries the torch' it doesn't imply that he is 'lit up' or drunk, but girl-less. His steady has quit him for another or he is lonesome for her. **1932** L. GOLDING *Magnolia Street* I. xi. 189 He had sometimes hoped that in Max a son was born to him who would take the torch from his dying hand and jump on to the platform he had vacated. **1953** L. Z. HOBSON *Celebrity* vi. 78 Jim's still carrying a torch for Roosevelt. **1959** *Manch. Guardian* 16 June 5/2 She was carrying a torch for someone. **1969** J. GROSS *Rise & Fall Man of Lett.* iv. 104 Dante was the poet of Catholicism, who handed over the torch to Shakespeare, the poet of Feudalism, who passed it on to Milton, the poet of Protestantism. **1977** H. FAST *Immigrants* v. 305 Maybe you got a torch for her, maybe not. But we both got her interest at heart.

c. = *blow-torch* s.v. *BLOW-.

1909 WEBSTER, *Torch,* 3... Any of various devices for emitting a hot flame, as for vaporizing oil to start an oil engine, burning off old paint, melting solder, or the like. **1931** *Writer's Digest* Oct. 28 A keister torch is an acetylene torch which can be carried in a suitcase. **1961** *Sheet Metal Industries* XXXVIII. 613/1 The high rating of the water cooled models..is made possible by the design which permits the circulation of cooling water right to the tip of the torch. **1978** S. BRILL *Teamsters* vi. 225 Our theory is that the car was hidden there and then cut up with torches and carted out.

d. An arsonist. *U.S. slang.*

1938 *Reader's Digest* Mar. 71/1 The torch is now serving a 20-year sentence. **1977** *Time* 31 Oct. 28/3 Blazes are set by quasi-professional 'torches' hired by landlords, real estate brokers, store owners, or welfare tenants who want to be relocated.

3. *torch battery, -flare*; *torch-lighted* ppl. adj.; **torch-carrying** *vbl. sb.* (*fig.*), the harbouring of (esp. unrequited) love (see sense 1 b above); **Torch Commando** *S. Afr.*, (see quots.); **torch igniter** (see quots.); **torch singer** orig. *U.S.*, a singer of torch songs; **torch singing** *vbl. sb.* (orig. U.S.), the singing of torch songs; **torch song** orig. *U.S.*, a popular song on the subject of unrequited love; a sad sentimental or romantic song.

1926–7 *Army & Navy Stores Catal.* p. xxii/3 (Index), Batteries, Torch. **1957** C. SMITH *Case of Torches* x. 128 Bring in the..report on the torch batteries. **1970** E. R. JOHNSON *God Keepers* (1971) iii. 26 When does the torch-carrying stop..and work itself into hate? **1951** *Sun* (Baltimore) 9 Nov. 13/1 South Africa's Torch Commando, an organization of war veterans pledged to uphold the Dominion Constitution, is building up into a potent opposition to Prime Minister Daniel F. Malan's Nationalist Government. **1971** L. BLACKWELL *Blackwell Remembers* xviii. 158 The Torch Commando, a militant organization which strongly opposed the policy of the Nationalist Government relating to the coloured voters at the Cape. **1910** W. DE LA MARE *Three Mulla-Mulgars* xv. 205 All the Men of the Mountains came out with their little ones in the starlight and torch-flare to see them go. **1959** E. POUND *Thrones* cii. 82 Lit by the torch-flare. **1948** *Jrnl. R. Aeronaut. Soc.* LII. 170/2 The simple expedient of fitting an igniter plug in the flame tube was not sufficient to cater for the more arduous duties of ignition, such as under flight conditions at over 20,000 feet. The torch igniter was designed..to get over these problems. This unit was an ordinary igniter plug, with a subsidiary supply of fuel to it. The fuel was injected through a small hole on to the plug points. **1970** *Gloss. Aeronaut. & Astronaut. Terms* (*B.S.I.*) VIII. 17 *Torch igniter,* a combined igniter plug and fuel atomizer for initiating combustion when starting the turbine. **1881** 'MARK TWAIN' *Prince & Pauper* xxxii. 365 We find the torch-lighted galleries already filling up with people. **1975** R. H. RIMMER *Premar Experiments* (1976) ii. 164 In every direction you looked, torchlighted faces were swaying to the music. **1934** J. O'HARA *Appointment in Samarra* vii. 210 Taking that dame out, that torch singer. **1973** *Times* 15 Dec. 10/1 She is sometimes a movie vamp, or a torch singer. **1947** E. JENKINS *Young Enthusiasts* 163 Jazz bands, torch singing and swing. **1983** *Listener* 9 June 35/4 If this is 'torch' singing, then Julie London is not a flimsy key-ring flashlight. **1927** *Vanity Fair* (N.Y.) Nov. 132/3 'Sing a torch song' is commonly used in Broadway late-places as a request for a ballad in commemoration of the lonesome state. Tommy Lyman is said to have created the slang and he announced one night: 'My famous torch song: "Come To Me, My Melancholy Baby".' **1939** G. GREENE *Lawless Roads* x. 256, I was grateful for the darkness and the torch songs. **1977** *Listener* 13 Oct. 481/2 The songs are pleasant parodies of Nashville, of torch songs and even of grand opera.

torch, *v.*[1] Add: **1. b.** To set alight, to set fire to, *esp.* in order to claim insurance money. *slang* (orig. and chiefly *U.S.*).

1931 *Writer's Digest* Oct. 29, I had just lit a match to torch the squib when I heard steps behind me. **1971** *Wall St. Jrnl.* 16 Aug. 1/3 Two bombs were planted in a university dormitory, part of a Belfast soccer stadium was torched, and snipers attacked army patrols. **1977** *Time* 31 Oct. 34/1 Griffith relied on an arsonist turned informant..who worked as a 'broker' for landlords eager to torch their property. **1979** *Arizona Daily Star* 22 July E 4/4 BIA police suspected a night of violence..when a group of people ran a car into Pike Creek... The car was then torched. **1983** *Granta* VII. 37 Halfway through the first pint of coffee, I torched a cigarette. Mmm, tasted good.

to·rcher[3]. *U.S. slang.* [f. TORCH *sb.* + -ER[1].] = *torch singer* s.v. *TORCH *sb.* 3.
1940 R. CHANDLER *Farewell, my Lovely* xli. 317 A handsome..torcher who could sing as if she meant it. **1975** J. GORES *Hammett* xxii. 147 A colored band..was backing a torcher.

torch-light. c. (Earlier example.)
1837 *New Yorker* 30 Sept. 441/3 A Loco-Foco 'Torch-Light Meeting', auxiliary to the larger concern in Tammany, was held in the Park on Thursday Evening.

torchon. Add: **torchon lace** (earlier example).
1865 F. B. PALLISER *Hist. Lace* iv. 53 But Venice point is now no more. The sole relic of this far-famed trade is the coarse torchon lace of the old lozenge pattern offered by the peasant women of Palestrina.

torchy, *a.* Restrict *rare* to sense in Dict. and add: **2.** Of, pertaining to, or characteristic of a torch song or torch singer. *colloq.* (orig. and chiefly *U.S.*).
1941 W. C. HANDY *Father of Blues* xxi. 285 The torchiest of all torch songs, *Melancholy Baby*. **1962** [see *SLINKY *a.*]. **1977** *Time* 25 July 60/2 He is married to Actress Diahnne Abbott, whose torchy rendition of *Honeysuckle Rose* in *New York, New York* upstages Liza Minnelli's belting.

tordion: see TURDION in Dict. and Suppl.

toreador. Delete ‖ and add: **c. toreador pants** chiefly *U.S.*, women's tight-fitting trousers, tapering to mid-calf.
1956 E. BAIN *Mugger* x. 83 She wore a white blouse, and black toreador pants, which tapered down to her naked ankles and feet. **1960** 'A. BURGESS' *Right to Answer* ii. 22 Veronica..went off, slim as a blade in toreador pants. **1974** R. B. PARKER *God save Child* vi. 48 She was dressed for a bull fight. Tight gold toreador pants... A ruffled red shirt,..a bronze wide-brimmed vaquero hat.

torenia (torī·niă). [mod.L. (Linnæus *Nova Plantarum Genera* (1751) 45), f. the name of the Rev. Olof *Torén* (1718–53), chaplain to the Swedish East India Company + -IA[1].] An annual herb of the genus of this name, belonging to the family Scrophulariaceæ, native to sub-tropical or tropical Africa and Asia, and bearing racemes of yellow, blue, or purple flowers.
1840 *Curtis's Bot. Mag.* LXVI. 3715 *(heading)* Heart-leaved Torenia. **1902** L. H. BAILEY *Cycl. Amer. Hort.* IV. 1822/1 Torenias are of easy cultivation. **1978** *Detroit Free Press* 16 Apr. (Gardening Guide) 12/1 Torenia or wishbone flower and browallia perform well in considerable shade.

tore-out (tōᵊ·raut). [f. *tore*, dial. pa. pple. of TEAR *v.*[1] + OUT *adv.*] A small inferior type of sailing-boat.
1923 *Yachting Monthly* Jan. 145/1 Wave was of the genus usually referred to by East Coast watermen as 'little old toreouts', being, in fact, a small converted ship's boat. **1956** A. DAVISON *My Ship is so Small* ii. 19 Most of the boats in the yard were old tore-outs like the one I lived in. **1979** *Yachts & Yachting* 9 Nov. 1443/3 Let it be hastily explained that the Sirens in the title of this book are all boats: old toreouts, yachts and ultimately a 117ft ex-trading schooner.

torgoch. (Later examples.)
1924 *Glasgow Herald* 8 Feb. 8 Among the fish got in the Clyde at that time (about 1840) was the..torgoch or char. **1936** J. T. JENKINS *Fishes Brit. Isles* (ed. 2) 237 The Torgoch..inhabits two lakes near Llanberis.

torgsin (tǫ·ɹgsin). Also **Torgsin.** [a. Russ., contraction of *vsesoyuznoe ob"edinenie po torgovle s inostrantsami*, the All-Union Association for Trade with Foreigners.] A Soviet trading organization in the 1920s and 1930s which sold goods only in return for foreign currency. Used *attrib.*
1933 *Sun* (Baltimore) 24 Nov. 18/5 Sale of 200,000 pounds of bacon to the 'torgsin' stores, which cater only to foreigners in Soviet Russia, has been announced by Polish exporters. **1934** H. G. WELLS *Exper. Autobiogr.* II. ix. 819 All over Moscow and Leningrad you can bribe with foreign currency because of the absurd *Torgsin* system. **1968** *Listener* 3 Oct. 434/2 It was fairly easy for us because of those Torgsin shops where you could really get everything.

Torgut (tǭ·ɹgut). Now *Hist.* Also **Torgod, Torgot, Torgud.** [Native name.] A migratory Mongol people now absorbed into China; a member of this people. Also *attrib.*
1883 *Encycl. Brit.* XVI. 745/1 It was with no great difficulty..that his brother Ki Wang detached the greater part of the Kerait tribes from his banner, and founded the Torgod chieftainship. *Ibid.*, The position of the Torgod at this time..was rapidly becoming unbearable. **1947** AUDEN *Age of Anxiety* (1948) v. 103 The Timurids and Torguts. **1957** *Encycl. Brit.* VIII. 351/1 Some of them [*sc.* the western Mongols], notably the Torgots (Torgud) migrated as far west as the Volga, whence they returned, and their descendants are settled in the Ili district. **1962** E. SNOW *Other Side of River* (1963) xix. 142 In the past three centuries there had been no similar armed migration of a nation in Asia, with the exception of the amazing Flight of the Torgut from the Caucasus to Mongolia.

toric, *a.* Add: Also with pronunc. (tǫ·rik). (Further examples.) *spec.* in *Ophthalm.*, applied to a lens with one surface curved like part of a torus, the radius of curvature having a minimum value in one direction and a maximum value in the direction at right angles to it; also as *sb.*, such a lens.
1890 *Trans. Amer. Ophthalm. Soc.* V. 708 Such toric surfaces are concave, and, when sunk in a plate of glass, afford typical examples of concavo-plane toric lenses. **1954** S. DUKE-ELDER *Parsons' Dis. Eye* (ed. 12) iv. 41 A regularly astigmatic surface is said to have a toric curvature. **1962** L. S. SASIENI *Princ. & Pract. Optical Dispensing* x. 264 'Commercial' torics of minus powers are usually transposed to the form which provides a plus cylinder. **1973** *Nature* 21/28 Dec. 479/2 A toric segment of bore diameter *d*, generator circle diameter *D* and length *s* measured along the central axis. **1978** J. PARR *Introd. Ophthalmol.* ii. 44/1 A cylindrical curvature can be combined with a spherical curvature in a lens which is then called a toric surfaced lens. In astigmatism the surface of the cornea is toric instead of spherical.

‖ **torii** (tǫ·ri,i). Also **tori, torij.** [Jap., f. *tori* bird, fowl + *i* to sit, perch.] A ceremonial gateway in front of a Japanese Shintō shrine, consisting of two uprights and two cross-pieces of which the lower is straight and the upper usu. curved and projecting. Also *attrib.*
Occas. erron. interpreted as *pl.*
1727 J. SCHEUCHZER tr. *Kæmpfer's Hist. Japan* III. ii. 208 At the entry of the walk, which leads to the temple, stands..a particular fashioned gate, called *Torij*, and built either of stone or wood. **1874** C. HOEY tr. *Humbert's Japan & Japanese* I. ii. 14 A long avenue of fir-trees, headed by a sacred gate called a Tori. **1874** *Trans. Asiatic Soc. Japan* II. 116 The *torii* gradually assumed the character of a general symbol of *Shintô*. **1904** D. SLADEN *Playing the Game* II. v. 231 Tall torii, those mystic arches of Japan. **1911** *Encycl. Brit.* XV. 182 Originally designed as a perch for fowls which sang to the deities at daybreak, this torii subsequently came to be erroneously regarded as a gateway characteristic of the Shintō shrine. **1960** B. LEACH *Potter in Japan* ii. 55 Torii gateway leading to cryptomeria-shaded steps climbing to little empty Shinto Shrines. **1977** *Amer. Speech 1975* L. 69 Mills..must be almost as exotic to most younger Americans as torii or dagobas.

‖ **toril** (torī·l). Pl. **toriles.** [Sp.] One (*spec.* the last) of a series of pens in which a bull at a bullfight is confined before being released into the ring. Also *attrib.*
1893 CHAPMAN & BUCK *Wild Spain* v. 65 The noble bulls will be lured in their company away from their native plains,..to the entrance of the fatal *toril*. **1932** E. HEMINGWAY *Death in Afternoon* vi. 61 The alguacils ride up to under the president's box to ask for the key to the red door of the toril where the bull is waiting. **1961** *Times* 8 July 10/6 The *toril* gates open and out bounds the animal. **1974** *Encycl. Brit. Macropædia* III. 477/1 The *presidente municipal*..throws down to one of the *alguaciles* the key to the *toriles* or bull pens.

Torinese (tǫrinī·z), *a.* and *sb.* Also **Turinese.** [a. It. *Torinese*, f. *Torino* Turin: see -ESE.] **A.** *adj.* Of, pertaining to, or characteristic of the city of Turin in Piedmont, north-west Italy, its natives and inhabitants, or their dialect. **B.** *sb.* **a.** A native or inhabitant of Turin. **b.** The dialect of Italian spoken in Turin.
1883 H. JAMES *Little Tour in France* (1885) xix. 132 The shops are probably better than the Turinese, but the people are not so good. **1886** WEBSTER, Torinese *a.* and *sb.* **1960** A. COLQUHOUN tr. *di Lampedusa's Leopard* i. 19 The Piedmontese... Wouldn't things be just the same? Just Torinese instead of Neapolitan dialect; that's all. **1975** R. COBB *Paris & its Provinces* 2 The famous café..that unkind Torinese have sometimes called *il caffè della mennapausa*. *Ibid.* 3 Two louts engage the auburn beauty in the coarsest Torinese. **1977** *Times* 26 Mar. 10/1 Turinese cooking. **1980** *Times* 16 Oct. 7/2 As the five acts of the *opera* drifted their way onwards the Torinese decided they had had enough.

‖ **torista** (torī·sta). [Sp.] An enthusiast for bullfighting who is chiefly interested in the performance of the bull.
1957 A. MACNAB *Bulls of Iberia* p. xii, The more solid Spanish *aficionados*, especially those known as *toristas* because their primary interest is in the Bull rather than the Bullfighter. **1967** MCCORMICK & MASCAREÑAS *Compl. Aficionado* ii. 31 The torista exalts the toro over the torero to the point where he will ignore and despise the man's best achievements.

torma (tǭ·ɹmă). Pl. **torma, tormas.** [a. Tibetan.] A sacrificial offering burned in a Tibetan Buddhist ceremony.
1895 L. A. WADDELL *Buddhism of Tibet* xii. 297 Another food-offering is a high conical cake of dough, butter and sugar, variously coloured, named *tormā*.., that is, holy food. It is placed on a metal tray supported by a tripod. **1929** D. MACDONALD *Land of Lama* xvii. 205 Everyone makes offerings in the temples, while the monks of the monastery prepare *torma*, symbolic emblems made of butter, on thin wooden or leather backing, often eight or ten feet high. **1958** *Illustr. London News* 13 Dec. 1041/1 A set of such figures, known as *torma* and representing divine personages, spirits and demons, as well as offerings of various forms, are required for every rite conducted by lamas. **1970** R. D. TARING *Daughter of Tibet* x. 135 On a certain day they burnt *tormas* (cone-shaped religious sweets). **1979** J. NORBU *Horseman in Snow* 46 The grass.. yields a red dye that is used to colour sacrificial offerings called tormas.

tormented, *ppl. a.* Add: **2.** *U.S. slang.* Used adjectivally and adverbially as a mild equivalent of DAMNED *ppl. a.* 4.
1825 J. NEAL *Brother Jonathan* I. 138 They hadn't come such a tormented long piece. **1867** J. R. LOWELL *Biglow Papers* 2nd Ser. p. lix, *Tormented*, euphemism for damned, as, 'not a tormented cent'. **1903** G. S. WASSON *Cap'n Simeon's Store* 86 It don't look right for nobody.. to take and hang on to them tormented ole witch-bridles so-fashion! **1938** M. K. RAWLINGS *Yearling* xi. 119 'Look at him,' she said. 'Tormented Yankee. His feet drag like a 'gator's tail.'

tormentor. Add: **3. f.** Freq. a device for squirting liquid (further examples).
1894 A. MORRISON *Tales of Mean Streets* 34 The ladies' tormentors are larger, and their contents smell worse than at any other fair. *Ibid.* 36 Billy bought a ladies' tormentor and began to squirt it at Lizerunt. **1912** J. MASEFIELD *Widow in Bye St.* 19 One's so safe with such a son to con her Through all the noises and through all the press, Boys daredn't squirt tormenters on her dress.

torn, *ppl. a.* Add: **c. torn-down** (examples in literal sense).
1933 S. SPENDER *Poems* 40 Through torn-down portions of old fabric. **1953** K. REISZ *Technique Film Editing* i. 35 Other fragments of the torn-down statue of the Czar reassembling.

tornadoed (tǫɹnē̆ⁱ·dōᵘd), *ppl. a. nonce-wd.* [f. TORNADO + -ED[2].] Affected by tornadoes. (In quot. *fig.*)
1851 H. MELVILLE *Moby Dick* III. i. 19 Even so, amid the tornadoed Atlantic of my being, do I myself still for ever centrally disport in mute calm.

toro (tǫ·ro, ‖ to·ro). [Sp.] A bull used in bullfighting. Also, a child's bullfighting game.
1660 in T. Mathews *Collection of Lett.* 172 But, in a word, me-thinks, that not onely in their sports of Cannas and Toros, but even in some more solemn and serious things than those, they are not free from having still somewhat of the Moor. **1846** R. FORD *Gatherings from Spain* xxi. 291 The young urchins in the streets play at '*toro*', as ours do at leap-frog. **1932** R. CAMPBELL *Taurine Provence* 66 Novillos (bulls that are full grown but lack the ultimate footsureness of the toros). **1958** L. VAN DER POST *Lost World Kalahari* i. 29 The rhinoceros, angry like a pricked toro with the rosette of blood that comes to it in adolescence vivid on the flank. **1967** MCCORMICK & MASCAREÑAS *Compl. Aficionado* i. 4 He might be compared to the actor but for the fact that he writes his own script, in collaboration with the *toro*.

toroid (tǫ·roid). [f. TOR(US + -OID.] An object having the shape of a torus (sense *4); a toroidal object.
1886 G. S. CARR *Synopsis Elem. Results Pure & Applied Math.* I. II. 932/1 (Index), Toroid. **1903** *Astrophysical Jrnl.* XVIII. 339 Each reflecting surface..would be part of a parabolic toroid. **1916** G. KAPP *Princ. Electr. Engin.* I. xi. 211 The term 'toroid' in this connection means a circular coil of *n* turns of wire wound so that the cross-section is a circle. **1954** *Electronic Engin.* XXVI. 196 Magnetic toroids could..be used..for random access information storage at the rate of one core per digit. **1973** *Nature* 15 June 386/2 This field is supplemented by an additional field produced by a coil wound on the toroid.

toroidal, *a.* Add: (Earlier and later examples.) Also = TORIC *a.* in Dict. and Suppl.
1881 *Phil. Trans. R. Soc.* CLXXII. 609 By 'toroidal functions' are understood functions which satisfy Laplace's equation and which are suitable for conditions given over the surface of tores. **1946** [see *POLOIDAL *a.*]. **1948** *Electronic Engin.* XX. 28 The problem..was solved by using a very few turns of concentrically wound copper tape and achieving the neccessary self-inductance by winding on a high permeability toroidal core. **1962** CORSON & LORRAIN *Introd. Electromagn. Fields* v. 200 *(caption)* Toroidal coil of square cross section carrying a current *I*. **1973** *Sci. Amer.* Aug. 111/1 Optical surfaces are far from spherical these days; even our spectacle lenses are toroidal. **1975** *New Yorker* 12 May 84/2 Wind instruments were bolted to a toroidal buoy.

Hence **toroi·dally** *adv.*
1961 *Technology* Mar. 72/1 A variable-ratio toroidally-wound transformer. **1970** *Nature* 26 Sept. 1299/1 Toroidally contained fusion plasmas. **1978** *Gramophone* Aug. 396/3 To the right of the PCB is a massive, toroidally wound mains transformer.

Torontonian (torǫntōᵘ·niăn), *sb.* [f. *Toronto*, capital of the province of Ontario in Canada + *-n-* + -IAN.] A native or inhabitant of Toronto.
1875 *United Service Mag.* Dec. 500 'No great thing after all!' exclaimed a Quebecker or Torontonian. **1967** *Economist* 29 July 396/3 Torontonians are often suspected of believing that money decides everything. **1975** *Globe & Mail* (Toronto) 16 July 7/3 Many Torontonians are probably not aware of the Western Guard's propaganda.

torp (tǭɹp), slang abbrev. of TORPEDO *sb.* 2 and *torpedo juice* s.v. *TORPEDO *sb.* 4. Cf. *TORPS.

1929 *Papers Mich. Acad. Sci., Arts & Lett.* X. 330 *Torp*, a torpedo. **1945** J. BRYAN *Diary* 23 Apr. in *Aircraft Carrier* (1954) 193 Someone brought a pint of torp. **1967** B. KNOX *Blacklight* ii. 42 If anyone does find a stray torp, then they'll make damn' sure it stays lost.

torpedo, *sb.* Add: **2.** (Earlier example.)

1776 J. THACHER *Military Jrnl.* (1823) 75 Mr. Bushnell gave to his machine the name of American Turtle or Torpedo.

b. See *aerial torpedo* s.v. *AERIAL *a.* 5. Also without specifying adj.

1922 W. RALEIGH *War in Air* I. 467 The hope of using the torpedo, launched from the air, against ships which are sheltered and protected from naval attack, was never long absent from the minds of those who directed the activities of the Royal Naval Air Service. **1943** *Jane's Fighting Ships 1942* 5, 18 inch torpedoes are used by the torpedo bombers of the Fleet Air Arm.

3*. *slang.* **a.** *U.S.* A professional gunman. **b.** A tablet or capsule of a narcotic drug.

1929 G. L. HOSTETTER *It's a Racket!* 241 *Torpedo*, a professional gunman or bomb tosser. **1940** R. CHANDLER *Farewell, my Lovely* xxxvi. 239 There's yellow cops and there's yellow torpedoes. **1971** *Go ask Alice* (1972) 28 He introduced me to torpedoes on Friday and Speed on Sunday. **1973** P. EVANS *Bodyguard Man* iii. 24 Ask Al Capone. Mention his torpedoes to most people and they conjure up mental sketches of middle-aged heavyweights. **1978** M. RUSSELL *Daylight Robbery* xv. 154 The phial.. contained more tablets... He tried to estimate how long.. it took a couple of the torpedoes to send him off.

3.** = *torpedo-body*. Also, a car with such a body.

1909 *Daily Chron.* 13 Nov. 9/6 There is a general tendency..to utilise the form of body known as the 'torpedo'. **1930** V. PALMER *Passage* III. i. 213 Another car coming! They..watched with strained eyes as the dusty torpedo shot into view. **1968** *Compl. Encycl. Motorcars* 624 *Torpedo*,..an open touring car with an unbroken line from bonnet to windscreen, and from windscreen right through to the back of the car, the seats being flush with the body sides. Bodies of this design began to appear in about 1910.

4. (sense 2) *torpedo bomber, coxswain, gunner, plane, ship*; *torpedo-carrying, -proof* adjs.; **torpedo-body** (example); **torpedo destroyer** (earlier example); **torpedo juice** *slang*, intoxicating liquor extracted from torpedo fuel; any strong home-made alcoholic liquor; **torpedo-tube** (earlier example); **torpedo vessel** (earlier example).

1924 *Motor* 21 Oct. 630 (*caption*) A handsome torpedo body, on a Voisin chassis, by H. J. Mulliner. **1930** *Flight* 16 May 535/2 The aircraft equipment consists of..two flights of two-seater fleet torpedo bombers. **1970** *Times* 24 Mar. 2/4 (*caption*) Using engine cylinders taken from an exhibit at the Imperial War Museum, the last airworthy Swordfish torpedo bomber in the Royal Navy. **1922** W. RALEIGH *War in Air* I. 466 The torpedo-carrying aeroplane or seaplane would outrival the submarine as a weapon of offence against enemy shipping. **1903** *Windsor Mag.* XIX. 6/2 Speakin' as a torpedo-coxswain,..I presume we fall in. **1918** KIPLING *Land & Sea Tales* (1923) 107 If his torpedo-coxswain had ever allowed anyone to look there. **1896** *World* 12 Feb. 29/1 It would not cost us much—not so much, in the long run, as a single torpedo-destroyer. **1903** *Windsor Mag.* XIX. 9/2 What's a torpedo-gunner more or less to a full lootenant? **1928** C. F. S. GAMBLE *Story N. Sea Air Station* xiv. 234 The crew consisted of the pilot, the observer, the torpedo-gunner, and a machine-gunner for the back seat. **1946** *Seafarers' Log* 31 May 13/5, I have known many Navy men who were chronic drinkers at sea as well as ashore. Some have gone blind from drinking torpedo juice. **1961** *Guardian* 26 Sept. 9/5 Torpedo juice is a combination of these [*sc.* bush beer and toddy] and acquires its name from its lethal effect. The original torpedo juice was the neat alcohol extracted from torpedoes during the war by American servicemen and sometimes mixed with local bush beers to soften the blow. **1917** *Flying* 1 May 317/2 Admiral Fiske declared that torpedo-planes in the battle of Jutland would have given a tremendous advantage to the side employing them. **1981** G. MACBETH *Kind of Treason* xi. 106 The *Prince of Wales* and the *Repulse* had been sunk by Japanese torpedo planes. **1914** H. H. ASQUITH *Let.* 27 Oct. in M. Gilbert *W. S. Churchill* (1972) III. Compan. I. 220 Torpedo-proof harbours and refuges. **1873** *Illustr. London News* 29 Mar. 294/2 It is also proposed to build a small torpedo-ship of 214 tons burden by way of trying experiments. **1911** *Q. Rev.* Oct. 476 This gradual merging of the essential features of the gun-ship and the torpedo-ship is now about to find expression in the submarine. **1893** *Souvenir World's Fair: Naval Exhibit*, The battery mounted comprises..two Gatling guns, and six torpedo tubes or torpedo guns. **1877** *Illustr. London News* 16 June 556 Steel Torpedo-vessel used by the Russians on the Danube.

torpex (tǭ·ɹpeks). [Blend of TORPEDO *sb.* + EXPLOSIVE *sb.*] An explosive consisting largely of T.N.T., cyclonite, and aluminium, used for depth charges.

1948 *Jane's Fighting Ships 1947–48* 6/1 These charges could be set to explode at any depth, the former [*sc.* hedgehog] employing torpex, and the latter minol. **1974** [see *RDX].

‖ **torpilleur** (tǭɹpiyöɹ). *Obs.* exc. *Hist.* [Fr., f. *torpille* torpedo.] A torpedo boat or destroyer in the French navy.

[**1894** W. LE QUEUX *Great War in England in 1897* xiv. 88 The reinforcements consisted of the French battleships ..together with nine cruisers, and thirty-eight *torpilleurs de haute mer.*] **1950** *Jane's Fighting Ships 1949–50* 181/2 (*caption*) 3 ex-German Type (Classed as *Torpilleurs*.)

torps (tǭɹps), slang abbrev. of *torpedo-lieutenant* s.v. TORPEDO *sb.* 4. Cf. *TORP.

1914 'BARTIMEUS' *Naval Occasions* xxiv. 237 The Torpedo Lieutenant (hereinafter known as 'Torps') was awakened by the June sunlight. **1943** C. S. FORESTER *Ship* 20 Torps and Lightfoot, the Officers of the Watch.

torque. Add: **c. torque converter,** a device that varies or multiplies torque; **torque meter, torquemeter** = *torsionmeter* s.v. *TORSION 3; **torque motor** *Electr. Engin.*, an electric motor designed to exert a torque without continuous rotation; **torque wrench,** a device to set and adjust the tension of nuts and bolts.

1934 WEBSTER, Torque converter. **1944** *Machine Design* July 117 The Lysholm-Smith torque converter.. incorporates multiple-stage turbine blading. **1970** *Commercial Motor* 25 Sept. 65/3 Its 190 bhp is passed through a two-stage torque-convertor which in its hydraulic stage multiplies the engine torque by 4·7 and in its mechanical stage has a ratio of 1·046 to 1, a slight overdrive. **1911** H. M. HOBART *Dict. Electr. Terms* II. 564/1 Torque meter. **1955** *Electronic Engin.* XXVII. 430/1 Several types of torquemeter are known but..it has sometimes proved difficult to obtain reliable results in this particular application [*sc.* in aircraft]. **1926** *Gloss. Terms Electr. Engin.* (Brit. Engin. Stand. Assoc.) 54 Torque motor. **1946** *Nature* 13 July 54/2 As a torque motor, the machine was required to operate on 333 c./s. and works continuously under standstill conditions, with a temperature rise at 20 volts/phase of about 30°C. **1979** *Engin. Materials & Design* Oct. 43/1 Torque motors are those which are designed to provide their maximum torque under the conditions of 'stall' or 'locked rotor'. **1948** A. W. JUDGE *Automobile Engine Overhaul* (ed. 3) x. 187 It is important to tighten each nut a little at a time... A torque wrench is here an advantage. **1979** G. HAMMOND *Dead Game* v. 55 Janet was still working on the hydraulics of the tractor... She pulled gently on the torque-wrench.

torque, *v.* [f. TORQUE².] *trans.* To apply torque to. So **to·rquing** *vbl. sb.*

1954 *Fasteners* IX. v. 3 The subject of bolt torquing. **1960** D. A. HALPERIN *Building with Steel* xii. 163/2 He then checks the bolts to verify that they have been torqued to at least specified minimum tension. **1978** *Nature* 12 Oct. 517/1 Perhaps these radio galaxies are systems where a pre-existing central black hole is gradually being torqued into alignment with the angular momentum of newly supplied fuel that has reactivated the nucleus. **1981** *Ibid.* 24 Sept. 261/2 Drilling conditions were rugged... Cave-ins and torquing finally caused them to abandon the hole well above their oceanic crustal target.

torquey (tǭ·ɹki), *a.* [f. TORQUE² + -Y¹.] Of the engine of a motor vehicle: producing plenty of torque; able to pull well.

1977 *What Car?* Apr. 59/1 Tractable, torquey engine. **1981** *Motor* 27 June 9/2 The torquey, sweet engine.

torr (tǭɹ). *Physics.* Also **Torr.** [f. the name of *Torricelli* (see TORRICELLIAN *a.*).] A unit of pressure used chiefly in measuring partial vacuums (see quot. 1958); 133·32 newton/sq. metre.

1949 S. DUSHMAN *Sci. Foundations Vacuum Technique* i. 4 In German literature, 1 Tor (or 1 Torr) is used to designate 1 mm Hg pressure. **1958** *Gloss. Terms Vacuum Technol.* (*B.S.I.*) 7 *Torr*, a unit of pressure defined by the relationship: 760 torr = 1 standard atmosphere (atm) = 1 013 250 dyn/cm² exactly. 1 torr is equal to the conventional barometric millimetre of mercury..within 1 part in 7×10^6. *Ibid.* 20, 1 torr = 1·333 22 millibar (mb) approximately. **1981** J. B. ADAMS in J. H. Mulvey *Nature of Matter* vii. 151 It is necessary to achieve a very low pressure in the vacuum chamber; pressures of 10^{-11} Torr are essential.

Torrens (Tǫ·rĕnz). The name of Sir Robert *Torrens* (1814–84), first Premier of South Australia, used *attrib.* in *Torrens system*, a system of land title registration devised by him, and adopted in Australia and elsewhere outside the U.K.

1863 R. R. TORRENS (*title*) Transfer of land by 'registration of title', as now in operation in Australia under the 'Torrens system'. **1905** J. E. HOGG (*title*) The Australian Torrens system. *Ibid.* p. v, The system of land transfer and registration known as the Torrens system has now been in operation in Australasia more than forty-six years. **1976** S. R. SIMPSON *Land Law & Registration* v. 68 Outside Great Britain the system of registering title..is widely known as the 'Torrens system', for it was Sir Robert Torrens who in 1858 introduced registration of title into South Australia, the first jurisdiction (at least of jurisdictions using English land law) to establish such a system.

torreyite (tǫ·riˌəit). *Min.* [f. the name of John *Torrey* (1796–1873), U.S. scientist + -ITE¹.] A hydrated basic sulphate of magnesium, manganese, and zinc, $(Mg, Mn)_5Zn_2SO_4(OH)_{12}.4H_2O$, found as massive aggregates of white to colourless monoclinic crystals.

1949 J. PREWITT-HOPKINS in *Amer. Mineralogist* XXXIV. 595 A new name, torreyite, is proposed to replace the name delta-mooreite. **1979** *Ibid.* LXIV. 952/2 Torreyite in fine-grained aggregates resembles hardened granular sugar.

Torricellian, *a.* (Earlier example of *Torricellian vacuum.*)

1753 *Phil. Trans. R. Soc.* XLVII. 371 The Torricellian vacuum then occupied a space of about thirty inches.

Torridon (tǫ·ridǫn). *Geol.* The name of Loch *Torridon* on the NW. coast of Scotland, used *attrib.* to designate Torridonian rocks (see next), which are well exposed there.

1873 *Q. Jrnl. Geol. Soc.* XXIX. 334 The lowest conglomerate bed of the Torridon sandstone is seen in fine section in a cliff north-west of Brochel castle. **1896** [see next]. **1930** PEACH & HORNE *Chapters Geol. Scotl.* iii. 83 The various groups of Torridon Sandstone are not equally developed along the belt from Cape Wrath to Skye. **1963** D. W. & E. E. HUMPHRIES tr. *Termier's Erosion & Sedimentation* i. 7 In this field the studies of British scientists.. extend over rocks of all ages back to the Torridon Sandstone (Precambrian).

Torridonian (tǫridōᵘ·niăn), *a.* *Geol.* [f. prec. + -IAN.] Of, pertaining to, or designating the later of the two main series of Pre-Cambrian rocks in NW. Scotland, which occur in a narrow belt running from Cape Wrath to Skye and consist chiefly of sandstones, grits, and shales; also the time of their deposition. Also *absol.*, the Torridonian series.

1896 J. W. JUDD *Student's Lyell* xxviii. 435/1 The Torridon Sandstone or Torridonian. *Ibid.* 435/2 The Cambrian strata being found lying on every portion of the Torridonian series. **1934,** etc. [see *MOINE]. **1938,** etc. [see *MOINIAN *a.*]. **1952** *Geol. Mag.* LXXXIX. 70 The possibility of a Torridonian age for this very isolated outlier should not be excluded. **1969** BENNISON & WRIGHT *Geol. Hist. Brit. Isles* iii. 46 Resting with marked unconformity upon the Lewisian of the foreland is the Torridonian Series, an enormous thickness of dominantly arenaceous rocks. **1971** *Country Life* 18 Nov. 1349/3 The fertile oolite soil gives way to Torridonian sandstone just north of James Gillie's croft. **1976** T. R. OWEN *Geol. Evolution Brit. Isles* ii. 19 Radiometric datings (1000–800 m.y.) now confirm that the Torridonian and the Moine are the lateral equivalents of one another.

torry (tǫ·ri), *v.* [ad. Sp. *torear* to fight (a bull), to be a bullfighter.] *trans.* To provoke and fight (a bull).

1936 R. CAMPBELL *Mithraic Emblems* 52 The white Torero—him who took the toss Sky-high upon the black horns of the Cross, For torrying the hornèd prince of Death. **1957** A. MACNAB *Bulls of Iberia* viii. 81 To give passes to a bull is not the same as to 'torry' it (*torear*). *Torear* means to exercise control over the bull at all times, and to work on it as desired. *Ibid.* 263 *Torear*, to 'torry', neologism..adopted from Roy Campbell..who has used it in print for twenty years.

torsade. (Earlier example.)

1872 *Young Englishwoman* Nov. 593/1 The black velvet bonnet is trimmed with a torsade of violet faille ribbon.

‖ **Torschlusspanik** (tōᵊ·ɹʃluspa:nik). [Ger. lit. 'shut door (or gate) panic'.] A sense of alarm or anxiety (said to be experienced particularly in middle age) caused by the suspicion that life's opportunities are passing (or have passed) one by; *spec.* that manifested in an ageing woman who longs to (re)discover the (sexual) excitement of youth, and who fears being left 'on the shelf'.

1963 P. BRACKEN *I Hate to Housekeep Bk.* ix. 92 The random housewife is often prone to Torschlusspanik, or fear of being locked in the park at night, after the gates are closed. **1977** *Time* 8 Aug. 21/3 She was haunted by *Torschluss-panik* (mid-life crisis). **1980** *Times Lit. Suppl.* 14 Mar. 287/2 She [*sc.* Mme de Staël] is perhaps history's most outstanding case of *Torschlusspanik*: the panic at the shutting of the door.

torsiograph (tǭ·ɹʃiogrɑf). *Mech.* [f. late L. *torsiō* (see TORSION) + -GRAPH.] An instrument for measuring torsional oscillations of the crankshaft of an engine.

1930 *Engineering* 25 Apr. 551/3 The handiest instrument, and therefore the most widely used, is the torsiograph. **1950** *Ibid.* 1 Sept. 204/1 It was decided..to carry out torsiograph tests on the engines under specially standardised conditions with specified instrumentation.

torsion. Add: **1. e.** *Math.* The degree to which a curve departs from being planar at any given point, measured by the rate of change of the angle of the osculating plane or the binormal with respect to distance along the curve; *radius of torsion*, the reciprocal of this.

1862 G. SALMON *Treat. Analytic Geom. Three Dimensions* xi. 269 The angle made with each other by two consecutive osculating planes..we shall call the angle of torsion, and denote by $d\eta$. *Ibid.* 270 Following the analogy of the radius of curvature which is $ds/d\theta$, the later French writers denote the quantity $ds/d\eta$ by the letter r, and call it the radius of torsion. **1939** BURINGTON & TORRANCE

Higher Math. vi. 711 Torsion is agreed to be positive when the rotation (with *s* increasing) of the binormal increases in the same sense as that of a right-handed screw traveling in the direction of **t**. **1978** E. C. YOUNG *Vector & Tensor Analysis* ii. 106 The torsion of a plane curve is zero, just as the curvature of a straight line is zero.

f. *Zool.* The twisting of the visceral hump of gastropod molluscs through 180 degrees when the embryo reaches a certain stage of development.

1888 ROLLESTON & JACKSON *Forms Animal Life* (ed. 2) 475 In..the *Streptoneura*, the posterior union of the visceral nerves..is situated dorsally to the intestine, and the loop is therefore twisted with the torsion of the visceral dome. **1930** G. R. DE BEER *Embryol. & Evol.* vii. 53 The limpet develops into a more or less symmetrical Veliger larva which suddenly undergoes a twist through 180°, the process of torsion occupying two or three minutes. **1972** M. S. GARDINER *Biol. of Invertebrates* ii. 59/2 Torsion appears to be a reversible process, for in some genera the anus and the organs on either side of it lie posteriorly and the nerve commissures are untwisted.

g. *Chem.* Restricted rotation of an atom or group about a bond joining it to another atom.

1932 *Physical Rev.* XL. 445 (*heading*) The torsion oscillator-rotator in the quantum mechanics. **1978** *Nature* 14 Dec. 674/1 Although in some cases, rotation of a rigid molecular structure cannot lead to superposition, this may be possible as a result of torsion about certain bonds.

3. torsion bar, a bar that is subject to torque; *spec.* one in the suspension of some motor vehicles, fixed to the frame at one end and the wheel assembly at the other so that up-and-down motion of the latter tends to twist the bar and is thereby absorbed; **torsionmeter, torsion meter**, an instrument which measures the torsion in a rotating shaft, thus providing information about the power output of the engine driving it; **torsion test** *Engin.*, a test in which a material is subjected to torsion (see quot. 1936).

1937 *Daily Herald* 15 Jan. 16/6 The action of the torsion-bar controlled shock-absorbers preventing roll and pitch. **1978** L. PRYOR *Viper* viii. 150 He'd nodded and set to work ordering adjustments to the tires, wings and torsion bars. **1983** *Sci. Amer.* Jan. 120/2 The strength of the gravitational force is measured from the magnetic force that is required to prevent the rotation of a torsion bar when an additional mass is brought close to it. **1905** *Engineering* 7 Apr. 440 (*heading*) Denny and Johnson's torsion meter. **1970** *Jrnl. Physics E* III. 105/1 The only practicable way to measure the power [of a ship's main engine] is by the use of a torsionmeter, ie an instrument that measures the twist put in the propeller shaft by the torque it transmits. **1891** W. G. KIRCALDY *Strength & Properties of Materials* vii. 196 Some examples of Twisting, or torsion, tests have been given to show in a graphic way the behaviour of different metals. **1936** P. F. FOSTER *Mech. Testing of Metals & Alloys* vii. 115 Torsion tests are carried out to determine the modulus of rigidity of a material..or to ascertain its ultimate torisional strength. **1969** DIVAKARAN & GARG *Strength of Materials* i. 27 In a torsion test on the same specimen the angle of twist was found to be 0·43°.

torso. Add: **2.** (Earlier example.)

1825 T. MOORE *Life R. B. Sheridan* xvi. 534 And exhibit little more than the mere *Torso* of his eloquence.

3. *Comb.*: **torso-tosser** *slang*, a hootchy-kootchy dancer.

1927 *Vanity Fair* (N.Y.) XXIX. 134/2 A kootch or hootchie kootchie dancer is a 'torso tosser'. **1954** F. P. KEYES *Royal Box* 361 Barbara Villiers, a torso-tosser who got to be no less than the Duchess of Cleveland.

torte. Restrict †*Obs.* to sense in Dict. and add: **2.** Pl. **torten** or **tortes.** [a. G. *torte*, of same origin.] An elaborate sweet cake or tart.

1748 H. GLASSE *Art of Cookery* (ed. 3) viii. 142 To make a Tort. First make a fine Puff-paste. **1957** [see *PASTRY 1 c]. **1967** V. NABOKOV *Speak, Memory* (rev. ed.) x. 205 Wedges of slightly salty mokka *torte* with whipped cream. **1972** F. B. MAYNARD *Raisins & Almonds* 20 Mama produced meringues..puff paste..tortes layered with nut creams and Turkish delight.

tortellini (tǫːtĭlīˑni), *sb. pl.* Also *erron.* **tortelloni.** [a. It., pl. of *tortellino*, dim. of *tortello* cake, fritter, dim. of *torta*: see TORTE.] Small squares of pasta rolled round a filling and then formed into a ring shape.

1937 M. MORPHY *Good Food from Italy* 5 One of the characteristic features of Italian soups is their garnish..—*ravioli, tortellini, gnocchi* and plain dumplings or forcemeat dumplings. **1954** E. DAVID *Italian Food* 102 Although tortellini are always to be had in the restaurants of Bologna, in private houses they are still the great dish for Christmas Eve. **1975** J. CLEARY *Safe House* iv. 172 Charlie Lincoln ate the now-just-warm tortelloni he had bought. **1980** *Times* 18 Oct. 11/8 The Bolognese invented tagliatelle, tortellini and lasagne.

tortie (tǭ·ɹti). [dim. of TORTOISE-SHELL.] = *tortoise-shell cat* s.v. TORTOISE-SHELL 4 b. Also *attrib.*

1948 P. M. SODERBERG *Cat Breeding* 312 The three colours required in the Tortie are black, red and cream. **1958** E. F. DAGLISH *Pet-Keeper's Man.* 1 Tortoise shell cats are almost invariably females... Anyone owning a male 'tortie' may pride himself on the possession of a feline rarity. **1960** *Times* 17 Mar. 1/4 (Advt.), Must find home for beautiful tortiecat. **1976** POND & SAYER *Cats* 25 Bi-Colours, bred from Tortie and White mothers,..could be produced.

tortillon (tǭɹti·lyoṅ). [a. F. *tortillon*, f. *tortiller* to twist, twirl.] = STUMP *sb.*[2]

1885 F. FOWLER *Drawing in Charcoal and Crayon* ii. 12 The other form of paper stump, known as the tortillon, is made of strips of paper rolled to a point like spills. **1895** *Army & Navy Co-op Soc. Price List* 674/2 Stumps for chalk drawing... Tortillons, White. **1970** *Oxf. Compan. Art* 1111/2 *Stump*, also called *tortillon*. A short tapered stick usually of cork or tightly rolled leather or paper, used to soften the edges of a drawing or spread the chalk, crayon, or pencil in shading. It was used in 18th-c. France.

tortoise. Add: **4.** *tortoise-shaped* adj. (later example); *tortoise-like* adj. and adv. (later examples); *tortoise-fashion* adv.; **tortoise core** *Archæol.*, a core (CORE *sb.*[1] 5) resembling a tortoise in shape; **tortoise race,** a race in which the last person home wins.

1919 R. A. SMITH in *Man* July 101 Tortoise-cores have been found on the bank of the ancient river to the south-east. **1972** K. P. OAKLEY *Man the Tool-maker* 52 Viewed on its outer face an oval flake thus detached from a tortoise-core has the appearance of a flat, finely worked hand-axe. **1894** A. BEARDSLEY *Let.* Oct. (1971) 75 The Tannhaüser gets on tortoise fashion but admirably for all that. **1921** W. DE LA MARE *Crossings* 71 Ann slowly thrusts her head out of the snow-house, tortoise-fashion. **1956** P. H. JOHNSON *Last Resort* xxiii. 143 His aged, stilted stride, his tortoise-like out-thrusting of the head. **1982** 'J. Ross' *Death's Head* iv. 22 The traffic once more moving, though at a tortoise-like crawl. **1913** Tortoise race [listed in Dict]. **1914** ROWE & WEBB *Guide to Study of Eng.* iii. 126 This is a 'tortoise' race, the last man to receive the prize. **1911** *Archæologia* LXII. II. 523Tortoise-shaped cores. This is perhaps the most striking group in the enormous series from Northfleet.

b. (With capital initial.) A proprietary name for a type of solid-fuel-burning stove.

1884 *Trade Marks Jrnl.* 5 Nov. 1025 The Tortoise... Slow combustion stoves. Charles Portway & Son, 'Tortoise' Stove Works, and High Street, Halstead, Essex; Stove Manufacturers. **1895** *Army & Navy Co-op Soc. Price List* 336 (*heading*) 'Tortoise' heating stoves. **1948** J. BETJEMAN *Few Late Chrysanthemums* (1954) 10 The Tortoise stove is lit again. **1981** *Country Life* 12 Feb. 411/3 (Advt.), The old world appeal of the Tortoise Ornamental Stove... Accepts woods, coal or smokeless fuel.

tortoise-shell. Add: **4. b. tortoise-shell ware** (examples).

1879 [see *agate-ware* s.v. *AGATE 6]. **1975** *Country Life* 9 Oct. 898/2 (*caption*) 19th-century teapot similar to Whieldon's tortoiseshell ware.

5. *tortoise-shell worker.*

1903 [see *CEMENTER]. **1931** P. A. S. PHILLIPS (*title*) John Obrisset Huguenot: carver, medallist, horn and tortoiseshell worker.

Tortolan (tǫɹtōˑlăn), *a.* and *sb.* [f. *Tortola* + -AN.] **A.** *adj.* Of or pertaining to Tortola, the largest of the British Virgin Islands. **B.** *sb.* A native or inhabitant of Tortola.

1923 C. F. JENKINS *Tortola* xi. 67 Captain Tittley, the commander of the Tortolan navy. **1953** *Caribbean Q.* III. II. 112 Most of Tortola's exports go to St. Thomas and most of her imports come from the island, and Tortolans go frequently by sloop or launch merely to do their marketing. *Ibid.* 113 In the Tortolan countryside..no one is seen at work between ten and four o'clock. **1980** *Washington Post* 20 July K6 Almost certainly, the government worker is a native St. Thomian, the taxi driver a Tortolan by birth.

Tortoni (tǭɹtōᵘ·ni). Also **tortoni.** The name of an Italian café-owner in Paris in the 18th cent., used *attrib.* and *absol.* to designate a kind of ice-cream.

1911 LEITER & VAN BERGH *Flower City Cook Bk.* xxiv. 128 *Tortoni pudding*, Scald 1 pint milk..; add 1 tablespoon of flour..; 1 egg and 1 cupful sugar... Add ½ pound chopped almonds, 7 macaroons..and a little vanilla. Cool. Add 1 pint whipped cream. Freeze. **1958** *Sunday Times* 27 Apr. 22/4 A raspberry Tortoni (raspberries plus cream, macaroons and a touch of kirsch). **1979** *Tucson Mag.* Sept. 61/2 Then try tortoni (made on the premises).

Tortonian (tǭɹtōᵘ·niăn), *a. Geol.* [ad. G. *Tortonien* sb. (K. Mayer 1857, in *Verhandl. der allgemeinen schweiz. Ges. für die gesammten Naturwiss.* 171), f. *Tortona*, name of a town in N. Italy: see -IAN.] Of, pertaining to, or designating a stage of the upper (or middle) Miocene in Europe. Also *absol.*, the Tortonian age.

1885 A. GEIKIE *Text-bk. Geol.* (ed. 2) 873 Italy... The Tortonian stage (3) is made up [of] blue marls, reaching the great thickness of 3900 feet. **1931** GREGORY & BARRETT *Gen. Stratigr.* xii. 192 The volcanoes of the Rhine began in the Tortonian. **1974** *Nature* 22 Mar. 312/2 We suggest that the separation of Calabria from Sardinia took place in the middle Miocene, and that Tortonian deformation in Sicily indicates a collision that terminates this phase of separation.

torture, *v.* Add: **3. b.** Also with *into.*

1789 J. MOORE *Zeluco* I. ix. 80 What he said was excusable; to endeavour to torture it into mutiny would be absurd. **1840** POE *Tales of Mystery* (1905) 365 An unredeemed dreariness of thought which no goading of the imagination could torture into aught of the sublime. **1956** E. H. HUTTEN *Lang. Mod. Physics* vi. 232 It is possible to torture almost any statement into the logical form of an implication.

torula. Add: Hence **torulo·sis** *Path.* [-OSIS] = *CRYPTOCOCCOSIS.

1929 *Jrnl. Amer. Med. Assoc.* 9 Feb. 438/1 Acute miliary torulosis of the lungs follows a blood stream dissemination of the torula organisms from some chronic lesion. **1974** S. L. ROBBINS *Pathologic Basis of Dis.* xxxii. 1494/1 European blastomycosis is known more commonly as cryptococcosis or torulosis... It is caused by a blastomyces known as *Cryptococcus hominis* or *Torula histolytica.*

† **torulin.** *Biochem. Obs.* [f. TORUL(A + -IN[1].] = *THIAMINE 3.

1912 E. S. EDIE et al. in *Biochem. Jrnl.* VI. 242 The substance isolated we propose to call Torulin. **1931** SHERMAN & SMITH *Vitamins* (ed. 2) ii. 81 The symptom of opisthotonus in pigeons appears to be due to excess of lactic acid in the brain and is cured most quickly by injecting concentrated preparations of torulin locally.

torus. Add: **4.** In mod. use, a surface or solid conceived of as generated by the circular motion of a circle about an axis outside itself but lying in its plane; also, any body topologically equivalent to this, having one hole in it but not necessarily circular in form or cross-section. (Further examples.)

1958 *Times* 25 Jan. 4/5 The Zeta apparatus is essentially a ring-shaped metal tube, or torus,..containing deuterium gas at low pressure. **1966** E. H. SPANIER *Algebraic Topology* 148 The surface with one handle is topologically the torus. **1976** *Offshore Platforms & Pipelining* 49/1 The base structure consists of a torus through which the piles are placed. **1977** *Time* 6 June 54/3 Tokamaks are toruses, or doughnut-shaped chambers, surrounded by huge electromagnets.

Tory, *sb.* and *a.* Add: **A.** *sb.* **4. b.** During the American civil war, applied in the Confederate states to a Union sympathizer.

1862 *Southern Confederacy* (Atlanta, Georgia) 3 May 3/1 The other prisoners..are all sharp, intelligent-looking men—no hard looking cases like Yankee prisoners, and East Tennessee tories usually are. **1866** W. REID *After the War* 402 Ef you fetch any d— tories heah, that went agin their State, and so kin take the oath,..'twill soon be too hot to hold 'em. **1953** T. C. BRYAN *Confederate Georgia* ix. 152 In the fall of 1864 bands of Tories were plundering northeast Georgia.

C. 3. a. (Earlier example.)

1867 LD. SALISBURY in *Q. Rev.* CXXIII. 539 It was not till the earlier struggles of the session were over..that the project of Tory democracy, which had been so long and so sedulously concealed, was at last given to the world.

b. Tory Democratic *a.* (earlier example).

1885 E. W. HAMILTON *Diary* 15 June (1972) II. 885 It was R. Churchill's way of protesting publicly against a revival of the old Tory Cabinet..without any infusion of fresh (Tory-democratic) blood.

Tosa (tōᵘ·să), *sb.*[1] The name of an aristocratic Japanese family of court painters used *attrib.* to designate (the products of) a school of painting characterized by the use of traditional themes and techniques, which flourished from the mid-fifteenth to the late-nineteenth century.

1879 *Trans. Asiatic Soc. Japan* VII. 355 The reputation of the Tosa school was maintained during the progress of the Kano riu. **1909** L. BINYON *Jap. Art* ii. 10 The typical Tosa picture was a long scroll (makimono) portraying scenes of battle, adventure, scenes of court life, or the lives of saints. **1952** L. WARNER *Enduring Art of Japan* vi. 64 It had been appropriate enough, for narrow Tosa scrolls..to use small patches of opaque colour set in cells of black ink. **1972** *Times* 18 May 21/5 An album of hand paintings of the Tosa school..dating from the turn of the seventeenth and eighteenth centuries.

Tosa (tōᵘ·să), *sb.*[2] [a. *Tosa*, the former name of a province on the island of Shikoku, Japan.] A black, tan, or brindle mastiff of the breed of this name, originally developed as a type of fighting dog in Japan. Also *attrib.*

1945 C. L. B. HUBBARD *Observer's Bk. Dogs* 191 The Tosa..has been known for at least six centuries. **1966** 'G. BLACK' *You want to die, Johnny?* ii. 39 Taro, my Japanese Tosa hound..is a big brindle fighting dog. **1971** DANGERFIELD & HOWELL *Internat. Encycl. Dogs* 309/2 Little effort has been made to keep the Tosa purebred until quite recently. *Ibid.*, The modern Tosa dogs are about 28 inches tall..and weigh well over 100 lb.

tosh (tǫʃ), *sb.*[3] *slang.* [Cf. *TOSHER[1].] Items of value retrieved from drains and sewers.

a **1852** [see *TOSHER[1]]. **1974** J. AIKEN *Midnight is Place* v. 164, I am at present engaged in fishing for tosh in the sewers of Blastburn.

tosh (tǫʃ), *sb.*[4] *slang.* Also **tush.** Abbrev. of *TOSHEROON. Also used *loosely* for two shillings, money.

1912 J. W. Horsley *I Remember* xii. 253 'Tush', for money, would be an abbreviation of 'tusheroon', which in old cant, and also in tinker dialect, signified a crown. **1937** *Night & Day* 22 July 14/3 A couple of grafters had the courage..to bat for a straight tush. **1961** J. Maclaren-Ross *Doomsday Bk.* I. v. 63 Here's a tosh to buy yourself some beer. **1964** A. Prior *Z Cars Again* ix. 74 'You can give me three blacks for a tush,' he said. 'Two blacks for half a dollar,' was Mr. Thistlethwaite's reply.

tosh (tǫʃ), *sb.*[5] *slang.* [Origin uncertain; perh. f. Tosh *a.* (*adv.*).] Used as a neutral or joc. form of address.

1954 E. Hyams *Stories & Cream* 175 'Ere, tosh, you bin at Cha'ham? **1978** M. Kenyon *Deep Pocket* vi. 75 'Sortin' you out for a start, tosh!' came a voice.

tosher[1]. Add: **b.** One who searches for valuable refuse in drains and sewers.

a **1852** H. Mayhew *London Labour* (1861) II. 150/2 The sewer-hunters were formerly, and indeed are still, called by the name of 'Toshers', the articles which they pick up in the course of their wanderings along shore being known amongst themselves by the general term 'tosh', a word more particularly applied by them to anything made of copper. **1870** D. J. Kirwan *Palace & Hovel* xxi. 331 These men..search the sewers..for..whatever is of value... They are called 'Toshers' or 'Shore-men'. **1974** J. Aiken *Midnight is Place* v. 154 Gudgeon's your mate, boy, he's my other tosher.

toshing (later example).

1974 J. Aiken *Midnight is Place* vi. 180 You tend to the toshing, let Mester Hobday tend to the dealing.

tosheroon (tǫʃərū·n). *slang.* Also **tusheroon.** [Etym. unknown.] Half-a-crown; a coin of this value (in quot. 1859 erron. said to be a crown).

1859 Hotten *Dict. Slang* 112 *Tusheroon*, a crown piece, five shillings. **1933** 'G. Orwell' *Down & Out in Paris & London* xxix. 214 A tosheroon (half a crown) for the coat, two 'ogs for the trousers. **1960** 'A. Burgess' *Doctor is Sick* xvi. 125 'I haven't got three nicker,' said Edwin, 'nor one nicker, nor half a bar, nor a tosheroon, nor,' he added, 'a solitary single clod. I can't buy anything.' **1978** *Daily Mirror* 18 Feb. 19/1 All sorts of things, places and creatures we believed were everlasting have vanished, like trams, tosheroons and Constantinople.

Tosk (tǫsk), *sb.* and *a.* Also **Toshke.** [a. Alb. *Toskë*.] **A.** *sb.* (A member of) one of the major ethnic groups of Albania, living mainly in the south of the country. Also, the Albanian dialect spoken by this people. **B.** *adj.* Of or pertaining to the Tosks or their language. Cf. *Gheg.

1835 [see *Gheg]. **1900** 'Odysseus' *Turkey in Europe* ix. 397 The Southern Albanians differ from the Northerners. ..Their generic name is Tosk. *Ibid.* 401 The whole of the Tosk country has been strongly influenced by Greece. **1908** T. G. Tucker *Introd. Nat. Hist. Lang.* ix. 195 A number of dialects, usually grouped under the two heads *Ghegh* (to the north) and *Tosk* (to the south), spoken by the Albanians..are admitted to belong to the Indo-European stock. **1939** L. H. Gray *Foundations of Lang.* 331 The language [*sc.* Albanian] falls into two groups, each with a number of sub-dialects: *Geg* (with colonies in Dalmatia) to the north and *Tosk* (with colonies in Greece, Italy, and Sicily) to the south of the Shumbi River. **1958** [see *Gheg]. **1966** E. P. Hamp in Birnbaum & Puhvel *Anc. Indo-Europ. Dial.* 98 Rosetti, however, mistakenly repeats the myth that some Tosk dialects show Geg characteristics. **1980** *Word 1979* XXX. 27 Within Albania the proportion of northerners (Gegs) to southerners (Tosks) is almost equal. *Ibid.* 41 The imposition of Tosk upon a population that was not entirely Tosk-speaking. **1983** *Ibid.* XXXIV. 26 Arvanítika is the form of Tosk Albanian spoken in Greece; it is closely related to the southernmost variety of Albanian.

toss, *sb.*[1] Add: **3. b.** *to take a toss*, to suffer a fall from a horse; also *fig.*

1917 [see *half *sb.* 7 h]. **1926** Galsworthy *Silver Spoon* I. xiv. 101 The Government had 'taken their toss' over the Editor. **1949** M. Steen *Twilight on Floods* iv. x. 699 By Jove, old boy, she's taken a toss for you! **1966** [see *league sb.[1] 1 e]. **1973** 'M. Innes' *Appleby's Answer* v. 47 The red-haired Lady Curricle, who had 'taken a toss', you will remember, over a hedge.

c. *U.S. slang.* A search (of a building or person) conducted by the police. Cf. *toss *v.* 1 c.

1970 L. Sanders *Anderson Tapes* xciv. 220 The author was allowed to attend as an observer but not active participant in the search. The toss of the above premises.. was..conducted with professional skill. **1972** J. Mills *Report to Commissioner* 86 You wanta give her a toss, give her a toss, but let's not stand here all night.

4. b. A spread of fall (of hair).

1946 D. C. Peattie *Road of Naturalist* i. 13 My wife lay hiding from the light in the toss of her hair. **1978** J. Updike *Coup* (1979) vi. 233 Ezana looked at her and saw beyond the brassy toss of her hair.

6. b. *to argue the toss*, to dispute a decision or opinion.

1925 Fraser & Gibbons *Soldier & Sailor Words* 288 *Toss, to argue the*, to dispute: wrangle: to have too much to say. **1945** *Penguin New Writing* XXIV. 84 Poetry was never much in my line, except Shelley, and Terry didn't think much of him, so..we argued the toss about it. **1958** *Economist* 11 Jan. 92/2 The Prime Minister's..venture.. cannot do more than clear the way... More is involved than just arguing the tosses of the moment. **1978** 'M. Underwood' *Crooked Wood* iv. 61 He was not in a strong position to argue the toss.

c. *fig.* In negative contexts: a jot, a whit, a very small amount. Usu. in phr. *not to care* (or *give*) *a toss. colloq.*

1876 [see sense 6 in Dict.]. **1925** P. Gibbs *Unchanging Quest* xviii. 132 She..didn't care a toss what people thought of her. **1973** *Time Out* 2–5 Mar. 13/1, I don't give a toss whether he's black, white or purple. **1979** *Bull. Yorks. Dial. Soc.* No. 26. 11 Ah deean't odd wi them as mooan As prices mak em cross. Then spend ther brass on eeaps o things Wat isn't woth a toss.

7. (Earlier example.)

1882 J. L. Burgess *Homing Fancier's Ann.* 11 The intermediate tosses were Redhill, 184 miles from Brussels, and Worcester, 280 miles.

11. toss-off. An act of masturbation. Cf. *toss *v.* 12 d. *coarse slang.*

1735 *Rake's Progress* iii. 19 Or loudly sing some bawdy Song, Then drops into St. *D—n*'s *C—h*, And take a *Toss-off* in the Porch.

12. *Comb.*: **toss pillow** *U.S.* = *scatter cushion* s.v. *scatter *v.* 7 b.

1956 *Sears, Roebuck Catal.* Fall & Winter 897 (*heading*) Toss pillows..new colors..styles..shapes. **1978** *Washington Post Mag.* 26 Mar. 20/2 (Advt.), Matching toss pillows $10 each.

toss, *v.* Add: **I. 1. c.** *U.S. slang.* To search (a building or person) in the course of a police investigation. Cf. *toss *sb.*[1] 3 c.

1939 *Fortune* July 102/2 [He] sent a couple of detectives across town to 'toss their flat' (i.e. search their apartment). **1969** 'P. Kavanagh' *Such Men are Dangerous* vii. 82 They tossed the room while I had breakfast. **1972** B. Garfield *Line of Succession* iii. 186 He had been tossed seven times..but no drugs had been found on him. **1980** 'E. McBain' *Ghosts* iii. 56 We ought to try for an order to toss his apartment.

3. e. In cookery, to stir or turn (food) over, esp. so as to coat it with butter, oil, etc.

1723 J. Nott *Cook's & Confectioner's Dict.* No. 107a Artichokes with cream... Toss them up with butter. **1877** E. S. Dallas *Kettner's Bk. of Table* 120 The fillets..are to be lightly tossed in butter, taking care not to colour them. **1913** C. M. Pearse *Kitchen Garden & Cook* 197 Separate the endive into tufts. Toss these in the salad dressing. **1952** G. W. Brace *Spire* (1953) viii. 69 The salad was tossed amid murmurs of pleasure. **1976** 'Trevanian' *Main* (1977) v. 109 You don't stir a salad. You toss it.

III. 9. c. To wager with (a person) on the toss of a coin. Usu. const. *for* (something).

1851 H. Mayhew *London Labour* I. 196/1 To 'toss the pieman' is a favourite pastime with costermongers' boys. ..If the pieman win the toss, he receives 1*d.* without giving a pie. **1858** G. H. Lewes *Sea-Side Stud.* iv. i. 271 We used to 'toss' the pieman for epicurean slices of pudding—a vulgar, but seductive form of juvenile gambling. **1942** Wodehouse *Money in Bank* (1946) xv. 128 He was in the frame of mind when he would have patted a small boy on the head and given him sixpence, though it is probable that a moment later he would have tossed him for it and won it back again. **1983** 'D. Shannon' *Exploit of Death* (1984) i. 18 'I'll toss you for the job.' Conway produced a quarter and flipped it.

d. To release (a homing pigeon) in a race or trial flight. Cf. Toss *sb.*[1] 7.

1882 J. L. Burgess *Homing Fancier's Ann.* 10 Five hundred and eighty-nine birds were tossed at 4 a.m. **1911** *Encycl. Brit.* XXI. 596/2 Training..consists in taking it [*sc.* the bird] out in a closed wicker basket and liberating or 'tossing' it at gradually increasing distances from its loft.

IV. 11*. toss in. To finish, to give up. *N.Z. slang.*

1956 D. M. Davin *Sullen Bell* ii. iv. 128 I'd toss it in for tonight, Miss Sim. It's an ugly night and you should get your train home. **1971** *N.Z. Listener* 19 Apr. 56/5 In the end they saw some hogsbacks up above the col so they tossed it in and glissaded down back to their bivvy.

12. toss off. c. To do or make easily, without effort. **d.** *trans.* and *intr.* To masturbate. *slang.*

1874 L. Troubridge *Life amongst Troubridges* (1966) 80 A new rage..for painting the panels of the shutters of our bedrooms..and they only take a jiffy to toss off. **1879–80** *Pearl* (1970) 258, I don't like to see, though at me you might scoff, An old woman trying to toss herself off. **1915** L. Strachey *Let.* 12 Mar. in P. N. Furbank *E. M. Forster* (1979) II. i. 16 À propos of Maurice tossing himself off..you say—'He knew what the price would be—a creeping apathy towards all things.' **1927** Joyce *Let.* 25 July (1966) III. 162 The verb 'to toss off' an expression for 'to masturbate'. **1937** M. Hillis *Orchids on your Budget* (1938) vi. 109 Any man worth anything could toss off a rarebit or an omelet. **1969** *Jeremy* I. iii. 22/1 All they want to do is toss off in the cottage while they look at my prick. **1979** *Church Times* 17 Aug. 7/1 [These books] do not provide bibliographical support for the learned references tossed off in the articles. **1981** 'D. Kavanagh' *Fiddle City* iv. 82 Would you like me to toss you off?.. It's ten if you're worried about the price.

tossed, *ppl. a.* Add: Of a salad: stirred or turned, esp. so as to be coated with dressing. See *toss *v.* 3 e.

1947 M. Given *Mod. Encycl. Cooking* II. 1315 Whole meal tossed salad... Wash and clean all vegetables, chill thoroughly. **1962** H. Hood in R. Weaver *Canad. Short Stories* (1968) 2nd Ser. 207 It was a good hot-weather supper, tossed greens with the correct proportions of vinegar and oil. **1978** H. C. Rae *Sullivan* i. ii. 15 Artichokes, tossed green salad and cold lake trout.

tosser. Add: **1. b.** [Prob. f. sense *12 d of the vb.] A term of contempt or abuse for a person; a 'jerk'. Cf. Bugger *sb.* 2 b. *slang.*

1977 *Zigzag* Apr. 40/3 She came on in a big mac and flashed her legs like an old tosser before throwing it off. **1983** P. Inchbald *Short Break in Venice* xviii. 172 It's a right pig's job... Poor little tosser. As if he wasn't suffering enough already.

3. A penny, a coin of small value. Cf. Toss *v.* 9, *toss *sb.*[1] 6 c.

1935 [see *carve-up]. **1964** J. Aiken *Black Hearts in Battersea* (1965) vi. 70 Shall we play for money?..I haven't a tosser to my kick. **1966** *New Statesman* 4 Nov. 662/1 There's no one mumming today whose opinion is worth a tosser on the cut of a dressing-gown. **1980** J. Gerson *Assassination Run* xi. 158 Your people don't give a tosser for me!

tostada, tostado (tǫstā·dă, -o). [a. Sp., pa. pple. of *tostar* to toast.] A deep-fried cornmeal pancake topped with a seasoned mixture of beans, mincemeat, and vegetables.

1945 E. Fergusson *Mexican Cookbk.* (ed. 2) p. v, Mexican food has, even since the 'American Occupation', been a part of the Southwestern diet... In every Southwestern town *tostados* are served with cocktails. **1958** *McCall's Mag.* Aug. 9/2 The tortilla is the basis of many famous Mexican dishes: Enchiladas, Tacos, Tostadas. **1972** *Times* 6 May 12/7 Wait for the crunch of tostados—for the next culinary invasion..will be Mexican. **1975** 'S. Marlowe' *Cawthorn Journals* xxiv. 235 Maruja fed tostadas into the hot splattering oil.

‖**toston** (tǫstǫ·n). [(Amer.) Sp.: cf. Teston, testoon.] A silver coin formerly in use in various Latin American countries; in Mexico, equivalent in value to half a peso.

1884 A. R. Conkling *Appleton's Guide to Mexico* xv. 61 Mexico has followed the example of Spain in adopting the decimal system of coinage, of which the *real* is the basis. The current coins are as follows: *Silver.* One *peso*, or dollar, containing 8 *reales*, or 100 cents. Four *reales*, or one *toston*, 50 cents. **1932** H. Crane *Let.* 22 Apr. (1965) 412 The telegraph office paid us off in six hundred and some odd 'Tostons' (about like getting it all in dimes) and neither the Ward Line office nor the official Banco de Mexico would accept them. **1947** M. Lowry *Under Volcano* vii. 240 Laying a tostón on the counter. **1980** in S. Terkel *Amer. Dreams* 6 My father's father came from Mexico... He paid a *toston*, a half-dollar. That automatically made him a U.S. citizen.

tosudite (tōᵘ·siūdəit). *Min.* [ad. Russ. *tosudit* (V. A. Frank-Kamenetsky et al. 1963, in *Zap. Vsesoyuz. Min. Obshch.* XCIII. 563): see quot. 1964 and -ite[1].] A blue mixed-layer clay mineral (see quots.).

1964 *Mineral. Abstr.* XVI. 549/2 This newly characterized mixed-layer mineral consisting of unusual aluminian chlorite and montmorillonite is named tosudite, in honour of Toshio Sudo, who described the Japanese occurrences. **1976** *Clays & Clay Minerals* XXIV. 142/1 The name tosudite is usually used for a regularly interstratified mineral with dioctahedral or di-trioctahedral chlorite component.

tosyl (tǫ·sil). *Chem.* [a. G. *tosyl* (Hess & Pfleger 1933, in *Ann. d. Chemie* DVII. 48), f. *to*luol*sulfonyl*: see *Toluol* s.v. Tolu-, *sulphonyl.] The *para* isomer of the univalent radical toluenesulphonyl, $H_3C{\cdot}C_6H_4{\cdot}SO_2$—.

1938 *Jrnl. Amer. Chem. Soc.* LX. 398/1 The unimolar tosylation of *α*- and *β*-methyl-*d*-glucosides in pyridine solution with tosyl chloride, followed by acetylation results in the formation of 6-tosyl-triacetyl-*α*-methyl-*d*-glucoside. **1975** *Nature* 30 Oct. 763/1 There is no evidence for a hydrophobic binding pocket or tosyl hole as seen in the *α*-chymotrypsin structure.

Hence **to·sylate** *sb.*, an ester of the tosyl group; *v. trans.*, to introduce a tosyl group into (a compound) or add one to (an atom); **to·sylated, to·sylating** *ppl. adjs.*; **tosyla·tion,** the process of tosylating.

1938 *Jrnl. Amer. Chem. Soc.* LX. 1203/2 The structure of this compound may be considered proved since it is identical with that obtained..upon tosylating 2,3,4,2′,3′-pentaacetyl-*β*-methylcellobioside. **1938** [see *tosyl above]. **1963** I. L. Finar *Org. Chem.* (ed. 4) I. xxv. 612 Tosylates are useful for preparing, *e.g.*, ethers. **1972** *Jrnl. Chem. Soc.: Chem. Communications* 1148/1 We have found that *N*-methyl-*N*-tosylpyrrolidinium perchlorate..can be used as a selective tosylating reagent. *Ibid.* 1149/1 We assumed that only nitrogen would be tosylated if both amino- and hydroxy-groups were present in the substrate. **1974** *Jrnl. Org. Chem.* XXXIX. 635/2 A greater chemical shift difference was observed for the C-2 ring protons adjacent to the tosylated nitrogen. *Ibid.*, Tosylation was carried out with tosyl chloride in the usual basic media of pyridine or aqueous sodium bicarbonate. **1978** J. M. & D. J. Cram *Essence Org. Chem.* vi. 150 The name *p*-toluenesulfonyl group (Ar—SO_2—) is shortened to the 'tosyl' group, and the ester is ethyl tosylate.

tot, *sb.*[3] Add: Also *gen.*, the total number or amount. (Earlier examples.)

1755 C. Charke *Narr. Life Mrs. C. Charke* 260 The above-mentioned notable Gentleman, with his wife and a young Fellow, besides our two selves, made up the whole *Totte.* **1857** *Londonderry Standard* 26 Feb. 2/2 Forty monopolists whose numerical 'tot' is so oddly coincident with the history of Ali Baba. **1866** *Times* 28 Apr. 5/6 He added up the gross 'tots' of the several poll books himself.

tot, *sb.*^{4} Add: **4.** *Comb.*: **tot lot** *N. Amer.*, a playground for small children; **tot system** *S. Afr.*, a system of paying agricultural workers, esp. in vine-growing districts, part of their wages in 'tots' (usu. mugs) of wine.

1944 *Sun* (Baltimore) 15 July 13/3 (*heading*) Pall Mall tot lot open daily except Saturday. **1968** *Daily Colonist* (Victoria, B.C.) 6 Dec. 41/4 Snow fails to stop Gold River children from enjoying recently completed tot-lot behind the community hall. **1977** *Ottawa Citizen* 19 May 2/2 The plan includes..a 'tot lot' for pre-schoolers. **1926** *Eastern Province Herald* (Port Elizabeth) 12 Feb. 7 (*heading*) Liquor bill under fire—evils of the tot system. **1953** P. Abrahams *Return to Goli* II. 77 The vicious 'tot'-system which obtains in the wine-growing Cape valley..is ruining the health..of a very large number of Coloureds. **1974** *Sunday Times* (Johannesburg) 24 Feb. 14 Asked whether he made use of the tot system, Mr. — said: [etc.].

tot, *v.*^{2} Add: **totting** *vbl. sb.* (later simple and *attrib.* examples with *up*).

1963 *Guardian* 2 May 5/1 The 'totting up' procedure is a new principle, and Mr Marples explained that its sole purpose was to make anyone who had two endorsements in two years drive extra carefully. **1976** *Deeside Advertiser* 9 Dec. 24/1 Hamilton had been disqualified by Chester City Magistrates in October for six months under the totting up procedure because of previous endorsements on his licence. **1978** R. Mark *Office of Constable* xxii. 273 'Totting up'..is the arrangement under the 1972 Road Traffic Act authorizing the endorsement of a driving licence after conviction for any one of a number of offences. The endorsement lasts three years and two further endorsements during that period mean mandatory disqualification from driving for a minimum of six months.

tot (tǫt), *v.*^{4} [Back-formation f. *totting* s.v. Tot *sb.*^{5}] *intr.* To pick anything saleable from a dustbin or tip; † to pick up bones.

1884 J. Greenwood *Little Ragamuffins* xiv. 121 'P'r'aps he's going a-tottin'' (picking up bones,) said Ripston. **1922** Joyce *Ulysses* 422 On a step a gnome totting among a rubbishtip crouches to shoulder a sack of rags and bones. **1969** *Guardian* 6 Feb. 5 The right to tot or sell salvage is the cause of a 10-day-old strike of 267 dustmen. **1976** M. Russell *Double Deal* iv. 32, I could earn as much, totting for the corporation.

total, *a.* Add: **2. b.** *total heat* (Physics): = *enthalpy; *spec.* (see quot. 1853).

1851 *Phil. Mag.* II. 4 We often hear of the total heat of bodies, and of gases and vapours in particular, this term being meant to express the sum of the sensible and latent heat. **1853** *Trans. R. Soc. Edin.* XX. 172 If to the latent heat of evaporation at a given temperature, is added the quantity of heat necessary to raise unity of weight of the liquid from a certain fixed temperature (usually that of melting ice) to the temperature at which the evaporation takes place, the result is called the total heat of evaporation from the fixed temperature chosen. **1927, 1962** [see *enthalpy].

c. *total impulse* (Astronautics): (see quot. 1949).

1949 G. P. Sutton *Rocket Propulsion Elements* i. 18 The impulse (often called total impulse) is the integral of the thrust over the firing duration. For a constant thrust it is the product of thrust and duration. **1979** J. W. Cornelisse et al. *Rocket Propulsion & Space Flight Dynamics* vi. 115 The specific consumption is defined as the ratio of propellant weight consumed and the total impulse delivered.

3. a. *total recall*: see *recall *sb.*^{1} 2.

c. Complete in nature; involving all resources; manifesting every characteristic or the whole nature of an activity, person, etc.; all-encompassing, all-inclusive; fully co-ordinated or integrated; *total diplomacy*, diplomacy conducted with the consent or participation of all citizens and institutions; *total institution* (see quot. 1962); *total theatre*, (*a*) a theatre designed for maximum involvement of performers and audience; dramaturgy which achieves this; (*b*) theatre involving a wide range of techniques and conventions; *total war*, a war to which all resources and the whole population are committed; loosely, a war conducted without any scruples or limitations; *total woman*, spec. a woman who conforms to the female 'ideal' or stereotype of complete self-abnegation and devotion to the interests of a man.

1935 W. Gropius in S. Giedion *W. Gropius* (1954) I. 61 The aim of this 'Total Theater' is to draw the spectator into the drama. All technical means have to be subordinated to this aim and must never become ends in themselves. **1937** W. L. Shirer *Berlin Diary* (1941) 86 Total war means the complete and final disappearance of the vanquished from the stage of history! **1940** Graves & Hodge *Long Week-End* i. 13 The philosophy of 'total war', that a war can best be won by complete ruthlessness, was of German origin. **1942** Total war [see *people's war* s.v. *people *sb.* 9]. **1950** *World-Telegram-Sun* (N.Y.) 14 Mar. 12 He [*sc.* D. Acheson] defines 'total diplomacy' as the full use of Congress, ..government agencies, as well as business, labor and agriculture. **1951** E. A. Walsh (*title*) Total empire: the roots and progress of world communism. **1957** *Sat. Rev.* (U.S.) 26 Jan. 22/1 M. [Jean-Louis] Barrault..describes it as follows: ' "Total Theatre" is simply the true and traditional theatre, the one which makes use of man "in his totality", his gestures, pantomime, dances, breath, cries, articulation, speech, poetry, and singing.' **1957** J. D. MacDonald *Man of Affairs* iii. 43, I did not see how any platonic relationship between Mike and this total woman would be possible. **1957** E. Goffman in *Symposium on Preventive & Soc. Psychiatry* 44 [These institutions'] encompassing or total character is symbolized by the barrier to social intercourse with the outside that is often built right into the physical plant: locked doors, high walls, barbed wire, cliffs and water, open terrain, and so forth. These I am calling total institutions. **1962** —— *Asylums* p. xiii, A total institution may be defined as a place of residence and work where a large number of like-situated individuals, cut off from the wider society for an appreciable period of time, together lead an enclosed, formally administered round of life. **1963** I. Fletcher in B. Sewell *Two Friends* 63 *Spiritual Poems* is a fine example of 'total art', its paper and typography reflecting the eclecticism and scholarly caprice of content. **1966** *Listener* 29 Dec. 959/2, I still think the best kind of Christmas show for children is pantomime. It is a form of total theatre—story, spectacle, ballet, song, revue sketch, comedians' jokes, audience-participation, even circus acts. **1966** Schwarz & Hadix *Strategic Terminology* 132 *War, total*, conflict in which the issue is a threat to survival and in which all weapons of the combatants are used. Many modern definitions of total war used the term for war involving nuclear weapons or the direct confrontation of the great powers on the assumption that it would be unlimited or become unlimited. **1967** *Boston Sunday Herald* 26 Mar. I. 34/2 Rather he is thought of as a human being who needs dentistry badly and one for whom total care is now available. **1969** *Times* 17 Oct. 17/4 Carlo Palazzi, who is a past-master of the total look..had all his men wearing saffron coloured clothes which mixed and, of course, matched. **1972** A. Bryant *Bless this House* iv. 44 Marabel Morgan..talked about her course entitled 'The Total Woman'. **1973** M. Morgan *Total Woman* (1975) iv. 60 A Total Woman caters to her man's special quirks, whether it be in salads, sex, or sports. **1973** *Times* 30 July 20/3 They became convinced that developers and local authorities ought to concern themselves with engineering a 'total' environment for a community, of which the buildings themselves are only a part. **1974** *Howard Jrnl.* XIV. 86 Most total institutions leave their mark on those who devote their lives to them—the colonel, the sea captain, the public school headmaster, the monk and the nun are popular cultural stereotypes. **1975** *Times Lit. Suppl.* 2 May 477/5 The approach throughout is scholarly and thorough, no one period receiving less attention than any other. As one might expect, Roman and medieval features are fully treated, but so too are post-medieval and recent... This is total archaeology at its best. **1977** *N.Y. Rev. Bks.* 27 Oct. 46/3 (Advt.), Professional man, 60, needs slender, total woman over 30 for September, 1978, fortnight Alaskan cruise. **1978** *New Yorker* 7 Aug. 45/1 In the past few years the Dutch have been the most thrilling [soccer] side to watch, playing a running game—'total football', it is called—with players interchanging positions and functions but always pressing forward on the attack. **1980** R. Moody *Devil you Don't* iv. 45 In the fight against Hitler, we progressed to the concept of Total War, no quarter given, no humanity expected, victory at any price.

5*. *total float* (see quot. 1967).

1964 K. G. Lockyer *Introd. Critical Path Anal.* v. 49 *Total float*, the time by which an activity can expand. **1967** S. Woodgate in Wills & Yearsley *Handbk. Management Technol.* 80 Total float is..the maximum amount of spare time which can be made available to any activity.

B. *sb.* **b.** *in total*, all together, entirely.

1965 *Listener* 7 Jan. 3/1 Does the Government mean incomes in total cannot go up by more than production..? Or does it mean that all incomes should go up by the same percentage? **1969** R. Buckminster Fuller *Operating Man. Spaceship Earth* iv. 52 We have not been seeing our Spaceship Earth as an integrally-designed machine which to be persistently successful must be comprehended and serviced in total.

total, *v.* Add: **2.** Also with *out*. *U.S.*

1966 *Word Study* Dec. 2/2 How long did I control on fly-by-wire?..That is something we want to total out. **1977** *New Yorker* 13 June 30/1 We weren't going to wait until the Police Department could total out what it would cost them.

3. To damage beyond repair (esp. a motor vehicle, in an accident); to destroy, to demolish, to wreck; to kill or injure severely; also *fig.* Also with *out*. Freq. in *pass.* and as *pa. ppl.* Chiefly *N. Amer.*

1895 W. Rye *Vocab. E. Anglia* 232 *Totald* [sic], killed or injured. **1954** *Amer. Speech* XXIX. 103 Bob totaled his car last night. **1965** *Ibid.* XL. 159 Her son was hospitalized because of an automobile accident and..his car was 'totalled'. **1966** *Newsweek* 13 June 48c/3 Amazingly, no drivers were 'totaled'. **1966** *Current Slang* (Univ. S. Dakota) Summer 4 *Totalled out*, intoxicated... Tom was *totalled out* by midnight. **1966** *Ibid.* Winter 8 *Totalled*, adj., mentally upset... After one semester, he was *totalled*. **1970** E. Segal *Love Story* iii. 24 Did you at least total the guy that hit you? **1971** *Wall St. Jrnl.* 17 Mar. 1/1 He has had 44 planes, three of which were 'totaled' in accidents. **1971** *New Yorker* 28 Aug. 81 Townshend did total his instrument during his last song. **1971** M. Tak *Truck Talk* 169 *Total it out*, to wreck a truck completely. **1972** C. Weston *Poor, Poor Ophelia* x. 52 You think it's a fantasy my car's totaled? **1973** *New Yorker* 16 July 34/3 A streak of sudden tire skids,..a totalled car at the bottom of a ravine. **1974** *Publishers Weekly* 1 Apr. 50/1 Water from fire engines and hydrants cascaded into the burning ruins. Eighteen businesses were totaled. **1974** J. Goldman *Man from Greek & Roman* xxiii. 211 'Totalled out.'.. Big gash along the side, hood all barged up. **1975** *Times Lit. Suppl.* 12 Dec. 1486/5 'The Execution of Lady Jane Grey'... Lady Jane is about to be totalled by the axe. **1977** *Time* 10 Jan. 42/2 He can still total a liquor store in the course of rescuing hostages. **1979** *Yale Alumni Mag.* Apr. (Suppl.) cn10/3 Little Robert was totaled by a bus that ran a red light but escaped with fractures of collar bone and right hand. **1979** G. Swarthout *Skeletons* 98 I'm too totalled to hate anyone... This has been the worst week of my life. **1981** J. D. MacDonald *Free Fall in Crimson* xx. 230 'He's the one that beat the old man to death.'..'They *think* he totaled the movie lady.' **1982** *Guardian* 26 Oct. 8/7 Daddy's BMW which she can drive any time she wants as long as she doesn't total it.

to·talist, *sb.* (and *a.*). [f. Total *a.* and *sb.* + -ist.] One who inclines to treat or regard things as a whole; one concerned with the whole social environment, esp. as a means of thought-control; one concerned with the whole person. Also *attrib.* or as *adj.*

1956 J. S. Bruner et al. *Study of Thinking* v. 128 The totalists have wanted to stay as close as possible to the whole cortex as an explanation, and it is only with the greatest reluctance that they will subtract any of its attributes as irrelevant. **1961** R. J. Lifton *Thought Reform* xxii. 420 Through this milieu control the totalist environment seeks to establish domain over not only the individual's communication with the outside.., but also ..over what he may speak of as his communication with himself. *Ibid.* 422 Ideological totalists do not pursue this approach *solely* for maintaining a sense of power over others. **1964** R. Wilkinson *Gentlemanly Power* xiii. 184 A 'totalist ideology'..refers to any doctrine which attempts a complete, unified explanation of world and society. **1969** *Political Q.* XL. 472 Only that which is known by the 'whole being' is sound and healthy... The origins of this totalist view of knowledge..are no doubt various.

So **totali·stic** *a.*

1932 H. H. Price *Perception* vi. 151 The perceptual act still has this totalistic character. **1942** *Mind* LI. 316 Some writers are frightened by the word *intuition*, and admittedly it has bad associations... Again, under, I believe, Croce's influence, it has come to mean the apprehension of a whole as a whole, a 'totalistic' apprehension. **1976** *Brit. Jrnl. Sociol.* XXVII. 88 A totalistic rejection of the contemporary order is not encountered. **1979** *Jrnl. R. Soc. Arts* Nov. 772/1 The idea of collage city was dualism itself, an incorporation of opposite qualities which Modern city planning in its utopian, or totalistic phase, had denied.

totalitarian (tō^{u}tælitē^{ə}·riăn), *a.* and *sb.* [f. Totality + *-arian, after It. *totalitario* complete, absolute; totalitarian.] **A.** *adj.* Of or pertaining to a system of government which tolerates only one political party, to which all other institutions are subordinated, and which usu. demands the complete subservience of the individual to the State. Also *transf.* Cf. *total *a.* 3 c.

1926 B. B. Carter tr. *Sturzo's Italy & Fascismo* ix. 220 Anti-Fascism..has, however, a positive sense if it is taken to represent an element antagonistic to the 'totalitarian' and absolute position of Fascism. **1929** *Times* 2 Nov. 7/5 A reaction against parliamentarism..in favour of a 'totalitarian' or unitary state, whether Fascist or Communist. **1936** E. Underhill *Worship* xii. 251 This cultus is, in origin, an acknowledgement of the corporate and totalitarian character of the Christian response to God. **1937** E. Pound in *Germany & You* 25 Apr. 95 (*heading*) Totalitarian scholarship and the new paideuma. *Ibid.* 96/2 In 1937 we are concerned with the reintegration of the arts in totalitarian synthesis. **1940** *Hutchinson's Pictorial Hist. War* 2 Oct.–26 Nov. 183 We have all heard lately about total or totalitarian war. It has been defined as conflict between nations taking the place of armed forces. Every citizen is in a sense a combatant and also the object of attack. **1951** H. Arendt *Burden of Our Time* III. x. 303 Totalitarian movements aim at and succeed in organizing masses—not classes. **1964** H. Marcuse *One Dimensional Man* i. 3 'Totalitarian' is not only a terroristic political coordination of society, but also a non-terroristic economic-technical coordination which operates through the manipulation of needs by vested interests. **1977** M. Walker *National Front* i. 15 The totalitarian society is a single-minded structure. It mobilizes all its resources under one authority to achieve one goal.

B. *sb.* A leader or member of a totalitarian party; an advocate or supporter of totalitarianism.

1938 *Times* 20 Oct. 15/3 The new methods of the totalitarians. **1944** A. Huxley *Let.* 10 Apr. (1969) 504 The Left-wing Intellectuals and the Labour Party are eager totalitarians. **1958** R. Liddell *Morea* II. vi. 149 Sparta has one of the finest romantic backgrounds in Greece; this is not surprising, for only romantics can successfully be totalitarians. **1978** L. Deighton *SS-GB* xiv. 115 The totalitarians of right and left have constantly to describe the faith they have in common.

Hence **totalita:rianiza·tion,** the action or process of rendering totalitarian; the fact of becoming totalitarian.

1941 'G. Orwell' in *Partisan Rev.* July–Aug. 321, I don't believe that the ordinary man cares a damn about the totalitarianisation of our economy. **1954** *Encounter* Dec. 32/2 Professor Hayek originated the phrase, 'the Road to Serfdom', to describe the progressive totalitarianisation of a whole *society* by a government that only wanted at first to control the *economy*, but finds more and more human obstacles to this aim. **1958** M. Fainsod *Smolensk under Soviet Rule* xxiii. 446 The stately procession includes urbanization, industrialization, collectivization, secularization, bureaucratization and totalitarianization.

totalita·rianism. [f. prec. + -ism.] Totalitarian theory and practice; the advocacy of totalitarian government. Also *loosely*, authoritarianism; *transf.* monolithic character.

1926 B. B. Carter tr. *Sturzo's Italy & Fascismo* ix. 233 This would mark the end of Fascist 'totalitarianism' and the renewal of political dualism. **1937** *Times* 9 Nov. 12/6 Nothing could be worse than to introduce totalitarianism into literature and to try to breed in a single country races of men and women fundamentally incapable of understanding one another. **1944** J. S. HUXLEY *On Living in Revolution* iii. 31 It [*sc.* Japan] has transformed itself from tribal and feudal totalitarianism to a modern technological totalitarianism. **1952** J. L. TALMON *Origins of Totalitarian Democracy* 6 The starting-point of totalitarianism of the Left has been and ultimately still is man, his reason and salvation, that of the Right totalitarian schools has been the collective entity, the State. **1967** G. STEINER *Lang. & Silence* 408 Soviet totalitarianism is most extreme not in the claims it makes on the utopian future, but in the violence it would do to the past, to the vital integrity of human remembrance. **1974** *Guardian* 2 Dec. 14/1 Most Swedish companies must have at least two elected representatives of workers on their boards of directors. . . Yet there was general agreement that the work place is the last bastion of totalitarianism in an otherwise democratic society.

totalizator. Add: **1.** Add to *spec.* def.: also, on each greyhound, etc., in a race; also, a system of betting based on the totalizator.

1910 *Encycl. Brit.* III. 827/1 On all French racecourses .., a system of betting known as the *Pari-Mutuel* or Totalizator, is carried on. **1935** *Encycl. Sports* 321/1 In 1931 and 1932 most of the licensed tracks in England were equipped with the most up-to-date all-electric totalisators; but in the February of 1933, following a High Court decision of December 17, 1932, that a totalisator on a greyhound track constituted a place within the meaning of the Act, these machines ceased to operate. **1975** *Oxf. Compan. Sports & Games* 445/2 Punters betting with a totalisator endeavour to select the dog or dogs they think will either win or obtain a place.

2. *Comb.*: **Totalizator Agency Board,** in Australia and New Zealand, an official organization, with local offices, for off-course betting on horses.

1950 *N.Z. Statutes 1949* 496 There shall be a board to be known as the Totalizator Agency Board. **1957** D. GLOVER *Since Then* 16 We are equals all in the sight of the Lord And the Totalizator Agency Board. **1957** *Weekly News* (Auckland, N.Z.) 6 Nov. 48/1 With the virtual extermination of the illegal bookmaker in the Dominion and the establishment of the Totalisator Agency Board as a firm medium for off-course bettors. **1983** *Austral. Encycl.* (ed. 4) X. 75 In Australia, the Totalizator Agency Boards are the government agencies which control legal off-course betting in the respective States and in the Australian Capital Territory.

totalness. (In Dict. s.v. TOTAL *a.* and *sb.*) For *rare*$^{-0}$ substitute *rare* and add example.

c **1864** E. DICKINSON *Poems* (1955) II. 619 All I may, if small, Do it not display Larger for the Totalness—'Tis Economy To bestow a World And withold a Star.

tote, *sb.*[1] **2.** For 'in *Australian colloq.*' read '*colloq.* (orig. *Austral.*)' and add: (further examples); also *loosely*, a lottery; hence also *tote board, double, ticket.*

1926 *Spectator* 9 Jan. 45/2 The 'tote' goes steadily on and the bookies do a roaring trade secretly. **1927** *Glasgow Herald* 30 Apr. 9 Information will be given on the legal and practical aspects of the 'tote'. **1930** *Cambridge Daily News* 25 Sept. 5/7 In the Tote Double on the 2.30. . the winning dividend was £10 13s. 9d. **1933** *Sun* (Baltimore) 3 May 14/4 (*heading*) Ticket a second expected of electric 'tote' at racing meet. **1945** *Daily Herald* 31 Aug. 3/4 A fraud by which a considerable sum. . was obtained with forged Tote tickets at Harringay Greyhound Stadium. . is thought to have been carefully planned by a gang. **1950** *Amer. Speech* XXV. 304/2 A tote board is a board where odds, payoffs, time of race and numbers of winners are posted in electric lights. **1966** *Listener* 27 Oct. 605/1 Further along there was a board showing the latest stock prices on Wall Street:. . Zurichers watch them in much the same spirit as race-goers watch the tote. **1974** *Times* 26 Nov. 16/4 Young women were selling tote tickets through the window. **1975** *Ox. Compan. Sports & Games* 495/2 The Tote also operates 'doubles', 'trebles', and 'jackpot' prizes for correct forecasts. **1976** *Star* (Sheffield) 30 Nov., The money was raised through totes and the fund is being wound up with a final pay-out because income was not enough to keep it going. **1977** *N.Z. Herald* 5 Jan. 2–8/4 The tote at Ellerslie, in line with the general trend this year, was up 22 per cent.

tote, *sb.*[4] (In Dict. s.v. TOTE *v.*) Add: **b.** *ellipt.* = *tote bag* below.

1959 *Sears, Roebuck Catal.* Spring–Summer 68 Cowhide Bag... 2 side zip pockets in this top-zipper tote. Rayon lined. **1967** *Observer* 24 Dec. 15/7 A Twiggy Fashion Tote, 'for shopping and surfing'. **1979** *Kingston* (Ontario) *Whig-Standard* 5 Apr. 24/6 Remember that an open bag, like a tote may make access to its contents easier for you, but it also means access is easier for a pickpocket.

c. tote bag, a large hand-bag or shoulder-bag; **tote box,** a portable box for small items.

1900 in *N. & Q.* (1904) 27 Aug. 162/1 The Watson Tote Bag. . best thing. . for carrying coat, camera,. . lunch, &c. **1969** *Daily Colonist* (Victoria, B.C.) 24 Sept. 2/6 Tote Bags —Great for knitting supplies, shopping. **1982** M. MILLAR *Mermaid* x. 108 A girl entered, carrying an oversized canvas tote bag with the name Gretchen printed on it. **1917** *Machinery* (N.Y.) July 957/1 The New Britain Machine Co. . . makes these tote boxes of steel, and they are designed in such a way that they may be stacked up to economize in floor space. **1951** URQUHART & BOYLE *Materials Handling Case Bk.* 7/1 If the parts are small and are handled in a tote box, then each operator must: 1. Position the totebox of pieces to be worked [etc.]. **1966** *Guardian* 18 Apr. 6/1 Tote boxes are also available with cushion tops and back cushions.

tote, *v.* For *U.S. colloq.* read '*colloq.* (orig. *U.S.*)' and add: **a.** Also, to wear or carry regularly as part of one's equipment; to take (a person) with one; (further examples); *to tote fair* (earlier example).

1823 J. A. QUITMAN in J. F. H. Claiborne *Life Quitman* (1860) I. 85 The belles. . 'tote' their fans with the air of Spanish señoritas. **1828** J. HALL in *Western Souvenir for 1829* 269 This is a poor shooting-iron. . it might do for young men to 'tote' in a settlement, but it is of no use in the woods. **1866** C. H. SMITH *Bill Arp, so Called* 147, I don't think you tote fair. **1909** R. PARRISH *My Lady of South* viii. 95 Thar warn't many Danielses left able ter tote a gun. **1909** H. G. WELLS *Tono-Bungay* II. iii 194 The old merchant used to tote about commodities. **1952** C. DAY LEWIS tr. *Virgil's Aeneid* IV. 89 One who, men say, totes round his home-gods Everywhere. **1975** *Nation* 20 Dec. 659/1 Others wear official-looking uniforms and tote service revolvers. **1977** C. McCULLOUGH *Thorn Birds* vi. 110 He toted the infants with easy familiarity. **1979** *Chatelaine* (Canada) Jan. 24/3, I toted a canvas bag over one shoulder. **1983** E. REVELEY *In Good Faith* iii. 59 They still tote the two original evangelists around with them but I think that's mostly so's they can keep getting money from the mother church.

totem. Add: **1. d.** *ellipt.* = *totem-pole*, esp. in *low on the totem. colloq.*

1974 K. MILLETT *Flying* (1975) II. 167 Counting on faculty privilege. Almost too low on the totem even to deserve it. **1977** D. BAGLEY *Enemy* xviii. 148 'What's your status here?' 'Low man on the bloody totem... I have a line into the Embassy but that's for emergency use only.'

2. *totem ancestor* (examples); **totem-pole,** (*a*) (earlier examples); also *fig.*, esp. in colloq. phr. *low on the totem pole*, of lowly status (see also sense *1 d); (*b*) *Electronics*, an arrangement of two output transistors or valves in which one takes the place of the load of the other, the output being taken from between the two.

1937 *Jrnl. Anthrop. Inst.* XL. 413 It is thus clear that the gi is nothing other than the totem-ancestor. **1949** J. CAMPBELL *Hero with Thousand Faces* 390 An unconscious identification took place, and this was finally rendered conscious in the half-human, half-animal, figures of the mythological totem-ancestors. **1880** S. JACKSON *Alaska & Missions on North Pacific Coast* ix. 263 Daylight found us near Fort Tongas... From the water there seemed to be a whole forest of. . *totem* poles. **1897** B. W. JAMES *Alaska* 75 It has ever been an unanswerable question as to the origin of these totem poles. **1940** L. MACNEICE *Last Ditch* 18 And under the totem poles—the ancient terror—between the enormous fluted Ionic columns There seeps. . The guttural sorrow of the refugees. **1945** *Sun* (Baltimore) 3 Sept. 1/7 The lowest brass to sign the surrender documents was Colonel L. Moore Cosgrave... 'He's low man on the totem pole,' murmured an Australian correspondent. **1967** *Electronics* 6 Mar. 155/2 High leakage of the multiple-emitter transistor may load a circuit excessively. To offset this. . the totem pole output stage is used. **1973** 'B. MATHER' *Snowline* iii. 36 Just how far up the Departmental totem pole was Hallaby? **1978** *Jrnl. R. Soc. Arts* CXXVI. 456/2 In looking at the heritage of ideas or values we are looking at the totem poles of the heritage, symbols that are of more importance to us for what they represent than for themselves. **1978** D. BAGLEY *Flyaway* xxxiii. 311 Kissack . . was pretty low on the totem pole—a hired hand. **1981** P. M. CHIRLIAN *Analysis & Design Integrated Electronic Circuits* v. 114 The load resistance of Fig. 5–10 has been replaced by an enhancement MOSFET. This 'load' is called an active load or active pull-up... The circuit is also called a totem pole because the elements are drawn one above the other in the schematic diagram.

totemic, *a.* (Earlier example.)

1846 H. R. SCHOOLCRAFT *Notes on Iroquois* 79 It will be necessary to go back, and examine. . the curious and intricate principles of the Totemic Bond.

totemistic, *a.* (Earlier example.)

1873 *Fortn. Rev.* May 631 They have lost whatever meaning their totemistic forefathers may have had.

‖ **Totenkopf** (to·tĕnkǫpf). [Ger., = 'death's head'.] Used *attrib.* and *absol.* to designate (a member of) one of the divisions of the SS in Nazi Germany, having a death's head as its badge; *spec.* in the war of 1939–45, designating a unit (*Verband*) of concentration-camp guards.

1943 W. NECKER *German Army of To-day* iv. 164 During the war some formations of the *Totenkopf-Verbände* or *Death's-head* (*Skull*) *Detachments* were incorporated into the *Waffen-SS*. Originally, these formations were guards at concentration camps. *Ibid.* 167 The *Totenkopf-Division*, or 'Death's Head' Division. **1953** G. REITLINGER *Final Solution* ii. 43 Later there developed a strong distinction between the *Totenkopfverbaende* and the SS *Totenkopf* Division, which. . became a field division like any other. **1975** tr. *Melchoir's Sleeper Agent* II. 81 You and me both know what those *Totenkopf* bastards are. Concentration camp guards, that's what! **1977** D. JAMES *Spy at Evening* vii. 45 Eicke was. . a *Waffen SS* divisional commander... He commanded The Death's Head, Totenkopf division. **1981** 'E. TREVOR' *Damocles Sword* xv. 149 The Totenkopf and the Gestapo keep extensive records.

‖ **Totentanz** (to·təntants). Also 8 **Toden Tans**; (*hist.*) **Todtentanz.** [Ger.] = *dance of death* s.v. DANCE *sb.* 6 c. Also *fig.*

1789 *Emblems of Mortality* p. xxiv, He [*sc.* Holbein] also engraved several things upon wood, among which are his *Scripture Cuts*, and *Dance of Death*, vulgarly called *Toden Tans*. **1937** *Jrnl. Archæol. Assoc.* I. 249 Switzerland, which was once rich in representations of the Dances of Death, has suffered grievous losses. All that remains are a few. . fragments in Museums. The earliest of these—the Klingental Totentanz at Basle—. . was destroyed. . about 1850. **1950** A. WILSON *Such Darling Dodos* 144 (*heading*) Totentanz. *Ibid.* 163 Your first big reception, duckie, shall be a Totentanz. **1964** W. G. RAFFÉ *Dict. Dance* 50/1 The popular play and mime dance of the *Todtentanz* was then [*sc.* in 1535] still extant in its ritual or miracle play form. **1966** J. FOWLES *Magus* xix. 113 Dupes of the reality of war, of the ultimate *Totentanz*. **1982** P. DICKINSON *Last House-Party* (1983) ii. 18 Time emerged. . no friendly old gaffer with a scythe, but close kin to the skeleton reaper of the *Totentanz*.

tother, *pron.* and *a.* Add: **A. 1. a.** Phr. *to tell tother* (or *t'other*) *from which* (joc.), to tell one from the other or (loosely) another; to distinguish or tell apart.

1874 M. CLARKE *His Natural Life* (1975) III. xxii. 24 You're so much alike one can't tell t'other from which. **1904** KIPLING *Traffics & Discoveries* 258 We've mixed the whole show up. . till you can't tell t'other from which. **1979** D. FRANCIS *Whip Hand* ii. 27 He calls them all Tommy, because he doesn't know tother from which.

B. 1. c. *tother school, 'un* (Public School slang), a preparatory school, a school one attended before one's public school.

1880 TROLLOPE *Dr. Wortle's School* (1881) I. ii. 34 The old prescribed form of education. . must be followed,—a t'other school, namely, then Eton... Therefore Bowick was chosen as the t'other school. **1940** M. MARPLES *Public School Slang* 179 'Where's your t'other 'un?' a question generally addressed to new boys. **1958** *Sunday Times* 25 May 8/3 Mr. Kenward's totherun (if the reviewer may be permitted to adopt, for the moment, his own public-school terminology) is named Ripple.

C. tothersider, delete *nonce-wd.* and add: *spec.* of Australia (earlier and later examples).

1896 H. LAWSON *Let.* 3 Sept. (1970) 62 W.A. is a fraud. . . The old Sand-gropers are the best to work for or having dealings with. The Tothersiders are cutting each other's throats. **1903** 'T. COLLINS' *Such is Life* (1944) 276 The ancient t'other-sider [*sc.* Vandemonian Jack] oscillated his frame-saw. **1929** J. RAESIDE *Golden Days* 224 The population of Hannans, although mostly composed of t'othersiders, included not a small sprinkling of West Australians. **1949** *Geographical Mag.* Feb. 373 *Tothersider*, a Western Australian. **1950** K. S. PRICHARD *Winged Seeds* 30 Unemployed from all over the country swarmin' here, t'other siders as well as W.A. blokes. **1963** X. HERBERT *Disturbing Element* 2 My parents. . were what were called T'othersiders, meaning people who had come to West Australia from the other side of the continent.

‖ **totidem verbis** (tǫ·tidem vɜ̄·ɹbīs), *adv. phr.* [L.] In so many words.

1659 N. HARDY *First Ep. John* VI. 101 We do not read (*totidem verbis*) in the Scripture that the Apostle Baptized Infants, yet it is very probable. **1704** SWIFT *Tale of Tub* 64 'Tis true, said he, there is nothing here in this Will, *totidem verbis*, making mention of Shoulder-knots. **1844** MILL *Ess. Pol. Econ.* ii. 47 This object, under the varying names of an extensive demand, a brisk circulation, a great expenditure of money, and sometimes *totidem verbis* a large consumption, was conceived to be the great condition of prosperity. **1902** L. A. BURD in *Cambr. Mod. Hist.* (1907) I. vi. 202 These [fundamental beliefs or hypotheses] are rarely stated *totidem verbis* in any passage, though implied in nearly all.

totipotent, *a.* Add: Also, able to differentiate into any other related kind of cell; so **totipo·tency** = *totipotence* s.v. TOTIPOTENT *a.*; **totipote·ntial** *a.* = TOTIPOTENT *a.* in Dict. and Suppl.

1918 *Jrnl. Exper. Zool.* XXV. 500 Totipotency is restricted to those girdle-forming cells which become implanted along with the limb bud. **1934** *Discovery* Aug. 220/1 There must be some power which controls and regulates the powers of these turbulent totipotential cells and this is exactly what Driesch called the 'entelechy'. **1942** M. M. WINTROBE *Clin. Hematol.* i. 30 According to the monophyletic school. . the lymphocyte of lymphatic tissue is identical with the primitive blood cell and is thus totipotential, giving rise under proper stimulation to any other type of blood cell. **1959** W. ANDREW *Textbk. Compar. Histol.* xii. 458 These cells are 'totipotent' and, according to need, can give rise to any other type of cell in the body of the sponge. **1967** *Amer. Jrnl. Med.* XLII 932/1 Yoffey and Courtice. . believe that a major function of the small lymphocyte is that of a circulating totipotential cell. **1979** *Sci. Amer.* Apr. 93/2 Totipotency equivalent to that of early embryonic cells was thereby established unequivocally for individual embryonal carcinoma cells.

toto[1] (tōᵘ·to). [ad. Swahili *mtoto* offspring, child.] In East Africa: a child; a baby; a young animal; a young servant.

1916 *Chambers's Jrnl.* Nov. 719/2 Poor little 'toto', bereft of his mother. **1927** *Ibid.* Nov. 762/1, I was a 'toto' then. How old I cannot say. In my tribe there is no record of birth or death. **1937** K. BLIXEN *Out of Africa* IV. 336, I was. . a long way in front of the waggons, with Farah, my dog Dusk and the Toto who looked after Dusk. **1964** C. WILLOCK *Enormous Zoo* v. 90 At first he ran out in front as is the custom with white rhino *totos*. **1979** *Observer* (Colour Suppl.) 9 Sept. 43/1 We hear goat-bells, and tiny herd-boys emerge cautiously from the bush. 'Give those *totos* a bowl of maize meal,' Thesiger orders.

toto^{2} (tō^{u}·to). *Mil. slang* (of the 1914–18 war). [a. Fr. mil. argot.] A louse.

[**1917** G. Clover *Stop at Suzanne's* (1919) 223 They were all covered with lice—*les totos* they call them.] **1918** *Radiator* 30 May 1 Dr. Kent Hagler..saw no evidence of flea or toto. *a* **1919** in E. C. Garrett *Trench Ballads* (1919) 78 Some people call 'em Totos—Some people call 'em lice. **1929** Hall & Niles *One Man's War* 46, I do not know who developed lice first, but I noticed them on that march. We called them 'totos'.

Totonac (totŏnæ·k). Also † **Totonaca.** [ad. Sp. *Totonaca*, f. Nahuatl *Totonacatl*, pl. *Totonaca.*] An Indian people of east central Mexico; a member of this people. Also, their language. Also *attrib.*

1787 C. Cullen tr. *Clavigero's Hist. Mexico* II. viii. 18 Five men..said in Mexican..that they were of the nation of the Totonacas, and sent by the lord of Chempoalla. **1852** B. Mayer *Mexico* I. iii. 29 The Tlascalans were not so easily won as his allies, the Totonacs. **1900** *Proc. Davenport Acad. Sci.* VIII. 187 Some of the..Totonac women in the Plaza..are really gay with hair ribbons. **1908** F. Starr *In Indian Mexico* xx. 245 In Tlaxco, a small village in this *municipio*, four idioms are spoken—Aztec, Otomi, Totonac and Tepehua. **1940** F. Johnson in C. L. Hay et al. *Maya & their Neighbors* vi. 109 The area on the map in which Totonac was spoken remains practically identical with that originally drawn by Orozco y Berra. **1948** A. L. Kroeber *Anthropol.* (rev. ed.) xviii. 794 Along the Gulf coast in Tabasco and Vera Cruz, a series of peoples known as Olmec, Totonac, and Huastec, in order from south to north. **1977** T. A. Sebeok *Native Lang. Americas* II. 153 The Totonac..were the first to become allies of Cortez when he disembarked on the coast of Veracruz and set out to conquer Mexico. **1977** *Language* LIII. 262/2 The publication of these volumes..makes Totonac an unusually well-documented language.

Hence **Totona·can** *a.*, of or pertaining to the family of languages that comprises Totonac and Tepehua.

1933 J. E. Thompson *Mexico before Cortez* viii. 259 The Tajin pyramid is in Totonacan linguistic territory. **1940** F. Johnson in *Maya & their Neighbors* vi. 109 (*heading*) Totonacan family [of languages]. **1977** T. A. Sebeok *Native Lang. Americas* II. 153 There are..well over 130,000 speakers of Totonacan dialects in Veracruz and Puebla.

totora (totō^{ə}·ra). [a. Quechua, Aymara.] A perennial bulrush, *Scirpus totora*, native to alpine lakes in Peru and Bolivia. Also *attrib.*

1936 *Discovery* Dec. 372/2 The 'totora'..is still used by the Indians of Lake Titicaca to make nets and cordage. **1958** A. Toynbee *East to West* vi. 17 The cattle wade out, breast-deep, to crop the tender shoots of the totóra reed. **1971** P. Crampton tr. *Heyerdahl's Ra Exped.* vi. 110, I knew that the *totora* reed in America was capable of long sea voyages. **1974** T. Morrison *Land above Clouds* 142 For centuries, the Indians around Titicaca have used the Totora for making their reed boats.

‖ **tot siens** (tǫt sins). *S. Afr.* Also **totsiens.** [Afrikaans *tot (weer)siens* 'until we meet again', f. Du. *tot* until + *zien* to see.] A formula of farewell: au revoir, till I see you again.

1937 S. Cloete *Turning Wheels* ix. 142 'Tot Siens. Tot siens,' they cried, their voices growing fainter. **1948** H. V. Morton *In Search S. Afr.* ii. 52 We said good-bye, with a *tot siens* or two and one 's' long folks'. **1963** A. Delius *Day Natal took Off* 72 This is, then, not good-bye, only totsiens. **1974** *Argus* (Cape Town) 30 July 22/9 Tot siens! May you come back to Britain soon.

totsy (tǫ·tsi). *slang.* [f. Tot *sb.*^{4} + -sy.] = *totty *sb.* 2.

1938 G. Greene *Brighton Rock* iv. i. 142 The atmosphere of innumerable roadhouses, of totsies gathered round swimming pools.

Tottenham. Add: **b.** *Tottenham pudding*, feed for pigs or poultry, consisting of sterilized kitchen waste.

1944 Halnan & Garner *Princ. & Pract. Feeding Farm Animals* (ed. 2) xvi. 329 In the process of cooking the waste..sets to a firm..'pudding' which finds a ready market for feeding to pigs and poultry. Since this pudding was first produced in..Tottenham..such prepared food is known as 'Tottenham Pudding'. **1966** K. Nicholson *Hook, Line & Sinker* viii. 91 He's a Large White... In the winter, he has his quota of Tottenham Pudding—that's concentrated swill, sterilised by steam. **1980** *Good Housekeeping* Dec. 226/6 The days of muck and mystery, when poultry were fed on 'Tottenham Pudding'—kitchen waste from hotels and restaurants, boiled up and sterilised.

tottle, *v.*^{1} Add: **tottlish** *a.* (earlier example); **to·ttly** *a.* = *tottlish* adj.

1835 *Knickerbocker* VI. 6 Had she not been obliged..to steady her tottleish bark with the paddle which now loitered behind the stern. **1905** *Eng. Dial. Dict.* VI. 203/1 *Tottly*,..ready to fall, unstable. **1910** Kipling *Rewards & Fairies* 155 My legs was pretty tottly, but I made shift to go on deck.

totty, *sb.* Add: **2.** *slang.* A girl or woman, *esp.* a 'good-time' girl.

1890 Barrère & Leland *Dict. Slang* II. 368/2 *Tottie*.., a girl, a fast girl. **1914** Joyce *Dubliners* 29 He asked us which of us had the most sweethearts. Mahony mentioned lightly that he had three totties. **1957** J. Braine *Room at Top* xxviii. 230 She has a pal, some old tottie that lends her a flat. **1968** 'O. Mills' *Sundry Fell Designs* viii. 86 All Dan's Manchester-type ladies were only totties. This marriage wasn't going to make any difference to them. **1977** C. Watson *One Man's Meat* iv. 34 Showing off. Certainly, why not? There were a couple of totties just behind.

3. *Comb.*: **totty-pot** = *potty *sb.* 1.

1966 'L. Lane' *ABZ of Scouse* II. 83 *Potty* or *totty-pot*, a child's chamber-pot. **1971** *Daily Tel.* (Colour Suppl.) 22 Oct. 17/2 Room in boot for pram, pushchair, totty-pots, picnic gear.

‖ **tou** (dō^{u}, tō^{u}). *Chinese Antiq.* [Chinese *dòu.*] A hemispherical pedestalled bowl with a lid of similar shape, used as a container for food.

1899 S. W. Bushell *Oriental Ceramic Art* xvii. 491 The twelve bowls (*pien*) on the right being made of closely woven slips of bamboo, lacquered yellow, the twelve (*tou*) on the left of carved wood, gilded. **1909** B. Laufer *Chinese Pottery of Han Dynasty* iv. 122 The ears are not essential to the type of the *tou*, as there are also bronze *tou* which lack them. **1973** *Genius of China* 52/2 Red Pottery tazza *tou*, with undulating ornament painted in black.

Touareg, var. *Tuareg.

touch, *sb.* Add: **II. 8. c.** (Earlier example.)

1816 Jane Austen *Emma* II. viii. 147 Having so much to ask and to say as to tone, touch, and pedal.

12. (Earlier example.)

1857 [see *play *sb.* 10 d].

III. 13. d. *out of touch* (examples).

1891 G. Moore *Impressions & Opinions* 88 He is out of touch with them; he cannot make them understand. **1969** H. Perkin *Key Profession* i. 4 By then Newman was out of touch with what universities were becoming. **1980** D. Lodge *How Far can you Go?* iv. 121 Most of them had been out of touch with him for many years, but he spoke to them as if it was only yesterday.

18. b. (*fig.* from senses 8 b, 10 b.) A person's characteristic skill or aptitude in any activity, *spec.* a sport; *to lose one's touch, to be out of touch*, not to show one's customary skill; similarly *to be in touch.*

1927 *Sat. Rev.* 9 July 60/1 But in the extended character-drawing of Ferdinand Banting and Tom Lord, who are not indigenous to the King's Cross scene, he seems to lose his touch. **1933** *Times* 18 Nov. 5/7 Success depended on being in touch for his drop shots, and yesterday his touch failed him. *Ibid.* 8 Dec. 6/2 He lost his touch and made but one more ace before the match was over. **1939** *Punch* 4 Oct. 378/1 That fatal hour when Hitler lost his touch. **1955** *Times* 13 July 8/5 It is one of the signs of greatness to be able to stay in for a long time without finding touch, and yet without looking exactly like getting out. **1959** *Times* 29 May 4/2 Nicholls, who has been out of touch, is a tall, stylish player. **1976** *Liverpool Echo* 6 Dec. 17/2 It was..stalemate until Ipswich found the touch which produced the winner 15 minutes from the end. **1977** *World of Cricket Monthly* June 28/3 The presence of Kallicharran in his best touch for the series..encouraged a little West Indian optimism entering the last day. **1979** A. Morice *Murder in Outline* v. 44 She may not be in the pink of health, but she has not lost her touch.

19. b. Also *a touch of the sun*, a mild attack of sunstroke.

1890 Kipling *Life's Handicap* (1891) 165, I judge no man this weather... He had a touch of the sun, I fancy. **1915** R. Brooke *Let.* Apr. (1968) 680 When I had a touch of the sun, in Egypt. **1965** M. Spark *Mandelbaum Gate* v. 118 'A touch of the sun,' Freddy said. Amnesia, was the doctor's conclusion... Nonsense, I'm suffering from sunstroke.

20. b. Add after 'person': esp. by persuasion or glib talk; *to make a touch*, to obtain money thus. (Earlier and further examples.)

1846 *Nat. Police Gaz.* (U.S.) 18 July 390/1 Ingenious Touch... Phillsburg..felt for his money, and..found in its place another pocket-book filled with newspaper instead of money. *Ibid.* 25 July 389/1 The Read Street Touch Case. Ann Henry, the keeper of a den of infamy and..one of her syrens, have been fully committed on the charge of robbing Townsend W. Hetherington. **1865** *Leaves from Diary of Celebrated Burglar & Pickpocket* xv. 48/2 The most splendid 'touch' of the campaign was already in our grasp! *Ibid.* xvii. 58/2 They took a furnished room in..Seven Dials, until a lucky 'touch' came off, when they took larger apartments. **1896** Ade *Artie* v. 43 Next day they had to make a hot touch for a short coin so as to get the price of a couple o' sinkers and a good old 'draw one'. **1914** *Automobile Topics* 4 July 638/3 His story of not being able to find employment..has enabled him to make many a successful 'touch'. **1939** R. Chandler *Big Sleep* xvi. 114, I figure it's a good time to..make a quick touch on the Sternwoods for travel money. **1953** *Essays in Crit.* III. 111 The poet might regard the patron as an intimate,..or simply as a public Maecenas, good for a 'touch' of three guineas a dedication. **1964** C. Chaplin *Autobiogr.* xvii. 299 It seemed obvious from the tone of the letter that it was all leading up to a 'touch'. So I thought I would take along $500.

c. *soft* or *easy touch*: a person easily manipulated; *spec.* one easily induced to part with money; also, a task or opponent easily handled. *colloq.*

1940 J. O'Hara *Pal Joey* 44 You get the reputation of being a soft touch. **1945** *Sun* (Baltimore) 4 Oct. 1/1 Newhouser.., who figured to be the outstanding pitcher of the season, proved..to be the softest sort of a touch for Manager Charlie Grimm's National Leaguers. The second Cub to bat belted him cleanly. **1955** H. Kurnitz *Invasion of Privacy* (1956) xii. 80 Dorsey's appetite for easy money..was honed to a razor edge... He sensed a vast soft touch. **1959** H. P. Tritton *Time means Tucker* vi. 45/1 He was an easy touch for any hard-luck story. **1972** *Police Rev.* 1 Dec. 1562/2, I would also warn any university student regarding the Police as a 'soft touch' for graduates. **1976** *Eastern Even. News* (Norwich) 29 Nov., Caravan dwellers are on the increase and they will keep on increasing while Norwich remains an easy touch; the complacency regarding this problem is alarming.

d. *to cut up (old) touches*: see *cut *v.* 59 f.

V. 28. *in* or *out of touch*: see also sense *18 b.

touch, *v.* Add: **I. 2. a.** Also = *to touch up*, sense 34 c (*b*) below; *refl.*, to masturbate.

1903 Farmer & Henley *Slang* VII. 177/2 *Touch*... verb... (or *to touch up*), to grope a woman. **1927** F. Harris *My Life & Loves* (1934) IV. ix. 182 You want to know if I have touched myself. Sure, all girls have. **1973** *Family Circle* July 114/1 Little girls are told not to touch or play with themselves, and later their sexual parts are associated with urination and menstruation, which are considered 'dirty'.

5. Also *fig.* in pa. pple., = *touché b. *rare.*

1853 E. Sewell *Experience of Life* xviii. 183 'I dislike this kind of bantering very much, Horatia,' I said... Horatia laughed merrily. 'Touched, I declare!'

7. Also, *pass.*, to be slightly affected by drink. *colloq.*

1834 C. Brontë *My Angria & Angrians* in W. Gérin *C. Brontë* (1967) vi. 84 Two bottles of..ale, and a double quart of Porter..and I'm not a bit touched—only light and smart and active. **1888** 'R. Boldrewood' *Robbery under Arms* II. xi. 180, I wasn't no ways drunk; but I must have been touched more or less, because I felt myself to be so sober.

11. a. Also in legal formula *to touch and stay.*

?**1796** in *Eng. Reports* (1927) CLXX. 471 Liberty to sail to, touch and stay at any port or ports whatsoever on her passage out..without prejudice to the insurance. **1895** W. Gow *Marine Insurance* iii. 59 The liberty to touch and stay is limited by its close application to the main object of the voyage. **1969** E. R. H. Ivamy *Marine Insurance* xiii. 142 It was formerly held that 'liberty to touch and stay' did not permit of trading at the port of call.

16. b. (Examples of sense 'to obtain a loan or gift of money from' without const., and of sense 'to rob'.)

1807 H. Tufts in E. Pearson *Autobiogr. of Criminal* (1930) ii. iv. 293 *Touching a cly*, robbing a pocket. **1888** in Farmer & Henley *Slang* (1903) VII. 177/1 A dip [*sc.* pickpocket] touched the Canadian sheriff for his watch and massive chain while he was reading the Riot Act. **1928** [see* knock *v.* 13 d]. **1950** *Austral. Police Jrnl.* Apr. 110 To touch a person is to steal from him, but to touch him for a loan is to ask him for one. **1951** G. Greene *End of Affair* v. iv. 197 'If you would lend me a pound.'..Had she 'touched' Henry once too often? **1963** T. Parker *Unknown Citizen* i. 32 He wants some money... Don't you send it to him, let him touch somebody else for a change.

23. b. Also in phr. *touched in the head* or *the upper story.*

1867 Trollope *Last Chron. Barset* I. xx. 172 We tried to get him through as being a little touched in the upper story. **1902** E. Nesbit *Five Children & It* ii. 61 Touched in the head, eh?.. All the more shame to you boys dragging the poor afflicted child into your sinful burglaries.

III. 30. touch down. b. *Aeronaut. intr.* To alight on the ground from the air; to land; also *transf.* Also (*rare*) *trans.*, to land (an aircraft).

1935 C. Day Lewis *Time to Dance* 41 M'Intosh touched her down. **1938** *Jrnl. R. Aeronaut. Soc.* XLII. 498 A successful flight down the beam..gives the feeling that if the ceiling had been only 50 feet one could have held on..longer before finally touching down. **1942** P. Brennan et al. *Spitfires over Malta* (1943) ii. 55, I touched down and swung my aircraft away from the pitted landing path, braking violently. **1955** *Times* 22 Aug. 5/4 The first aircraft to touch down brought an official party from Kallang. **1962** *Listener* 8 Feb. 260/2, I send this dove from the ark Where she must never touch down. **1970** N. Armstrong et al. *First on Moon* xiv. 369 At 12.45 a.m. Houston time, Apollo 12's lunar module Intrepid touched down on the moon. **1979** *Arizona Daily Star* 1 Apr. E 9/1 14 persons were injured when a tornado touched down near Glasgow, Ky.

32. touch off. b. (Earlier example.) Also *fig.*, to provoke (a reaction), to spark off.

1884 'Mark Twain' *Huck. Finn* xxviii. 282 It does seem most like setting down on a kag of powder and touching it off. *a* **1934** in Webster s.v., These terms..have become push buttons which touch off emotional reflexes. **1943** *Sun* (Baltimore) 12 Feb. 6/2 Senator Truman touched off the debate with a speech in which he assailed the supplanting of Lou Holland as chairman of the SWPC. **1950** *N.Y. Times* 20 Apr. 1/6 The surprise proposal..touched off several outbursts of denunciation of the Soviet action. **1958** *Listener* 29 Nov. 813/1 The Bundestag declaration has touched off a chain-reaction of inquiry, proposal, examination, plan. **1966** *Ibid.* 10 Feb. 221/2 All these insights the piano touched off with its single hollow note struck over and over again. **1979** *Tucson* (Arizona) *Citizen* 20 Sept. 5c/1 A $1·8 million error may touch off a legal challenge.

34. touch up. b. Also, to exert influence upon; to rouse the emotions of.

1811 Jane Austen *Sense & Sens.* III. iv. 88 We must touch up the Colonel to do something to the Parsonage. **1817** M. Edgeworth *Harrington* I. iii. 55 You will see..how cleverly I will get myself out of the scrape with her. I know how to touch her up. **1846** Dickens *Let.* 28 Mar. (1977) IV. 528, I hope you mean to go to the General Theatrical Fund Dinner on Monday Week... Let me know, that I may touch up the Committee to place you near me. *c* **1863** T. Taylor in M. R. Booth *Engl. Plays of 19th Cent.* (1969) II. 140 The roughs adore music..and as for sentiment and sensation, if you could hear Miss St. Evremond touch them up with the 'Maniac's Tear', the new sensation ballad [etc.]. **1884** E. W. HAMILTON *Diary* 10 Mar. (1972) II. 573 Slavery is a matter which specially touches up the British public.

c. † (*a*) (See quot. 1785.) *Obs.* (*b*) To finger or caress so as to excite sexually. *slang.*

1785 GROSE *Dict. Vulgar T., To touch up a woman,* to have carnal knowledge of her. **1903** [see sense 2 a above]. **1923** J. MANCHON *Le Slang* 318 *To touch up a woman,* caramboler une femme. **1961** H. S. TURNER *Something Extraordinary* vii. 135 She..went in for a crass practice..known as 'touching up'. It is..a quick flick, in passing, from the crotch upwards... When a girl 'touches up' a boy it seems to be a very casual signal,.. nowhere near a definite proposition. **1966** P. WILLMOTT *Adolescent Boys E. London* iii. 49 They would often try to move on from kissing to sexual play: as they put it, they ..went up her skirt or 'touched her up'. **1973** C. EGLETON *Seven Days to Killing* iv. 48 Good-looking tart... I wouldn't have minded her touching me up.

touch-. Add: **1. a.** *touch-sensation* (earlier example), *-stimulus*; *touch-sensitive* adj. **b.** **touch-dancing** orig. *U.S.*, dancing in which the partner is held close; hence (as a back-formation) **touch-dance** *v. intr.*; **touch-finder** *Rugby Football,* one who or a kick which succeeds in driving the ball into touch (TOUCH *sb.* 12); so **touch-finding** *vbl. sb.* and *ppl. a.*; **touch football** *U.S.*, a form of American football in which a player carrying the ball may be stopped simply by touching him, instead of tackling; **touch-kicking** *Rugby Football,* the action of kicking the ball into touch (TOUCH *sb.* 12); hence (as a back-formation) **touch-kick** *v. intr.*; so **touch-kick** *sb.*; **touch-mark**, an official stamp on pewterware, esp. one identifying the maker; cf. TOUCH *sb.* 5 b; **touch pad** *Computers,* a computer input device in the form of a small touch panel; **touch panel,** a panel containing different areas that need only to be touched to operate an electrical device; **touch preparation** *Microscopy,* a preparation made by lightly touching cultured or freshly cut tissue with a slide so that a thin layer of cells adheres to it; **touch rugby** or **rugger,** a version of rugby football in which touching takes the place of tackling; **touch screen** *Computers,* a VDU screen that is also an input device operated by touching it; **touch shot** *Lawn Tennis,* a shot without any force; **touch spot** *Physiol.*, one of the spots on the skin specially sensitive to touch or pressure; **Touch-Tone** *U.S.*, a proprietary name for telephone apparatus in which push-buttons take the place of a dial; **touch-typing,** the art of typing without looking at the keys; hence (as a back-formation) **touch-type** *v. intr.*; so **touch-typist**; **touch-writer** = *touch-typist* above.

1972 *Harper's Bazaar* Oct. 72/1 Dance experts agree that, as the East goes, so goes the nation, and what you've heard by now is true—'touch', 'partner', 'ballroom' dancing is back. *Ibid.* 72/3 Freddie doesn't touch dance at all. **1974** *Courier-Mail* (Brisbane) 23 Feb. 18/4 The latest craze among young people in the U.S. is 'touch dancing', which their mums and dads used to call 'dancing cheek-to-cheek'. **1939** *Daily Tel.* 18 Dec. 11/1 Jenkins..alternated long touch-finders with sliced shots. *Ibid.*, Ellis was allowed a lot of latitude in..putting in touch-finding kicks. **1960** *Times* 30 Nov. 3/6 The small, durable halves were dedicated touch-finders. **1976** *Leicester Mercury* 14 Oct. 46/1 It was a very solid display of good catching, good touch-finding and some probing entries into the line. **1933** *Jrnl. Health & Physical Educ.* Oct. 41/1 Touch football is now a scientific and standardized game. **1951** J. STEINBECK *Burning Bright* i. 37, I was..just playing around with some of the fellows—touch football. **1977** *Transatlantic Rev.* LX. 119 You often see Winterville kids playing touch football along the parkway. **1954** J. B. G. THOMAS *On Tour* vi. 71 They..saved and counter-rushed and touch-kicked with unerring accuracy. **1960** *Times* 31 Oct. 4/4 Long touch-kicks. **1978** *Morecambe Guardian* 14 Mar. 11/3 Glover took a while to find his usual accuracy with his touch kicks. **1936** *Times* 9 Jan. 4/3 Some excellent touch-kicking by Morris forced the Navy back into their own '25'. **1904** H. J. L. J. MASSÉ *Pewter Plate* xiv. 190 The touch-marks usually were the initials of the maker of the pewter, and various other devices such as the Company's quality mark. **1959** L. GROSS *Housewives' Guide to Antiques* viii. 103 Some, but not all, pewter will be found with a touch-mark. **1974** L. KOENIG *Little Girl* iii. 34 A pewter tankard..seemed to demand examination. She ..turned it over to study the touchmark. **1980** *Displays* I. 206/1 These experimental studies, conducted during the development of the Touch-pad, demonstrate the viabiity of an off-display touch input device. **1983** *Your Computer* Aug. 32/2 Once out of its package the Wizzard takes on the appearance of a quite simple, compact unit, complete with two joysticks, touch pads and firing buttons. **1974** *Physics Bull.* June 225/2 One of these is a touch panel made of a glass plate on which capacitors are thinly etched in copper. A TV tube behind the panel 'names' the capacitors in an array of 4×4 and these 'buttons' can be 'pushed' by merely touching the panel. **1981** J. B. ADAMS in J. H. Mulvey *Nature of Matter* vii. 156 The operator..can send instructions to any component of the machine by means of a touch panel, which identifies the component, and one knob, which determines the required action. **1956** *Nature* 7 Jan. 47/1 Touch-preparations of spleen and lung on slides were fixed in 95 per cent ethanol at 37°C. for 30 min. **1975** *Ibid.* 17 July 225/2 Spleens were sectioned sagittally and touch preparations were made and stained with the Wright–Giemsa stain or benzidine. **1977** *Arab Times* 14 Dec. 9/7 Both [games] entail constant running, both in defence and attack, especially touch rugby. **1942** C. MILBURN *Diary* 16 Dec. (1979) 161 He talks of hockey, soccer and touch-rugger, describing the latter game. **1974** *Management Informatics* III. 70/1 As a first step, a prototype touch screen was designed and constructed in our Laboratory by Mr. Stephen Salter. **1983** *Austral. Personal Computer* Aug. 60/2 The touch-screen and light-pen both have the limitation that the user must first identify the location that has to be touched, and then a physical movement has to be made... Also, touch screens do get finger-marked. **1865** S. HODGSON *Time & Space* ii. 78 A combination of a whole series of touch-sensation into a solid whole is apparently possible..in grasping a small object, where the fingers meet each other. **1969** *Bull. Radio & Electr. Engin. Div. Nat. Res. Council Canada* July–Sept. 15 (*heading*) An *X-Y* touch sensitive position encoder for computer input. **1979** *Washington Post Mag.* 25 Mar. 5/3 The clavichord changed. Its keyboard widened... 'It got louder and more touch-sensitive,' says Tom. **1983** *Listener* 12 May 3/2 You controlled your route by pressing buttons on a touch-sensitive screen. **1959** Touch shot [see [*DINK *sb.*[2]]. **1969** *New Yorker* 14 June 56/2 A loose, liberal, infuriating touch shot. **1906** C. S. SHERRINGTON *Integrative Action of Nervous System* ix. 324 The retina is thus a group of glorified 'warm-spots,' and the cochlea a group of glorified 'touch-spots'. **1927** HALDANE & HUXLEY *Animal Biol.* v. 122 The fineness of discrimination for touch depends mainly on the closeness of touch-spots. **1968** D. F. HORROBIN *Med. Physiol. & Biochem.* xxv. 150/2 There are touch spots, cold spots and warm spots, each particularly sensitive to one modality. **1927** HALDANE & HUXLEY *Animal Biol.* xii. 268 Most..of the group possess nerves, and at least scattered sense-organs for perceiving touch-stimuli. **1962** *Official Gaz.* (U.S. Patent Office) 19 June TM 122 American Telegraph and Telephone Company, New York... *Touch-Tone.* For providing telephone communication service. **1970** O. DOPPING *Computers & Data Processing* xi. 163 If the telephone is of the touch-tone type, the same buttons that are used for dialling can be used also for putting questions, expressed in numerical form, to the computer. **1972** *Sci. Amer.* Sept. 112/3 The first telephone switching systems were actuated by human operators; today the job is done automatically by means of a dial or 'Touch-Tone' terminal on the user's telephone. **1976** *National Observer* (U.S.) 10 Apr. 9/4 Touch-tone converters. This device changes your dial telephone to a touch-tone telephone. **1962** *Punch* 8 Aug. 191/1 If you will learn to touch-type, I will give you a new, feather-light portable. [**1897** in *Story of Typewriter* (1923) 113 Omaha has become the storm centre of the commotion over the touch method of typewriting.] **1947** K. JAEDIKER *Tall, Dark & Dead* viii. 117 All I know about touch-typing is that there are home keys and if you don't put your fingers on them, you go haywire. **1976** 'J. FRASER' *Who steals my Name?* iv. 46 Many coppers had done touchtyping courses. **1929** *Telegr. & Telephone Jrnl.* XVI. 13/1 Attention was concentrated upon touch-typing with the object of turning out highly-skilled touch-typists. **1972** 'J. & E. BONETT' *No Time to Kill* vii. 90 I'm not a touch typist. Very few writers are. **1915** *Literary Digest* (N.Y.) 21 Aug. Advt. p. i, Great numbers were so-called touch-writers—yet there has hardly been a single one who hasn't doubled or trebled his or her speed and accuracy.

2. a. touch-back: (examples); also, a similar action in some other ball games; **touch-last,** a children's game, = TOUCH *sb.* 1 g.

1891 W. CAMP *Amer. Football* 172 A touch-back is made when a player touches the ball to the ground behind his own goal, the impetus which sent the ball across the line having been received from an opponent. **1941** *Daily Progress* (Charlottesville, Va.) 14 Jan. 11 This used to be an automatic touchback and the ball was placed in play on the 20-yard line. **1976** *Webster's Sports Dict.* 455/2 *Touchback.* Speedball. A situation in which the ball is driven over the end line by an offensive player without scoring. **1825** JAMIESON Suppl. II. 568/2 *Tig,* a game among children, in which one strikes another and runs off... This game in S[cotland] is the same with Touchlast in E[ngland]. **1902** [see *HE *pers. pron.* 6 b]. **1927** *Sunday Express* 17 July 8/2 The younger and sprightlier guests..played 'touch last' on the lawn. **1951** E. GRAHAM *My Window looks down East* iv. 29 He walkes sideways away from her, like a child playing 'touch-last'.

touchable, *a.* Add: Hence also **touchabi·lity,** suitability to be touched.

1937 L. MACNEICE in *Essays & Stud.* XXII. 157 Spender..believes in 'touchability'... It means..the belief that people in themselves are worth knowing and touching, just as for Auden facts are worth remembering. **1944** [see *MARRIAGEABILITY].

tou·chdown. [TOUCH- 2 a.] **1.** (In Dict. s.v. TOUCH- 2 a.) Also in *American Football.*

1876 in P. H. Davis *Football, Amer. Intercollegiate Game* (1911) 462 A match shall be decided by a majority of touchdowns. **1949** *Desplaines Valley News* (Summit, Illinois) 28 Oct. 7/3 Harvard could not push across a touchdown in the first half. **1977** *New Yorker* 9 May 122/2 A figure holding hands overhead like a referee indicating a touchdown.

2. *Aeronaut.* The action of coming into contact with the ground during landing.

1935 P. W. F. MILLS *Elem. Pract. Flying* vii. 102 [The purpose] of causing the actual touchdown, when it takes place, to take place with the aeroplane in its natural position on the ground. **1948** *Sun* (Baltimore) 3 Nov. 11/3 You are 50 feet above glide path and one quarter of a mile from touchdown. **1961** H. H. KOLBE *Handbk. Astronaut. Engin.* XXVII. 7 The term *landing,* when used in a discussion of space flight, actually can be considered as four phases: i.e., the exit from orbit, the reentry, the letdown, and the touchdown. **1975** *Daily Tel.* 11 Aug. 11/4 One vehicle will make a soft touchdown on Mars while the large spacecraft which carried it on its journey will remain in orbit.

‖ **touché** (tuʃe), *int.* Occas. *fem.* **touchée.** [Fr., pa. pple. of *toucher* to hit.] **a.** *Fencing.* An exclamation used to acknowledge a hit.

1904 *Red Book* Feb. 382/1 *'Touché!'* Jarsac growled sharply. **1958** A. WEST *Princ. & Persuasions* 202 These cosy thrusts will never slip between the ribs into the lungs; the weapons are not rapiers but buttoned foils that will bend double against a jacket and at most produce a murmur of *'Touché'*.

b. A pleasant admission of a valid point or justified accusation made by another person.

1907 *Everybody's Mag.* XVI. 221/1 They did not cry *touché,* but the House cheered to the echo. **1912** E. C. BENTLEY *Trent's Last Case* xv. 322 *'Touché',* Trent said, with a dry smile. **1928** *Sat. Rev.* 17 Nov. 649/1 Touché—I apologize to Messrs. Brown and Phillips for my lack of technical discernment. **1952** H. INNES *Campbell's Kingdom* I. iv. 81 'I'd my own reasons, the same as you have.' ..'Touchée,' she said softly. **1981** A. PRICE *Soldier no More* 50 *'Touché...'* he nodded, accepting the rebuke.

touched, *ppl. a.* Add: **touched proof** (earlier example).

1831 J. CONSTABLE *Let.* 13 Apr. (1966) IV. 348, I send you the *twelve pounds,* and a touched proof of the Heath.

toucheous, var. *TOUCHOUS *a.*

toucher. Add: **1. d.** One who † robs or seeks to obtain gifts or loans of money for himself. *slang.*

1849 G. G. FOSTER *New York in Slices* 25 The other places in the cotillion are occupied by a notorious kracksman [*sic*] with his 'pal'—a celebrated 'toucher'. **1904** *Chicago Tribune* 30 Oct. (Worker's Mag.) 4/2 The salaried clerk who keeps his wife..at a fashionable hotel is, usually, a toucher of the kind that makes a good front. **1919** WODEHOUSE *My Man Jeeves* 91 Many's the time in London, I've hurried along Piccadilly and felt the hot breath of the toucher on the back of my neck. **1961** 'F. O'BRIEN' *Hard Life* xii. 101 The streets aren't crawling with touchers like Dublin.

4. b. *as near as a toucher* (earlier example). Also *within a toucher,* within an inch *of* doing something (only in Wodehouse).

1827 W. CLARKE *Every Night Bk.* 73 The cock which takes your fancy..is..to all appearance, right-thorough bred, or 'as near it as a toucher'. **1932** WODEHOUSE *Doctor Sally* viii. 78, I came within a toucher of saying, 'pause before it is too late!' **1954** —— *Jeeves & Feudal Spirit* xviii. 173 The hand of doom within a toucher of descending.

touching, *vbl. sb.* Add: **1. c.** (Examples with *up*: see TOUCH *v.* 34 in Dict. and Suppl.)

1902 [in Dict., sense 1 d]. **1936** *Burlington Mag.* May 208/1 The artist's later touching-up. **1957** *Practical Wireless* XXXIII. 558/1 'Look Back to Lyttleton' was a novel by Caryl Brahms, which had been laid aside for touching up and taken out as suitable material for a radio play. **1973** C. MULLARD *Black Britain* vii. 87 Both employees had for some months been practising a mild form of homosexuality—'touching up'. **1980** J. SCOTT *Gospel Lamb* iii. 51 Touchings-up were frequent—the girls seemed as eager as the boys.

4. *touching-distance*: hence *touching-distant* adj. (*poet.*).

1881 W. WHITMAN *Leaves of Grass* (new ed.) 352 Thy touching-distant beams.

touch-line. Add: Also **touchline. 3.** Also in some ball games other than rugby football, and *fig.*

1932 AUDEN *Orators* II. 46 The two-faced, the obscure and amazed, the touch-line admirers. **1964** *Sunday Times* 25 Oct. 22/5 A charming touchline companion called the [hockey] match 'grotty'. **1973** PARK & FAHEY *Team Handball* 50 The Boundary-Lines on the long sides shall be termed the Touch-lines. **1973** *Nature* 9 Nov. 108/2 From the touchlines the editor does, however, bias the issue by setting H. G. Haas's article on 'Active Ion Transport' immediately before that on the sinoatrial node.

touch-me-not, *sb.* **3. b.** (Earlier example.)

1817 M. EDGEWORTH *Harington* I. v. 112 Lady de Brantefield, the *touch-me-not* mistress of the mansion.

touchous (tʌ·tʃəs), *a. dial.* Also **toucheous.** [f. TOUCH *sb.* or *v.* + -OUS.] Easily offended, sensitive, touchy.

1867 P. KENNEDY *Banks of Boro* xxv. 190 By the time I got home, however, I was very cross and *touchous.* **1933** C. MILLER *Lamb in his Bosom* iv. 28 The ill-temper worked in her body like a slow fever... Lonzo called her toucheous **1960** H. LEE *To kill Mockingbird* viii. 72 He said Atticus was still touchous about us and the Radleys and it wouldn't do to push him away. **1973** *N.Y. Times* 3 June L-19/1 [In the Caribbean] an overly sensitive person is 'touchous', not touchy.

toudang, var. *TOERING.

tough, *a.* Add: **1. b.** Phr. *tough as* (*old*) *boots* or *leather.* Freq. *fig.*, implying sense 4.

1843 As tough as leather [in Dict.] **1870** As tough as old boots [see BOOT *sb.*³ 1 b]. **1946** J. B. PRIESTLEY *Bright Day* iv. 111 Joe Ackworth's more the type. He's as tough as old leather. **1967** *Listener* 7 Dec. 765/1 This is no sweet old dolly.. She is tough as old boots, working for a living. **1981** M. HATFIELD *Spy Fever* I. iii. 31 Colonel Theakston was..as the saying goes, as tough as old boots.

5. b. Resolute in dealing with opposition; vigorously uncompromising; severe; esp. in phr. *to get tough* (cf. *GET *v.* 73 d). *colloq.* (orig. *U.S.*).

1906 U. SINCLAIR *Jungle* i. 11 He affects a 'tough' aspect, wearing his hat on one side and keeping a cigarette in his mouth all the evening. **1930** E. H. LAVINE *Third Degree* ii. 17 A conscientious, or 'tough', [police] sergeant was assigned to a west-side precinct. **1935** WODEHOUSE *Blandings Castle* vi. 151 In all villages, of course, there must..be an occasional tough egg. **1938** E. AMBLER *Cause for Alarm* vii. 116 Vagas got tough. They had a showdown. **1964** in Hamblett & Deverson *Generation X* 10 The funniest thing was seeing the cops getting tough. If they want a fight we'll give it to them. **1972** J. SYMONS *Bloody Murder* xii. 159 The behaviour of the private detective may be tough, but is based on ethical standards. **1978** J. IRVING *World according to Garp* i. 14 They initiated a get-tough policy with Jenny Fields. It was a staff decision—'for her own good', of course. **1984** *N.Y. Times* 12 Feb. (Late City Final) I. I. 35/1 My policy is to be tough but fair with the gaming industry... Federal law-enforcement officials have greater access to data on Nevada.

c. Of laws or rules: strict, inflexible. Of an institution: marked by strict enforcement of discipline.

1961 in WEBSTER s.v., When the law gets too tough the courts don't convict. **1971** J. OSBORNE *West of Suez* I. 42 Father decided I needed 'toughening up' at a really tough school. **1977** *National Observer* (U.S.) 22 Jan. 1/1 Reformers want a tougher code of ethics for Presidential appointees. *Ibid.*, The environmentalists want a tougher line on automobiles that pollute.

6. c. Of circumstances, etc.: imposing hardship, distress, or injustice. *colloq.* (orig. and chiefly *U.S.*).

1890 *Stock Grower & Farmer* 8 Mar. 4/2 The recent blizzard..was pretty tough on range cattle. **1901** S. E. WHITE *Claim Jumpers* 256 I've been a little tough on you occasionally. **1929** WODEHOUSE *Mr. Mulliner Speaking* i. 34, 'I suppose it's because I'm rather an out-size and modelled on the lines of Cleopatra.' 'Tough!' 'You bet it's tough. A girl can't help her appearance.' **1933** P. GODFREY *Back-Stage* xvii. 216 The 'tough breaks' in their gipsy life soon weed out the weaklings. **1942** E. PAUL *Narrow St.* xxix. 265 You know you're likely to be bumped off? ..Things are tough down there, and they won't get any better. **1959** H. P. TRITTON *Time means Tucker* (1965) i. 11 Work was scarce and wages low, and conditions all round were tough. **1962** J. H. CUTLER *Honey Fitz* xx. 291 Joe [Kennedy] made his children stay on their toes... 'He would bear down on them and tell them, "When the going gets tough, the tough get going."' **1982** *Church Times* 30 Apr. 11/1 The life of a nun is extremely tough and involves a lot of physical hard work.

d. *tough luck* (colloq., orig. U.S.), hard luck, misfortune; esp. as an expression of (sometimes ironic) commiseration; also (chiefly *U.S. slang*) *tough shit, stuff,* or *tiddy* (*titty*).

1912 Tough luck [see *old top* s.v. *OLD *a.* 8 a]. **1932** *Kansas City* (Missouri) *Times* 14 Jan. 18 It may be Mr. Hoover's tough luck to be both renominated and re-elected. **1934** J. T. FARRELL *Calico Shoes* 143 You have to take your chances, and if you can't swim, you sink. It's just your tough tiddy. **1944** in A. M. Taylor *Lang. World War II* 198 Beachhead chaplains are carrying a special 'tough stuff' ticket these days which they issue to guys with complaints about which nothing can be done. **1946** *Amer. Speech* XXI. 249 [Army vocabulary.] *Tough shit*, something which is unfortunate, but about which nothing can be done. **1958** S. A. GRAU *Hard Blue Sky* ii. 89 'And the whole building near to going down with the next strong wind.' 'Tough titty, man.' **1971** 'A. BURGESS' *MF* ii. 32 [I got] robbed and rumpled.—Tough titty she said with little sympathy. **1974** *Black World* Jan. 10/2 Is Mr. Gayle exasperated by the fact that I do not give clear-cut answers to these questions? Tough luck: I do not have them. **1976** *New Yorker* 1 Mar. 74/2 I'm awfully sorry to hear about your tough luck. **1978** J. CARROLL *Mortal Friends* II. v. 200 Tough shit, Lady! Morning wears to evening and hearts break.

9. Restrict † to sense in Dict. **b.** In an uncompromising, aggressive, or unyielding manner.

1943 R. CHANDLER *Lady in Lake* iv. 25 You fellows [*sc.* cops] ever flash a buzzer—or is acting tough all the identification you need? **1968** *Globe & Mail* (Toronto) 3 Feb. 7/5 Saskatchewan's Premier Ross Thatcher, while he talks tough in private, is apparently willing to make at least a gesture.

9*. As an epithet of commendation: very good, 'great'. *U.S. slang* (orig. *Blacks'*).

1937 [see *CATCH *v.* 35 b]. **1960** R. G. REISNER *Jazz Titans* 167 *Tough*, great. **1965** MRS L. B JOHNSON *White House Diary* 3 June (1970) 282 'Pat N gent..he's just tons, Mother—he's a tough guy!' ("Tough' means great, wonderful, nice, attractive, it seems.) **1972** J. HUDSON in T. Kochman *Rappin' & Stylin' Out* 422 Now my singing ain't none too tough, but I can sell some dope.

10. a. tough baby, boy *slang* (orig. *U.S.*), a person given to hard-headed, violent, or lawless behaviour; **tough guy** *colloq.* (orig. *U.S.*), a person not easily injured or thwarted; freq. *attrib.*; **tough movement** *Transformational Grammar*, a transformation applied to a sentence moving words of a certain class (of which *tough* is one), from one part of the sentence to another (e.g. *to convince John is hard*: *John is hard to convince*); **tough nut** *colloq.* (orig. *U.S.*), a person difficult or dangerous to deal with; **tough pitch**, substitute for def.: commercially pure copper in which the amount of cuprous oxide was reduced by poling to the value at which it would produce minimum brittleness; usu. *attrib.* or as *adj.*; (examples).

1932 E. WALLACE *When Gangs came to London* xxiii. 234, I've had real tough babies on their knees to me in a police station, begging me to be put in a cell. **1946** WODEHOUSE *Joy in Morning* ii. 12 Scanning the roster of the females I've nearly got married to in my time, we find the names of some tough babies. **1958** F. NEWTON in P. Gammond *Decca Bk. Jazz* v. 68 It is no use being censorious about the atmosphere of..tough boys and sleezy vaudevilles in which the great blues singers were nurtured. **1974** T. P. WHITNEY tr. *Solzhenitsyn's Gulag Archipelago* I. I. vii. 294 The interrogators and their tough-boy helpers dashed in from the interrogation prison. **1932** Tough guy [see *CLEAN *v.* 6 b]. **1938** L. MACNEICE *Mod. Poetry* viii. 149 E. E. Cummings, the 'tough-guy' American poet. **1946** R. CHANDLER *Let.* 30 May (1981) 75 Bogart, of course, is..much better than any other tough-guy actor... Ladd is..a small boy's idea of a tough guy. **1946** H. CROOME *Faithless Mirror* vii. 75 Tough guys with a heart of gold. **1981** J. DUNNING *Deadline* (1982) xix. 187 At the bottom of that tough-guy facade, you're just like all the rest... Scared to death. **1971** P. M. POSTAL *Cross-Over Phenomena* iii. 27 There is a class of adjectives in English, *hard, tough, easy, difficult, impossible, simple,* which have played a prominent role in discussions of the need for a transformational grammar of English... The contrast between sentences like ..*a* Throneberry is easy to please. *b* Throneberry is eager to please..is by now well known... There is a special rule defined for this class ..which involves the movement of an NP out of the predicate of the complement sentence. Let us refer to this rule as tough-movement. **1977** *Canad. Jrnl. Linguistics* 1976 XXI. 157 Consider (24), resulting from Passive, and (25), resulting from Tough-Movement, as answers to the question 'Why was John arrested?' (24) That he robbed a store was reported in the newspaper. (25) That he robbed a store is hard for us to believe. **1862** in E. W. Pearson *Lett. from Port Royal* (1906) 81 There are a great many men of twenty-five to forty, 'tough-nuts' many of them. **1892** 'MARK TWAIN' *Amer. Claim.* xxv. 263 His father was rather a tough nut. **1922** E. O'NEILL *Hairy Ape* viii. 83 Say, yuh're some hard-lookin' guy, ain't yuh? I seen lots of tough nuts dat de gang called gorillas, but yuh're de foist real one I ever seen. **1950** *Times* 12 May 7/7 For the 'tough nut' the youth club as at present constituted offered no fold. **1977** C. MCCULLOUGH *Thorn Birds* x. 236 Meggie was going to be a tough nut to crack and he couldn't afford to frighten or disgust her... He'd woo her the way she obviously wanted. **1903** *Engineering* 4 Dec. 753/3 When the right amount of oxygen is present, the copper is said to be 'tough-pitch'. **1949** P. C. CARMAN *Chem. Constitution & Properties Engin. Materials* vii. 220 The product is a 'tough-pitch' copper of over 99·9% purity. **1964** H. HODGES *Artifacts* iv. 70 Correctly poled copper, tough pitch copper, still contains a little cuprous oxide.

b. *tough-hided* (in quots. *fig.*), *-necked*, *-skinned* (*fig.* example).

1925 D. H. LAWRENCE *St. Mawr* 158 She felt a peculiar tough-necked arrogance in him. **1930** R. LEHMANN *Note in Music* VI. 249 It would take a good deal..to harm a tough-hided old hippopotamus like Uncle Tom. **1933** C. S. LEWIS *Pilgrim's Regress* VII. v. 146, I always think it is possible for a place to be *too* bracing. They call it the land of the tough-minded—tough-skinned would be a better name. **1964** *Listener* 30 Apr. 731/3 A tough-hided, soft-centred, north-country, working-class dramatist.

B. *sb.* **1.** For *U.S.* read 'orig. *U.S.*' and substitute for def.: A person given to rough or violent behaviour. (Later examples.)

1929 'G. DAVIOT' *Man in Queue* iii. 25 The missing man ..was, in the opinion of the Durham inspector, a tough. **1946** R. LEHMANN *Gipsy's Baby* 145 Can't think how your parents put up with it—all that gang of young toughs in and out all day. **1972** E. GRIERSON *Confessions of Country Magistrate* ix. 86 Certainly the treatment of the teenage tough..is a problem to which no one has ever hazarded an optimistic answer. **1982** I. HAMILTON *Robert Lowell* (1983) ii. 16 He graduated to the status of school tough via a series of spectacular playground victories.

2. A person of uncompromising or aggressive views.

1928 C. CONNOLLY *Let.* July in *Romantic Friendship* (1975) 321, I am becoming a tough, an anglophobe, and reverting to intolerance and intellectual pride. **1931** H. NICOLSON *Diary* 21 Aug. (1966) 89 The latter asked whether Tom would join him and the Tory toughs in opposition. **1980** *Times* 23 June 31/1 The so-called 'toughs' who support Mrs Thatcher's policy—like Sir Keith Joseph.. against the 'wets' led by Jim Prior.

tough (tʊf), *v. slang* (orig. and chiefly *U.S.*). [f. TOUGH *a.*] **a.** intr. *to tough it* (*out*): to withstand (to the end) difficult conditions or adverse circumstances without flinching. Cf. *to rough* (*it*) *out* s.v. ROUGH *v.*¹ 4 b.

1830 *Mass. Spy* 27 Jan. (Th.), Judy with whom he had toughed it three years. **1852** *Knickerbocker* XXXIX. 26 You don't need no medicine; you'll tough it out, I dare say. **1873** C. THAXTER *Isles of Shoals* 64 (Th.), Our brave little schooner 'toughed it out' on the distant ledge. **1939** L. M. MONTGOMERY *Anne of Ingleside* xviii. 121 She darkly opined that it would be a miracle if he toughed it out till spring. **1956** T. RADDALL *Wings of Night* (1957) xxxii. 241 She was a great ol' lady... Just kep' her chin up and..toughed it out to the end. **1982** H. LIEBERMAN *Night Call* xvi. 94 We'll tough it out, but sacrifices will have to be made.

b. *trans.* With obj. in place of *it*: to withstand to the end.

1974 *Newsweek* 20 May 23/2 Everybody..was pressed into service denying that Mr. Nixon planned to quit; his daughter Julie vowed that he would tough out the impeachment process to its end in the Senate. **1979** *Courier-Mail* (Brisbane) 27 Sept. 1/6 Mr. Sinclair signalled he would try to tough out the crisis. **1981** *Observer* 26 Apr. 15/4 Fraser, it is assumed, will tough out this latest crisis.

toughie (tʊ·fi), *sb.* (and *a.*) *colloq.* (orig. *U.S.*). Also **toughy**. [f. TOUGH *a.* + -IE, -Y⁶.] **1.** A tough person. **a.** = *tough guy* s.v. *TOUGH *a.* 10 a. **b.** A person of aggressive or uncompromising views.

1929 *Princeton Alumni Weekly* 24 May 981/2 The *toughie* is the man of the hour when the policeman's whistle blows. It is always nice to be close to him when the riot calls are turned in. **1938** *New Republic* 21 Sept. 188/1 Getting the toughies off the street. **1940** R. CHANDLER *Farewell, my Lovely* xxvii. 168 A toughie..came in and showed me a blackjack. **1959** *She* May 65/2 Luxury-lovers had better stick to planes or boats. A trip in the 'Bombay Bus' is definitely one for the toughies. **1960** *Sunday Express* 24 July 16/5 Mr. Butlin is a toughie too... A man who has learned to cater for the mood of the people and take full advantage of their longer purses... I think he will continue to prosper despite credit squeezes, Chancellors, the rain, and other vexations. **1971** J. MANDELKAU *Buttons* x. 121 A group of bikers riding out for kicks every Friday and Saturday night, getting drunk and swinging back and forth over the white line behind the toughie they would call 'our leader'. **1980** I. MURDOCH *Nuns & Soldiers* I. 84 Daisy had women friends.. 'Women's Libbers', and left wing toughies. **1984** *Observer* 8 Apr. 12/4 Mondale may think that he makes a good political toughie.

2. A difficult problem, enterprise, or contest.

1945 *Good Housekeeping* June 230/2 How about the $80 question?..Think now. This is a toughie. **1947** *Sun* (Baltimore) 18 Jan. 1/7 West has another toughie for Congress... Would it be O.K. if the District used tax money to buy uniforms for the policemen's band? **1972** J. L. DILLARD *Black English* vii. 281 Children who speak Standard English may react to words like *island*,..with 'That's a toughie!' **1972** D. LEES *Zodiac* 6 It sounded, as Harry put it, 'a doddle', but even if it had looked a toughy the Riviera would have sold it.

3. *attrib.* or as *adj.*

1962 *John o' London's* 9 Feb. 138/4 The nice, 'toughie' Irishman. **1974** *Times Lit. Suppl.* 14 June 644/3 Admirers of Stephen Becher's urbane *When the War is Over* will be surprised at the toughie metaphysics of the opening of his new novel. **1977** *Film & Television Technician* Jan. 9/3 Bob was one of those 'toughie' production managers, greatly concerned not only with the budget, but with the film and the people working on it.

tough-mi·nded, *a.* In the philosophy of William James: marked by a purely empirical, sceptical, non-metaphysical approach to questions; opp. *TENDER-MINDED *a.* Hence more widely: free from excessive sensitivity, realistic, unsqueamish, etc. Also *absol.*

1907 W. JAMES *Pragmatism* i. 12 You will..recognize the two types of mental make-up that I mean if I head the columns..*The Tender-Minded.* Rationalistic (going by 'principles'), Intellectualistic, Idealistic, Optimistic, Religious, Free-willist, Monistic, Dogmatical. *The Tough-Minded.* Empiricist (going by 'facts'), Sensationalistic, Materialistic, Pessimistic, Irreligious, Fatalistic, Pluralistic, Sceptical. **1927** J. S. HUXLEY *Relig. without Revelation* iv. 116 Youth wakes to the fact of social inequality, and, if not one of the tough-minded, to remorseful distress of its own privileged position. **1945** AUDEN *Coll. Poetry* 123 Tough-minded men get mushy in their sleep. **1952** C. P. BLACKER *Eugenics* 240 The scientist, or at least the scientist's camp-followers, may become tough-minded and contemptuous: the word 'mysticism' expresses what they most passionately abjure. **1960** *Guardian* 17 Dec. 6/2 The tough-minded and unromantic pragmatism of the new President. **1974** *Sci. Amer.* Jan. 113/2 Tough-minded skeptics. **1980** F. K. PROCHASKA *Women & Philanthropy in Nineteenth Cent. Eng.* vi. 191 Reclaiming prostitutes was a daunting prospect for charitable women however tough-minded.

Hence **tough-mi·ndedness.**

1907 W. JAMES *Pragmatism* vii. 267 One misunderstanding of pragmatism is to identify it with positivistic tough-mindedness. **1936** *Mind* XLV. 218 The sort of tough-mindedness which, on principle, excludes ethical, aesthetic and religious considerations from metaphysical thinking, is wilfully blind. **1961** *Guardian* 3 Apr. 12/7 The first fruits of tough-mindedness [in U.S. policy in Laos] are..encouraging. **1975** *Nature* 10 Apr. 470/2 In addition to being careful in this way, we have also to be sensitive and observant, and not to react with a preconceived pattern of tough-mindedness.

‖**toughra** (tu·grǎ). Also **toghra, tughra, tuğra.** [a. Turkish *tura, tuğra.*] An ornamental monogram incorporating the name and title of the Sultan.

1888 S. LANE-POOLE *Turkey* 36 [1365] It s said that Murād signed the treaty, for lack of a pen, with his open hand, over which he had smeared some ink, in the manner of Eastern seals. This veritable sign-manual is believed to be the origin of the *tughra* or Sultan's cipher, which has ever since appeared on the coinage and the official documents of the Turks. **1903** *Amer. Jrnl. Numismatics* Jan. 73 The principal device on the gold coins of the present Sultan..is the imperial *toghra.* **1954** *Stamp Lover* XLVI. 136/1 Turkey was introduced by an official document of 1840 bearing the manuscript Toughra or signature of the

Sultan. **1962** R. A. G. CARSON *Coins* 488 The tughra, the monogram of the sultan's names and titles which is a feature of later Turkish coinage.., appeared for the first time under Suleyman I. **1974** *Encycl. Brit. Macropædia* III. 664/2 A distinctive *tuğra* was created for each sultan and affixed to imperial decrees by a skilled calligrapher.

‖ **toujours** (tuʒūr), *adv.* (and *sb.*) [Fr., = always.]

1. *toujours gai* (ge), 'always cheerful'; cheerful under all circumstances; also as *sb.*, an unfailingly cheerful disposition. Occas. partially anglicized as *toujours gay*.

1711 ADDISON in D. Piper *Eng. Face* (1957) vii. 163 A certain smirking Air..bestowed indifferently on every Age and Degree.. The *Toujours Gai* appeared even in Judges, Bishops and Privy-Counsellors. **1899** KIPLING *From Sea to Sea* I. viii. 263 They [*sc.* prostitutes] spoke of themselves as 'gay'... A night's reflection has convinced me that there is no hell for these women in another world... It was my duty to watch through the night a patient—gay, *toujours* gay, remember—quivering on the verge of the 'jumps'. **1927** D. MARQUIS *archy & mehitabel* xiv. 56 Well archy the world is full of ups and downs but toujours gai is my motto. **1972** M. KENYON *Shooting of Dan McGrew* xxi. 174 He was 'toujours gai' (I wonder is he on drugs?).

2. *toujours perdrix* (pɛ̄rdrī), lit. 'always partridge', an allusive phr. used to imply that one can have too much of a good thing. [For an explanation see A. M. Hyamson *Dict. Eng. Phrs.* (1922) 346/1.]

1818 *Blackw. Mag.* Feb. 569/2 A partridge is a good thing; and yet even '*Toujours Perdrix*' is not to be borne. **1877** L. W. M. LOCKHART *Mine is Thine* (1879) xvii. 163 He wanted a rest, a change from this *toujours perdrix* of ladies' society, polite small-talk, boredom. **1927** D. H. LAWRENCE *Let.* 12 Dec. (1962) II. 1026 I'm sick of Jesus. .. We might have somebody else born for a change. *Toujours perdrix!*

3. Used simply: always.

1902 G. MEREDITH *Let.* 19 Jan. (1970) III. 147 If it is *toujours* Goethe, that is because I share the *culte*.

touladi, var. *TULADI.

Toulousain (tūlūzæ̃n), *sb.* and *a.* Fem. **-aine** (-ɛn). [Fr., f. *Toulouse* + *-ain* -AN.] **A.** *sb.* A native or inhabitant of Toulouse, in SW France. **B.** *adj.* Of, pertaining to, or characteristic of Toulouse.

1883 H. JAMES in *Atlantic Monthly* Oct. 461/1 A big, brown, expansive woman... This terrible Toulousaine of today. *Ibid.* 462/1 Saint-Sernin..dedicated to Saint Saturninus—the Toulousains have abbreviated—is, I think, alone worth the journey to Toulouse. **1970** *Sat. Rev.* (U.S.) 3 Oct. 45/1 A young Toulousaine from the local tourist office. **1972** R. COBB *Reactions to Fr. Revolution* iii. 119 To do the opposite to what the Bordelais did was an ancient rule of Toulousain conduct. **1980** 'M. HARRIS' *Treasure of Ste. Foy* v. 54 Serge Gaspar is a Toulousain, dark, with a Spanish look to him. *Ibid.* 55 She is the same Toulousain type as Gaspar, with dark hair..and a clear olive complexion.

toungya, var. *TAUNGYA.

toup (tūp), slang abbrev. of TOUPEE in Dict. and Suppl.

1959 P. BULL *I know the Face* viii. 138 'Say, Padre, is that a toup?' he naïvely enquires. **1973** R. HAYES *Hungarian Game* xxxiv. 205 He picked a blond wig... He slipped the toup over his gray hair and adjusted it to cover the high forehead.

toupee. Add: No longer *rare* in the sense 'a patch of false hair or small wig to cover a bald place'. (Later examples.)

1973 M. AMIS *Rachel Papers* 81 My hair hung on my head as if it were a cut-price toupée. **1980** V. S. PRITCHETT *Tale Bearers* 20 He is having his toupee fixed and his hair dyed.

tour, *sb.* Add: **I. 1.** Freq. in *tour of duty*. Also, with pronunc. (taʊᵊɹ), in *Oil Industry*. (Further examples.)

1800 WELLINGTON *Suppl. Desp.* (1858) I. 464 This tour of duty to commence at morning parade on halting days. **1903** *Dialect Notes* II. 345 The morning *tour* lasts from midnight until noon. **1939** D. HAGER *Fund. Petroleum Industry* ix. 212 These men work in shifts or 'tours' (pronounced *towers*) of 6 or 8 hrs. **1946** *R.A.F. Jrnl.* May 153 The existing Editor having performed his tour of duty and taken up other duties in the Service. **1975** L. CROOK *Oil Terms* 60 The Driller is responsible for his crew and the running of the rig during his eight or twelve hour 'tour'. **1981** 'J. ROSS' *Dark Blue & Dangerous* xxvii. 158 He's too soft, and..I don't know how he did the rest of his tour of duty without showing it on his face.

2. b. *Dancing.* Also with pronunc. (‖tūr). In a cotillion, a circular movement by the dancers. In *Ballet*, a turn by a solo dancer; *tour en l'air*, such a turn while leaping in the air.

1841 MRS. GASKELL *Lett.* (1966) 822 The cotillion was so pretty—such amusing & graceful *tours*. **1930** CRASKE & BEAUMONT *Theory & Pract. Allegro Class. Ballet* 94 (*heading*) Series of tours en dedans en diagonale. **1948** A. H. FRANKS *Approach to Ballet* iii. 45 Used sparingly, *tours* can become most effective highlights in a male solo. **1958** [see *PLIÉ]. **1960** M. WOOD *Advanced Historical Dances* 93 The refrain had been replaced by a fixed series of movements called Tours, forming a framework into which the figures were fitted. The Tours in order of performance were these: (1) Grand Rond. All take hands in a ring and go round both ways. [Etc.] **1963** *Times* 29 May 13/4 Mr. Flindt..can produce effortless, waist-high *cabrioles*, yet is often constricted, even rough, in *tours*. **1977** *Times* 5 May 11/8 The skill with which she sustained the series of *tours en l'air* in her solo.

3. a. Also, † an account of such a journey.

1812 [in Dict.]. **1817** JANE AUSTEN *Sanditon* (1925) viii. 110 He read all the Essays, Letters, Tours & Criticisms of the day. **1821** BYRON *Don Juan* v. lii. 161 Nature..Resigns herself with exemplary patience To guide-books, rhymes, tours, sketches, illustrations.

III. 12. *tour bus, director, guide, operator, party*.

1952 *Galaxy* June 56/2 I'm the tour director. Can I help you? **1965** J. A. MICHENER *Source* (1966) 22 That afternoon the first excursionists stopped at the tell, asking to see the Candlestick of Death, and the next morning a tour bus arrived. **1971** M. MCCARTHY *Birds of America* 107 Their tour director, who had met them at Le Havre. **1973** P. THEROUX *Saint Jack* xviii. 219 The tour-guide had started his spiel. **1976** J. SNOW *Cricket Rebel* 47, I could only wait anxiously for the announcement of the names of the tour party to visit the West Indies that winter of 1967–68. **1981** *Sunday Express Mag.* 11 Oct. 9/1 (Advt.), We've taken more British holiday-makers here than any other tour operator. **1981** M. KENYON *Zigzag* xi. 67 He was agonizingly shy... Guiding tour parties petrified him.

tour, *v.* Add: **4.** Also with a performer as obj.

1920 *Glasgow Herald* 10 June 7 Mr. Quinlan..recently toured Madame Tetrazzini and Signor Caruso. **1922** JOYCE *Ulysses* 92 The idea is to tour the chief towns... Mary Anderson is up there now... Louis Werner is touring her.

touring *ppl. a.* (earlier and *Theatr.* examples).

1832 F. TROLLOPE *Dom. Manners Amer.* II. xxxiii. 236 To this frail shelter..nearly all the touring gentlemen.. find their way. **1867** *Harper's Mag.* Dec. 96/1 As railways have multiplied, the formation of what are called Touring-parties, for the purpose of giving concerts and operas in the provinces, has become the business of many. **1895** ROBERTS & MORTON *Adventures Arthur Roberts* xiii. 159 Whether from preference or economy,..this touring company generally slept at night on the beach. **1969** G. GREENE *Travels with my Aunt* I. xi. 105 The touring company..came after my Paris days. It was in Paris that I was spotted by Mr Visconti... 'He was a great amateur of..the stage.' **1983** *Times* 7 Sept. 3/4 Scunthorpe is a regular stop-off point for touring companies.

touraco. Delete ‖ and add: Now usu. spelt turaco. (Later examples.)

1932 *Discovery* Jan. 25/1 Colies, turacos, various doves and barbets..throng to the Amani plantations. **1965** G. B. SCHALLER *Year of Gorilla* ii. 69 A black-billed turaco flew up, flashing its brilliant crimson wings. Then this crow-sized bird hopped along a branch, chattering like a squirrel. **1977** *Daily Colonist* (Victoria, B.C.) 9 Oct. 23/4 You will see..exotic birds—bee-eaters, love-birds, sunbirds and turacos.

‖ **Tourangeau** (turɑ̃ʒō), *sb.* and *a.* Pl. **-x.** [Fr.] (A native or inhabitant) of Touraine, a former province of France corresponding more or less to the modern department of Indre-et-Loire, or of Tours, its chief town.

1883 H. JAMES in *Atlantic Monthly* July 25/1 The real Tourangeau will not make an effort..to go in search of a pleasure. **1969** B. ARTHAUD tr. *Martin-Demézil's Loire Valley* 9 The Tourangeaux gave it the wonderful name of '*le Jardin de France*'. **1973** *Listener* 22 Mar. 372/3 Motifs from this Tourangeau château or that, from Florentine palazzi or Classical temple architecture.

‖ **Tourangeois** (turɑ̃ʒwa), *a.* and *sb.* [Fr.] = prec.

1857 C. KINGSLEY *Two Years Ago* III. vi. 155 Balzac's old Tourangeois judge. **1958** C. COCKBURN *Crossing the Line* ii. 37, I took a terrible chance by recommending to him—a Tourangeois—a certain Catalan wine I had discovered.

tourbillion, tourbillon. 2. Delete '*Obs.* exc. as French' and add: Also, an eddy, a whirlpool; also *fig.* (Further examples.)

1891 'MARK TWAIN' *Lett.* (1917) II. xxxi. 557 We were allowed to go through the wrong arch, which brought us into a tourbillon below which tried to make this old scow stand on its head. **1931** R. GRAVES *To whom Else?* 19 Such portents are not to be wondered at Being tourbillions in Time made By the strong pulling of her bladed mind Through that ever-reluctant element. **1972** J. WAIN in Cox & Dyson *20th-Cent. Mind* I. xi. 374 In the history of any art there are unexpected eddies and tourbillions.

3. (Earlier example.)

1749 *Descr. Machine for Fireworks* 15 Tourbillons..88.

tour de force. (Earlier examples.)

1802 LD. ELGIN *Let.* 18 Feb. in *Paget Papers* (1896) II. 41 To exult over what is styled a *tour de force* of the British Influence here. **1802** M. BERRY *Jrnl.* 16 Mar. (1865) II. 137 Women now dance in the style of men, that is to say, with all the difficult steps and *tours de force* possible.

‖ **Tour de France** (tūr də frɑ̃s). [Fr., lit. 'tour of France'.] The name of an annual cycling stage race on the public roads of France (with some crossing into adjoining countries), now typically over about 4,000 kilometres including mountainous terrain.

1922 *Times* 24 July 7/5 The 'Tour de France' cyclist competition..ended to-day. **1926** E. HEMINGWAY *Sun also Rises* III. xix. 247 Bicycle road-racing was the only sport in the world, he said. Had I ever followed the Tour de France? **1967** *Guardian* 14 July 1/2 Tommy Simpson, the British cyclist, died early this evening after collapsing during a mountain stage of the Tour de France. **1978** *Listener* 6 July 15/1 These days find Paris in a sort of limbo... There is, it is true, the Tour de France to distract us in the weeks ahead.

‖ **tour d'horizon** (tūr dorizɔ̃). [Fr., lit. 'tour of the horizon'.] An extensive tour. Usu. *fig.*, a broad, general survey.

1952 *Ann. Reg. 1951* 181 General Eisenhower, returning from his European *tour d'horizon*, was able to give Congress..a report. **1964** *Economist* 5 Sept. 929/1 A fascinating *tour d'horizon* of the main theories. **1979** T. SKYRME *Changing Image Magistracy* xii. 162 Lord Widgery, in the course of a *tour d'horizon* in 1973 said: [etc.]. **1984** *Oxf. Univ. Gaz.* 22 Mar. 584/1, I hope it is not invidious, in an avowedly personal *tour d'horizon*, to single out here the museums for mention.

tourdion: see TURDION in Dict. and Suppl.

tourer (tūᵊ·rəɹ). [f. TOUR *v.* + -ER¹.] **1. a.** A touring-car.

1927 *Sunday Pictorial* 28 Aug. 8/4 Two and five-seater tourers will be £495. **1948** G. H. JOHNSTON *Death takes Small Bites* v. 102 Through a great rent in the tourer's flapping hood she could see Cavendish hunched over the wheel. **1978** *Hot Car* June 91/3 The *Munster Koach*, a wild '27 Model T tourer with a gung-ho Cobra engine.

b. A kind of caravan for touring.

1970 *Guardian* 25 Apr. 15/3 There are three basic types of caravans... There are tourers tacked on to the back of family cars, [etc.].

2. One who tours or goes on tour.

1931 *Times Lit. Suppl.* 1 Oct. 746/3 Mürren..tends to breed racers, the other [*sc.* Malója] 'tourers'. **1981** *Beautiful British Columbia* Summer 5 The first thing that bicycle tourers learn about British Columbia is that it is all up and down.

touring, *vbl. sb.* Add: **b.** *touring bag, centre*; touring-car (earlier example).

1903 *Encycl. Amer.* II. s.v. *Automobile*, Gasoline touring cars. **1930** *Cycling* 4 July p. iii, Touring bag. **1978** *Exchange & Mart* (South ed.) 20 Apr. 133/3 (Advt.), Motor cycle tank touring bag. **1981** *Nordic Skiing* Jan. 4/2 A group of Appalachian Mountain Club members went for a hike on trails established by a touring center for cross country skiing.

tourism. Add: Also ‖ **tourisme** (turīz'm). (Further examples.) Also, the business of attracting tourists and providing for their accommodation and entertainment; the business of operating tours.

1910 *Blackw. Mag.* Feb. 207/2 He thus inaugurated veritable aerial tourism. **1930** *Time & Tide* 2 May 555 The office of the commissioner of *tourisme* in France..was organized to clip as many petty annoyances as possible from the routine activities of visitors. **1954** H. F. M. PRESCOTT *Jerusalem Journey* v. 127 A mosque, to the Christian pilgrim, was forbidden ground, unless..he were ready to risk martyrdom in the cause of 'tourisme'. **1955** *Times* 24 May 9/3 In addition to the importance of the Kariba project for power and irrigation, emphasis is being laid on its potentialities with regard to fishing and tourism. **1976** J. ARCHER *Not a Penny More, Not a Penny Less* xii. 128 Tourism is the chief source of income for the Principality, and the Monégasques take the welfare of their visitors very seriously. **1981** I. MCEWAN *Comfort of Strangers* i. 12 They dutifully fulfilled the many tasks of tourism the ancient city imposed, visiting its major and minor churches, its museums and palaces, all treasure-packed.

tourist. Add: **a.** (Earlier example.) Also *spec.* a member of a touring sports team (usu. *pl.*).

1780 *Ode to Genius of Lakes in North of England* 3 (Advt.), He throws the piece only into the way of *actual tourists*. **1975** *Cricketer* May 11/2 On the fourth day Julien joined the feast, hitting a scintillating 101 and helping the tourists to an 87-run first-innings lead.

a*. *ellipt.* = *tourist class* (see sense b below).

1936 [see *cabin class* s.v. *CABIN *sb.* 8]. **1939** T. S. ELIOT *Family Reunion* 42, I was down in the Tourist..and you could see the corner of the upper deck. **1939** G. GREENE *Lawless Roads* 297 A middle-aged American woman, who should have been travelling tourist. **1976** V. CANNING *Doomsday Carrier* vii. 117 A few men could fly tourist to any country and plague would fly in with them. **1981** J. RATHBONE *Base Case* i. 8 The service in tourist had been appalling.

b. (i) *tourist agent, attraction, board, bureau, bus, camp, circuit, hotel, industry, office, resort, route, season, shop, tax, ticket* (example), *trade, traffic, visa*; *tourist-crowded* adj.; **tourist cabin,** (*a*) the tourist-class accommodation on a ship; (*b*) a cabin for tourists; **tourist-car** (earlier example); **tourist card,** an identity card substituting for a passport or visa for a short visit to certain countries; **tourist centre,** a place much frequented by tourists; **tourist class,** a low-charge class of passenger accommodation in a ship, aircraft, etc.; also *attrib.*; also adverbially, in the class of accommodation so designated; **tourist court** *U.S.*, a group of self-contained living units with service buildings, for tourists; **tourist flight,** a flight in the tourist class of a passenger aircraft, or in an aircraft which has only tourist-class seating; **tourist guide,** (*a*) = *tour guide* s.v. *TOUR *sb.* 12; (b) a guide-book which introduces tourists to a region or locality; **tourist park** *U.S.*, a park or camp-site with facilities for overnight campers, etc.; **tourist track,** (*a*) a route from place to place frequented by tourists; (*b*) *N.Z.*, a track through the bush for walkers; **tourist trap,** (*a*) a type of object sold to tourists at an excessively high price; (*b*) a place where tourists are exploited; **Tourist Trophy,** the name of a trophy awarded to the winner of motor-cycle races held annually on the Isle of Man since 1907; freq. *attrib.*; also *ellipt.* one of these races; usu. abbrev. as TT (see *T II. 6).

1884 *Queen* 16 Feb. (Advt.), Mr H. Laurence..Oculist Optician... Testimonials from..Thomas Cook, Esq., the well-known tourist agent, [etc.]. **1918** E. POUND *Pavannes & Divisions* 41, I knew a tourist agent, one whose art is To run such tours. **1959** A. H. MCLINTOCK *Descr. Atlas N.Z.* p. xix, The..geysers and boiling pools have long been a tourist attraction. **1978** *Times* 5 Aug. 5/6 Belsen had become almost a tourist attraction for visitors to Germany. [**1948** *Wales* (Tourist & Holidays Board Wales) 3 The Tourist and Holidays Board for Wales and Monmouthshire has pleasure in presenting its second Annual National Holiday Guide.] **1957** JACK & BLAIR *Chambers's Guide to Scotland* 13 An excellent publication (2s. 6d.) of the Scottish Tourist Board. **1972** 'R. CRAWFORD' *Whip Hand* I. viii. 44 Ballycroom might be as pretty in summer as the Tourist Board said all Kerry was. **1935** G. GREENE *Basement Room* 108, I opened a tourist bureau. Trips to the London underworld. Limehouse and all that. **1978** J. IRVING *World according to Garp* vi. 122 'I am from the Tourist Bureau,' Father announced. **1964** L. DEIGHTON *Funeral in Berlin* xvii. 105 In Horse Guards Avenue.. tourist buses were parked. **1928** H. CRANE *Let.* Dec. (1965) 332, I have been the only native American in the whole tourist cabin. The rest being Britishers, Canadians, Australians, [etc.]. **1937** A. HUXLEY *Let.* 7 May (1969) 421 Are now at Del Rio, on the Mexican frontier, in a tourist cabin. **1943** J. S. HUXLEY *TVA* ix. 61 Cove Lake Inn, with its group of tourist cabins,..has become..an important overnight stopping place for tourists. **1923** *Outlook* Aug. 591/3 The University of Iowa has published a bulletin on the tourist camps of that State. **1968** C. BURKE *Elephant across Border* vi. 217 Tourist camps with hot and cold running. **1895** J. C. WAIT *Car-Builder's Dict.* 134 *Tourist car*, a car roughly built and furnished for the transportation of men alone, such as bodies of troops, parties of excursionists, emigrants, etc. **1971** *Daily Nation* (Nairobi) 10 Apr. 5/3 Visitors now travelling to several Latin-American countries like Mexico require only a Tourist Card, which is issued by an airline authorised by the respective government. **1922** W. J. LOCKE *Tale of Triona* xxvi. 292 The hiring garages, in anything like tourist centres, found their resources strained. **1978** N. FREELING *Night Lords* xxvi. 123 The Loire country.. a centre for tourism... Normandy..another natural tourist centre. **1962** E. SNOW *Other Side of River* (1963) lxxv. 577 The city is after all on the main 'tourist circuit'—Peking–Shanghai–Hankow–Canton. **1936** *New Yorker* 22 Feb. 63/2 In Tourist Class, too, you find typical American standards. **1939** F. SCOTT FITZGERALD *Let.* Aug. (1964) 107 Only the rich now can do the things you and I once did in Europe—it is a tourist-class world. **1951** *Word Study* Feb. 5/1 People sailed to Europe *cabin class* or *tourist class*. **1952** *Shell Aviation News* No. 164. 4/2 Tourist class fares are being introduced and are going to lead to a doubling of passenger air travel in two years. **1964** MRS. L. B. JOHNSON *White House Diary* 20 Jan. (1970) 55, I left early this morning..tourist class on a commercial airline for New York. **1978** J. A. MICHENER *Chesapeake* xii. 712 At the Sunday meal many of the first-class passengers came down to the tourist class..to urge that Paxmore conduct the services. **1937** *Amer. City* Oct. 115 (*heading*) House trailer and tourist court regulations. **1979** R. THOMAS *Eighth Dwarf* iii. 27 A cluster of fishing shacks..and the odd tourist court. **1872** R. BROUGHTON in *Temple Bar* XXXVI. 340 The great glaring Schweizerhof, with its colonnaded, tourist-crowded porch. **1959** A. HUXLEY *Let.* 9 Jan. (1969) 861 The tourist flights are relatively cheap and I will treat you to the ticket. **1969** G. LYALL *Venus with Pistol* xxxii. 207 Maybe old Georgy-boy used to pop over to Germany on the cheap tourist flights. **1924** R. CUMMINS *Sky-High Corral* 15 You cut me down because you leased eighty acres of Hay Fork Meadow to that measly tourist guide to fence for horse feed. **1925** W. DEEPING *Sorrell & Son* iii. 26 Medlum.. kept the book-shop and sold..pretty-pretty art tourist guides. **1977** J. VAN DE WETERING *Japanese Corpse* (1978) xi. 109 He speaks English fairly well. He used to be a tourist guide. **1927** G. ADE et al. *Let.* 4 Mar. (1973) 118 We went to a most attractive tourist hotel above the town [*sc.* Gibraltar]..surrounded by palms and tropical plants. **1980** R. CONNOLLY *Sunday Kind of Woman* xxix. 194 She was staying in an ordinary tourist hotel just off Gloucester Road. **1938** *United Empire* Sept. 398 With peace achieved, the Government is fostering the tourist industry. **1977** *Times* 5 Apr. 16/6 The stately homes of England have been..making an important contribution to the tourist industry. **1875** *Cooks Continental Timetable* (1973) Mar. p. iv/1 (Advt.), Cook's Waterloo Coach Tickets..may be obtained at any of their tourist offices. **1977** *Times* 14 May 12/5 The tourist office put us in touch with the guest house association. **1927** F. F. VAN DE WATER *Family Flivvers to Frisco* iii. 52 There is money in well-run tourist parks. **1977** *Chicago Tribune* 2 Oct. XII. 27/8 (Advt.), Facility has been updated with boat launch, tourist park and public beach nearby. **1906** 'MARK TWAIN' *Autobiogr.* (1924) II. 215 Mr. Richmond had become possessed of Tom Sawyer's cave in the hills three miles from town, and had made a tourist-resort of it. **1959** A. H. MCLINTOCK *Descr. Atlas N.Z.* 74 New Zealand ..has roads of high quality leading to the principal tourist resorts. **1874** *Cooks Continental Timetable* (1973) Mar. p. ii/2 (Advt.), List of the Principal Hotels on the chief Tourist Routes in Europe. **1976** BOTHAM & DONNELLY *Valentino* xx. 147 He and Natacha followed the tourist routes to Windsor Castle, the Tower of London, Hampton Court, the theatre. **1884** MRS. F. F. MILLER *Harriet Martineau* viii. 135 Hunters of celebrities were wont, in the tourist season,..to walk round her garden. **1980** I. MURDOCH *Nuns & Soldiers* ii. 139 Now the tourist season's starting it's better to have someone there, like a caretaker. **1969** 'E. LATHEN' *When in Greece* x. 112, I call Athens... I have business with the tourist shops there. **1946** P. BOTTOME *Lifeline* vi. 61 It was two years since Mark had seen them, two years of grinding poverty under the [Nazi] Tourist tax. **1963** *Times* 21 Jan. 5/4 The tourist tax proposal appears to have had its brief, controversial highland fling. **1977** *Times* 22 Aug. 13/2 Proponents of a tourist tax really mean for it to be imposed only on foreign tourists. **1887** M. CORELLI *Thelma* I. xiii. 288 She wad send a' her relations there wi' tourist tickets, not available for the return journey. **1912** 'SAKI' *Chron. Clovis* 137 Continental travel..away from the great tourist tracks, was a favoured hobby. **1959** M. SHADBOLT *New Zealanders* 110 Ted..moved about the country from season to season..sheelite-mining in the Alps, cutting tourist tracks at Milford sound. **1969** *Guardian* 7 July 8/3 The Piazza Navona, right on the Roman tourist track. **1936** *Discovery* Sept. 264/1 That trade which cannot survive without peace—the tourist trade. **1946** J. S. HUXLEY *Unesco* ii. 53 An unregulated tourist trade in 'curios'. **1979** V. S. NAIPAUL *Bend in River* xv. 254 London is destroying itself for its tourist trade. **1892** KIPLING & BALESTIER *Naulahka* xiii. 156 Some towns might think we had a little tourist traffic now. **1979** *Tucson Mag.* June 54/1 Some extremists might seek out.. Hell on Earth. But, judging by the light tourist traffic into El Paso, these extremists are a small minority. **1939** G. GREENE *Lawless Roads* iv. 117 Different stations had their different tourist traps—at Apizaco hideous hand-painted clubs..at Rinconada little grey stone mortars. **1942** E. PAUL *Narrow St.* xxvii. 241 The Oubliette Rouge was a small tourist-trap..where..the drinks were watered to such an extent that temperance was automatically accomplished. **1967** O. WYND *Walk Softly, Men Praying* x. 157 The village..[was] now a tourist trap almost entirely given over to eating houses and souvenir shops. **1981** C. STORR *Vicky* xiv. 99 Vicky's eye was caught by something in one of the tourist-trap shop windows. **1907** *Motor Cycle* 1 May 358/1 Cash prizes will be awarded to the drivers of machines taking part in the International Auto Cycle Tourist Trophy Race. **1913** [see TT s.v. *T II. 6]. **1968** S. E. ELLACOTT *Everyday Things in England 1914–68* V. xii. 174 The Isle of Man..Tourist Trophy races.. began in May 1907. **1973** S. JACKMAN *Guns covered with Flowers* iv. 40 The Immigration Officer...issued him with a Tourist visa.

(ii) Of a foreign language: of that degree of proficiency required by a tourist or to communicate with a tourist.

1938 E. AMBLER *Cause for Alarm* ii. 30, I have seen six gentlemen before you. Three of them could speak tourist French and insisted that most Italians would understand it. **1953** S. BEDFORD *Sudden View* I. iii. 36, I had a small deposit of past tourist Spanish..equal to ordering the *comida corrida*, the table d'hôte luncheon. **1975** A. WORBOYS *Lion of Delos* ii. 23 Most of the [Greek] people you will come across talk Tourist English.

Hence **tou·rist** *v. intr.*, to travel for pleasure, as a tourist; **touristy** *a.*, also, designed for or likely to appeal to tourists, consisting of tourists, frequented by tourists; freq. with derog. connotation, superficial, trashy.

1953 E. M. FORSTER *Hill of Devi* 27, I continued my tour—I was touristing—and I did not expect to see my delightful host again. **1971** K. WHEELER *Epitaph for Mr. Wynn* xxviii. 364 He wasn't just touristing around. **1937** A. CHRISTIE *Death on Nile* vi. 86 This trip..feels somehow, so much less touristy—as though we were really going into the heart of Egypt. **1958** *Listener* 25 Sept. 454/1 Its rushing rivers leaping with salmon; its canyons; its glaciers;..steam from thermal springs..all these are perhaps the 'touristy' things. **1961** I. FLEMING *Thunderball* xii. 125 A tepid, touristy breakfast on his balcony. **1967** [see *STRIP *sb.*[2] 1 h.] **1969** E. MCGIRR *Entry of Death* iii. 59 There's a little 'ostelry wot only the helite know of. None of yer touristy trash. **1973** *Daily Tel.* (Colour Suppl.) 16 Feb. 31/3 They've turned out so many phoney things—touristy things about the Civil War, say.

touristic, *a.* Add: **touri·stically** *adv.*, from the point of view of a tourist; as regards tourists or tourism.

1928 *Sunday Dispatch* 16 Dec. 4/2 Asked to show a young French boy of fifteen the 'sights' of London... But he had one ambition, touristically, and one only. **1959** *Encounter* May 30/2 The girls..go anywhere, do anything sexually or touristically interesting. County Dublin, Positano, Ibiza, Tangier. **1971** *Daily Tel.* 10 Sept. 14/4 Replicas of the castle could also be erected not only in London but at touristically under-privileged places like Leeds and Merthyr Tydfil. **1983** *Which?* Nov. 515/1 The qualities I look for in a country house hotel—a tranquil location in a touristically rewarding area, [etc.].

tourmaline. Add: **b*.** (See quot. 1957.)

1957 J. H. F. STEVENSON *Mink in Britain* (ed. 2) 101 *Tourmaline*, EMBA [*sc.* Mutation Mink Breeders of America] brand name for high quality natural pale beige mutation mink skins. **1959** *Vogue* 1 Oct. 188/3 You'd see the all-important minks..from the very dark ranch mink through the lighter, lovely Emba mutations to the pales, which include a pearly blondness, 'Tourmaline'. **1959** *Official Gaz.* (U.S. Patent Office) 27 Oct. TM 127 Mutation Mink Breeders Association... Tourmaline. For Mink Fur Pelts. First use Dec. 11, 1956. **1965** P. O'DONNELL *Modesty Blaise* iii. 32 A Dior-designed mink coat in embL tourmaline.

c. *tourmaline mink.*

1959 *Vogue* Dec. 25 (Advt.), Tourmaline mink coat. **1973** 'R. MACDONALD' *Sleeping Beauty* x. 51 Elizabeth Somerville came to the front door in a tourmaline mink which almost matched her blonde head.

tourmalinize, *v.* (In Dict. s.v. TOURMALINE.) Add: (Examples.) Hence **tou·rmalinized** *ppl. a.*, **tou·rmalinizing** *vbl. sb.*; **tou:rmaliniza·tion,** the process or state of being tourmalinized.

1899 *Bull. Geol. Soc. Amer.* X. 23 As the vein widens the tourmalinizing of the schist becomes less and less marked. *Ibid.*, Fragments of this tourmalinized schist are thickly strewn along both sides of the road. *Ibid.* 24 A more intense tourmalinization is to be noticed in the immediate vicinity of the veins. *Ibid.* 26 The hornfels..has been tourmalinized on both sides of the vein. **1946** *Geol. Survey Nigeria Bull.* No. 17. 56 The altered country-rock on the hanging-wall has been recrystallized and tourmalinized to form a rock composed of brown biotite..and tourmaline. **1982** D. S. SUTHERLAND *Igneous Rocks of Brit. Isles* xxiii. 318/2 The second stage of tourmalinization followed the second stage of greisening, using the same channels. *Ibid.* 524/1 The tourmalinized varieties of the granitic rocks are of such striking appearance that they have given rise to several special names.

‖ **tourmente** (turmɑ̃t). [Fr.: see TORMENT *sb.*] A whirling storm or eddy (of snow): see TORMENT *sb.* 5.

[**1843** J. D. FORBES *Trav. through Alps* 187 The strong west wind..raises the snow into fearful eddies, called *tourmentes* in the French.] **1847, 1909** [see TORMENT *sb.* 5]. **1924** J. BUCHAN *Three Hostages* xii. 177, I could see that it was blowing hard, for my glass showed me little *tourmentes* of snow. **1928** *Blackw. Mag.* May 601/1 Above the howl of the *tourmente* came the crash of falling rocks.

Tournai. Now the usual form of TOURNAY. Used *attrib.* and *absol.* to designate products of the town, *esp.* the porcelain manufactured there from 1751.

1873 C. SCHREIBER *Jrnl.* (1911) I. 207 He..prides himself upon his Tournai. **1874** *Ibid.* 292 One Tournai plate, gold marked. **1907** C. H. WYLDE *How to collect Continental China* 119 Birds..had always been a favourite subject as a *motif* of decoration on Tournay porcelain. **1959** *Listener* 22 Jan. 179/1 The more familiar tombstone of a bishop in Tournai 'marble'. **1980** *Times* 5 Feb. 16/5 A Tournai shaped oval dish of about 1765..made £11,000.

Tournaisian (tūəɹnē·ziăn), *a. Geol.* [ad. Fr. *tournaisien* of Tournai: see prec., -IAN.] Of, pertaining to, or designating the lower of the two divisions of the Lower Carboniferous (Dinantian) in Europe. Also *absol.*

1910 *Rep. Brit. Assoc. Adv. Sci. 1909* 187 A minute exposition of the coral sequence in the Tournaisian. *Ibid.*, The Tournaisian Beds of this fine coast section. **1923** L. D. STAMP *Introd. Stratigr.* ix. 129 The lower three zones constitute the Tournaisian or Lower Carboniferous Limestone, the upper zones the Visean or Upper Carboniferous Limestone. **1969** BENNISON & WRIGHT *Geol. Hist. Brit. Isles* ix. 187 The Tournaisian is..exposed in a continuous section in the gorge of the River Avon. *Ibid.* 205 The Upper Old Red Sandstone may be in part of Tournaisian age.

tournament, *sb.* Add: **3*.** *Math.* A set of points each of which is joined to every other point by a line having a direction. Also *tournament graph.*

1959 F. HARARY in *Management Sci.* V. 398 Consider a tournament in which there are *n* players, every pair of players play each other once, and none of the games ends in a draw. For brevity let us call the resulting digraph *D* itself a tournament. **1972** R. J. WILSON *Introd. Graph Theory* vii. 108 Let *T* be a tournament on $n+1$ vertices, and let *T'* be the tournament on *n* vertices obtained by removing from *T* a vertex *v* and every arc incident to *v*. **1980** *Sci. Amer.* Mar. 18/3 Tournament graphs provide a convenient means of modeling a person's pairwise preferences for any set of choices, such as brands of coffee or candidates in an election.

Tournay: see also *TOURNAI.

‖ **tournedos** (turnədo). *Gastronomy.* [Fr., f. *tourner* to turn + *dos* back: acc. to Littré and Robert, so called because the dish is traditionally not placed on the table, but is passed behind the backs of the guests (see quots. for this and another account).] A fillet steak of beef with a surrounding strip of fat; *tournedos Rossini*, such a fillet served with a *croûton* and pâté, and a Madeira sauce.

1877 E. S. DALLAS *Kettner's Bk. of Table* 460 A tournedos is a thin collop, which..is done on one side before the cook has had time to turn round. **1937** G. FRANKAU *More of Us* v. 53 Italy! Twice ten thousand special pleaders Present your case—and tournedos Rossini, Whose rich appeal 'spite facial controlling Still sets these eyes in a fine frenzy rolling. **1958** *Times* 29 Nov. 7/6 Tucking into scampi and tournedos. **1966** P. V. PRICE *France: Food & Wine Guide* 124 About [1869]..the word tournedos came into use... Rossini was dining at the Café Anglais and..suggested an alternative method of cutting and preparing the steak... The horrified *maître d'hotel* announced that he could not..present a dish that was..unpresentable. 'Very well,' said Rossini, 'then don't let us see you do it—I'll turn my back' (*tourne le dos*). **1979** C. Curzon *Leaven of Malice* xi. 126 *Tournedos Rossini* with salad and a reasonable Valpolicella.

tournee (tūᵊ·ɹni), ‖ **tournée** (turne). [a. F. *tournée* round.] A round, circuit, tour.

1794 B. Wynne *Diary* 8 Oct. (1952) xiii. 163 We did today what is called the *Tournee* and which is visits to all the ministers and *Grand* Families. **1834** W. F. Tolmie *Jrnls.* (1963) 298 Made an unsuccessful tournee in the S. plain in quest of deer. **1961** *Times* 13 Oct. 10/5 When Louis Armstrong and Dave Brubeck come to Germany their tournées take them to sold-out concert halls.

tournette (tūᵊɹne·t). *Archæol.* [a. Fr., f. *tourner* to turn.] A rotating disc resembling a potter's wheel. Also *attrib.*

1927 Peake & Fleure *Peasants & Potters* iv. 47 The pots were made on a tournette, a slow wheel turned by hand. **1952** V. G. Childe *New Light on Most Anc. East* xi. 235 Centrally perforated stone discs some 20 cm. in diameter have been called 'tournettes'. **1964** H. Hodges *Artifacts* i. 27 Ring or coil-built pots are generally flat-bottomed since they are frequently formed on a turntable, or tournette. **1977** *Antiquaries Jrnl.* LVII. 317 The upper fills of such pits can often be seen as discarded rubbish relating to the use of clay: pot sherds,..loom-weight, and tournette fragments.

tourney, *sb.*¹ Add: **1. c.** = Tournament *sb.* 3.

1890 J. Rayner *Chess Problems* 15 If..one should creep into a problem deemed by him..to be fit for a tourney, it will be useful..to know that the German school of problematists is less puritanical than the English. *Ibid.* 28 In solution and problem tourneys..it is necessary to throw aside all conventionalities. **1950** *Sun* (Baltimore) 20 June 21/6 It was really rather astonishing to watch this youth club his way through the tourney to a sturdy victory..in a 36-hole grind. **1951** *Sport* 30 Mar.–5 Apr. 10/2 J. Parsons..outscored Billy McHale, newly-crowned Northern Counties A.B.A. champion, in the miners' divisional tourney. **1971** *Rand Daily Mail* 4 Sept. 2/9 The Government's new sports policy..has guaranteed a welcome for all teams for next year's Federation Cup tennis tourney. **1976** *Star* (Sheffield) 3 Dec. 28/8 Last week with the results boosted by the netball tourney..there were 140 results in the Hotline columns.

tournure. Add: **3.** (Earlier example.)

1827 Disraeli *Vivian Grey* III. v. xv. 299 Touched in with freedom—a grand *tournure*—great *goût* in the swell of the neck.

4. Also, a kind of corset. (Earlier examples.)

1831 H. Granville *Let.* Jan. (1894) II. 75 Very fat, but squeezed into a *tournure.* **1872** *Young Englishwoman* Dec. 646/2 The tournure is high indeed behind... It has superseded the crinoline.

Tourte² (tūᵊɹt, ‖ turt). The name of the French violin-bow maker François *Tourte* (1747–1835), who perfected the modern bow, used *attrib.* and *absol.* to designate bows made according to his model.

1889 Grove *Dict. Mus.* IV. 155 The Tourte bow greatly facilitated the new development of violin music. *Ibid.* 156 A very fine Tourte has been recently sold for £30. **1896** H. Saint-George *Bow* vi. 51 What a marvellous thing a fine Tourte is! What a revelation the first time a player handles one! **1908** *Sears, Roebuck Catal.* 233/2 This [professional violin] outfit includes:..One Tourte model bow, full German silver trimmings and best quality Brazil wood stick. **1950** *Musical Q.* Jan. 16 French and Italian bows shown in early 18-century sources seem lighter in construction than the Tourte bows. **1980** *Early Music* Apr. 200/1 Illus. 1c shows a genuine Tourte bow and 1d an English bow stamped forster..one of the types of so-called 'transitional' bows in vogue about 1775, some ten years before the invention of the Tourte.

tourtière (tūᵊɹti,ēᵊ·ɹ, ‖ turtyɛ̄r'). [a. Fr., lit. 'tart-tin', f. *tourte* Tourte tart.] **a.** *Fr. Canad.* A kind of meat pie traditionally eaten at Christmas. **b.** A tart-tin or round baking-sheet.

1953 Wattie & Donaldson *Nellie L. Pattinson's Canad. Cookbk.* (rev. ed.) xxv. 467 Tourtière (Pork Pies). These pies are traditional Christmas Eve fare. **1959** J. Donon *Classic French Cuisine* ix. 303 Pour into a well-buttered *tourtière*, or pie plate. **1960** E. David *French Provincial Cooking* 69 *Tourtière*, a shallow tart tin... In former times a *tourtière* was a heavy iron or earthenware dish, much deeper than a tart tin, in which many things besides pastry could be cooked. **1975** *Globe & Mail* (Toronto) 3 Dec. s8/5 A meat pie of Christmas Eve fame in Quebec, the tourtiere is traditional fare at the reveillon after midnight mass. **1978** *N.Y. Times* 29 Mar. c 8/6, I like to bake crust in flan rings set on round black baking sheets called tourtières.

tousle, touzle, *sb.* Add: The spelling *touzle* seems now to be obsolete. **3.** *touslehead.*

1900 M. Hewlett *Life & Death Richard Yea-and-Nay* ii. xi. 364 The townsmen of Gratz, hoarse-voiced touzle-heads mostly, dīvined her to be an anchoress. **1981** *Sunday Express Mag.* 7 June 12/1 The breathlessness of a touslehead at a school concert.

tously, *a.* Add: Also formerly **touzly.** (Earlier example.)

1832 *Chambers's Edin. Jrnl.* I. 193/2 Ye may be as touzly as ye like i' the outside o' your claes.

‖ **Toussaint** (tusæ̃ń). [Fr., f. *tous*, pl. of *tout* all + *saint* saint.] The feast of All Saints (1 November).

1930 K. Boyle *Plagued by Nightingale* (1931) xxv. 246 They would linger in the country..perhaps even until the *Toussaint.* **1955** *Caribbean Q.* IV. ii. (*verso front cover*) In many West Indian Islands, especially but not exclusively those under Catholic influence, it is customary to keep the Festival of All Saints, or Toussaint. **1979** N. Freeling *Widow* xxxiv. 210 The flowers for mum's birthday or the Toussaint.

tousy, towsy, *a.* Add: Also **touzie, -y. 1.** Also *transf.* and *fig.*

1873 A. G. Murdoch *Lilts* 57 Tell him, when in the touzie key, A nicht wi' him I wadna gie. **1897** H. Ochiltree *Out of Shroud* xxiv. 331, I was oot gey late ae nicht—a touzie nicht it was. **1925** G. B. Cumming *A'anside Lilts* 71 The times then were touzie to live in. **1955** *Times* 9 May 6/3 A campaign that is already showing signs of developing into a tousy fight. **1972** *Listener* 27 July 104/3 (*heading*) Glory goals rock tousy Rangers.

2. Abundant, prolific; *esp.* in *Comb.*, **tousy tea**, a knife-and-fork tea, high tea.

1835 *Glasgow Jrnl.* 31 Oct. 44 Mrs Stewart had laid what she styled a 'touzie tea'. **1895** H. Ochiltree *Redburn* ix. 90 It's no very great place for yits or barley, but a gye tousie place for gress. **1934** T. Smellie *Tea-Party* 12 Next to a touzie tea there's naething like maesic tae soothe a savage beast.

tout, *sb.*¹ Add: **5.** A spy; an informer. Cf. Tout *v.*¹ 2. *N. Ireland* and *Sc.*

1959 I. & P. Opie *Lore & Lang. Schoolch.* x. 189 The tell tale is ..a tout, traitor, quisling, or widemouth. **1973** *Times* 6 June 1/5 The body of a young man..was found.. shot through the head 800 yards from the southern Irish border... A label with the word 'Tout' written on it was attached to his neck. **1977** W. McIlvanney *Laidlaw* xl. 186 'What's his business?' 'Same as any tout's. Other people's.'

‖ **tout** (tu), *adv.*, *sb.*⁴, and *a.* [Fr.] **A.** *adv.* Quite, entirely: *tout au contraire* (tut o koǹtrɛ̄r'), quite the contrary; *tout court* (tu kūr), in short, in little, simply, without qualification or addition; *tout de suite* (tu də swīt) [*de suite* in sequence], at once, immediately; cf. *toot sweet; *tout seul* (tu sœ̄l), quite alone, on its (or his, etc.) own; *tout simple, simplement* (tu sæ̃pl', sæ̃pl'mań) quite simply, just that.

1841 M. Edgeworth *Let.* 23 Mar. (1971) 590 Scandal but not by any means ill natured tout au contraire. **1982** E. Dewhurst *Whoever I Am* i. 18 'You find it obvious that I've been on the amateur stage?' '*Tout au contraire...* But I know.'

1747 H. Walpole *Let.* 26 June (1955) XIX. 420 My eagle is arrived—my eagle *tout court*, for I hear nothing of the pedestal. **1888** Kipling *Wee Willie Winkie* 38 Judy was officially 'Miss Judy'; but Black Sheep was never anything but Black Sheep *tout court.* **1928** C. Dawson *Age of Gods* xii. 262 There are grave objections to the identification *tout court* of the Nordic race with the Indo-European stock. **1958** *Oxf. Mag.* 15 May 435/1 Hove, instead of asking for Psychology *tout court*, has a course by a Harley Street psychiatrist. **1981** J. Sutherland *Bestsellers* xxiv. 240 Len Deighton's..history *tout court* of the Second World War (*Bomber* and *Fighter*).

1895 E. Dowson *Let.* c 13 Nov. (1967) 319 If you see Moore tell him that I am writing tout de suite. **1971** *Ink* 12 June 14/3 Some of the underwriters quietly told their clients to resell their shares *tout-de-suite.*

1926 H. Crane *Let.* 19 Aug. (1965) 273, I have encountered him in the road, talking again tout seul and examining pebbles. **1954** *Essays in Criticism* IV. 272 The danger in self-exploration *tout seul* is that it can lead to loss of urgency.

1930 *Harvard Law Rev.* XLIII. 881 Strict or liberal construction or interpretation is therefore the ordinary process of interpretation, *tout simple.* **1977** *Times* 14 Apr. 14/6 The event was listed as a variety show, *tout simple.* **1939** *Burlington Mag.* Mar. 142/2 The most probable explanation..is, *tout simplement*, faulty recollection. **1973** E. Berckman *Victorian Album* 114 There it was. There, *tout simplement*, as they say, was my murder.

B. *sb.*⁴ and *a.* All: *tout compris* (tu koǹprī), all included, inclusive; *tout ensemble*: see Ensemble *sb.* 1; *tout le monde* (tu lə mońd), all the world, everyone; (*le*) *tout Paris* (lə tu parī), all Paris, i.e. Parisian society; also *transf.*, of other cities, social circles, etc.

1901 Ld. Milner *Let.* in J. A. Smith *John Buchan* (1979) 34/2 You will have to pay your own way out—about £60 *tout compris.* **1960** *Harper's Bazaar* Aug. 63/1 A day in one of these hotels..can cost under 15 shillings, *tout compris.*

1825 H. Wilson *Memoirs* III. 110 Tout le monde seemed so very much to admire my person. **1944** Auden *Sea & Mirror* in *For Time Being* iii. 29 She invites..just *tout le monde* to drop in at any time.

1894 G. du Maurier *Trilby* III. vii. 15 'Tout Paris' passed them; but they were none the wiser, and agreed that the show was not a patch on that in Hyde Park during the London season. **1921** G. Bell *Let.* 5 May (1927) xx. 480 'Le tout' Bagdad was there—the Arab world. **1965** N. Freeling *Criminal Conversation* ii. xix. 183, I married her..for the introduction she could give me into what I thought of as 'the club'. Le tout-Paris. **1975** P. Moyes *Black Widower* ii. 21 *Tout Washington* tends to arrive late at diplomatic cocktail parties. **1980** T. Morgan *Somerset Maugham* iii. 221 He wanted a hostess, who knew the tout-Londres. **1982** *Times* 14 Jan. 15/3 It is the talk of le tout Paris in the French business world. Who will be getting the plum jobs?

tout, *v.*¹ Add: **3. b.** *trans.* (*a*) To importune (a person) in a touting manner; (*b*) to solicit custom for (a thing), to try to sell; also (*U.S.*) in extended sense, to recommend.

1920 S. Lewis *Main Street* xvi. 199 Why, you're always touting these Greek dancers. **1928** *Daily Tel.* 5 May 9/6 It strikes one as..unfair for bankers to tout their clients for..investment business. **1930** R. H. Mottram *Europa's Beast* vii. 164 He was involved in the ghastly job of touting motor cars. **1948** M. Laski *Tory Heaven* i. 14 Touting vacuum-cleaners at back doors. **1974** *Nature* 11 Jan. 81/1 Such deposits of geothermal energy have long been touted as potential sources of power. **1978** *Detroit Free Press* 2 Apr. 6E/1 Any team that touts Jerry Augustine as the ace of its staff is in serious trouble.

Hence **tout·ed** *ppl. a.* (*U.S.*), (usu. with qualifying advb.) vaunted, extolled.

1953 *Manch. Guardian Weekly* 5 Feb. 3 The much touted Nationalist 'offensive' on the Chinese mainland. **1978** *Sci. Amer.* Aug. 32/2 The highly touted system of separating isotopes by laser excitation.

toutou (tū·tū). [Fr. nursery term.] A pet name for a dog, esp. a lap-dog. Cf. *loulou.

1894, 1916 [see *loulou].

‖ **tou ts'ai** (tū tsai). *Ceramics.* Also **doucai.** [Chinese (Wade-Giles), *duǒcǎi* (Pinyin), lit. 'multi-coloured', f. *tou* many + *ts'ai* colours.] Used *attrib.* and *absol.* of a kind of enamel painting on Chinese porcelain, developed in the reign of Ch'êng Hua (1465–87), and of (pieces of) porcelain so decorated.

1953 S. Jenyns *Ming Pottery & Porcelain* vi. 90 Another problem piece is the famous Kitchener bowl... Brankston is uncomfortably non-committal. 'There are some points', he says, 'on which it differs from other known Ch'êng Hua *tou ts'ai* pieces.' **1960** H. Hayward *Antique Coll.* 285/1 *Tou ts'ai* ('*contrasting colour*') *enamels*, delicate, sparing designs on Chinese porcelain in underglaze blue, set off by transparent enamel colours. **1972** *Trans. Oriental Ceramics Soc.* 109 A globular jar..painted in *tou-ts'ai* style in underglaze blue. **1980** *Catal. Fine Chinese Ceramics* (Sotheby, Hong Kong) 104 A rare doucai (tou ts'ai) Vase, brightly enamelled with a formal pattern of lotus scrolls.

tovarish, tovarich (tovā·riʃ). Also **tav-; -isch, -ishch, -istch, -itch.** Pl. **-i.** [ad. Russ. *továrishch* comrade.] In the U.S.S.R., comrade (freq. as a form of address).

1918 C. E. Russell *Unchained Russia* ii. 95 After the Revolution everybody in Russia was 'tavarisch'. **1930** E. Pound *XXX Cantos* xxvii. 127 And these are the labours of tovarisch, That tovarisch lay in the earth, And rose, and wrecked the house of the tyrants. **1935** N. Mitchison *We have been Warned* iii. 236 I'm rather looking forward myself to the first time someone calls me tovarish... It seems much more romantic in Russian. **1938** E. Hemingway *Fifth Column* iii. ii. 86 Hurry up, Tovaritch, and tape good the mouths. **1968** L. Smith *Fear & Dead Man* x. 80 The Russian grinned slyly. 'Now you know I cannot tell you why I wanted you brought here, *tovarich*.' **1976** M. Barak *Secret List of Heinrich Roehm* xi. 120 The KGB Chairman shrugged. 'Very well... We shall take care of Tovarishch Joe Gonen.' **1977** *Time* 28 Feb. 12/3 To compensate for her lost lover, she found at least one more torrid *tovarish.*

tove (tōᵘv). A factitious word introduced by 'Lewis Carroll' (see quot. 1855²).

Quot. 1855¹ also occurs in the first verse of 'Jabberwocky' in *Through the Looking-Glass* (1871) i. 21.

1855 [see *slithy *a.*]. **1855** 'L. Carroll' *Rectory Umbrella & Mischmasch* (1932) 142 Tove, a species of Badger. They had smooth white hair, long hind legs, and short horns like a stag: lived chiefly on cheese. **1928** [see *slithy *a.*]. **1937** G. Frankau *More of Us* 2 While the free-versifier gyres and gimbles The slithy tove—with his own 'private symbols'.

tow, *sb.*¹ Add: **3*.** A bundle of untwisted natural or manmade fibres.

1950 B. E. Hartsuch *Introd. Textile Chem.* viii. 237 The filaments from several coagulating baths or cabinets (acetate) are combined to form a thick strand known as tow. **1969** [see *prepreg *sb.* (*a.*)]. **1971** *New Scientist* 8 July 68/2 The material [*sc.* carbon fibres] was in the form of 'tows'—14 inch long bundles containing 10 000 filaments each of 1½ denier. **1973** *Materials & Technol.* VI. iv. 302 In the case of viscose rayon the thick tows are sometimes supplied to mills which desire to do their own cutting into staple lengths.

4. a. *tow-card* (earlier example), *-linen*, *-sack*, *string* (examples). **c.** **tow-head** (examples); *spec.*: for *Mergus* read *Lophodytes*; also (*U.S.*), a sand-bar or other obstruction causing ripples in a river or stream; **tow-headed** *a.* (earlier example).

1655 *Essex County, Mass. Probate Rec.* (1916) I. 201 A pair of tow cards, 1s. **1829** S. Cummings *Western Pilot* 7 There are..a great number of tow-heads and sand-bars. **1830** A. Royall *Southern Tour* I. 92 One insolent little tow-head. **1883** 'Mark Twain' *Life on Miss.* xxiii. 262 A large town which lay shut in behind a tow-head (*i.e.* new island). **1888** G. Trumbull *Names & Portraits of Birds* 75 The name Tow-Head..was heard in one of our Southern States. **1901** A. H. Rice *Mrs. Wiggs of Cabbage Patch* vii. 95 Little Europena, with baby wisdom, put her tow head under the cloth. **1960** *Guardian* 5 Nov. 1/6 The abominable tow-head from Massachusetts. **1977** *Verbatim* Dec. 6/2 Even the most casual student of American literature should have no trouble with..*tow-head* ('sand bar with cottonwoods'). **1850** S. Judd *R. Edney* xlix. 450 Bronze-faced and tow-headed Wild Olive boys. **1779** *New Jersey Archives* (1906) 2nd Ser. III. 154 [A] blue long elk saddle cloth lined with tow linen. **1884** 'MARK TWAIN' *Huck. Finn* xx. 196 Some of the children didn't have on any clothes but just a tow-linen shirt. **1921** J. BUCHAN *Path of King* xiii. 259 He wore an old skin shirt and a pair of tow-linen pants. **1930** W. FAULKNER *As I lay Dying* 48 The soaked towsack tied about his shoulders. **1976** J. LEE *Ninth Man* 243 He anchored the tow-sack bundle on his left arm. **1806** *Balance* V. 5/3 Our worthy old friend..sometimes wears a tow string round his hat. **1892** *Harper's Mag.* Mar. 649/2 What was known as the 'tow-string survey' offered him an excellent opportunity for the display of his peculiar talents.

tow, *sb.*[4] Add: **2. b.** (Earlier example.) Also *in tow* (*with*) in extended sense: in company (with), accompanying, following.

1722 *New-England Courant* 17–24 Sept. 1/1 Their eager and amorous Emotions of the Body, occasion'd by taking their Mistresses *in Tow*, they call'd *wild Steerage*. **1907** C. S. Ross *Early Otago* 169 He had got in tow with a young lady. **1937** C. DAY LEWIS *Starting Point* I. 14 Oh, he's got one of his Swedish blondes in tow. **1965** M. SHADBOLT *Among Cinders* xiv. 117 I'm in tow with my parents. **1979** S. BRETT *Comedian Dies* i. 18 'Come along, Paul.' And Walter Proud, with his writer in tow, hurried along to join them.

3. Also, a string of barges that is pushed rather than pulled.

1976 *Sci. Amer.* July 124/3 The U.S. has a network of inland waterways that carries roughly a sixth of all the nation's freight in multiple-barge 'tows' that are usually pushed, rather than pulled, by powerful tugs. **1977** *Washington Post* 4 Sept. A12/1 They [*sc.* towboats] push the barges ahead of them. But the nest of barges that is pushed is called the 'tow'.

4. a. *tow hook, -horse* (example), *-truck*; **tow-bar,** a bar used in towing; *spec.* the bar by means of which a trailer, caravan, etc., is attached to the vehicle that tows it; **tow-boating** *U.S.*, the piloting or operating of a tow-boat; **towfish,** a housing with measuring or detecting instruments in it or attached to it and designed to be towed underwater behind a ship; **tow-plane,** an aircraft that tows gliders; **tow-start** *v. trans.*, to tow (a motor vehicle) in order to start the engine.

1956 *Archit. Rev.* CXIX. 259 Small trucks are coupled to it by a quick-action towbar. **1959** *'Motor' Manual* (ed. 36) xiii. 270 Don't be misled by the Unladen Weight which is stamped on the towbar. **1960** *Guardian* 19 Sept. 2/4 For sailing families, boat-cradle, mast support, and long tow-bar can be bought as extras. **1980** *West Lancs. Even. Gaz.* 5 June 16/4 (Advt.), Tow-bars supplied and fitted with electrics to suit every caravan and trailer requirement. **1887** *Courier-Jrnl.* (Louisville, Kentucky) 7 Feb. 3/3 Theodore Brooks..will try his hand at tow-boating this season. **1977** *Amer. N. & Q.* XV. 153/1 For more than 300 years its [*sc.* New London's] people were involved in just about every activity related to the sea including fisheries,..towboating, [etc.]. [**1973** *Jrnl. Marine Res.* XXXI. 73 An alternative solution..is the replacement of the weighted fish with a lighter tow body having a controllable fin.] **1975** *McGraw-Hill Yearbk. Sci. & Technol.* 292/1 The..towfish..continuously monitors the depth of a preselected isotherm by towing at about 5 knots..two depth-controlled instrument packages which bracket an isotherm. **1876** KNIGHT *Amer. Mech. Dict.* 2604/2 Tow-hook, an artillery-man's hook, used in unpacking ammunition-chests. **1971** M. TAK *Truck Talk* 170 *Tow hooks,* hooks, generally found on a tractor's bumper, by which it can be towed or pulled. **1978** J. MCNEIL *Consultant* xx. 180 He unclipped the tow hook from the back of the car. **1865** *Harper's Mag.* Apr. 571/1 It requires as much judgment to drive tow-horses up the Alleghany as to pilot a steamboat down the Mississippi. **1940** *Aeronautics* Nov. 42/1 If the glider is more heavily loaded than the towplane, the latter will unstick first. **1973** 'A. HALL' *Tango Briefing* viii. 107 The change in the engine-note of the tow-plane. **1976** A. SCHROEDER *Shaking it Rough* i. 4 We passed a trio of youths trying to tow-start an old Chevrolet. **1957** Tow-truck [see *shopping plaza* s.v. *SHOPPING *vbl. sb.* 2]. **1972** *Sat. Rev.* (U.S.) 17 June 6/2 A tow truck..came for the crippled car.

b. With advbs.: **towaway** *U.S.*, the towing away of an illegally parked vehicle; freq. *attrib.* as *towaway zone*, an area from which such vehicles may be towed away; **tow-out,** the action of towing a drilling platform out to an oil-field at sea.

1956 *Sun* (Baltimore) 31 Jan. 32/6 Such cars parked in the 'tow-a-way' zones would be hauled off to the police impounding lot. **1967** *N.Y. Times* 5 Mar. 75 Despite the published warnings about illegal parking—towaways averaged close to 200 cars daily during February. **1975** *Petroleum Rev.* XXIX. 303/1, 56 steel cylinders..provide buoyancy during tow-out. **1977** *Offshore Engineer* July 55/2 Initial plans were for flat tops to the storage tanks, but these were redesigned to increase the deck loading capacity, at tow-out, by 10,000t, to 24,000t.

towable (tōᵘ·ăb'l), *a.* [f. Tow *v.*[1] + -ABLE.] That may be towed.

1927 *Glasgow Herald* Jan. 7 The dock..is towable to any part of Australia. **1967** [see *DRACONE, DRACONE]. **1982** *Social Trends 1983* viii. 114/2 Towable caravans and house-boats.

towel, *sb.* Add: **1. b.** Phr. *to throw* (*chuck,* or *toss*) *in the towel*: to admit defeat. orig. *Boxing.* Cf. SPONGE *sb.*[1] 1 c.

1915 E. CORRI *30 Yrs. Boxing Ref.* 223 In the nineteenth round Storbeck's seconds 'threw the towel' in literally. **1916** C. J. DENNIS *Moods of Ginger Mick* 132 I've done me limit, an' tossed in the tow'l. **1923** WODEHOUSE *Inimit. Jeeves* xv. 192 He had found the going too hard and had chucked in the towel. **1952** [see *DINGO *v.*]. **1979** M. RUSSELL *Touchdown* II. 90 'Don't give up.'..'Have no fear... I shan't throw in the towel, I promise you.'

2. c. = *sanitary towel* s.v. *SANITARY *a.* 3. Also *ellipt.*

1896 *Eng. Illustr. Mag.* Aug. (Advts. Section) 8/2 A sample of the improved 'towel' will be sent free to any lady applying to the Lady Manager. **1907** *Yesterday's Shopping* (1969) 1264 Full-sized towels reduced by pressure, packed in tiny boxes. **1979** *Guardian* 27 Mar. 9/5 A campaign for free sanitary protection through the NHS started in 1973 when the Government imposed VAT on towels and tampons.

4. *towel-covered* adj.; **towel-horse** (earlier example); **towel rail, ring,** a rail or ring on which to hang towels.

1916 H. G. WELLS *Mr. Britling sees it Through* I. i. 19 A towel-covered can of hot water. **1947** *Nation* 22 Feb. 214/1 The crooked towel-covered table. **1833** J. C. LOUDON *Encycl. Cottage, Farm, & Villa Archit.* 349 A Towel Horse has generally one rail at top... It..should..be painted, for the reasons given when speaking of fixed towel rails. **1961** *Times* 24 July 13/5 The civilized English custom of having heated towel-rails has not reached the United States. **1895** *Montgomery Ward Catal.* Spring & Summer 126/3 Towel Ring. Consists of polished hardwood ring with brass chain and hook. **1977** *Times* 30 July 10/6 Rough towels..towel rings..and all manner of taps.

towel, *v.* Add: **1. c.** *absol.* for *refl.* Also with *down, off.*

1972 M. CRICHTON *Terminal Man* IV. ii. 141 One of the girls got out of the pool lithely and began toweling off. **1977** P. MOYES *To kill Coconut* viii. 118 Emmy emerged from the shower, towelling vigorously. **1977** G. FISHER *Villain of Piece* iii. 29, I towelled down, dressed.

2. Also (*Austral.*) with *up*; also *fig.*

1941 BAKER *Dict. Austral. Slang* 78 *Towel up, to,* to beat, thrash. **1951** CUSACK & JAMES *Come in Spinner* 372, I think you deserve the V.C. for the way you towelled Old Mole up. **1973** A. BUZO *Rooted* 42 Gary got his big serve working, I chipped in at the net and we were laughing. Towelled them up in no time.

Hence **tow·elled** *ppl. a.*, wrapped in a towel.

1920 T. S. ELIOT *Ara Vus Prec* 23 Doris towelled from the bath Enters padding on broad feet. **1940** G. ARTHUR *Concerning W. S. Churchill* 8 Standing at the edge of a deep swimming pool a junior boy mistook a towelled, stocky figure for a contemporary and playfully pushed him into the water. **1978** C. TOMLINSON *Shaft* 3 The towelled head next.

towelette (tauĕle·t). [f. TOWEL *sb.* + -ETTE.] A small towel.

1902 in W. Forrester *Great-Grandmama's Weekly* (1980) iv. 84/1 Artmann's Hygienic towelettes. Superior to any other Sanitary Towels. **1926** *Blackw. Mag.* Apr. 528/1 Drying ourselves on pretty hand-woven towelettes. **1981** *Times* 16 Sept. 9/4 On board, someone opened my milk carton for me and someone else explained the uses of my towelette.

tower, *sb.*[1] Add: **I. 1. a.** For earlier examples of *Tower of Silence* see SILENCE *sb.* 2 c.

3. Freq. in *tower of strength.* See also *IVORY TOWER.

1549 *Bk. Common Prayer* fol. xvᵛ, O lorde..Bee vnto them a tower of strength. **1594** SHAKS. *Richard III* v. iii. 12 Besides, the King's name is a Tower of strength. **1852** TENNYSON *Ode on Death of Duke of Wellington* 7 O fall'n at length that tower of strength. **1866** MRS GASKELL *Wives & Daughters* II. xxii. 224 But, my dear Cynthia,—how soon Roger will be back,—a tower of strength. **1956** A. WILSON *Anglo-Saxon Attitudes* II. iii. 394 She's been such a tower of strength all this time. **1970** NEW ENGLISH BIBLE *Prov.* xviii. 10 The name of the Lord is a tower of strength, where the righteous may run for refuge. **1981** P. H. JOHNSON *Bonfire* II. i. 84 He put his arms round Agnes... She thought of him as a 'tower of strength'.

5. d. A railway signal-box. *U.S.*

1900 *Everybody's Mag.* II. 442/2 The tower from which the traffic entering and leaving the Grand Central Station in New York city is directed, is located just outside the station itself. **1910** H. A. FRANCK *Vagabond Journey* 328 A man in the neighbouring tower opened the block, and the diminutive freight screamed by us. **1946** [see *tower house,* sense 10 a below].

e. = *PYLON 4.

1930 *Engineering* 9 May 603/2 There are four standard types of tower for the single-circuit lines. **1946** D. C. PEATTIE *Road of Naturalist* iv. 42 The car lamps picked up out of vacancy the marching towers of the power lines. **1963** A. LUBBOCK *Austral. Roundabout* 72 The electric pylons, or towers, as they are called here, stalk up and down great rides cut through the trees, carrying the cable in their upflung arms.

f. See *control tower* s.v. *CONTROL *sb.* 5. Also *ellipt.*; *transf.*, the flight-control staff.

1958 'N. SHUTE' *Rainbow & Rose* i. 7 I'll come up to the Tower when we land. **1971** A. DIMENT *Think Inc.* xii. 201 Captain Roberts..asked tower, politely, for permission to taxi. **1977** *Time* 11 Apr. 23/2 The tower ordered KLM to taxi the full length of the runway.

g. *ellipt.* = *tower block,* sense 10 e below.

1970 *Times* 6 July 6/5 The towers, cheerless in their four tones of dun-colour. **1975** M. BRADBURY *History Man* i. 11 Higher on the hill grow the new concrete towers.

IV. 10. a. *tower house* (later example), *mill, silo.* **e. tower apartment,** an apartment in a tower block, a high-rise flat; **tower block,** a tall block of flats, a high-rise building, a sky-scraper; **tower bolt** = *barrel bolt* s.v. *BARREL *sb.* 11; **tower crane** (see quot. 1940); **tower karst** *Geomorphol.* [tr. G. *turmkarst* (H. von Wissmann 1954, in *Erdkunde* VIII. 122/1)], a type of karst characterized by isolated steep-sided hills; **towerman,** one who works in a tower; *spec.* (*U.S.*) (*a*) a railway signalman; (*b*) a look-out for forest fires; **Tower musket** *Hist.*, a tower-proof musket; **tower-shell** = *turret-shell* s.v. TURRET *sb.*[1] 5; **tower skull** = *oxycephaly* s.v. OXY- 1.

1961 Tower apartment [see *MAISONNETTE 2]. **1966** *Atlantic Monthly* Oct. 127 Tower blocks can be accused of leading to eardrum degeneration, owing to constant use of high-speed elevators. *a* **1974** R. CROSSMAN *Diaries* (1975) I. 82 The jack-block building in Coventry, a fifteen- or sixteen-storey tower block built by a new technique of jacking each storey up after it has been erected. **1982** *Listener* 23/30 Dec. 58/4 Most American film crews refuse to take rooms higher than the second floor of towerblock hotels since this picture. **1911** Tower bolt [see *barrel bolt* s.v. *BARREL *sb.* 11]. **1906** *Electr. World* XLVII. 743 An illustrated description of an electrically-operated rotating tower crane for the Dublin docks. **1940** *Chambers's Techn. Dict.* 856/1 *Tower crane,* a rotatable cantilever pivoted to the top of a steelwork tower, either fixed or carried on rails. **1967** *Listener* 27 July 111/1 A tower crane on our university building site. **1946** E. B. THOMPSON *Amer. Daughter* 124 We climbed the little ladder to the railroad tower house. **1954** *Erdkunde* VIII. 122/1 Of the various formations of kegelkarst, two widely differ in appearance from one another... **2.** A river plain, dotted with groups or swarms of limestone towers or castles... This is the tower karst. **1977** A. HALLAM *Planet Earth* 83/2 Hills with slopes of 70° and more occur, the relief being called tower karst. **1895** Tower man [see *ROUNDHOUSE *sb.* 4]. **1947** *Sun* (Baltimore) 18 Oct. 7/1 Towermen..serve as the eyes of the fire fighters. **1951** Towerman [see *GOLD-FISH b]. **1888** Tower mill [see SMOCKMILL]. **1933** *Times Lit. Suppl.* 14 Dec. 891/1 Even in brick or stone tower-mills the sweeps may be caught in the rear..by a suddenly veering storm. **1979** *Jrnl. R. Soc. Arts* Dec. 3/1 The viewer is taken inside one of the last remaining working tower mills. **1832** A. EARLE *Narr. Residence in N.Z.* (1966) 170 He had with him a beautiful double-barrelled gun, and a very good Tower musket. **1947** Tower musket [see *DANE GUN]. **1888** *Cassell's Encycl. Dict.*, Tower-shell. **1927** HALDANE & HUXLEY *Animal Biol.* xii. 300 One fossil tower-shell stands nearly five feet high. **1959** A. C. HARDY *Open Sea* II. v. 118 The tall slender *Turritella*, or tower-shell, is another common gastropod burrowing just below the surface. **1939** J. R. MCCALMONT *Silo Types & Construction* 2 Silos may be divided roughly into above-ground—tower or upright—and the below-ground—pit or trench—silo, either of which may be built for temporary or continued use. **1982** *Daily Tel.* 19 Apr. 9/3 Tower silos, standing as they do up to some 60 feet high and painted in various..colours are not particularly attractive features of our rural areas. **1905** *Trans. Ophthalm. Soc.* XXV. 364 (*heading*) Oxycephaly or 'tower skull'. **1918** J. H. PARSONS *Dis. Eye* (ed. 3) xxxiii. 620 Bilateral proptosis occurs in exophthalmic goitre..as a result of diminished orbital volume in oxycephaly or 'tower-skull' and leontiasis ossea. **1969** EDINGTON & GILLES *Path. in Tropics* x. 379 Patients with sickle-cell anaemia tend to have a certain type of habitus, with tower-skull, parietal bossing, and long slender, limbs.

tower, *v.* **I. 3. c.** (Earlier example.)

1799 COLERIDGE *Notebks.* (1957) I. entry 564 Partridges towering after being shot is a certain Proof that they are mortaly wounded.

towing, *vbl. sb.*[1] Add: **b.** *towing bracket.*

1959 [see *LITTLE MAN 2]. **1977** *West Briton* 25 Aug. 17/1 (Advt.), All types of caravan repairs undertaken,..towing brackets supplied and fitted.

‖ **towkay** (tau·kēⁱ). [ad. Malay *tauke.*] A Chinese businessman or employer, esp. in Malaysia.

1854 *Jrnl. Indian Archipelago* VIII. 16 Country born Chinese have a club called Sip Gee Seeah; they elect 12 Towkays or trustees. **1900** W. W. SKEAT *Malay Magic* v. 253 The Malay *pawang* may squeeze a hundred or perhaps two hundred dollars out of the Chinese *towkay* who comes to mine for tin in Malaya. **1948** *Straits Times* 7 July 4/5 Our lives were probably saved by a Chinese towkay from Karak who used to keep us supplied with fresh fruit and tinned milk. **1966** D. FORBES *Heart of Malaya* iii. 41 Nancy, the fourth daughter of Lee Kwan Bock, the sawmill *towkay*, was a schoolteacher.

towl (taul), *v. dial.* [Imit.] *intr.* To yowl.

1906 KIPLING *Puck of Pook's Hill* 283 Dan and Una found a couple of them [*sc.* beagles] towling round the kitchen-garden after the laundry cat. **1930** *Punch* 30 Apr. 478/2 They make reverent overtures to our Siamese Pugsie, who hates them and scurries towling with nerves from their outstretched hands.

town, *sb.* Add: **8. b.** *fellow about town* (earlier example); *man about town* (earlier example); also *woman about town.*

1734 in *15th Rep. R. Comm. Hist. Manuscripts* App. vi. 146 in *Parl. Papers 1897* (C. 8551) LI. 1 Though being what is called an idle man about Town, I generally read all that is writ on both sides. **1752** M. W. MONTAGU *Let.* 16 Feb. (1967) III. 6 One of the most disagreable Fellows about Town, as odious in his outside as stupid in his conversation. **1927** *Manch. Guardian Weekly* Jan. 75/1 Another surrender to the woman-about-town who wants a different kind of entertainment. **1979** 'S. KEMP' *Goodbye, Pussy* xii. 160 Zoë had been an 'actress'. Actress, model, woman-about-town.

c. *woman* (also *lady*) *of the town* (later examples).

1873 G. H. LEWES *Diary* 1 Jan. in *Geo. Eliot Lett.* (1956) V. 357 Trollope came to lunch. Told me of his trouble with Harry wanting to marry a woman of the town. **1886** *Lantern* (New Orleans) 20 Oct. 2/2 Orders were issued to the police to remove all women-of-the-town. **1982** C. CASTLE *Folies Bergère* i. 37 At the back of the stalls..the notorious 'ladies of the town'..plied their trade.

f. *to go to town*: to do something energetically, enthusiastically, or without restraint; *spec.* to make a great fuss. Freq. const. *on*. *colloq.* (orig. *Jazz slang*). See also sense 8 a in Dict.

1933 [see *GET *v.* 62 l]. **1940** E. S. GARDNER *Case of Silent Partner* xii. 222 Chocolate creams are one of the fondest things I am of [*sic*]. I was feeling low, and I went to town. **1946** J. B. PRIESTLEY *Bright Day* viii. 252 He surveyed me with mock admiration. 'The only writer who ever made..Gruman pay him a royalty on the gross. .. And did we go to town with it, I'll say we did.' **1947** J. BERTRAM *Shadow of War* 238 'Skeleton's' in a bad mood; he's going to town on 'em. **1958** A. HOCKING *Epitaph for Nurse* ix. 159 The local papers naturally went to town over the murder of Sister Biggs. **1960** N. HILLIARD *Maori Girl* II. ix. 128 'It's funny as hell to see girls fight.'.. 'They're really tough sorts, and boy! do they go to town. And swear! Punching and spitting and pulling hair.' **1972** P. M. HUBBARD *Whisper in Glen* vii. 67 Whoever had painted the thing, he had gone to town on his picture. **1980** *Times Lit. Suppl.* 14 Mar. 290/2 Professor MacAndrew goes to town on this novel, deciphering the code which she believes Henry James to have set up.

9. c. *town-builder* (example); *-loving* adj. (examples); *town-dark*, *-tied* (earlier example) adjs.

1859 S. R. STUMBO *Let.* 11 Jan. in L. R. Hafen *Colorado Gold Rush* (1941) 214 The reports you see in the papers.. are put in circulation by town builders for speculative purposes. **1918** D. H. LAWRENCE *New Poems* 26 Gay birds of the town-dark sea. **1960** R. WILLIAMS *Border Country* 10 It was dark..town dark. **1900** F. W. MAITLAND *Let.* 18 Feb. (1965) 211 The Spaniard of the middle class is a town-loving animal. **1941** *Mind* L. 396 A statement which no purely town-born, town-bred, town-loving person can..verify. **1845** E. A. POE in *Broadway Jrnl.* 13 Sept. 155 We poor town-tied denizens..can revel in scenes which we may never be able to visit, and snuff up in imagination the incense of the flowers, which only bloom for us through the painter's art.

10. town and country planning, the preparation and construction of plans in accordance with which the development of towns and countryside is to be regulated; cf. TOWN-PLANNING *sb.*; **town ball** *U.S.*, a game resembling baseball; **town belt** *N.Z.*, a belt of public land reserved chiefly for recreational purposes in or round a town; **town car** *U.S.*, a four-door motor car having a passenger compartment which is permanently enclosed and a driver's compartment which is not; **town centre,** a place or a collection of buildings forming a central point in a town (see *CENTRE *sb.* 6 a); **town clown** *U.S. slang*, a policeman working in a village or small town; **town gas,** gas manufactured and supplied for domestic or commercial use, based on coal gas; **town-head** (example); **townhithe** *rare*$^{-1}$, a haven or landing-place in a town; **townhome** *U.S.* = *TOWN-HOUSE, TOWN HOUSE 2 b; **town-miss,** a young woman who lives in a town: *spec.* a prostitute; **town-mouse** (earlier example); **town-plat** (earlier examples); **town-site** (earlier example); **town trail,** a route through a town for tourists or walkers linking features of interest, which are described and interpreted by explanatory notices, printed leaflets, or a guide; **town-traveller,** a commercial traveller whose operations are confined to the town which is his employer's place of business; **town twinning,** the establishment of regular contacts between two towns in different countries; cf. *TWIN *v.*^{2} 2.

1933 P. ABERCROMBIE (*title*) Town & country planning. **1941** J. S. HUXLEY in *Times Educ. Suppl.* 6 Dec. 581/2 It is here that adult education, enlightened town and country planning, and deliberate encouragement by the State and local authorities of living art, music, drama and all other branches of cultural life, must be called on to do most of the bridging of the gap. **1972** *Whitaker's Almanack 1973* 1177/2 The Town and Country Planning Act 1971 (consolidating earlier Acts) contains very far-reaching provisions affecting the liberty of an owner of land to develop and use it as he will. **1852** *California Dispatch* 18 Jan. 2/4 A game of 'town ball' which was had on the Plaza during the week, reminded us of other days and other scenes. **1909** *Collier's* 8 May 12/1 In America the corresponding game generally went under the name of 'rounders', and because it was played at the time of town meetings, 'townball'. **1975** E. WIGGINTON *Foxfire 3* 466 We'd go out and play town ball. **1851** E. WARD *Jrnl.* 3 Jan. (1951) 98 We afterwards went on to the Town Belt and Riccarton. **1889** W. DAVIDSON *Stories N.Z. Life* 61 The native bush which covers a large portion of the 'town belt'. **1907** *Horseless Age* 16 Oct. 589/3 There will be [from Ford Motor Co.] an enclosed town car, which is to be an exact copy..of the Renault town car. **1929** *Vanity Fair* (N.Y.) Mar. 89 (*caption*) The Blackhawk, a smaller and lower edition of the Stutz, is represented here by a town car of dignified proportions. **1968** G. N. GEORGANO *Compl. Encycl. Motorcars* 621 *Coupé de ville*,.. Some 'de ville' bodies had folding rear quarters as in the landaulette. In America they were more often known as town cars. **1932** T. SHARP *Town & Countryside* x. 203 But even if the naturalistic style could be quite perfectly carried out in the perfect replica of a romantic natural scene, what..is the purpose of such a scene in a sensibly-sized town, when..genuine countryside [is] accessible within a few minutes' walk of the town centre. **1966** *Guardian* 10 Sept. 14/1 A recently started town-centre housing scheme. **1980** P. LIVELY *Judgement Day* iii. 26 The street plan of the town centre, an elongated triangle enclosing an open space. **1927** *Amer. Speech* II. 387/1 The town clown's badge is called a *tomato can.* **1931** 'D. STIFF' *Milk & Honey Route* i. 20 There should always be some retreat, preferably a thicket, into which the hobos can flee, should they receive an unwelcome visit from the 'town clown', or the law enforcer of the community. **1908** F. E. JUNGE *Gas Power* ii. 31 The price for town gas has been gradually reduced during this period. **1958** *B.S.I. News* Aug. 16 Flexible tubing and connector ends for appliances burning town gas. **1973** C. CALLOW *Power from Sea* iv. 85 The number of people who have been inconvenienced is small compared with the total number converted from town gas to natural gas. **1805** G. MCINDOE *Poems & Songs* 62 Some b—h frae the town head has stown't. **1922** JOYCE *Ulysses* 379 Once her in townhithe meeting he to her bow had not doffed. **1976** *Washington Post* 19 Apr. C18/2 (Advt.), Rockshire Townhome w/3 bedrms., 2 ½ baths, English pub rec.rm., den, show well. **1979** *Arizona Daily Star* 22 July H 4/1 Accordingly, when what used to be called 'row houses'—attached houses—became economically desirable, they were at first called 'town houses' and are now in the process of being renamed 'town homes'. **1749** J. CLELAND *Mem. Woman Pleasure* II. 98, I was not at all out of figure to pass for a modest girl. I had neither the feathers, nor *fumet* of a tawdry town-miss. **1921** D. H. LAWRENCE *Sea & Sardinia* vi. 245 Two town-misses in fur coats. **1750** *Student* 31 May 190 Town-mice, he knew, luxurious were. **1656** *Public Rec. Colony of Connecticut* (1850) I. 282 Thos persons that cohabitt in the towne platte. **1723** *Proprietors' Rec. Waterbury, Connecticut* (1911) 121 To settle the old Town platt Lotts. **1821** *Canad. Courant* 17 Jan. 1/2 There are about fourteen acres cleared for a Town site but not a single house in a finished state. **1973** *Nature* 11 May 105/2 The local College of Education has sponsored the idea of 'town trails' in Leicester. **1980** *Jrnl. R. Soc. Arts* CXXVIII. 303/1 Its 140 pages of practical advice on ..town trails, heritage centres and other 'media' are not aimed at the general reader. **1850** DICKENS *D. Copperfield* xi. 114 He was a sort of town traveller for a number of miscellaneous houses. **1930** A. BENNETT *Imperial Palace* x. 59 A town-traveller in tinned comestibles. **1960** *Sunday Express* 16 Oct. 9/6 Town twinning between cities of highly developed and under-developed countries. **1981** *Times* 23 Mar. 4/4 The question of Dundee's association with Nablus would be raised with the Scottish Town Twinning Association.

11. Townswomen's Guild, an urban organization of women, engaging in educational and social activities.

1929 *Times* 26 Nov. 19/4 Lady Cynthia Colville, the president of the Townswomen's Guild Appeal..spoke of the great need there was in small towns and residential suburbs for the new Townswomen's Guilds, which are to fulfil a role similar to that played by the women's institutes in the rural areas. **1933** *Ludlow Advertiser* 25 Feb. 6/4 The Townswomen's Guild held a whist drive on Monday night in the Guild Room in Broad Street. **1960** J. STROUD *Shorn Lamb* vii. 79 Miss Dashforth stumped the whole area addressing Mothers' Unions, Townswomen's Guilds, Parent-Teacher Associations and so on. **1977** *Belfast Telegraph* 19 Jan. 3/5 Bloomfield Collegiate School—Knock Townswomen's Guild, talk on community relations, 7.45 pm.

townee, *sb.* Add: (Later examples.) Now usu. as distinguished from a country-dweller. Freq. pejorative. Cf. TOWNY *sb.* 1.

1929 S. KAYE-SMITH in H. C. Minchin *Legion Bk.* 195 The æsthetic week-ender is like other townees in that he generally fails to realize that the real country-dweller.. is a very mass of conventions. **1939** AUDEN in *I Believe* (1940) 18 We frequently admire the 'goodness' of illiterate peasants as compared with the 'badness' of many townees. **1976** J. I. M. STEWART *Memorial Service* xv. 245 Janet as a child had been a townee like myself.

B. *adj.* Of, pertaining to, or characteristic of town-dwellers or the town.

1935 H. H. BASHFORD *Lodgings for Twelve* 110 For the townee, as he called him, and townee pursuits, he had a quite unconcealed if tolerant contempt. **1936** AUDEN *Look, Stranger!* 55 The identical and townee smartness. **1960** W. MILLER *Russians as People* 60 It is all fascinating to the foreigner trying to sniff out 'Russian life', but to the townee Russian it is the shabby side of the familiar. **1972** *Daily Tel.* (Colour Suppl.) 24 Nov. 18/1 The Australians are far and away the most urbanised and townee of all nations.

towney: see TOWNY *a.* and *sb.* in Dict. and Suppl.

town hall. Add: **2.** *Comb.*: **town-hall clock(s)** = MOSCHATEL.

1900 DICKINSON & PREVOST *Gloss. Dial. Cumberland* (rev. ed.) p. xcv, *Adoxa moschatellina.* Town-hall clock (Carlisle). **1968** F. WARNER *Garland* 13 The red herb-Robert twined a bridge With celandine and town-hall-clocks. **1980** *Country Life* 28 Feb. 589/3 The countryman's name for the four-faced pale green woodland flower moschatel is..'Town Hall Clocks'.

town-house, town house. Add: **1. b.** (*a*) (Earlier and further examples.)

c **1870** in *Dict. Amer. Eng.* (1944) IV. 2341/2 *Town-house*, an almshouse.—Conn. **1889** R. COOKE *Steadfast* 28 Just as soon as the road settled she should 'cart her off to the town-house'.

2. a. (Earlier example.)

1771 SMOLLETT *Humph. Cl.* I. 185 He has his town-house, and his country-house, his coach, and his post-chaise.

b. = *terrace house* s.v. *TERRACE *sb.* 7. orig. *U.S.*

Often in multiple units designed in a stylish or adventurous manner.

1965 *Daily Progress* (Charlottesville, Va.) 13 July 13 The City Planning Commission..is to receive a proposed ordinance permitting the development of privately owned town houses. **1968** *Globe & Mail* (Toronto) 17 Feb. 5/3 It would include 1,800 dwellings comprising apartments, maisonettes and townhouses for 5,600 people. **1971** *Rand Daily Mail* (Home Owner) 27 Mar. 7/2 City dwellers are gravitating towards high density living (flat complexes, town houses). **1971** *Ideal Home* Apr. 69/2 Something become apparent is that..the modern terrace, even under the pretty name of 'town house', is not popular. **1977** *Telegraph* (Brisbane) 28 Oct. 49/3 The townhouse is a two-storey 'unit' which features a separate courtyard and more privacy than a home unit. **1977** *Detroit Free Press* 11 Dec. 1-B/2 One east side developer, ..would like very much to build a community of townhouses along one of the canals that leads to the Detroit river. **1982** *Habitat Catal. 1982/83* 28/3 Room 2 has a 'metropolitan' style associated with townhouse living.

townie: see TOWNY *a.* and *sb.* in Dict. and Suppl.

town-major. Add: **d.** An officer responsible for liaison between troops stationed in a town and the townspeople. (No longer current.)

1917 A. G. EMPEY *Over Top* 312 *Town major*, an officer stationed in a French town or village who is supposed to look after billets, upkeep of roads, and act as interpreter. **1919** A. P. HERBERT *Bomber Gipsy* 19 Town-major jobs that break men's hearts, and billets at the Base.

townscape. Delete *nonce-wd.* and add: **1.** (Later examples.)

1959 *Sunday Times* 18 Jan. 16/8 These townscapes display, in short, the internal contradictions which also mark this painter's portraits of the aged rich. **1962** *Listener* 4 Oct. 515/2 The tranquillity of his land- and town-scapes.

2. The arrangement and overall appearance of the buildings, spaces, and other physical features of a town.

1937 *Evening News* 23 Apr. 10/4, I prefer a townscape with human figures to a landscape with trees. **1939** *Archit. Rev.* LXXXVI. 235/2 That universal Croydon towards which the townscapes of England are tending. **1953** *Ibid.* CXIV. 33 If I were asked to define Townscape I would say that one building is architecture but two buildings is Townscape. For as soon as two buildings are juxtaposed the art of Townscape is released. Such problems as the relationship between the building and the space between the buildings immediately assume importance. **1972** *Oxford Times* 27 Oct. 2/6 Mr John Ashdown, the city's conservation officer, said the monument would add to the townscape and be particularly attractive when seen by people walking up Turl Street. **1983** *Listener* 20 Jan. 27/3 The tall, usurping factor of Aurungzeb's mosque, dominating the townscape that some remember.

Hence **tow·nscaper,** one who plans townscapes; **tow·nscaping,** the planning of townscapes.

1949 *Archit. Rev.* CV. 249 Though the townscaper may welcome the contribution of street publicity to the urban scene there is one pitfall he must avoid—impropriety. **1953** *Ibid.* CXIV. 251 The townscaper's box of tricks—enclosure, escape, claustrophobia, surprise, delight, relief. **1959** *New Statesman* 16 May 686/2 All over the unbuilt ground surface of the Churchill Gardens estate there is evidence of an attitude indistinguishable from Townscaping. **1961** *Guardian* 18 Jan. 10/6 This cool new piece of townscaping.

Townsend (tau·nzend). *Physics.* The name of Sir John *Townsend* (1868–1957), Irish physicist, used *attrib.* with reference to certain phenomena and concepts related to his work on the conduction of electricity through gases, as **Townsend discharge,** a dark, low-current electric discharge in a gas that depends on an external source of ionization for its continuance.

1932 K. K. DARROW *Electr. Phenomena in Gases* ix. 293 The relative importance of the various processes of ionization and electron-expulsion..which figure in the 'Townsend discharge'. **1956** *Nature* 25 Feb. 391/1 The possibility of using the Townsend electron avalanche process in a gas in a stage-by-stage system to give a highly stable electron-multiplication factor. **1968** ROMANOWITZ & PUCKETT *Introd. Electronics* xiv. 563 As the voltage is increased from zero, the dark current (called Townsend current..) increases slowly until the voltage approaches that at which the tube operates with a glow discharge. **1978** J. H. INGOLD in Hirsh & Oskam *Gaseous Electronics* I. ii. 23 At extremely low currents, on the order of microamperes and less, the discharge is a Townsend discharge, with little or on visible light emanating from the discharge tube. **1982** *Nature* 28 Oct. 774/1 The main agents of discharges are eelctrons that participate in Townsend avalanches.

township. Add: **6. a.** Also in New Zealand.

1857 R. B. PAUL *Lett. from Canterbury, N.Z.* iv. 72 Malvern Hills, where Mr Cass thinks there is a site suited for a township. **1911** W. H. KOEBEL *In Maoriland Bush* xviii. 241 Half an hour later the street of the township opens out before the rider. **1977** *N.Z. Herald* 8 Jan. 4-1/5 (Advt.), From Henderson Township take Swanson Rd for 1 mile.

b. In South Africa, an area set aside for non-White occupation.

1934 *Lovedale Sol-fa Leaflet* No. 17.4 When the Bantu Township of Nancefield or Klipspruit (eleven miles West of Johannesburg) was first settled as a Suburb of the Rand Municipality, the late Enoch Sontonga..was a teacher in one of the Methodist Mission Schools. **1946** P. ABRAHAMS *Mine Boy* viii. 98 This side of the township had mostly Coloured people. The other side was where the native people were. **1964** L. NKOSI *Rhythm of Violence* 15 Which black township would you go to? **1971** *Sunday Express* (Johannesburg) 28 Mar. 6/1 The non-Whites..are not going to be satisfied much longer with leading third-rate lives in third-rate townships. **1984** *Observer* 9 Dec. 12/2 The flood [of people] has overflowed the inadequate African townships built by apartheid planners.

9. township trustee (earlier example).

1836 *New-Yorker* 30 Apr. 92/1 The vote (by general ticket) for Township Trustees is stated as follows.

Townsville (tau·nzvil). The name of a town on the coast of Queensland, Australia, used *attrib.* in **Townsville lucerne, stylo** [abbrev. *Stylosanthes* (see below and STYLO-)] to designate an annual or perennial leguminous plant with trifoliate leaves, *Stylosanthes humilis*, now used as a pasture plant in northern Australia and other tropical regions.

1937 *Jrnl. Council Sci. & Industr. Res.* (Australia) X. 201 The so-called wild or Townsville lucerne..was introduced accidentally into north Queensland. **1968** *Times* 23 Jan. (Austral. Suppl.) p. xiv/4 Several decades ago a plant, now called Townsville lucerne, drifted ashore from a South American ship at the port of Townsville and took root. **1977** A. V. BOGDAN *Trop. Pasture & Fodder Plants* 402 *Stylosanthes humilis* was known as Townsville lucerne until about 1968–9 when the Queensland Herbage Plant Liaison Committee recommended that the name should be changed to Townsville stylo in order to avoid confusion with species of *Medicago*.

towny, *sb.* Add: **1.** In first quot. for **1828** (ed. 3) 223 read **1827** (ed. 2) 227 and add later examples.

1934 [see *BUSHY *sb.*]. **1942** C. BARRETT *On Wallaby* i. 13 A sundowner's life was better than that of the 'townie' who had to work hard for a living and wear clean collars and shirts. **1959** I. & P. OPIE *Lore & Lang. Schoolch.* iv. 62 The 'towney' touches the leaf gingerly. **1972** P. LIVELY *Driftway* vi. 85 He was a real townie, didn't care for walking at all. **1984** *Times* 13 Feb. 2/8 Farmers know and care far more about conservation than meddlesome townies.

2. a. (Earlier example.)

1852 *Deseret News* (Salt Lake City) 7 Aug. 1/1 'O, nothing,' replied the 'towney'.

b. *N. Amer. Circus slang.* A town-dweller, as opp. to a person travelling with a circus or carnival. Cf. *TOWNEE *sb.*

1937 [see *REUB, RUBE]. **1951** *N.Y. Times Bk. Rev.* 8 Apr. 7/5 A fight [of carnival workers] with the townies. **1971** *Islander* (Victoria, B.C.) 19 Dec. 6/4 Everything had been set up for the show and tickets were being sold when several 'townies' attempted to crash the gate.

3. (Earlier example.)

1834 *Knickerbocker* IV. 279 Five or six fellows, whom I knew were friends and 'townies' of his.

tow-path. (Earlier example.)

1788 G. WASHINGTON *Diary* 2 June (1925) III. 361 A tow path on the Maryland side.

toxaphene (tǫ·ksăfīn). *Chem.* [f. TOX-¹ + *-a-* + *cam)phene* s.v. CAMPH-.] Chlorinated camphene used chiefly as an insecticide for pests of crops and livestock.

1947 *Jrnl. Econ. Entomol.* XL. 79/1 The chlorinated bicyclic terpene, now designated *Toxaphene* is an insecticide developed cooperatively by Hercules Powder Company and University of Delaware entomologists. **1975** *Nature* 9 Oct. 475/2 Over the past ten years toxaphene has been used in the USA in larger quantities than any other insecticide.

toxi-. Add: **toxige·nic** *a.* [*-GENIC] = *toxicogenic* adj. s.v. TOXICO-; so **toxigeni·city,** toxigenic property.

1930 J. A. ARKWRIGHT in *Syst. Bacteriol. in Relation to Med.* (Med. Res. Council) I. xi. 344 The new form present may be a variant which makes less growth than a more serviceable strain, or may be less toxigenic though equally prolific. **1979** *Nature* 8 Feb. 453/1 Toxigenic strains of *E. coli* elaborate two types of toxins. **1929** TOPLEY & WILSON *Princ. Bacteriol. & Immunity* II. xlii. 626 The same association of phenomena, which occurs in the case of virulence, may hold in the case of toxigenicity. **1977** *Lancet* 19 Mar. 649/2 A half antitoxin Naglar plate was prepared..for use in toxigenicity testing with specific antiserum.

toxic, *a.* Add: **2. a.** *toxic shock syndrome*, an acute bacterial illness observed esp. in women using tampons, characterized by fever, vomiting, diarrhoea, muscle pain, and some peeling of the skin, and in severe cases followed by shock.

1978 TODD & FISHAUT in *Lancet* 25 Nov. 1117/2 The acute illness we have described and called the toxic-shock syndrome seems to affect older children. **1982** *Brit. Med. Jrnl.* 29 May 1586/1 There is no justification at present for any suggestion that women should avoid using tampons, since the risk of developing toxic shock syndrome is extremely small.

toxicant, *a.* and *sb.* Restrict *rare* to the adj. and add further examples of the sb.

1951 *Ann. Rev. Plant Physiol.* I. 311 The injury [to vegetation] has economic significance only in 'heavy' smog when..the concentration of the toxicants is raised materially above the usual 'smog' level. **1982** *Nature* 14 Jan. p. xvii/3 The system measures the effect of toxicants on the light output of a special strain of luminescent bacteria.

toxin. Add: **b.** *toxin-antitoxin* (used *attrib.*).

1904 [see TOXIN b]. **1910** HISS & ZINSSER *Text-bk. Bacteriol.* xiii. 204 This work..showed that the element of time entered into the toxin-antitoxin reaction, just as it enters into reactions of known chemical nature. **1923** *Daily Mail* 16 Feb. 5/2 Since May in that borough 250 children have been tested and protection has been conferred on 70 by injection of the toxin-anti-toxin mixture. **1951** WHITBY & HYNES *Med. Bacteriol.* (ed. 5) vi. 70 Toxin-antitoxin mixtures become highly toxic if frozen. **1975** E. NNOCHIRI *Med. Microbiol. in Tropics* iii. 43/1 Large visible floccules may be produced following a toxin-antitoxin reaction.

toxo-². Add: **toxophore** *a.* (earlier and later examples); also as *sb.*, a toxophoric group; [ad. G. *toxophor* adj. (P. Ehrlich 1898, in *Deutsch. med. Wochenschr.* 22 Sept. 599/2)].

1899 Toxophore [see *HAPTOPHORE]. **1951** KIRK & OTHMER *Encycl. Chem. Technol.* VII. 121 In World War I, derivatives of trivalent arsenic received considerable attention, the structure —As= being considered a toxophore.

toxocara (tǫksokæ·ră). *Vet. Sci.* [mod. L. (C. W. Stiles 1905, in *Bull. Bur. Animal Industry* (U.S. Dept. Agric.) No. 79. 150), f. TOXO-¹ + Gr. κάρα head.] **a.** A nematode worm of the genus of this name, which includes species parasitic in cats and dogs; also in *pl.* sense. **b.** = *TOXOCARIASIS.

1940 A. C. CHANDLER *Introd. Parasitol.* (ed. 5) xxii. 388 Toxocara males have a small finger-like process at the tip of the tail. **1962** *Lancet* 6 Jan. 35/1 Duguid has now recorded 28 cases of children with retinal granuloma endophthalmitis due to toxocara. **1968** *New Scientist* 4 Apr. 41/1 The nematode is toxocara, of which there are two important species. **1976** *Milton Keynes Express* 16 July 1/2 Toxocara, a 'rare and horrific' disease caught from dog-dirt, has infected a Bletchley boy.

So **toxoca·ral** *a.*; **toxocari·asis** [*-IASIS], infection with *Toxocara* nematodes.

1930 E. C. FAUST *Human Helminthol.* 613/2 (Index), Toxocariasis. **1966** *Arch. Dis. in Childhood* XLI. 222/1 The diagnosis of toxocariasis is essentially a clinical one. **1968** *Brit. Med. Jrnl.* 16 Mar. 677/2 Persistent eosinophilia, hepatomegaly, choroiditis, and pulmonary infiltration are mentioned together or separately as indicating possible toxocaral infection. **1976** *Ibid.* 19 June 1486/2 Of human toxocariasis virtually nothing was known until about 12 years ago. **1981** *Ibid.* 18 July 192/1 A case of arthritis and arthralgia associated with toxocaral infestation.

toxophily. (In Dict. s.v. TOXOPHILITE.) For *nonce-wd.* read *rare* and add later examples.

1970 M. GILMORE *World Away* 75 Mervyn had become fascinated by toxophily, and he returned with very beautiful equipment for us all. **1983** *N.Z. Listener* 19 Nov. 67 *Toxophily*,..a very exclusive and fancy word for the shooting of bows and arrows.

toxoplasma (tǫksoplæ·zmă). *Zool.* Pl. **-plasmata.** [mod.L. (coined in Fr. by Nicolle & Manceaux 1909, in *Compt. Rend.* CXLVIII. 371), f. TOXO-¹ + PLASMA.] A micro-organism of the genus of this name, which comprises crescentic uninucleate sporozoans that are parasites of vertebrates. Also in pl. sense.

1926 C. M. WENYON *Protozoology* II. II. 1042 Mayer.. discovered a parasite which appeared to be a toxoplasma in the spleen and liver of a bird. *Ibid.*, Though some of the toxoplasmata may be merozoites of hæmogregarines or coccidia, this cannot apply to such an organism as *Toxoplasma gondii*. **1937** *Science* 2 Apr. 336/1 Toxoplasma have been described as the causative agents of various pathologic conditions in birds and mammals, including man. **1962** *Lancet* 6 Jan. 23/2 Only when a woman is initially infected with toxoplasma during pregnancy can she pass the infection to her fœtus. **1973** *Times* 31 Oct. 14/3 It is thought that toxoplasma infection may occasionally lead to abortion, or to some cases of mental abnormality in the child.

Hence **toxopla·smic** *a.*; **toxopla·smin** [-IN¹], an antigenic preparation of toxoplasma; **to:xoplasmo·sis** [-OSIS], infection with or a disease caused by toxoplasma, which may vary from symptomless to fatal.

1934 *Biol. Abstr.* VIII. 972/2 This is the first observation of incidence of toxoplasmosis in canary birds in Argentina. **1937** *Science* 2 Apr. 337/2 It is not known how toxoplasmic infection is transmitted in nature. **1948** J. K. FRENKEL in *Proc. Soc. Exper. Biol. & Med.* LXVIII. 639/2 The preparation of toxoplasmin, a skin testing antigen made of toxoplasma has been described. **1962** *Lancet* 6 Jan. 23/2 At the end of the third month of pregnancy, all women should be tested by the toxoplasmin skin test, which is cheap and simple. **1971** *Physics Bull.* July 409/2 Recurrent toxoplasmic chorioretinitis, leading to satellite lesions about a scar caused by cysts, presents a serious ocular threat. **1977** *Rolling Stone* 24 Mar. 24/5 Roy Harper, popular British singer and guitarist, almost had to delay a tour of Britain when he caught a rare (in humans), flulike virus called toxoplasmosis while giving mouth to mouth resuscitation to a pregnant sheep.

toy, *sb.* Add: **II. 7. c.** (Earlier example.)

1826 *Sessions Papers* 21 Sept. 546/2 James Boyce.. said 'The b—g—r has got no *toy*'; I had no watch.

d. *U.S. slang.* A small tin or jar containing opium; the quantity of opium held in such a container.

1934 *Detective Fiction Weekly* 21 Apr. 114/1 *Toy*, small receptacle for opium. **1951** *Suggestions for Teaching Nature & Effects of Narcotics* (U.S. Board of Education) 9 It [*sc.* opium] is usually sold in round tin salve containers, about the size of a five-cent piece, and is known as a 'toy'. **1955** *U.S. Senate Hearings* (1956) VIII. 4161 The containers thereof are known as 'toys' (small jars or like containers). **1961** *Dissent* VIII. 349 Opium itself is often available. However, it is expensive ($15–20 for a *toy*, a ball about the size of a large pea).

9. a. (Earlier example.)

1876 *All Year Round* 15 Jan. 377/1 'Toys' repose on velvet cushions.

b. (Earlier example.)

1855 [see *HYACINTH 3 b].

10*. *pl.* At Winchester College, a bureau or desk; hence, a cubicle used as a study.

1816 *Hist. Colleges Winchester, Eton & Westminster* 43 Besides his scob, every boy has, in the chamber to which he belongs, another receptacle for his books, with convenience for writing, &c. denominated, in the language of the place, Toys. **1901** *Public School Mag.* VII. 158/1 A series of small compartments, semi-secluded, but answering in their way to private studies. Each of these little dens is known as 'Toys'. **1974** K. CLARK *Another Part of Wood* ii. 74 We all sat in the same large enclosure, round the walls of which were small partitions (known as toyes) like uncomfortable polling booths, with just enough room for two shelves, one to serve as a seat and the other as a desk.

III. 11. a. *toy pistol.*

1883, 1889 [see *AMORCE]. **1978** N. FREELING *Night Lords* ii. 11 The bandits..were pathetic imbeciles armed with toy pistols.

c. (Earlier example.)

1806 M. LEWIS *Jrnl.* 1 July in *Orig. Jrnls. Lewis & Clark Expedition* (1905) V. 178 [Barking squirrels] will generally set and bark at you.., their note being much that of the little toy dogs.

d. toy book *U.S.*, a children's book; **toy-getter** (earlier example); *toy-getting* (example); **toy soldier,** a small model of a soldier; also *fig.*; **toy theatre,** a miniature theatre in which the characters are represented by printed pictures mounted on card or wood; also *fig.*; **toy time,** at Winchester College, time allocated for work in toys (see sense 10* above). See also *TOYTOWN.

1801 M. L. WEEMS *Let.* 10 Mar. in E. Skeel *M. L. Weems* (1929) II. 177, I sell the Primers & toy books wholesale at great discount. **1865** Toy book [in Dict.]. **1879** *Macmillan's Mag.* Oct. 502/1 The following people used to go in there—toy-getters (watch-stealers), magsmen [etc.]. **1896** A. MORRISON *Child of Jago* xxiv. 239 The gains of the toy-getting trade were poor, except to the fence. **1850** DICKENS in *Househ. Words* Extra Christmas No. 291/2 The lazy-tongs that used to bear the toy soldiers. **1922** M. ARLEN *Piracy* III. xi. 232 Poor Hugo.. has gone clucking back for to be a toy soldier at Aldershot. **1980** *Listener* 19 June 796/1 A shopful of toy soldiers cast from the same lead mould. **1850** DICKENS in *Househ. Words* Extra Christmas No. 292/1 Out of this delight springs the toy theatre,..with its familiar proscenium, and..boxes. **1931** A. C. WARD *Found. Eng. Prose* iii. 98 Stevenson loved to play with toy-theatres, and all his novels, with one exception, are reflected through the toy-theatre temperament: life is not in them. **1978** A. & P. MIALL *Victorian Christmas Bk.* 30 The toy theatre..was similar to the kind..still being made by Pollocks of London. The printed figures and scenery were cut out and applied to wooden backings. **1881** W. H. DAVID in C. E. Pascoe *Everyday Life in our Public Schools* 84 The clock marking 7, each junior retires to his 'toys' or bureau, for an hour and a half—during what is known as 'toy-time', when the work of the next morning and the week's composition have to be prepared. **1901** *Public School Mag.* VII. 158/1 Thus we find that from seven o'clock to half-past eight is 'toy time'.

toyable (toi·ăb'l), *a. nonce-wd.* [f. TOY *v.* + -ABLE.] Fit for toying with.

1922 JOYCE *Ulysses* 213 Phedo's toyable fair hair.

Toynbeean (toi·nbīăn), *a.* [f. the name of Arnold Joseph *Toynbee* (1889–1975), British historian + -AN.] Of or pertaining to Toynbee, his style, or his theories of the rise and decline of civilizations.

1954 W. K. HANCOCK *Country & Calling* viii. 221 Even when he has attained these two virtues of attachment and justice, the historian still needs a third, which I call *span*. This resembles the Toynbean quality of remoteness. **1962** *Listener* 8 Feb. 240/1, I would translate your words into Toynbean English, namely an answer to a challenge. **1966** *New Statesman* 18 Feb. 230/3 A remark..that 'the mature societies of Europe..in numerous ways..responded to the challenge' has the authentic Toynbeean stamp. **1975** *Asian Affairs* LXII. 239, I speak of dominance in the Toynbeean sense of a dominant civilization.

toy-shop. Add: **2.** (Earlier example.)
1796 *Boston Directory* 232 Butler, Mary, crockery and toy shop.
3. (Earlier example.)
1813 *Theatrical Inquisitor* II. 124 Her arms..drop inanimate like the..limbs of a toy-shop harlequin.

toytown (toi·taun), *sb.* (and *a.*) Also **toy-town.** [f. TOY *sb.* + TOWN *sb.*] A model of a town used as a plaything; *fig.* a small or insignificant town; also (with capital initial) the name of a town featured in a series of books and radio plays for children by S. G. Hulme Beaman (1887–1932). Also *attrib.* or as *adj.*
1836 [see TOY *sb.* 11 a]. **1864** R. BROWNING *Let.* 22 Aug. in G. R. Hudson *Browning to his American Friends* (1965) 145 A toy-town with boulevards traced through the sand-hills. **1897** 'S. GRAND' *Beth Book* (1898) xxiii. 207 The place..[had] a look of having been..set in order like a toy-town. **1928** S. G. H. BEAMAN *Tales of Toytown* 53 'Did you tell him I am busy?' the Mayor asked, laying down the copy of the *Toytown News* he had been reading. **1941** *Sun* (Baltimore) 27 Nov. 10/7 The demonstration, in the [chemical warfare] school's 'toytown' buildings which simulate actual city conditions, is a regular part of the two-week course at the school. **1964** W. MARKFIELD *To Early Grave* (1965) xi. 191 Platters of marzipan cookies shone with a toytown brilliance. **1971** R. FALKIRK *Chill Factor* iv. 38 Austurvollur Square was still toytown with the little white Lutheran Cathedral. **1972** *Daily Tel.* (Colour Suppl.) 27 Oct. 19/4 The slums of Kingston are horrendous: hovels of cardboard and plywood, tiny packing-case houses like a stricken toytown. **1972** 'S. WOODS' *They love not Poison* vii. 97 She..was..listening to a Toytown play on the Children's Hour. **1973** *Times* 15 Nov. 25/6 The Treasury are also fairly unimpressed by it; they refer to it internally as 'toytown money'. **1979** *Theatre Australia* Apr. 30/1 A *faux naif* toytown set of kitchen cupboard colours clashed dismally with furniture. **1984** *Times* 13 Mar. 17/1 This toytown situation became the occasion for a number of serious-looking people (all men, as it happened) in serious-looking suits to respond in a serious way to the questions of a sombre moderator.

trabacolo. (Earlier example.)
1800 E. C. KNIGHT *Let.* 9 Aug. in *Autobiogr.* (1960) 221 Had we sailed, as was first intended, in the imperial [Russian] frigate, we should have been taken by eight trabaccoli, which the French armed on purpose at Pisaro.

trabant. Restrict 'Now chiefly *Hist.*' to sense in Dict. and add: **2.** *Cytology.* = *SATELLITE *sb.* 9.
1926 C. D. DARLINGTON in *Jrnl. Genetics* XVI. 248 A portion thus narrower than the main body of the chromosome seems to require the name of satellite or trabant; such an element, having an attraction for the parent body proportionally less than a larger element, is naturally more subject to external forces, hence the common appearance of flying out. **1967** C. P. SWANSON et al. *Cytogenetics* ii. 26 The region of the chromosome distal to the nucleolar gap is called a trabant or satellite. **1980** *Caryologia* XXXIII. 207 In three individuals we observed different thickness of the intercalary trabant.

trac (træk). *Basketry.* [Etym. unknown.] In full *trac border.* A basketwork border made by taking the remaining length of an upright and weaving it in and out of the following uprights before repeating the process with the next.
1924 C. CRAMPTON *Cane Work* 13 *Back trac*, an additional border worked with the remaining ends of a three-rod plain border. **1959** D. WRIGHT *Baskets & Basketry* ii. 57 A Foot-Border... This is a trac border used for securing stakes to a wooden base with holes in it... Other tracs may also be used. **1964** H. HODGES *Artifacts* x. 146 In the trac border one stake at a time was bent and woven in completely.

trace, *sb.*[1] Add: **6. a.** Also *to sink without trace*: see *SINK *v.* 1 a.
c. Also in *Meteorol.* (see quot. 1930).
1908 *Observer's Handbk.* (Meteorol. Office) I. 35 Falls [of rain] of less than ·005-inch should be noted in the register by entering the word 'trace'. **1930** *Meteorol. Gloss.* (ed. 2) (Meteorol. Office) 177 The word 'trace' is entered in the daily record sheet when some rain (or other form of precipitation) is known to have fallen and the amount in the gauge is not large enough to be measured. **1974** *Nature* 25 Oct. 694/2 The measurements were made in very light snowfall (which never exceeded a 'trace' in equivalent precipitation rate).
d. *Psychol.* A change in the brain as a result of some mental experience; the physical after-effect *of* such.
1690 LOCKE *Essay Hum. Und.* II. i. 41 The memory of Thoughts, is retained by the impressions that are made on the Brain, and the traces there left after such thinking. *Ibid.* x. 67 There is no reason why the sound of a Pipe should leave traces in their [*sc.* birds'] Brains. **1892** G. F. STOUT *Man. Psychol.* I. I. ii. 76 Mental development would be impossible unless previous experience left behind it persistent after-effects to determine the nature and course of subsequent experience. These after-effects are called..traces or dispositions. **1927** G. V. ANREP tr. *Pavlov's Conditioned Reflexes* iii. 39 The stimulus this time is not the actual disappearance of an external agent, but the trace left by the action of the agent on the central nervous system after the agent itself has been removed. **1930** W. KÖHLER *Gestalt Psychol.* ix. 232 Learning and those processes the traces of which make reproduction and recognition possible. **1940** *Brit. Jrnl. Psychol.* XXX. 193 This process..works in conjunction with and through the trace-column, the masses of traces, ultimately of a chemical nature, left by past experience. **1978** TARPY & MAYER *Found. Learning & Memory* ii. 22 In trace conditioning, the CS does not impinge directly upon the sense receptors.
e. *Linguistics.* In transformational grammar, a phonetically null element considered to have been left in the position from which another element has been moved by a transformation, and to retain some influence on the resultant sentence.
1975 N. CHOMSKY *Logical Struct. Linguistic Theory* 22 Transformations that move expressions leave a 'trace' in the position from which the item was moved. **1977** *Stud. in Eng. Lit.: Eng. Number* (Tokyo) 95 Traces make it possible to define permissible transformations correctly. **1978** *Language* LIV. 412 S-initial sentential complements are base-generated in topic position.., and are linked to an empty subject position (actually a trace in subject position..) by a general rule of interpretation.
8. b. The luminous line or pattern on the screen of a cathode-ray tube.
1937 G. PARR *Low Voltage Cathode Ray Tube* ii. 28 The effect on the trace on the screen is..to break up the line into a series of light and dark patches. **1966** D. BAGLEY *Wyatt's Hurricane* vi. 156 He blinked them open again and stared at the radar screen, following the sweep of the trace as it swept hypnotically round and round. **1975** D. G. FINK *Electronics Engineers' Handbk.* VII. 30 This trace is displayed continuously until erased, so long as the flood beam is maintained in operation.
11. *Math.* The sum of the elements in the principal diagonal of a matrix.
1938 A. A. ALBERT *Mod. Higher Algebra* iv. 80 We call $T(A)$ the trace of A. **1958** *New Scientist* 10 July 364/2 If A is a matrix it is usual to denote the transpose of A by A′ or A*, and the trace of A by tr A. **1972** *Jrnl. Physics* B. V. 990 Evaluating the constant of proportionality by taking the trace of each side of the result for the particular case of complete recapture.
12. a. *Computers.* The detailed examination of the execution of a program or part of one (usu. to investigate a fault) with the aid of another program that can cause individual instructions, operands, and results to be printed as they are reached by the first program; the analysis so obtained; also, a trace program. Freq. *attrib.*, as *trace program, routine.*
1957 M. V. WILKES et al. *Preparation of Programs for Electronic Digital Computer* (ed. 2) 96 A useful error-diagnosis subroutine..prints the function letters of orders as they are executed... The printed sequence of function letters is sometimes known as a trace. **1960** GREGORY & VAN HORN *Automatic Data-Processing Systems* iii. 82 (*caption*) Trace of operations in read-write loop using an index register. *Ibid.* viii. 271 A trace routine is used to observe how the object program..operates while it is being executed. **1966** Trace program [see *SNAPSHOT *sb.* 2 b]. **1980** N. RUSHBY in Meek & Heath *Guide to Good Programming Practice* iii. 84 Some debugging compilers provide a trace, which can be used simply to follow the program flow from statement to statement, or can include details of each assignment. **1982** GHEZZI & JAZAYERI *Programming Language Concepts* vii. 221 After the program has terminated, a trace and an indication of the cause of failure can be produced.
b. A request for information to be sought concerning a particular person or thing; an investigation which traces this information (freq. to discover the source of a telephone call).
1974 M. PENOYRE *Breach of Security* i. 4, I might put in a trace to London to see if my Office has got anything on him. **1976** G. SEYMOUR *Glory Boys* iv. 49 Very professional. No possibility of a trace on a call of the length they've been using. **1978** R. LUDLUM *Holcroft Covenant* xxviii. 331 There are men following me... I think it's called a 'trace'. Put out by *you*? **1981** D. BOGGIS *Time to Betray* xxi. 114 He..got the index number... 'Get me a trace through Yard liaison.'
II. 13. *attrib.* or as *adj.* Present or required only in traces.
1950 *N.Z. Jrnl. Agric.* Sept. 195/1 The control..of peat scours by copper in trace amounts. **1956** *Sun* (Baltimore) 1 May 12/7 The oysters..are loaded with trace minerals. **1962** *Listener* 16 Aug. 243/2 It is the selected drug that is actually the effective agent and not trace amounts of some as yet unrecognized contaminant. **1965** G. J. WILLIAMS *Econ. Geol. N.Z.* vi. 63/2 To place these figures in petrogenetic perspective we must realize that gold is a trace-metal—even where concentrated in a payable reef. **1978** *Sci. Amer.* Dec. 124/1 It is the trace ions (those at least 1,000 times less abundant than hydrogen and helium) that serve to control the nebula thermostatically, maintaining the nebular temperature generally between 5,000 and 15,000 degrees. **1979** *Brit. Med. Jrnl.* 15 Dec. 1529/1 Most trace minerals and other micronutrients required for survival are known.
b. Special Comb.: **trace element,** an element that is present (esp. in the soil) or required only in minute amounts; also *fig.*; **trace fossil** *Palæont.* [tr. G. *spurenfossil* (K. Krejci-Graf 1932, in *Senckenbergiana* XIV. 21)], a fossil that represents the burrowing or similar activity of an animal rather than the animal itself.
1932 *Yale Jrnl. Biol. & Med.* IV. 501 Investigation as to the occurrence and function of 'trace' elements in both plant and animal life is now very active. **1954** R. L. PARKER tr. *Niggli's Rocks & Mineral Deposits* i. 9 Fundamental rock chemistry need consider only comparatively few elements... This does not mean that relatively rare elements or even the so-called trace elements lack importance. **1970** *Nature* 17 Oct. 251 Trace element analyses of flint show statistically valid differences between products of major British and European Neolithic flint mines. **1976** *Church Times* 16 July 7/2, I found little that has not been said already by many radical Christian writers. There are trace-elements of Marxism, but hardly more than that. **1956** *Q. Jrnl. Geol. Soc.* CXII. 475 A consideration of the..morphology of the fossil, permits its interpretation as a trace-fossil resulting from the driving of a system of branching tunnels in the sea-bed sediment. **1974** *Nature* 22 Mar. 328/2 It is generally agreed that the earliest metazoan animals were soft-bodied forms which are rarely preserved but have left tracks, trails and burrows, collectively known as trace fossils.

trace, *v.*[1] Add: **6. b.** (Earlier example.)
1876 *Rep. Vermont Board Agric.* III. 107 The farmer loses sight of the fact that the character of the calf..may 'trace back', as it is termed, to a remote ancestor.
7. c. To make a tracing of (a listed item); to derive (a tracing) *from* an index or catalogue; see *TRACING *vbl. sb.*[1] 1 b.
1905 *N.Y. State Library Bull.* No. 95. 578 See that every secondary card is traced on one or both main cards. **1914** [see *TRACING *vbl. sb.*[1] 1 b]. **1926** *Amer. Speech* II. 93 The catalog cards are 'main entry' cards and 'secondary entry' cards, the latter being 'traced' from the former.
8. c. *Computers.* To subject (a program) to a trace (*TRACE *sb.*[1] 12 a).
1959 M. H. WRUBEL *Primer of Programming for Digital Computers* v. 107 When a program is traced, the machine produces a record of each instruction as it is performed. **1967** KLERER & KORN *Digital Computer User's Handbk.* I. i. 23 The location limits of the program segments to be traced enter as initial parameters to the trace program. **1981** L. A. HILL *Structured Programming in FORTRAN* iii. 73 The program is traced in Table 3–6 with Rule 4 relaxed.

trace, *v.*[3] Add: **1.** Also with *up.*
1884 *Vermont Agric. Rep.* VIII. 285 The ears thus selected should be 'traced up' and hung away to dry. **1941** *Old Farmer's Almanac* 70 In the early fall the farmers would speak of 'tracing up' the yellow ears of corn to hang from the beams of the woodshed.

traceless, *a.* Add: **2.** *Math.* Having a trace equal to zero.
1966 *Rev. Mod. Physics* XXXVIII. 220/1 To each representation belongs a traceless tensor. **1973** *Nature* 14 Sept. 78/1 A view of the Earth from Polaris, with W representing the pole of the traceless part of the nutation tensor. **1979** J. C. POLKINGHORNE *Particle Play* iv. 63 There is a triplet representation of SU(3) which is called the fundamental representation because all other representations..can be constructed by mathematical manipulations on these three fundamental objects. The mathematical operations involved are direct products, symmetrizing, and making traceless.

tracer[1]. Add: **2.** (Further examples.) **c.** A substance (as a radioactive isotope or a dye) with distinctive properties that is introduced into a system so that its subsequent distribution may be readily followed. Freq. *attrib.*
1938 *Encycl. Brit. Bk. of Year* 320/2 The use of deuterium as a tracer in biochemical studies has been important. **1946** *Nature* 12 Oct. 527/1 The attempt..to correlate by radioactive-tracer techniques the localization of heavy metals in the body and their chemotherapeutic activity. **1952** *New Biol.* XIII. 63 One method..involves injecting into such mammals as sheep and rats a very minute dose (called a 'tracer dose') of the isotope. **1960** P. DAUDEL tr. *Eisner's Radioactive Tracers in Chem. & Industry* v. 164 The Russian workers..have investigated the action of modifying agents in the extraction..of metals..using radioactive tracers. **1962** O. HOCKWIN in A. Pirie *Lens Metabolism Rel. Cataract* 423 We investigated the metabolism of nucleotides and carbohydrates by ion exchange using labelled inorganic phosphate as a tracer. **1963** G. L. PICKARD *Descr. Physical Oceanogr.* vi. 81 Radioactive materials seem attractive as tracers of water movement... A very convenient artificial tracer is the red dye rhodamine-B. **1971** *Physics Bull.* Jan. 22/2 Satellites also have their use in the determination of wind. A tracer moving with the wind and identifiable from the satellite is required; there are two suitable tracers, cloud elements and balloons. **1979** *Sci. Amer.* Apr. 130/1 (Advt.), Using beryllium-7 as a tracer of stratospheric ozone, our scientists found that such ozone is distributed *throughout* high pressure weather systems. **1979** *Nature* 26 July 299/2 Sunspots have long been used as tracers to determine the rotation rate of the Sun.
4. a. Bullets or shells whose course is made visible by the trail that they emit during flight; occas. in *sing.* sense. Orig., the trail produced by these.
1910 *Blackw. Mag.* July 6/2 The projectiles of airship guns may possibly give out a jet of flame and a smoke 'tracer' on discharge. **1922** *Encycl. Brit.* XXX. 120/2 For night use, the tracer shows a luminous spark, for day use the tracer gives a smoky trail. **1937** *Times* 16 Apr. 8/6 This was a most spectacular demonstration, the machine-guns using tracer and the new smoke observation projectiles. **1957** P. KEMP *Mine were of Trouble* ix. 173 A minute later bursts of tracer flew over us from high ground on our right. **1967** *Boston Sunday Globe* 23 Apr. 16/4 Helicopter gunships tried to protect the other busy helicopters by circling in pairs, one with a light on to draw a stream of enemy tracers. **1970** L. DEIGHTON *Bomber* xxiii. 335 He was in the nose watching ropes of red and yellow tracer curve towards them and fall away. **1983** 'W. HAGGARD' *Heirloom* xv. 169 He'd seen..appeals for death..that airman with tracer burning his lungs out.

b. *attrib.* and *Comb.*

1916 'TAFFRAIL' *Pincher Martin* xv. 278 A thin trail of dim light climbed skywards in a curve as a tracer shell hurtled its way through the air. **1918** 'BOYD CABLE' *Air Men o' War* 22 Tracer bullets emit smoke and flame to allow the shooter to follow their flight. **1928** C. F. S. GAMBLE *Story of North Sea Air Station* xii. 179 When about 1,500 feet below the airship, he fired two trays of explosive and tracer ammunition from his Lewis gun into her. **1943** *Sun* (Baltimore) 3 Aug. 4/6 During this exchange of fire, a Japanese plane had managed to get on the tail of Captain Walter's Warhawk. Tracer bullets were flying past him, but none hit. **1944** *Return to Attack* (Army Board, N.Z.) 18/1 The flash and crack of the high-velocity tank guns, the low parabola of the tracer shell. **1969** G. MACBETH *War Quartet* 40 Tracer-filled In open air-space. **1973** M. WOODHOUSE *Blue Bone* xii. 135 A machine-gun stammered and tracer bullets began to draw graceful curves in space. **1976** A. WHITE *Long Silence* vii. 58, I saw a lone fighter come in from the west... Sudden streams of tracer fire came from him.

tracery. Add: **2.** *stump tracery*: see STUMP *sb.*[1] 18.

tracheide. Add after **-id**: (the usual spelling).

1907 D. P. PENHALLOW *Man. N. Amer. Gymnosperms* vi. 88 Such tracheids are invariable features of the ray in all the higher Coniferæ. **1910** J. M. COULTER et al. *Textbk. Bot.* I. iv. 241 Tracheids are single cells thus formed. **1948** [see *COLLAPSE *sb.* 4]. **1974** *Sci. Amer.* Apr. 59/1 Tracheids predominate in softwoods, which have no vessel cells or libriform fiber cells.

tracheostomy (trē^{i}kiˌǫ·stŏmi). *Surg.* [f. TRACHEO- + *-STOMY.] **a.** The operation of making an opening in the trachea near its upper end, so that the patient can breathe through it; also, the opening so made.

1945 W. V. MULLIN in F. Christopher *Textbk. Surg.* (ed. 4) xix. 774/2 Tracheostomy may be necessary to facilitate the operation. **1961** *Lancet* 7 Oct. 819/2 He spoke of the need for asepsis in managing a tracheostomy, especially during cleaning and replacement of the tube. **1976** *National Observer* (U.S.) 18 Dec. 16/4 Siegel underwent a tracheostomy 2½ months ago. **1977** *Proc. R. Soc. Med.* LXX. 160/1 He was then able to breathe spontaneously and the tracheostomy was allowed to close.

b. tracheostomy tube, a curved tube which can be inserted into the trachea via a tracheostomy.

1961 *Lancet* 7 Oct. 819/2 There was less chance of stenosis of the trachea after removal of the tracheostomy tube. **1977** *Ibid.* 19 Mar. 636/2 Indwelling urinary catheters, endotracheal tubes, and tracheostomy tubes put the patient at special risk.

tracing, *vbl. sb.*[1] Add: **1. b.** The procedure of making a list of all the headings under which a given item occurs in an index or catalogue; an entry in such a list.

1905 *N.Y. State Libr. Bull.* No. 95. 582 Make slip under personal name as in 14*a*, following same method of tracing. **1914** *N.Y. State Libr. School Cataloging Rules* 32 Trace added entries on the back of the main card. Write the tracing for other cards toward what will then be the lower right corner. **1953** R. L. COLLISON *Indexes & Indexing* I. 73 Since revision [of an index]..may sometimes be necessary, it is a good policy to enter 'tracings' of any references made on the main slip. **1978** FOTHERGILL & BUTCHART *Non-Book Materials for Libraries* iv. 191 Then the primary name heading and tracings for added entries and references can be given.

c. The following of the course of the cutting stylus by a reproducing stylus; usu. in *tracing distortion*, distortion that occurs when the stylus does not describe exactly the same path as the groove owing to its size in relation to the groove.

1942 *Jrnl. Acoustical Soc. Amer.* XIII. 276/1 (*heading*) Tracing distortion in the reproduction of constant amplitude recordings. **1959** *Listener* 26 Mar. 542/1 Turning now to the gramophone record, we find a sound source which suffers from certain well-known inherent defects, among the most important being..tracing distortion. **1961** G. A. BRIGGS *A to Z in Audio* 208 These delicately balanced arms which permit good tracking and tracing at extremely light weights give the best available quality from the finest pickups. **1975** G. J. KING *Audio Handbk.* viii. 192 Incorrect adjustment of the lateral and vertical tracking of the pickup can also aggravate distortion; but that resulting from 'normal' errors is generally less than tracing distortion.

d. *Computers.* The process of performing a trace (*TRACE *sb.*[1] 12 a). Also *attrib.*, as *tracing routine*.

1959 M. H. WRUBEL *Primer of Programming for Digital Computers* v. 107 Tracing is an important technique in testing programs, but it must be used in moderation. **1967** KLERER & KORN *Digital Computer User's Handbk.* I. i. 23 It is possible to build in a tracing structure into any given program. **1969** P. B. JORDAIN *Condensed Computer Encycl.* 539 It is important that the tracing routine leave intact the natural operation of the subject program.

5. tracing table, a table with a translucent top illuminated from underneath; **tracing-wheel** (examples).

1953 A. H. ROBINSON *Elements Cartogr.* v. 82/2 (*caption*) A tracing table with fluorescent illumination. **1978** *N.Y. Times* 30 Mar. B-21/8 (Advt.), Nuarc lighted tracing table, 5 drawer blueprint files. **1894** J. E. DAVIS *Elem. Mod. Dressmaking* i. 7 Tracing the fitting-lines of the pattern through the doubled lining only..is now almost entirely done by tracing-wheel. **1969** *Guardian* 30 Sept. 11/2 Singers..stock everything for dressmaking..hem markers, tracing wheels, fastenings.

track, *sb.* Add: **I. 1. a.** *spec.* in *Particle Physics*, a line marking the path taken by an atomic or sub-atomic particle.

1912 *Proc. R. Soc.* A. LXXXVII. 277 It has now been found possible to photograph the tracks of even the fastest β-particles. **1942** J. D. STRANATHAN *Particles Mod. Physics* i. 43 The ions formed directly by the alpha particle must all have been of very low speed; otherwise the track would not be as narrow and sharply defined. **1955** *Sci. News Let.* 12 Feb. 103/1 When exposed to the special photographic plates, particles from the radioactive samples leave a distinct pattern, known as tracks, on the emulsion. **1973** L. J. TASSIE *Physics Elementary Particles* vi. 50 The forked track, *ab*, in Fig. 23.1 was due to the decay of a heavy neutral particle.. into two charged particles.

d. A line on the skin made by the repeated injection of an addictive drug. Usu. *pl. slang.*

1964 H. RODRIGUEZ in Larner & Tefferteller *Addict in Street* 34 Tracks are marks,..like a long black streak coming down your arm directly over your vein; that comes from hitting in the same place so much. **1965** *Life* 26 Feb. 86/4 In summer, they [*sc.* addicts] alone wear long sleeves (to cover their 'tracks'—needle marks). **1972** J. MILLS *Report to Commissioner* 104 Whaddya mean, lemme see your tracks? I'm a pros, man, I shoot up in my thighs. **1977** *Rolling Stone* 13 Jan. 14/3 The coroner found four fresh needle marks but no tracks, indicating that Bolan was not a junkie. **1979** R. B. PARKER *Wilderness* i. 10 'Junkie,' he said. The white trooper said, 'Tracks?'..The black trooper nodded, 'All up and down her right arm.'

4. d. *Aeronaut.* The projection on the earth's surface of the (actual or intended) course of an aircraft; the representation of this on a chart.

1919 S. F. CARD *Air Navigation* i. 6 The straight line on the map or chart joining the two places will be called the desired track. **1943** REDPATH & COBURN *Air Transport Navigation* viii. 176 Measurement of the line must give us the groundspeed, since track and groundspeed go hand in hand. **1970** TAYLOR & PARMAR *Ground Stud. for Pilots* II. i. 13 Plot in the places carefully on the chart.. and join them up, putting the two arrows on the line.. to indicate the Track you wish to follow over the Earth's surface.

e. The plane in which the blades of a propeller are intended to rotate.

1920 W. E. PARK *Treat. Airscrews* xii. 206 The relative position of corresponding points in opposite blades..in the side elevation is considered as the 'track' of the blade. **1948** C. E. CHAPEL *Aircraft Power Plants* xv. 323/2 This and the several other methods of field checking the track of the propeller are rough methods only. **1956** W. A. HEFLIN *U.S.A.F. Dict.* 81/2 A blade is said to be *in*, or *out of*, *track*.

f. = *LINE *sb.*[2] 19 c.

1931 *Flight* 23 Jan. 73/1 Each fuselage moves along the track to the next [stage]..until at the end of the track the machine is complete. **1979** *Daily Tel.* 3 Aug. 2 The jobs of about 1,000 workers will be affected at British Leyland's Rover saloon car plant..by plans to cut production tracks from three to two. **1981** B. WALSH *Live Bait* ix. 85 Me and Brian work on the track... The assembly line.

g. *U.S. Educ.* = *STREAM *sb.* 6 d. Usu. *attrib.*

1959 *Washington Post* 17 May E 4/2 The extension of the track system to District junior high and elementary schools ought to benefit most pupils, but the School Board should make certain that Superintendent Carl F. Hansen's 3-track plan for children below the senior high school level is as flexible as possible. **1964** B. FINE *Stretching their Minds* 19 'Acceleration' became fashionable—meaning either old-fashioned 'skipping' or the modern 'multiple-track' plan (in racing terms, a slow track for the average student, a fast track for the superior). **1968** *Economist* 7 Dec. 47/2 It ordered the end of the track system (which divided children according to academic ability, with most Negroes landing inevitably in the lowest track). **1983** *N.Y. Times* 13 Nov. XII. 71/2 There could be different rooms for learners and spurners. If a traditional track system is preferred, there could be a class for those who are on the track and another for those who have derailed.

6. a. Delete '(now *U.S.*)'. *Esp.* a single pair of rails, in contrast to a line (which may denote the route and comprise one or more tracks: cf. LINE *sb.*[2] 26 b). Also (*U.S.*) with following number, denoting the line served by a particular platform or gate.

1869 *Bradshaw's Railway Man.* XXI. 390 The length of this line is 94 miles... Of the whole only 33 are 'double track'. **1911** *Encycl. Brit.* XXII. 820/2 The Stockton & Darlington railway... This line..was in the first instance laid with a single track. **1955** J. L. AUSTIN *How to do Things with Words* (1962) v. 57 Passengers are warned to cross the track by the bridge only. **1967** [see *double-tracked* s.v. *DOUBLE *a.* C. 1]. **1978** R. LUDLUM *Holcroft Covenant* i. 12 He had learned before the announcement that the train for Zurich would leave from track twelve. **1984** *Financial Times* 27 Jan. 2/8 Yesterday, Breton farmers suspended their disruption of rail traffic and removed the barriers they had placed across the tracks in Brittany.

b. (Earlier examples.)

1836 *Spirit of Times* 20 Feb. 5/3 And he will run a match against either, or a sweepstakes with both, one, two, three, or four mile heats, over any good track in East Tennessee. **1851** *Fraser's Mag.* June 657/1 A barouche and four does not differ more from a trottingwaggon..than an English race-course from an American 'track'.

c. The distance between a wheel on one side of a vehicle and the corresponding wheel on the other side.

1850 *Western Jrnl.* IV. 96 This distance will, therefore, vary in different sections of the country according to the usual 'track' of wagons. **1910** J. GUNN *Practical Design Motor Cars* viii. 219 The wheel base and wheel track of a motor car require consideration. **1928** [see *ROADABILITY]. **1948** J. D. RITTENHOUSE *Amer. Horse-Drawn Vehicles* 1 The term 'track' refers to the extreme width of the vehicle as measured from outside rim of one wheel to the outside of the rim of the opposite wheel, measured at the bottom of the wheel. **1969** *Gloss. Aeronaut. & Astronaut. Terms* (*B.S.I.*) v. 12 *Track*, the distance between the outer points of contact of the port and starboard main undercarriages.

d. Each of the endless bands on certain heavy vehicles, esp. tanks, passing round and driven by wheels and facilitating travel over rough or soft ground. Cf. *CATERPILLAR 1 b.

1884 *Patent 269,998* in *Specifications & Drawings* (U.S. Patent Office) 15 Apr. 1384/1 This invention relates to certain improvements in that class of road-engines in which the driving and pilot or guiding wheels are connected by a chain or series of links, which together form an endless track which the wheels traverse in the movement of the engine. **1926** *Encycl. Brit.* Suppl. III. 723/2 The track..was carried all round the tank; this track was driven from the engine through a two-speed gear box. **1931** G. LE Q. MARTEL *In Wake of Tank* 83 The whole of the engine power could be transmitted to the track on the one or the other side of the tank as desired. **1971** *Power Farming* Mar. 13/2 Before the development of the large rubber tyre it was possible to transmit high power to the soil only through tracks. **1974** 'W. HAGGARD' *Kinsmen* viii. 82 A simple crane on a pair of tracks was well within his modest competence.

e. (Without article.) The branch of athletics in which a running track is used; track athletics, track events; *track and field* (also *attrib.*), athletics in general. orig. *U.S.*

1905 *Outing* XLVI. 490/1 Track and field sport has been working out its own spontaneous solution. **1934** T. V. WILDER *Heaven's My Destination* 66, I was captain of track and basket-ball. **1936** *Nat. Geogr. Mag.* LXIX. 799/2, I progressed the next year to my class squads in football and track. **1964** A. WYKES *Gambling* iv. 102 As for athletics, or 'track and field' sports, there are practically no places where public betting..flourishes to any extent. **1972** *N.Y. Times* 4 June 4/3 The Oregon Track Club is very active in promoting track in the area. **1978** G. A. SHEEHAN *Running & Being* viii. 107 Despite the detailed and accurate statistics of track and field, the scientists consistently underestimate the human body and its potential. **1979** R. JAFFE *Class Reunion* (1980) II. viii. 265 'Do you have a favorite sport?' 'Track.'

f. A ballroom or dance-hall. *U.S. slang.*

1945 L. SHELLY *Hepcats Jive Talk Dict.* 19/2 *Track*, hall for dancing. **1960** WENTWORTH & FLEXNER *Dict. Amer. Slang* 553/2 The Savoy Ballroom in N.Y.C.'s Harlem was widely known as 'The Track' to hepsters. **1965** 'MALCOLM X' *Autobiogr.* xvi. 315, I dig your holding this all-originals scene at the track. **1972** T. KOCHMAN *Rappin' & Stylin' Out* 163 The place where the movement can occur is appropriately termed the 'track', whether the place is a dance hall.., the street.., or, as used figuratively, the life span.

g. A metal or plastic strip designed to carry the sliding fittings from which a curtain is hung, or on which an electric (spot)light may be positioned. Cf. *track lighting* in sense 13 below.

1971 *Guardian* 18 Aug. 9/6 Curtain tracks and pelmets. **1976** *N.Y. Times Mag.* 15 Aug. 47 Installation of the track on the ceiling is tricky, and, in most instances, involves hiding the wires from the ceiling to the light switch. **1979** D. BRIERLEY *Cold War* iv. 39, I checked plugs, sockets..the track for the curtain across the window.

h. *Cricket.* = WICKET 3 c.

1976 J. SNOW *Cricket Rebel* 102 Deliveries..that pitched half way down the track and went through above head high. **1977** *Grimsby Even. Tel.* 31 May 12/6 Fast bowler Robert Herkes again gave a good account of himself and his figures of two for 33 off 16 overs was no mean feat on a track that did not give him a shred of help. **1983** *Daily Tel.* 3 Sept. 12 The commentators—particularly the professional cricketers (active or retired)—use a vocabulary peculiarly their own: the pitch is a 'track', good or bad.

8*. a. = *GROOVE *sb.* 2 c (now *rare* or *Obs.*); hence, a single recorded item (esp. of popular music), which on a long-playing record is a band bounded on both sides by an area of widely-spaced grooves.

1904 S. R. BOTTONE *Talking Machines & Records* 60 We must have some means of controlling or varying the pressure of the stylus of the reproducer on the record, so as to enable it to follow correctly every indentation in the 'track'. **1949** *Playback* Oct.–Nov. 4/2 This took the form of a 10″ record with two 'tracks' or 'grooves' impressed on each side. **1956** *Gramophone* Dec. 265/1 None of the tracks lives up to the promise of the star-studded personnel. **1957** [see *BAND *sb.*[2] 9 b]. **1958** *Observer* 28 Dec. 6/7 All the tracks had been released as singles in the era of seventy-eight r.p.m. **1967** A. DIMENT *Dolly Dolly Spy* xii. 160, I wandered over to the juke box and selected a Dylan track for relaxation. **1970** *Honey* June 53/4 Their first LP is so polished. There are some great original tracks. **1980** *Oxford Times* 1 Feb. 23/3 On tracks like 'Rock Music' they seem to want to be a hard rock 'n' roll band... On several other tracks their aim is vague and visionary.

b. *Cinemat.* = *sound track* s.v. *SOUND *sb.*[3] 7 b.

1931 B. BROWN *Talking Pictures* x. 226 To a certain extent surface noise is due to irregularities in the sensitive film used for recording the track. **1976** *Oxf. Compan. Film*

203/1 'Dolbyized' tracks sound 'cleaner' and clearer than ordinary tracks.

c. A lengthwise strip on magnetic tape consisting of a single sequence of signals; more widely, a linear path in any information storage device or medium that accommodates one sequence of signals or corresponds to one head.

Orig. identical with prec. sense.

1947 *Jrnl. Soc. Motion Picture Engineers* XLVIII. 9 A magnetic recording track..on 16-mm film. **1951** *Audio Engin.* Sept. 40/2 The recording medium is an endless polyvinyl-chloride [magnetic] tape with 56 parallel sound tracks spaced at the ordinary rate of four tracks per millimeter. **1951** *Proc. Inst. Electr. Engineers* XCVIII. II. 29/1 As the drum rotates the surface is carried past a fixed magnetic recording and reading head... Many separate tracks can be recorded side by side. **1957** *Practical Wireless* XXXIII. 697/1 Rotation of VR1 should cause it to click in and out as a certain point on the track is passed. **1962** *Times* 5 July 15/6 Some tapes have two tracks, others (in stereo) have four, and a four-track recorder will not produce the best results on a two-track tape. **1969** P. B. Jordain *Condensed Computer Encycl.* 305 Data are addressed on a drum by specifying the track number and word number within the drum. **1970** O. Dopping *Computers & Data Processing* iii. 57 Readers and punches for paper tape can easily be adjusted to different numbers of tracks. **1977** *Time* 4 July 4 (Advt.), There's a film to watch—a recent release—8 tracks of stereo to listen to, free naturally, and plenty of room to stretch out or stroll about. **1983** *Austral. Personal Computer* Aug. 62/1 Files stored on a disk are located by means of a directory set up on a particular grouping of tracks.

9. *in one's tracks* (earlier and later examples); delete (*U.S.*); *on the right track*, having the right idea; heading in the right direction; also *on the* (or *a*) *wrong track*; *the wrong side of the tracks*, the socially inferior part of town; so *to cross the tracks* and similar phrases; *on the track* (Austral.), tramping from place to place in search of work; *on track* (U.S.), on course; achieving or doing what is required; *to comb the tracks*: see *comb *v.*[1] 4 c; *to jump the track*: see Jump *v.* 6 c.

1824 T. D. Arnold in M. James *A. Jackson* (1937) 156 He failed to shoot 'Jackson dead in his tracks'. **1873** J. C. F. Johnson *Christmas on Carringa* 19 'Tis Christmas Eve again to day, and I am on 'the track'. **1886** C. M. Yonge *Chantry House* I. xiii. 116 This had done more to convince my father that he was on the right track than the having found him on his knees. **1889** J. K. Jerome *Three Men in Boat* iii. 37 You know we are on a wrong track altogether. We must not think of the things we could do with, but only of the things that we can't do without. **1896** H. Lawson *While the Billy Boils* 207 I've been knocking round for five years, and the last two years constant on the track, and no show of getting off it unless I go for good. **1915** A. Huxley *Let.* Oct. (1969) 84 These maximal horrors of war are really too unthinkably appalling; but things I trust are on the right track now for health. [**1929** T. Smith *Stray Lamb* iv. 29 In most commuting towns..there are always two sides of which the tracks serve as a line of demarcation. There is the right side and the wrong side. Translated into terms of modern American idealism, this means, the rich side and the side that hopes to be rich.] **1945** S. Lewis *C. Timberlane* (1947) xxxiv. 230, I thought at first that she was from the wrong side of the railroad tracks, but she seems to have settled down to being a nice little lady and a good war worker. **1953** 'Caddie' *Sydney Barmaid* xliv. 255 It would have been impossible for him to maintain the home on a dole ration... He was going on the track. **1954** I. Murdoch *Under Net* xi. 141 What I saw as I opened the door made me stop dead in my tracks. **1956** W. H. Whyte *Organization Man* xxi. 269 The boy from Shantytown was going to have less chance than ever of crossing over the tracks. **1965** E. Lambert *Long White Night* 12 His clothes clearly proclaimed him as a man who had been on the track, one of that tattered, aimless, wandering band which the Depression threw up. **1973** *Times* 19 May 6/6 'The Government may fall,' Mr Caulfield reportedly said, complaining: 'Everybody else is on track but you.' **1977** *Listener* 13 Oct. 478/2 Eva Duarte Peron.. came from the wrong side of the tracks. **1978** *Detroit Free Press* 16 Apr. F 3 (Advt.), We're looking for a professional who can keep us on track by making contributions that improve efficiency. **1978** *Time* 24 Apr. 20/2 If we can reach a salt agreement..that will begin to change the whole character of the relationship, put it on the right track again. **1979** B. L. C. Johnson *Pakistan* xiii. 199/1 The whole area has something of a 'beyond the tracks' character about it. **1984** *Gainesville* (Florida) *Sun* 3 Apr. 10 B/5 Three weeks ago, Mondale won the Illinois primary and said his comeback was on track.

III. 13. (sense *6 e) *track coach, event* (examples), *meet* (*U.S.*), *shirt, shorts, team*; also *track-mounted* adj.; **track-bed** = Bed *sb.* 12 e; **track circuit**, an electric circuit formed by the two rails of a railway line, so that the short-circuit produced by the presence of a train can be used to control the signals protecting it; so **track-circuit** *v. trans.*, to equip with or make into a track circuit; **track circuiting** *vbl. sb.*; **track-in**, the movement of a film or television camera towards the subject; **track-layer**, (*a*) (earlier example); (*b*) one who lays the trail in training dogs to track criminals; (*c*) a tractor or other vehicle which travels on endless tracks (sense 6 d above); **track-laying** *sb.*, (*a*) (earlier example); (*b*) in film editing, the putting together of the sound track that is to accompany a picture; *adj.*, (*b*) (of a vehicle) having endless tracks (sense 6 e above); **track lighting**, lighting in which the lights are fitted on to tracks, allowing variable positioning (see sense 6 g above); **track-man**, (*b*) a track athlete; **track record** (examples); also *fig.*, known facts about past achievements or behaviour taken as a guide to future performance; **track rod**, a rod that connects the two front wheels of a motor vehicle and transmits the steering action from the steering column to the stub axle of each wheel; **track-shoe**, (*b*) = *running shoe* s.v. *running *vbl. sb.* 17 a; **track suit**, a loose two-piece garment (elasticized at the wrists and ankles) worn by athletes while training and before and after contests; hence **track-suited** *a.*; **track system** *U.S. Educ.* (see sense 4 g above).

1962 *Mod. Railways* Apr. 278/2 The jack, which had been left projecting from the track bed, did considerable damage to the gear underneath the cars. **1978** W. Hjortsberg *Falling Angel* xliv. 217, I followed the trackbed of the downtown express, measuring my pace to the spacing of the ties. **1911** *Encycl. Brit.* XXV. 76/2 At points the track circuit is run through a circuit breaker, so that the 'opening' of the points sets the signal for the section. **1931** E. T. MacDermot *Hist. G.W.R.* II. 498 Track circuits, whereby the signals protecting an occupied section of line are electrically locked at Danger, were first introduced in August 1907. **1935** *Economist* 22 June 1419/1 If every mile of line in use were 'track-circuited'.. a blunder by a signalman would be impossible; no train could be signalled forward unless the line really was clear. **1983** *Internat. Railway Jrnl.* May 8/1 The Landskut box controls 125 signals, 83 points and 110 track circuits. **1931** *Times Lit. Suppl.* 10 Dec. 999/1 Exactly the same argument might be heard to-day against the introduction of track-circuiting or automatic train control. **1956** *Railway Mag.* Nov. 793/1 Track circuiting at both home and starting signals can be used to give additional safeguards. **1962** A. Lurie *Love & Friendship* x. 199 Hal Humphrey, the track coach. **1977** J. F. Fixx *Compl. Bk. Running* vii. 85 It has been attributed to..Lauri Pihkala, a pre-World War I Finnish runner, and George W. Orton, at one time Penn State's track coach. **1912** *Times* 29 June 13/1 In the track events, all of which must be held in the Stadium..there are 95 entries. **1928** *Daily Sketch* 10 Aug. 2/4 There are bound to be fine finishes in the international track events. **1973** C. Bonington *Next Horizon* ix. 138 He had always been a brilliant natural athlete, excelling at almost every game and track event in which he took part. **1954** *Encounter* Aug. 53/1 Her abject jealous misery has been..conveyed by the camera's slow track-in to close-up of her anguished face. **1961** *Listener* 2 Nov. 716/1 A track-in suggests an increase in intensity. *a* **1861** T. Winthrop *Life in Open Air* (1863) 234 'Wanted, experienced track-layer!' was the word along the files. **1928** *Daily Express* 19 Sept. 2 Coastguards..acted as track-layers for the open police dog trials. **1934** Webster s.v., The tracklayer is used especially where tractive conditions are poor. **1952** J. W. Day *New Yeomen of England* viii. 96 In all there are 45 tractors (including 6 track-layers), 4 moto-carts for hauling and odd jobs, and 8 combine harvesters. **1971** *Power Farming* Mar. 13/2 Use of the tracklayer was now mainly restricted to heavy clay soils and industrial duties where its higher costs could still be justified. **1857** R. G. Payne *Rep. Condition Railroads Tennessee* 7 The track-laying is progressing from the southern end of the road. **1920** *Sci. Amer.* 2 Oct. 335 (*caption*) Typical tractors of the wheeled and track-laying species now employed for agricultural and other purposes. **1957** *Times Lit. Suppl.* 27 Dec. 781/3 They resemble (as it says on driving licences) a 'track-laying vehicle steered by its tracks'. **1957** Manvell & Huntley *Technique Film Music* iv. 178 The four technical branches of film production, i.e., design..photography..sound.. and editing (including assembly cutting, track-laying, laboratory liason, and post-production processes). **1962** A. Nisbett *Technique Sound Studio* xii. 206 Track-laying systems, where a whole series of tracks can be recorded individually on a single broad tape and then scanned together. **1972** *Times* 30 Nov. 18/1 Ceiling mounted spotlights and..track lighting systems. **1980** D. Francis *Reflex* iii. 41 In the sitting room, white walls.. track lighting. **1972** *N.Y. Times* 4 June 4/2 An illegal water-jump area has impaired the credibility of the three fastest steeplechase performances by American trackmen. **1977** *Evening Gaz.* (Middlesbrough) 11 Jan. 14/2 Teesside Clarion's top trackmen..were among those honoured at their club's annual presentation in the Normanby Hotel last Friday. **1904** *Cap & Gown* (Chicago) IX. 215 Track Meets and Scores, 1903... Second Annual Interscholastic Meet, at Marshall Field. **1976** *Columbus* (Montana) *News* 27 May 1/4 Absarokee and Columbus scored first and second respectively in the Southern C Divisional track meet on May 20. **1977** *Time* 21 Feb. 34/2 He would be inclined to forgo continued development of a mobile U.S. nuclear missile launcher (the MX) if the Soviet Union will abandon deployment of its track-mounted launcher (the SS-20). **1951** *Publ. Amer. Dial. Soc.* XVI. 66 *Track record*, the best time made by a horse over a certain distance on a certain track. **1965** *Life* 15 Jan. 56 A/1 Wilder has had a series of extremely successful pictures... We were betting on his track record that this one would be too. **1972** *Observer* 30 Apr. 12/5 The airlines have over the years had enough confidence in our track record to be perfectly happy about this procedure. **1974** *Spartanburg* (S. Carolina) *Herald* 18 Apr. C 2/5 Charles Mathis..set a new track record at Northwestern with a 149′6″ in the discus. **1976** *Milton Keynes Express* 25 June 51/3 Houghton Rip.. came fourth behind the Irish dog, whose track record was smashed by last year's Derby consolation winner Shamrock Point. **1976** *Time* 20 Dec. 17/1 A lot of the women candidates..have no management track records to be judged on. So they keep being passed over. **1983** *Daily Tel.* 23 Mar. 21 The Trustee Savings Banks, which plan to go public towards the end of next year, badly need to establish a good track record on profits. **1926** *Amer. Speech* I. 686/2 The following list of automobile terms in American and English nomenclature appeared in a 'special' from the Boston News Bureau early in the present year... [American] Tie rod [English] Track rod. **1930** *Engineering* 12 Sept. 326/3 Each pair of steering pivots is connected by a track rod at right angles to the chassis centre line. **1976** *Flintshire Leader* 10 Dec. 25/10 (Advt.), New springs for Land Rovers and most cars, 1935–70, towing brackets,..new kingpins, trackrods. **1977** J. F. Fixx *Compl. Bk. Running* x. 121, I bought them all inexpensive track shoes and University of Southern California track shirts just like Daddy's. **1978** *Detroit Free Press* 5 Mar. A 19/1 (Advt.), Juvenile to teen male track shirts, hooded sweatshirts. **1961** Webster, Track shoe. **1970** G. Jackson *Let.* 28 May in *Soledad Brother* (1971) 261 We're wearing track shoes. **1983** 'J. le Carré' *Little Drummer Girl* ii. 45 Kids in summer rig and track shoes. **1946** C. McCullers *Member of Wedding* I. 4 She wore a pair of blue track shorts. **1974** *Index-Jrnl.* (Greenwood, S. Carolina) 23 Apr. 7/6 Smith describes his actions as mild, temporary schizophrenia, or Clark Kent in track shorts. 'When I pole vault..I'm like a complete different person.' **1955** R. Bannister *First Four Minutes* 46 Not having had the importance of warming up explained to me I did not wear a track suit. **1980** *Times Lit. Suppl.* 7 Nov. 1258/4 His..wife..memorably fetching in her pink towelling track suit. **1965** R. T. Bickers *Scent of Mayhem* iv. 42 His sweaty, track-suited figure. **1907** *St. Nicholas* (N.Y.) XXXIV. 693/2 Hammond has a track team, but we have n't. **1976** *Billings* (Montana) *Gaz.* 30 June 7-E/1 Aams was also an outstanding performer on the basketball and track teams at East Bay.

track, *v.*[1] Add: **I. 1. d.** Also (*U.S.*) of a horse: to walk with the fore and hind feet placed in the same straight line. Of the feet: to be placed thus.

1857 R. Glisan *Jrnl. Army Life* (1874) xxvii. 382, I observed..that he does not 'track' (step his hind foot straight after the fore one). **1897** E. Hough *Story of Cowboy* 34 His feet, in the vernacular of the range, do not 'track', but cross each other weakly.

e. *intr. Electronics.* Of a tunable circuit or component: to vary in frequency in the same way as another circuit or component, so that the frequency difference between them remains constant.

1932 [implied at *tracking *vbl. sb.*[1] 3]. **1939** [see *padder *sb.*[2] 3]. **1948** Slurzberg & Osterheld *Essent. Radio* vi. 271 In order to obtain the maximum fidelity, selectivity, and sensitivity..it is necessary that all the tuning circuits track together over the entire range of the receiver. **1975** D. G. Fink *Electronics Engineers' Handbk.* XIII. 40 The tuned circuits must track across the frequency band, and in the case of the superheterodyne, tracking of the local oscillator is necessary so that a constant frequency difference..is maintained.

f. *trans.* To follow the course of (a distant object) by means of a telescope, radar, or the like.

1950 in Webster Add. **1959** *Listener* 18 June 1057/2 The Jodrell Bank telescope and the smaller one at Bedford, Massachusetts, were tracking the moon. **1966** M. Woodhouse *Tree Frog* viii. 64 In order to track it [*sc.* a pilotless plane]..during flight trials..we've had to fit travelling wave reflection amplifiers under the wings. **1971** *Daily Tel.* 20 July 8/8 Every commercial and military aircraft flying over Europe can be tracked by radar. **1976** *Nature* 16 Sept. 216/1 An ITT FW 130 (S20) photomultiplier..was mounted about 40 feet above the ground on a radar dish programmed to track the star.

g. *intr.* To enjoy a rapport or 'get on' *with* another person; to take things in. *U.S.*

1972 *Newsweek* 17 July 22/3 He tracks better with reporters than did his phlegmatic predecessor. **1977** C. McFadden *Serial* (1978) xvi. 38/1 She's practically out of her mind. Like, she isn't even tracking. **1978** J. L. Hensley *Killing in Gold* ix. 116 Mom didn't track very well after the second stroke... It didn't mean anything to her any more.

2. c. (Earlier and later examples.) Also, *to track up* (a floor, etc.); to bring *in* (dirt, etc.) on one's feet (also const. preps.). Also *fig.*

1838 C. Gilman *Recoll. Southern Matron* xviii. 127 Miss Neely, one buckra woman want for track up all de clean floor. **1866** *Harper's Mag.* Jan. 271/2 The snow had been tracked in till it lay pretty thick on the floor. **1901** Merwin & Webster *Calumet 'K'* vi. 117 There's going to be a law passed about tracking mud inside the railing. **1915** *Century Mag.* Aug. 496/2 A good live boy..is a drug in the market. There seems to be a general feeling that they track in dirt. **1919** J. Reed *Ten Days that shook World* i. 11 The mud underfoot was deep, slippery and clinging, tracked everywhere by heavy boots. **1944** S. Bellow *Dangling Man* 100 Tracked your mat up. I'm sorry. **1950** M. Mead *Male & Female* xvi. 338 Floors do not need to be polished so often when there are no children's feet to track them up. **1980** R. Hill *Killing Kindness* ix. 87, I was trying not to track my work into the house too much. **1981** *Farmstead Mag.* Winter 50/2 Birds really use the trees to nest in, and small rabbits revel in tracking up fresh snow.

3. a. (U.S. examples.)

1843 R. Carlton *New Purchase* xxvii. 254 I'll track round a little—I wants any how to go over to the post-office. **1868** *Putnam's Mag.* June 670/1 We tracked through the dirty streets till we got to the house.

c. *Austral.* To keep company *with* (a person of the opposite sex, esp. a woman); *to track square* (see quot. 1919).

1916 C. J. Dennis *Songs of Sentimental Bloke* 51, I swear I'll never track wiv 'er no more. **1919** W. H. Downing

Digger Dialects 50 *Track square*, to pursue an amorous enterprise with honorable intentions. **1926** K. S. Prichard *Working Bullocks* 47 Combo's what they call a man tracks round with a gin in the nor'-west. **1933** N. Lindsay *Saturdee* 239 Who are you trackin' with now? **1949** A. Marshall *How Beautiful are thy Feet* 64 He wants me to track square with him. To look at him you'd never think he could talk seriously. **1954** T. A. G. Hungerford *Sowers of Wind* 270, I bet it's that cross-eyed harlot he's been tracking with. **1964** G. Johnston *My Brother Jack* 161 He's been at me for years about how irresponsible I am, and the first time I come back with a girl I'm tracking square with, I get hoisted!

d. Of a stylus or pick-up: to follow the wave-form of a record groove. Also *trans.*, with the record, the groove, or the sound represented as obj.

1929 Wilson & Webb *Mod. Gramophones* vi. 129 As the needle tracks in the groove it is gradually worn to a chisel point. **1937** *Electronics* Nov. 21/2 The test was stopped when the records had been played 185 times each and the quality had become very bad indeed. The needles still would track the grooves, however, showing that complete breakdown of the walls had not yet occurred. **1850** *Audio Engin.* Aug. 15/2 In ordinary recorded music, the inability of the stylus to track at high groove curvatures leads to objectionable high-frequency distortion. **1957** *Records & Recording* Nov. 20 It is these grooves which must be tracked with absolute accuracy by the pickup needle. **1977** *Gramophone* June 10/2 (Advt.), This cartridge successfully tracks all types of records at forces even lighter than one gram. **1978** *Ibid.* June 128/3 There is a solo flute passage which could only just about be tracked at 1 gram. **1981** *Popular Hi-Fi* Mar. 7/4 The DT1 tracks exceptionally well and retrieves more informations from the grooves.

e. Of a film or television camera, or its operator: to move (esp. *back* or *in*) in relation to the subject being filmed.

1959 *Listener* 30 Apr. 772/1 After we had seen Mac in close-up, the camera suddenly tracked right away. **1960** N. Kneale *Quatermass II* ii. 61 Track in on him fast. Fade in end music. **1961** G. Millerson *Technique Television Production* iii. 26 If..he is tracking backwards through an archway at too high an elevation, he might severely injure himself, as more than one cameraman has found. **1962** *Movie* June 5/2 Track into close-up of irrelevant detail; cut to close-up irrelevant detail of new setting; track out and begin sequence. **1975** *Radio Times* 22 May 66/3 Tufano starts a close shot on the broken walls of a bombed house. He then tracks back and pans across the blitzed street.

III. 5. *Comb.* **track-ball** *Computers*, a VDU input device in the form of a small ball that is rotated in a holder to move a cursor on the screen; = *tracker ball* s.v. *TRACKER[1] 2.

1969 M. H. Mehr in *Internat. Symposium Man-Machine Systems* V, Positioning to 0·1% of the screen diameter could be accomplished in 3–4 seconds which compares favorably with the published track ball data. **1972** *Acta Crystallogr.* A. XXVIII. S 253/2 The operator can interact with the display by means of a track-ball cursor. **1983** *Austral. Personal Computer* Aug. 60/2 Lisa's engineers are sometimes criticised for selecting the mouse rather than other quick data input devices—notably the trackball, touch-screen and light-pen.

trackability (trækăbi·lĭti). [f. Track *v.*[1] + Ability; cf. *-bility.] The ability of a stylus or cartridge to track adequately (*track *v.*[1] 3 d).

1972 Anderson & Jenrick in *Jrnl. Audio Engin. Soc.* XX. 162 (*heading*) A practical high-frequency trackability test for phono pickups. **1978** *Gramophone* May 1970/1 Not only does it check trackability, but also the tone-arm resonance over the frequency range of 4–12Hz.

tracked (trækt), *a.* [f. Track *sb.* + -ed[2].] **1.** Of a vehicle: having endless tracks (*track *sb.* 6 d).

1926 *Westm. Gaz.* 26 Jan. 6/2 'Tracked' vehicles, or, as most people would say,..'caterpillar' or roadless tractors. **1950** *Times* 17 Feb. 8/5 With a few bulldozers and grabs and tracked trucks, even the intimidating Snowdonian slate-tips could be put on the road to recovery. **1979** *Daily Tel.* 3 Dec. 3/1 A tracked armoured personnel carrier.

2. Of a hovercraft: confined to a fixed track.

1967 *Jane's Surface Skimmer Systems 1967–68* 52 (*heading*) Tracked air cushion vehicles. **1971** *New Scientist* 24 June 756/1 This time it is the £3·5 million tracked hovercraft project which is coming under attack.

tracker[1]. Add: **2.** Special Combs.: **tracker ball** *Computers* = *track-ball* s.v. *track *v.*[1] 5; **tracker dog**, a dog trained to pick up and follow a scent, esp. a police dog trained to track people; cf. *sniffer dog* s.v. *sniffer 3 b.

1969 *Advance in Electronics: Proc. 16th Electronics Congr.* 484 The input devices..vary from scheme to scheme but common ones are keyboards, light pens and tracker balls. **1982** *Internat. Conf. Radar-82* (Inst. Electr. Engineers) 306/1 A Maintrace Section..distributes the radar signals to the displays and an Intertrace Section..generates the video maps and provides interactive keyboard/tracker-ball facilities. **1962** 'J. le Carré' *Murder of Quality* iv. 51 We've got to rely on laboratories, tracker dogs and nation-wide searches. **1979** *Sunday Express* 16 Dec. 11 Police with tracker dogs will resume the search to-day for farmer's wife. **1984** *Times* 27 Feb. 8/1 Searching for..explosions with the eagerness of a tracker dog from the bomb squad.

tracking, *vbl. sb.* (In Dict. s.v. Track *v.*[1].) Add: **I. 1.** (Further examples, corresp. to senses of *track *v.*[1])

1932 *Jrnl. Sci. Instruments* IX. 288 The best tracking conditions are reached by choosing the position of the axis about which the tone arm rotates by the method shown. **1937** *Discovery* Nov. 330/2 The operators of the electron cameras receive their instructions through telephones, so that they can advance or withdraw their cameras (tracking) or swing them sideways (panning) as planned by the producer. **1958** *Listener* 4 Dec. 908/2 The manufacture of the satellite and its instruments, with the associated tracking and computing systems. **1959** *Cambr. Rev.* 24 Oct. 73/1 The technique in this section cuts right across Bazin's distinction between classic Eisenstein montage, and more realistic modern methods of tracking, panning, and so on, on a wide screen. **1969** *Times* 16 July 4/1 The radio tracking instruments spread around the globe for keeping in continuous contact with the spacecraft. **1975** G. J. King *Audio Handbk.* viii. 184 Tracking ability thus takes account of the compliance, effective tip mass and mechanical resistance.

II. Specific senses. **2.** The formation or occurrence of conducting paths for electricity over the surface of an insulating material.

1931 H. Warren *Electr. Insulating Materials* iii. xix. 239 The surface carbonization, or what is commonly called 'tracking'.., of these materials is their most serious electrical handicap. **1945** *Electronic Engin.* XVII. 600 Moisture..very soon causes..tracking between the connecting tags. **1967** M. Chandler *Ceramics in Mod. World* iv. 115 The electrical properties that matter most are high volume and surface resistivity, high puncture strength, and good tracking resistance. **1970** K. Ball *Fiat 600, 600D Autobook* iii. 34/1 Examine the distributor cap for cracks or signs of carbonisation (tracking).

3. *Electronics.* The maintenance of a constant difference in frequency between two or more connected circuits or components.

1932 *Electronics* Aug. 250/1 (*caption*) Deviation from exact tracking at various intermediate frequencies. **1971** [see *padder *sb.*[2] 3]. **1975** [see *track *v.*[1] 1 e].

4. *U.S. Educ.* = *streaming *vbl. sb.* f.

1967 *N.Y. Times* 23 June 36 Tracking can be a useful educational device if tests are frequently administered and if movement from one track to another is made easy. **1974** *Florida FL Reporter* XIII. 29/3 School would simplify their task if they could separate those students who want to learn to speak the new dialect from those who do not... This would not be a matter of 'tracking'.

III. 5. Special Combs.: **tracking error**, the error that occurs in gramophone reproduction when the tone-arm is pivoted, so that in general the axis of the cartridge is not in line with the groove; **tracking shot** *Cinemat.* and *Television*, a shot during which the camera tracks (*track *v.*[1] 3 e); **tracking snow** *N. Amer.*, snow sufficiently deep to enable hunters to track animals; **tracking station**, an establishment set up to track objects in the sky; **tracking weight**, the weight with which a stylus rests on a gramophone record.

1924 *Gramophone* Sept. 129/2 The 'tracking error'. **1930** *Wireless World* 26 Mar. 340/1 The mean between the highest and lowest deviations..gives a slightly smaller maximum tracking error. **1975** *Gramophone* Jan. 1424/1 Tracking error at all points across the record was within 2° overall. **1940** *Chambers's Technical Dict.* 857/1 Tracking shot. **1957** Manvell & Huntley *Technique Film Music* ii. 33 There follows a continuous tracking shot lasting in all for 2 minutes 22 seconds. **1973** D. Osmond-Smith tr. *Bettetini's Lang. & Technique of Film* ii. 95 Another narratively effective element is the 'tracking shot'; this consists of moving the whole cine-camera on a mechanical device known as a 'dolly'. **1971** W. Hillen *Blackwater River* ii. 17 Water running, little hope for tracking-snow. **1981** *Northeast Woods & Waters* Jan. 12/1 Coos County showed the largest increase (87%) where sportsmen had tracking snow for the entire season. **1963** *Ann. Reg. 1962* 445 The tracking station in Great Britain held the signal for only a few moments. **1972** *Daily Tel.* 14 Apr. 4/6 The TV signal is received from the Moon..at the Goldstone tracking station in the Mojave Desert. **1978** G. Greene *Human Factor* iv. i. 197 America maintains a guided missile tracking station and a space tracking station in the Republic. **1962** A. Nisbett *Technique Sound Studio* iv. 87 Recordings played under a tracking weight of about 1½ oz. were reckoned to have a life of about a dozen playings. **1978** *Lancashire Life* Sept. 131/1 The pick-up arm itself should have an adjustment to enable you to set the correct tracking weight for the cartridge.

tracklement (træ·k'lmĕnt). [Origin obscure. Dorothy Hartley claimed to have invented this word. She also claimed that her use of it in this sense was a *spec.* application of an older word, prob. *dial.*, meaning 'appurtenances, impedimenta', but no evidence of such a word has been found.] An article of food, *spec.* a jelly, prepared to accompany meat.

1954 D. Hartley *Food in England* v. 161 (*heading*) Mutton tracklements and condiment. **1959** *Times* 24 Aug. 11/4 A pleasantly astringent, smokily flavoured jelly as a 'tracklement' with mutton. **1971** R. Condon *Vertical Smile* (1973) xxxvii. 259 A saddle of lamb..delicate enough to accept only such a tracklement as rowan jelly. **1978** *Observer* 26 Feb. 35/9 Various salads and tracklements are included in the cold table.

trackster (træ·kstəɹ). *U.S.* [f. Track *sb.* + -ster.] A track athlete.

1974 *Hartsville* (S. Carolina) *Messenger* 22 Apr. 3A/6 The Hartsville High School Cindermen..won a 67-63 victory over the Hillcrest High tracksters. **1979** *Tucson Mag.* Apr. 70/2 The University of Arizona tracksters host two triangular meets at the Stadium.

tract, *sb.*[1] Add: **I. 3. b.** *Tracts for the Times*: also used in *sing.*, with small initials, of any literary work put out to meet a particular need of the times.

1927 A. H. McNeile *Introd. N.T.* 95 The Tübingen conception of the book [*sc.* the Acts of the Apostles] as a tract for the times mediating between the Judaic and the Pauline factions. **1979** E. H. Gombrich *Sense of Order* ii. 41 As a tract for the times the *Seven Lamps* failed to achieve Ruskin's aim of bringing the conditions of the Middle Ages back to industrialized England.

c. *tract society* (earlier example).

1760 Pratt in J. Adams *Wks.* (1850) II. 97, I should be very sorry to have the Tract Society dissolved.

tract, *sb.*[3] Add: **3. b.** (*a*) (Earlier and later examples.) Cf. *fibre tract* s.v. *fibre *sb.* 8.

1681 S. Pordage tr. *Willis's Remaining Med. Wks.: Treat. No. 4: Anat. of Brain* xiii. 101 Out of the same tract of the oblong Marrow, lesser paths are carried outwardly, here and there, by particular Nerves, arising from the same, within the Skull. **1803** C. Bell *Anat. Human Body* III. i. iii. 115 It [*sc.* the olfactory nerve] takes its origin by three medullary tracts. **1959** W. Andrew *Textbk. Compar. Histol.* xiv. 566 As one ascends the vertebrate scale, the bundles of white matter or 'tracts' make their appearance running through the gray. **1974** M. C. Gerald *Pharmacol.* x. 189 Ascending nerves transmit sensory impulses up the spinal cord, whereas descending tracts send instructions to effector cells via motor fibers.

c. *U.S.* A plot of land with definite boundaries, esp. one for development; hence, an estate. So *tract home, house.*

1912 *Oregonian* 20 Oct. iv. 6/2 Trading in farm land last week was devoted chiefly to small tracts. There were, however, several large parcels. **1940** S. L. McMichael *Selling Real Estate* (rev. ed.) i. 4 An owner who had a tract of land ripe for development would call in a surveyor. **1954** F. L. Wright *Natural House* i. 108 The plan..was for a housing project on a 100 acre tract near Pittsfield. **1963** D. Hughes *Expendable Man* iii. 72 Raw green tract houses seemed to have taken over the country-side. **1972** Tract home [see *realty[2] 4]. **1973** *N.Y. Law Jrnl.* 31 Aug. 1/7 The defendants..were developing a tract with cooperative apartments to be constructed on one part. **1977** *New Yorker* 6 June 99/1 Most of his customers live in tract houses that have tiny bedrooms. **1979** *Tucson* (Arizona) *Citizen* 20 Sept. 1B/1 The Lopezes gave up a nice home on the Northwest Side on an acre lot for a nice house on a cramped lot in one of the tracts that have sprung up in south Tempe during the last two years. **1980** *Times Lit. Suppl.* 19 Sept. 1020/4 An amiable, moderately licentious fellow who readily settles down..in a newly built tract home.

traction. Add: **1. e.** *Med.* A sustained pull applied to a part of the body to maintain the positions of fractured bones following reduction of the fracture; the state of being subjected to such a pull; so *in traction.*

1885 *Boston Med. & Surg. Jrnl.* CXII. 545/1 The high pulleys..were used, as before, for oblique traction from the knee bands. **1939** W. C. Campbell *Operative Orthopedics* ii. 97 The majority of apparatus for either suspension or traction of the upper extremity is extremely cumbersome. **1962** *Lancet* 13 Jan. 61/1 The patient had previously been treated by neck traction and by prolonged physiotherapy, without benefit. **1973** 'D. Shannon' *Spring of Violence* (1974) iii. 46 They had one leg in traction. **1981** R. S. H. Browne *Basic Facts in Orthopaedics* 95 Traction is used to overcome painful muscle spasm.

3*. *Physical Geogr.* The rolling and bumping of particles along the ground by a stream or the wind.

1914 G. K. Gilbert in *Prof. Papers U.S. Geol. Surv.* No. 86. 15 This second division of current transportation is called by certain French engineers *entraînement* but has received no name in English. Being in need of a succinct title, I translate the French designation..by the word *traction*. **1954** W. D. Thornbury *Princ. Geomorphol.* iii. 48 Traction involves the partial support of the material being transported by the buoyancy of the water or air but consists chiefly of the rolling, pushing, and dragging along of rock particles which are too large to be lifted. **1968** R. W. Fairbridge *Encycl. Geomorphol.* 319/2 Wind carries rock and organic debris by traction, saltation and suspension. **1972** R. J. Small *Study of Landforms* ii. 40 In areas where..chemical weathering is very active, streams may contain much of their load in solution, and traction, saltation and suspension may be correspondingly small.

4. traction motor, an electric motor designed for use in traction; **traction splint** (examples).

1900 Parshall & Hobart *Electr. Generators* i. 232 For satisfactory commutation, traction motors are designed with very high magnetisation at full load. **1950** *Times Rev. Industry* Sept. 25/1 The other two [locomotives] will have single-phase a.c. traction motors of special design. **1969** R. W. Smeaton *Motor Applic. & Maintenance Handbk.* viii. 5 Traction motors are very ruggedly built. **1935** *Sun* (Baltimore) 5 Apr. 3/2 The remedy..is use of 'traction splints', devices for automtically pulling ends of broken bones together and holding them. **1976** M. Machlin *Pipeline* xl. 443 He's got a bad break there. You'd better put that leg in a traction splint.

tractlet. (Earlier example.)

1889 E. Dowson *Let.* 27 Oct. (1967) 112, I have still a soul above tractlets.

tractor. Add: **2. c.** Also in mod. use, a rugged, powerful motor vehicle for drawing farm machinery, esp. one with large rear wheels and an elevated driving seat.

1905 *Sci. Amer. Suppl.* 4 Nov. 24948/3 At the recent show of the British Royal Agricultural Society great interest was centered in the Scott motor tractor... The motor in this tractor is a 24-horse-power..standard Aster engine. **1910** *Sci. Amer.* 15 Jan. 51/2 American motor tractors used for plowing and threshing usually develop from 12 to 35 horse-power. **1917** *Isle of Ely & Wisbech Advertiser* 28 Nov., This Tractor will operate on any land... It maintains a firm grip without injuring the lightest surfaces. **1932** [see *COMBINE *sb.* c]. **1958** *Economist* 11 Jan. 94/2 Antarctica's native inhabitants, on seeing the tractor marks in the snow, may well..ask themselves what will happen next. **1972** R. ADAMS *Watership Down* xix. 111 Few places are far from human noise—cars, buses, motor-cycles, tractors, lorries.

d. *Aeronaut.* An airscrew mounted at the front of an aircraft so as to exert a pull; an aircraft having this. Usu. *attrib.* (see sense 4 below). Cf. *PUSHER 2 c.

1903 *Work* 18 Apr. 171/1 A screw..working in front and acting as a tractor. **1909** [see *KITE *sb.* 3 c]. **1914** *Sphere* 7 Mar. 302/3 The Short and Sopwith tractors. **1980** H. F. KING *Sopwith Aircraft 1912–20* 20 Concerning the two early Naval Sopwith tractors, it seems worth recording that a demi-official drawing once existed showing just such a machine.

e. The driving section of an articulated lorry.

1926 *Encycl. Brit.* II. 987/2 Another combination for heavy merchandise transportation consisted of a road tractor, which was merely a foreshortened truck chassis, and a semi-trailer. **1951** [see *landing-gear* s.v. *LANDING *vbl. sb.* 8]. **1977** [see *PRIME MOVER 3]. **1982** *New Scientist* 11 Nov. 339/2 A lorry that has been loaded quite legally will tend to become overloaded on the drive axle (the rear of the two axles on the tractor) if it is gradually unloaded from the rear.

f. The mechanism that draws the paper through a printer.

1970 *U.S. Patent 3,511,354* 2 A switch is operated to reduce the speed of the tractor whenever..an excess of forms queued between the tractor and the stacker is such that a forms jam is imminent. **1983** *Austral. Micro-computer Mag.* Sept. 88/3 The TDS-13 daisy wheel printer handles paper up to 15in wide and has variable tractors and a friction platen to accommodate both continuous forms and sheets.

4. *attrib.* and *Comb.*, as (sense *2 c) *tractor-driver, -station; tractor-drawn, -mounted* adjs.; (sense *2 d) *tractor aircraft, airscrew, biplane, machine, monoplane, propeller, screw, seaplane*; **tractorman**, one who drives a farm tractor; **tractor-trailer** *U.S.*, an articulated lorry; cf. *trailer-truck* s.v. *TRAILER *sb.* 9.

1969 K. MUNSON *Pioneer Aircraft 1903–14* 110/1 A very early British Breguet bore the legend 'B. 3' on the rudder, the prefix letter indicating a tractor aircraft. **1932** *Rep. & Mem. Aeronaut. Res. Committee* No. 1522. 1 The magnitude of the retardation of air flow..has a mean value of 0·05 for a tractor airscrew in front of a medium body. **1912** S. F. WALKER *Aviation* iv. 28 In the later form of biplane, known as the tractor biplane, the engine and propeller are placed in front. **1969** K. MUNSON *Pioneer Aircraft 1903–14* 98/1 Antoinette III was the alternative title of the Ferber IX, a tractor biplane.. which was abandoned after only a few trial flights in.. 1908. **1943** J. S. HUXLEY *TVA* 43 (*caption*) Terraces, like the one being thrown up by a tractor-drawn grader.. retain from 85 to 90 per cent. of the rainfall. **1971** *Power Farming* Mar. 57/1 The machine is tractor-drawn. **1945** H. J. MASSINGHAM *Wisdom of Fields* x. 208 The tractor-driver despises the hard work of the older countryman and soon..he will need an elevator to lift him on his seat. **1969** R. BLYTHE *Akenfield* 17 Most modern farms need..a good tractor-driver or two, as once they needed good ploughmen. **1928** C. F. S. GAMBLE *Story North Sea Air Station* iv. 67 He was then of the opinion that 'pusher machines' were superior to 'tractor machines'. **1980** H. F. KING *Sopwith Aircraft 1912–20* 20 With a tractor aeroplane that was only a little faster than one of his motor-boats..Sopwith could hardly be content. **1946** J. W. DAY *Harvest Adventure* xiii. 210 Grover, the head tractorman. **1976** *Northumberland Gaz.* 26 Nov., Farmers appreciate the difficulties faced by shepherds and tractormen, he said. **1960** Tractor monoplane [see *MONOPLANE]. **1960** *Farmer & Stockbreeder* 12 Jan. 83/2 Tractor-mounted rotary tiller. **1979** *Internat. Pest Control* Nov./Dec. 139/1 Larger units to fit tractor-mounted spray booms. **1910** R. FERRIS *How it Flies* xx. 473 *Tractor propeller*, a propeller placed in front, so that it pulls the machine through the air, instead of pushing, or thrusting it from behind. **1910** C. C. TURNER *Aerial Navigation of To-day* viii. 127 In many monoplanes a single screw in front is used. It *pulls* the machine, and is often called a 'tractor' screw. **1969** K. MUNSON *Pioneer Aircraft 1903–14* 12 A Sopwith tractor seaplane. **1958** *New Statesman* 5 Apr. 423/2 The state is going to sell..some 20 billion roubles worth of farm machinery at present in the garages and parking lots of some 8,000 machine and tractor stations. **1965** M. MICHAEL tr. *J. Myrdal's Report from Chinese Village* (1967) I. 44 We hire one [tractor] from the tractor station at Yenan. **1949** Tractor-trailer [see *JACK-KNIFE *v.*]. **1977** D. E. WESTLAKE *Nobody's Perfect* xi. 143 A large tractor-trailer was..trying to back into position.

Hence **tra·ctored** *ppl. a.*, ploughed or cultivated by tractors; **tra·ctoring** *vbl. sb.*, activity involving a farm tractor. Also **tra·ctorcade** [*-CADE], a procession of tractors.

1949 E. COXHEAD *Wind in West* iii. 69 One [man] got out the tractor... When the tractoring was finished Les..got himself a fork from the byre. **1966** AUDEN *About House* 37 A house backed by orderly woods, Facing a tractored sugar-beet country. **1977** *Detroit Free Press* 11 Dec. 13-A/3 State and local police said there were no reports of traffic problems or arrests as a result of the so-called 'tractorcade'. **1981** *Observer* 22 Nov. 11/1 Towns throughout Northern Ireland will be choked with 'tractorcades' and marches.

tractotomy (træktǫ·tŏmi). *Surg.* [f. TRACT *sb.*[3] + -O + -TOMY.] An operation in which certain nerve tracts in the brain are severed or destroyed.

1938 O. SJÖQVIST in *Acta Psychiatrica* (Copenhagen) Suppl. 17. 95 Section of the tract could be performed without accessory lesions or other disadvantages to the patients... The term *trigeminal tractotomy* is proposed for this operation. **1974** R. M. KIRK et al. *Surgery* iv. 61/2 Patients with intractable pain may be helped by division of the posterior nerve roots, spinothalamic tractotomy, and prefrontal leucotomy. **1980** *Daily Tel.* 27 Nov. 3/2 The operations being carried out on the four patients.. was a stereo tractotomy, which involved the destruction of brain tissue at points the size of a pinhead by implanting radioactive particles.

trad (træd), *sb.* and *a. colloq.* **A.** *sb.* **1.** Short for *traditional jazz*. Also *attrib.*

1956 *Melody Maker* 12 May 8 (*heading*) The great trad battle. **1957** *Observer* 13 Oct. 3/5 Lyttelton, who found 'trad' (traditional jazz) became play-acting and a dead-end, has travelled far from the revival days. **1963** *Times* 4 May 13/3 In an ideal world all 'trad' bands would have a good gritty surface noise built in to give an air of authenticity to their records. **1965** G. MELLY *Owning-Up* xv. 194 In 1960 the Trad boom at its height, and a riot at Beaulieu. **1973** G. BEARE *Snake on Grave* viii. 41 The French like good trad and this was real old stuff out of..old Chicago. It was black men's music. **1979** *Globe & Mail* (Toronto) 14 June 13/6 Molson's Brewery is holding a Canadian Jazz Festival July 21 and 22. Fourteen trad bands will take the stand. **1985** *Church Times* 8 Feb. 6/3 A fresh cause for barriers to be raised between the trads and the trendies.

2. Abbrev. of TRADITIONALIST.

1956 *Melody Maker* 12 May 8/4 The 'trads' belong to a strange sort of exclusive society. **1957** S. TRAILL *Concerning Jazz* 11 Those devoted to the older form of the music are referred to by the monstrous and unlovely nickname 'trads', (short for traditionalists). **1960** *Guardian* 11 Jan. 5/2 The ski world is divided to-day between 'trads' and 'modernists'.

B. *adj.* Abbrev. of TRADITIONAL *a.*

1958 *Spectator* 25 July 133/2 A raucous trad-jazz group struck up 'Basin Street Blues'. **1964** *Harper's Bazaar* Nov. 110/2 For people who like to furnish as trad as possible. **1967** E. GRIERSON *Crime of one's Own* xiii. 108 What's going to happen to dear Dave when even his.. dirty books seem tradder than *The Times'* fourth leader? **1974** C. O. BUCHANAN in R. C. D. Jasper *Eucharist Today* ii. 24 The Commission remained resolutely 'trad' until the Liturgical Conference of February 1966. **1981** *N.Y. Times Sunday Mag.* 4 Apr. 90/2 The British fashion press reports London's new look is that of the 'trad English gentleman'.

tradable, *a.* Add: (Later examples.)

1960 *Farmer & Stockbreeder* 5 Jan. 4/1 For good milling qualities around 25s per cwt, delivered, was the tradeable basis. **1975** *Accountancy* Sept. 32/2 It [*sc.* government spending] signifies a transfer of resources from the tradeable to the non-tradeable sector, which would literally kill the productive section of the economy.

Hence **trad(e)abi·lity**.

1979 B. BROWN *Money Hard & Soft on Internat. Currency Markets* 2 A *sine qua non* of currency hardness is free tradability. Residents of the country of issue are permitted to buy and sell a freely tradable currency for foreign exchange. **1983** *Times* 16 Aug. 14/1 The BNOC argument is that Brent crude has a higher 'tradability'.

trade, *sb.* Add: **I. 5. a.** *in trade*, following a mercantile occupation, *spec.* that of a shop-keeper.

1813 [in Dict.]. **1816** JANE AUSTEN *Emma* II. vii. 118 On the other hand, they were of low origin, in trade, and only moderately genteel. **1865** TROLLOPE *Can you forgive Her?* II. xv. 113 There was a little prejudice, because of his being in trade. **1932** LADY DUFF GORDON *Discretions & Indiscretions* v. 60, I could never be presented at Court, because I was in 'trade'. **1953** M. SHARP *Gipsy in Parlour* xii. 125 His father was in trade, and Frederick snubbed him. **1974** 'W. HAGGARD' *Kinsmen* x. 98 When he'd made a great fortune Duncan Gregg had gone up the ladder a little. But not very much, he was still in trade. **1979** A. MCCOWEN *Young Gemini* 53 Living in the Royal Borough of Tunbridge Wells, my father was made to feel over-conscious of being 'in trade'.

6. a. (Earlier examples of the sense 'those engaged in the liquor trade'.)

1846 H. BRETT *Let.* 17 Oct. in *Licensed Victuallers' Guide & Almanack* (1848) 2, I enclose a copy of the Permit..suggesting that a reprint of it in your Almanack would be highly appreciated by the Trade. **1868** *Era Almanack* (Advt. Suppl.), Licensed Victuallers' Protection Society, instituted October, 1833, for the protection of the person and property of the licensed victualler, and for the promotion of the best interests of the trade.

c. Prostitution. *slang.* [Cf. TRADER 1 b.]

1680 OLDHAM in Rochester *Poems* 122 He Heav'n, one large Seraglio, made, Each Goddess, turn'd a glorious Punk, o' th' Trade, And all that sacred place, Was filled with Bastard Gods, of his own Race! **1937** PARTRIDGE *Dict. Slang* 905/2 *The trade* is prostitution: late C. 18–19. **1962** K. A. PORTER *Ship of Fools* 33 Two inordinately dressed-up young Cuban women, frankly ladies of trade, had been playing cards together in the bar for an hour before the ship sailed.

d. The Submarine Service of the Royal Navy. *slang.*

1916 KIPLING *Sea Warfare* 97 No one knows how the title of 'The Trade' came to be applied to the Submarine Service. **1942** G. HACKFORTH-JONES *One-One-One* xviii. 169, I remember in 1919 listening to and looking at the young submarine captains, most of whom had served their four years of war in the 'Trade'. **1982** A. MELVILLE-ROSS *Trigger* xv. 161 It had been tacitly established in 'The Trade' that you did not mourn friends... The Submarine Service referred to itself as 'The Trade'.

e. The Secret Service. *slang.*

1966 'A. HALL' *9th Directive* xviii. 170 'How long,' I asked her, 'have you been in the trade?'..'Three years, on active ops.' **1977** J. GARDNER *Werewolf Trace* x. 87 Heather had that smart plummy voice which spoke of a cut-glass background. The kind of girl the trade enjoyed using: the kind they called a *lady*. **1977** *3rd Rep. R. Comm. Intelligence & Security: Abridged Findings* (Austral.) 4 In the trade, people talk of the 'intelligence cycle'.

9. *spec.* (*N. Amer.*), an exchange of players between two sports clubs or teams.

1913 *Outing* XLII. 133/1 My first big trade was a success. **1968** *Globe & Mail* (Toronto) 10 July 27/5 Riders made another trade, sending Larry De Graw and Bill Cline to Regina Roughriders for Tom Beynon. **1976** *National Observer* (U.S.) 12 June 14/3 The Yankees, who had been spying on Randolph for a year, picked him up last winter in a trade that sent Doc Medich to Pittsburgh for Randolph, Dock Ellis and Ken Brett.

11. b. A prostitute or pick-up used by a homosexual; a homosexual partner; also, such people collectively. *slang.*

1935, etc. [see *rough trade* s.v. *ROUGH *a.* 21 a]. **1941** G. LEGMAN in G. W. Henry *Sex Variants* II. 1177 Trade, generic for male prostitutes to homosexuals, or for heterosexuals to whom homosexuals prostitute themselves. **1968** *Globe & Mail Mag.* (Toronto) 13 Jan. 7/4 If a hustler is not himself homosexual, or maintains the belief that he is not, he is called 'trade'. **1969** *Jeremy* I. III. 23/1 These are men who because they are too old, or unattractive, cannot pick up free 'trade'. **1975** *Daily Tel.* 24 July 3/6 Many of the boys became male prostitutes... They became known as 'rent boys' and were also referred to as 'trade'.

13*. A trade paper or magazine of the entertainment world. orig. and chiefly *U.S.*

1960 G. MARX *Let.* 21 Mar. in *Groucho Lett.* (1967) 270, I assume the trades are shoved under your door each morning. **1969** [see *PLANT *sb.*[1] 7 b]. **1978** *Guardian* 11 Dec. 7/2 In Hollywood the two newspapers which report the entertainment industry are known simply as 'the trades'.

14. a. (sense 5) 'of or pertaining to a trade or calling', as *trade journal, magazine, paper, press*; 'caused by or arising out of one's trade', as *trade disease* (example); (sense 8) *trade agreement, association, attaché, balance, boom, delegation, depression, fair, figure* (usu. *pl.*), *relation* (earlier example), *ship* (later example), *token* [TOKEN *sb.* 11].

1934 WEBSTER, Trade agreement. **1940** *Economist* 23 Mar. 514/2 Three agreements between the British and Spanish Governments, a Loan Agreement, a Payments Agreement and a Trade Agreement, were signed in Madrid **1977** *Whitaker's Almanack 1978* 929/1 Portugal has signed a Trade Agreement with EEC. **1909** WEBSTER, Trade association. **1928** *Britain's Industr. Future* (Liberal Industr. Inquiry) II. viii. §3. 98 Trade Associations are Associations of Traders, Producers, or Employers. **1984** *Economist* 18 Feb. 22 The BBC, IBA and the ITV companies' trade association are all off to Dublin to discuss such an Anglo-Irish deal. **1970** 'D. HALLIDAY' *Dolly & Cookie Bird* vi. 79 The trade attaché moved a bit nearer. **1980** A. COPPEL *Hastings Conspiracy* xxxvii. 227 He was a trade attaché... He would know with whom to speak to provide a friend of the Soviet Union with friendship. **1909** WEBSTER Trade balance. **1928** *Britain's Industr. Future* (Liberal Industr. Inquiry) I. iii. §4. 26 The increased volume of imports, together with a diminished volume of exports, has made the visible trade balance much less favourable. **1984** *Times* 28 Nov. 13/7 Our trade balance sags under imports of consumer goods. **1925** *Scribner's Mag.* July 59 Nothing in the nature of a 'trade boom' could be discovered. **1928** Trade boom [see *trade cycle*, sense 15 below]. **1961** 'J. LE CARRÉ' *Call for Dead* ix. 93 If Blondie was a carrier, it is exceptional..that he should use a trade delegation as a staging post. **1978** R. V. JONES *Most Secret War* liii. 520 He had somehow made contact with the Russian Trade Delegation. **1928** Trade depression [see *trade cycle*, sense 15 below]. **1908** W. JAMES *Mem. & Stud.* (1911) xiii. 322 Priggishness is just like painter's colic or any other trade-disease. **1970** 'D. HALLIDAY' *Dolly & Cookie Bird* iv. 45 One was the commercial attaché..and the three others were straight from Moscow on a trade-fair excursion. **1927** *New Republic* 12 Oct. 194/2 The Washington government is alarmed at the growing hostility toward us in Central and South America, which is beginning to be reflected in our trade figures. **1975** in R. Crossman *Diaries* I. 40 The First Secretary and the Chancellor continued to grapple with the trade figures and to lament the unhappy state of the pound. **1878** *Brooklyn Monthly* Apr. 118/2 The editor of a certain trade journal in New York. **1910** H. G. WELLS *Hist. Mr. Polly* vii. 218 Every issue of every trade journal has its four or five columns of abridged bankruptcy proceedings. **1981** P. VAN GREENAWAY *'Cassandra' Bell* ii. 27 I'm a special features writer for a trade journal—cosmetics. **1907** *Electr. World* XLIX. 674/1 And in other cases space in the trade magazines has been used as before. **1973** E. MCGIRR *Bardel's Murder* iv. 90 Forrest's desk was..bare except for a trade magazine. **1903** E. L. SHUMAN *Practical Journalism* 100 Sometimes the easiest line of approach to these coveted posts is through the avenue of the trade paper or technical journal. **1918** A. BENNETT *Roll-Call* I. ix. 208 It was a chap from the *Builder*, or I wouldn't have seen him. Can't trifle with a trade paper, you know. **1971** *Guardian* 1 July 11/2 The trade papers try to introduce retailers to modern marketing. **1907** *Electr. World* XLIX. 674/1 In some cases the house organ has taken the place of advertising in the trade press. **1973** 'D. HALLIDAY' *Dolly & Starry Bird* x. 147 She could announce it in the trade press. **1888** E. BELLAMY *Looking Backwards* xiii. 198 A basis of agreement as to what staples shall be accepted..for settlement of accounts, being a preliminary to trade relations. **1935** *Discovery* Feb. 61/2 Last January there were only 49 deep-sea square-rigged trade ships in the world. **1889** G. C. WILLIAMSON (*title*) Trade tokens issued in the seventeenth century. **1933** J. O. MANTON (*title*) Buckinghamshire trade tokens issued in the seventeenth century. **1971** J. R. S. WHITING *Trade Tokens* 11 Broadly speaking I have kept to the strict definition of the term *trade token* (tokens issued for trading purposes, ie as currency).

15. trade allowance (earlier example); **trade binding** (see quot. 1971); **trade book,** a book published by a commercial publisher and intended for general readership; **trade card,** a tradesman's card bearing his name, the designation of his trade, and place of business; **trade counter,** an area in a shop or business where sales are made only to members of the trade; **trade cycle,** a recurring alternation of a period of increased economic activity with one of reduced activity; **trade discount,** a discount allowed by one trader to another, usually one in the same kind of occupation; also *fig.*; **trade dispute,** any dispute between employers and workers, or between different groups of workers, that is connected with the employment or non-employment of any person, with the terms or conditions of employment, or with certain related matters; **trade edition,** (*b*) an edition of a book intended for general sale through bookshops, in contrast to special editions or those sold through book clubs or specialist suppliers; **trade effluent,** effluent produced in the course of a trade or industry; any effluent other than domestic sewage; **trade gap,** the extent by which a country's imports exceed its exports; cf. *trade surplus* below; **trade language:** delete † and add later examples; **trade-last** *U.S.*, a compliment offered in exchange for one that is directed towards the speaker; also, in weakened sense, a compliment, whether reciprocal or not; **trade mission,** a mission sent to another country to promote trade with it; **trade plate,** a temporary number-plate for an unlicensed vehicle; usu. *pl.*; **trade price** (earlier example); **trade-rat,** a pack rat (lit. and fig.); **trade reduction** = *trade-discount* above; **trade-route** (earlier example); **trade-sale** (earlier example); **trade secret,** a device or technique used in a particular trade or (*transf.*) occupation and giving an advantage because not generally known; **trade show** *Cinemat.*, a private showing of a new film to the trade, before release; so **trade-show** *v. trans.*; **trade surplus,** the extent by which a country's exports exceed its imports; cf. *trade gap* above; **trade term,** an expression largely confined to a particular trade; **trade test** (see quot.); hence **trade-test** *v.*, to subject to or carry out a trade test; **trade war,** a situation in which governments act aggressively in international markets to promote their own countries' trading interests; **trade waste** = *trade effluent* above; **trade-weighted** *a.*, esp. of exchange rates, weighted in relation to the importance of the trade conducted with the various countries included.

1837 DICKENS *Let.* ? 21 Apr. (1965) I. 250, I want at the usual trade allowance..a complete set of the Standard Novels up to this time. **1952** J. B. OLDHAM *English Blind-Stamped Bindings* 3 Copies already bound in what are usually called 'trade bindings'. **1971** L. M. HARROD *Librarians' Gloss.* (ed. 3) 645 *Trade binding.* 1. The binding in which a publisher issues a book... 2. Plain calf or sheep bindings which were used in England by publishers from the fifteenth–eighteenth centuries... Until the nineteenth century, purchasers usually bought books unbound or enclosed in wrappers. **1962** Y. MALKIEL in Householder & Saporta *Probl. Lexicography* 9 Other short word-lists..include,..on the tradebook market, glossaries accompanying contemporary novels and short stories. **1977** *Globe & Mail* (Toronto) 17 May 16/7 Last year 39 percent of the company's sales came from elementary school texts, 7 per cent from university texts and 19 per cent from trade books for the general public. **1927** B. C. LANDAUER (*title*) Early American trade cards. **1979** *Early Music* Oct. 475/1 The instrument was certainly rebuilt by Taskin in 1783–4, as attested by his two inscriptions, his trade card glued inside the bentside, and his characteristic workmanship throughout. **1977** *Wandsworth Borough News* 7 Oct. 21/3 (Advt.), Young person required by Builders' Merchants in Battersea to assist on trade counter and learn trade. **1979** P. WAY *Sunrise* vi. 61 David Marriott entered the newspaper building, via the trade-counter door. **1928** *Britain's Industr. Future* (Liberal Industr. Inquiry) v. xxviii. §2. 411 The trade booms..and trade depressions..which were so prominent a feature of the pre-war 'trade cycle'. **1976** *Scotsman* 20 Nov. 3/3 The industry was notoriously vulnerable to the trade cycle, and, at present, world supply of shipbuilding capacity was about twice the level of world demand. **1898** G. VAN DE LINDE *Bookkeeping & Other Papers* 414 *Trade Discount*, see 'Cash Discount'. **1901** *Windsor Mag.* Dec. 199/2 Barclay is simply a surly brute, I never liked him, so you can take the usual trade discount off my estimate. **1977** C. RUNDLE *Accountancy for Everyone* vi. 54 The same rate of trade discount must be taken off the return value as was allowed off the original price. **1875** *Act* 38 & 39 *Vict.* c. 86 §3 An agreement or combination by two or more persons to do or procure to be done any act in contemplation or furtherance of a trade dispute between employers and workmen shall not be indictable as a conspiracy if such act committed by one person would not be punishable as a crime. **1926** *Brit. Gaz.* 12 May 2/1 No trade dispute has been alleged or shown to exist in any of the unions affected except in the miners' case. **1980** *Illustr. London News* Mar. 19/2 In that case it was held that the interpretation of section 13 was subjective, and that a person was protected provided he honestly thought that his action might help one of the parties to a trade dispute to achieve their objectives, and did it for that reason. **1930** A. HUXLEY *Let.* 8 Mar. (1969) 332 With regard to subsequent unlimited trade editions, I imagine you wouldn't have the organization. **1949** R. CHANDLER *Let.* 3 May (1981) 174 Houghton Mifflin..want to publish a trade edition collection of my old stories. **1959** L. M. HARROD *Librarians' Gloss.* (ed. 2) 160 *Large paper copy*, or *edition*, an impression of a book printed on larger and better quality paper than the usual trade edition. **1930** *Engineering* 11 July 47/2 (*heading*) Trade effluents and sewers. **1976** *Eastern Even. News* (Norwich) 9 Dec. 16/6 (Advt.), The post will involve the routine implementation of trade effluent control. **1961** *Listener* 16 Nov. 816/1 Britain's 'trade gap' narrows during October. **1977** P. JOHNSON *Enemies of Society* v. 55 These fresh supplies of bullion bridged the trade-gap between West and East until western industry was sufficiently developed to mass-produce textiles for export. **1840** Trade language [see CHINOOK]. **1907**, etc. [see *MOBILIAN *sb.*]. **1937** M. COVARRUBIAS *Island of Bali* p. xxiii, Malay was the trade language between Balinese and foreigners. **1968** W. J. SAMARIN in J. A. Fishman *Readings Sociol. of Lang.* 661 *Trade language* (*langue de traité*) is usually used for some language not included among the world's majority languages and which is used by some people as a second language in commercial situations. **1891** KIPLING in *Author* July 42 Some day they'll be a Public—not a girl's school swapping Trade-lasts. **1895** *Inlander* Nov. 61 *Tradelast*, n., compliment. **1920** F. SCOTT FITZGERALD *This Side of Paradise* i. 12 It was based upon some 'trade-lasts' gleaned at dancing-school, to the effect that he was 'awful good-looking'. **1935** H. DAVIS *Honey in Horn* iv. 41 The compliment was pointed enough. Uncle Preston looked pleased but not overwhelmed. He was used to trade-lasts from the ignorant. **1949** M. MEAD *Male & Female* 456, I set myself to collect varieties of little-known folk-customs like trade-lasts. **1975** I. SHAW *Nightwork* v. 57 'While on the subject,' she said, 'let me give you a t.l.' 'What's a t.l.?' '..T.l. stands for trade last. A compliment. You gave almost the best performance of anyone I've slept with in this town.' **1964** S. BELLOW *Herzog* 172 Through a Japanese trade mission she also met Mr. Nasser and Mr. Sukarno. **1973** *Times* 24 Apr. (São Paulo Suppl.) p. viii/4 The Japanese presence is very real in São Paulo, and on average two trade missions visit the city every week. **1953** J. WAIN *Hurry on Down* v. 99 The other [formality] was to unscrew the trade plates which the cars carried in place of the regulation number plates they would have when licensed. **1978** J. FLEMING *Day of Donkey Derby* 110 I've got two sets of number plates, and just for luck, two lots of trade plates. **1805** SCOTT *Let.* 29 Mar. (1932) I. 244 He will of course expect what every author is entitled to—half profits upon the trade price when an edition shall be disposed of. **1912** R. A. WASON *Friar Tuck* xxiv. 239 Either the pack-rat reformed into a trade-rat, or else he sold out his claim to a trade-rat. **1948** F. BLAKE *Johnny Christmas* II. 79 Johnny slept that night..disturbed neither by Gitt's snoring nor the scuttle of secretive trade-rats over the packed earth floor. **1970** R. SYMONS *Broken Snare* xxiii. 157 He knew pack rats—trade rats some people called them. They would always make a trade for anything they took. **1852** MRS. GASKELL *Let.* 22 Nov. (1966) 213 Your Uncle Langshaw is to have the trade reduction of price. **1873** T. T. COOPER *Mishmee Hills* 33 Calcutta Chamber of Commerce convened a meeting 'for the purpose of discussing the subject of overland trade-routes with China'. **1791** J. LACKINGTON *Memoirs* xxxi. 230, I purchased very large numbers..at trade-sales of all sorts, as bankrupt sales, sales of such as had retired from business, [etc.]. **1895** *Atlantic Reporter* XXX. 521/1 (*heading*) Injunction—use of trade secrets. **1928** R. B. MCKERROW *Introd. Bibliogr.* II. x. 235 Some of the best [facsimiles] are, I believe, produced by a process of lithography, but the details are probably a 'trade secret'. **1942** *R.A.F. Jrnl.* 13 June 36 The chemicals used to produce this foam are a trade secret, so I am not able to tell you what they are. **1978** G. GREENE *Human Factor* II. iii. 82 They have secrets too—trade secrets. **1919** *Biogram* 8 Mar. 3 (Advt.), If you want a film that will pack your house nightly, book The Bride's Awakening... Trade show will be announced shortly. **1919** *Honey Pot* I. iv. 44 The picture will be trade shown during next February. **1927** G. B. SHAW in *Illustr. London News* 3 Dec. 1004/1 If you have ever been to what is called a 'trade show' and seen all the exhibitors there, [etc.]. **1946** R. CHANDLER *Let.* 30 May (1981) 75 The picture has not even been trade-shown. **1962** N. STREATFEILD *Apple Bough* xv. 214 I'll look out for you at the trade show of the picture. **1984** *Listener* 15 Mar. 8/1 For the other six nights, orchestral works give way to pop, dance.., conferences, trade shows and sport. **1977** *Time* 12 Dec. 18/2 Riding the crest of a gigantic trade surplus, which last week led to a Japanese Cabinet shake-up.., the yen has risen 22% against the dollar so far this year. **1946** O. JESPERSEN *Mankind, Nation & Individual* 164 Some of these trade-terms may have originally sprung up as slang. **1977** *Drive* Sept.–Oct. 113/2 He may remember to avoid such obvious trade terms as *hole in the roof* for sunshine roof. **1934** WEBSTER, *Trade test*, a test of proficiency in a given trade, such as plumbing. **1946** *R.A.F. Jrnl.* May 147 Those who were A.C.2s or A.C.1s will be trade-tested immediately on remustering to their trade. **1960** I. JEFFERIES *Dignity & Purity* vi. 122 Once it had become apparent that I wasn't trade-testing..they [*sc.* the workmen]..did me the favour of answering the questions I..put. **1909** *Cambr. Mod. Hist.* VI. ii. 49 The tariff-war was often the precursor of the trade-war. **1975** J. DE BRES tr. *Mandel's Late Capitalism* xiv. 472 The use of currency manipulations to gain short-term export advantages threatens to turn into a general trade war. **1902** *Encycl. Brit.* XXXII. 525/1 We may..enumerate some of the principal trade wastes; these are from dye-works, print works, [etc.]. **1976** *Financial Times* 11 Feb., Sterling fell to its lowest level ever against major currencies yesterday, with the Bank of England calculation for its trade-weighted average depreciation widening to 30·4 per cent from 30·3 per cent. **1984** *Times* 31 Mar. 21/8 Sterling's trade-weighted value against a basket of currencies fell to the lowest for a year yesterday.

trade, *v.* Add: **6. e.** *to trade down*: to buy or sell cheaper goods, usually in larger quantities; to sell something and buy a cheaper replacement; similarly *to trade up*. Also *fig.*

1942 *Sun* (Baltimore) 22 July 3/2 Catering to the masses, the fur trade is 'trading down', Green said, offering practical furs..in economical designs. **1959** *Wall St. Jrnl.* 14 Apr. 18/3 Americans have followed the traditional pattern of 'trading up' in foods as well as in other goods and services. **1963** *Guardian* 8 May 7/2 It pays to trade up rather than cater for the masses. **1975** *Times* 14 Mar. (Small Car Suppl.) p. vi/7 The phenomenon of trading up from small to bigger cars is well known... In 1974..as many buyers..traded down as traded up. **1977** *Times* 22 June 23/7 Graduates are being given first crack at the jobs in preference to school-leavers. In other words, companies are trading up. **1982** *Nat. Westminster Bank Q. Rev.* Feb. 3 People..may well 'trade up' at various times by increasing their mortgage in order to move into better property.

9. a. (Examples of sense 'to exchange' other than in commerce and barter.) *to trade off*: (earlier example); also *fig.*, to give up in exchange for something else, esp. as a compromise.

1793 in *Mass. Hist. Soc. Coll.* (1810) III. 1 Good crops of corn and rye, which they trade off for spirituous liquors. **1917** *Dial. Notes* IV. 402 *Trade*,..also 'to exchange' in general sense... 'Trade places with me.' **1949** F. FERGUSSON *Idea of Theater* i. 21 In the next part of the fight the opponents trade blow for blow. **1951** *N.Y. Herald Tribune* (Paris) 29 Nov. 3 (*heading*) Insults traded in Commons in 20-hour 20-minute session. **1956** S. SEELY *Radio Electronics* xv. 440 Pulse-duration modulation and pulse-position modulation trade bandwidth for an improvement in signal/noise ratio. **1958** L. URIS *Exodus* I. ix. 55 No American Jew would trade places with a Negro or a Mexican. **1972** *Sci. Amer.* June 22/3 Warheads can be traded off for either ABM penetration aids or increased range. **1974** *Times Lit. Suppl.* 8 Mar. 242/5 The bourgeoisie has 'traded off' some of its control to the armed forces acting in their interests. **1978** M. HESSE in Hookway & Pettit *Action & Interpretation* 6 The pragmatic criterion trades these difficulties for others. **1983** *Times* 29 Apr. 8/7 Punches and insults were traded at a rally addressed by..the South African Prime minister. **1984** *Times* 26 Mar. 2/1 Another skinhead leaned from a window and traded insults with seven youths in the street.

b. *spec.* in *N. Amer. Sport.* Of a club or team: to exchange (one of its players) *for* one or more from another club. Also, to exchange (players) between clubs or teams.

1899 *N.Y. Times* 5 Mar. 8/5 There was very little trading of players during the meeting. **1955** *Sports Illustr.* 7 Mar. 38/3 Branch Rickey..traded Southpaw Paul La Palme to the St. Louis Cardinals for Ben Wade, a relief pitcher. **1972** 'E. LATHEN' *Murder without Icing* vi. 62 Nashville wouldn't be forever. I'd be traded sooner or later. And as long as I shoot those goals in, I can get what I want. **1982** *Philadelphia Enquirer* 13 May 1-c/1 The former UCLA star was traded by the Knicks to New Orleans for Jim Barnett and Neal Wala in 1975.

10. *to trade in*, to give (a used car, etc.) in part payment or exchange *for* a new one. Also *transf.* and *fig.* orig. *U.S.*

1926 G. HUNTING *Vicarion* i. 22 'Don't say you're trying to guard my young innocence, dear,' murmured Carol. 'I traded it in long ago for the new model.' **1955** W. GADDIS *Recognitions* III. ii. 752 You trade in your goddam car, you trade in your goddam wife, and the minute you get used to the goddam thing some bastard puts out a new model. **1973** R. TRAVERS *Murder in Blue Mountains* x. 95 Butler traded in his old black hat for the new one. **1975** D. LODGE *Changing Places* iii. 105 Shall I trade it in for a new one while it's still working? **1977** C. MCCULLOUGH *Thorn Birds* II. vi. 106 Bluey Williams traded in his lovely draft horses and his massive dray for a truck.

11. *intr. Comm.* Of a share: to be bought and sold (*at* a price, etc.).

1976 *Honolulu Star-Bull.* 21 Dec. c-7/1 A 125,000 share block of the stock traded at 17⅛. **1981** *Times* 23 May 19/8 Its shares will start trading on June 1. *Ibid.* 8 June 16/1 The huge discount to net assets at which insurance shares have been trading.

tradeable, var. TRADABLE *a.* in Dict. and Suppl.

tradecraft. Add: **b.** *spec.* Skill in espionage and intelligence work; cf. *TRADE *sb.* 6 e.

1961 'J. LE CARRÉ' *Call for Dead* v. 56 He was suddenly alert... Was it the latent skill of his own tradecraft which informed him? **1979** *Observer* 30 Dec. 7/7 At every juncture of the break-in he made decisions that proved catastrophic, applied 'trade craft' that was ludicrous, and misled his accomplices about matters that were either incriminating to himself or strategic to the break-in's failure.

traded, *ppl. a.* Add: **I. 3*.** *traded option,* an option on a stock exchange (see OPTION 4) which can itself be bought and sold.

[**1973** *Business Week* 16 June 78/1 The Chicago Board of Trade's new Options Exchange is drumming up interest in trading options to buy and sell stock—puts and calls.] **1978** *Daily Mail* 11 Mar. 39 In a month, we shall see the opening in Amsterdam and London of markets in traded options, an innovation which took Chicago by storm in April 1973. **1984** *Daily Tel.* 24 Apr. 16/2 Privately Stock Exchange officials are furious that.. a major development in the traded options market has been marred by such uncertainty.

trade-in (tre^{i}·dˌin). [f. vbl. phr. *to trade in* s.v. *TRADE *v.* 10.] **1. a.** A transaction in which something is traded in; a part exchange. **b.** An item traded in, esp. a used car; also *fig.* **c.** A sum allowed in return for a trade-in.

1917 *Horseless Carriage* 1 Aug. 28 A used car in a trade-in. **1934** J. O'HARA *Appointment in Samarra* ii. 39 That Studebaker sedan, the black one. The one we took on a trade-in from Doc Lurie. **1945** *Word Study* Dec. 3/1 So useful and practical is English becoming that the time may not be far off when many small nations.. may consider some sort of 'trade-in' with their national language for the English language. **1954** P. HIGHSMITH *Blunderer* (1956) xxii. 140 Since he hadn't the money for a brand-new car, Kimmel preferred to keep his ancient one rather than acquire something slightly newer on a trade-in. **1960** V. PACKARD *Waste Makers* xiii. 137 The high trade-in proved to be enormously effective in luring prospects. **1969** F. SARGESON *Joy of Worm* ii. 33 He would sell his machine to Jeremy cheap, and.. accept as part of the transaction the trade-in of two push bikes in reasonably good condition. **1970** D. G. ALEXANDER *Retailing in England during Industr. Revol.* v. 143 Refurbished footwear which had been received as 'trade-ins' on new footwear. **1972** J. BELFRAGE in G. W. Turner *Good Austral. Eng.* vi. 115 Second-hand car dealers who.. beg you to take as-new late models off their hands.. for ultra-generous trade-ins on your old bombs. **1980** G. HAMMOND *Reward Game* iv. 46 There's a wee sports car that I took as a trade-in.

2. *attrib.*

1927 *Ladies' Home Jrnl.* Dec. 65/1 Buyers.. took prompt advantage of the liberal trade-in allowance on their old equipment. **1929** *Collier's* 12 Jan. 9/2 If more than one third of his.. transactions.. is represented by trade-in cars. **1946** *Sun* (Baltimore) 27 Jan. 22 (Advt.), No more 'tired power' or expensive engine repair. Extra value at trade-in time. **1958** *Economist* 8 Nov. 535/2 A general move in this direction would shave dealers' profit margins and might affect the trade-in values they could offer. **1974** P. FLOWER *Odd Job* iv. 29 They could get new trade-in jobs on HP... He wouldn't take any more old fridges. **1977** *Cork Examiner* 8 June 14/5 (Advt.), Typewriters all makes, new and secondhand, good trade-in allowance. **1980** *Sunday Express* 24 Aug. 22/1 (Advt.), You could get an exceptional trade-in price for your old car.

trade-mark. Substitute for the parenthesis: (secured by legal registration or, in some countries, established by use).

b. (Earlier example.) Also *attrib.* as *adj.*

1869 'MARK TWAIN' *Innocents Abroad* xxiii. 238 We see other monks looking tranquilly up to heaven, but having no trade-mark. **1977** *South China Morning Post* (Hong Kong) 13 Apr. 7/2 Jimmy Shtoow'd, to phonetically adopt his trademark drawl, has an unnerving 'look' for interviewers. **1983** *Daily Tel.* 18 Mar. 17/2 Fans need not worry: her trademark French rayon jersey made up at least half the collection.

tra·de-marked *ppl. a.*

1936 E. B. WHITE *Let.* 24 Dec. (1976) 146 Your public approval of a trademarked product and your influence can be bought at a price. **1983** P. DEVLIN *All of us There* xi. 133 The old [pub].. with its great copper-banded barrels and old trade-marked mirrors.

trade-off (trē^{i}·dǫf). [f. vbl. phr. *to trade off* s.v. *TRADE *v.* 9.] A balance achieved between two desirable but incompatible features; a sacrifice made in one area to obtain benefits in another; a bargain, a compromise.

1961 *Hovering Craft & Hydrofoil* Oct. 32/2 Propulsion system integration allowing trade-offs between the requirements of lift and forward thrust can be achieved in a variety of ways. **1968** *Economist* 21 Sept. 38/1 It may be that the old argument of the 'trade-off' between inflation and unemployment will be superseded. **1970** A. TOFFLER *Future Shock* xx. 425 To provide data on the social and economic costs of various goals, and to show the costs and benefits of proposed trade-offs. **1972** *Sci. Amer.* June 22/3 Although its nominal range of about 2,500 nautical miles is the same as that of the *A-3*, a trade-off between range and payload is always possible. **1975** *New Yorker* 7 Apr. 55/3 Whether it is prudent, let alone safe, for Congress to try for a trade-off between these two priorities—the environment and the economy—remains a question. **1976** *Nature* 27 May 279/2 The alternative strategy of increasing the protein content of cereals would be a difficult task due to the yield/protein content 'trade-off'. **1976** P. R. WHITE *Planning for Public Transport* ii. 48 The household location may be a compromise rather than a trade-off related solely to a place of employment in the central area. **1978** *Jrnl. R. Soc. Arts* CXXVI. 255/1 A quite significant proportion of judgements in life are a trade-off between safety and cost. **1983** *Times* 3 Sept. 7/2 In the long run, there is no trade-off between inflation and unemployment. **1983** *Listener* 8 Dec. 23/3 The trade-off between housing and other objectives of policy has changed.

tradesman. Add: **2. b.** *tradesmen's entrance* (or *door*): a minor or side entrance to a property for use by tradesmen or workmen.

1892 A. W. PINERO *Magistrate* III. i. 113 We're in the scullery, Guv; let's try and find the tradesmen's door. **1904** E. NESBIT *Phoenix & Carpet* vii. 131 At the side of the house.. there is a green gate labelled 'Tradesmen's Entrance'. **1946** 'J. TEY' *Miss Pym Disposes* xiii. 143 'Shouldn't you be going in by the other door?'.. 'I do not take well to tradesmen's entrances.' **1982** M. HINXMAN *Telephone Never Tells* iii. 21 A well-trodden path that wound round to the rear suggested.. that the tradesmen's door was a more familiar mode of entry and not only for tradesmen.

c. *tradesman's token* = *trade token* s.v. *TRADE *sb.* 14 a. Usu. in *pl.*, *tradesmen's tokens.* Cf. TRADE *sb.* 11.

1660 *CSP Dom.* 6 Oct. (1860) 307 Proposition by Sir Wm. Parkhurst.. to meet the necessity for small money, and obviate the inconvenience of tradesmen's tokens. **1757** *Gentl. Mag.* XXVII. IX. 498/2 The best account of the money called Tradesmen's Tokens.. is to be drawn from.. Mr Leake's hist. account of English money, London 1745. **1849** J. Y. AKERMAN *Tradesmen's Tokens* p. i, Notwithstanding the dictum of Pinkerton, many persons are yet found who collect Tradesmen's Tokens. **1892** J. ATKINS *(title)* The tradesmen's tokens of the eighteenth century.

trade-union, trades-union. Add: Now usu. written as two words (without hyphen) except when used *attrib.* **b.** *attrib.*; **trade(s) union congress,** *(a)* a national delegate conference of British trade unions, held annually since 1868; *(b)* (with capital initials) the national confederation of British trade unions, originally formed to organize the annual congress.

1831 LADY E. BELGRAVE *Let.* Feb. in G. Huxley *Lady Elizabeth & Grosvenors* (1965) iv. 97 The tremendous Trade Union Club there [in Manchester]... I wish it could be put down and that someone would shoot O'Connell and Cobbett. **1868** F. HARRISON *Let.* 11 Nov. in *Geo. Eliot Lett.* (1956) IV. 483 Since July I have been quite immersed in my Trades-Union work. [**1878** *Chambers's Encycl.* X. 757/1 The Trades' Congress.. holds an annual conference in the different leading towns.] **1888** *Encycl. Brit.* XXIII. 501/2 An annual trades union congress is held in some great centre of industry and population.. at which delegates from almost all the trade unions in the realm are present. **1895** *Nat. Review* XXVI. 163 The Trade-Union Congress.. has made itself a really representative body by adopting the principle of one vote one value. **1911** C. E. PERSONS et al. *Labor Laws & their Enforcement* 115 One of its members, Edward H. Rogers, a trade union leader, made some half-hearted recommendations. **1920** *Times* 11 June 17/2 The majority of trade union leaders.. have deserted to the camp of the capitalists. **1926** *Brit. Gaz.* 12 May 1/4 Every man who does his duty by the country and remains at work or returns to work during the present crisis will be protected by the State from loss of trade union benefits. **1926** A. CONAN DOYLE *Hist. Spiritualism* I. xiii. 299 The conduct of conjurers [towards mediums] seems to have been usually determined by a sort of trade union jealousy, as if the results of the medium were some sort of breach of a monopoly. **1926** *Law Rep. Chancery Div.* 540 No trade dispute does or can exist between the Trades Union Congress on the one hand and the Government and the nation on the other. **1927** CARR-SAUNDERS & JONES *Social Struct. England & Wales* 51 Trade-union officials. *Ibid.* 77 Trade-union membership advances in waves. **1936** G. B. SHAW *Millionairess* III. 174 You might as well ask me to pay trade union wages as do all that the inspector wants: I should be out of business in a week. **1941** E. WILSON in *Atlantic Monthly* Apr. 486/2 The trade-union leadership is represented only.. by an unscrupulous spellbinder. **1964** T. B. BOTTOMORE *Elites & Society* i. 9 Representatives of new social interests or classes (e.g. trade union leaders). *a* **1974** R. CROSSMAN *Diaries* (1975) I. 335, I am pretty used to Conference now, and being hardened I just opt out of the evening entertainments and the endless trade-union dinners. **1974** P. DICKINSON *Poison Oracle* iv. 100 The hoarse bellowings of an old-style trades union agitator trying to whip an apathetic strike meeting into action. **1975** *Economist* 4 Jan. 75 Mr Gill has been cutting quite a dash since his election as the only communist on the general council of the Trades Union Congress. **1976** *Daily Tel.* 20 July 2/5 When will the British public, 81·5 per cent of whom have no trade union affiliation, realize how rapidly our freedoms are being eroded.

Hence **trade-unionese** *colloq.*, the style of language supposed to be characteristic of public statements by trade-union officials; **trade(s)-unionism** (earlier example); **trade(s)-unionist** (earlier example); **trade-unionize** *v. trans.*, to enrol in a trade union, to form a trade union from among; **trade-unionized** *ppl. a.*

1834 *Times* 10 May 5/4 Is it not somewhat unreflecting on the part of trades' unionists to imagine that they can.. set up an opposition monopoly? **1867** *Blackw. Mag.* June 726/2 When Socialism and Communism in all their various forms died out, Trades-unionism.. took their place. **1927** A. P. HERBERT in *Times* 12 Jan. 13/5 There should be prizes for Essays in the Socialist Language, and polysyllabic Resolutions in Trade Unionese. **1960** *Times* 9 Feb. 14/2 *(heading)* Should artists be trade unionized? **1969** H. E. BATES *Vanished World* xii. 156 Nowadays.. we are near-suffocated by tradeunionese, councilese and Americanese, the new extensions of stodge-pudding language that have joined Johnsonese, journalese and politicalese. **1976** *Carn* Feb. 6/1 Public attention has been diverted from the Bretons to the jailed conscripts who tried to trade-unionise the French army. **1982** *Economist* 17 Apr. 51/3 Buy-outs by employees of bust and heavily trade-unionised businesses.

trading, *vbl. sb.* Add: **a.** *trading down, up* (see quot. 1963 and *TRADE *v.* 6 e).

1963 *Gloss. Managem. Terms* (Brit. Inst. Managem.) (Typescript), *Trading down*, a seller's practice of handling cheap or low-grade products in order to secure higher volume sales (usually at a low rate of profit with a high stock turn). *Ibid., Trading up*, a seller's practice of handling expensive or high-grade products in order to gain prestige and secure a better class of trade (usually at a high rate of profit with a low stock turn). **1971** *Daily Tel.* 13 Mar. 20/5 This second house is almost certain to be more expensive... Any capital gain on the first home will almost certainly be more than devoured by the additional cost of this 'trading up'. **1976** *Times* 6 Nov. 18/8 When prices increase.. there is a strong tendency to.. buying in smaller quantities or items of poorer quality. This is known in advertising jargon as 'trading down'.

b. *trading-boat, goods* (example), *-scow, vessel* (example), *voyage* (earlier example); **trading account,** an account showing the revenue from sales during a period, the cost of those sales, the stock at the beginning and end of the period, and the resulting gross profit or loss; **trading estate,** an area of land specially developed to accommodate light industry; **trading floor,** the area in a stock exchange where the dealing is done; **trading-house** (earlier and later examples); **trading-place,** *(b)* (examples); **trading profit,** profit as shown in a trading account; gross profit; **trading-rat** = *trade rat* s.v. *TRADE *sb.* 15; **trading stamp** orig. *U.S.*, an adhesive stamp given by a retailer to a customer when he buys goods of a certain value and exchangeable in quantity for goods from the company issuing the stamp.

1920 Trading account [see *cost account* s.v. *COST sb.^{2} 6]. **1978** J. KELLOCK *Elements of Accounting* x. 174 In the final form, accounts are divided into two sections referred to as the trading account and the profit and loss account. **1738** W. STEPHENS *Jrnl.* 15 June in A. D. Candler *Colonial Rec. State of Georgia* (1906) IV. 156 An Indian Trading Boat arrived. **1867** J. N. EDWARDS *Shelby* xx. 364 Marmaduke.. hoped to capture a trading-boat, and thus put an immediate quietus on the cotton trade. **1923** 'R. DALY' *Enchanted Island* xv. 154 I'm trying to figure out our chances of being picked up if we stay here. It's not on the track of any regular trading-boats. **1937** *Ann. Reg. 1936* 8 The Commissioner for the Special Areas of England and Wales.. issued a report... His chief object now, he said, was to establish in the Special Areas what he called 'trading estates' for the purpose of attracting to these areas fresh industries, particularly of the lighter type. **1981** B. HINES *Looks & Smiles* 31 They.. caught a bus out to the Ring Road where a Trading Estate was being developed to attract new industries to the city. **1947** *Encycl. Brit.* XXI. 422/1 As a market place, the trading floor of the New York Stock exchange affords exactly the same fundamental facilities that a public market does for the housewife. **1971** *Sunday Australian* 8 Aug. 13/9 He also suggested.. greater use of electronic equipment, culminating in the elimination of the current trading floor. **1981** *Times* 19 July 22/1 The trading floor appeared unusually empty. **1984** *Christian Science Monitor* 2 Mar. 10/3 They have to figure out what stocks to buy when the bulls return to the trading floor. **1796** *Saskatchewan Jrnls.* (Hudson's Bay Rec. Soc.) (1967) 73 Sent four men with ten horses to Buckingham House for trading goods. **1637** in *Mass. Hist. Soc. Coll.* (1863) VI. 215 They say he came from a trading howse which Plymouth men have at Qunnihticut. **1726** S. PENHALLOW in *New Hampsh. Hist. Soc. Coll.* (1824) I. 21 Trading-houses in several places were hereupon engaged. **1899** H. B. CUSHMAN *Hist. Indians* 478 A trading house for the accommodation of the Chickasaws has been established at the Bluffs. **1755** L. EVANS *Geogr. Ess.* 10 The situation of Indian Villages, trading Places, the Creeks [etc.]. **1883** W. E. HOWE *Country Town* xv. 84, I had never been to Twin Mounds, as there was a post-office and a small trading place several miles nearer. **1940** *Economist* 25 May 936/1 A double record of trading profits and also of true net profits has been kept. **1966** *Daily Tel.* 30 June 1/5 Sears Engineering made trading profits of £2,344,000. **1895** *St. Nicholas* Apr. 501/2, I would like to write an entire paper on the droll ways of certain distinguished members of the Wood-rat, Pack-rat, Trading-rat, or Bush-rat genus. **1875** 'MARK TWAIN' in *Atlantic Monthly* Feb. 219/2 He ran over the steering-oar of a trading-scow. **1897** *Catal. Title Entries of Bks.* (Office Reg. Copyright, Libr. of Congr.) No. 326. 21 Trading stamp book issued by Washington Trading Stamp Company. (Received Sept. 30, 1897.) **1901** *Daily Colonist* (Victoria, B.C.) 30 Oct. 2/4 The city council.. have passed a by-law prohibiting the use of trading stamps or coupons within the municipality. **1933** *Parl. Papers 1932–3* XII. 387 (Cmd. 4385) 12 A trading stamp company sells collecting books and stamps to retailers. **1964** S. BELLOW *Herzog* 121 Postage stamps and trading stamps soaking on the formica counter. **1977** *Times* 10 May 15/1 The Tesco supermarket chain.. has just decided to withdraw from the trading stamp business. **1895** C. M. YONGE *Long Vacation* xviii. 181 He.. set her up at Rockquay with the tobacco-shop. She had chosen that place on account of American trading-vessels putting in there. **1745** *Roxana* 427 He.. told me, he could help me to a Share in two Ships, one was going a trading Voyage to the Coast of Africa, and the other a Privateering.

trading post. orig. *U.S.* [f. TRADING *vbl. sb.* + POST *sb.*^{3}] **1.** A place occupied for purposes of trade, esp. in a region not fully developed.

1796 in *Coll. Georgia Hist. Soc.* (1916) IX. 15 The land.. has been recommended..as proper for a trading post. **1837** [in Dict. s.v. TRADING *vbl. sb.* b]. **1936** D. MCCOWAN *Animals Canad. Rockies* xxi. 190 The fur trading posts of the far North. **1976** *Sat. Rev.* (U.S.) 30 Oct. 23/1 Lamu—a tiny coral island off the Kenya coast..once a prosperous trading post of Omani Arabs.

2. One of the posts or positions on the trading floor of a stock exchange, where stocks assigned to that location are bought and sold.

1951 G. L. LEFFLER *Stock Market* xii. 178 There are now 18 active trading posts... The present posts are horse-shoe or U-shaped stations, occupying 100 square feet... A total of 12 clerks can work inside. **1970** *Toronto Daily Star* 24 Sept. 13/1 A bald man in a red jacket leans heavily against a quiet trading post. His eyes are closed. Another sits on a small seat, one of many which can be pulled down from the sides of the trading posts. **1971** *Reader's Digest* (U.S.) Oct. 58/2 Hundreds of brokers were swarming around 17 horseshoe-shaped trading posts to execute the overnight accumulation of orders to sell, sell, sell.

tradish (trē^i·diʃ), *a. nonce-wd.* [f. TRAD(E *sb.* + -ISH^1.] Of or suggestive of trade or tradesmen.

1803 D. WORDSWORTH *Jrnl.* (1941) I. 243 The houses.. have a tradish look, as if they might have been off-sets from Glasgow.

tradition, *sb.* Add: **7. tradition-directed** *a.*, applied to persons whose behaviour and goals are largely directed by social conventions; cf. *inner-directed* adj. s.v. *INNER *a.* (*sb.*^{2}) 1 n, *other-directed* adj. s.v. *OTHER *adj. pron.* (*sb.*) D. 2.

1950 D. RIESMAN *Lonely Crowd* i. 9 The society of high growth potential develops in its typical members a social character whose conformity is insured by their tendency to follow tradition: these I shall term tradition-directed people and the society in which they live a society dependent on tradition-direction. **1959** *Times* 3 Sept. 13/5 He insists warmly on the importance of establishing three main categories of social character among writers... There are the inner-directed..the other [*printed* outer]-directed..and the tradition-directed. **1970** E. FLORES in I. L. HOROWITZ *Masses in Lat. Amer.* ix. 333 In countries ruled by tradition-directed, ignorant landlords,..it is impossible to apply sophisticated redistributive policies.

traditional, *a.* Add: **1. c.** Applied to a style of post-war jazz inspired chiefly by the bands of the earliest period of jazz, as opposed to *modern jazz* s.v. *MODERN *a.* 3 a. Cf. *TRAD *sb.* 1.

1950 *Downbeat* 28 July 10/1 This..has been the particular gripe of the traditional jazz adherents. **1980** J. WAINWRIGHT *Man of Law* i. 7 A mutual fanaticism for traditional jazz... The small-group combinations beloved of three decades ago.

traditionalist. Add: **b.** One who plays, appreciates, or supports traditional jazz (see *TRADITIONAL *a.* 1 c). Also *attrib.* or as *adj.*

1951 *Jazz Jrnl.* Sept. 15/1 First, the bands... The stars of the Traditionalist show were 'The Saints'. *Ibid.* 15/2 Why did he have to spoil what was otherwise an excellent job of compering by making his usual crack at the traditionalists? **1962** [see *MODERNIST 6]. **1983** *New Oxf. Compan. Music* I. 990/1 Parker..laid his influence on virtually everything and everyone except the dedicated 'traditionalists'.

traditionalize, *v.* (in Dict. s.v. TRADITIONAL *a.* (*sb.*).) Add: Also, to imbue with or constrain by tradition. Chiefly as **tradi·tionalized** *ppl. a.*, **tradi·tionalizing** *ppl. a.* and *vbl. sb.*

1951 R. FIRTH *Elements of Social Organization* iv. 134 The price system..may be..of a highly traditionalized type, with relative inflexibility in rates over long periods, and considerable resistance on the part of producers and consumers to variation in these rates. **1960** C. GEERTZ *Relig. Java* i. 11 The more traditionalized peasants and their proletarianized comrades in the towns. **1976** *World Politics* XXVIII. 250 There may indeed be a traditionalizing role for military rulers in Africa. **1978** *Econ. Devel. & Cultural Change* XXVI. 763 The presence of the petroleum-extraction industry in the desert region surrounding Augila was having the simultaneous effects of modernizing and 'traditionalizing' oasis life. **1982** *Dædalus* Winter 101 What these revolts appear to have in common..is their class basis and their traditionalizing, but nontraditional, ideologies.

Hence **tradi:tionaliza·tion,** the process of making or becoming traditional; adherence to tradition.

1966 A. R. WILLNER *Neotraditional Accommodation to Political Independence* 3 At the microscopic level, the process of traditionalization, as it is described here for Indonesia, involves the increasing influence of indigenous and particularistic rather than modern, rational criteria on the way in which public officials fulfil their prescribed roles. **1977** *Social Problems* XXV. 135 In the Yom-Kippur War, traditionalization emphasized the centrality of the feminine family roles. **1981** R. & M. M. LAROSSA *Transition to Parenthood* i. 24 The practical implications of traditionalization following birth should also not be ignored. **1981** *Stud. in Compar. Internat. Devel.* Fall–Winter 65 The absorption of h.s. immigrants can be described as entailing not modernization, but rather 'traditionalization'.

traditioned, *a.* For *rare*$^{-1}$ read *rare* and after 'of a kind' add 'or to a degree'. (Further example.)

1940 W. DE LA MARE *Pleasures & Speculations* 14 One of the most ancient and richly traditioned cities of Denmark.

traductor. Restrict † to sense in Dict. (s.v. TRADUCT *v.*) and add: **2.** A device on the side of a railway carriage that picks up and deposits mail bags while the train is in motion.

1959 C. J. ALLEN *Mod. Railways* xv. 187 The sacks [of mail]..are then suspended from hinged traductor arms at the van side. **1970** *Railway Mag.* Oct. 545/2 Post Office Sorting van; has letter sorting racks and some vehicles also have nets and traductor arms. **1978** O. S. NOCK *Gt. Western in Colour* 147/1 Most of these trains had vans fitted with the traductor apparatus for picking up and setting down mails at speed.

Trafalgar. Add: **b.** Special Comb.: **Trafalgar chair** (see quots. 1934, 1969); **Trafalgar Day,** 21 October, the anniversary of the battle of Trafalgar; **Trafalgar Square** *v. trans. joc.*, to harangue (from the practice of 'soap-box' oratory in such public places).

1822 R. BROWN *Rudiments of Drawing Cabinet & Upholstery Furnit.* (ed. 2) p. xii, Many cabinet-makers, for the sake of notoriety, ridiculously give names to furniture quite inconsistent, such as Trafalgar chairs, Waterloo feet, &c. **1934** M. JOURDAIN *Regency Furnit. 1795–1830* 48/2 The well-known Trafalgar chair..was designed as a light 'parlour' chair, and made normally of beech..with caned seat and loose squab cushion. **1969** J. GLOAG *Short Dict. Furnit.* (rev. ed.) 674 *Trafalgar chair.* Various types of single and elbow chairs, with nautical symbols such as anchors and coiled ropes in the backs, were made after the Battle of Trafalgar in 1805... Apart from the incorporation of such ornament these chairs were usually of the graceful Regency type with sabre legs. **1979** E. CAVE *Blood Bond* I. ii. 22 A Trafalgar chair with a tapestry seat. **1918** A. HUXLEY *Let.* 30 Oct. (1969) 167 On Trafalgar Day this year Cobby made precisely the same remarks about Lord Nelson and Lady Hamilton as last year. **1977** *Navy News* Sept. 24/1 The Exeter Flotilla's Trafalgar Day service will be held in Exeter Cathedral on Sunday, October 23. **1895** A. PINERO *Notorious Mrs Ebbsmith* II. 103, I assure you, dear fellow, I was within three feet of her when she deliberately Trafalgar Squared me. **1944** J. AGATE *Ego 6* 35 But not until I had taken the floor and Trafalgar Square'd K as blisteringly as I could.

traffic, *sb.* Add: **2. e.** In phr. (*as much as*) *the traffic will bear* or *stand* and varr.: (as much as) the trade or market will tolerate, as much as is economically viable. Also *fig.*

1931 L. STEFFENS *Autobiogr.* v. ii. 853 His wage-earners had their rents raised to all the traffic would bear. **1936** L. C. DOUGLAS *White Banners* vii. 155 We've had all the worry about you that the traffic will stand. **1964** L. DEIGHTON *Funeral in Berlin* xlvii. 294 How much? That's difficult. What do you think the traffic will bear? **1972** *Guardian* 22 May 14/5 The landlord demands a deposit of anywhere from £3 to £150: this is based on what he thinks the traffic will stand. **1976** *Billings* (Montana) *Gaz.* 4 July 2-E/2 The invariable custom is to hire as many deputy superintendents, associate superintendents, assistant superintendents and administrative assistants as the traffic will bear. **1982** T. FITZGIBBON *With Love* I. v. 32 The small neighbourhood shops were..willing to give credit up to a pound, but no more. They knew to a penny what the traffic would bear.

5. a. Also with reference to air travel (usu. prefixed by *air*, and in *Comb.*: see sense 6 below); also *concr.*, the vehicles, etc., collectively.

1911 E. H. HODGKINSON *Tyranny of Speed* viii. 107 He should hear the traffic coming behind him. **1920** H. B. PRATT *Commercial Airships* vii. 72 Terminal Stations will comprise a landing ground or aerodrome, and will be provided with housing sheds, mooring towers.., with traffic offices, gas generating and storage plant, [etc.]. **1930** W. S. MAUGHAM *Cakes & Ale* ii. 34 There was none of the congested traffic of Jermyn Street. **1935** C. G. BURGE *Compl. Bk. Aviation* 136/1 The cheaper way at intermediate towns or where traffic is light, is to assemble the passengers at a central point, and deal with them at the airport. *Ibid.* 402/2 They were convinced that air traffic would only succeed as a new means of transport if.. international co-operation existed. **1938** [see *traffic control*, sense 6 below]. **1951** R. CAMPBELL *Light on Dark Horse* xvi. 223 The traffic used to collect [in London], like lumber on a river. **1974** J. A. FOSTER in G. P. Howard *Airport Econ. Planning* 5 The data to be collected should not only cover the physical facilities of the airport, but should also indicate the degree of utilization, the volume and composition of traffic, [etc.]. **1982** S. SPENDER *China Diary* 104 There was only one line of traffic in each direction.

d. *Telecommunications.* The messages, signals, etc., transmitted through a communication system; the flow or volume of such business.

1878 *Telegraphic Jrnl.* VI. 15/2 A monopoly of cable traffic to America. **1889** *Telephone* 15 Oct. 476/2 A Pacific Cable... The line..would find traffic enough to pay a fair interest on the investment. **1922** W. F. FRIEDMAN in *Bull. U.S. Signal Office Signal Corps* 1 Oct. 15 In modern military operations, a considerable volume of traffic is available for interception by the enemy. **1935** *Times* 26 Oct. 18/7 These are the busiest hours of the day, during which more than two-thirds of the daily traffic is handled. **1947**, etc. [see *ERLANG 2]. **1977** *Times Lit. Suppl.* 25 Feb. 222/5 British Intelligence could decipher German high-grade cipher traffic. **1978** T. ALLBEURY *Lantern Network* iii. 39 He's got his own W/T operator, but sometimes you may have to take his traffic.

6. (sense 5) *traffic area, block* (earlier example), *congestion, consciousness, flow, noise, stack, stream*; *traffic-conscious, -free* adjs.; instrumental, as *traffic-choked, -crammed* adjs.; **traffic analysis** *U.S.*, in Cryptography, the obtaining of information through analysis of patterns of communication without the decipherment of individual messages; hence **traffic analyst; traffic artery** orig. *U.S.*, a main or arterial road; **traffic circle** orig. and chiefly *U.S.*, a traffic roundabout; **traffic control,** the regulation of traffic movement through the use of signals or direct commands from authorized persons; a service with this responsibility; in *Aeronaut.*, also as *air traffic control* (see *AIR *sb.*^{1} III. 1); hence **traffic controller; traffic cop** *colloq.* (orig. *U.S.*) = *traffic policeman* below; **traffic court** orig. *U.S.*, a court of law with jurisdiction over motoring offences; **traffic engineer** orig. *U.S.*, one who deals with the design and planning of roads and the control of traffic; hence **traffic engineering; traffic island,** a raised or marked area in a road to direct traffic and provide refuge for pedestrians crossing the road; **traffic jam** orig. *U.S.*, a condition in which road traffic cannot proceed freely and comes to a standstill; a stoppage of traffic caused by this, or the vehicles caught in it; also *fig.*; hence **traffic-jammed** *a.*; **traffic lane,** a road carriageway for a single line of moving vehicles; an air or sea route designated as a set course for traffic in order to avoid collisions; **traffic light,** † (*a*) a light used for the guidance of aircraft (*obs. rare*); (*b*) freq. in *pl.*, (one of) a set of lights (usu. red, amber, and green) used for automatic control of road traffic, esp. at junctions; **traffic offence,** an infringement of the law by the driver of a motor vehicle; **traffic officer** = *traffic policeman* below; **traffic pattern,** (*a*) *Aeronaut.* (see quot. 1956); (*b*) the characteristic distribution of traffic on a route; also *fig*; **traffic police,** that branch of the police force concerned with road traffic control; hence **traffic policeman; traffic-proof** *a.*, of a horse or pony: that can be ridden safely in traffic; so **traffic-proof** *v. trans.*; **traffic sign,** a roadside sign conveying information, warnings, etc., to drivers of motor vehicles; **traffic signal(s** = *traffic light* (*b*) above; **traffic snarl:** see *SNARL *sb.*^{1} 2 b; **traffic ticket** *U.S.*, an official notification of a traffic offence, issued by a traffic warden or the police; **traffic warden,** a person employed to enforce regulations about the parking of motor vehicles and the use of parking meters.

1937 *Hist. Communications Intelligence in U.S.* (Naval Cryptologic Veterans Assoc.) (1982) 29 Information is obtained from communications by..methods short of cryptanalysis, i.e., traffic analysis. **1979** W. J. HOLMES *Double-Edged Secrets* iii. 18 But until the way was cleared by Rochefort we never discussed the subject of traffic analysis. *Ibid.*, Traffic intelligence summaries were produced each day by two traffic analysts. **1933** *Act* 23 & 24 *Geo. V* c. 53 §27 It is expedient that the existing traffic areas under the Road Traffic Act, 1930,..should be varied. **1977** *Chicago Tribune* 2 Oct. XI. B (Advt. Suppl.) 7/4 Washable—great for traffic areas. **1927** *New Masses* June 7/4 In a side street, close to one of the main traffic arteries of the city of the Angels. **1969** *New Scientist* 13 Mar. 560/1 These additional costs of assimilating a traffic artery into an existing urban area are themselves a massive community burden. **1977** E. V. CUNNINGHAM *One-Penny Orange* (1978) xi. 180 In the twenties..Sunset Boulevard was a quiet carriage road and not the major traffic artery it is today. **1896** *Chambers's Jrnl.* 26 Dec. 822/2 The slow speed and traffic blocks in crowded streets are atp to tell considerably against electricity. **1977** *Listener* 23 June 809/3 An uneventful march from Speakers' Corner to a rally in Trafalgar Square. No one who took part that day was ever out of sight of one or more of the scores of so-called traffic cameras that blanket central London and, on these occasions, are connected to the Operations Room [at Scotland Yard]. **1971** *New Scientist* 1 July 5/1 In traffic-choked cities the slender bike is the fastest means of getting from A to B. **1942** *Policy on Rotary Intersections* (Amer. Assoc. State Highway Officials) 1 The name 'traffic circle' is commonly applied to any intersection design based on the one-way movement of vehicles around a central area. **1970** *Rand Daily Mail* 28 Feb. 7/5 When South Africans say 'traffic circle' for the Englishman's 'roundabout', they give precision to the language. **1934** *Punch* 6 June 634/3 Sir William..urged traffic-congestion which six-line bridge would bring about in Strand, and reminded his adversaries that old bridge was as much national monument as Cenotaph. **1968** E. A. POWDRILL *Vocab. Land Planning* iii. 55 The case for urban renewal might be based on one or more of the following factors:..traffic congestion, [etc.]. **1948** C. GREATREX in B. Vesey-Fitzgerald *Bk. of Dog* I. 116 The problem of making a dog traffic-conscious is exceedingly difficult to solve... Far more dogs now possess an inborn instinct of some practical dimension, and as a result show caution and traffic consciousness. **1979** G. N. KNIGHT *Indexing* xiii. 176 An entry such as 'London, its happiness before the invention of Coaches and Chairs' induces a wry smile in our traffic-conscious age. **1936** *Spectator* 10 Jan. 56 The British vice-consulate at Varna, Bulgaria, protests that 'traffic-consciousness' is a horrid word. **1931** *Hansard* (Commons) 6 May 385 Installations of automatic traffic control signals. **1935** *Discovery* Jan. 2/2 Col. O'Gorman appeals to Science for aid in assessing the improvement due to any change of traffic control, of road layout, or of road code, etc. **1938** *Encycl. Brit. Bk. of Year* 33/1 Increasing volume of traffic forced the development of airport traffic control systems... Experiments in traffic control began almost 20 years ago (using signal lights). **1962** E. SNOW *Other Side of River* (1963) lxxi. 548 How many policemen do you have in New York? Most of ours are for traffic control. **1971** *Flying* Apr. 13/2 With 10 airplanes on the hook in a traffic-control sector that usually has a couple. **1978** L. DEIGHTON *SS-GB* xxiv. 225 The six-ton mobile command-centre—on hand for traffic control during the funeral procession. **1930** *Engineering* 25 July 106/3 Highfield automatic traffic controller... At present the three-light system appears to be most widely favoured. **1938** *Encycl. Brit. Bk. of Year* 33/1 A glass-enclosed tower is usually provided..to give the traffic controller a full view of the airport and its surroundings. **1973** *Times* 20 Mar. 8/4 The statement also referred to the month-long strike by French air traffic controllers. **1963** *Times* 20 Feb. 14/6 As a contrast to her decorative elegance there was the traffic-controller—I hesitate to say policewoman. **1977** G. MARKSTEIN *Chance Awakening* lxvii. 209 'Some big shot?' asked the RAF squadron leader... 'Guess so,' said the traffic controller. **1908** S. FORD *Side-Stepping with Shorty* xiv. 227 It'll be some time before Langdon'll be pestered anymore by the traffic cops. *a* **1930** D. H. LAWRENCE *Phoenix II* (1968) 425 One God is relative to another God until he gets into a machine; and then it's a case for the traffic cop! **1961** B. CRUMP *Hang on a Minute, Mate* 23 They..returned to the truck to find a traffic cop standing by it. **1975** R. BUTLER *Where all Girls are Sweeter* vi. 63 There was the usual jam on Putney Bridge... A traffic cop sorted us out. **1919** *Evening Star* (Washington, D.C.) 11 Mar. 24/1 Approval was given last night..to the plan..to establish a traffic court in this city. **1972** R. HOOD *Sentencing Motoring Offender* v. 105 The remainder [*sc.* motoring offences] would be dealt with at Traffic Courts. **1973** *Times* 17 Oct. 20/3 A traffic court is where a motorist pays to give harmless vent to his frustrations with his car, with traffic jams and wardens, with parking regulations and with authority in general. **1959** P. BULL *I know Face* ix. 164, I arrived at dusk in Casablanca and was driven at breakneck speed to Marrakesh along a traffic-crammed road, stiff with the results of accidents. **1916** *Proc. 8th Nat. Conf. City Planning* (U.S.) 69 The Traffic Engineer's duties are along two definite lines. **1959** *Daily Tel.* 8 May 23/3 All the committees were acting independently or their work overlapped. None was able to use the traffic engineers who were being used so effectively in the United States... There seems to be lacking in London the kind of adequately-staffed traffic engineering department which has proved essential in our large cities. **1978** *Jrnl. R. Soc. Arts* CXXVI. 425/1 Increasing the throughput of vehicles on an existing highway..is a field in which traffic engineers have notched up considerable successes as the demand has increased. **1931** *Roads & Streets* Dec. 506/1 A new..occupation has been created in the last few years—that of traffic engineering. **1959** Traffic engineering [see *traffic engineer* above]. **1970** P. LAURIE *Scotland Yard* ii. 54 They are initiated into the mysteries of traffic engineering. **1940** R. S. LAMBERT *Ariel & all his Quality* vi. 146 Broadcasting House..is responsible for a big inward and outward traffic flow; yet there is nowhere to park a car. **1978** *Dumfries Courier* 20 Oct. 10/3 The traffic operation and parking areas have been designed to ensure maximum traffic flow at all times. **1968** R. K. COX *Retail Site Assessment* xii. 140 The unfortunate word *pedestrianization* means the stopping-up of existing streets ..and their conversion into traffic-free areas for use by pedestrians. **1979** R. PERRY *Bishop's Pawn* viii. 137 Dieter was taken..towards Zurich along..relatively traffic-free roads. **1931** E. E. CUMMINGS *Let.* 7 Jan. (1969) 119 I've just returned from the place de la Concorde.. where waited on a traffic-island for $2\frac{1}{2}$ hours. **1935** L. MACNEICE *Eclogue for Christmas* in *Poems* 16 On all the traffic-islands stand white globes like moons. **1982** 'C. AIRD' *Last Respects* x. 101 The driver negotiated the traffic islands with impatience. **1917** I. CRUMP *Boys' Bk. Policemen* iii. 55 He plunged into the traffic jam at the next street. **1926** *Sunset* Mar. 38 (*heading*) Traffic jams: how Western cities are trying to reduce congestion on down-town streets. **1939** W. PLOMER *Dorking Thigh* (1945) 20 With a traffic-jam outside (for they turned up in scores). **1957** *Economist* 21 Dec. 1038/1 The Home Universities conference could hardly have chosen a more important subject for discussion last week than the traffic jam of students which piles up every summer when school leavers put in their bids for university places. **1976** *Liverpool Echo* 7 Dec. 1/1 A Buckingham Palace spokesman said she had travelled from Sandhurst and there had been heavy traffic jams. **1964** *Economist* 1 Aug. 476/1 They sit traffic-jammed in the intractable streets. **1983** *Listener* 1 Sept. 16/1, I was still sitting in my traffic-jammed car five minutes later. **1905** KIPLING *Actions & Reactions* (1909) 150 You could not hoist the necessary N.U.C. lights on approaching a traffic-lane because your electrics had short-circuited. **1937** *Times* 13 Apr. p. x/1 An elaborate Memorandum on the Construction and Lay-out of Roads, covering many subjects, including safety, standard widths, curves, gradients, traffic lanes. **1948** *Jrnl. R. Aeronaut. Soc.* LII. 90 The American omni-directional range which defines..traffic lanes..between zones of air traffic control at the airports of departure and arrival. **1972** *Daily Tel.* 5 May 3 The Government is taking powers to prosecute masters of British ships caught travelling the wrong way in traffic lanes through the Straits of Dover. **1912** Traffic-light [see *landing-tower* s.v. *LANDING *vbl. sb.* 8]. [**1920** W. P. ENO *Sci. Highway Traffic Regulation* viii. 19 (*heading*) Traffic regulation lights.] **1929** *Sat. Even. Post* 16 Nov. 145/1 T is for Traffic Light, bane of all motorists. **1934** *N. & Q.* 3 Nov. 314/1 These signals somewhat resembled our current traffic lights. **1958** J. CANNAN *And be a Villain* i. 5 Pulling up for the traffic lights at the turning into the High Street. **1973** D. BARNES *See Woman* I. 111 Stryker travelled northbound, cursing the traffic engineer who had planned the traffic-light sequence. **1978** S. WILSON *Dealer's Move* vii. 116 There were road works ahead, with temporary traffic lights. **1971** 'G. BLACK' *Time for Pirates* vii. 112, I..paused to listen, hearing nothing but traffic noises. **1960** *Daily Tel.* 29 Jan. 23/4 A 'ticket' system of optional fixed fines for minor traffic offences. **1981** C. DEXTER *Dead of Jericho* xxxii. 176 Cheque for £6, being the penalty fixed for the traffic offence detailed on the ticket. **1915** *Policeman's Monthly* Oct. 5/1 Traffic officers in the center of the street are subjected to many hardships. **1971** *Rand Daily Mail* 4 Sept. 5/2 Johannesburg traffic officers will still attend motor accidents in which there is only minor damage. **1956** W. A. HEFLIN *U.S. Air Force Dict.* 531/1 *Traffic pattern*, a pattern in the air above or about an airdrome, which is normally followed under visual conditions either by aircraft prior to touchdown or by aircraft after takeoff. **1968** L. O'DONNELL *Face of Crime* viii. 106 They landed at Kennedy at 8:32..having been delayed half an hour in the traffic pattern. **1977** *Mod. Railways* Dec. 461/3 These gentlemen cannot both be correct so, for the benefit of those of us who are not familiar with traffic patterns of these routes, would somebody please produce some evidence to prove the point one way or the other? **1977** *Chicago Tribune* 2 Oct. XI. 14/3 But the 'island' arrangement—placing furniture in the middle of a room (if it's large enough), thereby leaving space to walk around it—is a good way to create a traffic pattern. **1978** S. SHELDON *Bloodline* vi. 87 The private Boeing 707-320 was making its final approach to Kennedy Airport, gliding out of the stacked-up traffic pattern. **1906** *Collier's* 20 Jan. 22/3 The effort to find out how it feels to be 'regulated' by the traffic police of New York. **1959** *New Statesman* 3 Jan. 6/3 He also disliked anything that gave traffic police more discretion or wider powers. **1980** E. LEATHER *Duveen Let.* xi. 134 The Renault..would most certainly receive the attentions of the ever alert Traffic Police. **1917** *Wells Fargo Messenger* Mar. 115/3 The traffic policeman at Norman is still in doubt as to what it was that went by. **1940** AUDEN *Another Time* 91 Let the traffic policemen wear black cotton gloves. **1980** *Listener* 13 Nov. 653/1 Some of my best friends are traffic policemen. **1971** *Pony* Mar. 347/1 A few months ago I was given the task of traffic-proofing a pony. **1977** *Horse & Hound* 14 Jan. 40/4 (Advt.), Gelding..Viceless, traffic proof. **1915** *Policeman's Monthly* Oct. 5/1 Certain of the cities have given a great deal of thought and attention to traffic signs and signals. **1936** C. DAY LEWIS *Noah & Waters* 15 Do not be deceived by the two-faced traffic signs. **1973** J. WAINWRIGHT *Devil you Don't* 42 McGuire threaded the Jag. through the city streets. He obeyed every traffic sign. **1917** *Harper's Mag.* June 70/2 The Bostonian, supposedly sesquipedalian of speech, has reduced 'a pedestrian who crosses streets in disregard of traffic signals' to the compact *jaywalker*. **1934** *Archit. Rev.* LXXV. 184 Traffic signals did not come to Hyde Park Corner until 1932. **1981** 'J. ROSS' *Dark Blue & Dangerous* x. 57 A traffic signal which turned red as he approached it. **1963** L. DEIGHTON *Horse under Water* lii. 219 It's the Seville Traffic Control Zone... If it [*sc.* a plane] gets mixed into that traffic stack I'm not sure that I'll be able to sort it out. *a* **1930** D. H. LAWRENCE *Last Poems* (1932) 264 The minorities that still see the gleam of life Submit abjectly to the blind mechanical traffic-streams of..The stone-blind bourgeois, and the stone-blind bolshevist. **1981** H. R. F. KEATING *Go West, Inspector Ghote* xiii. 155 The monster car, slipping easily from one traffic stream to another. **1950** J. D. MACDONALD *Brass Cupcake* iii. 31 Every time you get into that car of yours, you'll get a traffic ticket. **1979** *Tucson Mag.* Apr. 33/2 The typical suburbanite..never goes downtown except for an occasional Community Center event or a traffic ticket to contest. **1984** *Miami Herald* 6 Apr. 18A/1 The judge's bill suggests that, by putting a thumb print on the traffic ticket, the scofflaw might be more easy to trace. **1959** *Punch* 25 Feb. 274/1 Any supposed similarity of function between the police and the newly-proposed traffic wardens vanished with the official statement that the wardens 'would help motorists to find parking space'. **1980** J. MCNEIL *Spy Game* xx. 197 It was a Ford, parked by the opposite kerb on..double yellow lines. A traffic warden was..preparing to write a ticket.

trafficator (træ·fikēˈtəɹ). [f. TRAFFIC *sb.* + INDIC)ATOR.] A signal arm attached in former times to either side of a motor vehicle which could be raised and illuminated to indicate the direction in which the vehicle was about to turn; also applied loosely to modern indicators (see *INDICATOR 3 g).

1933 *Autocar* 13 Oct. 733/1 (*caption*) The Lucas Trafficator is concealed when not in use. **1935** *Times* 17 Oct. 8/4 The least expensive Morris Eight is the two-seater which sells at £118, or £120 10s. with bumpers and trafficators. **1945** *Autocar Handbk.* (ed. 18) x. 196 The Trafficator arm is generally retained by some positive catch arrangement so long as it lies within its sheath, though other patterns leave the arm free so that it may be pulled out without injury. **1976** J. I. M. STEWART *Memorial Service* x. 167 He had actually flicked up a hand—jerkily, like an old-fashioned 'trafficator' on a car—in greeting. **1982** N. J. CRISP *Brink* i. 28 Jenkins signalled a right turn... The trafficators clicked.

‖ **tragédie lyrique** (traʒedi lirik). [Fr., lit. 'lyric tragedy'.] A name given to serious French opera of the seventeenth and eighteenth centuries. Cf. *opéra comique* s.v. OPERA 3.

1901 W. F. APTHORP *Opera Past & Present* vi. 117 If the Grand Opera—called *tragédie lyrique* when the libretto conformed to the rules of the classic French *tragédie*—was..a quasi-academic adaptation of the Italian *opera seria* to French taste, the *opéra-comique* may be called the natural growth..of..the Italian *opera buffa*. **1947** A. EINSTEIN *Mus. Romantic Era* xix. 358 In France, there was *tragédie lyrique* and *opéra-comique*. **1976** *Early Music* July 285 In 1966, came a virtually complete recording of Rameau's first and perhaps greatest tragédie-lyrique, *Hippolyte et Aricie*.

tragedize, *v.* Add: **3.** (Earlier example.)

1754 D. GARRICK *Let.* 31 July (1831) I. 57 Not like those paltry blasts of art employed in raising storms in a teacup, such as tragedizing trivial or even ludicrous situations.

tragedizing *vbl. sb.* (examples).

1780 T. FRANCKLIN tr. *Lucian's Works* I. 390 Several of them..fell insensibly into the tragedizing vein. **1813** *Theatrical Inquisitor* II. 182 Ye fair, an *Amateur* before you view, Whose love of tragedising sprung from you.

tragedy. Add: **5.** *tragedy-queen* (earlier examples).

1755 C. CHARKE *Life* 192 Though it was a valuable Gift, but more proper to ornament the Neck of a Country-Housewife, than a Tragedy-Queen. **1819** [see *SAIL *v.*[1] 5 b].

trageremics (trēˈgərīˑmiks), *sb. pl.* (const. *sing.*). *Linguistics.* [f. *Trager* (see *TRAGER–SMITH), after *phonemics*.] A mock-technical term for the approach to phonemic analysis characteristic of the American linguist George L. Trager. Hence **tragere·mic** *a.* (see quot. 1967).

1963 R. I. MCDAVID *Mencken's Amer. Lang.* 249 About 1950 E. Bagby Atwood coined *Trageremics* to designate phonemics according to the specifications of George L. Trager. **1967** —— in *Publ. Amer. Dial. Soc.* XLVII. 4 There does seem to be unnecessary virtuosity in displaying for individual entries the whole range of trageremic differences in the low-front vowel range. *Ibid.* 20 By *trageremic* (a term coined by Atwood) I refer to George Trager's analysis of all English syllable nuclei as composed of nine vowels and three semivowels. **1978** *Amer. Speech* LIII. 171, I mastered Trageremics in the middle 1950s.

Tragerian (trēˈgiᵊ·riăn), *a.* (*sb.*) *Linguistics.* [f. *Trager* (see next) + -IAN.] Of, pertaining to, or characteristic of the approach to linguistic analysis of George L. Trager. Occas. as *sb.*, an adherent of this method.

1962 R. P. STOCKWELL in *Texas Conf. Probl. Linguistic Analysis in Eng.* 10 The Tragerian pronunciation of *baa* that you wondered about. **1965** *Language* XLI. 168 His phonemics is Tragerian, though he makes tentative use of acoustic distinctive features. **1966** A. A. HILL *Promises & Limitations Newest Type Gram. Analysis* 6 Tragerians always began the description of language with phonemes, and ended it..with syntax. **1974** *Amer. Speech 1971* XLVI. 126 Since I have usually employed a Tragerian transcription in previous publications on English phonology, it will be adhered to in this paper.

Trager–Smith (trēˈ·gəɹ smi·þ). *Linguistics.* The names of George L. *Trager* (b. 1906) and Henry L. *Smith* (b. 1913), American linguists, co-authors of *An Outline of English Structure* (1951); used *attrib.* with reference to the method of linguistic analysis and phonemic transcription exemplified in this monograph. See also *SMITH–TRAGER.

1955 *Language* XXXI. 313 The Trager–Smith phonology..is the most nearly successful attempt at a statement of the English phonemic system that has yet been made. **1959** WIMSATT & BEARDSLEY in *PMLA* LXXIV. 586 The relation between meter and Trager–Smith linguistics. **1961** *Dissert. Abstr.* XXII. 1990 From the tapes the words were transcribed phonemically according to the Trager–Smith notation. **1962** *Amer. Speech* XXXVII. 154 A Trager–Smith analysis of the Middle English long mid vowels. **1965** A. H. ROBERTS *Statistical Linguistic Analysis of Amer. Eng.* v. 35 The system of notation in the count of French, Carter, and Koenig uses only one character to represent a diphthong, the Trager–Smith system uses two.

tragic, *a.* Add: **3. b.** *tragic flaw* = *HAMARTIA.

1913 L. COOPER *Aristotle on Art of Poetry* ii. 40 For Mary, the tragic flaw of the hero, described as an 'error of judgment', or a 'shortcoming', needs immediate illustration. The single Greek word, *hamartia*, lays the emphasis upon the want of insight within the man, but is elastic enough to mean also the outward fault resulting from it. **1950** W. FARNHAM *Shakespeare's Tragic Frontier* i. 4 In Brutus then, Shakespeare discovered the noble hero with a tragic flaw. By that discovery he made it possible for English tragedy to reach a greatness hitherto attained only by Greek tragedy. **1970** *English Studies* LI. 235 This flaw in the Hegge Pilate..approximates very closely what is generally meant in dramatic criticism as 'tragic flaw', and the Hegge Pilate may be the first tragic hero in English drama.

tragico-. Add: **tragico-farcical** *a.*, combining tragic and farcical elements; **tragico-historical**

a., combining tragic and historical elements.
1913 E. F. Benson *Thorley Weir* vi. 206 Tragico-farcical situations. **1919** T. S. Eliot in *Times Lit. Suppl.* 13 Nov. 637/3 In *Catiline* Jonson conforms, or attempts to conform, to conventions..of tragico-historical drama.

‖ **trahison des clercs** (traˌizoṅ de klɛ̄r). [Fr.] The title of Julien Benda's work *La Trahison des Clercs* (1927), used to denote a compromise of intellectual integrity by writers, artists, and thinkers. Cf. *treason of the clerks* s.v. *treason *sb.* 1 b.
1935 *New Statesman* 26 Oct. 598/1 Is it one more proof that the intellectual should always advise but never govern? Is it one more case of the *trahison des clercs*? **1952** E. Hyams *Soil & Civilization* 127 True, there has been some reaction away from this state of mind among a few intellectuals, a kind of uneasy, if wholesome, *trahison des clercs*. **1968** J. M. Ziman *Public Knowledge* vi. 123 The aim of Science is understanding, not the accumulation of data and formulae... To fail to construct the building, to leave all the bricks lying round in untidy piles, is the *trahison des clercs* of today. **1978** *Listener* 4 May 559/3 Look, they say, terrorism is a phenomenon of our times. Let us..acknowledge that a diplomat..is fair game... I find this *trahison des clercs*.

trail, *sb.*^{1} Add: **II. 9.** (Further examples.) Also *N.Z.* and *Austral.* Cf. *nature trail* s.v. *nature *sb.* 15 a.
1860 J. Burnett *Let.* 15 Mar. in H. F. von Haast *Life & Times Sir Julius von Haast* (1948) viii. 85 Crossed the Alexander stream and struck Mackay's last year's trail. **1939** *WPA Guide to Florida* (1984) i. 117 In Hillsboro River State Park..are overnight cabins, trails, roads, and a museum. **1958** *Tararua* XII. 25 A trail seems to be something narrow and perhaps rather hard to follow—a way marked only by blazes or worn by animals, usually deer. A track seems to be something broader, cut or formed by man. **1968** Mrs. L. B. Johnson *White House Diary* 2 Oct. (1970) 714 A system of urban and rural trails, including the Pacific Coast Trail from Mexico to Canada. **1968** K. Weatherly *Roo Shooter* 47 The ancestors of the roos used this path. It was miles wide and invisible... When this country is closely settled and these trails are sealed, the red kangaroos will die out. **1977** *Times* 23 Apr. 12/5 There are well marked trails for independent hikers. *Ibid.* 12/7 The benefit of camping and picnic grounds, walking and hiking trails. **1982** G. M. Fraser *Flashman & Redskins* 161 From Santa Fe to Algodones on the river the trail was dotted that night with emigrant camp-fires.

10*. *Radio* and *Television.* A piece of advance publicity (often an excerpt) broadcast prior to the transmission of a programme. Cf. *trail *v.*^{1} 3*; *trailer *sb.* 4 b.
1973 *Listener* 6 Dec. 798/1 Accidentally switching on early..on Radio 3..I heard..off-putting trails. **1980** *Broadcast* 7 July 24/3 The TV Presentation Department.. make hundreds of commercials every year in the form of programme trails.

V. 16. *trail-blazer* (later *fig.* examples), *-blazing* vbl. sb. and ppl. adj., *-breaking* vbl. sb. and ppl. adj., *-cutter, -herd, -herder, -man*; **trail bike** orig. *U.S.*, a motor-cycle designed for use on country tracks rather than on roads; **trail boss** *U.S.*, a foreman in charge of a cattle-drive; **trail head** *N. Amer.*, the beginning of a trail for walkers (occas. also for skiers); an organizational centre at such a place; **trail-hound,** (*a*) [*hound *sb.*^{1} 4 e] = *trail-blazer* above; (*b*) a small hound bred for the sport of hound trailing; **Trail of Tears** *U.S.* (see quot. 1930); **trail-riding,** motor-cycling with a trail bike; **trail-rope,** (*a*) substitute for def.: *U.S.*, a long rope used for tethering animals loosely; (earlier example); **trailway** *N. Amer.*, a route through rough country cleared and maintained for recreational walking.
1969 *Time* 12 Sept. 17 Anyone hoping to escape the.. cities for the quiet beauty of our woods, mountains or deserts is in for a rude shock. He is greeted by the rattling snarl of trail bikes, dune-buggies and the like. **1972** *Fairbanks* (Alaska) *Daily News-Miner* 3 Nov. 23/5 (Advt.), Extended bumper on rear for snowmobile, trail bikes. **1976** *New Motorcycling Monthly* Oct. 4/4 Yamaha, of course, have reincarnated the good old 500cc four-stroke single, but in trail-bike trim. **1937** *Discovery* July p. lix/1 Trail blazers of science. **1972** *Daily Colonist* (Victoria, B.C.) 3 Feb. 8/1 Agriculture Minister Shelford lauded his party as being trailblazers in humanity through fiscal astuteness during the throne speech. **1934** Webster, Trail blazing. **1957** V. Packard *Hidden Persuaders* xxi. 233 *Tide*, the merchandisers' journal, admonished America's merchandisers to pay attention to this trail-blazing development as it might be 'tomorrow's marketing target.' **1968** *Globe & Mail* (Toronto) 3 Feb. 43/3 (Advt.), Acres of wonderful wood for trail blazing and riding. **1971** *Advocate-News* (Barbados) 17 Sept. (Guyana Suppl.) p. iv/3 Volunteers..cleared the last few feet of bush for their historic meeting on top of a hill called Point Jason (after a trail-blazing pioneer who supervises the project). **1973** C. Bonington *Next Horizon* xxi. 279 We all agreed that it [*sc.* a climb] was as hard as anything we had ever done, with very little to show for each day's trail-blazing. **1890** *Stock Grower & Farmer* 21 Jan. 6/3 Trail bosses bronzed from exposure..are familiar sights. **1921** [see *pile *v.*^{2} 3 c]. **1977** *Daily Mirror* 15 Mar. 24/1 What was the name of the actor who played the trail boss in the TV Western series 'Rawhide'? **1912** L. J. Vance *Destroying Angel* xviii. 232 'Must I make talk, then?' she demanded. 'If we must, I suppose—you'll have to show the way. My mind's hardly equal to trail-breaking to-day.' **1965** T. A. Sebeok in *Language* XLI. 80 In this trailbreaking paper, he [*sc.* Trubetzkoy] reduced the supposed multiplicity of vowel patterns to a small number of symmetrical models. **1971** C. Bonington *Annapurna South Face* xiii. 171 Even in descent it took him an hour, and without his trail-breaking from above Martin and Mike Thompson would have had an exhausting time forcing the route from below. **1858** *Brit. Colonist* (Victoria, B.C.) 11 Dec. 2/4 The majority of the Lillooet trail cutters would have remained had it not been grossly mismanaged. **1903** A. Adams *Log of Cowboy* vii. 88 Four..strange men..representing themselves as trail cutters. **1958** *Edmonton* (Alberta) *Jrnl.* 24 June 46/1 The trail-cutters work a four-month season in the winter. **1971** *Islander* (Victoria, B.C.) 30 May 12/4 Another satisfactory water supply can be found at the southern end of the beach, just past the trail head. **1976** *Stillwater* (Montana) *News* 1 July 12/3 Backpackers, fishermen, day hikers, or anyone else using outdoor trails, should sign in on the log book at the trailhead where these are available. **1981** *Nordic Skiing* Jan. 48/2 The Warming Hut on Butternut Lake serves as the trailhead where a skier can..arrange for instruction, rentals, accessories, [etc.]. **1885** *Weekly New Mexican Rev.* 18 June 1/3 The trail herds in Colfax county must go forward or turn back at once. **1962** G. MacEwan *Blazing Old Cattle Trail* i. 1 Ever since the Patriarch, Abraham,.. stockmen have been driving trail herds to far places. **1890** *Stock Grower & Farmer* 19 Apr. 3/3 Cattle inspectors of New Mexico were holding up trail herders for one and one-half cents per head. **1931** *Times Lit. Suppl.* 29 Oct. 839/2 The writer is what in her mountaineering vernacular might be called 'a trail hound'. **1972** *Shooting Times & Country Mag.* 27 May 27/1 From all this evolved the trail hound, a smaller, lighter type altogether than his near relative, the Fell foxhound. **1978** R. Hill *Pinch of Snuff* vii. 73 She [*sc.* a cat] was born on a Cumberland farm and reckons she's a trail-hound. **1858** *Brit. Colonist* (Victoria, B.C.) 27 Dec. 3/2 The man..was no trail-man but a stranger. **1891** *Harper's Mag.* Nov. 886/2 The trail-men are sent out to cut what in general parlance would be called a path. **1930** E. Ferber *Cimarron* 40 Tears came to his own eyes when he spoke of that blot on southern civilization, the Trail of Tears, in which the Cherokees, a peaceful and home-loving Indian tribe, were torn [1838–9] from the land which a government had given them by sworn treaty, to be sent far away on a march which, from cold, hunger, exposure, and heartbreak, was marked by bleaching bones from Georgia to Oklahoma. **1978** *Peace News* 6 Oct. 7/2 It was named after the many Long Walks since the Andrew Jackson presidency, including walks like the Trail of Tears in which the Indian people were forced to trek vast distances overland as an expansionist government laid claim to their traditional homelands. **1984** *Miami Herald* 6 Apr. 6A/2 Tribal leaders are calling the reunion the most important event for the Cherokee Nation since the Indians were driven from their southern lands in the 1838 'Trail of Tears'. **1931** C. Aldin in Hunloke & Aldin *Riding* vi. 105 Trail riding..gives us a day's riding *with* a picnic, and teaches us where the side tracks and bypaths on a place like Exmoor lead to. **1979** *Daily Tel.* 13 Jan. 8 These tracks..provide great scope for that non-competitive and gentle form of motor-cycling known as trail-riding. **1826** G. C. Sibley *Diary* 15 Mar. in A. B. Hulbert *Southwest on Turquoise Trail* (1933) 162, I have paid away the following sums, since I left Sta. Fee ..14 trail ropes, 14·00. **1939** *Appalachian Trailway News* July 6/2 The matter of foremost importance was..to obtain the state recognition and interest in the Trailway project. **1940** *Ibid.* Jan. 20/1 The Appalachian Trail or Trailway is entirely a voluntary amateur project. **1972** E. Wigginton *Foxfire Bk.* 276 We'd gone walkin' along th' trailway. **1978** *Globe & Mail* (Toronto) 15 Feb. 1/7 About one-third of the route is already owned by the province and the draft plan calls for the gradual acquisition of a 60-foot-wide 'trailway' from present landowners.

trail, *v.*^{1} Add: **I. 1. d.** Phr. *to trail one's coat*, to seek to pick a quarrel; to be provocative in one's conduct. Cf. *to drag his coat-tails, so that some one may tread on them* s.v. Coat-tail.
[**1864**: see Trailer 1.] **1877** C. M. Yonge *Womankind* xxv. 216 Party spirit is equally ready to give offence and to watch for it. It will trail its coat like the Irishman in the fair. **1923** *Daily Mail* 7 Feb. 6 This risk [of war] is greatly increased by the presence of British troops at Constantinople and Chanak. Why should we thus be 'trailing our coats' before the Turks? **1950** D. Divine *King of Fassarai* xxxii. 291, I wouldn't put it in a report!.. I don't trail my coat. **1974** *Times* 4 Nov. 15/1 Nobody trails his coat for another election... There is to be no Commons division on the crisis in agriculture. **1980** J. Ditton *Copley's Hunch* i. ii. 35, I was trailing my coat... Trying to get the Luftwaffe to come up and fight.

3. a. Also, to cause (a person) to accompany or follow one, esp. reluctantly.
1914 W. Owen *Let.* 24 May (1967) 253 Tofield..is married, and trails a French wife about with him, from Berlitz School to Berlitz School. **1977** 'D. Rutherford' *Return Load* i. 21 Sally..trailing a reluctant Josie, was heading for the exit.

3*. To give advance notice of (a radio or television programme). Also *transf.* Cf. *trail *sb.*^{1} 10*, *trailer *sb.* 4 b.
1941 *B.B.C. Gloss. Broadcasting Terms* 33 *Trail* (*v. trans.*), to draw the attention of listeners to a forthcoming programme or other event of broadcasting importance by means of announcements, recorded excerpts, or other methods calculated to make it widely known. **1942** 'G. Orwell' *Diary* 14 Aug. in *Coll. Essays* (1968) II. 443 Horrabin was broadcasting today... This had been extensively trailed and advertised beforehand. **1960** *Guardian* 8 Nov. 7/2 It remains to me an object of mystery..why the BBC trailed this programme..as unsuitable for young people. **1976** *Daily Tel.* 20 Dec. 8 Powell blamed newspapers for having ignored his embargo—journalists usually receive copies of his speeches a day or two beforehand—but for years his speeches have been 'trailed' without complaint. **1978** *Times* 7 Aug. 12/5 At least by trailing their message on the envelope the senders have..reduced wear on my paper knife. **1980** *Musicians Only* 26 Apr. 11/5 Released to trail a three album blockbuster.

II. 6. c. Also with *in. U.S.*
1875 *Fur, Fin & Feather* (ed. 3) 112 Light and drink; drop off and trail in. **1907** S. E. White *Arizona Nights* xvi. 234 With exultant cackles of joy they'd trail in, reachin' out like quarter-horses.

7. b. (Later examples.)
1967 W. Styron *Confessions of Nat Turner* I. 32, I heard Hark's voice trail off in something like a stifled laugh, a gurgle of satisfaction. **1982** *Times* 16 June 17/1 The export expansion should trail off substantially this year.

III. 9. a. Also in *gen.* use, to follow.
1915 H. L. Wilson *Ruggles of Red Gap* (1917) iv. 79 Think of those two poor fellows trailing you over Paris yesterday trying to save you from yourself. **1925** H. L. Foster *Trop. Tramp Tourists* 70 We trailed the other steamer. We trailed her through the *Boca Chica*... We trailed her past the little forts. **1945** B. MacDonald *Egg & I* (1946) xxiii. 228 Sport and the puppy trailed me everywhere, whining and begging me to explain the smoke and excitement. **1957** 'R. Farre' *Seal Morning* ii. 16 No sooner was she past infancy than Lora [*sc.* a seal] started to waddle after me round the croft and trail me over to the byre.

b. To lag behind (someone or something), in a contest, comparison, etc. Also *intr.*
1957 *Times* 6 Sept. 13/2 Hansen's best work came after he had trailed for the first four rounds. **1961** *Wall St. Jrnl.* 24 Mar. 1/1 The value of contracts for residential building awarded last month trailed February, 1960, by 12%. **1972** *Guardian* 10 Aug. 2/3 The Harris Poll today shows that Senator McGovern now trails President Nixon by 23 points. **1979** *Sci. Amer.* Nov. 56/1 Diabetes mellitus and its complications are now thought to be the third leading cause of death in the U.S., trailing only cardiovascular disease and cancer. **1980** *Times* 3 Nov. 2/1 Most MPs seem to expect Mr Silkin to come third with between 30 to 40 votes and Mr Shore to trail with between 20 and 30. **1983** *Times* 19 Feb. 8/4 A few months ago..she was trailing Mr Daley.

IV. 15. *trans. Bowls.* To force (the jack) further up the green with one's bowl.
1908 J. M. Pretsell *Game of Bowls* xi. 194 If a bowl trail the jack through between, and past the line square to the back of, the stationary bowls, it shall score 3. **1923** J. A. Manson *Bowling* 84 The Bowler is required to trail the jack, his own bowl accompanying or 'hugging' it, between the stationary bowls over both of the horizontal lines. **1975** *Oxf. Compan. Sports & Games* 97/2 Occasionally a bowler delivers a bowl which runs on to the jack and stays with it while pushing it a foot or so farther up the green. Basically this is a draw shot delivered with a marginal increase of strength with the object of trailing the jack to a more advantageous position.

trai·lable, *a. U.S.* and *Austral.* [f. Trail *v.*^{1} + -able.] Of a boat: that may be towed on a trailer behind a motor vehicle; = *trailerable *a.*
1976 *N.Y. Times* 5 Sept. v. 11 As slip and mooring space becomes more difficult to find, the trailable boat represents an alternative—it can be dry sailed from a boatyard or moored at home. **1977** *Herald* (Melbourne) 17 Jan. 19/2 On the Saturday afternoon trailable yachts, Flying Fifteens, Fireballs and International Cadets will compete.

trailed, *ppl. a.* Add: **2. b.** *trailed slip* (Ceramics), a slip used for decorating pottery by applying it through a nozzle or spout.
1957 Mankowitz & Haggar *Conc. Encycl. Eng. Pott. & Porc.* 15/1 Staffordshire trailed slip posset-pots. *Ibid.* 223/1 They are decorated with 'trailed slip'. **1971** *Country Life* 27 May 1303/1 Trailed slip is the method of pouring out from a cone or can exactly as good cooks decorate birthday cakes with icing sugar. **1974** Savage & Newman *Illustr. Dict. Ceramics* 294 Lead-glazed ware decorated with trailed slip.

3. Publicized in advance. Usu. prefixed by advbs. Cf. *trail *v.*^{1} 3*.
1958 *Spectator* 22 Aug. 247/2 A much-trailed BBC investigation. **1981** *Economist* 20 June 14/1 Ministers at this week's well-trailed cabinet meeting listened to her lectures on the need to cut their spending.

trailer, *sb.* Add: **4. a.** Also *fig.*
1898 J. London *Let.* 6 Dec. (1966) 8 Sent out in this mail, 'trailers' after articles I mailed last September. **1941** H. G. Wells *You can't be too Careful* iii. i. 114, I join with Mrs Richard Tewler in deploring the inaudibility of Mrs Humbelay. If only we could have heard those lost trailers of hers, we might have benefited greatly from her ..wisdom. **1952** G. Raverat *Period Piece* vi. 112 This remark was..a sort of trailer, which she hoped might lead to more information.

b. orig. in *Cinematogr.* An excerpt of a film, broadcast, etc., used as advance publicity. Also *transf.* and *fig.*
1928 *N.Y. Times* 11 Mar. viii. 6 *A trailer*, a few hundred feet of film announcing a forthcoming picture. **1930** *Dancing Times* July 360/2 In a 'trailer' advertising the film, it is announced that the producers have aimed more at entertainment than historical accuracy. **1941** *B.B.C. Gloss. Broadcasting Terms* 33 *Trailer*, microphone announcement or short descriptive broadcast, designed to advertise a forthcoming programme or other event of broadcasting importance. **1942** *Punch* 4 Mar. 169/1 The war..has only just started. The trailer will have given you an idea of what it will be like. **1959** *New Statesman* 21 Mar. 403/2 A quasi-newscaster, giving verbal trailers

of coming attractions, does not fulfil this function. **1959** *Washington Post* 26 Dec. A19/2 Then some wisenheimer from the agency decided we needed a trailer. **1966** *Listener* 19 May 737/1 Whether there is much point in playing a section of a work, except as a trailer, is another matter. **1971** *Daily Tel.* 28 Jan. 1/1 Mr Barber, Chancellor of the Exchequer, used a lunch-time speech yesterday as a 'trailer' for the White Paper on Public Expenditure.. which is to be published this afternoon. **1977** J. AIKEN *Last Movement* i. 9 The evening's sunshine was only a trailer for spring. **1978** *Radio Times* 28 Jan.–3 Feb. 70/1 Once upon a time, in the cinema of my youth, there were trailers—unblushingly commercial attempts to lure in the customers by juxtaposing all the dangerous and sexy bits of the film and overlaying them with the most blatant sales pitch of plots and star appeal.

6. a. Now usu. an unpowered vehicle towed behind a car or truck, etc.; *spec.* (chiefly *U.S.*) = CARAVAN 4 in Dict. and Suppl.

1926 *Kansas City* (Missouri) *Star* 11 June, On the Victory highway most any day now one may see the migratory harvesters—a few walking,..more with their families in cars, and a trailer behind, carrying tents, bedding, and cooking utensils. **1931** J. H. STONE *Caravanning & Camping-Out* x. 64 These trailer-caravans are made so exceedingly light..that a low-power motor can draw them with ease. A trailer runs on two wheels or four. **1951** W. FAULKNER *Requiem for Nun* 246 Living now (with now a wife..and..after that a wife and children) in automobile trailers or G.I. barracks on the outskirts of liberal arts colleges. **1966** *Listener* 9 June 839/3 The first motor-diesel vessel to carry caravans—or, as the Americans call them, trailers—across the ocean is now being designed here in San Francisco. **1976** *New Yorker* 17 May 31/1 The miniature control room of a big white mobile broadcast trailer. **1977** P. WAY *Super-Celeste* I. 44 Family men from Sydney..on a fishing weekend—their wives.. in the trailers in the park.

c. *trailer-on-flatcar*, used to denote a system of freight transport whereby trailers (and other unaccompanied road freight vehicles) are carried on railway cars. Cf. *PICK-A-BACK *adv. phr.* (*a.*, *sb.*) b (*b*). orig. *U.S.*

1954 [see *PICK-A-BACK *adv. phr.* (*a.*, *sb.*) b (b)]. **1964** [see *TOFC* s.v. *T* 6 a]. **1979** *Railway Gaz. Internat.* Aug. 719/2 Piggyback, otherwise known as trailer-on-flatcar (TOFC), has proved to be an area of strong.. growth.

9. *attrib.* and *Comb.*, as (sense 4 b) *trailer film*; (sense 6 a) *trailer caravan*, *hitch* [HITCH *sb.* 6], *-wagon*; **trailer camp** *U.S.*, an area where caravans may be temporarily or permanently parked; similarly **trailer court, park**; cf. *caravan park, site* s.v. *CARAVAN *sb.* 4; **trailer home** *U.S.* = *mobile home* s.v. *MOBILE *a.* 1 h; also **trailer house**; **trailer tent**, a tent which is attached to and erected on a trailer; **trailer-truck** *U.S.*, an articulated lorry; cf. *tractor-trailer* s.v. *TRACTOR 4.

1921 *Outing* Apr. 39/2 (Advt.), Union Trailer Camp... Whether a week-end jaunt or a vacation tour, this outdoor palace makes it a real one... Your car can draw it easily. **1980** M. GORDON *Company of Women* (1981) III. 254 Mothers bringing their children up in trailer camps. **1930** *Motor Body Building* LI. 98/1 There are, of course, already a considerable number of trailer caravans standardised by body builders specialising in this type of vehicle. **1931** [see sense 6 a above]. **1979** W. H. CANAWAY *Solid Gold Buddha* xi. 77 The trailer..served him as living quarters and producer's office... He woke to find the trailer-caravan in darkness. **1939** E. S. GARDNER *D.A. draws Circle* (1941) xiv. 273 How about taking these folks down to the trailer court, Bill? **1979** *Arizona Daily Star* 5 Aug. (Advt. Section) 14/5, 56 space Travel Trailer Court on Wetmore near new shopping center. Can be converted to regular trailer court. **1941** *Electronic Engin.* XIV. 412 The 'trailer' film, interspersed with regular features, has been recognised by a number of manufacturers as a valuable advertising medium. **1953** C. ARMSTRONG *Catch-as-catch-Can* viii. 69 Do you understand how a trailer hitch operates? **1972** D. E. WESTLAKE *Bank Shot* viii. 58 It has a trailer hitch... It doesn't have any wheels. **1940** H. G. WELLS *New World Order* 180 In such large open countries as the United States there has been a considerable development of the mobile home in recent years. People haul a trailer-home behind their cars and become seasonal nomads. **1979** T. GIFFORD *Hollywood Gothic* xxx. 303 He followed her into the neat little trailer home. **1954**, **1969** Trailer house [see *MOBILE *a.* 1 h]. **1975** *Budget* (Sugarcreek, Ohio) 20 Mar. 16/2 They move into a trailer house located on his son-in-law, Ben Peachys farm. **1947** *Daily Oklahoman* (Oklahoma City) 21 Sept. D-6/1 The verdict may well point to a bust in the boom enjoyed this year by the nation's tourist camps, hotels, motels, trailer parks,..and restaurants. **1979** *Arizona Daily Star* 5 Aug. B1/6 A talented cook and editor of her trailer-park newsletter, Rosaaen said she knows why so many women like her are working today. **1971** *Rand Daily Mail* 4 Sept. 10/4 The largest selling trailer tent in Scandinavia... Independent suspension,..easy towing and light weight make it easy on your car. **1981** *West Lancs. Even. Gaz.* 25 Apr. 9 (Advt.), Trailer tent. **1958** A. BUDRYS *Edge of Sea* in Aldiss & Harrison *Decade the 1950s* (1976) 54 A long-haul trailer-truck driver. **1976** Trailer-truck [see *RIG *sb.*^{6} 3 b]. **1904** Trailer-wagon [in Dict., sense 6 a].

trai·ler, *v.* [f. the sb.] **1.** *trans.* **a.** To advertise or publicize in advance, esp. by the use of excerpts.

1965 *Observer* 5 Sept. 36/1 French 1964 vintages..are already trailered in some American liquor stores as 'the most heralded vintage of the century'. **1977** *Time Out* 28 Jan.–3 Feb. 5/4 Originally scheduled for broadcast last April and 'trailered' on the air, it has never in fact been run. **1979** *Internat. Jrnl. Sociol. of Law* Feb. 99 The book is reminiscent of a Hollywood film, in the sense of its having been extensively trailered. **1983** *Daily Tel.* 27 Aug. 29/2 *The Winds of War Preview*, excerpts from the series which does not start for another fortnight and has already been heavily trailered.

b. Chiefly *N. Amer.* and *Austral.* To transport on a trailer.

1971 *Islander* (Victoria, B.C.) 31 Jan. 7/2 For most of us, snowmobiling requires that we frequently trailer our machines from where we live to more suitable operating locales. **1976–7** *Sea Spray* (N.Z.) Dec./Jan. 55/3 Cover for a vessel while being trailered may be overlooked. **1977** *Austral. Sailing* Jan. 48/1 (Advt.), A little ship like the Marieholm is easy to trailer. **1984** *Gainesvillle* (Florida) *Sun* 27 Mar. 6B/1 An end to being trailered, to wearing halters, bridles, bits and saddles.

2. *intr.* **a.** To travel or live in a trailer. **b.** To give advance publicity.

1974 *Listener* 17 Jan. 93/3 [They] give up trailering around and settle back near the old folks. **1975** *Time Out* 22 Aug. 3/3 Trailering with stuff like 'The Leisure Press At Bay'.

Hence **trai·lered** *ppl. a.*, towing a trailer, having a trailer (sense *6 a) attached.

1965 'W. HAGGARD' *Hard Sell* ix. 97 The oil came up from Genoa in convoys of trailered lorries.

trai·lerable, *a.* Chiefly *N. Amer.* and *Austral.* [f. TRAILER *sb.* 6 + -ABLE.] Of a boat: that may be transported on a trailer attached to a motor vehicle; = *TRAILABLE *a.*

1971 *Austral. Sailing* Jan. 6/1 (Advt.), The new standard for small yachts. Eyecatching new trailerable mini ocean racer. **1976–7** *Sea Spray* (N.Z.) Dec./Jan. 112/1 (Advt.), 7m Flybridge trailerable Cruiser. **1980** *Outdoor Life* (U.S.) (Northeast ed.) Oct. 152/3 (Advt.), Boat kits—22 trailerable models.

trai·lering, *vbl. sb.* *N. Amer.* [f. *TRAILER *v.* + -ING^{1}.] The act or practice of travelling with or living in a caravan.

1938 *Amer. Speech* XIII. 196 Trailering..Galahading.. newspapering. **1967** (*title*) Woodall's trailering parks and campgrounds. *Ibid.* 33/1 Along Highway 190 from Oaxaca lies the..colonial village of San Cristobal... A bit of off-beat trailering, well worth the trip. **1973** *Daily Colonist* (Victoria, B.C.) 12 Oct. 25/1 A friend of theirs who had retired to a life of trailering told them of his experiences. **1978** *Sunday Sun-Times* (Chicago) 1 Jan. 122/2 Proper weight distribution is essential to insure safe trailering and should be checked before pulling out of the driveway.

trailerite (trē^{i}·lərəit). *N. Amer.* [f. TRAILER *sb.* + -ITE^{1}.] One who lives in or travels by caravan.

1940 *Capital* (Topeka, Kansas) 28 Jan. 16B/5 Many trailerites, caught unprepared by Florida's worst cold spell. **1977** *Globe & Mail* (Toronto) 7 Mar. 8/7 Your average trailerite has to be a..jack-of-other-trades to get along while prowling the highways and byways.

trailing, *vbl. sb.* **1. c.** Delete quots. 1873 and substitute earlier example. Now *Obs.*

1775 *Ann. Gaming* viii. 105 What now gives the peculiar advantage to the mace over the cue, is what has been artfully introduced by professed players, under the name of trailing, which is following the ball with the mace to such a convenient distance from the other ball as to make it an easy hazard.

d. A form of bowling played on Scottish greens, the object being to trail or carry the jack into a semicircle drawn beyond two bowls placed three feet apart.

1902 *Encycl. Brit.* XXVI. 329/2 In trailing, two bowls are laid on the turf..and a jack is then deposited equidistant from each bowl... A semicircle is then drawn behind the bowls with a radius of nine feet from the jack. **1923** J. A. MANSON *Bowling* 84 Trailing is the section of the Points game which is most worthy of attention.

e. *Ceramics.* A method of decorating pottery by applying slip or glaze through a nozzle or spout. (See also quots. 1960, 1968.)

1940 B. LEACH *Potter's Bk.* vi. 145 Glazes are applied by dipping, double dipping..dripping, splashing and trailing. **1960** C. WINICK *Dict. Anthropol.* 543/2 *Trailing*, a technique of making broad incised lines in pottery. **1968** J. ARNOLD *Shell Bk. Country Crafts* xix. 241 Glazes are applied in a liquid state, either by immersion or by brush-work; this is called trailing. *a* **1977** *Harrison Mayer Ltd. Catal.* 18/2 Slip decoration: trailing, feathering. Slip can be applied by all the usual painting, pouring, trailing and dipping methods.

f. The advance broadcasting of excerpts of films, programmes, etc., as a form of publicity. Cf. *TRAIL *v.*^{1} 3*.

1961 *Listener* 17 Aug. 254/3 The trailing of future programmes by announcement or sampling..now seems to be overdone—especially those repeated alluring snippets of coming films which could equally well be false starts of the next programme. **1978** *Broadcast* 20 Nov. 19/3 Intensive trailing on radio and TV.

trailing, *ppl. a.* Add: **1. b.** Also in the names of plants with a trailing habit; *trailing arbutus* = *New England mayflower* s.v. *NEW ENGLAND b; also *fig.*

1784 *Mem. Amer. Acad. Arts & Sci.* I. 413 *Cuscuta*... Trailing Cockspur... Borders of brooks and ditches. **1785** H. MARSHALL *Arbustrum Americanum* 42 Trailing Arbutus..grows naturally upon northern hills, or mountains. **1813** H. MUHLENBERG *Catalogus Plantarum Amer. Septentrionalis* 91 *Salix prostrata.* Trailing willow. *Ibid.* 93 *Juniferus prostrata.* Trailing juniper. **1855** Trailing arbutus [see *New England mayflower* s.v. *NEW ENGLAND b]. **1861** *Trans. Illinois Agric. Soc.* IV. 462 We have on the lake shore a beautiful trailing evergreen—the Trailing Juniper. **1878** R. T. COOKE *Happy Dodd* 347 A profusion of trailing pine had been stored away in the barn cellar, before frost came. **1899** M. GOING *Field, Forest, & Wayside Flowers* 251 The lycopodiums..under the name of.. 'club-moss', or 'trailing-evergreen', are familiar to almost every one who has summered in New England. **1939** WODEHOUSE *Uncle Fred in Springtime* i. 18 The male, Barny, was calling me a trailing arbutus..and The Subject was talking about horsewhips. **1979** *United States 1980/81* (Penguin Travel Guides) 633 Among the many woodland trails are no less than 600 varieties of flowering plants—including the trailing yew, unique to this island.

2. c. *trailing vortex* (see quot. 1969).

1929 *Proc. R. Soc.* A. CXXIII. 440 The flow behind the screw is the same as if the screw surface formed by the trailing vortices was rigid. **1949** O. G. SUTTON *Sci. of Flight* iv. 112 The trailing vortices actually spring from two wing-tip vortices which, in flight, form just inside the wing tips. **1969** *Gloss. Aeronaut. & Astronaut. Terms* (*B.S.I.*) iv. 15 *Trailing vortex*, a vortex extending downstream from the surface of a body.

trailing edge. [TRAILING *ppl. a.*] **1.** The rear edge of a moving body; *spec.* in *Aeronaut.*, that of a wing or other part of an aircraft.

1909 *Flight* 3 July 390/1 These ribs overlap the rear spar and form a flexible trailing edge. **1934** *Flight* 8 Feb. 123/1 The split trailing edge flaps effect a big reduction in landing speed and length of glide. **1962** [see *RIBLET]. **1969** *Daily Tel.* 12 Nov. 14/6 Warning red lights mounted in the interior trailing-edge of the doors come on when a door is opened. **1971** I. G. GASS et al. *Understanding Earth* xix. 263/1 The newly generated crust and its upper mantle is effectively welded to the plate's trailing edge.

2. *Electronics.* The part of a pulse in which the amplitude diminishes.

1945 *Nature* 15 Sept. 319/2 The end or 'trailing edge' [of the pulse] marks the beginning of an invaluable clear period in which the radar echoes..can be received free from the overlaying and interfering effect of the primary signal. **1967** *Electronics* 6 Mar. 160/1 Nearly all of the earlier logic systems were based on trailing-edge triggering, so many engineers consider it normal. **1973** *Sci. Amer.* May 109/2 The trailing edge of the next pulse, the third in the series, causes flip-flop A to change state.

trailside, *a.*^{2} (and *sb.*) [f. TRAIL *sb.*^{1} + SIDE *sb.*^{1}] Situated at the side of a man-made trail. Occas. as *sb.*, the side of a trail.

1943 F. GARDNER *Philippine Indic Stud.* v. 43 A bamboo letter is fastened in a cleft stick and placed by the trailside. **1980** *Beautiful Brit. Columbia* Summer 33 By now the crowd of hikers has thinned out into an ambling string, leisurely pacing themselves with time to..lie back on a trailside carpet of heather and dwarf spirea. **1981** *Nordic Skiing* Jan. 4/3 These are generally outlined on a board at the touring center, on trail maps, or on trailside signs.

train, *sb.*^{1} Add: **III. 12. b.** Freq. in *train of thought.* (Further, including *techn.*, examples.)

1651 HOBBES *Leviathan* I. iii. 8 By Consequence, or Trayne of Thoughts, I understand that succession of one Thought to another, which is called (to distinguish it from Discourse in words) Mentall Discourse. **1770** G. WHITE *Let.* 19 Feb. in *Selborne* (1789) II. iii. 125 Your observation..struck me so forcibly, that I naturally fell into a train of thought that led me to consider whether the fact was so. **1899** W. JAMES *Talks* xv. 190 Our habitual associations of ideas, trains of thought, and sequences of action, might thus be consequences of the succession of currents in our nervous systems. **1912** *Proc. R. Soc.* LXXXVII. 93 The electric disturbance produced by a lightning discharge..is probably either a solitary wave or a very short train of waves. **1948** *Proc. IRE* XXXVI. 1457/1 A train of reset pulses is applied to the shift register. *a* **1953** E. O'NEILL *Hughie* (1959) 34 [*stage direction*] His train of thought interrupted, irritably. **1955** F. O'CONNOR *Wise Blood* i. 13 Mrs. Hitchcock lost her train of talk. 'I guess you're on your way to visit somebody?' she asked. **1959** F. ASTAIRE *Steps in Time* (1960) i. 6 It is the easiest thing in the world to become discouraged by a well-meant suggestion which may throw you off your original train of thought. **1967** *Electronics* 6 Mar. 130/2 The circuit will oscillate, simultaneously generating a sawtooth wave and pulse train. **1978** *Nature* 4 May 57/1 When the current with one channel present was recorded for a longer time, characteristic trains of short impulses were observed, separated by relatively long intervals when the channel did not conduct.

16. a. *armoured train*: see *ARMOURED *ppl. a.* 2a; *train de luxe*: see LUXE 2.

c. *to pull a train*: see *PULL *v.* 11 g.

IV. 20. b. (Earlier example.)

1783 *Quebec Gaz.* 22 May 2/1 No person shall come with traines, carts or other carriages, loaded with hay, straw or wood within the limits of the market-place.

22. b. *train crash, crew, fare, hostess, ride, station* (U.S.), *-time* (earlier example), *travel, whistle, -wrecker* (earlier example), *-yard*; **train-boy**, (*b*) (earlier example); **train call** *Theatr.*, (a notice of) the time for touring performers to catch a train to the next tour stop; † **train caller**, a railway official who announces the destinations of departing trains (see quot. 1921) (*obs.*); **train-jumper**

orig. *U.S.*, one who travels by train without paying the fare; so **train-jumping** *vbl. sb.*; **train master, trainmaster** *U.S.*, a person in charge of a train or trains; *spec.* a railway official responsible for the movement of all trains over a certain stretch of line; † **train porter**, a railway official in charge of a train over a single-line section of railway (*obs.*); also *attrib.*; **train set**, (*a*) a set of trains, tracks, etc., required for a model railway; (*b*) a set of wagons or carriages, sometimes with an engine, coupled together; **train-sick** *a.* (earlier example); **trainside** *a. U.S.*, at the side of or near a train, taking place next to a train; **train smash** *Naut. slang*, cooked tinned tomatoes, usu. with bacon; **train-staff**, (*a*) (earlier example); **train-stop**, (*b*) the state of a train's being at a stop; a place at which a train stops; **train ticket**, (*a*) a ticket delivered to an engine-driver as authority to travel over a single-line section of railway; cf. *train staff* (a), *staff and ticket* (*system*) s.v. *STAFF *sb.*[1] 26; (*b*) a ticket enabling a passenger to travel on a train.

1869 *Atlantic Monthly* July 73/2 [He] prevailed upon me to be his train-boy. **1912** C. MACKENZIE *Carnival* (ed. 5) iv. 41 A pal wouldn't let you sleep over the train-call on a Sunday morning. **1933** P. GODFREY *Back-Stage* xvi. 206 He packs his dress-basket, notes down the time of the train-call from the notice-board by the stage door. **1921** *Dict. Occupational Terms* (1927) §706 *Train caller*; a porter whose only duty is to call out destination of a departing train..; also calls out name of own station on arrival of trains. **1939** *WPA Guide to Florida* (1984) I. 5 Seminole names..were even more plentiful before the railroads interceded in behalf of train callers. **1957** D. DU MAURIER *Scapegoat* x. 133 A train-crash north of Lyons. **1979** P. THEROUX *Old Patagonian Express* xix. 293, I don't want to be in a train crash. But I have a very bad feeling about this train. **1904** *McClure's Mag.* Apr. 617/1 As for the train crew, we never had any more trouble with them than if they had been so many sheep. **1976** P. R. WHITE *Planning for Public Transport* viii. 162 If a train is stopped because of a derailment, blockage, etc. between signal boxes..it is necessary for the train crew to protect the trains with emergency lamps. **1905** J. JOYCE *Let.* 15 Oct. (1966) II. 122, I will send you 100 crowns to pay your trainfare. **1983** *U.S.A. Today* 19 Apr. 3A/1 In New York, trainfare and bagels were free as 90,000 suburban commuters got their trains back after a six week strike. **1963** *Times* 2 May 16/4 Why don't we have train hostesses like air hostesses..who visit every carriage and see if we are comfortable and happy? **1971** *N.Z. News* 10 Mar. 5 Train hostesses who serve the needs of passengers on New Zealand Railways' 'Southerner' express trains between Christchurch and Invercargill pose in their distinctive transit red uniforms. **1909** WEBSTER, Train jumper. **1930** *Times Lit. Suppl.* 5 June 482/3 Setting out on his trek across the continent,..as hobo, 'train jumper',..and cook in a Great Lakes freighter. **1965** H. P. TRITTON *Time means Tucker* i. 18, I..silently cursed myself for being fool enough to take on train-jumping. **1978** *Sunday Mail Color Mag.* (Brisbane) 22 Oct. 6/2 Now, in the early years of this century, train-jumping was an unknown art in Australia. **1880** *News & Press* (Cimarron, New Mexico) 9 Sept. 3/2 Mr. Frank Fulton, train master on this Division,..gave the following information concerning the damage. **1907** J. W. SCHULTZ *My Life as Indian* xviii. 210 Berry declared that he would do no more freighting to the mines with his bull train; he would either sell it or employ some one as a train-master. **1983** *Mod. Railroads* Apr. 18/1 Along with the yardmaster and trainmaster we observed the handling. **1859** *Rep. Accidents on Railways 1858* 17 in *Parl. Papers* XXV. 601 The system..of working by means of a train porter. **1873** *Returns Railways Companies Connections* 11 in *Ibid.* LVII. 765 Single Lines of Railway..Worked under the Train Porter System. **1932** W. FAULKNER *Light in August* vi. 132 Perhaps he remembered suddenly the train ride and the food. **1980** *Listener* 4 Sept. 296/2 The train ride down the Peninsula is boring: rubber, rubber, grey rubber trees. **1939–40** *Army & Navy Stores Catal.* 826/1 This excellent train set..comprises a No. 1 Special Locomotive..two No. 1 Pullman Coaches..and rails. **1959** G. F. ALLEN *Brit. Railways Today & Tomorrow* vii. 133 The Rosters usually indicate the preceding and succeeding use to which each coach of a train set is to be put. **1980** J. CARTWRIGHT *Horse of Darius* xi. 158 He was playing with his train set... He..passed his days in a world of trains and model airplanes. **1982** WHITEHOUSE & ALLEN *E. Treacy—Railway Photographer* 42 The all-maroon train-set of the northbound 'Flying Scotsman' leaving Copenhagen Tunnel. **1905** E. M. FORSTER *Where Angels fear to Tread* vi. 163 They crossed the Apennines with a train-sick child. **1932** *Sun* (Baltimore) 21 Sept. 1/6 He [*sc.* F. D. Roosevelt]..jollying trainside crowds with localized pleasantries. **1940** *Ibid.* 24 July 1/5 In a series of train-side and platform talks..he [*sc.* W. L. Wilkie] lashed out against leading Democratic party machines by name. **1941** *Weekly Tel.* (Sheffield) 13 Sept. 16/1 The boys of the Navy have a lot of slang... They have given the name 'train smash' to a tomato and bacon breakfast. **1978** *Daily Mirror* 19 June 9/1 Train smash is our nickname for tinned tomatoes with bacon. **1859** *Rep. Accidents on Railways 1858* 17 in *Parl. Papers* XXV. 601 To make the train staff the means of opening the train-ticket box. **1955** W. GADDIS *Recognitions* II. iii. 422 Go to a train station yourself..or a bus station. **1981** *N.Y. Times Mag.* 21 June 10/3 When was the last time you heard a young, rich-affluent-wealthy type use the phrase *railroad station?* Upper-class use is now *train station.* **a 1963** S. PLATH *Ariel* (1965) 43 It is a trainstop, the nurses Undergoing the faucet water. **1977** H. FAST *Immigrants* 10 The food, brought to them at train stops, was a dismal, unchanging diet of cold sausage and stale bread. **1859** *Rep. Accidents on Railways 1858* 17 in *Parl. Papers* XXV. 601 If another engine or train is intended to follow in succession, a train ticket, stating 'staff following', will be given to the person in charge of the leading train, the staff itself being given to the last. **1941** B. SCHULBERG *What makes Sammy Run?* x. 256 A letter arrived with a train ticket and travelling expenses. **1977** *Lancashire Life* Dec. 60/1 He..showed early business acumen by taking orders for Wakes Week train tickets, sleeping-out on the doorstep of Thomas Cook's the night before the ticket sale to save others' queueing. **1877** F. M. A. ROE *Army Lett.* (1909) 163 From then on to train time, Hal was patted and petted and given dainties. **1979** P. THEROUX *Old Patagonian Express* xiii. 200 The difficulties of train travel in Latin America. **1927** R. LEHMANN *Dusty Answer* III. i. 128 A far train-whistle roused her. **1981** V. MEHTA *Vedi* (1982) i. 3, I remember the train whistle. It blew with a rush of steam. **1883** *Manch. Examiner* 28 Nov. 4/6 It is supposed that the would-be train wreckers were plotting against the Premier's life. **1930** J. DOS PASSOS *42nd Parallel* I. 16 Dumping grounds, trainyards. **1973** T. PYNCHON *Gravity's Rainbow* I. 171 Out the windows..are a row of bare Army-colored poplars, a canal, a snowy trainyard.

train, *v.*[1] Add: **III. 6. d.** (Earlier example.)

1832 S. AUSTIN tr. *Pückler-Muskau's Tour of German Prince* III. iv. 74, I kept race-horses myself, and had a Newmarket jockey for a time in my service... It amused me greatly to see this fellow 'training' himself.

7. b. *train on* (earlier *fig.* and later examples).

1767 G. SELWYN *Let.* 29 Dec. in *15th Rep. R. Comm. Hist. Manuscripts* App. VI. 225 in *Parl. Papers 1897* (C. 8551) LI. 1, Lord Beauchamp trains on well, as they say, but *il n' a pas le moyen de plaire.* **1789** *Loiterer* 6 June 7 He *trained on famously* well, and would soon be a very *dashing man.* **1937** *Daily Tel.* 15 Oct. 23/3 He..trained on into a first-rate College oar. **1976** *Horse & Hound* 10 Dec. 48/2 (Advt.), A good sire of fast 2-year-olds that train on.

IV. 9. c. To associate, ally, or co-operate *with*, (*dial.* also *along of*). *N. Amer. colloq.*

1871 J. HAY *Pike County Ballads* 22 It gravels me like the devil to train Along o' sich fools as you. **1889** *Cent. Dict.* s.v. *train*[1], I don't *train* with that crowd. **1892** 'MARK TWAIN' *Amer. Claimant* i. 5 Have you been training with that ass again? **1907** *Methodist Rev.* Nov. 984 He does not train with the extreme radical theologians. **1935** H. DAVIS *Honey in Horn* i. 4 A couple of bad-acting sons who got drunk, fought and trained around with thieving half-breeds. **1945** 'L. FORD' *Philadelphia Murder Story* ix. 146 She knew as well as I know now—and I don't train with lawyers—that Malone wasn't going to search the house.

11. b. (Earlier example.)

1856 LD. GRANVILLE *Let.* 12 Feb. in Ld. Fitzmaurice *Life Granville* (1905) I. vii. 163 After acting as godfather, I trained up to town for the Committee of Privileges.

trainability (trēⁱnăbi·lĭti). [f. TRAINABLE *a.* + -ILITY.] Aptness or capacity for being trained.

1955 G. A. N. LOWNDES *Brit. Educ. System* ii. 40 High trainability is a delicate plant. **1960** *Times* 20 Jan. 9/7 The fine quality of the Northern Ireland labour force, its trainability. **1980** *Observer* 4 May 26/6 If a degree indicates intelligence or trainability.

‖**trainante** (trẹnānt), *a.* Now *rare.* Also **traînante.** [a. F. *traînante* (fem.), f. pres. pple. of *traîner* to drag, as in *voix traînante*, etc.] Of vocal or musical sounds: dragging, drawling.

1818 C. MORGAN *Let.* 16 Sept. in Lady Morgan *Autobiogr.* (1859) 104 The music..possesses here and there fine strains of melody: *per contra*, it is *trainante* often too scientific and old-fashioned in its phrases. **1865** 'OUIDA' *Strathmore* I. x. 170 The tranquil *trainante* tones in which he always spoke his rudest things. **1899** *Westm. Gaz.* 5 Oct. 3/1 Talking in their pleasant, *traînante* tones to and of each other.

trainee. Add: Of a person, not now usu. correlative to *trainer*. (Earlier and later examples.) Also *attrib.* or as *adj.*

1841 *Fistiana* 112 An early, light, and nutritive supper would greatly benefit the trainee. **1927** *Daily Tel.* 8 Feb. 13/7 The number of new trainees is now so small that a workshop smaller than that which we are now using will suffice. **1932** *Sun* (Baltimore) 19 July 15/6 (*heading*) Trainees at Meade using machine guns. **1942** *Yank* 4 Nov. 11 Basic trainees beat the softball pitching. **1951** *Good Housek. Home Encycl.* 37/1 The majority of nursery training schools do not make any hard-and-fast rule regarding the work which their trainees should take over. **1953** *Manch. Guardian Weekly* 6 Aug. 7/3 A rice paddy..through which trainee squads are sent, as on a Korean patrol. **1956** *B.B.C. Handbk. 1957* 138 Sixteen trainee broadcasters. **1962** *Lancet* 1 Dec. 1156/2 The trainee assistant scheme is on the right lines, but there have been complaints that the scheme has occasionally been abused by trainers who used their trainees as ordinary assistants. **1977** *Grimsby Even. Tel.* 31 May 5/7 Miss Sally Dixon, a trainee nurse, was announced as the hospital's Jubilee representative following a ballot. **1978** *West Lancs. Even. Gaz.* 23 Feb. 17 (Advt.), Vacancies for able young persons as trainees.

Hence **trainee·ship**, the position of a trainee, a post as a trainee.

1961 *Listener* 14 Dec. 1021/2 Some management traineeship schemes in industry and commerce. **1964** *New Statesman* 13 Nov. 747/1 Bourgeois and ambitious parents..thrust their sons into low-paid traineeships with prospects of eventual power and wealth. **1966** *Rep. Comm. Inquiry Univ. Oxf.* II. 193 The category 'other' includes general traineeships and postgraduate apprenticeships. **1980** *Nature* 14 Feb. 610/1 The universities hope that the administration can be persuaded to contribute more than $150 million..to provide a national support programme of grants, traineeships and fellowships.

trainer. Add: **1. a.** Also *attrib.*

1973 *Philadelphia Inquirer* 7 Oct. 13 (Advt.), Convertible or girls sidewalk bike. Trainer wheels included. **1976** *Milton Keynes Express* 2 July 25/1 (Advt.), Baby walker, babycare bath mat and toddler trainer seat £2, or will sell separately. **1977** *Austral. Sailing* Jan. 46/1 For the very young, the best way into sailing is through a sailing club in a trainer class like the Sabot or Manly Junior.

c. An aircraft used in training pilots or other aircrew.

1932 AUDEN *Orators* II. 59, 1 Moth trainer fully equipped for advanced training. **1950** *Hansard Commons* 21 Mar. 1771 The introduction of the Prentice as the basic trainer has enabled instrument flying instruction to be improved considerably. **1977** 'J. LE CARRÉ' *Honourable Schoolboy* xvi. 368 A row of single-engined military trainers.

d. A soft running shoe without spikes; a training shoe.

1978 *Guardian* 22 Dec. 9/3 The Poynton Jemmers, a women's morris dance side..are in mufti tonight... But no trainers or pumps: it's clogs or nothing. **1982** *New Society* 4 Mar. 344/2 Skinny teenage boys in the ubiquitous parkas, jeans and trainers. **1983** *Listener* 28 July 19/1 Dr. Garrow is welcome to don trainers and join the ladies I run with on Saturdays.

training, *vbl. sb.* Add: **2. c.** (Earlier example.)

1786 W. COWPER *Let.* 1 May (1981) II. 531 When you come, I shall talk you into training, as the jockeys say, I doubt not that I shall make a nimble and good walker of you in a short time.

5. *training camp, centre, department, -ground* (earlier example), *prison, programme, session, shoe*; **training-school,** *spec.* (*b*) *N. Amer.*, a vocational institution for juvenile delinquents.

1894 T. B. ALDRICH *Two Bites at Cherry* 216, I don't fancy he heard a gun fired, unless it went off by accident in some training-camp for recruits. **1980** *Washington Star* 10 Dec. C6, I felt like a rookie again in training camp. **1926** *Encycl. Brit.* Suppl. III. 819/2 (*heading*) War training centers. **1962** E. SNOW *Other Side of River* (1963) lxxi. 549 Shanghai and Manchuria have been the biggest training centers for China's modernization. **1906** *Rep. Brit. Assoc. Adv. Sci.* 271 To take a course of training in some existing training college or training department. **1644** in *Early Rec. Dedham, Mass.* (1892) III. 102 From the Trayning ground to the Cart Bridge. **1950** Training prison [see *OPEN *a.* 2 d]. **1977** *Herald* (Melbourne) 17 Jan. 2/6 The prisoners were transferred after a security review at country jails following four escapes from Geelong Training Prison in a week last month. **1971** L. B. JOHNSON *Vantage Point* (1972) iv. 81 Our manpower training programs focused on preparing unskilled men and women for jobs. **1977** *Offshore Engineer* June 36/1 Pilots are selected from employees who show diving aptitude with a full mechanical understanding, and are put through a rigorous training programme. **1905** *First Ann. Rep. N.Y. State Training School for Girls* 4 The Penal Code was amended..so as to authorize the commitment of delinquent girls under the age of sixteen..to the New York State Training School for Girls. **1978** *Globe & Mail* (Toronto) 11 Jan. 7/3 If training schools are closed, then some group homes will have to have a custodial aspect. **1951** *Sport* 6–12 Apr. 12/2 Most clubs have selected their spot-kicker after careful tests during training sessions. **1977** J. M. JOHNSON in Douglas & Johnson *Existential Sociol.* viii. 242 A worker in Unit One said she had decided to record her time spent in training sessions on line C of the report. **1973** *People's Jrnl.* (Inverness) 4 Aug. 20/2 (Advt.), Training shoes. **1984** *Nutshell* (Gainesville, Florida) Spring 61/1 (Advt.), A remarkable new training shoe designed to take all the wear and tear high-mileage runners can give it.

trainman, train man. 2. For *U.S.* read 'orig. *U.S.*' and add earlier and later examples; *spec.* (see quot. 1982).

1877 J. D. MCCABE *Hist. Great Riots* 48 These motives have been misunderstood, and..produced the present troubles amongst our trainmen. **1960** [see *SHOPMAN 3]. **1964** [see *secondman* s.v. *SECOND *a.* 7 a]. **1967** *Guardian* 4 Dec. 1/3 British Rail's intention is to replace them [*sc.* firemen and guards] by a new type of railwayman—a 'trainman'. **1982** *Daily Tel.* 19 June 2/7 The six productivity concessions..include..the introduction of 'train men' to combine the duties of guards and travelling ticket inspectors.

trai·n-spotter. [TRAIN *sb.*[1] 16.] One (esp. a small boy) whose hobby is observing trains and recording railway locomotive numbers. Hence **trai·n-spotting** *vbl. sb.*; **trai·n-spot** *v. intr.*

1958 *Spectator* 11 July 70/3 A prize of six guineas is offered for a Train Spotters' Anthem. *Ibid.* 1 Aug. 179/1 Many of them must simply spend their time train-spotting. **1959** *Manch. Guardian* 22 July 2/6 British Railways..announced a ban on train-spotting..on about twelve main-line stations. **1969** *Times* 1 Nov. (Saturday Rev. Suppl.) p. iii/4 A train-spotting recluse, primed with exact information on lines that have rusted into the ground. **1974** P. MCCUTCHAN *Coach North* ii. 15 'I reckon you're all past train spotting.'..The old man didn't look as though he'd ever train spotted. **1978** D. WILLIAMS *Treasure up in Smoke* xiv. 126 The Governor appeared to have graduated from train-spotter to Lord Protector in one short morning.

traist, *a.* Restrict † *Obs.* to other senses and add: **3.** (Later *poet. arch.* examples.)

1919 E. POUND *Quia Pauper Amavi* 11 She has her lover till morn, Till the traist man cry out to warn Them. **1955** —— *Classic Anthol.* I. 21 Shall no one be traist? Mother of Heaven, Shall no one be traist?

trait. Add: **6. a.** (Further examples of a culture or social group.) Also *attrib.*

1916 *Amer. Jrnl. Sociol.* Mar. 656 In maize culture as practiced by American farmers we have a fine example of a borrowed culture trait. *Ibid.* 659 The colonists took over all the essential parts of the trait-complex. **1936** R. LINTON *Study of Man* xvi. 280 During this [trial] period both the new trait and the old trait or traits with which it is competing become Alternatives within the total culture complex. *Ibid.* xxii. 397 Every trait is intimately associated with some other trait or traits to form a larger functional unit commonly known as a *trait complex.* **1947** G. MURPHY *Personality* xxi. 506 Most of the trait names that are used represent general action tendencies; and as soon as they are applied to oneself, or..to others, they stimulate a trait psychology in their user. **1976** A. HALEY *Roots* vii. 21 Kunta would always turn and walk away, thus displaying the dignity and self-command that his mother had taught him were the proudest traits of the Mandinka tribe. **1977** R. HOLLAND *Self & Social Context* v. 165 Trait models of professions attempt to list the characteristics of professional activity..as though some essential quality will be revealed by describing and comparing the many examples.

‖**trait d'union** (trę dünyoṅ). [Fr., lit. 'hyphen'.] A connection between or amongst otherwise unattached characteristics or parties.

1912 J. BUCHAN *Moon Endureth* IV. 127 He had established no *trait d'union* between the intellect..and the senses. **1934** A. TOYNBEE *Study of Hist.* I. II. 190 In the British Empire..this medieval incarnation of political unity [*sc.* the Crown] has latterly acquired a new and unforeseen institutional value as the *trait d'union* between the States Members of the British Commonwealth of Nations. **1959** *Times* 7 Jan. 11/7 M. Moktar Ould Daddah likes to think of his country [*sc.* Mauritania] as a *trait-d'union*, or link, between the Maghreb and West Africa.

Trajanic (trēᶦdʒæ·nik), *a.* [f. L. *Trāiān-us* + -IC.] Of or pertaining to the Roman emperor Trajan (A.D. 53–117), esp. to the style of triumphal art associated with him.

1906 *Athenæum* 27 Jan. 113/2 The *extispicium* scene probably represents the nuncupatio votorum before Trajan set out on his Dacian campaign, and is Trajanic in style. **1933** *Times Lit. Suppl.* 9 Nov. 780/3 He finds no sign in either the Trajanic or the Aurelian column of a Court art. **1978** *Antiquaries Jrnl.* LVIII. 82 The Dacian victory is perhaps the most significant of all the triumphal themes in Trajanic art.

trajectory, *sb.* Add: Also with pronunc. (træ·dʒĕktǒri).

Trakehner (trakē·nəɹ). In sense 2 also **trakehner, trakena, trakener.** [a. Ger., f. the name of the Trakehnen stud.] **1.** A saddle horse belonging to a breed first developed at the Trakehnen stud in east Prussia.

[**1905** W. RIDGEWAY *Origin & Influence Thoroughbred Horse* iv. 472 The extraordinary tractability of the Prussian Trakehnen breed..is a well known feature.] **1926** A. TOPHAM *Chron. Prussian Court* i. 16 The carriages.. had been waiting in the shade, each with its four splendid Trakehner horses. **1975** *Islander* (Victoria, B.C.) 13 July 5/1 The Trakehner breed of horses is fairly new in North America, but is famous and long prized in Europe where the breed originated in the areas of Eastern Prussia and Poland. **1980** G. HENSCHEL *Illustr. Guide Horses & Ponies* 155/3 Trakehners often make top-grade show jumpers.

2. A type of fence in the cross-country section of an equestrian three-day event, etc. (see quot. 1973).

1958 S. WILLCOX *Three Days Running* xvii. 174 We made our way up the incline towards a big trakena fence. **1959** R. S. SUMMERHAYS *Encycl. for Horsemen* (rev. ed.) 306/2 *Trakener*, a type of fence used in Cross-country... It is a ditch spanned by rails in the centre. **1973** C. STRATTON *Encycl. Show-Jumping & Combined Training* 271/1 A trakener is a cross-country obstacle made of a 'knife rest' construction, built on a ditch, with a second rail attached to the cross pieces. **1977** *Horse & Hound* 10 June 25/1 Fences 5 (a trakehner over a dry ditch) and 6 (a sloping palisade followed by a bank and ditch) caused most of the trouble across country.

tralucent, *a.* Delete † *Obs.* and add later examples.

1914 C. MACKENZIE *Sinister St.* II. IV. iv. 932 The benign trees that hung down with tralucent green sprays in the lamplight. **1951** —— *Carnival* (rev. ed.) viii. 81 Her hands were long and white; her lips very crimson and tralucent.

tram, *sb.*² Add: **V. 8.** *tram-beam* (*fig.* example), *-fare* (also *transf.*), *-horn, horse, -refuge, ride, stop, -top, -track, -train, -wagon* (earlier example).

1879 G. M. HOPKINS *Poems* (1967) 81 Or to-fro tender trambeams truckle at the eye. **1909** J. R. WARE *Passing Eng.* 249/2 *Tram-fare* (*London Streets'*, 1882), twopence. **1922** JOYCE *Ulysses* 696 *Debit*... Tramfare [£.s.d.] 0.0.1. **1978** M. DE LARRABEITI *Rose beyond Thames* 87 He bought ..me a second-hand bike so that I could cycle to school and save the tram fare. **1922** *Blackw. Mag.* Apr. 447/1 The blowing of tram-horns. **1891** J. L. KIPLING *Beast & Man in India* viii. 206 (*caption*) Bombay tram-horse wearing horse-cap. **1938** *All England Law Rep. Annotated* I. 339 An illuminated bollard at one end of a tram refuge had been damaged in an accident. **1919** R. FRY *Let.* 3 Nov. (1972) II. 465 Marseilles is only one and a half hours tram ride. **1977** *Lancashire Life* Dec. 57/2 One summer's day he changed the routine and took us a tram ride into the country. **1930** R. LEHMANN *Note in Music* I. 19 They arrived at the tram-stop to find a solid wedge of humanity struggling to get aboard. **1980** P. HARCOURT *Tomorrow's Treason* I. iv. 58 It was a long walk to the nearest tram stop. **1895** G. B. SHAW *Let.* 23 Mar. (1965) I. 504 We..went to her sister's..by tramtop. **1916** JOYCE *Portrait of Artist* ii. 70 He heard the mare's hoofs clattering along the tramtrack on the Rock Road. **1911** R. FRY *Let.* 15 Apr. (1972) I. 347 A two hours' journey by a tram-train to the slopes of Mt Olympus. **1824** F. WITTS *Diary* 6 May (1978) 38 The tram waggons now may be made to travel without horses by steam.

Traminer (tramī·nəɹ). [a. Ger., f. *Tramin* (It. *Termeno*), the name of a village in N. Italy.] The name of any of several varieties of vine and grape widely grown in Germany, Alsace, and elsewhere; the white wine with perfumed bouquet produced from this grape. Also *attrib.*

1851 C. REDDING *Hist. & Descr. Mod. Wines* (ed. 3) ii. 48 Then there is the *Traminer* with a small berry, sweet, and fond of a marly soil. **1872** THUDICHUM & DUPRÉ *Treatise on Origin, Nature, & Varieties of Wine* ix. 281 German wines—... Riesling... Forster Traminer. *Ibid.* xvi. 541 There are also some so-called Franconia grapes, which we will describe as white Traminer. **1948** 'J. TEY' *Franchise Affair* xiii. 144 There is a Traminer for dinner. **1960** *Spectator* 13 May 714 Yugoslav traminer came on to the British market during 1959. **1972** *Guardian* 4 May 13/5 The local variety of the Traminer grape called the Savagnin.

tram-line. Add: Also **tramline. 2.** *pl.* Either pair of parallel lines bordering the side of a lawn-tennis court, the inner of each pair marking the boundary of the court for singles and the outer for doubles. Occas. *sing.*, one of this pair of lines. *colloq.*

1937 PARTRIDGE *Dict. Slang* 906/1 *Tram-lines*, the 4½ ft. wide area on each side of a (doubles) lawn-tennis court: sporting: from ca. 1929. Esp. *down the tram-lines*, i.e. more or less straight along this strip of the court. **1959** *Times* 31 Aug. 12/1 It passed an inch outside the tramline. **1978** G. FORBES *Handful of Summers* ix. 180 Cliff.. hit a two-hander down Rodney's tramlines.

3. *transf. fig.* Chiefly *pl.*, inflexible, predetermined or restrictive courses of action, principles, etc.

1948 D. WELCH *Brave & Cruel* 68, I ran it [*sc.* a nail-brush] up and down his back until I'd made harsh red tramlines. **1955** H. SPRING *These Lovers fled Away* iv. 113 One [obstacle] was..his addiction to social tram-lines. As things had been, they should, in a well-organised world, remain. **1967** *Times Rev. Industry* Oct. 60/2 Tramline thinking..delays improvement in the quality of the trade union movement itself. **1976** *Listener* 22 July 85/3 The government..is forced..more and more on to orthodox, predictable tramlines, and protestations that imagination, vision and radical policy must await more prosperous days. **1979** J. WAINWRIGHT *Duty Elsewhere* vii. 28 Most chief constables tend to run on tram-lines... They feel safer.

Hence **tra·m-lined** *a.*, furnished with tramlines.

1924 W. J. LOCKE *Coming of Amos* xiii. 171 He stepped into the car and..drove at break-neck speed down the tram-lined hill. **1932** AUDEN *Orators* III. 89 Tudor from the tram-lined town.

trammie, trammy (træ·mi). *colloq.* (esp. *Austral.* and *N.Z.*). [f. TRAM *sb.*² + -Y⁶, -IE.] A tram-conductor or tram-driver.

c **1926** 'MIXER' *Transport Workers' Song Bk.* 23 Then he slathers up the 'trammies', As the conductor goes through. **1934** L. G. GIBBON *Grey Granite* III. 192 The conductor had seen Alick and caught his arm... The trammie held fast, a squat, buirdly bird with a face like a badly-made barn door. *Ibid.*, That shortened the run, in a minute the Docks, the trammie slowed down at a bend. **1945** F. RYLAND in *Coast to Coast 1944* 166 The soldier sprang wildly to his feet and knocked the trammie in the mouth. **1972** *Guardian* 6 Dec. 13/5 Trammies, truckies and wharfies (Australian for tram and bus conductors and drivers, truck-drivers and dockers). **1979** *Jrnl. Lancs. Dial. Soc.* Jan. 5 At heart I will always be a trammie, for somehow the outlandish humour of those days was born in trams and synonymous with them.

tra·mming, *vbl. sb.* [f. TRAM *v.*¹ 2 + -ING¹.] Conveyance (of coal, ore, etc.) by a tram or trams.

1875 *Stock Exch. Observer* 9 Feb. 3/1 So much for breaking, tramming and carriage by rail. **1983** *New Scientist* 21 Apr. 162 The next operation is 'tramming', or the actual removal of the ore to the surface using wagons.

trammy: see *TRAMMIE.

tramp, *sb.*¹ Add: **1. b.** More fully *axle tramp.* Alternate bouncing of wheels on the same axle.

1935 *Story of Knee Action* (General Motors Corp.) 3 Such erratic wheel movements as 'shimmy' and 'tramp' should be eliminated. **1959** *Motor Manual* (ed. 36) v. 121 Independent rear suspension..offers the advantages of reduction of unsprung weight and the elimination of axle tramp and patter. **1977** *Drive* Sept.–Oct. 120/2 Banging and jumping from the rear axle..on fast take-offs from rest or in mid-corner (a condition called 'axle tramp'). **1982** *Motor* 3 July 39/4 Brisk starts are noticeable for their lack of tramp.

3. (N.Z. examples.)

1966 *Weekly News* (N.Z.) 3 Aug. 7/4 Two-day tramps from the Milford Hotel up to the Sutherland Falls. **1984** *N.Z. Woman's Weekly* 30 Apr. 121/2 Day tramps are popular.

4. b. *slang* (orig. *U.S.*). A sexually promiscuous woman.

1922 E. O'NEILL *Anna Christie* I. 119 Sure—and another tramp with her. **1936** D. POWELL *Turn, Magic Wheel* I. 60 A wayward, double-crossing, lying little tramp. **1959** 'J. WELCOME' *Stop at Nothing* ii. 28 You can usually tell..the nice girls from the tramps. **1971** *Sunday Nation* (Nairobi) 11 Apr. 19/2 Even in these permissive times the girl of your age who can't say 'no' can pretty soon earn the title of tramp among her contemporaries. **1979** R. JAFFE *Class Reunion* I. v. 49 Who could blame Richard, so young at prep school, for fooling around with the local tramp?

5. c. An aircraft plying commercially according to demand. Also *attrib.*

1905 KIPLING *Actions & Reactions* (1909) 141 These heavy freighters fly down to Halifax direct... They are the biggest tramps aloft. **1948** *Shell Aviation News* No. 115 8/3 At present the majority of freight charters are on a direct 'out-and-home' basis, but the time is coming when, with the parallel development of the Baltic and heavy duty tramp aeroplanes, 'time charter' will be as commonplace as it is with shipping. **1952** 'J. TEY' *Singing Sands* ix. 130 Most of us fly scheduled routes, but some fly tramps. Take anything anywhere.

7. (see also *5 c); (in sense 4) *tramp-woman.*

1902 HARDY *Time's Laughingstocks* (1909) 11 (*poem title*) A trampwoman's tragedy.

trampdom (earlier example).

1891 *Contemp. Rev.* Aug. 257 The tramp also finds it convenient to use the highways, but this is not..common ..for it is on the railroads that Trampdom thrives as an institution.

tramp, *v.*¹ Add: **4. a.** *N.Z. spec.* to walk for long distances in rough country.

1935, etc. [implied in *TRAMPING *vbl. sb.*]. **1984** *N.Z. Listener* 28 Apr. 62/1 One of my correspondents tramping with her husband, referred to the 'benched out' track they were following up the hillside.

b. (Earlier example.)

1846 *Swell's Night Guide* 134/2 *Tramp*, to wander as a beggar.

6. b. To transport goods by road to varying destinations as the load requires.

1959 [implied in *TRAMPING *vbl. sb.*]. **1968** in P. G. Hollowell *Lorry Driver* vi. 152 She [*sc.* a lorry driver's wife] didn't like it when I was on tramping... When you're tramping you never know where you're going and when you're coming back.

tramping *vbl. sb.* (further examples).

1935 J. GUTHRIE *Little Country* xxi. 319 The members of the Tem Tramping Club. **1959** A. MCLINTOCK *Descr. Atlas N.Z.* 74 New Zealanders are a people who take full advantage of these open spaces for all manner of recreational activity, including..shooting and fishing, and tramping and mountaineering. **1959** *Times Rev. Industry* June 45/3 Abolition of tramping and conduct of all long-distance movement through ..regular trunk services with sufficient terminal arrangements. **1963** *N.Z. Woman's Weekly* 17 June 18/3 [At Jackson Bay] we have the best deer shooting, tramping country and scenery in New Zealand. **1968** P. G. HOLLOWELL *Lorry Driver* iii. 71 Tramping, in contrast to the monotony of trunking, is mainly liked for the variety it affords, both in the types of loads carried, the different parts of the country which are seen, [etc.]. **1975** *N.Z. News* 9 July 5/2 Proper equipment enabled a six-strong tramping party..to survive near freezing temperatures in the rugged Pouakai Ranges. **1984** *N.Z. Woman's Weekly* 30 Apr. 121/2 Tramping, mountaineering and trout fishing are other attractions in the Nelson Lakes National Park.

tramper. Add: **2.** *N.Z. spec.* a person who walks long distances in rough country for recreation.

1960 B. CRUMP *Good Keen Man* 60, I sent my men, who were more likely to lose themselves than find lost trampers, up and down a branch of the stream looking for boot-prints. **1977** G. SCOTT *Hot Pursuit* x. 87 One of the temporary shelters for trampers that are dotted about the New Zealand bush. **1984** *N.Z. Field & Stream* Apr./May 46/3 Wool is excellent for New Zealand conditions, and is widely used by trampers and climbers.

trampolin, -ine, *sb.* Add: Now usu. with spelling **-ine** and pronunc. (-īn). Substitute for def.: A base of elastic material used as a springboard and landing area in acrobatic exercises and displays; now *spec.* a sheet of canvas, nylon mesh, or the like, held in a frame by springs. Also *attrib.* and *fig.* (Further examples.)

1799 *Times* 1 June 3/4 He positively leaps over a large tilted waggon..and does not make use of a spring board or trampoline. **1928** *Daily Express* 13 June 13 A trampoline act, a wire act..in fact,..a complete vaudeville programme. **1930** *Observer* 1 June 21 They perform on the apparatus resembling a spring mattress, which has been dubbed the 'trampoline'. **1938** N. STREATFEILD *Circus* *is Coming* vii. 109 The things they did when on the trampoline were breath-taking.., shooting up.., then coming down in amazing twists and somersaults. **1960** *Times Lit. Suppl.* 1 July 418/4 [D. H.] Lawrence has been bounced up and down on the trampoline of literary fashion more than most writers. **1961** *U.S. Patents Quarterly* CXXIX. 210/2 As applied to tumbling devices, 'Tram- poline' is completely generic. **1975** *Oxf. Compan. Sports & Games* 1044/2 The trampoline has a steel frame, braced in such a way as to ensure that a landing in the bouncing area ..may be made without fear of hitting any structural members.

trampolin(e *v.*, substitute for def.: to perform on a trampoline; also *fig.*; (later examples); **tra·mpolining** *vbl. sb.*, the practice or sport of performing on a trampoline; **tra·mpolinist,** a performer on the trampoline.

1843 in M. W. Disher *Greatest Show on Earth* (1937) 196 (*in illustration*) Mr. W. T. Twist the Trampolinist... Astley's Royal Ampitheatre 1843. **1953** *People & Places* (Chicago) Mar. 6/1 (*caption*) When performing the back turn-over or cannonball, a trampolinist attains a tuck or pike position on takeoff. *Ibid.* 6/2 Descended from a centuries-old European circus art, trampolining is one of the newest..sports to be adopted by the nation's colleges, high schools and private athletic clubs. **1972** *Guardian* 11 Apr. 15/4 Children fenced, trampolined, played volleyball and football. **1973** *Times* 1 Feb. 16/6 It proved.. difficult..to trampoline at all except at a speed dictated by gravity. **1978** R. Hill *Pinch of Snuff* xiv. 142 Isn't she..a trifle overdressed for trampolining? *Ibid.* xiv. 148 Estelle, the teenage trampolinist.

trance, *sb.*[1] Add: **4.** *trance faculty, -mediumship, music, -personality, speaker, -state* (examples), *-subject, -utterance, -writing*; *trance-bound* (example), *-eyed* adjs.

1860 J. G. Whittier *Home Ballads* 90 Shine on us with the light which glowed Upon the trance-bound shepherd's way. **1957** C. Day Lewis *Pegasus* 15 A bright bewildered April, a trance-eyed summer. **1909** W. James *Mem. & Stud.* (1911) viii. 190 All the resources of the automatist, including his or her trance-faculty of telepathy. **1870** *Spiritualist* 14 Jan. 37/3 One feature running through the whole range of trance-mediumship, is the fact that the media..feel symptoms of the death pains of the communicating spirits. **1961** Trance-mediumship [see *control *sb.* 4 b]. **1970** *Guardian* 5 June 9/4 The records cover the whole range of Ethiopian music..through cow milking songs to Moslem trance music. **1890** W. James *Princ. Psychol.* I. viii. 211 The poor passive trance-personality had stuck for weeks in the stagnant dream. **1920** Trance speaker [see *automatist 2]. **1890** W. James *Princ. Psychol.* II. xxvii. 601 The suggestion-theory may therefore be approved as correct, provided we grant the trance-state as its prerequisite. **1978** *Amer. Speech* LIII. 59 Felicitas Goodman describes behavior in trance states accompanying glossolalia in congregations mostly in Mexico. **1880** Trance-subject [see *associate *sb.* 7]. **1890** W. James *Princ. Psychol.* I. x. 394 One curious thing about trance-utterances is their generic similarity in different individuals. **1980** 'S. Woods' *Weep for Her* 51 So many things are involved...telepathy, clairvoyance, trance utterance, [etc.]. **1911** W. F. Barrett *Psychical Res.* xv. 218 The group of controls..manifested themselves also in the trance-writings.

tranche. Delete ‖ and 'Now only as a loan-word from French' and add: Now also semi-anglicized as (trɑ̃nʃ). **2.** *transf.* and *fig.*, esp. in *Econ.*, *spec.* an instalment of a loan, a quota, a block of bonds or (esp. government) stock.

1930 *Economist* 10 May (Suppl.) 10/1 The first business of the bank will be the arrangement of a loan to raise $300 million... The first *tranche* of the combined loan is expected to be offered about the end of May. **1953** *Ibid.* 15 Aug. 470/2 The gas stock (and a few other tranches, too) remains to be sold. **1962** C. A. R. Crosland *Conservative Enemy* v. 83 It is true that, as in Soviet Russia, or any industrial society, the top managerial executives belong to the highest social *tranche* in terms both of income and prestige. **1963** *Ann. Reg. 1962* 477 On 9 May a further tranche, amounting to £300 million, of 5 per cent Treasury Stock 1986–89 was issued at £84½ per cent. **1964** S. Brittan *Treasury under Tories* iv. 123 The 'gold tranche' represents the portion of British credit facilities automatically available without conditions. **1966** *Listener* 11 Aug. 206/1 It laid down political conditions which Egypt would have to fulfil in order to get the second *tranche* of the loan. **1973** *Times* 19 Dec. 17/6 To meet the load growth in the meantime, the board says, a 'large tranche of reliable nuclear plant' is required. **1974** *Times* 6 Mar. 15/2 Names have rarely been published except in the cases of the biggest tranches of aid [*sc.* Government aid to private industry]. **1977** *Observer* 3 Apr. 10/2 His second tranche of income-tax cuts. **1978** 'L. Black' *Foursome* v. 40 Later, the next tranche of old houses would be knocked down so that the Brickyard Lane estate could be doubled in size. **1980** *Times* 18 Jan. 19/4 Why not approach the institutional or wholesale money market for funds in large tranches rather than continue with the costly exercise of collecting money from a multitude of smaller savers?

3. ‖ **tranche de vie** [lit. 'slice of life'], a representation of quotidian existence, *spec.* in literature or painting; also *attrib.*

1934 in Webster. **1957** N. Frye *Anat. Criticism* 285 This idolatrous form of mimesis is rare, but the thin line of its tradition can be traced from Classical mime writers like Herodas to their *tranche-de-vie* descendants in recent times. **1958** *Spectator* 11 July 52/1 This *tranche de vie* came into my mind while I was talking. **1959** *Times* 1 Sept. 11/7 The static, informal *tranches-de-vie* landscapes of his Antwerp period. **1970** *New Yorker* 12 Dec. 193/1 It is the hand-held camera..that is designed to deal with the matter of obtaining *tranches de vie*.

‖ **tranchet** (trɑ̃nʃe). [Fr., f. *trancher* to cut.] **1.** (See quot.)

1858 P. L. Simmonds *Commercial Dict. Trade Products* 387/2 *Tranchet* (French), a shoemaker's heel knife.

2. *Archæol.* A flint with a chisel-shaped end, found in some mesolithic and neolithic cultures.

1899 R. Munro *Prehistoric Scotl.* ix. 332 Among the stone relics are small axes (*tranchets*), precisely similar to those found in the Danish Kjökkenmöddings, knife-flakes, scrapers, &c., but no polished objects. **1926** *Guide to Antiquities of Stone Age* (British Museum) (ed. 3) 150 One of the main flint forms..is the *tranchet*, or Shell-mound type of axe-head. **1977** G. Clark *World Prehist.* (ed. 3) v. 214 New forms such as tranchets or miniaturized cleavers.

b. *attrib.* and *Comb.*, designating chisel-shaped implements; **tranchet blow,** (a mark made by) a hard stroke at right angles to the main axis of an implement.

1931 *Antiquity* V. 579 An explanation of the tranchet axe. **1949** *Proc. Prehistoric Soc.* XV. 25 Near the base were also found two rather thick roughly made oval hand-axes with a tranchet blow at one end. **1957** V. G. Childe *Dawn Europ. Civilization* (ed. 6) i. 11 Stone tools (including tranchet celts) from high strands on the Norwegian coasts. **1975** J. G. Evans *Environment Early Man Brit. Isles* v. 103 The chisel-ended, or tranchet, arrowhead, specifically designed for immobilizing birds and other small game.

trank[2] (træŋk). Also **tranq.** Slang abbrev. of Tranquillizer (in Dict. and Suppl.).

1967 *Wentworth & Flexner's Dict. Amer. Slang* Suppl. 708/2 *Trank*,.. a tranquilizer, a pill or capsule containing a tranquilizer. **1973** M. Amis *Rachel Papers* 196 As late as four fifteen, mother flaked out: either the party had aggravated her sense of intraspecific alienation, or her tranqs, all day neutralized by adrenalin, had hit her together in one clammy punch. **1976** B. Bova *Multiple Man* xvii. 196 'Y'all got a buzzful of trank in yew, boy.' ..I [was] feeling like my head was numb with Novocain. **1980** A. Skinner *Mind's Eye* iv. 34 We'll have to go back to slipping tranks into his coffee.

Hence **tranked** (træŋkt) *a.*, drugged by tranquillizers.

1972 M. Crichton *Terminal Man* iv. i. 135 He was tranked out of his skull with thorazine. **1974** *Observer* 17 Mar. 34/7 Lulling drugs are prescribed; tots shamble eerily about, tranked.

tranny, trannie (træ·ni). Colloq. abbrev. of **transistor radio* s.v. *transistor *sb.* 3. Also *attrib.*

1969 *Courier-Mail* (Brisbane) 28 Oct. 14/4 Salt and sand have..been eroding the trannie set rather badly. **1969** *Nova* Nov. 144/3 'How do you feel about the Love Generation now?'..'Sick to my stomach,' he replied, tuning into *The Archers* on his tranny to get back in touch with decent values. **1976** *Listener* 5 Aug. 152/2 The Controller surely had her tranny in the shed with her. **1978** D. Murphy *Place Apart* viii. 158 A solitary, yawning customs officer sitting beside a hideously wailing 'trannie'.

tranq, var. *trank[2].

tranquillityite (træŋkwi·lĭti,ait). *Min.* [f. the name of the Sea of *Tranquillity* on the Moon, where the mineral was first collected: see -ite[1].] A silicate of ferrous iron, titanium, zirconium, and yttrium, $Fe_8(Zr,Y)_2Ti_3Si_3O_{24}$, occurring as dark red laths with a hexagonal crystal structure and found only on the moon.

[**1970** *Sci. Jrnl.* May 23/3 'Tranquilite' is the name Professors Paul Ramdohr and Josef Zaeringer..have given a new mineral they discovered in Moon rock samples collected by *Apollo 11* astronauts.] **1971** J. F. Lovering et al. in *Proc. 2nd Lunar Sci. Conf.* (*Geochim. & Cosmochim. Acta* Suppl. II) I. 39 Tranquillityite.., a completely new silicate mineral, was first recognized in Apollo 11 basalt rocks as a possible new phase 'A'. **1981** P. H. Cadogan *Moon* iii. 181 Of all lunar minerals, tranquillityite is perhaps the most important carrier of the naturally radiogenic elements, uranium and thorium.

tranquillizer. Add: Also (*U.S.*) **-ilizer.** (Earlier and further examples.) Now *spec.* any of a large class of drugs in widespread use since the 1950s for the reduction of tension or anxiety and the treatment of psychotic states; also *fig.*

1800 F. Burney *Jrnl.* 7 Mar. (1973) IV. 402, I find, however, *useful* employment the best tranquiliser, &..I have less of the violent emotions which have hitherto torn me. **1824** E. Sutleffe *Med. & Surg. Cases* I. 2, I invited the attention of the medical world by introducing this herbaceous tranquillizer [*sc.* ground ivy] to their notice. **1956** A. Huxley *Let.* 21 Jan. (1969) 787 Our impressions of the cutting short of the mescalin experience by this new tranquillizer. **1956, 1957** [see *ataractic *a.* b]. **1958** G. Greene *Our Man in Havana* iv. ii. 176 He found himself taking to truth like a tranquillizer. **1974** *Encycl. Brit. Macropædia* XVIII. 595/1 The antipsychotic tranquillizers act solely on the brain itself, whereas anti-anxiety agents act on the spinal cord as well. **1975** *N.Y. Times* 28 Nov. 37/2 Proposed reforms are only tranquilizers offered in place of the fiscal surgery needed.

b. *attrib.*

1958 *Times* 1 Aug. 7/7 Tranquillizer drugs have cured many animals of the zoo of 'emotional strain and anti-social behaviour'. **1961** *Daily Tel.* 13 Sept. 19/4 Inside the needle is a tranquilliser solution which, when aimed accurately into an unruly dog.., makes the animal docile. **1979** *Globe & Mail* (Toronto) 16 Apr. 9/3 Humane society inspectors arrived and captured the animal with the help of a tranquillizer gun.

tranquillizing, *vbl. sb.* and *ppl. a.* Add: Also (*U.S.*) **-ilizing.** (Further examples.)

1827 E. Sutleffe *Ess. Insanity* 13 Extract. Glecomæ constituted my principal remedial source. Its tranquillising effects became immediately operative. **1954** *Proc. N.Y. Acad. Sci.* LIX. 41 Reserpine, like *Rauwolfia*, acts well in combination with other hypotensive drugs. Perhaps because of its peculiar tranquilizing, sedative effect, it smooths the course of the hypotensive response of such drugs. **1955** *Sci. Amer.* Oct. 80/1 The new tranquilizing drugs have introduced a new regime in the management of patients in mental hospitals. **1962** R. Carson *Silent Spring* ii. 13 When the public protests..it is fed little tranquilizing pills of half truth. **1974** K. Clark *Another Part of Wood* vi. 223 'Never let the Tories get ye, Kenneth' he [*sc.* Ramsay Macdonald] would say, as Lady Londonderry offered him a Tranquillising pill.

tranquillo, *adv.* Add: Also *adj.* and *sb.*, (a movement or section) played in a tranquil style or tempo.

1939 J. Harrison *Brahms & his Four Symphonies* x. 204 Brahms changes the..shape of the phrases in a *Tranquillo* section. **1976** *Gramophone* May 1766/3 The 'Rondes printanières' in the first part, together with *tranquillo* woodwind melody that frames them, seems to me to be taken..rather too slow. **1980** *Daily Tel.* 17 Mar. 11/2 The 'Serenade'..by..Gerard Schurmann..tested the acoustics of the hall, the 'presto' and 'tranquillo' being at times almost inaudible from the middle of the hall.

tranquilly, *adv.* (Earlier example.)

1756 [see *emanate *v.*].

trans (trɑnz). *colloq.* Also **trans.** (with point). [Abbrev.] **1.** = Translation 2. *U.S.*

c **1877** E. Dickinson in *Poems* (1955) III. 1055 I dare not write until I hear—Intro without my Trans. **1922** H. Crane *Let.* *c* 18 June (1965) 91 *Physique L'Amour*, which I am lately reading in trans. **1955** E. Pound *Section: Rock-Drill* xciv. 97 No full trans Till 1811.

2. = *trans-continental *sb. Austral.*

1937 E. Hill *Great Australian Loneliness* xxviii. 225 The 'Trans' and its people are a little world sufficient to themselves, a remarkable colony of government servants living in progress and contentment in the desert. **1976** K. Thackeray *Crownbird* v. 85 The next day they got to Kalgoorlie..and changed onto the 'Trans', a long, streamlined diesel.

3. = Transmission d.

1954 *Amer. Speech* XXIX. 103 *Trans*,..transmission. **1976** *Billings* (Montana) *Gaz.* 30 June 9-d/5 (Advt.), Plymouth Fury II, 440 high performance, (highway patrol), trans out, $300 firm. **1981** *Pop. Hot Rodding* Feb. 20/3, I own a '68 Datsun pickup and would like to install a 327 Chevy small-block engine with a 350 turbo trans.

trans-, *prefix.* Add: **5.** *transabdominal, -antral* [Antrum], *-capillary, -cervical, -cutaneous, -duodenal, -epithelial, -glottal, -granular, -ovarial, -ovarian, -placental, -pyloric.*

The examples given below are cited here despite the note in Dict. after sense 6, since they did not call for the elaborate treatment of a main entry.

1956 *Nature* 18 Feb. 330/2 Although transabdominal puncture of the uterus has been carried out often for therapeutic and experimental reasons without accidents, mere curiosity does not justify the procedure. **1957** *Laryngoscope* LXVII. 566 The degree of orbital tension present in the severe forms of exophthalmos is correlated with the degree of recession obtained by the transantral decompression. **1974** *Nature* 31 May 495/3 Transcapillary and transepithelial water transport. **1963** *Lancet* 19 Jan. 165/2 Transcervical fractures. **1977** *Ibid.* 7 May 983/1 We believe that local warming of the skin and of the capillary blood under the electrode increases P_{CO_2}; the transcutaneous P_{CO_2} values are therefore higher than those found in arterial blood. **1908** Transduodenal [see *retro-duodenal* s.v. *retro- 3. b.]. **1975** H. J. Burhenne in Najarian & Delaney *Surg. Liver, Pancreas & Biliary Tract* 104 Percutaneous cholangiography will probably be supplanted by transduodenal cannulization. **1974** Transepithelial [see *transcapillary* above]. **1964** J. C. Catford in D. Abercombie et al. *Daniel Jones* 31 The trans-glottal air-jets of voice superimpose a periodic fluctuation on the mean air pressure behind the articulatory stricture, resulting in..hiss. **1970** *Language* XLVI. 313 The human..larynx is so constructed that the fundamental frequency of phonation is a function of both the transglottal air pressure drop and the tensions of the laryngeal muscles. **1962** *Science Survey* III. 329 Occasionally the cracks are transcrystalline (trans-granular). **1946** E. A. Steinhaus *Insect Microbiol.* viii. 439 Transovarial transmission of the virus takes place by the viruses penetrating the walls of the ovary and thence entering the developing ovum. **1971** P. C. C. Garnham *Progr. Parasitol.* iii. 34 The tick..may carry over into subsequent generations by transovarial passage. **1954** *Jrnl. Infectious Dis.* XCV. 178/2 The distribution of antibodies in different small age groups of wild birds is further evidence of the transovarian passage of neutralizing antibodies. **1980** *Nature* 7 Feb. 568/2 Another event occurring during oogenesis is trans-ovarian transmission of symbiotic bacteroids..from females to the oocytes. **1902** *Brit. Med. Jrnl.* 17 May 1198/1 Alterations in the transplacental interchanges. **1977** *Lancet* 9 Apr. 795/1 The transplacental leak of fetal red blood-cells. **1905** C. Addison *Ellis's Demonstrations of Anat.* (ed. 12) vi. 298 This plane, from its traversing the pyloric end of the stomach, is called the transpyloric. **1977** *Lancet* 28 May 1157/2 The gastric distension..can be relieved by passing an open-ended nasogastric tube, and adequate nutrition maintained by intravenous or continuous transpyloric feeding.

b. In derived advbs.: *transabdominally, -duodenally, -ovarially, -placentally.*

1962 *Lancet* 8 Dec. 1208/2 A needle passed transabdominally into the liver. **1955** *Radiology* LXIV. 325 When the sphincter of Oddi is sectioned transduodenally, a plastic tube can be inserted into the main pancreatic duct. **1954** *Jrnl. Infectious Dis.* XCV. 168/1 Neutralizing antibodies to western equine encephalitis (WEE) and St. Louis encephalitis (SLE) viruses may be transmitted transovarially. **1979** *Amer. Jrnl. Trop. Med. & Hygiene* XXVIII. 1064 Spores developing in transovarially infected mosquitoes. **1965** *Dorland's Med. Dict.* (ed. 24) s.v. *Listeria*, A septicemic disease which may be transmitted transplacentally in pregnant women.

7. a. *trans-Alleghanian* (earlier example), *-Alleghany, -Mississippian* (example), *-Pyrenean.*

1814 *Deb. Congress U.S.* 14 Feb. 1422 Even then the trans-Alleganean wilderness was rustling with the preparation of the savage. **1825** C. D. Colden *Mem.* 93 Why should the trans-Allegany States have remained united with those on the Atlantic? **1831** A. Wilson *Amer. Ornithology* IV. 31 In the trans-Mississippian territories of the United States, the burrowing owl resides. **1875** *Harper's Mag.* Mar. 572/2 The subdivision..into the Trans-Alleghany, Valley, Middle, and Tide-water districts. **1934** A. Toynbee *Study of Hist.* II. 203 Musa had completed the Arab conquest..by occupying the Transpyrenaean province of Septimania along the Gallic coast between the Pyrenees and the Rhône.

b. in substantives with the sense 'the region beyond' or 'one dwelling beyond or on the other side of', as *trans-Alleghanian, -Mississippi, -Mississippian.*

1774 J. Adams *Diary* 23 Oct. in *Wks.* (1850) II. 401, I went to the Baptist Church and heard a trans-Alleghanian, a preacher from the back parts of Virginia. **1883** *Century Mag.* Nov. 142/1 If the President was to attempt to reach the Trans-Mississippi at all,..he should move on at once. **1898** *Ibid.* Oct. 844/2 The trans-Mississippians have entered upon no line of rural industry with a more intelligent determination to make it a great success than upon dairying. **1949** Beebe & Clegg *U.S. West* 10 Anyone approaching the *matière* of the trans-Mississippi in the nineteenth century as an exploiter of new material is either deluded or an imposter.

8. *trans-Antarctic, -Canada, -Pyrenean* (earlier example), *-Saharan* (examples), *-Sierran, -Tasman.*

1846 R. Ford *Gatherings from Spain* iv. 31 Newfangled transpyrenean reforms, innovations, and botherations. **1888** *Times* 20 Sept. 3/6 Denham, Clapperton, Barth, and other trans-Saharan travellers. **1908** *Busy Man's Mag.* Apr. 95 The Proposed Route of the Trans-Canada Railway. **1916** R. K. Wood *Tourist's N.W.* 315 A campaign for the improvement and construction of roads which.. shall in combination form a trans-Canada motor route. **1933** *Geogr. Jrnl.* LXXXII. 470 Mr. Lincoln Ellsworth.. will then make the Transantarctic flight, which is the sole object of the expedition. **1935** E. B. Buckbee *Saga of Old Tuolumne* 385 The road survived until the State of California came to look with favor upon its possibilities as a tran-Sierran [*sic*] road. **1938** *Times* 17 Feb. 13/4 The flying-boat Centaurus showed her unsuitability for trans-Tasman traffic. **1950** *Pacific Discovery* Mar.–Apr. 4/1 Did you know that a trans-Sierran highway is now being built in Madera County? **1963** P. Drackett *Motor Rallying* iv. 62 The Trans-Canada and Canadian Winter Rallies have not yet reached the lofty eminence of the Safari. **1965** E. McCourt *Road across Canada* 199 The Trans-Canada Highway is an engineering, communications, and scenic marvel. **1966** N. Marsh *Black Beech & Honeydew* viii. 175 In..1928 the trans-Tasman steamer sailed..into Cook Strait. **1978** *Times Lit. Suppl.* 25 Aug. 957/4 Shackleton's unsuccessful transantarctic expedition. **1978** J. Updike *Coup* (1979) i. 4 The capital is Istiqlal, renamed in 1960, upon independence, and on prior maps called Cailliéville, in honor of the trans-Saharan traveller of 1828.

9. a. *Chem.* (Also without hyphen as a quasi-adj. Usu. printed in italic.) Designating a compound in which two atoms or groups are situated on opposite sides of some plane passing through the molecule; hence (of a bond or a reaction), characterized by such a relationship.

[**1888**: see *cis- 3.] **1892** *Jrnl. Chem. Soc.* LXII. 1213 The anhydride of the cis modification invariably melts at a lower temperature than that of the trans form. **1937** *Nature* 3 July 25/1 The trans form of ethylene bromide is considered to be the more 'stable' (preferred) form, even at high temperatures. **1951** C. R. Noller *Chem. Carbon Compounds* xvii. 316 It has been proved that *cis*-2-butene is the isomer boiling at 3·73° and *trans*-2-butene is that boiling at 0·96°. **1956** D. J. Cram in M. S. Newman *Steric Effects in Org. Chem.* vi. 306 The terms *cis* elimination will be used whenever the leaving groups depart from the same side of the incipient double bond, and *trans* elimination when they leave from the opposite side of the incipient double bond. **1972** R. A. Jackson *Mechanism* i. 7 Bromine adds across an olefinic double bond in a *trans* manner. **1976** *Sci. Amer.* Jan. 124/2 Nearly all peptide bonds are trans and planar, meaning that hydrogen and carbonyl oxygen (CO) are on opposite sides of the bond.

b. *transf.* in Genetics, with reference to the location on different chromosomes of dominant alleles of two or more genes or cistrons.

1941 J. B. S. Haldane *New Paths in Genetics* i. 17 There are two geometrically isomeric types of rabbit (to use a chemical analogy) heterozygous for recessive white *c* and recessive yellowfat *y*... The trans-rabbit $+y/c+$ is derived from the crossing of a white-fatted coloured rabbit and a yellow-fatted white. **1957** [see *cistron]. **1973** R. G. Krueger et al. *Introd. Microbiol.* xiii. 385/1 In the diploid the two mutants [*sc.* mutant genes] are said to be trans to one another because they are on different chromosomes.

10. *Biochem.* and *Biol.* In sbs. with the sense 'transfer', as *transacetylase, -amination, -genosis, -methylation, -peptidation* (see as main entries).

11. *Physics.* In adjs. and sbs. with the sense 'having a higher atomic number than; beyond (in the periodic table)'.

1952 *Chem. & Engin. News* 21 Jan. 237/2 The transcalifornium elements. **1969** *Nature* 26 Apr. 323/1 Dr Glen Seaborg..was able to proclaim that element 104 is the first of the 'trans-actinide' elements. **1973** *Q. Jrnl. R. Astron. Soc.* XIV. 121 The existence of transbismuth elements in nature.

transacetylase (trɑnzæ̆se·tilēⁱz). *Biochem.* [f. *trans- 10 + *acetyl + *-ase.] Any enzyme that catalyses the transfer of an acetyl group from one molecule to another.

1950 Stadtman & Barker in *Jrnl. Biol. Chem.* CLXXXIV. 788 The arsenolytic decomposition of acetyl phosphate by the cell-free extracts of *C[lostridium] kluyveri* can be represented in an analogous way..if it is assumed that the reaction is catalyzed by an acetyl transferring enzyme or trans-acetylase. **1966** *Jrnl. Molecular Biol.* XIX. 576 (*heading*) Transposition of the *lac* region of *Escherichia coli*. II. On the role of thiogalactoside transacetylase in lactose metabolism. **1976** *Ann. Rev. Microbiol.* XXX. 329 To illustrate genetic transfer, Hedges..cites the gene for chloramphenicol transacetylase.

transact, *v.* **2.** (Further examples.)

1883 R. L. Stevenson *Silverado Squatters* 122 With so strong a helper, the business was speedily transacted. **1950** R. Macaulay *World my Wilderness* xxii. 158 What careful, crafty affairs had they transacted in the Hall of the Haberdashers? **1970** D. Jacobson *Rape of Tamar* ii. 14 Gathering together around the king, while he transacts the business of the state.

transactional, *a.* Add: **c.** *Psychol.* Relating to or involving interpersonal or social communication viewed as transactions of attitude between the participants; *spec.* in *transactional analysis,* psychotherapeutic analysis based on the attitudes revealed in such transactions (esp. those of parent, adult, and child); abbrev. T.A. (see *T 6 a); hence *transactional analyst.*

1961 E. Berne (*title*) Transactional analysis in psychotherapy. *Ibid.* 12 Transactional analysis, the social aspect of structural analysis, reveals several different types of 'crossed transactions'. **1969** T. A. Harris *I'm OK—You're OK* i. 13 Transactional Analysis is the method of examining this one transaction..and determining which part of the multiple-natured individual is 'coming on'. *Ibid.* 15 Transactional Analysts claim to have found some of these regularities [of language]. **1976** *Listener* 5 Feb. 141/3 Discussing Basil Fawlty in terms of transactional analysis: as to whether, at certain times, Basil was behaving as a parent, or as a child.

Hence **transa·ctionalist,** one who believes in a theory of social transactions; also *attrib.*

1972 R. E. Ornstein *Psychol. of Consciousness* ii. 32 (*heading*) The transactionalists. *Ibid.* 37 Some of the most relevant psychological experiments have been performed by Jerome Bruner and by the transactionalist group. **1977** P. Johnson *Enemies of Soc.* xv. 202 Then there is a series of schools, associated with the Americans H. S. Becker and Edwin Lemert, known variously as social-control theorists, social-reaction theorists, transactionalists or labelling theorists.

transalpine, *a.* Add: **2. b.** That crosses the Alps, built across the Alps.

1908 *Chambers's Jrnl.* Sept. 647/1 The Simplon is the least steeply graded..of any transalpine railway.

transa·minase. *Biochem.* [f. next: see quot. 1940 and *-ase.] Any enzyme that brings about transamination.

1940 P. P. Cohen in *Jrnl. Biol. Chem.* CXXXVI. 566 Since the original term *Umaminierung*..has been accepted with the English (and French) equivalent of *transamination*..it is suggested here that the enzyme (or possibly enzymes) catalyzing the transfer of amino nitrogen be termed *transaminase.* **1970** R. W. McGilvery *Biochem.* xvii. 354 Much of the nitrogen of the amino acids sooner or later appears in the form of glutamate because of the action of transaminases.

transamination (trɑ:nzæminēⁱ·ʃən). *Biochem.* [a. F. *transamination* (Schaeffer & Le Breton *L'Action Spécifique des Protides* (1938) 143): see *trans- 10, *amino-, -ation.] The transfer of an amino group from one organic molecule to another, esp. from an amino-acid to a keto-acid.

1939 *Nature* 8 Apr. 609/1 The reversible transfer of amino groups between aminodicarboxylic acids and α-keto-acids, or 'trans-amination'..is of almost universal occurrence in biological objects. **1946** *Ibid.* 12 Oct. 515/2 Not until it reaches the root cells does the transformation of aspartic acid take place (through deamination, transamination, etc.). **1959** A. White et al. *Princ. Biochem.* (ed.2) xx. 514 In addition to transamination reactions involving L-α-amino acids, transamination of..aldehydes ..has also been observed. **1982** T. I. Diamondstone in T. M. Devlin *Textbk. Biochem.* xi. 546 Virtually every protein amino acid undergoes transamination at some point in its metabolic breakdown.

Hence (as back-formations) **transa·minate** *v. intr.*, to undergo transamination; *trans.*, to deprive of an amino group; to change by transamination; **transa·minated** *ppl. a.*, **transa·minating** *ppl. a.* and *vbl. sb.*

1940 *Ann. Rev. Biochem.* IX. 284 The experiments.. disclose the possible operation of the transaminating enzymes within the animal body. **1940** *Jrnl. Biol. Chem.* CXXXVI. 573 Braunstein reports that these amino acids are transaminated to the extent of 17 to 21 per cent. **1955** A. Meister in McElroy & Glass *Amino Acid Metabolism* i. 14 L-Alloisoleucine and its keto analogue.. transaminate at somewhat slower rates than L-isoleucine. **1959** A. White et al. *Princ. Biochem.* (ed. 2) xx. 517 The discovery of the transaminating mechanism. **1970** R. W. McGilvery *Biochem.* xvii. 355 Any other amino acid that will transaminate with α-ketoglutarate may be deaminated in the same way. **1972** *Nature* 8 Sept. 101/2 The group..included amino-acids..that are not transaminated or oxidized in myocardium and those..that can be transaminated and used for energy production. **1974** I. B. R. Bowman in K. Elliott et al. *Trypanosomiasis & Leishmaniasis* 268 It is likely that glutamate is transaminated to α-oxoglutarate.

trans,a·nnular, *a.* *Chem.* [f. Trans- 3 + Annular *a.*] Situated, existing, or occurring between non-adjacent atoms forming a ring.

[**1926** de Barry Barnett & Matthews in *Ber. Deut. Chem. Ges.* LIX. 1429 Es dürfte deshalb angezeigt sein, diese besondere Art tautomerer Umwandlungen unter dem allgemeinen Begriff 'Transannular-Tautomerie' zusammenzufassen.] **1926** *Chem. Abstr.* XX. 3003 The name '*trans*-annular tautomerism' is suggested for those cases..where the H migrates across the ring. **1941** *Nature* 21 June 776/1 As the carbon atoms concerned..are components of a cyclic system.., the resulting tautomeric change would be a transannular one and involve the formation of a bridge linkage from C_3 to C_5. **1978** *Further Perspectives Org. Chem.* (CIBA Symposium) 119 This reaction undoubtedly involves fission of the transannular bond.

transat (trɑ·nzæt). *colloq.* [Abbrev. of Transatlantic *a., sb.*] A type of large deck-chair (see quots.).

1968 *Daily Tel.* (Colour Suppl.) 29 Nov. 76 (Advt.), A few days flat-out on a 'transat'—a long couch like those on the decks of ocean liners—at the Tahiti beach did the trick. **1978** *N.Y. Times* 30 Mar. c8/1 Along with the regular-sized deck chairs,..there's..a transat..—a chair with an attached foot rest that slides neatly under the seat when you don't need it.

transaxle (trɑ·nzæks'l). orig. *U.S.* [f. Trans(mission + Axle[2].] In a motor vehicle: an integral driving axle and differential gear.

1958 *N.Y. Times* 1 June x. 21/4 The engineers call the new system a 'transaxle' or a 'traxle'. **1967** P. H. Smith in L. Holmes *Odhams New Motor Man.* vi. 160/1 When access is required to the clutch or gearbox on cars having unitary construction of engine and transaxle,..the complete unit must be removed from the vehicle. **1983** *Fortune* 7 Mar. 110/2 Some of the..contracts for high-margin items like engines, transaxles, and sophisticated electronics are going abroad.

trans-ba·y, *a.* *U.S.* [f. Trans- 3 + Bay *sb.*[2]] That crosses a bay, *spec.* San Francisco Bay.

1965 *Newsweek* 19 July 71/1 The most challenging and vital element of all, the Trans-Bay Tube, will be begun next year when a 30-foot-deep trench will be dug across San Francisco Bay. **1966** T. Pynchon *Crying of Lot 49* v. 130 She tailed him..back..to the trans-bay bus terminal, where he bought a ticket for Oakland. **1975** *New Yorker* 10 Jan. 29/3 Meanwhile, 1,200 commuters are stranded in a BART train in the collapsed trans-bay tube.

trans-border, *a.* Add: Also, on or from the other side of the border; crossing a border or borders.

1976 *Globe & Mail* (Toronto) 16 Feb. 9/1 It was detonated..where the DC-8 came to rest after the eight-hour, trans-border ordeal. **1976** *Southern Even. Echo* (Southampton) 1 Nov. 1/2 'We have undertaken hot pursuit operations as a result of trans-border aggression by terrorists,' the communique said. **1980** *Times* 26 Mar. 23/4 Restrictions are imposed by various countries on what is becoming known as 'transborder data flow'.

transbus (trɑ·nzbɒs). *U.S. temporary.* [f. Trans- (or Trans(it *sb.*) + Bus *sb.*[2]] A bus with special design features, including lower floors to give the elderly and disabled easier access.

1973 *Britannica Yearbk. Sci. & Future 1974* 335/1 The three proposals for the so-called Transbus would have several common features, in addition to length... Lower profile, plus further automatic lowering at stops. **1975** *General Motors Transbus* (Gen. Motors Truck & Coach Div.) I. 24 The use of the pantograph entrance on the Transbus allows use of the wheelchair elevator. **1977** *Time* 5 Dec. 34 He expects that the high cost of the transbuses (as much as $50,000 more than a regular bus) will halt the expansion of the special van service.

transceiver (trɑnsī·vəɹ). [f. Trans(mitter + Re)ceiver[1].] An instrument combining a radio transmitter and a radio receiver.

1934 *Electronics* Sept. 273/1 The increasing sales of so-called 'transceivers',..usually one or two-tube affairs operating from batteries, is an indication that the early days of radio may be re-enacted. **1952** *Times* 4 Dec. 7/4 Nowhere except on the transceiver network operated from Alice Springs is it possible for the scholars to play an active part by question and answer to their distant teacher. **1977** *Time* 10 Jan. 44/3 Sales of Citizens Band transceivers were boosted dramatically by gutted prices on current 23-channel gear.

transcendency. b. (Earlier example.)

1902 W. James *Let.* 14 Dec. (1920) II. 179, I believe that the 'transcendency' of the object will not recover from your treatment.

transcendental, *a.* **3.** Add: **e.** *transcendental meditation*: a method of relaxation and meditation based on the theory and practice of yoga popularized in the West by the Maharishi Mahesh Yogi; abbrev. TM (see *T 6 a); hence *transcendental meditator*.

A proprietary term in the U.S.

1966 C. F. Lutes in M. M. Yogi *Sci. of Being & Art of Living* 13 The system on which Maharishi's teaching is based—a simple method of transcendental meditation.. —is indeed systematic and produces measurable and predictable results and is therefore scientific. **1973** *Times* 30 June 14/3 Transcendental meditation is becoming popular as a way of coping with the stress of modern life. *Ibid.* 14/5 Transcendental meditators do not like to publicize the possible dangers inherent in mind-bending techniques. **1975** *Physics Bull.* Sept. 397/2 The aim was to measure the breathing rate and lung ventilation of 15 transcendental meditators before, during and after meditation and compare the values with those obtained for 15 non-meditators. **1976** *Early Music* Oct. 467/1 The place of meditation and mantra made familiar to the West by the practitioners of Transcendental Meditation and similar Yoga techniques. **1976** *Official Gaz.* (U.S. Patent Office) 3 Aug. TM77/2 Class 41—Education and Entertainment. 1,045,673. World Plan Executive Council—United States, Los Angeles, Calif... Transcendental Meditation. **1980** *Times* 27 May 1/8 Transcendental meditation, as taught by the Maharishi's World Government of the Age of Enlightenment..involves learning the techniques of meditating.

transcendible, *a.* Delete † *Obs.* and add later example.

1953 G. M. Young *Victorian Eng.* xx. 118 Such a body of permitted belief as makes the barriers between England and Rome transcendible.

transˌco·de, *v.* [f. Trans- 2 + Code *v.*] *trans.* and *intr.* To convert from one form of coded representation to another; to change the code of. Hence **transˌco·ding** *vbl. sb.*, the action or result of such conversion.

1962 *Language & Speech* V. 18 A common feature of linguistic and biological information is the ease with which it can be repeatedly transcoded resulting in a multiplicity of codes. *Ibid.*, Print, translation, shorthand and Braille are among many other examples of transcoding. **1965** *Guardian* 24 Mar. 5/6 It is technically possible to 'transcode' from one [television] colour system to another. **1972** *Computers & Humanities* VI. 150 In using either punched-card or paper-tape equipment one has to delegate the transcoding of the special input codes to the computer. **1984** *What Video?* Aug. 5/4 The only course open to you is to have the existing NTSC—standard tape transcoded to UJ—standard PAL 625.

transconductance (trɑnsˌkǒndɒ·ktăns, -nz-). *Electronics.* [f. Trans(fer *sb.* + *conductance.] The ratio of the (change in) current at one electrode or terminal of an active device, esp. the output, to the (change in) voltage at another, esp. the input; *spec.* = *mutual conductance* s.v. *mutual *a.* 1 f.

1933 K. Henney *Radio Engin. Handbk.* viii. 203 The coefficient showing the effect of plate voltage on the grid current has been termed inverse mutual conductance, or the plate-grid transconductance. **1944** *Electronic Engin.* XVI. 318 The transconductance between these two grids is negative. **1950** *Electronics* Feb. 107/1 In push-pull amplifiers, triodes using this type of neutralization compare favorably with pentodes of the same transconductance as wideband amplifiers. **1981** J. C. Sprott *Introd. Mod. Electronics* vii. 159 At the operating point [of a field effect transistor] the value of the forward transconductance,..and the output resistance,..can be determined.

transˌconfe·ssional, *a.* [f. Trans- 3 + Confessional *a.*] Extending across religious denominations; interdenominational.

1975 R. R. Williams in *Critique of Eucharistic Agreement* i. 11 The agreements we have here are by no means the only trans-confessional agreements of modern times. **1983** *Times Lit. Suppl.* 7 Oct. 1103/1 Edward Schillebeeckx..has been much read beyond the bounds of the Roman Catholic community to which he belongs. He has accepted the title of 'transconfessional' theologian.

transˌconforma·tion. *Chem.* [f. Trans- 1 + Conformation.] A change in the conformation of a molecule, esp. a protein; freq. *attrib.*

1954 Lumry & Eyring in *Jrnl. Physical Chem.* LVIII. 110/1 The bulk of denaturation changes consist of changes in secondary bonds... Such rearrangements of the secondary-bonded structure are defined as changes in conformation... We shall thus speak of transconformation reactions rather than denaturation reactions. **1979** *Nature* 18 Jan. 244/1 Besides the folding of the isolated polypeptide chains, additional transconformation reactions occur after the association of the native quaternary structure has taken place.

transconjugant (trɑnsˌkǫ·ndʒŭgănt). *Biol.* [f. Trans- 1 + Conjug(ate *v.* + -ant[1].] A plasmid or a bacterial cell which has received genetic material by conjugation with another bacterium.

1974 *Jrnl. Bacteriol.* CXX. 1187/2 Transfer frequencies were calculated from the number of transconjugants formed per donor cell in the mating mixture... (Transconjugants are cells of the recipient strain that have received genetic material by conjugation.) **1977** *Nature* 10 Feb. 560/2 Plasmid transconjugants which combine octopine utilisation of the donor and antibiotic resistance of the recipient grow well on this medium.

trans-continental, *a.* (*sb.*) Add: Now freq. as one word without hyphen. (Earlier example.)

1853 *Harper's Mag.* Feb. 550/2 A company..to construct a trans-continental railroad.

B. *ellipt.* as *sb.* A trans-continental railway, a trans-continental train. Chiefly *Canad.*

1907 *Eye Opener* (Calgary) 18 July 3/3 Dealing with the immense expenditure on the G.T.P. transcontinental. **1920** J. M. Gibbon *Conquering Hero* 147 At Winnipeg the transcontinental was boarded by..a rancher on his way back to the foothills. **1955** *Standard* (Shawinigan Falls, Que.) 12 Jan. 2/2 A rate [for carrying grain] fixed..shortly after the first trans-continental opened for business. **1964** J. Carroll *Shy Photographer* 6 You heard the one about the squaw on the transcontinental?

transcribe, *v.* Add: **1. c.** *Biol.* To synthesize a nucleic acid (usu. RNA) using an existing nucleic acid (usu. DNA) as a template, so that the genetic information in the latter is copied. Const. *into* (with the template as obj.), *from, off* (with the new acid as obj.).

1962 *Proc. Nat. Acad. Sci.* XLVIII. 544 Only one strand of the DNA is transcribed as functional messenger-RNA. **1973** *Sci. Amer.* Apr. 34/3 Their chromosomes are in a greatly enlarged and uncoiled 'lampbrush' stage where we might be able to see structural details of DNA being transcribed into messenger RNA. **1979** D. R. Hofstadter *Gödel, Escher, Bach* xvi. 517 When mRNA is transcribed off of DNA, the transcription process operates via the usual base-pairing. **1981** L. L. Mays *Genetics* ii. 65 Once RNA is transcribed from DNA, it is cut to its final size, modified in specific ways, and sent to its site of action.

2. b. Also *intr.* for *pass.*

1976 *Gramophone* June 61/1 Vocal ensemble music should transcribe well for brass.

6. a. To make a copy of (a gramophone recording) from a secondary source, not the master recording.

1931 *Gramophone* Dec. 264/1 The Philadelphians have recorded the Fifth Symphony of Beethoven complete on a single 12-in. disc and..thirty-two other discs..have been announced on which existing works..have been 'transcribed'.

b. *Broadcasting.* To record for subsequent reproduction; to broadcast in this form.

1941 W. Abbot *Handbk. Broadcasting* 245 These are inserted into transcribed programs or into a live program.

transcribed *ppl. a.* (further examples).

1961 J. Updike in *New Yorker* 17 June 31/1 A transistor radio somewhere in the sand releases in a thin, apologetic gust the closing peal of a transcribed service. **1981** L. L. Mays *Genetics* ii. 57 Sometimes the transcribed RNA is the final product.

transcriber. Add: **2.** An item of office equipment on which dictation cannot be recorded, but which replays dictated matter for transcription by an (audio) typist.

1931 *Times* 16 Mar. 1/6 All-electric Dictaphone with Shaver and Transcriber: good condition. **1976** *Southern Even. Echo* (Southampton) 3 Nov. (Advt.), Duties will include shorthand or use of transcriber, typing, correspondence, filing, [etc.].

transcript, *sb.* Add: **3.** *Biol.* A length of RNA or DNA which has been transcribed from a DNA or RNA template (respectively).

1961 Jacob & Monod in *Jrnl. Molecular Biol.* III. 352 The molecular structure of proteins is determined by specific elements, the structural genes. These act by forming a cytoplasmic 'transcript' of themselves, the structural messenger. **1972** *Sci. Amer.* Jan. 33/3 We have uncovered evidence that cancer-causing RNA viruses can produce a DNA transcript of the viral RNA. **1982** *Nature* 13 May 130/2 Transcripts initiated further upstream than position −675 will yield a protected fragment of ~1,375 nucleotides.

transcriptase (trɑnˌskrɪ·ptēɪz). *Biochem.* [f. Transcript(ion + *-ase.] The polymerase responsible for transcription, which catalyses the formation of RNA from a DNA template; *reverse transcriptase*, the polymerase responsible for reverse transcription, which catalyses the formation of DNA from an RNA template.

1963 Spiegelman & Hayashi in *Cold Spring Harbor Symp. Quantitative Biol.* XXVIII. 162/1 The transcribing DNA-dependent-RNA-polymerase which produces RNA complements will be referred to as a transcriptase. **1965** *New Scientist* 18 Mar. 713/2 An enzyme exists in cells (called 'RNA polymerase' or sometimes 'transcriptase') which is capable of reading the genic code. **1970** *Nature* 26 Dec. 1255/1 Research..on reverse transcriptases in animal cancer viruses and human cancer cells. **1976** *Ann. Rev. Microbiol.* XXX. 23 Kates & McAuslan..initially demonstrated transcriptase in poxvirus cores isolated from infected cells.

transcription. Add: **5. a.** A gramophone record made from a secondary source, not the master recording.

1931 *Gramophone* Dec. 264/2 'Transcriptions', too, for which our unkind readers used to prefer the phrase 'faked records', are not very popular over here. **1968** *Jazz Monthly* Feb. 4/1 Numerous 'pirate' labels also issuing EPs and LPs,..tend increasingly to concentrate on air shots and transcriptions from a variety of sources.

b. *Broadcasting.* The recording of a broadcast for subsequent reproduction; a record or broadcast so made. Also *attrib.*

1932 *B.B.C. Year-bk. 1933* 290 The relaying of the Empire station by overseas transmitters cannot for various reasons be assumed to be possible as a regular practice and therefore the recording of programmes on gramophone discs becomes an important subsidiary method of programme circulation... American programmes are already circulated by this method, which is termed 'electrical transcription'. **1936** *Communication* Mar. 5 (*heading*) The growing importance of transcription broadcasting. *Ibid.* 6/2 The transcriptions in every-day use in broadcast stations include both lateral-cut and vertical-cut recordings. **1943** *B.B.C. Year-bk.* 23 An important broadcasting activity little known in this country is the projection overseas, by means of recordings, of the culture and wartime life of Britain... Known collectively as the London Transcription Service, the activity has been undertaken by the BBC for the Empire since the beginning of the war, and for foreign countries for nearly two years. **1956** *B.B.C. Handbk. 1957* 42 English by Radio lessons..reach an audience of several millions by direct transmission from London, by relays, and by transcription recordings. *Ibid.* 133 Among other transcriptions, the special service for Colonial schools.. proved successful. **1978** *A–Z of BBC* (ed. 2) 225/2 Transcription services are the BBC's channel for selling Radio Programmes to stations overseas.

c. Used *attrib.* to designate equipment used in professional recording or broadcasting transcription, or *gen.* of a standard or type so used.

1936 *Communication* Mar. 8/2 Noise in the output of a transcription equipment is often caused by pickup of the motor vibration. **1943** *Proc. I.R.E.* Feb. 52 (*heading*) The measurement of transcription-turntable speed variation. **1957** *Long Playing Record Library Catal. & Handbk.* 10 The only answer..is the use of a 'transcription motor', implying a high standard of design and finish and individual care in manufacture. **1962** A. Nisbett *Technique Sound Studio* 271 The large transcription tape decks are normally equipped to play either type. **1965** *Wireless World* Aug. 6 (Advt.), The Goldring-Lenco GL 70 transcription unit with its integrally mounted transcription arm continues to be the first choice of discriminating record lovers with custom-built equipment. **1978** *Lancashire Life* Nov. 110/1 (Advt.), All the illustrated units are complete music centres with Dolby cassette deck-belt driven transcription unit.

6. *Biol.* The process by which genetic information represented by the sequence of nucleotides in the DNA of a cell or virus is copied into molecules of RNA, which are synthesized with the DNA serving as a template; *reverse transcription*, the reverse process, occurring in some RNA viruses, by which DNA is synthesized from an RNA template.

1961 Jacob & Monod in *Cold Spring Harbor Symp. Quantitative Biol.* XXVI. 193/1 The second process, which we shall call transcription, allows the gene to perform its physiological function. **1970** *Nature* 27 June 1198/1 For the past twenty years the cardinal tenet of molecular biology has been that the flow or transcription of genetic information from DNA to messenger RNA and then its translation to protein is strictly one way. **1971** [see *promoter 1 g]. **1973** *Sci. Amer.* Apr. 34/2 In prokaryotes, which include the many species of bacteria, transcription and translation of messenger RNA occur at the same time and place. **1977** *Nature* 8 Sept. 122/1 Until recently.. most groups studying reverse transcription *in vitro* found the DNA products to be small relative to the size of the RNA templates.

transcriptional *a.* (examples in *Biol.*); **transcriptionally:** also, in *Biol.*, in a transcriptional way; (further examples).

1970 *Nature* 29 Aug. 910/1 A similar mechanism controls gene expression at the transcriptional level during bacterial sporulation. **1975** *Ibid.* 5 June 462/2 This transcriptionally active DNA represents r-protein genes. **1981** L. L. Mays *Genetics* ix. 416 The prokaryotic systems that operate via transcriptional control often utilize different control systems. **1983** *Nature* 23 June 677/1 Transcriptionally active chromatin.

transcriptionist (trɑnˌskrɪ·pʃənɪst). *U.S.* [f. Transcription + -ist.] An audio typist.

1977 *Chicago Tribune* 2 Oct. xii. 67/6 (Advt.), 60 wpm typing, plus 1 year experience as a medical transcriptionist, or training in this field qualifies you. **1978** *Detroit Free Press* 16 Apr. F 5/5 (Advt.), Medical transcriptionist. For out-patient clinic in university setting. Accurate typing & Medical Terminology necessary.

transcriptor. Restrict † *Obs.* to sense in Dict. and add: **b.** = *transcriber 2.

1957 *Practical Wireless* XXXIII. 532/2 Tape transcriptors are also supplied by Collaro. **1958** *Punch* 17 Sept. 366/3 Anita types. You scarcely see The neat transcriptor at her ear. The tape turns confidentially, And no one else can overhear.

trans,cry·stalline, *a.* [f. TRANS- 5 + CRYSTALLINE *a.*] Of a fracture: passing through individual crystals of a metal rather than following grain boundaries.
1916 H. M. HOWE *Metallogr. Steel & Cast Iron* xxviii. 489 (*caption*) Intergranular and trans-crystalline rupture. **1956** M. C. SMITH *Princ. Physical Metall.* x. 379 The usual fracture of a metal is transcrystalline. **1978** E. LEPA tr. *S. Kocańda's Fatigue Failure Metals* v. 271 The brittle crack propagates..along cleavage planes, yielding a cleavage transcrystalline fracture, or along the grain boundaries, forming an..intercrystalline fracture.

trans,cu·ltural, *a.* [f. TRANS- 3, 4 + CULTURAL *a.*] Transcending the limitations or crossing the boundaries of cultures; applicable to more than one culture; cross-cultural; spec. *transcultural psychiatry*, psychiatry applied to disorders due to migration from one cultural environment to another.
1958 *Internat. Jrnl. Social Psychiatry* III. 245 (*heading*) Some problems of transcultural psychiatry. **1964** I. L. HOROWITZ *New Sociology* 37 Social science is interdisciplinary because social problems are transcultural. **1973** *Observer* (Colour Suppl.) 28 Oct. 34/5 Sailing ships are gone but the sea shanty is still sung: the function is altered but the song remains: the stuff is transcultural. **1976** *Daily Tel.* 27 Apr. 2/8 The congress, on transcultural psychiatry, is being organised by the university and the World Federation for Mental Health. **1978** *Church Times* 3 Feb. 6/5 The resolution of the problem suggested depends on a distinction between meanings which are universal and transcultural and the understanding and expression of those meanings which are limited historically and culturally.

trans,cultura·tion. [f. TRANS- 3 + CULTURE *sb.* + -ATION.] = *ACCULTURATION.
1941 B. MALINOWSKI *Sci. Theory Culture* (1944) ii. 14 Practical problems—such as..the difficulties of culture contact, and transculturation—problems that legitimately belong to anthropology. **1949** *Psychiatry* XII. 184 This paper..has shown that the process of transculturation is not really a process of adaptation to a culture but to a political situation. **1970** R. STAVENHAGEN in I. L. Horowitz *Masses in Lat. Amer.* vii. 287 We use the terms 'transculturation' and 'acculturation' interchangeably.

transcurrence. Restrict † *Obs. rare* to sense in Dict. and add: **2.** *Geol.* The phenomenon of transcurrent faulting.
1971 *Geol. Mag.* CVIII. 40 His [*sc.* S. W. Carey's] concept of megashears is essentially that of transcurrence as defined here. **1979** *Nature* 1 Mar. 12/2 Such transcurrence juxtaposed features whose dissimilarity had instead suggested to many an oceanic gap.

transcurrent, *a.* Add: **3.** *Geol.* Designating or pertaining to a fault which is primarily due to horizontal displacement; *esp.* one of large dimensions and with a nearly vertical inclination; usu. in *transcurrent fault* (see quots. 1942[2], 1971[1]).
1942 E. M. ANDERSON *Dynamics of Faulting* i. 1 The term 'Blatt' [used by Suess] will be translated as transcurrent fault. *Ibid.* v. 54 The name Transcurrent Faults has been adopted in this memoir for members of the class which are distinguished by lateral movement, with inclinations which, according to theory, are nearly vertical. **1965** G. J. WILLIAMS *Econ. Geol. N.Z.* i. 2/1 Movement along the Alpine Fault..is still going on in the form of major clockwise transcurrent movement with a 300 mile shift. **1971** *Geol. Mag.* CVIII. 33 Transcurrent faults are large-scale strike-slip faults which operate between lithosphere plates. **1977** [see *tear-fault* s.v. *TEAR *sb.*[2] 4].

trans,denomina·tional, *a.* [f. TRANS- 3 + DENOMINATIONAL *a.*] = *TRANSCONFESSIONAL *a.*
1972 *Clergy Rev.* Sept. 658 The first transdenominational church union to take place in Britain in modern times. **1976** *Christian* III. 168 There is a growing hunger for transdenominational eucharistic celebration.

trans,deriva·tional, *a.* *Transformational Gram.* [f. TRANS- 3 + DERIVATIONAL *a.*] Relating to or involving more than one derivation (see *DERIVATION[1] 6 c).
1977 *Language* LIII. 137 One way in which the notion 'superficially optional/obligatory element' could be handled would be by means of a transderivational rule, i.e. a rule referring to another derivation in which the optional element does not occur either in semantic or in superficial representation. **1979** *Trans. Philol. Soc.* 12 In French, by contrast, reflexive deletion is subject to a further transderivational condition.

trans,determina·tion. *Biol.* [f. TRANS- 1 + DETERMINATION.] An alteration of the course of development of an imaginal disc during the culture of *Drosophila* tissue so that it gives rise to a structure that normally develops from a different disc.
1965 E. HADORN in *Genetic Control of Differentiation* (Brookhaven Conf. Rep. BNL-C-44) 157 Since the allotypic organs appear in the offspring of cells which have been first autotypically determined, a change in determination must be postulated. We call this event transdetermination. **1978** *Nature* 2 Feb. 403/2 In general their state of determination (leg, wing, genital, and so on) is conserved during culture, but occasionally a so-called transdetermination occurs whereby a certain type of disk changes to another state of determination.

trans,discipli·nary, *a.* [f. TRANS- 3 + DISCIPLINARY *a.*] Of or pertaining to more than one discipline or branch of learning; interdisciplinary. So **trans,disciplina·rity.**
1972 E. JANTSCH in *OECD: Interdisciplinarity* II. i. 105 The ultimate degree of co-ordination in the education/innovation system,..which may be called *transdisciplinarity*, would..depend on a common axiomatics... The whole education..system would be co-ordinated as a *multi-level, multi-goal* system, embracing a multitude of.. interdisciplinary two-level systems, which..will be modified in the transdisciplinary framework. **1977** R. HOLLAND *Self & Social Context* ix. 267 It is therefore possible to assert three promising criteria for new work: reflexivity, transdisciplinarity and the subversiveness of discovery. **1979** *Nature* 3 May 1/2 A recent workshop jointly sponsored by the American Association for the Advancement of Science and the US Department of Energy has been attempting to lay transdisciplinary foundations for a federally supported research programme on the impact of increasing atmospheric carbon dioxide content.

transduce (trɑnsdiū·s, -nz-), *v.* [Back-formation from next.] **1.** *trans.* To alter the physical nature or medium of (a signal); to convert variations in (a medium) into corresponding variations in another medium.
1949 L. L. BERANEK *Acoustic Measurements* xiv. 637 The dynamic range of a microphone is the range of levels of input signals which can usefully be transduced by the instrument. It is..limited at high levels by the amount of distortion which can be tolerated in the transduced signal. **1971** *Nature* 19 Feb. 530/2 Rhodopsin, a visual pigment found in vertebrate retinal rods, transduces light into a neural message. **1973** *Sci. Amer.* Sept. 87/1 (Advt.), It transduced a heart's faint signals into a squiggly line that the doctor could compare with those produced by other hearts. **1977** *Listener* 22–29 Dec. 857/4 Carbon granules..to do their delicate work of transducing sound waves into varying electric currents.
2. *Microbiology.* Of a virus: to transfer (genetic material) from one bacterium to another; also used with the first bacterium as obj. Also, to transfer (a genetic characteristic) from one bacterium to another using a virus.
1952 *Jrnl. Bacteriol.* LXIV. 687 *FA* [*sc.* filterable agents] from each of the three LT-7 auxotrophs could transduce the other two. **1965** *Virology* XXVII. 290 (*heading*) Variation in composition of chromosome fragments transduced by phage P22. **1973** R. G. KRUEGER *Introd. Microbiol.* xiv. 404/2 In contrast to the specialized transducing phages, the viruses P1 and P2 can transduce a variety of genes in the bacterial genome. **1977** *Lancet* 9 July 94/2, 47 *gen-r* (ex 8799) was a resistant transductant produced by transducing the gentamicin resistance from strain 75/8799 to propagating strain (PS) 47.
Hence **transdu·ced, transdu·cing** *ppl. adjs.*; **transdu·cible** *a.*, susceptible to transduction.
1952 *Jrnl. Bacteriol.* LXIV. 686 All of the transduced cells were still streptomycin resistant. *Ibid.* 687 Several galactose-negative mutants were transducible to galactose-positive by *FA* [*sc.* filterable agent] from their parental wild type. **1952** *Physiol. Rev.* XXXII. 414 The chemical composition of transducing agents has important implications, if they can be regarded as purified genes. **1962** R. GOLDMAN *Ultrasonic Technol.* iii. 67 A transducing crystal must also be mounted in some sort of holder. **1971** G. S. STENT *Molecular Genetics* xiv. 416 Upon closer examination of the clones of transduced bacteria or transductants..it was found..that all the Gal^+ transductants were either actively lysogenetic.., or were at least immune to infection. **1973** Transducing [see sense 2 above].

transducer (trɑns,diū·səɹ -nz-). [f. L. *transdūcere* to lead across, transfer, f. *trans* TRANS- + *dūcere* to lead: see -ER[1].] Any device by which variations in one physical quantity (e.g. pressure, brightness) are quantitatively converted into variations in another (e.g. voltage, position).
1924 K. S. JOHNSON *Transmission Circuits for Telephonic Communic.* vii. 46 A structure which, when inserted in a circuit, enables this maximum possible power to be absorbed in the receiving circuit is called an ideal transducer. **1948** [see *QUANTIZER]. **1957** *New Scientist* 12 Dec. 30/2 The excitation of sensory [nerve] endings, physiological 'transducers' of mechanical changes into electrical signals. **1965** *Wireless World* July 31 (Advt.), Racal Magnetic Transducer..converts rotational movement to a pulse output without physical connection to the shaft under test. **1973** M. WOODHOUSE *Blue Bone* ii. 11 We designed and sold a capacitative transducer head for somebody else's flowmeter. **1976** A. HOPE *Hi-Fi Handbk.* 88 Although we have so far considered only moving coil-moving cone loudspeakers, there are other types of 'transducer' on the market which convert electrical energy into sound in different ways. **1980** *Jrnl. R. Soc. Arts* May 348/2 Huxley and Simmons use extremely fast-acting motors and transducers to record force changes in small fractions of a millisecond.

transductant (trɑns,dʊ·ktănt, -nz-). *Microbiology.* [f. TRANSDUCT(ION + -ANT[1].] A cell into which genetic material has been transduced.
1963 *Exper. Cell Res.* XXX. 252 When the histidine-requiring mutants..are crossed by transduction, $1/10^6$ recipient cells become stable his^+ transductants. **1978** *Nature* 1 June 355/2 RNA polymerase was therefore isolated from two transductants, differing only at the *alt* locus.

transduction. Restrict *rare* to sense in Dict. and add: **2.** The action or process of transducing a signal.
1947 *Jrnl. Acoustical Soc. Amer.* XIX. 307/1 It is rather interesting..that the direct method of electronic transduction, instead of the indirect method of employing a conventional transducer and then amplifying the output with a vacuum tube, has not been developed. **1970** J. EARL *Tuners & Amplifiers* iv. 87 Low impedance pickup cartridges..using the moving-coil principle of transduction. **1975** *Nature* 17 Apr. 625/1 The transduction of light energy into neural signals is mediated in all known visual systems by a common type of visual pigment.
3. *Microbiology.* The transfer of genetic material from one cell to another by a virus or virus-like particle.
1952 ZINDER & LEDERBERG in *Jrnl. Bacteriol.* LXIV. 681 To help the further exposition of our experiments, we shall use the term transduction for genetically unilateral transfer in contrast to the union of equivalent elements in fertilization. **1960** [see *F III. 1 l]. **1971** *Nature* 18 June 466/1 It has been suggested that transduction of genes by viruses was an important mechanism in evolution for spreading useful mutations between organisms not formally related. **1977** *Lancet* 9 July 94/2 These were derived by selection of sensitive variants from gentamicin-resistant strains or by transduction of this resistance to sensitive strains.
Hence **transdu·ctional** *a.*, of or pertaining to (genetic) transduction.
1956 *Genetics* XLI. 845 (*heading*) Linear inheritance in transductional clones. **1980** *Jrnl. Gen. Microbiol.* CXIX. 51 Transductional analysis revealed that one of the four mutations carried by strain T-693 was responsible for constitutive synthesis of both isoleucine and threonine biosynthetic enzymes.

transductor. Restrict ‖ to sense in Dict. and add: **2.** *Electr.* [See quot. 1939.] A reactor (sense *2 a) having a d.c. winding to control the saturation of a core and an a.c. winding whose impedance is thereby changed, so that a small change in direct current produces a large change in alternating current.
1939 U. LAMM in *ASEA Jrnl.* XVI. 71/2 We should like to introduce some explanation of the word 'transductor'... The purpose of this word is actually to express the idea that as regards the mutual action between its two windings the apparatus resembles a transformer whilst, however, at the same time functioning in the A.C. circuit as a reactor or inductor, *i.e.* a conductor. **1975** *IEEE Trans. Nuclear Sci.* XXII. 1277/1 At Fermilab, transductors are used as current measuring devices in the main accelerator quadrupole power supply feedback loop.

trans,ea·rth, *a.* *Astronautics.* [f. TRANS- 2 + EARTH *sb.*[1]] Of or pertaining to spaceflight or a trajectory towards the earth from the moon or another planet.
1965 *New Scientist* 1 July 12/3 The navigation of the injection into a transearth orbit and the transearth coast are similar to the outward parts of the voyage. **1970** N. ARMSTRONG et al. *First on Moon* xiii. 320 'Now we have only one more thing to worry about.' (She meant trans-earth injection—the big burn that would let the world know 'Here we come!')

transect (trɑ·nsekt), *sb.* [f. the vb.] **a.** A line or a belt of land along which a survey is made of the plant or animal life or some other feature; a survey of this kind.
1905 F. E. CLEMENTS *Research Methods Ecol.* iv. 176 When longer transects are desired, as in the case of forest formations, tapes of 500 or 1,000 meters should be used with eyelets a meter apart. **1939** [see *QUADRAT 3]. **1974** *Environmental Conservation* I. 57/2 A second transect in an area of high-centred polygons..exhibited less than 2% differences in total thaw by season's end. **1979** *Rescue News* Dec. 4/2 A transect was plotted from the highest corner of the field to the source of the Gypsey Race. Along this over 20 one-metre square trial holes were dug.
b. *attrib.*, as *transect count, line, strip.*
1971 *Country Life* 23 Sept. 739/1 The puffin study, involving transect counts of occupied burrows on the island's vertiginous slopes, had been hazardous. **1973** J. J. MCKELVEY *Man against Tsetse* iii. 175 Certain rounds were arranged to follow transect lines according to compass bearings. **1953** SCOTT & FISHER *Thousand Geese* 220 It was not possible to maintain a constant width of transect-strip.

transempirical, *a.* (Earlier example.)
1904 W. JAMES in *Mind* Oct. 465 Whether there be a trans-empirical reality or not.

transepted (trɑ·nseptĕd), *a.* *Archæol.* [f. TRANSEPT + -ED[2].] Having chambers resembling transepts; *spec.* designating a type of gallery grave (see quot. 1956).
1939 G. E. DANIEL in *Proc. Prehist. Soc.* V. 143 The present writer defined a type of megalithic burial chamber which was there called the transepted gallery grave. **1956**

R. J. C. ATKINSON *Stonehenge* v. 149 The tomb has..two pairs of chambers opening off its sides, in the manner of transepts in a church; for this reason the type is known technically as a transepted gallery-grave. **1963** [see *gallery grave* s.v. *GALLERY *sb.* 12 b].

transeunce, etc.: see *TRANSIENCE, etc.; **transexual,** etc.: see *TRANSSEXUAL *a.* and *sb.*, etc.

transfection (tranſfe·kʃən, -nz-). *Microbiology.* [f. TRANS- or TRANS(FER *sb.* + IN)-FECTION.] The introduction of free viral nucleic acid into a cell.

1964 FÖLDES & TRAUTNER in *Zeitschr. für Vererbungslehre* XCV. 61 Infection of cells by the isolated nucleic acid from a virus, resulting in the production of a complete virus will be termed Transfection. **1975** *Nature* 5 June 446/2 The rescue of proviral DNA of Rous sarcoma virus in mammalian cells by 'transfection' to permissive chicken cells. **1980** OLD & PRIMROSE *Princ. Gene Manipulation* i. 7 Transformation of a cell with DNA from a virus is sometimes referred to as transfection.

So **transfe·ct** *v. trans.*, to infect (a cell) with free viral nucleic acid; **transfe·cted** *ppl. a.* (said of the cell and of the acid).

1964 *Zeitschr. für Vererbungslehre* XCV. 61 For the plating of transfected cells it is essential to use tryptone plates. **1966** *Ann. Rev. Microbiol.* XX. 394 It appears that the genetic basis for the ability to be transformed or transfected is similar. **1974** *Nature* 22 Nov. 319/2 We tried to transfect ΦX-DNA to various bacteria belonging to the *Enterobacteriaceae.* **1983** *Sci. Amer.* Jan. 58/2 Investigators have 'transfected' cultured cells by exposing them to naked foreign DNA.

transfer, *sb.* Add: **2. c.** *Psychol.* (More fully *transfer of practice, training.*) The carrying over of the effects of training or practice from the learning of one function to the learning of another. Cf. *negative transfer* s.v. *NEGATIVE *a.* 8 c; *positive transfer* s.v. *POSITIVE *a.* 8 d.

1901 THORNDIKE & WOODWORTH in *Psychol. Rev.* VIII. 386 There is no inner necessity for improvement of one function to improve others closely similar to it, due to a subtle transfer of practice effect. **1924** *Psychol. Rev.* XXXI. 157 There is no evidence for such transfer of training among rats. **1948** E. R. HILGARD *Theories of Learning* ii. 29 The theory proposes that transfer depends upon the presence of identical elements in the original learning and in the new learning which it facilitates. **1970** HALSTEAD & RUCKER in W. Byrne *Molecular Approaches to Learning & Memory* 6 (*heading*) Behavioral modification, née transfer of training.

d. The transference of a worker or player from one location, sphere, sports club, etc., to another; a change of place of employment within an organization.

1895 *Football News* (Nottingham) 2 Nov. 1/6 It is stated that the Forest have offered £70 for Bruce's transfer. **1923** J. D. HACKETT *Labor Terms in Management Engineering* May, *Transfer*, the shifting of a worker from one occupation to another. **1937** [see *DOTTED *ppl. a.* 1 c]. **1970** *Times* 13 Oct. 15/3 Trevor Gould..has been given a free transfer by Coventry City. **1973** J. THOMSON *Death Cap* xiii. 176 'I've been thinking again about putting in for a transfer,' Holbrook said... Finch..wished now that he could have satisfied the Sergeant over the question of his transfer... A good local policeman meant a lot to a small community.

3. For '(*rarely*, a person)' read 'or a person' and add further examples of people.

1929 *Daily Express* 7 Nov. 12/4 The prizes will hardly be glittering enough to attract the best 'transfers'. **1970** *Globe & Mail* (Toronto) 26 Sept. 35/6 The Mustangs have six experienced transfers who must be fitted in. **1979** *Arizona Daily Star* 1 Apr. C 9/1 The return of 33 lettermen —five senior-college transfers, most of whom will likely start—and 10 junior-college transfers.

4. b. (Examples.)

1883 I. M. RITTENHOUSE *Maud* (1939) 187 The sun was just coming up as we crossed the river on the transfer. **1892** S. HALE *Let.* 28 Apr. (1919) 269, I mounted a cable, took a transfer, and went..out into the suburbs. **1903** A. B. HART *Actual Govt.* 207 In most cities there is a system of free transfers, so that, starting from one suburb, one may often travel for a single fare 5, 10, or 15 miles to another suburb.

5. *transfer agent, -boat* (earlier example), *-company* (earlier example), *-deed* (example), *list, market, office* (later example), *payment, price, pricing*; **transfer case,** (*a*) a case in(to) which materials are transferred; (*b*) *Mech.*, (the housing of) a mechanism for dividing the power between a number of axles in a motor vehicle with two or more driving axles; **transfer chamber,** the chamber in which the material is initially heated in transfer moulding; **transfer effect(s),** the result(s) of transfer of training (see sense 2 c above); **transfer factor** *Immunol.*, a substance released by antigen-sensitized lymphocytes and capable of transferring the response of delayed hypersensitivity to a non-sensitized cell or individual into which it is introduced; **transfer fee,** (*a*) (example); (*b*) *Football*, a sum of money paid by one club to another for the transfer of the services of a professional player; **transfer function,** a mathematical function relating the output or response of anything to the input or stimulus; also *transf.*; **transfer line** *Engin.*, a line of work-stations along which a part is automatically conveyed to be subjected to a sequence of automatic machining operations; **transfer machine** *Engin.*, a composite machine that performs a series of operations without the intervention of the operator; **transfer mould** *sb.*, the mould cavity in transfer moulding; also (with hyphen) as *v. trans.*, to make by means of transfer moulding; **transfer moulding,** a moulding process used chiefly for thermosetting plastics in which the material is softened in a heated chamber and then forced by a plunger into an adjacent closed, heated mould cavity where it sets; **transfer orbit** *Astronautics*, an orbit that touches two given orbits and therefore provides a trajectory by which a spacecraft can pass from one of them to the other; **transfer-paper** (earlier example); **transfer pot** = *transfer chamber* above; **transfer-printed** *a.* (examples); **transfer RNA** *Molecular Biol.*, RNA that collects particular amino-acids in the cytoplasm of a cell and conveys them to a ribosome, where they are assembled to form part of a polypeptide or protein molecule; **transfer station:** delete (*U.S.*) and add example.

1869 *Bradshaw's Railway Man.* XXI. 430 All certificates [shall] be signed by both the transfer agent and register. **1978** A. MALING *Lucky Devil* xix. 103 You are the transfer agent for Lucky Devil Minerals. **1882** *Uncle Rufus & Ma* 52 We ferried over in a transfer boat. **1923** H. A. MADDOX *Dict. Stationery* 77 *Transfer Case*, a Binding Case or file for receiving the matter transferred periodically from the live file or loose leaf book. **1949** I. FRAZEE et al. *Automotive Fundamentals* vi. 378 The transfer case is located behind the transmission. **1970** *Southerly* XXX. 216 Gear box and transfer case and differentials growled a deep throated work song with power to spare. **1983** *Judge of Election Handbk.* (*Board of Election Comm., Chicago*) 11/1 Open the transfer case and check that the official ballot cards are for the proper precinct. **1946** DUBOIS & PRIBBLE *Plastics Mold Engin.* 353 It is common practice to standardize on the size and design of the transfer chamber and plunger used with hand molds. **1977** *Times Educ. Suppl.* 21 Oct. 29/5 There has been at least one case of a transfer chamber exploding. **1879** H. T. WILLIAMS *Pacific Tourist* 262/1 The Transfer Company will carry baggage alone for 50 cents. **1869** *Bradshaw's Railway Man.* XXI. 63 Certificates must accompany transfer deeds. **1931** R. PINTER *Educ. Psychol.* xii. 268, I feel sure that actual measurements of the transfer effects would be very disappointing to me as a teacher. **1955** T. H. PEAR *Eng. Soc. Differences* ix. 194 For a time there was a general tendency to be sceptical concerning any claim of transfer-effects. **1963** *Rep. Comm. Inquiry Decimal Curr.* xi. 109 in *Parl. Papers 1962–3* (Cmnd. 2145) XI. 195 Psychologists have advised us that giving an old name to a new currency unit could result in serious 'transfer effect' difficulties. **1977** *Language* LIII. 340 'Transfer effects' may reverse the natural order of the acquisition of a sound or structure. **1956** *Jrnl. Exper. Med.* CIV. 328 The above experiments suggest that release of the transfer factor from sensitive cells may occur under relatively mild circumstances. **1978** J. A. BELLANTI *Immunology II* xiii. 333 Attempts to detect antibody in the transfer factor have always been negative, and since its small molecular weight became known, this possibility has been excluded. **1983** *Oxf. Textbk. Med.* I. v. 10/2 Therapy with transfer factor may ..find an accepted place in the management of a limited number of clinical situations. **1869** *Bradshaw's Railway Man.* XXI. 63 Transfer fee, 2*s.* 6*d.* each. **1901** *Football News* (Nottingham) 9 Mar. 6/3 New Brighton offered Everton £135 for my transfer, and Burnley were prepared to pay £200, but neither offer came to anything. Consequently I had to come South out of the reach of transfer fees. **1911** A. BENNETT *Card* xii. 296 How are you going to get new blood, with transfer fees as high as they are now? You can't get even an average good player for less than £200. **1976** *Western Mail* (Cardiff) 27 Nov., The three Welsh clubs..could also release experienced players to Somerton Park on a loan basis, should Newport be able to obtain transfer fees for any of their own professionals. **1948** BROWN & CAMPBELL *Princ. Servomechanisms* i. 18 The system behaviour may be represented in terms of transfer functions *KG* (*jω*), which are complex functions of the frequency variable *ω*. **1963** R. W. DITCHBURN *Light* (ed. 2) viii. 304 The transfer function constitutes a better evaluation of the performance of the optical system than a statement of the resolving power. **1971** *Nature* 20 Aug. 564/1 McFarland and Budgell found a transfer function for key pecking by thirsty birds in response to modulations of ambient temperature. **1977** *Gramophone* June 122/1 The speaker converts an electric signal into an acoustic wave and..may be regarded as a 'black box', with a particular transfer function representing its overall response in terms of sound waves. **1981** D. J. FISK *Thermal Control of Buildings* i. 9 The transfer function of a room..is not unique but depends on where heat is input ..and where its output temperature is measured. **1956** E. MOLLOY *Automobile Engineer's Ref. Bk.* III. 210 Only one head is used at the next station. This is at the right of the transfer line, and is a plunge-cut horizontal milling head for milling the bearing-retaining slots. **1975** *Sci. Amer.* Feb. 25/1 Under mass-production conditions..the engine block is conveyed automatically along a transfer line. **1951** *People* 3 June 6/7 Still on Spurs' transfer list at a fee is Cyril Toulouse. **1976** *Star* (Sheffield) 29 Oct. 28/6 Terry Eccles..is on the transfer list at his own request. **1951** *Treat. on Milling & Milling Machines* (ed. 4) xvii. 723 In order to reduce handling time, it is often advantageous to perform a number of different machining operations.. with a multiple-station automatic machine... Such machines are also known as transfer machines. **1977** *Sci. Amer.* May 89/1 (Advt.), Transfer machines finish rough castings into complex pieces such as engine blocks. **1970** *Globe & Mail* (Toronto) 25 Sept. B 7/4 Both see what is called the transfer market—the hundreds of thousands of Canadians who move from one community to another each year—as increasingly important. **1976** *Evening Times* (Glasgow) 1 Dec. 32/2 Partick Thistle could be involved at both ends of the transfer market before the weekend. **1933** *U.S. Patent 1,919,534* 5/1 A device of the class described for transfer molding an infusibly thermosetting resinous material. **1942** J. SASSO *Plastics for Industr. Use* iii. 36 Figure 13 shows an example of a transfer mold with a transfer plunger entering the transfer well. **1963** H. R. CLAUSER *Encycl. Engin. Materials* 165/1 Radio and television cabinets weighing up to four pounds have been transfer-molded from phenolic materials. **1971** E. W. DUCK *Plastics & Rubbers* iv. 56 Transfer moulds..can be regarded as very crude injection moulds, since they first pre-heat the plastic in the transfer cavity. **1940** J. DELMONTE *Plastics in Engin.* xi. 319 The term, transfer molding, has been used to designate specifically the injection of thermosetting materials. **1963** H. R. CLAUSER *Encycl. Engin. Materials & Processes* 164/1 In the transfer-molding process..the mold is completely closed and under clamping pressure before the material is injected into the mold cavity. This results in little or no flash and accurate control of dimensions. **1869** *Bradshaw's Railway Man.* XXI. 430 All the stock registered in New York at the transfer office now kept by Duncan, Sherman, and Co., shall also be registered at another office. **1961** W. T. THOMSON *Introd. Space Dynamics* iv. 66 Transfer between coplanar circular orbits can be effected by an elliptic orbit with perigee and apogee distances equal to the radii of the respective circles... The cotangential ellipse is known as the Hohmann transfer orbit. **1964** *Listener* 7 May 748/1 Once the transfer orbit has been entered, the probe will be moving in free fall, and no further thrust need be applied. **1841** *Brit. Pat. 9002* 18 Obtaining several copies of marks by the use of surfaces of transfer paper. **1964** S. M. MILLER in I. C. Horowitz *New Sociology* 301 In our country, the redistribution of income takes place to a large extent in transfer payments of welfare and social assistance. **1973** *Times* 9 June 19/2 A transfer payment is a payment made by the scheme of a former employee to the scheme of the employee's present employer in consideration of which the new employer's scheme takes over the responsibility for benefits in respect of the service with the former employer. **1976** *Hansard* (Canada) 17 Mar. 11881/1 The balance of $22 billion was in the form of transfer payments to persons, provinces and corporations for subsidies, and so on. **1963** H. R. CLAUSER *Encycl. Engin. Materials & Processes* 164/2 When the mold is opened, the small amount of material remaining in the transfer pot..is removed. **1971** B. SCHARF *Engin. & its Lang.* vi. 38 The mould (die) consists of two sections, an upper transfer chamber (transfer pot)..and a lower mould. **1969** J. ARGENTI *Managem. Techniques* 76 As the complexity and size of the company increases..the task of preparing a budget becomes highly intricate due to such problems as transfer prices and allocation of central overheads. **1974** *Terminol. Managem. & Financial Accountancy* (Inst. Cost & Managem. Accountants) 17 *Transfer price*, a price related to goods or other benefits transferred from one process or department to another or from one member of a group to another. **1971** D. C. HAGUE *Managerial Economics* III. x. 220 The problem of how to price a product as it leaves one department for another—the problem of transfer pricing—is one that has troubled accountants and managers for many years. **1979** *Abacus* (Sydney) XV. 3 International transfer pricing is concerned with the pricing of goods and services transferred between a company's domestic divisions and foreign subsidiaries or among those foreign subsidiaries themselves. **1869** LADY C. SCHREIBER *Jrnl.* 15 Sept. (1911) I. 37 We bought a couple of transfer-printed Wedgwood plates. *Ibid.* 17 Sept. 39, I coveted a small transfer-printed leaf. **1938** *Burlington Mag.* May p. xvii/2 Some rare Liverpool transfer-printed mugs. **1976** *Times* 24 July 9/3 Whieldon plates..and transfer-printed creamwares. **1961** *Ann. Reg. 1960* 402 It was thought a further kind of RNA, called 'Transfer' RNA, might be necessary to link the amino acids into a protein molecule. **1977** *Time* 4 Apr. 39/2 Aaron Klug..first determined the crystalline structure of transfer RNA (tRNA), the molecule that brings amino acids to the ribosome for assembly into protein. **1869** *Bradshaw's Railway Man.* XXI. 198 The negotiations with the South Eastern in reference to a new transfer station at Waterloo.

b. Chiefly *Electronics.* Used *attrib.* to designate a ratio of two quantities measured simultaneously at two different points of a circuit or device.

1933 [see *MUTUAL *a.* 1 f]. **1943** F. E. TERMAN *Radio Engineers' Handbk.* iii. 200 The transfer impedance is defined as the ratio of the voltage E_1 applied in mesh 1 to the resulting current I_2 of mesh 2. **1966** *McGraw-Hill Encycl. Sci. & Technol.* III. 429/2 The transfer characteristic *H* of the controller mathematically relates the controller M_1 to its input *E*: $M_1 = HE$. **1975** HAVILL & WALTON *Elem. Electronics* iv. 69 For the particular case of the transistor, the output and transfer characteristics are almost linear over substantial regions of the normal operating range. **1980** J. R. O'MALLEY *Circuit Analysis* xix. 467 The most popular of these transfer functions are the transfer impedance.., the transfer admittance.., the transfer voltage ratio or voltage gain.., and the transfer current ratio.

transferable, *a.* Add: *transferable vote*, (in systems of proportional representation) a vote that is transferred to a second or further competing candidate if the candidate for whom it is first cast is eliminated in one of the succession of counts or has more votes than are needed for election; esp. as *single transferable vote* (abbrev. S.T.V. s.v. *S 4 a).

1885 W. E. SMITH *Fair Representation* vi. 32 (*heading*) The single transferable vote. **1909** [in Dict.] **1954** B. & R. NORTH tr. *Duverger's Pol. Parties* II. iii. 358 We must distinguish between the result of proportional representation and the consequences of list-voting, which generally coincides with it (except in the transferable Irish vote). **1972** *Guardian* 19 June 10/4 Mr Whitelaw's reintroduction of the single transferable vote in Ulster local government is likely to please minority groups.

transferase (tra·nsfĕrēɪz, -nz-). *Biochem.* [f. TRANSFER *v.* + *-ASE.] Any enzyme that catalyses the transfer of some particular group or molecule from one molecule to another.

1948 *Jrnl. Biol. Chem.* CLXXII. 12 It may be that similar 'transferase' phenomena will be found to be of general occurrence with other types of hydrolases. **1974** [see *OXIDOREDUCTASE]. **1981** *Sci. Amer.* June 70/3 In *Penicillium chrysogenum* an acyl transferase then catalyzes the replacement of this side chain by one derived from a utilizable precursor, such as phenylacetic acid.

transference. Add: **1. b.** *Psychoanal.* [tr. G. *übertragung*.] The transfer to the analyst by the patient of re-awakened and powerful emotions previously (in childhood) directed at some other person or thing and since repressed or forgotten; the process or state of such a transfer; *loosely*, the emotional aspect of a patient's relationship to the analyst; also *transf. negative transference*: see *NEGATIVE *a.* 8 c; *positive transference*: see *POSITIVE *a.* 8 d.

[**1895** S. FREUD in Breuer & Freud *Studien über Hysterie* iv. 266 Die Uebertragung auf den Arzt geschieht durch falsche Verknüpfung. **1910** tr. *Freud's Orig. & Devel. Psychoanal.* in *Amer. Jrnl. Psychol.* XXI. 215 Every time that we treat a neurotic psychoanalytically, there occurs in him the so-called phenomenon of *transfer* (Uebertragung), that is, he applies to the person of the physician a great amount of tender emotion, often mixed with enmity.] **1911** *Amer. Jrnl. Psychol.* XXII. 434 The reason why the physician is so often the object toward which the transference is made is that the Œdipus complex is almost invariably present in the patient. **1916** C. E. LONG tr. *Jung's Analyt. Psychol.* 245 What has disgusted you in hypnotism is at bottom nothing but the so-called 'transference' to the doctor. **1920** E. JONES *Treatm. Neuroses* 40 He is..reacting not toward the physician, but rather toward the other person who has been brought together ('identified') with the latter in his mind, an occurrence technically known as 'transference'. **1937** A. S. NEILL *That Dreadful School* xi. 155 If you tell a child any vital truth, or if it confides its troubles to you, he or she gets a transference, that is you get all the child's emotions showered on you. **1973** A. JANOV *Primal Scream* xiv. 246 Since I believe that the transference *is* the neurosis, I think that doing anything else with the patient other than helping him to feel his Pain is to render him a disservice.

3. *attrib.* and *Comb.*, as (sense *1 b) *transference feeling, situation*; **transference neurosis** *Psychoanal.*, a neurotic stage during transference frequently encountered during analysis and considered beneficial to the therapy; **transference number** *Physical Chem.* (chiefly *U.S.*) = *transport number* s.v. *TRANSPORT *sb.* 6.

1964 GOULD & KOLB *Dict. Soc. Sci.* 557/1 Freud's aim in treatment gradually changed..to the interpretation and modification of 'transference feelings' and their underlying unconscious conflicts. **1977** R. HOLLAND *Self & Social Context* iv. 76 The Freudian analyst is prepared to hold the transference feelings, and possible acting out behaviours, long enough for the client to re-experience and go beyond them. **1916** A. A. BRILL *tr. Freud's Three Contributions to Theory of Sex* (ed. 2) iii. 77 Psychoanalysis of the so-called transference neuroses (hysteria and compulsion neurosis) offers us here a reliable insight. **1968** H. RACKER *Transference & Countertransference* i. 15 In the transference neurosis,..the return of the relations to the parents implies the return of the neurotic conflicts with them. **1898** *Jrnl. Chem. Soc.* LXXIV. II. 553 The values were found to be almost independent of the concentration .., the transference numbers for the anions being given by the expressions [etc.]. **1909** [see *HITTORF]. **1966** *McGraw-Hill Encycl. Sci. & Technol.* XIV. 18b/2 The two procedures for determining transference numbers by which most of the available data in the literature have been obtained are the Hittorf method and the moving boundary method. **1933** W. GALT *Phyloanalysis* 72 Only this intense transference-situation as it exists socially, however disguised, can account for the extremes of emotional stimulation and response constantly elicited in the process of phyloanalysis upon the slightest, most trivial occasion. **1977** C. STORR *Tales from Psychiatrist's Couch* 41 A probing of his feelings towards me as a mother figure, an exploration of the transference situation.

transferral. (Earlier example.)

a **1790** J. H. BEATTIE *Ess. & Fragments* (1794) III. 295 Instead of reference, preference, commitment..say *referral, preferral*..and the *transferral* of property, instead of the transferring of property.

transferred, *ppl. a.* (In Dict. s.v. TRANSFER *v.*) Add: *transferred epithet*, an epithet grammatically qualifying a noun other than (though contextually associated with) the noun to which it literally applies.

1866 A. BAIN *Eng. Comp. & Rhet.* 24 The *Transferred Epithet* is a common figure in Poetry. The shifting of an epithet from its proper subject to some allied subject.. is seen in... 'Hence to his *idle bed*.' **1947** C. BROOKS *Well Wrought Urn* ix. 159 One can..justify the adjective as a transferred epithet on the model of Vergil's *maestum timorem*. **1958** C. BROOKE-ROSE *Gram. Metaphor* iii. 57, I have not found this transferred epithet in the later texts.

transferrin (trɑnsfe·rin, -nz-). *Biochem.* [f. TRANS- + L. *ferr-um* iron + -IN[1].] Any of several beta globulins found in blood serum which bind and transport iron; = *siderophilin* s.v. *SIDERO-[1] 2.

1947 HOLMBERG & LAURELL in *Acta Chemica Scandinavica* I. 950 We suggest that the new metal-combining protein (iron-binding component) in serum be called transferrin. **1962** H. HEATH in A. Pirie *Lens Metabolism Rel. Cataract* 364 Ascorbic acid has been shown to be necessary for the transfer of plasma-bound iron, transferrin, into the liver and its incorporation into ferritin. **1971** [see *siderophilin* s.v. *SIDERO- 2]. **1977** *Jrnl. R. Soc. Arts* CXXV. 699/1 These transferrin genes show much genetic diversity within herds.

trans,fi:naliza·tion. *Theol.* [f. TRANS- 3 + *FINALIZATION.] The change in purpose or function undergone by bread and wine at the Eucharist through transubstantiation, expressed in terms of finality or teleology. Cf. *TRANSIGNIFICATION.

1965 *Pope Speaks* X. 311 It is not permissible..to discuss the mystery of transubstantiation without mentioning what the Council of Trent had to say about the marvelous conversion of the whole substance of the bread into the Body and the whole substance of the wine into the Blood of Christ, as if they involve nothing more than 'transignification' or 'transfinalization' as they call it. **1966** *Worship* XL. 337 In the eucharist we ought to be concerned with an interpersonal relationship between Christ and us,..in which Christ gives himself to man by means of bread and wine which, by this very gift, have undergone a transfinalization and an ontological and therefore radical transignification. **1975** E. L. MASCALL in *Critique Eucharistic Agreement* v. 73 The writers who introduced the notions of transfinalization and transignification were worried that the term 'transubstantiation' as commonly understood suggested a notion both insufficiently dynamic and insufficiently human.

transfixture. For *rare*[−1] read *rare* and add later example.

1955 W. DE LA MARE *Beginning* 215 In this transfixture, a single commonplace word came sallying nonchalantly up out of his memory.

transfluence (trɑ·nsfluĕns). *Geomorphol.* [ad. G. *transfluenz* (A. Penck *Die Alpen im Eiszeitalter* (1909) III. 804), f. L. *-fluentia* flow: see TRANS-.] The flow of glacial ice in quantity across a preglacial watershed with consequent severe erosion.

1949 *Scottish Geogr. Mag.* LXV. 123 The ice-flow thus set up across the divides is termed diffluence or transfluence. **1955** *Sci. News* XXXVIII. 55 At the present time transfluence is occurring at the edge of the Greenland ice-cap. **1970** R. J. SMALL *Study of Landforms* xi. 374 Glacial transfluence is found where the impeded ice cuts out of a valley system not by a lateral distributary but at the very head of the valley.

transfluent, *a.* Restrict *rare* to sense in Dict. and add: **b.** *spec.* in *Geomorphol.*, applied to glacial ice undergoing transfluence.

1951 *Trans. Inst. Brit. Geographers* Pub. No. 15, 2 Like Penck he clearly recognised that where a pass was crossed by diffluent or transfluent ice it was markedly eroded by it. **1968** R. W. FAIRBRIDGE *Encycl. Geomorphol.* 429/2 Many of the breaches made by transfluent ice involve considerable arrangement of the drainage pattern.

transfluxor (trɑnsflʌ·ksəɹ, -nz-). *Electronics.* [f. *TRANS- 10 + FLUX *sb.* + -OR.] (See quots.)

1955 RAJCHMAN & LO in *R.C.A. Rev.* XVI. 303 A novel device which is based on the fact that completely new switching and storing functions become possible when two or more apertures are made in the rectangular hysteresis loop cores, thereby creating a number of distinct legs and flux paths in the magnetic circuit. The new device operates by the controlled transfer of flux from leg to leg in the magnetic circuit and was consequently named 'Transfluxor'. **1963** [see *LADDIC]. **1972** G. J. KLIR *Introd. Methodol. Switching Circuits* v. 185 Interesting properties are exhibited by a magnetic core which has several holes with windings. This element is called a transfluxor.

transform, *sb.* Add: **2.** *Transformational Gram.* A syntactic structure derived by the application of a transformation.

1955 N. CHOMSKY *Transformational Analysis* (Ph.D. Dissertation, Univ. Pennsylvania) v. 26 It seems most natural to characterize these sentences in terms of some notation of grammatical transformation, regarding these sentences as transforms of certain sentences which are derived on the level *P* and which do have *P* markers. **1957** —— *Syntactic Structures* (1962) viii. 88 This sentence [*sc.* I found the boy studying in the library] was a transform..of 'I—found studying in the library—the boy'. **1964** R. H. ROBINS *Gen. Linguistics* vi. 243 The collocational compatibilities..between the particular words of any sentence and its transform are likely to be substantially the same. **1972** R. D. EAGLESON in G. W. Turner *Good Austral. Eng.* v. 98 We can see them [*sc.* two versions of a sentence]..as related to the same underlying structures and as different transforms of it. **1976** *Word 1971* XXVII. 253 There is an embedded sentence corresponding to sentence 7 b, a transform derived from sentence 8 b by a movement of the Aux *haben* ('have').

3. *Geol.* = *transform fault*, sense 4 below.

[**1965** J. T. WILSON in *Nature* 24 July 343/1 A junction where one feature [marking a mobile belt] changes into another is here called a transform.] **1971** *Geol. Mag.* CVIII. 27 It appears that there is a mechanical advantage in overcoming overall transtension by stepped transforms. **1978** *Nature* 16 Feb. 617/1 (*caption*) The three transforms are shown by dashed lines and their possible extensions by dotted lines.

4. *Comb.*: **transform fault** *Geol.*, a transcurrent fault terminating abruptly at both ends, *esp.* one that connects two segments of an oceanic ridge; also, any transcurrent fault associated with two lithospheric plates sliding past one another; hence **transform faulting.**

1965 J. T. WILSON in *Nature* 24 July 343/2 It is proposed that a separate class of horizontal shear faults exists which terminate abruptly at both ends, but which nevertheless may show great displacements... The name transform fault is proposed for the class. **1973** *Ibid.* 10 Aug. 341/2 The boundaries between the rigid plates which make up the Earth's crust are..of three distinct kinds: ridges..; trenches..; transform faults, along which plates may slip relative to each other. **1976** *Ibid.* 4 Mar. 14/1 There are several transcurrent faults in solid continental rocks which, because they happen to terminate at structural features which 'absorb' their motion, must also be termed 'transform faults' according to Wilson's strict definition. **1980** *Guardian* 20 Nov. 13/4 There are fault boundaries, known as transform faults, along which the plates merely slide past each other. **1971** *Geol. Mag.* CVIII. 27 The sinuous zone of fission as it extends the length of the north and south Atlantic Ocean is necessarily in many places oblique to the direction of spreading. This situation is generally..accommodated by transform faulting.

transform, *v.* Add: **1. c.** More widely, to subject (any mathematical entity) to a transformation (TRANSFORMATION 2 c in Dict. and Suppl.). Also *absol.*

1972 M. KLINE *Math. Thought* xix. 427 Finding it difficult to evaluate in rectangular coordinates, he transformed to spherical coordinates. **1982** D. M. SCHNEIDER et al. *Linear Algebra* v. 181 The function *f* defined by the equation $f(x) = x^2$. This function transforms a real number into a real number, namely its square.

f. *Molecular Biol.* To change (a bacterial cell) into a genetically distinct kind by the introduction into it of DNA from another cell of the same or a closely related species.

1928 *Jrnl. Hygiene* XXVII. 150 An R strain is most readily transformed into the S variety when the killed culture used is of the same serological type as that from which the R strain was derived. **1947** *Jrnl. Exper. Med.* LXXXVI. 449 Repeated attempts both *in vitro* and *in vivo* to transform D39/Int53 to pneumococcus Type III were unsuccessful. **1981** L. L. MAYS *Genetics* vi. 274 Pieces of DNA of molecular weight less than $1{\cdot}5 \times 10^7$ daltons cannot transform *Haemophilus influenzae*.

g. *Cytology.* To cause (a eukaryotic cell) to undergo transformation (*TRANSFORMATION 3 i).

1959 *Jrnl. Nat. Cancer Inst.* XXIII. 1035 (*heading*) Clonal analysis of variant cell lines transformed to malignant cells in tissue culture. **1982** *Sci. Amer.* Mar. 72/1 Analysis of the DNA of the Rous sarcoma virus has revealed a single gene capable of transforming cells.

2. Delete 'Now *rare*' and add later examples.

1893 HARKNESS & MORLEY *Treat. Theory of Functions* i. 14 If $w = u + iv$ be a one-valued monogenic function of $x + iy$, the systems of orthogonal straight lines $x = a$, $y = b$ transform into systems of orthogonal curves in the *w*-plane. **1970** PASSMORE & ROBSON *Compan. Med. Stud.* II. xxii. 9/2 The function of antigen at the surface of the lymphocyte is to induce it to transform and proliferate into active antibody-producing cells. **1971** *Nature* 26 Nov. 187/1 The larva then transforms to a pupa. **1982** *Suppl. to O.E.D.* III, *Pseudoscalar* sb., a quantity that transforms as a scalar under rotation but changes sign under reflection.

transformant (trɑnsfǭ·ɹmănt, -z-). *Biol.* [f. TRANSFORM *v.* + -ANT[1].] **a.** A transformed bacterium (see *TRANSFORM *v.* 1 f). **b.** = *transformed cell* s.v. *TRANSFORMED *ppl. a.* b.

1957 *Biochimica & Biophysica Acta* XXVI. 71 The yield of transformants is determined by the prior state of competence of a pneumococcal culture. **1959** *Jrnl. Exper. Med.* CIX. 437 Capsulated transformants producing type II polysaccharide have been obtained by reactions between a number of R mutants of type II pneumococcus. **1971** *New Scientist* 8 Apr. 83/2 Cells selected from a population of transformants by virtue of their resistance to agglutination by concanavalin A, grow to a density expected of untransformed rather than transformed cells. **1980** *Amer. Jrnl. Trop. Med. & Hygiene* XXIX. 1045/1 (*caption*) Transformant clones were plated in duplicate.

transformation. Add: **2. c.** (Further examples.) Also, a change of any mathematical entity in accordance with some definite rule or rules; the rules themselves; *spec.* = *MAPPING *vbl. sb.* 2.

1908 [see *LORENTZ]. **1909** *Proc. Section Sci. K. Akad. van Wetenschappen te Amsterdam* XI. 798 A continuous one-one transformation in itself of a singly connected, onesided, closed surface leaves at least one point invariant. **1941** BIRKHOFF & MACLANE *Surv. Mod. Algebra* vi. 128 The 'similarity' transformations of space—those one-one transformations which multiply all distances by a constant factor. **1949** S. LEFSCHETZ *Introd. Topol.* i. 29 If *f* is one to one and bicontinuous (both *f* and its inverse f^{-1} continuous), *f* is said to be a topological transformation or a homeomorphism. **1952** E. T. BELL *Mathematics* vi. 354 The numerical value of f(t) is unaltered when we replace the variable *t* by the linear expression $t+1$... Thus, the value of the function is invariant under a particular linear transformation. **1958, 1964** [see *MAPPING *vbl. sb.* 2]. **1964** [see *FOURIER]. **1966** S. BEER *Decision & Control* vi. 109 It is possible to specify a transformation that will map the infinite set of natural numbers on to this other finite set. **1982** D. M. SCHNEIDER et al. *Linear Algebra* v. 181 If *V* and *W* are vector spaces, a function or transformation *T* from *V* into *W* is a rule that associates with every vector *x* in *V* a unique vector in *W*.

3. g. *Physics.* Change of one element into another, whether artificially induced or by spontaneous decay. Cf. *TRANSMUTATION 3 a.

1902 RUTHERFORD in *Phil. Mag.* IV. 395 These changes must be occurring within the atom, and the radioactive elements must be undergoing spontaneous transformation. **1926** R. W. LAWSON tr. *Hevesy & Paneth's Man. Radioactivity* xxi. 150 Similar attempts to influence the velocity of transformation of uranium and radium D, by subjecting them to the action of radiation, have also led to a negative result. **1958** O. R. FRISCH *Nucl. Handbk.* IV. 4 In each unit of time a certain definite fraction of the total number of the atoms present will disintegrate but there is nothing to indicate the moment at which a given atom will undergo the radioactive transformation. **1969** *Times* 12 Mar. 4/8 It is to be assumed that the uranium and thorium in the galaxy were created by the nuclear transformation within densely packed matter at high temperatures.

h. *Molecular Biol.* The genetic alteration of a bacterial cell by the introduction or absorption of extraneous DNA (see *TRANSFORM *v.* 1 f).

1928 F. GRIFFITH in *Jrnl. Hygiene* XXVII. 154 Experiments with culture heated at temperatures higher than 60 °C. have rarely been successful in causing transformation of type. **1960** *New Biol.* XXXI. 72 The first clear demonstration of transformation was made in 1928 by Griffith, who discovered that an avirulent and normally harmless strain of pneumococcus was changed into a virulent strain when injected into mice together with some virulent pneumococci that had been thoroughly killed by heating. **1970** AMBROSE & EASTY *Cell Biol.* x. 346 Transformation is a very inefficient process but has proved useful for gene mapping in bacteria where a suitable transducing phage is not known. **1980** *Sci. Amer.* Feb. 36/2 In another process, known as transformation, DNA released by cell death or other natural processes simply enters a new cell from the environment by penetrating the cell wall and membrane.

i. *Cytology.* The modification of a eukaryotic (nucleated) cell so that it comes to possess some or all of the characteristics of a cancer cell.

1943 *Jrnl. Nat. Cancer Inst.* IV. 202/1 The cell transformations appeared after a definite latent interval of several weeks following intitial exposure to the carcinogen. **1967** *Nature* 8 July 171/2 The concept of contact inhibition has attracted particular interest since the advent of tissue culture investigations on neoplastic transformation. **1982** *Sci. Amer.* Mar. 71/1 Transformation..is due to the action of a gene, which must be expressed continuously to maintain the cancerous state.

j. *Linguistics.* An operation by which one syntactic structure is converted into another by the application of specific rules; a rule converting deep structure to surface structure (see *deep structure* s.v. *DEEP *a.* IV c, *surface structure* s.v. *SURFACE *sb.* 6 d); the process by which surface structures are generated.

1955 N. CHOMSKY *Transformational Analysis* (Ph.D. Dissertation, Univ. Pennsylvania). 27 A sentence *X* is related to a sentence *Y* if, under some transformation set up for the language, *X* is a transform of *Y* or *Y* is a transform of *X*. **1957** —— *Syntactic Structures* (1962) v. 44 Let us call each such rule a 'grammatical transformation'. **1957** Z. S. HARRIS in *Language* XXXIII. 283 We can proceed to define transformation..based on two structures having the same set of individual co-occurrences. This relation yields unique analyses of certain structures and distinctions which could not be analyzed in ordinary linguistic terms. **1964** *Word* XX. 429 Transformations..may be thought of as manipulations—reordering, combination, addition, deletion—performed on fully formed sentences. **1964** R. H. ROBINS *Gen. Linguistics* vi. 242 Transformation is a method of stating how the structures of many sentences in languages can be generated or explained formally as the result of specific transformations applied to certain basic sentence structures. **1967** D. G. HAYS *Introd. Computational Linguistics* viii. 153 Such a transformation can break down the structure of one sentence and insert all or part of it at a specified place in the structure of the other. **1977** *Canad. Jrnl. Linguistics 1976* XXI. 156 The traditional assumption that transformations do not change meanings.

5. transformation (playing) card, a playing card on which the suit signs are incorporated into a design or picture.

[**1848** W. A. CHATTO *Facts & Speculations on Origin & Hist. Playing Cards* iv. 260 In 1811 two different packs of caricature cards, imitated..from the picture-cards in Cotta's Almanack, appeared in England... On the wrapper of both packs the inscription is the same: 'Metastasis. Transformation of Playing-cards.'] **1931** H. T. MORLEY *Old & Curious Playing Cards* 152 Transformation cards, 1828. A pack of 52 cards,..printed from wood blocks. **1960** H. HAYWARD *Antique Coll.* 286/2 *Transformation playing cards,* first issued in London 1808... Making transformation cards from ordinary packs became a fashionable pastime, pen and ink converting cards into designs of topical or personal association. **1966** S. MANN *Collecting Playing Cards* viii. 164 Transformation cards are a rather different case... Their aim is to 'transform' an ordinary pip card into a picture by means of incorporating the pips in their standard positions in a larger overall design.

transformationist, (*b*) = *TRANSFORMATIONALIST *sb.*

1962 J. SLEDD in Householder & Saporta *Probl. Lexicogr.* 145 The transformationists..have little interest in pedagogic problems. **1965** *Language* XLI. 124 A Czech study on the structure of German sentences..is contrasted with a study on the same subject by an American transformationist.

transformational, *a.* (In Dict. s.v. TRANSFORMATION.) Add: *spec.* in *Linguistics,* of or pertaining to a transformation or transformations (sense 3 j); (more fully *transformational-generative* adj.) designating, of, or pertaining to a linguistic model or method of analysis based on the generation of surface structures from underlying structures by transformations; cf. *GENERATIVE *a.* 2 b and TG s.v. *T 6 a.

1955 N. CHOMSKY (*title of Ph.D. Dissertation, Univ. Pennsylvania*) Transformational analysis. **1957** —— *Syntactic Structures* (1962) v. 46 Corresponding to the level of phrase structure, a grammar has a sequence of rules of the form $X \rightarrow Y$, and corresponding to lower levels it has a sequence of morphophonemic rules of the same basic form. Linking these two sequences, it has a sequence of transformational rules. *Ibid.* ix. 101 The similarity between active-passive, negation, declarative-interrogative, and other transformational relations would not have come to light if the active-passive relation had been investigated exclusively in terms of such notions as synonymity. **1961** P. H. MATTHEWS in *Archivum Linguisticum* XIII. 196 (*heading*) Transformational grammar. **1963** F. G. LOUNSBURY in J. A. Fishman *Readings Sociol. of Lang.* (1968) 48 One result of transformational analysis..is to lead linguistics a step closer to a general model for the syntax of language. **1964** R. H. ROBINS *Gen. Linguistics* p. xviii, One of the most striking developments in linguistics in the last few years has been the increasing recognition of the transformational model of linguistic statement. *Ibid.* p. xix, Some transformationalists, as the adherents of transformational-generative grammar are called. **1964** E. A. NIDA *Toward Sci. Transl.* iv. 60 There are some psychological confirmations of transformational theory which seem to have special significance. **1965** *N.Y. Times* 29 Dec. 32 Transformational grammar grew in part from M.I.T. computer experiments to produce mechanical translations of foreign languages. **1966** T. F. MITCHELL in C. E. Bazell *In Memory of J. R. Firth* 354 One cannot help but be puzzled by the refusal of American transformational-generative grammarians to incorporate in their valuable work collocational study of the kind envisaged here. **1966** Y. BAR-HILLEL in *Automatic Transl. of Lang.* (NATO Summer School, Venice, 1962) 7 Transformational grammars seem to have a much better chance of being both adequate and practical. *Ibid.* 12 The fifth aspect of syntactic complexity is, then, transformational history. **1967** [see *GENERATIVIST]. **1968** CHOMSKY & HALLE *Sound Pattern Eng.* ii. 15 These observations suggest a general principle for the application of rules of the phonological component, namely, what we shall call the principle of the 'transformational cycle'. **1972** *Language* XLVIII. 442 Arens fails to show..the essential ideas and assumptions underlying transformational-generative theory. **1973** *Amer. Speech 1969* XLIV. 220 The discussion of Middle English grammar and phonology is based on a transformational-generative view of language. **1973** *Archivum Linguisticum* IV. 35 Presumably, in transformational terms, transitive, intransitive, perfective, imperfective..are here surface structure categories. **1976** J. HOOPER *Introd. Natural Generative Phonol.* i. 4 The phonological rules..apply in sequential order... Each rule may apply only once, and is assigned a particular place in the sequence or is said to be *ordered* with respect to other rules. The theory with this general form will be referred to as transformational generative phonology. **1977** *Dædalus* Fall 119 The proper division of theoretical labor between rewriting and transformational rules (in particular, how to limit the power of the transformational rules in intuitively reasonable ways) has been a central concern of those who have worked with this conception of grammar. **1980** *Word 1979* XXX. 132 Some degree of exposure to transformational-generative grammar, case grammar and other theoretical approaches is evident in several [Vietnamese] works. **1980** *Canad. Jrnl. Linguistics* XXV. 1. 1 The standard theory referred to as transformational generative phonology. **1980** *English World-Wide* I. 1. 133 Transformational grammar has shown itself unable to handle the problem of the description of varieties which are as apparent in the 16th and 17th centuries as at the present day.

Hence **transforma·tionalism** *Linguistics,* transformational theory; **transforma·tionalist** *sb. Linguistics,* an adherent of transformational theory; also *attrib.* or as *adj.*; **transforma·tionally** *adv. Linguistics,* by means of transformation(s), according to transformational rules.

1963 *Amer. Speech* XXXVIII. 240 These attributives can be related transformationally to predications. **1964** E. BACH *Introd. Transformational Gram.* viii. 187 The transformationalists have provided elegant and powerful tools for the description of particular languages. **1969** *Neuphilologische Mitteilungen* LXX. 221 Chomskyan transformationalism rejects a scientific approach for an anti-scientific one. **1973** *Amer. Speech 1970* XLV. 125 A question that challenged the structuralist linguistic theory..and that seems no more amenable to a transformationalist solution. **1976** *Archivum Linguisticum* VII. 155 It is interestingly novel, however, within the framework of contemporary transformationalism in America. **1977** *Dædalus* Fall 119 If the interrogative sentence 'Are the men here?' is derived transformationally from the phrase structure underlying the declarative sentence 'The men are here', it would seem to imply that a speaker first thinks of the declarative sentence and then transforms it into the interrogative form. **1978** *Language* LIV. 174 Raimo Anttila's 'Revelation as linguistic revolution'..reads like an extemporaneous sermon on the wickedness of the transformationalists. **1980** *English World-Wide* I. 268 The neglect of the results of earlier scholarship on the part of young linguists, especially of the transformationalist school.

transformative, *a.* Add: **b.** *Linguistics.* = *TRANSFORMATIONAL *a.*, *spec.* in *transformative-generative* adj.

1962 P. STREVENS *Papers in Lang.* (1965) v. 73 The three major modern linguistic theories (*i.e.* phoneme-morpheme grammar, transformative-generative grammar, and system-structure grammar). **1965** *Language* XLI. 213 Recent interest taken by transformative-generative linguists in unidirectional transformations and unique derivations.

transformed, *ppl. a.* Add: **b.** *transformed cell* (Cytology), a eukaryotic cell which has undergone transformation (*TRANSFORMATION 3 i).

1956 *Science* 23 Mar. 503/2 The malignant nature of the transformed cells was demonstrated by the production of sarcomas when the cultures were inoculated into animals of the same strain. **1979** ARMS & CAMP *Biology* xvi. 247 Transformed cells often undergo drastic changes in morphology and metabolism such that they become unresponsive to the normal controls over cell division.

transformer. Add: **2. a.** (Further examples.) In mod. use, a static apparatus in which an alternating or pulsating current in one winding induces an alternating current in a second winding, usu. with different values of voltage and current.

1911 *Encycl. Brit.* XXVII. 173 A continuous current transformer is an appliance which effects a similar transformation for continuous currents, with the difference that some part of the machine must revolve. **1947** R. LEE *Electronic Transformers & Circuits* vii. 187 Line impedance changes abruptly, and transformers may be necessary for good power transfer. **1955** *Sci. News Let.* 15 Oct. 248/3 A transformer is a device very widely used to increase or lower the voltage of an electric current.

b. transformer oil, a high-grade oil with a low sludge content used to cool and insulate transformers and other electrical equipment.

1904 *Electric Club Jrnl.* I. 228 By transformer oil is meant an oil in which the transformer is completely immersed, forming a homogeneous insulation. **1957** E. B. JONES *Instrument Technol.* III. 1. 19 The variable resistance at the transmitter end is immersed in transformer oil which keeps it free from dirt. **1979** *Electr. Rev. Internat.* 7 Dec. 47/3 Transformer oil becomes highly viscous at low temperature.

transfo·rmerless, *a.* [-LESS.] That does not have a transformer; also, produced without the use of a transformer.

1949 B. GROB *Basic Television* xxii. 498 (*heading*) Transformerless television receiver. **1975** *Physics Bull.* Feb. 81/2 This has been achieved by using a transformerless supply and an aluminium casting for the frame.

transforming, *ppl. a.* Add: **b.** *transforming principle* (Biol.), a substance that genetically transforms bacterial cells (*TRANSFORM *v.* 1 f).

1944 *Jrnl. Exper. Med.* LXXIX. 155 If the results of the present study on the chemical nature of the transforming principle are confirmed, then nucleic acids must be regarded as possessing biological specificity the chemical nature of which is as yet undetermined. **1965** PEACOCKE & DRYSDALE *Molecular Basis Heredity* iii. 13 The transforming principle has two properties characteristic of genes, namely, determination of a specific inheritable property and self-reproduction.

transfusion. Add: Hence **transfu·sional** *a.*, occurring as a result of or by means of transfusion.

1965 *Endocrinology* LXXVII. 954 (*heading*) Effect of natural and synthetic corticoids on transfusional shock in the rat. **1974** R. ZELEDÓN in K. Elliott et al. *Trypanosomiasis & Leishmaniasis* 70 Besides the normal mechanism of transmission by the insect, two other modes, the transfusional and transplacental, may be epidemiologically important in the maintenance of the disease. **1982** *Jrnl. Pharm. & Pharmacol.* XXXIV. 730 (*heading*) Pyridoxal complexes as potential chelating agents for oral therapy in transfusional iron overload.

transgenosis (trɑnsdʒĕnōᵘ·sis, -nz-). *Genetics.* [f. *TRANS- 10 + GENE + -OSIS.] The transfer of genes to an unrelated organism and their subsequent expression.

1973 C. H. DOY et al. in *Proc. Nat. Acad. Sci.* LXX. 723/1 The overall phenomenon of transfer and subsequent expression has been termed transgenosis. **1979** I. H. HERSKOWITZ *Elem. Genetics* xiii. 192 Such transgenosis experiments usually involve either the uptake of naked bacterial DNA or the injection of phage DNA into eukaryotic cells.

trans,glo·bal, *a.* [f. TRANS- 3 + GLOBAL *a.*] That travels across or round the world.

1953 [see *HOSTESS 2 c]. **1981** *TV Times* 25–31 July 29/3 Prince Charles talks about The Transglobal Expedition.

transgress, *v.* Add: **2. a.** (*b*) *spec.* in *Geol.* Of the sea: to spread over (the land). Cf. *TRANSGRESSION 2.

1909 *Bull. Geol. Soc. Amer.* XX. 479 There are periodic recurrences of extensive emergences of the continents and..each one is later invaded or transgressed by continental seas. **1978** *Nature* 13 July 131/1 The down faulted and transgressed blocks on Fig. 1 have been numbered to show the sequence and time when the block was first transgressed.

transgressed, *ppl. a.* (Later example in *Geol.*)

1978 [see *TRANSGRESS *v.* 2 a (*b*)].

transgressible, *a.* For *rare*⁻⁰ read *rare* and add example.

1851 H. L. MANSEL *Proleg. Logica* 100, I..consider the results of my experience as contingent only and transgressible.

transgression. 2. Substitute for def: The spread of the sea over the land, as evidenced by the deposition of unconformable marine sediments. (Later examples.)

1908, etc. [see *REGRESSION 7]. **1975** J. G. EVANS *Environment Early Man Brit. Isles* iii. 67 Minor changes of sea level and coastal configuration have continued well beyond the main period of marine transgression.

transhisto·rical, *a.* [f. TRANS- 4 + HISTORICAL *a.*] (Having significance) that transcends the historical; universal or eternal.

1909 W. R. INGE in *Q. Rev.* Apr. 602 It is not the province of faith to flout scientific knowledge, nor to contaminate the material on which science works by intercalating what M. Le Roy calls 'transhistorical symbols'—myths in fact—which do not become true by being recognised as false, as the new apologetic seems to suggest. **1963** J. A. T. ROBINSON *Honest to God* i. 24 In order to express the 'trans-historical' character of the historical event of Jesus of Nazareth, the New Testament writers used the 'mythological' language of pre-existence, incarnation, [etc.]. **1976** T. EAGLETON *Crit. & Ideology* v. 178 Even where literary science would deem a work to have 'justly' survived, there is no call for materialist embarrassment about the 'metaphysical' quality of such transhistorical status.

transhuman, *a.* Delete *rare* and add further examples.

1936 E. UNDERHILL *Worship* xii. 251 Gazing on the Saints in their manifest humanity, their heroic virtue and 'spiritual persuasiveness', he shares their trans-human experience. **1957** *Economist* 9 Nov. (Suppl.) 12/1 This intensification of life—reaching towards a 'transhuman' level. **1968** S. ROSEN in *PN Rev.* (1979) No. 10. 15/2 We cannot return..to Greek, Jewish, Christian, or any other trans-human gods, whose meaning has been effectively destroyed by the decay of the values they represented.

transhumance (trɑnshiū·măns, -nz). [a. Fr., f. *transhumer*, ad. Sp. *trashumar* (f. L. *trans* across, over + *humus* ground, soil).] The transfer of grazing animals to summer pastures and back, often over substantial distances.

1911 M. I. NEWBIGGIN *Mod. Geogr.* vii. 179 The summer drought makes it difficult for even these hardy animals to obtain food, and necessitates in many regions a curious form of nomadism, to which the name of transhumance is given. Transhumance, still well developed in Spain, is the periodic and alternating displacement of flocks and herds between two regions of different climate. **1931** C. F. JONES *South America* 366 Government concessions to permanent ranchers, who do not desire the migrating flocks,..are reducing transhumance. **1954** M. BERESFORD *Lost Villages* vi. 204 Sheep which knew transhumance were not averse to being shepherded a score of miles over to a new pasture. **1975** J. G. EVANS *Environment Early Man Brit. Isles* vi. 133 We do not know to what extent these Bronze Age people were nomadic, or were practising transhumance, or were settled farmers.

Hence **transhu·mant** *a.*, migrating between regions with differing climates; of or pertaining to transhumance.

1932 E. H. CARRIER *Water & Grass* 78 The transhumant flocks. **1967** *Listener* 30 Mar. 426/3 The Sarakatsani—transhumant pastoralists of the Balkans. **1976** *Times Lit. Suppl.* 26 Mar. 353/2 The longer transhumant routes from the Pyrenees southwards to Catalonia.

trans,hydro·genase. *Biochem.* [f. *TRANS-10 + *HYDROGENASE.] Any enzyme which catalyses the transfer of hydrogen from one organic substrate to another. Cf. *DEHYDROGENASE.

1952 S. P. COLOWICK et al. in *Jrnl. Biol. Chem.* CXCV. 95 It is shown that the enzyme catalyzes a transfer of electrons (or hydrogen)... The enzyme will therefore be referred to here as 'pyridine nucleotide transhydrogenase'. **1978** *Jrnl. R. Soc. Med.* LXXI. 171 About 60% of insulin entering the liver is inactivated by liver enzymes, such as glutathione insulin transhydrogenase.

transience. Add: Also (in sense 2) **transeunce.**

1906 S. S. LAURIE *Synthetica* I. I. i. 6 The difficulties that arise in connection with the transeunce. **1914** C. D. BROAD *Perception* ii. 105 Leibniz and Lotze would have overlooked the immanence in the whole system,..and fastened on the transeunce within it with respect to its various elements.

transiency. Add: Also (in sense 2 of TRANSIENT *a.*) **transeuncy.**

1942 *Mind* LI. 137 Spinoza's central causal theory refers to the world of adequate knowledge as it is directed to *entia in se*, and its application to transeuncy must be governed by derivation therefrom.

transient, *a.* (*sb.*) Add: **1. a.** *spec.* in *Electr.* (cf. sense B. 3 below).

1853 *Proc. Philos. Soc. Glasgow* III. 285 (*heading*) On transient electric currents. **1870** *Phil. Mag.* XXXIX. 428 The galvanometer takes account of the induced transient current as a whole. **1962** *Newnes Conc. Encycl. Electr. Engin.* 821/2 The transient current consequent upon the switching-on of a filament lamp. **1969** J. J. SPARKES *Transistor Switching* v. 124 With the pulse steering circuits added..a transient current may flow.

b. *transient equilibrium* (Nuclear Sci.), the condition in which the half-life of a parent isotope is greater than that of the daughter but comparable to the period of observation, so that after an initial increase the total radioactivity decays with the parent's half-life and the ratio of parent atoms to daughter atoms remains constant.

1912 MAKOWER & GEIGER *Practical Measurement in Radioactivity* viii. 111 The name transient equilibrium has been given to this state of apparent equilibrium, which exists whenever the life of a product is not negligibly short compared with that of the preceding substance which controls the decay. **1961** G. R. CHOPPIN *Exper. Nucl. Chem.* vi. 84 For a parent with a 1 month half life, observation over a few days will seem to be secular equilibrium, whereas observation over a 3 month period will show transient equilibrium.

2. (Further examples of *transeunt.*)

1903 F. C. S. SCHILLER *Humanism* iv. 64 The impossibility of explaining such transeunt causation compels to the inference that things are not really separate and independent. **1933** *Mind* XLII. 155 The more responsive P_n is to P_m the more transeunt action there is between the two. **1942** R. G. COLLINGWOOD *New Leviathan* xx. 140 It [*sc.* the process of ruling] is *transeunt* when that which rules rules something other than itself. **1949** H. W. B. JOSEPH *Lect. Philos. Leibniz* iii. 107 That is the difficulty of transeunt causation—an effect produced in one thing by what is just another.

4. (Further *spec.* examples.) Also *transf.*, for transient guests, short-stay.

1818 H. B. FEARON *Sk. Amer.* 44 Boarding..is 8 dollars a week, for what is termed 'a transient man'. **1879** F. R. STOCKTON *Rudder Grange* xi. 121 We had no accommodations for them, neither had we any desire for even transient visitors. **1891** *Fur, Fin & Feather* Mar. 185 The transient rate for travelers at the Hilsabeck Hotel in Springfield is $1 a day. **1903** *N.Y. Even. Post* 19 Oct. 3 A 12-story transient hotel. **1906** *Springfield* (Mass.) *Weekly Republican* 9 Aug. 16 They will then rent apartments with or without board to transient and permanent guests. **1942** E. PAUL *Narrow St.* xxii. 175 Would that..some Turk would..rush me to a transient hotel. I am past that age, and never enjoyed a clandestine situation. **1976** *Times* 29 May 1/8 Was placed in transient barracks, a form of solitary confinement. **1981** *Sci. Amer.* Nov. 37/3 More intensive canvassing of places such as pool halls and transient hotels was done in an attempt to include a greater proportion of people who have no permanent address.

6. *U.S.* (Esp. of printed matter) occasional, isolated, individual.

1831 *Boston Transcript* 18 Apr. 2/3 We shall use all patrons alike, whether they are annual or transient advertisers. **1841** *Lowell* (Mass.) *Offering* I. 245 The clerk asked her if it was a transient paper. **1857** *Harper's Mag.* Feb. 403/1 The prepayment of postage on transient printed matter has been made compulsory. **1857** *Lawrence* (Kansas) *Republican* 28 May 1 All transient advertisements must be paid for in advance. **1904** *Philadelphia Friends' Intelligencer* 15 Oct. p. ii, For transient advertisements, 5 cents per line.

B. *sb.* **2.** For *U.S. colloq.* read '*colloq.* (orig. *U.S.*)' and add: Also, a traveller, a tramp, a migrant worker. (Further examples.)

1941 H. G. WELLS *You can't be too Careful* II. xv. 104 Whenever Doober's had rooms to spare a card was put into the ground floor window, and there would be transients for three or four days. **1946** W. S. MAUGHAM *Then & Now* vi. 33 Piero and the courier were to share a straw mattress in a corridor along with a number of transients only too glad to have a roof over their heads. **1959** M. RENAULT *Charioteer* vi. 114 A respectable tenement full of transients in a time of flux. **1963** C. D. SIMAK *They walked like Men* iii. 17 He was snoring gently and he looked..like a transient who might have wandered in to find a place to sleep. **1978** *Beautiful British Columbia* Winter 17 Transients pile in each winter to work the oil patch as soon as the muskeg freezes.

3. *Physical Sci.* A transient variation in current or voltage, or in any waveform; a transient condition.

1911 C. P. STEINMETZ *Elem. Lect. Electr. Discharges* i. 2 The transient..appears as intermediate between two permanent conditions. **1911** —— in *Jrnl. Franklin Inst.* CLXXII. 41 Transients are not a specifically electrical phenomenon, but occur in any system of forces, where energy storage occurs. **1936** *Physical Rev.* XL. 522/1 Thus *I'* is of importance only in determining the initial transients but not the steady rate of absorption. **1947** R. LEE *Electronic Transformers & Circuits* iv. 102 Transients occur when the load is applied..or removed..causing respectively a momentary drop or rise in plate voltage. **1970** V. M. ALBERS *World of Sound* ix. 143 The transients from percussion instruments and a piano are quite severe. **1972** *Nature* 21 Apr. 384/1 Total surface fields of over 100 gammas have been observed when large solar field transients pass the Moon. **1979** *Guardian* 25 Oct. 20/1 Accidental abrupt changes of conditions in reactors—these are called transients.

attrib. **1962** A. NISBETT *Technique Sound Studio* 248 In such [microphone] designs..there are minimal inertial effects and therefore a very good transient response. **1975** G. J. KING *Audio Handbk.* v. 117 A useful signal for transient appraisal is the square wave provided its rise time is significantly smaller than that of the amplifier.

transignification (trɑːnsignifikēⁱ·ʃən). *Theol.* Also **trans-signification.** [f. TRANS- 3 + SIGNIFICATION.] The change in the significance of bread and wine at the Eucharist through transubstantiation, expressed in terms of sacramental symbolism. Cf. *TRANSFINALIZATION.

1965, etc. [see *TRANSFINALIZATION]. **1968** J. M. POWERS *Eucharistic Theology* iv. 170 It is sometimes proposed that the idea of transsignification is presented as an alternative to the traditional theological idea of transsubstantiation. **1983** M. F. WILES *Faith & Mystery of God* iii. 38 The approach in terms of trans-signification or establishment of new meaning can make the same point in a more constructive way.

transillu·minator. [f. TRANSILLUMINATE *v.* + -OR.] **a.** An instrument for examining the conjunctiva and the sclerotic of the eyeball by shining light through them. **b.** An instrument for making visible spots on chromatography plates and electrophoresis gels by shining ultraviolet light through them.

1906 *Ophthalmic Record* XV. 209 (*heading*) Transillumination of the eye in the differential diagnosis of intraocular tumors, with the description of an ocular transilluminator. **1925** B. LANG *Routine Examination of Eye* III. 150 The most important use of the transilluminator is to examine the interior of the globe, particularly in cases of detachment of the retina. **1954** S. DUKE-ELDER *Parsons' Dis. Eye* (ed. 12) vi. 87 For this purpose, special transilluminators may be employed. **1973** *Nature* 16 Feb. 473/2 Both the short-wave and long-wave transilluminator ultraviolet lamps were used for detection. **1978** *Ibid.* 17 Aug. 715/2 (*caption*) Gels were stained with ethidium bromide solution and visualised on an ultraviolet transilluminator.

trans,indivi·dual, *a.* [f. TRANS- 4 + INDIVIDUAL *a.*] Not confined to any particular thing or person, more than individual. Cf. *TRANSPERSONAL *a.*

1936 *Psychol. Monogr.* XLVII. I. 8 In Scholastic philosophy these realities are regarded as subsisting in the realm of ideas; they are trans-individual. **1938** *Mind* XLVII. 482 The right answer to the question 'What are numerical propositions?' is that they predicate a peculiar kind of trans-individual quality applicable only to groups. **1973** S. HEATH in *Screen* Spring/Summer 105 The transindividual system or code..of elements and rules underlying and assuring individual messages. **1977** A. SHERIDAN tr. *Lacan's Écrits* iii. 49 Its domain is that of concrete discourse, in so far as this is the field of the transindividual reality of the subject.

transistor (trɑnsi·stəɹ, -nz-), *sb.* [Blend of TRANSFER *v.* and *RESISTOR.] **1.** A semiconductor device, usu. having three terminals and two junctions, in which the load current can be made to be proportional to a small input current, so that it is functionally equivalent to a valve but is much smaller and more robust, operates at lower voltages, and consumes less power and produces less heat.

1948 *N.Y. Times* 1 July 46/3 A device called a transistor, which has several applications in radio where a vacuum tube ordinarily is employed, was demonstrated for the first time yesterday. **1948** BARDEEN & BRATTAIN in *Physical Rev.* 15 July 230/1 (*heading*) The transistor, a semi-conductor triode. **1949,** etc. [see *junction transistor* s.v. *JUNCTION *sb.* 4]. **1952** *Electronic Engin.* XXIV. 42 Although it is unlikely that the transistor will ultimately displace the electronic valve, there is no doubt that for many electronic applications the transistor..will be preferred because of its robust and compact form. **1953,** etc. [see *field-effect transistor* s.v. *FIELD *sb.* 21]. **1957** *Observer* 1 Sept. 9/7 A novelty now gaining respectability is small-scale radio, with tiny medium-wave sets using printed circuits, and transistors instead of valves. **1962** [see *point contact* s.v. *POINT *sb.*[1] B. 14]. **1970** J. EARL *Tuners & Amplifiers* iv. 78 Transistors, particularly the bigger power devices, are regarded as being current-operated... Valves, on the other hand, are often regarded as voltage-operated devices. **1973** *Sci. Amer.* Aug. 48/1 The MOS technology produces transistors of the unipolar type in contradistinction to earlier junction transistors, which are bipolar.

2. *ellipt.* = *transistor radio*, sense 3 below.

1961 *Daily Tel.* 13 July 12/2 Few seaside authorities are likely to risk driving away transistor-addicted visitors to other resorts. **1966** J. Betjeman *High & Low* 50 The endless anonymous croak of a cheap transistor Intensifies the loneliness I feel. **1977** *Rep. Comm. Future of Broadcasting* (Cmnd. 6753) iii. 23 Car radios and portable transistors have made radio one of the nation's major daytime diversions.

3. *Comb.*, as (sense 2) *transistor-addicted* adj.; **transistor radio**, a small portable radio having transistors and other solid-state devices in place of valves; **transistor set**, a radio or television set having transistors instead of valves; **transistor-transistor logic**, logic in which transistors take the place of many of the coupling resistors; abbrev. TTL s.v. *T 6 a.

1961 Transistor-addicted [see sense 2 above]. **1958** *Spectator* 1 Aug. 167/2 The new miniature transistor radios. **1965** Auden *About House* (1966) 15 Nobody I know would like to be buried with..A transistor radio. **1957** *New Yorker* 13 July 19/1 The kid got one of those compact transistor sets for his birthday, and is absolutely fascinated by it. **1961** *Ann. Reg. 1960* 451 Television became more than ever an intrinsic part of Japanese life, and transistor sets of compact size made its penetration possible everywhere. **1963** Transistor-transistor logic [see TTL s.v. *T 6 a]. **1977** *McGraw-Hill Yearbk. Sci. & Technol.* 282/2 I²L is transistor-transistor logic (TTL) compatible.

transistorize (trɑnsi·stəraiz, -nz-), *v.* [f. prec. + -ize.] *trans.* To design or make with transistors (rather than valves). Chiefly as **transi·storized** *ppl. a.*, employing transistors; also *fig.*

1953 *Sci. News Let.* 7 Feb. 86/1 Because of their ruggedness, 'transistorized' amplifiers should eliminate many an electronic headache under the restless sea. **1959** *Listener* 28 May 930/1 The compactness of transistorized equipment and their small power requirements make them suitable for use in telephone exchanges. **1963** T. D. Towers *Transistor T.V. Receivers* viii. 125/1 The line output stage has proved to be the most difficult part of the line time base to transistorise. **1963** *Daily Tel.* 5 Oct. 8/2 What Mr. Wilson has done is to lift the whole nationalisation issue..out of its traditional context and give it a streamlined, transistorized modern setting. **1972** *Ibid.* 31 July 3/1 Both are powered by a new six cylinder, 2·8 litre twin-cam engine with transistorised ignition and electronic fuel injection. **1976** A. Hope *Hi-fi Handbk.* 27 When the craze for transistorising everything got under way, in the 1960s, very few true hi-fi enthusiasts would touch a transistor amplifier with a barge pole. **1980** J. Gardner *Garden of Weapons* ii. ii. 132 The screech-boxes looked like..radio sets. They were in fact transistorised transmitters.

Hence **transi:storiza·tion**, the use of transistors in electronic apparatus.

1957 *Trans. Soc. Instrument Technol.* IX. 41/1 One feels that 'transistorization' is bound to be introduced rapidly, thus reducing cost, weight and power consumption. **1969** *Radio Times* 4 Dec. 68 (Advt.), The Ferguson Colourstar is brilliantly designed for reliability with full transistorisation and modular construction.

transit, *sb.* Add: **1. c.** *spec.* Public passenger transport; freq. *attrib.* Chiefly *N. Amer.*

1873, etc. [see *rapid-transit* s.v. *rapid *a.* 6]. **1967** *Boston Sunday Globe* 23 Apr. 8/2 Legislature to launch a 10-year, $300 million urban transit program. **1971** *Rand Daily Mail* 27 Mar. 11/1 White bus drivers employed by a transit authority in an unnamed South African city. **1979** *Tucson* (Arizona) *Citizen* 20 Sept. 1 c/3 The Canadian city has good mass transit.

5. (see also sense *1 c) *transit-line, -time* (examples in *Electronics* and *Med.*); **transit camp**, a camp for the temporary accommodation of servicemen awaiting posting, refugees, prisoners-of-war, etc.; **transit lounge**, a waiting-room for transit passengers at an airport; **transit man** *N. Amer.*, a surveyor who uses a transit-compass; **transit passenger**, a passenger making a brief stop at an airport in transit to another destination; **transit visa**, a visa permitting the holder to pass through a country but not to stay there.

1943 G. Greene *Ministry of Fear* ii. ii. 144 The place was as comfortless as a transit camp. **1946** E. Linklater *Private Angelo* xiii. 151 [He] made his escape..from a transit camp for prisoners of war near Bari. **1956** Wallis & Blair *Thunder Above* (1959) xi. 113 There were 25,000 East German refugees in West Berlin, living in transit camps built to accommodate 13,000. **1980** D. Lodge *How Far can you Go?* i. 7 Purgatory was a kind of penitential transit camp on the way to the gates of Heaven. **1894** Hardy *Life's Little Ironies* 179 For South Wessex, the year [*sc.* 1851] formed in many ways an extraordinary chronological frontier or transit-line, at which there occurred what one might call a precipice in Time. **1962** J. Fleming *When I grow Rich* iii. 43 After the arrival of the jet, the transit lounge had filled up with people. **1983** *Jetaway* (Air New Zealand) Sept.–Oct. 28/2 Transit lounge for 500 passengers who are transferring flights or have no need to go through customs. **1873** Transit man [*packer¹ 3 c]. **1971** *Islander* (Victoria, B.C.) 8 May 12/1 Harry, a young transit man, had his bed roll next to the Bella Coola trapper. **1955** E. Bowen *World of Love* xi. 223 They let the transit passengers off first. **1972** J. Potter *Going West* 17 Transit passengers were encouraged to alight for the stopover. **1948** Martin & Hynes *Clin. Endocrinol.* iv. 70 The intestinal transit-time is decreased with the production of loose stools or frank diarrhœa. **1962** Simpson & Richards *Physical Princ. Junction Transistors* vii. 117 When operation at higher frequencies is considered these complexities increase many-fold due chiefly to transit-time effects in the flow of minority carriers. **1974** *Brit. Med. Jrnl.* 19 Jan. 108/2 Constipation is best thought of not in terms of transit-time through the gut..but rather the type of faeces produced. **1975** D. G. Fink *Electronics Engineers' Handbk.* vii. 27 Transit time is a large factor in considering the upper frequency limitation of electron tubes. **1925** C. Connolly *Let.* May in *Romantic Friendship* (1975) 81, I..had got as far as sending my passport up for some transit visas. **1979** W. H. Canaway *Solid Gold Buddha* xx. 134 Miller went to the Burmese Embassy..and got his transit visa.

transitation. Delete † *Obs.*, for '(In quots. *humorous.*)' read '(In early quots. *humorous.*)', and add later example.

1915 D. H. Lawrence *Rainbow* vii. 187 Containing birth and death, potential with all the noise and transitation of life, the cathedral remained hushed.

transition. Add: **1. b.** *Physics.* A change of an atomic nucleus or an orbital electron from one quantized state to another, with the emission or absorption of radiation of a characteristic wavelength.

1913 *Phil. Mag.* XXVI. 18 We consequently observe an absorption of radiation which is not accompanied by a complete transition between two different stationary states. **1922** tr. *Bohr's Theory of Spectra* iii. iv. 118 Emission lines of the X-ray spectra due to transitions between the stationary states corresponding to these energy levels. **1930** *Science* 10 Oct. 376/2 Very little is known about nuclear properties of atoms because of the difficulties inherent in excitation of nuclear transitions in the laboratory. **1962** [see *level *sb.* 3 e]. **1977** *Whitaker's Almanack 1978* 1035/2 By varying the frequency, a detailed analysis of a particular x-ray transition was made.

4*. *Molecular Biol.* The occurrence in a nucleic acid of one purine in place of another, or of one pyramidine in place of another. Cf. *transversion¹ 3.

1959 E. Freese in *Proc. Nat. Acad. Sci.* XLV. 630 Each base analogue can induce the transitions..in both directions (from A–T into G–H and vice versa). **1981** Pai & Marcus-Roberts *Genetics* xv. 477 Substitutions of bases are further classified as transitions or transversions.

5. a. *transition area, belt, period, point, region, state* (examples), *zone.*

1831 Carlyle in *Fraser's Mag.* Mar. 144/2 *Don Karlos*, a work of what may be called his transition-period, the turning-point between his earlier and his later period. **1841** J. S. Buckingham *America* I. 461 Baltimore..appears from the very first to have been peopled by a race that never had this transition-state to pass through. **1907** E. A. Mearns *Mammals Mexican Boundary* 135 This station lies in the Transition Zone, the highest peaks extending well into the Canadian or lowest section of the Boreal Zone. **1940** *Chambers's Tech. Dict.* 860/1 *Transition region*, the portion of the axis of a young plant in which the change from root structure to shoot structure occurs. **1950** *Texas Studies in Eng.* XXIX. 254 The transition area (where both [s] and [z] are used), is relatively narrow to the west of Philadelphia. **1957** *Publ. Amer. Dial. Soc.* xxvii. 5 The net effect being to create a transition belt. **1969** J. J. Sparkes *Transistor Switching* i. 15 This results in a narrowing of the collector transition region and a widening of the base region. **1972** H. Kurath *Studies in Area Linguistics* iii. 44 The transition area between the North and the Midland reflects partly the complicated history of the settlement. **1977** *Nature* 14 Apr. 662/1 It is becoming increasingly apparent that FMO interactions are even more important in transition states than they seem to be on inspection of isolated reactant orbitals. **1977** A. Hallam *Planet Earth* 11/3 Based on its density distribution, the mantle has been divided into three parts: the upper mantle, which extends to a depth of 400km..; the transition zone, which extends from 400 to about 700km..; and the lower mantle. **1978** D. Joy *Railways in Lancashire* 81/1 This view shows the transition period with the new station completed but the old one not yet demolished. **1982** *Amer. Speech* LVII. 293 A discussion of isoglosses and transition belts.. underpins Chambers and Trudgill's theory of urban dialects.

b. Special Combs.: **transition element** *Chem.*, † (*a*) any of the nine metallic elements forming group VIII of the periodic table (see quot. 1922); cf. *transitional element* s.v. *transitional *a.* c; (*b*) any of a large class of metallic elements making up groups IIIA–VIIA, VIII, and IB of the periodic table (groups 3–11 in the new notation), which are characterized by partly filled *d* orbitals and commonly exhibit variable valency and an ability to form coloured complexes; also extended to include elements having partly filled *f* orbitals (see quots. 1962); **transition fit** *Engin.*, a fit between two mating parts such that, within the specified tolerances, there may be either interference or clearance between them; **transition flow** (see quot. 1969); **transition metal** *Chem.* = *transition element* (*b*) above; **transition probability** *Physics*, the probability of a transition between two given states of a system, *spec.* an atom; **transition temperature** *Physics*, the temperature at which a substance acquires or loses some distinctive property, esp. superconductivity.

1922 E. J. Holmyard *Inorganic Chem.* xxx. 530 (*heading*) The 'transition elements'.—Iron, cobalt, nickel; ruthenium, rhodium, palladium; osmium, iridium, platinum. **1953** de Barry Barnett & Wilson *Inorganic Chem.* i. 6 Transition Elements. This term was originally used by Mendeleef for the three triads of elements forming Group VIII of his periodic table.., but this meaning of the term has long since been abandoned. **1962** Cotton & Wilkinson *Adv. Inorganic Chem.* xxiv. 493 The transition elements may be strictly defined as those which, *as elements*, have partly filled *d* or *f* shells. Here we shall adopt a slightly broader definition and include also elements which have partly filled *d* or *f* shells in any of their commonly occurring oxidation states. *Ibid.* 494 The large number of transition elements is subdivided into three main groups: (*a*) the main transition elements or *d*-block elements, (*b*) the lanthanide elements, and (*c*) the actinide elements. **1965** Phillips & Williams *Inorganic Chem.* I. ii. 52 The valences of the transition and lanthanide elements. **1974** *Encycl. Brit. Macropædia* XVIII. 600/2 The so-called transition elements constitute a group of 56 (the majority of the 105 known elements). **1919** Transition fit [see *interference fit* s.v. *interference 5]. **1971** B. Scharf *Engin. & its Lang.* xi. 111 Transition fits are so designed that either clearance or interference may occur when the mating parts are assembled. Push fits may be tolerance fits. **1969** *Gloss. Aeronaut & Astronaut. Terms* (*B.S.I.*) iv. 11 *Transition flow*, the flow of gases under conditions intermediate between laminar viscous flow and molecular flow. **1942** *Ann. Reg. 1941* 356 Potter..investigated the resistivity..of pure samples of the transition metals. **1970** *New Scientist* 3 Sept. 457/2 The chemistry of the transition metals..is dominated by their complex compounds. **1926** E. Condon in *Physical Rev.* XXVIII. 1185 The theory of transition probability which will now be developed is an outgrowth of a picture proposed by Franck. **1942**, etc. [see *Markov]. **1978** Pasachoff & Kutner *University Astron.* xxiv. 598 Even though this transition probability is so very low, there are so many hydrogen atoms in space that enough 21-cm radiation is given off to be detected. **1930** *Sci. Abstr.* XXXIII. 697 In all these cases, at temperatures below the transition temperature, increasing the intensity of the magnetic field to a certain value..causes the superconductivity to disappear. **1966** C. R. Tottle *Sci. Engin. Materials* vi. 127 For the compound Nb_3Sn the transition temperature is as high as 18·2°K. **1982** *Sci. Amer.* May 30/1 Ferroelectric and ferromagnetic transition temperatures.

transitional, *a.* Add: **c.** Chem. *transitional element* = *transition element* (*a*) s.v. *transition 5 b.

1887 C. M. Tidy *Handbk. Mod. Chem.* (ed. 2) ii. 54 In Group VIII. three elements occur. These are termed by Mendeleef 'transitional elements', that is, elements occurring between the even and the odd series of a long period. **1921** J. R. Partington *Text-bk. Inorganic Chem.* xlviii. 972 The transitional elements.—The eighth group of the Periodic System comprises three sub-groups, with three elements in each, forming the termination of the even series 4, 6, and 8, and connecting the elements of these series with those of the odd series following. For this reason they were called by Mendeléeff the transitional elements.

transitive, *a.* Add: **1.** (Later U.S. example.)

1906 *Springfield* (Mass.) *Weekly Republican* 8 Mar. 6 At present he is in a transitive state.

6. (Earlier and later examples.) [ad. G. *transitiv* (S. Lie *Theorie d. Transformationsgruppen* (1888) I. 212).]

1888 *Amer. Jrnl. Math.* X. 297 If.. a G_r in *xy* can transform every ordinary point of the plane to every other ordinary point of the plane, the G_r is said to be transitive. **1968** [see *primitive *a.* 5 d]. **1971** L. Dornhoff *Group Representation Theory* A. xxxvi. 215 Nontrivial normal subgroups of primitive permutation groups are transitive.

7. *Math.* and *Logic.* Of a relation: such that if it holds between a first and second item, and also between the second and a third, it necessarily holds between the first and the third.

1856 A. de Morgan in *Trans. Cambr. Philos. Soc.* IX. 104 The first is what I shall call *transitiveness*, symbolized in $X—Y—Z = X—Z$; meaning that if *X* stand in the relation denoted by — to *Y*, and *Y* to *Z*, *X* therefore stands in that relation to *Z*. Very many copulæ exist in which this transitive relation is seen. **1870**, etc. [see *intransitive *a.* 3]. **1903**, etc. [see *reflexive *a.* 7]. **1936** A. J. Ayer *Lang., Truth & Logic* iii. 79 As each of these relations is symmetrical..and also transitive..it follows that the groups of visual and tactual sense-contents which are constituted by means of these relations cannot have any members in common. **1956** E. H. Hutten *Lang. Mod. Physics* iv. 143 We take as axiom the statement that the thermal equilibrium is a transitive relation, i.e. if two bodies in thermal equilibrium are in equilibrium with a third body, all three bodies have a common property, that is, the same temperature. **1976** *Nature* 29 Apr. 773/1 Whether or not the young child can make transitive inferences..is still a controversial issue. **1979** Georgacarakos & Smith *Elem. Formal Logic* ix. 330 Many comparative adjectives provide transitive relations, such as *it is taller than*.

transitively, *adv.* Add: **c.** *Math.* and *Logic.* (See senses 6 and *7 of Transitive *a.*)

1889 [see *intransitive *a.* 4]. **1971** C. W. Curtis in Powell & Higman *Finite Simple Groups* iii. 139 Any two bases of a root system Δ are conjugate by an element of the Weyl group (i.e., $W(\Delta)$ acts transitively on the set of bases).

transitiveness. (Further examples, corresp. to *transitive *a.* 7.)

1850 A. DE MORGAN in *Trans. Cambr. Philos. Soc.* (1856) IX. I. 104 The first [copular condition] is what I shall call *transitiveness*. **1903** B. RUSSELL *Princ. Math.* xxvi. 218 Relations may be divided into four classes, according as they do or do not possess either of two attributes, transitiveness and symmetry. **1955** A. N. PRIOR *Formal Logic* III. i. 220 It is as if one presented a study of transitiveness under the guise of a 'logic' of the relation of ancestorhood.

transitivism (trɑ·nsitiviz'm). *Psychiatry.* [f. TRANSITIVE *a.* (*sb.*) + -ISM.] A mental state or condition in which a patient attributes to others his own experiences and sensations.

1924 A. A. BRILL tr. *Bleuler's Textbk. Psychiatry* ii. 38 The splitting off of parts of a personality in *transitivism* proceeds in a different manner; here the patient's own experiences become detached from him, and are ascribed to another person... Transitivism is an almost common occurrence in schizophrenia. **1960** R. F. C. HULL tr. *Jung's Coll. Wks.* III. 134 The representation of one's own complexes by strange actors in dreams is well known.. in psychopathology we know it in the form of 'transitivism'. **1971** *Internat. Jrnl. Psycho-Anal.* LII. 237 The schizophrenic delusion of transitivism, which relates to the loss of ego boundaries, represents a regression of ego development.

transitivity. Add: Also in senses 2 and *7 of TRANSITIVE *a.* (Examples.)

1897 *Monist* Jan. 211 Not only is the relative of correspondence transitive, but it also possesses what may be called antithetic transitivity. **1928** *Mod. Lang. Rev.* Apr. 144 The following chapters [of Jespersen's *Modern English Grammar*] are concerned with..transitivity and predicatives. **1942** J. C. COOLEY *Primer Formal Logic* viii. 339 The generalized postulate for the transitivity of the relation, *older than*, could not be expressed without variables. **1969** J. C. WELLS *E.U.P. Concise Esperanto & Eng. Dict.* 17 Many English verbs are of varying transitivity, since they can be used either transitively or intransitively. **1980** A. J. JONES *Game Theory* iv. 194 To prove the theorem it is only necessary to verify the three defining properties of an equivalence relation... Reflexivity... Symmetry... Transitivity.

transitivize (trɑ·nsitivaiz, -nz-), *v. Gram.* [f. TRANSITIVE *a.* + -IZE.] *trans.* To make (a verb) transitive. So **tra:nsitivi·zing** *ppl. a.*; **tra:nsitivi·zer**, an affix that makes a verb transitive.

1964 *Language* XL. 76 With the transitivizing stem formative—cʔi the resulting stem..means 'he sets it down'. **1972** J. L. DILLARD *Black English* iii. 98 Pidgin characteristics, like the *-um* (*-em*) transitivizer. **1978** *Language* LIV. 125 An appropriate transitivizing suffix. **1979** *Trans. Philol. Soc.* 128 The causative **hanjāmaya-* would transitivize a 'joining' that was expressed by *han-gam-*, and thereby allow the past participle *hangmata-* to be used for English 'joined' in both its intransitive and passive sense.

transitron (trɑ·nsitrɒn). *Electronics.* [f. *TRANS(CONDUCTANCE + *-i-* + *-TRON.] A pentode in which the suppressor grid is used as the control grid so that the valve exhibits negative transconductance.

1939 C. BRUNETTI in *Proc. IRE* XXVII. 88/2 For the sake of brevity it has been found desirable to provide a name for the retarding-field negative-transconductance device... The name 'Transitron' is suggested. **1945** *Electronic Engin.* XVII. 383 Those devices such as.. transitrons, whose negative resistance characteristic can be measured by d.c. tests. **1957** *Practical Wireless* XXXIII. 523/1 The timebase employed in the oscilloscope is of the transitron type.

Transjordanian (trɑːnsdʒɔːdēⁱ·niăn, -nz-), *sb.* and *a.* Also (in non-*spec.* senses) **trans-Jordanian.** [f. *Trans-Jordan* (see TRANS- 7), *Transjordan(ia)* (see below) + -IAN, -AN: see *JORDANIAN *a.* and *sb.*] **A.** *sb.* A person from beyond the river Jordan (see *JORDAN²); also *transf.*; *spec.* (now *Hist.*) a native or inhabitant of Transjordan (Transjordania), a territory east of the Jordan, now part of the Hashemite kingdom of the Jordan. **B.** *adj.* Of or pertaining to the land beyond the Jordan; *spec.* (now *Hist.*) of or pertaining to Transjordan. Cf. *trans-Jordan, -ic* s.v. TRANS- 7.

The emirate of *Transjordan(ia)* was established under British mandate in 1921. The name was retained for the short-lived kingdom (1946–9), now Eastern Jordan.

1920 G. SAINTSBURY *Notes on Cellar-bk.* iv. 52 Gentiles, as it were, or at least trans-Jordanians to the pure Israel of Medoc. **1922** G. BELL *Let.* 18 Dec. (1927) II. xxii. 660 The conquest of Hayil..will bring Ibn Saud into the theatre of trans-Jordanian politics. **1965** M. SPARK *Mandelbaum Gate* iv. 97 He disliked the Lebanese and wished all the Arabs were Palestinian or Transjordanian. **1979** R. THOMAS *Eighth Dwarf* xxvi. 251 The Jews are going to have to fight..the Syrians and the Egyptians and..the Transjordanians.

Transkei, *sb.* (*a.*) Add to def.: From 1910 the Cape Colony formed part of the Union of South Africa, which became the Republic of South Africa in 1961; in 1976 the Transkei was the first Black homeland to be given a measure of independence. **Transkeian** *a.* (further examples); (*b*) *sb.* a native or inhabitant of the Transkei.

1974 *Standard Encycl. S. Afr.* X. 564/1 All Transkeian taxpayers over the age of 18 and all other Transkeian citizens over 21..to whom certain disqualifications do not apply are entitled to register as voters. **1976** *Times* 17 Feb. 7/6 The Transkeians want to make independence a success. **1976** *Times* 25 Oct. 13 Tonight the South African flag will be lowered in Umtata and the Transkeian flag will be raised. **1979** J. DRUMMOND *Patriots* ii. 15 The Transkeian labour problem. *Ibid.* iii. 23 Nearly all those who lost their jobs were Transkeians.

translate, *v.* Add: **I. 1. e.** *intr.* To undergo translational motion.

1964 *Amer. Jrnl. Physics* XXXII 261/1 If frame *β*, thus translates rigidly with velocity *α* as measured in *α* then frame *v* translates rigidly with velocity — *v* as measured in *β*. **1979** *Sci. Amer.* Jan. 76/2 One is therefore forced to conclude that these deep structures do indeed constitute the lower portions of the continental plates and that they have been translating coherently with the crust for hundreds or even thousands of millions of years.

II. 2. d. *Biol.* To use (genetic information in messenger RNA) to determine the amino-acid sequence of a protein during its synthesis; also with the RNA as obj.

1961 *Cold Spring Harbor Symp. Quantitative Biol.* XXVI. 101/2 This finding implied that the information encoded in DNA must somehow be transmitted to the ribosomes where it is translated into the amino acid sequence of a polypeptide chain. **1971** *Nature* 24 Sept. 234/2 Messenger RNAs transcribed in the nuclei of eukaryotic cells have to be transported to the cytoplasm to be translated. **1972** *Sci. Amer.* Jan. 25/2 A length of RNA representing a gene is then translated into a particular protein, a molecule constructed with a 20-letter alphabet, the 20 amino acids. **1977** D. E. METZLER *Biochemistry* xv. 936/2 The ribosome faithfully translates the genetic message, adding amino acids to the peptide chain until a stop codon is reached.

IV. 7. *intr.* Const. *into*. To result in, to be converted into, to manifest itself as.

1975 *Lamp* (Exxon Corporation) Winter 11/2 Any delays in bringing fields into production could quickly translate into lower government revenues and an adverse impact on the balance of payments. **1976** *Sci. Amer.* June 69/1 For maneuvers executed early in a mission this uncertainty translates into an error at the target planet on the order of one kilometer. **1977** *Time* 8 Aug. 42/2 The price of raw coffee could gradually decline to about $1 per lb. on the New York market, which would translate into a retail price somewhere in the $2 range.

translatese (trɑns,lēⁱtī·z, -nz-). [f. TRANSLA-T(ION + -ESE.] = *TRANSLATIONESE. Cf. *TRANSLATORESE.

1967 *Listener* 8 June 762/1 He..has couched it in the luke-warm translatese of one of his own more unurgent renderings. **1977** *Times Lit. Suppl.* 25 Feb. 202/1 Paralysing woodenness ('I am concerned to determine'), the dull thud of translatese ('Here is the place to mention Pirandello finally'). **1979** *Studies in Eng. Lit.: Eng. Number* (Tokyo) 228 To the very last his Japanese did not get rid of a 'translatese' completely.

translation. Add: **I. 2. c.** *Biol.* The process by which genetic information represented by the sequence of nucleotides in messenger RNA gives rise to a definite sequence of amino-acids in the protein or polypeptide that is synthesized.

1963 *Cold Spring Harbor Symp. Quantitative Biol.* XXVIII. 352/1 Polarity mutations affect the RNA to protein translation. **1968** H. HARRIS *Nucleus & Cytoplasm* iv. 83 In higher cells translation and transcription are not closely coupled. **1970, 1973** [see *TRANSCRIPTION 6]. **1977** P. B. & J. S. MEDAWAR *Life Science* xii. 95 This translation of genetic into structural information is irreversible, so there is no known..method by which germinal DNA could be imprinted with information acquired in an organism's own lifetime.

IV. 7. *translation-equivalent, process, theory*; **translation loan(-word)** = *loan-translation* s.v. *LOAN *sb.*¹ 5.

1963 J. LYONS *Structural Semantics* iv. 70 It may be impossible to find even a 'roughly equivalent' term in another language.., even though we can find satisfactory translation-equivalents for most..of its hyponyms. **1977** *Language* LIII. 295 Thai *khon* and its (near) translation-equivalents in many languages denote 'people'. **1954** KOESTLER *Invisible Writing* xi. 132 At which stage of the translation-process all these blessings had slipped in, we could not tell. **1967** M. ARGYLE *Psychol. Interpersonal Behaviour* v. 90 Social interaction..depends on the existence of a learnt store of central translation processes. **1900** E. BJÖRKMAN *Scand. Loan-Words in M.E.* I. 12 What I should like to call 'translation loan-words'... Thus..*wæpen̄zetæc* 'vote of consent expressed by touching weapons; district governed by such authority'..distinctively English in form, although..of Scandinavian introduction..*wæpen-* having been put instead of the Scand. *vápn*. **1922** O. JESPERSEN *Language* xi. 215 (*heading*) Translation-loans. *Ibid.*, Besides direct borrowings we have also indirect borrowings or 'translation loan-words,' words modelled more or less clearly on foreign ones, though consisting of native speech-material. **1958** Translation-loan [see *CALQUE]. **1974** R. QUIRK *Linguist & Eng. Lang.* vi. 101 We should add here the use of *bower* which is clearly a translation-loan. **1936** J. R. KANTOR *Objective Psychol. of Gram.* v. 59 No doubt in the translation theory it is these social and cultural factors that have been unnecessarily converted into psychic guides of bodily action. **1978** C. HOOKWAY in Hookway & Pettit *Action & Interpretation* 27 Given the underdetermination of translation theory by possible observations, we are invited to conclude that in the field of translation, there is no objective fact of the matter. **1980** *Times Lit. Suppl.* 12 Sept. 992/3 An academic researcher in translation-theory,..one of the very few people in the world..working in this field—had undertaken a questionnaire on the subject and now revealed some of its findings.

translational, *a.* Add: Hence **transla·tionally** *adv.*, (*a*) as regards language translation; (*b*) as regards, or by means of, translational motion.

1916 M. A. S. RIACH *Air-Screws* i. 8 The depth of the cylinder will then represent the distance advanced through translationally by the point, and therefore by the whole air-screw, at each revolution. **1923** C. D. BROAD *Sci. Thought* xi. 433 A rotating physical object which is translationally at rest. **1959** *Archivum Linguisticum* XI. 152 It is..no use trying..to measure range of content as the 'number of meanings'..of translationally equivalent words. **1978** J. DUNN in Hookway & Pettit *Action & Interpretation* 172 A translationally adequate science of human meanings must in principle be pragmatically accessible. **1981** C. H. LLEWELLYN-SMITH in J. H. Mulvey *Nature of Matter* iii. 55 If momentum is conserved then the underlying laws must necessarily be translationally invariant.

translationese (trɑns,lēⁱ:ʃənī·z, -nz-). [f. TRANSLATION + -ESE.] The style of language supposed to be characteristic of (bad) translations; unidiomatic language in a translation; = *TRANSLATESE, *TRANSLATORESE.

1957 R. W. ZANDVOORT *Handbk. Eng. Gram.* IX. ii. 313 The suffix [*-ese*] may be added in a derogatory sense..to denote a mannered diction or style: ..*journalese, translationese*. **1961** *Times Lit. Suppl.* 17 Feb. p. iv/5 Translationese in a version from Hebrew is not always easy to detect. **1964** *Listener* 3 Dec. 911/2 The kind of unthinking 'translationese' which has so often..imparted to translated Russian literature a distinctive, somehow 'doughy' style. **1972** C. DAY-LEWIS in G. W. Knight *Jackson Knight* 11 When I had lapsed into translationese, he never failed to point it out. **1984** *Times* 21 Mar. 17/5 A useless mixture of mushy colloquialisms..and translationese.

translator. Add: **1. c.** *Computers.* A program that translates from one (esp. programming) language into another.

1958 A. J. PERLIS et al. (*title*) Internal translator (IT) a compiler for the 650. **1959** [see *LANGUAGE *sb.* 1 d]. **1972** *Computer Jrnl.* XV. 229/1 General parsing algorithms..used in actual translators are characterised by the use of classes of grammars which are subsets of the class of context free grammars. **1981** POHL & SHAW *Nature of Computation* vi. 193 Language processors, such as translators and interpreters, are called systems programs or systems software because they are normally part of the total computer system presented to a user.

4. b. A relay set or station which receives television signals and retransmits them without demodulating them.

1958 *New Scientist* 25 Sept. 898/2 Instead of receiving signals, demodulating them to visual or aural form and then re-transmitting, it just passes on the original signals. The BBC calls it a translator. **1960** *Practical Wireless* XXXVI. 330/2 Tentative plans are being considered for a considerable number of additional TV 'translator' stations of very low power. **1966** *Daily Tel.* 17 Oct. 9/5 TIE may have solved the problem with a television translator powered by sunlight... The translator set on a high point would receive and re-transmit signals to isolated communities.

translatorese (trɑns,lēⁱ:tŏrī·z, -nz-). [f. TRANSLATOR + -ESE.] = *TRANSLATIONESE. Cf. *TRANSLATESE.

1915 *Morning Post* 15 Apr. 2/4 The worst 'journalese' is more English than schoolmasters' 'translatorese'. **1967** *Times Lit. Suppl.* 11 May 399/1 There is even a recognizable variant of pidgin English known as 'translatorese'. **1982** I. HAMILTON *Robert Lowell* (1983) xvi. 292 Critics might more damagingly have quoted the limp translatorese that crops up throughout *Imitations*.

translocate, *v.* Delete *rare* and add: **a.** Esp. in reference to the transfer of wild animals. (Later examples.)

1971 *Nature* 6 Aug. 374/2 As long ago as 1928 the possibility of translocating rhino from Zululand to other parts of their former range was suggested by the naturalist Herbert Lang. **1980** *Cape Times* 19 Aug. 5/3 The present objective is to translocate as many black rhino as possible to as many of their original areas.

b. (Examples.)

1931 E. C. MILLER *Plant Physiol.* xii. 696 It appears that the mineral nutrients absorbed by the roots on one side of a plant are, in a large measure, translocated to and used by the trunk, limbs, and leaves directly above them. **1959** *New Scientist* 12 Nov. 931/3 Substances may be translocated through the fungal threads and be accumulated into the fungal tissue which surrounds the root. **1976** *Sci. Amer.* Sept. 124/3 (Advt.), When the proper rate is applied to the weeds' well-grown foliage, the compound is translocated throughout the plant.

2. *Genetics.* To move (a portion of a chromosome) *to* a new position, esp. on a non-homologous chromosome.

1936 *Discovery* Sept. 269/1 In one of the new races the left ends were removed from both the second chromosomes and translocated to a third chromosome. **1949** DARLINGTON & MATHER *Elem. Genetics* v. 102 A piece may be taken out of a chromosome and inserted or translocated wherever else the same or another chromosome may be broken. **1975** *Nature* 3 Jan. 13/3 Genes translocated to positions close to heterochromatin seem in many species to become inactivated.

3. *intr.* To move, change location.

1977 *Lancet* 2 July 15/2 Others..had demonstrable abnormalities of receptor function, such as failure of the receptor hormone complex to translocate to the nucleus.

Hence **transloca·ted** *ppl. a.*; **transloca·table** *a.*, able to be translocated.

1930 *Jrnl. Genetics* XXII. 313 Offspring..will then have an excess (triple amount) of genes of the sort present in the proximal portion of the translocated piece. **1975** *Nature* 4 Dec. 384/1 Discrete translocatable elements (transposons) may constitute relatively common genetic units in bacteria. **1976** *Ann. Rev. Microbiol.* XXX. 517 One must also be aware of the prevalence of insertion sequences..and the newly discovered translocatable sequences..discovered in enteric microorganisms. **1980** R. P. WAGNER et al. *Introd. Mod. Genetics* x. 289/2 The two normal chromosomes move to one pole while the two translocated chromosomes go to the other.

translocation. Add: **1. a.** Esp. in reference to the removal of wild animals. (Later examples.)

1962 *Oryx* VI. 215 By translocation is meant the transfer of wild animals from one area to another. **1969** J. FISHER et al. *Red Bk.* 123/2 Several countries have already used the drug and translocation method to introduce or re-introduce rhinos.

b. (Examples.)

1887 H. M. WARD tr. *J. von Sachs' Lect. Physiol. Plants* xxi. 347 For starch also is found at places in the tissue where it has neither been originally produced nor is employed, and thus in a condition of translocation towards the places where it is made use of. **1951** *Chambers's Jrnl.* Aug. 457/1 In the case of these perennial weeds with persistent root-stocks the chlorate acts by the method of translocation, working downward, cell by cell, from the sprayed tops to the lowest root-tip. **1976** NOGGLE & FRITZ *Introd. Plant Physiol.* xii. 357 Translocation of sugars in the phloem is through living sieve elements.

2. *Genetics.* A transposition (sense *7), esp. to a position on a non-homologous chromosome; also, a portion of chromosome that is translocated.

1923 *Anat. Rec.* XXIV. 426 *(heading)* The translocation of a section of chromosome-II upon chromosome-III in Drosophila. **1924** [see *TRANSPOSITION 7]. **1937** C. D. DARLINGTON *Rec. Adv. Cytol.* (ed. 2) vii. 265 They may also arise with translocation of a segment from one chromosome to another or from one arm of a chromosome to another. **1956** [see *ANEUPLOIDY]. **1962** *Lancet* 8 Dec. 1229/2 In all cases diagnosed confidently as having Down's syndrome we have found an excess of material of chromosome no. 21, either as an additional chromosome in the regular trisomic type or as a translocation. **1977** *Nature* 3 Nov. 10/3 It is thought that interaction between the two inverted sequences plays an important part in this translocation.

Hence **transloca·tional** *a.*

1930 *Jrnl. Genetics* XXII. 312 *(caption)* Translocational parent. **1965** *Jrnl. Cellular & Compar. Physiol.* LXV. 280/2 There was virtually no translocational movement in the partially rounded individuals.

translunar, *a.* (In Dict. s.v. TRANSLUNARY *a.*) Add: **1.** (Examples.)

1927 W. B. YEATS in *Monthly Criterion* June 292 Being dead, we rise, Dream and so create Translunar Paradise. **1962** F. I. ORDWAY et al. *Basic Astronautics* v. 201 Mechta was instrumented to gather data on cosmic and solar radiations in cis- and translunar space.

2. *Astronautics.* Of or pertaining to spaceflight or a trajectory from the earth or another planet towards the moon.

1965 *New Scientist* 1 July 12/2 Corrections will be made several times during the translunar phase..based on measurements made by Earth stations..and..by astronauts. **1969** *Daily Mail* 14 Jan. 1/2 Everybody had built up that burn, and of course it was critical. But so was translunar injection, so was re-entry. **1972** *Daily Tel.* 8 Dec. 1 The correction was the result of a manoeuvre which put Apollo on a trans-lunar trajectory 15 minutes earlier than planned.

trans,ma·rginal, *a.* [f. TRANS- 4 + MARGINAL *a.*] Beyond the margin of normal consciousness; subliminal.

1902 W. JAMES *Var. Relig. Exper.* xx. 511 The exploration of the transmarginal field has hardly yet been seriously undertaken. **1915** J. H. TUCKWELL *Relig. & Reality* xi. 220 In the larger transmarginal or subliminal region of consciousness..nothing is ever really forgotten. **1968** W. E. BROEN *Schizophrenia* viii. 201 The level of stimulation necessary to produce the transmarginal inhibition is said to be lower in individuals with weaker.. nervous systems. **1973** T. PYNCHON *Gravity's Rainbow* I. 48 Send them over into one of the transmarginal phases, past borders of their waking selves.

trans,me·mbrane, *a.* [TRANS- 3.] Existing or occurring across a cell membrane.

1961 *Amer. Jrnl. Physiol.* CC. 1252/1 Transmembrane resistance measurements were made by putting a rectangular voltage pulse in series with the microelectrodes. **1974** *Ann. N.Y. Acad. Sci.* CCXXVII. 98 *(heading)* The separation of electrons and protons during electron transfer: the distinction between membrane potentials and transmembrane gradients.

transmental, *a.* (Earlier example.)

1905–6 W. JAMES in R. B. Perry *Thought & Char. W. James* (1935) II. lxxvii. 446 That an idea represents an 'object' may mean that it represents something..Transmental altogether, as when it is said to be altogether 'unknowable'.

transmethylation (trɑːns,meþilēⁱ·ʃən, -nz-). *Chem.* [f. *TRANS- 10 + METHYL + -ATION.] The transfer of a methyl group from a molecule of one compound to one of another.

1940 *Jrnl. Biol. Chem.* CXXXIV. 787 It was realized that direct proof of the transfer of the methyl group (transmethylation) was highly desirable. **1976** SMYTHIES & CORBETT *Psychiatry* v. 45 Schizophrenia might result from some disorder of transmethylation.

transmission. Add: **b.** *spec.* in *Radio* and *Television* (see *TRANSMIT *v.* 3 b); also, a series of electric signals or electromagnetic waves transmitted, a broadcast.

1907 *Rep. Brit. Assoc. Adv. Sci.* 731 To determine how many oscillations..take place in a certain wireless transmission. **1921** *Wireless World* IX. 52/2 In Surrey and Kent the transmissions were easily read. **1923** *Radio Times* 5 Oct. 15/2 Transmission from London of Dance Music by Savoy Orpheans. **1929** [see *television transmission* s.v. *TELEVISION 3 a]. **1959** *Viewpoint* July 10 A few days before transmission the final camera script will be typed. **1962** A. NISBETT *Technique Sound Studio* v. 99 We have.. wide-range hi-fi, demanding not only high-quality transmissions but also a wide dynamic range. **1966** *Listener* 11 Aug. 204/2 *The Black and White Minstrel Show*.. has just completed eighty-five transmissions. **1977** *Rep. Comm. Future of Broadcasting* (Cmnd. 6753) ii. 8 The Government..has to regulate the strength of the transmissions to prevent interference with other stations.

e. transmission electron microscope, an electron microscope in which the electrons are detected after they pass through the specimen; *spec.* one in which all parts of the image are formed at the same time; so **transmission electron microscopy; transmission line,** a conductor or set of conductors designed to carry electricity (esp. on a large scale) or electromagnetic waves with minimum loss and distortion; also *transf.*; **transmission loss,** dissipation of electrical or acoustic power during its passage from one point to another; **transmission print** (see quot. 1960).

1969 *Jrnl. Ultrastructure Res.* XXVII. 403 The resolution of the scanning instrument is an order of magnitude less than that of present transmission electron microscopes. **1971** *Sci. Amer.* Apr. 26 The transmission electron microscope is analogous to a conventional light microscope. **1972** [see *scanning electron microscope* s.v. *SCANNING *vbl. sb.* 5]. **1968** *Jrnl. Electron Microscopy* XVII. 164/1 Experimental procedures to determine the direction and the sign of the Burgers vector..of a dislocation by means of transmission electron microscopy are described. **1974** *Encycl. Brit. Macropædia* XII. 137/2 Recently, scanning instruments have been used for transmission electron microscopy, with the advantage over the conventional transmission instrument that very low magnification..may be used. **1906** Transmission line [in Dict.]. **1922** GLAZEBROOK *Dict. Appl. Physics* II. 862/1 The problem of finding the transmission loss due to a piece of apparatus inserted in..a telephone line is the problem of finding out how the current entering the receiving side is altered by the inserted or bridged apparatus. **1934** *Discovery* Dec. 348/1 The transmission loss in steel framing is only one decibel per 1,000 feet, a loss which is acoustically negligible. **1946** *Jrnl. Inst. Electr. Engineers* XCIII. IIIA. 33/1 It has become the common..practice to restrict the term 'wave guide' to devices employing a single hollow conductor, and to reserve the term 'transmission line' to devices employing two conductors. **1960** O. SKILBECK *ABC of Film & TV* 137 *Transmission print*, positive copy of a film intended for T.V. showings. **1970** *New Scientist* 15 Oct. (Suppl.) 13/1 The basic elements in microwave circuits are always some form of transmission lines. **1971** *Sci. Amer.* Sept. 235/1 (Advt.), This..guide is ..suited for use as an optical transmission line, carrying laser beams in any direction it is bent. **1975** D. G. FINK *Electronics Engineers' Handbk.* XVIII. 67 The transmission loss [of a radio circuit] is usually expressed in decibels. **1976** *Broadcast* 29 Nov. 18/2 Once 'shot' the film has to be 'processed'... A transmission print is achieved several generations later.

Hence **transmi·ssional** *a.*; **transmissionist** (earlier example).

1899 J. A. THOMSON *Sci. Life* xvi. 226 The Lamarckians and Buffonians..believe in the transmission of acquired characters or modifications. They are sometimes, though not elegantly, called 'transmissionists'. **1930** *Observer* 4 May 26 Sometimes the music sounded ghostly. There were a few transmissional hiccoughs too.

transmissivity (trɑns,misi·vĭti, -nz-). *Physics.* [f. TRANSMISSIVE *a.* + -ITY.] The degree to which a medium allows electromagnetic radiation to pass through it.

1913 *Electr. World* LXII. 426/2 The connection between cloudiness and transmissivity. **1928** *Proc. R. Soc.* A. CXXII. 314 The transmissivity of the telescope could then be calculated. **1946** *Nature* 21 Sept. 422/2 The optical efficiency, that is, the sum of the reflectivity and transmissivity, expressed as a percentage of the incident light intensity, is practically 100 for the interference films, owing to the negligible absorption. **1971** *Sci. Amer.* Sept. 89/1 The flux of solar radiation received at the ground is highly variable..because of the variable transmissivity of the atmosphere and the changing degree of cloudiness.

transmissometer (trɑns,misǫ·mĭtəɹ, -nz-). [f. L. *transmiss-*, ppl. stem of *transmittere* to TRANSMIT *v.* + -OMETER.] An instrument for measuring the degree to which light is transmitted through a medium without absorption.

1955 *Sci. News Let.* 24 Sept. 197/1 Other equipment the Weather Bureau plans to purchase includes:... Ceilometers and transmissometers, instruments that tell cloud ceiling height and visibility. **1966** *McGraw-Hill Encycl. Sci. & Technol.* X. 172/1 Reflectometer. This instrument, also called a transmissometer, combines integrating spheres and barrier-layer cells... The transmittance can be measured by placing a sample of the material in the opening between the two spheres. **1975** *Nature* 3 Apr. 414/2 A volumetric concentration [in the sea] on the order of 0·01–1%, obtained from the acoustic data, enabled us to carry out a first-cut check of acoustic and transmissometer readings.

transmit, *v.* Add: **3. b.** To send out electric signals or electromagnetic waves corresponding to (an image, a programme, etc.).

1877 [see *FACSIMILE 2 a]. **1923** *Radio Times* 28 Sept. 2/1 The first occasion..on which the voice of a public man had been transmitted simultaneously through six wireless stations hundreds of miles apart. **1946** *B.B.C. Year Bk.* 93 A fourth European programme network..allowed four different languages to be transmitted simultaneously. **1969** [see *FACSIMILE 2 a]. **1979** *Financial Times* 18 Sept. (Telecommunications Suppl.) p. vii/2 A related system, generically called teletext, uses the same basic format, but the information is transmitted on spare capacity of the normal television broadcast channels.

II. 4. *Radio.* The infin. used, freq. *attrib.*, in the sense 'transmission'; so *on transmit*, of a transceiver: in the state of being able to transmit radio signals, with the transmitter switched on; **transmit button, switch,** the button or switch used to activate the transmitter; also *ellipt.*

1968 J. SANGSTER *Touchfeather* xiv. 146 The radio suddenly crackled into life... Marvin flipped the transmit switch. **1973** 'A. HALL' *Tango Briefing* xii. 155, I hit the transmit. *Tango.* She answered straight away. **1976** L. HENDERSON *Major Enquiry* xiv. 89 Keep your personal radio on transmit, don't try to talk but keep the channel open. **1976** K. THACKERAY *Crownbird* vi. 122 He pressed the transmit button. 'Listen carefully.' **1980** *Basildon Recorder* 12 Sept. 1/4 Leaving his personal radio on 'transmit', so officers below could hear what was going on.

transmittance. Restrict *rare* to sense in Dict. and add: **2.** *Physics.* The ratio of the transmitted luminous flux to the incident luminous flux.

1919 *Technologic Papers U.S. Bureau of Standards* No. 119. 10 The transmittance T is defined as the fraction of radiant power transmitted by the first surface which is incident on the second surface. **1960** [see *REFLECTANCE]. **1980** *Nature* 29 May 313/1 We had to use a shorter pathlength (970 m at Riverside and 750 m at Claremont) because of the poor optical transmittance of the polluted atmosphere at our observation sites.

Hence **transmi·ttancy,** the ratio of the transmittance of a solution to that of a similar body of solvent.

1925 *Jrnl. Optical Soc. Amer.* X. 177 *(table)* T_{sol}/T_{sov} = transmittancy. **1936** *Plant Physiol.* XI. 229 The transmittancies were obtained with a Bausch and Lomb visual spectrophotometer. **1959** H. BARNES *Apparatus & Methods Oceanogr.* i. 26 A calibration can then be set up relating transmittancy and concentration from which the concentrations of unknowns may be read when their transmittancies have been determined.

transmitter. Add: **b.** (Earlier and further examples.) Now *esp.* an apparatus for transmitting radio or television signals.

1844 *Brit. Patent* 10,257 2, I have an instrument which I denominate a transmitter... If the operator turns a handle fixed to the wheel any number of discharges..may be passed from London to Liverpool. **1859** [see *PRINTER 2 a]. **1898** *Ludgate* Nov. 79 The Marconi Transmitter. **1912** *Chambers's Jrnl.* Jan. 60/2, I had got our receiver into 'tune' with the transmitter on board a steamer. **1913** E. C. BENTLEY *Trent's Last Case* ii. 18 Sir James looked at the telephone..and took up the receiver... Presently, as he listened, he..spoke quickly to Mr. Silver over the top of the transmitter. **1934** J. H. REYNER *Television* xvii. 191 It is conceivable that the introduction of some new scanning system may reduce the width of the band needed by a television transmitter providing plenty of detail. **1955** *Radio Times* 22 Apr. 3/2 Unless the listener lives very close to the nearest F.M. transmitter he will need to install a V.H.F. aerial. **1974** G. MARKSTEIN *Cooler* lv. 196 They've all been trained to rig up a wireless transmitter secretly, and send messages under the nose of the Gestapo. **1978** *Sci. Amer.* Mar. 58/2 A typical instrument consists of a handset, containing a transmitter and a receiver, that is connected to the base with an extendable cord.

d. *Physiol.* = *NEUROTRANSMITTER.

1930 *Jrnl. Physiol.* LXX. 142 The only hint as to the chemical nature of the transmitter is provided by the physiological similarity to the action of adrenaline. **1937** J. C. ECCLES in *Physiol. Rev.* XVII. 539 The actual transmission across the intercellular gap of the junctional region must depend upon one or more special factors—which will henceforth be called the synaptic or neuromuscular transmitter. **1954** MARTIN & HYNES *Clinical Endocrinol.* (ed. 2) vii. 168 It has now been shown..that *nor*adrenaline is the sympathetic transmitter-substance. **1970** *Nature* 5 Sept. 1006/2 Enzymes which synthesize transmitter. **1974** *Ibid.* 6 Sept. 14/3 L-Glutamate serves as the neuromuscular transmitter substance of arthropods, taking the place of acetylcholine in vertebrates in this respect.

2. Special Comb.: **transmitter-receiver** = *TRANSCEIVER.

1950 *Encycl. Radio & Television* 638/2 *Transmitter-receiver*, assembly comprising a sender and a receiver with provision for changing from send to receive, usually by means of a switching system. **1964** *Discovery* Oct. 23 (Advt.), The BBC 81 mobile VHF transmitter-receiver is so compact that the whole unit can be fitted under the dashboard of almost any vehicle. **1978** R. V. Jones *Most Secret War* xxxvi. 313 He had been parachuted back into France with six radio transmitter-receiver sets for distribution to his sub-agents.

transmitting, *vbl. sb.* and *ppl. a.* (In Dict. s.v. Transmit *v.*) Add: *transmitting station*, a building or establishment from which radio or television signals are transmitted.

1923 *Radio Times* 28 Sept. 26/3 The 2LO transmitting station. **1977** *Whitaker's Almanack 1978* 759/1 There are two shortwave transmitting and receiving stations in Freetown.

trans,mo·rtal, *a.* Chiefly *poet.* [f. Trans- 4 + Mortal *a.*] Beyond what is mortal, immortal.

1932 Blunden *Halfway House* 67 That much I saw without transmortal talk. *a* **1963** C. S. Lewis *Poems* (1964) 97 Thou art Lord of the unbreathable transmortal air Where mortal thinking fails.

transmural, *a.* Add: **2.** *Med.* Existing or occurring across the (entire) wall of an organ or blood vessel.

1951 Burton & Yamada in *Jrnl. Appl. Physiol.* IV. 330 It will be convenient..to call this difference of pressure the transmural pressure. **1968** *Amer. Jrnl. Obstetr. & Gynecol.* CII. 29/2 Hyalinization of vein walls became more patchy and occasionally transmural. **1977** *Lancet* 24/31 Dec. 1331/1 Transmural electrical stimulation of intestinal structures.

transmutation. Add: **3. a.** Also in *Physics*, the (actual) change of one element into another, esp. by irradiation or bombardment (as opposed to spontaneous decay). Cf. *TRANSFORMATION 3 g.

1897 *Electrician* 10 Dec. 214/1 Theoretically, if the modern doctrine as to the ultimate constitution of matter be accepted, the transmutation of the elements is a scientific possibility. The fierce atomic bombardments inside a Crookes tube or an electric furnace would seem the most probable of known conditions whereby the operation might be carried on. **1915** K. Tornberg tr. *Rasch's Electric Arc Phenomena* viii. 184 Since the electrons are ultra-atomic..the electric arc provides a means for the splitting up of matter, which perhaps makes the synthesis or transmutation of chemical elements not entirely beyond possibility. **1926** R. W. Lawson tr. *Hevesy & Paneth's Man. Radioactivity* xxi. 147 Up to the present we only know of one method that permits us to resolve the nuclei of the atoms artificially, and thus to achieve..the transmutation of the elements. **1969** Bennison & Wright *Geol. Hist. Brit. Isles* i. 5 The rate of 'decay' or transmutation of radioactive minerals. **1974** *Physics Bull.* Dec. 585/2 The process of transmutation ('neutron burning'), as applied for several years now to radioactive waste, where certain isotopes are transmuted to isotopes with shorter half lives or even to stable ones.

4. transmutation glaze (example).

1904 [see *flambé *a.* 1].

transmute, *v.* Add: **1. b.** (Further examples.) Also in *Physics*, to change (one element or isotope) *into* another by irradiation or bombardment; to change (one sub-atomic particle) *into* another.

1897 *Electrician* 10 Dec. 214/1 Only the other day we were told how many centuries it would require to 'transmute' a milligram or two of one element into another, in a Crookes tube. **1926** R. W. Lawson tr. *Hevesy & Paneth's Man. Radioactivity* xxi. 148 This method of transmuting elements is still far from being of any practical importance. **1956** A. H. Compton *Atomic Quest* i. 52 The naturally occurring atoms of U-238 and Th-232 can be transmuted into sources of atomic fuel. **1977** *Mod. Railways* Dec. 474/1 Vinyl chloride monomer.. leaves by rail for Barry, where it is transmuted into PVC and heavy-duty plastic items. **1979** *McGraw-Hill Yearbk. Sci. & Technol.* 267/2 The pions can produce only a single-charge exchange by transmuting a proton into a neutron. **1981** *Sci. Amer.* Feb. 85/1 Cosmic rays transmute nitrogen 14 in the upper atmosphere into the radioactive isotope carbon 14. **1981** C. H. L. Smith in J. H. Mulvey *Nature of Matter* iii. 72 In this case, quarks would very occasionally be transmuted into electrons.

c. Delete † *Obs. rare*$^{-1}$ and add later examples.

1962 D. G. Cogan in A. Pirie *Lens Metabolism Rel. Cataract* 294 The morgagnian globules..finally transmute into homogeneous milky fluid. **1970** A. Romer *Radiochem. & Discovery of Isotopes* 127 The radiothorium, transmuting into thorium X.., would gradually disappear. **1978** *Nature* 29 June 707/1 In the weak interaction of radioactivity it has been known for many years that the neutrino turns into an electron or that an up quark transmutes into a down. **1983** *Penthouse* Sept. 169 Do you think capitalism is an eternal system, or will it transmute into something else?

trans,na·tional, *a.* (*sb.*) [f. Trans- 3, 4 + National *a.*] Extending or having interests extending beyond national bounds or frontiers; multinational. Also *ellipt.* as *sb.*, a transnational company.

1921 N. Angell *Fruits of Victory* ii. 63 Much of Europe lives by virtue of an international, or more correctly, a trans-national economy. **1941** J. S. Huxley *On living in Revolution* (1944) 144 The outstanding case of what we may call a transnational natural region—an industrial area cutting right across national boundaries—is the great concentration of industry in North-Western Europe. **1941** J. Macmurray *Challenge to Churches* 59 The Christian religion is the only possible force which can conceivably create the condition of a transnational, non-racial democratic polity. **1956** P. C. Jessup *Transnational Law* i. 2, I shall use, instead of 'international law', the term 'transnational law' to include all law which regulates actions or events that transcend national frontiers. **1968** *Economist* 13 July 65/2 To these three [*sc.* the ethnocentric, the polycentric, and the geocentric types of multi-national company], Professor Galbraith has added a fourth type, the transnational company, with international stock ownership. **1973** *Reader's Digest* Apr. 167/1 Terrorism..is 'transnational' in scope—that is, there is a kind of global brotherhood of terrorists who share basic beliefs and techniques. **1977** *Irish Democrat* Mar. 3/5 The Brussels dictators would probably just tolerate a secession provided the transnationals continued to rule the roost economically. **1980** *Telegraph* (Brisbane) 5 Sept. 2/2 Now that multinational has become a dirty word,..multinationals are..known as transnationals. **1983** *Church Times* 6 May 10/4 It will fall to your lot to assess the transnational corporations..and see whether in fact they do promote Third World development.

Hence **trans,na·tionally** *adv.*; **trans,na·tionalism.**

1921 N. Angell *Fruits of Victory* i. 14 Transport and credit, operating trans-nationally. *Ibid.* 300 The old individualist 'trans-nationalism'. **1973** *Listener* 20 Dec. 845 The reality of transnationalism, at any rate in the non-Communist world, simply cannot be denied. **1976** *Times* 13 Feb. 15/6 Surely, a peaceful world needs respect for the rule of law, not only nationally but transnationally.

transnormal, *a.* (Earlier example.)

1853 Max Müller in C. Bunsen *Outl. Philos. Univ. Hist.* (1854) I. 282 Pott adds a fourth class, which he calls *transnormal* or *incorporative*, i.e. the polysynthetic American dialects.

trans,o·cean, *a.* [f. Trans- 3 + Ocean *sb.*] = Trans-oceanic *a.* 2.

1901 *Daily Record & Mail* 31 Aug. 3 Besides a free trans-ocean passage, passes are issued from Quebec or Montreal to eastern points of the States. **1950** *Travel Topics* Dec. 11 Trans-ocean trips. **1978** J. A. Michener *Chesapeake* 102 Steed found it difficult to clarify the difficulties of transocean trading.

transoid (trɑ·nzoid). *Chem.* [f. Trans- + -oid.] Designating a compound, group, or structure in which two unlike atoms or groups are situated in the *trans* position relative to one another.

1959 I. L. Finar *Org. Chem.* (ed. 3) I. xvii. 387 (*caption*) Staggered (transoid). **1965** *Tetrahedron* XXI. 3121 The optical rotatory dispersion of seven other transoid dienes has been determined. **1970** *Nature* 3 Jan. 36/1 Acetylcholine..in a 'transoid' conformation. **1978** *Ibid.* 29 June 785/1 Bathorhodopsin is a common intermediate between pigments based on two different *cis* isomers and thus must itself contain a 'transoid' chromophore.

transom. Add: **3. e.** (Examples.)

1907, 1927, 1955 [see *nose *sb.* 14 e].

g. (Earlier examples, in the context of a ship.)

1847 H. Melville *Omoo* lxxxii. 373, I would find the ship's articles on the cabin transom. **1851** — *Moby Dick* I. xvi. 91 Seated on the transom was what seemed to me a most uncommon and surprising figure.

transonic (trɑnsǫ·nik). *a.* Also **trans-sonic.** [f. Trans- 3 + *sonic *a.*, after *supersonic, ultrasonic.*] Pertaining to, involving, capable of, or designating speeds close to that of sound, at which some of the flow round a body is supersonic and some subsonic and there are characteristic changes in the behaviour of an aircraft.

1946 *Britannica Bk. of Year* (U.S.) 833/2 *Trans-sonic*, speeds ranging from 550 to 760 m.p.h. **1946** *Jrnl. R. Aeronaut. Soc.* L. 436/1, I propose to say a little about 'supersonic' aerodynamics first, and then to return to the so-called 'transonic' region, which presents the most difficult problem of all. **1948** 'N. Shute' *No Highway* xii. 294 The forces on the structure [of an aircraft] were still very much a matter of guesswork in the trans-sonic range. **1966** *New Scientist* 20 Jan. 135/1 A critical phase is reached as the aircraft goes 'transonic'; that is, as it accelerates through the speed band from just below to just above the speed of sound. **1977** *Jrnl. R. Soc. Arts* CXXV. 347/1 Notable examples [of development] since World War II have been jet propulsion, transonic and supersonic aerodynamics, [etc.].

transparency. Add: **1. b.** *Linguistics.* The state or quality of being transparent (sense *2 c). With reference to a phonological rule, opp. *opacity 3 c.

1971 [see *opaque *a.* 3 c]. **1975** *Canad. Jrnl. Linguistics* XX. 175 Rules tend to be ordered so as to become maximally transparent, where *transparency* is the opposite of *opacity*. **1981** *Ibid.* XXVI. 73 Transparency of the base word is an important factor in determining speakers' choice of neologism.

c. Of reproduced sound: the state or quality of being transparent (sense *3).

1982 E. Greenfield et al. *New Penguin Stereo Record & Cassette Guide* p. ix/2, Disc reproduction continues to offer a marginally greater range of sound and a more subtle inner transparency of detail than the equivalent tape. **1983** *What Hi-Fi?* Dec. 102/3 This £129 speaker offers a high quality of finish and a transparency and accuracy of sound that can compete with models twice the price.

d. The state or quality of transmitting or allowing the passage of sound waves without distortion (see *transparent *a.* 1 b).

1983 *What Hi-Fi?* Dec. 113/3 The most impressive [feature] was the sheer transparency of the design. **1984** *Gramophone* Mar. 1086/1 The effect (emphasized by the transparency of the CD medium) is of sitting in a small room, very close to the cello and with the lid of the piano wide open.

2. b. (Earlier examples.)

1785 J. Woodforde *Diary* 21 June (1926) II. 196 Went to Bunns Gardens... There was tolerable good Music, indifferent singing, some pretty transparencies and tolerable fire Works. **1801** *Sporting Mag.* XIX. 49/1 A transparency, in which a gardener at Hammersmith exhibited a Flower-pot, during the illuminations.

c. (Earlier and later examples.)

1866 *Brit. Jrnl. Photogr.* 1 June 264/1 Many of these lantern transparencies had been enlarged from spots of these originals. **1965** Mrs. L. B. Johnson *White House Diary* 9 Feb. (1970) 239 The transparency I have.. shows a real John Singleton Copley, of the best early American period. **1969** 'E. Lathen' *When in Greece* v. 49 He had brought slides..a veritable library of transparencies. **1973** 'H. Howard' *Highway to Murder* iv. 46 Like transparencies flashed on a screen I saw pictures of long ago.

transparent, *a.* Add: **1. b.** More widely, allowing the passage of any specified kind of radiation. Also, allowing the passage of sound waves without distortion.

1947 *Physical Rev.* LXXII. 1114/1 At sufficiently high energies the nucleus begins to be transparent to the bombarding particles. **1962** *Listener* 3 May 770/1 The needles..would be effective only in centimetre wavelengths—to which..the ionosphere is virtually transparent. **1962** A. Nisbett *Technique Sound Studio* ii. 41 Note that rack (as well as table surface) should be made of acoustically transparent mesh. *Ibid.* 269 The rack itself should be transparent to sound. **1974** *Nature* 13 Dec. 613/2 Their seismic data are said to 'reveal a distinct basement ridge' blanketed by acoustically transparent sediments which 'thin subtly near the crest of the buried ridge'. **1976** *Gramophone* Apr. 1682/2 The latter consists of a thin framework carrying two stand-off ribs to give a three-faced appearance when the black, acoustically transparent, stockinette cloth is stretched over it. **1978** *Nature* 21 Sept. 175/1 A container of superfluid ^{4}He whose walls are transparent to neutrons with velocity of 450 ms^{-1}. **1980** *Sci. Amer.* July 56/1 The interstellar medium is highly transparent to gamma rays. **1982** *Nature* 9 Sept. 122/1 The ocean is transparent to sound.

2. c. *Linguistics.* Obvious in structure or meaning; that can be extrapolated from surface structure; of a phonological rule: that can be extrapolated from every occurrence of the phenomenon, in which every context implies the rule (opp. *opaque *a.* 3 c).

1974 [see *opaque *a.* 3 c]. **1975** [see *transparency 1 b]. **1977** *Language* LIII. 820 A compound may be highly transparent semantically when it is coined. **1980** *Amer. Speech* LV. 38 The hydronymic element *-kill* and names formed from it are semantically opaque, whereas *creek* and *brook* are transparent. **1981** *Canad. Jrnl. Linguistics* XXVI. 73 They..show no preferences either way if both word boundary and formative boundary derivations are transparent.

3. Of reproduced sound: clear, without tonal distortion, not blurred, with each element distinct.

1950 *Audio Engin.* Sept. 33/2 The sound is then said to be *transparent*..; no *acoustic fog veils* the ensemble, and each instrument stands out with *clarity*.

transpecific, var. *transspecific *a.*

transpeptidation (trɑːnspeptidēⁱ·ʃən, -nz-). *Biochem.* [f. *trans- 10 + *peptide + -ation.] Any reaction in which a peptide bond is broken and the free carboxyl (or amino) group joined to the amino (or carboxyl) group of another molecule so as to form a new peptide bond.

1950 J. S. Fruton in *Yale Jrnl. Biol. & Med.* XXII. 264 Reactions of this type may be termed 'transpeptidation' or 'transamidation' processes. **1975** *Nature* 10 Apr. 482/2 Various cell-free transpeptidation systems are now known to be sensitive to penicillin.

So **trans,pe·ptidase** [*-ase], any enzyme that catalyses transpeptidation.

1952 C. S. Hanes et al. in *Biochem. Jrnl.* LI. 25/1 The enzyme will be referred to as γ-glutamyl transpeptidase. **1981** *Sci. Amer.* June 68/1 The vulnerable enzymes are either transpeptidases (which cross-link one peptide chain of new peptidoglycan to another by displacing a terminal D-alanine) or D-carboxypeptidases (which remove a terminal D-alanine by hydrolysis without cross-linking taking place).

trans,pe·rsonal, *a.* [f. TRANS- 4 + PERSONAL *a.*] That transcends the personal, trans-individual; *spec.* designating a form of psychology or psychotherapy which seeks to combine elements from many esoteric and religious traditions with modern ideas and techniques.
1905–6 W. JAMES in R. B. Perry *Thought & Char. W. James* (1935) II. 445 That an idea represents an 'object' may mean that it represents something either:—1. Trans-*personal*—as when my object is also your object; [etc.]. **1955** *Bull. Atomic Sci.* Apr. 109/1 Science provides the model of a free society of reasonable men co-ordinating themselves voluntarily in the light of a transpersonal standard. **1968** *Jrnl. Humanistic Psychol.* VIII. 77 Transpersonal (or Fourth Force) Psychology is the title given to an emerging force in the psychology field by a group of psychologists and professional men and women.. who are interested in those *ultimate* human capacities and potentialities [etc.]. **1972** *Science* 16 June 1203/2 Experiences of ecstasy, mystical union,..and transpersonal knowledge..are simply not treated adequately in conventional scientific approaches. **1980** R. HERINK *Psychotherapy Handbk.* 684 Transpersonal Psychotherapy can be said to have evolved..as the inner or esoteric teachings of all the great spiritual traditions.

transphasor (transfē¹·zəɹ, -nz-). *Electronics.* [f. *TRANS(IST)OR *sb.* with PHAS(E inserted.] A semiconductor device in which one light beam can be modulated by another.
1979 MILLER & SMITH in *Optics Communications* XXXI. 101/2 We report the first realisation of an optically bistable device in a semiconductor crystal as well as observation of differential gain both in one beam and, via the modulation of the transmission of one laser beam by a second, in a two beam system. This latter device is analogous to the three terminal transistor and, operating by transferred phase thickness, we term it a 'transphasor'. **1984** *Sunday Times* 18 Mar. 80/1 In a transistor a small electrical current can be used to switch an electrical voltage between a high and a low value... The transphasor does exactly the same thing with laser beams.

trans,pheno·menal, *a. Philos.* [f. TRANS- 4 + PHENOMENAL *a.* (*sb.*).] That transcends or goes beyond the phenomenal. Hence **trans,phenomena·lity.**
1897 W. M. URBAN *Hist. Princ. Sufficient Reason* vi. 87 The validity of this logical postulate in trans-phenomenal usage. **1904** [see *DEREALIZE *v.*]. **1954** W. DESAN *Tragic Finale* ix. 178 Sartre claims that the existence of the external *transphenomenal* being is the condition of my *phenomenal* perception. **1957** H. E. BARNES tr. *Sartre's Being & Nothingness* p. l, The phenomenon of being.. is an appeal to being; it requires as phenomenon, a foundation which is transphenomenal. The phenomenon of being requires the transphenomenality of being.

trans,pho:sphoryla·tion. *Biochem.* [f. *TRANS- 10 + *PHOSPHORYLATION.] The transfer of a phosphate group from a molecule of one compound to one of another.
1943 *Jrnl. Biol. Chem.* CXLVIII. 119 Transphosphorylation from adenosine diphosphate to glucose also results in the liberation of 1 acid equivalent. **1970** *McGraw-Hill Yearbk. Sci. & Technol.* 62/2 A transphosphorylation reaction..transfers the phosphate from the hydroxyl of the adjacent nucleotide to the hydroxyl of the pyrimidine sugar, giving a cyclic phosphate.

transpire, *v.* Add: **4.** Also *impers.*
1903 G. B. SHAW *Man & Superman* 209 We had hardly recovered from the fruitless irritation of this discovery when it transpired that the officers' mess of our most select regiment included a flogging club presided over by the senior subaltern. **1922** W. GERHARDI *Futility* III. vi. 173 It transpired that four regiments composing the division had gone over to the enemy. **1966** D. J. ENRIGHT *Conspirators & Poets* I. 16 But then, to our surprise, it transpires that he doesn't think much of our critics, either. **1982** I. HAMILTON *Robert Lowell* (1983) x. 144 Yaddo, it transpired, had been under FBI surveillance for some time.

b. Delete sentence beginning 'App. began in U.S. about 1800' and quot. 1802 and add earlier example.
1775 A. ADAMS *Let.* 31 July in J. & A. Adams *Familiar Lett. Revolution* (1876) 91 There is nothing new transpired since I wrote you last.

transplant, *sb.* Add: **1. a.** *spec.* in *Surg.*, etc., an organ, tissue, etc., which has been transplanted into another person or animal.
1913 *Arch. f. Entwicklungsmech. d. Organismen* XXXVII. 254 The homoeoplastic transplants in guinea pigs 5 and 8 were removed for microscopic examination. **1952, 1963** [see *heart transplant* s.v. *HEART *sb.* 56]. **1977** J. GILLIS *Killers of Starfish* x. 81 Look a little closer. This hair hat of mine is a transplant... I'm a lot older than Trevor.

b. One who is not native to his place of permanent residence. *U.S.*
1961 M. BEADLE *These Ruins are Inhabited* (1963) v. 73 If she's a good English wife, she doesn't tell him. If she's an American transplant, she does. **1973** T. TOBIN *Lett. G. Ade* 2 The bustling city [of Chicago], which was comprised of numerous rural transplants too busy with the business of living to establish traditions. **1979** *Tucson* (Arizona) *Citizen* 20 Sept. 1B/3 Traffic and the heat are two things the transplants mentioned.

3. *Surg.* An operation in which an organ, tissue, etc., is transplanted from one person or animal to another.
1951 *Sun* (Baltimore) 14 Mar. 34/1 He decided to try a transplant [of a tooth]. **1971** *Daily Tel.* 3 May 1/4 Prof. Christian Barnard..is standing by to carry out his first transplant for two years. **1982** *Sunday Times* 2 Sept. 16/2 It is a type of pneumonia usually found only where there are known causes for a breakdown in the immune system, as in cancer chemotherapy or transplants.

4. *attrib.*
1963 *Guardian* 22 Mar. 1/3 Surgeons at St Bartholomew's Hospital, London, this week carried out the hospital's first kidney transplant operation. **1967** *New Scientist* 7 Dec. 584/3 This [*sc.* the immune reaction] is the problem that bedevils the whole of transplant surgery. **1968** *Observer* 7 Jan. 1/1 After that we can think about further selection of transplant patients. **1977** P. B. & J. S. MEDAWAR *Life Science* i. 8 The anxious question of whether or when a potential transplant donor..can be regarded as dead.

transplantable, *a.*, **transplantability.** (Later examples of each in *Med.*)
1913 *Jrnl. Exper. Med.* XVII. 482 (*heading*) Transplantability of tissues to the embryo of foreign species. *Ibid.*, Much has been added to our knowledge of..tissue grafting in warm blooded animals through the study of the transplantable tumors. **1973** *Nature* 18 May 163/1 These tumours are transplantable and have been transplanted for up to six consecutive passages. **1977** *Ibid.* 6 Jan. 56/1 Increased malignancy of lymphoma cells [was] expressed by serial transplantability and capacity for widespread metastases.

transplanter. Add: **1. b.** *spec.* in *Surg.*, a surgeon who carries out transplant operations.
1970 *Daily Tel.* 15 June 13/2 For Prof. Roy Calne,.. pioneer liver transplanter, there is only one problem: not enough organs are being transplanted. **1971** *Nature* 24 Dec. 440/3 To the transplanter it may well be that if an antibody to a particular antigen can be elicited.. certain typing mismatches may be of no consequence. **1977** *Time* 7 Mar. 43 (*caption*) Kidney transplanter Stubenbord with patient Jose Serrano after surgery. **1984** A. SMITH *Mind* v. xv. 299 The needs of the transplanters formed a prime motive for redefining death.

transplendency. (Later example.)
1915 C. MACKENZIE *Guy & Pauline* 163 The clouds.. suddenly melted in a wild transplendency of gold.

trans,pluto·nium, *a. Physics.* [f. *TRANS- 11 + *PLUTONIUM 2 b.] Of a chemical element: having a higher atomic number than plutonium (i.e. 95 or over).
1955 *Physical Rev.* XCIX. 1048/2 It [*sc.* the alpha radiation] was due to a transplutonium element. **1977** *Sci. Amer.* Mar. 29/2 In the absence of fast-neutron reactors..it would be impossible to completely burn the plutonium and its transplutonium derivatives produced by the slow-neutron plants.

transponder (trɑnspǫ·ndəɹ, -nz-). [f. TRANS(MIT *v.* + RES)POND *v.* + -ER¹.] = *RESPONDER 2 b.
1945 *Army & Navy Jrnl.* 18 Aug. 1534/4 *Transponder.* The unit in the IFF system which receives the challenge and automatically transmits the reply. **1945** *Electronic Engin.* XVII. 735/3 It became clear that such a 'transponder'..could set up at any convenient place and would act as a beacon. **1957** [see *RESPONDER 2 b]. **1967** R. J. SERLING *President's Plane is Missing* (1968) iii. 55 Henderson pushed the transponder button... The new identifying transponders were hooked to the altimeter. **1974** *Nature* 16 Aug. 558/2 The position of the Archimède was known within 10–200 m, depending on her distance from the nearest of the acoustic transponders. **1983** *Listener* 8 Sept. 6/1 The transponder code ought to have immediately alerted ground controllers.

transpontine, *a.* Add: **2.** [f. L. *pontus* sea.] That is across the sea; on or from the other side of the ocean, *spec.* the Atlantic, i.e. North American.
1891 R. L. STEVENSON *Let.* Oct. (1923) XXII. 414 The last four chapters of *The Wrecker*!.. Ours is such rude, transpontine business. **1920** *Times Lit. Suppl.* 15 Apr. 232/2 She [*sc.* an American writer] has investigated her subject with typical transpontine enthusiasm. **1922** JOYCE *Ulysses* 416 Thou sawest thy America, thy lifetask, and didst charge to cover like the transpontine bison.

transport, *sb.* Add: **3.** (Later examples with *a* and *pl.*)
1920 D. H. LAWRENCE *Women in Love* i. 12 She experienced a keen paroxysm, a transport, as if she had made some incredible discovery. **1953** E. JONES *Sigmund Freud* I. xi. 275 A female patient suddenly flinging her arms round his neck in a transport of affection. **1978** A. S. BYATT *Virgin in Garden* xviii. 185 Almost she expected him to rouse himself and roar out transports of self-reproach or self-referring ecstasy, either of which would have embarrassed her profoundly. **1981** A. SCHLEE *Rhine Journey* ix. 111 She had gone on to describe..the gentle transports she would expect her sensitive nature to endure, the blameless pious raptures.

4. Cf. *tape transport* s.v. *TAPE *sb.*¹ 4. Also = *transport plane* below.
1940 *Times* (Weekly ed.) 7 Aug. 23 German tactics in attacking aerodromes, from the first attempt to divert the fighters to the arrival of low bombers and the landing of parachutists and troop transports are now well known. **1943** C. MILBURN *Diary* 11 Apr. (1979) 174 Forty transports going to supply the Axis were brought down. **1970** *Nature* 15 Aug. 655/2 The project to build a supersonic transport has run into renewed complaints from the environmentalists. **1974** C. RYAN *Bridge too Far* II. i. 79 Transports to carry paratroops and tow-planes to pull the gliders must be diverted from their normal task of supplying the advancing armies and grounded.

6. *transport officer, -wagon* (examples); **transport café**, a roadside café for lorry-drivers; **Transport House**, the name of the headquarters of the Labour Party, used as a synonym for the Labour Party leadership; **transport number** *Physical Chem.*, the proportion of a current flowing through a particular electrolytic solution which can be attributed to the movement of any given ion species; = *transference number* s.v. *TRANSFERENCE 3; **transport plane** *Mil.*, an aircraft used for transporting troops, supplies, etc.
1938 'J. CURTIS' *They drive by Night* i. 15 At St. Albans a lorry-driver was sitting hunched up at the counter of a transport café. **1959** *Manch. Guardian* 29 July 14/3 On the London–Birmingham motorway..there will be.. two transport cafés, but only one restaurant. **1978** C. A. BERRY *Gentleman of Road* xiii. 130 A welcome stay at the transport café..on the strength of two cups of tea. **1937** *New Statesman & Nation* 11 Sept. 364/2 This new orientation fits in exactly with that of the political wing of Transport House. **1958** *Spectator* 31 Jan. 124/2 On the Labour side, it does not appear as though Transport House is even thinking of coming to grips with reality. *a* **1974** R. CROSSMAN *Diaries* (1975) I. 72 If we as a Cabinet have neglected our relationship with the Parliamentary Party we have equally neglected our relations with Transport House and the Party outside. **1897** M. M. P. MUIR tr. *Lüpke's Elem. Electro-Chem.* I. iii. 43 A Cu ion will pass over two of six spaces, and a SO_4 ion will pass over four in the same time. The quotients $\frac{2}{6}$=0·33 and $\frac{4}{6}$=0·66 are called by Hittorf the transport-numbers (die Überführungszahlen) for the kation Cu and the anion SO_4, respectively. **1978** P. W. ATKINS *Physical Chem.* xxv. 843 The following are brief summaries of the three methods used to measure transport numbers of ions and, through them, individual ion conductivities and mobilities. **1917** W. OWEN *Let.* 4 Feb. (1967) 431 It doesn't necessarily mean a job as Transport Officer straight away. **1945** R. J. OAKES in *Coast to Coast 1944* 99 He had six wounded men to load into the transport plane. **1977** M. SOKOLINSKI tr. *Merle's Virility Factor* xv. 307 The jeep..led us straight into the maw of a transport plane that swallowed the truck. **1866** J. LEYLAND *Adventures Far Interior S. Afr.* 11, I travelled by a Dutch transport waggon. **1936** in N. Rouillard *Matabele Thompson* ii. 46, I found myself at no great distance from a transport waggon, laden with goods intended for a trader in the north.

transportable, *a.* Add: **1. a.** *spec.* of a computer (see quots.).
1982 *Byte* Nov. 6 Portable..refers to a small, transportable computer on which you can touch-type. **1983** *Times* 31 May 20/4 The new breed of portable computers makes some of the older machines..look immovable by comparison... Once known as portable computers, these machines are now dubbed transportable computers, to distinguish them from smaller machines that are more easily moved. **1985** *Pract. Computing* Jan. 70/3 Although called the Portable, the machine is..what is more normally termed transportable. That is, it is a mains-powered unit which..is too heavy to be carried around all the time.

b. Of software: that can be used on more than one kind of machine.
1972 *Rep. Nat. Res. Council Canada* No. 13659 (ERIC Rep. No. 160126) 4 Facilities for producing 'transportable' computer based course materials. **1977** *Proc. Internat. Symp. Computer Aided Seismic Analysis* 121/1 PAL, through its structured logic and easily transportable software, provides a framework which will readily accept modification and expansion. **1983** *Mini-Micro Systems* Feb. 71/3 DEC is encouraging software producers in Europe to make software transportable between countries.

B. *sb.* A transportable television set, computer, etc. *spec.* one which is heavier than a 'portable' appliance.
1959 *Daily Tel.* 27 Aug. 11/3 The transportable [*sc.* a television] is something comparatively new. It has a carrying handle, yet is too heavy to be classed as a lightweight portable. **1971** *Radio Times* 25 Nov. 35 (Advt.), The Deccavision Executive 17" transportable—a black-and-white TV that gives big, bold performance wherever there's a mains point. **1983** *Observer* 19 June 21/1 Although perception of portability differs radically, three categories can be discerned... These are the handhelds, the true portables, and the transportables. **1983** *Austral. Microcomputer Mag.* Nov. 76/1 Despite the provision of a high level of computing power in such recent hand-held portables.., there always should be room for larger transportables.

transportation. Add: **3.** (Earlier example.)
1853 J. L. MCCONNEL *Western Characters* 163 He furnished his own 'transportation', and selected his own encampment.

5. *transportation agent* (example), *-wagon.*
1819 J. A. QUITMAN in J. F. H. Claiborne *Life J. A. Quitman* (1860) I. 36, I went to the agent of a train of transportation-wagons. **1825** in T. L. McKenney *Memoirs* (1846) I. 299, I was appointed transportation agent for the United States at St. Louis. **1866** 'MARK TWAIN' *Lett. from Hawaii* (1967) 274 Her transportation wagons will be the freight cars of the Pacific Railroad.

transporter. Add: **2.** Also, a vehicle used to transport other vehicles or large pieces of machinery, etc., by road.

a **1944** K. Douglas *Alamein to Zem Zem* (1946) xi. 68 The tanks were to move by transporter. **1976** L. Deighton *Twinkle, twinkle, Little Spy* xxi. 206 In the Sahara there were only Peugeots, and Landrovers, and the smart little cars that came in by transporter.

transposable, *a.* Add: (Earlier example.) Also **transposible.**

1835 J. B. Robertson tr. *Schlegel's Philos. of Hist.* I. iii. 95 Instead of the regular art of printing with transposeable letters..this people [*sc.* the Chinese] make use of a species of lithography, which, to all essential purposes is the same. **1847** A. De Morgan *Formal Logic* vi. 122 The whole term is always transposible.

transpose, *sb.* Restrict † *Obs. rare* to sense in Dict. and add: **2.** *Math.* A matrix got from a given matrix by interchanging each row and the corresponding column.

1937 [see *similar *a.* 3 c]. **1939** A. C. Aitken *Determinants & Matrices* i. 15 The resulting matrix is called the transpose of *A* and is denoted by *A'*. (In the less recent literature the word *conjugate* is used.) **1961** [see *Hermitian *a.*]. **1978** *Nature* 13 Apr. 605/2 The transpose of the eigenvector matrix of climatic data.

transposed, *ppl. a.* (in Dict. s.v. Transpose *v.*). Add: *spec.* in *Math.*, applied to the transpose of a given matrix.

1858 *Phil. Trans. R. Soc.* CXLVIII. 32 A matrix compounded with the transposed matrix gives rise to a symmetrical matrix. **1907** M. Bôcher *Introd. Higher Algebra* ii. 21 Two square matrices..of which either is obtained from the other by interchanging rows and columns are called conjugate to each other. [*Note*] Sometimes also transposed. **1972** M. Kline *Math. Thought* xxxiii. 807 The transverse (transposed or conjugate) matrix is defined as the one in which rows and columns are interchanged.

transposition. Add: **2. a.** (Examples in *Math.*)

1965 J. J. Rotman *Theory of Groups* iii. 35 Of all the permutations, surely the transposition, which merely interchanges two points, is the simplest. **1972** A. G. Howson *Handbk. Terms Algebra & Anal.* x. 51 Any permutation can be expressed as a product of transpositions. **1981** *Sci. Amer.* Mar. 19/2 If you are willing to let cycles share members, however, any cycle can be further broken up into 2-cycles (called transpositions, or sometimes swaps).

b. *Math.* The interchange of each row of a matrix with the corresponding column.

1858 A. Cayley in *Phil. Trans. R. Soc.* CXLVIII. 31 Two matrices such as $\begin{vmatrix} a, b \\ c, d \end{vmatrix}, \begin{vmatrix} a, c \\ b, d \end{vmatrix}$, are said to be formed one from the other by transposition. **1955** *Geophysics* XX. 300 The transposition of the ξ_{12}' matrix was necessary to reveal the trend in the *u*..direction.

6. *Electr.* An alteration of the relative positions of power lines or telephone lines at intervals along their length, in order to minimize effects of mutual inductance and capacitance.

1911 A. B. Smith *Mod. Amer. Telephony* xxii. 616 Transpositions are unnecessary when there is but one circuit on a pole line. **1959** K. Henney *Radio Engin. Handbk.* (ed. 5) xxviii. 26 In the case of pairs used for high frequencies, the locations of the transpositions must be quite precise. **1975** R. L. Freeman *Telecommunication Transmission Handbk.* iv. 164 The dipole type of LP antenna is fed by a balanced transmission line with 180° transpositions at alternate dipole elements.

7. *Genetics.* The transfer of a chromosomal segment to a new position on the same or another chromosome.

1924 *Hereditas* V. 174 In his case of transposition (or translocation) a piece of one of the second chromosomes has been fastened to one of the third chromosomes. **1954** B. P. Kaufmann in A. Hollaender *Radiation Biol.* I. ii. ix. 650 The viable types of intrachromosomal rearrangement include inversions and transpositions. **1978** *Nature* 20 July 211/3 The subsequent transposition of tetracycline resistance from this engineered plasmid must therefore be due to the transposition of the toxin gene.

transpositively, *adv.* (Example.)

1946 *Mind* LV. 323 If we accept the premises..that *fa* and ~*fa* severally imply (∃*x*)..then we must accept the consequences..that they do not have contradictories; or, transpositively, if we want our universal propositions to be non-existential..we must repudiate the proposition that *fa* implies (∃*x*)*fx*.

transposon (trɑnspōᵘ·zɒn, -nz-). *Genetics.* [f. Transpos(ition + *-on¹.] A chromosomal segment that can undergo transposition (sense *7); *spec.* a segment of bacterial DNA that can be translocated *en bloc* between chromosomal, phage, and plasmid DNA in the absence of a complementary sequence in the host DNA.

1974 Hedges & Jacob in *Molecular & Gen. Genetics* CXXXII. 38 We designate DNA sequences with transposition potential as transposons (units of transposition). **1978** *Nature* 11 May 171/3 The determinants of resistance to at least seven different antibiotics form part of independent structures several kilobase-pairs long, called 'transposons', which can jump between the genomes of bacteria, plasmids and phages of widely different base compositions. **1980** *Sci. Amer.* Sept. 87/3 Some transposons carry genes for traits such as drug resistance that are clearly advantageous to a bacterial host under some circumstances. **1982** *Nature* 21 Oct. 676/1 Transposons, familiar enough in bacteria.., have been identified in..eukaryotic genomes principally because their DNA sequences can crop up at different places.

trans,provi·ncial, *a.* [f. Trans- 3 + Provincial *a.*] That crosses a province.

1916 R. K. Wood *Tourist's N.W.* 316 A trans-provincial highway is building through southern British Columbia from the mountains..to Hope in the Fraser River Valley. **1952** D. F. Putnam *Canadian Regions* 338/1 They have not..been able to get the Ontario Government to construct adequate transprovincial highways.

transpulmonary, *a.* Add: *transpulmonary pressure*, the difference between the pressure in the lungs and that in the intrapleural cavity.

1957 *Jrnl. Appl. Physiol.* X. 191/1 Measurements of the mechanical properties of the lungs depend on the separation of transpulmonary pressure into separate elastic and flow-resistive components. **1977** *Lancet* 3 Sept. 510/1 When airway collapse does occur, transpulmonary pressure rapidly increases with only a small resultant increase in inspiratory gasflow.

transputer (trɑnspiū·təɹ, -nz-). *Electronics.* [f. *Trans(istor *sb.* + Com)puter.] A chip that incorporates all the functions of a microprocessor, including memory.

1978 I. M. Barron in D. Aspinall *Microprocessor* vi. 343 The word 'transputer' has been coined to describe the computer on a chip. The word is derived from..'computer' and 'transistor'. **1983** *Times* 2 Nov. 3 Alice [*sc.* Applicative Language Idealized Computer Engine] will incorporate 64 transputers running in parallel, each in itself a 'computer on a chip'. **1984** *Times* 17 Feb. 10/4 The 'transputer' which Inmos, Britain's state-backed chip company, hopes to begin manufacturing in about a year's time,..includes processor, memory and communications on a conventional-sized chip.

trans,ra·cial, *a.* [f. Trans- 3 + Racial *a.*] Across or crossing racial boundaries.

1971 *Time* 16 Aug. 46 The Merediths' decision is part of a growing phenomenon known in sociologists' jargon as transracial adoption. **1976** *Indian Jrnl. Social Work* XXXVII. 152/1 The trend..is now moving towards transracial adoptions.

transreceiver (trɑːns,rɪsī·vəɹ, -nz-). [f. Trans(mitter + Receiver¹.] = *transceiver.

1942 *Electronic Engin.* XV. 239/2 Inside the Transreceiver there is a small moving coil mechanism. **1956** 'N. Shute' *Beyond Black Stump* ii. 46 David had a radio transreceiver for use with the Flying Doctor service.

trans,se·xual, *a.* and *sb.* Also (A. 1, B.) **transexual,** (esp. A. 2) **trans-sexual.** [f. Trans- 3 + Sexual *a.*] **A.** *adj.* **1.** Of or pertaining to transsexualism; having physical characteristics of one sex and psychological characteristics of the other.

1957 *Amer. Jrnl. Psychotherapy* XI. 85 Other kinds of secondary experiences might give rise to transsexual tendencies. **1963** A. Heron *Towards Quaker View of Sex* 68 In men..the trans-sexual urge occasionally reaches the point of completely assuming the female role. **1969** *Nature* 2 Aug. 448/2 Cases of transsexual children brought up in unusually close contact with their mothers, who were the dominant members of families in which the fathers were ineffectual characters. **1970** [see *sex change* s.v. *sex *sb.* 5]. **1977** *Proc. R. Soc. Med.* LXX. 792/1 He may sustain sexual relations..by transexual fantasy.

2. Of or pertaining to both sexes. Also, intersexual.

1977 G. Melly *Rum, Bum & Concertina* viii. 105, I came into her... We made love.., but crossing the trans-sexual barrier didn't convert me overnight. I continued for some years to prefer boys. **1978** *Logophile* VIII. 8/1 The word 'clerk' *sounds* acceptably undiscriminatory and trans-sexual.

B. *sb.* A transsexual person. Also, one whose sex has been changed by surgery.

1957 *Amer. Jrnl. Psychotherapy* XI. 84 Marriage, motherhood, and a husband are a woman's life and he wants that as a fulfillment of his femininity. These persons form the group aptly termed 'transsexuals'. **1966** *New Scientist* 8 Dec. 577/1 Transsexuals..are a..group of individuals 'who have a burning and overwhelming desire to be of the sex opposite to what they are anatomically'. **1971** *Daily Tel.* (Colour Suppl.) 10 Dec. 21/3 Adult transexuals are so resistant that psychological treatment and even aversion therapy is virtually hopeless so far as they are concerned. **1976** *Washington Post* 26 Jan. A2/8 Britain's state-run health service has started a night school for transsexuals where men who have changed their sex can learn to face the world as women. **1977** *Times* 18 Aug. 6/2 Dr Renée Richards, aged 42, a transsexual who was a man until 1975.

trans,se·xualism. Also **trans-sexualism, transexualism.** [f. Trans- 3 + Sexualism.] The state or condition of being transsexual (see *transsexual *a.* 1), manifested in an overwhelming desire to belong to the opposite sex.

1953 H. Benjamin in *Internat. Jrnl. Sexology* Aug. 12/1 Transvestitism..is the desire of a certain group of men to dress as women, or of women to dress as men. It can be.. overwhelming, even to the point of wanting to belong to the other sex and correct nature's anatomical 'error'. For such cases the term Transsexualism seems appropriate. **1954** *Amer. Jrnl. Psychotherapy* VIII. 220 Transsexualism..denotes the intense and often obsessive desire to change the entire sexual status including the anatomical structure. **1963** K. Walker in G. Turtle *Over Sex Border* 11 Transexualism was only defined with any clarity in 1954. **1969** *New Scientist* 24 July 183/1 The very difficult clinical problem of trans-sexualism. **1974** *Adolescence* Spring 71 The increasing rate of transsexualism. **1977** E. J. Trimmer et al. *Visual Dict. Sex* (1978) iii. 46 It is impossible for an ordinary person to be propelled into the condition of transsexualism, as it has nothing to do with free will or voluntary choice.

So **trans,se·xualist** *sb.* and *a.* = *transsexual *sb.*, *a.* 1.

1954 *Amer. Jrnl. Psychotherapy* VIII. 220 The transsexualist is always a transvestite but not vice-versa.... The transsexualist only lives for the day when his hated sex organs can be removed. **1966** *Punch* 28 Dec. 968/1 The transexualist..told us, in a pleasant baritone, how happily married 'she' was—after surgery. **1976** Smythies & Corbett *Psychiatry* xi. 211 Transexualists believe that a 'mistake' has been made and they really wish to actually become the opposite sex. **1977** A. Sheridan tr. *Lacan's Écrits* vi. 209 A trans-sexualist practice, in no way unworthy of being compared with 'perversion'.

trans,sexua·lity. Also **trans-sexuality, transexuality.** [f. Trans- 3 + Sexuality.] = *transsexualism; *loosely*, bisexuality.

1941 O. Legman in G. W. Henry *Sex Variants* ii. 1149 *Homosexuality*..is more widely used than any other of the many terms that have been proposed, such as.. *transsexuality.* **1955** J. F. Oliven *Sexual Hygiene & Pathol.* xxi. 397 Primary transvestism. *Synonyms:* Idiopathic transvestism... Transsexuality or transsexualism. **1957** *Amer. Jrnl. Psychotherapy* XI. 85 Homosexuality, transsexuality and transvestism. **1973** J. Marks *Mick Jagger* 142 Jagger's trans-sexuality is just one of the things which makes him qualify as our great hero. **1977** *Lancet* 6 Aug. 261/1 We have investigated 60 patients treated with high doses of methyltestosterone for transsexuality or impotence.

trans-Sibe·rian, *a.* (and *sb.*) [f. Trans- 8 + Siberian *a.*] That crosses Siberia. Also *ellipt.* as *sb.*, the trans-Siberian railway or express.

1896 [in Dict. s.v. Trans- 8]. **1911** *Daily Colonist* (Victoria, B.C.) 1 Apr. 14/1 Return from or go to the Coronation via the great Trans-Siberian. **1939** C. Isherwood *Goodbye to Berlin* 278 We'd stop a few days in Warsaw... Then on to Moscow, and take the trans-Siberian. **1964** S. Bellow *Herzog* 168 She..was repatriated via the Trans-Siberian Railroad. **1974** *Times* 4 Oct. 10/7 The present Trans-Siberian runs for thousands of miles..almost flush with the Chinese frontier. **1977** *Belfast Tel.* 17 Jan. 8/4 Two days out of Moscow on its seven-day journey to Vladivostock, the Trans-Siberian express was two minutes early.

transsignification, var. *transignification. **trans-sonic,** var. *transonic *a.*

trans-speci·fic, *a.* *Biol.* Also **transpecific.** [f. Trans- 3 + Specific *a.*] Passing from one species to another.

1963 E. Mayr *Animal Species & Evolution* xix. 586 The proponents of the synthetic theory maintain that all evolution is due to the accumulation of small genetic changes,..and that transpecific evolution..is nothing but an extrapolation and magnification of the events that take place within populations and species. **1964** *Discovery* Oct. 29/2 Communication may be trans-specific. This is particularly true of alarm signals.

trans-syna·ptic, *a.* *Physiol.* Also **transynaptic.** [f. Trans- 5 + Synaptic *a.*] Involving transmission of a nerve impulse across a synapse. Hence **trans-syna·ptically** *adv.*

1954 Penfield & Jasper *Epilepsy & Functional Anat. Human Brain* v. 211 Under deep barbiturate anesthesia.., transynaptic conduction is sufficiently impaired so that spikes recorded beyond a synapse are prolonged by temporal dispersion into slower waves. *Ibid.*, Under light anesthesia..the temporal dispersion of transynaptically conducted spikes may be scarcely detectable. **1974** *Nature* 11 Jan. 112/1 These findings suggest that the rise in T-OH activity elicited by reserpine is mediated trans-synaptically through an increase in ganglionic transmission. **1977** *Proc. R. Soc. Med.* LXX. 671/2 Trans-synaptic regulation and adaptation (both orthograde and retrograde) in the brain.

transtage (trɑ·nsteɪdʒ, -nz-). *Astronaut.* [f. Trans- + Stage *sb.*] A final stage of a multistage rocket that can be restarted in order to change the flight path or orbit.

1965 *Daily Progress* (Charlottesville, Va.) 6 May 20 After one 90-minute circuit of the globe in the initial orbit, the transtage was to re-start its engines and swing into an elliptical path. **1975** *Daily Colonist* (Victoria, B.C.) 21 May 1/7 Air force officials said the 'transtage' of the Titan III-C rocket and the two 1,200-pound satellites connected to it began rolling and tumbling out of control.

Transtainer (trɑns,tēᶦ·nəɹ, -nz-). *U.S.* [f. Trans- + *Con)tainer.] A proprietary name for a mobile gantry crane.

1964 *Official Gaz.* (U.S. Patent Office) 21 July tm 115/1 Pacific Coast Engineering Company, Alameda, Calif... Transtainer. For mobile gantry cranes. First use June 15, 1960. **1969** *Jane's Freight Containers 1968–69* 51 This Transtainer has a 35 foot span and straddles two rows of containers plus a truck roadway. **1977** *Hongkong*

Standard 12 Apr. (Business Suppl.) 4/4 This includes a quay crane costing $102 million, four new transtainers valued at $33 million [etc.].

trans,thoracic, *a.* *Med.* [f. Trans- 5 + Thoracic *a.* (*sb.*).] Occurring or carried out through the wall of the thorax or across the thoracic cavity.

1905 J. F. Binnie *Manual Operative Surg.* III. xii. 429 Close the wound in the diaphragm with sutures introduced by the transthoracic route. **1965** *Dis. Chest* XLVIII. 297/1 Suction aspiration of the lung (transthoracic lung puncture). **1973** *Sci. Amer.* Feb. 11/1 (Advt.), A plug-in module monitors respiration from a set of skin electrodes that detect changes in transthoracic impedance due to respiration.

transuranic (trɑns,iuræ·nik, -nz-), *a.* *Physics.* [f. *trans- 11 + Uran(ium + -ic 1 b.] Of a chemical element: having a higher atomic number than uranium (i.e. 93 or over), the highest-numbered element to occur naturally in any but trace amounts.

1935 *Proc. R. Soc.* A. CXLIX. 553 Our hypothesis that the 13-minute and 100-minute induced activities of uranium are due to transuranic elements seems to receive further support. **1958** *Times* 29 Aug. 6/3 The..isolation of the transuranic elements. **1976** *Jrnl. R. Soc. Arts* CXXIV. 586/1 Seventy-two of the ninety-two naturally occurring elements are metals. If one includes the man-made transuranic elements the proportion remains about the same.

Also **trans,ura·nian** (*rare*), **-ura·nium** *adjs.*, in the same sense; also *fig.*

1938 R. W. Lawson tr. *Hevesy & Paneth's Man. Radioactivity* (ed. 2) xxvi. 289 'Trans-uranium' elements were first prepared by Fermi. **1946** [see *americium]. **1947** Crowther & Whiddington *Science at War* iii. 129 He [*sc.* Fermi] concluded that he had made new atoms.. and supposed that these must be 'trans-uranian' atoms. **1965** C. Brooke-Rose in J. Turner *Fourth Ghost Bk.* 181 The rumour spreads..through live material like a transuranian element decaying..into lead. **1971** *Nature* 6 Aug. 366/1 Seaborg..expressed the desire to return to California to resume his research on transuranium elements. **1978** N. Freeling *Night Lords* xxiv. 112 Night is what? A trans-uranium element, perhaps. **1979** *Monitor* (McAllen, Texas) 10 June 11-H/3 A person of almost transuranium energy.

trans,ure·thral, *a.* *Surg.* [f. Trans- 5 + Urethral *a.*] Carried out via the urethra. Hence **trans,ure·thrally** *adv.*

1933 R. Howard *Practice of Surgery* (ed. 4) xxxvi. 1266 (*heading*) Transurethral endothermy. **1934** [see *resectionist]. **1951** [see *resectoscope]. **1972** J. P. Mitchell *Princ. Transurethral Resection & Haemostasis* xxvii. 227 It is difficult to..photograph the act of resecting transurethrally. **1980** *Brit. Med. Jrnl.* 29 Mar. 937/3 A very reasoned argument in favour of transurethral resection for the majority of benign enlarged prostates.

transvalue, *v.* (Earlier example.)

1899 G. B. Shaw in *Sat. Rev.* 13 May (Suppl.) p. iii/1 Nietzsche..'transvalued' our moral valuations.

transverse, *a.* Add: **1. d. transverse alliteration,** in the early verse of some Germanic languages, alliteration of the patterns *abab* or *baab* (the usage of scholars varies somewhat); **transverse flute**: see Flute *sb.*[1] 1; (now the usual name when specification is required; see also *cross-flute* s.v. *cross B, *German flute* s.v. German *a.*[2] 4, *Querflöte 1, *traverso, etc.); **transverse Mercator,** the name of a map projection obtained like the Mercator but with the globe turned through 90 degrees relative to the cylinder, so that the great circle where they meet is a pair of meridians rather than the equator; **transverse myelitis** *Path.*, myelitis which extends across a section of the spinal cord.

1900 O. F. Emerson in *Jrnl. Eng. & Gmc. Philol.* III. 127 (*heading*) Transverse alliteration in Teutonic poetry. **1920** R. J. Menner *Purity* p. lvi, Transverse alliteration —abab—appears in 515 For I *se wel* þat hit is *sothe* þat alle mannez *wyttez*. **1942** J. C. Pope *Rhythm of Beowulf* 154 Transverse alliteration occurs once with the whole-line pattern bx/ax/ax/bx. **1949** P. F. Baum in *Mod. Philol.* XLVI. 146 The most interesting of these minor variations is the crossed or transverse alliteration *ab ab*. **1879** Grove *Dict. Mus.* I. 536/1 It is held obliquely towards the right side of the player, like the modern transverse flute. **1959, 1976** [see *Querflöte 1]. **1980** *Early Music* July 313/1 Byzantine musical culture decisively influenced much of the corpus of musical instruments, including..the organ, transverse flute and the bowed instruments. **1921** Deetz & Adams *Elem. Map Projection* 104 In latitudes above 60° where the meridional parts of a Mercator projection increase rather rapidly, charts covering considerable area may be constructed.. on..a transverse Mercator, if the locality has predominating north-and-south dimensions. **1969** [see *national grid 2]. **1974** *Encycl. Brit. Macropædia* XI. 476/1 Among the variations of cylindrical projections is the Transverse Mercator, in which the axis of the cylinder is parallel to the Equator, a treatment which has advantages in drawing maps that are long in the north-south direction. **1879** *N.Y. Med. Jrnl.* XXX. 387 (*heading*) Transverse myelitis. **1903** Tubby & Jones *Mod. Methods in Surg. Paralysis* i. 33 Transverse myelitis in adults is more likely to be confused with the rare condition of poliomyelitis. **1964** J. J. Walsh *Understanding Paraplegia* iii. 16 Approximately 30% of the patients at the National Spinal Injuries Centre develop paraplegia from causes other than injury. Of these a proportion result from infections of various kinds, and are usually grouped under the heading of 'myelitis' or 'transverse myelitis'.

transversion[1]. Restrict *rare* to sense in Dict. and add: **2.** *Logic.* (See quot. 1933.) *Obs.* or *rare.*

1890 E. E. C. Jones *Elements Logic* xix. 143 These may be called *Mixed Eductions*, or *Transversions*. *Ibid.* 148 In Transversion, the most interesting points are that all Inferentials and Alternatives may..be fully and accurately expressed in Categorical form. **1933** C. A. Mace *Princ. Logic* vii. 121 A transversion may be defined as an immediate inference from a proposition of one logical form to another proposition which contains the same 'material content' but is of a different logical form.

3. *Molecular Biol.* The occurrence in a nucleic acid of a purine in place of a pyrimidine or vice versa. Cf. *transition 4*.

1959 E. Freese in *Proc. Nat. Acad. Sci.* XLV. 631 The mutagenic effect of the second kind involves the 'transversion' of a nucleotide pair, in which a purine is replaced by a pyrimidine. **1980** *Nature* 8 May 82/2 All the point mutations are transversions in the second position of each of four codons.

Transverter (trɑnsvɜ̄·ɹtəɹ, -nz-). *Electr. Engin.* Also **transverter.** [f. Trans(former + Con)verter.] An apparatus for converting alternating current into high-voltage direct current, and vice versa. (A proprietary name in the U.S.)

1916 *Official Gaz.* (U.S. Patent Office) 16 May 1070/1 *Transverter*... Electric motors, electric generators, and electric-motor generators. **1924** *Glasgow Herald* 17 June 9 The machine..is called a transverter... It both transforms, by raising the pressure and converts into direct current. **1975** *Oxford Times* 5 Dec. 15/4 Mr Geoff Day..spoke..about a 384MHz amplifier for use with a 23cm transverter.

trans,ve·sical, *a.* *Med.* [f. Trans- 5 + Vesical *a.*] Passing or performed through the bladder.

1926 Young & Davis *Young's Practice of Urol.* I. ii. 52 It is most important to empty the bladder at the end of the test period, to determine from this transvesical urine how much, if any, phthalein has escaped outside the catheters into the bladder. **1976** *Lancet* 4 Dec. 1221/2 An uneventful transvesical prostatectomy was done.

transvestic (trɑnsve·stik, -nz-), *a.* [f. *transvestism or *transvestite *sb.* and *a.*: see -ic.] Of or pertaining to transvestism; transvestite.

1961 in Webster s.v., Patients with transvestic tendencies. **1966** *Internat. Jrnl. Psycho-Anal.* XLVII. 384 (*heading*) The mother's contribution to infantile transvestic behaviour. **1976** *National Observer* (U.S.) 16 Oct. 10/3 Its basic elements are meticulous screening, designed to exclude applicants who are primarily homosexual, transvestic or psychotic.

So **transve·sticism** (-isiz'm) (now *rare*) = *transvestism.

1937 *Times Lit. Suppl.* 27 Feb. 145/2 By his 'transvesticism'..the mother's brother identifies himself with the mother and all she stands for. **1959** *Times* 31 Oct. 8/7 A group of four from the choir are not difficult to name in spite of temporary transvesticism.

transvestism (trɑnsve·stiz'm, -nz-). [ad. G. *transvestismus*, f. L. *trans* Trans- + *vestīre* to clothe: see Transvest *v.*, -ism.] The action of dressing in the clothes of the opposite sex; the condition of having an abnormal desire to dress in the clothes of the opposite sex.

1928 [see *Eonism]. **1938** *Spectator* 2 Dec. 962/1 So unimportant is the sexual element that transvestism is common in many dance-forms [in Bali] and produces no feeling of embarrassment. **1959** *Listener* 2 July 31/2 The transvestism which is part of the witch/fairy tradition. **1977** E. J. Trimmer et al. *Visual Dict. Sex* (1978) xix. 199 The most common cases of transvestism are heterosexual men leading otherwise conventional sex lives.

Hence **transve·stist** *sb.* and *a.* = *transvestite *sb.* and *a.*

1944 'M. Innes' *Weight of Evidence* viii. 88 One of those portraits of her in page's costume. She must have been what they call a transvestist nowadays. **1959** P. Bull *I know Face* xi. 197, I played the part of Miss Eve Ashley's mother, and the gentleman dressers at Lime Grove were not unpleased by this transvestist carry-on. **1961** *Guardian* 27 Jan. 8/7, I tired of all those transvestist photographs. **1972** *Daily Tel.* 23 Mar. 8/1 He was a clothes fetishist and eventually a transvestist.

transvestite (trɑnsve·stəit, -nz-), *sb.* and *a.* [ad. G. *transvestit*, f. L. *trans* Trans- + *vestīre* to clothe: see -ite[1].]

A. *sb.* A person with an abnormal desire to wear the clothes of the opposite sex.

[**1910** M. Hirschfeld (*title*) Die Transvestiten.] **1922** J. van Teslaar tr. *Stekel's Bi-sexual Love* ii. 69 Among the transvestites (personifiers) we find the most pronounced examples of marked homosexuality and stressed bi-sexuality. **1937** *Human Biol.* IX. 501 The transvestite must attempt to duplicate the behavior-pattern of his adopted sex. **1964** in W. H. Goodenough *Explorations Cultural Anthropol.* 490 The *bate*, male transvestites,.. excelled women in butchering, tanning, and other domestic tasks. **1976** Smythies & Corbett *Psychiatry* xi. 211 Transvestites wear the clothing of the opposite sex to obtain sexual gratification.

B. *adj.* Of or pertaining to transvestism or transvestites; of a person: who wears the clothes of the opposite sex.

1925 A. L. Kroeber *Handbk. Indians California* xxxiii. 497 The transvestite sexual perverts recognized by all North American tribes. **1937** *Human Biol.* IX. 501 An almost senile singer, said to be the last person to know the transvestite initiation songs. **1957** *Observer* 29 Dec. 9/1 According to scholarship, the principal boy in our transvestite pantomimes is a Saturnalian hangover. **1971** *Times* 16 Sept. 12/6 He moves as a suburban schoolmaster between the male aggression of his classroom and the frou-frou of his transvestite boudoir.

transvestitism (trɑnsve·stitiz'm, -nz-). [ad. G. *transvestitismus*, f. *transvestit*: see prec., -ism.] = *transvestism.

[**1913** M. Hirschfeld in *Neurol. Zentralblatt* XXXII. 946 (*heading*) Ein Fall von Transvestitismus bei musikalischem Genie.] **1934** in Webster. **1949** [see *Mohave]. **1976** *Jrnl. Amer. Psychoanal. Assoc.* XXIV. iii. 545 The analysis of a patient with the presenting symptom of transvestitism revealed a prominent set of fantasies of being 'initiated' and taught by a seductive and glamorous woman..in the art of dressing and make-up. **1983** *Financial Times* 4 Oct. 13 If there is a true sub-text to this farcical evening, devoted to voluntary or involuntary transvestitism, it is the satirical reference to psychiatrists' belief that simple things are all the consequence of serious, probably sexual, stimuli.

So **transvesti·tic** *a.* = *transvestite *a.*; **transve·stitist** *rare* = *transvestite *sb.*

1936 A. Huxley *Eyeless in Gaza* xviii. 233 Beppo giggled. 'Yes, those transvestitists!' he had to admit rapturously. **1977** *Gay News* 24 Mar. 13/1 Thus hetero-sexual, homosexual..transvestitic, and dozens of other special relationships hold the potential of working well. **1980** *Jrnl. Sex & Marital Therapy* Summer 124 Individuals rarely seek treatment for..transvestitic problems.

trans-wo·rld, *a.* [f. Trans- 3 + World *sb.*] That travels across the world; world-wide.

1955 R. J. Schwartz *Compl. Dict. Abbrev.* 178/2 *TWA*,..Trans World Airlines, Inc. **1959** I. & P. Opie *Lore & Lang. Schoolch.* i. 7 It seems that the schoolchild underground also employs trans-world couriers. **1962** *B.B.C. Handbk.* 50 The BBC Television Service is now looking forward to..transatlantic and even to trans-world television broadcasting.

Transylvanian (tran,silvē[i]·niăn), *sb.* and *a.* [f. *Transylvania* (see below) + -an.] **A.** *sb.* A native or inhabitant of Transylvania, formerly the eastern portion of Austria-Hungary, now part of Romania.

1644 Milton *Areopagitica* 30 Nor is it for nothing that the grave and frugal Transilvanian sends out yearly.. their stay'd men, to learn our language and our *theologic* arts. **1757** A. Butler *Lives Saints* III. 867/1 The vizir with one hundred and fifty thousand Turks (besides Hungarians, Transylvanians and Tartars) sat down before Vienna. **1927** [see *cartel *sb.* 3 d]. **1976** P. Henissart *Winter Quarry* xvi. 157 The only smart people in this country [*sc.* Hungary] are the Jews and the Transylvanians.

B. *adj.* Of or pertaining to Transylvania; *spec.* applied to a kind of deep red Turkish rug or carpet frequently found in Transylvanian churches.

1843 *Penny Cycl.* XXV. 165/1 The German universities are frequented by a considerable number of Transylvanian students, especially for divinity. **1875** *Encycl. Brit.* III. 116/1 The Transylvanian Highlands extend over Transylvania..into Moldavia and Wallachia. **1915** *Guide to Collection of Carpets* (Victoria & Albert Museum) ii. 45 It seems probable that these 'Transylvanian' carpets were made in Anatolia. **1929** E. G. Metcalfe *Metcalfe Coll. Oriental Rugs* vii. 31 This is an excellent specimen of the finest Transylvanian prayer rugs. **1957** *Encycl. Brit.* XIX. 624/1 (*caption*) So-called 'Transylvanian' rug, Asia Minor, 17th century. **1978** R. Westall *Devil on Road* x. 64 The [dog's] collar..had as many studs as a Transylvanian torture-implement.

transynaptic, var. *trans-synaptic *a.*

tranylcypromine (trɑ:nəil,səi·prŏmīn). *Pharm.* [f. *trans*-2-phen*ylcyclopropylamine*, the systematic name, f. *trans- 9 a + Phenyl + *cyclo- 2 + Propyl + Amine.] A monoamine oxidase inhibitor, $C_9H_{11}N$, used in the treatment of severe depression (usu. in the form of the sulphate).

1959 *Proc. Soc. Exper. Biol. & Med.* CII. 380 (*heading*) Some pharmacological observations on tranylcypromine (SKF *trans*-385). **1964, 1965** [see *Parnate]. **1976** *Lancet* 27 Nov. 1164/1 Six patients with neurogenic orthostatic hypotension were treated with a chemical preparation of tyramine and tranylcypromine.

trap, *sb.*[1] Add: **1. d.** A device which allows a pigeon to enter but not to escape from a pigeon loft.

1876 R. Fulton *Illustr. Bk. Pigeons* 274 Let the board, upon which the birds alight (when the trap is closed and admission only to be obtained through the bolting wires) be carried upon a pair of hinges. **1912** W. E. Barker *Pigeon Racing* i. 5 Others..swear by a steeply sloping roof..to compel the birds to drop upon a trap or alighting board. **1961** H. Blunt *Tackle Pigeon Racing this Way* iii. 30 The trap can be made of stout galvanized wire,..curved to facilitate use by the birds without injury.

2. a. (Earlier and later examples in *Theatr.* use.)
1800 in S. Rosenfeld *Temples of Thespis* (1978) x. 149 Theatre traps and cutting out bricks. **1977** S. Brett *Star Trap* xiii. 142 The stage..had been equipped with the full complement of trap doors... Downstage were the corner traps, small openings used for the appearance or disappearance of one actor... Then there was the Grave Trap centre stage..always used for the Gravediggers' scene in Hamlet.

b. The mouth, esp. in phrr.: *shut your trap!* be quiet!; *to keep one's trap shut*, to remain silent. *slang.*
1776 E. Gibbon *Let.* 19 Dec. (1896) I. 298 You may say in general in the family (if any should bark) that you are satisfied with my conduct, and order them to shut their trap. [**1785, 1860**: see *potato-trap* s.v. Potato *sb.* 7.] **1866** J. T. Staton *Rays fro' Loominary* 90 Shut thy trap, fayther. **1899** *Star of Hope* 12 Aug. 1/1 Why in h— don't those recruits..keep their traps shut? **1939** A. Huxley *After Many a Summer* II. i. 187 If only the rest were silence! But that's the trouble with poets... They will not keep their traps shut, as we say in the Western hemisphere. **1959** J. Braine *Vodi* xxiv. 255 'Shut your bloody trap,' Dick said. **1981** M. Duffy *Gor Saga* II. 48 If Emily should open her great trap and spill the lot she could find herself deep in trouble.

4. b. In greyhound-racing, the compartment from which a dog is released at the start of a race.
1928 A. R. D. Cardew *Greyhound Racing* 13 The owner ..is invited..to attend the draw for trap places 1 to 6, No 1 being the inside trap. *Ibid.* 18 (*caption*) Leaving the starting trap. **1954** R. Dahl *Someone like You* 251 The traps went up and the dogs flew out. **1977** *Listener* 30 June 847/3 The dogs barked in their traps. Then the hare was running..and the dogs were out.

5. *to be up to trap* (U.S. examples).
1837 W. Irving *Capt. Bonneville* II. i. 15 The beaver now being completely 'up to trap', approaches them cautiously. **1877** J. Habberton *Jericho Road* xix. 170 You needn't come any of your..moral tricks on me. I'm up to trap.

6. (Further Austral. and S. Afr. examples.) Now only *Austral. slang.*
1812 J. H. Vaux *Vocab. Flash Lang.* in *Mem.* (1964) 275 *Traps*, police officers, or runners, are properly so called; but it is common to include constables of any description under this title. **1882** T. Sheffield *Story of Settlement* 85 Amusing tales are told of how the excisemen or 'traps' sent to try to obtain evidence of illicit dealing were hoodwinked. **1935** L. Mann *Human Drift* xxviii. 185 Suddenly there came a cry 'The traps, look out, the — traps. The Joes, Joes.' He turned and saw a cordon of mounted and foot-police endeavouring to surround the crowd which scattered away from them. **1945** [see *Demon[2] 1]. **1970** *Sunday Mail Mag.* (Brisbane) 18 Jan. 14/6 After the arrests Derrincourt and Wilson were kept apart. Little did the former know that the latter was telling the traps how William Derrincourt had engineered the whole business.

8. c. *Geol.* An underground rock formation in which an accumulation of oil or gas is trapped; so *oil trap.*
1920 *Econ. Geol.* XV. 249 Trap structures contain the majority of the important accumulations of oil. **1938** D. Hager *Pract. Oil Geol.* (ed. 5) iii. 56 Areas of heavily metamorphosed rocks are unfavorable for gas and oil accumulations, unless the oil has migrated to traps in such rocks. **1946** *Nature* 28 Dec. 931/2 In considering the distribution of structures which might act as oil-traps, the field of inquiry may be limited to those geological formations which provide some indication of the presence of oil. **1969** Bennison & Wright *Geol. Hist. Brit. Isles* xii. 282 Salt-dome structures..commonly give rise to oil traps, salt being capped by gypsum. **1977** *Offshore Engineer* May 38/1 Seismic evidence suggests thick deeply buried deposits onlapping old ridges which may form hydrocarbon traps.

d. *Radio.* A resonant circuit used as a rejector or acceptor circuit to block or divert signals of a specific frequency, esp. to reduce interference in a receiver tuned to a nearby frequency; = *wave trap* s.v. *Wave *sb.* 10.
1927 B. F. Dashiell *Pop. Guide to Radio* xii. 236 A properly designed trap should not affect the tuning of the set to any great degree. **1957** *Practical Wireless* XXXIII. 570/1 Should there be any I.F. break-through traps, they should be done [*sc.* aligned] next. **1974** Harvey & Bohlman *Stereo F.M. Radio Handbk.* v. 113 The low-pass filter is followed by a 38 kHz trap..to remove any residual 38 kHz component.

9. d. *Golf.* = *Sand-trap 2. Cf. Bunker 4 a in Dict. and Suppl. Chiefly *U.S.*
1890 H. G. Hutchinson *Golf* xiii. 313 That little round trap of a Strath's bunker not three yards nearer you. **1903** J. L. Low *Concerning Golf* ix. 173 Bunkers..refuse to be disregarded, and insist on asserting themselves... That little bunker on the seventeenth green at St. Andrews..that 'trap' bunker at the third green at North Berwick. **1933** F. Ouimet *Game of Golf* xvi. 236 Billy waded into the sand and blasted his ball out of the trap. **1952** B. Cerf *Good for Laugh* 173 How many shots did you have in that trap? **1971** 'D. Halliday' *Dolly & Doctor Bird* xv. 215 Wallace Brady..landed in the long, pale trap in front of the green and stayed there doing explosive shots with a sand-wedge.

10*. *Physics.* A site in a crystal lattice which is capable of temporarily immobilizing a moving electron or hole.
1945 *Proc. R. Soc.* A. CLXXXIV. 366 Thermoluminescence and long-period phosphorescence arise from the release of electrons from metastable levels or traps. **1971** *Physics Bull.* Oct. 579/1 Laboratory studies use UV, X ray or corpuscular..excitation to fill the traps, which are then emptied on heating. **1980** *Cambr. Encycl. Archaeol.* 426/2 In the structure of the crystal lattice of most minerals there are defects or imperfections known as traps.

11. trap-bat (earlier example); **trap boat** *N. Amer.*, a boat used for fishing with trap-nets; **trap-drum, drummer**: see *Trap *sb.*[7] 3; **trap-gun**, (*a*) (see quot. 1964); (*b*) a shotgun used in trap-shooting; **trap-house**, a shelter from which clay pigeons are released for trap-shooting; **trap-line**, (*b*) *N. Amer.*, a series of hunter's traps; **trap-nest** orig. *U.S.*, a nesting-box which a hen can enter but cannot leave until released; also as *v. trans.*; hence **trap-nesting** *vbl. sb.*; **trap-net** (earlier example); **trap-point** (earlier example); **trapshoot** *N. Amer.*, a trap-shooting contest or event; **trap-shy** *a.*, of an animal: reluctant to approach a trap; hence **trap-shyness; trap skiff** *N. Amer.* = *trap boat* above; **trap-yard**, an enclosure into which animals such as horses, sheep, etc. are driven and confined.
1842 Dickens *Let.* 15 July (1974) III. 271 [I play] some most riotous game at trap-bat and ball in the Garden with the children. **1894** *Rudder* Aug.–Sept. 201/1 She was invited to sail over a course with a fleet of Richibucto's famous trap boats. **1974** F. Mowat *Boat who wouldn't Float* iv. 38, I was to join the four-man crew of a trap boat. She was a big, broad-beamed skiff powered by a five-horsepower, 'jump-spark' single-cylinder engine. **1801** J. Barrow *Travels Interior S. Afr.* I. vi. 360 A *stell-roar* or trap-gun, set by a Hottentot. **1947** J. Stevenson-Hamilton *Wild Life S. Afr.* xxxv. 307 Crocodiles are sometimes shot by trap guns. **1964** H. L. Peterson *Encycl. Firearms* 323/1 *Trap gun, trip gun.* 'Trap' as here used, has nothing to do with the sport of trapshooting; it refers to devices designed to shoot automatically at men or animals that come into the line of fire. Many of these trap guns are set off by the tripping of a wire or cord. **1976** *Shooting Times & Country Mag.* 16–22 Dec. 47/2 (Advt.), Nikko 5,000-II o/u trapgun. **1980** *Outdoor Life* (U.S.) (Northeast ed.) Oct. 90/2 None of the major arms makers offered specialized trap guns in 16-gauge, but ammo makers did make a special $2\frac{3}{4}$-dram-equivalent $1\frac{1}{8}$oz. 16-gauge load for trap shooting. **1942** *Tee Emm* (Air Ministry) II. 75 We hear that 50 yards is not the best distance between the two traphouses, if the 'Plus' trap is being used. **1979** G. Hammond *Dead Game* xvi. 206 The local club have put up a tower for high birds [*sc.* clay pigeons]..and built some trap-houses. **1926** *Daily Colonist* (Victoria, B.C.) 7 July 3/5 The disappearance of Charles Olson from his trap line on the headwaters of the Parsnip River in Northern British Columbia remains as much a mystery as when it was first reported. **1954** W. Faulkner *Fable* 82 He had no more doubt of where he was than would the old wolf or lynx when he was near a trap-line. **1970** *Islander* (Victoria, B.C.) 10 May 6/1 The men were absent on the trapline and only the women and children were home. **1901** G. M. Cowell in *Rep. Marine Agric. Exper. Station 1900* XVI. 97 It was a prime necessity to ascertain the exact record of the eggs produced by each individual. This led to devising the trap nest. **1908** *Ann. Rep. N.Y. Agric. Exper. Station, Ithaca, 1907* 261 For the poultry-man..who..will trap-nest conscientiously..we think there is a large reward. **1910** W. W. Broomhead *Poultry & Profit* iii. 33, I asked Mr. Tapley if he had his fowls trap-nested. **1960** *Farmer & Stockbreeder* 29 Mar. (Suppl.) 3/1 Three hundred pullets are trapnested ..each year. **1973** *Animal Behaviour* XXI. 98/1 When given access to trapnests the domestic hen has a characteristic behaviour associated with oviposition. **1906** *Reliable Poultry Jrnl.* XIII. 353/1, I read an editorial dealing with this problem of trap-nesting. **1956** Wilson & Card *Farm Poultry Production* iii. 60 The best way to get complete records is by trap nesting. **1865** Trap net [see *pound net* s.v. *Pound *sb.*[2] 6]. **1885** E. B. Ivatts *Railway Managem. at Stations* 555 It is common to speak of a *catch siding* and *catch points*, of a *trap siding* and *trap points*. **1926** *Daily Colonist* (Victoria, B.C.) 17 July 12/2 Big Trapshoot at Colwood on Sunday. One of the biggest shoots of years is to be held tomorrow. **1976** *Billings* (Montana) *Gaz.* 18 June 4-D/1 (*heading*) Trapshoot set at Huntley. **1922** *Contemp. Rev.* July 90 After a time the rat grows poison-shy and trap-shy. **1947** *New Biol.* II. 19 A population which is thus immune to trapping is sometimes called 'trap-shy'. We do not know what trap-shyness is in terms of rat behaviour, but it is a very real phenomenon. **1968** K. Weatherly *Roo Shooter* 39 The rabbits had become trap-shy. **1934** *Geogr. Jrnl.* LXXXIV. 44 There were some trap-skiffs jigging for cod on the shoal. **1969** Trap skiff [see *Jack *sb.*[1] 25]. **1906** *Chambers's Jrnl.* 12 May 380/1 There are..two means of capturing these horses... The first is to build a strong trapyard on their line of retreat, and endeavour to run them into it. **1936** Trap yard [see *Crush *sb.* 4 c].

trap, *sb.*[5] **b.** Add: *trap-dike* (earlier example).
1839 [see *Intrusion 1 b].

trap, *sb.*[7] Add: **2. a.** (See *Traps *sb. pl.* 2.)

b. *Comb.* **trap-drum**, (*a*) a drum forming part of a set of traps (*Traps *sb. pl.* 2) as opposed to a drum used in an orchestra or military band; (*b*) *pl.* = *Traps *sb. pl.* 2; hence **trap-drummer**, a musician who plays the trap-drums.
1924 see *Plastered *ppl. a.* 2]. **1929** T. Wolfe *Look Homeward, Angel* xiv. 180 Mr. Buckner..officiating at the trap drum and tambourine. **1959** W. F. Nolan *Dark Encounter* in H. Q. Masur *Murder Most Foul* (1973) 125 The sharp, sweet cry of horns could be heard above the rolling trap drums. **1978** *West Africa* 16 Oct. 2042/2 Trap-drums, double-bass, guitar. **1903** *Med. Rec.* (N.Y.) 14 Feb. 268/1 Trap-drummer's neurosis: a hitherto undescribed occupation-disease... The man's occupation was to beat a drum by the operation of a pedal which is manipulated with the right foot, while with his hands he plays the other drums, triangle, and the various traps. **1926** H. V. Morton *Nights of London* 168 We entered [the night club]. A trap drummer crouched over his instruments. **1977** *New Yorker* 20 June 93/1 When its complete personnel finally arrived onstage, the Ensemble consisted of two trap drummers.., a reedman who doubled on percussion.., a conga drummer.., a bassist.., and a singing pianist.

trap, *v.*[1] Add: **1. b.** (Later examples with inanimate obj.)
1936 *Discovery* Nov. 349/1 Its dust-particle content is.. trapped in the volume of liquid. **1952** E. R. Janes *Flower Garden* 49 Cloches were used in conjunction with hotbeds, but their efficacy for forwarding purposes depended chiefly upon their ability to trap solar heat. **1970** L. Deighton *Bomber* xxiii. 342 This cold still air trapped smoke from the furnaces and factories and held it like a grey woollen blanket.

2. (Earlier and later examples.)
1831 J. O. Pattie *Personal Narr.* 142 We set 40 traps, and..caught 36 beavers... We concluded..to travel slowly, and in hunters phrase, trap the river clear; that is, take all that could be allured to come to the bait. **1940** *Sun* (Baltimore) 2 Feb. 14/7 We plan to trap only a small part of our marshes. **1969** I. Kemp *Brit. G.I. in Vietnam* v. 105, I would usually go flat on the ground in case the door was trapped with a grenade or claymore mine.

4*. a. *Baseball.* (*a*) To catch (the ball) just after it has hit the ground; (*b*) to hem (a runner) between two fielders.
1892 *Chicago Herald* 16 May 2 Meehan trapped grounders by wholesale. **1912** C. Mathewson *Pitching in a Pinch* viii. 181 A Boston batter tapped one to Merkle which I thought he trapped, but Johnstone, the umpire, said he caught it on a fly. **1939** D. E. Jessee *Baseball* iv. 41 The second baseman will have many opportunities to participate in 'run-down' plays in which a base runner has been 'trapped' between first and second or second and third. **1959** E. Allen *Baseball Play & Strategy* v. 105 As a general rule all fly balls are caught... When a runner retreats toward a base with less than two outs, some fly balls may be purposely trapped and two players retired. **1967** R. Merkle *Concentrated Baseball* 105 On a rundown play between second and third, the trapped runner should be allowed to advance about half the distance toward third base.

b. *Cricket.* To cause (a batsman) to be dismissed leg before wicket.
1919 *Times* 4 July 8/6 The wicket..was nothing like so difficult as made out when once..you had gauged the bowler's spin without being trapped by Trumble's straight one. **1969** *Wisden's Cricketers' Almanack* 679 The use of pads instead of the bat was prevalent with six batsmen trapped leg before in the first innings. **1977** *Sunday Times* 27 Feb. 28/6 Lever broke through in his third over when Sri Lanka batted, trapping Fernando lbw at 16.

c. *Assoc. Football.* To receive and control (the ball), esp. between the foot and the ground.
1950 N. Cardus *Second Innings* 146 When it [*sc.* the football] was passed to him and it fell at his feet he would 'trap' it and lever it to an inch of where he wanted it. **1976** *Times* 2 Dec. 12/1 The ball was cleared from the United penalty area, Dobson trapped it with his left thigh, and hit it with his right foot, and the ball bounced just in front of Stepney and into the net.

trap-door. Add: **c*.** *Computers.* A method of surreptitiously gaining unauthorized access to data belonging to other users of a computer.
[**1976** D. B. Parker *Crime by Computer* xii. 112 The Trojan horse had been rolled into the fortified city and fully accepted. In the unsuspecting environment a trap-door in its belly opened, and out popped the soldiers.] **1977** *New Yorker* 29 Aug. 61/1 The nature of a trapdoor is that, while it is known to and usable by a penetrator, it is unrecognized by and unknown to other users of the system —even to the audit-trail mechanism. **1981** *Courier-Mail* (Brisbane) 27 July 5/5 'Trapdoors' allow people sharing a computer to slip into the confidential data streams of other users. **1982** S. F. X. Dean *Such Pretty Toys* xiv. 191 He just entered the girl's name into the computer..as some sort of routing key or trapdoor to cut off any trace.

c.** *Cryptography.* A piece of secret information that makes it easy to solve an otherwise very difficult code. Freq. *attrib.*
1978 *Communications Assoc. Computing Machinery* XXI. 128 They are called 'trap-door' functions since the inverse functions are in fact easy to compute once certain private 'trap-door' information is known. **1982** Beker & Piper *Cipher Syst.* 376 The general name given to this type of function (i.e. for which there does not appear to be a polynomial time algorithm but for which there is one so long as the method of application is known) is a trapdoor function. In our situation it is intended that the genuine receiver should be the only person who knows how to 'open' the trapdoor. **1984** *IEEE Trans. Information Theory* XXX. 595/1 It is this presence of trapdoors that makes some of the attacks on the additive knapsack cryptosystems feasible.

trapes, traipse, *v.* Add: (The usual spelling now is *traipse.*) **1. a.** Also in gen. use, to tramp or trudge, to go about.

1926 A. HUXLEY *Let.* 4 Mar. (1969) 268, I don't want to spend unnecessarily on traipsing round the continent. **1968** V. S. PRITCHETT *Cab at Door* xii. 238, I traipsed for a year from one paint shop to the next round Paris, selling glue, shellac and, for a hungry period, ostrich feathers and theatre tickets. **1976** *National Observer* (U.S.) 9 Oct. 5/4, I spent one day traipsing after Thomson, but his limousine disappeared at very high speed over a hill and by the time my rented sedan got to the other side he had disappeared. **1978** R. V. JONES *Most Secret War* xix. 159 For days we had to traipse for water down six flights of stairs and hundreds of yards to a stand pipe in the road.

2. c. Causatively: to carry or take about in a trailing way.

1814 H. CAPEL *Let.* July (1955) 53 St. Francis, the tutelary Saint of Brussels who had been previously trapsed round the town with the most astonishing pomp & splendour. *a* **1974** R. CROSSMAN *Diaries* (1976) II. 399 Suddenly I saw a picture of the tiny little woman looking upwards and seeing the soles of the feet of the statues above her as she was traipsed miles and miles around on the red carpet.

trapeze. Add: **1. b.** *Sailing.* (See quot. 1961.)

1961 F. H. BURGESS *Dict. Sailing* 211 *Trapeze*, in sailing dinghies, a sliding support used by the crew for outboard balancing when they lay up to windward. **1969** *Daily Tel.* 25 Oct. 7/7 The work covers the origins of the trapeze (a means of crew support to help in holding a light dinghy level in a breeze). **1977** *Modern Boating* (Austral.) Jan. 43/3 Try looking at the race with your head upside down sometime when you are..flat out on the trapeze.

2. b. (See quot. 1968); = *trapeze-line*, sense 3 below.

1958 *Spectator* 13 June 761/2 Miss Lee is the only lady member to have adopted the new short skirt..and none of them has so far ventured upon the trapeze. **1968** J. IRONSIDE *Fashion Alphabet* 30 The trapeze was a wide, stiff full-skirted tent shape stopping at the knees and moulding the figure to a high bust in front while falling free from the shoulders at the back. Trapeze was short for trapezium..but somehow a circus trapeze seemed to describe it more visually and the fashion magazines showed dresses on, under or in front of them.

3. *Comb.*, as **trapeze artist**, one who performs acrobatics on a trapeze; **trapeze harness** *Sailing* (see quot. 1981); **trapeze-line** [*LINE *sb.*² 14 b], a fashion style in which the outline of the garment resembles that of a trapezium (cf. sense 2 b above).

1938 *Amer. Mag.* CXXV. 90 Mother Millette started as a trapeze artist. **1981** W. STRATHERN *Don't look for Me—I'm Dead* iii. 52 The lean and sinewy strength of a trapeze artist. **1946** *Yachts & Yachting* 20 Aug. 383/2 (Advt.), All G.R.P., well equipped boat Needlespar, trolley, cover, certificate, lifting rudder, trapeze harness, ready to race. **1981** B. WEBB *Schult's Sailing Dict.* 297/2 *Trapeze*, gear fitted to fast racing dinghies and some keelboats to enable the crew to put all his weight outboard to windward. The crew wears a trapeze harness or belt with a hook, which he slips into a ring on the lower end of the trapeze wire. **1958** *Vogue* Mar. 119 His [*sc.* Yves St Laurent's] wedge-shaped silhouette—called..the Trapeze Line—is flared from narrow shoulders to a smooth wide hemline. **1975** 'M. FONTEYN' *Autobiogr.* II. iv. 173 A 'sack' dress,..a development of Christian Dior's 'Trapeze' line which had been..worn by so many wrong-shaped ladies.

trapezist. (Earlier example.)

1875 T. FROST *Circus Life* x. 179 The first female trapezist appeared.

trapezium. Add: **1. c.** (This sense is the one that is standard in the U.S., but in practice *quadrilateral* is used rather than *trapezium.*) (Further examples.)

1901 T. F. HOLGATE *Elem. Geom.* i. 74 If only two sides of a quadrilateral are parallel, the figure is called a trapezoid. If no two sides of a quadrilateral are parallel, the figure is called a trapezium. **1959** G. & R. C. JAMES *Math. Dict.* 400/2 *Trapezium*, a quadrilateral, none of whose sides are parallel.

trapezoid, *sb.* Add: **1. b.** For ? *Obs.* read 'Now *U.S.*' (Further examples.)

1901 [see *TRAPEZIUM 1 c]. **1925** F. E. SEYMOUR *Plane Geom.* II. 103 If the non-parallel sides of a trapezoid are equal, the trapezoid is called an isosceles trapezoid. **1972** *Whitaker's Almanack 1973* 902/2 Flag [of Kuwait].—Three horizontal stripes of green, white and red, with black trapezoid next to staff. **1975** *Sci. Amer.* Jan. 110/3 The matrix is stretched to a trapezoid, then the artist copies the picture by filling in the trapezoidal cells. **1977** *Monitor* (McAllen, Texas) 6 Jan. E-2/4 The Incas apparently adopted many things from the Mollos, of which the trapezoid is only one.

trapezoidal, *a.* Add: **a.** (Further examples.) The sense 'trapeziform' is standard in the U.S.

1955 *Sci. Amer.* Mar. 101/2 The temple has a trapezoidal central pyramid. **1973** *Nature* 21 Sept. 160/1 Trace brightness was modulated by a periodic trapezoidal waveform.

Trapezuntine (træpĭzu·ntəin), *sb.* and *a.* [f. L. *Trapezunt-, Trapezus*, Gr. τραπεζόντ-, τραπεζοῦς Trebizond + -INE¹.] **A.** *sb.* A native or inhabitant of the city of Trebizond or Trabzon in north-eastern Turkey.

1900 'ODYSSEUS' *Turkey in Europe* vi. 269 After the conquest of Trebizond in 1461, many noble families migrated from that town to Constantinople, and naturally aspired to the Patriarchate..thus producing another element of discord among the unhappy Greeks, who were now rent by the factions of Trapezuntines and Constantinopolitans. **1956** R. MACAULAY *Towers of Trebizond* viii. 79 We went out to explore, and the first thing we saw in the street was the B.B.C. van taking records, and round it stood a crowd of Trapezuntines staring.

B. *adj.* Of or pertaining to Trebizond, its natives, or inhabitants.

1926 W. MILLER *Trebizond* i. 11 A conspicuous landmark of Trapezuntine history. **1969** A. C. BANDY in *Ibid.* (new ed.) p. ix, The Trapezuntine Empire..continues to interest scholars and students of Greek civilization. **1980** *Times Lit. Suppl.* 4 July 763/5 Trapezuntine princesses married into the Byzantine imperial house and into other Orthodox ruling families.

trapped, *ppl. a.*¹ **2.** (Earlier example.)

1872 F. ROGERS *Specifications Pract. Archit.* II. ii. 106 To put to the water-closet in the basement-story a strong cast-iron trapped basin.

Trappist, *sb.*¹ (*a.*) **1. b.** (Earlier examples.)

1836 [in Dict., sense 1 a]. **1837** J. BINNS *Miseries & Beauties of Ireland* II. xiii. 298 The superintendant of the Trappist Settlement at Mount Melleray.

Trappistine. 1. For '*attrib.*' read '*attrib.* and as *adj.*' and add earlier example.

1869 P. G. HAMERTON *Wenderholme* III. xi. 96 He observed a Trappistine silence during the repast.

2. (Examples.)

1877 E. S. DALLAS *Kettner's Bk. of Table* 279 Trappistine, distilled by the good fathers of the Grace of God in the Doubs. **1920** G. SAINTSBURY *Notes on Cellar-Book* ix. 138 Benedictine; Trappistine; a certain 'Père Kermann' ..and others will occur.

trappy, *a.*¹ (Earlier example.)

1882 *Daily Tel.* 13 Nov. 2/5 The fences might have been increased in size, however, without being made 'trappy'.

traps, *sb. pl.* Add: **2.** *colloq.* (orig. *U.S.*). In a jazz or dance band, percussion instruments or devices (e.g. wood-blocks, whistles) used to produce a variety of special effects; these together with the standard jazz or dance band drum-kit. Cf. *trap-drum* s.v. *TRAP *sb.*⁷ 2 b.

1903 [see *trap-drummer* s.v. *TRAP *sb.*⁷ 3]. **1925** F. SCOTT FITZGERALD *Great Gatsby* iii. 56 A great number of single girls dancing individualistically or relieving the orchestra for a moment of the burden of the banjo or the traps. **1938** *Oxf. Compan. Music* 948/2 *Traps*,.. The origin of the word may be from the nineteenth-century colloquial 'traps' meaning baggage of which the individual in question [*sc.* the trap-drummer] has necessarily a good deal. **1947** J. STEINBECK *Wayward Bus* xvii. 278 It's a rubber drum that you beat with a sponge. It's for the drunks that want to play traps in the orchestra. **1967** *Crescendo* May 26/2 When one packed up after a gig, one simply stuffed the snare drum, stand, pedal and traps—all the bits and pieces were known as 'traps' in those days—inside the open side of the B.D. [*sc.* bass drum]. **1982** B. FANTONI *Stickman* ii. 19 Dance-band drummers, beats me why dames go goofy on them. I played the traps a little myself once.

trapunto (trăpu·nto). Also **Trapunto.** [a. It., = quilting.] A kind of quilting in which the design alone is padded (see quot. 1967).

1929 *Sewing for Profit* (Woman's Inst. Domestic Arts & Sci., U.S.) 73 Besides the usual kind of quilting..there is the trapunto, or Italian, quilting. **1936** *Home Arts Needlecraft* Jan. 5 (*heading*) Quilting in the Trapunto manner. **1967** E. SHORT *Embroidery & Fabric Collage* ii. 47 In the case of Trapunto, areas of the design are padded where required by splitting the backing and inserting wadding, after which the backing is sewn up again. **1972** *N.Y. Times* 3 Nov. 7/2 (Advt.), Leather-look..coat..with trapunto embroidery. **1979** *Guardian* 25 Apr. 11/8 The needlework designs..used in the country from which the garment hails: embroidery, applique, quilting, trapunto, smocking.

‖ **trascinando** (traʃinæ·ndo). *Mus.* [It., pres. pple. of *trascinare* (see next).] (See quots.); = RALLENTANDO.

1876 STAINER & BARRETT *Dict. Mus. Terms* 438/2 *Trascinando* (*It.*), dragging, delaying the time. **1947** E. BLOM *Everyman's Dict. Music* 632/2 *Trascinando* (It.), dragging. **1983** *New Oxf. Compan. Music* 1842/1 *Trascinando* (It.), 'dragging', i.e. holding back, *rallentando*.

trascine (trasī·n), *v. nonce-wd.* [ad. It. *trascinare* to drag, pull.] *trans.* To carry, to drag.

1922 JOYCE *Ulysses* 48 She trudges,..drags, trascines her load.

‖ **trasformismo** (trazfǭrmi·zmo). Also **Trasformismo.** [It.; cf. TRANSFORMISM.] In Italy, a system of shifting political alliances, or of changes of allegiance, to form a stable administration or a workable policy. Cf. OPPORTUNISM.

1925 A. SOLMI *Making of Mod. Italy* vii. 144 The parliamentary phenomena..called *trasformismo*. **1943** C. J. S. SPRIGGE *Devel. Mod. Italy* ii. 57 A struggle between *Trasformismo* and groups which endeavoured to gain power in the name of definite principles. **1957** M. CARLYLE *Mod. Italy* ii. 55 Depretis..with his policy of shuffling and reshuffling of cabinets (*trasformismo*) created the dictatorship of the Cabinet. **1964** *Economist* 27 June 1462/2 This change of heart looked like the wildest sort of *trasformismo*. **1973** P. A. ALLUM *Politics & Society in Post-War Naples* iv. 116 The Piedimonte cobbler was able to fit fascism into his life experience, the classic *trasformismo* of southern boss politics. Before the March on Rome, everyone was socialist, afterwards, they were all fascists.

trash, *sb.*¹ Add: **1. a.** *spec.* in the U.S., domestic refuse, garbage.

1906 H. DE B. PARSONS *Disposal of Municipal Refuse* iii. 21 Rubbish is discarded trash, composed principally of all kinds of paper, wood, rags, mattresses, bedding, boxes, ..tin cans,..bottles,..and the like. **1925** *Amer. City* Jan. 54/2 The collection of garbage and trash may be made by the city with its own organization. **1931** W. G. MCADOO *Crowded Years* i. 12 The abandoned..building... Its steps were littered with trash, and many..windows were broken. **1962** A. LURIE *Love & Friendship* vii. 127 Mother used to get up at five in the morning..to sweep the front porch and carry the trash out. **1977** *New Yorker* 24 Oct. 128/3 Truckloads of trash were taken to the prison dump.

4. (Later examples applied to individuals.) *white trash* (earlier and later examples); now also used outside the Southern States of America and in *attrib.* use. Cf. *WHITE *a.* 4 a.

1831 H. J. FINN *Amer. Comic Ann.* 88 'You be right dere,' observed Sambo, '..else what fur he go more 'mong niggers den de white *trash*?' **1833** F. KEMBLE *Jrnl.* 6 Jan. (1835) II. 112 The slaves themselves entertain the very highest contempt for white servants, whom they designate as 'poor white trash'. **1863** 'E. KIRKE' *My Southern Friends* 55 The poor trash..scratched a bare subsistence from a sorry patch of beans and collards. **1901** W. CHURCHILL *Crisis* I. i. 7, I..put a bullet past his ear, just to let the trash know the sound of it. *Ibid.* II. x. 211 It was not even a wild dream that white-trash Lincoln would be elected. **1932** W. FAULKNER *Light in August* xvi. 363 Who told you I am a nigger, you little white trash bastard? **1942** B. ROBERTSON *Red Hills & Cotton* viii. 189 If that was the sort of good-for-nothing trash she was, then she could just leave. **1945** E. WAUGH *Brideshead Revisited* I. viii. 180 Who are all this white trash, anyway? **1973** *Sunday Times* 10 June (Colour Suppl.) 51/4 He said that all the Australians were white trash. **1977** J. DIDION *Bk. of Common Prayer* IV. i. 158 'Lower that white-trash voice,' Warren said.

5. a. (See sense 1 a above) *trash basket, -bin, can, collection, collector, compactor, container, pickup*; **trashbag** (*a*) (further example); (*b*) chiefly *U.S.*, a rubbish bag; **trashman** *N. Amer.* = DUSTMAN 1.

1792 S. BURDY *Life of Late Rev. Philip Skelton* 161 He had a trash bag, as they call it, in which he kept needles, thread, and such like articles, to put a few stitches, if necessary, in his clothes. **1934** WEBSTER, Trash bag. **1960** *Guardian* 2 Feb. 5/1 The provision..of brown paper 'trash bags' for free issue to picnic parties. **1978** *Sci. Amer.* Feb. 158/3 Some household materials are also suitable: wrapping paper, brown paper bags and plastic trash bags (the kind used to line the inside of garbage cans). **1895** *Dialect Notes* I. 395 *Trash-basket*, waste-paper basket. N.Y. City. **1959** *Listener* 5 Mar. 411/2 The trash basket in his mother's bedroom. **1972** *New Yorker* 26 Aug. 21/3 Trash baskets stood in ranks on the empty sand, like sentinels. **1955** W. GADDIS *Recognitions* I. i. 38 Janet came in a few minutes later to find him sifting through the kitchen trashbin. **1966** *Punch* 9 Mar. 331/2 How many mushroom enterprises leave the customer with equipment fit only for the trash-bin or the attic? **1976** *Columbus* (Montana) *News* 27 May 1/1 Members of the Columbus High School..have 'bicentennialized' the fire hydrants and trash bins. **1929** *Sci. Amer.* May 445/3 A prominent member of Washington society last winter rolled 25,000 dollars worth of diamonds in a chamois bag and carelessly left the bag on a table where her little son found it and carried it to the trash can. **1936** W. STEVENS *New Caravan* 74 A trash can at the end of the world. **1960** *Times* 14 Sept. 12/7 Our dustbins—sorry, trash cans. **1981** 'P. MALLORY' *Killing Matter* xvii. 173 A shaggy dog, working the trash cans. **1967** MRS. L. B. JOHNSON *White House Diary* 26 Jan. (1970) 480 One of the Mayors said that his budget for trash collection and cleaning had tripled in the last two years. **1979** *Arizona Daily Star* 5 Aug. I. 12/3 (Advt.), A continuous city-wide program of trash collection was implemented in 1974. **1967** *Boston Sunday Herald* 26 Mar. I. 34/1, I have a bone to pick with the Dedham trash collectors. **1973** *Washington Post* 13 Jan. E 16/3 (Advt.), Optional trash compactors and tub enclosures. **1977** *Chicago Tribune* 2 Oct. XII. 11/7 (Advt.), Kitchen complete with all appliances including disposal and trash compactor. **1968** MRS. L. B. JOHNSON *White House Diary* 17 Jan. (1970) 617 We came out loud and strong for one more trash pickup a week..and for more trash containers. **1965** *Amer. Psychologist* Dec. 1014/2 A good idea was translated into banalities about..the friendly postman and trashman. **1971** *Daily Colonist* (Victoria, B.C.) 9 July 26/7 We used to organize regular expeditions..early on the mornings before the trashman came. **1968** Trash pickup [see *trash container* above]. **1978** *Detroit Free Press* 16 Apr. (Parade Suppl.) 31/1 You should see Beverley Hills on trash pickup day.

b. *attrib.* or as quasi-*adj.*, designating that which is worthless or of poor quality. Chiefly *U.S.*

In quot. 1843 perh. short for TRASHY *a.* 1.

1843 DICKENS *Let.* 7 Aug. (1974) III. 537 We were obliged at the last moment to alter an excellent bill; and the entertainments were very trash. **1940** *Sun* (Baltimore) 23 Jan. 5/1 Flocks of ducks—mostly 'trash' ducks like Black Bay coots and shelducks. **1944** *National Geogr. Mag.* Jan. 27/1 Trash fish and tons of discarded shrimp offal are now valuable in making fertilizer. **1966** 'H. MACDIARMID' *Company I've Kept* xiii. 270 That availability to Yankee trash-culture which has developed apace. **1967** G. STEINER *Lang. & Silence* 103 The serious novel has had to choose topics formerly exploited by trash-fiction. **1971** *Times* 27 Nov. 3/3 The so-called 'trash mail' service, the delivery of unaddressed circulars [by postmen]. **1973** *Daily Colonist* (Victoria, B.C.) 4 Oct. 31/3 Two inventors say they have a great new food product, but the name leaves something to be desired. It's 'trash fish' sausage. **1977** *Amer. N. & Q.* XV. 108/2 The image of Latin America in some German 'trash' novels of the twentieth century. **1979** R. BARNARD *Posthumous Papers* xiii. 127 The offspring of shopkeepers, who bribed him with trash food. **1983** *New Yorker* 5 Dec. 160/2 About seven tons of trash fish eventually turned belly-up—Sacramento suckers, hardheads.

trash, *v.*³ Add: **3. a.** To vandalize (property or goods), esp. as a means of protest. Occas. *intr.*, to perform such acts of destruction. Also *fig. colloq.* (chiefly *U.S.*).

1970 *Guardian* 14 May 2 On Sunday night a small gang went out to trash but a sudden rainstorm stopped the attack. **1971** *Time* 22 Mar. 26 Backstage at *Comes a Day* he got drunk and trashed his dressing room. **1974** H. L. FOSTER *Ribbin', Jivin', & Playin' Dozens* vi. 266 Students or unauthorized visitors who are physically attacking someone, 'ripping off' school equipment, 'trashing', attempting to burn or blow up a building, or otherwise interfering with instruction or threatening a student or worker with physical harm. **1975** 'S. MARLOWE' *Cawthorn Jrnls.* (1976) xix. 174 The room..had been trashed..by either the patrons..or by the police. **1976** *Globe & Mail* (Toronto) 24 Aug. 29/8 Mine was one of a group of offices trashed at Trinity College in early June. Trashed, not burglarized. Nothing stolen. Art works smashed. Manuscripts and notes left alone, but books soaked in wine or worse. Furniture ripped, ceiling tiles torn. **1984** *New Yorker* 20 Feb. 43/1 They've trashed the laws.

b. To injure seriously, destroy or kill (someone or something). *U.S. colloq.*

1973 W. MCGIVERN *Reprisal* 196 Don't be squeamish... Remember that Jules Levy, a Jew, trashed the pusher who murdered your son. **1977** C. MCFADDEN *Serial* (1978) l. 107/1 Harvey threatened Spenser with grievous bodily harm... 'Whaddaya wanna trash me for?'

c. To reduce or impair the quality of (a work of art, etc.); to expose the worthless nature of (something), to deprecate. *colloq.* (chiefly *U.S.*).

1975 *New Yorker* 12 May 114/2 In Hollywood, the writer is an underling whose work is trashed, or, at best, he's a respected collaborator without final control over how his work is used. **1976** *Time* 5 Apr. 42/2 The presentation is ignorant, cluttered and coarse, and it trashes the sculpture. Works that need to be walked around..can only be seen frontally. **1977** *Saturday Night* (Toronto) May 72/1 With *Ghost Fox*, I thought, Houston would trash all the melodramatic comic-book stuff about Indians with one neat blow. **1981** *London Rev. Bks.* 2–15 July 12/1 She writes..yet another trashing of radical chic. This might be more gripping had she herself not trashed radical chic already.

trashed (træʃt), *ppl. a. colloq.* (chiefly *U.S.*). [f. *TRASH *v.*³ 3 + -ED¹.] Bungled, spoiled; ill-treated or injured; run-down. Freq. with advbs.

1926 *Spectator* 22 May 857/1 We don't want any trashed-up peace. **1977** *Sounds* 9 July 30/2 Guthrie was real folk, born (1912) and raised in Oklahoma,..a trashed-on Okie farmer's son when that didn't mean you droned on about being proud of your bigoted ignorance. **1979** *Tucson* (Arizona) *Citizen* 20 Sept. 7B/6 'I've sat through this movie three times.'..'In this trashed-out theater? The picture's that good?' 'It's a lousy picture! I can't get my feet unstuck from the floor!!' **1980** *Dirt Bike* Oct. 14/1 Track-N-Trail has just come up with a solution to the age-old problems of mud, cold, rain, and trashed knuckles for you offroaders.

trasher. (In Dict. s.v. TRASH *v.*³) Add: **2.** A vandal or wrecker. Cf. *TRASH *v.*³ 3 a. *colloq.*

1970 *Guardian* 19 Sept. 9/5 The trasher mixes with the non-violent student. **1975** *Time* (Canada ed.) 9 June 8/2 'As a lifelong Tory and ranking member of the legal establishment,' reports Time Canada's Toronto Bureau Chief Robert Lewis, 'Maloney also is not about to pursue his office like a trasher.'

trashing, *vbl. sb.* (In Dict. s.v. TRASH *v.*³) Add: **2.** The action of *TRASH *v.*³ 3 a; vandalism or an instance of this. *colloq.* (chiefly *U.S.*).

1970 *N.Y. Times* 29 Apr. 40/1 The new breed of campus revolutionaries..are now turning to what they call 'trashing'—the setting of fires, hurling of rocks, smashing of windows. **1971** *Publishers' Weekly* 4 Oct. 24/1 Student riots and trashings of college stores. **1973** D. MARTIN *Tracts against Times* v. 47 The 'trashing' activities which damaged all property within a half-mile radius of the University of Wisconsin. **1979** *Listener* 3 May 614/2 'Trashing', the destruction of buildings and property, became commonplace.

trashy, *a.* Add: **3.** Of people: worthless, disreputable. *colloq.*

1862 'E. KIRKE' *Among Pines* vii. 167 He regarded the white man as altogether too 'trashy' to be treated with much ceremony. **1898** B. KIRKBY *Lakeland Words* 148 Of bad habits sairy man. Dick, Ah's flait he's nobbut trashy. **1931** H. NICOLSON *Diary* 31 Dec. (1966) 100, I am thought trashy and a little mad. I have been reckless and arrogant. **1935** [see *piney-woods cracker* s.v. *PINEY WOOD]. **1977** *Detroit Free Press* 11 Dec. 13-C/1, I honestly couldn't believe such things happened except in low class trashy families.

trat(t (træt), colloq. abbrev. of next.

1969 R. AIRTH *Snatch!* xv. 149 We stopped off at a little trat Bruno knew of..and had a last one. **1969** *Queen* 17–30 Sept. 18/3 Luigi..who served you dinner in last week's trendy tratt. **1970** *Guardian* 6 Mar. 9/5, I have been thinking about trattorias. Mostly I mean the white-tiled tratts of SW 1, 3, and 7.

trattoria (tratorī·a, tratɒ°·riˌă). Pl. **-ias,** ‖ **-ie.** [a. It., f. *trattore* host, f. *trattare* to treat.] **a.** In Italy, an eating house, a takeaway, a restaurant. **b.** Outside Italy, a restaurant serving Italian food.

1832 W. GELL *Pompeiana* I. iv. 49 A trattoria and coffee-house. **1873** 'OUIDA' *Pascarel* I. II. iv. 169 Then he would pass methodically across the piazza to his favourite trattoriâ. **1922** [see *FETTUCCINE]. **1955** E. POUND *Section: Rock-Drill* xci. 74 'Dodici Apostoli' (trattoria). **1966** *Punch* 20 July 112/1 The High Street sees a new Restaurant, a new Trattoria or a new Bistro opening every week. **1971** 'A. BURGESS' *MF* ix. 101 The Great Giro..was piling cold plates together like a *trattoria* waiter. **1973** *Times* 25 Aug. 12/7 An insipid stew (*veau Berichonne*), with tough meat, that one would get in lesser known London trattorie. **1975** FELTON & FOWLER *Best, Worst & most Unusual* 216 Pizzas of all shapes and varieties are served in restaurants and trattorias throughout Italy.

trauma. Delete ‖ and add: Now also with pronunc. (trɑu·mă). Pl. **traumas, traumata.**

2. a. *Psychoanal.* and *Psychiatry.* A psychic injury, esp. one caused by emotional shock the memory of which is repressed and remains unhealed; an internal injury, esp. to the brain, which may result in a behavioural disorder of organic origin. Also, the state or condition so caused.

1894 W. JAMES in *Psychol. Rev.* I. 199 Certain reminiscences of the shock fall into the subliminal consciousness, where they can only be discovered in 'hypnoid' states. If left there, they act as permanent 'psychic *traumata*', thorns in the spirit, so to speak. **1895** [in Dict.]. **1896** *Brain* XIX. 402 The author thought that the painful area on the thigh increased in size with the accession of fresh 'psychical traumas'. **1927** BRYAN & STRACHEY tr. *Abraham's Sel. Papers* i. 47 He [*sc.* Freud] assigns a secondary rôle to sexual traumas in youth and assumes the presence of an abnormal psychosexual constitution. **1927** HENDERSON & GILLESPIE *Textbk. Psychiatry* iii. 56 Trauma may produce mental symptoms in one of two ways. Either it causes structural injury to the brain, or it causes emotional disturbances... In the first instance the mental reaction is of the organic type..in the second the result is usually a psychoneurosis. **1941** S. H. KRAINES *Therapy of Neuroses & Psychoses* xv. 343 Simple trauma to the brain does not produce psychotic symptoms. **1950** *Brit. Jrnl. Psychol.* June 235 Complexes can be regarded as 'dissociated partial psyches'..the dissociation being produced by traumata, moral conflicts, etc. **1954** W. MAYER-GROSS et al. *Clin. Psychiatry* x. 398 Mental disease due to brain trauma is only rarely a cause of admission to mental hospital. **1967** H. P. LAUGHLIN *Neuroses* iv. 184 The specific trauma or event is not the *raison d'etre*, the cause of the depression. **1980** *Daily Tel.* 6 Dec. 12/3 Among the many shops and houses which advertise 'Counselling' (i.e., fortune-telling), I came across a handwritten notice which said 'Traumas Treated'.

b. In general and *fig.* use.

1977 H. GREENE *FSO-1* x. 96 We know the trauma you suffered..but you've gone about it all wrong. **1977** *Mod. Railways* Dec. 486/2 Because of the trauma in the American rapid transit vehicle business—caused largely by the dilution of the market by the aerospace companies and the absence of long runs of standard designs—only two firms had put in tenders. **1978** S. BRILL *Teamsters* vi. 248 Much of that trauma had come not from the real damage Dorfman had done but from the way the press had misstated or exaggerated it. **1981** *Daily Tel.* 30 Oct. 1/1 This is a sensible deal. It will mean that we do not have to go through the trauma of possible strike action.

traumatic, *a.* Add: Now also with pronunc. (trɑumæ·tik). **2. a.** *Psychoanal.* and *Psychiatry.* Of, pertaining to, or caused by a psychic wound or emotional shock, esp. leading to or causing behavioural disturbance.

1889 T. SAVILL tr. *Charcot's Clin. Lect. Dis. Nervous Syst.* III. 388 The existence of traumatic psychosis [*psychose traumatique*] adds still more to the gravity of the prognosis. **1909** A. A. BRILL tr. *Freud's Sel. Papers Hysteria* i. 1 It is quite evident that in 'traumatic' hysteria it is the accident which evokes the syndrome. **1929** *Times Lit. Suppl.* 4 July 528/2 The Freudian traumatic theory. **1941** S. H. KRAINES *Therapy of Neuroses & Psychoses* xv. 352 In the traumatic psychoses, damaged brain tissue is irreparable. **1979** A. STORR *Art of Psychotherapy* x. 94 Women who react to traumatic events with depression are generally contending with a variety of difficulties.

b. In general use: distressing, emotionally disturbing.

1962 A. HUXLEY *Let.* 17 June (1969) 935 Memories of traumatic events in childhood. **1965** M. NAYLOR *Your Money* ix. 54 You will only have sacrificed one-seventh of your original capital. This is depressing enough, of course, but it is a good deal less traumatic than losing half. **1973** *Howard Jrnl.* XIII. 287 It was felt by some that this would..make leaving prison at the end of the sentence less traumatic. **1977** E. HEATH *Travels* viii. 167 Whatever the outcome, the impact on the United States of the decade of war in Vietnam was traumatic. **1984** *Daily Tel.* 2 Feb. 2/3 We see manufacturing industry only feebly recovering from the traumatic experience of the last five years.

3. Bot. *traumatic acid*, a plant hormone that is found in damaged tissue in some plants and promotes its repair; dodec-2-ene-1,12-dioic acid, $HOOC(CH_2)_8CH{:}CHCOOH$.

1939 J. ENGLISH et al. in *Science* 6 Oct. 329/2 It would seem appropriate and convenient to refer to this substance as 'traumatic acid'. **1966** R. M. DEVLIN *Plant Physiol.* xvii. 427 The effect of traumatic acid on inducing cells to divide does not appear to be general. **1971** J. Z. YOUNG *Introd. Study Man* xii. 160 In plants..injured cells release a..traumatic acid.

Hence (in sense 2 b) **trauma·tically** *adv.*

1972 D. BLOODWORTH *Any Number can Play* viii. 56 His patriotic and anti-communist postures are almost traumatically compulsive. **1976** *Listener* 11 Nov. 615/1 A view of life, of being, that would lead me ineluctably into false hopes and traumatically real disappointments.

traumatism. Add: **2.** *Psychol.* and *Psychiatry.* A morbid condition of the psyche resulting from repression to the unconscious of emotional wounds or shock which are unacceptable to the conscious mind. Also *loosely* in general use, a shock or unpleasantly startling experience.

1898 H. ELLIS in *Alienist & Neurologist* XIX. 610 They may be said to have shown conclusively, what has already been more or less hesitantly suggested by others, that the most typical hysteria is really a 'psychic traumatism'. **1926** J. I. SUTTIE tr. *Ferenczi's Theory & Technique Psycho-Anal.* 77 A certain amount of infantile sexual experience (that is to say, a little 'sexual traumatism'). **1973** D. MATIAS tr. C. Metz in *Screen* Spring/Summer 51 The actor gave the impression of reciting a sparse and laconic text which cut across the preceding silence producing a minor aesthetic traumatism for the spectator.

traumatize, *v.* (In Dict. s.v. TRAUMATISM.) Add: **1.** (Further examples.)

1929 *Jrnl. Amer. Med. Assoc.* 13 July 116/2 The white bands disappeared promptly when care was taken not to traumatize the fold of skin with the orangewood stick. **1954** S. DUKE-ELDER *Parson's Dis. Eye* (ed. 12) xxii. 361 In this way they may be severely traumatized; and at the same time the wave of pressure, striking the retina and choroid, may do considerable damage.

2. To inflict an emotional wound or shock upon; to impair or damage psychologically. Also *fig.*

1949 M. MEAD *Male & Female* xvi. 336 Two bitter little rivals may otherwise spend hours quarrelling and traumatizing each other. **1958** *Spectator* 28 Feb. 255/1 A Roman Catholic lad who traumatised me by telling me that God was always about. **1965** *New Statesman* 17 Dec. 960/2 In the intervening period, 34 people were killed..1,032 were injured... The event has traumatised California. **1970** A. TOFFLER *Future Shock* x. 194 The year 2000 is closer to us in time than the great depression, yet the world's economists, traumatized by that historic disaster, remain frozen in the attitudes of the past. **1974** *Sci. Amer.* Aug. 56/2 For children who come from environments in which the capacity of the family to function has been most severely traumatized by such destructive forces as poverty, ill health and discrimination, the consequences for the child are seen [etc.]. **1979** P. THEROUX *Old Patagonian Express* (1980) xiii. 264 The passengers were either asleep or sitting silently, traumatized by the heat.

Hence **traumatiza·tion; trau·matized, trau·matizing** *ppl. adjs.*

1935 *Proc. Soc. Exper. Biol. & Med.* XXXII. 1249 If profound and fatal shock is to be obtained in the intact dog by traumatization, the severity of tissue injury must be very much greater than is required to induce shock symptoms in the equally healthy and vigorous animal lacking adrenal glands. **1935** *Amer. Jrnl. Physiol.* CXI. 430 Such traumatized animals lacking adrenals die within 24 hours or less. **1949** M. MEAD *Male & Female* v. 118 Two inexperienced adolescents had a first sex-affair..and became traumatized by their own clumsiness. **1950** E. H. ERIKSON *Childhood & Society* (1951) i. 37 The condition started with such damage, or at least with momentary traumatization. **1966** *Lancet* 31 Dec. 1464/1 Fat from traumatised adipose tissue can on occasion enter the circulation and produce fat-embolisation. **1971** K. MILLETT *Sexual Politics* (1972) II. iv. 180 We perceive that the traumatizing circumstance of being born black in a white racist society invests skin color with symbolic value. **1977** M. SOKOLINSKY tr. *Merle's Virility Factor* xvi. 330 There is an excess of love..an instinct that, in women, is no longer stifled by the traumatizing sense of her social inferiority. **1979** *Daily Tel.* 31 Oct. 15/2 Thousands of traumatised survivors of the Pol Pot horrors were starving and dying. **1979** *Nature* 13 Dec. 727/1 It was important to ascertain whether our surgical procedure led to any transient denervation or traumatisation of synapses made by the soleus nerve.

traumato-. Add: **traumatology** (examples); in mod. use, the branch of medicine concerned with the treatment of wounds and serious injuries and with the disabilities they cause; hence **traumato·logist,** a specialist in this.

1935 *Dorland's Med. Dict.* (ed. 17) 1427/2 Traumatologist. **1948** *Excerpta Medica Section IX* II. 944 Traumatologists must devote themselves not only to special treatment, but also to the prevention of injuries. **1981** *Sci. Digest* Aug. 52 'Half a million out of eighty million accident cases a year need Shock Trauma's services,' says one veteran traumatologist. **1948** *Excerpta Medica Section IX* II. 944 The necessity for special traumatology is caused by the progress of civilization. **1964** *Acta Universitatis Carolinae Medica Suppl.* XIX. 296 Modern scientific experiences and results of research of many teams offer more and more effective and better means to traumatology and raise the standard of its work. **1977** *Lancet* 30 Apr. 961/2 A national institute of traumatology in the United Kingdom cannot be put off any longer. **1980** R. OWEN et al. (*title*) Scientific foundations of orthopaedics and traumatology.

traumatropism. Add: Also **traumato-tropism.**

1965 Bell & Coombe tr. *Strasburger's Textbk. Bot.* 380 Galvanotropism, traumatotropism and thermotropism.. are possibly only special forms of chemotropism.

trautonium (trautō^u·niŏm). [f. the name of Friedrich *Trautwein* (1888–1956), German scientist and inventor of the instrument, after Euphonium.] An electronic musical instrument, capable of producing notes of any pitch.

1931 *Electronics* July 18/2 The 'Trautonium' is a recent development at the Radio Research section of the Berlin Academy of Music... Paul Hindemith..is himself an excellent Trautonium player and has written music specially for it. **1936** *Discovery* July 224/2 The Trautonium, due to Dr. Trautwein and developed at the Charlottenburg Music High School (Conservatoire), where it so interested Hindemith that he not only wrote for it but even himself learnt to play it. **1959** *Chambers's Encycl.* V. 131/2 Instruments such as the theremin and the trautonium derive music directly from the tuned circuits in oscillation and have no mechanical vibrator except the diaphragm in the loud-speaker. **1978** P. Griffiths *Conc. Hist. Mod. Music* viii. 111 Hindemith wrote a concertino for trautonium and orchestra in 1931.

travail, -aille, *sb.*[3] (Earlier example.)

1801 A. Henry *Jrnl.* 13 Oct. in E. Coues *New Light on Greater Northwest* (1897) I. iv. 190 Chamanau arrived from the hills, bringing his deceased wife on a travaille to be buried here.

‖ **travaux préparatoires** (travo preparătwār), *sb. pl. Law.* [Fr., lit. 'preparatory works'.] Drafts, records of discussions, etc., pertaining to legislation or a treaty under consideration (see quot. 1980).

1935 *Harvard Law Rev.* Feb. 562 French courts exhibited the tendency to limit recourse to *travaux preparatoires.* **1957** H. F. Jolowicz *Roman Foundations Mod. Law* ii. 16 No text appears to deal with *travaux préparatoires*, but it is in accordance with the civilian tradition that resort to drafts, speeches in Parliament, and similar evidence is usually allowed more widely on the Continent than in England. **1962** *Listener* 15 Mar. 456/1, I am thinking about our rule which excludes the so-called *travaux preparatoires*; that is to say, statements made in negotiation, prior to the treaty, which might throw light on its meaning. **1980** *Oxf. Compan. Law* 1231/1 *Travaux préparatoires*, materials used in the preparation of, and having formative effect on, the ultimately adopted form of an agreement, or legislation, or an international treaty. Such materials include, in the domestic sphere, reports, proposals and technical advice, in the legislative sphere, Select Committee or Royal Commission or other reports, academic studies, Green Papers, White Papers, and the like, and in the international sphere reports of expert committees, discussions and proposals, drafts, and the like.

travel, *sb.* Add: **5.** *travel bag, -book* (earlier example), *film, literature, permit, poster, ticket, time, voucher, warrant*; *travel-minded* adj.; objective, as *travel editor, -writer* (later examples); instrumental, as *travel-wearied* adj.; **travel agency,** a firm which makes arrangements for the transport, accommodation, etc., of travellers, and which acts as an agent for tour-operators (see *tour *sb.* 12); **travel agent,** one who owns or works for a travel agency; **travel allowance,** (*a*) the amount of money given to a traveller to cover the expenses of a journey; (*b*) under the Exchange Control Bill, the maximum amount of money travellers were allowed to take out of the U.K. during the period 1946–80; **travel brochure,** a booklet advertising travel and describing the features and amenities of holiday resorts or other places of travel; **travel bug** *colloq.*, a strong urge to travel (cf. *bug *sb.*[2] 4 a); **travel bureau** = *travel agency* above; **travel document,** a document required for travel; *spec.* a document allowing foreign travel, held by one not entitled to a passport; **travel folder** = *travel brochure* above; **travel sickness,** nausea induced by the motion of a vehicle; carsickness; hence **travel-sick** *a.* affected by travel sickness; **travel trailer** *U.S.*, a variety of caravan.

1927 *World Travel* Oct. 39/2 (Advt.), Imperial Airways. Daily Services Between London Cologne Brussels Paris... Book through any Travel Agency or direct with the Company. **1975** B. Bainbridge *Sweet William* iii. 79 He was going to get brochures from a travel agency. He thought they should all go to Spain. [**1902** *Encycl. Brit.* XXVII. 227/2 Cook, Thomas (1808–1892), travelling agent, was born at Melbourne in Derbyshire.] **1925** *Times* 1 May 2/2 (Advt.), write to-day for your copy of 'Economy Tours to America', to..leading Travel agents. **1980** S. Brett *Dead Side of Mike* vi. 61 Toby Root played a travel agent. **1937** Travel allowance [see *second *a.* 6 b]. **1951** *Ann. Reg. 1950* iv. 453 The basic annual travel allowances were increased in December to £100 for adults. **1978** A. Waugh *Best Wine Last* xviii. 237 In 1947..the meagre travel allowance was again reduced. **1939–40** *Army & Navy Stores Catal.* 875/2 Popular travel bag, with.. passport pocket. **1968** L. Deighton *Only when I Larf* i. 9 Umbrella in one hand, travel bag in the other, he marched off. **1843** Dickens *Let.* 2 Nov. (1974) III. 591 The travel-book, if to be done at all, would cost me very little trouble. **1953** P. Scott *Alien Sky* i. vi. 75 A plan I have to issue highly coloured travel brochures with a photo of myself on an elephant. **1972** F. Warner *Maquettes* 42 A copywriter for the travel brochures. **1976** P. Cave *High Flying Birds* i. 13 The travel bug. Ants in your suitcase. **1930** E. Waugh *Labels* iii. 51 Their speech is rich with the words of the travel bureau's advertising manager. **1966** A. K. Train *Spoken like Frenchman* 94 (*heading*) At a travel bureau. **1963** *Listener* 14 Feb. 281/2 Soblen, provided with an Israeli travel document valid for travel to any country except Israel, left by air. **1980** E. Behr *Getting Even* xiv. 166 He was not to volunteer information about the man's travel documents. **1910** *Bradshaw's Railway Guide* Apr. 1054/2 'Clonsilla' En Pension... Recommended by Travel Editor of 'Queen'. **1977** *Chicago Tribune* 2 Oct. iv. 19/5 Travel Editor Holt was born and reared in West Virginia. **1922** Travel film [see *scenic *sb.* 2]. **1978** A. Waugh *Best Wine Last* ix. 107 Marrakesh has been a subject of many articles and travel films. **1955** W. Gaddis *Recognitions* ii. v. 488 A tour from a travel folder. **1980** D. Bloodworth *Trapdoor* xii. 68 The secluded Kahala Hilton with its sun-swept beach ..could have been torn straight out of a travel folder. **1934** Travel literature [see *courtesy card* s.v. *courtesy *sb.* 12]. **1955** E. Blunden *Addresses on General Subjects* 285 It is an example of the prolific travel-literature of England. **1932** Travel-minded [see *minded *ppl. a.* 4 c]. **1962** *John o' London's* 1 Mar. 202/1 Everyone these days is travel-minded. **1942** M. Cable *Gobi Desert* 245 It was no longer he who issued the travel permits and received official visits. **1978** T. Willis *Buckingham Palace Connection* v. 96 The British Vice-Consul..had promised to get her the necessary travel permit. **1958** *Times Lit. Suppl.* 10 Jan. 22/5 This is no excuse for a travel-poster jacket and flamboyant title. **1979** R. Jeffries *Murder begets Murder* xv. 91 Sun from dawn to dusk just like the travel posters had promised. **1959** *Times* 13 July 9/1 Some of the children will be travel-sick. **1978** *Times* 30 Dec. 4/4, I felt travel sick as we were driving along the lane. **1900** Dorland *Med. Dict.* 710/2 *Travel-sickness...* Same as *Car-sickness.* **1941** W. Graham *Night Journey* xx. 246, I was talking to your husband on the problem of travel sickness. **1979** R. Perry *Bishop's Pawn* i. 15, I was going to swallow a handful of travel sickness pills. **1949** Dylan Thomas *Let.* 1 Dec. (1966) 341, I must..hurry everything up, as visas, travel-tickets, etc., cannot be too easy to procure. **1980** *Daily Tel.* 26 Jan. 17/3 Auckland..is not the place to buy travel tickets, as there is a 10 per cent tax on them there. **1946** Travel time [see *flying time* s.v. *flying *vbl. sb.* 3]. **1976** P. R. White *Planning for Public Transport* viii. 160 Over routes of about 200 to 250 m.. total travel times by air and rail are similar. **1961** *Mobile Home Jrnl.* Dec. 21/1 Harold Martin..is now the proud owner of a twenty-seven foot Yellowstone travel trailer... The twenty-seven foot model is the largest in the Yellowstone line of travel trailers. **1978** *Sunday Sun-Times* (Chicago) 1 Jan. 122/1 Travel trailers are of two types: The conventional, rectangular-shaped unit constructed of aluminum or molded fiberglass over wall studs, and the fifth-wheel trailer. **1964** L. Deighton *Funeral in Berlin* iii. 21 The travel vouchers and tickets are ordered. **1978** P. Bryers *Cat Trapper* xxviii. 180 His travel vouchers were made out for the motel at Kishinev. **1952** 'R. West' *Meaning of Treason* (ed. 2) i. vii. 156 A travel warrant issued by the Ministry of Labour. **1919** W. de la Mare *Flora* 40 Noonday to night the enigma of thine eyes Frets with desire their travel-wearied brain. **1927** W. B. Yeats *October Blast* 22 Cease to remember the delights of youth, travel-wearied aged man. **1969** C. Graves *Ireland Revisited* viii. 125 Every travel-writer and poet who has visited the Lakes of Killarney has made some attempt to do justice to their loveliness. **1972** W. Garner *Ditto, Brother Rat!* xi. 80 A guest! A famous travel writer.

travel, *v.* Add: **2. d.** (Earlier example const. *in.*) Also, const. *for* the concern for which a commercial traveller works (later examples).

1841 Thackeray in *Fraser's Mag.* Sept. 330/2 I've got a place—a tip-top place..to travel in the West of England in oil and spermaceti. **1872** Geo. Eliot *Middlem.* III. vi. lx .336, I travelled for 'em, sir, in a gentlemanly way—at a high salary. **1922** Joyce *Ulysses* 111, I travelled for cork lino. **1964** 'J. Melville' *Murderers' Houses* ii. 46 He travels for Associated Boxes. It's the big firm on the London Road.

f. *to travel light*: to travel with little luggage. Also *fig.*

1921 E. O'Neill *Emperor Jones* i. 166, I travels light when I wants to move fast. **1931** 'Grey Owl' *Men of Last Frontier* 13 As he has also to break his own trail, he travels light, taking only a sheet of canvas for a windbreak and one blanket. **1954** I. Murdoch *Under Net* xviii. 252, I just couldn't help making money, and I don't want that. I want to travel light. **1977** *Time* 19 Dec. 18/2 West German terrorists are especially difficult to fathom because ideologically they travel light.

3. e. (Later examples.)

1911 G. Stratton-Porter *Harvester* v. 74 Betsey.. wants to meander along the road with a loaded wagon... Betsey, you must travel! **1970** M. Kenyon *100,000 Welcomes* xxi. 178 Mercy, the lorry's travelling. Foot down.

5. b. *Theatr.* To take (costumes, equipment, etc.) with one from place to place.

1930 E. Wallace *Lady of Ascot* i. 15 She had sapphire rings and clips..of an incredible value, and she 'travelled' them, as they say in theatrical circles. **1966** 'J. Hackston' *Father clears Out* 123 The taller of these two guests travelled a broken concertina with him.

c. *Publishing.* To take (books) from place to place in order to promote and sell them. Cf. sense 2 d in Dict. and Suppl.

1937 V. Woolf *Let.* 10 Feb. (1980) VI. 106 We're taking Tuesday off at Rodmell to travel our books in Sussex. **1977** B. Colloms *Victorian Country Parsons* xi. 219 [George Routledge] liked to travel his own books in the north country so that he could keep in touch with booksellers.

travel(l)ator: see *Travolator.

travelled, traveled, *ppl. a.* Add: **1.** (Later examples.)

1966 *Listener* 11 Aug. 210/1 Synge, already a travelled man when Yeats suggested to him that he'd find the Aran Islands more to his liking than Paris was a foreigner in his own country. **1978** G. Greene *Human Factor* ii. i. 51 We need travelled gentlemen like you to deal with foreign affairs.

3. (Earlier examples.)

1845 J. C. Frémont *Rep. Exploring Expedition* 163 [To Fort Hall] along the travelled road from the town of Westport..is 1,323 miles. **1869** *Bradshaw's Railway Man.* XXI. 433 The travelled route through this country crosses formidable ranges of mountains.

4. *travelled blood* (see quots.).

1962 'J. le Carré' *Murder of Quality* iii. 41 There's a lot of what we call travelled blood..that's to say, blood spurted from an open artery. **1981** *Event* 9–15 Oct. 29/4 *Travelled blood...* A pathologist's description of blood that has spurted from a severed artery.

traveller, traveler. Add: **1. b.** (Earlier and later Austral. examples.) Also, a gypsy.

1868 M. Clarke in *Australasian* 5 Sept. 305/3, I remember at one station, situated on the main road for 'travellers', that the unhappy cook was 'put on the fire' by a crowd of these gentry. **1891** 'F. W. Carew' *No. 747* ii. 18 A little commercial transaction—known among 'travellers' as 'trucking'. **1945** [see *passage *sb.* 1 e]. **1967** *New Scientist* 7 Dec. 582/3 The question is whether or not gypsies (who call themselves Travellers) are members 'of the Romany race'. **1971** *New Society* 1 July 18/2 Scotland's 2,000-odd itinerant tinkers—or, as they prefer to be called 'travellers'... Some claim descent from the roving Irish tinsmiths or Scottish outlaws, others from the true romany gypsies.

3. (Earlier example.)

1790 J. Wedgwood *Let.* 13 July (1965) 328 Such distinguished favours cannot but make a deep impression on my mind. Nor will they be forgotten by the travellers.

5. a. (Earlier U.S. example.)

1828 A. Sherburne *Mem.* iii. 61 He and other officers contrived to haul the men ashore... He fixed a traveller on the rope, by which he first went ashore, so that he could not wash off.

f. A craftsman's tool used for measuring circumferences, esp. of wheels (see quots.).

1879–81 G. F. Jackson *Shropshire Word-Bk.* 454 *Trindle*, a disc used by blacksmiths for measuring the circumference of wheels—a 'traveller'. **1923** G. Sturt *Wheelwright's Shop* xxiii. 122 The new tyre..had to be measured, as also had the wheel it was meant for. Blacksmiths kept a special implement for this purpose —a 'traveller' or 'tyre-runner'. The traveller was a thin circular disk of iron, six or seven inches across, which the smith would hold out, waist-high, at right angles to himself, and run round wheel and tyre in turn. **1969** G. E. Evans *Farm & Village* xiv. 148, I cut the band to the exact circumference of the stone. I find this with a device I made... It's called a *traveller*... It's a metal wheel. I roll this round the stone and count the revolutions... (This device works on the same principle as the measuring wheel used by the old road surveyors—a trundle wheel or way-wiser.) **1976** *National Observer* (U.S.) 10 July 9/1 'This here is called a traveler,' he says..displaying a round, flat device used to measure the perimeter of a wagon wheel... 'You won't find too many of them left.'

5*. A suitcase, trunk, or travelling bag. Chiefly *U.S.*

1895 *Montgomery Ward Catal.* Spring & Summer 564/3 Canvas Traveler... Large square box made of the best basswood, covered with extra heavy duck... A most handsome ladies' trunk. **1965** *Harper's Bazaar* Dec. 89/1 Cosmetic traveller lined with silk for girls who are on the go all day. **1983** *Country Life* 1 Dec. 1677 (Advt.), Travel-bag—this great, waterproof traveller holds three leakproof bottles.

6. b. traveller's cheque orig. *U.S.*, a cheque for one of several specified amounts of money, which can be cashed at a bank in most countries, or used in payment for goods, on the holder's endorsement against his original signature; also written *travellers(') cheque.*

1891 (*title no. 24775 in Library of Congress copyright registration bk.*) American Express Company, Travelers Cheque. Ten Dollars. **1894** *N.Y. Tribune* 11 July 5/2 The American Express Company's travellers' checks are of great assistance to tourists abroad. **1907** M. Rollins *Money & Investments* 218 Express companies have made a speciality of issuing 'travellers' cheques'. **1922** F. Scott Fitzgerald *Beautiful & Damned* ii. i. 150 On his dressing-table were spread a number of articles..their tickets to California, the book of traveller's checks. **1957** D. du Maurier *Scapegoat* iii. 32 Twenty-five pounds of travellers' cheques still uncashed. **1969** *Times* 15 Nov. 7/7 The counterfeiting of travellers cheques. **1981** 'E. Lathen' *Going for Gold* iii. 29, I assume these foreign traveler's checks work like American Express?

Hence **travellership** *rare*, in various *nonce* usages.

1920 Joyce *Let.* 20 Aug. (1966) iii. 17 Giorgio has been offered a position here in an American Trust Agency which would develop into a secretaryship and travellership for same. **1961** *Times* 24 June 9/6 We left early..accompanied in somewhat distant travellership by an austerely demeanoured delegation from Communist China.

travelling, traveling, *vbl. sb.* Add: **b.** *travelling expenses* (earlier and later examples); *travelling bag* (earlier U.S. example), *cap* (earlier U.S. example), *case, cloak, clock* (earlier example), *dress* (earlier example), *rug, trunk* (later examples); **travelling scholarship** (examples).

1838 C. GILMAN *Recoll. Southern Matron* ii. 18 He.. called the little boy who held the travelling bag a 'black-faced nigger'. **1790** *Pennsylvania Packet* 2 Jan. 4/2 (Advt.), Trimmings..for Gentlemens Travelling Caps. **1744** H. PUREFOY *Let.* 26 Feb. (1931) I. 119, I desire you will send mee an allarum to pull up together with a Travelling Case. **1895** *Montgomery Ward Catal.* Spring & Summer 257/2 Ladies' and men's toilet and traveling cases. **1984** A. PRICE *Sion Crossing* iv. 48 He walked meekly to the nearest bench..tucking his travelling case beside him. **1854** E. B. BROWNING *Plea for Ragged Schools of London* 1 If she shakes a travelling cloak, Down our Appian roll the scudi. **1944** A. CLARKE *Coll. Plays* (1963) 245 A figure appears, tall and handsome, in travelling cloak with tricornered hat. **1860** C. M. YONGE *Hopes & Fears* II. xii. 236 Phœbe was strongly tempted to answer, but the little travelling clock struck. **1815** J. MAYNE *Jrnl.* Feb. (1909) xii. 282 We ran off, the instant we arrived, in our travelling dresses, were in the theatre at eight o'clock. **1793** J. WOODFORDE *Diary* 23 Oct. (1929) IV. 75 Travelling Expenses..amounted in the whole—78.19.7. **1907** G. B. SHAW *John Bull's Other Island* I. 13 An advance on his salary—for travelling expenses. **1977** D. FRANCIS *Risk* xvii. 230 He'd invented travelling expenses to the races for horses which..had never left the yard. **1911** *Daily Colonist* (Victoria, B.C.) 23 Apr. 18/3 (Advt.), *Lost*—Travelling rug and overcoat, between Empress Hotel and the outer wharf. **1977** C. MCCULLOUGH *Thorn Birds* iii. 66 The big tartan traveling rugs all the suitcases bore on their outsides. **1911** R. BROOKE *Let.* 1 Mar. (1968) 282 Benians, of John's, is staying in Munich a week on his way round the world on one of these Kivet Kahn Travelling scholarships. **1967** E. LEMARCHAND *Death of Old Girl* i. 13 I'm certainly going to mention the art department's successes, especially Miss Cartmell's travelling scholarship. **1854** *Rep. Trans. Pennsylvania State Agric. Soc.* 97 Their very handsome riding saddle and russet traveling trunk. **1981** *Christian Sci. Monitor* (Midwestern ed.) 12 Feb. B4 A 'traveling trunk' program, in which the institute sends out to schools actual trunks of touchable Texas gear.

travelling, traveling, *ppl. a.* Add: **1. b.** (Earlier and later U.S. examples.)

1775 F. ASHBURY *Jrnl.* 6 Nov. (1821) I. 124 At this meeting we admitted F.P.T.F. and J.H—y as travelling preachers. **1874** E. EGGLESTON *Circuit Rider* xxvii. 252 The incessant activity of a traveling preacher's life.

e. Physics. *travelling wave*, a wave in which the nodes and antinodes travel (cf. *standing wave* s.v. *STANDING *ppl. a.* 11 e); freq. *attrib.*, as *travelling wave tube*, an electron tube in which a guided electromagnetic wave is amplified by interaction with a beam of electrons travelling at about the same velocity.

1908 C. P. STEINMETZ *Gen. Lect. Electr. Engin.* 273 Where a traveling wave is reflected, the combination of the reflected wave and the incoming wave produces a standing wave or oscillation, that is, a wave in which the voltage maxima and the zero points or nodes have fixed positions on the line. **1946** *Wireless World* Nov. 371/3 The travelling wave tube..consists..of..a long and straight helix of wire supported in an evacuated glass envelope containing also an electron gun for producing an electron beam and a collector. **1963** G. TROUP *Masers & Lasers* (ed. 2) v. 66 For the travelling wave maser, the gain coefficient..is [etc.]. **1967** *Oceanogr. & Marine Biol.* V. 25 A travelling wave is an essential feature of surge phenomena in the North Sea. **1974** Traveling-wave tube [see *PLASMA 5*].

2. Special collocations. *travelling exhibition*; **travelling circus,** (*a*) a circus which travels from place to place giving performances; (*b*) *Mil. slang*: in the war of 1914–18, a mobile military unit; a squadron of aeroplanes (cf. *CIRCUS 2 d); also *fig.*; **travelling library,** a library which is transported from place to place and serves remote rural communities, hospitals, etc.; a mobile library; **travelling salesman** = TRAVELLER, TRAVELER 3; **travelling salesman problem** *Math.*, the problem of determining the shortest route that passes through each of a set of given points once only and returns to the starting point; **travelling stock** *Austral.* and *N.Z.*, livestock which is driven from place to place; freq. in Comb., as *travelling stock road, route*; **travelling stock reserve,** land decreed as stock-routes; cf. *stock-route* s.v. STOCK *sb.*¹ 63.

1883 *Harper's Mag.* June 137/1 The travelling circus.. had journeyed on and left her. **1917** [see *CIRCUS 2 d]. **1919** F. A. MCKENNA *Battery A—103rd Field Artillery in France* 36 Field Marshal Von Hindenburg's troops, nicknamed by the Yanks, 'The Traveling Circus', composed of the famous Prussian Guards and picked Turkish storm troops, were reported in the sector opposite. **1946** *Happy Landings* (Air Ministry) July 1/1 Among the latest exhibits added to the Directorate's 'travelling circus' are components from a Sabre engine. **1974** G. MITCHELL *Javelin for Jonah* xi. 137 He had been with a travelling circus for some time, but they dismissed him. **1937** *Discovery* Aug. 236/1 A travelling exhibition which will penetrate into the remotest country districts. **1977** J. R. L. ANDERSON *Death in City* vi. 87 Bringing 'Pictures to the People' in the form of travelling exhibitions. **1910** A. E. BOSTWICK *Amer. Public Library* 108 Traveling libraries are simply collections of books sent to communities, associations, or individuals for circulation. **1960** *Library Assoc. Rec.* Aug. 262/2 *Travelling Library*, a vehicle of small size..shelved or otherwise equipped to provide a rural service to villages and isolated farms and houses. **1982** H. INNES *Black Tide* v. i. 220 The *Mabinogion*... She'd got it from the travelling library. **1885** *South Florida Sentinel* (Orlando) 1 July 3/3 The popular traveling salesman..will leave in a few days. **1954** *Jrnl. Operations Res. Soc. Amer.* II. 393 Little is known about the traveling-salesman problem. **1960** G. A. W. BOEHM *New World Math.* 114 Equally exasperating is the travelling salesman problem, with which a good many mathematicians have wrestled unsuccessfully for more than twenty years. **1978** I. B. SINGER *Shosha* v. 105 Baskets and boxes accumulated from the time Zelig was a traveling salesman. **1979** PAGE & WILSON *Introd. Computational Combinatorics* iv. 79 These are very interesting paths and circuits as they can be generalised into the well-known 'travelling salesman' problem. **1891** R. WALLACE *Rural Econ. Austral. & N.Z.* xxvi. 364 Should the land [of a sheep station] be mountainous or a travelling-stock road pass through it, the numbers [of employees] require to be increased. **1930** L. G. D. ACLAND *Early Canterbury Runs* 1st Ser. viii. 196 There was a travelling stock reserve there, and it was in the hut belonging to it that the man was murdered. **1977** C. MCCULLOUGH *Thorn Birds* vi. 120 There was an official Travelling Stock Route or TSR winding its way near the Barwon River.

travelogue (træ·vělǫg). orig. *U.S.* [f. TRAVEL *sb.* + -LOGUE, after MONOLOGUE *sb.*] An (illustrated) lecture about places and experiences encountered in the course of travel; hence a film, broadcast, book, etc., about travel; a travel documentary.

1903 *Daily Chron.* 16 Apr. 6/7 Mr. Burton Holmes, an American entertainer new to London, delivered last evening the first of a series of 'Travelogues'. **1921** *Glasgow Herald* 7 Nov. 10 The..Travelogue film, 'With Allenby in Palestine and Lawrence in Arabia'. **1927** H. E. FOSDICK *Pilgrimage to Palestine* p. vii, Some [books] are simply travelogues in which the successive experiences of the traveler furnish the strand for the narrative. **1931** [see *SPONSOR *v.* 2]. **1932** [see *DOCUMENTARY *a.* 4]. **1935** R. MACAULAY *Personal Pleasures* 67 Dido and her court feasted Æneas and his warriors, and after supper listened to his mournful travelogue. **1956** S. ERTZ *Charmed Circle* 78 Reality lay wholly within the boundaries of the United States, and..what she saw in Europe was a sort of illustrated travelogue. **1976** A. DAVIS *Television* 119 There were 700 programmes and the travelogues of Armand and Michaela Denis. **1983** *Listener* 20 Jan. 27/2 It is part travelogue, part autobiography.

traversa: see *TRAVERSO.

traversal (trăvə̄·ɹsăl, træ·vəɹsăl). [f. TRAVERSE *v.* + -AL.] = TRAVERSE *sb.* 2.

1909 in WEBSTER. **1936** [see *line frequency* s.v. *LINE *sb.*² 32]. **1955** J. A. WHEELER in W. Pauli *Niels Bohr* 171 The increase of α in the traversal of the fission barrier will be of the order of unity. **1982** *Times* 22 Oct. 10/5 As he began on Wednesday the traversal of all Beethoven's sonatas..it was piercingly evident that here was someone who does far more than play the piano. **1984** *Observer* 15 Jan. 49/8 Speed—the traversal of the maximum space in the minimum time—was a disturbing obsession.

traverse, *sb.* Add: **3.** (Earlier example.)

1804 M. LEWIS in *Orig. Jrnls. Lewis & Clark Exped.* (1905) VI. 232 A Circumferentor..has also been employed in taking the traverse of the river.

16. Also *spec.* a pair of right-angled bends in a trench for protection against enfilading fire. (Later examples.)

1767 STERNE *Tr. Shandy* IX. xxvi. 115 Uncle Toby.. got his wound before the gate of St. Nicolas, in one of the traverses of the trench. **1802** C. JAMES *New Mil. Dict.* s.v. *Trenches*, On the angles or sides of the trench, there are lodgments or epaulements, in form of traverses, the better to hinder the sallies of the garrison. *a* **1917** E. A. MACKINTOSH *War, the Liberator* (1918) 136 As MacTaggart turned back at the corner of the traverse he felt strangely comforted by the sight of MacRae. **1957** P. KEMP *Mine were of Trouble* iv. 76 It struck me that the trenches were very badly constructed, being..dug almost in a straight line instead of with traverses. **1971** S. HILL *Strange Meeting* ii. 139 The men had been getting their mid-day meal in this traverse when the bomb had landed in the middle of them.

traverse, *v.* Add: In British (but not American) English the vb. is now often stressed on the 2nd syllable, and this has influenced the pronunciation of its derivative forms. The sb. is still normally stressed on the 1st syllable.

traverso (trăvə̄·ɹso). *Mus.* Also **traversa.** [a. It.] = *transverse flute* s.v. *TRANSVERSE *a.* 1 d.

[**1776** J. HAWKINS *Gen. Hist. Sci. & Pract. Mus.* II. IV. iv. 452 It seems that the invention of the traverse flute is not to be attributed either to the Germans or the Helvetians.] **1801** BUSBY *Dict. Mus.* s.v. *Traversa*, (Ital.) a German flute. **1884** GROVE *Dict. Mus.* IV. 163/1 *Traverso*, (Ger. *Querflöte*), the present form of flute, held *square* or *across* (*à travers*) the performer... In Bach's scores it is called Flauto traverso, Traverso, and Traversiere. **1932** C. S. TERRY *Bach's Orchestra* iv. 79 Bach's treatment of the traverso has peculiar interest. **1938** *Oxf. Compan. Mus.* 949/1 *Traversa, traverso* (It.); traversière (Fr.); Traversflöte (Ger.). **1979** *Early Music* July 357/1 Open and forked fingerings..are basically the same on oboe and traverso.

travesty, *sb.* **2.** Chiefly *Theatr.* **a.** Delete *rare* and add later examples. *Spec.* (dressing in) the attire of the opposite sex. Freq. (*en*) *travesti*.

The phr. *en travesti(e)*, which is not recorded in Fr., represents a misinterpretation of the F. pa. pple. as a sb.

1850 THACKERAY *Pendennis* II. x. 102 He went into the pit, and saw..that eminent buffo actor, Tom Horseman, dressed as a woman. Horseman's travestie seemed to him a horrid and hideous degradation. **1957** G. B. L. WILSON *Dict. Ballet* 212 *Petipa*, Marie S. .. Her husband created for her a dance, *The Little Moujik*, in which she appeared en travesti. **1959** *Times* 3 Nov. 15/5 Defrance's troupe leaders and the girls in *travesti* receiving their last-minute counsels remain unaffectedly convincing. **1975** *New Yorker* 12 May 131/1 Nero, Otho, Tamerlane, and Julius Caesar will still have to be played by women *en travesti* or by countertenors. **1980** *Daily Tel.* 15 Dec. 10/1 Shapely young women have been showing off their legs *en travesti* since they were allowed on the English stage.

b. *Comb.* **travesty role,** a role designed to be played by a performer of the sex opposite to that of the character represented.

1958 *Listener* 5 June 955/3 Michel Sénéchal handled the *travesti* role of Platée with tact and sang the difficult music in an accomplished style. **1978** *Times* 23 Aug. 11/4 At the Coliseum Dennis Wicks makes the most of his travesty role.

travisher (træ·viʃəɹ). [Origin uncertain: *travish* is recorded as a dial. form of *traverse* (*Eng. Dial. Dict.*).] A carpenter's shave used for the final smoothing of chair seats.

1929 *Architects' Jrnl.* LXIX. 138/1 The travisher was invented—a spokeshave with a curved cutting iron, to be used, after the adze, in making the seat more comfortable. **1953** A. JOBSON *Household & Country Crafts* xx. 182 Of the four remaining tools, the top two are travishers, for finishing off the elm seats after adzing. **1968** J. ARNOLD *Shell Bk. Country Crafts* 133 Smoothing off follows with a succession of shavers:—the travisher, the smoothing-off iron and a devil.

travois, -voise, *sb.* Add: Also † **travoi, try-voy,** etc. (which represent an older form). (Earlier and later examples.)

1847 K. CARSON in W. F. Cody *Wild West* (1888) 349 The Tlamaths ..prevented his body from falling into our hands by drawing it away on a travoi. **1879** J. G. BOURKE *Diary* VIII. 847 (MS.), [He] says he will stick with the column if he has to be hauled on a travois. **1926** C. S. WALGAMOTT *Reminisc. Early Days* 26/2 George..found.. five head of horses with two riders the other three horses dragging either lodge poles or try-voy, possibly both. **1959** E. TUNIS *Indians* 86/1 Those Indians trained their dogs to help with the transport job by carrying packs or by dragging tent poles and small travois on which burdens could be lashed. **1974** J. A. MICHENER *Centennial* iv. 149 The travois, that primitive but functional invention for hauling goods, was constructed always from two poles used otherwise to support the tipi.

Travolator (træ·vǫlēⁱtəɹ). orig. *U.S.* Also with small initial, and **travelator, travellator.** [f. TRAVEL *v.*, after *ESCALATOR.] The proprietary name of a moving pavement designed for use at railway stations, airports, shopping centres, etc. (see quot. 1955).

1955 *Sci. News Let.* 8 Oct. 232/3 A moving sidewalk with cleated escalator treads had been developed by the Otis Elevator Company... Designers foresee use of the moving platform, called 'Trav-o-lator', for such congested areas as airports, subway stations, [etc.]. **1957** *Country Life* 13 June 1186/3 Travolators..represent an improvement on the moving-staircase principle, since they will possess a flat surface along which the passengers can walk while they are moving. **1957** *Economist* 28 Sept. 1043/1 Two 300 foot 'travelators'—stepless escalators that carry pedestrians along slight gradients—are expected to be in operation at the Bank underground station in London towards the end of next year. **1958** *Trade Marks Jrnl.* 26 Feb. 196/1 *Trav-o-lator*..Passenger-carrying conveyors (machines). Otis Elevator Company..260, Eleventh Avenue, New York..United States of America; Merchants and manufacturers. **1959** *Official Gaz.* (U.S. Patent Office) 19 May TM98 Otis Elevator Company, New York, N.Y. Filed Nov. 28, 1958. *Trav-o-lator.* For Endless Conveyors. First use July 28, 1955. **1959** *Archit. Rev.* CXXVI. 321 Victorian Street, which is a rather dead shopping area, receives wedges of new shops, with rear servicing, on both sides of the travellator system. **1967** 'W. HAGGARD' *Conspirators* iv. 40 He bought a ticket from the coin-machine, going down to the train on the travolator. He didn't walk but let it carry him. **1967** *New Scientist* 19 Oct. 180/3 Whether all the oceans are continually in movement, like giant travolators. **1977** B. COCKS *Mid-Victorian Masterpiece* xx. 195 Members found that even without a travelator they could reach the Chamber within the six minutes allowed before the lobby doors are locked for a division. **1980** [see *TERMINAL *sb.* 5 a].

trawl, *sb.* **I. 2.** Restrict † *Obs.* to sense in Dict. and add: **b.** *fig.* An act of 'trawling' in order to find a person or persons (esp. a new employee) from among a larger population.

1971 *Daily Tel.* 2 Mar. 3/3 A 'trawl' is being made among civil servants to find a suitable man and an appointment is expected within two months. **1980** C. MOORHEAD *Fortune's Hostages* v. 97 The generals..rounded up 4,000 suspected leftists. They did very well in the trawl. **1984** *Times* 5 Apr. 1/8, I am going to make a serious trawl through the profession and see if I can find circuit judges whom I can safely appoint.

III. 4. *trawl-line* (earlier example).
1867 G. E. Clark *Seven Years of Sailor's Life* 308 The old mother fish, full of spawn, are snaked on, to their miles of trawl line.

trawl, *v.* Add: **1. c.** (Later *fig.* examples.)
1979 'J. le Carré' *Smiley's People* (1980) xix. 234 Kirov dutifully trawls the émigrés, but without result. **1984** *Observer* 8 Apr. 32/6 We trawled Britain, the United States, Australia and South Africa for a chief executive.

trawler. 3. trawler-man: delete † and add later examples.
1934 *Sun* (Baltimore) 8 Oct. 7/5 Trawlermen of Hampton, Phoebus, Portsmouth and nearby harbors are planning a union. **1958** *Times* 9 Oct. 11/6 The distant water trawlermen..are doing work that for its hazards, long hours, and gruelling conditions would be difficult to compare with any job ashore. **1976** 'W. Trevor' *Children of Dynmouth* i. 9 A few boys became trawler-men, but life was easier and richer at the fish-packing station. **1984** *Times* 20 Feb. 1/4 As the son of a trawlerman..he wanted to see the very highest level of safety of people crewing vessels of all kinds.

Traxcavator (træ·kskăvēɪtəɹ). orig. *U.S.* Also **traxcavator.** [Blend of Track *sb.*, Tractor, and Excavator.] The proprietary name of a type of mechanical excavator which moves on endless steel bands or tracks (see quot. 1940).
1940 *Official Gaz.* (U.S. Patent Office) 30 Apr. 1035/2 *Traxcavator.* For excavating, grading and loading machinery—namely high shovels, tractor shovels, tractor loaders, bull-dozers, graders, and the like. Claims use since Jan. 22, 1940. **1952** *Law Rep. Queen's Bench Div.* II. 608 A traxcavator, a tracked vehicle with a speed of 2½ miles an hour turned this corner and stopped. **1956** *Trade Marks Jrnl.* 22 Feb. 181/2 *Traxcavator*... Machines for mechanical handling. Caterpillar Tractor Co..; 800, Davis Street, San Leandro, State of California, United States of America; manufacturers. **1968** *Industrial Tribunals Reports* III. 176 The material was excavated by mechanical diggers and a traxcavator. **1977** *N.Z. Herald* 5 Jan. 2–17/10 (Advt.), Morton Brown Asphalt Ltd., paving Auckland's carparks, drives, etc since 1948. Own traxcavators, graders, rollers and pavers.

tray, *sb.*[2] Add: **1. a.** Also *spec.* a tray of food brought to one not able or not wishing to eat at table; hence (*loosely*), a light snack.
1914 L. S. Woolf *Wise Virgins* xiv. 296 I'll ask them to bring you up a tray. What would you like? A little beef-tea and fish—or chicken? **1939** E. F. Benson *Trouble for Lucia* ix. 199 My maid would bring me a tray instead of dinner. **1951** L. Hellman *Autumn Garden* ii. ii. 88 You have had no dinner? I have made a tray for you. **1982** J. S. Borthwick *Case of Hook-Billed Kites* (1983) xxiv. 72 Mrs. Brent and Miss Fellows had had trays in their room.
d. = *sand-box 2 e.
1938 F. MacCunn *Cats* ii. 33 The tray, or pan, should have a low side all round it; put it in a dark corner—not close to the cat's bed. **1948** P. M. Soderberg *Cat Breeding* 178 Once the use of the tray has been taught in the house it is an excellent plan to encourage the kitten to go out-doors. **1969** 'A. Gilbert' *Missing from Home* vii. 103 You really can't have a cat in the flat, there's no outlet, and I think..a tray is unhygienic. I don't care how often it's changed.
e. *Austral.* The part of a truck on which goods are carried.
1960 'N. Shute' *Trustee from Toolroom* v. 100 The semi-trailer stood by the aircraft with the sausage-like component on the tray swathed in hessian. **1980** P. Davis *Australians on Road* xiv. 125/2 Ford management conceived the idea of producing a vehicle which could be said to be an essential part of farm equipment, yet was still comfortable enough for the farmer to take his wife out for an evening in town. The result was a passenger-type cab, married to an enclosed load tray; it was called the coupé utility, later corrupted to 'ute'.
4. tray-cloth (examples); **tray lunch(eon),** lunch served on a tray; a light lunch; **traymobile** *Austral.* and *N.Z.* [*-mobile], a small wheeled table or stand on which food, etc., may be transported; a tea-trolley; **tray stand,** a small table on which to rest a tray; **tray supper,** supper served on a tray; a light supper; **tray top,** (*a*) a rimmed table top which can be removed and used separately as a tray; (*b*) *Austral.* a truck with a pick-up body.
1889 *Cent. Dict.*, Tray-cloth. *c* **1909** D. H. Lawrence *Collier's Friday Night* (1934) iii. 59 Beatrice Wyld sits in the armchair, and Nellie Lambert on the sofa, the latter doing drawn-thread work on a white tray-cloth. **1971** *Islander* (Victoria, B.C.) 25 Dec. 5/2 The very best cups and saucers..were set on a hemstitched linen traycloth in a large, round wicker tray. **1970** V. Canning *Great Affair* iv. 58 The steward..served our tray lunches. **1936** P. Bottome *Level Crossing* xvi. 193 After what Nelly called a 'tray luncheon', she suggested showing Deidre the house. **1948** V. Palmer *Golconda* xx. 169 Her attention was on the traymobile the girl had wheeled in beside her. She began to pour out the tea. **1965** G. McInnes *Road to Gundagai* v. 79 Against the vacant wall is the 'dumb waiter' or 'traymobile' on which food and crockery come in from the kitchen. **1844** T. Webster *Encycl. Domestic Econ.* 241 A tray-stand..formed of two frames and girth to fold up. **1895** *Army & Navy Co-op. Soc. Price List* 15 Sept. 311 Cairo Tray Stand. **1825** H. Wilson *Mem.* I. 43 Amy gave us merely a tray-supper, in one corner of the drawing-room. **1933** H. Edwards *All Night at Mr. Stanyhurst's* 23 Me and you were going to the play, and coming home to a tray supper. **1962** M. Carleton *Dread Sunset* (1963) ii. 36 Her own tray suppers looked deceptively simple. **1934** Webster, Tray-top table. **1951** *Catal. Exhibits, South Bank Exhib., Festival of Britain* 144/1 Occasional table with removable tray top. **1969** *Northern Territory News* (Darwin) *Focus '69* 97/3 It is a relief for the semi or tray top crews when they reach Alice—and the bitumen of the Stuart Highway. **1979** *Truck & Bus Transportation* (N.S.W.) Sept. 46/1 The general cartage fleet comprises..three Albions with tray-top bodies.

treacle, *sb.* Add: **III. 5.** *treacle pud(ding, toffee, -well* (earlier example); **treacle-posset** (earlier example); **treacle sleep** *colloq.*, a deep, unbroken sleep (later example).
1739 E. Smith *Compl. Housewife* (ed. 9) 319 Those who can't afford mountain-whey, may drink treacle-posset. **1974** I. Murdoch *Sacred & Profane Love Machine* 314 What about some treacle pud, it's awfully good here. **1861** Mrs. Beeton *Bk. Househ. Managem.* 688 *Rolled treacle pudding*..suet crust..treacle..grated ginger. **1973** 'H. Howard' *Highway to Murder* x. 117, I slept a treacle sleep from nine p.m. until the alarm clock went off..next morning. **1885** R. Holland *Gloss. Words County of Chester* 367 *Traycle toffy, s.*, sometimes called *toffy sticks*, a very favourite sweetmeat amongst Cheshire school children. **1924** 'R. Crompton' *William—the Fourth* viii. 124 William was..deeply engrossed in his treacle toffee. **1983** 'A. T. Ellis' *Other Side of Fire* xx. 133 Think what fun it will be..parkin and treacle toffee. **1865** 'L. Carroll' *Alice's Adventures in Wonderland* vii. 107 The Dormouse..said, 'It was a treacle-well.'

treacle, *v.* Add: **2. b.** Also *intr.*
1915 H. G. Wells *Boon* iv. 124 Going round with the lantern when one is treacling for moths. **1941** —— *You can't be too Careful* iii. xxii. 218 As moth hunters treacle for moths.
3. (Later example.)
1966 J. Betjeman *High & Low* 25 *In blest Bethesda's limpid pool* Comes treacling out of Sunday School.

treacly, *a.* Add: *fig.* (Examples in musical contexts.)
1930 J. B. Priestley *Angel Pavement* iv. 176 The organ was shaking out cascades of treacly sound. **1947** Auden *Age of Anxiety* (1948) i. 26 A doomed Sodom dancing its heart out To treacly tunes. **1980** S. Brett *Dead Side of Mike* xiii. 143 Treacly, undistinguished music.

tread, *sb.* Add: **III. 10. b.** (Examples with reference to motor transport.) Also *spec.* the thick moulded surface of a pneumatic tyre, which runs in contact with the ground (as opp. to the sidewalls). Cf. *retread *sb.* 1.
1902 C. L. Freeston in A. C. Harmsworth *Motors & Motor-Driving* 237 *The Collier*... this type is provided with an unusually stout tread. **1913** *Sci. Amer.* 11 Jan. 53/1 The tread is made up independently of the tire by laying up narrow strips of rubber..in such a way that the center of the tread is thicker than the edges. **1929** *Rubber & Tyre Rev.* Jan. 148/1 On pneumatic tyres for buses an average of 6,000 miles per ⅛ in. tread thickness can be safely assumed. **1964** *Amer. Speech* XXXIX. 275 *Tread, n.*, the outer, final component of the assembled tire. It is made up of the cap which contacts the road surface and the sidewall. **1982** M. Russell *Rainblast* iv. 28 People come along fast... The treads find they've a little extra to do.
11. c. *Geomorphol.* The approximately horizontal part of each of the step-like parts of a glacial stairway or similar landform.
1904 [see *stairway b]. **1930** F. E. Matthes *Geol. Hist. Yosemite Valley* 95/2 Rock structure, or, more broadly, rock resistance,..determines in large measure at what points in a given canyon the individual sills and treads shall develop. **1954** *Jrnl. Glaciol.* II. 421 Fig. 2..shows a *roche moutonnée* of step-like form... The contrast between the smoothed upper tread and the irregular 'plucked' riser can be seen. **1968** R. W. Fairbridge *Encycl. Geomorphol.* 467/1 Where the overdeepened treads are undrained, there are rock-cut depressions or partly moraine-dammed pools... They are known as paternoster lakes.
IV. 12. (sense 4) *tread-mire*; **tread plate,** (*a*) a footplate or runner which forms or protects the step on a vehicle; (*b*) (see quot. 1967); **tread-trap** *Archæol.*, a wooden device for trapping an animal by the foot.
1888 G. M. Hopkins *Poems* (1967) 105 Stanches, starches Squadroned masks and manmarks treadmire toil there Footfretted in it. **1949** *Automobile & Carriage Builders' Jrnl.* CIV. 59 (*heading*) P-G-P aluminium treadplate. **1967** *Gloss. Sanitation Terms* (*B.S.I.*) 57 *Tread plate.* 1. Glazed ceramic, or other hard wearing, edging to the floor finish adjacent to the channel of a urinal. 2. Glazed ceramic, or other hard wearing, non-slip footrests on each side of a squatting W.C. pan. **1952** J. G. D. Clark *Prehist. Europe* ii. 51 A type of tread-trap..appearing for the first time in the Late Bronze Age..symbolizes the part still played by trapping in the closing stages of European prehistory.
Hence **trea·ded** *a.* [-ed[2]], of a tyre: having or furnished with a moulded tread; **treadless** *a.* [-less], having no tread or treads (esp. of tyres).
1906 *Westm. Gaz.* 6 Mar. 4/2 The substitution of single pneumatic tyres for the present double-treaded ones. **1968** A. Diment *Great Spy Race* x. 186 The treadless tyres teetered on tiptoe across the road. **1973** 'D. Rutherford' *Kick Start* vi. 139 The bike canting at a steep angle, we were holding on to the road surface by the treaded edge of the competition tyre. **1974** *Observer* 3 Nov. (Colour Suppl.) 27/2 Wearing treadless shoes, [we] were let into a dusty attic with a forged key. Another prisoner followed us, replacing anything we might move.

tread, *v.* Add: **A. 2.** *pa. t.* Also: **treaded** (only in phr. *treaded water*: see sense 7).
1944 *Stars & Stripes* (London ed.) 1 May 3 While Huie and four crewmen clambered into the liferaft, three others treaded water for three hours before succeeding in blowing up another raft by lung power. **1947** H. E. Bates *Purple Plain* x. 113 He treaded water for a moment or two. **1974** J. Irving *158-Pound Marriage* viii. 193 He said nothing; he treaded water.
B. 3. b. *to tread on air* (earlier examples); cf. *to walk upon air* s.v. Walk *v.*[1] 5 l.
1796 R. M. Roche *Children of Abbey* I. viii. 154 Such were the ideas of the innocent and romantic Amanda; ideas, which made her seem to tread on air. *a* **1817** Jane Austen *Northanger Abbey* (1818) II. xi. 223 If Wednesday should ever come!..It came—it was fine—and Catherine trod on air.
4. c. *to tread on the gas*: see *gas *sb.*[2]
7. *to tread water*: also *fig.*, to withhold oneself from progressive action, to 'mark time'.
1942 J. Lees-Milne *Ancestral Voices* (1975) 46 Although they miscalculated in assuming that the campaign would be over before last winter, they have been treading water since then, and merely keeping up their line. **1967** *Guardian* 24 May 9 In the absence of the Secretary-General, the UN delegations were treading water. **1980** N. Marsh *Photo-Finish* vi. 180, I am really..treading water until the police arrive.

treadle, *sb.* Add: **4. treadle mat,** a mat or casing which activates a mechanism when stepped on or otherwise depressed.
1937 *Times* 13 Apr. p. xvi/4 Pneumatic treadle mats cover the steps so that the doors when released by the driver may be automatically opened by passengers standing on the steps. **1966** *Electronics Weekly* 16 Mar. 3/1 The passage of the wheels over a treadle mat causes the light to change to red.

treadmill, *sb.* Add: **trea·dmiller,** a person who is 'on the treadmill' (*fig.*), esp. one who follows a dull and arduous working life.
1923 D. H. Lawrence *Kangaroo* viii. 164 Better a 'wicked creature' any day, than a mechanical treadmiller of a careerist. **1956** H. Gold *Man who was not with It* (1965) viii. 66, I even thought of..that shy treadmiller Joy.

treason, *sb.* Add: **1. b.** *treason of the clerks* = *trahison des clercs.
1940 W. Empson *Gathering Storm* 34 Treason of the clerks, boys, curtains that descend, Lights becoming darks, boys, waiting for the end. **1970** C. C. O'Brien *Camus* iii. 61 The proposition that failure to take an anti-communist stand constituted 'the treason of the clerks' of which Benda spoke. **1979** *Guardian* 6 June 14/7 Ex-King's men will be revealed as those whose bogus liberalism led them to 'the treason of the clerks'.
4. a. *treason trial.*
1930 *Economist* 6 Dec. 1054/2 Treason trials are the grand elixir of revolutionary régimes; and for years the Soviet Government, like competent theatrical producers, have managed to stage a series of such performances in almost uninterrupted succession. **1979** A. Melville-Ross *Two Faces of Nemesis* viii. 47 Treason trials don't help the national image.

treasure, *sb.* Add: **2.** Also as an affectionate term of address.
1920 'K. Mansfield' *Let.* 31 Oct. (1977) 194 But, my treasure, my life is ours. You know it. **1967** N. Freeling *Strike Out* 40 Next week, treasure, we're going to make a cruise... Go and buy yourself some clothes.
4. *treasure-box* (earlier example), *-hunter* (earlier and later examples), *-seeker*; **treasure-hunt** (examples); freq. *fig.* and *transf.*, a game in which hidden objects are searched for, often by following a trail of clues; **Treasure State** *U.S. slang*, the State of Montana.
1876 Treasure-box [see *powder keg* s.v. *powder *sb.*[1] 5 b]. **1913** J. Vaizey *College Girl* xii. 166, I was thinking..c1a treasure hunt!..lots of presents, stowed away in odd corners. **1919** E. H. Jones *Road to En-Dor* (1920) vi. 58 A treasure-hunt has a glamour of its own. **1939** T. S. Eliot *Family Reunion* ii. ii. 110 You have a long journey ... Think of it as like a children's treasure hunt. **1977** M. Green *Children of Sun* 22 One of those Twenties' treasure hunts, in which people drove..across all England, in search of some otherwise unprocurable item. **1851** H. Melville *Moby Dick* II. xxxvi. 241 He proceeds very heedfully, like a treasure-hunter in some old house, sounding the walls to find where the gold is masoned in. **1983** S. Vizinczey *Innocent Millionaire* xiii. 111 Maybe I was meant to be a treasure-hunter. **1890** J. G. Frazer *Golden Bough* II. iv. 367 The treasure-seeker places the rod on the ground after sundown, and when it rests directly over treasure, the rod begins to move as if it were alive. **1982** 'C. Aird' *Last Respects* viii. 81 There are treasure-seekers, Inspector, who would..not care that they were destroying priceless marine archaeology. **1934** M. H. Weseen *Dict. Amer. Slang* 412 Treasure State, Montana. **1976** *Billings* (Montana) *Gaz.* 20 June 6-c/1 A solid century of mining has failed to put much of a dent in the state's gold, silver, copper and coal reserves. So the slogan, 'Treasure State', which used to grace Montana license plates, is still appropriate.

treasury, *sb.* Add: **3. c.** *pl.* Treasury bills.
1922 *Daily Tel.* 12 June 2/1 New secondhand Treasuries were dealt in at 2¼ per cent. **1930** *Daily Express* 6 Oct. 14/4 The banks bought short-dated Treasuries at 2 per cent.

6. treasury-bench (earlier example); **treasury note,** (*a*) for *U.S.* read chiefly *U.S.*; = *currency note* s.v. *CURRENCY 6; (earlier and later examples); (*b*) (in Dict. s.v. *treasury letter*) (earlier example); **treasury tag** = *India tag* s.v. *INDIA 6; formerly consisting of a length of lace with a blunt pin at one end which was secured through a socket at the other.

1775 F. E. BOSCAWEN *Let.* 28 June in C. Aspinall-Oglander *Admiral's Widow* (1942) 64 Our cruel patriots.. would willingly wade through blood, provided it led to the Treasury Bench. **1756** in S. M. Hamilton *Lett. to Washington* (1898) I. 202 Who is hereby required to pay the same in Treasury Notes, to be emmitted by Virtue of the said Act of Assembly. **1820** *Kaleidoscope* 25 July 30/1 Or (summoned by a Treasury-note) Night after night to sit and vote. **1923** A. HUXLEY *Antic Hay* iii. 50 It was with reluctance that Gumbril parted from his Treasury notes. **1974** *Encycl. Brit. Micropædia* X. 103/2 *Treasury note,* government security, usually marketable, with maturity ranging from one to five years. **1912, 1963** Treasury tag [see *India tag* s.v. *INDIA 6]. **1975** 'M. SINCLAIR' *Long Time Sleeping* iv. 48 A little tray of pins, paperclips and little bits of coloured string known as Treasury tags.

treat, *sb.*[1] Add: **5. a.** (Earlier example.)

1770 J. WEDGWOOD *Let.* 13 Oct. (1965) 98 Your stay here..was a most agreeable treat to us and all your friends in this part of the world.

b. Delete *vulgar* and add earlier and later examples. Also adjectivally.

1898 [see *DUKE *sb.* 7]. **1942** *R.A.F. Jrnl.* 18 Apr. 10 We..set light to a ..dump of Iraqi petrol which went up a fair treat. **1959** A. SILLITOE *Loneliness of Long-Distance Runner* iii. 185 The sports ground looked a treat: with big tea-tents all round and flags flying. **1960** *Guardian* 23 Dec. 7/2 He had a stroke..but he's come on a treat. **1984** *New Yorker* 17 Sept. 56/1, I knew this floor had life left in it... It's come up a treat.

treat, *v.* Add: **7. d.** Colloq. phr. *to treat 'em rough,* to manhandle (people, etc.), to treat harshly or aggressively. As a motto: see quot. 1918. Also (hyphened) as *attrib. phr.* Chiefly *U.S.*

1918 W. H. ALLEN *Stories of Americans in World War* 162 The men in the tank service have chosen 'Treat 'Em Rough' as their slogan, and a huge black cat as the emblem and mascot. Any cat that looks black enough and fierce enough is apt to be kidnapped and adopted by some tank battalion. **1930** *Amer. Speech* VI. 83, I never have the same girl twice; I take 'em young and treat 'em rough. **1962** *Times* 6 July 15/4 A treat-'em-rough warden of the old school.

treatabi·lity. [f. TREATABLE *a.*: see *-BILITY.] The quality of being treatable; responsiveness to medical or psychotherapeutic treatment.

1957 *Rep. Committee on Homosexual Offences* v. 32 in *Parl. Papers 1956–57* (Cmnd. 247) XIV. 85 The question of treatability. **1959** B. WOOTTON *Social Sci. & Social Pathol.* viii. 241 If treatability is taken as the test of responsibility, it follows that those who cannot or will not be treated must be regarded as liable to punishment. **1976** *Economist* 21 Aug. 18 The importance of treatability as a criterion. **1982** *Daily Tel.* 29 Oct. 18/6 The inclusion of 'treatability' among criteria for admission.

treatable, *a.* **1. b.** Delete † and add: *Obs.* exc. in *Med.* (Later examples.)

1974 E. AMBLER *Dr. Frigo* II. 141 Muscular dystrophy ..is to some extent treatable and controllable. **1978** *Bull. Amer. Acad. Arts & Sci.* Feb. 29 Heart disease and strokes are related to..potentially treatable but undetected hypertension.

treatise, *sb.* Add: **4.** *Comb.*, as **treatise poem,** a didactic poem of the eighteenth century.

1936 C. S. LEWIS *Allegory of Love* vi. i. 233 In our Augustan period we find a form which has not yet been named and which is only less dominant than satire. I mean the long Treatise Poem (if I may risk the invention of a name where one is badly needed) as practised by Thompson, Armstrong, Young, Akenside, Cowper, and the like. **1980** *Times Lit. Suppl.* 1 Aug. 863/3 The eighteenth-century treatise-poem of Akenside and the rest.

treatment. Add: **5. b.** *Cinemat.* A preparatory version of a screenplay, including descriptions of sets and of the camerawork required.

1928 L. NORTH *Parasites* i. 33 We always make treatments of our stories—it's a sort of synopsis suggestin' what to use an' what to put in the discard. **1938** A. HUXLEY *Let.* 18 Nov. (1969) 437 I've done a fair amount of work: a 'treatment', as they call it in the jargon of the films, of the life of Mme Curie for Garbo. **1959** HALAS & MANVELL *Technique Film Animation* 342 *Treatment,* preliminary stage to writing script. Assembling ideas and situations for the film in hand. **1981** L. DEIGHTON *XPD* xxix. 240 We asked the FO to request a copy of the treatment... They would have got a copy of the script too.

c. *the full treatment,* the most elaborate manner of dealing with a subject, 'the works', esp. in phr. *to give* (or *get*) *the full treatment.* Also (often less emphatically) without *full. colloq.*

1950 E. HEMINGWAY *Across River* xxiv. 170 We'll give breakfast the full treatment. **1958** *Sunday Express* 9 Nov. 17/4 In *No Concern of Mine* it gets the full treatment in a first act which is brilliantly contrived. **1959** *Listener* 4 June 999/2 This programme was admirably free from the piety or boost which seems to be unavoidable when some celebrities are given the treatment. **1967** MRS. L. B. JOHNSON *White House Diary* 25 June (1970) 539 She seemed impressed with the kitchen when we took her through. Betty gave her the full treatment about the washer and dryer and disposal. **1973** R. HILL *Ruling Passion* I. iii. 26 I'm really getting the treatment, thought Pascoe. What does he expect from me?

8. *attrib.*, as *treatment plant, room.*

1963 A. LUBBOCK *Austral. Roundabout* 114 These were the trucks which transport the ore from the mine to the treatment plant. **1975** *Petroleum Rev.* XXIX. 315/1 A treatment plant for the removal of impurities. **1961** I. FLEMING *Thunderball* iv. 43 It was a white cubicle treatment-room like all the others. **1977** J. A. KOTARBA in Douglas & Johnson *Existential Sociol.* ix. 259 These conversations occurred in the waiting room, double occupance treatment rooms..and occasionally over coffee.

treaty, *sb.* **3. a.** For 'b.' read 'b and in phr. *private treaty*: see *PRIVATE *a.* 7 f'.

6. *treaty-money* (Canad. examples); **treaty Indian** *N. Amer.* (now chiefly Canad.), an Indian whose tribe or band has signed a treaty with the Government, a ward of the Government; **treaty-port** (earlier example); **Treaty stone,** the stone on which the Treaty of Limerick (3 Oct. 1691) was reputedly signed (see quot. 1866).

1876 R. I. DODGE *Black Hills* 139 Every year since the treaty was signed has witnessed more or less pillage, depredation, and murder, by the treaty Indians. **1936** B. BROOKER *Think of Earth* I. v. 59 He wore the shoddy black clothes, moccasins and red neckerchief which the Treaty Indians of the neighbourhood had affected years before. **1973** 'M. CAMPBELL' *Halfbreed* ii. 18 Grandma Dubuque was a treaty Indian woman. **1933** *Beaver* June 53 Upon the arrival of the Indian agent, the payment of the treaty money is usually first proceeded with. **1956** H. S. M. KEMP *Northern Trader* (1957) iii. 35 Had he been on the books as an Indian, he would have been considered a ward of the Government, drawn his Treaty Money and supplies, [etc.]. **1863** *Times* 24 Nov. 9/6 (*heading*) The Yang-tze-Kiang and the new Treaty Ports. **1842** J. P. LAWSON *Gazetteer of Ireland* 602/2 It is said by tradition that this famous document was signed by both parties on a large stone near Thomond Bridge,..which is locally designated the *Treaty Stone.* **1866** M. LENIHAN *Limerick* xxxiv. 271 The treaty is said to have been signed..near the Red Gate... Tradition does not admit that it was signed on what has been called the 'Treaty Stone', which has occupied a place on the North side of Thomond Bridge for many years, and which was originally a stone, used by country people for getting on horses when leaving town. **1922** JOYCE *Ulysses* 324 Remember Limerick and the broken treatystone. **1977** *Irish Democrat* Mar. 6/3 In the breach of death my Donal fell and he sleeps near the Treaty Stone.

treble, *sb.* Add: **I. 2. f.** (Earlier example.)

1872 *Young Englishwoman* Oct. 555/1 *Crochet rosette*.. 3rd row:..work 11 treble on each chain scallop.

g. *Racing.* (*a*) A total of three races won by the same horse; (*b*) a bet on three horses to win the respective races in which they are entered (the usual sense).

1924 C. HAWTREY *Truth at Last* xix. 226 Many [*sc.* starting-price bookmakers] have further altered that rule, now limiting the odds to 50 to 1 for the double event, and 100 to 1 for treble. **1931** *Daily Express* 21 Sept. 15/4 Peacock wound up a fine week in Scotland, where Nevett landed a treble for him on Saturday. **1951** [see *ACCUMULATOR 4]. **1964** A. WYKES *Gambling* viii. 194 (*caption*) The bettor has staked a total of 27s. 6d. on his four chosen horses with 11 separate bets of 2s. 6d.—the bets consisting of six 'doubles', four 'trebles', and an 'accumulator' bet. **1981** P. INCHBALD *Tondo for Short* vi. 70 Cigars, liqueurs, brandy—has he won a big treble or something?

h. *Darts.* A throw into the narrow space between the two middle circles on a dart-board, worth three times the single score for the sector in which the dart lands; the space itself.

1936 [see *DOUBLE *sb.* 3 s]. **1981** R. LEWIS *Seek for Justice* ii. 53 The first dart flicked into the treble twenty. It was followed by a second... The microphone boomed: ..'Can he nail a third treble?..He's done it'.

i. *Assoc. Football.* The winning of three national or international competitions by one football club during a season.

1959 *Listener* 19 Feb. 331/1 The treble of League, Cup, and European Cup seemed to be at least a possibility. **1977** *News of World* 17 Apr. 21/2 That would make me unique, the only player who has done the double and treble.

j. A drink of spirits of three times the standard measure.

1968 J. F. STRAKER *SIN & Johnny Inch* 131 Sinclair poured yet another whisky. Like the others, it came well up the glass. A good treble, Johnny reckoned. **1979** M. BABSON *So soon done For* ii. 12 Crispin poured drinks for himself and Kay. Jeremy, he noted, had given himself a treble.

treble, *a.* Add: **1. c.** Also of a drink of spirits: constituting three times the standard measure.

1964 L. DEIGHTON *Funeral in Berlin* xxiii. 126 He.. ordered three treble brandies. **1977** 'J. D. WHITE' *Salzburg Affair* xvi. 137 Hendryks..raised an urgent hand for the waiter. 'A treble scotch.'

3. *treble agent,* a spy who works for three countries, his superiors in each being informed of his service to the other, but usu. with actual allegiance only to one; *treble chance,* a form of football pool in which various points are awarded for a draw, an away win, and a home win; *treble X,* a brand or strength of beer.

1967 *Punch* 11 Oct. 542/1 A list of our treble agents in Bulgaria. **1978** W. WINGATE *Bloodbath* i. 12 He wants out. Reckons he's earned it as a double, or treble, agent. **1951** 'M. INNES' *Operation Pax* II. iv. 64 'Heard what was last week's treble chance?' he asked. 'Ninety-eight thousand.' **1972** M. JONES *Life on Dole* II. i. 102 Luck..seems as evasive as the treble-chance. **1856** GEO. ELIOT in *Westm. Rev.* Jan. 5 German ennui must be something as superlative as Barclay's treble X. **1858** C. M. YONGE *Christmas Mummers* vii. 95 They began to sing at the next house as loud as if they thought they should get..more than three times treble XXX ale! **1880** E. W. HAMILTON *Diary* 7 Dec. (1972) I. 85 The Irish 'soup' (as Mr. Gladstone terms it) is 'thickening' and becoming what the brewers would call 'Treble X'.

tree, *sb.* Add: **B. 1. d.** = CHRISTMAS-TREE.

[**1838** H. MARTINEAU *Retrospect* III. 182, I was present at the introduction into the new country of..the German Christmas-tree... The tree was the top of a young fir, planted in a tub.] **1851** E. RUSKIN *Let.* 28 Dec. in M. Lutyens *Effie in Venice* (1965) II. 236 They wanted me to come in the evening when the tree was lighted to see the presents all divided. **1945** N. MITFORD *Pursuit of Love* iii. 23 We got back late for the tree... Uncle Matthew..was struggling into his Father Christmas clothes! **1979** M. MCCARTHY *Cannibals & Missionaries* i. 19 Distribution of presents..and the darned crèche and parish-house tree to set up.

6. b. (*b*) More widely, any branching system of vessels or organs in the body; (*e*) (further examples); (also in *Linguistics,* etc.) a set of items that can be represented by such a diagram; (*f*) *Oil Industry* (see quot. 1954); cf. *CHRISTMAS-TREE 2, quot. 1930.

1881, etc. [see *ROOT *sb.*[1] 14 c]. **1930** T. S. ELIOT tr. *St.-J. Perse's Anabasis* 59 You shall see me for long time unspeaking under the female tree of my veins. **1952** [see *CAVITATION 2]. **1954** *Time* 11 Jan. 3/2 (Advt.), These *trees of steel,* with their long *metal roots* extending thousands of feet into the earth, are actually assemblies of valves and fittings which control the flow of oil from reservoirs. Oilmen call them 'trees' or 'Christmas trees' because of the many unusual patterns and designs obtained when this wellhead equipment is put together to control wells of various kinds, varying pressures, and unique producing characteristics. **1958** W. H. BURGE in *Information & Control* I. 183 The tree used is a hierarchical network with a finite number of points arranged in levels. **1959** *Nuovo Cimento* Suppl. XIII. 499 The restriction on the number of symbols that can be rewritten in a single rule guarantees that given a terminal string..it will be possible to discover the associated tree or trees. **1972** *Computers & Humanities* VII. 5 With the use of a light gun the linguist can select from alternative expansions in phrase structure trees. **1973** C. W. GEAR *Introd. Computer Sci.* vii. 294 If it is necessary to trace through a tree in order frequently, it is worth storing the trace path. **1976** *Canad. Jrnl. Linguistics* XXI. 129 The psychological reality of aspects of deep structure and surface structure trees is open to interpretation in several respects. **1976** *Offshore Engineer* Mar. 6/3 Shell Expro is going ahead with subsea completion of a stepout well on the Brent field this summer and will be using one of the most sophisticated underwater trees in the world... The tree is described as 'wet, diverless', and flowline connection can be carried out from a rig or a drillship. **1977** *Lancet* 4 June 1187/1 Angiography has made it possible to assess with reasonable confidence the state of the cerebral vascular tree. **1977** *Ibid.* 6 Aug. 278/1 After cholecystectomy for gallstones, it is not unusual for a stone to be left behind in the biliary tree. **1978** *Nature* 24 Aug. 745/1 The amount of work involved in searching a tree of moves is B^D, where B (the branching factor) is the average number of alternatives throughout the tree, and D is the depth of search.

7. a. *money* (etc.) *does not grow on trees* (orig. *U.S.*): money (etc.) is not easily obtainable; *out of (one's) tree* (U.S. slang) (see quot. 1971).

1669 'POOR ROBIN' *Almanack* sig. B8, Minc'd Pyes do not grow upon every tree, But search the Ovens for them, and there they be. **1750** W. CHANCELLOR *Diary* Nov. in *Pennsylvania Mag. Hist. & Biogr.* (1968) XCII. 471 Africa, where tis so falsly said, that Gold grows on the Trees. **1787** *Amer. Museum* II. 383 When the new government is established, 'money will grow upon the trees'. **1833** F. MARRYAT *Peter Simple* in *Metropolitan Mag.* Aug. 302/2 *Clothes* don't grow upon trees in ould Ireland. **1932** W. MCFEE *Harbourmaster* xxi. 371 Can I make money? Does it grow on trees out there? **1964** J. AIKEN *Black Hearts in Battersea* (1965) iv. 51 You'll be wanting it yourself come dinner-time. Sausages don't grow on trees in London. **1977** 'S. WOODS' *Thief or Two* 118, I don't imagine these things [*sc.* jewels] grow on trees.

1966 *Current Slang* (Univ. S. Dakota) Fall 6 *Tree,* n., mind, esp. in the expression 'drive one out of one's tree.'.. She drives me right out of my tree. **1971** E. E. LANDY *Underground Dict.* 143 *Out of one's tree,* expression meaning (1) be thinking, talking or acting in an irrational way —e.g. *You are talking out of your tree* or (2) be in an unfamiliar place. **1976** N. THORNBURG *Cutter & Bone* ii. 45 'We is duh [= the] loan*ees*.' 'You're out of your tree.'

b. *tree of life,* (*d*) a schematized representation of a tree or shrub used as an artistic motif, esp. in oriental work; freq. *attrib.*

1880 G. C. M. BIRDWOOD *Industrial Arts India* 336 The tree of life represented on modern Yarkand rugs is always a pomegranate tree. **1931** A. U. DILLEY *Oriental Rugs &*

Carpets Pl. 57 (*caption*) Beluchistan Prayer Rug with Rectangular Niche and Tree of Life. **1960** B. Snook *Eng. Historical Embroidery* 81 Hangings worked in polychrome,..with flowing stems or a Persian 'Tree of Life' rising from a ground of grass-grown mole hills. **1972** *Islander* (Victoria, B.C.) 28 May 5/2 A most recently finished piece [of weaving] is done in the universal tree-of-life symbol. **1977** *Times* 25 June 2/3 A Kashan silk Tree of Life rug..made £3,000.

9. a. *tree-belt* (example), *-crop, -fork, -fruit* (later examples), *-growth, -shadow* (example). **b.** *tree-felling* (earlier example), *-planting* (examples); *tree-shadowing* adj. **c.** *tree-arched, -bound, -grown, -hung, -lined* (examples), *-planted* (examples), *-scattered, -screened, -shaded* (examples), *-shadowed, -surrounded, -tangled, -wrapt* adjs.

c **1857** J. R. Lowell *Power of Sound* in *Uncoll. Poems* (1950) 123 A parson's son, through tree-arched country ways, I rode. **1936** W. Faulkner *Absalom, Absalom!* ix. 365 They walked up the rutted tree-arched drive. **1962** E. Snow *Other Side of River* (1963) lxvi. 502 Another tree belt had been more than half planted over a length of 720 miles. **1886** Hardy *Mayor of Casterbridge* I. iv. 49 From the centre of each side of this tree-bound square ran avenues. **1951** L. MacNeice tr. *Goethe's Faust* II. 202 Through a great plain Peneios freely takes His bush-bound, tree-bound course through quiet lakes. **1943** J. S. Huxley *TVA* 102 An unusual line of TVA research concerns the development of so-called tree-crops. **1958** *Times* 22 Aug. 12/4 Tree-crops, small fruits, grains, seeds, and livestock are the main farming interests. **1759** *Crit. Rev.* Sept. 178 Why, for example, should we be so complaisant to the French, as to use their terms of *carcasse,..abbattement..*, and *coup de main*; when we can say *fire-ball,.. tree-felling,..*and *bold stroke*? **1922** Joyce *Ulysses* 191 A runaway in blighted treeforks from hue and cry. **1946** Dylan Thomas *Deaths & Entrances* 22 A she bird sleeping..Within the nested treefork. **1946** *Nature* 2 Nov. 605/1, I presented the fundamental and elementary culture of the Mediterranean based on a combination of cereal agriculture and tree-fruit crops. **1970** D. Waterfield *Continental Waterboy* i. 8 A family could make a living off ten acres by growing tree-fruits. **1846** J. G. Whittier *Poems* (1849) 321 Ghosts of old Beliefs still flit and moan..O'er tree-grown barrow and gray ring of stone. **1978** *Detroit Free Press* 5 Mar. (Parade Suppl.) 15/3 Tree-grown cherries..demand years of tender care. **1917** *Amer. Forestry* XXIV. 732 (*caption*) Comparison of 43 years of rainfall and tree growth. **1956** *Nature* 21 Jan. 124/1 The variety and abundance of insect life as a whole rapidly fall off beyond the limits of tree-growth. **1927** J. Elder *Thomasina Toddy* xii. 118 Leafy backwaters, sunny fields, and tree-hung banks to suit all tastes. **1981** *Sunday Express* 11 Oct. (Colour Suppl.) 23/2 There is a little, tree-hung, irregular village square with an island of greenery at its hub. **1910** *Bradshaw's Railway Guide* Apr. 1123 (Advt.), The smartest bijou hotel in London... Situate in wide tree-lined thoroughfare. **1978** R. Ludlum *Holcroft Covenant* xi. 130 He..drove rapidly through the peaceful, tree-lined suburban area. **1879** C. M. Yonge *Magnum Bonum* III. xl. 904 The broad tree-planted streets of the old Quaker city. **1962** E. Snow *Other Side of River* (1963) lxx. 539 Strolling down a tree-planted street of new apartment houses I chose one to enter. **1872, 1902** Tree-planting [see *Arbor Day]. *a* **1974** R. Crossman *Diaries* (1975) I. 67 Today I was busy with Pritchett about tree-planting on the bends of the Cherwell between Upper Prescote and Prescote. **1980** P. Lively *Judgement Day* vii. 90 He..had refused to contribute to the Tree Planting Fund. **1951** Tree-scattered [see *river-winding* s.v. *river *sb.*[1] 4 g]. **1923** Kipling *Irish Guards in Great War* II. 163 A close and blind land of woods, copses, farms, mills and tree-screened roads. **1909** *Westm. Gaz.* 20 Oct. 4/1 Matthew Arnold's tree-shaded grave lies to the south-east of the church. **1958** O. Caroe *Pathans* xvii. 285 A place he loved, covered with green turf, tree-shaded beside the broad stream. **1954** J. R. R. Tolkien *Fellowship of Ring* I. iii. 87 As silent as tree shadows. **1952** S. Spender *Learning Laughter* ix. 117 Ben Shemen is a charming, tree-shadowed place. **1912** E. Pound *Ripostes* 37 In streams and tree-shadowing Forests on hill slopes. **1915** W. B. Yeats *Reveries over Childhood & Youth* ii. 16 Next to Merville where I lived, was another tree-surrounded house. **1925** A. Huxley *Those Barren Leaves* II. v. 125 Round as a fruit, tree-tangled, shines The moon. **1886** W. B. Yeats *Mosada* 3 Whose dwelling was a tree-wrapt island.

10. a. tree box, any of several larger varieties of the common box, *Buxus sempervirens*; **tree-climber** = Liana, liane; cf. Tree-creeper 2; **tree-daisy** = *olearia; **tree-fuchsia,** a shrub or small tree, *Fuchsia excorticata*, native to New Zealand and bearing pendent reddish-purple flowers with blue pollen; cf. *konini; **tree lucerne** (see quot. 1965); **tree pæony, peony** = *moutan.

1731 P. Miller *Gardeners Dict.* s.v. Buxus, All the Varieties of the Tree or large Box are proper to intermix in Clumps of Ever-greens. **1785** G. Washington *Jrnl.* 13 Apr. (1925) II. 360, 12 Horse Chestnut Trees..and an equal number of cuttings of the Tree Box. **1858** J. A. Warder *Hedges & Evergreens* II. 240 Where a moderate or low hedge is needed,..nothing can be better than the Tree-box. **1864** J. A. Grant *Walk across Afr.* 339 A tree-climber (*Landolphia florida*?) lay with its trunk winding like a huge snake. **1926** Tree-daisy [see *daisy-tree* s.v. *daisy 7]. **1958** Cockayne & Turner *Trees N.Z.* (ed. 4) 142 Weeping tree daisy..common in Central Otago. **1906** Laing & Blackwell *Plants N.Z.* 294 (*heading*) Fuchsia excorticata (the tree fuchsia). **1910** L. Cockayne *N.Z. Plants* iii. 29 The tree-fuchsia..offers a transition to the scrambling habit. **1970** *S. Afr. Panorama* Feb. 35/3 Below the platform a minute sunbird with iridescent blue plumage hovered before the crimson blooms of a tree-fuchsia. **1933** *Bulletin* (Sydney) 14 June 25/1 Tree lucerne is very hardy and easily grown from seed. **1965** *Austral. Encycl.* V. 383/1 The white-flowered tagasaste of Teneriffe (*Cytisus proliferus*), which is a very large broom, is often known in Australia as tree lucerne, a name strictly applicable to the yellow-flowered bush *Medicago arborea*. **1981** *Southern Horticulture* (N.Z.) Spring 53/1 Weather conditions could influence the situation, as too could the presence of tree lucerne near-by. **1811** W. T. Aiton *Hortus Kewensis* (ed. 2) III. 315 Chinese Tree Pæony. Moutan. Nat[ive] of China. **1880** [see *moutan]. **1962** I. Murdoch *Unofficial Rose* I. 44 The more intense evening light against a long bed of yuccas and tree peonies. **1980** R. Grounds *Private Life Plants* xxiii. 133 As many as 3,000 flowers have been counted on a tree peony.

b. tree-fly (example); **tree-partridge** (earlier example); **tree-runner,** a brightly coloured Australian nuthatch of the genus *Neositta*, esp. *N. chrysoptera*; **tree-spider,** any of many spiders that live on the trunks or branches of trees; **tree squirrel,** an arboreal squirrel, distinguished from a ground squirrel.

1834 *Chambers's Edin. Jrnl.* III. 357/3 Much wood.. during warm and summer months, raining down great store of tree-flies. **1864** J. A. Grant *Walk across Afr.* 93 The..tree-partridge resembles the painted one of India, has yellow legs, beautiful plumage, and weighs about a pound. **1901** A. J. Campbell *Nests & Eggs Austral. Birds* I. 337 The true home of the Orange-winged Sittella or Tree Runner is Eastern Australia. **1964** A. L. Thomson *New Dict. Birds* 545/2 The so-called 'treerunners' or 'sitellas' are widely distributed in Australia. **1904** W. H. Hudson *Green Mansions* ii. 33 The shaft reveals a tangle of shining silver threads—the web of some large tree-spider. **1910** W. de la Mare *Three Mulla-Mulgars* iii. 45 They sat and ate..with scorpions and speckled tree-spiders watching them. **1934** A. Russell *Tramp-Royal in Wild Austral.* xxxviii. 249 So strong and thickly-woven are the webs of the Central Australian tree or orchid spider that small birds are often caught in them. **1822** J. Woods *Two Years' Residence Eng. Prairie* 193 Tree-squirrels are of two or more sorts, and are eaten here. **1872** *Routledge's Every Boy's Ann.* 614/1 Dennis climbs like a tree squirrel. **1968** *Ecol. Monogr.* XXXVIII. 31 (*title*) The adaptive nature of social organisation in the genus of tree squirrels *Tamiasciurus*.

c. tree-box, a frame used to protect a young tree; **tree-bridge,** (*b*) (earlier example); **tree-coral,** a branching coral; **tree diagram** = sense 6 b (*e*) in Dict. and Suppl.; **tree doctor** = *tree surgeon* below; **tree farm** orig. and chiefly *U.S.*, an area of forest managed in a way that ensures the regular production of timber; hence **tree farmer, farming; tree-feeder,** an animal that feeds on the foliage of trees or the insects living on leaves or bark; **tree-house,** (*a*) (earlier example); (*b*) a child's playhouse (sense *2 a) built in a tree; **tree-limit,** the line beyond which trees do not grow, with reference to either altitude or latitude; cf. *tree-line* (*a*); **tree-line,** (*a*) (earlier examples); (*b*) a row of trees; the edge of a wood; **tree-nest,** a nest built in a tree, in contrast to one built at ground level; **tree-path,** the track of an arboreal animal; **tree-people,** in fantasy or fiction: (*a*) persons that live in trees; (*b*) animated trees; **tree preservation order,** an order prohibiting the felling or removal of a tree or group of trees; **tree-pruner** (example); so **tree-pruning** (also *transf.*, the removal of branches from a tree diagram); **tree-ring,** an annual growth ring in the trunk of a tree; hence **tree-ring analysis, dating** = *dendrochronology; **tree-road** = *tree-path* above; **tree-rune** (earlier example); **tree search,** a search in which a situation or entity is represented by a tree diagram, e.g. to facilitate efficient searching; **tree stool,** the stump of a fallen tree as preserved in a peat bog; **tree structure,** a structure in which there are successive branchings or subdivisions; cf. *tree diagram* above; **tree surgeon,** a practitioner of tree surgery; **tree surgery,** the pruning, repair, and preservative treatment of ornamental trees, first professionally organized by John Davey (1846–1923), American landscape architect.

1876 'Mark Twain' *Tom Sawyer* ii. 27 [Tom] sat down on the tree-box discouraged. **1896** J. C. Harris *Sister Jane* 157 Whittling away with his pocket-knife on the tree-box, against which he was leaning. **1805** T. E. White *Jrnl.* 20 July (1904) 26, I..cross'd the creek on a tree bridge an came through the woods. **1871** *Harper's Mag.* June 28 On the confines of this channel may be seen in clear water a perfect forest of coral—tree-coral, we call it, on account of its great size. **1915** E. R. Lankester *Diversions Naturalist* 11 Great tree-coral of these waters—the Paragorgia. **1965** N. Chomsky *Aspects of Theory of Syntax* i. 14 A tree-diagram of a sentence. **1978** *Language* LIV. 15 In a tree diagram, only the configuration of nodes matters, not the length of branches and sub-branches. **1776** tr. *Béardé de l'Abbaye's Ess. in Agriculture* vi. 37 There was a person, who assumed the title of Tree doctor. **1908** *Harper's Weekly* 5 Dec. 15/1 The services of the tree doctor are needed. **1976** 'M. Albrand' *Taste of Terror* xx. 115 The tree doctor..took a look at the willow. **1941** *N.Y. Times Mag.* 9 Nov. 13/2 Instead of reseeding sketchily over immense areas, the industry is laying out 'tree farms'. **1942** *Jrnl. Forestry* XL. 596/2 Tree farmers.. should be eligible for the same..treatment as other farmers. *Ibid.*, Tree farming appears to be off to a good start. **1962** Tree-farming [see *clear-fell* s.v. *clear *a.* D. 3]. **1973** P. A. Whitney *Snowfire* ii. 21 Julian had gone into tree farming. *Ibid.* xii. 231 He told me..about the controlled growth..on a tree farm. **1984** *New Yorker* 23 Jan. 78/3 Tree farms [in China] have also begun to experience problems with theft. **1914** *Chambers's Jrnl.* Jan. 75/1 A species of rhinoceros..was particularly a tree-feeder. **1953** N. Tinbergen *Herring Gull's World* vii. 66 Great Tits..being tree-feeders, they do not peck at the ground. **1867** J. C. Patteson in C. M. Yonge *Life J. C. Patteson* (1874) II. xi. 275, I am high and dry, and have ..a broad ladder—up to my house. The Mahaga lads and I call it my tree-house. **1949** A. Wilson *Wrong Set* 128 Go see if she's in the Tree House... It's a kind of funny old place she and Hamish made when they were kids. **1979** R. Jaffe *Class Reunion* I. iv. 40 She couldn't go up in the tree house anymore. **1934** *Discovery* June 167/1 They extend well above the local tree-limit. **1953** D. Bannerman *Birds Brit. Isles* I. 209 The typical Swedish race..and the west European race..have a very wide distribution on the continent of Europe, where their combined range extends north to the tree-limit. **1893** *Outing* Aug. 346/1 We struck the tree-line again in the immense ravine between them. **1903** Kipling *Five Nations* 53, I camped above the tree-line—drifted snow and naked boulders. **1936** F. Clune *Roaming round Darling* xiv. 123 The trail..wended down the Barwon, branching off at the various blazed tree-lines to the numerous creeks where they settled. **1977** D. Harsent *Dreams of Dead* 23 In single file the women left the treeline, a flicker at the corner of his eye. **1924** J. A. Thomson *Sci. Old & New* x. 55 A..Tineid caterpillar, found in the tree-nest of one of the Termites. **1953** D. A. Bannerman *Birds Brit. Isles* I. 16 These tree-nests [of crows] are often most conspicuous. **1897** J. L. Allen *Choir Invisible* xv. 227 The grass-path or the tree-path of the cougar. **1954** J. R. R. Tolkien *Fellowship of Ring* II. vi. 355 That was the custom of the Elves of Lórien, to dwell in the trees... Therefore they were called the Galadrim, the Tree-people. **1964** *Listener* 24 Dec. 1003/1, I think an intelligent plant would be large and virtually immobile; the tree-people in Olaf Stapledon's *Star Maker* might just qualify. [**1943** *Act* 6 & 7 *Geo. VI* c. 29 §8 If it appears to any interim development authority that it is expedient..to make provision for the preservation of trees or woodlands..they may..make an order (in this section referred to as an 'interim preservation order') with respect to such trees.] **1947** L. Silkin in *Hansard* (Commons) 22 Apr. 779 One hundred and six tree preservation orders have been submitted for my approval. **1976** *Leicester Mercury* 16 July, A tree preservation order has been made by the Harborough District Council to protect trees in and around the grounds of Little Bowden Rectory. **1887** *Illustr. Catal. Garden Furniture* (J. B. Brown & Son) 83 The 'standard' tree pruners. **1933** R. Tuve *Seasons & Months* iv. 160 February-by-the-fire has been crowded out by putting an extra tree-pruning picture into the series. **1966** *Math. Linguistics & Automatic Translation* (Harvard Univ. Computation Lab. Rep. No. NSF-17) IV-1 (*heading*) A proposal rule of tree-pruning. **1976** J. S. Gruber *Lexical Structures in Syntax & Semantics* II. iii. 365 We will have the following four derived trees... Each of these will undergo tree-pruning. **1919** A. E. Douglass *Climatic Cycles & Tree-growth* iii. 23 The plan of using tree-rings for the general purpose of a check on astronomical and meteorological phenomena was first formulated in 1901. **1946** F. E. Zeuner *Dating Past* i. 6 Tree-ring analysis is based on a well-known structural feature of wood, namely the annual growth-rings. *Ibid.* 11 The scope of tree-ring dating is extending rapidly. **1977** *Times* 20 July 13/4 Tree-ring analysis—or..dendrochronology—can..help to date..old paintings on oak panel. **1982** *Nature* 6 May 28/1 Others have sought an explanation of..variations in tree rings. **1895** Kipling *Second Jungle Bk.* 218 When he tired of ground-going he threw up his hands monkey-fashion to the nearest creeper,..he would follow a tree-road till his mood changed. **1863** J. M. Mitchell *Mesehowe* 49 The six tree Runes form the word *Arrier*. **1970** O. Dopping *Computers & Data Processing* xxii. 362 Tree search and heuristic programming cover a wide field of problems and are in principle well suited for automatic computation. **1980** *Daily Tel.* 26 May 10/6 In a complex game, a computer normally moves after conducting a 'tree search' of all possible moves, a process which if unlimited by time, would take billions of years. **1898** *Geogr. Jrnl.* XI. 431 The deeply submerged peats and tree-stools indicated..that the post-glacial recovery brought the land-level almost to normal pre-glacial conditions. **1975** J. G. Evans *Environment Early Man Brit. Isles* vi. 140 Peat now covers these hills, but..they..were once forested as is shown by the presence of tree stools at the base of the peat. **1965** N. Chomsky *Aspects of Theory of Syntax* i. 12 The most obvious formal property of utterances is their bracketing into constituents of various types, that is, the 'tree structure' associated with them. **1971** *Computers & Humanities* V. 292 Special language facilities in the fields of list processing, string processing, tree structure operations. **1983** *Austral. Microcomputer Mag.* Aug. 51/2 WangNet's cable topology is a duplicated tree structure. **1908** *Harper's Weekly* 5 Dec. 15/1 The attention given by the tree surgeon to the aged and decaying historical trees of the country..is equal to that given a wealthy invalid by his physician. **1978** *Cornish Guardian* 27 Apr. 19/1 (Advt.), Tree Surgeons. Fully qualified and insured for all felling, planting, pruning and repair work. **1902** J. Davey *Tree Doctor* 14 Learn to do your own tree surgery, or direct it personally. **1973** *Country Life* 7 June 1706/3 (Advt.), Southern Tree Surgery Company (Consultants and Tree Surgeons).

treeless, *a.* (Earlier example.)

1794 W. B. Stevens *Jrnl.* 19 Nov. (1965) II. 205 On your Tree-less Coast indeed You can have no falling leaves to warn you of the approach of Winter.

treen, *a.* Restrict *Obs.* exc. *dial.* to senses in *Dict.* and add: **B.** as *sb.* = Woodware, esp. when regarded as antiques. Const. as *pl.*

1927 H. V. MORTON *In Search of England* i. 7 'Before people used pewter for plates and tankards,' he explained, 'wooden trenchers, drinking cups and bowls—called 'treen'—were used by everyone.' 1949 E. H. PINTO *Treen* 3 The small useful woodware of to-day is the treen of to-morrow... The turnery side of treen-making is much more alive than most people realise. 1971 *Canadian Antiques Collector* Apr. 22/1 Articles ranging from ladles to snuff boxes, candlesticks to combs, may be included in the group known as treen. 1980 *Daily Tel.* 26 Feb. 13/3 Hand-turned treen are a joy to look at and a great pleasure to use. 1981 *Rescue News* Mar. 2/6 The site has also yielded a great deal of domestic material, including a rich collection of pottery, pewter and treen.

treescape. Delete *rare* and add later examples.

1950 *Archit. Rev.* CVIII. 53 (*caption*) A lovely, casual treescape at Marsh Lock..another fine treescape at Cookham Dean. 1960 *Guardian* 15 July 7/1 The treescape seen from inside appears to be part of the walls. 1969 B. PATTEN *Notes to Hurrying Man* 62 Above treescapes the fawn smells black Smoke drifting. 1978 *Times* 5 June 12/8 This particular polished granite..has a very high reflectivity, and will tend to mirror the treescape of Euston Square.

tree-top, tree top. Add: **b.** *attrib.* passing into *adj.* Of or pertaining to tree-tops; in the tops of trees. Also *fig.*

1896 R. L. STEVENSON *In South Seas* III. iii. 246 The folk of the town streamed by us intermittingly... In the first grey of the morning, and again late in the afternoon, these would straggle past about their tree-top business.. and vanish from the face of earth. 1945 *New Yorker* 10 Feb. 23/3 Bombers went to critical missions, at tree-top level. 1961 *Sunday Express* 26 Feb. 5/3 A tree-top hotel ..in the Aberdare Mountains. 1977 *Daily Mail* 24 Sept. 15/6 One man with a few machines can run a dawn-to-dusk radio station. Britain's few fugitive tree-top pirates do the same on the odd Sunday afternoon. 1979 P. NIESEWAND *Member of Club* xxi. 165 Colonel Winter heard the jets flash over; just above tree-top height.

‖**tref** (trev). *Wales.* [W., hamlet, home, town.] A social unit that was once traditional in Wales, consisting of a hamlet or homestead or the community occupying it (see quot. 1889).

1841 A. OWEN tr. *Anc. Laws & Institutes of Wales* 1004/2 *Trev, a vill*:—A territorial division of land containing four gavaels or 256 erws. 1889 H. LEWIS *Anc. Laws Wales* I. iii. 57 In modern Welsh 'trev' means a village or town, in ancient times it is said to have meant a single house or homestead... In..laws we have a frequent use of trev in a sense having reference to the land of the joint family, that is to their settlement and group of dwellings. 1895 *Wales* July 304/2 There was a good deal of feasting amongst the hillside *trefs*. 1900 RHYS & BRYNMOR-JONES *Welsh People* vi. 218 We now turn to consider briefly the law relating to property in or possession of land... The cymwd was thus divided: Four *erwau* in every *tyddyn* (homestead),..four *gafaelion* in every *tref* (vill or township). 1968 [see *GWELY].

trefa, trifa. Add: Also **trayf, treff, treife, trifah,** etc. (Earlier example.) Chiefly *attrib.* or as *adj.*, not prepared according to the Law, applied to any food. Also *transf.*

1837 *Brit. & Foreign*] *Rev.* V. 424 The Jews call..*treff* all that is prohibited to be used as food. 1892 I. ZANGWILL *Childr. Ghetto* I. 88 Even pious people eat *tripha* cheese and butter. *Ibid.* III. 39 Their money is *kosher*; they are *tripha*. 1907 —— *Ghetto Comedies* 68 The *tripha* meat cooked in Simon's mess-tin. 1961 A. W. MOSS *Valiant Crusade* vi. 81 If more than one cut is necessary..the carcase is rejected as 'Trifah', i.e. unfit for Jewish..food. 1966 H. KEMELMAN *Saturday the Rabbi went Hungry* (1967) xix. 115 When a utensil becomes tref, the way you cleanse it is to bury it in the earth. 1975 G. MEIR *My Life* i. 5 He served in the Russian army for another thirteen years, and never..did he touch *treife* (non-kosher) food. 1978 I. B. SINGER *Shosha* ix. 168 To me he's as *trayf* as pork.

‖**treffend** (tre·fĕnt), *a.* [Ger.] Apposite, fitting, pertinent.

1850 S. AUSTIN *Let.* 21 Jan. in J. Ross *Three Generations* (1888) I. 244 It is perfectly and thoroughly *treffend*. 1900 W. JAMES *Let.* 13 Mar. (1920) II. 119 His surface thoughts ..of a scientific order, were extraordinarily *treffend* and clearly expressed.

trefid: see *TRIFID *a.* b.

trehalase (trĭhā·lēˡz). *Biochem.* [ad. F. *tréhalase* (E. Bourquelot 1893, in *Bull. de la Soc. mycologique de France* IX. 194): see TREHALA and *-ASE.] An enzyme which catalyses the hydrolysis of trehalose to two molecules of glucose.

1893 *Jrnl. Chem. Soc.* LXIV. 451 The author proposes to call the special ferment trehalase. 1926 WAKSMAN & DAVISON *Enzymes* x. 182 Trehalase has been demonstrated in the intestinal secretions of certain animals (horse, cattle), certain fishes, in malt, in various fungi, in yeasts and in certain bacteria. 1977 *Lancet* 5 Nov. 982/2 Sucrase, trehalase and lactase activities were absent.

treille. b. (Earlier example.)

1865 F. B. PALLISER *Hist. Lace* vii. 119 The thick 'treille' and scanty flowers of the old laces [in West Flanders].

trek, *sb.* For 'S. Africa' read 'orig. S. Afr.' **1. a.** Restrict def. to S. Afr. use and add: Now in gen. use elsewhere, a long journey or expedition, esp. one overland involving considerable physical effort.

1941 I. L. IDRIESS *Great Boomerang* i. 6 Risky treks against hazards different from those of the general Australian bush. 1968 R. M. PATTERSON *Finlay's River* 168 There they made camp, cached their canoe and load, and sorted out what they wanted to take for their next overland trek—this time a hunting trip. 1972 D. CRAIG *Double Take* i. 8 The trekking lesson always ended like this... The other members of the trek looked at Brian.

2. trek Boer, (*a*) a Boer who moved his family and grazing stock from place to place; (*b*) = VOORTREKKER; also, a participant in a later migration of Afrikaners; **trek-bok,** *pl.* **bokke(n),** an antelope, esp. a springbok, in a migrating herd; **trek-cart,** a light cart used by (boy) scouts for transporting stores, etc.; **trek chain** (examples); **trek-farmer** = *trek Boer* (*a*) above; **trek fever,** an insatiable longing for travelling or wandering in the veld; **trek-net** = SEINE *sb.*[1]; hence **trek-netter; trek path,** a right of way across the land of another farmer; **trek sheep,** sheep driven or carried a long way for pasturage.

1835 A. STEEDMAN *Wanderings S. Afr.* II. III. iii. 53 The next day we met a Trek Boor, with his cattle. 1847 in C. Pettman *Africanderisms* (1913) 513 All the most intelligent of the *Trek Boers* whom I have seen, look forward with dread to the course the Government are pursuing. 1882 C. DU VAL *With Show through Southern Afr.* I. 106 Abolition of slavery was the primary cause of the movement of these 'trek Boers'. 1929 D. REITZ *Commando* xxiv. 281 We moved north through country thinly occupied by Nomad Boers (Trek Boers), who spend their lives going from one well to another with their flocks. 1941 C. W. DE KIEWIET *Hist. S. Afr.* 17 When the Trekboers entered it with their flocks and tented wagons, they left the current of European life. 1981 *Times Lit. Suppl.* 13 Feb. 159/2 The Afrikaner remains, according to Lambley, the atavistic, insular, racially arrogant *trekboer*. 1824 *S. Afr. Jrnl.* I. 72 On the approach of the *Trek-Bokken* or migrating spring-boks, the grazier makes up his mind to look for pasturage elsewhere. 1827 G. THOMPSON *Trav. & Adv. S. Afr.* II. vi. 274 The destructive flocks of *trek-bokken*, or migratory springboks, pressed by the long droughts, occasionally inundate the northern parts of the Colony. 1896 H. A. BRYDEN *Tales S. Afr.* ix. 215, I have passed across these plains through a herd of trek-bokken ..three or four miles broad. 1966 E. PALMER *Plains of Camdeboo* ix. 157 The springbuck migrations..are something we shall never see again. Colonists called them 'trekbokke' or 'travellingbuck'. 1928 R. A. KNOX *Footsteps at Lock* v. 43 The bigger boys had gone..with the trek-cart to bring our stores over. 1977 *Drive* Jan.-Feb. 15/2 Boy scouts' trek-cart needed. 1878 H. A. ROCHE *On Trek in Transvaal* 332 Our oxen were free, walking off a yard or two with our *tree-disselboom* and trek-chain. 1972 *Farmer's Weekly* (S. Afr.) 21 Apr. (Advt.), Chain traces 55c each; Trek chains R1.55. 1912 *East London Daily Dispatch* 1 May 5 (Pettman), The desirability of amending the railway tariff for trek-sheep to enable trek farmers to avail themselves of the railway. 1966 E. PALMER *Plains of Camdeboo* vii. 128 The mountain bush had housed the first trek-farmers in hard and stormy weather. 1980 FIRST & SCOTT *Olive Schreiner* i. 28 Boer trek-farmers moved away from British control. 1897 J. P. FITZPATRICK *Outspan* 3 When..this instinct awakens,..it becomes a madness, and they call it trek-fever. 1943 D. REITZ *No Outspan* viii. 106 Gauko-Otawi, the 'Rustplaats' or resting place of the Trekkers. Here it was that in 1878 they had built a church, their trek-fever temporarily stilled. 1913 W. W. THOMPSON *Sea Fisheries Cape Colony* ii. 46 The seine, or 'trek-net', has from the very earliest period of the European occupation of the country been the type of net generally adopted. 1970 *Cape Argus* 24 Dec. 2 They had cast trek nets in the surf. 1956 J. L. B. SMITH *Old Fourlegs* i. 9, I..lived with the coastal trek-netters. 1934 WEBSTER, Trekpath. 1936 *Cape Argus* 18 Mar. 13 The trek-path controversy has led many men to fence their farms. 1955 L. G. GREEN *Karoo* xii. 142 A trek path is a definite route which a farmer is entitled to follow when leading his sheep to new pastures. 1912 Trek sheep [see *trek-farmer* above].

trek, *v.* For '*S. Africa*' read 'orig. *S. Afr.*' **1. a.** Restrict orig. use to *S. Afr.* and add examples of further *transf.* applications elsewhere (see *TREK *sb.* 1 a). Freq. in trivial use.

1911 C. E. W. BEAN '*Dreadnought' of Darling* xxxviii. 342 When the police first saw them they were trekking through the scrub. 1912 [in Dict.]. 1943 *Sun* (Baltimore) 11 June 13/2 The hungry pilot trekking over the tundra should beware of the liver of the Polar bear. 1955 [see *TREKKING *vbl. sb.*]. 1976 *Oadby & Wigston* (Leics.) *Advertiser* 26 Nov. 7/6, I was surprised as I trekked from shop to shop how much prices varied. 1977 C. McCULLOUGH *Thorn Birds* xvii. 438 It would mean trekking down to the kitchen again, and..no one appreciates the patter of my little feet.

trekker. (In Dict. s.v. TREK *v.*) Add: **1.** (Earlier and later examples.)

1851 R. GRAY *Jrnl. Bishop's Visitation Tour through Cape Colony in 1850* 27 Only a few of the latest trekkers have a friendly feeling towards the English government. 1973 *Sunday Times* (Johannesburg) 9 Dec., Many Coloureds..trekked to..the Cape Flats, but unlike other trekkers before them there was no promised land.

2. A person travelling a long distance, esp. on foot; *spec.* a rambler or hiker. Cf. *pony-trekker* s.v. *PONY *sb.* 6 b.

1932 *Sun* (Baltimore) 7 Jan. 2/5 The main body of the small army marching from Pennsylvania..is not expected until late tonight... The trekkers..found no difficulty in obtaining admission to the gallery. 1939 R. GODDEN *Black Narcissus* iv. 39 It isn't even on the route that the trekkers take. 1968 *Punch* 14 Aug. 234/2 The Association has 'on call' about seventy ponies—for sixty trekkers, six experienced guides, and a few spares. 1977 *Times Lit. Suppl.* 13 May 595/2 It will just about go into the side pocket of your rucksack, and no intelligent trekker should go off to Gurung country without one. 1984 *Times* 18 Feb. 14/1 In their hearts trekkers are all pilgrims.

trekkie (tre·ki). [f. TREK *sb.* + -IE.] **1.** *S. Afr.* A small group of trekkers.

1888 J. BIRD tr. *D. P. Bezuidenhout's Narrative* in *Annals of Natal* I. 367 Five men were first sent forward to seek a road to the Drakensberg... A small 'trekkie' (party of emigrants) had preceded us. 1953 J. COLLIN-SMITH *Locusts & Wild Honey* I. i. 10 It was a bright autumn morning when we had inspanned the sixteen oxen, and the wagon wheels had turned, and the little trekkie had started away.

2. Also **Trekkie.** An admirer of the U.S. science fiction television programme *Star Trek*; hence, a space-traveller; one interested (trivially) in space travel.

In S. Africa the form *trekker* is also used for this sense.

1976 *New Yorker* 16 Feb. 39 (*caption*) Of course, I didn't know George was a Trekkie when I married him. 1977 *Time* 15 Aug. 50/2 Berry admits that his first trekkies would not know where they might emerge or if they would ever get back. 1978 *Sunday Sun* (Brisbane) 17 Sept. 45/3 Fans—called Trekkies—still number in their tens of thousands. 1981 *Space World* Aug.-Sept. 6/3 Many of the [L-5] society's other members were considered space Trekkies more interested in social experimentation than in technology. 1983 *Oxf. Univ. Press (N.Y.) Spring Catal.* 27 The audience for science fiction now runs the gamut from the high school 'trekkie' to the serious literary scholar.

trekking, *vbl. sb.* and *ppl. a.* (In Dict. s.v. TREK *v.*) Add: (Later examples.) *spec.* = *pony-trekking* s.v. *PONY *sb.* 6 b.

1942 ZUCKERMAN & BERNAL in S. Zuckerman *From Apes to Warlords* (1978) vii. 143 The situation in Hull has been somewhat obscured..by the occurrence of trekking, which was made possible by the availability of road transport. 1955 *Times* 22 July 9/6 About 35,000 came last year, and more are expected this summer... They come to fish and shoot or to trek in the mountains. 'Only the English like trekking,' one agent said. 1962 *Times* 21 Apr. 11/3 There is also a list of trekking and riding holiday centres which have been awarded a certificate of approval. 1968 *Punch* 14 Aug. 234/3 While some of the ponies probably would be kept in any case..the majority are now kept principally for the revenue from the trekking. 1972 [see *TREK *sb.* 1 a]. 1976 *Horse & Hound* 3 Dec. 42/4 His book is well illustrated and there are some useful appendices, though that claiming to list a brief selection of trekking centres in fact is so brief as to be almost comic. 1984 *Times* 18 Feb. 14/1 Trekking has an aura which is irresistible to the romantic.

trek-tow. Add: Also **tracktoe, trektou(w).** (Earlier and further examples.)

1822 W. J. BURCHELL *Trav. Interior S. Afr.* I. 151 The trektouw (draw rope or trace), is a long rope made of twisted thongs of raw hide, made fast by a hook to the staple at the end of the pole, and having iron rings attached to it at proper distances, into which rings the yokes are hooked. 1835 A. SMITH *Diary* 8 June (1940) II. 60 In this river the crocodile abounds; one carried off and swallowed a tracktoe belonging to a trader. [*Note*] Trektouw, or draught rope. 1939 S. CLOETE *Watch for Dawn* ii. 26 As the wagon topped the rise they trotted down with slack trek-tous. 1972 A. SCHOLEFIELD *Wild Dog Running* 214, I didn't know how many had been in the pride but two bullocks had been killed where they stood. A third had been dragged some yards from the *trektou*, the strong leather thong around his neck snapped like cotton.

trellis, *sb.*[2] Add: **1. e.** Short for *trellis stitch*: see *3.

1912 L. F. PESEL *Stitches from Old Eng. Embroideries* 19 (*caption*) Trellis with cross-stitch couching. 1921 A. G. I. CHRISTIE *Samplers & Stitches* v. 57 Trellis is used for solid fillings.

3. trellis stitch, in embroidery or knitting, an arrangement of stitches between parallel lines to give a lattice effect.

1921 A. G. I. CHRISTIE *Samplers & Stitches* v. 57 The thread for working Trellis stitch should be untwisted for the best effect to be gained. 1974 *Guardian* 26 Jan. 15/2 Trellis, moss and blackberry stitch by which..Aran mothers recognise their drowned sons.

trellised, *ppl. a.* Add: **2. c.** *Physical Geogr.* Of a drainage pattern: resembling the pattern of a vine growing on a trellis, with tributaries flowing in a direction approximately at right angles to the stream they join and bends in the main stream being approximately right-angled.

1895 *Monogr. Nat. Geogr. Soc.* No. I. vi. 186 (*caption*) On the head waters of Bluestone River..the branches are adjusted to tilted hard and soft beds, forming an example of 'trellised' drainage. 1937 WOOLDRIDGE & MORGAN *Physical Basis Geogr.* xiv. 192 In all such cases, whether the network of major valleys is rectangular or rhomboidal, the drainage plan may be described as 'trellised'. 1970 R. J. SMALL *Study of Landforms* vii. 227 The weaker strata are gradually eroded to form strike vales, separated by cuestas associated with the more resistant rocks, and are occupied by tributary streams which, with the passage of time, form an increasingly dominant component of the trellised pattern.

Tremadoc (trĭmæ·dǒk). *Geol.* The name of a village in Gwynedd, N. Wales, used *attrib.* to designate a series of Tremadocian rocks (see next) about 300 metres thick that form the top of the Harlech Dome and comprise mudstones, shales, and slates; also, more widely, = next.

1847 A. SEDGWICK in *Q. Jrnl. Geol. Soc.* III. 145 The anomalous position of the Tremadoc rocks,..and the dislocation of the beds above noticed along the Merioneth coast, were probably all produced by the same set of disturbing forces. *Ibid.* 157 The Festiniog or the Tremadoc group. **1882** A. GEIKIE *Text-bk. Geol.* 655, 12 species of lamellibranchs from the Tremadoc beds of Ramsay Island and St. David's. **1885** C. LYELL *Student's Elem. Geol.* (ed. 4) xxviii. 448 Mr. Callaway has shown that the Shineton shale of Shropshire is of Lower Tremadoc age. *Ibid.*, *Orthoceras sericeum* and *Cyrtoceras præcox* are of the Upper Tremadocs. **1938** A. K. WELLS *Outl. Hist. Geol.* iii. 20 The graptolites..had made their first appearance in Tremadoc (Upper Cambrian) times. **1970** R. M. BLACK *Elements Palaeont.* xiv. 222 Primitive pterobranchs are found in rocks of Tremadoc age. **1974** *Encycl. Brit. Micropædia* X. 108/3 Important Tremadoc sequences are..known from Australia.

Tremadocian (tremădǫ·kiăn), *a. Geol.* [f. prec. + -IAN.] Of, pertaining to, or designating a stratigraphic series typified by the Tremadoc beds, orig. placed in the Upper Cambrian but now sometimes regarded as Lower Ordovician. Also *absol.*

1910 W. G. FEARNSIDES in Monckton & Herries *Geol. in Field* xxxii. 795 Across the denuded edges of Tremadocian and Olenidian rocks rest the basal members of the great Arenig series. **1927** *Q. Jrnl. Geol. Soc.* LXXXVIII. 145 The order of that succession is applicable in all its detail to the type-area of the Tremadocian in the western parts of Wales. **1950** DAVID & BROWN *Geol. Commonw. Austral.* I. iii. 135 By Tremadocian time graptolites had begun to make their appearance in Victoria. **1974** *Nature* 18 Oct. 575/1 None of the formal papers included any discussion of the boundaries of the Ordovician, most speakers making it clear whether they regarded the Tremadocian as Cambrian (as in English usage) or Ordovician.

trematode, *sb.* (Earlier and further examples.)

1859, 1877 [see *BILHARZIA, BILHARZIA]. **1962** J. D. SMYTH *Introd. Animal Parasitol.* xiii. 138 The great majority of digenetic trematodes are inhabitants of the vertebrate alimentary canal or its associated organs.

tremblant (tre·mblănt), *a.* [f. TREMBLE *v.* + -ANT[1].] Of an ornament, jewel, etc.: incorporating springs or fine projecting wires which tremble or vibrate when affected by movement.

1970 *Times* 26 Mar. 12 A very fine diamond tremblant brooch in the shape of a five-petalled flower brought the same price. **1973** *Country Life* 13 Dec. (Suppl.) 32b A late 18th Century diamond head ornament, the sunburst tremblant. **1979** *Ibid.* 3 May (Suppl.) 56/1 A mid Victorian ruby and diamond tremblant spray brooch.

tremblement. Add: ‖**3.** *Mus.* (trañbləmañ) = SHAKE *sb.*[1] 5, TRILL *sb.*[2] 1b.

[**1883** GROVE *Dict. Music* III. 479 Shake or trill (Fr. *trille*, formerly *tremblement*).] **1884** F. NIECKS *Conc. Dict. Mus. Terms* s.v., *Tremblement* (Fr.), a snake. **1893** E. DANNREUTHER *Mus. Ornamentation* I. xiv. 100 In the Méthode the tremblements are generally marked [*sign given*]. **1915** A. DOLMETSCH *Interpret. of Music of 17th & 18th Centuries* iv. 163 The 'Tremblement et Pincé' is a shake with a Turn as termination. **1946** E. BLOM *Everyman's Dict. Music* 482/1 *Tremblement appuyé* = prepared shake. **1978** *Early Music* Oct. 517/2, I have left aside certain details, for example, whether the *tremblement* is to be played slowly at first and increasing in speed, or is to be trilled equally throughout.

trembler. Add: **4.** Also, such a blade used as a make-and-break sensitive to physical disturbance.

1943 N. BALCHIN *Small Back Room* xv. 185 It was the terminals I had to get wires on to, not the trembler. **1958** A. B. HARTLEY *Unexploded Bomb* ii. 13 When the bomb struck its target..the shock caused the trembler to function and electrically to ignite the flash-pellet in the base of the fuze. **1973** J. DRUMMOND *Bang! Bang!* xii. 26 A Banx is an anti-personnel device... Set it for time-fuse, or a trigger-action, even a trembler. **1978** R. JANSSON *News Caper* 8, I held the control column rock steady, as if it were a bomb with a trembler fuse.

trembleuse, *a.* or *sb. attrib.* Add: Also as *sb. absol.*

1869 C. SCHREIBER *Jrnl.* 17 June (1911) I. 13 A pair of Trembleuses and Stands, ruby glass, with white Smalto inside..£7.

trembling, *ppl. a.* Add: **trembling poplar** (earlier example).

1731 P. MILLER *Gardeners Dict.* s.v. Populus. The Trembling Poplar, or Aspen-Tree.

tremblingly, *adv.* (Earlier and later examples of the collocation *tremblingly alive.*)

1733 POPE *Ess. Man* I. 11 Or touch, so tremblingly alive all o'er, To smart, and agonize at ev'ry pore? **1818** C. R. MATURIN *Women* I. ii. 40 Ignorant of music as a science, but 'tremblingly alive' to its influence, he listened.

tremblor (tre·mblǫɹ). orig. and chiefly *U.S.* [Alteration of Sp. *temblor* shudder, (in Amer. Sp.) earthquake, influenced by Eng. TREMBLER.] An earthquake or earth tremor.

1913 C. C. GOODWIN *As I remember Them* 193 He.. received the sobriquet of 'Earthquake' Stewart, because of the theory that he put out, that the tremblors in California were caused..by..electrical disturbances in the air and in the earth near the surface. **1925** *N.Y. Times* 1 July 2/2 Dr. U. S. Grant..does not agree with Prof. Goode that the same tremblors shook Montana and California. **1926** *Daily Colonist* (Victoria, B.C.) 1 July 1/5 Today's shocks occurred in areas more than 100 miles removed from the lower coast line, where tremblors were felt yesterday. **1977** *Chicago Tribune* 2 Oct. 1. 10/5 Californians, long accustomed to earthquake jitters, have become concerned over a rapid-fire series of minor tremblors along a 20-miles stretch of the mysterious San Andreas Fault.

tremendous, *a.* Add: Also *dial.* and nonstandard **tremenj(i)ous, treminjous**, etc. **2.** (Further examples.) Also as quasi-*adv.*

1835 [see *LATHERING *vbl. sb.*]. **1886** R. D. BLACKMORE *Springhaven* in *Harper's Mag.* Oct. 755/1 Makes us pay tremenjious for 'most everything. **1888** KIPLING *Phantom 'Rickshaw* 92 Then ten men with bows and arrows ran down that valley, chasing twenty men with bows and arrows, and the row was tremenjus. **1892** 'Q' *I saw Three Ships* v. 97 'Ay, naybours all,' broke in Farmer Tresidder... 'I shudn' wonder if ye was to see me trottin' to Parlyment House in a gilded coach..I be so tremenjous rich.' **1901** M. FRANKLIN *My Brilliant Career* xvii. 150, I thought them straps couldn't break only onder a tremenjous strain. *Ibid.* xix. 162 'How are you enjoying yourself?'.. 'Treminjous intoirely, sor.' **1952** M. ALLINGHAM *Tiger in Smoke* ii. 39 'Was it fun?' 'Tremenjous.' **1977** E. W. HILDICK *Loop* vii. 37 She had 'tremenjous powers of seeing the future'.

‖**tremendum** (treme·ndǝ̆m). [Shortened from *MYSTERIUM TREMENDUM.] The overwhelming awe which can be part of religious experience.

1923 J. W. HARVEY tr. *Otto's Idea of Holy* iv. 12 (*heading*) The analysis of 'tremendum'. *Ibid.* 16 The elements which unfold as the 'tremendum' develops. **1930** A. G. HEBERT tr. *Brilioth's Eucharistic Faith & Practice* ii. 65 It is an expression for the awfulness of the holy, the *tremendum*, which belongs to all deep religion. **1950** [see *NUMINOSUM]. **1960** R. F. C. HULL tr. *Jung's Coll. Wks.* III. 260 The originally chaotic or frightening impression is replaced by the picture, which, as it were, covers it up. The *tremendum* is..made harmless and familiar.

tremis. Substitute for entry:
tremissis (trĕmi·sis). Also erron. **tremis(s.** Pl. **tremisses.** [late L., gen. sing. of *trēmis*, f. *trēs* three, after *sēmis* half an as: cf. *SEMIS[1].] A late Roman or early Byzantine gold coin, the third part of a solidus; a Merovingian or other imitation of this.

1706, 1756 [in Dict.]. **1952** *Antiquity* XXVI. 77 All the coins from Sutton Hoo are tremisses (thirds of solidi). **1962** H. R. LOYN *Anglo-Saxon England* ii. 74 The *solidus* (or sou) was..essentially..the imperial coin reformed by Constantine; more frequent in Gaul was the *tremissis* (or *triens*), the third part of a sou. **1976** *Anglo-Saxon England* V. 176 Small Merovingian gold tremisses..had been penetrating the south-east of England. *Ibid.* 177 There is considerable circumstantial evidence for the equation of a Merovingian tremissis with an Anglo-Saxon gold shilling. **1983** *Times* 6 Apr. 16/4 The discovery of a remarkable Visigothic *tremiss* minted in gold in Southern Gaul in AD 455–475, in the final levels of one site excavated in late 1982, shows that some form of 'urban' life continued until nearly the end of the fifth century.

tremolist (tre·mǒlist). [f. TREMOLO + -IST.] One who uses the tremolo.

1927 *Proc. Musical Assoc. 1926–7* 18 The soprano tremolist is no longer tolerated. **1952** B. ULANOV *Hist. Jazz in Amer.* (1958) vi. 63 The first boogie-woogie crew, who must have influenced the second wave of C-major tremolists, the famous Chicagoans.

tremor (tre·mǫ̆ɹ), *v.* [f. the sb.] *intr.* To be agitated by a tremor or tremors; to shake or tremble.

1921 *Chambers's Jrnl.* XI. 858/1 The ship tremored, vibrated like mad. *Ibid.* 860/2 Her voice had tremor'd.. with urgency. **1926** M. WALSH *Key above Door* x. 113 His strong, big jowl was..tremoring with the chill. **1928** —— *While Rivers Run* vi. 68 His car was purring and tremoring. **1963** A. SMITH *Throw out Two Hands* xvi. 162 They [*sc.* zebras] went by in droves, and the earth tremored beneath them.

tremorine (tre·mǒrīn). *Pharm.* [f. TREMOR + -INE[5].] A crystalline compound, 1,4-dipyrrolidino-2-butyne, $C_{12}H_{20}N_2$, capable of inducing the symptons of Parkinsonism and used in research into this disease.

1956 G. M. EVERETT in *Federation Proc.* XV. 420/2 'Tremorine', when given in doses of 5–20 mg/kg by all routes, produces a marked sustained tremor. **1970, 1972** [see *OXOTREMORINE]. **1976** *Nature* 15 July 221/2 Tremorine, which is oxidised *in vivo* to oxotremorine by mammals, showed only slight activity against ticks.

trench, *sb.* Add: **2. b.** An elongated channel in the sea-bed; *spec.* one of the very long ones, several kilometres deep, that run parallel to the edge of a continent or an island arc and are believed to mark subduction zones.

1936 *Amer. Jrnl. Sci.* CCXXXI. 401 Recent discoveries of many valley-like trenches that interrupt the outer steeper slopes ('continental slopes') of continental shelves are truly startling. **1948** F. P. SHEPARD *Submarine Geol.* xi. 283 A series of deep trenches skirt the Pacific. **1963** G. L. PICKARD *Descriptive Physical Oceanogr.* ii. 10 The greatest depths in the oceans occur in these trenches. **1972**, etc. [see *SUBDUCTION 5]. **1975** *Offshore Engineer* Sept. 60/1 The Norwegian trench is a pitfall that has always tempered Norway's oil future. Crossing it is beyond the current state of pipeline technology. **1977** A. HALLAM *Planet Earth* 94 The island arcs and ocean trenches that border the northwest and southeast Pacific.

3. d. (Later examples.)

1970 G. JACKSON *Let.* 23 Mar. in *Soledad Brother* (1971) 188 I've been living in the trenches where it's understood that it's us against them, hide and seek. **1977** *Rolling Stone* 24 Mar. 13/2 He has been in the trenches too long not to be a master at mixing sincerity with evasiveness.

8.* *ellipt.* for *trench-coat*, see sense 9 below.

1972 *New Yorker* 14 Oct. 1 (Advt.), Bonwit's velvet rain trench plays matinees and evenings. **1974** [see *MIDI-]. **1978** *N.Y. Times* 30 Mar. A9/3 (Advt.), Three styles for sizes 8 to 16. Double breasted trench for reg. and petite.

9. *trench kit, life, light, raid, raiding, rifle, strafing, system, war*; *trench-stale, trench-to-trench* adjs.; **trench boot**, (usu. in *pl.*) combined boot and leggings; **trench-coat**, a waterproofed overcoat worn by officers in the trenches; a long, belted raincoat for civilian use; hence **trench-coated** *adj.*; **trench fever**, an epidemic louse-borne rickettsial disease that was common among soldiers in the war of 1914–18, causing splenomegaly and recurrent fever; **trench foot, feet**, a painful condition of the feet caused by prolonged immersion in cold water or mud, marked by swelling, blistering, and some degree of necrosis; **trench-knife**, a knife with a double-edged blade, orig. used in trench raids; **trench mortar**, a small mortar designed to propel bombs from a front trench into enemy trenches; hence as *v. trans.*; **trench mouth**, Vincent's angina of the mouth (see *VINCENT[2]); **trenchoscope** = next; **trench-periscope**, a kind of tube-and-mirror apparatus used in trench warfare (see quot. 1918 for *trenchscope* below); cf. prec. and *PERISCOPE 3; **trench-rat**, the brown or Norway rat, *Rattus norvegicus*; **trenchscope** = *trench periscope* above; cf. also *trenchoscope* above; **trench warfare**, hostilities carried on by means of or in trenches; also *fig.*, a protracted dispute or conflict in which the parties seek to maintain their entrenched positions while launching persistent attacks upon their opponents; cf. *trench war* above.

1933 J. BUCHAN *Prince of Captivity* II. i. 132 He wore a tattered trench waterproof and..ancient trench-boots. **1973** *Country Gentlemen's Mag.* Mar. 184/2 Officer's brown leather calf length trench boots..practically new. **1916** W. OWEN *Let.* 16 Aug. (1967) 405 My poor troops were wet to the bone. (But I had my Trench Coat.) **1918** E. FERBER in *Best Short Stories of 1917* 209 Jo Hertz, in one of those pinch-waist belted suits and a trench coat..was a sight for mirth or pity. **1944** M. LASKI *Love on Supertax* xi. 107, I got a job in a trench-coat factory in Manchester. **1978** W. F. BUCKLEY *Stained Glass* xi. 109 A young man dressed in an old army trenchcoat walked slowly out, dragging his wooden leg like a ball and chain. **1941** N. ALLEY *I Witness* xxxv. 296, I compensated my desire with the wishful thought that I'd be running across his familiar trench-coated figure some time later. **1980** *Listener* 29 May 697/3 A trench-coated Micawberish librarian. **1915** *Lancet* 25 Sept. 734/1 The case of a twice-inoculated soldier suffering from trench fever, whose case was diagnosed as pyrexia. **1917** G. S. GORDON *Let.* 22 May (1943) 77 He says I've got what they call vaguely 'Trench' Fever. **1933** J. BUCHAN *Prince of Captivity* I. iii. 85 Blown-up, buried, dysentery, trench-fever, and most varieties of wounds. **1976** *West Lancs. Even. Gaz.* 13 Dec. 7/1 After convalescing in England from trench fever, he successfully applied for a commission. **1915** *Lancet* 17 Apr. 812/2 The term trench-foot appears to us to be the most suitable for a condition which has practically only been met with in those who have had to remain for long periods in the trenches. **1916** W. S. CHURCHILL *Let.* 6 Jan. in M. Gilbert *Winston S. Churchill* (1972) III. Compan. II. 1359, I wish you wd write for me a brief description of your 'trench feet routine'. *a* **1918** W. OWEN *Poems* (1920) 23 But never..fever, trench-foot, shock, Untrapped the wretch. And death seemed still withheld. **1940** *War Illustr.* 12 Jan. 603/1 Though the men had plenty of food all were suffering from exposure and trench feet when they landed at a South Coast port. **1969** [see *immersion foot* s.v. *IMMERSION 5]. *a* **1976** A. CHRISTIE *Autobiogr.* (1977) v. ii. 239 Half our patients seemed to be trench feet cases. **1982** *Times* 31 May 5/3 There have been cases of exposure and trench foot. **1914** *War Illustr.* 19 Dec. 416/1 He inspected their trench kit of goatskins and strawbags. **1926** *Scribner's Mag.* Aug. 194/2 A Boche lad I killed with me trench-knife. **1979** R. BLYTHE *View in Winter* iv. 188, I had a trench knife in one hand and a pistol in the other. **1917** W. OWEN *Let.* 15 Aug. (1967) 484

Nothing like his [*sc.* Sassoon's] trench life sketches has ever been written. **1977** A. WILSON *Strange Ride of R. Kipling* vii. 298 What he [*sc.* Kipling] saw of trench life.. horrified him. **1918** G. FRANKAU *Judgement of Valhalla* 18 Downwards, and on, where trench-lights shone—For *we*, we might not rest. **1915** D. O. BARNETT *Let.* 19 May 143 In the afternoon we had a trench-mortar duel with the Allymans. **1920** *Chambers's Jrnl.* 20 Mar. 254/1 He shelled it; he trench-mortared it, he raided it. **1973** M. WOODHOUSE *Blue Bone* xii. 129 What looked like a three-foot metal pipe with a rectangular base... 'Five-centimeter trench mortar,' said Yancy. **1918** *Evening Mail* 1 May 3/4 We have trench mouth, just as we have trench feet. Otherwise known as ulcero-membranous stomatitis, or Vincent's disease. **1946** J. LEES-MILNE *Diary* 1 Jan. (1983) 3 Went to the dentist who said it *is* trench mouth that I am suffering from. **1981** G. PRIESTLAND *Priestland's Progress* 8 Chris Rees had to take to his bed with a rare attack of trench mouth. **1915** *Morning Post* 11 Feb. 3/5 The Adams trenchoscope is the latest periscope for use in the trenches. **1915** Trench-periscope [see *hyposcope* s.v. *HYPO- II]. **1917** A. G. EMPEY *Over Top* 313 *Trench raid*, several men detailed to go over the top at night and shake hands with the Germans, and, if possible, persuade some of them to be prisoners. **1961** W. VAUGHAN-THOMAS *Anzio* i. 5 A struggle in the mud, complete with duck-boards, trench-raids and patrols in no-man's-land. **1974** A. PRICE *Other Paths to Glory* II. viii. 213 It's a sawn-off Lee Enfield... Used for trench raiding... The trench rifle had been Jarras's newest toy. **1916** G. FRANKAU *Guns* 22 The trench-rats patter And nibble among the rations. **1917** A. G. EMPEY *Over Top* 308 There are three things in this world that Tommy loves: a slacker, a German, and a trench-rat. **1918** E. S. FARROW *Dict. Mil. Terms* 629 *Trenchscope*, a simple periscope, used in the trenches (permitting a safe view to the front), consisting of parallel mirrors in a long wooden box, both set 45° to the long axis of the box. **1915** KIPLING *France at War* v. 55 One understood after a while the nightmare that lays hold of trench-stale men. **1931** *Times Lit. Suppl.* 22 Oct. 822/1 The squadron was required to assist the hard-pressed infantry by..'trench strafing'. **1918** E. S. FARROW *Dict. Mil. Terms* 629 *Trench system*, all the field-works included in a defense zone. **1923** KIPLING *Irish Guards in Gt. War* I. 227 Some half-wiped-out German trench-systems. **1975** P. FUSSELL *Gt. War & Mod. Memory* ii. 36 From the winter of 1914 until the spring of 1918 the trench system was fixed. **1923** KIPLING *Irish Guards in Gt. War* II. 143 There are certain analogies between trench-to-trench attack and 'soccer'. *Ibid.* I. 20 The trench-war was solidifying itself. **1918** F. M. FORD *Let.* 6 Jan. (1965) 86, I could do a very good one [novel] about trench warfare. **1973** *Times* 7 Dec. 18/3 In industry we have had continuing trench warfare deriving from low pay, and authoritarian and remote management. **1978** F. MACLEAN *Take Nine Spies* iv. 125 He had fought at Dixemude.. before settling down later that winter [in 1914] to the horrors of trench warfare. **1980** R. BARNARD *Death in Cold Climate* vii. 69 Sterile trench-warfare with colleagues over matters of principle.

trencher[1]. Add: **5.** (Later U.S. example.)

1889 *Harper's Mag.* Jan. 238/2 He next binds his [beaver] trap to a flat stone 'about the size of a teakettle', opens the jaws, and arranges the 'trencher', as the pan is called, pressure on which springs the trap.

7. trencher-bread (later *Hist.* examples); **trencher-salt**: delete † and add later examples; **trencher table**, a table at which members of domestic staff were seated at meal times.

1882 F. MICHEL *Crit. Inquiry into Scottish Lang.* iii. 54 [Edinburgh] citizens had four different kinds of wheaten bread: the finest called *manchet*, the second *cheat* or *trencher* bread. **1974** Trencher-bread [see *JUMBAL, JUMBLE]. **1967** *Times* 24 Feb. 14/6 The most unusual objects in a silver sale at Sotheby's yesterday were two miniature trencher salts, 1½in. diameter and weighing only to 10 dwt. by George Middleton, 1864. **1970** *Canad. Antiques Collector* Mar. 23/1 Salt cellars were made in many shapes, starting with plain, round or oblong, so-called trencher salts in the early 1700's. **1968** *Ibid.* June 9/1 Dinner..was served on two tables. One was at floor level—the 'trencher' table—where the steward, the curate, the governess and members of the staff were seated. **1977** D. E. WESTLAKE *Nobody's Perfect* II. iii. 110 Ratty pieces of living-room furniture..and an old trencher table.

trenching, *vbl. sb.* **b.** Add: *trenching-spade* (earlier U.S. example), *-tool* (examples).

1866 *Harper's Mag.* Oct. 636/1 Rough-boarded warehouses crammed with..gun-carriages,..trenching spades, and axes. **1779** in *9th Rep. R. Comm. Hist. MSS.* App. III. 148 in *Parl. Papers 1910* (Cd. 5038) XXXV. 675 A large quantity of trenching tools, etc., had been put on board. **1809** A. HENRY *Trav. & Adventures Canada* xv. 130 The most common way of taking the beaver is that of breaking up its house, which is done with trenching-tools. **1979** R. BLYTHE *View in Winter* iv. 172 They was now shellin' like anything... I got my trenchin'-tool out.

tre·nchless, *a.* [f. TRENCH *sb.* + -LESS.] Applied to pipe-laying and draining machinery, etc., that dispenses with the cutting of a trench.

1969 [see *PIPE-LAYER]. **1971** *Power Farming* Mar. 60/1 This is a dual-purpose trenchless drainer. **1979** *Daily Tel.* 31 Dec. 15/5 There is the so-called trenchless machine which, in one operation, can lay the pipe without any soil being removed.

trench-plough, *sb.* Add: Also used for trench-making in warfare.

1918 E. S. FARROW *Dict. Mil. Terms, Trench-plough*, a kind of plough for opening land to a greater depth than that of common furrows; a plough used in trench making.

trend, *sb.* Add: **4. b.** Now freq. with qualifying word and without const. (Later examples.)

1902 G. W. E. RUSSELL *Londoner's Log-Book* xiv. 243 Beyond doubt, Bounderley's local popularity is waning. The 'trend' is pointing in another direction. **1928** *Granta* 3 Feb. 240 Show me a play that's Russian with a psychosymbolical trend. **1930** M. A. MAGEE (*title*) Materials for the study of business trends in location of the women's clothing industry. **1967** SINGHA & MASSEY *Indian Dances* i. 38 This can be regarded as a healthy trend since it has aroused a consciousness of the dance.

c. *spec.* in *Educ.* (See quots.)

1960 *Where?* III. 18/1 '*Trend*', *the*, jargon for the increasing tendency of pupils to stay at school beyond the compulsory school-leaving age. **1962** A. SAMPSON *Anatomy of Britain* xii. 185 Since the war more children are staying on voluntarily than had been expected..(the phenomenon known to schoolteachers as 'Trend'). **1969** H. PERKIN *Key Profession* v. 208 The 'trend', that is, the growing demand on the part of the young and their parents for higher education expressed in the tendency to stay on at school beyond the statutory leaving age.

5. *Geol.* A geological formation which is a source of oil or gas. Cf. sense 4 a in Dict.

1939 *Bull. Amer. Assoc. Petroleum Geologists* XXIII. 860 The Jackson trend continued to lead in the number of discoveries with 16 new [oil] fields. **1977** *Time* 5 Dec. 59/1 In Louisiana, the 'trend' (main potential gas-producing formation) lies four miles beneath the green bayous and sugar-cane fields.

6. Special Comb.: **trend analysis**, analysis of (esp. statistical) data in order to detect or study any trend represented in them; **trend line**, a line indicating the general course or tendency of something (as a geographical feature or a set of points on a graph); **trend-spotter**, one who observes (or seeks to predict) the changing tide of fashion, in dress, ideas, etc.; **trend surface**, a mathematically defined surface computed as a best fit to the sampled values of some parameter over an area of interest; so *trend surface analysis*.

1934 M. SASULY *Trend Analysis of Statistics* i. 6 The primary purpose of this book is to derive formulas and computation schedules that will simplify..practical trend analysis. **1964** M. ARGYLE *Psychol. & Social Probl.* xv. 183 For purposes of trend analysis it is not particularly interesting to know how particular people have changed, since this confuses developmental with historical trends—we want to compare groups of people today with equivalent groups at a previous date. **1971** *Jrnl. Gen. Psychol.* LXXXIV. 107 Trend analysis showed that performance under steady illumination did not vary over wavelength. **1912** *Q. Rev.* Apr. 532 The trend-lines of mountain systems are the results..of something more than a lateral pressure. **1930** M. EZEKIEL *Method of Correlation Analysis* xvi. 239 The residuals from the final trend line might be again plotted against the other curves, to see if any further changes were necessary. **1959** *Listener* 2 Apr. 581/2 The almost level trend-line of coal production. **1965** G. J. WILLIAMS *Econ. Geol. N.Z.* iii. 30/2 The lateral displacements are as much as 95 ft from the trend-line of the lode. **1976** *National Observer* (U.S.) 6 Nov., If you slow growth, it means that the trend line for the production of automobiles, refrigerators, houses, and so forth will begin to taper down. **1965** *Punch* 21 Apr. 570/2 As trend-spotters will have spotted, the sweet-and-twenty blonde, who was last year selling us Scotch, shirts and motor-cars from the hoardings is increasingly yielding place to little winsome children. **1980** *Times Lit. Suppl.* 21 Nov. 1316/4, I don't deny that ideology can be adopted as a fashionable mode, but ideas, real ideas, do not make their appearance and disappearance merely to satisfy the shaping whims of trend-spotters; and to pretend that they do is to become a trend-spotter yourself. **1956** R. L. MILLER in *Jrnl. Geol.* LXIV. 425 The problem of defining and analyzing contemporary environments of sedimentation is approached from the point of view of mapping 'trend surfaces'. **1959** *Jrnl. Geophysical Res.* LXIV. 823 Trend surface analysis is a procedure for separating the relatively large-scale systematic changes in mapped data from essentially non-systematic small-scale variations due to local effects. **1978** B. CHAPMAN *Clarke's Analytical Archaeol.* (ed. 2) x. 455 (*caption*) The location of the cultural assemblages in the Central Plains which have been analysed by trend-surface analysis.

Trendelenburg (trende·lĕnbɒɪg). *Med.* Also (*erron.*) **-berg.** The name of Friedrich *Trendelenburg* (1844–1924), German surgeon, used in the possessive and *attrib.* to designate certain phenomena observed and medical procedures invented by him, as **Trendelenburg('s) position**, an operating position in which the patient lies supine on a tilted table or bed with the pelvis higher than the head; **Trendelenburg('s) test**, (*a*) a test for disorders of the hip joint or gluteus muscles in which the patient stands on one leg and raises the other, a dropping of the pelvis on the unsupported side being a positive sign (*Trendelenburg's sign*); (*b*) a test for varicose veins in which the leg is raised to drain it of blood and then quickly lowered, immediate and rapid distention of the leg veins indicating valve incompetence.

1892 KEEN & WHITE *Amer. Text-bk. Surg.* II. III. viii. 948 The further manipulations within the pelvis will be much facilitated by the elevation of the pelvis.., the position being known as Trendelenburg's position. **1907** *Practitioner* Aug. 288 The abdomen is opened with patient in the extreme Trendelenburg position. **1912** A. H. TUBBY *Deformities* (ed. 2) I. III. ix. 586 Trendelenburg's sign is this: If the patient stands on the affected limb and flexes the hip of the second side..the pelvis slips downwards on the sound side. **1923** JONES & LOVETT *Orthopedic Surg.* xxvii. 556 The so-called Trendelenburg sign.. is very characteristic and explains a good deal of the curious gait. **1930** H. BAILEY *Demonstrations of Physical Signs in Clin. Surg.* (ed. 2) xxi. 214 Trendelenburg's test is not diagnostic of congenital hip disease. **1967** G. M. WYBURN et al. *Conc. Anat.* vi. 170/2 With paralysis of gluteus medius or minimus the pelvis drops on the unsupported side when standing on the affected limb (Trendelenberg's sign). **1974** J. D. MAYNARD in R. M. Kirk et al. *Surgery* xi. 239 Trendelenburg test... Confirmation of retrograde flow in the superficial veins is carried out. **1975** *Year Bk. Ear, Nose & Throat* 116 The patient is placed in the 8-degree reversed Trendelenburg position.

trendily (tre·ndili), *adv.* [f. *TRENDY *a.* + -LY[2].] In a fashionable or 'trendy' manner; modishly. Also in *Comb.* with *ppl. adjs.*

1967 *Guardian* 24 Apr. 4/4 A trendily dressed couple. **1971** *Rolling Stone* 24 June 3/1, I passed a trendily-attired Mendelsohn in front of Bullock's Westwood. **1974** *Listener* 21 Nov. 685/1 His young, trendily radical mistress. **1980** S. BRETT *Dead Side of Mike* ix. 101 A trendily-dressed blonde teenager of thirty-seven.

tre·ndiness. [f. *TRENDY *a.* + -NESS.] The uncritical following of fashionable modes of thought, dress, etc.; the quality of being trendy.

1966 *Guardian* 11 Oct. 6/2 Trendiness seemed worse than going to the common hordes. **1968** *Listener* 26 Dec. 871/2 Its breathless combination of trendiness and self-righteousness. Admittedly, *How It Is* is not alone in turning civil rights, say, into a fashion; and fashion.. into a tyranny. **1972** J. MCCLURE *Caterpillar Cop* iii. 42 The homes..were modest bungalows succumbing..to an ill-becoming trendiness; bright colours had been painted over the exterior woodwork. **1974** *Economist* 5 Jan. 13/1 As a result of yesterday's trendinesses, we have now created in the developed world an unfortunate excess of both birth control devices and anti-pollution controls. **1982** S. RADLEY *Talent for Destruction* x. 70 Indeed he is! A very popular Rector, I put it down to the fact that he's not trendy. Trendiness doesn't do in a parish like Breckham Market.

trending, *ppl. a.* (In Dict. s.v. TREND *v.*) (Later example.)

1968 D. L. CLARKE *Analytical Archaeol.* VI. v. 274 Once again we have six trending variables, each with three crude attitudes.

tre·nd-setter. [f. TREND *sb.* + SETTER *sb.*[1]] One who or that which establishes trends in dress, thought, etc.

1960 *Guardian* 17 Mar. 4/3 Powerful trend-setters, outstanding personalities. *Ibid.* 7 Dec. 6/3 The magazines.. are the chief trend-setters. **1966** *Listener* 2 June 814/1 The music and aesthetics of modern Italy's musical trend-setter, Casella. **1973** *Times* 24 Apr. 10/2 His big shouldered jackets are important trendsetters. **1979** D. HURD *End to Promises* ii. 26 My strongest feeling was satisfaction that the experts, the know-alls, and the trend-setters had been confounded.

Hence (as back-formation) **tre·nd-set** *v. intr.*; **tre·nd-setting** *ppl. a.*

1960 *House & Garden* Oct. 172 The big news from.. those trend-setting couturiers. **1965** *Punch* 7 July 34/3 That hairstyle, do you think it will trend-set? **1971** M. LEE *Dying for Fun* v. 42 Pollie Potter, dress designer, had been trendsetting now for two years. **1976** *Times* 26 Aug. 13/2 The trend-setting intellectuals of our day.

trendy (tre·ndi), *a.* and *sb.* [f. TREND *sb.* + -Y[1].] **A.** *adj.* Fashionable, up to date, following the latest trend. (Sometimes dismissively.)

1962 *Punch* 7 Nov. 654/3, I saw the headline 'The Trendiest Twin Set'. **1965** *Sun* 20 May 7/6 The BBC's Debussy film..must have been the first to use the screen credit 'Art Nouveau Consultant'... This is trying to be trendy: what's wrong with art-adviser? **1972** *Lancet* 20 May 1104/1 Pathobiology (a trendy name for general pathology) seems to be a fashionable subject in the United States. **1977** B. PYM *Quartet in Autumn* viii. 74 That was how it had always been and how it would go on in spite of trendy clergy trying to introduce so-called up-to-date forms of worship. **1982** *Chicago Sun-Times* 11 Nov. 88 (*heading*) Bargains still available in trendy neighborhoods.

B. *sb.* One who follows the latest trends or fashions.

1968 J. FLEMING *Kill or Cure* xi. 143 She was well in with what is now called the Chelsea set.., there are trendies and *personae non gratae* amongst them. **1971** *New Scientist* 26 Aug. 450/1 Amphetamine..to the young trendy..provides a means of staying awake all night. **1974** *Courier-Mail* (*Brisbane*) 30 Mar. 8/3 Some of us have fought all our lives to be trendies. **1982** *Listener* 16 Dec. 20/2 The 'trendies'' concern for the individual seems to relate more to his place in society than to his soul.

tre·ndyism. [f. prec. + -ISM.] = *TRENDINESS.

1977 *Spare Rib* July 4/1 The coy use of Christian names ..reminds me of the clubby, in-group atmosphere of competitive trendyism I found so depressing at the last WLM conference. **1981** *Observer* (Colour Suppl.) 13 Dec. 66/1 An encroaching tide of trendyism.

trepan, *v.*[1] Add: **c.** *Engin.* To cut an annular groove or hole in (something) by means of a crown saw or other tool; to make (a hole) thus, the core being removed as a solid piece.

1909 in *Cent. Dict.* Suppl. **1919** A. G. Robson *Engin. Machine Tools & Processes* ix. 195 With the cutters at hand it was impossible to get a feed greater than 1/200 inch per revolution when trepanning steel from the solid without breaking the cutter. **1953** G. S. Schaller *Engin. Manufacturing Methods* xiii. 221 The solid forging is trepanned instead of being bored in the conventional manner. **1970** I. Bradley *Myford ML10 Lathe Man.* xi. 64 The smaller holes are best bored, but large holes can be trepanned in order to save a useful piece of material.

trepanning *vbl. sb.* (further examples).

1880 M. P. Bale *Woodworking Machinery* xvii. 168 A Mr. Murdock, in 1810, took out a patent for an improved machine for forming wooden or stone pipes. For boring wood he employed a hollow cylinder, fitted at its extremity with a circular trepanning saw. **1949** W. S. Churchill *2nd World War* II. II. xviii. 319 Trepanning consisted of making a hole in the bomb casing in order to deal with the explosive contents. **1974** *Sci. Amer.* Jan. 36/2 In trepanning a hollow cathode shaped according to the specified pattern lifts parts of complex shape and uniform thickness from a metal slab.

trepa·nger. [f. Trepang + -er[1].] A trepang-fisher.

1912 A. Searcy *By Flood & Field* xlviii. 302 Our confrere then informed us that as soon as the famous hunter gained his liberty he had purchased a ketch, fitted her up with the requirements of a trepanger, and sailed away. **1934** *Bulletin* (Sydney) 14 Mar. 33/1 The trepangers with their long, sharp iron spears will soon be working the Rowley Shoals.

trepanner[1]. Add: **2.** *spec.* in *Coal Mining* (see quot. 1967).

1956 Atkinson & White in D. L. Linton *Sheffield* 269 Intensive efforts are being made to replace the hand-loading of coal..by mechanical power-loaders and..considerable success is being achieved with..Gloster Getters, Trepanners,..and Huwood Slicers. **1967** *Gloss. Mining Terms* (*B.S.I.*) viii. 27 *Trepanner*, a longwall power loader, usually double ended, the main cutting element of which is a trepanning wheel. **1971** [see *plough, plow *sb.*[1] 5 i]. **1974** P. Wright *Lang. Brit. Industry* xiv. 145 He may..hear..shearer and trepanner for types of coal-cutters.

trephine, *sb.* Add: **2.** = *trephination* s.v. Trephine *v.*

1958 F. G. Slaughter *Daybreak* I. ii. 13 A patient should be more than a chart number..even to a neurosurgeon performing a preliminary trephine. **1976** *Lancet* 9 Oct. 769/2 Bone-marrow aspirate and trephine confirmed acute myeloid leukæmia.

trepidant, *a.* (Earlier example.)

1891 [see *abasia].

treponema (treponī·mă). *Biol.* and *Med.* Pl. **-ne·mata.** Also anglicized as **tre·poneme.** [mod.L. (coined in Ger. by F. Schaudinn 1905, in *Deutsch. med. Wochenschr.* 26 Oct. 1728/1), f. Gr. τρέπ-ειν to turn + νῆμα thread.] An anærobic spirochæte of the genus of this name, the members of which are parasitic or pathogenic in man and warm-blooded animals and include those causing syphilis and yaws.

1908 [see *spirochæte* s.v. *spiro-]. **1922** *Nature* 20 May 667/2 Existence of the treponeme in the cytoplasm of the nerve cells of the cerebral cortex. **1949** M. A. Jennings in H. W. Florey et al. *Antibiotics* II. xxxi. 1011 In a patient with concurrent typhoid fever the treponemata disappeared but the typhoid infection ran its usual course. **1970** *New Scientist* 19 Mar. 543/1 Late in the disease, dormant treponemes persist in some instances in lymph nodes and other tissues. **1981** *Brit. Med. Jrnl.* 18 Apr. 1312/1 Walt Disney's serried ranks of gonococci and treponemes.

Hence **trepone·mal** *a.*, of, pertaining to, or caused by treponemes; **treponemato·sis** (pl. **-oses**), infection with, or a disease caused by, treponemes.

1913 Castellani & Chalmers *Man. Trop. Med.* (ed. 2) xliv. 1191 These drugs seem to act in frambœsia more quickly and powerfully than in any other spirochætal and treponemal condition. **1927** *Jrnl. Laboratory & Clin. Med.* XII. 670 In this paper we are using the term 'treponematosis' to include syphilis and the condition called yaws. **1970** *New Scientist* 19 Mar. 543/1 Venereal syphilis of adults is rare in tropical regions where the endemic treponematoses, yaws and pinta, prevail. *Ibid.*, The results of a quarter of a century's experience with penicillin in the treatment of treponemal disease, notably syphilis, are now available. **1980** *Nature* 7 Feb. 573/2 Treponemal infection in irradiated mice.

treponemicidal (tre:pŏnīmisəi·dăl), *a.* [f. prec. + -i- + -cid(e + -al.] Of, pertaining to, or causing the destruction of treponemata.

1933 J. E. Moore *Mod. Treatment of Syphilis* xxvi. 382 In early meningeal neurosyphilis..the desideratum of treatment is treponemicidal effect applied as powerfully as possible. **1970** *New Scientist* 19 Mar. 543/1, 2·4 mega-units of long acting benzathine penicillin can maintain a treponemicidal blood and tissue level for three weeks or more.

‖**très** (trę), *adv. colloq.* [Fr.: see Tres-.] With English adjs.: very. Usu. with reference to a fashionable or modishly superior quality, freq. as *très snob*, very 'posh'.

[**1815** F. Burney *Let.* 10 July (1980) VIII. 285 He is *très* what those on the other side the question call *exalté*.] **1819** Keats *Let.* 3 Jan. (1931) I. 292 A full, true, and très particular account of Miss M's ten Suitors. **1939** 'N. Blake' *Smiler with Knife* iv. 63 It's a sort of county club. Très snob. On the Thames. **1959** A. Sinclair *Breaking of Bumbo* v. 74 The continental millionaires, who thought it *très snob* to bring out their young in the last society in Europe. **1968** A. Diment *Gt. Spy Race* viii. 126 *Très, très, très* sexy. It was fairly obvious..which section of 'trad' spy-craft Mrs Omega was going to test. **1976** *Publishers Weekly* 8 Mar. 67/2 The picture on the cover, a *très* cool modern kid who doesn't look a bit like the novel's hero. **1978** J. Sherwood *Limericks of Lachasse* xii. 140 Students..who were of good family and *très snob.*

Trevira (trəvīᵊ·ră). Also **trevira.** The proprietary name of a type of artificial fibre or the fabric made from it (see quots.).

1959 *Official Gaz.* (U.S. Patent Office) 24 Nov. TM160/1 Trevira. Owner of German Reg...dated Mar. 21, 1956.. For table linen and bed linen; net, lace, woven and mesh fabrics; textile ribbons, textile trimmings; carpets and rugs; mats; curtains; flags; and felt. **1960** *Trade Marks Jrnl.* 21 Dec. 1650/2 *Trevira*... All goods included in Class 24. Farbwerke Hoechst Aktiengesellschaft Vormals Meister Lucius & Brüning..45, Brüningstrasse, Frankfurt-am-Main—Hoechst, Germany; Manufacturers and Merchants. **1964** *Which?* Aug. 253/3 *Polyester*... Brand names: *Dacron* (USA), *Tergal* (France), *Terlenka* (Holland), *Terylene*, *Trevira* (W. Germany). **1967** *Daily Tel.* 30 Oct. 11/3 Now there's another new test-tube fibre name to memorize... Trevira will pop into Britain's fashion shops from December. **1972** *Guardian* 22 Aug. 9/2 Trevira/rayon shirt. **1977** *N.Z. Herald* 5 Jan. 2-18/3 (Advt.), Lincoln Fabrics... Plain and fancy crimps and treviras.

trevorite (tre·vŏrəit). *Min.* [f. the name of T. G. *Trevor* (1865–1958), South African geologist and mining official + -ite[1].] A black, magnetic, isometric oxide of nickel and ferric iron, $NiFe_2O_4$, belonging to the spinel group.

1921 A. F. Crosse in *Jrnl. Chem., Metallurgical & Mining Soc. S. Afr.* XXI. 126/2 One of the most interesting mineralogical discoveries..in the Transvaal..is an extraordinarily rich nickel ore... This ore is as far as I am able to judge a new and undescribed mineral... I should like to call it 'Trevorite' after Major T. G. Trevor, Mining Inspector for the Pretoria District. **1976** *Mineral. Abstr.* XXVII. 252/2 Microprobe analyses of grains of ferroan trevorite from a serpentine massif in south-western China reported Ni 3·4–8·8% but no Ti.

trews, *sb. pl.* Add: **b.** Trousers in general (tartan or otherwise), including close-fitting trousers worn by women.

1847 H. S. Riddell *Poems* 19 When I brought ben your clase, Sae beaten with the weather, And gae the trews a wee bit touch, Out flew goud guinea frae ae pouch. **1883** F. Sutherland *Sunny Mem. Morayland* 57 The soor-moo'd limmer wears the trews. **1917** N. Munro *Poetry* (1931) III. 51 His body unadorned by Highland raiment, Trammelled, for glorious hours, in Saxon trews. **1931** E. Linklater *Juan in America* II. iv. 94 His Tyrolean costume made evident that even his knees were comely—strong, round, and rosy under their brief leather trews. **1958** *Woman's Own* 5 Mar. 16/3 They make a handsome pair, when she's wearing a blouse with matching tapered trews in printed wool. **1959** H. Hobson *Mission House Murder* i. 5 She was wearing tartan trews, a black cashmere sweater and a short red duffle-coat.

trey, *sb.* Add: **2.** (Earlier and further examples.) *spec.* in the U.S., a three-dollar packet of a narcotic.

[**1859** Hotten *Dict. Slang* 204 Tray saltee, threepence.. tre soldi.] **1887** J. W. Horsley *Jottings from Jail* i. 3 And he who 'does a tray' (serves three months' imprisonment) therein, borrows his word from our Gallican neighbours. **1944** D. Burley in A. Dundes *Mother Wit* (1973) 214 A deuce or tray of haircuts ago. **1960** 'A. Burgess' *Doctor is Sick* xiii. 98 'I know all about you. You did a tray on the moor.'..'It wasn't a tray..it was only a stretch.' **1967** [see *nickel bag* s.v. *nickel sb. 3 a]. **1972** J. Mills *Report to Commissioner* 98 She wants to buy two treys, $3 bags of heroin. He says he has treys, but wants $3.50 for them. **1977** *National Times* (Austral.) 17 Jan. 11/3 Service of the kind just described is as rare these days as finding a trey in the Christmas pudding.

3. trey-bit (freq. **tray-bit**) *Austral.* and *N.Z. slang* (now *Hist.*), a three-penny piece; also *trey-piece*.

1898 *Bulletin* (Sydney) 1 Oct. 14, 3d. a 'traybit'. **1901** *Bulletin Reciter* (Sydney) 181 Den I socked me bit upon 'er—Ev'ry tray-bit I could bring. **1937** F. Sargeson in *Tomorrow* 17 Mar. 310/2, I upend them to collect the tray bits. **1953** A. Upfield *Murder must Wait* xviii. 162 I'll bet my job against a trey bit you're right. **1977** *Sunday Sun* (Brisbane) 1 May 16 When it comes to unique competitions the people of outback Winton reckon they're the full quid—and you can bet your last zac or traybit on it! **1899** *Bulletin* (Sydney) 14 Jan. (Red Page), We have here [*sc.* in Tauranga, N.Z.]..slang words for..3d.—*thrum, half-tiz, tray*, or *tray-piece*.

trez, var. Tray *sb.*[4]

tri-, *prefix.* Add: **I. 1. a. trialle·lic** *Genetics*, having three different alleles of a gene; **tricontine·ntal,** embracing three continents; **trifu·nctional** *Chem.*, having three functional groups in the molecule; hence **trifu·nctionally** *adv.*; **trilaminar:** also in *Cytology* (examples); **trinu·cleotide** *Biochem.*, an oligonucleotide in which the number of nucleotides is three; **tripare·ntal** *a. Microbiology*, involving or resulting from the infection of a bacterium by three different bacteriophages at the same time; **trisensory** (earlier example).

1944 S. S. Atwood in *Proc. Nat. Acad. Sci.* XXX. 70 Because suitable terms to describe multiple alleles in autotetraploids would facilitate the discussion, the following new terminology is suggested and will be used in this paper:..Triallelic. **1975** *Nature* 24 July 310/2 Triallelic plants..cannot be obtained by any normal form of inheritance and their appearance is strong evidence for the occurrence of an unusual genetic transfer process. **1962** M. Hardwick *Sherlock Holmes Compan.* 199 Watson's astonishing statement about his tri-continental experience of women. **1966** *Economist* 22 Jan. 299/1 The tricontinental conference held in Havana..will increase the prestige of Dr Castro. **1929** W. H. Carothers in *Jrnl. Amer. Chem. Soc.* LI. 2550 Among compounds having more than one functional group, those of the type x—R—y may be called bifunctional, $R''x_3$, trifunctional, etc. **1975** *Nature* 10 Apr. 482/2 An essential feature is that some of these amino acids are trifunctional. **1941** *Jrnl. Amer. Chem. Soc.* LXIII. 3085/2 (*caption*) Schematic representation of a trifunctionally branched three-dimensional polymer molecule. **1889** *Cent. Dict.*, Trilaminar. **1971** *New Scientist* 1 Apr. 24/1 (*caption*) Electron micrographs of mitochondrial membranes reveal a trilaminar or railway track appearance. **1977** *Jrnl. Protozool.* XXIV. 18/1 The trilaminar construction of the ciliate cortex. **1918** *Jrnl. Chem. Soc.* CXIV. I. 48 The simultaneous liberation of the trinucleotide, triphosphonucleic acid, and the mononucleotide, uridine-phosphoric acid, indicates that the three constituent mononucleotides in triphosphonucleic acid must be combined in a different manner from the uridine-phosphoric acid in the parent molecule of yeast-nucleic acid. **1974** *Nature* 25 Oct. 734/2 The two RNAs are known to contain an identical trinucleotide at their 5′ terminal. **1951** *Cold Spring Harbor Symp. Quantitative Biol.* XVI. 471/2 Important information about genetic recombination comes from experiments in which the frequency of triparental recombination is measured. **1961** *Genetics* XLVI. 1314 Occurrence of triparental recombinants between two Hfr and one F⁻ has been demonstrated in *E. coli* K–12. **1976** *Ann. Rev. Microbiol.* XXX. 517 Nonconjugative plasmid transfer by such triparental matings may occur under ideal laboratory conditions. **1894** Trisensory [see *bisensory *a.*].

b. *tri-county, state.*

1974 *News & Courier* (Charleston, S. Carolina) 19 Apr. 6-A/1 A municipal scramble for federal recreation funds is under way in the tri-county. **1978** *Detroit Free Press* 5 Mar. 13/2 These centers cater to some 150,000 deaf adults in the tri-county area. **1963** *Times* 15 Jan. 9/6 A tri-state transportation committee is carrying out a survey..of New York, New Jersey, and Connecticut. **1983** *Listener* 22 Sept. 5/2 The attractions of the US market—and the New York tri-state area in particular—have been appreciated for a long time.

II. 4. b. tri-·axle, a trailer or articulated lorry with three (rear) axles; **triplane** (further examples); **trivoltine:** also **trivoltin** (example). **c. tri-car** (earlier example); **tri-·mix,** a breathing mixture for deep-sea divers composed of nitrogen, helium, and oxygen.

1971 M. Tak *Truck Talk* 173 *Triaxle*, a semi with three rear axles and consequently a greater weight-carrying allowance. **1978** *Detroit Free Press* 16 Apr. F 8/1 (Advt.), Trailer: 1967 Ravens 29′ dump on 34′ frame, tri-axle with air-lift. **1981** *Daily Tel.* 10 Dec. 9 (*caption*) A..38-tonne tri-axle lorry. **1903** *Motor* 6 May 279/1 (*heading*) The new Rex 'Tricar'. **1976** *Jrnl. Appl. Physiol.* XL. 605/2 Each subject..breathed either air or a mixture of 36% helium, 21% oxygen, and 43% nitrogen (tri-mix) during cycles of immersed work. **1981** *New Scientist* 12 Feb. 390 Last week a team of divers..broke the world record for a simulated dive, experiencing pressures equivalent to those 686 metres beneath the sea surface... Part of the secret of the test's success was that the divers breathed a recently developed gas mixture, called trimix. **1909** Triplane [see *quadruplane]. **1920** *Glasgow Herald* 10 July 5 The Pullman triplanes of the British Company carry 18 people. **1977** J. Cleary *High Road to China* ii. 47 'What did you fly?'..'Albatros D's and Fokker Triplanes. I was with von Richthofen.' **1888** Trivoltin [see *bivoltine *a.*].

III. 5. a. trite·rpane, a terpane with the formula $C_{30}H_{60}$, analogous to the triterpenes; **trite·rpene,** any of the group of terpenes of formula $C_{30}H_{48}$, found in plant gums and resins; also, a triterpenoid; **trite·rpenoid,** a triterpene or a derivative of one.

1902 F. J. Pond tr. *Heusler's Chem. Terpenes* 432 Several well characterized compounds which occur in elemi-resin belong to the class of triterpenes. **1932** *Chem. Abstr.* XXVI. 3244 (*heading*) Contribution to the accurate determination of the empirical formulas of several triterpenes and triterpenoids. **1945** Triterpene [see *isoprenoid *a.* and *sb.*]. **1965** *Proc. Nat. Acad. Sci.* LIV. 1406 We wish to report now the isolation and identification of..a C_{30}-pentacyclic triterpane from the branched-cyclic alkane fraction of the Green River Shale. **1978** Triterpene [see *stevioside]. **1978** *Nature* 16 Mar. 217/1 Polycyclic triterpenoids are found in petroleum and their presence was at first taken as evidence of non-marine contribution, as they had been detected in the lipid extract of ferns. **1981** *Jrnl. Chromatogr. Sci.* XIX. 156/1 This study deals with the apparent effect that maturation has on the relative concentration of individual triterpanes [*etc.*].

b. triethylene, containing three non-contiguous ethylene radicals in the molecule.

1920 *Jrnl. Chem. Soc.* CXVII. 1090 (*heading*) Triethylene tri- and tetra-sulphides. **1953,** etc. [see *thiotepa* s.v. *thio- 1]. **1962** H. Burn *Drugs, Med. & Man* xix. 193

Tri-ethylene melamine..is used in the textile industry... It is now widely used in the treatment of Hodgkin's disease.

c. **tributyl phosphate,** an oily liquid, $(C_4H_9O)_3PO$, that is a solvent used as a plasticizer and in the solvent-extraction of nuclear fuels; **tricre·syl phosphate** [Cresyl], a colourless liquid, $(CH_3C_6H_4O)_3PO$, used as a fuel additive, plasticizer, and fire retardant; **tri:ethano·lamine** [*ethanolamine], an oily alkaline liquid alcohol, $(HOCH_2CH_2)_3N$, used as a solvent and a stabilizer; **trihydroca·lcite** *Min.* [ad. Russ. *trigidrokal'tsit"* (P. N. Chirvinsky 1906, in *Ezhegodnik" po Geol. i Mineral. Rosīi* VIII. 241/1)], a trihydrate of calcium carbonate, $CaCO_3.3H_2O$, the natural occurrence of which is uncertain; **tri:iodo-thy·ronine** *Biochem.* [*thyronine], a thyroid hormone similar to thyroxine (tetraiodothyronine) but having greater potency; $HO{\cdot}C_6H_3I{\cdot}O{\cdot}C_6H_2I_2{\cdot}CH_2CH(NH_2)COOH$.

1930 *Brit. Patent* 330,228 1/2 The excess of alcohol and later the tributyl phosphate are distilled off in vacuo. **1957** *Financial Times Ann. Rev. Brit. Industry* 69/1 The concentrate is dissolved in nitric acid..where it is extracted with tributyl phosphate, producing uranium. **1882** *Jrnl. Chem. Soc.* XLII. 839 The authors have thus obtained triphenyl, tri-β-naphthyl and tricresyl phosphate from the corresponding phenols. **1959** *Economist* 10 Jan. 153 (Advt.), The Ignition Control Additive based on tricresyl phosphate..was developed..to overcome serious problems of power loss and rough running. **1962** *Punch* 15 Aug. 218/3 Tricresyl phosphate was a chemical similar to triorthocresyl phosphate. **1897** *Jrnl. Chem. Soc.* LXXII. 314 (*heading*) Triethanolamine (trihydroxytriethylamine). **1939** *Jrnl. R. Aeronaut. Soc.* XLIII. 617 Strips of brass sheet were..immersed respectively in pure glycol, commercial glycol and commercial glycol treated with triethanolamine phosphate. **1976** *New Yorker* 8 Mar. 67/1 (Advt.), Its mild 'heavy-molecular' triethanolamine-base formulation is chemically balanced to remove surface dirt and makeup without penetrating and robbing the sub-layers of the skin. **1910** *Mineral. Mag.* XV. 432 Trihydrocalcite... Hydrated calcium carbonate, $CaCO_3.3H_2O$, occurring as a mould-like encrustation on chalk-marl near Nova-Alexandria. **1928,** etc. Trihydrocalcite [see *pentahydrocalcite* s.v. *penta-]. **1952** *Lancet* 1 Mar. 439/1 (*heading*) The identification of 3:5:3′-L-triiodothyronine in human plasma. **1975** *Jrnl. Endocrinol.* LXIV. 573 In the present culture system the thyroid hormones (tri-iodothyronine and thyroxine) inhibited the action of PTH.

triac (trəi·æk). *Electronics.* [f. *tri(ode *a.* and *sb.* + *A.C.* s.v. *A III.] A three-electrode semiconductor device that will conduct in either direction when triggered by a positive or negative signal at the gate electrode.

1964 E. K. Howell in *IEEE Internat. Convention Record* XII. ix. 86/2 To simplify the control of AC power, a completely new silicon semiconductor has been developed. 'Triac' is a generic term coined for this *tri*ode *AC* switch. **1975** *Hi-Fi Answers* Feb. 78/2 The light pulses from the led are picked up by a photo-conductive cell, and applied to the..triggering circuit of the triac. **1981** *Computer-Aided Design* Jan. 7/1 During the past two decades the application of triacs and thyristors in the control of power and machines with complex feedback arrangements has rapidly replaced the use of their conventional counterparts in almost all sectors of industry and public services.

triacetate (trəiˌæ·sĭtēⁱt). *Chem.* [f. Tri- + Acetate.] † **a.** A compound in which an acetate group is combined with three atoms or molecules of a base. *Obs.*

1860 [see Tri- 5 a].

b. A compound containing three acetate groups in the molecule; *spec.* cellulose triacetate, in which acetate groups replace hydrogen atoms in (notionally) all three hydroxyl groups in each constituent glucose molecule; a man-made fibre made from this.

1895 C. F. Cross et al. *Cellulose* i. 35 Heated at 180° in a sealed tube, in the proportion by weight of 1 of cellulose to 6 of the anhydride, the cellulose is converted into the triacetate. **1921** *Jrnl. Soc. Chem. Industry* 31 Jan. 8T/2 If the ratio of chlorine to sulphur dioxide be nearer to unity then the product is mainly cellulose triacetate. **1956** W. J. Roff *Fibres, Plastics, & Rubbers* 25 A method of preparing fully acetylated triacetate possessing exceptionally good electrical properties. **1960** *Which?* Jan. 19/1 Triacetate is very similar to ordinary acetate, but not so soft to handle; it will take permanent pleats and creases. **1978** *Lancashire Life* Mar. 113/3 Each item can be bought separately—the triacetate and nylon shirt at about £13.50.

triacid (trəiˌæ·sid), *sb.* and *a.* [f. Tri- + Acid *a.* and *sb.*] **A.** *sb.* [partial tr. G. *triacidlösung* 'three-acid solution'.] A biological stain consisting of methyl green, orange G, and acid fuchsin. Also *attrib.*

1896 A. B. Lee *Microtomist's Vade-Mecum* (ed. 4) xviii. 223 Ehrlich's Triacid Mixture.—According to a custom which, I believe, originated with Ehrlich himself, and which would, perhaps, be better honoured in the breach than the observance, the name of Triacid ('Triacidlösung') has been given to a mixture of the same three dyes as in the Ehrlich-Biondi mixture, but in such proportions that the 'acid' colours therein have a larger share assigned to them. **1899** [see *polychromatic a. 2]. **1929** Slider & Downey in C. E. McClung *Handbk. Microsc. Technique* vii. 248 The triacid stain is used for five minutes. *Ibid.*, Triacid contains methyl green, orange G and acid fuchsin. **1976** P. Collard *Devel. of Microbiol.* v. 54 In 1880 he [*sc.* P. Ehrlich] published an account of his famous tri-acid stain for the differential staining of leucocytes.

B. *adj.* Of a triglyceride: containing three different acid radicals in the molecule.

1945 Chen & Daubert in *Jrnl. Amer. Chem. Soc.* LXVII. 1256/1 'Triacid triglycerides' is used in this report to describe those triglycerides consisting of three different fatty acids. **1977** *Appl. Spectrosc.* XXXI. 122/1 Seven diacid and five triacid saturated triglycerides have been investigated by infrared spectroscopy.

triactor (trəiˌæ·ktəɹ). *Canad.* [Tri- 4 c.] A form of betting on race-horses (see quot. 1979); freq. *attrib.*

1976 *Telegraph-Jrnl.* (St. John, New Brunswick) 23 Aug. 12/2 *Charlottetown*—Two big triactor payoffs..highlighted a 10-dash harness racing card here Saturday. **1979** *Beautiful Brit. Columbia* Winter 36 The triactor bettor..had to name the first three finishers, in order, in the last race each day and lived in hopes of making up to $1,000 for his $2 bet. **1984** E. Wright *Smoke Detector* iv. 124 It is sometimes nearly as helpful if you know which horse *can't* win a race... It helps with the triactor, anyway.

triad. Add: **2. c.** (Earlier examples.)

[**1809** W. Blake in *Compl. Writings* (1972) 560 Three Ancient Britons overthrowing the Army of armed Romans ..From the Welch Triades.] **1838** [see *afanc].

j. *Path.* A group of three symptoms or signs.

1899 E. Lang in T. L. Stedman *20th Cent. Pract.* XVIII. 267 Since the work of Hutchinson, who looked upon a keratitis parenchymatosa in conjunction with a frequently observed deafness and anomaly of the incisors as an expression of hereditary syphilis (Hutchinson's triad), affections of the cornea are numbered among the most frequently occurring manifestations of syphilis. **1908,** etc. [see *Hutchinson]. **1909** G. Dock in Osler & McCrae *Syst. Med.* VI. xvii. 439 The early idea that the disease [*sc.* exophthalmic goitre] was characterized by a 'triad' of symptoms gives way slowly. **1948** [see *Tridione]. **1954** D. Nabarro *Congenital Syphilis* ii. 14 He pointed out that interstitial keratitis and notched incisor teeth were frequently associated with 8th nerve deafness —the three signs being known as the Hutchinsonian triad. **1982** *Sci. Amer.* Aug. 82/2 The classic triad of the inflammatory reaction is redness, warmth and swelling.

3. *Triads*: also, secret societies, freq. of a criminal character, into which the Triad Society has become divided, and which flourish among overseas Chinese. Also in *sing.* Freq. *attrib.*

1960 D. Whitehead *Journey into Crime* (1961) 27 Triad gangs poured into the streets..and fought the police. **1962** M. & G. Gordon *Journey with Stranger* (1963) xxiv. 139 The Triads, those secret criminal societies that sought to monopolize every kind of racket. **1975** D. Bloodworth *Clients of Omega* vii. 64 A rival society buried your body, it seems. The 18-K Triad. **1976** *Spectator* 14 Feb. 3/2 Chinese Triad gangs made their mark in London by kicking to death a man in a Soho gambling club. **1976** *Daily Colonist* (Victoria, B.C.) 2 Mar. 3/1 A heroin smuggling racket that may be linked with the world-wide Chinese secret society known as Triad. **1977** *Hongkong Standard* 14 Apr. 5/1 As far as triad influence in these committees was concerned, Mr Lam admitted his department had received complaints in the past. **1978** *Daily Tel.* 3 Apr. 3/3 Yard chiefs concerned about the increasing violence between rival triads ..have ordered a further big crackdown.

Triadist. Restrict *Welsh Lit.* to sense in Dict. and add: **2.** *pl.* Members of the Triad Society (see Triad 3). *rare.*

1855 *North-China Herald* 17 Mar. 132/2 The Triadists, who so recently held Shanghae.

triage. Add: **2.** Also with Fr. pronunc. (triɑ̄ʒ). **a.** The assignment of degrees of urgency to wounds or illnesses in order to decide the order or suitability of treatment. Freq. *attrib.* Hence (*rare*) as *v. trans.* (see quot. 1977).

1930 F. A. Pottle *Stretchers* 222 A special triage officer at once surveys the patients to determine the urgency of their injuries. **1945** *Jrnl. R. Army Med. Corps* LXXXIV. 125 The word 'triage', literally 'assessment according to quality', has recently been adopted to describe the process. **1973** *Parade* 18 Feb. 8/1 Chicago's Michael Reese Hospital ..has instituted a 'triage', or selection system, whereby incoming patients are evaluated by an RN as to their degree of urgency, and sent to the appropriate area. **1973** N. Meyer *Target Practice* viii. 95 And presto, we were all second-lieutenant navy doctors. For six months I worked in *triage* there, operating sometimes around the clock. **1975** *Observer* 11 May 6/7 Hundreds of 'borderline' cases have been at the mercy all this week of 'triage' panels trying to sort out patients desperately in need of care. **1976** *Lancet* 15 Nov. 1061/1 Triage at an early stage can label the patient with coma as surgical or medical. **1977** M. Herr *Dispatches* 82 He was so bad that the doctor triaged him, passed him over to treat the ones that..could still be saved. **1978** *Tucson Mag.* Dec. 55/1 An extremely efficient triage nurse, an RN, greets new arrivals and determines the severity of the problem.

b. *transf.*

1974 *Time* 11 Nov. 80 In the West, there is increasing talk of triage, a commonsense if callous concept that teaches that when resources are scarce, they must be used where they will do most good. **1975** *Globe & Mail* (Toronto) 3 Nov. 7/2 The concept should now be applied to countries crippled by food shortages, famine and over-population. 'The triage discussions now seek to classify nations into those what do not need help, those that are capable of responding to help and those "broken back" states that are in such difficulty that they cannot be helped,' says Mr Hopper. **1979** *Guardian* 18 Oct. 5/8 There is [*sc.* in New York] an unofficial 'triage' system in which teachers and school administrators concentrate their limited resources on helping those students who seem to be capable of succeeding.

triagonal, *a.* (Earlier examples.)

1665 Hooke *Micrographia* 158 Piggs-hair (A) is somewhat *triagonal*, and seems to have neither pith nor pore. **1794** A. Thomas *Newfoundland Jrnl.* (1968) 121 Its shape is Triagonal and it measures Three Hundred and Fifty Miles in length.

trial, *sb.*[1] Add: **1. a.** Also *transf.* in phrr. *trial by television* or *the media*, subjection of a public figure under some cloud to discussion of his case on television or in the media, usu. in such a way as to imply his guilt.

1960 J. Freeman in *New Statesman* 15 Oct. 556/1 A group of Labour MPs had..written to *The Times* complaining that my questions to Mr. Foulkes, in the BBC programme *Panorama*, about specific..allegations of malpractice in his union amounted to public trial by television. **1968** *Punch* 6 Mar. 327/1 Urged to stop 'trial by television', the Postmaster-General..said..he himself had no power over the content of programmes. **1979** *Broadcast* 4 June 10/1 There have been predictable references to 'trial by the media', 'trial by television'.

2. a. Applied *spec.* in *pl.* to a boat's trial run (see sense *13 a below).

1921 *Daily Colonist* (Victoria, B.C.) 25 Mar. 17/2 On Friday the Traveller was taken out for her trials... Slight trouble arose in the main bearings and the vessel returned to the dock for adjustments. **1969** F. Mowat *Boat who would not Float* (1970) vii. 70 Seamen refer to the first tentative voyage of a newly commissioned ship as her trials.

c. A contest designed to test the capabilities of motor-cyclists or (formerly) car-drivers and their vehicles, in which riding or driving takes place over long distances or rough terrain. Freq. in *pl.* Cf. *reliability trial* s.v. *reliability 3.

1926 [see *scramble *sb.* 2 b]. **1935** *Encycl. Sports* 429/1 Among the more famous English trials that have been run for many years are the London–Edinburgh run, the London–Exeter run, the London–Land's End Trial and the London–Gloucester Run. **1950** *Oxf. Jun. Encycl.* IX. 328/2 The famous Scott Trial in Yorkshire was the first of such rough-riding fixtures [in motor-cycling contests]. **1963** P. Drackett *Motor Rallying* i. 10 The Thousand Miles Trial of 1903 went several steps nearer to the rally as we know it to-day, with road sections and timed hill-climbs. **1976** *Southern Even. Echo* (Southampton) 3 Nov., Trials enthusiasts will be out in force in Hampshire this weekend to watch the Hood Trophies and Perce Simon Trials—two major events in the British motor cycle calendar.

4. a. *trial and error*, (*a*) also in non-mathematical contexts, the process of succeeding by repeated trying with or without improvement of method by learning from failures; (*b*) *spec.* in *Psychol.*, with reference to the theory that a primitive form of learning results, over a series of trials, from erroneous random responses to a problem being replaced by the correct response, rather than from insight. Freq. (with hyphens) *attrib.*

1894 C. L. Morgan *Introd. Compar. Psychol.* xiv. 241 Such a proceeding can be completely explained in terms of sense-experience. The process was throughout one of trial and error. **1898** E. L. Thorndike in *Psychol. Rev. Monogr. Suppl.* II. viii. 105 If the method of trial and error, with accidental success, be the method of acquiring associations among the animals, the slow progress of primitive man..becomes suggestive. **1900** C. L. Morgan *Animal Behaviour* iv. 139 The method of varied trial and error with the utilization of chance success, is a lengthy and somewhat clumsy process; but it suffices. **1940** Hilgard & Marquis *Conditioning & Learning* x. 252/2 The behavior of animals in the trial and error situation yields evidence of more intelligent behavior than is implied in the simple process of stamping in correct responses and stamping out wrong ones. **1951** Parsons & Shils *Toward Gen. Theory of Action* ii. ii. 129 Invention may be..trial-and-error learning. **1957** J. S. Huxley *Relig. without Revelation* ix. 230 Scientific hypotheses.. are better organisations for coping with our experience of physical phenomena than are trial-and-error methods. **1962** *Listener* 15 Nov. 796/1 There had been fitful, trial-and-error attempts to create a National Assembly. **1967** M. Dobb *Capitalism, Devel. & Planning* v. 242 In the Lange trial-and-error process..it was variable prices (accounting prices) that were fixed by the top-level authorities. **1972** *New Yorker* 26 Aug. 32/1 The American psychologist Edward L. Thorndike..is credited with the first rigorous investigation of trial-and-error, or instrumental, learning.

6. b. *Sport.* A match held to select players for a major team; esp. in *Rugby Football.* Cf. *trial match*, sense 13 in Dict.

a **1914** J. E. Raphael *Mod. Rugby Football* (1918) 249 E. W. Baker played for the South and in other important trials. **1921** E. H. D. Sewell *Rugby Football* 337 He was nominated to play on the wing in the third Trial. **1950** [see *SIGNING *vbl. sb.* 1 b]. **1978** *Rugby World* Apr. 5/2 Jeeps was the man who instigated the new system of trials which operated this season, involving games between England's regions and divisions.

c. A contest in which horses, dogs, etc., are put through various tests and assessed on their performance.

1942 R. B. KELLEY *Animal Breeding* xvi. 145 The second kind of trial endeavours to set out a course during which the dog is required to perform the tasks of everyday life. **1946** M. C. SELF *Horseman's Encycl.* 196 Working hunter trials. Jumps 4 feet to 4 feet 6 inches. On special course. Details of course to be withheld until one hour before class. **1960** J. STROUD *Shorn Lamb* xv. 175, I was..flitting round the suburbs like a sheepdog at a Trial. **1974** *Encycl. Brit. Micropædia* I. 723/3 The park [at Badminton] is also well-known for its horse trials.

13. a. *trial flight, marriage* (examples), *night, pit, separation* [SEPARATION 3]; **trial balance** (examples); † **trial ball** *Cricket*, a practice ball which a bowler was formerly allowed to bowl before beginning his first over (*obs.*); **trial balloon** = *BALLON D'ESSAI; **trial-bred** *a.*, of a dog bred: to compete in trials (*TRIAL *sb.*[1] 6 c); **trial court** (earlier example); **trial eight** (examples); **trial judge** (example); **trial jury** (example); **trial lawyer** (examples); **trial run,** a preliminary trip given to a new vessel or vehicle, to test its performance; freq. *transf.* or *fig.*; **trial trench** *Archæol.*, an exploratory trench dug on a site; hence *trial-trench* vb. intr.

1838 Trial balance [see *balance-sheet* s.v. *BALANCE *sb.* 22]. **1910** *Encycl. Brit.* IV. 227/1 A *trial balance* is thus no very adequate safeguard against fraud. **1978** *Detroit Free Press* 5 Mar. c 16/5 (Advt.), Local Co. needs a mature individual for full-charge bookkeeping thru trial balance. **1830** in R. S. Holmes *Hist. Yorks. County Cricket* (1904) 25 It is usual for a bowler, before he commences, to bowl a trial ball at one of his colleagues. **1870** *Times* 1 Sept. 10/4 The former [bowler] preluded his successes..with three trial balls. **1939** *Sun* (Baltimore) 21 Apr. 3/4 Congressional moves to bar alliance members from relief funds are in the 'trial balloon' stage. ?**1949** Q. HOWE in W. Safire *New Lang. Politics* (1968) 454/1 He [*sc.* Theodore Roosevelt] also originated the 'trial-balloon' technique and gave favored correspondents 'off-the-record' statements that they attributed to 'authoritative sources'. If the statement caught on, Roosevelt would make it his own. If it fell flat, he would drop it. *a* **1974** R. CROSSMAN *Diaries* (1976) II. 590 Since I'd been wanting to launch a trial balloon on this subject, I aired my views at length. **1948** J. A. REID in B. Vesey-Fitzgerald *Bk. Dog* 749 The 'trial-bred' collie. **1960** *Farmer & Stockbreeder* 9 Feb. 91/3 Many collies lie down almost instinctively and, among trial-bred dogs, getting them to stay on their feet is far more difficult. **1890** *U.S. Rep.* (Supreme Court) CXXXVII. 347 On review in this court, the rulings of the trial court were sustained. **1873** C. C. KNOLLYS *Oxf. Univ. Challenge Races* p. iii, The crews of the Trial and University Eights. **1900** W. E. SHERWOOD *Oxford Rowing* 63 In 1858..considerable alterations were made..the most important perhaps being the establishment of the Trial Eight Race. **1909** F. ASH *Trip to Mars* xii. 89, I only took my trial flight in it yesterday! **1892** *U.S. Rep.* (Supreme Court) CXLI. 562 The conclusion of the trial judge was that the second claim of the reissue was an enlargement of the single claim of the original patent. **1884** *Pacific Reporter* IV. 255 A trial jury in this territory is a body of 12 men, possessing the requisite qualifications, duly summoned, and sworn to well and truly try the questions of fact submitted to them by the court, and a true verdict render according to the law and the evidence. **1929** R. R. MORTON *What Negro Thinks* 146 His practice is seldom that of a trial lawyer, but rather as an adjuster of cases and an adviser in civil processes. **1983** 'E. LATHEN' *Green grow Dollars* vi. 48 She..had steered Wisconsin Seedsmen into the arms of the right trial lawyer. **1906** E. C. PARSONS *Family* vii. 142 *Trial-marriage* is a variety of time-marriage, it being distinctly agreed that the relationship may be dissolved by either man or woman at any time. **1930** *New Statesman* 27 Dec. 355/2 The Bishops of Miss Dunbar's Church recently gave an episcopal blessing to birth control, one prominent clergyman approving trial marriage. **1977** *Time* 4 Apr. 11/2 For the moment, the Liberals and Labour are only committed to keep their trial marriage going until the end of this parliamentary session in November. **1825** P. EGAN *Life of Actor* vii. 253 Our hero received a letter, offering him a *trial night* in Hamlet. **1904** W. D. ADAMS *Dict. Drama* I. 187/2 At last in 1817 he was granted, through the influence of friends, a trial-night at Covent Garden. **1905** D. MACKENZIE *Let.* in *Observer* (1962) 11 Feb. 11/3 The many preliminary trial-pits sunk in the early years of the excavation. **1966** Trial pit [see *soil survey* s.v. *SOIL *sb.*[1] 10]. **1903** *Trans. Inst. Naval Archit.* XLV. 295 Some twenty trial runs..were made under various conditions as to speed. **1909** *Chambers's Jrnl.* 25 Sept. 675/1 The first great trial-run of a number of motor-cars. **1949** *Sun* (Baltimore) 22 July 1/2 The House rejected the proposal for a 'trial run' of the Brannan farm program for a period of two years. **1962** *Rep. Comm. Broadcasting 1960* 4 in *Parl. Papers 1961–2* (Cmnd. 1753) IX. 259 Two trial runs of local sound broadcasting were arranged for us. **1974** D. SEAMAN *Bomb that could Lip Read* xviii. 177 The government desperately wants the new [Irish] Assembly to have a peaceful trial run. **1968** *Listener* 4 Oct. 439/2 We are telling our friends that he's not around because we've agreed to a trial separation. **1978** M. TRIPP *Wife-Smuggler* ii. 20 When I suggested..a trial separation she said..I didn't have the guts to make a clean break. **1947** *E. African Ann. 1946–7* 67/2 Once trial trenches had been cut, it became obvious that the site was even more important than we had at first believed. **1954** M. BERESFORD *Lost Villages* App. III. 416 The position of each house is clearly visible, thus precluding the need to trial-trench to find structures. **1980** *Rescue News* Sept. 2/3 In the first small trial trench was found a rim of Saxo-Norman pottery.

b. *attrib.* in *pl.* (cf. sense 2 c above), as *trials bike, rider, riding*, etc.

1969 *Daily Tel.* 25 Oct. 8/8 Quite a few leading trials riders are farmers... Light-weight two-stroke machines are now favoured for trials work. **1976** Trials enthusiast [see sense 2 c above]. **1976** *Southern Even. Echo* (Southampton) 10 Nov. 21/1 The cream of British trials riders left their native Yorkshire and came south to compete in rain and mud in the National Perce Simon and Hoad Trophy Trials. **1976** *Norwich Mercury* 19 Nov. 12/1 Trials riding is the cheapest form of motor cycle sport. **1977** *West Briton* 25 Aug. 10/3 The new trials bike group.. have raised half the £180 for their trials machine by a sponsored walk.

trialist (trəi·ălist), *sb.*[1] [f. as TRIAL *a.* + -IST.] One who advocates or follows trialism (sense 2); used *spec.* with reference to a proposed German–Magyar–Slav state. Also *attrib.*

1931 J. A. R. MARRIOTT *Europe 1815–1923* 429 On one detail of their programme the 'Trialists', as they began to be called, were not unanimous. **1935** H. A. L. FISHER *Hist. Europe* III. xxviii. 1097 Would it not be possible.. to substitute for the dual monarchy, resting on the dominion of the Magyars and the Germans, a trialist state founded on the equal fellowship of Slav, Magyar, and German? **1980** *Times Lit. Suppl.* 4 Jan. 22/2 *The Southern Slav Question* builds up to a plea for a modified 'trialist' state of Austrian, Hungarian and Slav units.

tri·alist, *sb.*[2] Also **triallist.** [f. TRIAL *sb.*[1] + -IST.] **1.** One involved in a judicial trial (TRIAL *sb.* 1).

1967 *Guardian* 17 Nov. 11/1 Letter from trialists' relatives. The 'Guardian' received..a copy of a letter addressed to the Prime Minister by the relatives of the 50 Greeks whose trial begins in Salonika today. **1979** J. DRUMMOND *Patriots* vii. 48 The Treason Trialists were acquitted.

2. a. One who takes part in a preliminary match or contest, with a view to being selected for a major team. Cf. *TRIAL *sb.*[1] 6 b.

1960 D. STOREY *This Sporting Life* I. ii. 37, I took this to mean he was watching me, though there were four other trialists in the team. **1961** *Listener* 19 Oct. 628/1 The contestants [*sc.* bridge-players] are all international trialists. **1971** *Daily Tel.* 15 Sept. 12 An Olympic trialist, who was training in the same pool. **1977** *Western Morning News* 1 Sept. 10/7 Richmond include..Dave Whibley, their England triallist full-back.

b. One who takes part in a contest or competition, esp. a motor-cycle trial (*TRIAL *sb.*[1] 2 c).

1961 *Times* 5 Oct. 4/5 The American motor cycle trialist. **1971** *Daily Tel.* 18 Oct. 22/8 Griffiths, this season's leading time trialist, covered the [cycle] course in 5hr 54min 14sec. **1980** *Observer* (Colour Suppl.) 12 Oct. 54 (*heading*) Alan Road reports on the bumpy world of the triallist. **1982** *Daily Tel.* 24 Nov. 3 The future of two top Welsh international sheep dog trialists hangs in the balance after an allegation that they tried to influence the selection of a competition judge.

c. One who takes part in clinical tests or trials of new drugs, etc.

1977 *Lancet* 17 Sept. 595/2 The conditions of a trial can be adjusted so that only the most dramatic results emerge with the statisticians' stamp of approval, though trials conducted under such harsh discipline would yield neutral results more often than not and triallists would fade away through frustration. **1983** *Glaxo Group News* Mar. 1/1 The..programme, attended by nearly 800 doctor-delegates (mainly triallists and specialists in infectious diseases) from more than 30 countries, included 83 presentations.

triallelic: see *TRI- 1 a.

triamcinolone (trəiămsi·nŏlōᵘn). *Pharm.* [f. *triamcin-* (etym. unkn.) + *PREDNIS(-OLONE.] A synthetic glucocorticoid which resembles prednisolone in its effects but is a more potent anti-inflammatory agent; 9α-fluoro-16α-hydroxyprednisolone, $C_{21}H_{27}O_6F$.

1957 *Jrnl. Amer. Med. Assoc.* 7 Dec. 1821/1 The purpose of this clinical study was to evaluate the anti-inflammatory and antipruritic properties of a new steroid compound, Aristocort diacetate (also known as triamcinolone diacetate). **1961** *Lancet* 12 Aug. 347/2 Some children with nephrosis do not respond to high doses of prednisolone, but they do respond to 'equivalent' doses of triamcinolone. **1979** *Nature* 13 Dec. 736/2 The glucocorticoids dexamethasone, triamcinolone,..stimulated interferon production more than 20-fold.

triangle, *sb.* Add: **1. c.** Esp. a love-relationship in which one member of a married couple is involved with a third party; freq. as *eternal triangle.*

1907 [in Dict.]. **1913** KIPLING *Diversity of Creatures* (1917) 358 The couples had rearranged themselves or were re-crystallizing in fresh triangles. **1919** G. B. SHAW in F. Harris *Contemp. Portraits* 2nd Ser. 332 For the modern drama, with its eternal triangle and so forth, he claims nothing, but that it proves adultery to be the dullest of subjects. **1938** H. G. WELLS *Apropos of Dolores* iv. 162 He was much more substantial than in the days of our romantic triangle. **1955** H. KURNITZ *Invasion of Privacy* (1956) vi. 48 The details of the story, the way the husband and wife first met..the other woman in the triangle. **1963** A. HERON *Towards Quaker View of Sex* iv. 39 Most examples of the 'eternal triangle' are produced by boredom and primitive misconduct. **1979** J. PHILIPS *Why Murder?* (1980) II. ii. 90 A husband, a wife, a lover—the classic triangle.

d. *North Atlantic Triangle*: a name given to the tripartite alliance between Great Britain, Canada, and the United States.

1945 J. B. BREBNER (*title*) North Atlantic Triangle. **1957** H. HEATON in L. B. Pearson *Where do we go from Here?* 2 Canada was one of the three points in 'the North Atlantic Triangle'—the others were Great Britain and the United States. **1978** J. HUTCHESON *Dominance & Dependency* i. 12 The nationalistic position..has been complicated by Canada's location in the North Atlantic Triangle.

2. a. *the Bermuda* or *Devil's Triangle*: a name given to an area of sea between Bermuda and Florida credited with a high number of unexplained disappearances of boats and aircraft; hence used allusively; *the golden triangle*, an area at the meeting-point of Burma, Laos, and Thailand, where much opium is grown.

1964 V. GADDIS in *Argosy* Feb. 28 (*heading*) The deadly Bermuda triangle. *Ibid.* 116/2 Draw a line from Florida to Bermuda, another from Bermuda to Puerto Rico, and a third back to Florida through the Bahamas. Within this area, known as the 'Bermuda Triangle', most of the vanishments have occurred. **1973** *Bangkok Post* 22 Apr. 1 Both the opium and the morphine base almost certainly originated in the so-called 'golden triangle' where the opium poppy grows in abundance. **1975** *Collier's Encycl. Year Bk. 1976* 161 The Atlantic region known as the Bermuda, or Devil's, Triangle. **1978** *Times* 23 Jan. 2/6 The increasing importance of South-East Asia's 'golden triangle' as a source of narcotics. **1979** A. PRICE *Tomorrow's Ghost* vi. 99 [She] had stepped out for a breath of fresh air..and she hadn't been seen again... She had turned a quiet piece of English countryside into a Bermuda Triangle. **1983** *Times* 12 Feb. 4/8 Drugs from the Golden Triangle were in heavy demand in Europe before 1979.

p. A triangular warning sign placed on the road to mark the presence of a broken-down vehicle or vehicles.

1969 B. WEIL *Dossier IX* ii. 8 There's your red breakdown triangle... They're obligatory in France. **1971** H. PACY *Road Accidents* i. 33 Utilize the special warning triangles larger trucks carry for this purpose. **1977** 'J. FRASER' *Hearts Ease* ii. 12 Superintendent Bill Aveyard braked his car when he saw the flashing torches and warning triangles at the side of the road.

4. (sense *1 c) *triangle drama*; (sense 2 j) *triangle-player*; **triangle inequality** *Math.*, the statement that the modulus of the sum of two quantities is less than or equal to the sum of their moduli; (so called from the analogy with the distances between the vertices of a triangle).

1931 E. A. ROBERTSON *Four Frightened People* i. 22 Just another triangle drama. **1961** *Times* 13 May 5/2 In an all too successful attempt to turn Shakespeare's tragedy into a conventional triangle-drama, Rossini's librettist, Berio, built up Rodrigo. **1941** BIRKHOFF & MACLANE *Survey Mod. Algebra* vii. 183 In any Euclidian vector space, length has the following properties:.. $|\xi+\eta| \leq |\xi|+|\eta|$ (the triangle inequality). **1972** M. KLINE *Math. Thought* xlvi. 1083 Schwarz's inequality and the triangle inequality are proved for the norm. **1906** J. JOYCE *Let.* 4 Oct. (1966) II. 170 AE ought now to write some..dreamy thing about a ..Triangle-player. **1971** D. E. WESTLAKE *I gave at Office* 24 Arnold dropped an occasional word in, like the triangle player at the Philharmonic.

triangulable (trəi,æ·ŋgiŭlăb'l), *a. Math.* [f. TRIANGUL(ATE *v.* + -ABLE.] Of a topological space: capable of undergoing triangulation (sense *2 b).

1940 *Proc. Nat. Acad. Sci.* XXVI. 359 *Triangulable manifold*, a topological manifold which can be subdivided into the cells of a complex. **1975** I. STEWART *Concepts Mod. Math.* xii. 184 We know that *S* is triangulable, so there exists a map on *S* (with triangular faces).

triangular, *a.* (*sb.*) Add: **3.** (Later examples.) Also *spec.* with reference to the 'eternal triangle' (see *TRIANGLE *sb.* 1 c).

1880 HARDY Fellow-Townsmen v. 44 The triangular situation—himself, his wife, Lucy Savile—was the one clear thing. **1908** *Times* 9 July 15/5 [The Australians] were unable to take part in the suggested triangular contest in this country next year. **1914** W. L. GEORGE *Dramatic Actualities* 39 The difficulties of matrimony, triangular or other, financial or monetary entanglements. **1968** S. HYNES *Edwardian Turn of Mind* vi. 181 The hero [is] involved in a triangular situation that Shaw took from his own amatory experience. **1976** *Southern Even. Echo* (Southampton) 13 Nov. 13/7 The Mid-Hants (Southampton) girls' netball teams had a successful time in a triangular tournament against Derbyshire and Berkshire at Reading. **1977** *Gay News* 24 Mar. 24/4 Husband, wife and female lodger involved in a triangular relationship.

4. c. triangular trade, a multilateral system of trading in which a country pays for its imports from one country by its exports to another; *spec.* (Hist.) in the slave trade (see quots.).

1934 C. M. MACINNES *England & Slavery* iii. 39 After the Restoration a great triangular trade developed between England, the West Coast of Africa and the West Indies or the continental colonies. **1948** T. S. ASHTON *Industrial Revolution 1760–1830* ii. 47 Cloth, firearms, hardware, and trinkets were sent to Africa and exchanged for slaves, who were shipped to the West Indies to pay for the luxuries and raw material which constituted the final cargo in this disreputable, triangular trade. **1971** C. & D. PLIMMER *Damn'd Master* ii. 26 With the profits from the sale of the slaves in the West Indies they bought sugar..which, back in Europe, they sold for a second profit with which in turn they bought more goods... This became known as the triangular trade.

triangularly, *adv.* **b.** (Earlier example.)
1890 KIPLING in *Pioneer Mail* 15 Jan. 92/3 We nodded triangularly in all good will and swore eternal friendship.

triangulated, *ppl. a.* and *a.* **2.** (Lit. example.)
1969 G. C. DICKINSON *Maps & Air Photographs* ii. 40 From about 1750 onwards a few of the better cartographers had begun to accept the need, for accuracy's sake, of providing a full triangulated framework for their county maps.

triangulation. Add: **1.** *spec.* by measuring the angles and one side of each triangle (cf. *TRILATERATION). Freq. *attrib.*, as *triangulation point* (also *fig.*).
1923 *Geogr. Rev.* XIII. 465 The recent remarking of the Meades Ranch Station calls attention to the unique importance of this triangulation point. **1947** A. R. HINKS *Maps & Survey* (ed. 5) ix. 172 The methods of trigonometrical survey..divide themselves into the following sections: 1. Determination of mean sea level... 9. Transference of the triangulation points to the plane-table sheets. **1977** *Times Lit. Suppl.* 22 Apr. 494/1 Dispassionate yet sensitive, his *Lenz*..deservedly became the triangulation-point for a whole generation.
2. b. *Math.* (See quot. 1956); also, the result of such a process.
1940 *Proc. Nat. Acad. Sci.* XXVI. 360 This result is but one of the implications of a triangulation. **1956** E. M. PATTERSON *Topology* v. 89 Triangulation..is the process of dividing up a [topological] space into pieces which are homeomorphic with the interior of a triangle or its analogues in other dimensions. **1974** *McGraw-Hill Yearbk. Sci. & Technol.* 412/2 These developments [in topology] were highlighted by the solutions in 1969 of the annulus conjecture..and of the triangulation problem for manifolds. **1977** *Sci. Amer.* Oct. 113/1 A triangulation that represents a minimal five-chromatic map cannot have any vertices with fewer than five neighbors.

triangulator. Add: (Example.) Also, an instrument used in triangulation.
1933 *Geogr. Jrnl.* LXXXII. 444 Norway, Poland, Romania, and the United States are the most active triangulators. **1938** *Ibid.* XCII. 434 In this exhibition there were also shown..a radial triangulator.

triathlon (trəiˌæ·þlǫn). [f. Gr. τρι- TRI- + ἆθλον contest, after *decathlon*, etc.] An athletic or sporting contest composed of three different events.
1973 *Daily Tel.* 21 July 14 A new event..called the 'Triathlon'. In this all four members of a team have to demonstrate their prowess in clay pigeon shooting, fly fishing and riding a handy hunter-course over jumps. **1981** *Austin* (Texas) *Amer.-Statesman* 28 Mar. (Time Out section) 8 The Triathlon consists of a 2·5 mile surf swim, followed by a 112-mile bike race, followed by a full marathon. **1983** *Times* 26 Feb. 22/1 The word 'triathlon' is the label that has been attached to the so-called 'Iron Man contests' which..basically consist of a swim in the open sea, a long cycle ride of up to 100 miles and then a marathon run.

triatomid (trəiˌæ·tǫmid), *a.* (*sb.*) [f. mod.L. family name *Triatomidæ*, f. generic name *Triatoma* (F. L. Laporte 1832, in *Mag. Zool.* II. IX. 11), f. TRI- + Gr. τέμνειν to cut, in allusion to the antennæ of the insects: see -ID[3].] Of or pertaining to the family Triatomidæ, now usually included in the family Reduviidæ. Also as *sb.*, a blood-sucking assassin bug of the family Triatomidæ, which includes several vectors of disease.
1955 *Sci. News Let.* 29 Oct. 280/1 The blood-suckers are triatomid bugs and are known to carry the germs from animals, such as opossums, to man. **1961** E. R. & G. A. NOBLE *Parasitol.* xv. 726 Some triatomids..obtain meals by tapping the blood-engorged bodies of other arthropods. **1971** P. C. C. GARNHAM *Progress in Parasitology* iii. 30 In the State of São Paulo..the writer saw typical dwellings in which the incidence of the infection was 19 per cent in the dogs, 16 per cent in the cats, and nearly 100 per cent in the triatomid bugs. **1974** F. PIFANO in K. Elliott et al. *Trypanosomiasis & Leishmaniasis* 77 The source of food of the triatomids captured in the palm trees was investigated with the precipitin test.

triatomine (trəiˌæ·tǫmīn), *a.* (*sb.*) [f. mod.L. subfamily name *Triatominæ* (see prec. and -INE[1]).] = *TRIATOMID *a.* (*sb.*), when the group is considered as a subfamily of the family Reduviidæ.
1962 GORDON & LAVOIPIERRE *Entomol. for Students of Med.* xxxix. 237 Triatomine bugs are almost entirely American in distribution. **1974** *Nature* 29 Nov. 392/2 The triatomine bugs..are medically important as vectors of Chagas' disease in the Americas. **1978** *Ibid.* 27 Apr. 820/2 The second type (type II) was found in acute and chronic cases of Chagas' disease, cats, house mice, rats and guinea pigs, from houses infested by the domiciliated triatomine *Panstrongylus megistus*. **1979** *Pharmacol. & Therapeutics* VII. 86 *T. rangeli* is a non-pathogenic trypanosome with a wide range of hosts which is also transmitted by triatomine vectors.

triaxial, *a.* (In Dict. s.v. TRIAXAL *a.*) Add: (Further examples.) Also, occurring or responding in three mutually perpendicular directions.
This, rather than TRIAXAL *a.*, is the usual term.
1924 J. G. A. SKERL tr. *A. Wegener's Origin of Continents & Oceans* xiii. 202 In his latest work Helmert infers, from the distribution of the force of gravity on the earth's surface, that the earth is a triaxial ellipsoid. **1951** *Engineering* 14 Dec. 746/2 A state of triaxial stress, according to its severity, suppresses deformation by shear and makes cleavage more probable. **1975** *Nature* 31 Jan. 327/2 A single range triaxial fluxgate magnetometer capable of measuring fields up to 10 gauss along each orthogonal axis. **1978** *Sci. Amer.* Jan. 48/2 The criterion of triaxial motion meant that a ball-and-socket arrangement would be the best means of achieving a mechanical interlock between components.
Hence **tri:axia·lity**, triaxial nature; **tria·xially** *adv.*
1970 *Nature* 14 Mar. 1008/2 Because of triaxiality the Moon theoretically has three free oscillations with periods of about 1, 40 and 800 months in the directions of its axes. **1972** *Physics Bull.* Nov. 669/1 There are clearly cases when the micromode of fracture is dependent on triaxiality of stress and very sensitive to temperature or strain rate. **1982** *Sci. Amer.* May 116c/1 (Advt.), By means of a triaxially stabilized altitude control system, it..directs the solar panels towards the sun.

tri-axle: see *TRI- 4 b.

tribadism. Add to def.: *spec.* in modern use (see quots.).
1965 *New Statesman* 26 Mar. 492/3 The first [technique of lesbian intercourse], known as 'tribadism', consists in one woman lying on top of the other and simulating the movements of heterosexual intercourse in such a way as to stimulate the clitoris of each. **1970** G. GREER *Female Eunuch* 293 The prevalence of tribadism as the principal lesbian mode of lovemaking argues the relative unimportance of the masculine fantasy.

tribal, *a.* Add: **1. b.** Characterized by the tendency to form groups or by strong group loyalty.
1951 H. ARENDT *Burden of Our Time* II. viii. 227 Tribal nationalism always insists that its own people is surrounded by 'a world of enemies', 'one against all'. **1970** G. GREER *Female Eunuch* 182 In the tribal teenage situation there are some boys with whom one does not go out. **1977** *Time* 10 Oct. 113/1 A Jew in this rural, tribal and fiercely Christian heartland [*sc.* Savannah, Georgia] is a wanderer indeed.
c. As *sb.*, a member of a tribal community (usu. in *pl.*). Chiefly *Indian English*.
1958 *New India: Progress through Democracy* III. vi. 378 Illiteracy is almost universal among tribal peoples... Tribals are being trained as teachers. **1964** *Economist* 18 Apr. 261/1 More are arriving daily, among them Christian and Buddhist tribals. **1971** *Illustr. Weekly India* 25 Apr. 42/2 An elaborate welfare scheme..reached both the settlers and the tribals. **1973** *Country Life* 14 June 1715/2 A ceremonial bag of five tigers slain by tribals in Nagaland in 1964. **1979** *South China Morning Post* 28 Dec. 3/1 Teams of mountain tribals are to join the search for three Singapore Air Force Skyhawks which disappeared over the northern Philippines eight days ago.
2. Special collocations: *tribal council*, the organ of internal self-government of a recognized U.S. Indian tribe, since the Indian Reorganization Act of 1934; *tribal mark*, a scar resulting from the traditional or ritual cutting of the face practised among certain African tribes; hence *tribal marking*; also *tribal scar*, *scarring*; *tribal territory*, an administrative division of the Northwest Frontier Province of Pakistan (formerly of India).
1948 *Salt Lake Tribune* 17 Dec. 16/5 Other tribal council members, speaking in Navajo.., agreed with Mr. Akeah. **1976** *Billings* (Montana) *Gaz.* 5 July 1-D/4 The Northern Cheyenne Tribal Council has launched a drive for redesignation of the air quality level on the southeastern Montana reservation. **1980** *New Age* (U.S.) Oct. 5/1 Through CERT and the tribal councils, thousands of acres of traditional tribal land have been turned over to mining companies searching for uranium and coal. **1897** M. H. KINGSLEY *Trav. in W. Afr.* xxiii. 530 The cicatrices are sometimes tribal marks, but sometimes decorative. **1965** W. SOYINKA *Road* 73 Are you sure you know who I mean? Sort of tall but a little on the short side. Tribal marks, but beginning to wear off. **1925** W. D. HAMBLY *Hist. Tattooing & its Significance* iii. 176 Are there among the accounts of tribal markings any present-day accounts or ancient legends, which reveal that these marks have.. an important social significance? **1973** 'A. HALL' *Tango Briefing* xx. 251 The carved teakwood statuette..was obviously a god, wide nosed and with tribal markings on the forehead. **1977** P. RAYMOND *Matter of Assassination* iii. 23 An expressionless Negro face marked with tribal scars across the cheeks. **1982** D. WILTSE *Wedding Guest* ii. 33 The ritual scars..had been worked..into her cheeks with a needle... The tribal scarring had been outlawed for thirty years. **1908** *Imperial Gazetteer India* XIX. 166 In tribal territory, besides the tribes already alluded to, the Torwāl and Garhwī reside in the higher ranges of Swāt. **1951** KHAN & STARK *Young Pakistan* xxiv. 199 In the far north, an observer standing on the high mountains can in fact look down on five different lands—Afghanistan..and Pakistan (Tribal territory) in the south west. **1974** *Encycl. Brit. Macropædia* XIII. 256/2 Between the settled districts to the south and the Afghan border is the tribal territory, whose inhabitants enjoy a large measure of independence.

tribalism. Add: **b.** Loyalty to a particular tribe or group of which one is a member.
1955 *Times* 30 Aug. 9/7 If a stable parliamentary democracy is to be introduced one stable political party, avoiding if possible the extremes of tribalism and anti-tribalism, would seem necessary. **1969** *Busara* (Nairobi) II. II. 56 According to Reinhold Niebuhr, 'the chief source of man's inhumanity to man seems to be the tribal limits of his sense of obligation to the other man'. In *tribalism* Niebuhr includes race, language, religion, class and culture as important traits. **1976** *Drum* (E. Afr. ed.) Apr. 3/1 Tribalism? Isn't it true that in some firms about 75 per cent of the employees come from one tribe—depending, of course, on which tribe the bosses come from. **1978** *Times Lit. Suppl.* 1 Dec. 1390/5 His call for a fusion or integration of cultures is one that commits him to the course of liberal tolerance, and sets him against closed systems of thought such as Marxism and tribalism.

tribalist. Restrict *rare* to sense in Dict. and add: **b.** An advocate or practitioner of tribalism (sense *b). Also *attrib.* or as *adj.* (cf. next).
1960 *Times* 29 Sept. (Nigeria Suppl.) p. iv/4 Opponents have accused him of being a tribalist. **1970** J. D. CAUTE *Fanon* vi. 70 The Nationalist Parties drove the political opposition into retrograde, tribalist forms.

tribalistic (trəibăli·stik), *a.* [f. TRIBAL *a.* + -ISTIC.] = TRIBAL *a.* 1 a, b in Dict. and Suppl. Also, characterized by tribalism. Cf. *TRIBALIST b.
1961 in WEBSTER. **1976** *Daily Sketch* (Ibadan) 26 Oct. 1/2 They..recommended that Nigeria's future President should not be arrogant, tribalistic but should be consistent. **1980** in S. Terkel *Amer. Dreams* 320 It [*sc.* a cocktail party] was a tribalistic ritual. I was the meat on the altar.

tribalize (trəi·băləiz), *v.* [f. as prec. + -IZE.] *trans.* To render tribal, to unite on a tribal basis; to imbue with tribal loyalty. So **tri·balized** *ppl. a.*; **tri:baliza·tion.**
1927 *Other Lands* Jan. 59/2 The United Free Church worked more among the tribalized communities. **1959** *Times Lit. Suppl.* 6 Mar. 127/5 There are still many who share Mary Kingsley's predilection for 'tribalized' peoples. **1964** M. MCLUHAN *Understanding Media* (1967) xxiv. 249 The war had fraternalized and tribalized us. **1984** *Times* 16 Oct. 14/6 The main effect [in Poland] has been the tribalization of politics..the bike boys, the punks..the hippies..the tough and the meek.

tribe, *sb.* Add: **4. b.** A gang of criminals or delinquents. Also, in recent use, a group of hippies or other drop-outs.
1914 JACKSON & HELLYER *Vocab. Criminal Slang* 85 *Tribe*, used principally by yeggs and begging bums, though current, too, amongst grafters who operate in cliques. A gang; a class. **1955** D. W. MAURER in *Publ. Amer. Dial. Soc.* XXIV. 83 In general, [pickpocketing] mobs are also known as *tribes*. **1968** *Guardian* 29 Apr. 7/5 The fifteen hundred 'Tribes' of San Francisco..beg their food and sleep where they can. **1973** R. C. DENNIS *Sweat of Fear* vii. 44 A room with wall-to-wall mattresses. Sprawled about were a half-dozen members of the tribe.

tribo- (trəi·bo, tri·bo), comb. form repr. Gr. τρίβος rubbing, as **tri:boelectri·city** [ad. F. *triboélectricité* (O. D. Chwolson *Traité de Physique* (1913) IV. I. ii. 268)], electricity generated by friction; so **triboele·ctric** *a.*, **-ele·ctrically** *adv.*; **tri:boelectrifica·tion,** the production of triboelectricity; **tri:bonuclea·tion** (see quot. 1967); **tri·bophysics,** the physics of friction; hence **tribophy·sical** *a.*; **tribosphenic** (-sfī·nik) *a.* *Palæont.* [Gr. σφήν wedge] (see quots. 1936, 1975[2]); **tribo-the:rmolumine·scence,** thermoluminescence produced in a material as a result of friction.
1917 *Nature* 27 Dec. 337/1 The research provides an explanation of the well-known readiness with which materials change their tribo-electric character. **1967** W. R. HARPER *Contact & Frictional Electrification* v. 77 The notorious difficulty of performing triboelectric experiments in damp weather proclaims the importance of adsorbed water. *Ibid.*, Glass cleaned with alkalis became triboelectrically ⊕ve with respect to metals. **1972** *Sci. Amer.* Mar. 54/3 Yarns, plastic films, paper and kindred materials moving at high speeds inevitably lead to triboelectric troubles. **1979** *Adv. Colloid & Interface Sci.* XI. 64 The roles of tribo-electricity in everyday life and in industry are numerous both as a nuisance and hazard and as a phenomenon to be exploited. **1938** G. P. HARNWELL *Princ. Electr. & Magn.* i. 1 The production of electrification by the frictional process of rubbing is known as triboelectrification. **1967** W. R. HARPER *Contact & Frictional Electrification* v. 85 The loosely bound ions are available to diffuse to another surface brought into contact with the one under consideration, and might be important..for triboelectrification. **1967** *Brit. Jrnl. Appl. Physics* XVIII. 641 If a solid body such as a stirrer rod

is rubbed against the inner wall of a vessel containing either a supersaturated solution of a salt or a supercooled liquid, the nucleation of crystals is likely to occur at the point of contact. This phenomenon is known as tribonucleation ('nucleation by rubbing'). **1974** *Nature* 20 Dec. 696/1 One mechanism for the production of micronuclei in man, tribonucleation, has been suggested by Ikels. **1977** *Jrnl. Catalysis* L. 542/1 The catalyst produced by the tribophysical procedure is more active longer than the conventional one. **1950** *Engineering* 17 Mar. 303/3 The new Division of Tribophysics has developed from a section which, during the war, evolved some interesting theories regarding the fundamental nature of friction and lubrication. **1976** *Sci. Amer.* Apr. 30/2 Sanders, who is chief research scientist in the Tribophysics Division, heads a group that is engaged in studying the reactivity of metallic surfaces, relying mainly on electron microscopy. **1936** G. G. SIMPSON in *Dental Cosmos* LXXVIII. 797/1 At this stage the upper molar is implanted by two external and one internal root, the latter generally largest, and the lower molars are implanted by two sub-equal roots, one beneath the trigonid and one beneath the talonid... In order to have a single word..by which this type of molar dentition can be unequivocably..designated, I propose to call it 'tribosphenic'. **1975** *Nature* 31 July 402/1 Therian mammals with tribosphenic molars were probably in existence at the beginning of the Cretaceous. *Ibid.*, Tribosphenic molars have an additional cusp on the upper molars (protocone) which fits into a basin (talonid) on the matching lower molar. **1930** NYSWANDER & COHN in *Physical Rev.* XXXVI. 1257 The term tribothermoluminescence has been given to the phenomenon under consideration which involves the process of grinding followed by application of heat. **1971** *Nature* 23 July 257/2 Thermoluminescence (TL) of fossil bones and of various kinds of recent biological material has been reported by Jasińska and Niewiadomski, who suggest that such materials could be used for dating purposes, but draw attention to difficulties which arise due to tribothermoluminescence (TTL, which is thermoluminescence derived from the mechanical energy of grinding).

tribology (trəibǫ·lŏdʒi). [f. *TRIBO- + -OLOGY.] The branch of science and technology concerned with interacting surfaces in relative motion and with associated matters (as friction, wear, lubrication, and the design of bearings).

Mr. H. P. Jost (see quot. 1968), chairman of a working group of 'lubrication engineers', corresponded with me in 1965 about the need for a new term and accepted *tribology*, a word suggested by Mr. C. G. Hardie of Magdalen College.—Ed.

1966 (Feb.) *Lubrication* (*Tribology*) (Dept. Educ. & Sci.) 4 Tribology is defined as follows: Tribology is the science and technology of interacting surfaces in relative motion and of the practices related thereto. **1968** H. P. JOST in *New Scientist* 8 Feb. 292 After consultation with the English Dictionary Department of the Oxford University Press—the publishers of the *Oxford Dictionary*—we chose the term 'tribology'. **1969** *Sunday Times* 30 Nov. 30/2 Two chairs of tribology have been established, one at Leeds and another at Salford. **1975** *Sci. Amer.* July 50/3 This field of study is known, more commonly in Britain than in the U.S., as tribology. **1980** *Canada Weekly* 19 Nov. 4/1 As Canada's main centre of expertise on tribology..the..laboratory examines the problem of wear and failure of rails and wheels.

Hence **tribolo·gical** *a.*, of or pertaining to tribology; **tribo·logist**, an expert or specialist in tribology.

1966 *New Scientist* 19 May 423/1 They suggested that the Institution of Mechanical Engineers should organize 'professional institution activities in the tribological sphere'. **1969** *Lubrication Engin.* Feb. 88/3 (*heading*) Dr. Finkin named chief tribologist. **1973** *Nature* 6 Apr. 361/3 The tribological problems the centre has tackled have ranged from making gas bearings to designing window hinges for high rise flats. **1974** *Globe & Mail* (Toronto) 18 Apr. 45/2 Tribologists believe they can save Canadians several hundred million dollars a year. **1977** *Engin. Materials & Design* Aug. 35/2 This compound layer has excellent tribological properties under dry running as well as lubricated conditions.

tribrachic, *a.* (Earlier example.)

1852 J. S. BLACKIE *Pronunciation of Greek* 43 The tendency to the ineffective tribrachic and even proceleusmatic accent in the termination of our polysyllables.

tribunal, *sb.* Add: **2. c.** Any of various local boards of officials empowered to settle disputes, esp. between an individual and a government department, to adjudicate on fair rents, exemption from military service, etc.; *industrial tribunal*, a board arbitrating in disputes arising out of employment, such as complaints of unfair dismissal. Also (in full *tribunal of inquiry*), a board set up by the government to investigate some matter of public concern.

1916 *Act* 5 & 6 *Geo. V* c. 104 § 2 An application may be made at any time before the appointed date to the Local Tribunal established under this Act..for a certificate of exemption from the provisions of this Act. **1921** (*title of Act*) Tribunals of inquiry (evidence) act. **1932** L. GOLDING *Magnolia Street* II. iv. 321 The Baritone, at least, managed to convince tribunal after tribunal that it would be a mistake to put him into khaki. **1945** [see *RENT *sb.*[1] 4 c]. **1949** *Britannica Bk. of Year* 309/2 Public interest was focused upon the judicial tribunal set up, under the chairmanship of Mr. Justice Lynskey, to inquire into allegations of corrupt practices involving several ministers and public servants. **1962** L. GOLDING *Dict. Local Govt.* 158 A Committee..was set up to consider..the constitution and working of administrative tribunals, particularly those dealing with the compulsory purchase of land. **1971** *Mod. Law Rev.* XXXIV. 657 The industrial tribunal may only recommend reinstatement. *Ibid.*, The tribunals may award..compensation. **1974** M. MEACHER *Scrounging on Welfare* iii. 38 In 1971 the Supplementary Benefits Commission reported 153 cases to a Tribunal under Section 12/1.

tribune, *sb.*[1] Add: **2. b.** (with capital initial.) The title of a British weekly journal, founded in 1937, advocating radical left-wing policies: used *attrib.* with reference to this type of socialism, esp. as *Tribune group*, a group of Labour MPs sharing these views.

1952 *Ann. Reg. 1951* I. ii. 33 *One Way Only*, a *Tribune* pamphlet published on 9 July. **1968** *Times* 9 July 9/6 The trade unionists who are moving against the Government are not, as the *Tribune* group supposes, moving to the left. *a* **1974** R. CROSSMAN *Diaries* (1975) I. 562 They were really completely answered by Raymond Fletcher, a left-winger from the Tribune group. **1975** *Times* 16 July 14/7 Those who regarded themselves as the keepers of the socialist conscience—the Tribune group. **1976** A. PRICE *War Game* I. viii. 165 Not even the Tribune Group will be able to complain about the high cost of security. **1976** [see *TRIBUNISM]. **1977** *Times Lit. Suppl.* 3 June 685/1 Orwell..was a Tribune-style socialist (egalitarian, libertarian).

Hence **Tri·bunism**, socialist policies of the type advocated by the *Tribune*; **Tri·bunite**, a member of the Tribune group (freq. *attrib.*).

1970 *Times* 18 Nov. 12 Frank Allaun, the Tribunite M.P. *Ibid.* 7 Dec. 2 The second day took in a debate led by..Mr. Stan Orme, the redoubtable Tribunite, and Mr. Neil McBride. **1976** *Times* 15 Mar. 13/2 The influx of new MPs..has probably weakened Tribunism rather than reinforced it. But a new generation of Tribune men is beginning to assert its influence. **1977** *Listener* 28 July 125/2, I do not believe that the Tribunite view..goes by default. **1981** *Times* 22 June 2/7 Neither have Tribunites north of the border made any open moves to become involved.

tributary, *a.* and *sb.* **A.** *adj.* **2.** (Earlier example with reference to a stream.)

1823 C. B. VIGNOLES *Observations upon Floridas* 56 The Choctawhatchie river, and all its tributary streams discharge into the eastern end of this bay.

B. *sb.* **2. a.** (Earlier example.)

1822 W. H. SIMMONS *Notices of East Florida* iii. 29 [The] appearance [of bonnet leaf]..indicates from a distance, the influx of some tributary of the main stream.

tribute, *sb.* Add: **2. b.** A praiseworthy thing attributable *to*, a testimony *to*.

Often (as by Fowler in quot. 1926) regarded as an incorrect use.

1926 in H. W. Fowler *Dict. Mod. Eng. Usage* 662/2 The debate on the whole was a tribute to the good taste and good form of the House of Commons. **1937** W. H. S. SMITH *Let.* 3 May in *Young Man's Country* (1977) ii. 69 Are the Guildford's using their old Coronation Robes? If so, it's a tribute to Lady G.'s figure. **1961** *New Statesman* 8 Feb. 198/1 Perhaps..the gusty vigour of the heroes of the period from Grant to McKinley is a tribute to the American character.

4. tribute rice *Chinese Hist.*, a grain tax paid in kind.

1853 *North-China Herald* 26 Mar. 134/4 (*heading*) Destruction of the Che Hien's House and tribute rice. **1959** P. FLEMING *Siege at Peking* v. 61 Tungchow, whose prosperity depended on its status as an entrepot for tribute-rice brought by canal from the interior, had economic as well as ideological motives for disliking the railway.

tributyl phosphate: see *TRI- 5 c.

tricarballylic (trəi:kāɹbăli·lik), *a. Chem.* [f. TRI- + *carballylic acid* s.v. CARB-.] *tricarballylic acid*: a crystalline tribasic acid found in immature beets and produced synthetically; propane-1,2,3-tricarboxylic acid, $HOOC{\cdot}CH(CH_2COOH)_2$.

1865 M. SIMPSON in *Jrnl. Chem. Soc.* XVIII. 334 This body has been named by Kekule carballylic acid...I propose..in order to avoid confusion, to call it *tri*-carballylic acid. *Ibid.* 335, I have prepared and analysed several of the salts and ethers of tri-carballylic acid. **1950** I. L. FINAR *Org. Chem.* xvii. 348 Tricarballylic esters have been used as plasticisers. **1980** *Polish Jrnl. Chem.* LIV. 1681 In the course of biological studies on new potential anticonvulsants, a number of substituted tricarballylic acids..were synthesized.

tricarboxylic (trəi:kāɹbǫksi·lik), *a. Biochem.* [f. TRI- + CARBOXYL + -IC.] *tricarboxylic acid*: any acid with three carboxyl groups in each molecule; *tricarboxylic acid cycle*, the Krebs cycle (see *KREBS).

1894 PERKIN & KIPPING *Org. Chem.* I. xiii. 246 Citric acid is a tricarboxylic acid, and..forms three classes of salts. **1938** G. H. RICHTER *Textbk. Org. Chem.* xvi. 302 Aconitic acid is an example of an unsaturated tricarboxylic acid. **1945** *Jrnl. Biol. Chem.* CLXI. 413 (*heading*) Fatty acid oxidation and the Krebs tricarboxylic acid cycle. **1947** *Ibid.* CLXXI. 446 Tricarboxylic acids may be formed in plants by a process involving the addition of CO_2 to an α-ketoglutarate. **1950** [see *KREBS]. **1974** B. A. NEWTON in K. Elliott et al. *Trypanosomiasis & Leishmaniasis* (Ciba Symp. No. 20) 299 Some of the changes which occur during the development of T. cruzi, such as the activity of the tricarboxylic acid cycle enzymes.., may only be quantitative changes. **1982** M. S. OLSON in T. M. Devlin *Textbk. Biochem.* vi. 278 Various investigators defined many of the enzymes and di- and tricarboxylic acid intermediates in this pathway, but it was Krebs who pieced together these components in his formulation of the 'Krebs cycle'.

Tricel (trəi·sel). Also **tricel.** [f. TRI- (in **triacetate*) + CEL(LULOSE *sb.*] A proprietary name for a man-made fibre made from cellulose triacetate, and for material made from this.

1954 *Trade Marks Jrnl.* 22 Dec. 1300/2 *Tricel*... Raw or partly prepared artificial fibrous textile materials not being yarns or threads. British Celanese Limited, Celanese House.., London W.1; manufacturers. **1956** *Official Gaz.* (U.S. Patent Office) 20 Nov. 88/1 *Tricel*... For staple fibres made wholly or partially of cellulose derivatives. **1965** *Guardian* 31 Mar. 13/2 The two fabrics looked identical, but 'Tricel' had got something that the other hadn't got—easy-care properties. **1969** W. J. BURLEY *Death in Willow Pattern* i. 13 Susan..put on a simple short-sleeved Tricel dress. **1977** *Lancashire Life* Feb. 22/2 A top cup of cotton embroidered nylon tricel.

tricesimo-secundo: see *-MO.

trichinelliasis (trikinelǝi·ăsis). *Med.* [f. mod.L. *Trichinella*, generic name superseding TRICHINA (f. L. *-ella*: see -EL[2]) + *-IASIS.] = TRICHINOSIS.

1907 *Allbutt's Syst. Med.* (ed. 2) II. II. 914 The girl had evidently died, not of enteric fever as was supposed, but of trichinelliasis. **1930** E. C. FAUST *Human Helminthol.* xxiii. 327 The disease trichinelliasis or, more familiarly, trichinosis, may be divided into three stages. **1977** SCHMIDT & ROBERTS *Foundations of Parasitol.* xxiii. 424/2 *Trichinella spiralis* is the only species in the family ..and is responsible for the disease variously known as trichinosis, trichiniasis, or trichinelliasis.

Also **trichinello·sis** [-OSIS], in the same sense.

1958 *Excerpta Medica* IV. 479, 209 wild rats..and 21 domestic rats..were examined for trichinellosis. **1965** *Jrnl. Amer. Med. Assoc.* 13 Sept. 182/1 So-called meat inspection..provides no mechanism for detection of trichinellosis. **1971** P. C. C. GARNHAM *Progress in Parasitol.* v. 64 In the Mau Mau emergency the youth went wild on Mount Kenya, ignoring the ancient tribal taboo regarding the consumption of the flesh of certain animals and devoured uncooked wild pig: a severe outbreak of trichinellosis, with many deaths, was the result.

Trichinopoli. Add: *Trichinopoli chain.*

1879 *Encycl. Brit.* IX. 163/2 Round plaited gold chains of fine wire, such as are still made by the filigree workers of India, and known as Trichinopoly chains.

trichlor-, trichloro-. Add: **trichlo:ro-, tri:chloraceta·ldehyde** = CHLORAL.

1921 J. S. CHAMBERLAIN *Textbk. Org. Chem.* 226 The tri-chlor acet-aldehyde then reacts with an alkali present yielding chloroform. **1964** N. G. CLARK *Mod. Org. Chem.* x. 189 Acetaldehyde..may be chlorinated to chloral (trichloroacetaldehyde..), an important intermediate in the manufacture of 'D.D.T.'.

trichloroethylene (trəiklōᵊ:roe·þilīn). *Chem.* Also **trichlorethylene.** [f. TRI- + CHLORO-[2] + *Ethylene* s.v. ETHYL.] A liquid organochlorine compound, C_2HCl_3, used as a solvent, analgesic, and anæsthetic. Cf. *TRILENE.

1889 G. M'GOWAN tr. *Bernthsen's Text-bk. Org. Chem.* 60 (*table*) C_2HCl_3, Tri-chloro-ethylene. **1930** *Engineering* 26 Dec. 814/2 The use of chemical cleaners, such as petrol ..and trichlorethylene, is more effective. **1955** *Ann. Reg. 1954* 411 Midwives should be allowed..to use a new pain-relieving vapour called trichlorethylene B.P. **1976** *National Observer* (U.S.) 17 July 2/3 The Food and Drug Administration said it will ban use of a chemical once used in decaffeinated coffees and some beers. The chemical, trichloroethylene, has been found to cause liver cancer in mice.

tricho-[1]. Add: **trichoma·niac** *nonce-wd.*, a hair fetishist; **trichomo·nal** *a.*, of, pertaining to, or caused by trichomonads; **tri:chotillo-ma·nia** [ad. F. *trichotillomanie* (H. Hallopeau 1889, in *Ann. de Dermatol. et Syphilol.* X. 441), f. Gr. τίλλεσθαι to pull out (hair)], a compulsive desire to pull out one's hair; hence **tri:chotilloma·niac**, a person with this.

1949 R. GRAVES *Common Asphodel* 303 From descriptions in his poems it is clear that the first thing that he [*sc.* Milton] saw in a woman was not her bright love-darting eye (as it was to practically all his contemporaries), but her hair. He was, in fact, a trichomaniac. **1948** *Jrnl. Amer. Med. Assoc.* 18 Sept. 231/2 The diagnosis and treatment of trichomonal vaginitis may not always be as simple as depicted. **1970** G. GREER *Female Eunuch* 259 Cases of incurable trichomonal infection are all due to a combination of fear, superstition and doctors' sloppiness. **1905** *Rep. Soc. for Study of Dis. in Children* V. 28 (*heading*) A case of trichotillomania. **1980** *Brit. Med. Jrnl* 29 Mar. 881/2 The loss is patchy and must be distinguished from.. trichotillomania, in which the child pulls out his or her hair and may eat it. **1962** *Woman* 26 May 9 (*heading*) Don't be a trichotillomaniac! That is, in simple terms, someone who tears out hair!

trichome. Add: **2.** *Ent.* In myrmecophilous insects, a tuft of hairs near a gland producing a secretion attractive to ants.

1911 E. JACOBSON in *Tijdschr. Ent.* LIV. 177 The bug possesses a very curious tuft of yellow hair (a trichome) which apparently secretes some substance with a flavour agreeable to the ants. **1923** W. M. WHEELER *Social Life among Insects* v. 227 The trichomes surround the openings of singular glands, the aromatic, volatile secretions of which..are licked off by the ants. **1971** E. O. WILSON *Insect Societies* (1972) xx. 390/2 The *Cremastocheilus* adults are furnished with tufts of golden hairs ('trichomes') at the anterior and posterior corners of the thorax.

trichomoniasis (tri:komǫnəi·ăsis). *Med.* and *Vet. Sci.* [f. mod.L. *Trichomonas*, generic name (coined in Fr. as *Trico-monas* by A. Donné 1836, in *Compt. Rend.* III. 386), f. TRICHO-[1] + *-MONAS: see *-IASIS.] Infection with trichomonads, which in man is often symptomless; *esp.* (*a*) a venereal disease of women caused by *Trichomonas vaginalis*, in which there are vaginal irritation and a discharge; (*b*) a venereal disease of cattle caused by *T. fœtus*, characterized by abortion, pyometra, and sometimes sterility.

1915 *N.Y. Med. Jrnl.* CI. 886/2 (*heading*) Clinical and experimental trichomoniasis of the intestine. **1972** *Daily Colonist* (Victoria, B.C.) 19 May 2/2 Another common cause of persistent or recurrent discharge is a parasitic infection called trichomoniasis. **1980** *Trop. Med. & Hygiene News* Dec. 25 Investigations on trichinellosis, hydatid disease and trichomoniasis.

trichoplax (tri·koplæks). [mod.L. (F. E. Schulze 1883, in *Zool. Anzeiger* VI. 92), f. TRICHO-[2] + Gr. πλάξ plate.] A minute marine animal with a body formed of three layers of cells, formerly included in the genus of this name but now usually considered to be a modified form of a hydrozoan planula.

1897 PARKER & HASWELL *Text-bk. Zool.* I. iv. 220 Trichoplax is a compressed plate-like body of irregular and extremely variable shape, but circular in the resting condition. **1940** L. H. HYMAN *Invertebrates* iv. 243 *Trichoplax* and *Tetroplax* were found actually to be modified planulae of Hydroidea.

trichothecin (triko-, trəikoþī·kin). *Biochem.* [f. mod.L. *Trichothec-ium*, name of a genus of fungi (H. F. Link 1809, in *Mag. d. Ges. Naturforschender Freunde zu Berlin* III. 18), f. TRICHO-[1] + THECIUM: see -IN[1].] A crystalline trichothecene, $C_{15}H_{19}O_3{\cdot}O{\cdot}CO{\cdot}C_3H_5$, that is an ester of butenoic acid produced by the fungus *Trichothecium roseum* and is toxic to some other fungi.

1948 FREEMAN & MORRISON in *Nature* 3 July 30/1 Antagonistic activity to other fungi by *Trichothecium roseum* Link..has been reported... The name 'trichothecin' is suggested for the active substance. **1981** COLE & COX *Handbk. Toxic Fungal Metabolites* v. 152 Examples of trichothecenes that do not contain a carbonyl function at C-8 are T-2 toxin,..and trichothecin.

Hence **trichothe·cene**, any of a class of sesquiterpenoids based on a tetracyclic ring system $C_{15}H_{22}O_2$.

1971 *Analytical Biochem.* XLIII. 327 The trichothecenes are a family of closely related tetracyclic sesquiterpenoid metabolites of various strains of *Fusarium*, *Trichoderma*, *Trichothecium*, *Myrothecium*, and other species of imperfect fungi commonly found in soil, and on grains and other foods and feeds. **1978** *Experientia* XXXIV. 1333/1 Samples from 2 lots of corn in France suspected of causing infertility, hyperestrogenic signs and feed refusal in swine were analyzed for zearalenone and trichothecenes. **1982** *Daily Tel.* 24 Mar. 18 Trichothecene toxins should be seen as the murderous successors to mustard gas.

trichromasy (trəikrō͡u·măsi). *Ophthalm.* Also **-chromacy**. [f. TRI- + Gr. χρῶμα colour: see -Y[3].] Colour vision in which three pure colours, in different combinations, are required to match all the colours that can be perceived (as in normal vision).

1911 *Amer. Jrnl. Psychol.* XXII. 371 Guttmann.. identifies color-weakness with anomalous trichromacy. **1923** *Proc. R. Soc.* CII. 359 Trichromasy, in my experience, seems to approach monochromasy directly without passing through dichromasy as an intermediate stage. **1973** [see *PROTANOMALY]. **1980** *Nature* 27 Mar. 306/1 Our trichromacy has a 'blue' channel that is about 100 times less sensitive than the 'red' and 'green' channels.

trichromat (trəikrō͡u·mæt). *Ophthalm.* Also † **-ate**. [f. TRICHROMAT(IC *a.*] An individual with trichromasy, esp. an anomalous form of it.

1906 *Arch. Ophthalm. & Otol.* XXXV. 27 A thorough study was made of only two normal and two abnormal trichromates. **1925** M. COLLINS *Colour-Blindness* i. 14 It is customary to divide these anomalous trichromates into..deuteranomalous trichromates..and protanomalous trichromates. **1940** *Nature* 17 Aug. 226/2 It might happen that a building matched its background for the normal person, yet, for the anomalous trichromat, the two would be distinct. **1978** J. PARR *Introd. Ophthalm.* iii. 69/2 The normal individual requires a minimum of three primaries and is said to be a trichromat.

trichromatism. Add: (*c*) = *TRICHROMASY.

1910 M. GREENWOOD *Physiol. Special Senses* 239/1 (Index), Trichromatism. **1925** M. COLLINS *Colour-Blindness* i. 13 Nagel rejects the term colour-weakness as being too wide, and prefers the term anomalous trichromatism. **1946** [see *PROTANOMALY]. **1956** *Jrnl. Optical Soc. Amer.* XLVI. 1075/1 The commonest form of aberrant color vision, namely anomalous trichromatism.

trichrome (trəi·krō͡um), *a.* [f. TRI- + Gr. χρῶμα colour.] = TRICHROMATIC *a.*; *spec.* applied to a stain and method of staining in which different kinds of tissue are stained in one or other of three different colours.

1918 H. CROY *How Motion Pictures are Made* xiii. 289 To show the trichrome pictures a special projecting-machine was needed. **1929** *Jrnl. Technical Methods* XII. 83 Sections intended for the trichrome stain—Hæmalum, Erythrosin–Saffron, should previously undergo a collodionisation. **1931** *Museum Jrnl.* XXII. 213 The artist had at his disposal monochrome, bichrome and trichrome decorations of pleasing though simple geometric designs. **1938** *Amer. Jrnl. Path.* XIV. 237 Trichrome methods are rapidly replacing the ancient hematoxylin-eosin technique so largely used in pathology. **1939** *Times* 10 Mar. 17/6 A number of trichrome jars of varying shapes. **1975** *Nature* 6 Nov. 71/2 Material for histological examination was fixed in neutral formal saline, embedded in wax and sections were stained with haemalum and eosin or Masson's trichrome stain.

Trichuris (trikiū̆·ris). *Zool.* and *Med.* Also **trichuris.** Pl. **Trichurides** (-idiz). [mod.L., f. Gr. τριχ -, θρίξ hair + οὐρά tail.] A nematode worm of the genus of this name, which comprises filamentous worms (whipworms) several centimetres long that are intestinal parasites of man and higher animals.

[**1799** *Mem. Med. Soc. London* V. 226 It is now five years since I first discovered a new species of worm..but it was not till lately that I found that the same worm was first mentioned by Roederer, in the year 1760... By him it was first called Trichuris, and under that name I have described it.] **1807** *Edin. Med. & Physical Dict.* II, s.v. *Worms*, Dr. Hooper has seen upwards of twenty trichurides in some fæces of a child of six years old. **1929** E. R. STITT *Diagnostics & Treatm. Tropical Dis.* (ed. 5) xlii. 517 Of the cosmopolitan round worms *Ascaris* and *Trichuris* are the most common. **1951** P. KOURÍ in R. B. H. Gradwohl et al. *Clin. Tropical Med.* xxxvii. 842 A great number of Trichuris were found attached to the prolapsed and congested [rectal] mucosa. **1962** [see *ASCARIS]. **1977** SCHMIDT & ROBERTS *Foundations Parasitol.* xxiii. 421/1 (*caption*) A male *Trichuris*. Note the slender anterior end and the stout posterior end.

Hence **trichuri·asis** [*-IASIS], infection with such worms, which in man may be inapparent but can cause diarrhœa and other symptoms.

1921 *Amer. Jrnl. Tropical Med.* I. 375 (*heading*) The treatment of trichuriasis with leche de higueron. **1970** PASSMORE & ROBSON *Compan. Med. Stud.* II. xix. 29/2 All these species [of worms] are cosmopolitan, though ascariasis and trichuriasis are probably less common in Britain than they used to be. **1981** M. CHEESBROUGH *Med. Lab. Man. Tropical Countries* I. xxi. 266/1 The laboratory diagnosis of trichuriasis is by finding the characteristic eggs in stool specimens.

trick, *sb.* Add: **I. 1.** *trick of* (or *o'*) (*the*) *loop*, a cheating game; = FAST AND LOOSE a, *strap-game* s.v. STRAP *sb.* 17. Also *fig.* *Anglo-Irish.*

1886 M. B. BUCKLEY *Diary of Tour in Amer.* 16 The thimble-rigger and trick-o'-loop man are nowhere to be found. **1907** J. M. SYNGE *Playboy of Western World* III. 57 And he after bringing bankrupt ruin on the roulette man, and the trick-o'-the-loop man. **1922** JOYCE *Ulysses* 318 Norman W. Tupper bouncing in with his peashooter just in time to be late after she [*sc.* his wife] doing the trick of the loop with officer Taylor. **1974** *Listener* 21 Feb. 239/1 Their cities were..crowded..with pilgrims, curiosity-mongers, refugees from justice and trick-of-the-loop men [in medieval Ireland].

2. a. *trick or treat*, a traditional formula used at Hallowe'en by children who call on houses threatening to play a trick unless given a treat or present; also as *sb.*, this practice. Hence *trick-or-treating* vbl. sb. and ppl. adj. orig. and chiefly *U.S.*

1947 *Amer. Home* Oct. 150/2 The household larder needs to be well stocked on October 31, because, from dusk on, the doorbell rings, bright eyes peer through crazy-looking masks, and childish voices in ghostlike tones squeal, croak, or whisper, 'Trick or Treat!' **1950** *Sun* (Baltimore) 31 Oct. 12/1 So let the kids go out tonight and have a grand time with their masquerading and trick-or-treating. **1954** *Ibid.* 22 Oct. 18/4 Now that the 'Trick or Treat' season is upon us, let us hope that thoughtful parents will discourage the practice. **1968** MRS. L. B. JOHNSON *White House Diary* 31 Oct. (1970) 731 He and his mother had stopped by the office on their way to 'trick or treating' at some friends' houses. **1973** M. CROWELL *Greener Pastures* 64 Trick-or-treat begins at Grandma Latimer's down the road in the little green house. **1974** *New Yorker* 25 Feb. 112/2 Like a horde of trick-or-treating children who have suddenly been turned middle-aged and paunchy by a wicked witch. **1982** *Daily Tel.* 29 Oct. 3/1 A tradition of allowing children out on Halloween 'trick-or-treat' expeditions.

3. *bag of tricks*: see *BAG *sb.* 17.

5. b. A robbery, theft; chiefly in phr. *to turn a trick*, to commit a successful robbery or theft. *U.S. slang.*

1865 *Leaves from Diary of Celebrated Burglar & Pick-pocket* xxvii. 94/2 Directly he had done the trick he 'namased' with his booty. **1904** 'No. 1500' *Life in Sing Sing* 254/1 *Trick*, a theft. *Ibid.* 258/1 *Turning a trick*, accomplishing a theft. **1904** H. HAPGOOD *Autobiogr. of Thief* v. 104, I am hounded for the old trick; and the detectives are looking everywhere for these negotiable bonds. **1926** *Flynn's* 30 Jan. 843/1 Ewing was a thief, who..had settled in Chicago... He did not ply his trade here, but after 'turning a trick' outside of the city, would return to Chicago to plan the next excursion into the country. **1935** *Jrnl. Abnormal Psychol.* XXX. 365 *Trick, go on a*, to commit a robbery. **1956** [see *SCORE *sb.* 15 c]. **1979** D. MACKENZIE *Raven settles Score* 70 Campbell's claim was that he hadn't turned a trick in a year but the money had to be coming in from somewhere.

c. In Negro folk-magic or hoodoo: a spell cast on a person; an object used to 'conjure' a person or put him under a spell. Cf. *trick-doctor* s.v. TRICK *sb.* 13.

1893 [see *door-stone* s.v. *DOOR 8]. **1895** A. M. BACON in A. Dundes *Mother Wit* (1973) 367/1 Either after or before the cure of the patient is well under way, the doctor will make an effort to find the 'trick' or 'conjure' and to identify the miscreant who has caused the trouble. **1962** [see *ROOT *sb.*[1] 3 c]. **1966** D. J. CROWLEY *I could talk Old-Story Good* ii. 17 Stories about the return of spirits, murder or curing through obeah, love-potions, 'tricks' (aggressive magic) and 'guards' (protective charms) are all traditional in theme. **1977** J. DILLARD *Lexicon Black Eng.* vii. 119 The conjure doctor..is involved in the performance of *tricks*. To *trick* the victim is the frequently recorded phrase.

6. c. Applied playfully to a small or amusing person, animal, or child. *U.S.* and *Austral. colloq.*

1887 *Century Mag.* May 113/1 We uns played tergether w'en we wuz little tricks. **1890** *Stock Grower & Farmer* (Las Vegas) 29 Mar. 7/1 Down in the Panhandle..I used to ride a little trick named Dandy. **1907** H. B. WRIGHT *Shepherd of Hills* iv. 39 She ain't had no mother since she was a little trick. **1941** BAKER *Dict. Austral. Slang* 78 *Trick*, an amusing person or child, esp. the latter. **1945** S. LEWIS *Cass Timberlane* xxiv. 156 'What kind of a girl he marry?' 'Cute little trick, bright's dollar.' **1951** H. GILES *Harbin's Ridge* ii. 7 She was a little trick of a person. **1963** *Sunday Mail* (Brisbane) 10 Mar. 19/1 My wife was mystified when somebody in Brisbane described our daughter Sally, who is nearly five, as a 'trick'.

II. 7. *at* or (now more usually) *up to one's* (*old*) *tricks*, misbehaving or plotting mischief in one's characteristic way. Cf. quot. 1581 in Dict.

1823 SCOTT *St. Ronan's Well* II. i. 15 Aweel, I trust he is not at his auld tricks again, goodwife? **1863** H. E. P. SPOFFORD *Amber Gods* 206 'You are at your old tricks again!' said he. **1898** G. B. SHAW *Man of Destiny* 181 What do you mean? Eh? Are you at your tricks again? Do you think I dont know what these papers contain? **1935** *Time* 7 Jan. 55/1 She and Dill are soon up to their old tricks.

9. b. *U.S. slang.* A term of service on a ship. Also, a term in prison.

1933 *Amer. Speech* VIII. III. 32/2 *Trick*, a prison term. **1939** *Sun* (Baltimore) 28 Jan. 20/6 After serving a few tricks in the penitentiary they might turn State's evidence. **1942** *Ibid.* 19 Mar. 15/1 He reenlisted as a corporal, a rank he held at the end of his former trick. **1975** J. GORES *Hammett* i. 16 He got caught..and did a little trick at Quentin.

9*. a. An instance of the sexual act or any of its variations; usu. *spec.* a prostitute's session with a client. Esp. *to turn a trick*, to perform a sexual act with a casual partner, usu. for money. *slang* (orig. and chiefly *U.S.*).

In quot. 1926 the context concerns repeated sexual acts.

1926 C. VAN VECHTEN *Nigger Heaven* 252, I said, Now, daddy, do you know any more tricks? **1946** MEZZROW & WOLFE *Really the Blues* 30 'Turning a trick' was how they described one session with a john. **1956** B. HOLIDAY *Lady sings Blues* (1973) iii. 30, I had decided I was through turning tricks as a call girl. **1962** A. LURIE *Love & Friendship* xv. 300 Twenty-four dollars a time. That's pretty cheap for a girl like you... In New York, with the right connections, I bet you could get at least a hundred a trick. **1974** *Telegraph* (Brisbane) 16 July 14/2 She said in June: 'I'm lucky if I turn five to 10 tricks a week now.' **1975** J. F. BURKE *Death Trick* ii. 20 It was a true lovers' tryst, not a trick. **1977** *Time* 28 Nov. 45/1 Some of the young prostitutes live at home and turn tricks merely for pocket money.

b. A casual sexual partner; usu. *spec.* a prostitute's client. *slang* (orig. and chiefly *U.S.*).

1925 in Odum & Johnson *Negro & his Songs* 189 Lawd, I went to my woman's do' Jes' lak I been doin' befo'; She says, 'I got my all-night trick, baby, An' you can't git in.' **1931** B. L. REITMAN *Second Oldest Profession* viii. 118 Lillian has four children. Billy, her man, is a fourth-rate taxi-driver pimp. Billy goes out and gets 'tricks', and she takes care of them in the home where her children are. **1968** B. TURNER *Sex Trap* xv. 148, I doubt there's one trick in twenty who isn't a married man. **1973** [see *JOHN 1 f]. **1979** *Globe & Mail* (Toronto) 2 July 10/1 Young male prostitutes vie for tricks, the street name for a client.

V. 12. b. Also (chiefly *U.S.*) *to turn the trick*. **c.** *to miss a trick*, to fail to take advantage of an opportunity or notice something important; esp. *he* (or *she*) *never misses* (*does not miss*, etc.) *a trick* (see *MISS *v.*[1] 5 d; earlier examples). *colloq.* (orig. *U.S.*). **d.** *how's* (less freq. *how* are) *tricks?* how are things? how are you getting on? *colloq.* (orig. *U.S.*).

b. [**1872** Trollope *Eustace Diamonds* (1873) II. xxxvii. 134 Then the boy was done with and was carried away. She had played that card and had turned her trick.] **1933** *Sun* (Baltimore) 20 Apr. 10/3 It is our hope and prayer that Mr. Farley may turn the trick. We should be glad to see any administrator make a go of the postal service. **1942** *R.A.F. Jrnl.* 3 Oct. 24 But it was the Old Man who really turned the trick. **1960** I. Wallach *Absence of Cello* 230 It takes many years to live without a deliberate confusion about anyone's wants, including our own. Some people never turn the trick. **1976** *Springfield* (Mass.) *Daily News* 22 Apr. 39/2 A couple of American college products turned the trick for the Whalers. North Dakota graduate Alan Hangsleben and New Hampshire alumnus Cap Raeder shared the hero's role in the triumph.

c. [*a* **1916** H. James *Sense of Past* (1917) IV. iii. 266 It was..for him to have kept it as..she preferred it. He had begun so..and how..came it therefore that he now repeatedly missed that trick?] **1922** S. Lewis *Babbitt* xix. 241 'I'll bet..you were a bad old egg when you were a kid!' 'Well, I wasn't so slow!' 'I bet you weren't! I'll bet you didn't miss many tricks!' **1943** N. Coward *Middle East Diary* (1944) 11 He is a highly intelligent man and doesn't miss a trick... He had clear, alert views on the most diverse subjects. **1957** 'J. Wyndham' *Midwich Cuckoos* xii. 99 He went on, with a puzzled frown on his brow as he realised that somewhere he had missed a trick; something had been kept from him. **1965** *Weekly News* (Auckland, N.Z.) 10 Mar. 49/1 The fact that the Wellington [boxing] association could match three Auckland fledgling professionals with three unknown Australians and make a profit points to someone else missing a trick.

d. **1915** J. London *Jacket* xiii. 149 'How's tricks?' I asked finally. **1924** W. Holtby *Crowded Street* i. 21 'Well, Mrs. H., how's tricks?' His wife flushed slightly at the vulgarity of his phrase. **1934** D. Runyon in *Collier's* 24 Nov. 8/4 Meyer Marmalade and I are glad to see her looking so well, and we ask her how are tricks. **1959** 'A. Fraser' *High Tension* ix. 91 'Well,' he greeted me, 'how's tricks?' **1980** N. Marsh *Photo-Finish* ii. 36 'Gidday,' said Les Smith. 'How's tricks, then, Bert?'

13. (sense 5) *trick-flying, -rider; trick-leap* vb.; (sense 11) *trick-score, -taking;* **trick-cycling,** (*b*) *humorously,* psychiatry (cf. *trick-cyclist* (*b*) below); **trick-cyclist,** (*a*) (earlier example); (*b*) humorous alteration of Psychiatrist; **trick-film,** a film using trick photography; **trick photography,** photography using montage and other technical devices to create visual illusions; **trick picture** = *trick-film* above; **trick question,** a question designed to elicit more information than it appears to on the surface, or to trick the respondent into giving a wrong answer; **trick shot,** (*a*) in golf, etc.: a particularly clever or devious shot; (*b*) a camera shot made by means of trick photography; **trick wheel,** an auxiliary steering wheel on a ship.

1951 G. Frankau *Oliver Trenton* xvi. 139, I picked it up from one of our surgeons, who's rather keen on trick-cycling. **1966** G. B. Mair *Kisses from Satan* vii. 79 Don't try and sell that stuff about trickcycling to someone with rheumatism and gall stones. **1897** *Nat. Police Gaz.* 26 May 14/4 That noted trick cyclist, Lee Richardson, left London for America on Saturday. **1930** H. Wolfe *Uncelestial City* III. 112 A trick-cyclist gravely reassembling The features of the ectoplasmic dead. **1971** P. Scott *Towers of Silence* v. iii. 345 That's why the trick-cyclist wallah insists on coming. **1977** *Listener* 31 Mar. 414/3 Is neurotic, inadequate, unhappy..is up in Harley Street being sorted out by a trick cyclist. **1912** F. A. Talbot *Moving Pictures* xix. 207 The achievements of Méliès and Paul set a very high standard of excellence in trick pictures. Their popularity precipitated a 'trick film' fever. The market became flooded with so-called magic pictures. **1914** *Chambers's Jrnl.* 6 June 429/2 A certain number of these craft [*sc.* aeroplanes] are kept..for..trick-flying, &c. **1932** E. Wallace *When Gangs came to London* xxii. 198 You used to do trick flying. **1922** Joyce *Ulysses* 428 Bloom trickleaps to the curbstone. **1913** *Technical World* XIX. 464 It merely accomplishes what is known as 'trick photography'. **1928** R. Knox *Footsteps at Lock* xxiv. 238 His cousin was fond of trick photography. **1984** *Listener* 2 Feb. 37/3 He achieved the crucial transformation scenes without the help of trick photography on cutaways. **1912** Trick picture [see *trick film* above]. **1939** R. Stout *Red Threads* xv, in *Mystery Bk.* 516, I could easily ask you some trick questions that would put sweat on your brow. **1954** N. Tomalin in J. Philip et al. *Best of Granta* (1967) II. 139 He plugs away at trick questions..like: 'You *did* say you were giving the money to Dr Barnardo's didn't you sir?' **1978** P. Niesewand *Underground Connection* 86 The journalists ..filed out... He had not expected any trick questions, and none came. **1902** *Billboard* 31 May 18/1 (Advt.), The motor wonders Arthur Stone and Joe Judge pace Frank Armstrong (who knows no fear as a trick rider). **1976** *National Observer* (U.S.) 24 July 18/4 Keitel calmly saying, 'Hi, Joy,' to a trick rider flashing past slung from the side of her horse. **1929** Trick-score [see *overtrick]. **1938** J. Culbertson *Contract Bridge for Beginners* vii. 71 A three-bid in no-trumps will produce a trick-score of 100 points. **1924** C. J. Tolley *Mod. Golfer* 229 He tried to recover by the aid of a trick shot. **1926** *Daily Colonist* (Victoria, B.C.) 20 Jan. 11/3 He told me that Joe Kirkwood, the marvelous trick-shot golfer had just given an exhibition. **1933** *Jrnl. Soc. Motion Picture Engineers* XX. 319 If the subject should contain more than the usual number of so-called 'trick' shots..the shooting time will easily run from 125 to 150 hours. **1981** *Sunday Times* 23 Aug. 54 At an exhibition they expect you to play about 10 frames [of snooker] and then to do some trick shots like hitting a ball into someone's handkerchief. **1983** J. Gardner *Elephants in Attic* xii. 110 My one experience of the film world had been devising trick shots for Alexander Korda. **1936** E. Culbertson *Contract Bridge Complete* xxxvii. 398 The low cards in long and short suits have their own trick-taking power. **1977** *Jrnl. Playing-Card Soc.* May 23 Reversis is historically important as the earliest known negative complex trick-taking game. **1942** *Sun* (Baltimore) 18 June 8/4 Men were stationed at the 'trick wheel'—an auxiliary wheel situated deep inside the ship, where it was operated by hand. **1972** L. M. Harris *Introd. Deepwater Floating Drilling Operations* 244 The emergency steering wheel and trick wheel.

trick, *v.* Add: **I. 1. e.** To put a spell on (a person), 'conjure'. Cf. *trick *sb.* 5 c. *U.S. dial.* (esp. in the speech of *U.S. Blacks*).

1829 *Virginia Lit. Museum* 25 Nov. 384 And, amongst the degraded and ignorant part of our own population, the notion of '*tricking*' or bewitching is universally.. received. **1895** L. Herron in A. Dundes *Mother Wit* (1973) 360/2 The conjure doctor's business was of two kinds: to conjure, or 'trick', a person, and to cure people already conjured. **1970** H. M. Hyatt *Hoodoo-Conjuration-Witchcraft-Rootwork* I. 688 Well, if a man is got de skill upon 'im tuh make a man do 'jes whut he want 'im to do without *hurtin'* 'im, dat's *trickin'* a man. **1977** [see *trick *sb.* 5 c].

3. b. To have casual sexual intercourse, esp. for money; chiefly const. *with.* Cf. *trick *sb.* 9* a, b. *U.S. slang.*

1965 C. Brown *Manchild in Promised Land* (1966) vi. 163 Since her mother was laying so many cats, why shouldn't she be tricking. **1967** C. Himes *Black on Black* (1973) 133 He was trying to get his old lady, Tang, to go down into Central Park and trick with some white man so they could eat. **1973** J. Wambaugh *Blue Knight* xii. 207 He tricked with a whore the night before in the Orchid Hotel. **1978** A. Maling *Lucky Devil* xxix. 154 'You *know* him?' I asked. 'We've tricked,' he replied.

IV. 8. *trick and tie* (*trick* app. = to take one's turn at something; cf. Trick *sb.* 9), to be equal or even *with* someone or something; chiefly as *adj.* (sometimes hyphened); occas. as *sb.*

1825 C. M. Westmacott *Eng. Spy* I. 241 Trick and tie you know is fair play. **1829** P. Egan *Boxiana* 2nd Ser. II. 132 The Grecian, in order to make 'trick and tie' with his opponent, put his best foot foremost, and pursued him. **1883** W. H. Cope *Gloss. Hampshire Words & Phr.* 96 *Trick-and-tie*.., equal to each other. **1890** Barrère & Leland *Dict. Slang* II. 374/1 *Trick and tie* (sport). To be *trick and tie*, or touch and go, is to be equal in a race, or other athletic performance. **1905** *Eng. Dial. Dict.* VI. 234/1 [Wiltshire] 'I'll keep trick-and-tie wi' un', will keep even or level with him, in mowing or standing pots of beer or anything else.

trick, *a.*[2] *U.S. colloq.* [f. the sb.] = Tricky *a.* 2; liable to give way unexpectedly, defective, unreliable.

1961 in Webster. **1968** *Punch* 21 Feb. 256/2 He would have been out there himself, he said, only he had this trick knee, had it since he was a kid, gave him hell. **1977** *Time* 8 Aug. 14/1 Private Citizen Henry Kissinger has a trick back like millions of other Americans. **1977** *Hot Car* Oct. 42/1 Best upholstery went to Sandy Ventriglin for her work on a very trick Viva.

trickeration (trikəreɪ·ʃən). *U.S. Blacks.* [f. Tricker(y + -ation.] A trick or stratagem (see also quots. 1940, 1970).

1940 *Music Makers* May 37/3 *Trickeration*, struttin' your stuff, muggin' lightly and politely. **1946** Mezzrow & Wolfe *Really the Blues* ix. 138 History was laying some trickeration on us. **1951** L. Hughes *Montage of Dream Deferred* 18, I believe my old lady's pregnant again! Fate must have some kind of trickeration to populate the cullud nation! **1970** C. Major *Dict. Afro-Amer. Slang* 116 *Trickeration*, to show off.

trickle, *sb.*[1] Add: **2.** Special Comb.: **trickle charger** *Electr.*, a device for charging a storage battery at a low rate over a long period; hence **trickle-charge** *sb.* (in quot., *attrib.*) and *v. trans.*; **trickle-charged** *ppl. a.*; **trickle-charging** *vbl. sb.*; **trickle irrigation** (see quot. 1969); hence (as back-formation) **trickle-irrigate** *v. trans.*

1959 *Times* 11 Sept. 7/4 It is ideal for trickle-charge operation. **1974** *Undercurrents* July–Aug. 3/3 This.. produced a few hundred milliamps at about 10 volts in a fair breeze—enough to trickle-charge a small battery. **1938** *Proc. Physical Soc.* L. 422 The driving, demultiplying, and amplifying circuits were operated by trickle-charged batteries. **1927** *Observer* 24 July 4/5 A fool-proof set..is provided with a 'trickle charger' for keeping the filament battery up to strength. **1977** *Film & Television Technician* Mar. 11/3 Complete with its internal rechargeable batteries and a built-in trickle charger, the D34 weighs in at only 12 lbs. **1960** E. L. Delmar-Morgan *Cruising Yacht Equipment & Navigation* xvi. 175 This 'trickle charging' is..harmful for the type of batteries used in yachts. **1971** *World Bk. Sci. Ann. 1972* 255 Vast areas in the Negev Desert of Israel are now trickle-irrigated. **1969** *Gloss. for Landscape Work (B.S.I.)* v. 13 *Trickle irrigation*, a method of supplying water by means of a restricted, controlled flow to the surface of a growing medium (usually at discrete points, one to each plant). **1975** *N.Z. Jrnl. Agric.* Sept. 43/1 The research workers.. are hopeful that trickle irrigation, by maintaining even soil moisture, will give some help.

trickle, *v.* Add: **1. c.** Also used facetiously for 'to make one's way, go'. Cf. *ooze *v.*[1] 2 c.

1912 R. Brooke *Let.* Feb. (1968) 357, *I* wrote to *her*, about her perhaps trickling down to Rugby. **1936** Wodehouse *Laughing Gas* iii. 32 In these circs, it seemed to me that the best way of passing the time would be to trickle over to the table where the drinks were and brace myself with one or two. **1961** —— *Service with Smile* (1962) vii. 100 He headed for the lake. I trickled after him. **1983** *Country Life* 5 May 1194/3 Trickling through morning traffic..it [*sc.* a car] showed its docility by contentedly running in fifth.

3. c. *Sport.* To cause (a ball) to travel slowly over the ground, esp. in golf. Also *to trickle a putt.* Also *absol.*

1902 *Daily Chron.* 20 Aug. 7/3 He can..trickle the ball away to fine-leg with a delicate turn of the wrist. **1903** *Westm. Gaz.* 6 Feb. 3/2 If you bolt at the hole, you will not need to make the same allowance for incline as if you trickled. **1927** *Daily Tel.* 14 Mar. 13/1 'I will trickle the.. putt up to the hole.'..It certainly was a trickle..for the ball stopped five feet short of the hole.

4. *Comb.*: **trickle-down** *a.*, of or based on the theory that economic benefits to particular groups will inevitably be passed on to those less well off; also *transf.* as *sb.*, a filtering down (of money or ideas). orig. and chiefly *U.S.*

[**1931** W. Rogers in *Tulsa Daily World* 12 July IV. 7/3 What about the old Boys here on the home grounds? Well maybe this thing will eventually reach him in some beneficial way. Lord knows what way it may trickle down to him some day.] **1944** *Antioch Rev.* Summer 192 In agriculture, as in business, they are devotees of the trickle-down philosophy. **1949** H. S. Truman in *Sun* (Baltimore) 6 Jan. 6/1 We have rejected the discredited theory that the fortunes of the nation should be in the hands of a privileged few. We have abandoned the 'trickle-down' concept of national prosperity. **1954** *Sun* (Baltimore) 13 Feb. (B ed.) 2/1 The Administration has already offered us a trickle-down tax program. Now, we are presented with a trickle-down housing program. **1962** C. Walsh *From Utopia to Nightmare* i. 18 There has been a trickle-down [of ideas] and permeation. **1971** *Publishers' Weekly* 6 Dec. 17/2 It is to be hoped that textbook writers come in contact with frontier thinkers or their writings and translate some of the results into educational materials. This is known as the 'trickle-down' process. **1977** *Time* 16 May 38/2 It's classic trickle-down economics. **1980** *Jrnl. R. Soc. Arts* July 508/2 The theory that if you build the industrial capability and increase the GNP of the country there will be a trickle-down to people at subsistence level. **1981** Plate & Darvi *Secret Police* ii. 42 If the sovereign himself is corrupt or family and relatives are corrupt, there can be a trickle-down effect into the ranks. **1984** *New Yorker* 16 Apr. 82/2 To Fink this often sounded suspiciously like Republican trickle-down economics.

trickless (tri·klės), *a.* [f. Trick *sb.* + -less.] Possessing no tricks (*spec.* in *Cards*).

1927 *Observer* 29 May 25 If he finds his partner trickless, he must go down enormously. **1977** *Times* 17 June 12/1 Anyone who regularly makes preemptive opening bids on hands which are trickless in defence has only himself to blame.

trickling, *vbl. sb.* Add: **b. trickling filter** = *percolating filter* s.v. *percolating *vbl. sb.*

1903 W. J. Dibdin *Purification of Sewage & Water* (ed. 3) p. xv, I think it is quite practicable to deal with Leeds sewage on trickling filters without antecedent septic treatment. **1976** *Ann. Rev. Microbiol.* XXX. 266 Bacterial and viral aerosols are generated..and bacteria have been detected at least 0·8 mile from a trickling filter.

tricky, *a.* **2.** (Earlier example.)

1868 C. L. Eastlake *Hints Househ. Taste* vii. 176 Chromo-lithography..accustoms the eye to easily rendered and therefore *tricky* effects of colour which falsify rather than illustrate nature.

tricolour, tricolor, *a.* and *sb.* **A.** *adj.* **1.** Delete '(in form **tricolor**)'. Esp. in reference to a black, white, and tan dog. (Later examples.)

1922 R. Leighton *Compl. Bk. Dog* viii. 113 At Cruft's in 1913 an especially nice tricolour puppy named Jason was placed high above Lerwick Jarl. **1971** F. Hamilton *World Encycl. Dogs* 103 The coat is smooth and short and the colors are tricolor, black, tan and white.

3. a. Employing or pertaining to the use of the three primary colours. Cf. *three-colour *a.*

1898 A. C. Austin (*title*) Practical half-tone and tricolor engraving. **1909** *Chambers's Jrnl.* 27 Mar. 268/1 A remarkable new development..promises to revolutionise the art of printing in photogravure. The process is three-colour; and..the results..are far in advance of anything that has yet been attempted in tricolour printing. **1937** J. S. Mertle *Photolithography & Offset Printing* 101 Three-color photography proper is based on the photographic separation of the colored original into three primary color-record (separation) negatives, which are obtained by exposing three separate color-sensitive plates through what are termed 'tri-color' filters. *Ibid.* 103 Tri-color images. **1968** *Gloss. Terms Offset Lithogr. Printing (B.S.I.)* 17 *Tricolour filter*, a colour filter that transmits a primary band of the spectrum, i.e., red, green or blue.

b. *gen.* Three-coloured.

1979 *Washington Post* 20 Oct. F7/2 Even the large sculptures are hard to find among the visual chaos—amid blaring tricolor trashcans, telephone booths, [etc.]. **1983** *Christian Sci. Monitor* 14 Nov. B12/1 Almost anything Chinese—whether Tang Dynasty tricolor jars, Ming molded gourds, or cheap jade trinkets—can be bought in Hong Kong.

B. *sb.* **2. a.** (Earlier example.)

1797 *Political Censor* Mar. 84 To strut and hector over the poor fallen *Tricolor*, and to call on your readers to 'unite under their *own flag*'..entitles you to but very little praise.

b. The green, white, and orange Irish Republican flag.

1969 *Listener* 28 Aug. 268/2 The tricolour had been raised in Bogside once before. **1977** *Belfast Tel.* 22 Feb. 5/5 No Irish tricolours were displayed.

3. A black, white, and tan dog.

1905 J. Watson *Dog Bk.* lxvi. 724 The tricolour has been neglected in the fashion for black and tans. **1971** F. Hamilton *World Encycl. Dogs* 97 Two tricolors can produce a pure golden-sable.

4. A combination of the three primary colours.

1978 *SLR Camera* Dec. 88/3 In theory, the yellow, magenta-red, and cyan-blue tricolour forming the image of the slide should each perfectly reflect two-thirds of the spectrum of white light.

tricoloured, -colored, *a.* (Later example.)

1913 F. T. Barton *Toy Dogs* ix. 41 The Ruby and Tri-coloured, or Prince Charles Spaniels, have a separate classification.

tricontinental: see *tri- 1 a.

tricot². Add: Also, a pair of close-fitting knitted tights. (Earlier and later examples.)

1859 L. Wraxall tr. *Robert-Houdin's Mem.* II. ix. 259 And the whole [false stomach] being concealed beneath a flesh-colour *tricot*, appeared to form part of his body. **1893** [in Dict.]. **1926** *Spectator* 6 Feb. 219/1 Let us hope that the odious 'tricot', or tights, which create, by emphasizing, indecency have disappeared for ever—at any rate in Paris [music-halls].

‖ **tricoteuse** (trīkotøz). Also **Tricoteuse.** [Fr.] **1.** A woman who knits; applied *spec.* to women who, during the French Revolution, sat and knitted at meetings of the Convention or at guillotinings. Also *transf.*

1830 Hazlitt *Life of Napoleon Buonaparte* I. vi. 284 It was this [popular fury] that inspired the Furies of the Guillotine, and sat and smiled in the galleries of the Convention with the *tricoteuses* of Robespierre! *a* **1886** M. B. Chesnut in C. V. Woodward *M. Chesnut's Civil War* (1981) viii. 183 Jenny Barron, Jenny Cooper and Mary Hammy have gone to have their photographs taken as 'Tricoteuses', each armed with their knitting. **1905** Baroness Orczy *Scarlet Pimpernel* i. 8 The old hags, 'tricotteuses' [*sic*] as they were called, who sat there and knitted, while head after head fell beneath the knife. **1940** M. Dickens *Mariana* viii. 309 The eyes of the *tricoteuses* nearly came out of their heads, and the less hardened of them dropped a stitch. **1961** *Guardian* 19 Apr. 10/6 Is it fair that the Conservative Women's Conference should ..be thought of as..a collection of elegant Tricoteuses? **1972** R. Quilty *Tenth Session* 1. 66 The inner circle around the victim, the eager *tricoteuses* who always collected at any drama on the streets. **1973** *Listener* 22 Nov. 727 The wife of the production manager..sits sourly knitting on set like a *tricoteuse* at the guillotine.

2. *Antiques.* (See quot. 1960.)

1960 H. Hayward *Antique Coll.* 287/2 *Tricoteuse* (Fr.), a term probably of 19th-cent. origin, applied to a small work-table surrounded by a gallery, part of which can be lowered to contain sewing materials. **1973** *Country Life* 30 Aug. (Suppl.) 72/2 Mahogany Tricoteuse with black line inlay. English, circa 1810.

Tricotine (tri·kŏtīn). Also **tricotine.** [f. Tricot² + -ine⁴.] A worsted fabric with a double twill.

A proprietary term in the U.S.

1914 *Official Gaz.* (U.S. Patent Office) 27 Oct. 1236/2 'Tricotine'...Woolen, Worsted, Silk, Mohair and Cotton Piece Goods and Piece Goods Made of a Combination of Two or More of Those Fibers. **1920** G. Bell *Let.* 10 Oct. (1927) II. xviii. 502 I've got bills for tricotine and things which Elsa kindly bought for me. **1921** *Daily Colonist* (Victoria, B.C.) 5 Oct. 8/6 Smartly fashioned dresses..of Tricotine and Serge, comprise this special offering. **1930** *Daily Express* 6 Oct. 6/1 (Advt.), Smart in every sense of the word in a tricotine finished faced-cloth.

Tricouni (trəikū·ni). Also **tricouni.** [Swiss trade name, app. f. Tri- + Co- + Uni-.] The proprietary name for a kind of climbing-boot nail with a serrated edge. (Now *disused.*)

1914 O. Eckstein in *Climbers' Club Jrnl.* Mar. 77 (*title*) The Tricouni Nail. *Ibid.*, A new nail, bearing the above name, has lately been invented by a Swiss climber, Mr. F. Genecand; it is intended for nailing boots used on mountains. **1920** G. W. Young *Mountain Craft* ii. 82 An even better nail appears to be the lately invented Tricouni nail. **1934** *Trade Marks Jrnl.* 3 Oct. 1276/1 Tricouni... Boot and shoe nails; and cleats and calks; all of ordinary metal. Tricouni S.A..., Geneva, Switzerland; manufacturers. **1946** J. E. Q. Barford *Climbing in Britain* ii. 20 Tricounis are better on snow and ice because the sharp edges bite in well. **1957** J. Masters *Far, Far the Mountain Peak* 143 They had spent those eight hours hanging by fingertips and tricounis over the Bowl. **1972** M. Woodhouse *Mama Doll* ii. 4 Boots nailed with what ..are..called tricounis.

tri-county, tricresyl phosphate: see *tri- 1 b, 5 c.

tricycle, *sb.* Add: **2. b.** A three-wheeled motorized invalid carriage.

1974 *Guardian* 26 Mar. 32/4 Disabled drivers' tricycles should be replaced with modified production cars. **1976** *Times* 24 July 1/7 Invalid tricycles are to be phased out... The existing 21,265 tricycle drivers will be able to keep their vehicles until they wear out.

c. An aeroplane with a three-wheeled undercarriage.

1942 *Tee Emm* (Air Ministry) II. 95 The pilot..strikes the sea at the normal three-point landing attitude (slow landing attitude for tricycles).

3. *Comb.* **tricycle undercarriage** *Aeronaut.*, a three-wheeled undercarriage; also **tricycle landing-gear.**

1938 *Sun* (Baltimore) 26 Sept. 13/5 The 'tri-safety' tricycle landing gear, with a nose wheel under the pilot's cockpit. **1960** *Economist* 31 Dec. 1382/2 Development of the tricycle landing gear has been the greatest single factor in making a flier out of a businessman. **1937** *Flight* 18 Nov. 483/1 (*heading*) Simplified control system for all-metal pusher with tricycle undercarriage. **1966** D. Francis *Flying Finish* x. 129 The bump from the tricycle undercarriage as we touched down. **1976** *Official Programme Farnborough Internat. Exhib.* 28 The aircraft has a fixed tricycle undercarriage.

tricyclic, *a.* Add: **2. b.** *spec.* in *Pharm.*, designating or pertaining to a group of antidepressant drugs based upon a molecular structure of three fused rings; also as *sb.*

1966 *Internat. Jrnl. Neuropharmacol.* V. 299 (*heading*) Association between biochemical and behavioral actions of tricyclic antidepressants. **1972** *Daily Tel.* 4 Mar. 32/3 He said pregnant women should steer clear of all drugs if possible, particularly drugs known as tricyclic antidepressants. **1973** *Sci. Amer.* Sept. 121/2 The chemical structures of these two classes of antidepressants—the monamine oxidase inhibitors and the tricyclics—are quite different. **1980** J. Wainwright *Man of Law* i. 18, I suggested..a good tricyclic antidepressant.

tridentate, *a.* Add: **2.** *Chem.* Of a ligand: forming three separate bonds (usu. but not necessarily with the same central atom). Of a molecule or complex: formed by such a ligand.

1925 *Jrnl. Chem. Soc.* CXXVII. 2030 Werner also identified groups capable of treble attachment to metallic atoms, such tridentate residues containing three fused chelate groups. **1966** Phillips & Williams *Inorg. Chem.* II. xxvii. 347 The cyclopentadienyl and benzene ligands are best regarded as tridentate and their transition-metal complexes are strongly stabilized in the sandwich symmetry only.

tridimensional, *a.* Add: (Earlier example.)

1858 *Q. Jrnl. Math.* II. 182 An analogous method of transformation is applicable to tridimensional space.

Hence **tridime·nsionally** *adv.*

1919 R. T. Browne *Mystery of Space* vii. 240 Trace out the biologic development of each mental faculty..and it will be found that..the nature of each of these has been to express itself tridimensionally. **1956** H. Read *Art of Sculpture* v. 102 One of the most striking developments in our time has been in the direction of linear sculpture, another apparent contradiction of terms that can be justified in so far as the lines are used tridimensionally to indicate volume.

Tridione (trəidəi·ōᵘn). *Pharm.* [f. Tri- + *-dione.] A proprietary name for an analgesic agent (also called *troxidone*).

1944 Richards & Everett in *Federation Proc.* III. 39/2 Preliminary clinical investigations have shown that Tridione is an effective analgesic. **1948** *Official Gaz.* (U.S. Patent Office) 24 Feb. 607/1 *Tridione*... For anticonvulsant intended for use in treatment of the petit mal triad and other convulsive disorders. **1948** *Trade Marks Jrnl.* 25 Feb. 141/2 *Tridione*... Therapeutic compounds being alkyl derivatives of diketo oxazolidine. Abbott Laboratories.., City of North Chicago,..manufacturers. **1974** M. C. Gerald *Pharmacol.* xi. 212 Trimethadione (Tridione) was originally synthesized as an aspirin substitute; however, its lack of dependable analgesia caused it to be rapidly discarded for this purpose. **1979** R. Jaffe *Class Reunion* 1. ix. 95 Time to get to the pharmacy.., fill her prescriptions for Dilantin and Tridione.

tri-dominium. Add: Also applied to the former rule of Great Britain, Greece, and Turkey in Cyprus.

1955 *Times* 25 July 7/7 The second scheme is, broadly, that the island should be turned into some form of 'tri-dominium' with, perhaps, a British Governor and one Greek and one Turkish deputy Governor, and with all three national flags flying over Government House. **1958** *Times* 20 June 11/2 The next stage may be independence, condominium, or even the perpetuation of tridominium, but it can scarcely be absorption by either Greece or Turkey.

triduum. b. (Earlier example.)

1873 G. M. Hopkins *Jrnl.* 9 Feb. (1959) 230 Began a triduum.

tried, *ppl. a.* Add: **3. b.** Phr. *tried and true*, proved reliable by experience.

1954 W. Faulkner *Fable* 352 His enslavement to the demonic progeny of his own mechanical curiosity, from which he will emancipate himself by that one ancient tried-and-true method by which slaves have always freed themselves: by inculcating their masters with the slaves' own vices. **1967** *Listener* 6 Apr. 474/3 Miss Aukin had had the good sense to use the tried and true concealment gambit by which eventually two young officers, bent on cuckolding a greengrocer, were compelled to hide in the same grandfather clock. **1979** *Tucson Mag.* Apr. 47/1 A beautifully made 'period' movie, written and directed by tried-and-true Michael Crichton.

triene (trəi·īn). *Chem.* [f. Tri- + -ene.] Any organic compound containing three double bonds between carbon atoms.

1917 *Chem. Abstr.* XI. 3031 These hydrocarbons give exaltations greater than those of the aromatic series: with the trienes the difference is proportionally greater than with the dienes. **1936** [see *diene value* s.v. *diene b]. **1976** *Nature* 22 Apr. 726/2 We recorded the laser Raman spectrum of vitamin D_3 (in CCl_4), which has a conjugated triene structure.

trier. 10. (Further examples in gen. use.)

1927 C. A. Wilson *Empire's Junior Partner* 227 There are many opportunities to acquire land on easy terms, very many farmers' trading concerns which are ready to back a 'trier'. **1942** *Tee Emm* (Air Ministry) II. 133 One day his Instructor said 'That chap's a trier' and sent him to a Squadron. **1955** *Times* 10 June 4/7 Pritchett has always been a real trier, and his game has looked more mature since his return from the United States.

Triestine (tri,e·stīn), *sb.* and *a.* [f. *Trieste*, name of a city and province in north-eastern Italy + -ine¹.] **A.** *sb.* A native or inhabitant of Trieste. **B.** *adj.* Of Trieste or its inhabitants.

1905 J. Joyce *Let.* 12 July (1966) II. 93 Nora can speak about thirty words of Triestine dialect. *Ibid.* 24 Sept. (1966) II. 112 Two little Triestines went into a hallway and laughed till they beat each other. **1921** *Contemp. Rev.* July 46 Sig. Scaramanga, was a Triestine, and therefore an ex-Austrian subject. **1975** 'D. Rutherford' *Mystery Tour* iv. 69 Maria, his homely and chubby Triestine wife.

triethanolamine, triethylene: see *tri- 5 c, b.

trifecta (trəife·ktă). *N. Amer.*, *Austral.*, and *N.Z.* [f. Tri- + *per)fecta.] (See quot. 1977.) Also *fig.*

1974 *Daily News* (N.Y.) 6 Feb. 46 The money that is bet on gimmick races like the trifecta is placed in a separate pool from the straight win, place, and show wagering. **1975** *Cleveland* (Ohio) *Plain Dealer* 6 Apr. 13-c/1 Before acting on the request for trifecta wagering..the ORC must advertise in affected counties 30 days before the hearing. **1977** *Daily Colonist* (Victoria, B.C.) 26 Nov. 32/1 To win the trifecta, a bettor must select the first, second and third place horses in order. **1979** *Sunday Mail* (Brisbane) 19 Aug. 6/5 A new bride on Thursday, a $50,000 win in the New South Wales lotteries on Friday and a winning day at the races on Saturday. That's last week's trifecta for Sydney's biggest bookmaker. **1984** *N.Z. Truth* 23 May 6 The T.A.B. is accepting trifecta and quinella on this feature event which is also the 1st leg of the Double and Treble.

triffid (tri·fid). Also **Triffid.** [f. Tri-, prob. after Trifid *a.*, as the plant was supported on 'three bluntly-tapered projections extending from the lower part' of the body.] In the science-fiction novel *The Day of the Triffids*, by John Wyndham (1903–69), one of a race of menacing plants, possessed of locomotor ability and a poisonous sting, which threaten to overrun the world. Hence used allusively of vigorous plants, or *transf.* of anything invasive or rapid in development.

1951 'J. Wyndham' *Day of Triffids* ii. 46 A catchy little name originating in some newspaper office as a handy label for an oddity—but destined one day to be associated with pain, fear and misery—*triffid*. *Ibid.* 54 He had also established that the infertility rate of triffid seeds was something like ninety-five per cent. **1965** *New Scientist* 11 Mar. 619/3 Ninety per cent of British households have television..and neither bindweed, triffids, nor dragon's teeth grew more rapidly than the angular aerial. **1972** S. Hughes in M. Bygrave et al. *Time Out's Bk. of London* ix. 90/1 The south is sprouting with tall dark buildings like triffids. **1977** *Times* 10 Feb. 5/2 Roots and suckers started appearing all over our gardens... They were like 'Triffids'. **1978** R. H. Lewis *Antiquarian Bks.* iv. 86 Books 'taking over' in Triffid style is a common experience.

Hence **triffi·dian** *a.*; **tri·ffid-like** *a.* and quasi-*adv.*

1951 'J. Wyndham' *Day of Triffids* ii. 49 It was assumed..that their characteristic of suddenly losing their immobility and rattling a rapid tattoo against the main stem was some strange form of triffidian amatory exuberance. **1971** *Daily Tel.* 16 Jan. 10/6 This cactus had run wild and, Triffid-like, had taken over thousands of square miles of good agricultural land. **1971** *New Scientist* 9 Sept. 589/3 Even the departure of four million..inhabitants..did not appear to check the spread of the Triffid-like condition.

trifid, *a.* Add: **c.** Also **tref(f)id.** Designating a type of antique spoon (see quot. 1977). Also *absol.* as *sb.*

1892 C. J. Jackson in *Archaeologia* LIII. 1. 138 The stem of this [Puritan] spoon is as wide as that of the trifid-ended form which immediately succeeded it. **1911** —— *Hist. Eng. Plate* II. xvii. 521 The earliest *Trifid Spoon* known to the author is one bearing the Dublin hallmarks for 1663. **1927** N. GASK *Old Silver Spoons of England* ix. 96 (*heading*) Lobed-ends, variously called Trifids, Trefoils, Split-ends or Pieds-de-Biche. **1932** *Antique Collector* Nov. 394/1 The Trifid type of handle, introduced with the Restoration, appears to have been evolved in turn from the Puritan. **1952** G. E. P. HOW *Eng. & Scottish Silver Spoons* I. II. xiv. 325 The Trefid Spoon, in its fully-developed form, was apparently introduced to London from the Continent at the Restoration of the Monarchy. **1956** G. TAYLOR *Silver* v. 111 The so-called Puritan spoon seems to be the starting-point for more decorative developments. The plain square end was hammered out into a thin leaf-shaped blade which is most commonly notched on either side of the pointed end to form a simple trefoil... Such spoons are therefore described as 'trefid' (or 'trifid')... Larger trefid spoons with the same characteristics, but a much longer stem, are found. **1974** [see *RAT-TAIL 3 b]. **1977** FLEMING & HONOUR *Penguin Dict. Decorative Arts* 802/1 *Trifid* or *Trefid spoon*, a C17 English type of spoon with a flat handle widening towards the end which is divided into three parts by deep notches.

trifle, *sb.* **6. b.** (Earlier example.)

1755 H. GLASSE *Art of Cookery* (ed. 5) xvi. 285 Trifle. Cover..your Dish..with Naples Biscuits..Mackeroons..and Ratafia Cakes..wet them..with Sack, then make a good boiled Custard..pour over it..then put a Syllabub over that.

trifluoperazine (trəiflūoˌpeˑrăzīn). *Pharm.* [f. TRI- 5 + FLUO- + *PI)PERAZINE.] A phenothiazine derivative used as a tranquillizer and anti-emetic (usu. administered as the hydrochloride); 10-[3-(4-methylpiperazin-1-yl)propyl]-2-trifluoromethylphenothiazine, $C_{21}H_{24}F_3N_3S$.

1958 *Amer. Jrnl. Psychiatry* CXIV. 747 (*heading*) Triflupromazine and trifluoperazine: two new tranquilizers. *Ibid.* 747/2 The chlorine atom of the phenothiazine nucleus has been replaced by carbon trifluoride... This differentiates..trifluoperazine from prochlorperazine. **1965** [see *STELAZINE]. **1977** *Lancet* 15 Oct. 816/2 A 65-year-old woman had been taking 'Parstelin' tablets (tranylcypromine 10 mg, trifluoperazine 1 mg), one three times daily for a depressive illness for 4 years. **1984** *Brit. Med. Jrnl.* 8 Sept. 612/1 He was diagnosed as having an anxiety neurosis and was prescribed trifluoperazine together with orphenadrine.

trifocal (trəifōᵘ·kăl), *a.* and *sb.* [f. TRI- + FOCAL *a.*] **A.** *adj.* † **a.** (See quot.) *Obs.*

1826 J. I. HAWKINS in *Repertory Patent Inventions* III. 386 When three pairs [of glasses] are worn in one frame..which I denominate trifocal spectacles, the opening should be a circle of one inch diameter.

b. Of a lens: having three parts with different focal lengths. Of spectacles: having such lenses.

1921 *Amer. Jrnl. Ophthalmol.* IV. 406/2 The writer does not claim that every presbyope should have a pair of trifocal spectacles. **1928** W. S. DUKE-ELDER *Pract. Refraction* xxiii. 343 For some purposes tri-focal lenses are advocated. **1969** K. VONNEGUT *Slaughterhouse-Five* v. 93 She was wearing tri-focal lenses in harlequin frames.

B. *sb.* A trifocal lens; usu. *pl.*, trifocal spectacles.

1899 J. THORINGTON *Refraction* xi. 283 Trifocals.—Occasionally, a patient is not content with bifocals, but will demand a focal point somewhere between infinity and his working distance. **1946** BERENS & ZUCKERMAN *Diagnostic Examination of Eye* I. xii. 319 (*caption*) Double-segment panoptik trifocal for sculptors. **1962** L. S. SASIENI *Optical Dispensing* vii. 172 Where the gardener does not need a distance correction, the best combination may be reading and weak intermediate. A trifocal is the obvious alternative. **1973** R. HAYES *Hungarian Game* xxiv. 147 He was a pallid man with eyes that were weirdly distorted by trifocals.

trifunctional, -ally: see *TRI- 1 a.

trifurcate, *a.* Add: **tri·furcating** *vbl. sb.*, in *trifurcating box* (see quot. 1940).

1922 *B. I. Handbk.* (Brit. Insulated & Helsby Cables Ltd.) (ed. 3) 447 (Index), Trifurcating boxes. **1940** *Chambers's Techn. Dict.* 864/2 *Trifurcating box*, a cable dividing box for enclosing the joints between a three-arc or triple concentric cable and three single-core cables or conductor terminals.

trig, *sb.*[2] Add: *to toe the trig*: see *TOE *v.* 2.

trig, *a.*[2] and *sb.*[5] Colloq. abbrev. of TRIGONOMETRICAL *a.*, TRIGONOMETRY. Freq. as *trig point, station.*

1862 *McLean Papers* (MS.) XX. 87 Mr Swainson informs me that the Trig Station pulled down was not one erected by him. **1895** W. C. GORE in *Inlander* Nov. 65 *Trig.* n., trigonometry. **1924** P. MARKS *Plastic Age* 36 Kane announced the textbook, and when Hugh caught the word 'trigonometry' he actually thrilled with joy. He had had trig in high school. **1926** J. DEVANNY *Lenore Divine* xx. 184 They reached the trig station at the top, two thousand five hundred feet above sea-level. **1936** H. S. L. WINTERBOTHAM *Key to Maps* iii. 28 On the ordnance maps and plans you will find..little triangles with dots inside... Each one represents a place fixed by careful instrumental measurement, and the sum total represents the skeleton..upon which all our maps depend... 'Trig. Points', represented by the triangles, control the map in plan, 'Bench-marks' in height. **1959** J. BRAINE *Vodi* vi. 92 I've not done those trig. problems. **1968** G. R. CRONE *Maps & their Makers* xi. 143 Transference of the trig. points to the sheets issued to the plane tablers. **1976** J. LEE *Ninth Man* I. 48 Andy flunked trig for the second time (damn higher mathematics, anyway). **1981** *Times Lit. Suppl.* 22 May 577/1 Surveyors had to be trained [for Ordnance Survey mapmaking]; trig-points and bench-marks established.

trigenic, *a.* Add: **2.** *Genetics.* [cf. *GENIC *a.*] Involving or controlled by three genes.

1941 [see *POLYGENIC *a.* 3]. **1979** *Experientia* XXXV. 172/2 The trigenic ratios have been reported here for the first time for the above-mentioned characters.

trigger, *sb.*[1] Add: **3.** (Earlier examples of *quick on the trigger* and further *fig.* examples.)

1808 M. L. WEEMS *Let.* 22 Apr. in E. E. F. Skeel *M. L. Weems: Works & Ways* (1929) II. 377, I trust that all your Aids will be quick on the trigger. **1842** C. M. KIRKLAND *Forest Life* II. xlvii. 223 'Pretty quick on the trigger!' muttered Uncle William. **1887** G. H. DARWIN in *Leisure Hour* May 354/2 The attraction of the moon or the variation in atmospheric pressure pulls the trigger. **1946** *Lancet* 19 Jan. 97/1 A theory of the nervous initiation of contraction—the trigger without which voluntary muscle remains inert. **1961** M. LASKI *Ecstasy* ii. 16 Of the circumstances in which they found themselves when ecstasy took place, they identified certain objects, events, and ideas as standing in some kind of a causal relationship to their ecstatic experiences. These objects, events, and ideas I am calling *triggers*. **1977** J. L. HARPER *Population Biol. of Plants* 64 Triggers to development which predict a changing environment will generally be more efficient than those that are themselves the changed conditions.

3*. *Electronics.* **a.** A trigger circuit or trigger tube.

1945 *Electronic Engin.* XVII. 329/1 The charging circuit producing the used forward stroke operates continuously even through the flyback period when the trigger is conducting. **1946** [see *FLIP-FLOP *sb.* e]. **1962**, etc. [see *SCHMITT]. **1969** J. J. SPARKES *Transistor Switching* v. 126 The reasons should be understood for always using a negative-going trigger to drive *npn* transistors off rather than a positive one to drive them into the conducting state. **1981** J. C. SPROTT *Introd. Mod. Electronics* x. 239 The Schmitt trigger is useful..for generating square waves from a sinusoidal input.

b. A momentary signal or change in signal level that causes a change of state in a trigger tube or other device.

1948 *Gloss. Computer Terms* (Mass. Inst. Technol. Servomechanisms Lab. Rep. R-138) 11 *Trigger.* See *trigger pulse.* **1953** *Electronic Engin.* XXV. 143/1 A trigger derived from the phantastron is used to initiate the multivibrator circuit. **1979** M. M. MANO *Digital Logic & Computer Design* vi. 210 Asynchronous flip-flops ..require an input trigger defined by a change of signal level... Clocked flip-flops are triggered by pulses.

3.** A fission bomb built into a fusion bomb in order to initiate the fusion reaction.

1955 *Times* 13 Aug. 5/4 It was a question of arranging the proper conditions, and there was no reason why fusion energy should not be obtained without the use of a fission bomb as 'the trigger'. **1969** *Listener* 5 June 773/3 It's necessary to have a trigger made of an ordinary fission bomb, and there is good evidence that this must consist of fissile uranium or uranium-235 and not fissile plutonium. **1982** *New Scientist* 2 Sept. 642/1 The X-rays produced by the triggers are absorbed and re-emitted by an ellipsoidal casing of ^{238}U, and the fraction which is re-emitted inwards goes on to strike the main bulk of the thermo-nuclear fuel.

4. *trigger-action, effect, question, switch, word; trigger-pulling* adj.; **trigger circuit** *Electronics*, a circuit that behaves like a trigger tube; also, a circuit for producing a trigger pulse; **trigger-fish:** for 'the genus *Balistes'* substitute 'the family Balistidæ'; (earlier example); **trigger-happy** *a. colloq.* [*-HAPPY], over-ready to shoot at anything at any time or on slight provocation; also *transf.* and *fig.*; hence **trigger-happiness; trigger man** *slang* (chiefly *U.S.*), a gunman; a hired thug or bodyguard; also *fig.*; **trigger-point,** (*b*) *U.S.*, a price level at which price controls are imposed or re-imposed; **trigger price** *U.S.*, a minimum selling price for steel imported into the U.S., such that any steel imports below that price incur investigation to ensure that dumping is not taking place; **trigger pulse** *Electronics*, a pulse that acts as a trigger (sense 3* b above); **trigger tube** *Electronics*, a vacuum tube that has two operating states and changes rapidly from one to the other in response to a momentary application of, or change in, a signal.

1915 W. M. BAYLISS *Princ. Gen. Physiol.* x. 304 The difference between what is sometimes called 'trigger action' and catalysis. *Ibid.*, Supersaturated solutions are cases of 'trigger action'. They remain indefinitely as such until infected with a crystal, and then the rate of crystallisation is independent of the amount of crystals added. **1950** A. HUXLEY *Lett.* (1969) 623 Trivial acts of selfishness and wantonness may release, as though by a kind of trigger action, a huge avalanche of tragic destiny. **1938** *Rev. Sci. Instruments* IX. 223/1 Another trigger circuit which has inherent possibilities as a counting circuit is shown in Fig. 2. **1951, 1962** [see *BISTABLE *a.*]. **1974** A. VAN DER ZIEL *Introd. Electronics* xi. 262 (*caption*) Transistor monostable circuit with trigger circuit. **1931** *Prof. Papers Inst. Post Office Electr. Engineers* No. 136. 19 The adjustments were such as to avoid definitely the 'trigger' effect. **1949** M. MEAD *Male & Female* x. 218 In the..patterning of a woman's sexual receptivity now one part of the body, now another,..may be sensitive enough to develop a trigger effect. **1849** H. MELVILLE *Mardi* I. xlviii. 131 The rank and file of the Trigger-fish—so called from their quaint dorsal fins being set in their backs with a conical curve, as if at half-cock. **1945** C. BURNEY *Dungeon Democracy* III. 82 There was much trigger-happiness, men shooting each other, shooting themselves and shooting into thin air. **1970** *Daily Tel.* 23 Mar. 16 The trigger-happiness with which workers are now ready and eager to enforce their fantastically increased claims by industrial action..leaves Britain with the choice between being ruined by runaway inflation or by a series of disastrous strikes. **1978** N. FREELING *Night Lords* xxi. 95 Suddenly she said 'Have you killed people?'..I thought it the usual accusation of trigger-happiness. **1943** F. J. BELL *Condition Red* 190 Yes, they missed us, and the *G* hereby absolves whoever it was along that section of coast that got a little trigger-happy early one December morning. **1946** *Archit. Rev.* CI. 47/1 On the Acropolis itself a group of trigger-happy gendarmerie lounged with an assumed nonchalance by the lower entrance. **1957** *Time* 2 Sept. 19/1 Some trigger-happy U.S. radio commentators ..helped confuse it further by proclaiming that Syria was already Russia's newest satellite. **1971** H. WILSON *Labour Govt.* xxxvi. 937 It was fairly clear that the main issues now were relief and the avoidance of atrocities, which, if they occurred, would be most likely to be caused by trigger-happy young soldiers. **1974** F. WARNER *Meeting Ends* I. ii. 7 If only you knew how trigger-happy he is when he gets a dialling tone. **1984** *Miami Herald* 6 Apr. 12 A/2 We have a president who is trigger-happy and who commits troops for impossible missions. **1930** *Amer. Mercury* Dec. 458/2 *Trigger man*, an assassin; a body guard. 'He's trigger man for Big Tony.' **1934** *Sun* (Baltimore) 22 Aug. 13/1, I was the triggerman in both hold-ups. **1954** 'N. BLAKE' *Whisper in Gloom* iii. 42 A graceful, self-possessed, cat-like walk..the tread of the trigger-man. **1974** *Times* 2 May 6/5 P[resident]... You feel that really the trigger man was really Colson on this thing? D[ean] No... He was just in the chain. **1977** *Hongkong Standard* 12 Apr. 9/3 He was said to be a senior triggerman—an overseer of 'hit men'—for reputed mob boss Anthony 'Big Tuna' Accardo. **1981** W. SAFIRE in *N.Y. Times Mag.* 1 Mar. 9/3 The triggerman of this slim but explosive volume is described on the cover as 'formerly professor of Romance languages and literatures at Harvard University, where he is now emeritus professor'. **1952** *N.Y. Times* (Late City Ed.) 12 Aug. 32/6 The federation estimates that at the beginning of suspension the average of current prices was 69.39 per cent of their 1951 highs, which meant that they could rise a little more than 15 per cent before reaching the so-called 'trigger-point'. **1979** H. KISSINGER *White House Years* ix. 330, I had to learn an entire vocabulary of international trade, such as 'export subsidy techniques' as well as the arcane complexity of 'trigger points' (at which restraints would go into effect). **1978** *Business Week* 23 Jan. 25/2 (*heading*) Steel trigger-prices start sowing discord. *Ibid.* 26/3 Jack Meyer, assistant director of the Council on Wage & Price Stability, which devised the trigger-price system. **1981** *Economist* 24 Jan. 88/1 The renewal of trigger prices last October coincided with a recovery in demand for, eg, tubes for the oil and gas industry, plates and girders for process plant and construction. **1924** J. A. THOMSON *Sci. Old & New* xix. 105 A current of air is necessary as the trigger-pulling stimulus. **1946** *Radar: Summary Rep. & Harp Project* (U.S. Nat. Defense Comm., Div. 14) 144/2 *Trigger pulse*, a pulse which starts a cycle of operations. **1956** *IRE Trans. Electronic Computers* V. 124/1 For trigger pulses of a few mμsec duration there will be little or no interference between the trigger pulse and the change of voltage at the cathodes of the EFP-60's. **1981** J. D. LENK *Handbk. Digital Electronics* ii. 84 The circuit changes state only when both the input pulse and a clock pulse are present simultaneously. (The clock pulse is also known as a gate pulse or trigger pulse.) **1927** J. ADAMS *Errors in School* 213 In external written examinations, where..the clever pupil..is led astray by expecting a question, and then treating one of the questions actually set as the one he expected. These 'trigger questions', as they may be called, set off the candidate on the wrong track. **1973** T. PYNCHON *Gravity's Rainbow* (1975) I. 147 Hyperkinetically, waiting only the right trigger-question to start blithering 200 words a minute about their special, terrible endowments. **1952** 'J. WYNDHAM' in *Galaxy Sci. Fiction* July 72/1 He brought the cutter up, and pressed the trigger-switch. **1894** *Electrician* 15 June 188/1 Zehnder's trigger tube. **1939** H. J. REICH *Theory & Applications of Electron Tubes* vii. 208 A single pentode may also be used as a trigger tube. **1978** R. V. JONES *Most Secret War* viii. 69 My first step was to take the electronic trigger tube down to my former colleagues at the Admiralty Research Laboratory, to get them to evaluate its performance. **1975** *Listener* 17 July 74/1 Those of us who work in radio..rely on trigger words, Pavlovian clichés which become a kind of bogus mental shorthand.

trigger (tri·gəɹ), *v.* [f. TRIGGER *sb.*[1]] **1.** *trans.* To act as a 'trigger' (sense 3) for, causing another event (esp. a chain reaction) to occur; to stimulate or 'set off'; to activate, to bring about; to spark *off* (an idea, etc.). Also *lit.*, to pull (depress, etc.) the trigger of (a gun or other device).

1930 R. CAMPBELL *Adamastor* 94 When life is triggered by a hair And stands upon the peak of death. **1938** *Sun* (Baltimore) 18 Apr. 8/5 Denmark, whose people thrive on thrift, milk, bacon and eggs, and never need 'triggering' into activity by shot-in-the-arm spendings of borrowed billions. **1948** *Sat. Even. Post* 20 Mar. 39/3 There is certainly no lack of evidence that the typical glaucoma patient has a nervous temperament and that emotional episodes will increase the pressure within the eyeball and even trigger off acute attacks. **1949** *Sun* (Baltimore) 26 Sept. 4/1 The strike..was triggered by two rival AFL unions. **1950** *Ibid.* 21 July 14/3 A system by which the powers are prepared but lie dormant until triggered into action by specific congressional action is the ideal. **1958** W. J. H. SPROTT *Human Groups* 163 May it not be that a crowd is 'triggered off' by people whose 'thresholds of mob-involvement'..are low? **1958** *Spectator* 19 Sept. 379/1 But as a space-veteran who once triggered a ray-gun with Flash Gordon, let me advise you to read on. **1958** *Listener* 23 Oct. 648/2 Artists like Joan Mitchell, Al Leslie..have all been triggered by de Kooning's example. **1959** *Ibid.* 18 June 1083/2 Sir Faithful Fortescue..whose loyalties were so finely triggered that he rode across from Parliament side to Royalist. **1968** J. D. McCAWLEY in Bach & Harms *Universals in Linguistic Theory* 168 Chomsky..in effect asserts that all lexical insertion takes place in the base component unless triggered by other transformations. **1972** *Amateur Photographer* 12 Jan. 42/2 (*caption*) Recently there have been a number of flash meters on the market which, when placed at the subject position read out the correct f/stop to use when the flash is triggered. **1973** C. BONINGTON *Next Horizon* xiii. 190 We tiptoed up the snow, hardly daring to talk, as if the resonance of our voices might trigger off an avalanche. **1977** *New Yorker* 5 Sept. 80/3 Before I improvise, I just listen, and that triggers me. **1978** S. SHELDON *Bloodline* xlii. 361 His eyes were fixed on the ribbon that the girl was wearing around her neck. It triggered a memory. **1978** *New York* 3 Apr. 10/1 The Israeli invasion of Lebanon and the mass murder that triggered it have nearly obliterated from the public consciousness the killing of Egyptian editor Yousef el-Sebai. **1981** *Times* 5 May 15/7 The fact that no danger signals were triggered during the growth of Norton Warburg has alarmed the City.

2. *Electronics.* **a.** To initiate a change of state or a cycle of behaviour in (a device).

1937 *Proc. Cambr. Philos. Soc.* XXXIII. 551 In order that it may be used in a scale-of-two counter, it is necessary to provide some simple means of triggering the circuit, that is to say changing from one stable state to the other. **1945** *Electronic Engin.* XVII. 473 A differential circuit and pulse generator which triggers a thyratron. **1967** *Electronics* 6 Mar. 160/1 A d-c flip-flop is triggered by the leading edge and clamped until the pulse is removed. **1974** A. VAN DER ZIEL *Introd. Electronics* xi. 262 A monostable multivibrator is a circuit that goes through a complete wave form when triggered.

b. *intr.* Of an electronic device: to change state in response to a momentarily applied signal.

1933 *P.O. Electr. Engineers' Jrnl.* XXVI. 63/2 A tube is now manufactured capable of 'triggering' both 'on' and 'off'. **1967** [see *SCHMITT].

Hence **tri·ggered** *ppl. a.*, furnished with or activated by a trigger; **tri·ggering** *vbl. sb.* (freq. *attrib.*) and *ppl. a.*

1944 *Electronic Engin.* XVI. 380 The harmonics generated in the circuit provide standard frequencies.. for..high speed triggering etc. **1945** *Electronic Industries* Sept. 226 *Triggered spark gap*, a fixed spark gap in which the discharge passes between two electrodes and is struck (started) by a subsidiary electrode, the trigger, to which low power pulses are applied at regular intervals from a pulse amplifier, thus closing the switch. **1958** K. AMIS *I like it Here* xii. 152 The sight of it at this moment must have had some triggering effect on Bowen's alimentary canal. **1962** *Listener* 3 May 770/2 This would involve installing a 'triggering' device in the vehicle. **1967** *Ibid.* 30 Nov. 694/1 The triggered responses which might deter me..no longer apply. **1972** *Language* XLVIII. 299 Identity-of-reference deletions involve two coreferential NP's, a vanishing NP and a triggering NP. I propose that the rule of deletion..superimpose the vanishing NP over the triggering NP, keeping both NP nodes. **1977** J. L. HARPER *Population Biol. Plants* xviii. 520 Most of these annuals have a precisely triggered transition from the vegetative to reproductive phase depending on photoperiod. **1977** SAVAGE & RUMBAUGH in D. M. Rumbaugh *Language Learning by Chimpanzee* xvi. 289 Hockett.. defined communication as an act by which one individual 'triggered' the behavior of another ('triggering' in this sense implies that the energy expended during the output of a communicative pattern is unrelated to the energy of the response).

triggerable (tri·gərăb'l), *a.* [f. *TRIGGER *v.* + -ABLE.] Susceptible to triggering.

1964 *Anesthesiology* XXV. 200/1 You will need both triggerable and automatic respirators. **1973** *New England Jrnl. Med.* 4 Oct. 735/1 If such triggerable foci, in which spontaneous activity can be either initiated or terminated by the appropriately timed arrival of a propagated impulse, exist in depressed areas of the heart they might well serve to initiate or sustain fibrillation.

trigonal, *a.* (*sb.*) Add: **1. c.** *Chem.* Characterized by three orbitals lying in a plane and directed to the corners of an equilateral triangle.

1939 L. PAULING *Nature Chem. Bond* 429/2 (Index), Trigonal bond orbitals. **1961** A. STREITWIESER *Molecular Orbital Theory* i. 20 Linear combinations of *s*- and two of the *p*-orbitals result in three trigonal sp^2-orbitals. **1979** B. M. GIMARC *Molecular Struct. & Bonding* iv. 79 These complexes are mainly trigonal bipyramidal..in structure with the bonds to the axial ligands..being slightly longer than those to the equatorial ligands.

trigonally *adv.*, restrict *rare*$^{-0}$ to sense in Dict. and add: (*b*) *Chem.*, in a trigonal manner.

1962 P. J. & B. DURRANT *Introd. Adv. Inorganic Chem.* xviii. 590 (*heading*) Compounds in which the carbon atom is trigonally hybridised. **1982** *Nature* 25 Feb. 658/1 The borates, where trigonally and tetrahedrally bonded atoms may occur.

trigonitis (tri-, trəigonəi·tis). *Med.* [f. TRIGON(E + -ITIS.] Inflammation of the trigone of the bladder.

1900 in DORLAND *Med. Dict.* **1912** R. GUITERAS *Urology* II. lxiii. 508 Gonorrhea of the neck of the bladder, trigonitis, is not uncommon. **1974** J. D. MAYNARD in R. M. Kirk et al. *Surgery* viii. 178/1 In young women, urethral trauma from intercourse commonly leads to recurrent attacks of urethritis and trigonitis.

trigonometrical, *a.* Add: *trigonometrical point, station*, a reference point on high ground, usu. marked by a small pyramidal structure, used in triangulation.

1860 Trigonometrical station [in Dict.]. **1886** T. P. WHITE *Ordnance Survey of U.K.* iv. 68 In very many cases the old trigonometrical points were again observed to or from. **1949** T. W. BIRCH *Maps* vi. 56 The *trigonometrical points* or *stations* determined by theodolite are accurately plotted on the plane-table sheet.

trigram. Add: **a.** *spec.* in *Psychol.*, a (nonsense) word of three letters used in the study of learning or memory (see esp. quot. 1960).

1960 E. J. ARCHER in *Psychol. Monogr.* LXXIV. x. 1/2 This study is a re-evaluation of the meaningfulness of all possible three-letter combinations of the Roman alphabet of the form consonant-vowel-consonant... It is herewith proposed to call these combinations 'trigrams', and in view of their form to further specify them as 'CVC trigrams'. **1970** *Jrnl. General Psychol.* LXXXIII. 214 The study..assumes that an object elicits a given number of mediating responses with which a CVC trigram can be associated. **1973** *Jrnl. Genetic Psychol.* CXXIII. 15 Correct recognitions of trigrams on test trials.

b. Also *spec.*, a figure traditionally used in the Chinese philosophy of the I Ching for the purposes of divination.

1877 J. LEGGE in *Encycl. Brit.* VI. 263/2 The *Yih King* ..the rudiments of which are assigned to Fuh-hsi in the 30th century B.C. Those rudiments, however, are merely the 8 trigrams and 64 diagrams, composed of a whole and a broken line. **1923** J. P. BRUCE *Chu Hsi & his Masters* vi. 127 The Grand Terminus..produced the two elementary Forms. These two Forms produced the four Symbols, which, again, produced the eight Trigrams. The eight Trigrams served to determine the good and evil issues of events. **1957, 1965** [see *I CHING]. **1974** *Sci. Amer.* Jan. 108/2 There are two ancient ways of displaying the eight trigrams in a circle.

trigrammatic, *a.* For quot. 1834 substitute: **1824** T. YOUNG in *Suppl. Encycl. Brit.* IV. 43/1 The 'trilinguar' or rather trigrammatic Stone of Rosetta.

trihybrid (trəihəi·brid), *a.* [f. TRI- + HYBRID *sb.* and *a.*] **1.** *Genetics.* Of or pertaining to a hybrid that is heterozygous with respect to three independent genes.

1918 *Genetics* III. 591 The undepleted litters in our trihybrid ratio show a suggestive order or arrangement of frequencies.

2. Involving or pertaining to a descent from three different races or types that interbred.

1941 TINDALE & BIRDSELL in *Records S. Austral. Museum* VII. i. 6 The Australian aboriginal no longer may be considered as a pure race of unusual homogeneity, but a well-blended group of at least dihybrid and probably trihybrid origin. **1969** A. A. ABBIE *Original Australians* xi. 215 My own observation on Aborigines in many parts of Australia have not disclosed the physical differences the 'trihybrid theory' demands. **1979** *Nature* 15 Nov. 298/2 In spite of an earlier model postulating a trihybrid origin, a theory favouring a homogeneous colonising stock had gained some acceptance.

trihydrocalcite: see *TRI- 5 c.

trihydrol (trəihəi·drǫl). *Chem. Obs.* exc. *Hist.* [f. TRI- + *HYDROL.] A supposed trimer of water, $(H_2O)_3$, formerly thought to be present especially in ice.

1900 [see *HYDROL 2]. **1932** *Proc. Nat. Acad. Sci.* XVIII. 136 (*heading*) The physiological effect of trihydrol in water. **1957** [see *HYDROL 2]. **1972** H. S. FRANK in F. Franks *Water* I. xiv. 531 Many of the detailed models ..have been overtaken by events and are now of hardly more than historical interest. Perhaps the classic example of such obsolescence is found in the theory put forward in 1900..representing water as a mixture of monohydrol (monomeric, steamlike), dihydrol (dimeric, intrinsically liquid), and trihydrol (trimeric, icelike) molecules.

triiodothyronine: see *TRI- 5 c.

tri-jet (trəi·jet). Also **trijet.** [f. TRI- + JET *sb.*[3]] An aircraft powered by three jet engines. Freq. *attrib.*, as *tri-jet airbus, transport.*

1968 *Economist* 20 Apr. 24/3 Last month Eastern Air Lines and Trans World Airlines jumped in with orders to the Lockheed Aircraft Corporation for 94 of the new-look tri-jet transports. **1969** *New Scientist* 13 Mar. 554/2 The tri-jet air bus to carry 350 is on the way. **1970** *Time* 19 Jan. 44 Originally designed for shorter-range routes than the 747, the trijets are now being offered in stretched intercontinental versions. **1979** *Daily Tel.* 17 Apr. 8/8 Boeing..will be extremely busy introducing two new twin-jet airliners and possibly a tri-jet as well.

trike. Colloq. abbrev. of TRICYCLE *sb.* and *v.* or (*rarely*) of TRICYCLIST. Hence **tri·ker**; **tri·king** *vbl. sb.*

1883 *Sporting Life* 22 Apr. 6/5 Londoners call bicyclists 'bikes' and tricyclists 'trikes'. **1884** *Wheel World* Apr. 495/2 The makers of his new trike. **1885** *N. & Q.* 14 Nov. 386/1 Do you *bike* or *trike*? **1890** BARRÈRE & LELAND *Dict. Slang* II. 374/1 *Trike*, (common) a tricycle; *triking*, cycling. Do you bike or trike? do you ride a bicycle or a tricycle? **1901** *Pall Mall Gaz.* 15 May 1, I was further gratified with the intimation that the peccant triker had been discovered. **1912** A. S. M. HUTCHINSON *Happy Warrior* III. v. 148 I'm all mixed up in this awful trike, you know. **1939** X. HERBERT *Capricornia* xiii. 185 There is no fixed time for those who wish to come by horse or trike. Just roll up when you like. **1939–40** *Army & Navy Stores Catal.* 827/1 *Trike*..for ages 3 to 7 years. **1972** *Oxford Times* 4 Feb. 17 An Oxford doctor has condemned the three-wheeled invalid trikes as 'tin coffins'. **1977** *Times* 9 Aug. 5/7 Many disabled people are now turning from the 'to trike or not to trike' argument. **1984** *N.Z. Farmer* 23 Feb. 31/2 (*caption*) Honda farm bikes and trikes remain one of the strongest sellers in Motor Holdings' lineup.

b. A kind of ultralight aircraft.

1981 M. A. MARKOWSKI *Ultralight Aircraft* 45 The trike appears to be a viable approach to ultralight flight and allows thousands of hang gliders to be powered, as desired. **1982** *Sci. Amer.* July 63/1 A trike (from tricycle) is a pyramidal tubular frame that holds the engine, the pilot's seat and the landing gear.

Trike, var. *TRIQUE *sb.* and *a.*

trikini (trəikī·ni). Also **tri-kini, Tri-Kini.** [f. TRI-, after *BIKINI b, with reference to BI-[2].] Any of various designs of ladies' swimsuit which consist of three main areas of fabric (as pants and a separate covering for each breast).

1967 *Scottish Daily Mail* 7 June 12 Some ingenious fellow has just come up with a Tri-Kini, best described as a handkerchief and two small saucers. The saucers, say the manufacturers, stick on with Velcro, the stuff which fastens at a touch. **1968** *Sunday Truth* (Brisbane) 8 Sept. 1/2 She is wearing the new trikini swimsuit which is to make its debut in Australia next summer. **1970** *Telegraph* (Brisbane) 20 Feb. 15/5 When is a bikini a trikini? When it's a suntanner of a swimsuit like this..deeply decolette [*sic*] and, to put it briefly, even briefer.

trilateral, *a.* Add: **2.** Pertaining to or concerning three countries, parties, etc., esp. with reference to the relations between Europe, the United States, and Japan; *the Trilateral Commission* (see quots. 1973, 1981).

1965 *Economist* 20 Feb. 758/1 Ethiopia. A trilateral agreement is being negotiated with the object of harnessing German and American help in forming an Ethiopian frontier defence force. **1973** *N.Y. Times* 2 Mar. 35/1 A group of distinguished private citizens in the United States, Japan and Europe are now organizing what they call 'the trilateral commission' to study the common problems of these three power centers. **1977** *Times* 28 Apr. 7/4 Mr Jimmy Carter..really believes in what has been called the trilateral system of America, Europe and Japan. **1981** *Washington Post* 18 Mar. A1/2 For the record, the Trilateral Commission is a New York-based policy group formed by Rockefeller in 1973 in a reaction to the nationalistic foreign economic policy of President Nixon, which disturbed some traditional U.S. allies. **1984** *Times* 5 Mar. 12/2 It was thanks to the complicated trilateral arrangement worked out in secret..that he was taken to Pakistan.

Hence **trila·teralism; trila·teralist.**

1976 R. H. ULLMAN in *Foreign Affairs* Oct. 1 'Trilateralism'..is the latest attempt both to describe and to prescribe for the relationship between the United States and the other principal democratic, industrialized, market-economy states. **1977** *Studia Diplomatica* XXX. 231 Dr Kissinger can hardly be said to have been unaware of the 'Trilateralists'. **1977** *Foreign Policy* No. 29. 90 The original trilateralism, which links prominent citizens of the United States, Western Europe, and Japan in an international 'commission', arises from the shared ideological commitment of its members to liberal values and politics. The goals of Arab trilateralism, however, are not expressed in ideological terms. **1981** *Washington Post* 18 Mar. A1/2 Remember those dreaded, three-sided Trilateralists, the international conspirators headed by David Rockefeller who were going to take over the world? *Ibid.* A5/6 But old fears die hard, and the far right is ever-vigilant for signs of creeping Trilateralism within the citadel.

trilateration (trəilætĕrē[i]·ʃən). [f. TRI- + L. *later-, latus* side + -ATION.] A method of surveying analogous to triangulation in which each triangle is determined by the measurement of all three sides.

1948 *Bull. Géodésique* No. 10. 342 A network of triangles may be computed and adjusted from observed lengths of sides. The development of error in trilateration is different from that in triangulation..as the side error is not accumulative. **1952** G. BOMFORD *Geodesy* i. 34 It might be possible to use radar trilateration between ground points instead of ordinary geodetic triangulation. **1960** *Times* 4 Mar. 3/2 Experienced in first order triangulation, trilateration and astro-fixes. **1974** *Physics Bull.* Apr. 136/3 A geodetic network was established to an accuracy of 2 mm over the surface of the Laboratory II site using triangulation and trilateration.

trilby (tri·lbi). Also **Trilby.** Pl. **trilbies** or **trilbys.** [The title of a novel by George du Maurier published in 1894, and the name of its heroine.] **1.** *colloq.* **a.** A jocular name for the foot (with reference to Trilby's feet, which were objects of admiration). ? *Obs.*

1895 *People* 7 July, An American paper has spent its energy of psychological investigation on the foot (I beg pardon, the trilby). **1907** H. E. Dudeney *Canterbury Puzzles* 114 'Two feet—' he murmured. 'Somebody's Trilbys?' I inquired. **1932** U. Sinclair *Candid Reminiscences* I. v. 29 There was a book by the name of 'Trilby', which the ladies blushed to hear spoken of... I knew it had something to do with feet, because thereafter my father always called them 'trilbies'.

† **b.** A particular type of shoe. (Formerly a proprietary name in the U.S.) *Obs.*

1895 *Official Gaz.* (U.S. Patent Office) 16 Apr. 447/1 Boots, shoes and lasts. S. Weil & Co., New York... 'Trilby'. Essential feature—the word 'Trilby'. Used since October 1, 1894. **1895** *Montgomery Ward Catal.* Spring & Summer 509/3 The Trilby... The very latest in ladies' footwear. **1897** *Sears, Roebuck Catal.* 192/1 Our New Trilby... The accompanying cut is an exact reproduction of our new Trilby Shoe.

2. In full *trilby hat*: a soft felt hat, esp. one of the Homburg type with a narrow brim and indented crown; any hat of a similar shape.

[**1895** *Bradford Daily Argus* 12 Nov. 1/8, I have been puzzling my head to account for the reason of so many soft hats being worn at present, and at last I have hit it. It is another phase of the 'Trilby' complaint. In one of the illustrations of the book Little Billee is 'discovered' wearing a hat of this description, so it has been seized upon by those worshippers at the shrine of Trilby, whom nature will not assist in the cultivation of a Svenjali [*sic*] beard or Taffy whiskers.] **1897** *Daily News* 6 Feb. 6/5 In the struggle Mr. Bennett lost his hat, a black 'Trilby'... Mr. Carr..was also wearing a black 'Trilby' hat. **1915** E. Wallace *Man who bought London* iii. 33 He turned sharply to the young man in the trilby hat. **1927** W. Deeping *Kitty* v. 63 The window-sill being a low one Mrs Sarah had a good view of Vernor Street, and the passing of the khaki caps, bowlers, 'Trilbys' and cloth caps. **1958** *Observer* 9 Feb. 11/5 Three men in trilbies and a woman with straggly hair. **1978** *Lancashire Life* Apr. 67/1 Fred was a dapper dresser, and I like to remember him in Summer, wearing a medium-grey lightweight suit, black patent shoes, a beautifully-arranged lilac-coloured pure silk cravat with a massive diamond stick-pin, and a natural straw Trilby. **1979** 'J. le Carré' *Smiley's People* (1980) xxi. 258 Toby..had given him a trilby hat.

Hence **tri·lbied, tri·lby-hatted** *adjs.*, wearing a trilby hat.

1966 *Punch* 12 Jan. 45/2 'Tell him about Indonesia, Dave,' cried a small, trilbied man. **1975** M. Simpson *Chrome Connection* ii. 25 The trilby-hatted husband.. gave her a curious look.

Trilene (trəi·līn). *Pharm.* Also **trilene.** [f. *tri(chloroethy)lene.] A proprietary name for a medicinal grade of trichloroethylene, used as an analgesic and light anæsthetic.

1935 *Trade Marks Jrnl.* 13 Feb. 184/1 *Trilene*... Medicated preparations of trichlorethylene for human use. Imperial Chemical Industries Limited,..Millbank, London. *Ibid.* 20 Feb. 214/1 *Trilene*... Trichlorethylene for veterinary and sanitary purposes. Imperial Chemical Industries Limited. **1941** *Brit. Med. Jrnl.* 21 June 925/1 We..found that this firm was already manufacturing, under the trade name of 'trilene', a purified form of the substance specially prepared for medical purposes, though with no reference to inhalation or general anaesthesia. **1944** *Official Gaz.* (U.S. Patent Office) 18 Jan. 349/1 *Trilene* for anaesthetic for cleansing wounds and for the alleviation of pain. **1966** *New Statesman* 8 July 47/3 Where we had practised my wife was completely able to use the breathing for her own purposes, even under the sleepy drug. She never used her Trilene machine at all. **1971** H. Pacy *Road Accidents* ii. 51 Trilene inhalers.. provide mild analgesia and are used by the casualties themselves. **1979** G. Bourne *Pregnancy* (rev. ed.) xxiv. 365 The indications and the technique for Trilene analgesia are essentially similar to those described for nitrous oxide and oxygen analgesia.

tri-level, *a.* and *sb.* *N. Amer.* Also **trilevel.** [f. Tri- + Level *sb.*] **A.** *adj.* Having or consisting of three levels; (of a house, etc.) having three storeys or floors on three levels. Cf. *split-level *a.* **B.** *sb.* A tri-level house.

1960 V. Packard *Waste Makers* i. 8 Workingmen today..want their tri-level house in the suburbs. **1965** P. Wylie *They both were Naked* I. ii. 55 Coming down the staircase in Will's suburban home, a tri-level, if there's such a term. **1973** 'D. Shannon' *No Holiday for Crime* iii. 34 Pershing Square with the tri-level parking lot under it. **1974** *Car & Locomotive Cycl.* (ed. 3) S1-25/1 *Tri-level car*, a flat car designed with integral superstructure of posts, bracings and decking to permit triple level loading of automobiles. **1976** *Casper* (Wyoming) *Star-Tribune* 29 June 16/5 (Advt.), Stretch out in over 2000 sq. ft. of tri-level located on 1.8 acres. **1979** *Arizona Daily Star* 5 Aug. (Advt. Section) 16/7 This tri-level showplace home is ideal for entertaining and family living. **1979** *United States 1980/81* (Penguin Travel Guides) 432 Today this tri-level arcade features chic boutiques and restaurants.

trilingualism (trəili·ŋgwăliz'm). [f. Trilingual *a.* + -ism.] The ability to speak three languages; the use of three languages.

1934 H. V. Morton *In Steps of Master* i. 5 And as you go into Jerusalem, glancing at the trilingualism everywhere, the words of St. John come into the mind. **1956** *Nature* 18 Feb. 343/2 If we take into consideration languages read as well as written, no language group can to-day avoid even trilingualism if it wishes to attain the highest standards of culture and scholarship. **1976** *Word 1971* XXVII. 388 The scope of this article constrains us from adding still a third dimension, where more than a language pair is involved, such as the Yaqui-English-Spanish trilingualism of Pascua, near Tucson, Arizona.

trilinguar, *a.* **b.** (Earlier example.)

1824 [see *trigrammatic *a.*]

triliterality. (Earlier example.)

1864 *Ann. Rep. Smithsonian Inst. 1863* 109 Their [*sc.* the Semitic languages'] most fundamental peculiarity is the triliterality of their roots, every Semitic verbal root containing just three consonants.

trillet. (Earlier *lit.* example.)

1867 G. Meredith *Vittoria* I. ii. 25 We require to be refreshed with quavers and crescendos and trillets.

trillion. Add: The sense 'a thousand "billions", or 10^{12}' is now standard in the U.S. and is increasingly common in British usage. (Further examples.)

1919 *Evening Star* (Washington, D.C.) 12 Mar. 2/7 The consideration of reparations has introduced the word 'trillion' in recognizing money... In estimating the war losses of all the powers the first figures of one of the great powers aggregated a trillion francs and those of another power were slightly above a half trillion francs, namely, six hundred billion francs. **1971** *Daily Tel.* 30 Jan. 13 For the current calendar year the 'magic trillion' will be with us. The [American] budget assumed a 9 p.c. growth in GNP this year to $1,065,000 million. **1975** *New Yorker* 21 Apr. 48/1 About two trillion dollars' worth of insurance alone is currently in force. **1980** *Guardian Weekly* 30 Nov. 8/1 Plans to devote a trillion dollars to US military spending over the next five years. **1982** *Nature* 1 July 9/1 Compositions of many important trace species are in the parts per trillion (10^{-12}) by volume range.

trilobal, *a.* Delete *rare*$^{-1}$ and add: *spec.* applied to (man-made fibres having) a cross-section of this form.

1961 *Times Rev. Industry* Mar. 33/3 Bri-nylon 61.. owes its softness of handle and subdued, silky lustre to the trilobal cross-section of the individual filaments. **1965** *Guardian* 31 Mar. 13/4 In America textured yarns of heavier denier tri-lobal..nylon have made a big hit in dress jersey. **1979** *Men's Wear* 24 May 34/1 Tri-lobal polyester and viscose do much the same.

trilobe (trəi·lōᵘb), *a.* *rare.* [f. Tri- + Lobe.] Having three lobes, trilobate.

1931 *Antiquity* V. 272 One is reminded of the trilobe cranial amulet found in a La Tène context. **1950** A. L. Rowse *Expansion Elizabethan England* i. 36 Pendennis and St. Mawes castles,..the latter a perfect..specimen of a Henrician fort of trilobe design, both planned by a German military engineer.

trim, *sb.* Add: **I.** For 'Nautical' read 'Nautical and Aeronautical'. **2. f.** The position of a submarine with respect to the angle between its longitudinal axis and the horizontal.

1917 *Chambers's Jrnl.* Aug. 557/2 When his boat was diving he had to be careful how he changed his position; otherwise the 'trim' was in danger of being upset. **1935** *Sun* (Baltimore) 14 Feb. 8/2 All ballast and emergency fuel dump tanks in the after part of the ship were dropped, and gas was valved from the forward gas cells in an effort to regain the trim. **1942** *Gen* 1 Aug. 3/1 Once out of the harbour the submarine dives for trim and, having caught the trim, she surfaces again. **1974** M. Hebden *Pride of Dolphins* II. ix. 186 Navigation..is what you will be chiefly responsible for. Navigation and trim. *Ibid.* III. ii. 224 Addams did a trim dive before he left.

2*. The position of an aircraft with respect to the angle between its longitudinal axis and the horizontal; the condition of static balance of the aerodynamic forces on an aircraft in straight flight; a device or action used to maintain such balance. Freq. *attrib.*

1919 W. B. Faraday *Gloss. Aeronaut. Terms* 17 *Trim*, the inclination to the horizontal of the longitudinal axis when the aerostat is floating freely at rest. **1935** C. G. Burge *Compl. Bk. Aviation* 242/2 A trim of this kind may also be useful on a very powerful fighting aeroplane of small span. **1944** *Times* 3 Apr. 2/4 With the elevator trims gone, the Lancaster was tending to climb all the time. **1962** J. Glenn in *Into Orbit* 12 The enemy shell had knocked out part of my trim controls. **1968** M. Woodhouse *Rock Baby* xxvii. 250 Yancy corrected trim. We flew another mile. **1977** D. Beaty *Excellency* vi. 78 He studied the load and trim sheet. *Ibid.* 81 He took his right hand off the stick, grabbed the trim wheel to push it forward... He let go of the trim, brought his right hand back. *Ibid.* 82 With the aircraft so badly out of trim, the autopilot refused to cope. **1982** J. Savarin *Water Hole* 173 He found the trim to his liking, switched on the auto pilot and relaxed.

II. 3. d. (Later examples.)

1931 G. A. Foan *Art & Craft of Hairdressing* iii. 134/1 It must be realized, however, that this is a shingle *trim*, that the work must be done more lightly, and that..less hair will be removed. **1955** H. D. Steiner *Crowning Glory* iii. 30 The main business of the hair dresser is to see that both the trim and set accord with the natural convolutions of the hair. **1977** D. Bennett *Jigsaw Man* viii. 141 He left with two wigs and an appointment to come back for a trim. **1983** *Chicago Sun-Times* 15 Nov. 41/1 (*heading*) Too few trims in new budget.

e. Delete † *Obs.* (Later examples.)

1948 H. Pepin *Fund. Apparel Design* vi. 137/2 This asymmetrically balanced motif proved suitable for border trim on sleeve. **1964** [see *beading *vbl. sb.* 2 b]. **1982** W. Boyd *Ice-Cream War* I. i. 7 The women all wore white dresses with lacy trims and carried parasols.

g. *U.S.* A shop-window display.

1899 *Harman's Jrnl.* Feb. 7/1 The design for a [men's] furnishing trim..by Harry Harold of Milwaukee, Wis., a window trimmer, is a very clever arrangement. **1926** *Publishers' Weekly* 30 Jan. 328/1 A large red ribbon rosette, from which radiated white satin ribbons to a number of stands at each side of the trim. *Ibid.* 10 July 119/2 When Stone's trim was removed, Wheatly did his 'stuff'. **1945** J. Bradford *Retail Merchandiser's Handbk.* xi. 62 Try to liven up a window as much as possible by using new, bright, and flashy display trims.

h. Ornamental additions or finishings to a vehicle, piece of furniture, or other article; *spec.* the upholstery or interior lining of a motor car. Cf. *trimming *vbl. sb.* 2 c. orig. *U.S.*

1922 *Automobile Trimmer & Painter* Aug. 50/1 The Franklin trim is designed to give a maximum degree of resiliency and durability in order to match these qualities in the rest of the car. **1936** C. W. Seager *Upholstered Furniture* vii. 54 Trim serves the double purpose of concealing the raw edges and seams and supplying a decorative note. **1950** Pomeroy & Walkerley *Motor Year Bk.* 23 Throughout the range is an attractive style of trim incorporating contrasting piping round the edges of the seats. **1957** *Practical Wireless* XXXIII. 532/1 This model costs 98 guineas, and the bow-fronted cabinet is veneered in walnut with gilt trim. **1961** *B.S.I. News* Aug. 26/2 We have not had a single exhaust trim or exhaustor returned with a plating fault. **1962** *Which? Car Suppl.* Oct. 144/1 Leather upholstery and walnut trim. **1969** *Sears Catal.* Spring/Summer 6/2 Matching double handle handbag... Contrasting bar lightly touched with gleaming gold-color metal trim. **1971** 'D. Halliday' *Dolly & Doctor Bird* vi. 85 The sofa..was one of a facing pair in oatmeal with hide trim. **1977** *Time* 4 July 6/3 But the new Soviet President let it be known that he was not pleased with the color of the trim on the wagon's seats.

i. *Cinemat.* A piece of film cut out during editing; *spec.* a very short piece cut out during the final stage of editing. orig. *U.S.*

1934 in Webster. **1948** R. Spottiswoode *Basic Film Techniques* iii. 31/2 If he has to unwind rolls of *trims* (or cut-out sections of shots), he will let them hang on the bins. **1959** W. S. Sharps *Dict. Cinematogr.* 116/1 *Outs*, otherwise *Trims*, the material that is not included in the final edited version of a film. **1964** *Listener* 28 May 899/3 Theseus-Adonis and the Minotaur were separated by a film about Montreal made completely out of 'trims' from taped interviews and very rapid shots exemplifying the culture of cities. **1976** *Broadcast* 23 Aug. 6/2 The shop committee..will consider releasing the trims once it has seen all the documentation. *Ibid.* 6/3 Thames..could also satisfy the union curiosity about the sheer quantity of trims—60 cans.

6. *U.S. slang.* A woman; sexual intercourse with a woman.

1955 *Amer. Speech* XXX. 302 *Chick, crazy freak, local talent, neat job, snatch, talent, trim, unfair sex, n.*, girl, usually pretty. Often used to refer to a woman of loose morals. [**1961** Rigney & Smith *Real Bohemia* p. xvii, *Trim*, cunnilingus.] **1962** E. Lacy *Freeloaders* vi. 125 The broad isn't worth it, no trim is. **1974** H. L. Foster *Ribbin', Jivin', & Playin' Dozens* v. 191 Female student: 'Somebody always askin for some trim and haven't even got anything.'

7. Special Comb.: **trim tab**, (*a*) *Aeronaut.* = *trimming tab* s.v. *trimming *vbl. sb.* 7 b; (*b*) *Naut.*, a hinged tab fitted to the trailing edge of a keel or rudder to facilitate steering.

1944 H. F. Gregory *Anything a Horse can Do* 47 Elevator trim tab on an airplane—trimmed the craft so that when the hands were off the stick, the aircraft had no tendency to nose down or up. **1958** 'Castle' & 'Hailey' *Flight into Danger* vii. 96 The speed slowly dropped. At 160 George adjusted the trim tabs. **1977** *Encycl. Aviation* 188/3 Most airplanes have hinged trim tabs whose incidence is controlled from the cockpit. **1978** *Detroit Free Press* 5 Mar. C21/5 (Advt.), 1977 Sea Ray 24' 233 Merc cruiser..trim tabs—hydraulic.

trim, *v.* Add: **II. 9. b.** *fig.* or in fig. context. To cheat (a person) out of money; to 'fleece'. *slang.*

1600 [in Dict., sense 9 *fig.*]. **1604** Dekker *Newes from Graves-End* Ep. Ded. sig. C, Thou wouldst neuer haue gone to any Barbers in London..but haue bin trimd only there, for they are the true shauers, they haue the right Neapolitan polling. **1917** D. G. Phillips *Susan Lenox* I. vi. 95 Guileful women, bent on trimming him for anything from a piece of plated jewelry to a saucer of ice cream. **1926** *Flynn's* 16 Jan. 639/1, I had simply trimmed a sucker for a few kale seeds. **1940** Wodehouse *Eggs, Beans & Crumpets* 155 Hearing her elders discuss..some burgeoning scheme for trimming the investors. **1955** *Publ. Amer. Dial. Soc.* xxiv. 94 Some of the big circuses carried their own *whiz mobs* to trim the crowds along the way. **1962** J. Ludwig in R. Weaver *Canad. Short Stories* (1968) 2nd Ser. 254 Didn't she know he was going to get trimmed? But what did she care about money by that time?

c. *fig.* To reduce the size, amount, or number of; to eliminate (wasteful expenditure); to reduce the profits of. Also *absol.* orig. *U.S.*

1966 *Wall St. Jrnl.* 21 Nov. 2/2 General Motors Corp. will reduce previously scheduled overtime next month and trim its daily car production pace 3.7%. **1970** *Globe & Mail* (Toronto) 26 Sept. 33/2 If you really want to trim expenses, you can rent a camper. **1976** *National Observer* 13 Nov. 12/2 There is the argument over dollar levels of U.S. spending and what waste might be trimmed from the budget as well as what new items should be included. **1979** *Daily Tel.* 8 Nov. 21/1 Readicut trimmed. Readicut International reveals a 32·5 p.c. drop in interim pre-tax profits. **1981** *Times* 17 Apr. 1/4 British forces on the Continent are likely to be trimmed. **1982** *Times* 9 Jan. 17 (*heading*) American Telephone trims to compete.

10. Also, to defeat.

1927 S. LEWIS *Elmer Gantry* iii. 40 No, gee, Judson, I guess you got me trimmed! **1950** WODEHOUSE *Nothing Serious* 152 Surely..Rodney can trim a man with hay fever? **1977** *Chicago Tribune* 2 Oct. III. 16/9 Grand Valley of Michigan piled up 324 yards rushing and 90 yards passing to trim Northeastern Illinois 34–12.

11. b. (Earlier example.)

1783 G. CARTWRIGHT *Jrnl.* 8 Oct. (1792) III. 29 As those birds [*sc.* eider-ducks] trim the shore along in the flight-times.

13*. *Aeronaut.* **a.** To maintain or adjust the trim (sense *2*) or inclination of (an aircraft or spacecraft, or part of one). Also *absol.*

1909 *Aero Manual* 40 Some..device is necessary to damp any oscillations that may take place in the line of flight..but hand operation of the steering devices must also be used to 'trim' the machine occasionally. **1921** *Discovery* Apr. 95/2 When trimmed up by the bow, the airship will be found to ride satisfactorily. **1924** *Flight* 13 Mar. 149/2 The pilot trims the tail by operating a hand pump..to increase or decrease its angle of incidence. **1942** *Tee Emm* (Air Ministry) II. 85 If he trims it to fly at a certain speed and power, it should stay at that speed despite bumps. **1958** 'CASTLE' & 'HAILEY' *Flight into Danger* vii. 103 Put full flap on, bring your airspeed back to 110 knots and trim to hold you steady. **1976** B. LECOMBER *Dead Weight* i. 12, I ease the throttles back a fraction and trim the nose a touch lower. **1978** *Nature* 5 Oct. 415/1 The spacecraft gyros were trimmed to the Ganymede celestial motion and Io was subsequently manoeuvered into the large slot.

b. *intr.* (for *refl.* or *pass.*) of an aircraft.

1921 *Techn. Rep. Advisory Comm. Aeronautics 1917–18* III. 1023 It should be noted that the ability to trim at high speeds is the one essential point of difference between a seaplane and a racing motor boat. **1923** *Flight* 31 May 295/2 In order..that the machine would trim correctly..the pilot was placed ahead of the wing, in which position he balances the rest of the machine.

14. c. Freq. in phr. *to trim one's sails to the wind*, to adapt oneself to circumstances.

1928 L. STRACHEY *Elizabeth & Essex* viii. 112 Burghley, trimming his sails to the changing wind, thought it advisable..to take the side of Essex in the matter of the Spanish ransoms. **1934** J. E. NEALE *Queen Elizabeth I* xiv. 229 She preferred to trim the country's sails to the winds when and how they blew, rather than set them at once for a storm that might not come. **1940** F. L. ALLEN *Since Yesterday* x. 275 *Fortune*..trimmed its sails so skillfully to the winds of conservatism that it not only became a mine of factual material for future historians but subtly broadened reactionary minds.

trimaran (traɪ·măræn). [f. TRI- + CATA)-MARAN *sb.*] A boat with a central hull and a float on each side.

1949 *Sun* (Baltimore) 27 Sept. 22/3 A trimaran showed running speed but little drive to windward. **1959** *Engineering* 16 Jan. 86/2 The trimaran configuration, that is a main hull and two outriggers. **1966** T. PYNCHON *Crying of Lot 49* iii. 57 Metzger handed Oedipa aboard the about-to-be-hijacked vessel, a 17-foot aluminum trimaran. **1973** *Guardian* 18 May 18/1 [He] sailed out from England to New Zealand three years ago in a 22-foot trimaran, built and designed by himself.

trimeprazine (traɪme·prăzīn). *Pharm.* [prob. f. TRIME(THYL + PR(OPYL + *PHENOTHI)AZINE.] A phenothiazine derivative that is used for its sedative and antihistaminic properties (usu. in the form of the tartrate); dimethyl(2-methyl-3-phenothiazin-10-ylpropyl)amine, $C_{18}H_{22}N_2S$.

1959 *Canad. Med. Assoc. Jrnl.* LXXX. 125/1 (*heading*) A new drug for control of itching—trimeprazine. **1977** *Proc. R. Soc. Med.* LXX. 627/1 Mild sedation, e.g. trimeprazine tartrate, is usually required for a few days until the child becomes used to the apparatus.

trimer (traɪ·məɹ). *Chem.* [f. TRI- + *-MER.] A compound whose molecule is composed of three molecules of monomer.

[**1929** *Chem. Abstr.* XXIII. 3213 The supernatant liquid..yielded 180, 20, 11, and 4g. of the di-, tri-, tetra- and pentamer, resp.] **1939** [see *TETRAMER]. **1952** *Jrnl. Physical Chem.* LVI. 85 A reaction between 3 molecules of insulin of molecular weight 12,000..to give a 'trimer' of molecular weight 36,000..is postulated. **1969** W. R. R. PARK *Plastics Film Technol.* viii. 195 Even polystyrene films..can cause problems if they contain even relatively low percentages of residual monomers, dimers, or trimers. **1974** M. C. GERALD *Pharmacol.* xi. 198 This compound [*sc.* paraldehyde] is a trimer of acetaldehyde..., that is, three molecules linked in a ring.

Hence **trime·ric** *a.*; **tri:meriza·tion**, the formation of a trimer from smaller molecules.

1938 *Jrnl. Chem. Soc.* 11 Polymerisation of βγ-dimethylbutadiene by sulphuric acid dissolved in acetic acid gives dimeric, trimeric and other low-molecular products. **1954** *Adv. Protein Chem.* IX. 419 A similar free energy change might be expected on dimerization and trimerization. **1972** A. A. R. SAYIGH et al. in Stille & Campbell *Condensation Monomers* v. 382 The value of these catalysts is limited because the same substances can act as catalysts for the trimerization of isocyanates. **1975** *Nature* 18 Dec. 576/2 The functional significance of the trimeric nature of the molecule is obscure.

trimester. Add: *spec.* each of three such periods into which human gestation is divided.

1916 G. P. SHEARS *Obstetrics* ii. 27 Most writers divide pregnancy into three periods of three months each, three trimesters, as they are often called. **1938** A. L. MUDALIAR *Clin. Obstetrics* vi. 33 The signs and symptoms vary with the different periods of pregnancy, and we shall classify them into..the first, second and third trimesters of pregnancy. **1980** GATES & MECKEL *Newborn Beauty* (1981) iii. 79 During the first trimester you may feel nauseated, fatigued, and lose your appetite.

trimethoprim (traɪme·þoprim). *Pharm.* [f. TRIMETH(YL + O(XY- + *P(Y)RIM(IDINE, constituent parts of the systematic name (see quot. 1962).] An antibiotic, $C_{14}H_{18}N_4O_3$, that is usually given in conjunction with a sulphonamide, esp. in the treatment of malaria and of respiratory and urinary infections.

1962 *Jrnl. Medicinal & Pharmaceutical Chem.* V. 1107 Compound LXV, 2,4-diamino-5-(trimethoxybenzyl)-pyrimidine (B.W. 56–72, trimethoprim), has been selected for detailed study and clinical trial. **1968** *New Scientist* 17 Oct. 147/1 A tablet of Septrin actually contains two drugs, one old—a sulphonamide—and one 'new'—trimethoprim. **1974** R. M. KIRK et al. *Surgery* ii. 29/1 Trimethoprim acts synergistically with sulphonamides, since they interfere sequentially at two stages in bacterial synthesis of folic acid. **1977** *Lancet* 2 July 4/1 Much of the shigellosis could be successfully treated with ampicillin trihydrate and closely related antibiotics, or with co-trimoxazole (trimethoprim and sulphamethoxazole).

trimetrical, *a.* **b.** (Earlier examples.)

1835 *Chinese Repository* July 105 The Trimetrical Classic. **1853** *North-China Herald* 21 May 168/1 (*heading*) Pamphlets published by the Insurgents. The Trimetrical Classic. [*Note*] Each line containing three words, and each verse four lines.

Trimetrogen (traɪme·trogǫn). Also trimetrogon. [f. TRI- + *Metrogon* (see quot. 1944).] Used *attrib.* with reference to a technique in which aerial photographs are taken simultaneously by a camera pointing vertically downwards and two pointing obliquely in opposite directions.

1944 P. G. MCCURDY et al. *Man. Photogrammetry* (Amer. Soc. Photogrammetry) xiii. 648 In the United States the tri-lens system of map compilation is now usually designated as the 'Trimetrogon' method. The word 'Metrogon' is the commercial name of the kind of lens generally used, but the method of compilation is not affected by the kind of lens. *Ibid.*, Either the K-17 or K-3B type cameras are used in the trimetrogon assembly. **1952** *Chambers's Jrnl.* Feb. 84/1 The planes..carried the marvellous trimetrogon aerial cameras, developed during the War, which make possible a thousandfold increase of speed and show the landscape in stereoscopic detail. **1969** G. C. DICKINSON *Maps & Air Photographs* xv. 244 Something of the best of both worlds is obtained with photographs taken by multiple camera installations, the chief aim here being to reduce cost or time by increasing the area photographed during each run; well-known types are..the American Trimetrogon type where one vertical camera is flanked by two high oblique cameras giving continuous cover from horizon to horizon at each exposure.

trimmed, *ppl. a.* Add: **a.** *trimmed joist*, a joist which is tenoned into a trimmer (sense 4); cf. *trimming-joist* s.v. TRIMMING *vbl. sb.* 7.

1876 *Encycl. Brit.* IV. Plate facing p. 482, Trimmed Joists. **1945** H. C. BISSILL in N. W. Kay *Pract. Carpenter & Joiner* xvii. 361 (*caption*) Pictorial view of floor of a first-floor, with..bridging joists,..trimmer, trimming joist, and..trimmed joist. **1966** A. T. COLLINS *Newnes Complete Pract. Woodworking* 96/1 A further use for the stopped housing is to join trimmed floor joists to a trimmer.

b. In Comb. with advbs. and preps. forming adjs., as *trimmed-down*, *-up*.

1897 KIPLING *Capt. Cour.* ix. 198 It's great to have a trimmed-up meal again. **1971** *Wall St. Jrnl.* 22 July w1/3 Last month the White House vetoed a public works measure, but an administration spokesman said there are signs the President might accept a trimmed-down plan.

trimmer. Add: **4.** (Later examples.)

1897 F. C. MOORE *How to build Home* iii. 32 'Trimmer'-beams enter the wall on each side of the chimney. *Ibid.* viii. 113 All hearths shall be constructed with trimmer-arches extending 20 inches from the chimney-breast to a 'skew back'. **1953** *Archit. Rev.* CXIV. 364/1 With the exception of the assembly hall and gymnasia, which are on solid load-bearing walls, the structure is carried on reinforced raft foundations with ground trimmer beams at the edges.

6. Also (chiefly *Austral.* and *N.Z.*) a good or impressive thing or person, a 'smasher'.

1878 'IRONBARK' *Southerly Busters* 11, I thought thee a regular 'trimmer', I thought thee a generous man. **1943** N. MARSH *Colour Scheme* v. 92 'Running well, isn't she [*sc.* a car]?'..'She's a trimmer.' **1955** [see *LAIR *v.*]. **1962** [see *SHEILA]. **1970** *Private Eye* 13 Mar. 16 Jeez Valda Clissold, cripes she was a real little trimmer. **1970** *N.Z. Listener* 12 Oct. 13/5 Dave, you're a trimmer. You'll go places. Take a top seat.

10. *Electronics.* A small adjustable capacitor usu. used for the fine adjustment of a larger capacitor to which it is connected. Also *trimmer capacitor, condenser.*

1930 MOYER & WOSTREL *Radio Construction & Repairing* (ed. 2) xviii. 331 'Trimmer' condensers which are out of adjustment..will impair the quality of sound reproduction. **1939**, etc. [see *PADDER *sb.*[2] 3]. **1944** *Electronic Engin.* XVI. 362/2 This error can easily be compensated by the use of a two gang trimmer condenser across the two tuning condensers. **1965** *Wireless World* Sept. 422/2 The appropriate trimmer is first adjusted to give a low intermediate frequency. **1971** A. MARGOLIS *Mod. Radio Repair Techniques* (1974) vi. 83 Usually, padder capacitors are found only in oscillator circuits. Trimmer capacitors are found in the RF circuits, mixer circuits and oscillator circuits.

11. *Aeronaut.* = *trimming tab* s.v. *TRIMMING *vbl. sb.* 7 b.

1935 *Aircraft Engineering* Dec. 305/1 The effect of the trimmer on the drag of the whole tail must be kept in mind. **1947** A. C. DOUGLAS *Gliding & Advanced Soaring* ii. 48 If the quick release is the one used for winching, usually below the thrust line, the machine may tend to ride high, necessitating a continual forward pressure on the stick. This may be tiring on long tows unless elevator trimmers are fitted. **1964** G. LYALL *Most Dangerous Game* ix. 62 Watching my hands wander round the cockpit, checking and setting... Trimmers to takeoff, throttle nut tensioned.

trimming, *vbl. sb.* Add: **2. b.** Freq. in phr. *all the trimmings.* Also *fig.*

1927 D. PARKER in *New Yorker* 29 Oct. 93/1 He was praised, adored, analyzed, bestsold, argued about, and banned in Boston; all the trimmings were accorded him. **1946** M. DICKENS *Happy Prisoner* ix. 195 If he..had to start his illness all over again, with transfusions and penicillin and all the trimmings, it would be their fault. **1949** R. HARVEY *Curtain Time* 148 Turkey and all the trimmings. **1973** *Times* 25 Apr. 8/2 Those rich romantics or fantasists who still wish to enter matrimony with a gracious splash can hire for a day the ancestors, the family retainers, their own private stately home and all the trimmings, in the centre of London. **1981** 'W. HAGGARD' *Money Men* iii. 35 He had a passion for silverside, all the trimmings—carrots and onions and small sweet dumplings. **1984** *Times* 6 Apr. 21/2 Next week he unveils his..personal computer which is said to have all the trimmings but with a no-frills price.

c. The upholstery or interior lining of a motor vehicle. Cf. *TRIM *sb.* 3 h.

1938 *Motor* 8 Nov. 2/1 (Advt.), 1937, colour scheme green, suitable leather trimming, comprehensively equipped. **1948** *Ibid.* 3 Nov. 385/1 The windscreen is slightly vee'd. Interior trimming is grey leather and the price is £3,775.

7. b. trimming flap = *trimming tab* below; **trimming gear** *Aeronaut.*, apparatus for altering the angle of the tailplane of an aircraft; **trimming plane** *Aeronaut.*, a control surface used to trim an aircraft; **trimming tab** *Aeronaut.*, an adjustable tab or aerofoil attached to a control surface, and used to trim the aircraft; *spec.* one which can be adjusted by the pilot in flight; **trimming wheel** *Aeronaut.*, a control wheel used to trim an aircraft by its action on the tailplane.

1935 *Jrnl. R. Aeronaut. Soc.* XXXIX. 1038 The ailerons and elevators require trimming flaps sufficient to enable the airplane to be flown 'hands off'. **1922** *Flight* XIV. 416/1 The tail plane, for which a very substantial worm trimming gear is provided, has spars of straight taper, spindled out to an I section. **1933** *Aeroplane* 5 Apr. 606/1 There was some mechanical stiffness in the ailerons and no tail trimming gear had yet been rigged. **1921** *Flight* XIII. 325/2 A trimming plane is installed just ahead of the tail plane, which can be adjusted in flight from the pilot cabin by a wheel. **1935** *Aircraft Engineering* Dec. 297 The trimming tab is quite revolutionary in its simplicity. **1942** W. SIMPSON *One of our Pilots is Safe* II. 42 To twist the trimming tab controls for rudder and elevator. **1950** *Engineering* 29 Sept. 269/3 All the control surfaces are provided with trimming tabs. **1941** D. MASTERS *So Few* 99 The trimming wheel is a device which acts upon the tailplane in order to take the physical strain off the pilot. **1956** D. BARNHAM *One Man's Window* 153, I start turning the trimming wheel to ease me out of this dive.

trimodal (traɪmōᵘ·dăl), *a.* [f. TRI- + MODE *sb.* + -AL.] Of a frequency curve or distribution: having three modes (*MODE *sb.* 7 c). Of a phenomenon or property: described by such a distribution.

1927 *Jrnl. du Conseil* II. 354 Though the significance of the bimodal or trimodal selection in drift caught fish is open to argument, the fact of its existence is not. **1962** *Lancet* 5 May 968/1 The distribution of the values for 'relative incidence' is not a normal one but bimodal (or possibly even trimodal). **1978** *Nature* 3 Aug. 485/2 The results in Fig. 2 show a trimodal distribution when viability was determined after exposure to a standard dose of γ-radiation.

trimonthly, *a.* **a.** (Earlier example.)

1856 *Trans. Mich. Agric. Soc.* VII. 329 The Steamer Superior..made tri-monthly trips from Buffalo to Detroit.

tri-mo:tor. Also **tri-motor.** [f. TRI- + MOTOR *sb.*] An aeroplane fitted with three engines. Cf. *TRI-JET.

1923 *Glasgow Herald* 1 Jan. 8 The aeroplane which it is proposed to use will be a tri-motor. **1931** *Technol. Rev.* Nov. 66/2 The Ford trimotors are *tin geese*, an amphibian is often a *duck*. **1936** *New Yorker* 14 Mar. 25/1 His favorite machines are a tri-motor Junker and a silver-and-black steel Immelmann. **1965** C. D. EBY *Siege of Alcázar* (1966) 13 The pueblo of Getafe..in 1936 boasts the busiest airport in Spain, but there are only a few silent trimotors on the airstrips. **1977** H. FAST *Immigrants* IV. 226 He lay awake most of the night, reliving his experience on the big trimotor plane. **1981** R. THOMAS *Mordida Man* xviii. 158 The old gentleman said he had flown in everything from Ford trimotors to 747s.

tri-mo:tored, *a.* Also **trimotored.** [f. TRI- + MOTOR *sb.* + -ED².] Of an aeroplane: fitted with three engines.

1927 *Times* (Weekly ed.) 9 June 632/3 Tri-motored aeroplanes capable of landing on the water..were essential. **1929** *Sat. Even. Post* 7 Dec. 63/1 The giant tri-motored Ford planes of this line. **1968** MILLER & SAWERS *Technical Devel. Mod. Aviation* ii. 33 The totals..may suggest the general level of operating costs of the tri-motored aircraft in the United States in 1932–33. **1980** R. BUTLER *Blood-Red Sun at Noon* (1981) I. ii. 28 One of the big tri-motored Junkers.

Trimphone (tri·mfōᵘn). Also **trimphone.** [f. TRIM *a.* + PHONE *sb.*²] The proprietary name of a type of lightweight telephone with a high-pitched quavering (or 'warbling') ringing tone.

1965 *Times* 11 May 6/7 The new instrument is called a Trimphone and, in the words of the Post Office, it does not ring, it warbles. **1969** *Daily Tel.* 18 Apr. 23/2 The £1 charged is also removed from the cost of installing a Trimphone—the one that 'warbles'. **1973** *Trade Marks Jrnl.* 26 Sept. 1852/2 *Trimphone*..B 986,992. Telephones; telephone receivers; telephone transmitters; telephone dialling apparatus; and parts and fittings..for all the aforesaid..The Post Office. **1973** J. WAINWRIGHT *Pride of Pigs* 166 Quince hooked his fingers through the carrying handle of the Trimphone, telephone handset. **1977** J. GARDNER *Werewolf Trace* i. 18 The trimphone whistled and Greg picked it up, nodding at the voice in his ear.

‖ **Trimurti** (trimū·rti). Also **Tri-murti** and with small initial. [Skr., f. *tri* three + *-mūrti* consisting or formed of.] **1.** In Hinduism, the gods Brahma, Vishnu, and Shiva, conceived as aspects of one ultimate reality. Also *transf.* Cf. TRIAD 2 b.

1836 J. F. DAVIS *Chinese* II. xiii. 107 Their own *Tri-murti*, or Triad of *Brahma, Vishnu*, and *Siva*. **1877** MONIER WILLIAMS *Hinduism* vii. 87 These three gods are the first and highest manifestations of the Eternal Essence, and..constitute the well-known *Tri-mūrti*, or Triad of divine forms which characterises Hindūism. **1895** E. W. HOPKINS *Relig. of India* xvi. 447 The votaries of these subsects worshipped some, the rising sun, some the setting sun, while some again worshipped the noonday sun, and others, all three as a *tri-mūrti*. **1921** *Encycl. Relig. & Ethics* XII. 457/2 Serving as it does to reconcile rival monotheisms with one another and with the philosophic doctrine of the absolute, the theory of the Trimūrti presents no such close similarity to the Christian doctrine of the Trinity as to render derivation from Christian influences either necessary or probable. **1954** D. S. SARMA in K. W. Morgan *Relig. of Hindus* 34 The three most important functions of that Spirit, the creation, preservation, and destruction of the world, were associated with the great gods Brahmā, Vishnu, and Śiva. Thus arose the doctrine of the Hindu Trinity, the Trimūrti. **1980** M. GILBERT *Death of Favourite Girl* ii. 23 Brahma, the creator, with Vishnu, the preserver and Siva, the destroyer..form the Trimurti—that is, the great Hindu Triad.

2. A statue with three faces representing Brahma, Vishnu, and Shiva.

1877 MONIER WILLIAMS *Hinduism* vii. 87 There is a well-known Tri-mūrti sculptured out of the rock in the caves of Elephanta, at Bombay. **1920** E. B. HAVELL *Handbk. Indian Art* III. i. 203 The Bodhisattva holds in his right hand Vishnu's blue lotus, and his tiara bears the three jewelled sun-discs like the Vishnu in the Trimūrti sculpture of Elephanta. **1953** B. ROWLAND *Art & Architecture of India* xvii. 188 The treatment of the subjects, ranging from the *Trimurti*..to a panel like the Betrothal of Śiva and Pārvatī..reveal the extraordinary ability and scope of the Dravidian sculptor. **1981** G. PRIESTLAND *Priestland's Progress* viii. 123 A statue with three faces, like the sublime Hindu *trimurti* in the cave temples of Elephanta.

Trinidadian (trinidæ·diăn, -dēⁱ·diăn), *a.* and *sb.* [f. *Trinidad* + -IAN; see TRINIDADO.] **A.** *sb* A native or inhabitant of Trinidad.

1910 L. O. INNISS (*title*) Trinidad and Trinidadians. **1948** *Trinidad Guardian* 24 June 1/2 (*heading*) Trinidadian faces fraud indictment. **1957** [see the adj. below]. **1966** *Listener* 23 June 923/3 White men in Trinidad had only taught the Trinidadians how to play cricket because there were not enough of their own sort to make a team. **1978** 'A. YORK' *Tallant for Disaster* ii. 25 A Trinidadian by birth, he was tall and thin.

B. *adj.* Of or pertaining to Trinidad or its inhabitants.

1934 A. HUXLEY *Beyond Mexique Bay* 20 This appeal for Trinidadian autarchy was warmly applauded. **1957** *Amer. Anthropologist* LIX. 817 Trinidad's social structure ..shows these racial and national groups to be arranged in a hierarchy by Trinidadians... A consensus of Trinidadian opinion might arrange these groups as follows. **1971** *Advocate-News* (Barbados) 17 Sept. (Guyana Suppl.) p. iii/1 A Trinidadian sportsman has also been ordered to serve two six-month jail sentences. **1980** *Amer. Speech* LV. 31 Examples are Barbadian../basabasa/ 'fussy' and /kɔŋki/ 'boiled corn pudding', both also Trinidadian and Guyanese.

Trinil (trī·nil). The name of a village in Java, used *attrib.* to designate the fossil remains found there by Eugène Dubois in 1891, esp. those of a hominid, *Homo erectus* or Java man. Cf. *JAVA *a.*, *PITHECANTHROPUS 2.

1896 *Jrnl. Anthropol. Inst.* XXV. 245 The Trinil skull in form and size very closely resembles the type of the anthropoid apes. **1898** E. DUBOIS in *Sci. Trans. R. Dublin Soc.* VI. 9 The human form of the Trinil femur is not sufficient to prove that it did not belong to the same individual as the skull-cap. *Ibid.* 12 The Trinil individual, if a human being, ought to have been a microcephalic idiot... The Trinil cranium..very much approaches the type of Anthropoid Apes. **1933** A. S. ROMER *Man & Vertebrates* xi. 237 The teeth are essentially human in character but do not definitely settle the status of this Trinil man. **1960** C. WINICK *Dict. Anthropol.* 210/1 The Trinil man's teeth are large and his dental arch narrow. **1975** G. H. R. VON KOENIGSWALD in R. H. Tuttle *Paleoanthropology* 304 The famous hominid of the Trinil fauna is the classic *Pithecanthropus* or *Homo erectus*. *Ibid.* 305 It [*sc.* a skull] is not directly comparable to the Trinil skull cap.

trinitrotoluene (trəinəi:trotǫ·liu,īn). [f. TRINITRO- + *toluene* s.v. TOLU-.] Any of three isomeric nitro derivatives, $CH_3C_6H_2$-$(NO_2)_3$, of toluene, esp. the 2,4,6-isomer, used as a high explosive that is relatively insensitive to shock and can be conveniently melted. Abbrev. *T.N.T.* s.v. *T 6 a. Also † **trini:troto·luol** [*toluol* s.v. TOLU-], in the same sense.

1908 *Chem. Abstr.* II. 459 The trinitrotoluene is preferable because it leaves no poisonous gases after explosion..and can be added to safety explosives. **1910** Trinitrotoluol [see *TROTYL]. **1915** KIPLING *Fringes of Fleet* 21 We lay doggo in twelve-fathom water With tri-nitro-toluol hogging our run. **1916** *Yorkshire Post* 27 Mar. 5/1 Contact with tri-nitrotoluol may result in the occurrence of troublesome skin affections. **1917** *Causation & Prevention Tri-nitro-toluene (T.N.T.) Poisoning* (Nat. Health Insurance) 9 The material known commercially as T.N.T. is mainly composed of one of the three isomeric tri-nitro-toluenes. **1964** N. G. CLARK *Mod. Org. Chem.* xx. 402 All the existing substituents direct to one position in the nucleus, and the product is 2,4,6-trinitrotoluene, the well-known explosive TNT. **1973** 'A. HALL' *Tango Briefing* xviii. 227 It has the equivalent of one hundred tons of trinitrotoluene.

trinity. Add: **2. c.** (Later examples.)

1911 [see *Trinity Sunday*, sense 6 in Dict.]. **1981** BARTON & HALLIBURTON in *Believing in Church* iv. 90 From Trinity to Advent a series of *historiae* is appointed [to be read].

5. (Later examples.)

1874 K. H. DIGBY *Temple of Memory* iii. 39 To Cambridge he is gone..with comrades three, Bound like himself for Trinity. **1933** D. L. SAYERS *Murder must Advertise* i. 12 'He was at Trinity. Your Trinity, I mean, not ours.' (Mr. Hankin was a Cambridge man.) **1982** M. YOUNG *Elmhirsts of Dartington* ii. 20 He became a 'Trinity man' expected to assume a definite character..to distinguish him from King's men or Christ's men or John's men.

6. Trinity House (later examples); now chiefly concerned with the licensing of pilots and the erection and maintenance of lighthouses, buoys, and other aids to navigation, on the coasts of England and Wales.

1842 QUEEN VICTORIA *Jrnl.* 29 Apr. (1980) 17 The Trinity-House steamer goes with us. **1979** *Bull. Yorks. Dial. Soc.* Summer 9 The station at the time was controlled by the Hull Trinity House.

trinket, *sb.*¹ Add: **4.** *trinket-box* (earlier example).

1814 JANE AUSTEN *Mansfield Park* II. viii. 186 You would be..welcome to any other in my trinket-box.

trinket, *v.*² Add: Hence **tri·nketed** *ppl. a.* (*rare*).

1922 JOYCE *Ulysses* 433 Her hands passing slowly over her trinketed stomacher.

‖ **Trinkhalle** (tri·ŋkhalə). Also **trinkhalle.** [Ger., lit. 'drinking-hall'.] A place at a spa where medicinal water is dispensed for drinking; a pump-room. Also, an establishment at which (alcoholic) drink is served; a refreshment stall.

1873 G. H. LEWES *Diary* 16 Aug. in *Geo. Eliot Lett.* (1956) V. 427 Drinking seltserwasser at a Trinkhalle. **1971** D. MACKENZIE *Sleep is for Rich* vi. 189 Chalice was waiting in the *trinkhalle* in an aura of stale tobacco smoke and beer.

trinocular (trəi-, trinǫ·kiŭlăɹ), *a.* [After BINOCULAR *a.* and *sb.*: see TRI-.] Of a microscope or its body tube: having provision for a camera in addition to eyepieces for both eyes.

1960 *McGraw-Hill Encycl. Sci. & Technol.* VIII. 392/1 Trinocular bodies are binocular bodies with a third tube for a camera. **1970** R. P. LOVELAND *Photomicrography* I. iii. 121 The trinocular body tube can now be obtained from all of the microscope companies. **1972** *Sci. Amer.* Mar. 65/1 (Advt.), The ED-10 fits virtually any microscope. Whether monocular, binocular or trinocular.

trinomial, *a.* Add: **3.** Of the names of married women (esp. in the U.S.): consisting of three elements, the given, maiden, and husband's surname; also applied to those known by this style, whereby the maiden name is in some measure retained.

1966 *Listener* 2 June 806/3 A vast cast of trinominal cuckoos (Harriot Stanton Blatch, Carrie Chapman Catt, Elizabeth Gurley Flynn, Lucretia Coffin Mott, Rev. Anna Howard Shaw *et aliae*) flap across the stage, but hardly one is characterized by any human identifiable characteristic. **1981** *Economist* 28 Nov. 107/2 Mary Boykin Chesnut—and the reader cannot begin too soon to accustom himself to trinomial appellations.

trinucleotide: see *TRI- 1 a.

trio. Add: **3.** *Comb.*, as **trio-sonata** [cf. It. *sonata a tre*], a sonata written in three parts, and often performed on four instruments.

1884 BELL & FULLER-MAITLAND tr. *Spitta's Johann Sebastian Bach* II. IV. iii. 106 The accompaniment..is arranged by one of the master's best pupils..who did the same thing in a trio-sonata of Bach's. **1934** (*title*) J.-M. Leclair: Trio-Sonata in B flat major for 2 violins, violoncello (ad lib.) & Piano. **1958** *Listener* 11 Dec. 1010/2 Purcell wrote two splendid sets of trio-sonatas. **1978** *Early Music* Oct. 561/1, I have chosen the trio sonata in C major for recorder, flute and basso continuo.

triode (trəi·ōᵘd), *a.* and *sb.* [f. TRI- + *-ODE².] † **A.** *adj. Telegr.* Permitting or involving the transmission of three signals simultaneously. *Obs.*

1886 [see *HEXODE *a.*].

B. *sb. Electronics.* **a.** A thermionic valve having three electrodes (also *triode valve*); also, an analogous semiconductor device with three terminals.

1919 W. H. ECCLES in *Electrician* 18 Apr. 475/2 It seems very natural to call a vacuous space containing three electrodes a 'tri-electrode', or, for short, a triode. **1919** *Nature* 30 Oct. 178/2 The internal action of a triode valve. **1923** *Mod. Wireless* June 304/2 The amplifier used consisted of a single Western Electric triode. **1943** C. L. BOLTZ *Basic Radio* x. 155 The thing which is most striking about the triode is the effect of grid voltage on the anode current. **1948** *Physical Rev.* LXXIV. 230/1 (*heading*) The transistor, a semi-conductor triode. **1962** D. F. SHAW *Introd. Electronics* xi. 220 One of the most important uses of the triode valve is for the amplification of a voltage. **1962** SIMPSON & RICHARDS *Physical Princ. Junction Transistors* viii. 191 The second type of avalanching triode..is obtained by connecting a base lead to either the n_1 or p_2 sections of the diode in Fig. 8.22. **1974** A. VAN DER ZIEL *Introd. Electronics* ix. 216 The vacuum triode is hardly ever used as a small-signal amplifier except at high temperatures, but it is still the only way to develop very large powers.

f. Comb.: **triode-hexode**, a valve containing a triode and a hexode in a single envelope, with separate anodes but a common cathode; similarly **triode-pentode.**

1937 A. T. WITTS *Thermionic Valves Mod. Radio Receivers* viii. 164 (*caption*) Circuit for the triode-hexode. **1952** E. ARMITAGE *Wireless Fundamentals* xviii. 325 Sometimes the beat oscillator valve and the mixer valve are both inside a single glass envelope as in the triode-hexode. **1936** MOYER & WOSTREL *Radio Receiving & Television Tubes* (ed. 3) iv. 156 (*caption*) Characteristic curves of triode section of triode-pentode tube.

triose. Add: **2.** Special Comb.: **triose phosphate**, any compound in which a hydrogen atom in the hydroxyl group of a triose is replaced by a phosphate group (PO_3^{2-}).

1934 *Chem. Abstr.* XXVIII. 3746 Triosephosphate was sepd. by fractional pptn. with EtOH and Me_2CO. **1982** R. A. HARRIS in T. M. Devlin *Textbk. Biochem.* vii. 336 Triose phosphate isomerase then catalyzes the reversible interconversion of dihydroxyacetone phosphate and glyceraldehyde 3-phosphate to complete the splitting stage of glycolysis.

trioxan (trəi,ǫ·ksæn). *Chem.* Also **-ane** (-ēⁱn). [f. TRI- + *OX(A- + -ANE.] A cyclic trimer of formaldehyde, $(—CH_2·O—)_3$, obtained as colourless, pliant crystals that are combustible and very volatile at room temperature.

1915 P. E. SPIELMAN tr. *V. von Richter's Org. Chem.* I. 205 Hexachlorodimethyl Trioxan. **1919** *Decennial Index Chem. Abstr. 1907–16* 4643/2 *s*-Trioxane. **1964** [see *trioxymethylene* s.v. *TRIOXY-]. **1978** P. S. & C. A. BAILEY *Org. Chem.* x. 268 It [*sc.* formaldehyde] is usually sold and transported as low-molecular-weight polymers, such as 1,3,5-trioxane, formalin, and paraformaldehyde.

trioxy-. Add: **trioxyme·thylene** = *TRIOXAN.

1880 *Jrnl. Chem. Soc.* XXXVIII. 25 The distillate left a white amorphous residue..which proved to be identical with trioxymethylene, $C_3H_6O_3$. **1964** N. G. CLARK *Mod. Org. Chem.* x. 188 On distilling aqueous formaldehyde with a trace of sulphuric acid, trioxan ('trioxymethylene') is obtained.

trip, *sb.*¹ Add: **I. 3. g.** *colloq. this* (or *that*) *trip*: on this (or that) particular time; on the occasion specified.

1746 C. KNOWLES *Let.* 19 Sept. in J. S. McLennan *Louisbourg* (1918) x. 174 M. le Duc with all his force shan't have Louisbourg this Trip. **1902** S. E. WHITE *Blazed Trail* 188, I guess I'll let you off this trip. **1906** E. DYSON *Fact'ry 'Ands* ii. 18 Copped out that trip, didn't yeh?

h. *Racing.* The distance from start to finish of a race.

1959 *Times* 1 June 16/7 Dan Cupid is a stocky..colt with..little on public form to prove he can get the trip. **1969** *Australian* 24 May 34/5 Koranui: eighth to Deep Court over 14½f here last Sat. Looks tested at this trip from 24 yd. **1977** *Cork Examiner* 6 June 8/9 The highly fancied Pharly, who beat Crystal Palace three weeks ago in the Prix Lupin at Longchamp over a slightly shorter trip.

4*. *slang* (orig. and chiefly *U.S.*). **a.** A hallucinatory experience induced by a drug, esp. LSD. Cf. *down trip* s.v. *DOWN *a.* 1 e.

1959 N. MAILER *Advts. for Myself* III. 245, I took some mescaline... At the end of a long and private trip which no quick remark should try to describe, the book of *The Deer Park* floated into mind. **1960** J. GELBER *Connection* I. 23 All right, junkies. During our trip we will incorporate an allied art—the motion picture. **1966** *Daily Tel.* 10 Aug. 13/3 The tape-recorder picked up the horrifying moans and shrieks of one man who had made 33 pleasurable 'trips' with LSD and was encountering his first 'freakout,' or bad LSD experience. **1971** *Sci. Amer.* Sept. 240/3 One of the volunteers had a bad trip, entering a panicky and nearly psychotic state. **1975** I. MURDOCH *Word Child* 301 You were under the influence. He tried to talk to you... I said you were on a trip.

b. *transf.* and *fig.* An experience, esp. a stimulating one.

1966 *Time* 1 July 50 The Jefferson Airplane flies on weekends at a discothèque in Fillmore Auditorium, where projectors flash quivering, amoeba-like patterns on the walls to induce the dancers 'to take a 'trip'..without drugs'. **1968** L. W. ROBINSON *Assassin* (1969) xii. 128 Their passion was a long one.., as though they hated to come back, ever, from the rocking, tossing, sweet trip. **1970** *Time* 3 Aug. 32 Part of the message is in the drug argot that he [*sc.* Arthur Blessitt] raps out to his street audiences: 'You don't need no pills. Jes' drop a little Matthew, Mark, Luke, and John. Christ is the ultimate, eternal trip.' **1974** *Melody Maker* 13 July 3/7 The drums are bright shiny cab yellow by the way. It's a trip. **1978** G. VIDAL *Kalki* iv. 91 On the other hand, the shop itself was not only exotic, it was a trip, as the addicts say.

c. An activity, attitude, or state of mind, esp. one that is delusory or self-indulgent. Cf. *ego-trip* s.v. *EGO 5.

1967 WENTWORTH & FLEXNER *Dict. Amer. Slang* Suppl. 708/2 *Trip*,..any activity, outing, period of time, or way of life. Some beat and student use since c 1965. **1969** [see *BIT *sb.*[2] 4 i]. **1970** J. POPENOE *Inside Summerhill* 104 It [*sc.* a gang] was a great power trip for the 14-year-old boy who was the leader. **1972** V. FERDINAND in A. Chapman *New Black Voices* 470 It's an unbelievable trip to think that the absence of quality is the cause for the exclusion of Black writers when there is so much garbage being dumped on the heads of people by white publishers. **1974** K. MILLET *Flying* III. 282 Hoping is a trip, and it's hopeless anyway. **1977** *New Musical Express* 12 Feb. 8/2 Transcribed onto paper his words may sound like a speech by a musician with delusions of grandeur, but Piazzo ain't into that trip. **1979** R. L. SIMON *Peking Duck* xvi. 117, I shouldn't bother—politics was a sixties trip.

III. 8. b. *Nuclear Sci.* (See quots.)

1962 *Gloss. Terms Nucl. Sci.* (*B.S.I.*) 122 *Trip*, a reduction in reactor power initiated by any of the safety circuits of the reactor. **1978** *Times* 1 Feb. 4/7 Reactors suffer occasional unscheduled shut-downs or 'trips' from a wide range of causes, such as fail-safe faults on protective equipment, operator errors and faults in conventional non-nuclear equipment.

IV. 9. trip-bucket, a bucket used for raising water from wells in Arabia, operated by a tripping device and pulled by animals; **tripcock**, a device on a train which applies the brakes when engaged by a projection on the track, if the train is passing a signal set at danger; **tripmeter**, an instrument which may be set to record the distance travelled by a vehicle during each trip; similarly *trip* (*mileage*) *counter*, *trip* (*distance*, *mileage*) *recorder*; **trip slip** (examples); **trip switch** *Electr. Engin.* (see quot. 1924).

1926 T. E. LAWRENCE *Seven Pillars* (1935) xxxix. 229 He told me of the wheel over the well, with its machinery of leathern trip-buckets, raised by oxen upon an inclined path of hard-trodden earth. **1959** W. THESIGER *Arabian Sands* x. 190 Villagers in the Hadhramaut use camels and oxen to raise the trip-buckets from which they water their cultivation. **1906** *Railway Mag.* Apr. 341/2 These automatic signals have a trigger, which, when the signal is at danger, should engage with a trip cock on the vehicles of the train. **1968** O. S. NOCK *Railway Enthusiasts' Encycl.* VII. 274 Co-acting with each stop signal is a train stop, mounted beside the track... When the signal is at danger, the arm is raised. If a train overran a signal..a trip cock lever would strike the raised train stop arm. **1959** *Motor Manual* (ed. 36) vii. 195 Another difference with the trip counter is that it may be set to zero at any time. **1977** *Westworld* (Vancouver, B.C.) May–June 34/2 This gradual phasing-in of the changes means that by 1978 all instrumentation, speedometers, odometers and tripcounters will be entirely converted [to metric]. **1955** *Motor* 7 Dec. 765/1 (*caption*) Trip distance recorder re-setting (twist). **1966** T. WISDOM *High-Performance Driving* xi. 114 A driver..may..exchange his present speedo for a similar one with a trip meter. **1972** O. SELA *Bearer Plot* xxi. 134 Elmer hunched over the bicycling machine... The tripmeter read 5.2 kilometres. **1959** *Motor Manual* (ed. 36) vii. 195 When a trip mileage counter is also fitted this will be constructed on similar lines to the main counter. **1962** *Times* 8 May 16/5 The car is well equipped, and noteworthy points include..a trip mileage recorder, brake servo warning light, twin screenwashers. **1970** *Motoring Which?* Apr. 55/1 All six cars had a speedometer, mileage recorder, trip mileage recorder, fuel gauge. **1966** T. WISDOM *High-Performance Driving* xi. 114 Few speedometers these days are fitted with trip recorders. **1977** *Daily Tel.* 14 Dec. 12/6 Instruments include a rev. counter, speedometer trip recorder, and large clock. **1876** *Scribner's Monthly* Apr. 910/2 The conductor, when he receives a fare, will immediately punch in the presence of the passenger, A Blue trip slip for an 8 cent fare. *a* **1884** Trip-slip [see *bell-punch* s.v. *BELL *sb.*[1] 12]. **1924** S. R. ROGET *Dict. Electr. Terms* 275/2 *Trip Switch*, a switch for closing the tripping circuit of a circuit breaker. **1977** *Times* 15 July 8/5 The British system includes a series of trip switches, making it a simple matter for the engineer watching the various loads at any time to isolate a power failure.

Trip (trip), *sb.*[5] Colloq. abbrev. of TRIPOS 2 d.

1909 R. BROOKE *Let.* 18 May (1968) 170, I am a prisoner ..in a room where a hundred and eight damned fools are writing Greek verses for the classical Trip. **1925** W. DEEPING *Sorrell & Son* xxiv. 229, I want a first in the Science Trip. **1927** R. LEHMANN *Dusty Answer* III. i. 126 Trips. Labs. Lectures. Dons. Vacs. Chaperons. The voices gabbled on.

trip, *v.* Add: **I. 5. b.** *slang* (orig. *U.S.*). To experience hallucinations induced by a drug, esp. LSD. Also with *out*. Also *transf.* Cf. *TRIP *sb.*[1] 4* a.

1966 [see *PSYCHEDELIC *sb.* 2]. **1968** *Globe & Mail* (Toronto) 3 Feb. 25/1 'Trip with us,' coaxes Duke Edwards in a sandy voice... 'Trip with us—without the aid of LSD.' **1969** *Daily Tel.* 4 Sept. 23/2 He was asked if he took LSD, and answered: 'I have been tripping for three weeks.' **1971** [see *MANDY, MANDY]. **1976** H. FERGUSON *Confessions of Long Distance Acid Head* 13 The bunch with whom I used to trip out and smoke pot with were form-mates of my brother. **1980** J. SCOTT *Gospel Lamb* iii. 45 Some of the people here were tripping already. Seemed a pity not to bust 'em.

II. 6. b. Also *spec.* in U.S. Sport, to defeat.

1974 *State* (Columbia, S. Carolina) 15 Feb. 6-B/2 The Generals got goals from Mike Gaines and Eddie Hewbrank in the second overtime to trip Airport, 2-0. **1979** *Honolulu Advertiser* 8 Jan. c-2/4 In Rural AJA games, Wahiawa tripped Pearl Ridge 7-5.

III. 14. a. (Later examples.) Also more widely, to cause to operate or respond; *spec.* in *Electronics*, to cause (a bistable device) to change from one stable state to the other; *to trip out*, to render electrically disconnected, esp. as an automatic action.

1936 *Sun* (Baltimore) 25 Jan. 5/8 It was eleven minutes after the electrical apparatus operating the gas generating equipment was tripped before physicians pronounced Foster dead. **1937** *Rev. Sci. Instruments* VIII. 414/2 It is necessary that at each incident pulse the circuit shall be tripped from one equilibrium state to the other. **1950** *Engineering* 20 Jan. 79/3 The gap was in the form of an expulsion tube..this arrangement helping to extinguish quickly the power-follow current so that the transformer was not tripped out. **1953** C. A. LINDBERGH *Spirit of St. Louis* II. vi. 307, I tripped my safety-belt buckle..and rolled out over the high rim of the cockpit. **1961** *Ann. Reg.* *1960* 396 This light in turn tripped more atoms until none were left in the excited state. **1967** *Electronics* 6 Mar. 126/2 When the critical temperature is reached, the resistance of the thermistor changes to allow the proper value of current to flow, and this trips a relay. **1972** P. CLEIFE *Slick & Dead* xxviii. 233 Tripping the quick-release of my harness, I leapt from my seat. **1977** *Daily Tel.* 25 Oct. 2/1 'The damn thing didn't even trip our noise meters,' he was quoted as having said after last week's three days of test landings and take-offs at Kennedy Airport. **1978** *Sci. Amer.* Mar. 146/3 When I tripped the switch *S1*, the outputs from *Q* and *Q* of *IC 1A* changed states: the *Q* then produced a logical-1 signal. **1981** *New Scientist* 29 Oct. 295/2 Another tree..in East Sussex caused a similar fault, tripping out another 400 kV supergrid line feeding the south coast.

b. *intr.* Of a mechanism or the like: to undergo a sudden change of state; to operate or (also *trip out*) cease to operate.

1940 *Jrnl. Marine Res.* III. 73 When each water bottle trips there will be a sufficient jar..so that the recording stylus..will make a noticeable mark on the temperature depth trace. **1950** *Engineering* 20 Jan. 79/3 In the 14 years under review, sub-station transformers tripped out 140 times. **1977** *Times* 16 July 5/8 Three main power lines..were hit by lightning... This caused four more lines to trip out as the safety devices to stop them overloading came into action. **1980** *Sci. Amer.* Mar. 36/1 The main feedwater pumps in the lower level of the turbine building tripped, interrupting the removal of heat from the primary system. **1981** *New Scientist* 29 Oct. 295/2 As other parts of the grid tripped out, power stations in the South and South-West struggled to meet what demand they could.

15. *Bot. trans.* To operate the pollination mechanism of (certain flowers) by disturbing the keel so that the anthers and style spring out of it.

1909 *Bull. Bureau Plant Industry, U.S. Dept. Agric.* No. 24. 9 Only a slight pressure on the keel is necessary to trip the flower. **1930** *Jrnl. Amer. Soc. Agronomy* XXII. 782 The flowers were left exposed and not tripped artificially. **1978** *Nature* 7 Sept. 54/1 Most inbred lines show poor seed set unless their flowers are visited by bees or artificially manipulated (tripped) and are therefore called auto-sterile.

tripack (trəi·pæk). *Photogr.* Also **tri-pack**, † **-pak**. [f. TRI- + PACK *sb.*[1]] A set of three superimposed plates or films with different colour sensitivities and kept in contact, so that three separation negatives can be obtained at one exposure; also (*integral tripack*), a film having three such emulsions on the one base.

1911 *Brit. Jrnl. Photogr.* 3 Mar. (Suppl.) 19 (*heading*) The Ives Tripak system of colour photography. **1924** *Ibid.* Sept. (Suppl.) 36/1 It is fundamentally impossible to obtain satisfactory results by the tri-pack system. **1931** [see *separation negative* s.v. *SEPARATION 14]. **1953** [see *INTEGRAL *a.* 2]. **1957** R. W. G. HUNT *Reproduction of Colour* v. 47 (*caption*) Sensitization of the layers in Kodachrome, Ektachrome, Kodacolor and other similar integral tripacks. **1973** D. A. SPENCER *Focal Dict. Photogr. Technol.* 606 The coloured positive images may be produced..*in-situ* by using integral tripack material.

triparental: see *TRI- 1 a.

tripa:rtisa·n, *a.* [f. TRI- + PARTISAN *a.*] Of, representing, or composed of members of, three (political or other) parties.

1959 *Economist* 14 Mar. 950/2 Candidates deliver brief speeches of equal length to an invited bi-partisan or tripartisan audience. **1965** *Ibid.* 20 Feb. 731/1 The cross-currents of party strife over what should be a tripartisan policy. **1972** D. DAKIN *Unification of Greece* v. 76 Otho accepted a tripartisan cabinet of seven who had been recommended by Makriyannis.

tripartism (trəipā·ɹtiz'm). [f. TRIPART(ITE *a.* + -ISM.] **1.** Division into three political parties or other groups. Also *transf.*

1954 B. & R. NORTH tr. *M. Duverger's Pol. Parties* II. i. 222 A tripartism analogous to that in England at the same period where the Socialist party was taking up a position alongside the two 'bourgeois' parties. **1964** *Listener* 1 Oct. 505/1 If different types of secondary school really were 'separate but equal', the attacks upon tripartism would lose much force.

2. A system under which representatives of three groups engage in consultation, negotiation, or joint action; *spec.* a system of economic planning by representatives of government, employers, and trade unions.

1961 *Guardian* 14 June 18/6 The Soviet insistence on tripartism and triunity. **1974** *Government & Opposition* IX. 405 The British flirtation with planning throughout the 1960s could be characterized as toothless tripartism. **1980** *Times* 17 May 14/3 Meetings with Ministers are not the 'tripartism' that the TUC wants.

tripe[1]. Add: **1. c.** ‖ *tripe(s) à la mode de Caen*, a traditional French dish of tripe cooked with carrots, onions, and cow heels in cider or white wine. Also *tripe à la mode* (*du pays*).

1859 THACKERAY *Virginians* II. iii. 26 'And an orchard ..and a dish of tripe *à la mode du pays*!'..Museau would ..return to the subject of Normandy, and cyder, and '*trippes* [sic] *à la mode de Caen*.' **1936** E. WAUGH *Waugh in Abyssinia* ii. 71 From time to time she would placard the town with news of some special delicacy—*Grand Souper. Tripes à la mode de Caen.* **1968** E. HYAMS *Mischief Makers* ii. 20 An improbable garden-restaurant where we sat eating *tripe à la mode*. **1970** SIMON & HOWE *Dict. Gastronomy* 376/2 The classical way of preparing tripe in France is *Tripe à la mode de Caen*.

3. Now applied esp. to artistic work, opinions, conversation, or the like: worthless stuff, rubbish.

1892, 1895 [in Dict.]. **1902** 'T. LE BRETON' *Mod. Christian* viii. 80 She puts in six or seven pages of her own tripe. **1927** C. CONNOLLY *Let.* Aug. in *Romantic Friendship* (1975) 313 Ordinary talk is such ghastly tripe once voice and gesture are removed. **1935** I. MILLER *School Tie* xiv. 277 'I've tried hard, sir; really I have.' 'Tripe! You've tried to get out of work.' **1952** W. STEVENS *Let.* 24 Oct. (1967) 763 Non-objective art without an aesthetic basis seems to be an especially unpleasant kettle of tripe. **1963** [see *CODSWALLOP]. **1973** W. H. CANAWAY *Harry doing Good* I. ii. 22 The group of girls who were watching some tripe on television.

4. *tripe sausage*; **tripe-hound** *slang*, (*a*) an unpleasant or contemptible person; also *spec.* a newspaper reporter or an informant; (*b*) a contemptuous term for a dog; *spec.* in Austral. and N.Z., a sheep-dog.

1923 J. MANCHON *Le Slang* 320 *Tripe-hound*,..un sale cabot, un clebs à poubelles. **1928** D. L. SAYERS *Unpleasantness at Bellona Club* xv. 176 If you'll call off your tripe-hounds, we'll let you have an interview and a set of photographs. **1933** L. G. D. ACLAND in *Press* (Christchurch, N.Z.) 23 Dec. 15/7 *Tripe-hound*, slang for sheep dog. This was common on South Canterbury stations in the 'nineties, and I always thought it a New Zealand word until I came across it in an English novel the other day, 'Early Closing', I think. In the novel the word was applied to a spaniel! **1935** J. BUCHAN *House of Four Winds* iv. 98 If your tripe-hounds had been worth their keep they would have seen me meet him. **1937** N. MARSH *Vintage Murder* viii. 87 You damned little tripe-hound. **1946** B. MARSHALL *George Brown's Schooldays* 123 Draw, you sorry tripehound, draw. **1966** 'L. LANE' *ABZ of Scouse* 111 *Tripe-hound*, a mongrel dog. Also applied to a racing greyhound that persists in putting up a disappointing performance. **1966** P. V. PRICE *France* II. 219 *Andouilles limousines*. Tripe sausages, usually served grilled. **1981** 'M. HEBDEN' *Pel is Puzzled* viii. 73 Andouillettes, the tripe sausage of the region.

triped (trəi·ped). [ad. L. *tripēs*, *-ped-is*, three-footed, three-legged, f. *tri-* TRI- + *pēs* foot.] A three-legged animal.

1916 *Daily Colonist* (Victoria, B.C.) 2 July 4/5 A three-legged chicken is the pride of a brood of a dozen hatched last week... The triped is quite lively and is putting lots of joy into the life of the Simpson barnyard. **1954** W. K. HANCOCK *Country & Calling* 14 Peter [*sc.* a horse] went permanently lame after a week or two of work; he was a triped, William said, and no use to a bush minister in his professional capacity. **1971** I. BROWN *Old & Young* xiv. 220 The small child is a quadruped... Then comes the erect and active biped. At last the codger limps along using a stick for an extra limb. As one who has reached the triped stage I am denied the pleasure of..exercise.

tripelennamine (trəipele·nămīn). *Pharm.* [f. TRI- + P(YRIDYL + E(THY)LEN(E + AMINE.] An antihistamine drug, $C_{16}H_{21}N_3$, given orally as the crystalline hydrochloride or citrate.

1947 *Jrnl. Amer. Med. Assoc.* 31 May 454/2 Granulocytopenia is believed not to have been described hitherto among the untoward side effects of tripelennamine hydrochloride, 'pyribenzamine' (N.N.R.) (N'-pyridyl-N'-benzyl-N-dimethylethylenediamine hydrochloride), therapy. **1962, 1974** [see *PYRIBENZAMINE].

tripey (trəi·pi), *a. colloq.* Also **tripy**. [f. TRIPE[1] + -Y[1].] Inferior, trashy, rubbishy, worthless.

1955 E. BLISHEN *Roaring Boys* IV. 239 How you can tell them to paint in the same tripey way as me, I don't know. **1962** L. DAVIDSON *Rose of Tibet* x. 177 'Don't you like any of our books?..What do you think of this one?' 'It looks a bit tripy to me.' **1968** R. JEFFRIES *Traitor's Crime* iv. 49 It's a case of the more tripey, the more relaxation. **1971** 'M. UNDERWOOD' *Trout in Milk* xiv. 145 The jury'll never convict on the tripey evidence the prosecution have brought.

trip-hammer. (Earlier examples.)

1781 S. PETERS *Gen. Hist. Connecticut* 265 Anchor-making is done by water and trip-hammers. *a* **1817** T. DWIGHT *Trav. New-Eng.* (1821) II. 15 Here he built a shop; and set up the first trip-hammer in this part of the country.

triphibian (trəifi·biăn). [Irreg. f. TRI- + AM)PHIBIAN *sb.*] One who or that which is capable of existing or operating in three different spheres, esp. on land, on water, and in the air. (An occasional word.)

1935 *Sun* (Baltimore) 26 Oct. 1/2 Constantinos Vlachos' invention, which he had intended should travel on the ground, in the air and on water, collapsed upon him in flames today as he was demonstrating it on the lawn of the Library of Congress. The device, which Vlachos, a resident of Washington, called a triphibian, has never been off the ground, his wife said. **1943** W. S. CHURCHILL in *Amer. Speech* (1944) XIX. 14/2 He [*sc.* Lord Mountbatten] is what I venture to call a complete triphibian. **1943** *Punch* 8 Sept. 197 (*caption*) Looking Eastward. Mr. Punch's portrait of a 'Triphibian'. **1977** H. OSMOND in A. Huxley *Moksha* viii. 39 Soon my dear friend [*sc.* A. Huxley], the wise and gentle triphibian, for that was his own definition of man, was no more.

triphibious (trəifi·biəs), *a.* [Irreg. f. TRI- + AM)PHIBIOUS *a.*] Capable of living or operating on land, on water, and in the air; *spec.* of or pertaining to military operations involving land, sea, and air forces. Hence **triphi·biously** *adv.* (*rare*).

1941 L. HORE-BELISHA in *Times* 4 Nov. 2/3 Whether or not amphibious—or rather triphibious—raids at unexpected points along the extensive coastline..would at this stage seriously distract the enemy was doubtful. **1950** A. DE SEVERSKY *Air Power* (1952) ii. 25 Either we shall continue to divide our national potential three ways to support an outlived triphibious method of war-making, or we shall concentrate it. **1964** D. MACARTHUR *Reminiscences* VI. 166 Ground, air, and sea operations were thoroughly co-ordinated. It was a new type of campaign —three-dimensional warfare—the triphibious concept. **1978** *Sci. Amer.* Dec. 29/2 In southeastern Asia, however, some 50 species of frogs have lengthened toes, arrayed in a still wider web, and swim the air—triphibiously. **1982** *Contemp. Rev.* Jan. 51 Their service is universal and triphibious.

tripho:sphopy·ridine nu·cleotide. *Biochem.* [f. TRI- + PHOSPHO- + PYRIDINE + *NUCLEOTIDE.] = *nicotinamide-adenine dinucleotide* s.v. *NICOTINAMIDE b.

1937 *Chem. Abstr.* XXXI. 718 (*heading*) Oxidation of Robison's ester with the aid of triphosphopyridine nucleotide. **1951** *Sci. News* XXII. 80 This reaction, which uses di- or tri-phosphopyridine nucleotide as a hydrogen carrier may thus be a key reaction in photosynthesis. **1962** [see *DIPHOSPHOPYRIDINE NUCLEOTIDE].

triping (trəi·piŋ). *Sc.* [Perh. f. TRIPE[1] + -ING[1].] Coal as brought to the pit-head, not yet cleaned or graded.

1886 J. BARROWMAN *Mining Terms* 68 *Triping*, a kind of drossy coal. **1921** *Glasgow Herald* 21 Apr. 5 A 'triping' ton..represents about 55 per cent. of round coal, 40 per cent. of dross, and 5 per cent. of dirt. **1923** *Ibid.* 22 Dec. 5 The miner produces what is known in the trade as 'triping'. **1924** *Ibid.* 6 Oct. 8 The coals are filled in the hutches at the coal face as 'triping'—large and small mixed.

tripla. Delete † *Obs.* and add later examples.

1944 W. APEL *Harvard Dict. Mus.* 608/2 Nominally, this proportion was *proportio tripla* (another name for such a *Nachtanz* was *Tripla*). **1980** *Early Music* Jan. 120/2 Whilst I applaud the attempt to maintain a definite relationship with the main pulse, the required effect might sometimes be a stately *sesquialtera* rather than a hectic *tripla*.

tripla: pl. of *TRIPLUM.

triple, *sb.* **1. b.** Delete † *Obs. rare* and add later examples.

1966 D. BENNETT *Stranger in his Grave* viii. 66, I wanted to..lie naked in an air-conditioned room with a triple of aspirins inside me. **1981** *Northeast Woods & Waters* Jan. 11/2 We finally settled down and started to pick individual targets and stopped shooting at triples or whole flocks.

2. d. *Chem.* A group of three atoms or ions.

1952 *Jrnl. Chem. Physics* XX. 685/2 I_{123} is an integral involving a triple of atoms arranged as in the figure. **1977** *Sci. Amer.* July 95/2 (*caption*) A sodium cation (Na^+) might attract to its vicinity two independent solvated electrons, forming an 'ion triple'.

e. *Horseracing.* = *TRIFECTA.

1972 *Britannica Bk. of Year* 733/3 *Triple, specif.*, a system of betting on races in which the bettor must pick the first, second, and third horses in this sequence in a specified race in order to win. **1976** *N.Y. Times* 21 Aug. 22 They had hit on a triple (picking the first three horses in the right order), and it was the young woman's turn to collect.

6. *Baseball.* A hit which enables the batter to reach third base.

1880 *Chicago Inter-Ocean* 21 June 8/4 In the fifth Farrell's two-baser, Ward's triple hit, Bradley's triple hit, and Walker's fumbled grounder gave the Champions two earned runs. **1887** *Chicago Tribune* 3 May 3/1 He made in succession a single, double, triple, and home run. **1926** [see *HOME *a.* 4]. **1949** *Milwaukie* (Oregon) *Rev.* 4 Aug. 4/4 The hard working first sacker collected his first triple of the year. **1974** *Birmingham* (Alabama) *Post-Herald* 29 June A 14/2 With two out, Bill North singled and scored on Campaneris' triple.

7. = *TREBLE *sb.* 2 j.

1981 W. H. HALLAHAN *Trade* v. 153 He poured himself another drink—a triple. **1981** G. MARKSTEIN *Ultimate Issue* 174 Welk poured them all triples. 'Salut,' he toasted.

triple, *a.* (*adv.*) Add: **A.** *adj.* **5.** *triple agent* = *treble agent* s.v. *TREBLE *a.* 3; *triple alliance*: also, an alliance of trade unions representing miners, railwaymen, and transport workers; *triple bond* (Chem.) [*BOND *sb.*[1] 13 e], a bond in which the two atoms 'share' three pairs of electrons rather than one pair; hence *triple-bonded* adj.; *triple concerto*, a concerto with three solo parts; *triple cross*, the act of betraying one party in a transaction by pretending to betray the other, or of betraying a person who has betrayed another; so *triple-crossing*; *triple crown*, (*b*) also applied to several other instances of winning three victories in of the Kentucky Derby, the Preakness Stakes, and the Belmont Stakes, and, in Rugby Union and hockey, the winning by England, Ireland, Scotland, or Wales of victory over each of the other three in the same season; *triple entente* (earlier example); *triple jump*, an athletic long jump event, also known as the hop, step, and jump (cf. HOP *sb.*[2] 3 a in Dict. and Suppl.); *triple junction* (Geol.), a region at which the boundaries of three lithospheric plates meet; (Petrogr.), a point where three grain boundaries meet at angles of approximately 120 degrees; *triple mirror* = *three-way mirror* s.v. *THREE-WAY *a.* a; *triple play* (earlier example); *triple point*, (*b*) (Physics), the temperature and pressure at which the solid, liquid, and vapour phases of a pure substance can coexist in equilibrium; the point representing this state in a phase diagram (marked by the junction of three lines); more widely, an analogous state or point for any three phases of a substance; (*c*) (Petrogr.), an invariant point involving three phases, e.g. where kyanite, andalusite, and sillimanite are stable in the system $Al_2\ SiO_5$; *triple spacing*, the spacing of typewritten or other text so that two blank lines separate adjacent lines of text (see *triple-spaced*, sense C. 1 a below); *triple time*: also *transf.* in prosody; *triple tonguing*, the use of the tongue to achieve rapid articulation in groups of three notes on the flute and brass instruments; hence (as back-formation) *triple-tongue* vb. intr.; *triple vaccine* (Med.), (*a*) a vaccine containing three species of the *Salmonella* bacteria, used as a prophylactic against typhoid and paratyphoid; (*b*) a vaccine containing diphtheria and tetanus toxoids and the killed whooping cough organism, administered in early childhood as a prophylactic against conditions caused by these.

1968 J. WAINWRIGHT *Web of Silence* 94 Jackson figures he's created a double-agent. We don't agree. The way we see it, Schneller's maybe a triple-agent. **1982** T. HEALD *Masterstroke* viii. 159 Something in Intelligence. Our Intelligence. Theirs too... A triple agent at least. **1915** *Times* 9 Oct. 3/1 The conference of the Miners' Federation of Great Britain..adopted unanimously the scheme of a triple alliance between railwaymen, transport workers, and miners. **1974** *Times* 8 Jan. (Europe Suppl.) p. ii/2 As Christmas approached, a state of affairs was fast developing reminiscent of that which occurred when the 'triple alliance' of miners, dockers and railwaymen sprang into being during the run-up to the General Strike of 1926. **1889** G. M'GOWAN tr. *Bernthsen's Organic Chem.* i. 55 The constitutional formula for acetylene, C_2H_2, is assumed to be CH≡CH, according to which the carbon atoms are joined together by a triple bond. **1971** *Nature* 10 Dec. 333/2 The CO molecule has a very stable triple bond which is difficult to dissociate. **1937** *Jrnl. Amer. Chem. Soc.* LIX. 2091/2 The carbon–oxygen bond [in BH_3CO] presumably involves resonance between double- and triple-bonded structures. **1965** PHILLIPS & WILLIAMS *Inorg. Chem.* I. xiii. 484 In the most extreme cases there is some reason for saying that oxygen is triple-bonded. **1879** GROVE *Dict. Mus.* I. 389/1 Sometimes concertos are written for more than one solo instrument, and are then known as double, triple, etc., concertos as the case may be. **1932** *Daily Tel.* 8 Oct. 8/3 In March a triple concerto for flute, clarinet, bassoon and orchestra by J. R. Heath will be introduced. **1985** *Daily Tel.* 22 Jan. 9 The London Sinfonietta..had played the Triple Concerto on the first night of the Tippett birthday celebration week. **1971** J. AIKEN *Nightly Deadshade* vii. 76, I..resolve to set a few subliminal tests for my fellow-conspirators.. in case they are working the triple-cross. **1978** *Times* 25 Jan. 11/5 Anthony Price is a master of the double (or even triple) cross. **1922** S. LEWIS *Babbitt* xix. 236 'Kind of double-crossing.' 'It ain't. It's triple-crossing. It's the public that gets double-crossed.' **1899** *Whitaker's Almanack 1900* 648/2 In their last match at Cardiff against Wales, Ireland won by a try to nothing, securing the triple crown with three straight victories as in 1894. **1946** M. C. SELF *Horseman's Encycl.* 413 Race horses which win the Kentucky Derby, the Preakness and the Belmont are said to win the Triple Crown. **1953** *Times* 10 Apr. 4/5 A victory for England [over Scotland at hockey] will mean that the meeting of Ireland and England in Dublin on April 18 will be a fight for the triple crown. **1974** *Sunday Tel.* 7 Apr. 36/7 Hockey history was made on the Cardiff University ground at Llanrumney where Wales won the Championship and took the Triple Crown for the first time since the quadrangular tourney began in 1903. **1976** *National Observer* (U.S.) 22 May 6/4 She may never win a Triple Crown race herself—no woman ever has—but she says she'll 'definitely ride again; it's in my blood'. **1978** *World of Tennis* (BP Yearbk.) 179 The Virginia Slims Championship is the first event in the Triple Crown (Wimbledon and Forest Hills are the others) which has replaced the Grand Slam at the pinnacle of achievement in women's tennis. **1979** M. BOYCE *I was There!* 47/2 Twelve..the number of times Wales have won the Triple Crown. **1979** *Harvard Gaz.* 23 Feb. 2 Zoo Captain Bill Renke is the only person to have won the tiddlywinks Triple Crown—the Singles, Pairs, and Team Championships. **1910** *Encycl. Brit.* IX. 949/1 (*heading*) The Triple entente and the Triple Alliance. **1964** M. WATMAN *Encycl. Athletics* 150/1 Basically, the rules for the triple jump (formerly known as the hop, step and jump) are identical with those governing the long jump. **1972** *N.Y. Times* 4 June 4/7 The runner-up in the voting was John Craft, who set an American triple-jump record of 55·5. **1969** *Nature* 11 Oct. 125/2 Evolution of such triple junctions can produce many of the changes which would otherwise appear to have been caused by a change in the direction or magnitude of the relative motion between plates. **1976** R. H. VERNON *Metamorphic Processes* v. 137 Three grains meet at a point ('triple junction'), the interfacial angles closely approximating 120°. **1979** MALLORY & CARGO *Physical Geol.* xvii. 437 Examination of these triple junctions shows that the three branches of the junction may involve convergence, divergence, or translational (sideways) movement. **1982** ARAMAKI & UI in R. S. Thorpe *Andesites* iii. 260/1 Japan and the surrounding islands form three chains of island arcs which meet at a trench-trench-type triple junction located at *c.* 34° N and 142° E. **1907** *Yesterday's Shopping* (1969) 110/2 Triple folding mirrors..Size of glass, 9 by 9 in.—20/3. **1920** S. LEWIS *Main Street* xiv. 164 A real dressing-table with a triple mirror. **1967** 'K. O'HARA' *Unknown Man* iv. 29 She adjusted the triple mirror and took up the eye-liner. **1869** *De Witt's Official Base Ball Guide* 42 Remarks concerning double and triple plays will apply to the third baseman as much as to either of the other base-players. **1872** J. THOMSON in *Rep. Brit. Assoc. Adv. Sci. 1871* II. 32 We must suppose three curves (namely, the line between gas and liquid, the line between liquid and solid, and the line between gas and solid) to meet in one point... This point of pressure and temperature for any substance may then be called the triple point for that substance. **1879** [see *ice line* s.v. *ICE *sb.* 8]. **1955** *Sci. Amer.* Mar. 52/3 In another change, the absolute temperature scale was redefined in terms of a single fixed reference point—the triple point of water. **1964** J. H. BROPHY et al. *Thermodynamics of Structure* ii. 20 If the specified temperature and pressure are the coordinates of point *D*, all three phases coexist in equilibrium with one another. Point *D* is called the *triple point.* **1966** [see *ice-point* s.v. *ICE *sb.* 8]. **1978** *Nature* 14 Dec. 696/2 One possible reason..is that a solid–solid–liquid triple point could exist near 10^7 Pa..in the proposed phase diagram [of carbon]. **1979** K. G. COX et al. *Interpretation of Igneous Rocks* iii. 47 Figure 3.1 shows a one-component phase diagram for a substance such as H_2O. It consists of three fields in each of which a single phase exists. Each pair of fields meets in a curve along which two phases co-exist, and the three fields meet in a point U (so-called triple point) at which all three phases co-exist. **1983** D. S. BARKER *Igneous Rocks* iii. 28 The 'triple point' where liquid, vapor, and solid coexist in equilibrium has yet to be experimentally located for any silicate. **1957** A. C. LLOYD et al. *Gregg Typewriting for Colleges* 2/1 In triple spacing, typing appears on every third line with 2 blank lines between the typed ones. **1978** *Brit. Med. Jrnl.* 16 Dec. 1724/3 Typing should be on one side of the paper, with double or triple spacing between the lines. **1880** G. M. HOPKINS *Let.* 5 Sept. (1935) 107 So far as I know triple time is in English verse a shy and late thing. **1951** W. MORUM *Gabriel* I. i. 7

He triple-tongued up the scale to high C. **1967** *Crescendo* Feb. 23/3 The band stopped for several bars, and Charles *triple-tongued*—at breakneck tempo—and never faltered or slowed down once. **1879** GROVE *Dict. Mus.* I. 459/2 Triple tongueing is also possible. **1951** W. MORUM *Gabriel* II. vi. 211 You could rattle out triple-tonguing stuff when you was a kid. **1961** C. W. MONK in A. Baines *Mus. Instruments* xi. 280 Rapid passages are managed by alternating 't' and 'k' in 'double-tonguing' and fast triplets by 'triple tonguing' 'ttk' (or 'tkt, ktk'). **1917** *Jrnl. Amer. Med. Assoc.* 22 Sept. 100/2 The reaction following the inoculation of the triple vaccine was no different than when the typhoid vaccine was alone used. **1947** *Ann. Rev. Microbiol.* I. 327 A reinvestigation of the antigenicity of the strains routinely used for the preparation of typhoid and 'triple' vaccine..resulted in the introduction of strains rich in somatic antigen. **1970** PASSMORE & ROBSON *Compan. Med. Stud.* II. xxii. 22/2 The injection of the triple vaccine may be combined with three oral doses of poliomyelitis vaccine. **1982** *Times* 8 Sept. 1/4 Kate is to have her third triple vaccine against whooping cough, diphtheria and tetanus today.

C. 1. a. *triple-barrelled, -hummocked, mirrored, -tiered*; **triple-spaced**, typed or formatted so that two blank lines separate adjacent lines of text; also as quasi-*adv.*; (see *triple spacing*, sense A 5 above).

1934 W. S. CHURCHILL *Marlborough* II. xxv. 561 Between their squadrons appeared the triple-barrelled guns, which opened a rapid fire. **1977** *Navy News* Sept. 2/3 Up, up, and away goes H.M.S. Salisbury's Squid triple-barrelled mortar, the last firing mounting in the Royal Navy. **1876** G. M. HOPKINS *Poems* (1967) 64 The triple-hummocked Giant's Stool. **1939** R. CHANDLER *Big Sleep* vii. 45 There was perfume on the triple-mirrored dressing table. **1970** R. RENDELL *Guilty Thing Surprised* iii. 38 Between the two mirrors stood a triple-mirrored dressing table. **1946** R. CHANDLER *Let.* 6 Oct. (1981) 80 The silly little triple-spaced half pages I type on. **1966** F. STEWART *Deadly Nightcap* iii. 40 There were margins of twenty degrees on either side of the typescript, and it was triple-spaced. **1978** M. H. CLARK *Stranger is Watching* xix. 81, I typed them triple-spaced. **1807** J. BARLOW *Columbiad* VII. 267 Flames, triple tier'd, and tides of smoke, arise, And fulminations rock the seas and skies. **1962** E. SNOW *Other Side of River* (1963) ii. 23 A balcony overlooking the Outer City gave a view of the distant, triple-tiered, blue-glazed round roofs of the Temple of Heaven. **1972** M. J. BOSSE *Incident at Naha* i. 11 He.. went to his triple-tiered pipe rack.

b. *triple-action, -digit, -expansion* (earlier example), *-threat*.

1934 WEBSTER 725/2 A *triple-action die*, when in operation, has a movement, produced by springs or a triple-action press, of two punches, two matrices, or a punch and a matrix, within either the upper or lower half of the die. **1960** *Farmer & Stockbreeder* 29 Mar. (Suppl.) 11/1 From Steiner comes news of two brand new hair aids. The first is Pearl Foam, a triple-action shampoo which cleanses, adds lustre and protects the hair from the weather. **1974** M. TAYLOR tr. *Metz's Film Lang.* ix. 233 This triple-action construction gives the ending of the film..its true meaning. **1976** *N.Y. Times* 7 Mar. III. 15/6 The foot-dragging is caused by Argentina's triple-digit inflation. **1979** *Time* 28 May 12 The cost of living for April had jumped a shocking 8·7%, more than 100% if projected over the entire year. The admission provoked howls of alarm that the country could be heading toward uncontrollable triple-digit inflation. **1882** *Engineering* 12 May 474/1, I may mention that within the last few weeks there has been a steamer completed to work at a pressure of 150 lb. per square inch with triple expansion engines very similar to those fitted in the Aberdeen. **1939** W. H. BAUMER *Sports as taught & played at West Point* 40 Any backs who possess the three qualifications of being a good runner, passer and kicker to a marked degree are triple-threat men. **1972** J. MOSEDALE *Football* v. 67 Football no longer requires the triple threat back—the player who can run and kick as well as punt.

2. a. *triple-locked, -quick*.

1974 HAWKEY & BINGHAM *Wild Card* xiv. 123 The triple-locked door to his apartment. **1951** L. MACNEICE tr. *Goethe's Faust* 226 How triple-quick we spirits fly!

c. with vbs., as *triple-lock*.

1876 'MARK TWAIN' *Tom Sawyer* xxxii. 251, I had its big door sheathed with boiler iron..and triple-locked. **1976** B. BOVA *Multiple Man* xvi. 177 The first thing I did was..to make certain I was alone..after triple-locking the front door.

triple, *v.* Add: **4.** *Baseball.* To hit a triple (see *TRIPLE *sb.* 6).

1908 *Sporting News* 17 Sept. 4/5 The very next day he tripled with the bases full. **1972** *N.Y. Times* 4 June 3/1 Danny Thompson tripled, and consecutive singles by Rod Carew, Harmon Killebrew, Steve Braun and Bobby Darwin gave the Twins a 2-0 lead.

tri·ple-decker *a.* [f. TRIPLE *a.*, after DOUBLE-DECKER.] **1.** Of sandwiches: consisting of three layers of bread and two layers of filling.

1946 *New Yorker* 16 Mar. 21/2 We are the land of the between-meals snack, of the triple-decker sandwich. **1973** *Cookery Year* (Reader's Digest Assoc.) 133/5 *Club sandwiches*, one of the best inventions of the American kitchen is this triple-decker sandwich.

2. Of bunk beds: arranged one above another in threes.

1979 *Arizona Daily Star* 5 Aug. A 8/2 Rosenthal walked into a tin-roofed quonset hut jammed with triple-decker bunk beds. **1980** *Nat. Geographic* June 866 Those who need rest..retire..to homemade triple-decker triple beds.

triple-hea·der. *U.S.* Also **tripleheader.** [f. TRIPLE *a.*, after DOUBLE-HEADER.] **1.** In baseball, etc., a sporting event at which three consecutive matches are staged. Also *transf.* and *fig.*

1961 in WEBSTER. **1970** *New Yorker* 3 Oct. 34/2 Anybody who can't straighten out a plain old two-league, six-division distribution of twenty-six teams, each of which plays games both inside and outside its own division..isn't in shape for a single Sunday TV triple-header. **1979** *Honolulu Advertiser* 8 Jan. C-2/3 Sheridan Midas Mufflers..annihilated Manoa 15-5 in the opener of a Honolulu AJA Senior Baseball tripleheader yesterday.

2. A situation, occurrence, etc., having three aspects or involving three participants.

1976 *New Yorker* 29 Mar. 16/1 In his first attempt at a tripleheader (writer-director-star) he gets bogged down in an overelaborate production. **1977** *Ibid.* 4 July 23/1 The Cooper-Hewitt Museum, which this year has been throwing new exhibitions at us almost faster than we can catch them, has most recently unveiled a triple-header. **1977** *Washington Post* 13 Jan. C 1/3 Sens. Donald Riegle (D-Mich.), Lowell Weicker (R-Conn.) and Herman Talmadge (D-Ga.) made it a triple-header with their divorce announcements—getting it done before the new congressional session began and, of course, a few months after election time.

tripler (tri·plər). *Electronics.* [f. TRIPLE *v.* + -ER^1.] Any device for producing an output whose frequency or whose voltage is three times that of the input.

1924 S. R. ROGET *Dict. Electr. Terms* 244/2 *Static frequency-changer*... Also called doublers and triplers in the cases of twice and three times the original frequency. **1947** L. B. YOUNG in C. G. Montgomery *Technique of Microwave Measurements* vi. 371 In this frequency range the push-pull tripler of Fig. 6.22 is used. **1973** G. J. KING *Newnes Colour Television Servicing Man.* I. i. 29/2 The final 24 kV potential is developed only when the tripler e.h.t. output is connected to the tube final anode.

triplet. Add: **2. j.** *Poker.* (See quot. 1864.)

1864 W. B. DICK *Amer. Hoyle* 164 *Triplets* are three cards of the same denomination, and rank higher than two pairs. For example;—three Deuces beat a pair of Aces and Kings. **1887** J. W. KELLER *Game of Draw Poker* 14 Full Hand—(Triplets accompanied by a pair)... A full hand beats a flush. **1950** [see *SANDBAGGER 2].

k. (i) *Physics* and *Chem.* A multiplet (sense *a) composed of three lines or energy levels. Freq. *attrib.*, esp. designating an atom with two unpaired electrons and $S=1$.

1879 *Proc. R. Soc.* XXX. 29 The flame spectrum of magnesium was examined, a green triplet was observed. **1922** [see *SINGLET 3 a]. **1934, 1937** [see *INTERCOMBINATION]. **1950** G. HERZBERG *Spectra of Diatomic Molecules* (ed. 2) v. 216 Molecules with an even number of electrons have odd multiplicities (singlets, triplets, ...) since *S* is integral. **1977** *Nature* 3 Nov. 15/1 The Earth has an atmosphere containing diatomic triplet oxygen..essential for life.

(ii) *Particle Physics.* A multiplet (sense *b) of three sub-atomic particles.

1937 [see *SINGLET 3 b]. **1961** M. GELL-MANN in Gell-Mann & Ne'eman *Eightfold Way* (1964) 12 We have a triplet ρ of vector mesons coupled to the isotopic spin current and a singlet vector meson ω^0 coupled to the hypercharge current. **1968** [see *OCTET, OCTETTE 3 c]. **1975** *Sci. Amer.* Oct. 40/1 The pion is a triplet with an average mass of ·137 GeV and three charge states: +1, 0 and −1.

3. triplet code *Genetics*, the accepted version of the genetic code in which amino-acids are specified by three successive nucleotides in a nucleic acid molecule.

1957 *Proc. Nat. Acad. Sci.* XLIII. 687 Such triplet codes..have an excess of information, since there are sixty-four different triplets for the twenty amino acids. **1976** P. COLLARD *Devel. Microbiol.* viii. 107 The correctness of the triplet code was soon verified by the elegant experiments of Nirenberg.

triplex, *a.* (*sb.*) Add: **1. b.** *triplex board*, a type of cardboard consisting of three layers felted together by pressure without the use of adhesive.

1921 H. A. MADDOX *Dict. Stationery* 78 *Triplex board*, a cheap class of pasteboard or ticket board which derives its name from the fact that it comprises three layers. **1962** F. T. DAY *Introd. to Paper* iv. 46 In the case of Triplex boards one grade of pulp is used for the middle while the two outside sheets are made of a thinner substance to make up the finished board.

2. *Genetics.* Of a polyploid individual: having the dominant allele of any particular gene represented three times.

1921, etc. [see *NULLIPLEX *a.*]. **1929** *Jrnl. Genetics* XXI. 138 If we assume 14/16 to be triplex for Y the unexpected ivory plant could then have arisen by (1) non-disjunction.., or (2) irregularity of disjunction in the equational division.

3. (Usu. with capital initial.) The proprietary name of a type of toughened or laminated glass, orig. *spec.* consisting of two layers of glass and a layer of celluloid between them.

1923 *Trade Marks Jrnl.* 28 Nov. 2495 Triplex. Use claimed from 2nd August 1912... Safety Glass in sheets. The Triplex Safety Glass Co. Ltd. **1927** M. ARLEN *Young Men in Love* II. 128 'I live in such a glass house, Peter!' 'Well, so does everyone else.' 'Oh, no, other people's are made of Triplex!' **1930** *Times Educ. Suppl.* 27 Dec. (Home & Classroom Suppl.) p. i/3 The car was fully equipped with three speeds,.. Triplex glass screen, windscreen wiper,..side curtains, and hood bag. **1935** L. MACNEICE *Poems* 40 Chromium dogs on the bonnet, faces behind the triplex screens. **1970** P. DICKINSON *Seals* i. 26 Even through that grimy and half-opaque triplex, the harbour had seemed awkwardly placed.

4. a. An apartment or other residence on three floors. Chiefly *U.S.*

1932 E. FERBER in *Hearst's Internat.* Mar. 18/1 Photographs in the magazines showed her glamorous apartment—triplex, with balcony overhanging the East River. **1978** *New York* 3 Apr. 91 (Advt.), 40' converted mansion, elevator, magnificent owner's triplex plus high income apartments. **1981** *Times* 3 Aug. 10/5 A 21-room 'triplex' (ie, on three floors) going for 'only' $9 million.

b. A building containing three self-contained residences or suites of rooms; also, one of the dwellings in such a building. Cf. *DUPLEX *sb.* 1. Chiefly *N. Amer.*

1962 *Maclean's Mag.* (Toronto) 10 Mar. 37/1 They wanted to build three triplexes. 'Definitely not,' Reeve Fred Hall told Norman. **1971** A. BLAISDELL *Practice to Deceive* i. 2 She lived in one unit of a triplex. **1971** *Rand Daily Mail* (Home Owner) 27 Mar. 7/2 City dwellers are gravitating towards high density living (flat complexes.. duplex and triplex..and so on). **1976** *Billings* (Montana) *Gaz.* 30 June 7-D/1 (Advt.), Accelerated depreciation is still available on this new brick tri-plex. This unit features a fantastic view. **1979** *Arizona Daily Star* 5 Aug. B 1/6 She observes construction workers working on a triplex where her display company's warehouses once stood.

Triplice (tri·plitʃe). Also with small initial. [a. It. *triplice* triple; cf. TRIPLEX *a.* (*sb.*).] The Triple Alliance (see TRIPLE *a.* 5) of Germany, Austria-Hungary, and Italy, formed in 1882 against Russia and France. Also *transf.*

1896 *Daily News* 15 Dec. 5/3 The same demand has been made to the other members of the Triplice. **1897** *Ibid.* 6 Sept. 5/2 The Triplice desires peace at any cost. **1901** *Speaker* 20 Apr. 74/2 It would be misleading to call the *Triplice* a League of peace. **1908** *Daily Chron.* 30 July 3/6 A suggestion for a new alliance, a triplice of Britain, France, and Germany, in the interests of peace, was made by Mr. Prust, of Launceston. **1911** DJAVID BEY *Let.* 28 Oct. in R. S. Churchill *Winston S. Churchill* (1969) II. Compan. II. xvii. 1368 The attack of one of the triple alliance powers on our territory has turned the public opinion greatly against the triplice. **1947** *Hist. of The Times* III. x. 250 The conclusion that the Triplice.. was weak as an Alliance, was forced to the forefront of Wallace's mind. **1979** E. INGRAM *Beginning of Great Game* ix. 263 The tsar forestalled Palmerston's attempt to erect a near-eastern triplice [of Britain, Austria and France].

Hence **Tri·plicist**, a supporter of the Triplice; also *attrib.* or as *adj.*

1923 J. BUCHAN *Nations of To-day: Italy* 172 It was able to give a decidedly 'Triplicist' aspect to the enterprise. **1924** *Glasgow Herald* 15 Jan. 7 It is all to the credit of the Triplicists..and very little to that of the Allies.

triploid, *sb.* Restrict *rare.* ? *Obs.* to sense in Dict. and add: **B.** *adj.* *Genetics.* [Cf. *-PLOID.] (Made up of somatic cells) containing three sets of chromosomes. Also as *sb.*, a triploid organism.

1911 *Ann. Bot.* XXV. 933 There is not, so far as I am aware, a single case of a species whose sporophyte has the triploid number of chromosomes. **1927** *Jrnl. Genetics* XVIII. 183 These five are all the configurations which have been seen among several hundred trivalents of triploids..in *Datura* and *Canna*. **1930** *Times Lit. Suppl.* 10 July 578/3 Triploid apples (e.g., Bramley's Seedling) fruit well. **1957** R. A. BEATTY *Parthenogenesis & Polyploidy in Mammalian Devel.* iv. 59 Three of the young [rabbits] lived nearly a year, being the two 'triploids' and a presumed diploid male. **1971** [see *DIPLOID *a.*]. **1973** [see *OCTOPLOID *a.* (*sb.*)].

Hence **tri·ploidy**, the state of being triploid.

1916 *Genetics* I. 237 It seems probable that we have in these plants examples of triploidy (21 chromosomes). **1961** *Lancet* 5 Aug. 318/1 A malformation syndrome associated with triploidy. **1976** *Cytogenetics & Cell Genetics* XVII. 144 Triploidy or diploid/triploid chimerism has been reported in man. **1982** *Annals Human Genetics* XLVI. 223 Human triploidy is a common condition.

‖ **triplum** (tri·plum). *Mus.* Pl. **tripla.** [med. L., neut. of *triplus* TRIPLE *a.*; cf. TREBLE *sb.* 4.] In thirteenth- and fourteenth-century polyphonic vocal music, the third voice part, next but one above the tenor.

1782, 1884 [see TREBLE *sb.* 4]. **1944** W. APEL *Harvard Dict. Mus.* 223/1 *Triplum, quadruplum* are other parts above the tenor, frequently of the same range as the duplum. **1954** *New Oxf. Hist. Music* II. xi. 354 The motet 'Salve virgo virginum/Est il donc ainsi/Aptatur' has 202 notes in the *triplum* (highest voice), 173 in the *motetus* (middle voice), and only 103 in the tenor. **1977** *Early Music* Apr. 185 A glance through the tripla and dupla of 13th-century motets is enough to show that rhythmic styles could be tolerated in music which made a nonsense of poetic scansion.

tripod, *a.* **1.** (Later examples.)

1939 *Oxoniensia* IV. 101 Thirty-seven base and body fragments of tripod pitcher..buff ware, uniform in colour throughout, fairly well fired and hard. **1963** E. M. JOPE in Foster & Alcock *Culture & Environment* xiii. 342 Regional styles are still discernible among these glazed jugs, such as the tripod-pitchers of the twelfth century.

Tripoli. Add: **2.** A large, mild onion; also, the plant producing a bulb of this kind. Also *attrib.*

1822 J. C. LOUDON *Encycl. Gardening* III. i. 715 Tripoli, the largest onion grown; oval, light-red, tinged with green and brown, soft and mild. **1873** *Young Englishwoman* Sept. 446/2 The best varieties [of onion] for autumn sowing are the Tripoli, Giant Madeira, [etc.]. **1932** *Times Educ. Suppl.* 27 Feb. (Home & School Suppl.) p. iv/1 The following crops should be started as soon as possible:.. tripoli onions, shallots, [etc.]. **1951** *Dict. Gardening* (R. Hort. Soc.) III. 1425/2 Such onions as the Roccas, White Lisbon, and Tripoli..are of no value for storing.

Tripoline, *a.* Add: **2.** [f. *Tripoli*, the name of a city and port in North Africa.] Of or pertaining to Tripoli, now the capital of Libya. Also as *sb.*, a native or inhabitant of Tripoli. Cf. next.

1819 A. SALAMÉ *Narr. Exped. Algiers* 6 We found she was a Tripoline polacca, (I am sorry that she was not an Algerine). **1843** *Penny Cycl.* XXV. 256/1 The Tripoline cruisers seldom allowed a ship at sea to escape them if they thought they could make a prize of her with impunity. *Ibid.* In 1832, Yussuf, the last basha of the Caramanli family,..having lost the affection of the Tripolines, after a reign of forty years,..was obliged to abdicate. **1909** [see *TRIPOLITAN *a.*].

Tripolitan (tripǫ·lităn), *a.* (and *sb.*) [ad. It. *tripolitano* (in sense a); in sense b, f. *Tripolitania* (see next).] **a.** = TRIPOLINE *a.* 2. **b.** = TRIPOLITANIAN *a.* Occas. as *sb.*

1783 MISS TULLY *Let.* 3 July in *Narrative Ten Years' Residence at Tripoli* (1817) 5 The Tripolitan dresses, almost covered with gold and silver,..make a most superb appearance. *Ibid.* 3 Sept. 24 The Tripolitans carry the right hand from the breast to the forehead..where they mean to be respectful. **1888** *Encycl. Brit.* XXIII. 575/2 The Tripolitan pirates soon became the terror and scourge of the Mediterranean. **1896** *Geogr. Jrnl.* VII. 150 The Tripolitan range of hills. **1909** G. W. FURLONG *Gateway to Sahara* i. 8 'Tripolitans' signifies the people of the territory, 'Tripoline' a dweller in the town of Tripoli. **1913** R. G. USHER *Pan-Germanism* xii. 184 From the ports on the Tripolitan coast..a flank attack could be directed upon the English communications with Suez. **1928** V. G. CHILDE *Most Anc. East* ii. 25 In the very heart of the Sahara at In-Ezzan, just south of the Tripolitan borders.

Tripolitanian (tripǫlitēⁱ·niăn), *sb.* and *a.* [f. *Tripolitania*: cf. -IAN.] **A.** *sb.* A native or inhabitant of Tripolitania, the region surrounding Tripoli in North Africa. **B.** *adj.* Of or pertaining to Tripolitania. Cf. prec., sense b.

1942 [see *CYRENAICAN *a.*]. **1943** G. CASSERLY *Tripolitania* 5 When this book was begun no enemy stood on Tripolitanian soil. **1963** M. KHADDURI *Modern Libya* ii. 48 Native Tripolitanians were soon to enter the service and their number steadily increased. **1969** J. WRIGHT *Libya* v. 55 The Roman empire has been called 'a federation of municipalities' and the Tripolitanian townsmen derived more benefit from Roman rule than the countryman. **1978** A. MELVILLE-ROSS *Blindfold* x. 60 The Tripolitanians are very much afraid of the nomads. **1981** T. BARLING *Bikini Red North* i. 29 Do what you can with your Tripolitanian argot.

Tripolye (tripǫ·lyĕ). Also **Tripolje.** The name of a village near Kiev in Russia, used *attrib.* to denote a neolithic culture typified by remains found there, which flourished in the western Ukraine and in eastern Romania during the late fourth and third millennia B.C.

1913 [see *PLOSHCHADKA]. **1935** *Jrnl. R. Anthrop. Inst.* LXV. 113 In successful search for painted pottery of the Tripolye type. **1937** *Discovery* Jan. 27/1 The Tripolje culture, so called from the site in Southern Russia on which it was first found, has as its most characteristic feature painted pottery. **1957** G. CLARK *Archæol. & Society* (ed. 3) vi. 190 Significant differences have been noted between the composition of animal remains from sites of the Tripolje culture marked by painted and grooved pottery and from those of the neighbouring Ousatovo culture. **1970** BRAY & TRUMP *Dict. Archaeol.* 237/2 Tripolye culture came to an end with the expansion westwards of steppe cultures of kurgan or Single-Grave type.

‖ **tripot** (trī·po). [Fr.] A gaming-house, a gambling-den.

1864 W. H. AINSWORTH *John Law* I. II. v. 290 The person before us..is a suspected sharper, and a constant frequenter of tripots. **1883** 'OUIDA' *Wanda* I. vii. 264 A winner at a *tripot*, what a hero for you, mother mine. **1909** R. NEVILL *Light come, Light Go* viii. 236 The gaming-resorts of old Paris were filled with people whose reputations for probity were generally a good deal more than doubtful. In one of the best of these *tripots* a gentleman..delayed the game by insisting on searching for a few pieces of gold which he had dropped on the floor. **1930** A. BENNETT *Imperial Palace* xlv. 319 The loss of sixty pounds odd..in a Paris *tripot*.

‖ **tripotage** (trīpotā·ʒ). [Fr.] **a.** Underhand dealings, intrigue. Also *fig.* **b.** *rare.* Pawing, handling, fingering.

In quot. 1853 perh. used mistakenly for *tripotée* large quantity.

1779 DR. WARNER *Let.* Mar. in J. H. Jesse *George Selwyn & his Contemporaries* (1844) IV. 38 An infinite deal of lying, on all sides, and *tripotage*. *Ibid.* 42 But it is all of a piece, such a cursed *tripotage*! **1853** C. BRONTË *Villette* III. xxxvi. 131 At last I got through my list. The patterns for the slippers, the bell-ropes, the cabas were selected—the slides and tassels for the purses chosen—the whole 'tripotage', in short, was off my mind. **1895** *Nineteenth Cent.* Oct. 548 The recent exposures of political *tripotage*. **1932** *Times Lit. Suppl.* 12 May 343/3 Beau Nash, though dabbling deeply in the *tripotage*, deprecated sensational ruins and suicides. **1958** J. LODWICK *Bid Soldiers Shoot* ii. 41 The freshly shaved Hirsch..cornered the two women and subjected their not unwilling flesh to expert *tripotage*.

trippage (tri·pėdʒ). [f. TRIP *sb.*¹ + -AGE.] The act or process of making a series of short journeys over the same route; the number of such journeys made.

1941 *Sun* (Baltimore) 16 Oct. 7/2 Dairy officials pointed out that the new system would eliminate 'back trippage of drivers' and make for 'straight trippage'. Under the old system, most drivers made early morning deliveries and then, on collection days, repeated the routes to collect the money. The second trip will be eliminated under the daylight delivery system. **1972** *Daily Tel.* 5 Apr. 19/4 If milk distribution costs are to be stabilised, some means must be found to push up the trippage rate [of milk bottles]. **1979** *Ibid.* 6 Aug. 2/6 The average milk bottle makes 23 trips to and from the dairy and customer before it is lost or broken... Bottles are still used because their high trippage more than offsets other costs.

tripped (tript), *ppl. a.* [f. TRIP *v.* + -ED¹.] **1.** *Bot.* Of a flower whose pollinating mechanism has been activated by tripping.

1914 *Bull. U.S. Dept. Agric.* No. 75. 5 In artificially tripped flowers..12 out of 34 tripped set seed. **1956** *Nature* 18 Feb. 334/2 The number of tripped florets was recorded and calyces marked each day. **1980** *Sabrao Jrnl.* XII. 104 The seed set of tripped flowers indicates the level of self-fertility.

2. Operated or caused to respond by contact with a projection or other object.

1921 *Conquest* Jan. 130/1 A roller which reacts the 'tripped' brushes or wipers. **1977** R. LUDLUM *Chancellor Manuscript* xxx. 320 Don't worry, there's a set of electronically tripped windows..with..bulletproof glass.

3. *tripped-out*: under the influence of a hallucinogenic drug, esp. LSD. *slang.*

1973 *Listener* 15 Nov. 680/3 The tripped-out nudes in the penthouse flat. **1976** H. FERGUSON *Confessions of Long Distance Acid Head* 11 Everyone was gathered round talking about the arrangements they would make for their 'excursion' the following day. They cared so little for my tripped-out state that they turned out the light and left me in the darkened room.

tripper, *sb.* Add: **5.** (Examples.)

1882 J. D. MCCABE *New York by Sunlight & Gaslight* 244 The 'trippers', as those men are called who only run three-quarters of a day, get $1·50. **1950** *Reading* (Pennsylvania) *Times* 28 Feb., They had refused to operate 'tripper' or extra, runs because five members of the union had been furloughed. The company said this situation resulted in the failure of nine 'tripper' runs to be made.

7. *slang* (orig. *U.S.*). One who experiences hallucinations induced by a drug, esp. LSD.

1966 T. LEARY in *Playboy* Sept. 110/2 These episodes can be dealt with easily by an experienced guide who recognizes where the LSD tripper is caught. **1968** *New Scientist* 3 Oct. 38/3 LSD 'trippers'..need no sleep. **1972** *Village Voice* (N.Y.) 1 June 78/4 When I returned several days later, Wheeler's was in an uproar over the discovery of a dead tripper. **1979** B. MALAMUD *Dubin's Lives* i. 29 One of the swamis there, a secret acid tripper, got on my nerves.

tripper (tri·pəɹ), *v. colloq. rare.* [f. the sb.] *intr.* To behave like a tripper (sense 4); to take trips or excursions.

1959 G. JENKINS *Twist of Sand* ii. 41 Trippering up and down the coast. **1974** 'S. HARVESTER' *Forgotten Road* iii. 37 They trippered around Istanbul for some days.

tripperish (tri·pəriʃ), *a. colloq.* [f. TRIPPER *sb.* + -ISH¹.] = *TRIPPERY *a.* So **tri·pperishness.**

1898 M. SADLER *Let.* 26 Sept. in M. Sadleir *Michael Ernest Sadler* (1949) x. 166 Stromness is prim little grey stone place of about 2,000 people—quite unspoiled... No obtrusive tripperishness. **1931** E. WAUGH *Remote People* iv. 89 Do you think..it would be very vulgar and tripperish to make them scramble for them [*sc.* coins]? **1934** M. ALLINGHAM *Death of Ghost* xxi. 245 Nothin' tripperish about them. **1960** 'J. & E. BONETT' *No Grave for Lady* xi. 170 The atmosphere was rather tripperish. **1975** S. LAUDER *Killing Time on Corvo* iii. 26 She was very sharp.. and tripperish.

trippery (tri·pəri), *a. colloq.* [f. TRIPPER *sb.* + -Y¹.] Of, pertaining to, or characterized by the presence of trippers (sense 4); touristy (somewhat *derog.*).

1924 C. CONNOLLY *Let.* 22 Dec. in *Romantic Friendship* (1975) 41 Italy is so trippery in Spring. **1926** W. J. LOCKE *Old Bridge* ii. 18 'But let us see all we can to-night.'.. 'That wouldn't be fair to Florence. It's a bit trippery, isn't it?' **1928** *Daily Express* 11 Apr. 9/4 Venice,..the Queen of the Adriatic in its most trippery and least attractive garb. **1969** M. PUGH *Last Place Left* xix. 145 Wordsworth had complained of trippery overcrowding in this belt, more than a hundred years before. **1970** *Nature* 4 July 11/1 The trippery appurtenances and atmosphere which have been established in the neighbourhood [of the Niagara Falls]. **1971** *Country Life* 20 May 1234/3 All that is missing are the monkeys: even though Iguazu is very definitely far from trippery, they have taken themselves off.

tripping, *vbl. sb.* Add: **1.** (Examples in *Bot.*)

1909 *Bull. Bureau Plant Industry, U.S. Dept. Agric.* No. 24. 8 If fertile seed is to be produced in any quantity it is necessary that a certain explosive mechanism within the flower be released. The release of this mechanism, whether it be accomplished by insects or otherwise, is popularly called 'tripping'. **1930** *Jrnl. Amer. Soc. Agronomy* XXII. 782 When the flowers were left exposed and not tripped artificially the gain was 1:1·7 in favor of artificial tripping. **1978** *Nature* 7 Sept. 54/2 In artificial field bean pollination, manual tripping of open flowers is a recommended practice for increasing seed set in auto-sterile lines.

2. (Examples in sense *5 b of the verb.)

1968 L. W. ROBINSON *Assassin* xii. 128 Their passion was a long one..as though they hated to come back..from the rocking, tossing, sweet trip... But no, the sweet tripping was not over. **1970** K. PLATT *Pushbutton Butterfly* vi. 59 The girls weren't wearing brassieres... The skinnier ones just looked flat. Tripping didn't solve everything. **1980** *Times Lit. Suppl.* 24 Oct. 1203/4 When Christiane F. was thirteen years old, she began to frequent a youth club run by the Protestant Church in an overcrowded district of West Berlin. There she started smoking hashish, taking 'uppers and downers' and 'tripping' on LSD.

trippkeite (tri·pkiˌəit). *Min.* [ad. G. *trippkeit* (G. vom Rath 1880, in *Sitzungsber. d. Niederrheinische Ges. f. Natur- und Heilkunde* 209), f. the name of P. *Trippke* (1851–80), Polish or German mineralogist, its discoverer: see -ITE¹.] An oxide of copper and arsenic, $CuAs_2O_4$, found as soft greenish blue tetragonal crystals.

1881 *Jrnl. Chem. Soc.* XL. 551 Minerals from the Veins of Copper-ore near Copiapo, in Chili.—*a.* Trippkeite. A cupric arsenite..occurring in small bluish-green crystals, in druses of a thick bed of red copper-ore mixed with malachite and copper pyrites. **1976** *Mineral. Abstr.* XXVII. 300/1 The crystal structure of synthetic trippkeite..was refined to R = 0·059.

trippy (tri·pi), *a. colloq.* (chiefly *U.S.*). [f. TRIP *sb.*¹ + -Y¹.] Of, pertaining to, or resembling a hallucinatory experience induced by a drug. Hence **tri·ppiness.**

1969 FABIAN & BYRNE *Groupie* (1970) xiv. 101 Joe asks if it's trippy, and I tell him that it is a bit. **1975** *Harper's Mag.* June 9 In my trippy daze, dope was the filter for the movie camera in my mind, the regulator of my psychic jets. **1976** *New Yorler* 19 Jan. 48 Robert Wise directed with tame, impersonal good taste; there's none of the blissful trippiness of being carried in the belly of a zeppelin, and none of the carnival vulgarity of the recent disaster thrillers. **1976** LOGAN & WOFFINDEN *Illustr. New Musical Express Encycl. Rock* 96/1 In 1966 they [*sc.* The Grateful Dead] chose their name; in keeping with the band's image, it was a decision made under the influence of various drugs... The band thought it seemed vaguely appropriate, and certainly it had trippy connotations. **1978** *Maclean's Mag.* 13 Nov. 78 The trippy optimism of the '60s lent importance to such things as creativity and communication, which in the '70s have given way to matters of a homelier urgency. **1980** *New Age* (U.S.) Oct. 54 (Advt.), Trippy music for meditation, massage, free-form movement, tantric loving, and a relaxing environment.

triptane (tri·ptēⁱn). [f. TRI- + -*p*- + *BU)-TANE.] A liquid branched paraffin used as a high-octane aviation fuel; 2,2,3-trimethylbutane, $CH_3C(CH_3)_2CH(CH_3)CH_3$.

1943 *Chem. & Engin. News* 25 Sept. 1561/1 Triptane is the most powerful hydrocarbon known for use in internal combustion engines. **1970** M. SMITH *Aviation Fuels* x. 65 Some of the best hydrocarbons, such as triptane, do not occur naturally in significant amounts.

tripton (tri·ptǫn). *Biol.* and *Oceanogr.* [ad. G. *tripton* (J. Wilhelmi 1917, in *Arch. für Hydrobiol.* XI. 115), f. Gr. τριπτόν, neut. of τριπτός that which is rubbed or pounded, f. τρίβειν to rub or pound.] The non-living part of the fine particulate matter suspended in water. Cf. *SESTON.

1931 R. N. CHAPMAN *Animal Ecol.* xvi. 325 The dry organic matter has been selected as the measure because it eliminates a large amount of detritus ('Tripton' of Wilhelmi, 1917). **1957** G. E. HUTCHINSON *Treat. Limnol.* I. xvii. 897 The phytoplankton, or possibly bacteria associated with organic tripton, produce a good supply of thiamin. **1978** *Nature* 21 Sept. 194/1 As spring and summer pass, decaying organic matter (tripton) from the overlying water accumulates on or near the chemocline where its continued decomposition removed any dissolved oxygen from the overlying water mass.

triptych. Add: **3.** *transf.* **a.** A set of three operas or pieces of music intended to be performed together.

1925 R. A. STREATFEILD *Opera* (ed. 5) xiii. 304 Puccini's last work is a so-called 'triptych', consisting of three one-act operas. **1928** *Grove's Dict. Mus.* (ed. 3) IV. 283/2 In this triptych the composer's technique is more elaborate than in 'Butterfly'. **1959** *Listener* 31 Dec. 1176/3 Any music that makes a strong visual suggestion like the Debussy orchestral triptychs. **1976** *New Yorker* 1 Mar. 90/1 This season, the triptych has been reassembled: a new 'Tabarro' and 'Suor Angelica' join the 1974 staging of 'Gianni Schicchi'. **1976** *Gramophone* Sept. 424/2 Ormandy's version (which offers 24 minutes' extra music in the form of *Feste romane*, the still more luridly coloured third leaf of the triptych) will do very nicely.

b. *Cinemat.* A sequence of film designed to be shown on a triple screen, using linked projectors.

1976 *Oxf. Compan. Film* 494/2 After the first presentation it [sc. *Napoléon*] was released in a truncated version from which the triptych sequences had been removed: Gance, disappointed by the poor reception, destroyed much of the original footage, including some of the triptych. **1980** *Times* 5 Dec. 11/5 The great triptych—Gance called it Polyvision—in no respect falls short... From the breath-catching moment when the screen is suddenly multiplied to reveal a great panorama of the Grand Army on the Alps, Gance's use of the triptych is light years in advance of anything three-projector Cinerama ever achieved. *Ibid.*, Sometimes the triptych image is a continuous panorama; sometimes it is split into different images. There are superimpositions and mirror images, the whole orchestrated with passion.

‖ **tripudium** (tripiū·diŏm). *Rom. Antiq.* [L.; see TRIPUDIATE *v.*] A ritual dance (see quots.). Also *transf.* and *fig.*

1909 in WEBSTER. **1922** W. R. HALLIDAY *Lect. Hist. Roman Relig.* iii. 46 A feature of this procession was the dancing of the armed priests... Their leaping dance, the *tripudium* or three step, was accompanied by the clashing of rods or spears against the shields. **1922** JOYCE *Ulysses* 50 The foot that beat the ground in tripudium. *Ibid.* 559 He runs to the piano and takes his ashplant, beating his foot in tripudium. **1923** L. PULLAN *Relig. since Reformation* viii. 239 The Tübingen school attempted..at the same time 'to force Christian history into the Hegelian *tripudium* of thesis, antithesis, and synthesis'. **1938** B. SCHÖNBERG tr. *C. Sachs' World Hist. Dance* vii. 246 The weapon dances of the warriors and the priests of Mars who were grouped together under the name of *Salii*, which is equivalent to *saltantes* or dancers... The *Salii* stamped..in repetends of three beats... From this tripedal character their dance takes the name of *tripudium*. As a choral dance..it had a dance leader whose movements were answered by the two choruses of older and younger men as they walked around in a circle to the rhythmical beating of the shields. **1949** *Oxf. Classical Dict.* 789/1 At certain spots they [*sc.* the Salii] halted and performed elaborate ritual dances (*tripudium*, cf. Plut. *Num.* 13), beating their shields with their staves.

tripuhyite (tripū·i,əit). *Min.* [f. *Tripuhy*, name of a locality near Ouro Prêto, Minas Gerais, Brazil, where the first specimen was found: see -ITE[1].] An oxide of ferrous iron and antimony, $FeSb_2O_6$, found as aggregates of translucent, yellowish to dark brown, tetragonal crystals.

1897 HUSSAK & PRIOR in *Mineral. Mag.* XI. 302 From these schists, doubtless, is also derived the tripuhyite, although as yet this new mineral has only been found in fragments loose in the gravel. **1968** [see *ORDOÑEZITE].

tripus. Restrict ‖ *Obs. rare* to sense in Dict. and add: **2.** *Zool.* A bone in the Weberian ossicles of cypriniform fishes, linking the ear and the swim-bladder.

1893 T. W. BRIDGE in *Phil. Trans. R. Soc.* B. CLXXXIV. 83 The horizontal process moves backwards or forwards with the lateral motion of the tripus. **1962, 1970** [see *INTERCALARIUM 2].

tri·p-wire. Also **trip wire, tripwire.** [f. TRIP *sb.*[1] or *v.* + WIRE *sb.*] **1. a.** A wire stretched near the ground in order to trip up enemies, trespassers, etc. Hence, a wire placed so that contact with it operates a weapon, flash-light, or other device.

1916 A. KNEBWORTH *Let.* 24 Feb. in Ld. Lytton *Antony* (1935) i. 21 He walks forward, he has found his landmark. He thinks he knows where the Huns are. He is coming to the Hun trip wire. He has cut the German trip wire. **1928** *Daily Mail* 3 Aug. 8/3 Trip-wires to ensnare the enemy. **1928** *Daily Tel.* 16 Oct. 18 A flash-light operated by means of a 'trip wire'. **1941** *Illustr. London News* 22 Feb. 233/1 (*caption*) The mine can be fired by various methods such as electric contact or time fuse—trip wire or impact. **1947** D. M. DAVIN *Gorse blooms Pale* 124 They had time..to lace the stumps with barbed tripwires. **1960** C. DAY LEWIS *Buried Day* v. 100 The window-cleaner's tricycle was built up to represent a German tank, which was laagering in a dell I had privily surrounded with trip-wires. **1974** *Times* 21 Jan. 12/5 There's a series of trip wires which set off rockets and flares if they are touched. **1978** 'F. PARRISH' *Sting of Honeybee* vi. 83 Dan wondered about dogs, electric fences, trip-wires, gin-traps.

b. *transf.* and *fig.*

1971 P. O'DONNELL *Impossible Virgin* vi. 117 He was operating on more than one level. He may have meant his offer, but he was laying trip-wires at the same time. **1976** LD. HOME *Way Wind Blows* xiv. 195 A Prime Minister..is well-advised to search every question for the trip-wire which is usually well-concealed, but almost sure to be there, and to think up the riposte which will turn the tables on the Opposition. **1979** P. NIESEWAND *Member of Club* ix. 63 One other type of sensor..sets up an invisible light beam... If someone walks across it, they interrupt the beam. It's a kind of optical tripwire.

2. *fig.* A comparatively weak military force employed as a first line of defence, whose involvement in hostilities will trigger the intervention of stronger forces. Freq. *attrib.* orig. *U.S.*

1957 *Observer* 1 Sept. 8/3 The German electorate are baffled as to whether Nato is meant to defend their soil, or provide the tripwire for a Soviet–American suicide pact. **1960** *Washington Post* 4 Apr. A 19 Stans suggested that a switch be made to the 'trip-wire' defense theory which would require but one American division. **1966** SCHWARZ & HADIK *Strategic Terminology* 115 Advocates of this modification ridicule the simple tripwire concept by saying that to all intents and purposes a single U.S. soldier could act as tripwire. **1969** *New Statesman* 11 Apr. 500/3 He [*sc.* King Hussein] is anxious to make a separate peace with the Israelis on the basis of a demilitarised West Bank, with an Israeli military tripwire on the Jordan. **1976** LD. HOME *Way Wind Blows* xii. 167 There was, however, a running argument among the professionals as to whether the line between the Warsaw Pact and the NATO forces should be thinly held (by a tripwire) or more strongly manned. **1979** *Jrnl. R. Soc. Arts* CXXVII. 550/2 From the mid 1950s to the late '60s, the West relied on the so-called 'tripwire' strategy. Stated simply, this meant that any aggressive adventure on the part of the Soviet Union would be met by an overwhelming nuclear response. **1980** *Times* 24 May 15/2 What is profoundly discouraging is to find our work impeded by the old discredited trip-wires of the Cold War.

Trique (trī·ke), *sb.* and *a.* Also **Trike, Triqui.** [Native name.] **A.** *sb.* **a.** An Indian people of Oaxaca, Mexico. **b.** The Mixtecan language spoken by this people. **B.** *adj.* Of or pertaining to this people or their language.

1891 D. G. BRINTON *Amer. Race* III. 148, I do not doubt that Orozcoy Berra was right in placing the Triquis in the same [Tequistlatecan] family. **1900** F. STARR in *Proc. Davenport Acad. Sci. 1899–1900* (1901) VIII. 142 Belmar gives in his *Essays* a brief sketch of the grammar, a list of phrases in Spanish and Triqui and a Spanish-Triqui vocabulary. *Ibid.*, The towns he mentions are none of them Triqui. *Ibid.*, San Andres Chicahuastla is the Triqui town where our work was done. **1911** *Bull. U.S. Bureau Amer. Ethnol.* No. 44. 52 Trike. This language, which belongs to the Zapotecan family, is spoken by a small tribe residing in the central part of the Mixtec area. *Ibid.* 53 Professor Starr..says none of the towns mentioned by Orozco y Berra are Trike..and that the real district of the Trike is situated in the high mountains of the districts of Tlaxiaco and Juxtlahuaca... They form a little island of Trike speech in the midst of the Mixtec area. **1952** J. R. SWANTON *Indian Tribes N. Amer.* 639 Trique, a tribe entered by Mason and Johnson as a substock of their Otomanguean stock. **1957** [see *MAZATEC *sb.* and *a.*]. **1965** *Language* XLI. 67 The identifier tagmeme in Trique noun phrases. **1974** *Encycl. Brit. Micropædia* X. 130/1 *Trique*, Indians of Oaxaca, Mex., speaking a Mixtecan language... Some Trique men work outside the community as labourers... Trique religion includes both ancient Indian and Roman Catholic rites. **1977** T. A. SEBEOK *Native Languages Americas* II. 370 Trique. Mixtecan; 4,000 in Oaxaca (1952).

triquetral, *a.* Add: *triquetral bone*, also, an approximately pyramidal bone of the wrist that articulates with the pisiform bone; = *cuneiform bone* (*a*) s.v. CUNEIFORM *a.* 1; also *ellipt.* as *triquetral*.

1913 *Cunningham's Text-bk. Anat.* (ed. 4) 223 An exceptional case..in which the centres for the capitate and triquetral bones were already present [at birth]. **1961** S. ZUCKERMAN *New Syst. Anat.* I. iv. 84 The triquetral bone forms a conspicuous prominence distal to the head of the ulna on the medial border of the dorsum of the hand. **1980** *Gray's Anat.* (ed. 36) 371/2 The palmar and dorsal surfaces of the carpal bones, apart from the triquetral and pisiform, are rough for the attachment of ligaments.

triradius (trəirēⁱ·diŏs). Pl. **-radii.** [f. TRI- + RADIUS.] In dermatoglyphics, a point from which the dermal ridges radiate in three directions at angles of approx. 120 degrees.

1960 *New Scientist* 14 July 129 (*caption*) A finger-print on which a white line has been drawn joining the core of the pattern..to the associated triradius. **1965** *Ibid.* 11 Feb. 345/2 There are discontinuities [in the fingerprint pattern], known technically as 'triradius points', where three ridges meet at a single junction. **1970** [see *LOOP *sb.*[1] 4 h]. **1971** J. Z. YOUNG *Introd. Study Man* xxxix. 570 For genetic analysis counts are made from the triradius to the centre of the pattern. **1977** *Sci. Amer.* Dec. 141/1 The resulting patterns are known to the dermatologist respectively as loops, triradii and whorls.

tris (tris), *sb. Chem.* Also **Tris.** [f. TRIS-.] **1.** [f. *tris*hydroxymethylaminomethane.] The crystalline compound $(HOCH_2)_3CNH_2$, 2-amino-2-(hydroxymethyl)propane-1,3-diol, used as a buffering agent. Also *tris buffer*.

1959 *Science* 20 Mar. 783/1 This compound is commonly known as 'trishydroxymethylaminomethane' or 'tris buffer'. **1964** *Biochim. & Biophysica Acta* XCII. 133 A uniform suspension of ghosts in 0·5 mM Tris. **1979** *Sci. Amer.* Mar. 102/2 The sodium current in a squid axon is abolished by applying a sizable dose of tetrodotoxin (and also replacing the sodium in the bathing medium with 'Tris' buffer).

2. [f. *tris*-2,3-dibromopropylphosphate.] The organophosphorus compound $(Br_2C_3H_5)_3PO_4$, which is used as a flame retardant.

1976 *St. Louis* (Missouri) *Globe-Democrat* 17 Sept. 6 B/1 A chemical nicknamed 'tris' that clothing manufacturers use as a flame retardant in children's pajamas causes mutations in the genes of bacteria. **1981** M. C. GERALD *Pharmacology* (ed. 2) xxx. 578 To date there is no evidence that Tris causes cancer in humans.

trisazo (trisæ·zo), *a. Chem.* [f. TRIS- + AZO-.] Containing three azo groups in the molecule.

1904 *Jrnl. Chem. Soc.* LXXXVI. I. 700 Black trisazo-dyes are obtained by diazotising acetyl-*p*-phenylenediamine, [etc.]. **1948** KIRK & OTHMER *Encycl. Chem. Technol.* II. 247 Naphthogene Blue 4R.., a trisazo dye. **1966** [see *DISAZO-]. **1970** R. L. M. ALLEN *Colour Chem.* v. 62 Three of the various types of trisazo structure are of principal importance.

Triscuit (tri·skit). Also **triscuit.** [f. TRI-, irregularly after *biscuit*.] The proprietary name of a savoury cracker or biscuit.

1906 *Official Gaz.* (U.S. Patent Office) 27 Mar. 1324/2 Biscuit or crackers. The Natural Food Company..The word 'Triscuit'. **1919** 'G. CUMBERLAND' *Set down in Malice* xiv. 174 They have..studios..where one has triscuits for breakfast. **1932** *Trade Marks Jrnl.* 23 Mar. 383/1 *Triscuit*..Solid food products. The Shredded Wheat Company, Limited, Welwyn Garden City..Manufacturers. **1937** G. FRANKAU *More of Us* viii. 93 Stern strong business-men Whom Shredded Wheat or Triscuit made that hearty They rarely failed to catch the ten-past-ten. **1980** *Times* 22 Dec. 12/7 Ketchup in a bottle, salt in a shaker, triscuits (a savory snack biscuit) in the box.

tri-service (trəisɔ̄·ɹvis), *a.* Also **tri-Service, Tri-Service.** [f. TRI- + SERVICE[1] 5 b.] Of, pertaining to, or representing the three armed forces, Army, Navy, and Air Force.

1959 *Times* 18 June (Queen in Canada Suppl.) p. vii/7 A unique experiment in military education, a tri-service college. **1977** *Globe & Mail* (Toronto) 1 Feb. 7/6 Much has been made of the damage supposedly done by unification. The opponents of it, both in the services, and in groups on the outside such as TRIO (Tri-Service Identities Organization), concentrated on this one issue. **1979** *Navy News* Feb. 1/5 The survey, which will be tri-Service, will cover all personnel, including Servicewomen. **1982** *Daily Tel.* 15 Dec. 24/4 The White Paper confirmed the maintenance of a sizeable tri-service garrison in the South Atlantic.

trishaw (trəi·ʃǭ). Also **trisha, tri-sha, tri-shaw.** [f. TRI- + RICK)SHAW.] In the Far East, a light three-wheeled vehicle propelled by pedalling, freq. used as a taxi.

1946 *Sun* (Baltimore) 9 July 5/6 (*heading*) Trishaws may replace Singapore Rickshaws. *Ibid.*, The Rickshaw Association has asked permission for 2,000 additional trishaw licences to provide employment for former rickshawmen. **1955** [see *PEDAL *v.* b]. **1961** *Guardian* 30 May 7/3 The Chinese trishaman..who failed to move out of his way. **1971** *Carry Singapore in your Pocket* (Singapore Tourist Promotion Board) (ed. 3) 71 *Trishaw*, a pedal bicycle with side-car attached. This typically Oriental mode of transport is fast dying out in Singapore but a short 'trishaw ride' is certainly worthwhile. **1972** *Daily Colonist* (Victoria, B.C.) 26 Mar. 49/3 The Chinese introduced a souped-up version of the jinricksha in the form of the tri-sha. These bicycle-powered two-seaters weave their way through George Town traffic, as common as taxis are to the streets of other cities. **1977** P. THEROUX *Consul's File* 79 The cycling noises approached... It was a trishaw, cruising for fares. **1979** R. CASSILIS *Arrow of God* IV. vi. 119 The tri-shaw man came over to help him.

trishtubh, var. *TRISTUBH.

triskaidekaphobia (tri:skəidekăfōᵘ·biă). Also **triske-, -decaphobia.** [f. Gr. τρεῖσκαιδεκα thirteen + -PHOBIA.] Fear of the number thirteen.

1911 I. H. CORIAT *Abnormal Psychol.* II. vi. 287 Fear of the number thirteen (triskaidekaphobia). **1953** *N.Y. Times* 8 Nov. E2 A discussion in the U.N. last week on the number of members on a committee raised the question of triskaidekaphobia. **1967** *Daily Tel.* 14 Jan. 18/8 Thirteen people, pledged to eliminate triskaidecaphobia, fear of the number 13, today tried to reassure American sufferers by renting a 13ft plot of land in Brooklyn for 13 cents (10½d) a month. **1976** *Sunday Mail Color Mag.* (Brisbane) 1 Aug. 7/1 Mrs. Ratcliffe suffers from triskedekaphobia..the name psychologists have given for an inexplicable dread of a Friday falling on the 13th of the month. **1979** *Guardian* 13 July 11/6 I'm tempted to diagnose triskaidekaphobia or allergy to 13.

triskele. Add: (Later examples of form *triskelion*.)

1973 T. PYNCHON *Gravity's Rainbow* (1975) I. 150 Pins, brooches, opalescent scorpions (her birth sign) inside gold mountings in triskelion. **1977** *Sci. Amer.* Dec. 168 (*caption*) Below, at the left, is another fragment of side-link mold with a decorative whorl and, at right, a triskelion decoration for a chariot linchpin.

trisome (trəi·sōᵘm). *Cytology.* [f. TRI- + *-SOME[4].] A chromosome which is represented three times in a chromosomal complement; also, a trisomic individual.

1921 [see *DISOME]. **1926** L. W. SHARP *Introd. Cytol.* (ed. 2) xvii. 388 Such $2n+1$ forms are called 'simple trisomic' mutants; they have 11 disomes (normal pairs) and one trisome. **1944** [see *MONOSOME 1]. **1979** *Nature* 27 Sept. 280/2 The failure to form trisomes indicates.. that on intact RNA3 stable ribosome binding does not occur simultaneously at both the site near base 29 and the site near base 70.

trisomic (trəisōᵘ·mik), *a.* (*sb.*) *Cytology.* [f. as prec. + -IC.] Of or pertaining to a trisome. Also as *sb.*, a trisomic chromosome, cell, or individual.

1921 A. F. BLAKESLEE in *Amer. Naturalist* LV. 259 If the Globe and Poinsettia [*sc.* 'mutant' forms of *Datura stramonium*] could be combined to form a mutant with 3 chromosomes each in two of the 12 sets, such a mutant would be called a double trisomic mutant. **1924** *Genetics* IX. 194 Super-enlarged in general bears the same relation to enlarged as round-leaf globe to globe; i.e., the tetrasomic is an accentuated expression of the trisomic. **1939** *Jrnl. Genetics* XXXVIII. 382 Trisomics are of frequent occurrence and are known in almost every genus employed in genetic work. **1957** R. A. BEATTY *Parthenogenesis & Polyploidy in Mammalian Devel.* v. 79 Since the only abnormality would be the presence of one extra chromosome, the trisomic might have greater viability than the full triploid. *Ibid.* vi. 102 In triploid or trisomic *Drosophila*, the position of the centromere has been assessed in this way. **1974** *Nature* 1 Mar. 54/2 Aneuploid embryos found in this study included uniform monosomics and trisomics.

So **tri·somy**, trisomic state; freq. with following numeral denoting the chromosome concerned, as *trisomy-21* (associated with Down's syndrome).

1930 *Bibliographia Genetica* VI. 15 Further observations..disclosed a high degree of intraspecific variation resulting in polyploidy, trisomy, fragmentation of chromosomes [etc.]. **1961** G. ALLEN et al. in *Lancet* 8 Apr. 775/2 Several others [of the undersigned] believe that this is an appropriate time to introduce the term 'trisomy 21 anomaly' which would include cases of simple trisomy as well as translocations. **1963** [see *DERMATOGLYPHICS]. **1965** [see *DOWN'S SYNDROME]. **1970** PASSMORE & ROBSON *Compan. Med. Stud.* II. xxxi. 19/1 The relative frequency of trisomy 13–15 in abortuses indicates that it is less compatible with normal intra-uterine development than either trisomy 17–18 or mongolism. **1977** *Nature* 6 Jan. 65/2 Case 2..showed an excess of α-globin synthesis smaller than expected for functional trisomy of the α-globin genetic region. **1979** *Ibid.* 4 Jan. 57/1 Although the patient had no features of the trisomy 21 syndrome, two first-degree cousins of his father had given birth to children with Down's syndrome.

Tristanesque (tristănε·sk), *a.* [f. the name *Tristan*, the hero of Wagner's opera *Tristan und Isolde* (1865), + -ESQUE.] Resembling the music of *Tristan und Isolde*; *spec.* characterized by tonal ambiguity and chromaticism.

1942 *Scrutiny* XI. 5 Similarly the diatonic system decayed into the deliquescence of feeling and tonal instability which marks the Tristanesque music of the late nineteenth century. **1948** [see *IMPRESSIONIST 2]. **1957** W. MELLERS *Man & his Music: Romanticism & 20th Cent.* I. ii. 46 (Consider the Tristanesque opening of the second piece). Liszt the romantic lover here recollects in tranquillity. **1962** *Times* 26 Jan. 16/5 The debt to Wagner was incurred a little later, in the thoroughly Tristanesque love duet towards the end of *A Village Romeo and Juliet*.

tri-state: see *TRI- 1 b.

tristful. Add: Hence **tri·stfulness.**

1909 HARDY *Time's Laughingstocks* 152 In the bearing of each a passive tristfulness. **1914** C. MACKENZIE *Sinister Street* II. IV. ii. 877 For a whim of tristfulness, for the luxury of consummating the ineffable depression the house created in him.

tristimulus (trəisti·miŭlə̆s). [f. TRI- + STIMULUS.] Each of three reference colours (as red, green, and blue) which can be combined additively in specified proportions (*tristimulus values*) to produce any given colour. Usu. *attrib.*

1933 *Jrnl. Optical Soc. Amer.* XXIII. 359/2 The specification [for matching any given colour stimulus] consists of giving the amounts of each primary stimulus required for the match. This is known as the tristimulus system of color specification. **1937** G. S. MONK *Light* xvii. 336 The tristimulus values of the recommended standard source..for wave-length 4800 angstroms are given by the ordinates at that wave-length of the three curves. **1962** H. C. WESTON *Sight, Light & Work* (ed. 2) vii. 212 The vertical scale labelled Y refers to one of the tristimuli and the horizontal scale labelled X refers to another. **1976** C. REYNOLDS *Photoguide to Filters* 227 The CIE system is the tristimulus specification most widely used, and is ideally suited to defining the colour of filters.

tristubh (tri·ʃtub). Also **trishtubh.** [Skr. *triṣṭubha*.] A Vedic metre of eleven syllables (see also quot. 1939).

1869, etc. [see *JAGATĪ]. **1939** *Jrnl. Amer. Oriental Soc.* LIX. 159 Ordinarily, the Hindu metricians mechanically define any metrical pāda of eleven syllables as 'triṣṭubh', and any of twelve syllables as 'jagatī'. This cannot be accepted... What we shall call a triṣṭubh may have anywhere from ten to thirteen syllables, a jagatī from eleven to at least thirteen (possibly more). The distinction between the two is solely based on the cadence; a triṣṭubh always ends ˘ – x..in western terms..in a catalectic diiambus. **1965** *Language* XLI. 11 Three instances are accounted for by the pāda..two by the triṣṭubh cadence. **1971** *Ibid.* XLVII. 64 The last pada of the stanza in question is incontrovertibly triṣṭubh.

tritanopia (trəitănōᵘ·piă). *Ophthalm.* [mod. L., ad. G. *tritanopie* (J. von Kries 1911, in *Helmholtz's Handbuch der Physiol. Optik* (ed. 3) II. 341), f. *trit-*, var. TRITO- + AN- 10 + *-OPIA.] A form of dichromatic colour-blindness marked by reduced sensitivity and discrimination in the blue and green parts of the spectrum. Hence **tri·tanope,** one who has tritanopia; **tritano·pic** *a.*

1915 J. H. PARSONS *Introd. Study Colour Vision* II. i. 159, I shall adopt his [*sc.* v. Kries's] terms, viz., protanopes, deuteranopes, and tritanopes, corresponding respectively with v. Helmholtz' red-, green-, and blue-blind. *Ibid.* ii. 180 Cases of tritanopia or so-called blue-blindness are rare and mostly due to disease. *Ibid.* 304/1 (Index), Tritanopic vision. **1937** [see *DEUTERANOPE]. **1955** *Jrnl. Optical Soc. Amer.* XLV. 614/1 The tritanopic luminosity function..does not indicate any major shift in excitation peaks of the receptor substances. **1959** [see *DICHROMAT, DICHROMATE *sb.*²]. **1965** *New Scientist* 14 Oct. 134/3 Tritanopic defects are described as autosomal dominant while tritanomaly is considered to be more or less recessive sex-linked. **1974** *Jrnl. Optical Soc. Amer.* LXIV. 1246/1 The tritanope's targets were formed of checks of pale violet and yellow–green and were compared to a blank field of violet. **1978** *Nature* 23 Nov. 390/1 When the eye has been adapted to a bright yellow light, a marked loss of sensitivity to short-wavelength stimuli may be recorded immediately after the extinction of the adapting field. This phenomenon..was termed transient tritanopia by Mollon and Polden.

triterpane, -pene, -penoid: see *TRI- 5 a.

tritiated (tri·tiēᶦtėd, -ʃiēᶦtėd), *a. Chem.* [f. *TRITI(UM + -ATE³ + -ED².] Containing tritium; having had an atom of ordinary hydrogen replaced by tritium. So **tritia·tion,** the introduction of tritium into a compound or molecule in place of ordinary hydrogen.

[**1947** M. D. KAMEN *Radioactive Tracers in Biol.* vi. 127 A few drops of triterated water may be recovered.] **1956** *Nature* 25 Feb. 379/2 Analyses for tritium were carried out by combustion of the organic compound and conversion of the tritiated water to tritium. **1961** G. R. CHOPPIN *Exper. Nuclear Chem.* xi. 180 The Wilzbach method of tritiation involves the exposure of the unlabeled compound to a multicurie atmosphere of tritium gas for periods of time as long as two weeks. **1978** *Bull. Amer. Acad. Arts & Sci.* Feb. 11 He further developed novel methods for the accurate determination of tritiated compounds in tissues.

triticale (tritikēᶦ·li). Also **Triticale.** [f. mod.L. generic names *Tritic(um* wheat + *Se)cale* rye.] A hybrid cereal grass, of the genus × *Triticosecale*, produced by crossing various species or varieties of wheat and rye.

1952 *New Biol.* XIII. 44 A cross between wheat and rye..is known as Triticale. **1968** *New Scientist* 24 Oct. 181/2 (*caption*) Triticale, a hybrid of wheat and rye developed at the University of Manitoba. **1974** A. J. HUXLEY *Plant & Planet* xxvii. 309 New races of the great seed plants..have been created in the last few years, including a promising wheat/rye hybrid called triticale. **1979** *McGraw-Hill Yearbk. Sci. & Technol.* 414/1 Although triticale plants were first described in 1876, only in the mid-1960s did they begin to receive great interest from scientists and farmers. **1983** *New Scientist* 13 Jan. 98/1 From a slow start in the 1950s..triticale is now growing on more than half a million hectares, in the USSR, Europe, the United States and South America.

tritish, *a.* Delete *rare*⁻¹ and add: Also triteish.

1980 *Times* 5 June 11/3 A good, if triteish, situation.

tritium (tri·tiə̆m). *Chem.* [mod.L., f. Gr. τρίτ-ος third + -IUM.] **1.** A radioactive heavy isotope of hydrogen, having two neutrons as well as a proton in the nucleus, which constitutes one part in 10^{18} of the naturally occurring element and is produced for use in fusion reactors and as an isotopic label. Symbols ^3H (H^3), T. Cf. *DEUTERIUM, *PROTIUM.

1933 UREY & MURPHY in *Jrnl. Chem. Physics* I. 513/2 If the H^3 isotope is discovered, we would recommend to the discoverer the consideration of the name tritium for it. **1959** *Sci. News* LI. 12, ^3He is obtained from the decay of tritium which in turn is the product of nuclear reactions involving neutrons from a reactor. **1962** [see *SUPERHEAVY *a.* b]. **1972** *Sci. Amer.* Oct. 104/3 Large amounts of tritium (hydrogen 3)..are stockpiled for nuclear weapons and for research in fusion power. **1976** *Nature* 9 Sept. 103/1 Tritium ($t_{\frac{1}{2}}$ = 12·3 yr) is present on the Earth's surface mainly as HTO.

2. *attrib.* and *Comb.*

1934 *Sun* (Baltimore) 6 Oct. 20/6 Tritium water could be formed by the addition of two more atoms of hydrogen to the heavy water. **1953** J. BLISH in E. Crispin *Best SF* (1955) 345 The U.N.'s police would be glad to know that they could have access to a virtually inexhaustible stock of tritium bombs. **1966** *McGraw-Hill Encycl. Sci. & Technol.* XIV. 113/1 Tritium oxide, T_2O, has been prepared by oxidation of tritium gas with hot copper oxide. *Ibid.* 113/2 Tritium-labeled compounds may be prepared by ordinary synthetic chemical methods. **1979** *McGraw-Hill Yearbk. Sci. & Technol.* 153/2 Tritium-helium dating will eventually prove very useful in studying those physical processes which transport or redistribute substances in oceans.

trito-. Add: **tritano·maly** *Ophthalm.* [ANOMALY], a rare form of anomalous trichromatism marked by a reduced sensitivity to blue; hence **tritano·malous** *a.*, having tritanomaly.

1943 *Jrnl. Optical Soc. Amer.* XXXIII. 572/1 These [subjects] are diagnosed by most other tests as tritanomalous or blue-yellow blind. *Ibid.* 574/2 These plates are invalid for the detection of tritanomaly. **1946** W. D. WRIGHT *Res. on Normal & Defective Colour Vision* xxiv. 297 The tritanomalous observer has poor hue discrimination in the blue-green wavelengths. **1956** *Jrnl. Optical Soc. Amer.* XLVI. 1075/1 Tritanomaly, discovered by Engelking, seems to be very rare. **1965** Tritanomaly [see *TRITANOPIA].

tritoma. Add to etym. after mod.L. (J. B. Ker 1804, in *Curtis's Bot. Mag.* XX. 744). Add to def.: = *KNIPHOFIA. (Earlier examples.)

1804 *Curtis's Bot. Mag.* XX. 744 (*heading*) Glaucous-Leaved Tritoma. **1854** [see *KNIPHOFIA]. **1871** J. C. PATTESON *Let.* 8 Mar. in C. M. Yonge *Life J. C. Patteson* (1874) II. xii. 514, I like both the red and the yellow tritoma.

tritomite (tri·tŏməit). *Min.* [ad. G. *tritomit* (P. H. Weibye 1850, in *Ann. d. Physik u. Chem.* LXXIX. 299), f. Gr. τρίτομος thrice-cut, in allusion to the shape of the cavities left by the crystals: see -ITE¹.] **a.** A borosilicate, fluoride, and hydroxide of cerium earths, calcium, and thorium found as brown trigonal crystals. **b.** *tritomite-Y*: an analogue of this in which yttrium largely replaces cerium.

1856 *Edin. New Philos. Jrnl.* III. 60 The tritomite here analysed was sent me by M. Wiborg of Brevig, labelled as thorite, which it also very closely resembled in appearance. **1962** *Amer. Mineralogist* XLVII. 9 Tritomite, a rare, metamict boro-silicate..is known only from the nepheline syenite pegmatites of Låven, Brevik, and Barkevik, in..southern Norway. **1966** *Ibid.* LI. 156 The terms..spencite, [etc.]. should be dropped... Respectively, these minerals would be known as..tritomite-(Y), [etc.]... The Commission [on New Minerals and Mineral Names of the International Mineralogical Association] has approved this nomenclature.

triton² (trəi·tǫn). *Physics.* [f. *TRIT(IUM + *-ON¹.] A sub-atomic particle composed of one proton and two neutrons, the nucleus of the tritium atom.

1942 *Physical Rev.* LXII. 115/1 The nucleus Li^7 is pictured on the alpha-particle model as built up from an alpha-particle group and a triton (H^3) group. **1965** *Wireless World* Sept. 446/2 Semiconductor devices can be employed for counting other types of ionizing particles such as protons, deuterons, tritons, fission fragments, etc. **1976** *Nature* 29 Apr. 749/3 There have been rather few studies of the interactions of tritons with nuclei, mainly because tritons are highly radioactive, with a half-life of about 12 years.

tritonality (trəitonæ·lĭti). *Mus.* [f. TRI- + TONALITY.] The simultaneous use of three keys in a musical composition. Hence **trito·nal** *a.*

1931 *Music & Lett.* Oct. 323 Atonalities, bitonalities, tritonalities and their peers are best heard and not seen. **1944** *Scrutiny* XII. 121 The Lydian [mode]..is harmonically treacherous owing to its imperfect tritonal fourth. **1963** *Listener* 17 Jan. 141/2 The third movement is at the opposite tritonal pole, F sharp.

Tritoness. (Later example.)

1956 K. CLARK *Nude* vii. 271 A small tritoness,.. recently emerged from the excavations in Ostia.

trit-trot. (Earlier example.)

1818 M. EDGEWORTH *Let.* Sept. (1971) 89 The drollest trit-trot little walk she has.

triumphal, *a.* (*sb.*) Add: Hence **triu·mphally** *adv.* Cf. TRIUMPHANTLY *adv.*

1897 F. THOMPSON *New Poems* 109 Thou dost thy dying so triumphally. **1984** *Miami Herald* 6 Apr. 2B/1 Mike Zeck returns triumphally as..the local kid who actually did break into the business.

triumphalism (trəi,ɒ·mfăliz'm). [f. TRIUMPHAL *a.* + -ISM.] The sense of pride (often linked with ostentation) in the rightness and achievements of one's Church (used *pejoratively*). Also in extended sense.

1964 R. McA. BROWN *Observer in Rome* 27, I am greatly impressed by the recognition of human failings in this prayer and by its exclusion of the 'triumphalism' that has often seemed to characterize the church. **1968** *N.Y. Times* 12 Jan. 25 Wayne H. Cowan, managing editor of the liberal Protestant journal, Christianity and Crisis, said the pastoral 'mutes the triumphalism of the past, but still places great emphasis on the mystery and infallibility of the church'. **1972** *Catholic Herald* 9 June 4 Nostalgia for the pre-Conciliar years of exclusivity and triumphalism. **1975** *New Yorker* 10 Mar. 83/1 This contrast is understandable, given what critics of the regime have labelled 'triumphalism'—something that goes way beyond mere ostentation on a colossal scale. **1977** P. JOHNSON *Enemies of Society* iv. 47 The loss of interest and confidence in the human mind and spirit is, to some extent, concealed by the gigantic triumphalism of late imperial architecture. **1981** G. PRIESTLAND *Priestland's Progress* i. 17 John V. Taylor, Bishop of Winchester,..is right when he seeks to turn us from shallow triumphalism or the reshuffling of old dogmas. **1983** *Times* 31 May 13/2 There would probably be an initial outbreak of Tory triumphalism, which would be distasteful and unnecessary.

Hence **triu·mphalist** *a.* and *sb.*, **triumphali·stic** *a.*

1967 H. CHADWICK *Early Church* 285 Towards such triumphalist assumptions a twentieth-century Christian is likely to be cool and reserved. **1967** *Times* 22 Apr. 12/5 The anxieties of the lingering triumphalists are increased. **1967** R. McA. BROWN *Ecumenical Revolution* vi. 115 It must be acknowledged that later Protestants themselves became as triumphalistic about their own confessions and traditions and denominations as they ever accused the

Roman Catholic Church of being. **1970** *Daily Tel.* 2 Dec. 12/7 Elgar's unashamedly triumphalist setting of the National Anthem sounded a defiantly anachronistic note. **1973** *Listener* 19 Apr. 512/1 The busy, businesslike, triumphalist, materially successful France of today. **1980** *Focus* Summer 24/1 The triumphalist tends to interpret what God has done as his own achievement. **1982** *Sunday Tel.* 30 May 9/2 Churches have been stripped of baroque or Italianate furnishings, altars have been heaved forward, 'triumphalist' pictures and symbols stashed away. **1983** *Observer* 28 Nov. 8/3 The journalists ..fed readers and viewers a diet of triumphalistic pap.

trivalent, *a.* Add: **2.** *Cytology.* That is (part of) a trivalent.

1921 *Proc. Nat. Acad. Sci.* VII. 200 In the 8 remaining prophase or metaphase figures, not all the trivalent chromosomes could be distinguished from the bivalents or univalents into which they had divided, or from which they were composed. **1929** [see *QUADRIVALENT *a.* 2]. **1976** *Genetical Res.* XXVIII. 55 We present data pertaining to..chromosome XVII trisomics of *S*[*accharomyces*] *cerevisiae* which demonstrate that trivalent meiotic association occurs with a high frequency.

3. *Immunol.* Of a vaccine: giving immunity to three forms of a disease.

1959 *New Scientist* 19 Feb. 395 (*caption*) Transfer of single strain vaccine pools to tanks to form final trivalent vaccine. **1961** *Guardian* 25 Oct. 3/5 A 'trivalent' form of vaccine will be used. This contains polio virus of all three types.

B. *sb. Cytology.* With pronunc. (tri·vălĕnt). A multivalent consisting of three chromosomes.

1922 *Amer. Naturalist* LVI. 341 There are 12 sets of three united chromosomes each, and these trivalents can be arranged according to the size formula. **1936** *Hereditas* XXI. 305 In triploid hybrids..there was a high frequency of trivalents. **1975** [see *QUADRIVALENT *sb.* 2].

Hence also **triva·lency.**

1888 *Jrnl. Chem. Soc.* LIV. 1071 The formula for benzene [was]..afterwards given up owing to the difficulty of explaining the trivalency of carbon which it involved. **1927** N. V. SIDGWICK *Electronic Theory of Valency* xv. 271 Trivalency [of carbon]..only arises under extreme compulsion, and is excessively unstable.

trivia (tri·viă), *sb. pl.* [mod.L., pl. of L. *trivium* (see TRIVIUM), infl. in sense by TRIVIAL *a.* 6.] Trivialities, trifles, things of little consequence.

1902 L. P. SMITH (*title*) Trivia. **1920** *Glasgow Herald* 21 July 8 His [*sc.* Mr. Bennett's] method suggests the amount of human interest and knowledge that may lurk in the trivia of holiday experience. **1929** E. LINKLATER *Poet's Pub* xv. 175 He packed an attaché case with a few shirts,..some toilet trivia. **1947** AUDEN *Age of Anxiety* I. 20 Farouche they appear,..loitering through the..Nocturnal trivia. **1961** B. PYM *No Fond Return of Love* xix. 191 The rooms were furnished in a luxuriantly Victorian style, and filled with such nostalgic trivia as waxed fruit under glass, paper-weights, shell and seaweed pictures, and stuffed birds. **1978** *Sunday Times* 26 Feb. 33/7 Besides, trivia has its importance too. Or to put it another way, trivia have their importance too.

trivial, *a.* Add: **6. b.** *Math.* Of no consequence or interest, e.g. because equal to zero; satisfying a given relation on a set with every member of the set; *spec.* applied to a subgroup of a given group that either contains only the identity element or is identical with the given group.

1915 R. D. CARMICHAEL *Diophantine Analysis* ii. 28 We have thus established the fact that Eq. (2) has at least one integral solution which is not trivial. **1941** BIRKHOFF & MACLANE *Surv. Mod. Algebra* vi. 135 The reflexive property is trivial (every group is isomorphic to itself by the identity transformation). **1949** S. KRAVETZ tr. *H. Zassenhaus' Theory of Groups* i. 10 $\mathfrak{G}$ and *e* are trivial subgroups of $\mathfrak{G}$. **1953** [see *PROPER *a.* 5 c (ii)]. **1957** L. FOX *Two-Point Boundary Probl.* vii. 192 If *y* vanishes at $x = 1$ then all the derivatives, if finite, are also zero, giving the trivial solution. **1971** G. GLAUBERMAN in Powell & Higman *Finite Simple Groups* i. 35 These subgroups..will therefore be non-trivial when *P* is not trivial. **1979** *Proc. London Math. Soc.* XXXVIII. 508 Strong spectrality is trivial since $A(K) = A$.

7. c. *Chem.* Of the name of a chemical species: not systematic; often used in preference to the systematic name for reasons of convenience or tradition, as *neohexane* (systematic name *2,2,dimethylbutane*) or *formaldehyde* (systematic name *methanal*). Cf. *SYSTEMATIC *a* 7.

1892 *Nature* 19 May 58/1 The extent to which familiar trivial names shall be retained in the official system [of chemical nomenclature] is therefore a matter of great importance. **1951** *Chem. & Engin. News* 23 July 3036/2 The alchemists used fanciful names; we would class them as 'trivial' names today. **1979** CLARK & MCKERVEY in Barton & Ollis *Comprehensive Org. Chem.* I. ii. 40 Several of these trivial names are still universally accepted... However, trivial names for alkanes containing multiple branching can become cumbersome.

trivialization (triviălaizēi·ʃən). [f. TRIVIALIZE *v.* + -ATION.] The act or process of trivializing.

a **1866** J. GROTE in *Jrnl. Philol.* (1874) V. 153 A still more important law..is that of *evaporation* or *trivialization*; by which I mean the gradual blunting of the force of a word. **1927** H. G. WELLS in *Sunday Express* 26 June 12 The greater danger of promiscuity and the trivialisation of the sexual life lies in a delayed marriage. **1949** KOESTLER *Insight & Outlook* xxviii. 380 By this process of trivialization and smug understatement, the universe itself becomes a silly thought. **1981** *Times* 21 May 4/7 The growing under-use of human abilities through trivialization of work and through unemployment is damaging to those who suffer from them.

trivializer (tri·viălaizəɹ). [f. TRIVIALIZE *v.* + -ER[1].] One who trivializes.

1960 F. RAPHAEL *Limits of Love* III. vi. 369 There was.. nothing the happy man thought about less than death, but nor was there anything the trivialiser was more eager to forget. **1980** *Times Lit. Suppl.* 12 Dec. 1405/3 Taylor has been a popularizer without being a trivializer.

trivializing (tri·viălaiziŋ), *ppl. a.* [f. as next + -ING[2].] That trivializes.

1961 *New Left Rev.* Mar./Apr. 13/2 Berger would..see all 'abstract' art as the product of a trivialising despair. **1966** *Economist* 28 May 970/3 He has serious doubts about the power of literary studies, as now practised, to act as a counterweight to the trivialising forces of our society. **1970** *Radio Times* 8 Oct. 66 It's true that television is endemically a trivialising medium, but it doesn't follow that it *has* to be it.

tri·vializing, *vbl. sb.* [f. TRIVIALIZE *v.* + -ING[1].] The action of TRIVIALIZE *v.*

1963 A. HERON *Towards Quaker View of Sex* v. 44 There is an almost overwhelming urge throughout society towards the trivializing of sexual actions. **1979** *Listener* 16 Aug. 220/3 Any such trivialising of the sacred backfires. The gods will not be mocked.

trivially, *adv.* Add: **2. b.** Chiefly *Math.* In an inconsequential or uninteresting way.

1941 BIRKHOFF & MACLANE *Survey Mod. Algebra* vi. 148 The conclusion is trivially true. **1956** E. M. PATTERSON *Topology* ii. 35 Conditions (T.1) and (T.3) are satisfied trivially. **1977** *Language* LIII. 353 But it is trivially true that *all* features characteristic of creole speech will be removed if decreolization is carried far enough.

tri-weekly, *a.* and *adv.* Add: **A.** *adj.* **b.** Also *absol.* as *sb.*, a tri-weekly journal. orig. *U.S.*

1851 C. CIST *Sk. Cincinnati in 1851* 74 These are all dailies, tri-weeklies, and weekly reissues of dailies. **1884** *U.S. Census* VIII. 111 Three months only the *Spy* ran as a tri-weekly, and but three months longer as a semi-weekly. **1978** D. DAICHES *Edinburgh* vi. 110 The *Caledonian Mercury* (a tri-weekly founded in 1720).

B. *adv.* **b.** (Earlier example.)

1837 J. M. PECK *Gazetteer Illinois* (ed. 2) III. 180 The mail..arrives here tri-weekly.

trizonal (trəizōᵘnăl), *a. temporary.* [f. TRI- + ZONAL *a.*] Of, pertaining to, or consisting of three zones; *spec.* with reference to the British, French, and American zones of occupation in West Germany at the end of the war of 1939–45. So **trizo·nia,** an area of three zones; *spec.* (with capital initial) West Germany as occupied by the Allies.

1947 *Sun* (Baltimore) 21 Nov. 2/8 Advance indications were that a stalemate at London would bring efforts to expand the present American–British occupation area in Western Germany into a 'trizonia' with France. **1947** *Richmond* (Va.) *Times-Dispatch* 28 Dec. II. 2-B/1 It [*sc.* the German Socialist party] views the proposed establishment of 'Trizonia' with many misgivings. **1948** *Times* 10 Jan. 4/4 Pending steps towards tri-zonal fusion, administrative reorganization must go on in the bizone to secure greater efficiency. **1948** *Sunday Times* 7 Mar. 1 Establishment of a trizonal régime in Western Germany. **1948** *News Chron.* 28 Aug. 1 He said the West German political situation, particularly the question of the formation of a trizonal area was discussed.

trizzie (tri·zi). *Austral. slang.* Also **trizzy.** [Orig. uncertain: perh. f. TREY *sb.* + -IE.] A threepenny piece.

1941 BAKER *Dict. Austral. Slang* 78 *Trizzie*, a 3d. piece. **1959** G. HAMILTON *Summer Glare* 31 My greatest pal now was John 'Trizzie' Peele... He always had a threepenny bit in his pocket which gave him his nickname. **1966** *Sunday Truth* (Brisbane) 23 Dec. 22/1 When you peppered the Christmas pud. with trey-bits this year we hope you remembered they will be scarcer next Yuletide and unless you hoard some there will be no trizzies at all for..the 1968 plum-duff... A trey-bit or a trizzy is Aussie slang for a three-penny-bit.

Troadic (trōᵘˌæ·dik), *a.* [(f. *Troad*, name of the region about Troy,) f. L. *Trōad-, Trōas*, a. Gr. *Τρωάδ-, Τρωάς* (contr. of *Τρωϊάς*) Trojan + -IC.] Of or pertaining to ancient Troy and its surrounding regions.

1932 *Antiquity* VI. 77 In the second half of the third millennium, the culture which we may call Troadic spread over a large part of Asia Minor. **1977** G. CLARK *World Prehistory* (ed. 3) IV. 157 That Troadic forms reaching Greece were transmitted by way of the Cyclades is confirmed by the occurrence on the mainland of..the ceramic fictiles of 'hour-glass' form.

Trobriand (trōᵘ·briˌănd). Used *attrib.*: Of, pertaining to, native to, or produced in the *Trobriand* Islands, a small group of coral islands in the Solomon Sea, now forming part of Papua New Guinea; **Trobriand Islander** = *TROBRIANDER.

1922 B. MALINOWSKI *Argonauts W. Pacific* ix. 221 The big bay of Gatu, where once the crews of a whole fleet of Trobriand canoes were killed and eaten. **1935** —— *Coral Gardens & their Magic* II. VI. v. 232 The Trobriand phenomenon of a language of magic..fits into our theory of language. **1937** R. H. LOWIE *Hist. Ethnol. Theory* xiii. 231 The reader becomes saturated with the Trobriand atmosphere. **1951** E. E. EVANS-PRITCHARD *Social Anthropol.* iv. 74 Malinowski came to know the Trobriand Islanders well. **1956** R. REDFIELD *Peasant Society & Culture* 35 The many interrelations of custom, institution, and human need in Trobriand life. **1974** *Country Life* 11 Apr. 838/1 The bronze..can be appreciated..by anyone—atheist, Hottentot, Eskimo, Trobriand Islander.

Trobriander (trōᵘ·briˌændəɹ). [f. *Trobriand* (see prec.) + -ER[1].] A native or inhabitant of the Trobriand Islands.

1922 B. MALINOWSKI *Argonauts W. Pacific* ix. 220 The Trobrianders will sail deep, shaded bays. **1969** *Times* 22 Jan. 12/8 The difficulty of disentangling the Trobrianders' original beliefs from what they have been taught by Europeans.

trochaical, *a.* (Later *fig.* example.)

1930 R. CAMPBELL *Poems* 10 Jack Squire through his own teardrops sploshes In his great flat trochaical goloshes.

trochanter. Add: **trocha·nteral** *a.*

1961 in WEBSTER. **1967** J. H. SUDD *Introd. Behaviour Ants* ii. 15 The coxal and trochanteral joints.

trochotron (trǫ·koˌtrǫn). *Electronics.* [f. TROCHO(IDAL *a.* + *-TRON.] A type of magnetron in which there are a number of anodes at different angular positions around the central cathode, with the electron beam able to be switched from one anode to another.

1947 ALFVÉN & ROMANUS in *Nature* 1 Nov. 614/1 Research on valves with cycloidal or trochoidal electronic motion has been carried out... The development of the valves, which are called 'trochotrons', has been carried out by G. Hambraeus and..T. Wallmark. **1962** *Jrnl. Brit. Inst. Electr. Engineers* XXIII. 99/1 The Trochotron is a hot-cathode multi-electrode tube containing a number of open box electrodes and operating in a constant magnetic field. **1980** *Jrnl. Nuclear Materials* XCIII–XCIV. A. 352/2 The property of stigmatic focusing used in the trochotron mass spectrometer..is conserved in this device.

‖ **trockenbeerenauslese** (trǫ·kənbērənau:s-lēzĕ). Pl. **-lesen.** [Ger., f. *trocken* dry + *beeren* pl. of *beere* BERRY *sb.* grape + *auslese* selection, choice (wine).] (A) sweet German white wine of superior quality, made from individually selected grapes affected by noble rot.

1963 *Times* 8 Feb. 12/5 Beerenauslesen and Trockenbeerenauslesen. These latter terms mean, respectively, wines made from selected over-ripe single grapes and those made from over-ripe single grapes which are in effect sun-dried raisins, in a state of *pourriture noble*. **1964** *Harper's Bazaar* Nov. 146/3, I do not think a white wine, except a Trockenbeerenauslese..should be expected to last so long. **1972** W. GARNER *Ditto, Brother Rat!* i. 5, I drank so many good wines my tastebuds stopped performing for anything less than a *Trockenbeerenauslese*.

troepie: see *TROOPIE.

trog (trǫg). *slang.* [Abbrev. of TROGLODYTE.]

1. A speleologist. *rare.*

1955 *People* (Austral.) 7 Sept. 23/3 These are the trogs, as they cosily call themselves,..members of the Sydney Speleological Society, the Sydney University Speleological Society, [etc.].

2. One of a despised social group; a lout, a boor, a hooligan, an obnoxious person.

1956 L. MCINTOSH *Oxford Folly* 15 This charm school would have been rather a brilliant thing to do... After all, these trogs lead such dreary lives. **1957** J. I. M. STEWART *Use of Riches* I. ii. 23 You've been listening to some disgusting trog being beastly about Rupert, and now you're parroting him. **1960** D. POTTER *Glittering Coffin* vi. 89 Trinity..infrequently admits a 'trog' (in other words a grammar school boy). **1961** M. DICKENS *Heart of London* III. 277 Nobody mixes, I mean really *mixes* with the trogs. **1962** J. FLEMING *When I grow Rich* xv. 173 One of the trogs appointed himself foreman. **1967** *Guardian* 30 May 2/4, I am thoroughly disgusted. Yesterday I saw two long-haired trogs, one with a ribbon in his hair, wearing the red frock-coats of the Chelsea Pensioners. **1981** M. DUFFY *Gor Saga* 87 He'd given her the morning after pill and the little trog had just kept it... She would stick him with a paternity order. **1983** *Granta* VII. 17 The scowling vandals, bus-stop boogies, and soccer trogs malevolently lining the streets.

3. (See quot. 1958.) *N.Z.*

1958 *Tararua* XII. 28 For shelter, hillmen may seek a *trog*, a large overhanging boulder or bluff giving shelter like a cave. **1971** *N.Z. Listener* 19 Apr. 56/5 They found a possie in a bit of a trog and boiled-up.

4. A teenager who camps out or lives in caves. *temporary.*

1965 *Sun* 8 June 7/7 For Mods and Rockers you can now read Trogs and Thunderbirds... A teenager I know explained it to me yesterday: 'Mods do a lot of sleeping out, camping.' **1966** *Daily Tel.* 14 Apr. 23/3 The young people, who called themselves 'trogs' after the word troglodyte, cave dweller, could be found in the caves at weekends with about 50 permanent 'residents'.

troglo- (trǫ·glo), combining form of Gr. τρώγλη hole, used in the names of various groups of organisms found in caves, as **troglobi·on(t)**, **tro·globite** [a. G. *troglobie* (J. B. Schiner in A. Schmidl *Grötten und Höhlen von Adelsberg* (1854) 240), f. Gr. βιῶν living], an animal living entirely in the dark parts of caves; hence **troglobi(o)·tic** *a.*; **tro·glo-phil(e)** [a. Ger. (J. B. Schiner *loc. cit.*: see -PHIL, -PHILE], a cave-dwelling animal that does not live entirely in the dark; **tro·gloxene** [a. Fr. *trogloxène* (E. G. Racovitza 1907, in *Arch. Zool. Expér. & Gén.* 4th Ser. VI. 437), f. Gr. ξένος guest], an animal that spends occasional short periods in dark caves.

1924 *Glasgow Herald* 13 Dec. 4 Permanent cave-dwellers (the troglobions), like the Dalmatian Proteus newt. **1927** *Ibid.* 2 July 4 The three groups have received various names, such as troglobionts, troglophils, and trogloxenes. **1982** MOYLE & CECH *Fishes* xxxi. 444 Most cave waters containing troglobiotic fishes have at least intermittent connections to the outside. **1953** HAZELTON & GLENNIE in C. H. D. Cullingford *Brit. Caving* ix. 268 The family Dendrocoelidae includes a large number of troglobites. *Ibid.* 270 The genus *Candona*..includes many troglobite species. **1971** WEBSTER Add., Troglobitic. **1924** *Glasgow Herald* 13 Dec. 4 We include many of the bats as troglophils. **1947** *Sci. News* V. 52 The troglophili actively seek out and prefer the underground dark. **1953** HAZELTON & GLENNIE in C. H. D. Cullingford *Brit. Caving* ix. 268 Only those species which find the cave temperature suitable can become troglophiles. **1965** B. E. FREEMAN tr. *Vandel's Biospeleology* vii. 66 Its grey colour and the presence of eyes indicate that this planarian is a troglophile. **1927** Trogloxene [see *troglobiont* above]. **1965** B. E. FREEMAN tr. *Vandel's Biospeleology* ix. 142 Until quite recently all crabs which had been found in caves were trogloxenes or at most troglophiles.

troika. Add: **2.** A group or set of three persons (*rarely* things) or categories of people associated in power; a three-person commission or administrative council. Also *attrib.*

1945 [see N.K.V.D. s.v. *N II. 1]. **1954** C. P. SNOW *New Men* xl. 286 Faith, hope, and hate: that was the troika which rushed him on. **1957** *Times Lit. Suppl.* 15 Nov. 682/1 The so-called *troika*, or commission of three, which authorized summary executions. **1961** *Guardian* 6 June 1/2 Experience of the United Nations action in the Congo..had convinced the Soviet Government of the need for the troika principle to be applied to all international action. **1961** *New Statesman* 9 June 901/2 Krushchev's central doctrine of the 'Troika', the principle of triple-harness—Communist, western and uncommitted—in the administrative, as well as in the policy-making, organs of the UN. **1969** A. ARENT *Laying on of Hands* (1971) ix. 91 The landed gentry. Part of the troika who, with the army and the Church, run Spain. **1971** *Nature* 26 Feb. 585/1 Every chemistry department, after all, is now at least a troika of inorganic, physical and organic chemistry. **1974** T. P. WHITNEY tr. *Solzhenitsyn's Gulag Archipelago* I. I. vii. 281 Real scope entered the picture with the twenties, when *permanently* operating *Troikas*—panels of three, operating behind closed doors—were created to bypass the courts permanently. **1976** *Church Times* 23 Jan. 9/1 The editorship is now a troika consisting of David Jenkins, John Drury and James Mark. **1976** M. J. LASKY *Utopia & Revolution* (1977) ii. 92 Ideas, images, and ideology never quite manage to be harnessed into a controllable troika.

troilism (troi·liz'm). [Perh. f. F. *trois* three: see -ISM.] Sexual activity in which three persons take part simultaneously. Also *transf.* Hence **troi·list** *a.*

[**1941** *Dorland's Med. Dict.* (ed. 19) 1544/2 Troilism,.. a psychotic sexual manifestation in which the patient desires the sexual partner of the person for whom he has homosexual yearnings.] **1951** *Ibid.* (ed. 22) 1622/2 *Troilism*,..paraphilia practised by three persons, by two women and a man, or by two men and a woman. **1973** *Sunday Times* 14 Oct. 18/4 Wife-swapping and troilism are mostly in the writers' imaginations, not part of their life. **1976** *Times Lit. Suppl.* 20 Feb. 191/1 The troilist encounter in the film *Performance* is breathlessly mentioned as taking place in 'a great big bed'. **1983** V. GLENDINNING *Vita* 197 Emotional troilism always attracted her.

Trojan, *a.* and *sb.* Add: **1. b.** *Trojan horse*: according to epic tradition, the hollow wooden horse in which Greeks were concealed to enter Troy; *fig.* a person, device, etc., insinuated to bring about an enemy's downfall; a person or thing that undermines from within; also *attrib.*

1574 [in Dict.]. **1837** S. S. PRENTISS in G. L. Prentiss *Memoir of S. S. Prentiss* (1858) I. viii. 188 He cannot so easily introduce his Trojan horse within these walls [seating of contested members in Missisipi House]. I, for one, will hurl a spear against its hollow sides. **1940** *Sun* (Baltimore) 13 May 1/4 Alarmed by the success of Germany's 'Trojan horse' and parachute-troop tactics. **1963** *Listener* 17 Jan. 112/2 The strengthening of the 'special links' between London and Washington made Britain's possible entry into the Common Market 'more than ever likely to be that of a Trojan horse'. **1974** *Datamation* Jan. 57/1 A 'Trojan Horse' technique was used to compromise the security of a campus time-sharing computer system... A computer operator used it..erasing all trace of the illicit Trojan Horse code. **1979** A. BOYLE *Climate of Treason* iii. 96 This ambitious Trojan Horse strategy called for the recruitment and indoctrination of compliant intellectuals. **1981** *Courier-Mail* (Brisbane) 27 July 5/4 The 'Trojan horse' technique involves smuggling into a computer system an illegal set of instructions.

2. *Astr.* The epithet of two groups of asteroids which are at the same distance as Jupiter from the sun and approximately 60 degrees ahead of it and 60 degrees behind it in their orbit, so that with the sun and Jupiter they occupy positions of stability at the corners of two equilateral triangles. [So called because the first ones to be discovered were named after heroes of the Trojan War.]

1913 *Jrnl. Brit. Astron. Assoc.* XXIII. 214 Masculine names are reserved for [minor] planets of peculiar interest, viz., those that pass very near the Earth..or have the same period as Jupiter (the Trojan group). **1918** *Mem. R. Astron. Soc.* LXII. 79 The four asteroids—Achilles, Patroclus, Hector, and Nestor—are the Trojan planets. **1979** *Daily Tel.* 17 Apr. 8/6 (*caption*) Troy is one of the two groups of so-called Trojan satellites which always form equilateral triangles between themselves, the sun and Jupiter.

B. *sb.* **4.** *Astr.* A Trojan asteroid.

1918 *Mem. R. Astron. Soc.* LXII. 80 The inclinations of the orbits of the Trojans and Jupiter vary through a quite considerable range. **1954** C. PAYNE-GAPOSCHKIN *Introd. Astron.* (1956) ix. 234 The theory of the 'Trojans' is a beautiful special application of the dynamical 'Problem of Three Bodies'. **1979** *Icarus* XL. 341/1 There seem to be three times more Trojans at the leading Trojan point.

5. *U.S.* The proprietary name of a make of contraceptive sheath.

First registered as a proprietary term in the U.S. on 26 Apr. 1927.

1951 *Official Gaz.* (U.S. Patent Office) 17 Apr. 757/1 Trojan... For Prophylactic Membranous Articles for the Prevention of Contagious Diseases. **1962** A. LURIE *Love & Friendship* xiv. 264 'Why "Trojans"?' she asked, picking up a small box... 'They lost the war, after all.' **1973** M. AMIS *Rachel Papers* 202 After some neck-ricking soixante-neuf and a short period inside her unsheathed, I clawed at the little pink holder and took its final trojan.

troland (trōᵘ·lǎnd). [The name of L. T. *Troland* (1889–1932), U.S. psychologist and physicist.] A unit of retinal illumination, being the illumination produced by a surface with a luminance of one candela per square metre when the pupil has an area of one square millimetre; orig. called a *photon* (*PHOTON[1] 1).

1944 *Jrnl. Optical Soc. Amer.* XXXIV. 254/2 [Report by the Committee on Colorimetry.] A special unit of retinal illuminance, the photon, was introduced by Troland in 1917 and has been employed to some extent, but its use is circumscribed by the danger of confusion with the elementary quantum of radiant energy which is generally called the photon. The renaming of the unit of retinal illumination as the troland, in honor of Dr. L. T. Troland, its originator and chairman of the Committee..in 1921–22, is recommended. **1976** *Nature* 19 Feb. 570/1 We have..measured sensitivity to short wavelengths after adaptation to retinal illuminances that varied over the range 1·1–6·0 log trolands.

troll, *sb.*[2] Add: **b.** Also Comb. *troll-like* adj.

1954 J. R. R. TOLKIEN *Two Towers* iv. 66 A large Man-like, almost Troll-like, figure. **1978** *Trans. Yorks. Dial. Soc.* LXXVIII. 18 Joseph is a troll-like figure, the foil to Heathcliff's gigantic, elemental being.

troll, *v.* Delete '*arch.* and *dial.*' and add: **I. 1.** Delete † *Obs.* and add later examples; *spec.* (*slang*) of a homosexual: to walk the streets, or 'cruise', in search of a sexual encounter; cf. sense 13.

1942 E. LANGLEY *Pea Pickers* I. iii. 41 Past rows of hawthorn hedges in leaf, but lacking flowers, we trolled. **1967** A. WILSON *No Laughing Matter* III. 201 At first..I just got myself picked up... But later I started trolling. **1967** *Listener* 21 Dec. 814/3 They all come trolling on in form-hugging black and do evocative things with chairs and ladders and planks of wood. **1981** R. BARNARD *Sheer Torture* xi. 120, I trolled off quite happily and entered the house.

III. 6. (Later example.)

1819 SCOTT *Ivanhoe* II. vi. 88 Come, trowl the brown bowl to me.

IV. 10. (Further examples.) Cf. TROLLY-LOLLY *int.*

1881 R. L. STEVENSON *Virginibus Puerisque* 283 But let him feign never so carefully, there is not a man but has his pulses shaken when Pan trolls out a stave of ecstasy and sets the world a-singing. **1933** H. ALLEN *Anthony Adverse* III. IX. lxiv. 1190 At Anthony's suggestion they left off the doleful ballads which at first engrossed them and took to trolling more cheerful lays. **1951** N. M. GUNN *Well at World's End* xiv. 99 He felt like a voyageur.. trolled a note or two and lifted his tweed hat as if it were a sombrero. **1977** *Rolling Stone* 16 June 69/2 When the Diamonds trolled 'Them Never Love Poor Marcus', I was moved.

12. (Later examples.)

1948 J. BERRYMAN *Dispossessed* 77 Now Tell me. Troll me the sources of that Song—Assigned last week—by Blake. **1971** K. MILLETT *Sexual Politics* (1972) II. iii. 137 The old scholar chuckles while trolling the more rakish passages of Catullus.

V. 13. (Later *fig.* examples.)

1966 E. LINDALL *Time too Soon* iv. 51 Kamindo had rebuffed him when he had trolled for information. **1984** *Monitor* (McAllen, Texas) 1 May 6A/3 It will troll the Earth's upper atmosphere for magnetospheric, atmospheric and gravitational data.

trolley, trolly, *sb.* Add: **2. b.** In fig. phr. *off one's trolley*, crazy. Cf. ROCKER[1] 2 c. *slang.*

1896 ADE *Artie* x. 92 Any one that's got his head full o' the girl proposition's liable to go off his trolley at the first curve. **1903** A. H. LEWIS *Boss* xix. 264 She's off her trolley. She toins sick; an' in a week she croaks. **1949** N. R. NASH *Young & Fair* II. ii. 66 If you suspect Patty, you're off your trolley! **1976** *National Observer* (U.S.) 4 Sept. 13/3 Anybody who buys a luxury liner for use as a floating hotel is off his trolley. **1983** *Times* 5 Feb. 3/1 The London college gym mistress who is suing her former lover for libel in the High Court, heard a lawyer say yesterday that she had 'gone off her trolley' about the affair.

c. A small table or stand on wheels or castors for use in serving food, transporting light objects, luggage, etc. Freq. as the second element in Combs. *supermarket trolley*: see *SUPERMARKET 2 b; also *ellipt.*

1937, etc. [see *tea-trolley* s.v. *TEA *sb.* 9 c]. **1944** D. WELCH *In Youth is Pleasure* ii. 39 Some [waiters] carried trays poised high in the air; others trundled chromium trolleys with glass shelves, on which brilliant little cakes were piled. *a* **1948** —— *Voice through Cloud* (1950) iv. 39 When the porters..started to wheel him out of the ward, he sat up on the trolley, so that the red blankets fell off him. **1949** S. SMITH *Holiday* xiii. 173 The semolina pudding came in on the trolly. **1963** [see *hostess trolley* s.v. *HOSTESS 4]. **1973** J. WILSON *Truth or Dare* ii. 24, I couldn't help noticing what she'd got in her trolly: sausages, luncheon meat *and* a tub of marge. **1977** *Lancs. Life* Nov. 107/1 (*caption*) A good trolley is an invaluable aid to efficient hostessmanship. **1982** *Amer. Speech* LVII. 154 *Trolley*, surgical dressing cart (British).

4. trolley-bus († **trolli-bus**), a trackless passenger vehicle that gets its power from an overhead cable by means of a pole and trolley (see 3); also *attrib.*; **trolley shop**, a trolley (see *2 c) from which goods are sold, esp. in a hospital.

1921 *Daily Colonist* (Victoria, B.C.) 13 Oct. 11/7 The trolley-buses..are of the single-deck type, with seats for twenty-four passengers. **1927** *Daily Express* 20 July 9/6 The 'trolli-bus' traffic receipts last week..were £400 more than the receipts for the corresponding week last year. **1939** J. B. PRIESTLEY *Let People Sing* i. 13 He climbed into a trolley-bus, which after a mile or so stopped at a large gateway. **1961** C. WILLOCK *Death in Covert* xii. 224 A clang and ring that reminded him incongruously of vibrating trolley-bus wires. **1978** *Country Life* 13 Apr. 956/2 The nearly extinct tram and trolley bus will be revived. **1958** *Times* 7 July (Suppl.) p. xix/1 Volunteer nurses..still give invaluable aid in hospital wards; volunteers take round trolley-shops. **1974** *Country Life* 4 Apr. 797/1 We [*sc.* the Red Cross] organize out-patients' canteens. Trolley shops. Libraries.

trolley *v.* (further *trans.* examples); **trolley-ful** (earlier example).

1889 KIPLING *From Sea to Sea* (1899) II. xxvii. 34 The cans..were..slidden along by the trolleyful. **1936** 'M. INNES' *Death at President's Lodging* xiii. 234 Ah, well, my picture of Håveland trolleying his own bones plus corpse up the garden path was no doubt, as you suggested, a bit steep. **1978** P. MCCUTCHAN *Blackmail North* vi. 69 Stocks being trolleyed in from freighter aircraft.

trolling, *vbl. sb.* Add: **4. trolling motor** *U.S.*, a motor suitable for a boat used in trolling (see TROLL *v.* 13 c); **trolling pole** *N. Amer.*, a horizontal pole rigged on each side of a fishing boat in order to keep the lines clear of the propeller.

1964 M. WEEKS *Compl. Boating Encycl.* 530/1 *Trolling motor*, a low-powered, slow-speed motor used for trolling. **1980** *Outdoor Life* (U.S.) (Northeast ed.) Oct. 26/1 The latest high-thrust, 12-volt electric trolling motor, Thruster Plus from Mercury Marine, is the most efficient that I've tested to date. **1960** M. SHARCOTT *Place of Many Winds* v. 97 Fishermen cut their trolling poles from the forest... The poles must be between thirty and fifty feet long.

trollius (trǫ·li,ŏs). Also **Trollius.** [mod.L. (J. C. Buxbaum *Plantarum Minus Cognitarum Centuria I* (1728) 15): see TROLL FLOWER.] A perennial herb of the genus of this name, belonging to the family Ranunculaceæ, native to Europe, Asia, and North America, and bearing yellow or orange globe-shaped flowers. Also *attrib.* Cf. *globe-flower* s.v. GLOBE *sb.* 10 b.

1899 in E. T. Cook *Century Bk. Gardening* 142/1 It must be a sorry garden that fails to satisfy the Trollius. **1952** BATES & LOWTHER *Breeding Birds Kashmir* 191 We found one [*sc.* a wagtail's nest] in a tuft of *trollius* leaves. **1962** R. PAGE *Education of Gardener* viii. 236 We planted its [*sc.* a stream's] banks..with..clumps of different varieties of yellow trollius. **1978** R. GORER *Growing Plants from Seed* vi. 76 Plants with hard, shiny seeds, such as..trollius, tiarella, and saxifraga all do best if sown outside in autumn.

trollop, *v.* (In Dict. s.v. TROLLOP *sb.*) Restrict *Sc.* to sense (a) and add: (*b*) *spec.* to walk in a slovenly way, to slouch; (earlier and later examples).

1854 M. DODS *Early Lett.* (1910) 63, I felt deeply moved for her, thinking she would trollop away home. **1870** 'OUIDA' *Puck* I. vii. 113 There's allus a lot of..bad wimmin a trolloping about. **1925** *Chambers's Jrnl.* 23 May 397/2 We'll go very slow and he can trollop behind.

Trollopian (trǫlǭu·piǎn), *a.* and *sb.* Also -ean. [f. the name *Trollope* (see below) + -IAN.] **A.** *adj.* **1.** Of, pertaining to, or characteristic of the English novelist Frances Trollope (1780–1863) (mother of Anthony) or her writings.

1847 W. HOWITT in *Howitt's Jrnl.* 9 Jan. 18/1 Mrs. Trollope was introduced to the court circles—everything was shown to her, and the urbane minister was so particularly polite, that, instead of a Trollopean laughter, there was nothing but laudation.

2. Of, pertaining to, or characteristic of the English novelist Anthony Trollope (1815–82) or his writings.

1903 G. GISSING *Private Papers Henry Ryecroft* 213 Any Trollopean work that lay upon the counter. **1907** HARDY *Let.* 29 Sept. in *One Rare Fair Woman* (1972) 134 *Our Fatal Shadows*..shows I think a great advance upon your previous novels... It is quite Trollopian. **1939** C. S. LEWIS *Let.* 24 Nov. (1966) 171 The Curé and the whole cathedral surroundings in Tours are almost Trollopian. **1957** *Times Lit. Suppl.* 25 Oct. 637/4 A Trollopean setting and situation, a cathedral town and a Dean's daughter about to be married. **1980** *Daily Tel.* 12 July 9/2 The 'Strangers and Brothers' sequence..was a conscious effort to write a social history in novel form on a Trollopian scale. **1983** M. DUGGAN *Runcie* xii. 173 The paper's Trollopian report next day—' "Good Heavens!" cried the chaplain.'

B. *sb.* A student or admirer of Anthony Trollope or his writings.

1910 A. D. GODLEY *Reliquiae* (1926) II. 316 In Trollope one remembers the characters, but I never met more than one Trollopian who knew the plots apart. **1946** *N. & Q.* 23 Feb. 67/1 We receive..from the University of California Press the first number of '*The Trollopian*: A Semi-annual Journal Devoted to Studies in Anthony Trollope and His Contemporaries in Victorian Fiction'. **1969** J. GROSS *Rise & Fall Man of Lett.* ix. 245 Michael Sadleir..well known as biographer, bibliographer, Trollopean, and author of *Fanny by Gaslight*.

trolly. Add: **2.** [Perh. a different word: cf. *trolleywags* trousers (Barrère & Leland *Dict. Slang*).] *pl.* Ladies' drawers or knickers. *dial.* and (*schoolgirls'*) *slang*.

1891 J. BARON *Blegburn Dickshonary* (rev. ed.) 68 *Trollys* (female underclothing). That's as near as th' payson'll come to th' meeanin' o' this word; aw co'em wimmen's treawsis, an' he co's 'em drawers, which is *wheere* they're kept. **1934** B. PYM *Diary* 8 Jan. in Holt & Pym *Very Private Eye* (1984) I. 33, I bought a peach coloured vest and trollies to match. **1971** M. WOBER *Eng. Girls' Boarding Schools* vi. 148 Items of clothing earned names, thus 'trolleys' for underwear, 'B squared' for brassieres.

trolly (trǫ·li), *sb.*² *dial.* [Alteration of TROLLOP *sb.*: cf. also TRULL.] = TROLLOP *sb.* 1. Also *comb.* in **trolly-mog, trollimog** [cf. MOGGY 2] in the same sense.

1851 T. STERNBERG *Dial. & Folk-Lore Northants.* 117 *Trolly-mog*, a dirty, slovenly female. **1854** A. E. BAKER *Gloss. Northants. Words & Phrases* II. 357 Oh! what a *trolly* she is! **1876** J. HARTLEY *Yorksher Puddin* 164 He's pickt up some idle trolly. **1901** F. E. TAYLOR *Folk-Speech S. Lancs.* s.v. *Troll, Trolly*, a loose woman; a trull. **1925** W. DE LA MARE *Broomsticks* 130 That old trollimog what lives in Hogges Bottom. **1974** P. WRIGHT *Lang. Brit. Industry* xvii. 163 Untidy housewives abound, judging by all the so-called *slatterns, trolly-mogs, slovens* and *tosspots*.

‖**tromba marina** (trǫ·mbă mărī·nă). [It., = marine trumpet.] = *trumpet marine, marine trumpet* s.v. TRUMPET *sb.* 2 b.

The identification in quot. 1776 is erron.

1776 [see SEA-TRUMPET 2]. **1838** [see TRUMPET *sb.* 2 b]. **1948** G. B. SHAW *How to become Mus. Critic* (1960) 325, I should rather like to hear the *tromba marina*. **1976** D. MUNROW *Instruments Middle Ages & Renaissance* 30/2 A French sculpture of the twelfth century gives us our first glimpse of the tromba marina: the three-sided body is about four feet long and tapers towards the pegbox... By the fifteenth century it had acquired two strings of unequal length.

Trombe (trǫmb, ‖troṅb). *Archit.* The name of Felix *Trombe*, 20th-c. Frenchman, used *attrib.* and in conjunction with that of his collaborator J. *Michel* to designate a masonry wall of a kind designed by him, having glass sheeting fixed a small distance in front of it so as to absorb solar radiation, and usu. ventilated internally to release the heat into the building.

1978 *Washington Post* 4 Nov. E33/2 One of its simple forms is the Trombe wall. This consists of a masonry wall just inside a large south-facing glass wall or window. **1980** *Family Handyman* Sept. 83/1 Since these shutters can be motor-controlled from a remote position, you can install them in front of a trombe wall or other passive solar heat collector. **1980** J. J. GREENLAND in H. J. Cowan *Solar Energy Applications in Design of Buildings* v. 130 A recent development which makes use of solar energy and thermal inertia without excessive loss of heat through glass is the Trombe–Michel solar wall. **1984** *Christian Sci. Monitor* 14 Feb. 21/3 A 'Trombe wall' solar-heating system..helps warm the big structure's lab.

trombiculid (trǫmbi·kiulid), *a.* (and *sb.*) [a. mod.L. family name *Trombiculidæ*, f. generic name *Trombicula* (A. Berlese *Acari Nuovi* (1905) IV. 155), f. *Trombi-dium* (see TROMBIDIID *a.* and *sb.*) + -CULUS: see -ID³.] Of or pertaining to a mite of the family Trombiculidæ, which includes several species having parasitic larvæ which cause or transmit disease in man and other mammals. Also as *sb.*, a mite of this kind.

1950 R. MATHESON *Med. Entomol.* (ed. 2) iv. 133 Trombiculid mites and disease: The attacks of various species of mites..usually result, in man, in a marked dermatitis accompanied by intense itching. **1957** *New Scientist* 14 Nov. 33/1 A trombiculid does not feed on a mammal more than *once* in its lifetime. **1962** GORDON & LAVOIPIERRE *Entomol. for Students of Med.* xlv. 267 The association of trombiculid mites with scrub typhus had been suspected well over a century ago by the Japanese physician Ohtomo. **1978** *Jrnl. R. Soc. Med.* LXXI. 507 The causative organism..is transmitted by the larvae (or chiggers) of several species of trombiculid mites.

trombone. Add: **3.** A green or yellow pear-shaped pumpkin belonging to the Australian variety of this name.

1946 *Jrnl. Agric.* (S. Austral.) Jan. 275 The trombone is not such a good cropper unless it can be watered in hot weather. **1969** *Ibid.* Jan. 208 By far the most popular pumpkin variety in South Australia is the Trombone. It is typically pear-shaped with a curved neck. **1978** *Guardian* 10 Nov. 21/8 According to one reader, a trombone is a non-spherical pumpkin much used in chutneys and pickles. Another, equally well versed in Australian horticulture, tells me that it is a long-necked marrow with a bulbous end (hence the name) which is cooked and treated exactly like vegetable marrow.

trombone, *v.* Restrict *rare* to sense 1 in Dict. and add: **2.** (Earlier and later examples.) So **trombo·ning** *vbl. sb.*

1864 J. A. GRANT *Walk across Africa* ix. 196 When standing here, the hoarse tromboning of the hippopotamus, wishing to come out to graze, echoed from out these rushes. **1866** J. MACGREGOR *Thousand Miles in Rob Roy Canoe* (ed. 2) iii. 48 Crowds of gaping peasants..jostled against bands drumming and tromboning.., and marching in a somewhat ricketty manner over the undoubtedly rough pavement. **1958** R. HARRIS in P. Gammond *Decca Bk. Jazz* iii. 44 There was one man..who created a legend of tail-gate tromboning—the one and only Kid Ory. **1960** *New Oxf. Hist. Music* III. xii. 426 'Die pusauner pusaunoten über einnander mit dreyen stymmen, als man sunst gewonlichen singet' ('the trombonists tromboned together in three parts as one is otherwise accustomed to sing'). **1967** *Listener* 26 Jan. 144/3 A contentious fugal start and imperious tromboning herald the story-telling with a piquant sense of expectation.

tromino (trǫ·mino). [f. TR(I- + D)OMINO by deliberately false analogy (see quot. 1961).] Any planar shape formed by joining three identical squares by their edges.

1954 S. W. GOLOMB in *Amer. Math. Monthly* LXI. 676 It is impossible to cover the checker board with 21 *straight* trominoes, and a monomino in the upper left-hand corner of the board. **1961** [see *PENTOMINO]. **1979** *Sci. Amer.* Apr. 19/1 The games played with the two 3-cell animals (the trominoes) are slightly more difficult to analyze.

tromp (trǫmp), *v.* Var. (orig. and chiefly *U.S.*) of TRAMP *v.*¹ Hence **tro·mping** *vbl. sb.*

1892 *Dial. Notes* I. 234 Tromp = tramp. **1895** S. CRANE *Red Badge of Courage* x. 105 Yeh wanta go trompin' off. **1902** *Dial. Notes* II. 248 He *tromped* my toe. **1929** W. FAULKNER *Sanctuary* (1981) viii. 95 You'll tromp on a loose boa'd and find yoself downstairs befo you know hit. **1940** J. STUART *Trees of Heaven* 251 Somebody has.. tromped the vines into the ground. **1952** E. FERBER *Giant* xx. 334 You want to look out, Bick, she don't get tromped the way they're milling around today. **1953** R. MAIS *Hills were Joyful Together* I. xi. 109 White-robed figures..sang hymns and clapped their hands, and some shook tambourines, and they tromped, jumping and grunting rhythmically. *Ibid.*, And while the singing and tromping was going on on the river bank, the initiates for baptism came down one by one from a high rock. **1962** J. STEINBECK *Trav. with Charlie* I. 12 About that time hurricane Donna was reported tromping her way out of the Caribbean. **1968** J. CRIST *Private Eye, Cowboy & Very Naked Girl* 193 Beatniks tromping grapes in the buff. **1974** J. IRVING *158-Pound Marriage* v. 117 Edith heard Frau Reiner and the Chetniks whispering and tromping about in the living room. **1975** *New Musical Express* 24 May 20/1 Heat and noise and darkness and a steady, muffled tromping that you can feel through your feet. **1976** M. MACHLIN *Pipeline* xlvii. 491 He wouldn't care who he tromped on to get there, either. **1979** *United States 1980/81* (Penguin Travel Guides) 501 Tromping through the ice plants is a botanical education in itself.

‖**trompe l'œil** (troṅp lǭʸ). Also **trompe-l'œil**, *erron.* **d'œil.** [Fr., lit. 'deceives the eye'.] Deception of the eye, an illusion, *spec.* in *Art* with regard to the material reality of the object(s) represented, a (usu. still-life) painting, plaster ornament, etc., intended to give an illusion of reality. Also *fig.* and *attrib.* passing into *adj.*

1889 C. H. STRANAHAN *Hist. French Painting* vii. 457 The public of connoisseurs who care not for any tricks of 'trompe l'œil', but for art. **1926** A. HUXLEY *Ess. New & Old* 171 Their taste ran to *trompe l'œil* pictures of fighting giants. **1927** E. BOWEN *Hotel* x. 118 The hill..by some *trompe-l'œil* of twilight seemed to topple. **1928** *Observer* 19 Feb. 5/1 The nearest approach to realistic treatment is Mr. Cedric Morris's picture of a luxurious flowery meadow in North Africa, but this realism is not carried to the point of a *trompe l'œil*. Paint is made to tell as paint, and not as a substitute for the thing represented. *a* **1934** R. FRY *Last Lect.* (1939) 207 The carefully exposed reflection of the fallen soldier in the retina of his shield, which is very much in agreement with the puerile stories of *trompe-d'œil*—like that of the 'Grapes of Zeuxis'—which were the stock in trade of art critics like Pliny. **1936** A. HUXLEY *Eyeless in Gaza* xviii. 231 And the Museum of Sexology: such photographs and wax models—almost too *trompe-l'œil*. **1957** *Listener* 24 Oct. 658/3 Details may be solid, trompe l'œil, or flat. **1961** E. TAYLOR *In Summer Season* i. 11 Facing her, as she turned the stairs, was a *trompe-l'œil* panel, designed to lengthen the passage into an endless arcade. **1964** S. SONTAG in *Evergreen Rev.* Dec. 76 Plato's view that all art is an elaborate *trompe l'œil*, and therefore a lie. **1968** *Ideal Home* Nov. 31 The dining-room has *trompe l'œil* marbling. **1970** *New Scientist* 11 June 530/1 *Trompe d'œil* effects such as false perspectives painted on walls are common. **1974** G. BUTLER *Coffin for Canary* xii. 147 Olivia had told her own story and had told it badly... She had led those who listened to her up to a blank wall and confronted them with a *trompe l'œil*. **1978** R. BARNARD *Unruly Son* xv. 155 Shelves and books had been painted on the wall, making a perfect *trompe l'œil*.

-tron (trǫn), *suffix. Physics.* The ending of *ELECTRON² (but cf. Gr. -τρον instrumental suffix), used: **a.** in the names of some kinds of thermionic valves and other electron tubes, as *kenotron* (1915), *pliotron* (1915), *ignitron* (1933); **b.** in the names of a few sub-atomic particles, as *positron* (1933), *negatron* (1934), *mesotron* (1938): cf. *-ON¹; **c.** in the names of devices and machines, *spec.* particle accelerators, as *cyclotron* (1935), *betatron* (1941), *phantastron* (1943), *levitron* (1960).

1939 *Nature* 8 Apr. 602/1 *-tron* should be restricted to signify either an instrument or a particle, but not both... *-on* taken by itself..seems the most natural ending for a particle. **1949** *Ibid.* 13 Aug. 263/2 The Amsterdam conference [of the International Union of Physics] attempted to dispose of the curious modern theory that the ancient Greek termination for a fundamental particle was '-tron'. It blessed the word 'meson' as against its rivals.

tronc (trǫŋk, ‖troṅ). [a. Fr., = collecting box.] In hotels and restaurants, a common fund into which tips and service charges are paid for distribution to the staff. Also *attrib.*

1928 *Observer* 15 Jan. 6/1 The staff are paid on the tronc, or pooling system, whereby all tips are divided. **1960** *Times* 15 Jan. 9/3 The value of a point was set each week according to the amount in the *tronc*. **1964** *Observer* (Colour Suppl.) 13 Dec. 33/1 In all *troncs* (pooled tips, which the *tronc* head waiter distributes according to the number of points each waiter has) they declare an average figure to the Income Tax. **1976** *Rhyl Jrnl. & Advertiser* 9 Dec. 20 (Advt.), Chef—Royal Lido, Prestatyn. Applications are invited for this permanent post at a salary in accordance with Miscellaneous grade 6..plus an annual supplement of £312 and a percentage of tronc. **1981** *Times* 11 June 14/6 The money was massaged by managements and distributed on their behalf to staff..or paid into an independent tronc fund.

trondhjemite (trǫ·ndhẽⁱmait). *Petrogr.* [ad. G. *trondhjemit* (V. M. Goldschmidt 1916, in *Skrifter udgivna af Vidensk. i Christiania* (Matem.-Naturv. Klasse) No. 2. 77), f. *Trondhjem* (now *Trondheim*), name of a city in western Norway: see -ITE¹.] Any leucocratic tonalite, esp. one in which the plagioclase is oligoclase.

1922 *Jrnl. Geol.* XXX. 406 The acid phase is represented by 'trondhjemite' (new name) which Kjerulf calls an oligoclase-granite, and which might as well be characterized as a granodiorite. **1978** *Nature* 12 Oct. 538/2 The metabasaltic sequences may be of considerable thickness and in many areas are associated with intrusive cumulate gabbros, trondhjemites and minor developments of serpentinised peridotites. **1979** F. BARKER *Trondhjemites, Dacites, & Related Rocks* i. 1 The author suggests that the IUGS definition of trondhjemite as leucotonalite be followed, except that andesine-bearing leucotonalite be termed calcic trondhjemite, and that albite-bearing leucotonalite, as well as the oligoclase variety, be termed trondhjemite.

troop, *sb.* Add: **1. c.** *esp.* A group of apes or monkeys.

1929 R. M. & A. W. YERKES *Great Apes* vii. 71/1 Some observers assert that troops [of gibbons]..will abandon a wounded comrade. **1951** R. CAMPBELL *Light on Dark Horse* v. 84, I blundered into the middle of a huge troop of baboons. **1965** *Listener* 10 June 863/1 Another of the characteristic features of the primates is the size of the group or 'troop' as it is called.

2. b. *pl.* The members of a mob or gang collectively. *U.S. slang.*

1932 *Daily Progress* (Charlottesville, Va.) 7 Apr. 4/4 *Troops*, mob or gang. **1963** *Listener* 4 Apr. 585/2 On the trip back he was met by 'the troops'. With quick dispatch they placed four bullets in the back of his head, disposed of the weapon in a nearby alley, and were gone.

3. c. A company of Scouts comprising not less than three patrols of six Scouts each.

1908, etc. [see *PATROL *sb.* 3 b]. **1959** E. H. CLEMENTS *High Tension* x. 167, I ran a Scout Troop in that town and he was one of my troop. **1980** W. MAXWELL *So Long, see You Tomorrow* iii. 28 Were we in the same Boy Scout troop?

5. troop-carrier, a large aircraft or armoured vehicle for transporting troops; hence **troop-carrying** *a.*

1923 *Daily Mail* 23 June 5 Among landplanes there are huge new troop-carriers capable of carrying 25 fully equipped soldiers. **1958** *Ibid.* 18 July 1/1 Israel's permission to ferry troop-carriers through her air-space was not..fully cleared. **1964** L. DEIGHTON *Funeral in Berlin* vi. 38 A Volkspolizei troop carrier was parked at the roadside. **1976** A. WHITE *Long Silence* ix. 84 We could hear..the engines of motor-cycles, lorries and troop-carriers. **1937** L. HART *Europe in Arms* iii. 32 A force of 1200 men together with 150 machine-guns and 18 light field-guns was carried 100 miles in troop-carrying aircraft. **1977** M. GILBERT *Winston S. Churchill* IV. Compan. I. 654 The first use of troop-carrying aeroplanes during a military campaign took place on 21 February 1923.

trooper. Add: **1. b.** (Earlier example.)

1739–40 RICHARDSON *Pamela* (1740) I. 239 She curses and storms at me like a Trooper.

c. A brave or stalwart person. *colloq.*

1951 R. CAMPBELL *Light on Dark Horse* 230 Nina Hamnett (she was a fine trooper).

3. a. (Earlier example.)

1830 *Hist. Rec. Austral.* (1922) 1st Ser. XV. 770 The Mounted Police, which at present consists of about 68 Troopers.

b. *U.S.* A mobile state policeman. More fully *state trooper.*

1911 *Ann. Rep. 1910* (Pennsylvania Dept. State Police) 16 On arrival of the detail, the mob of foreigners proceeded to stone and shoot at Troopers... Three of the Troopers.. fired at their assailants, wounding two Italians. **1941** [see *STATE *sb.* 38 e]. **1977** *New Yorker* 3 Oct. 43/1, I slowed the car and pulled over..and a state trooper pulled up behind us... The trooper said, Do you need any help.

c. A paratrooper. orig. *U.S.*

1942 *Yank* 14 Oct. 2 English neighbors tasted this clannishness soon after the troopers settled in their midst. **1974** C. RYAN *Bridge Too Far* III. iii. 156 Of the sixteen paratroopers, pilot and co-pilot, only Johnson and two other troopers got out.

4. (Later examples.)

1942 *R.A.F. Jrnl.* 16 May 11, I saw the empty trooper, scrubbed and waiting. **1981** J. BARNETT *Firing Squad* II. 114 First objective, a decent cabin on the trooper.

Hence **troopere·ss** (*rare*), a female trooper.

1924 GALSWORTHY *White Monkey* II. iv. 152 When she was..lying to them like a trooperess. **1927** *Daily Express* 2 Sept. 3 The stories related of the coarse, swearing 'trooperess' are astounding.

troopie (trū·pi). *colloq.* Also (*S. Afr.*) **troepie.** [f. TROOP *sb.* + -IE.] In South Africa and Rhodesia (Zimbabwe): a private soldier, esp. a national serviceman without rank.

1972 *Eng. Use in S. Afr.* May, Some of the troopies with particularly dirty habits..receive the title *vuilgat.* **1976** [see *request programme* s.v. *REQUEST *sb.*[1] 11]. **1980** *Observer* 3 Aug. 10/1 The FN rifle carried by troopies in the bush.

tropane (trōᵘ·pēⁱn). *Chem.* Also † **tropan.** [ad. G. *tropan*, f. *tropeïn* TROPEINE: see -ANE 2 b.] A saturated bicyclic tertiary amine which is a basic liquid obtained from various plants and the parent of a series of compounds which includes atropine, cocaine, and related alkaloids; 8-methyl-8-azabicyclo-[3.2.1]octane, $C_8H_{15}N$.

1919 *Chem. Abstr.* XIII. 592 The residual sirup solidifies in a few days to needles, somewhat deliquescent in air of the HCl salt of tropan. **1923** *Ibid.* XVII. 1643 (*heading*) The spectrochemistry of derivatives of tropane. **1951** A. GROLLMAN *Pharmacol. & Therapeutics* i. 34 The alkaloids of the atropine group of drugs may be considered as derived from a combination of a piperidine and pyrrolidine ring designated as tropane. **1981** *Phytochemistry* XX. 497/1 Tropane alkaloids are known to occur in *Anthocercis littorea* [etc.].

trope (trōᵘp), *v.* [f. TROPE *sb.* 5.] *trans.* To introduce (a trope) as an embellishment; to embellish with a trope or tropes; to add as a trope to. Hence **troped** *ppl. a.*

1894 W. H. FRERE *Winchester Troper* p. xv, The Winchester Tropers..originally contained only a long jubilum on *per*manebit, but later in MS. CC the words were added and the trope troped. **1922** MADAN & CRASTER *Summary Catal. Western Manuscripts Bodleian Library* II. I. 149 These flyleaves I understand from Mr. Bannister to come from a non-monastic breviary, and, as he does not find a troped office for St. K. in English breviaries, I should have supposed them French. **1959** *Listener* 24 Dec. 1134/3 The final word 'portum', set to a long melisma, is troped 'portum in ultimo, da nobis iudicio'. **1977** *Gramophone* Sept. 469/3 The choir missed a golden opportunity by not singing *O come, O come, Emmanuel* in its original fifteenth-century French Franciscan version, as a two-part troped litany.

troph-, var. *TROPHO- before a vowel.

trophallaxis (trǫfălæ·ksis). *Ent.* [f. *TROPH- + Gr. ἄλλαξις exchange.] The mutual exchange of food material by adult insects and larvæ. Hence **trophalla·ctic** *a.*

1918 W. M. WHEELER in *Proc. Amer. Philos. Soc.* LVII. 322 In *Belonogaster* the feeding of adults and larvæ is reciprocal... As the relationship is clearly coöperative or mutualistic, I suggest the term *trophallaxis.* **1919** W. OSLER *Old Humanities* ii. 13 The nursing function..is really trophallactic... The larva is provided with..an ambrosia greedily lapped up by the nurse. **1931** W. C. ALLEE *Animal Aggregations* xix. 388 'Trophallaxis' is the bond that unites parent and offspring in the social insects. **1940** *Jrnl. Compar. Psychol.* XXIX. 456 This process.. may be represented as the outcome of a simple conditioned response based upon trophallactic relations in the bivouac. **1978** R. J. ELZINGA *Fund. Entomol.* vii. 186 Trophallaxis plays a greater role in ants than it does in the social wasps.

trophic, *a.* (*sb.*) Add: **1. b.** *Ecol.* Of or pertaining to the feeding habits of, and the food relationship between, different types of organisms in the food-cycle; so *trophic level*, any of a hierarchy of levels of an ecosystem, each consisting of organisms sharing the same function in the food-web, and the same relationship to the primary producers.

1942 *Ecology* XXIII. 407/2 Food-cycles rarely have more than five trophic levels. **1957** *Ecol. Monogr.* XXVII. 55 (*heading*) Trophic structure and productivity of Silver Springs, Florida. **1974** R. H. BRITTON in R. Goodier *Natural Environment of Shetland* 123 The nutrient poor categories (dystrophic and oligotrophic) are by far the most numerous and..eutrophic and brackish lochs are rather rare... The lochs within each trophic category can be further subdivided according to their superficial area. **1976** *Nature* 22 July 284/1 The trophic base of the arthropod fauna is wind-blown detritus. **1980** *Jrnl. R. Soc. Arts* Feb. 140/2 While they are trophic levels—top carnivore, herbivore, plants, microorganisms—none is dominant.

3. Of a hormone: stimulating the production of another hormone from a specific gland; = *TROPIC *a.* 4 b.

1945 I. S. KLEINER *Human Biochem.* xxiii. 503 Another hormone of this gland which produces its effect by influencing a different structure, i.e., a 'trophic' hormone, is the adrenotrophic factor. **1965** LEE & KNOWLES *Animal Hormones* ii. 19 The site of production of the trophic hormone controlling the adrenal cortex is still in doubt. **1975** *Nature* 27 Nov. 340/2 The existence of a human cell line showing severalfold stimulation by androgens in a defined system, free from the effects of other trophic hormones, should provide a useful reagent for the further study of the mechanism of androgen action.

-trophic (trōᵘ·fik, trǫ·fik), *suffix.* [See TROPHIC *a.*] **1.** Forming adjs.: (*a*) with the senses 'characterized by nutrition (of a certain kind)', 'finding nourishment in', as in *autotrophic* adj. s.v. *AUTO-[1], *HETEROTROPHIC, *LECITHOTROPHIC *adjs.*, *psychrotrophic* adj. s.v. *PSYCHRO-; also 'controlled by', as in *NEUROTROPHIC *a.*; (*b*) with the sense 'maintaining or supporting (a gland, tissue, etc.)' and hence 'regulating', esp. in the epithets of hormones, as *GONADOTROPHIC, *SEBOTROPHIC *adjs.* Cf. *-TROPIC.

1943 *Endocrinology* XXXIII. 407 The use of -tropic as in *gonadotropic*..reverses and confuses a clear, practical pre-established usage in the broad field of biology... -Trophic, even if not perfectly apt, is close enough in meaning and is free from confusion. **1950** *Lancet* 2 Dec. 708/2 It is becoming current practice to speak of the action of a hormone in controlling an endocrine gland as trophic (e.g., thyrotrophic hormone..)... This is surely a misuse of words, from a confusion between trophic action..which is concerned with nutrition,..and tropism .., which connotes control... Is it too late to revert to thyrotropic..and the like? **1971** *Ibid.* 25 Sept. 701/2 For good or ill, -trophic is all but universal [in the names of hormones], though I saw corticotropic recently in a new edition of a student's biochemistry book from the States.

trophied, *a.* **2.** (Earlier example.)

1805 SOUTHEY *Madoc* II. 197 He sits upon a throne of trophied skulls.

tropho-. Add: Also, before a vowel, **troph-.** **trophe·ctoderm** *Embryol.* = *trophoblast*; hence **trophectode·rmal** *a.*; **trophobi·ont** *Ent.* [f. Gr. βιουντ-, βιων living], an insect which produces a secretion used as food by another; † **tropho-chro·matin** *Cytology* [f. *CHROMATIN: cf. G. *trophochromatisch* (W. Lubosch 1902, in *Ergebnisse Anat. und Entwicklungsgeschichte* XI. 783)], chromatin which was thought to be concerned only with the regulation of the metabolism and growth of the cell, and not with its reproduction (*obs.*); **tropholy·tic** *a.* [*-LYTIC], (of part of a lake) characterized by the decomposition of organic matter; opp. *TROPHOGENIC *a.* 2; **trophonu·cleus** *Zool.*, a large nucleus present in some flagellated protozoa, esp. trypanosomes, which regulates the metabolism and growth of the cell; **trophothy·lax** *Ent.* [f. Gr. θύλακ-ος pouch] (see quot. 1971).

1932 M. T. HARMAN *Textbk. Embryol.* vii. 134 Supposedly the troph-ectoderm produces an enzyme which digests the maternal tissue until the embryo is entirely imbedded. **1980** *Nature* 10 Apr. 550/2 It was recently found that the inner cell mass of the early blastocyst is also totipotent and can form trophectoderm when isolated by immunosurgery. **1978** *Ibid.* 7 Sept. 10/3 The strange distribution of this determinant does not fit in with any preconceived notions of trophectodermal formation or differentiation. **1913** E. WASMANN in *Ann. Rep. Smithsonian Inst. 1912* 464 We distinguish..trophobionts or food-producing animals of the ant. **1978** R. J. ELZINGA *Fund. Entomol.* vii. 173 These trophobionts are protected by their hosts and are analogous to domestic cows, for they yield food sugar solutions..upon request. **1909** *Q. Jrnl. Microsc. Sci.* LIII. 282 Mesnil ('05) uses a terminology which also has a physiological foundation..; trophochromidia, for chromidial structures of a vegetative function; idiochromidia, for chromidia which enter into the formation of gametes. [*Note*] Cf. Lubosch's ('02) terms, 'trophochromatin' and 'idiochromatin'. **1947** *Ann. Rev. Microbiol.* I. 2 In amœboid forms special interest attaches to the structure and division of the nucleus. A distinction may be made between the 'trophochromatin' which stains intensely with iron haematoxylin, but takes no part in the formation of the chromosomes, and the 'idiochromatin' out of which the chromosomes are formed. **1957** Tropholytic [see *TROPHOGENIC *a.* 2]. **1975** G. A. COLE *Textbk. Limnol.* ii. 10/1 Below the trophogenic layer is a darker tropholytic region..where respiration and decomposition predominate. **1906** H. M. WOODCOCK in *Q. Jrnl. Microsc. Sci.* L. 182 This is revealed..in the sharp resolution of the nuclear material into trophic and kinetic constituents, which are practically separate and independent, at any rate, during the trypanosome phase... The fertilisation spindle or definitive nucleus is to be regarded as representing the trophic portion, and it will be convenient, therefore, to distinguish it as the trophonucleus. **1964** M. HYNES *Med. Bacteriol.* (ed. 8) xxviii. 436 Stained preparations [of *Trypanosoma gambiense*] show two nuclear structures; the one, larger and centrally placed, is known as the macronucleus or trophonucleus and the other, smaller, placed at the posterior end, is known as the micronucleus or kinetoplast. **1920** WHEELER & BAILEY in *Trans. Amer. Philos. Soc.* XXII. 258 The sternal portion of the first abdominal segment is transversely elliptical..and furnished with a food-pouch, the trophothylax. **1971** E. O. WILSON *Insect Societies* iv. 55/1 The nurse worker first pushes the fragment deep within the trophothylax, the special food pouch located on the lower surface of the thorax just behind the head (and found only in pseudomyrmecine [ant] larvae).

trophogenic (trǫfo-, trōᵘfodʒe·nik), *a.* [f. TROPHO- + *-GENIC.] **1.** *Ent.* Arising from an insect's feeding habits or diet.

1928 W. M. WHEELER *Social Insects* viii. 193 The castes may be blastogenic..in some groups of social insects, and trophogenic..in others. **1980** *Insectes Sociaux* XXVII. 80 The autogenic determination which separates queen and worker castes is succeeded by the larval trophogenic determination which is also at the origin of the soldiers.

2. Of part of a lake: characterized by the photosynthetic production of oxygen and organic matter. Opp. *tropholytic* adj. s.v. *TROPHO-. [tr. G. *trophogen* (E. Naumann *Limnologische Terminol.* (1931) 696).]

1957 G. E. HUTCHINSON *Treat. Limnol.* I. ix. 583 Oxygen, produced by photosynthesis in the trophogenic layers of the lake, and methane, produced by anaerobic decomposition in the tropholytic layers. **1979** *Ecol. Modelling* VI. 1 (*heading*) The modelling of ^{32}P kinetics within the trophogenic zone of a small lake.

So **tropho·geny**, the determination of an insect's development by its feeding habits.

1923 W. M. WHEELER *Social Life among Insects* vi. 253 It was formerly supposed that all termite eggs were alike and therefore produced young larvae which..took on the various caste characters as a result of differences in feeding (trophogeny). **1938** *Times Lit. Suppl.* 5 Mar. 159/1 Are the castes of ants determined by the diet of the larvae, that is, trophogeny, or in the egg, that is blastogeny?

tropic, *a.*[1] Add: **II. 4.** In this sense usu. pronounced (trōᵘ·pik).

b. Of a hormone: = *TROPHIC *a.* 3.

1955 R. M. DE COURSEY *Human Organism* xviii. 433 The hypophysis or pituitary gland has been called the master gland of all the endocrines because through its tropic hormones it exerts a regulatory effect over the activity of other endocrine glands. **1965** LEE & KNOWLES *Animal Hormones* ii. 19 The hormones secreted by the adenohypophysis may be divided into those which control the secretion of other endocrine glands and are named trophic (or tropic) hormones; the remainder act without the mediation of another endocrine gland. **1982** *Jrnl. Clinical Endocrinol. & Metabolism* LIV. 367/1 Rates of [^{14}C]acetate incorporation into steroids are increased by tropic hormones.

-tropic (trǫ·pik, trōᵘ·pik), *suffix.* [f. Gr. τροπή turning (sb.) + -IC.] Forming adjs. with the senses: (*a*) 'turning or attracted towards', as in GEOTROPIC, HELIOTROPIC, *SYMPATHICOTROPIC *adjs.*; (*b*) 'affecting', as in *NEUROTROPIC, *PSYCHOTROPIC *adjs.* (in epithets of hormones used interchangeably with *-TROPHIC, q.v.).

tropical, *a.* Add: **2. b.** (Further examples.)

1934 *Discovery* July 207/1 The practical certainty of infection from tropical anaemia or 'hookworm'. **1944** *Living off Land* v. 101 The most insignificant scratch or wound should be tended carefully—it might cause immediate infection and numerous large tropical sores. **1969** EDINGTON & GILLES *Path. in Tropics* x. 435 Tropical splenomegaly syndrome may in some patients end up in lymphosarcoma. **1974** Tropical bubo [see *LYMPHOGRANULOMA]. **1980** F. A. NWAKO *Textbk. Paediatric Surg. in Tropics* lxv. 368/1 The acute tropical ulcer may be complicated by tetanus and gas-gangrene.

d. Of clothing, fabric, etc.: suitable for wearing or using in hot climates; lightweight and porous; also more fully *tropical weight*. Of a (weight of) fabric freq. in *attrib.* use.

1792 W. BLIGH *Voy. to South Sea* ii. 26, I gave orders for their light tropical clothing to be put by, and made them dress in a manner more suited to a cold climate. **1920** W. J. LOCKE *House of Baltazar* x. 121 The tropical drill material which had clothed the troops in Hong Kong. **1924** R. MACAULAY *Orphan Island* ii. 31 [We] can be ready in a fortnight. It will take us about that to get our tropical outfit. **1925** in C. Allen *Tales from Dark Continent* (1979) iii. 43 Tropical weight dress coat. **1931** E. WAUGH *Remote People* 150 They dried themselves, combed their hair, put on smart tropical suits, and called for dinner. **1938** —— *Scoop* I. iii. 57 William had acquired..six suits of tropical linen. **1942** R. CHANDLER *High Window* iii. 24 A tropical worsted suit. **1945** E. WAUGH *Brideshead Revisited* II. i. 200, I discarded the experiences of those two years with my tropical kit. **1966** P. O'DONNELL *Sabre-Tooth* i. 8 He wore the tropical uniform of the United States Army. **1971** 'J. MAYO' *Asking for It* v. 18, I unpacked a cream shirt, my tropical-weight brown suit and put them on. **1972** 'W. HAGGARD' *Protectors* viii. 93 He wore a tropical suit and a spotted bow tie. **1978** L. BLOCK *Burglar in Closet* i. 4 My suit was a tropical worsted. **1981** G. MACBETH *Kind of Treason* xviii. 178 Mountbatten..was..in immaculate tropical kit.

B. *sb. pl.* Tropical clothes (see sense A. 2 d above).

1934 G. B. SHAW *Too True to be Good* III. 85 Aubrey, in white tropicals, comes strolling along the beach. **1980** J. HONE *Flowers of Forest* III. i. 221 Dressed in immaculate linen tropicals and some kind of old boy's tie.

tropicalize, *v.* Add: **2.** To make suitable for use under tropical conditions. Chiefly in *pass.* or as *pa. pple.*

1941 W. S. CHURCHILL *Second World War* (1950) III. 760 The German tanks recently captured by the Tobruk garrison... Are they tropicalised, desert-worthy, and fitted for use in the very hot weather? **1947** *Short Wave Mag.* V. 234/1 All components are tropicalised. **1972** *Daily Tel.* (Colour Suppl.) 20 Oct. 50 All the woodwork in a Rolls..is 'tropicalised' by three coats of lacquer making it impervious to changes in temperature and humidity. **1978** *Gramophone* Jan. 1335/3 The massive mains transformer is fully tropicalized and the primary winding is adjustable for input voltages of 110–120 and 220–240V AC. **1981** *Hi-Fi Answers* Jan. 7/2 The manufacturer of the British amplifier made a 'Point' of claiming that his equipment had been tropicalised.

Hence also **tro:picaliza·tion.**

1944 *Sun* (Baltimore) 24 Sept. 5/4 For a year past our modern battleships have been undergoing a further measure of modernization and tropicalization to meet the rapid wartime changes in technical apparatus. **1980** *Nature* 7 Feb. p. xii/1 Virtually any required type of impregnation, tropicalisation, potting or moulding (in epoxy, polyester or polyurethane) can be supplied.

tropicana (trǫpikā·nă), *sb. pl.* [f. TROPIC *sb.* and *a.*[1] + ANA *suff.*] Things associated with or characteristic of tropical regions; objects from the tropics.

1960 *Spectator* 1 July 12/2 Cockfighting is part of the exotic tropicana Haiti offers to American tourists. **1969** 'G. BLACK' *Cold Jungle* xii. 165 An astonishing display of tropicana, palms, bamboo, a couple of flame trees. **1976** *Listener* 29 Jan. 121/3 'That slice of the mind which is pure tropicana'—a mixture of Kipling and Maugham.

tropism. Add: Also with the pronunc. (trōᵘ·piz'm).

tropo (trōᵘ·po), colloq. abbrev. of *TROPOSCATTER.

1966 [see *BILL-BOARD, BILLBOARD 2]. **1976** *Offshore Engineer* July 5/1 There is little hope of a similar development in the UK sector, since the Post Office has provided the tropo facility and would be reluctant to offer an alternative.

tropo-. Add: **tropoco·llagen** (trōᵘ-) *Biochem.* [so called from its being able to turn into collagen], the molecular constituent of collagen fibrils, formed of three supercoiled polypeptide chains; **tropota·xis** (trōᵘ-) *Biol.* [mod.L., coined in Ger. (A. Kühn *Die Orientierung der Tiere im Raum* (1919) 60)], a taxis in which an animal's movement is in response to the difference in stimulation of two symmetrically placed receptors; hence **tropota·ctic** *a.*, **-ta·ctically** *adv.*

1954 J. GROSS et al. in *Proc. Nat. Acad. Sci.* XL. 679 We adopted the term 'tropocollagen' to denote the thin, long particles. *Ibid.*, In the present paper is summarized the evidence..that the various morphologically distinguishable forms of collagen are mutually interconvertible and that the unit of collagen structure involved in these changes of aggregation is the tropocollagen particle. **1971** *Nature* 16 Apr. 437/1 It is usually accepted that collagen is composed of tropocollagen molecules 2900 Å long, 15 Å wide. **1982** J. F. VAN PILSUM in T. M. Devlin *Textbk. Biochem.* xxi. 1050 The above classifications of collagens are based on the amino acid sequence and composition of the peptide chains in the tropocollagen molecule. **1940** FRAENKEL & GUNN *Orientation of Animals* vii. 89 Arthropods..are, above all, the animals which have eyes suitable for tropo-tactic behaviour. **1979** *Experientia* XXXV. 1457/1 Widely separated nares..would appear to be an adaptation for tropotactic olfactory perception. **1940** FRAENKEL & GUNN *Orientation of Animals* vii. 78 The paired receptors of an animal which behaves tropotactically have been compared with the paired reins of a horse. **1934** Tropotaxis [see *TELOTAXIS]. **1979** *Experientia* XXXV. 1457/2 Tubenosed fruit bats locate ripe fruit from among unripe fruit by olfaction, and since detection..has to be made while on the wing, it seems likely that tropotaxis is beneficial.

tropolone (trǫ·pŏlōᵘn). *Chem.* [f. TROP(ILIDINE + -OL + -ONE.] A water-soluble, colourless crystalline compound, $C_7H_6O_2$, which is an enolic ketone whose molecule is formed by a ring of seven carbon atoms and which is the parent of a series of compounds derived from various plants (as colchicine and the thujaplicins); also, any derivative of this.

1945 M. J. S. DEWAR in *Nature* 13 Jan. 51/1 If stipitatic acid actually has the resonating structure (I) or (II), it represents a new type of aromatic system; the parent *cyclo*heptatrienolone might be termed 'tropolone'. **1964** *New Scientist* 4 June 613/1 One group of compounds extracted [from timber], the tropolones, was found to be comparable in fungicidal effect to the synthetic fungicides. **1981** *Tetrahedron* XXXVII. Suppl. No. 9. 426/1 The 1,3,2-benzodioxaarsole ether of tropolone..illustrates the possibility of modelling extremely rapid rearrangements.

tropomyosin (trǫpo-, trōᵘpomai·ŏsin). *Biochem.* [f. TROPO- + MYOSIN.] Any of a group of crystallizable proteins related to myosin; *esp.* one found together with troponin in the thin filaments of myofibrils which is instrumental in the mechanism of muscle contraction.

1946 K. BAILEY in *Nature* 23 Mar. 369/1 The exact relation of tropomyosin to myosin itself is equally obscure, but the analytical and structural similarities indicate that it is a species of myosin differing mainly in the length of the polypeptide chain. In proposing the present name, we have deemed it desirable to retain the word 'myosin' and to add a prefix which suggests this specific relationship. **1973** *Nature* 5 Oct. 235/3 The finding of non-muscle tropomyosins, of course, raises more questions than it answers. **1979** *Sci. Amer.* May 94 (*caption*) In muscle cells tropomyosin regulates the ability of actin filaments to form cross bridges with adjacent myosin filaments. **1982** J. F. VAN PILSUM in T. M. Devlin *Textbk. Biochem.* xxi. 1006 Tropomyosin is a rod-shaped molecule found associated with the actin filaments.

tropone (trōᵘ·pōᵘn). *Chem.* [TROP(ILIDINE + -ONE.] A viscous hygroscopic oil, C_7H_6O, which is a cyclic ketone of aromatic character and of which tropolone is the hydroxylated derivative.

1951 *Jrnl. Amer. Chem. Soc.* LXXIII. 876/1 We wish to report the synthesis of 2,4,6-cycloheptatrien-1-one (tropone)..and evidence bearing on its aromatic character. **1981** *Jrnl. Org. Chem.* XLVI. 3575/1 The cycloadducts from 8-azaheptafulvenes and sulfenes, as well as those from tropone and arylsulfenes, readily undergo metalation.

troponin (trōᵘ·pǫnin, trǫ·-). *Biochem.* [f. *TROPO(MYOSIN + *-n-* + -IN[1].] A globular protein complex consisting of three subunits (*troponin C, I,* and *T*) which is related to and occurs with tropomyosin in the thin filaments of muscle tissue and is important in the mechanism of muscle contraction.

1966 EBASHI & KODAMA in *Jrnl. Biochem.* (Tokyo) LIX. 425/1 Tropomyosin-like protein, or 'native' tropomyosin..has been shown to consist of two different proteins, *viz.*, tropomyosin of Bailey type and a globular protein promoting the aggregation of tropomyosin, named troponin. **1982** *Sci. Amer.* June 52/3 Troponin *c* is probably found only in cardiac and skeletal muscle; the troponinlike protein in other tissues is calmodulin.

tropopause (trǫ·pŏ-, trōᵘ·popǭz). *Meteorol.* [f. *TROPO(SPHERE + PAUSE *sb.*] The upper limit of the troposphere, separating it from the stratosphere, at which the lapse rate falls to zero.

1919 *Geophysical Mem.* (Meteorol. Office) No. 13. 59 The terms 'tropopause' and 'lapse-limit' have been suggested to denote the plane of cessation of the vertical temperature gradient. **1922** *Encycl. Brit.* XXXI. 930 In a cyclone the tropopause is low, in an anticyclone high. **1947, 1971** [see *JET STREAM a]. **1982** *New Scientist* 17 June 788/1 Venus's tropopause..is much higher than that of the Earth,..some 70 kilometres above the Venusian surface.

troposcatter (trǫ·po-, trōᵘ·poskætəɹ). [f. *TROPO(SPHERIC *a.* + SCATTER *sb.*] The scattering of radio waves by clouds and local variations in the troposphere so as to extend the range of radio communication.

1959 *Britannica Bk. of Year* 547/1 Tropo-scatter. **1962** *Aeroplane* 7 June 19/2 For VHF ground-air improvements the team suggested the investigation of mountain-top sites and tropo-scatter methods to provide better coverage. **1967** *Technology Week* 23 Jan. 45/1 (Advt.), The Pacific Scatter System..uses ionoscatter, troposcatter, microwave, and vhf. **1976** *Times* 26 May 16/8 High levels of production of oil from the North Sea are dependent on advances in the use of troposcatter.

troposphere (trǫ·pŏ-, trōᵘ·posfīᵊɹ). *Meteorol.* [f. TROPO- + SPHERE *sb.*] The lowest region of the atmosphere, extending to a height of 8 to 18 km. and marked by convection and a general decrease of temperature with height.

1914 *Q. Jrnl. R. Meteorol. Soc.* XL. 108 M. Teisserenc de Bort discovered that the atmosphere is divided into two parts, the troposphere, which extends from the surface to about 7 miles, and the stratosphere, which lies above. **1922** *Nature* 2 Feb. 141/1 In the lower layer, called the troposphere, the atmospheric gases are kept well mixed up by winds and convection. **1951** [see *exosphere* s.v. *EXO-]. **1982** *New Scientist* 21 Jan. 151/1 Dust in the troposphere, the lowest layer of the atmosphere, is soon washed out by rain.

Hence **tropospheric** *a.*, of, pertaining to, or involving the troposphere; *tropospheric scatter* = *TROPOSCATTER.

1939 *Proc. IRE* XXVII. 634 It is believed that most of the tropospheric reflections occur at air-mass boundaries or other similar discontinuities. **1955** *Ibid.* XLIII. 1336 (*heading*) Some tropospheric scatter propagation measurements near the radio horizon. **1966** *Electronics* 17 Oct. 137 The system..is a wideband tropospheric scatter and microwave network consisting of 100 sites. It hops across the Mediterranean from the center of Spain to eastern Turkey, covering 6,000 miles and five nations. **1973** *Guardian* 18 May 18/5 With tropospheric fallout there is a steep rise in the level of iodine 131 in milk.

troppo (trǫ·po), *a. Austral. slang.* [f. TROPIC *sb.* and *a.*[1] + *-O[2].] Mentally ill through spending too much time (orig. on war service) in the tropics; (hence simply) crazy, mad. Esp. in phr. *to go troppo.*

1943 G. JOHNSTON *New Guinea Diary* 222 'A man must be going troppo,' he remarks quietly. **1958** R. STOW *To Islands* i. 19 'Terry thinks he's going troppo.' 'Troppo?' 'It's not in the Nurse's Encyclopaedia. Means going queer from being too long in the tropics.' **1968** S. L. ELLIOTT in E. Hanger *Three Austral. Plays* I. i. 33 Only fourteen months here and he's troppo... Know what he does this morning?.. Gets out of bed at reveille and goes off to shave with his spoon and fork. **1975** *Sun-Herald* (Sydney) 30 Nov. 131 Aunty Jack..could bring a badly-needed fresh burst of local comedy (in a troppo way) to our screens.

tropylium (trŏpi·liŏm). *Chem.* [f. *TROP(OLONE + -YL + -IUM.] The cation $C_7H_7^+$ consisting of a ring of seven =CH— groups. Usu. *attrib.*

1954 *Jrnl. Amer. Chem. Soc.* LXXVI. 3204/2 The value ..indicates that the tropylium ion is about as strongly acidic as acetic acid when water is the reference base. **1982** T. W. G. SOLOMONS *Fund. Org. Chem.* xi. 375 Tropylium bromide, C_7H_7Br, is insoluble in nonpolar solvents but dissolves readily in water.

trot, *sb.*[1] Add: **I. 1. d.** *on the trot,* (*b*) in uninterrupted sequence, in succession; (*c*) on the run, escaping from confinement, etc.

1952 M. TRIPP *Faith is Windsock* vii. 106 Two kites on the trot with crook engines. **1956** *People* 13 May 13/5, I want to be between those posts again when Manchester City reach Wembley next year for the third time on the trot! **1958** M. PUGH *Wilderness of Monkeys* 176, I eloped with one of the boys and we went on the trot from the approved school. Then it came time for his National Service and he went on the trot from the Army. **1973** *Times* 12 Apr. 12/6 Bookmakers lost money for five weeks on the trot. **1982** G. LYALL *Conduct Major Maxim* ii. 16 'He's on the trot,' Maxim guessed. 'Oh *Christ*, Jim, you can get a district court for that, aiding a deserter.'

e. *the trots* († *trot*), diarrhœa; also *fig. colloq.* Cf. *RUN *sb.*[1] 14 f.

1808 E. WEETON *Let.* 10 June in *Jrnl. of Governess* (1969) I. 94, I should perhaps be running over to Mr. Ridyard's so *very* often, that ten to one my brother would be..asking what was the matter with me that I was so *often hastily taken*; saying he was sure I was ill of the trot. **1904** in P. Fleming *Bayonets to Lhasa* (1961) xv. 205 He suffers continually from the trots (diarrhoea) which have completely shattered his nerves. **1936** J. G. COZZENS *Men & Brethren* II. 181, I often used to have to hot-foot it over to chapel—a kind of spiritual trots—and pray fervently. **1977** C. MCCULLOUGH *Thorn Birds* xi. 249 'Go easy on the water at first,' he advised. 'Beer won't give you the trots.'

2. Delete *rare* and add earlier and later examples. In *pl.* (*colloq.*, orig. *Austral.* and *N.Z.*), a series of trotting-races held at a fixed time on a regular course.

1856 *Porter's Spirit of Times* 25 Oct. 128/2 Nothing would have given the lovers of the trotting turf more pleasure than to witness a trot of three miles. **1899** *Bulletin* (Sydney) 21 Jan. 24/2 At the recent big M.L. trots horses well-known this side carried off their full share of prize-money. **1905** A. C. RICE *Sandy* 215 Nelson wants the fellow to drive for him at the fall trots. **1934** T. WOOD *Cobbers* ii. 19 We're proud of the Trots in Perth. It's the best course in the world. **1959** *N.Z. Listener* 16 Jan. 14/4 An oddball like myself, wholly uninterested in racing, even night trots. **1968** *Globe & Mail* (Toronto) 17 Feb. 43 Sixth race—Trot, mile. Purse $3,000. **1976** *National Observer* (U.S.) 2 Oct. 7/1 He won the Empire Trot at Syracuse two weeks ago. **1977** *New Yorker* 19 Sept. 131/1 No doubt remembering the crush of more than forty thousand when the trots opened at Meadowlands a year ago, many people stayed away.

5. (Examples.)
1924 P. Marks *Plastic Age* 299 I'm talking about the copying of math problems and the using of trots. **1975** B. Meggs *Matter of Paradise* (1976) vii. v. 173 Somebody suggested..that he get a trot. An absolutely forbidden interlinear translation. The Latin on one line; the English right below it. **1984** *Times Lit. Suppl.* 27 Apr. 44/2 The translations are rarely better than lame trots.

5*. *Austral. colloq.* A sequence, a succession, esp. in a game of chance; a run of luck of a specified kind. See 1 d above.
1911 L. Stone *Jonah* 216 A trot or succession of seven tails followed, and the kip changed hands rapidly. **1919** W. H. Downing *Digger Dialects* 51 *Trot*, an experience (e.g. 'a rough trot'; 'a bad time'). **1937** J. A. Lee *Civilian into Soldier* 99 Sometimes a man would succeed daringly, doubling up and breaking the ring with a long run of heads, 'throwing a trot'. **1949** L. Glassop *Lucky Palmer* 177 He was 'Lucky' Palmer, having a bad trot at the moment, admittedly, but still 'Lucky' Palmer. **1966** P. Mathers *Trot* 90 He..had had a tough trot, humped the bluey, been through it all. **1974** D. R. Stuart *Prince of my Country* v. 33 He's had a damn good trot, old Marney.

II. 6. b. *Naut.* (See quot. 1976.)
1923 *Man. Seamanship* (Admiralty) II. 107 When several targets are secured in line to a trot, only the ends of the trot need be marked by lights. **1950** G. Hackforth-Jones *Worst Enemy* iii. 202 The old ship parted her moorings and drifted down on to a destroyer trot. I had to let go two Admiralty-pattern anchors that were last used in the Crimean War. **1976** *Oxf. Compan. Ships & Sea* 893/1 *Trot*, a multiple mooring for small boats or yachts. The base mooring is laid in a straight line and from it individual moorings rise at intervals spaced to allow the boats room to swing with the tide.

III. 7. trot-boat (see quot. 1955); **trot-line** (earlier example).
1945 'N. Shute' *Most Secret* vi. 124, I can get the trot boat down each evening. **1955** *N. & Q.* Sept. 402/2 A 'trot-boat' is a boat of any size which makes routine visits to discharge or embark passengers, stores, etc., at ships secured to the buoys. **1826** 'Nonius Nondescript' *The* —— 18 Feb. 10 As full of noozes and strings as a fisherman's trot line.

Trot (trǫt), *sb.*³ and *a.* Colloq. abbrev. of *Trotskyist *sb.* and *a.*, *Trotskyite *a.* and *sb.*
1962 D. Lessing *Golden Notebk.* iv. 451, I was a hundred per cent party member, and there was Harry, a dirty Trot, so there were high words and we parted for ever. **1970** G. Greer *Female Eunuch* 22 The most telling criticisms will come from my sisters of the left, the Maoists, the Trots. **1976** *Times* 29 Dec. 8/8 A true *Trot* ought to believe in worldwide revolution. **1983** 'J. le Carré' *Little Drummer Girl* iv. 80 Some kind of loony Trot splinter group.

trot, *v.* Add: **2.** Freq. with specifying adv. or advb. phr.; *absol.* also (contextually) to depart, to leave. (Further examples.)
1847 C. Brontë *Jane Eyre* II. viii. 203 In case I married Miss Ingram, both you and little Adèle had better trot forthwith. **1862** in N. Longmate *Hungry Mills* (1978) viii. 108, I..trot down to a butcher in a better neighbourhood. **1899** O. Wilde *Importance of being Earnest* ii. 74 *Chasuble*... At what hour would you wish the ceremony performed? *Jack.* Oh, I might trot round about five if that would suit you. **1954** J. R. R. Tolkien *Fellowship of Ring* i. ix. 166 No time for talking. I must be trotting. **1960** *Cambr. Rev.* 7 May 506/2 It is not true to suppose that the setting-up of machinery for psychiatric consultation merely encourages the 'neurotic' to trot along to the psychiatrist at the least excuse. **1984** *Your Computer* May 25/2 You can..trot up to the Registry with that reference number and get a copy of his death certificate very quickly.

4. d. *to trot out*: also (*N.Z.*) simply *trot*.
1946 F. Sargeson *That Summer* 33 I've got a job in a grocer's shop and I'm trotting a sheila. **1964** B. Crump in *Weekly News* (Auckland) 21 Oct. 46/6, I didn't know she was going steady with you... If I'd known you were trotting her [etc.].

f. To bid against at an auction in order to force up the price; to make or accept a spurious bid for (an item at auction) in order to force up the price. Also with *up*. *slang.*
1864 Hotten *Slang Dict.* 262 *Trot*, to 'run up', to oppose, to bid against at an auction. *Ibid.*, 'We *trotted* him up nicely, didn't we?' *i.e.*, we made him (the private buyer) pay dearly for what he bought. **1955** W. Mankowitz *Make me an Offer* viii. 64 'But it's no good to you?'.. 'Only if it goes reasonable—not if the reserve is high. And not..if it's trotted.' 'We don't do that sort of thing in the country, you know.'

g. *to be able to trot a mouse on it* and varr.: said of particularly strong or thick liquid food or drink. *dial.*
1936 'N. Blake' *Thou Shell of Death* xiii. 229 A cup of tea, sir, after your journey... It's nice strong tea, so it is. Ye could trot a mouse on it. **1970** H. McLeave *Question of Negligence* i. 3 That's the way they make it [*sc.* tea] in Scotland... Sweet as a sheep's eye and strong enough to trot a mouse on. **1975** *Times* 17 May 10/8 A bowl of parsnip soup—'so thick you could trot a mouse on it', as the country saying goes.

Trotskyism (trǫ·tski,iz'm). Also † **Trotskysm**, † **Trotzkyism.** [f. Leon *Trotsky*, the assumed name of Lev Davidovich Bronstein (1879–1940), Russian revolutionary and politician + -ism.] The political or economic principles of Trotsky; a form of Marxism urging world-wide revolution, as advocated by Trotsky.
1925 tr. Trotsky in *Times* 30 Jan. 11/4, I cannot.. accept the accusation of trying to pursue my own line of policy (Trotskyism). **1925** —— in M. Eastman *Since Lenin Died* 155, I can nowise accept, however, the accusation that I have pursued a special line (Trotskysm) and tried to revise Leninism. **1930** W. H. Chamberlin *Soviet Russia* iv. 76 There would seem to be little political future in Russia for Trotzkyism. **1942** E. Waugh *Put out More Flags* 48 She believed in a People's Total War; an uncompromising girl whom none of them liked; a suspect of Trotskyism. **1963** [see *capitulationism]. **1977** *Belfast Tel.* 24 Jan. 9/8 Trotskyism is installed as official doctrine and the pro-Soviet sympathies of some of our trade union leaders go unrebuked.

Trotskyist (trǫ·tski,ist), *sb.* and *a.* Also **Trotskist**, † **Trotzkyist.** [f. *Trotsky* (see prec.) + -ist.] **A.** *sb.* A follower or supporter of Trotsky or Trotskyism. **B.** *adj.* Of, pertaining to, or characteristic of Trotsky or Trotskyism.
1927 *Daily Tel.* 22 Nov. 9/2 The adoption of the word 'Russia' by the Trotskyists. *Ibid.* 6 Dec. 11 The struggle between the Trotskists and the Stalinites. **1930** W. H. Chamberlin *Soviet Russia* iv. 74 The Party Congress.. laid down the rule that adherence to the views of the Trotzkyist opposition was inconsistent with membership in the Communist Party. **1937** Koestler *Spanish Testament* ix. 178 The P.O.U.M.—the Trotskyist Party—was even more unrestrained in its agitation. **1949** [see *diversionist]. **1959** *Daily Tel.* 15 Apr. 17/5 The recently formed Trotskyist organisation known as the Socialist Labour League. **1973** 'I. Drummond' *Jaws of Watchdog* x. 136 Trotskyists, anarchists and the lunatic fringe of the Underground. **1980** *Washington Post* 6 July c1/2 On the left there are well over 40 different organizations—Leninist, Stalinist, Trotskyist.

Trotskyite (trǫ·tski,ait), *a.* and *sb.* Also **Trotskiite.** [f. *Trotsky* (see *Trotskyism) + -ite[1].] = *Trotskyist *sb.* and *a.*
1919 *Mr. Punch's Hist. Great War* 210 Which am I.. Pro-German or Pro-Trotskyite? **1920** [see *Leninite *a.* and *sb.*]. **1953** *Encounter* Nov. 30/2 Young X. starts as a Communist, is soon disillusioned, founds a Trotskyite opposition group of ten people [etc.]. **1957** V. Nabokov *Pain* vii. 184 Russian emigration was made to mean by astute communist propaganda a vague and perfectly fictitious mass of so-called Trotskiites (whatever these are), ruined reactionaries, [etc.]. **1977** M. Walker *National Front* viii. 210 The Trotskyite parties..are too small and too dependent upon the intelligentsia to present any credible revolutionary threat. **1978** *Jrnl. R. Soc. Arts* CXXVI. 671/1 Their activities were compared to those of the Trotskyites in 1923.

trottie, *sb.* (In Dict. s.v. Trot *sb.*¹ 4.) (Example.)
1924 'L. Malet' *Dogs of Want* vii. § 6 Darling girls, from the time when they were the tiniest trotties till now.

trottie, var. *Trotty *a.*

trotting, *vbl. sb.* Add: (Example corresp. to *trot *v.* 4 f.)
1969 *Daily Tel.* 5 May 19/2 The most common is 'trotting'—taking non-existent bids to force up the price.
b. *trotting-match* (earlier example.)
1822 *Sunday Times* 20 Oct. 3/2 The roan trotting match for 500 sovereigns.

trottoir. (Earlier example.)
1792 A. Young *Trav. France* I. 150 The streets..are wide, and very well paved, with the addition, uncommon in France, of *trotoirs*.

trotty (trǫ·ti), *a.* *colloq.* Also **trottie.** [f. Trot *sb.*¹ + -y¹.] **a.** Of daintily small proportions. **b.** Of a person: agreeable, amenable.
1891 'L. Malet' *Wages of Sin* II. v. i. 165 Some of the little silk shifties and night-i-gowns were simply too trottie for words. *a* **1913** F. Rolfe *Desire & Pursuit of Whole* (1934) xi. 109 'I can't tell you how trotty we think it of you!'..bibbled the woman. **1928** Galsworthy *Swan Song* i. i. 4 Trotty little ladies with dresses tight blown about trotty little figures.

trotyl (trōᵘ·til). [f. *trini)trot(oluene + -yl.] = *trinitrotoluene.
1910 *United Service Mag.* Feb. 554 A new explosive for shells, mines and torpedoes is being manufactured... It is known commercially as 'Trotyl', its full name being Trinitrotoluol. **1922** *Encycl. Brit.* XXXI. 50 Trinitrotoluene (TNT) which is known officially as Trotyl is..very similar in its action to picric acid and had been discovered by Wilbrand in 1863. **1981** *Chem. Abstr.* 7 Sept. 121/2 (*heading*) Initial phase of the initiation of the detonation process in pressed trotyl.

trouble, *sb.* Add: **1. e.** *my troubles*, a dismissive exlamation: 'don't worry about me': 'I don't care'. *Austral. colloq.*
1895 C. Crowe *Austral. Slang Dict.* 89 *My troubles*, what do I care. **1905** N. Spielvogel *Gumsucker on Tramp* 90 Off again; round Leuwin Cape; rough seas; My Troubles! I'm coming home. **1947** G. Casey *Wits are Out* 44 'You better lay off Kitty while the old man's about, or there'll be one more out-of-work motor salesman kicking round the city,' Syd suggested. 'My troubles!' Jerry jeered.
f. Usu. with qualifying noun: faulty working of apparatus or machinery, esp. on a motor vehicle; a problem caused by this (*engine trouble*, etc.). Also applied *transf.* to personal relations, as *wife trouble*.
1902 *Trans. Inst. Naval Archit.* XLIV. 213 Although it seems to fit the water tube troubles, it does not answer so well with the furnace troubles. **1909** *Westm. Gaz.* 26 Oct. 2/1 The only other serious difficulty [with the Wright biplane] seems to be what is known, generically, as 'engine trouble'... The forms that this 'engine trouble' takes are various, as every motorist knows. **1981** P. Audemars *Gone to her Death* iii. 61 The local garagist..has wife trouble, because she has the money he needs.
g. *trouble and strife*, rhyming slang for: (*a*) 'life' (*rare*); (*b*) 'wife'.
1908 'Doss Chiderdoss' in *Sporting Times* 11 July 1/3, I shouted, 'Your "bees", or your "trouble and strife"!' Like the hero in 'Highwayman Harry'. **1929** J. B. Priestley *Good Companions* iii. ii. 611 The old trouble-and-strife, eh? **1949** A. Wilson *Wrong Set* 62 'Thanks for looking after my old trouble and strife' said Bruce. **1959** J. Osborne *Paul Slickey* ii. x. 86 My posh trouble-and-strife, I'll be hers. **1977** G. Fisher *Villain of Piece* i. 7 It's the old trouble and strife—wife. I want to see her all right.
2. b. *the troubles, the Troubles.* Any of various rebellions, civil wars, and unrest in Ireland, *spec.* in 1919–23 and (in Northern Ireland) since the early 1970s.
1880 W. H. Patterson *Gloss. Words Antrim & Down* 109 *Troubles, the*, the Irish rebellion of 1641. **1922** Joyce *Ulysses* 237 Times of the troubles... Somewhere here Lord Edward Fitzgerald escaped from major Sirr. *Ibid.* 613 He vividly recollected when the occurrence alluded to took place..in the days of the land troubles..early in the eighties. **1923** *Times Lit. Suppl.* 11 Oct. 661/3 A weak Government.., a new wave of nationalist exaltation, an untrained army of youths brought up on war rations..—these factors were sufficient to account for the troubles of 1919–21. **1942** E. Waugh *Put out More Flags* iii. 235 The ruins of a police barracks, built to command the road through the valley, burnt in the troubles,..were one green with the grass. **1949** C. Graves *Ireland Revisited* vi. 57 'This was where Michael Dwyer was in keeping during the Troubles,' Mackey vouchsafed. ('In keeping' means being on the run.) **1959** *Listener* 2 July 32/1 The complicated political and personal passions inspired by 'the troubles'. **1968** M. Collis *Somerville & Ross* xxv. 258 As the Troubles were over more than ten years before [1936], how came it that Admiral Boyle, living in quiet retirement and much liked by high and low, was singled out? **1981** M. Kenyon *Zigzag* i. 6 Before the new Troubles..he had fallen in love with romantic Ireland.
3. *to take the trouble* (earlier example).
1830 R. J. Raymond *Oh! Men what Silly Things You Are* (song) 3 She marks you down, fly where you will.. Can wing you, feather you or kill, Just as she takes the trouble.
5. a. Also *to ask for trouble*: see *ask *v.* 16 b. Similarly, *to look for* (or *seek*) *trouble*.
1901 Merwin & Webster *Calumet 'K'* 134 We've got to build the belt gallery—and we'll have no end of a time doing it if the C. & S.C. is still looking for trouble. **1905** *N.Y. Even. Post* 29 Aug. 2 In the possible chance of rounding up all who might be seeking trouble, the police temporarily sequestered and searched 140 Chinamen. **1912** 'Aurora' *Jock Scott, Midshipman* xiv. 165 But if you are artful you don't often get 'bowled out', unless one of the 'crushers' has a 'down' on you, and is 'looking for trouble'. **1922** E. O'Neill *Anna Christie* (1923) i. 25, I ain't looking for trouble. **1947** W. Motley *Knock on Any Door* 152 Swollen out in their own importance they walked along West Madison looking for trouble.
7. *trouble-maker* (examples), *-shirker*; *trouble-making* ppl. adj. and vbl. sb.; **trouble-hunter** (examples); *spec.* = *trouble-shooter 1; also **trouble hunting** *vbl. sb.*; **trouble lamp, light** *N. Amer.*, a portable lamp (esp. one carried on a motor vehicle), by the light of which roadside repairs, etc., can be done; **trouble man** *U.S.* = *trouble-shooter 1; **trouble spot,** a place where difficulties frequently occur; a scene of (impending) conflict.
1910 Trouble-hunter [see *hell-bent *a.* and *adv.*]. **1924** *New Eng. Telephone Topics* XVIII. 288 Repairmen, the 'trouble hunters', are at work constantly. **1882** T. D. Lockwood *Pract. Information for Telephonists* 135 Every movement made for an accurate preliminary test frequently saves an hour of happy-go-lucky trouble hunting. **1916** *Daily Colonist* (Victoria, B.C.) 9 July 12/4 If a car is not equipped with an extension trouble lamp, it is well to provide among the accessories a pocket flash lamp. **1927** W. Faulkner *Sartoris* iii. 196 He was doing something to the engine of it [*sc.* a car] while the house-yard-stable-boy held a patent trouble-lamp. **1952** *Sun* (Baltimore) (B ed.) 5 Jan. 7/4 Their headlights went out... A door slammed shut and cut the wire on the trouble light. **1979** *Arizona Daily Star* 1 Apr. h3/1 He just happened to have a siphon hose; also a trouble light with a cord that seemed long enough to reach back to his home in Mexico City. **1923** *Time* 28 May 1/2 (*heading*) Chief trouble maker. **1931** Kipling *Limits & Renewals* (1932) 191, I took stock o' them, to spot the funny-men an' trouble-makers. **1955** 'A. Gilbert' *Is She Dead Too?* ii. 40 A snooper, or trouble-maker, that was Margaret Reeve. **1981** W. Ebersohn *Divide Night* xiii. 175 A more disciplined age where trouble-makers who went against the government would be dealt with firmly. **1920** S. Lewis *Main St.* xvi. 202, I certainly hope you don't class yourself with a lot of trouble-making labor-leaders! *a* **1974** R. Crossman *Diaries* (1975) I. 77 Manny wouldn't allow it, for fear—as he put it—that the questions raised would be used for trouble-making. **1889** *Cassell's Family Mag.* June 410/1 A special band of what the Americans call 'Trouble-men', who are prepared to attend at once to sudden calls for assistance. **1953** *Herald* (Belle Glade,

Florida) 13 Feb. 1/1 According to Florida Power & Light district manager C. A. Chase, FPL's 'Troubleman' J. J. McCarley located the difficulty, and repair crews worked until 2 am Wednesday repairing broken circuits and restoring service. **1908** A. S. M. HUTCHINSON *Once aboard Lugger* v. vii. 268 These light-hearts, these trouble-shirkers. **1956** M. E. W. Goss in R. K. Merton *Student-Physician* IV. 258 The regular duties..included the unwritten obligation to assist in..assessing the 'trouble-spots' and suggesting possible solutions. **1963** *Listener* 7 Feb. 260/2 Sir David Eccles wants £200,000,000 a year pumped into the trouble-spots [*sc.* areas of heavy unemployment]. **1981** T. BARLING *Bikini Red North* ii. 41 It should be quiet enough, being so far from Montmartre and the other trouble spots.

trou·ble-shooter. orig. *U.S.* [f. TROUBLE *sb.* + SHOOTER.] **1.** A person who traces and corrects faults in machinery and equipment (orig. *spec.* on a telegraph or telephone line). Cf. *trouble-hunter, man* s.v. *TROUBLE *sb.* 7.

1905 *Strand Mag.* Mar. 268/1 A good looking young 'trouble-shooter'—as a mender of telephone lines is called—had..asked her to marry him. **1913** *Red Cross Mag.* Jan. 34/1 Among them are..the 'trouble shooters', highly trained men who are responsible for the repairing of any breaks in the plant or equipment. **1931** B. STARKE *Touch & Go* xv. 248 A trouble-shooter for the telephone lines. **1945** H. D. SMYTH *Gen. Acct. Devel. Atomic Energy Mil. Purposes* xi. 121 Particularly in the early stages of operation the Berkeley men stationed at Clinton were invaluable as 'trouble shooters' and in instructing operators. **1951** *Engineering* 2 Feb. 133/2 Manufacture..by fully-automatic machine shops..with only a few skilled men as 'trouble-shooters'. **1959** H. HOBSON *Mission House Murder* xxi. 140 A post office electronics expert and trouble-shooter.

2. One who specializes in removing or solving difficulties; esp. a mediator in diplomatic or industrial affairs.

1927 *Sat. Even. Post* 15 Jan. 153/3 With the 'Trouble-Shooters' of the North Atlantic Icebergs... Locating and destroying them is the perilous and never-ending duty of the United States Coast Guard cutters. **1933** R. C. MAYER *How to do Publicity* xi. 134 The 'trouble-shooters' in publicity deal mostly with such emergencies. **1940** R. S. LAMBERT *Ariel & all his Quality* iii. 77 The light had gone out of the Talks... His successors were chosen to be what Americans call 'trouble shooters'. **1953** W. R. BURNETT *Vanity Row* iii. 21 He needed an expert trouble-shooter, untainted by police politics. **1962** R. BUCKMINSTER FULLER *Epic Poem on Industrialization* 24 Self-helpless old fashioned business War forced to call in ..Professional Trouble-shooters. **1971** H. WILSON *Labour Govt.* ix. 136 The appointment of an industrial relations 'trouble-shooter' for the industry.

Also **trou·ble-shooting** *vbl. sb.* and *ppl. a.*; hence (back-formation) **trouble-shoot** *v. trans.* and *intr.*, to solve (a problem), to repair; to mediate.

1918 V. W. PAGÉ *Aviation Engines* 9 Special attention has been paid to instructions on tool equipment, use of tools, trouble 'shooting' and engine repairs. **1938** E. B. WHITE *Let.* 18 Nov. (1976) 186 This place teems with trouble of one sort and another. I am up every morning at twenty past six, trouble shooting. **1941** *Daily Progress* (Charlottesville, Virginia) 19 Aug. 1 (*heading*) Judge Rosenman..is now in capital, trouble-shooting the bottle-neck. **1957** V. PACKARD *Hidden Persuaders* xviii. 208 One firm that provides psychological bug-hunting services to industry cited the service it performed in trouble-shooting an employee problem in Ohio. **1964** S. BRITTAN *Treasury under Tories* ii. 53 The Cabinet's *Economic Policy Committee*.., over which the Chancellor presides, is mainly a trouble-shooting body. **1969** *Daily Colonist* (Victoria, B.C.) 8 June 2/7 (Advt.), Analyst—reporting to the President—required for troubleshooting all facets of the Victoria winery operation. **1977** P. DICKINSON *Walking Dead* IV. ii. 255 His official status in the Company was a string of vague general nouns, but his job was trouble-shooting. **1978** R. LEWIS *Inevitable Fatality* i. 19 I'm a business consultant... My forte is to troubleshoot, to get in and out again.

trough, *sb.* Add: **1. d.** *fig.* A place where food is provided, *spec.* a dining-table; hence, a meal. *colloq.*

1901 'H. MCHUGH' *John Henry* 95 We left the mob just as all hands were paddling off to the ice-cream trough. **1915** F. M. HUEFFER *Good Soldier* I. iii. 38 Why shouldn't we all eat out of the same trough—that's a nasty New York saying. **1930** WODEHOUSE *Very Good, Jeeves!* iv. 96 The Bellinger..had sung us a few songs before digging in at the trough. **1965** *New Statesman* 14 May 777/1 Things are a bit different at the old trough these days. **1981** 'M. INNES' *Lord Mullion's Secret* viii. 68 If he didn't stir his stumps he would be late for the trough.

e. In various *fig.* phrases applied to a ready source of income, esp. one shared by unscrupulous persons. *colloq.*

1906 J. LONDON *Let.* 20 Oct. (1966) 212 All I can tell you is, that you've got your feet in the trough. **1971** P. TAMONY *Americanisms* (typescript) No. 28. 2 Local pimps and fast-buck boys who had hustled to the troughs for fat-staff salaries. **1974** L. DEIGHTON *Spy Story* iv. 47 I'm going to find out what it's costing. We can't go on eating our heads off at the public trough. **1981** J. D. MACDONALD *Free Fall in Crimson* xvi. 186 The money would come..to Josie, and you would be able to stay in the trough.

6. b. Also *absol.* (Later *fig.* examples.)

1942 C. S. LEWIS *Let.* 20 Jan. (1966) 199 Sorry you're in a trough. I'm just emerging..from a long one myself. **1958** *Sunday Times* 9 Nov. 15/3 E. Nesbit..has therefore been 'in the trough'—widely read, ardently admired, but neglected as a subject for critical appraisals. **1977** *Listener* 28 July 123/3 At the moment his [*sc.* E. M. Forster's] reputation is in the trough; it is said that he is a slight talent, overpraised for extraneous reasons.

d. *Econ.* The lowest level of economic activity or prosperity reached during a recession.

1916 G. B. SHAW *Androcles & Lion* Pref. p. lxvi, Basing..our whole industrial system on successive competitive waves of overwork with their ensuing troughs of unemployment. **1930** *Economist* 29 Mar. 691/1 We are, in fact, in the trough of a depression. **1960** *Ibid.* 8 Oct. 161/2 Even if the recession does not reach its trough until well into the spring. **1981** *Daily Tel.* 9 July 1/6 There is now firmer evidence that the trough in the recession has been reached, said the Treasury yesterday.

e. Hence, the lowest point in a period of any varying quantity; the time when this occurs. Also, the representation of this state on a graph; a point in a wave-form at which the varying quantity is a minimum. Cf. *CREST *sb.*^{1} 7 e, *PEAK *sb.*^{2} 5 e.

1938 *British Birds* XXXII. 214 This is followed by a more or less distinct trough, after which numbers rapidly increase to a higher autumn peak by mid September. **1958** *Listener* 16 Oct. 605/1 Absence of distortion and the avoidance of marked peaks and troughs in the amplitude-frequency characteristic. **1971** *Physics Bull.* Aug. 462/2 Such currents tend to pile electrons in the potential troughs of the wave and denude the crests. **1976** *Daily Tel.* 22 Mar. 7/1 Chromatography splits the sample into its volatile chemical constituents, and draws an alpine graph with heady peaks and troughs to represent the chemicals coming through.

7. trough garden, a miniature garden comprising a group of small plants, often alpine ones, grown in a trough-like container of real or imitation stone; cf. *sink garden* s.v. *SINK *sb.*^{1} 14.

[**1923** *Times* 31 May 10/7 Mr. Clarence Elliott's attempt at providing miniature alpine gardens in old stone troughs ..would undoubtedly provide much interest where space was too limited for real gardening.] **1935** C. ELLIOTT *Rock Garden Plants* 288 An invaluable small thing for spilling about and filling up odd sunny corners, and perfect on the trough rock garden. **1950** W. E. SHEWELL-COOPER *Home, Window & Roof Gardening* viii. 70 The Trough Garden..can be a great joy to the rock garden lover. **1979** M. SOAMES *Clementine Churchill* xxviii. 471 Here Clementine made a 'trough' garden.

trounce, *v.*^{1} Add: **3. c.** To defeat heavily at a sport. *colloq.*

1942 BERREY & VAN DEN BARK *Amer. Thes. Slang* § 649/5 *Defeat decisively*,..trample (on), trounce, walk on [etc.]. **1951** *Sport* 27 Jan.–2 Feb. 3/1 He was omitted from the side trounced 4–0 at Reading. **1972** J. MOSEDALE *Football* v. 64 Green Bay teams had trounced AFL entries the previous two years.

trouncer. Add: Also *spec.* an assistant to a carman, drayman, or lorry-driver. (Later examples.)

1913 M. S. REEVES *Round about Pound a Week* i. 2 Some of the more enviable and settled inhabitants of this part of the world [*sc.* Kennington]..generally are somebody's labourer, mate, or handyman. Painters' labourers ..trouncers for carmen, are common amongst them. **1923** *Weekly Dispatch* 30 Sept. 3 It was stated that a 'trouncer' was a coal carman's assistant. **1953** *Word for Word* (Whitbread & Co.) 35/2 *Trouncer*, the drayman's mate; so-called because, before the improvement of roads under Telford and MacAdam, he had to 'trounce', i.e., push and manhandle the dray over the innumerable potholes and hazards.

trouper (trū̆·pəɹ). Also **trooper.** [f. TROUPE + -ER^1.] **1.** An actor or performer belonging to a troupe.

1890 B. HALL *Turnover Club* 160 As the 'troupers' come into the station where I sat, they were a sorry-looking lot. **1912** L. J. VANCE *Destroying Angel* (1913) vi. 77 I'm as superstitious as any trooper in the profession. **1946** *Boston Transcript* Sept. 6/2 A little knot of interested troupers were looking on as Joe and I met. **1973** 'D. RUTHERFORD' *Kick Start* i. 8 A good trouper can still shimmy in her fifties.

2. *transf.* A reliable, uncomplaining person; a staunch supporter or colleague. Freq. with qualifying adj., as *good trouper*. *colloq.*

1959 P. BULL *I know Face* xi. 194 The phrase 'she's a trouper' now has an old-fashioned and faintly derogatory air and is usually bandied about when someone continues to play with a high temperature or a shattering bereavement. **1961** *Times* 6 July 5/5 Chapman is a good trouper, and..he has a fine record of consistency in match and stroke play. **1976** D. FRANCIS *In Frame* iv. 70, I don't think you're selfish at all. In fact, Maisie, I think you're a proper trouper.

trousers, *sb. pl.* Add: **2. c.** (Earlier example.)

1820 M. WILMOT *Let.* 3 May (1935) 57 Catharine..has not one frock, or pair of trousers fit to wear, now that summer is coming.

d. Applied to the hair on the hind legs of certain dogs, esp. those of long-coated breeds.

1948 C. L. B. HUBBARD *Dogs in Britain* 464 Trousers.—The hair on the hindquarters of any dog. **1949** L. E. NAYLOR *Poodles* v. 44 They [*sc.* poodles] enjoy having any kind of smart clip, because they dislike their trousers being muddy. **1962** R. H. SMYTHE *Anat. Dog Breeding* vii. 133 The loose trousers wrinkled round the knees and pasterns of the Dachshund.

2*. In various colloq. phrases. **a.** *anything in trousers*, etc.: any man, whether eligible, suitable, or not.

1887 *Lantern* 14 May 3/1 They go crazy over everything that wears trousers. **1979** A. PRICE *Tomorrow's Ghost* i. 9 Anything in trousers was as much Target for Tonight to Marilyn Francis as Marilyn Francis was for anything in trousers.

b. *not in these trousers*: certainly not.

1920 P. GIBBS *Realities of War* IV. vii. 189 'Come up and have a look, Jack,' he said to one of the blue-jackets. 'Not in these trousers, old mate!' said that young man. **1929** R. C. SHERRIFF *Journey's End* III. ii. 71 She said, 'Not in these trousers'—in French. **1939** J. CARY *Mister Johnson* 247 You think perhaps we leave the money in the till and you tief 'em. Not in these trousers, Mister Poldedoodle.

c. *to wear the trousers*: to be the dominant member of a household. Also *transf.* Cf. BREECH *sb.* 2, *PANTS *sb. pl.* 1 e.

1931 R. CAMPBELL *Georgiad* i. 11 It is you must 'wear the trousers' now. **1959** J. L. AUSTIN *Sense & Sensibilia* (1962) ii. 15 It is essential to realize that here the notion of perceiving *in*directly wears the trousers. **1963** A. HERON *Towards Quaker View of Sex* iii. 33 A married couple where the woman 'wears the trousers'.

d. (*to catch*) *with one's trousers down*: in a state of embarrassing unpreparedness. Cf. *PANTS *sb. pl.* 1 c. *slang.*

1966 *Guardian* 31 Mar. 14/8 Catch them with their trousers down. **1967** 'F. CLIFFORD' *All Men are Lonely Now* II. vii. 234 By that time the shooting will seem to be as haphazard as can possibly be, as if we'd almost been caught with our trousers down. **1980** J. GARDNER *Garden of Weapons* II. vii. 186 A job... Took us by surprise: with the trousers down.

4. *trouser-fly, -pocket* (earlier example), *-seat*; **trouser-bottoms** *pl.*, the lower parts of the legs of a pair of trousers; **trouser-clips** *pl.*, clips (of various kinds) used by cyclists to confine the trousers round the ankles; **trouser-cuff,** the turn-up on a trouser-leg; **trouser suit,** a woman's suit consisting of matching jacket and trousers; hence **trouser-suited** *a.*; **trouser zip,** a zip used as a fastening, usu. at the front of a pair of trousers.

1920 D. H. LAWRENCE *Women in Love* xxiv. 388 He.. pulled on his boots. They were sodden, as were his socks and trouser-bottoms. **1973** A. ROSS *Dunfermline Affair* 116 My trouser bottoms were wet. **1895** *Army & Navy Co-op. Soc. Price List* 1379/2 Lucas's Trouser Clips. Per pair 0/3. **1908** H. G. WELLS *War in Air* ii. 33 A small, dissolute-looking shop in the High Street, adorned with.. a display of bells, trouser-clips, oil cans..and other accessories. **1970** K. GILES *Death in Church* i. 11 Horace Drood adjusted his trouser clips and resentfully pedalled off. **1931**, etc. Trouser-cuff [see *CUFF *sb.*^{1} 2 d]. **1942** C. BARRETT *On Wallaby* v. 90, I had fifteen-inch trouser cuffs, while my coat sleeves were about half-mast high. **1982** H. ENGEL *Murder on Location* (1983) xxiii. 207, I squeezed water from my shoes and trouser cuffs. **1922** JOYCE *Ulysses* The slits of his buttoned trouserfly. **1852** J. S. COYNE *Box & Cox married & Settled* 9, I demand your card, sir?..You'll find it in my left-hand trowsers' pocket. **1923** D. H. LAWRENCE *Ladybird* 243 He would have slid the whole way down on his trouser-seat. **1960** WODEHOUSE *Jeeves in Offing* viii. 90 Gives a woman a start, naturally, to come into her son's bedroom and observe an alien trouser-seat sticking out from under the dressing table. **1939** *Vogue* Dec. (Advt., verso front cover), Digby Morton, famous tailleur, created this trouser suit in a bright tartan 'Viyella'. **1975** D. LODGE *Changing Places* v. 174 She was waiting for him..in a cream-coloured trouser-suit. **1973** 'D. HALLIDAY' *Dolly & Starry Bird* iv. 47 The girls were thin, trouser-suited and purposeful, with Pat Nixon hairdos. **1966** *Olney Amsden & Sons Ltd. Price List* 44 Lightning Trouser Zipps. **1976** P. DICKINSON *King & Joker* vi. 70 'Shall I show you something, little girl?' he whispered. His hand was at his trouser-zip.

trouserettes, (*b*) short trousers; **trouserless** *a.* (earlier example).

1924 W. DE LA MARE *Ding Dong Bell* 30 A little boy in velveteen trouserettes. **1961** *New Statesman* 28 Apr. 658/2 The huge arthritic waiters stared..at Mart's rather strange check pantaloons. A party of secure business people were eating lobsters, and one of them..giggled at these semi-tropical trouserettes. **1848** A. H. CLOUGH *Bothie of Toper-na-Fuosich* v. 33 A heavy pea-coat his trouserless trunk enwrapping.

trousies (trau·ziz), *sb. pl.* Also **trowsies.** Dial. or colloq. var. of TROUSERS *sb. pl.* 2 a.

1886 H. BAUMANN *Londinismen* 219/2 *Trousies*,.. trousers. **1913** H. KEPHART *Our Southern Highlanders* xiii. 285 The ancient syllabic plural is preserved in beasties (horses), nesties, posties, trousies (these are not diminutives). **1924** H. DE SELINCOURT *Cricket Match* viii. 200 Mind now, or you'll spill the beer over your trousies. **1958** A. HUNTER *Gently through Mill* v. 52 It spoils the set of my nice new trousies! **1974** J. AIKEN *Midnight is Place* v. 146 You'll want clothes..canvas trowsies and some old slops of shoes.

Trousseau^2 (truso). *Med.* [The name of A. *Trousseau* (1801–67), French physician, who described the sign in 1862 (*Clin. Med. de l'Hôtel-Dieu de Paris* II. xliv. 113).] *Trousseau's sign*: spasm of a muscle evoked by pressure on the nerve supplying it, as seen in cases of tetany.

1887 VICKERY & KNAPP tr. *A Strümpell's Text-bk. Med.* 748 Another very characteristic symptom [of tetany] was discovered by Trousseau—'Trousseau's sign'.

It is..this: a fresh paroxysm can at any time be artificially excited by pressure upon the larger arteries and nerves of the arm. **1981** *Brit. Med. Jrnl.* 14 Nov. 1315/2 Trousseau's sign, while dramatic for the doctor, is very painful for the patient.

trout, *sb.*[1] Add: **3. lake trout** (earlier U.S. example); **yellow trout**, a name used in Scotland for the brown trout.

1830 *Cabinet Nat. Hist.* I. 147 In the outlet..from the lake, none of the lake trout were ever found. **1794** *Statist. Acct. Scotland* XIII. xxiii. 345 Fish are not plenty in this river; a few salmon, sea trout, yellow trout, and flounders, are caught in it. **1839** T. T. STODDART *Songs & Poems* 51 Is the yellow trout at feed? **1884** *Sat. Rev.* 12 July 61/1 Mr. Thomson caught one sixteen-pounder, which seized a yellow trout he was playing.

4. b. *old trout*: a derogatory term for an old woman. Cf. TROT *sb.*[2]

1897 'S. GRAND' *Beth Book* (1898) xxxix. 364 They said ..they were blessed if they'd go near the old trout again. **1914** D. BEATTY *Let.* 16 Feb. in W. S. Chalmers *Life & Lett. David, Earl Beatty* (1951) vi. 127 There were some funny old trouts and some spritely young ones, but no raving beauties. **1932** S. GIBBONS *Cold Comfort Farm* xvi. 224 'Serve her right, the old trout,' muttered Flora. **1956** 'A. GILBERT' *And Death came Too* ii. 33 She and her husband always went south to stay with her mother-in-law, an old trout called Lady Dingle. **1972** V. CANNING *Rainbird Pattern* iii. 50 She wasn't such a bad old trout. For all her money and position, life hadn't been all good to her.

5. a. *trout-hole* (example), *-hook* (earlier example), *-pond*, *-rod* (earlier example), *-stream* (earlier examples); *trout-fisher* (examples).

1751 FIELDING *Amelia* I. III. xii. 271 It is placed among Meadows washed by a clear Trout Stream. **1770** S. FOOTE *Lame Lover* I. 15 Oh! clear as a trout-stream. **1839** *Spirit of Times* 15 June 170/3 Surely a trout rod of fourteen ounces is not likely to fatigue (by the difference of weight in ash and willow) in the last hours of fishing. **1840** *Ibid.* 5 Sept. 319/1 Get a couple of dozen of trout hooks of assorted sizes. *Ibid.* 319/2 They know every trout hole or deer stand within twenty miles. **1842** W. P. HAWES *Sporting Scenes* I. 189 A scow, chiefest for a trout-pond. **1849** THOREAU *Week Concord Riv.* 323 Trout-fishers from distant cities had arrived before us. **1887** in W. Whitman *Daybks. & Notebks.* (1978) II. 509 A trout pond formed the boundary. **1936** *Discovery* Feb. 43/1 It is common knowledge to most trout-fishers that the May Fly has steadily decreased over many parts of the country in recent years.

b. trout-lily *U.S.*, the yellow dog's-tooth violet, *Erythronium americanum*; cf. *ERYTHRONIUM; **trout-line**, (*a*) a line used in trout fishing; (*b*) *U.S.* = *trot-line* (TROT *sb.*[1] 7).

1909 *Cent. Dict.* Suppl. 729/2 *Trout-lily*, the yellow dog-tooth violet. **1943** R. PEATTIE *Great Smokies* 275 The spring beauties and trout lilies..herald the blooming season. **1975** M. C. DAVIS *Near Woods* ix. 148 Almost all the trout-lilies emerging had but single leaves. **1789** J. WOODFORDE *Diary* 15 July (1927) III. 121 Busy..in making up some new Trout lines and for Eels. **1839** *Spirit of Times* 13 July 217/1 We have..bought an assortment of trout-lines and flies. **1912** *Dialect Notes* III. 592 *Trout-line, n.*, a trot-line. *Trout-line* has grown from the belief that there was something incorrect about *trot-line*. The line, of course, is not used in catching trout. **1934** *Sun* (Baltimore) 9 July 11/3 Crabs are reported to be so scarce that trout-line crabbers are able to catch only two barrels daily.

Trouton (trautǝn). *Physics.* [The name of F. T. *Trouton* (1863–1922), Irish physicist, who published the observation in 1884 (*Phil. Mag.* XVIII. 54).] *Trouton's law* or *rule*: the observation that for many substances the latent heat of vaporization of one mole, divided by the absolute temperature of the boiling point, is a constant (*Trouton('s) constant*) equal to approximately 88 joules per kelvin.

1899 J. WALKER *Introd. Physical Chem.* xii. 124 If the substance is in the state of vapour, the heat of vaporisation must be added to the thermochemical data for the liquid. This correction is often considerable, amounting approximately to one-fourth of the value of the boiling point of the substance on the absolute scale (Trouton's rule). **1901** *Jrnl. Chem. Soc.* LXXX. II. 372 The author states that if the heat of fusion is added to the heat of vaporisation for the determination of Trouton's constant, the quotient then obtained agrees with that found for dissociation. **1922** GLAZEBROOK *Dict. Appl. Physics* I. 561/2 It was shown by Despretz in 1823 that some relationship of the form given above by Trouton held, and later Pictet (1876), Ramsay (1877), rediscovered it independently, but it is now generally referred to as Trouton's law. **1966** [see *POLAR *a.* 3 b]. **1982** A. M. LESK *Introd. Physical Chem.* iv. 71 Enthalpies of vaporization of unassociated substances follow Trouton's rule.

trove. Add: Hence, a source of treasure, a reserve or repository of valuable things.

1976 *Publishers Weekly* 13 Sept. 97/1 Reaching back to the fifth century and up to today, the authors find a trove of artists whose work merits acknowledgment. **1982** *Sci. Amer.* Aug. 30A/1 Kingdon has himself visited 105 of those areas. He returns with his trove of image and understanding.

trowel, *sb.* **1. d.** (Earlier example.)

1845 G. DODD *Brit. Manuf.* 4th Ser. v. 128 The workman holds in his right hand a kind of trowel, consisting of a long narrow blade, about a foot in length, decreasing in width towards one end, and having at the other a handle which bends back over the blade. With this trowel..the workman draws the paint over the canvas, smoothing it repeatedly.

troxidone (trǫ·ksidōᵘn). *Pharm.* [f. TR(I- + OX- + *-ID(INE + -ONE, elements of the systematic name (see quot. 1952).] An anticonvulsant drug, $C_6H_9NO_3$, used chiefly in treating petit mal epilepsy. Cf. *TRIDIONE.

1952 *Brit. Pharmaceutical Codex 1949* Suppl. 78 Troxidone... *Synonym*: Trimethadone. Troxidone is 3:5:5-trimethyloxazolidine-2:4-dione. **1970** PASSMORE & ROBSON *Compan. Med. Stud.* II. v. 60/1 In patients undergoing electroconvulsion treatment the seizure patterns are not modified by troxidone as they are by phenobarbitone and phenytoin.

truant, *sb.* (*a.*) Add: **C.** *Comb.* **truant officer** *U.S.* = *truant-inspector*; **truant-school** (earlier example).

1872 C. L. BRACE *Dangerous Classes N.Y.* 348 The Massachusetts system of 'Truant-schools'—that is, Schools to which truant officers could send children habitually truant—does not seem so applicable to New York. **1911** G. F. WARD in S. M. Kingsbury *Labor Laws* 181 The truant officer finds that no certificate has been issued from the central office. **1972** T. KOCHMAN *Rappin' & stylin' Out* 249 What do you do when you ditch school and..a truant officer walks up.

Trubenized (trū·bĕnǝizd). [f. *Tru-*, of unknown origin + *-ben-*, said to be f. the name of *Benjamin* Liebowitz, inventor of the process + -IZE + -ED[1].] A proprietary name for clothing, esp. shirt collars, made durably stiff by a special process in manufacture.

No longer a proprietary name in the U.S.

1933 *Official Gaz.* (U.S. Patent Office) 26 Dec. 879/2 S. Liebovitz & Sons, Inc., New York... *Trubenized* for dress and negligee shirts and collars. **1939** *Trade Marks Jrnl.* 26 July 1051 *Trubenised*... All goods included in Class 25. Trubenising Limited,..High Holborn, London. **1955** *Radio Times* 22 Apr. 27/3 Shirt..25/6d. with soft collar (or 26/6d. with 'Trubenised' collar). **1969** A. J. HALL *Stand. Handbk. Textiles* (ed. 7) i. 45 Actually this solubility is not a serious disadvantage..for it enables acetate fibres to be employed in the 'Trubenised' process.

Trubetzkoyan (trūbetskoi·ăn), *a.* Also **Trubetskoyan.** [f. the name of Nikolai Sergeevich *Trubetzkoy* (1890–1938), Russian linguist + -AN.] Of or pertaining to Trubetzkoy or his theory and methodology.

1940 *Language* XVI. 248 The first part is very largely Trubetzkoyan. **1951** *Ibid.* XXVII. 333 Martinet presents an outline of fairly orthodox Trubetskoyan phonology. **1964** R. H. ROBINS *Gen. Linguistics* iv. 177 Without the use of further Trubetzkoyan concepts like neutralization. **1977** *Language* LIII. 427 The Trubetzkoyan era, however, was to be closed in a most dignified manner by his virtually finishing the manuscript of his famous encyclopaedic *Grundzüge der Phonologie*.

truce, *sb.* Add: **1. g.** A temporary pause or respite during a game. Hence, used to demand such a truce (cf. sense 2 b in Dict.).

1870 [see *FAIN *v.*[2]]. **1959** I. & P. OPIE *Lore & Lang. Schoolch.* viii. 142 Children were sensitive to the difference between making a truce and surrendering.

4. b. *truce-breaker* (later example).

1949 KOESTLER *Promise & Fulfilment* II. v. 265 The Egyptians having officially been branded as truce-breakers.

trucial (trū·ʃiăl), *a.* [f. TRUCE *sb.* + -IAL.] Of, pertaining to, or bound by a truce; used only with reference to the maritime truce made in 1835 between the British Government and certain Arab sheikhs of the Oman Peninsula.

The truce was renewed several times. In 1853 it was succeeded by a Treaty of Perpetual Peace, but the territories to which it had applied continued to be known as the *Trucial States* until 1971, when they became the United Arab Emirates.

1876 *Aitchison's Coll. Treaties* (ed. 2) VII. 44 The possessions of the so-called trucial Chiefs of the maritime tribes of the Persian Gulf. **1891** G. N. CURZON *Persia* II. 452 Adjoining the Trucial states upon the West is the rugged promontory of El Katr. **1911** L. FRASER *India under Curzon* 82 We..bound them by a truce..so that to this day they are known as the Trucial Chiefs of Oman. **1927** P. Cox in *Lett. Gertrude Bell* II. 506 We had treaties of old standing..with the Sheikhs of the Pirate (now the Trucial) Coast of Oman. **1930** A. RIHANI *Around Coasts of Arabia* 354 In Trucial Oman also the five independent Sheikhs agree not to enter into correspondence or agreement with any power other than the British Government. **1957** *Times* 24 Aug. 5/4 The Government are prepared to prop up even the ailing and backward sheikhs of the Trucial coast. **1971** *Daily Colonist* (Victoria, B.C.) 15 Aug. 1/4 The announcement of independence had been expected for some time—ever since six of the seven trucial coast emirates agreed to federate without Bahrain when the British military forces depart at the end of this year.

truck, *sb.*[1] Add: **3. a.** (Later examples.) Now usu. in negative contexts: *to have no truck with* (a person or thing), etc.

1899 R. WHITEING *No. 5 John Street* xxvi. 259 Fust time in 'er life..she's ever 'ad any truck with any of them sort. **1929** H. S. WALPOLE *Hans Frost* III. iii. 333, I don't want to have any truck with the world at all. **1938** M. K. RAWLINGS *Yearling* xi. 112 Mebbe your Ma's right. Mebbe you hadn't ought to have no truck with the Forresters. **1948** *Mind* LVII. 17 Others will have no truck with images, and declare that when we remember we are directly apprehending the past occurrence. **1952** J. L. WATEN *Alien Son* 97 She would have no truck with so-called midwives who practised spells and incantations. **1960** 'J. & E. BONETT' *No Grave for Lady* i. 13 Wasn't there a story going about..that Lotte Liselotte was having truck with him? **1975** S. HEANEY *North* II. 58 We tremble near the flames but want no truck With the actual firing.

5. *truck-farm*, *-farmer*, *-farming*: later examples; **truck crop** *U.S.* = sense 4 c.

1895 *U.S. Dept. Agric. Yearbk. 1894* 133 Soils having over 10 or 12 per cent of clay are too heavy and too retentive of moisture for the early truck crops. **1937** *Sun* (Baltimore) 17 Feb. 7/8 Payments for truck-crop growers have been increased. **1972** R. G. KAZMANN *Mod. Hydrol.* (ed. 2) iv. 109 Higher-valued crops such as truck crops are valuable enough to justify far more than this expenditure. **1969** *Observer* (Colour Suppl.) 19 Jan. 8/3 It was a truck farm, which you call a market-garden, don't you, or a nursery? **1976** *New Yorker* 17 May 34/1 Sold their.. duplex and moved to a coöperative truck farm. **1979** *Amer. Poetry Rev.* Mar./Apr. 24/1 A few children of Japanese truck farmers and some of us from Youngstown and White Center helped preserve what I snobbishly prefer to think of as peasant vitality. **1973** *Publ. Amer. Dial. Soc.* LX. 10 Raised and lives in Williston, an unincorporated community..mainly devoted to fishing, tugboating, and truck farming.

truck, *sb.*[2] Add: **3. g.** A motor vehicle for carrying goods, troops, etc., by road. Cf. *LORRY *sb.* 1 b. orig. *U.S.*

1916, etc. [see *motor-truck* s.v. *MOTOR *sb.* 5 a]. **1930** [see *LORRY *sb.* 1 b]. **1932** G. GREENE *Stamboul Train* I. i. 3 The passengers cross the quay..round..abandoned trucks. **1950** *Times* 27 Apr. 6/7 Many soldiers in the last war will remember that 'gas' might or might not be petrol and a 'truck' might or might not be a lorry. So it is to-day with 'gearbox', 'transmission', and many others. **1961** L. VAN DER POST *Heart of Hunter* vii. 112 One of the foremost ranchers near Gemsbok Pan was in the Union and coming back by truck across the desert. **1976** *Economist* 16 Oct. 92/1 Of European sales nearly 200,000 were glorified cars, about 400,000 medium-sized vans (up to 3.5 tonnes) and some 240,000 trucks (over 3.5 tonnes). **1984** *Times* 8 Feb. (Energy Suppl.) p. iv./2 This step by the manufacturers to put electric vans and trucks into serious production..has vindicated the enthusiasm of the.. Electric Vehicles Association. **1984** *N.Z. Truth* 23 May 33/3 The new ERF M16, ERF's bid for sales in the mid-size truck market, is on its way to becoming a big seller in Europe.

h. An axle unit of a skateboard to which the wheels are attached.

1976 A. CASSORLA *Skateboarder's Bible* 12 The average board came with trucks featuring one cushion rather than two. **1977** *Montgomery Ward Catal.* Spring–Summer 509/1 Heavy duty double-action die-cast trucks. **1978** *Globe & Mail* (Toronto) 15 Aug. 5/2 The wheels are lined with fibrous or plastic material to reduce noise, and steerable axles called trucks are supposed to eliminate squealing on curves and costly wear on rails.

3*. *U.S.* A popular dance (see quots.). Cf. *TRUCK *v.*[2] 5, *TRUCKING *vbl. sb.*[2] 3.

1935 *Sun* (Baltimore) 15 Nov. 14/6 The truck, or truckin', that jerky yet rhythmic dance which combines a bend of the body, a tightening of the hand muscles and a slight strut with the legs, hit the theaters, sidewalks, gin taverns and dance floors of Harlem last summer. **1937** *N.Y. Amsterdam News* 4 Sept. 12/2 Add a bit of the Shag, the new dance sensation that has pushed the 'Truck' out of the limelight, throw in a bit of the Suzi-Q for a spice and then top it all off with the 'Truck'.

4. *truck-driver* (examples in sense *3 g), *-horse* (earlier example); **truck-end** *slang rare*[−1], the buttocks; **truck frame** *U.S.*, the frame of a bogie; **trucklot** *N. Amer.*, a quantity of goods sufficient to fill a truck and sold at a lower rate than a smaller quantity; **truck mixer** (see quot. 1954); **truck stop** chiefly *U.S.*, an establishment which provides refreshments for truck-drivers and fuel and servicing for their trucks.

1931 E. WILSON *Axel's Castle* viii. 278 At Marseilles, he manages to live by unloading cargo and helping truck-drivers. **1973** 'R. MACLEOD' *Burial in Portugal* iii. 71 A truck driver leaned out of his cab and shouted a greeting. **1913** D. H. LAWRENCE *Sons & Lovers* iii. 53 But six shillin' wearin' his truck-end out on a stool's better than ten shillin' i' th' pit. **1850** *Rep. Comm. Patents 1849* (U.S.) I. 164, I claim the shapes and combinations of the truck frame pieces. **1942** W. FAULKNER *Go down, Moses* 145 He nudged the log to the edge of the truckframe. **1839** *Spirit of Times* 27 July 246/1 Indeed many of their truck horses are equal to those used on the road. **1943** *Sun* (Baltimore) 15 July 12/3 The regulation covers sales of berries at country shipping points, effective July 13, and carlot and trucklot sales at any receiving point. **1970** *Toronto Daily Star* 24 Sept. 16/3 (Advt.), Attention! all Trucklot Buyers!!.. Prices in this section apply on normal mixed truckloads. **1954** *Gloss. Highway Engin. Terms (B.S.I.)* 49 *Truck mixer*, a concrete mixer mounted on a self-propelled chassis, capable of mixing materials during transit from a batching plant to the point of placing. **1976** *Milton Keynes Express* 9 July 16/1 (Advt.), Experienced class II H.G.V. driver required to operate a truck mixer in the Milton Keynes area. **1961** *Amer. Speech* XXXVI. 271 Somewhere on your *run* you will spend some time at a *truck stop*..while the *hasher* serves your *diesel* or *Joe* or

Java. **1973** P. BERTON *Drifting Home* vi. 91 Now it is a hodge-podge: tavern, gas station, motel, snack bar, grocery store. Carmacks has become a truck stop.

truckful (earlier example).
1836 DICKENS *Pickw.* xxi. 213 He had moved in all his furniture—it wasn't quite a truck-full.

truck, *v.*² Add: **1.** (Later examples.) Now usu. with reference to *TRUCK *sb.*² 3 g.
1935 *Motion Picture* Nov. 80/3 The heavy electrical equipment was trucked in. **1943** *Sun* (Baltimore) 28 Apr. 8/3 The fighters are trucked in crated from cargo ships. **1954** [see *FAT *sb.*² 1 b]. **1969** A. LURIE *Real People* 108 He has trucked all his equipment..up here at considerable expense. **1982** L. KALLEN *C. B. Greenfield* iv. 47 The produce, trucked in daily from their own up-state farm, was fresh.

2. (Example with reference to *TRUCK *sb.*² 3 g.)
1976 M. MACHLIN *Pipeline* xi. 135 If he stayed with the private contractors who were trucking for Denali, it was improbable he would be recognized.

3. a. *U.S. slang.* Of a vehicle: to proceed. Hence of a person: to go (by truck or otherwise); to move or stroll.
1925 C. R. COOPER *Lions 'n' Tigers* v. 109 One by one the big wagons were trucking toward the first smoking torch at a corner of the grounds. **1938** *Better English* Nov. 51 *Truck, truck on down,* to go somewhere. **1941** STEINBECK & RICKETTS *Sea of Cortez* xxiv. 237 We said good-by to Tiburoñ and trucked on down toward Guaymas. **1970** T. WOLFE *Radical Chic & Mau-Mauing Flak Catchers* 131 They would truck around in the pimp style, too. **1979** *United States 1980/81* (Penguin Travel Guides) 148 You'll still find plenty of people trucking through the streets in flannel shirts, blue jeans, cowboy hats, and boots.

b. Slang phr. *to keep on trucking,* to persevere: a phrase of encouragement.
1972 *Sat. Rev.* (U.S.) 28 Oct. 12 One poster..shows the famous R. Crumb cartoon characters and bears the caption: 'Let's Keep on Truckin'.' **1976** *Southern Even. Echo* (Southampton) 6 Nov. (Advt. Suppl.) 5/4 'To keep in business he's just got to keep on truckin'.' For Karl, and his kind, that can mean upwards of 200,000 miles a year. **1977** *New Yorker* 27 June 79/1 Feels like I frosted the ends of my toes a bit, but they're far from my heart, so I'll keep on truckin.

4. *Cinematogr.* = *TRACK *v.*¹ 3 e.
1929 [see *DOLLY *sb.*¹ 4 h]. **1942** *Amer. Cinematographer* June 283/2 The camera would start at a long shot, and truck rapidly down toward the background. **1948** A. HUXLEY *Ape & Essence* (1949) 151 Dr. Poole and Loola enter the shot, and the Camera trucks with them as they come striding down the slope. **1961** G. MILLERSON *Technique Television Production* iii. 25 (*caption*) Two methods of trucking sideways are shown.

5. To dance the truck. *U.S. slang.*
1937 *Amer. Speech* XII. 183/1 Only negroes can really truck. **1966** M. & J. STEARNS in A. Dundes *Mother Wit* (1973) 614/2 Sweetie May trucks provocatively onstage. **1972** W. M. ESTES *Streetful of People* vii. 238 Toward the end of the number, the girls turned rosy red and started truckin'.

Hence **trucked** *ppl. a.*; *trucked-in* adj., brought by truck.
1940 *Sun* (Baltimore) 16 Apr. 15/5 Offerings during forenoon rounds in the sheep pens consisted of a few lots of trucked-in native spring lambs. **1966** T. PYNCHON *Crying of Lot 49* iii. 56 The trucked-in white sand. **1977** *Time* 7 Mar. 54/3 Lack of green grazing land and hay is also forcing cattlemen either to sell off their thin animals at low prices or fatten them on expensive trucked-in feed.

truckage². (Earlier example.)
1830 W. S. MOORSOM *Lett. from Nova Scotia* iii. 80 Away scamper a dozen proud nags waiting for truckage.

trucker². Add: **1.** (Earlier example.)
1853 DICKENS *Down with Tide* in *Househ. Words* 5 Feb. 484/2 The Truckers..whose business it was to land more considerable parcels of goods than the Lumpers could manage.

2. A (long-distance) lorry-driver. orig. and chiefly *U.S.*
1961 *Amer. Speech* XXXVI. 273 A fast-driving trucker. **1963** *Times* 2 Feb. 9/6 'Truckers, the real night drivers, are a race apart and 99 per cent honest,' said Taffy. **1966** B. H. DEAL *Fancy's Knell* (1967) vi. 84 There was the barbecue and good coffee. Truckers often stopped here. **1971** *Maclean's Mag.* Sept. 72/3 Most truckers..name their rigs after their girl friends. **1978** S. BRILL *Teamsters* i. 14 The special nature of their work gives these truckers and warehousemen a stranglehold on the nation's economic life. **1984** *Gainesville* (Florida) *Sun* 30 Mar. 11A/1 The chase started when truckers on I-75 radioed troopers about a late-model Chevrolet station wagon that was weaving on the highway. **1984** *More* (Auckland) May 81/3 And then there are some hardcore longterm truckers who have seen several seasons come and go.

truckie (trʊ·ki). *Austral.* and *N.Z. colloq.* [f. TRUCK *sb.*² + -IE.] = *TRUCKER² 2.
1958 *Coast to Coast 1957–8* 201 The truckie looked upwards. 'Whaddya want, mate?' **1968** *Sunday Mail* (Brisbane) 9 June 5/3 Since April last year, more than 50 truckies had appeared in the courts in Queensland on 'pep' pill charges. **1970** P. CARLON *Souvenir* vi. 56 In the truckies' café..the waitress remembered them. **1970** *N.Z. Listener* 21 Dec. 8/4 Another time you'll thumb a truck—truckies will generally stop for you. **1976** *Telegraph* (Brisbane) 24 June 20/2 Detectives have begun a blitz on interstate truckies in a bid to catch color television thieves. **1978** O. WHITE *Silent Reach* viii. 83 We are evacuating this camp... Regular truckies stand to their vehicles.

trucking, *vbl. sb.*² (In Dict. s.v. TRUCK *v.*²) Add: **2. a.** Lorry-driving; *spec.* the conveyance of goods by means of a lorry or other motor vehicle. orig. and chiefly *U.S.*
1947 [implied at *PARLAY *v.* 2]. **1955** *Amer. Speech* XXX. 91 In trucking, *twin screws* mean that there are two sets of rear wheels that are powered. **1961** *Ibid.* XXXVI. 271 Both the [lumbering] industry and the comparative isolation encourage trucking. **1968** *Globe & Mail* (Toronto) 3 Feb. B5/1 Parts one and two of the act, introduced last year, have been implemented and deal mainly with railways. Part three, dealing with trucking, has not yet become law. **1978** *New York* 3 Apr. 88/1 (Advt.), Quick (but careful) Trucking—Immediate Service.

b. *attrib.*
1947 Trucking firm [see *PARLAY *v.* 2]. **1955** *Amer. Speech* XXX. 91 Some of the words and terms of the trucking industry have been carried over from earlier days of teamsters and steamboat men. **1962** 'E. MCBAIN' *Heckler* iv. 35, I..work for the trucking company. **1969** G. LYALL *Venus with Pistol* ix. 50 I'm in the trucking business. **1978** S. BRILL *Teamsters* i. 14 He had negotiated a national trucking contract.

3. The action of dancing the truck. *slang.*
1935 [see *TRUCK *sb.*² 3*]. **1938**, etc. [see *SUSIE-Q]. **1944** C. CALLOWAY *Hepsters Dict.* in *Of Minnie the Moocher* (1976) 260 *Trucking,* a dance introduced at the Cotton Club in 1933. **1959** 'F. NEWTON' *Jazz Scene* iv. 60 The Black Bottom, Charleston, Lindy Hop, Big Apple, Truckin' and the rest..have been mainly temporary crazes. **1971** E. BULLINS in W. King *Black Short Story Anthol.* (1972) 70 The dancers upon the concrete were blocks away, souls in time to the trotting and trucking of the savage song of the threshing floor.

4. *Cinematogr.* (In sense *4 of the vb.) **trucking shot** = *tracking shot* s.v. *TRACKING *vbl. sb.* 5.
1948 A. HUXLEY *Ape & Essence* (1949) 46 We..enjoy a trucking shot of mortuary gazebos. **1959** W. S. SHARPS *Dict. Cinematogr.* 91/2 *Dollying,* otherwise *Tracking, Travelling* or *Trucking,* the moving of a camera on a *dolly* or *camera truck* during *shooting.*

truckster. (Earlier and later examples.)
1843 *Knickerbocker* XXII. 38 All relics of a former age.. exposed for sale in the windows of the trucksters. **1916** H. J. LASKI in *Holmes–Laski Lett.* (1953) I. 40 It gets very nauseating to have the measure of progress taken as a commercial truckster might measure it. **1931** A. UTTLEY *Country Child* v. 69 He had a pack on his back containing ..all the odds and ends of the truckster.

Trudeaumania (trūdōᵘmēⁱ·niă). [f. the name of Pierre Elliott *Trudeau* (b. 1919), former Prime Minister of Canada + -MANIA.] Enthusiastic or exaggerated admiration for Trudeau.
1968 *Listener* 4 July 5/1 With the phenomenal climb to power of Mr Trudeau a tremendous cult has developed among younger Canadians. It's known as Trudeaumania or Trudolatry. **1971** *Maclean's Mag.* Oct. 28/1 Far more accomplished than Pierre Trudeau, who merely observed the phenomena named Trudeaumania and was shrewd enough to take advantage of it. **1976** *Time* 22 Mar. 32/1 Trudeaumania has long since faded away in Canada.

true, *a.* (*sb., adv.*) Add: **A.** *adj.* **3. e.** Phr. *true for you* [after Ir. *is fíor duit*]: an expression of assent to something said by another. (Stressed on *for.*) *Anglo-Ir.*
1835 R. M. BIRD *Hawks of Hawk-Hollow* I. xix. 247 'You are Tapes, the pedler.'.. 'True for you, captain Gilbert!' cried the other, with a stare. **1901** J. BARLOW *From Land of Shamrock* 63 They would not, thrue for you. **1980** J. O'FAOLAIN *No Country for Young Men* xv. 329 You're right there... True for you.

f. Purporting to be true. Freq. in collocations used *attrib.* to designate popular magazines which contain (remarkable) stories which purport to be true, as *true confessions, story*; also *true-life story,* etc.
1926 A. HUXLEY *Jesting Pilate* IV. 260 He walked up and down the train..peddling..True Story Magazines. **1937** [see *pulp magazine* s.v. *PULP *sb.* 5 c]. **1957** C. MACINNES *City of Spades* II. x. 170 Barbara was..reading a 'true story' magazine. **1958** *Times Lit. Suppl.* 7 Feb. 72/3 She writes well, and—somewhat unusually for a social worker—quotes poetry. She seasons her facts with many 'true-life' stories. **1965** M. SPARK *Mandelbaum Gate* vii. 303 Love, love-affairs, men and women and true-life stories formed the daily entertainment and talk of their week's travelling. **1967** 'T. WELLS' *What should you know of Dying?* ii. 30 [She] was reading a true confessions magazine. I didn't think they even printed them any more.

g. Colloq. phr. *so* (..) *it isn't true* and varr.: to an almost incredible extent.
1963 *Daily Herald* 25 Apr. 7/6 The Princess was so calm it wasn't true. She was so relaxed. **1964** 'A. GARVE' *Ashes of Loda* i. 14 He's..so incompetent about ordinary day-to-day living it's just not true. **1970** R. RENDELL *Guilty Thing Surprised* ix. 103 You may be only thirty-six but you're so dead old-fashioned it isn't true. **1982** BARR & YORK *Official Sloane Ranger Handbk.* 8/1 Sloane Britain is so heavily weighted towards the South and the West it's not true.

4. e. *true to life* (earlier and later examples). Also *true to type.*
1835 *Athenæum* 16 May 372/1 Another character—true to life—is Mrs. Hollis, the fruiterer. **1872** J. M. LANGFORD *Let.* 11 Mar. in *Geo. Eliot Lett.* (1956) V. 254 One feels them all to be true to life. **1929** *Oxford Poetry* 10 Say he died true to type: and then erect A cenotaph; he liked to be select. **1960** *Farmer & Stockbreeder* 1 Mar. 80/2 This was indeed a true-to-type Devon: a good, compact animal with nice fleshing and conformation. **1980** K. FOLLETT *Key to Rebecca* xvii. 193 His preference for 'true-to-life' murders, as opposed to implausible country-house killings.

i. Of bearings: measured relative to true North.
1834 [see AZIMUTH 2 a]. **1912** [see *PROJECTION *sb.* 7 b]. **1969** G. C. DICKINSON *Maps & Air Photographs* viii. 125 Bearings measured relative to true north are called true bearings.

j. Of the ground or other surface prepared for ball games: free from unevenness, level and smooth.
1851 in W. G. Grace *W. G.'s Little Bk.* (1909) i. 5 A man is but half a player who is only prepared for true grounds. **1895** H. G. HUTCHINSON *Golf* (ed. 5) xii. 309 The putting-greens are very good and true. **1934** W. J. LEWIS *Lang. Cricket* 297 It [*sc.* the wicket] is said, with regard to its condition, to be *hard* when firm..*plumb* or *true* when it is perfectly level and the ball behaves normally. **1965** L. R. BENAUD *Young Cricketer* 86/1 Pitches of today seem to have changed from those of Bulli soil days..when..one played on a true, black, shiny strip as hard as concrete.

5. d. *true left* (or *right*): the side which is on the left (or right) as one looks down from a hill or mountain, or downstream.
1910 J. BUCHAN *Prester John* x. 177 We followed a narrow shelf on its left side (or 'true right', as mountaineers would call it). **1929** —— *Courts of Morning* III. iv. 344 Six men were perched high up among the rocks on the right side (what mountaineers would call the 'true left') of the couloir. **1971** *N.Z. Listener* 19 Apr. 55/2 An acquaintance asked..what the reporter had meant by the 'true left' bank of the river. I explained that it was the one on the lefthand side as you looked downstream.

B. *sb.* **3.** (Earlier and later examples.) Now usu. without *the.* Hence *out-of-true* sb., the extent to which a part is out of exact alignment. Cf. TRUTH *sb.* 6 in Dict. and Suppl.
1876 J. ROSE *Compl. Pract. Machinist* vi. 86 If the face plate of the lathe is a trifle out of true, the eccentric will only be out to an equal amount. **1895** J. T. USHER *Mod. Machinist* xxi. 199 The eccentric is..held on the arbor while it is being turned in precisely the same way as it is held on the crank-shaft or axle of the engine, thereby avoiding the tendency to spring it out of true after it is turned, which often happens when it is held for turning by other means. **1970** K. BALL *Fiat 600, 600D Autobook* vi. 59/1 The out-of-true at bearing seats must not exceed ·0008 inch.

C. *adv.* **3. b.** (Later examples.)
1912 *Chambers's Jrnl.* Dec. 810/2 Each variety breeds 'true' in breeders' parlance. **1967** *Listener* 3 Aug. 142/1 But there are two regularities which are equally impressive: organisms breed true, and their structures are orderly.

D. Combinations. **1. d.** Appositively: **true–false** *a. Educ.* and *Psychol.,* denoting a type of test question constructed so that only the words 'true' or 'false' (or another pair of opposites) are acceptable responses; characterizing a test that uses this technique.
1923 P. B. BALLARD *New Examiner* vii. 80 The new examination comprised three tests, the first of which was of the True–False type. **1957** D. L. BOLINGER in *Publ. Amer. Dial. Soc.* XXVIII. 24 Yes–no Qs are essentially true–false Qs. **1965** N. E. GRONLUND *Measurement & Eval. in Teaching* viii. 127 Some of the variations..deviate considerably from the simple true–false pattern. **1974** in H. G. Macintosh *Techniques & Probl. Assessment* iii. 25 Other word pairs relating to the statement such as 'greater than–less than'..'faster–slower' and so on. It is the possibilities offered by these other pairs which make the true/false form a particularly useful one.

trueish (trū·iʃ), *a. colloq.* Also **true-ish.** [f. TRUE *a.* + -ISH¹.] Partly true, almost true.
1980 I. MURDOCH *Nuns & Soldiers* v. 326 'So you think it's true?' 'I think it may be trueish. There's something.' **1981** T. HEALD *Murder at Moose Jaw* iv. 44 'True,' said Bognor. 'Or at least true-ish.'

truffle. Add: **1. b.** **truffle-dog** (earlier example); **truffle hound** = *truffle dog.*
1855 S. WHITING *Heliondé* ii. 47 'If they should see you digging into the surface of the Sun' (he might have added 'like a truffle dog') 'they will certainly think you are demented.' **1975** J. GRIGSON *Mushroom Feast* 134 There is the whole business of truffle pigs and truffle hounds.

2. A type of confectionery made of a mixture of chocolate and cream, freq. flavoured with rum, shaped into a ball and covered with powdered chocolate.
1926–7 *Army & Navy Stores Catal.* 54/2 Chocolates.. Truffles—lb. 4/3. *c* **1938** *Fortnum & Mason Price List* 8/1 Truffles, with fresh cream (perishable)..Truffles, Rum Flavoured. **1944** D. WELCH *In Youth is Pleasure* iv. 61 He imagined the aromatic acrid dust..sticking to [the heart] and coating it..as bright-coloured bitter cocoa powder clings to the rich dark truffle. **1951** *Good Housek. Home Encycl.* 407/1 (*heading*) Chocolate truffles. *Ibid.* 675/1 Turkish delight and marshmallows, chocolates and truffles. **1974** J. STUBBS *Painted Face* xiii. 168 [His] only acquaintance with truffles had been the chocolate variety.

‖ **truite au bleu** (trwīt o blö). *Cookery.* [Fr., lit. 'trout in the blue'.] Trout cooked with vinegar, which turns it blue.

[**1861** MRS. BEETON *Bk. Househ. Managem.* 44 *Au-bleu*, fish dressed in such a manner as to have a *bluish* appearance.] **1935** M. MORPHY *Recipes of All Nations* 37 *Truite au bleu*...One of the most popular ways of cooking them is 'au bleu'—the boiling vinegar in which they are plunged turning them a vivid blue. **1966** B. GLEMSER *Dear Hungarian Friend* iv. 76 He offered her blue trout, *truite au bleu Duna.* **1978** *Chicago* June 236/2 The Chicago branch of the Paris house offers wonderful dishes like truite au bleu (trout are killed immediately before poaching and sauced with hollandaise at the table).

‖ **truite bleue** (trwīt blö). Also *erron.* **truite bleu.** [Fr., lit. 'blue trout'.] = prec.

1907 E. GLYN *Three Weeks* i. 18 She ate a delicate *truite bleu.* **1948** WODEHOUSE *Uncle Dynamite* iv. 56 It was a relief when the waiter, arriving with *truite bleue*, broke a tension which had begun to be uncomfortable. **1980** 'M. HARRIS' *Treasure of Sainte Foy* ix. 123 The prix-fixe is Truite Bleue, then Cassoulet..salad, fruit, and cheese.

‖ **trullo** (tru·lo). Pl. **trulli.** [It.] In Apulia, a small round house built of stone, with a conical roof.

1909 in WEBSTER. **1925** L. V. BERTARELLI *Southern Italy* iii. 380 *Alberobello* is a curious village of 'trulli'... These are round huts of stone without mortar, with conical roofs. **1932** *Antiquity* VI. 408 Away in the distance another trullo is visible... No stables or barns are these. We have arrived in 'trulli land'. These trulli are human habitations. **1958** P. KEMP *No Colours or Crest* xii. 252 We lived in a *trullo*, one of the beehive-shaped dwellings that are typical of the Apulian hill country. **1968** S. JAY *Sleepers can Kill* xiii. 134 Those round Trulli houses they have in Southern Italy. **1981** *Italy* (Michelin Tourist Guide) 243 The *Trulli*.—In these..can be seen traces of prehistoric Saracen and Christian civilisations, similar to the *nuraghi* of Sardinia.

truly, *adv.* (*sb.*) Add: **4. b.** *well and truly* (examples); now also for colloq. emphasis: decisively, 'good and proper' (*GOOD *adv.* d).

1458 J. JERNYNGAN *Let.* 1 June in N. Davis *Paston Lett.* (1976) II. 341 There was not so gret a batayle vpon þe se þis xl wyntyr; and for sothe we were wele and trewly bette. **1477** in *N. & Q.* (1975) July 290/2 The forme of this present lettre whiche ben wel and truly correct. **1521** B. ANSLAY tr. *C. de Pisani's Bk. Cyte of Ladyes* I. xiii, He shall rewarde them that well and truely maynteyneth hym. **1760** STERNE *Tristram Shandy* I. xv. 82 The said intended marriage..to be well and truly solemnized and consummated. **1895** *Funk's Standard Dict.* s.v. *well* adv., *Well and truly* (Law), conformably to duty; heedfully; used in oaths and affirmations. **1935** *Discovery* Oct. 314/1 The great principle is laid well and truly down—not to attempt to hurry. **1948** G. V. GALWEY *Lift & Drop* iv. 72, I am—well and truly married. **1971** D. POTTER *Brit. Eliz. Stamps* iii. 41 As soon as the cup was well and truly won by England. **1973** *Guardian* 16 Feb. 13/8 British Brussels is well and truly split on the issue of the TUC's participation in Europe.

Truman (trū·măn). The name of Harry S. *Truman* (1884–1972), U.S. President 1945–53, used *attrib.* in **Truman Doctrine,** the principle first enunciated by Truman in March 1947 that the United States should 'support free peoples who are resisting attempted subjugation'.

1947 *Sun* (Baltimore) 2 Apr. 18/1 At some time, at some point, the Soviet may not take kindly to our extension of the 'Truman Doctrine' to areas bordering upon her claimed sphere of influence. **1948** *Labour Monthly* Aug. 237 The Truman Doctrine aims at making Europe safe against socialism. **1958** *Polit. Sci. Quarterly* LXXIII. 321 The broad terms of the Truman doctrine merely claimed a broad right to intervene, even though there was no intention to exercise this right in full. **1964** MRS. L. B. JOHNSON *White House Diary* 10 Mar. (1970) 82 President Truman..said, 'It [*sc.* the Truman Doctrine] was all the Marshall Plan... It's just that the Greeks like the Jews and the Irish can holler louder than anybody else, if you have heard more about the Truman Doctrine than you have the others.' **1977** *Time* 6 June 14/1 By early 1947 Soviet adventurism had inspired the Truman Doctrine, with its pledge of military help to any free people threatened by Communist aggression.

trumeau (trü·mo). Pl. **trumeaux.** [Fr., lit. 'calf of the leg'.] **1.** Also *trumeau mirror.* A pier-glass.

1883 J. W. MOLLETT *Illustr. Dict. Art & Archæol.* 327/1 *Trumeau*, a pier looking-glass. **1941** *Amer. Speech* XVI. 27 'Über dem Kamin..ist ein Trumeau-Spiegel.'..Cf. 'Trumeau' in Cent. Dict., also in Webster's; not in NED. Nowhere do I find any reference to 'Trumeau Mirror'. **1969** *Canad. Antiques Collector* May 11/1 The trumeau at the left is one of a pair flanking the dining room entrance. **1974** S. SHELDON *Other Side of Midnight* xiv. 278 From mantel top to ceiling rose a heavily carved trumeau mirror.

2. *Archit.* A stone pillar supporting the middle of the tympanum of a doorway, esp. in a church.

1890 C. H. MOORE *Gothic Archit.* vii. 262 After the eleventh century the principal portals of great monastic and cathedral churches were commonly divided into two openings by *trumeaux*, or pillars of stone, affording place for sculpture, which consisted usually of a statue with more or less subordinate carving. **1936** A. W. CLAPHAM *Romanesque Archit.* iv. 100 The 'trumeau' at Moissac, also with its superimposed pairs of lions, stands parent to the extraordinary creation at Souillac. **1968** M. JAY tr. *Bazin's Hist. World Sculpture* (1970) vii. 266 (*caption*) *Trumeau* of the old portal, church of Souillac. **1977** *New York Rev. Bks.* 12 May 8/4 The only other Romanesque church with two portals, which originally included trumeaux, is St. Lazare at Autun.

trump, *sb.*[2] Add: **2. a.** *to turn up trumps* (earlier example).

1819 M. WILMOT *Let.* 3 Sept. (1935) 17 A little converted Jew..who received us into his house at a moderate rate and has turned up such *trumps* that I must introduce him to you.

3. b. *Austral.* and *N.Z. slang.* A person in authority.

1937 PARTRIDGE *Dict. Slang* 912/2 *Trump of the dump, the,* anyone in authority: New Zealanders': in G[reat] W[ar]. **1941** BAKER *Dict. Austral. Slang* 78 *Trump,* a commanding officer. Diggers' slang. **1950** *Landfall* (N.Z.) IV. 126 The hoops are on the last cask by 11.45, and the trump calls out all hands to load the railway wagon. *Ibid.* 127, The trump comes in and calls us gentlemen and wishes us the very best. **1974** D. STUART *Prince of my Country* xiv. 142 There's a blackfeller or two knows which is which, shafters, and pin, and body, and leaders, the trump says.

4. trump signal (example); also at Bridge.

1901 C. J. MELROSE *Bridge Whist* 41 His partner must.. be on the alert to lead trumps through the opponent's strength, and to look out for a trump signal from his partner. **1964** FREY & TRUSCOTT *Official Encycl. Bridge* 634/1 Some players use the trump signal whenever they hold three trumps.

† **trumpa** (trɒ·mpă). *Obs.* [ad. F. *trumpeau, trumpo.*] = SPERM WHALE.

1625 PURCHAS *Pilgrimes* III. 471 The third sort of Whale is called Trumpa, being as long as the first, but thicker forwards. **1851** H. MELVILLE *Moby Dick* I. xxxi. 215 This [sperm] whale, among the English of old vaguely known as the Trumpa whale.

trumped *ppl. a.* (Earlier examples.)

1728 FIELDING *Love in Several Masques* v. xii. 76, I know my Title to be secure, it must be some trumped-up Cheat. **1777** *Sixteenth Ode of Third Bk. Horace Imit.* 21 A Pamphlet fill'd with trump'd-up stories.

trumpet, *sb.* Add: **2. e.** = *HORN *sb.* 14* a. Now *Hist.*

1899 *Strand Mag.* Dec. (Advt.), p. xxxv/1 The Gramophone. Berliner's Patent... Length of Trumpet 16 inches. **1904** *Science Siftings* 26 Mar. 353/1 These are again transferred into sound..and transmitted to the audience through a huge trumpet. **1922** S. A. MAYCOCK *Handbk. Gramophone* iii. 18 The hornless models certainly look neater than the instruments which are fitted with trumpets. **1947** F. W. GAISBERG *Music on Record* vi. 81 For the first time they heard sibilants emerge from the trumpet, loud and hissing!

3. *to blow one's own trumpet* (examples).

1854 MAYNE REID *Young Voyageurs* v. 71 They may live to 'blow their own trumpet' a long while yet. **1887** W. S. GILBERT *Ruddigore* I. 12 You must stir it and stump it, And blow your own trumpet. **1952** A. BUCKERIDGE *Jennings & Darbishire* ii. 27, I vote we're not allowed to vote for ourselves because my father says it's swanking to blow your own trumpet. **1983** P. ROBERTS *Tender Prey* xiv. 165, I was not averse to blowing my own trumpet. Modesty is a fool's game.

6. f. *Metallurgy.* A vertical tube with a bell mouth and a refractory lining, through which metal is poured into runners in uphill casting.

1923 HARBORD & HALL *Metallurgy of Steel* (ed. 7) I. i. 37 At one time it was generally considered that sounder ingots could be obtained by bottom casting, but opinions are now much divided as with bottom pouring there is.. some danger of the refractory lining of the trumpet.. being carried into the steel. **1929** W. LISTER *Pract. Steelmaking* xxxviii. 370 In this trumpet no wet clay or ramming is used and no weights or clamps are required. **1973** *Times* 12 Feb. (Anchor Project Suppl.) p. ii/6 Mould preparation will be done in a separate bay which is well designed for mould cooling and equipped for..preparation of trumpets and runners for up-run teeming.

7. b. *trumpet-twisted* adj.; **c. trumpet creeper** (earlier example); **trumpet-gall** (examples); **trumpet honeysuckle** (earlier example); **trumpet-leaf** (earlier example); **trumpet-lug** *Archæol.*, a type of tubular handle with expanded ends, found on British neolithic pottery; **trumpet medium,** a spiritualistic medium in whose seances a trumpet megaphone is used; **trumpet pattern,** in medieval art: a shape resembling that of a horn; **trumpet seance,** a spiritualistic seance in which a trumpet megaphone is used; **trumpet-snail** = *RAM'S HORN 6; **trumpet spiral** (see quot. 1959); cf. *trumpet pattern* above; **trumpet style** *Jazz*, a style of piano-playing imitative of a trumpet; **trumpet-vine** (later examples); **trumpet-weed,** (*b*) (earlier example).

1818 W. P. C. BARTON *Compendium Floræ Philadelphicæ* II. 43 Trumpet Creeper... Flowers red and orange. **1879** Trumpet-gall [see *nail-gall* s.v. *NAIL *sb.* 14 a]. **1908** V. L. KELLOGG *Amer. Insects* 470 Trumpet-galls on leaves of California white oak. **1731** P. MILLER *Gardeners Dict.* s.v. *Periclymenum*, Trumpet Honeysuckle... We have but one species of this Plant at present,..Virginian Scarlet Honeysuckle. **1861** A. WOOD *Class-Bk. Bot.* (ed. 10) 222 *S. Gronovii.* Trumpet-leaf..in swampy pine woods. [**1932** S. PIGGOTT in *Archaeol. Jrnl.* LXXXVIII. 76 The horizontally perforated lug..exhibits a 'trumpet-ended' variety at Windmill Hill and Hembury.] **1937** —— in *Antiquity* XI. 450 More important was the occurrence of a type of lug or tubular perforated handle with expanded ends, which the writer distinguished as a 'trumpet-lug' in 1932... At Hembury it was present as a recurrent feature. **1972** L. ALCOCK *By South Cadbury* v. 109 These suspension tubes—trumpet lugs to give them their technical name—are seen again on pottery from sites like Windmill Hill in Wiltshire. **1912** *Nash's Mag.* July 553/2 Last year the wonderful trumpet medium, Mrs. Wreidt, spent some time at 'Julia's Bureau'. **1968** B. STEIGER *Voices from Beyond* iii. 58 Trumpet mediums always seem to be popular at Spiritualist camps. **1937** *Burlington Mag.* Feb. 99/1 We find that admirable curling trumpet-patterns..in the brilliant manuscripts of the early Church in Ireland and Northumbria. **1954** M. RICKERT *Painting in Brit.: Middle Ages* 232 *Trumpet pattern,* two whorls.. joined across the open side by a curved line. **1965** L. N. VALENTINE *Ornament in Medieval Manuscripts* 51 '*French horn*', a trumpet pattern combined with a helix shape. **1912** *Nash's Mag.* July 544/1 The sitting took place at 'Julia's Bureau'. It was a Trumpet Séance, and Mrs. Wreidt..was the medium. **1931** *Daily Express* 15 Oct. 7/3, I am aware you are giving trumpet seances. **1968** B. STEIGER *Voices from Beyond* iii. 58 At trumpet seances—almost invariably conducted in the dark—the horn rises, ostensibly lifted by spirit hands. **1901** E. STEP *Shell Life* 320 The Ram's Horn or Trumpet-snail, so frequently introduced in fresh-water aquaria. **1965** tr. *H. Janus' Young Specialist looks at Land & Freshwater Molluscs* iv. 70 Family Planorbidae (Ram's-horn or Trumpet Snails). **1936** A. W. CLAPHAM *Romanesque Archit.* i. 9 Certain Celtic motives such as the trumpet-spiral. **1959** E. A. FISHER *Anglo-Saxon Archit. & Sculpt.* 73 Both single and double spirals were common in Celto-British art... Sometimes the connecting C-line would be double and wider apart in the middle resembling two trumpets joined at their wide ends—hence the term *trumpet spiral.* **1946** R. BLESH *Shining Trumpets* xiii. 320 Hines's trumpet style..was based on Louis Armstrong's trumpet phrasing. **1959** 'F. NEWTON' *Jazz Scene* vii. 130 Players attempted the feat of adapting the piano to the vocalising style of the other instruments (the so-called 'trumpet style'). **1977** *New Yorker* 6 June 120/1 The so-called trumpet style of jazz piano playing, which Earl Hines originated in the late twenties, consists of hornlike single-note melodic lines in the right hand and on-and-off-the-beat chords, single notes, and countermelodic lines in the left hand. **1895** W. B. YEATS *Poems* 12 Many a trumpet-twisted shell. **1883** *Peterson Ladies' Nat. Mag.* June 460/2 The great porch in front..[was] destitute of railing or ornament, but the creeping trumpet vine. **1978** *Detroit Free Press* 16 Apr. (Gardening Guide) 14/2 Trumpet vine is another woody vine that bears striking flowers. **1830** *Huntingdon* (Pa.) *Courier* 15 Sept. 4/5 American Remedies Wanted..Gravel Wort or Trumpet Weed.

trumph (trɒmf). Sc. and north. var. of TRUMP *sb.*[2] Phrases: † *to play trumph about* (obs.): to vie in achievements *with*; *what's trumph?* what is happening? what is the news?

1777 R. FORBES *Ulysses' Answer* 29 Achilles played na' trumph about Wi' him, he says; but judge ye. **1819** J. BURNESS *Plays, Poems* 286 Again Will deals the cartes about Says he, Lads, hearts is trumph. **1895** J. NICHOLSON *Kilwuddie* (ed. 3) 173 A lass that has that wi' the lads should be trumph. **1908** E. M. SNEYD-KYNNERSLEY *H.M.I.* iii. 30 Corners denoted the 'Jack of trumph'. **1955** W. P. MILNE *Eppie Elrick* xxx. 272 Fat's lickly tae be trumph noo? **1969** J. T. R. RITCHIE *Golden City* 76 Ye turn the tope card over to see what's to be trumph.

truncate, *v.* Add: **c.** *Math.* To cut short or approximate (a series, etc.) by ignoring all the terms beyond a chosen term. Also *absol.*

1955 M. LOÈVE *Probability Theory* xvi. 233 We truncate X [*sc.* a random variable] at $c > 0$..when we replace X by $X^c = X$ or 0 according as $|X| < c$ or $|X| \geq c$. **1966** J. H. CADWELL *Topics Recr. Math.* xiv. 157 Because of the steadily decreasing terms, when the series is truncated the error incurred is of smaller magnitude than the first term omitted. **1968** P. A. P. MORAN *Introd. Probability Theory* ii. 78 It is also sometimes useful to exclude more than one of the possible values of i, and in this case it is more often necessary to truncate at the other end. **1981** *Nature* 5 Nov. 14/3 The series in equation (1) should extend to $m = n = \infty$, but in practice the series is truncated at a maximum value..of m and n, usually in the range 8 to 15.

truncated, *ppl. a.* Add: **2. e.** *Statistics.* Of a frequency distribution or sample: obtained by disregarding values of the variate greater than or less than some chosen value. Of a variate: treated in this way.

1931 R. A. FISHER *Truncated Normal Distribution in Math. Tables* (Brit. Assoc. Adv. Sci.) I. p. xxxiii, The frequency of the truncated distribution in the range dx. **1952** A. HALD *Statistical Theory with Engin. Applications* vi. 146 The cumulative distribution functions of three truncated distributions..with degrees of truncation of 10, 30 and 50% respectively. **1971** C. R. HEATHCOTE *Probability* v. 240 Truncated variables are often easier to handle than the original ones, and..under wide conditions, the two sequences have the same asymptotic behaviour.

f. Of soil: having lost the upper horizon(s) as a result of rapid erosion.

1938 A. B. YOLLAND tr. *A. de Sigmond's Princ. Soil Sci.* xiv. 206 These truncated forest soils possess a peculiar dynamics of their own. **1941** H. JENNY *Factors of Soil Formation* v. 100 Owing to differences in color of the *A* and *B* horizons, truncated profiles are often readily discernible on freshly plowed slopes. **1976** L. F. CURTIS et al. *Soils Brit. Isles* 315 Truncated podzols. Here the surface soil has the characters of a B horizon.

truncation. Add: **2. c.** *Statistics.* The cutting off of a frequency distribution at a certain value of the variate.

1937 YULE & KENDALL *Introd. Theory of Statistics* (ed. 11) vi. 103 We can picture it as a slightly skew distribution which has been cut off on the left owing to the inadmissibility of negative values of the variate. Discontinuous variates not infrequently give rise to this effect of truncation. **1952** [see *TRUNCATED *ppl. a.* 2 e].

d. The loss or removal of the upper horizon(s) of a soil by erosion.

1941 H. JENNY *Factors of Soil Formation* v. 100 An example of widespread truncation is provided by the Cecil series of the Piedmont Plateau. **1972** J. G. CRUICKSHANK *Soil Geogr.* iv. 133 Loss of surface horizons by erosion (truncation) is more common in Oxisols [than in Spodosols].

e. *Math.* The cutting short of a numerical computation or expression before its natural end (if any). Usu. *attrib.* in *truncation error.*

1952 D. R. HARTREE *Numerical Analysis* x. 223 The solution of the set of equations..is not, of course, the solution of the partial differential equation on account of the truncation error of the approximation. **1968** FOX & MAYER *Computing Methods for Scientists & Engineers* x. 205 For the fourth-order Runge–Kutta method the truncation error is the factor h^5 multiplying a rather complicated expression involving derivatives of $f(x, y)$. **1973** [see *ROUNDING *vbl. sb.*[1] 1 c].

trundle, *v.* Add: **1. c.** (Earlier and later examples.)

1849 *Punch* 14 July 12/1 In those Days..they did moderately trundle the Ball under-hand; but now they fling it over-handed from the Elbow. **1861** *Baily's Mag.* July 140 Such bowling as was trundled by Mr. Lyttelton and Mr. Salter in this innings is rarely witnessed in a University match. **1870** *Ibid.* Dec. 213 Six out of the eleven have trundled the ball. **1898** G. GIFFEN *With Bat & Ball* iii. 47 The bowlers, too, trundled with that specially placed on-field in their mind's eye. **1959** *Punch* 3 June 747/2 Four of the team bowl leg-spinners.., and Gupte is reported to be the best of his type now trundling.

trundling *vbl. sb.* (earlier examples in sense 1 c of the vb.)

1861 W. J. PROWSE in *Bell's Life* 10 Nov. 6/3 But however good their trundling—pitch or pace, or break, or spin—Still the monarch of all bowlers, to my mind, was Alfred Mynn! **1862** *Baily's Mag.* Apr. 260 The Eleven then commenced batting to the trundling of Moore and Conway.

trundler. b. (Earlier example.)

1871 [see *SNICK *v.*[2] 2 b].

trunk, *sb.* Add: **I. 1. d.** (see quot. 1950). Cf. *trunk dial,* sense 18 in Dict.

1899 F. J. BRITTEN *Old Clocks and Watches* 316, I am able to give an engraving of a very early specimen of a long-case clock... This case is of oak and panelled. The head is fixed on the trunk, and will not take off. **1950** D. DE CARLE *Watchmakers' & Clockmakers' Encyclopædic Dict.* 188/1 *Trunk,* refers to the body or main part of the case of a long-case clock. The case is formed of three parts, the trunk, the Hood..and the Plinth. **1978** *Times* 17 June 9/5 A dial clock is basically a clock with a round dial which hangs on the wall, or a round dial with a trunk underneath, which is called a trunk dial or drop dial.

4. c. *Teleph.* (*a*) A telephone line connecting two exchanges a long way apart or in different telephone areas; also (*U.S.*), a line connecting exchanges within the same area (cf. *toll call* s.v. *TOLL *sb.*[1] 3); (*b*) a line connecting selectors or the like of different rank within an exchange.

1889 PREECE & MAIER *Telephone* 249 This switchboard is required to distribute the trunks between the different offices [*sc.* exchanges], and also to enable the testing of all the trunk and subscribers' lines to be carried on from one central point. **1908** *Jrnl. Inst. Electr. Engineers* XLI. 120 In America the *local* term remains the same, the *junction* is called 'trunk', and our *trunk* is called a 'toll' or 'long-distance' line. **1921** W. AITKEN *Autom. Telephone Syst.* I. 4 The designation of the lines interconnecting apparatus at different switching stages..is somewhat confusing. The American generally speaks of these as trunks, which practically is equivalent to our junctions... For example, the circuits between first and second preselectors,..second and third selectors, and third selectors and connectors, are all trunks or junctions... Very commonly the lines between exchanges in this country [*sc.* Britain], and for the use of which an extra charge is made.., are known as trunks. For these the American terms toll line or long-distance line is used. **1925** WRIGHT & PUCHSTEIN *Telephone Communication* ii. 33 It is necessary in central-energy systems to serve districts of more than ten thousand lines by means of a number of central offices connected by trunk circuits or trunks. **1966** *McGraw-Hill Encycl. Sci. & Technol.* XIII. 433/1 When the extension user dials the first digit, the wipers of the first selector step upward to the level corresponding to the digit dialed, and automatically step around in a horizontal arc..until they find an idle trunk. **1978** *Sci. Amer.* June 90/2 A modern telephone exchange is connected not only to its own subscribers but also, through special lines called trunks, to other exchanges serving other subscribers. **1978** P. H. SMALE *Telecommunication Syst. I* vii. 60 There are various grades of exchange in order of importance... There are also various grades of interconnecting line, for example subscribers lines, junctions and trunks, and again the number gets fewer as length, importance and cost increase.

(ii) *pl.* The operators who deal with trunk calls. *colloq.*

[**1889** PREECE & MAIER *Telephone* xx. 353 As the trunk operators had too much to do..a special plan was arranged by which a subscriber requiring a connection to another town mentions the word 'trunk' to the ordinary operator.] **1947** N. CARDUS *Autobiogr.* III. 233 He rang me up at my Manchester house; he was speaking from Harrogate. When 'trunks' gave me notice of his call I expected something urgent. **1977** C. McCULLOUGH *Thorn Birds* ix. 203 Give me trunks, please, switch... I want to put an urgent call through.

II. 7. b. *N. Amer.* The luggage compartment of a motor vehicle; = *BOOT *sb.*[3] 4 c.

[**1929** *Hearst's Internat. Mag.* Nov. 210 (Advt.), Six wire wheels and trunk rack standard equipment. **1930** *Automobile Topics* 6 Dec. 359/3 Rear-end trunks were larger and more prevalent. In one line of cars they were designed into the rear of the body itself.] **1931** *Amer. Home* Apr. 197 The luggage belongs in the trunk on the rear of the car. **1937** *Sat. Even. Post* 2 Oct. 28/3 The enlarged trunks will hold enough luggage to carry you around the world. **1951** J. W. VALE *Mod. Auto Body & Fender Repair* xiii. 162 The deck compartment, sometimes referred to as the rear trunk compartment or the turtle back..may be repaired in the same way. **1960** *Times* 14 Sept. 12/6 When we hired a car in California we found that a car..bristles with surprises. You..find the spare wheel in the trunk. **1964** MRS. L. B. JOHNSON *White House Diary* 24 Apr. (1970) 119 Lyndon had transferred to an open convertible. Along the way he made three unscheduled stops, standing on the trunk of his car. **1968** *Globe & Mail* (Toronto) 17 Feb. 49/9 (Advt.), Extra lighting inside, in hood, in trunk. **1975** N. LUARD *Robespierre Serial* v. 34 The Belgian unlocked the trunk, stood by the porter while he lifted out two suitcases.

10. i. *U.S.* A floodgate or sluice controlling the flow of water into and out of rice-fields.

1856 in *Documentary Hist. Amer. Industr. Society* (1910) I. 120 Trunk-minders undertake the whole care of the trunks. **1903** 'P. PENNINGTON' *Woman Rice Planter* (1913) i. 8 Each field has a very small flood-gate (called a trunk), which opens and closes to let the water in and out. **1939** *Sat. Even. Post* 10 June 37/2, I opened all my rice-field trunks, so that the flowed field inside would equalize the pressure from the flood outside, thus saving my banks.

IV. 17. c. For *U.S.* read 'orig. *U.S.*' and add later examples. *swimming trunks*: see *SWIMMING *vbl. sb.* 6.

1941 BAKER *Dict. Austral. Slang* 78 *Trunks,* swimming shorts. **1956** P. SCOTT *Male Child* I. vi. 86 Except for a pair of swimming trunks he was naked. **1964** L. DEIGHTON *Funeral in Berlin* xviii. 107 A blond man in very small knitted swimming-trunks. **1982** S. B. FLEXNER *Listening to Amer.* 61 Men's *trunks* had been in use by professional swimmers and athletes since the 1880s.

d. Knickers; underpants with short legs.

[**1926–7** *Army & Navy Stores Catal.* 705/1 Gent's underwear..Trunk drawers—18/6.] **1936** [see *ankle-sock* s.v. *ANKLE *sb.* 3]. **1970** *Kay & Co.* (Worcester) *Catal.* *1970–71* Autumn–Winter 452 *Meridian trunks.* New style with shorter leg and continental front.

V. 18 (sense 4 a) *trunk route, -wire* (earlier example); (sense *4 c) *trunk circuit*; (senses 6, 7) *trunk room, -seller, strap*; (sense 15) *trunk-nosed* adj. (earlier example); **trunk-cabin** (example); **trunk-deck** (example); **trunk dialling** (see quot. 1971); **trunk murder,** a murder after which the body is hidden in a trunk; also **trunk murderer**; **trunk-road** (further examples); *spec.* in *Grand* (also *Great*) *Trunk Road,* the great highway between Calcutta and Amritsar constructed during the British Raj; **trunk-work** (later example in allusion to quot. 1611). See also *TRUNK LINE.

1878 F. O. DAVENPORT *On Man-of-War* 197 The captain had a small trunk cabin, a little higher and abaft ours. **1896** Trunk circuit [see *TRUNKING *vbl. sb.*[2] 2]. **1921** *Jrnl. Inst. Electr. Engineers* LIX. 390/2 (*caption*) Trunk circuits radiating from London to provincial towns. **1896** *Nautical Mag.* LXV. 1076 Oscar II..a trunk deck vessel of the type invented by Mr. W. Hök. **1952,** etc. Trunk dialling [see *subscriber trunk dialling* s.v. *SUBSCRIBER 3]. **1959** *Ann. Reg. 1958* 505 Trunk dialling from Bristol began in December. **1971** *Gloss. Electrotechnical, Power Terms* (*B.S.I.*) III. ii. 20 *Trunk dialling,* control of an exchange's automatic switching equipment from an exchange in another multi-exchange area over trunk or toll circuits. **1976** *Times* 20 Dec. (Istanbul Suppl.) p. iv/3 Although international trunk-dialling is promised..it can take anything up to 15 minutes to get a dialling tone..in Istanbul. **1905** *Daily Mail* 15 Apr. 5/4 (*heading*) The trunk murder. How the bodies were found. **1936** G. GREENE *Journey without Maps* I. i. 11 Another clue in a trunk murder case. **1976** S. HYNES *Auden Generation* v. 136 The crimes..are actual-sounding crimes: a trunk murder at Paddington station, a girl killed on Streatham Common. **1925** P. SELVER tr. *K. Capek's Lett. from Eng.* 54 At Madame Tussaud's..in the catalogue I found..Arthur Devereux, hanged 1905, known as the 'trunk murderer', because he hid the corpses of his victims in trunks. **1962** G. BUTLER *Coffin in Oxford* xiv. 176 Discovered your trunk murderer yet? **1887** KIPLING *From Sea to Sea* (1899) I. 114 The Englishman..took off his hat to the tun-bellied, trunk-nosed God of Good-Luck. **1851** *Ret. Public Works India* 146 in *Parl. Papers* XLI. 513 Documents..report the progress of the works on the Great Trunk Road. **1848** J. BOURNE *Let.* 24 Apr. in *Railways in India* (ed. 2) 19 The grand trunk road, connecting Calcutta with the north west provinces..is already a railway all but the rails. **1888** KIPLING *Departmental Ditties* (1890) 19 All those hairy gentlemen..Swaggered down the Grand Trunk Road into Bow Bazar. **1931** J. W. GREGORY *Story of Road* xviii. 274 In 1839 it was decided to construct a metalled road, the Grand Trunk Road, from Calcutta to Delhi.. By 1849 about £300,000 had been spent on it. **1937** *Archit. Rev.* LXXXI. 155 The Trunk Roads Act comes into operation on April 1st. **1974** *Listener* 2 May 574/3 Bentinck's Governor-Generalship..was not a complete failure, as the Great Trunk Road shows. **1698** J. VERNEY *Let.* 16 June in M. M. Verney *Verney Lett.* (1930) I. iii. 31 The little long room that is under the Trunk room of the Purple Chamber. *a* **1752** LD. VERNEY *Will* in *Ibid.* II. xxxiii. 246, I give to her..all the money & Jewels in the cabinet in the Trynk Room. **1860** J. G. HOLLAND *Miss Gilbert's Career* (1866) 293 Cheek was..led to the trunk-room of the lodging-hall. **1952** E. WILSON *Lilly's Story* i, in *Equations of Love* 133 A trunk-room full of the trunks which accompany a large English family in migration. **1970** *Times* 2 June (Container Suppl.) p. i/5 Container ships,..capable of carrying as much general cargo in a year on a trunk-route shuttle service as an entire fleet of traditional break-bulk cargo liners. **1855** TROLLOPE *Warden* xvi. 264 He remembered the shop distinctly; it was next door to a trunk-seller's. **1887** KIPLING *From Sea to Sea* (1899) I. 40 Jey Singh..would have hanged those Globe-trotters in their trunk-straps. **1970** *Country Life* 31 Dec. 1296/2 The hood, when up, was secured to the front mudguards by two stout trunk straps. **1885** *List of Subscribers, Classified* (United Telephone Co.) (ed. 6) 8 The very great cost of running and maintaining the Trunk wires between the different Exchanges. **1920** 'K. MANSFIELD' *Let.* 25 Sept. (1928) 46, I heard again from Methuen to-day. They now say they'd like 2 books for next spring. I think there must have been some trunk work, some back stair work in this on your part.

trunker (trʌ·ŋkəɹ). [f. TRUNK *sb.* or *v.*[2] + -ER[1].] **1.** (See quot. 1921). Cf. TRUNK *v.*[2] 2.

1881 *Instructions to Census Clerks* (1885) 84 Copper miner... Trunker. **1921** *Dict. Occup. Terms* (1927) § 056 *Trunker,* separates slimes from ore by running mixture into and out of a long box, launder or trunk.

2. a. A long-distance lorry-driver; *spec.* one who drives at night, and is not responsible for loading or unloading his vehicle.

1954 in P. G. Hollowell *Lorry Driver* (1968) vii. 192 *Trunker,* night driver. **1958** *Times* 12 Apr. 7/6 The long-distance night lorry driver, or trunker. **1959** *Manch. Guardian* 20 July 2/3 We night trunkers..pull out of the depot at seven or eight in the evening. **1968** P. G. HOLLOWELL *Lorry Driver* vii. 176 Although the trunker is a long distance driver and a night worker he is for the most part able to organize his leisure life as he has regular runs. He is not as able to do this as is the shunter who has the greatest rate of participation in associational groupings.

b. A lorry used for long journeys along trunk roads.

1965 M. RUSSELL *No Through Road* 20, I could see the..cars on the A.1 highway and hear the scream of the all-night trunkers. **1969** *Jane's Freight Containers 1968–69* 10 (Advt.), By freight-liner any number of Abel Air containers are carried by rail to terminals where they are readily transferred to trunker or local delivery units. **1979** *Navy News* Sept. 34/1 (Advt.), Driving artics., trunkers or vans or sorting and loading back at base.

trunking, *vbl. sb.*[2] Add: **1. b.** *spec.* a system of ducts or trunks (sense 10), esp. for cables or purposes of ventilation.

1923 *Man. Seamanship* (Admiralty) II. 284 The quantity of air supplied by a fan depends greatly on..the size and tortuosity of the trunking. **1950** *Engineering* 3 Feb. 123/1 Forced draught fans..arranged to draw air..and discharge it to the boilers through suitable trunking. **1963** *Times* 11 May 8/1, 60 electricians were dismissed for refusing to work on the trunking of electric cables on the frigate Mohawk. **1977** *Timber Trades Jrnl.* 17 Dec. 36/2 To blow the by-products from the hopper into a storage silo via trunking is..becoming a more common practice.

d. The driving of lorries on long journeys along trunk roads.

1968 P. G. HOLLOWELL *Lorry Driver* iii. 64 Trunking, being a night driving job, is heavy on the eyes, and also requires quick response to meet crises particularly on runs where the schedules are tight. **1974** P. WRIGHT *Lang. Brit. Industry* ii. 31 *Trunking* used to mean only night driving, but now, because of improved roads and speeds enabling travel to and from a far unloading point in one day, it includes *day-trunking.*

2. *Teleph.* [f. TRUNK *sb.*] The use or arrangement of trunks (sense *4 c). Freq. *attrib.*

1896 *Jrnl. Inst. Electr. Engineers* XXV. 639 Facilities for through trunking—*i.e.,* connecting two or more trunk circuits at intermediate offices to provide communication between towns not directly connected. **1933** *Discovery* Apr. 132/2 When all the direct junctions to an exchange are engaged, subsequent calls to that exchange are passed (or 'routed') through a central exchange. This feature of the system is termed 'alternative trunking'. **1947** *Electronic Engin.* XIX. 66 Automatic telephony is dealt with almost entirely by means of trunking diagrams and trunking calculations. **1979** DANIELSON & WALKER *Telecommunications Systems for Technicians I* ix. 79 A trunking diagram showing the connection of a subscriber to a desired number in a four-digit (up to 9999) exchange.

trunk line. 1. (In Dict. s.v. TRUNK *sb.* 18.) (Earlier examples.)

1843 R. WILSON *Let.* 13 Jan. in W. F. Cooke *Electric Telegraph* (1857) I. 219 Mr. Cooke's first object..would be to get the Telegraph laid down on the Croydon or some other trunk line. **1851** DICKENS *Our School* in *Househ. Words* 11 Oct. 81/1 The Railway had cut it up... A great trunk-line had swallowed the playground.

2. *Teleph.* = *TRUNK *sb.* 4 c (*a*).

1883 *Pall Mall Gaz.* 6 Dec. 12/2 The cost of laying a trunk line overhead averages about £25 a mile. **1893**

PREECE & STUBBS *Man. Telephony* xxi. 336 The main trunk lines—those connecting [London] with the various provincial exchanges—are invariably metallic. **1926** T. E. LAWRENCE *Seven Pillars* cxi. 590 Young and I cut the telegraph, here an important network of trunk and local lines. **1964** M. McLUHAN *Understanding Media* xxx. 306 Radio's use of the telephone in a glorified form of the old trunk-line wire-tapping. **1980** *Wall St. Jrnl.* 26 Nov. 10/2 The Federal Communications Commission voted to authorize American Telephone & Telegraph Co. to install an optical-fiber telephone trunk line between Washington and N.Y.

3. A large or main pipeline for oil or gas, esp. one from a production field to a refinery or terminal.

1896 REDWOOD & HOLLOWAY *Petroleum* II. VII. 475 As soon as the well is found to yield, the tank is connected by a 2-inch pipe with the trunk line. **1925** A. B. THOMPSON *Oil-Field Exploration & Devel.* II. xix. 1092 Long-distance trunk lines entail nearly as much work in surveys and construction as a railway. **1975** *Offshore* Sept. 195/2 The compressor will push the gas shoreward through a 67 mile, 42 inch diameter trunkline to a platform in West Cameron block 167 offshore Louisiana.

trunnel. Add: **trunnel-head** *U.S.* (earlier examples).

1819 E. EVANS *Pedestrious Tour* 270 The cogs, wallower, the trunnel-head and the stones [of a grist-mill]. **1839** *Knickerbocker* XIII. 345 Mill-wheels, and trunnel-heads.

truscottite (trɒ·skǫ̆təit). *Min.* [ad. Du. *truscottiet* (P. Hövig 1914, in *Jaarboek van het Mijnwezen in Nederlandsch Oost-Indië* XLI. 202), f. the name of S. J. *Truscott* (1870–1950), English mining engineer: see -ITE[1].] A hydrated basic silicate of calcium and manganese occurring as crystals of the hexagonal system that are typically pearly white.

1925 *Mineral. Mag.* XX. 466 Truscottite... Pearly white scales from the Lebong Donok gold-silver mine, Benkulen, Sumatra. **1979** *Ibid.* XLIII. 333/1 Truscottite and reyerite are of interest not only as natural minerals, but also because of their potential formation in cements hydrated at elevated temperatures and pressures, as in the casings of deep geothermal wells.

truss, *sb.* Add: **8. truss-block** (example).

1883 *Man. Seamanship for Boys' Training Ships R. Navy* (Admiralty) (1886) 26 Trestletrees are two pieces of hard wood, standing fore and aft... On their after ends an eye-bolt is driven from the lower side, for attaching the truss blocks to.

trusser. 2. c. (Earlier example.)

1857 A. MATHEWS *Tea-Table Talk* II. 96 It [*sc.* a chicken] had apparently made a vigorous struggle for continued existence, which struggle had evidently distorted its form out of the power of the trusser to regulate.

trust, *sb.* Add: **5. e.** *on trust*: (of a dog) obeying the command to trust (see *TRUST *v.* 1 b). Also *to play 'Trust'*.

1932 C. MORGAN *Fountain* i. 4 In Lewis's compartment were two former sergeants of marine, Lapham and Shordey, upright in opposite corners like dogs on trust. **1939** C. DAY LEWIS *Child of Misfortune* 196 Eve was trying to teach her puppy to play 'Trust' with a piece of biscuit. **1970** [see *PAID *ppl. a.* 4 a].

7. b. (Earlier example.)

1877 J. WANAMAKER in J. H. Appel *Business Biogr. John Wanamaker* (1930) x. 137 Why should not individual ownership be permitted to grow peaceably and equally with industries that are bunched into trusts?

8. a. *trust-fund* (earlier examples).

1780 J. FIFE *Let.* 29 Feb. in A. & H. Tayler *Lord Fife & his Factor* (1925) v. 121 After his death, you know how I was involved in a trust-fund. **1862** *Harper's Mag.* Aug. 337/1 Mr. Pennington has a considerable practice as a lawyer and a handsome private estate. He has, as a consequence, many trust funds.

b. trust-buster *colloq.* (orig. *U.S.*), one who works for the dissolution of trusts (sense 7 b); *spec.* a government official responsible for the enforcement of legislation against trusts; hence **trust-busting** *vbl. sb.* and *ppl. a.*; **trust corporation** *Law*, a corporation empowered to act as a trustee; **trust deed** (earlier examples); **Trust House**, a hotel owned by a company called Trust Houses, which was founded in 1903 to restore the traditional high standards of the best of the old coaching inns, and merged with Forte Holdings Ltd. in 1970 to form Trusthouse Forte; **trust officer** *N. Amer.*, an officer of a trust company or similar institution who has direct responsibility for the institution's activities as a trustee; **Trust Territory**, a territory administered by a nation acting on behalf of the United Nations Organization; cf. *TRUSTEESHIP 2 b.

1903 *Chicago Chron.* 11 Apr. 2 Mr. Knox is surprising everybody by his zeal as a trust-buster. **1949** *Time* 9 May 34/3 U.S. trustbusters were still locked in stalemate with the Zaibatsu. **1979** *N.Y. Times Mag.* 30 Sept. 60/2 'Fighting the oil and gas lobby'..was soon to become more fashionable among liberals than it had been since the turn of the century, when the muckrakers and the trust-busters were riding high. **1911** *Daily Colonist* (Victoria, B.C.) 22 Apr. 13/5 Clark McClercher..has been appointed special assistant to the attorney-general with 'trust-busting' duties. **1944** *Chicago Daily News* 8 May 10/1 So we have a faint revival of 'trust busting' to give color to the stuff. **1973** *Business Week* 13 Jan. 32/1 The Administrative Council for Economic Defense (ACED)..claims to be the only trustbusting agency in Latin America. **1925** *Act* 15 *Geo. V* c. 18 § 30. 422 Where there is a sole personal representative, not being a trust corporation, it shall be obligatory on him to appoint an additional trustee. *Ibid.* § 117. 491 'Trust corporation' means the Public Trustee or a corporation either appointed by the court..or entitled by rules made under..the Public Trustee Act, 1906, to act as custodian trustee. **1967** E. RUDINGER *Wills & Probate* 12 The Public Trustee is a government department which can be appointed to be your executor, as can some trust corporations. *a* **1754** P. GRANT *Decisions of Court of Session* (1813) II. 490 The Lords *nem. con.* found action competent upon the trust-deed. **1812** *Dramatic Censor 1811* 400 The creditors on the trust deed, consisting of authors, performers, tradespeople, and others, had due to them 52,611 *l.* [**1900** EARL GREY in *Econ. Rev.* (1901) XI. 101 Arrangements have already been made for the formation of a Public-house Trust Company (Limited) for the county of Northumberland.] **1902** EARL OF CARLISLE in *Monthly Rev.* Feb. 36 This decision..may affect the reformed trust houses. **1915** *Nineteenth Cent.* Jan. 68 The whole atmosphere of these Trust Houses..is essentially different to that of the average Trade house. **1928** *Evening News* 18 Aug. 11/7 No attempt was made to define 'disinterested management', but one gathered..that it is supposed to be found in 'trust houses'. **1942** E. WAUGH *Put out More Flags* i. 22 Basil will be covered with medals while your silly old yeomanry are still messing in a Trust House. **1972** 'M. DELVING' *Shadow of Himself* i. 17, I ..looked up hotels. There was a Trust House there, the White Swan. **1905** KIRKBRIDE & STERRETT *Mod. Trust Company* iii. 41 The trust officer must have full authority over his department. **1965** H. HOOD in R. Weaver *Canad. Short Stories* (1968) 2nd Ser. 221 You're doing splendidly. You have all your friends in the office and inside of two years you'll be a trust officer. **1976** *Globe & Mail* (Toronto) 16 Feb. 15/6 One prominent trust officer calculated that the increase would cost his company an additional $84,000 a year. **1945** *U.N. Charter* xii. § 75, in *Times* 27 June 8/5 The United Nations shall establish under its authority an International Trusteeship System for the administration and supervision of..Trust Territories. **1970** *Internat. & Compar. Law Q.* XIX. 218 New Guinea was a Mandated Territory... Its change of status in 1946 to become a Trust Territory [etc.]..have not affected section 16.

c. Passing into *adj. Soc. Psychol.* Applied to activities in which an individual is required to display trust or confidence, esp. as *trust game*. Also with reference to techniques aimed at measuring or achieving trust.

1967 J. B. ROTTER in *Jrnl. Personality* XXXV. 653 (*heading*) Construction of the interpersonal trust scale. **1972** *Psychol. Report* XXX. 850 The authors recognize that it is inappropriate to call this particular activity a trust exercise. **1975** *Psychol. Abstr.* LIII. 1181/1 Behavior ..was related to choice in the 'competition' game but not in the 'trust' game. **1978** *Peace News* 25 Aug. 10/2 As I see it, trust games (for example) don't produce trusting groups any more than brooms sweep floors.

trust, *v.* Add: **1. b.** Imperative: an instruction given to a dog, requiring it to wait for a reward, usu. in a begging position with a titbit placed on its nose. Cf. *TRUST *sb.* 5 e.

1854, etc. [see *PAID *ppl. a.* 4 a]. **1921** W. DE LA MARE *Mem. Midget* xlix. 331 Finger and thumb outstretched above the cringing little dog... 'Trust, Plum, trust!' **1930** M. ALLINGHAM *Mystery Mile* xiv. 132, I put a bit of sugar on his nose and said 'Trust'. **1974** G. BUTLER *Coffin for Canary* ix. 104 David was throwing him biscuits as to an old dog and saying 'trust'.

trusteeship. Add: **2. a.** The function of a colonial power or other dominant people as protectors of a subject people.

1936 *Internat. Labour Rev.* June 856 Something must be done at once to remedy a state of affairs which.. constitutes a flagrant breach of that ideal of trusteeship of Native races not yet able to stand by themselves under the strenuous conditions of the modern world. **1943** *Ann. Reg. 1942* 88 The old ideas of exploitation [of colonial possessions] had of recent years given place to the new doctrine of trusteeship. **1944** J. C. SMUTS in H. G. Wells *'42 to '44* II. 71, I remember Cecil Rhodes used to say that the proper relation between Whites and Blacks in this country [*sc.* S. Africa] was the relation between guardian and ward. This is the basis of trusteeship. Much later, this principle of trusteeship was put into the Covenant of the League of Nations. **1946** *Ann. Reg. 1945* 9 The whole House was committed to the doctrine of trusteeship, and beyond that of partnership.

b. The administration of a territory by a nation acting on behalf of the United Nations Organization. Freq. *attrib.* Cf. *Trust Territory* s.v. *TRUST *sb.* 8 b.

1945 *U.N. Charter* xii. § 79, in *Times* 27 June 8/5 The terms of trusteeship for each territory..shall be agreed upon by the States directly concerned. **1946,** etc. [see *MANDATE *sb.* 4 b]. **1952** *Times* 5 Aug. 3/7 The corporation is a Government-sponsored body set up by the Nigerian Government to develop 250,000 acres of plantations, formerly owned by Germans before the war, in the Cameroons territory, which was formerly under British mandate and is now under United Kingdom trusteeship. **1959** *Listener* 19 Nov. 880/1 The Belgian trusteeship territory of Ruanda-Urundi, Central Africa. **1962** *Observer* 14 Oct. 40/1 Sir Hugh Foot, Britain's representative in the United Nations on colonial and trusteeship questions, resigned.

trustify, *v.* Add: **trustified** *ppl. a.* (later examples); **trustification** (later examples).

1920 A. C. PIGOU *Econ. of Welfare* II. vii. 182 The marginal social net product of activities devoted to bringing about any widespread 'trustification' of industry is likely to be smaller than the marginal trade net product. **1922** *Encycl. Brit.* XXXII. 506/2 The large-scale and 'trustified' American capitalist system. **1938** L. HOGBEN *Science for Citizen* xiii. 653 Edison's later inventions sponsored the far-flung trustification of American industry. **1965** B. PEARCE tr. *Preobrazhensky's New Economics* 152 When there is trustification or syndication of important branches of production within a certain country, prices systematically..deviate from value in the upward direction. **1969** P. WORSLEY in Ionescu & Gellner *Populism* 223 Petty farmers..wanted a freer, more competitive, less trustified, market economy.

trusty, *a.* (*sb.*) Add: **A.** *adj.* **2. a.** Also *spec.* (orig. *U.S.*) designating a well-conducted convict to whom special privileges are granted.

1856 *Democratic State Jrnl.* (Sacramento, Calif.) 28 Oct. 2/3 The 'trusty guards', (commanded by Pete, Scotty acting as first lieutenant,) have recovered from the effects of their stolen debauch of Saturday. **1926** J. BLACK *You can't Win* iv. 40 A trusty prisoner appeared at my side. 'Come on, you.' **1968** *Listener* 15 Feb. 209/2 At this prison, the 200 guards are all trusty prisoners.

B. *sb.* **a.** (Earlier and later examples of sense 'a well-conducted convict to whom special privileges are granted'.) For 'in *U.S.*' read 'orig. in *U.S.*'

1855 *San Francisco Citizen* 2 Oct. 2/3 Two 'trusties' named Scottie and Greene, escaped in a whale boat from the State Prison grounds on Sunday night. **1912** in J. SANDILANDS *Western Canad. Dict. & Phrase-Bk.* **1926** J. BLACK *You can't Win* iv. 38 He told me to stay there till he could get a 'trusty' to take me upstairs. **1958** *People* 4 May 6/4 He was a trustie working in our records office. **1963** T. & P. MORRIS *Pentonville* ii. 27 The 'outside' men who go beyond the prison walls are selected 'trusties'. **1969** *Telegraph* (Brisbane) 29 May 2/7 (*heading*) Trusties plan no trouble. **1973** R. TRAVERS *Murder in Blue Mountains* x. 100 The Chief of Police banned all general visitors to Butler's cell and a trusty was put in with him to guard against any attempt at suicide.

truth, *sb.* Add: **II. 6.** So *out-of-truth* sb. Cf. TRUE *sb.* 3 in Dict. and Suppl.

1967 L. HOLMES *Odhams New Motor Man.* viii. 189/1 Out-of-truth produces irregular tyre wear.

7*. *Particle Physics.* = *TOP *sb.*[1] 17*. [An arbitrary choice of name.]

1977 *Sci. Amer.* Oct. 74/2 If the two new quarks do exist, there must also be two new properties of matter, which some physicists have taken to calling 'truth' and 'beauty'. **1978** [see *TOP *sb.*[1] 17*]. **1979** *Nature* 6 Dec. 546/2 They have included evidence for the 'gluon' (the photon of the quark-quark force), and excited states of the upsilon (which contains a beauty quark and its anti-particle), but 'truth' (the quark beyond and pairing with beauty) remains to be found.

III. 8. c. (Also with capital initial.) A game in which players have to answer truthfully questions put by the others or, in some forms of the game (called *truth, dare, promise*, etc., according to the rules), fulfil an alternative requirement.

1868 L. M. ALCOTT *Little Women* I. xii. 191 Do you know 'Truth'?..The person who draws at the number has to answer truly any questions put by the rest. **1928** *Sat. Even. Post* (U.S.) 29 Sept. 7/1 The ancient game of truth had begun. 'What's your favorite color, Bill?' **1959** I. & P. OPIE *Lore & Lang. Schoolch.* xviii. 377 In 'Truth, Dare, and Promise' each player has to agree either to tell the truth, accept a dare, or promise to do as he is told. **1969** —— *Children's Games* ix. 265 In Kidderminster the game is occasionally called 'Truth, Dare, Promise, or Kiss'; in Peterborough and Swansea, 'Do, Dare, Kiss, or Promise'; in Gloucester, 'Truth, Dare, Warning, Love, Kiss, or Marriage';..in Aberdeen, 'Truth, Dare, Force, or Promise'... At Spennymoor,..the game is called 'Truth, Dare, Will, Force, and Command'. **1970** *Times* 8 July 2/7 On one occasion she said, Carole Hanson..stripped to her panties during a game of 'truth, dare and promise'. **1980** G. M. FRASER *Mr American* xiii. 270 Playing truth or consequences in..Sir Charles's drawing-room.

V. 14. a. *truth-claim, -frequency, -relation.* **c.** *truth-searcher*; *truth-bending, -compelling, -loving* (earlier example), *-seeking* (earlier and later examples) sbs. and adjs.

1977 P. JOHNSON *Enemies of Society* xvii. 232 The title [*sc. Travesties*] reveals the fact that the whole play is an elaborate exercise in truth-bending and symmetrical confusion. **1979** *Tucson* (Arizona) *Citizen* 20 Sept. 2c/6 Tucson is..about to have a Liar's Contest to call its very own... Big Jim Griffith, banjo plucker, anthropologist, impresario, folklorist, Ph.D and himself no slouch in the truth-bending dept., phoned with the news. **1909** W. JAMES *Meaning of Truth* xiv. 273 Good consequences.. are proposed rather as the lurking *motive* inside of every truth-claim. **1977** A. GIDDENS *Stud. in Social & Polit. Theory* i. 78 An 'empirical intersection' subject to disputation in respect of truth claims. **1925** JOYCE *Let.* 27 Sept. (1957) I. 233, I am still under the influence of the 'truthcompelling' drug, scopolamine. **1936** *Mind* XLV. 501 The most complete and ingenious defence of the 'truth-frequency' interpretation of probability statements. **1949** A. PAP *Elem. Analytic Philos.* ix. 169 The truth-frequency of a form of influence is the limit approached by the ratio of the number of cases making both premisses and conclusion true to the number of cases making the premisses true. **1828** CARLYLE in *Foreign Rev.* II. 439 He has every feature also of a just, quiet, truth-loving man. **1947** H. REICHENBACH *Elem. Symbolic Logic* iv. § 33.178 The truth-preserving property of derivational processes. **1969** *Aristotelian Soc. Suppl. Vol.* XLIII. 77 It is tempting to generalize and actually define logical rules as truth-preserving grammatical rules. **1907** W. JAMES *Meaning of Truth* (1909) vii. 165 It is *between* the idea and the object that the truth-relation is to be sought and it involves both terms. **1952** *Mind* LXI. 193 The truth relation is repeatedly defined by Peirce in straightforward old-fashioned correspondence terms. **1928** A. HUXLEY *Point Counter Point* xxvi. 443 Truth-Searchers become just as silly..as the boozers. **1828** Truth-seeking [see *open-minded* adj. s.v. *OPEN *a.* 22 c]. **1896** W. JAMES in *New World* V. 345, I..cannot see my way to accepting the agnostic rules for truth seeking.

d. Special Combs.: **truth-condition** (see quot. 1937); **truth drug**, any substance that is administered to a person in the supposition that it will prevent him from lying; **truth-function** (see quots.); hence **truth-functional** *a.*, **truth-functionality**; **truth-functionally**; *adv.*; **truth game** = sense 8 c above; also *transf.*; **truth serum**, a truth drug in the form of an injection; **truth set** (see quot. 1966); **truth squad** *U.S. Politics*, a group of people with the task of questioning the truth of statements made by members of an opposing party; **truth-table**, a tabular representation of the truth or falsity of a complex proposition as determined by the possible combinations of truth-values of its components; also *transf.*, esp. in *Computer Sci.*; **truth-value** [ad. G. *wahrheitswert(h)*], the value of truth (or falsehood) assigned to propositions, esp. those of two-valued logic; also *transf.* and *attrib.*

1922 tr. *Wittgenstein's Tractatus* 95 The proposition is the expression of its truth-conditions. **1937** *Mind* XLVI. 191 Propositional complexes which are definable by reference to truth conditions *i.e.*, to propositions whose truth-values are logically *determined* by the truth-values of their arguments. **1978** P. PETTIT in Hookway & Pettit *Action & Interpretation* 48 Incompatible sentences have truth conditions which we cannot conceive of as being simultaneously fulfilled. **1931** 'A. ABBOT' *Murder of Geraldine Foster* xiii. 179 Neither the lie detector nor the truth drug have ever been officially adopted by the Police Department. **1947** *Lancet* 4 Jan. 39/1 If an attempt were made to use a 'truth drug' against an accused person in an English criminal court, the judge would reject its results as an involuntary confession. **1969, 1973** [see *PENTOTHAL]. **1976** T. SHARPE *Wilt* xiii. 140 You can put me on a lie detector. You can pump me full of truth drugs. **1909** W. JAMES *Meaning of Truth* i. 41 The reader will easily see how much of the account of the truth-function developed later in *Pragmatism* was already explicit in this earlier article. **1910** WHITEHEAD & RUSSELL *Principia Math.* I. i. 8 We may call a function $f(p)$ a 'truth-function' when its argument p is a proposition, and the truth-value of $f(p)$ depends only upon the truth value of p. **1967** *Encycl. Philos.* V. 76/2 *Truth-function*, a function whose arguments and values are truth-values. **1981** *Sci. Amer.* Oct. 155/1 A complete account of how the truth value of a compound sentence is determined by its constituent sentences is called a truth function, and logicians customarily display the evaluation of the truth function in an array called a truth table. **1947** *Mind* LVI. 237 A modern extensional logic containing the ordinary truth-functional modes of statement-construction. **1968** CHOMSKY & HALLE *Sound Pattern Eng.* 387 We note there that certain truth-functional conditions are required for the phonological rules. **1950** W. V. QUINE *Methods of Logic* (1952) § 2.8 The property of truth-functionality.. is thus enjoyed by negation, conjunction, and alternation. cases, to a semantic component based on truth-functionality. **1950** W. V. QUINE *Methods of Logic* (1952) § 7.37 in which it is used in linguistics—unrelated, in many cases, to a semantic component based on truth-functionality. **1950** W. V. QUINE *Methods of Logic* (1952) § 7.37 The one statement implies the other truth-functionally. **1935** F. SCOTT FITZGERALD *Taps at Reveille* 66, I thought you might want to know... I thought maybe you thought I liked somebody else. The truth game didn't get around to me the other night. **1941** 'N. BLAKE' *Case of Abominable Snowman* xviii. 198 Since we seem to be playing the truth game..did you kill Elizabeth Restorick? **1980** G. MITCHELL *Whispering Knights* iv. 42 'Why don't we play the Truth Game?' 'Because nobody will tell the truth.' **1925** F. J. REYNOLDS *Marvels of 1924* 44 Dr. House believes truth serum should be a part of every court and prison equipment. **19..** [see *SCOPOLAMINE]. **1977** J. CROSBY *Company of Friends* vi. 43 Acetol is the strongest truth serum there is. Do you remember talking, talking, talking? **1963** Truth set [see *solution set* s.v. *SOLUTION *sb.* 12]. **1966** *Britannica Bk. of Year* 807/2 *Truth set*, a mathematical or logical set containing all the elements that may be substituted in a given statement of relationships without altering the truth of the statement (the equation $x + 7 = 10$ has as its *truth set* the single number 3). **1952** *Tuscaloosa* (Alabama) *News* 3 Nov. 12/5 The Republican 'Truth Squad' after trailing President Truman across the country on his campaign trips, passed down its final verdict today that the President was 'guilty of over 100 lies, half-truths and distortions.' **1980** *Washington Star* 31 Oct. B1/1 GOP leaders formed what they called a 'truth squad' to campaign this week because they said Democrats have avoided the issues. **1921** E. POST in *Amer. Jrnl. Math.* XLIII. 166 The general notion of truth-table is not introduced [in *Principia Mathematica*]. *Ibid.* 167 So corresponding to each of the 2^n possible truth-configurations of the p's a definite truth-value of f is determined. The relation thus effected we shall call the truth-table of f. **1937** *Mind* XLVI. 191 Truth-tables which analytically exhibit the logical conditions under which a given truth-function..would be true, together with those under which it would be false. **1962** SIMPSON & RICHARDS *Physical Princ. Junction Transistors* xvi. 401 The above results may be most easily summarized for two transistors with two inputs A and B in the form of so-called truth tables, two of which are shown below. **1965** P. CAWS *Philos. of Sci.* xvi. 122 A decision procedure..for the sentential calculus..consists of constructing a truth-table for the *wff* in question. **1970** O. DOPPING *Computers & Data Processing* i. 26 From the truth table we can then derive a logical equation, which can be used as a basis for the program. **1977** *Sci. Amer.* Sept. 84/2 The first step in the design of the circuit is the construction of a truth table that gives the desired output for every possible combination of inputs. [**1891** G. FREGE in *Funktion, Begriff, Bedeutung* (1975) 26 Ich sage nun: 'der Wert unserer Funktion ist ein Wahrheitswert' und unterscheide den Wahrheitswert des Wahren von dem des Falschen.] **1903** B. RUSSELL *Princ. Math.* 502 There are, we are told.., three elements in judgment: (1) the recognition of truth, (2) the Gedanke, (3) the truth-value (*Wahrheitswerth*). **1932** LEWIS & LANGFORD *Symbolic Logic* vii. 215 In this calculus, it is important to distinguish the truth-*values*, 1, ?, and 0, from the truth-functions, *p*, *Mp*, and *Np*. **1936** WIRTH & SHILS tr. *Mannheim's Ideology & Utopia* 13 The truth-value of human knowledge in general. **1966** S. BEER *Decision & Control* viii. 165 Then this formulation is subjected to a truth-value analysis. **1978** J. MCDOWELL in Hookway & Pettit *Action & Interpretation* 129 Dummett's realist is attempting, with the truth-value-link manoeuvre, to respect that principle. **1981** A. BORN tr. F. Lasson in *Dinesen's Lett. from Afr.* p. xiv, The presumed documentary truth-value of the letters.

try, *sb.* Add: **III. 7.** *attrib.* and *Comb.*, as (sense 4 b) *try-getter*, *-getting*, *-scorer*, *-scoring*.

1954 J. B. G. THOMAS *On Tour* iv. 43 The two wings, were the try-getters. **1977** *Western Mail* (Cardiff) 5 Mar. 3/3 England could well feel the backlash of these frustrated Welsh try-getters. **1954** J. B. G. THOMAS *On Tour* 12 Without complete forward supremacy try-getting was like needle-hunting in the proverbial haystack. **1930** *Daily Express* 8 Sept. 10/5 Try-scorers for the tourists in the first half were Rew and Jones-Davies. **1976** *Scotsman* 27 Dec. 11/1 Earlier try-scorers for Gala were Gordon Dickson and George Telfer. **1974** *Times* 4 Feb. 7/2 With try-scoring so difficult, Wales missed a golden opportunity of taking a decisive lead midway through the first half.

try, *v.* Add: **5. d.** *to try out*: to test the advantages, possibilities, or qualities of (a material or immaterial thing); also, to test (a person). orig. *U.S.*

1888 *Judge* (N.Y.) 29 Dec. 190/1 Tried Out By Fire. **1899** *N.Y. Jrnl.* 30 July 34/6 Britain will try out heavy motor wagons. **1906** *N.Y. Evening Post* 26 Oct. 1 The new rules have been but partially tried out. **1974** A. PRICE *Other Paths to Glory* III. 254 He was being tried out on someone else's problem.

6. c. To submit (a case) for the judgment of a court of law. *U.S.*

1905 S. W. MITCHELL *Constance Trescot* 166 'Do you still feel that all chance of settlement is out of the question?' 'Yes; I am instructed to try the case.' **1931** *N. Amer. Rev.* Jan. 22 This is one of his jokes; he knows I can't afford to try criminal cases. It's been fifteen years since I've been in a criminal court.

7. e. To put (a person) to the test to ascertain the truth of what is asserted or believed of him or her. Freq. in imp. *try me.*

1970 V. CANNING *Great Affair* xi. 193 'You'll not like it.' 'Try me.' **1971** *Scope* (S. Afr.) 19 Mar. 124/2 'Miss Blandish..ahem..I take it that you can keep a secret?' 'Try me, Mr Stone.' Her voice was like a soft caress. Her suggestion to 'try her' scared J.B. **1984** A. PRICE *Sion Crossing* vi. 106 'I think maybe you won't like it, Oliver.'..'Try me.'

11. e. To test the effect of (a thing) *on* (a person, thing, etc.). *to try it on the* (or *a*) *dog*: to test the effectiveness of something on someone regarded as being of lesser consequence than those for whom it is ultimately intended; *Theatr.*, to test the possibilities of a play, etc., by performing it as a matinée or before a provincial audience. *colloq.* (orig. *U.S.*).

1890 in Barrère & Leland *Dict. Slang* II. 377/1 'Bootle's Baby' will on the 7th of May be produced somewhere in the provinces. This is what the Americans call trying it on a dog. **1897** *Daily Tel.* 4 Feb. 9/1 If any enterprising person desires to make money from a play or a composition of music he does not boldly attempt the experiment upon the public. His shrewd suspicion that they would avenge the torture induces him to adopt the preliminary precaution of 'trying it on the dog'—a creature of delicate susceptibilities, and very amenable to the influences of Teutonic bands and street-corner cornet solos. **1922** H. CRANE *Let.* 29 Sept. (1965) 101, I want to try *Dial* [a literary review] on 'F and H', before it goes anywhere else. **1941** G. HEYER *Envious Casca* xiv. 261 Mathilda had never felt less inclined to listen to a dissertation on the benefits of experience to an actress, and she very rudely told Paula to try it on the dog.

f. *to try in* (Dentistry): to place (a denture or prosthesis) in the patient's mouth to test the fit. [From the prepositional use illustrated in quot. 1896.]

[**1896** C. J. ESSIG *Amer. Textbk. Prosthetic Dentistry* xi. 408 After the teeth of a full upper denture have been tried in the mouth and found to be correct, a protective rim is to be made.] **1921** D. GABELL *Prosthetic Dentistry* viii. 199 The dentures should be placed in tepid water with some pleasant antiseptic,..and then each separately tried in. **1968** NEILL & NAIRN *Compl. Denture Prosthetics* 101/2 When trying in the waxed-up dentures initially the opportunity is taken to..check the jaw relationships.

g. *try anything once*: a cliché indicating (often somewhat unexpected) willingness on the part of a speaker to attempt or experience something new.

1921 *Ladies' Home Jrnl.* July 20/1 This slogan runs, 'Try anything once'. **1959** N. MAILER *Advts. for Myself* (1961) 160 'I am sort of curious about the film. I've never seen one [*sc.* a pornographic film], you know.' 'Try anything once, is that it?'

h. *try-your-strength*, *try-your-weight*: used *attrib.* to designate an apparatus at a fair or the like which tests or measures a person's strength or weight.

1929 J. B. PRIESTLEY *Good Companions* I. iv. 135 One o' these try-your-strength things..—down with the 'ammer and up she goes and rings the bell. **1930** R. LEHMANN *Note in Music* v. 214 A try-your-strength machine that gave him his money back. **1932** *Radio Times* 29 July 241/1 Everything to make them feel at home..try-your-weight machines, 'diddlers', peeps-at-Paris. **1963** WODEHOUSE *Stiff Upper Lip, Jeeves* iii. 24 There was plenty and to spare of the Rev. H. P. Pinker. Even as a boy..he must have burst seams and broken try-your-weight machines. **1977** 'E. CRISPIN' *Glimpses of Moon* vi. 97, I want to try the Try-Your-Strength machine.

try-. Add: **1. try-pot** (earlier example); **try-works** (earlier example).

1795 R. MURRY *Jrnl.* 12 Oct. in R. McNab *Hist. Rec. N.Z.* (1914) II. 523 The try pot and steam were as they were left. **1792** Z. MACY *Jrnl.* 15 May in *Mass. Hist. Soc. Coll.* (1810) III. 157 The oil [was] boiled out in the try works at sea.

2. try-in *Dentistry* [*TRY *v.* 11 f], the experimental trial of a denture or prosthesis in a patient's mouth as a preliminary to any further work; also, the prosthesis itself; **try-on,** (*a*) (earlier example); **try-out,** for '(*U.S. slang* or *colloq.*)' read '*colloq.* (orig. *U.S.*)' and add: (further examples); also, an experimental trial, a test of performance, a trial run or period, *spec.* of a play, etc., in a provincial theatre, etc.; also *attrib.*

1939 R. O. SCHLOSSER *Compl. Denture Prosthesis* xvi. 244 One of the dentures..may be completely processed, and a final try-in made while the opposing denture is still in the wax model state. **1963** C. R. COWELL et al. *Inlays, Crowns, & Bridges* iii. 26 Immediately before the try-in the temporary dressing must be removed. **1970** J. M. BUCHANAN *Atlas Compl. Denture Prosthesis* xix. 100/2 Replace the characterized mandibular try-in in the patient's mouth. **1977** M. M. HUDIS *Dental Lab. Prosthodontics* iv. 99 The teeth are arranged on the occlusion rims so that they may be returned to the dentist for a try-in. **1823** 'J. BEE' *Slang* 181 *Try-on*,..an essay or endeavour to do a thing. **1903** *Sci. Amer.* 30 May 414/1 Cup challengers in their try-outs in British waters. **1915** *Literary Digest* (N.Y.) 21 Aug. 361/2 The new Grinnell Sprinkler equipment..has already had its initial tryout. **1923** *N.Y. Times* 7 Oct. IX. 2/6 *Try out*, an experimental hearing of a new act, usually far away from Broadway. **1928** *Evening News* 18 Aug. 9/3 The play will not be given the provincial 'try-out'. **1933** P. GODFREY *Back-Stage* vi. 76 Had this play not first been produced at a 'try-out' theatre..its author might still be sending it round. **1941** B. SCHULBERG *What Makes Sammy Run?* i. 4 Sammy was getting a three-week tryout. **1963** A. ROSS *Australia 63* viii. 157 Davidson's final try-out in the nets was watched over..by two selectors, Bradman and Seddon. **1970** A. GLYN *Blood of Britishman* xxi. 275 Brief try-outs of plays before they arrive in London's West End. **1976** A. DAVIS *Television* 89 It is as difficult to predict which comedy series will succeed as to forecast which records will top the hit parade charts, and that is one of the reasons for the development of try-out series. **1983** *Listener* 17 Mar. 29/3 *Gilgamesh* was chosen to give the new technology a try-out.

trying, *vbl. sb.* **b. trying-pot** (earlier example).

1843 E. DIEFFENBACH *Trav. N.Z.* I. ii. 51 The blubber is..immediately put into the trying-pots.

trypaflavine (tripăflēⁱ·vīn). *Pharm.* [f. TRYPA(NOSOMA (see quot. 1954) + L. *flāv-us* yellow: see -INE⁵.] = *ACRIFLAVINE.

1913 *Chem. Abstr.* VII. 2944 Trypaflavine..and KCN.. give 3,6-diamino-N-methyl-ms-cyanoacridane,..partially converted back into trypaflavine by heating with conc. H_2SO_4. **1954** *Thorpe's Dict. Appl. Chem.* (ed. 4) XI. 381/2 Amongst purely organic substances, Acriflavine..was originally introduced as a trypanocide under the name *Trypaflavin*. **1975** *Biol. Abstr.* LX. 50/1 (*heading*) Investigation of the interaction between trypaflavine and nucleic acid components.

trypan. Add: **trypan blue** [rendering G. *trypanblau*], a diazo dye used as a vital stain and in the treatment of trypanosomiasis and other protozoan infections.

[**1909** *Parasitology* II. 187 Trypanblau and Trypanrot are highly efficient remedies in the treatment of canine piroplasmosis.] **1911** *Chem. Abstr.* V. 3495 (*heading*) Tryparosan, trypan red, trypan blue and parafuchsin in immunization against rabies. **1980** *Nature* 8 May 110 (*caption*) Viable cells (trypan blue exclusion) at 16 h after infection normally contained approximately 10% bi- and multinucleated heterokaryons.

trypanocidal (tri:pǎnosəi·dǎl), *a.* [f. TRYPANO(SOMA + -CIDE 1 in Dict. and Suppl. + -AL.] That is fatal to trypanosomes.

1909 *Practitioner* Feb. 248 Trypanocidal substances. **1946** A. A. MORTON *Chem. Heterocyclic Compounds* xii. 339 Crude dichloro ortho-para fuchsin proved less toxic but more trypanocidal than para fuchsin, methyl violet, and like compounds. **1976** P. COLLARD *Devel. Microbiol.* v. 55 Atoxyl is a very effective trypanocidal agent.

So **trypa·nocide**, a trypanocidal agent; = *trypanosomacide* s.v. TRYPANOSOMA.

1917 in STEDMAN *Med. Dict.* (ed. 4) 1012/2. **1956** *Nature* 31 Mar. 604/2 Contributions on trypanocides, antimalarials, amœbicides and on the chemotherapy of virus infections. **1977** *Lancet* 8 Oct. 769/1 On its own, S.H.A.M. is ineffective as a trypanocide in vivo, but when combined with glycerol it temporarily clears bloodstream trypanosomes in rodents infected with *T. brucei*.

trypanolysis (tripǎnǫ·lisis). [f. as prec. + *-LYSIS.] Destruction of trypanosomes; **trypanolytic** *a.* (in Dict. as main entry) (further example).

1905 *Index Medicus* 2nd Ser. III. 200/1 (Index), Trypanolysis. **1936** *Ann. Trop. Med. & Parasitol.* XXX. 377 Trypanolysis by mouse immune serum is very rapidly effective in the presence of added haemolytic complement. **1979** *Infection & Immunity* XXIV. 691/1 Eleven anti-*T[rypanosoma] brucei* and five anti-*T. congolense* IIg preparations were tested in the trypanolysis assay for the presence of trypanolytic factors.

trypanosome (in Dict. s.v. TRYPANOSOMA). Add: **b.** Used *attrib.* to designate trypanosomes and related hæmoflagellates at a stage in their life cycle when they have an elongated body with the flagellum arising from the posterior end. Cf. *TRYPOMASTIGOTE.

1924 HEGNER & TALIAFERRO *Human Protozool.* v. 151 Once these crithidial forms [of *Trypanosoma* spp.] are established in the salivary glands they probably form a permanent source for the production of the infective trypanosome forms. **1949** C. A. HOARE *Handbk. Med. Protozool.* xi. 171 The developmental stages through which trypanosomes pass in the course of their life-cycle.. comprise the trypanosome, crithidial and leishmanial forms, and occasionally also the leptomonad form. **1967** A. W. JONES *Introd. Parasitol.* xxix. 412 *Trypanosoma*.. may include all forms, and it parasitizes insect and vertebrate hosts. In the latter host, only the trypanosome form occurs.

trypanosomal *a.* (examples of the sense 'trypanosomid'); **trypanoso·mid** *sb.* and *a.* [ad. mod. L. *Trypanosomidæ* (F. Doflein *Die Protozoen als Parasiten und Krankheitserreger* (1901) 57): see -ID[3]], (pertaining to or designating) a member of the family Trypanosomidæ, which comprises trypanosomes and related species of flagellate protozoans which at some stage in their life cycle have an elongated body with one nucleus and a single flagellum arising from a kinetosome; also **trypanoso·matid** *sb.* and *a.* (corresponding to the synonymous family name Trypanosomatidæ).

1942 D. L. BELDING *Textbk. Clin. Parasitol.* xi. 144 The species..of the genus *Herpetomonas* have four stages in their life cycle, appearing as leishmanian, leptomonad, crithidial and trypanosomal forms. **1956** *Nature* 11 Feb. 279/2 (*heading*) A synthetic growth medium for the trypanosomid flagellate *Strigomonas* (*Herpetomonas*) *oncopelti*. *Ibid.*, This trypanosomid..is parasitic in the digestive tract of Hemiptera. **1962** *Jrnl. Protozool.* IX. 53/1 Because certain species of horseflies..have been incriminated in the transmission of trypanosomes of animals, a study of their own trypanosomatid parasites has a particular interest for students of insect flagellates. **1963** F. G. WALLACE in J. Ludvík et al. *Progr. in Protozool.* 70 The criteria that have been used most in the definition of genera among the trypanosomatids of insects have been morphological. **1971** MARKELL & VOGE *Med. Parasitol.* (ed. 3) vii. 115 In both the Gambian and Rhodesian forms of African trypanosomiasis, the parasites occur in the blood stream and central nervous system in the trypanosomal form. **1975** *Nature* 8 May 157/1 Calcium may be responsible for the control of flagellar activity in a trypanosomid flagellate, *Crithidia oncopelti*. **1977** C. D. BECKER in J. P. Kreier *Parasitic Protozoa* I. x. 370 Trypanosomes of fish appear to be similar to related trypanosomatids from the blood of other vertebrates.

tryparsamide (tripā·ɹsǎməid). *Pharm.* [f. TRYP(ANOSOMA + ARS(ENIC *sb.*[1] + AMIDE.] An arsenical organic compound, $C_8H_{10}AsN_2NaO_4 \cdot \frac{1}{2}H_2O$, used to treat trypanosomiasis and syphilis of the central nervous system.

1921 *Jrnl. Exper. Med.* XXXIII. 193 (*heading*) Therapeutic action of N-phenylglycineamide-*p*-arsonic acid (tryparsamide) upon experimental infections of *Trypanosoma rhodesiense*. **1935** *Lancet* 26 Jan. 193/2 After one injection of reduced tryparsamide the trypanocidal titre of the urine rapidly rose to an enormous level. **1974** *Trypanosomiasis & Leishmaniasis* (Ciba Foundation) 310 The problem of drug resistance has become of less importance since the discontinuance of tryparsamide for the treatment of established cases, and its replacement by melaminyl derivatives of arsenic such as melarsoprol and melarsonyl potassium.

trypomastigote (tripomæ·stigōᵘt). *Zool.* [f. Gr. τρυπ-ᾶν to bore + -O + Gr. μαστῑγ-, μάστιξ whip + -ώτης (see -OT[2], -OTE).] A stage in the life cycle of trypanosomes (see quot. 1966). Cf. *TRYPANOSOME b.

1966 HOARE & WALLACE in *Nature* 17 Dec. 1386/1 We have devised the following new terms...(3) Opisthomastigote.., for former 'trypanosome'..stage, represented..by forms with postnuclear kinetoplast; flagellum arising near it and emerging from its anterior end...(5) Trypomastigote.., for the true 'trypanosome' stage, represented by forms with postnuclear kinetoplast; flagellum arising near it and emerging from the side of the body to run along a long undulating membrane. **1980** J. N. FARMER *Protozoa* vi. 225/1 Trypomastigotes reproduce in the vertebrate host by means of longitudinal binary fission except in the case of *Trypanosoma* (*S.*) *cruzi*.

trypsinize (tri·psinəiz), *v. Biochem.* [f. TRYPSIN + -IZE.] *trans.* To treat with trypsin. So **try·psinized** *ppl. a.*, **try·psinizing** *vbl. sb.*

1952 *Jrnl. Immunol.* LXIX. 688 The cultures prepared with trypsinized tissue were inoculated on the 8th day of incubation. **1959** *Virology* VIII. 396 Because these cultures sometimes contained tissue lumps which interfered with plaque production, they were usually trypsinized. **1971** *Nature* 30 July 312/2 After 10–14 days, wells containing single colonies were trypsinized. **1974** F. WARNER *Meeting Ends* I. vi. 25 Oh my head! I'm trypsinized, pepsinized, falling to bits. **1979** *Experientia* XXXV. 244/2 When the cells reached confluency standard trypsinizing procedures were used to remove them from the flask surface.

Also **trypsiniza·tion**, treatment with trypsin.

1959 *New Scientist* 19 Feb. 396/1 (*caption*) Trypsinization of monkey kidney for tissue-culture. **1980** *Parasitology* LXXX. 374 They were removed from the T-75 flask by trypsinization.

tryptamine (tri·ptǎmīn). *Biochem.* [f. *TRYPT(OPHAN + AMINE.] An amine, $C_8H_6NCH_2CH_2NH$, related to tryptophan, from which it is produced by decarboxylation and which itself is oxidized to indoleacetic acid.

1929 R. A. GORTNER *Outl. Biochem.* xx. 445 Tyramine, histamine, and tryptamine, all have a powerful physiological action. **1963** *Lancet* 19 Jan. 127/1 Indole and tryptamine are formed by the action of bacteria on unabsorbed tryptophan in the colonic lumen. **1980** G. GUROFF *Molecular Neurobiol.* ix. 127 An overload of tryptophan and/or an amine oxidase inhibitor is required to produce pharmacological evidence for tryptamine formation [in brain tissue].

tryptophan (in Dict. s.v. TRYPTIC *a.*). Also **tryptophane.** Add: **a.** An amino-acid essential in the diet of vertebrates; *β*-3-indolylalanine, $(C_8H_6N)CH_2CH(NH_2)COOH$. (Earlier and later examples.) [a. G. *tryptophan* (R. Neumeister 1890, in *Zeitschr. f. Biol.* XXVI. 3).]

1890 *Jrnl. Chem. Soc.* LVIII. 804 The term tryptophan is suggested for the substance which is formed during pancreatic digestion from proteïds, and which gives a reddish-violet coloration with bromine. **1922** *Sci. Amer.* July 42/3 Certain of the amino acids, of which about 19 have been found in proteins, are absolutely essential for growth and maintenance, among which are lysine, cystine and tryptophane. **1945, 1949** [see *CO-FACTOR 2]. **1956** *Nature* 3 Mar. 422/2 Supplementation of the [rats'] diet with either nicotinic acid or tryptophan had no effect on this depressed growth-rate. **1978** *Detroit Free Press* 5 Mar. (Parade Suppl.) 13 (Advt.), Pay less for more protein potency! A whole and complete protein derived from soybean. 0% carbohydrates, 325 mg tryptophane, 26 grams protein with lecithin and papain. **1979** *Time* 2 Apr. 42/2 Only a small dose of tryptophan—which is found in many foods, notably milk—seems to ease the insomniac to sleep.

b. Special Comb.: **tryptophan synthetase**, a bacterial enzyme that synthesizes tryptophan.

1955 C. YANOFSKY in Colowick & Kaplan *Methods in Enzymol.* II. I. 233 Tryptophan synthetase from *Neurospora*... This enzyme has also been called tryptophan desmolase... The name tryptophan synthetase was suggested by the editors of this volume. **1976** *Ann. Rev. Microbiol.* XXX. 413 Where this has been specifically tested—with tryptophan synthetase subunits in *Escherichia coli*..homologies have not been found.

Hence **try·ptophanase** [a. Jap. *tryptophanase* (K. Kurono et al. 1932, in *Jrnl. Agric. Chem. Soc. Japan* VIII. 82): see *-ASE], an enzyme catalysing the breakdown of tryptophan into ammonia, indole, and pyruvic acid.

1932 *Chem. Abstr.* XXVI. 5107 (*heading*) Tryptophan-decomposing enzyme, tryptophanase. **1963** *Lancet* 19 Jan. 128/1 Glucose reduces indole formation by inhibiting tryptophanase synthesis.., but does not affect the activity of tryptophanase already present. **1976** *Ann. Rev. Microbiol.* XXX. 421 Tryptophanase from *Escherichia coli* can catalyze the reversal of its normal function, forming L-tryptophan from indole, pyruvate, and ammonia.

Tsaconian, var. *TSAKONIAN *sb.* and *a.*

tsaddik (tsa·dik). *Judaism.* Also **tsadik, tzaddik, tzaddiq, zaddik,** etc. Pl. **-kim, -ks.** [a. Heb. *ṣaddīq* just, righteous.] A man of exemplary righteousness; a Hasidic spiritual leader or sage.

1873 *New Era* (N.Y.) III. 75 These zadiks, or leaders, have no fixed salary. **1881** [see *REBBE]. **1904** *Jewish Encycl.* VI. 253/2 The Hasidim were, however, particularly noted for the exalted worship of their 'holy' zaddikim. **1907** I. ZANGWILL *Ghetto Comedies* 409 A *Tsaddik* (wonder-rabbi) was killed in the last *pogrom*. **1933** S. BIRNBAUM *Life & Sayings Baal Shem* p. iii, Chassidism..is characterized..by a new psychic and material organization of comprehensive scope, at whose center of crystallization stand the *tzaddikim*, the 'righteous ones', the masters of the souls of men. **1941** G. G. SCHOLEM *Major Trends in Jewish Mysticism* ix. 338 The existence of the Zaddik or saint as the actual proof of the possibility of living up to the ideal. **1964** M. WOHLGELERNTER *I. Zangwill* vii. 111 The numerous sects that mushroomed all over Europe, each with its own *Zaddik* performing untold 'miracles'. **1968** *Observer* 10 Nov. 26/5 He was bound to end up..a great chassidic *Tsadik*. **1974** *Encycl. Brit. Micropædia* X. 225/3 In the..movement known as Ḥasidism, the Jewish religious leader (*tzaddiq*) was viewed as a mediator between man and God. Since the *tzaddiq*'s life was expected to be a living expression of the Torah, his behaviour was even more important than his doctrine. **1982** *Times* 18 June 13/3 The world has much need of such *tsaddiks* (righteous men).

Tsakonian (tsǎkōᵘ·niǎn), *sb.* and *a.* Also **-c-, Tz-.** [f. *Tsakon*, a region in the eastern Peloponnese, Greece + -IAN.] (Of or pertaining to) a modern Greek dialect spoken in an area of the south-eastern Peloponnese, containing ancient elements not derived from the koinē.

1902 *Encycl. Brit.* XXIX. 102/2 Certain peculiar dialects, such as the Tzakonian in the south-eastern Morea. **1925** P. RADIN tr. *Vendryès's Language* ii. 46 For the present Tsaconian still seems to use it [*sc.* digamma]. **1933** C. D. BUCK *Compar. Gram. Gk. & Lat.* 20 The present Tsaconian dialect, spoken in a small portion of Laconia,..is in part the offspring of ancient Laconian. **1939** A. J. TOYNBEE *Study of Hist.* VI. 71 This 'Tsakonian' *patois* is the only surviving form of spoken Greek that is not derived from the Attic κοινή. **1972** W. B. LOCKWOOD *Panorama Indo-Europ. Lang.* 7 Tsakonian is the outlandish dialect of perhaps as many as 10,000 speakers in an area difficult of access along the forbidding coast of the Peloponnese between the Parnon Range and the Gulf of Argolis.

tsamba. Add: (Earlier example.) Also **tsampa, tsumpa.**

1852 *Dublin Rev.* XXXIII. 12 As tsamba is not a very toothsome affair, we used to make three or four balls of it, with our tea. **1937** H. W. TILMAN *Ascent Nanda Devi* iv. 31 The Tibetan tsumpa—barley, or wheat, which has been parched and then ground into meal. **1952** MORIN & SMITH tr. *Herzog's Annapurna* v. 78 Khangsar was very poor: not a pound of tsampa to spare. **1979** P. MATTHIESSEN *Snow Leopard* ii. 86 The two outcasts dip up tsampa, the roasted maize or barley meal, ground to powder and cooked as porridge or in tea.

tsamma (tsæ·mǎ). Also **(t)sama.** [a. Hottentot *t'sama*.] A wild water-melon, *Citrullus lanatus*, native to parts of southern Africa. Also *attrib.*

1886 G. A. FARINI *Through Kalahari Desert* vii. 106 We came across the first sama I had seen... It is the 'wild water-melon', resembling the cultivated variety in appearance, both internally and externally. **1933** *Times Lit. Suppl.* 16 Mar. 175/2 Ground melons (tsamas) provide the only water supply for the wandering tribes of bushmen. **1937** A. J. H. GOODWIN in I. Schapera *Bantu-Speaking Tribes S. Afr.* ii. 39 The tsama melon..supplies liquid to men and beasts. **1948** L. G. GREEN *To River's End* i. 16 The dunes topped by their t'samma melons..only form a background. **1958** L. VAN DER POST *Lost World Kalahari* ix. 212 A middle-aged woman sat diligently pounding the seeds of the tsamma. **1974** *Stand. Encycl. S. Afr.* X. 640/2 The name 'tsamma' is used mainly in the Kalahari, and is derived from a Bushman name for the plant.

tsampa, var. *TSAMBA.

‖ **tsantsa** (tsa·ntsǎ). Also **tzantza.** [Jivaro.] A human head shrunk as a trophy by the Jivaros of Ecuador.

1923 R. KARSTEN *Blood Revenge* 14 That the blood feuds which take place within the tribe have an entirely different character from the wars of extermination waged against foreign tribes also appears from the fact that only in the latter case..the victors make trophies (*tsantsas*) of the heads of their slain enemies. **1957** *Encycl. Brit.* XIII. 70/1 The finished 'tsantsa' is about the size of the head of a small monkey, and preserves strikingly the human expression. **1966** J. M. WOODMAN in *Fodor's Guide to S. Amer.* 177 The famed Jívaro shrunken heads or *tzantzas* are extremely rare. Many good imitations are for sale in almost every gift shop in Ecuador, and a good goat-hide imitation *tzantza* usually costs around $2.60. **1977** *New Yorker* 25 July 81/2 Another is the stealthy sale by dubious chaps of shrunken heads (tsantsa), war trophies of the Jivaro head-hunters.

‖ **ts'ao shu** (tsɑu ʃu). Also **cao shu, tsaou shoo.** [Chinese *cǎoshū*, f. *cǎo* hasty + *shū* writing.] In Chinese calligraphy, a cursive script developed during the Han dynasty (206 B.C.–A.D. 220) from the 'official' script.

1876 *Encycl. Brit.* V. 655/2 The *Tsaou shoo* or 'grass character'. **1910** *Ibid.* VI. 220/2 Out of the 'official script' two other forms were soon developed, namely the..*ts'ao shu*, or 'grass character', [etc.]. **1974** J.-F. L. CHANG in T. C. Lai *Chinese Calligraphy* (1975) p. xiii, Ts'ao Shu or Cursive Script..was originally developed as a quicker version of the Official Script during the second century

A.D. **1978** *Nagel's Encycl.-Guide: China* 326 *Cao shu* is a style in which the characters are abbreviated, giving free reign to the movement. The economy of style is often such that it is hard to read for all but the initiated.

tsatske (tsǫ·tskə), **tchotchke** (tʃǫ·tʃkə). *U.S. colloq.* [Yiddish, f. Slavonic (cf. Russ. *tsatska*).] A trinket or gewgaw; *transf.*, a pretty girl. Also **tsa·tskeleh** [Yiddish *-le* dim. suff.], an affectionate diminutive of *tsatske*.

1964 W. MARKFIELD *To Early Grave* (1965) v. 101 He was no *tsatskeleh*, Leslie, he was in certain respects far from being trustworthy. **1968** L. ROSTEN *Joys of Yiddish* 408 *Tsatske* and *tchotchke* are used interchangeably... At one time..West End Avenue in New York had an inordinately high proportion of *tchotchkies*. **1970** S. ELLIN *Man from Nowhere* (1971) xix. 94 He looked Elinor over appraisingly... 'A real *tsatskeh*,' he said with approval. **1972** M. GLENNY tr. *Solzhenitsyn's August 1914* (1974) viii. 77 True, she never did anything to cross him, never even put on her expensive clothes and her *tsatski* (diamonds) at home because he disapproved of it. **1974** *N.Y. Times* 12 July 31 'Décor doesn't add to the glamour of a suit,' an owner pointed out. 'You're not buying the rugs or the lamps or the tsatskes.' **1977** *New Yorker* 1 Aug. 14/1 A..boutique, to the left of the entrance, stocked with a careful selection of New York's best tchotchkes. These include thirteen-inch-long matchbooks.

Tsaubwa, var. *SAWBWA. **Tschaikowskian,** var. *TCHAIKOVSKIAN. **tschee,** var. STCHI in Dict. and Suppl.

Tschermak (tʃɜ̄·ɹmæk). *Min.* The name of Gustav *Tschermak* (1836–1927), Austrian mineralogist, used *attrib.* and in the possessive to designate the synthetic pyroxene CaAl(AlSi)O_6 as a hypothetical component of natural pyroxenes, or the part Al(AlSi)O_6 of this.

1943 *Amer. Mineralogist* XXVIII. 73 The substitution Al_2/MgSi is that by which the 'Tschermak molecule' is derived from diopside. **1962** *Jrnl. Petrol.* III. 355 The Cs may also be traced to the Tschermak's molecule in the high-CaO titaniferous clinopyroxene. **1970** *Nature* 26 Sept. 1337/1 Omphacite (diopsidic clinopyroxene in which jadeite predominates over Tschermak's molecule). **1974** *Encycl. Brit. Macropædia* XV. 322/1 Ferric diopsides contain ferri-Tschermak's molecule ($CaFe_2SiO_6$).

Hence **tsche·rmakite**, an amphibole end-member of the hornblende group, $Ca_2Mg_3Al_4Si_6O_{22}(OH)_2$, that is rich in aluminium; also, any member of the series this forms with ferrotschermakite (the other end-member). Hence **tschermaki·tic** *a.*

1945 A. N. WINCHELL in *Amer. Mineralogist* XXX. 29 Hallimond notes that the second of these formulas is often called the Tschermak molecule; the writer would suggest that it be called tschermakite. **1963** W. A. DEER et al. *Rock-Forming Minerals* III. 272 Tschermakitic hornblendes. **1966** —— *Introd. Rock-Forming Minerals* II. 168 Compositions approaching those of the edenite and tschermakite end-members are rare, and the compositions of the majority of the hornblendic amphiboles are intermediate between the two end-member series, tremolite–ferroactinolite and pargasite–ferrohastingsite. **1976** *Nature* 22 Apr. 673/2 The generally tschermakitic-pargasitic nature of all the amphiboles is like that of amphiboles produced synthetically from hydrous basaltic melts.

tschernozem, var. *CHERNOZEM.

tsetse. Add: **2.** *attrib.* and *Comb.*, as *tsetse-bitten, -conveyed, -free, -infested, -poisoned* adjs.; **tsetse country, district,** an area infested by the tsetse fly; **tsetse-fly disease** = *NAGANA.

1906 RIDER HAGGARD *Benita* x. 138 Meyer..had already decreed the death of the tsetse-bitten cattle. **1917** *Nature* 18 Oct. 127/2 The tsetse-conveyed sleeping sickness is being got well in hand. **1853** D. LIVINGSTONE *Jrnl.* 23 May (1960) iv. 139 There is only one small strip of Tsetse country to hinder one going westward. **1877** T. BAINES *Gold Regions S.E. Afr.* 89 Persons travelling must seek for the *latest* information..when approaching the borders of a Tsetse country. **1851** D. LIVINGSTONE *Jrnl.* 29 Aug. (1960) ii. 64 Several Englishmen have lost all their cattle horses & dogs by being led into a Tsetse district. **1895** Tsetse fly disease [see *NAGANA]. **1932** C. FULLER *Louis Trigardt's Trek* ii. 28 They..were compelled to desist..on account of tsetse-fly disease among their cattle. **1948** T. A. M. NASH *Tsetse Flies in Brit. W. Afr.* I. 7/1 Inside this huge area there are only three districts which are tsetse-free. **1977** *Times* 22 Apr. 10/2 The ever-spreading erosion and desertification wreaked by over-stocking of domestic cattle in tsetse-free areas. **1948** T. A. M. NASH *Tsetse Flies in Brit. W. Afr.* I. 13/1 Should..the river flow from tsetse-infested country northwards, it would be wiser not to plant up the banks. **1977** *Times* 22 Apr. 10/4 Vast tsetse-infested tracts of Nigeria. **1906** RIDER HAGGARD *Benita* x. 138 The time was to come when she would swallow that hard, tsetse-poisoned flesh.

Tshi: see *TWI.

T-shirt (tī·ʃɜɹt). orig. *U.S.* Also **tee-shirt.** [f. the letter T (see below) + SHIRT *sb.*] A simple kind of garment, orig. a man's undershirt, typically short-sleeved, round-necked, buttonless and made from knitted cotton fabric, and forming the shape of a letter T when spread out flat; now a similar garment of various designs, widely worn as a shirt by men, women, and children for sport or as casual wear.

1920 F. SCOTT FITZGERALD *This Side of Paradise* I. i. 25 Amory, provided with 'six suits summer underwear.. one sweater or T shirt..' set out for New England, the land of schools. **1944** *Survey Graphic* Aug. 368/3 We have been slow to realize that the high school crowd needs to sit in with us, with all their jive talk, their 'T' shirts and 'sloppy joes'. **1948** *Sun* (Baltimore) 2 Aug. 6/2 A ragged looking pair of trousers and as dark a shirt [as] possible or an old 'tee' shirt. **1957** J. BRAINE *Room at Top* xxv. 203 Roy..was wearing blue suède shoes, blue linen slacks, an orange T-shirt, and white sunglasses. **1958** *Daily Express* 4 Mar. 3/7 Lord M—..wore a striped tee-shirt. **1973** C. BONINGTON *Next Horizon* xiv. 202 Sebastian,.. presented a sharp contrast to myself, already scruffy in T-shirt and jeans. **1980** *Times* 7 Feb. 13 There will be pop music and phone-ins, tee-shirts and car stickers.

Hence **T-shirted, tee-shirted** *adjs.*, wearing or clothed in a T-shirt.

1957 J. KEROUAC *On Road* (1958) II. vi. 134 His muscular neck, T-shirted in the winter night. **1959** *Times* 21 Oct. 11/3 T-shirted trippers perched on tubular steel chairs. **1973** *Philadelphia Inquirer* (Today Suppl.) 14 Oct. 27 (*caption*) A funeral parlor..is guarded by tee-shirted gang members outside. **1979** *Guardian* 3 Sept. 11/8 The jeaned and tee-shirted young.

tsimmes, -is, varr. *TZIMMES.

Tsimshian (tʃi·mʃən), *sb.* and *a.* Also **Tsimpshian,** etc. [Tsimshian self-designation *čamsián*, lit. inside of the Skeena River.] **A.** *sb.* **a.** An Indian people of the north Pacific coast of N. America; also, a member of this people. **b.** Their language. **B.** *adj.* Of or pertaining to this people or their language.

1836 D. FINLAYSON *Let.* 29 Sept. in E. E. Rich *McLoughlin's Fort Vancouver Lett.* 1st Ser. (1941) 323 The Pearl Harbour, and Skeenah Indians called the Chimmesyan tribe. **1888** [see *COPPER *sb.*[1] 4 b]. **1890** *Rep. Brit. Assoc. Adv. Sci. 1889* 853 The Olala is confined to the southern Tsimshian tribes. **1911, 1934** [see *NASS]. **1966** [see *CHILKAT]. **1972** *Language* XLVIII. 390 Geographically or genetically contiguous languages which share many features of the proposed analysis, e.g. Squamish and Tsimshian.

tsine. For *sondaicus* substitute *banteng*. Also, = *BANTENG. (Earlier example.)

1880 [see *BANTENG, BANTING].

‖ **tsipouro** (tsi·puro). Also **tsippouro, tsipuro.** [mod.Gr., prob. a. Turk.] A rough and local kind of Greek spirituous drink.

1947 J. MULGAN *Report on Experience* viii. 98 We cheered each other in Fourna, passing *tsippouro*—a lower-class cousin of *ouzo*—across the fire. **1953** X. FIELDING *Stronghold* i. 4 [*Tsidoukhia*,] The local name for raki, similar to the *tsipouro* of Epirus, which is distilled from what is left of the grape after it has been pressed for wine. **1969** [see *RAKI]. **1981** J. BOWMAN *Crete* (ed. 5) 46 On Crete the men are distinguished from the boys by drinking *raki*, a stronger unflavoured version [of ouzo] (and known in Crete as *tsipouro* or *tzikoudhia*).

tsitsith (tsi·tsis, -it), *sb. pl.* and *collect. sing.* *Judaism.* Also **tzitzit(h), zizith.** [a. Heb. *ṣīṣīṯ*.] The tassels of twisted and knotted cord worn by orthodox Jewish males on the corners of certain garments, esp. the tallith; cf. FRINGE *sb.* 1; also, a small rectangular garment, with a large hole in the middle and with tassels attached to each corner, worn over the vest but under the shirt.

Translated as 'fringes' in A.V. and R.V. and as 'tassels' in N.E.B. (see Numbers xv. 38, Deut. xxii. 12).

1675 L. ADDISON *Present State of Jews* xiii. 99 The wearing of the Zizith or Fringe, they collect from Exodus. **1738** 'GAMALIEL BEN PEDAHZUR' *Bk. Relig. of Jews* 4 The Fringe on each Corner is of eight worsted Threads double twisted [*marg.* Called Zizith]. **1816** J. ALLEN *Mod. Judaism* xvii. 305 Every male is required to have a quadrangular vestment, which they call *Talleth*... Its principal denomination, Tsitsith,..it receives from the fringes upon which all its sanctity is supposed to depend. **1854** *Asmonean* X. 198/1 In every corner is a string of plaited thread, called *zizis*, or *ziziths*. **1881** *Living Age* CIL. 418/1 The *tzitzis*, or fringes..of the boy's garment have been neglected. **1891** M. GOLDSMITH *Rabbi & Priest* 29 Shall he earn a few paltry kopecks in making tzitzith (fringes for the praying scarfs)? **1907** I. ZANGWILL *Ghetto Comedies* 389 These fellows..wear fuses under their waistcoats instead of *Tsitsith* (ritual fringes). **1920** J. A. ROBERTSON *Hidden Romance N.T.* viii. 173, I see you are a Jew, like myself... But you don't wear the Zizith any more than I do. **1962** *New Jewish Encycl.* 475/1 The Tallit is rectangular in shape,..with *Tzitzit* (fringes) at each of its four corners. The Tzitzit is the important part of the Tallit. **1962** *Encounter* Sept. 21/2 They didn't buy ice-cream from the carts in the streets because it wasn't kosher; they never took their caps off in class..they wore *tzitzith* under their vests... They were heroic, absurd, and maddening. **1967** C. POTOK *Chosen* i. 16 They all wore the traditional undergarment beneath their shirts, and the tzitzit, the long fringes appended to the four corners of the garment, came out above their belts. **1968** L. ROSTEN *Joys of Yiddish* 418 *Tzitzit* are meant as reminders of one's duty to the laws of Judaism. **1973** *Times* 16 June 9/4 The distinctive features of Jewish dress—the *tsitsith* (tassels) [etc.].

tsk, *int.* Also **tsck,** and redupl. **tsk-tsk.** [Alveolar click formed by suction: cf. TCHICK *sb.*, TCK *int.*] A sound expressing commiseration; an exclamation of disapproval or irritation. So **tsk-tsk** *v. intr.*, to make this sound or utter this exclamation; also *trans.*, to say disapprovingly.

1947 K. L. PIKE *Phonemics* ii. 41/1 Do you get..a sound resembling the noise of commiseration which is sometimes written in literature as 'tsk-tsk', or 'tut-tut'? **1952** S. KAUFFMANN *Philanderer* (1953) xvii. 277 'When she doesn't like a writer or a composer, it sort of dampens my..activity about him. I'm henpecked.' 'Tsk, tsk,' said Ed extra clearly. **1958** L. DURRELL *Mountolive* xvi. 307 Balthazar..walked slowly..making the little clucking noise he always made with his tongue..*Tsck, tsck.* **1962** A. LURIE *Love & Friendship* xiv. 273 'Poor Carolyn Hastings is officially engaged to that dreadful Cowie boy.' 'Tsk.' **1966** M. AVALLONE *Fat Death* 47 'Mr. Noon,' he *tsk-tsked* reprovingly. 'You really pretend not to know?' **1968** *Punch* 20 Mar. 428/3 No amount of tsk-tsking indignation and bitter wit will turn a buy into a bargain. **1976** *New Yorker* 26 Apr. 102/2 She tsk-tsks over Momma. **1983** M. GEE *Sole Survivor* iv. 32 The constable went tsk, tsk and looked at us sadly. There was nothing he could do so he sent us home.

Tsonga (tsǫ·ŋgă), *sb.* and *a.* Also **Thonga.** [Native name: cf. *TONGA[4].] **A.** *sb.* An African tribal group chiefly inhabiting the Transvaal area of the Republic of South Africa and parts of southern Mozambique; the Bantu language spoken by this people. **B.** *adj.* Of, pertaining to, or designating this people or their language.

1905 *Jrnl. Afr. Soc.* V. 12 There are three main Native languages in South Africa: Zulu, Suto and Thonga. **1907** H. A. JUNOD in C. W. Chatelain *Pocket Dict. Thonga (Shangaan)* (1909) 3 The Shangaan language, which would be more scientifically called the Thonga language. **1912** —— *Life S. Afr. Tribe* I. 13 The Thonga tribe is composed of a group of Bantu peoples settled on the Eastern coast of South Africa. **1933** *Bantu Stud.* VII. 4 The languages of the South-eastern [*sc.* Bantu] zone fall into four clusters, the 'Nguni', the 'Sotho', the 'Venda' and the 'Thonga'... In the Thonga cluster [are] three main groups, Ronga, Thonga and Tswa. **1937** R. H. LOWIE *Hist. Ethnological Theory* xii. 225 The Northern Thonga of Portuguese East Africa use a single word for the maternal uncle, the maternal uncle's son, and the mother's father. **1940** A. A. JAQUES in *Bantu Stud.* XIV. 259 It should be noted that it is not correct to spell the name of this people [*sc.* the Shangana-Tsonga] *Tonga* or *Thonga*... Since the recent decisions taken by the Tsonga Language Board concerning orthography, there should be no difficulty in adopting the form *Tsonga*. **1955** M. GLUCKMAN *Custom & Conflict in Afr.* iii. 63 Among the Tsonga of Mozambique..witchcraft passes..from women to their children, so that men can carry it, but not transmit it. *Ibid.* v. 116 Take this description of the Tsonga ritual which organizes the moving of a village. **1970** *Standard Encycl. S. Afr.* II. 106/2 The Tsonga group is often also called the Shangana group. These languages are spoken by the descendants of the Zulu chief Soshangana. *Ibid.* 306/1 The first portions of Scripture in Tsonga..appeared in 1883. **1973** 'S. HARVESTER' *Corner of Playground* III. ii. 181 A Swazi king in eighteen-fiftyfour raided the Tsonga to find boys..to sell to the Boers. **1974** *Encycl. Brit. Micropædia* IX. 967/3 Although many Thonga are Christian, a substantial proportion adhere to their own traditional, highly ritualistic religion. **1979** *Jrnl. Imperial & Commonwealth Hist.* VII. 255 The provision of food, lodging and security to Tsonga migrants proved beneficial to Natal.

‖ **Tsongdu** (tsǫ·ŋ,du). Also **Tsong-du.** [ad. Tibetan *t'sogs du*, lit. 'an assembly meets'.] The Tibetan National Council or Assembly.

1905 *Spectator* 18 Feb. 243/2 When the expedition started we had two parties in Lhasa against us,—the Dalai Lama, with his adviser Dorjieff, who urged a breach in the traditional exclusiveness of the State in favour of Russia; and the Tsong-du, or Council, who were for the maintenance of the old system against Russia and Britain alike. **1970** R. D. TARING *Daughter of Tibet* vi. 68 A meeting of the *Tsongdu* (the National Assembly).

‖ **tsores** (tsǫ·rəs), *sb. pl.* (sometimes const. as *sing.*) *U.S. colloq.* Also **tsouris, tsuris, -us, (t)z-,** etc. [Yiddish *tsores*, pl. of *tsore* trouble, woe, a. Heb. *sārāh*.] Trouble(s), worries.

1901 M. WOLFENSTEIN *Idyls of Gass* viii. 143 I have other *Zores* (troubles). **1905** W. WITTIGSCHLAGER *Minna* I. i. 15 We have no money..nor do we propose ever to experience such *zorus*, (trouble). **1929** J. D. ROSENBERG *Kosher Americans* xvii. 165 Ve had plenty *tso-res* (troubles) before. **1941** B. SCHULBERG *What makes Sammy Run?* iv. 70, I had a notion that a little of Billie and Sammy Glick might not be such a bad idea, if only to get my mind off my own tsurus. **1950** *Commentary* X. 67/2 He had enough *tzores* without politics. **1956** 'T. BETTS' *Across Board* 103 During a long streak of tzuris (misery) with cards and horses. **1968** L. ROSTEN *Joys of Yiddish* 412 Oh, have I got *tsuris*! **1972** J. CAINE *Hamlet, my Boy* vi. 71 It's no *tsooras* for a child. **1975** *N.Y. Times Bk. Rev.* 16 Mar. 31 She has a bad back..and miscellaneous medical tsouris.

tsotsi (tsǫ·tsi). *S. Afr.* [Origin uncertain: freq. said to be a corruption of *zoot suit*.] An African street thug or hoodlum, usu. from the Black townships and distinctively dressed in narrow trousers or in garments of exaggerated cut. Also in extended sense. Also *attrib.* Hence **tso·tsi-ism.**

1949 *Cape Argus* 20 July 8/9 (*heading*) Tsotsi gangs who hate Bantu students. **1949** *Cape Times* 10 Sept. 8/6 The 'Tsotsi' may be distinguished by his exceedingly narrow trousers which hardly reach his shoes, or else by his 'zoot suit'. **1952** B. Davidson *Rep. Southern Afr.* II. v. 121 The conditions out of which have grown such strange and horrible manifestations of maladjustment as *tsotsi-ism.* **1956** H. Bloom *Episode* xv. 273 One could tell they were *tsotsis* by their fancy clothes, by the way they took command... They led the mobs. **1971** *Sunday Times* (Johannesburg) *News Mag.* 28 Mar. 9/7 We do not want agitators to give hooligans and tsotsis the chance to plunder shops and businesses. **1979** A. Brink *Dry White Season* I. vii. 70 'You may be a *lanie*'—his red tongue caressed the syllables of the taunting *tsotsi* word—'but you've got it right here.'

tsouris, var. *tsores.

‖ **tsu** (tsū). *Anthrop.* [Chinese.] A patrilineal kinship group in pre-revolutionary China (see quot. 1939).

1939 H.-T. Fei *Peasant Life in China* v. 84 According to accepted principle, all the patrilineal descendents and their wives that can be traced to a common ancestor within five kinship grades consider themselves as belonging to a kinship group called Tsu. **1957** in K.-C. Chang *Archaeol. Anc. China* (1963) vi. 168 *P'i* (grandmothers and female ancestors) was partnered to *tsu* (grandfathers and male ancestors). **1966** M. Freedman *Chinese Lineage & Society* i. 5 Almost all *tsu* (lineage) relatives in the village are related through a grandfather.

‖ **tsuba** (tsū·bă). Pl. **tsuba, tsubas.** [Jap., shortened f. *tsumiha, -ba,* f. *tsumi* to stop + *ha* (enemy's) blade, sword.] A Japanese sword-guard.

1889 J. J. Rein *Industries Japan* III. vii. 432 The sword-shell, or guard, Tsuba, is as old as the sword. It is an oval metal plate..with an opening in the middle to admit the blade of the sword. **1909** J. Masefield *Multitude & Solitude* ii. 35 Melyard collected tsuba, and fenced archæologically at the Foil Club. **1970** *Times* 11 Mar. 12/5 Sotheby's held a similar sale, mainly devoted to Japanese sword guards or tsubas. **1976** *Times Lit. Suppl.* 16 Jan. 48/4 (*caption*) Examples of the *tsuba,* or hand-guard, of Japanese swords. 'On them..may be found illustrated the whole of the mythology, customs, legends, folklore, famous scenes, characteristics and celebrated personages and events of the history of Japan.'

‖ **tsubo** (tsū·bo). Pl. **tsubo, tsubos.** [Jap.] A Japanese unit of area, equivalent to approximately 3.95 square yards (3.31 square metres).

1727 J. G. Scheuchzer tr. *Kæmpfer's Hist. Japan* I. iv. iii. 292 Woods and forests pay a ..Ground-rent, which differs according to the number of *Tsubo's,* and the goodness and fruitfulness of the soil. **1902** *Encycl. Brit.* XXXIII. 810/1 Tsubo... Japan... 3·0306 [? *an error for* 3·306] sq. metres. **1972** P. M. Bartz *South Korea* viii. 123/2 In crowded Korea, urban land is sold by the *pyong* (35·6 square feet), the equivalent of the Japanese *tsubo* (3·3 square metres).

tsuica (tsū·ikă). Also **tuica, ţuica, tzuica.** [a. Rum. *ţuică.*] A Romanian plum brandy.

1927 *Sunday Express* 26 June 17/5 Will you come into the house and have a talk over a glass of tuica? **1938** *Times* 1 Jan. 11/1 The improvement of the facilities for the making of *ţsuica* (plum brandy, which is a national drink). **1960** O. Manning *Great Fortune* I. 52, I make my own red wine, white wine, *ţuică,* and martini. **1965** A. Sichel *Penguin Bk. Wines* III. 221 Various fruit cordials, such as plum brandy, are also exported from Rumania; there are two types, called Tzuica and Slibovitza. **1971** T. E. B. Clarke *Wrong Turning* xv. 105 She was drinking red wine with sodawater, he was having beer: there was laughter..at Jean's insistence in sticking to tuica. **1977** 'A. Stuart' *Snap Judgement* 51 She was choking—with emotion? With ţuica? Both she and the room smelt strongly of plum brandy. **1981** B. de Breffny *My First Naked Lady* i. 29 Grandfather made me sip a Rumanian liqueur called Tsuica.

‖ **tsukemono** (tsūkimōᵘ·no). Also **tsuki-mono.** [Jap., f. *tsukeru* to pickle + *mono* something.] (See quots.)

1885 *Trans. Asiatic Soc. Japan* XIII. 8 *Tsukemono,* the preserved roots or leaves of certain vegetables. **1920** *Japan Advertiser* 22 Aug. 5/3 Most Japanese meals..are accompanied by vegetable dishes... Tsuki-mono stands for the pickle that accompanies the rice at the end of the meal and is made from vegetables in season, such as cucumbers, eggplant, melon, etc. **1968** P. S. Buck *People of Japan* xiv. 167 *Tsukemono,* the pickled vegetables served with any meal.

‖ **tsukuri** (tsukūᵊ·ri). [Jap.] In Judo, preparatory action taken to facilitate the breaking of one's opponent's balance. Cf. *kuzushi.

1941 M. Feldenkrais *Judo* 25 Thus you have performed the 'fitting movement' (*Tsukuri*). **1968** [see *kuzushi].

tsumebite (tsū·mĕbəit). *Min.* [ad. G. *tsumebit* (K. Busz 1912, in *Festschr. gewidmet den Teilnehmern der 84. Versammlung Deutsch. Naturforscher und Ärzte in Münster von der Med.-Naturwiss. Ges. in Münster* 182), f. *Tsumeb,* name of a town in Namibia: see -ite¹.] A basic phosphate and sulphate of lead and copper, $Pb_2Cu(PO_4)(SO_4)OH$, found as crusts of transparent green monoclinic crystals.

1913 *Mineral. Mag.* XVI. 373 Tsumebite... Hydrated basic phosphate of lead and copper..found as small, emerald-green, monoclinic crystals on white calamine at Tsumeb, Otavi, German South-West Africa. **1966** *Amer. Mineralogist* LI. 267 Due to the extreme tendency of tsumebite to occur as intimately intergrown crystals, considerable difficulty was encountered in obtaining a suitable, single crystal.

tsumpa, var. *tsamba.

‖ **tsun** (tsun). [Chinese.] A style of Chinese vessel, either wide-mouthed or animal-shaped (see quot. 1974). Also *attrib.*

1958 W. Willetts *Chinese Art* I. iii. 144 The Sung cataloguers proceeded to identify as *tsun* various animal-shaped vessels known to them. **1974** *Encycl. Brit. Micropædia* X. 162/3 *Tsun,*..generic term ('sacrificial vessel') for a wide range of Chinese vessel shapes, generally of the Shang (*c.* 1766–*c.* 1122 BC) and early Chou (*c.* 1122–*c.* 900 BC) dynasties, all of which have an ample interior volume probably meant for containing wine. There are two essential varieties of *tsun*: one is shaped like a much enlarged *ku*; the other consists of various animal shapes, often densely embellished with animal decoration. **1977** Kwang-Chih Chang *Archaeol. Anc. China* (ed. 3) vi. 222 Pottery *li* tripods and large-mouthed *tsun* beakers began to appear in significant numbers.

tsunami (tsunā·mi). Also (repr. a strict transliteration of the Jap. form) **tunami.** [a. Jap. *tsunami, tunami,* f. *tsu* harbour + *nami* waves.] A brief series of long, high undulations on the surface of the sea caused by an earthquake or similar underwater disturbance. These travel at great speed and often with sufficient force to inundate the land; freq. misnamed a *tidal wave* (see Tidal *a.* 1 b). Also *fig.* and *attrib.*

1897 L. Hearn *Gleanings in Buddha-Fields* i. 24 '*Tsunami*!' shrieked the people; and then all shrieks and all sounds and all power to hear sounds were annihilated by a nameless shock..as the colossal swell smote the shore with a weight that sent a shudder through the hills. **1904** *Publ. Earthquake Investigation Comm. Foreign Lang.* (Japan) XIX. 6 Records and reports of earthquakes and '*tsunamis*'. **1938** *Nature* 12 Nov. 881/2 The authenticity of the reports of earthquakes mentioned in these catalogues is weighed..with records of tunamis. **1956** *Jrnl. Earth Sci. Nagoya Univ.* IV. 2 The tunamis associated with strong earthquakes are frequent in Japan. **1967** *Technology Week* 23 Jan. 34/1 This system would predict ..tsunami run-up floods. **1970** *Daily Tel.* 27 Nov. 11/7 A *tsunami* generated off Chile by the 1960 earthquake crashed into Japan on the other side at 400 m.p.h. **1972** *Science* 11 Aug. 502/1 The Food and Drug Administration ..is currently swimming through a tsunami of comments generated by its announced intention to alter the regulations concerning the dispensation of methadone. **1981** *Monitor* (McAllen, Texas) 30 Jan. 3A/3 The National Weather Service..issued a *tsunami* warning. **1984** W. Golding *Paper Men* viii. 89 It seemed to me that I could feel the indifferent threat of the earth through the soles of my feet, the volcanoes, earthquakes, tsunamis, terrors of nature's fact.

tsuris, -us, etc., varr. *tsores.

‖ **tsutsugamushi** (tsū:tsugămu·ʃī). *Path.* [Jap., f. *tsutsuga* trouble, illness + *mushi* insect.] = *scrub typhus* s.v. *scrub sb.¹ 6. Usu. *attrib.* in *tsutsugamushi disease.*

1906 *Index Medicus* IV. Index 216/1 Tsutsugamushi disease. **1908** *Philippine Jrnl. Sci.* B. III. 1 (*heading*) A comparative study of *tsutsugamushi* disease and spotted or tick fever of Montana. **1929,** etc. [see *scrub typhus* s.v. *scrub *sb.*¹ 6]. **1937** *Med. Jrnl. Australia* 21 Aug. 300/1 The absence of a local intradermal lesion speaks against the virus being of the spotted fever or *tsutsugamushi* types of Rickettsia. **1978** *Jrnl. R. Soc. Med.* LXXI. 507 The Japanese synonym, tsutsugamushi disease, clearly had precedence, but the name, scrub typhus, became fully established through widespread use in World War II.

‖ **tsutsumu** (tsūtsū·mū). [Jap., to wrap.] The Japanese art of wrapping or packaging items in an attractive and appropriate way.

1975 *N.Y. Times Mag.* 9 Feb. 56 Each of the 300 packages in the show (called 'Tsutsumu, The Art of the Japanese Package') was purchased in 1974 in Japan, where an object's wrapping can be as important as the object itself.

Tswana (tswā·nă), *sb.* and *a.* Also **Chwana.** [Native name.] **A.** *sb.* **a.** = *Bechuana (for which *Tswana* is now the usual term). **b.** The Bantu language of this people (cf. *Sechuana). **B.** *adj.* Of or pertaining to this people or their language.

1930 *Bantu Studies* IV. 211 It is therefore probable that they may be still more widespread, at least among the Sotho-Tswana tribes. **1932** D. Jones *Outl. Eng. Phonetics* xxix. 227 Strong stress without accompanying loudness is a common feature of the Chwana language of South Africa. **1937** *Bantu Studies* XI. 137 The orthography set out in the present pamphlet represents the latest result of a prolonged series of efforts made..by the Education Departments..to arrive at a uniform orthography of Tswana. **1948** M. Guthrie *Classification Bantu Lang.* iv. 68 In Tswana the verbal has the extra suffix -ŋ. **1949** I. Schapera in M. Fortes *Social Structure* 104 In contrast to most other Bantu-speaking peoples of southern Africa, the Tswana tribes of the Bechuanaland Protectorate have remarkably few marriage prohibitions. **1957** [see *Sotho]. **1973** J. J. McKelvey *Man against Tsetse* i. 16 Cumming went..down to the hunting grounds of the Limpopo against the advice of the local people, the Tswanas. **1975** 'D. Jordan' *Black Account* xviii. 96 A girl came down the steps..she was blonde, and slim and tall... 'I thought you were all Tswana here,' I said and she laughed... She explained she worked in Bantu Affairs. **1980** First & Scott *Olive Schreiner* i. 37 Basotho and Tswana refugees.

t test (tī·test). *Statistics.* [f. *t* chosen arbitrarily as a symbol.] = *Student's (t) test* s.v. *Student².

[**1924** R. A. Fisher in *Proc. Internat. Math. Congr.* (1928) II. 498 If for the accurate standard deviation we substitute an estimate based on *n* degrees of freedom we have $t = x\sqrt{n}/\sqrt{S(x^2)}$. **1925** 'Student' in *Metron* V. 105 The present tables have..at Mr. Fisher's suggestion been constructed with argument $t = z\sqrt{n}$.] **1932** R. A. Fisher *Statistical Methods for Research Workers* (ed. 4) v. 116 The validity of the *t*-test, as a test of this hypothesis, is therefore absolute. **1958** M. Argyle *Relig. Behaviour* iii. 16 The 't' test..is generally used when equal measurement units are involved, otherwise various non-parametric methods are available. **1968** *Brit. Med. Bull.* XXIV. 220/2 A selection of commonly required significance tests is available, including paired and unpaired *t* tests, correlation coefficients..and analysis of variance. **1974** *Florida FL Reporter* XIII. 73/1 Correlated one-tailed t-tests were run for both the differences between the two groups.

‖ **tuak** (tū·æk). [Malay.] A locally-distilled Malaysian or Indonesian palm- or rice-wine.

[**1850** *Jrnl. Indian Archipelago* IV. 179 Liquid sugar.. is obtained by boiling the juice extracted from the *loutar* or *tuak* palm.] **1852** *Ibid.* VI. 317, I could not learn that they prepared any fermented liquor, not even sago-weer or tuak. **1920** C. Lumholtz *Through Central Borneo* II. xxxi. 335 On the Upper Samba the custom still prevails of drinking tuak from human skulls. **1961** P. Kemp *Alms for Oblivion* vii. 119 *Tuak* drinking is a favourite pastime of the elderly men. *Tuak,* or toddy, is brewed from the juice of the sugar palm; it looks and tastes somewhat like farm cider,..though not so intoxicating. **1966** *Festival Malaysia 1966: Calendar of Events* 10/1 Tuak (locally distilled rice-wine) is the drink of the occasion [*sc.* a Dyak Gawai]. **1977** *Borneo Bull.* 7 May 4/5 The main cultural show was at an open night for all participants at the Rest House which would have been even more fun if the tuak had not run out early.

tuan (tuā·n). Also **Tuan.** [Malay.] A master, a lord, formerly esp. a European as spoken to or of by Malays; freq. used as a title of respect or form of address, = 'sir', 'mister'.

1779 T. Forrest *Voy. New Guinea* I. ii. 27, I found Tuan Hadjee in high spirits. **1864** J. T. Thomson *Some Glimpses Life Far East* xxi. 106 'Why,' said he, '*tuan,* these two rows belong to the East India Company's chief official.' **1885** E. Innes *Chersonese* I. ii. 21 Before the Tuan's (master's) marriage, all his mending is cheerfully done for him by his 'boy'. **1900** Conrad *Lord Jim* i. 3 They called him Tuan Jim: as one might say—Lord Jim. **1937** G. Frankau *More of Us* xvi. 166 There is nothing frets your gent, your sahib, your tuan,.. Like having some old donah near his new one. **1958** J. Slimming *Temiar Jungle* ii. 25 'Greetings, Tuan!' His voice is quiet and gentle. **1978** L. Heren *Growing up on The Times* iv. 136 British conscript soldiers were expected to keep the enemy at bay in Malaya while the *tuans* made their piles.

Tuareg (twā·reg), *sb.* and *a.* Also 9 **Tawarek, Tuari(c)k.** [Native name.] **A.** *sb.* (A member of) a nomadic people of the western and central Sahara. Also, the Berber language of this people. **B.** *adj.* Of or pertaining to this people or their language.

1821 G. F. Lyon *Narr. Trav. N. Afr.* iii. 112 The nearest Tuarick to Fezzan are at Ghraat. **1826** Denham & Clapperton *Narr. Trav. & Disc. N. & Central Afr.* p. l, The greater number of Tuaricks follow the nomadic life. *Ibid.* p. lxv, They..laughed heartily at our blundering out a few Tuarick words. *Ibid.* 83 He was dressed in a light blue cotton tobe, with a white muslin turban, the shawl of which he wore over the nose and mouth, in the Tuarick fashion. *Ibid.* App. 160 Under the government of the Tawarêk. **1882** [see *Kabyle]. **1933** L. Bloomfield *Language* iv. 67 The *Berber* branch of Semitic-Hamitic.. is represented today by various languages, such as *Tuareg* and *Kabyle.* **1955** *Sci. News Let.* 4 June 3 Called the 'People of the Veil', the Tuaregs are a nomadic people who live in the central part of the Sahara desert. **1973** *Times* 19 Mar. 6/3 The tracks..did lead to some Tuareg nomads, and to water. **1977** *Time* 3 Oct. 2/2 The peregrinations of the Tuareg in Niger, Mali and Upper Volta and the nomadic Masai in Kenya and Tanzania frighten their respective governments.

‖ **Tuatha Dé Danann** (tūᵊ·hă dē da·năn). Also (*erron.*) **Tuatha de Danaan,** etc. [Ir., f. *tuatha,* pl. of *tuath* Tuath + *dé* + *Danann,* name of the mother of the gods (app. formerly gen. sing. of *Danu,* but later used as nom).] In Irish mythology, a people who inhabited prehistoric Ireland.

1682 P. Walsh *Prospect State of Ireland* f. b2, He has not the least mention of Tuatha-De-Danainn, though a powerful People. **1876** [see *Nemedian]. **1893** W. B. Yeats in *Bookman* May 43/1 The berries were the food of the *Tuatha de Danaan*, or faeries. **1980** J. O'Faolain *No Country for Young Men* ii. 41 Ever hear of the prehistoric rulers of Ireland and how they fought their wars? The Tuatha De Danaan? They wrapped themselves in a cloud and withdrew into the hills..and turned into fairies.

tub, *sb.* Add: **1. c.** (Earlier example.)

1853 E. Clacy *Lady's Visit Gold Diggings Austral.* 116 Great wooden tubs are filled with the dirt and fresh water.

g. A tub-shaped carton, *spec.* one containing a portion of ice-cream; the contents of a carton.

1939 'G. Orwell' *Coming up for Air* iv. iii. 248, I watched the floats rocking up and down among the ice-cream tubs and the paper bags. **1955** 'C. Brown' *Lost Girls* xii. 139 You bought these ices from a fat woman holding out a podgy hand and saying, 'Two tubs, ducks?' **1981** P. Vansittart *Death of Robin Hood* iv. i. 183 The sallow ground was strewn with..ice-cream tubs, empty tins and ruined shoes.

2. (Earlier example.)

1776 H. Newdigate *Let.* in A. E. Newdigate-Newdegate *Cheverels* (1898) i. 11 To-night I can use my warm Bath..which I cannot at present do conveniently at home having neither Tub nor dressers.

6. d. A fire-engine. *U.S. slang.*

1864 *Student & Schoolmate* Jan. 3 The rope was only half manned and wishing to make myself useful..I joined the party in charge of the 'tub'. **1906** J. D. Lovett *Old Boston Boys* vii. 67 A boy without a 'tub', as they were called in the vernacular, was like a man without a country.

e. A bus; *to work the tubs*, to pick pockets on buses or at bus-stops. *slang* (chiefly *Underworld*).

1929 G. Dilnot *Triumphs of Detection* iv. 52 Snatches of their conversation..told that they were on their way to 'work the tubs'—in other words, to pick pockets at omnibus stopping-places. **1933** C. E. Leach *On Top of Underworld* x. 141 *Tub*, omnibus. **1974** P. Wright *Lang. Brit. Industry* x. 85 Inland transport comes along with *tubs* for buses.

10. tub-bass, a bass string instrument made from a tub; **tub garden,** an area containing plants grown in tubs; **tub-oarsman** (example); **tub-size** *v.*: hence **tub-sized** *ppl. a.*; **tub-wheel** (earlier example).

1958 P. Oliver in P. Gammond *Decca Bk. Jazz* i. 23 Parallels have been drawn between the tub-bass and the African earth-bow, but that the former is a folk memory of the other seems unlikely. **1974** N. Marsh *Black as he's Painted* i. 62 She spent a good deal of time in the tub garden at the back of the house. **1845** E. J. Wakefield *Adventure N.Z.* I. xi. 318 The common men have nothing to do but to ply their oars according to orders; except one, called the *tub oarsman*, who sits next to the tub containing the whale-line, and has to see that no entanglement takes place. *a* **1912** Tub-sized [see A.T.S. s.v. *A III]. **1967** E. Chambers *Photolitho Offset* xvi. 250 Surface-sized or tub-sized paper is made by passing the moist paper (15–18% moisture) through a trough containing starch solution. **1815–16** *Niles' Weekly Register* IX. Suppl. 182/2 Many mill owners have laid aside their tub wheels.

tuba[1]. Delete ‖ and add: **2. b.** (Earlier example.)

1858 J. A. Symonds *Let.* Nov. (1967) I. 174 The stops of the organ were unusually fine—Tuba, [etc.].

tuba[3]. Add: **1.** For *Dalbergia* substitute *Derris.* (Earlier examples.)

1839 T. J. Newbold *Straits of Malacca* II. xii. 189 The Malays sometimes resort to unfair means of securing the finny tribe, by inserting at low water the roots of the Tuba..into the holes and fissures of the coral reefs. **1890** [see *derrid, derride].

2. (Earlier example.)

1704 in A. & J. Churchill *Coll. Voy.* IV. 447/2 Their Wine or Liquor is drawn from the Palm, or Coco-Tree... The Poor put into it some Bark of Trees which give it a Colour, and a hotter Tast, and then it is call'd Tuba.

tubal, *a.* Add: **2.** *tubal ligation*, ligation of the Fallopian tubes, esp. as a method of sterilization.

1948 H. S. & R. J. Crossen *Operative Gynecol.* (ed. 6) 991/2 (Index), Tubal ligation. **1961** *Biol. Abstr.* XXXVI. 5391/2 (*heading*) Histological studies on the change of the adrenal cortex by means of the oophorectomy and tubal ligation in rabbits. **1975** *New Yorker* 29 Sept. 84/3 Mrs. Santana had intended to get a tubal ligation after Gabriel's birth.

tubbable (tʊ·băb'l), *a.* [f. Tub *v.* + -able.] Of garments, etc.: washable in a tub; suitable for laundering in a tub or (domestic) washing-machine.

1929 *Chicago Daily Tribune* 20 May (Advt.), Tubbable Wearable Suitable Cotton! **1960** *News Chron.* Mar. 229 Synthetic fibres..permanently pleated and tubbable. **1982** *Sunday Express* 25 July 17/1 Children's clothes this week—cute, sharp and tubbable they come in easy-care cotton.

tubbily (tʊ·bili), *adv.* [f. Tubby *a.* + -ly[2].] In a tubby manner; with an appearance of tubbiness.

1924 D. H. Lawrence in M.M. *Mem. Foreign Legion* 12 He stuck his front out tubbily, like a bird. **1935** H. Nicolson *Let.* 4 Dec. (1966) 229 Winston rose tubbily and stretched out great arms. **1957** M. Spark *Comforters* ix. 220 He watched the movements of a young fat woman on a houseboat moored nearby... But she did emerge again, with a cup of tea. She drank it propped tubbily on the tiny bridge of the boat.

tubby, *a.* Add: **2.** Also, of general acoustic quality.

1940 *Chambers's Techn. Dict.* 869/2 *Tubby*.., characterised by reverberant booming for frequencies which are familiar when barrels are struck. **1962** A. Nisbett *Technique Sound Studio* 243 *Boomy*, subjective description of a sound quality which has resonances in the low frequencies, or a broad band of bass lift. Expressions with similar shades of meaning are tubby or, simply, bassy. **1981** *Popular Hi-Fi* Mar. 81/3 Drum sound was tubby on both decks.

tube, *sb.* Add: **I. 2. g.** *Electronics.* A sealed container, evacuated or gas-filled, containing two or more electrodes between which an electric current can be made to flow; *spec.* (*a*) a cathode-ray tube; (*b*) (chiefly *U.S.*) a thermionic valve. Freq. in *Comb.* with preceding sb., as *discharge, electron, picture, vacuum tube*, qq.v.

1859, etc. [see *vacuum tube 2]. **1898,** etc. [see *discharge *sb.* 3 b]. **1905** *Electrician* 16 June 335/1 The phosphorescent spot on the screen of the tube follows strictly any changes which occur in the strength of the field. **1915** *Ibid.* 21 May 241/2 In the X-ray tube..the space charge effects are very much exaggerated. **1922** C. W. Taussig *Bk. of Radio* ix. 111 The tubes used are 5 watt transmitting tubes. **1940** H. M. Watson et al. *Understanding Radio* v. 223 As you experiment with this one-tube set, you will hear many stations faintly. **1947** R. Lee *Electronic Transformers & Circuits* i. 3 The limitations which inhere in transformers often influence the choice of amplifier tubes. **1973** G. J. King *Newnes Colour Television Servicing Man.* I. i. 29/2 The output direct from the tripler is too high an impedance to accommodate the normal beam current swings of the tube without serious voltage fluctuations. **1981** Nashelsky & Boylestad *Devices* iv. 128 Production rose from about 1 million tubes in 1922 to about 100 million in 1937.

h. *inner tube*: see *inner *a.* 1 i. Also *ellipt.*

1894 Albemarle & Hillier *Cycling* 471 The outer arch is removed, the inner tube carefully examined, the hole discovered—if necessary, by inflating the tube and immersing it in water. **1904** A. B. F. Young *Complete Motorist* (ed. 2) xi. 246 When the tube and cover are both in place..the air chamber is inflated by means of a pump. **1979** *United States 1980/81* (Penguin Travel Guides) 367 You can buy tubes..at gas stations and stands along the route.

i. A telephone. Cf. sense 7 a and Speaking-tube. *colloq.* or *slang.*

[**1873** C. M. Yonge *Pillars of House* II. xiii. 38 Mr. Underwood breathed through a mysterious tube, and Edgar appeared.] *c* **1899** C. H. Chambers in M. R. Booth *Eng. Plays of 19th Cent.* (1973) III. 401 (*Rings off, and hangs up tube.*) That is another mistake—that telephone. **1959** *Esquire* Nov. 70 *Tube*, can be television, but usually telephone. Example: Buzz me on the tube. Call me up.

j. A type of skate (see quot.).

1923 E. Jessup *Snow & Ice Sports* 220 The 'tubes' are a comparatively recent departure in skate design... The blade..is set in a long hollow tube. Similar but wider tubes support the heel and front plates.

k. *the tube*, television, a television set; also, *the boob tube* [see *boob *sb.* 3]; cf. *the box* s.v. *box *sb.*[2] 3 j. *colloq.* (orig. and chiefly *U.S.*).

1959 [see sense 2 i above]. **1965** *Sunday News* (N.Y.) 4 Oct. 2 She..is making a name for herself as a singer on the tube. **1966** *Current Slang* (Univ. S. Dakota) Fall 1 Let's catch the late show on the boob tube. **1972** *Observer* 31 Dec. 24/1 Turning to the tube in order to redress the balance with a spot of the old festive vulgarity. **1977** M. French *Women's Room* (1978) ii. 115, I sit and watch the stupid boob tube. **1979** *Radio Times* 11–17 Aug. 19/1 'I see you on the tube a lot,' an American said to me recently in a pub. 'Oh really,' I replied, 'the Piccadilly line?' 'No,' he said, 'the *tube*, the dream machine.'

l. *down the tube*(*s*), lost, finished, in trouble; freq. in *to go down the tube*(*s*) = *to go down the drain* s.v. *drain *sb.* 1 e. *slang* (orig. *U.S.*).

1963 *Amer. Speech* XXXVIII. 168 To fail to pass an examination:..*go down the tubes.* **1975** *New Yorker* 5 May 32/1 It would be ludicrous to end on a note of Chris going down the tube. **1977** J. D. MacDonald *Condominium* xii. 122 We've got too many goodies tucked into the Marliss Corporation to take a chance of it going down the tube. **1982** *Listener* 16 Dec. 35/3 The smile on Sir Freddie's face the week before it was revealed that he was down the tubes to the extent of something over £270 million was the smile of a consummate actor.

m. A bottle or can of beer. *Austral. colloq.*

1969 *Listener* 24 Apr. 588/2 This..extrovert chunders..his way through the kangaroo valley of Earl's Court..buoyed up by innumerable tubes (bottles) of Foster's Beer. **1980** R. Hill *Killing Kindness* xx. 187 'What do you want to do?'..Mow my lawn and then cool off with a tube of lager, thought Pascoe.

4. b. A cigarette. *slang.*

1946 P. Larkin *Jill* 16 Christopher, extending his silver cigarette[-case], said with an uneasy smile: 'Tube for anyone?' **1975** *High Times* Dec. 11/2 (Advt.), Filter tipped tubes give a smoother smoke to the very end.

5. a. (Later example.)

1897 Kipling in *Times* 17 July 13/6 Heathen heart that puts her trust In reeking tube and iron shard.

7. b. Also, any tunnel or tubular bridge for a railway. (Earlier example.)

1847 Queen Victoria *Jrnl.* 15 Aug. (1868) 72 We passed the famous *Swilly Rocks*, and saw the works they are making for the tube for the railroad.

II. 9. c. The penis. *slang.*

1922 Joyce *Ulysses* 750, I suppose the people gave him that nickname [*sc.* Mr de Kock] going about with his tube from one woman to another.

11. b. *Surfing.* The hollow curve of a breaking wave.

1962 *Austral. Women's Weekly* 24 Oct. (Suppl.) 3/4 *Tube*, the area of a dumping wave between the breaking crest and the trough. **1968** *Surfer Mag.* Jan. 89/1 You get back inside the tube and the whole tunnel is glowing. **1979** *Nat. Geographic Mag.* Feb. 235 (*caption*) Shootin' the tube, a surfer threads the eye of a breaker.

12. b. Tube Alloys, the code name of a section of the Department of Scientific and Industrial Research formed in 1940 and concerned with research into the production of an atomic bomb; **tube counter** *Physics*, the now usual form of Geiger counter, as contrasted with the point-counter; **tube curare,** curare kept or transported in bamboo tubes; **tube-fed** *a.*, fed, sometimes forcibly, by passing nourishment through a tube into the stomach; so **tube-feed, tube-feeding** *vbl. sb.*; **tube journey,** a journey in a tube, *spec.* a journey by underground railway; **tube-lift,** a lift for the conveyance of passengers from street-level to an underground railway or vice versa; **tube map,** a map of an underground-railway system; **tube shelter,** an underground tube station used as an air-raid shelter; also *attrib.*; **tube skate** = sense 2 j above; **tube sock,** an elasticized sock with no shaping for the heel; **tube steak** *slang*, a hot dog, a frankfurter; **tube top,** a women's close-fitting elasticated top reaching from the waist to under-arm level; **tube-worm** (later examples).

1942 J. Anderson in M. Gowing *Britain & Atomic Energy 1939–45* (1964) App. iii. 437 When you asked me to take over the supervision of work on the project known as 'Tube Alloys', it was contemplated that..a full scale production would be expected in this country. **1945** W. S. Churchill *Victory* (1946) 221 Imperial Chemicals Industries Limited agreed to release Mr. W. A. Akers to take charge of this directorate, which we called, for purposes of secrecy, the Directorate of 'Tube Alloys'. **1978** R. V. Jones *Most Secret War* xxxv. 309 The British 'Tube Alloys' project, as our own nuclear bomb effort was called. **1930** Tube-counter [see *coincidence 7 a]. **1938** R. W. Lawson tr. *Hevesy & Paneth's Man. Radioactivity* (ed. 2) i. 17 We shall only discuss the two [counters] that are most important.., viz. the point-counter and the tube-counter, both of which were introduced by Geiger. **1898** *Jrnl. Chem. Soc.* LXXIV. i. 284 Paracurara, or tube curara, is imported in bamboo tubes, and is the variety now usually met with in commerce. **1974** *Encycl. Brit. Micropædia* III. 300/3 Preparations have been classified according to the containers used for them: pot curare in earthenware jars; tube curare in bamboo; and calabash curare in gourds. **1909** *Westm. Gaz.* 23 Oct. 3/2 Tube-fed Suffragettes. **1964** *Lancet* 26 Dec. 1349/2 Most babies were getting their first tube-feed within 2 hours of birth. *Ibid.* 1351/1 Tube-feeding is a very much simpler procedure. **1974** *Brit. Med. Jrnl.* 19 Jan. 108/1 The ethical problems of prolonged tube-feeding. **1980** *Ibid.* 21 June 1493/1 More work is needed to assess the relative merits of these proprietary diets compared with the tube feeds prepared in hospitals. **1866** Geo. Eliot *Felix Holt* I. 2 Posterity may be shot, like a bullet through a tube, by atmospheric pressure from Winchester to Newcastle... The tube-journey can never lend much to picture and narrative. **1972** C. Fremlin *Appointment with Yesterday* i. 5 No one could guess..that there is one..that has left its identity behind not just for the duration of the tube journey, but for ever. **1915** E. Wallace *Man who bought London* ii. 19 The 'tube' lift was crowded. **1935** E. Farjeon *Nursery in Nineties* 428 Once she had ventured into a tube-lift—'But never again, my dear Eleanor!' **1962** J. Braine *Life at Top* xxiii. 256, I used to have a Tube map on my bedroom wall when I was at College? **1977** *Times* 15 Nov. 17/8 The Bakerloo line on the tube map. **1942** N. Balchin *Darkness falls from Air* xi. 196 We went..by tube... I wanted to see how the tube shelter business was working out. **1943** C. E. Milburn *Diary* 4 Mar. (1979) 170 There was a terrible accident at a tube shelter last night after the sirens had sounded in London. **1962** *Times* 23 Jan. 13/4 Henry Moore's Tube-Shelter drawings. **1923** E. Jessup *Snow & Ice Sports* 230 'Tube' skates. **1975** *Kingston* (Ontario) *Whig-Standard* 19 Dec. 12/3 As a reporter who has covered various classifications of professional hockey since the invention of tube skates, it is my considered opinion that Robert Earle Clarke is one of the most adept ankle-tappers in the history of the game. **1976** *N.Y. Times Mag.* 18 Jan. 4/2 Monday morning I bought a striped blue pair of training shoes,..tube socks, a sweatband and a book called 'On the Road to Self Improvement: The Joy of Jogging'. **1963** *Amer. Speech* XXXVIII. 272 Frankfurters are *tube steaks.* **1978** *Boston Globe* 15 Aug. 1/1 The food isn't bad which is mainly tube steaks (hot dogs). **1974** *News & Reporter* (Chester, S. Carolina) 24 Apr. 4-c (Advt.), Calico-print elasticized tube tops! **1984** *New Yorker* 23 Apr. 42/1 She was wearing khaki shorts and a lime-green tube top. **1928** Russell & Yonge *Seas* viii. 194 The case of the concealed animals, such as the Piddock or the Tube-worm,..presents almost equal difficulties. **1981** *Sci. Amer.* May 90/3 Occasionally a crab would climb the stalk of a tube worm, presumably to attack its plume.

tube, *v.* Add: **4.** *trans.* and *intr.* To fail, to perform poorly (in). *U.S. slang.*

1966 *Current Slang* (Univ. S. Dakota) Summer 5 *Tube*, to fail; to do a poor job. College students, both sexes. Midwest. 'He tubed every test last week.' **1979** *N.Y. Times Mag.* 30 Sept. 10/3 In time, surfers used the verb 'to tube' to mean 'to do poorly'.

tubectomy (tiūbe·ktŏmi). *Surg.* [f. TUBE *sb.* + *-ECTOMY.] = *salpingectomy* s.v. *SALPINGO-.

1925 STEDMAN *Med. Dict.* (ed. 8) 1057/2 *Tubectomy*, salpingectomy. **1975** *Lancet* 27 Sept. 567/1 (*heading*) Tubectomy by paraprofessional surgeons in rural Bangladesh. **1977** *Time* 7 Feb. 45/3 The government is pushing birth control programmes: 6 million people underwent vasectomies or tubectomies in six months last year.

tubed, *ppl. a.* Add: **2.** Of a race-horse: having a metallic tube inserted in the air-passage.

1925 W. & A. J. DAY *Racehorse in Training* 13 Tubed horses are rather a nuisance, as the tube should be taken out and disinfected occasionally. **1955** *Times* 13 May 3/3 In the absence of Defender, the tubed steeplechaser Remy was made favourite for the long-distance race, against four opponents.

tubercular, *a.* Add: **B.** *sb.* A person having tuberculosis.

1952 *Sun* (Baltimore) 2 July 14/3 Maryland has three State institutions for the chronically sick, four hospitals for tuberculars, and four for the mentally ill. **1980** I. HUNTER *Malcolm Muggeridge* x. 177 In 1949 Orwell left the Isle of Jura to enter a convalescent home for tuberculars at Cranham in Gloucestershire.

tuberculin. Add: **b.** *attrib.* and *Comb.*, as *tuberculin reaction*, † *treatment*; **tuberculin test**, the injection of tuberculin, usu. intradermally, as a test for the past or present existence of tubercle bacilli in the individual; also as *vb. trans.*; hence **tuberculin-tested** *ppl. a.* (see quot. 1950).

1906 *Review of Reviews* Sept. 366 [It] showed no tuberculine reaction. **1955** *Sci. News Let.* 1 Oct. 221/1 The tuberculin test is a skin test. A tuberculin reaction means that tuberculosis germs have invaded the person's body and sensitized it to proteins of the TB germ. **1900** DORLAND *Med. Dict.* s.v. *Tests*, Tuberculin-test. **1908** *Med. Annual* 662 Tuberculin Test.—This test, prepared by the Pasteur Institute of Lille, claims to be diagnostic of tuberculosis in man. **1950** J. G. DAVIS *Dict. Dairying* 721 Three forms of the tuberculin test have been evolved —the ophthalmic, the subcutaneous and the intradermal. **1966** Tuberculin test [see *intradermic* adj. s.v. *INTRA- 1]. **1937** *Amer. Rev. Tuberculosis* XXXV. 598 A classification of the 56,688 persons tuberculin-tested according to age disclosed the fact that boys and girls between ten and nineteen years of age comprised almost two-thirds of the groups reported. **1936** Tuberculin-tested [see *CERTIFIED *ppl. a.* b]. **1950** J. G. DAVIS *Dict. Dairying* 721 *Tuberculin-tested milk*, milk which is derived solely from a herd of tuberculin-tested cows under licence and kept pure and unmixed with other non-tuberculin-tested milk. **1982** M. YOUNG *Elmhirsts of Dartington* xi. 277 Nielsen admitted to disposing of a small quantity of milk as Tuberculin Tested when it was not. **1908** *Med. Annual* 47 Roemisch thinks that tuberculin treatment gives good results in a class of chronic phthisical patients, in whom the ordinary treatment with fresh air and rest at first gives marked improvement.., but after a time no further improvement can be obtained. **1912** *Nature* 12 Dec. 427/2 The mortality of the phthisical under sanatorium and tuberculin treatments.

tuberculo-. Add: **tube:rculo-pro·tein**, protein from the tubercle bacillus, *Mycobacterium tuberculosis*; **tube:rculosta·tic** *a.* [*-STATIC], inhibiting the multiplication of the tubercle bacillus, *Mycobacterium tuberculosis*.

1912 HAMMAN & WOLMAN *Tuberculin in Diagnosis & Treatm.* III. 231 Tuberculocidin represents the attempts by Klebs to purify tuberculin by alcohol and bismuth precipitation... He also produced tuberculo-protein and tuberculo-sozin. **1954** S. DUKE-ELDER *Parsons' Dis. Eye* (ed. 12) xvi. 218 In many cases the presence of sensitivity can be demonstrated by skin-reactions to tuberculoprotein or streptococci. **1945** *Jrnl. Immunol.* L. 159 Sera, either from rabbits sensitized with a purified tuberculin protein preparation or from tuberculous rabbits, possessed tuberculostatic activities in the chick membrane. **1971** *Nature* 4 June 301/1 We recently proposed structure (I) for the tuberculostatic antibiotic viomycin.

tuberculoid, *a.* Add: **a.** Also *Path.* (Example.)

1974 *Trypanosomiasis & Leishmaniasis* (Ciba Foundation Symp.) 163 In localized forms we often saw epithelioid or tuberculoid nodules, surrounded by a thick infiltration of lymphoid cells.

b. *Path.* Designating one of the two principal forms of leprosy, characterized by a few well-defined lesions similar to those of tuberculosis, often with anæsthesia.

1938 *Leprosy Rev.* IX. 20 No progress can be made.. unless it is frankly admitted that at the Manila Conference [in 1931] the significance and extent of the tuberculoid phases of leprosy were not fully appreciated. *Ibid.*, Anaesthesia is by no means the sole preserve of tuberculoid leprosy. **1948** E. MUIR *Man. of Leprosy* ix. 49 The term 'tuberculoid' is given on account of the histological resemblance of this type to chronic lesions in tuberculosis. It is a somewhat unfortunate term, as it is often confused with 'tubercular', the word formy used for the severeerl form, now called lepromatous. **1971** [see *lepromatous* adj. s.v. *LEPROMA].

tuberculome. Add: More commonly as mod.L. **tuberculo·ma** (pl. **-omas, -omata**).

1897 *Lippincott's Med. Dict.* 1076/1 Tuberculoma. **1908** E. A. PETERS in T. N. Kelynack *Tuberculosis in Infancy & Childhood* vii. 55 Seward has collected a hundred cases of other forms of tuberculosis of the nose—*e.g.*, tuberculoma and ulcer—from a great many sources. **1954** S. DUKE-ELDER *Parsons' Dis. Eye* (ed. 12) xxx. 508 Intracranial tumours (including neoplasms and such lesions as tuberculomata) produce two sets of symptoms. **1974** J. D. MAYNARD in R. M. Kirk et al. *Surgery* x. 215/1 A tuberculoma, a round focus over 1 cm in diameter, which has failed to disappear after adequate chemotherapy.

tubero-. Add: **tu:bero-hypophyseal, -ial** *a. Anat.* = next; **tu:bero-infundi·bular** *a. Anat.*, relating to the tuber cinereum and the infundibulum; *spec.* applied to a tract of nerve fibres that includes those running from the infundibular and related nuclei of the hypothalamus to the infundibulum.

1962 Tubero-hypophyseal [see *tubero-infundibular* below]. **1969** TRUEX & CARPENTER *Human Neuroanat.* (ed. 6) xix. 494/2 The connections of the hypothalamus with the posterior lobe of the hypophysis are well established for man... A smaller bundle [of nerve fibres], the tuberohypophysial tract, is contributed by the medial cells of the tuber cinereum. **1962** J. SZENTÁGOTHAI in J. Szentágothai et al. *Hypothalamic Control of Anterior Pituitary* ii. 45 This system corresponds to the tubero-hypophyseal tract of Spatz (1951) and Nowakowski (1951). Since it terminates in the median eminence and in the proximal part of the stalk, it would be better to term it tubero-infundibular tract. **1980** *Gray's Anat.* (ed. 36) 966/1 The tuber cinereum around the base of the infundibulum is raised to form a median eminence which ..is superficially marked by a shallow tubero-infundibular sulcus.

tuberose, *a.* Add: *tuberose sclerosis* = *tuberous sclerosis* s.v. *TUBEROUS *a.* 2.

1933 W. R. BRAIN *Dis. Nervous Syst.* ix. 487 Beyond the fact that tuberose sclerosis is due to a congenital abnormality..little is known about its aetiology. **1963** *Lancet* 12 Jan. 67/2 When in the Royal Air Force during the war I saw a man with tuberose sclerosis it was not unexpected to find in his son evidence of the same, genetically determined, disorder.

tuberous, *a.* Add: **2.** *tuberous sclerosis*, a rare, hereditary, usu. fatal disease in which there are hard swellings on the brain and elsewhere, with symptoms including mental deficiency and epilepsy.

1898 C. K. MILLS *Nervous Syst. & its Dis.* v. 503 Tuberous Sclerosis. An interesting form of sclerotic pseudotumor is sometimes found in the brain, especially among the idiotic..and epileptic. **1954** S. DUKE-ELDER *Parsons' Dis. Eye* (ed. 12) xviii. 313 Tuberous Sclerosis (Bourneville's Disease), occurring in young individuals, is associated with nodular lesions in the central nervous system and the skin, particularly on the face (adenoma sebaceum). **1975** SWAIMAN & WRIGHT *Practice of Pediatric Neurol.* II. xxxii. 739/1 Tuberous sclerosis is best identified by cutaneous signs associated with neurologic deterioration and myoclonic seizures.

tubi-. Add: **tu·bifex** [mod.L. (J. B. P. A. de M. de Lamarck *Hist. Nat. Animaux sans Vertèbres* (1816) III. 224)], a red oligochæte worm of the genus of this name, found in mud at the bottom of rivers or lakes and used as live food for aquarium animals; also *attrib.*; **tubi·ficid** [mod.L. family name *Tubificidæ*: see prec.], an aquatic oligochæte worm of the family Tubificidæ; also as *adj.*

1952 J. CLEGG *Freshwater Life Brit. Isles* xi. 156 *Tubifex* worms lay their eggs in oval capsules and breed very rapidly. **1972** *Sci. Amer.* Oct. 115/1 Among the more commonly viewed organisms are tubifex worms. **1976** *Daily Tel.* 3 Dec. 18 The river is now almost too clean. It has led to a decrease in the tubifex worm population, on which waterfowl feed. **1950** M. GORDON in E. J. Farris et al. *Care & Breeding Lab. Animals* xiv. 382 Tubificids are usually most plentiful about one-half mile downstream from the spot where raw pollution is dumped. **1971** *Nature* 26 Feb. 596/1 Tubificid worms..are typical bottom dwelling animals of all fresh-water lakes and reservoirs. **1971** *Oxf. Bk. Invertebrates* 114/1 Tubificids will emerge, tail upwards, to undulate their bodies gently in the water for respiratory exchange. **1978** *Nature* 17 Aug. 644/2 Chironomid midge larvae and tubificid worms have replaced a previously rich fauna.

tubify (tiū·bifəi), *v. nonce-wd.* [f. TUBE *sb.* + -IFY.] *trans.* ? To give a tubular form to.

1928 D. H. LAWRENCE *Lady Chatterley's Lover* xviii. 347 'I don't think Vulcan has a figure that interests me.' 'Not even if it was tubified and tittivated up?'

tubing, *vbl. sb.* Add: **b.** (See quot. 1976.) *U.S.*

1975 *Newsweek* 3 Feb. 69 But the big rage of the ski year—and the most painful—is a pastime called 'tubing'. For experts, the idea is to take a running start and then execute a belly-flop onto an ordinary inflated inner tube. **1976** *Webster's Sports Dict.* 464/1 *Tubing*, the sport or pastime of riding down a river or of sliding down a snow-covered slope on an inflated automobile inner tube. **1979** *United States 1980/81* (Penguin Travel Guides) 367 *Tubing*—Arizona's most popular summer sport. On any given weekend, as many as 20,000 residents strap beer-filled ice chests and their behinds to old inner tubes and float down the five or ten miles of free-flowing Salt River below Saguaro Lake.

Tubism (tiū·biz'm). [f. TUBE *sb.* + -ISM, after *CUBISM.] A style of painting characterized by cylindrical and other mechanistic forms, *spec.* that developed by the French artist Fernand Léger (1881–1955). So **Tu·bist** *a.*

1923 *Weekly Dispatch* 11 Feb. 9 He [*sc.* Gregory Brown] first took up applied art, working in metal. Turning his attention to poster work, he..became one of the pioneers of what was jocularly known as the Tubist School. **1955** *Times* 18 Aug. 13/1 'Tubism' serves well to describe the brand of Cubism that Léger made peculiarly his own. Out of the several possibilities indicated by Cézanne's famous remark about the geometrical basis of natural forms he selected the cylinder, and though he admitted other forms, a tubular tendency runs through most of his compositions. **1960** *Twentieth Cent.* Dec. 526 Léger's 'tubist' portraits. **1978** N. GOSLING *Paris 1900–1914* 165 Fernand Léger.. attracted by the Cubist experiments..developed a variety of his own, based on interlocking cylinders—a style which was nicknamed 'Tubism'.

tubocurarine (tiūbo,kiūᵊ·rărīn). *Pharm.* [ad. G. *tubocurarin*, f. *tubocurare* tube curare (see TUBO-, CURARE): see -IN[1].] An isoquinoline alkaloid that is the active ingredient of tube curare and whose chloride, $C_{37}H_{42}Cl_2$-N_2O_6, is used as a muscle relaxant.

1898 *Jrnl. Chem. Soc.* LXXIV. I. 284 Paracurarine (tubocurarine). **1935** *Nature* 23 Mar. 470/1 The quaternary alkaloid tubocurarine..has now been crystallised for the first time. **1973** *Reader's Digest* Apr. 206/1 They paralysed him with 70 milligrams of tubocurarine chloride. **1977** *Lancet* 19 Mar. 650/2 Three drugs used in clinical anæsthesia consistently cause arterial hypotension in patients with essential hypertension—halothane, *d*-tubocurarine, and verapamil.

tuboplasty (tiū·boplæsti). *Surg.* [f. TUBO- + -PLASTY.] The surgical repair of one or both Fallopian tubes.

1961 *Obstetr. & Gynecol.* XVII. 504/2 The combination of tuboplasty and metroplasty was indicated as an attempt to overcome sterility factors and minimize the possibility of subsequent miscarriage. **1976** *Daily Colonist* (Victoria, B.C.) 14 Apr. 2/3 A few pregnancies have resulted from tuboplasty procedures—as for unblocking a tube —but generally the results here, too, have been disappointing. **1977** *Lancet* 5 Feb. 284/2 Regular ovulation and a positive postcoital test were confirmed in each patient before tuboplasty.

tub-thumper. Add: So also (as a back-formation) **tu·b-thump** *v. intr.*; **tu·b-thu:mpery.**

1920 'SAPPER' *Bulldog Drummond* iv. 117 The sort of type one sees tub-thumping in Hyde Park. **1927** *Observer* 28 Aug. 11/4 Fanny Hawthorne's refusal to be made an honest woman..may still be regarded as advanced in ethics, even if its expression is not without a suspicion of tub-thumpery. **1933** DYLAN THOMAS *Let.* (1966) 75 And thank you for..heeding my dogmatic tub-thumpery. **1934** E. POUND *ABC of Reading* 113 A bad reader of fourteeners is almost certain to tub-thump.

tubular, *a.* Add: **1.** *tubular bells*, a series of tuned metal tubes of graded length vertically suspended and struck by hammers; *tubular goods* (Oil Industry) (see quot. 1922); *tubular steel*, steel tubing, esp. as used in the manufacture of furniture; also *attrib.*

[**1884** J. HARRINGTON *Provisional Spec. 14,270* (Patent Office) (1885) 1 Instead of employing the costly gongs or bells hitherto employed, I employ metallic tubes which I suspend vertically by means of catgut, cord or other suitable material... I arrange the hammers so as to strike the same at their upper parts above the point of suspension thereof.] **1919** A. T. BASSETT *S. Barnabas', Oxford* iii. 25 The original bell of S. Barnabas'..did service until 1890, when a set of tubular bells was hung in the tower, and a chiming machine added. **1922** D. T. DAY *Handbk. Petroleum Industry* I. 300 The term 'tubular goods' generally covers all classes of pipe, casing and tubing used in drilling or operating oil or gas wells, and comprises the following distinct types: casing, tubing, drive pipe, line pipe and rotary drill pipe. **1930** *Melody Maker* Jan. 69/1 Tubular bells are often considered 'a bit of a bore' by drummers. **1933** *Archit. Rev.* LXXIV. 78/3 Four double tubular-steel legs shaped like hair-pins. **1946** R. GRAVES *Poems 1938–45* 35 Among box-files and tubular steel chairs. **1957** *Times* 2 July (Agric. Suppl.) p. viii/3 The gate and posts are made of tubular steel. **1962** *B.S.I. News* May 19/2 Glockenspiel, xylophone, tubular bells, celesta. **1981** *Times* 3 July 14/7 Marcel Breuer, the Hungarian-born architect..created the first tubular steel furniture..and in 1926 he equipped the new Bauhaus buildings with furniture of this type.

4. c. *Ophthalm.* Applied to a visual field which is restricted to a small area surrounding the fixation point; *tubular vision* = *tunnel vision* s.v. *TUNNEL *sb.* 5.

1903 HANSELL & SWEET *Text-bk. Dis. of Eye* xviii. 488 When his sight had improved the visual fields were still contracted.., showing the so-called 'tubular' field of hysteria. **1927** H. M. TRAQUAIR *Introd. Clinical Perimetry* v. 49 A special form of concentric contraction is the 'tubular' field. The depression is severe and involves the whole field with the exception of an area surrounding the fixation point, producing a great and often extreme contraction... Such fields are obviously of functional origin. *Ibid.* xii. 222 Hysteria. The typical field change.. is concentric contraction... The field is..tubular in type, a form which is necessarily of subjective origin. **1934** *Amer. Jrnl. Ophthalmol.* XVII. 384/2 (*heading*) Transient tubular vision in postencephalitic Parkinson's disease. **1956** *New Gould Med. Dict.* (ed. 2) 1319/2 *Tubular v[ision]*, a hysterical phenomenon in which the constricted visual field defies the laws of physical projection and maintains a uniform small size..: popularly called gun-barrel v[ision]; tunnel v[ision].

B. *ellipt.* as *sb.* **1.** = *tubular bridge.*

1861 A. J. Symonds *Let.* 9 Aug. (1967) I. 303 We took a nice walk..to Bangor. We saw 2 trains go through the Tubular—one each way.

2. *pl.* = *tubular goods.*

1975 *North Sea Background Notes* (Brit. Petroleum Co.) 27 Most of each top deck will be occupied by a skid-mounted, electrically-driven drilling rig with appropriate storage for tubulars. **1979** *Shell Trade in Eastern Europe* (Shell Internat. Petroleum Co.) 5 Shell companies' purchases from countries in Eastern Europe include oil, chemicals and some metals and materials and equipment such as tubulars, rotary drilling hose, and items for sale in Shell filling-stations.

tubularia (tiūbiŭlēᵊ·riă). [See Tubularian *a.* and *sb.*] = Tubularian *sb.*

1912–13 A. S. Pringle-Pattison *Idea of God* (1917) iv. 72 The Tubularia, a kind of sea-anemone, re-grows its flower-like head. **1924** *Glasgow Herald* 19 June 258/4 The tubularia and the sea-urchin. **1971** *Oxf. Bk. Invertebrates* 8/2 Tubularia, richly-coloured, with long, drooping polyps, is common locally and found at low tide under rocky overhangs.

tubularian, *a.* (Earlier example.)

1856 Geo. Eliot *Jrnl.* 8 May–26 June in *Lett.* (1954) II. 243 G..brought home several varieties of Polyps..—Tubularian, Plumularian and Sertularian.

tubulin (tiū·biŭlin). *Biochem.* [f. Tubule + -in¹.] Either or both of two similar proteins that are the main constituent of microtubules.

1968 H. Mohri in *Nature* 16 Mar. 1054/1 We believe that the microtubule constituent is a different protein, for which we propose the name 'tubulin'. **1977** *Jrnl. Protozool.* XXIV. 4/1 Microtubules are composed of 2 subunits, termed α and β tubulins, which form dimers and then polymers that are essentially infinitely long. **1978** *Bio Systems* X. 93/1 Tubulin..can undergo self-assembly in the absence of other macromolecules to form a microtubule. **1982** J. F. Van Pilsum in T. M. Devlin *Textbk. Biochem.* xxi. 1042 Tubulin..comprises about 14% of the total protein found in mammalian brain.

T.U.C. (tī,yū,sī). Also **TUC.** Abbrev. of *trade(s) union congress* s.v. *trade-union, trades-union b.

1910 W. J. Davis *Brit. Trades Unions Congress* I. 105 The Chairman of the Parliamentary Committee presented to the Secretary..an ornate address... The monogram 'T.U.C.'..with the motto..were..beautifully inscribed. **1926** *Manch. Guardian* 4 May 12/4 His Majesty's Government..before it can continue negotiations, must require from the T.U.C...an immediate and unconditional withdrawal of the instructions for a general strike. **1947** *Radio Times* 2 May 16/3 George Woodcock, Assistant General Secretary of the T.U.C. **1955** *Times* 2 May 20/1 It is extraordinary that the T.U.C. should actually be advocating an increase in the tax on distributed profits. **1976** F. Zweig *New Acquisitive Society* ii. i. 81 Three decades of incomes policies have enormously enhanced the status of the TUC and unions at large.

tuchas, var. *tochus.

‖ **tuchun** (dudʒün, tū·tʃun). *Hist.* Also **Tuchün, Tu Chün.** [Chinese *dūjūn*, f. *dū* govern + *jūn* military.] In China at the time of the Three Kingdoms, the title of a military leader; later, in the early years of the Republic of China, the highest military leader in a province; a warlord.

1917 S. Couling *Encycl. Sinica* 213/2 During the disturbances of the last few years it has frequently happened that the post of Governor has been combined with that of 'Tu Chün'..or Military Governor. This latter is the principal military official of the province. **1920** *Nineteenth Cent.* Dec. 942 Nowadays, a *tuchun* or military governor, ..will address the foreigner in a patchwork of stilted literary phrases jumbled together. **1943** J. T. Pratt *War & Politics in China* xii. 194 After the death of Yuan Shih Kai China for several years presented a sorry spectacle of politicians quarrelling and Tuchuns waging civil war. **1977** J. Cleary *High Road to China* i. 15 He was a Confucian, but he had a more immediate master, the *tuchun*, the war lord, in Hunan.

Hence **tu·chunate,** the rule of tuchuns, the office of tuchun.

1923 *Times Lit. Suppl.* 23 Aug. 558/1 At present the Tuchuns control their respective armies and are giving endless trouble. It would not, however, be sufficient to abolish the Tuchunate. A national army is necessary.

tuchus, var. *tochus.

tuck, *sb.*¹ Add: **1.** Also *fig.*

1878 'Mark Twain' in *Atlantic* Jan. 17/2 We had an iron-clad chicken... He ought to have been put through a quartz mill until the 'tuck' was taken out of him. **1910** *N.Y. Evening Post* 10 Nov. 1 The sight of a wounded man lying on the pavement seemed to take the tuck out of the mob.

7*. In diving, gymnastics, etc., (the adoption of) a tuck position (see sense 8 below). Also, in downhill skiing, a squatting position (see quot. 1976).

1951 *Swimming* (Eng. Schools Swimming Assoc.) v. 81 The seat is drawn up and the head dropped slightly forward on the tuck, causing the body to spin. **1956** Kunzle & Thomas *Freestanding* vi. 81 The tuck and open out, as in the backward somersault, should be sharp and distinct movements. **1964** *Trampolining* ('Know the Game' Series) 31/1 It is better to learn the action slowly and then the tuck can be added later for effect and for faster rotation. **1976** *Webster's Sports Dict.* 464/1 *Tuck*.., a position in which the skier squats forward and holds his ski poles under his arms and parallel to the ground that is usually used to minimize wind resistance in downhill racing. **1981** 'E. Lathen' *Going for Gold* xvii. 186 There was..no discontinuity between being earthborne and airborne, no jerking resolution of the hunched-over tuck into the aerial float high over the heads of the spectators. *Ibid.* xxi. 232 Tilly..hunched into the tightest tuck that Dick had ever seen, increased her speed to flat-out downhill velocity.

8. tuck box, a box for storing eatables etc., esp. at a boarding-school (see sense 6); **tuck-comb** *U.S.* = *tucking-comb* s.v. Tucking *vbl. sb.*¹ 5; **tuck position,** in diving, gymnastics, etc., a position in which the thighs are pulled close to the chest, the knees bent, and the hands clasped round the shins; **tuck-stitch,** a stitch used in making a tuck; also *attrib.*; so **tuck-stitched** *a.*

1934 I. W. Hutchison *North to Rime-Ringed Sun* xviii. 207 Tuck-boxes were then opened and supper cooked and demolished. **1978** G. Greene *Human Factor* ii. ii. 70, I used to steal out at night from my dormitory and take him tins of sardines from my tuck-box. **1824** Tuck comb [see *side-comb]. **1870** E. Eggleston *Queer Stories* viii. 63 Sukey's way of doing up her hair in a great knot, behind, with an old-fashioned tuck comb. **1931** *Morning Post* 7 Aug. 14/2 All you have to do is hang on to your 'tuck', or 'balled-up' position a little longer. **1964** *Trampolining* ('Know the Game' Series) 32/2 Allow knees to bend to give a loose tuck position here and this helps to speed rotation. **1974** *Encycl. Brit. Macropædia* XVII. 864/1 In the tuck position, the body is gathered tightly into a ball with the hands grasping the shins firmly. **1926** J. Chamberlain *Hosiery, Yarns & Fabrics* vi. 121 The tuck-stitch is a defect in the plain fabric, but if produced systematically, forms many classes of designs. **1971** *Guardian* 7 Sept. 9/1 Tuck-stitch slipover vest in lambswool. **1922** Joyce *Ulysses* 171 In tuckstitched shirt sleeves.

tuck, *v.*¹ Add: **8.** Freq. with *away*; also *fig.*; also, to hit (a ball) to the desired place.

1912 [in Dict.]. **1936** J. Buchan *Island of Sheep* v. 99 My first business must be to tuck him away comfortably somewhere out of the road. **1958** *Observer* 6 July 24/4 There was greater punch in Miss Gibson's game once she had the first set safely tucked away. **1959** *Times* 29 May 4/6 His low forehand, as he tucks the ball away, is a special weapon of execution. **1966** *Listener* 12 May 702/3 What a pity that it should be tucked away into that most unlikely of all listening hours, the end of a Saturday evening. **1977** *Times* 7 Feb. 7/3 Tueart..outpaced a scattered defence and efficiently tucked away a rebound after Shilton had superbly blocked his first attempt.

tu·ck-away, *a.* [f. the vbl. phr. *to tuck away*: see Tuck *v.*¹ 8 in Dict. and Suppl.] That may be tucked away.

1935 *Sun* (Baltimore) 9 Nov. 1/3 The clipper's spick-and-span tuckaway galley producing hot bouillon, fried chicken and fruit. **1968** *Harrods Christmas Catal.* 5/3 Satin evening pochette with gilt tuck-away chain handle. **1979** *Arizona Daily Star* 1 Apr. (Advt. Section) 9/3, 1968 International 18' high cube van trucks with tuck away tailgates.

tucked, *ppl. a.* **1.** (Example with *in.*)

1963 R. N. Frye *Heritage of Persia* v. 198 The nomadic background of the Parthians may be seen in some equestrian features of dress, such as leggings *cum* boots with tucked-in trousers.

tucker, *sb.* Add: **6.** Also *N.Z.*

1864 J. C. Richmond *Let.* 12 May in *Richmond-Atkinson Papers* (1960) II. 111 It is very hard work humping your blankets and tucker. **1870** *Append. Jrnls. House Representatives N.Z.* D. xl. 4 Tucker Flat..has been looked upon as containing worse than 'tucker' ground. **1911** W. H. Koebel *In Maoriland Bush* xxi. 275 If they had obtained no wages for the first six months or so, they would have obtained their 'tucker' free. **1972** M. Shadbolt *Strangers & Journeys* iii. 43 Later Ned got the tucker cooking. It was stew and spud, like most nights.

Hence **tu·ckerless** *a.* (*Austral.* and *N.Z.*), without food.

1937 E. Hill *Great Austral. Loneliness* x. 82 The rind of the pods..makes an acrid but nourishing food..that tides over the tuckerless white man to the next out-camp. **1946** A. P. Harper *Mem. Mountains & Men* xvi. 162 We were left almost 'tuckerless' on Christmas Day.

tucker (tʊ·kəɹ), *v.*² *colloq.* (orig. and chiefly *Austral.* and *N.Z.*). [f. Tucker *sb.* 6.] **1.** *trans.* To supply with food. Also *refl.*

1899 *Bulletin* (Sydney) 21 Jan. 14/3 An oldish widower with three sons..goes out to work with Son No. 1, leaving the other two mites at home to mind the 's'lection' and tucker themselves. Old man comes home every month or so. **1920** B. Cronin *Timber Wolves* 40, I got a friend hereabouts that tuckers me when I'm along this way. **1940** E. I. Lord *Old Westland* xi. 137 He 'tuckered' many a down and out digger. **1964** B. Wannan *Fair Go, Spinner* (1965) iv. 126 In those days, the shearers had to provide their own food supplies—'to tucker themselves', as they put it.

2. *intr.* To eat, to have a meal. Also with *up.*

1903 H. B. King *Bill's Philosophy* 24 I'm sick of starving, when a cove can tucker free. **1940** F. D. Davison *Woman at Mill* 143 We were counting on it [*sc.* a money order] to tucker up with in Bairnsdale. **1959** H. P. Tritton *Time means Tucker* (1965) v. 64 We tuckered at the house and Mrs. Craig fed us till we couldn't eat another thing. **1963** *Weekly News* (Auckland, N.Z.) 5 June 37/2 The cowboy was tuckering at the cookshop on his own.

tu·ck-in, *a.* [f. the vbl. phr. *to tuck in*: see Tuck *v.*¹ 9.] That may be tucked in; *spec.* of a woman's blouse, etc., designed to have its lower edge tucked into the skirt.

1929 *Daily Express* 7 Nov. 5/2 Two [blouses] are 'tuck-in', and the other comes over the skirt. **1965** *Harper's Bazaar* June 65 Slashed tuck-in top.

tucking, *vbl. sb.* **5. tucking-comb** (earlier example).

1822 in *Dict. Amer. Eng.* (1944) IV. 2369/1 Mr. Pettigrew Bot of D McDowell one tucking Comb at $4.50.

tu·ck-up. [f. the vbl. phr. *to tuck up*: see Tuck *v.*¹ 6, 9.] † **1.** A fold or plait of hair. *Obs.*

1749 J. Cleland *Mem. Woman Pleasure* I. 186 His hair, which was of a perfect shining black, play'd to his face in natural side-curls, and was set out with a smart tuck-up behind.

2. A boat of a particular construction (see quot. 1889).

1887 *Forest & Stream* 24 Feb. 94/1 The tuckup could swing 300 sq. ft. if desired. **1889** W. P. Stephens *Canoe & Boat Building* (ed. 4) 239 The peculiar name 'tuckup' is derived from the fact that in building, the flat keel is not carried out straight from the stem to sternpost..but it..'tucks up'..to the height of the waterline.

3. The action or an act of tucking someone up in bed.

1915 H. L. Wilson *Ruggles of Red Gap* iv. 81, I was strangely a little warmed at thinking I might not have seen the last of Cousin Egbert, whom I had just given a tuckup.

Tudeh (tū·de). [a. Pers., lit. 'mass'.] In full *Tudeh party.* The Communist Party of Iran. Also *attrib.*

1946 *Civil & Milit. Gaz.* 16 Mar. 2/2 The Tudeh (Proletarian) Party in Azerbaijan, or what is left of it in Persia. **1966** S. Zabih *Communist Movement in Iran* iii. 73 In its first phase the Communist movement assumed the characteristics of a democratic front... Its organizational expression was the Tudeh party of Iran, formed in early October, 1941. **1979** *Economist* 8 Sept. 60/3 There are about a dozen leftist groups (three Chinese, two Trotskyists), all in opposition except for Tudeh, the official Communist party. **1980** J. Cartwright *Horse of Darius* x. 145 They have eliminated two hundred Tudeh Communists and Russian agents in the last few months. *Ibid.* 153 Let us concentrate on the Tudeh. Does our man in Iran know what they are up to?

Tudesco (tude·sko). Also **Tedesco.** Fem. **Tudesca.** [Ladino, = Sp., Pg. *tudesco* German.] A colloq. term among Sephardic Jews for an Ashkenazic Jew.

1897 I. Zangwill *King of Schnorrers* i. 12 You are a Tedesco. *Ibid.* v. 116 A Sephardi marry a Tedesco! Shameful. **1932** C. Roth *Hist. of Marranos* viii. 234 They accentuated the superficial differences..between them and the *tudescos*, from Germany and Poland, or even the *italianos* and *berberiscos* whose antecedents were nearer to their own. *Ibid.* xii. 316 Jacob Israel Bernal..desired to marry a *tudesca*—a member of the despised German and Polish community. **1949** *Spectator* 4 Nov. 595/1 Not so long ago English Sephardic families used to sit in mourning if one of their members married, not a Goy (or non-Jew), but a Tudesco (or Ashkenazi Jew). **1964** M. Wohlgelernter *Israel Zangwill* ii. vi. 85 The intended union of Menasseh's daughter with a Polish Jew excites..horror in..the *Mahamad*. A Tedesco did not pronounce Hebrew as they did, hence he was inferior.

Tudor, *a.* Add: **2.** (Further examples of buildings not belonging to the Tudor period, = mock Tudor.) Also of interior decoration. Also *Tudor-style* adj.

1902 G. E. Mitton *Hampstead & Marylebone* 23 There is the police-station..and adjacent an interesting Tudor house, which, though not old, is well built. **1928** Kipling *Bk. of Words* 267, I have only to leave the Tudor grill-room, take the electric lift upstairs. **1953** R. Lehmann *Echoing Grove* 177 A chintzy Tudor-style hotel. **1955** M. Gilbert *Sky High* viii. 116 They had a glass of sherry in the Tudor Bar, followed by a meal in the Jacobean Dining-Room. **1970** *Globe & Mail* (Toronto) 26 Sept. 42/6 (Advt.), Charming Tudor bungalow with pretty garden. **1978** J. Pudney *Thank Goodness for Cake* 82 Their Tudor-style manor house. **1979** R. Jaffe *Class Reunion* ii. iv. 156 Would they like this Tudor house, or that Spanish one?

B. *sb.* **a.** Mock-Tudor style. **b.** *N. Amer.* A house in mock-Tudor style.

1939, etc. [see *Stockbroker's Tudor* s.v. *stock-broker, stockbroker b]. **1961** 'J. le Carré' *Call for Dead* iv. 37 The Fountain Café..was all Tudor and horse brasses. **1969** E. Sandon *View into Village* 93 At the Somerton corner is the Boxted and Hartest Club erected..in 1888, in red brick Tudor, with two gigantic oriel windows. **1969** P. ZELVER *Honey Bunch* vii. 35 The Swopes lived on one side of the McKittricks in an English Tudor. **1980** *News & Observer* (Raleigh, N. Carolina) 28 Oct. WA-5/5 This tudor is located on a circular street with many trees.

Tudorbethan (tiū:dǭɪbī·þăn), *a.* (and *sb.*). [Blend of TUDOR *a.* and ELIZABETHAN *a.*] Mock Tudor; imitative of Tudor and Elizabethan styles. Also *ellipt.* as *sb.*

1933 LEAVIS & THOMPSON *Culture & Environment* 32 The outbreak of 'Tudorbethan' villas. **1958** *Spectator* 4 July 13/1 The 'mediæval character' of their 1930-Tudorbethan neighbours. **1960** *House & Garden* June 66/2 Proper treatment can make bearable the most vulgar stockbroker's 'Tudorbethan'. **1975** *Times* 13 Aug. 10/4 [Liberty's] store was rebuilt in 1924 to the Tudorbethan designs of E. T. and E. S. Hall. **1977** *Guardian Weekly* 29 July 19/2 A flash of black-and-white Tudorbethan pastiche.

Tudory (tiū·dǭri), *sb.* [f. TUDOR *a.* + -Y³.] Mock-Tudor architecture or decoration.

1959 P. BULL *I know Face* viii. 144 The atmosphere of old Tudory and brass ornaments brings my bile to boiling-point. **1973** R. HILL *Ruling Passion* I. i. 11 Above the thatched roof a flock of television aerials..sang their triumph over charm and Tudory.

Tudory (tiū·dǭri), *a.* [f. TUDOR *a.* + -Y¹.] Imitative or suggestive of Tudor style.

1970 A. FOWLES *Dupe Negative* xi. 141 The Tudory dining room. **1974** R. INGHAM *Yoris* xiii. 41 The May Pole..was beamy and Tudory and phony.

Tudric (tiū·drik). [App. f. TUD(OR *a.* + CYM)RIC *a.*] The proprietary designation of a type of pewter (see quots.).

1902 (*title*) 'Cymric' gold and silverwork jewellery and 'Tudric' pewter (Liberty & Co.). **1904** *Jrnl. Soc. Arts* 10 June 638/1 For pewter..only modifications of Celtic forms were used, and these were soon supplemented by floral and plant motives to which the distinguishing name of 'Tudric' was given. **1922** *Trade Marks Jrnl.* 7 Feb. 232 *Tudric*... Pewter Ware. Liberty & Co. (Cymric) Limited, 16, Hylton Street, Birmingham; manufacturers of pewter wares. **1963** *Archit. Rev.* CXXXIII. 108/2 Two or three years afterwards, he was to add the range of 'Tudric' pewter to his enterprises. **1977** FLEMING & HONOUR *Penguin Dict. Decorative Arts* 468/2 From 1894 he [*sc.* Sir Arthur Liberty] produced silver in an Art Nouveau version of the Celtic style which he termed 'Cymric' and from 1903 a new type of pewter, with a high proportion of silver in the alloy, which he called 'Tudric'.

tuff-tuff (tɒf,tɒf). Anglicized f. *TEUF-TEUF.

1902 E. GLYN *Refl. Ambrosine* v. 62 The tuff-tuff-tuff of a motor car was heard, and it drew up at our gate. **1903** *Daily Chron.* 1 July 3/2 'When one has steered one's "tuff-tuff" all day,' said a Parisian..'or been driven through the clouds in a balloon.' **1982** N. FREELING *Wolfnight* 98 He managed..with a tufftuff to Kehl..and walked across the Europa Bridge.

tufted, *a.* Add: **1. b.** *spec.* Of a carpet, carpeting, etc. (see quot. 1960). Also *ellipt.* as *sb.*

1960 *Textile Terms & Definitions* (Textile Inst.) (ed. 4) 152 Tufted Carpet consists essentially of a pile yarn of tufts or loops which is inserted into a pre-woven backing and secured by means of a bonding material. **1963** *Which?* Mar. 70/2 Tufted carpets..are easier and cheaper to make than Wiltons or Axminsters. *Ibid.*, Tufteds may have cut or loop pile. **1965** *Guardian* 31 Mar. 14/1 Poor performance fibres..tended to give tufteds such an unwelcome reputation in the 1950s. **1970** *Which?* Sept. 265/2 There is a..labelling code..which requires that the label gives..the type of construction (eg Axminster, Wilton or tufted). **1981** *Times* 10 Aug. 16/1 The company..played the pioneering role in introducing the cheaper-to-make tufted carpet to a British market dominated by traditionally woven Axminster or Wilton.

tufting, *vbl. sb.* Add: **1. a.** (Later examples.)

1967 E. SHORT *Embroidery & Fabric Collage* iii. 68 There is no reason why good designs should not be carried out in candlewick cotton, using either tufting or couching and surface stitchery. **1976** *Daily Tel.* 21 Oct. 17/2 Knitting, crochet,..tufting and soft-toy making.

c. The process of making tufted carpeting, etc. Also *attrib.*

1965 *Guardian* 31 Mar. 14/1 In inserting the pile vertically rather than horizontally as in weaving, tufting has been limited as to the range of effects which can be produced. *Ibid.*, Tufting machines are exclusively American and British developments. **1970** *Encycl. Americana* XXIII. 763 In tufting, a preconstructed backing is used for the basic carpet structure... As the backing fabric moves through the machine, the pile yarns are stitched through it by a long bank of needles working simultaneously. **1974** J. GRAY *Canvas Work* 121 (*heading*) Turkey (Single Knot Tufting)... This stitch, like all tufting stitches, is best worked from bottom to top of the area. **1976** J. MESSENT *Designing for Embroidery from Anc. & Prim. Sources* I. 28/1 Stumpwork, raised work, high padding and quilting are among some methods of creating a protruding area of interest from an otherwise flat surface, as is a highly textured area such as a shaggy pile or tufting.

tug, *sb.* Add: **3. c.** *tug of love*, a conflict of affections; *spec.* a contest for custody of a minor; also (with hyphens) *attrib.*

Perh. infl. by the title of a comedy 'The Tug of Love' by I. Zangwill (1907).

1973 *Times* 9 Nov. 20/7 The Houghton committee was set up after some highly-publicized 'tug of love' cases, and recommended making it easier for long-term foster-parents..to adopt. **1977** *Daily Mirror* 21 Mar. 13/1 Back home in the arms of her mother, a tiny tug-of-love girl sleeps peacefully. The girl..had been taken to California after being snatched by her father. **1984** *Times* 12 Oct. 2/2 'Tug of love' cases where a child is seized by one parent from another.

4. g. A rope. *U.S.*

1805 M. LEWIS *Jrnl.* in *Lewis & Clark Exped.* (1904) I. 369 The white perogue..[was] refitted in a few minutes with some tugs of raw hides and nales. **1852** H. C. WATSON *Nights in Block-House* 445 They took a strong tug, made from the raw hide of the buffalo or elk. **1910** W. M. RAINE *B. O'Connor* xiv. 216 He stopped as if to fasten a tug.

6. b. Any other towing craft or vehicle, *spec.* (*a*) = *tug aircraft* below; (*b*) a tractor used to tow aircraft on the ground or unpowered road vehicles.

1942 *Jrnl. R. Aeronaut. Soc.* XLVI. 7 Aircraft towing as a method for launching high-performance gliders is a relatively recent development. Up till now, no specially designed aircraft 'tug' has become available. **1945** *Amer. Speech* XX. 227/2 *Tug*, a four- or six-wheeled tractor used for towing planes on the ground or for towing warehouse trailers. **1960** *Times Rev. Industry* Nov. 20/3 A..tractor can be a tug for two..vans. **1981** *Times* 14 Dec. 22/8 Tugs could not move the big jets because of ice.

7*. [Perh. a different word.] *Public School slang.* At Eton College, a student on the foundation, a colleger as distinguished from an oppidan. In wider use, a studious or academic type, a swot.

1864 *Eton School Days* ii. 21 That building on the right is Tuggery, where the Tug-Muttons live; you'll hate the Tugs like anything: all the Oppidans hate the Tugs. **1922** S. LESLIE *Oppidan* iv. 48 *Tugs* or Scholars were separated from Oppidans by the same gulf that lay between Professionals and Gentlemen in the world of sport. **1976** R. POUND *A. P. Herbert* i. 23 In Wykehamist parlance, he was a 'tug', a clever chap, whose achievement was held worthier than any playing-field victory. **1977** A. J. AYER *Part of My Life* ii. 34 Traditionally, the Oppidans despised the Collegers, who tended to come from a lower social stratum, and spoke of them as Tugs, because they were believed to engage in tugs of war for the few pieces of mutton which was all that they were given to eat. **1982** BARR & YORK *Official Sloane Ranger Handbk.* 71/1 Swots are weeds (at Eton: 'tugs don't wash').

8. tug aircraft, a powered aircraft used to tow a glider or train of gliders; **tug-boating** *U.S.*, working on a tug-boat; † **tug-mutton** = sense 7* above; **tug pilot,** the pilot of a tug aircraft; **tug-rope:** for † read '*obs.* exc. *U.S.*' (later examples).

1931 *Flight* 26 June 578/2 The tug aircraft, as it will probably be called. **1962** [see *parachute aircraft* s.v. *PARACHUTE *sb.* 5]. **1976** J. COLVILLE *Footprints in Time* xxxiii. 185 Soon there were fleets of gliders too. As each was released over the river, its tug-aircraft turned steeply away for home. **1941** E. P. O'DONNELL *Great Big Doorstep* xxi. 310 If it wasn't for rain, I wooden have a job to hole down. You'd see me tugboatin on the river or some kinda ordinary work. **1973** *Publ. Amer. Dial. Soc.* LX. 1 The coastal fringes are ideally suited to those who make their living from the sea—fishing, whaling.., boatbuilding, tugboating. **1864** Tug-mutton [see sense 7* above]. **1948** PARTRIDGE *Dict. Forces' Slang* 197 *Tug pilot*, the pilot of an aeroplane towing a glider. (Colloquial.) **1978** A. WELCH *Bk. of Airsports* iii. 48/2 When experienced as a tug pilot, you will probably be given the occasional cross-country retrieve from a field or private airstrip. **1852** J. REYNOLDS *Pioneer Hist. Illinois* 236 They often pack their meat..by running a tug rope through each piece. **1891** *Century Mag.* Mar. 774/2 We began by eating the rawhide tug ropes and parfleches.

Hence **Tu·ggery** *Eton College slang*, the collegers' boarding-house; the position or status of a colleger.

1864 [see TUG *sb.* 7*]. **1883** J. BRINSLEY-RICHARDS *Seven Yrs. at Eton* xii. 112 [A boy] who had come from Aberdeen 'to try for Tuggery'—that is, to try and pass on to the foundation as a King's scholar.

tug (tɒg), *a.* *Public School slang.* [Origin uncertain: cf. TUG *sb.* 7*.] (Esp. at Winchester College) ordinary, commonplace.

1890 BARRÈRE & LELAND *Dict. Slang* II. 378/2 *Tug* (Winchester College), usual, ordinary, common, stale, as tug-clothes, every-day clothes. **1907** *Wykehamist* Mar. 387/1 Accounts of events, 'tug' to the average reader, but recorded in print for the sake of the past and the future. **1951** C. P. SNOW *Masters* vi. 53 No one on earth could call Jago tug... He's the least commonplace of men.

tug, *v.* Add: **7. b.** To tow (a glider) by means of a powered aircraft.

1942 W. S. CHURCHILL *Second World War* (1951) IV. 800 The Whitley aircraft..is unsuitable for tugging gliders.

tugged (tɒgd), *ppl. a.* [f. TUG *v.* + -ED¹.] *tugged-at*: pulled at.

1930 AUDEN *Poems* 25 The tugged-at teat. **1962** I. MURDOCH *Unofficial Rose* xxxiv. 320 Tugged-at leaves and whirling branches knew that summer was defeated and departing.

tughra, tuğra, varr. *TOUGHRA.

tugrik (tū·grik). Also **tukhrik.** [Mongolian.] A monetary unit of Mongolia, equal to one hundred mongos.

1935, etc. [see *MONGO²]. **1978** *Financial Times* 10 Jan. 21/2 The Mongolian tugrik has lately been reported to stand at an official commercial rate of 0·225 Russian roubles.

tugtupite (tɒ·gtɒpəit). *Min.* [f. the name of *Tugtup* agtakôrfia in southern Greenland, where it was first found + -ITE¹.] A tetragonal aluminosilicate and chloride of sodium and beryllium, $Na_4AlBeSi_4O_{12}Cl$.

1962 H. SØRENSEN in *Meddelelser om Grønland* CLXVII. I. 219 At the oral presentation of the mineral, it was suggested that it should be termed tugtupite, because it clearly differs from sodalite. **1977** *Mineral. Mag.* XLI. 130 Tugtupite..has a distorted sodalite type of structure.

tuhseel, var. *TAHSIL.

tui. (Earlier example.)

1832 A. EARLE *Narr. Residence in N.Z.* 174 The only sounds which broke the calm were the wild notes of the tooe (or New Zeland blackbird).

tuica, ţuica, varr. *TSUICA.

Tuileries (twīlĕri). *Hist.* [Fr., so called because built on the site of an ancient tile-works: see TUILLE, TUILE.] A palace in Paris begun by Catherine de Medici in 1564 and destroyed by fire in 1871. It stood on the site between the Champs Elysées and the Louvre, now occupied by the Jardin des Tuileries, and was a residence of the court in royal and imperial France: hence, the royal or imperial family, the court, the administration.

1814 M. BIRKBECK *Journey through France* 81 Every paragraph in the public journals is modelled and pared down to suit the temper of the Tuilleries. **1863** [see POLITESSE]. **1885** H. JAMES *Little Tour in France* xi. 80 The gardens..are the promenade—the Tuileries—of the town [*sc.* Bourges]. **1967** *Listener* 25 May 678/1 By the end of the next decade, [Victor] Hugo..had become ..the tame poet of the Tuileries. **1972** T. ARONSON *Queen Victoria & Bonapartes* x. 126 The coolness between Windsor and the Tuileries.

tuille, tuile. Add: ‖ **2.** As **tuile.** A thin curved biscuit, usu. made with almonds. Also *attrib.* and with defining addition.

1943 A. L. SIMON *Conc. Encycl. Gastron.* IV. 133/1 *Tuiles d'oranges.* Cream 1 oz. butter, add 1½ oz. castor sugar and cream together. Add 1½ oz. chopped blanched almonds, 1½ oz. chopped candied peel, dessertspoonful flour, dessertspoonful milk. **1966** *Observer* (Colour Suppl.) 3 Apr. 41 In France the biscuits shown below are called 'tuiles'—which is French for roof tiles. These thin, crisp biscuits contain chips of almond. **1972** P. V. PRICE *Eating & Drinking in France Today* II. 276 *Tuiles* from Amiens (thin chocolate and orange biscuits). **1976** *Times* 2 Oct. 10/3 The coffee ice was served in a tuile basket. **1979** *Harper's & Queen* Apr. 42/1 Sorbets..in a fragile basket of crisp, sweet, *tuiles*, made without almonds.

Tuinal (tiū·inăl). *Pharm.* [f. *tuin-*, of unkn. origin + *-al* in *AMYTAL, *SECONAL.] A proprietary name for a combination of the two barbiturates quinalbarbitone and amylobarbitone, used as a sedative-hypnotic.

1949 *Trade Marks Jrnl.* 25 May 453/2 *Tuinal*... Medicinal preparations composed of sodium propyl-methyl-carbinyl allyl barbiturate and sodium isoamyl ethyl barbiturate. Eli Lilly and company,.. Indianapolis,.. United States of America. **1952** *Martindale's Extra Pharmacopœia* (ed. 23) I. 259 Tuinal (*Lilly*). 1½ or 3 gr. capsules containing equal parts of Seconal Sodium and Sodium Amytal. **1980** *Daily Tel.* 5 Nov. 3/1 She was drunk and they went on to a party at a friend's house. He saw her take two Tuinal tablets during the night.

tuition. Add: **2. c.** = *tuition-fee. U.S.*

1828 WEBSTER, s.v., In our colleges, the tuition is from thirty to forty dollars a year. **1940** W. FAULKNER *Hamlet* II. i. 101 Your tuition will be paid. **1979** *Arizona Daily Sun* 19 Apr. 1/6 Wettaw..was given the award for his opposition to increases in university tuitions.

tuitionary *a.* (earlier example).

1816 J. B. GILCHRIST (*title*) The orienti-occidental tuitionary pioneer to literary pursuits [etc.].

tukal, var. *TUKUL. **tukhrik,** var. *TUGRIK.

tukul (tu·kŭl). Also **tukal, tukl.** [Native name.] In Ethiopia and some adjacent regions: a dwelling shaped like a beehive, and constructed with a thatched roof.

1901 H. VIVIAN *Abyssinia* vii. 174 The capital is rather a camp than a town, and there is no particular trouble in rooting up a tukul and planting it elsewhere. **1920** *Blackw. Mag.* Nov. 675/2 The tukls were strongly built of rough stone. **1936** E. WAUGH *Waugh in Abyssinia* v. 188 The office was a small, lightless *tukal* a hundred yards or so off the road. **1958** *Spectator* 18 July 111/1, I would not like my daughter to become the mistress of a *kraal* or a *tukl.* **1971** *Daily Tel.* 12 June 11/1 Rough compounds of mushroom-like *tukals*—round, mud-walled thatched peasant huts. **1981** E. NORTH *Dames* i. 5 Thatched huts known as *tukuls*, some now with corrugated roofs.

tuku-tuku (tu·ku,tu·ku). *N.Z.* Also (as one word) **tukutuku, tuku tuku.** [Maori.] (See quots. 1946 and 1958.)

1936 [see *KAKAHO]. **1946** *Jrnl. Polynesian Soc.* June 160 *Tukutuku*, ornamental lattice-work of toetoe-reeds (kakaho) cross-laced in various patterns with narrow strips of flax and pingao: a panel of tukutuku was placed between every pair of poupou on the whare walls. **1950** *N.Z. Jrnl. Agric.* Aug. 187/3 The tuku tuku (decorative reed panels) [on the meeting house] are admirable examples of Maori art. **1958** *Listener* 20 Nov. 825/2 The tuku-tuku, a weaving of a wall-covering with split, or rather halved, bamboo as the warp. **1977** *N.Z. Herald* 5 Jan. 1-4/7 The old tukutuku or woven panel walls will in most cases be restored and cleaned.

tuladi (tūlădi·). Also **toledi, touladi.** [a. Canad. Fr., f. Algonquin, Micmac.] = NAMAYCUSH.

1846 C. L. HATHEWAY *Hist. New Brunswick* 61 The Toledi..weighs from five to twenty-five pounds,..and is a very voracious fish. **1856** C. LANMAN *Adv. Wilds U.S.* II. 79 The principal fish which it yields are the common trout, tuladi or great gray trout, and a small species of white fish. **1896** *Trans. R. Soc. Canada* II. 135 The Mackinaw trout of the great lakes [is]..the touladi of the country of the Micmacs. **1957** *Field & Stream* (N.Y.) May 90/2 A fourth kind of trout called touladi..the French-Canadians say, is a natural cross between the lake trout and the brook trout.

tularæmia (tiūlărī·miă). *Path.* Also (chiefly *U.S.*) **-emia.** [f. mod.L. *tular-ensis*, specific epithet of the causative organism (f. the name of *Tulare* Co., California) + Gr. αἷμα blood + -IA[1].] An acute infectious febrile disease of man and domestic animals caused by the bacterium *Francisella tularensis*, endemic among wild rodents in N. America and elsewhere, and transmitted to man by biting insects and by other means, producing very variable symptoms.

1921 E. FRANCIS in *Public Health Rep.* (U.S.) 29 July 1731 The names thus far used for this disease are strictly vernacular and do not lend themselves to international usage as easily as a name in Latin form. Accordingly, the name tularæmia is proposed as a technical international name. **1925**, etc. [see *rabbit fever* s.v. *RABBIT *sb.*[1] 4]. **1949** A. HUXLEY *Ape & Essence* 30 On the pressure-tanks of one army are painted the words *super tularemia*; on those of their opponents, *improved glanders*. **1961** R. D. BAKER *Essent. Path.* ix. 183 Tularemia is acquired, usually, from the handling of infected rabbits.

tule. Add: Also **toolie, tulé, tuley. a.** (Earlier and further examples.)

1837 P. L. EDWARDS *Jrnl.* 20 July (1932) 26 Driving her along the margin of a bulrush or Tule pond she turned about. **1845** J. C. FRÉMONT *Rep. Exploring Expedition* 252 They..live principally on acorns and roots of the tulé, of which also their huts are made. **1850** W. R. RYAN *Personal Adv. Upper & Lower Calif.* I. 298 The Indians of the party were despatched to hunt up the banks of the river for toolies. **1892** *Outing* Jan. 329/2 Arriving at a small patch of tuleys about the middle of the lake.

b. **tule fog** *U.S.*, fog over low-lying ground.

1899 *Monthly Weather Rev.* Dec. 536/2 Connected with this pressure distribution was the prevalence of tule fog in the great valleys of California... This ground or tule fog was so dense as to seriously inconvenience farming operations. **1934** S. E. WHITE *Folded Hills* 340 A *tule* fog lay thick over the bottomlands. **1980** M. G. EBERHART *Casa Madrone* vi. 81 The evening breeze freshened, yet was still moist... Scott said..'The tule fog is coming in.'

tulgey (tʊ·ldʒi), *a.* Also (*erron.*) **tulgy.** A factitious word introduced by 'Lewis Carroll' applied to a wood; (usu. interpreted as) thick, dense, and dark; also *fig.*

1871 'L. CARROLL' *Through Looking-Glass* i. 22 The Jabberwock, with eyes of flame, Came whiffling through the tulgey wood. **1936** J. R. R. TOLKIEN in *Proc. Brit. Acad.* XXII. 250 The jabberwocks of historical and antiquarian research burble in the tulgy wood of conjecture, flitting from one tum-tum tree to another. **1949** E. TAYLOR *Wreath of Roses* xiv. 216 You came out of that tulgy wood? **1972** K. BONFIGLIOLI *Don't point that Thing at Me* viii. 71, I battled..with Professor Aschloch's tulgey prose—only German poets have ever written lucid German prose. **1976** *Times Lit. Suppl.* 23 Jan. 71/5 A suitable backcloth to the dark, thick gothic forest of his own tulgey forebodings. **1982** *Ibid.* 10 Dec. 1352/4 The tulgey wood of semiotics.

tulip. Add: **2. b.** (Examples.)

1847 *Punch* 16 Oct. 148/1 This, my tulip, is a *salle de danse*. **1895** 'G. MORTIMER' *Tales from Western Moors* iii. 67 'Cos for this, my tulip,..work and me fell out a long time back.

3. b. An explosive charge used to destroy a length of railway track. Now *Hist.*

1918 T. E. LAWRENCE in *Lett.* (1938) 250 A gang of four men can lay twenty 'tulips' in an hour on easy ballast, and for each two slabs (and single fuse) you ruin a sleeper, a yard of bank and two rails. **1920** *Blackw. Mag.* May 599/2 J. and I tried our prentice hands at the new game of 'planting tulips'. **1956** *Railway Mag.* Mar. 167/1 'Tulips', so called because of the appearance of the track after they had 'flowered', were the most effective means of derailing a train.

5. *tulip-bed* (examples), *-field, -glass* (later examples), *-time*; **tulip break(ing)**, the variegated colouring of certain tulip flowers, caused by a virus infection; **tulip fire**, a fungus disease of tulips, caused by *Botrytis tulipæ* and producing speckled, discoloured leaves and flowers.

1822 T. G. WAINEWRIGHT in *London Mag.* June 552/2 A delicate Schiavone, various as a tulip bed with rich broken tints. **1939** JOYCE *Finnegans Wake* 526 Or tulipbeds of Rush below. **1958** *Manch. Guardian* 28 May 6/3 These changes of colour are symptoms of the virus disease known as tulip break. **1929** *U.S. Dept. Agric. Yearbk. 1928* 596 (*heading*) Tulip 'breaking' is proved to be caused by mosaic infection. **1969** G. LYALL *Venus with Pistol* vii. 38 Amsterdam was cold... Carlos told me..not [to] stop off to look at any tulip fields. **1931** *Pamphl. Seale-Hayne Agric. Coll.* XXXVI. 27 Several suggestions have been made as possible methods for the control of Tulip Fire. **1976** *Homes & Gardens* June 131/2 Tulips are particularly susceptible to tulip fire; this produces malformed leaves and shoots, which wither and stop growing. **1952** M. ALLINGHAM *Tiger in Smoke* ii. 49 He was carrying two large tulip glasses which he had overfilled. **1976** D. FRANCIS *In Frame* v. 83 When Jik opened the champagne he poured it into shining tulip glasses. **1954** L. MACNEICE *Autumn Sequel* 41 Its tuliptime and playtime.

tulle. Add: **b.** *tulle gras* (gra) [F. *gras* fatty], a gauze dressing for the skin impregnated with petroleum jelly.

1933 *Jrnl. R. Army Medical Corps* XL. 353 The 'Tulle Gras' dressing..was first placed on the market..by a French firm some years ago. It consists..of a fairly large-mesh gauze net, impregnated with vaseline containing 1 per cent. of balsam of Peru, supplied in sections of about four inches by five inches in size. **1974** R. M. KIRK et al. *Surgery* v. 75 A partial thickness burn, or one that is of doubtful nature, is treated by removing debris, pricking and emptying the blisters, and covering the area with tulle gras..which is non-adherent.

tullibee. (Earlier examples.)

1789 A. SHAW *Let.* 16 Dec. in L. F. R. Masson *Bourgeois de la Compagnie du Nord-Ouest* (1889) I. 33, I take a walk to my traps, return to the house, eat *Tollibees* about nine. **1823** J. FRANKLIN *Narr. Journey to Shores of Polar Sea* II. 711 The Cree name of this fish, ottonneebees, has been corrupted by the traders into tullibee.

tulp (tŭlp). *S. Afr.* Also **tulpe.** [a. Du. *tulp* tulip.] Any of several bulbous plants of the genus *Homeria* or *Moræa* of the family Iridaceæ, esp. *Homeria breyniana* or *Moræa polystachya*, which are native to southern Africa, bear yellow, pink, or blue flowers, and are extremely poisonous to cattle.

[**1795**: see *SUIKERBOS.] **1835** T. H. BOWKER *Jrnl.* 10 May (MS.), Lots of Bullocks sick with eating Tulp. **1844** J. BACKHOUSE *Narr. Visit Mauritius & S. Afr.* xviii. 276 Among the grass, on the south side, there was an abundance of the species of *Moræa*, known in the country by the name of Tulip or Tulpe, which is very destructive to cattle. **1871** T. BAINES *Diary* 28 May (1946) III. 601 Tulp, a plant poisonous to cattle, grew at Blauwe Krantz. **1896** R. WALLACE *Farming Industries Cape Colony* iv. 96 Cattle bred on the ground do not eat tulp unless they are very hungry. **1958** *Cape Times* 23 Aug. 11/6 Poisonous plants, such as tulp,..led to illness among animals. **1973** *Grocott's Mail* (Grahamstown, S. Afr.) 19 June 3 An abundance of the highly poisonous tulp plant..could mean stock losses for unsuspecting farmers.

tulwar. (Earlier example.)

c **1810** W. HICKEY *Mem.* (1960) xv. 252 In about half an hour after the first grand attack had thus been made, an alarm was given that the mob armed with *tulwars* (scimitars) had forced the sentries.

tum (tʊm), *sb.*[2] *joc.* Short for *TUMMY. Cf. *TUM-TUM *sb.*[4]

1869 W. S. GILBERT *Bab Ballads* 121 They can reduce a bulging tum To measures fair By taking air And exercise in plenty. **1890** A. JAMES *Diary* 18 July (1965) 129 That dissipated organ known in the family as 'Alice's tum'. **1937** G. FRANKAU *More of Us* xiv. 153 Chilled all those suns for which we oiled the raw tum Or boracized the blistering shoulder blade. **1977** *Time* 14 Feb. 33/2 To re-establish old wisdom and simple certitudes: hot chestnuts in the hand, calories in the tum.

tuman (tumā·n). [Var. TOMAN[1].] A tribe of Baluchis or Pathans.

[**1816** H. POTTINGER *Trav. Beloochistan* iv. 62 An assemblage of these Ghedans [*sc.* tents] constitute a Toomun, or village, and the inhabitants of it a Kheil, or society.] **1907** *Baluchistan District Gazetteer Ser.* III. 372 A tribe is not responsible for the actions of any person who takes up his abode temporarily with it for purposes of cultivation or for grazing. In this case his heirs and his own *tuman* is responsible for his acts. **1950** *R. Central Asian Jrnl.* XXXVII. 284 There are nine Baloch tumans (tribes) of Dera Ghazi Khan. **1974** *Encycl. Brit. Micropædia* I. 773/3 Each tribe (*tuman*) consists of several clans and acknowledges one chief, even though in some *tuman* there are clans in habitual opposition to the chief.

So **tumanda·r**, a Baluchi or Pathan chief.

1907 *Baluchistan District Gazetteer Ser.* III. i. 78 Among the Baloch..a chief or *tumandár* may invite contributions on the occasion of a marriage. **1932** *Cambr. Hist. India* VI. xxv. 455 Casting all fear on one side, he boldly advanced into their mountain retreats and made friends with the tribal chiefs or tumandars. **1979** *Indo-British Rev.* (Madras) VIII. 1–11. 52/2 The Tumandars, or chiefs of the unadministered territory, had come in for their annual reunion with..the political Agent.

tumângong, var. *TEMENGGONG. **tumbaga**, var. TOMBAC in Dict. and Suppl.

tumble, *sb.* Add: **2. d.** *to take a tumble* (*to oneself*): to realize the facts of one's situation; to wake up *to* something, to tumble. *slang* (orig. *U.S.*).

1877 [see *ON TO, ONTO *prep.* 2]. **1928** F. HURST *President is Born* xiv. 182 An iron negro boy, with a hitching ring in his fist, stood..at the curb... Once, some townwag..had hung a pasteboard tag about his neck, 'Take a tumble to yourself, Joe.' **1944** *Living off Land* v. 106 At one goldfield where malaria broke out virulently no one took a tumble why for a long time. **1949** J. R. COLE *It was so Late* 65 The woman, taking a tumble to our set up, gave me the come on. **1959** M. GEE in C. K. Stead *N.Z. Short Stories* (1966) 267 After a while I give up, and I take a tumble to what's happening. I'm getting the bum's rush. **1973** 'J. PATRICK' *Glasgow Gang Observed* viii. 79 Ma wee brother will learn sense; he'll take a tumble tae hissel'.

e. A sign of recognition or acknowledgement, a response; chiefly in phr. *to give a tumble. U.S. slang.*

1921 H. C. WITWER *Leather Pushers* xi. 282 Neither of 'em give him a tumble. **1934** J. O'HARA *Appointment in Samarra* (1935) vii. 208, I went in his office and started kidding around... I noticed I wasn't getting a tumble from him, so I finally broke down and asked him, I said what was the matter. **1935** D. RUNYON in *Cosmopolitan* Jan. 160/3 He never lets on he knows me, and naturally I do not give Mr. Labez any tumble whatever. **1953** *N.Y. Times Book Rev.* 8 Feb. 17 If the right boy won't give you [*sc.* a girl] a tumble, you've got a problem. **1976** *Washington Post* 19 Apr. c3/6 Der Bingle took a subway ride in New York over the weekend and not a soul gave him a tumble. Bing Crosby said he knew what it meant to be just another straphanger.

4. *slang.* An act of sexual intercourse; a woman giving opportunity for this; chiefly in phr. *to give* (or *get*) *a tumble.*

1903 FARMER & HENLEY *Slang* VII. 224/2 *To do a tumble* (of women) = to lie down to a man. **1934** H. MILLER *Tropic of Cancer* 297 She's a big, healthy bitch... I wouldn't mind giving her a tumble. **1954** J. TRENCH *Dishonoured Bones* iii. 110 He was..giving la Vitrey a tumble somewhere. **1970** 'J. & E. BONETT' *Sound of Murder* xiii. 172 Most men think that a woman who has been loved by a married man is an easy tumble. **1976** P. CAVE *High Flying Birds* iii. 45 'Back-pay', he said, 'plus an advance on a quick tumble tomorrow night.'

tumble, *v.* Add: **II. 3. e.** Of laundry: to be tossed about in the revolving drum of a tumble-drier (or washing-machine).

1970 *Which?* Aug. 240/1 Too much foam will certainly stop your clothes from tumbling freely and so getting clean. **1975** C. WESTON *Susannah Screaming* (1976) i. 9 Rees..watched his laundry tumbling inside the barrel of the dryer.

7. b. *to tumble up*: to make haste, orig. (*Naut.*) from below deck. *slang.*

1826 W. N. GLASCOCK *Naval Sketch-Bk.* I. 8 The command was repeated by the boatswain and his mates, who were piping and roaring down the hatchways—'Tumble up, tumble up from below.' **1832** [see sense 7 a in Dict.]. **1838** DICKENS *Nicholas Nickleby* (1839) viii. 65 'Now, Nickleby, come; tumble up, will you?' Nicholas.. 'tumbled up' at once, and proceeded to dress himself. **1842** J. F. COOPER *Wing-and-Wing* I. viii. 125 This sight produced a great commotion in the ship, even the watch below 'tumbling up', to get another sight of a craft so renowned. **1858** TROLLOPE *Three Clerks* II. ii. 40 'Mr. Tudor to attend in the board-room immediately,' said a fat messenger... 'All right,' said Charley—'I'll tumble up and be with them in ten seconds.'

9. b. To have sexual intercourse with. *slang.*

1602, 1698 [see sense 9 a in Dict.]. **1772** T. BRIDGES *Burlesque Transl. Homer* I. 4 What priest beside thyself e'er grumbl'd To have his daughter tightly tumbl'd? **1922** JOYCE *Ulysses* 502 Beware of the flapper and bogus mournful... Tumble her. **1971** 'R. MACDONALD' *Underground Man* xxxii. 225 He had tumbled the prettiest girl, and got her with child, and Albert and Fritz had taken the rap for it. **1973** *Guardian* 21 June 10/1 A hip young girl who tumbles him when his wife is away. **1976** R. LEWIS *Witness my Death* v. 166 Tommy Elias had tumbled the schoolgirl in the ferns.

10. b. (Earlier example.) Also const. *that.* Also *trans.*, to detect, see through.

1846 *Swell's Night Guide* 58, I..officed Bet, she tumbled to the fake, and stalled off to the dossery. **1901** 'J. FLYNT' *World of Graft* iii. 104 Women..tumble more guns 'n all the coppers in existence. **1926** *Variety* 29 Dec. 7/4 The pincher would never tumble that 'nice people' meant an act that kicked in more than the usual vaudeville agent's legitimate commission. **1936** G. INGRAM *Muffled Man* iii. 49 You can't go on for ever at any game, and not get tumbled some time or other. **1938** F. D. SHARPE *Sharpe of Flying Squad* xxvi. 262 We thought you wouldn't tumble us, Guv'nor. **1962** *New Statesman* 21 Dec. 899/1 By the time you tumble that your drum has been turned over, we're miles away. **1974** *Times* 7 Feb. 3/7 John Rodger..heard the radio and said: 'They have tumbled us.' **1981** J. BARNETT *Firing Squad* vi. 57 Have to have words with Simonson, in case he has tumbled the tattoo.

tumble-. Add: **1. tumble-action**, the tumbling action of a tumble-drier; **tumble-bug** (earlier example).

1958 *Sunday Times* 9 Mar. 22/6 Here [in an electric washing machine] tumble-action replaces a wringer. **1976** *National Observer* (U.S.) 11 Dec. 9/1 Do not use tumble-action dryer. **1805** R. PARKINSON *Tour Amer.* 362 A kind of beetle, called a tumble-bug,..in the summer forms a cave in the earth.

2. tumble home: also *transf.* of a motor

vehicle; **tumble-up,** substitute for def.: a tumbler designed to be placed upside down on the neck of a carafe.

1924 *Motor* 7 Oct. 450/2 The body is of particularly pleasing lines, with a V windscreen and tumble-home stern. **1968** *Motor Industry Res. Rep.* IX. 25/1 Decreases due to increasing the canopy tumble-home.

tumble-dri·er. Also **-dryer.** [f. TUMBLE *v.* + DRIER, DRYER.] A machine for drying washing in a heated drum that turns about a horizontal axis. So **tumble-dry** *v. trans.* (also *absol.*), **tumble-drie·d, -dry·ing** *ppl. adjs.*

[**1952** *Gas Age* 8 May 62/1 The tumbler-type of clothes dryer.] **1962** J. T. MARSH *Self-Smoothing Fabrics* xiv. 228 Different results may be obtained according to whether the fabric is dried on a line or on one of the tumble-drying machines. *Ibid.* xx. 347 Fabrics with wet recovery only cannot be tumble-dried with satisfaction but need line-drying. **1969** *Which?* Nov. 372/2 (*caption*) Line dry or Tumble dry. **1972** J. MCCLURE *Caterpillar Cop* vi. 98 The lady next door has a tumble drier so you put your clothes outside and I'll take them round. **1976** *Ilkeston Advertiser* 10 Dec. 12/1 (Advt.), Don't have wet clothes hanging around, buy a Tumbledryer. **1977** 'M. YORKE' *Cost of Silence* v. 36 Mrs Costello hung her tumble-dried washing round the kitchen. **1982** A. PRICE *Old Vengeful* vi. 86 We can do your things... Clarkie can wash them, and tumble dry them, and iron them.

tumbler. Add: **5. b.** An inexperienced window-cleaner.

1960 'A. BURGESS' *Doctor is Sick* i. 8 Me, I clean windows... I've seen these young ones just starting—'tumblers' we call them—get froze stuck up there on a ladder. **1972** *Times* 20 Sept. 3/2 Forty years ago..novice window cleaners starting at the bottom of the ladder were known in the cold-blooded jargon of the trade as tumblers.

6. c. (Earlier example.)

1850 DICKENS in *Househ. Words* 21 Dec. 289/2 The Tumbler with his hands in his pockets, who wouldn't lie down.

13. j. *ellipt.* for *tumbler-drier* below.

1947 W. L. CARMICHAEL et al. *Callaway Textile Dict.* 360/1 *Tumbler,* a clothes-drying device consisting of a revolving cage in which hot air is circulated. **1961** *Listener* 30 Nov. 951/2 The most trouble-free and quick-to-use kind of dryer, the electric 'tumbler'.

14. *tumbler-glass* (earlier example), *-screw* (earlier example); **tumbler-drier, -dryer** = *TUMBLE-DRIER; **tumbler-punch** (earlier example).

1956 *Good Housek. Home Encycl.* 13/2 Electric Tumbler Dryers dry by means of a revolving drum in a heated cabinet. **1969** *Which?* Nov. 352/2 Generally all the tumbler driers were easy to use. **1795** J. WOODFORDE *Diary* 14 Oct. (1929) IV. 234 The third [remarkable fact] was, of a Man drinking half Pint Tumbler Glass of Beer and eat the Glass after it. **1843** *Act relating Militia State of Vermont 1842* 80 Each squad of ten men, a wire and tumbler punch. *Ibid.*, Order in which the lock is taken apart... 9. The tumbler screw.

tumbling-. Add: *tumbling girl* (earlier example).

1854 DICKENS *Hard Times* vii. 52 Tom Gradgrind's whim, ma'am, of bringing up the tumbling-girl.

‖**tumbok lada** (tu·mbǫk lā·dă). [Malay, lit. 'pepper-crusher', f. *tumbok* to thump, pound + *lada* pepper.] A small Malayan dagger.

1839 T. J. NEWBOLD *Straits of Malacca* II. xii. 212 The Battas of Sumatra, wear..knives called tombak lada. **1911** *Encycl. Brit.* XVII. 477/1 The Malays use..short stabbing daggers called *tumbok lada.* **1936** G. B. GARDNER *Keris* viii. 113 A nasty ripping knife is sometimes made by fixing an old razor blade into a *tumbok lada* hilt. **1967** J. CLEARY *Long Pursuit* i. 25 He..took from his belt the *tumbok lada,* the small Malayan knife.

tumbu fly (tu·mbu fləi). [f. Bantu name of the insect + FLY *sb.*[1]] A yellow fly with grey markings, *Cordylobia anthropophaga,* found in sub-Saharan Africa, where its larva is a parasite of man and other animals.

1911 A. ALCOCK *Entomol. for Med. Officers* x. 155 The notorious species is..the Tumbu-fly, the larva of which is a subcutaneous parasite of man and other animals. **1930** *Discovery* Aug. 265/1 Wild beasts..and tumbu flies abound. **1979** C. ALLEN *Tales from Dark Continent* i. 5 There was the *tumbo* [sic] fly..whose worm manifested itself as a large boil.

tumeler, var. *TUMMLER.

tumesce (tiume·s), *v.* [Back-formation from TUMESCENCE or f. L. *tumēscere* (see TUMESCENT *a.*).] *intr.* = TUMEFY *v.* 2. Also *fig.* Hence **tume·scing** *ppl. a.*

1966 *New Statesman* 10 June 853/3 Forming open alliances which were secret before, exposing sexual and ethical weaknesses as they tumesce under the threat of death. **1976** *Theriogenology* V. 261 Those [monkeys] that tumesced before they were 3 years old tended to be heavier than their peers, but were not necessarily heavier than older, nonswelling females. **1976** *New Scientist* 9 Sept. 528/2 Other aids to prediction [of eruptions]... As a volcano tumesces the distance between fixed points increases, and these distances can be measured accurately with optical instruments using laser beams. **1980** *Sci. Amer.* Feb. 86/1 In a tumescing system such as the Yellowstone one the ring fractures could propagate downward, eventually penetrating the main magma chamber.

tumescence. Add: *spec.* the swelling of a volcano as a result of increasing pressure of magma inside it.

1943 *Amer. Jrnl. Sci.* CCXLI. 243 Easterly tilt has long been known to indicate tumescence of Mauna Loa accompanying the rise of magma pressure preceding eruption. **1976** P. FRANCIS *Volcanoes* x. 310 The tumescence of the Hawaiian volcanoes, however, is slight, only one metre or so at the summit.

tummied (tʌ·mid), *a.* [f. *TUMMY + -ED[2].] In parasynthetic combs., having a stomach (of a specified kind).

1975 T. HEALD *Deadline* iv. 72 He..wondered if she had to wear a corset. She was remarkably flat tummied. **1975** *Times* 5 July 10/5 A carved, fat tummied elephant.

tummler (tu·mləɹ). Also **toomler, tumeler.** *colloq.* (orig. and chiefly *U.S.*). [Yiddish, f. G. *tummeln* stir.] Someone who acts the clown, a prankster; *spec.* a professional maker of amusement and jollity at a hotel or the like.

1966 ADAMS & TOBIAS *Borscht Belt* iv. 41 If Mrs. Rappaport complained about not getting her third portion of blueberries or Mrs. Davidoff was scrounging fruitlessly for a dancing partner.. it was the Toomler to the rescue. **1968** L. ROSTEN *Joys of Yiddish* 413 It is the *tummler*'s job to guarantee, to the blasé (but insatiable) patrons of a summer resort, that most dubious of vacation boons: 'Never a dull moment!' **1970** L. M. FEINSILVER *Taste of Yiddish* iii. 345 Danny Kaye and other entertainers got their starts as tumelers in the Catskills. **1977** *New Yorker* 12 Sept. 86/3 A summer job as part-time social director and tummler at a hotel in Lake Hopatcong, New Jersey. **1984** *Times* 20 Mar. 12/3 Why should she not believe the agents and promoters, the spivs and *tummlers*?

tummy (tʌ·mi). *colloq.* [Repr. a childish alteration of *stomach*: see -Y[6].] The stomach or intestine.

1869 W. S. GILBERT *Bab Ballads* 200 Why should I hesitate to own That pain was in his little tummy? **1884** KIPLING *Let.* ? Sept. in Ld. Birkenhead *Rudyard Kipling* (1978) vi. 74, I felt the cramps in my legs dying out and my tummy more settled. **1922** JOYCE *Ulysses* 356 Cissy poked him..out of fun in his wee fat tummy. **1936** N. STREATFEILD *Ballet Shoes* iii. 40 Laughing so much that they fell on the floor, and their tummies ached. **1962** V. NABOKOV *Pale Fire* 191 That was Dad's tummy, I think —not a spook. **1979** *Beautiful British Columbia* Fall 14 The bucks..lie napping with heads tucked against tummies like so many dogs.

2. An abdominal pain or complaint. Freq. with preceding place-name: diarrhœa suffered by visitors there.

1888 KIPLING *Story of Gadsbys* (1889) 21 He has nothing more than a wet weather tummy. **1937** F. STARK *Let.* 25 Oct. in *Coast of Incense* (1953) 177, I am spending these five days rather tiresomely in hospital with a *tummy.* **1939** R. GODDEN *Black Narcissus* vi. 77 'Sister Briony..thinks it must be some local infection, as we all have it.'..'Darjeeling tummy,' said Mr. Dean. **1943**, etc. [see *GIPPY 1 c]. **1959** L. DURRELL *Spirit of Place* (1969) 423 The Mediterranean affliction of high summer known to us all as 'tummy' (Egyptian, Greek or Naples tummy). **1970** N. MARSH *When in Rome* iv. 97 A sudden onslaught of the affliction known to tourists as Roman Tummy..necessitated an immediate withdrawal. **1979** A. V. BADGLEY *Rembrandt Decisions* (1980) ix. 119 He's sick... Says he's got 'Bombay Tummy'.

3. *attrib.* as *tummy muscle, pain, rumble, trouble, upset*; **tummy ache,** an abdominal pain; **tummy bug,** (a germ causing) a disorder of the stomach; **tummy-button** = NAVEL *sb.* 1.

1926 GALSWORTHY *Silver Spoon* III. viii. 284 Kit had tummyache this morning. **1979** L. & J. BROWN *Our Miracle called Louise* iii. 35 'I've got a tummy ache,' I told her. 'It will be gone in the morning,' she said. **1969** M. PUGH *Last Place Left* xvii. 121 We're rather below strength... Some sort of tummy bug. **1945** A. HUXLEY *Time must have a Stop* ii. 13 Everybody's tummy-button grew inwards like that. **1974** G. BUTLER *Coffin for Canary* x. 133 My waist and tummy muscles are really taut. **1924** J. BUCHAN *Three Hostages* xvi. 238 He really has had a bad tummy pain. **1947** G. GREENE *Nineteen Stories* 192 It was the doctors who called his complaint Borborygmi: in England we usually call it just 'tummy rumbles'. **1982** N. MARSH *Light Thickens* iii. 91 His tummy rumbles are positively deafening. **1937** W. H. S. SMITH *Let.* 12 Jan. in *Young Man's Country* (1977) ii. 51 My tummy trouble persisted for several days after my return to Madaripur. **1926** A. HUXLEY *Let.* 21 Oct. (1969) 274 Matthew meanwhile flourishes..in spite of a tummy upset.

‖**tu-mo** (du mo). Also **Tu Mu.** [Chinese *dū mài.*] In Chinese medical theory, the chief passage through which the vital energy circulates, located within the spine; *spec.* in acupuncture.

1972 DA LIU *T'ai Chi Ch'uan & I Ching* (1974) i. 9 In meditation one learns to focus and direct energies which are usually squandered in the mundane perceptions of the five senses. In Taoist meditation these energies are directed through two main channels: *Tu Mu,* a channel along the spinal column..and *Jen Mu,* a channel which passes down the front of the body to the genital region. **1974** *Barefoot Doctor's Man.* iv. 105 The governing 'tu-mo' meridian.

tumorigenic (tiūmǒɹidʒe·nik), *a. Med.* Also **tumo(u)r(o)-.** [f. TUMOUR, TUMOR + -I-, -O + *-GENIC.] Capable of causing tumours.

1948 *Cancer Res.* VIII. 410/1 It is thought that they [*sc.* these observations] afford an example of the tumorigenic action of..follicle-stimulating hormone. **1965** *Dissertation Abstr.* XXVI. 1300/2 (*heading*) The salivary gland chromosomes of a tumorigenic strain of *Drosophila melanogaster.* **1971** *New Scientist* 24 June 732/2 Tumourgenic hybrids had 80 chromosomes instead of the expected 116. **1979** *Nature* 11 Oct. 486/1 The significance of EBV [*sc.* a virus] as a tumorigenic agent in humans could be finally established if it were possible to prevent tumours by vaccination. **1980** *Ibid.* 21 Feb. 777/1 The present experiments show that human diploid cells can be transformed *in vitro* into tumorogenic cells by X-ray-irradiation.

So **tu·morigen** (and varr.), a tumorigenic agent; **tumorige·nesis,** the production or formation of a tumour; **tu:morigeni·city,** tumorigenic property.

1948 *Cancer Res.* VIII. 397 (*heading*) Hormonal imbalances in tumorigenesis. **1952** J. E. GREGORY *Pathogenesis of Cancer* (ed. 2) xii. 147 These elements [*sc.* coal tar, etc.] are called carcinogens. We now know that if the virus was present cancer would develop, but if it was not present only benign tumors and hyperplasia would develop as a result of the irritation. This latter fact makes it appear that a better name for these substances might have been tumorgens, instead of carcinogens. **1967** *New Scientist* 25 May 478/2 More than 50 per cent of the tumorigenicity of 24-hour condensate..was due to stable, non-volatile carcinogens. **1970** *McGraw-Hill Yearbk. Sci. & Technol.* 217/2 Other studies have shown..the dominance of tumorogenicity, and the characteristics of polyoma transformation in hybrids between transformed and nontransformed cells. **1971** *Nature* 17 Sept. 195/1 Irradiated hamster foetal cells protect male hamsters against SV40 tumorigenesis. **1978** *Brit. Med. Jrnl.* 11 Mar. 649/2 It would be a disservice to the public to allow marketing of a compound which is a demonstrated tumorigen. **1980** *European Jrnl. Cell Biol.* XXII. 491 The tumorigenicities of RBCF-1 cells.

tumour, tumor. Add: **5. tumour virus,** a virus that causes tumours.

[**1934** *Lancet* 21 July 117/2 Neutralising antibodies can be shown to be formed against fowl-tumour viruses.] **1950** *Amer. Jrnl. Med.* VIII. 495/2 There is no proof that tumor viruses are of a different nature from other viruses. **1982** *Sci. Amer.* Mar. 69/3 Some tumor viruses are oncogenic (that is, they induce tumors) only in animals that are not their host in nature, whereas other tumor viruses are oncogenic in their natural host.

tump, *sb.* Restrict *local* to senses in Dict. and add: **4.** *fig.* Trivial writing, bad prose.

1917 KIPLING *Divers. Creatures* 172 It's the most vital, arresting and dynamic bit of tump I've done up to date. **1933** D. L. MURRAY *Eng. Family Robinson* ii. 36 Did you ever read such tump as our parish magazine?

tump-tump (tʌmp,tʌmp). [Echoic.] A short sound as of water slopping without splashing, or a large ball being kicked.

1917 [see *PUNT-ABOUT]. **1983** *Listener* 20 Oct. 26/3 The one creation that is seen in innumerable moods is the Fenland water—rising to the tump-tump of the water-pumps.

tum-tum (tʌ·m,tʌm), *sb.*[4] *joc.* [Redupl. *TUM *sb.*[2]] = *TUMMY.

1864 G. MEREDITH *Let.* 1 Mar. (1970) I. 245, I hope hope your tum-tum is stronger, old boy? **1894** G. DU MAURIER *Trilby* II. IV. 6 Many other unaccustomed good things, so bad for their little French tumtums. **1930** [see *icky-boo* adj. s.v. *ICKY *a.* and *sb.*]. **1981** P. MALLORY *Killing Matter* ii. 22 Make some toast and coffee. My tum-tum's empty.

tuna[2]. Add: Also with pronunc. (tiū·nă). Substitute for def.: Any of several large marine food and game fishes of the family Scombridæ, belonging to the genus *Thunnus, Euthynnus, Katsuwonus,* or a closely related genus and found in Atlantic, Pacific, and Mediterranean seas. Cf. *SKIPJACK *sb.*[4], TON[4], and TUNNY. (Earlier and later examples.)

1881 *Proc. U.S. Nat. Mus.* IV. 45 Another *Orcynus,* known as the 'tuna', exists about Santa Cruz Island. **1911** *Chambers's Jrnl.* Jan. 63/2 My Californian friends might well possess their disappointed souls in patience if there were any promise of such compensation..for the loss of the tuna. **1949** *Manch. Guardian Weekly* 24 Mar. 11/2 Water you can't swim in, and good tuna and jacks you can't eat. **1970** *Nature* 19 Dec. 1141/2 Tuna is a fisheries term for the larger tunny species.

b. *attrib.,* as *tuna bait, boat, fisherman, fishing, fleet, meat, packer, packing, salad, sandwich, school*; **tuna clipper** *U.S.,* a powered fishing boat with facilities for catching and storing small fish; **tuna fish,** the flesh of the tunny as food.

1901 *McClure's Mag.* Feb. 370/1 Vincente..is just taking the tuna bait from his gill-nets. **1968** *National Fisherman* July 18-c/2 Much squid was used for tuna bait. **1903** C. F. HOLDER *Big Game Fishes* iv. 59 The tuna boats of Catalina Island are designed for the purpose. **1956** *Fishery Bull.* LVII. 195/1 (*heading*) Grounds fished by tuna boats operating in the Inner South Seas. **1929** *Pacific Fisherman* Sept. 39/1 The 100-ft tuna clipper 'Enterprise' was driven ashore. **1970** *National Fisherman* Sept. 1-B/2 A tuna clipper is a vessel equipped to carry small fish alive for use as bait; capable of being trimmed in such a way as to bring her stern rail as low as possible in the water; and fitted with a system which permits her to hold her catch for long periods of time. **1917** M. GREEN *Better Meals for Less Money* xvi. 130 (*heading*) Tuna fish salad. **1922** *Guardian* 27 June 6/2 Tinned goods..are the most suitable for storing... 1 tin 'tuna' fish or crayfish. **1978** *Amer. Poetry Rev.* Nov./Dec. 16/3 To a tunafish gray on a bruised, greenish blue. **1982** J. GARDNER *For Special Services* viii. 64 Tuna fish sandwiches were hardly Bond's style. **1919** *Pacific Fisherman Yearbk.* 64/2 The tuna fishermen return to port each evening. **1901** *McClure's Mag.* Feb. 370/1 The rods and reels in tuna fishing are of the finest description. **1926** G. FRANKAU *My Unsentimental Journey* xvii. 222 His hobby—he told me at once—is tuna-fishing. **1980** *Times* 4 Nov. 18/4 [In Peru] tuna fishing..has now virtually ended. **1932** M. MILLER *I cover Waterfront* xvii. 97 The only people who know of him are the two men who live on the island and the crews and skippers of the tuna fleet. **1968** *National Fisherman* Apr. 2-A/2 Commander, a steel-hulled, 20-year-old veteran of the Southern California tuna fleet, sank off Mexico. **1923** A. WARD *Encycl. Food* 537 Very little tuna meat is sold fresh in our markets. **1951** TRESSLER & LEMON *Marine Products of Commerce* (ed. 2) xx. 448 A machine for molding blocks of tuna meat the exact size for the can is in operation in some canneries. **1922** *Pacific Fisherman* May 43/1 Prominent tuna packers. *Ibid.*, Mr. Ambrose was one of the organizers of the first tuna packing plant in California. **1967** *Commercial Fisheries Rev.* Nov. 64/2 Japanese tuna packers.. switched from fruit canning to tuna packing in September. **1953** *Special Sci. Rep.* (U.S. Fish & Wildlife Service, Fisheries) No. 104. 32 [Chunk tuna] was especially suited to the preparation of tuna salads. **1977** C. MCFADDEN *Serial* (1978) xiii. 32/2 He left Fred's, absent-mindedly leaving her to pay for his tuna salad special. **1957** HESELTINE & DOW *New Basic Cook Bk.* 718 (*heading*) Tuna sandwiches. **1977** C. MCCARRY *Secret Lovers* iii. 42 The passenger compartment of the BMW smelled..of bay rum, Brylcreem, tuna sandwiches. **1930** *Pacific Fisherman* Apr. 41/1 In search of distant tuna schools. **1967** *Trans. Amer. Fisheries Soc.* XCVI. 127/1 Purse seines capture only about half the number of tuna schools upon which they are set.

tuna[3]. Substitute for def.: Either of two freshwater eels, *Anguilla dieffenbachii* or *A. australis schmidtii*, found in New Zealand. (Earlier and later examples.)

1843 E. DIEFFENBACH *Trav. N.Z.* II. III. 389/2 *Tuna*, eel. **1851** J. C. RICHMOND *Let.* 25 Mar. in *Richmond-Atkinson Papers* (1960) I. ii. 79 They set off..to catch crawfish & tuna, the eels of the country. **1966** *Encycl. N.Z.* I. 565/1 These are the common freshwater eels called tuna by the Maoris.

tunability (tiūnăbi·lĭti). [f. next: see *-BILITY.] The capability of being varied in frequency and wavelength.

1969 *Sci. Jrnl.* Apr. 57/3 Spectroscopy is one of the most obvious fields for exploitation of laser tunability. **1977** *Jrnl. R. Soc. Arts* CXXV. 766/2 Tunability and the time-compression of laser energy into very short pulses.. represent considerable technological achievements.

tunable, tuneable, *a.* **2.** Delete *rare*⁻⁰ and add: *spec.* capable of having its operating frequency and wavelength varied.

1934 E. LITTLE *Mod. Rhythmic Drumming* (rev. ed.) 26 No outfit is complete without at least one tomtom. The 'tuneable' models are the best, because any dampness in the atmosphere can be counteracted by the use of the tensioning handles. **1943** C. L. BOLTZ *Basic Radio* xii. 195 It is seen that the aerial is not tunable. **1957** *Proc. IRE* XLV. 1467/2 The system [*sc.* for a maser] is 'tunable'; i.e., the useful frequency can be adjusted. **1969** R. B. FULLER *Operating Man. Spaceship Earth* v. 67 The macrocosmic irrelevancies are all the events too large and too infrequent to be synchronizably tuneable in any possible way with our consideration. **1969** *Sci. Jrnl.* Apr. 53/3 Lasers capable of producing megawatts of power and tunable right through the visible spectrum. **1971** *Daily Tel.* (Colour Suppl.) 22 Oct. 57 (Advt.), The VHF radio has pushbutton programme selection and each programme is separately tunable. **1979** *Jrnl. R. Soc. Arts* Jan. 106/2 In conjunction with a tunable x-ray monochromator, anomalous scattering experiments can be performed close to absorption edges.

Tunbridge (tʌ·nbridʒ). **a.** Used *attrib.* to designate water from the chalybeate spring at Royal Tunbridge Wells in Kent.

a **1661** FULLER *Worthies* (1662) Kent 62 Tunbridge-water... Good for Splenitick distempers. **1678** T. BROWNE *Let.* 1 May (1946) 92 He may hopefully drink Tunbridge waters..if they passe well. *c* **1702** C. FIENNES *Journeys* (1947) 125 Tunbridge waters whose property is to retrieve lost limbs that are benumbed. **1967** E. S. TURNER *Taking Cure* iii. 46 Nothing was to be gained from the Tunbridge waters unless the person who drank them was facetious, merry..and jovial.

b. Also **Tonbridge.** Used *attrib.* (rarely *absol.*) to designate wooden articles with a characteristic mosaic decoration, made in and about Royal Tunbridge Wells and nearby Tonbridge by slicing cross-sections from a bundle of thin strips of differently coloured wood glued together, to obtain identical copies of the pattern for sticking on the article to be decorated; chiefly in *Tunbridge ware.*

1773 R. GRAVES *Spiritual Quixote* I. II. xiii. 101 His Tunbridge-ware tobacco-dish. *c* **1795** *Advt. C. Fellows's Circul. Library, Salisbury,* With various Articles in Tunbridge, Ivory, and Morocco. **1816** JANE AUSTEN *Emma* III. iv. 50 A pretty little Tunbridge-ware box. **1842** MARRYAT *Perc. Keene* I. ix. 98 In the front windows ..were..prints, caricatures, and Tonbridge ware. **1888** *Encycl. Brit.* XXIII. 607/1 Tunbridge ware..includes work tables, boxes, toys, &c. **1901** J. BLACK *Illustr. Carpenter & Builder Ser.: Home Handicrafts* 61 Developments of the art of what may be termed 'wood mosaic', and amongst these may be reckoned 'Tarsia work' and 'Tonbridge work'. **1934** N. MARSH *Man lay Dead* xiii. 237, I suddenly remembered..a funny Victorian casket made out of inlaid wood... Antique dealers call those caskets.. Tunbridge boxes. **1973** *Times* 25 Aug. 11/5 It has a Tunbridge-ware change-tray and an Edward VII crown set into the base.

tund, *v.* **1.** (Earlier example of the vbl. sb.)

1866 *School Life at Winchester Coll.* iii. 38 When I was a big Inferior, I have more than once received..a 'Tunding' (thrashing with a stick).

tun-dish, tundish. Restrict 'Now *local*' to sense in Dict. and add: In mod. use, a broad, open container with one or more holes in the bottom, used in various industrial processes, e.g. to feed molten metal into an ingot mould so as to avoid splashing and give a smoother flow.

1926 *Jrnl. Iron & Steel Inst.* CXIV. 74 This tun-dish is provided with one large hole or several smaller holes, dividing the stream of metal into several smaller streams. **1957** *Technology* Aug. 223/1 Plugged into the base of a fireclay tundish..fed with liquid metal from an electric furnace, is a vertical die of..graphite. **1965** *Economist* 25 Dec. 1437/2 In the new [spray steelmaking] process, the liquid iron flows from the bottom of a tundish (a container used to keep a constant head of metal). **1975** *Petroleum Rev.* XXIX. 118/1 The tank vent pipes have now been fitted with tundishes to collect condensate.

tundrite (tʊ·ndrəit). *Min.* [ad. Russ. *tundrit* (E. I. Semenov *Mineralogiya Redkikh Zemel'* (1963) 209), f. Russ. *túndra* tundra (from its being first found on the Lovozero tundra near Murmansk): see -ITE[1].] A silicate and carbonate (essentially) of cerium (normal tundrite, tundrite-(Ce)) or neodymium (tundrite-(Nd)), sodium, and titanium found as triclinic brownish- or greenish-yellow crystals.

1965 *Amer. Mineralogist* L. 2098 Tundrite occurs in 3 nepheline syenite pegmatites of Mt. Nepkha, Lovozero tundra, Kola Peninsula. **1974** *Ibid.* LIX. 633/2 Infra-red study of tundrite from a new locality in the Khibina massif showed bands of carbonate; this was confirmed by spectra of the Greenland mineral.

tune, *sb.* Add: **2.** Hence (from the proverb) *to call the tune*, to hold the initiative, to have control of events.

1928 A. HUXLEY *Point Counter Point* xii. 211 Lucy insisted, when she was with men, on doing as much of the paying as possible. Paying, she was independent, she could call her own tune. **1948** W. S. CHURCHILL *Second World War* I. I. x. 182 If Britain had used her naval power, closed the Suez Canal, and defeated the Italian Navy in a general engagement, she would have had the right to call the tune in Europe. **1963** A. ROSS *Australia 63* iii. 92 A match throughout which, despite frequent fluctuation, England had called the tune. **1978** *Lancashire Life* Nov. 70/1 The Listers had called the local tune ever since the reign of Henry IV, although it was not until 1797 that the head of the family was ennobled.

e. (Earlier example.) Also *the tune the cat died of.*

1820 M. WILMOT *Let.* 4 May (1935) 60, I am made laugh heartily three times a week..when they cut capers in the air with solemn faces, to the tune which *the old Cow died of.* **1943** H. C. BAILEY *Mr. Fortune finds Pig* xxxvi. 140 What are they singing?..It sounds like the tune the cat died of.

tune, *v.* Add: **I. 1. c.** *spec.* To make (a radio or television) sensitive *to* a chosen signal frequency or wavelength; to adjust (any device or component) by varying its operational frequency. Also *absol.*

1899 *Notices Proc. R. Inst.* XV. 475 It is easy to transmit many messages in any direction at the same time. It is only necessary to tune the transmitters and receivers to the same frequency or 'note'... Tuning is very easy. **1900, 1904** [in Dict.]. **1915** W. H. ECCLES *Wireless Telegr.* 304 The primary—*i.e.*, the antenna—is tuned to the incoming waves. **1943** C. L. BOLTZ *Basic Radio* xii. 192 At the transmitter..the LC circuit is tuned to produce free oscillations at a chosen frequency. **1972** *Daily Tel.* (Colour Suppl.) 3 Mar. 17 For several months an 85 foot radio telescope, tuned to 21 centimetres, was aimed at the stars *Tau Ceti* and *Epsilon Eridani.* **1974** *Guardian* 23 Mar. 10/1 The kind of programme listeners tune to, broadcasters respect, and disc critics certainly rarely miss. **1975** D. G. FINK *Electronics Engineers' Handbk.* XIII. 74 Solid-state microwave masers can be tuned over a wide range of frequencies by adjustment of an external magnetic field.

d. Restrict *local* to sense in Dict. In mod. use, to adjust (an engine or part) to improve its efficiency or some other attribute; also with the vehicle or craft as obj.

1916 R. T. NICHOLSON *Bk. of Ford* 151 You know now how to 'tune' your carburetter for the best results. **1931** T. E. LAWRENCE *Let.* 10 June (1938) 724 The R.A.F. detached me to Hythe on special duty, to test and tune their new-type speed-boats for the Schneider Cup. **1955** *Times* 23 Aug. 7/6 The Rootes Group have chosen..an engine..and have tuned it for economy and longevity rather than maximum efficiency. **1978** R. WESTALL *Devil on Road* i. 3, I can strip her [*sc.* a motor-bike] in a day *and* put it all back. Tuned her like Yehudi Menuhin's violin.

5*. *intr.* Of a radio, etc.: to be capable of being tuned.

1922 *Wireless World* 1 July 435/1 Will the Reinartz Tuner tune to any wavelength by means of external coils? **1930** J. H. REYNER *Testing Radio Sets* iv. 55 It may be found that the circuit does not tune correctly when the aerial is connected to its proper terminal. **1970** J. EARL *Tuners & Amplifiers* i. 23 The f.m. section will..tune over Band II, usually from about 88 to 108MHz.

6. tune in. b. *trans.* and *intr.* To tune a radio or television to (a particular station or transmission, or a particular frequency). Freq. *to tune in on* or *in to.* Also *transf.*

1913 *Wireless World* Apr. p. xxxviii/1 It is possible to tune out one ship or station and tune in others. **1919** *Ibid.* May 105/2 Operators at the various Government wireless stations in and about town, who promptly 'tuned in' and listened. **1922** *Westm. Gaz.* 12 Dec., While listening-in on a Lincoln wireless company's apparatus..Mr. H. Mawer was successful in tuning in to an American broadcasting station. **1929** S. CHENEY *Theatre* xxiv. 536 A million or so people may..sit in their parlors and 'tune in' on a song by Al Jolson or a scene from *Twelfth Night.* **1935** S. LEWIS *It can't happen Here* 52 He tuned in on a program of old songs. **1936** AUDEN & ISHERWOOD *Ascent of F6* (1937) II. iii. 102 Turn off the wireless. Tune in to another station. **1956** R. M. LESTER *Towards Hereafter* 18 This higher range of inspirational thought is constantly being radiated, and each one of us in his own capacity can tune into it. **1957** A. C. CLARKE *Deep Range* xii. 104 This was a simple enough task for the sub's frequency converters; if he wished, Franklin could tune in to any sounds from almost a million cycles a second down to vibrations as sluggish as the slow opening of an ancient, rusty door. **1964** MRS. L. B. JOHNSON *White House Diary* 12 Jan. (1970) 42 We tuned in on my TV appearance in '*The Week That Was*'. **1976** *Shooting Times & Country Mag.* 16–22 Dec. 30/3 The Indians when on a hunt think of anything but their quarry, as they believe that the hunted can 'tune in' on their thoughts. **1977** 'J. FRASER' *Hearts Ease in Death* vii. 61 You make it sound like a radio serial. Tune in next week for the latest episode.

c. *fig.* To become mentally receptive to, or aware of; to comprehend. Const. as prec. sense.

1926 *Variety* 29 Dec. 5/4 Those fortunate individuals who can tune in on the conversation of a flock of cannons and follow it without the aid of a central office dick or an interpreter. **1961** A. MILLER *Misfits* ii. 18 His mind is constantly trying to tune in on the world, but the message is never clear. **1977** R. GADNEY *Champagne Marxist* xiii. 84 He'd been so slow in tuning in to the presence of an intruder.

d. *fig.* To harmonize *with.*

1938 L. MACNEICE *I crossed Minch* ii. 25, I had a passion for the wild... This tuned in with my other passions for the antique, the fantastic,..and the Irish.

7. tune off. b. *trans.* = *tune out* (sense 7* below); also *intr.* Also *fig. rare.*

1926 MAINES & GRANT *Wise-Crack Dict.* 14/1 *Tune off that station*, change the conversation. **1931** F. A. ARNOLD *Broadcast Advertising* 140 The public has its own method of self protection. The listener may..tune off and find some program less offensive. **1957** *Practical Wireless* XXXIII. 721/1 When the input signal decreases, as one tunes off the station, the valve will conduct.

7*. tune out. *trans.* To eliminate reception of (a radio signal of a particular frequency) by tuning.

1908 *Rep. Brit. Assoc. Adv. Sci. 1907* 621 It is easy to hear the ships in the Channel, but it is also easy to tune everything out and listen to the desired station alone. **1913** [see sense 6 b above]. **1957** *Practical Wireless* XXXIII. 722/1 When..the signal is tuned out, the voltage at point A drops. **1970** J. EARL *Tuners & Amplifiers* ii. 47 The filter tunes out the 19kHz pilot carrier. **1981** G. MACBETH *Kind of Treason* xiii. 124 Strand was kneeling at the radio. He found the station and tuned the static out.

b. *fig.* To disregard; to cease listening to.

1928 T. E. LAWRENCE *Let.* 1 May (1938) 599 In the East..you hear everything that's happening, and a great deal more. The selective ear tunes out the false news. **1969** *Sat. Rev.* (U.S.) 5 July 28 If you don't like what I say, you can tune me out. **1970** E. G. OLIM in S. Rogers *Children & Language* (1975) v. 322 He learns, as a result of failure and frustration in school, either to tune out the school or to adopt a defiant, rebellious attitude towards it. **1978** G. A. SHEEHAN *Running & Being* iii. 38, I have the ability to tune out what is going on around me.

8. tune up. b. Now usu. *absol.*

1869 W. S. GILBERT *Bab Ballads* 182 He requested them to tune up and begin. **1929** W. FAULKNER *Sound & Fury* 31 'Now you got to tune up.' Dilsey said. **1981** A. SCHLEE *Rhine Journey* xii. 154 Already the orchestra was tuning up for the next waltz.

tuned, *ppl. a.* Add: **2. a.** *Electronics.* Adjusted so as to resonate at a particular frequency; forming part of a circuit so adjusted. Also *transf.*

1899 J. J. FAHIE *Hist. Wireless Telegr.* 182 The circuits are said to be in resonance, or to be electrically tuned. **1928,** etc. [see *LITZ]. **1936** *Discovery* June 197/2 This is of importance in short-wave technique, seeing that condensation is constantly varying the capacity of the tuned circuit. **1962** SIMPSON & RICHARDS *Physical Princ. Junction Transistors* xiv. 328 Two types of high-frequency amplifiers are in general use, tuned amplifiers and untuned wide-band or video amplifiers. **1971** *Nature* 3 Dec.

256/1 In *Diptera*, the antennae are the principal organs of hearing and are tuned and directional. **1980** K. J. Bohlman *Colour & Mono Television* I. viii. 97 At Band 4 and 5 frequencies, conventional *L, C* tuning circuits are not practical... Fortunately..it is possible to use tuned transmission lines.

b. Having one's radio or television tuned (*in*) to a particular station; esp. in imp. phr. *stay tuned*, go on listening to this station.

1956 *Amer. Speech* XXXI. 258 Stay tuned for Roy Neal and his program. **1970** *Wall St. Jrnl.* 15 June 1/1, 13 million American homes are tuned in via ABC-TV to a previously taped episode of Mr Welk's 15-year-old show. **1972** *Guardian* 8 Jan. 8/3 Our own Keith Dewhurst ..had stayed tuned for this unique blend. **1977** 'E. Crispin' *Glimpses of Moon* viii. 152 She fiddled with volume control in order to get him satisfactorily tuned in.

c. *tuned in* (fig.): (*a*) in rapport with, in harmony with; const. *to, on*; (*b*) (*slang*) = *switched on* s.v. *switched *a.* and *ppl. a.* 3 b.

1958 *Oxf. Mag.* 1 May 398/1 It took us some time to get tuned in... Everyone was saying how much better the second half was than the first... Had we just begun to get the wave-length?.. A minor triumph in the difficult art of getting acquainted. **1963** N. Marsh *Dead Water* (1964) i. 29, I miss..the way people think. All the same, it's fun trying to get tuned-in. **1968** P. Brook *Empty Space* iii. 85 It is perhaps for this reason that..the pop tradition in England has such wide appeal: non-political, unaligned, it is none the less tuned in on a fragmented world in which bombs, drugs, God, parents, sex, and private anxieties, are inseparable. **1972** D. Haston *In High Places* xii. 143 I'd walk alone, slowly shaking off the delights of civilization and getting completely tuned in once again to a mountain environment. **1976** *National Observer* (U.S.) 14 Aug. 12/2 This is a regional museum tuned in to the story of man's relationship to the wilderness. **1977** *Hudson Rev.* Spring 69, I thought he'd be some kind of *creep*, instead I meet this really sweet cat... He's really tuned in.

tune-in (tiū·n,in). *U.S.* [f. vbl. phr. *to tune in*: see *tune *v.* 6 b.] **a.** The state of being tuned to a particular station or channel. **b.** The size of the audience for a station or channel.

1931 in F. A. Arnold *Fourth Dimension* 141, I hit the high spots between 7:00 and 10:00 p.m. four evenings a week with a tune-in on the biggest features that come occasionally. **1951** *Sun* (Baltimore) (B ed.) 20 Mar. 1/7 No figures were available for the afternoon telecasts, but ..the average tune-in from 12 noon to 6 P.M. here is about twelve per cent. **1970** *T.V. Guide* (N.Y. Metro ed.) 8 Aug. A1/1 The network is abandoning..long familiar Sabbath half hours..in favor of occasional hour-long specials to be scheduled late Sunday afternoon when tune-in is higher than it is at midday.

tunellite (tʊne·ləit). *Min.* [f. the name of George *Tunell* (b. 1900), U.S. geologist + -ite[1].] A hydrated borate of strontium, $SrB_6O_{10}.4H_2O$, found as colourless or white monoclinic crystals.

1961 R. C. Erd et al. in *Prof. Papers U.S. Geol. Survey* No. 424-C 294/1 Tunellite was first noted..in some samples collected in 1957 from a ventilating shaft in the Jenifer mine, Kramer borate district, California. **1964, 1968** [see *nobleite]. **1978** *Mercian Geologist* VI. 263 Tunellite ..has been found only in the lower part of the borate zone in the Emet deposits in the clay layers in the Kirka deposits [in Turkey].

tuner. Add: **3.** Any device for varying the frequency to which a radio or television is tuned; *spec.* a separate unit for detecting and preamplifying the programme signal and supplying it to an audio amplifier. Also *tuner unit*.

1909 J. Erskine-Murray *Handbk. Wireless Telegr.* (ed. 2) 148 Another instrument..has been designed quite recently (1908). It is called the tuner and contains the inductances, capacities, and coupling arrangements required in a tuned receiving station. **1925** W. Greenwood *Text-bk. Wireless Telegr. & Telephony* vi. 122 (*heading*) The tuner portion of a receiving circuit. *Ibid.* 124 The various tuning inductances and condensers are often assembled in a separate box called the 'tuner'. **1953** E. T. Canby *Home Music Syst.* iii. 37 There are separate units that combine numerous functions: AM-FM radio tuners; ..separate AM tuners and FM tuners; [etc.]. **1959** *Listener* 26 Mar. 541/2 There is no substitute for a high-quality FM tuner unit. **1967** *Ibid.* 30 Mar. 424/1 Some parts of the [television] receiver, such as..the tuner unit, and the box, will cost no more than in a black-and-white receiver. **1970** *Which?* Apr. 115/1 Most of the tuners had a device to show when you were exactly tuned to a station. **1976** K. Thackeray *Crownbird* vi. 127 Priest rotated the tuner on his receiver until he was listening to the police frequency.

4. Special Comb.: **tuner-amplifier**, a combined radio tuner and amplifier; cf. *receiver[1] 7 c; also abbrev. **tuner-amp.**

1970 J. Earl *Tuners & Amplifiers* i. 21 The tuner-amplifier is a new breed of hi-fi equipment. **1975** *Hi-Fi Answers* Feb. 49/1 Your choice of possible tuner-amps is limited by your requirement for an MW section. **1979** J. Gardner *Nostradamus Traitor* xi. 37 A big reel-to-reel tape machine..was linked to a tuner/amplifier set to a pre-selected clear channel.

Tunesin(e), obs. var. *Tunisine *sb.* and *a.*

tunesmith (tiū·n,smiþ). *colloq.* (orig. *U.S.*). [f. Tune *sb.* + Smith *sb.*] A composer of popular music or songs; *derog.*, a composer of unoriginal or trifling music.

1926 Whiteman & McBride *Jazz* viii. 171 Jazz..is the hardest of all to write, the tunesmiths say. **1959** E. S. Turner *Court of St. James's* xxiii. 256 A modern lyric writer and tunesmith in Tin Pan Alley. **1962** *Times* 24 Aug. 11/6 How else does it happen that Bellini, dismissed for years as a vapid tunesmith, has become admired in our own day as a master of poised classical music-drama. **1976** *Gramophone* Nov. 843/3 How dare he dismiss Duke Ellington as a mere 'tunesmith'!

tunesome, *a.* For *rare*$^{-1}$ read *rare* and add later example.

1921 W. de la Mare *Crossings* iii. 82 As neat a brace of nightingales as ever I heard. Shy, but tunesome.

tunester (tiū·nstəɹ). Chiefly *U.S.* [f. Tune *sb.* + -ster.] A song-writer or singer; a musician, composer.

1903 R. Hughes *Love Affairs of Great Musicians* I. xii. 126 (*heading*) A few tunesters of France and Italy—Peri, Monteverdi, et al. **1935** *Amer. Speech* X. 154/2 Singers are now tunesters to advertisement writers for vaudeville and other entertainments. **1936** *N.Y. World-Telegram* 22 Aug. 14/4 At that studio, too, are Mack Gordon and Harry Revell, best known of all movie tunesters. **1983** *Washington Post* 9 May B11/1 Luigi Proietti as a tour guide is pretty lively and alert, like a merry tunester at a funeral.

tune-up (tiū·n,ʊp). orig. *U.S.* [f. vbl. phr. *to tune up*: see Tune *v.* 8 in Dict. and Suppl.]

1. The action, or an act, of tuning up (*lit.* and *fig.*).

1933 *Automotive Electrician* Nov. 16 (*heading*) Analyzing the need for winter tune-up. **1959** [see *hot rod]. **1962** *Daily Tel.* 17 Jan. 20/5 Parties begin on election tune-up. ..Preliminary moves to 'tune-up' the Conservative and Labour party machines for the next general election have already begun. **1968** 'E. Lathen' *Stitch in Time* viii. 71 He always does the tune-ups on Dr Neverson's sports cars. **1977** *Rolling Stone* 16 June 12/1 They still take ten-minute tuneups between songs.

2. *Sport* (chiefly *U.S.*). An event that serves as a practice for a subsequent one.

1934 *Collier's* 11 Aug. 48/3 Webb..intended starting Black Gold in a few tune-up races. **1940** *Sun* (Baltimore) 19 Aug. 20/5 The rain..spoiled several attempts to stage an informal flying exhibit as a tuneup for the annual meet. **1946** *Richmond* (Va.) *Times-Dispatch* 10 Apr. 16/3 A couple of Purple Heart fighters..went along fine in easy tuneups. **1962** *Times* 25 Apr. 4/5 Warburg, who must have benefited from his thorough tune-up against Hughes. **1979** E. Newman *Sunday Punch* xx. 181 'When's Tyner?' 'In about four months. I have a tune-up in Pittsburgh first.'

tuney, tune-y, var. Tuny *a.*

tung (tʊŋ). [a. Chinese *tóng*]. **1. a.** Any of three trees of the genus *Aleurites* or *Vernicia* (family Euphorbiaceæ), *A. fordii*, *A. cordata*, and *A. montana*, which are native to China and Japan and are cultivated there and elsewhere for the oil from their seeds. So *tung tree*.

1889 *Cent. Dict.*, Tung-tree. **1914** N. Shaw *Chinese Forest Trees* I. ii. 70 Tallow, tea-oil trees, and tung grow wild in these hills. **1921** *Outward Bound* Jan. 42/1 The *tung* tree was the abode of the phoenix. **1959** E. Pound *Thrones* xcix. 52 Phoenix to *t'ung* tree A mirrour to flowers, as water is to the moon. **1965** J. Ch'ên *Mao & Chinese Revolution* (1967) I. vii. 138 The mountains are covered..with *t'ung*-trees. **1974** *Tropical Agriculture* LI. 10 This series of trials has shown that nitrogen is the most important nutrient for tung in Malawi.

b. The oil extracted from seeds of the tung tree, used chiefly in the manufacture of inks, paints, and varnishes; = Wood-Oil (*c*).

1911 *Encycl. Brit.* XX. 46/1 (*table*) Name of oil... Tung. **1950** *Caribbean Q.* I. iii. 42 A trial should be made with a settlement of 200 families, beginning with pigs and poultry and proceeding to tree crops (coffee, cocoa, citrus, tung). **1962** H. G. Champion *Streets's Exotic Forest Trees Brit. Commonw.* II. 173 The oil [of *Aleurites montana*] is known commercially as Tung.

2. *attrib.*, as *tung nut*; **tung oil**, a drying oil obtained from the seeds of tung trees and used in varnishes, paints, and inks; so *tung oil tree*; cf. Wood-oil.

1937 R. Frost *Let.* 5 Jan. (1964) 287 We will probably end our days growing Tung nuts in northern Florida. **1881** Tung-oil [see Wood-oil]. **1913** E. H. Wilson *Naturalist in W. China* II. vii. 64 'T'ung Oil tree'.. produces this valuable oil. **1937** A. F. Hill *Econ. Bot.* ix. 213 The United States uses so much tung oil that trees of the latter species have been introduced. **1951** R. Mayer *Artist's Handbk.* iii. 112 Tung Oil..is highly valued as an ingredient of industrial paints and varnishes. **1972** *Guardian* 16 Feb. 15/3 American businessmen..are confronted with increasing difficulties in obtaining soya beans, bristles, tung-oil and egg products from China. **1973** *Times* 21 Mar. (China Trade Suppl.) p. xiv/5 Huge tracts of hillside had only recently been terraced for planting with..tung oil trees.

Also **tung-yu** [Chinese *yóu* oil], tung oil.

1788 tr. *Grosier's Gen. Descr. China* I. iv. vi. 449 The work is..daubed over with a kind of oil, which the Chinese call *tong-yeou*. **1913** E. H. Wilson *Naturalist in W. China* II. vii. 66 'T'ung-yu' is the chief paint oil throughout the Chinese Empire. **1973** T. R. Tregear *Chinese* iv. 89 The Yangtze valley is noted for its production of..*tung yu* (wood oil), which forms the basis of paints and varnish.

Tungan (tʊ·-, tu·ŋgan; dʊ-, du·ŋgan), *sb.* and *a.* Also †**Tungani** *sing.* and *pl.*; **Dungan.** [ad. Jagatai *Döngan*.] **A.** *sb.* A member of a Muslim people in China and in Russian Central Asia of Chinese descent. **B.** *adj.* Of or pertaining to the Tungans.

1875 Bellew & Chapman in T. D. Forsyth *Report Mission Yarkund* ii. 81 The Kara Khitay, the Khitay, and the Tungani. **1908** Lady Macartney *Diary* 12 July in *Eng. Lady in Chinese Turkestan* (1931) xi. 166 Tunganis and Kirghiz, noticeable by reason of their big fur hats. **1927** Cable & French *Through Jade Gate* xxxvii. 221 A stranger on first seeing a Tungan youth would probably say: 'What a handsome Arab boy.' *Ibid.*, Whereas the Tungan speaks Chinese, the Turki has his own tongue. **1965** K. P. S. Menon *Many Worlds* xiv. 201 A young Tungan General. **1974** *Encycl. Brit. Micropædia* V. 190/3 Some Chinese Muslims, called Dungans, have settled in the Soviet Union in the villages and towns of the Uzbek Soviet Socialist Republic, and the Alma-Ata *oblast* (region) of the Kazakh S.S.R.

Tungar (tʊ·ŋgāɹ). *Electronics.* [f. Tung(sten + *ar(gon.] A type of low-voltage discharge tube filled with argon and having a heated cathode of thoriated tungsten, used as a rectifier for currents of a few amperes. (A proprietary name in the U.S.)

1917 *Official Gaz.* (U.S. Patent Office) 4 Dec. 270/1 General Electric Company... *Tungar*... Rectifying apparatus. Claims use since October, 1916. **1935** Nilson & Hornung *Practical Radio Communication* xv. 710 The Tungar battery charger..is a device for charging storage batteries from an alternating-current line. **1966** *McGraw-Hill Encycl. Sci. & Technol.* VI. 61/1 Hot-cathode gas tubes... Three representative types may be distinguished, (1) the Tungar..; (2) the phanotron; and (3) the thyratron.

Tungkingese, -quinese, obs. varr. *Tonkinese *sb.* and *a.*

tungsten. Add: **3.** *tungsten filament*; **tungsten carbide**, either of two compounds of tungsten and carbon, WC and W_2C, that are very hard and are used for cutting tools and abrasives.

1899 *Jrnl. Chem. Soc.* LXXVI. ii. 104 On heating a mixture of tungstic anhydride.., iron.., and petroleum coke.., an iron tungsten carbide..is obtained. **1930** *Engineering* 14 Nov. 634/2 The enhanced cutting properties of the newer cutting steels, such as the tungsten-carbide tools. **1963** C. R. Cowell et al. *Inlays, Crowns, & Bridges* iii. 12 Penetrate to just within the dentine, using a small round tungsten-carbide bur. **1973** *Sci. Amer.* July 42/1 Tungsten carbide, a cermet, has long been used as a cutting tool. **1922** Glazebrook *Dict. Appl. Physics* II. 379/2 From 1904..it became obvious that the future of the incandescent lamp for some time to come would be with the tungsten filament lamp. **1962** V. Nabokov *Pale Fire* 192 The dead, the gentle dead—who knows?—In tungsten filaments abide.

tungstenite. Add: **3.** A tungsten sulphide, probably WS_2, that occurs as both hexagonal and rhombohedral polytypes in dark grey scaly aggregates that mark the fingers.

1917 Wells & Butler in *Jrnl. Washington Acad. Sci.* VII. 596 It is..a pleasure to announce the discovery of tungsten sulphide..from..Utah... On account of the apparent resemblance to molybdenite in formula and some of its properties the new mineral has been named tungstenite. **1970** *Canad. Mineralogist* X. 731 It is virtually impossible to distinguish the *x*-ray powder pattern of a given polytype of molybdenite from the same polytype of tungstenite... Consequently it is quite possible that tungstenite is more widespread than the literature indicates.

Tungus (tu·ŋus, tuŋū·s). Forms: 6 **Tingus,** 6–7 **Tongu(e)se**, 8 **Toongus.** [Yakut name of a people called by themselves Evenki.] **a.** (A member of) a people of eastern Siberia. Also *attrib.*

1625 Purchas *Pilgrimes* III. iii. vii. 527 The people.. signified..that they were called *Tingoesi*, and that their dwelling was vpon the banke of the great Riuer Ieniscè. *Ibid.* x. 543 These *Tingusses* report, that there is another huge Riuer. **1698** tr. *A. Brand's Embassy Muscovy into China* 48 The Tongueses..have of late years been conquered by the Victorious Arms of the Czars of Muscovy, unto whom they pay a yearly Tribute. **1698** [see Shaman *sb.*]. **1763** J. Bell *Trav. from St. Petersburg* I. iii. 225 The Tongusy, so called from the name of the river, who live along its banks, are the posterity of the ancient inhabitants of Siberia. *Ibid.* 229 When a Tonguse kills an elk or deer, he never moves from the place, till he has eat it up. **1799** W. Tooke *View Russian Empire* II. 98 That the Tunguses originally composed one people with the Mandshee, is apparent not only from the resemblance of features..but also chiefly from the agreement of their languages. **1841** *Penny Cycl.* XXI. 459/2 The whole region..has been abandoned to the Toonguses, who get their subsistence by the chace. **1882** A. H. Keane *Asia* 478 Conterminous on the north with the Buriats are the Tunguses. *Ibid.* 479 The Tungus race. **1914** M. A. Czaplicka *Aborig. Siberia* 52 The Nomadic Tungus are cattle-breeders. **1931** M. Burr *Bolshevik Siberia* 154 When a Tungus hits off the spoor of one of these grand beasts. **1948** A. L. Kroeber *Anthropol.* (rev. ed.) x. 429

The Manchu, the Mongols, and the still earlier Tungus conquerors of China lost their own cultures there. **1974** J. R. Baker *Race* x. 174 The Tungus and Kalmuks (Tungid subrace of Mongolids) are said to be devoid of axillary smell.

b. An Altaic language or group of languages related to Manchu, spoken in parts of Siberia, and since 1931 set down in an alphabet based on the Russian alphabet. Also *attrib.* Cf. *Manchu-Tungus.

1822 tr. *Malte-Brun's Universal Geogr.* I. xxiii. 571 The Tunguse is a dialect of the Mantchou. **1888** *Encycl. Brit.* XXIV. 1/2 An exuberance..of verbal forms, which in Osmanli, Finnish, Magyar, Tungus, and Mordvinian may be said to run riot. **1961** L. F. Brosnahan *Sounds of Language* viii. 177 The area of the simple stress accent.. includes..the Mongolian, Tungus and Paleosiberian languages of eastern Asia. **1977** C. F. & F. M. Voegelin *Classification & Index World's Languages* 335 The Tungus languages are bifurcated into two groups... Northern Tungus..= Evenki... Southern Tungus.

Hence **Tungu·sian** *a.*, of or pertaining to this people or language; *sb.*, a Tungus; also, the Tungus language; **Tungu·sic** *a.*, Tungusian; *sb.*, the Tungus language.

1706 tr. *E. Y. Ides's Trav.* 27 Subject to the Jurisdiction of this City are several Tunguzian Heathens. **1706** [see Shaman *sb.*]. **1763** J. Bell *Trav. from St. Petersburg* I. iii. 231 From all the accounts I have heard..of the natives of Canada..they..resemble..the Tongusians. **1799** W. Tooke *View Russian Empire* II. 100 At that time [*sc.* 1607] many tungusian stems owned the paramount supremacy of the Buriats who had shortly before been expelled from Mongolia. **1839** *Jrnl. R. Geogr. Soc.* IX. 198 The Tungusian, though confined to the eastern extreme of the ancient continent, contains some words common to it with languages spoken in Europe. **1854** Max Müller in C. Bunsen *Christianity & Mankind* III. 277 Some of them are certainly widely distant; as, for instance, the dialects of the Finnic nations in the west, and of the Mongolic and Tungusic tribes in the east. **1855** H. D. Seymour *Russia on Black Sea & Sea of Azof* v. 49 The Tungusians extend on the east from the Yenisei to the Sea of Okhotsk. **1864** *Ann. Rep. Smithsonian Inst. 1863* 111 The rank of the Scythian languages..is but an inferior one... They diminish in value eastward, the Tungusic being the poorest of all. **1885** J. Byrne *Struct. Lang.* I. 391 The Tungusian dialect. *Ibid.* 398 The verb *bi*, which in Tungusian takes *hi* in the present. **1888** *Encycl. Brit.* XXIV. 2/2 Turkic lies much closer to Mongolic than it does to Samoyedic and Tungusic. **1890** [see *Gilyak]. **1914** [see *Palæo-Siberian *sb.*]. **1951** W. K. Matthews *Languages U.S.S.R.* iv. 54 Of the three branches of Altaic the easternmost and least significant numerically is the Manchurian or Tungusic. This comprises two subdivisions, viz. the declining Manchu of Northern Manchuria (Manchukuo), with the related languages..and the more primitive and vigorous Tungus (Evenki) and its cognates. **1956** J. Whatmough *Language* ii. 32 The great belt of Mongolian and Tungusian..is connected with the Turkic languages further west, and with Yakut to the North, reaching through Siberia to the Arctic. **1977** *N.Y. Rev. Books* 14 Apr. 3/1 Founded in 947 as a capital of the Khitan Mongols' Liao dynasty, it [*sc.* Peking] had been used similarly by the Tungusic Chin dynasty 1122–1234.

tunic. Add: **5.** Also **tunic shirt**, a long loose-fitting shirt worn outside the trousers; cf. Caftan, *kaftan.

1918 G. Frankau *One of Them* xxx. 234 Smart bosom itch in horsehair tunic-shirts. **1930** *Daily Express* 6 Oct. 5/1 (Advt.), Men's tunic shirts made of the balloon fabric. **1971** 'D. Halliday' *Dolly & Doctor Bird* viii. 104 Mr Tiko, in a blue tunic shirt and blue trousers.

tunica[1] (tiū·nikă). *Anat.* [L.: see Tunic.] = Tunic 4 a in various mod.L. collocations, as *tunica adventitia* [see Adventitious *a.*], an outer sheath, esp. of a blood-vessel; *tunica albuginea* [L. *albūgin-is* white spot], a white fibrous layer, esp. of the penis or testes; *tunica vaginalis*, a serous membrane covering much of the testis.

1698 W. Cowper *Anat. Humane Bodies* sig. Aa, The tunica albuginea, or proper membrane of the testes. **1828** J. Quain *Elem. Anat.* 530 The tunica vaginalis, or serous covering derived from the peritonæum. **1890** *Gray's Anat.* (ed. 12) 48 The arteries are composed of three coats: internal or endothelial coat (tunica intima of Kölliker); middle muscular coat (tunica media); and external cellular coat (tunica adventitia). **1963** *Lancet* 5 Jan. 19/2 The two layers of the tunica vaginalis, which normally invest the testis alone, extend upwards to cover the whole epididymis and the cord, sometimes as high as the inguinal canal. **1977** *Proc. R. Soc. Med.* LXX. 645/1 They observed degenerative changes mainly in the progressive thickening of the tunica adventitia. **1980** *Gray's Anat.* (ed. 36) 1152/1 The fibrous layer of the eyeball..consists of an opaque, posterior part, the tunica sclera, and a transparent, anterior part, the tunica cornea.

Tunica[2] (tiū·nikă). Also [† **Tonica, Tonika.** [ad. F. *Tonika, Tounika*, perh. ad. Tunica *tóniku* the man.] (A member of) an American Indian people of the lower Mississippi valley; their language, now extinct. Hence **Tu·nican**, † **To·nikan**, a postulated linguistic family of which Tunica was the chief member.

1806 J. Sibley in *Message from President of U.S., communicating Discoveries made in exploring Missouri by Capts. Lewis & Clark* 83 Tunicas. These people lived formerly on the Bayan Tunica..on the Mississippi, east side... Their native language is peculiar to themselves. **1891** D. G. Brinton *Amer. Race* I. v. 91 The Tonicas are frequently mentioned in early French accounts of the colony of Louisiana. **1891** J. W. Powell *Indian Linguistic Families* 125 The distinctness of the Tonika language, has long been suspected, and was indeed distinctly stated by Dr. Sibley in 1806. *Ibid.*, The Tonika are known to have occupied three localities. **1902** *Encycl. Brit.* XXV. 374/1 [Linguistic families of North America] Tonikan, Miss. **1911** J. R. Swanton *Indian Tribes Lower Miss. Valley* 19 The method of distinguishing masculine and feminine pronominal forms is also decidedly unlike, Taënsa employing a suffix while Tunica uses entirely distinct forms. **1947** *Romance Philol.* I. 145 (*title*) Some French loan-words in Tunica. **1965** *Canad. Jrnl. Linguistics* Spring 100 Tunican (comprising Tunica, Atakapa, and Chitimacha).

tuning, *vbl. sb.* Add: **1. c.** Also, the process of making adjustments to the engine of a motor vehicle so as to improve its performance.

1916 R. T. Nicholson *Bk. Ford* 151 With proper 'tuning', you ought..to get from 25 to 30 miles per gallon on give-and-take roads. **1939** W. Hassan in Earl Howe et al. *Motor Racing* (Lonsdale Libr. XXVII) xv. 181 One of the most important items in the tuning of a racing car is the correct interpretation and application of the rules of the race for which it is being prepared. **1971** C. Williams *Car Conversions for Power & Speed* v. 127 The most advanced tuning of all is found on racing engines, where the average small capacity unit may be producing more than twice the power of an equivalent engine in a road car.

d. The adjustment of a transmitter or receiver to a particular signal frequency or wavelength; variation of the resonant frequency of an oscillatory circuit. Also *tuning in*, the action of adjusting a radio set to a desired frequency; the selection (of a frequency) by this process; also *transf.*; *tuning out*, the cutting out (of a radio transmission) by tuning.

1899 [see *tune *v.* 1 c]. **1908** *Rep. Brit. Assoc. Adv. Sci. 1907* 622 The various self-inductions and other arrangements for effecting tuning are similarly wound. **1927** W. E. Collinson *Contemp. Eng.* 113 If they have heard through a friend's set they..will have some inkling of the mysteries of tuning in and tuning out. **1929** *Radio Times* 8 Nov. 386/1 Only three knobs..one for tuning, one for volume and one for wavelengths. **1934** H. Jackson *Maxims Bks. & Reading* 9 Reading is nothing but tuning oneself in to a book in a spirit of reverential subjection. **1940** *Amer. Speech* XV. 247 He allows nobody else to have anything to do with the *tuning-in* and the *tuning-out* (or the *turning-off*) of the radio programs. **1970** J. Earl *Tuners & Amplifiers* iii. 73 Very accurate tuning is essential for good stereo reception. **1975** D. G. Fink *Electronics Engineers' Handbk.* xxi. 11 The transmitter is designed for a minimum of tuning adjustment, and..all tuning can be performed from the front panel using only two controls. **1977** *Listener* 17 Mar. 344/1 A furtive tuning-in to Radio 3.

4. (sense *1 d) *tuning circuit, coil, condenser, indicator, inductance, knob, meter*; **tuning-slide** (examples).

1943 C. L. Boltz *Basic Radio* xii. 195 We then put a coil in the aerial to earth circuit, and couple this inductively to the coil of the tuning circuit. **1923** *Popular Wireless* 13 Oct. (Suppl.) 1 Many wireless amateurs experience considerable difficulty in estimating the maximum wavelengths of their tuning coils. **1978** F. Maclean *Take Nine Spies* iv. 148 The copper wire needed for the tuning coils he managed..to buy in Tokyo. **1913** *Wireless World* Apr. p. xxix, If the aerial tuning condenser was set to its previous value and the tuning-switch (not the aerial tuning inductance) put to the second stop, the maximum signals were again obtained. **1937** F. E. Terman *Radio Engin.* (ed. 2) xiii. 559 A more recent development in tuning indicators is a special miniature cathode-ray tube. **1913** Tuning inductance [see *tuning condenser* above]. **1981** *Sunday Express* (Colour Suppl.) 12 July 33/4 For a monthly subscription fee the tuning knob of a British domestic TV set could then offer a dozen or more channels. **1978** *N.Y. Times* 30 Mar. B11/1 (Advt.), Model STA-52.. includes..tuning meter and a cabinet that's made of genuine walnut veneer. **1885** Tuning-slide [see *shank *sb.* 5 w]. **1961** A. Baines *Mus. Instruments* 358 *Tuning slide*, in wind instruments, a part of the tubing that is made extensible for the purposes of tuning.

Tunisian (tiūni·ziăn), *sb.* and *a.* [f. *Tunis* + -ian, or *Tunisia* + -an (see below): cf. the earlier *Tunisine *sb.* and *a.*] **A.** *sb.* **a.** A native or inhabitant of the country of Tunisia in North Africa (or of its capital Tunis), or of the former Barbary state of Tunis which preceded it. **b.** The demotic speech of the Tunisians. **B.** *adj.* Of, pertaining to, or belonging to Tunisia, or Tunis.

1825 J. C. Loudon *Encycl. Agric.* I. vi. 175 The Tunisians are much more agriculturists than their neighbors either of Tripoli or Algiers. **1843** *Penny Cycl.* XXV. 361/1 Grain is frequently imported into the Tunisian territory. **1891** O. Wilde *Pict. Dorian Gray* xi. 199 Yellow-shawled Tunisians plucked at the strained strings of monstrous lutes. **1902** *Encycl. Brit.* XXXIII. 483/2 No doubt in vulgar Tunisian a good many Berber words remain. **1926** A. Huxley *Let.* 31 Dec. (1969) 279, I hope the children's Tunisian dates will arrive fairly soon. **1958** *Ann. Reg. 1957* 325 The Franco-Tunisian customs union. **1973** 'A. Hall' *Tango Briefing* xvii. 217 There was a police guard ..a young Tunisian with a peaked cap.

Tunisine (tiū·nisīn), *sb.* and *a.* ? *Obs.* Also **Tunesin(e), Tunis(s)een.** [f. *Tunis* + -ine[1]: see prec.] **A.** *sb.* A native of Tunis, a city and former Barbary state in North Africa; esp. a pirate from Tunis. **B.** *adj.* Of or belonging to Tunis.

c **1670** J. Verney *Let.* in M. M. Verney *Mem.* (1899) IV. v. 159 [The ship was taken] by the Tunisseens. **1738** T. Shaw *Trav. Barbary & Levant* 155 The Tuniseens, are the most civilized Nation of Barbary. **1764** A. Anderson *Origin Commerce* I. iii. 126 The Genoese grew very uneasy, lest the Tunesins..should seize on all their effects. **1843** *Penny Cycl.* XXV. 360/1 Susa..is..one of the wealthy cities of the Tunisine state. *Ibid.* 364/2 The Tunisines in general, like the Algerines, are a mixed race of Turks, Moors and Jews. *Ibid.* 366/2 The Tunesine corsairs continued their excursions at sea until 1655.

tunket (tʊ·ŋkėt). *U.S. dial.* or *colloq.* Sometimes with initial capital. Also **tunkett.** [Origin doubtful.] Euphem. for *hell*; chiefly *who* (*what, why*, etc.) *in tunket*.

1871 *Scribner's Monthly* II. 630 What in tunket are you making such a to-do about it for? **1894** *Life* 4 Jan. 13/2 What in the name o' Tunkett makes all boys so crazy to leave the old farm? **1905** G. S. Wasson *Green Shay* iii. 37 'Who in tunket is it backs up the old creetur', anyways?' asked Master Fairway. **1922** Joyce *Ulysses* 420 Golly, whatten tunket's yon guy in the mackintosh? **1951** E. Graham *My Window looks down East* vii. 59 'And why not, in tunket?' she says. **1971** H. A. Smith *View from Chivo* xix. 192, I cannot forego the use of harsh language when I think of him; he makes me madder'n tunket.

tunku (tʊ·ŋkʊ). Also ‖ **tengku** (te·ŋkʊ). [Malay.] A title of rank in certain states of Western Malaysia; = 'prince'.

1879 in C. W. Harrison *Council Minutes, Perak, 1877–79* (1907) 63 Toh Puan, the chief wife of the former Tengku Mentri. **1897** D. C. Boulger *Life Sir Stamford Raffles* x. 314 He also goes on to say that Tunku Long, a native rajah, arrived from Rhio, and that Raffles thereupon acknowledged him as Sultan of Johore. **1911** R. J. Wilkinson *Papers Malay Subjects: Malay Hist.* v. xi. 34 His son, Tengku Antah, on claiming the throne, was opposed by a Sumatran prince. **1956** *Britannica Bk. of Year* 283/2 Tengku Abdul Rahman was to head a delegation to London early in 1956. *Ibid.* 284/1 On Dec. 28–29, less than a week before he left for the London talks, the Tengku..met Chin Peng, secretary of the Malayan Communist Party. **1961** *Listener* 23 Nov. 866/2 The Tunku is in this country to discuss with the British Government proposals for a Federation of Malaysia. **1977** P. Theroux *Consul's File* vi. 48 A boy vaguely related to the Sultan..known locally (but inaccurately) as 'Tunku', The Prince. **1977** *Times* 31 Aug. (Malaysia Suppl.) p. viii/8 When someone is a Tengku or Tunku..his blood is very blue indeed, or very white, as the Malays put it; unless..he comes from Perak where a Raja is usually higher.

tunnel, *sb.* Add: **1. b.** (Example.)

1873 [see *crib *sb.* 10 b].

4. a. (Earlier example.)

1765 T. Lowndes *Let.* 1 July in *Hist. Inland Navigations* (1766) I. 41 Mr. Brindley..is driving a large tunnel through the center of this hill.

g. Applied fig. to a prolonged period of difficulty, suffering, etc. Freq. in phr. *light at the end of the tunnel* and the like: a long-awaited sign that a period of hardship or adversity is nearing an end. *colloq.*

1879 Geo. Eliot *Let.* 7 July (1956) VII. 178 Though I am getting out of the tunnel into daylight, this renewal of weakness..makes it seem as if we should be wiser to defer the visit. **1899** H. James *Awkward Age* x. xxxvii. 437 We've worked through the dark tunnel of artificial reserves. **1922** J. M. Murry *Let.* in A. Alpers *Life K. Mansfield* (1980) xx. 359, I begin to feel that the horror may move away and that there is a big round spot of real daylight at the end of the tunnel. **1943** J. B. Priestley *Daylight on Saturday* xxxv. 283 The work..seemed to him a long way off,..seen at the end of a tunnel. It had retreated from him. **1971** *Guardian* 6 Sept. 2/5 The world has reached a crucial point in its drive to reduce illiteracy, UNESCO reports today. There is now 'light at the end of the tunnel'. **1975** Ld. Robbins *Against Inflation* (1979) xviii. 89, I confess I do not understand the suggestion.. that there is any strong light at the end of the tunnel, the way we are going now.

h. *Aeronaut.* A wind tunnel (*wind *sb.*[1] 31).

1911 A. P. Thurston *Elem. Aeronautics* viii. 84 The *wind tunnel* consists of a tube, passage or tunnel, through which air may be forced or drawn by means of rotating fans, steam jets, or the like. The tunnel may be vertical or horizontal. Sir Hiram Maxim used a horizontal tunnel... Dr Stanton used a wind tunnel..in which the current was vertical and downwards. **1930** Nayler & Ower *Aviation* 116 Essentially, the tunnel consists of a large tube..along which the air is drawn by means of a motor driving a fan. **1972** *Nature* 18 Aug. 379/2 A low density tunnel for simulating supersonic and hypersonic flight at altitudes of 20 to 70 miles.

i. *Sport.* A subway or covered passage by which players pass to or from the field of play.

1950 *Sport* 24–30 Mar. 3/3 He..made for the tunnel under the impression that the game was over. **1976** *S. Wales Echo* 22 Nov., He..threw it towards the players' tunnel where the police were escorting the referee.

5. *tunnel-making, worker* (earlier example); *tunnel-like* (earlier example); **tunnel-back** *local*, the rear extension of a house, containing the scullery and other functional rooms; a house built in this style; **tunnel diode** *Electronics*, a two-terminal semiconductor device, consisting of a heavily doped *p–n* junction, which has negative resistance at low voltage due to quantum-mechanical tunnelling and is principally used as a high-speed switching device; **tunnel effect** *Physics* = *TUNNELLING *vbl. sb.* 2*; **tunnel-kiln** (examples); **tunnel of love**, a fairground amusement involving a train- or boat-ride through a darkened tunnel, intended for courting couples; **tunnel vision**, a condition in which there is a major loss of peripheral vision; also, one in which anything away from the centre of one's field of view escapes attention; also *fig.*, inability to see more than a single or limited point of view; hence **tunnel-visioned** *a.*

1957 R. HOGGART *Uses of Literacy* i. 20 They have, almost city by city, their own recognizable styles of housing—back-to-backs here or tunnel-backs there. **1981** C. DEXTER *Dead of Jericho* vi. 52 No tunnel-backs to the houses, and so the bicycles had to be left outside. **1959** *Proc. IRE* XLVII. 1204/1 The tunnel diode has a very high admittance. **1982** J. E. UFFENBECK *Introd. Electronics* i. 24 This switching property of the tunnel diode makes it suitable for digital applications. **1932** J. FRENKEL *Wave Mech.* iii. 111 (*heading*) Transition through a potential energy mountain (tunnel effect). **1974** G. REECE tr. *Hund's Hist. Quantum Theory* xiv. 187 A barrier is not completely impenetrable. In fact it allows..the 'tunnel effect'. **1901** Tunnel kiln [see *continuous kiln* s.v. *CONTINUOUS 3]. **1961** M. KELLY *Spoilt Kill* i. 11 We have gas-fired tunnel kilns now... There's very little coal firing left in the [pottery] industry. **1880** 'MARK TWAIN' *Tramp Abr.* xlvi. 530 One of the shows of the place was a tunnel-like cavern, which had been hewn in the glacier. **1910** Tunnel-making [see *road-building* s.v. *ROAD *sb.* 11 a]. **1954** J. R. R. TOLKIEN *Fellowship of Ring* 31, I know of no tunnel-making. **1954** *New Yorker* 8 May 100/2 'And the lights!.. There are thirty-eight hundred on that ride alone. Why, even the World's Fair in its heyday—' he cried, and then for a moment, words failed him. 'And yet it's only a Tunnel of Love!' **1968** [see *loop-the-loop* sb. s.v. *LOOP *v.*[1] 6]. **1976** 'W. TREVOR' *Children of Dynmouth* i. 13 The Hall of a Million Mirrors and the Tunnel of Love and Alfonso's and Annabella's Wall of Death were in the process of erection. **1949** SNYGG & COMBS *Individ. Behav.* vi. 110 It has often been observed that in emotional experiences there exists a very high degree of attention sometimes referred to as 'tunnel vision'. *Ibid.* vii. 125 This narrowing of the field is particularly likely to occur when the individual feels he is threatened. The effect has sometimes been called 'tunnel vision'. **1962** *Times* 3 Apr. 17/2 One of the dangers of 'tunnel vision' in driving was brought home to a motorist who recently took the test of the Institute of Advanced Motorists. **1967** *Freedomways* VII. 137 The confused black college graduate, thrust out into a hostile racist society and handicapped by tunnel vision and a self-negating perspective. **1968** *New Scientist* 29 Aug. 449/3 The alternative theory, that of 'Tunnel Vision'. The idea here is that a high level of arousal causes the brain to select very narrowly from among the signals reaching the eyes. **1979** *Daily Tel.* 7 Apr. 3/2 He was now registered as blind. He had tunnel vision, but even this was imperfect... There was some brain damage. **1980** T. BARLING *Goodbye Piccadilly* viii. 169 Prebble had the ghetto mind and the tunnel-vision of a committed social climber. **1985** *Observer* 10 Mar. 5/1 Only someone with Tony Benn's tunnel vision could see the strike as 'a turning point in the battle against monetarism'. **1968** J. LOCK *Lady Policeman* vi. 50 What happened to the juvenile after the Court's decision was not really in our province but we would have been tunnel-visioned indeed if we had never felt any concern. **1903** Tunnel worker [see *sand-hog* s.v. *SAND *sb.*[2] 10 a].

tunnel, *v.* Add: **4. d.** *intr.* Physics. Of a sub-atomic particle: to pass *through* a potential barrier by tunnelling (*TUNNELLING *vbl. sb.* 2*).

1938 S. DUSHMAN *Elem. Quantum Mech.* iii. 66 The probability that a particle coming up to the boundary at $x = 0$ shall 'tunnel' through the barrier. **1966** D. G. BRANDON *Mod. Techniques Metallogr.* iv. 181 Electrons may be able to 'tunnel' through to the far side. **1978** P. W. ATKINS *Physical Chem.* xiii. 402 An electron is able to tunnel through even quite high potential barriers (for example, they can escape from the powerful forces inside nuclei, and emerge as β-rays).

tunnelling, -eling, *vbl. sb.* Add: **I. 2*.** *Physics.* The quantum-mechanical process whereby a particle has a non-zero probability of penetrating a finite potential barrier even if it has less energy than the height of the barrier.

1938 S. DUSHMAN *Elem. Quantum Mech.* iii. 68 The 'tunneling effect'..is one of the most important deductions contributed by the new quantum mechanics. **1970** *New Scientist* 1 Oct. 38/2 Tunnelling is a phenomenon particular to quantum mechanics. **1978** P. W. ATKINS *Physical Chem.* xiii. 402 The particle might be found on the outside of a container, even though according to classical physics it has insufficient energy to escape. This passage through classically forbidden zones is called tunnelling.

tunny. Add: **b.** *tunny boat, fishing* (hence *-fish* vb. intr.); **tunnyman**, a boat engaged in tunny fishing.

1934 *Yachting Monthly* LVII. 24/1 An ever-interesting panorama is provided by the sardiniers and tunny boats [at Concarneau]. **1974** 'J. GRAHAM' *Bloody Passage* xiii. 173 There are a hell of a lot of tunny boats scattered around. **1977** C. WATSON *One Man's Meat* viii. 78 He was with me, tunny-fishing off Scarborough. **1971** 'D. HALLIDAY' *Dolly & Doctor Bird* v. 66 Between its [*sc.* a bridge's] arches tunny-fishing boats were constantly sprinting. **1930** *Sea Breezes* Dec. 94 Whilst the motor is making rapid headway amongst the sardine luggers and crabbers, at present the tunnymen are unaffected. **1961** A. J. R. FRASER TAYLOR *Diary* 13 Aug. in *Roving Commissions 1962* (1963) 123 The following day a slow passage to Bermeo, tying up late in the evening alongside a tunnyman.

tup, *v.* Add: **1. a.** *transf.* Also of a man: to copulate with (a woman). *coarse slang.*

1970 B. W. ALDISS *Hand-Reared Boy* 96 In Derbyshire's dull dorms... When lesser souls abused themselves, outclassed, Our Dancer, saint and patron, he upped and tupped the matron. **1976** R. JEFFRIES *Two-Faced Death* xviii. 210 You wouldn't tup her?.. Neither of us cut out for adultery.

tupaiid (tupai·id). [a. mod.L. family name *Tupaiidæ*, f. TUPAIA + -ID[3].] A tree-shrew of the family Tupaiidæ.

1885 T. GILL in J. S. Kingsley *Riverside Nat. Hist.* (1888) V. 141 The proper diet of the Tupaiids is small insects. **1972** T. A. VAUGHAN *Mammalogy* vi. 70/1 Paleontological evidence indicates that tupaiids were derived from the Insectivora and not from the Primates.

tupaioid (tupai·oid), *a.* (*sb.*) [a. mod.L. superfamily name *Tupaioidea*, f. TUPAIA + -OID.] Of or pertaining to the superfamily Tupaioidea, or resembling a member of this group. Also as *sb.*, an arboreal mammal of the superfamily Tupaioidea.

1912 *Rep. Brit. Assoc. Adv. Sci.* 583 Its Tupaioid ancestor took to an arboreal life. **1972** W. C. O. HILL *Evolutionary Biol. Primates* ii. 18 The order is remarkable for the persistence..of living forms that illustrate several successive evolutionary steps..from tupaioids to man.

Tupamaro (tupămā·ro). [f. the names of the Inca leaders *Tupac Amaru* I (d. 1571) and *Tupac Amaru* II (d. 1781).] A member of a left-wing guerrilla organization in Uruguay. Also *attrib.*

1969 *N.Y. Times* 23 Jan. 12/2 The Tupamaros represent a new approach to guerrilla warfare in Latin America. *Ibid.* 12/4 Tupamaro intelligence sources. **1970** *Guardian* 11 Aug. 11/3 The Tupamaros..would like to see a Cuban-style revolution in Uruguay. **1973** G. JACKSON *People's Prison* xxiv. 194 Tupamaro hideouts were even then notoriously subterranean. **1977** *Time* 31 Jan. 54/3 Urban guerrilla movements, such as the extinct Tupamaros of Uruguay, may have seen their day.

‖ **tupan** (tu·pæn). [Chinese.] The civil governor of a Chinese province under the Republican regime.

1925 *Glasgow Herald* 31 Aug. 9 Another mandate appoints General Feng's associate, Sun Yueh, Tupan of Shensi. **1928** T. F. MILLARD *China* 28 That process grew the crop of tuchuns, tupans, field marshals, and what not, so much heard of in these times. As originally used, the word 'tuchun' was distinctly a military term, and 'tupan' meant an officer who exercised civil authority; but in late years the terms are used indiscriminately. **1936** P. FLEMING *News from Tartary* vi. ii. 250 Chin Shu-Jen was succeeded by the present *tupan*, General Sheng Shih-tsai. **1949** F. MACLEAN *Eastern Approaches* (1951) i. v. 98 The intention was that I should go to Urumchi, the capital of Sinkiang, to contact the Tupan, or Provincial Governor.

Tupi. Add: Also pronounced (tupī·). **a.** Also, the group of tribes speaking this language; a person belonging to one of these tribes. Also *attrib.*

1842 [see THE *dem. adj.* and *pron.* B. 3 b]. **1863** [see *JACITARA]. **1911** *Encycl. Brit.* XXVII. 410/2 Latham makes the Tupis members of the Guarani stock. **1950** C. LÉVI-STRAUSS in J. H. Steward *Handbk. S. Amer. Indians* VI. 475 The fruit of a Bignoniaceae..was used as a comb by the *Tupi* and other tribes. **1950** C. O. SAUER in *Ibid.* 499 The peanut was..important in Tupí economy.

b. *Tupi-Guarani* (gwăranī·), also unhyphened: a South American linguistic and ethnic stock of which Tupi and Guarani are the most prominent members; a person belonging to this ethnic stock. Also *attrib.* Cf. *GUARANI 1.

1850 R. G. LATHAM *Nat. Hist. Varieties of Man* 443 The Guarani. Synonyms.—Tupi, Brazilian, Guarani-Brazilian, Tupi-Guarani. **1876** *Encycl. Brit.* IV. 235/1 They [*sc.* the tribes of Brazil] belong..to one original stock, called by ethnographers, the Tupi-Guarani. **1901** *O.E.D.* s.v. *Jaguar*, According to writers on Tupi-Guarani, *jaguara* or *jagua* is orig. a class-name for all carnivorous beasts. **1933** L. BLOOMFIELD *Language* iv. 73 In South America, we note..the Tupi-Guarani [family of languages], stretched along the coast of Brazil. **1956** E. HAUGEN *Bilingualism in Americas* ii. 15 Tupí-Guaraní is taught in some Brazilian schools. **1968** M. GILBERT *Cork in Bottle* in *Ellery Queen's Christmas Hamper* (1975) 231 The three mestizos..were Tupi-Guaranis, half Indian, half Spanish. **1977** G. CLARK *World Prehistory* (ed. 3) x. 449 Polychrome pottery closely resembling the Tupi-guarani ware of East Brazil.

Tupian *sb.* and *a.* (examples).

1902 *Encycl. Brit.* XXV. 374/1 [Linguistic families of America] Tupian, Amazon R. **1948** A. L. KROEBER *Anthropology* (rev. ed.) xviii. 833 A Tupian tribe, the Chiriguano, having conquered an Arawakan one, the Chané, pushed on westward. **1974** *Encycl. Brit. Micropædia* X. 187/1 *Tupians*, South American Indians who speak languages of the Tupian linguistic group. Tupian-speaking peoples were widespread south of the Amazon.

tupik. Add: Also 9 **toupik, tupic; tubik.** (Earlier and later examples.)

1864 C. F. HALL *Life with Esquimaux* I. ix. 176 On my way,..just outside the angeko's tupic, I noticed an oar of a kia[k] stuck upright in a drift of frozen snow. **1878** C. HALLOCK *Sportsman's Gazetteer* (ed. 4) 700 *Toupik*, an Esquimaux summer lodge of poles covered with seal-skins. **1895** KIPLING *Second Jungle Bk.* 152 One of their hunters came across a *tupik*, a skin-tent. **1920** W. T. GRENFELL *Labrador Doctor* vi. 129 Wooden huts had largely replaced the former 'tubiks', or skin tents.

Tupinamba (tupinæ·mbă, *prop.* tupinambā·). Also † **Tupinambo.** [Native name; cf. F. *Topinambou* (1578 in form *Tououpinambaoults*) and TUPI.] A group of extinct tribes on the coast of Brazil; a person belonging to one of these tribes. Also *attrib.*

1810 SOUTHEY *Hist. Brazil* I. viii. 229 Nobrega learnt from the Tupinambas that two persons..taught them the use of the mandioc. **1819** SHELLEY *Let.* 3 Nov. (1964) II. 140 An Otaheitan or a Tupinambo. **1863** H. W. BATES *Naturalist on River Amazons* I. vii. 285 The old historians relate that the island of Tupinambarána was colonised by a portion of the great Tupí or Tupinámba nation, who were driven from the sea-coast near Pernambuco, by the early Portuguese settlers in the 16th century. **1949** WAGLEY & GALVÃO *Tenetehara Indians of Brazil* i. 5 The Portuguese..found the Island of Maranhão inhabited by the Tupí-Guaraní Tupinambá. **1974** *Encycl. Brit. Macropædia* XVII. 124/1 The Tupinamba shaman fumigates his rattle with tobacco.

-tuple (tiŭp'l), *a.* and *sb.* Chiefly *Math.* [The ending of QUINTUPLE *a.* and *sb.*, etc.] With preceding algebraic symbol: (an entity or set) consisting of as many parts or elements as indicated by the symbol.

1863 *Phil. Trans. R. Soc.* CLIII. 457 The curve m is a $(m-1)n$-tuple line on the scroll $S(m^2, n)$. **1910** *Encycl. Brit.* I. 615/2 We may regard it as a (2^n-1)-tuple linear algebra. **1938** *Jrnl. Symbolic Logic* III. 151 Each function is defined over a subset..of the n-tuples of natural numbers. **1963** J. LYONS *Structural Semantics* ii. 12 In so far as words can be segmented into morphemes, the lexeme can be defined extensionally as the set of all the ordered n-tuples ($n \geq 1$) of morphemes (each n-tuple being a word) which are grouped together in setting up the paradigm. **1972** *Computer Jrnl.* XV. 232/1 A structure of a string A is an ordered n-tuple T.

Tupperism. (Earlier example.)

1870 J. R. LOWELL *Among my Books* 114 The gradual degeneration of a poetic faith into the ritual of unimaginative Tupperism.

Tupperware (tʌ·pəɹwēᵊɹ). [Trade name, f. Earl S. *Tupper*, President of the Tupper Corporation + WARE *sb.*[3]] The proprietary name of a range of plastic vessels, containers, etc., sold exclusively at 'parties' in private homes to which potential purchasers are invited. Freq. *attrib.*; also in allusive use.

1956 *Official Gaz.* (U.S. Patent Office) 12 June TM 53 Tupperware... For Molded Plastic Tumblers, Canisters, Pitchers, Dispensers; Empty Condiment Holders... Empty Soap, Hair Massage and Tooth Brush Boxes [etc.]. First use Mar. 3, 1950. **1961** *Trade Marks Jrnl.* 23 Aug. 1162/1 Tupperware... Small domestic utensils and containers..; combs and sponges; brushes.., Rexall Drug and Chemical Company.., City of Los Angeles, State of California, United States of America; manufacturers. **1965** *Which?* Dec. 373/1 Are more expensive brands [of food container], in particular Tupperware, better than cheaper brands at storing foods? *Ibid.*, You can't buy Tupperware in the shops. It is sold through local 'dealers'... The dealer gets a housewife to be the hostess at a party. **1966** T. PYNCHON *Crying of Lot 49* i. 9 Mrs Oedipa Maas came home from a Tupperware party whose hostess had perhaps put too much kirsch in the fondue. **1971** N. STACEY *Who Cares?* viii. 131 We were not training a group of people to give Tupperware parties or sell cosmetics to housewives. **1979** T. BARLING *Olympic Sleeper* i. 15 There were too many cowboys on the Thames nowadays, playing sailors in their Tupperware boats.

tur (tūᵊɹ). [a. Russ.] A greyish-brown wild goat, *Capra caucasica*, native to south-eastern Russia.

1894 C. PHILLIPPS-WOLLEY *Big Game Shooting* II. iii. 51 The tûr is the mountain beast, *par excellence*, of the Caucasus. **1894** R. LYDEKKER *Royal Nat. Hist.* II. 235 There occur in the Caucasus range..wild goats, known locally as tur. **1925** G. BURRARD *Big Game Hunting* 87 The East Caucasian tur..is an undoubted goat. **1965** D. MORRIS *Mammals* 428 There are several other species which are also called Ibex. These include the Tur, or Caucasian Ibex.

turaco: now the usual spelling of TOURACO (in Dict. and Suppl.).

Turanian, *a.* Add: **1.** (Earlier examples.)

1788 *Asiatick Researches* I. 7 A Turanian pronunciation. **1841** J. C. PRICHARD *Res. Physical Hist. Mankind* (ed. 3)

I. i. 16 A great number of roots are thus to be traced in veral of the Turanian languages.
2. (Earlier example.)
1836 J. C. PRICHARD *Res. Physical Hist. Mankind* l. 3) I. iv. 267 The skulls of the Esquimaux..bring them to the same class of human races with the Kalmuk d other Turanian nations.
Hence **Tura·nianism,** the principle of unitg speakers of Turanian or Ural-Altaic lanıages (esp. Turkish); cf. *pan-Turanianism* v. *PAN- I.
1922 *19th Cent.* Nov. 835 The seeming paradox of the olshevist *régime* cementing Islamism and Turanianism a widespread brotherhood.

uranose (tiūᵊ·rănōᵘz). *Chem.* [ad. Russ. *ranoza* (A. Alekhina 1889, in *Zhurnal usskago fiziko-khim. Obshchestva* XXI. 418), ter Pers. *Turān* Turkistan, place of origin the manna used to prepare this: see -OSE².] he reducing disaccharide sugar $C_{12}H_{22}O_{11}$, ormed by partial hydrolysis of melezitose; -α-D-glucopyranosyl-D-fructose.
1890 *Jrnl. Chem. Soc.* LVIII. 733 Melezitose, on inveron with dilute mineral acids, yields at first turanose and extrose; the former is a new saccharose of the formula $_{12}H_{22}O_{11}$. **1927** M. BODANSKY *Introd. Physiol. Chem.* ii. Turanose (fructose+glucose) is obtained by hydrolyzg the trisaccharide melicitose. **1975** *Nature* 10 July 128/1 altose was slightly more effective, and sucrose, turanose, ojibiose, trehalose and melezitose all inhibited binding significantly lower concentrations than glucose.

turba (tūᵊ·rbă). *Mus.* [L., = crowd.] A ame given to the chorus in Passions and other eligious oratorios in which crowds particiate in the action. (See also quot. 1889.)
1876 STAINER & BARRETT *Dict. Mus. Terms* 443/1 *urbæ (Lat.)*, the chorus part or voice of the multitude a Passion-music. **1889** *Cent. Dict.* s.v., *Turba*, the chorus mediaeval passion-plays, representing the Jewish opulace. **1947** A. EINSTEIN *Music in Romantic Era* xiii. 73 It is a work with fanatic *turbae*, the 'crowds', as in the assions. **1962** *Listener* 15 Feb. 317/3 The Roman hurch's dramatic Passions now come into view with ictoria's and Byrd's settings of the *turba*.

urban, *sb.* Add: **8. turban squash** (examles); **turban tumour** *Path.*, a rare benign umour, probably of sweat glands, that preads over the scalp or thorax in grape-like lusters.
1902 L. H. BAILEY *Cycl. Amer. Hort.* IV. 1713/1 The urban Squashes..have a 'Squash within a Squash'. **1949** *'at. Geogr. Mag.* Aug. 162/2 Several years ago a North akota horticulturist bred a small variety of turban quash. **1981** *Farmstead Mag.* Winter 38/3 The last of the x types to be mentioned is the turban squash. **1903** I. RADCLIFFE-CROCKER *Dis. of Skin* (ed. 3) II. viii. 961 arcoma Capitis, or Endothelioma Capitis (Turban ımours). A peculiar form of tumour, in rare instances ttacks, and is limited to the hairy scalp; in extreme cases, overing the whole scalp like a wig. **1974** J. D. MAYNARD R. M. Kirk et al. *Surgery* ix. 196 Turban tumour... hese rare tumours are sub-epithelial basal cell carcinoıas, usually of sweat-gland origin which grow steadily nd slowly, without ulceration or metastasis, on the scalp, ace and thorax.
turban(n)y *a.*, resembling or suggestive of turban.
1912 A. HUXLEY *Let.* 13 May (1969) 42 The banner earers..wear marvellous uniforms—usually consisting f a..sort of turbanny object or a cocked hat..white reeches and highly polished top-boots. **1924** E. BOWEN *Spectator* 5 July 11/1 Yes, but haven't you got *any* oldish sort of turbany thing?

urban, *v.* Add: **b.** To wind in the form of a urban.
a **1861** T. WINTHROP *John Brent* (1883) xvi. 151 A strip f old white blanket..was turbaned askew about his ead. **1969** *Daily Tel.* 20 Jan. 11 A long white and cream ilk scarf turbanned round the head and floating free.

urbaned, *a.* Add: Also **turbanned. a.** (Later examples.)
1968 T. STOPPARD *Real Inspector Hound* (1970) 12 Mrs. Drudge is the char, middle-aged, turbanned. **1976** G. S. Fox in M. Drabble *Genius of Thomas Hardy* III. 172 A urbanned Indian.
b. Arranged to form a turban. (In quot., *ransf.*) *poet. rare.*
1924 E. SITWELL *Sleeping Beauty* vi. 28 The..shore Where curled and turbanned waves sigh 'Nevermore'.

turbary. Add: **3. b.** [tr. G. *torf-*.] Applied to kinds of domesticated sheep and pig of prehistoric times that were first found in turbaries in Swiss lake-dwellings.
1908 R. PUMPELLY *Explorations Turkestan* I. I. v. 57 The turbary sheep (Torfschaf) and..the turbary pig Torfschwein)..appear towards the end of the neolithic period. **1912** R. LYDEKKER *Sheep & its Cousins* vii. 150 An apparently pure-blooded breed of small sheep inhabiting Crete..is identified by Dr. Keller with the turbary sheep. **1920** J. RITCHIE *Animal Life Scotl.* 40 Even in Neolithic times the Turbary or Peat Sheep..was widely distributed in Scotland. **1936** *Antiquity* X. 203 We find a small sheep with erect horns,..the so-called 'goathorned' or turbary sheep. **1963** F. E. ZEUNER *Hist. Domesticated Animals* x. 257 In the earlier group of Neolithic lake-dwellings the small turbary pig (*Sus palustris* Rütimeyer) occurs beside the ordinary European wild pig. There is no doubt that this turbary pig was introduced into Switzerland by Neolithic man from the East. *Ibid.* 258 According to Kuhn, the turbary pig has survived to the present day in some of the Alpine valleys. **1972** *Science* 12 May 656/2 With regard to sheep and pig, he believes that the well-known turbary type..is a natural product of malnutrition and poor care.

turbidimeter (tɜ̄ɹbidi·mĭtəɹ). *Chem.* and *Biol.* [f. TURBID *a.* + -I- + -METER.] An instrument for determining the turbidity of a liquid from the decrease in the intensity of a beam of light passing through it.
1905 *Water Supply & Irrigation Papers* (U.S. Geol. Survey) No. 151. 26 The needs of the Survey were found to be met in a satisfactory manner by the use of a turbidimeter devised by Mr. Daniel D. Jackson. **1920** *Jrnl. Biol. Chem.* XLII. 191 Turbidimeters and nephelometers are instruments designed for practically the same purpose. **1973** *Sci. Amer.* June 112/1 Extinction turbidimeters are doubtless the simplest instruments that have been devised for measuring the concentration of solids in suspension. They are based on the principle that turbidity is inversely proportional to the minimum length that a column of fluid must have in order to extinguish at one end of the column a source of light at the other end.
Hence (all also **turbido-**) **turbidime·tric** *a.*, obtained with or employing a turbidimeter; **turbidime·trically** *adv.*; **turbidi·metry,** the use of a turbidimeter, esp. for the quantitative analysis of turbid solutions.
1911 *Jrnl. Industr. & Engin. Chem.* III. 554/1 The discrepancies between the turbidimetric and gravimetric results..were..thought to be caused by the presence of nitrates in the solutions examined. **1918** *Jrnl. Biol. Chem.* XXXVI. 33 This reagent gives quite good results used either turbidometrically or nephelometrically. **1920** *Ibid.* XLII. 196 With several of the substances which have already been standardized for turbidimetry we can multiply the accuracy. **1943** *Jrnl. Bacteriol.* XLVI. 377 Applications of turbidimetry to the study of *in vitro* penicillin effects. **1971** Turbidimetric [see *nephelometric* adj. s.v. *NEPHELO-]. **1975** D. H. BURRIN in Williams & Wilson *Biologist's Guide to Princ. & Techniques Pract. Biochem.* v. 145 Very dilute suspensions may be assayed by turbidometry. **1981** *Jrnl. Protozool.* XXVIII. 371/2 Growth was determined turbidimetrically.

turbidite (tɜ̄·ɹbidəit). *Geol.* [f. TURBID(ITY + -ITE¹.] A sediment or rock deposited, or presumed to have been deposited, by a turbidity current. Hence **turbidi·tic** *a.*
1957 P. H. KUENEN in *Jrnl. Geol.* LXV. 231/1 The term 'turbidite' for all deposits of turbidity currents is more appropriate, and the writer accepts this verbal suggestion of C. P. M. Frijlinck. **1973** *Nature* 9 Feb. 389/2 The lowest (Unit I)..has at the base a phyllitic formation..followed by turbiditic sandstones. **1977** A. HALLAM *Planet Earth* 204/1 The thick clastics and turbidites of the upper Devonian of the Yukon seem to be derived from an oceanic zone of uplift.

turbidity. Add: **2.** Special Comb.: **turbidity current,** an underwater current flowing swiftly downslope owing to the weight of sediment it carries.
1939 D. W. JOHNSON *Origin of Submarine Canyons* iii. 27 By analogy those [currents] due to turbidity will here be called *turbidity currents*. **1950** *Jrnl. Geol.* LVIII. 91/1 The most important types of graded bedding appear to have been produced by the action of turbidity currents of high density on the sea floor. **1977** A. HALLAM *Planet Earth* 54/2 An unusual but geologically very important type of suspension deposit is that produced by a turbidity current.

turbidometric, etc., varr. *TURBIDIMETRIC *a.*, etc.

turbine. Add: Also with pronunc. (-əin). **1. a.** (Earlier example.)
1838 *Railway Mag.* IV. 51 Turbine.—An instrument under this name has lately been invented by M. Fourneyron, worked by water-pressure, which is said to have made a great sensation in Germany. *Ibid.*, It is said that a turbine, only thirteen inches diameter,..under a vertical pressure of water of 118 yards, revolved 2,300 times in a minute, and..realized a power, which estimated in steam, would be equal to that of sixty horses.
d. = *gas-turbine* s.v. *GAS *sb.*¹ 7.
1904 *Proc. Inst. Mech. Engineers* Oct. 1078 Some or all of the available heat energy of the gas can be converted into kinetic energy before causing it to act on the turbine. **1940** A. W. JUDGE *Aircraft Engines* I. vii. 231 An alternative method of driving the supercharger is to couple it directly to an exhaust turbine of the de Laval type. **1950** E. T. VINCENT *Theory & Design Gas Turbines & Jet Engines* vi. 161 The power-plant turbine can be divided into the following units: (1) compressor, (2) combustion chamber, (3) turbine, and (4) regenerator. **1971** B. SCHARF *Engin. & its Lang.* xv. 215 After expansion in the turbine, the combustion gases escape at high velocity through the jet pipe, thus providing the forward thrust for the aeroplane.
2. *turbine blade.*
1911 *Encycl. Brit.* XXV. 843/2 The general arrangement of the steam nozzle and turbine blades is illustrated. **1977** *R.A.F. News* 11–24 May 18/2 A pair of turbine blades from an Orpheus jet engine.

turble, var. *TURRIBLE.

turbo. Add: **3. b.** = *TURBOCHARGER; also, a motor vehicle equipped with this device. Also *attrib.*
1957 *Motor* 6 Mar. 168/1 General Motors have built four turbo vehicles. The 370 b.h.p. Firebird I..had single-stage centrifugal compressor and two-stage turbine layout. **1978** *Country Life* 17 Aug. 460/1 While turbo is a term associated with power, the Saab 99 Turbo has no shortcomings in terms of comfort. **1980** *Daily Tel.* 23 Jan. 14/4 Driving it in Portugal last week, I found it impressively smooth and quiet, with a quicker throttle response from low speeds than usual with a turbo.

turbo-. Add: *turboblower, -compressor*; **tu·rbocar,** a motor car powered by a gas-turbine engine; **turbo-co·mpound** *a.*, applied to a piston engine in which the exhaust gases drive a turbine coupled to the crankshaft; hence **turbo-compou·nded** *a.*, **-compou·nding** *vbl. sb.*; **tu·rbodrill** *Oil Industry*, a drill in which the drilling bit is rotated by a turbine situated next to it in the drilling string and driven by the upflow of mud; also as *v. trans.*; hence **tu·rbodrilled** *ppl. a.*, **tu·rbodrilling** *vbl. sb.*; **turbo-ele·ctric** *a. Engin.*, involving or employing electricity generated by means of a turbine; **turbomole·cular** *a. Physics*, applied to a type of high-vacuum pump in which momentum is imparted to molecules by a high-speed rotor inside a stator, both of which possess inclined slots or blades designed so as to cause the molecules to move axially towards the outlet; **tu·rbopump,** a pump that incorporates a small turbine to provide the necessary mechanical power, used esp. in aircraft and rockets; **turbora·mjet** *Aeronaut.*, any of a class of jet engines combining the operations of a turbojet and a ramjet, either as a turbojet with provision for afterburning, or as a ramjet containing a turbojet which is shut down at high velocities; **tu·rboshaft** *Engin.*, used *attrib.* and *absol.* to designate a gas turbine engine in which the turbine drives a shaft other than a propeller shaft; **tu:rbosu·percharger** *Engin.* = *TURBOCHARGER; hence **tu:rbosu·percharged** *ppl. a.*, **-su·percharging** *vbl. sb.*; **tu·rbotrain,** a train powered by a gas-turbine engine.
1911 *Trans. Inst. Mining Engineers* XL. 580 *(heading)* Turbo-blowers and turbo-compressors. **1947** *Jrnl. R. Aeronaut. Soc.* LI. 95/1 For high altitude cruising the application of turbo-blowers has received much consideration. **1979** *Truck & Bus Transportation* (Austral.) Feb. 41/2 With a turboblower, you literally shovel the air in. [**1950** *Motor* 15 Mar. 183/1 *(caption)* The Rover turbine car easily reached 90 m.p.h.] **1956** *Times* 3 July 4/6 The Rover turbocar..was timed at 152 m.p.h. **1974** D. NYE *Motor Racing Mavericks* xix. 190 This turbine car sparked off a terrific controversy... Wallis was taken on..to build two cars similar to his 'STP Turbocar'. **1954** *Economist* 11 Sept. 11/3 Turbo-compound; piston compound. A combination of gas turbine and reciprocating engine. **1955** C. E. CHAPEL et al. *Aircraft Power Plants* (ed. 2) xvii. 339/2 Aircraft powered by the Wright turbo-compound engine are the Douglas DC-7, the Lockheed Super Constellation, [etc.]. **1983** *Truck & Bus Transportation* (Austral.) July 60/2 Whilst the turbocompound diesel has progressed to the operational stage..the benefits of this concept can be more fully realised and cost justified when used in conjunction with an adiabatic or insulated engine. **1978** *Automotive Engin.* Aug. 85/1 In a turbocompounded engine..the exhaust gases are expanded in a turbine and the power generated is transmitted back to the crankshaft. Turbocompounding can be incorporated in naturally aspirated, as well as turbo-charged engines. **1911** Turbo-compressor [see *turbo-blower* above]. **1922** *Daily Mail Year Bk. 1923* 75/1 By the development of a mechanism known as a 'turbo-compressor', he has enabled aero-engines to maintain their power in the thin air of upper altitudes. **1979** A. L. LYDERSEN *Fluid Flow & Heat Transfer* xi. 327 Turbo-compressors are used for vapour recompression of large vapour volumes..while steam ejectors are used in many smaller installations. **1948** *Oil & Gas Jrnl.* 3 June 58/3 During initial field tests conducted in May.., the new Edco Turbodrill penetrated 950 ft. of shallow section in a wildcat test drilling. *Ibid.* 61/1 Photoclinometer and hole-section surveys showed a total drift of 3 ft. or 10½ minutes from vertical through the section turbo-drilled. **1981** 'D. RUTHERFORD' *Porcupine Basin* iv. 66 We're developing a new turbo-drill on a flexible string which can be reeled out on a drum. **1949** *World Oil* 1 July 88/1 Electric logs..were run after the turbodrilled section was completed. **1955** *World Petroleum* XXVI. 84/3 The advantages of turbodrilling stem from the fact that only the bit is actually involved in the rotating effort. **1977** *Offshore Engineer* May 20/1 (Advt.), Our turbodrilling and directional drilling engineers and equipment are at your service. **1904** Turbo-electric [in Dict.]. **1930** *Engineering* 18 Apr. 513/3 Turbo-electric propulsion must exhibit an overwhelming superiority in reliability and maintenance cost to overcome the disadvantages. **1974** *Encycl. Brit. Macropædia* XVII. 752/2 On most nuclear submarines reduction gears are used between the turbines and the propeller shaft; however, a few incorporate turbo-electric drive. **1969** *Gloss. Terms Vacuum Technol.* (*B.S.I.*) 17 *Turbo-molecular pump*, a molecular drag pump in which the rotor has inclined slots or blades moving between corresponding slots or blades in a stator. **1976** *Physics Bull.* Nov. 499/2 The vacuum system is kept

at 10^{-7} Torr by about 650 sputter ion pumps and 80 turbomolecular pumps. **1903** Turbo-pump [in Dict.]. **1947** *Aircraft Engin.* Aug. 254/2 The turbo-pump assembly consists of a shaft carrying a single stage impulse steam turbine, on each side of which is a centrifugal pump. **1962** F. I. ORDWAY *Basic Astronautics* x. 411 The turbopump proves to be the best means of pressurizing the propellants for large liquid rocket engines. The bi-propellant turbopump consists of two centrifugal pumps and a gas turbine that supplies the driving power for the pumps. **1979** *Nature* 11 Jan. 84/1 A fire in the high pressure turbo-pump that feeds oxygen into the combustion chamber caused the engine to explode. **1948** *Aviation Week* 23 Feb. 36/2 Turboramjet—A conventional turbojet engine with provision for reheating the gas between the turbine discharge and the exhaust nozzle. **1971** P. J. MCMAHON *Aircraft Propulsion* iii. 119 At the moment the most promising fields of use for the turboramjet would seem to be those in air-breathing boosters for the launching of space vehicles. **1958** P. H. WILKINSON *Aircraft Engines of World 1958/59* 31 Bristol-Siddeley Engines Ltd... is specializing in advanced turbojets, turboprops, turboshafts, [etc.]. **1967** *Jane's Surface Skimmer Systems 1967–68* 130/2 The GE LM1500 turboshaft engine is the result of a company investment in a programme to adapt the J79 jet engine to a free power turbine for commercial use. **1977** I. M. CAMPBELL *Energy & Atmosphere* vi. 127 The gas turbine engine used in aircraft under the names of turbojet, turboprop or turbofan, or in industrial or marine settings as a turboshaft engine. **1944** P. H. WILKINSON *Aircraft Engines of World 1944* 34 The Boeing Flying Fortress B-17 (powered with a turbo-supercharged engine). **1978** *Financial Times* 20 Dec. 21/5 At the moment, Mercedes is unique in marketing a turbo-supercharged diesel car. **1938** A. SWAN *Handbk. Aeronaut.* (ed. 3) II. IV. 206 The inherent advantages of the turbo supercharger are mainly centred around the fact that it possesses remarkable flexibility of speed control. **1971** P. J. MCMAHON *Aircraft Propulsion* xi. 319 From the turbo-supercharger, it is a logical step to develop the fully compound engine. **1979** *Financial Rev.* 14 June 29/1 Turbosupercharging is very much in as far as motoring is concerned these days. **1966** *Time* 27 May 52/3 Canadian National Railways..has now ordered five of the turbotrains developed by the U.S.'s United Aircraft Corp... These light-weight, low-slung, turbojet-powered whiz-bangs should be able to clip nearly an hour off the present five-hour Montreal–Toronto run. **1978** *Times* 9 June 1/8 The turbo-train between Strasbourg and Lyons.

turbocharger (tɜ̄·ɹbo,tʃɑ̄ɹdʒəɹ). *Engin.* Also **turbo charger.** [f. *turbo(super)charger* s.v. *TURBO-.] A supercharger driven by a turbine powered by the engine's exhaust gases.

1934 *Jrnl. R. Aeronaut. Soc.* XXXVIII. 182 After explosion, the first exhaust valve which is connected to the turbo charger, opens. **1961** *Engineering* 9 June 786/1 The advantages obtained by applying turbochargers to diesel engines are well known. **1980** 'D. RUTHERFORD' *Turbo* viii. 107, I gently depressed the accelerator. The turbocharger came in with its characteristic whine and the Saab swept quickly to 120 m.p.h.

Hence (as a back-formation) **tu·rbocharge** *v. trans.*, to equip with a turbocharger; **tu·rbocharged** *ppl. a.*, **tu·rbocharging** *vbl. sb.*

1961 *Engineering* 10 Mar. 370/1 The cycle for the Ford 704 engine of 300 hp rating may be described as a turbo-charged gas turbine. *Ibid.* 9 June 786/1 Turbocharging has brought with it the reduced weight and space requirements. **1970** *Commercial Motor* 25 Sept. 97 Ford offers a turbocharged version of its 360 cu. in. engine,.. while Perkins has turbocharged the 6·354. **1971** *Farmer & Stockbreeder* 23 Feb. 21/3 The combination of air cooling and turbocharging is said to reduce engine noise and smoke emission. **1981** *Sci. Amer.* May 41/2 Turbocharging automotive diesels has made possible fuel-economy advances of between 10 and 15 percent. **1981** D. BOGGIS *Time to Betray* x. 54 The Skylane..was turbocharged, with retractable gear.

turbofan (tɜ̄·ɹbofæn). *Aeronaut.* Also with hyphen. [f. TURBO- + FAN *sb.*[1].] **a.** A fan connected to or driven by a turbine. **b.** Used *attrib.* and *absol.* to designate a jet engine employing such a fan for additional thrust; = *fan-jet* (*engine*) s.v. *FAN *sb.*[1] 11.

1911 *Trans. Inst. Mining Engineers* XL. 580 The smaller efficiency of the turbo-fan. **1949** *Gloss. Aeronaut. Terms* (*B.S.I.*) II. 17 *Ducted-fan turbine engine, turbo-fan*, a gas turbine engine in which a portion of the net energy is used to drive a ducted fan. **1959** *Wall St. Jrnl.* 7 July 10/1 The turbofan engine is the latest in the family of jet power plants. **1961** [see *double-flow* s.v. *DOUBLE *a.* C. 2 a]. **1970** *Daily Tel.* (Colour Suppl.) 13 Nov. 14/4 Large turbofan engines of the Spey type tend to expel ingested objects along the cold fan duct, so that they do not enter the engine core. **1980** R. L. DUNCAN *Brimstone* x. 261 A cruise missile..propelled by a jet turbofan.

turbojet (tɜ̄·ɹbodʒet). *Aeronaut.* Also with hyphen. [f. TURBO- + *JET *sb.*[3] 5 c.] Used *attrib.* and *absol.* to designate (an aircraft having) a type of jet engine in which the jet gases also power a turbine-driven compressor for compressing the air drawn into the engine.

1945 *Aeronautics* Mar. 28/2 The turbo-jet shows definite advantages in comparatively light aircraft designed to operate at high speeds. **1950** *Ann. Reg. 1949* 424 Propelled by..turbo-jets,..the Comet flew at an altitude of 35,000 feet. **1958** *Times Rev. Industry* Dec. 50/2 Within five years it is probable that over 1,300 turbo-jet and turbo-prop aircraft will be in service. **1962** E. SNOW *Other Side of River* (1963) i. 17, I had flown halfway around the world and landed at Peking in a Soviet turbojet manned by a Chinese crew. **1977** *Sci. Amer.* Feb. 23/2 A turbojet engine exhausts its gases at 1,450 degrees, whereas a turbofan engine, because of turbulent mixing at the outlet, exhausts them at 600 degrees.

turbopause (tɜ̄·ɹbopǭz). *Meteorol.* [f. TURB(ULENCE + -O + PAUSE *sb.*] The outer limit of a turbosphere, where the distribution of constituents is due equally to diffusion and turbulent mixing.

1951 S. CHAPMAN in *Jrnl. Atmospheric & Terrestrial Physics* I. 201 The diffusive tendency becomes increasingly effective at greater heights, and it may be (but it is not certain) that at some level diffusion becomes dominant over the turbulent mixing. The name turbopause is suggested for this level. **1967** R. W. FAIRBRIDGE *Encycl. Atmospheric Sci. & Astrogeol.* 5/1 Above the turbopause, which [on earth] lies between 100 and 130 km, diffusion is more important than turbulent mixing in distributing the constituents. **1979** *Nature* 17 May 221/1 The δ-bands, present in the Earth's twilight and night time airglow spectra,..indicate a significant population of atomic nitrogen at or below the Venus turbopause.

turboprop (tɜ̄·ɹboprǫp). *Aeronaut.* Also **turbo-prop.** [f. TURBO- + *PROP *sb.*[6]] Used *attrib.* and *absol.* to designate (an aircraft having) a jet engine in which a turbine is used as in a turbojet and also to drive a propeller; = *prop-jet* s.v. *PROP *sb.*[6] 2 b. Also **tu:rboprope·ller.**

1945 H. H. ARNOLD *Third Rep. Commanding General U.S. Army Air Forces* in *War Reports* (1947) 464 This war has evolved six distinct methods of utilizing atmospheric oxygen for propulsion, such as:..*turboprop*—a gas turbine plus propeller. **1946** *Shell Aviation News* No. 102. 5/2 The following..types of planes will be..powered by turbo props. **1947** *Aircraft Engin.* Mar. 79/1 The question can turbo-jets or turbo-propellers be used in transport is timely. **1957** *Times* 17 Dec. 13/2 There has been an increasing demand for equipment for civil aircraft, particularly those employing turbo-propeller engines. **1958** *Daily Mail* 3 Mar. 5/2 The more economical turbo-props could be used to force down the price of air travel. **1958** [see *TURBOJET]. **1968** MILLER & SAWERS *Technical Developments Mod. Aviation* vi. 205 A turbopropeller-driven airliner will have an advantage over a jet if they both seat significantly fewer than 50 passengers on stage lengths exceeding 200 miles. **1972** *Physics Bull.* Oct. 580/3 The four turboprops which will power the biggest ship at speeds up to 120 mph are located on the tail spars. **1978** *N.Y. Times* 30 March B19/1 (Advt.), Mechanics... Exp on..air research turboprop engines.

turbosphere (tɜ̄·ɹbosfɪ̄ᵊɹ). *Meteorol.* [f. TURB(ULENCE + -O + SPHERE *sb.*] A region of a planetary atmosphere in which mixing occurs predominantly through turbulence.

1951 S. CHAPMAN in *Jrnl. Atmospheric & Terrestrial Physics* I. 201 Throughout the lower atmosphere, and up to at least 60 km height, turbulence suffices to mix the permanent constituents effectively, overcoming the diffusive tendency for each to distribute itself independently of the others, according to its molecular weight... It is suggested that this whole region be called the turbosphere. **1979** J. K. HARGREAVES *Upper Atmosphere & Solar-Terrestrial Relations* iv. 52 The well mixed part of the atmosphere, in which composition does not change with height, can be called the turbosphere.

turbostratic (tɜ̄ɹbostræ·tik), *a. Physics.* [f. L. *turb-ātus*, pa. pple of *turbāre* to disturb, disorder + -O + STRAT(UM + -IC.] Of or pertaining to a material (esp. one allotrope of carbon) having a structure intermediate between amorphous and crystalline, consisting of stacked disordered layers.

1942 BISCOE & WARREN in *Jrnl. Appl. Physics* XIII. 370/1 Carbon black is a simple and definite example of an intermediate form of matter, which is distinctly different from both the crystalline and the amorphous states. The term 'turbostratic' (unordered layers) is suggested as a name of this particular class of mesomorphic solids. **1966** *R. Inst. Chem. Lect. Ser.* V. 12 The so-called 'turbostratic' boron nitride is still basically the hexagonal form. **1975** *Physics Bull.* June 260/1 This model is distinctly different from the traditional, 'turbostratic' model..in which crystallites comprise flat, graphite layer planes in disordered stacking.

turbulence. Add: **c.** Of fluid flow (see *TURBULENT *a.* 2 c).

1907 F. W. LANCHESTER *Aerodynamics* ii. 53 When a certain critical velocity is exceeded the continuity is broken and the phenomenon of turbulence manifests itself. **1922** GLAZEBROOK *Dict. Appl. Physics* I. 299/2 The important part played by turbulence in reducing the time of explosion in actual engines, and thus rendering high revolution speeds practicable. **1928** N. SHAW *Man. Meteorol.* II. vi. 284 The variation of wind with height is now treated as the effect of turbulence or eddy-motion in the moving air. **1935** *Discovery* Oct. 390/2 This is remedied either by small fans or, automatically, by injecting some cold air from the dehumidifier with the heated air, causing a form of turbulence in the enclosure. **1980** R. P. BENEDICT *Fund. Pipe Flow* iv. 141 A stability theory has been given that explains the origin of turbulence in terms of arbitrary small disturbances which initiate instabilities in the laminar boundary layer.

turbulent, *a.* Add: **2. c.** Of, pertaining to, or designating flow of a fluid in which the velocity at any point fluctuates irregularly and there is continual mixing rather than a steady flow pattern.

Turbulent flow was earlier called *sinuous* or *eddying flow*.

1895 H. LAMB *Hydrodynamics* xi. 574 The resistance, in the case of turbulent flow, is found to be sensibly independent..of the viscosity of the fluid. **1907** F. W. LANCHESTER *Aerodynamics* ii. 53 When this critical velocity is reached the parallel flow breaks up, and is replaced by an irregular turbulent motion. **1926** H. R. RICARDO *Engines of High Output* 63 In the actual engine cylinder..the mixture..is being whirled about very rapidly; it is, in fact, in a highly turbulent condition. **1930** *Engineering* 7 Mar. 319/3 Hence, when viscous flow changes to turbulent flow the dissipation of energy is increased. **1947** [see *Reynolds stress* s.v. *REYNOLDS]. **1956** A. A. TOWNSEND *Struct. Turbulent Shear Flow* i. 3 In turbulent motion..the motion at any point influences the motion at other distant points. **1968** [see *LAMINAR *a.* 2 a]. **1982** *Sci. Amer.* July 99/1 When the bore of a tube flares gradually (as the aortic lumen does in an incipient aneurysm), the fluid near the wall slows down, generating turbulent flow.

Turcification: see TURKIFICATION in Dict. and Suppl.

Turco-, Turko-. Add: **a.** *Turco-Bulgarian* (example), *-German*, *-Persian*, *-Russian*, *-Tartar*, *-Tatar*, *-Tataric*.

1854 MAX MÜLLER in C. Bunsen *Christianity & Mankind* III. 279 The still undivided 'Turko-Tataric' speech. **1854** J. H. NEWMAN *Lect. Hist. Turks* 62 The ancient Turco-Tartar empire..extended to the Caspian and towards the Indus. **1880** A. H. SAYCE *Introd. Sci. Lang.* II. viii. 190 The whole Turanian family..may be divided into five branches, the Finno-Ugric, the Turko-Tatar, the Samoyedic, the Mongolian, and the Tungusian. **1909** G. DRAGE in *Cambr. Mod. Hist.* (1921) XI. ix. 276 The settlement of the Turco-Persian frontier question. **1915** W. S. CHURCHILL in M. Gilbert *Winston S. Churchill* (1972) III. Compan. I. 421 The Turco-German fleet. **1923** G. BUCHANAN *My Mission to Russia* I. vi. 64 The Turco-Bulgarian agreement. **1948** D. DIRINGER *Alphabet* 567 Turco-Tatar and Caucasian languages. **1969** V. N. DATTA *Jallianwala Bagh* 5 The Turco-German organisation at Berne. **1982** M. BINGHAM *Princess Lieven* xiii. 189 The Turco-Russian conflict rumbled on.

b. Turcoce·ntric *a.*, centred round Turkey or the Turks; hence **Tu:rcocentri·city; Turcologist:** delete *nonce-wd.* and add later examples; also **Turcolo·gical** *a.*, **Turco·logy; Turcophi·lia** = *Turcophilism*.

1964 *Jrnl. R. Central Asian Soc.* LI. 72 A Turco-centric history. **1969** *Middle Eastern Studies* May 173 The passage is worth noting for Gökalp's turcocentricity: 'Europeans committed an historical sin by translating Attila's title..as "Scourge of God".' **1952** *Round Table* Dec. 25 The well of Turcological study. **1951** W. K. MATTHEWS *Languages U.S.S.R.* iv. 63 Gyula Németh, the Hungarian turcologist. **1976** *Times Lit. Suppl.* 3 Sept. 1077/3 The Russians..began to produce excellent Persianists, Turcologists, Mongolists. **1918** *Q. Rev.* Apr. 513 The transformation of the *Medresses*..into 'National' schools for the teaching of Turkology. **1951** W. K. MATTHEWS *Languages U.S.S.R.* iv. 64 This uses phonetic as well as morphological data, and has received the sanction of Soviet turcology. **1908** J. MORLEY *Recoll.* (1917) II. 245 Am I quite wrong in suspecting a degree of Turcophilia in you? **1967** C. SETON-WATSON *Italy from Liberalism to Fascism* x. 376 William II was impressed. His Turcophilia of the previous autumn had by now quite vanished.

Turcoman. Add: **1. b.** (Later examples.) Cf. *TURKMEN, TÜRKMEN.

1888 *Encycl. Brit.* XXIV. 1/1 Ural-Altaic Languages.. *Turkoman* (*Turkmenian*), west Turkestan, north Persia, and Asia Minor. **1908** [see *JAGATAI]. **1954** PEI & GAYNOR *Dict. Ling.* 222 *Turkoman*, a Near-Eastern language; it belongs to the Southern Turkic group of the Altaic subfamily of the Ural-Altaic family of languages.

3. (Earlier example.) Also, a Turcoman carpet or rug.

1881 C. C. HARRISON *Woman's Handiwork in Mod. Homes* I. 57 Turcoman, when ravelled, produces a superb fringe, like soft chenille. **1962** C. W. JACOBSEN *Oriental Rugs* I. vi. 63 Up until 1940, all rugs known as Turkomans or Bokharas..came from Turkestan. **1975** P. SOMERVILLE-LARGE *Couch of Earth* iv. 54 On the floor..were good carpets, mostly small Turcomans.

4. Turcoman carpet (example), **rug** (examples).

1901 J. K. MUMFORD *Oriental Rugs* xii. 235 One division of these Turkoman carpets, which avoids on the one hand close adherence to the Bokhara device, and on the other the latch-hook style of the Yomuds, is called Beshir. **1922** H. CLARK (*title*) Bokkara, Turkoman and Afghan rugs. **1975** *Oxf. Compan. Decorative Arts* 791/1 A design peculiar to Turcoman rugs is that known as katchli.

turd. Add: **1. a.** (Later examples.)

1922 JOYCE *Ulysses* 649 The horse..added his quota by letting fall on the floor..three smoking globes of turds. **1928** in A. W. Read *Class. Amer. Graffiti* (1935) 81 Now and then a fart is heard Mingling with a dropping turd. **1968** *Listener* 1 Aug. 152/2 His protest at the killing in Vietnam is at least original: he parcels up a rich turd and mails it to the White House. **1981** N. GORDIMER *July's People* 35 It was true that it was difficult to get the children to remember to bury the paper along with the turd.

c. (Later examples as a term of execration or contempt.) Cf. SHIT *sb.* 1 b.

1936 A. HUXLEY *Eyeless in Gaza* xxii. 315 'But why not?' the poor old turd kept asking. **1944** D. WELCH *In*

Youth is Pleasure viii. 152 Somebody called Woods a dirty old sod, another called him a great turd. **1965** HOWARD & WEST *Making of Prime Minister* xiii. 204 A purple-faced steward walked up to a scrawny, pale heckler and yelled, 'Shut up, you ignorant turd!' **1978** B. FREEMANTLE *Clap Hands* ix. 66 The man..could make everyone else feel a turd.

2. *turd-coloured* (later example), *-eating* adjs.

1978 in R. Quirk *Style & Communication in Eng. Lang.* (1982) ii. 33 Lofty structures of turd-coloured brick.. seemed to be deserted. **1969** Turdeating [see *cock-sucking* ppl. adj. s.v. *COCK *sb.*[1] 23]. **1978** J. KRANTZ *Scruples* x. 295 Those turd-eating Mexican border guards'll put you away.

Hence **tu·rdish** *a.*, characteristic of a 'turd' or contemptible person.

1936 A. HUXLEY *Eyeless in Gaza* xxii. 315 'Turds to the core,' he said. 'So they can't think anything but turdish thoughts.' **1966** *Punch* 12 Jan. 64/2 An aristocratic, even Byronic work which finds strident anti-communism turdish.

turdion. Delete † *Obs. rare* and add later examples in revived use, in Fr. forms *tordion, tourdion.*

1895 L. GROVE *Dancing* viii. 244 The 'Danse basse' was very grave... It was performed to the accompaniment of psalms. It consisted of three parts—(1) the *Danse basse* proper, (2) the *Retour*, (3) the *Tourdion.* **1914** T. & M. W. KINNEY *Dance* iii. 54 The *Tordion* is another dance of lively origin. Sometimes it was made a vehicle for the grotesque. **1924** SHARP & OPPÉ *Dance* 15 The Tordion was danced with the same steps as the Galliard but more quietly, without spring. **1957** G. B. L. WILSON *Penguin Dict. Ballet* 267 *Tordion*, third section of the Basse Danse. **1974** *Early Music* July 164/2 The tordion, a restrained form of galliard.

turf, *sb.*[1] Add: **4. b.** *transf.* The road or street as the milieu of prostitutes, tramps, etc.; esp. *on the turf*, engaged in prostitution. *slang.*

1860 HOTTEN *Dict. Slang* (ed. 2) 241 *On the turf*, one who occupies himself with race course business; said also of a street-walker. **1899** 'J. FLYNT' *Tramping* I. ii. 28 The road proper, or 'the turf', as the people who toil along its stretches sometimes prefer to call it, is low life in general. **1936** H. ASBURY *French Quarter* xii. 369 During [Kate Townsend's] early years 'on the turf', as the saying went, she was..thrifty and ambitious. **1962** PARKER & ALLERTON *Courage of his Convictions* v. 179, I wouldn't let her go out on the turf, because of this thing I've got about not poncing. **1984** J. O'DONOGHUE *Sergeant Horn's Murder Trap* vi. 41 'I might have been one of Ma Dolma's brasses for all you know.'..'Come off it. You've never been on the turf.'

4*. Usu. with substantive in possessive case or with possessive adj. orig. and chiefly *U.S.* **a.** The streets controlled by a juvenile street-gang and regarded by them as their territory.

1953 CRAMER & KARR *Teen-Age Gangs* i. 4 He had looked forward to drifting pleasantly through the Emerald turf—the term currently used in Brooklyn instead of territory. *Ibid.* 6 No War Hawk was safe if caught on the turf of the Emeralds. And no Emerald was safe on the turf of the War Hawks. **1959** H. SALISBURY *Shook-Up Generation* i. 19 These blocks constituted the 'turf' of a well-known street-gang. **1964** [see *CHIPPY *sb.* 4]. **1973** 'J. PATRICK' *Glasgow Gang Observed* xx. 189 Like most American adolescent gangs..the Young Team attached enormous importance to territory and used the same word 'turf' for it.

b. The part of a city or other area within which a criminal, detective, etc., operates. Cf. *PATCH *sb.*[1] 3 e.

1962 *Sat. Even. Post* 28 Apr. 30/2 Her [*sc.* a social worker's] turf: the lower Bronx. **1966** 'J. ASHFORD' *Consider Evidence* iii. 23 She [*sc.* a prostitute] claimed she could make a hundred quid a week on her turf. **1971** *N.Y. Times* 10 Jan. xx-1/1, I came to Beverly Hills..to see the stars' home turf. **1976** D. BENNETT *Jigsaw Man* (1977) viii. 153 Special Branch would not want to be involved in a killing so far from their own turf. **1978** S. BRILL *Teamsters* ii. 48 As both men sat in prison, they were dividing up Teamsters turf.

c. *transf.* and *fig.* A person's sphere of influence or activity.

1970 *Sat. Rev.* (U.S.) 17 Oct. 67/3 The lives of all our children and the very mindedness of society itself cannot be made whole as long as educators are obsessed by indecent needs to defend their own turfs. **1973** *Family Circle* Apr. 120/1 Male occupations are a turf from which women are excluded. **1977** J. F. FIXX *Compl. Bk. Running* xiii. 157 Dogs, he explained, are assiduous defenders of turf. **1982** 'E. LATHEN' *Green grow Dollars* vii. 55 They think that, on their own turf, they can overawe Ackerman and Werzel.

5. a. *turf-barge, -house* (later examples), *-wall* (earlier example); *turf-coloured* adj.; **c.** *turf-grown* (earlier example).

1922 JOYCE *Ulysses* 218 Father Conmee saw a turf-barge... Father Conmee reflected on the providence of the Creator who had made turf to be in bogs where men might dig it out and bring it to town. **1916** —— *Portrait of Artist* (1969) i. 54 He had skin the same colour as the turf-coloured bogwater in the..bath. **1867** J. G. WHITTIER *Tent Beach* 10 Above..turf-grown wall They saw the fort flag rise and fall. **1789** J. WESLEY *Jrnl.* 26 May (1916) VII. 502 Part of them [*sc.* his congregation] were sheltered by a spacious turf-house, and the rest little regarded the rain. **1967** H. HARRISON *Technicolor Time Machine* (1968) v. 50 Smoke still drifted down from the chimney hole of the squat, turf house. **1849** THOREAU *Week Concord Riv.* 168 But as it were, by a turf wall this valley was concealed.

d. *turf-knife* (example); **turf-line,** a line formed from turf; *spec.* in an archæological excavation, a layer of soil representing former grassland.

1841 THOREAU *Jrnl.* 20 Apr. in *Coll. Wks.* (1906) VII. 251 The ditching spade and turf knife may be engraved on the coat-of-arms of his posterity. **1935** E. H. W. MEYERSTEIN *Verse Lett. to Five Friends* (1954) 11 One joy.. To take the turf-line of the Pilgrim Road. **1936** *Proc. Prehist. Soc.* II. 214 Well marked turf lines isolated these ditches from the Iron Age above them. **1957** V. G. CHILDE *Dawn Europ. Civilization* (ed. 6) i. 3 Fossil turf-lines of Atlantic age. **1975** J. G. EVANS *Environment Early Man Brit. Isles* vi. 119 At the surface of the buried soil is a thin stone-free horizon or turf line... This is caused by earthworm sorting.

turf, *v.*[1] Add: **4.** *trans.* To throw or kick (a person, etc.) forcibly *out* (occas. *off*); also *transf. colloq.* Without const. (*Public School slang*), to kick.

1888 KIPLING *Only Subaltern* in *Under Deodars* 97 The Colonel will turf you out of that in double quick time. **1905** H. A. VACHELL *Hill* ii. 32 Sorry I turfed that little ass so hard... [*Note*] To 'turf', *i.e.* to kick—*Harroviana.* **1925** WODEHOUSE *Carry on, Jeeves!* 90 The old boy turfed me out, Bertie, because he said I was a brainless nincompoop. **1930** J. B. PRIESTLEY *Angel Pavement* viii. 410 She'd bought hundreds of them [*sc.* magazines]. I've just had them turfed out. **1957** C. MACINNES *City of Spades* II. iv. 128 The guv'nor tried turfing them all out at first..but he's given up the struggle. **1976** J. I. M. STEWART *Memorial Service* iv. 58 These people have become my colleagues. If you use that sort of language about them I'll have to turf you out myself. **1977** 'O. JACKS' *Autumn Heroes* iv. 60 The plane's loaded... I can't turf off passengers.

Turfanian (tṽɹfēⁱ·niăn). [f. *Turfan* in Chinese Turkestan + -IAN.] A name given to the western dialect of Tocharian, otherwise known as Tocharian A. Also **Tu·rfan, Turfane·se.**

1939 Turfanese [see *KUCHAEAN, KUCHEAN]. **1958** PRIEBSCH & COLLINSON *German Lang.* (ed. 4) I. i. 6 Another extinct group of I.E. dialects is..Turfan (Turfanian, W. Tocharian or Toch. B). **1972** W. B. LOCKWOOD *Panorama Indo-Europ. Lang.* 254 Tocharian A was spoken at Karashahr and Turfan; it is sometimes called Turfanian.

turfite. (Earlier example.)

1836 [see *BOOK-MAKING 3].

Turinese, var. *TORINESE.

Turing machine (tiūᵊ·riŋ). [Named after A. M. *Turing* (1912–54), English mathematician, who described such a machine in 1936.] A notional computing machine for performing simple reading, writing, and shifting operations in accordance with a prescribed set of rules, invoked in theories of computability and automata.

It is represented as a scanner that has a number of internal states and moves left or right along a tape on which is a sequence of symbols. The symbol read and the state of the scanner determine (in accordance with the rules) what replacement symbol is written, what new state the scanner enters, and what move it makes along the tape before the cycle is repeated.

1937 A. CHURCH in *Jrnl. Symbolic Logic* II. 43 [Abstract of Turing's paper.] Certain further restrictions are imposed on the character of the machine, but these are of such a nature as obviously to cause no loss of generality—in particular, a human calculator, provided with pencil and paper and explicit instructions, can be regarded as a kind of Turing machine. **1955** *Sci. Amer.* Apr. 62/1 To understand a Turing machine we need only know its table of commands. **1961** *Proc. Symposium Appl. Math.* XII. 39 A Turing machine plus random elements is a reasonable model for the human brain. **1969** P. B. JORDAIN *Condensed Computer Encycl.* 550 No Turing machine has ever been physically constructed or realized in hardware as a device for its own sake, but general-purpose digital computers have been programmed to simulate Turing machines. **1984** *Sci. Amer.* May 70/1 Beginning with the intuitive idea that a method is an algorithm—a procedure that can be mechanically carried out without creative intervention—he [*sc.* A. M. Turing] showed how the idea can be refined into a detailed model of the process of computation in which any algorithm is broken down into a sequence of simple, atomic steps. The resulting model of computation is the logical construct called a Turing machine.

‖ **turismo** (tūᵊri·zmo). [Sp., It.] Tourism as an industry or dedicated pursuit (in the Latin countries of Europe).

1926 R. MACAULAY *Crewe Train* I. v. 29 Poor Humphrey is looking quite sick and wan, either with turismo, the motion of the Andorran diligences, or *l'amour.* **1959** *Times Lit. Suppl.* 20 Nov. 679/4 His descriptions of the countries he collected on his speedometer seem more often to be drawn from the handbooks of *Turismo* than from fresh observation. **1977** J. I. M. STEWART *Madonna of Astrolabe* xii. 179 Ravello hadn't changed much... *Turismo* hadn't gained its hoped-for grip.

‖ **turista** (tūᵊri·stă). [Sp., lit. = tourist.] A name for a form of traveller's diarrhœa affecting visitors to Mexico.

1970 *New Scientist* 8 Jan. 47/1 An intestinal attack known as gyppy tummy..in the Middle East;..Montezuma's revenge..and turista in Mexico. **1976** M. MILLAR *Ask for me Tomorrow* v. 40 *Turista* is bad enough..but infectious hepatitis is worse. **1980** *Jrnl. R. Soc. Arts* Jan. 90/1 Even avoiding water does not entirely protect me against turista.

Turk, *sb.*[1] Add: **2. e.** Also *transf.* (sometimes with small initials): any group of young or relatively young men full of new ideas and impatient for change; esp. a radical or 'progressive' element in a political party. Occas. *sing.*

c **1929** in W. Safire *New Lang. Politics* (1968) 496/2 These new Republican warriors were called the Young Turks, a band of about 20 who had mutinied against the feeble leadership of the Old Guard. For Senators they were young men (average age: 56). **1953** W. S. CHURCHILL in *Ibid.* 497/2 You're just like the Young Turks in my government. **1963** D. OGILVY *Confessions Advert. Man* (1964) ii. 24 In hiring, the emphasis will be on *youth.* We are looking for young turks. **1971** A. MIZENER *Saddest Story* 331 E. E. Cummings and Pound..were writers little calculated to attract the Young Turks, for whom they would seem elder statesmen of the modern movement. **1981** J. DUNNING *Deadline* (1982) xvii. 160 Malcolm Dawes had been a career man. He was a young turk, graduating from the FBI Academy in 1952.

4. b. A person of Irish birth or descent. *slang* (usu. *depreciatory*). Chiefly *U.S.*

In this sense perh. really a derivative of Ir. *torc* boar, hog, as suggested by W. A. McLaughlin (*Dialect Notes* (1914) IV. 147–8); but cf. *TURKEY *sb.*[2] 5* b.

1914 in *Dialect Notes* IV. 148 You Italians have the votes, but it takes us Turks to run the government. **1945** MENCKEN *Amer. Lang.* Suppl. I. 603 *Turk* is used among Roman Catholic priests in the United States to designate a colleague of Irish birth. **1959** *Observer* 1 Mar. 10/1 Their backs are to the wall in a desperate tyre-chain feudal war to protect the integrity of their declining manor against the invasion of 'bubbles and squeaks' (Greeks and Cypriots), 'turks' (Irish) and 'spades' (coloureds). **1971** S. HOUGHTON *Current Prison Slang* (MS.) 17 *Turk*, Paddy, Irishman.

6. c. A Turkish cigarette.

1926 'SAPPER' *Final Count* iii. 65 Why the devil don't you smoke a Corona Corona, you fool! Put out that Turk. **1935** N. MARSH *Enter Murderer* vi. 71 Cigarette? These are Turks. **1965** 'R. ERSKINE' *Passion Flowers in Business* v. 60 Fat, oval Turks in a Wedgwood box.

Turkana (tṽɹkā·nă). [Native name.] (A member of) an East African tribe living between Lake Rudolph and the Nile; their language. Also *attrib.*

1902 H. JOHNSTON *Uganda Protectorate* II. xx. 887 Turkana has a few more words in it betraying Hamitic.. affinities. **1911** [see *KARAMOJO]. **1930** C. G. SELIGMAN *Races of Africa* vii. 161 The Masai and Turkana are nomadic herdsmen. **1959** A. MOOREHEAD *No Room in Ark* vii. 137 The local tribesmen—people like the Karamojong and the Turkana—have not taken to western civilization in the way nearly all other Africans are doing. **1963** *Times* 7 June 12/3 Thirty-two Turkana tribesmen and women have been killed in inter-tribal fighting in Kenya's Eastern Region. **1977** H. INNES *Big Footprints* I. 26 He's a Turkana. He was born up there and he's been back to Lake Rudolph many times. *Ibid.* 27 'Is that Turkana you're talking?'..'No. A mixture of Samburu and Swahili.'

Turkey[1]. Add: **3. c. Turkey rug** = *Turkish rug* s.v. TURKISH *a.* 2 b; **Turkey sponge,** a superior grade of commercial sponge from the Mediterranean and Adriatic.

1881 C. C. HARRISON *Woman's Handiwork in Mod. Homes* III. 143 The hardwood floors are stained dark, with Turkey rugs. **1920** F. G. ELLERTON *Let.* 25 Feb. in J. Bailey *Lett. & Diaries* (1935) 201 Now stamp up and down your Turkey rugs. **1902** D. SALOMONS in A. C. Harmsworth *Motors* vi. 94 A large Turkey sponge is best for cleaning the body and wheels of the car. **1968** *Canad. Antiques Collector* Nov. 21/1 A fine piece of Turkey sponge was soaked in this mixture [*sc.* aromatic vinegar] and enclosed in a small container called a vinegar box or vinaigrette.

turkey[2]. Add: **2. d.** *to talk turkey* (earlier example of sense 'to say pleasant things'); now usu. (in this sense also *to talk cold turkey*) to speak frankly and without reserve; to talk hard facts, get down to business. (No longer restricted to N. Amer.)

1824 *Little Bit of Tid-Re-I* II. 109 So that, all things considered, I hope neither the Indian, whom the Yankey could not cheat in the division of their game (a turkey and a buzzard,)..will accuse me of *not talking Turkey* to them in this article. **1903** *Dialect Notes* II. 333 *Talk turkey*, v.phr., to talk plainly: 'I'm going to *talk turkey* with him and see if I can't get him to mend his ways.' **1919** E. HOUGH *Sagebrusher* xiv. 125 Do you know when he got rattled he began to talk Dutch to me? Well, I talked turkey to him. **1928** *Daily Express* 4 Jan. 11/5 She talked cold turkey about sex. 'Cold turkey' means plain truth in America. **1939** A. HUXLEY *After Many a Summer* II. x. 279 'I'll make it worth your while,' he said. 'You can have anything you care to ask for.'.. 'Ah,' said Dr. Obispo, 'now you're talking turkey.' **1946** E. HODGINS *Mr. Blandings builds his Dream House* (1947) xv. 196 The boss painter..wanted to talk turkey about..the final colours. **1967** A. CHRISTIE *Endless Night* ix. 67 Send for a high powered lawyer and tell him you're willing to talk turkey. Then he fixes..the amount of alimony. **1982** T.

Berger *Reinhart's Women* xix. 270 Maybe I'll be in a position to talk turkey about an arrangement that would work out for us both.

e. *cold turkey*: a method of treating drug addicts by sudden and complete withdrawal of the drug, instead of by a gradual process. Also *attrib.* and as *advb. phr.*; also *transf.* Hence *cold-turkey* vb. trans., to cure of drug addiction by 'cold turkey' treatment. *slang* (orig. *N. Amer.*).

1921 *Daily Colonist* (Victoria, B.C.) 13 Oct. 15/6 Perhaps the most pitiful figures who have appeared before Dr. Carleton Simon..are those who voluntarily surrender themselves. When they go before him, they [*sc.* drug addicts] are given what is called the 'cold turkey' treatment. **1936** *Amer. Speech* XI. 120/1 *Cold turkey*, treatment of addicts in institutions where they are taken off drugs suddenly without the 'tapering off' which the addict always desires. **1941** W. C. Handy *Father of Blues* xviii. 243 We went on 'cold turkey' that morning without a rehearsal. **1951** *N.Y. Times* 27 June 19 She tried it 'cold turkey' once, which she explained meant merely stopping completely, without any attendant medication. **1960** *Times Lit. Suppl.* 16 Sept. 589/4 *The Scene* is written by a junkie..who was snitched by a flip, busted by the nailers and after a stretch in the pen cold turkeyed..that is to say, was once a dope addict; he was arrested and.. managed to break himself of his addiction. **1962** 'K. Orvis' *Damned & Destroyed* xi. 72, I made one cold-turkey cure and it near killed me. **1976** S. George *Fatal Shadows* 154 She took a cold turkey, no methedrine, no sedatives, nothing, just off.

3. b. *plain turkey, scrub turkey*: humorous names for swagmen who haunt, respectively, the Australian plains and the bush [perhaps with partial allusion to the 'turkey' (sense 5 below) which they carry]. *Austral. slang.*

1955 A. Marshall *I can jump Puddles* 152 Father.. was familiar with the ways of swagmen... The bearded men who kept to the bush he called 'Scrub Turkeys' and those who came down from the plains he called 'Plain Turkeys'. **1973** F. Huelin *Keep Moving* 178 *Scrub Turkey*, bagman who has gone Bush. Usually slightly mental or eccentric.

5. Applied more generally to bundles or hold-alls carried by other itinerant workers, vagrants, etc. Also *Canad.* and *Austral.*

1909 *Outlook* 2 Jan. 19/1 A [Colorado] desert miner calls his valise a 'turkey'. **1912** G. H. Gibson *Ironbark Splinters* 6 So you 'pack' your bloomin' turkey, and you take the northern train. **1931** 'D. Stiff' *Milk & Honey Route* 216 *Turkey*, a bundle, a suitcase or a canvas bag. **1945** Baker *Austral. Lang.* v. 104 Expressions to describe being on the tramp...[*to*] *coil one's turkey* (strictly this applies to the rolling of a swag) [etc.]. **1963** R. Symons *Many Trails* v. 54 The cowboys' 'turkeys'—as they called their bedrolls, in which were wrapped their personal possessions such as tobacco—when the outfit was on the move. **1973** in B. Broadfoot *Ten Lost Years* ii. 19, I took to the road with..my poor clothes tied together with two leather thongs, and that is what they call a turkey.

5*. *U.S. slang.* **a.** An inferior or unsuccessful cinematographic or theatrical production, a flop; hence, anything disappointing or of little value.

1927 *Vanity Fair* (N.Y.) XXIX. 132/3 'A turkey' is a third rate production. **1939** G. Marx *Let.* 27 Oct. (1967) 21 The boys at the studio have lined up another turkey for us... I saw the present one the other day and didn't care much for it. **1941** J. M. Cain *Mildred Pierce* 176 The beach..was studded with rocks and was therefore unsuitable to swimming. For all ordinary purposes it was simply a turkey. **1962** *Movie* June 18/1 With *The Four Horsemen*, Minnelli was once more landed with a turkey, an old one, too. **1977** H. Fast *Immigrants* iii. 201 'Have you ever thought of selling the place?' Jake asked... 'Oh? And who the hell would buy this turkey?'

b. = *Turk *sb.*[1] 4 b; *spec.* an Irish immigrant in the U.S.

1932 J. T. Farrell *Young Lonigan* i. 31 Dooley was one comical turkey, funnier than anything you'd find in real life. **1966** [see *salt water B. c].

c. A stupid, slow, inept, or otherwise worthless person.

1951 in Wentworth & Flexner *Dict. Amer. Slang* (1960) 556/2 So, if you got a collector [of internal revenue] through the civil service system who was a real turkey, you'd be stuck with that turkey practically until he died. **1969** C. Burke *God is Beautiful, Man* (1970) 105 You better get real strong like so that you won't be a turkey. **1978** *Time* 3 July 13/3 'Come on, you turkeys! Let's speed this show up!' cries an irreverent observer. **1984** *Tampa* (Florida) *Tribune* 5 Apr. 4D/3, I decided I had had enough of that turkey.

6. *turkey dinner, farm, farmer, -gobbler* (earlier example), *meat, -tail, -wing* (earlier example); **turkey-bush**, an evergreen shrub, *Myoporum deserti*, native to Australia and bearing white flowers followed by purple berries; **turkey-foot**, (*b*) applied to other things resembling a turkey's foot (in quot. 1957, a weaving pattern); **turkey-shoot** (examples); **turkey-trot** (earlier example); also, a fast jogging trot like that of a turkey; hence **turkey-trotting** *a.*; **turkey vulture** (earlier example).

1911 W. R. Guilfoyle *Austral. Plants* 265 'Turkey-bush'..evergreen shrub..reputed poisonous and injurious to stock. **1936** F. Clune *Roaming round Darling* xvii. 163 Shrubs..mingled with turkey-bush flower—white and small, having five petals to each bloom, like an English daisy. **1965** *Austral. Encycl.* IX. 59/2 Turkey-bush, one of several names applied to the inland shrub *Myoporum deserti* because wild turkeys or native bustards have been observed to eat the berried fruits. **1953** G. W. Brace *Spire* xiii. 125 'Turkey dinner, eh?' 'With gravy,' Sylvia said. **1977** 'W. Trevor' in D. Marcus *Best Irish Stories* II. 78 The Bulrush Café has a turkey dinner advertised. **1952** *Turkeys* Nov. p. ix. (Advt.), Beale's turkey farm. **1959** *Ibid.* July–Aug. 29 (Advt.), One of Norfolk's leading turkey farmers. **1972** K. Bonfiglioli *Don't point that Thing at Me* iv. 40 A rich turkey-farmer in Suffolk. **1932** Simpson & Weir *Weaver's Craft* xii. 126 *Turkey Foot* (24 threads).—Each pedal should be used six times in the following order: 4, 2, 3, 1; repeat. **1935** M. Moore *Sel. Poems* 71 The firs stand in a procession, each with an emerald turkey-foot at the top. **1836** W. T. Porter in *Spirit of Times* 9 July 162/1 They seemed to me about the size of a big Christmas turkey gobbler. **1901** A. H. Rice *Mrs. Wiggs of Cabbage Patch* ii. 24 If you ain't never et turkey meat you don't know how good it is. **1972** *Country Life* 30 Nov. 1507/1 The promoters of turkey-meat sales. **1845** S. Judd *Margaret* i. 62 Its succedanea..were a turkey shoot the next day, and a ball. **1898** H. Frederic *Deserter* 81 The farther of the two was now so far away that he seemed a mere dark speck, like the object seen from the gun-line of a turkey-shoot. **1980** *Outdoor Life* (U.S.) (Northeast ed.) Oct. 92/2 Saturday afternoon turkey shoots used to be popular in my community. **1851** J. J. Hooper *Widow Rugby's Husband* 84 Betsy dodged behind the wild turkey-tail which she carried by way of a fan. **1936** M. Mitchell *Gone with Wind* xviii. 318 Girls who laughed from behind turkey-tail fans. **1839** *Southern Lit. Messenger* V. 337/1 May-be I didn't set up a high turkey-trot, and peeled it like thunder. **1895** F. Remington *Pony Tracks* 187 He would run me off the plantation at a turkey trot if I did shoot. **1908** W. G. Davenport *Butte & Montana beneath X-Ray* 42 The light fantastic, the turkey trot and the pazamala were indulged in by all to a late hour. **1859** H. E. Taliaferro *Fisher's River Scenes & Characters* 36 You're a purty set uv ill-begotten, turkey-trottin' pukes, to raise a quarrel with a peaceubble man, and then run like a gang uv geese. **1823** E. James *Acct. Exped. Rocky Mts.* I. 4 At evening we..saw..several turkey vultures. **1872** Mrs. Stowe *Sam Lawson's Oldtown Fireside Stories* 4 'I'll sweep up the coals now,' he added, vigorously applying a turkey-wing to the purpose.

Turkey-carpeted, *a.* (Earlier example.)

1831 M. Edgeworth *Let.* 29 Mar. (1971) 505 The library at Eton College is the most *comfortable* I ever was in—turkey carpetted.

Turkey red. Add: **c. Turkey red oil** (also **Turkey-red, turkey Red Oil**), sulphonated castor oil, principally used with alizarin to produce the colour Turkey red.

1879 *Jrnl. Chem. Soc.* XXXVI. 187 This 'Turkey-red oil' is a mixture of sulpho-ricinoleate and sulpho-pyroterebate of sodium. **1903** [see *oil tanning* s.v. *oil *sb.*[1] 6 c]. **1980** K. G. Ponting *Dict. Dyes & Dyeing* (1981) 172/2 John Mercer did a great deal of research on the production of the necessary turkey red oil produced by the action of sulphuric acid on castor oil.

Turkicize (tɜ̄·ɹkisəiz), *v.* Also **turkicize.** [f. Turkic *a.* + -ize.] *trans.* To render Turkic or Turkish. Hence **Tu:rkiciza·tion; Turkicized** *ppl. a.*

1939 C. S. Coon *Races of Europe* vii. 233 The Magyars were Ugrians from the region between the Volga and the Urals, who had been partially Turkicized by the Petchenegs and others. **1951** W. K. Matthews *Languages U.S.S.R.* iii. 17 A tiny remnant of a mostly turkicised tribe living in the Turkic-speaking country north of the Altai range. **1964** *Language* XL. 301 It was long believed ..that Chuvash was a Turkicized Finnic language. **1964** G. Wheeler *Mod. Hist. Sov. Central Asia* ii. 24 The Turkicization of the Mongol rulers appears to have started very early after the Mongol state was established.

Turkification. Add: (Later examples.) Also **Turcification.**

1922 Buxton & Conwil-Evans *Oppressed Peoples & League of Nations* v. 132 The Armenians..resisted all attempts at 'turcification'. **1949** J. Parkes *Hist. Palestine* xii. 241 Unhappily at this point the new policy of Turcification caused the government to maintain the deposition [of the Patriarch Damianus], as they had no intention of supporting what appeared—and was—an Arab demonstration. **1976** *Economist* 4 Sept. 45/1 The demographic Turkification of the north will soon be complete.

Turkish, *a.* (*sb.*) Add: **A.** *adj.* **2. b.** *Turkish cigarette* (or *cig*), *tobacco*; **Turkish carpet** = Turkey carpet; **Turkish coffee,** the strong (usu. sweet) black coffee commonly drunk in the East, in which the ground beans are boiled thrice over and the liquid is served with the grounds; a cup of such coffee; **Turkish crescent** *Mus.* = *Chinese pavilion* s.v. Chinese *a.* 2; cf. *jingling Johnny* (*a*) s.v. *jingling *ppl. a.*; **Turkish delight,** substitute for def.: a sweetmeat consisting of gelatine boiled, cubed, and dusted with sugar, *rahat lokum; (earlier examples); cf. *delight *sb.* 4; **Turkish slipper,** a soft heelless slipper with turned-up toe, a babouche; **Turkish trousers,** baggy oriental pantaloons.

1886 S. W. Mitchell *Roland Blake* v. 42 The room.. was luxuriously comfortable with a heavy-piled Turkish carpet and easy-chairs. **1977** Fleming & Honour *Penguin Dict. Decorative Arts* 805/2 Turkish carpets.. differ from Persian carpets..stylistically in that their design seems invariably to have been created by weavers rather than painters. **1897** Kipling *Captains Courageous* i. 6 Any gen'elman got a real Turkish cig on him? **1903** A. Bennett *Truth about Author* xii. 172 The aroma of coffee, the odour of Turkish cigarettes. **1950** G. Greene *Third Man* vii. 56 The Turkish cigarettes that Harry always smoked. **1982** T. Keneally *Schindler's Ark* ix. 102 Oskar Schindler—in his coat with the fur lapels.. reaching for another Turkish cigarette. **1854** F. Duberly *Let.* 17 Aug. in E. E. P. Tisdall *Mrs. Duberly's Campaigns* (1963) ii. 54 Rum and water till bedtime, or the very strongest Turkish coffee. **1898** G. B. Shaw *Arms & Man* ii. 22 (*stage direction*), A small table..is laid for breakfast with Turkish coffee pot, cups, rolls, etc. **1958** L. Durrell *Mountolive* xiv. 267 She was sitting in the lounge of Shepheards Hotel under the clock with an untouched Turkish coffee before her. **1978** H. Kaplan *Damascus Cover* xv. 155 Ari ordered a second cup of thick Turkish coffee. **1891** C. R. Day *Descr. Catal. Mus. Instruments R. Military Exhib., London, 1890* xii. 233 There were specimens of the old Turkish Crescent (*chapeau chinois*), once a favourite adjunct to military bands, and known in former years by the familiar nick-name of 'Jingling Johnny'. They consisted of brass hoops, hung with little bells.., and ornamented with gilded crescents and long streaming tails of horse-hair. They were carried upon poles. **1938** *Oxf. Compan. Mus.* 965/1 *Turkish crescent* or *Turkish jingle*.., a noise maker introduced into military bands..at a time when there was a craze for 'Turkish music'. **1961** J. Blades in A. Baines *Mus. Instruments through Ages* xiv. 338 The middle of the eighteenth century when European military bands were being increased to include percussion instruments on the lines of the Turkish military music—bass drum, cymbals, triangle, and sometimes also tambourine and the Jingling Johnny or Turkish Crescent. **1877** *Porcupine* 31 Mar. 843/2 Arabs and Greeks vended Turkish delight (horrible compound). **1888** *Boy's Own Paper* Summer 38/1 Instead of the usual boxes of..Turkish delight,..there was little to tempt the youthful appetite but piles of fruit. **1865** Dickens *Our Mutual Friend* II. iii. i. 3 Mr. Fledgeby's appearing erect at the foot of the bed in Turkish slippers, rose-coloured Turkish trousers..and a gown and cap to correspond. **1971** 'D. Halliday' *Dolly & Doctor Bird* v. 65 He [*sc.* a Turkish dancer] wore a cinnamon tunic and trousers with gold Turkish slippers. **1827** M. Wilmot *Let.* 10 Oct. (1935) 305 If you add a *pipe* and some turkish tobacco..you will have the portrait of most of our beaux. **1981** A. Mackay *Death on Eno* 68 The Turkish tobacco is added for aroma. [**1612** W. Strachey *Trav. Virginia* (1849) v. 66 A kynd of leather breeches and stockings, all fastened together..which they tye and wrappe about the loynes after the fashion of the Turkes or Irish Trouses.] **1821** Byron *Don Juan* iii. lxxii. 39 Her orange silk full Turkish trowsers furl'd About the prettiest ankle in the world. **1865** [see *Turkish slipper* above]. **1928** V. Woolf *Orlando* iv. 140 The Turkish trousers which she had hitherto worn. **1973** *Guardian* 10 Apr. 13/2 Twinsets.. allied to jersey wrapover skirts, loose lopped-off pants, Turkish trousers.

B. *sb.* **2.** (Earlier example of sense 'Turkish tobacco'.)

1859 A. J. Munby *Diary* 2 Mar. in D. Hudson *Munby* (1972) 24 Long clays also, & a tall jar..of real Turkish.

turkle (tɜ̄·ɹk'l), U.S. dial. var. Turtle *sb.*[1] and *sb.*[2] Hence **tu·rkling** = Turtling.

1861 O. W. Holmes *Elsie Venner* 384 Don' wan' no snappin'-turkles in my stable. **1893** H. A. Shands *Some Peculiarities of Speech in Mississippi* 65 *Turkle*, Negro for *turtle*. *Turkle-dove* is the common name given by negroes to the *turtle-dove*. **1929** W. Faulkner *Sartoris* ii. 64 It wuz jes' like shootin' turkles in a slough. **1941** J. Still *Proud Walkers* in *Sat. Even. Post* 10 May 112/3 The hours crawled turkle-slow. **1978** J. A. Michener *Chesapeake* p. ix, *Turkling*: State Senator Frederick C. Malkus, the region's premier turtle trapper, took me turkling, as that sport is called.

Turkmen, Türkmen (pl. *-mens*), varr. Turcoman.

1927 W. M. Ramsay *Asianic Elements Gk. Civilization* viii. 86 The Turkish term *ova* and the Turkmen *oba*... The distinction between the Turks and the Turkmens or Nomads. **1953** O. Caroe *Soviet Empire* xiv. 235 Yet Uzbeks, Kazaks and Turkmens persist in abstract praises of their 'motherlands'. One Turkmen even had the insolence to write a poem 'My Turkmenistan'. **1962** A. Tietze in Householder & Saporta *Probl. Lexicogr.* 267 Other languages of the Southern Turkic or Oghuz subgroup, as Azerbaijani or Türkmen. **1978** *Times* 18 Oct. 16/8 [In] Uzbekistan..many..speak Tadzhik, Turkmen and other Asian languages.

Turk's cap. Add: **3.** Also, any of several other members of the genus *Cactus*. (Earlier and later examples.)

1731 P. Miller *Gardeners Dict.* s.v. *Melocactus*, The common or large Melon-Thistle, commonly call'd Turk-cap or Pope's-Head in the West-Indies. **1926** Fawcett & Rendle *Flora of Jamaica* V. 283 Turk's Head, Turk's Cap, Pope's Head, Melon Thistle. **1951** *Dict. Gardening* (R. Hort. Soc.) I. 345/2 The Turk's Cap. The species [of *Cactus*] are characterized by the formation of a woolly cap or cephalium when the plants reach flowering size.

turmoil, *v.* **2.** Delete † *Obs.* and add later examples (in quot. 1900 in humorous mock-solemn use). Now *rare.*

1900 W. Sewell in W. Tuckwell *Reminisc. Oxford* xiii. 237 Garlic, deadlier without question E'en than hemlock: oh digestion... What is this, that still so deep here, Keeps turmoiling in my chest? **1981** T. Holme *Funeral of Gondolas* v. 216 The noise of the storm receded. Outside, where it still turmoiled, was a long way away.

turn, *sb.* Add: **I. 2. d.** *turn of the screw*: an additional twist to tighten up the hold; an extra twist given to a thumbscrew by way of increasing the torture (in quots. *fig.*).

1796 [see SCREW *sb.*[1] 2 a]. **1853** DICKENS *Bleak House* xxiv. 331 (*heading*) A turn of the screw. **1898** H. JAMES *Turn of Screw* 4 If the child [in a ghost story] gives the effect another turn of the screw, what do you say to *two* children? **1940** *Manch. Guardian Weekly* 1 Mar. 175 Even more far-reaching schemes of increasing direct taxation.. are certain to be realised..whenever the psychological ground is favourable for this further turn of the screw. **1973** *Listener* 14 June 785/2 The first turns of the screw on the car commuter are already being prepared. The GLC wants to put up parking fines from £4 to £20.

6. *Naut.* A twist of rope round a mast, etc.

1886 R. BROWN *Spunyarn & Spindrift* vii. 91, I.. jumped to let go of the main-sheet. But Lord! we was in the white water almost before I could cast the turns off. **1930** *Sea Breezes* 74 Brushing off the snow and hammering gasket turns warmed my hands.

7. c. (Later examples.)

1932 G. F.-H. BERKELEY *Italy in Making* I. xviii. 268 At suitable points were inset 'turns', similar to those used in convents, so as to enable the servants to hand in food for both the cardinals and their attendants, without themselves entering the isolated wing. **1966** M. C. LORANG *Footloose Scientist in Mayan America* 90 Food was passed into the dining room through a '*turn*'..—a hollow roller set into the wall so that when one side is open, the other side is closed.

II. 8. d. *Cards.* The dealing or inversion of two cards in faro; hence *to call the turn*, to guess the order of the last three cards in the pack. Also *fig.*

1864 W. B. DICK *Amer. Hoyle* 207 The two cards drawn from the dealer's box—one for the bank and the other for the player..constitute a turn. **1889** *Cent. Dict.* s.v. *faro*, The showing of two cards constitutes a 'turn'. After each turn new bets are made for another, down to the last three cards of the pack; the only betting allowed after this is on 'calling the turn', or guessing which will show first. **1901** H. JAMES *Sacred Fount* 44 The face of Guy Brissenden, as recognizable at a distance as the numbered card of a 'turn'. **1908** *Sat. Even. Post* 5 Dec. 18/2 Ye-e-s, but this Wallingford person called the turn. **1940** D. W. MAURER *Big Con* viii. 257 The odds are always greater on the last turn, and anyone who wins on that play may make a young fortune. **1964** A. WYKES *Gambling* vii. 169 When three [cards] are left (the 'last turn'), players bet on the order of their appearance.

e. *Cricket.* A deviation of the ball's course after pitching; = BREAK *sb.*[1] 5.

1900 P. F. WARNER *Cricket in Many Climes* 190 The Newlands ground is the most difficult to make runs on in the whole of South Africa, the bowlers always being able to get considerable turn on the ball. **1977** *Observer* 30 Jan. 23/8 A deficit of even 50 runs..could pose problems for England because the spinners have already begun to extract a lot of turn.

11. d. *Golf.* The point in the course (after the ninth hole) at which the players begin the return journey.

1899 *Golf Illustrated* 1 Sept. 336/2 The hole was halved, as were also the eighth and ninth... The match..was all square at the turn. **1930** *Cambridge Daily News* 24 Sept. 7/3 Compston, who went out in 37 and was five up at the turn, won by seven and five.

III. 18. c. The point at which one named period of time gives way to the next; the beginning or end *of* a named period of time, regarded in relation to the transition point between it and the preceding or following period; *spec.* (*a*) *turn of the century*, the beginning or end of the century under consideration; also (usu. with hyphens) *attrib.* or as *adj.*; (*b*) *turn of the year*, the end of winter and the beginning of spring; also, the beginning of the calendar year.

1853 R. S. SURTEES *Mr Sponge's Sporting Tour* lxxi. 395 Who doesn't know the chilling feel of an English spring, or rather of a day at the turn of the year before there is any spring? **1859** [in Dict., sense 18 a]. **1926** O. BARFIELD *Hist. in Eng. Words* xi. 195 Just before the turn of the century there burst..upon England that strange explosion..the Romantic Movement. **1934** J. C. POWYS *Autobiogr.* vii. 300 How well I remember watching out the turn of the centuries—the nineteenth becoming the twentieth—in the little dining-room at Court House. **1935** *Discovery* Oct. 310/2 It is interesting to compare Dr Burr's notes, dating back to the turn of the century, with present conditions. **1947** R. CHURCH in M. Balcon et al. *Eng. Lang. & Lit.* xii. 200/2 Blatant imperialism shouted with a loud voice round the turn of the last Victorian years. **1947** W. H. LEWIS in *Ess. presented to C. Williams* 140 If they reached the port at the turn of the year,..the galleys, stripped to their hulls, would be emerging from their winter hibernation. **1952** G. SARTON *Hist. Sci.* I. xx. 512 We know that Autolycos was the teacher of..Arcesilaos of Pitane (315–240)... This suggests that he resided in Pitane and fixes the date approximately, the turn of the century. **1955** E. BLISHEN *Roaring Boys* IV. 251 The school lavatories..were a product of turn-of-the-century parsimony. **1955** I. & P. OPIE *Oxford Dict. Nursery Rhymes* 4 Romantic lyrics of a decidedly free nature..which were carefully rewritten to suit the new discrimination at the turn of the last century. **1955** *Time & Tide* 19 Nov. 1503/1 Can those who were young in the nineteen-twenties..remember the favourites as vividly as their elders recollect the tunes of the century's turn? **1961** I. MURDOCH *Severed Head* xiii. 120, I brought to mind that it was New Year's eve. Some nearer bells took up the peal... Soon it would be the turn of the year. **1961** *Times* 29 Dec. 11/7 Mr. William Brodie's sets, vaguely turn-of-the-century. **1965** C. E. POCKNEE *Parson's Handbk.* (ed. 13) p. xiv, At the turn of this century there were many who were in that state. **1968** A. M. FARRER *Interpretation & Belief* (1976) 190 It was as a doctrine of free will that Neo-Platonism was embraced by St Augustine at the turn of the fourth to the fifth century. **1970** *New Scientist* 17 Sept. 563/1 The latest estimates suggest that the area will be short of..1 270 000 cu.m. a day in 1981, and more than three million cu.m. a day by the turn of the century. **1970** H. BRAUN *Parish Churches* i. 22 At the turn of the millennium the monastic churches were quite enormous. **1970** *Daily Tel.* 26 Feb. 6/2 It was inevitable that at the turn of the decade there should appear yet more 'condition of Britain' analyses. **1971** *Ibid.* 23 Aug. 8 At the turn of the year, Kuala Lumpur officials talked confidently of reduced Communist terrorism along the Thai-Malaysia border. **1976** *National Observer* (U.S.) 29 May 9/1 Her modest, turn-of-the-century home on a quiet street in Indianapolis. **1976** *Church Times* 9 July 6/2 He begins with a splendid assembly of Church of England men all earnestly proclaiming, at the turn of the eighteenth and nineteenth centuries, doctrines then trendy. **1977** K. M. E. MURRAY *Caught in Web of Words* xv. 282 In 1897 James had set himself the target of completing half the letters of the alphabet by the turn of the century. **1979** *Sci. Amer.* Dec. 96/1 The evolutionary significance of the original Neanderthal discovery and of other human remains uncovered at Paleolithic sites was not apparent until the turn of the 20th century. **1981** 'W. HAGGARD' *Money Men* xi. 122 What was still called the parlour..was vintage turn of the century.

V. 28. b. (*e*) *out of* (*one's*) *turn*: out of one's due order or place in a series; *to talk* or *speak out of* (*one's*) *turn*: to say more than one ought to say, to speak inadvisedly or tactlessly.

1888 *Rules of Golf* 5 Playing out of turn. **1930** 'SAPPER' *Finger of Fate* 186 Well, old boy, our Lady Carrington was talking a little out of her turn. I don't blame her—it's a bit disconcerting to lose a thing like that. **1939** I. BAIRD *Waste Heritage* vi. 79 Easy, Eddy, I shouldn't have spoken out of turn there. **1945** J. B. PRIESTLEY *Three Men in New Suits* i. 7 I'm talking out of my turn, I expect—as usual. **1969** P. ROTH *Portnoy's Complaint* 14, I voluntarily and out of my turn set the table. **1978** P. VAN GREENAWAY *Man called Scavener* ix. 123 I'm going to talk out of turn and you'll be welcome to tell me I should mind my own business.

29. b. (Earlier examples.)

1715 D. RYDER *Diary* 19 Sept. (1939) 101 There was rope dancing and tumbling... There were now and then some good humorous turns came in that made us laugh with a just pleasure. **1861** E. COWELL *Diary* 16 Apr. in M. W. Disher *Cowells in America* (1934) 293 Mr. Ogden, not appreciated and evidently uncomfortable, would not sing a second 'turn'. **1889** G. B. SHAW *London Music in 1888–89* (1937) 234 Five out of six of the 'turns' are of the deadliest dulness.

VII. 37. b. (Later examples.)

1862 M. D. COLT *Went to Kansas* 99 Have just been to the spring for my turn of water. **1981** *Publ. Amer. Dial. Soc.* LXVIII. 48 *Turn of water*.., a container in each hand.

c. (Earlier example.)

1792 G. CARTWRIGHT *Jrnl. Coast of Labrador* I. p. xvi, *Turn of timber*, So much as a man can carry on his shoulders.

39. (Earlier examples.)

1857 *Sat. Rev.* 18 Apr. 348/2 Nobody understands the turn of the market better than Tomkins. **1870** J. K. MEDBERY *Man & Mysteries Wall Street* 78 This neat profit is called a 'turn'.

VIII. 41. turns (*rarely* **turn**) **ratio** *Electr.*, the ratio of the number of turns on the primary of a transformer to the number on the secondary, or vice versa.

1927 R. E. BROWN *Alternating-Current Machinery* iii. 66 The turn ratio of a transformer may be obtained from the designer or may be approximately measured by determining the ratio of the indications of two voltmeters. **1965** *Wireless World* Sept. 431/2 The number of turns on each coil, the turns ratio and the inductances are in no sense critical. **1976** RYDER & THOMSON *Electronic Circuits & Systems* xii. 286 A loudspeaker of 4 Ω can be made to appear as 400 Ω on the primary side if we use a transformer with the turns ratio $a = \sqrt{(400/4)} = ..10$.

turn, *v.* Add: **II. 4. a.** (Earlier *absol.* example.)

1796 JANE AUSTEN *Let.* 1 Sept. (1952) 8 Frank..enjoys himself here very much, for he has just learnt to turn.

5. d. *to turn an honest penny*: see HONEST *a.* 4 b; *to turn a profit* (U.S.): to earn or make a profit.

1969 *Time* 21 Jan. 44 Partly because of the competition from IBM it is unlikely to turn a profit before 1970. **1976** *National Observer* (U.S.) 14 Aug. 4/1 The iron rule of business dictates staying open anytime there's a decent chance to turn a profit.

IV. 13. c. *Cricket.* Of the bowler: to cause the ball to 'break' (BREAK *v.* 32 b). Also *intr.* of the ball: to break or turn in its course after pitching.

1898 G. GIFFEN *With Bat & Ball* iii. 47 There are very few men bowling at Mac's pace who can turn the ball on the Adelaide Oval. **1909** W. G. GRACE *W.G.'s Little Book* iii. 33, I don't know the moment he delivers the ball which way it will turn on pitching. **1928** *Morning Post* 2 July 15/1 Garland-Wells is slow right, and can turn the ball both ways. **1930** *Ibid.* 16 July 11/6 The bowlers were making the ball turn more than before luncheon. **1955** [see *FLIGHT *v.* 7].

17. c. In *Assoc. Football*, etc., to get round (an opponent at close quarters) by making it necessary for him to change direction.

1976 E. DUNPHY *Only a Game?* (1977) iv. 121 He turns full backs, he does unusual things on the ball, he creates unusual situations. **1980** *Times* 3 Apr. 13/2 Francis.. turned Buchan and sent in a stinging shot.

V. 29. Restrict †*Obs.* to senses in Dict. and add: **c.** To induce or persuade (a person) to act against his country, former associates, etc., esp. as a spy.

1971 C. EGLETON *Last Post for Partisan* xvi. 162 'How did they turn you?' 'I was shopped... They said I could save my neck if I helped them, and so I agreed.' **1973** T. ALLBEURY *Choice of Enemies* vii. 32 It's my assessment that this officer gave no information to the Russians and was not turned by them. **1979** A. BOYLE *Climate of Treason* ix. 309 The process of cornering and 'turning' the Fifth Man made such limited sharing of the secret almost inevitable. **1982** *Times* 27 Aug. 2/4 Several have been 'turned' only after being shown evidence from another 'supergrass'.

30. c. Also of a criminal, to become an informer, to 'grass'.

1977 *Chicago Tribune* 2 Oct. I. 24/3 Like many other informants, Bompensiero 'turned' in order to avoid jail. **1982** *Times* 27 Aug. 2 (*heading*) Pressures that lead a man to 'turn'.

VI. 39. b. Freq. as *pa. pple.* modifying a sb.

1945, etc. [see *POACHER[1] 1 b]. **1964** *Eng. Studies* XLV. 382 Their Scandinavian conquerors-turned-neighbors. **1973** E. SCHUMACHER *Small is Beautiful* I. iii. 44 The economist-turned-econometrician is unwilling..to face the question. **1982** *Times Lit. Suppl.* 10 Sept. 968/3 Jerome's father was a Nonconformist preacher, turned architect, turned mine-owner.

VII. Phrases. (For *to turn the* (*other*) *cheek* see *CHEEK *sb.* 2 b.)

51. turn one's coat (later examples).

1946 G. MILLAR *Horned Pigeon* ix. 130 Like good policemen all over the world, they were only too willing to turn their coats (to keep law and order, of course). **1981** *Times Lit. Suppl.* 2 Jan. 7/5 What prompted Sohō, Japanese intellectuals have endlessly debated, to 'turn his coat' in the 1890s?

c. *trans.* and *intr.* Also *turn aloose.* To let go (of), to leave hold (of). *U.S. dial.*

1906 *Dialect Notes* III. 162 *Turn loose*,..to get rid of, let go. **1910** *Ibid.* 457 *Turn it loose*,..let go of it. **1929** W. FAULKNER *Sound & Fury* 199 He turned my hands loose. **1934** C. CARMER *Stars fell on Alabama* 139, I jus' *got* to hold you now. I *can't* turn you aloose. **1935** T. WOLFE *Of Time & River* III. xlii. 376 You git his other hand, Jim, an' try to make him turn a-loose. *a* **1938** —— *Web & Rock* (1947) 34 'You turn loose of me,' the captive panted, 'I'll show you who's the cry-baby!' **1966** R. PRICE *Generous Man* (1967) i. 63 'Safe! We're in awful danger. Turn loose, old fool!' He turned loose and lay flat, small on the ground.

VIII. In combination with adverbs. **66*. turn around.** (See simple senses and AROUND *adv.*) = *turn round*, sense 78 in Dict. and Suppl. orig. *U.S.*

1880 'MARK TWAIN' *Tramp Abroad* xiii. 119, I could see the dim blur of the windows, but in my turned-around condition they were exactly where they ought not to be. **1919** E. O'NEILL *Moon of Caribbees* 114 Smitty does not turn around. **1925** F. SCOTT FITZGERALD *Great Gatsby* i. 9 Turning me around by one arm. *Ibid.* ix. 208 He opened it at the back cover and turned it around for me to see. **1932** W. FAULKNER *Light in August* xiv. 315 When he sat up he found that the sun..now shone upon him from the opposite direction. At first he believed that he was merely turned around. Then he realised that it was now evening. **1945** DYLAN THOMAS in *Horizon* Feb. 83 The weather turned around. **1963** J. JOESTEN *They call it Intelligence* I. iv. 45 A spy..caught..usually is given a chance to switch sides..such a helpless foreign agent is being 'turned around'. **1967** V. C. WELBURN *Johnny So Long* II. ii. 63 He shakes his hands high at the crowd, then turns around and does it to Judy. **1971** *Sci. News* 13 Feb. 108 Children..with severe behavioral problems.. are treated in a 'family' situation... An innovative school program helps 'turn youngsters around'. **1971** *Black World* Mar. 54/1, I felt so sorry for them and they wuz so turned around that one day over to Tony's crib I got high wid em. **1972** B. MOORE *Catholics* i. 21 Order them to turn that boat around and send it back for him. **1976** *National Observer* (U.S.) 29 May 3/4 This thing is so close, so fragile, that anything could happen tomorrow to turn it around. **1977** J. D. MACDONALD *Condominium* xxxiii. 322 We're past our marker... More than a mile. We can turn around. **1978** *Globe & Mail* (Toronto) 16 May 5/1 The Ontario Government has announced a..campaign to turn around the image Ontarians have gained as boorish and unfriendly hosts to foreign visitors.

69. turn back. b. For † *Obs.* read '*Obs.* exc. *U.S.*' and add later example.

1927 *Publishers' Weekly* 12 Feb. 610 We felt that the only course open to us in view of the authors' feelings in the matter was to offer to turn back the book to them, subject to their disposal.

71. turn down. c. For ? *Obs.* read '*Obs.* exc. *U.S.*' and add later examples.

1876 'MARK TWAIN' *Tom Sawyer* vi. 71 He took his place...in the spelling class, and got 'turned down', by a succession of mere baby words. **1946** G. WILSON *Fidelity Folks* 136 We had regular places in the line and turned down those who could not spell a word.

d. For *U.S. slang* read 'orig. *U.S. slang*' and add further examples.

1915 J. CHURCHILL *Let.* 11 Aug. in M. Gilbert *Winston S. Churchill* (1972) III. Compan. II. 1128 Everybody seemed to have 'turned it down'. **1927** A. CONAN DOYLE *Case-Bk. Sherlock Holmes* x. 261 A quarter's rent..in advance and no arguing about terms. In these times a poor woman like me can't afford to turn down a chance like that. **1951** *Sport* 7–13 Jan. 17/1 Many of our suggestions are turned down. **1956** A. H. Compton *Atomic Quest* iii. 202, I had been approached with regard to college and university presidencies... I had..turned them down. **1958** P. Gibbs *Curtains of Yesterday* xxvii. 214 Many nations..put forward plans for a gradual process of disarmament, and each plan was turned down by the other delegations. **1979** R. Jaffe *Class Reunion* I. vii. 70 A lot of attractive, eligible men kept asking Annabel for dates, and she didn't like having to turn them down.

g. Also, to lower the temperature of (an electrical appliance, heating system, etc., and *transf.*, that which it heats or cooks), orig. by turning a knob or switch; to reduce the volume of sound from (a radio, record-player, etc.), usu. by turning a knob or switch; to turn (a knob or switch) in order to reduce the temperature, volume of sound, etc. Cf. sense 80 m below.

1941 N. Marsh *Death & Dancing Footman* (1942) xv. 277 'To get back to the wireless.'..'I turned it down.'..'You turned it *down*... Not off. Down.'..'I turned it down, and five minutes later somebody turned it up.' **1950** B. Pym *Some Tame Gazelle* x. 111 The beef..would be roasted to a cinder by now, unless Emily had had the sense to turn down the oven. **1961** J. Stroud *Touch & Go* v. 48 'Excuse me if I just turn my liver down?'..She hustled back into the kitchen. **1966** P. Willmott *Adolescent Boys* ix. 170 He was alone, playing records... He said, 'Just a minute, I'll turn this down.' **1969** 'D. Rutherford' *Gilt-Edged Cockpit* vi. 93 Could you turn that transistor down a bit? **1970** 'A. Gilbert' *Death wears Mask* ix. 138 Miss Buxton's client..began to fidget under her drier and call out something about it being too hot. 'Turn it down, dear,' said Miss Buxton crisply. **1970** J. Porter *Dover strikes Again* ii. 30 Old Mr Revel..switched on the television set. Miss Kettering..turned the volume control right down. **1975** *Guardian* 21 Jan. 5/1 Turn down your heating a couple of degrees. **1975** 'M. Sinclair' *Long Time Sleeping* xii. 143 He stopped to turn down the potatoes.

g*. To let down with a winch or the like.

1929 [see sense 80 r* below].

j. Of business or economic activity or fortune: to decline, worsen.

1960 *Economist* 8 Oct. 261/1 Wall Street has shown an impressive record of moving ahead of business activity. In the recession of 1957–58..it turned down in July, one month before the index of industrial production; and turned up again in December, four months before production did. **1980** *Daily Tel.* 23 July 19 Unemployment is rising fast in all the major economies, partly because the economic cycle is turning down.

72. turn in. a. (Further examples.) Also, to hand in or over; *spec.* to betray or surrender to the police; to trade in; to give up, to stop (freq. with *it*). Also, to register, to produce (a result or performance, etc., of a specified kind).

1830 R. Dawson *Present State of Australia* v. 201, I asked him..the reason of his having been 'turned in', as they call it, to government. **1912** *Technical World Mag.* June 403/1 When they discover any part of the track..which they cannot readily repair they turn in a signal that summons the roadmaster. **1919** in F. A. Pottle *Stretchers* (1930) 359 Tomorrow we will turn in what few articles of equipment we have not left at Merritt. **1926** J. Black *You can't Win* vii. 85 If either of you gets grabbed..and thinks he can get a light jolt by turning me in, he's wrong. **1931** H. Crane *Let.* 15 July (1965) 376 I'm very glad that you spoke about the check... I couldn't figure it out any other way than that you had waited until the following month before turning it in. **1938** F. A. Pottle *Boswell & Girl from Botany Bay* 17 Bligh published a book..and Edwards turned in a report to the Admiralty. **1947** A. Huxley *Let.* 27 July (1969) 573 Jessica Tandy..is a first-rate actress and seems to be likely to turn in a performance which will make most of the more celebrated Hollywood stars look merely silly. **1948** C. Day Lewis *Otterbury Incident* iii. 23 'I'll kill myself, then.' 'Turn it in, Nick!' Ted punched him in a friendly way. **1952** L. Durrell *Let.* 4 Nov. in *Spirit of Place* (1969) 114 I've turned in my resignation and we are clearing off in December. **1958** *Listener* 23 Oct. 632/2 This company, in common with many others, turned in a sizeable loss. *Ibid.* 13 Nov. 777/1 They didn't have to pay anything really [*sc.* for a new car];..they've turned in their old one..and that only left a £50 balance. **1968** *Globe & Mail* (Toronto) 13 Jan. 39/5 Doug Acomb and Frank Hamill scored two goals each as their line turned in one of its best performances of the season. **1971** *Sci. Amer.* July 5 It turns in the kind of performance that delivers up to 25 miles per gallon. **1973** L. Meynell *Thirteen Trumpeters* iv. 66 'Turn it in, Hooky,' he advised himself. 'Go while the going's good.' **1977** M. Sokolinsky tr. *Merle's Virility Factor* xii. 236 If she'd gone to bed with you, she would have enjoyed it—and then she'd have turned you in. **1978** 'M. Yorke' *Point of Murder* iii. 35 His Ford Escort..was being turned in for an older car with a higher mileage on the clock. **1979** *SLR Camera* Mar. 53/3 At full aperture the 75mm f2.8 optic turned in a surprisingly good performance. **1982** *Sunday Tel.* 1 Aug. 5/3 It [*sc.* the year 1981–82] has seen Sotheby's turn in its first loss in over 20 years.

73. turn off. d. (Later example.)

1888 'R. Boldrewood' *Robbery under Arms* I. i. 8 You can have..anything you like..you unfortunate young beggar, until you're turned off.

h. Also *transf.* of an electrical appliance, a recording or broadcast, etc. Also *fig.*, esp. (*colloq.*) to put (a person) off, to repel, to disillusion, to cause to lose interest.

1965 *Harper's Bazaar* Apr. 173 *Turned off*: Humperdinck turns me off. **1966** P. Willmott *Adolescent Boys* iii. 51 You can always get a bit if you want it, with the girls with the big mouths... But that sort of thing turns you off after a while. **1967** B. Patten *Little Johnny's Confession* 33 Until death comes and turns me off. **1968** J. Hudson *Case of Need* II. vi. 128, I was just turned off, I wasn't paying attention. **1969** J. Gaskell *Sweet Sweet Summer* 70 Or for the water and electric to stay on all the time, instead of being turned off after midnight. **1971** *Radio Times* 18 Nov. 80, I wonder how many viewers turned off the play, as we did. **1972** *Daily Tel.* 5 Feb. 14 [He] is kinky for short-back-and-sides and turned off by long-haired television performers. **1973** *Sci. Amer.* Dec. 14/2 Having become 'turned off' by economics, I was not sure what I wanted to be. **1975** *Nature* 20 Nov. 228/1 The male [cichlid fish] has bright colour patterns which he can turn on and off quickly. **1977** I. Shaw *Beggarman, Thief* I. viii. 101 School was a big part of his life and he couldn't just turn it off because it would be unimportant to grown-ups at this time. **1979** *Financial Rev.* 24 Oct. 10/1 Many voters were turned off by a strike in the last moment of the campaign. **1982** *Times* 21 Oct. 3, I had three frigates badly turned off in terms of capability. We were running out of steam.

74. turn on. a. (Earlier and later *fig.* examples.) *to turn the tap(s) on*, to start weeping; *to turn it on*, to make a particular effort, esp. to be charming. Also *transf.* of an electrical appliance, a recording or broadcast, etc.; *to turn on the heat*: see *HEAT *sb.* 12 b.

In quot. 1877 of piped music.

1866 'Mark Twain' *Screamers* (1871) xxix. 149 There was a good deal of honest snickering turned on this time. **1877** *Punch's Almanack for 1878* 14 Dec. 3/1 Now, recollect, Robert, at a quarter to nine turn on 'Voi che sapete' from Covent Garden. **1883** *Daily Tel.* 8 Feb. 3/2 When she had finished her song she fell a crying... She can turn the taps on at a moment's notice. **1930** A. P. Herbert *Water Gipsies* iii. 23 They had the wireless, which they turned on often for the 'jazz' bands. **1930** R. Macaulay *Staying with Relations* iii. 43 They turned on a gramophone and danced. **1948** M. Laski *Tory Heaven* i. 7 'Don't turn it on till the eleven o'clock news,' Janice called out. **1966** *Listener* 24 Nov. 779/1 Thomas could turn it on and brilliantly, when he wanted to. **1976** E. Dunphy *Only a Game?* (1977) ii. 52 But Preston, who knows? They could turn it on under the floodlights. **1981** T. Heald *Murder at Moose Jaw* xii. 144 She used to be some looker... And she could turn it on. But not any more.

c. To excite, interest, fill with enthusiasm; to intoxicate with drugs, to introduce to drugs; to arouse sexually. Also const. *to* the object of interest, etc. *slang* (orig. *U.S.*).

1903 H. James *Ambassadors* xxii. 291 One of his sisters..had observed her somewhere with me. She had spoken to her brother—turned him on. **1953** W. Burroughs *Junkie* ii. 31 We kept the weed in Marian's apartment, turned her on for all she could use, and gave her a 50 per cent commission on sales. **1965** *Harper's Bazaar* Apr. 173 Bach really turns me on. **1966** *Current Slang* (Univ. S. Dakota) Winter 8 *Turn on*,..to excite sexually. **1966** *Guardian* 18 Apr. 13/4 Police in New York said that they had seized enough of the drug LSD to 'turn on' the entire population of New York if it was put in the water supply. **1967** J. Hayes *Deep End* 16 The excitement in her eyes deepened. 'You turn me on, man.' **1967** *Melody Maker* 29 July 10/6 There is a compulsive beat so maybe even the nation's half-wits may be turned on to Lloyd. **1972** J. Brown *Chancer* iv. 53 It must be about this time he turns her on too—onto heroin. **1975** J. I. M. Stewart *Gaudy* ix. 173 It's a funny thing..how quite sure I was she wasn't going to turn me on. **1976** *News of World* 14 Mar. 5/3 Dinner jacket, wing collar, and bow tie may not sound the sort of gear to turn on a teeny bopper. **1976** *National Observer* (U.S.) 10 Apr. 14/5 My work is important. When I can turn on a student or write a good paper, I'm really happy, I'm elated. **1979** S. Wilson *Glad Hand* I. v. 30 Well..it's probably God's way of saying He takes a rather dim view of what turns you on.

d. *intr.* To become intoxicated; to take drugs. Also with *to*, to become interested in. *slang* (orig. *U.S.*).

1955 [see *POD *sb.*² 1 c]. **1967** *Sunday Truth* (Brisbane) 2 Apr. 63/2 According to Dr. Timothy Leary, the avowed leader of the LSD set, you can turn-on without using drugs. **1969** *Gandalf's Garden* IV. 9/1 It was about this time I had turned on to Zen. **1970** *New Scientist* 12 Nov. 314/1 Young people who turn on by sniffing the vapour of airplane glue..sometimes..drop dead. **1971** *Nature* 12 Feb. 462/2 Increasingly scientists are 'turning on' to the human environment. **1976** *Maclean's Mag.* 17 May 22/3 More and more teen-agers..are turning on with alcohol. **1979** R. Jaffe *Class Reunion* III. iii. 242 She walked in while I was turning on so I offered her some [marijuana].

75. turn out. h. (Earlier example.)

1813 J. Taylor *Arator* 117 The phrase 'the land is killed and must be turned out', has become common over a great portion of the United States.

q. *spec.* (*Austral. slang*) to become a bushranger.

1862 *Western Post* 24 Sept. 2/2 He was immediately told by the robber they ought to turn out. **1888** [in Dict.]. **1910** J. Cameron *Spell of Bush* 131 [The bush] had been his home; for even before he had 'turned out', four walls had never held Michael Moran for long.

77. turn over. h. (Further examples.)

1925 W. L. Cross *Life Sterne* I. 175 Robert Dodsley had just turned over the management of his business to his brother. **1930** *Publishers' Weekly* 5 Apr. 1896 By retiring and turning the business over to his son. *Ibid.* 1917 Columbia University has just come into possession of the famous collection of works on economics which Professor E. R. A. Seligman..has turned over..for a price of one-half, or less. **1930** *Harper's Mag.* July 196 My German instinct to care for my own child kept me from turning her over to someone else.

i. Also in extended sense.

1971 *Nature* 24 Dec. 483/2 *Sminthopsis crassicaudata* turns over water at about three times the rate of *Dasycercus cristicauda*. **1976** *Ibid.* 22 July 280/1 This indicates that the bulk of dentinal protein is not turned over.

i*. To search; to ransack (usu. in order to commit robbery). *Criminals' slang.*

1859 Hotten *Dict. Slang*, *Turned over*, to be stopped and searched by the police. **1925** [see *DRUM *v.* 9 b]. **1960** *Observer* 25 Dec. 7/6 The drummers, those squalid daytime operators who turn over empty semi-detached villas while the housewives are out shopping. **1971** [see *GOON 2]. **1981** L. Meynell *Hooky goes to Blazes* vi. 83 What about that girl's bedroom that got turned over?

i.** To distress, upset, affect with nausea. Cf. sense 80 k in Dict. *colloq.*

1865 Dickens in *All Year Round* 7 Dec. 47/2 The discovery turned me over. **1962** N. Streatfeild *Apple Bough* ix. 126 Proper turned me over, you did. I don't want to lose my old man yet. **1972** *New Society* 11 May 302/1 Escalope I had, though what they do to those calves turns me over.

i*.** To cause (an engine, propeller, etc.) to revolve.

1913 *Autocar Handbk.* (ed. 5) vii. 143 The motor should be able to turn the engine over at not less than 150 r.p.m. **1927** C. A. Lindbergh *We* v. 75 Learning how to turn the propellers over in starting the engine. **1976** P. Alexander *Death of Thin-Skinned Animal* xx. 209 He..pulled the wires away from the ignition switch and tied them together. This turned the [car] engine over but she wouldn't start without the choke. She was..cold.

i**.** *Printing.* To carry over (a letter, part of a word, etc.) to the next line.

1925 *Hart's Rules for Compositors & Readers* (ed. 27) 64 In most divisions it is the consonantal letter that should be turned over. **1981** I. A. Gordon in *N.Z. Listener* 14–20 Feb., The fragmented word is 'turned over' into the following line.

i***.** *U.S. Sport.* To lose possession of (the ball) to the opposing team.

1971 *Tuscaloosa* (Ala.) *News* 29 Jan. 8/5 We knew we could force Kentucky to turn the ball over and we did. **1979** *Honolulu Advertiser* 8 Jan. C-4/1 We turned over the ball and we just didn't score.

l. Of a body or part of a body or any collective whole: to replace or renew its constituent parts, to renew itself or be replaced.

1956 *Planning* XXII. 155 The entire research staff has turned over on an average about every three years as the various studies have been completed. **1971** J. Z. Young *Introd. Study Man* xii. 151 The body..has some parts that turn over very little..while others turn over so efficiently that we do not normally think of them as suffering wear. **1973** *Times* 17 Apr. 4/7 Nearly three-quarters of the men..have stayed. The other 27 per cent have 'turned over' several times.

m. Of an engine, etc.: to revolve.

1978 T. Gifford *Glendower Legacy* (1979) 281 He..heard the engine turning over;..the boat quivered.

78. turn round. b. (Examples of *fig.* phrases.)

1802 F. Burdett *Let.* 18 Aug. in H. Maxwell *Creevey Papers* (1903) I. i. 3, I have scarcely time to turn round, but will not defer sending a line in answer to your very kind letter. **1911** A. Bennett *Hilda Lessways* (ed. 2) III. ii. 226 He simply walked out of the office!..Didn't give me time to turn round. **1969** *Listener* 14 Aug. 217/2 Before my parents could turn round and ask what I was going to do for a living, I went back and announced I'd already got a job as a ship's musician.

c. (Earlier example with *on.*)

1846 Dickens *Dombey & Son* (1848) v. 38 You're a good little thing..; and yet you turn round on me, because there's nobody else.

g. In *pa. pple.* Confused, disorientated. *U.S. dial.*

1877 R. I. Dodge *Plains Great West* 46 To me, Detroit is always in Canada, and New Orleans always on the right bank of the Mississippi, because I happened to be 'turned round' when I first arrived in those cities.

h. To prepare (a ship, aircraft, etc.) for its return journey. Cf. *TURN-ROUND 1.

1942 *R.A.F. Jrnl.* 16 May 13 Cleanliness also shortens the time it takes to turn a ship round. **1972** *Nature* 21 Apr. 363/1 Is there..a chance that supersonic aircraft can be turned round at international airports with the speed that will be necessary if operators are to make..the fullest use of their capital investment?

i. = sense 29 c above.

1966 *New Statesman* 6 May 657/2 SOE's intrigues included..'turning round' captured agents. **1974** 'J. le Carré' *Tinker, Tailor* xxi. 180 All right. The Russians have turned Tarr round... What sort of plant can he be when we don't believe a word he says?

80. turn up. d. Also, to shorten (a garment or part of one) by increasing the width of the hem or by making a hem; to increase the width of (a hem).

1918 E. & M. Wallbank *Dress-Cutting & Making* xiv. 89 To turn up the skirt to the required length, a skirt gauge..may be used. *Ibid.* xxi. 126 Turn up the hem, fell down the pleats. **1958** M. Johnson *Sewing the Easy Way* (1960) 127 Turn up the hem, matching seam upon seam. **1976** J. Tate tr. *Bodelsen's Operation Cobra* xi. 54 Margrethe had borrowed a skirt from her mother and was busy turning it up. **1979** R. Rendell *Make Death love Me* iii. 29 Pam turned up the hem of an evening skirt.

g. *to turn up trumps*: see TRUMP *sb.*² 2.

k. (*fig.* examples.)

1932 S. Gibbons *Cold Comfort Farm* xii. 178 Turns you up, don't it, seein' ter-day's dinner come in 'anging round someone's neck? **1968** M. WOODHOUSE *Rock Baby* i. 11 You don't like the rules. Well, well, Giles. Do you know, sometimes you science boys turn me up.

m. Also, to raise the temperature of (an electrical appliance, heating system, etc., and *transf.*, that which it heats or cooks), orig. by turning a knob or switch; to increase the volume of sound from (a radio, record-player, etc.), usu. by turning a knob or switch; to turn (a knob or switch) in order to increase the temperature, volume of sound, etc. Cf. sense 71 g above.

1941 [see sense 71 g above]. **1962** A. NISBETT *Technique Sound Studio* 259 The volume can be turned up louder. **1967** 'E. LINDALL' *Time too Soon* v. 57 Put on your hi-fi... Just turn it up a bit more. **1971** M. LEE *Dying for Fun* ix. 53 The producer of the radio magazine programme turned up his loudspeaker. **1976** W. CORLETT *Dark Side of Moon* II. 85 It *is* colder... I must turn up the central heating. **1978** *Sci. Amer.* Apr. 67/1 The microscope [operating] is then turned up to high magnification (25 or 40 diameters).

p. Also *imp.* with *it*, stop it!

1945 J. B. PRIESTLEY *Three Men in New Suits* i. 6 Turn it up, will you... You're arguing with yourself. **1948** M. ALLINGHAM *More Work for Undertaker* (1949) x. 127 Turn it up... Keep it for your reminiscences. **1961** J. B. PRIESTLEY *Saturn over Water* xvii. 240 'Are you sure you can trust her?' 'Yes, Joe. So turn it up.'

r. (Earlier example.)

1782 in *Ann. Reg. 1783* (1785) 122/2 The main-sail a-back; all hands turned up; the main-clue garnets manned.

r*. To draw up with a winch or the like.

1911 D. H. LAWRENCE *Prussian Officer* (1914) 282 The winding-engine rapped out its little spasms. The miners were being turned up. **1929** —— *Pansies* 82 My father was a working man And a collier was he, At six in the morning they turned him down And they turned him up for tea.

s. Also *fig.*

1974 *Nature* 22 Feb. 514/2 Lillie presented preliminary evidence that the zodiacal light spectrum turns up below 2,500 Å. **1977** *Evening Post* (Nottingham) 27 Jan. 4/5 The rate of inflation has turned up again and we must expect to see some further deterioration in the next few months.

v. Also, to arrive or present oneself (with no connotation of unexpectedness or casualness); freq. *neg.*, to fail to arrive when expected. *colloq.*

1903 SOMERVILLE & 'ROSS' *All on Irish Shore* i. 18 And if you'll believe me, the two chaps there had never turned up at all. **1939** G. B. SHAW *Geneva* III. 52 The judge himself hasnt turned up. **1977** *Arab Times* 14 Dec. 2/5 Let women everywhere from this day on encourage men to have the courage not to turn up for war. **1979** J. COOPER *Class* iv. 84 At prep schools they insist you turn up [at sports days] and then ignore you. **1981** R. HAYMAN *K* iv. 38 They..turned up in large numbers to the general meetings.

turn-. Add: **turn-and-bank, turn-and-slip** *Aeronaut.*, used *attrib.* and *absol.* to designate an indicator which shows the pilot his rate of turn and correctness or error in banking; **turn-furrow** (earlier example); **turn indicator,** (*a*) *Aeronaut.* (see quot. 1930); (*b*) = *INDICATOR 3 g; **turn-plough** (examples); **turn-row** (earlier example); **turn-screw** (earlier example); **turn signal** *U.S.* = *INDICATOR 3 g; **turn-turtle** *a.* (*nonce-wd.*), in which one turns turtle and dies.

1933 *Jrnl. R. Aeronaut. Soc.* XXXVII. 930 If operating in daylight, they must have a complete set of instruments including duplicate turn and bank indicators, compass, air speed indicator, [etc.]. **1981** *Pilot* Jan. 45/1 A Motorola low-frequency transceiver with..altimeter, turn-and-bank and a clock. **1955** LIPTROT & WOODS *Rotorcraft* iii. 25 Further instruments include..turn-and-slip indicator. **1978** A. WELCH *Bk. of Airsports* ii. 36/2 The instruments used to cope with cloud flying are either a turn-and-slip indicator or an artificial horizon, or both. **1810** in Thirsk & Imray *Suffolk Farming 19th Cent.* (1958) ii. 77 Various sorts of mould boards, turn furrows or breast plates. **1919** *Nature* CIV. 183/2 A trustworthy turn-indicator and improved compass made accurate navigation through clouds possible. **1930** P. M. HENSHAW *Air Questions & Answers* 180 A Turn Indicator is an instrument that warns a pilot when the machine is turning right or left in circumstances (at night or in a cloud) when he would not be aware of it. **1953** C. A. LINDBERGH *Spirit of St. Louis* II. vi. 303, I glance at the turn indicator, kicking rudder slightly as I do so. The needle jumps over to the side. Yes, it's working properly. **1959** *Motor Manual* (ed. 36) vi. 183 Flashing turn indicators are operated either by a switch..mounted on the steering column, or by an independent switch mounted within easy reach of the driver. **1970** *Motoring Which?* July 88/2 All had warning lights for ignition, turn indicators and headlamp main beam. **1854** G. N. JONES *Florida Plantation Rec.* (1927) 104, I think you will read about 10 turnplowes. **1907** T. F. HUNT *Forage & Fiber Crops* 352 The land having been plowed with an ordinary mold board or turn plow. **1885** 'C. E. CRADDOCK' *Prophet Gt. Smoky Mts.* 3 A young man..came to a meditative halt in the turn-row. **1778** J. WOODFORDE *Diary* 4 June (1924) I. 226 For a turn screw and picker for a gun pd 0. 1. 0. **1949** *N.Y. Times* 20 Mar. II. 19/5 Mechanical turn signals must be standard equipment on all new motor vehicles sold in Minnesota after July 1. **1977** J. WAMBAUGH *Black Marble* (1978) vi. 79 He started the Plymouth, flicked on his turn signal,..then pulled into traffic. **1951** DYLAN THOMAS in *World Rev.* Oct. 66 Dolphins dive in their turnturtle dust.

turnable, *a.* (Later examples.)

1935 E. R. EDDISON *Mistress* xiii. 262 What's good in Lessingham is right sense..and a wit so turnable for all things alike. **1972** C. MUDIE *Motor Boats & Boating* 37 This grill in some units is turnable to direct the jet in any required direction.

turnabout. h. (Earlier example.)

1789 J. BYNG *Torrington Diaries* 1 June (1938) IV. 109 There was (today) a little Fair, and a Stall, and a Turnabout to make the children sick after their Gingerbread.

turnaround (tɜ̄·ɹnăraund). Also **turn-around.** orig. and chiefly *U.S.* [f. the verbal phr. *turn around* (*TURN *v.* 66*).] **1.** = *TURN-ROUND 1.

1936 *Sun* (Baltimore) 20 Aug. 11/6 The dirigible Hindenburg landed..at the Naval Air Station tonight for what was expected to be the quickest turn-around in transatlantic airship service. **1946** *Ibid.* 9 Apr. 17/6 Another feature of the day's market was the turn-around of two loads of 100-pound Iowa wooled lambs which brought $18.55. **1952** *Ibid.* 9 Oct. 5/4 At present the two queens have a 48-hour turnaround at Southampton. **1971** D. BAGLEY *Freedom Trap* ix. 202 The skipper was returning in the tender. It seemed as though they intended a faster turnaround than Gibraltar. **1974** T. P. WHITNEY tr. *Solzhenitsyn's Gulag Archipelago* I. II. i. 497 So that the prisoner shouldn't attempt to escape during the moment he was in the toilet, and also for a faster turnaround, the door to the toilet was not closed. **1977** *Sci. Amer.* Jan. 127/1 Ships designed to carry a unitized cargo, for ease of transshipment, quick turnaround, low damage and low longshore labor costs.

2. = *TURN-ROUND 2.

1941 *Sun* (Baltimore) 30 Dec. 15/1 Many [railroad bonds] had been depressed to the lowest level since 1938 prior to the turn-around late last week. **1961** *N.Y. World-Telegram* 15 Mar. 31/2 Yet this would mean a turn-around in the trend of residential construction. **1972** M. WILLIAMS *Inside Number 10* iv. 82 He was found an office and in the general turnaround the Private Secretary..was shifted from the study..to a large room on the first floor. **1975** *N.Y. Times* 19 May 18/4 The migration to the Arkansas countryside is part of a national turnaround in population. **1984** *Times* 13 Jan. 13/1 Associated Newspapers..yesterday disclosed a £5m turnaround from loss to profit.

3. A space for vehicles to turn round in, often at the end of a drive or cul-de-sac.

1954 C. ARMSTRONG *Better to eat You* vi. 63 He..ran across the turn-around and the parking apron. **1969** 'F. RICHARDS' *Risky Way to Kill* (1970) vi. 68 She swung the Volks in the graveled turnaround, so that it headed back the way it had come. **1975** *New Yorker* 31 Mar. 29/3 Then they..got into the truck, circled the turnaround, and drove straight off. **1984** *Ibid.* 7 May 57/3, I turned up my driveway and parked in the turnaround.

4. The action or fact of turning round; a point in a team-game at which the teams change ends to play in the opposite directions.

1959 I. & P. OPIE *Lore & Lang. Schoolch.* vii. 116, I can do the splits, I can do the turn-arounds, I can do the kicks. **1960** T. MCLEAN *Kings of Rugby* 212 Then, at the turnaround, when the Lions now had the northerly wind at their backs, the change which came over the game was remarkable. **1962** A. SHEPARD in *Into Orbit* 108, I could feel the capsule begin its slow, lazy turnaround to get into position for the rest of the flight.

5. *attrib.*

1944 *Sun* (Baltimore) 15 Aug. 12/5 The 'Big Inch' line..has done the work of 23,000 tank cars operating on an 18-day turn-around schedule. **1946** *Ibid.* 27 Dec. 6/1 Ease of maintenance and servicing will cut costs and turn-around time. **1950** *Ibid.* 14 Aug. 10/6 The harbor to be built at Lake Washington will consist of a turn-around area 1,000 feet square. **1959** *Wall St. Jrnl.* 29 July 6/3 He described the current period as a 'turn-around year' leading to higher sales and earnings next year. **1976** *National Observer* (U.S.) 17 July 7/3 There ought to be some turnaround time to get into a system different than the one that has existed for nearly 40 years.

turnaway (tɜ̄·ɹnăwēⁱ), *sb.* and *a.* Also **turn-away.** [f. the verbal phr. *turn away* (TURN *v.* 68).] **A.** *sb.* The action or an act of turning away or deviating (from a course, etc.).

1922 *Encycl. Brit.* XXXI. 666/1 The British battle fleet turned away two points to port... This was the 'turn-away' which has given rise to considerable controversy. **1976** *Nature* 27 May 278/2 The complete turn-away from crop uniformity by employing mixed varieties or multilines, which are heterogeneous for disease resistance and other characters, may be of advantage only where there is severe and continuous disease present.

B. *adj.* Of a crowd: so large that part of it has to be turned away. Also *transf.*, of business, trade, etc.

1943 *Life* 1 Nov. 76 Since the beginning of her radio show she has enlarged her audience 34%, business at the Persian room is turnaway. **1950** *Richmond* (Va.) *News-Leader* 27 Oct. 11/2 In death, as in life, Al Jolson drew a turnaway crowd. **1968** *Punch* 18 Sept. 395/2 Sunday evensong—a service that always did turn-away business. **1977** *Oxford Times* 22 July 16/5 A French restaurant..opened at the end of June, and has been enjoying a turn-away trade ever since.

turnback, *sb.* and *a.* Add: Also, an act of turning back. **A.** *sb.* (*b*) (Earlier example.) (*c*) The return of something borrowed or rented. (*d*) A reduction in price; a reversal.

1843 *Vermont Militia Act 1842* 61 Coat—dark blue, double breasted;..the skirts to reach to the bend of the knee, with buff kerseymere turnbacks. **1943** *Daily Progress* (Charlottesville, Va.) 19 Nov. 4/1 (*heading*) 13 billion dollar turnback... The War Department is returning to the Budget Bureau more than 13 billion dollars..from its 1943 appropriation. **1949** *Sun* (Baltimore) 18 Mar. 1/2 (*heading*) Second auto turnback. **1967** *Electronics* 6 Mar. 351/2 A rise in turnbacks of rented machines in recent years has Japanese computer makers uneasy. **1977** *Sunday Times Mag.* (Perth, Austral.) 16 Jan. 6/5 When the turn back came on the last three days of trading, it was the farm leaders in particular that held their gains.

turncoat, *sb.* and *a.* Add: **A.** *sb.* **c.** Also, a reversible coat.

1958 *Vogue* Oct. 163 Givenchy's barrelled and narrowing turn-coat, in pearl grey wool reversing to off-white.

turncoating *vbl. sb.* (later example).

1965 *National Observer* (U.S.) 11 Jan. 2 He told Mr. Watson he didn't 'think much of turncoating' when Mr. Watson announced for the House in 1962.

turn-down, *a.* and *sb.* Add: Also **turndown. B.** *sb.* **2. b.** *U.S.* A person who is 'turned down' or rejected, esp. as unfit for military service.

1945 *Daily Progress* (Charlottesville, Va.) 30 Jan. 4/1 The high proportion of turndowns among Negro registrants. **1977** *Sat. Rev.* (U.S.) 23 July 14/1 We've gotten a lot of turndowns, yeah; but we've gotten guys who're willing, too.

3. = *DOWN-TURN, DOWNTURN *sb.*

1957 *Economist* 26 Oct. 283 This slow-down in expansion is not the same thing as a turn-down in activity. **1960** V. PACKARD *Waste Makers* (1961) xiv. 153 How far Americans could continue running up debts..during an economic turndown was not clear. **1979** *Daily Tel.* 5 May 23/2 Shares in EMI were sent reeling yesterday after a warning by the company of likely..losses..following an unforeseen and severe turndown in its music division. **1980** *Jrnl. R. Soc. Arts* Mar. 208/2 The industry..is fearful of a turn down in the volume of work.

turned, *ppl. a.* Add: **3. b.** *U.S. colloq.* Of a person: disposed, natured. Cf. TURN *sb.* 34 a.

1931 *Amer. Speech* VII. 94 *Quar-turned*, droll-natured. **1949** H. HORNSBY *Lonesome Valley* 334 She's the best turned girl I ever talked to. She's as friendly turned as anybody! **1951** L. CRAIG *Singing Hills* 70 A nicer-turned man you never saw when he ain't in liquor. **1972** J. S. HALL *Sayings from Old Smoky* 138 Turned, etc. Having a disposition (of a certain kind)... 'She's a mild-turned girl.' She has a mild disposition.

8. *turned-around, -off, -on, -out* (earlier example).

1880 Turned-around [see TURN *v.* 66*]. **1958** T. STANWELL-FLETCHER *Clear Lands* 156 The two missionaries, each in black clerical garb and turned-around collars. **1966** T. PYNCHON *Crying of Lot 49* v. 117 She thought she saw a turned-around collar but took no chances. **1911** 'O. ONIONS' *Widdershins* iv. 35 The dripping of water from an imperfectly turned-off tap. **1972** D. E. WESTLAKE *Bank Shot* xiii. 97 [He] stared moodily at the turned-off television set. **1976** *Washington Post* 19 Apr. A3/2 Camejo hopes to capture votes of turned-off blacks and blue-collar workers. **1967** *Wall St. Jrnl.* 9 Feb. 1/4 The turned-on generation..will beat a path to your door. **1971** *Guardian* 25 May 8/1 Is it merely a difference in style between Huxley's experience and that of the turned-on teenager? **1977** E. J. TRIMMER et al. *Visual Dict. Sex* (1978) vi. 62 The most obvious change in the turned on male is erection of the penis. **1722** DEFOE *Plague* 272 Some of the Dissenting turn'd out Ministers staid, and their Courage is to be commended.

turner[1]. Add: **III. 8.** Also, a member of a *TURNVEREIN.

1854 *Calif. Chron.* 16 May 7/3 We..paid a hasty visit to Russ' Gardens, where the Turners and their compatriots had resumed the sports of the previous day. **1913** *N.Y. Times* 13 Oct. 12/4 There was a big gathering of Turners and guests at the North German Lloyd Line Pier.

Tu·rner[3] (tɜ̄·ɹnəɹ). The name of James *Turner*, eighteenth-century London colour-maker, used *attrib.* and in the possessive to designate a yellow pigment patented by him in 1781; = *mineral yellow* s.v. MINERAL *a.* 5 b.

[**1792** *Act* 32 *Geo. III.* c. 73 The yellow colour invented by the said James Turner, and which is composed of British materials only, has been found to be far superior to the foreign.] **1835** [see *Montpellier yellow* s.v. *MONTPELLIER]. **1886** H. C. STANDAGE *Artists' Man. Pigments* iv. 46 Turner Yellow, Cassel Yellow,..Mineral Yellow. **1951** R. MAYER *Artist's Handbk. Materials & Techniques* ii. 63 *Turner's yellow*, lead oxychloride... Patented by James Turner, England, 1781. **1970** R. D. HARLEY *Artists' Pigments* viii. 92 Accounts of the legal proceedings give no indication of the place where Turner's yellow was made, although, according to one authority the pigment was manufactured at..Walker-upon-Tyne where it was sold as Turner's Patent Yellow.

Turner[4] (tɜ̄·ɹnəɹ). *Med.* The name of Henry Hubert *Turner* (b. 1892) U.S. physician, used in the possessive (less commonly *attrib.*) to designate a syndrome he described in 1938 which affects females and is characterized by developmental abnormalities including an absence of ovaries, underdeveloped breasts and womb, and shortness of stature, and is usu. caused by a missing X chromosome in normally XX cells.

1942 *Amer. Jrnl. Med. Sci.* CCIV. 641 Dr. Lawson Wilkins..showed one of the authors a patient who..has both coarctation of the aorta and webbing of the neck. He called the authors' attention to 'Turner's syndrome'. **1961** *Lancet* 23 Sept. 711/2 It had taken more than 50 years from the recognition of the sex chromosome to the discovery that children with Turner's syndrome had just one X chromosome, and Klinefelter's syndrome 2Xs and a Y. **1970** [see *KLINEFELTER]. **1977** *Lancet* 19 Mar. 649/2 There have been conflicting reports about the level of amniotic-fluid α-fetoprotein (A.F.T.) when a fetus has Turner syndrome.

Turneresque, *a.* Add: (Earlier example.)

1846 LADY TREVELYAN *Let.* 7 Oct. in J. Brown *Lett.* (1912) 417 It is in his boundless prodigality of thought that Turner differs from other painters, and that the more Turneresque he was..the more full of meaning every bit of his work became.

Turnerian *a.* (earlier example); **Turnerism** (earlier example).

1851 Turnerism [see *RAPHAELITE]. **1857** GEO. ELIOT *Scenes Clerical Life* (1858) II. 87 Her cheeks..loomed through a Turnerian haze of net-work.

turn-in (tɜ̄·ɹn,in) *sb.* (*a.*) [f. the verbal phr. *turn in* (TURN *v.* 72).] **1.** An edge of material that is folded inwards, as at a seam; *spec.* in *Bookbinding* (see quot. 1952).

1873 *Young Englishwoman* Mar. 147/2 Pin the edge.. allowing an inch and a half for the turn in. **1901** [see *JOINT *sb.* 4 c]. **1931** *N. & Q.* 28 Feb. 146/1 Showing the price on the 'spine' of the jacket instead of at the foot of the front turn-in. **1933** J. E. LIBERTY *Practical Tailoring* v. 52 It should be remembered that the first turn in is not as an ordinary *turned-in* edge, the turn being on the top and not underneath. **1952** J. B. OLDHAM *English Blind-Stamped Bindings* 66 *Turn-in*, the portion of leather that shows along the edges on the inside of the covers.

2. An entrance, a way by which one may turn in, a road or passage leading off another road.

1959 *Cape Times* 7 July 9/2 What could be more pleasing than the old 'leafy lane' road..to the left of the High Constantia gateway? One wonders what this new and awkward turn-in is going to cost. *Ibid.* 26 Oct. 6/4 The accident..occurred on the Port Elizabeth–Uitenhage road at the Despatch turn-in. **1973** E. LEMARCHAND *Let or Hindrance* xiii. 157 'Look, there's a turn-in at the side of the office.'..Toye negotiated the narrow entry.

3. *attrib.* or as *adj.*

1955 J. E. LIBERTY *Practical Tailoring* (ed. 2) v. 66 Baste the silesia edge to the turn-in edge across the top, and sew it. **1973** S. JENNETT *Making of Books* (ed. 5) xii. 195 It [*sc.* the leather] must be pared thin on all turn-in edges.

turning, *vbl. sb.* Add: **6.** (Earlier example of sense 'a part of something folded over'.)

1886 *Girl's Own Paper* 25 Dec. 202/3 All paper patterns ..are of medium size... No turnings are allowed.

12. *turning off, round* (later example).

1940 *Amer. Speech* XV. 247 He allows nobody else to have anything to do with the..*tuning out* (or the *turning-off*) of the radio programs. **1973** *Black Panther* 5 May 2/1 It is hard to understand how any Oakland residents could have missed some exposure to the..campaign... But turning off can be a total thing. **1976** 'W. TREVOR' *Children of Dynmouth* iv. 84 The abrupt turning-off of the kitchen radio, and the bang of the door. **1966** M. R. D. FOOT *SOE in France* viii. 190 Among [Pierre] de Vomécourt's achievements, this successful turning round again of Mme Carré stands second only to his indispensable contribution towards getting organized resistance going at all.

13. turning circle, the smallest circle within which a ship, motor vehicle, etc., can be turned round completely; **turning-machine** (earlier example); **turning-mill** (earlier example); **turning radius,** the radius of a turning circle.

1903 KIPLING *Traffics & Discoveries* (1904) 39 The endurance, armament, turning-circle, and inner gear of every ship in the British Navy. **1928** *Motor Man.* (ed. 27) 219 *Turning circle*, the minimum diameter of circle within which a car can be turned round completely. **1959** [see *LOCK *sb.*[2] 15 b]. **1963** *Listener* 21 Feb. 339/2, I cannot myself..accept the suggestion..that Admiral Tryon confused radius and diameter of the ship's turning circle ...Diameter is so inseparable in the mind of a seaman with 'turning circle' that the phrase 'turning circle' is commonly and loosely used to mean its diameter. **1980** *Jrnl. R. Soc. Arts* July 513/2 The dimensions of a ship's turning circle vary approximately in proportion to ship's length. **1983** *Sunday Tel.* (Colour Suppl.) 20 Mar. 18 Although over three feet longer than the Golf, the Volvo's turning circle is seven inches smaller. **1849** E. CHAMBERLAIN *Indiana Gazetteer* 429 There are..one foundry and several turning and carding machines, all driven by water. **1844** *Knickerbocker* XXIV. 184 The uplifted arm of Labor.. meets his eye everywhere, in the paper-mill and grist-mill, and..turning-mill. **1967** *Jane's Surface Skimmer Systems 1967–68* 79/1 Characteristics... Turning radius at cruising speed 1,640 ft (500 m). **1973** T. PYNCHON *Gravity's Rainbow* I. 105 She's fed back who knows how many reams' worth of Most Secret flimsies.., squadron numbers, fueling stops, spin-recovery techniques and turning radii.

turning, *ppl. a.* Add: **7. turning pitch** *Cricket*, a pitch on which the ball turns or deviates on delivery; **turning plough** (earlier example).

1956 N. CARDUS *Close of Play* 31 Parkin had no superior at off-breaks on a turning pitch. **1959** *Listener* 19 Mar. 516/1 Slow and turning pitches. **1850** in J. A. Turner *Cotton Planter's Man.* (1865) 118 Many planters here say they scrape with the turning-plough as well.

turning-point. Add: **1.** (Later examples.)

1956 *Railway Mag.* Mar. 165/2 Katrane ..is the only turning point (a triangle) for engines between Amman and Ma'an. **1977** *Wandsworth Borough News* 16 Sept. 9/3 London Transport should be asked to stop using Medfield-street as a turning-point for their buses.

2. (Earlier example.)

1836 J. KEBLE *Wks. R. Hooker* I. p. li, In the annals of the Church,..we may from time to time mark out what may be called *turning points*.

turnip, *sb.* Add: **4. a.** *turnip-head* (*lit.* and *fig.* examples); *turnip-faced* (cf. sense 3 b).

1939 F. THOMPSON *Lark Rise* iii. 49 The old turnip-faced watches which descended from father to son. **1869** D. G. ROSSETTI *Let.* 1 Mar. (1965) II. 689 The turnip-head falls off the broomstick. **1931** S. KAYE-SMITH *Susan Spray* III. 281 He..saw her standing there..fooling all those turnip-heads, who wanted to be fooled. **1962** *Spectator* 2 Nov. 684 Pop..has become the divisive symbol between the turnip-heads and the giant intellects.

b. turnip greens (earlier example, in *sing.*).

1796 J. WOODFORDE *Diary* 9 Feb. (1929) IV. 262 Dinner to day, fryed Pork & Turnip Green.

turnkey. Add: **2. b.** (Earlier example.)

1855 P. T. BARNUM *Life* vi. 91 The pseudo-dentist went to work, and by dint of hammer, pincers, and 'turnkeys', he extracted the twenty teeth.

3. Used *attrib.* to designate a contract, system, etc., whereby the contractor undertakes to supply or install a complete product or service that is ready for immediate use.

1934 WEBSTER, Turn-key job. **1958** *Times* 16 Dec. 6/5 The station, which is to supply the colony's rapidly growing needs, is being built on a 'turnkey' contract by the English Electric Company, which is supplying all the electrical plant. **1964** *Times Rev. Industry* Feb. 48/2 It now has a reputation for successful completion of contracts on a 'turnkey' basis, starting from a survey of the geology of the country concerned and ending with the handing over of a complete factory with trained staff. **1966** *Economist* 5 Mar. 925/1 The so-called 'turnkey' factories, bought ready to go into production and wholly on credit. **1979** *Personal Computer World* Nov. 32 (Advt.), We offer a variety of turnkey systems. **1980** *Nature* 24 Apr. 657/2 A standard PWR reactor of the type sold by Westinghouse all over the world under turn-key contract. **1984** *Christian Science Monitor* 2 Mar. 17/1 One likely institutional change is the construction of 'turnkey' nuclear power plants.

turn-off (tɜ̄·ɹn,ǫf). Also **turnoff.** [f. the verbal phr. *turn off* (TURN *v.* 73 in Dict. and Suppl.).] **1.** A turning off a main road; a side road; a junction where a track or road branches off a main road.

1881 'R. BOLDREWOOD' *Robbery under Arms* (1888) III. xvii. 255 It's the wrong turn-off that makes a man lose his way. **1894** J. WINSOR *Cartier to Frontenac* 151 The turn off at Lake Athabasca..would have conducted him to the northern tributaries of the Columbia. **1949** F. SARGESON *I saw it in my Dream* xv. 237 The boss managed to keep the sheep nicely bunched together until he'd pushed them past the turn-off. **1955** E. BOWEN *World of Love* xi. 221 The road due soon to go on without them to Galway, for soon would be coming the Turn Off. **1977** *Times of Zambia* 7 Sept. 5/5 The premises situate at Lukashya turn-off, Mungwi Road. **1980** *Beautiful British Columbia* Summer 20 Access to Golden Ears Park is from a turnoff at Haney.

2. Disposal (of cattle) at market; the number or quantity marketed.

1960 *Times* 1 Oct. 7/7 The Territory's annual turn-off of 150,000 cattle. **1961** in *Webster* s.v. *turnoff*, Average annual turnoff of fat bullocks. **1969** *Northern Territory News* (Darwin) *Focus '69* 30/3 Last year the turn-off from the Alice Springs pastoral district was more than 20,500 head, earning more than $2,750,000.

3. The action or an instance of turning (something) off, stopping, or causing to cease functioning.

1967 *Technology Week* 23 Jan. 52/1 (Advt.), Each satellite was cycled through turn-off, cold soak, and restart during approximately 53 eclipses of the sun. **1970** *Globe & Mail* (Toronto) 25 Sept. 1/1 'It's inconvenient, but it's bearable,' she said of the electricity turnoffs. **1974** R. S. BRAY in *Ciba Symposium* No. 20. 97 Another possible mechanism for the 'turn off' of the cellular immune system is a viraemia. **1978** S. BRILL *Teamsters* iii. 104 Hicks attributed Kleindienst's unusual turnoff of the investigation to 'the love affair between Fitzsimmons and Nixon'.

4. Something that repels, disgusts, or 'turns one off' (see *TURN *v.* 73 h). *colloq.*

1975 *N.Y. Times* 1 Nov. 18/1 Patrons dined on cervelle Grenobloise. 'Sounds better in French,' said the chef... 'Brains is a turn-off.' **1976** *National Observer* (U.S.) 13 Mar. 6/6 Should it become unpleasant or prove a turn-off to either, they stop the game. **1982** *Listener* 23 & 30 Dec. 48/1 At first impression, this uneasy blend of piano quintet and violin sonata..was a gigantic, four-square turn-off.

turn-on (tɜ̄·ɹn,ǫn). [f. the verbal phr. *turn on* (TURN *v.* 74 in Dict. and Suppl.).] **1.** The action or an instance of turning something on; activation.

1962 SIMPSON & RICHARDS *Physical Princ. Junction Transistors* vii. 145 It thus produces a further delay in the turn-on of the transistor. **1967** *Technology Week* 23 Jan. 12/2 Availability of the eight new satellites in orbit, assuming proper operation after turn-on..should provide the U.S. with an estimated 95% certainty of continuous service for shorter path lengths and about 89% for longer-haul traffic. **1969** A. M. CAMPBELL *Episomes* ii. 19 Gene *Q* is not required for DNA synthesis, but is necessary for normal turn-on of late phage genes.

2. The action or an instance of turning somebody on; a drug-taker's 'trip'; something which or someone who arouses interest, enthusiasm, or sexual response. *slang.*

1969 FABIAN & BYRNE *Groupie* (1970) xxi. 138 There is enough in one bottle for two turn-ons. **1969** *Telegraph* (Brisbane) 3 June 12/2, I think I'm more of a turn-on now than I ever was when I was trying to conform to that curvy image. **1969** *Sunday Mail Mag.* (Brisbane) 22 June 11/5 Other turn-ons are music.., qualities of appearance or character.., and straight-out sex. **1975** *N.Y. Times* 1 Nov. 15/3 A museum spokesman said nearly 50,000 people visited the galleries during the first 25 days. 'It's been a real turn-on,' she said. **1978** J. KRANTZ *Scruples* iii. 81 Masturbation isn't a great big turn-on in my life. **1982** D. HOCKNEY in S. Spender *China Diary* 189 A medieval city is unstimulating to me, whereas to others it might be a great turn-on.

3. *attrib.*

1967 *Electronics* 6 Mar. 133/2 A desirable feature of this circuit is that the turn-on time of the relay is very sharp. **1972** G. S. HOLT in T. Kochman *Rappin' & Stylin' Out* 204 This 'turn-on' ability in terms of communication style.

turn-out, *sb.* (*a.*) Add: Also **turnout. 3.** *spec.* (The number of) those who turn out to vote in an election.

1970 *Guardian* 20 June 15/5 Only one of the five polls gave full weighting..to differential turnout—the question of how many Labour or Conservative supporters will in fact bother to vote. **1976** *New Yorker* 15 Nov. 204/2 Only eighty per cent of the Democratic turnout voted for Carter. **1976** *Honolulu Star-Bull.* 21 Dec. A-2/4 He called his committeemen into party headquarters on the day after elections and made them account for the turnout in their wards.

turn-over, *sb.* and *a.* Add: Also **turnover.**

A. *sb.* **1. b.** The point at which it is necessary to turn over a gramophone record; a break in play at the end of a side of a record.

1931 *Times Educ. Suppl.* 12 Dec. 1/3 With almost incredible perversity the engineers have made the turn-over not at the beginning of the Scherzo, but at the *più mosso*. **1976** *Gramophone* Apr. 1603/3 Now that DG have put the whole work on to one disc,..there is a turn-over in the 'Gretchen' movement (it comes at the beginning of the fourth bar after letter G).

3. d. *Printing.* (See quots.)

1938 L. M. HARROD *Librarians' Gloss.* 652 *Turn-over*, an extension of printed matter, beyond the space allotted. **1956** *Bookman's Conc. Dict.* 44/1 *Break line*, the last line of a paragraph not spaced full out to the measure; also known as..Turn Over. **1981** I. A. GORDON in *N.Z. Listener* 14–20 Feb., I am well aware that newspaper columns are narrow and that words must consequently be broken up into two bits, joined by a hyphen at the end of the first line. This necessity is known by printers as the 'turn-over'.

6. a. Also in extended sense, the amount or number of anything (or of persons) dealt with, processed, etc.; the throughput; *turnover tax*, a tax on the turnover of a business.

1911 G. B. SHAW *Doctor's Dilemma* Pref. p. xxvi, The sixpenny doctor, with his low prices and quick turnover of patients,..makes much more than you do. **1920** *Manch. Guardian* 28 Dec. 11/5 A turnover tax operates whether the transaction is a profit or a loss. **1938** *Sun* (Baltimore) 13 Sept. 3/1 Under the old paper-ballot system the turnover was many times faster. **1944** *Ibid.* 15 June 20/8 It is only by speeding up the rate of turnover that, with our depleted staff, we are able to deliver practically as many babies as in [a] normal period. **1973** E. OSERS tr. *Waldheim's Austrian Example* ii. 30 Economic recovery required..the application of a severe austerity programme which involved..the introduction of a turnover tax. **1976** *Howard Jrnl.* XV. I. 43 The subject-matter is the frequency of remands for medical reports.. in relation to the total turnover of magistrates' courts.

b. The simultaneous synthesis and degradation of a substance in a living organism; *turnover rate, time* (see quot. 1943).

1943 *Jrnl. Gen. Physiol.* XXVI. 326 *Turnover.*—This term refers to the process of renewal of a given substance. ..*Turnover rate*..is the amount of the substance that is turned over by that tissue per unit of time... *Turnover time*..is the time required for the appearance or disappearance of an amount of that substance equal to the amount of that substance present in the tissue. **1961** *Times* 3 Feb. 19/7 In health the myelin sheath is a stable tissue element with little or no evidence of metabolic turnover. **1967** M. E. HALE *Biol. Lichens* iv. 58 Slow rates of protein turnover might well be a characteristic of all lichens. **1977** P. B. & J. S. MEDAWAR *Life Sci.* x. 84 The turnover rate of bodily constituents varies widely from tissue to tissue. **1982** S. G. CHANEY in T. M. Devlin *Textbk. Biochem.* xxv. 1180 The turnover of body protein is a normal process.

c. The number of employees leaving a workforce and being replaced, change of staff.

1955 *Times* 7 June 7/3 The plan was also expected to reduce labour turnover since a qualifying period would be—or should be—needed to secure the guarantee. **1956** W. H. WHYTE *Organization Man* I. v. 58 Employees like it and absence and turnover are low. **1963** E. P. THOMPSON *Making of Eng. Working Class* viii. 246 The labour turnover in the early engineering workshops was prodigious; Galloway, who employed eighty or ninety men in 1824, claimed to have had between 1,000 and 1,500 men pass through his works in the previous twelve years; that is more than a total turnover of the labour force *per annum.* **1977** W. B. Eberhard in Bond & McLeod *Newslett. to Newspapers* II. 149 Postal rates soared..and personnel turnovers were unusually high.

7. *U.S. Sport.* The (unintended) loss of possession of the ball to the opposing team.

1969 *Eugene* (Oregon) *Register-Guard* 3 Dec. 1 D/3 Not often does a team commit 27 turnovers and win, but South Eugene did just that. **1975** *New Yorker* 7 Apr. 108/2 Similarly, in their other defensive ploys the Knicks' object was to harass their opponents into committing turnovers—that is, losing the ball by making wayward passes or committing technical infractions. **1979** *Tucson* (Arizona) *Citizen* 20 Sept. 11D/2 Four turnovers took the Ducks out of the contest.

B. *adj.* (Earlier and further examples.) *turn-over collar* (earlier example); **turnover article** = sense 3 c; **turnover board** *Founding*, a flat board on which a flat-bottomed pattern or half-pattern may be stood for sand to be rammed round it; **turnover cartridge,** a gramophone cartridge with a pivoted mounting for two styluses for use at different speeds.

1605 P. Erondelle *French Garden* i. sig. D 8ᵛ, Send for the shoomaker that he may haue againe these turnouer shooes, for they be too high. **1747** H. Glasse *Art of Cookery* ii. 25 Close the two Ends of your Paper as you do a Turnover Tart. **1836** Dickens *Sk. Boz* 1st Ser. I. 238 Soiled buff boots with turnover red tops. *a* **1861** T. Winthrop *Life in Open Air* (1863) 318 In jacket and turn-over collar. **1888** *Lockwood's Dict. Mech. Engin.* 391 *Turn over board*, a board used for ramming a pattern upon. **1928** W. Rawlinson *Mod. Foundry Operations & Equipment* xiii. 168 A method adopted in certain instances of repetition work..is that of a 'turnover board', also termed 'bottom board' or 'joint board'. **1944** *Penguin New Writing* XXII. 142 *Moby Dick* marks the turnover point where balance was perhaps precariously achieved. **1952** H. Herd *March of Journalism* vi. 82 The third column had a turnover article giving a retrospect of political events since the beginning of the year. **1958** *Spectator* 20 June 795/1, I was glad to see *The Times* coming out so strongly, in Monday's 'turnover' article, against recent abuses by the courts of their Contempt powers. **1958** *Practical Wireless* XXXIV. 57/2 (Advt.), Latest type lightweight crystal pick-ups with turn-over cartridge. **1962** A. Nisbett *Technique Sound Studio* 264 The pick-up head may consist of a turnover cartridge having styli for coarse and fine groove records on the two sides. **1964** S. Crawford *Basic Engin. Processes* (1969) x. 238 The flat face of the pattern is placed on a turnover board and a suitable size moulding box..is placed over it. **1978** *Rugby World* Apr. 59/2 (Advt.), Best quality stretch nylon socks in plain colours and turn-over tops.

turnpike, *sb.* Add: **I. 5. a.** Now *Hist.* exc. *U.S.* (Later examples.)

1950 *Sun* (Baltimore) 2 June 10/5 One route will be recommended for the turnpike. **1965** *New Statesman* 5 Nov. 713/1 The good, fast, safe roads are toll roads, called in New England by the old name of turnpikes. **1977** *New Yorker* 3 Oct. 43/1 Halfway up the Connecticut Turnpike, I slowed the car.

III. 9. turnpike gate, (*b*) (earlier example); **turnpike sailor** (earlier example).

1793 J. Woodforde *Diary* 21 July (1929) IV. 45 We got to Bruton Turnpike Gate. **1839** H. Brandon *Poverty, Mendicity & Crime* 165/1 Turnpike sailors.

turnpike *v.* (earlier example).

1791 J. Hiltzheimer *Diary* 17 Sept. (1893) 172, I took Mr. Francis..to view the road, from Vine Street to Vanderen's Mill, six miles, which it is proposed to turn-pike.

turn-round (tɜ̄·ɹnˌraund). [f. the verbal phr. *turn round* (Turn *v.* 78 in Dict. and Suppl.).]

1. The arrival, unloading, and preparation for the return journey of a ship, aircraft, goods vehicle, etc.; the time taken for this. Also *gen.*, the course of receiving, processing, and sending out again; progress through a system.

1913 A. Bennett *Regent* x. 291 She's going to do the quickest turn-round that any ship ever did... She'll leave at noon to-morrow. **1929** *Evening News* 18 Nov. 5/5 In these cabin ships the engines do not take up nearly as much space..nor is it necessary to provide for such a rapid turn-round at the terminal ports. **1951** *Engineering* 1 June 658/1 An exceptional amount of sickness among the key and other operative staff, resulting in a slower turn-round of wagons. **1958** *Daily Mail* 3 July 4/3 An efficiency service that is..capable of..achieving a quicker turn-round in the hospitals. **1963** *Times* 9 Feb. 9/4 The campaign for quicker 'turnround'..is being conducted jointly by the Road Haulage Association and British Road Services. **1972** L. Lamb *Picture Frame* xiv. 125 The expertness of the waiters in getting a quick turn-round of occupants at their tables. **1974** *Physics Bull.* Apr. 142/2 The total time which the material spends in the office including editing time, turn-round of proofs and any waiting time is usually not more than a month. **1976** *Southern Even. Echo* (Southampton) 12 Nov. 3/4 Heavy demands were made on her [*sc.* QE2], particularly with the short turn-rounds which were the pattern today. **1976** P. R. White *Planning for Public Transport* viii. 156 On the railways,..increases in average speed..coupled with much quicker turnround of stock, have improved utilization of rolling stock on all-year service, by about 100 per cent. **1979** *Dan-Air In-flight Mag.* Winter 15 His [*sc.* the captain's] is the responsibility for the proper turn-round of an aircraft at its outward destination.

2. The reversal of a trend, a change to an opposite direction, opinion, etc.

1963 *Times* 29 Jan. 14/5 There is a growing feeling in market quarters that..the end of the upswing is in sight and a turnround may be near. **1976** *Listener* 22 Jan. 86/4 Critics in Britain are much more often attacked these days for their indiscriminate praise of everything new than for their obscurantism. To be fair, there is some perception of this turn-round. **1981** *Times* 22 May 19/2 Associated Engineering's £12.2m turnround from first half profits of £10.5m last year to a loss of £1.7m this time shows how bad conditions are in engineering. **1984** *Daily Tel.* 1 Feb. 18/5 There was a notable turn-round in leading engineers. GKN, down to 201p at the opening, were finally a shade better at 208p.

3. *attrib.*

1920 *Glasgow Herald* 16 Aug. 8 The strike has arisen from a dispute about special payment for quick turn-round voyages. **1969** *Times* 5 Nov. 23/6 Turnround time on orders has been cut from 15 to six days. **1977** *Modern Railways* Dec. 462/1 A turnround time of about 5min would permit the running of a half-hourly service with only the barest of margins.

turnstile. Add: **b.** (Examples with sense 'resembling or shaped like a turnstile'.)

1952 D. G. Fink *Television Engin.* (ed. 2) vii. 367 Decoupling in the antenna itself is accomplished by separating the elements of the turnstile antenna..into two orthogonal groups and connecting these groups in a bridge circuit. *Ibid.* 371 The appearance of two horizontal dipoles at right angles has given rise to the descriptive term turnstile radiator. **1959** K. Henney *Radio Engin. Handbk.* (ed. 5) xx. 76 Many forms of vertical arrays have already been evolved using magnetic dipoles, turnstile elements, or current sheets. **1971** *Gloss. Electrotechnical Power Terms* (*B.S.I.*) III. vii. 16 *Turnstile aerial*, aerial consisting of one or more tiers, each tier being a combination of two horizontal dipoles arranged in the form of a right angled cross. **1978** *Nature* 5 Oct. 375/2 The VHF system consists of duplicate transponders and a four-element turnstile antenna.

turn-table. Add: Now usu. **turntable. 2.** (*e*) The rotating plate on which a gramophone record is placed to be played; the unit housing this plate.

1908 *Sears, Roebuck Catal.* 195/2 The Type FH Harvard Disc Talking Machine... The turntable, of a special composition metal, is 10 inches in diameter. **1921** P. A. Scholes *Learning to Listen by Means of Gramophone* 157 The motor should be wound up fully for each record played, in order that the turntable can rotate at its normal and even speed. **1960** *Practical Wireless* XXXVI. 421/2 Wedge the turntable so that it does not move. **1962** *Times* 5 July 15/7 The disc had been standing on the turntable for a few minutes before playing. **1979** L. Kallen *Introducing C. B. Greenfield* xiii. 166 An old armoire..held his recordings and the turntable.

turn-up, *sb.* and *a.* Add: **A.** *sb.* **2.** *spec.* The turned-up cuff of a trouser-leg.

1925 *Minister's Rep. of Fashion for Gentlemen* Feb. 8/2 Permanent turn-ups are still worn for outdoor wear. **1933** J. E. Liberty *Practical Tailoring* vi. 77 For turned-up bottoms, called permanent turn-ups, go down on the seam from the mark the width of turn-up required..and make a straight line across the bottom. *a* **1944** K. Douglas *Alamein to Zem Zem* (1946) xiii. 81 He had..beautifully cut narrow trousers of fawn cavalry twill, without turn ups. **1969** B. Malamud *Pictures of Fidelman* (U.K. ed.) i. 25 His blue gabardine suit—a one-button jacket affair, the trousers a little frayed at the turn-ups. **1972** G. Durrell *Catch me a Colobus* vii. 142 She..nosed round our legs eagerly, searching in our turn-ups to see whether she could find anything to eat.

3. a. *fig.* Also, an unexpected occurrence, a surprise. Cf. sense 3 b in Dict. and Suppl.

1942 Berrey & Van den Bark *Amer. Thes. Slang* § 178/1 *Surprise*..bob-up, springer, turn-up. **1961** R. Park *Hole in Hill* (1962) x. 79 'Well, this is a turn-up,' said Dunk in disgust. 'How do we get out?' **1972** *Jazz & Blues* Oct.26/3 What a turn-up then to find there's another version.

b. Freq. in phr. *a turn-up for the book*(*s*); also in *gen.* use (*colloq.*), an unexpected turn of fortune, a surprise.

1948 'J. Tey' *Franchise Affair* xviii. 209 Won by a length and a half on a tight rein; and was that a turn up for the book! **1951** *People* 3 June 2/2 What a Derby Day it was! And what a turn up for the books! **1959** P. Bull *I know Face* ii. 35, I reported my findings to Mr Huth, who said..perhaps I would like to write the script. Now this was quite a turn-up for the book, as very few people..are allowed to say what they write. **1968** 'C. Franklin' *Escape* viii. 104 This was indeed a turn up for the book. 'Penelope!' he exclaimed. **1978** J. Wainwright *Jury People* v. 16 A bit of a turn up for the book, isn't it? Murder, I mean. **1983** *Daily Tel.* 13 Oct. 8/7 Even..the Labour group's spokesman..could not hide his surprise... 'This is a real turnup for the books. I am quite amazed by it..,' he said.

5. The curve of the projecting lower jaw of a bull-dog.

1905 [see *lay-back 1]. **1922** R. Leighton *Compl. Bk. Dog* v. 64 It [*sc.* a type of bulldog] has certain well-defined characteristics, notably the extreme width and turn-up of underjaw. **1973** J. F. Gordon *Bulldog* (rev. ed.) iv. 53 (*caption*) Nice head and skull, good 'turn-up'.

turnverein (tɜ̄·ɹnˌvəɹain). [Ger., f. *turnen* to do gymnastic exercises + *verein* society, club.] In the United States, a gymnastic society, orig. for German immigrants, on the model of those instituted by Jahn (see Turner¹ 8). Also *attrib.*

1852 *San Francisco Herald* 1 Nov. 2/2 The Turnverein Society held another of their fetes yesterday. **1949** *Minnesota Hist.* Mar. 26 The Cincinnati Turnverein built the first Turner Hall in the United States in 1850. **1959** R. Condon *Manchurian Candidate* (1960) xxvii. 267 Petitions and documentations were submitted to the Resolutions Committee by farm lobbies, labour unions,..and national manufacturers' Turnvereins. **1974** *Encycl. Brit. Micropædia* X. 202/1 Turnvereins continue to foster citizenship and cultural programs together with health and physical-education activities, particularly gymnastics.

turpentine, *sb.* Add: **4.** *turpentine wood* (earlier example); **turpentine moth,** substitute for first part of def.: any of several leaf-roller moths of the family Tortricidæ; (example); **Turpentine State** (earlier example); **turpentine still** (examples); **turpentine weed:** also, any of several other herbs containing an aromatic sap; (earlier and later examples).

1842 T. W. Harris *Insects Injurious to Vegetation* 350 Turpentine-moths..injure pines and firs. **1850** Mayne Reid *Rifle Rangers* I. v. 46 The danger is, we may stick in the Turpentine State. **1799** *Wilmington* (N. Carolina) *Gaz.* 12 Dec. 2/1 Will be sold..at Public Sale... Two turpentine stills. **1935** Z. N. Hurston *Mules & Men* I. iv. 86 One woman had killed five [men] when I left that turpentine still where she lived. **1819** *Western Rev.* I. 95 Among the most remarkable and singular [plants of Kentucky is].. *Silphium therebinthaceum*, Turpentine weed. **1913** W. C. Barnes *Western Grazing Grounds* 236 There is a little green weed (*Gutierrezia*) known locally as snakeweed, fireweed, turpentine weed. **1931** G. H. Vansell *Nectar & Pollen Plants Calif.* 14 Turpentine weed..is also visited freely by bees for nectar. **1890** *Philadelphia Inquirer* 1 June 1/4 He would find there every interest and every occupation of the period fully depicted, from the forests of Maine to the turpentine woods of North Carolina.

turpentining, *vbl. sb.* (Examples.)

1910 C. Van Hise *Conservation Natural Resources of U.S.* iii. 229 (*heading*) Reduction of loss in turpentining. **1971** *Forest Products Jrnl.* Feb. 53/2 The Southeastern Forest Experiment Station conducted a ..study to determine the effect of turpentining on..yields of butt peeler blocks.

turps. Add: **2.** *Austral. slang.* Intoxicating liquor, esp. beer.

1945 Baker *Austral. English* 168 Australians have a fair selection of terms to describe drinking and drinking bouts, such as *a beer-up*,..and to *bash the turps*. **1962** Marshall & Drysdale *Journey among Men* 84 The Sergeant alleged that Ah Fong was a notorious drunkard, forever on the 'turps'. **1973** J. O'Grady *Survival in Doghouse* 57 He's humping a dozen cans with him. Ice cold. And he gets a great welcome. Not only because of the turps, but because with him there we can have a four-handed game.

turquoise, *sb.* (*a.*) Add: Now freq. with pronunc. (tɜ̄·ɹkwoiz). **II. 5. c.** *turquoise-coloured* (earlier example), *turquoise-gemmed, -studded* (earlier example).

1823 C. J. Mathews *Jrnl.* 13 Nov. in Dickens *Life Charles J. Mathews* (1879) I. iv. 93 The beautiful turquoise-coloured bay. **1862** G. M. Hopkins *Poems* (1967) 9 One bound o'er dripping gold a turquoise-gemm'd Circlet of astral flowerets. **1901** Kipling *Kim* xiv. 361 A fair-coloured woman with turquoise-studded headgears.

turr (tɜ̄ɹ), *sb. Newfoundland.* Also †**tuir, turrh.** [Prob. imit.] = Murre.

1794 A. Thomas *Newfoundland Jrnl.* (1968) x. 144 Here are..Penguins, Hegdowns, Muirs and Tuirs, Ice Birds.. and a number of other Sea Fowl. **1853** *Trans. Lit. & Hist. Soc. Quebec* IV. 334 Among the sea birds are *Mernettes*, Moyocks, Gulls,..Turrhs, Paraquets, Penguins, and divers others. **1960** L. M. Tuck *Murres* 34 A common vernacular name for the murre in Newfoundland is 'turr'. **1974** *Nat. Geographic* Jan. 122/2 The seabirds here called stearin, turr, and tickle-ace are the birds known elsewhere as tern, murre, and kittiwake.

turret, *sb.*¹ Add: **2. b.** Also, a similar structure on a tank, armoured car, or aircraft.

1914 E. A. Powell *Fighting in Flanders* iii. 70 The earlier armoured cars used by the Belgians..consisted of a circular turret, high enough so that only the head and shoulders of the man operating the machine-gun were exposed, covered with half-inch steel plates and mounted on an ordinary chassis. **1933** *Gloss. Aeronaut. Terms* (*B.S.I.*) IV. 27 *Turret*, a form of cockpit primarily intended for the use of a gunner. **1942** *Tee Emm* (Air Ministry) II. 140 Give yourself a few minutes each day in the training turrets so that your turret manipulation is absolutely one hundred per cent. *Ibid.* 141 For most of the trip your hands will be on the turret controls. **1969** G. Macbeth *War Quartet* 26, I stretched Across my turret, thinking. **1978** J. Irving *World according to Garp* i. 15 This ball turret was a metal sphere with a glass porthole; it was set into the fuselage of a B-17 like a distended navel—like a nipple on the bomber's belly.

4. a. (Examples.)

1898 H. S. Wilson *Pract. Tool-Maker & Designer* vi. 58 Knurling fixtures for both the slide and turret. **1963** [see *semi-automatic *sb.* 1]. **1975** Bram & Downs *Manuf. Technol.* vii. 200 The turret is then indexed to perform a number of drilling, reaming, tapping and counter-sinking operations.

b. *Cinematogr.* and *Television.* = *lens turret* s.v. *lens *sb.* 3.

1951 R. Spottiswoode *Film & its Techniques* iii. 64 On almost all cameras..the lenses are mounted in clusters of three or four on a turret, a revolving device which serves to bring the wanted lens in front of the aperture. **1960** O. Skilbeck *ABC of Film & TV* 138 *Turret*, a circular mounting of several lenses held in readiness for use on the front of a camera. **1961** G. Millerson *Telev. Production* iii. 34 The internal complexity of a zoom lens makes it bulkier than a turret assembly. **1965** J. Von Sternberg *Fun in Chinese Laundry* (1966) vii. 184 We illuminated every possible retreat he might find, and more cameras, turrets, and various lenses were employed. **1976** A. Davis *Television* 27 The turret camera with a revolving disc offering the choice of several lenses of different focal lengths, and the single zoom lens of variable focal length ..were still to come.

5. (sense 1) *turret-room* (earlier example); (senses 2 and 4 b) *turret-mounted* adj.; (sense 4 b) *turret-mounting*; **turret-lathe** (examples); **turret-light**, a light on top of a police car, ambulance, etc., which flashes to signal an emergency.

1898 H. S. Wilson *Pract. Tool-Maker & Designer* vi. 58 The variety of work that may be executed on a screw machine or turret lathe. **1939** *Daily Tel.* 18 Dec. 12/3 (Advt.), Experience should include the setting up and tooling of automatic and turret lathes. **1975** Bram & Downs *Manuf. Technol.* v. 129 The vertical turret-lathe is a chucking machine only. **1972** 'G. North' *Sergeant Cluff rings True* i. 14 A small van..carried a turret-light on its roof and had, 'Police,' lettered on its sidepanels. **1961** *Observer* 21 May 5/1 (Advt.), Twin lenses, standard and telephoto, turret mounted to whisk you smoothly from close-up to long shot. **1963** *Times Lit. Suppl.* 31 May 394/5 The loss of the Captain..marked the end of the attempt to combine a full set of sails with steam propulsion and turret-mounted guns. **1923** F. A. Talbot *Moving Pictures* 86 Behind this turret-plate is a second and fixed disk or 'turret-mounting' of identical diameter, but having only two openings, corresponding to the photographing and focussing apertures respectively. **1966** 'A. Hall' *9th Directive* ix. 83, I set it [*sc.* a camera] up on a tripod with a turret-mounting that was rigid enough for the weight. **1803** *Lett. Miss Riversdale* III. 368, I have been removed from the turret room I occupied, to a bed room on the ground floor.

turrible, turble, dial. (chiefly U.S.) varr. Terrible *a.*, esp. in sense 3.

1893 H. A. Shands *Some Peculiarities of Speech in Mississippi* 65 *Turrible*... A pronunciation of *terrible* very common among the illiterate, and sometimes heard in the conversation of the educated. **1897** Kipling *Captains Courageous* vii. 148 Jason was tur'ble praoud of his boy. **1903** K. D. Wiggin *Rebecca of Sunnybrook Farm* xxviii. 305 It's a turrible risk splittin' up families. **1912** J. Masefield *Everlasting Mercy* 20 You must be turble strong. **1929** H. W. Odum in A. Dundes *Mother Wit* (1973) 183 Had some turrible times in France. **1966** J. Aiken *Trouble with Product X* vii. 123 'Tis a long pull up from the village and turble weather. **1971** *Black World* Apr. 67 You musta done somethin turble to aggravate me like that.

turriform, *a.* For *rare*$^{-1}$ read *rare* and add further examples.

1959 E. A. Fisher *Anglo-Saxon Archit. & Sculpture* 57 Turriform churches. These were not uncommon and are so-called as they were built in the form of towers. **1970** H. Braun *Parish Churches* iii. 33 The structural nucleus of every Byzantine church is a central turriform structure with four..arches rising from four tall and massive piers.

‖ **turron** (turō·n). Pl. **turrones, turrons.** [Sp. *turrón*.] A Spanish sweetmeat resembling nougat, made from almonds and honey; a piece of this.

1918 *Chambers's Jrnl.* Jan. 33 The best hams of Montanchez, the finest turron from Jijona. **1950** E. David *Bk. Mediterranean Food* 153 In the winter there are..the sugar-plums of Nice; Spanish nougats and *turrons*; *pralines* from Aix-en-Provence. **1976** E. P. Benson *Bulls of Ronda* xvi. 100 Their desserts were to his taste... 'You can bring me some *turrones*.' He selected two of the creamiest.

turtle, *sb.*[1] Add: **1. c.** *Rhyming slang.* = *turtle-dove 3. (Usu. in *pl.*)

1893 P. H. Emerson *Signor Lippo* xiv. 55 A long sleeve cadi on his napper, and a pair of turtles on his martins finished him. **1936** 'J. Curtis' *Gilt Kid* 24 Got any turtles? The Gilt Kid, having no gloves, answered: 'No, but I'll buy a pair.' **1962** *John o' London's* 25 Jan. 82/1 Of course he [*sc.* the criminal] takes the precaution of wearing *turtles* (short for *turtle-doves*, rhyming slang for gloves).

turtle, *sb.*[2] Add: **2. b.** (Earlier examples of *to turn the turtle*.) (See also quot. 1818.)

1818 'A. Burton' *Johnny Newcome* II. 69 John..in the next week..would take Twice calling, to be once awake; They turned the turtle, cut him down. *Ibid.* 254 *Turn the turtle*, to get under a hammock, and lift it up in the middle, thus pitching the sleeper out on one side of it. **1830** *United Service Jrnl.* June 709 The chance on some equally squally night of 'turning the turtle', as Jack facetiously calls upsetting.

5. turtleburger, a kind of hamburger made from turtle; **turtle-deck**: (*a*) also applied to a similar structure on an aircraft; (*b*) = *turtle-back 1 b; **turtle-frolic** (earlier example).

1946 *Amer. Speech* XXI. 67/1 While in Florida Keys in the service in the Spring of 1940 I came across a road stand selling turtleburgers. **1979** *Daily Tel.* 29 Nov. 18 It must be admitted that the meat can be tasteless and fibrous, but its strength is its versatility: 'turtleburgers', for example, are delicious. [**1912** *Flight* 26 Oct. 966/2 The fabric is..stretched over light formers above the girder so as to provide a kind of turtle-back deck.] **1913** *Flight* 31 May 586/2 The comfort of the pilot has been carefully studied and he is well sheltered behind an aluminium turtle deck. **1937** *Jrnl. R. Aeronaut. Soc.* XLI. 7 It was customary for the pilot to carry the parachute in the cockpit with the cable laid along the turtle deck and fastened securely with adhesive tape. **1954** *Amer. Speech* XXIX. 103 *Turtledeck*, the trunk or turtleback of a roadster. **1967** A. Shennan *Sopwith Snipe Described* 17 To this basic structure was affixed a turtledeck structure of plywood formers and stringers. **1750** F. Goelet *Jrnl.* 2 Oct. in *New-England Hist. & Geneal. Reg.* (1870) XXIV. 53 Had an Invitation to day to Go to a Turtle Frolick.

turtle, *v.*[2] Add: **2.** (Examples.)

1838 in G. C. Anderson *Laws of Bahamas* (1843) 119 If any person..be found turtling, or fishing, against the provisions of this Act. **1952** E. Hemingway *Old Man & Sea* 15 He never went turtle-ing. That is what kills the eyes.

3. Also *intr.*

1920 [see *careen *v.* 4 b].

4. b. *intr.* To act in a manner characteristic of a turtle (perh. *spec.* to bridle or show indignation). Also with *up*. ? *nonce-wd.*

1914 D. H. Lawrence *Widowing of Mrs. Holroyd* I. ii. 28 *Clara*: Turning-out time, Laura. *Laura* (*turtling*): I'm sorry, I'm sure. **1920** —— *Lost Girl* v. 64 It was most curious to see Miss Pinnegar turtle up at the mention of this scheme... She blurted, bridling and ducking her head..like an indignant turkey.

turtle-back. Add: **1. b.** A rounded projecting boot on a motor vehicle; the lid of this. *N. Amer.*

1941 'A. A. Fair' *Double or Quits* iii. 33 He raised up the turtleback in the car. **1971** D. Conover *One Man's Island* 23 The right fender fell off and rolled into a ditch. I stuck it disgustedly in the turtleback and in the village asked Lloyd at the garage to put it back on.

3. (Earlier example.)

1898 G. B. Shaw *Let.* 18 Oct. (1972) II. 68 They all.. betrayed gross ignorance on the points they were most cocksure about, such as riding on turtleback and the like follies.

3*. A land form likened to the shell of a turtle.

1913 *Geogr. Jrnl.* XLII. 149 Thick forests..alternate with tall grassland and bare and rocky turtlebacks. **1928** *Amer. Speech* IV. 126 'Hog-back' and 'turtle-back' are common names for hills or ridges suggesting those forms. **1938** *Bull. Geol. Soc. Amer.* XLIX. 1875 Three turtleback areas have been recognized in the Black Mountains [of Death Valley, California]. They prove to be structural as well as topographic features.

turtle-dove. Add: **3.** *Rhyming slang.* A glove. (Usu. in *pl.*) Cf. *turtle *sb.*[1] 1 c.

1857 'Ducange Anglicus' *Vulgar Tongue* 23 *Turtle doves*, ..gloves. **1935** A. J. Pollock *Underworld Speaks* 127/1 *Turtle doves*, a pair of gloves. **1959** I. & P. Opie *Lore & Lang. Schoolch.* xiv. 320 'Turtle doves' for gloves, and so on, normally associated with cockneys, is neither confined to the metropolis, nor to the shift-for-a-living class. **1972** *Lebende Sprachen* XVII. 8/4 *Turtle dove*, glove.

Hence as *v. trans.*, ?to show affection for (another), like a turtle-dove for its mate. *nonce-use.*

1922 Joyce *Ulysses* 196 Take her for me... Jove, a cool ruttime send them. Yea, turtledove her.

tu·rtle-neck, *sb.* (and *a.*) orig. *U.S.* [Turtle *sb.*[2]] **1. a.** A close-fitting roll or band collar, now usu. one intermediate in height between a crew-neck and a polo-neck; formerly also = *polo-neck* (*a*) s.v. *polo[1] 3. **b.** A shirt or jersey with such a collar.

1897 *Sears, Roebuck Catal.* 217/3 Turtle Neck Sweater. Extra heavy knit, all wool, turtle neck. **1939** M. B. Picken *Lang. Fashion* 102/3 (*caption*) Turtle Neck. **1957** *New Yorker* 5 Oct. 112/2 The roll at the round neck suggests a turtleneck, and little inverted tucks do nice things for the bosom. **1960** *Daily Express* 30 Aug. 5/3 Back buttoning turtle necks of matching fabric. **1970** E. Tidyman *Shaft* xiii. 170 Tall, young men in..turtlenecks, leatherjackets. **1977** *New Yorker* 3 Oct. 40/2 Dr. Sayles.. asks me to take off my shirt, a turtleneck. **1982** J. Gardner *For Special Services* xvi. 174 Bond, clad now in dark slacks, a black turtle-neck and short jacket.

2. *attrib.* or as *adj.*, esp. as *turtle-neck sweater*.

1895 *Montgomery Ward Catal.* Spring & Summer 483/1 The Turtle Neck Shirt or Sweater, double from waist up, one of the most desirable garments ever invented for cold-weather shooting. **1896** F. D. Roosevelt *Let.* 14 Oct. (1947) 47, I should very much like a red turtle neck sweater for skating and coasting. **1905** *Outing* Mar. 743/1 Shape the coat like a turtle-neck sweater. **1926** *Daily Colonist* (Victoria, B.C.) 7 Jan. 18/4 (Advt.), Balbriggan Turtle-Neck Pull-Overs of fine quality, finished with ribbed band at the waist. **1938** J. Steinbeck *Long Valley* 95 The younger wore a blue turtle-neck sweater. **1946** Wodehouse *Joy in Morning* vi. 42 He dresses like a tramp-cyclist, affecting turtle-neck sweaters and grey flannel bags. **1952** M. McCarthy *Groves of Academe* (1953) xiii. 266 He..signalled to a tall blonde girl in a tight turtle-neck sweater. **1964** *McCall's Sewing* xi. 182/2 Turtle-neck collar. A wide true bias band that stands up from the neck edge and then rolls back over the neckline seam. **1978** G. Greene *Human Factor* II. i. 53 She wore brown trousers and a turtle-neck sweater.

Hence **tu·rtle-necked** *a.*

1931 G. S. Chappell *Gardener's Friend* 7 When long-haired athletes in turtle-necked sweaters were the idols of the hour. **1954** *Encounter* Feb. 47/1 Long-haired men in turtle-necked sweaters marched into the room. **1978** J. Wainwright *Jury People* iii. 13 He wore a cheap wind-cheater over a turtle-necked sweater.

Tuscan, *a.* and *sb.* Add: **A.** *adj.* **d.** Also *Tuscan grass, hat.* (Earlier examples.)

1830 in A. Adburgham *Shops & Shopping* (1964) iv. 38 Chip and Tuscan Hats. **1833** in *Ibid.* 40 A new bonnet, composed of Tuscan Grass and prepared whalebone.

B. *sb.* **b.** (Later examples.)

1857 J. F. Maguire *Rome* xxi. 245 Tuscans only, or their descendants to the third generation, are received into the society. **1901** M. Carmichael *In Tuscany* i. 9 Certainly the Tuscan has some real love of the English-man.

d. The golden-yellow colour of Tuscan straw.

1887 [see sense d of *adj.* in Dict.]. **1912** *T. Eaton & Co. Catal.* Spring & Summer 3/3 Draped Toque..Colors Black, Navy or Tuscan, with corded silk in colors to harmonize. **1923** *Daily Mail* 16 Apr. 1 Colours:..Old Gold, Tuscan, Mastic.

C. *Comb.* **Tuscan lamb**, a variety of processed lambskin, used mainly to make head-wear.

1956, 1962 [see *Lucca]. **1970** *Guardian* 24 Nov. 9/4 A Tuscan Lamb Hat (in black or white) complete with ear muffs.

Tuscarora (tɒskărǭ·ră). [Iroquois, = hemp-gatherer.] An Iroquoian tribe, originally inhabiting Carolina, which, after moving to upper New York State, joined the Iroquois Confederacy of North American Indians, commonly called the Five Nations (thereafter Six Nations), in 1722; a member of this tribe; their language. Also *attrib.*

1650 E. Bland *Jrnl.* 28 Aug. in *Discovery New Britaine* (1651) 3 An Englishman, a Cockarous hard by Captaine Floods, gave this Indian Bells..to lay downe to the Tuskarood King. **1713** in *N. Carolina Colonial Rec.* (1886) II. 2 An order from ye Government of New Yorke to Caution ye Tuscaroras against going to warr with ye English here. **1785** T. Jefferson *Notes Virginia* 390 The Monacans or Tuscaroras..were taken into the confederacy.., making the sixth [nation]. **1878** *Jrnl. R. Soc. Arts* 10 May 537/2 He wants one of my improved phonographs to preserve the accents of the..Tuscaroras, who are dying out. **1910** F. W. Hodge et al. *Handbk. Amer. Indians N. of Mexico* II. 842 The Tuscarora..possessed in early times the 'country lying between the sea shores and the mountains, which divide the Atlantic States'. **1915** J. Buchan *Salute to Adventurers* ix. 137 All this land ..is Sioux country... But cheek by jowl is a long strip held by the Tuscaroras. **1933** L. Bloomfield *Language* iv. 72 The Iroquoian family was spoken in a district surrounded by Algonquian; it includes..the languages of the Iroquois type (Mohawk, Oneida,..Tuscarora). **1976** W. L. Chafe in T. A. Sebeok *Native Languages of Americas* I. 532 The Northern Iroquoian languages which are still spoken are six in number. They include the very closely related languages of the original Five Nations of the Iroquois..plus Tuscarora, now the Sixth Nation, a language somewhat more divergent. **1979** *United States 1980/81* (Penguin Travel Guides) 654 The Tuscarora Indian Reservation is nearby.

tusche (tu·ʃə). orig. *U.S.* Also **tushe.** [Ger., back-formation from *tuschen*, f. F. *toucher* to touch.] A greasy black liquid composition used in lithography and other printing techniques; lithographic drawing ink. Also *attrib.*

1885 *Lithographer & Printer* 24 Jan. 114/1 By the term autography we designate..everything that is written with lithographic tushe on transfer paper in order to enable it to be transferred to the lithographic stone. We use the word 'tushe', for though specially coined, it has been adopted by the entire craft of lithographers in this country. **1912** W. C. Brown *Practical Textbk. Lithography* iii. 26 The most useful of all inks for writing or drawing on stone come under the name tusche. **1940** R. Mayer *Artist's Hand-bk.* xii. 440 Lithographic crayons and tusche are always black, regardless of the color in which the final proof is to be printed. *Ibid.* 460 (*heading*) Tusche-wash-out method. **1965** Zigrosser & Gaehde *Guide Coll. Orig. Prints* iv. 49 The crayons used [in lithography]—and their liquid equivalent, tusche or lithographic ink—are made of a mixture of grease, wax, soap, and lampblack... Many technical manipulations are possible:..tusche effects with pen, brush, drybrush or spatterwork, [etc.]. **1967** V. Strauss *Printing Industry* v. 274/2 If lithographic tusche is used as a painting medium [in serigraphy], glue can serve as blocking medium as it will be repelled by the fatty lithographic tusche which is, of course, water-repellent.

tush (tuʃ), *sb.*[4] *slang* (chiefly *N. Amer.*). Also **tushie, -y.** [Abbrev. or dim. of *tochus.] = Backside 3.

1962 *Amer. Speech* XXXVII. 205 Another bilingual children's diminutive, *tushie*—from Yiddish *toches* or *tuches* 'rump'—has appeared in phrases like *tushie slide* 'a slide down a slope on one's bottom', the delights of which a group of Midwestern Jewish children have, I am told, expressed to their Gentile social workers. **1969** P. Roth *Portnoy's Complaint* 47 You'd think I was a twenty-one-year-old girl; you'd think I hadn't wiped your backside and kissed your little tushy for you all those years. **1970** *Pix* (Austral.) 26 Dec. 11/4 Pretty young girls who walk around with..their tushes out there asking for it. **1973** *N.Y. Times* 10 June II. 1/3, I felt a fork hanging from the seat of my pants. I threw it off, just like Stanley would, and the audience went wild. I mean, there were 1,100 people there, looking at me with a fork up my tush! **1977** *Detroit Free Press* 11 Dec. 23-A/1 Eight hundred guests danced their tushies off on the world's largest discotheque floor. **1981** G. V. Higgins *Rat on Fire* xxviii. 170 Her tush is tight and she's got great boobs. **1984** *Miami* (Florida) *Herald* 6 Apr. 4B/6 (*caption*) So what's a damp tush between good friends?

tush (tuʃ, tʊʃ), *v.*² orig. *dial.* [Origin unknown.] *trans.* To pull or drag (a heavy object, esp. a log) along the ground.

1841 C. H. Hartshorne *Salopia Antiqua* 602 *Tush*,.. to draw a heavy weight, as *tushing* timber. **1879** G. F. Jackson *Shropshire Word-bk.* 458 'Can yo' carry them faggits to the 'ŏŏd-pil?' 'I dunna know, but if I canna carry 'em, be'appen I can *tush* 'em alung.' **1953** H. L. Edlin *Forester's Handbk.* xv. 238 Felled logs are *tushed*, or drawn over the ground, butt-end foremost, by hauling chains attached to a tractor, a horse-team or a winch, until the nearest hard road is reached. **1963** *Times* 12 Feb. 12/7 Dolgelly's eight oak pillars had originally been snaked or tushed by oxen 10 miles over the mountains from Dinas Mawddwy, where they had been grown.

tushery. Add: Now usu. *gen.*, sentimental or romanticizing writing.

1921 H. S. Walpole *Young Enchanted* I. ii. 42 In literature her great period had been during the Romantic Tushery of 1895 to 1905. **1932** *Times Lit. Suppl.* 21 Apr. 292/4 Unlike many novelists who set their scene in Japan, Mr. John Paris indulges in no sentimental tushery about the Japanese. **1967** *Guardian* 16 May 7/5 What a wonderful vanished world of tushery is brought back by 'The Desert Song'. **1981** *Times* 14 Oct. 13/4 The *Idylls* wound their endless way... Such Arthurian tushery seems far removed from..*In Memoriam*.

tusk, *sb.*³ Now the usual spelling of Torsk. (Later examples.)

1925 J. T. Jenkins *Fishes Brit. Isles* 164 The Torsk or Tusk..is moderately elongate and covered with very small scales. **1926** *Glasgow Herald* 19 Oct. 3 The inhabitants fit out boats for the..tusk fishing. **1935** *Fisheries Notice* (Min. Agric. & Fisheries) XXIII. 6 Suggested Trade Name. Tusk. **1977** *Grimsby Even. Tel.* 26 May 18/5 Principal sorts were..monk 28, tusk 20.

tussie-mussie: see Tuzzy-muzzy in Dict. and Suppl.

tussock, *sb.* Add: **5. tussock land** *Austral.* and *N.Z.*, uncultivated grassland used for sheep-grazing.

1881 W. Bateman *Colonists* x. 186 The tussock land abounds in the Middle Island..Prior to breaking up the tussock land the native grass is first burnt. **1928** 'Brent of Bin Bin' *Up Country* ii. 17 The journey started across tussock land alive with purling streams. **1941** Baker *N.Z. Slang* v. 41 The tussock lands are a peculiar feature of this country.

tussock-grass. Add: **1.** (*c*) (Earlier example.) Freq. in *Comb.*, as *tussock-grassland*.

1848 J. White *Jrnl.* 13 Mar. 266 (MS.), The top [of the house] is of the nikau leaf and tussock grass. **1867** J. T. Thomson *Rambles with Philosopher* v. 25 The natural tussock-grass lands..stretched beyond the narrow precincts of incipient colonization. **1959** A. H. McLintock *Descr. Atlas N.Z.* p. xiv, Some pockets of beech forest still survive..along with a depleted tussock grassland

tut, *v.* Add: **2.** *trans.* To express disapproval of by the exclamation 'tut'; to say disapprovingly.

1972 *Times* 10 Nov. 7/2 He [*sc.* President Nixon] felt sure some of his ideas would be 'tut-tutted' by 'the Georgetown cocktail set'. **1975** *Nature* 3 Jan. 1/2 The authors never address the problem, instead tut-tutting that university geology courses are unsuited to the demands of petroleum geology. **1984** A. Carter *Nights at Circus* III. vii. 239 But when he embarrassedly confessed there'd been no bang nor damage because the dynamite was damp, I'd 'tut-tutted' his inefficiency.

Hence **tu·tting** *vbl. sb.* and *ppl. a.*

1929 J. B. Priestley *Good Companions* I. i. 25 Ted.. was shaking his head and..making a loud tut-tutting noise. **1947** *Manch. Guardian Weekly* 30 Oct. 8/3 Great and glossy cars rolled up in smooth procession. Into this a taxi-cab had strayed, to be hurriedly diverted with much tutt-tutting by police officers into the unimportant wastes of Millbank. **1962** *John o' London's* 19 Apr. 386/2, I simply could not see what all the tutting was about. **1976** T. Heald *Let Sleeping Dogs Die* ix. 183 She sucked her teeth and made little tutting noises. **1984** *Times* 11 June 6/6 There was much tut-tutting and an agreement that something should be done.

tute (tiūt). Colloq. abbrev. of Tutor *sb.* and *v.* or *tutorial *sb.*

1895 W. C. Gore in *Inlander* Nov. 65 *Tute*, tutor. **1934** Webster, *Tute*, v.t. & i. **1942** Berrey & Van den Bark *Amer. Thes. Slang* § 197/9 *Tute*, tutor, to give private instruction. **1955** J. I. M. Stewart *Guardians* III. ii. 217 Jones is my tutor, and this happened at my first tute this term. **1957** D. Balsdon *Oxford Life* 169 But the College tutor's public lecture is an interruption in a week otherwise devoted to teaching pupils in his rooms, listening to their essays and talking about them. These are 'private hours'—'tutes', as undergraduates call them, or tutorials. **1982** T. Heald *Masterstroke* iii. 64 We did political theory tutes together.

tutee (tiutī·). orig. *U.S.* [f. Tut(or *v.* + -ee¹.] A university student (in relation to his tutor); a pupil of a private tutor.

1927 *Amer. Speech* II. 214/1 *Tutee*, English 'pupil'. I met this queer coinage in two academic publications. **1937** *Life* 7 June 58/2 Wolff at work is a two-hour torrent of words covering the high spots of a whole college course. Tutees take hasty notes, try to remember what he says overnight. **1952** M. McCarthy *Groves of Academe* (1953) i. 6 He was feeling more than half tempted to take the letter over to the main hall and post it on the faculty bulletin board, before the arrival of the eleven-o'clock tutee. **1975** D. Lodge *Changing Places* i. 19 His girl tutees suddenly began to dress like prostitutes.

tutor, *sb.* Add: **4. a.** Also used in other British universities and other further education establishments. Also, in Cambridge and some other universities and colleges, a member of the teaching staff assigned responsibility for the general well-being of a student (cf. *moral tutor* s.v. *moral *a.* 3 d).

1933 *Times Lit. Suppl.* 14 Dec. 889/3 He [*sc.* Sir John Sandys] was for long Senior Tutor of his college, a different thing in Cambridge from Oxford. **1980** L. P. Wilkinson *Century of King's* p. xiv, *Tutor*, a Fellow responsible for a student's general welfare. Every student has one.

6. (Later examples.) Now chiefly applied to books of instruction in playing a musical instrument.

1918–19 *T. Eaton & Co. Catal.* Fall & Winter 383/6 Bellak Piano Tutor..one of the best tutors in use. **1956** F. Reidy in S. Traill *Play that Music* 108 Any tutor I have ever read says that the tip of the reed should be struck with the tip of the tongue. **1981** Ld. Harewood *Tongs & Bones* iii. 60, I wanted to learn the clarinet... A beautiful Boehm arrived together with an English 'tutor'.

tutor, *v.* Add: **5.** *intr.* To study under a tutor. *U.S.*

1900 C. C. Munn *Uncle Terry* 55, I tutored some, read law, and was admitted to the bar. **1920** [see *flunk *v.* 1b].

tutordom. (Further example.)

1957 G. Avery *Warden's Niece* xi. 214 There will be a storm to-night, a very suitable end to my tutordom.

tutorial, *a.* Add: **B.** *sb.* **a.** A period of individual instruction given by a college or university tutor to pupils, either singly or in small groups.

1923 G. Saintsbury *Second Scrap Bk.* 27 For 'Mods' Logic one went to Professor Wall's University lectures and Mr. Sidgwick's tutorials. **1927** W. E. Collinson *Contemp. Eng.* 124 In regard to teaching within the University the only terms worthy of notice are the use of Oral (where some universities use Viva..) and tutorials (practical classes for recapitulating the formal lectures). **1932** C. Bailey in *Handbk. Univ. Oxford* 128 During term each man will attend a 'tutorial', as post-war Oxford has agreed to name it, at least once a week. **1953** A. Moorehead *Rum Jungle* i. 19 Old Jack or Geoff with whom I had attended tutorials at the university. **1966** *Rep. Comm. Inquiry Univ. Oxf.* II. 450 A 'tutorial' is to be taken to mean teaching of not more than three people at one time. **1979** *Washington Post* 26 Oct. B4/1 Windt did not show up for her 11:15 math tutorial that day.

b. Any period of tuition or training; a printed account or explanation of a subject intended for private study.

1978 *Sci. Amer.* Feb. 99/1 (Advt.), You'll find our tutorials on hardware and software invaluable reading, also our reports on home applications and evaluative reviews based on experiences with home computer products. **1980** *Amer. Banker* 15 Jan. 6/1 The 1980 conference will feature state-of-the-art developments to help assure the integrity of information systems. The schedule includes 10 tutorials, three general sessions, [etc.]. **1980** *Washington Post* 5 July B2/1 Sonny Stitt, that world-traveling, one man be-bop workshop, is holding tutorials at the One Step Down through tonight.

tutorship. Add: **2. b.** A post as a tutor, *spec.* in a university.

1925 C. Connolly *Let.* 9 Mar. in *Romantic Friendship* (1975) 62, I don't expect your tutorship will be till April. **1929** S. Leslie *Anglo-Catholic* xviii. 262 Colley had taken a travelling tutorship in Switzerland. **1980** *Daily Tel.* 19 Feb. 14/2 The following elections have been made: Magdalen: Official Tutorship as Tutor in Law, [etc.].

‖ **tutoyant** (tütwayaṅ) *a. rare.* [a. F. *tutoyant*, pres. pple. of *tutoyer* Tutoyer *v.*] Intimate, affectionate; suggesting a degree of familiarity sufficient to 'tutoyer'.

1899 'A. Leslie' *Some Players* 110 He turns facile and covert scorn upon the pretty tutoyant affection of happily wedded woman and man. **1975** *Times Lit. Suppl.* 14 Mar. 274/4 Many of her [*sc.* Lady Tennyson's] letters to her fiancé and husband have been destroyed, but there are enough affectionately *tutoyant* letters to her 'Ally' to show the nature of their correspondence.

Tutsi (tu·tsi). [Native name.] = *Watusi 1.

1950 Huntingford & Bell *E. Afr. Background* (ed. 2) 123/2 (Index), Tutsi. **1965**, etc. [see *Hutu]. **1972** *Times* 8 May 13/2 The Tutsi feudal regime was destroyed in massacres in Rwanda. **1976** *Daily Times* (Lagos) 3 Nov. 1/2 At the heart of the conflict and Burundi's general political malaise lay the fact that the Tutsi, tall cattle herders who make up only 14 per cent of the population, politically and economically dominate the Hutu who number 85 per cent of the population. **1979** 'D. Grant' *Olympic 5000* i. 27 Ochengwe was a Tutsi... In 1964.. the Hutu massacred several thousand Tutsis, the traditional ruling caste of Rwanda.

tutti. (Earlier example of sense 'a passage or movement'.)

1816 G. F. Graham *Acct. First Edin. Festival* 105 The flowing and cantabile style of the subject is well contrasted with the spirited *tutti* beginning at the 28th bar.

tutti-frutti (tu·tiˌfru·ti). [It., = all fruits.] **a.** A confection of mixed fruits; *spec.* a mixture of chopped preserved fruits, nuts, etc., used to flavour ice-cream; ice-cream so flavoured. **b.** (**Tutti Frutti, Tutti-frutti.**) A proprietary name for a chewing-gum with a mixed fruit flavouring. **c.** *attrib.* and *transf.*

1834 *Knickerbocker* IV. Sept. 232 *Tutti Frutti*, (all fruits) is the cognomen of an Italian ice, composed of, or rather flavored with, various fruits. **1876** M. J. Henderson *Cooking* 313 *Tutti Frutti*. When a rich vanilla cream is partly frozen, candied cherries, English currants, chopped raisins,..or any other candied fruits chopped rather fine, are added. **1885** *Official Gaz.* (U.S. Patent Office) 30 June 1564/1 *Chewing-gum.*—Adams and Sons, New York, N.Y... The words '*Tutti Frutti*'. **1888** A. Randall-Diehl *Two Thousand Words* 210 *Tutti-frutti*, a compound of many kinds of sliced fruits mixed with sugar and alcohol, also the name of a chewing gum. **1898** A. M. Binstead *Pink 'Un & Pelican* v. 125 Most of my readers will very well remember old Bob Bignell, who kept the Argyll rooms, and, after the powers put a stop to the dancing and tutti-frutti business, turned the place into the cheery old Trocadero. **1916** *Daily Colonist* (Victoria, B.C.) 4 July 9/1 The pleasing tang of its mellow fruit flavors alone was always sufficient for you to prefer Adams Tutti frutti gum. **1924** *Official Gaz.* (U.S. Patent Office) 21 Oct. 478/1 *American Chicle Company*, Long Island City, N.Y... *Tutti-frutti*. Particular description of goods.—Chewing gum. Claims use since October 1882. **1951** *Good Housek. Home Encycl.* 516/1 *Tutti Frutti*: Add chopped pistachio nuts, cherries and angelica. **1974** D. Chantler *Man who followed in Front* II. 60 'And look at them fuckin' ice cream machines,' he said. 'Tell the waiters..the Tutti-Frutti is off.' **1976** *Listener* 29 Jan. 121/3 Felix Mendelssohn and his Hawaiian Serenaders, and all those kitsch tutti-fruttis which drop like coconuts from a set of plastic palm trees.

‖ **tutti quanti** (tu·ti kwa·nti). [It.] Everyone, everything, all (of this, that, kind).

[**1671** Mme de Sévigné *Let.* 1 Apr. (1862) II. 135 M. et Mme de Duras, a qui j'ai fait vos compliments, MM. de Charost et de Montausier, et *tutti quanti*, vous les rendent au centuple. **1676** —— *Ibid.* 29 July IV. 545 Enfin *tutti quanti*: vous savez ce que c'est que de recevoir un mot de tout ce qu'on trouve en chemin.] **1772** Ld. Chesterfield *Let.* 10 Sept. (1932) VI. 2937, I hope you and *tutti quanti* are in a better plight. **1814** *Edin. Rev.* Jan. 403 All the heretical sects are active partisans of Passion, and furiously inimical to Reason, and to all his adherents, *tutti quanti*. **1864** J. A. Symonds *Let.* 6 July (1967) I. 488 If you come with Green & me you will have all the published Dramatists, tutti quanti, to read at pleasure. **1934** H. James *Art of Novel* xv. 274 Whether 'Daisy Miller',.. 'Julia Bride' and *tutti quanti* do in fact conform to any such admonition would be an issue by itself. **1948** J. Flanner in *New Yorker* 8 May 43/1 The idea..was to bring over from New York..Barrymore, Bankhead, Hayes, *e tutti quanti*.

tutu¹. Add: **a.** (Earlier examples.)

1845 E. Meurant *Diary* 4 Oct. (typescript, Alex. Turnbull Library, Wellington) 24 Bullocks..had been eating the tutu bush wich [*sic*] is poisonous to cattle. **1849** [see *slash *v.* 1 c].

b. Phr. *to eat* (one's) *tutu* or *toot*, to become acclimatized, *spec.* to colonial life in New Zealand (see quots.). *N.Z. slang* (now *Obs.* exc. *Hist.*).

1857 R. B. Paul *Lett. from Canterbury* ii. 26 [The newly arrived settlers] passed..through the crisis of unreasonableness, false pride, and grumbling, which old settlers call 'eating their tutu'... The tutu, or 'toot',..is a native shrub the leaves of which may be eaten with safety by cattle gradually accustomed to its use, but are often fatal to newly-landed animals. **1889** [in Dict.]. **1941** Baker *N.Z. Slang* iii. 27 *To eat toot* was the pioneer way of describing the period during which new immigrants settled down to the cold facts of New Zealand life. More correctly the expression was *to eat tutu*..the poisonous plant. **1966** G. W. Turner *Eng. Lang. in Austral. & N.Z.* viii. 165 The early colonial phrase 'to eat one's tutu' meaning 'to become acclimatized to colonial life'.

Hence **tu·tued** *a.*, poisoned by eating tutu.

1874 A. Bathgate *Colonial Experiences* xv. 211 Flock-owners have sometimes to contend with a poisonous plant called the tutu (*Coriaria ruscifolia*), commonly pronounced toot... Those [sheep] feeding amongst it..are apt to be affected by it, or be, as the phrase is, 'tutued'. **1878** E. S. Elwell *Boy Colonists* 34 When they [*sc.* bullocks] were 'tutu'd' the only cures were either to bleed them or to put ammonia on the tip of the tongue.

tutu² (tu·tu). Also **tu-tu.** [a. F. *tutu*, childish alteration of *cucu*, dim. of *cul* Cul.] A ballet skirt made up of layers of stiff frills, reaching halfway between the knee and the ankle (*romantic tutu*) or very short and standing out from the legs (*classic tutu*). Also *attrib.*

1910 E. F. SPENCE *Our Stage & its Critics* ix. 196 She wished to exhibit what in technical slang is called *le tutu*, a term descriptive of the abbreviated costume and possessed also of a secondary meaning. **1913** A. E. JOHNSON *Russian Ballet* 56 Columbine..attired in a scanty *tu-tu*. **1934** A. L. HASKELL *Balletomania* 26 An old-fashioned ballet for this old-fashioned tragedy of naked footlights and a dancer's *tutus*. **1947** N. NICOLAEVA-LEGAT *Ballet Educ.* III. 49 To make a tutu skirt, the basque should first be cut. **1949** CHUJOY & MANCHESTER *Dance Encycl.* 486/1 The classic tutu reaches to a little above the knee, the romantic to the ankle. **1958** L. GIBBS *Gowns & Satyr's Legs* xii. 82 Four miniature ballet-girls, each poised gracefully on one toe and wearing a diminutive *tutu*. **1970** B. CARTLAND *We danced All Night* vii. 196 A snow-white figure in a fluffy *tutu*. **1980** 'M. FONTEYN' *Magic of Dance* 239 The soft, full ballet skirt Marie Taglioni had introduced climbed to just below the knee, then to mid-thigh. As it was shortened, it was made fuller and stood out more and more stiffly until it became the modern tutu.

Tuvaluan (tuvalū·ăn, tuvā·lū̆ăn), *sb.* and *a.* [f. *Tuvalu* (see def.) + -AN.] **A.** *sb.* A native or inhabitant of the Commonwealth State of Tuvalu, formerly the Ellice Islands, in the south Pacific. **B.** *adj.* Of or pertaining to Tuvalu.

1975 *Pacific Islands Monthly* Dec. 15/2 The Tuvaluans, known before October 1 as the Ellice Islanders. **1978** *Daily Mirror* 20 Feb. 6/4 In 1975 the Polynesian Ellice Islanders voted to part peacefully from the Micronesians on the Gilberts... Today the Tuvaluans rely on coconuts for food and exports. **1978** *Daily Tel.* 30 Sept. 17/6 On Sunday, Tuvalu will become a constitutional monarchy, with the Queen as Head of State represented by a Tuvaluan Governor-General.

tux (tɒks). Also **Tux.** *U.S.* colloq. abbrev. of *TUXEDO.

1922 S. LEWIS *Babbitt* i. 11 Everyone knows I can put on as expensive a Tux. as anybody else. **1951** W. C. WILLIAMS *Autobiogr.* xii. 61, I agreed to take her to a dance and showed up in a tux. **1974** K. MILLETT *Flying* (1975) III. 322 Daddy doing his tux. First the black tie. Next the studs.

tuxedo (tɒksī·do). orig. and chiefly *U.S.* Also **Tuxedo.** [Named from *Tuxedo* Park, N.Y., where the jacket was first introduced at the country club in 1886.] **1.** In full *tuxedo coat, jacket.* A short jacket without tails, for formal wear; a dinner-jacket.

1889 *Sartorial Art Jrnl.* Aug. 18/1 The low-roll, silk-faced sack, variously called the 'Cowes' coat, the 'Tuxedo' coat, and the Dress Sack, is undoubtedly popular. *Ibid.* Dec. 97/1 The 'Tuxedo' or dress sack is steadily growing in favor for dress negligee purposes. **1900** ADE *Fables in Slang* 130 A jimmy little tuxedo. **1925** H. L. FOSTER *Trop. Tramp with Tourists* 333 Dress coats and tuxedo jackets were removed. **1931** *Times Lit. Suppl.* 12 Nov. 888/4 Bert..is to pose in public as a successful lover,..in the traditional Tuxedo, with the ribbon of the Garter pinned across his bosom as a Right Honourable. *a* **1944** K. DOUGLAS *Alamein to Zem Zem* (1946) vi. 47 Beneath the oil stains their white tuxedos and seductive dresses shone. **1950** J. VEDEY *Band Leaders* p. xiii, The budding maestro must make up his mind whether he will present his band in orthodox tuxedos or in some distinctive style of uniform. **1971** 'A. BURGESS' *MF* viii. 93 He was in a white tuxedo with black floppy tie.

2. Special combinations. † **tuxedo net,** a kind of net veiling (*obs.*); **tuxedo sofa,** a sofa of a style having back and arms the same height; also *tuxedo-style sofa*; **tuxedo (trade) unionism** (see quot. 1965).

1895 *Montgomery Ward Catal.* Spring & Summer 79/1 Black silk tuxedo net veiling, 13 inches wide. *c* **1900** in *Amer. Mail Order Fashions* (1961) 19, 28 in. tuxedo net. Entirely new pattern in black, white and navy. **1961** WEBSTER, tuxedo sofa. **1965** *Economist* 6 Feb. 537/2 Critics accuse him of having become aloof from the rank and file of his union and of practising what they call 'tuxedo trade unionism'... As a 'labour statesman' he associates freely with leading officials in both the government and the steel companies. **1965** *Amer. Home* Mar. 43/1 (*caption*) Curved Tuxedo sofa..illustrates the graceful, softer look for 1965 Modern. **1972** *N.Y. Times* 29 Oct. 85/5 (Advt.), Tuxedo-style sofa. **1977** *Time* 17 Jan. 48/2 Sadlowski calls McBride's style 'tuxedo unionism'. **1977** *Chicago Tribune* 2 Oct. I. 45 (Advt.), An elegant and timeless tuxedo sofa with loose pillows and arm bolsters in a rich champagne beige velvet.

Hence **tuxe·doed** *a.*, wearing a tuxedo.

1934 J. T. FARRELL *Young Manhood Studs Lonigan* xviii. 284 They..passed the tuxedoed orchestra, which was playing wildly on a dais. **1973** E. MCGIRR *Bardel's Murder* ii. 45 Near him was Jack Prat, tuxedoed, urbane.

tuzzy-muzzy, *sb.* (*a.*) Restrict *Obs.* exc. *dial.* to other senses and add: **a.** Revived in 20th. cent., usu. in form *tussie-mussie.*

1958 J. G. CONWAY *Encycl. Flower Arrangement* vi. 104 Tuzzy-muzzy, a small, neat arrangement with flowers in repeated circular lines, edged with foliage or lace. **1960** V. WILLIAMS *Walk Egypt* 180 He gave her a hand bouquet of lemon-colored roses which smelled like lemon too, a sour-sweetness that matched the morning. He said, 'A tussie-mussie... I figured you belonged to have something, a day like this.' **1968** *Herb Grower Mag.* XXI. I. 1 From a little Tussie-mussie to a formal garden at the White House, the warmth of herbs reaches across the miles. **1973** *New Yorker* 7 Apr. 126/3 (Advt.), Tussie-mussies... Delightful bouquets of fragrance herbs, cooking herbs,..and medicinal herbs. A full-color limited edition portfolio.

TV (tīvī·). Abbrev. of *TELEVISION.

1948 *Fortune* May 82/1 It is not where TV has gone,.. but the pace at which it is going that causes all the excitement. **1948** *Time* 25 Oct. 82/2 TV is not only color-blind; its eye is astigmatic. **1957** *Times Lit. Suppl.* 29 Nov. 722/3 He knows 'most of the tricks of popular journalism, films, radio, TV'. **1962** V. NABOKOV *Pale Fire* 35 The gauzy mockingbird..Returning to her perch —the new TV. **1964** M. ARGYLE *Psychol. & Social Probl.* iv. 47 Is the effect of showing violence in films or on TV to arouse or to satiate aggressive feelings? **1977** *R.A.F. News* 22 June–5 July 2/3 (*heading*) TVs for hospital.

b. Freq. *attrib.* and *Comb.* **TV dinner,** a prepared frozen meal that needs only to be heated and is suitable for eating while watching television (formerly a proprietary name in the U.S.).

1948 *Fortune* May 83/1 The average capital investment for a TV station is about $375,000. **1950** 'A. GILBERT' *Is She Dead Too?* vii. 135 That's the best of livin' in a village. It's like livin' on a TV screen. **1953** A. HUXLEY *Let.* 25 Jan. (1969) 663 One must read 100% in order to be able to leave out 99%, as has to be done in this medium and for a TV audience. **1954** TV aerial [see *SHOW-OFF *sb.* (*a.*) d]. **1954** *Official Gaz.* (U.S. Patent Office) 27 July 735/2 C. A. Swanson & Sons, Omaha, Nebr... TV Dinner. .. For frozen Turkey Dinner, Including Turkey, Dressing, Giblet Gravy, Sweet Potatoes, and Green Peas. **1955** *Radio Times* 22 Apr. 39/3 Gilbert Harding's outspoken autobiography..the frank, personal story of the popular Radio and T.V. personality. **1955** *Times* 9 Aug. 4/5 Mr. Leon Goodman, chairman of T.V. Commercials, Ltd. **1955** H. KURNITZ *Invasion of Privacy* (1956) iii. 26 He's been in two flops on Broadway and in five T.V. shows. **1958** *New Statesman* 5 July 1/2 The argument about the third TV network. **1961** P. FRANKAU *Pen to Paper* 21 '*That's it!*' as the T.V. announcer snaps at the winning point of the tennis match. **1961** *Times* 18 May 9/7 One TV antenna. **1962** L. DEIGHTON *Ipcress File* xvi. 92 A girl featured weekly in a badly made TV series. **1962** N. STREATFEILD *Apple Bough* xv. 216 They went all the way to the T/V studio on a bus. **1963** H. A. HARGREAVES in *New Worlds Science Fiction* Dec. 62 It would have to be a TV satellite. **1964** L. DEIGHTON *Funeral in Berlin* vii. 51 Spectacles swung the TV receiver around so that I couldn't see it. *Ibid.* x. 66 The very same people who made the great little TV film..paid for by the TV company, N.B.C. **1964** J. MASTERS *Trial at Monomoy* x. 292 TV dinners, and everything quick frozen, dehydrated and prepacked. **1964** M. MCLUHAN *Understanding Media* (1967) I. i. 19 If the TV tube fires the right ammunition at the right people it is good. *Ibid.* II. xiii. 140 The combined radio and TV channels in the United States. *Ibid.* II. xvii. 176 The cartoon is clue to understanding the TV image. *Ibid.* II. xxxi. 334 The TV camera does not have a built-in angle of vision like the movie camera. **1969** TV licence [see *radio licence* s.v. *RADIO *sb.* 7]. **1970** KOENIG & DIXON *Children are Watching* (1971) i. 6 Inside the stove glinted four TV dinners..nested in silver-aluminum trays,.. identical portions of gray pot roast, dinner roll, wrinkled peas and rigid mashed potatoes under foil. *Ibid.* 7 These dinners..she wheeled across the hall into the TV room. **1974** *Guardian* 23 Mar. 10/6 It was dense, thick, primeval onion soup. But it was not a TV play. **1974** *Broadcast* 11 Nov. 16/3 The bulk of the population..needs effortless entertainment... The theatre mogul, the film-maker, and now the TV programme producer, have found the truth of this platitude. **1975** D. LODGE *Changing Places* ii. 49 He filled the micro-refrigerator with TV dinners. **1976** B. BOVA *Multiple Man* xix. 209 TV crews were rolling their cameras in. **1976** *Liverpool Echo* 7 Dec. 3/1 The Wirral TV mast saga. For more than two years the B.B.C. have been seeking to erect a 200 ft. mast on Wirral.

tvorog (tvǭ·răk). [a. Russ. *tvórog.*] A soft Russian cheese similar to cottage or curd cheese.

1918 DOANE & LAWSON *Varieties of Cheese* (U.S. Dept. Agric. Bull. No. 608) 59 Tworog. This is a sour-milk cheese made in Russia..on a large scale by Russian farmers. **1960** K. DAVYDOVA *Good Food from Russia* 107 The following recipes have as their main ingredient, tvorog, the Russian version of cottage cheese. *Ibid.* 109 Tvorog Pudding with candied peel. **1973** S. SKIPWITH *Eat Russian* i. 16 Cottage cheese and curd cheese are the nearest equivalent to the Russian Tvorog which is dry but not 'cheesy'. **1981** J. TRENHAILE *Kyril* xxiv. 180 He ate only a biscuit smothered with *tvorog*, the stodgy cottage cheese of the peasants. **1982** L. CHAMBERLAIN *Food & Cooking of Russia* (1983) 245 By Good Friday several pounds of *tvorog* (curd cheese) would have been sitting for at least 24 hours under a wooden press to extract..the last drops of whey.

twa(a)-gras(s) (twā·grɑs). Also **dwa-, toa-grass.** [f. *umTwa* name used by Bushmen + GRASS *sb.*[1]] Any of several species of the genus *Aristida*, which includes several tall feathery grasses native to southern Africa.

1857 A. WYLEY *Rep. Min. Struct. Namaqualand* 44 Twa-grass..grows from two to three feet in height, from a small bushy base... When it is green, oxen, horses, and sheep all thrive upon it. **1896** R. WALLACE *Farming Industries Cape Colony* v. 100 'Twa-gras' is the most abundant grass..in the Kalahari region. **1897** EDMONDS & MARLOTH *Elem. Bot. S. Afr.* xvii. 185 The Dwa-grass or Toa-grass. **1920** F. C. CORNELL *Glamour of Prospecting* xv. 246 We lit fires of dry *toa* grass. **1946** L. G. GREEN *So Few are Free* I. x. 137, I can hear the 'twaa grass' crackling in the wind. **1949** K. L. SIMMS *Sun-Drenched Veld* i. 10 Because they [*sc.* plains] are thickly peppered with drought-resisting bushes and tufts of toa grass, they constitute wonderful ranching country. **1974** *Stand. Encycl. S. Afr.* X. 367/1 In the times of occasional rain Bushman grass and twa grass..will spring up.

Twaddell. (Earlier example.)

1853 URE *Dict. Arts* (ed. 4) II. 828 The patentee employs diluted sulphuric acid, at 105° Twaddle.

twaddlesome, *a.* (in Dict. s.v. TWADDLE *sb.* (*a.*)). Delete *nonce-wd.* and add later examples.

1892 G. MEREDITH *Let.* 25 Apr. (1970) II. 1080 *Dorothy Penrose*, an enormous bulk, is uninterruptedly twaddlesome. **1966** K. S. SORABJI in 'H. MacDiarmid' *Company I've Kept* ii. 65 The twaddlesome sentimentalities about trusting the ultimate judgement and good sense of the public.

twain, *numeral a.* Add: †**2. c.** *U.S. Naut.* Two fathoms. Esp. in phr. *mark twain*, the two fathom mark on a sounding-line. Cf. MARK *sb.*[1] 12 b. *Obs.*

1799 J. W. RUSSELL in R. D. Paine *Romance Old Time Shipmaster* (1907) iii. 43 The man in the chains suddenly sung out 'quarter less twain', and we instantly struck. **1863** 'MARK TWAIN' in A. B. Paine *Mark Twain* (1912) I. xl. 221, I want to sign my articles..'Mark Twain'. It is an old river term, a leads-man's call, signifying two fathoms—twelve feet. **1947** E. M. MACK *Mark Twain in Nevada* xv. 228 How many times when he was on the River had he heard the leadsman..call out, 'By the mark, twain!'

Twainian (twē̆i·niăn), *a.* [f. the name of 'Mark *Twain*' (S. L. Clemens), American writer (1835–1910) + -IAN.] Of, pertaining to, or characteristic of 'Mark Twain' or his work.

1938 *Times Lit. Suppl.* 27 Aug. 551/4 When stimulated by the potentialities of human sacrifice or the vapourings of a politician, it [*sc.* the pen] moves to a Twainian climax. **1968** *Word Study* Feb. 2/1 Here is such a Twainian reference, appearing in the late novel *The American Claimant.* **1977** *Time* 28 Feb. 53/1 They contain their share of Twainian 'stretchers', or exaggerations.

Twana (twā·nă). [ad. Twana *tuwáduxq*, in an earlier pronunciation that had *n* for *d.*] **1.** A Salishan people of western Washington; a member of this people. Also *attrib.* Cf. *SALISH, *SALISHAN.

1838 J. DOUGLAS *Let.* 18 Oct. in E. E. Rich *McLoughlin's Fort Vancouver Lett. 1825–38* (1941) 262 [*in a list*] Too a nook. **1889** M. EELLS in *Ann. Rep. Board of Regents Smithsonian Inst. 1887* 605 The name of the Twanas is spelled Too-au-hooch, in their treaty. The Klallams pronounce it Tu-an'-hu. The Twanas say Tu-ád-hu... These various pronunciations have been shortened into Twana, now used in all governmental reports. It is said to mean a portage, and to be derived from the portage between the head of Hood's Canal and the main waters of the Sound, where the Indian, by carrying his canoe 3 miles, avoids rowing around a peninsula 50 miles long. **1960** W. W. ELMENDORF in *Research Stud.* (Washington State Univ.) Sept. Monogr. Suppl. No. 2. 281 Few non-Twana cared to learn the Twana language. **1978** *Amer. Poetry Rev.* Sept./Oct. 19/1 The Twana of Puget Sound maintained that if a woman in seclusion touched her head with her fingers, it would at once rot away.

2. The language of this people. Also *attrib.*

1886 M. EELLS *Ten Yrs. Missionary Work* vi. 34 The Twana language..is said to be so difficult to learn that no intelligent Indian advised me to learn it. *Ibid.* 37 We have often sung in English, Chinook jargon, Twana, and Nisgually, on the same Sabbath. **1960** W. W. ELMENDORF in *Research Stud.* (Washington State Univ.) Sept. Monogr. Suppl. No. 2. 280 Twana seems a unique case among all Coast Salishan tongues in its features of areally simple distribution restricted to a single inlet and its fresh-water drainage, and very slight heterogeneity of dialects. **1971** *Language* XLVII. 844 Twana (Salish, Puget Sound area) uses duplication of the root vowel.

† **twang** (twæŋ), *sb.*[4] *Austral. slang. Obs.* [perh. back-formation from TWANKAY.] Opium.

1898 *Bulletin* (Sydney) 1 Oct. 14/3 A few more W.Q. [*sc.* West Queensland] slang words... Opium 'twang', a Chinaman a 'canary' [etc.]. **1910** O'BRIEN & STEPHENS *Material for Dict. Austral. Slang 1900–10* (typescript), *Twang*, opium. **1945** T. RONAN *Strangers on Ophir* (1966) 68 The honest Chinese limits himself to his one pipe of 'Twang' per night. **1966** BAKER *Austral. Lang.* (ed. 2) 157 Opium was once known as *twang* in bush slang (the later use of *treacle* was noted earlier).

twanka-pang, twank-a-pank. An imitation of the sound of a banjo or guitar.

1929 J. B. PRIESTLEY *Good Companions* I. vi. 201 This banjo..was being *played.* The night retreated hastily before its impudent twanka-pang, twanka-pang. **1980** M. GILBERT *Death of Favourite Girl* i. 6 Twank-a-pank... The guitar quickened to a livelier tempo.

twat. Delete † *Obs.* and add pronunc. (twǫt). Also **twot(t. 1.** (Later examples.)

1919 E. E. CUMMINGS *Let.* 18 Aug. (1969) 61 On Tuesday an Uhlan To her twat put his tool in. **1934** H. MILLER *Tropic of Cancer* 55 A man with something between his legs that could..make her grab that bushy twat of hers with both hands and rub it joyfully. **1959** N. MAILER *Advts. for Myself* (1961) 101 The clothes off, the guards are driving them into the other room, and smack their hands on skinny flesh and bony flesh, it's bag a tittie and snatch a twot. **1970** G. GREER *Female Eunuch* 39 No woman wants to find out that she has a twat like a horse-collar. **1973** P. WHITE *Eye of Storm* iii. 137 This young thing with the swinging hair and partially revealed twat.

2. A term of vulgar abuse. Cf. *TWIT *sb.*^{1} 2 b and *CUNT 2.

1929 F. MANNING *Middle Parts of Fortune* II. xv. 383 Yes, they let a bloody twat like 'im off. **1933** M. LOWRY *Ultramarine* i. 16 He can't help it if you're just a bloody, senseless twat. **1958** H. WILLIAMSON *Love & Loveless* i. 27 Looked a proper twott to me. **1969** P. ROTH *Portnoy's Complaint* 211 Here comes another dumb and stupid remark out of that brainless twat. **1978** J. UPDIKE *Coup* (1979) iii. 123 Divorce me and you'll have a slot for this new twat, what's her name. **1979** R. FIENNES *Hell on Ice* ix. 134 Sterns not prows, you twot.

3. *U.S. dial.* The buttocks.

1950 *Publ. Amer. Dial. Soc.* XIII. 20 *Twat*,..the buttocks. **1964** M. KELLY *March to Gallows* xii. 132, I could tell her what to do with her twat if she's frightened to sit on it.

tweak, *v.* Add: **4.** *Cricket. colloq.* Of a bowler: to impart spin to (the ball).

1958 D. BRADMAN *Art of Cricket* 94/1 My pal.. R. W. V. Robins, tweaked his leg breaks so hard that he left the ground altogether with both feet.

5. To make fine adjustments to (a mechanism).

1966 *Punch* 16 Feb. 233/1 He has been running a Morris 1100 'tweaked so it'll do nearly 100'. **1971** *Daily Tel.* 13 Oct. 11/1 The three-litre V6 engines..have been 'tweaked' to produce eight per cent. more power. **1978** *Gramophone* May 1960/1 It was possible to improve its performance very considerably by 'tweaking' the internal pre-set controls.

tweaking *vbl. sb.*: also in senses *4 and *5 of the vb.

1949 E. M. WELLINGS in *Boys' Bk. of Cricket* 78/1 Most right-handed off-break bowlers do their spinning largely with the forefinger. Personally I do not even have that finger resting on the ball when bowling an off-break. My 'tweaking' is done by the middle finger. **1975** *Drive* Nov.–Dec. 90/3 These engine hiccups are the result of carburettor tweaking that has been necessary to bring cars in line with current exhaust emission regulations. **1983** *Australian Personal Computer* Sept. 123/1 Most parallel [daisy-wheel] printers should work with a little tweaking.

tweaker. Add: **2.** *Cricket. colloq.* **a.** A bowler who spins or 'tweaks' the ball, esp. a left-arm leg-spinner. **b.** A ball bowled with spin.

1948 C. SLY *How to bowl them Out* ii. 17 The slow bowler should have great patience... There should also be an element of precision in his brain—a slapdash fellow will never make a good 'tweaker'. **1956** R. ALSTON *Test Commentary* 12 Johnson's insidious 'floaters' were likely to be more penetrative than Ring's 'tweakers'. **1961** *Times* 12 June 3/6 Lancing's leg tweaker came on too late. **1976** J. SNOW *Cricket Rebel* 40 When I came into the side Ron Bell, a left-arm spinner, was the only genuine tweaker of the ball on the staff. **1982** *Guardian* 26 July 19/3 The fragile left-arm tweakers of Steele.

twee (twī), *a.* (and *sb.*) *colloq.* [f. *tweet*, an infantile pronunciation of *sweet*.] **1.** Originally: 'sweet', dainty, chic. Now only in depreciatory use: affectedly dainty or quaint; over-nice, over-refined, precious, mawkish.

1905 *Punch* 8 Mar. 178/1, 'I call him perfectly twee!' persisted Phyllis. **1917** M. T. HAINSSELIN *Grand Fleet Days* xv. 91 *Girl*: Oh, here's another little gun; isn't it a darling! Isn't it just too twee for words! **1947** E. HYAMS *William Medium* viii. 164 'Isn't he *twee*!' said Mary, and pinched his cheek. **1956** G. DURRELL *Drunken Forest* x. 193 'What twee individuals?' 'Those knowledgeable sentimentalists who are forever telling me that it's cruel to lock up the poor wild creatures in little wooden boxes.' **1962** *Observer* 25 Mar. 25/3 She has a small and, it must be said, pretty twee cottage. **1967** E. SHORT *Embroidery & Fabric Collage* iv. 102 The best of our designers who have abandoned the rather 'twee' decorative type of embroidered picture. **1973** G. ROBYNS *Wimbledon* xxix. 192 There is..a twee Arcadian outdoor studio complete with white trellis and plastic flowers. **1983** *Listener* 21 July 33/1 Mike Nichols's thriller-fantasy about dolphins should be as nauseatingly twee as the worst Disney—but it isn't.

2. *ellipt.* as *sb.*

1957 *Daily Mail* 29 Oct. 12/8, I cannot understand why television's handling of fashion in evening programmes has never got past the twee.

Hence **twee·ly** *adv.*, in a twee manner; **twee·ness.**

1958 *Spectator* 2 May 565/3 He manages..to resist the temptation to play up the tweeness and tell the English what they expect to hear. **1962** *Guardian* 12 July 7/1 The..highly commendable idea of importing bulk grains ..and passing them, tweely packaged, to cage-bird fanciers. **1973** *Observer* 18 Nov. 36/2 'And no doubt, if the bride is awake and has peeped out through the curtains..,' he speculated tweely. **1981** *Radio Times* 7–13 Nov. 21/2 The word 'herbs'..seems to have become associated with tweeness.

tweed. Add: **b.** *tweed mill* (example); *tweed-jacketed, -skirted* adjs.

1928 A. HUXLEY *Point Counter Point* iii. 46 This huge bent old man, pipe-smoking and tweed-jacketed. **1949** C. GRAVES *Ireland Revisited* x. 156 The only really interesting person..was Robert Miller, to whose tweed mill he directed us. **1957** C. MACINNES *City of Spades* II. v. 138 The recalcitrant bowler-hatted or tweed-skirted natives.

tweeded (twī·dėd), *a.* [f. TWEED + -ED^{2}.] Clad in tweed.

1921 G. B. SHAW *Back to Methuselah* II. 38 *The tweeded gentleman*. (Coming in very slowly.) I have something on my mind. **1949** N. MITFORD *Love in Cold Climate* II. v. 241 Why are the English roads always so covered with these tweeded stumpers? **1979** M. RUSSELL *Touchdown* i. 14 Her companion..was nursing on a tweeded lap..a Thermos flask.

‖ **Tweede Nuwejaar** (twīᵊ·də nǖvəyā·ɹ). Also **Tweede Nuwe Jaar, Tweedenuwejaar.** [Afrikaans, lit. = second New Year.] The second of January, a public holiday in Cape Province, celebrated especially by the Black population.

1947 *Cape Times* 30 Dec. 14 The Coons are ready for the New Year—and tweede nuwejaar—that extra holiday which is taken only in the Cape. **1953** *Ibid.* 1 Jan. 1/6 There will be no issue of the *Cape Times* to-morrow, January 2 (*Tweedenuwejaar*). **1959** *Ibid.* 3 Jan. 7/3 The coons have enjoyed fine weather for New Year and the Tweede Nuwe Jaar and we have enjoyed them too. **1978** *Argus* (Cape Town) 29 Dec. 3 Normal editions of The Argus will be published on Tuesday January 2, Tweede Nuwejaar.

tweedle (twī·d'l), *sb. Criminals' slang.* [See *TWEEDLE *v.*^{2}] A counterfeit ring; hence, a swindle (involving counterfeit goods); a 'fiddle', 'racket'.

1890 BARRÈRE & LELAND *Dict. Slang* II. 383/2 *Tweedle* (thieves), a spurious ring, used to swindle jewellers and pawn brokers. **1938** F. D. SHARPE *Sharpe of Flying Squad* xxvii. 275 One of the oldest methods of crime is the Tweedle... The Tweedler spots a ring worth a lot of money in a jeweller's shop and goes..to have an exact.. replica made. He goes in..and when the assistant isn't looking very carefully substitutes the fake for the real thing. **1959** J. GOSLING *Ghost Squad* ix. 122 A bloke's tried to pull a tweedle on me with a load of jargoons. **1963** H. SLESAR *Bridge of Lions* (1964) 2 'What's 'is tweedle?' the youth asked suspiciously. **1982** *New Society* 2 Dec. 382/3 Then it was back to the shop for the 'tweedle'—for the switch.

tweedle, *v.*^{2} *Criminals' slang.* [prob. f. *tweedle*, var. TWIDDLE *v.*^{1}, in sense 2 b of the latter.] *trans.* To counterfeit, swindle, practise a confidence trick on. Hence **twee·dler,** one who tweedles; **twee·dling** *vbl. sb.*

1925 E. JERVIS *Twenty-Five Years in Six Prisons* i. 17 Some of the boys go 'tweedling'. I am afraid that the knowing author of the 'cracking-a-crib' book would be flummoxed by 'tweedling'. *Ibid.* 18 The chain is handed over in tissue-paper, and the 'tweedler' departs. **1959** J. GOSLING *Ghost Squad* ix. 114 The tweedler will flog you sawdust cigarettes or dummy diamond rings. **1975** P. G. WINSLOW *Death of Angel* iv. 94 'Tweedling'—small con jobs, mostly against the old and weak. *Ibid.* ix. 195 He was always blubbing to Joss, a tweedler like that has to make himself big to a woman. **1980** 'D. KAVANAGH' *Duffy* ii. 30 Big bad villain. Girls, smokes, bit of smack, mossing, tweedling.

tweedy (twī·di), *a.* [f. TWEED + -Y^{1}.] **a.** Consisting of or relating to tweed cloth. **b.** Characterized by or given to wearing tweeds. **c.** *fig.* Characteristic of those (e.g. the country gentry) who wear tweeds; heartily informal, exclusively clannish, etc.

1912 R. BROUGHTON *Between Two Stools* xiv. 107 Iris stood before them in tweedy brevity of skirt and pertness of tam-o-shanter. **1928** *Sunday Dispatch* 5 Aug. 17/3 In Scottish country houses you rarely get away from the tweedy atmosphere until the afternoon has worn on. **1930** J. B. PRIESTLEY *Good Companions* II. vii. 445 An angel of a woman, very erect, y'know, and tweedy, and straight out of the Old Moated Grange. **1946** G. D. KLINGOPULOS in *Scrutiny* XIV. II. 144 The only excuse for noticing this tweedy sequel [*sc.* V. Sackville-West's *The Garden*]..is that we need to be reminded..that, in Courses of English, 'The Land' is still too often the substitute for modern poetry. **1949** L. P. HARTLEY *Boat* 80 She nodded very perceptibly in the direction of the tweedy group who were talking to each other as members of the same family do. **1978** I. MURDOCH *Sea* 164 He is a big stout man, always dressed..in tweedy suits with waistcoats. **1980** *Daily Tel.* 20 Mar. 14/5 Miss Foster, who seems to have been a perfectly splendid, large and tweedy lady.

Hence **twee·dily** *adv.*, **twee·diness.**

1964 C. P. SNOW *Corridors of Power* xxiv. 195 Roger.. lolloped tweedily along between them. **1965** *Listener* 27 May 788/1 The exotic tweediness of little Phyllis Benton, so despised by Mr Amis. **1978** R. HILL *Pinch of Snuff* x. 100 He would have classified her as genuine English county with a good seat but not erring on the side of tweediness. **1980** 'A. SKINNER' *Mind's Eye* I. 10 An old James Bond movie relayed rather tweedily from the mainland.

tweek (twīk). (*Radio.* [Echoic.] A type of whistler which is heard as a short, high-pitched chirruping noise.

1933 BURTON & BOARDMAN in *Proc. IRE* XXI. 1479 Two varieties of distinct musical atmospherics have been observed and given the onomatopœic names 'swish' and 'tweek'. **1953** *Phil. Trans. R. Soc.* A. CCXLVI. 114 The 'short whistler', 'tweek', or 'chink'..is the short (about 20 ms) musical tone produced by repeated reflexion between the earth and the ionosphere of the waves from a distant lightning flash. **1981** *Jrnl. Atmospheric & Terrestrial Physics* XLIII. 1271 The appearance of tweeks on whistler sonograms has been discussed in terms of VLF wave propagation through the land-sea and ionospheric waveguide.

tweely, tweeness: see *TWEE *a.*

tweeter (twī·təɹ). [f. *tweet* vb. s.v. TWEET *sb.* and *int.* + -ER^{1}.] A small loudspeaker designed to reproduce accurately high-frequency sounds whilst being relatively unresponsive to those of lower frequency. Cf. *SQUAWKER, *WOOFER.

1934 *Nature* 25 Aug. 294/1 The extension of the range of acoustic fidelity permitted by the 'tweeter'—the high frequency auxiliary speaker—is a boon. **1952** *Electronic Engin.* XXIV. 583/3 The..Tweeter Unit is of the moving coil pressure type and is similar to that used in the 10in. and 12in. concentric Duplex loudspeakers. **1957** *Times* 3 May 13/4 Bearded young men talk of Beethoven in terms of baffles and tweeters. **1959, 1975** [see *SQUAWKER 3]. **1982** *Hi-Fi Answers* Oct. 77/1 These drive units are pretty unusual beasts, and the NS1000M sports two: a 30mm dome tweeter and a 8·8cm dome midrange unit.

tweeze (twīz), *v.* [Back-formation from TWEEZERS *sb. pl.*] *trans.* To pull out (hair) with tweezers. Also, to pull as with tweezers. Hence **twee·zing** *vbl. sb.*

1932 V. WOOLF *Common Reader* 2nd Ser. 153 He.. tweezed out hairs with a silver tweezer. **1956** *Sun* (Baltimore) 13 June B 12/4 Before tweezing, apply to brow area a soft cloth wrung out in hot water. **1968** B. HINES *Kestrel for Knave* 29 So he tweezed the lashes between his finger and thumb and drew the lid down. **1979** M. MCMULLEN *But Nellie was so Nice* I. i. 9 The mouth was scarlet, the brows tweezed to an almost invisible line. **1982** *Chicago Sun-Times* 20 Nov. 19 When Gordon finished, makeup artist Gloria Percival tweezed Schaefer's brows.

twelfth, *a.* Add: **1. c.** (Earlier example.)

1816 SCOTT *Antiquary* III. ix. 196 'I must be prepared for Lord Glenallan's moors on the twelfth, sir,' said M'Intyre. 'Ah, Hector! Thy great *chasse*, as the French call it.'

d. *ellipt.* The 12th of July, celebrated by Protestants in Northern Ireland as the anniversary of the Battle of the Boyne (1 July (Old Style) 1690) at which William III defeated James II.

1896 M. HAMILTON *Across an Ulster Bog* vi. 57 The greatest excitements of her life—next always to 'the twelfth'—had been occasional Methodist or Plymouth Brethren meetings. **1936** *Ann. Reg. 1935* 115 The Orange celebrations of 'The Twelfth' were on a bigger scale than ever, but the atmosphere was highly charged, and in the evening there were serious riots. **1957** *Belfast News-Letter* 2 July 6 (*heading*) Record 'Twelfth' parades expected. **1978** D. MURPHY *Place Apart* xiii. 269 The Twelfth festivities commemorate the victory at the Boyne.

4. *twelfth man* (Cricket), a twelfth player selected as reserve to the team of eleven.

1876 *Haygarth's Scores* VI. 20 Mr. E. Arkwright..was first choice out of the [Harrow] Eleven, or 'twelfth man' in 1858. **1928** J. BUCHAN *Runagates Club* vii. 195, I saw you play at Lord's. I was twelfth man for Harrow that year. **1976** J. SNOW *Cricket Rebel* 26 There were just a couple of minutes to the off when the two twelfth men appeared on the field, the horses lined up as we gathered round the radio.

twell (twel), *prep.* and *conj.* Also **twel.** U.S. dial. and Black English var. of TILL *prep.*, *conj.*, *adv.*

1837 A. SHERWOOD *Gazetteer Georgia* (ed. 3) 72 *Twell*, for till;—twell night—twell next week. **1893** H. A. SHANDS *Some Peculiarities of Speech in Mississippi* 65 *Twel* (twel). Negro for *till*. **1901** W. CHURCHILL *Crisis* I. iv. 38 Dis ole woman'll wuk fo' you twell de flesh drops off'n her fingers, suh. **1938** W. FAULKNER *Unvanquished* vi. 229 Uncle Cash that druv the Benbow carriage twell he run off with the Yankees two years ago.

twelve, *numeral a.* and *sb.* Add: **B. II.** *sb.* **3. c.** A flower-pot eleven inches in width, of which there were twelve in a cast.

1802, etc. [see *SIXTEEN *sb.* 5]. **1852** G. W. JOHNSON *Cottage Gardeners' Dict.* 392/2 Eleven-inch..[Old name] 12s.

III. c. twelve-note, -tone *attrib. Mus.*, (of the technique of musical composition developed by Arnold Schœnberg (1874–1951) using the twelve notes of the chromatic scale so that none is dominant, as opposed to basing composition on the seven notes of the diatonic scale; cf. *note-row, -series* s.v. *NOTE *sb.*^{2} 21, *SERIAL *a.* h, *tone-row* s.v. *TONE *sb.* 11; hence **twelve-toner,** a composer employing the twelve-tone technique.

1928 C. GRAY *Hist. Music* vi. 96 A reaching out towards the chromatic or twelve-note scale of to-day. **1959** *Times Lit. Suppl.* 16 Oct. 588/5 The most interesting letters are those in which Schoenberg speaks about his own work and his theory of composition. There is one to the Viennese composer Josef Hauer, in December, 1923, in which are discussed the rival claims of the two composers to have invented the twelve-note system. **1975** *Gramophone* Jan. 1329/3 Moses is an uncompromisingly twelve-note composition. [**1923** A. SCHOENBERG *Let.* 1 Dec. in *Briefe* (1958) 108 Mir handelt es sich ausgesprochen dabei um gar keine anderen Theorien, als um die Methoden der 'Komposition mit 12 Tönen', wie ich das—nach vielen Irrtümern und Abschweifungen—heute (hoffentlich endgültig) nenne.] **1926** *Mod. Music* Mar.–Apr. 6 He (*sc.* Schoenberg), too, is convinced that no tone of the twelve tone system should dominate and that the new structural elements should be sought in sequence of twelve tones. **1956** AUDEN & KALLMAN *Magic Flute* (1957) 58 A *Geist* whose music was composed from *Angst*, at International Festivals enjoys An equal status with the Twelve-Tone Boys. **1980** *Times* 4 Sept. 12/5 There was an almost missionary zeal in the Schoenberg circle to spread the Twelve-Tone gospel of the master. **1966** N. ROREM *Paris Diary* II. 215, I despair of twelve-toners: they have lost the need for pleasure. **1977** Y. MENUHIN *Unfinished Journey* viii. 165 Bartók pours them [*sc.* chromatic sequences] out with a lavishness of invention which the twelve-toner, working away with his slide rule, will never know.

Twelver[2] (twe·lvəɹ). *Islam.* [f. TWELVE + -ER[1].] A member of the larger of the two Shiah sects (the 'Twelvers' and the 'Seveners'), a follower of the twelve Imams or prophets (cf. IMAM 2 b, SHIAH).

1876 R. D. OSBORN *Islam under Arabs* II. i. 167 The Ismailiens, like the Twelvers, make profession of an exclusive attachment to Ali and his descendants. **1934** R. STROTHMANN in *Encycl. Islām* IV. 353/2 We shall consider the main branch somewhat more fully, the Imāmīs or 'Twelvers'. **1979** *Sunday Tel.* (Colour Suppl.) 27 May 25/4 In Iran the Shias are divided essentially into two sects, the Twelvers and the Seveners.

twentieth, *a.* Add: **1. d.** (Earlier example.)

1888 E. BELLAMY *Looking Backwards* xxvii. 432 My thoughts made better music than even twentieth century orchestras discourse.

e. Special Comb.: **twentieth century cut** *Diamond-cutting* (see quots.); **Twentieth Century (Limited)** the name of an express train running between Chicago and New York from 1902 to 1967.

1903 W. R. CATTELLE *Precious Stones* 63 The 'twentieth century' is a new form of cutting lately introduced. The number of facets is greater than in the brilliant-cut and they are differently shaped and arranged. **1925** KRAUS & HOLDEN *Gems & Gem Materials* vii. 77 The '*twentieth century' cut* has eighty or eighty-eight facets. **1970** E. BRUTON *Diamonds* x. 164 Jubilee or twentieth century cut (40+40=80 facets). **1902** *N.Y. World* 16 June 7/2 The 'Twentieth Century Limited', the new fast train,.. yesterday afternoon at 2.45 o'clock pulled out of the Grand Central Station. **1913** E. WHARTON *Custom of Country* III. xxii. 332 The Twentieth Century's generally considered the best route to Dakota. **1980** M. G. EBERHART *Casa Madrone* iii. 39 The Twentieth Century made a record run of eighteen hours from New York to Chicago. .. It is a very good train.

twenty, *numeral a.* and *sb.* Add: **A.** *adj.* **1.e.** Phr. *twenty-four hours a day*, all the time, incessantly.

1914 G. B. SHAW *Misalliance* p. xl, If we were habitually underworked and overfed, our notion of heaven would be a place where everybody worked strenuously for twenty four hours a day and never got anything to eat. **1942** *R.A.F. Jrnl.* 13 June 15 The least useful man..is the ..type, who is belligerent 24 hours a day. **1951** W. FAULKNER *Requiem for Nun* II. i. 143 Shut up in that room twenty-four hours a day. **1980** J. BARNETT *Palmprint* xiv. 149 There are American military planes over the Caribbean twenty-four hours a day.

2. c. Also *twenty-first* with ellipsis of *birthday*; cf. *TWENTY-FIRSTER.

1873 C. M. YONGE *Pillars of House* I. xi. 229 Here was his twenty-first not very far off. **1937** 'M. INNES' *Hamlet, Revenge!* I. i. 23 Celebrating a daughter's twenty-first by dressing her in white satin. **1975** 'J. LYMINGTON' *Spider in Bath* vii. 121 My daughter's twenty-first tomorrow. I should have collected a watch from the jeweller.

B. *sb.* **2. b.** (Earlier and later examples.)

1839 *Spirit of Times* 8 June 162/2 We had the gratification of seeing it [*sc.* his jockeyship] rewarded by more presents of odd fifties and twenties than probably Daniel ever saw in his lifetime. **1977** *Transatlantic Rev.* LX. 140 'God knows neither of you can call me ungrateful.' He put a twenty in front of each of them.

4. (Examples with reference to the third decade of the twentieth century; also *attrib.*)

1898 KIPLING in W. Nicholson *Almanac of Twelve Sports* July, The child of the Nineties..in pursuit of a girl whom The Twenties will dub a 'last-century heirloom'. **1930,** etc. [see *roaring twenties* s.v. *ROARING *ppl. a.* 4]. **1956** A. S. C. ROSS in M. Black *Importance of Lang.* (1962) 97 At Oxford in the late twenties the use of the surname..was a known *gaucherie*. **1969** *Listener* 26 June 903/1 A scandalous title, of course, for a book which was, in the Twenties manner, meant to scandalise. **1976** J. GRENFELL *Joyce Grenfell requests Pleasure* (1977) i. 21, I see us now,..our peculiar Twenties figures forced flat by bust-bodices.

C. a. *twenty-minute* (fig. example). **b.** *twenty-five-pounder.* **d.** Special Comb.: **twenty-first century** *attrib.* or as *adj.*, living in the twenty-first century; characteristic of the imagined conditions of the twenty-first century; **twenty-four carat** *a. colloq.*, (*a*) thoroughgoing, unalloyed, out-and-out; (*b*) genuine, flawless, trustworthy; **twenty-four-hour** *attrib.*, (*a*) lasting twenty-four hours; (*b*) of or pertaining to a system of reckoning the time whereby the hours of the day are numbered from one to twenty-four; (*c*) operating all day and all night, round-the-clock; **twenty questions,** a parlour game in which one party is allowed twenty questions (answered by either 'yes' or 'no') to discover the object of the other's thoughts; *spec.* the name of a popular radio panel game; **Twenty-six Counties,** the counties which by the Irish peace agreement of 1921–2 formed the Irish Free State, now the Republic of Ireland; cf. *Six Counties* s.v. *SIX *a.* 1 d; **twenty-twenty** (also **20/20**) *Ophthalm.*, the Snellen fraction for normal visual acuity, expressed in feet; *colloq.* used to denote good eyesight; also *fig.*; **twenty-two carat** *a. colloq.* = *twenty-four carat* (*b*) above; also *ellipt.* as *twenty-two*.

1964 D. FRANCIS *Nerve* iii. 37 He was what I pictured twenty-first century man should be—intensely alive, curiously innocent. **1979** D. BRIERLEY *Cold War* v. 49 The computer...it's very big, very expensive, very twenty-first century. **1980** *Jrnl. R. Soc. Arts* July 467/2 Everyone in the country must adapt to twentyfirst-century living and working patterns. *a* **1944** K. DOUGLAS *Alamein to Zem Zem* (1946) 10, 25-pounders and quads, Bofors guns in pits with their crews lying beside them. **1983** J. MASTERS *Man of War* xx. 264 Now came the first shell from the 25-pounders. **1900** Twenty-four carat [in Dict.]. **1965** D. FRANCIS *Odds Against* iii. 40 It is you.. who is the dyed-in-the-wool, twenty-four carat, unmitigated bastard. **1968** *Times* 21 Dec. 2/3 The legs in thigh-length boots are still lissom, 24 carat. **1974** G. JENKINS *Bridge of Magpies* v. 71 I'd accepted her story as 24-carat. **1984** *Times* 7 Mar. 28 The rest..had to work up real 24-carat grins. **1908** Twenty-four hour [in Dict.]. **1919** in *Cook's Continental Time-Table* (1973) Mar. p. vi/2 Cook's Continental Time-Table...Based on the 24-Hour System. **1947** CROWTHER & WHITTINGTON *Science at War* 7 A continuous twenty-four-hour watch for strange aircraft started. **1975** C. EGLETON *Skirmish* xvii. 169 He had located a twenty-four hour service station and had had the tyre repaired. **1978** H. KEMELMAN *Thursday the Rabbi walked Out* (1979) xxix. 141, I got sick. It was this twenty-four-hour bug. **1978** G. VAUGHAN *Belgrade Drop* i. 11 A clipboard..contained dates, 24-hour clock times, and a short, neatly typed entry against each. **1939** WODEHOUSE *Uncle Fred in Springtime* xi. 150 No matter how suave her manner for the nonce, she is at heart a twenty-minute egg. **1786** H. MORE *Lett.* (1925) 107 Mrs Fielding and I..diverted ourselves with teaching Sir Joshua and Lord Palmerston the play of twenty questions. **1846** R. BELL *Life of Rt. Hon. George Canning* x. 255 Canning proposed that they should play at 'Twenty Questions'. They had never heard of this game. **1930** 'HAY' & WODEHOUSE *Baa, Baa, Black Sheep* I. ii. 21 All right, a vicarage garden. What are we playing at? Twenty Questions, or something? **1979** E. H. GOMBRICH *Sense of Order* iv. 104 This can be done by a simple series of yes or no answers which allows a questioner to locate an item on a given grid as in the game of Twenty Questions. **1922** *Times* 6 June 16/2 The requirement that Ulster shall deliberately 'contract out' of the arrangements made between Great Britain and the twenty-six Southern counties. *Ibid.*, If Mr. Griffith is right in claiming all but two per cent. of the population in the twenty-six counties as supporters of the Treaty. **1949** C. GRAVES *Ireland Revisited* viii. 102 The Bantrymen have always provided a strong contingent in the Government of the Twenty-six Counties ever since 1922. **1978** [see *SOUTH *sb.* 2 a]. **1979** W. NELSON *Minstrel Code* vi. 45 The garage..belonged to a brother-in-law of one of the Sinn Fein leaders in the Twenty-Six Counties... O'Hagan explained that, within the IRA, no one talked of the 'Irish Republic' by any term other than this. **1875** T. LONGMORE *Man. Instructions Army testing Vision* (ed. 2) iii. 46 The 20-feet types are read at 20 feet, the 30-feet types at 30 feet; then V.=20/20 or 30/30, and the acuteness of vision is normal. **1945** L. SHELLY *Jive Talk Dict.* 35 *Twenty twenty*, excellent. **1951** E. F. TAIT *Textbk. Refraction* ii. 16 The visual acuity of healthy corrected eyes may be much better or considerably worse than that represented by the 6/6 or 20/20 standard. **1956** 'E. McBAIN' *Cop Hater* (1958) iii. 21 Having 20/20 vision without glasses..he..had been appointed a patrolman. **1962** *Flight International* LXXXI. 426/2 Perfect eyesight is denoted as 20/20 vision, and the newest expression in the US air transport business—ruefully coined, we believe, by somebody in Convair—is 20/20 hindsight. Hindsight, of the 20/20 kind, abounds in plenty. But the aviation business is more interested in 20/20 foresight, because it can prevent people from losing a lot of money. **1977** H. GREENE *FSO-1* ix. 83 We're looking back with twenty-twenty hindsight, now. **1981** P. TURNBULL *Deep & Crisp & Even* ix. 162 He had 20:20 vision... He glimpsed a black shape. **1962** R. COOK *Crust on its Uppers* iv. 45 You come out twenty-two carat. *Ibid.* 47, I tell you they're absolutely twenty-two. **1974** W. J. BURLEY *Death in Stanley Street* ii. 46 I've got a twenty-two carat alibi. **1981** J. BARNETT *Firing Squad* vi. 61 Lady Lowderton was no nutter and her title was twenty-two carat.

twenty-firster (-fɜ̄·ɹstəɹ). *slang.* [f. *twenty-first* (sc. *birthday*) + *-ER[6].] A twenty-first birthday party (until 1970 in the U.K. celebrating the coming-of-age), or one who celebrates this. Also, a twenty-first birthday present.

1912 *Isis* 17 Feb. 204/1 There always are, or seem to be, celebrations of a sort on a twenty-firster. **1930** R. LEHMANN *Note in Music* IV. 129 'What a lovely case!' 'Yes, it was a twenty-firster.' **1964** C. MACKENZIE *My Life & Times* III. 166 The conventional Twenty-Firster at one of the Oxford hotels or clubs. *Ibid.* 214 Our rendez-vous with the rest of the Twenty-firsters was for supper. **1975** J. I. M. STEWART *Young Pattullo* iii. 69 The contraption itself was familiar to me, Ninian once having brought one home from the twenty-firster of an older friend.

twenty-five. Add: **1.** Also in Hockey.

1895 [see *BULLY *sb.*[2] 2]. **1930** *Times* 14 Mar. 7/4 With 12 minutes to go, Home worked his way to the German '25' and then suddenly sent in another long shot.

2. (Earlier example.)

1870 'CAVENDISH' (*title*) The Pocket Guide to Spoil-Five, Twenty-Five and Forty-Five.

twentyish (twe·ntiˌiʃ), *a.* [f. TWENTY + -ISH[1].] **a.** Of a person, (looking) approximately twenty years old. **b.** Characteristic of the 1920s.

1928 *Daily Express* 20 July 4 On the other hand, her blazer-clad, twentyish escort was impressed. **1940** GRAVES & HODGE *Long Week-End* viii. 125 The discovery ..of the unrifled tomb of the Pharaoh Tutankhamen was given typical Twentyish publicity. Ancient Egypt suddenly became the vogue. **1975** L. DICKSON *Radclyffe Hall at Well of Loneliness* 9, I try to show her as the unique personality she was, part of a 'twentyish scene now vanished in the clearer if harsher light of our times. **1981** 'J. ROSS' *Dark Blue & Dangerous* viii. 43 The woman.. wasn't twenty-ish..or startlingly beautiful.

twenty-one. [TWENTY A. 1 b.] = VINGT-ET-UN, VINGT-UN. Cf. *BLACK JACK, BLACK-JACK 10; *PONTOON *sb.*[2]

1790 E. WYNNE *Diary* 11 Mar. (1952) 30 My aunt winned 80 livers in playing at twentyone. **1917** [see *PONTOON *sb.*[2] a]. **1977** *Time* 21 Nov. 44/2 New croupiers are taught the 'theory of craps', while Twenty-One dealers are told to slap their hands and hold them upward when they leave their posts to show that they are not concealing any chips.

twenty-three. [TWENTY A. 1 b.] Ellipt. for *twenty-three skidoo*: see *SKIDOO *v.* 2 b.

1930 J. DOS PASSOS *42nd Parallel* 72 We want to take a look at this burg an then twentythree. **1933** L. BLOOMFIELD *Language* xxiv. 443 One suspects that the queer slang use, a quarter of a century ago, of *twenty-three* for 'get out' arose in a chance situation of sportsmanship, gambling, crime, or some other rakish environment.

twenty-two. [TWENTY A. 1 b.] A twenty-two calibre rifle; = **two-two* (a) s.v. *TWO IV. 2. Also *attrib.*, as *twenty-two rifle*.

a **1930** D. H. LAWRENCE *Phoenix II* (1968) 464, I went back to the house, and got the little twenty-two rifle. **1937** J. STEINBECK *Red Pony* 13 Jody took his twenty-two rifle up to the cold spring at the brush line. **1958** 'E. McBAIN' *Killer's Payoff* (1960) xiii. 134 I've got three guns. A shotgun, a twenty-two, and a big-game rifle. **1967** K. S. PRICHARD in *Coast to Coast 1965–66* 182 Quick as light, Mac swung his twenty-two.

twerp (twɜ̄ɹp). *slang.* Also **twirp.** [Of uncertain origin. See quots. 1944, 1957; T. W. Earp of Exeter College, Oxford, matriculated in Michaelmas Term, 1911.] A despicable or objectionable person; an insignificant person, a nobody; a nincompoop.

1925 FRASER & GIBBONS *Soldier & Sailor Words* 292 *Twerp*, an unpleasant person. **1934** J. O'HARA *Appointment in Samarra* iv. 87 'And what a husband.' 'Exactly!.. That little twirp.' **1936** WODEHOUSE *Laughing Gas* xxv. 265 You're simply a lot of low twerps who kidnapped me in order to cash in. **1944** J. R. R. TOLKIEN *Let.* 6 Oct. (1981) 94 He lived in O[xford] at the time when we lived in Pusey Street (rooming with Walton, the composer, and going about with T. W. Earp, the original twerp). **1945** [see *RAT *sb.*[1] 3 a]. **1955** E. POUND *Section: Rock-Drill* xcv. 105 Among all these twerps and Pullizer sponges no voice for the Constitution, No objection to the historic blackout. **1957** R. CAMPBELL *Portugal* 87 T. W. Earp (who gave the English language the word twirp, really twearp, because of the Goering-like wrath he kindled in the hearts of the rugger-playing stalwarts at Oxford, when he was president of the Union, by being the last, most charming, and wittiest of the 'decadents'). **1960** S. BARSTOW *Kind of Loving* I. iv. 91 If she turns me down I'll look more of a twerp than ever. **1973** B. BROADFOOT *Ten Lost Years* xxvii. 309 The R. B. Bennetts of Canada and that despicable little twerp Mac. **1980** *National Times* (Austral.) 21 Dec. 30/3 Kendig's former boss..is a twerp. His offices contain a gallery of framed photographs of [himself]: there he is with John Wayne, with Nixon, [etc.].

Twi (twī, tʃwī). Also **Tshi** (tʃī). **a.** The chief language spoken in Ghana, consisting of several mutually intelligible dialects. **b.** The speakers of Twi. Also *attrib.*

1874 J. G. CHRISTALLER *Dict. Eng., Tshi-Asànté-Akra* p. iv, Tshi is the prevailing language of the Gold Coast. *Ibid.* p. ix, In the publications of the Basel missionaries, the language is called Tw̃i, pronounced as *Chwee* would be in English. **1887** A. B. ELLIS (*title*) The Tshi-speaking peoples of the Gold Coast. **1920** A. W. CARDINALL *Natives N. Territories Gold Coast* 113 There are in the Gold Coast and its dependencies..two great languages: Twi,..and a language which in its simplest form is spoken by the Moshi. **1931** *Times Lit. Suppl.* 17 Sept. 692/3 The author's argument that the Twi people originally came from the grass country. **1955** [see *FANTI *sb.* and *a.*]. **1972** *Bk. Thousand Tongues* (rev. ed.) 441/1 The administrative term 'Akan' is used to denote all forms of Twi (Fante, Asante, and Akuapem)... In the 1850's, when Johannes Christaller translated the Bible into 'Twi', he chose..a form of the language which fell phonetically between the linguistic extremes of Fante and Asante-Akyem... Thus Scriptures were finally provided for the Twi. **1978** *Language* LIV. 458, I would like to enumerate the contributions in terms of the languages treated:..one paper each on Bambara (David Dwyer), Twi (Lynette Nyaggah), Nupe (Isaac George), [etc.].

twi-, twy-, *prefix.* Add: **a.** *twi-natured* (later

example). **c.** *twi-nature.* **e. twi-minded.** Delete '?' and add later examples.

1886 E. Dowden *Let.* Jan. in *Fragments from Old Lett.* (1914) I. 176 You raise..a difficult general question concerning the destruction of old letters. As usual, *I* am twi-minded. **1932** V. Woolf *Common Reader* 2nd Ser. 174 From the first he [*sc.* Hazlitt] was a twy-minded man. **1897** W. B. Yeats *Secret Rose* 178 Then the twy-nature faded. **1916** G. Saintsbury *Peace of Augustans* viii. 287 The cat was a nymph and the nymph was a cat; the two lines fit the twynatured creature in both its natures.

twice, *adv.* (*sb.*, *a.*) Add: (Examples of *dial.* forms *twicet, twict.*)

1789, etc. [see *once *adv.* A. γ]. **1895** *Dialect Notes* I. 375 Some other words reported individually are...onct, twict. **1922** Joyce *Ulysses* 453 And he interfered twict with my clothing. **1926** R. Hughes in *Hearst's Internat.* Feb. 44/2 Wha'd' you say, Kid, if I'd 'a' matched Coily up wit' some old vet'ran twicet his weight wit' twicet his ring-gener'lship. **1940** H. G. Wells *Babes in Darkling Wood* II. i. 137 'Seems like Hitler's thinking twicet,' said a gentleman behind him. **1958** E. Birney *Turvey* v. 48, I los all my good time for climbin the fence twicet.

1. e. (Earlier examples.)

1623 W. Painter in *Oxf. Dict. Eng. Proverbs* (1970) 263/1 Thinke twise, then speak, the old Prouerbe doth say. **1640** R. Brathwait *Ar't Asleepe Husband?* vii. 277 You thinke twice before you speake, and may be demanded twice before you answer. **1818** Scott *Heart Midl.* in *Tales my Landlord* 2nd Ser. IV. viii. 180 If a fule may gie a wise man a counsel, I wad hae him think twice or he mells wi' Knockdunder. **1853** C. Brontë *Villette* I. viii. 147, I saw in her countenance a something that made me think twice ere I decided.

5. b. In combination with advbs., forming compound advbs. or adjs. (and sbs.), as *twice-nightly, -weekly, -yearly.*

1929 D. H. Lawrence *Pansies* 133 And let the nodding tempests of verbosity Weekly or twice-weekly whistle round your bottles. **1949** M. Steen *Twilight on Floods* IV. vi. 611 There was English's.., the first of the twice-nightlies, down in Hackney. **1976** 'W. Trevor' *Children of Dynmouth* v. 102 The cartoonist responsible..was now, in the sunset of his life, himself the recipient of twice-weekly Meals on Wheels. **1980** M. Babson *Queue here for Murder* iv. 30 The twice-yearly Sales.

twice-laid, *a.* **b.** (Earlier and later examples.)

1777 P. Thicknesse *Year's Journey* II. xlvi. 110 My entertainment..was half a second-hand roasted turkey, or, what the sailors call, a *twice-laid* dish, i.e. one which is *done over* a second time. **1937** G. P. Low *Sea made Men* ii. 35 Bread that had been on one long voyage and had been baked over again. It was called by sailors 'twice laid bread', and poor at that.

twicer. Add: **3.** A crook, liar, cheat; a deceitful or cunning individual.

1924 *Truth* (Sydney) 27 Apr. 6 *Twicer*, a deceitful fellow. **1925** Fraser & Gibbons *Soldier & Sailor Words & Phrases* 292 *Twicer*, a cunning fellow. **1949** E. Wingfield-Stratford *King Charles & King Pym* IV. ix. 262 The recent dismissal..of that elderly twicer, Sir Harry Vane.

twiddle, *sb.* (Later *Mus.* examples.)

1908 [see *dynamics 3]. **1975** *New Yorker* 21 Apr. 115/1 She adds to Rossini's tense exclamations a cascade of pretty twiddles.

twiddle-twaddle. Add: Hence as *v. intr.*, to chatter foolishly (*nonce-wd.*).

a **1930** D. H. Lawrence *Phoenix II* (1968) 480 All you can do now is to twiddle-twaddle about golden boughs.

twiddly, *a.* (In Dict. s.v. Twiddle *v.*[1]) Add: Also **twiddley.** (Later examples.) Freq. in Comb. *twiddly bit*, a fancy or intricate embellishment; a detail.

1912 C. Mackenzie *Carnival* viii. 83 That's no tune to dance to. You want something to show off the twiddly-bits. **1922** H. Jenkins *Mrs Bindle* ii. 52, I like them little twiddley bits wot you been puttin' into that 'ymn. **1935** 'G. Orwell' *Let.* Sept. in *Coll. Ess.* (1968) I. 152, I have three more chapters and an epilogue to do, and then I shall spend about two months putting on the twiddly bits. **1964** V. S. Naipaul *Area of Darkness* x. 255 He was tall and thin,..and had a brisk, twiddly walk. **1974** *Guardian* 23 Mar. 14/4, I was..enchanted by the dining car, all wood panelling and twiddly bits. **1982** Barr & York *Official Sloane Ranger Handbk.* 148/1 Sloane windows need curtains with a capital C: with pelmets, twiddly bits, bands, tassels, tie-backs, edging.

twig, *sb.*[1] Add: **5. c. twig girdler** (examples); **twig-pruner,** substitute for def.: = *oak pruner* s.v. *oak 9 (examples).

1874 *Rep. U.S. Dept. Agric. 1873* 153 The twig girdler, *Oncideres cingulatus*... The insects girdle the twig before depositing their eggs. **1972** Swan & Papp *Common Insects N. Amer.* xx. 452 The Twig Girdler..is rough-surfaced, grayish brown or yellowish brown. **1974** *Ridge Citizen* (Johnston, S. Carolina) 18 Apr. 6/3 The twig girdlers deposit their eggs in the portions of the branches that fall to the ground. **1928** Metcalf & Flint *Destructive & Useful Insects* xix. 664 Maple and oak twig pruner. **1972** Swan & Papp *Common Insects N. Amer.* xx. 446 Twig Pruner..Brown, clothed with irregular patches of grayish yellow pubescence.

twiglet (*b*), (with capital initial) the proprietary name of a crisp, savoury snack in the shape of a twig.

1932 *Trade Marks Jrnl.* 15 June 766 *Twiglets*... Biscuits. Peek, Frean & Company, Limited,..London, S.E. 16; manufacturers. **1962** M. Frayn *Day of Dog* 57 A cheese twiglet slips from my fingers. **1980** J. Melville *Chrysanthemum Chain* 103 Walker set out a..drinks tray ..and opened a tin of imported Twiglets.

twig, *v.*[1] Add: Hence **twi·gging** *vbl. sb.*

1916 Joyce *Portrait of Artist* iv. 174 To flee from noise which caused him painful nervous irritation such as the sharpening of knives..and the twigging of the carpet.

twig(g)age (twi·gėdʒ). *Literary. rare.* [f. Twig *sb.*[1] + -age.] Twigs collectively.

1923 *Glasgow Herald* 11 Dec. 6/8 Even the umbered purple loom of the birch twigage and its stem washes of amethystine-cream were but enhanced. **1964** *Listener* 16 Apr. 633/3 The dry stuff's best To start with, twiggage and haulm and herby tops.

twiggery (twi·gəri). [f. Twig *sb.*[1] + -ery.] Twigs collectively. Also *fig.*

1909 in Webster. **1922** *Contemp. Rev.* Feb. 255 Something that was not merely discursive wooden twiggery. **1931** *Observer* 11 Oct. 26 In the winter of 1929 it was only the twiggery that was killed. The main stems broke out into bud... The numerous end-twigs do habitually suffer in winter. **1980** *Washington Post* 6 July K2/3, I would walk into the apartment..warm myself at the fire, admire my twiggery, [etc.].

twiggy, *a.* Add: Hence **twi·gginess,** the condition or quality of being twiggy.

1927 *Smallholder* 26 Mar. 105/1 Pea sticks ought to last through two seasons. Of course, in the second year they lose most of their twigginess. **1981** *Country Life* 1 Jan. 39/2 *Potentilla fruticosa*... Its winter-brown twigginess should match the tawny beech.

twilight, *sb.* Add: **3. a.** *twilight of the gods* (later examples); also *transf.* Cf. *Götterdämmerung, *Ragnarök.

1888 R. Garnett (*title*) The twilight of the gods and other tales. **1944** *Sun* (Baltimore) 22 July 2/1 The German nation is split wide open... The twilight of the gods has begun. **1979** A. R. Peacocke *Creation & World of Science* ii. 55 Under the pressure of experimental facts and the bold and convincing analyses of Planck and Einstein, there was, as Karl Heim puts it, a 'twilight of the gods' of absolute space, time, object, and determinism.

4. a. *twilight glow*, a diffuse glow in the sky at twilight; *spec.* in *Meteorol.*, that caused by spectroscopic emission in the upper atmosphere from atoms excited by solar radiation; *twilight vision*, vision in which colours are hardly perceptible owing to the dimness of the light; scotopic vision.

1819 Byron *Don Juan* II. clxxxviii. 213 The twilight glow, which momently grew less. **1955** *Sci. Amer.* Sept. 150/3 There is also a twilight glow, about 100 times as intense as the nightglow but not detectable by the eye because of the brighter sky. **1972** *Ibid.* Jan. 80/3 The spectrum of the twilightglow differs from the nightglow spectrum in that certain features disappear shortly after the end of twilight and others are markedly stronger in twilight than they are during the night. **1980** F. H. Ludlam *Clouds & Storms* iv. 77/1 The twilight glow continues to fade and its upper border to descend more rapidly than the sun, but it does not disappear below the horizon until the sun's depression exceeds about 16°, and astronomical twilight ends. **1921** Twilight vision [see *rod vision* s.v. *rod *sb.*[1] II c]. **1924,** etc. [see *scotopic *a.*]. **1950** *Sci. News* XV. 17 It has been suspected for many years that the coloured pigment 'visual purple', found in the retinas of such animals as frogs, is associated with twilight vision. This supposition has recently become a certainty.

e. Special Combs.: **twilight area** = *twilight zone* (*a*) below; **twilight home,** (*a*) a home (see Home *sb.* 8) for old people or animals; (*b*) = *twilight house* below; **twilight house,** a house in a twilight zone (see *twilight zone* (*a*) below); hence **twilight housing; twilight night** *Baseball* = *twi-night; **twilight shift,** a shift worked between the day shift and the night shift; **twilight sleep** [tr. G. *dämmerschlaf* (C. J. Gauss, *c* 1905)], a state of amnesia and partial analgesia induced by the administration of morphine and scopolamine (hyoscine), esp. to lessen the pains of childbirth; **twilight world,** (*a*) a shadowy region; (*b*) a world characterized by uncertainty, obscurity, or decline; (*c*) the world which comes to life after sunset, characterized by merry-making or criminal activities; **twilight zone,** (*a*) *spec.*, an urban area in which housing is becoming decrepit; (*b*) *gen.*, an indistinct boundary area combining some of the characteristics of the two areas between which it falls (cf. sense 4 b in Dict.); (*c*) occas., a dimly illuminated region.

1960 *Daily Tel.* 18 June 8/3 Where debate begins and should be encouraged is over the question whether re-development of what Sir Keith Joseph called the 'twilight areas' must wait entirely on these other two housing operations. *a* **1974** R. Crossman *Diaries* (1975) I. 44 A Labour Minister should impose central leadership, large-scale state intervention, in these blighted areas of cities, the twilight areas, which were once genteelly respectable and are now rotting away. **1934** Webster, *Twilight home*, a charitable institution providing a home for aged people. *Colloq., Australia.* **1966** 'K. A. Saddler' *Gilt Edge* v. 74 Twilight homes for retired beach donkeys. **1968** *Guardian* 5 Apr. 1/6 A plan to modernise Britain's four million twilight homes has been agreed by the Cabinet. **1978** I. Murdoch *Sea* 493 [I] arranged for her mother to be packed off to a comfortable and expensive 'twilight home'. **1971** *New Society* 1 July 20/2 There were 600,000 'slums' and about two million 'twilight' houses. *Ibid.*, A current comparison of slum and twilight housing. **1971** *Mod. Law Rev.* XXXI. vi. 698 He has sections on ..houses in disrepair, on planning blight and on twilight housing areas. **1949** P. Cummings *Dict. Sports* 478/1 *Twilight-night. Baseball.* A double-header, the first game played late in the afternoon, the second in the evening under lights. **1953** *Sun* (Baltimore) 28 Oct. (B ed.) 21/2 There can be none of those frisky twilight-night double headers. **1970** 'C. Aird' *Late Phoenix* x. 115 He didn't come home last night after the twilight shift at his factory. **1977** *Wandsworth Borough News* 7 Oct. 18/2 (Advt.), Laundry workers evening shift, 5.30–9.30 p.m. We require a number of part-time workers for clean and simple work on our twilight shift, Monday–Friday. **1912** F. W. Hewitt *Anæsthetics & Administration* (ed. 4) ix. 278 As a matter of actual experience in hospital practice by no means all patients achieve the state of *dammerschlaf*, or 'twilight sleep', which foreign authors advocate. **1922** Joyce *Ulysses* 159 Twilightsleep idea: queen Victoria was given that. **1971** D. D. Moir *Pain Relief in Labour* i. 5 Twilight sleep is seldom used today because it causes respiratory depression in the new-born and tends to cause delirium and restlessness in the mother. **1981** J. Gardner *License Renewed* xiv. 161 A nice mix—Scopolamine with morphine: twilight sleep, like having a baby. **1887** Twilight world [see sense 4 c in Dict.]. **1954** Koestler *Invisible Writing* xxvi. 281, I mention this episode as one example of the ambiguities of the twilight world in which we lived. **1963** *Times* 8 May 6/7 But in this unhappy twilight world in which we live in a state of truce—neither peace nor war. **1970** C. Major *Dict. Afro-Amer. Slang* 117 *Twilight world*, the world of all-night parties. **1977** D. Seaman *Committee* 116 The twilight world of the mentally ill. **1977** 'J. D. White' *Salzburg Affair* v. 45 The twilight world that exists in every city.. the doctor who will tend a bullet wound, the hotel that will provide accommodation without papers. **1909** *Arena* XLI. Mar. 273/2 Such organization will leave no 'twilight zone', no 'no man's land', for railway corporation dodgers. **1918** *Policeman's Monthly* June 30/1 There still remain twilight zones in most centers of population. **1920** J. G. Frederick *Great Game of Business* iii. 23 Be aware that the test of real 'honesty' comes in the 'twilight zone' between what is quite clearly honest and dishonest. **1938** *Jrnl. Royal Aeronaut. Soc.* XLII. 492 The twilight zone extends to about 20° either side of the equi-signal zone centre. **1960** *Daily Tel.* 20 June 17/6 There are many towns with 'twilight zones' of shabby and outdated houses. **1969** *Times* 29 Jan. 10/7 It lives between 300 and 500 metres below the surface of the ocean, in the region to which light penetrates with such difficulty that it may be considered as a kind of twilight zone. **1981** *Washington Post* 26 Apr. A1/1 Several key officials charged with formulating foreign policy remain in a bureaucratic twilight zone almost 100 days after Reagan's inauguration.

Hence **twilight** *v. trans.* (earlier example).

1819 Keats *Song of Four Fairies* in R. M. Milnes *Life, Lett. & Lit. Remains J. Keats* (1848) II. 275 And the beams of still Vesper..Are shed thro' the rain..And twilight your floating bowers.

twilly, *a.* and *sb.*[1] Add: **b.** *sb.* (*b*) (see quot. 1948); so *twill(e)y hole*, a hole left in the centre of a wattle hurdle for the insertion of a pole on which several hurdles may be carried simultaneously.

1893 A. Kennard *Diogenes' Sandals* vi. 90 A 'twilley' hole, is left in the centre of each hurdle for the insertion of the..pole, on which the shepherds carry them. **1948** E. J. Stowe *Crafts of Countryside* iii. 24 About two-thirds of the way up from the bottom of the hurdle there are two important rods. They are known as 'twillies' (a country name for twisted rods), and are twisted about each other and around the upright sails one by one across the hurdle. *Ibid.* 128 *Twillies*, two twisted rods woven across wattle hurdles just above the twilly hole. **1959** *Times* 2 June 12/7 The split rods are twisted until the complete hurdle is ready with the twilly hole in the middle. **1971** *Country Life* 25 Feb. 424/1 These hurdles differ slightly from sheep hurdles which had a gap or twilly hole in their middle through which a shepherd put his stick to carry a load to the next enclosure.

twin, *a.* and *sb.* Add: **B.** *sb.* **3. d.** *ellipt.* for *twin aerial, bed, -city, -cylinder car, -cylinder engine, -engined aeroplane, -town*, etc. (see C. in Dict. and Suppl.).

1928 [see *sun arc* s.v. *sun *sb.* 13 a]. **1930** *Times* 14 Mar. 12/3 As soon as the B.B.C. 'twins' came into use and two wave-lengths were available. **1938** O. Nash *I'm a Stranger here Myself* 85 A double bed or twins. **1944** G. L. Nute *Lake Superior* III. xii. 277 Superior had hoped to be the terminus of the first railroad to the head of the lake, but when one came, in 1870, its terminal was Duluth rather than the other twin. **1955, 1963** [see *single *sb.* 3 o]. **1975** B. Meggs *Matter of Paradise* vi. ii. 167 Nice..room, double bed... Should have made a point to ask for twins. **1976** R. Barnard *Little Local Murder* i. 11 They've done one before—for a town in Essex with a twin in Canada. **1976** B. Lecomber *Dead Weight* iii. 45 If I was going into the charter business I had to have a twin—and she was.. the only twin on the whole airport that I could afford.

C. *Comb.* **a.** *twin-burner, -cylinder* (earlier example), *-engine, -float, -fuselage, -track.* **b.** *twin-engined, -tyred, -walled.* **e. twin aerial** (*temporary*), a twin-wire aerial; **twin bed,** one of a pair of matching single beds; hence **twin-bedded** *a.* (*a*) tucked up in a twin-bed (*nonce* *use*); (*b*) furnished with twin beds; **twin bedstead,** one of a pair of matching single bedsteads; **twin-bill** *Baseball* = *DOUBLE-HEADER c; **twin carburettor,** one of a pair of carburettors in the same engine; so **twin carb.**; **twin city,** (*a*) *N. Amer.*, either of two cities that are very close neighbours; *spec.* in *pl.* (*U.S.*) St. Paul and Minneapolis, (*Canad.*) Fort William and Port Arthur; (*b*) occas. used of a city in the sense of *twin town* below; **twin double,** a system of betting (on horse-races, etc.) in which the winners of four successive races must be selected (i.e. two *doubles* in sequence); **twin floats,** a pair of floats (*FLOAT *sb.* 8 e) on a seaplane; **twin-jet** *a. Aeronaut.*, having two jet engines; also *ellipt.* as *sb.*, a twin-jet aircraft; **twin lamb disease,** a pregnancy toxæmia in sheep, apparently caused by malnutrition; **twin-lens** *a.*, designating a camera with two identical sets of lenses, either for taking stereoscopic pictures, or (more commonly) with one forming an image for viewing and the other an image to be photographed; **twin paradox** *Physics*, in relativity theory, the conclusion that if one of a pair of twins makes a long journey at high speed and then returns, he will have aged less than the twin who remains behind; **twin plate** *Glass Manufacture*, plate glass which is ground and polished on both sides at once; also *attrib.*; **twin prime** *Math.*, each of a pair of prime numbers whose difference is 2; **twin set** (also with hyphen and as one word), a woman's matching jumper and cardigan; **twin soul,** a kindred spirit; also as *attrib. phr.*; **twin species** *Biol.* [tr. F. *espèce jumelle* (L. Cuenot 1929, in *Reunion Plénière de la Soc. de Biol. et de ses Filiales, 17–18 Mai* 85], two species which are morphologically identical but which are separated by reproductive isolation; cf. *sibling species* s.v. *SIBLING 3; **twin town,** one of a pair of towns (usu. in different countries) that have established official links; **twin-tub** *a.*, (of a washing machine) having two separate top-loading drums, one for washing and the other for spin-drying; also *ellipt.* as *sb.*

1913 *Wireless World* June 211/2 The ordinary 'twin' aerial used by the Marconi Company on most of their ship-stations. **1928** J. Frost *Wireless Man.* iv. 17 A twin aerial, or aerial of two wires. **1919** G. B. Shaw *Heartbreak House* p. xxxviii, If the twin flats and twin beds produce a guinea more than Shakespear, out goes Shakespear. **1940** Graves & Hodge *Long Week-End* xi. 181 Twin-beds replaced the old..double-bed for married couples. **1973** E.-J. Bahr *Nice Neighbourhood* i. 8, I pictured her.. slipping into bed beside her husband... Of course, they may have had twin beds. **1937** G. Frankau *More of Us* xiii. 138 O happy nests (nest's best!) where Bob and Bill Sleep (sleep?) twin-bedded by their spawn-glad spouses. **1960** *News Chron.* 27 July 4/3 The writer asked for the best twin-bedded room, with private bathroom. **1981** 'E. Lathen' *Going for Gold* iii. 29 The twin-bedded cubicle. **1900** *Heal & Son Catal.: Guest's Room: Paris Exhib.* 4 Twin bedsteads. Each 3 feet by 6 feet 6 inches. **1930** *Heal & Son Catal.: Matter of Taste in Furnit.* 17 Twin bedsteads in limed oak. **1939** in E. J. Nichols *Hist. Dict. Baseball Terminol.* (Ph.D. thesis, Pennsylvania State Coll.) 81 Twin bill. **1974** *Anderson* (S. Carolina) *Independent* 19 Apr. 5B/1 Virginia's Cavaliers invade Clemson Friday afternoon for a 1:30 Atlantic Coast Conference twin-bill. **1907** *Yesterday's Shopping* (1969) 219/2 A twin-burner Stove, strongly recommended as a boiler and heater. **1974** *Country Life* 5 Dec. 1772/1 Refrigerator, twin-burner stove..stainless-steel sink. **1967** *Autocar* 5 Oct. 47/1 New car called TC (for Twin Carb.), retaining all the special equipment of the basic model. **1973** 'R. MacLeod' *Burial in Portugal* v. 93 The Lancia had..a high compression alloy engine which sucked fuel through twin carburettors. **1856** *Rock Island* (Illinois) *Argus* 23 Apr., The church bells of the twin-cities [*sc.* Rock Island, Ill. and Davenport, Iowa] rang out their joyous notes in honor of the achievement [*sc.* bridging the Mississippi]. **1883** *Harper's Mag.* June 73/2 The twin cities [*sc.* St. Paul and Minneapolis, Minn.] ..emulate each other in metropolitan airs. **1912** J. Sandilands *Western Canad. Dict. & Phrase Bk.*, *Twin Cities*, when spoken of in Canada, usually refer to Port Arthur and Fort William, neighboring cities and ports in Ontario. **1949** *St. Paul Pioneer-Press* 12 Aug. 1/3 Fog and clouds gave the Twin Cities respite from the hot weather for a few hours Thursday morning. **1968** A. Hailey *Airport* (1969) iii. iii. 319 Detroit and Windsor, the twin cities straddling the [U.S.–Canada] border. **1973** *Guardian* 13 Apr. 10/5 Manchester ..is what they, laughingly I trust, call the 'twin city' of Leningrad. **1980** *Quilt World* Sept./Oct. 28/3 A learning-packed three-day seminar..will be held at a camp on the shores of Silver Lake in the Twin Cities. **1846** T. Craddock *Chemistry of Steam-Engine* 91 The loss..as that shown by the expansive curve, induced me to devise the arrangement I have designated the Twin-Cylinder Engine. **1960** *N.Y. Times* 25 Oct. 43/7 The new method, called the twin double, requires a fan to pick four consecutive winners from the sixth through the ninth races. **1979** *Internat. Herald Tribune* 31 Oct. 23/4 There were seven more races, four more swingers, two daily doubles and a jackpot, or twin double, still to come. Plenty of chances to get well. **1931** *19th Cent.* Feb. 155 Twin-engine Farman 'Goliath' seaplanes. **1916** *War Illustr.* 1 Jan. 474/1 The twin-engined Caudron biplane. **1942** *R.A.F. Jrnl.* 27 June 1 The aircraft employed..were..twin-engined Handley-Page bombers. **1974** E. Ambler *Dr. Frigo* III. 190 There was a small twin-engined plane waiting. **1913** *Flight* 19 Apr. 436 (*caption*) One of the floats on the twin-float Breguet. **1942** E. Sargent *Every Boy's Bk. Aircraft* viii. 39 A good example of a military seaplane ..is the Fairey Seafox... It has twin floats. **1977** G. R. Duval *World Float Planes* (*caption*), The Fairey Flycatcher was the standard Fleet Air Arm fighter from 1923 to 1934... The land undercarriage was readily interchangeable with twin floats. **1980** P. Lewis *Brit. Bomber since 1914* v. 204 During 1933 another Fairey twin-float biplane made its appearance as the Fox Mk. IVM. **1931** *19th Cent.* Feb. 159 The twin-fuselage Blériot 125 mono-plane. **1980** *Jane's Encycl. Aviation* II. 305/1 *Blackburn T.B. Twin* (*UK*), large twin-fuselage twin-engined seaplane designed to attack Zeppelin airships with incendiary steel darts. **1946** *Jrnl. R. Aeronaut. Soc.* L. 348/1 It may therefore be possible to make more advanced explorations into the transonic region with similar twin-jet installations. **1953** *Ann. Reg. 1952* 405 An English Electric Canberra B5 twin-jet bomber made history on 26 August by completing a double crossing of the Atlantic in a single day. **1961** E. Brown *Wings on my Sleeve* 85 We had a standing date to go back to Grove and pick up the first of the Arado 234 B twin jets. **1945** J. F. H. Thomas *Sheep* v. 93 When in-lamb ewes have a diet which is protein-adequate,..twin lamb disease is never a serious cause of loss. **1974** *Country Life* 28 Mar. 740/1 Twin-lamb disease..is often fatal. **1894** *Country Gentlemen's Catal.* 158/3 Hand-Cameras... The 5 × 4 Twin Lens Artist Magazine or dark slides—£15 15s. od. **1911** *Encycl. Brit.* XXI. 505/1 (*heading*) Twin-lens and reflex cameras. *Ibid.* 505/2 Stereoscopic cameras are another form of twin-lens cameras. **1977** J. Hedgecoe *Photographer's Handbk.* 19 The twin lens reflex design is much older than the SLR and was one of the most popular 'advanced' types of camera prior to World War II. **1957** *Nature* 5 Jan. 35/2 The 'twin paradox' is not even qualitatively discernible in any experiment that does not involve relative accelerations. **1982** W. R. Rindler *Introd. Special Relativity* iii. 51 If the twins A and B, in the twin-paradox 'experiment'.., visually observe the regular ticking of each other's standard clocks, describe quantitatively what each sees as B travels to a distant point Q and back. **1939** *Archit. Rev.* LXXXV. 104 Twin-plate has arrived to supersede ordinary plate glass. **1962** *Gloss. Terms Glass Industry* (*B.S.I.*) 28 *Twin-plate process*, a process for making polished plate glass in which rolling, annealing and grinding are carried out on a continuously produced ribbon of glass without first cutting it into sections and in which top and bottom surfaces are ground simultaneously. **1930** T. Dantzig *Number* iii. 49 It has been shown that the so-called twin-primes, such as (3,5), (5,7),..(41,43), etc., become rarer and rarer as the numbers increase. **1981** *Sci. Amer.* Feb. 19/2 The largest pair of twin primes given in the December column has now been surpassed by an even larger pair discovered in 1980. **1937** *New Yorker* 9 Jan. 62 Here you will find sweater classics—twin sets of the conventional type. **1944** M. Laski *Love on Supertax* iii. 35 I've got a Worth frock.. I swopped..for my cashmere twin-set. **1970** *Listener* 27 Aug. 289/2 Sophia Loren wandering in a tidy twinset across the USSR. [**1868** Twin soul: in Dict., sense A. 5.] **1927** Wodehouse *Meet Mr Mulliner* vi. 172 It seemed to him so plain a proof that they were twin souls that he decided to offer her his hand and heart without delay. *a* **1930** D. H. Lawrence *Mod. Lover* (1934) v. 37 You know, love isn't the twin-soul business. **1931** *Archivio Zool.* XV. 289 During his studies upon evolution the A. has been led to propose some neologisms that seemed to him useful and he reunites in this study, defining precisely the sense of them. Those neologisms are: statistic adaptation, homochromy, preadaptation, differentative death, differentative fecundity, twin species. **1971** *Biol. Abstr.* LII. 11353/2 (*heading*) Study of 2 twin species of parasitic copepods. **1955** *Harrogate Advertiser* 18 June 8/3 In the afternoon they met in the Council Chamber to discuss Le Monde Bilingue Twin Town Scheme. **1976** *Southern Even. Echo* (Southampton) 2 Nov. 2/2 Wickham entertained 11 French visitors from their proposed twin town of Villers-Sur-Mer at the Kings Head. **1960** Twin-track [see *Speed-walk* s.v. *SPEED *sb.* 11 c]. **1983** *Listener* 13 Oct. 3/2 When the 'twin-track' approach to European nuclear weapons was devised by NATO (make preparations to deploy, but hold arms control talks at the same time) no one seems to have remembered Euclid's principle that parallel lines can never meet. **1962** *Which?* May 139/1 We carried out washing tests..in a twin-tub washing machine. **1970** *New Scientist* 15 Oct. 134/1 An overnight soak and a wash (in a twin-tub), did remove some..stains. **1916** *Chambers's Jrnl.* Dec. 829/1 The twin-tired commercial vehicle. **1913** D. H. Lawrence *Love Poems & Others* 26 As if..the twin-walled darkness had bled In one great spasm of birth.

twin, *v.*^{2} Add: **2. a.** Also *spec.* to cause (towns) to be twinned (chiefly in *pass.*): see *TWINNED *ppl. a.* 2 c.

1957 *Harrogate Advertiser* 16 Mar. 13/5 Harrogate was the first town in the country to be twinned with a French town—Luchon. **1983** *Guardian Weekly* 6 Feb. 13/5 One thousand towns and villages from each country have been twinned.

b. *spec.* Of a town or city: to become twinned *with* (another).

1973 *Daily Tel.* 1 Feb. 1/4 Liverpool is to go ahead with a plan to 'twin' with the port of Haiphong in North Vietnam. **1977** *Cornish Times* 19 Aug. 15/5 Pleyber-Christ, the Breton town with which it is proposed that Lostwithiel should 'twin'.

twindle (twi·nd'l), *v.*^{2} *nonce-wd. intr.* Used by G. M. Hopkins: prob. a blend of Twist *v.* and Dwindle *v.*

1881 G. M. Hopkins *Poems* (1967) 89 A windpuff-bonnet of fáwn-fróth Turns and twindles over the broth Of a pool so pitchblack, féll-frówning.

twing twang. (Later examples.)

1922 Joyce *Ulysses* 436 Their paler smaller negroid hands jingle the twingtwang wires. **1953** *John o' London's* 23 Jan. 75/3 Central in the 'orchestra' was a guitar making a lazy twing-twang of sound.

twingy (twi·ndʒi), *a. rare.* Also **twingey.** [f. Twinge *sb.* or *v.*^{1} + -y^1.] Experiencing twinges of pain.

1865 N. Hogg *Poet. Lett. tu es Brither Jan* (ed. 5) 52 And then tha litt'l pigs wid zook, an twinjy in tha jaw wis took. **1915** V. Woolf *Voyage Out* ix. 120 Aunt E. cheerful, though twingy, she says. **1974** D. Sears *Lark in Clear Air* (1976) xv. 187 Hearing that song made me feel twingey and kind of lonesome.

twi-night (twəi·nəit). *Baseball.* [Blend of Twilight *sb.* and Night *sb.*] (See quot. 1955.) Freq. *attrib.*, as *twi-night double-header* (cf. *DOUBLE-HEADER c). Hence **twi-·nighter,** in same sense.

1939 *Amer. Speech* XIV. 5 Blending..has proved practical in the formation of useful compounds where a combination of ideas is desired; as in..'brunch', 'twinight', 'Anglamerican'. **1953** *Sun* (Baltimore) 28 Oct. (B ed.) 21/2 (*heading*) Twi-nighters? **1955** M. Reifer *Dict. New Words* 214/2 *Twinight*, *n. Baseball*, a double-header game which begins in the afternoon and continues into the night with artificial illumination. **1975** *New Yorker* 17 Nov. 148/2 The pitching left something to be desired, but the next afternoon, in the opener of a twi-night doubleheader, Frank Tanana struck out seventeen Texas batters. **1980** *N.Y. Post* 4 Aug. 56 The Mets are still—again—two games under .500 and twi-night double-header here tonight..opens another five-game series against the division-leading Expos.

twinkle, *sb.* Add: **4.** A ballroom dance (step), danced to slow Blues music. Also *twinkle step.*

1920 A. E. W. Mason *Summons* xxi. 220 'Do you know the fox-trot?' 'A little.' 'The twinkle step?' 'Not at all.' **1936** A. Moore *Ballroom Dancing* v. 214 A Twinkle is a figure of three steps. The feet are closed..on the 2nd step and the weight is changed, and the 1st and 3rd steps are both taken in a forward direction or both in a backward direction. **1962** L. K. Engel *Fred Astaire Dance Bk.* xv. 47 The Open Twinkle is a slight variation of the basic One Step. **1975** G. Howell *In Vogue* 9/2 We got syncopated music and what to do to it—the Baleta, the Maxina, the Twinkle, the Jog Trot, the Vampire, [etc.].

5. *Comb.*, as **twinkle-dress** *poet. nonce-wd.*, a sparkling party dress; **twinkle roll** *Aeronautics*, an aerobatic stunt (see quot. 1962); **twinkle-toed** *a.*, light-footed, nimble; (of a dance) quick, requiring agility.

1960 S. Plath *Colossus* 59 When on tiptoe the schoolgirls danced, Blinking flashlights like fireflies And singing the glowworm song, I could Not lift a foot in the twinkle-dress. **1962** *Flight International* LXXXII. 269/2 Highlights of an outstanding presentation by the Lightnings were the 'twinkle roll' in which the two wingmen of a three-aircraft formation rolled individually on either side of their leader as they passed low and fast in front of the crowd. **1978** R. Jansson *News Caper* 7 The fighter..slid over our port wing and did a twinkle roll in front of our nose. **1960** *Farmer & Stockbreeder* 29 Mar. (Suppl.) 10/2 Hand-in-hand with about six other youngsters she was scampering through a twinkle-toed dance which she later informed me is called 'the shuffle'. **1961** *Sunday Express* 7 May 14/3 Abandoned, twinkle-toed dancers leaping about. **1978** *Lancashire Life* Nov. 129/1 John Travolta doesn't have the monopoly of twinkle toed addicts.

twinkle, *v.*^{1} **4.** *intr. Dancing.* To perform the twinkle step. *temporary.*

1920 *Punch* 10 Nov. 366/2 *Chassée* to the left, two steps forward, two steps back, twinkle each way. *Ibid.*, I quite enjoyed that twinkling business. **1928** *B.B.C. Handbk.* 1929 201 Wireless dance music is often heard from houses where no one has ever 'twinkled' or 'hesitated' or 'glided' or 'dragged'.

twinkly, *a.* Add: **2.** *Comb.*, as *twinkly-eyed* adj.

1926 G. Frankau *My Unsentimental Journey* x. 135 A very self-possessed if somewhat twinkly-eyed young woman. **1974** P. Gzowski *Bk. about this Country* 11/2 Professor Hiebert..made twinkly-eyed, flirtatious remarks to Edith.

twinly (twi·nli), *adv. rare.* [f. Twin *a.* and *sb.* + -ly^2.] To an equal extent, doubly; in an identical degree.

1913 A. O'Connor *Poems* 50 A spot for man, bearing his cross, to seek, Where night and day are healers twinly bright. **1981** C. Dexter *Dead of Jericho* xxii. 123 Even if, in his boyhood, Sergeant Lewis's parents had been twinly blessed with privilege and wealth, it seems unlikely that their son would have won a scholarship to Winchester.

twinned, *ppl. a.* Add: **2. c.** Of a city, town, etc.: linked *with* another (in a different country) for the purpose of friendship and cultural exchange. Usu. *predic.* Cf. *twin town* s.v. *TWIN *a.* and *sb.* C e.

[**1923** E. Conybeare *Highways & Byways Cambr. & Ely* iii. 51 William of Wykeham..first conceived the idea of twinned colleges, in the provinces and at the University.] **1957** *Harrogate Advertiser* 16 Mar. 13/5 The congress is to talk about problems facing twinned towns, and report on the progress of the twinning. **1960** *Guardian* 25 Feb. 5/5 About 68 towns in Britain are now 'twinned' with towns abroad. **1976** *Times* 5 July 13/6 Leicester city is twinned with Krefeld and a most encouraging friendship has grown up between the two cities. **1980** *Times* 11 July 14/8 Delegates pay visits to twinned cities.

twinning, *vbl. sb.* Add: **2. b.** The linking (of two towns or of one town *with* another) for the purpose of friendship and cultural exchange. Cf. *TWINNED *ppl. a.* 2 c.

Occas. (as in quot. 1975) used of similar links between institutions such as schools.

1956 *Harrogate Advertiser* 9 June 8/3 French week celebrates the town's pioneer contribution to Le Monde Bilingue in its 'twinning' with Luchon, the spa town in the Pyrenees. **1962** *Guardian* 10 Mar. 16/3 The British Bi-Lingual Association..exists to promote the 'twinning' of towns in Britain with towns abroad. **1973** *New Society* 8 Feb. 284/2 Twinning [of towns]—a translation of the French term *jumelage*—became popular after the second world war, and reached a zenith of municipal goodwill in the late 1950s. **1975** *Globe & Mail* (Toronto) 12 Sept. 5/2 Students in Ontario and nine Caribbean countries and the Bahamas will have a chance to learn more about one another's lives through a new twinning program launched by the Ontario Ministry of Education. **1983** *Listener* 6 Jan. 4/1 There is the twinning of cities.

twirl, *sb.* Add: **c.** *Criminals' slang.* A skeleton key. Cf. *TWIRLER b.

1879 *Autobiogr. of Thief* in *Macmillan's Mag.* Oct. 502/2 It was now that I got acquainted with the use of twirls (skeleton-keys). **1923** J. C. GOODWIN *Sidelights* xxvi. 165 In the room Bill cracked with his twirls we piped a pater. **1980** P. KINSLEY *Vatchman Switch* x. 82 She scarcely heard him open the old lock..with the set of 'twirls'.

d. *slang.* A prison warder.

1891 J. BENT *Criminal Life* 272 Will you go and tell Dutch Doll to come up to try and get me a right twirl (good warder)... There is a twirl here from another stir. **1933** G. INGRAM *Stir* xi. 160 I'm standing orderly on this landing and the twirl'll do anything for me. **1962** *John o' London's* 25 Jan. 82/2 Prison officers..are sometimes referred to as *twirls*.

e. A cake in the shape of a twirl.

1973 E.-J. BAHR *Nice Neighbourhood* ii. 20 My Viennese aunt's recipe for butter twirls. **1979** M. INGATE *Tomb of Flowers* i. 8 All kinds of rolls and buns..twirls that went round and round with currants in between.

twirler. Add: **a.** Also *spec.* (*N. Amer.*), one who leads a marching band; a drum-major or drum-majorette. Cf. *TWIRLING *vbl. sb.*

1949 R. L. LEE *Baton* 2 A twirler must 'sell' himself to the audience..having..a big natural smile. **1965** *Daily Progress* (Charlottesville, Va.) 21 May 9/2 Twirlers from Maryland, Ohio, Pennsylvania, [etc.] will compete in the individual events [in a baton-twirling competition]. **1980** *Times* 7 Aug. 12/7 British twirlers tend to call themselves Majorettes.

b. *Criminals' slang.* = *TWIRL *sb.* c.

1921 J. C. GOODWIN in *Chambers's Jrnl.* 24 Sept. 680/1 Skeleton-keys, or 'twirlers', as the thieving fraternity call them. **1935** R. T. HOPKINS *Life & Death at Old Bailey* ii. 64 In a burglar's kit of tools will be found a jemmy, a bunch of skeleton keys, known as 'twirlers',..wedges, glass-workers' diamond, and a 'treacle plaster'. **1974** 'J. ASHFORD' *Colour of Violence* iv. 34 Weir, who was an expert with the twirlers, forced the lock in six seconds.

twirligig. (Earlier and later examples.)

1902 H. BELLOC *Path to Rome* 58 Investigating the twirligigs of the brain to find out where the soul is. **1942** R. KNOX *In Soft Garments* ii. 11 Take those twirligigs in our brains which are concomitant..of our thoughts. **1980** *Washington Post Bk. World* 2 Nov. 9/4 The dress with an orange twirligig pattern worn by Mrs Umphelby.

twirling, *vbl. sb.* (In Dict. s.v. TWIRL *v.*[1]) (Examples in sense of manipulating a baton as the leader of a marching band.)

1938 BENNER & PAINTER *Art of Baton Spinning* I. ii. 4/1 All actions of baton spinning may be divided into four categories: Looping, Twirling, Spinning and Throwing. **1945** F. H. RODGERS *Keokuk High School Marching Band Student's Handbk.* II. 11 It is not necessary that the drum major do any twirling. **1974** *Cleveland* (Ohio) *Plain Dealer* 26 Oct. 6-D/3 They got fancier with their twirling and began to do tricks. **1980** *Times* 7 Aug. 12/7 The United States Twirling Association..[wants] to have twirling recognized as a full Olympic sport.

twirp, var. *TWERP.

twisel, twissel, *sb.* (*a.*) **3.** Delete † and add later *poet.* example.

1956 [see *PENELOPIZE *v.*].

twist, *sb.*[1] Add: **II. 10.** (Earlier example.)

1830 G. COLMAN *Random Rec.* II. iii. 78 But plague upon their *bapps*..a doughy sort of something, between a roll and a *twist*.

11*. A curled piece *of* lemon (or other citrus) peel used to flavour a drink. Also (colloq.) *ellipt.*

1958 A. L. SIMON *Dict. Wines* 58/1 *Merry Widow*, 50 per cent Byrrh Wine; 50 per cent Dry Gin. Fill glass with ice; stir and strain in cocktail glass; twist of orange peel and serve. **1968** *Spirits* ('Know the Drink' Series) 36/1 *Cuba Libre*, 2 oz. light rum, 1 tablespoon unsweetened lime juice. Pour over ice in glass, top up with Coca-Cola, add a twist of lime or lemon rind. **1971** G. V. HIGGINS *Friends of Eddie Coyle* (1972) viii. 55 He ordered a vodka martini on the rocks with a twist. **1973** [see *LILLET]. **1981** W. SAFIRE in *N.Y. Times Mag.* 2 May 18/3 A *twist* is of course a twist of lemon skin.

III. 12. c. A dance in which the body is twisted from side to side; *spec.* a dance of this kind popular in the early 1960s. Also, music for such a dance.

1894 in *Sunday Times* (1962) 11 Mar. 42/5 They're ready an' willin', An' fair at Kadrillin', But my little Flo does the twist. **1898** J. D. BRAYSHAW *Slum Silhouettes* 239 An' there's no kid abaht it, they can both on 'em darnce. Kitty took fust prize..at the contest at that there 'all in Bow. You orter see 'er do the twist. **1928** *Daily Tel.* 11 May 11/1 'The Twist', created by M. Camille de Rhynal..is designed to cultivate gliding and swaying movements. **1961** *Guardian* 4 Nov. 6/3, I have read recently that a new dance has been introduced in America called 'The Twist'. **1965** M. SPARK *Mandelbaum Gate* iv. 116 My mother makes a party for the girls to do the Twist. **1966** *Crescendo* Nov. 6/1 'Manchild'..is an exciting, driving twist. **1978** S. NAIPAUL *North of South* I. iv. 102 Modishly dressed African men and women dancing what I assumed to be the twist.

15. a. Also, a spiral ornament in the stem of a wine-glass. Usu. with defining word, as *air-twist*, *colour twist* (see under the first elements), *enamel twist*, and freq. *attrib.*; also *transf.*, a glass with this kind of stem.

1897 A. HARTSHORNE *Old Eng. Glasses* 275 The stems are of opaque-white twists of many threads. **1923** H. J. POWELL *Glass-Making in Eng.* iv. 61 A goblet with enamel-twist stem. **1927** W. A. THORPE *English & Irish Glass* 18 Enamel-twists in white or coloured enamels. **1930** T. ROHAN *Old Glass Beautiful* 72 A Norwich twist glass. **1961** C. M. ELVILLE *Collector's Dict. Glass* 81 Those glasses in white monochrome included ales and glasses with straight-sided and bucket-shaped bowls, most of which had enamel-twist stems. **1965** P. M. HUBBARD *Hive of Glass* iv. 42 Have you anything in the way of drinking glasses?.. A twist for choice. **1973** *Guardian* 17 Mar. 18/6 A wine glass with an opaque twist might be worth £25, but with a blue spiral as well £200. A goblet with coloured twists would be worth upwards of £500. **1979** *Radio Times* 7–13 Apr. 25/2 We don't normally touch chipped [glass] items—though we did have a very fine colour twist with a slight chip which went for £800... You can still get a little opaque twist of the 1750s for £20–£30.

c. (Earlier example.)

1880 E. W. HAMILTON *Diary* 30 Nov. (1972) I. 83 The Irish land question evidently weighs heavily on Mr. G... He is afraid of Forster 'getting a twist'. Forster is evidently in favor of very strong measures.

d. *the twist*: cheating, dishonesty; treachery; also in phrs. *on, at the twist*. *Criminals' slang.*

1933 C. E. LEACH *On Top of Underworld* x. 141 *Twist, at the*, double-crossing. **1938** F. D. SHARPE *Sharpe of Flying Squad* 334 *Twist (the)*, to change something written or said from right to wrong. Sometimes called 'the Oliver Twist'... A dishonest bookmaker..would say: 'Put the Oliver on it', instead of..'Put the Twist on it'—which might be understood by the 'Mug'. **1977** J. WAINWRIGHT *Day of Peppercorn Kill* 29 Silver-smiths,.. one of 'em on the twist. **1979** —— *Duty Elsewhere* x. 36 If I'd wanted you picked up—if I'd wanted to work a twist—would I be here, now? *Ibid.* xxv. 67 Who the hell's poor? *Really* poor? Poor enough to merit going on the twist?

e. Slang phr. *to get one's knickers in a twist*: to become unduly agitated or angry (*joc.*).

1971 *Morning Star* 26 June 2/1 Britain's Foreign Office mandarins have had their knickers in a twist for the past fortnight. **1982** *Brand New York* (Lit. Rev. special issue) 118/3 There is no reason to get one's knickers in a twist and believe the revolution is nigh.

20. c. An unexpected development of events, esp. in a work of fiction; a change from usual procedure.

1941 B. SCHULBERG *What makes Sammy Run?* ii. 31 It's a comedy with a helluva twist in it... *she* kidnaps *him*. **1943** B. SMITH *Tree grows in Brooklyn* (1947) xxvi. 145 She did not report happenings truthfully, but gave them colour, excitement and dramatic twists. **1962** [see *SNAPPER *sb.*[1] 2 e]. **1974** 'E. LATHEN' *Sweet & Low* xii. 125 Well, there's a new twist for you... I wonder how much it's costing Dreyer to go on network TV and remind us all that they specialize in murder, as well as chocolate. **1978** *Navy News* Oct. 3/1 Portraying a sailor came almost naturally to Peter O'Toole when he played Robinson Crusoe in 'Man Friday', which provides a new twist to the Daniel Defoe classic. **1982** M. YOUNG *Elmhirsts of Dartington* ix. 227 The fact that he was nephew to..a staunch opponent of theirs was a twist that..appealed to them both. He got the job.

d. *round the twist* = *round the bend* s.v. *BEND *sb.*[4] 10 c. *slang.*

1960 D. ABSE *House of Cowards* in *Plays of Year 1960–61* XXIII. 190, I knew he was barmy. I knew that man was round the twist, sayin' things like that. **1971** 'F. CLIFFORD' *Blind Side* IV. iii. 178, I ask you. Enough to send you round the twist. **1977** D. BAGLEY *Enemy* v. 38, I swear Ogilvie thought I was going round the twist.

IV. 22. twist grip, a control operated manually by twisting, *spec.* one which serves as a hand-grip, and alters the throttle on a motor cycle or scooter, or the gears on a bicycle; **twist-lock**, a locking device for securing large containers to the trailers on which they are transported; **twist-off**, (*a*) *Oil Industry* (see quot. 1932); (*b*) *attrib.*, that may be removed manually by twisting.

1954 J. MASTERS *Bhowani Junction* i. 13, I was bending over the handlebars, turning the twist-grip throttle. **1962** *Engineering* 2 Nov. 584 Travel controls consist of a twist-grip (the amount of twist governing the speed of travel) and a steering wheel. **1975** *Which?* May 143/4 Twistgrip gear change. **1980** *Outdoor Life* (U.S.) (Northeast ed.) Oct. 26/1 Several times I've bumped that twist grip accidentally, turning the motor on. **1969** *Jane's Freight Containers 1968–69* 137/2 'Tie-down' devices..are designed to mate with the bottom corners of the containers, which are fitted with twist-locks. **1977** *Grimsby Even. Tel.* 26 May 4/8 (Advt.), One new Crane Freuhauf 40 ft PSK twistlock trailer, available for hire, £35 per week. **1932** *Amer. Speech* VII. 271 *Twist-off*.., a breaking off of the rotary drill pipe in the hole by torsional stress. **1964** *Supermarket & Self-Service* May/June 19/2 The new twist-off cap. **1970** W. SMITH *Gold Mine* xiii. 38 The whole rig was seconds away from a twist-off. **1974** P. L. MOORE et al. *Drilling Practices Manual* ii. 14 Other limitations have to be considered such as..pipe wear and the danger of twist-offs. **1981** A. LOPEZ *Compl. Course in Canning* (ed. 11) I. viii. 183 (*caption*) 'Twist-off' or Lug cap.

twist (twist), *sb.*[3] *slang* (chiefly *U.S.*). [short for *twist-and-twirl* (also used), rhyming slang for *girl*.] A girl, a young woman (freq. depreciatory).

1924 *Truth* (Sydney) 27 Apr. 6 *Twist and twirl*, a girl. **1926** *Clues* Nov. 162/2 *Twist*, a girl. **1927** *Dialect Notes* V. 466 *Twist*, n., a loose woman. **1932** [see *DOG-HOUSE b]. **1953** 'R. MACDONALD' in H. Waugh *Merchants of Menace* (1969) 93, I hate to see it happen to a pretty little twist like Fern. **1956** H. GOLD *Man who was not with It* (1965) xvii. 154 I'm just as good as any of those Pittsburgh twist-and-twirls. **1979** [see *PROPOSITION *sb.* 7 b].

twist, *v.* Add: **III. 9. d.** *to twist the tail* (of a person): to annoy, to coerce (someone). *to twist the lion's tail* (U.S.): to provoke the resentment of British people.

1895 *Lit. Digest* 25 May 112/2 Papers in the U.S. take to shouting 'Hands off!' to England... Twisting the lion's tail is a regular electioneering maneuver. **1909** 'O. HENRY' *Roads of Destiny* xvi. 259 [He] twisted the tail of a Connecticut insurance company that was trying to do business contrary to the edicts of the great Lone Star State. **1926** E. L. ABBEY *Twist of Lion's Tail* 9 John Bull takes the lion for his emblem... Twist the lion's tail and how he hollers! **1935** 'N. BLAKE' *Question of Proof* v. 91 Revenge seems to me least likely. Grown men don't kill boys just because they've had their tails twisted by them. **1956** A. WILSON *Anglo-Saxon Attitudes* I. iv. 173 I get a good deal of amusement twisting both their 'advanced' tails, particularly the egregious parson's. **1965** P. O'DONNELL *Modesty Blaise* vi. 72 So they were going to twist his tail for a while. Well,..the side-effects would have to be accepted stoically. **1979** E. NEWMAN *Sunday Punch* vii. 58, I took a silent vow never again to twist the lion's tail editorially.

e. *to twist* (someone's) *arm*: to force or persuade someone to do something. Also used *joc.* when no coercion is needed, esp. with reference to drinking.

1953 *Word for Word* (Whitbread & Co.) 36/2 *Twist one's arm*, to 'persuade' one to have a drink, when no persuasion is needed. **1953** BERREY & VAN DEN BARK *Amer. Thes. Slang* (1954) § 221/2 *Force; compel*... twist one's arm. *Ibid.* § 223/5 *Induce; persuade*..twist one's arm. **1968** C. COOPER *Thunder & Lightning Man* iv. 65 The National Trust, in their genteel fashion, are beginning to twist my arm. The property must be made to pay its way. **1972** G. BELL *Villains Galore* v. 57 'That looks a very nice little pub over there.'..'All right—you've twisted my arm enough,' admitted Boote. **1977** G. SCOTT *Hot Pursuit* xii. 108 If you'd twisted my arm I would have had to admit that it was even important enough to justify the risks. **1982** H. ENGEL *Ransom Game* xxv. 154, I let him twist my arm into taking a Scotch with water.

12. d. *trans.* To cheat, to defraud. *slang.*

1914 JACKSON & HELLYER *Vocab. Criminal Slang* 95 They had to learn awareness in the school of cold, hard facts, having been..'twisted'..times innumerable. **1956** *People* 13 May 2/3 Don't imagine that all the boys in the trade are out to twist you. **1967** P. RYAN *How I became Yorkshireman* xv. 95 He were..content to be twisted daft wi'out mekking a mouse-squeak after value for his brass.

e. *trans.* and *intr. Insurance.* To induce someone to change a policy from one company to another. Cf. *TWISTING *vbl. sb.* 5.

1924 WEBSTER Add., *Twist, v.t. Life Insurance.* To induce (a person) to drop a policy already in force in a company other than that of the twisting agent for one in the agent's company.—*twister, n.* **1936** *Sun* (Baltimore) 29 July 16/2 He expressed the hope that any agent found 'twisting' or attempting to discourage policyholders in the Pacific Mutual not to retain their insurance would be reported to the Insurance Division.

IV. 14. b. (Earlier example.)

1816 W. LAMBERT *Instructions & Rules for playing Cricket* 20 The Ball may be twisted by the usual mode of under-armed Bowling.

c. *intr.* To dance the twist (*TWIST *sb.*[1] 12 c).

1961 *Guardian* 30 Dec. 5/3 It is a week with only one new film, a small loud monstrosity called 'Hey, Let's Twist'. **1968** J. UPDIKE *Couples* ii. 166 Frank was grotesquely Twisting..opposite Carol Constantine.

15. b. In Vingt-et-un, to receive a card dealt face upwards; also, to deal a card in this manner. Occas. *trans.* and as *imp.* Also *fig.* Cf. *STICK *v.*[1] 6 e.

1921 P. ALSTON *Card Games* 121 If it is not desired to buy, the usual expression is to say 'Twist'. *Ibid.* 122

Having bought a player can then twist; but once having twisted, a card cannot be bought. **1939** Phillips & Westall *Compl. Bk. Card Games* 194 The player can either buy cards or can have them 'twisted'..; a card twisted is turned face upwards. *Ibid.*, B has a 9 and a 5; he says 'twist me one'. **1963** G. F. Hervey *Handbk. Card Games* 285 He can twist: that is to say he elects to receive a card face upwards. **1972** *Guardian* 12 Oct. 1/3 Every pontoon player will understand the dilemma of the Tory chiefs. They are undecided whether to stick or twist on a relatively modest hand of cards. **1976** J. Archer *Not a Penny More, Not a Penny Less* xii. 136 The young man on Harvey's left also drew a ten and asked the dealer to twist again.

16. (Earlier example.)

1800 T. Boxall *Rules & Instructions for Playing Cricket* 18 When the ball goes out of a bowler's hand he must endeavour to make it twist a little.

twisted, *ppl. a.* Add: **2. c.** Of the stem of a wine-glass: having a spiral ornament inside. Cf. *twist *sb.*[1] 15 a.

1897 [see *air-twisted* s.v. *air *sb.*[1] II]. **1897** A. Hartshorne *Old Eng. Glasses* 61 The glasses which we know generically as those with 'twisted stems', that is, with thin air-threads, and opaque white spiral lines in their standards. **1929** W. A. Thorpe *Hist. English & Irish Glass* I. 199 Between 1714 and 1745..twisted stems are rare. **1970** G. Gros-Galliner *Glass* iv. 108 A twisted stem decoration could be achieved by rib-moulding and rib-twisting.

3. b. Of a person: neurotic, emotionally unbalanced; perverted. Also *transf.* and with *up*.

1900 *Dialect Notes* II. 68 [College words.] *Twisted*, pp. as adj. 1. Wrong. 2. Crazy. 3. Confused. **1956** R. M. Lester *Towards Hereafter* xiv. 165 Those who had held to the twisted idea that all psychical phenomena and spirit communication was 'the work of the devil' began to think again. **1963** *Times Lit. Suppl.* 25 Jan. 64/3 Alan..who is as extroverted as Paul is twisted up. **1963** A. Heron *Towards Quaker View of Sex* iii. 34 The emotional strains ..produce the twisted embittered woman, only too familiar to psychiatrists. **1971** A. Morice *Death of Gay Dog* v. 72 Old Roger..does so enjoy having lots of money; not like that twisted-up Nancy. **1978** S. Sheldon *Bloodline* xlii. 360 Snuff films..would have been made to be shown privately to wealthy individuals who got their pleasure in twisted, sadistic ways.

4. twisted pair *Teleph.*, a pair of insulated conductors twisted about each other, as in a flex or by alternating their positions on successive telegraph poles.

1923 T. E. Herbert *Telephony* xxiii. 651 The disturbing effect of a twisted pair in good condition is relatively minute when compared with a single wire. **1979** *Sci. Amer.* Aug. 9/2 (Advt.), Each link can be up to five miles long, and uses a single, shielded, twisted pair cable.

twister, *sb.* Add: **4. b.** Also, a dishonest person, a crook. *slang.*

1863 *Once a Week* IX. 568/2 One swags all that the palmer purchases, and stays outside to render the 'twister' any assistance he may need. **1915** *Film Flashes* 4 Dec. 1 'Twisters'..endeavour to put German films in the picture houses, under the pretext that they were made in a neutral, Continental country. **1930** J. B. Priestley *Angel Pavement* vii. 367 If you ask me, he looks a rotten twister—bit of a crook or something. **1937** [see *spiv *sb.*]. **1940** E. Pound *Cantos* lv. 53 And Liu-hoei said Ngan was a twister. **1966** [see *knuck 3]. **1976** *Milton Keynes Express* 23 July 7/3 He was said to have called two women teachers 'cheats and twisters' and had refused to apologise for his remarks.

c. (Earlier example.)

1832 P. Egan *Bk. Sports* I. 348/2 The batsman now his weapon rais'd To meet a puzzling twister.

d. Delete 'In the Mississippi region'. (Further examples.)

1903 G. S. Wasson *Cap'n Simeon's Store* vi. 108 He see in his paper where the English ship Falls of Ettrick was plunked on the Diamond Shoal and had went to pieces in that ole twister of a breeze there was a spell ago. **1930** Neff & Henry *Folk-Say Regional Misc.* 48, I never did see so many of them little twisters all a-goin at one and the same time. **1955** *Sci. News Let.* 18 June 388/2 A Weather Bureau meteorologist is making miniature tornadoes in a small box in the hope of learning more about what causes 'twisters'. **1967** *Boston Sunday Globe* 23 Apr. 1/2 The most vicious twisters in the history of the Midwest, striking heavily-populated sections of Northern Illinois and Western Michigan, left 53 dead. **1974** V. Nabokov *Look at Harlequins* (1975) iv. ii. 162 A group of fifteen schoolchildren..were safe in the sudden darkness of that sturdy building when the twister struck. **1977** J. Cleary *Vortex* iv. 93 You hear the twister warnings, too?

f. A grossly exaggerated tale; a lie. *Naut. slang.* ? *Obs.*

1834 W. N. Glascock *Naval Sketch-Bk.* 2nd Ser. I. 235 I'm an even-minded man..that's providin' I wasn't provok'd by lying lip,—but if the best man in the sarvus was to come up to me,..to tell *me* such a thund'ring twister..why I'd just..floor the feller as flat as a flounder. **1850** H. Melville *White Jacket* II. xxviii. 184 Among innumerable 'yarns and twisters' reeled off in our maintop during our pleasant run to the north, none could match those of Jack Chase. **1873** [in Dict., sense 6].

g. A type of handcuff (see quot. 1939).

1910 [see *nipper *sb.*[1] 4 c]. **1939** *Fortune* July 104/1 A style of handcuff, sometimes called 'twisters', used by the New York police instead of the old bracelet type. It consists of a short length of chain with a T-bar at each end. The policeman wraps it around the prisoner's wrist, twists the two T's like a tourniquet as tightly as necessary to make the prisoners come along like a lamb.

h. A key. *twister to the slammer*: (see quot. 1940). *U.S. slang.*

1940 *Music Makers* May 37/3 *Twister to the slammer*, the key to the door. **1941** J. Smiley *Hash House Lingo* 55 *Twister*, key. **1944** D. Burley in A. Dundes *Mother Wit* (1973) 208 Give the jivers a break and substitute the phrase, 'twister to the slammer', for the word 'key'. **1970** C. Major *Dict. Afro-Amer. Slang* 117 *Twister*, doorkey.

i. = Twitch *sb.*[1] 3 b (*spec.* sense). *U.S.*

1940 W. Faulkner *Hamlet* iii. ii. 223 He..reached down from its nail in the wall a short, smooth white-oak stick eyed at the end with a loop of hemp rope—a twister which Houston had used with his stallion. **1948** *Richmond* (Va.) *Times-Dispatch* 23 Aug. 4/4 A mean horse may take up to eight hours to shoe, using rope harnesses to tie up the leg being worked on, or even a 'twister' for the horse's nose. **1968** R. F. Adams *Western Words* (ed. 2) 334/1 *Twitch*, a small loop of cord with a stick through it used to punish a held horse. The loop is placed vertically around the animal's upper lip and then tightened by twisting the stick. Also called *twister*.

j. One who dances the twist (*twist *sb.*[1] 12 c).

[**1942** Berrey & Van den Bark *Amer. Thes. Slang* § 583/27 *Hip dancer*...twister, wiggle dancer, wiggler.] **1966** 'K. Nicholson' *Hook, Line & Sinker* viii. 97 'I just go on Twist nights, don't I, Di?' 'She's a jolly good twister too.' **1977** J. Wilson *Making Hate* ii. 21 He'd been the runner-up in the Champion Twister competition at the Palais.

6. (Earlier examples.) Also (*dial.*), a blow which makes the victim twist or writhe; also *fig.* in U.S. colloq. phr. *to knock* one *the* (or *a*) *twister*.

1835 in *Amer. Speech* (1965) XL. 133 So, low each pill was a twister. I swallow'd about three Doctor's shops. **1843** J. R. Planché *Fortunio* I. ii. 9 Ha, ha! I think that was a twister! **1886** F. T. Elworthy *W. Somerset Word-bk.* 783 *Twister*.., a blow with a whip or other instrument. **1896** G. Ade *Artie* vi. 55 That's what knocked me the twister. I thought this fellow was all right. **1908** G. Sanger *70 Yrs. a Showman* xvii. 59, I got a twister well home under his ribs that sent him grunting and staggering. **1934** G. Ade *Let.* 15 Mar. (1973) 181, I was, to use an old slang phrase, 'knocked a twister' when I received your letter [etc.].

8. *Insurance.* An insurance salesman or agent who unscrupulously induces a holder to switch his policy from one company to another. orig. *U.S.*

1924 [see *twist *v.* 12 e]. **1979** *Telegraph* (Brisbane) 24 Sept. 24/2 The industry calls it twisting. Presumably its practitioners are called twisters. The industry says that life insurance consumers are being ripped off by its practice.

9. *U.S. slang.* In various senses with reference to the taking of drugs (see quots.).

1936 [see *marijuana addict* s.v. *marijuana 3]. **1936** *Amer. Speech* XI. 127/1 *Twister*. 1. A feigned spasm. **1938** *Ibid.* XIII. 192/1 *Twister*. 3. A speed-ball or whiz-bang [vein-shot of mixed drugs]. 4. A bit of violent retching or vomiting of blood or mucus during withdrawal distress. 5. A ration of narcotics. **1951** *Even. Sun* (Baltimore) 27 Mar. 4/1 A powerful combination of 'bernice snorting' and heroin 'shooting' was called 'blowing speed balls' or 'twisters' or 'whiz bangs'. **1959** J. E. Schmidt *Narcotics* 185 *Twister*, an intravenous injection of a potent narcotic taken by a drug addict, esp. a dose composed of heroin or morphine and cocaine.

10. Var. *twistor 1.

11. Comb. **twister's cramp** *Path.*, pain in the hands or fingers produced by twisting or wringing.

1923 E. W. Hope *Industr. Hygiene & Med.* viii. 516 This process of knotting [the warp threads] is done by a peculiar rolling motion of the fingers. The constant repetition of the movement..gives rise in certain operatives to a peculiar trade affection known as 'twister's cramp', the symptoms of which are pain, usually referred to the base of the thumb, tenderness of the muscles, and sometimes swelling at the base of the thumb. **1967** *Punch* 29 Mar. 458/3 Twister's Cramp can still be acquired by any housewife who is eccentric enough to wring clothes by hand.

twisteroo (twiːstĕrūˑ). *colloq.* [f. *twist *sb.*[1] 20 c; cf. *-eroo.] (A narrative with) an unexpected twist.

1963 *Punch* 13 Feb. 237/1 The story was a twisteroo, a variation, of the legend of King Midas. **1965** J. P. Carstairs *Concrete Kimono* xxx. 251, I think when you hear me out the twisteroo will appeal to you. **1970** M. Pei *Words in Sheep's Clothing* iii. 23 There is in the field [of 'weasel' words used on the screen] one suffix which may be described as derogatory, and that is the -eroo of 'twisteroo'.

twistical, *a.* (Earlier U.S. example.)

1805 T. G. Fessenden *Democracy Unveiled* v. 158 *Certain* sages, learn'd and *twistical*... Have prov'd what's wonderful.

twistify (twiˑstifəi), *v. U.S. dial.* and *colloq.* ? *Obs.* [f. Twisty *a.* + -fy. Cf. Twistification.] *trans.* To make twisty (*lit.* and *fig.*); to twist. Hence **twiˑstified, twiˑstifying** *ppl. adjs.*

1835 R. M. Bird *Hawks of Hawk Hollow* I. xix. 254 The path is astonishing twistified, and not fit for horse. **1843** 'J. Slick' *High Life in N.Y.* I. 148 There was the fat nigger a twistifying his whip-lash round the horses' heads. **1845** in C. Cist *Cincinnati Misc.* I. 167, I knew..an individual..who possessed this twistifying talent in high perfection... Many amusing stories of his faculty of shifting have been told me. **1872** *Newton Kansan* 17 Oct. 4/3 [The Republicans] repudiate his twistified explanations now.

twisting, *vbl. sb.* Add: **5.** *Insurance.* (See quots.) Cf. *twister *sb.* 8. orig. *U.S.*

1906 *Even. Post* (N.Y.) 20 Jan. (Financial Section) 7/1 By 'twisting' is meant the persuading of policyholders in one company to transfer their insurance to another. **1962** L. E. Davids *Dict. Insurance* 205/2 *Twisting*, practice of inducing any policyholder to lapse or cancel a policy for the purpose of replacing such policy with another to the detriment of the policyholder. The practice is considered to be unethical as well as illegal. **1979** *Telegraph* (Brisbane) 24 Sept. 24/2 In simple terms twisting works like this. A life insurance agent sells you a policy when he is working for company X... Three years later he switches allegiance to company Y. To make life easier he retraces his steps..to tell you that the policy from company X is outdated.

twistor (twiˑstəɹ). [f. Twist *v.* + -or.] **1.** *Computers.* Also **-er.** A non-volatile memory element consisting of an insulated copper wire wound helically round with a wire of readily magnetized material. Freq. *attrib.*

1957 A. H. Bobeck in *Bell Syst. Technical Jrnl.* XXXVI. 1319 Three methods have been developed for storing information in a coincident-current manner on magnetic wire. The resulting memory cells have been collectively named the 'twistor'. **1962** *Flight Internat.* LXXXII. 170/1 A permanent twistor memory and a ferrite-core scratch-pad memory are vital to reliability, assuring continuous operation until an attacking missile is intercepted and destroyed. **1975** D. G. Fink *Electronics Engineers' Handbk.* xxii. 19 A twister memory is used as the semipermanent memory constituting a major portion of the program store in central control.

2. *Physics.* A type of spinor used in some descriptions of space-time (see quots. 1967, 1973).

1967 R. Penrose in *Jrnl. Math. Physics* VIII. 346 Twistors are..the 'spinors' which are relevant to the six-dimensional space whose (pseudo-) rotation group is isomorphic with the conformal group of ordinary Minkowski space-time. The simplest (non-scalar) twistors constitute a four-dimensional, four-valued representation of the restricted conformal group... The general twistor is then a many-index quantity constructible from the above basic twistors by means of the usual 'tensor type' rules. **1973** —— & MacCallum in *Physics Rep.* VI. 244 Twistors (that is to say, the original flat-space twistors about which these notes are mainly concerned) are actually the reduced spinors for the proper pseudo-orthogonal group SO(2,4) which is locally isomorphic with, and 2-1 homomorphic with, the restricted conformal group of flat space-time. *Ibid.*, A twistor (of the simplest type) can be pictured 'classically' as effectively a zero rest-mass particle in free motion, where the particle may possess an intrinsic spin. **1979** *New Scientist* 31 May 737 Twistor theory is incomplete, but it offers considerable hope for a quite new approach to the basic problems of theoretical physics.

twisty, *a.* (*sb.*) Add: **c.** = *twisted *ppl. a.* 2 c.

1929 L. P. Hartley in *Mercury Story Bk.* 206 The glasses with twisty stems were there.

twit, *sb.*[1] Add: **2. b.** A fool; a stupid or ineffectual person. *slang.*

1934 E. Linklater *Magnus Merriman* xvi. 178 He was..a false hero who flaunted himself in fine colours when he was drunk and dwindled to a shabby twit when sober. **1960** F. Raphael *Limits of Love* i. iii. 34 Don't be a twit, Sid. **1964** *Spectator* 10 Apr. 493/1 By making his psychologists a dim bunch of twits he weakens his statements. **1970** N. Fleming *Czech Point* i. 20 No one but a prize twit or Captain Oates would have ventured out in this weather. **1977** C. McCullough *Thorn Birds* xviii. 467 There's no need to get so worked up about it, you twit. **1984** *Observer* 4 Mar. 7/7, I hear and read such phrases as 'geriatric old twit': an expression which would hardly have sprung to the lips of the pious Aeneas.

twit, *int.* and *sb.*[3] **2.** (Later example.)

1922 T. S. Eliot *Waste Land* (1923) iii. 15 Twit twit twit Jug jug jug jug jug jug So rudely forc'd. Tereu.

twitch, *v.*[1] Add: **3.** (Later example with *off.*)

1934 T. S. Eliot *Rock* i. 28 As he names them they twitch off their caps and kneel.

8. Also said of a smile.

1930 'Sapper' *Finger of Fate* 31 The faintest suspicion of a smile would twitch round his lips.

twitched, *ppl. a.* (In Dict. s.v. Twitch *v.*[1]) Add: Also *spec.*, twitchy, irritable, 'rattled'. *slang.*

1959 P. Townend *Died o' Wednesday* xii. 216 He or she is likely to be..worried..'twitched to the eyebrows' as the flying boys have it. **1981** S. Jackman *Game of Soldiers* i. i. 16 The C.O.'s in there and he's a bit twitched.

twitcher. Add: **4.** A bird-watcher whose main aim is to collect sightings of rare birds. So **twiˑtching** *vbl. sb.*

1977 *Birds* Summer 59/3 Twitchers are difficult to identify because they are polymorphic. Best clues are behavioural including carrying Zeiss binoculars and *Where to Watch Birds*... Known to have nested in Wandsworth and possess a sense of humour. **1978** *Sunday*

Times 19 Feb. 5/1 (*caption*) The people in the picture are 'twitchers'—birdwatchers. **1980** [see *TICKER^{3} 2]. **1980** L. BROWN in Howard & Moore *Compl. Checklist Birds of World* p. vii, Certainly, knowing what a bird is and where it occurs is the first step towards the wider interest that may stem from merely ticking a bird off on a list—twitching, as the vulgar parlance has it. **1982** *Times* 15 June 10/4 Twitchers are only interested in spotting rarities to claim they have seen them. Ornithologists are serious students, who despise and distrust twitchers. **1982** *Brit. Birds* LXXV. 537 The word 'twitcher' has, over the last decade, gained widespread use, meaning a person who 'chases' rare birds... I first heard the term from Bob Emmett at Beachy Head in 1968, when it was used to mean anyone who got 'twitchy' when southeast winds blew and headlands bristled with Pied Flycatchers and Redstarts.

twitchety (twi·tʃėti), *a.* Also **twitchetty.** [f. TWITCH *v.*^{1} or *sb.*^{1} + *-et* + *-Y*^{1}, perh. after *crotchety, fidgety*, etc.] Twitchy, nervous; of things, moving back and forth.

1859 HOTTEN *Dict. Slang, Twitchetty*, nervous, fidgetty. **1936** W. GREENE *Death in Deep South* III. 214 When I heard the buzzer, I wuz' mos' asleep and I wait two three minutes... It didn't ring again, but I git up anyways and look at the elevator and see where Number One gone twitchety. **1973** *Nature* 28 Sept. 225/3 Variables are, apparently, pulsating, eruptive, symbiotic, eclipsing or twitchety.

twi·tchily, *adv.* [f. TWITCHY *a.*^{1} + -LY^{2}.] Nervously, in a twitchy manner; displaying nervous energy.

1934 in WEBSTER. **1964** J. BRAINE *Jealous God* iii. 70 A girl..who was pretty in an acceptable way, not tartish, not twitchily refined. **1978** J. UPDIKE *Coup* (1979) iii. 108 She no longer moved like the great-granddaughter of a leopard, but more electrically, twitchily, like a modern woman connected to a variety of energy-sources.

twitchy, *a.*^{1} Add: **1.** Also said of a smile.

1924 W. M. RAINE *Troubled Waters* xx. 221 When she said goodbye to him it was with a wan twitchy little smile on her face.

Hence **twi·tchiness**, the state or condition of being twitchy; nervousness, fidgetiness, irritability.

1933 J. THURBER *My Life & Hard Times* p. xv, This type of writing is..the manifestation of a twitchiness at once cosmic and mundane. **1984** *Times* 23 Mar. 12/6 (*heading*) Twitchiness in the president's camp.

twitteration. For *nonce-wd.* read *Obs. rare* and add earlier example.

1820 G. COLMAN *X.Y.Z.* I. iii. 26 A female hand! bless me, I'm all over in a twitteration!

twittering, *ppl. a.* **2.** (Later example.)

1936 T. S. ELIOT *Coll. Poems 1909–35* 189 Not here Not here the darkness, in this twittering world.

twizzle, *v.* **2.** (Earlier examples.)

1788 E. PICKEN *Poems & Epistles* Gloss. 248/1 Twisle, to twist, fold. *c* **1840** LADY WILTON *Art of Needle-Work* xvi. 255 In vain she cut and screwed the thread, she burnt it in the candle..she twizled it between her finger and thumb..but enter the eye of the needle it would not.

two, *a.* and *sb.* Add: **B. I.** *adj.* **1. a.** *two cents' worth* (U.S.): = *TWO PENNYWORTH (fig.); cf. *two-cent* adj. in sense IV. 2 below; *no two ways about it*: see WAY *sb.*^{1} 14 j.

1942 *Short Guide Gt. Brit.* (U.S. War Dept.) 18 You will hear..Britons openly criticizing their government... That isn't an occasion for you to put in your two-cents worth. **1954** *Sun* (Baltimore) 20 Dec. (B ed.) 14/7 The discussion concerning writers about old age in your column..impels me to add my 2 cents' worth.

2. a. Phr. *that makes two of us*, colloq. formula of agreement: the same is true of me, I am in the same position, I agree.

1956 H. KURNITZ *Invasion of Privacy* x. 71 'He was an amnesia victim.' 'That makes two of us,' said Zorn bitterly. **1974** P. DICKINSON *Poison Oracle* ii. 37 She wanted reassurance. That makes two of us, he thought. **1980** A. E. FISHER *Midnight Men* ix. 116 'She barely understands anything that is g-going on.' 'That makes two of us,' he said.

3. c. *two-thirds*: *spec.* in *Fashion*, applied to a garment that is shorter than the standard full length by about a third.

1963 *Harper's Bazaar* Oct. 56/2 This dreamy two-thirds coat. **1980** *Washington Post* 4 Dec. D3 The writers are really more interested in who's being reassigned to the Ottawa bureau than in whether two-thirds stockings are a trend or not.

5. b. *two-three*: for *dial.* read 'chiefly *dial.* and *U.S.*' (Further examples.)

1930 W. FAULKNER *As I lay Dying* 83 It'd taken them two-three days to get her to town in the wagon. **1949** L. HUGHES *One-Way Ticket* 40, I knock on your door About two-three A.M. **1962** J. F. STRAKER *Coil of Rope* ii. 13 You'll have to wait two-three days if you don't go now. **1976** A. PRICE *War Game* I. viii. 159 The last two-three years he's been working on a post-graduate thesis.

c. (Later examples.)

1818 SCOTT *Heart Midl.* III. ix. 229, I will explain to you in two words the connection betwixt this young woman and me. *a* **1845** S. SMITH *Sk. Moral Philos.* (1850) Lect. xix. 280, I never could find any man who could think for two minutes together. **1956** N. MARSH *Off with his Head* (1957) v. 92, I wonder if I may have two words with Dame Alice Mardian?

II. *sb.* **1. a.** (Earlier example of *to put two and two together.*)

1849 LYTTON *Caxtons* II. XII. i. 254 If they saw that, in proportion to their civility to me, they were depopulated by you, they would put two and two together and renounce my acquaintance.

2. g. Also *in two ups* (Austral. colloq.) = *in two shakes* s.v. SHAKE *sb.*^{1} 2 h in Dict. and Suppl.

1934 T. WOOD *Cobbers* iii. 25 He said we'd be there in two ups. **1941** BAKER *Dict. Austral. Slang* 79 *Two ups, in*, in a brief space of time. **1967** J. MORRISON in *Coast to Coast 1965–6* 133 Too close to dark now, Mister, but we'll have you out of that in two ups in the morning.

IV. 1. a. *two-bar, -base, -bearing, -beat* (also *ellipt.* as *sb.*), *-bed, -berth, -blade, -car, -centre, -channel, -colour* (also *fig.*), *-column, -component, -cultures* (cf. *CULTURE *sb.* 5 c), *-deck* (later example), *-digit, -dollar* (also *fig.*), *-door, -drift* (*DRIFT *sb.* 2 f), *-electrode, -front, -hour* (earlier example), *-income, -lane* (*LANE *sb.* 2 d), *-level, -light* (earlier example), *-member, -pack, -part, -pedal, -person, -piano, -pin, -place, -point, -position, -reel, -seat, -sex, -shilling* (earlier example), *-stage, -story* (earlier example; also *-storey*), *-stripe, -term, -tier* (usu. *fig.*), *-topsail, -track* (also *fig.*), *-volume, -wheel* (earlier example), *-wire, -word.* **b.** *two-armed, -banked, -bedded* (earlier examples), *-columned, -decked, -engined, -fingered, -forked, -framed, -fronted, -gunned, -horsed, -named* (later example), *-pronged* (also *fig.*), *-seated, -storied* (earlier example; also *-storeyed*), *-stranded, -sworded, -termed, -tiered, -toothed* (earlier example), *-winged* (later examples). **c.** *two-hitter* (U.S.), *-mover* (earlier example), *-parter, -reeler, -striper* (see *STRIPER 1). **e.** *two-and-a-half striper* (see *STRIPER 1), *two-and-two* (cf. sense I. 2 d in Dict.), *two-in-oneness, two-plus-two, two-to-one.*

1861 'R. HARRINGTON' *Swimming* p. iii, They [*sc.* school children] often passed a river when out for a miserable two-and-two walk. **1957** J. S. BRUNER *Beyond Information Given* (1974) i. 35 The experiment is done on a conventional two-armed bandit, the subject having the task of betting on whether a light will appear on the left or on the right. **1935** L. MACNEICE *Poems* 25 Poetry is not only the bridging of two-banked rivers. **1967** 'M. HUNTER' *Cambridgeshire Disaster* x. 65 He warmed his hands briefly at the two-bar fire. **1880** N. BROOKS *Fairport Nine* 184 Ned made a fine two base hit which brought Watson home amidst great excitement. **1974** J. H. SUBAK-SHARPE et al. in Carlile & Skehol *Evolution in Microbial World* 132 Correlations exist between three-base sequences (that is codons) in messenger RNA and two-base sequences in the DNA coding for that Messenger RNA. **1922** *Times* 20 June 8/5 A short two-bearing auxiliary shaft. **1960** E. L. DELMAR-MORGAN *Cruising Yacht Equipment & Navigation* i. 20 The principle.., as with all two-bearing fixes, attains its best accuracy when the position lines are 90 deg. to each other. **1938** *Swing* July 18/2 *Two-beat swing*.., swing in which the accent is on the second or fourth beats. **1978** *Detroit Free Press* 16 Apr. 11 c/2 Chet Bogan plays two-beat, Dixiebelle sing same. **1792** H. NEWDIGATE *Let.* Feb. in A. E. Newdigate-Newdegate *Cheverels* (1898) viii. 110 She..shew'd me a neat 2 bed Garret where I dare say we shall sleep as well as in a Palace. **1962** E. SNOW *Other Side of River* (1963) lx. 461 Bachelor quarters varied from small two-bed to larger four-bed and six-bed rooms. **1784** H. NEWDIGATE *Let.* in A. E. Newdigate-Newdegate *Cheverels* (1898) iv. 59 We have obtained to Sleep to-night in a tollerable two bedded Room. **1788** J. WOODFORDE *Diary* 19 May (1927) III. 26, I slept at the Kings Head, in a two bedded Room. **1969** M. PUGH *Last Place Left* xxi. 164 He made out sleeper tickets for us..and we shared a two-berth compartment. **1967** *Jane's Surface Skimmer Systems 1967–68* 9/1 Propulsion is provided by two two-blade metal variable pitch propellers. **1983** *Flight Internat.* 10 Sept. 703/1 A pair of two-blade teetering rotors are mounted 50° apart. **1927** *Sat. Even. Post* 9 Apr. 89 This is a two-car country. **1961** M. BEADLE *These Ruins are Inhabited* (1963) viii. 105 Two-car families are rare in England. **1964** J. W. LINNETT *Electronic Struct. Molecules* ix. 152 Sovers showed that a very good description of the excited states could also be achieved by employing two-centre bonding and anti-bonding orbitals only. **1939** *Florida* (Federal Writers' Project) I. 75 Two-channel highways divided by a parkway to reduce the menaces of bright lights and head-on collisions. **1973** G. TALBOT *Ten Seconds from Now* (1974) xvi. 203 A blaring juke-box and two-channel television. **1979** H. KISSINGER *White House Years* xx. 827 The two-channel system and its significance. **1907** *T. Eaton & Co. Catal.* Spring & Summer 43/1 Men's fancy Sweaters,..medium weight, two color effect. **1925** I. A. RICHARDS *Princ. Lit. Crit.* xxvii. 211 *Macbeth*..is a highly successful, easily apprehended, two-colour melodrama. **1967** E. CHAMBERS *Photolitho-Offset* xv. 236 The wide use of lithography for colour work has resulted in the development of two-colour machines. **1916** E. WALLACE *Let.* 13 Nov. in M. Gilbert *Winston S. Churchill* (1972) III. Compan. II. 1583 Do a two column story. **1922** JOYCE *Ulysses* 465 Tom Rochford..jumps from his two-columned machine. **1956** *Nature* 18 Feb. 328/2 Only two-component solvent systems were investigated. **1966** *Listener* 1 Sept. 297/1 As Margaret Mead puts it: 'The recent two-cultures discussion is essentially a lament about..lack of communication.' **1960** *Farmer & Stockbreeder* 29 Mar. 93/1 Sending the farm two-deck lorry to the south-west and back. **1883** *Man. Seamanship for Boys' Training Ships* (Admiralty) (1886) 2 A two-decked ship. So named from having two gun decks below the upper deck. **1963** *Rep. Comm. Inquiry Decimal Currency* 9 in *Parl. Papers 1962–3* (Cmnd. 2145) XI. 195 People find considerably greater difficulty in remembering and manipulating three-digit numbers than two-digit numbers. **1793** *Deb. Congr. U.S.* 3 Jan. (1849) 788 The miserable two-dollar men who were raised for a six months' service. **1873** T. B. HAZARD *Nailer Tom's Diary* (1930) 414/2 Went to Thomas Rodmans Store to get a two dollar bill changed. **1929** *Century Mag.* Autumn 68 He hated what he called 'two-dollar words' and 'high hat' manners. **1908** *Sears, Roebuck Catal.* 61/1 The two-door automatic Model 'A' desk cabinet. **1982** *Sunday Tel.* 1 Aug. 6/2 You can get a 1.8 litre, two-door, four-seat sports saloon for £5,950. **1926** H. MACPHERSON *Mod. Astron.* 156 The results of this study of stars of very large proper motion, scattered all over the sky, were strongly in support of the two-drift hypothesis. **1921** *Wireless World* IX. 187/1 The two-electrode Fleming valve. **1931** *19th Cent.* Feb. 154 The standard two-engined type. **1966** D. FRANCIS *Flying Finish* v. 64 Small two-engined job..cost nearly thirty-five pounds per flying hour to hire. **1910** W. DE LA MARE *Three Mulla-Mulgars* 47 A behemothian bull-Ephelanto..wound his long, two-fingered trunk round Nod's belly. **1978** *Church Times* 27 Jan. 5/3 What she was doing was making a kind of 'I'm as good as you, see if I'm not' two-fingered gesture of defiance at society. **1981** H. CARPENTER *W. H. Auden* (1983) II. iv. 341 He was an adequate two-fingered typist. **1934** DYLAN THOMAS in *Criterion* Oct. 28 The two framed globe that spun into a score. **1946** *New Yorker* 23 Mar. 74/2 One of those two-front wars which 'Mein Kampf' had sensibly argued couldn't be won. **1856** J. G. WHITTIER *Panorama* 12 The two-fronted Future... To-day, your servant, subject to your will; To-morrow, master, or for good or ill. **1936** DYLAN THOMAS *Twenty-Five Poems* 44 And from the windy West came two-gunned Gabriel. **1949** *Time* 10 Oct. 47/2 Accompanied by a grim, 200-lb., two-gunned Big Spring sheriff. **1974** *State* (Columbia, S. Carolina) 26 Apr. 4-B/3 Paul Splittorff pitched a two-hitter for seven innings. **1939** W. B. YEATS *On Boiler* 31 There in a two horsed carriage..Great bladdered Emer sat. **1880** 'MARK TWAIN' *Tramp Abr.* xix. 171 A two-hour pedestrian excursion. **1969** *Guardian* 31 Mar. 2/1 The two-income family spends 15 per cent more on alcohol. **1895** HARDY *Jude* VI. ii. 404 O my comrade, our perfect union—our two-in-oneness—is now stained with blood! **1957** J. KEROUAC *On Road* (1958) II. viii. 156 On a two-lane highway to Baton Rouge in purple darkness. **1957** H. WHITEHALL in N. Frye *Sound & Poetry* II. 142 Metrical patterns..based on the two-level contrast of stressed versus unstressed syllables. **1981** *Beautiful Brit. Columbia* Summer 23/1 A glassed-in two-level public seating area provides a view of busy False Creek. **1845** S. R. GLYNNE *Notes Churches of Cheshire* (Chetham Soc.) (1894) 56 There are large gargoyles at the angles..; in the second stage a two-light window. **1924** O. JESPERSEN *Philos. Gram.* xxii. 306 Every sentence is said to be composed of two parts, Subject and Predicate... Besides such two-member sentences..we may have one-member sentences. **1967** R. S. CHURCHILL *Winston S. Churchill* II. viii. 261 The city of Dundee in 1908..was, like Oldham, a two-member, primarily working-class, constituency. **1868** *Westm. Chess Club Papers* I. 47 A two-mover now knocks me down. **1931** R. GRAVES *To Whom Else?* 17 Two-named one, how shall I call you without duplicity? **1952** V. WILKINS *King Reluctant* I. ix. 131 The involved two-pack patience game known as 'Maréchal Saxe'. **1977** *Listener* 10 Mar. 295/2 He is a two-pack smoker, drinks on occasion to keep going. **1928** *Daily Tel.* 11 Dec. 17/4 'Two-part tariffs' will be introduced by the County of London Electric Supply Co. Ltd. from Jan. 1 for domestic and business consumers. **1939** F. SCOTT FITZGERALD *Let.* 8 June (1964) 106, I have..over half-finished what will be a two-parter for *The Saturday Evening Post.* **1984** J. WAIN in *Listener* 28 June 30/2 They are making two plays out of it, or, perhaps more exactly, a three-hour two-parter. **1961** *New Scientist* 5 Jan. 50/3 Mr. Saunders's two-pedal system..interested me, so I tried it on my car. **1920** D. H. LAWRENCE *Lost Girl* vii. 134 Madame and the German did a screaming two-person farce. **1977** *New Yorker* 17 Oct. 93/1 A new playwright..made a pleasing début on Broadway..with a harsh little two-person comedy. **1952** S. KAUFFMANN *Philanderer* xv. 242 Turning the phonograph very low, he played the Mozart two-piano concerto. **1978** LD. DROGHEDA *Double Harness* x. 92 During the two years that she had been in America, Joan had become a very active pianist, giving a considerable number of two-piano concerts with her partner Harold Triggs. **1894** D. SALOMONS *Electr. Light Installations* (ed. 7) II. vi. 233 The plug to be used with this connector is of the two-pin type. **1962** *B.S.I. News* Feb. 24/1 Three proposals were considered for a standard two-pin plug for use with all-insulated and double-insulated appliances. **1948** H. REICHENBACH *Elem. Symbolic Logic* § 17. 83 Both functions are two-place functions; i.e. they possess two arguments. **1963** W. V. QUINE *Set Theory* § 1. 13 Suppose the only primitive predicate of some theory is a two-place predicate. **1966** *Publ. Amer. Dial. Soc. 1964* XLII. 10 *Two-plus-two*,..two-seater with capacity to hold two additional passengers in back. **1977** *Lancashire Life* Mar. 118/3 The 104ZS is cramped in the back and is more of a two-plus-two than a proper four seater. **1960** *Farmer & Stockbreeder* 1 Mar. 131/1 Experience has proved this two-point system. **1972** J. POTTER *Going West* 180 The plane made a jerky two-point landing. **1951** Two-position [see *BISTABLE *a.*]. **1960** *Farmer & Stockbreeder* 8 Mar. 108/2 Two-position Hitch. Easy for field or transport. **1919** W. S. CHURCHILL in M. Gilbert *Winston S. Churchill* (1977) IV. Compan. I. 535 With Mr Balfour's approval, I made the following two-pronged proposals. **1925** O. CAROE *Pathans* xxiii. 375 The success of the two-pronged advance by the Khaibar and the Kurram. **1929** WODEHOUSE *Mr. Mulliner Speaking* ix. 301 Come on, let's beef in or we'll be missing the educational two-reel comic. **1978** *Radio Times* 18–24 Mar. 15/1 Within the next couple of years he made over 20 two-reel Westerns. **1928** *Sunday Express* 3 June 4 The British Screen two-reeler 'Homes of Our King'. **1979** *Guardian* 4 Aug. 9/2 He had made a few modest pictures, two-reelers mostly. **1895** *Montgomery Ward Catal.* Spring & Summer 580/2 Two-seat business wagons. **1880** W. WHITMAN *Daybks. &*

Notebks. (1978) III. 642 Heavy two-seated covered voitures. **1936** G. B. Shaw *Six of Calais* 89 Between them, near the King's pavilion, is a two-seated chair of state for public audiences. **1933** O. Jespersen *Essent. Eng. Gram.* xix. 192 When a special indication of sex is wanted with one of the two-sex words, this can always be done by the addition of the adjectives *male* and *female*, respectively: *a male reader, a female cousin*, . . etc. **1973** Talamini & Page *Sport & Society* v. 271 To note [sport's] emergence as a two-sex activity . . should not obscure the persistence in sport of male domination, male prejudice, and discrimination against girls and women. **1789** J. Woodforde *Diary* 11 June (1927) III. 112 Briton also went into the 2 Shilling Gallery. **1944** R. V. Jones *Most Secret War* (1978) xlv. 460 A two-stage rocket of about 150 tons starting weight could deliver a 1 ton warhead to nearly 3,000 miles range. **1963** *Ann. Reg. 1962* 183 The Skybolt was a two-stage solid fuel missile. **1979** *Dædalus* Summer 50 'Hypocrisy displayed', then, is a two-stage process, a masking followed by an unmasking. **1854** M. S. Cummins *Lamplighter* iii. 13 A decent two-storied house. **1874** W. Black *Princess of Thule* (ed. 2) I. i. 12 It was a square, two-storeyed substantial building of stone. **1977** P. G. Winslow *Witch Hill Murder* II. xvi. 212 The lovely, two-storeyed drawing-room. **1796** *Aurora* (Philadelphia) 15 Apr., That certain one-story Frame shop in front, and Two Story Frame messuage. **1866** A. D. Richardson *Secret Service* ii. 38 We took a two-story car of the Baronne street railway. **1977** *Times* 9 Sept. 2/3 Spacious late-nineteenth-century two-storey terrace houses. **1982** W. Boyd *Ice-Cream War* (1983) II. ii. 120 He passed the . . two-storey building. **1851** H. Melville *Moby Dick* I. ix. 65 Shipmates, it is a two-stranded lesson. **1976** P. Collard *Development Microbiol.* v. 64 Synthetic two-stranded RNA polyinosinic acid-polycytidylic acid. **1918** *Jrnl. R. Naval Med. Service* IV. 317 A 'two-stripe doctor'. **1860** W. Whitman in *N.Y. Times* 27 June 2/1 The Princes of Asia, swart-cheek'd princes, First comers, guests, two-sworded princes. **1933** A. N. Whitehead *Adventures of Ideas* xv. 230 Also we may well ask whether there are not subtle variations of meaning stretching far beyond the competence of the two-term vocabulary—Judgment, Proposition. **1964** R. H. Robins *Gen. Linguistics* i. 26 A two-term relation between the word and the referent. **1968** Fox & Mayers *Computing Methods for Scientists & Engineers* i. 4 A better approach is to observe that, with a single integration by parts, we can find the two-term recurrence relation. **1981** *Times* 6 Aug. 8/7 A programme which can be implemented only by a two-term Government. **1933** *Mind* LXII. 45 If we consider *Russia is happy, England fears France, Germany prefers England to France, Italy believes that Germany prefers England to France*, we see that these facts form a series in that the first is one-termed, the second two-termed, the third three-termed and the fourth four-termed. **1964** E. Bach *Introd. Transformational Gram.* vii. 157 Prepositional phrase in English is usually a two-termed relation. **1932** *Times* 26 Nov. 12/3 If their system were a two-tier system, the element of uncertainty was reduced to a minimum. **1933** [see *stack *sb.* 1 d]. **1937** *Burlington Mag.* Oct. 194/1 Ionic impost capitals, . . two-tier capitals. **1969** *Punch* 1 Jan. 26/3 It is now working a good deal harder and will work even harder still when the reforms with their two-tier system of voting and non-voting but speaking Peers come into force. **1975** J. P. Morgan *House of Lords & Labour Govt.* ii. 75 The House can be persistent when an issue catches its imagination—favourites of the 1966–70 Parliament were decimal currency, the two-tier postal service, and the anti-Stansted campaign. **1969** *Listener* 23 Jan. 103/2 The debate is two-tiered: the violence of Chicago . . and the violence of the TV shows. **1979** *Arizona Daily Star* 5 Aug. D2/2 The Natural Gas Policy Act of 1978 . . wiped out the two-tiered pricing structure. **1910** *Motor Man.* (ed. 12) iii. 75 The layshaft is driven by a chain instead of the usual two-to-one gear wheels. **1975** *New Yorker* 17 Nov. 117/1 The Court of Appeals for the District of Columbia Circuit, in a two-to-one vote, upheld the claim. **1742** W. Ellis *Mod. Husbandman* Sept. xxvi. 124 These are the right profitable sort for Fatting, and not the two-toothed sheep. **1811** *Boston Patriot* 23 Jan. 3/2 A two top-sail sch[ooner] was at H Hole on Saturday. **1944** J. Masefield *New Chum* 137 There used to be that kind of schooner. She was called a 'two-topsail schooner' or a 'maintopsail schooner'. **1934** *New Statesman* 27 Oct. 602/2 It is useless approaching these circles with two-track class-war propaganda. **1961** G. A. Briggs *A to Z in Audio* 200 Regular supplies of high quality 7½"/sec pre-recorded stereo tapes will be available, giving twice the playing time of previous two-track issues. **1977** *N.Y. Rev. Bks.* 13 Oct. 18/1 Had President Kennedy been pursuing a 'two-track' policy of offering Castro friendship while plotting his murder? **1925** I. A. Richards *Princ. Lit. Criticism* 1 In a pamphlet or in a two-volume work. **1978** *Early Music* Oct. 544/1 Silvestro Ganassi's two-volume treatise on the viol . . is perhaps the most interesting and significant instrumental tutor to have survived from the 16th century. **1744** W. Ellis *Mod. Husbandman* Jan. i. 16 He plowed up the Surface . . with a two-wheel pecked Share-Plough. **1918** D. H. Lawrence *New Poems* 41 Who then sees the two-winged Boat down there? **1949** E. Pound *Pisan Cantos* lxxvi. 45 Benecomata dea Under the two-winged cloud. **1974** *Encycl. Brit. Macropædia* V. 819/1 Diptera, the two-winged, or 'true', flies. **1930** *Engineering* 28 Feb. 278/3 Power distribution is at 230 volts in the two-wire system. **1961** W. F. Leopold in Saporta & Bastian *Psycholinguistics* (1961) 357/1 Two-word verbs of the type 'wake up'. **1977** N. Sahgal *Situation in New Delhi* xi. 115 They had labelled him with destructive little one and two-word flourishes that could smear an image for millions of readers.

2. **two-address** *a. Computers*, having two addresses (see quot. 1953); **two and eight** *Rhyming slang*, a state (of agitation); **two-backed beast** = *the beast with two backs* s.v. *beast *sb.* 4 b; **two-bagger** *N. Amer. Baseball*, a hit that enables the batter to reach second base safely; **two-bit** *a. U.S.* [*bit *sb.*² 8 b], (*a*) of the value of a quarter of a dollar; (*b*) *fig.*, cheap, petty, worthless (*slang*); **two-body** *a. Physics*, involving or pertaining to two objects or particles; **two-by-four** orig. *U.S.*, a post or batten measuring 2 inches by 4 in cross-section; also (*U.S.*) *fig.* in *attrib.* use: small, insignificant; **two-cent** *a. U.S.*, (*a*) of the value of two cents; (*b*) *fig.* = *two-bit* (*b*) above (*slang*); **two cheers**, catch phr. expressing qualified enthusiasm *for* something, as opposed to the traditional three cheers (see *three *a.* 1 g); **two-China(s)** *a. U.S. Pol.*, designating a proposal or policy for admitting to the United Nations representatives of both Communist China and Taiwan; **two cultures**: see *culture *sb.* 5 c; **two-egg** *a.* = *dizygotic *a.*; **two-eyed stance** *Cricket* (see quot. 1924); **two fingers**, two fingers made into a V-sign as a coarse gesture of contempt; **two-fisted** *a.*, (*b*) *U.S. colloq.*, tough, aggressive; vigorous; (*c*) *Tennis*, of a backhand stroke: played with both hands on the racket; **two-holer** *N. Amer.*, a privy or lavatory accommodating two people; **two-horse** *a.* (earlier example); (*b*) (of a race or other contest) in which only two of the contestants are likely winners; **two-line** *a.*, (*b*) occupying two lines, being two lines long; (*c*) underlined twice; *spec.* applied to a notice of forthcoming parliamentary business in which the attendance of members is requested with two underlines, indicating less urgency than a three-line whip (now the strongest one); **2LO** (tū̆ˌelˌōᵘ·) [*Lo*(*ndon*)], the call-sign of a radio station established in London in 1922 and taken over the same year by the newly-formed British Broadcasting Company, which used it as call-sign until 1924 and as a name of a programme service until 1930; the station itself; **two-meal**, (*a*) (earlier example); **two(-) minute(s') silence** = *silence *sb.* 2 e; **two nation(s)**, used, chiefly *attrib.*, with reference to two irreconcilable groups or factions within a nation; **two-one**, a place in the upper division of the second class in a degree class-list; (a graduate having) an upper-second-class degree; also represented as 2(1), etc.; **two-piece** *a.* and *sb.*, (a suit) consisting of two garments (as a jacket and trousers, or coat and dress) matching or meant to be worn together; (a swimming costume) consisting now of a brassière and briefs, a bikini; also (*U.S.*) **two-piecer**; **two-place** *a.*, applied to an aeroplane with seats for two people; so **two-placer**; **two-power standard** (see quot. 1910); **two-revolution** *a. Printing*, applied to a cylinder press in which the impression cylinder rotates continuously, alternately printing and delivering sheets as the forme moves to and fro; abbrev. **two-rev** (also *absol.*); **twos and threes**, a children's chasing game for six or more players; **two-seater**, something (as a vehicle or settee) that has two seats; freq. *attrib.*; **two shoes** (earlier example); **two-shot**, a cinema or television shot of two people together; **two-spot** *U.S.*, (*a*) a playing card with two pips, a deuce; (*b*) a two-dollar banknote; (*c*) *transf.*, an insignificant or worthless person; a two-year prison sentence; **two-star** *a.*, (*a*) given two stars in a grading system in which more stars indicate higher quality (cf. *star *sb.*¹ 10 c); (*b*) having or being a military rank that has two stars on the shoulder-piece of the uniform, e.g. major-general or rear-admiral in the U.S. (cf. *star *sb.*¹ 6 c); **two-state** *a.*, capable of existing in either of two states or conditions; **two-step**: (*a*) also as *v. intr.*, to dance a two-step; (*b*) *a.*, having or consisting of two successive actions; two-stage; **two-sticker** *Canad. colloq.*, a two-masted boat; **two-suiter**, (*a*) *Bridge* (see quot. 1923); (*b*) orig. *U.S.*, a suitcase large enough to hold two suits and accessories; **two-tailed** *a.*, (*a*) having two tails; (*b*) *Statistics*, applied to a test that tests for deviation from the null hypothesis in both directions; cf. *one-tailed* adj. s.v. *one *numeral a., pron.*, etc. B. 33; **two-tone** *a.*, (*a*) in two colours or two shades of the same colour; (*b*) being or producing two notes, usu. alternately at intervals; also *fig.*; so **two-toned** *a.*, in the same sense; **two-tooth** *a.* (later example); *sb.* (examples); **two-two**, (*a*) (usu. represented as .22), used *attrib.* and *absol.* to designate (ammunition for) a gun with a calibre of 0.22 inch; (*b*) (also represented as 2(2), etc.), a place in the lower division of the second class in a degree class-list; see also sense II. 2 g; **two-week** *dial.*, a fortnight; **two-year** *a.*, (*b*) lasting or valid for two years; also *transf.*

1948 Two-address [see *three-address* adj. s.v. Three *a.* and *sb.* III. 2]. **1953** *Computers & Automation* Dec. 22 *Two-address*, in programming, a system of instructions whereby each complete instruction includes an operation and specifies the location of two registers, usually one containing an operand and the other the result of the operation. **1961** [see *sequencing *vbl. sb.*]. **1982** G. Lee *Hardware to Software* xx. 339 With 3-address instructions (as for 2-address), it is not necessary to have an accumulator. **1938** 'J. Curtis' *They drive by Night* ix. 103 Give us a hand out, will you? I'm in a right two and eight. **1960** M. Cecil *Something in Common* 129 Poor old Clinker! Bet she's in a proper two-and-eight! *a* **1693** Two-backed beast [see *beast *sb.* 4 b]. **1925** G. Greene *Babbling April* 5 The two-backed beast went trotting in my head. **1939** Dylan Thomas *Map of Love* 63 Here dwell, said Sam Rib, the two-backed beasts. He pointed to his map of Love. **1973** L. Snelling *Heresy* II. i. 60 Hubby got on to us. Came within an ace of catching us making the two-backed beast in his car. **1880** *Globe* (San Francisco) 16 May 1/4 Willigrod, Smith and J. Whitney led at the bat, the two former getting in each a two-bagger. **1946** *N.Y. Herald Tribune* 24 Mar. VIII. 19/1, I hit a two-bagger with the bases full. **1802** J. Drayton *View South-Carolina* 215 Hence the origin of this society; which, from the contributions, being a sum of money called *two bitts*, became known by the appellation of the *two bitt* club. **1873** *Harper's Mag.* May 799 Thompson's Two-bit House, Front St. **1928** S. Lewis *Man who knew Coolidge* I. 51 There's a man . . always got a good story and a two-bit cigar for you. **1932** E. Caldwell *Tobacco Road* xvii. 208 Tom said she used to be a two-bit slut. **1978** T. Willis *Buckingham Palace Connection* viii. 155 Some other two-bit General will try shooting us up. **1956** *Nature* 11 Feb. 268/2 A principal aim of the theory is to show that, using only such two-body forces, one can achieve nuclear separation. **1978** Pasachoff & Kutner *University Astron.* xxvi. 648 The effects that the planets have on each other are much less than the effect that the sun has on each, and the mutual interactions of the planets are treated as small deviations . . from the situation that would be present if only the sun-planet two-body problem had to be solved. **1884** E. W. Nye *Baled Hay* 23 The managing editor of the mill lays out the log in his mind, and works it into dimension stuff, shingle bolts, slabs, edgings, two by fours. **1897** 'O. Thanet' *Missionary Sheriff* 13 'That how she makes a living?' 'Yes—little two-by-four bakery.' **1916** 'B. M. Bower' *Phantom Herd* v. 77 Houses . . bald behind as board fences save where two-by-fours braced them from falling. **1939** J. B. Priestley *Let People Sing* i. 3 A little two-by-four provincial agency . . giving itself airs now! **1978** *Maledicta* II. 7 You hit him over his ossified skull with a two-by-four. **1979** J. van de Wetering *Maine Massacre* xix. 226 De Gier saw a tableau made out of barn boards, framed neatly by weathered two-by-fours. **1859** L. A. Wilmer *Our Press Gang* 42 The Express was a two-cent cash paper. **1899** 'J. Flynt' *Tramping* I. v. 119 The next higher type of the town tramp is the 'two-cent dosser'—the man who lives in stale-beer shops. **1902** [in Dict., sense IV. 1 a]. **1908** Two-cent [see *gunk 3]. **1951** E. M. Forster (*title*) Two cheers for democracy. **1977** *Times* 5 Sept. 6/7 Two cheers for . . the National Theatre's debut in community drama. **1962** E. Snow *Other Side of River* (1963) xx. 149 Mao and other Chinese continued to respect Chiang Kai-shek for one thing, however: he had declined to support the 'two-Chinas' plan aimed at removing Taiwan from the sovereignty of China. **1979** H. Kissinger *White House Yrs.* xviii. 719 This was close to the two-China solution always vehemently rejected by both Taipei and Peking. **1959** *Listener* 29 Oct. 728/2 Two-egg twins . . are derived from the separate eggs fertilized by two different sperms. **1971** Two-egg [see *multiple birth* s.v. *multiple *a.* 4 c]. **1924** A. C. MacLaren *Cricket Old & New* viii. 73 What is called 'the two-eyed stance' or the turn of the head to enable the batsman to see the ball with as full a face as possible but without taking the left shoulder off the line of the ball. **1977** *Sunday Times* 3 July 28/2 Hughie Trumble . . condemned the two-eyed batting stance. **1971** G. Ewart *Gavin Ewart Show* III. 50 Meanwhile on the roof of the Playboy Club . . one Bunny Flag. Two ears, like sensual man's two-fingers-up to Culture. **1977** *Zigzag* June 24/1 There's nothing more the kids want to see than The Pistols at the top of the chart, two fingers pointed at the TV, radio, printing firms and council officials who've tried to stifle them. **1774** P. V. Fithian *Jrnl.* (1900) 223 He was Director, and appointed a sturdy two-fisted Gentleman to open the Ball with Mrs. Tayloe. **1908** [see *clean *v.* 4 c]. **1925** E. E. Cummings *Let.* 3 Sept. (1969) 108 [I] was not made to match wits with twofisted go-getters. **1960** *Times* 16 June 18/6 The two-fisted backhand of Australia's Howe. *Ibid.* 16 Sept. 52 Hamdinger . . being, as the menu says, 'for two-fisted appetites'. **1978** *Times* 4 July 19/4 Miss Kruger, a steady and tenacious competitor with a two-fisted backhand. **1979** *Tucson Mag.* Mar. 18/3 Bonanno . . is going to have a two-fisted fight on his hands. The U.S. Criminal Justice system is also bearing down on Bonanno. **1971** *Islander* (Victoria, B.C.) 3 Jan. 12/2 Gone were the woodshed and the two-holer discreetly removed from the house. **1974** S. Alsop *Stay of Execution* II. 224 The house . . is a shooting lodge, built in 1929. . . There is one bathroom for the ladies, and one for the men, each with a two-holer. *c* **1780** 'J. H. St. J. de Crèvecœur' *Sk. 18th-Cent. Amer.* (1925) 138 You have often admired our two-horse waggons. **1976** *Newmarket Jrnl.* 16 Dec., [Darts] With White Lion beating Wellington 7-2 it seems to be a two-horse race at the top. **1977** *Evening Gaz.* (Middlesbrough) 11 Jan. 14/1 [Association football] The two-horse race in Division B looks like continuing. **1984** *Times* 22 Feb. 1/5 If, as is expected, he comes second in New Hampshire, it could turn into a two-horse race. **1901** G. B. Shaw *Admirable Bashville* in *Cashel Byron's Profession* (rev. ed.) Pref. 288, I like the melodious sing-song, the clear simple one-line and two-line sayings, and the occasional rhymed tags. **1958** Wilding & Laundy *Encycl. Parl.* 603 Sir Wilfrid Lawson explained pithily that a one-line whip meant 'you ought to attend'; a two-line whip 'you should attend'; a three-line whip 'you must attend'. **1962** W. Nowottny *Lang. Poets Use* v. 110 One usually expects of couplets that the sense of the passage will fall into two-line chunks. **1976** H. Wilson *Governance of Britain* iii. 46 The chief whip then indicates the kind of whip he will issue for each day—one-line, two-line or three. **1978** W. White in W. Whitman *Daybks. & Notebks.* I. 121 'Roaming in Thought' is a two-line poem, published in the 1881 *Leaves of Grass.* **1923** *Radio Times* 28 Sept. 3/1 (*heading*) A recent talk broadcast from 2LO. **1924** A. R. Burrows *Story of Broadcasting* viii. 59 A station known as 2LO, a 100-watt set contained in a small teak cabinet, and housed in the cinema theatre on the top floor of Marconi House, London. **1961** E. Williams *George* xxvi. 415, I would sit for an hour while the faint dream-sounds of 2LO echoed in my head. **1969** *Listener* 17 Apr. 514/3, 30 years after the introduction of broadcasting from 2LO, radio was the dominant or only means of electronic communication. **1981** S. Briggs *Those Radio Times* 9/2 The pre-Savoy Hill 2LO studio at Marconi House. **1741** W. Ellis *Mod. Husbandman* May vii. 112 It is generally made with half skim, and half new; or what is more properly called Two-meal Cheese. **1919**, etc. Two(-)minute(s') [see *silence *sb.* 2 e]. [**1711** Addison in *Spectator* 24 July, There cannot a greater Judgment befall a Country than such a dreadful Spirit of Division as rends a Government into two distinct People, and makes them greater Strangers and more averse to one another, than if they were actually two different Nations.] **1845** Disraeli *Sybil* I. ii. v. 149 Two nations; between whom there is no intercourse and no sympathy; who are as ignorant of each other's habits, thoughts, and feelings, as if they were..inhabitants of different planets... The rich and the poor. **1913** *Times* 8 May 10/3 Rightly or wrongly, the Protestants of Ulster hold to the 'two nations' theory. **1958** O. Caroe *Pathans* xxvi. 434 Only when the British Government's move to bring British authority to an end acquired a momentum so unmistakable that even the unbelieving were compelled to read the signs..was the two-nation theory translated into practical politics. **1976** *Equals* Oct./Nov. 1/5 In contemporary Britain the Two Nations are not so obviously the rich and the poor or the blacks and the whites or the townspeople and the country people, as the urban deprived and the rest of us. **1937** 'M. Innes' *Hamlet, Revenge!* I. ii. 34 Gott with his tutor's instinct was placing this young lady's mind provisionally among the good Two-ones. **1963** *Times* 10 May 6/4 The survey showed that 10 per cent of the firsts and 25 per cent of the 2.i (upper second) were earning less than £1,250 a year. **1964** *Guardian* 23 Oct. 14/2 It is argued..that examiners who can award 'two ones' are less ready to give firsts. **1969** M. Kelly *Write on Both Sides of Paper* 17 He was..a two-one graduate. **1976** *Times* 6 Sept. 10/5 For quite a number of years, New Hall got more firsts and 2/1s combined than any other college. **1984** *Oxf. Univ. Gaz.: Suppl.* 16 Feb. 506/1 It [*sc.* division of the second class] will..greatly help the II(1) in competition with officially recognized II(1)s from other universities. *c* **1880** in *Amer. Mail Order Fashions* (1961) 11 A very neat little two-piece suit of calico. **1895** *Montgomery Ward Catal.* Spring & Summer 501/2 Bathing Suits... Two-piece suits. Consisting of quarter sleeve shirts and knee pants. **1933** Auden *Dance of Death* 8 Revealing handsome two-piece bathing suits. **1956** *Times* 28 May 13/3 The two-piece, which has now become the generic term for a dress with a matching jacket, has to a great extent replaced the suit for special occasions. **1978** L. Deighton *SS-GB* iii. 29 She was dressed in a tailored two-piece of pink wool. **1963** *New Yorker* 1 June 110 Soak up the sun in our beautifully brief, terry two-piecer. **1978** *Detroit Free Press* 5 Mar. (Spring Fashion Suppl.) 17 (Advt.), The Pierrot collared two-piecer has a gently shirred skirt, with side pockets. **1916** Hall & Niles *One Man's War* (1929) 160 He was flying a two-place fighter. *Ibid.* 190 It wasn't long until Luf spied a two-placer. **1971** *Flying* Apr. 35/2 The jet works the same as a two-place trainer. **1901** *To-Day* 26 Sept. 280 In men and ships..the British Navy is distinctly above the 'two-Power standard'. **1910** *Encycl. Brit.* IV. 613/2 It has..been accepted as a fundamental axiom of defence that the British navy should exceed in strength any reasonable combination of foreign navies which could be brought against it, the accepted formula being the 'two-power standard', *i.e.* a 10% margin over the joint strength of the next two powers. **1914** G. B. Shaw *Fanny's First Play* iii. 223 Your honest and sensible statesmen demand for England a two-power standard. **1980** Two-rev [see *stop cylinder* s.v. *stop *sb.*[2] 29]. **1902** *Encycl. Brit.* XXXII. 5/2 The two-revolution cylinder..makes two revolutions to each impression and can be made to produce 1500 or more impressions on a large sheet in one hour. **1967** *Elsevier's Dict. Printing* 328/2 The cylinder on a two-revolution press constantly rotates, printing a sheet on its first revolution and delivering the sheet on its second. **1896** E. Turner *Little Larrikin* xxiii. 279 The frantic rushes of the game of 'twos and threes'. **1935** N. Mitchison *We have been Warned* iii. 236 After dinner there were games with the crew... They had fox-and-geese and twos-and-threes. **1983** G. Mitchell *Greenstone Griffins* ii. 14 Some traditional party games were played... A game of Twos and Threes was in progress. **1891** H. C. Bunner *Zadoc Pine* 172, I climbed into his 'two-seater', and sat behind talking to Mrs. Tom. **1906** Two-seater car [see Seater 2]. **1918** T. E. Lawrence *Lett.* (1938) 248 Our Bristol Fighter the same day brought down a German two-seater in flames. **1931** *Daily Express* 31 Jan. 7/4 The two-seater airplane which crashed in Bushy Park. **1973** R. Ludlum *Matlock Paper* xviii. 150 He sat in the Early American two-seater in the outer office. **1977** P. Hill *Fanatics* 145 The helicopter..was a two-seater. **1979** R. Jaffe *Class Reunion* (1980) iii. i. 305 Emily..drove to her analyst..in the little two-seater Mercedes. **1858** Geo. Eliot *Scenes Clerical Life* I. 166 Little Bessie Parrot, a flaxen-headed 'two-shoes', very white and fat as to her neck. **1949** N. Streatfeild *Painted Garden* xxi. 228 Movies are made with a long shot, a two-shot and a close-up of each person, each taken separately. **1978** *Broadcast* 27 Mar. 8/3 Two grey-suited figures, held in two-shot, recapped results interminably. **1885** *Narragansett Hist. Reg.* III. 213 We were shown a play-card, the two-spot of clubs. **1896** Ade *Artie* vi. 50 You're nothin' but a two-spot. **1901** 'J. Flynt' *World of Graft* 184 They convicted me at last and I got a two-spot. **1909** 'O. Henry' *Roads of Destiny* xviii. 305 We get the heelers out with the crackly two-spots. **1936** H. Hagedorn *Brookings* v. 73 He knew..when to be discreet and when to bluff on a two-spot. **1951** *Observer* 27 May 4/5 He cannot do better than buy the Michelin Guide to France and tour the two- or even three-star restaurants. **1960** *John o' London's* 7 Apr. 403/1 The unknown two-star general..accumulated power for himself in the name of France. **1976** *Daily Mail* (Hull) 30 Sept. 11/3 The Galant..will do over 35 miles to the gallon on two-star petrol. **1982** 'E. Lathen' *Green grow Dollars* ii. 16 Two-star generals are less accustomed to being balked than most men. **1959** G. Troup *Masers* iii. 35 The two-state molecules under consideration. **1971** J. H. Smith *Digital Logic* i. 1 Although most digital devices are 'two state', the essential requirement of a digital device is that it should change from one discrete state to another and not settle into any intermediate state or position. **1910** *Punch* 30 Mar. 223/2 But when the maid my signal sees She 'two-steps' by like winking. **1929** S. Lewis *Dodsworth* i. 9 The aristocracy of Zenith were dancing... They two-stepped on the wide porch. **1940** *Chambers's Techn. Dict.* 874/1 Two-step relay. **1948** A. C. Clarke *Across Sea of Stars* (1959) 13 The A. 20 was a two-step rocket. **1978** *Bull. Amer. Acad. Arts & Sci.* Feb. 13 The two-step mechanism of translocation of estradiol finds a precise counterpart in the action of other steroid hormones. **1895** Two-sticker [see *Jack *sb.*[1] 25]. **1931** *Canad. Geogr. Jrnl.* II. 391/1 Our 'two-sticker with a kicker' lies in Sandy Bay harbour, Nova Scotia. **1923** M. C. Work *Auction Bridge of 1924* vi. 60 A hand containing two suits both strong enough to bid is called a 'two-suiter'. **1958** *Which?* Winter 25/1 The boot accommodated one two-suiter and one week end case, or three week-end cases. **1979** *Arizona Daily Star* 5 Aug. i. 12/1 North had to have a monstrously powerful major two-suiter for his repeated cue-bids, and they invariably took a preference to six spades. **1981** L. Deighton *XPD* xxvii. 223 Stuart lifted a Samsonite two-suiter onto the bed. **1904** *Oxford Mag.* 16 Mar. 275/2 When imported Labour Yellow should eliminate the Fellow, And the Head of every College be a two-tailed Mandarin! **1922** Joyce *Ulysses* 491 His twotailed black braces dangling at heels. **1931** *Times Lit. Suppl.* 1 Oct. 747/2 They [*sc.* Norman clerks] used a two-tailed capital F. **1945** *Biometrics Bull.* I. 70 If querist has other alternatives to be considered, he may be interested in the two-tailed test discussed in following answers. **1976** *Lancet* 30 Oct. 922/1 Data were analysed by Student's two-tailed *t* test. **1906** Goodchild & Tweney *Technol. & Sci. Dict.* 800/2 *Two tone*,..a term applied to lace composed of cotton of the natural colour (ecru) interspersed with objects of white. **1940** R. Chandler *Farewell, My Lovely* xviii. 115 A couple of very nice two-tone Buicks. **1963** *Listener* 21 Feb. 349/2 There are signs, in the two-tone sketchiness of some of the scenes..that the book was written at speed. **1965** G. McInnes *Road to Gundagai* x. 167 The sad two-tone cadence of the mopoke or Australian owl. **1966** *Statutory Instruments 1966* III. 3501 'Two-tone horn' means an instrument or apparatus which, when operated, automatically produces a sound which alternates at regular intervals between two fixed notes. **1977** *Harpers & Queen* Sept. 51/2 The usual luxury touches like electric windows, two-tone horns. **1981** *Country Life* 22 Jan. 226/3 Deep burgundy *bouclé* jacket..two-tone belt. **1897** *Sears, Roebuck Catal.* 238/1 Striped Undershirts... Neat two toned shades, silver gray predominating. **1951** T. Sterling *House without Door* v. 47 A two-toned gong rang... He opened the door. **1982** R. Ludlum *Parsifal Mosaic* xviii. 271 He climbed out of the two-toned coupé. **1945** N. Marsh *Died in Wool* viii. 180 A couple more dirty two-tooths for the herd to shear. **1962** *Coast to Coast 1961–62* 26 Kangaroos, goannas and two-tooth ewes constitute the characteristic fauna of Coorabin. **1972** P. Newton *Sheep Thief* iii. 26 As two-tooths they all go out to Cow Creek with the ewes. **1980** D. Hart-Davis *Heights of Rimring* xviii. 212 'What the hell's a two-tooth ewe?' 'A hogget—a second-year ewe. The best mutton there is.' **1895** *Army & Navy Co-op. Soc. Price List* 921 The Remington single shot rifle. Shooting the ·22 rim fire American Cartridge. **1944** 'N. Shute' *Pastoral* i. 11 A little gun, his own. Two-two. **1973** 'M. Hebden' *Dark Side of Island* xvi. 134 'What sort was it? Shotgun?' 'No. Two-two.' **1976** J. H. Spencer *Surgenor Campaign* i. 11 His own Tripos degree class in history, a Two-Two in place of the expected First, had been a disappointment. **1981** Ld. Harewood *Tongs & Bones* v. 90, I..at least got a II: ii..; in those days the only respectable thing was either a First or a Third. **1900** H. Sutcliffe *Shameless Wayne* 119 It's a two-week come yesterday sin' they fought i' th' kirk-yard. **1927** A. H. McNeile *Introd. Study N.T.* v. 141 St. Paul returned [to Ephesus] for his two-year visit. **1962** E. Snow *Other Side of River* (1963) i. 19 There were six of them..on their way to serve two-year contracts as technical advisers in China. **1975** *Whitaker's Almanack 1976* 802 Institutions of higher education include universities, colleges, professional schools, and two-year colleges.

two-dime·nsional (*also* tū·-), *a.* **1.** Having or appearing to have length and breadth but no depth.

1883 [see Dimensional *a.* 2]. **1898** [in Dict. s.v. Two *a.* and *sb.* IV. 1 b]. **1954** M. Rickert *Painting in Britain: Middle Ages* viii. 201 Two-dimensional compositions for glass panels. **1967** E. Short *Embroidery & Fabric Collage* i. 8 Without realising what effect they will have when translated into a two-dimensional design.

2. *fig.* Lacking depth or substance; shallow, superficial.

1934 C. Lambert *Music Ho!* v. 310 It is possible to detach Stravinsky's methods from their contents and apply Stravinsky scoring to any piece of music. Like everything else in his music, it is two-dimensional. **1959** *Times Lit. Suppl.* 9 Oct. 573/4 By comparison *Heart to Heart* seems both shallow and hollow, a two-dimensional manufactured thing for an obvious mass market. **1977** *Broadcast* 7 Nov. 13/1 'Hard Times'..is less a novel than..a strip cartoon with two-dimensional characters.

Hence **two-dimensionality**, the property of being two-dimensional; **two-dimensionally** *adv.*, in, or in terms of, two dimensions; **two-dimensionalness** (*rare*).

1926 H. Read *Eng. Stained Glass* i. 11/1 Two-dimensionality. No attempt is made to put the scene in strict spatial perspective. **1956** *Essays in Criticism* VI. 219 The two-dimensionality of the canvases. **1958** S. Spender *Engaged in Writing* 116 Her general two-dimensionalness permitted her to appear different on each side. **1961** Webster, Two-dimensionally. **1968** *Jrnl. Physical Soc. Japan* XXV. 934/1 The computations were made two-dimensionally. **1975** I. Stewart *Concepts Mod. Math.* ii. 22 It is a consequence of the two-dimensionality of the plane that any rigid motion is uniquely specified by what it does to a (non-degenerate) triangle. **1978** *Spectator* (New Canaan High School, Connecticut) 65 The world has become two-dimensionally black and white. **1979** *Jrnl. R. Soc. Arts* July 509/1 The criticisms..that Ruskin saw architecture only two-dimensionally, and that he never seems to have looked at a building structurally, are refuted with ample quotations.

twoer. (Earlier and further examples.)

1887 W. S. Churchill *Let.* 3 May in R. S. Churchill *Winston S. Churchill* (1967) I. Compan. i. iv. 131 We had a game of Cricket this afternoon, I hit a *twoer*, as the expression goes, my first runs this year. **1899** C. Rook *Hooligan Nights* iv. 64, I..went froo the till. It wasn't much of a 'aul... I don't fink there was more'n free twoers worf to be nicked. **1970** G. F. Newman *Sir, you Bastard* iii. 98 Sneed flipped the notes without undoing the band. 'A twoer there,' Doleman said.

twofer (tū·fəɹ). *U.S. colloq.* Also **too-, -fah, -for, -fur.** [f. Two *sb.* + (representation of) For *prep.*] **1.** A cigar sold at two for a quarter; hence, any cheap cigar.

a **1911** D. G. Phillips *Susan Lenox* (1917) I. xx. 351 He smoked five-cent cigars instead of 'two-furs'. **1922** S. Lewis *Babbitt* v. 63 'I do like decent cigars—not those Flor de Cabagos you're smoking—' 'That's all right now! That's a good two-for.' **1923** Wodehouse *Inimitable Jeeves* xiii. 143, I found him..lying on the bed with his feet on the rail, smoking a toofah. **1943** *Sun* (Baltimore) 3 Feb. 24/6 The latest items on the list of wartime shortages are the 'toofer', the 'nickel cigar' and the '10-center'.

2. a. A coupon that entitles a person to buy two tickets for a specified theatre show for the price of one.

1948 *N.Y. Herald Tribune* 9 Aug. 8/1 Twofers, as they are called in the slang of the trade, entitle the holder to two seats for a given show for the price of one. **1959** P. Bull *I know Face* iii. 56 It was a constant embarrassment to me to watch a nice customer..buy two expensive stalls for 27*s.*, only to be followed by a 'twofer' lady who got the same thing for 13*s.* 6*d.* **1971** *It* 2–16 June 11/3 Me and the missus got twofers for the show. **1982** *Eastern Province* (S. Afr.) *Herald* 5 Aug. 17/2 Twofers are usually available only for near-to-flop shows or those looking tatty after a long run.

b. *transf.*; also *spec.* a Black woman appointed to a post, the appointment being seen as evidence of both racial and sexual equality of opportunity.

1969 *Britannica Bk. of Year* (U.S.) 801/1 *Twofer*, *specif.*, a blazer with matching trousers. **1978** *N.Y. Times* 29 Mar. A11/2 (Advt.), Another terrific two-for. This sun dress..becomes city-smart when you float the boxy jacket over it. **1977** *Time* 3 Jan. 36/1 By appointing her, Carter got a kind of 'twofer': as a black and as a woman, she is proof that the President-elect is trying to open his Cabinet to both groups. **1979** *Daily Tel.* 2 June 10 Personnel departments [in the United States] are told always to try and hire a 'toofer'. **1982** *Record Business* 11 Jan. 2/1 Ian Miles..had best-sellers with..a Wout Steenhuis twofer and a Harry Secombe–Moira Anderson album of duets.

two-footed, *a.* Add: **2.** Of a footballer: able to kick equally well with either foot.

1948 *Sporting Mirror* 19 Nov. 6/2 He's a fine two-footed defender, very speedy in recovery and cool under pressure. **1969** *Listener* 3 Apr. 473/3 Arsenal's Jimmy Robertson, naturally two-footed. **1978** *Sunday Express* 19 Mar. 29/5 Robson drafted the inexperienced but talented, two-footed Russell Osman into his depleted defence.

twofor, var. *twofer.

two-forked, *a.* (Later example.)

1923 D. H. Lawrence *Birds, Beasts & Flowers* 113 He ..flickered his two-forked tongue from his lips.

twofur, var. *twofer.

two-handed, *a.* Add: **6.** *U.S. colloq.* Generous, open-handed.

1929 D. Runyon in *Cosmopolitan* July 57/1 Miss Missouri Martin..puts the blast on her plenty for chasing a two-handed spender..out of the joint. **1933** G. Ade *Let.* 12 Sept. (1973) 173 He was..a two-handed drinker who could not carry his rum because he was too frail and intellectual.

Hence **two-handedly** *adv.*, with or in both hands; **two-hander**, (*b*) *Theatr.*, a play with a cast of two.

1927 Kipling *Verse 1885–1926* 730 Two-handedly tossing me jewels. **1976** *Listener* 20 May 648/3 The play was..a two-hander, finely acted by Maurice Denham and Colette O'Neil. **1981** H. Baldry *Case for Arts* 9 The ever-diminishing casts of the plays which our theatre directors can afford to present... This is the time of the three-hander and the two-hander. **1981** M. Kenyon *Zigzag* xxi. 143 Peckover, pickaxe two-handedly poised..stepped towards him.

two-legged, *a.* Add: Also *fig.*

1930 W. K. Hancock *Australia* i. 28 In the very best wheat country the farmer will keep a flock of sheep, not only to make his economy 'two-legged', but also because sheep are an essential agricultural implement. **1976** *Milton Keynes Express* 16 July 39 Whereas last season the winners and runners-up of each section met in the semi finals, the winner and runner-up of the one league will meet in a two-legged final.

two natures, *sb. pl. Theol.* The divine and human natures united in the person of Christ. Also (hyphened) *attrib.*

1600, 1651 [see Hypostasis 5]. **1797** *Encycl. Brit.* VII. 43/1 He [*sc.* Eutyches] appeared to allow of two natures, even before the union. **1874** J. H. Blunt *Dict. Sects, Heresies* 332/2 The Monophysites held that the two Natures were so united, that although the 'One Christ' was partly Human and partly Divine, His two Natures became by their union only one Nature. **1946** E. L. Mascall *Christ, Christian & Church* iii. 49 In no case is the divine nature seen acting in separation from the human. The two natures are distinct and their union is unimaginably intimate. **1977** D. Cupitt in J. Hick *Myth of God Incarnate* vii. 136 Liddon..did not see in the full two-natures doctrine any threat to the unity of Christ's person. **1982** *Church Times* 24 Dec. 8/3 The doctrine of the 'two natures' in the one person of Christ..does not mean that Jesus was in any sense schizophrenic, acting at one moment as man and the next as God.

twopence. Add: Since the introduction of decimal coinage in Britain in 1971 also pronounced (tū pens) when a sum of money is meant (as in senses 1, 2, and 6).

3. a. Also *for twopence*, very easily, with the smallest encouragement.

1934 R. H. Mottram *Bumphrey's* I. 37 I'm all heavy with that stuff. I could go to sleep for tuppence! *a* **1960** E. M. Forster *Maurice* (1973) xxvi. 132 I'd jump out of the window for twopence.

c. *twopence coloured* adj. phr.: orig. with reference to prints of characters for toy theatres that were sold in the early nineteenth century at one penny (1d) for black and white ones and two pennies (2d) for coloured ones; hence, excessively theatrical; cheap and gaudy.

1859, etc. [see *penny plain* adj. s.v. *Penny 12 c]. **1879** R. L. Stevenson *Trav. with Donkey* 82 If landscapes were sold, like the sheets of characters of my boyhood, one penny plain and twopence coloured, I should go to the length of twopence every day. **1887** *Art Jrnl.* Apr. 105/1 Picturesque melodrama..has given place to every-day drama..unsusceptible of twopence coloured treatment. **1908** E. Terry *Story of my Life* x. 243, I never cared much for Henry [Irving]'s Mephistopheles—a two-pence coloured part, any way. **1911** G. K. Chesterton *Innocence of Father Brown* xi. 304 It was a twopence coloured sort of incident. **1926** W. de la Mare *Connoisseur* 311 My American adventure..is of the 'twopence coloured' variety, rather than the 'penny plain'. **1932** *N. & Q.* 27 Feb. 151/2, I have two very unusual specimens of the twopence coloured. They..have very little brushwork, being decorated in every possible part with foil of different colours. **1948** *Eng. Stud.* I. 95 The Rape of Heraclide is a magnificent specimen of the 'twopence coloured' style. **1966** A. L. Coburn *Autobiogr.* iv. 48 The toy theatre of Stevenson's childhood and mine. A penny plain and twopence coloured. **1968** *Economist* 9 Nov. p. v/1 Almost too much painful detail, which is of no intrinsic interest except by double proof of the horror of the whole; and perhaps slightly two twopence-coloured; but brilliantly readable. **1978** *Guardian Weekly* 24 Sept. 20/3 A penny-dreadful dramatisation..that has been bumped up into a tuppence-coloured theatrical event by sheer production values.

6. (Further examples. Cf. *Twopenny *a.* 1 a.)

1972 J. Wilson *Hide & Seek* ii. 28 Alice found she had a two-pence piece in the pocket of her jeans. **1976** Deakin & Willis *Johnny go Home* ii. 50 Annie called him from a coin box..using a two-pence piece that had been given her. **1979** M. Page *Pilate Plot* vi. 94 Dick Goddard pushed a two-pence coin into the slot.

two-penneth, -pennorth, -penn'orth, colloq. contractions of *Two pennyworth.

twopenny, *a.* and *sb.* Add: **A.** *adj.* **1. a.** *twopenny piece*, any coin of the value of twopence (cf. Twopence 2); in mod. use (freq. pronounced (tū·peni)), a bronze coin first issued in Britain with the introduction of decimal currency in 1971.

1607 E. Topsell *Foure-Footed Beasts* 358 A round peece of leather, as broad as a two penny peece. **1907** [in Dict.]. **1972** A. Ross *London Assignment* 65 The old witch outside began to rap on the glass door [of the telephone kiosk] with her tuppenny pieces. **1974** [see *Phone *v.* a]. **1976** *Daily Tel.* 5 Nov. 13/6 There were plastic bags of tuppenny pieces from current juniors who had held raffles in 'break'. **1979** J. Scott *Clutch of Vipers* viii. 141 The chunk as the Twopenny piece fell.

d. Also *ellipt.* for *twopenny post* or *letter.*

1818 Keats *Let.* Oct. (1931) I. 263 Haslam..has taken all the Letters except this sheet, which I shall send him by the Twopenny. **1832** Dickens *Let.* ?Aug. (1965) I. 9 The place has no other name, but a twopenny directed as above will no doubt find us.

† **f.** *twopenny rope*: a cheap lodging-house (see quot. 1836). *Obs.*

1836 [see *Rope *sb.*[1] 2 f]. **1850** [see *lie-down* s.v. *Lie *sb.*[2] 6].

g. *twopenny library* (Hist.): a lending library, usu. operated from a shop, from which a book could be borrowed for twopence a week.

1935 W. G. Taylor in J. Hampden *Bk. World* 85 That the 'reading public' is growing rapidly seems evident from the growth of the 'twopenny library'. **1942** J. B. Priestley *Black-Out in Gretley* iii. 23 Twopenny libraries bright with book jackets. **1963** 'R. Findlater' *What are Writers Worth?* 7 The 'twopenny libraries' which spread rapidly throughout the country before the war, and have vanished nearly as quickly in the past decade. **1978** S. Hodges *Gollancz* v. 115 The twopenny libraries..had come into their own..in the mid-thirties.

2. a. *esp.* in phr. (*not*) *to care* (or *give*) *a twopenny damn* (or *hang*); also *ellipt.*

1897 W. S. Maugham *Liza of Lambeth* xi. 215, I don't care a twopenny 'ang for all them blokes. **1898** R. Fry *Let.* 5 Sept. (1972) I. 172 The date for Bissolo's death, for which I don't care just now a tuppenny damn. **1924** Lawrence & Skinner *Boy in Bush* 58, I don't believe she cares a tuppenny for 'em. **1980** D. K. Cameron *Willie Gavin* ix. 86 It was rich in its lairds, men who.. gave not a tuppeny damn..for anybody.

b. *twopenny upright*, a prostitute. *slang.*

1958 L. Durrell *Balthazar* ii. 41 A little old tart, button-eyed and razor-nosed—a tart of the Waterloo Bridge epoch, a veritable Tuppeny Upright. **1978** *Maledicta* II. 258 At the turn of the century, an Iowa woman was awarded $200 for being called a 'whore', while in England, at about the same time, a woman was denied any award for being called a 'two-penny upright'.

B. *sb.* **4.** *slang.* The head. [See quot. 1931.]

1859 in Hotten *Dict. Slang.* **1889** W. S. Gilbert *Gondoliers* II. 34 A Lord High Archbishop might tell a Lord High Chancellor to tuck in his tuppenny, but certainly not a cook. **1906** Galsworthy *Man of Property* III. iv. 321 Fast after him walked George. If the fellow meant to put his 'twopenny' under a bus, he would stop it if he could! **1928** C. E. Montague *Action* 150 'Into it, Jemmy', I yelled. 'Into the sewer and tuck in your tuppenny.' **1931** 'G. Orwell' *Coll. Essays* (1968) I. 71 The hop-pickers..also used the abbreviated rhyming slang, e.g. 'Use your twopenny' for 'Use your head'. This is arrived at like this: head, loaf of bread, loaf, twopenny loaf, twopenny.

two pennyworth (tū:pe·niwə̆þ), contr. **two-penneth, -penn'orth, -pennorth** (-pe·nəɹþ). As much as is worth or costs twopence. Freq. *fig.*, a small or contemptible amount. See Pennyworth.

1851 H. Mayhew *London Labour* I. 75/2 Two penn'orth for a whet. **1865** 'L. Carroll' *Alice's Adv. Wonderland* x. 160 Who would not give all else for two p (rhyme with 'soup') ennyworth only of beautiful Soup? **1870** *Punch* 5 Nov. 194/1, I walked down the street with just two-penn'orth of swagger on. **1896** G. B. Shaw *Let.* 5 Dec. in *Ellen Terry & Shaw* (1931) 134 You thought two pennorth of flattery all that the occasion demanded. **1924** Wodehouse *Leave it to Psmith* vi. 90 Within reason—and if undetected—I see no objection to two-pennorth of crime. **1965** G. Melly *Owning Up* ix. 105 After it [*sc.* the band] broke up I used to go along every other Tuesday to 'The Three Brewers'..and put in what Mick would call 'my two penn'orth'. **1979** *SLR Camera* Mar. 16/1 No meter, only years of experience and twopenneth of glass.

two-pi·pe, *a.* **a.** Applied to a system of hot-water heating in which a flow pipe supplies the radiators and a separate return pipe receives water from them.

1897 F. Dye *Hood's Pract. Treat. Warming Buildings* (ed. 3) xviii. 328 The arrangement of pipes is on the ordinary two-pipe principle. A flow and return is carried in different directions almost from a central point. **1970** [see *One-pipe *a.* a].

b. Applied to a system of plumbing in which separate waste-pipes and soil-pipes are employed.

1946 E. Molloy *Plumbing & Gas-Fitting* x. 203 The 'dual' or 'two-pipe' system, in which the removal of excretal matters..is effected by a pipe connected direct to the drain, and the removal of waste water..effected by a second pipe..discharging..over or into a properly trapped gully. **1972** T. A. Tompson *Guide Sanitary Engin. Services* vii. 226 The two-pipe system of sanitation is rarely used today and has been largely replaced by a more economic design.

twos (tuz), *v. U.S. colloq.* [f. Two sb.] *intr.* To keep company with a person of the opposite sex. Hence **two·sing** *vbl. sb.*

1920 S. Lewis *Main Street* 2 She played tennis,..went 'twosing', and joined half a dozen societies for the practice of the arts. **1924** *Dialect Notes* V. 291 *Twosing*,..going in couples. **1940** W. Faulkner *Hamlet* II. ii. 119 They chose one another monotonously in the twosing games.

twosome, *sb.* and *a.* For 'Chiefly *Sc.*' read 'orig. *Sc.*' and add: **A.** *sb.* (Later examples.) Also, a pair of lovers.

1926 [see *Foursome B. *sb.* 2]. **1945** L. Shelly *Jive Talk Dict.* 19/2 *Twosome*,..lovers. **1959** *Manch. Guardian* 12 Aug. 6/2 For the leaders of the nations..the rule is two by two. What is one to think of these twosomes? **1972** *Guardian* 4 Dec. 12/1 Government in Australia and New Zealand has become a socialist twosome. **1973** L. Snelling *Heresy* I. i. 8 Shockley and..Rosamund became a definite twosome in Rome. **1978** J. Irving *World according to Garp* xii. 232 Along came another Land Rover, as if they were a separated twosome from a column of an army on the move. **1982** H. Engel *Ransom Game* xvii. 101 Eddie Milano..used to spend a lot on her. They didn't keep house..—there's a Mrs. Milano out in Fort Erie, I think—but they were known as a twosome in the joints.

2. A game, dance, etc. for two persons.

1911 in *Conc. Oxf. Dict.* **1977** *Washington Post* 3 Sept. D7/4 Irwin and Weiskopf..had to roll in 25-foot birdie putts at the 18th in the last twosome of the day. **1983** *Ibid.* 6 Nov. C2/1 The [golf] competition..also includes two some matches.

two-·stroke, *a.* (and *sb.*) [Stroke *sb.*[1] 12 c.] Working mechanically by means of a succession of reciprocal movements, in and out or up and down; applied *esp.* to (vehicles having) internal-combustion engines in which the power cycle is completed in one upward and one downward stroke of a piston. Also as *sb.*, a two-stroke engine or vehicle.

1855, 1900 [in Dict. s.v. Two IV. 1 a]. **1902** P. N. Hansluck *Automobile* vi. 113 Motors of the four-stroke cycle consume less fuel than motors of the two-stroke cycle. **1936** *Economist* 2 May 234/1 In a two-stroke engine, each cylinder gives an impulse at every revolution of the crankshaft. **1963** L. Deighton *Horse under Water* xiv. 59 Fernie propped his two-stroke against the baker's shop. **1972** J. McClure *Caterpillar Cop* ii. 19 The lights pulsed to the quick beat of the two-stroke. **1975** D. Malouf *Johnno* x. 109 All one scorching summer I blazed from suburb to suburb on a Fanny Barnet two-stroke. **1982** *Sunday Tel.* 1 Aug. 6/1 It [*sc.* a free-wheel device] was..also used by Saab, mainly on its two-stroke models.

twot: see Twat in Dict. and Suppl.

two-·time, *a. slang* (orig. *U.S.*). **1.** [f. *two times* adv. phr. s.v. Two B. 1 d.] Characterized by something that has happened or been done twice; *two-time loser*: see *Loser 4.

1897 R. M. Johnston *Middle Georgia* 113 Is a widder, even a two-time widder, got nothin' else to do but..go about grievin' for them that's gone? **1960** *Guardian* 14 July 9/1 A threat to unseat one man..for his two-time allegiance to Eisenhower. **1972** *Publishers' Weekly* 3 Jan. 9 This book by a two-time ABC Master Tournament winner. **1979** A. V. Badgley *Rembrandt Decisions* (1980) xv. 212 Maybe they won't go [*sc.* be stolen] any more... Maybe it was just a two-time snatch.

2. [f. the vb.] Double-crossing, two-timing.

1937 E. S. Gardner *Case of Dangerous Dowager* xii. 231 You think I'm a two-time, chiseling crook.

two-·time, *v. slang* (orig. *U.S.*). *trans.* To deceive (esp. a person to whom one owes loyalty); to be unfaithful to (a spouse or lover); to double-cross. Also *absol.* or *intr.*

1924 J. Edwards in P. Oliver *Screening Blues* (1968) ii. 64 She'll two-time you like she double-crossed me. **1926** E. Hemingway *Sun also Rises* I. vii. 66 The drummer shouted: 'You can't two time—'. **1937** Wodehouse *Summer Moonshine* (1938) xxiv. 287, I can tell you it pretty near broke me up when I found you were two-timing me that way. Letting another guy send you jewellery. **1959** 'M. M. Kaye' *House of Shade* v. 63 You can't go two-timing the police and skipping out of the country on a stolen passport. **1959** M. Renault *Charioteer* vi. 117 In return you've done nothing but two-time me. **1975** *Time Out* 10 Jan. 65/2 Do all attractive slim girls think it clever to lie and two-time? **1981** *Sunday Times* 8 Mar. 8/2 Judith Exner..two-timed the late President John Kennedy with a leader of organised crime.

Hence **two-timing** *vbl. sb.* and *ppl. a.*; also **two-timer,** one who double-crosses or is unfaithful.

1927 K. Nicholson *Barker* I. ii. 53 You dirty two-timer, you can't get away with that. **1927** 'C. Woolrich' *Children of Ritz* viii. 149 Two-timing was what they called that, when a wife went out in other company. **1927** *Columbia Record Catal.* 205/2 My two-timing papa. **1935** *Discovery* Nov. 346/2 His criticism of the hypocritical quakers and 'two-timing' politicians..is too strong. **1942** *Daily Mirror* (N.Y.) 7 Aug. 5/4 The girl had a gun..and told McNaughton: 'You're a two-timer and no good... I'm going to kill you.' **1959** N. Marsh *False Scent* (1960) i. 36 You little, two-timing, double-crossing, dirty rat. **1974** G. Jenkins *Bridge of Magpies* xii. 182 I'd written him off as a two-timer who'd run away to save his own skin. **1982** N. Painting *Reluctant Archer* iii. 36 Goneril's two-timing of her worthy but dull husband. **1984** *Listener* 26 Jan. 31/3 Rogers plays a chorus girl out to make a show business reputation by confessing to the murder of her two-timing lover.

two-·up, *sb.* and *adv.* (*a.*) [Up *adv.*[2]] **A.** *sb.* **1.** *Austral.* and *N.Z.* A gambling game played by tossing two coins, bets being laid on the showing of two heads or two tails.

1898 *Bulletin* (Sydney) 3 Sept. 32 At 'loo he'd lately scooped the pool; He'd simply smashed the two-up school. **1898** [see *Kip *sb.*[6]]. **1911** L. Stone *Jonah* vi. 213 He marked pak-a-pu tickets, took the kip at two-up, and staked his last shilling more readily than the first. **1916** G. Thornton *Wowser* viii. 108 Forty young men..

were..playing that favourite but not intellectual game of chance, 'two-up'. **1936** 'R. HYDE' *Passport to Hell* viii. 137 Two dozen mounted police charged the two-up schools, involving a heavy loss of stakes as the men scattered. **1948** V. PALMER *Golconda* iv. 27 A fellow of some power, a fellow who had been used to handling the rough crowds of two-up rings. **1952** J. CLEARY *Sundowners* 229 Who's for a game of two-up? Got just the place out the back? **1960** P. WILSON in C. K. Stead *N.Z. Short Stories* (1966) 129 Some had a two-up school going on in the corner. **1965** B. WANNAN *Fair Go, Spinner* IV. 192 The landlord of the pub, who ran the two-up school, roared out to them, 'Stay where you are, around the ring, but put your dough outa sight!' **1980** *Courier-Mail* (Brisbane) 19 June 3/4 Two-up is banned in Queensland. **1982** G. GREER in *Observer* 8 Aug. 21/3 Two-up is Australia's very own way of parting a fool and his money.

2. two-up (and) two-down, a house with two reception rooms downstairs and two bedrooms upstairs. Also *attrib.* or as *adj. phr.* So *two-up-and-two-downer.*

1958 *Listener* 7 Aug. 212/1 The microphone popped in and out of the two-up-and-two-downers. **1962** *Radio Times* 2 Aug. 37/2 Recalling such local institutions [in Liverpool] as 'the two-up, two-downs'. **1970** J. SANGSTER *Touchfeather, Too* v. 125 A smart little two up and two down somewhere in the suburbs. **1973** *Times* 18 May 4/5 Long, straight terraces of miners' cottages, typically two up, two down. **1978** *Times* 18 May 18/4, I am a poor cotton town boy who grew up in a two-up two-down. **1978** M. KENYON *Deep Pocket* vi. 71 The two-up, two-down brick and dinginess of Ensign Terrace.

B. *adv.* Two at a time, two together.

1926 [see *DOUBLE-BANK *v.* 2]. **1967** COX & GROSE *Organization & Handling Bibl. Rec. by Computer* II. 25 Master output for photo-litho reproduction 'two-up'.

two-va·lued, *a.* Chiefly *Logic.* Able to take one or other of only two values; characterized by the usual two truth-values, i.e. truth and falsity.

1918 C. I. LEWIS *Survey Symbolic Logic* iv. 222 The first procedure..interprets the elements of this system as propositions, and adds to it a postulate which holds for propositions but not for logical classes. The result is what has been called the 'Two-valued Algebra'. **1933** *Mind* XLII. 269, I attempt to show that there are fourteen different meanings of implication in a two-valued logic. **1946** *Nature* 14 Sept. 357/1 Ordinary symbolic logic..represents two-valued logic. **1965** N. CHOMSKY *Aspects Theory Syntax* 232 We can regard..number [in German grammar] as a two-valued dimension. **1970** O. DOPPING *Computers & Data Processing* i. 26 All logical connections between two-valued variables can be expressed by means of the three functions NOT, AND, and OR.

two-way, *a.* and *sb.* Add: **1. b.** Of a plug or adaptor: able to accommodate two plugs at the same time.

1923 *T. Eaton & Co. Catal.* Spring & Summer 357 Two-way socket plug. **1977** *Times* 24 Sept. 22/2 You can use two or three-way adaptors..but do be careful not to overload your current supply.

c. Of a loudspeaker: having two separate drive units for different frequency ranges.

1950 *Audio Engin.* Aug. 15/2 Many loudspeakers are two-way: that is, the frequency range is divided and each portion is handled by separate radiating systems. **1960** [see *THREE-WAY *a.* b]. **1978** *Detroit Free Press* 16 Apr. 18A/1 (Advt.), Two-way bass reflex speaker system. 8-in. woofer, 3-in. tweeter.

2. Delete *Math. two-way stretch* attrib. phr., designed to stretch in both length and width; also *ellipt.* such an elastic corset.

1932 [see *GIRDLE *sb.*[1] 1 d]. **1959** *News Chron.* 19 Aug. 3/8 A girdle of Ellen Terry's—'I mean a sash, not a two-way stretch.' **1964** *Observer* 22 Mar. 3/1 Mr Clutson invented the two-way stretch elastic. **1977** *Summit* (Austin Reed, Ltd.) Autumn 44 Men's two-way stretch riding breeches from £18.

3. *Electr.* Of a switch, wiring, etc.: that enables a light or other device to be switched on or off at either of two points.

1893 W. P. MAYCOCK *Electric Lighting & Power Distribution* III. xv. 382 Fig. 240 shows a double-pole, 2-way switch, which would be connected in a parallel circuit in the manner illustrated. **1903** [see sense 1 in Dict.]. **1933** D. L. SAYERS *Murder must Advertise* vii. 113 The hall-light..was fitted with two-way wiring. **1960** *Practical Wireless* XXXVI. 395/1 A two-way switch is provided so that C9 may be connected to either.

4. a. Involving or permitting movement or communication in each of two opposite directions; (of a radio) capable of both transmitting and receiving.

1922 *Encycl. Brit.* XXXII. 1027/2 A problem of practical importance is that of two-way radiotelephony enabling two communicators to speak and hear simultaneously. **1927** *Glasgow Herald* 16 Apr. 7 The purpose.. is to strengthen the direct connection between Great Britain and the Middle Western group of American States by increasing the two-way tonnage exchange clearing through the Virginian ports. **1938** *Radio Times* 1 July 6/3 A two-way broadcast arranged by the BBC and the Columbia Broadcasting System of America. **1957** L. F. R. WILLIAMS *State of Israel* viii. 144 There is a growing two-way traffic in literature between Israel and other countries. **1971** A. PRICE *Alamut Ambush* x. 127 He was fixing up the two-way speaker in the porch..so that I could answer the door from here. **1976** L. DEIGHTON *Twinkle, twinkle, Little Spy* xxi. 207 Has he got a two-way radio in the car? **1967** 'R. STARK' *Damsel* (1968) II. 47 Eight lanes of two-way traffic were flanked by broad swaths of green grass. **1981** R. HAYMAN *K* xii. 156 A solitude which was unbroken by the two-way traffic in fantasies that went on in his correspondence.

b. Occurring or existing in two directions; reciprocal; *two-way street* (fig.), a situation of mutual action; something that works both ways.

1950 J. JENKS *From Ground Up* ii. 17 The agri-cultural relationship is, like all vital relationships, two-way. **1951** *Sun* (Baltimore) 14 Dec. 5/6 'An amendment..provided that if any company..gave so much as a cigar to a Government employé, the contract should be cancelled... Do you think that should be made stronger?'..'Yes, it is a two-way street.' **1959** *Times* 19 Sept. 6/3 In sharp contrast with other days this week the market was more 'two way'—that is, there was more buying to offset the selling. **1968** H. WAUGH *Con Game* xi. 101 'Our aim in this racket is to use you.' 'I prefer to think of it as a two-way street.' **1969** T. F. TORRANCE *Theol. Sci.* ii. 67 The relation between God and the creature is a two-way relation. **1975** *Language for Life* (Dept. Educ. & Sci.) xiv. 214 Some will have had very little sustained two-way conversation in the home. **1975** *Times Lit. Suppl.* 21 Nov. 1392/5 Tolerance..was a two-way street: if the Germans were to learn to live with the Jews, so too must the Jews learn to live with the Germans. **1982** *Times* 12 Jan. 12/3 The jobbers..encountered a fair amount of two-way business.

c. *two-way mirror,* a mirror which lets through enough light for an observer at the back to see through it, without being seen from the front.

1967 J. GARDNER *Madrigal* i. 3 They directed total concentration through the sighting side of a two-way mirror. **1974** *Times* 23 Jan. 2/5 Everyone laughed at a show business party when looking through a two-way mirror at couples having sexual intercourse. **1982** R. HILL *Who guards a Prince* I. viii. 57 Locking doors was an empty gesture in these days of two-way mirrors.

B. *sb.* A two-way radio.

1963 'W. HAGGARD' *High Wire* v. 54 There's an operator with a two-way somewhere near the junction. I'm picking up his message. **1974** V. BROME *Day of Destruction* v. 51 We've just received a message over the two-way to say he's stuck..in the middle of a swamp.

two-year-old, *sb.* Add: **b.** As the type of a youthful and energetic person.

1912 *Punch* 19 June 470/1 Feeling as he did like a two-year-old, he was convinced that an immeasurable advantage to the country would be gained by placing the ballot in the hands of babies. **1928** GALSWORTHY *Swan Song* III. xvi. 342 Mr. Forsyte was a proper wonder—went at it like a two-year old. **1936** [see *STINKER 6 c].

Tyburnia (təibɝ·ɹniă). [mod.L., f. TYBURN + -IA[1].] A former literary name for the residential district built in the nineteenth century and extending along the Bayswater Road from Marble Arch to Lancaster Gate and northwards.

1848, *a* **1852** [see *BELGRAVIA]. **1878** A. J. C. HARE *Walks in London* II. 104 Tyburn still gives a name to the white streets and squares of *Tyburnia*, which are wholly devoid of interest or beauty. **1902** G. W. E. RUSSELL *For Better? For Worse?* iv. 58 The most gorgeous mansion in Cromwell Road or Tyburnia could never for a moment be quoted as supplying the place of the Hall or the Manor. **1973** *Country Life* 15 Nov. 1528/1 By the mid-1830s in Tyburnia stucco was replacing brick-facing.

Hence **Tybu·rnian** *a.*

1850 THACKERAY *Pendennis* II. xi. 104 The great lawyers are giving grand dinner parties at their houses in the Belgravian or Tyburnian districts. **1860** *Once a Week* 28 July 124/2 The gallows, called 'Tyburn Tree'..had been for years a standing fixture on..the Edgware Road, ..but this was..the second Tyburnian location of the gallows. **1973** *Country Life* 15 Nov. 1528/1 The circular turrets..contemporary with the earliest Tyburnian example..appear in Victoria Square.

tychism (təi·kiz'm). [f. Gr. τύχη chance + -ISM.] The doctrine that objective account must be taken of the element of chance in (philosophical, cosmological, etc.) reasoning.

1892 C. S. PEIRCE in *Monist* II. 533, I endeavored to show what ideas ought to form the warp of a system of philosophy, and particularly emphasised that of absolute chance..which it will be convenient to christen *tychism* (from τυχη, chance). **1926** J. LAIRD *Study in Moral Theory* viii. 173 The theory that every event..is necessary (or *must* occur precisely as it does occur) I shall call *determinism*... The opposite theory I shall call *tychism*, such tychism being either general or restricted. **1978** *Sci. Amer.* July 18/1 At a time when determinism dominated physics Peirce's doctrine of 'tychism' maintained that pure chance—events undetermined by prior causes—are basic to the universe.

tycoon. Delete ‖ and add: **1.** (Earlier examples.)

1857 T. HARRIS *Diary* 28 Oct. (1930) 406 Today, I am told *Ziogoon* is not the proper appellation of their ruler, but that it is *Tykoon*. *Ziogoon* is literally 'Generalissimo' while *Tykoon* means 'Great Ruler'. **1858** *Times* 9 Nov. 7/1 This treaty, in the first place, engages that there shall be perpetual peace and friendship between Her British Majesty and the Tycoon of Japan.

2. An important or dominant person, esp. in business or politics; a magnate. Also *attrib.* orig. *U.S.* (as a nickname of Abraham Lincoln).

1861 J. HAY *Diary* 25 Apr. in *Lincoln & Civil War* (1939) 12 Gen. Butler has sent an imploring request to the President to be allowed to bag the whole nest of traitorous Maryland Legislators. This the Tycoon..forbade. **1886** *Outing* (U.S.) IX. 164/1 The tycoon of the baggage car objected to handling the boat. **1926** *Time* 14 June 32/3 *Married.* Fred W. Fitch, 56, rich hair-tonic tycoon. **1947** AUDEN *Age of Anxiety* (1948) 36 With diamonds to offer, A cleaned tycoon in a cooled office, I smiled at a siren. **1952** *Manch. Guardian Weekly* 3 July 7/3 Warren has.. been the preferred choice of..oil and aviation tycoons with delusions of grandeur. **1958** [see *TYCOONISH *a.*]. **1960** R. W. MARKS *Dymaxion World of B. Fuller* 62/1 Pictures of his latest projects appear regularly on the front cover of the magazines which symbolize the tycoon press. **1982** M. RUSSELL *Rainblast* iii. 21 She has a thing going with Marcus Hicks, the stores tycoon.

Hence **tycoo·nery** [-ERY], the behaviour or status of a tycoon or tycoons; a group of businessmen; **tycoone·ss,** a female tycoon (sense *2); **tycoo·nish** *a.*, characteristic of a tycoon (sense *2); **tycoo·nship,** the status or position of a tycoon (sense *2); the fact of being a tycoon.

1956 *Time* 24 Dec. 47/2 Instead of making a budget, Falk decided to indulge in a bit of extracurricular tycoonery. **1958** *Times* 3 Dec. 6/4 Tycoons are not quite as tycoonish as they were before. **1959** *Times* 19 Nov. 15/5 This immensely long..novel gives us a new Tom Sawyer and takes him up to tycoonery. **1960** *Guardian* 28 Oct. 8/4 A high-powered tycooness must have sharp claws within the velvet paw. **1962** *Punch* 26 Sept. 443/3 The *Express* group stands alone among the major press tycooneries. **1964** R. WARD *Penguin Bk. Austral. Ballads* 15 Rugged individualists separately thrusting their ways.. to an industrial tycoon-ship. **1965** 'R. ERSKINE' *Passion Flowers in Business* iv. 48, I..thought it tycoonish in an exciting way. **1970** 'D. HALLIDAY' *Dolly & Cookie Bird* viii. 119 Janey's father..had..several irritating habits of tycoonery. **1976** 'M. INNES' *Gay Phoenix* iii. 43 Business affairs... A high degree of continuity in their direction was..a *sine qua non* of successful tycoonship. **1983** *Listener* 27 Oct. 34/3 He was busy trying to set up a rival consortium to buy the Sunday Times, competing with (and losing to) Murdoch in tycoonery.

tyee, tyhee. Add: **1.** For *U.S.* read *N. Amer.* and add earlier and later examples.

1792 in E. HEALEY *Hist. Alert Bay* (1958) 15 The Ty-ee, or chief, of the village paid us an early visit. **1866** J. K. LORD *Naturalist in Brit. Columbia* I. 161, I was presented to the chiefs as a Hyas tyee (great chief), one of 'King George's' men. **1877** *Puget Sound* (Washington) *Argus* 23 Nov., With the coming of the military among us came a big church 'tyhee', who told us that the soldiers were come to protect us. **1880** D. M. GORDON *Mountain & Prairie* 117 We were surprised to find, at the head of Stewart Lake, a well-stocked farm, owned and worked by the Indian 'tyhee'. **1927** [see *HIGH-MUCK-A-MUCK]. **1963** *Brit. Columbia Digest* Oct. 54/2 A British officer..may have told the Chief that he was now the great Tyee of the country. The Indian took the words literally and elevated himself to top position. **1966** H. MARRIOTT *Cariboo Cowboy* v. 54 The agricultural tyees in both Canada and the United States have taken a wise view.

tyen, obs. var. *T'IEN.

tyke. Add: **2.** Also (unreprovingly), a child, esp. a small boy; occas., a young animal. *U.S.*

1902 *Dialect Notes* II. 248 *Tyke, n.,* a child. **1930** W. FAULKNER *As I lay Dying* 30 'That poor boy,' Cora says. 'The poor little tyke.' **1942** H. K. SMITH *Last Train from Berlin* v. 174 If you think the present Gestapo is brutal, just wait until these little tykes..grow up and become the rulers of Victorious Germany. **1979** *Tucson* (Arizona) *Citizen* 20 Sept. 1E/4 The stripes are nature's way of protecting the tapir tyke until it's old enough to fend for itself. **1981** *Verbatim* VII. III. 23/2 What hours of chair-side fun await the tyke supplied with 'three 6-oz. cans of modeling compound'!

3*. [Assimilated or altered f. TEAGUE.] A Roman Catholic. *Austral.* and *N.Z. slang.*

1941 BAKER *Dict. Austral. Slang* 76 *Tike, tyke,* a Roman Catholic. **1948** R. PARK *Harp in South* xxi. 268 I'll do what I like without the interference of any bone-headed tike. **1961** P. WHITE *Riders in Chariot* viii. 232, I would never ever of suspected you Rosetrees of being tykes. Only the civil servants are Roman Catholics here, and the politicians, if they are anything at all. **1977** D. AITKIN *Second Chair* xviii. 172 Baxter's a tyke (you wouldn't think it from his name..) and he goes to mass each Sunday. **1981** M. GEE *Meg* xvii. 189 Once it fell to me to..explain to a pair of Jehovah's Witnesses that we were all good Catholics in this house... 'At least the tikes have got some style... Shall I nail a crucifix on the door?'

Hence **ty·kish** *a.*, characteristic of a tyke; **tykishness** (further example).

1888 G. M. HOPKINS *Let.* 20 May (1956) 392 There is an old Adam of barbarism, boyishness, wildness, rawness, rankness, the disreputable, the unrefined in the refined and educated. It is that I meant by tykishness (a tyke is a stray sly unowned dog)... Ancient Pistol is the typical tyke,..and the tykish element undergoing dilution in Falstaff and Prince Hall [*sic*] appears to vanish.. in Henry V as king.

tylectomy (təile·ktŏmi). *Surg.* [f. TYLO- + *-ECTOMY.] The excision of a lump or swelling, esp. a cancerous one.

1972 H. ATKINS et al. *Brit. Med. Jrnl.* 20 May 423/2 We are indebted to Dr. W. J. Mann, who has proposed the term 'tylectomy'..for excision of a lump and we use the term 'extended tylectomy' instead of 'wide excision' throughout the paper. **1978** *Jrnl. R. Soc. Med.* LXXI. 341 Stage I cases treated by tylectomy and HVT in the

Guy's Hospital trial..had local recurrence rates of 15% at three years and 20% at five years.

tylosin (təi·lǝsin). *Vet. Sci.* [Etym. unkn.; see -IN[1].] A macrolide antibiotic, $C_{46}H_{77}NO_{17}$, produced by *Streptomyces fradiæ* and used esp. to treat respiratory infections in animals.

1961 J. M. McGuire et al. in *Antibiotics & Chemotherapy* (N.Y.) XI. 326 Tylosin, a new antibiotic substance, has been obtained from soil isolates tentatively identified as strains of *Streptomyces fradiae* (Waksman and Curtis) Waksman and Henrici. **1968** [see *MACROLIDE]. **1981** *Antimicrobial Agents & Chemotherapy* XX. 214/1 Tylosin is a complex macrolide antibiotic which is produced commercially by a strain of *Streptomyces fradiae*.., it is also produced by strains of *Streptomyces rimosus*.. and *Streptomyces hygroscopicus*.

Tymba, var. *TEMBU. **tymbal,** var. TIMBAL in Dict. and Suppl.

tympani, var. *TIMPANI.

1876 in Stainer & Barrett *Dict. Mus. Terms.* **1917** *Lit. Digest* 25 Aug. 28/2 The thirty-seconds scored for the tympani in some of the modern Russian music. **1927** *Melody Maker* May 483/1 There has been much controversy concerning the practical use of tympani in the dance band, and many dance drummers have, owing to the infrequency of tympani passages in dance arrangements, regarded them as instruments unnecessary for dance work altogether. **1965** G. McInnes *Road to Gundagai* xi. 200 The man with the bass drum and tympani was responsible for the heavy artillery.

tympanist. Add: Now *spec.*, one who plays upon a kettledrum.

1930 *Melody Maker* Jan. 72/3 All that need trouble the tympanist in regard to the minor chords is [etc.]. **1955** L. Feather *Encycl. Jazz* 195/1 He studied with Saul Goodman, tympanist with the N.Y. Philharmonic.

tympano-. Add: **ty·mpanogram,** a graphical record of pressure changes obtained in tympanometry; so **tympano·graphy; tympano·metry,** the measurement, for diagnostic purposes, of changes in the compliance of the tympanic membrane as the air pressure is altered in the passage of the external ear; hence **ty:mpanome·tric** *a.*; **ty·mpanopla:sty** *Surg.* [-PLASTY], an operation to repair the middle ear; hence **ty:mpanopla·stic** *a.*; **ty:mpanosclero·sis** *Med.* [SCLEROSIS], thickening of the tympanic membrane, and of the connective tissue in the tympanic cavity; hence **ty:mpanosclero·tic** *a.*

1969 *Arch. Otolaryngol.* LXXXIX. 217/2 The tympanogram has a normal configuration. **1979** J. J. Knight in H. A. Beagley *Auditory Investigation* viii. 158 A flat tympanogram with a negative middle ear pressure is suggestive of serous otitis media. **1977** *Proc. R. Soc. Med.* LXX. 824/1 Surgery should not be undertaken until after tympanography has been done and tomograms taken to exclude abnormalities of cochlear anatomy. **1984** *Lancet* 19 May 1112/2 A sound case can be made for including tympanography in the routine screening tests at school entry. **1970** *Arch. Otolaryngol.* XCII. 255/2 Tympanometric characteristics provide information in analysis of the conductive pathological abnormality. **1984** *Jrnl. Speech & Hearing Res.* XXVII. 257 The influence that repeated tympanometric trials have on the aural-acoustic admittance characteristics of the middle-ear transmission system was studied in 24 young adults. **1956** H. Anderson et al. in *Acta Oto-Laryngol.* XLVI. 384 This method—for which we propose the name tympanometry—may..yield very important additional information for the diagnosis of hearing impairments. **1980** *Ibid.* LXXXIX. 480/1 The patients were regularly checked with audiometry and tympanometry. **1955** *Jrnl. Laryngol.* LXIX. 654 Of 110 tympanoplastic cases..60 per cent. have retained or regained 'social' hearing. **1977** *Lancet* 16 July 119/2 Tympanoplastic surgery is a logical development of the modified radical techniques and aims to avoid their main disadvantages—deafness and an open cavity in the mastoid—by creating a functioning middle ear in a healthy closed system. **1955** *Acta Oto-Laryngol.* XLV. 457 It seems advisable in some cases..to operate in two stages: first a conservative radical operation..and, secondly, tympanoplasty. **1960** J. Grant *Come again, Nurse* xvi. 97 Now a tympanoplasty is different again. That is a plastic repair to the middle ear with a skin graft, to help the sound waves. **1977** *Lancet* 16 July 119/1 Grafting the drum constitutes the simplest and most successful form of tympanoplasty. **1961** *Brit. Med. Dict.* 1491/1 Tympanosclerosis. **1965** I. B. Thorburn in W. G. Scott-Brown et al. *Dis. Ear, Nose & Throat* (ed. 2) II. xx. 454 Tympanosclerosis. Zöllner (1955) drew fresh attention to this condition which was first described as 'Paukensclerose' by von Tröltsch in 1873. *Ibid.*, On otomicroscopic examination a keratinizing appearance distinguishes cholesteatoma, whereas the white tympanosclerotic focus is covered by an intact healthy mucous membrane. **1978** *Jrnl. R. Soc. Med.* LXXI. 354 Scars and tympanosclerosis were only present in the ears with grommets. **1981** *Brit. Med. Jrnl.* 14 Feb. 501/1 Tympanosclerotic plaques are commonly seen in the drum after the use of grommets.

tympany. 1. Delete 'now *rare* or *arch.*' and add later examples.

1923 G. H. Wooldridge *Encycl. Vet. Med., Surg. & Obstetr.* II. 1023/2 Tympany is..a common accompaniment of rumenitis. **1970** W. H. Parker *Health & Dis. in Farm Animals* xiv. 186 The swelling in cases of tympany is primarily on the left.

Tyndall (ti·ndăl). The name of John *Tyndall* (see TYNDALLIZATION), used *attrib.* with reference to the scattering of a beam of light by small particles and the blue colour that the scattered light often has (described by Tyndall in 1869).

1910 H. H. Hodgson tr. *Pöschl's Introd. Chem. of Colloids* ii. 12 The Tyndall effect is the basis of ultra-microscopy. **1915** M. H. Fischer et al. tr. *Ostwald's Handbk. Colloid-Chem.* 8 Liquids which show no definite Tyndall light-cone..are molecular-disperse solutions. **1925** G. Barger tr. *Freundlich's Elem. Colloidal Chem.* 125 All colloidal solutions with colourless particles show a blue Tyndall light. **1939** H. B. Weiser *Colloid Chem.* xii. 160 There is no pigment in blue eyes; the color is a Tyndall blue which is more intense the finer the particles that give rise to the blue color. **1964** *Oceanogr. & Marine Biol.* II. 366 With the searchlights [of the bathyscaph] on, it is possible to discern very minute particles..by the Tyndall effect. **1966** *McGraw-Hill Encycl. Sci. & Technol.* XIV. 169/1 In aqueous gold sols..strong Tyndall cones are observed. **1971** *Nature* 19 Feb. 573/1 Drops smaller than 1 μm form a 'blue haze' due to selective Tyndall scattering of shorter light wavelengths.

Hence **Ty·ndallmeter** (also as two words), **Tyndallo·meter,** an instrument that makes use of the Tyndall effect for measuring aerosols and suspensions.

1919 Tolman & Vliet in *Jrnl. Amer. Chem. Soc.* XLI. 297 (*heading*) A Tyndallmeter for the examination of disperse systems. **1937** *Nature* 25 Sept. 553/1 The hygienic importance of the reduction of dust lends interest to means for its measurement, and the Tyndallometer shown by E. Leitz (London) provides a new and rapid means of its measurement. **1957** H. C. van de Hulst *Light Scattering by Small Particles* xix. 405 This problem, of obvious importance in the testing of gas masks, was studied by Gucker and by O'Konski. A Tyndall meter is insufficient for the concentrations of 10^{-9}g/liter and lower that have to be investigated.

Tyneside (təi·nsəid). [SIDE *sb.*[1] 7 a.] The area adjacent to the banks of the river Tyne in England, *spec.* the city of Newcastle-on-Tyne, used *attrib.* to designate things, esp. speech, characteristic of this area.

1824 R. Gilchrist *Coll. Original Songs* 9 Hail, Tyneside lads! in collier fleets. **1844** R. Nichols in M. A. Richardson *Local Historian's Table Bk.* II. 370 (*heading*) The Tyneside angler. **1872** T. & G. Allan (*title*) Tyneside songs. **1896** R. O. Heslop *Bibliogr. List Wks. Illustr. Dialect Northumberland* 6 Two tales of sixty years sin seyne, as related by the late Thomas Bewick, of Newcastle, in the Tyneside dialect. **1923** A. Herbert *Northumberland* viii. 127 In the Hancock Museum of Natural History may be seen the matchless collection of birds set up by the Tyneside naturalist, John Hancock. **1949** H. L. Honeyman *Northumberland* II. ii. 219 If there is anything that can be called a Tyneside type it is perhaps the rather small, wiry kind of man. **1955** P. Strevens *Papers in Lang. & Lang. Teaching* (1965) ix. 114 A uvular fricative *r*, similar to that used in Tyneside pronunciation of English or in Parisian French. **1978** *Early Music Gaz.* Oct. 3/3 The senior minstrel, aged about 12, gave his mates a good Tyne-side dressing-down for being late and playing wrong notes the night before!

Tynesider (təi·nsəidəɹ). [f. prec. + -ER[1].] A native or inhabitant of Tyneside. Cf. *CLYDESIDER, *MERSEYSIDER.

1895 *Tyneside* May 146/1 The Life of Sir Charles Palmer has been frequently written and is familiar enough to every Tynesider. **1923** A. Herbert *Northumberland* v. 69 The word 'keel' on Tyneside..was the name for an entire boat... It is the word for which all Tynesiders have most regard. **1950** S. Middlebrook *Newcastle upon Tyne* xviii. 222 In the 'forties the practice began of holding an annual skiff race..either between two local champions, or between a Tynesider and some challenger from the Thames. **1978** M. Stoppard in D. Abse *My Medical School* 173 Tynesiders were proud of their College.

type, *sb.*[1] Add: **6.** Also preceding a sb. with ellipsis of *of*, = type of. Cf. *-TYPE 2. *U.S. colloq.*

1966 *Word Study* Dec. 2/2 He could not pick out things like a bridge from 'this type distance'. **1979** *Nature* 22 Nov. p. xvii/1 The 110C systems may be used with virtually any type projector.

7. c. A person of a certain (specified or implicit) character; *one's type*, the sort of person to whom one is attracted (usu. in neg. or interrog. contexts). Also simply, a person; as a gallicism (also with pronunc. (‖tīp)) derogatory. *colloq.*

1922 [see *ABANDON *sb.*[3]]. **1930** Kipling *Limits & Renewals* (1932) 327, I played piquet with our schoolmaster... *That* was a type upon whom our War had done bad work. **1931** K. Boyle *Plagued by Nightingale* xv. 123 Luc could fish with Nicholas... It's exactly what the poor *type* would prefer anyway! **1933** 'G. Orwell' *Down & Out in Paris & London* xxix. 216 'Low types,' said the old Etonian, 'very low types.' **1934** F. B. Cuthrell *Innocent Bystander* vii. 130 Richardson did not interest her, he was not her 'type'. **1942** T. Rattigan *Flare Path* II. i. 127 You're the actor type, aren't you? **1948** 'N. Shute' *No Highway* ii. 41 It didn't do Fisher any good with the R.A.F. types. **1951** J. G. Fennessy *Sonnet in Bottle* I. v. 28 'Oh, by the way, do you know these types?' and he introduced the two men with him. **1956** 'A. Bridge' *Lighthearted Quest* 199, I went to look for Colin in that red-haired type's house. **1962** A. Lurie *Love & Friendship* xiii. 250 You wouldn't like him... He's not your type. He's a little fat man. **1965** R. & D. Morris *Men & Snakes* i. 16 Although an intrepid explorer type, he made a hasty exit. **1968** M. Jones *Survivor* iii. 51 'I'm asking you if you think she's at all his type.' Stuart shrugged. 'I shouldn't care to say what Martin's type is. Come to think of it, I'd say he has no type.' **1971** D. E. Westlake *I gave at Office* 136, I was not alone in the room. Three army types were there..tall, fat, khaki-uniformed. **1974** J. Aiken *Midnight is Place* iv. 142 That *type*... He is a brigand! **1979** R. Jaffe *Class Reunion* II. ii. 145 I've always thought you were very beautiful, Annabel. You always were just my type. **1979** A. Fraser *King Charles II* vii. 102 These were scarcely the types to risk life and limb. **1981** 'M. Hebden' *Pel is Puzzled* xi. 113 'Type over here... He recognises it.' The 'type over here' was a man about thirty-five with long blond hair.

8. b. Add to def.: *esp.* the specimen on which the first published description of a species is based. (Further examples.)

1893 O. Thomas in *Proc. Zool. Soc.* 242 The following are..the definitions now suggested for the different terms: A Type is a single specimen either unaccompanied by others at the time of description, or else deliberately selected as such by the author out of a series. **1951** G. H. M. Lawrence *Taxonomy of Vascular Plants* ix. 205 The term type, used alone and unqualified, generally refers to the holotype. **1964** *Internat. Code Zool. Nomencl.* xiii. 59 The 'type' affords the standard of reference that determines the application of a scientific name. **1970** *Watsonia* VIII. 156 A herbarium sheet stated..to be the 'type'.. is, however, quite different.

e. *Semiotics*, etc. A sign representing a category or set of instances, as opposed to the individual tokens by which the category is instantiated. Cf. *TOKEN *sb.* 1 f.

1908 [see *TOKEN *sb.* 1 f]. **1966** *Publ. Amer. Dial. Soc.* XLVI. 13 The incidence of tokens is..equal to the sum of all forms... The incidence of types..is equal to the number of different forms. **1976** *Biometrika* LXIII. 435 Shakespeare's known works comprise 884 647 total words, of which 14 376 are types appearing just one time, 4343 are types appearing twice, etc.

10. *type category, -character, description, index, -name, -tragedy*; in sense 9, *type-foundry* (earlier example), *size*; *type-founder* (earlier example); *type-creating* adj. (example); *type-marked* adj.; **type approval** (see quot. 1979); **type area,** (*a*) the part of a page covered by print; (*b*) the location of a type-specimen or an area taken as typical of a particular group; *Geol.* = *type site* below; **type-ball,** a spherical ball on certain kinds of electric typewriter on which all the type is mounted; = *golf ball* (b) s.v. *GOLF *sb.* b; **type basket,** the assembly of type-bars in a typewriter; **type-copy** *sb.* (*arch.*), a typewritten copy; so **type-copy** *v. trans.* (*arch.*); **type face,** a set of printing type of a particular design; cf. FACE *sb.* 22, FOUNT[2]; **type facsimile,** a copy of a piece of printing which is either a page-for-page copy using type as close as possible to the original or an exact photographic reproduction; **type-fallacy** *Logic*, the fallacy or mistake of including amongst the members of a type or category something belonging to another type or category (see quot. 1908); **type height** = *HEIGHT *sb.* 1 c; **type locality** = *type-area* (b) above, *type site* below; **type-psychology,** psychological study or theory based on the classification of people or phenomena by type; **type-script** *sb., a.*: hence **type-script** *v. trans.*, to record in type-script; **type-scripted** *ppl. a.*; **type-scripting** *vbl. sb.*; **type-setting** (earlier examples); **type site** *Archæol., Geol.*, etc., a site the features of which are used to define, or are paradigmatic of, a culture, stratigraphic level, etc.; **type-specimen,** (*b*) a printed sheet or booklet showing the variety of type-faces a printer or founder has available; **type test** *sb.* (esp. *Aeronaut.*), a test conducted to determine whether a new piece of equipment meets its specifications; also *attrib.*; hence **type-test** *v. trans.*; **type—token** *attrib.*, in *Semiotics*, etc., pertaining to types and tokens, involving the relationship of type to tokens (see *TOKEN *sb.* 1 f, sense 8 e above).

1967 *Economist* 15 Apr. 270/1 The Europeans are used to the 'type approval' on which most Continental governments insist before [motor] models can be sold. **1979** *Gloss. Terms Quality Assurance* (*B.S.I.*) 11/2 *Type approval*, the status given to a design that has been shown by type tests to meet all the requirements of the product specification and which is suitable for a specific application. **1916** W. H. Hazell et al. *Estimating for Printers* 19 Before an estimate..can be worked out, the following points must be decided: Number of words in bookwork..; size of type,..and type area of page. **1937** *Burlington Mag.* June 309/2 Consideration of primitive work as craftsmanship..is no more essential for an æsthetic evaluation than the geographical location of type-areas. **1969** *Proc. Geol. Soc.* Aug. 146 Customary stratigraphical usage should be maintained by placing the marker-points as near to the stratigraphical correspondence with traditional boundaries as possible, although not necessarily in the traditional type-area. **1973** S. Jennett *Making of Books* (ed. 5) xvi. 338 There is a theory that the type area should be about 50 per cent of the page area. **1975** Type area [see *type site* below]. **1971** *Computers & Humanities* VI. 43 The character set..is limited to the Selectric type-balls specified by the scanning service. **1977** *Daily Tel.* 3 Aug. 3/5 There has been a real search for a type ball from one of the IBM electric typewriters that were in the office. **1931** M. Crooks *Bk. of Underwood Typewriter* ii. 10 Above and behind the keyboard, occupying practically the centre of the framework, is the type—this part of the machine is known as the Type-Basket. **1968** *Typing* ('Know the Craft' Series) 4/1 Every machine has a type basket and a carriage. **1947** *Amer. Jrnl. Sociol.* LII. 293 Kinship, its relationships and institutions, are the type categories of experience and the familial group is the unit of action. **1931** *Times Lit. Suppl.* 5 Nov. 865/3 Mr. Strauss hits off the foibles of his type-characters with wit and acumen. **1890** H. James *Let.* 10 Nov. (1981) III. 307 A shorter story..which I am just sending off to be typecopied. **1893** *Ibid.* 2 July 416, I have determined to dispatch by the same post as this note, in another cover, a fresh type-copy of the said first act. **1854** Geo. Eliot tr. *Feuerbach's Essence Christianity* vii. 75 Mind presenting itself as at once type-creating, emotional, and sensuous, is the imagination. **1905** Type-description [see *protologue]. **1962** J. A. Ford *Quantitative Method for deriving Cultural Chronol.* iii. 16 Other workers have sought to achieve greater precision by dealing not with types but with various elements, attributes, or 'modes'.. that are usually hidden away in the type description. **1967** J. Deetz *Invitation to Archaeol.* 51 An artifact type description is..a statement of a set of somewhat variable attributes which can be observed to occur together in the majority of cases. **1887** T. B Reed *Hist. Old Eng. Letter Foundries* i. 40 It now remains to trace briefly the origin and development of the leading type-faces used in English Typography. **1923** S. Morison *On Type Faces* p. v, The choice of type face is always a matter of immediate and insistent importance. **1980** B. Crutchley *To be a Printer* v. 65 Bodoni..produced in his lifetime over four hundred type faces. **1900** (*title*) Type Facsimile Society. Publications of the Society for the year 1900. **1966** *Eng. Studies* XLVII. 298 It [*sc.* old spelling] does no harm, provided the reader is not misled into using the book as a type-facsimile. [**1908** B. Russell *Logic & Knowl.* (1956) 75 The division of objects into types is necessitated by the reflexive fallacies which otherwise arise. These fallacies.. are to be avoided by what may be called the 'vicious-circle principle'; i.e., 'no totality can contain members defined in terms of itself'.] **1935** *Mind* XLIV. 150 Now, of course, the word 'about' is very ambiguous; but, in one sense of it, to say that a proposition is about itself is to commit the simplest of type-fallacies. **1952** *Mind* LXI. 130 The type-fallacy that only moral goodness itself is good. **1967** *Philos.* XLII. 3 A transition from one to the other would then become tantamount to a category-mistake or type-fallacy. **1797** M. L. Weems *Let.* 13 July in *Works & Ways* (1929) II. 84 A letter was written.. containing an order on Mr. Baine the Type Founder for some money. **1809** T. Jefferson *Let.* 28 June in *Writings* (1904) XII. 295 The foundation of printing..is the type-foundry. **1905** C. T. Jacobi *Printers' Handbk.* (ed. 3) 22 There is some uncertainty as to what is type-height, and therefore all those engaged in supplying blocks..to the printer should remember that type-height is ·9175 inch. **1931** R. R. Karch *Printing & Allied Trades* iii. 9 Type heights differ in foreign countries. In England the height is ·917; France, Germany and Spain ·928. **1973** S. Jennett *Making of Books* (ed. 5) ii. 40 Type height, or height to paper, is not the same thing as height of face. **1943** *Mind* LII. 271 In *Principia* the need to avoid a small number of objectionable trains of argument is made the occasion for wholesale elaboration of symbolism (the introduction of type-indices). **1972, 1973** Type index [see *motif-index* s.v. *motif 4]. **1934** Webster, Type-locality. **1937** *Brit. Birds* XXXI. 10 Dr. Ticehurst has given as type-locality Lincolnshire. **1940** *Chambers's Techn. Dict.* 874/2 *Type locality*, the locality from which a rock, formation, etc., has been named and described, usually because of its characteristic occurrence there. **1962** Gordon & Lavoipierre *Entomol. for Students of Med.* liii. 325 The locality from which the holotype was collected is known as the 'type locality'. **1969** *Proc. Geol. Soc.* Aug. 159 Donovan..stated Watchet to be the type-locality of the index species of the zone, but gave no type-locality for the zone itself. **1866** G. M. Hopkins *Jrnl.* 16 May (1959) 137 Hawthorn especially when thrown up with may is very clearly type-marked. **1928** L. P. Smith *Words & Idioms* 40 Some of these type-names give evidence of the impression made on foreigners by the travelling Englishmen of rank. **1974** *Encycl. Brit. Micropædia* X. 219/2 *Type names*,..those names given by the dramatist to characters in his play so that their personalities may be instantly ascertained. **1932** *Brit. Jrnl. Psychol.* July 77 The considerable growth of 'type' psychologies has been a leading characteristic of recent psychological and clinical study and speculation. **1952** H. Read *Philos. Mod. Art* iv. 83 The science of typology—or type-psychology as it is more often called—is comparatively modern. **1976** *Amer. Speech 1974* XLIX. 19 H. Rex Wilson..was probably the first linguistic geographer to propose typescripting entire interviews. **1979** *Amer. N. & Q.* Mar. 106/1 Nor did Fisher ever mention to Crane or to me his *Plowshare* publications of Greenberg, which included 'The Charming Maiden' (June 1918) 'Serenade in Grey', 'Regret At Parting', and 'Where Sweepest Thou' (January 1920), all later typescripted by Hart Crane. **1980** *Amer. Speech 1976* LI. 204 A typescripted record represents several weeks of tedious work. **1981** *Ibid.* LVI. 258 The typescripting or computer-taping and indexing of LAGS field records are now considered supplemental descriptive components of the atlas. **1846** S. F. Smith *Theatrical Apprenticeship* ii. 30 She..would then dismiss us to our type-setting. **1848** *De Bow's Rev.* VI. 52 But the printer is too important..to have his usefulness set aside by the multiplication of type-setting and press-working machines. **1935** *Proc. Prehistoric Soc.* I. 6 The Late Bronze Age assemblage to which the type site offers no significant parallel. **1959** J. D. Clark *Prehist. Southern Africa* vi. 159 Bambata is the type site for the Stillbay Culture in Rhodesia. **1969** *Proc. Geol. Soc.* Aug. 157 Table 1..gives the sequence of stages so far defined for the Quaternary of the British Isles. The stage names are based either on type-sites or type-areas. **1975** J. G. Evans *Environment Early Man Brit. Isles* i. 8 Each interglacial is named after a type site or area where deposits of that stage occur. **1981** P. Salway *Roman Britain* 7 A 'type-site' is, in archaeological jargon, the site after which a culture is named, often the site at which it was first discovered or recognized as distinct. **1922** D. B. Updike *Printing Types* I. ii. 32 It [*sc.* the point system] placed type sizes upon a basis comprehensible to the meanest intelligence. **1978** *Early Music* Oct. 597/3 The physical presentation of *Clementi* is also gratifying. Type sizes are unusually ample. **1875** W. Blades *Some Early Type Specimen Bks.* 3 When printers were their own type-founders their works were their own type-specimen. **1922** D. B. Updike *Printing Types* I. xi. 133 A few 'type specimens' were issued by founders, and some by printers. **1922** *Flight* XIV. 267/1 The Bristol 'Lucifer' engine..has successfully passed its type-tests in accordance with British Air Ministry Type-Test Schedule of May, 1920. **1946** *Sun* (Baltimore) 17 May 6 (Advt.), For sale: Stinson cabin monoplanes... Have been type-tested and declared eligible for certification by CAA. **1978** *Proc. Internat. Conf. Noise Control Engin., San Francisco* 743 Because of the complexity and cost of conducting certification type tests, a study was undertaken to determine the feasibility of using an alternative scheme to obtain approach and takeoff noise levels. **1979** *Gloss. Terms Quality Assurance* (*B.S.I.*) 11/2 *Type test*, a test or series of tests directed towards approval of a design, conducted to determine whether an item is capable of meeting the requirements of the product specification. **1960** G. Herdan (*title*) Type-token mathematics: a textbook of mathematical linguistics. **1971** *Computers & Humanities* V. 133 A type/token ratio is computed for each text, where type is the number of different words occurring in the text and token is the total number of occurrences of all words in the text. **1979** *Sci. Amer.* Feb. 61/2 The type-token ratio, a parameter that reflects the size of the vocabulary employed by the author, was determined for each text. **1931** S. Beckett *Proust* 7 The tragedy of the Marcel-Albertine liaison is the type-tragedy of the human relationship whose failure is preordained.

type, *v.* Add: **4.** Also *trans.* with *out*, *up*.
1948 A. Keith *Three came Home* xv. 255 The news that came over the radio was typed out. **1961** 'E. Lathen' *Banking on Death* xvii. 135, I want you to..type up a copy of the Hoffman contract. **1981** C. Dexter *Dead of Jericho* xxxvi. 202 We've got to..get it down in writing, then typed up, and signed.

5. a. To assign to a particular type; to classify; esp. in *Biol.* and *Med.*, to determine the type to which (blood, tissue, etc.) belongs.
1900, etc. [see *typing *vbl. sb.* 1]. **1929** L. H. Snyder *Blood Grouping in Relation to Clin. & Legal Med.* iii. 13 They called attention to the fact that the methods used for typing an unknown blood are based upon the assumption that there are only four iso-agglutination groups and that the blood of every person belongs to one of the four. **1939** *Jrnl. Bacteriol.* XXXVII. 136 Sixty-seven of the double-zone strains have been serologically 'typed' by Lancefield or Plummer. **1946** Gerth & Mills *From Max Weber* (1947) iii. 56 Less 'rational' actions are typed by Weber in terms of the pursuit of 'absolute ends', as flowing from affectual sentiments, or as 'traditional'. **1959** *Times Lit. Suppl.* 3 Apr. 194/4 The simple character, long ago 'typed' and pigeon-holed, often turns out to be much more complex in the light of his correspondence. **1964** *McCall's Sewing* iii. 41/1 Zippers are typed according to their purpose. **1967** A. S. Byatt *Game* xi. 154 Her clothes ..typed her: grey pleated skirt, cable-stitch sweater, brogue shoes. **1968**, etc. [see *tissue-type* vb. s.v. *tissue *sb.* 9 b]. **1969** *New Yorker* 12 Apr. 85/1 The exobiologists have insisted that..the astronauts' microflora..have all been typed and catalogued for comparison later. **1977** *Time* 7 Mar. 43/2 The kidney was..then 'typed' so that doctors could choose a patient whose body tissue matched it. **1977** *Jrnl. R. Soc. Arts* CXXV. 87/1 We like to label periods in our history as we like to 'type' people.

b. = *type-cast *v.*
1933 *Sat. Even. Post* 17 June 14/3 The danger of being 'typed' by the producers, which, in turn, fixes you irrevocably in the public eye, is one of those haunting fears that an actor must meet and conquer. **1939** J. Gielgud *Early Stages* ix. 151 Refusing to be typed in 'silly society' parts, she [*sc.* Edith Evans]..achieved her greatest triumph as Millamant. **1959** *Times Lit. Suppl.* 27 Feb. 118/1 There is an inevitable tendency in novels about soldiers and sailors for characters to be typed; but though some of Mr. Armstrong's ship's company conform, others are distinct individuals. **1959** *Listener* 9 July 72/1 This was good documentary in that the characters were not in the least typed. **1960** *Guardian* 20 Oct. 8/7 They were in revolt against the whole Broadway system of typing actors and thus limiting their development.

-type, *suffix.* Add: **2.** [Type *sb.*^{1}] Appended to adjs. and sbs. or sb. phrs. forming adjs. with the sense 'of the specified type; typical or characteristic of (..), reminiscent or imitative of (..)'. Cf. *type *sb.*^{1} 6.
1887 [see New *a.* 10 b]. **1907** *Yesterday's Shopping* (1969) 97/2 *Australian*... Claret type..Burgundy type. **1922**, etc. [see *shell-type* adj. s.v. *shell *sb.* 39]. **1924** *Sat. Even. Post* 13 Sept. 80 (Advt.), Has the car you have in mind a European type, high compression motor? **1936** *Discovery* Aug. 237/2 Eight astronomical-type stainless steel mirrors. **1939** W. S. Churchill in *War Illustr.* 29 Dec. 522/2 The submarine had not long been in her patrol area before she sighted a big-type U-boat. **1940** *Illustr. London News* 28 Dec. 821 The outbreak of the war found the Fleet Air Arm using for the most part adapted land-type machines. **1949** *Here & Now* (N.Z.) Oct. 23/3 Following the old Spanish custom still prevalent at California-type barbecues, the meat can be served with some version of hot, tangy tomato sauce. **1959** *Chambers's Encycl.* IV. 693/2 The indulines and nigrosines are important azine type dyes. **1960** *Farmer & Stockbreeder* 8 Mar. 77/1 He showed slides of some of his farm-made, 'home-grown' Dutch-barn-type buildings which he believed in putting up. **1970** *Daily Tel.* 18 Aug. 11 Ocean Spirit is the biggest-type glass fibre boat ever made in this country. **1973** *New Statesman* 19 Oct. 557/3 Fifties-type social realist films. **1976** *Derbyshire Times* (Peak ed.) 3 Sept. 15/1 (Advt.), A very spacious older type house.

type-cast (təi·pˌkɑst), *a.* Also as one word. [f. Type *sb.*^{1} + Cast *ppl. a.*] **1.** Formed into type for printing.
1876 [in Dict. s.v. Type *sb.*^{1} 10].

2. Of an actor, etc.: that has been type-cast (see *type-cast *v.*); identified with a particular kind of part. Also *transf.* and in extended use.
1946 S. H. Adams *Alexander Woollcott* 314 He is type-cast if ever a man was. **1952** *Time* 2 June 92/2 Hollywood noticed Jules in 1938, changed his name to John Garfield, and launched him on a type-cast screen career of playing himself—the narrow-eyed, rock-hard underdog. **1964** L. Deighton *Funeral in Berlin* xxiv. 135 'So I am type-cast as the loser?' 'It's a one-horse race,' said Samantha. **1965** *Spectator* 29 Jan. 137/2 He is in danger of becoming typecast. **1971** *Daily Tel.* 9 June 13/5 David Shepherd is type-cast as the man who paints elephants and this bothers him. He wants to be known as 'a painter'. **1976** M. Gilbert *Night of Twelfth* xvi. 149 Naval Officers are deceptive people. They're usually type-cast as bluff simple extroverts... Actually, their training, and the lives they have to lead, are calculated to produce the most complex introverts. **1982** M. Babson *Death beside Seaside* v. 41 One gets the feeling she's typecast in her show. **1984** *Listener* 19 Jan. 37/2 It is only in New York, in my experience, that truly typecast events occur.

type-cast (təi·pˌkɑst), *v.* Also as one word. [Back-formation from *type-casting *vbl. sb.* 2.] *trans.* To cast (an actor) in a role or roles for which he appears to be physically or temperamentally suited or of a kind in which he has been successful; to allocate continually to the same type of part. Also *transf.* and *fig.*, and in extended use, to represent or regard as a stereotype.
1946, etc. [implied in *type-cast *a.* 2]. **1952** Granville *Dict. Theatr. Terms* 192 *Type cast*, to assign parts to artistes who approximate the type drawn in the play. **1958** R. Hoggart in N. Mackenzie *Conviction* 136 We.. will no longer type-cast regional accents by class or comedy. **1958** *Wall St. Jrnl.* 6 Nov. 6/2 Right-to-work has been type-cast as a villain in the public mind. **1959** *Times* 9 Nov. 6/4 Sir Thomas Beecham's gifts tend to typecast him as an interpreter of even-numbered Beethoven. **1971** *Country Life* 20 May 1252/1 But it is by using plants in this category as ornamentals in their own right instead of type-casting them purely as herbs for the herb garden that they become most useful in the garden. **1981** *N. & Q.* Oct. 448/2 Hardy's contemporaries, having type-cast him as a novelist, were dubious if not contemptuous of his poetry. **1982** *Daily Tel.* 16 July 15/4 People are not as likely to be typecast by their accents as they once were.

type-casting (təi·pˌkɑstiŋ), *vbl. sb.* Also as one word. [f. Type *sb.*^{1} + Casting *vbl. sb.*]
1. The forming of metal, wood, etc., into type for printing. Also *attrib.*
1864 T. L. Nichols *Forty Years Amer. Life* I. 381 By the use of type-casting machines a workman can cast ninety brevier types a minute. **1875, 1897** [in Dict. s.v. Type *sb.*^{1} 10]. **1967** V. Strauss *Printing Industry* ii. 66/1 Hot-metal machines are type-casting equipment.

2. The casting of an actor in a role or roles for which he appears to be physically or temperamentally suited or of a kind in which he has been successful; the fact of being so cast. Also *transf.* and in extended use, representation as a stereotype or stereotypes.
1927 *Observer* 25 Sept. 13/4 Please do not conclude that I believe in 'type-casting'; an actor should in his time play many sorts of part. **1947** A. Menen *Prevalence of Witches* xi. 190 He says..why pick on *him* to work a miracle? He says it's his beard..; he says its just type-casting, like they do in pictures. **1960** *Twentieth Cent.* Dec. 588 These Dickensian names suggest the general feeling of type-casting. **1977** 'E. Crispin' *Glimpses of Moon* iii. 38 Film-music composers are just as liable to type-casting as actors and actresses. **1979** D. Arkell *Looking for Laforgue* iii. 78 Laforgue was invariably given the part of Colline, the philosopher... It would appear to have been excellent type-casting.

typed, *ppl. a.* Add: **3.** Also with *out*, *up*.
1971 D. E. Westlake *I gave at Office* 200 They had this typed-out paper, and it would be everything you said... So you'd read it and sign it. **1977** A. Hunter *Gently Instrumental* viii. 116 Gently found Leyston glooming over the policewoman's typed-up notes.

typewriter. Add: **1.** (Earlier example.)
1868 C. L. Sholes et al. *U.S. Patent 79,265* 23 June 4 Thus made, the type-writer is the simplest, most perfectly adapted to its work.

2*. A machine-gun or sub-machine-gun. *slang.*
1915 A. D. Gillespie *Let.* 3 Mar. in *Lett. from Flanders* (1916) 31 The only typewriter here is the machine-gun—the men's nickname for it. **1930** *Sun* (Baltimore) 25 Oct. 10/3 When the 'typewriters', as machine guns are called,

rattle, it is natural for the police to suspect these 'independents' of even shooting each other. **1959** 'J. CHRISTOPHER' *Scent of White Poppies* vii. 101 'You associate typewriters with more than one guy.'..'Typewriters?' Bella asked. 'Submachine gun. Browning, maybe..firing automatic.' **1973** P. EVANS *Bodyguard Man* iii. 25 Al Capone['s]..torpedoes..were mean with a Thompson 'type-writer'.

3. *typewriter cover, ribbon.*

1903 *Christendom* 13 June 393 Please furnish..12 typewriter ribbons. **1934** WEBSTER, Typewriter cover. **1966** D. FRANCIS *Flying Finish* i. 8 Maggie's..typewriter cover askew. **1975** 'D. JORDAN' *Black Account* xiv. 74 She was busy..with her typewriter ribbon.

typewriting, *vbl. sb.* (In Dict. s.v. TYPEWRITE *v.*) (Earlier example.)

1867 *Sci. Amer.* 6 July 3/1 The subject of type writing is one of the interesting aspects of the near future.

typey (təi·pi), *a.* Also **typy.** [f. TYPE *sb.*[1] + -Y[1].] Of a domestic animal: exhibiting the distinctive characteristics of the breed; being a perfect specimen of the breed.

1931 *19th Century* Feb. 210 It is not registered bulls that are needed, nor 'typey' bulls, but proved bulls, whether registered or not. **1951** *Sun* (Baltimore) 9 Oct. (B ed.) 11/3 One bull might be as 'typy' (Angus argot for conforming to perfect physical standards) as another bull. **1976** *Horse & Hound* 10 Dec. 67/4 (Advt.), Pure Arabian filly... Very typey with large eyes and one of the best movers we have ever seen. **1980** *Hunting Ann. 1981* 107 (Advt.), Typey pups sired by our top studs and from matings within our own pack.

typhlo-. Add: **typhlograph,** also = *NYCTOGRAPH; (earlier example).

1891 [see *NYCTOGRAPH].

typho-. Add: **typhomalarial** *a.* (earlier example).

1863 J. J. WOODWARD *Outl. Chief Camp Diseases U.S. Armies* iii. 87 In all the cases of typho-malarial fever,.. three several trains of phenomena are to be noted: the malarial, the typhoid, and the scorbutic.

typhoid, *a.* Add: **3.** *Typhoid Mary*, nickname of Mary Mallon (d. 1938), Irish-born cook who transmitted typhoid fever in the U.S.A. Also *fig.*, a transmitter of undesirable opinions, sentiments, etc.

1909 *N.Y. Times* 17 July 3/5 Mary Mallon, known to fame as 'Typhoid Mary',..must remain at Riverside Hospital. **1961** S. P. HAYES in *Webster* s.v., Authoritarianism..is carried by Typhoid Marys, unwitting sources of infection. **1971** 'L. EGAN' *Malicious Mischief* (1972) vii. 118, I went to the library..and asked. And of course they looked at me as if I was—was Typhoid Mary. **1976** *Ann. Rev. Microbiol.* XXX. 438 During the next 15 years Typhoid Mary infected well over 200 persons. **1979** R. JAFFE *Class Reunion* II. vi. 180 Alexander's own misery was the most important thing in Alexander's life, and whatever he gave of it to others was unimportant to him; he was simply unaware. Alexander was the Typhoid Mary of angst.

typhoon. Add: Hence **typhoon** *v. trans.* (*nonce-word*), to batter with the force of a typhoon.

1953 DYLAN THOMAS *Under Milk Wood* (1954) 50 But with blue hazy eyes the fishermen gaze at that milkmaid whispering water with no ruck or ripple as though it blew great guns and serpents and typhooned the town.

typhus. Add: **c. typhus-louse,** a louse of the kind responsible for transmitting typhus.

1939 AUDEN & ISHERWOOD *Journey to War* 136 Their upholstery often contained typhus-lice.

typing, *vbl. sb.* Add: **1.** (Examples corresp. to *TYPE *v.* 5 a, b.)

1900 W. MYERS tr. *Ehrlich & Lazarus' Histol. of Blood* 32 The simple 'typing' of several hundred cells. **1927** H. W. JONES in *Osler's Mod. Med.* (ed. 3) V. 191 The institution of blood typing has made the operation of blood transfusion reasonably safe. **1928,** etc. [see *blood-typing* vbl. sb. s.v. *BLOOD *sb.* 19]. **1960** *Guardian* 3 Nov. 8/4 The rigid typing of her as a dumb blonde... Hollywood has destroyed..talent by typing. **1962** *Brit. Med. Bull.* XVIII. 64/1 (*heading*) The genetic basis of bacteriophage typing. **1965,** etc. [see *tissue typing* s.v. *TISSUE *sb.* 9 b]. **1971** *Nature* 9 July 141/2 Each centre coordinates the typing and distribution of cadaveric kidneys to and from a group of collaborating hospitals.

2. *attrib.* and *Comb.*, as *typing agency, bureau, course, error, paper, pool* (see *POOL *sb.*[3] 5 c), *purposes, school, speed.*

1973 W. M. DUNCAN *Big Timer* xi. 75, I should like.. a list of the typing agencies within say, roughly, a half-mile. **1935** D. L. SAYERS *Gaudy Night* v. 97 [She] ran what was ostensibly a Typing Bureau. **1974** R. RENDELL *Face of Trespass* i. 17 My friend Molly that I used to have my typing bureau with. **1952** LESLIE & PEPE *Methods Teaching Typing Simplified* (1954) 85 A slightly condensed verbatim report of an actual teaching period within the first week of the typing course. **1981** C. STORR *Vicky* xviii. 128 She'd taken a typing course and she had a job. **1936** A. DVORAK et al. *Typewriting Behavior* xiii. 395 Typing errors are signs of interference, due partly to drills on isolated letter strokes. **1979** M. PAGE *Pilate Plot* i. 21 He looked at it three times to make sure it was not a typing error. **1944** MRS. BELLOC LOWNDES *Let.* 4 June (1971) 249, I got a packet of *pre-war* typing paper—finest quality! **1889** Typing purposes[in Dict.]. **1966** 'G. BLACK' *You want to die, Johnny?* xii. 223 There are certainly duller jobs waiting for a graduate of typing school than being the secretary to a Regent. **1936** A. DVORAK et al. *Typewriting Behavior* xi. 286 Typing speed grows, but fast motions must also be present from the start. **1976** 'A. YORK' *Dark Passage* xiv. 182 Her typing speeds and general ability as a secretary were excellent.

typiste (təipī·st). [Alteration of TYPIST, with Fr. termination as in *modiste*, misinterpreted as fem.] A female typist.

1923 *Daily Mail* 26 Feb. 8 An actress who played the part of a typiste. **1969** *West Australian* 5 July 65/1 (Advt.), Shorthand typiste.

typo, *sb.* (*a.*) Add: **a*.** A typographical error.

1892 I. ZANGWILL *Childr. Ghetto* III. II. iii. 24 My men..don't like to pass anything till it's free from typos. **1945** E. B. WHITE *Let.* 10 July (1976) 266 As for the 'her'–'hen' typo, I guessed that it was a typo and that it would be caught. **1963** C. D. SIMAK *They walked like Men* vi. 36, I went through the story again and caught a couple of typos and fixed up another place or two to make language better. **1978** *Times Lit. Suppl.* 15 Sept. 1031/5 Since few proof-readers are perfect, a typo here and there is easily forgiven.

typo-. Add: **typophil** (examples of *typophile*).

1958 *Times Lit. Suppl.* 3 Jan. 12/3 It is only sad that the Typophile Chap Books are not more widely available. **1975** *Dalhousie Rev.* Summer 206 Berenson..was the recognized leader of an energetic group which included.. Bertram Goodhue, architect, book-designer and typophile. **1982** *Amer. N. & Q.* Jan./Feb. 89/2 It is good reading, at least for typophiles.

typographica (təipǒgræ·fikă), *sb. pl.* [see TYPOGRAPHIC *a.*] Examples of fine printing; in quot. 1949 used as the title of a journal dealing with typography.

[**1858** S. L. SOTHEBY (*title*) Principia typographica.] **1931** *Times Lit. Suppl.* 25 June (Salon Int. du Livre d'Art Suppl.) p. i/3 The former [publishing] house has issued a series of *feuillets d'imprimerie* which..are coveted by collectors of typographica. **1949** *Typographica* 1. 3 The first purpose of Typographica will be to present serious analyses of various aspects..of contemporary typography. **1959** *Times Lit. Suppl.* 15 May 289/4 Your account of the George A. Poole collection of typographica ..contains one inaccuracy.

typographist. (Earlier example.)

1851 *Tait's Edin. Mag.* Oct. 636/1 The public had a thousand or so of quarto pages for which they paid a folio price, nearly three-fourths of which price was a clear gain to the colluding typographists.

typological, *a.* Add: **3.** Also, pertaining to the study of the use of types in other disciplines or fields of study: see *TYPOLOGY 3.

1913 E. T. LEEDS *Anglo-Saxon Settlements* 28 A large amount of information can be obtained from the purely typological method. **1929** V. G. CHILDE *Danube in Prehist.* 246 By correlating the several stages in the evolution of celts, daggers,..&c...it is possible to divide the Bronze Age up into several typological phases. **1930** *Psyche* X. III. 80 (*heading*) Typological methods in experimental psychology. **1942** *Antiquity* XVI. 61 What typological evidence there is..confirms the standard view of the invasion in its secondary stages. **1964** R. H. ROBINS *General Linguistics* viii. 325 It is..possible to compare languages..simply by reference to any significant general features of form or structural organization that they share at any level of analysis... Comparison of languages on this basis is usually distinguished..by the title of *typological comparison.* **1968** *Internat. Encycl. Soc. Sci.* XVI. 178/1 Typological classification, as a subdivision of taxonomy, has characterized a considerable part of the culture of the social sciences. **1971** J. Z. YOUNG *Introd. Study Man* xxvii. 386 We are bound therefore to use arbitrary typological groupings, that is to say to put together those we think seem most alike in appearance or some other character. **1972** *Jrnl. Social Psychol.* LXXXVI. 55 The first definition refers to..the characteristics rather than the persons being used for typological identification. **1980** *Nature* 27 Mar. 341/1 Isaac has stated that it is likely that Olorgesailie may date to before 400 kyr BP and it is suggested on typological grounds that Namib IV is of similar antiquity.

Hence **typolo·gically** *adv.*, by means of, in terms of, or according to typology.

1895 in *Funk's Standard Dict.* **1921** M. C. BURKITT *Prehistory* vii. 94 If a series be made out they are found to grade on the one hand into what typologically are Mousterian points, and on the other into a sort of pseudo-Solutrean. **1943** C. L. WRENN *Word & Symbol* (1967) 134 Collingwood typologically demonstrates on historical artistic grounds that the inscription belongs to the close of the eighth century. **1964** R. H. ROBINS *General Linguistics* viii. 326 Languages are typologically classified according to the similarities of form they exhibit with other languages at any level or levels. **1976** G. W. H. LAMPE in M. F. Wiles et al. *Christian Believing* (C. of E. Doctrine Cmn.) 55 The Church continued to read it [*sc.* the Old Testament] in its supposed 'spiritual' sense, or typologically. **1980** *Nature* 27 Mar. 340/2 Typologically ..Namib IV may closely be paralleled by East African industries from Olorgesailie, Kilombe and Olduvai IV.

typologize (təipǫ·lǒdʒəiz), *v.* [f. TYPOLOGY + -IZE.] *trans.* and *intr.* To interpret or classify typologically. Hence **typo·logizing** *vbl. sb.*

1895 *Funk's Stand. Dict.* II. 1955/2 *Typologize*,..To interpret by types; treat typologically... To deal in or with types or figures. **1959** A. FARRER in *Proc. Oxf. Soc. Hist. Theol.* 8 Questions, which..theologians and exegetes are not going to let alone, whether they typologise or not:—for example, why St Mark put several paragraphs in the order in which he placed them. *Ibid.* 9 Here..is an example of the prefiguration scheme which the greatest enemy of typologising can scarcely deny. **1964** *Harvard Educ. Rev.* XXXIV. ii. 356 Then in a sort of neo-Jespersenian typologizing, we find that there are three sorts of monemes. **1969** P. WORSLEY in Ionescu & Gellner *Populism* 218 When actors see themselves as part of a shared tradition or organized movement..we are plainly dealing with a quite different kind of typologizing, based upon self-identification. **1976** *Times Lit. Suppl.* 12 Mar. 288/2 One might even say they [*sc.* the anthropologists Benedict and Radcliffe-Brown] shared the impulse to typologize. **1978** *Ibid.* 17 Feb. 217/1 It is possible to typologize military regimes.

typology. Add: **3.** The study of classes with common characteristics; classification, esp. of human products, behaviour, characteristics, etc., according to type; the comparative analysis of structural or other characteristics; a classification or analysis of this kind.

1886 *Academy* 8 May 332/1 In his former publications the learned writer gave too high a place to typology. **1929** V. G. CHILDE *Danube in Prehist.* p. vii, Where stratigraphical or geological evidence is lacking, we must have recourse to typology. This depends on the assumption that types evolved (or degenerated) regularly. **1930** S. CASSON *Archæol.* 43 Even after Schliemann archæologists are to be found who will still prefer a typology which is established by *a priori* methods. **1930** *Psyche* X. III. 82 Scheler..tries to construct a typology on a purely philosophical and phenomenological basis. **1937** J. R. FIRTH *Tongues of Men* i. 17 Language is the typology of the common elements in your speech and mine, yesterday, to-day, and to-morrow. **1950** T. W. ADORNO *Authoritarian Personality* xix. 744 Hardly any concept in contemporary American psychology has been so thoroughly criticized as that of typology. **1953** C. E. BAZELL *Linguistic Form* 80 There will therefore be different typologies of language according to the system which is taken as starting-point. **1959** J. J. MICHAELS in S. Arieti *Amer. Handbk. Psychiatry* I. xix. 358/1 The absence of a psychoanalytic typology may also be explained by the absence of a complete theory of character structure. **1962** [see *A-HISTORICAL *a.*]. **1964** M. ARGYLE *Psychol. & Social Probl.* i. 17 One typology in common use is that of mental disorders, largely derived from a classification due to Kraepelin. **1971** *New Scientist* 27 May 534/3 A sort of 'typology' of unsafe drivers, dividing them into groups. **1974** P. H. MATTHEWS *Morphology* 17 In some [languages], grammarians speak of a 'word' without internal grammatical structure: according to the first typologies these were 'isolating' languages... This typology has..been criticised and elaborated. **1977** H. C. TRIANDIS *Interpersonal Behav.* i. 21 The..most important function of the model is to guide investigations of typologies of behaviors, settings and people. **1977** *Dædalus* Summer 89 One direction in which the comparative analogical approach can lead is toward what might be called a typology of cultures and of process.

typothetae (təipǫ·pětī, təi:pǫ̌þī·tī), *sb. pl.* [mod.L., f. Gr. τύπος TYPO- + θετός, f. τίθεναι to set, place.] Master printers collectively; *spec.* the members of a N. Amer. association of master printers.

1825 T. C. HANSARD *Typographia* I. ii. 43, I cannot find that Gutenberg was encouraged in his labours by the smiles of royal influence. This is the more remarkable, as the then reigning sovereign of Germany, Frederic III, was a monarch 'deeply versed in the learning of the times'. ..The..emperor..permitted printers to wear gold and silver, and granted coat-armour to the *Typothetae* and *Typographi*, to perpetuate the honour of the discovery. This armorial bearing is still claimed by the professors of the art in Germany. **1865** *N.Y. Times* 22 Mar. 5/2 (*heading*) Inauguration of the Typothetæ. *Ibid.*, At a recent general meeting of master printers of this city, it was decided to organize a permanent association for the general benefit of the the trade and the improvement of the typographic art. A constitution was adopted and the name of 'Typothetæ' was given to the new association. **1888** (*title*) Banquet given by the Typothetae of New York to the delegates of the United Typothetae of America, September 20, 1888. **1915** E. G. GRESS in *Fifty Years Typothetae City of N.Y.* 6 The reign of Frederick III., who recognized the German Typothetae, was from 1440 to 1493. **1921** *Daily Colonist* (Victoria, B.C.) 30 Mar. 1/4 The Boston typothetae today announced a reduction of $4 a week in the pay of journeymen printers, and $3 a week in the pay of journeywomen printers.

typy, var. *TYPEY *a.*

tyramine (təi^ə·rămīn). *Biochem.* Also **tyramin.** [f. *TYR(OSINE + AMINE.] A crystalline sympathomimetic amine derived from tyrosine and occurring naturally in cheese and other foods, which can cause dangerously high blood pressure in people taking a monoamine oxidase inhibitor; 2-(*p*-hydroxyphenyl)ethylamine, $HO{\cdot}C_6H_4{\cdot}CH_2{\cdot}CH_2{\cdot}NH_2$.

1910 *Biochem. Jrnl.* V. 236 Tyramine,..an organic base which can be produced from tyrosine by action of certain bacteria. **1939** Tyramin [see *HYPERTENSIN]. **1974** PASSMORE & ROBSON *Compan. Med. Stud.* III. lxii. 22/2 Cheese, red wine, yeast extracts and pickled herrings may contain large amounts of tyramine, and this is normally metabolized by monoamine oxidase... In patients receiving MAO [*sc.* monoamine oxidase] inhibitors, tyramine is absorbed intact and releases the large amounts of stored noradrenaline causing a hypertensive crisis.

tyrannicidal, *a.* (Earlier example.)

1801 W. DUPRÉ *Lexicographia-Neologica Gallica* 282 Projet *tyrannicide*—A *tyrannicidal* scheme.

tyrannis (tiræ·nis). *Gr. Hist.* [L., a. Gr. τυραννίς rule of a despot.] = TYRANNY *sb.* 1. Also *transf.*

1878 T. D. WOOLSEY *Political Science* I. ix. 406 His [*sc.* Plato's] forms of polity..are..aristocracy, timocracy, oligarchy, democracy, and the *tyrannis*. Oligarchy arises from overgrown wealth, tyrannis from overgrown liberty. **1910** *Encycl. Brit.* XII. 446/2 Between the Roman principate and the Greek *tyrannis* there are two essential differences. **1920** *Glasgow Herald* 6 Apr. 6 D'Annunzio.. proceeded to establish a tyrannis quite on the classical model.

tyrannosaurus (tirænosǭ·rǒs). Also **tyra·nnosaur.** [mod.L. (H. F. Osborn 1905, in *Bull. Amer. Mus. Nat. Hist.* XXI. 259), f. TYRANNO- + Gr. σαῦρος lizard.] A large bipedal dinosaur of the genus of the same name, known from fossil remains found in North America. Also *fig.*

1906 H. F. OSBORN in *Bull. Amer. Mus. Nat. Hist.* XXII. 281 (*heading*) Tyrannosaurus, Upper Cretaceous carnivorous dinosaur. **1927** HALDANE & HUXLEY *Animal Biol.* xi. 240 The Tyrannosaur [was adapted] for preying on large animals. *Ibid.* xiii. 314 The Tyrannosaurus.. stood over twenty feet high. **1934** [see *ANKYLOSAURUS]. **1957** L. EISELEY *Immense Journey* 64 Tyrannosaurs, enormous bipedal caricatures of men, would stalk mindlessly across the sites of future cities. **1984** J. WAIN in *Listener* 23 Aug. 37/1 Peter Ustinov and Alec McCowen play two 19th-century American railroad barons—Cornelius Vanderbilt and Jay Gould... The two tyrannosaurs fought to a standstill.

2. *Tyrannosaurus rex*, the only species of the genus *Tyrannosaurus*; also *fig.*

1906 *Bull. Amer. Mus. Nat. Hist.* XXII. 284 Tyrannosaurus rex... The complete skeleton of this animal is restored. **1972** D. BLOODWORTH *Any Number can Play* viii. 56 A stupid, feudal autocrat..who believes in the divine right of all Kings, starting with tyrannosaurus rex. **1976** 'J. ROSS' *I know what it's like to Die* xxiv. 150 A crane, fancifully recognisable to him as an orange-painted *Tyrannosaurus Rex*, towered above a metal-crushing plant.

tyre, *sb.*[5] Add: **2. b.** *spare tyre*: see *SPARE *a.* and *adv.* 1 a (a).

3. *tyre-burst, cast, lever, mark, pressure, track, tread*; **tyre chain,** a chain fastened to a tyre to prevent wheel-skid, esp. in snow.

1935 'R. WEST' *Harsh Voice* ii. 91 A tyreburst made him turn towards the road. **1971** J. WAINWRIGHT *Dig Grave* 67 We're busy taking tyre-casts... Taking plaster of Paris casts of tyre-marks. **1958** L. DURRELL *Mountolive* iii. 80 His ears had caught the slither and scrape of tyre-chains on the frosty drive outside. **1927** *Cycling Man.* (ed. 7) (Advt.), Tyre levers. The famous 'Jiffy' has no rival. **1959** I. JEFFERIES *Thirteen Days* vii. 92 Once he found a receptive bitch he wouldn't leave her..until he was prized off with tyre-levers. **1936** 'N. BLAKE' *Thou Shell of Death* xiv. 258 They had stopped at a fork. Blount was out, scanning the road surface for tyre marks. **1971** Tyre mark [see *tyre cast* above]. **1931** *Man. Morris Minor Car* (Morris Motors, Ltd.) 50 Gauges for testing balloon tyre pressures can be bought from all reputable motor dealers. **1959** *Motor Manual* (ed. 36) v. 130 A word or two should be said on the subject of tyre pressures. The basic fact to be remembered is that it is the air that carries the load. **1931** D. L. SAYERS *Five Red Herrings* iii. 38 A fresh set of tyre-tracks in the dust showing where the car had been taken out. **1971** M. KELLY *Twenty-Fifth Hour* i. 23 There were tyre tracks, wide ones, in the shingle reef at each edge of the road. **1925** *Motor* 29 Dec. 1091/3 (*heading*) Oil grooves and tyre-tread grooves compared. **1978** R. WESTALL *Devil on Road* xi. 73 There were hoofprints in the dried-up mud... Wheeltracks too, but no tyre-treads.

Tyrian, *a.* and *sb.* Add: **C.** *Tyrian-dyed* adj. (earlier example).

1847 C. BRONTË *Jane Eyre* I. xi. 194 A wide arch.. hung..with a Tyrian-dyed curtain.

ty·ring, *vbl. sb.* [f. *tyre* vb. s.v. TYRE *sb.*[5] + -ING[1].] The action of furnishing with a tyre or tyres (= TIRING *vbl. sb.*[4]). Freq. *attrib.*

1923 G. STURT *Wheelwright's Shop* xxiii. 117 A great business was this tyring—if possible deferred..until a number of tyres could be put on in a batch, being 'hotted up' in one fire. *Ibid.* xxiv. 125 Armed with tyring dogs, the three of us watched, expectant. **1936** *Automobile & Carriage Jrnl.* Dec. 153/2 The exhibits will include the tyring platform and tyre-bending machine. **1945** *Daily Herald* 31 Aug. 4/2 (Advt.), Much of the work had lain in its adaptation to the tyring of tank bogie wheels. **1968** J. ARNOLD *Shell Bk. Country Crafts* 159 The construction of a wheel, before the tyring stage was reached, required long experience.

tyrocidine (tǝirosǝi·din, -dīn). *Pharm.* Also **tyrocidin.** [f. mod.L. *Tyro-thrix* (see *TYROTHRICIN) + -CID(E + -IN[1], -INE[5], after *GRAMICIDIN.] (Any of) a group of crystalline monocyclic decapeptide antibiotics which along with the gramicidins are the active components of tyrothricin, as *tyrocidine A* ($C_{66}H_{87}O_{13}N_{13}$), *tyrocidine B* ($C_{68}H_{88}O_{13}N_{14}$), *tyrocidine C* ($C_{70}H_{88}O_{13}N_{15}$).

1940 HOTCHKISS & DUBOS in *Jrnl. Biol. Chem.* CXXXVI. 803 This substance was described earlier under the name *graminic acid* before its low chlorine content was recognized; it will be referred to hereafter as *tyrocidine hydrochloride*. **1952** BATTERSBY & CRAIG in *Jrnl. Amer. Chem. Soc.* LXXIV. 4021/2 Crystalline tyrocidine hydrochloride is in fact a family of polypeptides... The major peptides have been called tyrocidine A, tyrocidine B, tyrocidine C according to their partition ratios in the solvent system. **1969** Tyrocidin [see *GRAMICIDIN]. **1977** J. S. GLASBY *Encycl. Antibiotics* 350/1 Most of the bacteriological examination has been carried out on the mixture of tyrocidins.

Tyrode (tǝi·rōᵘd). *Med.* Also **tyrode.** The name of Maurice Vejux *Tyrode* (1878–1930), American pharmacologist, used *attrib.*, in the possessive, and *ellipt.* as *Tyrode's*, to designate a type of physiological saline solution used to irrigate tissue and in laboratory work.

1923 *Jrnl. Pharmacol. & Exper. Therapeutics* XXI. 218 Lowering of pH values of the blood did not occur regularly after injection of..Tyrode's solution. **1962** HARRIS & GRUBER in A. Pirie *Lens Metabolism Rel. Cataract* 374 The cation transport can be measured reasonably well in a fairly simple medium. Originally, we used Tyrode's solution. **1964** W. G. SMITH *Allergy & Tissue Metabolism* iii. 36 These experiments..consisted simply of replacing the oxygenated tyrode solution in which the tissue was bathed with tyrode solution containing either 48/80, stibamidine protamine sulphate or toluidine blue. **1975** *Nature* 31 Jan. 353/1 The sperm were recovered from the albumin by centrifugation at 2,500*g* and washed once in Tyrode's.

Tyrolean, *a.* and *sb.* Add: Now usu. with pronunc. (tirolī·ăn). **a.** *adj.* (Earlier example.) *Tyrolean hat*, a soft felt hat with a brim turned up at the sides and usu. a feather cockade; (later example). **b.** *sb.* Also = *Tyrolean hat* above.

1805 *Times* 7 Nov. 2/3 The greatest part of those prisoners taken..belong to..the Tyrolian Chasseurs. **1957** M. B. PICKEN *Fashion Dict.* 361/2 *Tyrolean hat*, soft brimmed felt hat. **1973** T. PYNCHON *Gravity's Rainbow* III. 495 Von Göll tips an invisible Tyrolean to old ladies in black who've come out in pairs to get some sun.

Tyroler: also, the dialect of German spoken in the Tyrol; also as *adj.*, = *Tyrolean* a.

1887 M. HOWITT *Let.* 21 June in *Autobiogr.* (1889) II. ix. 345 Father Paul..has been ill.., but being able to say Mass this morning, he, a Tyroler Benedictine, remembered our Queen's Jubilee, and made it his intention. **1923** E. HEMINGWAY *Three Stories & Ten Poems* 18 Part of the time he talked in D'Ampezzo dialect and sometimes in Tyroler German dialect... Peduzzi decided to talk altogether in Tyroler. **1963** I. FLEMING *On H.M. Secret Service* (U.S. ed.) xxvii. 295 A dark-grey Tyroler outfit with the traditional dark-green trimmings and stag's-horn buttons.

tyrosin. Add: Now always **tyrosine** (-īn). An amino-acid that is the precursor of several hormones, including adrenalin; 3-(*p*-hydroxyphenyl)alanine. (Further examples.)

1926 [see *DEAMINATION]. **1955** *Sci. Amer.* July 75/2 The six virus strains were analyzed for their content of three amino acids: tyrosine, tryptophan and phenylalanine. **1965** LEE & KNOWLES *Animal Hormones* v. 91 Basically, thyroid hormone consists of iodine conjugated with tyrosine. **1982** [see *TYROSINASE].

tyrosinæmia (tǝirǒsinī·miă). *Med.* Also (chiefly *U.S.*) **-emia.** [f. prec. + Gr. αἷμα blood + -IA[1].] Any of several conditions marked by the presence in blood and urine of abnormally high amounts of tyrosine.

1965 J. GENTZ et al. in *Jrnl. Pediatrics* LXVI. 670/1 Tyrosinemia as defined in the present report is a disorder characterized biochemically by a continuous high urinary excretion of tyrosine and tyrosyl compounds and a high plasma tyrosine level, while the concentrations of other amino acids are normal or rather low. **1982** T. I. DIAMONDSTONE in T. M. Devlin *Textbk. Biochem.* xii. 589 Transient tyrosinemia of the newborn appears to be due to delayed development of tyrosine transaminase and/or *p*-hydroxyphenylpyruvate oxidase... Persistent tyrosinemia without liver or kidney disease has been reported in six patients, all of whom are retarded. **1983** *Oxf. Textbk. Med.* I. IX. 94/1 A single metabolic lesion to explain all the findings has not yet been identified, and it has been argued that Type I tyrosinaemia is not in fact primarily a disorder of tyrosine metabolism.

tyrosinase. Delete entry in Dict. and substitute:

tyrosinase (tǝiᵊ·rǒs-, tǝirǫ·sinēⁱz). *Biochem.* [a. F. *tyrosinase* (G. Bertrand 1896, in *Compt. Rend.* CXXII. 1216): see TYROSIN and *-ASE.] A copper-containing oxygenase found in many plants and animals which catalyses the formation of quinones from phenols and polyphenols (e.g. melanin from tyrosine) by the addition and then the oxidation of hydroxyl groups.

1896 *Jrnl. R. Microsc. Soc.* 430 In the root of the dahlia and beet, as well as in several fungi..M. G. Bertrand finds a hitherto undescribed diastase, to which he gives the name *tyrosinase*, from its connection with tyrosin. **1904** *Proc. R. Soc.* LXXIV. 313 An extract can be made from the skins of certain pigmented animals.., which will act upon tyrosin and produce a pigmented substance. This action suggests the presence of a tyrosinase. **1931** [see *PHENOLASE]. **1974** [see *polyphenol oxidase* s.v. *POLY- 2]. **1982** T. I. DIAMONDSTONE in T. M. Devlin *Textbk. Biochem.* xii. 614/2 Melanin is formed from tyrosine via L-dopa as intermediate; however, the enzyme that catalyzes the formation of L-dopa in this pathway is not tyrosine hydroxylase, but a copper-containing oxygenase known as tyrosinase.

tyrosine: see TYROSIN in Dict. and Suppl.

tyrosinosis (tǝirǒsinōᵘ·sis). *Med.* [f. *TYROSINE + -OSIS.] A rare condition of unknown ætiology in which there is increased excretion of the early metabolites of tyrosine but no liver or kidney damage; also (now *rare*) = *TYROSINÆMIA.

1932 G. MEDES in *Biochem. Jrnl.* XXVI. 938 The essential feature in our patient..consists in a complete stoppage of the oxidation of tyrosine at the stage of *p*-hydroxyphenylpyruvic acid... Thus results an excretion not only of *p*-hydroxyphenylpyruvic acid and..*l*-*p*-hydroxyphenyllactic acid, but also of tyrosine and.. *l*-3:4-dihydroxyphenylalanine. For this condition, the name tyrosinosis is proposed. **1942** [see *L-DOPA]. **1969** [see *homocystinuria* s.v. *HOMOCYSTINE]. **1974** PASSMORE & ROBSON *Compan. Med. Stud.* III. xlvii. 8/1 Formerly hypertyrosinaemia or tyrosinosis was considered to be a single, exceedingly rare abnormality. **1982** T. I. DIAMONDSTONE in T. M. Devlin *Textbk. Biochem.* xii. 589/1 Tyrosinosis and the tyrosinemias have certain biochemical features in common.

tyrothricin (tǝiroþrǝi·sin, -þri·sin). *Pharm.* [f. *Tyrothrix* (see quot. 1940), f. Gr. τυρό-ς cheese + θρίξ, τριχ- hair: see -IN[1].] A preparation of gramicidin and tyrocidine which has antibiotic properties, esp. against Gram-positive bacteria, and has been used externally to treat local infections.

1940 HOTCHKISS & DUBOS in *Jrnl. Biol. Chem.* CXXXVI. 804 Gramicidin will continue to be used as the name of the crystalline neutral substance described before. It is proposed here to apply the name tyrothricin to the bactericidal agent prepared as an alcohol-soluble, water-insoluble material and containing both gramicidin and tyrocidine. This name is derived from the word *Tyrothrix*, a generic name first used by Duclaux to designate sporulating aerobic bacterial species, several of which have since been found to exhibit antagonistic activity toward other microorganisms. **1959** *Sunday Graphic* 25 Jan. 4 (Advt.), Antibiotic throat lozenges contain the highly effective antibiotic tyrothricin. **1974** M. C. GERALD *Pharmacol.* xxvi. 453 Tyrothricin proved too toxic for systemic use in animals.

tystie, now the usual spelling of TEISTIE in Dict. and Suppl.

tyuyamunite (tiūyămū·nǝit). *Min.* [ad. Russ. *tyuyamunit'* (K. A. Nenadkevicha 1913, in *Izvestiya imper. Akad. Nauk"* VI. 945), f. *Tyuya Muyun*, name of a village near Osh, Kirgiziya, U.S.S.R.: see -ITE[1].] A hydrous uranyl vanadate of calcium, $Ca(UO_2)_2(VO_4)_2.5–8H_2O$, occurring as soft, yellowish orthorhombic crystals and mined for its uranium content.

1913 *Amer. Jrnl. Sci.* CLXXXV. 440 The calcium carnotite experimented with is probably identical with the tuyamunite of Nenadkevich. **1957** *Financial Times Ann. Rev. Brit. Industry* 39/3 Important secondary ore mineral[s]..are the calcium–uranium vanadate tyuyamunite, ..and tobernite. **1979** *Mineral. Abstr.* XXX. 362/1 The San Rafael mining area is situated along the east flank of the San Rafael Swell in east-central Utah... Coffinite is the most abundant primary ore mineral, and tyuyamunite is the most abundant secondary ore mineral.

tzaddik, -iq, varr. *TSADDIK. **Tzakonian,** var. *TSAKONIAN *sb.* and *a.* **tzantza,** var. *TSANTSA.

‖ **tzedaka(h)** (tsedǫ·ka). [Heb. *ṣ*ᵉ*dāqāh* righteousness.] Charity, the obligation to help one's fellow Jews.

1959 D. D. RUNES *Conc. Dict. Judaism* 225/2 *Tzedakah*, righteousness; charity. **1962** *New Jewish Encycl.* 87/1 The Jewish concept of 'charity' has..been refined to mean more than the mere giving of alms; it has been considered as 'Tzedakah', an act of justice and righteousness. **1968** L. ROSTEN *Joys of Yiddish* 417 Maimonides set down variously rated forms of *tzedaka*. **1973** *Synagogue Light* Sept. 30/1 To all who have helped our brothers overseas in the year 5733, let me say that there can be no finer act of Tzedakah. **1978** *Jewish Chron.* 6 Oct. 23/3 Acceptance of the mitzvot, the ritual acts of prayer, *tzedaka* and so on.

Tzeltal (tselta·l, tse·ltal; s-), *sb.* (and *a.*) Also **Tzendal, Tzental.** Pl. **-al, -ales** (-a·lès), **-als.** [a. Sp., earlier also *Tzendal, Sendal*, name of one of the three regions of Chiapas as divided by the Spaniards; ulterior origin uncertain.] (A member of) an Indian people inhabiting parts of southern Mexico; the

Mayan language of this people. Also *attrib.* or as *adj.*

1868 C. H. BERENDT in *Ann. Rep. Board of Regents Smithsonian Inst. 1867* 426, I visited the ruins of Palenque, and..was enabled..to collect vocabularies of the Putum and Tzental languages, both spoken in Chiapas. **1871** L. H. MORGAN *Systems of Consanguinity* II. vi. 263 The Chontal language is allied to the Maya of Yucatan. It also affiliates with the Chol and Tzental of Chiapa. **1875** H. H. BANCROFT *Native Races Pacific States N. Amer.* I. vi. 645 South of them [*sc.* the Chontales] in Chiapas are the *Choles, Tzendales, Zotziles,* [etc.]. *Ibid.* III. x. 760 Most..are related to..the Maya, of which a dialect called the Tzendal is said to be the oldest language spoken in any of these countries. **1927** O. LA FARGE in *Tribes & Temples* II. xv. 326 The language itself has been variously named Cendal, Tzendal, Cendales, Tzental, and Tzeltal. I have taken the latter form, as it most nearly represents the Indians' own form, *ts'eltal,* varied in careless speech to *tceltal. Ibid.* 325 They speak the Tzeltal language, belonging to that branch of the great Mayance stock more closely related to Maya. **1939** REDFIELD & VILLA in *Contrib. Amer. Anthropol. & Hist.* V. xxviii. 107 Mr. Villa..does not speak Tzeltal. *Ibid.* 110 Most Tzeltal communities are without beehives. **1949** [see *INTRANSITIVIZE *v.*]. **1964** E. A. NIDA *Toward Sci. Transl.* x. 239 Among the Tzeltals in Southern Mexico the coming of missionaries..resulted in the conversion of many hundreds of persons, who responded, in their eagerness to describe their spiritual experiences, by creating many new phrases. *Ibid.*, At the same time, the Tzeltal people were undergoing certain adjustments of experience to new elements of language. **1979** L. CAMPBELL in Campbell & Mithun *Lang. Native Amer.* 902 Examination of numerals shows every other one to be Tzeltal alternating with Tojolabal.

tzimmes (tsi·məs). Also **tsimmes, -is; tzimmas, -is, -us; (t)zimes.** Pl. same. [a. Yiddish *tsimes* of obscure origin.] A stew or casserole of sweetened vegetables or vegetables and fruit, sometimes with meat. Also *fig.*, a fuss, a confused affair.

1892 I. ZANGWILL *Childr. Ghetto* I. v. 136 Esther sometimes compounded *Tzimmus*, a dainty blend of carrots, pudding, and potatoes. **1893** *Pall Mall Mag.* Oct. 870 It was a good and simple meal of fish, fowl, and fruits, no 'borsch', no 'tabeches', no 'tzimmas'. **1903** *Jewish Encycl.* IV. 256/1 *Zimes*, or compote, consists generally of cooked fruits..or of vegetables, well spiced. **1923** A. YEZIERSKA *Children of Loneliness* 142 *Tzimmes—blintzes*—a golden-roasted goose swimming in its own fat ravished the senses. **1925** S. RAPHAELSON *Jazz Singer* 125 Brother Levy, I am the chairman of the Executive Committee. Make yourself a *tsimmes* from it... All right—*all* right. **1925** A. YEZIERSKA *Bread Givers* vi. 102 You ought to taste her *gefülte* fish! Her *tzimes*! **1946** D. RUNYON *Short Takes* 199 Why is he making a big tsimmis out of a grunt? **1958** J. GROSSINGER *Jewish Cookery* p. xi, Rosh Hashonah ..one of the many different styles of *tzimmes* is a regular part of the holiday's menu. **1968** L. ROSTEN *Joys of Yiddish* 411 Since making *tsimmes* took time and various mixings, the word came to mean:..A prolonged procedure; an involved business; a mix-up. **1970** S. ELLIN *Bind* xxxviii. 186 I'll be owing money before this *tzimmis* is over. **1970** [see *KISHKE]. **1974** R. L. SIMON *Wild Turkey* (1976) vii. 39 Why are you making such a *tsimmis*? Hecht is dead. **1975** G. MEIR *My Life* iii. 37 The Sabbath meal—chicken soup, *gefilte* fish, and meat braised with potatoes and onions, with a carrot-and-prune *tzimmes* on the side. **1978** *Times* 29 July 9/2 On a recent visit, latkes were greasy and tzimmis boring.

tzitzit(h), varr. *TSITSITH.

tzolkin (tsǫ·lkin, s-). [Mayan.] The cycle of two hundred and sixty days constituting the sacred calendar of the Maya.

1931 GANN & THOMPSON *Hist. Maya* viii. 208 After giving the position of a day in their sacred calendar or Tzolkin, as it was probably called, they proceeded to give the position in their 365-day year. **1948** A. L. KROEBER *Anthropol.* (rev. ed.) 549 The 260-day tzolkin..had heavy religious and astrological import. **1977** G. CLARK *World Prehistory* (ed. 3) viii. 374 The Maya maintained two distinct counts. For religious purposes they used a sacred year (*tzolkin*) made up of thirteen twenty-day units.

tzores, var. *TSORES.

Tzotzil (tsōu·tsil, tsōutsi·l; s-), *sb.* (and *a.*) Also **Zotzil.** Pl. **-il, -iles** (-*i*·lės), **-ils.** [a. Sp., ad. Tzotzil *sočil* bat people.] (A member of) an Indian people inhabiting parts of southern Mexico; the Mayan language of this people. Also *attrib.* or as *adj.*

1875 [see *TZELTAL]. **1927** O. LA FARGE in *Tribes & Temples* II. xv. 326 Their [the Bachajons'] immediate neighbors of the Highlands are the Zotzil. [They] speak a language differentiated from Tzeltal only by a shift of *a, e,* and *b* to Zotzil *o, i,* and *m.* **1939** REDFIELD & VILLA in *Contrib. Amer. Anthropol. & Hist.* V. xxvii. 110 Wheat is..grown in the Tzotzil towns of Chamula and Huistán. **1940** F. JOHNSON in *Maya & their Neighbors* vi. 108 The Chañabal, and Tzotzil Languages. **1964** E. A. NIDA *Toward Sci. Transl.* ix. 218 The same period may be spoken of in very different ways in diverse languages; e.g. the Biblical 'tenth hour' (or 4 P.M.) is called..'the sun is astride the mountain' (Tzotzil) and 'time for untying the oxen' (Bolivian Quechua). **1977** *Language* LIII. 464 Tzotzil is a Mayan language with more than 120,000 speakers, all living in the State of Chiapas, Mexico.

Tz'u Chou (tsu dʒu). Also **Cizhou.** [Chinese *Tz'u Chou* (Wade–Giles), *Cizhou* (Pinyin), place-name in northern China.] Pottery made at Tz'u Chou, or in similar styles elsewhere, from the Sui dynasty onwards.

1910 S. W. BUSHELL *Chinese Art* II. 22 The Ting-chou and Tz'u-chou porcelains. **1915** R. L. HOBSON *Chinese Pott. & Porc.* I. viii. 103 By far the largest group of the Tz'ŭ Chou family consists of the painted wares. Like the rest of the Tz'ŭ Chou pottery..these have a greyish buff body of porcellanous stoneware..covered with a transparent glaze... On this glaze..the painters executed rapid, bold..designs in shades of brown, varying from black to a soft sepia colour. **1934** *Burlington Mag.* May 214/2 The most characteristic Tz'ŭ Chou product is a buff or grey stoneware dressed with white slip. **1972** *Guardian* 15 Nov. 7/1 A firm of New York dealers.. yesterday paid £50,000 for a vase of Tz'ŭ Chou stoneware of the Sung dynasty at Sotheby's. **1980** *Sotheby's Preview Calendar of Sales* Apr.–May p. xxiii (*caption*) A Cizhou (Tz'u Chou) pillow... Jin (Chin) dynasty.

tzuica, var. *TSUICA. **tzuris,** var. *TSORES.

U

U. Add: **I. 1. b.** Now in wider, esp. U.S. commercial and Black, use. (Further examples.) *U-Haul* (U.S. proprietary name for) a small rented truck or a trailer.

1862 HARDY *Let.* 3 Nov. (1978) I. 2, I wish you wd tell me how u.r. when u. write. **1923** *Dialect Notes* V. 231 Call Tel-U-Where for our nearest distributor... Fits-U Eyeglasses. U All Kno After Dinner Mints. Uneeda Biscuit. **1924**, etc. [see *PUT-YOU-UP]. **1929** *Amer. Speech* V. 24 U-Bet-U It's Good Candy. *Ibid.*, U Drive It (cars for hire),..Shine While U Wait, Hats Cleaned While U Wait,..Motor Boats to Rent—U Drive,..Did U Eat? (card in window of restaurant). **1951** *Washington Yellow Pages Classified Telephone Directory* (Chesapeake & Potomac Telephone Co.) Nov. 846/3 Rent a 'U-Haul Co.' trailer. You can rent here and leave in other major cities. **1963** *Official Gaz.* (U.S. Patent Office) 26 Feb. TM 154/2 Arcoa Inc., Portland, Oreg... *U-Haul.* For Rental of Trucks and Automobile Freight Trailers. First use Oct. 15, 1945. **1970** S. SANCHEZ in S. Henderson *Understanding New Black Poetry* (1973) 275 U blew away our passsst. **1971** *Black World* June 48 That scag Reefers Wine That send u spinnen into witeness. **1972** *Guardian* 11 July 10/6 The..catalogue essay..is a masterpiece of myth-making, art history while-u-wait. **1974** R. M. PIRSIG *Zen & Art of Motorcycle Maintenance* I. iv. 48 It would probably be normal about this time to wonder what sort of U-Haul trailer all this is in. **1976** *Billings* (Montana) *Gaz.* 27 June 2-D/6 Roberts lost his gas station and is residing in a U-Haul propped on cinder blocks. **1980** 'D. SHANNON' *Felony File* viii. 193, I had the hell of a time getting hold of a U-Haul truck. **1981** M. C. SMITH *Gorky Park* III. iv. 356 Painted everywhere were signs: NO TRESPASSING THIS MEANS U and BEWARE OF DOGS.

2. a. *U-shaped* adj. (further examples); *spec.* designating or pertaining to a valley having such a cross-section, esp. as a result of glacial erosion.

1894 *Jrnl. Geol.* II. 350 Glacial cañons are..U shaped rather than V shaped in cross-profile. **1909** *Bull. Geol. Soc. Amer.* XX. 409 (*heading*) Striations and U-shaped valleys produced by other than glacial action. **1970** R. J. SMALL *Study of Landforms* xi. 367 Virtually all U-shaped valleys in glaciated areas have been produced by the glacial modification of pre-existing river valleys.

b. *U-bend, cross profile, -frame, -section* (hence *-sectioned* adj.), *-tube* (earlier example), *-turn* (also *fig.* and as *v. intr.* and *trans.*), *-valley* (see prec. sense).

1819 M. EDGEWORTH *Let.* 4 Mar. (1971) 177 Excellent lecture room well lighted with *gas* spouting from U tubes at the bottom of the gallery. **1884** W. J. MCGEE in *Proc. Amer. Assoc. Adv. Sci.* XXXII. 238 The effect of temporary occupancy of a typical water-cut cañon by glacier ice will be to..change the original V to a U cross profile. **1909** WEBSTER, *U section*, or *U-section.* **1928** BLUNDEN *Undertones of War* viii. 80 A support line was being made, and very nice and proper it looked..with its clean U-frames..and symmetrical wire anchorages. **1937** *Sun* (Baltimore) 27 July 6/3 He will enforce new ordinances barring U turns in the public square and regulating parking. **1947** AUDEN *Age of Anxiety* (1948) iii. 62 Let down From U-valleys like yarn, Waterfalls..Quietly encourage me on. **1950** 'S. RANSOME' *Deadly Miss Ashley* xi. 145 The driver U-turned into the wake of the police car. **1954** 'N. BLAKE' *Whisper in Gloom* xvi. 232 The armoured car ..made a sudden sweeping u-turn. **1958** R. STOUT *Champagne for One* vii. 82, I do the driving, and I wanted one [*sc.* a car] I could U-turn when the occasion arose. **1959** *Sunday Express* 17 May 6/1 His wife offered him a cup of tea... He U-turned again. **1959** *Times* 30 Sept. 13/6 (Advt.), We don't care *what* you call us so long as you *do* call us when you are in need of cold drawn precision tubes... Not to mention..'U' bends. **1961** WEBSTER, *U-turn*.., something held to resemble a U-turn (as a reversal of policy) < stated that the Administration is making an economic *U-turn*—T. R. Ybarra >. **1963** A. Ross *Australia 63* ii. 49 At weekends motor boats churn up the water and skiers make U-turns past the koala farm. **1969** E. H. PINTO *Treen* 26 Early folding umbrellas were heavy and clumsy... The most important patents were that of Henry Holland..and that of Samuel Fox & Co. of Stockbridge, Sheffield, for the lighter U-section steel rib in 1852. **1969** *Jane's Freight Containers 1968–69* 578/1 The Conjack is a U-frame container lifter and transporter. **1972** A. ROTH *Heath & Heathmen* i. 16 One of the things which surprised even close observers was the ease with which Heath made a complete U-turn between his first rightwing, or Mark I phase of 1970–1, and his second, leftwing or Mark II phase of 1971–2. **1974** 'A. GARVE' *File on Lester* xx. 93 His wife had once lost a ring down a wash basin waste pipe and it had stuck in a U-bend. **1974** H. MACINNES *Climb to Lost World* ix. 132 Don was carrying up more climbing gear, pitons and bongs—large U-sectioned pieces of alloy or steel..which, when hammered into cracks as climbing aids, emit a resounding 'bong-bong'. **1975** J. G. EVANS *Environment Early Man Brit. Isles* iii. 69 We cannot see..the U-valleys of Lakeland with their sheer rock walls..without feeling the drama and immediacy of the Pleistocene ice. **1977** *Western Morning News* 30 Aug. 2/3 Reg. Cann, F.S.V.A., will sell by Auction,..steel U-sections. **1981** R. LEWIS *Seek for Justice* iii. 81 The car ahead slowed, then turned in a wide U-turn.

c. (Earlier example.)

1873 J. H. BEADLE *Undevel. West* xxv. 521 Four miles from Wingate the valley makes a great U to the northward.

d. = *U-turn*, sense 2 b above.

1971 'G. BLACK' *Time for Pirates* iv. 80, I was gambling on the lane doing a U and coming down again beyond the building. **1973** J. GORES *Final Notice* xv. 95 Ballard went by, U-ed, came back into the parking area.

3*. Symbolic uses: *U* is a coefficient representing the rate at which heat is lost through a structure, in B.Th.U. per hour per square foot per degree difference in temperature between the two sides (or the metric equivalent). Also *U factor, value.*

1928 *Jrnl. Amer. Soc. Heating & Ventilating Engineers* XXXIV. 63 Let U = coefficient of heat transmission. **1958** *Times Rev. Industry* Sept. 24/1 To specify the standard the Ministry [of Power] has approved the U value of thermal transmittance coefficient. **1975** R. H. WARING *All about Home Heating* v. 40 For the same actual *thickness* of brick, an 11 inch cavity wall has a U factor of about 0·33, compared with a value of 0·43 for a solid brick wall. **1982** *New Scientist* 10 June 692/3 All the external walls are insulated... This should cut the 'U' value from 1·7 to 0·5.

II. 4. a. (All abbreviations given here with a full stop are frequently used without it; those without can also be used with.) *u* (Physics) [f. G. *ungerade* odd], used to designate functions, esp. wave functions, which change sign on inversion through the origin (cf. *ODD *a.* 4*), and atomic states, etc., represented by such functions; U, universal, designating (a certificate given to) films suitable for exhibition to audiences of all age-groups; also *ellipt.* and *fig.*; *u* (Physics), up, a quark flavour; U (= uranium): also with following or preceding numeral indicating the mass number of the isotope symbolized; U.A.B., Unemployment Assistance Board; U.A.E., United Arab Emirates; U.A.P., United Australia Party; U.A.R., United Arab Republic; U.A.W.(A.) (*U.S.*), United Automobile Workers (of America); UCCA (ʌ·kă), Universities Central Council on Admissions; U.C.D., University College, Dublin; U.C.L., University College London; U.C.L.A., University of California at Los Angeles; U.D.A., Ulster Defence Association; U.D.C., universal decimal classification; U.D.C., Urban District Council; U.D.I., unilateral declaration of independence (orig. of Rhodesia from the U.K.); UDN (*Vet. Sci.*), ulcerative dermal necrosis, a disease of fish; U.D.R., Ulster Defence Regiment; U.D.S.R. [F. *Union Démocratique et Socialiste de la Résistance*], Democratic and Socialist Union of the Resistance, a left-wing French party under the Fourth Republic; UEFA (yū,ēⁱ·fă), Union of European Football Associations; U.F., United Free (Church, of Scotland); also, a member of this; U.F.F., Ulster Freedom Fighters; U.G.C., University Grants Committee; UHF, uhf, ultra-high frequency; UHT, ultra heat treated; ultra-high temperature; U.I.L., United Irish League; UJ, universal joint; U.K.A.E.A., United Kingdom Atomic Energy Authority; ULCC, ultra-large crude carrier; ULMS, underwater long-range missile system; UMNO, Umno (ʌ·mno), United Malay(s) (*later* Malaysia) National Organization; U.N., United Nations; UNCTAD, Unctad (ʌ·ŋktæd), United Nations Conference on Trade and Development; UNDP, United Nations Development Programme; U.N.E.F., United Nations Emergency Force; UNEP, United Nations Environment Programme; UNESCO, Unesco (yūnes·ko), United Nations Educational, Scientific, and Cultural Organization; UNHCR, United Nations High Commissioner for Refugees; U.N.I.A. (*U.S.*), Universal Negro Improvement Association; UNICEF, Unicef (yū·nisef), United Nations International Children's Emergency Fund (now officially the United Nations Children's Fund); UNIDO, United Nations Industrial Development Organization; UNIDROIT, Unidroit [F. *Institut international pour l'unification du droit privé*], International Institute for the Unification of Private Law; UNIP, Unip (yū·nip), United National Independence Party (of Zambia); UNITA, Unita (yūnī·tă) [Pg. *União Nacional por Independência Total de Angola*], National Union for the Total Independence of Angola; UNO, Uno (yū·no), United Nations Organization; U.N.P., United National Party (of Sri Lanka (Ceylon)); UNREF, Unref (ʌ·nref), United Nations Refugee Emergency Fund; UNRRA, Unrra (ʌ·nră), United Nations Relief and Rehabilitation Administration; UNRWA(PRNE), United Nations Relief and Works Agency (*orig.* for Palestine Refugees in the Near East); U.P., United Party (*spec.* of South Africa); U.P., United Press; U.P., United Provinces (of Agra and Oudh, India), now, Uttar Pradesh; U.P.C., Uganda People's Congress; UPC, universal product code; U.P.I., United Press International; U.P.N.I., Unionist Party of Northern Ireland; u/s, U/S, U.S., u.s., unserviceable; U.S.A.A.F., United States Army Air Forces; U.S.A.F., United States Air Force; U.S.C., Ulster Special Constabulary; U.S.I.A., United States Information Agency; USM, unlisted securities market; U.S.N., United States Navy; U.S.O. (*U.S.*), United Service Organization; U.S. of A. (*colloq.*), United States of America; U.S.P., United States Pharmacopœia; U.S.S., United States Ship; U.S.S.R., Union of Soviet Socialist Republics (Russ. *Soyuz sovetskikh sotsialisticheskikh respublik*); U.T., Universal Time; U.U.U.C., United Ulster Unionist Council; U.V., ultraviolet; U.V.F., Ulster Volunteer Force; U.W.C., Ulster Workers' Council; UXB, unexploded bomb. See also *UFO.

1930, 1962 *u* (= *ungerade*) [see g s.v. *G III. f]. **1965** J. N. MURRELL et al. *Valence Theory* x. 143 Only if there is an odd number of electrons in *u* orbitals can a state of *u* symmetry (e.g. He_2^+) exist. **1922** *Times* 11 Mar. 8/2 An attempt may be made to secure a rather broader interpretation of the division of films into 'U' and 'A' classes. The former are passed for universal exhibition... The 'U' certificate is very difficult to obtain. **1929** M. ALLINGHAM *Mystery Mile* xxiv. 224 They collected the evidence: Datchett collected the blackmail. Not a certificate 'U' production. **1935** [see A, adult s.v. *A III]. **1958** *Spectator* 15 Aug. 221/3 *A Cry from the Streets* (..'U' certificate) is about children. **1968** *Guardian* 26 Sept. 15/2 About the only British medium-budget U showing in London's West End is 'Yellow Submarine'. **1972** D. BLOODWORTH *Any Number can Play* xviii. 182 This particular prophecy was to whom it may concern. U-certificate. Kitay, Americans, British, it didn't matter. **1977** *Punch* 21 Jan. 80 'Hell!' cried the priest. 'What kind of penitent *are* you? Did you at least make love to your wife, see a U film, buy *Reader's Digest*?' 'No,' said the confessant, 'none of those.' **1964**, etc. *u* (Particle Physics) [see *S 15]. **1975** *Sci. Amer.* Oct. 43/1 Just two of the quarks, the *u* and the *d*, suffice to explain the structure of all the hadrons encountered in ordinary matter. **1982** *McGraw-Hill Yearbk. Sci. & Technol.* 386/1 Neutron decay corresponds to a transition $d \to u$ and Λ^0 decay to a transition $s \to u$. **1938** R. W. LAWSON tr. *Hevesy & Paneth's Man. Radioactivity* (ed. 2) xxiii. 221 Uranium is a mixture of three isotopes, uranium I (^{238}U), uranium II (^{234}U), and ^{235}U. **1940** *Manch. Guardian Weekly* 10 May 367 The discovery of a natural substance whose chief characteristic is the release of great energy is announced... It is known as U-235. **1968** *Listener* 22 Aug. 230/3 But an analysis of the radioactive fallout associated with the bombs showed that they were made from U235 and not plutonium as had generally been expected. **1979** A. G. MADDOCK in Harbottle & Maddock *Chem. Effects Nucl. Transformations in Inorg. Systems* xxi. 388 In uranyl sulphate solution most of the ^{239}U appears as uranyl ion. **1937** 'G. ORWELL' *Road to Wigan Pier* v. 77 When a man's stamps are exhausted.. he receives twenty-six weeks' 'transitional benefit' from the U.A.B. (Unemployment Assistance Board). **1972** *Whitaker's Almanack 1973* 958/1 The United Arab Emirates (formerly the Trucial States) is composed of seven Emirates... The approximate area of the U.A.E. is 32,000 square miles. **1979** *Financial Times* 12 Jan. 3/4 The Iranian community based on the UAE, which, in the northern Emirate of Dubai, runs into thousands. **1936** *Age* (Melbourne) 4 May 8/5 The attitude likely to be adopted by the full-blooded protectionist members of the U.A.P. towards the Government's proposal for abolition of duty on cement from Great Britain. **1964** J. JUPP *Austral. Party Politics* vi. 130 The U.A.P. leader, R. G. Menzies, called a conference at Canberra in October 1944. **1958** *Spectator* 20 June 793/1 There is no more reason to think that they [*sc.* the Lebanese] want to join the UAR in the immediate future than there is that the UAR wants them to join it. **1966** M. WOODHOUSE *Tree Frog* xxv. 190 The U.A.R. were supposed to be developing a delta-wing of their own. **1981** *Economist* 24 Jan. 43/1 In

1963, when a second attempt was made at a UAR, this time a tripartite one, the Syrians and Iraqis spent weeks in Cairo arguing against Nasser's federal ideas. **1946** W. Weinstone *Case against David Dubinsky* iv. 35 They now have in Walter P. Reuther and the presidency of the U.A.W. a strong base from which to operate more effectively. **1970** *Toronto Daily Star* 24 Sept. 35/1 There is some possibility that the UAW strike at General Motors will reduce the number of UAW delegates. **1936** *Business Week* 5 Dec. 16/2 The U.A.W.A. has a remarkable story to tell of its growth. **1963** F. D. Fawcett *Cycl. Initials & Abbrev.* 149/1 *UCCA*, Universities Central Council for Admissions. **1971** *Where* Dec. 357/3 The particular sections on the UCCA form which need careful filling in. **1976** *Times Higher Educ. Suppl.* 6 Aug. 8/2 A Nigerian universities joint matriculation scheme, which includes a combined school leaving and university entrance examination, and a form of UCCA selection. **1955** R. J. Schwartz *Compl. Dict. Abbrev.* 179/2 *UCD*, University College, Dublin. **1962** B. Inglis *West Briton* vii. 123 The 'National', as U.C.D. was known in Trinity. **1979** U.C.D. [see T.C.D. s.v. *T 6 a]. *a* **1912** W. T. Rogers *Dict. Abbrev.* (1913) 192/2 *U.C.L.*,..University College, London. **1979** W. H. Canaway *Solid Gold Buddha* xiv. 101 Das had a first class degree in law..and had studied full-time for it at UCL. **1941** B. Schulberg *What makes Sammy Run?* viii. 185 We drove past Westwood Village, the home of UCLA..Hollywood's version of campus life. **1977** H. Fast *Immigrants* iv. 290 He asked how far it was to the U.C.L.A. campus at Melrose and Vermont. **1972** *Times* 15 May 2/6 One UDA man said today [etc.]. **1978** D. Murphy *Place Apart* vii. 134 The main loyalist paramilitary force, the UDA, is not illegal. **1935** *ASLIB Information* Dec. 4/2 (*heading*) English edition of the U.D.C. **1965** *Rev. Internat. Documentation* XXXII. 19/1 For many years the problems of indexing and retrieving information have involved the use of tree-structured classification schemes such as the UDC system. **1905** F. H. Collins *Author & Printer* 383/1 *U.D.C.*, Urban District Council. *a* **1974** R. Crossman *Diaries* (1977) III. 576 There were the C.C.A., the A.M.C., the London boroughs, the G.L.C., the U.D.C.s and R.D.C.s. **1965** *Economist* 8 May 634/1 They shrug off..the threat of Britain imposing sanctions if Mr Ian Smith's government made a unilateral declaration of independence ('UDI'). **1966** *Listener* 17 Feb. 251/3 The British often 'lean over backwards' in their determination to do justice to George Washington and the other U.D.I. heroes. **1972** A. Price *Col. Butler's Wolf* ix. 99 He lived in Rhodesia...left shortly after UDI. **1980** *Times* 30 July 13/2 Both he and his wife Avis are from Yorkshire—not quite the kind that think Yorkshire should declare UDI. **1968** Carbery & Strickland in *Irish Veterinary Jrnl.* XXII. 171/2 This paper describes the symptoms, gross and microscopic lesions, epizootiology and bacteriology of UDN. **1972** *Trout & Salmon* Feb. 9/1 The effects on spawning stocks of UDN..are dangers just as significant. **1969** *Times* 20 Nov. 5/5 The Bill provided the necessary legal framework for the establishment of the U.D.R. **1978** D. Murphy *Place Apart* iii. 53 No UDR, no British army patrols, nothing to flaw the impression of a traditional rural community. **1945** *Times* 25 Oct. 3/3 Joint Socialist and U.D.S.R. (*Union Democratique et Socialiste de la Résistance*) lists, 961, 704. **1965** F. R. Willis *France, Germany, & New Europe* vi. 138 The Pleven cabinet, a coalition of the four most 'European' parties in the Assembly (Socialists, MRP, Radicals and UDSR), hoped in this way to avoid a national German army and advance European integration at the same time. **1963** I. Wilkes *British Initials & Abbrev.* 102/2 *UEFA*, Union of European Football Associations, P.O. Box 16, Berne, 15, Switzerland. **1972** *Rothman's Football Yearbk.* 1972–73 808 Last season, the U.E.F.A. took over the running of this colourful competition, re-named it the U.E.F.A. Cup and clearly stated that only clubs which finished high in their respective domestic leagues will be accepted. **1982** *Daily Tel.* 23 Dec. 16/1 UEFA have joined FIFA in their condemnation of the referee clampdown. **1913** *Northern Whig* 3 Dec. 8/5 The Rev. John C. Ingles, minister of the North U.F. Church, Crieff. **1922** 'R. West' *Judge* I. i. 17 The snatching of the Church funds from the U.F.'s by the Wee Frees. **1973** *Times* 13 Nov. 2/6 The U.F.F...have claimed responsibility for at least 10 murders. **1947** *Universities Q.* Aug. 326 There is..another field of major importance which the UGC is not touching; the whole issue of the aims and methods of university teaching. **1979** *Jrnl. R. Soc. Arts* Oct. 707/2 In 1964..the U.G.C. lost its distinctive rôle of a body advising the Treasury directly. **1937** *RCA Rev.* II. 30 For low-power u-h-f transmitters and receivers, special tubes having low internal capacities..are available. **1939** *Amat. Radio Handbk.* 161/1 The devices of Fig. 16 are satisfactory for matching U.H.F. aerials to open wire lines. **1955** *Times* 27 July 9/6 Its task is confused by the haphazard growth of early v.h.f. (very high frequency) stations and the consequent need to resort to the u.h.f. (ultra-high frequency) band for many of the new licences. **1978** *Jrnl. R. Soc. Arts* CXXVI. 437/1 Chief Officer Rowe..remained with the lifeboats and maintained communication with the rescue vessels using portable UHF radio. **1968** *Sunday Truth* (Brisbane) 27 Oct. 32/3 Local sale of UHT milk. **1981** *Economist* 24 Jan. 49/3 The UHT process—sterilisation by heating to 132 degrees centigrade—produces milk that keeps for months without refrigeration, but tastes peculiar. **1983** *Times* 7 Feb. 10/2 A repellent whitish fluid ..known as ultra heat treated (UHT) milk. [**1963** J. F. Hogerton *Atomic Energy Handbk.* 569/1 (*heading*) Ultra high-temperature reactor experiment (UHTREX).] **1968** E. Pugh *Dict. Acronyms & Abbrev.* 174 *UHT*, ultra high temperature. **1901** *Notes from Ireland* 1 Dec. Suppl., A U.I.L. meeting in Longhrea. **1976** J. V. O'Brien *William O'Brien* viii. 194 UIL circles in America. **1970** K. Ball *Fiat 600, 600D Autobook* 165/2 UJ Universal joint. A coupling between shafts which permits angular movement. **1959** *Times Rev. Industry* Aug. 17/1 U.K.A.E.A. research section. **1983** *Listener* 24 Nov. 5/2 In 1955 a new quango, the UKAEA, was created from various research and production units of the Ministry of Supply. **1973** *Sunday Post-Herald* (Hong Kong) 20 May (Business sect.) 5/3 The European yards..worry that their..share of new orders for VLCCs and ULCCs will remain small. **1981** E. Corlett *Revolution Merchant Shipping* 26/1 The world was about to be presented with new initials, VLCC and ULCC—the very large and the ultra large crude carriers were at hand. **1970** B. Wedertz *Dict. Naval Abbrev.* 234/1 *ULMS*, Underwater Long-range Missile System. **1973** *New Scientist* 30 Aug. 483 The ULMS will have a greater range than either Polaris or Poseidon. **1946** *Malay Mail* 14 May 4/5 Delegates from the newly formed United Malays National Organization will..attend. A two-day conference..has just ended at which delegates from all over Malaya and Singapore passed and ratified a charter incorporating the U.M.N.O., as the new organization will in future be known. **1979** *Straits Times* 27 Nov. 1. 12/8 Umno Youth leader Haji Suhaimi bin Datuk Haji Kamaruddin. **1946** *N.Y. Times* 11 Apr. 1/6 If the U.N. remained at Hunter or went to Lake Success, it would have to erect an auditorium. **1946** J. S. Huxley *Unesco* I. iii. 14 Other U.N. agencies such as the F.A.O. and the World Health Organisation. **1978** L. Heren *Growing up on The Times* iii. 84 The assassination of the UN mediator had frightened most Israelis. The UN had been the indispensable midwife at the birth of their country. **1964** *Newsweek* 6 Apr. 31 UNCTAD..might very well lead to a major realignment of global power, with the world's poor nations in solid opposition to the rich. **1967** *Economist* 19 Aug. 670/1 Unctad, the United Nations body which tries to help the less developed countries. **1977** *Arab Times* 14 Dec. 6/6 A five-day session of an UNCTAD committee. **1966** *U.N. Monthly Chron.* Feb. 21/1 (*heading*) New Projects Approved by UNDP Governing Council. **1956** *N.Y. Times* 29 Nov. 12/6 The United Nations Emergency Force has been in Egypt.. two weeks... It may be..the UNEF, in terms of potential effectiveness.., must be rated as equivalent to a substantially larger military body. **1964** *Ann. Reg. 1963* 141 Owing to the continued failure of a number of Member States to pay their assessed contributions to the costs of the U.N. Emergency Force in the Middle East (U.N.E.F.) ..the financial situation remained serious. **1974** P. Gore-Booth *With Great Truth & Respect* 364 The Israelis had not helped their case by refusing to allow the UNEF to operate on their side of the frontier. **1973** *U.N. Monthly Chron.* Aug.–Sept. 84/1 The Council adopted..a resolution noting the report of the Governing Council of UNEP on its first session. **1980** *Africa* Jan. 43/2 UNEP's plans for the Red Sea. **1946** J. S. Huxley (*title*) UNESCO: its purpose and its philosophy. **1946** A. Huxley *Let.* 27 Oct. (1969) 551, I was delighted..to learn that all goes well with you and the infant Unesco. **1948** *Hansard Commons* 11 Mar. 1504 Someone was being brought from U.N.E.S.C.O. in order to help formulate an education policy. **1955** *Times* 17 June 5/2 The Universal Copyright Convention, which has been promoted by Unesco, will at last come into force on September 16. **1983** *Whitaker's Almanack 1984* 964 (*heading*) United Nations Educational, Scientific and Cultural Organization (UNESCO). *Ibid.*, In most Member States National Commissions serve as a link with Unesco. **1953** *U.N. Yearbk. 1952* 492/2 The report of the United Nations High Commissioner for Refugees (UNHCR)..dealt with the activities of the High Commissioner's Office. **1984** *Listener* 8 Mar. 12/2 The UNHCR includes Laotian and Kampuchean exiles in its total of 891,967 resettled up to the end of 1983. **1921** *Nation* (N.Y.) 28 Dec. 750/1 Any phenomenon among the colored population, like the U.N.I.A., white persons at first..regard as a huge joke. **1977** *Western Political Q.* XXX. 171 Thus we arrive at an understanding of the enhanced emotionality/reduced intellectuality characteristic of groups like the UNIA. **1948** *U.N. Bull.* 1 Mar. 184/2 The word UNICEF, pronounced 'Uni-sef', is now known far and wide in Europe. **1958** *Listener* 5 June 952/3 Danny Kaye's touching film.. about the part played by Unicef in conquering disease among children all over the world. **1982** *Whitaker's Almanack 1983* 962/1 United Nations Children's Fund (UNICEF). **1967** *Ann. Rep. Sec. Gen.* [*U.N.*] *16 June 1966–15 June 1967* xi. 145/1 The General Assembly decided that the United Nations Industrial Development Organization (UNIDO) should function as an autonomous organization. **1980** *Jrnl. R. Soc. Arts* June 440/2 At this moment, UNIDO III—the third conference of the UN International Development Organization—is in its final hours in Delhi. **1959** *Uniform Law Cases* (UNIDROIT) p. iii, One of the activities collateral to the unification of law, which the International Institute for the Unification of Private Law (UNIDROIT) has taken over, has been the study of the most appropriate measures to ensure uniformity in the interpretation of texts of uniform law. **1974** A. Watson *Legal Transplants* xv. 91 The work of the legal committees of the Council of Europe and of Unidroit is regarded as important as an indication of European trends. **1959** *Central African Post* 26 Oct. 1 (*heading*) Chona's Congress merges with U.N.I.P. **1961** *Times* 2 Nov. 9/2 Youth branches of Unip in the Western Province. **1977** *Times of Zambia* 7 Sept. 6/5, I see UNIP everywhere and I see it as one of the best organised parties in the world. **1967** *N.Y. Times* 17 Sept. 1. 17/3 Two Angolan nationalist organizations, the Popular Movement for the Liberation of Angola and the Unita, have been sending small guerrilla bands into eastern Angola from Zambia. **1972** J. Biggs-Davison *Africa—Hope Deferred* i. 9 U.N.I.T.A. of Angola and C.O.R.E.M.O. of Mozambique. **1978** *Guardian Weekly* 2 July 6 Secretary of State Cyrus Vance..defeated a move by President Carter's national security advisor, Zbigniew Brzezinski, proposing the covert sending of arms to UNITA guerrillas fighting in Angola against the Marxist Government of President Agostinho Neto. **1945** *Tuscaloosa* (Alabama) *News* 15 Nov. 4/4 The ideas range like this..let the United Nations Organization (UNO) handle it [etc.]. **1946** H. H. Henson *Let.* 14 May (1950) 181 The degraded haggling of the international market to which the cosmic idealism of U.N.O. has now degenerated. **1953** P. Scott *Alien Sky* I. ii. 32 An official observer from Uno or one of those dreary organisations. *a* **1974** R. Crossman *Diaries* (1976) II. 353 The arrival of the U.N.O. troops who are there to police the peace settlement between the Greeks and Turks. **1946** *Ceylon Daily News* 9 Sept. 4/2 The speech of Mr. D. S. Senanyaka, the leader of the State Council, at a meeting of the Executive Committee of the United National Party ..is..remarkable for its fairness and vigour... The leader delivered his speech under the auspices of the U.N.P. **1979** *Round Table* Jan. 49 No defeat in the annals of Sri Lanka's volatile parliamentary history is quite as comprehensive as that suffered by the rivals of the United National Party (UNP) in July 1977. **1954** *U.N. Yearbk. 1953* 845/2 *UNREF*, United Nations Refugee Emergency Fund. **1959** *Economist* 17 Jan. 229/2 In Austria, where the UN has a much freer hand than in Germany, the Unref building schemes are progressing much faster than government projects. **1943** *Times* (Weekly ed.) 24 Nov. 4 U.N.R.R.A. has already reached an agreement to share the cost by a levy of one per cent. on the national incomes of the contributing countries. **1943** *Times* 15 Dec. 5/6 The great success achieved by the United Nations Relief and Rehabilitation Administration (Unrra) conference. **1944** J. S. Huxley *On Living in Revolution* xiii. 139 UNRRA, the United Nations Relief and Rehabilitation Agency,..is preparing the vast stores we shall need to rush into Europe as soon as the 'cease fire' sounds—food and medical supplies, feeding-stuffs for the surviving livestock, seed and new breeding-stock. **1975** J. Cleary *Safe House* i. 23 The UNRRA parcels had began arriving from overseas. **1951** *U.N. Yearbk. 1950* 1014/3 *UNRWAPRNE*, United Nations Relief and Works Agency for Palestine Refugees in the Near East. **1955** *Times* 24 May 8/3 Some U.N.R.W.A. experts admit that the completion of the High Dam is necessary for the full realization of their scheme. **1943** *Cape Times* 29 July 4/7 The first election result to arrive at this office last evening was Major Piet van der Byl's at Bredasdorp—a smashing U.P. victory. **1959** *Ann. Reg. 1958* 101 On 10 November, the detention of 43 members of the U.P. was ordered after government allegations of a plot to assassinate Dr. Kwame Nkrumah, Prime Minister. **1971** *Progress* (Cape Town) May 1/2 Cutting the U.P. majority in North Rand by 1688 votes..Progressive candidate John Wilding has shown a considerable swing to the Progressive Party. **1915** *Oregon Daily Jrnl.* 13 Apr. 1/2 London, April 13.—(U.P.)—French aviators dropped bombs upon Hamburg..yesterday. **1943** C. Hollingworth *German just behind Me* v. 84 The Ministry of Propaganda issued a statement from the Ministry of Foreign Affairs which denied the U.P. story entirely. **1960** R. St. John *Foreign Correspondent* x. 222 We were forty-eight hours ahead of UP. **1908** *Resolution on Administration Famine Relief in United Provinces of Agra & Oudh 1907 & 1908* ii. 18 (*table*) Statement showing percentage outturn of the autumn harvest in terms of normal yield on normal area... Total, U.P. of Agra and Oudh. 39 31. **1919** *Indian Ann. Reg.* IV. 148 U.P. Provincial Conference. Special Session—11 Aug. 1918. **1947** G. Cunningham *Diary* in N. Mitchell *Sir George Cunningham* (1968) vii. 146 He has been in Kashmir (Uri front) for three-and-a-half-months with 200 of his 'fanatics' (mostly U.P. Muslims). **1963** *Listener* 21 Mar. 520/2 One would pass them [*sc.* Gurkhas] in the U.P. foothills. **1975** *Ibid.* 30 Oct. 558/3 Mrs Naidu, the famous poetess..was ..Governor of the UP. **1961** *Times* 22 Mar. 10/6 The U.P.C. has committed itself more emphatically to an East African Federation. **1980** *Economist* 9 Aug. 31/2 There are old grievances against the UPC. **1974** *McGraw-Hill Yearbk. Sci. & Technol.* 357/2 The Universal Product Code (UPC) is coming to the general merchandise store, too. **1982** *Sci. Amer.* Sept. 119/1 UPC bars are the set of thick and thin lines now printed on essentially all prepared-food items. **1958** *N.Y. Times* 25 May 1/4 The United Press Associations and the International News Service announced yesterday they had merged into a new agency called United Press International... The new U.P.I. agency announced that it would take over key I.N.S. employees. **1972** J. Belfrage in G. W. Turner *Good Austral. Eng.* vi. 103 You will find very likely that.. the UPI stories, and various others taken from agency sources are written with less colour..than local stories written by Australians for Australians. **1975** *Times* 22 Apr. 2/8 The leaders of the three power-sharing parties, Alliance, SDLP and UPNI. **1975** *Irish Times* 9 May 1/1 The standing orders committee—seven Loyalists, three S.D.L.P. members, and one member from each from the Alliance and U.P.N.I. **1942** *Tee Emm* (Air Ministry) II. 84 If your helmet is u/s, then your wireless mechanics have wasted their time. **1948** 'N. Shute' *No Highway* xii. 305 'What was the Machmeter showing?' 'I never look at that,' he said. 'It's no bloody good, that thing. Half the time it's U/S.' **1966** D. Francis *Flying Finish* v. 65 The de-icers were U.S. last week... It's O.K., I've checked them..since they were repaired. **1971** O. Norton *Corpse-Bird Cries* ii. 35 His brakes were u.s., I daresay. The usual story. **1978** M. Duffy *Housespy* v. 110 The device seems to have gone U.S. They're dodgy things because they're so small. **1943** *Times* 22 Dec. 4/5 The bombers, all of which returned safely, were escorted by U.S.A.A.F., R.A.F. and Dominion fighters. **1973** M. Calvert *Slim* 55/1 (*caption*) Brigadier-General Old (USAAF). **1947** *Air Force Times* 23 Sept. 1/2 The USAF is a reality! This first issue of Air Force Times..coincides with the birth of the independent Air Force. **1955** *Times* 24 Aug. 6/4 It makes the project the exclusive property of the United States Air Force. Regular progress reports are being made to the U.S.A.F.'s air research and development command headquarters at Baltimore. **1977** *R.A.F. News* 11–24 May 3/5 The Deputy Chief of Staff Personnel USAF, paid an official visit. **1963** I. Wilkes *Brit. Initials & Abbrev.* 106/2 *USC*, Ulster Special Constabulary. **1973** J. Callaghan *House Divided* vii. 91 They said that the USC had been the victim of a propaganda campaign. **1982** M. Wallace *Brit. Govt. Northern Ireland* ii. 28 The disbanding of the U.S.C. **1953** *U.S. Congr. House Hearings Comm. Govt. Operations Reorganization Plans 7 & 8* 43 USIA, which is United States Information Agency, will go through here [indicating the box marked 'State']. **1975** *New Yorker* 26 May 27/3 The Stanton panel, after working on the problem for over ten months and taking testimony from over a hundred witnesses, recommended that the cultural activities of the U.S.I.A. ..be combined with the cultural activities of the State Department. **1979**, etc. USM [see *unlisted *ppl. a.* 2 a]. **1863** *Rebellion Rec.* V. II. 177 All our fleet,..under Commodore Davis, U.S.N.,..was under way. *a* **1968** R. S. Churchill *Winston S. Churchill* (1969) II. Compan. I. 635 Rear Admiral Charles Davis, USN. **1974** L. Deighton *Spy Story* xviii. 189 We changed into U.S.N. khakis. **1941** *Christian Century* 30 Apr. 597/1 When on June 3 solicitation begins for $10,765,000 for the U.S.O. the public will

. . know that another organization is in the field. The letters stand for 'United Service Organization'. **1966** *Sunday Times* (Colour Suppl.) 4 Dec. 73/4 GI Jargon *USO*, United Services Organisation, nearest equivalent of ENSA. **1973** *Black World* Apr. 90 A Moslem man. . marries an Afro-American Catholic woman while on an extended visit to the u.s. of a. **1982** A. Melville-Ross *Trigger* xxiv. 284 You'll be told. . that won't be until you're back in the US of A under tight security wraps. **1909** *Cent. Dict.* Suppl. 1408/3, U.S.P. **1946** F. Schneider *Qualitative Organic Microanalysis* vi. 171 This technique is based upon the original U.S.P. directions in that the concentrations of the solutions are the same. **1961** R. D. Baker *Essent. Path.* viii. 129 The absorption of some of the substances by the ventral area [of a rat] denuded of skin is sufficient to cause death; specifically, alcohol (95 per cent) causes acute alcoholism and solution of hydrogen peroxide (U.S.P. half strength) causes gaseous cardiac embolism. *a* **1912** W. T. Rogers *Dict. Abbrev.* (1913) 194/2 *U.S.S.*, . . United States ship. **1957** 'N. Shute' *On Beach* i. 9 I'm posting you as liaison officer in the U.S.S. *Scorpion*. **1981** G. Markstein *Ultimate Issue* 17 The *USS Sharkfin* wasn't due to surface for another nine weeks. **1927** *19th Cent.* Nov. 653 The. . execution of two Italian anarchists in America stirred up the human soul far more than the mass executions, mass tortures, mass deportations, that have been taking place almost daily in the U.S.S.R. for ten painful years. **1959** E. H. Carr *Socialism in One Country* II. xx. 231 The year 1924 saw the constitution of the USSR in full operation on lines which were to remain substantially unchanged till 1936. **1982** *Whitaker's Almanack 1983* 961/2 There are five *permanent members* (China, France, U.K., U.S.A., U.S.S.R.). **1929** *Trans. Internat. Astron. Union* III. 224 The terms Greenwich Civil Time (G.C.T.), Weltzeit (W.Z.) and Universal Time (U.T.) denote time measured from Greenwich Mean Midnight, and are not ambiguous. **1974** *Nature* 1 Nov. 25/1 The balloon was launched at 0830 UT and it reached a ceiling height of 3.8 mbar. **1974** *Times* 22 June 1/3 Members of the Democratic Unionist Party, one of the three Protestant groups in the UUUC. **1982** M. Wallace *Brit. Govt. in Northern Ireland* vi. 125 The overall UUUC vote rose from 366,703 to 407,778. [**1925** E. H. & W. K. Russell *Ultra-Violet Radiation & Actinotherapy* 261/2 (Index), Veterinary uses of U.V.R.] **1928** *Moderna Språk* XXII. 188 Popularly one also hears U.V.-treatment, light treatment, light bath. **1940** A. L. M. Sowerby *Wall's Dict. Photogr.* (ed. 15) 431 Ultra-violet light is only present in sufficient amounts to be harmful on very clear days at sea-level, or at high altitudes. . . In such circumstances it should be excluded by a U.V. filter if it is desired to obtain photographs not showing the characteristics associated with the use of the ordinary yellow filter. **1979** *Nature* 29 Mar. 484/1 The ultraviolet region of the solar spectrum, which has somewhat arbitrarily been divided into three sections—UV-C (wavelength 200–290 nm), UV-B (290–320 nm) and UV-A (320–400 nm). **1913** *Northern Whig* 27 Nov. 8/5 They knew that the letters 'U.V.F.' stood for Ulster Volunteer Force. **1983** *Listener* 11 Aug. 3/1 The two supergrasses have helped to convict over 50 people they once worked with: Black in the IRA, Bennett in the UVF. **1974** *Times* 9 Sept. 2/2 Mr Murray resigned from the UWC but was later reappointed. **1975** *Irish Times* 30 May 4/6 The Ulster Loyalist Central Co-ordinating Committee (made up of the para-military groups, the U.W.C., and political representatives). **1955** R. J. Schwartz *Compl. Dict. Abbrev.* 184/3 *UXB*, unexploded bomb. **1979** P. Way *Sunrise* vii. 72 Once a UXB was in position—then, until this Unexploded Bomb had been dealt with, it was necessary to cordon off an entire block.

b. U, upper class, esp. with reference to linguistic usage; as *sb.*, U persons or characteristics collectively, U language. Hence *U-ness*. Cf. *non-U *a.* and *sb.*

1954, etc. [see *non-U *a.* and *sb.*]. **1956** *Times* 1 Mar. 11/5 He is what, in old-fashioned 'U' was called a 'rattle' and, in 'Non-U', a 'scream'. **1956** Auden *Making, Knowing & Judging* 15 Poets and scholars have one thing in common. They are not gentlemen. The U is that which both, being non-U, with passion worship. **1956** A. S. C. Ross in N. Mitford *Noblesse Oblige* 26 *Fault, also, Balkans*, . . are pronounced by the U as if spelt *fawlt, awlso, bawlkans*. **1957** E. Hyams *Speaking Garden* vi. 68 *Spinacia oleracea* of Linnaeus. . . I must say, at the risk of being accused of gastronomic U-ness. . is the only one I care to eat. **1958** *Oxf. Mag.* 15 May 432/2 He. . dropped the final 'g's' of his present participles in a manner then 'U'. **1959** *New Statesman* 17 Oct. 499/1 My own personal participation. . was to go and speak for Fenner Brockway at Eton and Slough. For me, he is a nostalgic figure of the old Labour Party into which I was born, and therefore more sympathetic than the later U intake. **1962** A. Lurie *Love & Friendship* ix. 166 'I don't think he's really U, though, do you?' 'Oh no. Shabby genteel, maybe.' **1968** *New Society* 22 Aug. 266/1 In London, Mayfair, once so very U, is still so in some sort, but few U people live there as it is so expensive. **1970** *Daily Tel.* (Colour Suppl.) 27 Nov. 12 The point is not so much that U-speech and U-behaviour are, by some absolute standard, superior but that they are indicators. If you want to be unobtrusive, or effective, in a U context, you must adopt U manners. **1977** D. Bennett *Jigsaw Man* xii. 225 He had spoken with a distinct English accent. Very U, indeed.

U² (*ū*, yū). [Burmese.] A Burmese honorific, used as the Burmese equivalent of Mr.

1930 *Outlook* 17 Dec. 607/2 Noting that the Burmese delegates were becoming restive, U Ba Pe, their chief, forced the issue. **1953** Stevenson & Eveleth *Judson's Burmese-English Dict.* p. vii, In 1893 Mr. Robert C. Stevenson, aided by U Si, U Thiri of Danubyu, U Pho U, and U San Ngyeing of Monywa, prepared an enlarged edition. **1971** *Whitaker's Almanack 1972* 813/2 *Secretary-General* (1966–71), U Thant (*Burma*).

uakari (wăkā·ri). Also **ouakari, wakari.** [a. Tupi.] A short-tailed monkey of the genus *Cacajao*, found in the upper Amazon basin, esp. *C. rubicundus*, which has a red face and shaggy reddish-brown fur.

1863 H. W. Bates *Naturalist on Amazons* II. v. 306 These red-faced apes belonged to a species called by the Indians Uakarí. **1894** H. O. Forbes *Hand-bk. Primates* I. 174 The Uakarí monkeys. . are at once recognised by their short tail. *Ibid.* 175 The Uakarís are arboreal monkeys, very gentle and timid. **1966** R. & D. Morris *Men & Apes* iii. 67 The curious uakari monkeys with their shaggy coats, abbreviated tails and sad, naked, almost human faces. **1975** *New Yorker* 12 May 46/2 He slew a wallaby and a lemur and a trio of ouakaris.

-ual *suffix* of adjs., repr. late L., med. L. *-uālis, -uāle*, as in *conceptual* (med.L. *conceptuālis*), *sensual* (late L. *sensuālis*); in adjs. formed from sb. stems in *-u-*, as *accentual* (L. *accentus*), *eventual* (L. *eventus*); and in adjs. derived from L. adjs. in *-uus*, as *individual* (med.L. *individuālis*, f. L. *individuus*), *perpetual* (L. *perpetuālis*, f. L. *perpetuus*). (Further information is given at -al *suffix*.)

‖ **U-bahn** ((y)ū·bān). [Ger., f. *U*, abbrev. of *untergrund* underground, + *bahn* railway.] The underground railway in any of several of the major cities of Germany and Austria.

1938 G. Conklin *All about Subways* x. 193 After the construction of the Paris subway came the *Untergrundbahn*, Berlin's thirty-nine-mile subway, which Berliners always refer to as the *U-Bahn*. **1957** S. Clark *All Best in Germany & Austria* ix. 117 Only in trips to East Berlin would I recommend the U-Bahn or S-Bahn, where you can lose yourself in crowds and feel at ease. **1964** L. Deighton *Funeral in Berlin* xl. 238 The U-bahn station across the road. **1974** P. Highsmith *Ripley's Game* v. 58 He gets off the U-bahn at the Steinstrasse station every day around six-fifteen. **1983** *Railway Mag.* Jan. 15/3 When I was in Vienna in April 1982, the prototype of the city's U-Bahn e.m.us was being *completely* rebuilt.

Ubaid (ubəi·d). *Archæol.* [f. the name of the tell Al *'Ubaid* near Ur in the Euphrates valley.] Used *attrib.* of the culture thought to have flourished throughout Mesopotamia in the fifth millennium B.C., and of the artefacts associated with it.

[**1927** Hall & Wooley *Ur Excavations* I. viii. 165 Two types of kiln were employed by the al-'Ubaid potter. *Ibid.* ix. 217 All of the al-'Ubaid skulls have assumed. . a reddish grey colour. **1936** S. Lloyd *Mesopotamia* ii. 40 The familiar greenish-painted pottery. . known as Al'Ubaid ware.] **1952** V. G. Childe *New Light on Most Anc. East* i. 13 Still older and purely prehistoric are villages of the Ubaid culture. **1961** G. Clark *World Prehist.* iv. 92 On the Ubaid foundation Sumerian civilization developed comparatively rapidly in the south. **1976** *Times* 3 Sept. (Qatar Suppl.) p. iv/6 Recently Ubaid pottery has been found farther down the Gulf in Saudi Arabia.

‖ **über alles** (ū:beɹ a·lès), *phr.* [Ger.] Above all else.

In quots. 1967 and 1983 prob. influenced by a misunderstanding of the opening words of the German national anthem, 'Deutschland über alles', as 'Germany supreme'.

1967 *Listener* 21 Sept. 365/3 Advertising. . is now advertising *über Alles*: it has become very big business indeed. **1979** *Guardian* 18 June 9/7 Monetarism, in the sense of giving precedence uber alles to restraining the growth of money supply. **1983** *Times* 22 Feb. 10/3 An exhibition. . presented. . by the British-Soviet Friendship Society. . . astronauts, Red Square, Lenin *über alles*.

‖ **Überfremdung** (ū̆bəɹfre·mduŋ). [Ger., f. *überfremden* to give foreign character to, f. *über* over + *fremd* foreign + *-ung* -ing[1].] The admission or presence of too many foreigners.

1965 *Economist* 27 Feb. 910/1 The vulgar prejudice against *Überfremdung* of which Dr Abs has recently chosen to become the spokesman. **1969** *Britannica Bk. of Year* 709 The issue of Überfremdung ('over-alienation'; i.e., the high percentage of foreign workers in Switzerland) continued to make news. **1970** *Time* 8 June 39 Nowhere in Europe have relations between guest and host become more acrimonious than in Switzerland. Uberfremdung (over-foreignization) has been a battle cry of the far right for the past five years.

‖ **überhaupt** (ū̆bəɹhau·pt), *adv.* [Ger.] In general, (taken) as a whole; as such; par excellence.

1875 W. James *Let.* 14 Nov. in R. B. Perry *Thought & Character W. James* (1935) I. 361 This element, which I suppose lawyers and men of society and business *überhaupt*, must necessarily lose. **1909** —— *Pluralistic Universe* 381 But what made them at all? What propels experience *überhaupt* into being? **1927** C. R. S. Harris *Duns Scotus* II. i. 50 It is only by supposing that universals have some reality which is quite independent of our thinking that the objectivity of thought *überhaupt* can be maintained. **1954** *Ethics* LXIV. 277/2 We seek. . the form of particular truths *überhaupt*. **1976** *Times Lit. Suppl.* 3 Dec. 1507/1 Psychology was regarded by Dewey as the philosophic science *überhaupt*, in the Hegelian sense.

‖ **Übermensch** (ū̆·bəɹmenʃ). Also **Ueber-.** Pl. **-menschen.** [Ger.: see Superman.] = Superman. Also in extended and weakened senses. Similarly **übermenschlich** (ū̆·bəɹmenʃliχʸ) *a.*, superior; like a superman, superhuman; **Übermenschlichkeit** (ū̆·bəɹme:nʃliχʸkəit), the quality of a superman, superhumanity.

1902 *Pall Mall* XXVI. 405/1 Where Bismarck exerted the full. . strength of the *Uebermensch*, Bülow always remains the polite orator. **1907** G. B. Shaw *Major Barbara* Pref. 152 It is assumed, on the strength of the single word Superman (Übermensch) borrowed by me from Nietzsche, that I look for the salvation of society to the despotism of a single Napoleonic Superman. **1911** J. Ward *Realm of Ends* xx. 451 The struggle for existence and the survival of the fittest. . will lead, he teaches, to a yet higher being, the *Uebermensch* or Över-man. **1920** D. H. Lawrence *Women in Love* xxix. 439 One really does feel übermenschlich—more than human. **1922** Joyce *Ulysses* 417 Mead of our fathers for the *Ubermensch*. **1931** W. Stevens *Harmonium* 131 If it were lost in Übermenschlichkeit Perhaps our wretched state would soon come right. **1939** L. MacNeice *Autumn Jrnl.* vii. 32 Take one's paltry measures against the coming Of the unknown Uebermensch. **1950** Blesh & Janis *They All played Ragtime* v. 85 A subtle but devastating caricature of the white *Übermensch*, employing the blackface like an African ceremonial mask. **1963** *Economist* 13 July 103/1 Doctor and detective *übermenschen*. **1977** *Times* 2 Sept. 11/4, I should like to know whether the Irish would be reckoned by him among the Übermenschen or the Untermenschen.

‖ **uberrima fides** (yu̇be·rimă fəi·dīz), *sb. phr. Law.* Also gen. **uberrimae fidei.** [L.] The utmost good faith.

1850 Macnaghten & Gordon *Rep. Cases High Court of Chancery* (1851) II. 243 The application for a special injunction is very much governed by the same principles which govern insurances, matters which are said to require the utmost degree of good faith, 'uberrima fides'. **1880** *Law Rep. Appeal Cases* 954 In policies of insurance, whether marine insurance or life insurance, there is an understanding that the contract is *uberrima fides*. **1899** *Law Rep. Queen's Bench Div.* I. 792 There are some contracts in which our Courts of law and equity require what is called 'uberrima fides' to be shewn by the person obtaining them. **1946** *Rep. Patent, Design, & Trade Mark Cases* LXIV. 6 The Petitioner must provide complete disclosure of all the circumstances and furnish all relevant accounts. .; the matter is one *uberrimae fidei*. **1959** Jowitt *Dict. Eng. Law* II. 1797/1 Contracts of suretyship and partnership, though not strictly contracts *uberrimae fidei*, are. . such as to require full disclosure and the utmost good faith. **1979** H. S. Kent *In on Act* iii. 37 He said that there was a very good relationship, based upon *uberrima fides*, the utmost good faith.

ubicity (yu̇bi·sĭti). *rare.* [f. L. *ubi* Ubi: see -icity.] Whereabouts.

1922 Joyce *Ulysses* 388 No man knows the ubicity of his tumulus. **1938** E. Pound *Let.* 9 Jan. (1971) 305 If letter via *Criterion* don't reach him, I will indaginare his ubicity.

ubiquinone (yu̇bi·kwĭnōᵘn, yū:bĭ,kwi·nōᵘn, -kwĭnōᵘ·n). *Biochem.* [Blend of Ubiquitous *a.* and Quinone.] Any of a class of dimethoxy-, methyl-, and polyisoprenyl-substituted quinones, (the number of isoprene units depending upon the biological source) which act as electron-transfer agents in cell respiration.

1958 R. A. Morton et al. in *Biochem. Jrnl.* LXVIII. 16P/2 Because of its widespread distribution. . and properties, the name *ubiquinone* is proposed. **1979** *Biochimica & Biophysica Acta* DLXXXII. 400 The ubiquinones in malaria parasites. . differ from those in mammalian cells. **1982** M. S. Olson in T. M. Devlin *Textbk. Biochem.* vi. 310 The final component of the mitochondrial respiratory chain, which is neither a nucleotide species nor a protein, is a lipophilic electron carrier called coenzyme Q or ubiquinone.

‖ **ubi sunt** (u·bi sunt). *Literary Criticism.* [L., lit. 'where are'.] An interrogatory phrase taken from the opening words or the refrain of certain mediæval Latin works, used chiefly *attrib.* to designate a mood or theme in literature of lament for the mutability of things.

1914 B. C. Williams *Gnomic Poetry in Anglo-Saxon* 45 The *ubi sunt* motivation is an old one, perhaps of equal age with riddle, charm, and spell. **1957** N. Frye *Anat. Crit.* 160 Themes of. . the wheel of fortune in social affairs, of the *ubi sunt* elegy. **1965** *English Studies* XLVI. 307 Cresseid's *ubi sunt* lament underscores the narrator's sympathy. **1969** Dunning & Bliss *Wanderer* 97 The adaptation of the *Ubi sunt* commonplace from a Latin *milieu* to an Anglo-Saxon one takes place in the sermon in much the same fashion as in *The Wanderer*. **1977** *Times Lit. Suppl.* 25 Feb. 224/4 The *ubi sunt* motif ('where are Caesar and Alexander [now]?'). **1977** M. McC. Gatch *Preaching & Theology in Anglo-Saxon England* 229/1 Characteristically, the device is employed in discussions of the brevity of life ('Brevis est hujus mundi felicitas, modica est hujus saeculi gloria, caduca est et fragilis temporalis potentia. Dic ubi sunt reges? ubi principes? ubi imperatores?. .'—Isidore of Seville, *Synonyma* II. 91. . . Ælfric's use of the rhetorical tag *ubi sunt?*, however, is quite different here. . . I know of no strict *ubi sunt?* passage in Ælfric.

ubity. Delete † *Obs.* and add later example.

1964 Auden in *Listener* 1 Oct. 525 Your influence is welcome at any hour in my ubity.

U-boat. Add: (Examples.) Also *attrib.*
1916 *Times* 11 July 6/4 The U boat is stated to be unarmed. **1918** *Glasgow Herald* 27 Aug. 4/6 The Maura Cabinet will stand firm in its attitude towards Germany on the question of the U-boat sinkings. **1928** C. MACKENZIE *Extremes Meet* 115 I'm frightened of what the Germans will do presently with their U-boats. **1943** J. B. PRIESTLEY *Daylight on Saturday* xxxi. 249 Sinking all the U-boats, putting out all the incendiaries, bombing the Ruhr. **1975** tr. *Melchior's Sleeper Agent* (1976) vii. 161 Two reporters..had walked boldly up and down Times Square clad in full Nazi U-boat commander uniforms. **1979** A. PRICE *Tomorrow's Ghost* ii. 22 The Atlantic is very big and a U-boat is very small.

Ubykh (ū·biχ). [Native name.] An almost extinct language of the North-West Caucasian group, now spoken only in Turkey.
1951 W. K. MATTHEWS *Languages U.S.S.R.* v. 87 A third type of North-West Caucasian is usually listed, viz. Ubykh, which is now almost extinct along the north-east coast of the Black Sea and survives chiefly in Asia Minor. **1965** W. S. ALLEN *Vox Latina* 9 The number of consonants..varies from 8 in Hawaiian..to 80 in Caucasian Ubykh. **1977** *Language* LIII. 450 Ironically, the language which has been the most extensively documented, Ubykh, is the most seriously moribund.

Uchee: see *YUCHI.

‖ **uchiwa** (ū·tʃiwă). [Jap. f. *utsu* to strike, shake + *ha* feather.] A flat Japanese fan (FAN *sb.*[1] 3) that does not fold.
1877 W. E. GRIFFIS *Mikado's Empire* II. xv. 518 Fukiu has a few shops where *ogi* (folding fans) and *uchiwa* (flat fans) are made. **1898** A. DIÓSY *New Far East* v. 268 The Japanese *uchi-wa*, or non-folding fan..is often decorated with a highly coloured print. **1970** J. KIRKUP *Japan behind Fan* 164 One should..carry in one's left hand an *uchiwa*, that broad, flat paper fan printed with cool summer subjects.

uckers (ʊ·kəɹz). Also **ukkers.** [Origin unknown.] A board game resembling ludo, played in the Navy.
1946 J. IRVING *Royal Navalese* 180 Uckers. A game very similar to Ludo, and played on a large board by teams of three or four men. **1976** C. CAUSLEY in *Cornish Short Stories* 63 The rest of the members of the mess—arguing, scuffling, singing, writing, playing uckers. **1978** *Navy News* Aug. 2/5 A 50-hour uckers match..raised £277 for the Spina Bifida Association. **1979** *Daily Tel.* 3 Dec. 20 That nautical form of ludo known as 'ukkers', and tombola, too, have given way in the patrol craft HMS Vigilant to war-games.

ucky (ʊ·ki), *a. colloq.* Also **ukky.** [Cf. *YUCKY *a.*] Sticky and dirty; disgusting.
1963 J. T. STORY *Something for Nothing* i. 7 It's ucky. That's what it is. It's ucky. **1969** *Sydney Morning Herald* 7 June 2/1 According to the organiser, Mrs Kemp, it will do away with 'ukky little pastel colours, fairy tales and endless nursery rhyme jingle stuff', replacing them with modern paintings, bright orange curtains and hi-fi sets playing classical music and jazz. **1974** 'D. FLETCHER' *Lovable Man* I. 61, I guess it would be awfully ucky... You know, sticky, muddy.

ud, var. *OUD. **udad,** var. *AOUDAD.

‖ **udarnik** (ūdā·ɹnik). Pl. **-i.** [Russ.] A shock-worker (*SHOCK *sb.*[3] 4 c).
1931 S. N. HARPER *Making Bolsheviks* vii. 162 *Udarnik* is the member of a 'shock brigade'. **1939** G. B. SHAW *Geneva* I. 25 In her youth she was a udarnik, what you call a shock worker. **1966** *Economist* 29 Oct. 464/1 Various forms of 'socialist competition' were gradually introduced, first with the aid of shock workers or *udarniki*, and then by the encouragement of Stakhanovites.

udder. **3.** For † *Obs.*[−1] read *rare* and add later example.
1933 DYLAN THOMAS *Let.* Nov. (1966) 53 Farmers' boys pressed amorously upon the udders of their dairy-maids.

udderful *a.*: also as *sb.*, as much (milk) as an udder will hold.
1922 JOYCE *Ulysses* 416 Drink, man, an udderful!

‖ **uddiyana** (udī·yana). [ad. Skt. *uḍḍīyana* rising up.] One of the physical exercises in Yoga (see quots.).
1949 S. KUVALAYÂNANDA *Popular Yoga* I. iii. 51 Uḍḍiyâna means *rising up* and Bandha means *contraction of particular anatomical parts*. This exercise is called Uḍḍiyâna-Bandha because the muscular contractions.. enable the spiritual force to rise up. Anatomically this Bandha may be called Uḍḍiyâna because it raises the diaphragm. **1960** J. HEWITT *Yoga* II. 42 *Uddiyana* can be counted as one of the physical exercises. **1960** KOESTLER *Lotus & Robot* iii. 117 Udiyama [*sic*]—drawing in the abdominal muscles, while forcing the viscerae and diaphragm upwards.

Udi (ū·di). [Native name.] An almost extinct north-east Caucasian language of Daghestan. Also *attrib.*
1948 [see *ALBANIAN *sb.*[3] 2]. **1951** W. K. MATTHEWS *Languages U.S.S.R.* v. 86 Udi, which is the language of two villages, in South-East Daghestan. **1974** *Encycl. Brit. Macropædia* III. 1013/2 One village of Udi speakers is located in Georgia. *Ibid.*, The Udi language is supposed to be one of the languages of ancient Caucasian Albania.

‖ **udon** (ū·dǫn). [Jap.] A kind of noodle made from wheat flour.
1920 *Japan Advertiser* 22 Aug. 5/2 Udon is an alternative for soba..but is made of wheat flour instead of buckwheat and is cut in thicker strings. **1959** *Encounter* Jan. 26/1 Bowls of *udon*, a kind of noodle-soup. **1978** *Chicago* June 236/2 There's also terrific chicken teriyaki, and reliable sukiyaki and udons ($1.75–2.25).

Uebermensch, var. *ÜBERMENSCH.

U-ey (yū·i). *Austral. slang.* Also **youee.** [f. U + -Y[6].] A U-turn.
1976 *Bulletin* (Sydney) 28 Feb. 27 Ted Heath, like Fraser, began as a professed opponent of big government but was soon 'doing a youee' (U-turn) all over the place. **1983** *Truckin' Life* Aug. 70/1 The turning circle is 15.2 m (49.8 ft). Not natural U-ey material but adequate for a six tonner.

uff (ʊf), *int.* An exclamation as of someone panting with exertion or difficulty.
1922 JOYCE *Ulysses* 244 O, my corns!..Come upstairs for goodness' sake till I sit down somewhere. Uff! Ooo! **1958** O. CAROE *Pathans* xxiv. 394 One day the fisherman caught—uff!—an enormous fish.

uffish (ʊ·fiʃ), *a.* [f. H)UFFISH *a.*] = HUFFISH *a.*
1871 'L. CARROLL' *Through Looking-Glass* i. 22 And as in uffish thought he stood. **1926** C. MACKENZIE *Fairy Gold* xviii. 200 I'm sorry if I was uffish. **1942** BERREY & VAN DEN BARK *Amer. Thes. Slang* § 301/6 *Arrogant, haughty*,..uffish. **1960** *Guardian* 5 Oct. 9/5 Watson looks a trifle uffish. **1977** *Times* 24 June 14/5 The infant Levin sat for a while in uffish thought.

UFO (yū·fo, yū,ef,o). orig. *U.S.* Also **U.F.O., Ufo, ufo.** [Acronym.] An unidentified flying object; a 'flying saucer'.
1953 D. E. KEYHOE in *Air Line Pilot* Oct. 9/3 The UFO was estimated to be between 12,000 and 20,000 feet above the jets. **1956** E. J. RUPPELT *Rep. Unidentified Flying Objects* 13 UFO is the official term that I created to replace the words 'flying saucers'. **1957** *Flying Saucer Rev.* III. vi. 9/2 Andrew Vaccari, of London Road, Neath, saw a crescent-shaped U.F.O. travelling at a terrific speed from the direction of Wern Mountain, Port Talbot, towards Mumbles. **1959** 'WYNDHAM' & PARKES *Outward Urge* ii. 86 Radar Watch here, sir..Two ufos observed approaching south-east by south. **1966** *New Statesman* 8 July 58/2 Flying saucers or Ufos..continue. They are now seen in all parts of the world and in increasing numbers. **1977** *New Yorker* 27 June 51/2 She talked to people who had seen strange sights—UFOs or sea monsters. **1983** *Out of Town* July 14/2 A relative of the marquess, celebrated for her obsession with flying saucers, scans the skies and..UFOs obligingly hover overhead.

Hence **U·FOish** *a.*, having characteristics of a UFO.
1973 G. S. HAWKINS *Beyond Stonehenge* vii. 117 We found no extraterrestrial artifacts. Nothing the least bit UFO-ish. **1978** J. UPDIKE *Coup* (1979) iv. 130 Steely, spherical UFOish IBM type elements.

ufology (yufǫ·lŏdʒi). [f. prec. + -LOGY.] The study of UFOs. Hence **ufolo·gical** *a.*, of or pertaining to ufology; **ufo·logist**, one who makes such a study.
1959 *Times Lit. Suppl.* 23 Jan. 44/4 The articles, reports, and bureaucratic studies which have been written about this perplexing visitant constitute 'ufology'. **1963** *New Scientist* 19 Sept. 613/2 Long before the frustrated ufologist has realised that even the finest binoculars do not help in finding ufos, he will have discovered that there are other sports and pastimes than ufology. **1966** *New Yorker* 9 Apr. 32 The ufological definition of a flap is a concentration of sightings in a small area within a short period. **1973** *Nature* 31 Aug. 582/1 He was not writing.. another addition to the burgeoning literature of Ufology. **1981** *Guardian* 29 Aug. 1/3 Cley Hill is the Loch Ness of the Ufologist. Flying saucers, it is claimed, cannot keep away from its flat top. **1984** *Spectator* 21 July 30/1 George Adamski..wrote, in collaboration with Desmond Leslie,..the first ufological best-seller, *Flying Saucers Have Landed*.

‖ **ugali** (ugā·li). [Swahili.] A type of maize porridge eaten in east and central Africa. Also *attrib.*
1970 *Kenya Farmer* Feb. 24/4 A maizemeal consumer in Kaloleni said that although the taste of the 'ugali' prepared from the new cereal was similar to that of 'ugali' prepared from ordinary granulated maizemeal, the new cereal was coarser and darker. **1974** *Sunday News* (Tanzania) 29 Sept. 4/7 We would get out early in the morning—work for a few hours before stopping at about ten thirty for an ugali break—then everyone would disperse and resume their normal jobs.

Uganda (yugæ·ndă). The name of a central African State used *attrib.*, as **Uganda kob**, a large brown waterbuck, *Adenota kob thomasi*, found in parts of Uganda.
1915 ROOSEVELT & HELLER *Life-Histories Afr. Game Animals* II. xvi. 511 The Uganda kob differs from the typical race by its larger size and darker coloration. **1964** C. WILLOCK *Enormous Zoo* ii. 30 Uganda kob stare from the tall grass.

Ugandan (yugæ·ndăn), *sb.* and *a.* [f. prec. + -AN.] **A.** *sb.* A native or inhabitant of Uganda. **B.** *adj.* Of or pertaining to Uganda or its people.
1962 *Times Index* Nov.–Dec. 79/1 Ugandan and Tanganyikan Prime Ministers to appeal to Mr. Macmillan. **1963** *Punch* 3 July 4/2 A tall Ugandan in his ankle-length white robe. **1969** *Times* 15 Sept. (Uganda Suppl.) p. i/3 One of the most delicate feats of balance facing the Ugandan Government. **1972** *Listener* 7 Sept. 291/2 A poll in the *Daily Express*..showed that only six out of every 100 people wanted to see the Ugandan Asians allowed in immediately. **1977** *Whitaker's Almanack 1978* 588/1 President Amin declared that neither he nor any other Ugandans would attend the Commonwealth Conference in London. **1982** *Daily Tel.* 4 Dec. 6/7 Anyone convicted of giving away examination papers to candidates will be liable to two years in jail..under a Bill approved by the Ugandan Parliament yesterday.

Uga:ndaniza·tion. [f. prec. + -IZATION.] In Uganda, the replacement of settlers and Asians by Ugandan Africans in government posts, the civil service, and other occupations.
1962 *Economist* 13 Oct. 132/1 The government's recent adoption of the term 'Ugandanisation' in place of 'Africanisation'. **1969** *Times* 15 Sept. (Uganda Suppl.) p. i/4 In filling new jobs, the Government has had to choose between Ugandanization, which allows Asian citizens to qualify, and Africanization, which looks at colour rather than citizenship. **1970** [see *KENYANIZATION].

Ugaritic (ūgări·tik), *sb.* and *a.* [f. *Ugarit*, the name of an ancient city in northern Syria + -IC.] **A.** *sb.* A pre-Phoenician Semitic language examples of which were first discovered at the site of Ugarit by Claude Schaeffer in 1929. **B.** *adj.* Of of pertaining to this language.
1936 H. L. GINSBERG in *Orientalia* V. 179 There is excellent reason for believing that Phoenician was almost identical with Ugaritic. **1938** A. GOETZE in *Jrnl. Amer. Orient. Soc.* LVIII. 266 The student who approaches the Ugaritic epics..is startled by the fact that the long narrative passages..are for the most part in the 'imperfect' (ygtl). **1951** A. M. HONEYMAN in H. H. Rowley *Old Testament & Mod. Study* 279 The precise linguistic affiliation of the Ugaritic tongue was for some time the subject of keen debate, Bauer and Goetze holding that.. Ugaritic cannot be classed as a Canaanite dialect. **1955** *Proc. Prehistoric Soc.* XXI. 177 There is a curious knife from Galilee which has a cuneiform inscription on the blade in the Ugaritic of the second half of the second millennium. **1963** *Listener* 31 Jan. 213/2 In northern Syria the thirty-letter Ugaritic cuneiform alphabet was already a precise instrument for recording phonetically several quite distinct tongues. **1973** A. R. MILLARD in D. J. Wiseman *Peoples of Old Testament Times* ii. 47 The tremendous impetus given to Hebrew studies by the recovery of the Ugaritic texts. **1981** *Word 1980* XXXI. 222 We have here an important isogloss for the chronological division of the Semitic languages into languages with *š* (Akkadian, Ugaritic, Eblaite,..), languages with *h* [etc.].

ugli (ʊ·gli). Also **uglifruit.** [Alteration of UGLY *a.*] A citrus fruit resembling a grapefruit with a thick mottled skin, developed as a hybrid of the grapefruit and the tangerine in Jamaica about 1930.
1934 *Daily Gleaner* (Kingston, Jamaica) 26 Feb. 19 Should the name of 'ugli' fruit be changed to a more beautiful name? **1943** WEBBER & BATCHELOR *Citrus Industry* I. 650 The Ugli is a very interesting fruit, probably a hybrid, that first came to the writer's attention.. in February, 1934. **1958** *Spectator* 13 June 770/2 Passion fruit, mangoes, uglifruit, and pomegranates. **1959** *Ibid.* 14 Aug. 196/3, I wonder who created the demand for uglis and Chinese gooseberries. **1975** *Austral. Post* 31 July 27/1 Prince Charles loves an ugli, so said the Queen when she opened London's new Covent Garden market recently.

ugly, *a.*, *adv.*, and *sb.* Add: **A.** *adj.* **3. e.** *ugly duckling*, a young person who shows no promise of the beauty, success, etc., that will come with maturity (in allusion to the story by Hans Andersen first translated into English in 1846). Also *transf.*
[**1871** GEO. ELIOT *Middlem.* (1872) I. p. vii, Here and there a cygnet is reared uneasily among the ducklings. **1877** M. W. CHAPMAN in H. Martineau *Autobiogr.* II. 151 Those early days..when she seems to have been like the 'ugly duckling' of Hans Christian Andersen.] **1885** A. EDWARDES *Girton Girl* I. xiv. 258 As a girl she never went through that chrysalis or ugly-duckling stage. **1927** M. SADLEIR *Trollope* 138 He [*sc.* Trollope] rose in the hierarchy of the Post Office... His ugly-duckling days were done. **1934** G. B. SHAW *Too True to be Good* Pref. 10 When one of their ugly ducklings becomes a revolutionist it is not because countryhouse life is idle, but because its activities are uncongenial. **1940** V. W. BROOKS *New England: Indian Summer* xxi. 440 He had grown up in a Boston family, a strange, alien, lonely child, a duckling, far from ugly, in whom perceptive eyes foresaw the swan. **1963** B. FRIEDAN *Feminine Mystique* xiv. 356 The feminine mystique..often forced the unhappy ones, the ugly ducklings, to find themselves while the girls who fitted the image became adjusted 'happy' housewives. **1977** D. RAMSAY *You can't call it Murder* I. 49 A big, gawky ugly duckling like me. **1978** *Nature* 26 Jan. 303/3 Mass spectrometers have been something of an ugly duckling in magnetospheric research. Initially too heavy, magnetically dirty and ill suited for hot plasma measurements, they have come of age and are now invited to all the best satellite projects. **1982** M. HINXMAN *Telephone never Tells* xviii. 134 The ugly duckling gawkiness of her youth had matured and mellowed.

4. b. *Ugly* (or *ugly*) *American* (in allusion to the title of the book: see quot. 1958), an American who behaves offensively abroad.

1958 LEDERER & BURDICK *(title)* The ugly American. **1965** *Atlantic Monthly* May 152 A host of odd and funny foreigners: bogus Russian counts, semi-aristocratic Slavic ladies, German officers, and an early type of the ugly American abroad. **1968** *Sat. Rev.* (U.S.) 9 Mar. 76 I don't think we were Ugly Americans; perhaps just unaware, or Unlettered. **1980** D. WILLIAMS *Murder for Treasure* x. 100 That awful man..thinks you're swinging the deal and he needs Edgar to blow it by acting the Ugly American.

C. *sb.* **3.** *the uglies* (slang), depression, bad temper; (see also quots. 1903 and 1974).

1846 *Swell's Night Guide* 77, I know as how I've got the uglies. **1903** FARMER & HENLEY *Slang* VII. 251/1 *Ugly*,.. In *pl.* = delirium tremens; the horrors. **1939** N. LAST *Diary* 18 Oct. in *N. Last's War* (1983) 20 A gloom seems over us all. I've shaken off my fit of the uglies, but I felt I'd just like to crawl into a hole. **1974** *Petroleum Rev.* XXVIII. 672/1 Nitrogen narcosis, popularly called 'raptures of the deep' but perhaps more accurately described as 'the uglies', is the malady caused by nitrogen under pressure, interfering with the normal function of the nervous system.

ugly *v.* (later example); also with *up*.

1946 *Sun* (Baltimore) 5 Feb. 8/7 Hands uglied by winter weather? **1965** *New Statesman* 26 Nov. 850/2 He uglies up the very places where one expects an opposite treatment. **1979** *Listener* 23 Aug. 248/2 Ever since *Grease* uglied up the Fifties..the nostalgia industry has taken a curiously tough turn.

Ugrian, *a.* (Earlier example.)

1838 *Jrnl. R. Geogr. Soc.* VIII. 390 He will investigate in that region the primitive as well as the present abodes of the nations belonging to the Ugrian race.

Ugric, *a.* Add: (Earlier example.) Also as *sb.* = UGRIAN *sb.* 2.

1854 MAX MÜLLER in C. Bunsen *Christianity & Mankind* III. 445 If we compare the Ugric and Tamulic Numerals. *Ibid.* 453 In Mandshu..we find juan for 10, the same root we met before in Ugric. **1964** J. ATKINSON tr. *Vuorela's Finno-Ugric Peoples* 2 Ugric comprising Vogul, Ostyak and Hungarian.

Ugro-. Add: *Ugro-Finn*; *Ugro-Tartarian* (earlier example).

1848 J. C. PRICHARD in *Rep. Brit. Assoc. 1847* 241 The Turanian, or as I shall term them, Ugro-Tartarian languages, or the languages of High-Asia and other regions... Ugro-Tartarian nations. **1862** *Temple Bar* Nov. 549 The Ugro-Finns, whom they have driven northwards. **1880** A. H. SAYCE *Introd. Sci. of Lang.* II. viii. 190 It is more than doubtful whether we can class the Mongols physically with the Turkish-Tartars or the Ugro-Finns.

uguisu (*ugwī·zu*). [Jap.] A bush warbler of delicate olive-green plumage, *Cettia diphone*, native to Japan.

1871 A. B. MITFORD *Tales of Old Japan* I. 37 The *uguisu*, by some enthusiasts called the Japanese nightingale. **1941** N. TAKATUKASA *Jap. Birds* 40 Pride of place among the native songbirds is therefore given to the *uguisu*. **1974** K. REXROTH *New Poems* 33 Maple leaves, an uguisu Sings as if in spring.

uh, *interj.* Add: **b.** *U.S.* Expressing hesitation: = *ER.

1962 J. D. MACDONALD *Only Girl in Game* vi. 85 'Are you cashing cheques?'..The man hesitated. 'Uh...Yes, we are.' **1973** *National Observer* (U.S.) 3 Feb., He wanted most awfully to see the one in the advertisement about being, uh, well, you know. **1977** *N.Y. Rev. Bks.* 4 Aug. 32/4 'Perhaps we should, uh, wait,' I said.

c. = *EH *int.* 3.

1977 'E. TREVOR' *Theta Syndrome* ii. 28 'Was it okay, Doc?' 'Uh?' 'The tube.' 'Oh, sure.' **1978** G. GREENE *Human Factor* v. iii. 272 'Weren't those my very words?' 'Uh,' Mr Barker said.

uh (*ɒ*), repr. the indefinite article in the speech of U.S. Blacks.

1893 H. A. SHANDS *Some Peculiarities of Speech in Mississippi* 65 *Uh*, the common negro form for the indefinite article *a*. This is generally written *er* by dialect writers, but no sound of *r* is ever apparent in the negro pronunciation. **1933** *Publ. Texas Folklore Soc.* XI. 105 Dey's jes' ez good uh fish in de creek ez evah been caught. **1973** *Black World* Oct. 74 Locking up folks lives For stealing less than uh hundred dollars.

uh-huh (*ɒ·hɒ*; see quot. 1982), *adv. colloq.* (orig. *U.S.*). [Imitative.] A spoken affirmative or non-committal response to a question or remark; 'yes', 'oh yes?'

1924 *Dialect Notes* V. 278 *Uh-húh*, yes. **1925** *Ladies' Home Jrnl.* May 22/3 The policeman behind the desk said to Buckbarrow: 'Here's something! A runaway kid.' ..'Uh-huh,' commented Buckbarrow. **1941** E. CARR *Klee Wyck* 111 'Uh huh,' he nodded. **1947** 'N. BLAKE' *Minute for Murder* v. 111 'You ought to go on the films, Blount.' 'Uh-huh?' **1969** D. DALBY in A. Dundes *Mother-Wit* (1973) 139/1 African usage can also explain the frequent use by Americans of the interjections uh-huh, for 'yes', and uh-uh for 'no'. Similar forms, especially for 'yes', occur in scattered parts of the world, but nowhere as frequently and as regularly as in Africa. **1978** J. A. MICHENER *Chesapeake* iii. 123 'You're to..mind your manners. This is your last chance.' 'Uh-huh,' Timothy grunted, staring with contempt at the wretched spot to which he was being taken. **1982** J. C. WELLS *Accents of English* III. vi. 556 There are also the grunts sometimes spelt *uh-huh* and *uh-uh* respectively. The first, 'yes', is phonetically [ˈə̃hə̃, ˈʌ̃hʌ̃, ˈmmm], hence nasal or nasalized; it usually has a rising tone pattern... The second, 'no', is [ˈʔəʔˈʔə, ˈʔʌʔˈʔʌ, ˈʔmʔˈm]..; it is not necessarily nasal, and has an accented final syllable, with an obligatorily falling tone pattern.

uh-uh (*ɒ,ɒ·*; see quot. 1982 in prec.), *adv. colloq.* (chiefly *U.S.*). [Imitative.] A spoken negative response to a question or remark; 'no'.

1924 *Dialect Notes* V. 278 *Ŭh-uh*, negation. **1930** D. HAMMETT *Maltese Falcon* xvi. 194 'Do you know who he is?'..'Uh-uh,' he said, 'but I'd guess he was Captain Jacobi.' **1970** H. WAUGH *Finish me Off* (1971) 133 She shook her head. 'Uh-uh. He's my daddy.' **1977** *Sounds* 9 July 19/1 Uh-*uh*. I thought not.

Uhuru (uhū·rū). Also **uhuru.** [a. Swahili, = freedom.] National independence of an African country, *spec.* Kenya.

1961 *Times* 4 Aug. 11/5 The British base in Kenya will be liquidated, all British troops evacuated, and the police totally Africanized. These are the basic conditions of *uhuru*. **1976** *Drum* (E. Afr. ed.) June 4/2 Kenya became independent in 1963. Much has been done to defend and demonstrate the hard-won uhuru. **1980** *Oxford Diocesan Mag.* Jan. 18/1 Any Christian struggle for *uhuru* in South Africa must involve the church as well as the state. **1982** D. BAGLEY *Windfall* xx. 192 The coming of Uhuru [to Kenya] must have been painful for the [club] membership who had to adapt to a determinedly multiracial society. **1984** *Listener* 24 May 11/1 An entire continent has seemed hell-bent on self-destruction, despite uhuru, despite the bright hopes of the many thousands who died seeking it.

Uigur, *sb.* and *a.* Add: **Uighur** is now the usual form. **A.** *sb.* **1.** (Further examples.)

1966 D. WILSON *Quarter of Mankind* vii. 89 Unlike the Tibetans, Mongols and Uighurs, these are relatively primitive people. **1969** *Listener* 3 July 6/2 There are millions of people living in the border areas, who speak neither Russian nor Chinese. They're Khazaks, Uzbeks, Uighurs, Tartars, many of them still leading nomadic lives, herdsmen born to the saddle. **1977** *Times* 4 July 5/4 The eight to ten million inhabitants of Sinkiang, the majority of whom are Uighurs and Kazakhs.

B. *adj.* (Earlier example.)

1747 *Astley's Gen. Coll. Voy.* IV. II. iv. 457/2 He says, they are the same with the Wigûr, Oygûr, or Jugur Characters.

uillean pipes (i·lyin), *sb. pl.* Also **-ann.** [See UNION PIPES *sb. pl.*] = UNION PIPES *sb. pl.* *Rarely* in *sing.*

The etymological relationship between the two terms is uncertain. This name is now the usual one.

[**1876**: see WOOLLEN *a.* 1 ¶.] **1906** *Grove's Dict. Mus.* (ed. 2) II. 509/1 The later bagpipe, the Uillean or Union pipe, blown with a bellows, became popular in Ireland. **1962** *Times* 16 Nov. 16/1 Ceilidh bands of the venerable Uilleann pipes. **1974** *Irish Democrat* Nov. 2/4 Irish concert in..Acton Town Hall... Tommy McCarthy (Uillean pipes and concertina). **1980** *Observer* 10 Feb. 14/8 The ensemble consists of two fiddles, flute, harp, a single-headed drum called the bodhran and the uillean pipes. **1984** *Listener* 3 May 28/1 Making extensive use of the most beautiful sound on earth, that of uilleann pipes in skilled hands, it was first and foremost a portrait of a contented man.

uintaite (yū,i·ntă,əit). *Geol.* Also **uintahite.** [f. the name of the *Uinta* Mountains, Utah + -ITE[1].] = *GILSONITE.

1888 [see *GILSONITE]. **1904** G. P. MERRILL *Non-Metallic Minerals* xiii. 373 The principal use of uintaite thus far has been in the manufacture of varnishes for ironwork and baking japans. **1951** E. N. TIRATSOO *Petroleum Geol.* xi. 291 The following are the principal bitumens found:—(a) Uintaite.., also called Gilsonite. **1974** *Encycl. Brit. Micropædia* IV. 546/2 *Gilsonite*, also called uintaite, lustrous, jet-black, natural bitumen.., an asphaltite.

‖ **ujamaa** (*ud*ʒ*amā·*). [Swahili, = consanguinity, brotherhood, f. *jamaa* family, a. Arab. *jamā'a* group (of people), community.] The name given by President Nyerere of Tanzania to a kind of socialism he introduced in that country in the 1960s, in which village co-operatives were established based on equality of opportunity and self-help; so *ujamaa village*.

1962 J. K. NYERERE *Ujamaa: Basis of African Socialism* in *Ujamaa: Ess. Socialism* (1968) 12 'Ujamaa', then, or 'Familyhood', describes our socialism. **1962** *Economist* 8 Sept. 892/2 Mr Nyerere's thesis that Ujamaa (familyhood) is the basis of African socialism. **1969** *Reporter* (Nairobi) 13 June 21/1 *Ujamaa* villages will be encouraged, to spread more wealth across the rural areas. **1970** *Drum* (E. Afr. ed.) Feb. 19/2 Tanzania is now well under way with its second Five-Year Development Plan, a £400 million investment programme tailor-made for the strengthening of ujamaa throughout the land. **1971** *Standard* (Dar es Salaam) 7 Apr. 1/8 A sum of 15,422/20 is to be spent by the government on drilling ten boreholes in various villages of Hanang district, including two ujamaa villages. **1979** *New African* Mar. 57/2 Out of Tanzania's total 16 m. population, more than 13 m. are living in about 8,000 *ujamaa* villages. **1983** *N.Y. Times* 15 Aug. C14/6 Most of the cast participate in the theater arts and black studies programs of Ujamaa.

‖ **uji** (*ū*·dʒi). [Jap.] In feudal Japan, a name indicating which ancestral noble family the bearer belonged to; a patriarchal lineage group comprising all those with the same *uji*.

1876 W. E. GRIFFIS *Mikado's Empire* (1877) I. xii. 117 The family name (*uji*) precedes the personal..name. **1896** F. BRINKLEY *Japanese-Eng. Dict.* 1555/1 Although the offshoots from these noble families took various names.., yet these were not, strictly speaking, the family names or *uji* in the now-accepted sense. **1931** G. B. SANSOM *Japan* I. ii. 36 The society consisted of patriarchal units called *uji*, which were communities formed of a number of households of the same ancestry. **1970** J. W. HALL *Japan* iv. 29 Being of the upper class the *uji* possessed surnames and bore titles of respect. **1974** *Encycl. Brit. Micropædia* X. 238/1 The *uji* members..were supported by the labour of common workers, who were organized into subunits of the *uji*... Imperial rule over the various autonomous *uji* remained weak until the adoption of centralized government in the early 8th century.

‖ **ujigami** (*ū*dʒigā·mi). [Jap., f. *uji* *UJI + *kami* good.] In feudal Japan, the ancestral deity of an *uji*; later, the tutelary deity of a particular village or area.

1897 L. HEARN *Gleanings in Buddha-Fields* i. 18 The peasants were going to celebrate their harvest by a dance in the court of the *ujigami*. **1931** G. B. SANSOM *Japan* I. ii. 36 The members of a clan all worshipped a guardian god, the *uji-gami*, or clan god. **1970** J. W. HALL *Japan* iv. 32 The *uji-gami* venerated by members of certain *uji* were human or totemistic progenitors.

ukata, var. *YUKATA.

uke[1] (yūk), colloq. abbrev. of *UKULELE.

[**1915** *N.Y. World* 18 July 2M/4 Those who pretend to know say that the euk did more than anything else to put the lulu in Honolulu.] **1921** *Quill* July 21 The music store of Gino Polluce on Blocker Street was raided by Inspector Bullem but no ukes were captured. **1949** L. FEATHER *Inside Be-Bop* i. 7, I fooled around with the uke. **1960** N. HILLIARD *Maori Girl* 133 A big grey hair. It looks just like a uke-string, it's that big. **1976** W. GOLDMAN *Magic* III. xiv. 227, I won't sing no more 'Cause I ain't got my uke.

‖ **uke**[2] (*ū*·ke). [Jap., f. *ukeru* to receive, be passive, defend.] In Judo, the passive partner, the one who is acted upon.

1956 [see *REAP *v.*[1] 2 e]. **1961** *New Statesman* 22 Sept. 402/2 The thrower's body is turned facing the same way as the Uke's... He gets both feet inside the Uke's. **1972** *Judo Illustrated* Sept. 48/2 Tori and uke should be friends and know each other's attitudes well. **1984** *Coaching Award Scheme* (Brit. Judo Assoc.) 6/2 If nage-no-Kata is mastered it vastly widens tori's repertoire, but just as vital, it will eliminate uke's fears of falling—right or left side.

ukeke (*ūkēi·kēi*). [a. Hawaiian *'ūkēkē*.] A Hawaiian stringed instrument consisting of a strip of wood with two or three strings that are played with the fingers and mouth.

1891 W. D. ALEXANDER *Brief Hist. Hawaiian People* xiv. 91 The *ukeke* was a strip of flexible wood or bamboo, mounted with two or three strings of *olona* or of cocoanut fiber. **1970** *Western Folklore* XXIX. 239 The guitar was introduced [into Polynesia]..in 1879 by Portuguese immigrants, the only native stringed instrument being the two- or three-stringed *ukeke*, which was never played with a slider. **1980** *New Grove Dict. Mus.* XIX. 323/2 There is no string instrument native to Hawaii other than the *ukeke*, a musical bow.

ukelele, var. *UKULELE.

‖ **ukemi** (*ū*·kemi). [Jap., f. *uke* *UKE[2] + *mi* body.] In Judo, the art of falling safely.

[**1942** C. YERKOW *Mod. Judo* ii. 26 *Ukemi* is the Japanese word and means 'to fall away'. The aim is to break the fall *before* the body reaches the mat or ground, so that no jar or shock is felt. Thus the equivalent for 'ukemi' might be *break*-falling.] **1956** K. TOMIKI *Judo* iii. 54 It is essential to learn the art of falling. This is called *ukemi* (breakfall). **1969** G. R. GLEESON *Anatomy of Judo* iv. 66 In spite of the much vaunted effectiveness of traditional ukemi..very few indeed considered they were capable of taking the falls in the last two sets of nage-no-kata. **1984** *Coaching Award Scheme* (Brit. Judo Assoc.) 29/2 No ukemi is asked as such, but in the first section, the candidate is required to act as Uke and Tori.

‖ **ukiyo-e** (*ūkī*yoyēi·). Also **ukiyo-we, -ye,** and without hyphen. [Jap., f. *ukiyo* fleeting world (f. *uku* to float, go by fleetingly + *yo* world) + *e* picture.] A Japanese art-form consisting of wood-block prints or paintings of scenes from everyday life simply treated; a picture belonging to this art-form. Usu. *attrib.*

1879 *Trans. Asiatic Soc. Japan* VII. 358 Its founder is still celebrated as the author of the *Ukiyo-we* or popular style. **1898** L. HEARN *Gleanings in Buddha-Fields* v. 115 The Ukiyo-yé artist drew actualities, but not repellent or meaningless actualities... He looked for dominant laws..for the order of the beautiful as it was and is. **1915** *Dial* LIX. 375/1 In the forty years or thereabout since the color prints by the Ukiyoe masters first came to the attention of art lovers..the circle of their ardent admirers has steadily widened. **1955** *N.Y. Times* 24 Apr. II-1. 9/1 Japanese tend to see things flatly. This is..most noticeable in the ukiyoe prints. **1957** *Encycl. Brit.* XII. 966/2

Ukiyo-e grew to be almost exclusively the art of the populace of Edo. **1971** *Times Lit. Suppl.* 20 Aug. 997/3 The 'Pictures of the Passing World', the *ukiyo-e*, which from the late seventeenth century constituted the latest and most inventive phase of the Popular School. **1983** *Sunday Tel.* (Colour Suppl.) 26 June 31/2 The tradition of the *Ukiyo-E* print, which had been bought by a Japanese public uninfluenced by Western work, was effectively dead by the 1880s.

ukkers, ukky, varr. *UCKERS, *UCKY.

Ukrainian, *a.* (Earlier example.)

1804 M. WILMOT *Jrnl.* 12 Aug. in Londonderry & Hyde *Russian Jrnls.* (1934) I. 124 His dress a jacket lin'd with Ukrainian sheeps' skin.

ukulele (yūkəlēⁱ·li). Also **ukelele.** [a. Hawaiian *'ukulele*, f. *'uku* flea + *lele* jumping: see quot. 1957.] A small four-stringed Hawaiian guitar that is a development of a Portuguese instrument introduced to the island *c* 1879.

1896 *Hawaiian* Feb.–Mar. 789 Then comes the twang of the *ukelele*, the soft, melodious cadence of the hula song. **1900** *Century Mag.* June 164/2 Kolomono..holds the ukulele, a stringed instrument which may or may not be indigenous to the island. **1913** R. BROOKE *Coll. Poems* (1918) 28 Somewhere an eukaleli thrills and cries. **1919** WODEHOUSE *Damsel in Distress* vi. 93 You see the handsome sophomore from Yale sitting beside her on the porch playing the ukalele. **1932** D. L. SAYERS *Have his Carcase* xii. 146 Campers..brought gramophones or concertinas or ukeleles. **1950** 'D. DIVINE' *King of Fassarai* xviii. 144 Queer the notions you get about South Sea islands,..all..hula-hula skirts..and ukeleles. **1957** *Amer. Speech* XXXII. 309 The machete was heard one day by the vice-chamberlain of King Kalakaua's court, who.. asked to be taught to play it... This vice-chamberlain was a British army officer named Edward Purvis; but the Hawaiians..called him *ukulele* because his lively playing and antics and his small build suggested a leaping flea. The new instrument became a great success,..and someone started calling them *ukuleles.* **1978** L. THOMAS *Ormerod's Landing* iv. 67 The simple boy produced a dramatic strumming chord on the ukelele.

ulalu, var. ULULU in Dict. and Suppl.

ulcerogenic (ʌlsĕro,dʒe·nik), *a. Med.* [f. ULCER + -O- + *-GENIC.] = ULCERATIVE *a.* I.

1959 *Amer. Jrnl. Digestive Dis.* IV. 903 (*heading*) Ulcerogenic drugs. **1971** *Nature* 15 Oct. 498/1 These results strengthen the hypothesis that nicotine sensitizes the duodenum to the ulcerogenic property of acid flowing from the stomach.

ule, var. *HULE.

‖ **ulendo** (ule·ndo). [Nyanja.] In central Africa: a trek, a safari.

1921 *United Free Church Miss. Rec.* June 189/1 The settlements near the missions may not be so interesting to visit as those one sees on ulendo or trek in the more backward districts. **1927** *Other Lands* Oct. 14/2 Two months on ulendo through Nyasaland would be an ideal holiday. **1971** *Countryman* Autumn 88 A month-long *ulendo* on foot into the western side of the Luangwa Valley in the wet season was one of the moments of my life. **1979** C. ALLEN *Tales from Dark Continent* vi. 79 Touring through the district, a process..known as a safari in East Africa, as *ulendo* in Central Africa and as 'going to bush' or 'going on trek' in West Africa.

uliginose, *a.* **2.** (Example.)

1967 V. NABOKOV *Speak, Memory* vi. 138 Pretty Cordigera, a gemlike moth, buzzed all over its uliginose food plant.

ulli, var. *HULE.

'ullo (ʌlo·), *int.* Also **ullo.** Colloq. or joc. pronunc. of *HULLO *int.*

1895 A. W. PINERO *Second Mrs. Tanqueray* III. 112 'Ullo, 'ullo! Whisky and potass! **1955** M. ALLINGHAM *Beckoning Lady* ii. 31 'Ullo, now what? **1968** P. DICKINSON *Skin Deep* iii. 36 Ullo, ullo! The other fellah caught in the nest, eh? **1980** *Daily Mail* 17 Jan. 4/1 [*Cartoon: policeman speaking*] 'Ullo, 'ullo, 'ullo..and where do you think *you're* going?

-ulose (-iŭlōᵘz), *suffix*². *Biochem.* [f. LÆV)ULOSE.] Used (in place of -OSE²) to form the systematic names of ketoses from the names of the corresponding aldoses, esp. ketoses having the carbonyl group at the second carbon atom; as *hexulose*, *RIBULOSE, *SEDOHEPTULOSE.

ulotrichous, *a.* Add: Hence **ulo·trichy,** woolly-hairedness.

1924 A. C. HADDON *Races of Man* (ed. 2) i. 5 *Ulotrichy*, or woolly hair. **1936** [see *CYMOTRICHY].

‖ **ulpan** (ulpa·n). Pl. **ulpanim** (-i·m). [mod. Heb. *ulpān.*] An intensive course in the Hebrew language, orig. for immigrants to the modern state of Israel; a centre providing such a course; also in extended use.

1950 *Israel Govt. Yearbk.* 119/1 The intensive Hebrew language courses (Ulpanim) are attended by lawyers, engineers, teachers, newspapermen..and senior officials. **1973** *Jewish Chron.* 19 Jan. 7/1 The erection of temporary classrooms and religious ulpanim. **1975** *Times* 27 May 2/3 The courses, run by the extramural department of the University of Wales, are a development of the Ulpan method of language teaching. **1977** *New Yorker* 9 May 42/3 You should go downtown ..where they got regular language factories... They even got an *ulpan*, like in Israel.

Ulster. Add: **3.** (Earlier examples.)

1876 L. TROUBRIDGE *Jrnl.* 31 Dec. in J. Hope-Nicholson *Life amongst Troubridges* (1966) 149 [I] came swaggering into Dulcie's bedroom..in an ulster, revealing the immortal check trousers. **1877** TROLLOPE *Amer. Senator* I. xx. 209 She once offered to lay an Ulster to a sealskin jacket.

4. b. Also *Ulsterwoman.*

1971 *Guardian* 18 Sept. 9/6 A lady assures us that she is proud to be an Ulsterwoman. **1981** A. T. Q. STEWART *Edward Carson* v. 87 An Ulsterwoman who was the wife of a high official.

c. *Ulster fry* (see quots.).

1941 J. D. CARR *Case of Constant Suicides* 43 That stuff that looks like slices of boloney is called Ulster Fry. **1978** J. GALWAY *Autobiogr.* (1979) v. 57, I remember eating liver and sausages, roast beef for dinner on Sunday and, of course, an Ulster fry for breakfast—bacon, eggs, potato and soda bread. **1979** *Guardian* 22 June 19/5 The notorious 'Ulster fry'—most things you can think of cooked in a pan.

Ulsterette (earlier example); hence also **U·lsterite** *temporary*, a native or inhabitant of Ulster; **Ulsteriza·tion,** the policy of replacing British security forces in Northern Ireland by Northern Irish ones; also in extended use.

1881 J. W. BUEL *Border Outlaws* 187 Each wearing a long linen ulsterette over a heavy fall coat. **1920** *Glasgow Herald* 11 Nov. 9 The amendment was criticised by a number of members in addition to the Ulsterites. **1921** LLOYD GEORGE *Let.* 24 Nov. (1973) viii. 195 The Irish negotiations have taken a turn for the worse... This time it is the Sinn Feiners. Last week it was the Ulsterites. **1925** J. O'CONNOR *Hist. Ireland 1798–1924* II. xx. 260 Southerners hope and think, and the Ulsterites fear and affect to think that the four counties could not stand by themselves. **1977** *Belfast Tel.* 28 Feb. 1/6 Attempts by the Government to move towards an 'Ulsterisation'..of the security forces. **1979** *An Phoblacht* 29 Sept. 1/3 Given Britain's Ulsterisation policy, then that increased repression is likely to be led by the RUC. **1980** *Times* 15 Sept. 12/3 One could be speaking about the ultimate 'Ulsterization' of the West Bank and Gaza.

ult. (Later examples.)

1935, 1962 [see *PROX.].

ultima (ʌ·ltimă). [L. *ultima* (sc. *syllaba*), fem. of *ultimus* last.] The last syllable of a word.

1913 [see *AFFECTION *sb.* I b]. **1964** *Language* XL. 24 PItW [*sc.* Proto-Italo-Western] posttonic syllables survived into Rhaeto-Romance (1) in paroxytones if the ultima was /a/. **1977** *Amer. Speech 1975* L. 46 It also occurs in unstressed position, for example, in the ultima of *always* and the penult of *annihilated.*

‖ **ultima ratio** (ʌ·ltimă rēⁱ·ʃio). [L.] Final sanction.

1848 MILL *Polit. Econ.* I. II. ix. 375 The Irish cottier.. protects himself by the *ultima ratio* of a defensive civil war. *a* **1902** S. BUTLER *Way of All Flesh* (1903) lxv. 292 There can be no doubt about faith and not reason being the *ultima ratio.* **1910** G. K. CHESTERTON *George Bernard Shaw* 26 The very logic of the Irishman makes him regard war or revolution as extra-logical, an *ultima ratio* which is beyond reason. **1933** *Times Lit. Suppl.* 29 June 436/4 The rod is still the *ultima ratio* of so many teachers. **1969** P. ANDERSON in Cockburn & Blackburn *Student Power* 226 The cultural limitations of bourgeois reason in England were thus politically rational: the *ultima ratio* of the economy founded both.

ultimate, *a.* Add: **2. e.** Applied to the values of a mechanical property corresponding to fracture or breakage of the object concerned.

1858 W. J. M. RANKINE *Man. Appl. Mech.* II. iii. 273 The Ultimate Strength of a solid is the stress required to produce fracture in some specified way. **1869** —— *Man. Machinery & Millwork* 485 The column headed 'Ultimate Extension' gives the ratio of the elongation of the piece, at the instant of breaking, to its original length. **1876** [see *STRESS *sb.* 5 c]. **1922** GLAZEBROOK *Dict. Appl. Physics* I. 156/2 The ultimate stress was in some cases greater when the extension was fast than when it was slow. **1962** READ & WATSON *Introd. Geol.* viii. 446 The properties which control the reactions of rocks are..the values of the elastic limit and the ultimate strength.

f. *ultimate Frisbee* U.S., a form of the game of Frisbee (see *FRISBEE, FRISBEE).

1972 in *Amer. Speech 1974* (1976) XLIX. 301 In *ultimate Frisbee*, two seven-man teams play on a field 60 yards by 40 yards each game lasting 48 minutes. **1980** *Boston Globe* 7 Mar. 32 The game of Ultimate Frisbee now is included on the list of activities accepted for academic credit at prestigious Worcester Polytechnic Institute, one of the nation's top five suppliers of engineers. **1984** *New Yorker* 9 Apr. 36/1 Ultimate Frisbee..bears only a slight resemblance to the mellow..Frisbee played on beaches.

B. *sb.* **1.** *the ultimate*, the best that can be achieved or imagined; the 'last word'; const. *in.*

1958 S. J. PERELMAN *Most of S. J. Perelman* 343 The Central Hotel,..advertised as the ultimate in gaiety and chic. **1971** *Hi-Fi Sound* Feb. 67/1 In the medium-cost category our ideal is a system in which the most attractive 'top' features are recognisable while the ultimate in power handling or 'monitoring' capability has been lost. **1981** P. DAVIES *Edge of Infinity* viii. 168 The ultimate in elaborate organization is the human body and mind. **1981** *Monitor* (McAllen, Texas) 8 July III. 1/1 Shop for your man on the first floor and yourself on the second. They have *the ultimate* in fashions.

ultimatory (ʌltimēⁱ·tŏri), *a.* [f. ULTIMATE *a.* + -ORY².] Having the character of an ultimatum.

1928 E. BLUNDEN *Undertones of War* xi. 127 The company..was..exhausted, and its commander appealed.. for relief in ultimatory terms.

u:ltimobra·nchial, *a. Anat.* [f. L. *ultim-us* last + -O + BRANCHIAL *a.*; so called because the gland develops from the most caudal pharyngeal pouches.] Applied to a gland in the neck which in many lower vertebrates regulates the calcium level in the body but in man and several higher vertebrates is absorbed into the thyroid during embryonic life.

1913 *Gray's Anat.* (ed. 18) 123 A pair of diverticula arise from the fifth branchial pouch and form what are termed the ultimobranchial bodies..: these fuse with the thyroid gland, but probably contribute no true thyreoid tissue. **1968** *New Scientist* 15 Feb. 375/2 The ultimobranchial glands are small and situated in the neck region in birds and reptiles, but are generally absent in mammals. **1976** *Path. Ann.* XI. 222 Parafollicular C cells are not restricted to the thyroid, but can also be found in other structures embryologically connected with the ultimobranchial body, ie, parathyroid IV and thymus IV.

ultion. (Later example.)

1901 G. B. SHAW *Admirable Bashville* III. 323 My mission here Is to wreak ultion for the broken law.

Ultisol (ʌ·ltisǫl). *Soil Sci.* [f. ULTI(MATE *a.* + *-SOL.] A type of highly weathered, leached, red-yellow or red acid soil marked by a clay-rich B horizon and found in warm, humid climates.

1960 *Soil Classification: 7th Approximation* (U.S. Dept. Agric.) xv. 226/1 The Ultisols include most soils that have been called Red-Yellow Podzolic soils, Reddish-Brown Lateritic soils, and Rubrozems in the United States. **1972** J. G. CRUICKSHANK *Soil Geogr.* iv. 132 In their geographical distribution, the Ultisols—otherwise known as red-yellow podsolics or ferruginous soils—merge into grassland soils on their arid margins and into Alfisols and Inceptisols (brown earths) on their cool humid margins (eg, in North America).

ultra, *sb.* **2.** (Earlier example.)

1823 H. MORE *Let.* in R. B. Johnson *Lett. Hannah More* (1925) 201 My friend F. is an ultra of the first magnitude. The poor must not only read English, but ancient history, and even the sciences are to be laid open to them.

ultra, *prep.* Add: **2.** (Earlier example.)

1876 *Law Times Rep.* XXXIV. 697/2 Here she was asked to do something which was no part of her service.. it being something *ultra* her service to go to the kitchen.

3. In the L. phr. *ultra crepidam* (kre·pidæm) [see ULTRA-CREPIDARIAN *a.* and *sb.*], on matters beyond one's knowledge.

1883 G. M. HOPKINS *Let.* 7 Nov. (1956) 332 Pope was the great master of metre of his day,..but..he was nothing *ultra crepidam.* **1895** *Econ. Jrnl.* V. 589 Meeker than the ancient master, he has refrained from breaking out against the criticisms which have been *ultra crepidam.*

ultra-, *prefix.* Add: **1. b.** *ultra-stellar.*

1906 [see *night-web* s.v. *NIGHT *sb.* 13 a].

2. c. With sbs. in this sense, as *ultrafiltration, -microscope*, etc. (qq.v. as main entries).

3. a. *ultra-beloved, -bourgeois, -Catholic, -cautious, -civilized, -clean, -clear, -clerical, -critical, -fast, -feminine, -generous, -German* (earlier example), *-intellectual, -left, -leftist, -militant, -miniature, -miniaturized, -nationalist, -nationalistic, -patriotic, -professional, -pure, -rapid, -rationalist, -respectable, -revolutionary* (later example), *-rightist, -romantic, -sentimental, -smart, -tropical* (earlier example), *-violent.*

1923 D. H. LAWRENCE *Birds, Beasts & Flowers* 183 Everybody so dear, and yourself so ultra-beloved. **1934** G. B. SHAW *On Rocks* Pref. 161 Even Lenin and his colleagues, all ultra-bourgeois (otherwise they would never have so absurdly overestimated the intellectual resources of the proletariat [etc.]). **1830** J. S. MILL *Let.* 20 Aug. in *Victorian Stud.* (1957) I. 143 Three were printers of an ultra-Catholic and royalist journal. **1930** G. B. SHAW *John Bull's Other Island* Pref., in *Works* XI. 71 The ubiquitous sodalities of that new ultra-Catholic Church called Socialism. **1946** *Mind* LV. 141 To suppose that no improvement can be effected by so doing is an ultracautious and conservative position. **1842** E. A. POE in *Graham's Mag.* Feb. 125/2 Hugh has grown to a stalwart man—the type of man *the animal*, as his father is of man the ultra-civilized. **1931** E. BLUNDEN *Votive Tablets* 170 Byron..with his ultra-civilised fraternisation with the gentlemen. **1970** Ultraclean [see *sonication* s.v. *SONICATE *sb.* and *v.*]. **1907** W. JAMES in *Jrnl. Philos., Psychol.*

& Sci. Methods IV. 295 Your letter is so ultraclear. **1938** *New Statesman* 23 July 162/1 Maria-Cristina's ultra-clerical court. **1907** W. JAMES *Pragmatism* v. 192 Common science or corpuscular philosophy, ultra-critical science..or idealistic philosophy, all seem insufficiently true. **1939** *Sun* (Baltimore) 28 Jan. 2/6 Ultrafast American two-engined light bombers, capable of being used for combat after they have dropped their bomb loads. **1977** J. HEDGECOE *Photographer's Handbk.* 41 Ultra-fast films are most useful for working in dim existing-light conditions. **1964** Ultra-feminine [see *SLIMLINE, SLIM-LINE *a.* a]. **1976** *Time* 27 Sept. 94/2 Melba Till Allen owes much of her success at the polls to her charming, ultrafeminine manner. **1903** W. JAMES *Let.* 8 Apr. in R. B. Perry *Thought & Char. W. James* (1935) II. 375 Your review..was as usual ultra-generous, and I thank you for it. **1837** E. A. POE in *Amer. Monthly Mag.* June 566 Young men..alive with an exaggerated sense of honour. They abound in the most ultra German opinions respecting the *duello*. **1927** T. S. ELIOT in *Seneca's Tenne Tragedies* p. xliii, It is assumed..that Shakespeare had acquired some extra- or ultra-intellectual knowledge superior to a philosophy. **1954** KOESTLER *Invisible Writing* xv. 186 He had discovered both its weaknesses as a play, and its ultra-Left tendency. **1977** P. JOHNSON *Enemies of Society* xviii. 240 Ulrika Meinhof.. became the ideological leader of the German Baader-Meinhof gang of ultra-Left terrorists. **1947** *Partisan Rev.* XIV. 398 Gorky's became an 'opposition school' for 'ultra-leftist' Bolsheviks. **1970** *Times* 11 Mar. 6 A new, ultra-militant shopkeepers' organization, known as the 'Tour du Pin Movement'. **1968** *Sci. News* 7 Dec. 573 An ultra-miniature vacuum pump..will be worn directly under the astronaut's chin. **1968** *World Book Sci. Ann. 1968* 215 Using a multitude of ICs, ultraminiaturized, working in parallel, together with functional circuits, he may build electronic devices tomorrow that seem like impossible dreams even today. **1927** H. DOBBS in *Lett. Gertrude Bell* II. 555 It had indeed alarmed the ultra-nationalist party to find a section of the British press averse from the extension of the alliance. **1977** *Time* 27 June 22/3 Some are concerned about Israeli intransigence and afraid that the new ultranationalist Premier-designate, Menachem Begin..may make a settlement all the harder to achieve. **1974** *Daily Colonist* (Victoria, B.C.) 1 Oct. 5/1 The Chinese call the Amur the Black Dragon River, and the Japanese named one of their most ultranationalistic societies after it in the days when they were itching to go to war with Russia. **1801** W. DUPRÉ *Lexicographia-Neologica Gallica* 283 Some ultra-patriotic writers and journalists have likened Bonaparte to the conquerors who plundered Greece. **1926** J. S. HUXLEY *Ess. Pop. Sci.* 159 Proud and ultra-patriotic Gods. **1928** E. O'NEILL *Strange Interlude* IV. 147 In his ultra-professional manner—like an automaton of a doctor. **1961** Ultra-pure [see *CONDUCTIVITY 2]. **1973** *Nature* 13 Apr. 482/3 The preparation, handling containment and analysis of ultrapure materials. **1921** *Sci. Amer.* 9 Apr. 288 Diagram of the multiple prism ring used for the ultra-rapid camera. **1969** *Jane's Freight Containers 1968–69* 445/1 The Boeing has three baggage/cargo compartments. Two, fully containerised for ultra-rapid ground handling. **1907** W. JAMES *Pragmatism* iii. 123 A mere mess of anarchy and confusion..will pragmatism often seem to ultra-rationalist minds in philosophy. **1925** T. DREISER *Amer. Trag.* (1926) II. i. 152 Older and more conservative families who constituted the ultra-respectable element of the city. **1958** *People* 4 May 2/3 The workers have captured even the ultra-respectable Royal Academy this year. **1974** tr. *Wertheim's Evolution & Revolution* i. 47 The ultra-revolutionary Red Guards in turbulent China,..the dissatisfied students in France or the rebellious young Negroes in the United States—all of them are..rebelling against the *status quo*. **1974** *Ann. Reg. 1973* 313 Whereas previously most criticism had accused him of being ultra-leftist, the media now argued that most of his faults were in fact ultra-rightist. **1846** E. A. POE in *Godey's Mag. & Lady's Bk.* Mar. 135/1 As a drama, we find 'Elfrida' faulty in the extreme. Its situations are ultra-romantic, or improbable. **1931** *Times Lit. Suppl.* 14 May 385/1 Young Browning in his period of ultra-romantic chaos. **1926** E. O'NEILL *Great God Brown* Prologue 11 The sound of the school quartet rendering 'Sweet Adeline' with many ultra-sentimental barber-shop quavers. **1904** *N.Y. World Mag.* 1 May 6/1 She is likewise one of the prettiest girls in society, and ultra-smart. **1939** O. LANCASTER *Homes Sweet Homes* 74 Ultra-smart householders who reacted instantaneously to every change of fashion. **1848** E. A. POE *Eureka* 83 On the Melville islands..we find traces of *ultra-tropical* vegetation. **1972** *Daily Colonist* (Victoria, B.C.) 3 Mar. 5/3 Another standard argument for the ultraviolent film is that in real life, violence is not the gunshot flash and quick dissolve, [etc.].

4. a. *ultra-Catholic, -feminist, -leftist, -modernist, -nationalist, -patriot, -rationalist, -rightist, -royalist* (earlier example); also with adj. used as collective sb., as *ultra-feminine, -left, -right.*

1837 J. S. MILL in *Westm. Rev.* XXVIII. 71 The ultra-Catholics with their bigotry and pretensions to priestly domination. **1907** *Cambr. Mod. Hist.* X. xvi. 530 Belgium ..was divided.., as it is still, into two irreconcilable parties, the ultra-Catholics or Clericals, and the Liberals. **1926** W. DE LA MARE *Connoisseur, & Other Stories* 184 Mr. Thripp indeed was no lover of the ultra-feminine. **1979** *Maledicta* III. 17 Even though many ultra-feminists have attacked you.., you still insist that women are superior to men. **1971** *New Scientist* 30 Sept. 740/2 The ultra-left found its voice by protesting against the new Tokyo international airport. **1971** *Time* 11 Oct. 13 As an ultra-leftist, of course, Wu would hardly expect a warm welcome from as revisionist a country as the Soviet Union. **1926** H. W. FOWLER *Mod. Eng. Usage* 709/1 Let us not be ultra-modernists & assume that *whence* & *whither*..are dead & buried. **1936** G. B. SHAW *Millionairess* Pref. 121 Only the stupidest or craziest ultra-Nationalists believe that people corralled within the same political frontier are all exactly alike. **1938** Ultra-patriot [see *samurai-minded* adj. s.v. *SAMURAI 2]. **1976** *Times Lit. Suppl.* 21 May 602/4 De Mille and the ultra-patriots who had been smearing the guild's president..for opposing the introduction of a compulsory loyalty oath. **1909** W. JAMES *Pluralistic Universe* 352 Mr. Bradley, for instance, is an ultra-rationalist. **1977** *Time* 21 Nov. 39/3 She's willingly making herself a stalking horse for the ultra-right. **1976** *New Yorker* 8 Mar. 28/1 In 1973, he [*sc.* Lin Piao] became an 'ultra-rightist'. **1817** *Ann. Reg. 1816* 109/2 The latter were accordingly eminently monarchical in their principles, and were invidiously branded with the title of *ultra-royalists*.

b. *ultra-leftism, -liberalism* (earlier example), *-marathon, -nationalism, -Protestantism* (earlier example), *-radicalism* (later example), *-rationalism, -speed, -supernaturalism, violence.*

1949 *Horizon* May 315 'Trotskyism' (i.e., ultra-leftism). **1835** J. E. ALEXANDER *Sk. Portugal* viii. 192 The priest.. seized a musket by the barrel and hit him a crack with the butt over the head to show his ultra-liberalism, (priests being generally suspected of being anti-constitutional). **1977** J. F. FIXX *Compl. Bk. Running* xxiv. 268 Corbitt knows as much about long races—ultramarathons, runners call them—as anyone alive. **1949** *Horizon* June 398 Men who have grown old in the ways of self-interest and ultranationalism. **1839** J. S. MILL *Let.* 27 Dec. in *Wks.* (1963) XIII. 415 The principal peculiarity of this school is hostility to what they call ultra-Protestantism. **1949** I. DEUTSCHER *Stalin* 405 The Comintern was now indeed engaged in a mock fight. Its ultra-radicalism was so unreal. **1899** W. S. CHURCHILL *Let.* 19 Jan. in R. S. Churchill *Winston S. Churchill* (1969) II. Compan. 1. p. xxvii, Who should draw the line where the maximum of human pain and doubt may be allayed and the minimum of ultra-rationalism be incurred? **1946** *Mind* LV. 109 This ultra-rationalism, as I may call it, put forward by Leibniz. **1963** C. R. COWELL et al. *Inlays, Crowns, & Bridges* ix. 103 Some operators..then undertake most of the rest of the preparation at ultra-speed. **1950** R. A. KNOX *Enthusiasm* i. 2 If I could have been certain of the reader's goodwill, I would have called my tendency 'ultrasupernaturalism'. For that is the real character of the enthusiast; he expects more evident results from the grace of God than we others. **1972** *Times* 6 May 9/2 It will serve as a textbook study of how to photograph acts of ultraviolence without giving offence. **1977** *Time* 24 Jan. 14/2 It was like an orgy of 'ultra-violence' from Stanley Kubrick's *A Clockwork Orange*... About 200 masked youths rioted last week in the industrial town of Mestre near Venice.

ultrabasic (ʌltrăbēⁱ·sik), *a.* (*sb.*) *Petrol.* [f. ULTRA- 3 + BASIC *a.*] Of an igneous rock: having a silica content that is lower than that of the basic rocks (cf. BASIC *a.* 2 b), *spec.* less than 45 per cent by weight. Also as *sb.*

1881 J. W. JUDD *Volcanoes* (ed. 2) 317 There are some rarer materials..that present a most wonderful resemblance to the stony portions of meteorites. These materials we may call 'ultra-basic rocks'. **1885** —— in *Q. Jrnl. Geol. Soc.* XLI. 354 Those rocks which contain an excessive proportion of the bases, especially magnesia and ferrous oxide, and are therefore composed largely of unisilicates, may be conveniently classed as ultra-basic rocks. **1893, 1898** [in Dict. s.v. ULTRA- 3 b]. **1938** R. W. LAWSON tr. *Hevesy & Paneth's Man. Radioactivity* (ed. 2) xxv. 274 Stone meteorites are still more strongly basic than the ultrabasic terrestrial rocks. **1964** *Economic Geol.* LIX. 804 In the low-lying regions the ultrabasics are largely masked by soil. **1970** *Nature* 28 Mar. 1227/2 Most of the volcanics were basic, but during the upper Cretaceous ultrabasics..were intruded. **1977** *Sci. Amer.* Mar. 96/3 In a typical greenstone belt early volcanic activity has produced ultrabasic and basic lavas.

ultracentrifuge (ʌltrăse·ntrifiŭdʒ), *sb.* [f. *ULTRA- 2 c + CENTRIFUGE *sb.*] A very high-speed centrifuge, now usu. generating over 100,000*g*, used to separate small particles and large molecules in a liquid and to determine their sedimentation rate (and hence their size).

1924 SVEDBERG & RINDE in *Jrnl. Amer. Chem. Soc.* XLVI. 2678 In analogy with the naming of the ultra-microscope and ultra-filtration apparatus we propose the name *ultra-centrifuge* for this apparatus. **1939** *Ann. Reg. 1938* 374 The ultracentrifuge showed the presence in plant juices of carbohydrates of well-defined molecular weight. **1948** *New Biol.* V. 33 Tiny air-driven turbine ultra-centrifuges which rotate at speeds up to 5,000 revolutions per second, giving forces equal to half a million times that of gravity, will stratify many of the finest cell inclusions. **1968** *New Scientist* 3 Oct. 6/3 A pilot plant for enriching uranium by the ultracentrifuge method. **1978** H. MCLEAVE *Borderline Case* (1979) xiii. 132 The laboratory..had everything, including..several ultracentrifuges.

Hence **u:ltracentrifugal** (stress variable) *a.*, involving or employing an ultracentrifuge; **u:ltracentrifugally** (stress variable) *adv.*, by means of an ultracentrifuge; with respect to the ultracentrifuge.

1930 *Jrnl. Amer. Chem. Soc.* LII. 2904 The ultracentrifugal study of gelatin solutions has been fruitful in revealing the heterogeneous nature of the sols. **1943** *Jrnl. Exper. Med.* LXXVII. 460 Gratia and Paillot had reported polyhedral bodies and ultracentrifugally purified material from jaundiced blood to be serologically unrelated to ultracentrifugally purified material from the blood of normal silkworms. **1953** *Jrnl. Amer. Chem. Soc.* LXXV. 67/2 Recently they succeeded in preparing an electrophoretically and ultracentrifugally homogeneous mucoprotein. **1962** M. RABAEY in A. Pirie *Lens Metabolism Rel. Cataract* 310 Ultracentrifugal analysis permitted us to classify this protein as a member of the so-called group of β-crystallins. **1977** *Lancet* 8 Oct. 742/1 A typical ultracentrifugal scan and the distribution of IgE in the corresponding fractions is shown.

ultrace·ntrifuge, *v.* [f. prec. sb.: cf. *CENTRIFUGE *v.*] *trans.* To spin in an ultracentrifuge. Chiefly as **ultrace·ntrifuged** *ppl. a.*, **-ce·ntrifuging** *vbl. sb.* Also **u:ltracentrifuga·tion,** the action or process of ultracentrifuging.

1934 *Proc. Soc. Exper. Biol. & Med.* XXXI. 707 (*heading*) Effect of ultracentrifuging on Paramecium. **1936** *Trans. Faraday Soc.* XXXII. 301 In this case again, analogous to those of viscometry and ultracentrifugation, the dilutest solutions yield the clearest result. **1946** *Nature* 5 Oct. 488/2 Virus can be separated by differential ultracentrifuging into fractions with widely different properties. **1947** *Ann. Rev. Microbiol.* I. 364 Ultracentrifuged concentrates of virus. **1971** *Nature* 18 June 447/1 The extract was spun at 25,000g for 20 min to remove large particles before being subjected to ultracentrifugation at 105,000g for 90 min to sediment out the microsomes and membrane fractions. **1974** *Ibid.* 13 Dec. 605/2 The injection of adult mice with ultracentrifuged heterologous γ globulin induces immunological unresponsiveness to a subsequent injection of the globulin. **1977** *Lancet* 8 Oct. 742/1 The distribution of radioactivity in a radiolabelled (^{125}I) myeloma IgE preparation ultracentrifuged under identical conditions.

u:ltraco·ld, *sb.* and *a.* [f. ULTRA- 3 + COLD *a.*, *sb.*] **A.** *sb.* Extreme coldness.

1967 *Britannica Bk. of Year* (U.S.) 804/3 *Ultracold*, excessive coldness especially near absolute zero. **1977** A. HALLAM *Planet Earth* 15/1 The Moon's atmosphere.. provides little protection from the direct heat of the Sun, and little insulation from the ultracold of space.

B. *adj. Nucl. Physics.* Of a neutron: having an energy of the order of 10^{-7} eV or less.

1969 *JETP Lett.* IX. 26 Ultracold neutrons are produced and propagate in accordance with the theoretical expectations. **1978** *Nature* 9 Mar. 127/1 Ultracold neutrons are slow neutrons with velocities of less than 7 m s^{-1}. **1979** *Sci. Amer.* June 106/1 A striking property of ultracold neutrons is their total reflection from solid surfaces.

u:ltracytoche·mistry. *Biol.* [f. *ULTRA (*structural* adj. s.v. *ULTRASTRUCTURE + *cytochemistry* s.v. *CYTO-.] Ultrastructural cytochemistry. So **u:ltracytoche·mical** *a.*; **u:ltracytoche·mically** *adv.*

1963 *Proc. Amer. Assoc. Cancer Res.* IV. 16/1 Ultracytochemical studies of the thymus of birds with myeloblastosis..revealed adenosinetriphosphatase activity. **1965** *Virology* XXV. 162/1 The technique for ultracytochemistry..was proved to be an effective method for investigating intracellularly developing viruses. **1981** *Physiol. Plant Path.* XVIII. 339 (*heading*) Phenolic ultracytochemistry of tobacco cells undergoing the hypersensitive reaction to *Pseudomonas solanacearum*. *Ibid.*, The objective of this study was to ultracytochemically determine if any phenolic deposition and PPO [*sc.* polyphenoloxidase] might be detected. *Ibid.* 343 With the ultracytochemical method, particulate as well as soluble activity can be demonstrated.

ultradian (ʌltrēⁱ·diăn), *a.* [f. ULTRA- + L. *di-ēs* day + -AN.] Designating cycles of physiological activity which recur with a period shorter than one day but longer than one hour. Cf. *CIRCADIAN *a.*

1961 F. HALBERG in *39th Rep. Ross Conf. Pediatric Res.* 15 Observations have been made on frequencies higher than circadian, yet lower than the respiratory or cardiac cycles (ultradian), and frequencies lower than circadian, but higher than the menstrual cycle (infradian). **1978** *Nature* 3 Aug. 490/1 In humans, REM sleep..occurs every 90–110 min and is presumed to be under the control of an underlying ultradian oscillatory mechanism.

ultrafiche (ʌ·ltrăfīʃ). [f. *ULTRA- 2 c + *FICHE.] A microfiche in which the linear reduction of the image size is of the order of 100 or more; documentary material of this kind.

1971 *Collier's 1971 Year Book* 322/1 (*caption*) On one card, over 3,000 pages are reduced to microscopic proportions... The cards, called ultrafiches or microfiches, are magnified in the reader. **1972** *Physics Bull.* Sept. 522/1 Flat sheets of film, known as ultrafiche and measuring 6 in × 4 in can contain more than 3000 pages of normal text. **1972** *Times* 1 Dec. (Suppl.) p. ii/6 Ultrafiches of the photochronic micro image process store up to 4,000 pages on a 4 in by 6 in film. **1975** *New Yorker* 22 Dec. 30/1 They brought out the Bible on an ultrafiche... The whole book on a piece of film two inches square. **1976** P. HARCOURT *Dance for Diplomats* xii. 135 The really vital thing is a bit of ultrafiche—that's some form of microfilm. **1981** JACOBSTEIN & MERSKY *Fund. Legal Res.* (ed. 2) 447 In some instances up to 1700 pages can be placed on a single sheet of ultrafiche.

ultrafi·ltrate. *Biol.* [f. next, after *filtration, filtrate*.] Liquid that has passed through an ultrafilter.

1928 *Biochem. Jrnl.* XXII. 633 There was slightly less inorganic phosphorus in the ultrafiltrate than in either the original or the residual plasma. **1957** G. E. HUTCHINSON *Treat. Limnol.* I. xv. 811 Two determinations of the copper content of ultra filtrates indicate that about 80 per cent of the so-called organic copper is associated with colloidal material. **1977** *Lancet* 18 June 1294/1 Ultrafiltrates of pepsin digests of the mucosa.

u:ltrafiltra·tion. *Biol.* [f. *ULTRA- 2 c + FILTRATION.] The action or process of filtration through a medium sufficiently fine to retain colloidal particles, certain viruses, or large molecules.

1908 *Chem. Abstr.* II. 1155 Ultrafiltration... Filtration of this type is accomplished by forcing under pressure the solutions through colloid membranes such as collodium, glacial acetic acid-collodium and hardened gelatin. **1946** *Nature* 9 Nov. 665/2 The blood pressure reduction cannot have augmented the osmotic pressure by more than.. about 3·2/1000 of the total osmotic pressure. This change is so small that ultra-filtration cannot play any considerable part in the formation of aqueous humor. **1959** *New Scientist* 15 Jan. 135/3 Most marine animals possess some type of ampullary excretory organ... It is probable ..that these organs produce an excretory fluid by a process of ultrafiltration. **1964** [see *GRADOCOL]. **1978** *Sci. Amer.* July 88/2 The pores of an ultrafiltration membrane are on the scale of 10^{-9} meter, or one nanometer; average pore diameters range from less than a nanometer to about 10 nanometers.

So **u·ltrafilter** *sb.*, a medium or membrane used for ultrafiltration; also as *v. trans.*, to subject to ultrafiltration; **ultrafi·lterable** *a.*, capable of passing through an ultrafilter.

1908 *Chem. Abstr.* II. 3183 (*heading*) Porosity of ultra filters. **1911** *Ibid.* V. 2 Ultrafiltration... A discussion of the merits of the Bechhold and Burian ultrafilters and of the author's modifications. **1920** *Biochem. Jrnl.* XIV. 539 The oxygenase remains on the ultrafilter. **1928** *Ibid.* XXII. 633 A large proportion of the inorganic phosphate of the plasma is ultrafilterable through cellophane. **1946** *Physiol. Rev.* XXVI. 586 The first indication that the adrenotrophic factor could be ultrafiltered was presented ..in 1934. **1961** *Lancet* 5 Aug. 284/2 The plasma was ultrafiltered. **1974** *Nature* 8 Nov. 176/1 The haemagglutinating activity in galactose..was found in the retentate and could be concentrated quantitatively and washed free of monosaccharide by ultrafiltration over an XM-50 ultrafilter (Amicon) which nominally retains proteins of molecular weight greater than 50,000. **1976** *Ibid.* 8 Apr. 487/1 The rise in brain tryptophan..correlates..with the fraction of tryptophan which is not protein bound (free or ultrafilterable). **1978** *Ibid.* 2 Mar. 65/2 The supernatant was ultrafiltered twice..to separate the proteins into three fractions with molecular weights..above 50,000, between 10,000 and 50,000 and below 10,000.

ultra-high (*ʊ*ltrăhəi·), *a.* [f. ULTRA- 3 + HIGH *a.*] **1.** *Radio.* Of a radio-frequency: in the range 300 to 3,000 megahertz. Abbrev. UHF s.v. *U 4 a.

1932 *Proc. IRE* XX. 95 Among the significant and comparatively recent developments in electrical engineering is the efficient and dependable production of ultra-high-frequency oscillating circuits. **1935** *Discovery* Sept. 278/2 Special valves are being developed suitable for direct signal amplification at the ultra-high frequencies. **1940** *Jrnl. R. Aeronaut. Soc.* XLIV. 216 Another application of ultra-high frequencies is to provide a system of instrument landing. **1951** *Electronic Engin.* XXIII. 452 The use of ultra high frequencies for communication purposes is a relatively new and rapidly developing branch of radio. **1978** *Dædalus* Spring 212 There is already a good deal of listening in the ultrahigh frequency radio bands.

2. *gen.* Exceedingly high; freq. in attrib. phr. in comb. with following sb.

1936 *Discovery* Mar. 88/1 The G.W.R. and the L.N.E.R. have been even more enterprising in introducing some ultra-high-speed expresses. **1962** F. I. ORDWAY et al. *Basic Astronautics* vii. 327 Ultrahigh-risk equipment. **1966** D. G. BRANDON *Mod. Techniques Metallogr.* iv. 184 Methods for obtaining ultra-high vacua (UHV) are now highly developed. **1972** D. HALBERSTAM *Best & Brightest* 558 At West Point he again had ultrahigh visibility and he impressed everyone. **1977** P. JOHNSON *Enemies of Society* i. 4 The extended family also dissociated procreation from the responsibility to maintain offspring, and so produced ultra-high birthrates. **1981** *Economist* 24 Jan. 49/3 How long can Britain go on protecting its farmers from competition from imported UHT (Ultra-High Temperature, or long-life) milk?

ultralight, *a.* and *sb.* [f. ULTRA- 3 + LIGHT *a.*[1]] **A.** *adj.* (Stress variable.) Extremely lightweight; *spec.* applied to a small, low-speed, inexpensive, usually one-seater aircraft that has a small engine but can also soar and whose fuselage is an open framework without an enclosed cockpit. **B.** *sb.* (Stressed *u·ltralight.*) An ultralight aircraft.

1974 *Soaring* Jan. 44/1 (Advt. heading), Ultralights. **1974** *Flying* Mar. 30/1 Hang gliders have been in the news. .. Sometimes called 'ultralight gliders', they represent the minimum machine capable of controllable sustained flight. **1974** *Nat. Geographic* Dec. 771/2 His ultralight 30-foot canoe was a perfectly balanced sailing machine. **1982** *Sci. Amer.* July 60/1 Only within the past few years has the conjunction of the hang glider and the small engine (Go-Kart or snowmobile) brought the long-sought objective into being as the ultralight airplane. **1982** *N.Y. Times* 22 Aug. I. 1/4 Swarms of these new craft—known to enthusiasts as ultralights—are filling the air. **1983** *Economist* 27 Aug. 47 First on the runway is likely to be Eipper Aircraft of California, the biggest maker of ultralights (almost the same as microlights in Europe).

ultramafic (*ʊ*ltrămæ·fik), *a.* (and *sb.*) *Petrol.* [f. ULTRA- 3 + *MAFIC *a.*] Of an igneous rock: composed chiefly of mafic minerals. Also as *sb.*

1933 R. A. DALY *Igneous Rocks & Depths of the Earth* ii. 31 The more important groups [of igneous rocks] are the granite clan.., the ultramafic clans, and the 'feldspathoidal' clans. *Ibid.* xxii. 565 Each of the ultramafic and ultrabasic species..treated in this chapter has its own unsolved problems. **1948** *Bull. Oregon State Dept. Geol. & Mineral.* XXXIX. 8 The ultramafics include bodies of dunite, pyroxenite, and gabbro which have been extensively altered to hornblendite and serpentine. **1965** G. J. WILLIAMS *Econ. Geol. N.Z.* x. 143/1 The useful non-metallic minerals are more abundant in those ultramafics which have been subjected either to metamorphic or metasomatic changes. **1967** P. J. WYLLIE *Ultramafic & Related Rocks* 1/1 Ultramafic monomineralic rocks composed of the following mafic minerals would certainly be ultrabasic..forsterite..fayalite..hornblende..biotite. **1971** I. G. GASS et al. *Understanding Earth* i. 23/1 Only in the ultramafic rocks..does Al_2O_3 fall to significantly lower values than those quoted.

ultramicro- (*ʊ*ltrăməi·kro), *prefix* and quasi-*adj.* *Chem.* [f. ULTRA- 2 + MICRO- 2 a, *8 b.] Formative element denoting chemical analysis or research which involves very minute quantities (of the order of a few microgrammes or less), as in *ultramicroanalysis*, *-analytical* adj., *-chemistry*, *-chemical* adj. Also used without a hyphen as an independent word.

1937 *Ann. Rev. Biochem.* VI. 90 The methods of capillary colorimetry are necessarily more difficult than the other ultramicro methods which have been discussed. **1940** *Ibid.* IX. 599 Drop analysis.—Ultramicrochemical methods have been advanced..in regard to the number of constituents determinable. **1946** *Chem. Abstr.* XL. 6017 (*heading*) Ultramicroanalysis. III. A method for enriching copper by selective adsorption and for destroying organic matter in the determination of copper. **1946** *Chem. & Engin. News* XXIV. 1195/2 The field which embraces the chemical study of material on this minute scale of operation has been given the name 'ultramicrochemistry' by P. L. Kirk, a pioneer investigator in the field of quantitative chemistry on the microgram scale. **1946** *Nature* 31 Aug. 313/1 (*heading*) Ultra-micro methods in nuclear chemistry. **1962** H. HEATH in A. Pirie *Lens Metabolism Rel. Cataract* 365 Ultra-microanalytical methods have to be used to detect the last traces of ascorbic acid. **1971** *Analytical Biochem.* XLIV. 503 (*heading*) Quantitative ultramicroanalysis of amino acids in the form of their DNS-derivatives. **1973** *Biol. Abstr.* LVI. 1717/1 (*heading*) Ultramicrochemical methods for the analysis of tissues and cells of the inner ear. **1979** MA & RITTNER *Mod. Organic Elemental Analysis* xi. 366 Since it is now possible to carry out organic synthesis at the microgram level, the applications of ultramicro analytical methods become apparent.

ultrami·crofiche. [ULTRA- 3.] = *ULTRA-FICHE.

1967 in WEBSTER Add. **1974** *Encycl. Brit. Macropædia* IX. 569/1 Film has not been used widely as a medium of primary distribution. One example is the Library of American Civilization, a retrospective collection on ultra-microfiche of the full original text of about 20,000 titles.

ultrami·croscope. [f. *ULTRA- 2 c + MICROSCOPE *sb.*, or a back-formation from next.] An optical microscope used to detect particles smaller than a wavelength of light by illuminating them at an angle, so that the light scattered by the particles (Tyndall scattering) can be observed against a dark background.

1906 *Jrnl. R. Microsc. Soc.* 366 The ultramicroscope is adapted to the determination of the identity and purity of oils. **1927** [see *polydispersity* s.v. *POLYDISPERSE *a.*]. **1936** *Discovery* Nov. 347/2 The ultramicroscope, which by specially illuminating fine particles so that they themselves shine with reflected light, makes them perceptible through an ordinary microscope when they would not otherwise be so. **1974** *Sci. Amer.* May 88/2 We examined samples of oil in an ultramicroscope.

Hence **ultramicro·scopy,** the art or practice of using an ultramicroscope.

1906 *Jrnl. R. Microsc. Soc.* 366 (*heading*) Ultramicroscopy of oleosole. **1910** [see *TYNDALL]. **1961** R. D. BAKER *Essential Path.* i. 7 Advances in histochemistry and ultramicroscopy are increasing the scope of pathologic anatomy as an investigative science.

u:ltramicrosco·pic, *a.* Formerly also with hyphen. [f. ULTRA- 2 + MICROSCOPIC *a.*] Of such minute size as to be invisible or indeterminate under the ordinary light microscope; of or pertaining to the use of the ultramicroscope.

1870, 1905 [in Dict. s.v. ULTRA- 2]. **1932** *Nature* 2 Jan. 21/1 Optical ultra-microscopic examination of.. films. **1946** F. SCHNEIDER *Qualitative Organic Microanalysis* iv. 103 An instrument for estimating the refractive index of particles of ultramicroscopic size. **1958** *Times Lit. Suppl.* 17 Jan. 33/2 A description of this extraordinary population of all shapes and sizes from rabbits to ultramicroscopic organisms. **1978** *Nature* 22 June 610/1 Proteolytic enzymes..are emitted through ultramicroscopic pores in the eggshell.

Hence **u:ltramicrosco·pical** *a.*, in the same sense; **u:ltramicrosco·pically** *adv.*

1904 *Jrnl. R. Microsc. Soc.* 711 There is a very disturbing adsorption effect of the glass planes on the ultramicroscopical particles. **1906** *Ibid.* 366 Fats and ethereal oils were treated with chlorides of the metals, and the products of reaction ultramicroscopically studied. **1929** A. S. C. LAWRENCE *Soap Films* v. 88 Microscopically, we see the actual particles; ultramicroscopically, we only see the light diffracted by particles themselves invisible. **1976** *Jrnl. Compar. Path.* LXXXVI. 516 Light and ultramicroscopical features of spontaneous glomerular lipoidosis are described. **1981** *Jrnl. Protozool.* XXVIII. 308 Thin sections of treated cells, examined ultramicroscopically, exhibited vacuolations..and severe mitochondrial damage.

ultrami·crotome. [f. *ULTRA- 2 c + MICROTOME.] A microtome for cutting sections thin enough for electron microscopy (typically about 300 nanometres thick).

1953 *Jrnl. Electron Microsc.* I. 44 (*heading*) A simplified thermal expansion type ultramicrotome. **1966** D. G. BRANDON *Mod. Techniques Metallogr.* 92 A plate glass or diamond knife ultramicrotome has proved to be the most successful method available for producing thin sections of biological specimens for electron microscope examination, and serious attempts have been made to adapt the technique to metallurgical specimens. **1980** *Amer. Jrnl. Tropical Med. & Hygiene* XXIX. 775/1 Ultra-thin sections..were cut with either glass knives or diamond knives on an ultramicrotome.

Hence **ultrami·crotomed** *ppl. a.*, sectioned with an ultramicrotome; **ultramicro·tomy,** the practice or technique of using the ultramicrotome.

1949 *Science* 15 July 66/2 A promising new development in ultramicrotomy is presented. **1976** *Nature* 8 Apr. 513/1 Detailed examinations of a Georgia kaolinite using high resolution electron microscopy of ultramicrotomed sections of the kaolinite mineral revealed not only the expected 7 Å (001) spacing, but also occasional 10 and 14 Å spacings. **1978** *Ibid.* 30 Mar. 433/1 Ultramicrotomy and ion beam thinning of films..have provided greater information on film morphology and composition. **1982** *Electrochimica Acta* XXVII. 245 Electron microscopy.. of stripped anodic films and ultramicrotomed sections of the aluminium substrate and the anodic film have been used to examine directly the general film growth over the macroscopic metal surface.

ultramontane, *sb.* **1. b.** (Earlier examples.)

1829 *Dublin Even. Post* 3 Oct. 3/1 Supposed that the Catholic Clergy in Ireland were *Ultramontanes* of the same class. **1845** J. H. NEWMAN *Ess. Devel. Christian Doctrine* ii. 129 An unbeliever, as Gibbon, assumes one hypothesis, and an Ultra-montane, as Baronius, adopts another. **1865** E. B. PUSEY *Eirenicon* 326 The present Ultramontanes have apparently changed the old Ultramontane doctrine of the inerrancy of the Pope.

ultra-sho·rt, *a.* Also **ultrashort.** [ULTRA-3.] **a.** *Radio.* Applied to radio waves significantly shorter than the usual 'short waves': in mod. use, shorter than 10 metres, corresponding to a frequency greater than 30 MHz (i.e. in the VHF range).

1926 E. V. APPLETON in *Proc. Cambridge Philos. Soc.* XXIII. 155 (*heading*) On the diurnal variation of ultra-short wave wireless transmission. [*Note*] The term 'ultra-short' is here applied to wave-lengths less than the critical band indicated by the magneto-ionic theory (i.e. about 200 meters). It seems desirable, for historical reasons, to retain the term 'short waves' for the broadcasting wave-lengths 200–600 metres. **1935** *Discovery* Sept. 278/1 A difficulty is..the limited range of these ultra-short wave-lengths, as we are dependent upon the direct waves propagated more or less parallel to the earth's surface. **1947** *Nature* 4 Jan. 16/1 The electrical interference from motor-car ignition systems..is a serious factor in the reception of ultra-short waves. **1974** *Radio Engin. & Electronic Physics* Dec. 20 (*heading*) Multiple diffractor amplification of ultrashort waves.

b. *gen.* Extremely short (in length or duration).

1962 R. H. SMYTHE *Anat. Dog Breeding* 29 An ultra-short loin. **1975** *Bio Systems* VII. 45 Accordingly, we may introduce an ultrashort time scale. **1977** *Jrnl. R. Soc. Arts* CXXV. 766/1 The same lasers can be used to generate ultra-short light pulses.

ultrasonic (*ʊ*ltrăsǫ·nik), *a.* [f. ULTRA- 2 + *SONIC *a.*] **1. a.** The more usual synonym of *SUPERSONIC *a.* 1.

1923 *Proc. & Trans. R. Soc. Canada* XVII. III. 145 The wave-lengths of ultra-sonic waves are very convenient for experiment. **1926** *Encycl. Brit.* III. 592/1 The utilisation of ultrasonic waves by Professor Langevin..in connection with deep-sea sounding. **1928** *Observer* 30 Dec. 3/6 This was the first occasion in this country on which the 'ultra-sonic' waves have been shown to an audience. **1938, 1948** [see *HYPERSONIC *a.* 1]. **1957** *New Scientist* 9 May 26/3 Owing to the restricted frequency response of the human ear, those organisms which produce ultra-sonic sounds, as do many insects and bats, for example, have in particular been thought of as 'dumb'. **1976** R. DAWKINS *Selfish Gene* iv. 67 The..song of the humpback whale, with..its frequencies spanning the whole of human hearing from subsonic rumblings to ultrasonic squeaks. **1985** *Sunday Times* 27 Jan. 80/8 An ultrasonic beam passed through liquid generates bubbles which act as a cleansing agent.

b. Employing or operated by sound waves or vibrations having a frequency above the range of human hearing (i.e. greater than 15–20 kHz); used esp. with reference to devices and techniques which make use of the reflected echo of an ultrasound pulse.

1923 *Proc. & Trans. R. Soc. Canada* XVII. III. 142 Two ultra-sonic generators..were placed facing one another, 60 cms. apart, in a large tank of water. **1935** [see *REFLECTOMETER]. **1949** A. R. WEYL *Guided Missiles* 25 Photo-electric, magnetic, acoustic (ultra-sonic) and other methods have been successfully used for proximity fuses. **1961** *Lancet* 30 Sept. 750/1 Ultrasonic methods have been described for the detection of intra-abdominal masses, breast tumours, [etc.]. **1976** *Offshore Platforms & Pipelining* 174/1 Ultrasonic inspection followed the completion of the welds.

2. Designating speeds above that of sound; supersonic. *rare*$^{-1}$.

1942 [see *INFRASONIC *a.* 2].

Hence **ultraso·nically** *adv.*, by means of ultrasound.

1955 *Sci. News Let.* 26 Mar. 206/3 Ultrasonically treated honey..showed no signs of crystallizing. **1968** *Amer. Mineralogist* LIII. 1558 Samples of the ash were cleaned ultrasonically. **1974** *Nature* 2 Aug. 410/2 Electrodeposition in an ultrasonically agitated solution.

ultrasonication (*ɒ*:ltrăsǫnikēi·ʃən). [f. *ULTRA- 2 c + *SONICATION.] = *sonication* s.v. *SONICATE *sb.* and *v.*

1965 *Dissertation Abstr.* XXV. 4366/1 Ultrasonication causes the complete shedding of the embryonic periderm leaving a residual layer of originally basal cells. **1979** *Chem. & Physics of Lipids* XXIV. 257 The solubility of the three steroid hormones..was measured after shaking and ultrasonication.

So **ultraso·nicate** *v. trans.* = *SONICATE *v.*; **ultraso·nicated** *ppl. a.*

1969 *Bot. Mag.* (Tokyo) LXXXII. 162 (*heading*) Electron microscopy of replicas from ultrasonicated *Chara* oosporangial walls. **1974** P. PULIDO in K. Elliott et al. *Trypanosomiasis & Leishmaniasis* (Ciba Symp. No. 20) 280 Lyophilized *T. cruzi* was resuspended in buffer and ultrasonicated. **1980** *Exper. Parasitol.* L. 360/1 Two milliliters of the suspension was ultrasonicated on ice.

ultrasonics (*ɒ*ltrăsǫ·niks), *sb. pl.* [f. *ULTRASONIC *a.*: see -IC 2.] **a.** Ultrasonic waves; ultrasound.

1924 *Ann. Rep. Canadian Nat. Research Council* 23 Ultra Sonics are sound vibrations of a pitch higher than those which are audible. **1931** *Nature* 21 Feb. 284/2 Prof. F. L. Hopwood discussed ultra-sonics or inaudible sounds. **1957** A. C. CLARKE *Deep Range* i. 10 Sub 5 was still close enough to the mother ship for radio to work, but before long he'd have to switch to the ultrasonics. **1960** *New Biol.* XXXI. 32 The bacteria which have been treated by ultrasonics..cannot multiply any more. **1972** R. E. ORNSTEIN *Psychol. of Consciousness* (1975) ii. 19 We normally consider that our senses are the 'windows' to the world... But such a view..is not entirely true, for a primary function of sensory systems taken as a whole is to discard 'irrelevant' information, such as X-rays, infrared radiation, or ultrasonics.

b. The branch of science and technology concerned with the study and use of ultrasonic waves. Const. as *sing.*

1940 [see *ASDIC]. **1959** *Sunday Times* 21 June 3/2 Ultrasonics has..been established for a number of years in submarine detection, underwater signalling, echo-sounding, fish location, flaw detection in metals and in many fields of industrial measurement and control. **1977** *Time* 28 Nov. 56/2 Since the original development of the technique for cardiology in the 1950s, ultrasonics has been used to explore other areas of the body, notably, the developing fetus in the mother's uterus.

ultrasonography (*ɒ*ltrăsonǫ·grăfi). *Med.* [f. ULTRA- (in *ultrasound*) + *SONO- + -GRAPHY.] A technique which makes use of echoes of ultrasound pulses to delineate objects or areas of different density within the body, esp. for diagnostic purposes.

1960 *Arch. Ophthalmol.* LXIV. 180/1 Ultrasonography is an invaluable aid in the diagnosis and management of orbital disease because it can visualize and localize the position of orbital lesions when all other tests are negative. **1967** *New Scientist* 26 Jan. 195/2 Ultrasonography..is capable of detecting pregnancy even before a woman's urine test becomes positive. **1980** *Brit. Med. Jrnl.* 29 Mar. 940/2 Serum luteinising hormone concentrations and serial ovarian ultrasonography are helpful screening procedures.

So **ultraso·nogram**, an image obtained by ultrasonography; **ultraso·nograph**, an apparatus for producing ultrasonograms. Also **ultrasono·grapher**, one who specializes in ultrasonography.

1958 *Arch. Ophthalmol.* LX. 266/2 The ultrasonogram represents a horizontal section, or planigram, through a level of the eye. **1975** *Proc. 2nd European Congr. Ultrasonics in Medicine* 129 Ultrasonographs employed to visualize internal eye structures use focusing systems which concentrate the ultrasonic beam into a small area. **1975** *Daily Tel.* (Colour Suppl.) 7 Feb. 21/1 Now the second generation of ultra-sonographs—some capable of using a computer to 'freeze' the movement of a single heartbeat—are extending the boundaries of medical knowledge. **1979** *Brit. Med. Jrnl.* 13 Oct. 934/2 They are not in conflict with the ultrasonographers' longitudinal data. **1981** *Daily Tel.* 24 Apr. 3/3 Hydrocephalus occurs in about two of every 1,000 babies. With the use of ultrasonograms..doctors can usually detect the condition while the foetus is developing.

ultrasound (*ɒ*·ltrăsaund). [f. *ULTRA- 2 c + SOUND *sb.*[3]] Sound waves or vibrations with frequencies greater than those audible to the human ear, or greater than 20,000 Hz; also, ultrasonic techniques.

1923 *Proc. & Trans. R. Soc. Canada* XVII. III. 143 When the electrical exciting sources were alternating in potential, the tonic trains of ultra-sound so produced—120 pulses per second—could be heard in the stethoscope. **1936** *Jrnl. R. Aeronaut. Soc.* XL. 25 Ultra-sound waves are generated by a quartz oscillator arc propagated through a surrounding liquid medium. **1953** J. Y. COUSTEAU *Silent World* 104 Are porpoises equipped with sonic or ultra-sound apparatus by which their squeaks give them the feel of unseen bottom topography? **1958** *Oxford Mail* 30 June 4/4 Some firms now use ultrasound to detect flaws in metal. **1968** *New Scientist* 16 May 347/1 The moth's sensitivity to ultrasound may have other uses. **1984** *Times* 16 Nov. 12/4 Any woman who is worried about malformations would be subject to a detailed ultrasound scan.

ultrastable (*ɒ*ltrăstēi·b'l), *a.* [f. ULTRA- 3 + STABLE *a.*] Stable against all subsequent disturbances, even those not taken into account in the design of the system. Hence **ultrastabi·lity.**

1952 W. R. ASHBY *Design for Brain* viii. 91 This process is most clearly shown in what I shall call an ultrastable system: one that is absolute and contains step-functions in a sufficiently large number for us to be able to ignore the finiteness of the number. *Ibid.*, The principle of ultrastability will be stated formally: an ultrastable system acts selectively towards the fields of the main variables, rejecting those that lead the representative point to a critical state but retaining those that do not. **1967** R. WHITEHEAD in Wills & Yearsley *Handbk. Management Technol.* 66 Cybernetics seeks to produce an ultra-stable solution between an organism and its environment. *Ibid.*, If self-regulation and ultra-stability are desirable things..then we must be prepared to learn from the systems that exhibit them. **1970** G. ORDISH tr. *R. Chauvin's World of Ants* 203 What do we mean here by the word 'adaptation'? It should mean a series of successive changes of tactics which only stop, as Ashby says, when the system reaches an 'ultrastable' state within the limits set by the physiology of the individuals in question. **1976** *Listener* 24 June 821/4 Such thought..would itself become an historical system—in the modern jargon, an 'ultra-stable' system, one which could take its own corrective action when things went wrong.

u·ltrastru:cture. [f. ULTRA- 2 + STRUCTURE *sb.*] Structure of biological material that is visible only under greater magnification than can be obtained with optical microscopy.

1939 F. O. SCHMITT in *Physiol. Rev.* XIX. 270 The term ultrastructure as used in this review denotes the submicroscopic organization of cellular and tissue components. **1948** *New Biol.* V. 34 Experiments with the centrifuge and micromanipulator show..that organised development can be interfered with by breaking up this ultrastructure, but as we have seen, it often reforms itself after such a breakdown. **1970** *Jrnl. Neurosurg.* XXXII. 142/2 The ultrastructure of the capillaries in human malignant brain tumors has been studied. **1977** J. L. HARPER *Population Biol. Plants* v. 131 A seed that is going to germinate may begin to show marked changes in the ultrastructure of its cells within 30 min of welting.

Hence **ultrastru·ctural** *a.*, of or pertaining to ultrastructure; **ultrastru·cturally** *adv.*, with regard to ultrastructure.

1939 *Physiol. Rev.* XIX. 270 To learn the details of the ultrastructural organization of such systems it is necessary to know the chemical composition and the physical and chemical properties of the molecules which compose the system. **1971** *Nature* 2 Apr. 334/2 Ultrastructurally, as well as by light microscopy, the human parafollicular cells were similar to those of other mammals. **1975** *Ibid.* 7 Aug. 459/3 Ultrastructurally, the size (diameter 600±150 Å), but not the number, of nuclear pores is remarkably constant in all eukaryotic cells. **1977** *Proc. R. Soc. Med.* LXX. 670/2 The anatomical, histological, ultrastructural and physiological aspects of normal peripheral nerves.

Ultrasuede (*ɒ*·ltrăswēid). *U.S.* Also **ultrasuede.** [f. ULTRA- + SUÈDE.] A proprietary name for a synthetic non-woven fabric resembling suede. Also as *sb.*, a garment made of this.

1973 *Official Gaz.* (U.S. Patent Office) 13 Mar. TM 96/2 Spring Mills, Inc., Fort Mill, S.C... *Ultrasuede.* For non-woven suede-like fabrics... First use Nov. 24, 1971. **1974** [see *MAN-MADE *a.*]. **1976** *National Observer* (U.S.) 2 Oct. 16/1 Rich chocolate-brown carpet, white ultrasuede couch, and..two pink ultrasuede armshairs. **1977** *Detroit Free Press* 11 Dec. 22-A/2 She dressed in Von Furstenberg shirtwaists and Halston ultrasuedes. **1981** A. CROSS *Death in Faculty* i. 8 Her suit, ultra-suede, was worn over a turtleneck knit.

ultrathi·n, *a.* Also **ultra-thin.** [f. ULTRA- 3 + THIN *a.*] Extremely thin; *spec.* in *Biol.*, applied to a section cut with an ultramicrotome.

1949 *Science* 15 July 68/2 The new technique provides an inexpensive, practical method for producing ultrathin sections of tissue in almost a routine fashion. **1961** *Technology* Feb. 52/4 Fabrics treated with an ultrathin coating of a polyamide..are said to retain the soft texture of wool, and yet may be washed repeatedly without shrinking. **1962** *Sci. Survey* III. 164 These ultrathin sections are today about 250 times thinner than the conventional sections used in light microscopy. **1969** *New Scientist* 16 Oct. 131/2 The new ultrathin transistor is particularly important for uhf applications. **1976** *Ann. Rev. Microbiol.* XXX. 116 (*caption*) Ultrathin section of cell from a diseased mushroom.

ultraviolation (*ɒ*:ltrăvəiŏlēi.ʃən). *slang.* [Humorous blend of *ULTRAVIOLET *a.* and *sb.* and VIOLATION.] Irradiation with ultraviolet light. So **ultravi·olate** *v. trans.*

1978 *Oxf. Univ. Gaz.* 23 Oct. Suppl. I. 167 (*heading*) Why does yeast die from ultra-violation? **1979** *Amer. Speech* LIV. 119 Ultraviolation. William J. Payne tells us that, when cells are subjected to ultraviolet radiation (for mutagenesis), they are said to have been ultraviolated. Editors..strike the term from papers submitted for publication, but scientists frequently use it in conversation. **1984** *New Scientist* 3 May 46/1 At Stanford University.. medical scientists no longer expose cells to UV light... They prefer to ultraviolate them.

ultra-violet, *a.* Substitute for entry s.v. ULTRA- 1 c:

ultravi·olet, *a.* and *sb.* Also with hyphen. [f. ULTRA- 1 c + VIOLET *sb.*[1]] **A.** *adj.* **1.** Lying beyond the violet end of the visible spectrum: the epithet of electromagnetic radiation (and of the part of the spectrum containing it) which has a wavelength shorter than that of violet light (about 420 nm.) and (in modern use) no shorter than that of the longest X-rays (of the order of 4 to 40 nm.).

1840 [see *LAVENDER *a.* 2]. **1870** J. TYNDALL *Nine Lect. Light* 36 As regards the ultra-violet rays; when they are permitted to fall upon certain substances..they render the substance luminous. **1875, 1887** [in Dict. s.v. ULTRA- 1 c]. **1904** *Sci. Siftings* 12 Mar. 320/2 These ultra-violet rays..are most effective in the treatment of such diseases as tuberculosis of the skin, *i.e.*, lupus. **1928** GALSWORTHY *Swan Song* I. xi. 84 They talk about these ultra-violet rays. Plain sunshine used to be good enough. **1935** *Discovery* Aug. 225/1 Those physical agents which have been found of service in the treatment of various diseases—such agents as ultra-violet and infra-red radiation. **1947** *Sci. News* IV. 43 Ultra-violet light is a strong bleacher. **1955** *Times* 2 July 7/7 Ultra-violet radiation is useful, both to the naked eye and by photography, to determine whether varnish has perished. **1979** T. B. AKRILL et al. *Physics* xviii. 248/1 The mercury vapour spectrum also includes a considerable amount of ultra-violet radiation.

2. a. Involving, producing, or pertaining to ultraviolet radiation or its use; *ultraviolet catastrophe*, an indefinite increase that the Rayleigh–Jeans law predicts should occur in the radiation emitted by a black body at successively shorter wavelengths (where the law in fact becomes invalid).

1922 [see *LAVENDER *a.* 2]. **1934** *Discovery* May 138/1 In the detection of forgery, the deciphering of illegible or faded documents, over-writing and the like..ultra-violet photography is the most useful process to employ. **1935** J. DOUGALL tr. *Born's Atomic Physics* vii. 189 We have here what is called the 'ultra-violet catastrophe'. **1958** *New Biol.* XXVII. 12 The conclusion reached on a chemical basis regarding the presence of lignin has been confirmed using the ultra-violet microscope for spectro-micrographic purposes. **1966** M. JAMMER *Conceptual Devel. Quantum Mech.* i. 17 A situation which was later, following Ehrenfest, referred to as the 'ultraviolet catastrophe'. [*Note*] P. Ehrenfest,..*Annalen der Physik* 36, 91–118 (1911). The fourth chapter of this paper is entitled 'Die Vermeidung der Rayleigh-Jeans-Katastrophe im Ultravioletten', where the term 'ultraviolet catastrophe' appeared for the first time. **1974** *Daily Tel.* 17 Jan. 17/6 An ultra-violet photograph taken from an Aerobee rocket..has revealed the development of a huge ball of hydrogen. **1976** *Progress in Sci. Culture* (E. Majorana Centre) Spring 20 The paradox is the ultraviolet catastrophe of the theory of black-body radiation, which was predicted on the basis of classical statistical mechanics and Maxwell's theory of radiation.

b. Sensitive to ultraviolet radiation.

1940 *Chambers's Techn. Dict.* 875/2 Ultra-violet cell. **1969** *Rev. Sci. Instruments* XL. 311 (*heading*) A secondary standard vacuum ultraviolet detector. **1975** J. TAYLOR *Superminds* iii. 52 At this point the primitive ultra-violet detector was used.

B. *ellipt.* as *sb.* The ultraviolet part of the spectrum; *near, far ultraviolet*, the part close to, or far from, the visible spectrum.

1887 [in Dict. s.v. ULTRA- 1 c]. **1931** *Discovery* Mar. 86/2 The possibility is discussed of extending the study of the spectrum of stars into the regions of the ultra-violet. **1954** *Jrnl. Amer. Chem. Soc.* LXXVI. 3847/1 Samples of barium and calcium titanates were sealed in quartz tubes containing phosphorus pentoxide for 72 hours and then exposed to ultraviolet. **1962** L. S. SASIENI *Optical Dispensing* xiii. 326 In snow glare protection is required against the ultra-violet. **1974** *Nature* 4 Jan. 44/1 At the molecular level, the effects of far-ultraviolet (< 300nm) and near-ultraviolet (300 to 420nm) on biological systems are quite different.

‖ **ulu**[1] (*ū*·l*ū*). Also **oo(d)loo.** [Eskimo.] An Eskimo woman's knife having a crescent-shaped blade.

1864 C. F. HALL *Life with Esquimaux* I. 291 One of the Innuit women slit them down with her oodloo till they did fit. **1940** *Beaver* (Winnipeg) Mar. 24 The women then take their semicircular knives or 'ooloos', and flench the hide from the blubber. **1958** W. WILLETTS *Chinese Art* I. ii. 77 They [*sc.* knives] are especially common in the North-western Eskimo area, where they occur as the 'woman's knife' or *ulu*, mounted in wood or ivory handles. **1964** *Nat. Geogr. Mag.* May 718/2 Some Eskimo women want their favourite ulu to be buried with them. **1972** S. BURNFORD *One Woman's Arctic* (1973) ii. 35 Tabitha.. hacked off some bannock with her round, razor-sharp ooloo.

‖ **ulu**[2] (*ū*·l*ū*). Also **Ulu.** [Malay (*h*)*ulu* head, upper part.] The upstream, interior part of Malaya; the Malayan jungle.

1878 F. MCNAIR *Perak & Malays* xxxv. 424 Futreu surveys will confirm this description of the Ulu—interior, or up-stream. **1936** R. H. BRUCE LOCKHART *Return to Malaya* II. iii. 108 In my time every healthy young man preferred the 'ulu' to the town, not merely because he found the life more attractive in itself, but also because it offered greater chances for promotion. **1963** J. KIRKUP *Tropic Temper* 106 In the ulu or deep jungle country, no Chinese would ever dare to look at a Malay girl. **1977** *Borneo Bull.* 7 May 4/3 The ulu people may now be less willing to flock into a town which can cope only primitively with big numbers of visitors.

ululance (ɒ·liulăns). *rare*⁻¹. [f. as ULULANT *a.*: see -ANCE.] Ululation.

1951 W. FAULKNER *Requiem for Nun* III. 244 At last, the last of silence too: the county's hollow inverted air one resonant boom and ululance of radio.

ululu. Add: Also **ulalu, ul-ul-loo, ululalu.**

1834 *Knickerbocker* IV. 15 Well may they raise the ul-ul-loo. **1889** W. B. YEATS *Wanderings of Oisin* 80, I must away by wood and sea And lift an ulalu forlorn And fling my laughter to the sun. *a* **1955** W. STEVENS *Opus Posthumous* (1957) 26 'Olu' the eunuchs cried. 'Ululalu.'

‖ **ulus** (ū·lūs). Also † **Oolooss.** [Turk.] In Afghanistan, a tribe.

1815 M. ELPHINSTONE *Caubul* II. ii. 159 The name of Oolooss is applied either to a whole tribe, or to one of these independent branches. The word seems to mean a clanish commonwealth. **1902** *East India (N.-W. Frontier) Mahsud-Waziri Operations* 125 in *Parl. Papers* (Cd. 1177) LXXI. 649 In return for the allowances, both Maliks and Levies are expected to serve Government, to control the body of the clansmen, the 'ulus', and to arrange that individual offenders are surrendered for trial. **1953** O. CAROE *Soviet Empire* iii. 35 The Mongol *ulus* or hordes.

ulvöspinel (ɒ:lvospine·l). *Min.* Also **ulvo-.** [ad. Sw. *ulvöspinell* (F. Mogensen 1943, in *Blad för Bergshandt. Vänner* XXVI. 135), f. the name of the *Ulvö* islands, Sweden: see SPINEL.] A mineral of the spinel group, Fe_2TiO_4, frequently found as lamellæ in magnetite.

1947 *Mineral. Abstr.* X. 6 X-ray examination shows two spinel phases with cell edges 8·40 and 8·47Å., close to the values for magnetite (8·37) and ferrous orthotitanate Fe_2TiO_4 or titanspinel (8·50). It is assumed that the ore contains a large amount (100,000 tons) of the latter which is named Ulvöspinel. **1963** D. W. & E. E. HUMPHRIES tr. *Termier's Erosion & Sedimentation* i. 6 The Curie point is 575°C. for pure magnetite and 675°C. for hematite; it alters in the solid solutions of magnetite (Fe_3O_4) and ulvo-spinel. **1970** *Sci. Jrnl.* May 32/3 If the lava lake was sufficiently enriched in titanium dioxide, its base would tend to collect concentrations of ilmenite, ulvospinel and pseudobrookite. **1971** *Nature* 3 Dec. 264/1 The rock contains relatively small amounts of the phases that we have found in other Apollo basalts (nickleliferous iron, troilite ulvöspinel, ilmenite, [etc.]).

ulys (yū·lis). *nonce-wd.* [Coined by W. de la Mare.] An imaginary mountain flower.

1912 W. DE LA MARE *Listeners* 58 The icy hills far off from me With frosty ulys overgrown.

Ulysses (yūli·sīz, yū·lisīz). [See ULYSSEAN *a.*] Used as the type of a traveller or adventurer; occas. also, of a crafty and clever schemer.

1611 CORYAT *Crudities* 160 Famous Sir Iohn Mandeuil our English Vlysses. **1876** GEO. ELIOT *Dan. Der.* II. III. xxii. 68 Klesmer was as versatile and fascinating as a young Ulysses. **1915** J. BUCHAN *Salute to Adventurers* iv. 68, I had been dreaming of foreign parts..and here on a Glasgow stairhead I had found Ulysses himself. **1959** T. H. WHITE *Godstone & Blackymor* 172 That Ulysses, that circumnavigator, that..cheated husband. **1981** P. VANSITTART *Death of Robin Hood* II. vii. 84 Richard [Lionheart]..was invisibly present, a resentful Ulysses marking his victims.

um, *int.* Add: **1.** (Later examples.)

1933 P. MACDONALD *Mystery of Dead Police* viii. 63 'I don't think,' she said, 'that you two know each other.. Mr. Revel—Captain Um-ha'. **1974** C. HAMPTON *Savages* v. 39, I publish, I mean I have had published, a few what we used to call slim volumes of verse, um, poetry, you know.

3. Used to indicate assent.

1913 J. VAIZEY *College Girl* vii. 98 'Shall I tell you?'.. 'Um!' 'Very well, then.' **1964** L. DEIGHTON *Funeral in Berlin* xlii. 271 'You knew I was working for the Israeli Intelligence.' 'Is that who you work for?' I said...'Um,' she said. **1974** N. FREELING *Dressing of Diamond* 49 'Um,' said Vera vaguely... The 'um' was only a symbol.

Hence as *v. intr.*, to make an utterance indicative of hesitation; also as *sb.*

1913 KIPLING *Songs from Books* 74 Sometimes in a smoking-room, through clouds of 'Ers' and 'Ums'. **1962** P. PURSER *Peregrination 22* vii. 35, I ummed in agreement. **1980** J. O'FAOLAIN *No Country for Young Men* iii. 67, I drink to doubt..and stutters and ums and ahs. Beware of the smooth-speaker.

Uma, var. *HUMA.

umangite (yū·mǎŋgəit). *Min.* [ad. G. *umangit* (F. Klockmann 1891, in *Zeitschr. f. Krist. und Min.* XIX. 265), f. the name of Sierra de *Umango* in Argentina: see -ITE¹.] A copper selenide, Cu_3Se_2, found as dark red, violet, or black tetragonal crystals.

1891 *Jrnl. Chem. Soc.* LX. 1435 The author has found three rare minerals of great interest... 2. Umangite.—Associated with eukairite, there occurs a mineral..which proved on analysis to be a variety of copper selenide... The new mineral occurs in finely granular masses. **1978** *Mineral. Abstr.* XXIX. 198/2 Umangite (Cu_3Se_2), berzelianite ($Cu_{2-x}Se$), and athabascaite ($Cu_{5.1}Se_4$) are found in fracture fillings in a carbonatized mafic intrusive rock from Christopher Island, Baker Lake, North West Territories.

Umayyad (uma·yæd), *sb.* and *a.* Also α **Umeiyad;** β **Om(m)ay(y)ad, Omeyyad, Ommiyan,** etc. [f. the name of *Umayya*, ancestor of Muhammad.] **A.** *sb.* A member of a Muslim dynasty which ruled the Empire of the Caliphate from 660 (or 661) to 750 and founded an emirate in Spain in 756. **B.** *adj.* Of or pertaining to this dynasty.

1758 tr. *de Marigny's Hist. Arabians* II. 331 The descendants of Abbas had always refused to acknowledge the Ommiyans as lawful Caliphs. *Ibid.* III. 5 Abdollah.. vented his rage on the tombs of the Ommiyan Caliphs. **1788, 1872** [see *ABBASID, -IDE *a.* and *sb.*]. **1907** D. S. MARGOLIOUTH tr. *Zaydán's Umayyads & 'Abbásids* ii. 63 The pivot on which the policy of the Umayyads turned.. was the recovery of the sovereignty which they had enjoyed in pagan days. *Ibid.*, The Umayyad desire for exclusive sovereignty..led them to commit many acts which blacken their memories. **1924** W. MUIR *Caliphate* (ed. 2) lx. 432 In passing from the Umeiyad to the 'Abbāsid Caliphate, we reach..a fresh departure... The first new feature is, that while the Umeiyad Caliphate.. was co-ordinate with the limits of Islām, this is no longer true of the 'Abbāsid. *Ibid.* 433 Of the Umeiyads, the Syrians remained the last support. **1927** D. HOGARTH in *Lett. Gertrude Bell* I. xiii. 353 Her journey was a pioneer venture which..cast much new light on the history of the Syrian desert frontiers under Roman, Palmyrene, and Ummayad domination. **1950** B. LEWIS *Arabs in Hist.* iv. 68 Umayyad society was based on the domination of the Arabs. *Ibid.* 78 The last of the Umayyads, Marwān II.., was a clever and capable ruler, but he had come too late to save the dynasty. **1975** F. HEER *Charlemagne & his World* viii. 106 In 750 the Ommayyad dynasty was overthrown by the Abbassids, descendants of Mohammed's uncle... One Ommayyad..escaped the massacre of his dynasty in Baghdad..and made his way to Spain, where he became emir. **1981** *Economist* 24 Jan. 43/1 It is taken for granted that present day Damascus and Baghdad automatically oppose each other because of the hostility between the Ummayad and Abbasid dynasties 1,200 years ago.

umbershoot (ɒ·mbəɹʃūt), *nonce-wd.* [Perh. fanciful formation f. UMBRELLA and SHOOT *sb.* Cf. UMBER *sb.*¹] (A word of obscure meaning.)

1922 JOYCE *Ulysses* 189 Crosslegged under an umbrel umbershoot he thrones an Aztec logos.

umbilical, *a.* and *sb.* Add: Also with pronunc. (ɒmbilǝi·kăl). **A.** *adj.* **2.** *umbilical cord.* **c.** *transf.* (*a*) *Astronaut.* A cable or other linking device supplying essential liquid or electrical services; *spec.* the connection between a guided missile and its launching equipment, or that joining a space-walking astronaut to his craft. Similarly *umbilical connection, pipe, tower,* etc.

1948 *Gloss. Guided Missile Terms* (U.S. Research & Development Board) 69 *Umbilical cord*, a cable fitted with a quick disconnect plug at the missile end, through which missile equipment is controlled and tested while missile is still attached to launching equipment or parent plane. **1958** *Times* 1 Mar. 6/3 The 'umbilical pipes' through which liquid oxygen was being pumped to top up its [*sc.* the missile's] fuel tanks. **1959** *Manch. Guardian* 3 Jan. 5 The 'umbilical cord' is a widely detachable cable through which the missile is powered and controlled while still on its 'ivory tower'. **1962** J. GLENN in *Into Orbit* 188 A special countdown started for dropping the umbilical cord which had been providing external power and cooling for the capsule until now. **1963** *Times* 31 May 19/4 The Apollo spacecraft and the three-stage Saturn MK.5 launch vehicle will be erected in the vertical position, together with the umbilical tower on a fabricated base. **1966** *Daily Tel.* 12 Oct. 21/5 The value of the umbilical tether employed on all space walks so far is being questioned. **1967** *Economist* 23 Dec. 1237/2 (*caption*) That grip of gold: umbilical cord linking astronaut to his space ship. **1970** N. ARMSTRONG et al. *First on Moon* vii. 147 We can see the LM umbilical connection quite well.

(*b*) A cable or pipe providing a deep-sea diver with essential electrical and similar supplies. Similarly *umbilical cable, link, pipe,* etc.

1968 *New Scientist* 17 Oct. 127/2 Helium-distorted speech, picked up through the microphone, is transmitted by shielded cables in the umbilical pipe. **1969** *Ibid.* 2 Oct. 11/2 Life support requirements have been provided by way of an umbilical link to a surface station. **1970** R. BARTON *Oceanology Today* v. 123 It submerges and then travels along the seabed on four large hydraulically driven wheels... Power is provided through an umbilical cable. **1975** *Offshore* Sept. 115/2 Moreover, the Globule has..an emergency life support of 96 hours and batteries which can be recharged when in operation through the umbilical cable and the induction cable. **1979** *Daily Tel.* 11 Aug. 2/5 The divers asked for their chamber to be lowered to the sea-bed by means of their life-support umbilical cord. **1981** *Times* 23 May 3/3 He found the umbilical lifeline to the [diving] bell..in tatters.

(*c*) In other misc. uses.

1962 *New Scientist* 9 Aug. 285/1 Steering was done from another car travelling behind and a little to one side of the crash car by an attachment which is referred to by the research workers as an umbilical cord. **1968** *Listener* 15 Aug. 200/1 Tiny portable cameras carried by stalwart chaps loaded with power packs and aerials and umbilical cords like a spaceman operating outside his spaceship. **1977** *Rolling Stone* 30 June 117/3 Their giant electrostatic Model One..was the first electrostatic speaker system I know of that got rid of that cumbersome 'umbilical cord' (the line cord you had to connect to a wall outlet to power its high-voltage polarizing supply).

B. *sb.* **2.** *transf.* and *fig.* (also in sing.).

1936 W. FAULKNER *Absalom, Absalom!* 259 That River which runs not only through the physical land of which it is the geologic umbilical. **1960** *Times* 18 Oct. 13/6 The umbilicals are..expendable power lines which nurture the bird (missile) while it is on the ground and vanish when it takes flight. **1966** J. A. CHAMIER *Cannonball* iv. 34 He picked up a microphone with its spring-spiral umbilical from its recess. **1974** *Petroleum Rev.* XXVIII. 674/3 Underwater vehicles may be..tethered (powered by an umbilical from a surface vehicle) or untethered (free swimming). **1977** *Times* 17 Oct. 14/7 On the humid roof sat batteries of television crews... Wires and umbilicals led..to a generator outside. **1982** D. HART-DAVIS *Level Five* i. 9 Newman held the end of the hot-water umbilical. .. The steady flow began, cold at first, then warm, then hot... He..felt the warm jets course through the [diving] suit.

umbilically, *adv.* Add: Also *transf.* and *fig.*

1936 D. GASCOYNE *Man's Life is this Meat* 19 Umbilically detached, of sorrowful mien and at the same time tricked out in cobwebs,—these vanquished ones, whose breathings propagate violence and fear. **1951** M. MCLUHAN *Mech. Bride* (1967) 51/1 The self-consciousness and uneasiness of those still umbilically attached to such guides. **1963** *Adv. Space Sci. & Technol.* V. 241 Mass transfer (gas, liquid, solid cargo, and personnel) can be done umbilically or by docking. **1979** G. MACDONALD *Camera* xiii. 187/2 After being linked umbilically to the visual arts for half of the last century, the cultural influence of the contemporary photograph is now slight.

umbiliciform, *a.* (Earlier example.)

1867 [see *AFTER-SHAFT].

umbracious, *a.* For *rare*⁻¹ read *rare*, and add later example.

1983 P. LEVI *Flutes of Autumn* i. 12 That scruffy umbracious margin where the town was just beginning to dissolve the countryside in its dark acid.

umbrell. Add: Also **umberell.** (Earlier and later U.S. examples.)

1816 U. BROWN *Jrnl.* 18 Aug. in *Maryland Hist. Mag.* (1916) XI. 151 Never was as wet in my Clothing, through Great Coat umbrell & all. **1910** G. B. MCCUTCHEON *Rose in Ring* I. i. 5 The drizzling rain..blew softly into the faces of the few who enjoyed the luxury of 'umberells'.

umbrella. Add: **5. c.** A screen of fighter aircraft or a curtain of fire put up as protection against enemy aircraft.

1941 [see *air umbrella* s.v. *AIR *sb.*¹ III. 2]. **1942** *Hutchinson's Pict. Hist. War* 18 Mar.–9 June 102 The task of a fleet working in confined waters is a most difficult one. It is eased if long-range fighters or aircraft-carriers..are available to provide a protective umbrella. **1945** *Sun* (Baltimore) 17 Mar. 2-0/5 The giant bombers of the United States 15th Air Force, continuing their methodical pounding of Germany's vital fuel sources, were escorted by an umbrella of fast American fighters. **1946** *Ibid.* 26 June 8/3 Gun crews pumped deadly umbrellas of anti-aircraft fire above the harbor. **1967** *Electronics* 6 Mar. 73 (Advt.), The Army's new Missile Mentors.. now provide major U.S. cities with air defense umbrellas.

6. d. *U.S. Mil. slang.* A parachute.

1933 C. K. STEWART *Speech Amer. Airman* 99 *Umbrella*, parachute. **1980** J. DITTON *Copley's Hunch* II. i. 117 It takes ages to come down on an umbrella... Then you have to get rid of the chute.

8*. Authority, protection, means of defence; controlling or unifying agency. Freq. in phr. *under the umbrella* and var.

1948 *Hansard Commons* 22 Jan. 388 Giving the smaller Powers a chance to evolve, under the umbrella of the Four Powers. **1949** *Ibid.* 24 May 1213, I am not taking away from the occupants of these flats the umbrella which the law intends to give them. **1952** *Sun* (Baltimore) 15 Feb. (B. ed.) 2/6 The big broad budgetary umbrella under which all manner of wasteful sin is committed. **1958** *Economist* 25 Oct. 297/2 The political division of Germany may become once more a looming *casus belli*, to be contested by the conventional forces that can regain their freedom of action under the atomic umbrella. **1962** H. E. BEECHENO *Introd. Business Stud.* xi. 93 What they have done is to bring all the operations, or most of them, under the umbrella of one firm and cut out various 'middlemen' as separate concerns. **1965** *Listener* 1 July 7/2 Europe seems unenthusiastic to exchange the American nuclear umbrella for a French one. **1973** E. BULLINS *Theme is Blackness* 7 Theater workers and institutions that presently work from under the Black umbrella. **1976** *Howard Jrnl.* XV. 1. 55 Many of the former approved schools continue in their former practices, albeit under a new umbrella. **1983** *Listener* 12 May 5/3 The harsh truth is that Sweden is not under the NATO umbrella.

9. a. *umbrella-stand* (earlier example); (sense *5 c) *umbrella barrage*; (sense *8*) *umbrella basis, policy.*

1944 T. H. WISDOM *Triumph over Tunisia* 134 There was..an intense umbrella barrage over the two Tunisian ports. **1961** *Wall St. Jrnl.* 30 Nov. 19/3 Companies with assembly plants, warehouses and other properties in 15 countries, for example, are realizing it is to their advantage to write insurance on an 'umbrella' basis. **1963** *Daily Tel.* 23 Sept. 21/6 Miss Hawkes said that CND's 'umbrella policy' of accepting any group simply because it had pacifist aims, was not acceptable to her. **1837** Dickens *Pickw.* xxxiv. 378 A mahogany umbrella stand.

b. *umbrella fern.*

1882 T. H. Potts *Out in Open* 53 There Cunningham's *Gleichenia* grows marvellously robust, its stiff many-branched fronds rise, tier above tier, in curved fan-like form—which habit, doubtless, induced settlers to call this species the 'umbrella fern'. **1959** A. McLintock *Descr. Atlas N.Z.* 30 Where the forest has been cleared and burnt, the resulting cover is all too often low scrub, rushes, and umbrella fern.

10. umbrella bridge, a temporary raised traffic lane with ramp approaches, in use while building work is conducted below; **umbrella defence,** in Amer. football, an alignment of the backs resembling the shape of an open umbrella; **umbrella field** *Cricket*, an arrangement of close fieldsmen (esp. in the slips) spread in a cordon about the batsman; **umbrella organization,** an organization which represents and protects separate member bodies; **umbrella type,** used (freq., with hyphen, *attrib.*) to denote any structure which resembles (part of) an umbrella in shape.

1962 *Daily Tel.* 14 Sept. 15/7 Supports will be sunk to take a steel 'umbrella' road bridge while the Oxford Circus underground station is rebuilt. **1973** *Times* 24 Mar. 2/8 A temporary 'umbrella' bridge is to be erected in the Charring Cross railway station forecourt. **1950** *Sun* (Baltimore) 23 Oct. 17/3 An umbrella backfield defense.. had no special name. It was..a formation to provide width and depth for pass defence. It has the general shape of an umbrella. **1972** J. Mosedale *Football* x. 145 Owen installed what was called 'the umbrella defense', so-called because the alignment of the defensive backfield resembled an open umbrella. **1954** Miller & Whitington *Gods or Flannelled Fools?* vi. 225 Hassett had been loath to set the..'Umbrella' field..with eight men stationed in an inner arc behind the batsman from backward point to square-leg. **1963** *Courier-Mail* (Brisbane) 21 Nov. 17/1 The conversation..consisted of snippets like..'in an umbrella field'. **1950** *Times* 8 May 2/7 The domestic poultry-keepers could also win independence, and it is doubtful whether either group needs an 'umbrella' organization set up at the Ministry of Agriculture. **1983** *Out of Town* Dec. 17/1 They [*sc.* naturalist rectors] showed an equally native disposition to flourish best as part of an amiable, protective institution. Today the BBC has replaced the Church as the umbrella organisation. **1913** *Wireless World* June 210/1 M.V...asks..whether the 'umbrella type' of aerial would be most suitable, or whether the use of another mast, 10 feet high,..would improve matters. **1940** *Chambers's Techn. Dict.* 876/1 *Umbrella-type alternator*.., a vertical-shaft alternator,..in which the field system is overhung and revolves around the stationary armature. **1962** *Daily Tel.* 4 Dec. 15/3 An open market..has been replaced by a modern covered market. It has an attractive umbrella-type roof. **1963** *Guardian* 27 Feb. 5/2 Why on a semisports car should the handbrake be of the 'umbrella' type? **1971** *Jamaican Weekly Gleaner* 17 Nov. 9/1 The promenade..would contain umbrella type shops and stalls to accommodate the present proliferation of peddlers.

11. *attrib.* passing into *adj.* Of words, names, etc.: covering a number of meanings or associated terms; general, catch-all.

1949 G. Ryle *Concept of Mind* vi. 198 The range of higher order acts and attitudes, which are apt to be inadequately covered by the umbrella-title 'self-consciousness'. **1957** *Listener* 8 Aug. 201/1 Cancer is one of the umbrella words. It covers a number of disease conditions. **1974** *Country Life* 5 Dec. 1723/1 The numerous [Ilex] hybrids which are gathered beneath the umbrella name of *I.* × *altaclarensis.* **1977** *Times Lit. Suppl.* 29 Apr. 530/3 Any one of half a dozen umbrella titles would equally well match the variety of the contents of this military miscellany, *War and Society.*

Umbrian. Add: **A.** *sb.* **2.** (Earlier example.)

1854 C. C. J. Bunsen *Christianity & Mankind* III. 91 In Umbrian, the *D* between two vowels passes into a specific *R*, expressed in the national alphabet by a peculiar letter, in Latin by *RS*.

B. *adj.* **2.** (Earlier example.)

1836 *Dublin Rev.* July 443 The continuous efforts of the Umbrian School, even after..the death of Perugino.

Umbro-. Add: *Umbro-Samnite* (earlier example).

1858 *Bibliotheca Sacra* XV. 99 The Latin stands related to all this Umbro-Samnite class of special dialects, as, in Greek, the Ionic to the Doric dialect.

umfaan (u·mfān). *S.Afr.* Also † **oomfaan, umfane.** [Afrikaans, ad. Zulu *umFana* small boy.] A young African boy, esp. one employed in domestic service.

1852 C. Barter *Dorp & Veld* xiv. 213 The Kaffir *umfane* (boy) when he becomes an *indola* (man), shaves his head, and *sews* into the scalp a circular coronet of reeds. **1878** H. A. Roche *On Trek in Transvaal* iii. 39 Your wife..if she be so lucky as to have floors at all, will make..that provoking '*Oomfan*' clean them for her. **1907** P. FitzPatrick *Jock of Bushveld* 194 Jim had fought at 'Sandhlwana, and could tell of an umfaan sent out to herd some cattle within sight of the British camp to draw the troops out raiding. **1932** F. W. Fitzsimons *Snakes* xiv. 173 No! Snakes do not suck milk from cows; but Kafir umfaans and pigs do. **1964** S. Milne *False Witness* xv. 167 'You have a servant on the premises?' 'Yes, an *umfaan.* He is sixteen years old.' **1977** J. McClure *Sunday Hangman* ii. 13 He'd strung himself up on a thorn tree... Some umfaans made a report.

umfundisi (umfu·ndisi, umfundi·zi) *S.Afr.* Also 9 **fundis, umfundis(e; mfundisi.** [a. Nguni *umFundisi, Mfundisi* teacher.] A teacher, a minister, a missionary; also used as a respectful form of address.

1825 W. Shaw *Diary* in C. Sadler *Never Young Man* (1967) 64 The Caffres knew me to be a 'Fundis' (teacher). **1833** S. Kay *Trav. Caffraria* iii. 73 Never have we been safe; but the *Umfundis* shall be our bush. *Ibid.* xii. 317 But if we neglect her, the *Umfundis* (Missionary) will be angry. **1837** F. Owen *Diary* 12 Oct. (1926) 44 We don't know what we have learned this morning, for the Umfundis (teacher) sent us away so soon. **1863** J. S. Dobie *S. Afr. Jrnl.* (1945) 78 Called at a kraal and got enlightened on road to the umfundisi (missionary). **1905** G. Calloway *Sk. Kafir Life* 9 Oh! Mfundisi; I am weak, I cannot work to-day. **1923** *Other Lands* Oct. 19/1 Their dear old *Umfundise* was the Moderator-elect. **1948** A. Paton *Cry, Beloved Country* I. ii. 14, I bring a letter, umfundisi. *Ibid.* iii. 21 They saw his clerical collar, and moved up to make room for the umfundisi. **1973** *Eastern Province Herald* 6 Aug. 6/7 Job's comforters are..the umfundisi and a cheerful scavenger from the municipal rubbish dump.

‖ **Umgangssprache** (u·mgaŋsʃprāχə). [Ger., = colloquial speech.] The vernacular language between standard and dialect speech customarily used as a means of communication within a linguistic community.

1934 Priebsch & Collinson *German Lang.* viii. 350 The schools..are playing a considerable part in removing the *Umgangssprache*..from local influences by basing the language of instruction more strictly upon the literary language. **1961** R. E. Keller *German Dialects* i. 8 Wherever the ideal of the standard has led to the abandonment of the native dialect a third form arises between the two: the *Umgangssprache.* **1976** *Amer. Speech 1973* XLVIII. 215 We assume that the Swiss immigrants on their arrival in Wisconsin used Swiss German as their 'Umgangssprache' and had at least some knowledge of standard German.

Umklapp (u·mklæp). *Physics.* Also **umklapp.** [tr. G. *umklappprozess* (R. Peierls 1929, in *Ann. d. Physik* III. 1073), f. *umklappen* to turn down or over.] Used *attrib.* to designate interactions in a crystal lattice in which their total momentum is not conserved, and the momentum of the initial excitations is reversed. Abbrev. *U-* or *u-process.*

[**1937** *Physical Rev.* LII. 690/1 These authors neglect transitions due to the '*Umklappprozesse*' of Peierls.] **1951** *Proc. R. Soc.* A. CCVIII. 90 Further measurements made on a corundum crystal confirm the importance of the 'Umklapp' processes, postulated by Peierls, in causing thermal resistance. **1960** J. M. Ziman *Electrons & Phonons* iii. 133 We shall refer to *U*-processes, and, where wave vector is conserved,..*N*-processes. **1974** H. E. Hall *Solid State Physics* viii. 207 An Umklapp process can be thought of as one in which a phonon is Bragg reflected simultaneously with absorbing or emitting another phonon. **1975** H. M. Rosenberg *Solid State* vi. 99 In a continuous medium u-processes cannot occur. **1976** F. Cap tr. *Busch & Schade's Lect. Solid State Physics* 67 At low temperatures the umklapp processes are essential for the establishment of thermal equilibrium in the crystal.

umlaut. Delete ‖ and add: **b.** The diacritical sign (¨) placed over a vowel to indicate that such a change has taken place.

1938 H. Faulk *Common-Sense German Course* 3 The so-called modified vowels are distinguished by the modification mark or umlaut(¨) on the vowel. **1952** M. Pei *Story of Lang.* I. ix. 93 English makes use of no subsidiary characters, save for the apostrophe. Many other languages use accent-marks, umlauts, cedillas. **1970** [see *computer 2 b].

Hence as *v. trans.*, to make such a change; **u·mlauting** *vbl. sb.* and *ppl. a.*

1938 W. F. Twaddell in *Monatschr. f. Deutschen Unterricht* XXX. 177 The *i, i,* or *j* which 'caused' the umlauting was no longer present in MHG. **1943** E. A. Nida *Handbk. Descriptive Linguistics* II. v. 84 What changes the stems so materially is the umlauting produced by the *e* vowel of *-et.* **1976** *Language* LII. 154 Moulton.. assumes that all instances of [a] were umlauted simultaneously to [ä]. **1977** *Ibid.* LIII. 18 As a result of this second rule, back vowels are created on the surface which, unlike all the other back vowels, fail to umlaut in umlauting environments. **1983** *Word* XXXIV. 120 The color of prothetic vowels, unless and until umlauted by the next syllable, was that of the laryngeal which was vocalized.

Umlimo, var. *Mlimo.

‖ **umma** (u·ma) Also **Umma, ummah.** [Arab. *'umma* people, community, nation.] **1.** The Islamic community, founded by Muhammad at Medina, comprising individuals bound to one another by religious ties on a tribal model.

1885 T. P. Hughes *Dict. Islam* 654/2 *Ummah*,..a people, a nation, a sect. The word occurs about forty times in the Qur'an. *Ummatu Ibrāhīm*, the people of Abraham ..*Ummatu Muhammad*, the people of Muhammad. **1919** H. U. W. Stanton *Teaching of Qur'an* vi. 71 The..term.. *ummah*, i.e. religious community. Of this it is said that mankind were originally one *ummah*, and that Allāh, had He pleased, could have kept them so. **1934** *Encycl. Islam* IV. 1015/2 Muhammad frequently discusses the question why mankind consists of a plurality of ummas and has not remained a unit. **1974** B. Lewis in Schacht & Bosworth *Legacy of Islam* (ed. 2) iv. 157 From the start, the Islamic *umma* had a dual character. On the one hand it was a political society..; on the other it was a religious community, founded by a prophet and ruled by his deputy. **1976** *Jrnl. R. Soc. Arts* CXXIV. 613/1 The flexibility of government in Islam goes back—doesn't it?—to the concept of 'Umma' in Islam, the idea that Islam came actually to build up an Umma, a community, rather than impose a doctrine. **1979** *Economist* 5 May 82/2 The governance of the Moslem community, the *umma.*

2. (With capital initial.) The name of a nationalist political party founded in the Sudan in 1945.

1946 *Economist* 9 Mar. 369/1 The western Sudanese.. speak through the Umma or nationalist party, which wants 'a union in which the two partners enjoy internal and external autonomy'. **1946** *Times* 30 Sept. 4/5 The Umma Party of Sudan. **1958** *Listener* 21 Aug. 256/2 Both these ministers are members of the Umma, the Mahdist party. **1965** K. D. D. Henderson *Sudan Republic* vii. 89 There emerges in March 1945 a new political party calling itself the *Umma*, the Community Party with the slogan of 'the Sudan for the Sudanese'. **1979** M. Deeb *Party Politics in Egypt* ii. 40 The defunct Umma Party. **1981** *Economist* 24 Jan. 43/2 There are parochial or communal parties which do not favour or are fearful of, absorption into larger units: these include the Christian Phalange in Lebanon, the Umma in Sudan, the Neo-Destour in Tunisia.

umohoite (yūmohō^u·əit). *Min.* [See quot. 1953.] A hydrous uranyl molybdate, $UO_2MoO_4.4H_2O$, found as monoclinic and orthorhombic, usu. dark-coloured, crystals.

1953 P. F. Kerr in *Rocks & Minerals* XXVIII. 480/1 The name 'umohoite' is given to the mineral by combining the chemical symbols U, Mo, H, and O with the mineral suffix 'ite'. **1980** *Mineral. Abstr.* XXXI. 82/2 Umohoite from Shinkolobwe, Shaba, Zaïre.., is regarded as a magnesian variety: dark green to black, 0·65% Mg, orthorhombic... Two other varieties are described.

ump (ʌmp), *slang* (chiefly *U.S.*). Abbrev. of Umpire *sb.*, *spec.* in baseball. Also **umps** (cf. *-s[2]).

1915 'High Jinks, Jr.' *Choice Slang* v. 74 Every time that Umps starts talking his tongue gets twisted around his eye tooth and he can't see what he's saying. **1942** *Sun* (Baltimore) 30 June 12/4 (*heading*) Durocher fined..for quarrel with umps. **1952** B. Malamud *Natural* 46 I'd've thrown him out too if I was the ump. **1975** *New Yorker* 17 Feb. 25/3 That's why Nick Colosi, National League ump, was a featured attraction at the Auto Show last week. **1979** *Arizona Daily Star* 8 Apr. C1/6 A few bad calls by the rookie umps will no doubt be cause for more outcries from the baseball world.

umpah, var. *oompah. **umph,** var. *oomph.

umpiring, *vbl. sb.* (Earlier example.)

1851 W. Clark in W. Bolland *Cricket Notes* vii. 149 Umpiring is a very arduous and often unthankful office.

umpteen (ʌ·m(p)tīn, ʌm(p)tī·n), *a.* and *sb. colloq.* Also **umteen.** [f. *ump(ty + Teen *sb.*[2] after *thirteen*, etc.] **A.** *adj.* An indefinite number, used in the sense 'many, several', etc. **B.** *sb.* Such a number in the abstract.

1918 *Blackw. Mag.* Mar. 290/1 Men from five continents and umpteen colonies. **1919** *Athenæum* 1 Aug. 695/1 As 'umpty' means 'dash', it is fairly evident that..'umpteen' (or 'umteen'), which means 'any number of times', comes from this source. **1922** *Public Opinion* 11 Jan. 48/2, I entered into it and prepared to drop umteen floors. **1923** [see *umpty *sb.*] **1930** J. B. Priestley *Angel Pavement* ii. 82 I've got umpteen things for him to sign. **1973** K. Giles *File on Death* ii. 39, I leave business to the Estate managers, six of 'em with umpteen clerks and typists. **1976** A. Price *War Game* I. viii. 141 A potential offender against section umpteen of the Road Traffic Act.

Hence **umpteenth** (stress variable) *a.*

1918 E. A. Mackintosh *War, the Liberator* 99 That's the umpteenth Bosche that I've killed today. **1921** *Blackw. Mag.* Apr. 475/1 It was our umteenth breakdown. **1952** M. Laski *Village* v. 89 'I always did say I'd go back if.. she needed me,' she said for the umpteenth time. **1980** P. Harcourt *Tomorrow's Treason* 19 For the umpteenth time I'm telling you. I haven't done anything.

umpty (ʌ·mpti), *sb.* and *a.* [A fanciful verbal repr. of the dash (—) in Morse code. Cf. *iddy-umpty.] **A.** *sb.* An indefinite number, usu. fairly large. (Often used on an analogy with *twenty*, etc.) *Mil. slang.*

1905 *Outing* July 389/2 The undergraduates..whisper to their guests, who stroked the crew in umpty-seven, the year we won by twenty lengths. **1919** W. Lang *Sea Lawyer's Log* 70 Umpteen or 'umpty', it should be explained, is to the Navy what x is to Euclid—the symbol of an unknown or unmentionable quantity. **1923** *Daily Mail* 3 Sept. 1 (Advt.), Umpteen to umpty Fahrenheit, Wolsey keeps you comfy, quite. **1924** Kipling in *Hearst's Internat.* July 16/2 The bettin' was even on my drawin' a V.C. or getting Number Umpty Rest-Camp.

B. *adj.* **1.** An indefinite number of this kind, in adjectival use.

1917 P. MacGill *Gt. Push* xii. 250 When I go back to blighty I'll go to bed and I'll not get up for umpty-eleven months. **1939** J. D. Carr *Black Spectacles* xx. 289 Again, once more, and for the umpty-umph time, we had been hocussed by still *another* of Chesney's ingenious tricks. **1959** W. Faulkner *Mansion* xv. 354 'I never got to Heidelberg,' Charles said. 'All I had was Harvard and Stalag umpty-nine.' **1974** R. L. Simon *Peking Duck* xi. 84 A drill press of umpty-ump kilotons' capacity.

2. *fig.* Of a person, place, or circumstance: unpleasant.

[**1925** Fraser & Gibbons *Soldier & Sailor Words & Phrases* 294 *Umpty iddy, to feel*, so so. Not very well. All upside down.] **1948** M. Allingham *More Work for Undertaker* xiii. 158 Things a bit umpty at home, I rather suspect. **1970** A. Draper *Swansong for Rare Bird* vii. 54, I was worried in case the guvnor was umpty about the night before. The last thing I wanted was a slanging match. **1974** N. Marsh *Black as he's Painted* iii. 76 Very umpty little dump. **1980** C. Fremlin *With no Crying* xix. 117 This rather umpty friend of his.

Hence **u·mptieth** *a.*

1917 'Contact' *Airman's Outings* 216 The umptieth squadron then had the only machines of this type in France. **1984** *Business Rev. Weekly* 25 Feb.–2 Mar. 92/2 Two hours later, after being wiped out for the umptieth time, frustration rears its ugly head.

umquhile, umwhile, *adv.* and *a.* Add: **A.** *adv.* **2.** (Further example.)

1832 F. Trollope *Dom. Manners Amer.* I. vii. 93 A drawing..representing Hebe and the bird, umquhile sacred to Jupiter.

B. *adj.* **a.** (Later examples.)

1934 J. Buchan *Free Fishers* ii. 40 What do you think of your umquhile pupil, Professor? **1976** *Times Lit. Suppl.* 21 May 606/3 The reference to the *ci-devant* Lord Stansgate is notoriously getting shorter and shorter;.. with further reduction en by en the umquhile peer will disappear completely.

‖ **umu** (*u*·m*u*). *N.Z.* [Maori.] = *hangi; also, the food prepared in this oven.

Also used in other Polynesian areas in the Pacific.

1845 E. J. Wakefield *Adventure in N.Z.* I. iv. 75 The tangi had terminated; the *umu* or 'cooking holes' were smoking away for the feast. **1889** S. P. Smith in *Trans. N.Z. Inst.* XXII. 98 An oven of stones, exactly like a Maori *umu* or *hangi*. **1950** *Landfall* IV. 85 The passage describes in detail the well-remembered lighting of the *umu* fires. **1972** M. Shadbolt *Strangers & Journeys* xxii. 474 Mother, grandmother, and children scattered around in vague blue smoke for their *umu*, or earth oven. **1974** T. Heyerdahl *Fatu-Hiva* i. 46 No banquet..can better regale guests than such a juicy, fresh..Polynesian *umu* served without cost..in the open air of a tropical night.

umutsha, var. *moocha.

‖ **Umwelt** (u·mvelt). Pl. **Umwelten.** [Ger., = environment.] The outer world, or reality, as it affects the organisms inhabiting it.

1964 M. King *Heidegger's Philos.* ii. ii. 96 One suggestion which Heidegger undoubtedly intends to convey with *Umwelt* is of a world that is closest and most familiar to man... We shall paraphrase *Umwelt* by 'the first and nearest world'. **1966** J. S. Bruner *Beyond Information Given* (1974) xviii. 318 Modern ethnological conceptions are centrally concerned with representation in such mechanisms as releasers and imprinting, much of it deriving from the originating idea of the *Umwelt* first proposed by von Uexküll. **1971** E. O. Wilson *Insect Societies* (1972) xi. 209/2 The various species of ants are generally similar to the honeybee in their *Umwelten*. **1977** A. Sheridan tr. *J. Lacan's Écrits* i. 4 To break out of the circle of the *Innenwelt* into the *Umwelt* generates the inexhaustible quadrature of the ego's verifications.

umzimbeet (umzimbī·t). *S.Afr.* Also **umzimbit(i).** [a. Xhosa *umSimbithi* ironwood.] A South African tree, *Millettia grandis* or *M. caffra* (family Leguminosæ), which bears clusters of pink or purple flowers, may be evergreen or deciduous, and has very heavy, hard wood; the wood itself.

[**1851** R. Gray *Jrnl. Bishop's Visitation Tour Cape Colony* II. 99 There are several kinds of valuable wood unknown in the colony. Two of the hardest and most useful are called by the natives 'Unizimbeti' and 'Umnebelala'.] **1870** C. Hamilton *Life & Sport S.-E. Afr.* 6 The wheels are made of the famous Natal wood called 'umsimbiti' or ironwood, from its strength and durability. **1902** G. S. Boulger *Wood* ii. 335 Umzimbit..Known also as 'White Ironwood'. **1907** T. R. Sim *Forests & Forest Flora Cape of Good Hope* 203 Umzimbeet is a light-demanding tree. **1950** [see *flat-crown* s.v. *flat *a.* 15]. **1955** W. Gaddis *Recognitions* ii. i. 293 Bird-of-paradise flowers..among the native white pear..and umzimbiti. **1972** Palmer & Pitman *Trees S. Afr.* II. 923 The umzimbeet is a medium to large tree of the coastal forests. *Ibid.* 925 The wood of the umzimbeet is extremely heavy, hard, and strong.

un-[1]. Add: **7. a.** (This and subsequent sections contain examples illustrating the recent formations that are best attested in the O.E.D. files.) *unadult*, *un-African*, *unairworthy*, *unambivalent*, *unarcadian*, *unarchæological*, *un-Australian*, *unbitchy*, *unblameworthy*, *unblasé*, *unbureaucratic*, *un-Byronic*, *uncerebral*, *uncharismatic*, *unchic* (also *absol.*), *un-Chinese*, *unchipper*, *unchoosy*, *un-Christmassy*, *uncomfy*, *uncomposite*, *uncomradely*, *unconscient*, *uncool* [esp. *cool *a.* 4 e] (also *absol.*), *uncooperative*, *uncosy*, *uncranky*, *uncreditworthy*, *uncuddlesome*, *uncuddly*, *un-Darwinian*, *undeducible*, *un-Dickensian*, *undimensional*, *undisastrous*, *undoctrinaire*, *undynamic*, *unecological*, *uneconomic*, *unecstatic*, *unecumenical*, *unegoistic*, *unegotistic*, *unegotistical*, *unerotic*, *unetymological*, *unexotic*, *unfaery* (poet.), *unfeline*, *unfeminist*, *unflamboyant*, *unflashy*, *unfond*, *unfresh*, *unfurtive*, *un-Gaelic*, *ungay*, *ungimmicky*, *unglamorous*, *ungroovy*, *unhep* (also *absol.*), *unhip* (also *absol.*), *unhors(e)y*, *unideological*, *unintrospective*, *unirksome*, *unironic*, *unironical*, *un-Islamic*, *un-Italian*, *un-Jamesian*, *un-Japanese*, *unjingoistic*, *unkeen* (also *absol.*), *unkosher*, *unlegendary*, *unlocal*, *unmarital*, *un-Marxist*, *unmawkish*, *unmeritocratic*, *unneurotic*, *unodoriferous* (earlier example), *unopen*, *unpacifist*, *unphonemic*, *unphon(e)y* (also *absol.*), *unphotogenic*, *unplatonic* (earlier examples), *unpolemical*, *unpolicemanly*, *unpositive* (earlier example), *unprestigious*, *unpriggish*, *unprivate*, *un-Proustian*, *unpugnacious*, *unradiogenic*, *unresilient*, *unrevolutionary*, *unrisky*, *unroadworthy*, *un-Russian*, *unscenic*, *unseductive*, *unselective*, *unsemantic*, *unsexy*, *un-Shelleyan*, *unsnobbish*, *unsorry*, *un-Spanish*, *unspecial*, *unspectacular*, *unstarchy*, *unsterile*, *unstiff*, *unstuffy*, *unsycophantic*, *unsymmetric*, *untendentious*, *untense*, *untherapeutic*, *unthistly*, *unticklish*, *untogether*, *untouristy* (also *absol.*), *untraditional*, *untrendy*, *unurgent*, *unutilitarian*, *unviable*, *un-Victorian*, *unviolent*, *unvisual*, *un-Western*, *un-with-it*, *unworthwhile*, *unyoung*.

1944 A. L. Rowse *Eng. Spirit* xxxiii. 229 There was something curiously unadult, ungrown-up about him. **1976** R. B. Parker *Promised Land* xxiv. 152 She's not a fool, but she's misled, maybe unadult. **1923** D. H. Lawrence *Birds, Beasts & Flowers* 31 An ultimate desperateness, un-African. **1979** *Guardian* 6 Sept. 11/7 Parliament [in Kenya] has just thrown out as 'unAfrican' a Marriage Bill which would have outlawed wife-beating. **1907** *Cornh. Mag.* May 617 For such a motion the machine would be longitudinally unstable, and, shall we say, 'unairworthy'—to coin an analogue for the word 'unseaworthy', as applied to ships. **1979** *Daily Tel.* 8 Nov. 3/5 A fine..has been imposed on Braniff International Airways for conducting hundreds of flights with aircraft that were allegedly in an 'unairworthy condition'. **1977** *Lancet* 2 July 36/2 We felt that obstetricians and midwives should remain unambivalent in their efforts to advise smoking mothers to give up the tobacco habit during pregnancy. **1981** *London Rev. Bks.* 5–18 Feb. 9/1 No such vision is likely to be utterly unambivalent, regret being as intrinsic to the human condition as is hope. **1962** Auden *Dyer's Hand* (1963) 350 If the landscape of New England is unarcadian, so is its social life. **1927** *Observer* 11 Dec. 16/5 The workmanship and designs of ancient Peruvian pottery..seemed, to my unarchaeological eye, so like the Etruscan as to be almost identical. **1965** J. A. Michener *Source* (1966) 890 Swinging his pick with unarchaeological vigor he felt its point bite through a thin layer of semi-rock and then leap forward into nothingness. **1965** G. McInnes *Road to Gundagai* v. 82 The larder was notable for two very un-Australian..gadgets. **1963** S. Farrar *Death in Wrong Bed* x. 148 You're the unbitchiest woman I know. **1973** *Country Life* 18 Oct. 1210/3 This most readable and unbitchy of biographies. **1966** S. Smith *Frog Prince* 78 Touch, where the feeling is most vulnerable, Unblameworthy. **1860** Queen Victoria *Let.* 6 June in R. Fulford *Dearest Child* (1964) 258, I like them extremely, so nice, natural, sensible, quiet and so unblasé. **1977** C. Wood *James Bond, Spy who loved Me* vii. 58 Only the most skilful and unblasé eye would be able to detect an unfamiliar outline. **1970** *Daily Tel.* (Colour Suppl.) 16 Oct. 68/1 The first stages..were remarkably easy, unbureaucratic, and free from the famous red tape. **1936** F. R. Leavis *Revaluation* vii. 270 The aesthete who achieved so un-Byronic and so un-Shelleyan a note in the contemplation of human suffering. **1959** *Times Lit. Suppl.* 23 Jan. 45/4 Even his forged confessions have an unbyronic slime about them. **1934** F. Scott Fitzgerald *Tender is Night* ii. i. 153 His criterion of uncerebral phrase-making was that it was American. **1971** P. Ziegler *King William IV* ii. 29 The Hanoverians had brought their own style of home-spun and singularly uncharismatic monarchy to England. **1960** *Guardian* 6 May 10/6 Anything thicker is totally unchic. **1975** *51 Newsmagazine* 12 Sept. 2/2 You'll read about New York's politics, events, labor, the chic and unchic. **1934** Webster, Un-Chinese. **1974** Dawa Norbu *Red Star over Tibet* xi. 176 Norzin-la occasionally uttered the words '*San fan, shuang jian*' in her un-Chinese accent before the uneducated masses. **1969** J. Fowles *French Lieutenant's Woman* lvii. 403 The evening that saw him so unchipper in his place of refreshment. **1948** M. Allingham *More Work for Undertaker* xiv. 177 The Fuller gang..made quite a name for themselves as being remarkably unchoosy. **1927** D. H. Lawrence *Let.* 12 Dec. (1962) II. 1026 The post is so tiresome here, and altogether one feels so unchristmassy. **1982** *Daily Tel.* 24 Dec. 1/6 The Leader of the Opposition ..was in a most unChristmassy temper. **1888** Kipling *Wee Willie Winkie* (1889) 51 I'm *so* uncomfy! Come and tuck me up. **1925** A. Huxley *Those Barren Leaves* iii. vi. 222 Such an uncomfy house! **1981** 'A. Hall' *Pekin Target* xvii. 181 Put it under my head..no need to be uncomfy. **1920** W. B. Yeats *Michael Robartes & Dancer* 3 It follows from this Latin text..that all beautiful women may Live in uncomposite blessedness. **1968** *Listener* 23 May 654/3 The foreign editor charges his chief with suppressing news vital to Party comrades: his chief has rebuked him to the extent of three columns for 'the anarchy of emotions and passions that give rise to uncomradely and irresponsible actions'. **1929** R. Bridges *Testament of Beauty* iv. 184 Like as in unconscient things whence conscience came, ther is also thru'out conscient life. **1953** W. Burroughs *Junkie* (1972) vi. 61 'It's better to meet alone like this.' His smile was ambiguously sexual. 'Nick is a very un-cool guy.' *Ibid.* xiv. 145, I learned the new hipster vocabulary..'cool', an all-purpose word indicating anything you like or any situation that is not hot with the law. Conversely, anything you don't like is 'uncool'. **1958** G. Lea *Somewhere there's Music* xx. 175 Like, buy my forthcoming book on what's uncool in American education. **1960** [see *daddy-o]. **1961** R. Russell *Sound* v. 101, I dunno, old man, to the average colored person the average gray acts like he's in a sweat most of the time. Hungup. Uncool. **1966** *Punch* 30 Nov. 824 The uncool in the audience clapped heartily. The hip young watched in stony contempt. **1968** *It* 1–14 Nov. 16/1 The whole place [*sc.* Turkey]..is very very uncool. The Turks seem to be ready to turn with a malicious vengeance on young Europeans for the least (often no) provocation. **1979** *Guardian* 5 July 9/3 Those men who keep their cool are dragged, willy nilly, into violence not of their making and are then tarred with the same brush as their uncool brethren. **1934** Webster, Uncooperative. **1944** J. S. Huxley *On Living in Revolution* xi. 114 The neighbours had at first been wholly unco-operative. **1970** *Morning Star* 11 May 4/4 The kindergarten teacher told me that she deals in the same way with unco-operative children. **1893** M. Beerbohm *Let.* 3 Dec. (1964) 82, I thought the streets would be rather un-cosy. **1976** *Times Lit. Suppl.* 26 Mar. 344/2 Paris, where they knew nobody, and where their *collègues de carrière* were, at the outset at least, singularly uncosy. **1935** E. Bowen *House in Paris* ii. vii. 159 Mrs. Michaelis joined two more un-cranky committees. **1941** *Scrutiny* IX. 376 Yet, if it is his weakness to seem unaware of the amount of uncreditworthy coinage he puts into circulation, at least he knows the problems which must beset anyone who writes poetry to-day. **1960** *Times* 29 Feb. 14/7 Cases which the banks would consider uncredit-worthy. **1946** M. Dickens *Happy Prisoner* vii. 122 Elizabeth..began to give Heather more help with the children, which she did on modern hospital lines, uncuddlesome, but extremely efficient. **1963** *Punch* 13 Nov. 693/1 Huge animals all around; gross, uncuddly. **1899** A. H. Japp *Cuckoo* iii. 162, I regard this phrase as in itself very unhappy—and, in fact, un-Darwinian. **1955** H. Hodgkinson *Doubletalk* 43 'The modern theory of mutations' is regarded as un-Darwinian. **1977** D. Cory *Bennett* iv. 121 If he..had evolved from a mere *something*..to a sentient personality, then Bennett in a most un-Darwinian way gave an opposite impression. **1854** Geo. Eliot tr. *Feuerbach's Essence Christianity* viii. 84 The *differentia specifica*..is always in the ordinary sense inexplicable, undeducible. **1952** *Mind* LXI. 267 What is unexpectable—or unpredictable or undeducible. **1948** F. R. Leavis *Great Tradition* iii. 133 The un-Dickensian subtlety—the penetrating analysis. **1982** *Times* 30 June 8/5 Damn un-Dickensian sentimentality. **1940** W. Faulkner *Hamlet* iii. i. 173 She owns no dimension against the lambent and undimensional grass. **1931** V. Sackville-West *All Passion Spent* iii. 218 He managed to be an undisastrous Prime Minister of England during five..difficult years. **1963** *Economist* 28 Dec. 1317/2 Moving..towards undisastrous answers. **1962** *Times* 4 Apr. 6/5 Her sensibility inclines her to an undoctrinaire approach. **1976** *Daily Tel.* 2 Dec. 18 He was sensible, undoctrinaire, moderate—a consensus man. **1960** C. Day Lewis *Burial Day* vii. 140 E., despairing..of so undynamic a lover..married a don. *a* **1974** R. Crossman *Diaries* (1975) I. 33 Their proposals..struck me as extremely undynamic and dull. **1976** N. Postman *Crazy Talk* 7 What is wrong with Orwell's advice is that it is unecological. It places language outside of any context in which it is used. **1909** Webster, Uneconomic. **1953** *Maori Affairs Act* (N.Z.) 71 For the purposes of this Part of the Act, the expression 'uneconomic interest' means a beneficial freehold interest the value of which..does not exceed the sum of twenty-five pounds. **1971** 'G. Black' *Time for Pirates* ii. 40 Vicious, totally uneconomic price cutting. **1858** Queen Victoria *Let.* 28 July in R. Fulford *Dearest Child* (1964) 125 With your..poetical, romantic mind how can you be so unecstatic? **1953** *Essays in Criticism* III. 95 A universe..forever beyond.. tomorrow's unecstatic nights at home. **1970** *Irish Jurist* V. 97, I have given these individuals the benefit of the doubt (if the phrase is not unecumenical). **1934** Webster, Unegoistic. **1942** E. Bowen *Bowen's Court* x. 270 Henry was unegoistic. **1939** D. Cecil *Young Melbourne* i. 25 She cared for few people; but these she loved with a strong, unegotistic affection. **1977** *Gramophone* Aug. 309/3, I should stress that this is a completely unegotistic performance, devoid of any mannerisms or interpretative point-making. **1932** E. Wharton in *Scribner's Mag.* Feb. 113/1 Like many perfectly unegotistical women Catherine Glenn had no subject of conversation except her own affairs. **1930** V. Sackville-West *Edwardians* vi. 275 Morning is bleak and unerotic. **1962** Auden *Dyer's Hand* (1963) 374 The personal relation was completely unerotic. **1876** *Fortn. Rev.* 1 Apr. 568 What is now called the etymological or historical spelling of words, is, in many cases, utterly unetymological and unhistorical. **1960** P. H. Reaney *Orig. Eng. Place-Names* i. 13 A similar unetymological *-ham-* appears in the early forms of Alphamstone, *Alfelmestune* 1086, *Alfhampston* 1318, 'Ælfhelm's farm'. **1934** Webster, Unexotic. **1951** 'J. Wyndham' *Day of Triffids* vi. 116 Her pleasant though unexotic countenance. **1983** *Out of Town* Dec. 16/3 For a haunt of Jungle Jims the BBC at Bristol is distinctly unexotic. **1885** W. B. Yeats in *Dublin Univ. Rev.* May 83/1 Peace, peace, the earth's a-quake. I hear Some barbarous, un-faery thing draw near. **1869** 'Mark Twain' *Innocents Abroad* ix. 87 Their unfeline conduct in eating up all the Tetouan cats aroused a hatred toward them in the breasts of the Moors. **1930** *Times Lit. Suppl.* 4 Sept. 698/3 Rachel, sweet and serene, destined to be the loyal and unfeline friend. **1924** *Blackw. Mag.* Jan. 73/2 It is only my retrograde feminine mind that *will* jump to these unfeminist conclusions. **1980** M. Drabble *Middle*

Ground 2 'I know my limitations,' said Kate. 'That's a very unfeminist remark,' said Hugo provocatively. **1934** Webster, Unflamboyant. **1962** *Times* 12 Nov. 4/1 Camberabero..had a neat and unflamboyant partner in Laforgue. **1981** J. Johnston *Christmas Tree* 6 The older ladies would wear hats, neat, unflamboyant hats. **1967** *Punch* 29 Nov. p. x/2, Unflashy surroundings designed to relax diners... Very good French cooking. **1979** *Guardian* 9 Oct. 19/8 King is a quiet, unflashy man. **1804** D. O'Connell *Let.* 20 Aug. (1972) I. 115, I know you are unfond of that expedition—But if I do go I solemnly pledge myself to you that I will not put my foot in other than Capt. O'Sullivan's own boat. **1964** *Punch* 11 Nov. 732/2 A medley of mutually unfond nationalities. **1980** *Country Life* 3 July 69/4 She was not un-fond of her children, but they stood in the way of..a full working life. **1854** C. M. Yonge *Heartsease* II. iii. iv. 164 In spite of clinging unfresh muslin and shrinking figure, with the unmistakable air of high breeding. **1976** J. Colville *Footprints in Time* xi. 63 The unfresh air of the Central War Room. **1967** J. Porter *Chinks in Curtain* vii. 68, I spun round and assumed as unfurtive an air as possible. **1949** St. J. Ervine *Craigavon* ii. lix. 278 His singularly un-Gaelic name. **1977** A. T. Q. Stewart *Narrow Ground* i. i. 28 The markedly un-Gaelic physical characteristics of the people now living in the Irish-speaking areas of the south and west. **1936** M. Franklin *All that Swagger* xxxv. 273 Laura and Humphrey, both big and ungay, would make a fine buggy pair. **1977** *Logophile* iv. 9/2, I have known some very, very un-gay homosexuals, and many gay heterosexuals. **1963** *Punch* 22 May 753/3 An ungimmicky, original writer. **1977** *Times* 15 Feb. 8/6 It is the goblet that captures me. I love the ungimmicky, familiar and simple lines. **1934** Webster, Unglamorous. **1960** *Times* 15 Jan. 16/4 Mr. David Tindle's unglamorous but sympathetically conceived 'Girl dressing'. **1967** P. Welles *Babyhip* (1968) viii. 73 They're so ungroovy but we have to do it this way. **1944** C. Calloway *Hepsters Dict.*, *Unhep*, not wise to the jive, said of an icky, a Jeff, a square. **1961** L. Hughes *Ask your Mama* xii. 84 *(heading)* Liner notes for the poetically unhep. **1940** *Music Makers* May 37/3 *Unhip*, not wise to the jive, an icky..a square. **1959** C. MacInnes *Absolute Beginners* 131, I climbed in the rear seat, with a fine view of their.. un-hip Jermyn street hair-dos. **1968** *Esquire* Apr. 88/2 There is nothing more detrimental to anything hip than to have it fall into the square hands of the hopelessly unhip. **1974** H. L. Foster *Ribbin', jivin', & playin' Dozens* v. 180 Because the teacher may be unhip and square middle class, he has no idea that the game is being run. **1931** Ld. Wodehouse in 'Marco' *Introd. Polo* p. v, Living in the 'unhorsey' atmosphere of ships. **1955** H. Smith *Horseman through Six Reigns* xvi. 163 A very unhorsy and rather ungainly lady. **1935** N. Mitchison *We have been Warned* iii. 298 Tom refused to admit that there is anything unideological about cafés. **1981** *Daily Tel.* 28 Nov. 12/5 To live as an ordinary, totally unideological private person. **1913** Webster, Unintrospective. **1931** *Times Lit. Suppl.* 26 Mar. 241/2 Such a straightforward lie was possible to so unintrospective an artist as Milton, but not to Donne. **1929** W. Faulkner *Sartoris* iii. viii. 259 And so there was another bond between them, but unirksome. **1938** G. Greene in *Spectator* 4 Nov. 782/2 Miss Richardson's unironic and undetached method. **1979** L. Lerner *Love & Marriage* i. 18 Poetry like this is essentially unironic. **1934** Webster, Unironical. **1942** *Scrutiny* X. 345 Shakespeare's power to present acceptably and movingly the unironical vision (for us given in Miranda and Ferdinand) goes with his power to contemplate the irony at the same time. **1958** O. Caroe *Pathans* i. 13 The un-Islamic flavour of the names of the two sons of Sarbanr..will not escape notice. **1984** *Times* 31 Mar. 4/8 Artificial methods of birth control are unislamic. **1934** Webster, Un-Italian. **1939** *Burlington Mag.* May. 227/2 Both of them have an un-Italian flavour. **1973** P. Evans *Bodyguard Man* iv. 36 The mainlanders.. think of the people from the islands as being un-Italian. **1931** T. H. Pear *Voice & Personality* iv. 35 The workings of the mind are..designated in single stark letters. Their messages are un-Jamesian and un-Proustian, but concise. **1979** F. Kermode *Genesis of Secrecy* iv. 81 This model,..a useful way of thinking about the relation of character to narrative structure..is a very un-Jamesian way. **1934** Webster, Un-Japanese. **1974** *Country Life* 28 Mar. 716/1 The more convincing the make-up, the more disconcerting are un-Japanese physiques. **1962** *Economist* 15 Sept. 990/2 A majority of the unjingoistic people in the country. **1978** Cadogan & Craig *Women & Children First* viii. 185 An honest picture of the practical, unjingoistic attitudes which characterized most RAF personnel. **1966** A. E. Lindop *I start Counting* iv. 67 Grandad was on edge until he'd settled his mice... Aunt Lucy had been a bit unkeen to have them. **1971** *Daily Express* 7 Dec. 1/5 Mrs. Indira Gandhi and Mrs. Golda Meir do make one feel tremendously unkeen on Women's Lib. **1983** Barr & York *Official Sloane Ranger Diary* 4/2 The Keen have to put up with the Unkeen. **1924** G. B. Stern *Tents of Israel* i. 20 For nearly fourteen years she must have been ..cooking for them unkosher food. **1965** *Guardian* 4 Aug. 6/4 The Israeli Embassy..had almost been faced with an Israeli parliamentary inquiry into its allegedly sinful un-kosher way of life. **1939** S. Spender *Still Centre* 97 In you The Caesars tamed by dying, fired again Their lives in the unlegendary sky. **1854** Geo. Eliot tr. *Feuerbach's Essence Christianity* xxii. 215 God sees..all locality in an unlocal manner. **1977** Unlocal [see *un-central *a.*]. **1876** Trollope *Prime Minister* III. iv. 65 That coarse un-marital and yet marital roughness. **1956** M. McCarthy *Sights & Spectacles* p. xii, The notion that abstract reasoning can crush a fact.., a wholly un-Marxist notion, was nonetheless the principle on which most of our criticism was practiced. **1966** *Punch* 13 Apr. 524/2 His exquisite black-and-white short *Shorts*.., with its touching yet unmawkish dwelling upon the hemline. **1966** *Guardian* 10 Oct. 16/8 The present pattern is in many ways strikingly unmeritocratic. **1938** D. Jones *Let.* 15 Feb. in R. Hague *Dai Greatcoat* (1980) ii. 85 The *only* time of day when I feel more or less un-neurotic..is after dinner. **1980** S. Brett *Dead Side of Mike* x. 113 A very balanced and unneurotic personality. **1856** Bagehot in *National Rev.* Oct. 365 If Miss Westbrook had married.. a gentleman, suppose, in the tallow line..her society would have been a gentle relief from unodoriferous pursuits. **1823** R. H. Froude *Let.* 12 Aug. in G. Battiscombe *John Keble* (1963) iv. 75 Keble..is neither positive on this subject nor un-open to conviction on any. **1981** 'A. Cross' *Death in Faculty* v. 47 The few older men..were so stuffy, so unopen to any views but their own. **1916** J. Buchan *Greenmantle* iii. 30 He got a brussels-sprout in the eye, at which..he swore in a very unpacifist style. **1976** S. Hynes *Auden Generation* vii. 195 The book is pacificist propaganda.., but the position he takes is an oddly belligerent and un-pacifist one. **1965** W. S. Allen *Vox Latina* i. 15 Such a complication..is 'unphonemic'. **1974** D. G. Scragg *Hist. Eng. Spelling* iv. 61 Mulcaster.. was frequently forced to compromise his endeavour to be guided by sound because what he calls custom favoured a flagrantly unphonemic spelling. **1959** *News Chron.* 19 Aug. 4/3 'I'm no intellectual,' he says with unphoney modesty. **1973** *Publishers' Weekly* 26 Mar. 61/3 Individually these British lads (and lass) are enjoyably unphony. **1982** *Listener* 11 Feb. 27/3 Let our final words honour the exceptionally unphoney—the first performance of Edward Cowie's..Concerto for orchestra. **1934** C. Lambert *Music Ho!* iv. 244 The present vogue for mechanical realism..is bound to disappear..as the Turneresque steam engine gives way to the unphotogenic electric train. **1977** R. Lacey *Majesty* 14 She is actually quite small.. and..really rather unphotogenic. **1749** J. Cleland *Mem. Woman Pleasure* II. 219 Our acquaintance..innocent, at first..changed nature, and ran into unplatonic lengths. **1866** J. S. Mill in *Edin. Rev.* CXXIII. 340 The answer of the Xenophontic Sokrates to the question of Hippias is very un-Platonic. **1934** Webster, Unpolemical. **1936** *Mind* XLV. 397 Philosophy, according to Jaspers, is 'unpolemical'. **1965** *Times Lit. Suppl.* 25 Nov. 1079/2 There is evidence of good, unpolemical work being done. **1936** 'M. Innes' *Death at President's Lodging* ix. 164 Appleby had brought out his notebook—not without a certain diffidence over the remains of the Dean's elegant and unpolicemanly luncheon. **1980** P. G. Winslow *Counsellor Heart* xi. 148 Manning..sitting quietly at his desk, might have been an accountant. For once his unpolicemanly appearance did not amuse Capricorn. **1865** Mill *Comte* 80 Political economy..he deems unscientific, unpositive, and a mere branch of metaphysics. **1968** 'D. Halliday' *Photogenic Soprano* xiv. 160 All the sordid and unprestigious details of your warm friendship with Kenneth. **1980** *Word* *1979* XXX. 197 Speakers of unprestigious urban dialects were sharply disadvantaged in education and employment. **1933** H. Walpole *Vanessa* iii. 484 She learnt now to be patient, tolerant and unpriggish. **1969** J. Clarke *Foxon's Hole* xxii. 133 Roger really was feeling rebellious, and Gawaine..found it much easier to tell this new, unpriggish Roger..about Mick. **1974** P. Gzowski *Bk. about this Country* 190 I'd..have to become what I call an unprivate person in relation to social issues. **1931** Un-Proustian [see *un-Jamesian* above]. **1981** *Times* 2 Mar. 6/2 Scott Moncrieff's unProustian style. **1934** Webster, Unpugnacious. **1962** Auden *Dyer's Hand* (1963) 305 As creatures go, he [*sc.* the ant-eater] is unpugnacious. **1981** *Daily Tel.* 18 July 28/3 He fought an uncomplicated, unpugnacious and honest campaign. **1968** *Earth & Planetary Sci. Lett.* V. 220/1 Hamilton invoked the melting of Lewisian rocks to account for the unradiogenic leads in the Skye acid rocks. **1949** St. J. Ervine *Craigavon* ii. lxvi. 296 Whose unresilient and unimaginative mind. **1963** *Times* 17 May 7/2 (Advt.), They took an ordinary piece of hard, unresilient plastic and 'let the air in'. **1976** *Gramophone* Mar. 1499/1 The music is steam-rollered into a kind of impersonal uniformity, its lines unphrased, its rhythms unresilient, and the subtle interaction of words and notes quite lost. **1974** Moore & Parry *Twentieth-Cent. Russ. Lit.* ii. 22 His unrevolutionary deed in surrendering to despair and killing himself. **1909** 'Mark Twain' *Is Shakes. Dead?* 13 When an unrisky opportunity offered..and he was feeling good, I showed it to him. **1934** Webster, Unroadworthy. **1955** *Times* 20 Aug. 5/1 The cars hired by correspondents to take them to the frontier were unroadworthy. **1978** N. Freeling *Night Lords* xxxii. 147 Being suddenly told your home is unhygienic and your car unroadworthy. **1919** tr. *Turgenev's Smoke* x. 73 A dandified air utterly un-Russian. **1976** W. Greatorex *Crossover* 159 She took in the flared tartan trousers... He looked so un-Russian she laughed. **1926** G. Frankau *My Unsentimental Journey* xiii. 178 And so away from Denver by this route which seems not so unscenic. **1978** J. Updike *Coup* (1979) vi. 219 His trip down from the Massif, by the unscenic highway. **1791** E. Inchbald *Simple Story* I. ii. 12 Nor upon that event did he think it necessary..to fly the roof of two such unseductive innocent females as Mrs. Horton and her niece. **1937** M. Borden *Black Virgin* ii. 26 He looked at..her neat unseductive clothes and thanked God she was like that. **1934** Webster, Unselective. **1956** *Nature* 10 Mar. 489/1 Government shooters co-operated in recording results of unselective shooting [of red deer] to make these data available. **1968** *Punch* 24 Jan. 105/2 Flat-rate, unselective welfare was possible when the vast majority of people were earning poor wages and when taxation was relatively light. **1933** L. Bloomfield *Language* x. 158 The situations of the several speakers contain some common features, and..the differences between these situations are irrelevant (unsemantic). **1968** *N.Y. Times* 21 Feb. 56/1 His barrage of blithely unsemantic bombast sweeps you up in such phraseology as 'the political hue that blightens the eye' and the oracular 'protocol takes precedence over procedure'. **1959** *News Chron.* 25 Aug. 6/6 He thought the most unsexy things a woman could wear were trousers, boat necklines, and high-heeled shoes. **1973** M. Amis *Rachel Papers* 193, I would get..a kind of hollow pressure at the back of my throat (..not unsexy) which nevertheless I had to lose, and the only way to lose it was to go on coughing. **1936** Un-Shelleyan [see *un-Byronic* above]. **1896** 'M. Rutherford' *Clara Hopgood* iv. 41 His unsnobbish, deferential behaviour.. showed that he understood who they were and that the little house made no difference to him. **1959** G. D. Painter *Proust* I. vii. 100 She was unmusical, non-political, and in the social sense unsnobbish. **1934** Webster, Unsorry. **1963** J. Fowles *Collector* ii. 195 I'm not really sorry. But I'm not absolutely unsorry. **1973** 'G. Butler' *Coffin for Pandora* viii. 163 Alice had departed.., not unsorry, I thought, to get away. **1846** R. Ford *Gatherings from Spain* xxiii. 330 Some muscular.. performer..screams forth his couplets..to the imminent danger of his own trachea, and of all un-Spanish acoustic organs. **1959** H. Thomas *Establishment* 15 Spain, where for four hundred years any idea..which had not existed in the golden sixteenth century has been automatically frowned upon as 'Un-Spanish'. **1970** T. Hilton *Pre-Raphaelites* v. 151 Here is a dull day, unspecial, cold and leaden, and yet a momentous day for those people who are leaving home. **1983** *Woman's Weekly* 8 Jan. 18/1 Anna, feeling very un-special indeed, agreed..that there was no point in looking back. **1926** *Public Opinion* 30 Apr. 433/3 An unspectacular honesty and a certain literary sobriety..mark this novel. **1977** M. V. Brian *Ants* 11 Most of the species have wide temperate Eurasian distributions and, though unspectacular compared with some tropical types, play an important part in terrestrial ecosystems. **1968** R. Marett *Through Back Door* iv. 37 The bluff, nautical and unstarchy Chief Press Censor. **1934** Webster, Unsterile. **1953** R. Lehmann *Echoing Grove* 29 But still the stones seemed rocked, the unsterile mounds, reimpregnated, exhaled dust's fever; a breath, impure, of earthbound anguish. **1977** *Lancet* 26 Mar. 688/1 Unsterile cystoscopes have been in use for years. c **1873** V. Montagu *Let.* in G. Battiscombe *Queen Alexandra* (1969) ix. 127 It is very jolly here indeed,.. very unstiff and only a certain amount of etiquette. **1958** J. Pope-Hennessy in *Lonely Business* (1981) iii. 248 They said above all she..was 'such a *darling*'—such fun —so unstiff. **1929** D. H. Lawrence *Pansies* 117 Space, of course, is alive. That's why it moves about; and that's what makes it eternally spacious and unstuffy. **1974** K. Clark *Another Part of Wood* vi. 220 To be one of Lady Cunard's regular guests was to have reached somewhere very near the top of unstuffy, new world society. **1933** H. Walpole *Vanessa* ii. 414 Will's love for [his master] Adam had been..protective, selfless, and also gay, simple, unsycophantic, man to man. **1964** *Punch* 23 Sept. p. xv, Cockney writers..are refreshingly unsycophantic. **1909** Webster, Unsymmetric. **1957** L. Fox *Numerical Solution Two-Point Boundary Probl.* iv. 103 In this case we would have to use some unsymmetric formula involving only internal points. **1935** J. Laird *Enquiry into Moral Notions* 10 In my view the times are propitious for attempting an untendentious comparison of ethical ideas ..with equity and..patience. **1962** *Times* 5 Dec. 17/6 *(heading)* Untendentious story of the Berlin Wall. **1934** Webster, Untense. **1959** *Punch* 25 Feb. 277/2 To become untense you must relax. **1974** *Times Lit. Suppl.* 8 Nov. 1248/4 A melodrama in a curiously untense key. **1961** *Lancet* 2 Sept. 549/1, I..support your editorial.. questioning the value of euthanasia... Justification for such untherapeutic therapy can rest only on a total lack of understanding of the nature..of Man. **1978** *Sci. Amer.* Feb. 50/2 Untherapeutic though many nursing homes are, living conditions in most of them are at least tolerable. **1906** Kipling *Puck of Pook's Hill* 6 They sat down in the unthistly centre of the Ring. **1953** Auden in R. Humphries *New Poems by Amer. Poets* 7 The water-scorpion finds it quite unticklish. **1969** Fabian & Byrne *Groupie* xxix. 206 As a group they are something else, but off-stage they're pretty untogether, and they need someone like me to get them to the top. **1976** Untogether [see *staggeringly *adv.*]. **1962** *Harper's Bazaar* Aug. 57/3 Basutoland is for the sophisticated traveller seeking the untouristy. **1979** *Homes & Gardens* June 23/2 Today more visitors bring their cars and instead of making an automatic beeline for London they venture into the most remote and 'untouristy' localities. **1934** Webster, Untraditional. **1958** *Times* 16 Dec. 11/1 We await the rest of the season with untraditional excitement. **1971** 'E. Ferrars' *Stranger & Afraid* xii. 187 The understanding that the university should be one of the new ones and as untraditional as possible. **1968** *Guardian* 26 Sept. 8/5 A BBC man, worried that Priestley might be too untrendy for the 'Wednesday Play'. **1978** *Times* 4 Sept. 13/2 My untrendy and doubtless outdated opinions about the high seriousness of political debate. **1934** Webster, Unurgent. **1939** C. Day Lewis *Child of Misfortune* ii. iv. 212 There was something intimate yet un-urgent in the touch. **1949** *New Yorker* 18 June 24/2 The mist incorporates the pulse, rapid but unurgent, of a motorboat. **1907** H. Rashdall *Theory of Good & Evil* I. vi. 158 Such an obviously unutilitarian precept as that which condemns cannibalism. **1955** S. Spender *Making of Poem* i. 16 Architecture..expresses the tension of the aesthetic against the useful. At the other extreme, music is completely unutilitarian. **1931** *Times Lit. Suppl.* 7 May 360/3 Courses which are ultimately impolitic though not formally 'unviable'. **1964** G. Wheeler *Mod. Hist. Soviet Central Asia* 234 The steady proliferation of independent although economically unviable states. **1982** M. Wallace *Brit. Govt. Northern Ireland* i. 18 The Irish negotiators..had clearly felt that a commission would so reduce the area of Northern Ireland that it would become unviable. **1916** L. Strachey *Let.* 25 Feb. in *Virginia Woolf & Lytton Strachey* (1956) 56 Oh, it's very, very unvictorian! **1981** F. Inglis *Promise of Happiness* v. 144 Ideal parents..so un-Victorian but also so excellently authoritative. **1934** Webster, Unviolent. **1963** *Listener* 3 Oct. 522/3 Even his rhetorical phrases..came out with a lack of ferocity which has great charm for people enamoured of unviolent politicians. **1980** U. Curtiss *Poisoned Orchard* x. 100 That tranquil, un-violent setting. **1931** V. Woolf *Waves* 168, I may find something unvisual beneath [the mind's eye]. **1943** H. Read *Education through Art* 147 This leaves two of our categories unaccounted for, the expressionist and the decorative, but a little consideration will show that one of these is *a priori* excluded from Bullough's apperceptive types, because it is essentially un-visual. **1903** *Lippincott's Monthly Mag.* Aug. 230 To tell the truth, Barrett's calm philosophy irritated her not a little. It was painfully un-Western. **1981** G. MacBeth *Kind of Treason* xii. 116 The Japanese were traditionally un-Western in their attitude to declarations of war. **1965** K. Amis *James Bond Dossier* ix. 88 These days there are few things more un-with-it than feeling..the slightest anti-American sentiment. **1977** *Grimsby Even. Tel.* 5 May 8/3 There is only one word for them, a word so passé, fuddy-duddy and un-with-it that one blushes to use it. **1959** *Economist* 23 May 716/2 The importation or maintenance of party ardours..must seem singularly un-worthwhile. **1974** *Nature* 19 Apr. 715/3 Contributions so speculative as to make such an effort unworthwhile. **1925** 'H. H. RICHARDSON' *Way Home* III. v. 281 Emmy with the hard and unyoung look her face assumed when she spoke of her stepmother. **1972** *National Observer* (U.S.) 27 May 12/1 An unyoung 'youth' leader travels about the country urging audiences to 'kill your parents'.

b. (*a*) *unactionable, unarrangeable, unbackable, unbilletable, unbiodegradable, unblinkable, unbroadcastable, unbudgeable, unbuggable, unbuildable, uncapturable, uncashable, unclaimable, unclearable, uncollectable, uncondonable, unconfessable, unconfusable, unconsortable, uncontactable, uncopyrightable, uncounterfeitable, uncrackable, undeflectable, undevelopable* (earlier example), *undeviable* [*DEVIABLE *a.*], *undiagnosable, undisseverable, undownable, undreamable* (also *absol.*), *unexorcizable, unexperienceable, unexploitable, unfak(e)able, unfalsifiable, unfaultable, unfilmable* (also *absol.*), *unfulfillable, unidentifiable, unignorable, uninterruptable, unjammable, unkinkable, unkissable* (also *absol.*), *unmanœuvrable, unmeltable, unoccupiable, unpatentable, unplaceable, unplumbable, unpoliceable* (also *absol.*), *unquantifiable* (also *absol.*), *unrecapturable, unregenerable, unrejectable, unreviewable, unruffl(e)able, unsayable* (also *absol.*), *unshar(e)able, unshockable, unskiable, unsmoothable, unsplinterable, unsplittable, unsquashable, unstageable, unstat(e)able* (further examples), *unstressable, unswallowable, untappable, untestable, untippable, untransmittable, unverbalizable, unvintageable, unweighable, unwettable, unwipeable, unwithstandable*; (*b*) *unputdownable, unswitchoffable, unwearoutable*.

(*a*) **1952** *Federal Suppl.* (U.S.) CVI. 1019/1 All this might still be unactionable but for the fact that [etc.]. **1980** *Times* 16 Nov. 3/1 The case was dismissed by the High Court in London in preliminary proceedings as 'unactionable in English law'. **1821** *Blackw. Mag.* X. 525 An unarrangeable mass of contraries and shades of difference. **1982** *Book Collector* Winter 457 Vivaldi was virtually unarrangeable. **1928** *Daily Express* 2 Aug. 13/1 Zahrat.. walked away from three moderate rivals in the Alexandra Handicap. She was..unbackable, odds of nine to two having to be laid on. **1973** *Nation Rev.* (Melbourne) 24–30 Aug. 1418/3 Who's Who was literally unbackable on form and treble figure odds ought to have been obtainable. **1940** *Daily Mirror* 17 Dec. 2/2 My wife was asked to give temporary lodging to some young girls who were described by the authorities as unbilletable. **1977** *Water SA* (S. Afr.) Jan. 18/1 The influent TKN [*sc.* Total Kjeldahl Nitrogen] is split into three fractions (i) an unbiodegradable fraction [etc.]. **1978** D. BLOODWORTH *Crosstalk* xxxi. 239 An imitation crocodile handbag in some unbiodegradable plastic. **1936** *Times Lit. Suppl.* 31 Oct. 884/4 A stark unblinkable picture of life as it is being lived somewhere to-day. **1966** *Guardian* 28 Dec. 7/2 There is, finally, the unblinkable fact that the [U.S.] Cabinet is weary. **1975** *Listener* 6 Feb. 163/1 The interview was quite unbroadcastable, due..to the Venerable brother's imperfect English. **1936** L. C. DOUGLAS *White Banners* iv. 73 'Now that's where you're wrong, Marcia.' Paul was kind, but unbudgeable. **1981** *Time* 7 Dec. 74/2 It is an almost unbudgeable popular belief..that cats and dogs have an instinctive rivalry. **1979** R. CASSILIS *Arrow of God* II. vi. 33 The Service's beautiful, new, and allegedly unbuggable headquarters. **1956** R. A. HEINLEIN *Door into Summer* v. 82 Take the great Leonardo da Vinci, so far out of his time that his most brilliant concepts were utterly unbuildable. **1851** H. MELVILLE *Moby Dick* II. xxxix. 274 The only spout in sight was that of a Fin-Back, belonging to the species of uncapturable whales, because of its incredible power of swimming. **1925** *Glasgow Herald* 7 Feb. 4 In the translation something elusive and..uncapturable has vanished. **1906** 'Mark TWAIN' *Autobiogr.* (1924) II. 288, I don't know what Dick got, but it was probably only un-cashable promises. **1978** *Daily Tel.* 28 Oct. 1/4 The £100,000 cheque handed to Korchnoi as defeated finalist in the World Chess Championship is uncashable until he signs a declaration that he has lost the title. **1884** W. JAMES in *Unitarian Rev.* XXII. 205 Whether the world be the better or the worse for having either chances or gifts in it will depend altogether on *what* these uncertain and unclaimable things turn out to be. **1955** *Bull. Atomic Sci.* Apr. 146/3 Most unfortunate is the cleared scientist who marries into an unclearable family. **1984** *Sunday Express Mag.* 26 Feb. 28/1 The RE major.. has abandoned whole fields and beaches as 'unclearable'. **1927** *Glasgow Herald* 18 July 10 They had huge outstanding accounts up country, which were uncollectable. **1981** *Sunday Tel.* 26 July 19/6 Some £12 million that is now officially designated as 'almost uncollectable'. **1935** W. DE LA MARE *Early One Morning* 136 Hatred of elderly and yet not wholly uncondonable cant. **1919** C. B. JORDAN tr. *Ibañez's Four Horsemen of Apoc.* I. v. 143 The infallible remedy for the most unconfessable of diseases. **1967** P. WHITE in *Coast to Coast 1965–6* 232 He lied smiling, ashamed..of his..unconfessable experience. **1934** WEBSTER, Unconfusable. **1935** W. DE LA MARE *Early One Morning* 533 Each is in accord with its writer's after-work, and unconfusable with the work of any other poet. **1907** JOYCE *Chamber Music* xxi, He who hath glory lost, nor hath Found any soul to follow his... That high unconsortable one. **1976** *Daily Tel.* 26 Oct. 1/6 The 3,500-ton Swiftsure class hunter-killer vessel is said to be 'uncontactable' beneath the Arctic ice-pack at the North Pole. **1926** WHITEMAN & MCBRIDE *Jazz* viii. 178 The earliest jazz was found uncopyrightable by certain judges. **1982** *Amer. Speech* LVII. 308 It seems possible that other dictionary makers may well have adopted this simple method of protecting their essentially uncopyrightable labors. **1912** E. POUND in *Poetry Rev.* Feb. 73 A man's rhythm must be interpretative, it will be, therefore, in the end, his own, uncounterfeiting, uncounterfeitable. **1932** *Blue Book Mag.* Sept. 12/1 He owned that uncounterfeitable trait which goes with what we call good birth. **1959** 'B. MATHER' *Achilles Affair* I. ii. 21 The code we were using was as near to uncrackable as any code can be. **1954** W. FAULKNER *Fable* 263 The forsaken ..betrothed pursuing,..undeflectable. *a* **1866** J. GROTE *Moral Ideals* (1876) xv. 371 The other kind of knowledge lies at the base.., insoluble and undevelopable. **1929** S. LESLIE *Anglo-Catholic* xiv. 199 This continuity stretching back beyond modern history, undeviating and undeviable. **1951** W. FAULKNER *Requiem for Nun* II. 210 Who am I..to set the puny appanage of my office in the balance against that simple undeviable aim? **1926** *Jrnl. Amer. Med. Assoc.* 20 Nov. 1721/2 Some intangible,.. undiagnosable sinus disease. **1978** R. BANNISTER *Brain's Clinical Neurol.* (ed. 5) p. iii, Disorders either undiagnosable or untreatable or both. **1897** H. JAMES *Spoils of Poynton* xiii. 152 Mona was undisseverable from her prey. **1957** *Sci. Amer.* Apr. 50/2 The undownable question remained: Why were tau and theta [particles] exactly alike in every respect except this one? **1978** J. UPDIKE *Coup* (1979) vi. 224 His motionlessness a mask for his suffocating struggle with the resurging, undownable fact of Sheba's absence. **1906** W. DE LA MARE *Poems* 81 In its future loomed the undreamable. **1957** L. MACNEICE *Visitations* 53 When the undreamable Dream comes clearer. **1922** *Blackw. Mag.* June 800/2 Because of those unexorcisable..Oriental ancestors of his, nothing will ever bring him to regard the game [*sc.* golf]..with the laconic reverence that a Scotsman..expects. **1909** W. JAMES *Meaning of Truth* p. xii, Things of an unexperienceable nature may exist ad libitum, but they form no part of the material for philosophic debate. **1976** *Word 1971* XXVII. 130 If grammar is 'autonomous and independent of meaning', then it is unexperienceable in the surface structure of sentences—therefore unlearnable, and therefore innate. **1923** *Blackw. Mag.* Sept. 398/1 A rich spring of natural oil, as yet unexploited, and perhaps, on account of the climate and neighbours, forever unexploitable. **1978** A. GILCHRIST *Cod Wars* vi. 42 Such resources were largely hidden or disregarded or unexploitable until modern techniques could be applied. **1955** P. LARKIN *Less Deceived* 41 You cannot always keep That unfakable young surface. **1977** H. OSBORNE *White Poppy* xxii. 160 That loud wah-wah voice that..was the unfakeable mark of an English gentleman. **1934** WEBSTER, Unfalsifiable. **1963** *Guardian* 25 Jan. 7/6 Any..existential statement which is unrestricted in scope and therefore unfalsifiable. **1977** P. JOHNSON *Enemies of Society* xi. 153 The proposition was left sufficiently vague to allow for it to be updated..in the light of scientific advances; it is thus a classic example of an unverifiable, or unfalsifiable, statement, and as such scientifically useless. **1965** *Punch* 21 Apr. 572/3 They plump for a return to this hotel, reminding each other of its unfaultable charms. **1928** *Sunday Express* 29 Apr. 4 'Piccadilly', Arnold Bennett's original story.., is said to be not wholly disconnected with his novel 'The Pretty Lady', the great unfilmed (and unfilmable). **1958** *Times Lit. Suppl.* 15 Aug. p. xxviii/4 Film studio executives sat up and took notice of the work of writers whom they had previously dismissed as unfilmable. **1963** E. HUMPHREYS *Gift* II. iv. 238 It didn't matter how unfilmable the book might be, other producers were after it. **1983** *Listener* 6 Jan. 28/1 Le Carré is on record as saying that it is unfilmable. **1934** WEBSTER, Unfulfillable. **1968** *Punch* 4 Sept. 337/1, I ended up spending the night with my friend.., after signing numerous, apparently unfulfillable bonds and promises for the Customs officer. **1982** H. KISSINGER *Years of Upheaval* vi. 197 A demand as seemingly reasonable as it was unfulfillable. **1909** WEBSTER, Unidentifiable. **1923** M. SADLEIR *Desolate Splendour* ix. 142 The small girl, in charge of her young uncle and the unidentifiable Margery, gambolled..across an uneven field. **1971** S. HILL *Strange Meeting* iii. 179 The hammering noise went on, only slightly muffled and then another, unidentifiable sound, though the voices had ceased. **1955** P. LARKIN *Less Deceived* 26 A tense, musty, unignorable silence. **1981** *London Rev. Bks.* 18 June–1 July 7 The speed, wit and range of the book make it unignorable and exhilarating. **1977** *Sociology* XI. 99 We would observe the syntactical momentum employed for an uninterruptable delivery. **1959** *Economist* 11 Apr. 140/2 The [Soviet] government fears that this information has already become unjammable. **1963** *Daily Tel.* 4 Mar. 1/7 Typhon is designed to knock down aircraft and winged missiles by homing on them with its 'unjammable' radar. **1935** *N. & Q.* 4 May 314/1 *Unkinkable.* A new cable-trade term, applied to a fresh and useful flexible electric cord, which is guaranteed not to ravel or ruck up when in use. **1977** *Offshore Engineer* May 16/2 (Advt.), The right rope for the job... H and T Multiplait is:..unkinkable. **1936** G. B. SHAW *Simpleton* II. 63 His poor little secret vice of cigaret smoking?..Faugh! The unkissable... The air poisoner. **1962** M. DRABBLE *Summer Bird-Cage* vi. 99, I was standing stock still and quite unmanoeuvrable. **1940** W. FAULKNER *Hamlet* II. ii. 141 He brought a gross with him in the suitcase, specially made up for him outen asbestos, with unmeltable snaps. **1922** JOYCE *Ulysses* 697 A thatched..2 storey dwellinghouse..with agreeable prospect..over unoccupied and unoccupyable interjacent pastures. **1854** *U.S. Reports* (U.S. Supreme Court) LVI. 132 If the inventor of printing had..claimed his art as something distinct from his machinery, the doctrine now advanced, would have declared it unpatentable to its full extent as an art. **1980** *TWA Ambassador* Oct. 21/3 Left unpatentable are elements of nature—a newly discovered wildflower, for instance—and laws of nature such as philosophical theories and mathematical principles. **1935** *Sun* (Baltimore) 10 Jan. 22/4 The increase in the number of unplaceable children taken under care. **1940** DYLAN THOMAS *Portrait of Artist as Young Dog* 117 We stood in the scooped, windy room of the arch, listening to the noises from the muffled town,..unplaceable sounds,..an engine coughing like a sheep on a hill. **1972** *Human World* Feb. 21 The absence of unplaceable graduates in Britain and the U.S.A. was one of the chief causes of the relative immunity of these countries to Marxism. **1984** *New Yorker* 9 Apr. 39/2 The music was unplaceable. It must have been a Russian idea of American pop. **1921** H. WILLIAMSON *Beautiful Years* 118 The man certainly was queer: he no longer thought as he had at first, that there was anything deep in his nature. Either that, or it was so deep as to be unplumbable. **1929** S. LESLIE *Anglo-Catholic* x. 122 The pitiless unplumbable spaces filled him with terrors. **1980** D. MORAES *Mrs Gandhi* viii. 116 While she usually answers complex and difficult questions fluently, perfectly innocuous queries seem to drive her back into unplumbable depths of silence. **1971** *Nature* 3 Sept. 2/2 This device let the Vienna agency escape from the invidious position of policing the unpoliceable into which it has been jockeyed. **1981** *Times* 25 July 5/1 Protests in other centres would render the rest of New Zealand unpoliceable. **1890** A. C. FRASER *Locke* 147 The idea of the *unquantifiable* is 'suggested' by the positive ideas of spaces and times which we have had in our sense experience. *Ibid.*, We are *as* remote from the unquantifiable infinite..as we were at the beginning of the process. **1979** *Financial Times* 2 Apr. 27/4 Job security is more generally regarded as unquantifiable. **1925** T. DREISER *Amer. Tragedy* I. II. xxii. 307 So wild and unrecapturable is the fever of youth. **1964** W. MCCORD in I. L. Horowitz *New Sociology* 428 We must eschew..the romanticism which longs for the virtues of an unrecapturable past. **1930** *Times Lit. Suppl.* 30 Oct. 884/3 The unregenerate and unregenerable realm of life. **1982** *Observer* 17 Jan. 31/9 It is typical of my unregenerable soul that I can only see this as a marvellous theme for a novel. **1934** WEBSTER, Unrejectable. **1963** M. DRABBLE *Summer Bird-Cage* viii. 127, I felt rather guilty.., as if I had been reading a diary instead of simply receiving unrejectable impressions. **1934** WEBSTER, Unreviewable. **1955** *Bull. Atomic Sci.* Apr. 129/3 With so much unreviewable power in the executive there is bound to be doubt whether the company is getting the information which it really needs. **1968** *Guardian* 15 Nov. 6/7, I find Mary McCarthy's account of her visit to North Vietnam almost unreviewable. **1960** E. W. SWANTON *West Indies Revisited* 226 Worrell, however, is unruffleable. **1981** F. INGLIS *Promise of Happiness* ii. 65, I read them for..the unrufflable, wholly impossible calm of big boys. **1870** W. KNIGHT *Colloquia Peripatetica* p. xii, The thought might penetrate into that shadowy region where language almost breaks down in the effort, as he put it, 'to say the unsayable'. **1905** E. F. BENSON *Image in Sand* vii. 99 The only things worth saying are just those which are unsayable. **1954** R. JARRELL *Pictures from Institution* IV. 150 Her name was not Rosenbaum on the [gramophone] records but her own real unsayable Russian name. **1979** 'J. LE CARRÉ' *Smiley's People* (1980) iv. 49 Strickland incanted the unsayable: 'No coat-trailing..No émigrés. No bugger all.' **1902** W. JAMES *Varieties Relig. Experience* xx. 499 That unshareable feeling which each one of us has of the pinch of his individual destiny. **1976** *Daily Tel.* 19 Oct. 2/1 He said the doctor's belief in independence was fostered by the ultimately unshareable responsibility he accepted for his patient. **1928** C. BELL *Civilization* vi. 173 At this time of day a civilized person, male or female, should be unshockable. **1980** FIRST & SCOTT *Olive Schreiner* iv. 132 The tenor of the history..was..cool and unshockable. **1950** *Times* 15 Feb. 7/5, I should like to ask Lord Montgomery what he does when the 'soft' snow is practically unskiable. **1978** *Detroit Free Press* 2 Apr. 17D/3 Help came in the form of the snow drought during the 1976–77 ski season that left Western and New England slopes unskiable. **1851** H. MELVILLE *Moby Dick* III. xxvii. 176 'Canst thou smooth this seam?'..'Aye, man, it is unsmoothable.' **1925** 'R. CROMPTON' *Still—William* xi. 207 William watched him, smoothing back his unsmoothable hair. **1924** *Motor* 21 Oct. 623/3 An M.E. rear screen with Triplex unsplinterable glass. **1962** L. S. SASIENI *Optical Dispensing* xiii. 329 Unsplinterable lenses are provided as protection. **1926–7** *Army & Navy Stores Catal.* 101/3 Shaving brushes..with unsplittable handles. **1945** R. KNOX *God & Atom* i. 13 It might be possible..to resolve the molecule into its component parts, but beyond that lay something smaller yet, completely indivisible; it was christened accordingly 'the atom'—the unsplittable thing. **1978** M. MIDGLEY *Beast & Man* (1979) x. 214 Language..seems an unmistakable, unsplittable single thing. **1956** M. STEWART *Wildfire at Midnight* ii. 26 He's little and round and quite, quite sorbo... Unsquashable. **1975** *Daily Tel.* 7 Apr. 9/1 Ghastly statistics about the vast number of totally unstageable scripts that come pouring through the post on to the desks of successful theatre people. **1981** *Times Lit. Suppl.* 13 Feb. 161/5 The work [*sc.* a Russian play] is unstageable today. **1955** P. HERON *Changing Forms of Art* p. xiv, Indeed, as with all good art, the whole truth is unstatable. **1963** *Times Lit. Suppl.* 24 May 376/4 This appeal to unstateable personal and inter-personal experience. **1972** *Language* XLVIII. 83 Of course, one can state rules in global grammar that are unstatable as transformations. **1950** D. JONES *Phoneme* 150 Semivowels, such as j and w, would appear to be essentially unstressable. **1968** *Economist* 14 Dec. 21/1 Shifting to the side of their cheeks some unswallowable differences, they agreed to put up common candidates in 1969's general election. **1910** *Chambers's Jrnl.* 10 Sept. 644/1 The secrecy provided by the use of cryptic combinations of meaningless consonants can be equally assured by the various methods used for rendering the electric waves 'untappable'. **1979** C. MCCARRY *Better Angels* II. ii. 115 'I found that a computer out there..knew some things that only our computer was supposed to know.'..'But I thought our equipment was untappable.' **1909** WEBSTER, Untestable. **1964** F. BOWERS *Bibliogr. & Textual Criticism* III. vii. 93 Generalized opinions that are not only untested ..but are also (usually) untestable. **1950** O. NASH *Family Reunion* (1951) 102 Where hotels and restaurants and service stations are operated by untippable unoffendable machinery. **1968** *Listener* 27 June 851/1 Even in Europe —where tipping started—there are such things as untippable taxis, though one has perhaps to go to Helsinki to find them. **1978** *Broadcast* 28 Aug. 19/2 This commercial ..took place in almost undecipherably muddy twilight. They can't really mean that, I thought..it looks untransmittable. **1953** J. S. WILKIE *Sci. Mind & Brain* iv.

41 Some things are virtually unverbalizable: is it at all credible that one could verbalize the face of a friend? **1978** *Language* LIV. 268 A variant of this position holds that experience, to be authentic, must be unverbalizable ('the idea, once expressed, is a lie'). **1877** O. Wilde in *Irish Monthly* Dec. 746, I stood by the unvintageable sea. **1915** Unvintageable [see *polyphloisbic *a.*]. **1909** Webster, Unweighable. **1938** R. W. Lawson tr. *Hevesy & Paneth's Man. Radioactivity* (ed. 2) xi. 132 A parent substance present in unweighable quantities. **1971** *Nature* 23 July 260/2 By trapping the effluent from gas chromatographic columns we have obtained unweighable samples (< 50μg) of the natural pheromone. **1955** *New Biol.* XVIII. 112 Flowers, if floating, must be more or less cup-shaped, and even if lifted above the water surface must, like the leaves, be unwettable. **1977** J. L. Harper *Population Biol. Plants* ii. 46 When light unwettable seed lands on water, it tends to become concentrated at the edges of the water. **1912** G. B. Shaw *Let.* 10 Dec. in *B. Shaw & Mrs. Campbell* (1952) 68 There would be some terrible breach of etiquette some unwipable-out insult, if she gave me a card for you. **1971** *Daily Tel.* (Colour Suppl.) 4 June 39/1 This little hole (felt-lined usually, and utterly unwipeable)..which they actually call a glove-box. **1981** *Times* 4 July 10/1 Tape costing a quarter of the price of these unwipeable tapes. **1931** *Times Lit. Suppl.* 12 Mar. 196/2 The episodes of Susan's life..and her ruthless imposition of herself upon..her third husband, and upon his Poor Christians as a kind of unwithstandable Deborah—are told with admirable spirit. **1970** R. Price *Gt. Roob Revolution* 5 The classic rube withstood the unwithstandable winter at Valley Forge.

(*b*) **1947** R. Chandler *Let.* 5 Jan. in *R. Chandler Speaking* (1966) 66, I found it absolutely..unputdownable. **1982** *Brit. Med. Jrnl.* 15 May 1466/2 The novel is highly readable and quite unputdownable. **1974** *Guardian* 21 Mar. 10/4 The immediacy which makes TV sometimes ..absolutely un-switch offable. **1984** *Listener* 10 May 38/1 Alfred Brendel's recording of Beethoven's Five Piano Concertos, with the Chicago Symphony Orchestra conducted by James Levine..is unswitchoffable. **1968** *Economist* 25 May 89/2 The engine..is a neat—and presumably unwearoutable—air-cooled flat-four unit in the back of the car. **1979** *Field* 3 Oct. 942/1 (Advt.), Almost unwearoutable socks.

c. *unbridegroomlike* (earlier example), *unbutlerlike, uncatlike, unpolicemanlike.*

1830 M. O'Brien *Jrnl.* 15 May (1968) xii. 114 Mary and Fanny exclaimed at this most unbridegroomlike proceeding. **1924** J. Sutherland *Circle of Stars* iii. 24 His manner was unimpeachable, his tone superlatively correct, but somewhere in his eyes was a most unbutler-like gleam. **1955** Auden *Shield of Achilles* i. 22 For an uncatlike Creature who has gone wrong, Five minutes on even the nicest mountain Is awfully long. **1978** D. Williams *Treasure up in Smoke* xx. 186 There was a most unpoliceman-like implication in the Chief Inspector's tone.

8. a. (*a*) *unacclaimed, unaddled, unaffrayed* (arch.), *unassessed, unattributed, unbeglamoured, unbobbed* [*bobbed *a.* b], *unbombed, unbothered, unbuffered, unbugged, unbypassed, uncaked, uncatalysed, uncloned, uncluttered, uncobbled, uncoded, uncopyrighted, uncouponed, undeafened, undepicted, undiffused, undisbursed, undistanced, unearmarked, unenhanced, unenthused, uneroded, unexploded, unfaked, unfattened, unfazed, unfilmed* (later example), *unflustered, unfocus(s)ed, unformatted, unfussed, ungrazed, ungritted, unhipped* [*hip *v.*[5]], *unhousetrained, uniced, uninjected, unkeepered, unladdered* [*ladder *v.* 2], *unlaundered, unlenited, unmonitored, unneutered, unoriented, unpackaged, unpadded, unphotographed, unplanned, unposed, unpowered, unprogrammed, unprovenanced, unrationed, unrattled, unseeded, unshingled* [*shingled *ppl. a.*[1] 3], *unsignposted, unslanted, unsliced, unslipped* [*slipped *ppl. a.*[3]], *unsourced, unspayed, unsponsored, unstaffed, unstreamed* [*streamed *a.* 2], *unstructured, unsupercharged, unsurfaced, untagged, untelevised, untenured, unupholstered, unvetted*; (*b*) *unacculturated, unactivated, unagglutinated, unallocated, uncalibrated, unchlorinated, undemarcated, unencapsulated, unexhilarated, unfractionated, unintegrated, unmotivated* (also *absol.*), *unmyelinated, unpatinated, unrefrigerated, unreplicated, unsegregated, unsublimated, unsyncopated* (later examples), *unvegetated*; (*c*) *unactualized, un-Americanized, unanæsthetized, unanatomized, un-Anglicized, unbowdlerized, uncolonized* (cf. Uncolonize *v.*), *undiphthongized, un-Hellenized, unindustrialized, unlemmatized, unnationalized, unnormalized, unparasitized, unpasteurized, unplasticized, unpoliticized, unpolymerized, unpressurized, unpublicized, unsclerotized, unsocialized, unstabilized, unstandardized* (also *absol.*), *unsterilized, ununionized, unvandalized, unverbalized.*

(*a*) *general.* **1921** W. de la Mare *Mem. Midget* xlvi. 314 That other less professional *début* which poor Mr. Crimble ..had left unacclaimed. **1899** *Leeds Mercury Weekly Suppl.* 5 Aug. (E.D.D.), We should call money that had been acquired without effort, 'unaddled brass'. **1935** W. de la Mare *Early One Morning* xiv. 179 Flattery of the young is so usual that it is remarkable that a child with a 'fine head' manages to keep the brains in it unaddled. **1935** T. S. Eliot *Murder in Cathedral* i. 20 Archbishop, secure and assured of your fate, unaffrayed among the shades. **1922** *Times* 15 Nov. 13/6 That unassessed quantity, the man in the street. **1970** *Jrnl. General Psychol.* LXXXII. 146 Ebbinghaus was faced with a similar problem of unassessed previous experience in learning phenomena. **1972** N. Freeling *Long Silence* ii. 233 He had been to look at a picture... The price was high, and might have been a great deal higher but that it was, as he pointed out, quite unattributed. **1901** G. B. Shaw *Three Plays for Puritans* Pref. p. xxix, A thing compared to which Falstaff's unbeglamored drinking and drabbing is respectable. **1927** *Blackw. Mag.* Nov. 601/1 By her own account the only unbobbed head in Hampstead. **1931** W. Faulkner in *Harper's Mag.* Sept. 394/2 The fine, soft cloud of her unbobbed hair gleamed like the chestnut's flank. **1928** M. Beerbohm *Variety of Things* 128 One likes to think of him there among the unbombed Lakes. **1980** A. Price *Hour of Donkey* iv. 63 One unbombed veteran to another obviously much-bombed one. **1912** W. Deeping *Sincerity* xxviii. 216 Wolfe..seemed to brush Turrell's arms aside as though they were mere sticks. His crisp, sinewy punches landed serenely. He looked unmarked, unbothered. **1965** J. A. Michener *Source* (1966) 794 Bagdadi, apparently unbothered by history, pressed on. **1936** *Nature* 7 Nov. 800/1 The native hæmoglobin of the horse, in unbuffered dilute salt solutions at the isoelectric point. **1966** *Punch* 2 Feb. 169/2 If any Tom, Dick or Harry can meet in a collapsible plastic balloon and chatter away unbugged, there is no knowing what they will say. We shall be back to the old, bad days of secret diplomacy. **1962** Simpson & Richards *Physical Princ. Junction Transistors* xi. 255 A better solution is to leave a portion of the emitter bias resistor un-by-passed, thereby introducing negative-current feedback. **1954** T. Gunn *Fighting Terms* 44, I..felt my body sweet, Uncaked blood in all its channels flowing. **1939** *Jrnl. Organic Chem.* IV. 434 No uncatalyzed addition has yet been observed. **1976** *Nature* 24 June 659/1 After the establishment of the kinetic orders of the catalysed and uncatalysed reactions a mechanism consistent with all the results was deduced. **1971** *Ibid.* 2 Apr. 276/1 If single-cell clones of cultured cells are derived from women heterozygous for *X*-linked genes determining enzyme variants, each clone shows the activity of only one of the two possible genes, whereas uncloned cultures derived from many cells show both. **1980** *Jrnl. Immunol. Methods* XXXIV. 153 Uncloned and cloned populations. **1925** *Glasgow Herald* 6 Nov. 8 The adjective uncluttered is an American term of strong commendation when used to describe a wall, a mantelpiece or even a whole room. **1960** J. Stroud *Shorn Lamb* xxii. 239 New modern houses.. with their plate-glass and uncluttered lines. **1980** *Times* 29 Feb. 26 (Advt.), Spring-time in Greece. Uncluttered beaches, [etc.]. **1922** Joyce *Ulysses* 422 An uncobbled tramsiding set with skeleton tracks. **1918** J. W. Gerard *Face to Face with Kaiserism* xx. 230 The bags were secretly opened and our uncoded despatches and letters read. **1971** B. Patten *Irrelevant Song* 24 A bleak and uncoded message whispers Down all the nerves. **1852** Mrs. Stowe *Let.* 27 Sept. in N. Spain *Mrs Beeton* (1948) i. iv. 51, I do not conceive that I have any *claim* on an English publisher for any of the profits of an uncopyrighted work. **1950** A. Lomax *Mister Jelly Roll* 292 He established *The Tempo-Music Publishing Company* to protect, publish, and push Morton's uncopyrighted and unpublished works. **1935** *Economist* 9 Nov. 930/1 They had actually harvested rather more than that quantity, but the balance, being uncouponed stock, had been carried forward to the current season's account. **1967** *Punch* 13 Sept. 388/1 Unfortunately the police caught him with several bales of uncouponed suit material. **1935** W. B. Yeats *Dramatis Personae* vii. 25 Only at pictures did he look undeafened and unblinded. **1979** *New Scientist* 17 May 537/2 It also sings normally next season, and goes through the usual subsong and plastic song again in the same way as undeafened birds. *c* **1884** E. Dickinson in *Poems* (1955) III. 1120 Bugles call the least of us To undepicted Realms. **1940** W. Faulkner *Hamlet* iii. ii. 212 That perfect marriage of will and ability with a single undiffused object. **1964** *Economist* 7 Mar. 917/3 Loans still undisbursed. **1951** W. Faulkner *Requiem for Nun* iii. 262 There is the clear undistanced voice as though out of the delicate antenna-skeins of radio. *a* **1868** [see *earmark *v.* 3]. **1971** *Oxf. Univ. Gaz.* 25 Feb. 709/2 That the Curators of the University Chest be authorized to expend from the unearmarked money in the Higher Studies Fund a sum of £10,000. **1934** Webster, Unenhanced. **1942** R. Frost *Witness Tree* 41 We gave ourselves outright..to the land vaguely realizing westward, but still unstoried, artless, unenhanced. **1963** *Punch* 9 Oct. 516/2 It [*sc.* industry] is markedly unenthused about the Tories. **1977** M. Kenyon *Rapist* ix. 109 Keane, unenthused, watched from the door. **1924** *Brit. Weekly* 13 Nov. 147/3, There is no 'basalt and bronze' for a Prime Minister like a still uneroded majority of 210. **1978** J. Updike *Coup* (1979) ii. 48 Its façade is topped with eight marble statues of an unreal whiteness, uneroded in this climate. **1889** *Cent. Dict.*, Unexploded. **1924** A. D. Sedgwick *Little French Girl* ii. i. 100 Their mutual secret..that Giles visualized as an unexploded bomb..liable at a touch to.. scatter the family happiness to fragments. **1952** A. Cohen *Phonemes of English* 28 We find that..in *nipped* [the [p] is] unexploded. **1981** B. Langley *Autumn Tiger* ii. 21 *Berlin, February 1945*...a sign in red paint which warned 'Danger! Unexploded Bomb.' **1902** Kipling *Let.* 30 Nov. in C. Carrington *Rudyard Kipling* (1955) xv. 369 A grey stone lichened house..with old oak staircase, and all untouched and unfaked. **1968** A. Diment *Bang Bang Birds* vi. 102 One of the Birds, gazing at them with apparently un-faked adoration. **1895** Hardy *Jude* i. viii. 58 Three young unfattened pigs had escaped from their sty. **1951** T. Capote *Grass Harp* ii. 50 'Of course they are nearer God,' he said, unfazed by the disapproving, sober faces around him. **1977** P. Roth *Professor of Desire* 55 They were all screaming at one another, but he just walked along, unfazed. **1928** Unfilmed [see *unfilmable*, sense 7 b above]. **1913** H. Walpole *Fortitude* ii. ii. 165 Beaming, calm, and unflustered as though he had just come from the next street. **1967** T. Stoppard *Rosencrantz & Guildenstern are Dead* ii. 58 (*He turns away.* GUIL *grabs him and spins him back violently.*) (*Unflustered.*) Now if you're going to be subtle, we'll miss each other in the dark. **1886** Hardy *Mayor of Casterbridge* II. xxii. 307 His eyes lighting on them with an unfocused gaze. **1939** H. Nicolson *Diary* 4 Feb. (1966) 390 V. and I go round to the Beales where there is a Television Set... Compared with a film, it is a bleary, flickering,..unfocused, interruptible thing. **1979** G. Macdonald *Camera* xii. 165/1 The greatest portraitist of Victorian England was the unfocussed Julia Margaret Cameron. **1967** E. R. Lannon in Cox & Grose *Organiz. & Handling Bibliogr. Rec. by Computer* iv. 82 The second type of data, sometimes called unformatted, takes on special meaning due to its surrounding elements. **1982** *Which Computer?* June 30/3 The M20 has..an on-line unformatted data storage capacity of 320 KB. **1907** T. Hodgkin *Let.* 27 Oct. in L. Creighton *Life & Lett. T. Hodgkin* (1917) xii. 282 When Christ..said that he would have us ἀμέριμνοι he meant almost what we mean by 'unfussed'. **1981** N. Freeling *One Damn Thing after Another* xxxii. 236 She phoned home. To hear Arthur's voice, unfussed and matter-of-fact. **1903** Kipling *Five Nations* 155 For the ungrazed upland, the untilled lea Cry, and the fields forlorn. **1972** J. L. Harper *Population Biol. Plants* 450 Within this zone of taller, ungrazed herbage the balance of competitive interactions is changed. **1977** *Belfast Tel.* 19 Jan. 1/2 Environment Department officials were caught napping today by the heavy overnight frost, which left a network of icy Ulster roads ungritted. **1938** *Amer. Speech* XIII. 314/2 *Jump salty*, implies an unexpected change in a person's..knowledge... An unhipped person may become hipped. **1944** D. Burley *Orig. Handbk. Harlem Jive* 90, I hunch the pinball layout, Jack, and it's an unhipped tilt. **1955** Auden *Shield of Achilles* iii. 66 Where should we be but for them? Feral skill, un-housetrained. **1967** A. Wilson *No Laughing Matter* iii. 232 He's doing PPE. Whatever that may be. It sounds very un-housetrained. **1864** Geo. Eliot *Let.* 8 Mar. (1956) IV. 138 Iced water is what I always long for ..while water *un*-iced is detestable to me. **1971** 'J. Bell' *Hole in Ground* iv. 53 A plate of scones and an uniced cake. **1934** Webster, Uninjected. **1946** *Nature* 31 Aug. 311/2 There are two natural folds of skin in cattle at..the root of the tail, and the uninjected fold serves as a control. **1977** P. Dickinson *Walking Dead* i. i. 20 He only injected three pairs of rats in a batch... Nor could he run uninjected rats. **1938** J. W. Day *Dog in Sport* xi. 143 There were partridges, naturally bred, more or less unkeepered. **1977** H. Douglas-Home *Birdman* vi. 71 Keepering established a balance which could not have existed in the earlier predator dominated times. Anyone who doubts this need only take a train from Edinburgh to Glasgow, unkeepered country today. **1956** 'C. Blackstock' *Dewey Death* v. 102 She was..her well-groomed self, with..unladdered stockings. **1978** J. Goodman *Last Sentence* i. 28 She and Cecil were entered..at the Streatham Locarno..and she *had* to have unladdered hose for that. **1895** *Montgomery Ward Catal.* Spring & Summer 36/3 Soft or Unlaundered Waists. **1965** T. Capote *In Cold Blood* ii. 125 Some bits of unlaundered laundry. **1978** 'R. Cassilis' *Winding Sheet* iii. 199 Politicians..should never be allowed to hear unlaundered secrets. It made them uncomfortable. **1953** K. Jackson *Lang. & Hist. in Early Britain* 554 Original unlenited Brit. *b.* **1977** *Word* 1972 XXVIII. 99 Three of the 7 semi-speakers showed switching between lenited and unlenited forms of *daor* 'expensive'. **1966** R. H. Rimmer *Harrad Experiment* (1967) 92 Locating my leopard coat under a heap of fur coats in the unmonitored cloak room. **1976** *Guardian* 23 July 15/6 Now at last it seems that a researcher from Stirling University may begin work, and both staff and inmates see this as a positive development, while regretting that the first years have slipped past largely unmonitored. **1962** G. Butler *Coffin in Oxford* ii. 38 The undying burning hate of one un-neutered tom for another. **1971** *Nat. Geographic* May 735/2 The Seigneur [of Sark]..exercises the right to keep the Island's only 'unneutered' bitch. **1931** V. Woolf *Waves* 205 Here am I marching up and down the terrace alone, unoriented. **1947** [see *oriented *ppl. a.* 2]. **1962** U. Weinreich in Householder & Saporta *Probl. Lexicogr.* 30 Features of a geographic area can be studied even from an unoriented map. **1969** W. R. R. Park *Plastics Film Technol.* ii. 33 Unoriented film is very brittle at below zero temperatures. **1948** A. N. Keith *Three came Home* xi. 199, 100 cigarettes, unpackaged and unlabelled. **1984** *Times Lit. Suppl.* 10 Feb. 148/1 Here is a manual for the unpackaged, mildly enterprising and tolerably well-heeled holidaymakers. **1923** A. Huxley *Antic Hay* x. 152 The wearing exhaustion to which long-protracted sitting on unpadded seats subjects them. **1979** A. Buck *Dress in 18th-C. Eng.* ii. 31 The coat was losing its stiffness, and the pleats of its skirts, now unpadded, were set further back. **1914** G. Bell *Let.* 21 Jan. (1927) I. xiii. 327 And we came at two o'clock to the last of the castles, Baîr, as yet unplanned and unphotographed. **1929** 'E. Queen' *Roman Hat Mystery* v. 86 You are by no means an unphotographed young lady—I saw your picture in the paper to-day. **1981** J. Wainwright *All on Summer's Day* 80 An inspection which (literally) left no square inch unsearched or unphotographed. **1909** Webster, Unplanned. **1914** [see *unphotographed* above]. **1942** J. S. Huxley in *Harper's Mag.* Sept. 346/1 The need for entering upon our revolution consciously.., deliberately guiding its course instead of allowing its blind forces to push and buffet our unplanned lives. **1959** *Listener* 4 June 981/1 These people are spontaneous in almost all they do. Children are 'unplanned'. **1961** 'J. le Carré' *Call for Dead* xvii. 186 The obviously unplanned and unproductive selection of files. **1973** *Times* 19 Apr. 19/2 Nearly half of *all* pregnancies are unplanned. **1981** N. Tucker *Child & Book* i. 45 A shoe.. may..house a large and almost certainly unplanned family. **1934** Webster, Unposed. **1960** *Guardian* 13 July 7/2 The best pictures of people are unposed and are taken while they are intent on what they are doing. **1968** E. Hyams *Mischief Makers* i. 12 This unselfconscious, unposed animation was not what I was used to. **1963** *Times* 26 Feb. 9/4 After being boosted to orbital speed, the 45ft. long Dyna-Soar will be capable of manoeuvering freely during reentry into the earth's atmosphere, and then making a horizontal landing. As it will be unpowered at that stage this will call for particular skill and judgment by the pilot. **1975** S. JOHNSON *Urbane Guerilla* III. 108 The canal..plunging..through a half-mile tunnel forbidden to unpowered craft. **1941** W. C. HANDY *Father of Blues* (1957) xiv. 194 Other New York composer-conductors were introduced here and there and asked to play unprogrammed numbers. **1953** *Sun* (Baltimore) 12 Mar. 2/1 The 'unprogrammed' funds referred to come to the Army from several sources. **1959** *New Biol.* XXVIII. 113 In order to keep such a process going in its most elementary form, some prearrangement, in the form of strings of unprogrammed material to be used, has been found necessary. **1974** *Sci. Amer.* May 61/2 When the machine is off or unprogrammed, the knob moves freely in all directions. **1976** H. WILSON *Governance of Britain* iv. 85 Apart from pre-arranged ministerial meetings with documents circulated and written and sometimes oral briefing, each day sees a number of often unprogrammed meetings with ministers. **1967** *Antiquaries Jrnl.* XLVII. 209 Another animal..is the springing canine with collar on an unprovenanced ?flagon handle also in the British Museum. **1919** A. P. HERBERT in *Punch* 22 Jan. 62/1 The free unrationed blotting-pad. **1940** C. E. MILBURN *Diary* 10 Mar. (1979) 26 To church..then home for the last unrationed meat dinner. **1982** T. FITZGIBBON *With Love* I. v. 31 We would have friends to dinner, and with food rationing becoming stringent, stuff and braise unrationed sheeps' hearts. **1934** WEBSTER, Unrattled. **1953** *Manch. Guardian Weekly* 20 Aug. 7 He was quite unrattled, in good physical shape. **1976** J. COLVILLE *Footprints in Time* xxvii. 144 His second-in-command at the Embassy..was unrattled by the crescendo of disaster to the allied cause. **1952** *N.Y. Times* 8 Sept. 27/5 The third-seeded player, Irene Rawcliffe of Nutley High, was eliminated by unseeded Lynn Anderson of Mount St. Mary's Academy 6-1, 6-1. **1977** *Washington Post* 9 Mar. D4, I think anybody, including the unseeded squads, has a chance to make the final. **1928** *Daily Express* 23 May 8/4 Among the fifty horsewomen only five have unshingled hair. **1933** A. G. MACDONELL *England, their England* xiv. 246 A network of narrow lanes, unsignposted. **1981** M. E. ATKINS *Palimpsest* ii. 12 Breakdowns *always* occurred in foul weather on unsignposted roads. **1964** F. BOWERS *Bibliogr. & Textual Criticism* vi. i. 165 With selected though unslanted evidence, a point should be reached at which our common-sense view of probability rebels at being asked to accept any more coincidence as the result of mere chance. **1974** J. IRVING *158-Pound Marriage* vi. 131 It was an old-fashioned, unslanted, glass windshield. **1889** *Cent. Dict.*, Unsliced. **1968** D. E. ALLEN *Brit. Tastes* iii. 77 Bread, being..made more by small local bakers, tends to be unwrapped (and..unsliced) more frequently than elsewhere. **1978** *Times* 15 Apr. 3/6 There will be bloomers, cobs,..sliced and unsliced, white and brown loaves on the shelves. **1940** R. E. SMITH in *Maya & Their Neighbors* xvi. 243 Unslipped jars with flaring necks. **1977** *Sci. Amer.* Mar. 130/2 The pots range from rough, unslipped pieces—'earthenware' in modern terminology—to thinner-walled pieces with smooth and glossy surfaces. **1851** H. MELVILLE *Moby Dick* III. xviii. 128 This ante-mosaic, unsourced existence of the unspeakable terrors of the whale. **1977** *Kuwait Times* 1 Nov. 6/3 In an unsourced report from Bucharest, the Egyptian agency also said that a decision whether to reconvene the Geneva conference would be made within the next two weeks. **1939** J. R. KINNEY *How to raise a Dog* vi. 144 During their periods the unspayed bitch is sometimes an aesthetic problem because of the discharge. **1979** 'J. Ross' *Rattling of Old Bones* ix. 83 The woman..[had] the sexual hunger of an unspayed cat in her eyes. **1930** E. RICE *Voyage to Purilia* i. 7 We wanted to travel quietly and unobtrusively... This could be done only if our voyage was unsponsored and unheralded. **1979** *Tucson* (Arizona) *Citizen* 20 Sept. 2D/1 The Patio Pools team amassed 4,882 pins..against Diamond Life and unsponsored Team No. 4 in the first round of action. **1934** WEBSTER, Unstaffed. **1957** [see *REMOTELY *adv.* 2 b]. **1979** V. L. PANDIT *Scope of Happiness* xxxvii. 288 The Embassy remained closed and unstaffed. **1962** *Guardian* 30 Mar. 10/4 A large *unstreamed* school in which these distinctions have no place. **1981** *Indexer* XII. 152/2 Six unstreamed classes in a local comprehensive school. **1936** F. & G. M. HEIDER tr. *Lewin's Princ. Topological Psychol.* xii. 134 If one puts a rat into the maze without food, he gets a chance to 'orient' himself, which means that what is first an unstructured field becomes structured. **1948** M. SHERIF *Outl. Soc. Psychol.* vii. 181 Psychological principles which are..applicable in the case of the individual facing an unstructured situation. **1965** *Times Lit. Suppl.* 25 Nov. 1049/3 This was..an anarchically 'unstructured' society. **1973** *Computers & Humanities* VII. 171 The current trend in elementary education is in the direction of open, unstructured classrooms. **1977** *Lancashire Life* Mar. 106/2 Spring coats are lean and unstructured, with their line emphasised with braid or other fabric trimming in contrast colour. **1984** *Guardian* 5 Mar. 11/4 Jackets are loose and unstructured. **1929** V. W. PAGÉ *Mod. Aviation Engines* I. xii. 343 A supercharged plane requires a somewhat larger propeller than an unsupercharged one. **1974** *Encycl. Brit. Macropædia* VII. 936/1 The loss in power suffered by unsupercharged engines at high altitudes can be largely restored [by supercharging]. **1953** W. MOORE *Bring Jubilee* (1955) ii. 13 It was impossible to maintain unsurfaced highways in good condition. **1971** D. POTTER *Brit. Eliz. Stamps* vi. 68 A few copies of the 10d on unsurfaced paper..were found in 1970. **1909** WEBSTER, Untagged. **1957** D. L. BOLINGER in *Publ. Amer. Dial. Soc.* XXVIII. 112 The evolution of the secondary towards tag-ness has not reached the point of admitting an untagged secondary on the second A of the most conducive intonation. **1967** *Oceanogr. & Marine Biol.* XVI. 440 The basis for this is an assumption that tagged and untagged fish are caught in the same proportions. **1962** *Punch* 11 Apr. 555/2 Shakespeare, untelevised and unrecorded, was never asked to take it all back and substitute some more ethical appeal. **1971** *Guardian* 25 Aug. 8/5 'Polaris—The Secret World' (Yorkshire) was wholly untelevised territory. **1969** *Federal Suppl.* (U.S.) 11 Dec. 1053/1 Person, even though untenured, may not be denied public employment for unconstitutional reason. **1981** 'A. CROSS' *Death in Faculty* v. 49 An untenured professor in search of 'contacts'. **1919** G. B. SHAW *Heartbreak House* I. 1 A row of books under the window provides an unupholstered window-seat. **1938** S. BECKETT *Murphy* v. 63 Two massive upright unupholstered armchairs. **1962** *Guardian* 15 Feb. 6/6 Unscripted, unvetted discussion programmes. **1979** T. WISEMAN *Game of Secrets* viii. 100 The company..in certain cases actually prohibited unsanctioned intercourse with unvetted outsiders.

(*b*) ending in *-ated*. **1969** *Nature* 26 July 419/1 European children, during their first year at school, were like unacculturated African tribal adults in that many failed to interpret the perspective features of a picture as representing depth. **1956** A. HUXLEY *Adonis & Alphabet* 156 The problem of what we may politely call 'unactivated sludge'. **1950** RACE & SANGER *Blood Groups in Man* iii. 34 Such points as..the shaking free of unagglutinated cells enmeshed in agglutinates are skilfully dealt with. **1979** *Jrnl. R. Soc. Med.* LXXII. 450 An unagglutinated suspension of the recipient's blood. **1869** *Bradshaw's Railway Man.* XXI. 183 Deducting all proper expenses and interest on the unallocated debt. *a* **1974** R. CROSSMAN *Diaries* (1977) III. 953 It looks to me as if he might find himself unallocated and put back into the pool. **1965** *Canad. Jrnl. Linguistics* Fall 45 The whole process is wasteful, much as if one were to work with a number of highly sensitive but quite uncalibrated scientific instruments. **1974** *Jrnl. Water Pollution Control* XLVI. 2153 (*heading*) Bacteriology of chlorinated and unchlorinated wastewater effluents. **1902** G. F. STOUT in H. Sturt *Personal Idealism* I. 42 All demarcated figure presupposes what we may call undemarcated figure. **1967** M. AYUB KHAN *Friends not Masters* x. 161 A similar situation could arise on our own undemarcated borders in the Sinkiang and Baltistan areas. **1965** *Amer. Jrnl. Clin. Path.* XLIII. 112/2 The tumor was..usually unencapsulated and often diffusely infiltrated the adjacent muscle. **1851** H. MELVILLE *Moby Dick* I. xxxiii. 235 He swings himself to the deck and in an even, unexhilarated voice, saying 'Dinner, Mr Starbuck,' disappears into the cabin. **1956** *Nature* 18 Feb. 326/2 The unfractionated polymer..gives crystals which are smaller and more opaque to electrons. **1889** *Cent. Dict.*, Unintegrated. **1920** R. R. MARETT *Psychology & Folk-Lore* vi. 121 An unintegrated or imperfectly rational type. *a* **1974** R. CROSSMAN *Diaries* (1977) III. 484 An absolutely self-perpetuating oligarchy of R.H.B.s completely unintegrated with the community services of the local authorities. **1922** J. RIVIERE tr. *Freud's Introd. Lect. Psycho-Anal.* iv. 48 They [*sc.* acts] also appear to be unmotivated, insignificant and unimportant. **1947** *Mind* LVI. 353 Witness the familiar sort of situation where someone has met with misfortune from a natural, apparently unmotivated, cause. **1953** E. SIMON *Past Masters* I. 18 The house..bleak despite a mass of unmotivated Victorian architectural curlicues. **1964** M. ARGYLE *Psychol. & Social Probl.* v. 70 A man with an unmotivated tendency to attack perambulators and handbags. **1973** *Sci. Amer.* July 22/3 A fairly simple change yielded a considerable response from a group of patients who had previously been characterized..as 'unmotivated' to seek postpartum checkups. **1977** P. STREVENS *New Orientations Teaching of English* i. 10 They are unmotivated towards learning English and sometimes even hostile towards doing so. **1978** H. R. F. KEATING *Long Walk to Wimbledon* II. 18 His world was at the mercy of the unmotivated. **1915** *Brain* XXXVIII. 384 The unmyelinated fibres of spinal nerves are distributed chiefly to the skin. **1980** *Jrnl. R. Soc. Med.* LXXIII. 268 Using the electronmicroscope, Frank..described unmyelinated nerve fibres in the inner third of fully formed human coronal dentine. **1926** *S. Afr. Jrnl. Sci.* XXIII. 785 The Earlier Stone Age implements are heavily patinated, the later are unpatinated or only slightly so. **1946** F. E. ZEUNER *Dating Past* vi. 193 The gravel has yielded..in a fresh, unabraded and unpatinated condition: a middle Levalloisian comparable with that found by Burchell. **1934** WEBSTER, Unrefrigerated. **1964** *Supermarket & Self-Service* (Johannesburg) Feb. 5/2 On the left is a 12 ft. long cabinet with three unrefrigerated shelves. **1968** D. E. ALLEN *Brit. Tastes* 234 Milk was scarce and the sealed, sterilised variety would stay fresh, though unrefrigerated, for seven days. **1971** *Nature* 25 June 491/3 This fact enabled Hill and Hillova to separate.. the newly replicated double helices..from unreplicated DNA. **1976** *Billings* (Montana) *Gaz.* 20 June 12-A/1 It would be 'almost criminal to look upon this unreplicated study as representative'. **1905** *Rep. Evolution Committee R. Soc.* II. 110 Some gametes are bearing r.p. [*sc.* the characters of both 'rose comb' and 'pea comb' together (in poultry)] unsegregated. **1954** *Harper's Mag.* Sept. 47/2 On the first day of the fall term, Amy Miller..was so apprehensive about entering an unsegregated school that she persuaded her father, a truck driver, to accompany her. **1977** *Listener* 17 Feb. 215/3 One of the motives..was to bring an unsegregated band to perform before an unsegregated audience. **1923** J. S. HUXLEY *Ess. Biologist* vii. 271 We may perhaps best say that a sublimated instinct has more and higher values attached to its satisfaction than one unsublimated. **1952** GERTH & MARTINDALE tr. *Weber's Anc. Judaism* v. 126 Acculturation is generally productive of entirely new..phenomena given the..compelling need of absorbing a mass of yet unsublimated ideas. **1967** N. MARSH *Death at Dolphin* iv. 94 An actor..was embarrassed rather than released by unsublimated chunks of raw association. **1922** W. J. LOCKE *Tale of Triona* ix. 97 A company of women groping ..after ideals in unsyncopated time. **1950** BLESH & JANIS *They all played Ragtime* (1958) ii. 44 The second and third themes, printed unsyncopated, cry out for syncopation when one plays them. **1953** K. JACKSON *Lang. & Hist. in Early Britain* 689 The AS. *Cerdic* seems to have been borrowed..from a syncopated Pr. W. **Car'dig*..side by side with unsyncopated *Ceredig*. **1939** *Geogr. Jrnl.* XCIV. 221 A high pyramid of unvegetated sand was a prominent landmark. **1970** *Nature* 2 May 429/2 The unvegetated mudflats of Sanderson's Gulf.

(*c*) ending in *-ized*. **1938** A. FARRER in T. E. Jessup et al. *Christian Understanding of Man* 211 Christianity asserts ..that there is a true nature of man..actual in the Divine mind and never wholly unactualized in men. **1875** A. J. C. HARE *Days near Rome* I. 1 The real, true, un-Anglicized, un-Americanized country. **1931** *Times Lit. Suppl.* 18 June 481/4 An un-Americanised..honest English England. **1950** O NASH *Family Reunion* (1951) 134 He undergoes the lecturing Like unanesthetized vivisecturing. **1934** BLUNDEN *Mind's Eye* IV. 256 A world as yet unanatomized by scientific accuracy. **1875** Un-Anglicized [see *un-Americanized* above]. **1964** B. TRNKA in D. Abercrombie et al. *Daniel Jones* 186 The French nasals in the occasionally un-Anglicized pronunciation of Modern French words. **1873** J. DAVIES *Hesiod, & Theognis* II. i. 130 The shape in which the poetry of Theognis has come down to us is as unlike the original form and drift as a handbook of maxims from Shakespeare is unlike an undoctored and un-Bowdlerised play. **1957** *Times Lit. Suppl.* 6 Dec. 738/2 A quarter of a century ago the complete, unbowdlerized edition of 1951 might have made a stir. **1862** J. S. MILL in *Westm. Rev.* XXII. 510 The vast uncolonized region of Arkansas, and Texas. **1979** *Jrnl. Brit. Interplanetary Soc.* XXXII. 222/1 The relative availability of uncolonized stars will be rapidly and dramatically restricted. **1921** E. SAPIR *Language* 176 The long undiphthongized *u* is still preserved in Lowland Scotch. **1951** W. K. MATTHEWS *Languages U.S.S.R.* iii. 35 Undiphthongised long *e* and *o*. **1907** G. MURRAY *Rise Greek Epic* ii. 55 It was a hard task for an island in that position to keep itself un-Hellenized. **1934** A. TOYNBEE *Study of Hist.* II. 79 This region remained unhellenized much longer than many places that were far more distant from the Aegean. **1960** C. S. LEWIS *Studies in Words* ii. 24 In defiance of chronology, we begin with some account of the Latin and English words in their un-hellenised condition. **1934** WEBSTER, Unindustrialized. **1962** *Rep. Constitution Commission, Pakistan 1961* iv. 40 The unindustrialized portion of Bengal. **1978** R. MITCHISON *Life in Scotland* viii. 154 The Scottish pattern of tall tenements..is to be found in older unindustrialized burghs. **1971** Unlemmatized [see *key-word-in-context* s.v. *KEY *sb.*[1] 17]. **1968** O. WYND *Sumatra Seven Zero* ii. 16 She'll have a handsome income for as long as the place stays unnationalized. **1957** L. FOX *Numerical Solution Two-Point Boundary Probl.* vii. 170 This constant is the reciprocal of the corresponding current estimate of λ, obtained as the ratio of successive unnormalized first components. **1889** *Cent. Dict.*, Unparasitized. **1949** *Proc. Soc. Exper. Biol. & Med.* LXX. 580/2 To make such values really comparable with those obtained for unparasitized blood it is necessary to know both the parasite count, and the proportions present of parasites of different sizes. **1909** WEBSTER, Unpasteurized. **1955** J. G. DAVIS *Dict. Dairying* (ed. 2) 789 Special fluting arrangements to prevent any unpasteurised milk seepages from reaching the outlet connection. **1975** *Listener* 14 Aug. 205/2 The beer here is unpasteurised, unassisted into the glass by CO_2. **1946** *Electronic Engin.* Feb. 54/3 Unplasticised polyvinyl chloride. **1982** SEARS & DARBY *Technol. of Plasticizers* v. 301 Rigid, unplasticized PVC..essentially obeys Hooke's Law for quite some distance. **1976** D. DAVIN *Woman-Work* (1978) ii. 57 Communist experience in the towns had been limited to clandestine work in which contact with the mass of unpoliticized women was very difficult. **1879** *Jrnl. Chem. Soc.* XXXV. 758 They [*sc.* terpenes] are ultimately rendered optically inactive, a considerable proportion remaining unpolymerised. **1976** *Jrnl. Molecular Biol.* CV. 527 Is there an appreciable amount of unpolymerized protein free within the cytoplasm, as there probably is for microtubules? **1958** A. TOYNBEE *East to West* 37 Even this unpressurized plane would fly high enough to make certain of that [*sc.* flying blind]. **1963** *Economist* 2 Feb. 413/2 Some of the best thinking had been done under pressure..far from..optimum conditions... Its case for an unpressurised future might have seemed stronger. **1974** P. GORE-BOOTH *With Great Truth & Respect* 57 But I did, between Chicago and Minneapolis, take my first aeroplane flight; nobody warned me what an unpressurized flight does to your ears. **1978** S. RADLEY *Death & Maiden* xiii. 123 The real, unpressurised Adnams Suffolk ale. **1978** *Detroit Free Press* 16 Apr. E2/4 (Advt.), Package of 3 Nassau brand unpressurized tennis balls. **1959** *Times* 28 May 16/6 Equally important is a constant, unpublicized two-way exchange. **1977** M. EDELMAN *Polit. Lang.* vii. 123 Both the publicized and the unpublicized aspects of policymaking processes have functions to serve. **1967** *Ann. Entomol. Soc. Amer.* LX. 1134/1 The second type of integument is found in the softer unsclerotized regions of the body. **1976** D. J. HORN *Biol. Insects* v. 212 Greater freedom of movement between sclerotized parts is afforded by thin, unsclerotized membranes at joints of moveable body parts. **1934** WEBSTER, Unsocialized. **1948** H. V. HODSON *Twentieth-Cent. Empire* x. 112 The still unstabilized and unsocialized citizens. **1964** P. MEADOWS in I. L. Horowitz *New Sociology* 451 Locating the sources of human hostility in.. unsocialized, primitive impulse, Freudian social theory provided the same kind of conservative blast at political and economic radicalism. **1948** Unstabilized [see *unsocialized* above]. **1960** *Times* 23 Feb. 12/2 The other [class of satellite] was a smaller unstabilized instrumentation package of 50 lb. **1975** *Petroleum Rev.* XXIX. 89/3 Unstabilised raw crude oil consisting of crude oil and natural gas liquids will be pumped at increasing rates of throughput to Teesside. **1909** WEBSTER, Unstandardized. **1920** S. ALEXANDER *Space, Time, & Deity* II. 262 Error is real only as possessed by the unstandardised believer. **1930** E. WEEKLEY *Adjectives & Other Words* 154, I need hardly say that he was one of the elderly and unstandardized—the sort of man..who says *onct* for *once*. **1909** WEBSTER, Unsterilized. **1945** *Mind* LIV. 327 Pasteur found that putrescible liquids exposed to unsterilised air..developed infusoria. **1979** *United States 1980/81* (Penguin Travel Guides) 333 The atmosphere in this 19th-century structure is distinctly unmodern..and unsterilized. **1973** *Guardian* 23 Feb. 17/2 The American unions seemed to accept a situation in which some 68 million workers..remained ununionized. **1984** *Listener* 1 Mar. 15/2 There is..an inability to see what this feels like from the point of view of people who may be unskilled workers who are still predominantly ununionised. **1968** P. DICKINSON *Skin Deep* iii. 42 There was still a telephone kiosk..momentarily unvandalised too. **1909** W. JAMES *Pluralistic Universe* 348 Its purity is only a relative term, meaning the proportional amount of unverbalized sensation which it [*sc.* experience] still embodies. **1977** P. STREVENS *New Orientations Teaching Eng.* xii. 149 The internalized, unverbalized rules according to which sentences are created.

c. *un-clued-up.*

1970 D. FRANCIS *Rat Race* ix. 116 The Derrydowns Six had been hired by an un-clued-up trainer. **1982** *Times* 20 Apr. 1/5 Cardinal Hume..said..'I am terribly unclued up on what constitutes a war.'

9. a. *unautumned, unaveraged, unbanked* (also *absol.*), *unbra-ed, unbrassièred, undentisted, ungated, ungoggled, unillusioned, unjacketed, unmooned, unpupilled, unrectored, unscripted, unspeeched* (later example).

1920 J. MASEFIELD *Enslaved* 6 The old un-autumned beauty that never goes away. **1905** WEBSTER, Unaveraged. **1924** G. B. SHAW *St. Joan* p. xli, The unaveraged individual, representing life..never at its merely mathematical average. **1965** *Economist* 19 June p. vii, One way of jerking the clearing banks into providing better facilities for the great unbanked public. **1980** *Daily Tel.* 9 Dec. 15 The banks are well aware that they can best pay their own wages bills by drumming up more business from the great unbanked. **1962** J. P. CARSTAIRS *Pardon my Gun* i. 20 The large cusp-like un-bra-ed bosom ..stood, prow-like. **1965** G. MCINNES *Road to Gundagai* ix. 148 He touched his hat to local Mums with shapeless unbrassiered bosoms. **1981** M. GEE *Dying, in Other Words* 74 She had pressed her unbrassièred breasts on his shoulders and said he was gorgeous. *a* **1916** H. JAMES *Sense of Past* (1917) 290 His perfect and soignées teeth..which that undentisted age can't have known the like of. **1954** *Norfolk Mag.* June 57/2 Immediately beyond the farmhouse is the now ungated entrance to the grounds. **1978** C. TOMLINSON *Shaft* 21 Did Eden Greet us ungated? **1914** M. BEERBOHM in *Eng. Rev.* Dec. 18 From time to time (for I too was ungoggled) I looked round to nod and smile. **1940** G. FRANKAU *Self-Portrait* lxii. 385, I drove like a fool, the car open and my eyes ungoggled. **1934** WEBSTER, Unillusioned. **1940** W. FAULKNER *Hamlet* II. ii. 130 The father, the lean pleasant shrewd unillusioned man..had been betrayed at the last. **1982** *London Rev. Bks.* IV. XXIV. 23/2 We competitors are unillusioned about the lipservice of the walls of leaning bodies and megaphone hands that we sprint between. **1925** *Times* 17 Aug. 6/2 A single unjacketed saucepan of a capacity equal to twice the amount of water to be put into it. **1970** D. DODGE *Hatchetman* iii. 52 They used lead bullets, unjacketed; illegal, under the Hague Convention. **1980** N. MARSH *Photo-Finish* iv. 86 He..came upon a book... It was unjacketed and the spine was rubbed. **1926** S. LESLIE *Cantab* (ed. 2) x. 115 The unmooned sky inked out the Universe. **1940** W. FAULKNER *Hamlet* II. ii. 127 The long return through night-time roads across the mooned or unmooned sleeping land. **1914** R. BROOKE *Let.* Mar. (1968) 568 They come to you by night,..& their eyes—unpupiled balls of white—fall out too, & they stink & shine. **1955** W. GADDIS *Recognitions* I. vii. 231 He did not move, nor did his unpupiled eyes betray any surprise. **1944** AUDEN *For Time Being* 31 She cannot conceivably tolerate in her presence..the rival..who does not rule but defiantly is the unrectored chaos. **1953** *Ann. Reg. 1952* 449 Previously an unscripted defamatory broadcast was treated as slander. **1966** G. N. LEECH *Eng. in Advertising* ix. 89 So far my remarks about the spoken language have applied mainly to unrehearsed and unscripted speech. **1922** JOYCE *Ulysses* 49 His mouth moulded issuing breath, unspeeched.

b. *unfootnoted.*

1964 *Economist* 19 Dec. 1356/1 A straightforward, unfootnoted historical narrative.

10. *unalloying, unarresting, uncompelling, unconflicting, unendearing, unenticing* (examples), *unexhilarating, unexpanding, unfascinating* (earlier example), *unflowering, unforfending, unforthcoming, unmatching, unminding* (cf. UNMINDING *vbl. sb.*), *unmourning, unselfpitying, unselfregarding, unselfseeking, unswinging* [*SWINGING *ppl. a.* 3 b, c], *unthreatening.*

1812 SHELLEY *Retrospect* in *Compl. Poet. Wks.* (1904) 970/2 When mountain, meadow, wood and stream With unalloying glory gleam. **1906** G. HIGGINS in A. Smith *Life of St. Agnes* p. viii, It may be objected..that a book treating of times and persons and occurrences of so ancient a date must be dull and unarresting. **1958** *Times* 25 Nov. 14/4 It was disconcerting to hear..so musically unarresting an account from her of so genial a work. **1920** W. J. LOCKE *House of Baltazar* xi. 130 We sought for possible imperative objectives, and one so apparently uncompelling as China never occurred to us. **1977** *Gramophone* Jan. 1139/3 How best to write about a set which is noteworthy but ultimately uncompelling? **1899** 'J. OXENHAM' *Rising Fortunes* xxvii. 182 His was a character of sharp contrasts—of perfect consistency, from his own point of view—of unconflicting opposites. **1938** F. SCOTT FITZGERALD *Let.* 18 Apr. (1964) 29 We are unconflicting on 90% of things. **1926** W. DE LA MARE *Connoisseur* 49 The eyes..were now peering vacantly..over a trim but unendearing moustache at the crumbs on his empty plate. **1981** F. INGLIS *Promise of Happiness* viii. 202 That is a lapse into avuncularity... In the novel..it is not unendearing. **1915** W. J. LOCKE *Jaffery* v. 63 Mountains.. were made for goats and cascades and lunatics..; and the more jagged and unenticing they are, the greater is their specious air of stupendousness. **1948** D. WELCH *Brave & Cruel* 95, I wondered that Mr. Mellon could show such fondness for Phyllis; she seemed so very unenticing to me. **1978** *Observer* 16 Apr. 38/1 The furniture was unenticing, but some American dealer would take a 40-foot container of assorted items. **1811** JANE AUSTEN *Sense & Sensibility* II. xiii. 253 The nature of her commendation..was..very unexhilarating to Edward. **1909** W. J. LOCKE *Septimus* x. 114 He walked to the window and looked out into the unexhilarating street. **1968** *Punch* 3 Jan. 32/2 With such an unexhilarating cast-list you'd expect a muted, subfusc drama. But there are surprises in store. **1905** *Spectator* 11 Mar. 363 Countries which exclude coloured labour,.. though possessing a larger area and..advantages of soil and climate, continue to suffer from..unexpanding revenue, heavy taxation, and a stationary population. **1957** 'O. EDWARDS' *Talking of Books* 231 The time came, alas —as it always must in the case of expanding collections of books and unexpanding homes—when something had to go. **1866** GEO. ELIOT *Felix Holt* III. xliii. 149 The love of this not unfascinating man. **1942** T. S. ELIOT *Little Gidding* iii. 12 Being between two lives—unflowering, between The live and the dead nettle. **1891** HARDY *Tess* III. lvii. 255 Their every idea was temporary and unforefending, like the plans of two children. **1920** 'O. DOUGLAS' *Penny Plain* xiv. 141 He might be so shy and unforthcoming that he would put people off. **1934** R. A. KNOX *Still Dead* xii. 152 He was certainly a very repressed, unforthcoming sort of boy. **1966** I. JEFFERIES *House-Surgeon* i. 13 Smiling uncomfortably and looking round for unforthcoming support from Grant. **1981** 'E. LATHEN' *Going for Gold* xvi. 183 They were guarding a secret... It tells us why Miss Deladier..was so unforthcoming when we spoke to her. **1939** D. WALLACE *E. Anglia* ii. 35 This unique church with its two unmatching towers. **1969** C. ARMSTRONG *Seven Seats to Moon* xiii. 119 A bottle and two unmatching glasses. **1945** DYLAN THOMAS in *Life & Lett.* July 28 Under the unminding skies. **1945** —— in *New Republic* 14 May 675/2 By the unmourning water Of the riding Thames. **1932** W. FAULKNER *Light in August* xi. 221 The hard, untearful and unselfpitying..yielding of that surrender. **1983** *N. & Q.* Dec. 576/1 The voice that emerges.. is that of a writer who is..generous in spirit, self-aware and unselfpitying. *a* **1945** E. R. EDDISON *Mezentian Gate* (1958) ii. 21 An ambiency of beauty that lived in her whole frame and posture, an easefulness and reposefulness of unselfregarding grace. **1982** W. J. WALSH *R. K. Narayan* i. 27 An oblique and as unself-regarding a treatment as anything like an autobiography could possibly be. **1931** W. S. CHURCHILL *World Crisis* VI. iii. 53 Fop, dandy, la-di-da; amiable, polite and curiously un-selfseeking. **1963** *Times* 7 June 7/3 Edward Grey, 'the most completely unselfconscious and unselfseeking politician I have ever known'. **1958** K. GOODWIN in P. Gammond *Decca Bk. Jazz* xiii. 153 Rumsey—himself a rather dull, plodding, completely unswinging bassist. **1967** *Punch* 23 Aug. 275/2 It only takes you a day or two in this utterly unswinging country to realise what a frightful crushing bore the legendary London Scene has become. **1969** *Daily Tel.* 29 May 22/7 An unswinging Anglo-Irishman who stands for the common decencies now so acutely unfashionable. **1972** *Jazz & Blues* Feb. 22/1 Marshall is a little unswinging in places but Weston is suitably solid. **1903** E. WHARTON *Sanctuary* I. i. 11 The very lifting of the cloud—remote, unthreatening as it had been.

11. *unarguably, unassessably, unboringly, unbridgeably, unconsciently, unhungrily, unidentifiably, unignorably, unprotestingly, unselectively, unurgently.*

1929 *Daily Express* 3 Jan. 8/6 'You know Mr. Umph, don't you?' with an intonation implying that not to know Mr. Umph leaves one unarguably in the certifiable class. **1978** *Nature* 20 Apr. 666/3 By excluding a sizable class of environmental variables, high within group heritability, unarguably does raise the probability of the remaining classes of possible explanations. **1937** J. R. R. TOLKIEN *Hobbit* xii. 231 Surely, O Smaug the unassessably wealthy, you must realize that your success has made you some bitter enemies? **1921** F. G. ELLERTON *Let.* 6 Sept. in *John Bailey* (1935) 214 You do his life most frightfully well and unboringly and your observes on *Paradise Lost* and *Paradise Regained* are most excellent. **1932** *Times Lit. Suppl.* 21 Jan. 33/3 The unique, the unbridgably different. **1979** *Church Times* 30 Nov. (Christmas Bk. Suppl.) p. xi/1, Christ and God are presented as living in a world unbridgeably remote. **1929** R. BRIDGES *Testament of Beauty* II. 51 So, tho' slowly and unconsciently, he remembereth. **1922** JOYCE *Ulysses* 172 His eyes unhungrily saw shelves of tins, sardines, gaudy lobsters' claws. **1965** 'R. MACDONALD' *Far Side of Dollar* xxiii. 204 Susanna broiled me a steak, and chewed unhungrily on a piece of it. **1934** F. M. FORD *Let.* 27 Sept. (1965) 235, I never guyed you either identifiably or unidentifiably. **1982** A. PRICE *Old Vengeful* ii. 42 The new voice..was.. unidentifiably classless. **1960** E. BOWEN *Time in Rome* ii. 41 No tribute to an assassinated uncle can have been ever more unignorably placed. **1953** R. LEHMANN *Echoing Grove* 80 'I didn't realize she was so completely your kept woman.' 'She wasn't,' he said unprotestingly. **1972** P. CAVE *Judas Freaks* xv. 104 She followed unprotestingly. **1929** A. N. WHITEHEAD *Process & Reality* 161 The pattern refers unselectively to any eternal objects. **1977** *Nature* 3 Nov. 15/2 Quantitative measurements.. show hydroxyl radicals..to interact unselectively with most biological molecules at rates which are practically diffusion controlled. **1980** V. CUNNINGHAM *Spanish Civil War Verse* 45 Jack Lindsay's Declamation now seems unurgently lengthy and even turgid.

12. *unaccentuation, unamaze, unamazement, unbook, unclarity, uncomfiness, uncountry, uncrackability, uncreditworthiness, undeath, undeathliness, undecrease, undeviation, uneducation, unenlightenment, unfreshness, unfulfilment, unglamorousness, unimportancy, unintelligentsia, uninterruptability, uninvolvement, unlight, unmeritocracy, unpriggishness, unrepose, unsurprise, unwettability.*

1879 G. M. HOPKINS *Let.* 27 Feb. in Hopkins & Dixon *Corr.* (1955) 22 Wherever there is an accent or stress, there there is also so much unaccentuation, so to speak, or slack. **1936** W. FAULKNER *Absalom, Absalom!* i. 8 Then in the long unamaze Quentin seemed to watch them. **1954** —— *Fable* 369 Thinking in a sort of quiet unamazement, Yes, I probably knew from the moment he sent for me what door I should have to emerge from. **1965** *Probl. Communism* July/Aug. 56 (*heading*) Another un-book. **1982** *Underground Grammarian* Nov. 5/1 Reading experts always need tricky new gimmicks to put in their unbooks. **1934** WEBSTER, Unclarity. **1936** *Mind* XLV. 503 Prof. Reichenbach's discussion of material, formal, and tautologous implication..suffers from the same unclarity. **1980** 'J. LE CARRÉ' *Smiley's People* v. 54 'Vladimir telephoned the Circus at lunch-time today, sir,' Mostyn began, leaving some unclarity as to which 'sir' he was addressing. **1914** L. S. WOOLF *Wise Virgins* ii. 39 'I hate being uncomfortable. But then I don't think I often am, except when I..cut my nails.' 'Oh, that sort of uncomfyness!' said Gwen. **1964** W. GOLDING *Spire* ix. 178 In this uncountry there was blue sky and light, consent and so sin. **1923** *Daily Mail* 10 Jan. 9 (Advt.), The Vitreosil Globe, because of its 'uncrackability', lies close to the mantle. **1966** *Economist* 22 Oct. 413/2 Even the unlucky companies mentioned above are..credit worthy enough: the depths of uncreditworthiness below remain murky indeed. **1933** L. RIDING *Poet* v. 125 The sum of the first and second sign Shall be undeath of the moon. **1974** *Globe & Mail* (Toronto) 24 July 13/4 There is, every now and then, a film that escapes this sort of un-death. **1922** JOYCE *Ulysses* 379 She prayed to God the Allruthful to have his dear soul in his undeathliness. **1898** HARDY *Wessex Poems* 5 Knowing that, though Love cease, Love's race shows undecrease. **1932** W. FAULKNER *Light in August* xix. 435 He was going fast too,..with..the implacable undeviation of Juggernaut or Fate. *a* **1936** G. K. CHESTERTON *Common Man* (1950) vii. 39 It is not their uneducation but their education that I scoff at. **1950** T. S. ELIOT *Cocktail Party* II. 110 While still in a state of unenlightenment, You could always say: 'he could not love any woman.' **1967** T. KENEALLY *Bring Larks & Heroes* xxii. 178 A creature of dish-eyed unenlightenment. **1897** ST. L. STRACHEY *From Grave to Gay* 288 We can keep the unfreshness of our eggs to ourselves, but not so the unfreshness of our jokes. **1969** J. CHEEVER *Bullet Park* vi. 79 She..exhaled the faint unfreshness of humanity at the end of the day. **1851** H. MELVILLE *Moby Dick* (U.S. ed.) lxxxi. 397 Oh! that unfulfilments should follow the prophets. **1881** 'L. MALET' *Counsel of Perfection* xiv. 323 There is a wonderful compensation in the unfulfilment of prophecy. **1978** F. KING *Action* ii. 12 The pathos of his unfulfilment. **1958** *Economist* 26 July 277 He has probably had to contend..also with the poor pay offered and the unglamorousness of the whole proceeding. *a* **1960** E. M. FORSTER *Maurice* (1971) xlvi. 226 Excuse me if I work at unimportancies for a bit now. **1930** G. B. SHAW *Philanderer* Pref., in *Works* VII. 68 That far more numerous body which may be called the Unintelligentsia was as unconscious of Ibsen as of any other political influence. **1964** R. H. ROBINS *Gen. Linguistics* v. 211 The unitary behaviour of such forms in sentences and their uninterruptability..are the grounds for ascribing single word status to them. **1966** *Punch* 2 Nov. 682/2 He remains an aloof catalyst. Yet his very uninvolvement has a value of its own. *a* **1973** J. R. R. TOLKIEN *Silmarillion* (1977) viii. 74 A cloak of darkness she wove about them ..an Unlight, in which things seemed to be no more, and which eyes could not pierce, for it was void. **1970** *New Scientist* 31 Dec. 586/2 Large families are not the prerogative of the feckless poor whether in the Third World or in the urban ghettoes of the unmeritocracy. **1955** S. SPENDER *Making of Poem* 75 There are standards of sensibility or of 'unpriggishness' which are a development of what Samuel Butler approvingly called 'being a nice person'. **1868** J. H. NEWMAN *Verses on Various Occasions* 312 The prison where they roam in hopeless unrepose. **1954** W. FAULKNER *Fable* 343 Thicker and denser than the stars in its concentration of anguish and unrepose. **1932** —— *Light in August* xvii. 371 He seemed to stand aloof,..thinking with a kind of grim unsurprise: 'Byron Bunch borning a baby.' **1955** W. GADDIS *Recognitions* II. iii. 393 A, M, D, G, sequence of unsurprise (Lao-tse's 84-year gestation), right Nicodemus? **1937** *Nature* 26 June 1107/2 The unwettability of natural cotton is generally ascribed to the existence of a film of wax or oil covering its outer surface.

13. *unforgetting.*

1930 AUDEN *Poems* 8 Unforgetting is not today's forgetting For yesterday.

14. (nonce-wds.) *unbloom, undie, unfulfil, untouch, unvision.*

1898 HARDY *Wessex Poems* 8 And why unblooms the best hope ever sown? **1952** DYLAN THOMAS *Coll. Poems* p. x, These seathumbed leaves That will fly and fall Like leaves of trees and as soon Crumble and undie. **1922** HARDY *Late Lyrics & Earlier* 37 Though duties due that press to do This whole long day I unfulfil. *Ibid.* 34 And time untouched me with a trace Of soul-smart or despair. **1917** —— *Moments of Vision* 207 I'll not unvision A shape which, somehow, there may be.

16. In telegrams *un-* is sometimes used in nonce formations with any part of speech to avoid a separate negative.

1936 E. WAUGH *Waugh in Abyssinia* 161 Cables were soon arriving... '*Require earliest name life story photograph American nurse upblown* [*sc.* bombed] *Adowa.*' We replied '*Nurse unupblown*,' and after a few days she disappeared from the news. **1967** *Observer* 8 Oct. 2/5 Regret expelled by Syrians after twenty-four hours unreason given. **1968** *Punch* 3 Apr. 485/3 All those compound words like 'unproceed'..in press cables.

un-². Add: **3.** *unbake, unban, unbatten, unbore, unclutter* (examples), *undip* [*DIP *v.* 6 d], *unendear, uninvent, unjumble, untape, untease.*

1864 G. M. HOPKINS *Poems* (1967) 15 Wasteful wide huge-girthèd Nile Unbakes my pores, and streams, and makes all fresh. **1968** *Guardian* 5 Sept. 9/2 Book censorship has eased since the Dail passed a law which un-bans a book after 12 years in purdah. **1983** *Bookseller* 4 June 2072/3 *Lady Chatterley's Lover*: unbanned in South Africa in 1980, it has been selling through Leserskring at a steady 1,000 a quarter. **1788** W. BLIGH in R. M. Bowker *Mutiny* (1978) iii. 90 Unbattened all the Hatchways. **1927** R. A. FREEMAN *Certain Dr. Thorndyke* iv. 62 Osmond..unbattened the doors, and, opening them, slid the wriggling captive down the ladder on to the cabin floor. **1922** M. A. VON ARNIM *Enchanted April* xiii. 213 Rose felt right down at her very roots that if you have once thoroughly bored somebody it is next to impossible to unbore him. **1930** *Times* 29 Nov. 13/6 Sadler's Wells..

appears to go farthest in uncluttering the conditions for witnessing the performance. **1977** A. Scholefield *Venom* III. 90 He liked to clear everything away, to unclutter the stage. **1966** T. Wisdom *High-Performance Driving* x. 104 Drivers..use their headlights badly. They do not undip them fast enough after meeting other traffic. **1865** G. M. Hopkins *Poems* (1967) 21 Still thou bind'st me to fresh fealty..for nothing here Nor elsewhere can thy sweetness unendear. **1962** *Guardian* 4 Oct. 6/5 It may not be possible to un-invent the motor-car. **1982** *Church Times* 22 Oct. 5/1 Nuclear weapons cannot be uninvented. **1966** J. Derrick *Teaching English to Immigrants* v. 206 Pupils can also be asked to unjumble and write out in correct order a series of sentences that should obviously follow a certain sequence (such as the description of a picture story or of a series of actions). **1979** J. Gardner *Nostradamus Traitor* xliii. 204 He's the bloody expert on Nostradamus. He's even..unjumbled the prophecies. **1968** 'R. Macdonald' *Instant Enemy* xxxiv. 217 He untaped my wrists and ankles. **1981** E. Ward *Baltic Emerald* xxi. 175 Henry untaped the envelope and photographs from my back. **1932** Auden in *Rev. Eng. Stud.* (1978) Aug. 287 A piece of paper, neatly Folded in a hexagon shape Which Sampson took and unteased and read.

4. a. *unblouse, undogcollar* (nonce), *unpearl* (nonce).

1922 Joyce *Ulysses* 254 Miss bronze unbloused her neck. **1953** Dylan Thomas *Under Milk Wood* (1954) 74 Esau,..undogcollared because of his little weakness, was scythed to the bone one harvest by mistake. **1936** A. E. Housman *More Poems* 18 For these of old the trader Unpearled the Indian seas.

b. *unzone* (later example).

1907 Joyce *Chamber Music* xi, Begin thou softly to unzone Thy girlish bosom into him.

5. *uncrate.*

1929 W. Faulkner *Sound & Fury* 235, I went on to the back, where old Job was uncrating them [*sc.* cultivators]. **1963** *Ann. Reg. 1962* 520 In addition, jet bombers, capable of carrying nuclear weapons, are now being uncrated and assembled on Cuba.

6. b. *unfather.*

1876 [see *unchild *v.*].

7. *unportal* (nonce).

1922 Joyce *Ulysses* 461 The Timepiece (*Unportalling.*) Cuckoo. Cuckoo. Cuckoo.

9. Another redundant or extended use (= 'peel off') exists in *unpeel*. Cf. Unpeeled *ppl. a.*

1904 W. James *Let.* 16 June in R. B. Perry *Thought & Character W. James* (1935) II. 487 The original 'that' may vanish in the infinitely regressive superposition of human 'whats'—we can't today unpeel them wholly. *a* **1914** in *Penguin Bk. Austral. Ballads* (1964) 122 Then the sheila raced off squealin', And her clothes she was un-peelin'. **1969** *Washington Post* 14 Apr. A27/3 Aides believe that the Kennedy ploy..will ultimately unpeel Republican Senators from the anti-ABM forces.

un, 'un[1]. (Later examples.)

1919 G. B. Shaw *Heartbreak House* III. 109 Right in the gravel pit: I seen it. Serve un right! **1932** D. L. Sayers *Have his Carcase* xi. 134 Soon as I come in sight of 'un, I zee un. **1977** P. Hill *Liars* x. 140 The ladies liked 'un.

un, 'un[2]. (Earlier example.)

c **1810** W. Hickey *Mem.* (1960) iv. 64 The young 'un there wanted to be off.

unabatable, *a.* (Earlier example.)

1788 T. Paine *Amer. Crisis* (1787) 170 The enmity is perpetual, unalterable, and unabateable.

unacceptable, *a.* Add: (Examples in phr. *the unacceptable face of—.*)

1973 E. Heath in *Hansard Commons* 15 May 1243 It is the unpleasant and unacceptable face of capitalism, but one should not suggest that the whole of British industry consists of practices of this kind. **1973** *Times* 5 June 1/6 He called the actions of the *News of the World* 'the unacceptable face of journalism'. **1975** A. Beevor *Violent Brink* vii. 210 Let us look at the unacceptable face of Communism. **1982** *Guardian* 8 Jan. 18/1 The unacceptable face of modern men's tennis was seen again during the Barratt world doubles championship..yesterday when Hank Pfister..swore at the match umpire and then accused him of cheating.

unaccountable, *sb.* **2.** (Later examples.)

1833 R. Dyer *Nine Yrs. Actor's Life* 66 His non-engagement in London is amongst the unaccountables of metropolitan management. **1961** 'J. le Carré' *Call for Dead* viii. 83 Of all the unaccountables in the case, that worried him most.

unaccustomedly, *adv.* (See small-type note s.v. Unaccustomed *ppl. a.*) (Examples.)

1963 *Economist* 2 Nov. 472/1 Unaccustomedly emotional language. **1980** H. Curtiss *Poisoned Orchard* iii. 22 She had put her car away, unaccustomedly, because of the sub-zero temperature forecast.

una corda (ū·nă kōᵊ·ɹdă). *Mus.* [It., = one string.] As a direction in music for the piano, etc.: use the soft pedal (which on grand pianos softens the tone by shifting the hammers so as to strike only one or two strings instead of two or three for each note). Also *attrib.*, designating such a pedal mechanism. Cf. *soft pedal *sb.*

1849 *Hamilton's Celebrated Dict.* s.v., *Una corda* (Italian). Implies that a passage is to be played upon only one string. **1876** Stainer & Barrett *Dict. Mus. Terms* 444/1 *Un, Una, Uno* (It.), one; as *Una corda*, one string. **1909** *Cent. Dict.* Suppl. s.v. *pedal* n., The direction *una corda* signifies simply the use of this [shifting] pedal. **1931** D. F. Tovey *Beethoven Sonatas for Pianoforte* xxix. 140 Beethoven's double shift from *tre corda* through *due corda* to *una corda*. **1961** [see *escapement 3]. **1979** *Sci. Amer.* Jan. 99/2 To prevent this the piano is equipped with the una corda pedal, whose mechanical function is to shift the entire keyboard so that a hammer strikes only two strings of a unison triplet.

unadopted, *ppl. a.* (Examples corresponding to *adopted *ppl. a.* 1 b.)

1938 [see *adopted *ppl. a.* 1 b]. **1963** *Times* 18 May 10/7 It is virtually undistinguished except for the number of roughly surfaced streets compelling a glance at signs proclaiming that they are unadopted. **1970** J. Burke *Four Stars for Danger* ii. 21 That road up to Bryncroeso Hall is unadopted. If the people at the Hall don't want to do anything about it, nobody's going to make them.

unaffectioned, *ppl. a.* (Later example.)

1911 K. Hare *Green Fields* 5 His tuneable unaffectioned voice that loved the matter Has in the grey room conjured up the sunshine.

unaffixed, *ppl. a.* Add: Also as *adj.* [Un- 9 a].

1964 R. H. Robins *Gen. Linguistics* vi. 260 In Japanese the formation of words..referring to more than one entity ..leaves the resultant words syntactically equivalent to unaffixed forms.

unaflow, var. *uniflow *a.*

unali·gned, *ppl. a.* [Un-[1] 8.] **1.** Not physically aligned.

1936 F. M. Ford *Let.* 2 July (1965) 254 This damned new machine—unaligned a's and all which means that it will have to go back to the shop. **1962** Corson & Lorrain *Introd. Electromagn. Fields* iii. 107 An unaligned dipole therefore has greater energy than an aligned one.

2. = *non-aligned *a.* Also *absol.* as *sb.*

1961 *Guardian* 28 Jan. 2/3 India and the 'unaligned nations'. **1962** C. B. Marshall in L. W. Martin *Neutralism & Nonalignment* ii. 13 (*heading*) On understanding the unaligned. **1965** *Listener* 10 June 851/1 Africans feel the need to be wholly African, unaligned, even in their form of government.

unali·ke, *a.* [Un-[1] 7.] Different; not alike.

1934 'L. G. Gibbon' *Grey Granite* 210 If Ewan had been as that other Ewan..and she paused... Was he so unalike? **1944** *Penguin New Writing* XX. 61 Arthur continued to wonder..how these two unalike girls had come to set up together. **1961** B. Vawter *Conscience of Israel* v. 127 If they are two prophets in agreement on fundamentals, they are also severely unalike in numerous ways. **1978** D. Murphy *Place Apart* xii. 250 Cycling is by far the best way to travel around the North where regions only twenty miles apart can be so very unalike.

unalive, *a.* Add: **b.** Lacking in vitality; not living. Also *fig.*

1905 M. Dods *Let.* 14 Apr. (1911) 176 How you can think yourself empty and unalive I don't know. **1931** H. S. Walpole *Judith Paris* II. v. 338 All the members of the Herries family, with whom she had so lately been, seemed unreal and unalive. **1935** E. Bowen *House in Paris* II. x. 209 The street reflected the blind windows and a strip of unalive wet sky. **1954** R. Speaight *George Eliot* iv. 51 The true criticism of Stephen is not that he is unattractive but that he is unalive.

unaltered, *ppl. a.* Add: Of an animal: not castrated.

1946 H. A. Smith *Rhubarb* ii. 28 An unaltered cat is by nature inclined to wildness. **1967** A. Lewin *Unaltered Cat* II. iv. 117 Have you ever tried keeping an unaltered cat in an apartment?

un-American, *a.* Add to def.: Contrary to the ideals and interests of the United States of America. (Further examples.)

1893 H. B. Fuller *Cliff-Dwellers* xviii. 242 Does it seem unreasonable that the State [*sc.* Illinois]..which has done most..to check alien excesses and un-American ideas, should also be the State to give the country the final blend of the American character and its ultimate metropolis? **1917** T. Roosevelt *Let.* 10 Jan. in *Proc. Congr. Constructive Patriotism* 172 Everything is un-American that tends either to government by a plutocracy or government by a mob. **1936** F. R. Marvin (*title*) Fools gold: an exposé of un-American activities and political action in the United States. **1938** *N.Y. Times* 27 May 2/2 The House..today passed a resolution providing for the appointment of a seven-man committee to investigate un-American propaganda in the United States. **1958** E. H. Clements *Uncommon Cold* iii. 97 Visas aren't handed out by Americans to anyone. They are averse to Communists, criminals, all un-American activities. **1980** in S. Terkel *Amer. Dreams* 363 The Red scare was on, the witch hunt. The House Un-American Activities Committee came to town.

un-Americanism (recent examples).

1955 C. L. Sewrey in *Comprehensive Dissert. Index* (1973) XXVIII. 116/3 The alleged 'un-Americanism' of the Church. **1960** *Guardian* 26 Aug. 5/1 To question either now seems tantamount to un-Americanism. **1978** *Amer. Speech 1975* L. 315 The sin is neither as recent a matter of concern nor as diagnostic of un-Americanism as Dwight Bolinger implies.

unamusing, *ppl. a.* (Earlier example.)

1794 F. Burney *Jrnl.* 2 Mar. (1973) III. 43 He found it very unamusing to have a Walk without any *but*.

unanalysable, *a.* Add: Hence **una:nalysabi·lity.**

1941 *Mind* I. 335 The sort of unanalysability which the P[ure] E[go] theory attributes to class (1) 'someone' sentences. **1973** E. Jong *Fear of Flying* i. 3 There were 117 psychoanalysts on the Pan Am flight to Vienna and I'd been treated by at least six of them... God knows it was a tribute either to the shrinks' ineptitude or my own glorious unanalyzability that I was now..more scared of flying than when I began my analytic adventures some thirteen years earlier.

unanalytic, *a.* (Earlier example.)

1865 *North Brit. Rev.* XLIII. 27 Reflective Realism is only a change in the unanalytic manner of thinking about objects.

Unani, var. *Yunani.

unanimism (yūnæ·nimiz'm). Also ‖ **unanimisme** (ünan*i*mism). [ad. F. *unanimisme*, f. *unanime* unanimous + *-isme* -ism.] A French poetic movement of the early twentieth century which emphasized the submersion of the poet in the group consciousness and which was characterized by simple diction, absence of rhyme, and strongly accented rhythms.

1931 [see *populism b]. **1936** *Times Lit. Suppl.* 7 Mar. 197/3 But Mr. Buchanan is not indulging in the fallacies of *unanimisme*. **1959** *Oxf. Compan. French Lit.* 724/1 *Unanimisme*, a 20th-century poetic movement which owes much to the Whitmanesque doctrine of universal brotherhood as well as to more modern psycho-philosophical theories of group emotion. **1964** *Listener* 27 Aug. 315/2 This man [*sc.* Apollinaire]..under the banner of Unanimism..had loudly and proudly identified himself with everything quick and living. **1971** J. Willett in A. Bullock *Twentieth Century* x. 235/2 Jules Romains, whose faith in the anonymous mass..inspired his short-lived doctrine of Unanimism.

¶ **unani·sm,** ‖ **unanisme.**

1919 W. B. Yeats *If I were Four-&-Twenty* (1940) ii. 4 There has been a development in various forms of literature—in French 'unanisme' for instance—towards the expression..of an emotional agreement with some historical or local group. **1958** *Times Lit. Suppl.* 4 July 383/1 A study..of unanism in the plays of Jules Romains.

unanimist (yūnæ·nimist), *sb.* (and *a.*) *Also* ‖ **unanimiste** (ünan*i*mist). [ad. F. *unanimiste*: see prec., -ist.] An adherent of unanimism. Also *attrib.* or as *adj.*

1915 A. Huxley *Let.* Dec. (1969) 88 This good man [*sc.* D. H. Lawrence]..proposes..to go to the deserts of Florida there..to found a sort of unanimist colony. **1918** [see *surrealist *a.* and *sb.*]. **1929** V. Payen-Payne in M. S. McLaren *Douze Sonnets de Varlet* 9 Varlet..has been classed among the Unanimists because of his friendship with Jules Romains and Georges Duhamel. **1938** *Times Lit. Suppl.* 10 Sept. p. iii/1 From such an incident does the writer, with something like the *unanimiste* technique of Jules Romains..develop a theme of nation-wide, or even world-wide, import. **1959** *Oxf. Compan. French Lit.* 724/2 The *unanimistes* had their own, fairly recognizable, technique of versification. **1974** *Encycl. Brit. Micropædia* X. 253/1 The Unanimiste theories of prosody..resembled those of the American poet Walt Whitman.

unappreciable, *a.* (Earlier example.)

1801 F. Burney *Let.* 29 Oct. (1975) V. 21 My dear Charlottina, whom I regard as an unappreciable consolation & delight to you.

unappreciative, *a.* (Earlier example.)

1840 J. S. Mill *Let.* 23 Dec. in *Wks.* (1963) XIII. 453 A man of Molesworth's sort of limitation has a natural tendency to be intolerant, because unappreciative of ideas & persons unlike him & his ideas.

unapprehended, *ppl. a.* **2.** (Later example.)

1977 *Daily Tel.* 5 Mar. 3/1 It included 341 multi-offenders and concluded with 60 unapprehended men wanted in Dallas this year.

unapropos (ʋnæprŏpōᵘ·, ʋnæ·prŏpōᵘ), *a.* and *adv.* [Un-[1] 7, 11 b.] Not apropos; irrelevant(ly); inappropriate(ly).

1840 H. Mozley *Let.* 13 Oct. in D. Mozley *Newman Family Lett.* (1962) III. 92, I have none of the un-a-propos propensities that would stand in the way of engagement with some ladies. **1940** J. Pope-Hennessy *Let.* in J. Lees-Milne *Ancestral Voices* (1975) 267 Christianity.. seems a clear and tranquil stream running parallel to but utterly detached from the turgid river of the war, and ..too unapropos for words. **1956** R. Robinson *Landscape with Dead Dons* xxi. 194, I was chatting to Christelow when it occurred to me quite unapropos that one of the things they had in common was *The Book*.

unarithmetic, *a.* Delete *Obs.*[-1] and add later example.

1953 *Trans. Amer. Inst. Electr. Engineers* LXXII. 597/2 The unarithmetic representation for zero is standard in the 2-out-of-5 code.

unarmed, *ppl. a.* Add: **1.** *transf.* Freq. in phr. *unarmed combat.*

1947 'N. Shute' *Chequer Board* ix. 262 'You went on to a course in unarmed combat. What did they teach you to do there?' 'We was taught how to attack an armed man just with our hands and feet.' **1957** J. Braine *Room at Top* xxx. 252 A hand on my shoulder..started the

Unarmed Combat reflexes working. **1973** J. R. L. ANDERSON *Death on Rocks* ii. 39 If I could get my hands on him—well, I'd been quite good at what the Army calls unarmed combat.

unartificial, *a.* **2.** (Later example.)
1982 *N. & Q.* Aug. 361/2 He demonstrates that Wordsworth considered a good epitaph to be an expression in unartificial language of the deep feelings of the bereaved for the dead.

unary (yū·nări), *a.* [f. L. *ūn-us* one + -ARY[1], after BINARY, TERNARY *adjs.*] **1.** *Chem.* Of a chemical system: consisting of a single component.
1923 A. C. D. RIVETT *Phase Rule* i. 25 For systems of one, two, three, four, five (and so on) components, one uses the terms unary, binary, ternary, quaternary, quinary (and so on), respectively. **1980** *Mineral. Abstr.* XXXI. 311/1 Sixteen possible configurations of phase diagrams have been deduced for unary four-phase multisystems.
2. *Math.*, *Logic*, and *Linguistics.* Of an operator, operation, or transformation: involving or operating on a single element.
1931 *Bull. Amer. Math. Soc.* XXXVII. 487 Let p be the result of an undefined unary operation on a K-element p, and $p+q$ the result of an undefined binary operation on the K-elements p, q. **1940** [see *SINGULARY *a.*]. **1961** *Jrnl. Assoc. Computing Machinery* VIII. 579 The five binary arithmetic operators (↑, ×, /, +, −), the two unary arithmetic operators (+, −). **1965** *Language* XLI. 270 Robert Stockwell has described rules that indicate the colorless patterns for kernel sentences and unary transformations. **1968** J. J. C. SMART *Betw. Sci. & Philos.* ii. 24 'Not' can be thought of as a unary sentence connective. **1973** C. W. GEAR *Introd. Computer Sci.* iii. 104 The unary arithmetic operators take precedence over all of the binary operators and must be performed first. **1976** J. S. GRUBER *Lexical Structures in Syntax & Semantics* II. i. 266 If the treatment is through a unary transformation that alters structure, the dependency of the transformation on apparently semantic factors becomes a matter of graver theoretical consequences.
3. Composed of a single item or element.
1968 P. M. POSTAL *Aspects Phonol. Theory* i. 13 Natural languages have structures which are such that the markers on every level can be looked upon as sets (sometimes unary sets) of strings of elements. **1968** *Amer. Documentation* Jan. 73/1 Items are either unary or multiple, depending upon whether they are composed of a single piece of information (which may itself be composed of any number of characters or words) or of two or more separate pieces of information.

unascended, *ppl. a.* (Earlier example.)
1820 SHELLEY *Prometh. Unb.* III. iv. 203 The loftiest star of unascended heaven.

unashamedly, *adv.* (See small-type note s.v. UNASHAMED *ppl. a.*) (Examples.)
1905 W. J. LOCKE *Morals of Marcus Ordeyne* iv. 50 She was wearing a deep red silk peignoir,..unashamedly Parisian, which clung to every salient curve of her figure. **1928** *Manch. Guardian Weekly* 10 Aug. 115/2 They break out..into dance measures of an unashamedly negroid vigour. **1983** M. GILBERT *Black Seraphim* iii. 35 Amanda ..was listening unashamedly.

unassailability. (See small-type note s.v. UNASSAILABLE *a.*) (Recent examples.)
1952 *Mind* LXI. 504 Its unassailability has been bought at the price of making no claim about the world. **1957** J. S. HUXLEY *Relig. without Revelation* i. 27 The unassailability of private property.

unassailableness. (Earlier example.)
1854 GEO. ELIOT tr. *Feuerbach's Essence Christianity* xiv. 136 The truth and unassailableness of their subjective feelings.

unate (yūnēi·t), *a. Math.* [f. L. *ūn-us* one + -ATE[2].] Of a logical function: containing no variable in both negated and unnegated forms. Hence **una·teness.**
1960 *Proc. IRE* XLVIII. 1336/1 The first of these, Theorem 1, gives one of the most easily recognized properties of a setting function, unateness... A unate function is defined as one from which one of each pair of complementary literals..can be eliminated. **1978** S. C. LEE *Mod. Switching Theory* iv. 118 Any threshold function is unate.

unatmosphe·ric, *a.* [UN-[1] 7.] That conveys no suggestion of tone or mood; that fails to evoke associations. Hence **unatmosphe·rically** *adv.*
1913 E. F. BENSON *Thorley Weir* iii. 68 Arthur..found this peremptory young savage slightly alarming. For himself he demanded that social intercourse should be conducted in a serene atmosphere of politeness, of manners... He thought he had seldom seen anybody so unatmospheric. *Ibid.* 69 Frank looked at him quite unatmospherically. **1938** *Scrutiny* VII. 179 His [*sc.* Roussel's] instrumentation is unatmospheric. **1963** *Listener* 28 Feb. 393/2 A couple of very stagy and unatmospheric outdoor sets. **1976** *Gramophone* Oct. 584/2 The 'Royal Hunt and Storm' begins unatmospherically, with the strings at once forceful and casual, carrying none of the sense of light slowly dawning on a classical landscape.

unattached, *ppl. a.* Add: Hence **unatta·chedness.**
1936 WIRTH & SHILS tr. *Mannheim's Ideology & Utopia* III. iv. 140 The 'unattachedness' of the intellectuals. **1981** M. WARNER *Joan of Arc* iv. 86 The..unattachedness of the displaced and the poor.

unattributable, *a.* (Later examples.)
1967 *Listener* 9 Nov. 594/2 The 'unattributable' story, which is valid information to be published as long as the source is not identified. **1972** T. LILLEY *K Section* xli. 229 The information is unattributable and for your ears only.

unauthentically, *adv.* (Later example.)
1975 *Daily Tel.* 17 Mar. 10/2 John Constable's amusingly, if probably unauthentically, informal continuo-comments.

unavailability. (See small-type note s.v. UNAVAILABLENESS.) (Examples.)
1855 D. G. ROSSETTI *Let.* 29 July (1965) I. 265 If Mr. Oakes should..be no longer in the above capacity,.. let me know at once of Mr. O.'s unavailability. **1967** *Listener* 13 July 61/2 In England the young composer is sadly hampered by the unavailability of one possible salvation—electronic equipment. **1980** J. KRANTZ *Princess Daisy* xvi. 267 *That's* what drives him crazy.. your essential *unavailability.*

unavailingly, *adv.* (Earlier example.)
1748 RICHARDSON *Clarissa* IV. 170 Must..those arms ..be used to repel brutal force; all their strength, unavailingly perhaps, exerted to repel it?

unavertible, var. of UNAVERTABLE *a.*
1897 J. L. ALLEN *Choir Invisible* vi. 78 Their own inescapable tombs, their own unavertible ruins. **1929** *Daily Tel.* 15 Jan. 11/7 The public is seldom concerned with the future until it has become an unavertible disaster.

unavoidability. (See small-type note s.v. UNAVOIDABLE *a.*) (Examples.)
1858 D. G. ROSSETTI *Lett.* (1965) I. 336 Three evenings a week at least are..used up away from work by unavoidabilities. **1938** *Mind* XLVII. 47 Arguments which seek to prove unavoidability by reference to determinism are to be dismissed as ridiculous.

unbated, *ppl. a.* **2.** Delete † *Obs.* and add later example.
1979 A. WILLIAMSON *Funeral March* xv. 81 'Do you know how Andersson died?'..'Well—I suppose it was the unbated spear?'

unbeautifully, *adv.* (Later examples.)
1879 GEO. ELIOT *Let.* 5 Mar. (1956) VII. 111 The margin seems perilously and unbeautifully narrow. **1922** *Daily Mail* 23 Nov. 8 A Frenchwoman would as soon be seen in shabby shoes as with wisps of hair escaping unbeautifully from her coiffure. **1984** A. PRICE *Sion Crossing* xi. 222 His lip twisted unbeautifully.

unbecoming, *ppl. a.* Add: **d.** Const. *to.*
1893 WILDE *Lady Windermere's Fan* III. 90 There is nothing in the whole world so unbecoming to a woman as a Nonconformist conscience. **1901** G. B. SHAW *Capt. Brassbound's Conversion* II. 245 Brandyfaced Jack: I name you for conduct and language unbecoming to a gentleman. **1980** *Washington Post* 1 June A17 But to set out to fix blame is..unbecoming to America. **1982** *Financial Times* 21 Aug. 4 Rumours flew about in a manner most unbecoming to the month.
e. *ellipt.* after a sb. in *conduct unbecoming* (*sc.* of a military officer); also *transf.*
1971 B. ENGLAND (*title*) Conduct unbecoming. **1976** *Time* 5 July 46/3 The Merchant Marine Academy, which classifies copulation in the barracks as conduct unbecoming and worthy of dismissal. **1976** *Times Lit. Suppl.* 6 Aug. 988/4 Conduct unbecoming in a man of letters must be reprimanded.

unbegot, *ppl. a.* Delete † *Obs.* and add later example.
1936 A. E. HOUSMAN *More Poems* 14 This is for all ill-treated fellows Unborn and unbegot.

unbeing, *vbl. sb.* Delete † *Obs.* and add later examples.
1935 G. BARKER *Janus* 16 The lighter bird of being, obstructing my line of sight, entirely conceals the form of the bird of unbeing. **1936** T. S. ELIOT *Coll. Poems 1909–35* 191 Love is itself unmoving... Caught in the form of limitation Between un-being and being. **1944** L. MACNEICE *Springboard* 17 From the lubber depths of my unbeing.

unbeknown, *ppl. a.* Add: **1.** (Later examples.)
1947 *Sun* (Baltimore) 31 Oct. 10/3 That this number is insufficient is being quietly demonstrated at the present time, unbeknown to the general public. **1952** J. L. WATEN *Alien Son* 121 Unbeknown to our parents we sneaked away from the street one summer day.
ellipt. **1901** J. BARLOW *From Land of Shamrock* 215 Openin' it at the breakfast-table, unbeknown, to set people passin' remarks, and risin' a laugh on him.
2. (Later example.)
1976 *Jrnl. Lakeland Dial. Soc.* No. 38. 39 Ah nivver really spock t' dialect proper, but Ah hev a gey lot ev dialect sayings Ah offen let slip oot, unbeknawen like!

unbeknownst, *a.* or *adv.* Add: Also, = UNBEKNOWN *ppl. a.* 1. (Earlier and later examples.)
Now of much wider currency than in the 19th. cent.
1848 MRS. GASKELL *Let.* 11 Nov. (1966) 61 You don't see me, but I often am sitting in the rocking-chair unbeknownst to you. **1907** J. M. SYNGE *Playboy of Western World* III. 70 Burying your poor father unbeknownst when..we could have given him a decent burial. **1932** W. FAULKNER *Light in August* i. 16 Interfering with his work unbeknownst to him. **1952** A. CHRISTIE *They do it with Mirrors* xiii. 122 One of those smart lads may have got out of the College buildings unbeknownst. **1979** *Dædalus* Summer 99 Here, illusion, unbeknownst to those who believed they had overcome it, made its most triumphant reentry. **1982** *London Rev. Bks.* 20 May–2 June 3 A whole other wife and children all unbeknownst to Ackerley until after his father's death.

unbelted, *a.* Add: (Further examples, of a seat belt.) Also *absol.* as *sb.*
1970 *Guardian* 24 Aug. 7/4 An unbelted driver can die (and has died) at speeds as low as 13 miles an hour. **1973** [see *NON-TRIVIAL *a.*]. **1977** *Times* 5 July 15/5 A higher proportion of belted than unbelted drivers remain in control of their vehicles.

‖**unberufen** (unbərū·fən), *int.* [Ger., unauthorized, gratuitous.] 'Touch wood!' (TOUCH *v.* 29 b).
1858 QUEEN VICTORIA *Let.* 10 Apr. in R. Fulford *Dearest Child* (1964) 88 Poor Leopold..bruises as much as ever but unberufen 1000 times—is free from any at present. **1911** BEERBOHM *Zuleika D.* xv. 225, 'I will choose ..whatever moment within my brief span of life shall seem aptest to me. *Unberufen,*' he added, lightly tapping Mr. Druce's counter. **1960** N. MITFORD *Don't tell Alfred* xvi. 180 'My point is that going to Eton will have minimized the danger of such extreme phases in the case of Charlie and Fabrice.' 'Unberufen,' said Alfred.

unbiolo·gical, *a.* [UN-[1] 7 a.] **a.** Not in accord with the findings of biology. **b.** Not such as occurs in the course of nature, as studied in biology.
1934 *Mind* XLIII. 519 Positivism and Kantianism were pre-evolutionary and unbiological. **1950** [see *STEREOTYPED *ppl. a.* c]. **1977** P. JOHNSON *Enemies of Society* xv. 197 Many of the central ideas of psychoanalysis are profoundly unbiological.

unbirthday. (Further examples.)
1930 W. DE LA MARE *On the Edge* 272 'Have you one really simple, lovely..trinket suitable for a lady?..An un-birthday present?' **1977** *Lancet* 2 July 31/2 A friend who has come to the front door, unexpectedly bearing a small unbirthday present.

unblinking, *a.* (See small-type note s.v. UNBLINKINGLY.) (Examples.)
1909 in WEBSTER. **1923** *Chambers's Jrnl.* 10 Nov. 791/1 John..could see only the unblinking stars. **1965** G. MCINNES *Road to Gundagai* xvi. 283 The unblinking stare of the lizard on the sun-baked rock.

unblissful, *a.* Add: Hence **unbli·ssfully** *adv.*
1849 C. BRONTË *Shirley* III. iv. 107 His whole nature seemed serenely alight: he stood..musing not unblissfully.

unblock, *v.* **1.** (Later examples.)
1969 H. PERKIN *Key Profession* v. 186 Even that..did not unblock the channels of advance. **1974** J. MANN *Sticking Place* ii. 30 She did not want to un-block drains or carry the dustbins.

unblushingly, *adv.* (Earlier example.)
1752 RICHARDSON *Let.* 18 Apr. (1964) 207 For the word *Love* has enabled some People to talk of a Passion fearlessly, unblushingly.

unbosom, *v.* Add: Hence also **unbo·soming** *vbl. sb.*
1910 *Blackw. Mag.* Jan. 57 And with a voice of growing strength renewed His vague unbosomings. **1935** DYLAN THOMAS *Poems* (1971) 46 Summer to him Is the unbosoming of the sun.

unbound, *ppl. a.*[1] Add: **4.** Also of a particle: = *FREE *a.* 14 b.
1971 *Sci. Amer.* June 25/1 Once a few unbound electrons are produced on the surface of the solid hydrogen isotope, these free electrons rapidly pick up energy from the incident oscillating electric field.

unboyish, *a.* (Earlier example.)
1838 S. G. GOODRICH *Fireside Educ.* 107 Charles, the eldest boy, with a patience most *unboyish,* was holding a skein of yarn for grandmamma to wind.

unbranning, *vbl. sb.* (Earlier example.)
1848 *Rep. Comm. Patents 1847* (U.S.) 373 In addition to the *unbraning* of the berry, the wheat undergoes an operation [etc.].

unbrave, *a.* Add: (Later and *absol.* examples.)
1896 *Godey's Mag.* Feb. 172/1 She saw before her his old self—strong, not unbrave, not disloyal. **1981** *London Mag.* Oct. 18 The sensible thing, as many unbrave realised at the time, would have been to opt for ground duties with the RAF.

unbreakable, *a.* (Examples corresponding to *BREAK *v.* 16 b.)
1929 T. M. JOHNSON *Our Secret War* iv. 180 Is there an unbreakable code? **1944** H. MCCLOY *Panic* 73 There's no such thing as an unbreakable cipher! **1963** R. V. JONES in Brown & Foote *Early Eng. & Norse Studies* 223 An unbreakable W/T code.

unbundle, *v.* Add: **2.** To introduce a system of separate charging for (items previously charged for collectively, esp. computer hardware and software).

1969 *Datamation* XV. 69 (*heading*) IBM 'unbundles' hardware/services charges... Will software be next? **1971** *New Scientist* 15 July 140/1 Programs, courses, computer maintenance and systems engineering would be priced separately (or 'unbundled') from the computers themselves. **1977** *Business Week* 18 Apr. 83/2 Banks may then be forced to unbundle costs and charge an additional 30¢ or so for each check processed. **1983** *Austral. Microcomputer Mag.* Dec. 40/3 The 8086 processor has been unbundled and is now an option.

Hence **unbu·ndling** *vbl. sb.*, (the introduction of) a policy of separate charging for related items.

1969 *Datamation* XV. 69/1 IBM 'expects to make changes in the way it charges for and supports its data processing equipment'. The word for it is 'unbundling'. **1971** E. F. SCHOETERS in B. de Ferranti *Living with Computer* viii. 72 These arguments are becoming academic in the light of separate pricing of hardware, software, support and staff training, commonly known by the unlovely name of 'unbundling'. **1981** *Economist* 11 July 65/2 Independent Japanese software houses, helped by separate pricing ('unbundling') of software and hardware by computer makers, are starting to write their own packaged programmes.

unbutton, *v.* Add: **1. c.** Also *fig.*

1956 N. STREATFEILD *Judith* III. 235 She definitely unbuttoned about her letters. **1978** O. WHITE *Silent Reach* ix. 97 If I cleared you, he'd probably unbutton.

unbuttoned, *ppl. a.* **2.** *fig.* (Earlier and later examples.)

1885 G. MEREDITH *Diana of Crossways* I. i. 8 He was careless of social opinion, unbuttoned, and a laughter [*sic*]. **1918** 'K. MANSFIELD' *Let.* 6 Feb. (1928) I. 124 On my life, I'd almost rather, like that English lady, not know whether my husband went to the lavatory or not, than be so unbuttoned. *a* **1967** J. R. ACKERLEY *My Father & Myself* (1968) 23 An unbuttoned stage of mellowness and ease. **1983** *Maledicta 1982* VI. 90 They are not by any means considered polite or even acceptable, except in a mood of broad and unbuttoned humor among close friends.

uncalled, *ppl. a.* **4.** (Earlier example.)

1869 *Bradshaw's Railway Man.* XXI. 199 The financial statement to same date... Discount on shares, 1837—£400,000... Uncalled—£619,525.

uncannily, *adv.* **2.** (Earlier example.)

1822 A. CUNNINGHAM *Traditional Tales* II. 267 He skirls sae uncannilie.

uncanopied, *ppl. a.* (Later example.)

1890 R. BRIDGES *Shorter Poems* III. xv. 61 Uncanopied sleep is flying from field and tree.

uncapped, *ppl. a.* (Examples corresponding to *CAP *v.*[1] 1 c.)

1955 *Times* 3 Aug. 4/6 (*caption*) The only uncapped player in the British Isles team to meet South Africa at Johannesburg on Saturday. **1977** *World of Cricket Monthly* June 92/2 The form of uncapped 24-year-old seamer Bill Bourne pierced the gloom like a ray of sunshine.

uncaring, *ppl. a.* Add: Hence also **unca·ringness.**

1930 A. HUXLEY *Brief Candles* 5 The superficial charm and good humour of the man seemed to overlie a fundamental hardness, an uncaringness, a hostility even. **1955** E. BOWEN *World of Love* iv. 78 Oh, how the vice of uncaringness had been hers; she had neither heart nor wish for a living creature.

uncentral, *a.* (Later examples.)

1911 R. BROOKE *Let.* Mar. (1968) 292 One's whole personality was there—only, somehow without the point. One was curiously *uncentral*. **1977** D. JONES *My Friend Dylan Thomas* iv. 40 This unlocal, uncentral world where the pubs are bad and the people are sly.

uncertain, *a.* Add: **4. b.** Phr. *in no uncertain terms*, emphatically, very clearly indeed.

1958 L. DURRELL *Balthazar* vi. 139 And what's more, I told Abdul so in no uncertain terms. 'Lay a finger on the girl..and I'll get you run in.' **1976** J. SNOW *Cricket Rebel* 132 Here we were bowling them out so that they could take advantage of it [*sc.* a green wicket]. They did that in no uncertain terms. **1977** *Time Out* 28 Jan.–3 Feb. 7/1 Five months after the programme was axed, Edmonds was told in no uncertain terms why it didn't fit.

c. Phr. *of uncertain age.*

[**1817**: see Dict.] **1877** F. H. BURNETT *Theo* v. 137 The blandishments of a single gentleman of uncertain age. **1930** A. CHRISTIE *Murder at Vicarage* iv. 33 There is no detective in England equal to a spinster lady of uncertain age with plenty of time on her hands. **1952** J. CANNAN *Body in Beck* vii. 152 The fair sex is very credulous, especially in the case of maiden ladies of uncertain age.

uncertainty. Add: **1. a.** Also, the quality of being indeterminate as to magnitude or value; the amount of variation in a numerical result that is consistent with observation.

1853 *Proc. R. Irish Acad.* V. 372 As to the sun and moon, it is more doubtful. In the transit they have larger probable errors than the stars. For the sun I obtained.. the first limb $\pm 0^{s}\cdot116$, the second $\pm 0^{s}\cdot087$;..while stars ..had but $\pm 0^{s}\cdot097$. This greater uncertainty arises from the strong contrast between the bright and dark surfaces whose boundary we take. **1861** G. B. AIRY *Theory Errors of Observations* I. 4 Strictly speaking, we ought..to use the word 'uncertainty' instead of 'error'. For we cannot at any time assert positively that our estimate or measure, though fallible, is not perfectly correct; and therefore it may happen that there is no 'error', in the ordinary sense of the word. **1930** RUARK & UREY *Atoms, Molecules & Quanta* xviii. 619 If a coordinate q is measured with an error of the order Δq, the uncertainty, Δp, of the conjugate momentum introduced by our measurement is such that $\Delta q \cdot \Delta p \cong h$. **1943** M. W. WHITE et al. *Practical Physics* i. 12 As applied to the final result of a measurement, the accuracy is expressed by stating the uncertainty of the numerical result, that is, the estimated maximum amount by which the result may differ from the 'true' or accepted value. **1974** G. REECE tr. *Hund's Hist. Quantum Theory* xii. 161 We thus have the relationship $\triangle E \triangle t \approx h$ between the uncertainty in the determination of energy and the evaluation of a point in time. **1975** *Physics Bull.* Apr. 165/2 The PTB developed a new measuring apparatus capable of accurate measurements of diameter on pistons of 850 mm and cylinders up to 1200 mm in diameter. The uncertainty in Q, dQ/Q, was estimated to be 3×10^{-5}.

4. *Econ.* (The quality of) a business risk which cannot be measured and whose outcome cannot be predicted or insured against (see quots. 1921 and 1964). Cf. *RISK *sb.* 2 a.

1921 F. H. KNIGHT (*title*) Risk, uncertainty and profit. *Ibid.* i. 20 A *measurable* uncertainty, or 'risk' proper, as we shall use the term, is so far different from an *unmeasurable* one that it is not in effect an uncertainty at all. We shall accordingly restrict the term 'uncertainty' to cases of the non-quantitative type. It is this 'true' uncertainty..which forms the basis of a valid theory of profit. **1929** G. O'BRIEN *Notes on Theory of Profit* ii. 17 The assumption of uncertainty is therefore a disutility and must be rewarded. Is uncertainty bearing on this account, entitled to rank as a separate factor of production. **1964** GOULD & KOLB *Dict. Social Sci.* 606/1 In its broadest definition the term uncertainty is used by economists to refer to any situation in which a set of alternative outcomes is not fully predictable. **1969** D. C. HAGUE *Managerial Economics* vii. 137 To conform to established terminology we shall, from now on, use the word uncertainty to mean the same thing as non-insurable risk.

5. (*Heisenberg's*) *uncertainty principle* (Physics), a principle of quantum mechanics implying that certain pairs of observables (e.g. the momentum and position of a particle, the energy and lifetime of a quantum level) cannot both be precisely and simultaneously known, and that as one of any pair is more exactly defined, the other becomes more uncertain. Also *transf.* Cf. *HEISENBERG, *principle of indeterminacy* s.v. *INDETERMINACY b.

The principle is usually stated as an inequality such that the product of the uncertainties of the pair of observables cannot be less than a quantity of the order of Planck's constant.

[**1928** *Physical Rev.* XXXII. 570 The principle of uncertainty is particularly clear in this [*sc.* Weyl's] system.] **1929** CONDON & MORSE *Quantum Mech.* i. 21 (*heading*) The quantum uncertainty principle. **1931** *Times Lit. Suppl.* 5 Nov. 852/4 Perhaps the most remarkable discovery that has been made in connexion with atomic theory is the so-called Uncertainty Principle. **1955** W. HEISENBERG in W. Pauli *Niels Bohr* 15 It was now [*sc.* in 1927] assumed in quantum mechanics that real states can always be represented as vectors in Hilbert space (or as 'mixtures' of such vectors). The uncertainty principle was the simple expression for this assumption. **1977** *Time* 14 Mar. 74/1 Even in the age of the Uncertainty Principle and culture fracture, Warren has not lost his sense of life as a sustained drama. **1982** A. M. LESK *Introd. Physical Chem.* x. 309 What Heisenberg's uncertainty principle asserts is that for *no* state of *any* system can *all* dynamical variables be arbitrarily well-determined.

uncertified, *ppl. a.* Add: **3.** Not certified insane.

1889 G. B. SHAW *London Music in 1888–89* (1937) 101 Brinio..is a patriotic Batavian with two sisters, one of whom is mad and the other sane... Ada, the uncertified one, is beloved by Aquilius. **1938** S. BECKETT *Murphy* ix. 161 There were a few such fortunate cases, certified and uncertified, enjoying all the amenities of a mental hospital. **1969** M. PUGH *Last Place Left* xiv. 102 Some uncertified genius had hit upon a new virus mutation method.

unchalked, *ppl. a.* (Later example.)

1938 J. STEINBECK *Long Valley* 113 The house was unscarred, uncarved, unchalked.

uncharge, *v.* **3.** (Later example.)

1902 *Infantry Training* (War Office) I. 119 Charging and Uncharging Magazines in two ranks.

uncharmed, *ppl. a.* Add: **2.** *Particle Physics.* Not possessing the property known as charm.

1972 *Physics Lett.* XXXIX. B. 349 Hadrons containing the fourth type of quark may be as low as 700 MeV above their uncharmed counterparts. **1975** *Physics Bull.* Apr. 181/1 If SU(3) symmetry were perfect, one should clearly distinguish a neutral octet member..from a singlet.., even though they are both neutral, non-strange and of course uncharmed. **1977** *Sci. Amer.* Oct. 68 Charm.. becomes manifest only in hadrons that include a charmed quark or antiquark in combination with uncharmed quarks. **1983** *Canad. Jrnl. Physics* LXI. 124/1 Uncharmed baryons.

unchartered, *ppl. a.* **2.** (Earlier example.)

1812 *Weekly Reg.* II. 19/2 Those planters..who should place confidence in the paper of unchartered banks.

unchild, *v.* Add: Hence **unchi·lding** *ppl. a.*

1876 G. M. HOPKINS *Wreck of Deutschland* xiii, in *Poems* (1967) 55 Wiry and white-fiery and whirlwind-swivelled snow Spins to the widow-making unchilding unfathering deeps.

unchildish, *a.* (Later examples.)

1888 F. H. BURNETT *Sara Crewe* I. 22 She spoke in a strange, unchildish voice. **1925** V. WOOLF *Common Reader* 169 An astonishing and unchildish story, *Love and Friendship*.

unchildlike, *a.* (Earlier contextual example.)

1833 J. S. MILL in *Monthly Repos.* VII. 62 This most grown-up and unchildlike age.

unchinked, *ppl. a.* (Earlier example.)

1819 *Niles' Reg.* XVII. 30/2 A year ago there were only 'five or six unchinked cabins' on the town plot.

unchurchly, *a.* (Earlier example.)

1815 J. MAYNE *Jrnl.* 1 Jan. (1909) 237 For although the most wretched, spiritless animals had been purposely selected, yet the novelty of the scene and the shouts of the people would sometimes elicit an unchurchly amble.

uncinate, *a.* Add: **b.** *uncinate gyrus*, the hook-shaped anterior part of the hippocampus involved in the perception of olfactory stimuli.

1883 *Gray's Anat.* (ed. 10) 487 The uncinate gyrus extends from the posterior extremity of the hemisphere to the fissure of Sylvius. **1980** *Ibid.* (ed. 36) 999/1 The tail [of the uncinate gyrus] separates the rest of the inferior surface of the uncus into an anterior uncinate gyrus and a posterior intralimbic gyrus.

c. Involving or affecting the uncinate gyrus: applied to a type of epileptic fit in which hallucinatory sensations of taste and smell are experienced.

1899 J. H. JACKSON in *Lancet* 14 Jan. 79/2 There is very often the Dreamy State in cases of this group of epileptic fits—the Uncinate Group. **1948** A. BRODAL *Neurol. Anat.* x. 338 An uncinate attack may be followed by an ordinary epileptic fit, in which case the uncinate attack represents an aura. **1974** E. NIEDERMEYER *Compendium of Epilepsies* v. 109 In human epileptic conditions, Jackson's term of 'uncinate epilepsy' corresponds with amygdaloid insular seizure manifestations.

uncirculated, *ppl. a.* Add: (Examples of money.) Also *absol.* as *sb.*

1938 J. COFFIN *Coin Collecting* viii. 100 It is highly doubtful just what price might be given for an 1804 silver dollar in uncirculated condition. **1962** L. BROWN *Coin Collecting* i. 17 Owing to modern methods of minting, where coins move along conveyor belts, slide down shutes and are packed into bags, it is almost impossible to obtain a modern coin..in anything like FDC [perfect mint state] condition and so the term 'uncirculated' was introduced. **1978** J. L. HENSLEY *Killing in Gold* v. 61 I'll stay with crisp uncirculateds..at least for type.

uncircumstanced, *ppl. a.* (Later example.)

1943 S. SASSOON in *Country Life* 25 June 1136/2 Cloud shadows..Dwell and dissolve; uncircumstanced they pause and pass.

uncivic, *a.* Add: Hence **unci·vically** *adv.*

1931 A. HUXLEY *Music at Night* II. 81 We do not admit ..that there should be citizens treated uncivically.

uncivilization. (Earlier contextual example.)

1880 W. MORRIS *Hopes & Fears for Art* (1882) 107 The attainment of these very comforts is what makes the difference between civilisation and uncivilisation.

uncivilized, *ppl. a.* Add: Also *absol.*

1900 tr. *J. Deniker's Races of Man* vii. 251 Among the uncivilised, it is not a question of absolute right, of absolute morality; everything is reduced to a very restricted altruism, not extending beyond kin and immediate neighbours.

unclassified, *ppl. a.* Add: (Examples corresponding to *CLASSIFIED *ppl. a.* b, c.) Also *absol.* as *sb.*

1935 *City of Oxford Council Rep.* 1 Mar. 401 It is recommended that the following programme be submitted to the Ministry of Transport..:—*Bridges... By-passes... Classified Roads... Unclassified Roads.* **1958** M. KELLY *Christmas Egg* III. 129 The road was lonely, unclassified... He must walk back to A260. **1972** O. SELA *Bearer Plot* iv. 28 He would swoop off the main roads onto undulating unclassifieds that sometimes were little more than dirt tracks. **1978** *Country Life* 8 June 1634/3 Of all the trackways of these Lincolnshire Wolds the most romantic is the Bluestone Heath Road, now an unclassified lane.

absol. **1952** *Manch. Guardian Weekly* 14 Feb. 13 My work is unclassified, but the fund out of which I am paid comes from a government agency. **1968** 'J. LE CARRÉ' *Small Town in Germany* v. 72 He's down here collecting the mail... Everything. Classified or Unclassified, it didn't make no difference. **1980** D. BLOODWORTH *Trapdoor* xxiii. 143 The file was not unclassified... It was marked Top Secret.

uncle, *sb.* Add: **1. f.** In B.B.C. Radio: formerly, a male announcer or story-teller for children's programmes. Cf. sense *2 b and *AUNTIE b (b).

1923 *Wireless Weekly* 8 Aug. 183/3 The Director of Programmes received me into the actual studio, where he and the other Uncles have so much fun over the Children's Hour. **1981** S. BRIGGS *Those Radio Times* 12/1 Long before the Corporation was called 'Auntie'..it had dozens of 'aunts' and 'uncles' on its staff. **1985** *Times Lit. Suppl.* 22 Mar. 330/3 Knight began to broadcast..after the war, becoming extremely popular as Uncle Max on the children's programme *Nature Parliament.*

g. *universal uncle*: see *UNIVERSAL *a.* 9 b.

h. A male friend or lover of a child's mother.

1962 *Listener* 31 May 935/2 His mother has never been married, has lived for some years at a time with a series of 'uncles' who have been the fathers of these siblings. **1968** *Ibid.* 1 Aug. 155/2 The play is a simple tale of a boy who, lacking a resident father, grows up under the influence of various temporary 'uncles'.

2. b. (Earlier and later U.S. examples and examples corresponding to senses 1 f, h above.)

1830 S. P. HOLBROOK *Sketches by Traveller* 111 In many families..the children are taught to address the older servant as *uncle* or *auntee*, and this is sometimes more than a figure of speech. **1876** 'MARK TWAIN' *Tom Sawyer* xxviii. 216 He let's [*sic*] me, and so does his pap's nigger man, Uncle Jake. **1923** *Radio Times* 28 Sept. 11/2 Children's Stories—Uncle Donald and Auntie Betty. **1937** PARTRIDGE *Dict. Slang* 337/1 Her children call him 'Uncle'. **1945** T. RATTIGAN *Love in Idleness* I. 280 Oh, don't call him sir, Michael. Call him—I know—call him Uncle John. **1962** W. FAULKNER *Reivers* ii. 30 His wife.. was Delphine, Grandmother's cook. At that time he was 'Uncle' Ned only to Mother. I mean, she was the one who insisted that all us children..call him Uncle Ned.

c. Also *ellipt.*; also, (the members of) a federal agency.

1849 *Placer Times* (Sacramento, Calif.) 1 Sept., Two Express Lines have been established between our City and San Francisco. Our old Uncle will have to 'stir his stumps' else his 'regular' arrangements will become a *dead letter.* **1950** H. E. GOLDIN *Dict. Amer. Underworld Lingo* 231/1 *Uncle*... (Plural) G-men; agents of the Federal Bureau of Investigation. **1953** W. BURROUGHS *Junkie* x. 98 'He belongs to Uncle, now,' said the [police] captain to my wife as they left the house. **1966** T. PYNCHON *Crying of Lot 49* i. 17 The well-known portrait of Uncle that appears in front of all our post offices. **1971** G. V. HIGGINS *Friends of Eddie Coyle* ii. 14 That's not working for uncle, Eddie. You got to put your whole soul into it. **1978** 'P. MANN' *Steal Big* ii. 8 The nerve I had. Uncle had made me prove it time and again.

e. *Uncle Tom Cobleigh* (or *Cobley*) *and all*: a name given to the last of a long list of persons (see quot. *c* 1800 for the ballad alluded to); a whole lot of people.

c **1800** *Widdicombe Fair* in G. Bantock *One Hundred Songs of Eng.* 72 Tom Pearce's old mare doth appear gashly white Wi' Bill Brewer, Jan Stewer, Peter Gurney, Peter Davy, Dan Whiddon, Harry Hawk, old Uncle Tom Cobleigh and all, Old Uncle Tom Cobleigh and all. **1933** E. A. ROBERTSON *Ordinary Families* xiii. 287 When Dru.. repeated to Margaret some gossip about an engagement, Margaret said casually, 'Oh, and to Uncle Tom Cobley an' all, I suppose!' **1941** J. D. CARR *Case of Constant Suicides* iv. 55 They're all here: the Fiscal, and the law-agent..and Uncle Tom Cobleigh and all. **1963** L. KLEIN *Fabian Tract No. 349* i. 2 We..are exhorted to pant along behind the industrious Germans, Japanese, Russians, Americans and Uncle Tom Cobley. **1966** *Guardian* 10 Sept. 14/8 It seems clear that a compromise, half-way solution had equally been ruled out by Government, Opposition, economists, press, TV, Uncle Tom Cobleigh and all. **1981** D. BOGGIS *Time to Betray* xxv. 130 Stupid little man, dragging in old Uncle Tom Cobley and all.

f. *Uncle Ned* (Rhyming slang), (*a*) bed (also ellipt. as *uncle*); (*b*) head.

1925 FRASER & GIBBONS *Soldier & Sailor Words* 294 *Uncle Ned*, bed. **1955** F. BROWN *Martians, go Home!* II. iii. 68 Hi *got* to speel or there's no weeping willow for my Uncle Ned. **1964** *Listener* 31 Dec. 1053/1, I have spent an hour fixing the big, loose curls on top of my Uncle Ned. **1974** J. GARDNER *Corner Men* xiv. 194 Get out of that Uncle Ned, slide into your threads, and come down the nick with us. **1982** J. SCOTT *Uprush of Mayhem* x. 105 'You did right, shoving him back in his uncle.'..Uncle. Uncle Ned, Cockney rhyming slang for bed.

3*. *to cry* (*holler, say*, etc.) *uncle*, to acknowledge defeat, to cry for mercy. *N. Amer. colloq.*

1918 *Chicago Herald-Examiner* 1 Oct. 11 Sic him Jenny Jinx—make him say 'Uncle'. **1939** *Amer. Speech* XIV. 267 'He hollered "calf rope" or 'He hollered "uncle",' are publishments of his defeat. **1941** B. SCHULBERG *What makes Sammy Run?* vi. 139 Kit was the one who did him some good. 'Okay,' I said. 'I'll cry uncle.' **1962** W. STEGNER *Wolf Willow* III. iii. 237 With good hay land and good range [we can] make this God darned country holler uncle. **1972** D. DELMAN *Sudden Death* v. 122 'Stop it, darling, please.' 'Say uncle.' 'Uncle.' **1980** *Amer. Speech 1976* LI. 281 Most American schoolboys are..familiar with the expression *cry uncle* or *holler uncle*, meaning 'give up in a fight, ask for mercy'. *Uncle* in this expression is surely a folk etymology, and the Irish original of the word is *anacol* (*anacal, anacul*) 'act of protecting; deliverance; mercy, quarter, safety', a verbal noun from the Old Irish verb *aingid* 'protects'... My unscientific sampling of English speakers in Britain a few years ago indicated that *cry uncle* is not familiar in England or Scotland.

4. *uncle-figure.*

1959 *Listener* 10 Sept. 375/1 To a majority of Americans, Adlai Stevenson is an uncle-figure—'good old Uncle Adlai'. **1975** *Times* 8 Mar. 7/4 Such an uncle-figure as Johnny Carson..on late night television.

Hence **u·ncle-ish** *a.*

1928 A. HUXLEY *Point Counter Point* x. 160 An occasional chaste uncle-ish kiss on the forehead. **1981** P. DICKINSON *Seventh Raven* xii. 166 He'd get much more mileage out of seeming friendly and uncle-ish.

uncleaned, *ppl. a.* (Earlier example.)

1854 MRS. GASKELL *North & South* (1855) I. xiii. 157 The uncleaned corners of the room.

Uncle Tom. orig. *U.S.* [UNCLE *sb.* 2 b.] The name of the hero of *Uncle Tom's Cabin*, a novel (1851–2) by Harriet Beecher Stowe, used allusively for a Black man who is submissively loyal or servile to White men. Also *transf.* and in extended use.

1922 [see *NEW NEGRO, NEW NEGRO]. **1942, 1960** [see *handkerchief-head* s.v. *HANDKERCHIEF b]. **1971** *Guardian* 15 July 3/1 Arafat was always attacked by the Marxist-orientated militants as being a Palestinian 'Uncle Tom', neither sufficiently radical or violent. **1972** M. J. BOSSE *Incident at Naha* i. 37 Some people consider him an Uncle Tom because he doesn't study Afro-American culture. **1975** M. BRADBURY *History Man* v. 84 The girl I'm living with..says I have a slave mentality... She says I'm an Uncle Tom. **1977** *New Yorker* 22 Aug. 66/3 Pryor goes through his part pop-eyed, playing Uncle Tom for Uncle Toms. **1978** *Church Times* 24 Feb. 2/4 Many parishes do have a youngster on the PCC, but... It's only tokenism. The youngsters are 'Uncle Toms', in a way. **1981** *Bull. Amer. Acad. Arts & Sci.* May 41 Uncle Tom's virtues as a worker change when the vices of his condition have to go.

attrib. **1953** BERREY & VAN DEN BARK *Amer. Thes. Slang* (1954) § 579/2 *'Straight jazz'*,..schmaltz,..unadulterated corn, Uncle Tom music. **1959** 'F. NEWTON' *Jazz Scene* v. 88 The savage hostility to 'Uncle Tom' musicians, which for the first time split the community of jazz players. **1960** [see *JIM CROW[1], JIM-CROW, JIM CROW 3]. **1971** *Black Scholar* Dec. 20 The harshest discrimination that I have encountered *in the political arena* is anti-feminism—from both males and brainwashed 'Uncle Tom' females. **1978** G. GREENE *Human Factor* III. iii. 127 Been to the African University in the Transvaal where Uncle Tom professors always produce dangerous students. **1979** *Guardian* 14 Apr. 8/8 You got an Uncle Tom figure there in your book?..You know, kinda creepy black always trying to ingratiate himself with the white folks.

Hence **Uncle Tom** *v. intr.*, to act in a manner characteristic of an Uncle Tom; also with *it*; **Uncle Tom(m)ery, Uncle Tom(m)ing** *vbl. sb.*, **Uncle Tom(m)ish,** *a.*, **Uncle Tom(m)ism.**

1937 Uncle Tomism [see *NIGGER *sb.* 1]. **1944** C. HIMES *Black on Black* (1973) 198 Here come a big Uncle Tomish lookin' cat in starched overalls. **1947** S. LEWIS *Kingsblood Royal* x. 52 Why, you gold-digging, uncle-tomming, old, black he-courtesan! **1950** PATTERSON & CONRAD *Scottsboro Boy* III. iv. 219 The prisoners clowned for the white folks—the guards, the prison heads, and their families. It looked like a lot of Uncle Tom-ing to me, and I didn't enjoy seeing whites laugh at the coloured guys' pranks. **1960** *New Left Rev.* Nov.–Dec. 49/1 Armstrong's clowning is just Depressing. It isn't that he 'uncle toms' but that the act is so automatic and lifeless. **1961** *Guardian* 1 Dec. 6/5 The Uncle-Tommish innocence of the..Negro. **1967** *Listener* 23 Feb. 264/2 Not all Jews will like it, though. One of my acquaintance finds it patronizing and demeaning, the Jewish equivalent of Uncle Tommism. **1967** *Punch* 9 Aug. 210 An obligation.. applies constantly to all underdog groups, constantly tempted by rewards to uncle-tom, to pull the forelock. **1968** *New Yorker* 17 Aug. 21 The guests will be arriving any minute now. Please, Amanda, try to Uncle Tom it a little just for tonight. **1972** *Guardian* 21 Oct. 9/2 The young black studies' teacher..was striking out against Uncle Tommery. **1976** *Gramophone* Feb. 1321/2 Now today it has almost the opposite effect from what was intended. Many blacks relate it to the era of Uncle Tom-ism. **1979** *N.Y. Times* 12 Feb. B13/1 To tell women that if they just behave nicer, if they shuffle and Uncle Tom a little more, that they will be more successful, is simply not accurate. **1981** *Cape Argus Mag.* 24 Oct. 2/2 With..that substantial brush of Uncle Tommery with which his opponents have tarred him, Dr Cedric [Phatudi] is a walking..paradox... He has none of the stridency of a Chief Buthelezi,..or the bombast of a Matanzima.

unclipped, -clipt, *ppl. a.* Add: **c.** Not fastened with a clip.

1922 JOYCE *Ulysses* 23 Buck Mulligan stood on a stone, ..his unclipped tie rippling over his shoulder.

uncock, *v.*[2] (Earlier example.)

1745 W. ELLIS *Mod. Husbandman* VII. II. 80 Then this Nobleman thought it high time to uncock all the wheat again.

uncognisant, *a.* Add: Also **uncognizant.** So **unco·gnizantly** *adv.*

1843 [see *pigeon-pie* s.v. *PIGEON *sb.* 5 a].

uncommendable, *a.* (Later examples.)

1959 I. & P. OPIE *Lore & Lang. Schoolch.* xviii. 377 Almost any group of 12-year-olds, asked what are their favourite after-dark games, will name doorbell-ringing, and similar uncommendable activities. **1983** T. DE VERE WHITE *Johnnie Cross* i. 12 The public had shown uncommendable restraint in the book shops.

uncommissioned, *ppl. a.* **2.** (Earlier example.)

1822 M. EDGEWORTH *Let.* 12 June (1971) 407 The Nelson—just finished but uncommissioned a first rate man of war 120 guns.

uncommitted, *ppl. a.* Add: **4.** (Further examples, esp. as between two power groups.) Also *absol.*

1956 BALL & KILLOUGH *International Relations* xxiii. 494 The Arabs had rejected association with the West and insisted on maintaining a 'neutral' position. Many Arab leaders regarded the Middle Eastern states as likely to be safer from Soviet attack if they remained uncommitted to the West. **1958** *Listener* 6 Mar. 390/2 It brings in not only countries committed to Western alignment, like the Philippines, Siam, and Pakistan, but also uncommitted countries of the neutral bloc, like India, Burma, and Indonesia. **1958** *Spectator* 22 Aug. 259/2 The key..lies..in a transformation of American relations with the uncommitted world. **1959** *Oxf. Mag.* 11 June 469/2 Islam is likely to gain far more of the uncommitted than is Christianity. **1959** *News Chron.* 10 July 4/2 The uncommitted voter. **1961** *Daily Tel.* 31 Aug. 10 Neutralism, Mr Foster Dulles once declared, is immoral. Nowadays, when the 'uncommitted' constitute a decisive, if not solid, phalanx in the United Nations, Western statesmen eschew such language.

uncomplimentary, *a.* Add: (Earlier example.)

1842 J. S. MILL *Let.* 25 Nov. in *Wks.* (1963) XIII. 558 People call you by various uncomplimentary names indicative of self-conceit.

Hence **u:ncomplime·ntarily** *adv.*

1909 'MARK TWAIN' *Is Shakes. Dead?* xi. 127 It would grieve me to know that any one could think so injuriously of me, so uncomplimentarily, so unadmiringly of me.

uncompromised, *ppl. a.* Add: Hence **unco·mpromisedness.**

1851 H. MELVILLE *Moby Dick* III. xxi. 145 This strange uncompromisedness in him.

uncompromisingly, *adv.* (Earlier example.)

1834 J. S. MILL in *Monthly Repos.* VIII. 527 The military tribunals..Mr. Abercromby..steadily and uncompromisingly opposed.

uncomputable, *a.* (Later examples.)

1906 SOMERVILLE & 'ROSS' *Some Irish Yesterdays* 51 Large statements as to her uncomputable value had not her tail in youth been shut into a stable door and given a double angle like a bayonet. **1979** *Sci. Amer.* Nov. 30/2 Consider a more traditional way of encoding the halting problem in an uncomputable irrational number.

uncondescending, *ppl. a.* (Later example.)

1969 *Guardian* 31 July 2/3 A performance that was obviously pleasing and uncondescending.

unconditional, *a.* (Earlier and later examples of *unconditional surrender.*)

1830 HAZLITT *Life Napoleon Buonaparte* IV. l. 119 We will have more, namely the original stake we played for; unconditional surrender of the right of nations to chuse their own government. **1901** H. CAMPBELL-BANNERMAN in *Hansard Commons* 14 Feb. 89 Unconditional surrender was our first and last word. **1930** G. B. SHAW *Apple Cart* II. 69 In plain terms we require from you an unconditional surrender. **1949** *New Statesman* 30 July 115/2 The sharp argument about 'unconditional surrender' in the House of Commons last week revealed much that was of more than historical significance... He [*sc.* Mr. Bevin] had not protested when Mr. Churchill brought back this fatal slogan from Casablanca. **1956** A. HUXLEY *Adonis & Alphabet* 81 The only completely unconditional surrender will come when everybody—but *everybody*—is a corpse. **1974** *Times* 20 Dec. 1/2 The Kuwait authorities insisted that the [hijackers'] surrender was 'unconditional'.

unconditioned, *ppl. a.* Add: **2. a.** (Earlier example.)

1796 F. A. NITSCH *Gen. View Kant's Princ. concerning Man* 127 Reason..produces the idea of an unconditioned Limitation.

b. *unconditioned reflex*, an inborn, instinctual reflex or reflex action (cf. *CONDITIONED *ppl. a.* 7 b). So *unconditioned stimulus.*

1906, 1927 [see *CONDITIONED *ppl. a.* 7 b]. **1937** *Discovery* Jan. 17/2 Its instincts, or, to use Pavlov's expression, its unconditioned reflexes. **1972** *New Yorker* 26 Aug. 32/3 In the vocabulary that Pavlov adopted to describe his findings, the meat powder was labelled an 'unconditioned stimulus'.

unconditionedness (earlier example).

1854 GEO. ELIOT tr. *Feuerbach's Essence Christianity* iv. 54 The metaphysical attributes of eternity, unconditionedness,..and the like abstractions.

unconducive, *a.* (Later example.)

1984 *Times Lit. Suppl.* 25 May 593/4 A number of local CIA men do seem to have taken steps unconducive to the success of Kennedy liberalism.

unconfirmed, *ppl. a.* **1.** (Later examples.)

1920 *Conference of Bishops of Anglican Communion* 30 The irregularity of admitting to Communion the baptized but unconfirmed Communicants of the non-episcopal congregations. **1977** R. L. WOLFF *Gains & Losses* II. ii. 122 Danger besets the unconfirmed girls... They find their own vicar crusty and aloof.

unconformity. 1. (Later example.)

1982 K. SMIDT (*title*) Unconformities in Shakespeare's history plays.

unco·njugated, *a. Med.* and *Gram.* [Un-¹ 8 a.] Not conjugated.

1909 in Webster (undefined). **1963** *Jrnl. Clin. Endocrinol.* XXIII. 820/2 Measurement of unconjugated cortisol in the urine affords a reliable index of the biologically active fraction of circulating cortisol. **1964** *Language* XL. 277 The description of pronoun position with verbal constructs..is simple and clear: where the unconjugated form precedes the conjugated, it is equated with the other elements that cause anteposition. **1977** *Proc. R. Soc. Med.* LXX. 598/2 Some patients do have an increase in biliary unconjugated bilirubin.

unconnected, *ppl. a.* **2.** (Earlier example.)

1745 Hume *Let. from Gentleman* (1967) 32 Suppose Mankind, in some primitive unconnected State [etc.].

unconscious, *a.* Add: **2. c.** *Psychol.* Applied to mental or psychic processes of which a person is not aware but which have a powerful effect on his attitudes and behaviour, *spec.* in Freud's psychoanalytic theory, processes activated by desires, fears, or memories which are unacceptable to the conscious mind and so repressed; also designating that part of the mind or psyche in which such processes operate. Freq. *absol.* Cf. *collective unconscious* s.v. *collective *a.* 2 e; *id².

a **1884** M. Pattison *Mem.* (1885) vii. 329, I cannot help observing the remarkable force with which the Unconscious—*das Unbewusste*—vindicated its power. *Ibid.* 330 By whatever name you call it, the Unconscious is found controlling each man's destiny without, or in defiance of, his will. **1912** Freud in *Proc. Soc. Psychical Res.* XXVI. lvi. 315 The term *unconscious*, which was used in the purely descriptive sense before, now comes to imply something more. It designates not only latent ideas in general, but especially ideas with a certain dynamic character, ideas keeping apart from consciousness in spite of their intensity and activity. *Ibid.* 318 The system revealed by the sign that the single acts forming part of it are unconscious we designate by the name 'The Unconscious', for want of a better and less ambiguous term... And this is the third and most significant sense which the term 'unconscious' has acquired in psycho-analysis. **1914** [see *co-conscious *a.* and *sb.*]. **1925** C. E. M. Joad *Mind & Matter* iv. 111 This greater part is known as the unconscious mind, or simply as 'the unconscious'. The theory of the unconscious is based mainly on the work of..Freud. **1946** *Mind* LV. 21 Perhaps further investigation following Wisdom's hint that philosophical views are the vehicles for expressing 'unconscious fantasies', will lead to an understanding of this point. **1956** R. F. C. Hull tr. *Jung's Symbols of Transformation* in *Coll. Wks.* V. ix. 443 The Miller case is a classic example of the unconscious manifestations which precede a serious psychic disorder. **1959** N. Mailer *Advts. for Myself* (1961) 216 To put it crudely, I would think I was dropping people when they were dropping me. And of course my unconscious knew better. **1977** A. Sheridan tr. *J. Lacan's Écrits* iii. 50 The unconscious is that chapter of my history that is marked by a blank or occupied by a falsehood: it is the censored chapter.

unconsiderable, *a.* Delete † *Obs.* and add later examples.

1914 W. J. Locke *Fortunate Youth* i. 19 Sky and grass and trees and white mass of ladies..and unconsiderable men and boys became a shimmering blur. **1976** *Brit. Jrnl. Sociol.* XXVII. 109/2 The rank and file of British Educationalists, sociologists of education and educational psychologists have concentrated their considerable energies and occasionally some not unconsiderable talents on devising arguments to legitimate the equalization of opportunity on moral grounds and to support it on scientific grounds.

unconstitutional, *a.* Add: **1.** (Earlier example.)

1734 *Country Jrnl.* 16 Nov. 1/2 Lest all other Provisions should be ineffectual to keep the Members of the House of Commons out of this unconstitutional Dependency..the Wisdom of our Constitution hath thought fit that the Representatives of the People should not have Time to forget that they are such; that they are empowered to act for the People, not against them.

Hence **unconstitu·tionalism.**

1920 *Glasgow Herald* 11 Dec. 7 It is the first area of dry land which has shown itself after the deluge of unconstitutionalism in that part of the country [*sc.* Ireland]. **1949** St. J. Ervine *Craigavon* ii. lxxvi. 344 He might have made an effective debating retort to the Ulstermen about unconstitutionalism.

uncontrollability. (See small-type note s.v. Uncontrollableness.) (Examples.)

1909 *Chambers's Jrnl.* June 342/2 Wherever horses are there must be unsanitary filth, and sometimes uncontrollability born of nerves or vice. **1980** *New Scientist* 31 Jan. 341/2 The uncontrollability of medical costs.

unconvincible, *a.* (Earlier and later examples.)

a **1747** J. Wesley *Wks.* (1829) V. xxxvii. 476 An unadvisable and unconvincible spirit. **1979** C. McCarry *Better Angels* ii. vii. 119 He made his argument to her, knowing that Patrick..was unconvincible.

uncoped, *ppl. a.* (Later examples.)

1972 J. G. Vermandel *Last Seen in Samarra* xii. 81 Wearing a housecoat, and with her red hair curlier than he'd ever seen it before. Uncoped with. **1981** E. North *Dames* i. 4 They..think back over life uncoped with.

uncorrectable, *a.* (Later examples.)

1970 *New Yorker* 30 May 26 A regularly scheduled airliner..radioed..to report..an undiagnosed and uncorrectable loss of power. **1970** *Time* 21 Sept. 57 For many years, facial paralysis has been uncorrectable.

uncorrectible, *a.* (See small-type note s.v. Uncorrectable *a.*) (Examples.)

1902 A. H. Buck *Ref. Handbk. Med. Sci.* (ed. 2) IV. 528/2 Finally the deformity becomes permanent and uncorrectible. **1952** G. Sarton *Hist. Sci.* I. xxi. 546 Superstition is of necessity more conservative than science, because it is uncorrectible and unprogressive.

uncountable, *a.* Add: **2. a.** *spec.* in *Math.*, infinite and incapable of being put into a one-to-one correspondence with the integers. Opp. *countable *a.* 2 c.

1952 R. L. Wilder *Introd. Foundation Math.* iv. 88 Some mathematicians do not admit the existence of an uncountable set of real numbers as a legitimate consequence of the argument. **1964** T. O. Moore *Elem. Gen. Topology* i. 16 The set *R* of all real numbers is uncountable. **1971** *Sci. Amer.* Dec. 98/1 If the final destination of the bird is not specified, an uncountable infinity of such graphs can start at *C* and end anywhere on the track between *A* and *B*.

4. *Gram.* That cannot be counted; invariable in number; *spec.* of a noun: that cannot form a plural or be used with the indefinite article.

1924 [see B below]. **1948** A. S. Hornby et al. *Learner's Dict. Current Eng.* p. x, The sign [U] is a warning that the noun..stands for a material, quality, etc. that is uncountable. The noun..may not be used with the indefinite article and must not be used in the plural. **1961** R. B. Long *Sentence & its Parts* ix. 225 There is a tendency to assign uncountable-plural status and *mumps are dangerous to adults* is heard alongside the preferred *mumps is dangerous to adults*. **1966** J. Derrick *Teaching Eng. to Immigrants* ii. 71 Foreign learners may misuse these 'uncountable' nouns by analogy with 'countable' ones and say such things as 'I want two milks', 'This is a rice', 'These are moneys', 'This is an ink', etc. **1980** *Chambers Universal Learners' Dict.* p. viii, *nu* This is short for *noun uncountable* and means that a noun (or a particular meaning) labelled in this way may not be used in the plural form.

B. *sb. Gram.* An uncountable noun or its referent.

1924 O. Jespersen *Philos. Gram.* xiv. 188 There is a class of 'things' to which words like one, two are inapplicable; we may call them uncountables, though dictionaries do not recognize this use of the word *uncountable*, which is known to them only in the relative sense 'too numerous to be (easily) counted'. **1965** K. Schibsbye *Mod. Eng. Gram.* ii. 100 Though uncountables are normally in the singular, some of these (nearly) always appear in the plural: *oats, riches.* **1981** *Fremdsprachen* XXV. 236 Modern grammarians often divide nouns according to their capacity to be used with numerical values into: countables and uncountables.

Hence **u:ncountabi·lity,** the property of being uncountable; **uncountably** *adv.* (later examples).

1952 R. L. Wilder *Introd. Foundation Math.* iv. 88 The proof of the uncountability of *R*. **1955** J. L. Kelley *Gen. Topology* iv. 122 The product of uncountably many topological spaces does not generally satisfy the first axiom of countability. **1977** *Sci. Amer.* Jan. 115/3 Conway's proof of the uncountability of Penrose patterns ..can be outlined as follows. **1981** *Ibid.* Nov. 29/1 Their number, however, will be uncountably infinite.

uncounterfeit, *v.* Add: Hence **uncou·nterfeiting** *ppl. a.*

1912 [see *uncounterfeitable* s.v. *un-¹ 7 b (a)].

uncouple, *v.* Add: **3. a.** *Biochem.* To separate the processes of (phosphorylation) *from* those of oxidation.

1948 *Jrnl. Biol. Chem.* CLXXIII. 808 These results indicate that DNP [*sc.* dinitrophenol] reversibly uncouples phosphorylation from oxidation. **1977** D. E. Metzler *Biochemistry* vii. 366/1 Arsenate is said to uncouple phosphorylation from oxidation.

b. *Physics.* To cause to cease to interact; to decouple (sense *2 a).

1980 *Chem. in Brit.* XVI. 456/2 This excited state may return to groundstate or undergo a chemical reaction or may uncouple two electron spins (intersystem crossing) to yield a triplet state.

uncoupled, *ppl. a.*¹ (Examples corresponding to *uncouple *v.* 3 a.)

1954 *Proc. Nat. Acad. Sci.* XL. 919 Mitochondria suspensions taken from thyroxine-treated animals remain uncoupled. **1981** *Plant Physiol.* LXVIII. 1485/1 The light saturated rate of photosystem I-dependent electron transport..was increased by a high concentration of DCMU added to broken and uncoupled chloroplasts.

uncoupled, *ppl. a.*² Add: **b.** *Physics.* Not physically interacting.

1965 W. T. Thomson *Vibration Theory & Applications* vi. 167 The two pendulums behave as if they were uncoupled and independent of each other. **1981** *Sci. Amer.* July 56/1 Wiesel's computer simulations of the evolution of the resonance begin with Io, Europa and Ganymede in uncoupled orbits and with Io driven outward by its tidal interaction with Jupiter.

uncoupler. Add: *spec.* in *Biochem.*, any agent that causes the uncoupling of oxidative phosphorylation.

1956 *Science* 22 June 1107/1 The factor specifically inhibits phosphorylation without affecting the oxidation of β-hydroxybutyrate and thus simulates the action of 2,4-dinitrophenol and other known uncouplers. **1976** *Sci. Amer.* June 44/3 Then we tried uncouplers: agents that allow electron transport to proceed but that in effect disconnect it from phosphorylation and thus from the ATP synthesis it usually accomplishes. **1979** *Nature* 8 Feb. 486/1 We have found that the rapid efflux of Ca^{2+} brought about by collapse of the membrane potential by uncouplers or antimycin A..is not affected by tetracaine.

uncoupling, *vbl. sb.* Add: **a.** (Examples corresponding to *uncouple *v.* 3 a, b.)

1954 *Proc. Nat. Acad. Sci.* XL. 919 As much thyroxine was carried down by rat mitochondria which did not show any appreciable uncoupling. **1983** *Nature* 10 Feb. 512/1 A progressive uncoupling of [bacterial] growth and H_2S production was observed during approach to the stationary state.

b. *attrib.* and *Comb.*, as *uncoupling chain, lever, pole, rod*; **uncoupling agent** *Biochem.*, = *uncoupler.

1956 *Jrnl. Biol. Chem.* CCXXII. 338 Certain uncoupling agents such as thyroxine and Ca^{++} caused rapid swelling of the mitochondria. **1981** *Arch. Microbiol.* CXXIX. 94/1 Inhibition was relieved by low concentrations of uncoupling agent. **1879** *Car-Builder's Dict.* 172/1 *Uncoupling-chain*, a chain by which the uncoupling lever of a Miller-coupler is connected with the coupling-hook or draw-bar. *Ibid.*, *Uncoupling-lever, for Miller-coupler*, a lever attached to the platform of a car, and connected by a chain with a Miller coupling-hook or draw-bar to disengage or uncouple it from the one on the adjoining car. **1895** *Ibid.* (ed. 3) 139/2 *Uncoupling-rod*,..a rod connecting the uncoupling-lever with the lock of an automatic coupler. **1976** A. White *Long Silence* ix. 88 Two trains were being worked... I counted five men walking about the yard with long un-coupling poles.

unco·very. [f. Uncover *v.*, after *discovery, recovery*, etc.: see -ery.] The action of uncovering or bringing to light.

1963 *Listener* 12 Sept. 377/2 When we indulge in.. deduction..the theorem contains the discovery (or, more exactly, the uncovery of something which was there in the axioms and postulates, though it wasn't actually evident). **1977** *Times Lit. Suppl.* 25 Mar. 336/1 Dr Ray's uncovery of a dusty trove of illustrated books in the basement of a London dealer recalls the accidental discovery of the golden bowl.

uncramp, *v.* (Examples of *intr.* use.)

1937 V. Woolf *Diary* 21 Apr. (1984) V. 80 What a mercy to use this page to uncramp in! after squeezing drop by drop into my 17 minute BBC. **1952** E. Hemingway *Old Man & Sea* 70 His left hand was still..tight... It will uncramp though, he thought.

uncredited, *ppl. a.* (Later examples.)

1959 *Times* 17 Aug. 12/6 This version (adapter uncredited) concentrated on the two main conflicts in the book. **1977** *Rolling Stone* 30 June 102/3 The uncredited musicians play sparely but with enough fire to make their presence, and this entire album, memorable.

uncre·olized, *ppl. a.* [Un-¹ 8.] Of a language or dialect: not creolized; that has not undergone creolization.

1980 *English World-Wide* I. i. 50 The greater contact with uncreolized English on the American mainland had altered the identity of this speech. **1982** D. Sutcliffe *Brit. Black Eng.* i. 23 And English—that is, uncreolized English—is also the official language in Jamaica.

uncri·nkle, *v.* [Un-² 7, 3.] **a.** *intr.* To lose crinkles, to become less crinkled. **b.** *trans.* To remove crinkles from.

1904 G. A. B. Dewar *Glamour of Earth* viii. 173 The tiny leaves will be uncrinkling in a day or two about the dark twiggy bole. **1911** W. De Morgan *Likely Story* v. 136 He uncrinkled a result of the shape of that letter-box. **1935** E. Bowen *House in Paris* ii. vii. 165 No one with him to smile and make his face uncrinkle.

uncrossed, *ppl. a.* **4.** (Earlier example.)

1882 [see *open cheque* s.v. *open *a.* 22 c].

uncrowned, *ppl. a.* Add: **2. b.** *uncrowned king* (*queen*), a man (woman) exerting autocratic influence over a specified sphere; a dominant man (woman). Const. *of.*

1917 J. W. Gerard *My Four Years in Germany* ii. 22 Heydebrand, is known as the 'Uncrowned King of Prussia'. *a* **1940** in *Harper's Bazaar* (1969) Oct. 36/3 Lady Dashwood, uncrowned Queen of Diabolo. **1978** 'S. Woods' *Exit Murderer* 154 The uncrowned King of the diamond smugglers. **1981** I. Boland tr. *Ginzburg's Within Whirlwind* ii. iv. 226 Old General Nikishov.. had this handsome lady living with him... the uncrowned Queen of Kolyma.

uncrushable, *a.* (Further examples.)

1929 *Daily Mail* 20 July 8/3 What are our scientists and inventors doing that they have not yet invented uncrushable linen? **1935** C. Ellis *Chem. Synthetic Resins* I. xxx. 641 Natural or artificial textile fibers can be given an uncrushable finish by the use of urea-formaldehyde resins condensed with alkalies. **1954** M. Stewart *Madam, will you Talk?* x. 78, I..shook out the green dress, thanking heaven and the research chemists for uncrushable materials. **1983** 'E. Anthony' *Company of Saints* i. 16 She..put on one of the long, uncrushable shifts that are a godsend to travellers.

uncushioned, *ppl. a.* (Earlier contextual example.)

1852 H. W. Dulcken tr. *Pfeiffer's Visit to Holy Land, Egypt, & Italy* i. 23 Uncushioned benches serve for seats by day and for beds by night.

uncustomary, *a.* Add: Hence **u:ncu·stomarily** *adv.*

1909 Webster, Uncustomarily, adv. **1966** *Punch* 2 Mar. p. viii/2 Functional, even austere decor, and uncustomarily fast service don't mark this splendid Chelsea restaurant as unluxurious. **1982** *Nature* 25 Feb. 642/1 Your uncustomarily superficial and misleading article.

uncut, *ppl. a.* Add: **5.** Also, without excisions or omissions.

1946 *Partisan Rev.* Nov.–Dec. 577 O'Neill's new play.. is guaranteed to last two-and-a-half hours longer than any other play, with the exception of the uncut *Hamlet.* **1953** K. Reisz *Technique Film Editing* xii. 193 The documentary or story-film editor's job..requires a subtler understanding and interpretation of the shades of meaning in the uncut shots. **1960** *News Chron.* 15 Mar. 8/3 His film 'India 1958', so far only seen in the uncut version at private showings. **1967** *Guardian* 9 May 5/3 (*heading*) Film director defends uncut 'Ulysses'. *Ibid.*, 'Ulysses' is due to be shown uncut at the Academy Cinema in London from June 1.

6. Undiluted, unadulterated.

1967 C. Drummond *Death at Furlong Post* vii. 104 All six of the Dancer's gaffs have been taken to pieces. Four ounces of uncut heroin. **1978** T. Williamson *Technicians of Death* vi. 43 They can produce very large amounts of uncut heroin.

undared, *ppl. a.* (Later example.)

1936 Auden *Look, Stranger!* 12 And into the undared ocean swung north their prow.

undation. For † *Obs. rare* read: *Obs. rare* exc. in **undation theory** *Geol.* [tr. Du. *undatietheorie* (1932)], the theory that selective internal heating of the earth's mantle causes large wave-like folds to appear in the crust.

1932 R. W. van Bemmelen in *Natuurk. Tijdschr. Nederlandsch. Indië* XCII. 93 The geologic history of the western part of the Sunda arc has been examined according to the Undation Theory. **1950** P. H. Kuenen *Marine Geol.* ii. 146 In his undation theory, van Bemmelen (1939) postulates a primary salsima layer formerly enveloping the whole earth and now forming the floor of the oceans. **1975** *Nature* 3 Apr. 386/1 The..hypothesis bears some resemblance to the minority view of Van Bemmelen.. and others, whose 'undation theory' proposes that selective high radioactive heating in the mantle produces warping of the overlying crust followed by lateral spreading under gravity.

undead, *a.* Add: Also, not quite dead but not fully alive, dead-and-alive. In vampirism, clinically dead but not yet at rest. (Later examples.) Also *absol.* as *sb.*

1897 B. Stoker *Dracula* xxvii. 381 There remain one more victim in the Vampire fold; one more to swell the grim and grisly ranks of the Un-dead. *Ibid.* 382 This then was the Un-Dead home of the King-Vampire. **1920** H. G. Wells *Outl. Hist.* 286/2 Presently by some amazing miracle he would become undead again and return, and set up his throne with much splendour and graciousness in Jerusalem. **1936** Dylan Thomas *Twenty-Five Poems* 4 They suffer the undead water where the turtle nibbles. **1949** D. L. Sayers tr. *Dante's Divine Comedy* I. viii. 118 Why walks this man, Undead, the kingdom of the dead? **1956** C. S. Lewis *Till we have Faces* xiv. 169 Shadow and monster in one, may be, a ghostly, un-dead thing. **1959** *Twentieth Cent.* Dec. 427 The vampire or 'undead' can only move about freely..between sunset and sunrise. **1972** P. H. Kocher *Master of Middle-Earth* (1973) iv. 62 They still inhabit their original bodies, but these have faded and thinned in their component matter until they can no longer be said to exist in the dimension of the living. Their flesh is not alive, not dead, but 'undead'. **1981** J. Sutherland *Bestsellers* v. 59 The good old folkloric remedies for killing the undead.

undeaf, *v.* (Later example.)

1933 W. de la Mare *Fleeting* 53 Fame with trump and drum Cannot undeaf the dumb.

undeca- (ʋndeˑkă), before a vowel **undec-**, comb. form of L. *undecim* eleven, as in Undecagon; cf. Hendeca- in Dict. and Suppl. In *Chem.* and *Biochem.* used to form the names of molecules that contain eleven carbon atoms or consist of eleven of the second element, as **unde·cane**, any of a series of isomeric hydrocarbons $C_{11}H_{24}$, *esp.* the liquid unbranched member $CH_3(CH_2)_9CH_3$; **u:ndecape·ptide**, any polypeptide composed of eleven amino-acids; **u:ndecyle·nic acid**, a yellow, water-insoluble carboxylic acid, $CH_2{:}CH(CH_2)_8COOH$, which is used as an antifungal agent.

1899 *Jrnl. Chem. Soc.* LXXVI. i. 816 The same substances were also detected in neutral creosote from paraffin oil; in this, undecane was found. **1971** E. O. Wilson *Insect Societies* xii. 237/1 Undecane and the mandibular gland substances..evoke the alarm response at concentrations of 10^9–10^{12} molecules per cubic centimeter. **1960** *Jrnl. Biol. Chem.* CCXXXV. 3645/2 Imidazole·heme undecapeptide exhibits a more complex behavior. **1979** *Nature* 8 Feb. 480/2 Several lines of evidence suggest that the undecapeptide, substance P, is involved in synaptic transmission in various areas of the central nervous system. **1879** *Jrnl. Chem. Soc.* XXXVI. 306 Undecylic acid, $C_{11}H_{22}O_2$, prepared by heating undecylenic acid with red phosphorus and hydriodic acid.., is a colourless transparent substance. **1952** S. Spender *Learning Laughter* xiii. 179 Castor oil plants can also be broken down into eneanthol and undecylenic acid. **1979** *Jrnl. Pharm. Sci.* LXVIII. 384/1 The antifungal activity of products containing undecylenic acid and its salts was demonstrated some time ago.

undecidable, *a.* Add: **b.** *Logic* and *Math.* Of a proposition, theorem, etc.: incapable of being either proved or disproved.

1937 *Mind* XLVI. 60 Gödel has shown that the particular sentence in question is undecidable, *i.e.*, neither it nor its negation is demonstrable. **1966** S. Beer *Decision & Control* x. 208 The network language which spans the gap between a problem situation and its conceptual model also contains undecidable sentences. **1979** *Sci. Amer.* Feb. 5/1 Logicians have been able to show that even simple and mathematically interesting statements may be undecidable.

Hence **u:ndecidabi·lity**, the property of being undecidable.

1942 *Mind* LI. 260 It therefore raises the issue of undecidability in the arithmetical as well as in the linguistic realm. **1967** S. C. Kleene *Math. Logic* v. 279 By the essential undecidability of S, S_2 is undecidable. **1971** *Sci. Amer.* Aug. 99/1 In contrast, the Platonists, who count among their number even Gödel himself, believe (like Einstein) that the undecidability in mathematics is a statement about the inherent limitations of our present axiomatic mode of investigation and not about the mathematical objects themselves.

undecided, *sb.* Add: **2.** An undecided person, one who has not made up his mind.

1968 *Listener* 31 Oct. 568/2 Who can decide what an undecided is going to do? **1974** *Times* 7 Oct. 4/4 The Labour Party is picking up more support from the undecideds than any other party.

undecision. Delete † *Obs.* and add later example.

1930 W. Faulkner *As I lay Dying* 13, I mislike undecision as much as ere a man.

undecylenic: see *undeca-.

undefeatable, *a.* Add: (Later examples.) Hence **undefea·tably** *adv.*

1938 J. W. Day *Dog in Sport* xvi. 218 Of great heart and wisdom, with courage undefeatable. **1943** —— *Farming Adventure* xvii. 192 All bids were overtopped by the undefeatable broad Norfolk of an aircraftman who bought recklessly. **1980** *Oxf. Diocesan Mag.* Mar. 19/2 A power which will work unceasingly and undefeatably until the kingdoms of the world become the Kingdom of God.

undefecated, *ppl. a.* (Earlier example.)

1812 *Dramatic Censor 1811* 325 We have not met with any thing on the stage, more abounding in pure, unalloyed, undefecated absurdity, than the '*Wood Dæmon*'.

undefe·ndable, *a.* [Un-[1] 7 b.] **a.** Of a place: that cannot be defended.

1931 W. S. Churchill *World Crisis* VI. viii. 126 Belgrade, the capital, stood actually upon the Danube at the frontier and was undefendable.

b. Of a person = Defenceless, defenseless *a.* 1.

1938 E. Bowen *Death of Heart* i. vi. 109 Her tears were like a flag lowered at once: she felt herself to be undefendable. **1977** W. M. Spackman *Armful of Warm Girl* 114, I never felt so undefendable and I didn't even know who you were.

undefinably, *adv.* (Earlier example.)

1796 F. Burney *Camilla* V. x. xi. 470 This reverie, poignantly agitating, yet undefinably soothing.

undelightfully, *adv.* (Earlier example.)

1749 J. Cleland *Mem. Woman Pleasure* I. 86 The extreme whiteness of her skin was not undelightfully contrasted by the smooth glossy brown of her lover's.

undelighting, *ppl. a.* **2.** (Later example.)

1984 *Times Lit. Suppl.* 27 Apr. 449/4 Trakl himself, whose cold, undelighting, unhuman speech, with its small, select and poisoned vocabulary, is like no other in German.

undema·nding, *ppl. a.* [Un-[1] 10.] Not rigorous or exacting; tolerant; easy. So **undema·ndingness.**

1939 'A. Bridge' *Four-Part Setting* xi. 143 'She..is the most unexacting person I ever met... She *asks* less of you than anyone I know.'..Rose Pelham..had not hit on that peculiar undemandingness. **1940** W. Faulkner *Hamlet* iii. ii. 180 [She] was loyal, discreet, undemanding, and thrifty with his money. **1958** *Times* 18 Dec. 14/1 An undemanding public can be blamed in these cases for spoiling art. **1971** Hindell & Simms *Abortion Law Reformed* v. 122 His publishing activities were fairly undemanding.

undenizened, *ppl. a.* (Later example.)

1887 G. M. Hopkins *Poems* (1967) 103 Undenizened, beyond bound Of earth's glory, earth's ease, all.

undenominationalist. (Earlier example.)

1879 T. Legge in A. Peel *Lett. to Victorian Editor* (1929) 323 Somerville Hall will belong to the undenominationalists.

under, *prep.* Add: **I. 4. a.** Also *under the counter*: see *counter *sb.*[3] 4 b; *under the table*: see *table *sb.* 5 e and 6 d.

b. (Later example.) Also, of a motor-cycle to the rider.

1942 [see *nip *v.*[1] 4 c]. **1980** *Dirt Bike* Oct. 57/1 If you're a specialist, you must think long and hard about the MAG 3. Especially if one knifes under you on a flat corner.

II. 10. e. (Earlier example.)

1846 S. Magoffin *Diary* 19 Sept. in *Down Santa Fé Trail* (1926) 135 He has been under the Doctor for some time.

f. *Mus.* = Conducted by.

1887 E. Dannreuther tr. *Wagner's On Conducting* 63 Fancies of this sort, however, were not permitted during the strictly classical performance, under the veteran Capellmeister, at the Munich Odeon. **1910** G. B. Shaw *How to become a Musical Critic* (1960) 278 A performance under Manns of a Mozart symphony. **1943** *N.Y. Times* 9 May ii. 5/5 The City Amateur Symphony Orchestra, under Judge Leopold Prince, will give its annual series of Summer concerts. **1962** *Listener* 12 Apr. 661/2 The BBC Northern Orchestra under Jacques-Louis Monod. **1976** Y. Menuhin *Unfinished Journey* (1977) xvi. 342 During Sir Thomas Beecham's sponsorship of it, I performed the Viotti A Minor Concerto with him—the last time I played under Sir Thomas's baton.

13. f. *Math.* With sbs. denoting an operation performed.

1901 L. E. Dickson *Linear Groups* ii. xi. 252 *G* contains..such conjugate cyclic subgroups, all of whose substitutions are conjugate under *G*. **1940** E. T. Bell *Devel. Math.* xx. 394 The constancy of the cross ratio of four collinear points under projection. **1956** E. M. Patterson *Topology* iv. 84 y_0 is the image of x_0 under the homeomorphism. **1974** *Encycl. Brit. Macropædia* XI. 657/1 A conic has a central projection that is another conic, but some properties are not preserved under projection.

IV. 22. b. Also prefixed to a number and used as a *sb. pl.* (usu. with *the*) to denote the class of persons who have not yet attained that particular age. Cf. *over- 13 b.

1937 E. Garnett *Family from One End Street* v. 98 John was hopping along..in a sack race for 'under tens'. **1939** E. R. Boyce *Infant School Activities* 201 As much provision as possible should be made for the sort of period suggested for the 'under-fives'. **1941** [see *cross-sectional *a.*]. **1953** K. Tennant *Joyful Condemned* xii. 100 He added her to the other two under-sixteens, Else and Violet. **1968** *Catholic Herald* 15 Mar. 12/5 The Cenacle, Grayshott... Retreat for the Under Thirties. **1973** M. Amis *Rachel Papers* 153 But then, you see, we did the sort of lyrically zany thing that the under-twenties do fairly often.

under, *adv.* Add: **3. d.** In a state of unconsciousness; below the level of consciousness; *spec.* under anaesthetic, in a trance. Also, under the influence of alcohol. *colloq.*

a **1936** 'G. Orwell' *Shooting Elephant* (1950) 28 Doctors..thinking it funny to start operating before you were properly 'under'. **1946** K. Tennant *Lost Haven* (1947) xix. 332 Well, one night when I was down at the pub, this cove..is beside me and he's well under. **1960** M. Spark *Bachelors* vii. 98 He attempted to question me while I was under the other night. **1979** D. Anthony *Long Hard Cure* xxvii. 207, I..stretched out on my bed, and let the music take me under.

4. c. *to get out* (*stand*, etc.) *from under*, to escape or get away from a dangerous or awkward situation. *colloq.* (orig. *U.S.*).

[**1857** *Chicago Times* 6 Oct., To enable me to stand from under the present crash, I shall offer my entire stock for the next 30 days at a great sacrifice.] **1861** *Cincinnati* (Ohio) *Commercial* 24 Apr. (*heading*) Stand from under. **1875** *Scribner's Monthly* Nov. 124/2 The system is rotten.. and, if the nation cares for its life, the quicker it gets 'out from under' the better. **1916** *Lit. Digest* (N.Y.) 8 Jan. 88/2 The next to 'get from under'. **1916** 'Taffrail' *Pincher Martin* iii. 35 Shouts of 'stand from under!' and empty bags came from the deck above. **1938** *New Statesman* 20 Aug. 298/2 The extension of anti-Semitic persecution in the business field [in Germany] has probably led to a certain amount of 'getting out from under' sales by Jews. **1951** H. McCloy *Alias Basil Willing* xiv. 178 I'll get out from under by going to the police myself before anyone else. **1966** 'H. Calvin' *Italian Gadget* ix. 143 Maybe you'll come some day... If I ever get from under Count Capucci. **1974** 'J. Ross' *Burning of Billy Toober* xvi. 157 I'll buy you a dinner when I get out from under.

under-, *prefix*[1]. Add: **I. 4. c.** *underredden.*

1866 G. M. Hopkins *Jrnls. & Papers* (1959) 138 The meadows yellow with buttercups and under-reddened with sorrel.

5. a. *under-bodice* (earlier example), *-shorts* (*U.S.*), *-slip*, *-waist* (*U.S.*).

1873 *Young Englishwoman* Apr. 194/1 (*heading*) Under-bodice of jaconet, insertion, and lace. **1960** 'E. McBain' *See them Die* (1963) iii. 28 Murchison..tugged at his undershorts, and wondered if it was any cooler upstairs. **1978** W. F. Buckley *Stained Glass* xii. 129 She had opened the door, exhilarated at the prospect of seeing Paul lying there as she so regularly came on him, dressed only in his undershorts. **1922** Joyce *Ulysses* 321 The bride..looked exquisitely charming in a creation carried out in green mercerised silk, moulded on an underslip of gloaming grey. **1968** B. Hines *Kestrel for Knave* 23 His mother was standing in her underslip, a lipstick poised at her mouth. **1857** in A. V. G. Allen *Life Phillips Brooks* (1900) I. vi. 209 Thick winter underwaists and socks. *a* **1911** D. G. PHILLIPS in *Hearst's Mag.* (1916) Feb. 137/1 She bought a pair of shoes for a dollar,..two underwaists for a quarter.

b. *underchin.*

1906 GALSWORTHY *Man of Property* I. iii. 44 Between the points of his stand-up collar,..the pale flesh of his underchin remained immovable. **1978** J. A. MICHENER *Chesapeake* 19 The geese [had]..jet-black head and neck, snow-white under-chin.

c. *underclearance, -deep, -mire, -structure.*

1930 *Engineering* 15 Aug. 197/3 The [U.S.] War Department..imposed the limiting conditions of 100 feet underclearance above the level of mean high water. **1967** *Jane's Surface Skimmer Systems 1967–68* 64/1 Riser bars may be used, depending on load underclearance. *a* **1930** D. H. LAWRENCE *Last Poems* (1932) 7 As if any Mind could have imagined a lobster dozing the under-deeps. **1913** —— *Love Poems & Others* 27 And even in the watery shells that lie Alive within the oozy under-mire, A grain of this same fire I can descry. **1943** *Mind* LII. 135 These instincts or reflexes are the second point of contact where behaviour science, factually though not methodologically, rests upon its biological understructure. **1980** *Dædalus* Spring 99 Stories about dreams..often deliberately obfuscate the understructure of common sense.

d. *under-dark, -dusk, -gold, -mist, -night, -pattern.*

1916 D. H. LAWRENCE *Amores* 137 Bright blue crops Surge from the under-dark to their ladder-tops. **1923** —— *Kangaroo* i. 8 It..was like a whole country with towns and bays and darknesses. And all lying mysteriously within the Australian underdark, that peculiar lost, weary aloofness of Australia. **1914** —— in *Eng. Rev.* Feb. 305 And lamps like venturous glow-worms steal among The shadowy stubble of the under-dusk. **1929** —— *Pansies* 17 Twilight thick underdusk..While darkness submerges the stones. **1922** —— in *Eng. Rev.* June 509 Fishes, with their gold-red eyes, and green-pure gleam, and under-gold. **1917** —— *Look! We have come Through!* 48 Over there is Russia—Austria, Switzerland, France, in a circle! I here in the undermist on the Bavarian road. *Ibid.* 120 Where the seed sinks in To the earth of the under-night Where all is silent. **1934** T. S. ELIOT *Elizabethan Essays* 190 What distinguishes poetic drama from prosaic drama is a kind of doubleness... The drama has an under-pattern, less manifest than the theatrical one.

II. 6. a. *under-boss, -matron, -waiter.*

1942 M. HARCOURT *Parson in Prison* 20 The whole school was assembled before the underbosses. **1964** *Amer. Speech* XXXIX. 305 Over each [Mafia] family presides a boss... Beneath the boss are an underboss, also known as *sotto capo*, and a *consiglieri*. **1972** *N.Y. Times Mag.* 4 June 95 In the restructured family on which Joe Colombo solidified his hold as boss, another tantalizing figure emerged, Charles (Charlie Lemons) Mineo... Mineo has become a unique kind of underboss. **1976** 'W. TREVOR' *Children of Dynmouth* ii. 42 The undermatron, Miss Tomm, had come into the dormitory and asked him to come with her to the study. **1880** Underwaiter [see *LANDLORD *sb.* 4]. **1921** E. M. FORSTER *Let.* 17 May in *Hill of Devi* (1953) 81 He worked like an underwaiter in a Soho restaurant.

9. a. *underself, -taste.*

1890 W. JAMES *Princ. Psychol.* I. viii. 206 Barring a certain common fund of information, like the command of language, etc., what the upper self knows the under self is ignorant of, and *vice versa*. **1914** W. DE MORGAN *When Ghost meets Ghost* II. xvi. 662 This underself of hers may have vibrated in response to the strange hints he had thrown out. **1908** H. JAMES *Spoils of Poynton* p. xxiii, An air of comedy comparatively free from sharp undertastes. **1980** R. B. KITAJ *Artist's Eye* (Nat. Gallery) 3 Their lives at the sinister heart of the Baudelairean city, the spell its compelling undertaste cast on them.

IV. 10. a. *under-calculate, -emphasize, -fulfil, -graze, -react, -recover; under-endowed, -equipped, -financed, -fulfilled, -funded, -garrisoned, -grazed, -gunned, -industrialized, -informed, -policed, -powered, -publicized, -researched, -stained, -stressed* ppl. adjs.; *under-funding, -grazing.*

1836 DICKENS *Let.* 8 Oct. (1965) I. 181 There really is not time, unless Hansard's people, have greatly undercalculated the quantity sent. **1910** *Practitioner* Feb. 152 Cough..is one of the..most significant symptoms of pulmonary tuberculosis... It is too often undercalculated by the patient and his friends. **1983** *Platt's Oil Marketing Bull.* 15 Aug. 1/1 It has been undercalculating its Windfall Tax payments. **1964** *Amer. Psychologist* XIX. 14/2 If I have seemed to underemphasize the importance of inner capacities..it is because I believe that this part of the story is given by the nature of man's evolution. **1909** H. G. WELLS *Ann Veronica* xvii. 344, I remarked that science was disgracefully under-endowed, and confessed I'd had to take to more profitable courses. **1969** N. W. PIRIE *Food Resources* viii. 191 They are almost all underendowed while money is squandered on projects with little bearing on the world's real needs. **1960** *Times Lit. Suppl.* 2 Sept. 553/4 Our teenagers are cast out into the world with boredom as the only memory of their ill-disciplined, under-equipped schooldays. **1923** *Daily Mail* 30 Jan. 4 This Department is under-staffed, underfinanced, unprovided with many of the safeguards it has itself demanded. **1977** M. EDELMAN *Political Lang.* v. 100 An under-financed and uncoordinated reaction to widespread destitution becomes a 'war on poverty'. **1950** A. LEE *Soviet Air Force* 77 Unlike the later Five Year Plans, the target for the first was 'underfulfilled'. **1964** *Ann. Reg. 1963* 230 According to Premier Široký..the plan as a whole had been underfulfilled by 1·2 per cent. **1982** T. J. BINYON *Swan Song* v. 32 The professor..accused me..of consistently underfulfilling the department's norms in teaching, research and administration. **1970** *Nature* 8 Aug. 551/2 It also suggests, perhaps intentionally, that the project is grossly underfunded. **1963** *Economist* 27 Apr. 342/1 Over-funding last year could be compensated by under-funding this year. **1981** *Daily Tel.* 17 Oct. 12/3 The continual underfunding of the Royal Shakespeare Company..was endangering its ability to..retain its talented staff. **1936** AUDEN & ISHERWOOD *Ascent of F6* I. ii. 24 We're under-garrisoned and underpoliced and..we're in a blue funk that the Ostnians will come over the frontier. **1977** J. L. HARPER *Population Biol. of Plants* xiv. 438 Swards were overgrazed in winter and spring and undergrazed in summer and autumn. **1960** *Farmer & Stockbreeder* 8 Mar. 71/1 Those swards which needed improvement were the undergrazed type. **1933** *Jrnl. R. Agric. Soc.* XCIV. 24 This plot was subjected to overstocking in winter and early spring, followed by gross undergrazing during the summer and autumn. **1974** *Times* 7 Jan. 12/3 To tear up large areas at once has led too often to undergrazing, drainage difficulties, [etc.]. **1928** C. F. S. GAMBLE *Story North Sea Air Station* xiii. 214 As a fighting machine the H.12 was under-gunned for her size. **1944** *Return to Attack* (Army Board, N.Z.) 8/1 The armoured brigades..were equipped with..both types [of tank] fast-moving but under-gunned compared with the German tanks. **1964** I. L. HOROWITZ *New Sociol.* 33 We cannot examine demography without basing our analysis on some definite correlation of..underindustrialized and overpopulated. **1968** *Punch* 31 July 141/1 The under-informed voter. **1936** Under-policed [see *under-garrisoned* above]. **1978** *N.Y. Times* 30 Mar. A20/5 Underpoliced and unkempt, [the bus terminal]..serves as headquarters for an ominous army of hookers, muggers and pimps. **1905** KIPLING *Actions & Reactions* (1909) 128 Under-powered craft..can ascend to the limit of their lift. **1980** 'M. HARRIS' *Treasure of Sainte Foy* i. 4 The small Renault is underpowered and rather cheaply built. **1971** H. WILSON *Labour Govt.* xxxvi. 739 One of the under-publicised achievements of comprehensive secondary education. **1965** Under-react [see *OVERREACT *v.*] **1982** *Economist* 5 June 37/2 The markets may, on average, have underreacted to the publication of the money figures. **1967** Under-recover [see *over-recovered* s.v. *OVER- 27 b]. **1942** M. MCCARTHY *Company she Keeps* v. 239 [He] went back to the public library; perhaps..the material was under-researched. **1982** *Pol. Sci. Q.* XCVII. 474 Rawlings's intervention, so sadly underresearched. **1941** Understained [see *HETEROCHROMATIN]. **1956** Understained [see *HETEROCHROMATIC *a.* 2]. **1900** *Phil. Mag.* L. 132 A lower factor of safety might..be used in such cases, where there is a large reserve of understressed material. **1928** *Observer* 17 June 8 It is a curious book. Colloquial and offhand, deliberately understressed in feeling and description, [etc.]. **1969** *Harper's Bazaar* Sept. 27/1 An expensive car must be one hundred per cent reliable, and this..means an under-stressed engine of the simplest possible kind.

b. *under-capacity, -emphasis, -fulfilment, -population, -recovery, -registration.*

1962 E. SNOW *Other Side of River* (1963) lxxxvi. 725 The American problem of abundance or overcapacity to produce commodities and undercapacity to consume them. **1916** E. POUND *Let.* 17 Apr. (1971) 76 In 'Impression', I don't think 'dissolved' is just the right word, though I recognize that you may have been aiming at a sort of restraint or under-emphasis which *can* be effective. **1977** M. EDELMAN *Political Lang.* v. 83 Hess and Torney found a repetitive emphasis in the schools on the values of loyalty, authority, and law, and an underemphasis on citizens' rights. **1962** E. SNOW *Other Side of River* (1963) vii. 58, I can't recall visiting any mine or factory where 'underfulfillment' was predicted. **1922** *Daily Mail* 29 Nov. 8/4 The absurd underpopulation of the country parts. **1966** *Times* 28 Mar. (Austral. Suppl.) p. xii/6 Faced with the difficulties of isolation and under-population, managements argue that secondhand top name overseas packages are a cheaper..investment. **1961** *Ann. Reg. 1960* 511 The Sugar Board..revealed a loss..; the deficit brought the Board's total 'under-recovery' to £7·1 million. **1952** C. P. BLACKER *Eugenics* 160 Lorimer gives good reasons for thinking that this discrepancy arose from under-registration of deaths, especially of infantile deaths, in the intervening period.

c. *under-luminous.*

1971 *Nature* 23 Apr. 517/1 With this value..Fig. 1 suggests that the primary is grossly underluminous for its mass.

under-, *prefix.*[2] Add: *under-ice, -strength.*

1966 *Times* 28 Feb. (Canada Suppl.) p. xvi/6, The submarine freighter..must have an under-ice capacity of 800 to 1,000 miles. **1976** *Jrnl. R. Soc. Arts* CXXIV. 638/2 BAS has undertaken surface sledge traverses for major anomalies and to interpret the under-ice rocks and principal structural features such as George VI Sound. **1959** *Encounter* Nov. 17/2, 175 divisions in the Red Army ..as against 14 under-strength divisions in the U.S. army. **1971** R. PETRIE *Thorne in Flesh* ix. 117 An understrength police force was at full stretch.

under-achie·ver. *Psychol.* Also as one word without hyphen. [UNDER-[1] 10 b.] Someone whose actual performance consistently fails to reach the level predicted by intelligence tests or other measures of ability. Cf. *OVER-ACHIEVER.

1953 *Jrnl. Abnormal Psychol.* XLVIII. 533/2 If his grades fell a full rank below prediction he was labelled an 'underachiever'. **1962** 'I. Ross' *Old Students Never Die* viii. 105 Nowadays we have a name for them: the kids with the high potential and the low grades. We call them 'under-achievers'. **1968** D. LAWTON *Social Class, Lang. & Educ.* i. 6 For a number of reasons working-class children tend to be under-achievers. **1973** E.-J. BAHR *Nice Neighbourhood* v. 47, I identify with the underachievers of this world. **1975** *Kingston* (Ontario) *Whig-Standard* 6 Sept. 27/6 The survey also found that those not using seat belts also were under-achievers in school.

So **under-achie·vement; under-achie·ve** *v. intr.*, **under-achie·ving** *ppl. a.* and *vbl. sb.*

1951 *School Rev.* LIX. 472 (*title*) Factors related to over-achievement and under-achievement in school. **1953** Underachieving *vbl. sb.* [see *OVERACHIEVING *vbl. sb.*]. **1954** *Jrnl. Educ. Psychol.* Oct. 322 It is virtually impossible for a pupil at or near the..first percentile [on an intelligence test] to 'under-achieve'. **1965** in M. Kornrich *Underachievement* 553 A role for the counselor may be to help the underachieving student. **1972** *Guardian* 21 July 12/5 Parents who want their children to go to a popular school may..encourage them to underachieve. **1982** *Secondary Educ. Jrnl.* XII. III. 1/2 Underachievement is not confined to pupils in secondary schools. *Ibid.*, Many of these pupils are..not achieving their full potential—in other words they are underachieving.

under-age, *a.* Add: **1*.** Carried on by someone below the legal age (for the activity).

1978 *Morecambe Guardian* 14 Mar. 19/8 He went on, about supervision on the rally site, and the danger of under-age drinking. **1983** *Sun* 8 June 15/3 He persuaded her to pose nude and sing about under-age sex.

u·nder-and-o·ver, *adj.* (and *sb.*) *phr.* Also unhyphened. [UNDER *adv.* I.] = *OVER-AND-UNDER *a.* Also *absol.* as *sb.*

1881 W. W. GREENER *Gun & its Development* 380 (*caption*) Under and over Wedge-fast Gun. **1911** *Encycl. Brit.* XXIII. 336/1 There is also Greener's 'under and over', the rifle barrel being topmost (usually 16-bore shot-gun barrel and ·450 rifle barrel). **1931** G. BURRARD *Modern Shotgun* I. ix. 235 (*heading*) The Woodward 'under and over' gun. **1958** *Spectator* 1 Aug. 163/1 The 'professionals'..tended to shoot with under-and-over guns. **1969** C. CHEVENIX TRENCH *Shooter & his Gun* viii. 97 (*caption*) Double-barrelled under and over.

under-arm, *a.* Add: **1. b.** In other sporting contexts. Also as *adv.*

1929 W. E. COLLINSON *Spoken Eng.* 90 I'll have to serve underarm, I've strained my wrist. **1960** E. W. SWANTON *West Indies Revisited* 230 An under-arm throw by Smith. **1974** MILLS & BUTLER *Tackle Badminton* v. 39 Take a good underarm swing, turning your left shoulder towards the net. **1976** *Times* 3 Feb. 9/4 When one recalls that most women of the period [*sc.* 1909] would have added a hat to the recommended [tennis] ensemble one can see why they had to serve under-arm.

3. *Dressmaking.* Of a seam: that edges the lower half of the arm-hole of a garment, or that joins the underside of a sleeve or the side of a bodice.

1908 M. E. MORGAN *How to dress Doll* (1973) v. 43 Put the seam of the sleeve a little to the front of the underarm seam. **1941** L. I. WILDER *Little Town on Prairie* ix. 85 Laura sewed the whalebone stays onto the underarm seams. **1964** *McCall's Sewing* xi. 161/1 Pin the underarm seam of bodice and sleeve. *Ibid.* 162/1 On the pattern there will be a slash marking at the curve of the underarm.

4. Of a bag or case: carried under the arm.

[**1925** *T. Eaton & Co. Catal.* Spring & Summer 279/1 Under-the-arm bag.] **1927** *Glasgow Herald* 21 Jan. 8 Whatever she carries about with her she keeps in an attaché case, an 'under-arm bag', or some other receptacle. **1974** *Harrod's Christmas Catal.* 19 Under-arm document case £27.50.

5. Applied to various items of personal care used on the armpit, as *under-arm deodorant, razor.* Also *under-arm odour.*

1947 H. M. MCLUHAN in *Horizon* Oct. 132 The means of defeating under-arm odour. **1968** A. DIMENT *Great Spy Race* viii. 122 At twelve, showered, shaved with her small under-arm razor..we were on the coast road. **1976** J. WAINWRIGHT *Walther P. 38* 21 You use under-arm deodorant.

u·nder-bark, *a.* (and *adv.*). [UNDER-[2].] Measured or taken without including the bark of a tree trunk. Also as *adv.* Cf. *OVER-BARK.

1911 C. L. HANSON *Forestry for Woodmen* xiv. 192 If it [*sc.* a log] is 16 inches over bark it will be taken as 15 inches under bark. **1927** *Forestry* I. 8 Sample plots..gave the age as 123 years..and the underbark quarter girth volume per acre over 8,000 cubic feet. **1953** H. L. EDLIN *Forester's Handbk.* xiv. 215 Under-bark measure is strictly the volume of the log as measured after the bark has been peeled off it; but in practice it is often taken as the over-bark measure less the customary bark allowance. **1967** SCOTT & PALMER *Hiley's Woodland Managem.* (ed. 2) ix. 130 Prices which are quoted for timber nearly always apply to the under-bark measurement.

underbed. (Further examples.)

1725 in F. Kidder *Exped. Capt. Lovewell* (1865) 93 A feather bed and under bed and bed furniture. **1778** *New Hampsh. Hist. Soc. Coll.* (1889) IX. 108 We have cut up all the sheets, table cloths, underbeds, towels, &c. **1868** G. G. CHANNING *Recoll. Newport* 254 The bed or underbed of straw was laid on cords, and the feather bed above. **1978** *Morecambe Guardian* 14 Mar. 6/5 You can buy beds already fitted with underbed drawers. **1982** *Habitat Catal. 1982/83* 122 Sturdy underbed storage on fixed nylon castors.

under-belly. Add: Also **underbelly. 1.** Now, the belly or underside of an animal. Also *transf.*, esp. of motor vehicles. Cf. UNDER-BODY 2, 3 b.

1960 *Times* 3 Mar. 8/6 Both propellers were buckled and the front underbelly was severely dented. **1963** *Listener* 10 Jan. 65/2, I creep along on my cat's underbelly Nursing the floor for smells. **1964** S. BELLOW *Herzog* 327 The great car got up the hill slowly, scraping its underbelly on rocks.

2. *fig.* **a.** A vulnerable part, esp. in phr. *soft underbelly.*

1942 W. S. CHURCHILL in *Hansard Commons* 11 Nov. 28 We make this wide encircling movement in the Mediterranean..having for its object the exposure of the under-belly of the Axis, especially Italy, to heavy attack. **1949** *Life* 31 Oct. 36/2 An all-out attack on the 'soft underbelly' of socialism. **1959** E. H. CLEMENTS *High Tension* vii. 130 The educational organisation..attacked the soft under-belly of the nation: the children. **1976** J. CROSBY *Snake* (1977) x. 45 She was..sticking her knife into the disgusting underbelly of male chauvinism, and..into the soft underbelly of capitalism. **1980** *Encounter* May 86/2 The plan was to..punch their way through the soft, unsuspecting underbelly of Iran.

b. The underside or inferior part of something, which is often unnoticed or concealed.

1962 *Listener* 6 Dec. 957/2 It is a picaresque language from the under-belly of a culture, the speech of people on the move..of the wagon, railroad, and camp. *Ibid.* 27 Dec. 1106/3 The many programmes of popular music, the under-belly, so to speak, of the broadcast structure. **1976** *National Observer* (U.S.) 21 Aug. 16/3 What we're seeing is the underbelly of some of the great legends of American history. **1981** 'D. JORDAN' *Double Red* ix. 97 The seamy underbelly of American capitalism.

underbid, *v.* Add: **4.** *Bridge.* To bid less on (a hand) than its strength warrants. Also *intr.*

1908 R. F. FOSTER *Auction Bridge* 29 It is a mistake to underbid the hand. **1945** 'S. J. SIMON' *Why you lose at Bridge* 58 The average player overbids his big hands and underbids his small ones. **1969** A. TRUSCOTT *Gt. Bridge Scandal* xii. 159 He had decided to underbid his hand. **1974** *Times* 16 Feb. 13/3 He did not wish to deny diamonds..nor could he afford to underbid by signing off in Three No Trumps.

u·nder-bid, *sb. Bridge.* [f. the vb.] **a.** A bid of a number of tricks insufficient to surpass the previous bid. *rare.* **b.** A lower bid than is warranted by the strength of a hand or of a partnership's combined hands.

1923 *Daily Mail* 6 Oct. 6/4 The under-bid of 2 spades is automatically raised to 3 spades by the fact of one of the opponents calling attention to it. **1945** 'S. J. SIMON' *Why you lose at Bridge* 96 Most of the time I make what seems to me the best bid in the circumstances, whether it is an overbid, an underbid, or even an anti-system bid. **1977** *Times* 10 Dec. 13/6 The response which is outstanding is a gross underbid of One No Trump.

underbidder. Add: **2.** *Bridge.* A player who under-bids.

1923 [see *OVERBID *v.* 2 c]. **1945** 'S. J. SIMON' *Why you lose at Bridge* 58 On the cancelled hands, both overbidder and underbidder remain oblivious of their enormities.

u·nderbit. *U.S.* [UNDER-[1] 5 b.] An earmark to indicate ownership, made on the lower part of the ear of cattle. Cf. UNDER-BITTED *ppl. a.*, UNDERKEEL.

1837 *Knickerbocker* X. 408 The young bridegroom boasted that he had taken an 'under bit out of his left ear'. **1869** *Overland Monthly* III. 126 A red mulley cow, with a crop and an underbit in the right [ear]. **1915** *Dialect Notes* IV. 185 *Under-bit*, a triangular cut from the lower side.

u·nderbite, *sb.* [UNDER-[1], after *OVERBITE.] The projection of the lower jaw or the lower incisors beyond the upper.

Not a term used in Dentistry.

1976 M. MACHLIN *Pipeline* xlvi. 484 Coutts was a big lantern jawed man with a pronounced underbite that gave his chin an appearance something like an Arctic icebreaker. **1982** *Guardian* 26 Oct. 8/6 You stick your jaw way out until it's almost as if you have an underbite.

u·nder-blanket. Also as one word. [UNDER-[1] 5 b and UNDER *a.* 2 a.] A blanket laid under the bottom sheet, as opp. to one used as a covering; now often an electric blanket.

[**1746**], **1819** [see UNDER *a.* 2 a]. **1930** *Daily Express* 6 Oct. 9/7 (Advt.), Under blankets. **1971** *Guardian* 12 July 3/1 (Advt.), Electric underblanket. Single size approx. 50″ × 26″. **1979** *Daily Tel.* 24 Jan. 14 A simple pin magnet together with a bag of corks placed between the under sheet and the underblanket has made me immune [from cramp].

under-body. Now usu. unhyphened. **1. b.** For *U.S.* read *U.S. dial.* and add example. Also, any undergarment for the body, esp. an under-bodice or under-shirt.

1873 in *Mag. Albemarle County* (Va.) *Hist.* (1963) XX. 57 She gave me some mighty pretty nansook to make an underbody. **1936** E. GLASGOW *Vein of Iron* I. i. 12 She hoped the minister couldn't see the top of her red flannel underbody, which would poke up at the neck, though it was sewed to her petticoat.

3. b. (Further examples.) Freq. *attrib.*, with reference to rust protection.

1956 *Autocar* 19 Oct. 596/1 Under-body sealing and sound-deadening compound. **1976** *Sci. Amer.* Feb. 77 (*caption*) Spot-welding robots..are used in assembling the underbodies of Chevrolet Novas, Pontiac Venturas and Buick Skylarks at the General Motors plant. **1976** *Time* 20 Dec. 56/2 (Advt.), The entire underbody is sealed against the elements. **1977** *R.A.F. News* 8–21 June 5/3 (Advt.), Like fitted front seat belts, full underbody seal and servo-assisted front disc brakes.

u·nder-bo:nnet, *a.* [UNDER-[2].] Pertaining to, situated, or occurring beneath the bonnet of a motor vehicle (i.e. in or of the engine).

1962 *Times* 24 Apr. 16/2 Oil supply, from an underbonnet tank. **1973** *Times* 3 May 35/2 A few pounds worth of sound damping material would probably work wonders in suppressing underbonnet and underfloor noise. **1977** *Custom Car* Nov. 13/3 Presumably, Ford believe that customers in that price bracket leave under-bonnet checks to a garage.

u·nderbrim. [UNDER-[1] 5 e.] The underside of the brim of a hat; a trimming or lining attached to this.

1908 *Sears, Roebuck Catal.* 1036/1 This child's hat is..made on wire frame with the entire upper and under brim very closely covered with shirred pink miliners' mull. **1922** JOYCE *Ulysses* 344 A hat of wide-leaved nigger straw contrast trimmed with an underbrim of eggblue chenille. **1923** *Daily Mail* 5 Mar. 15 A pretty girl's hat is a mushroom shape of rough biscuit straw with a flower-covered underbrim. **1935** BRAND & MUSSARED *Millinery* viii. 64 Tack the underbrim to the interlining at the headline, work from the centre-front in either direction.

underbrush, *sb.* Add: **a.** (Earlier U.S. example.)

1775 J. JEFFREY *Jrnl.* 3 Apr. in *Essex Inst. Hist. Coll.* (1914) L. 107 The fire ran among the leaves & dry underbrush for upwards of a mile.

b. *fig.*

1888 *Kansas State Hist. Soc. Trans.* (1890) IV. 274 The underbrush of forgetfulness has so grown that but few in Kansas know that Joel K. Goodin ever lived. **1927** *Bulletin* (Glasgow) 6 Apr. 16/1 Taking up a tarnished knife and fork, he pushed aside the underbrush of onions and came face to face with his steak. **1938** [see *PRETRIAL *sb.*]. **1968** *Med. World News* 20 Sept. 86/2 It drags the reader through dense verbal underbrush.

underbrush *v.* (earlier and later examples); **underbrushing** *vbl. sb.*

1824 *Canad. Mag.* III. 246 Every year we..have a quantity of wood land under-brushed. **1838** *Six Years in Bush* 80 Underbrushing consists in cutting and removing all the young trees and brushwood. **1863** Under-brushing [see *LINE *sb.*[2] 26 e]. **1933** D. G. CAMERON *Twigs from Oak* 124 That process..called 'underbrushing', was continued over a space about twenty yards wide. **1964** E. C. GUILLET *Pioneer Days Upper Canada* (ed. 2) 122 After underbrushing the piece of land the workers proceeded with logging.

underbush, *sb.* (Earlier examples.)

1849 S. C. BREES *Panorama N.Z.* 27 Crawling along the ground, among the underbush and trees. **1867** tr. *Guéranger's Life St. Austin* x. 97 Others grafting fruit trees, or thinning the underbush.

underca·pitalize, *v.* [UNDER-[1] 10 a.] *trans.* To furnish with insufficient capital (to achieve a desired result). Chiefly as **underca·pitalized** *ppl. a.*

1934 WEBSTER, Undercapitalize. **1962** E. SNOW *Other Side of River* (1963) lxvii. 509 The vicious paradox of China's undercapitalized economy. **1976** *Broadcast* Dec. 4/2 The External Services of both the BBC and these other broadcasting organisations are under-capitalised. **1982** J. FOX *White Mischief* i. 15 The early settlers..most of them were chronically undercapitalised.

under-carriage. Add: Now usu. unhyphened. **b.** The landing-gear of an aircraft.

1911 HARPER & FERGUSON *Aerial Locomotion* 92 The under-carriage was formed of wheels alone. **1922** *Aerial Age* Aug. 420/2 A shock-absorbing type of under-carriage. **1935** C. G. BURGE *Compl. Bk. Aviation* 160/2 In addition to the undercarriage, alighting gear includes subsidiary items such as tail skids, wing-tip skids, and floats. **1946** *Happy Landings* July 7/1 A characteristic fault of this aircraft made it necessary to operate the undercarriage lever two or three times. **1969** G. MACBETH *War Quartets* 71 One clutched the under-carriage Of a packed hospital-plane. **1977** D. BEATY *Excellency* vi. 80 The three green undercarriage lights, the two white engine lights, the red inverter lights.

u·ndercart. *slang.* [UNDER-[1] 5 b; cf. UNDER-CARRIAGE.] = *UNDER-CARRIAGE b.

1934 *Popular Flying* Sept. 295 (*caption*) The British Klemm 'Eagle'..going great guns, with undercart out of the way. **1939** J. L. RHYS *World owes me Living* xvi. 244 We've got de-icers, variable pitch airscrews, retractable undercart. **1948** 'N. SHUTE' *No Highway* v. 127 Honey had ruined a Reindeer at Gander by pulling up its undercart. **1958** 'CASTLE' & HAILEY *Flight into Danger* vii. 103 Look, Janet, I think you'd better work the undercart lever and call off the air-speed as the wheels come down. *a* **1963** J. LUSBY in 'B. James' *Austral. Short Stories* (1963) 225 Do remember that release-tit on the undercart-lever.

undercast, *v.* Restrict † *Obs.* to senses in Dict. and add: **4.** [UNDER-[1] 10 a.] *Theatr.* To allot (a part) to an inadequate player; to cast (a player) in an insufficient role.

1827 J. BOADEN *Mem. Mrs. Siddons* II. xiii. 66 The Anna, by Miss Wheeler, was rather under-cast. **1920** G. B. SHAW *Let.* in *Bernard Shaw & Mrs. Patrick Campbell* (1952) 206 Overcasting a part means undercasting an artist. **1957** *Observer* 12 May 15/2 [The part] is admittedly under-written; that is no reason why it should have been undercast. **1970** *New Yorker* 22 Aug. 59 Rossellini deliberately undercasts him, as he does everyone else. Colbert is made to look uninteresting and rather bourgeois. **1977** *Times* 9 July 10 The play was woefully undercast.

underchа·racterize, *v.* [UNDER-[1] 10 a.] *trans.* To depict or play with insufficient characterization or subtlety. So **under-cha·racterized** *ppl. a.*; **u:ndercharacteriza·tion.**

1960 *Times* 13 Jan. 6/6 Minor characters, either under-characterized..or over-characterized, but in both cases quite lifeless. **1963** *Times* 14 Feb. 8/1 The outer movements..sounded mechanical and under-characterized. **1968** *Time* 26 Apr. 50 *Couples* is flawed by overwriting and undercharacterization. **1970** *Times* 16 Dec. 11 In the wry second movement..the players needed more detailed help with phrasing, and the work as a whole was under-characterized. **1977** *Gramophone* Feb. 1270/1 Impressive as his playing is, in the last resort it is a degree under-characterized.

undercharge, *sb.* Add: Also, an adjustment made to correct an account (see quot. 1861).

1861 E. B. IVATTS *Handbk. Railway Station Managem.* 86 The undercharges or amounts that are afterwards added when the proper charge has not been made,—(when a charge has been once made on an invoice, the figures in English accounts are never altered, errors being corrected by undercharge or overcharge). **1920** *Rep. Departmental Comm. Industrial Assurance Companies* 3 If there is under-payment,..it is not due to any undercharge on the assured.

u·nder-chosen, *a. Sociology.* [UNDER-[1] 10 a.] Denoting those who, in a sociometric group study, are chosen by others as companion, fellow-worker, etc., significantly fewer times than average. Cf. *OVER-CHOSEN *a.*

1943, 1956 [see *OVER-CHOSEN *a.*]. **1968** LINDZEY & BYRNE in Lindzey & Aronson *Handbk. Social Psychol.* (ed. 2) II. xiv. 467 Persons who receive significantly more choices than would be expected by chance may be..pooled for comparison with a similarly selected group of under-chosen persons.

u·nderclass. [UNDER-[1] 5 b.] A subordinate social class; *spec.* [ad. Sw. *underklass*] the lowest social stratum in a country or community, consisting of the poor and the unemployed.

1918 J. MACLEAN in 'H. MacDiarmid' *Company I've Kept* (1966) iv. 124 The whole history of Society has proved that Society moves forward as a consequence of an under-class overcoming the resistance of a class on top of them. **1963** G. MYRDAL *Challenge to Affluence* iii. 40 Less often observed..is the tendency of the changes under way to trap an 'underclass' of unemployed and, gradually, unemployable persons and families at the bottom of a society. **1964** *Observer* 12 Jan. 10/7 The Negro's protest today is but the first rumbling of the 'underclass'. **1966** *New Statesman* 19 Aug. 247/2 The national economic growth has been bought at the expense of industrial workers and the poor (largely Negro) under-class. **1977** D. M. SMITH *Human Geogr.* x. 299 While in South Africa the black proletariat is large enough radically to change society on its own, the American under-class is in a minority and has much less potential power. **1981** D. G. GLASGOW (*title*) The Black underclass: poverty, unemployment and entrapment in ghetto youth. **1981** *New Statesman* 17 July 14 Many people... have warned of trouble if we went on creating a permanent underclass, and typing it by colour. **1982** *N.Y. Rev. Bks.* 12 Aug. 15/2 The distinctive feature of any underclass is that its members do not conform to the conduct expected of the poor. **1985** *Times* 11 Jan. 5/1 Modern Britain is fostering an underclass of unemployed and unskilled workers.

underclothes. Add: = UNDERCLOTHING. (Earlier examples.)

1835 R. M. BIRD *Hawks* I. 19 Under-clothes of some white summer-stuff. **1855** D. G. MITCHELL *Fudge Doings* I. 47 She supplies her cook with cast-off under-clothes.

underclu·b, *v. Golf.* [UNDER-[1] 10 a.] *refl.* To select (for oneself) a club which will not satisfactorily strike the ball the required distance. Also *intr.* and **underclu·bbed** *ppl. a.*, **underclu·bbing** *vbl. sb.*

1900 H. HILTON in *Outing* Sept. 654 A besetting sin of nearly all golfers is to what may be termed 'underclub themselves'. **1923** *Daily Mail* 8 May 12 When in doubt underclub yourself and hit hard. **1931** T. H. COTTON *Golf* vii. 56 There are more shots lost through underclubbing than anything else. **1936** P. A. VAILE *Short Game* 33 At least ninety-five per cent. of those that swing putters are grievously under-clubbed. **1955** *Times* 2 May 4/1 Burgess underclubbed at the 11th. **1961** *Times* 28 Mar. 4/2 Underclubbing at the 16th caused their opponents to take three putts. *Ibid.* 8 Sept. 4/1 Wolstenholme under-clubbed himself. **1975** D. LANGDON *How to talk Golf* 78 *Under-clubbing*, a drive which falls short of reaching the green at a short hole. **1979** *Tucson Mag.* Jan. 38/3 Everybody underclubs.

undercoat. Add: **4. a.** *Painting* and *Decorating.* A layer or layers of paint applied before the finishing or top coat; the paint used for this. Also *transf.* in electro-plating, cementing, etc.

1873 [see PRIMING *vbl. sb.*[1] 4]. **1901** *Decorators' & Painters' Mag.* I. I. 45 It is a rather risky experiment to use red lead as an undercoat for vermilion. **1927** W. DEEPING *Kitty* xxvi. 329 'The next job will be to paint 'em.' 'Couldn't I do that?' 'Don't see why you shouldn't, sir. Two good coats over an undercoat.' **1930** FIELD & WEILL *Electro-Plating* 90 The copper is soft and easily buffed, and this is required of the copper which forms the undercoat for nickel. **1958** [see *PRIMER *sb.*[2] 3]. **1960** *Farmer & Stockbreeder* 23 Feb. 76/2 Marley Mix is available..in the following mixes; fine concrete, bricklaying mortar, cement mortar, internal rendering, undercoat mix 1:2:4 concrete. **1976** *Handyman Which?* May 47/1 You'll get a better result by using two coats of primer/sealer beneath the gloss instead of one coat of the primer/sealer and one of undercoat.

b. = *UNDERSEAL *sb.*

1960 *Motor* 13 July 21 The Flintkote under-coat service is available in many countries. **1968** *Globe & Mail* (Toronto) 15 Jan. 19/7 (Advt.), Automatic transmission, power disc brakes, undercoat, [etc.].

Hence as *v. trans.*, (*a*) to apply an undercoat of paint to; (*b*) to coat the underside of (something, esp. a motor vehicle) with paint, sealant, or the like; **u·ndercoated** *ppl. a.*, **u·ndercoating** *vbl. sb.*

1922 *Decorator* Feb. p. xii (Advt.), Dixon's white paint inside glossy and flat undercoating. *Ibid.* Apr. p. xx (Advt.), The new semi-liquid flat white oil paint for undercoating paint or enamel. **1947** *Automobile Topics* Dec. 20/2 The future of the automobile undercoating business largely rests upon..a proper job of spraying. **1953** *Ibid.* Mar. 26/1 More than half of the nation's postwar automobiles have been undercoated. **1960** *Farmer & Stockbreeder* 23 Feb. 117/1 It can be brushed or sprayed—one coat being sufficient on suitably..primed surface—no undercoating being required. **1978** *Detroit Free Press* 5 Mar. c 22/2 (Advt.), BMW 2002, red,.. undercoated, 57,000 mi. **1979** P. WALLAGE *Restoration Post-War Cars* ii. 25/2, I once had to tackle one which had been undercoated and painted so well it was almost a shame to scrape it off.

under-consu·mption. *Econ.* [UNDER-[1] 10 b.] Insufficient consumption; a demand for goods and services exceeded by supply or insufficient to call forth the full potential supply. Cf. OVER-PRODUCTION.

1895 [see UNDER-[1] 10 b]. **1906** J. A. HOBSON *Evolution Mod. Capitalism* xi. 288 When the disease is at its worst, the activity of producer and consumer at its lowest, we have the functional condition of under-production due to the pressure of a quantity of over-supply, and we have a corresponding state of under-consumption. **1931** *Times Lit. Suppl.* 14 May 374/3 They are thus on the way, not only to disentangling the mesh of popular theory connected with the words 'over-production' and 'under-consumption' but to destroying the presupposition..that ..over-production..may..occur. **1961** *Economist* 22 Apr. 348/1 'Under-consumption' at the bottom of the social scale was apparent to a slight extent in dental and ophthalmic care. **1974** B. PEARCE tr. *Amin's Accumulation on World Scale* I. i. 112 After a certain level of development has been reached, possibilities of saving become greater than investment needs (governed by the volume of consumption). We have here a general theory of underconsumption.

Hence **underconsu·mptionist**, an advocate of a theory of underconsumption; also *attrib.* or as *adj.*

1936 A. L. ROWSE *Mr Keynes & Labour Movement* 41 In sympathy..with the attitude of the under-consumptionists all along. **1948** G. CROWTHER *Outl. Money* (ed. 2) v. 149 'Under-consumptionist' theories. **1974** M. B. BROWN *Economics of Imperialism* ix. 216 Some neo-Marxists..have accepted an underconsumptionist interpretation of Marx and therefore see the increase of surplus value and the search for its disposal as the main source of the continuing expansionism.

undercoo·l, *v.* **1.** [UNDER-[1] 8 c.] **a.** *trans.* = *SUPERCOOL *v.* a.

1895 C. S. PALMER tr. *Nernst's Theoret. Chem.* I. iii. 65 Probably the two curves would intersect asymptotically at abs. zero, if one could under-cool a liquid so far. **1962** *Zeitschr. f. Metallkunde* LIII. 600/2 Many molten metals slagged in Pyrex glass can be highly undercooled irrespective of the amount. **1977** *Scripta Metall.* XI. 253 Ingots..were under-cooled and solidified under increasing gravity-levels.

b. *intr.* = *SUPERCOOL *v.* b.

1969 *Cast Metals Research Jrnl.* V. 137/1 Cooling curves for ductile iron showed no distinct eutectic arrest but undercooled during eutectic solidification. **1977** *Scripta Metall.* XI. 253 The prepared boules were heated to 230°C, and allowed to undercool.

2. [UNDER-[1] 10 a.] *trans.* To cool insufficiently.

1983 *New Scientist* 13 Jan. 83/2 The continued loss of core-cooling water..meant that the reactor's core was seriously undercooled.

Hence **undercoo·led** *ppl. a.*; **undercoo·ling** *vbl. sb.*

1895 C. S. PALMER tr. *Nernst's Theoret. Chem.* I. iii. 65 The dotted line is the pressure curve of the under-cooled liquid substance, and forms the continuation of the pressure curve of the liquid. **1913** *Engineering* 10 Oct. 510/3 The under-cooled liquid phase can in many cases be retained in the metastable condition at temperatures far below the normal freezing-point by a process of under-cooling. **1936** *Forestry* X. 128 The point at which ice formation begins may be still further lowered by under-cooling. If water is kept absolutely still, it is possible to lower its temperature below the freezing point without ice formation... This undercooling often takes place in plants. **1980** *Sci. Amer.* Apr. 84/3 Above the glass temperature, in the undercooled liquid phase, the atoms are free to make extensive translational movements.

u·ndercount. *Statistics.* [UNDER-[1] 10 b.] An incomplete enumeration; *spec.* the amount by which the number enumerated in a census falls short of the actual number in the group.

1955 *Population Studies* (United Nations) No. 23. 11/2 Is there a possibility of an under-count in the 1950 census in the Vega Alta? **1964** *New Statesman* 13 Mar. 390/3 Allowing for a 5 per cent undercount in 1952 and for a 2 per cent increase per annum,..the Northern total was just about what had been expected. **1981** *Sci. Amer.* Apr. 70/1 Preliminary study of the raw census data now suggests that the 1980 census was remarkably complete: the undercount is turning out to be much smaller than had been projected.

Hence as *v. trans.*, to enumerate incompletely; **u·ndercounting** *vbl. sb.*

1955 *Population Studies* (United Nations) No. 23. 11/1 There was serious under-counting in the Southern States at the time of the 1870 census. **1970** *Daily Tel.* 22 Aug. 3/6 Mayor Lindsay is convinced that New York will be seriously undercounted in the 1970 census figures. **1978** *Guardian Weekly* 30 Apr. 17/1 In the United States, the Mexican-American population, which may have been severely undercounted in the 1970 census, is growing steadily.

under-cover, *a.* (and *sb.*). Also **undercover.** [UNDER-[2].] **A.** *adj.* **1.** That is situated or occurs under cover; sheltered.

1854 [see UNDER-[2]]. **1959** *News Chron.* 14 July 4/4 A good fun-fair and some under-cover amusements. **1971** *Engineering* Apr. 61/1 The first mentioned can be very useful when under-cover storage is not available.

2. a. Of a person: operating in secret within a community or organization, esp. as a detective or spy. Freq. as *under-cover agent, man.* Also applied to organizations or agencies.

1920 U. B. SINCLAIR *100%* 266 [Mrs. Godd] had written in a large, bland, girlish hand her opinion of 'under cover' men and those who hired them. **1932** W. FAULKNER *Light in August* ii. 41 Whiskey can be bought from Brown almost on sight, and the town is..waiting for him to.. produce from his raincoat and offer to sell it to an under-cover man. **1933** *B'nai B'rith Mag.* XLVIII. 108/1 German steamship lines were 'in the front ranks of Nazi-ism—active under-cover nests of conspiracy'. **1951** E. PAUL *Springtime in Paris* iii. 67 An undercover worker for the Party. **1958** *Spectator* 20 June 809/3 The Providence Island Company..which served as undercover organisation for the opposition to Charles I. **1970** *Toronto Daily Star* 24 Sept. 12/8 The undercover agent is the surest way of handling narcotics problems in factories.

b. Surreptitious, covert. Of an activity: conducted or existing in secret.

1933 *Light* Nov. 3/1 That undercover atheism which disguises itself under other names... The undercover atheism which so often sneaks by in the clothing of religion itself. **1935** R. MCKAY *'Intelligence' Game* 169 Perhaps they were made careless because they had an undercover 'tip' about the coming of the Austrian. **1953** M. MCCARTHY *Groves of Academe* iii. 50, I have been useful to them from time to time in various little under-cover jobs. **1960** *Times* 27 Aug. 7/3 The menace of recruitment to under-cover prostitution on a large scale cannot be ignored. **1979** N. MAILER *Executioner's Song* (1980) I. xvii. 285 Years ago, when a patrolman, Nielsen did some under-cover work in narcotics.

B. *sb.* An undercover agent. *slang.*

1962 'K. ORVIS' *Damned & Destroyed* vii. 50 The Horsemen have sneaked plants, undercovers, right inside here. **1972** J. MILLS *Rep. to Commissioner* p. x, She was a very good detective. She was a narcotics undercover.

undercure (stress variable), *v.* [UNDER-[1] 10.] *trans.* To cure (plastic or rubber) for less than the optimal period.

1916 [see *OVERCURE *v.*]. **1965** *Encycl. Polymer Sci. & Technol.* II. 53 To increase the bending capacity still more, the laminated sheets are usually slightly undercured.

So **un·dercured** *ppl. a.*, **undercu·ring** *vbl. sb.* Also **u·ndercure** *sb.*, the process or result of undercuring.

1912 *Jrnl. Soc. Chem. Industry* 16 Dec. 1100/1 Nos. (1) and (2) [*sc.* specimens of rubber] were distinctly undercured at 35 lb. **1915** *Ibid.* 15 Oct. 990/2 In the case of undercures the curve often breaks off too soon for this to be apparent. **1916** *Ibid.* 31 Aug. 872/2 If the impulse is insufficient..we have the condition of undercuring and the rod falls back, corresponding with a gradual deterioration of the vulcanised product. **1940** J. OSBORNE *Dental Mech.* xi. 128 Under-cured vulcanite is soft and weak, and permeable to mouth fluids and bacteria. **1952** [see *overcured* ppl. adj. s.v. *OVERCURE *v.*]. **1965** *Encycl. Polymer Sci. & Technol.* II. 53 This undercure slightly reduces the quality of the surface, but other advantages are gained so that today a substantial fraction of the total production of decorated, laminated sheet stock is plasticised. **1968** *SPE Jrnl.* Nov. 47/1 Undercured resins are inferior..but long cure times are uneconomical. **1969** *Jrnl. Paint Technol.* XLI. 702 (*heading*) Effect of undercuring on durability of siliconized polyester enamels with hexakis-(methoxymethyl) melamine.

undercurrent. 2. (Earlier example.)

1792 [see *REACTION 4 a].

undercut, *sb.* Add: **2. b.** *Dentistry.* A horizontal cut at the base of a tooth cavity; *esp.* one made to anchor a filling more securely.

1892 R. OTTOLENGUI *Methods of filling Teeth* i. 6 Many fillings have failed through the well-meant but unwise efforts of the operator to give great retentive strength to his cavity by deep undercuts. **1923** J. B. PARFITT *Operative Dental Surgery* (ed. 2) x. 87 The condition for retention, namely, some kind of 'undercut', has already been fulfilled. **1980** J. R. GRUNDY *Conservative Dentistry* vii. 41/1 Minor undercuts should be removed during cavity preparation.

c. *Mining.* A long, thin cut made under a vein of ore or a face of coal. Cf. *OVERCUT *sb.* c.

1892 *Trans. Federated Inst. Mining Engineers* I. 130 (*table*) Depth of undercut. **1902** A. S. E. ACKERMANN *Coal-Cutting by Machinery in Amer.* ii. 31 They hole about 2in. in the clay, and partly because of this and partly because of two dirt bands at the bottom, they got practically the whole of the coal taken out of the undercut. **1939** B. L. COOMBES *These Poor Hands* vii. 109 With such a large undercut there was the likelihood of it [*sc.* the roof] falling any second. **1959** G. D. MITCHELL *Sociol.* viii. 136 Gummers..clean out the undercut so that when the shot is fired the coal will have space in which to fall.

d. *gen.* A space formed by the removal or absence of material from the lower part of something.

1914 [see *INTERFERENCE 4* b (i)]. **1964** F. O'ROURKE *Mule for Marquesa* iii. 58 Fardan found an undercut in the south wall two miles from the mouth. **1971** *Country Life* 15 July 141/3 Some sickness has made them lie out of sight in one of those undercuts that sheep rub for themselves in an eroding bank of light soil. **1977** *Design Engin.* July 54/2 In load bearing applications, undercuts, knurls, lugs, and dovetails are used to provide the component with surfaces onto which the molten metal can lock as it shrinks.

3. A projection on a pattern corresponding to an undercut portion of the mould.

1909 in *Cent. Dict.* Suppl. **1935** *Die-Casting* (Machinery's Yellow Back Series No. 4) i. 10 To provide the undercut a collapsible core is necessary.

undercut, *v.* Add: **2. c.** Also in *Lawn Tennis*, to impart backspin to (the ball) by slicing down on it below the centre (in quot. *absol.*, to play a stroke which would have this effect).

1926 E. BOWEN *Ann Lee's* 86 Mr. Barlow..walked springily about..hacking, slashing, and under-cutting with his racquet at the air.

d. *Mining.* To cut away the under-part of (a vein of ore or a face of coal); to obtain (coal, etc.) in this way.

1883 [in Dict., sense 2 a]. **1892** *Trans. Federated Inst. Mining Engineers* I. 130 The function of all these machines is to undercut the coal in the same way as has hitherto been done by hand labour. **1939** B. L. COOMBES *These Poor Hands* vii. 108 It [*sc.* the coal-cutter] undercut the coal to the depth of the jib. **1945** D. H. ROWLANDS *Coal* xiii. 172 The very first coal-cutter was patented in the eighteenth century, and since then hundreds of inventors have worked on the problem of undercutting the coal-face. **1982** *Sci. Amer.* Sept. 66/1 By the end of World War II 90 percent of the coal mined in the U.S. was undercut by machine.

3. b. *fig.* To render unstable; to render less firm, to undermine.

1955 W. J. BATE *Achievement Sam. Johnson* ii. 81 In the very activity or process of wishing, there are inherent liabilities that are able to undercut the wish itself. **1976** *National Observer* (U.S.) 13 Nov. 1/3 Many vowed that their children would not grow up with the same sort of expectations and handicaps that had so undercut their own self-reliance. **1977** L. GORDON *Eliot's Early Years* iii. 63 The wry, derisive note..undercuts the posturing of Saint Narcissus. **1981** R. HAYMAN *K.* xi. 146 He was aware of undercutting all his gestures towards healthy living by starving himself of sleep.

undercut, *ppl. a.* Add: **2.** In *Lawn Tennis*, applied to a stroke which undercuts or imparts backspin to the ball.

1920 [see *CHOP *sb.*[1] 4 e]. **1977** *New Yorker* 10 Oct. 152/2 He shifted from his usual top-spin backhand to a sliced undercut backhand—a stroke that many of us had seen him use only rarely.

3. *Mountaineering.* Of a handhold: cut from below, and used esp. to maintain balance when climbing.

1950 tr. *Mountaineering Handbk.* (Assoc. Brit. Members Swiss Alpine Club) vi. 46 Hand and footholds make progress possible... They can be horizontal, oblique, vertical or undercut. **1965** A. BLACKSHAW *Mountaineering* vi. 161 Side-holds and undercut holds are valuable for maintaining balance or for moving 'in opposition'. **1975** W. UNSWORTH *Encycl. Mountaineering* 120/1 An undercut hold is one that is upside down, but it can be useful.

underda·mped, *a.* [UNDER-[1] 10 a.] Of a physical system: incompletely damped; damped to the extent of allowing only a few oscillations after a single disturbance. So **underda·mping** *vbl. sb.* Cf. *OVERDAMPED *a.*

1934 W. V. HOUSTON *Princ. Math. Physics* iv. 45 Write the expression for the work done by an under-damped oscillator against the damping force. **1951** [see *HUNT *v.* 7 b]. **1952** D. E. CHRISTIE *Intermediate College Mech.* xii. 297 We shall limit our discussion to what is called underdamping. **1976** *Water Resources Res.* XII. 71/1 In the underdamped case the water level oscillates about the equilibrium level.

u·nderdamper. [UNDER-[1] 5 b.] Any of the set of dampers in an upright piano of a type in which the dampers are placed below the hammers. Freq. *attrib.*

1870 E. BRINSMEAD *Hist. Pianoforte* 74 Square piano action, with under dampers, and a screw in each key. **1909** *Northampton Independent* 30 Oct. 29/2 (Advt.), A magnificent overstrung underdamper, upright iron grand. **1933** R. E. M. HARDING *Piano-Forte* iv. 56 The under damper is also found in connection with the Single Action. **1980** *Early Music* Apr. 241 (Advt.), After John Broadwood, 1801, a simple under-damper square fortepiano.

underdete·rmine, *v.* [UNDER-[1] 10 a.] *trans.* To account for (a theory or phenomenon) with less than the amount of evidence needed for proof or certainty. Freq. as *pa. pple.* Cf. *OVERDETERMINE *v.*

1966 J. J. KATZ *Philos. of Lang.* ii. 11 As in other sciences, the evidence underdetermines a generalization. **1977** A. GIDDENS *Stud. in Social & Polit. Theory* 11 Even in the most developed areas of the natural sciences, theories are underdetermined by facts. **1979** A. R. PEACOCKE *Creation & World of Science* ii. 73 It is salutary to remember that most cosmological theories are underdetermined by the facts. **1984** *Times Lit. Suppl.* 14 Dec. 1453/3 Early exploratory models will be drastically underdetermined by the data.

Also **u:nderdetermina·tion**, the state or quality of being underdetermined; **underdete·rmined** *ppl. a.*

1966 J. J. KATZ *Philos. of Lang.* iv. 114 Such underdetermination means that the slack must be taken up by considerations that have to do with the simplicity and generality of the hypotheses. **1977** A. GIDDENS *Stud. in Social & Polit. Theory* 11 The underdetermination of theories by facts in social science is certainly greater than in natural science. **1978** HOOKWAY & PETTIT *Action & Interpretation* p. xi, The argument is that with underdetermined theories as to someone's beliefs and desires, there is no language-independent realm of meanings in regard to which the theories differ.

under-deve·loped, *a.* [UNDER-[1] 10 a.] **a.** Incompletely developed, in various senses of the vb.

1892 [see UNDER-[1] 10 a]. **1910** H. G. WELLS *Hist. Mr. Polly* vii. 165 Mr. Polly felt himself the faintest underdeveloped simulacrum of man that had ever hovered on the verge of non-existence. **1944** *Ann. Reg. 1943* 328 A creed of this kind [*sc.* Fascist] will appeal to certain types of under-developed Europeans. **1975** *Gen. Systems* XX. 107/1 Anthropology is disorganized and crisis-ridden, yet vastly underdeveloped.

b. *spec.* designating a country or other region in which economic and social conditions fail to reach their potential level or an accepted standard. Cf. *DEVELOPING *ppl. a.* and *THIRD WORLD.

1949 H. S. TRUMAN in *Congressional Record* 20 Jan. 478/1 Fourth, we must embark on a bold new program for making the benefits of our scientific advances and industrial progress available for the improvement and growth of underdeveloped areas. **1950** *U.S. Dept. State Bull.* 25 Sept. 497 (*title*) Methods of financing economic development of underdeveloped countries. **1956** T. BALOGH in A. Pryce-Jones *New Outl. Mod. Knowl.* 519 The typical under-developed country even in the more recent past has only attracted capital for the exploitation of primary products. **1964** AUDEN in *Listener* 1 Oct. 525/2 It's heartless to forget about the under-developed countries. **1977** P. JOHNSON *Enemies of Society* xix. 253 Among the so-called underdeveloped countries, the group most likely to carry through industrialization are those which have profited from the 'energy crisis' which has given them truly gigantic quantities of investment capital. **1984** *Guardian* 5 Nov. 12/2 Few people begrudge the aid we send to the starving or merely under-developed regions of the earth.

Also **u:nderdeve·lopment**, incomplete development.

1891, 1892 [see UNDER-[1] 10 b]. **1927** H. G. WELLS in *Sunday Express* 20 Feb. 12/6 The development of Soviet flying is retarded by comparative poverty and the economic underdevelopment of the huge regions concerned. **1958** *Listener* 21 Aug. 274/1 It has for too long been.. assumed that inserting a technical skill into a different society will automatically overcome that aspect of underdevelopment to which it is applied. **1969** A. G. FRANKS *Latin Amer.* (1970) i. 3 Most studies of development and underdevelopment fail to take account of the economic and other relations between the metropolis and its economic colonies.

u:nderdiagno·sis. *Med.* [UNDER-[1] 10 b.] Failure, on a significant scale, to detect or correctly diagnose all the cases of a disease examined.

1966 *Gastroenterology* LI. 1074 (*heading*) Underdiagnosis of biliary tract disorders? **1971** *Brit. Med. Bull.* XXVII. 14/1 Under-diagnosis has also contributed to the apparently low incidence. **1982** *Brit. Med. Jrnl.* 29 May 1585/1 This low figure for Britain is unlikely to represent underdiagnosis.

So **underdi·agnose** *v. trans.*, **underdi·agnosed** *ppl. a.*

1974 *Med. Jrnl. Austral.* 12 Jan. 49/1 (*heading*) Cœliac disease: an underdiagnosed disorder with important implications. **1975** *Gut* XVI. 81 The condition may have been underdiagnosed in Britain. **1979** *Brit. Med. Jrnl.* 15 Dec. 1582/3 Surely this does not show general practitioners to be disgracefully underdiagnosing or undertreating hypertension, especially with regard to detection, as a great number of these people had not seen their doctor for some considerable time. **1983** *Ibid.* 17 Sept. 827/1 He considers the disorder to be seriously underdiagnosed.

u:nder-differentia·tion. *Linguistics.* [UNDER-[1] 10 b.] The incomplete differentiation of phonemic elements in a language, esp. in loanwords taken from a language in which certain phonemic distinctions do not correspond to those in the receiving language. Cf. *DIFFERENTIATION 1 b.

1953 U. WEINREICH *Languages in Contact* ii. 18 Underdifferentiation of phonemes occurs when two sounds of the secondary system whose counterparts are not distinguished in the primary system are confused. **1962** *Canadian Jrnl. Linguistics* VII. 82 These three types of substitution have been variously called..under-differentiation, overdifferentiation, and reinterpretation. **1976** *Amer. Speech 1973* XLVIII. 220 Underdifferentiation is the failure to distinguish two or more sounds of the donor language because of the existence of a single counterpart in the recipient language. **1983** *English World-Wide* IV. 53 The orthography gives near maximum representation of significant sounds but allows for underdifferentiation in spelling.

u:nder-dispe·rsion. [UNDER-[1] 10 b.] A reduced degree or amount of dispersion; *spec.* in *Ecol.*, a greater evenness in the distribution of individuals than would be expected on purely statistical grounds. Cf. *OVER-DISPERSION. Also **u:nder-dispe·rsed** *ppl. a.*

1935 *Ann. Bot.* XLIX. 794 There is significant under-dispersion or aggregation among the individuals of the population. **1940** *Proc. Linnean Soc. N.S.W.* LXV. 135 The distribution of individual species in the areas examined must be either random, or over- or under-dispersed. **1946, 1957** [see *OVER-DISPERSION]. **1962** D. R. COX *Renewal Theory* iii. 42 Expression..is less than one, so that there is apparent under-dispersion relative to the Poisson distribution. **1964** K. A. KERSHAW *Quantitative & Dynamic Ecol.* vi. 98 Several species showed either 'overdispersion' or 'underdispersion'. **1982** G. A. F. SEBER *Estimation of Animal Abundance* (ed. 2) xii. 479 The classification into overdispersed and underdispersed is not sufficiently fine.

underdo·ctored. *a.* [UNDER-[1] 10 a.] Chiefly of an area: insufficiently supplied with doctors; short of doctors.

1960 *New Left Rev.* May–June 23/2 There were..more than 3,500 people per doctor..and, in some underdoctored areas, many more. **1976** *Lancet* 9 Oct. 778/1 Too few graduates from British medical schools are willing to work in underdoctored areas. **1980** *Brit. Med. Jrnl.* 29 Mar. 951/2 Its working party's report on underdoctored areas.

underdog. Add: Hence **u·nderdogger**, one who supports the underdog in a contest; **underdo·ggery.**

1938 H. BELLOC in *Tablet* 1 Jan. 8/1 Anyhow, the difficulty and injustice of under-doggery is softened in all sorts of ways by the virtues of charity and humility. **1969** D. THOMSON *Aims of Hist.* 68 It was no doubt natural, perhaps inevitable, that the approach of early enthusiasts for economic history should be strongly tinged with under-doggery. **1970** *N.Y. Times* 17 Aug. 26/4 'We underdoggers have to try harder,' he [*sc.* Governor Rockefeller] explained to reporters. **1977** *Time* 3 Oct. 54 After three crushing defeats, *Australia*'s loyal underdoggers were busy recalling all the old familiar whiny excuses. **1978** *Times* 2 Sept. 7 The angel with the perfect smell, the innocent, the do-gooder, the outsider, the perfect stranger. I was a great underdogger. **1981** *London Rev. Bks.* 2–15 July 24/3 He bore a grudge for not getting the Nobel prize... Reviews..have made much of O'Hara's underdoggery.

underdrain, *v.* Add: Hence **underdrai·ning,** *vbl. sb.*

1805 [see UNDERDRAIN *v.*]. **1879** *Harper's Mag.* June 135/2 Other minor improvements have been made, such as the under-draining of a low tract. **1969** G. E. EVANS *Farm & Village* ii. 27 This is under-draining, sometimes called thorough-draining, the technique by which a hollow drain is made under the soil into which excess water can soak and be taken off.

u·nder-drawing. [UNDER-[1] 5 b.] A preliminary sketch, subsequently covered by layers of paint.

1934 *Burlington Mag.* Feb. 85/2 In the latter picture the under-drawing is done for effect and lacks entirely the astounding precision of Holbein's portraiture. **1968** *New Scientist* 3 Oct. 37/2 Mediaeval European paintings.. were made on wood... Preliminary designs were sketched ..with bone black or carbon black..and this underdrawing was then..covered with paint layers.

underdress, *sb.* **2.** (Earlier example.)

1806 E. WYNNE *Diary* 22 July (1940) III. viii. 291 My bridal array consisted of a white satin under dress and a patent net over it, with a long veil.

u·nderdrive. [UNDER-[1] 10 b.] An auxiliary speed-reducing gear in a motor vehicle which may be brought into operation in addition to the ordinary gears to provide an additional set of gear ratios.

1929 [see *OVERDRIVE *sb.* 1 a]. **1941** *Automobile Engineer* XXXI. 48/1 Chrysler's new 'underdrive' transmission, when coupled with the fluid drive and conventional clutch, is one of the outstanding mechanical innovations of the year. **1981** *Sunday Express* (Colour Suppl.) 4 Oct. /4 (Advt.), The only car with underdrive.

under-edge. Add: Also *spec.* in *Cricket*, the inside- or bottom edge of the bat.

1960 E. W. SWANTON *West Indies Revisited* 143 He.. dragged the ball into his stumps off the under-edge. **1977** *Sunday Times* 30 Jan. 30/4 Willis bowled Kirmani off the under-edge.

under-employ·ed, *a.* [UNDER-[1] 10 a.] Insufficiently employed, not used to the optimum capacity. Chiefly of persons or machinery.

1908 W. S. CHURCHILL in R. S. Churchill *Winston S. Churchill* (1969) II. Compan. II. xii. 852 We cannot distinguish between the unemployed and the under-employed. **1941** *Economist* 22 Feb. 241/1 The existence of idle or under-employed machinery—and labour—is sheer waste to the war effort. **1962** *Daily Tel.* 15 June 14/2 There is ample evidence of a progressively under-employed industry and of a turn to export business to employ spare capacity. **1980** *Jrnl. R. Soc. Arts* Feb. 150/2 No sensible organization keeps an expensive designer under-employed.

under-employ·ment. [UNDER-[1] 10 b.] Insufficient use of resources; *spec.* a situation in which the number of the unemployed exceeds the number of job vacancies, producing a labour surplus.

1909 S. & B. WEBB *Public Organization of Labour Market* (Minority Rep. Poor Law Commission II) iv. 185 The evil of Under-employment is shown in its most common form in the great class of Casual Labourers. **1926** GALSWORTHY *Silver Spoon* II. i. 112 To free the country from..under-employment, and over-population. **1944** A. L. ROWSE *Eng. Spirit* xxxii. 225 Carlyle [in *Past & Present*]..went on to point to the dilemma of over-production and under-employment which is a recurrent trouble of *laissez-faire* capitalism. **1961** *Times* 1 Dec. 13/6 This kind of underemployment is to be seen in many sectors of the economy. **1979** *Dædalus* Spring 90 Under-employment does exist, though, and..there are strategies to pay certain categories of women to take time off or to leave the labor market early.

u·nderfelt. [UNDER-[1] 5 b.] Felt used as an underlay, esp. beneath a carpet.

1895 *Harrod's Catal.* 1487 Paper and felt for laying under carpets—..Underfelts..0/10 and 1/1 per yard. **1907** *Army & Navy Stores Catal.* 270/4 Electric Illuminating Table Cloth. Is used as an underfelt and covered with a white table cloth. **1934** *Discovery* June 155/2 Carpets are much more effective as absorbents [of sound] at the lower frequencies when they are used with underfelts. **1975** N. LUARD *Robespierre Serial* xiii. 119 Carswell slept..in the hall, on a roll of underfelt which had been accidentally left behind.

u·nderfill, *sb.* *Metallurgy.* [f. UNDER-[1] 10 b, after *OVERFILL *sb.*] The condition of there being insufficient metal to fill the aperture between rolls, the impression of a die, etc., so that the desired shape is not taken; a bar or the like that is too small for the rolling it is to undergo.

1924 F. W. DENCER *Detailing & fabricating Struct. Steel* xxvii. 355 Underfills.—A defect of this kind may result from cobbling, and generally is cause for rejection of the pieces affected. **1929, 1957** [see *OVERFILL *sb.*]. **1970** *Welding Engineer* July 24/2 With three of four tetra axis welds inclined to the bottom plane, weld underfill would make conventional welding difficult without a special positioner.

under-filling, *vbl. sb.* Add: **II. 2.** *Metallurgy.* (Stressed *underfi·lling* and written without a hyphen.) [UNDER-[1] 10 a.] The action or result of causing an underfill.

1953 [see *OVERFILLING *vbl. sb.*]. **1968** R. N. PARKINS *Mech. Treatm. Metals* ii. 78 In designing a sequence of passes the critical factor is to ensure that each groove in turn is just filled with metal so that its form is accurate... Underfilling will produce an imperfect shape.

So **underfi·ll** *v. trans.*

1968 [see *OVERFILL *v.*].

u·nderfit, *a.* *Physical Geogr.* [f. UNDER-[1] 10 c, after *misfit.*] Pertaining to or designating a stream which, if its average flow in the past was at present-day levels, would be expected to have eroded a smaller valley than it has done. Cf. *OVERFIT *a.*

1913 W. M. DAVIS in *Ann. Assoc. Amer. Geographers* III. 3 Underfit Rivers.—The chief object of this paper is to call attention to an explanation recently suggested for the peculiar relation that is frequently observed between the small-curved meanders of a river and the larger-curved meanders of its valley, a relation that has been called 'underfit'. **1939** A. K. LOBECK *Geomorphology* vi. 199 The beheaded stream, having lost much of its volume, acquires mature characteristics. It develops small meanders not suited to the size of the valley. It becomes a misfit, or an underfit, stream. **1964, 1968** [see *MISFIT *sb.* 2]. **1970** R. J. SMALL *Study of Landforms* ii. 46 In post-glacial times, the old channels have been choked with alluvium, and the meandering valleys are now followed by 'underfit' streams, possessing insufficient power to effect further erosion.

Hence **underfi·tness**, the property or state of being underfit.

1913 *Ann. Assoc. Amer. Geographers* III. 24 The lower Seine in Normandy shows a slight underfitness.

1964 *Prof. Papers U.S. Geol. Survey* No. 452-A. 29/2 The underfitness of streams in incised meandering valleys can no longer be denied.

u·nderfloor, *a.* [UNDER-².] That occurs or is situated below floor level; also, operating below the surface of the floor, as *underfloor heating* (often by an electrical element embedded in a concrete floor).

1899 [see UNDER-²]. **1934** H. M. VERNON *Princ. Heating & Ventilation* v. 92 The scheme adopted took the form of under-floor heating by means of a pipe running round each room at a distance of about 4 in. from the walls. **1953** D. J. WARBURTON *ABC Commercial Vehicles* 8 An under-floor-engine passenger chassis. **1977** M. DRABBLE *Ice Age* I. 61 The flat she'd lived in with Len had had the lot: de luxe washing machine,..underfloor central heating, two bathrooms, shower... The lot.

underflow, *sb.* Add: **2.** The (more or less horizontal) flow of water through the ground, *spec.* underneath a river bed.

1890 *Rep. Secretary of Agric. 1890* (U.S. Dept. Agric.) 472 Papers on underflow and subterranean water. *Ibid.* 475 Mr. [J. W.] Gregory became convinced of the existence at moderate depths below the surface..of an almost continuous drainage supply, which he has termed the under-sheet or under-flow water. **1905** *U.S. Geol. Survey Water-Supply & Irrigation Papers* No. 140. 85 Such wells, several hundred feet in depth, with perforations opposite the best water-bearing material, would utilize a large part of the underflow which now escapes to the sea. **1951** H. E. THOMAS *Conservation of Ground Water* iii. 138 Underflow is the only method of movement in certain reaches of some streams, where the surface channel is dry. **1970** W. C. WALTON *Groundwater Resource Evaluation* vi. 375 Water leaving basins includes streamflow, evapotranspiration, and subsurface underflow.

3. *Computers.* [After *OVERFLOW *sb.* 2 d.] The generation of a number that is too small to be represented in the device meant to store it.

1959 E. M. MCCORMICK *Digital Computer Primer* xi. 155 A number which is too small (yet is not 0) will cause an 'underflow'. **1970** O. DOPPING *Computers & Data Processing* vi. 102 In machines with automatic floating-point arithmetic..there may also be indicators for overflow and underflow in the characteristic. **1985** *Personal Computer World* Feb. 182/2 Computer users pay far less attention to underflow than they do to overflow or rounding.

underflow, *v.* Add: **3.** *intr. Computers.* [Cf. prec., sense 3.] Of the result of an arithmetical operation: to become too small for the device meant to store it.

1965 *IBM Systems Jrnl.* IV. 32 If the exponent underflows or the result fraction is zero, the result should be treated as 'zero'. **1973** C. W. GEAR *Introd. Computer Sci.* ii. 73 Give examples of pairs of numbers A and B in internal form such that..A×B underflows in floating-point arithmetic.

underfo·cus. [UNDER-¹ 10.] The situation in which the beam of an electron microscope is focused to a point somewhat short of the specimen. So **underfo·cused** *ppl. a.*, **-fo·cusing** *vbl. sb.*

1953 C. E. HALL *Introd. Electron Microsc.* x. 268 The pattern appearing at the screen is an underfocused image. **1971** *Jrnl. Physics A* IV. 806 These large phase shifts can be exactly cancelled by underfocus of the objective lens. *Ibid.*, This underfocusing will produce a large chromatic aberration. **1979** *Nature* 17 May 227/1 The contrast of the images taken from very thin parts of crystal at about 700 Å underfocus is known to reflect approximately the projection of the structure; the dark dots show the sites of Re ions.

underfoot, *a.* **1.** (Examples of conditions underfoot, esp. applied to the state of the going in *Horseracing*.)

1976 *Eastern Even. News* (Norwich) 9 Dec., Underfoot conditions at Chelmsford made it difficult for everyone. **1979** *Oxford Times* (City ed.) 5 Jan. 6 They [*sc.* postmen] begin their round in darkness before underfoot conditions have a chance to improve.

underfoot, *adv.* Add: **5.** Of a person or persons: about one's feet, constantly (and irritatingly) present; 'in the way'. *colloq.*

1891 *Harper's Mag.* June 62/1 He muttered something about children being underfoot and staring at such times. **1922** S. LEWIS *Babbitt* xviii. 230 Kenneth Escott and she were always under foot. **1959** M. SCOTT *White Elephant* i. 3 It has been a trying month for her too, with Deryk always underfoot. **1981** 'S. WOODS' *Dearest Enemy* I. 38 It's really too much of a nuisance having him always underfoot when I'm trying to prepare my own meals.

u·nderfoot, *sb. rare.* [f. the adv.] The surface of the ground at the foot of a tree.

1910 W. DE MORGAN *Affair of Dishonour* iv. 50 This morning was no time for breakfast under the cedar trees. For all the underfoot, where grass grew, was no better than a sponge. **1959** E. COLLIER *Three against Wilderness* xxiv. 248 No flame could lick far into the forests so long as their underfoot was moist.

underfoo·ting. [f. UNDER FOOT *adv.*: see -ING¹.] **1.** *Ir.* In turf-cutting: (see quots.).

1942 E. E. EVANS *Ir. Heritage* xv. 136 In breast-work the digger stands facing the turf bank, and thrusts his spade horizontally, whereas in underfooting he stands on the bank and cuts vertically. **1957** —— *Ir. Folk Ways* xiv. 189 There are two methods of cutting, vertically or 'underfooting' and horizontally or 'breasting', and they tend to be used respectively on thin upland and deep lowland bogs. **1979** *Country Life* 27 Sept. 963/3 In some areas the [peat] turf is cut horizontally, known as breasting, but most turf is cut vertically, which is termed 'underfooting'.

2. The ground under foot, esp. with regard to its condition. Cf. FOOTING *vbl. sb.* 5.

1948 *Sun* (Baltimore) 29 Apr. 19/1 Shivaree..was timed in 1.12 3–5, which was excellent in the sloppy underfooting. **1961** L. MUMFORD *City in History* x. 309 Some three centuries before wheeled vehicles became common, the street lost its natural underfooting. **1976** M. & G. GORDON *Ordeal* (1977) xviii. 125 He slowed only when he encountered rough underfooting.

under-frame. Add: **a.** Also, the substructure of a motor vehicle. Cf. *sub-frame* (*b*) s.v. *SUB- 3 a.

1903 *Lanchester Motor & Carriage Descriptive Man.* I. 9 The transmission from the car frame to the front under-frame. **1954** D. J. WARBURTON *ABC Brit. Lorries & Road Services* 28 The underframe is also available for the construction of other lightweight bodies.

b. *Furnit.* The framework supporting a seat or table-top.

1934 *Burlington Mag.* Nov. 201/2 The armchair[s] of walnut..show in the carving on the top-rail and underframe..that they are closely connected with the Indian high-back chairs. **1952** HOARD & MARLOW *Cabinet-maker's Treasury* 266/2 *Underbracing*, arrangement of stretchers to brace the legs of chairs, tables... Also *Underframe*. **1982** *Habitat Catal. 1982/83* 53/1 The underframe and legs of the tables are in solid timber.

underframing (examples of furniture).

1902 *Carpet & Upholstery Trade Rev.* 1 Sept. 73/1 The chair..is of a different type... The underframing begins to resemble rather closely the style known as 'Louis Quatorze'. **1969** E. H. PINTO *Treen* xv. 218, I think that the underframing was cut down to support the top, which originally was a loose board.

u·nderfug. *Schoolboys' slang.* [UNDER-¹ 5 a + *FUG *sb.*] An undervest; also, underpants.

1924 H. DE SÉLINCOURT *Cricket Match* ii. 32 'I do hope you'll be sensible and wear your nice, warm undervest, John.'..'I'm not vain, Maria..But..I heard one of the toffs say..'My God! Look, he's wearin' an underfug.' **1946** B. MARSHALL *George Brown's Schooldays* iv. 18 The matron kept everybody's spare shirts, underfugs and towels and dished clean ones out once a week. **1967** *Listener* 2 Mar. 299/3 Felsted School calls radiators *fugs* and underpants *under-fugs*.

underfu·nction, *sb.* Chiefly *Med.* [UNDER-10.] = *hypofunction* s.v. *HYPO-. Hence as *v. intr.*, to exhibit underfunction; to have a diminished capacity for acting and responding; **underfu·nctioning** *vbl. sb.*

1941 *Trans. Assoc. Amer. Physicians* LVI. 51 The adrenal cortex is underfunctioning because of pituitary disease. *Ibid.*, The term 'hypoleydigism' is defined as underfunction of the cells of Leydig of the male gonad. **1964** M. ARGYLE *Psychol. & Social Probl.* vi. 74 The person suffering from a behaviour disorder is usually ineffective, underfunctioning in his work and social relations. **1979** *Brit. Med. Jrnl.* 15 Dec. 1582/2 It is not uncommon to diagnose pathological underfunctioning in the presence of values which may be above average for the population but which are known..to fall below the norm for that particular individual. **1981** *Pharmacopsychiatria* XIV. 3 An underfunction of nonadrenergic synaptic transmission in depression.

u·nderfur. [UNDER-¹ 5 d.] An inner layer of shorter fur on an animal.

[**1892** H. POLAND *Fur-Bearing Animals* 200 The under fur of this Seal is long compared with other species.] **1904** *Ann. & Mag. Nat. Hist.* XIII. 424 Underfur of back about 15 mm. in length. **1968** [see *OVERFUR]. **1971** *Nature* 4 June 331/1 The fur was very spiny with virtually no soft underfur.

undergird, *v.* Add: The *fig.* use is now dominant. (Further examples.)

1973 *Times* 30 July 20/6 It involves an understanding of the variety of sub-systems which undergird community life, health, education, welfare, [etc.]. **1975** *Church Times* 15 Aug. 16/5 Dr. Taylor believes that such smaller groups as these are going to become the essential sub-structure of Church life that is needed to undergird the larger congregation in the parish church. **1981** *Dædalus* Spring 19 'Why shouldn't people have these rights?' was the question that undergirded these laws. **1983** *Salisbury Rev.* Spring 18/1 The same instinct directing a man to preserve his life, undergirds his attachment to the institutions which inform his life as a participant in the historical stream of the national culture.

under-glaze, *a.* and *sb.* Add: **1. a.** Also in other collocations, as *under-glaze design*, *work*, etc. (Earlier and later examples.)

1879 J. C. L. SPARKES *Pottery Painting* 28 Oil mediums may be used for over-glaze and for under-glaze work. **1925** *Heal & Son Catal.: Table Wares*, A simple brush-work under-glaze design in blue and red. **1967** M. CHANDLER *Ceramics in Mod. World* ii. 49 (*caption*) Chinese porcelain bowl with blue underglaze design.

2. (Earlier and later examples.)

1879 J. C. L. SPARKES *Pottery Painting* 45 An underglaze flesh tint may be made of claret brown. **1947** J. C. RICH *Materials & Methods of Sculpture* ii. 49 An underglaze color is a concentrated pigmenting agent that depends upon the glaze subsequently applied over it for 'life' or gloss and brilliance. **1980** R. ADAMS *Girl in Swing* i. 11, I took out the Copenhagen plate, with its underglaze blue wave mark.

undergra·duacy. *rare.* [f. UNDERGRADUA(TE *sb.* + -CY.] The state or position of (being) an undergraduate in a university.

1927 C. CONNOLLY *Let.* 21 Apr. in *Romantic Friendship* (1975) 295 This sense of living in a sequel tends to be the canker gnawing at the heart of undergraduacy. **1964** *Economist* 11 Jan. 89/2 The rather unworldly cloister of undergraduacy.

undergra·duatish, *a.* [f. UNDERGRADUATE *sb.* + -ISH¹.] Characteristic of an undergraduate; undergraduate-like. Cf. UNDERGRADUATE *a.* 3.

1925 [see *FLOATER 5]. **1931** *Times Lit. Suppl.* 10 Dec. 1001/3 He seems, for example, to give way to an undergraduatish melancholy at Cambridge. **1980** W. ASH *Incorporated* iii. 33 You're more interested in undergraduatish cleverness than in pursuing an interest which ..unites us.

undergradue·tte. *colloq.* (now *rare*). [Altered f. UNDERGRADUATE *sb.*: see -ETTE.] A female undergraduate.

1919 *Observer* 23 Nov. 17/4 The audience was chiefly composed of under-graduates and under-graduettes. **1926** *Spectator* 23 Oct. 677/1 There are too many undergraduettes at Oxford. **1934** W. GERHARDIE *Resurrection* xcv. 355 A professor, a don, an undergraduette in black cotton stockings, a green-grocer's boy—all move on bicycles. **1940** GRAVES & HODGE *Long Week-End* viii. 123 The subject of the duel was reported in the London Press to be an 'undergraduette of Somerville'. **1972** J. POTTER *Going West* 70 He ostentatiously walked out arm-in-arm with the prettiest undergraduettes. **1980** *Listener* 23 Oct. 549/2 In the Oxford of 1939..I remember a red-headed 'undergraduette' (as we then rather quaintly would have called her).

u·ndergrip. [UNDER-¹ 5 b.] **a.** *Gymnastics.* A hold in which the hands pass beneath the horizontal bar, with the palms facing the gymnast. **b.** *Mountaineering.* = *UNDER-HOLD.

1920 NAYLOR & TEMPLE *Mod. Physical Education* 109 The starting position is reached as in Exercise 90, the hands being in 'under-grip'. **1955** J. E. B. WRIGHT *Technique of Mountaineering* iv. 76 (*caption*) An under grip. **1976** T. & J. COUSMINER tr. *Kaneko's Olympic Gymnastics* 214 Hang straight from the horizontal bar... If your palms face backwards, you are using the ***reverse grip*** (also called the ***undergrip***). **1977** D. LAW *Starting Mountaineering & Rock Climbing* vi. 67 In the ***under grip*** [hold] the hand is turned over, fingers pointing upwards; it is quite sufficient to maintain balance.

underground, *adv.* Add: **2. b.** Into hiding or surreptitious activity, esp. in phr. *to go underground*: applied chiefly to political organizations and their representatives which continue to operate in secret (and often subversively) after becoming officially unacceptable.

1935 *Ann. Reg. 1934* II. 198 The Socialist leaders.. decided that it was best to accept defeat: those leaders who were known made for the frontier, the others 'went underground' and began at once the organising of an illegal party. **1949** 'M. INNES' *Journeying Boy* xxiii. 285 There was nothing for it but a quick get-away and a going underground for good. **1960** E. BOWEN *Time in Rome* iv. 118 Like Resistance workers in the occupied countries, long-ago Christians, from time to time, strategically 'went underground'. **1977** *Times* 15 June 1/5 The crucial factor was the subsequent move underground by a handful of those people [*sc.* Soviet sympathizers], and the covers they assumed to mask their new role as agents.

underground, *a.* and *sb.* Add: **A.** *adj.* **1. d.** *underground mutton*, a rabbit; rabbit meat. *Austral. slang.*

1946 A. J. HOLT *Wheat Farms of Victoria* viii. 129 'Underground mutton' (rabbit) is almost always available for those who like it. **1965** E. LAMBERT *Long White Night* xv. 138, I thought a feed of underground mutton would go all right for my tea. **1979** D. R. STUART *Crank Back on Roller* 151 Maybe a rabbit, though I was never what y' could call over fond of the ole underground mutton meself.

2. c. (*a*) Also in other collocations, as *underground line*, *service*, etc. (now often *attrib.* uses of the sb.); (*b*) also *fig.*

(*a*) **1883** [see *METROPOLITAN *a.* 2 b]. **1926** *Times* 6 May 3/1 In London most of the tube and underground services were in force or others were expected to be to-day. **1926** *Daily Express* 11 May 1/3 The Underground trains yesterday showed no difference from any ordinary Monday morning. **1975** J. SYMONS *Three Pipe Problem* xviii. 204 He lost his way to the Underground station. **1982** G. LYALL *Conduct of Major Maxim* vii. 62 With the Underground map in his diary he worked out a route that involved two changes of train.

(*b*) **1868** C. M. YONGE *Chaplet of Pearls* I. xviii. 251 There was what in later times has been termed an underground railway amid the persecuted Calvinists. **1940** *Sun* (Baltimore) 14 Oct. 2/3 A so-called 'underground railway' delivering prominent scholars and writers from Nazi-dominated parts of Europe. **1979** R. LAIDLAW

Lion is Rampant xviii. 137, I could probably have got you smuggled to the Border via my 'Underground Railway'.

4. c. Designating (the activities of) a group, organization, or its representatives, working covertly to subvert the aims of a ruling (often occupying) power. Cf. *RESISTANCE I c.

1939 [see *RESISTANCE I c]. **1939** *War Illustr.* 9 Dec. 392/3 Even in the completely occupied territory there was underground activity. **1944** *Times* 18 July 2/3 An exhibition of the underground press of Europe. **1950** G. BRENAN *Face of Spain* v. 118 Until recently people suspected of Underground activity had been arrested and court-martialed. **1965** J. A. MICHENER *Source* (1966) 784 The night in the Belgian port when another English underground operative had called, 'One more place in the lorry. Look lively.' **1974** J. WHITE tr. *Poulantzas's Fascism & Dictatorship* IV. ii. 186 The KPD's underground apparatus turned out to be non-existent.

d. Of or pertaining to a subculture which seeks to provide radical alternatives to the socially accepted or established mode; *spec.* manifested in its literature, music, press, etc.

1953 *Observer* 13 Sept. 9/3 Its detached picture of barren tragic love..in a furtive fantastic 'underground' sector of London. **1962** *Movie* Dec. 4/2 Fuller is not an 'underground' director whose films actually *do* the opposite of what they overtly *say*. **1969** *Oz* May 36/1 He talked solidly for nearly forty-five minutes—he'd said it all before..to all the underground papers in the States. **1970** A. TOFFLER *Future Shock* xii. 248 The underground movie..is flourishing even more than the underground press. **1977** *New Yorker* 9 May 126/3 He is attracted to buying *Mainline* because of its history as a radical underground weekly.

e. *underground economy*, the economic sector of private business deals in which tax liability is not reported; the 'black' economy. Cf. *BLACK *a.* II c. *U.S.*

1978 *Business Week* 13 Mar. 74 Neither the government nor labour unions seem to have any control over the underground economy. **1980** *Economic Rev.* (Fed. Reserve Bank of Atlanta) Jan.–Feb. 8/2 It suggests increasing activity in the 'underground economy' (gambling, bartering, and other unreported income). **1982** *Christian Sci. Monitor* 1 July B-4/1 Local custom means heavy traffic in illegal drugs and prostitution, an underground economy that is left alone as long as there is no trouble. **1983** *Chicago Sun-Times* 9 Sept. 38/2 The 30 cents a pound is essentially tax-free, part of the underground (or curbside) economy.

B. *sb.* **3.** Esp. the one in London. Usu. with capital initial. (Earlier examples.)

1866 J. R. PLANCHÉ *Orpheus in Haymarket* III. 32 For Tartarus I happened to be bound, And was just starting by the Underground. **1875** L. TROUBRIDGE *Life amongst Troubridges* (1966) 123 Set off from Victoria Station by the Underground for Shepherd's Bush.

4. *fig.* **a.** A group or movement organized secretly to work against an existing regime, often by violent means; *spec.* an 'underground' resistance movement. Usu. with *the*.

1946 KOESTLER *Thieves in Night* 277 The Hebrew underground began as a purely political movement. **1946** AUDEN *Nones* (1952) 61 By night our student Underground At cocktail parties whisper round From ear to ear. **1958** L. URIS *Exodus* I. xii. 72 The Danes, by the middle of 1941, had established a small but determined little underground. **1966** A. SACHS *Jail Diary* iii. 30 With her husband Dennis on trial for his life for supporting the underground, she was hoping for some peace. **1973** T. PYNCHON *Gravity's Rainbow* I. 96 Captain must allow for the real chance she's a British spy, or member of the Dutch underground.

b. Any unofficial group or movement which seeks to provide alternatives to the forms of expression and action sanctioned by the society in which it exists.

1959 [see *TRANS-WORLD *a.*]. **1969** *Oz* Apr. 27/2 The underground's a great crowd really. We enjoy them as people..just being what they are. **1970** *Guardian* 28 Feb. 9/2 We are going to try..to establish a definition of the underground... The word applies to a life-style, to a group of people who live..outside the constraints of ordinary society..and who largely..have come to the realisation of this new life-style through the use of cannabis and LSD. **1974** M. C. GERALD *Pharmacol.* i. 13 On the one hand, he has been enticed by 'notes from the underground', exalting the wonders of 'acid';..simultaneously, he has often been subjected to..the lies and half-truths of the well-meaning establishment.

undergrounder (later examples).

1954 L. MACNEICE *Autumn Sequel* xv. 94 The hole becomes..a wide Doorway; the undergrounders burst and spout. **1974** K. MILLETT *Flying* IV. 380 This patron saint of all undergrounders.

u·nderground, *v.* [f. the adv.] *trans.* To lay (electricity or telephone cables) below ground level. So **u·ndergrou:nding** *vbl. sb.*

1889 in *Cent. Dict.* **1961** *Times Rev. Industry* Jan. 40/1 In..transmitting power, there are only two alternatives—the overhead and underground..and it's 16 times as dear to run [cables] underground... I think undergrounding is out of the question. **1964** *Times* 2 Sept. 11/6 We were recently obliged to underground three and a half miles of the Thorpe Marsh–Stalybridge line. **1971** P. GRESSWELL *Environment* 71 In the case of a line of pylons..he [*sc.* the citizen] needs to be told not simply how much undergrounding would cost..but how this relates to the total capital expenditure. **1977** *New Scientist* 27 Jan. 188/2 The CEGB spent £220,000 undergrounding 2 km..cable..to preserve the view of Oxford as seen from Elsfield.

u·nder-hold. *Mountaineering.* [UNDER-[1] 5 b.] A hold in which the hand grasps a downturned edge or point from beneath with the palm upwards, used esp. to maintain balance. Cf. *UNDER-GRIP b.

1920 G. W. YOUNG *Mountain Craft* iv. 162 A cling 'under'-hold keeps body and eyes free at the length of our arms, bent or straight according to our convenience. **1948** 'MOUNTAINEERS' *Mountaineers' Handbk.* ix. 68 In a cling under hold..the hands pull upward and exert a tension through the body against the feet, pressing them into the rock. **1965** A. BLACKSHAW *Mountaineering* vi. 175 (*caption*) Note the use of the under-hold..to permit a high reach with left hand.

under-insu·rance. [UNDER-[1] 10 b.] Insurance (of goods, property, etc.) at less than their real value.

1893 *Standard* (Boston) 20 May 518/1 Mr. Goodwin considers the tendency toward under-insurance of safe risks as the cause of the general requirement of the 80 per cent coinsurance clause. **1930** F. E. WOLFE *Princ. Property Insurance* ix. 147 Underinsurance is ignored if the practice is followed by fixing rates from time to time. **1949** R. S. SHARMA *Insurance Princ. & Pract.* xxiv. 268 One of the difficulties in arriving at a scientific basis of rating in fire insurance is of under-insurance. **1976** *Business Week* 5 July 24 The hazards of underinsurance ..exploded in Mississippi as a massive liquidity crisis triggered the..'bank holiday'.

under-insu·re, *v.* [UNDER-[1] 10 a.] *trans.* To insure at less than the real value. Also *intr.* or *absol.* Cf. *OVER-INSURE *v.*

1911 *Rep. Labour & Social Conditions in Germany* (Tariff Reform League) III. 145 If a person..under-insured to avoid the rates he would lose in case of fire. **1921** W. N. BAMENT *Co-Insurance* 3 The natural inclination..is to under-insure and take the chance of not having a total loss. **1982** *Economist* 18 Sept. 25 The problem is that the less well-off might underinsure.

So **under-insu·red** *ppl. a.* (also *absol.* as *sb.*).

1893 *Standard* (Boston) 20 May 518/2 The sufferers of slight and partial losses are able..to draw their full damage without reference to the insurance carried, which, in the case of small insurance in proportion to value carried, enables a person who is thus under-insured to draw more than an equitable portion. **1909** W. J. GRAHAM *Romance of Life Insurance* v. 66 Life, the great creator and conservator of the world's wealth, is grossly underinsured when compared with fire insurance. **1912** E. R. HARDY in H. P. Dunham *Business of Insurance* I. x. 179 In case of important properties where mortgage loans have to be protected..all such, although their property may not be subject to any greater loss than the under insured, are paying for the under insured property. **1947** P. GORDIS *How to buy Insurance* i. 8 We have established the inadvisability of being under-insured. **1962** A. LURIE *Love & Friendship* iv. 69 A regular fire-trap the whole house. Oh they're wild about it now... Underinsured, that's what it was. **1981** M. DUFFY *Gor Saga* II. 102 He was underinsured... His capital had been in his stock.

u·nderkill. *colloq.* (orig. *U.S.*). [f. UNDER-[1] 10 a, after *overkill*.] (The mobilization of) insufficient capacity, esp. of nuclear weapons, to kill and effect destruction to the level of strategic requirements. Freq. *fig.*

1964 *New Scientist* 10 Sept. 647/2 Mr Goldwater has engaged in a press war..over the future strength of United States' strategic retaliatory force—what for lack of a better description might be called the question of underkill. **1971** *Time* 5 July 13 Harvard's Paul A. Freund maintained that 'risk for risk, the law has opted for underkill in duels over publication'. **1984** *Financial Times* 20 Jan. 21/1 There is no limit to the silliness resulting when that director goes over the top and weds visual overkill to narrative and dramatic underkill.

u·nderlap, *sb.* [UNDER-[1] 5 b, after *overlap*.] † **1.** *Geol.* The fact or state of underlapping. *Obs. rare*$^{-1}$.

1883 J. G. GOODCHILD in *Geol. Mag.* Decade II. X. 226 Overlap, and its correlative Underlap, as it is here suggested to employ them, thus denote the stratigraphical relations of one part of a formation to another where the original extent of the lower part occupied a smaller area than that of the next higher members of the same series.

2. a. In warp knitting, the lateral movements of the guide bar made on the side of the needle remote from the hook.

1926 J. CHAMBERLAIN *Hosiery Yarns & Fabrics* vii. 170 The underlap may be at the back of any convenient number of needles. **1952** D. F. PALING *Warp Knitting Technol.* i. 4 The first movement is applied to the guide bars, and consists of a lateral motion in front of the needles ..known as the *underlap*. **1971** D. G. B. THOMAS *Introd. to Warp Knitting* iii. 24 In most modern machines, the underlap takes place when the needles are down. The underlap is sometimes called a *shog*.

b. A piece of material that extends beneath another fold or pleat.

1943 I. R. DUNCAN *Needles & Pins* xiv. 284 Stitch the two pieces together at the top and bottom for a dress.. to form an over and under lap for the placket. **1964** *McCall's Sewing* ii. 33/1 *Underlap*, a part of a garment that extends or laps under another pleat. **1979** *Tucson* (Arizona) *Citizen* 20 Sept. 2B/1 Put the coat on over a skirt or dress and button it closed. Place a pin at the desired new hem length at center front on both the overlap and underlap.

underlay, *sb.* Add: **2. e.** *gen.* A layer which underlies another; a substratum. Also as *fig.* use of next sense.

1876 W. WHITMAN *Jrnl.* 10 June in *Specimen Days* (1883) 87, I write..here by the creek... For underlay, trees in fulness of tender foliage—liquid reedy, long-drawn notes of birds. **1964** *Listener* 15 Oct. 572/1 The main characteristic of the new popular manner is an aggressive surface over a soft underlay; it is noisy..about minor issues, but takes good care not to tread any..controversial ground. **1977** C. MCCULLOUGH *Thorn Birds* (1978) II. vii. 174 'I do not intend to make a long eulogy,' he said in his clear, almost Oxford diction with its faint Irish underlay.

f. *spec.* (sheets of) material laid beneath a carpet (usu. felt or paper, or as an integral rubberized backing) or a mattress, for protection and support.

1907 *Army & Navy Stores Catal.* 275/2 Moth proof Cotton underlay to go between wire bottom of bed and mattress..4/8. **1923** *Daily Mail* 21 Feb. 8 (Advt.), Cedar Felt is an improved paper felt underlay for carpets. **1929** W. DEEPING *Roper's Row* xxi. 233 They'll do for underlays on the beds. I shan't waste them. **1959** *Spectator* 7 Aug. 165/2 Underlay adds to the life of a carpet, absorbs pressure from furniture and footsteps and acts as a sound absorber and insulator. **1980** D. ADAMS *Restaurant at End of Universe* xx. 117 The thin tufted nylon floor covering was black, and when they had lifted up a corner of it they had discovered that the foam underlay also was black.

4. *Early Mus.* The placing of text in relation to music. Cf. sense *1 e of the vb.

1969 G. REANEY in Reese & Snow *Essays in Musicology in Honor of Dragan Plamenac* xvi. 250 The most difficult type of underlay consists of a moderately large group of notes with rather fewer syllables. **1974** *Times Lit. Suppl.* 14 June 642/2 When Petrarch's lines are restored to their proper shape and order and deployed in reasonable fashion below the notes of the vocal part, most if not all of the problems of underlay disappear. **1980** *Early Music* Jan. 21/1 Directions for tempo and dynamics, and frequently for underlay also, are absent from manuscript and printed sources alike.

underlay, *v. trans.* Add: **1. e.** *Early Mus.* To place (the text of a song, etc.) in relation to the music.

1934 A. HUGHES *Anglo-French Sequelae* 7 Is there any satisfactory reason adducible to explain why the music of the Verba-passages should be underlaid with a text, and not the rest? **1949** W. APEL *Notation of Polyphonic Music 900–1600* (ed. 4) II. ii. 118 This composition also serves to illustrate the problem of text-underlaying in early music... The original frequently leaves considerable room for doubt..as to the 'correct' placing of the words. **1960** D. STEVENS *Hist. Song* 88 The text does not fit the ligatures of the tenor part... But it makes good sense when underlaid to the soprano part.

u·nderlayment *U.S.* [f. UNDERLAY *v.* + -MENT.] Carpet underlay; material laid beneath roofing tiles, etc.

1956 *Study of Installation Wood Block Finish Flooring* (U.S. Nat. Res. Council) 17 The sub-floor should be covered with an underlayment of 15 lb. asphalt impregnated felt. **1975** 'E. LATHEN' *By Hook or by Crook* x. 97 You'll be sure that the men have instructions about the underlayment.

u·nderlead. [UNDER-[1] 4 d.] *Bridge.* The lead of a low card in a suit of which a higher card is held by the player.

1934 E. CULBERTSON *Contract Bridge Red Bk. on Play* xli. 531 An Ace underlead not only has the advantage of the surprise effect on the enemy but it retains the control of the suit. **1947** C. H. GOREN *Better Bridge* ii. 101 This is one of the rare cases in which the under lead of an Ace is recommended. **1964** *Official Encycl. Bridge* 650/2 Another motive for an underlead is an urgent desire to get a particular lead from partner.

Also **underlea·d** *v. trans.*, to lead with a card of lower value than (another card of the suit held).

1945 PHILLIPS & REESE *How to play Bridge* III. 111 It is dangerous to underlead Aces against suit contracts. **1962** *Listener* 26 July 154/3 The question was whether East would risk underleading his queen of diamonds, to put partner in with the jack for a spade lead. **1973** *Daily Tel.* 13 Jan. 9/5 West should therefore underlead his ♡A (assuming he has it) for a second club ruff.

underleaf. Add: **2.** Also, a lower leaf.

1922 JOYCE *Ulysses* 220 The lychgate..showed Father Conmee breadths of cabbages, curtseying to him with ample underleaves. **1969** F. E. ROUND *Introd. Lower Plants* viii. 99 Yet another feature of this group is the basic conservatism of the organs; they differ in detail but vegetatively there are only three basic growth forms, (*a*).. (*b*) a dorsiventral leafy thallus with two rows of lateral leaves and a third modified row of 'underleaves'.

underline, *sb.* Add: **4.** The caption or text beneath a picture, esp. in a book, newspaper, etc.

1924 N. J. RADDER *Newspaper Make-Up & Headlines* vi. 109 Practice varies with respect to the underline below the cut... When the underline is brief it is much like the second deck of a headline and the copyreader must.. avoid repetition of words..in the overline. **1947** A. E. DAVIES in J. G. Herzberg *Late City Edition* xxii. 206 The editor writes captions to run above the picture, and the more detailed underlines to run below them. **1956** H. WILLIAMSON *Methods Bk. Design* p. xiii, In order to simplify the text pages, the underlines of the illustrations refer only to the specific points which are illustrated. **1971** Baskette & Sissors *Art of Editing* x. 203 Picture texts are known by many names—cutlines, captions, underlines (or overlines), legends.

underline, *v.*^{2} **2.** (Earlier examples.)
1825 P. Egan *Life of Actor* ii. 67 A file of old play bills which might do to bind, With only the play for next night—underlined. **1838** *Actors by Daylight* I. 5 A new burletta is underlined for this week.

underlining, *vbl. sb.* (Earlier example.)
1838 L. Hunt *Let.* July in *Lett. C. Dickens* (1965) I. 685, I have marked..my *most* favourite passages... The underlinings imply admiration.

underloaded (stress variable), *a.* [Under-^{1} 10 a, after *overloaded.*] Not loaded or burdened to capacity; *spec.* in *Geomorphol.* of a stream: carrying less than the maximum amount of sediment for the given conditions, and eroding its bed.
1898 I. C. Russell *River Development* iv. 68 But if the bottom current is underloaded, the material is carried slowly forward. **1942** O. D. von Engeln *Geomorphol.* xii. 234 A stream may be underloaded in which case it will ordinarily be downcutting, or it may be loaded to capacity. **1964** K. G. Lockyer *Introd. Critical Path Analysis* viii. 70 When too much work is required of a work source, the work source is said to be *Overloaded*, whilst if too little is needed it is said to be *Underloaded.* **1970** R. J. Small *Study of Landforms* ii. 57 At some times streams erode vertically (because they are underloaded), at others they erode laterally (because they are graded), and at others they deposit (when they change from a graded to an overloaded condition).

Hence **u·nderload,** an occurrence or state of being incompletely loaded.
1964 K. G. Lockyer *Introd. Critical Path Analysis* viii. 76 With experience, a great facility is obtained in viewing a histogram and..assessing whether a 'peak' (i.e. an overload) can be toppled into a 'valley' (i.e. an underload) in order to 'smooth out' the loading. **1971** *Cabinet Maker & Retail Furnisher* 24 Sept. 535/1 Unless the home market improves..APV could have..an underload position in some of their factories. **1981** *N.Y. Times Mag.* 8 Feb. 12/2 Conservatives are foolishly worrying about lithosphere underload.

u·nderlord. [Under-^{1} 6 a.] A subordinate or lesser lord; one in authority below another (opp. *overlord*).
1929 Belloc *Joan of Arc* ii. 39 The Kingdom was held in fealty from God alone of Whom Charles was Vassal and Under-Lord. **1937** F. L. Packard *Dragon's Jaws* 251 And if the old temple is the secret meeting place ..and Fan Chao-tao and his underlords..are to be there —what then? **1969** *Daily Tel.* 29 Oct. 16 In the sphere of the other main new overlord (Mr Benn) one nominated underlord has already resigned, presumably because he thinks it won't work. **1985** *Financial Times* 1 Feb. 21/5 The appointment of Lord Young..to the Cabinet as what he calls a kind of 'underlord' responsible for training matters.

Hence **u·nderlordship** *rare.*
1937 Belloc *Crusade* ii. 38 The title King meant that he had no overlord. He was the summit in a pyramid of overlordships and underlordships.

underlying, *ppl. a.* Add: **2.** *Linguistics.* Applied to a significant feature of a linguistic unit or structure which needs to be represented in its derivational or syntactic analysis, but which may not be apparent from the standard written or spoken form. Cf. *deep structure* s.v. *Deep *a.* IV. c.
1933 L. Bloomfield *Language* xiii. 210 By a feature of modulation common to nearly all constructions of English morphology, the underlying form keeps its stress, and the bound form is unstressed. **1958** C. F. Hockett *Course in Mod. Linguistics* xxviii. 241 If the underlying form in a secondary derivative is not a single morpheme, its structure is also covered by the classification. Thus the underlying form of *actress-* is the secondary derivative *actor-*. **1970** J. Lyons *Chomsky* 67 This system of phrase structure rules will generate a large (but finite) number of what we may call *underlying strings.* **1978** *Language* LIV. 387 Actually, rather than 'deep structure' we should think in terms of the 'underlying structure' of Generative Semantics, a highly abstract and universal level that is much more closely akin to the Freudian unconscious than is the 'deep structure' of classical transformational grammar.

Hence **underly·ingly** *adv.*
1973 A. H. Sommerstein *Sound Pattern Anc. Greek* i. 2 There is underlyingly a system of five short..and five corresponding long vowels. **1982** J. C. Wells *Accents of English* i. 76 It is possible to argue..that an occurrence of the phoneme /r/ is present underlyingly in the critical environments, but that it is obligatorily vocalized or deleted by rule so that it is not present phonetically.

underman. Add: **2.** [tr. G. *untermensch.*] *spec.* opp. *Overman *sb.* 4; a person with sub-human attributes.
1910 T. Common tr. *Nietzsche's Joyful Wisdom* III. 179 The inventing of Gods, heroes and supermen of all kinds, as well as co-ordinate men and undermen—dwarfs, fairies,..devils—was the inestimable preliminary to the justification of the selfishness..of the individual. **1936** A. N. Field *All these Things* vi. 206 Planned Economy calls for Supermen to control and Undermen to submit. **1963** L. Trilling in N. Frye *Romanticism Reconsidered* 92 *More life*: perhaps it was this boast of the Underground Man that Nietzsche recalled when he said, 'Dostoevsky's Underman and my Overman are the same person.' **1974** W. Kaufmann tr. *Nietzsche's Gay Science* III. 192 *Untermensch* (underman, for a subhuman man) is not rare.

3. *Railways.* A subordinate member of a gang of platelayers.
1921 *Dict. Occup. Terms* (1927) § 577 *Underman..*, a worker in a permanent way gang supervised by ganger. **1928** *Daily Express* 18 Feb. 7/3 Sidney Coleman, an underman platelayer, said he was one of the gang which was 'packing' sleepers on the down main line. **1931** *Cambridge Daily News* 5 Sept. 5/2 Andrew White, an underman.. said he shouted as hard as he could to warn the men that a train was approaching.

u·ndermass. *Geol.* [Under-^{1} 5 c.] An older, deformed body of rock overlain by younger, undeformed strata.
1942 O. D. von Engeln *Geomorphol.* ix. 168 The geomorphic significance of the abrupt, commonly marked in kind, transition between the materials above and below a plane of angular unconformity is indicated by the introduction of the terms cover mass and undermass. **1956** D. L. Linton *Sheffield* ii. 35 We..interpret it as the product of the cycle(s) of erosion which stripped away the presumed chalk cover, removed some hundreds of feet of the undermass, and saw the first group of adjustments of the superimposed streams to the underlying structures. **1966** [see *plate tectonics* s.v. *Plate *sb.* 20].

undermeaning. (Earlier example.)
1841 Ruskin *Let.* 12 Feb. in *Lett. to College Friend* (1894) vii. 87 Rhyme and rhythm are..thoroughly injurious where there is no mystery, when there is not some undermeaning.

underminingly, *adv.* (Later example.)
1832 F. Burney *Mem. Dr. Burney* III. 176 The accumulation of the whole had, slowly and underminingly, brought him into the state that has been described.

u:ndermodula·tion. *Radio* and *Cinemat.* [Under-^{1} 10 b.] Modulation that is less than it need be, so that the available capacity of a transmitter or medium is underused or the signal is too weak. So **undermo·dulate** *v. trans.*, **-mo·dulated** *ppl. a.*
1940 *Chambers's Techn. Dict.* 877/1 Undermodulation. **1962** A. Nisbett *Technique Sound Studio* v. 94 Programme meters... Its uses are:..(ii) to provide indications of levels which would result in under- or over-modulation at the recorder or transmitter. *Ibid.* 100 Reducing the effective service area of the transmitter by undermodulating a whole programme. **1974** *Listener* 2 May 573/3 Why are the transmissions on Radio 3 invariably under-modulated?

undermost, *a.* **1. b.** (Earlier example.)
1822 D. Wordsworth *Jrnl.* 22 Sept. (1941) II. 367 A girl, bare-legged, petticoats kilted to her undermost, of white flannel.

under-nou·rished, *a.* [Under-^{1} 10 a.] Having had insufficient nourishment, esp. over a sustained period; in a state of semi-starvation. Also *fig.*
1910 Galsworthy *Justice* IV. 98 He's under-nourished. It's very trying to go without your dinner. **1928** *Manch. Guardian Weekly* 10 Aug. 110/1 Most of the Indian children are badly under-nourished. *a* **1942** B. Malinowski *Sci. Theory of Culture* (1944) viii. 80 When African labour is drafted into European enterprise, whether mines, plantations, or factories, it is usually found that the workers are undernourished with reference to the efforts which they will have to put into their performances. **1962** E. Snow *Other Side of River* (1963) xxxix. 289, I asked one how he explained his fine white teeth if he had been undernourished. **1972** *Computer Jrnl.* XV. 200/1 The element of black magic in it satisfies one of our most undernourished psychological needs.

Also **u:nder-nou·rishment.**
1920 H. G. Wells *Outl. Hist.* 575/2 Scores of millions were suffering and enfeebled by undernourishment and misery. **1944** M. Laski *Love on Supertax* v. 62 Never before had he been brought into direct contact with under-nourishment. **1971** *Sci. Amer.* Oct. 20/1 A child who has suffered undernourishment very early and for an appreciable length of time will never reach normal size for his age.

u:nder-occupa·tion. [Under-^{1} 10 b.] The occupation of a dwelling or dwellings by fewer people than had been planned; *spec.* applied to local authority accommodation that is considered to be underused.
1961 *Guardian* 6 Nov. 2/4 There is a good deal of under-occupation. **1966** [see *one-person* s.v. *One B. IX. 32 a]. **1977** *Jrnl. R. Soc. Arts* CXXV. 116/2 Parallel with the so-called scandal of empty homes, we also hear of the scandal of under-occupation. It is all wrong, the critics say, for an elderly council tenant to occupy a three bedroom house, when she could be living in a one-room new council flat.

Also **under-o·ccupy** *v. trans.*, **under-o·ccupied** *ppl. a.*
1961 *Guardian* 28 Nov. 8/2 From the point of view of a local authority housing official a house with spare bedrooms is 'under-occupied'. **1966** J. Tunstall *Old & Alone* xiv. 281, 52.3 per cent of old people under-occupying housing were owner-occupiers, against 38.5 per cent who paid rent. **1970** *Times* 23 Mar. 5/1 To find room in this way for the elderly and others needing small homes would release seriously underoccupied large houses for bigger families. *a* **1974** R. Crossman *Diaries* (1975) I. 75 The interesting thing at Leicester..was the admirable way they are trying to deal with the problem of the people who grow elderly on their huge housing estates and then under-occupy their three-room council houses.

under-officered, *a.*^{2} (Earlier example.)
1856 *Tracts on Increase of Episcopate in Eng. & Wales* I. 3 In respect to her Bishops, the Church of England is, so to speak, under-officered.

underpaid, *ppl. a.* (Earlier example.)
1817 Ld. Colchester *Diary* 17 Feb. (1861) II. l. 604 This was objectionable, as giving currency to the vulgar opinion that public men..were overpaid, whereas, they were notoriously underpaid.

u·nderpainting. *Art.* [Under-^{1} 5 d.] (The application of) a layer of paint subsequently overlaid by another painted surface; a painting underlying a finished work. Cf. *Overpainting *vbl. sb.*
1866 [see Under-^{1} 5 d]. **1905** *Spectator* 25 Feb. 287/2 In much of his painting..Whistler seems to have begun with a cool grey underpainting. **1937** *Discovery* July 212/1 Constable himself did not disdain the use of a warm monochromatic under-painting. **1951** E. Paul *Springtime in Paris* iii. 63 There must have been an underpainting of that tone, because it showed also around the edges of the canvas. **1979** Ld. Clark in *Hist. Today* Nov. 725/1, I had it X-rayed, and there appeared an underpainting that was unquestionably the work of Filippino.

Also **u·nderpaint,** a layer of paint applied before another coat or finish.
1934 *Burlington Mag.* Jan. 19/2 There are indications of a dark grey underpaint. **1976** D. Francis *In Frame* ii. 38 A gloss on the lips..which one couldn't do until the under paint was dry.

u·nderpan. [Under-^{1} 5 b.] The protective metal covering fitted beneath the engine, clutch, and transmission of a motor vehicle.
1913 A. C. Clough *Dict. Automobile Terms* 275 *Sod pan*, a protective covering, fitted under the engine..and other parts of an automobile... Syn.: Pan, underpan. **1934** Webster *Under pan*, in automotive vehicles, a protective metal covering fitting under the engine, clutch, and transmission case. **1968** *Jane's Freight Containers 1968–69* 530/1 Hi-tensile pressed steel bottom rail with cross-members pressed into all welded leak proof underpan of great strength. **1977** *Drive* Mar.–Apr. 57/3 Opel's anti-rust measures include..a wax spray in box sections and over the underpan.

u·nderpants, *sb. pl.* [Under-^{1} 5 a.] An undergarment covering the lower part of the body (and part of the legs); short knickers, briefs. Cf. Pants *sb. pl.* 1 b.
1931 R. Campbell *Georgiad* I. 15 The living image of a country lover, In woolly underpants, a sort of Faun. **1955** J. Morrison in B. James *Austral. Short Stories* (1963) 144 Without having removed shirt or underpants, he shuffled down between the blankets. **1961** M. Beadle *These Ruins are Inhabited* iii. 37 The Salesman spread out an impressive..array of undershirts, underpants, knee-high wool socks..and red Rugby shirts. **1979** R. Jaffe *Class Reunion* I. xi. 105 Chris yanked off her..slip and bra and underpants.

under-pa·rted, *a. rare.* [Under-^{1} 10 a: cf. Underpart *sb.* 2.] Of an actor: cast in an insufficient role. Cf. *Undercast *v.* 4.
1890 G. B. Shaw in *Star* 2 May 2/3 Mr Coffin, being a handsome young man, and considerably under-parted to boot, had an easy time of it. **1898** —— *Our Theatres in Nineties* (1932) III. 290 Miss May Harvey..is almost dangerously underparted. **1984** *Daily Tel.* 14 Aug. 7/8 Only the underparted Andrew Cruickshank as the Abbot, with his hissed cry of 'heresy!' in a superb scene of denunciation, strikes the right balance between malevolence and outrageousness.

u·nderpass. orig. *U.S.* [Under-^{1} 5 b.] A (section of) road providing passage beneath another road or a railway; a subway. Cf. *Overpass *sb.*
1904 *Springfield* (Mass.) *Weekly Republ.* 16 Sept. 8 The need of an underpass at the union railroad station in this city. **1929** [see *Overpass *sb.*]. **1943** *Sun* (Baltimore) 29 Oct. 4/3 The Ponca-Lombard street bypass. is designed to bypass the Eastern underpass. **1959** *Manch. Guardian* 26 June 8/7 A four-lane underpass..would run under Euston Road. **1973** [see *Ringway].

underpay, *v.* Add: Also **underpay·ment.**
1848 Mill *Pol. Econ.* II. III. xiii. 87 There was an underpayment to one set of persons, and an overpayment to another. **1920** [see *Undercharge *sb.*]. **1972** *Accountant* 26 Oct. 507/3 He received eight changes of code number within..five months. He also received a notice alleging £42.67 underpayment of tax.

underperfo·rm, *v.* [Under-^{1} 10 a.] **1.** *intr.* To perform in a manner which falls below expectation.
1976 *Business Week* 26 Jan. 71/1 Institutions..underperform over the all-important long term. **1977** *Daily Mail* 17 Mar. 6/1 What's wrong with comprehensive schools..is..not that they fail to teach children properly. .. They just 'underperform'. **1984** *Observer* 26 Feb. 27/2 Our shares have underperformed since 1977. But this time we have performed.

2. *trans.* Of shares, etc.: to perform less well than (the general market).

1975 *Dun's Rev.* June 92/3 A company that fits the criteria..might underperform the market for several years before somebody wants to acquire it. **1979** *Daily Tel.* 18 July 21 The shares of Midland Bank have under-performed in an astonishing way..those of its rivals. **1984** *Amer. Banker* 14 Mar. 13/4 Further doubts could make bank stocks underperform even a downward moving stock market.

Hence **underperfo·rmance; underperfo·rmer.**

1975 *Forbes* 15 Aug. 82/3 Stocks like International Flavors, IBM..have all been underperformers in this bull market. **1976** *Business Week* 29 Mar. 86/2 The Japanese economy shows signs of continued underperformance. **1977** *Daily Mail* 17 Mar. 6/1 What's wrong with comprehensive schools, according to the Ministry inspectors, is 'widespread underperformance'. **1981** *Times* 18 May 18/6 Phillips & Drew has put it [*sc.* a named share] on its list of expected underperformers.

under-petticoat. (Later examples.)

1865 DICKENS *Our Mutual Fr.* II. iv. xvi. 295 Why one should go out to dine with one's own daughter..as if one's under-petticoat was a backboard. **1924** R. MACAULAY *Orphan Island* xiii. 156 Flora looked with interest at Rosamond's cami-knickers, Rosamond at Flora's under-petticoat of scarlet-dyed cocoa-nut cloth.

underpinning, *vbl. sb.* Add: **2. c.** *spec.* (*U.S. slang*), the legs. Chiefly in *pl.* Cf. UNDERPINNER[2].

1848 E. BENNET *Mike Fink* 9/2 Nothing like long under-pinins fur travel. **1895** *N.Y. Dramatic News* 5 Oct. 6/1 Do cigarette girls at work wear their dresses decollete at the bottom and show their underpinning? **1934** A. WOOLLCOTT *While Rome Burns* 48 There he was at last with his underpinnings shot from under him. **1974** R. B. PARKER *God save Child* (1975) xiii. 95, I learned Vic's technique for developing 'sinewy and shapely under-pinnings'.

under-pitched, *ppl. a.* Add: **2.** *Cricket.* Of a ball: pitched short of a length; = SHORT *a.* 16.

1927 *Daily Tel.* 14 June 6/1 Allen..began to pull Larwood's slightly under-pitched one—a manoeuvre which showed..that he meant to get close to the ball. **1963** *Times* 14 Feb. 3/1 Knight, it is true, is a disappointing fielder and looks vulnerable to the under-pitched ball.

underplant, *v.* Restrict *rare* to sense a. **b.** For def. read: To plant or cultivate the ground about (a tall plant) *with* smaller ones. (Examples.) Chiefly as **underpla·nted** *pa. pple.* and *ppl. a.*

1891 W. SCHLICH *Man. Forestry* II. iv. 244 Oak woods should be underplanted when the process of opening out has set in. **1959** *Geogr. Rev.* XLIX. 29 Clumps and spinneys were underplanted with evergreens. **1962** R. PAGE *Educ. of Gardener* iii. 101 There were a few old trees which Duchêne had underplanted with yews. *Ibid.* xi. 302 The cypresses are underplanted with sheets of the bright gentian blue echium. **1971** *Guardian* 17 Apr. 7/7 We plan..to underplant a bush of *Spirea arguta*..with the pale lemon tulip. **1980** *Amat. Gardening* 25 Oct. 24/2 Transform a corner into a mini-woodland garden with light foliage trees, such as silver birch, underplanted with small flowered daffodil varieties.

u·nderplanting, *vbl. sb.* [f. prec.] The planting or cultivation of smaller plants in between taller ones; a plant so grown; *spec.* in *Forestry*, the process of growing shade-bearing trees among taller ones which they may eventually replace.

1914 G. JEKYLL *Colour in Flower Garden* (ed. 3) ix. 86 [Variegated mint] is one of the prettiest things as an underplanting to anything of white or yellow colour. **1928** R. S. TROUP *Silvicultural Systems* xv. 170 Underplanting of the thinned coppice and standards should be carried out with shade-bearers only. **1953** H. L. EDLIN *Forester's Handbk.* vii. 108 As a rule the purpose of underplanting is to raise a successor crop, to supersede the present main one, which will gradually be eliminated. **1962** R. PAGE *Educ. of Gardener* iii. 99 The Shablikine roses share a terrace with an underplanting of agapanthus. **1978** *Country Life* 10 Aug. 367/1 There is an extensive pinetum in which the trees are sufficiently widely spaced to allow generous underplanting.

underplay, *v.* Add: **3.** *Theatr.* To underact (a part); to perform with deliberate restraint. Also *fig.* **a.** *intr.*

1896 G. B. SHAW *Let.* 16 Mar. (1965) I. 612 Waring.. will not exactly fail: he will only underplay, and all the papers will treat him with great politeness. **1962** *Movie* Dec. 10/2 In *Dawn Patrol* we underplayed, dispensing with the emoting and ham-acting. **1975** *New Yorker* 17 Nov. 159/1 Tiant..did not have full command of his breaking stuff and was forced to underplay.

b. *trans.*

1897 [see *ROUTINE *v.*]. **1941** B. SCHULBERG *What makes Sammy Run?* xi. 208 He came in quietly, underplaying the scene. **1976** *Daily Tel.* 11 Aug. 9/8 Whatever happened..to the amazing gift Mr Williams showed here for underplaying his lines?..In the Hancock world..he let the character..speak.

4. *fig.* To play down the importance of (something); to present less emphatically than usual.

1949 M. MEAD *Male & Female* v. 124 So among the Arapesh the six-year-olds are treated gently, their sex underplayed. **1965** *New Statesman* 16 Apr. 599/3 They slowly start approaching the peasants, buying provisions at high prices and..underplaying their communist identity. **1973** C. BONINGTON *Next Horizon* iii. 60 The others had tried to underplay my narrow escape, but she had heard them talk about it amongst themselves. **1980** *Amer. Speech* LV. 120 Scargill's book underplays, to some extent, the influence of America on Canadian English. **1983** R. SCRUTON *Aesthetic Imagination* ii. 15 The point of under-playing intention is to insist on the public character of the aesthetic object.

Hence **underplay·ed** *ppl. a.*, **underplay·ing** *vbl. sb.*

1896 G. B. SHAW *Let.* 16 Mar. (1965) I. 612 XYZ's underplaying will not hurt Janet. **1951** T. STERLING *House without Door* iii. 26 It was not much different from any other bar..but it had a kind of underplayed elegance which he liked. **1962** *Listener* 13 Dec. 1025/1 Kenneth More's easy underplaying adapts to the television screen much better than one might have thought. **1973** J. J. MCKELVEY *Man against Tsetse* ii. 83 Davies' analysis of the controversy stressed the underplayed contributions of Nabarro and Baker.

underpri·vilege. [f. next.] The state of being underprivileged; lack of what are considered the normal amenities of life.

1937 *Nation* 25 Sept. 324/2 The greater part of the book deals with the factors that underlie the spread and control of syphilis, its relation to poverty, underprivilege, [etc.]. **1966** P. SCOTT *Jewel in Crown* v. 207 He..had so obviously set his heart on lifting himself by his bootstraps from the state of underprivilege into which he had been born. **1976** *Times* 8 Nov. 3/2 The probation service..has a duty to oppose policies which intensify underprivilege.

underpri·vileged, *a.* (and *sb.*) [UNDER-[1] 10 b.] **1.** Less privileged than others; *spec.* experiencing a standard of living which falls short of an accepted norm, socially disadvantaged. Chiefly applied to persons.

1896 J. BARNES *Princetonian* xxxiii. 380 It was very quiet in the little square that was filled with nurse-maids and children moving about inside the railings—several little underprivileged ones peering in at them from the outside. **1935** Z. N. HURSTON *Mules & Men* 18 These people, being usually under-privileged, are the shyest. **1939** C. R. COOPER *Designs in Scarlet* ii. 27 Don't try to say that the problem is one of 'underprivileged districts', and not of such surroundings as yours. **1948** 'J. TEY' *Franchise Affair* xiii. 140 He wrote a..letter about her.. pointing out how under-privileged she had been. **1960** M. SPARK *Bachelors* viii. 109, I was definitely underprivileged by birth..though not delinquent. **1978** K. HUDSON *Jargon of Professions* iv. 96 Writers and speakers on education...refer..to..'underprivileged children'.

2. *absol.* as *sb.* with *the.*

1935 A. P. HERBERT *What a Word!* iii. 46 She had spent a long time persuading one of the 'underprivileged' to go to hospital to have an operation. **1945** 'L. LEWIS' *Birthday Murder* (1951) iii. 36 Not infrequently he got drunk, coming home late from some revel with the underprivileged. **1977** M. DRABBLE *Ice Age* I. 34 They did not read novels, or go to good films, or read the arts pages of newspapers, or listen to music or discuss the problems of the underprivileged.

under-rea·d, *v.* [UNDER-[1] 10 a.] **a.** *trans.* (See quot. 1934.) **b.** *intr.* Of a gauge, dial, etc.: to show a reading lower than the true one. **c.** *trans.* Of the reading public: to read (an author, a book, etc.) with less than normal frequency or with less than due appreciation.

1934 WEBSTER, *Underread*,..to take a reading below the correct reading of (a test); to read (a temperature, measurement, weight, etc.) as lower than that actually registered. **1975** *Daily Tel.* 7 May 12/4 Under an EEC directive..it would be illegal for speedometers to under-read at all. **1977** *Lancet* 30 Apr. 952/1 The device over-read the systolic pressure by an average of 2.7 mm Hg (S.D. 5.2) and under-read the diastolic pressure by an average of 2.4 mm Hg (S.D. 9.3). **1982** E. DIPPLE *Iris Murdoch* p. ix, Although the role of critic as evangelist may seem questionable, it strikes me as necessary, given the current tendency to under-read and underestimate Murdoch's work. **1984** *N. & Q.* June 274/2 Some progress is made towards consolidating that concept through isolating characteristic aspects of fiction by under-read, minor, and 'popular' novelists as well as by those more familiar names later accorded their separate chapters.

u·nderreamer. *Oil Industry.* [UNDER-[1] 5 b.] A drilling bit that can be used to drill a hole below the casing, of sufficient size for the casing to be lowered further. So **u·nderreaming** *vbl. sb.*

1912 Under-reamer [see *ROTARY *a.* 2 c]. **1922** D. T. DAY *Handbk. Petroleum Industry* I. 246 Underreaming is accomplished through the medium of an ingeniously designed bit (termed an 'underreamer,' because it reams under the casing). **1939** D. HAGER *Fund. Petroleum Industry* viii. 186 If for any reason the hole has been cased at a certain depth and it is necessary to carry the same diameter of hole deeper without removing the casing, an underreamer is used.

under-reco·rd, *v.* [UNDER-[1] 10 a.] *trans.* **a.** To make too few recordings of (a work or performer). Chiefly *pass.* **b.** To record using too low a signal, so that the sound is obscured by other sounds or by instrument noise. **c.** To record (data, information, etc.) insufficiently or inadequately. So **under-reco·rded** *ppl. a.*, **under-reco·rding** *vbl. sb.*

1958 P. GAMMOND *Decca Bk. Jazz* xv. 183 There was Teddy Weatherford, a most able but under-recorded musician. **1962** *John o' London's* 18 Jan. 66/3 Nobody can complain that Britain's favourite oratorio is under-recorded. **1968** P. OLIVER *Screening Blues* iii. 122 Though Sunnyland Slim's stentorian voice was under-recorded, his shouting style of blues singing could be heard outlining the vocal line with its exaggerated rise. **1971** H. WILSON *Labour Govt.* (1974) xxxv. 911 It became clear that for four or five years our national export figures had been increasingly under-recorded. *Ibid.* 913 In the autumn of 1970 the statisticians had discovered that the 1970 figures were still subject to substantial under-recording. **1977** *Gramophone* Mar. 1481/2 One can under-record to a peak of a few dB below zero on the VU meter. **1980** *Times Lit. Suppl.* 31 Oct. 1232/4 Such crucial problems as how to compensate for the under-recording of the activities of the poorer inhabitants of Halesowen.

under-rehea·rsal. [UNDER-[1] 10 b.] Insufficient rehearsal of a play, piece of music, etc., for performance. Hence **under-rehearsed** *a.*

1900 G. B. SHAW *Let.* 30 Dec. (1972) II. 215 The second performance has all the flatness of a second night plus the effects of under rehearsal. **1937** *Discovery* Nov. 331/1 The major difficulty with the B.B.C. transmissions is under-rehearsal. **1960** *Times* 24 Nov. 8/5 The performance itself had an air of under-rehearsal. **1963** *Times* 7 Mar. 15/5 Those under-rehearsed in the intrigues of the narratives can suck them out from his obliquities. **1982** J. SHERWOOD *Shot in Arm* vi. 51 The show was badly under-rehearsed.

under-repo·rt, *v.* [UNDER-[1] 10 a.] To fail to report (income, events, information, etc.) fully. So **under-repo·rted** *ppl. a.*, **under-repo·rting** *vbl. sb.*

1959 *Washington Post* 12 Nov. A2/1 Harrington..made public Tuesday night that new steps are needed to deal with the 'shocking' problem of under-reporting of income. *Ibid.*, Americans 'under-reported' their 1957 income by about $24 billion. **1972** *Science* 26 May 857/2 He found that people underreported both their use and knowledge of contraceptives. **1976** A. GREY *Bulgarian Exclusive* v. 35 Bulgaria's the most under-reported, unnoticed East European country of 'em all. **1980** *Sci. Amer.* Oct. 70/2 The actual total was surely higher, not only because of countries not included in the survey but also because of underreporting in the records of those countries that were included.

underri·de, *v.* [UNDER-[1] 4 b.] **a.** *trans.* To form the basis on which (something) occurs; cf. OVERRIDE *v.* 3 a. *rare.*

1956 M. DUGGAN in C. K. Stead *N.Z. Short Stories* (1966) 84 It underrode everything and was to him no more than suspected.

b. *Geol.* Of a mass of rock, water, etc.: to move underneath (another mass).

1970 *Bull. Geol. Soc. Amer.* LXXXI. 1665/1 The seismically active zone of movement..between the moving oceanic crust and upper mantle, and the relatively stationary material that it underrides. **1977** A. HALLAM *Planet Earth* 54/2 Sediment-charged rivers spread material out over the lake floor by under-riding the lake water.

under-ru·ff, *v.* *Bridge.* [UNDER-[1] 10 a, b.] *intr.* To undertrump. Also as *sb.*

1945 'S. J. SIMON' *Why You lose at Bridge* 151 He made a gallant attempt to avert the impending squeeze by under-ruffing with the seven of Hearts. **1960** T. REESE *Play Bridge with Reese* 185 The under-ruff to preserve possibilities is uncommon but worth noting. *Ibid.*, I under-ruff with the 5 of spades. **1964** R. L. FREY *Official Encycl. Bridge* 651/1 In the following deal an underruff was necessary at the third trick, because East could not spare any cards in the side-suits. *Ibid.*, East had a discard problem which he solved by underruffing with the diamond deuce. **1979** *Country Life* 4 Oct. 1127/3 The Rabbit ..underruffed with his Eight. *Ibid.*, Without the underruff the contract would have been secure.

underrun, *sb.* Add: **2.** [UNDER-[1] 10 b: see sense *4 of the vb.] (An instance of) underrunning; the extent to which a programme, project, etc., underruns.

1941 *B.B.C. Gloss. Broadcasting Terms* 34 *Underrun*, extent by which a programme falls short of its allotted time. **1967** A. BATTERSBY *Network Analysis* (ed. 2) xiv. 238 An example is shown in Fig. 14.2, which displays the extent to which the project is ahead of schedule or behind it, referred to respectively as 'over-run' and 'under-run'.

3. [UNDER-[1] 4 d.] The act of running under something, *spec.* (of a vehicle) under the back of the vehicle in front. Used *attrib.* and in *Comb.*, as **underrun bar, bumper,** etc., a guard attached to the back of a large-wheeled vehicle to prevent other vehicles running underneath.

1969 *Jane's Freight Containers 1968–69* 532/1 *Underrun bar*, at the rear of the chassis a massive bumper bar is provided. **1970** *Daily Tel.* 27 May 11/4 What are needed are under-run bumpers or similar protective structures at the rear of lorries, intended to catch a car that might run into them. **1973** *Care on Road* (RoSPA) Feb. 9/1 Referring to under-run accidents on motorways, the report says: 'There were severe and multiple fractures of skull and face with associated brain damage.' **1974** *Ibid.* Oct. 7/2 Some trailer-manufacturers do fit under-run bumpers. **1980** *Daily Tel.* 24 May 30/4 Under-run accidents are one of the most lethal types of collisions, particularly on motorways.

underrun, *v.* Add: **4.** [UNDER-[1] 10 a.] *intr.* Of a broadcast programme, item, etc.: to run for less than its allotted time.

1941 *B.B.C. Gloss. Broadcasting Terms* 34 *Underrun,* to fall short of the allotted time (of a programme). **1962** [see *OVERRUN *v.* 10 d].

5. Of a car: to run under a larger vehicle in front. Cf. *UNDERRUN *sb.* 3.

1972 *Care on Road* (RoSPA) Sept. 9/4 A carefully designed bumper is essential at the rear of every truck. It must be large enough to prevent the car under-running.

under-runner. Add: **3.** [UNDER-[1] 4 a.] A subterranean stream. *N.Z.*

1921 H. GUTHRIE-SMITH *Tutira* v. 34 At last there is created a subterranean stream, or, in shepherd's phrase, an 'under-runner'. **1949** F. SARGESON *I saw in my Dream* II. xiv. 211 It had been one of those under-runners, with the opening all grown over with biddy-bid. **1959** *Mother Earth* Jan. 428 On the down (lower) country, the problem is one of water retention rather than erosion, though there are some bad cases of the latter, consisting mainly of 'under-runners'.

undersa·turated, *ppl. a.* [UNDER-[1] 10 a.] **a.** Not saturated, falling short of being saturated; *spec.* (of a solution) not containing as much solute as is possible in equilibrium conditions.

1832 *Nat. Philos.* (Libr. Useful Knowl.) II. v. ii. 13/1 In a deficiency of fluid, or in matter under-saturated [with electric fluid]. **1957** G. E. HUTCHINSON *Treat. Limnol.* I. ix. 592 It appears that the surface of the lake is significantly undersaturated throughout the spring months. **1961** L. MARTIN *Clinical Endocrinol.* (ed. 3) ii. 56 The arterial blood is chronically under-saturated with oxygen. **1973** *Sci. Amer.* Jan. 105/2 When the bases of the clouds are fairly high and there is a thick layer of warm, undersaturated air below them.

b. *Petrol.* Of a rock or magma: containing insufficient free silica (or some other specified oxide) to saturate all the bases present; consisting wholly or partly of undersaturated minerals. Of a mineral: unable to form in the presence of free silica; unsaturated.

1913 S. J. SHAND in *Geol. Mag.* Decade V. x. 510 An undersaturated magma (i.e. one which on solidifying would give rise to a partsaturated or unsaturated rock) is capable of entering into chemical combination with the silica of invaded rock masses. **1947,** etc. [see *OVERSATURATED *ppl. a.*]. **1965** G. J. WILLIAMS *Econ. Geol. N.Z.* xi. 168/2 A very fine-grained phonolite or undersaturated trachyte of high soda content. **1983** D. S. BARKER *Igneous Rocks* xi. 259 All xenoliths for which a mantle origin seems likely have been found in silica-undersaturated rocks.

u:ndersatura·tion. [UNDER-[1] 10 b.] The state of being undersaturated.

1913 S. J. SHAND in *Geol. Mag.* Decade V. X. 510 It will also be desirable to distinguish partsaturated rocks.. from wholly unsaturated ones; as a general term to cover both partsaturation and unsaturation we may employ *undersaturation.* **1957** G. E. HUTCHINSON *Treat. Limnol.* I. ix. 595 Both supersaturations and undersaturations are likely to be recorded at the time of vernal circulation. **1978** *Nature* 19 Oct. 639/1 Magmas with increasing degrees of undersaturation can be produced only by progressively decreased amounts of partial melting of a peridotitic upper mantle if H_2O is the only volatile component present. **1981** *Jrnl. Chem. Physics* LXXIV. 5243/2 The theory predicts evaporation rates at any degree of undersaturation.

underscore, *v.* Add: **b.** *fig.* To point up, to emphasize, to reinforce; = UNDERLINE *v.*[2] 1 b.

1891 [in Dict.]. **1939** *Sun* (Baltimore) 17 Apr. 8/2 A look at the gold statistics underscores the fears which are so often expressed on this score. **1952** S. KAUFFMANN *Philanderer* (1954) iv. 58 He could feel the stupidity of what he was writing being underscored by the stupidity of what was being written in the editorial rooms next door. **1966** D. F. GALOUYE *Lost Perception* iv. 37 Headquarters would not be caught unawares. And, in the interest of underscoring that point, the International Guard detail had been tripled. **1979** *Nature* 13 Sept. 98/1 The near catastrophe this year at the nuclear plant at Three Mile Island, Pennsylvania, has underscored dangers which could arise even in the absence of war. **1984** *Toronto Star* 28 Mar. A 3/1 The report..underscores the common complaint made by several groups about institutional racism.

underscoring *vbl. sb.* (earlier and later examples).

1751 RICHARDSON *Clarissa* (ed. 3) VII. xcix. 386 You will perhaps, Mr. Walton, wonder at the meaning of the lines drawn under many of the words and sentences (*underscoring* we call it). **1941** [see *PURPLE *a.* 3]. **1983** *N. & Q.* Apr. 100/2 The use of an emboldening effect for titles makes the volume easier on the eye than does the usual method of underscoring.

underscrub. Add: **2.** (Earlier examples.)

1870 S. F. PRENTICE *Tale of N.Z.* (MS.) 56 To force a passage through lighter underscrub. **1891** [see *FALL *v.* 51 c].

Hence **u·nderscrubbing** *vbl. sb. N.Z.*, the cutting down of underscrub.

1935 N. R. MCKENZIE *Gael fares Forth* vi. 79 To the younger boys was assigned the task of 'under-scrubbing' or cutting the small trees, shrubs, vines..and other plants which grow so luxuriantly on the forest floor. **1948** D. L. G. MUNDY *There's Gold in Hills* ix. 83 The underscrubbing in New Zealand would be done for about 4s. to 5s.

u·nderseal, *sb.* Also **Underseal.** [UNDER-[1] 4 d.] A waterproofing material for use as a protective coating on the under-parts of motor vehicles; in the *U.S.*, a proprietary term for a particular brand of this.

1948 *Official Gaz.* (U.S. Patent Office) 14 Sept. 307/2 Minnesota Mining & Manufacturing Company... *Underseal* for rust, corrosion and abrasive resistant rubberized coating material. **1964** *Times* 7 Feb. p. iii/4 The wise motorist, for example, protects his new car with Underseal. **1968** BUSBY & HOLTMAN *Main Line Kill* v. 45 The professionals..bring it in pasted on the underneath of their cars with underseal. Jacks would never think of stripping off underseal looking for junk. **1973** *Sci. Amer.* Dec. 138/3 (Advt.), Underbody, wheel arches, longitudinal members and the underside of the luggage-compartment floor carry a thick coating of underseal.

u·nderseal, *v.* [f. prec.: see UNDER-[1] 4 a.] *trans.* To coat (the underbody of a vehicle) with waterproof material. Also *absol.* So **u·ndersealed** *ppl. a.*, **u·ndersealing** *vbl. sb.*

1958 *Autocar* 24 Oct. 658/1 Undersealing of cars. **1960** *Farmer & Stockbreeder* 12 Jan. 108/1 Unitary all-steel construction with undersealed bodies gives extra strength and durability. **1961** *Economist* 21 Oct. 252/2 The body is undersealed. **1963** N. FREELING *Gun before Butter* III. 141 He liked to get a car in good condition; he cursed the cheap peeling chrome..the corner-cutting factories that did not underseal. **1976** *Horse & Hound* 3 Dec. 66/1 (Advt.), These ex-Army Land-Rovers are undersealed from new and have heavy duty chassis, springs and suspension. **1980** *Motoring Which?* July 388/2 '*Rustproofed*', '*undersealed*' and 'Ziebarted' were the terms cropping up most frequently.

under-secretary. Add: *parliamentary under-secretary* (*of State*), a member in a department of State, ranking below a minister: see *PARLIAMENTARY *a.* 1; *permanent under-secretary*: see *PERMANENT *a.* 1 d; also used for various other ranks in the administrative civil service, esp. as a title next below *deputy secretary.*

1904 *Rep. War Office Committee* in *Parl. Papers* 9 (Cd. 1932) VIII. 101 The Council should consist of seven members—four military and three civil—with the Permanent Under-Secretary as Secretary. **1917** G. BELL *Let.* 20 July (1927) II. xvi. 420, I wish you would go and see Sir A. Hirtzel, the Permanent Under-Secretary. **1959** C. DIXON *Civil Service* v. 47 The Administrative Class is the top Class of the Civil Service. Direct entrants come in as Assistant Principals and then proceed by promotion to Principal; the next grades are Assistant Secretary and Under-Secretary (or Assistant Under-Secretary in some departments). **1980** KELLNER & CROWTHER-HUNT *Civil Servants* vii. 167 By the time a civil servant is ripe to join the highest ranks of the Service—Under Secretary, Deputy Secretary and Permanent Secretary—he needs to have acquired certain qualities. *Ibid.* 170 Where Assistant Secretaries handle the details of specific issues, Under Secretaries supervise wide areas of policy.

under-se·xed, *a.* [UNDER-[1] 10 a.] Having a lesser degree of sexual desire than the average; lacking in sexual feelings or desire, uninterested in sexual gratification.

1931 J. S. HUXLEY *What dare I Think?* ii. 61 Grafts and extracts of the reproductive glands have been used successfully in under-sexed cases. **1947** 'N. BLAKE' *Minute for Murder* ix. 207 Alice simply wouldn't understand the feeling of all-for-love. She's madly civilised. And she's under-sexed. **1965** *Mod. Law Rev.* XXVIII. v. 606 To use the words of the learned judge, 'the husband was undersexed'. **1972** H. J. EYSENCK *Psychology is about People* ii. 88 The introvert..is slightly 'under-sexed', but again not unhealthily so.

undershoot, *v.* Add: **1.** *fig.* Also *spec.* of financial performance.

1977 *Daily Tel.* 10 Mar. 21 Evidence that the public sector borrowing requirement is still firmly under control with only a month of the current financial year to go has added to signs that the money supply is also going to undershoot even the lower end of the target range. **1982** *Times* 23 Apr. 21/3 The public sector borrowing requirement in the financial year just ended undershot the Government's original estimate.

2. *trans.* and *intr.* Of an aircraft or pilot: to fail to reach (a designated landing-point) while attempting to land. Cf. *OVERSHOOT *v.* 1 d.

1918 W. G. MCMINNIES *Pract. Flying* v. 79 If he sees that he is going to undershoot, it is a good plan to make another circuit. **1938** *Sun* (Baltimore) 8 Jan. 3/2 He undershot storm-swept Newark airport. **1947** A. C. DOUGLAS *Gliding & Adv. Soaring* 68 If you are still high, wait a bit before turning round into wind, but it is always better to come in slightly high and then do gentle S turns into wind, than undershoot. **1969** *Gloss. Aeronaut. & Astronaut. Terms* (*B.S.I.*) II. 4 *Undershoot,* to land, or to follow an approach path which would cause an aircraft to land, short of the intended area.

Hence **undershoo·ting** *vbl. sb.*

1928 B. STUDLEY *Pract. Flight Training* xxiv. 293 Undershooting is always to be avoided. **1982** *Age* (Melbourne) 3/1 The Treasurer..also outlined 'savings' of $361 million made by the Government on earlier appropriation bills..because of normal undershooting of Budget outlay targets.

u·ndershoot, *sb.* [f. the vb.: cf. *OVERSHOOT *sb.*] The action or result of the vb.; *spec.* in *Electronics*, a small variation in signal immediately before, and in the opposite direction to, a sudden (larger) change.

1934 in WEBSTER. **1938** [see *power approach* s.v. *POWER *sb.*[1] 18]. **1956** AMOS & BIRKINSHAW *Television Engin.* II. i. 26 (*caption*) Waveform of a pulse with undershoot of the leading and trailing edges. **1959** *Listener* 26 Feb. 371/1 The score now stands at two undershoots by the United States to one powerful drive by the Russians. **1969** [see *OVERSHOOT *sb.*]. **1978** *Nature* 12 Oct. 550/1 One of them is a progressive rise in time of the overshoot and undershoot (for spikes following the first) amplitudes with nearly constant firing level. **1982** *Times* 23 Apr. 23/7 When one allows for the adverse impact on Government resources of the civil servants' dispute, the undershoot is larger still.

underside. Add: **2.** *Comb.* **underside-couching,** a form of couching (COUCH *v.* 4 b) in which the couched thread is drawn through the fabric to the underside by each of the couching stitches (cf. *surface couching* s.v. *SURFACE *sb.* 6 d); also **underside-couched** *a.*

1936 *Burlington Mag.* Oct. 182/1 Underside-couching is used for the metal threads, and also for some of the silk ones. *Ibid.* 187/1 The heraldic shields..are underside-couched throughout. **1964** tr. *A. Geijer's Textile Treasures Uppsala Cathedral* 24 Embroidery of multicoloured silk, in split stitch, and gold in underside couching forming a herringbone pattern.

undersle·pt, *ppl. a.* [UNDER-[1] 10 a: cf. *undersleep* vb.] Having had insufficient sleep; suffering from or characterized by lack of sleep.

1943 *Our Towns* (Women's Group on Public Welfare) ii. 23 It has become a commonplace to say that the town child is underslept. **1966** K. AMIS *Anti-Death League* III. 340 Lucy took an illustrated magazine to Churchill's bedside, but she too was underslept, and in a few minutes she nodded off. **1981** P. SHEA *Voices & Sound of Drums* ii. 14 A neglected, underslept appearance.

u·nderslung, *ppl. a.* [UNDER-[1] 4 a.] **a.** *Mech.* That is slung under (another part, etc.), or from the under part of (something).

1909 in WEBSTER. **1920** *Sci. Amer.* 30 Oct. 453/1 Those who have had to do with the handling of lumber have..discovered that..shapes long and narrow..are frequently best manipulated by the aid of an underslung carriage. **1924** S. R. ROGET *Dict. Electr. Terms* 282/1 Underslung Monorail Railway. See Suspended Railway. **1932** S. C. H. DAVIS *Motor Racing* v. 74 The whole of the front axle had parted from its underslung spring on one side. **1951** *Engineering* 14 Sept. 329/1 A marine Diesel engine has an under-slung crankshaft. **1968** *Gloss. Terms Materials Handling* (*B.S.I.*) IV. 8 *Under-slung crane,* a crane in which the travelling end carriage wheels run on the lower flanges of the gantry beams. **1982** *Daily Tel.* 24 May 5/6 Helicopters..hover to lift underslung loads.

b. In various *transf.* and *fig.* uses.

1931 'D. STIFF' *Milk & Honey Route* 216 *To get underslung,* means to ride under a train and have the *shacks* [brakemen] throw things at you, or to have them drag a piece of iron on a string under the car so that, bounding up and down, it will punish you plenty. **1931** F. L. ALLEN *Only Yesterday* vi. 130 Charles G. Dawes..entranced the newspaper-reading public with his picturesque language, his underslung pipe, and his broom-waving histrionics. **1940** *Amer. Speech* XV. 248 Though his figure is somewhat *underslung,* he is by way of being a sportsman. **1978** S. SHELDON *Bloodline* xii. 163 She had a tiny potbelly, and her derrière seemed—this was the only word Elizabeth could think of—underslung.

undersow, *v.* Add: **2.** [UNDER-[1] 4 a.] **a.** To sow (a later-growing crop) on land already seeded with another crop. **b.** To sow land already seeded with (one crop) *with* a second, later-growing crop. Also *absol.*

1950 *N.Z. Jrnl. Agric.* Aug. 145/1 In arable farming districts many spring-sown pastures are established with a cover crop, usually by undersowing the grass mixture on land which is carrying an autumn- or winter-sown cereal. **1951** P. OYLER *Feeding Ourselves* vii. 65 If the wheat has not been under-sown with ryegrass and clover ..the stubble will either be scarified..or it will be shallow ploughed. **1960** *Farmer & Stockbreeder* 5 Jan. 102/3 Also include (or undersow) 15lb per acre Westerwolths ryegrass. **1963** *Times* 10 June 7/2 High Mowthorpe..has grown barley for nine successive years, comparing the effects of giving additional nitrogen, undersowing with trefoil and ploughing in straw. **1981** *Daily Tel.* 21 Sept. 10/8 Partridges..lost a major source of food when the practice of undersowing barley with grass was abandoned from the mid-1960s onwards.

So **undersow·ing** *vbl. sb.*, **undersow·n** *ppl. a.*

1943 H. J. MASSINGHAM *Men of Earth* viii. 142 There was hardly a crop in the garden that was not undersown to another. **1960** *Farmer & Stockbreeder* 12 Jan. 107/2 What is your opinion of sowing seeds along with corn when undersowing is practised? *Ibid.* 1 Mar. 106/2 (Advt.), Particularly recommended for undersown crops. **1963** *Times* 10 June 7/1 Undersown cereals can be difficult to deal with in a wet year where the corn is slow to ripen. **1972** *Nature* 21 Jan. 135/2 Field experiments..using various types of undersowing on the levels of pest insects and their enemies.

underspe·nd, *v.* Add: **2.** [UNDER-[1] 10 a.] To spend less than (an estimate or budget).

Hence **underspe·nding** *vbl. sb.*; **underspe·nt** *ppl. a.*

1890 WEBSTER, Underspend. **1963** [see **overspending* vbl. sb. s.v. *OVERSPEND *v.*]. **1977** *Lancet* 14 May 1065/2 One of the big London authorities for instance, the North West Thames region, underspent its budget by £2.7 million. **1980** *Chem. in Brit.* XVI. 540/2 Sometimes sums of money are available at short notice—maybe several thousands of pounds of an underspent budget have to be allocated quickly. **1982** *Daily Tel.* 24 Mar. 2/7 Council leaders will seek to reassure Mr Heseltine by saying that they traditionally underspend budgets.

u·nderspend, *sb.* [f. the vb.] An amount (of a budget, etc.) unspent; a shortfall in the amount expected to be spent.

1982 *Jrnl. R. Soc. Arts* Apr. 269/1 The ability to seek to have certain categories of 'underspend' and excess receipts revoted into the following year. **1982** *Sunday Times* 25 Apr. 49/1 The underspend emerged suddenly, at the last moment. **1983** *Hansard Commons* 27 Apr. 868 It looks as though Sheffield might end up with an underspend this year.

understaffing, *vbl. sb.* [UNDER-[1] 10 a.] Inadequate staffing; employment of an insufficient number of staff.

1957 *Economist* 28 Dec. 1142/1 The strong feeling that understaffing lay at the root of the Windscale accident.. is confirmed by the report. **1963** *Times* 17 Apr. 5/2 One of the reasons for the present difficulties was the extreme understaffing in the Home Office forensic science laboratory. **1981** R. D. EDWARDS *Corridors of Death* xi. 48 The problems caused by new legislation, under-staffing and all those other obstacles to achievement.

understair(s. Add: **2.** Also *attrib.*

1976 *Cumberland & Westmorland Herald* 4 Dec. 16/3 (Advt.), Understairs cupboard. **1977** *36 Home Handyman Projects* (Austral. Home Jrnl.) 62 Understairs storage is invaluable, so..why not make use of it by modifying these ideas.

understandabi·lity. The quality of being understandable.

1934 in WEBSTER. **1947** [see *IDEAL *a.* 1 c]. **1976** *Economist* 31 July 4 Perhaps such a system would not be as statistically fair as some other suggestions but fairness would not be bought at the expense of understandability.

understa·ndably, *adv.* [f. UNDERSTANDABLE *a.*: see -ABLY.] For understandable reasons; in a manner that can be understood.

1921 in Dict. s.v. UNDERSTANDABLENESS. **1928** *Daily Tel.* 10 Jan. 10/6 The members of the Fascist Militia.. might understandably display an aggressive consciousness of their position and power. **1964** *Times* 11 Feb. 11/6 Though it is understandably difficult to find direct evidence, Mr. Wood and officials of both B.R.S. and the major haulage firms are certain that large-scale abuses of the existing laws and trade union agreements are taking place. **1979** A. MCCOWEN *Young Gemini* 75 There was a seventy-five year-old character man in the company who sulked understandably at having to play my son.

understanding, *vbl. sb.* Add: **5. b.** (Earlier example.)

1803 G. COLMAN *John Bull* III. ii. 37 Sit down, and compose yourself, my love; the gentleman and I shall soon come to an understanding.

6. a. (Earlier example.)

1789 G. PARKER *Life's Painter of Variegated Characters* v. 36 He [*sc.* a cobbler] had frequently furnished men of the first rank (bishops not excepted) with *understandings* of the best sort.

understanding, *ppl. a.* Add: **4.** Of a person, etc.: displaying sympathetic tolerance; of a forgiving nature or temperament.

1913 E. C. BENTLEY *Trent's Last Case* xiii. 251, I felt that..I must speak to you about this... Because you seemed to me an understanding person. **1929** E. BOWEN *Last September* xviii. 228 You had always been so understanding. **1959** G. FREEMAN *Jack would be Gentleman* v. 100 Oh thank you... You are understanding. **1974** 'R. TATE' *Birds of Bloodied Feather* iii. 64 Thank you for writing such an understanding note to me about my sister.

understated, *ppl. a.* [UNDER-[1] 10 a. Cf. UNDERSTATE *v.*] **a.** Stated below what is adequate or sufficient; that understates the truth.

1937 E. AMBLER *Uncommon Danger* xviii. 275 Zaleshoff gave a brief and, Kenton thought, grossly understated account of their night's adventure. **1978** *Language* LIV. 158 This is most clearly exemplified in his chapter on social class and language, where he discusses criticisms of the work of Bernstein (under the somewhat understated subheading, 'A small misunderstanding?'). **1982** BARR & YORK *Official Sloane Ranger Handbk.* 10/2 The royal family are pretty good here with their understated asides about 'living above the shop' and 'family business'.

b. Of clothes, appearance, etc.: unemphasized, modest; designed not to attract undue attention. Cf. QUIET *a.* 2 b.

1957 *Punch* 6 Feb. 224/1 The clothes..were in good taste, wearable and, to borrow a word much in vogue, *understated*—or, to use one's own word, dull. **1963** *Harper's Bazaar* Feb. 41 Catching up with fashion..in this era of understated looks. **1967** MRS. L. B. JOHNSON *White House Diary* 8 Oct. (1970) 578, I changed again into another quiet understated outfit. **1979** R. JAFFE *Class Reunion* (1980) 15 Emily had longed for a camel's hair coat like Daphne's—understated, sophisticated, collegiate.

understatement. Add: **b.** The quality of being understated (sense *b) or modest in design.

1967 *Guardian* 21 July 7/4 The kind of subtly simple dress..that 'Vogue' would call understated... Understatement is the thing. **1977** 'J. FRASER' *Hearts Ease in Death* xiii. 142 Her simple Hardy Amies dresses, designed with all the understatement..that had become the Queen's dressmaker's hallmark.

u·nderstater. [f. UNDERSTATE *v.* + -ER[1].] One who understates or avoids overstatement.

1957 *New Yorker* 2 Nov. 114/3 Mr. Sinatra..is probably not a natural-born understater. **1977** P. USTINOV *Dear Me* vii. 96 Britain had already supplied Hollywood with a whole battalion of elegant understaters, immaculate actors of the Du Maurier school, who..were able to play anything..without their assumed characters..being allowed to affect their performances.

understeer, *sb.* [UNDER-[1] 10 b.] A tendency in a motor vehicle to take too wide a turn when made to deviate from the straight.

1936 [see *OVERSTEER *sb.*]. **1957** S. MOSS *In Track of Speed* xii. 149, I..watched Castellotte sorting out his Ferrari, the front wheels on full understeer with the inside one off the ground. **1964** *Which?* Apr. 36/2 The *Bedford Romany* had light steering and very little understeer—it was hardly necessary to turn the steering wheel more when going faster round a bend. **1971** *Daily Tel.* 31 Mar. 11/5 A disadvantage of the bigger engine is the heavier steering and even more marked understeer, made worse by the steep roll angles in fast cornering. **1981** G. G. HILDITCH *Further Look at Buses* i. 8/2 You make your approach run perhaps changing down..and then wind on a bit of lock. The bus doesn't notice thanks to a wonderful degree of understeer so you add a few more degrees..and the resulting oversteer runs away with you.

understeer, *v.* Add: **2.** [Under-[1] 10 a.] *intr.* To exhibit understeer. Hence **u·ndersteering** *vbl. sb.* and *ppl. a.*

1936 *Proc. Inst. Automobile Engineers* XXX. 730 If a car under-steers, more rudder is required at the higher speeds. *Ibid.*, The under-steering of the parallel front road springs is..due to the lack of cornering power. **1948** R. DEAN-AVERNS *Automobile Chassis Design* ii. 49 Understeering vehicles,..when put into a turn, endeavour to straighten up and require constant *increase* of lock as the speed on the bend is increased. **1966** J. MILES in T. Wisdom *High-Performance Driving* v. 47 If the wheels are pointing exactly round the line of the circle some cars will actually travel in a wider circle. These are under-steering cars. **1970** *Motoring Which?* Apr. 45/1 Both tended to understeer (run wide of the corners). **1972** *Sci. Amer.* Aug. 20/2 Of the three characteristics understeering is the most desirable.

u·nderstorey. Also **-story.** [UNDER-[1] 5 d.] The (layer of) vegetation growing beneath the level of the tallest trees in a forest. Cf. UNDERWOOD 1. Also *attrib.*

1945 *Ecology* XXVI. 280/1 The setback in growth for the dominant trees..may occur because of too dense a hardwood understory. **1958** *New Biol.* XXV. 62 The removal of the dense shrub understorey of rhododendron and laurel from another catchment increased the yield of water. **1970** *New Scientist* 30 Apr. 212/1 The total removal of herb and scrub understory removes a habitat diversity which makes young conifer plantations so attractive to wildlife. **1975** W. CONDRY *Pathway to Wild* xi. 191 A woodland bird reserve needs a wealth of understorey shrubs for birds to nest in. **1983** M. GEE *Sole Survivor* xxi. 224 Although the sun spreads a watery light in the understoreys of the bush the cold stays on.

understudy, *v.* Add: **3.** *intr.* To act as an understudy.

1909 in WEBSTER. **1939** W. FORTESCUE *There's Rosemary* x. 74 He was very kind and encouraging, but assured me that I should only waste my time in London, understudying and playing small parts. **1962** J. MCCABE *Mr. Laurel & Mr. Hardy* i. 26 He went on as a single again..and understudied for *Home from the Honeymoon.*

undertaking, *vbl. sb.* **1. d.** (Earlier example.)

1843 DICKENS *Mart. Chuz.* (1844) v. 52 There's other businesses. Undertaking, now. That's gloomy.

underthru·st, *v. Geol.* [UNDER-[1] 4 b.] *trans.* To be forced underneath. Chiefly as **underthru·st** *ppl. a.*, **u·nderthrusting** *vbl. sb.*

1893 E. A. SMITH in *Amer. Jrnl. Sci.* CXLV. 306, I..suggest the following terms, *under fault, faulted under fold, underthrust fault*, as applicable to this type of structure. **1908** H. B. C. SOLLAS tr. *Suess's Face of Earth* III. ix. 396 Holmquist concludes that, owing to the continuous subsidence of the eastern part (i.e. of the shield or foreland) the overthrusting practically becomes an underthrusting. **1931** *Geol. Mag.* LXVIII. 39 The front of the underthrust mass will be concave towards the direction of underthrusting. **1965** G. J. WILLIAMS *Econ. Geol. N.Z.* xix. 350/1 The south-east flank is steep and in places faulted or underthrust. **1971** I. G. GASS et al. *Understanding Earth* xix. 286 The major mountain chains..occur where moving plates collide and one underthrusts the other. **1977** [see *RICHTER].

underti·p, *v.* [f. UNDER- 10 a + TIP *v.*[4]] To give an inadequate or insufficient gratuity to (one who has been of service). Hence **underti·pped** *ppl. a.*

1975 'A. HALL' *Mandarin Cypher* iv. 64, I got out and paid and under-tipped..but..he went away happy.. with a Hong Kong dollar. **1979** *Guardian* 4 Aug. 19/3 The undertipped taxi-driver who returned his passenger's gratuity. **1984** *New Yorker* 24 Dec. 37/1 My twenty-five-year-old daughter undertipped the airline porter.

undertone, *sb.* **1. a.** (Earlier example.)

1762 D. GARRICK *Let.* 24 Jan. (1831) I. 135 It naturally gives him a slow tremulous under-tone of voice.

u·ndertread. [UNDER- 5 d.] A layer of reinforcement in a rubber tyre.

1968 *Wall St. Jrnl.* (Eastern ed.) 29 Jan. 11 The new tire is made with a rubber impregnated mat of steel wire under the tread. Called a reinforced undertread, the mat contains about 80,000 pieces of wire. **1971** *Flying* Apr. 7/1 (Advt.), A deep undertread adds muscle... Next time you buy tires, ask for Goodyear's Flight Custom. **1982** *Coal Age* Apr. 140/2 An undertread or protective cushion of rubber can also be placed on all three tire designs between the tread..and body ply.

undertreat, *v.* Add: Also, to provide with insufficient (medical, etc.) treatment.

1908 H. JAMES *Portrait of a Lady* I. p. xxi, So early was to begin my tendency to overtreat, rather than undertreat..my subject. **1979** [see *underdiagnose* vb. s.v. *UNDERDIAGNOSIS].

u·ndertrial. *India.* [UNDER-[2].] A person held in custody awaiting trial.

1966 *Times of India* 5 May 9/4 An infuriated group of about 50 undertrials tore down the walls of the judicial lock-up. **1979** V. L. PANDIT *Scope of Happiness* xv. 102 The Allahabad District Jail..was used for under-trials or for those prisoners about to be released after completion of their term in other parts of the province.

u·ndertrick. *Bridge.* [UNDER-[1] 10 b.] A trick required to make up the number of the bid or contract, but not taken. Also *attrib.*

1908 *Laws of Auction Bridge* § 50 When he fails, his adversaries score, above the line, 50 points for each undertrick, *i.e.*, each trick short of the number declared. **1929** M. C. WORK *Compl. Contract Bridge* i. 4 Vulnerable.. seems appropriate enough when it increases the losses for undertricks. **1952** J. B. PICK *Phoenix Dict. Games* 266 Undertrick points—that is, penalty points when declarer fails to fulfil his contract—are scored by opponents above the line. **1981** REESE & DORMER *Bridge Player's Alphabetical Handbk.* III. 220 (*heading*) Penalties for undertricks. *Ibid.*, Not vulnerable, 50 a trick. Doubled, 100 for the first undertrick, 200 for each subsequent one.

under-u·se, *sb.* [UNDER-[1] 10 b.] Insufficient use (of a facility, etc.); use below the optimum level.

1960 *Guardian* 26 Nov. 2/7 There might, in some places, be a considerable 'under-use' of [parking] meters. **1971** *Country Life* 18 Feb. 348/2 Under-use leads to poor maintenance of roofs, gutters and party walls. **1975** *Physics Bull.* Sept. 411/3 A current wastage of communication in research (due to underuse of existing services) of the order of 9%.

under-u·se, *v.* [UNDER-[1] 10 a.] *trans.* To make insufficient use of (a facility, etc.); to use (something) below the optimum level. So **under-u·sed** *ppl. a.*

1960 *Farmer & Stockbreeder* 8 Mar. 51/2 Farming can have no overwhelming case to retain all its present land while it is so obvious that some of it is still under-used. **1970** *Guardian* 9 Nov. 10/2 A country can never recover by persistently under-using its resources, as Britain has done for too long. **1976** *Field* 18 Nov. 948/1 The substantial amount of derelict and under-used land which exists in urban areas..indicates that these transfers could be reduced to not more than 29,700 acres per year.

under-u·tilize, *v.* [UNDER-[1] 10 a.] *trans.* To make use of (equipment, resources, etc.) insufficiently or below the optimum level; to underuse. So **u:nder-utiliza·tion** *sb.*, **under-u·tilized** *ppl. a.*

1954 *Newsweek* 29 Nov. 89/1 Underutilization of capacity in some lines is inevitable for some time. **1958** *Economist* 18 Oct. 204/1 Mr Amory may go on living down to his..nickname of Derick-or-little-by-little this winter (when industrial capacity may be unnecessarily underutilised). **1964** K. G. LOCKYER *Introd. Critical Path Anal.* viii. 83 To increase utilization it is common practice to employ the under-utilized resources on another project. **1977** *Lancet* 2 July 26/2 The cause of the lactic acidosis is almost certainly both underutilisation of lactic acid as well as overproduction. **1978** *N.Y. Times* 30 Mar. A 15/1 The small-boat mariners have turned to the 'junk fish', or underutilized species like perch and pollock, while waiting out the 12-day Federal ban on cod.

underway·, *adv.* [The phr. *under way* s.v. WAY *sb.*[1] 38 taken as one word.] **a.** *Naut.* Of a vessel: under way; having begun to move through the water.

1934 W. NELSON *Seaplane Design* vi. 67 The depth of the step affects..the moment to change trim when underway near the planing speed. **1940** P. V. H. WEEMS *Marine Navigation* (1941) v. 82 Before getting underway the navigator should determine by azimuth or by a known true bearing of a prominent object whether any error exists in the compass reading. **1978** *Sunday Mail* (Brisbane) *Boating Suppl.* 26 Nov. 16/6 Technically a vessel is underway when not moored, at anchor or aground.

b. *transf.* Of a process, project, activity, etc.: having begun, in progress, being done or carried out. Of a person: having started doing something.

1935 *Sci. Amer.* Apr., 198/1 Uncle Sam now has underway one of his greatest construction projects. **1950** *Chem. Engin. Progress* XLVI. 112/1 Construction should be underway by 1952. **1955** [see *PROGRAM, PROGRAMME *sb.* 2 b]. **1973** M. AMIS *Rachel Papers* 23 Once underway, though, Gloria would have been able to detect few noteworthy points of contrast between sexual arousal and rabies. **1976** *New Scientist* 16 Dec. 660/2 Experiments.. with an electro-optically q-switched neodymium-glass laser are underway. **1981** W. BOYD *Good Man in Africa* II. ix. 124 They walked arm-in-arm into the club where the dance was underway.

underwear. (Earlier examples.)

1872 *Picayune* (New Orleans) 2 Apr. 6/1 (Advt.), Ladies' underwear... Best Merino Undershirts, fine finish;..fine French corsets. **1875** *Cassell's Family Mag.* I. 113/2 It will scarcely be necessary to give the address where the patterns of hygiene 'under-wear' are to be obtained. It would be more to the purpose to tell how the so-called 'under-wear' is made and trimmed in Paris.

underweight, *sb.* Add: **2. a.** The condition or quality of being lighter than average for one's height and build.

1935 H. S. DIEHL *Textbk. Healthful Living* x. 143 Both underweight and overweight are handicaps to employment,..for women overweight is a greater handicap than underweight. **1952** R. MACAULAY *Let.* 16 May (1961) 313, I suspect that thinness and under-weight may be a physical quality that you and I share.

b. [Absol. use of adj.] An underweight person.

1910 A. BRYCE *Laws of Life & Health* vii. 247 It is quite a common thing for underweights to live to eighty, ninety, or even a hundred. **1935** H. ROBERTS *Everyman in Health & Sickness* II. iv. 152 The longest lived are found among the underweights.

underwei·ght, *a.* Also **under-weight.** [UNDER-².] **a.** Not sufficiently heavy, lacking in weight; *spec.* of a person: lighter than average for one's height and build; too thin.

1899 [see *OVER-WEIGHT *a.*]. **1925** C. E. TURNER *Personal & Community Health* ii. 53 The underfed person drags himself about—underweight, pale,..and pessimistic. **1971** 'D. HALLIDAY' *Dolly & Doctor Bird* i. 5 He was a tall, underweight man in his early thirties. **1979** *Irish Times* 28 Sept. 3/6 Two British boats had been found to be underweight but no action was taken.

b. *fig.*

1960 T. REESE *Play Bridge with Reese* 15 Partner is sufficiently pleased with the result not to notice that I was under-weight for my medium no-trump. **1977** *Time* 26 Sept. 42/1 The plot of *Annie Hall* has the two underweight egos twine together, rose and briar. **1985** *Times* 11 Jan. 17/6 With many institutional investors still underweight, the price is set to move up.

underwhe·lm, *v. joc.* [f. UNDER-¹ 10 a, after OVERWHELM *v.*] *trans.* To leave unimpressed, to arouse little or no interest in. Chiefly as **underwhe·lmed** *pa. pple.* and *ppl. a.*, and **underwhe·lming** *ppl. a.*

1956 T. K. QUINN *Giant Corporations* viii. 61 He wrote..commending the action of one of the giant corporations for a..price reduction at a time when prices were rising. I was underwhelmed, and investigated. **1968** *Punch* 17 July 81/2, I agree that the wretched parents are not to be penalised till 1969 and I'm sure they are under-whelmed with gratitude. **1970** *Daily Colonist* (Victoria, B.C.) 3 July 47/1 Victoria Fair got off to a quite underwhelming start..with a concert in the University of Victoria gym. **1972** *Times Lit. Suppl.* 29 Dec. 1569/4 Both the prose and the play are underwhelming. **1978** *Ottawa Citizen* 2 Mar. 3/3 The Sparks Street post office ran out of applications..but a survey of other post offices ..showed the public was generally underwhelmed. **1984** *Observer* 15 Jan. 9/3 He was..fluent in speech and crashingly dull. If there was an opportunity to be underwhelming, he unfailingly seized it.

underwing. Add: **1. b.** The part of a bird's body concealed when the wings are folded.

1956 G. DURRELL *Drunken Forest* vi. 110 Two jacanas bathing, their underwings flashing buttercup yellow. **1977** C. MCCULLOUGH *Thorn Birds* iv. 75 Big pale-grey parrots with brilliant purplish-pink breasts, underwings and heads.

3. Also, situated or occurring beneath the wing of an aeroplane.

1946 TAYLOR & ALLWARD *Spitfire* 27 (*caption*) The Spitfire's eye—the underwing camera installation. **1947** *Shell Aviation News* No. 106 23/1 Underwing or integral fuelling of aircraft is receiving a great deal of attention in the United States and Great Britain. **1949** *Gloss. Aeronaut. Terms* (*B.S.I.*) II. 14 *Under-wing radiator*, a radiator fitted below a wing. **1979** J. GARNETT *Backfire is Hostile* xiii. 143 Aircraft are..carrying underwing stores.

underwooded, *a.* (Earlier example.)

1811 [see *oak barren* s.v. *OAK 9].

u·nderwool. [UNDER-¹ 5 a, d.] **1.** Wool used to make underwear; woollen undergarments. *rare*⁻¹.

1910 W. DE LA MARE *Private View* (1953) 223 The typical Englishman..a scorner of great-coats and underwool.

2. A layer of wool lying beneath the outer layer on an animal.

1939 J. S. HUXLEY in *Geogr. Mag.* Dec. 78/2 They [*sc.* Soay sheep] have..the same general colouration..with dense underwool. **1965, 1968** [see *QIVIUT].

underwork, *v.* **2. c.** (Earlier example.)

1869 H. SIDGWICK *Let.* 8 Mar. in A. & E. M. Sidgwick *Henry Sidgwick* (1906) 191, I am rather underworking.

underworld. Add: **4. a.** (Later *fig.* examples.)

1903 J. LONDON in *Ainslie's Mag.* Oct. 76/1 And without a word, when his *wanderlust* gripped him, he was off and away into that great mysterious underworld he called 'The Road'. **1913** C. J. HOGARTH (*title*) Dostoyevsky's Letters from the underworld. **1929** *Amer. Speech* IV. 337 The following word-list..does..record representative words and phrases commonly used by 'knights of the road', 'migratory workers', and denizens of the so-called 'underworld'. **1972** F. FITZGERALD *Fire in Lake* iii. 126 They managed to create an underworld of warlords, secret societies, and bandit groups.

b. *spec.* The world of criminals or of organized crime (usu. with *the*); hence, the inhabitants of this region.

1900 *McClure's Mag.* Aug. 356 (*heading*) True stories from the Underworld. *Ibid.*, Their life amongst them [*sc.* the criminal classes] is not to break laws, but to understand as thoroughly as possible the motives and methods of that great part of the community which they describe as 'The Under-World'. **1903** 'J. FLYNT' *Rise of R. Clowd* iv. 136 Susan was the accepted Queen of the local Under World. **1926** *Westm. Gaz.* 22 Mar., Four of the most dangerous women in London's underworld began long terms of imprisonment during the weekend. **1956** H. KURNITZ *Invasion of Privacy* xxiii. 146 Remember the code of the underworld and what happens to a squealer. **1977** *Time* 8 Aug. 16/2 He..was presumably executed by the underworld. **1981** M. MOORCOCK *Byzantium Endures* ix. 235 Through an acquaintance in the Podol underworld, I had two copies of my passport printed, complete with photographs.

c. The slang of the criminal underworld. *rare*.

1927 *Vanity Fair* (N.Y.) Nov. 132 'Taking him for a ride' is underworld for enticing a person to death.

5. *attrib.* and as *adj.* (esp. in sense *4 b).

1929 D. H. LAWRENCE *Pornography & Obscenity* 12 Genuine pornography is almost always underworld. **1955** D. W. MAURER in *Publ. Amer. Dial. Soc.* XXIV. 12 Perhaps the fact that underworld areas have not been traditionally considered 'respectable' for academic research has discouraged some investigators. **1977** *Time* 4 July 8/2 Widely believed to have underworld as well as high society connections, Riachi was found murdered in his apartment.

Hence **u·nderwo:rldling,** a member of an underworld.

1928 *Tablet* 21 Jan. 89/1 One of the points on which Protestant Underworldlings have agreed to blacken the Church. **1962** N. MARSH *Hand in Glove* v. 157 'What can I do for you, Super?' Moppett asked him with the slight smile of the film underworldling.

underwrite, *v.*¹ Add: **3.** (Further *fig.* examples.) Also, to support or reinforce (an idea, quality, etc.); to lend support to (a party, etc.).

1938 *Sun* (Baltimore) 5 Sept. 6/3 This sectional purpose in the bill was in effect underwritten by the new Administrator. **1962** *Listener* 15 Mar. 480/1 The fact that Hirst was at the Royal College of Art..at the time of that journalistically stimulated style known as 'New Realism', to some extent underwrites this basic quality of factualness in his work. **1965** *Ibid.* 10 June 851/2 We must not always find ourselves underwriting the regimes of yesterday while our opponents support those of tomorrow. **1978** *Jrnl. R. Soc. Arts* CXXVI. 439/1 Their sponsors (usually governments) underwrote the belief that an exhibition's ultimate social and economic benefits would outweigh its immediate costs.

4. c. (Later example.) Also *transf.*, to guarantee by military or other power.

1964 *Ann. Reg. 1963* 224 A free West Berlin could have its social system underwritten by the United Nations, and foreign troops could remain there 'for a certain period' under the U.N. flag. **1979** T. BENN *Arguments for Socialism* ii. 50 Big business..underwrote the cost of the campaign to keep Britain in the Common Market at the time of the 1975 referendum.

underwriting, *vbl. sb.*² *rare*⁻¹. [f. UNDERWRITE *v.*²] Writing with less than acceptable power or fervour, 'low-key' writing.

1938 O. SITWELL *Trio* 69 These days of 'under-writing', as of 'under-acting'.

undescended, *a.* Add: *spec.* in *Med.*, applied to a testis that has not descended into the scrotum from its fœtal position in the abdominal cavity.

1897 in *Lippincott's Med. Dict.* **1901** *Ann. Surg.* XXXIV. 234 The undescended testicle is an extremely interesting organ. **1908**, etc. [see *MALDESCENDED *a.*]. **1964** [see *MALDESCENT]. **1980** *Amer. Jrnl. Roentgenol.* CXXXV. 211/2 Until recently, localization of the undescended testicle has remained a clinical urologic problem.

undesire, *v.* Add: So **undesi·rer** (*rare*).

1945 DYLAN THOMAS in *Horizon* Jan. 13 In the name of the unborn And the undesirers Of midwiving morning's Hands or instruments.

undetectable, *a.* Add: Hence **u:ndetectabi·lity, undete·ctably** *adv.*

1960 *Jrnl. Amer. Chem. Soc.* LXXXII. 673/1 No step corresponding to equation 10 is included because of the undetectability of an uncatalyzed term. **1978** J. MCDOWELL in Hookway & Pettit *Action & Interpretation* 141 How can one derive, from confrontation with a detectable circumstance, an idea of what it would be for a circumstance of some kind to which it belongs to obtain undetectably? **1981** M. SPARK *Loitering with Intent* vi. 108 The point..was undetectably lost in a web of multisyllabic words.

undeveloped, *ppl. a.* Add: (Further examples.) Also, spec. of a film.

1870 DICKENS *Edwin Drood* iii. 18 Triumphs of engineering skill..are to change the whole condition of an undeveloped country. **1911** H. F. HOWARD *India & Gold Standard* p. iii, Conditions in India, as in other undeveloped countries, differ from those in the more advanced countries. **1939** EMANUEL & DASH *All-in-One Camera Bk.* 133 Once they have been exposed, colour films should not be left undeveloped too long. **1959** W. S. SHARPS *Dict. Cinematogr.* 137/2 *Undeveloped*, the term applied to film that has not yet passed through the development stage of processing. **1983** D. FRANCIS *Danger* iii. 39 It was..routine to send the undeveloped films..to the London office.

undies (*v*·ndiz), *sb. pl. colloq.* [f. UNDER- in UNDERGARMENT, UNDERWEAR, etc.] Articles of girls' or women's underclothing.

1906 *Punch* 30 May 384/3 She'd blouses for Sundays, And marvellous 'undies' Concocted of ribbons and lace. **1920** A. BENNETT *Our Women* i. 35 You have only to reflect..upon the astonishing public importance given to what are delicately known as 'undies'. **1939** A. RANSOME *Secret Water* xxvii. 321 Go on, Bridgie. Off with your things. Undies too. **1967** N. FREELING *Strike out where not Applicable* 107 Arlette..knows I'm not just belting off for the afternoon because of the black undies.

undilated, *ppl. a.* (Earlier non-dict. example.)

1858 R. BARNES *Placenta Praevia* iii. 96 At the same time undilated and rigid.

‖**unding** (u·ndiŋ). [Ger., = absurdity.] A non-thing, vague abstraction, or concept having no properties.

1932 H. H. PRICE *Perception* v. 132 It turns out to be a mere *Unding*, in short, to be nothing at all. **1941** *Mind* L. 249 The *bringing about*..is non-existent, an *Unding*. **1950** *Ibid.* LIX. 477 An object without properties is assuredly an *Unding*. **1955** C. S. LEWIS *Surprised by Joy* xiii. 199, I did believe (so far as one can believe in an *Unding*) in the Absolute.

Undinism (*v*·ndīniz'm). *Psychol.* [f. UNDINE (see also Baron F. H. C. La Motte Fouqué *Undine, eine Erzählung* 1811) + -ISM.] (A term proposed for) a strong interest in water and in the urinary function (see quots. 1928 and 1934). Now usu. = *UROLAGNIA.

1928 H. H. ELLIS *Stud. in Psychol. of Sex* VII. vii. 409 The peculiarities of those human water-folk with whom I am here concerned I propose to call by the rather arbitrary but convenient name of *Undinism*. **1933** —— *Psychol. of Sex* iv. 142, I have been accustomed to apply the term Undinism to the frequent presence of an early interest in water in general, and the urinary function in particular, persisting in later life. This interest, not amounting to a definite deviation of the sexual impulse.. is common, especially in women. **1959** *Times Lit. Suppl.* 6 Feb. 65/4 Mr. Collis also avoids the question of the earlier Undinism and Urolagnia. **1977** *Ibid.* 13 May 584/3 Ellis was not homosexual. His 'germ of a perversion' was Undinism (ie watching women pee).

undiplomatic, *a.* Add: Hence **undiploma·tically** *adv.*

1961 R. B. LONG *Sentence & its Parts* 479 He makes his points too undiplomatically. **1969** 'E. LATHEN' *When in Greece* xi. 118 Bill Riemer undiplomatically interrupted.

undipped, *ppl. a.* Add: **3.** Of (the beams of) a headlight of a vehicle: not lowered.

1960 *Guardian* 12 Sept. 2/3 One glaring, undipped.. headlight. **1969** 'A. HALL' *Striker Portfolio* ix. 112 My undipped heads catching the Mercedes full across the screen. **1983** *Times* 23 Dec. 3/6 Once the ignition is switched on the choice will be between dim-dip (dipped headlights with reduced light), full dip and undipped.

undiscriminated, *ppl. a.* Add: (Later examples.) Also with *against*.

1883 F. H. BRADLEY *Princ. Logic* 422 We begin here with a vague and undiscriminated unity. **1890** W. JAMES *Princ. Psychol.* II. xx. 146 All our sensations (however as yet unconnected and undiscriminated) are of extensive objects. **1981** *Observer* 27 Sept. 36/5 Those of my generation and younger who found ourselves undiscriminated against in our respective faculties. **1984** *Times Lit. Suppl.* 23 Mar. 306/3 A recurring topic was the inchoate, undiscriminated bulk of information and misinformation now being stored.

undismayable, *a.* (Later example.)

1940 W. FAULKNER *Hamlet* III. ii. 187 The face.., bent, in profile or three-quarters, sober and undismayable.

undisso·ciated, *a.* *Chem.* [UN-[1] 8 a.] Of a molecule: whole, not split into oppositely charged ions.
1899 *Jrnl. Physical Chem.* III. 284 The properties of this acid are therefore to be attributed almost solely to the undissociated molecule, CH_3·COOH. **1930** FIELD & WEILL *Electro-Plating* i. 14 The undissociated copper sulphate..takes no direct part in the plating process. **1965** PHILLIPS & WILLIAMS *Inorg. Chem.* I. vii. 237 At pressures around 1 atmosphere I_2 is largely undissociated at 1000 °K, but largely dissociated at 2000 °K. **1976** *Electrochimica Acta* XXI. 280/1 The activity coefficient of the undissociated acid is taken as unity.

undi·tch, *v.* [UN-[2] 5.] *trans.* To get (a vehicle, etc.) out of a ditch (by hauling, levering, or the like). So **undi·tching** *vbl. sb.* (usu. *attrib.*).
1920 *Blackw. Mag.* Feb. 272/1 The unditching beam could not be used. **1928** *Daily Tel.* 6 Mar. 9/7 All [the tanks] were either repaired or unditched. **1971** 'D. RUTHERFORD' *Clear Fast Lane* 40 In the [car's] boot were the spares and..a couple of unditching mats.

undivisible, *a.* Delete † *Obs.* and add later example.
1907 G. B. SHAW *John Bull's Other Island* Pref. p. xix, A supporter of Church and State one and undivisible.

undock, *v.* Add: Also *transf.*, to separate a lunar module from its command ship. Also *absol.*
1966 *Time* 23 Sept. 67 On the third day of the flight, Conrad undocked Gemini and used his thrusters to back slowly away from the Agena. **1969** *Observer* 2 Mar. 2/8 The astronauts..will crawl from the command ship through a tunnel into the LEM. They will then undock and separate the LEM from the command ship. **1970** N. ARMSTRONG et al. *First on Moon* xiii. 324 You can undock at your convenience.
Hence **undo·cking** *vbl. sb.*
1966 *Life* 14 Jan. 88 We discussed undocking, but we had to be sure that the tumbling rate at the instant of separation would be low enough to keep us from colliding. **1969** *Daily Tel.* 8 Mar. 1/2 The 'undocking' of the two [modules] was the first step in the dress rehearsal that will have to work equally faultlessly if two Americans are to step on to the moon later this year.

undocumented, *ppl. a.* Add: (Further U.S. examples in *spec.* sense 'not having the appropriate legal document or licence'.) Also *absol.*
1886 *Navigation Laws U.S.* 456 (Index), *Documents* Of vessels, or undocumented. **1919** *Statutes at Large U.S.A.* XL. 602 Every undocumented vessel, operated in whole or in part by machinery,..shall be numbered. **1977** *New Yorker* 23 May 112/3 On the list were, among other things, ..undocumented workers (illegal aliens). **1979** *Tucson* (Arizona) *Citizen* 28 Apr. 6 A/3 The bishop..sees it as an effective way to bring about social change for the elderly, undocumented, alcoholics and drug users. **1984** *New Yorker* 28 May 52/2 When undocumented workers are picked up, the Immigration Service encourages them to accept a sort of plea bargain.

undoing, *vbl. sb.*[1] Add: **5. b.** *Psychoanal.* The obsessive repetition of a ritualistic action as if to undo some previous event, action, or attitude, or to signify that it never happened, usu. a symptom of obsessional neurosis.
1927 L. P. CLARK tr. *Freud's Inhibition, Symptom & Anxiety* vi. 42 The precautionary measures are rational, the abolitions through undoing are irrational, magical in nature. **1960** HINSIE & CAMPBELL *Psychiatric Dict.* (ed. 3) 770/2 Expiatory acts, counter-compulsions, and some forms of compulsive ceremonials and counting compulsions are among the more frequent expressions of undoing. **1965** ROSEN & GREGORY *Abnormal Psychol.* iv. 75/2 A magical attempt to wipe out a real or fancied guilt is termed undoing. The individual engages in ritualistic behavior. **1972** H. J. EYSENCK *Encycl. Psychol.* III. 366/2 *Undoing*, an (inner) defense mechanism which allows appeasement of a guilt feeling about a forbidden motive gratification that has already occurred.

undomesticated, *ppl. a.* (Examples.)
1834 J. S. MILL in *Monthly Repos.* VIII. 411 To remain ..undomesticated and without a home. **1926** G. B. SHAW *Transl. & Tomfooleries* 9 Mrs Billiter, an elderly housekeeper, has something of the same undomesticated air as the room. **1972** P. M. NORTH *Mod. Law Animals* ii. 41 The second category is that of more normally peaceful, but undomesticated, animals.

undrawn, *ppl. a.*[1] Add: **4. c.** Of curtains, etc.: open, not drawn across the window.
1923 E. BOWEN *Encounters* 153 Here the curtains were undrawn and they could see the lights twinkling out in the windows of the other houses. **1940** M. SADLEIR *Fanny by Gaslight* II. 311 The curtains were undrawn and the daylight dim... She rang for the curtains to be drawn and the gas lit. **1954** 'M. COST' *Invitation from Minerva* 84 The Utrecht hangings of scarlet velvet and gold which.. festooned the lower floor windows..were undrawn. **1968** J. FLEMING *Kill or Cure* xv. 203 The thick velvet undrawn curtains.

undress, *sb.* **3.** (Earlier example.)
1777 P. THICKNESSE *Year's Journey* II. 231 You cannot dine, or visit after dinner, in an undress frock.

undre·ssable, *a.* Of a doll: that can be undressed.
1972 *Daily Tel.* 7 Jan. 13 His 6½-year-old sister, longing for a 'mod' but cuddly undressable doll. **1983** *Harrods Mag.* Christmas 194/2 Washable, undressable dolls.

‖ **und so weiter** (unt zo vaɪ·təɹ). Also *occas.* as one word. [Ger.] And so forth.
1885 A. EDWARDES *Girton Girl* I. xiv. 277 One gets beastly weather for this sort of thing. Festive gatherings, I mean, *und so weiter*. **1930** E. POUND *XXX Cantos* xii. 54 First lot mortgaged to buy the second lot, undsoweiter. **1972** J. WAIN in Cox & Dyson *20th-Cent. Mind* I. xi. 366 They..held meetings to study European magic and Eastern philosophy, the fourth dimension, Odic force, *und so weiter*.

undub, *v.* (Earlier example.)
1807 H. TUFTS in E. Pearson *Autobiogr. of Criminal* (1930) II. iv. 293 *Undub the jigger*, unlock the door.. *Undub the qua*, unlock the jail.

undulant, *a.* Add: **b.** *undulant fever*, in mod. use, a rarely fatal febrile disease, caused by bacteria of the genus *Brucella*, which may be chronic but intermittent or acute and chiefly affects the reticuloendothelial system; (human) brucellosis. (Earlier and later examples.)
1896 M. L. HUGHES in *Lancet* 25 July 239/2 It has occurred to me that the term 'Undulant Fever', by referring to the peculiar pyrexial curve so characteristic of the disease, might prove a serviceable name. **1930** J. T. DUNCAN et al. in *Syst. Bacteriol.* (Med. Research Council) V. ix. 404 There has been much controversy as to whether *Br. abortus*, so commonly found in cattle, is capable of producing undulant fever in man. **1968** PASSMORE & ROBSON *Compan. Med. Stud.* I. xviii. 75/1 *Br. melitensis* causes a similar infection in goats and is common in Mediterranean countries. In man it gives rise to a severe form of undulant fever called Malta fever.

undular, *a.* Add: **b.** Applied to a type of hydraulic jump consisting of a number of waves of diminishing size trailing downstream, with little difference in the water levels on either side of them.
1961 V. L. STREETER *Handbk. Fluid Dynamics* xxiv. 36 On the basis of Froude number..the hydraulic jump may be classified into five types... For $F_1 = 1$ to 1·7, the flow surface shows undulations; an undular jump is formed. **1982** *Sci. Amer.* June 134/2 Whether a particular bore is breaking or undular depends on the height of the tide, the depth of the river, [etc.].

undulator (ʊ·ndiŭlēɪtǝɹ). [f. UNDULATE *v.* + -OR.] **1.** *Telegr.* A device for recording Morse signals in which a line is traced on a roll of paper by a pen that is deflected sideways during the transmission of a dot or dash.
1910 *Post Office Electr. Engineers' Jrnl.* II. 312 The undulator is an instrument of considerable sensitiveness working with a current of ·5 milliampères, and is capable of recording 200, or slightly more, words per minute. **1921** *Wireless World* IX. 479/2, I have in addition two picture slides which illustrate the undulator of Messrs. Creed & Co. **1959** K. HENNEY *Radio Engin. Handbk.* (ed. 5) xxiv. 35 Reception..is effected by recording the incoming Morse signal on an ink recorder, or undulator.
2. *Physics.* A device in which a beam of particles is made to describe a sinusoidal path (and so emit radiation) by a series of transverse electric or magnetic fields of alternating polarity.
Orig. introduced as a means of generating microwaves of millimetre and submillimetre wavelength.
1951 H. MOTZ in *Jrnl. Appl. Physics* XXII. 529/2 We want to calculate the energy radiated by an electron riding through a succession of electric or magnetic fields of alternating polarity. We shall call the arrangement an undulator. **1963** A. F. HARVEY *Microwave Engin.* xii. 559 The electrons can be given a transverse motion by passage through an undulator. **1981** *McGraw-Hill Yearbk. Sci. & Technol.* 406/1 Multiperiod wigglers or undulators have also been used recently to make quasi-monochromatic photon beams.

undulose, *a.* Add: *undulose extinction*, extinction (sense *1 c (ii)) that occurs in strips which move across the field of view of the microscope as the stage is turned.
1889 [in Dict.]. **1975** *Nature* 10 Apr. 489/1 Granular xenoliths..show various strain effects, including undulose extinction.

uneager, *a.* Add: Hence **unea·gerness.**
c **1867** HARDY *Time's Laughingstocks* (1909) 83 Your intention seemed Converted by my false uneagerness To putting off for ever the caress.

uneared, *ppl. a.* (Later example in allusion to quot. *c* 1600.)
1922 JOYCE *Ulysses* 200 When he wants to do for him, and for all other and singular uneared wombs, the holy office an ostler does for the stallion.

unearned, *ppl. a.* Add: **2. b.** (Earlier example.)
1871 *Scotsman* 10 Aug. 3/7 But there is no doubt that the touch of his [*sc.* Scott's] pen does in many places form an important element of that unearned increment of value—that, I believe, is the scientific term—which Mr Stuart Mill and friends propose shortly to transfer from the lords of the soil to the Lords of the Treasury.
c. *unearned income*, (an) income derived from property, interest payments, etc., as opposed to one from a wage, a salary, or from fees.
1889 G. B. SHAW *Fabian Essays in Socialism* 189 A growing disposition to impose a tax of twenty shillings in the pound on obviously unearned incomes. **1912** P. SNOWDEN *Living Wage* xiii. 148 Even if the enforcement of a living wage lessened the spending power of the people who live on 'unearned incomes', that, too, would be for the national good. **1935** *Planning* 15 Jan. 5 In the case of a married couple the first 30s of unearned income is not taken into account. **1965** AUDEN *About House* (1966) 15 No unearned income Can buy us back the gait and gestures To manage a baroque staircase. **1970** *Times* 29 Jan. 27/5 Is it not about time that the starting point for the imposition of surtax on 'unearned' income be raised above £2,000 per annum?

unedge, *v.* (Later *poet.* example.)
1893 F. THOMPSON *Poems* 37 It seemed corrival of the world's great prime, Made to un-edge the scythe of Time.

unemancipated, *ppl. a.* (Earlier contextual example.)
1811 F. PLOWDEN *Hist. Irel. 1801–10* II. iv. 535 The Catholics remained unemancipated.

unembroidered, *ppl. a.* (Later example.)
1977 A. MORICE *Scared to Death* xxv. 168 They had heard of Bernard's elopement from Helena, whose white-washed account intrigued me far less than the unembroidered version from Farndale.

unembroiled, *ppl. a.* (Later example.)
1968 P. DICKINSON *Skin Deep* v. 111 Mr Tinker reacted into ferocious melodrama, swivelling round on the unembroiled Mr Green.

unemolumented, *a.* (Later example.)
1933 M. LOWRY *Ultramarine* iii. 135 'A name to conjure with.' You see, unemolumented but monumental.

unemotioned, *a.* (Later example.)
1929 E. BOWEN *Last September* xi. 138 As a rather perplexing system of niceties, Laurence saw it;..an unemotioned kindness withering to assertion selfish or racial.

unemployable, *sb.* (Further examples.)
1909 *Chambers's Jrnl.* Nov. 728/1 Every country has its shiftless element—its 'unemployables' as they are termed by the Salvation Army. **1944** L. MUMFORD *Condition of Man* vi. 209 The artist, who was the most courted figure of the fifteenth century, became ultimately the chronic unemployable of the nineteenth century. **1979** *Daily Tel.* 22 Sept. 20 You write about the employability of school-leavers. It is farcical to suppose that this depends on whether they have been beaten at school; otherwise Germany and Japan would be nations of unemployables.
unemployability (see small-type note) (examples).
1926 A. M. CARR-SAUNDERS *Eugenics* vii. 157 It is worthy of note that over half the men and over one-third of the women placed in the category of those 'verging upon unemployability' were sixty years of age or over. **1958** [see *FAINÉANTISME]. **1980** J. BOYD-CARPENTER *Way of Life* xi. 131 He was also receiving what was called Unemployability Supplement, an extra allowance intended to compensate war-disabled people whose disability prevented them from earning.

unemployed, *ppl. a.* and *sb.* **2. b.** (Earlier examples.)
1782 'J. H. ST. J. DE CRÈVECŒUR' *Lett. from Amer. Farmer* viii. 212 The means of procuring subsistence in Europe are limited..the manufacturer is overcharged with supernumerary hands; what then must become of the unemployed? **1817** T. BERNARD *Supply of Employment & Subsistence for Labouring Classes* 28 Our sea-coasts would swarm with adventurous fishing boats; new means of employment would be afforded to the..unemployed.

unemployment. Add: *unemployment benefit, insurance* (examples).
1909 *R. Comm. Poor Laws* App. XIX. 78 in *Parl. Papers* (Cd. 4795) XLIV. 1 Trade Unionists have..to consider the large number of fellow workmen who are in unions which cannot afford to pay unemployment benefit. **1923** *Spectator* 13 Jan. 47/2 From the point of view of the employer unemployment insurance is not less important. **1933** *Nation* (N.Y.) 4 Jan. 13 In the interests of economy the unemployment benefits would be reduced. **1967** N. FREELING *Strike out where not Applicable* 110 Applications for a building licence, claim for unemployment benefit..—the policeman can find gold in this. **1978** S. SHELDON *Bloodline* xxxix. 347 They were listed if they had paid taxes or drawn unemployment insurance or welfare funds.

unemptied, *ppl. a.* (Later examples.)
1952 M. LASKI *Village* vi. 106 Mrs. Robinson..went, leaving Miss Evadne to stare distastefully at..the empty flower-vases, the unemptied ash-trays. **1980** J. O'FAOLAIN *No Country for Young Men* i. 20 The house was full of.. smells of unemptied chamber-pots, a clutter of unassigned hats and macintoshes.

unended, *ppl. a.* **2.** (Later example.)
1935 T. S. ELIOT *Murder in Cathedral* i. 14 Meetings unended or endless At one place or another in France.

unenforceable, *a.* Add: Hence u:nenforce-abi·lity.

1935 *Columbia Law Rev.* XXXV. 94 More fundamental, however, is the inherent unenforceability of any statute.. attempting to prohibit an essentially private practice where all parties concerned are desirous of avoiding the restriction. **1973** I. M. SINCLAIR *Vienna Convention on Law of Treaties* v. 131 The unenforceability of any treaty contemplating genocide or the slave trade is further assured by the fact that such a treaty would contravene the Charter of the United Nations, which prevails in the event of conflict.

unentered, *ppl. a.* **4.** (Earlier example.)

1772 G. CARTWRIGHT *Jrnl.* 5 May (1792) I. 220 Having two couple of unentered hounds with me, I let them all loose to blood them, but the old dog following the first deer, I was not able to catch him again.

unenumerated, *ppl. a.* (Earlier contextual example.)

1799 G. BARNES *Rights Crown of Ireland Asserted* 47 The *un-enumerated,* equally with the enumerated articles.

unequal, *a.* and *adv.* Add: **5. b.** (*b*) Of treaties, etc.

1682 W. EVATS tr. *Grotius' Rights of War & Peace* II. xv. 184 Unequal leagues are often made, not only between the Conquerors and the Conquered..but also between people of unequal power. **1799** T. RUTHERFORTH *Inst. Nat. Law* (ed. 3) II. ix. 595 Unequal compacts, which lay the greater burden on the inferior party, are either such as diminish the sovereign power..or such as do not diminish this power. **1814** A. C. CAMPBELL tr. *Grotius' Rights of War & Peace* II. xv. 127 Unequal treaties may be made not only between the conquerors and the conquered, but also between mighty and impotent states, between whom no hostilities have ever existed. **1925** *China Yearbk.* 891 The 'most favoured nation clause'.. is the basis of the intercourse between China and most foreign countries. The 'most favoured nation clause' is unilateral and is the ground for the recent agitation against 'unequal treaties'. **1962** E. SNOW *Other Side of River* (1963) iv. 38 Under the unequal treaties foreign nationals had extraterritoriality rights which enabled them to reside and do business in China while remaining accountable only to their own courts. **1973** I. M. SINCLAIR *Vienna Convention on Law of Treaties* iv. 108 The Afro-Asian majority were extremely reluctant to countenance any material departure from the texts proposed by the Commission, particularly if it could be represented that the change was designed to keep in being so-called 'unequal' treaties.

unequality. Delete † *Obs.* and add later examples.

1939 *Sun* (Baltimore) 21 June 1/3 Industry went into case records today to present to a Senate committee studying proposed changes in the Wagner Act fourteen specific points of 'unequality' in that statute as it stands. **1973** *Nature* 8 June p. vi/1 The tools employed include linear programming and the calculus of variations, special attention being devoted to the use of Lagrangian multipliers for unequality constraints.

unenjoyed, *ppl. a.* (Later example.)

1984 H. SPURLING *Secrets of Woman's Heart* 101 She belonged to what my mother used to call the army of unenjoyed women... Margaret had a very unenjoyed look about her.

unequi·vocable, *a.* [irreg. f. UNEQUIVOC(AL *a.* + -ABLE.] Capable of only one interpretation; unambiguous.

1921 *Glasgow Herald* 30 Dec. 7/3 Yesterday 12 public bodies representative of the four provinces recorded in unequivocable language their conviction that the Treaty should be accepted. **1974** *Nature* 8 Feb. 397/2 Thereby providing unequivocable evidence for the former unity of the southern continents.

So **unequi·vocably** *adv.*

1917 W. J. LOCKE *Red Planet* xix. 234, I knew that for his own sake he would have unequivocably declined. **1980** *Daily Tel.* 6 Sept. 9/6 In 1980 Gdansk is unequivocably Polish.

unequivocalness. (Contextual example.)

1873 G. H. LEWES *Probl. Life & Mind* (Ser. 1) I. 58 The chief distinction between his [*sc.* the geometer's] probabilities and those of the physicist or biologist, lies in the greater simplicity or unequivocalness of his terms.

unerrable, *a.* (Later example.)

1984 *New Yorker* 12 Mar. 39/1 A submachine gun blasts at him from unerrable range.

Únětice (ūnye·tītsi). The Czech original of *AUNJETITZ. Hence **Úně·tician** *a.*

1947 V. G. CHILDE *Dawn Europ. Civilization* (ed. 4) vii. 121 In the classical phase of Únětice..these [pots] are transformed by flattening out the belly into keeled mugs. *Ibid.* (*caption*) Marschwitz and early Únětice pottery. *Ibid.* x. 194 Imitations of Únětician pins and Únětician gold ornaments..show that the fourth period of the Northern Stone Age did not even begin till the Early Bronze Age was well established in Central Europe. **1977** G. CLARK *World Prehist.* (ed. 3) iv. 176 On straight radiocarbon dating the Únětice bronze industry of Czechoslovakia and adjacent parts of Germany was active by the nineteenth century B.C. *Ibid.* 180 Wealth is indicated in outstanding burials such as the Únětician one of Leubingen.

uneuphonious, *a.* Add: Hence **uneupho·niously** *adv.*

1882 *Murray's Handbk. Wiltshire, Dorsetshire & Somersetshire* (ed. 4) 261/1 On the N. bank of the most uneuphoniously named *Puddle* or *Piddle,* from which unhappily the string of villages along its banks take their names. **1939** J. SQUIRE *Water-Music* ii. 38 The mother bird (if she indeed it was) by this time screaming uneuphoniously around my head.

un-European, *a.* (Earlier example.)

1846 R. FORD *Gatherings from Spain* xv. 175 A Spanish gentleman..suspects..that you are..considering his country as Roman, African, or in a word, as un-European.

uneven, *a.* Add: **4. c.** (Further examples.)

1905 R. BROOKE *Let.* 25 Mar. (1968) 19 It's not a bad number [of a magazine], a bit uneven of course; but then you can't expect the other men to ascend to my level. **1974** *Country Life* 7 Feb. 240/2 Almost no one was more uneven, as it is politely called, than G. F. Watts.

5. uneven-aged *a.,* (of a group of trees) containing individuals of different ages.

1905 *Terms Forestry & Logging* (U.S. Dept. Agric. Bureau Forestry) 14 Forests in which the trees differ considerably in age..uneven-aged forest. **1953** H. L. EDLIN *Forester's Handbk.* vii. 105 Woodlands may..be.. uneven-aged, with trees of various ages and therefore differing sizes.

unexcitability. (Earlier example.)

1882 W. JAMES *Let.* 13 Nov. (1920) I. 215 The traditional German professor in its highest sense..an absolute unexcitability of manner.

unfaceable, *a.* Restrict *dial.* to senses in Dict. and add: **c.** That cannot be faced or confronted.

1889 in *Cent. Dict.* **1966** M. RUSSELL *No Return Ticket* ix. 79 Suddenly the prospect of work was unfaceable. **1981** M. MCMULLEN *Other Shoe* (1982) xii. 111 Willett exchanged unfaceable reality for unconsciousness.

unfact. Add: **b.** *Pol.* A fact which is officially denied or disregarded.

1954 [see *UNPERSON]. **1959** *Economist* 8 Aug. 329/1 A government founded on the principle of treating as an unfact that bitter sequence of miscalculated events for which its leading members bore..responsibility. **1967** G. STEINER *Lang. & Silence* 379 Already, under the pressure of different truths, of 'un-facts' and history rewritten, the East German language is developing its own jargon and dialect.

unfailed, *ppl. a.* (Earlier example.)

1749 J. CLELAND *Mem. Woman Pleasure* II. 239 My breasts..unfail'd in firmness.

unfair, *a.* Add: **2. a.** (Examples of (business) competition.)

1891 *Federal Reporter* (U.S.) XLIV. 278 The relief sought is based on the charge that the denomination used is untrue, is calculated to deceive the public, and operates as an unfair and fraudulent competition against the business of the complainants. **1909** H. D. NIMS *Law Unfair Business Competition* 2 Unfair competition..exists wherever unfair means are used in trade rivalry. **1931** *Economist* 17 Jan. 103/1 The only recommendation..is that which would require road hauliers to be licensed.. with a view to eliminating unfair competition in the transport of goods by carriers who do not conform to decent standards of wages and hours. **1963** *Observer* 3 Nov. 33/1 'Unfair competition' is competition you cannot meet, and 'free enterprise' a condition where the Government regulations ensure that you make money. **1983** *Economist* 5 Feb. 62/1 They deplore the unfair competition between law-abiding and tax-evading firms, and the loss to the State.

unfamous, *a.* Restrict † *Obs.* to sense 2 in Dict. and add: **1.** (Later example.)

1980 R. CONNOLLY *Sunday Kind of Woman* xxiii. 162 The former escort of a couple of unfamous film stars.

unfancied, *ppl. a.* (Examples corresponding to *FANCY *v.* 8 c.)

1922 *Daily Mail* 3 Nov. 11 By turns the favourite, Flaming Sword, and Solace, a not unfancied 9 to 1 chance, put up a challenge. **1937** E. RICKMAN *On & Off Racecourse* i. 8 Horses who..are not seriously expected..to win, are said to be 'unfancied'.

unfasten, *v.* Add: **1. b.** *fig.* (Later example.)

1840 BROWNING *Sordello* I. 15 Not the more Is he unfastened from the earnest eyes Because that arras fell between!

2. (Later example.)

1963 [see *DEPRESSURIZE *v.*].

unfatherly, *a.* (Later example.)

1944 S. BELLOW *Dangling Man* 20 It might be considered unmanly or unfatherly to fall sick.

unfa·vourite, *a.* [UN-[1] 7.] Least favourite; disliked.

1934 WEBSTER, Unfavorite. **1951** N. COWARD *Star Quality* 232 *Love Child*..was my *un*favourite play of all time. **1962** 'R. FARRE' *Time from World* xii. 152 Belloc and Chesterton,..whom I number among my unfavourite authors. **1974** N. FREELING *Dressing of Diamond* 166 Carnations..were nearly her most unfavourite flower. **1979** *Listener* 15 Nov. 668/2 Perelman did..make frequent forays to California..to report on his unfavourite city.

unfeather, *v.* **1.** (Later example.)

1948 L. MACNEICE *Holes in Sky* 34 The foam..is a goose-quill That feathers—unfeathers—itself.

unfeeling, *vbl. sb.* Add: Also, an instance of this.

1919 V. WOOLF *Night & Day* xxiv. 331 The chaos of the unfeelings or half-feelings of life.

unfiltered, *ppl. a.* For (UN-[1] 8) read (UN-[1] 8, 9) and add later examples.

1976 'O. BLEECK' *No Questions Asked* iv. 48 Spivey produced a pack of unfiltered Camels, lit one. **1980** M. GORDON *Company of Women* (1981) II. v. 227 They both smoked unfiltered cigarettes.

unfit, *a.* (and *adv.*) Add: **5.** As *sb.* A person whose mental or physical health falls below a desired standard.

1912 *Q. Rev.* Apr. 496 The statistics..showing the enormous number of 'unfits', made clear the havoc wrought by the modern city. **1925** *Scribner's Mag.* July 7/2 By cutting off the reproduction of these social unfits,..we can go so far.

unfla·ppable, *a. colloq.* [UN-[1] 7 b.] Not subject to nervous excitement or anxiety; imperturbable.

1958 *Observer* 27 July 11/1 Six months ago even the unflappable Mr. Macmillan had his doubts and sometimes asked in bewilderment what he was doing wrong. **1963** *Times* 27 May 4/5 The Stowe captain looked a neat and unflappable batsman, and his 41 out of 62 was the yardstick of his value to the team. **1973** 'B. MATHER' *Snowline* iv. 47 He was a senior policeman, and as such deemed to be unflappable. **1980** L. BIRNBACH et al. *Official Preppy Handbk.* 34/2 Charm is the Preppy's suit of armor, the facade of unflappable gentility. **1984** *Listener* 20–27 Dec. 48/1 In other economic areas Japan appears equally unflappable, and with reason.

Hence **unflappabi·lity; unfla·ppably** *adv.*

1959 *Economist* 30 May 823/2 The Prime Minister..has no doubt been reflecting on the virtues of the legend of unflappability. **1965** C. FREMLIN *Jealous One* xxi. 169 The confident unflappability of the one who doesn't actually have to make the journey. **1966** *Guardian* 19 Aug. 8/6 An omission unflappably repaired by the BBC's music library. **1971** *Ibid.* 9 Sept. 9/6 Catering apparently unflappably for whole houses full of actors. **1982** J. ELLIOTT *Country of her Dreams* i. 14 Nicholas..had been roped in..as nanny to the British delegation..for his unflappability.

unfleshly, *a.* (Earlier example.)

1834 J. H. NEWMAN in *Brit. Mag.* Aug. 156 Our ample choir of holiest souls Are followers of the unfleshly seraphim.

unflown, *ppl. a.* Add: Also *absol.* (Later examples.)

1913 A. E. BERRIMAN *Aviation* p. xxi, Today, the great unflown is divided into two camps... 'I should love to go up.'.. 'Not I, at any price.' **1969** *Guardian* 13 Feb. 1/8 The backlog of unflown flights was, of course, appalling.

unfortunate, *a.* and *sb.* Add: **A.** *adj.* **1. c.** (Earlier example.)

1792 *Observer* 24 June 3/1 The great number of unfortunate young women, who nightly parade the streets of this immense metropolis, for the horrid purpose of.. prostitution of their persons.

B. *sb.* **2.** (Earlier example.)

1803 G. COLMAN *John Bull* II. ii. 20 *Frank.* Where is the reparation to the unfortunate he has deserted? *Shuffleton...* A great many unfortunates sport a stilish carriage.

unfortunately, *adv.* **a.** (Later example.)

1936 R. LEHMANN *Weather in Streets* I. ii. 36 Etty had not married—not even unfortunately.

unfouled, *ppl. a.*[1] (Later examples.)

1916 G. FRANKAU *Poet. Wks.* (1923) II. 3 The Killer-men of Valhalla looked up from the banquet-board At the unfouled breach of his rifle. **1929** D. H. LAWRENCE *Pansies* 74 The soul's first passion is for sheer life Entering in shocks of truth, unfouled by lies.

unfractured, *ppl. a.* (Later examples.)

a **1845** S. SMITH in S. Holland *Mem. Sydney Smith* (1855) I. xi. 387 To him..I owe unfractured integrity of limb. **1927** E. V. GORDON *Introd. Old Norse* 254 The *e* of verbs of the fourth and fifth conjs. remained unfractured. **1946** F. E. ZEUNER *Dating Past* ix. 286 The (fractured or unfractured) raw material is not directly shaped into the tool. **1982** W. J. WALSH *R. K. Narayan* ii. 29 A coherent and unfractured psyche.

unfreeze, *v.* Add: **1.** *fig. spec.* To make (assets, credits, etc.) realizable; to remove restrictions or rigid control from.

1933 *Kalends* (Williams & Wilkins Co.) May, Among other horrors..of our present adventure into fiscal delirium tremens, we discover the rise and growth of the monstrous verb, *unfreeze.* **1940** *Sun* (Baltimore) 3 Dec. 1/6 Great Britain and..Spain signed an agreement today designed to 'unfreeze' Spanish funds blocked in London. **1948** DYLAN THOMAS *Let.* 17 Nov. (1966) 323, I have already borrowed in advance from my fee..in order to unfreeze my Bank account. **1948** *Time* 22 Nov. 58/3 Thanks to improved domestic production of newsprint, circulation would be unfrozen Jan. 1. **1957** *Economist* 28 Sept. 1006/1 If Britain were to unfreeze the Egyptian working sterling account..President Nasser would be willing to discuss diplomatic relations. **1974** *Guardian* 23 Jan. 10/1 Building projects..were due to be unfrozen early this year. **1983** *Times* 20 June 6/1 The [EEC] leaders agreed..to unfreeze the aid package for Israel, blocked..after the Israeli invasion of Lebanon.

2. (Later examples.)
1918 *Scotsman* 6 Apr. 7/2 Their enthusiasms were reached only by tact and wise consideration... The atmosphere unfroze; and even the hotel people became polite and gentle. **1958** *Times* 11 Nov. 8/1 Members of his [*sc.* de Gaulle's] staff point out that he never expected educated Muslim opinion to 'unfreeze' all at once. **1968** K. O'HARA *Bird-Cage* xiii. 99 A small Scotch to his hand, a steak quietly unfreezing in the kitchen. **1981** P. VANSITTART *Death of Robin Hood* III. iii. 143 She slowly unfroze, motioning him to the damson ottoman.

un-French, *a.* (Earlier example.)
1803 *Lett. Miss Riversdale* II. 249 Madame de Sainval.. prides herself much upon being so *un*french as to admit it.

unfunny, *a.* Add: Hence **unfu·nnily** *adv.*; **unfu·nniness.**
1927 *Daily Mirror* 10 Dec. 4/1, I saw quite a lot of Mark Twain, and my chief astonishment was his regular unfunniness. **1958** N. MARSH *Singing in Shrouds* (1959) viii. 160 Could he hit quite such an all-time-low for unfunniness, do you suppose? **1963** V. NABOKOV *Gift* iv. 221 A student who unfunnily plays the fool. **1973** *Daily Tel.* 16 Mar. 14/4 The amiable progress began..at Harwich, which Mr Cutforth..unfunnily commended for being pleasant and rather empty. **1980** *Times Lit. Suppl.* 21 Nov. 1342/5 For me, it had all the wearisome unfunniness of back numbers of *Punch* perused in the dentist's waiting-room.

unfussy, *a.* Add: (Earlier example.)
1823 H. FROUDE *Let.* 12 Aug. in G. Battiscombe *John Keble* (1963) iv. 75 The unfussy way in which he [*sc.* Keble] goes on, and the complete indifference which he seems to feel to the opinions of people.
Hence **unfu·ssily** *adv.*; **unfu·ssiness.**
1960 *Guardian* 29 Oct. 5/6 The film..becomes what, unfussily, it tries to be: a genuine human document. **1968** D. E. ALLEN *British Tastes* iv. 95 The Welsh unfussiness about social class. **1977** K. BENTON *Red Hen Conspiracy* viii. 50 She handled the little car well, unfussily.

ungardened, (*ppl.*) *a.* (Later examples.)
1928 'BRENT OF BIN BIN' *Up Country* ix. 139 Shy, ungardened, but industrious and dependable, he's worked his sentence out without moral mishap. **1981** *Times Lit. Suppl.* 8 May 520/1 There were too..the un-gardened gardens, the unapologetic messes, too sodden in winter.. for any caller to beat a path to their owners' doors.

ungear, *v.* **1.** (N. Amer. examples.)
1846 T. L. MCKENNEY *Mem.* I. vii. 157 Wading into the stream, we ungeared the obstinate animal, and led him out. **1878** J. H. BEADLE *Western Wilds* xv. 237 At 2 p.m. we..ungeared the mules, and crawled under the wagon for shade. **1975** E. WIGGINTON *Foxfire 3* 235 When I come in at night I'd put m'mules up an' ungear 'em.
2. Also *fig.*
1931 GALSWORTHY *Maid in Waiting* xxii. 188 He'll almost certainly get up against something now he's back. If he does it will ungear him in no time.

ungenially, *adv.* (Earlier example.)
1814 F. BURNEY *Let.* 4 Sept. (1978) VII. 457 O drive, as fast as you can, this W[illia]m L[ocke] who has broken so ungenially upon your happiness, from your mind.

unglued, *ppl. a.* (Later and *fig.* examples: in a confused or incoherent state or condition.) Normally preceded by *come* or *become*.
1870 CROWN PRINCESS OF PRUSSIA *Let.* 15 Feb. in R. Fulford *Your Dear Letter* (1971) 261 All the woodwork comes unglued and the tilestones all cracked and bent. **1922** M. A. VON ARNIM *Enchanted April* xx. 322 Now that Mrs. Fisher too had at last come unglued,—Rose protested at the expression, and Lotty retorted that it was in Keats. **1971** *Wall St. Jrnl.* 13 Aug. 1/5 Already-negotiated agreements may come unglued. **1980** A. COPPEL *Hastings Conspiracy* xxviii. 181 What's gone wrong? You wouldn't be here if something weren't coming unglued.

ungood, *a.* (Later examples.)
1949 'G. ORWELL' *Nineteen Eighty-Four* I. 53 If you have a word like 'good', what need is there for a word like 'bad'? 'Ungood' will do just as well—better, because it's an exact opposite, which the other is not. **1964** W. GOLDING *Spire* viii. 150 Jocelin found the capstone ungood to look at.

ungovernable, *a.* (and *sb.*). Add: Hence also **ungo:vernabi·lity.**
1968 *Economist* 18 May 3/1 [Mr Wilson's] going might merely contribute to Britain's drift towards ungovernability. **1977** *Financial Times* 1 Apr. 22/8 Beyond the immediate question of the invasion perhaps the most serious problem is what has been termed Zaire's fundamental ungovernability. **1983** *Guardian Weekly* 16 Jan. 9/3 Now comes the threat the Germans call 'ungovernability'.

ungracious, *a.* Add: **5. b.** *ungracious living* (opp. *GRACIOUS *a.* 2 c).
1958 *Spectator* 4 July 13/2 He had gone straight to a bodge-you-up builder for a slab of ungracious living. **1976** R. RENDELL *Demon in my View* i. 11 The houses were warrens... Ungracious living was evinced by a row of doorbells, seven in an eight-roomed house.

ungraded, *ppl. a.* **1.** (Earlier example.)
1845 S. JUDD *Margaret* I. vi. 33 The roads rough, ungraded, and divided by parallel lines of green grass.

ungrammatical, *a.* Add: Hence also **u:ngrammatica·lity; ungrammaticalness** (later example).
1961 *Word* XVII. 6 On the other hand, sentences which are not universally rejected do not show ungrammaticality either total, or to a significant degree. **1967** R. W. LANGACKER *Language & its Structure* II. iv. 94 It is important not to confuse ungrammaticalness with excessive complexity that makes a sentence difficult or impossible to use. **1969** D. T. LANGENDOEN *Study of Syntax* ii. 8 Ungrammaticality arises not when there is merely internal contradiction within a linguistic object, but when it is felt that the object possesses some gross deformity in comparison with sentences in the language. **1975** *Language* LI. 579 The two sources of ungrammaticality in written texts are slips of the pen..and deliberate breaches of grammar.

ungra·ssed, (*ppl.*) *a.* [UN-[1] 8, 9.] Not sown with grass.
1934 in WEBSTER. **1947** *Sun* (Baltimore) 26 June 10/3 The visitors saw evidence of erosion in corn fields and former timberland, steep embankments along roadsides and ungrassed drainage ditches. **1974** R. ADAMS *Shardik* xlii. 339 At a little distance were four or five mounds of newly-turned earth, ungrassed and strewn with a few flowers.

ungrate, *a.* **2. a.** (Later *nonce* example.)
1922 JOYCE *Ulysses* 394 The men of the island, seeing no help was toward as the ungrate women were all of one mind, made a wherry raft.

un-Grecian, *a.* (Earlier example.)
1799 F. BURNEY *Let.* a 19 Nov. (1973) IV. 359 William there may see Noses to his mind—& if difficult already, make himself 10 times more so with every ungrecian one he sees.

ungroomed, *ppl. a.* (Earlier example.)
1829 G. GRIFFIN *Collegians* I. x. 216 Close behind..on that long-backed, ungroomed creature..rides the crafty Ulysses of the assemblage.

u·ngrown-up, *ppl. a.* and *sb.* [UN-[1] 8 c, 12.]
A. *adj.* Not grown-up; immature.
1937 *Mind* XLVI. 515 He may feel anxiety in the face of the infantile threats of his ungrown-up super-ego. **1945** A. L. ROWSE *Eng. Spirit* xxxiii. 229 There was something curiously unadult, ungrown-up about him. **1960** C. STORR *Marianne & Mark* x. 116 She thought this a very ungrown-up thing to do. **1980** J. LEES-MILNE *Harold Nicolson* xi. 201 To some extent he..remained ungrown-up in that his code of social behaviour was what he had imbibed from his..parents and schoolmasters.
B. *sb.* An ungrown-up person. *rare.*
1946 J. LEES-MILNE *Diary* 22 Feb. (1983) 21 J. just the same sweet ungrown-up he always will be.

unguardedness. (Earlier example.)
1818 T. BROWN *Brighton* III. i. 38 So also does he argue with ability, when unguardedness does not break in upon him.

unguent, *v.* (Later example.)
1918 A. QUILLER-COUCH *Foe-Farrell* xvi. 273 'I understand,' said I, looking up from my business of unguenting the stoker, who was not badly burnt.

u·nguent, *a. rare.* [f. UNGUENT *sb.* or *v.*] Of a person: emollient in manner, unctuous.
1931 BELLOC *Cranmer* ii. 30 He shrank, withdrew, was suave and unguent.

unhappen, *v.* Add: (Later example.) Also *trans.* To cause not to happen or to have happened.
1975 I. MURDOCH *Word Child* 135 All these things did happen. Keeping them secret isn't going to unhappen them. **1980** —— *Nuns & Soldiers* iii. 187 It's..so unreal. All this can unhappen. You can unhappen it just by saying we won't speak of it again.

unheaded, *a.* (Later examples, corresponding to HEADED *a.* and *pa. pple.* 6.)
1908 KIPLING *Lett. of Travel* (1920) 153 Even unheaded clippings from them [*sc.* various newspapers] declared their origin. **1970** R. JEFFRIES *Dead Man's Bluff* xix. 189 How did you know which hotel to come to today?..The letter was written on unheaded notepaper.

unhealthy. *a.* Add: **2. b.** *Mil. slang.* Dangerous.
1915 A. D. GILLESPIE *Lett. from Flanders* (1916) 266 All this place is 'out of bounds' to the troops, for it must be an unhealthy corner when shells are falling. **1930** E. RAYMOND *Jesting Army* I. vi. 93 The Gully Ravine..was now 'unhealthy': it was being sprinkled with shrapnel bullets.

unhear, *v.* For † *Obs.*$^{-1}$ read *rare* and add later examples.
1604 J. FRASER *Offer maid to Gentilman of Qualitie* 182 Many of ws hes done weal worse hauing condemned the kirk the spouse of Iesvs Christ vnhard hir, following the first that hes accused hir and praised him self. **1953** DYLAN THOMAS *Let.* 22 June (1966) 408 The woman next to me was stonedeaf so I spoke to her all the way more.. and more wildly.., and she unheard all my delirium with a smile.

unhearable, *a.* Add: Also *absol.* (Later examples.)
1841 T. CARLYLE *Let.* 19 July in T. Wemyss Reid *Life Lord Houghton* (1890) I. vi. 267 Drawing..things unspeakable into things unhearable. **1931** R. CAMPBELL *Georgiad* I. 10 With the Unhearable their ears we'll din.

unheedy, *a.* For † *Obs.* read 'Now *rare*' and add later example.
1919 R. BRIDGES in W. Caröe *Tom Tower* (1923) 112 Nor 'mong them was a single person..so void of scruple and unheedy.

‖**unheimlich** (u·nhəimliχ[y]), *a.* [Ger.] Uncanny, weird.
c **1877** W. JAMES in R. B. Perry *Thought & Character of W. James* (1935) I. xxix. 499 To human nature there is something uncanny, *unheimlich*, in the notion of a universe stripped so stark naked [as pure phenomenalism would have it]. **1900** G. BELL *Let.* 9 Apr. (1927) I. v. 81 But it is very strange—'unheimlich', some silly German said and it's not as silly as it sounds at first. **1945** B. RUSSELL *Let.* 20 Feb. in *Autobiogr.* (1969) III. i. 41 The new ways on the Campus make it strange and *unheimlich* to me.

unhelpful, *a.* Add: Hence also **unhe·lpfully** *adv.*
1889 in *Cent. Dict.* **1971** *Daily Tel.* 21 Apr. 12/3 The situations are promising, but the play becomes unhelpfully confusing.

unhistorically, *adv.* (Earlier example.)
1846 GEO. ELIOT tr. *Strauss's Life of Jesus* I. II. i. 310 We might..be led to the supposition that the words *for the remission of sins*..was commonly used in relation to Christian baptism, and was thence transferred unhistorically to that of John.

unholy, *a.* and *sb.* **2.** (Earlier example.)
1842 DICKENS *Let.* 24 Dec. (1974) III. 401, I am reminded of my promise to see to the Pantomime, and am called out at this unholy hour.

unhoodwinked, *ppl. a.* (Later example.)
1904 KIPLING *Traffics & Discoveries* 38 Let Zeus adjudge your landward kin,.. But ye the unhoodwinked waves shall test.

unhook, *v.* **1.** *fig.* (Later examples, corresponding to *HOOK *v.* 5 b.)
1966 *Guardian* 17 June 22/8 Girls who have been in trouble over drugs have been helped to stay 'unhooked'. **1977** B. GARFIELD *Recoil* xxxiii. 328 We..made a junkie out of her... I'll just get her unhooked.

unhope. (Later *poet.* example.)
1895–6 HARDY *Poems of Past & Present* (1902) 214 But death will not appal One who, past doubtings all, Waits in unhope.

unhuman, *a.* **3.** (Earlier example.)
1861 W. JAMES *Let.* Sept. (1920) I. 38, I have noticed fleeting shades of expression on her face..*unhuman*, ghoul-like, fiendish-cunning.

unh-unh (ɒ·ṅ,ɒṅ), *int.* Expressing negation or denial.
1951 J. CORNISH *Provincials* 38 'I guess no one'd buy *here*.' 'Unh-unh.' Gloom flooded back. **1963** M. MCCARTHY *Group* xi. 255 'I should think he would step in as a doctor,' Polly said mildly. Gus shook his head. 'Unh-unh,' he said. 'That's what they have to watch out for.' **1977** *New Yorker* 20 June 31/2 Unh-unh, I don't feel like it.

unhurrying, *ppl. a.* (Later examples.)
1918 *Glasgow Herald* 15 May 5/2 Through all this.. blaze of conflict the old Vindictive, still unhurrying, was walking the lighted waters towards the entrance. **1928** *Daily Express* 13 July 10/2 Others..detect something fine and typical of the national character in the mild and unhurrying dignity of this annual contest. **1972** P. D. JAMES *Unsuitable Job for Woman* iii. 107 Benskin arrived, unhurrying, imperturbable.

unhy·phenated, *ppl. a.* [UN-[1] 8.] **1.** Not joined by a hyphen; not written with a hyphen.
1934 in WEBSTER. **1960** *Amer. Speech* XXXV. 215 The authors seem to be unsure whether some forms occur as nicknames or as generic epithets... Some unhyphenated terms comprising two words have only the first capitalized. **1980** *Washington Post* 25 Apr. (Weekend Section) 4 [Noel Hume's]..double barreled name goes unhyphenated because such things are regulated by law as well as custom in his native Britain.
2. Not employing a hyphenated term (such as *French-Canadian*) in describing one's political or cultural allegiance. Of such allegiance, etc.: not divided. Cf. *HYPHENATED *a.* 2. *N. Amer.*
1970 L. B. PEARSON *Words & Occasions* 229, I am a Canadian who speaks English. There are millions [of others] who speak French... Others..have an ancestral language which they use. But we are all, or should be, Canadians—and unhyphenated with pride in our nation and its citizenship. **1973** *Saturday Night* (Toronto) Oct. 17/2 Many Canadians..were interpreting his One Canada to be on a par with the call for unhyphenated Canadianism. **1981** *Washington Post* 30 Jan. A15 Unhyphenated Democrats, at least those brave enough to acknowledge their political heritage, have a brand-new patron saint.

unhypocritical, *a.* (Earlier example.)
1854 GEO. ELIOT tr. *Feuerbach's Essence Christianity* 310 The unhypocritical, honest acknowledgment of sensual life is the acknowledgment of sensual pleasure.

uni (yū·ni). Also **Uni.** Chiefly *Austral.* and *N.Z.* Colloq. abbrev. of UNIVERSITY *sb.* 1. Also *attrib.* and *Comb.* Cf. *UNIV.

1898 *Bulletin* (Sydney) 17 Dec. (Red Page), The only classical idioms I have found..are *rotter, i.e.*, an adept in learning anything; and *panem agere*, Sydney Uni. slang for 'doing a loaf'. **1913** *Lincoln* (Nebraska) *Daily News* 28 Feb. 1/7 (*heading*) Uni. men depart to judge debates. **1929** K. S. PRICHARD *Coonardoo* 163 Stay in Perth, go to the uni, be a lawyer or doctor, or something? **1962** A. SEYMOUR *One Day of Year* 103, I think I might ditch my course. Leave Uni. **1966** 'L. LANE' *ABZ of Scouse* 112 *Uni-type*, a university student. **1975** M. BRADBURY *History Man* x. 169 All the girls at the uni, what she calls the uni, in her set talk about separating. **1984** *Metro* (Auckland) Mar. 15/2 The poor fool who sat the exam and got potted has been threatened with having his own accreditation cancelled and may be banned from sitting the exam for another two years—when he planned to go to uni in this year.

uni-. Add: **1. a.** *uniconsonantal, -segmental*; **unia·lgal** *Bot.* (see quot. 1914); **unicu·spid** *Zool.* = *unicuspidate* s.v. UNI- 1 a; **unifacial**, (*b*) *Archæol.*, of a flint tool, etc.: (worked) on one side only; cf. *BIFACIAL *a.*; also *absol.* as *sb.*; **unilinear**, (*b*) of an evolution, a theory, etc.: having a single line of development or progression; **unimodular** *Math.*, having a determinant whose value is 1; **uniovular**, substitute for def.: = *MONOVULAR *a.*; (further examples); **unipo·tent** *Med.* and *Biol.*, of a cell: capable of giving rise to only one type of cell or tissue; **univa·llate** *Archæol.*, having a single encircling rampart; cf. *MULTIVALLATE *a.*; **univa·riant** *Physical Chem.*, of a chemical system: having one degree of freedom (cf. *FREEDOM 10 b); **univa·riate** *Statistics*, involving or having one variate or variable.

1914 G. M. SMITH in *Trans. Wisconsin Acad.* XVII. 1173 According to the usage of some authors, a pure culture is one that contains only one algal species; others understand it to be a culture of single algal species that is also free from other organisms... To differentiate between the two I propose the term *unialgal culture* to designate one which contains but a single species of alga, but which may contain other organisms. **1946** E. G. PRINGSHEIM *Pure Cultures of Algae* vi. 79 The separation of the purification process into two stages, the first involving the preparation of unialgal or species-pure cultures, the second that of bacteria-free or absolutely pure cultures, is very helpful. **1979** *Nature* 27 Sept. 300/2 This infective filtrate caused the destruction of cultures of four unialgal strains of *M*[*icromonas*] *pusilla*. **1948** D. DIRINGER *Alphabet* ii. 60 The phonograms were bi-consonantal..or uni-consonantal. **1894** GOULD *Dict. Med.* 1572/1 Unicuspid. **1948** A. L. RAND *Mammals Eastern Rockies* 54 The skull when viewed from the side appears to hold only 3 unicuspid teeth. **1977** *Lancet* 17 Sept. 610/2 Surgical exploration.. revealed a unicuspid aortic valve with a 'horseshoe' appearance. **1951** *N. & Q. Anthropol.* (ed. 6) IV. 345 The distinction between tools made on cores and tools made on flakes or blades should be noted, and also that between tools flaked on both faces (so-called bifacials) and those flaked or retouched on one side only (unifacials). **1957** *Jrnl. R. Anthropol. Inst.* Jan. 119 A wide range of choppers and chopping tools, core, flake, bifacial and unifacial, is still in use. **1981** *Science* 4 Sept. 1115/2 Simple unifacial tools. **1910** *Athenæum* 12 Mar. 299 A worldwide unilinear evolution. **1939** *Mind* XLVIII. 369 It is an order in which the thoughts in the chains of reasoning are *not* linked in a unilinear, but in a 'global' fashion. **1974** tr. *Wertheim's Evolution & Revolution* i. 22 In Soviet Russia during the twenties..the issue of unilinear evolution also came in for serious discussion. **1852** J. J. SYLVESTER in *Cambr. & Dublin Math. Jrnl.* VII. 52 The linear-transformations are supposed to be always taken such that the modulus..is unity; or, as it may be phrased, the transformations are uni-modular. **1973** L. J. TASSIE *Physics Elementary Particles* xi. 136 The group *SU*(3) is the group of all unimodular unitary 3 × 3 matrices. **1948** 'M. INNES' *Night of Errors* ix. 102 The two men were uncommonly like each other—a most striking family resemblance. But then I suppose they were what are called uniovular twins—or triplets, I should say. **1965** J. POLLITT *Depression & its Treatment* vii. 91 Kallman..showed that 96 per cent of uniovular twins of manic-depressive partners were similarly affected. **1979** G. BOURNE *Pregnancy* (rev. ed.) xxx. 448 These babies will be identical, or uniovular twins since they have exactly the same genetic structure and the same chromosomes. **1974** *Brit. Jrnl. Haematol.* XXVI. 605 Stem cells are assayed by quantifying their progeny. In techniques measuring cells of one lineage this measurement reflects the number of unipotent stem cells. **1979** *Nature* 18 Jan. 177/1 Such a cell is unipotent and exclusively committed to maturation along the erythroid pathway. **1955** Uni-segmental [see *multi-segmental* s.v. *MULTI- 1 b]. **1977** *Word* *1972* XXVIII. 183 The data discussed there share with these data the fact of unisegmental modification. **1950** *Archaeol. Jrnl. 1948* CV. 56 The first univallate enclosure on Eddisbury Hill was preceded by a palisade structure. **1979** L. LAING *Celtic Britain* ii. 56 The simple univallate hillforts were in some cases given further ramparts. **1899** Univariant [see *INVARIANT *a.* b]. **1940** GLASSTONE *Text-bk. Physical Chem.* vi. 467 When two phases are in equilibrium..the conditions must correspond to a point on one of the lines..in Fig. 99: only temperature *or* pressure need be arbitrarily fixed.. in order to define the system, and the latter has one degree of freedom, i.e., it is univariant. **1978** P. W. ATKINS *Physical Chem.* vii. 181 The system is univariant when two phases are present; there is only one degree of freedom. **1928** *Biometrika* XXA. 32 Various writers struggled with the problems that arise when samples are taken from univariate and bi-variate populations. **1938** *Brit. Jrnl. Psychol.* XXIX. 451 (*heading*) The influence of univariate selection on factorial analysis of ability. **1973** *Nature* 16 Mar. 210/3 The wealth of mathematical forms with which we can express the frequency or probability distributions of univariate theory.

b. *uniface* (later examples), *-pivot*.

1911 H. M. HOBART *Dict. Electr. Engin.* II. 591/1 (*heading*) Unipivot measuring instrument. *Ibid.*, The chief advantage of the unipivot instrument is that, owing to the fact that the moving system is supported on a single jewel, it may be entirely lifted off when the instrument is out of use. **1940** *Chambers's Techn. Dict.* 878/1 *Unipivot instrument*, an instrument whose moving-coil system is balanced on a single pivot passing through its centre of gravity. **1944** *Antiquity* XVIII. 217 Amid the amazing expressions of the goldsmith's art which Scandanavia.. produced between the late 4th and mid-5th centuries, perhaps the most interesting is the bracteates, the pendent uniface medallions. **1977** *Signature* May/June 34/4 By October 1914 watermarked paper was produced and used. This had a uniface surface, as did the first issue. **1977** *Gramophone* Aug. 377 (Advt.), A unique system of magnetic stabilization on the unipivot bearings.

2. *unidimensionality, -linearism.*

1953 C. E. BAZELL *Linguistic Form* 3 Unidimensionality. There is only one dimension of succession. **1975** *Human Relations* XXVIII. 795 Another factor is the unidimensionality of the approach. **1964** P. WORSLEY in I. L. Horowitz *New Sociol.* 374 It will certainly have to eschew unilinearism and the West-European ethnocentrism of nineteenth-century schemas.

uniaxial, *a.* Add: **3.** Characterized by one axis of alignment or action.

1965 E. B. ATKINSON in P. D. Ritchie *Physics of Plastics* v. 250 The cube is subjected to a simple tensile stress normal to the *x* faces,..i.e. a state of simple uniaxial tension exists. **1969** W. R. R. PARK *Plastics Film Technol.* ii. 28 Uniaxial orientation takes place during the drawing of a filament. Here the polymer chains are aligned in one direction. **1982** *Jrnl. de Physique: Lettres* XLIII. 585 The dynamics of an amorphous polystyrene.. melt is studied..during stress relaxation following a uniaxial deformation.

Hence **unia·xially** *adv.*

1909 in WEBSTER. **1969** *Jrnl. Appl. Physics* XL. 1301 The coercive force for a pair of identical interacting uniaxially anisotropic dipoles of arbitrary bond angle is calculated. **1979** *Nature* 15 Mar. 222/2 The entire assembly would then be hot-pressed, either uniaxially or isostatically, at a temperature of 1,200–1,300°C.

unicameral, *a.* Hence **unica·meralism**, the system of having only one legislative chamber.

1924 *Fortn. Rev.* Oct. 742 With rare unanimity the civilized world has rejected the nostrum of unicameralism, and has decided that two legislative chambers are..necessary to a modern democracy. **1957** A. C. BRECKENRIDGE *One House for Two* i. 4 Unicameralism at best simply became a thing of historical interest.

† **uniceptor** (yū·ni,se:ptǫɹ). *Immunol. Obs.* [f. UNI- 2 + RE)CEPTOR.] In Ehrlich's theory of immunization, a receptor having only one combining or haptophoric group of atoms, by which it unites with the immunizing body but not with the complement. Cf. *AMBOCEPTOR.

1902 *Jrnl. Exper. Med.* VI. 281 According to the manner of action he distinguishes 'uniceptors' and 'amboceptors'. **1910** in *Lippincott's New Med. Dict.*

uniclinal: delete entry in Dict. s.v. UNI- 1 a and substitute:

uniclinal (yūniklǝi·năl), *a. Geol.* [f. UNI- + Gr. κλιν- (see CLINO-) + -AL.] Characterized by a uniform angle of dip; formed by uniformerly dipping strata; = *homoclinal* adj. s.v. *HOMOCLINE. (In quot. 1884 = *MONOCLINICAL *a.* b.)

1846 DARWIN *Geol. Obs. S. Amer.* vii. 197 The masses having these different inclinations, are separated from each other by parallel vertical faults.., often giving rise to separate, parallel, uniclinal ridges. **1884** A. J. JUKES-BROWNE *Student's Handbk. Physical Geol.* 342 When a set of horizontal beds is suddenly bent up or down into a sharp curve, and then continued horizontally at a higher or lower level, the flexure is called a monoclinal or uniclinal curve. **1921** A. W. GRABAU *Textbk. Geol.* I. xxii. 733 Thus a series of uniclinal ridges is produced, facing the center of the original anticline. **1937** WOOLDRIDGE & MORGAN *Physical Basis Geogr.* xii. 159 This general process of asymmetrical development [of valleys] is called uniclinal shifting. [*Note*] The word 'uniclinal'..is preferable to 'monoclinal', since the asymmetrical development of valleys bears no necessary relation to 'monoclines'. **1970** R. J. SMALL *Study of Landforms* xi. 402 Glacial streams which happen to be superimposed on to the slopes above a col will undergo 'uniclinal' shifting along the ice-rock contact towards the centre of the col. **1975** *New Oxf. Atlas* 106 Newer sediments..with gentle or moderate uniclinal dips.

unicycle. Add: For *U.S.* read orig. *U.S.* and add later examples. Hence as *v. intr.* and **u·nicycling** *vbl. sb.*

1897 *Wheelist Ann.* 15 It's all been so slow at Slochester Park, That of fun or of frolic I've not seen a spark, Until yesterday week, when we had a rare treat: The first *rocking-horse* and *unicycle* meet. **1978** J. IRVING *World according to Garp* vi. 123 There's no *tradition* of bears on unicycles here. *Ibid.* 127 The sullen animal unicycling in the lunatic's left-behind clothes. *Ibid.* 128 Even his one talent, unicycling, was irretrievable. **1980** *Radio Times* 23–29 Feb. 10/1 He rejects the 'pure' dumbshow of performers like Marcel Marceau, preferring to mix.. verbal humour, video, the odd spot of unicycling, and mask work.

unideal, *a.* **4.** (Earlier example.)

1838 E. FITZGERALD *Let.* 8 June (1979) 26 The best painter of the unideal Christ is, I think, Rembrandt.

unidentified, *ppl. a.* (Examples of *unidentified* (*flying*) *object*: cf. *UFO.)

1950 *Chambers's Jrnl.* Nov. 668/1 Project Saucer revealed that it had analysed 375 incidents of 'unidentified flying objects'. **1954** 'R. CRANE' *Hero's Walk* v. 81 Five unidentified objects were discovered last night..flying.. in the direction of Earth. **1966** *New Scientist* 14 Apr. 87/1 Community after community observed unidentified flying objects. There were the inevitable sightings by police. **1976** L. DEIGHTON *Twinkle, twinkle, Little Spy* i. 11 The strictly infra dig. pastime of looking for unidentified flying objects, or what the sci-fi freaks call ufology.

unidire·ctional, *a.* [f. UNI- 1 + DIRECTIONAL *a.*] Having or being motion in one direction; operating or functional in one direction only.

1883, 1894 [in Dict. s.v. UNI- 1]. **1946** *Nature* 9 Nov. 674/2 The simplified apparatus was..actuated by unidirectional air flow. **1955** O. G. SUTTON *Sci. of Flight* 36 The effect is to give an additional but unidirectional motion to the molecules of air. **1961** A. NISBETT *Technique Sound Studio* i. 23 Cardioids—sometimes called unidirectional microphones—have a heart-shaped response. **1962** Y. MALKIEL in Householder & Saporta *Probl. Lexicogr.* 13 The kernel of Howell's..*Lexicon tetraglotton* (1660) is a unidirectional dictionary providing for the translation of each English entry into French, Italian, and Spanish. **1971** I. G. GASS et al. *Understanding Earth* xiii. 174/2 The uni-directional flow of rivers is complicated by the development of meanders. **1975** *Sci. Amer.* Mar. 36/1 For years psychologists have been concerned with the effectiveness of unidirectional modes of communication such as highway signs, books, lectures and television programs. **1983** *Trans. Philol. Soc.* 6 The impression that [linguistic] evolution is neat, continual and unidirectional is a mirage. **1984** *What Video?* Aug. 59/1, 1·5 in. electronic viewfinder, unidirectional mike *but* it is heavy.

Hence **u:nidirectiona·lity; unidire·ctionally** *adv.*

1958 W. D. KINGERY *Ceramic Fabrication Processes* viii. 70/2 A much more suitable method is to apply pressure from all sides instead of unidirectionally. **1960** A. C. SPAULDING in Dole & Carneiro *Essays in Science of Culture* 454 Unidirectionality of formal changes through time is simply the idea of cultural evolution. **1968** *Science* 21 June 1365/3 The unidirectionality observation..may be placed in correspondence with certain findings concerning functional neuroanatomy of OKN [*sc.* optokinetic nystagmus]. **1970** *Proc. I.E.E.E.* Aug. 1252/1 Unidirectionality increases transducer conversion efficiency by 3 dB. **1976** *Nature* 10 June 516/1 Replication..proceeds either unidirectionally or bidirectionally away from this site. **1980** *English World-Wide* I. 1. 16 If there was initially unresolved conflict at the level of decision-making this lack of unidirectionality can be expected to re-emerge at the implementation stage.

unification. Add: **2.** *Comb.* **Unification Church**, an evangelistic religious and political organization (see quot. 1973) founded in 1954 in Korea by Sun Myung Moon, and subsequently known as a cult religion in the U.S. and elsewhere. Its adherents are sometimes contemptuously called *Moonies*.

1973 *Time* 15 Oct. 129/3 By 1954 he had founded the Holy Spirit Association for the Unification of World Christianity—known more simply as the Unification Church. **1975** *Americana Ann.* 481/1 A..group in Korea, called the Unification Church, claiming Christian origins and suggesting Messianic status for its leader, the Rev. Sun..Moon, engaged in evangelistic work in the United States. **1976** *Daily Colonist* (Victoria, B.C.) 18 Mar. 7/2 The fringe religious groups include..Unification Church, [etc.]. **1979** *Minutes Gen. Synod House of Bishops* 3 May 4 The Archbishop of York made a statement..relating to the Unification Church.

Hence **unifica·tory** *a.*, tending to unify.

a **1897** W. WALLACE *Lect.* (1898) 84 The monistic, if that means the unificatory, instinct is irresistible. **1932** W. T. STACE *Theory of Knowl.* vii. 156 The other chief logical character of unificatory constructions is that they ..are simply serviceable fictions. **1971** A. KIRK-GREENE in J. Spencer *Eng. Lang. W. Afr.* 143 In Nigeria, Hausa.. played the same unificatory role until its use was forbidden..during the 1939–45 war.

unified, *ppl. a.* Add: **2.** Special collocation. *unified* (*field*) *theory* (Physics): a field theory that describes two or more of the four interactions (orig. gravitation and electromagnetism) previously described by separate theories.

1935 E. A. MILNE *Relativity, Gravitation & World-Structure* i. 13 This view is in violent opposition to the demand for a 'unified field theory', a demand for further geometrical modification of the space used so as to be able to employ these modifications in describing electromagnetic phenomena. **1959** *Listener* 26 Mar. 544/2 The first unified field theory was produced not by Einstein but by Hermann Weyl, in 1918. **1979** *New Scientist* 1 Mar. 667/2 QCD is a particularly favoured theory because it is very similar to the 'field theories' of the other forces in nature, and this would be a great help in formulating 'GUTs', the grand unified theories of the strong, weak and electromagnetic forces which currently challenge theorists. **1983** *Nature* 27 Jan. 285/2 Minimal SU(5), one of the simplest of the 'grand unified theories', or GUTs, which links all the non-gravitational forces.

unifilarly (yūnifəi·lăɹli, -fi·lăɹli), *adv. Biochem.* [f. as UNIFILAR *a.* + -LY[2].] In a single strand of a DNA duplex.

1974 *Nature* 13 Sept. 156/2 The unifilarly substituted chromatids fluoresced more brightly than the bifilarly substituted sister chromatids. **1980** *European Jrnl. Cell Biol.* XXII. 552 Unifilarly-substituted DNA.

uniflow (yū·ni,flōu), *a.* Also una- (now *rare*). [f. UNI- 2 + FLOW *sb.*[1]] Involving flow in one direction only; *spec.* applied to: (*a*) a type of reciprocating steam engine in which the steam in the cylinder flows in one direction from inlet(s) to outlet; (*b*) scavenging in an internal-combustion engine in which there is a similar flow of waste gases in the cylinder. Also *ellipt.*, a uniflow steam engine.

1912 tr. *J. Stumpf's Una-Flow Steam-Engine* i. 1 Unaflow engines..may be made with a single expansion stage. **1913** G. F. GEBHARDT *Steam Power Plant Engin.* (ed. 4) ix. 379 A 20 × 30, 200 horse-power Nordberg uniflow engine using very wet steam. **1942** L. B. CHAPMAN *Marine Power Plan* (ed. 2) v. 127 The unaflow engine has been widely used for stationary work in both Europe and the United States. **1949** C. W. CHAPMAN *Mod. High-Speed Oil Engines* I. xi. 95 There are three main systems employed: cross scavenging, loop scavenging and uniflow scavenging. **1963** H. W. DICKINSON *Short Hist. Steam Engine* (ed. 2) viii. 156 The uniflow engine is a gallant attempt on the part of the reciprocating engine-makers to hold the field against the advance of the turbo-alternator and the electrical drive. **1963** R. R. A. HIGHAM *Handbk. Papermaking* vii. 184 Contraflow vat. This vat is similar in construction to the uniflow type. **1971** G. WATKINS *Textile Mill Engine* II. 74 The gearing of the waterwheel was destroyed by grit in a flood, and the uniflow then drove the whole until the mill was closed. **1981** BURGHARDT & KINGSLEY *Marine Diesels* iv. 62 Figure 4-8(d), illustrating an opposed piston engine, is another method of uniflow scavenging.

uniform, *sb.* Add: **2. d.** *transf.* The customary dress or mode of appearance characteristic of persons of a certain age, class, or lifestyle.

1930 G. B. SHAW *Apple Cart* I. 13 (*Pointing to his blouse.*) *Boanerges.* The uniform of Labor, your Royal Highness. **1967** *Listener* 17 Aug. 197/3 One day one had one's hair flopping down one's back, short skirts which barely cleared the knee. (Ironically that's the uniform of grown-ups nowadays, isn't it?) **1976** 'D. FLETCHER' *Don't whistle 'Macbeth'* 37 The discreet beads, the silver bracelet, ..court shoes..were identical with the uniform of hundreds of women..of the middle class.

3. a. For † *Obs.*[−1] read *rare* and add later examples.

1900 J. K. JEROME *Three Men on Bummel* ix. 208, I believe there is a heavy fine for joking with any German uniform. **1970** G. JACKSON *Let.* 24 Mar. in *Soledad Brother* (1971) 189 If a uniform denied some small request, we would take it to the counselor.

b. Short for *uniform branch* (see below).

1978 F. BRANSTON *Sergeant Ritchie's Conscience* i. 13 'Spoken to the Chief?' he said... 'Uniform have done that,' guessed Ritchie.

4. b. *spec.* in the police force, distinguished from the plain-clothes section, esp. in *uniform branch.* (Later examples.)

1938 F. D. SHARPE *Sharpe of Flying Squad* i. 15, I don't wish to detract from the valuable work carried out by the Uniform Section..but..the Flying Squad plays a leading part in this work. **1970** P. LAURIE *Scotland Yard* ii. 51 The school also provides instructors to train uniform officers. **1972** *Police Rev.* 17 Nov. 1509/1, I would like to express my gratitude..for the efforts of both the C.I.D. and the uniform branch to deal with crime. **1980** P. G. WINSLOW *Counsellor Heart* ii. 41 Uniform Branch have had complaints of noise... Late parties.

uniform, *v.* **3.** (Earlier U.S. examples.)

1861 O. W. NORTON *Let.* 8 June in *Army Lett.* (1903) 12 We are to be uniformed and equipped immediately. **1888** *Long Branch* (New Jersey) *News* 7 Apr., In our spirit of imitation do we not go too far when we talk of uniforming the shop girls in the big dry goods store.

uniformed, *a.* Add: *spec.* of police officers. See *UNIFORM *sb.* 4 b. (Later examples.)

1922 *Rep. Tax Cases 1913–21* VII. 176 Detective officers receive the same rates of pay as uniformed officers. **1945** *Law Rep. King's Bench Div.* 420 When they saw the uniformed officer they hurried in the opposite direction. **1973** 'E. PETERS' *City of Gold & Shadows* v. 81 Sergeant Comstock, of the uniformed branch..came from a long line of native fishermen.

uniformize, *v.* Restrict *rare* to sense in Dict. and add: **2.** *Math.* To transform (an equation or expression) so that each variable is expressed as a single-valued function of a new parameter; to parameterize.

1899 *Phil. Trans. R. Soc.* A. CXCII. 1 The only automorphic functions known hitherto which have been applied to uniformise forms whose genus is greater than unity, are [etc.]. **1940** E. T. BELL *Devel. Math.* xxi. 474 The circle $x^2+y^2=1$ is uniformized by $x=\sin t$, $y=\cos t$. **1972** M. KLINE *Math. Thought* xxxix. 938 The parametric equations (11) or (12) are said to uniformize the algebraic equation (10).

Hence **u·niformizing** *vbl. sb.* and *ppl. a.*; **u:niformiza·tion.**

1899 *Phil. Trans. R. Soc.* A. CXCII. 1 Comparatively little of the published work on automorphic functions..has been written in connexion with the uniformisation of algebraic forms. *Ibid.* 2 The analytical connexion between the uniformising variable *t* and the variables *u*, *z*, of the algebraic form. **1933** E. SAPIR in *Encycl. Social Sci.* IX. 160/2 Language acts as a socializing and uniformizing force. **1954** HODGE & PEDOE *Methods Algebraic Geom.* III. xvi. 112 A necessary and sufficient condition that *P* be a simple point of *V* is that there exist a set of uniformising parameters at *P*. **1972** M. KLINE *Math. Thought* xxxix. 938 Clebsch's results on the uniformization of curves of genus 1 by means of elliptic functions of a parameter made it possible to establish for such curves remarkable properties about points of inflection, [etc.].

u·nijunction. *Electronics.* Also **uni-junction.** [UNI- 1 b.] A negative-resistance device consisting of a rectifying *p–n* junction in the middle of a length of semiconducting material that has an ohmic contact at each end, used as a switching element.

1957 *Automatic Control* Feb. 24 The silicon unijunction transistor has characteristics resembling a neon light; it can be wired to a capacitor and a resistor to yield an oscillator. **1962** SIMPSON & RICHARDS *Physical Princ. Junction Transistors* viii. 192 A device whose regenerative property is obtained in a somewhat different manner..is the uni-junction transistor or double-based diode. **1981** NASHELSKY & BOYLESTAD *Devices* vii. 291 Recent interest in the unijunction transistor (UJT) has, like that for the SCR, been increasing at an exponential rate.

unilateral, *a.* Add: **I. 1. c.** Of car-parking: restricted to one side of the street.

1945 *Rep. Watch Comm. Oxf. City Council* 7 June, The Council desired to preserve the effect of the war-time Orders..relating to unilateral parking in King Edward Street. **1954** *Highway Engin. Terms* (*B.S.I.*) 57 *Unilateral waiting* (*prohibition of*), a system under which vehicles are prohibited from waiting on one side of a carriageway. The side may be fixed or alternated. **1959** *Listener* 14 May 841/2 Or, if it is unilateral parking, that you go to the side where parking is allowed.

II. 4. d. *unilateral disarmament*, disarmament (in recent use, *spec.* of nuclear weapons) by one state, irrespective of whether others take similar action. Also *unilateral disarmer.*

1929 *Times* 15 Nov. 14/3 Lord Salisbury agreed that unilateral disarmament had probably reached its limits. **1935** C. R. ATTLEE in *Hansard Commons* 22 May 375, I want to recall to the House what our position is as a party on the question of defence... We do not stand for unilateral disarmament. **1960** [see *DISARMER b]. **1969** PLANO & OLTON *Internat. Relations Dict.* 237 By demonstrating peaceful intentions rather than merely talking about them, unilateral disarmament theorists believe, one side could put the arms-race cycle into reverse by evoking reciprocation of its disarmament initiatives. **1980** *Observer* 14 Sept. 11 To adopt the unilateral disarmament option would be akin to behaving like a virgin in a brothel. **1980** *Times* 17 Nov. 15/3 Mr Foot..is a unilateral disarmer. **1984** S. TOWNSEND *Growing Pains A. Mole* 90 Went back to Pandora's and watched the Labour Party Conference vote for unilateral disarmament... If elected the Labour Party would chuck all their nuclear weapons away.

unila·teralism. [-ISM.] = *unilaterality* s.v. UNILATERAL *a.*; *spec.* (*a*) = *unilateral disarmament* s.v. *UNILATERAL *a.* 4 d; (*b*) *U.S.*, the pursuit of a foreign policy without allies or irrespective of their views.

1926 *Public Opinion* 30 Apr. 434/2 We must..surmount national and social unilateralism in the domain of the spirit. **1935** *Punch* 25 Sept. 354/2 Laugh heartily when politicians talk about 'unilateralism'. **1959** *Manch. Guardian* 20 July 6/2 He said that unilateralism would take Britain out of N.A.T.O. **1964** GOULD & KOLB *Dict. Social Sci.* 357/1 *Unilateralism* is now used to mean 'no alliances' while *isolationism* is more often used to mean an attitude of withdrawal. **1968** N. NICOLSON in H. Nicolson *Diaries* III. 385 The policy of unilateral renunciation by Britain of the atomic bomb had been advocated by Bevan... The Labour Party Conference had voted..for unilateralism. **1979** H. KISSINGER *White House Years* xxiv. 1089 From an early hostility to the American alliance with Japan..the Chinese leaders soon came..to view it a guarantee of America's continued interest in the Western Pacific and a rein on Japanese unilateralism. **1984** *New Statesman* 16 Nov. 10/1 After the Labour defeat at the General Election, the installation of Cruise missiles and a seemingly unequivocal Labour commitment to unilateralism, many CND activists are looking at the shape and direction CND needs to take in order to win the political debate on disarmament.

unila·teralist, *sb.* and *a.* [-IST.] **A.** *sb.* One who favours or adopts a policy of unilateral disarmament.

1927 *Daily Tel.* 14 Mar. 9/7 The lack of foresight on the part of the 'Unilateralists'..led..to the..postponement of Germany's entry into the League. **1959** *Guardian* 15 Oct. 10/4 Defeats among unilateralists were matched by defeats among believers in the 'great deterrent'. **1960** [see *multilateralist* adj. and sb. s.v. *MULTILATERAL *a.*]. **1980** *Times Lit. Suppl.* 14 Nov. 1277/2 For Bevan was emphatically no fellow-traveller, no isolationist, no unilateralist and certainly no pacifist.

B. *adj.* Of or pertaining to unilateral disarmament, or to unilateralists or their activities.

1959 *Manch. Guardian* 20 July 6/2 There is..little danger that it [*sc.* the Labour Party conference] will go along the unilateralist road. **1960** *News Chron.* 20 Sept. 6/1 By insisting that this country should abandon nuclear weapons and any alliance that possesses them, Mr. Cousins is taking up a unilateralist position. **1963** *Ann. Reg. 1962* 22 Mr Gaitskell's recapture of Labour Party defence policy from the hands of the Campaign for Nuclear Disarmament..had left him exposed as the chief target for unilateralist retaliation.

u:nilateraliza·tion. *Electronics.* [f. UNILATERAL *a.* + -IZATION.] Neutralization (sense *1 d), esp. of resistive as well as reactive feedback. So **unila·teralized** *ppl. a.*

1954 *IRE Trans. Circuit Theory* May 23/1 (*caption*) Lossless unilateralization. *Ibid.*, Suppose..that a number of active devices are to be placed in cascade, each being unilateralized with lossless coupling in order to avoid the problem of wave reflection back through the chain. **1962** [see *NEUTRALIZATION 1 d]. **1974** HARVEY & BOHLMAN *Stereo F.M. Radio Handbk.* v. 99 The winding direction of L_7 is such that signals at the lower end of this coil are in antiphase with the signals at the lower end of L_4. In this way the stage is unilateralized. **1981** E. OXNER in A. D. Evans *Designing with Field-Effect Transistors* iv. 144 The advantages of neutralization and unilateralization are that input and output are effectively isolated from each other and maximum stable gain results.

unili·neal, *a.* [f. UNI- 1 + LINEAL *a.*] **1.** *Anthropol.* Of or relating to a kinship system in which group membership, inheritance, etc., are established through either the father's or the mother's lineage. Opp. *MULTILINEAL *a.*

1935 A. R. RADCLIFFE-BROWN *Structure & Function Primitive Society* (1952) ii. 36 The problem..of the nature and function of the unilineal transmission of rights. **1947** *Advancem. of Sci.* IV. 219/1 This leads to the emergence of more stable groupings of kin according to a principle of unilineal affiliation. **1957** V. W. TURNER *Schism & Continuity in Afr. Soc.* x. 291 Nor is their polity one consisting of homologous unilineal descent groups. **1963** *Brit. Jrnl. Sociol.* XIV. 24 Both [patrilineal and matrilineal] kinds of lineage system are described as *unilineal.* **1964** GOULD & KOLB *Dict. Social Sci.* 367/1 In a double unilineal system, while both parents are severally members of the same group as their child, he has kinsmen..who are not members of either of his unilineal groups. **1976** *Times Lit. Suppl.* 6 Aug. 992/1 Positive marriage rules which established alliance relations between unilineal descent groups.

2. Of a theory, progress, etc.: that adheres to one line of development, *spec.* that of uniform stages in the evolution of culture.

1957 G. CLARK *Archaeol. & Society* (ed. 3) vi. 173 Those who believed in the unilineal progress of culture. **1962** M. S. ZENGEL in J. A. Fishman *Readings Sociol. of Lang.* (1968) 298 It can be said that the 100 word list shows no more validity for this type of unilineal study than the 200 word list. **1968** *Encycl. Brit.* IX. 519/2 In the second half of the nineteenth century a belief in unilineal social evolution and the passage of all peoples through successive and similar stages of development was generally held by anthropologists and was not limited to them. **1980** *Times Lit. Suppl.* 15 Aug. 911/5 Hallpike seems to be a unilineal evolutionist for one kind of cognitive operation (that studied by developmental psychology), and a permissive relativist in the sphere of practical wisdom.

Hence **unili·nealism**, adherence to unilineal views; **unili·neally** *adv.*, in a unilineal manner.

1947 *Advancem. of Sci.* IV. 219/2 Factors tending to produce both unilineal transmission of rights and status and groups of unilineally related kin. **1957** K. A. WITTFOGEL *Oriental Despotism* ix. 371 (*caption*) The spread of a 'Marxist-Leninist' neo-unilinealism. **1964** GOULD & KOLB *Dict. Social Sci.* 367/1 A kind of discrete..descent group which in certain respects resembles a unilineally constructed group. **1984** *Times Lit. Suppl.* 16 Mar. 279/1 Soviet Marxism, as it crystallized during the Stalin period, had a clear and sharp outline, with its theory of a single dominant historical highway... This celebrated unilinealism is easy to attack.

unilingual, *a.* Add: **2.** *absol.* as *sb.* = MONOGLOT *sb. rare.*

1956 *Publ. Amer. Dial. Soc.* XXVI. 9 A monolingual (also called a monoglot or a unilingual) is a person who knows only one language. **1976** *Word 1971* XXVII. 382 Swedish was usually spoken to unilinguals.

unimer (yū·niməɹ). *Chem.* [f. UNI- 2 + *-MER.] One of the single molecules (usu. macromolecules) that go to make up a multimeric aggregation. Cf. *MULTIMER.

1967 *Chimia* XXI. 53/1 Methods to determine the association of macromolecules and to calculate the molecular weight of the unimer..are discussed. **1972** [see *MULTIMER]. **1976** [see *POLYMOLECULAR *a.* d].

unimodal (yūni,mōu·dăl), *a.* [f. UNI- + MODE *sb.* + -AL.] Of a frequency curve or distribution: having one mode (*MODE *sb.* 7 c). Of a phenomenon or property: described by such a distribution.

1923 *Biometrika* XIV. 339 The distribution according to size of family..would be represented by one of the unimodal curves of the Pearson types. **1932** J. S. HUXLEY *Probl. Relative Growth* VII. i. 210 The frequency-curve for female body-length is unimodal. **1975** *Sci. Amer.* Feb. 70/2 The unimodal solar-day rhythms of organisms geared to the 24-hour solar day.

Hence **unimoda·lity**, the property or quality of being unimodal.

1934 in WEBSTER. **1967** *Ann. Math. Statistics* XXXVIII. 1296 (*heading*) A note on the unimodality of distribution functions of class *L.* **1978** *Nature* 3 Aug.

504/1 The switch from bimodality to unimodality (that is convergence of two peaks into one) is what is expected for X-chromosome inactivation.

u:nimole·cular, *a. Chem.* [f. UNI- 1 + MOLECULAR *a.*] **a.** [ad. F. *unimoléculaire* (J. H. Van 't Hoff *Études Dynam. Chim.* (1884) 8).] In chemical kinetics: having or pertaining to a molecularity of one; involving the fragmentation or internal transformation of a single molecule in the rate-determining step of a reaction (rather than the collision of a pair of molecules); in quot. 1901, first-order (see *ORDER *sb.* 10 f). Cf. *MONOMOLECULAR *a.* b.

1901 *Jrnl. Chem. Soc.* LXXX. II. 647 The reaction between ferric salts and metallic iodides is unimolecular for the iron salt and bimolecular for the iodide. **1946** [see *BIMOLECULAR *a.*]. **1972** R. A. JACKSON *Mechanism* i. 5 Unimolecular reactions occur as a result of reorganization of the bonds within a molecule, with or without rupture into fragments. **1978** P. W. ATKINS *Physical Chem.* xxvi. 863 Most reactions can be broken down into a sequence of steps that involve either a unimolecular reaction, in which a single molecule shakes itself apart or into a new configuration, or a bimolecular reaction.

b. = *MONOMOLECULAR *a.* c.

1925 *Proc. R. Soc.* A. CIX. 303 Unimolecular films are thus to be anticipated in those cases in which the surface of the adsorbate is not very active, *e.g.*, on diamond. **1942** S. BRUNAUER *Adsorption of Gases & Vapours* I. i. 6 When a surface can take up only one layer of adsorbed gas the adsorption is called *unimolecular.* [*Note*] I. Langmuir [proposing the concept in 1917] used the term *monomolecular.* However since this is a term of mixed Greek and Latin derivation the use of the term unimolecular is preferable. **1978** K. J. LAIDLER *Physical Chem. with Biol. Applic.* xi. 462 Ammonia molecules are rather strongly attached to such a surface, which may become completely covered by a unimolecular layer.

Hence **unimole·cularly** *adv.*

1901 *Jrnl. Chem. Soc.* LXXX. II. 647 Strontium and calcium iodides act unimolecularly. **1935** *Jrnl. Chem. Physics* III. 112 Suppose we have a non-linear molecule of *n* atoms decomposing unimolecularly. **1974** GILL & WILLIS *Pericyclic Reactions* vi. 203 Both 2,5-dihydrofuran and 1,4-cyclohexadiene are decomposed unimolecularly into hydrogen and respectively furan and benzene.

unimpressively, *adv.* (Earlier example.)

1832 J. S. MILL *Let.* 29 May (1910) I. 30 The opinions I have put forth in these different articles..are expressed so coldly and unimpressively that I can scarcely bear to look back upon such poor stuff.

unimprovability. (Earlier example.)

1814 H. C. ROBINSON *Diary* 28 May (1967) 34 The doctor's favourite opinion of the unimprovability of mankind met with no opposition from the Lambs.

unindicted, *ppl. a.* (Later examples.)

1978 *N.Y. Times* 30 Mar. B13/6 [He] had been named by a grand jury as an unindicted co-conspirator in a series of allegedly illegal break-ins. **1979** *N.Y. Rev. Bks.* 8 Feb. 8/1 The publishers of this chaotically dull..work of angry, apologetic confusion, should be named unindicted co-conspirators in this sinister effort to get those few left who read to switch to television.

unindividualized, *ppl. a.* (Earlier example.)

1844 POE in *Columbian Lady's & Gentleman's Mag.* Aug. 69/2 Man thus divested *would be* God—would be unindividualized.

unineme (yū·ni,nīm), *a. Cytology.* [f. UNI-1 + Gr. νῆμα thread.] Of a chromatid: having (as usual) just one duplex of DNA.

1963 *Proc. Nat. Acad. Sci.* XLIX. 794 Autoradiographic experiments..have yielded results conformable to a polyneme rather than a unineme structure of the chromosome. **1972** *Proc. R. Soc.* B. CLXXXI. 21 Most cytologists refused (and some still refuse) to accept the simplest and most direct deduction from Taylor's classical labelling experiment, namely that a chromatid, prior to replication, is unineme. **1981** *Chromosoma* LXXXII. 1 The unineme concept is supported by genetical data.

Hence **unine·mic** *a.*, in the same sense; **u·ninemy**, the state of having one duplex of DNA per chromatid.

1970 *Cold Spring Harbor Symp. Quantitative Biol.* XXXV. 533/1 The current usage of the hybrid word *uninemic* is, etymologically, quite incorrect. **1972** *Proc. R. Soc.* B. CLXXXI. 26 Another line of evidence for 'uninemy'..was provided a few years ago by Miller. **1980** *Tsitologiya* XXII. 83 Chromosomes are uninemic, i.e. each chromonema consists of a single DNA molecule (or a single chain of linked DNA molecules) whose ends are located in telomeres. **1981** *Chromosome* LXXXII. 1 (*heading*) Evidence for the uninemy of eukaryotic chromatids.

uninhi·bited, *ppl. a.* [UN-1 8.] Not inhibited; unrestrained.

1880 W. JAMES *Feeling of Effort* 24 The motor idea,.. uninhibited by remote associations,..discharges by the preappointed mechanism into the right muscles. **1929** B. RUSSELL *Marriage & Morals* x. 111, I think that uninhibited civilised people, whether men or women, are generally polygamous in their instincts. **1949** M. MEAD *Male & Female* xii. 263 'Why,' asks the uninhibited American child of 1949, 'does no one ever go to the bathroom in a book?' **1956** P. H. JOHNSON *Last Resort* xlv. 293 He coughed once or twice, blew his nose with an uninhibited trumpeting. **1971** S. HILL *Strange Meeting* II. 147 Hilliard stood, pitying them their lack of privacy.. yet envying them too, their carefully ordered life and clear uninhibited friendships and enmities. **1980** A. N. WILSON *Healing Art* xvi. 194 In the States..he was being, according to his own lights, uninhibited.

Hence **uninhi·bitedly** *adv.*

1959 *Times* 10 Jan. 7/6 An informal folk concert in which the audience uninhibitedly join. **1966** L. Ó BROIN *Dublin Castle & 1916 Rising* vi. 47 Birrell was accustomed to express himself thus uninhibitedly to Nathan about personalities. **1976** *New Society* 22 Jan. 147/1 If, as a child, things don't go your way and you're miserable, you can make the point by screaming, kicking or flinging your food on the floor. Adolescents and adults cannot show their unhappiness so uninhibitedly.

uninterested, *ppl. a.* Add: **3.** In this sense *disinterested* is increasingly common in informal use, though widely regarded as incorrect: see *DISINTERESTED *ppl. a.* 1. (Later examples.)

1980 G. GREENE *Dr Fischer* iv. 28, I wouldn't say that —he was totally uninterested in both of us. **1981** *London Rev. Bks.* 19 Nov.–2 Dec. 21 Classical historiography was on the whole uninterested in local provincial history. **1982** D. FRASER *Alanbrooke* iii. 53 He gave, at that time and later, a certain impression of being uninterested in people except at an agreeably superficial level, absorbed only in practical or professional pursuits.

uninterpreted, *ppl. a.* Add: *spec.* in *Logic*, applied to a calculus, formula, or symbol that has no meaning assigned to the symbol(s) independently of the calculus.

1898 A. N. WHITEHEAD *Universal Algebra* i. 5 When the marks and their rules of arrangement are such as appear likely to receive an interpretation..then the art of arranging such marks may be called..an uninterpreted calculus. **1947** H. REICHENBACH *Elem. Symbolic Logic* 165 The uninterpreted formula, regarded only as an aggregate of symbols equipped with certain structural properties. **1963** H. WANG *Survey Math. Logic* ii. 29 It is more correct to call the sentence-like expressions of Q statement schemata..because the symbols for predicate, functions, and individuals are uninterpreted.

uninterruptible, *a.* (Later example.)

1984 *Sunday Tel.* 22 July 13/8 He no longer discusses. He just gives uninterruptible lectures.

uninvitedly, *adv.* (Later example.)

1882 E. W. HAMILTON *Diary* 12 May (1972) I. 272 The Government..could not fail to take heed of information tendered to them uninvitedly.

union, *sb.*1 Add: **I. 1. f.** (Later example.)

1960 C. WINICK *Dict. Anthropol.* 554/2 *Ritual union*, sexual intercourse on special occasions, as part of a ceremonial.

II. 7. f. *India, Pakistan*, and *Bangladesh.* A local administrative unit comprising several rural villages. Freq. *attrib.*

1885 *Bengal Local Self-Govt. Act* ii. § 38 in *Acts of Lieutenant-Governor of Bengal in Council* (1886) 38 The Lieutenant-Governor may, by order in writing, constitute any village or group of villages into a Union; and may prescribe for such Union the number of members of which the Union Committee shall consist. **1959** *Pakistan Q.* Winter 14/2 Basic Democracy creates institutions at the Union, Tehsil, Divisional and Provincial levels... At the Union level the Panchayat or Council, has roughly ten elected and five nominated (non-official) members. **1964** R. W. GABLE in Inayatullah *District Admin. W. Pakistan* I. 15 Basic Democracies are characterized by a four-tier structure of councils... The councils operate, in ascending order, at the level of unions, or groups of villages; *tehsils* (in West Pakistan) and *thanas* (in East Pakistan); districts; and divisions. In urban areas there are Town Committees and Union Committees in place of Union Councils. **1977** *Bangladesh Times* 19 Jan. 1/8 Elections in 229 unions will be held today (Wednesday) in 18 districts of the country.

g. *Math.* The set that comprises all the elements (and no others) contained in any of two or more given sets; also, the operation of forming such a set.

1941, 1968 [see *INTERSECTION 3 b]. **1970** O. DOPPING *Computers & Data Processing* i. 28 The formation of the union is analogous to a logical addition... The union X ∪ Y (also written X+Y and spoken as 'X union Y') comprises all elements which are elements in set X, set Y, or both. **1972** *Computer Jrnl.* XV. 195/1 The character set handled by most of the systems programs is practically the union of all the characters available on the various devices.

V. 11. a. (*b*) *Union Army.*

1866 'F. KIRKLAND' *Bk. Anecdotes* 376 Colonel Bailey.. [believed] that their capture or destruction would involve the destruction of the Union army. **1931** E. O'NEILL *Homecoming* I, in *Mourning becomes Electra* (1932) 27 He wears the uniform of an artillery captain in the Union Army. **1973** A. DUNDES *Mother Wit* 562 The Union Army..was ostensibly fighting in part to end slavery.

c. *union baron, -basher, -card, dues, hours, house, negotiator, pay, scale, ticket; union-bashing, -busting* (also as *pres. pple.*).

1974 *Socialist Worker* 26 Oct. 11/5 There is a need for links with the other unions in the entertainment industry and beyond, not just Media Conferences where Labour MPs and union barons spout and TV directors nod approvingly. **1977** *Times* 14 Sept. 1/1 Voices in the Conservative Party arguing moderation rather than 'union bashing' in its approach to the closed shop... Sir Keith Joseph had been depicted as an 'enthusiastic union basher'. **1980** *Illustr. London News* Mar. 19/3 It [*sc.* the Employment Bill] is not revolutionary, it is not union-bashing, but it imposes some legal restraints on secondary strike activity and provides some stimulus to union democracy. **1913** J. LONDON *Valley of Moon* 198 They're all union-bustin' to beat the band. **1947** *Sun* (Baltimore) 26 June 1/7 Union-busting act. **1874** *Rep. Proc. Internat. Typographical Union N. Amer.* 84 The International Typographical Union shall issue..a card, with appropriate designs, to be called the 'Union Card'. **1977** 'W. HAGGARD' *Poison People* IV. 141 There's..an efficient Trade Union... You'll need a Union card. **1977** *Undercurrents* June–July 11/4 Being an anarchist I don't take dole nor can I afford union dues. **1945** Union hours [see *social disease* s.v. *SOCIAL *a.* 12]. **1937** F. M. FORD *Let.* 27 Mar. (1965) 277 Doing what I can to persuade any publishers..[to have] their printing done by union houses. **1964** *Mod. Law Rev.* XXVIII. III. 274 The local union negotiator (shop steward and the like, who is so vital to the operation of collective bargaining) will..usually be an employee. **1914** D. H. LAWRENCE *Widowing of Mrs. Holroyd* III. 75 Well, if he's badly hurt, there'll be the Union-pay, and sick-pay—we shall manage. **1976** *Honolulu Star-Bull.* 21 Dec. D-2/6 The artists will be paid union scale, and the Kennedy Center is donating the space, he added. **1891** A. FRENCH *Otto the Knight* 19, I went to two or three cities, but I couldn't get work, having no union ticket. **1908** KIPLING *Lett. of Travel* (1920) 167 It is difficult to get skilled labour into here?.. Even if he has his Union ticket? **1948** Union ticket [see *ANTE *v.*].

12. union catalogue, a catalogue of the combined holdings of several libraries; **union dye,** a dye that will satisfactorily dye the two materials of a union cloth, esp. cotton and wool, at the same time; so **union dyeing** *vbl. sb.*; **union list,** a union catalogue, esp. one giving details of periodical holdings in several libraries; **union purchases,** a method of cargo-handling (see quots.); **union shop** orig. *U.S.*, a shop, factory, trade, etc., in which employees must belong to or join a trade union; a post-entry closed shop (see *POST-ENTRY *a.*); **union suit**: restrict † to sense in Dict.; (*b*) chiefly *N. Amer.*, a one-piece undergarment reaching to the ankles; = COMBINATION 9; **union-wide** *a.*, that involves or encompasses the whole of a trade union (movement).

1897 *Libr. Jrnl.* Sept. 437 One of the latest examples of co-operative library work is the union catalog of medical literature recently completed in Denver. **1982** *Papers Dict. Soc. N. Amer. 1979* 83 Most union catalogs are made up from individual libraries' catalog cards and are created by dispensing with the subject element in the individual library catalogs. **1909** OWENS & STANDAGE *Dyeing & Cleaning Textile Fabrics* 36 Union dyes are..of more general adaptation to the renovating of garments than any other class of dyewares. *Ibid.* 38 Full directions are given later for union dyeing. **1963** A. J. HALL *Student's Textbk. Textile Sci.* iv. 191 Union dyes are a mixture of direct cotton dyes and neutral dyeing acid wool dyes. **1974** N. G. & T. E. HARRIES *Textiles* VI. 517 Two variations of piece dyeing are union dyeing and cross dyeing. **1885** *Libr. Jrnl.* X. 370 A union list of periodicals in these libraries. **1968** *Bodl. Libr. Rec.* VIII. 63 Union list of serials in the science area, Oxford. **1978** *Amer. N. & Q.* XVII. 9/1, I am initiating a union list of 19th century photographically illustrated books in library collections throughout the country. **1926** B. CUNNINGHAM *Cargo Handling at Ports* (ed. 2) v. 46 The principle of using the double line with a single hook for the combined process of lifting and slewing, called in this country [*sc.* Great Britain] the Union Purchase. **1961** *B.S.I. News* Mar. 13/1 Greater safety for stevedores handling cargo by the union purchase method (the operation of two ships' derricks in tandem). **1904** *McClure's Mag.* Feb. 370/1 Many stores, restaurants, and saloons display placards in their windows advertising the fact that they are strictly union shops. **1937** F. M. FORD *Let.* 27 Mar. (1965) 276, I will..ask the publisher..whether or not the Riverside Press, which prints this book, is or is not a union shop. **1977** *Time* 7 Mar. 28/2 The section permits states to ban the so-called union shop, which requires new employees to join unions. **1892** *Ladies' Home Jrnl.* Sept. 29/3 *Yes*, you will say to yourself, I know all about *union suits*, but *do* you? **1948** W. FAULKNER *Intruder in Dust* vii. 147 The sagging fences..by nightfall would be gaudy with drying overalls..and unionsuits. **1967** E. S. TURNER *Taking Cure* xii. 187 Smedley..urged the wearing of merino union suits for both adults and children. **1937** *Nation* 14 Aug. 165/1 Assuming..unionwide participation. **1981** *N.Y. Times* 24 Mar. 14B/4 The operators also gave up a unionwide arbitration review board.

‖ **Union Corse** (ünioṅ kǭrs). [Fr., lit. 'Corsican union'.] A criminal organization controlled by Corsicans, operating in France and elsewhere. Cf. next.

1963 I. FLEMING *On Her Majesty's Secret Service* v. 51 'The Union Corse', more deadly and perhaps even older than the Unione Siciliano, the Mafia..it controlled most organised crime throughout metropolitan France and her colonies. **1973** *Times* 21 May 14/3 A key figure was a former model..said to have been living with an Union Corse racketeer..before his death in a gun battle with Mexican police. **1978** W. GARNER *Möbius Trip* (1979) iii. 80 His signet ring featured the Moor's head and eagle of the official Union Corse.

‖ **Unione Siciliana** (ūniō·ne sitʃiliā·na). Also (*erron.*) **Unione Siciliano**, etc. [It., lit. 'Sicilian union'.] A criminal organization controlled by Sicilians, operating in Italy and the United States.

Similar but not equivalent to the Mafia. The Union's roots in the U.S. were apparently as a mutual protection society amongst early Sicilian immigrants.

1924 *Chicago Daily Tribune* 13 Nov. 5/5 At [Merlo's] death he was chairman of the board of the Unione Siciliana, with hundreds of thousands of members. **1924** *Chicago Herald Examiner* 13 Nov. 3/1 A guard also was maintained at the wake for Michael Merlo, head of the Unione Siciliano society. **1930** F. D. PASLEY *Al Capone* (1931) v. 231 Lombardo fell in his tracks, two dumdum bullets in his brain, the third president of the Unione Sicilione to die by the gun. **1956** C. COCKBURN *Discord of Trumpets* xvi. 218 He had recently been elected the President of the Unione Siciliano, a slightly mysterious, partially criminal society, which certainly had its roots in the Mafia. **1970** P. GEDDES *November Wind* iv. 35 The Trust..came into existence when the Mafia and *L'Unione Siciliana* were both on the slide.

unionism. Add: **a.** (Further examples relating to trade unions.)

1904 W. T. MILLS *Struggle for Existence* (ed. 8) xxxv. 487 The New Unionism of recent years has been continuously enlarging the number of those to be included. **1976** F. ZWEIG *New Acquisitive Society* I. v. 65 White-collar unionism has grown over the last two or three decades much faster than manual workers' unionism. **1978** S. BRILL *Teamsters* vii. 279 The appeal of unionism diminished, especially in the eyes of younger workers.

Unionist, *sb.* and *a.* Add: **A.** *sb.* **1. c.** The name remained the official designation of the alliance of Liberal Unionists and Conservatives until 15 January 1922, when the Irish Free State was established. The title is retained, however, by loyalist parties in N. Ireland (the official *Unionist*, *Ulster*, and *Democratic Unionist* Parties, etc.); also in the full name of the Conservative (and Unionist) Party, and in the Scottish Unionist Association (see quot. 1982 of the adj. *1 b).

1953 *Times* 23 Oct. 8/6 The Unionists were returned to power again in the general election in Northern Ireland. **1964** G. D. M. BLOCK *Source Book of Conservatism* 67 In Ulster and Scotland 'Unionist' has entirely carried the day, but in the Southern Kingdom the 'new term' of Conservative has survived as an official name of the Party. **1974** *Times* 18 Feb. 14/8 Opposed to them are three loyalist groups: the Rev Ian Paisley's Democratic Unionists, Mr William Craig's Vanguard Unionists, and Mr Harry West's Ulster Unionists.

B. *adj.* **1. b.** (Earlier and later examples.)

1885 *Cork Constitution* 1 Dec. 3/2 (*heading*) Unionist meeting. **1955** *Times* 16 May 3/5 The fact that Sinn Fein has put forward candidates for West Belfast, Mid-Ulster, and Fermanagh and South Tyrone may mean that a Unionist gain will be recorded. **1965** *Times* 6 Mar. 6/2 The Scottish Conservatives set the seal on their reorganization plans by approving a new constitution today... The title of the organization is to be changed from the Scottish Unionist Association to the Scottish Conservative and Unionist Association. **1974** *Times* 5 Sept. 2/5 Mr Brian Faulkner..launched his own political group yesterday. It is..called the Unionist Party of Northern Ireland. **1982** R. ROSE *Understanding United Kingdom* iii. 68 The Conservative Party officially styles itself the Conservative and Unionist Party. *Ibid.* 69 In Scotland, the party is organized separately. Its modern foundation dates from amalgamation in 1912 of Scottish Conservatives and the Liberal Unionist Association under the name of the Scottish Unionist Association.

unionize, *v.* Add: **2.** *intr.* To become unionized; to join or constitute a trade union.

1969 *Computers & Humanities* IV. 95 It would be especially inappropriate in this context to get into the question of whether scholar/teachers should unionize or professionalize. **1974** J. WHITE tr. *Poulantzas's Fascism & Dictatorship* VI. iv. 292 The agricultural protelariat unionized in massive numbers. **1978** J. L. HENSLEY *Killing in Gold* viii. 99 There is a new breed of schoolteachers... They unionize, they strike.

unioniza·tion (examples); **u·nionized** *ppl. a.* (examples).

1896 *Proc. Internat. Typogr. Union* 30/2, I am sure there would be little to gain in its unionization. **1900** *Amer. Review of Reviews* XXI. 651 This year [*sc.* 1900] the strikes were notably successful—New England papers reporting that nearly every 'unionized' town in that section has now the eight-hour workday for..building trades workmen. **1918** *World's Work* XXXV. 486 The issue of the strike being once more unionization. **1920** A. C. PIGOU *Econ. of Welfare* III. iv. 388 The facts..do not warrant us in supposing that local non-governmental Boards would fail if tried on the less completely unionised soil of the Continent. **1947** J. BERTRAM *Shadow of War* I. iii. 26 Under the reorganised National Government of 1946, the voluntary unionisation of labour in China is legalised in the country as a whole for the first time. **1957** W. H. WHYTE *Organization Man* 42 The employers..resisted unionization. **1978** S. BRILL *Teamsters* v. 159 He was..emphasizing the benefits of unionization. **1980** *Times* 23 Jan. 10/6 We should also ask whether big, bureaucratic, hierarchical, highly unionized, cumbersome and cautious local government machines are the best instruments for delivering social services. **1984** *Guardian* 5 Nov. 6/5 Mr Mondale's day started early yesterday with church in Memphis, just as it began on Saturday among unionised car workers outside Detroit.

unionized (ʊnˌaɪ·ŏnaɪz'd), *ppl. a.*[2] Also **un-ionized.** [UN-[1] 8.] Not ionized.

1900 B. D. JACKSON *Gloss. Bot. Terms* 283/1 *Unionized*, when the molecules are undivided. (J. F. Clark). **1915** *Chem. Abstr.* IX. 1412 Thus HX and YOH (un-ionized) may unite to form HX.YOH. **1962** D. H. CALAM in A. Pirie *Lens Metabolism Rel. Cataract* 439 At the low pH employed, only strongly acidic groups remain charged, most of the carboxyl groups are unionized. **1973** *Sci. Amer.* Apr. 57/1 Later neutral, or un-ionized, sodium was also found to be a constituent of the interstellar medium.

unipare·ntal, *a. Biol.* [UNI- 1.] Of, pertaining to, or derived from, one parent.

1900 K. PEARSON *Grammar of Sci.* (ed. 2) xi. 469 The algebraical discussion of this problem..involves no further assumptions than those already made for uniparental inheritance. **1963** E. MAYR *Animal Species & Evolution* ii. 27 Clandestine sexuality appears to be rather common among so-called asexual organisms. The expression 'uniparental reproduction' is being used increasingly, instead of 'asexual reproduction', to overcome this and other difficulties. **1975** *Nature* 29 May 401/2 This indicates that streptomycin resistance was transmitted in a non-Mendelian, uniparental way [in tobacco hybrids].

unipersonal, *a.* **2.** (Contextual example.)

1843 G. CRANE *Princ. Lang.* v. 207 Verbs, which thus express action without a definitely conceived subject, are called *impersonal*, or perhaps more properly *unipersonal*, verbs.

unipod (yū·nipǫd). *Photogr.* [f. UNI-, after TRIPOD *sb.* 4.] A one-legged support for a camera. Cf. *MONOPODE *sb.*

1935 *Camera* Feb. 361/2 The Unipod. Pocket models, which extend to 4ft. 3 ins. and 5 feet... This real aid to steadiness should meet with a universal sale. **1937** L. C. PELTIER in Fraprie & Jordan *Photographic Hints & Gadgets* 40 (*title*) Unipod made from flexible steel tape measure. **1951** G. H. SEWELL *Amat. Film-Making* (ed. 2) iii. 34 An alternative to the tripod is the 'unipod'. That is a single stick or rod, with a screw at the top for fixing the camera. **1979** *Mod. Photogr.* (N.Y.) Oct. 60/1 (Advt.), Now that you've steadied your camera on a conventional unipod, what are you going to do about your arms?

unipolar, *a.* (and *sb.*). Add: **1. a.** Also *unipolar induction*: electrical induction in which a continuous direct current is produced in a conductor joining a magnetic pole and equator by the rotation of either the conductor or the magnet. Cf. *HOMOPOLAR *a.* 2.

1884 S. P. THOMPSON *Dynamo-Electric Machinery* ix. 176 The same fundamental idea has been worked upon by Messrs. Siemens and Halske, who have produced a so-called 'unipolar' machine. [*Note*] This sounds like a *lucus a non lucendo*, for the machine has two poles. But the name is derived from the term 'unipolar induction', which Continental electricians give to the induction of currents by a process of 'continuous cutting'. **1888** [in Dict.]. **1982** *Astrophysical Jrnl.* CCLXII. 87 A potential drop $\sim 10^{19}$ volts is generated by the unipolar induction of a rotating accretion disk surrounding the black hole.

b. Also, involving, or operating by means of, unipolar induction.

1883, 1884 [in Dict.]. **1884** [see prec. sense]. **1920** *Whittaker's Electr. Engineer's Pocket-bk.* (ed. 4) 139 Unipolar machines have not been able to compete with heteropolar types. **1940, 1973** [see *INDUCTOR 3 b]. **1975** *Nature* 6 Feb. 416/2 The satellite Io acts as a unipolar inductor and a source of constant e.m.f. across the Io flux tube as it moves through the Jupiter magnetic field. **1975** A. SHADOWITZ *Electromagnetic Field* xi. 410 A unipolar generator (or motor) differs from a homopolar generator (or motor) in that the rotating disk or cylinder is also a uniform magnet.

3. *Electronics.* Of a transistor or similar device: involving conduction by charge carriers of a single polarity.

1952 W. SHOCKLEY in *Proc. IRE* XL. 1313/1 In order to distinguish between the more conventional transistors and the analog types, we propose to use the words *bipolar* and *unipolar*. *Ibid.* 1365/2 In a 'field-effect' transistor, the current flow is carried by one type of carrier only... For this reason the name 'unipolar transistors' is proposed. **1973** *Sci. Amer.* Aug. 48/2 Most integrated circuits produced in the 1960's were of the bipolar type, but production of the newer unipolar type is growing rapidly. **1981** J. C. SPROTT *Introd. Mod. Electronics* viii. 169 The bipolar transistor is so named because current is carried simultaneously by charges of both polarities (electrons and holes) rather than by a single species, as in the FET which is an example of a unipolar device.

4. *Psychol.* Of a psychiatric disorder: characterized by depressive but not manic episodes.

1965 *Acta Psychiatrica Scandinavica* Suppl. No. 180. 87 We..have assumed that 'middle age depressions' according to Stenbäck and 'unipolar depressions' according to Leonhard are merely different terms, which..cover the same nosographic entity. **1982** DONLON & ROCKWELL *Psychiatric Disorders* v. 76 Unipolar disorders are much more common than bipolar.

unipole (yū·nipōᵘl). *Radio.* [f. UNI- 2 + POLE *sb.*[2]] = *MONOPOLE[3] 2. Also *attrib.* or as *adj.*

1950 H. P. WILLIAMS *Antenna Theory & Design* II. v. 226 Fig. 5.13 (*b*) shows a folded unipole antenna which is suitable for mounting in an attic. **1958** *Engineering* 31 Jan. 157/3 It works into groundplane folded unipole aerials on top of 80 ft. masts. **1973** *Electronics Lett.* IX. 300/2 The input impedance of a coaxially fed short unipole can be brought to resonance by encasing the antenna in a slab of high-permittivity dielectric material.

unique, *a.* Add: **2. a.** (Later examples.)

1908 K. GRAHAME *Wind in Willows* viii. 168 'Toad Hall,' said the Toad proudly, 'is an eligible self-contained gentleman's residence, very unique.' **1912** CHESTERTON *Manalive* I. iii. 86 Diana Duke..began putting away the tea things. But it was not before Inglewood had seen an instantaneous picture so unique that he might well have snapshotted it. **1939** *Country Life* 11 Feb. p. xviii/2 (Advt.), Almost the most unique residential site along the south coast. **1960** [see *DIQUAT]. **1980** *Verbatim* Autumn 15/2 A high-ranking state Alcoholic Beverage Commission official said Friday that Wednesday's retroactive renewal and transfer of the beverage permit of the rural Bloomington Liars' Lodge by the Monroe County Alcoholic Beverage Board was 'unique but not uncommon'.

b. (Later examples.)

1934 G. B. SHAW *On Rocks* II. 262 You dont appreciate him. He is absolutely unique. **1938** [see *CHEF D'ÉCOLE].

un-Irish, *a.* (Earlier example.)

1829 G. GRIFFIN *Collegians* III. xli. 225 Suicide is a very un-Irish crime.

unirradiated, *ppl. a.* (Later examples.)

1955 *Radiation Res.* II. 364 When both haploid cells were unirradiated, zygote formation occurred in about 95% of the pairs. **1978** *Jrnl. R. Soc. Med.* LXXI. 670 Patients with grade III astrocytoma who were irradiated had greater 1–5 year survival rates than those unirradiated.

unirrigated, *ppl. a.* (Earlier example.)

1876 'MARK TWAIN' *Tom Sawyer* iv. 44 When he emerged from the towel, he was not yet satisfactory, for the clean territory stopped short at his chin... Below..there was a dark expanse of unirrigated soil.

uniselector (yū·niˌsīlektəɹ). *Teleph.* and *Electr.* [f. UNI- 2 + SELECTOR.] A selector (sense *c(*b*)) which has a wiper free to rotate about an axis but not to move along it.

1930 *Gloss. Terms Telegraphs & Telephones* (*B.S.I.*) 27 Uniselector. **1938** C. W. WILMAN *Automatic Telephony* (ed. 2) iii. 20 Single-motion switches are commonly termed uniselectors, lineswitches being known as subscribers' uniselectors. **1956** G. A. MONTGOMERIE *Digital Calculating Machines* ix. 181 The other major component of interest to us is the stepping switch or uniselector. **1971** J. H. SMITH *Digital Logic* i. 4 An electronic telephone exchange uses static switching, but..a conventional exchange..uses relays and uniselectors consisting entirely of moving parts.

u·nisex, *a.* and *sb.* [f. UNI- + SEX *sb.*] **A.** *adj.* Of, pertaining to, or characterized by a style (of dress, appearance, etc.) that is designed or suitable for either sex; not peculiar to one sex, sexually indeterminate or neutral.

1968 *Life* 21 June 87 With-it young couples..are finding that looking alike is good fashion as well as good fun. The unisex trend was launched by..the teen-agers. **1968** *Manch. Guardian Weekly* 21 Nov. 4 Greenwich Village..has just spawned the world's 'first unisex boutique for men and women from 16 to 25'. **1969** *New Yorker* 5 Apr. 99/1 Unisex metallic trouser suits. **1969** *Daily Tel.* 6 June 17 Unisex fashions have literally gone to children's heads, with look-alike brother and sister haircuts. **1970** P. CARLON *Death by Demonstration* vi. 71 A lot of the men..were friendly with her on a strictly unisex level. I mean there was nothing in the slightest degree like romantic attraction. **1972** *Sat. Rev.* (U.S.) 1 July 47/1 'How clean,' 'how Spartan,' 'how unisex' the Chinese appeared to be. **1976** J. I. M. STEWART *Memorial Service* xv. 262 A sexuality quite as strong as Anna's moved beneath the androgynous or 'unisex' persona she had created for herself. **1980** *Times Lit. Suppl.* 21 Mar. 320/1 A group of student actors, all with cropped hair, sallow cheeks and dressed in unisex denims, are warming up in front of a packed house.

B. *sb.* A condition or phase during which people of both sexes appear to be indistinguishable in dress and outward behaviour.

1969 *Sunday Mail* (Brisbane) 11 May 24/8 It's unisex where men and women have abandoned the old 'vive la difference' school of thought in dressing and added a fillip to the old guessing game of 'is it a he or a she?' **1972** *Nature* 28 Jan. 234/2 It could be pertinent to recall that, at the time these results were obtained, the adolescent trend towards unisex was strongly under way. **1976** T. SHARPE *Wilt* i. 5 Eva Wilt was too easily influenced..to be allowed out with a woman who believed that..unisex was here to stay.

unisexual, *a.* Add: **3.** = *UNISEX *a.*

1970 *Sunday Times* 29 Nov. 29/2 Adolescents of both genders strode along..with books and long flaxen unisexual hair. **1978** C. SYKES in R. Buckle *U & Non-U Revisited* 52 By the 1960s unisexual umbrellas were commonplace in Germany.

unisexuality. Add: **b.** In sense of *UNISEXUAL *a.* 3.

1971 *Daily Tel.* 13 Aug. 9/2 If he meant anything serious at all in his comedy..it can only have been the tedium arising from such coy and quaint treatments of unisexuality. **1973** *Ibid.* 25 Sept. 18 The notion of a blatant unisexuality such as she implies is not the aim of these anti-discrimination laws—or of the majority of feminists.

unit, *sb.* (and *a.*). Add: **1. c.** *spec.* one kilowatt-hour, as the unit used in measuring and charging for mains electricity; also, the unit used for metered telephone calls.

1891 *Minutes of Proc. Inst. Civil Engineers* CVI. 16 Fuel used..has..fallen from 12 lbs. to 7·9 lbs. per unit generated. **1926–7** *Army & Navy Stores Catal.* 344/3 Electric radiators... Two bars..consumes 2 units per hour when full-on. **1961** *Which?* Dec. 334/1 Local and trunk calls are divided into 2*d.* 'units', the amount of the time you get for your 2*d.* depending on the distance. **1972** *Daily Tel.* (Colour Suppl.) 12 May 15/1 Food freezers are inexpensive to run, using about 2 units of electricity for each cubic foot per week.

f. *unit of account*, a monetary unit in which accounts are kept; *spec.* in the European Economic Community (see quots. 1977 and 1982).

1882 R. Bithell *Counting-House Dict.* 311 *Unit of Account*, the unit of value in which accounts are kept. It may, or may not, coincide with any coin in circulation. .. The Anglo-Saxon unit of account was the shilling.. but no coin called a *shilling* was issued before the reign of Henry VII. **1959** A. H. Robertson *European Institutions* ii. 42 After offsetting these balances (measured in 'units of account' equivalent to the gold value of the U.S. dollar) against each other, Members are left with a credit or debit account *vis-à-vis* the [European Payments] Union. **1973** *Physics Bull.* Apr. 207/1 The four year allocation for direct research work amounts to 157·2 million units of account (UA, equal to the predevaluation US dollar, ie about £65m). **1977** *Times* 6 Dec. (Europa Suppl.) p. iii/6 *Units of account*, embryonic European currency used as a device for calculating the EEC budget, fixing farm prices and in certain transactions with non-Community countries. The value of the *unit of account* in national currencies depends on the purpose for which it is being used. **1982** J. Phillips *Dict. Trading Terms* 67 The unit of account is now equivalent to a group, or 'basket' of fixed amounts of European currencies, and is described as a 'basket unit of account'.

g. A basic measure of educational attainment credited to a student for completing the number of hours of study assigned to one section of an academic course. Cf. *credit *sb.* 13 d. *U.S.*

1894 *Univ. of Chicago Weekly* 4 Oct. 4/1 The system of majors and minors, units and flunks, is harder to understand than any other 'credit' method in operation among educational institutions. **1930** A. Flexner *Universities* ii. 47 When a college catalogue states that fifteen units of high school work are required for matriculation, a unit, as defined by the College Entrance Examination Board, represents one year's study in any one subject in a high school. **1945** C. V. Good *Dict. Educ.* 436/1 *Unit*..(3) a basic measure used in calculating the amount of credit to be assigned to any particular course or the number of graduation credits earned by a pupil or student in completing a course..(*a*) in secondary education, one *unit* equals approximately 120 hours of classroom or laboratory work in a given subject..(*b*) in higher education,..one *unit* may equal 1 hour of class or laboratory work per week during one term, semester, or school year. **1974** *Aiken* (S. Carolina) *Standard* 18 Apr. 4-C/3 Their required 18 units of study. **1981** D. Rowntree *Dict. Educ.* 335 *Unit*... 3 (US) In high school, one hour in class per day of a subject (for five days a week over the academic year) counts as one course unit of that subject.

h. The standard unit of quantity by which bread and petrol were rationed during and immediately after the war of 1939–45; a coupon of this value.

1939 *Punch* 18 Oct. 439 (*caption*), I can't move on—I've used up all my units. **1946** [see B.U. s.v. B III. b]. **1948** *Daily Tel.* 26 Oct. 5 Nine Hundred Petrol Units were stolen from an office at Swanley, Kent. **1963** S. Cooper in Sissons & French *Age of Austerity* ii. 41 The Bread Unit represented seven ounces of bread... A large loaf..would require four Units, one pound of flour three Units.

2. d. A group of buildings, wards, etc., in a hospital; *spec.* one equipped to provide a particular type of health care.

1893 D. Galton *Healthy Hospitals* xiii. 229 Separation of the ward unit has been the principal feature of modern hospital construction in Germany and..the United States. **1911** W. Osler in *Lancet* 28 Jan. 212/1 There might be, as at Berlin and Vienna, two or three medical and the same number of surgical units. **1927** J. E. Stone *Hospital Organization & Management* xiv. 287 The operating theatre unit is a very important part of a hospital. **1955** R. F. Bridgman *Rural Hospital* ii. 70 With the rural hospital as a base, mobile health-units may be organized, through which modern medical techniques can be taken to the villages in sparsely populated countries with poor communications. **1965** *Nursing Times* 5 Feb. p. vi/1 (Advt.), Plastic Surgery and Burns Unit..Regional Thoracic Surgical Unit. **1976** *Amer. Speech 1973* XLVIII. 195 The inhalation therapist, for example, supplies hospital floors, or units, with oxygen masks and in emergencies is summoned to start and operate O_2 tents 'oxygen tents'.

e. A piece of (esp. storage) furniture or equipment which may be fitted with other pieces to form a larger system, or which is itself composed of smaller complementary parts. Freq. *attrib.* Also *transf.* (see also *unit audio, construction*, sense 3 c below).

1912 L. Weaver *House & its Equipment* 44 The unit system of bookcases, by which they are built up of sections of standard size, and are thus capable of indefinite expansion. **1930** *N.Y. Times* 10 Aug. v. 14/4 He [*sc.* Franz Schuster] has developed a kind of 'unit' furniture. He reduces the shapes of chest and cabinet to their fundamental forms and by standardizing their measurements permits the combination of parts by the manufacturer. **1937** [see *kitchen unit* s.v. *kitchen *sb.* 5 c]. **1944** J. van Druten *Voice of Turtle* i. 3 The kitchen has an icebox, stove and sink in a combined unit in the left wall. **1958** *Engineering* 7 Mar. 320/2 The cooking unit ..is mounted on top of a storage cupboard with a sliding serving shelf. **1974** *Gramophone* Nov. 1009 The connoisseur takes pride in choosing separate units. **1978** [see *recliner 2]. **1981** M. E. Atkins *Palimpsest* ix. 92 I'm going to..start with the kitchen. I'll have units all round, a new sink and cooker.

f. An accommodation unit in a larger building or group of buildings, esp. in a block of flats or a motel. *U.S., Austral.*, and *N.Z.*

1932 F. L. Wright *Autobiogr.* ii. 223, I lingered in Los Angeles aided by my son Lloyd working on the new unit-block system. **1937** *Tourist Court Jrnl.* Oct. 6/2 Being separate units each cottage is assured of ample ventilation..through the windows on each side. **1953** *Hotel Monthly* Nov. 27/1 Additional units will be added to the Kahler Ranchotel. **1963** D. B. Hughes *Expendable Man* ii. 46 No one was waiting for him at the motel. No one stopped him at the door of his unit. **1971** 'A. Blaisdell' *Practice to Deceive* i. 2 She lived in one unit of a triplex. **1973** *Sun-Herald* (Sydney) 26 Aug. 103/1 We live in a unit in a delinquency-prone inner area. **1980** 'D. Shannon' *Felony Files* x. 230 It was a pleasant, unpretentious furnished apartment in a six-unit place.

g. = *film unit* s.v. *film *sb.* 7 c.

1959 E. H. Clements *High Tension* i. 13 The hectic urgency of everyone else in the unit. **1962** L. Davidson *Rose of Tibet* i. 26 Location work would have finished in Calcutta and..the unit would have moved up into the foothills of Everest.

3. c. Special Combinations. **unit audio**, a sound reproduction system which comprises separate matching parts; **unit cell** *Cryst.*, the smallest structural unit having the overall symmetry of a crystal, which by repetition in three dimensions gives the entire lattice; **unit character** *Genetics*, a character inherited according to Mendelian laws, esp. one controlled by a single pair of alleles; also, † the alleles themselves (see quot. 1966); **unit construction**, modular construction, esp. of buildings (cf. *modular *a.* 1 b); **unit cost** *Accounting*, the cost of manufacturing or otherwise processing one unit of production; **unit factor** *Genetics* = *gene (cf. *factor *sb.* 7 b); now *hist.*; **unit-holder**, one who holds securities in a unit trust; **unit-linked** *a.*, of a life assurance policy (see quot. 1979); **unit load**, a package of goods arranged for shipment, etc., as a single unit (esp. on a pallet) to facilitate handling; **unit matrix** *Math.* = *identity matrix* s.v. *identity 10; **unit membrane** *Biol.*, any lipoprotein membrane composed of two electron-dense layers enclosing a less dense layer, found enclosing many cells and cell organelles; **unit price**, the price at which a single unit of a commodity is sold; **unit pricing** (see quot. 1970); **unit train** *N. Amer.*, a train allocated to transport a single commodity (i.e. coal or grain) at special rates between two points; **unit trust**, an investment group investing combined contributions from many persons in various securities and paying them dividends in proportion to their holdings.

1966 *Hi-Fi News* Nov. 592/3 'Unit audio' is the name given to a new range of matching equipment... Two loudspeakers, a tuner-amplifier, an amplifier and a tape recorder..are available. **1976** *Gramophone* Nov. 880/1 People without expert knowledge will generally find it easier to buy a 'unit audio' system made up from matching units from the same manufacturer. **1915** W. H. & W. L. Bragg *X-Rays & Crystal Structure* viii. 116 Only calcium and carbon atoms are shown in their places in the unit cell of the structure. **1930** G. P. Thomson *Wave Mech. Free Electrons* iii. 40 Each unit cell of a crystal lattice contains the same amount of matter similarly arranged. **1966** C. R. Tottle *Sci. Engin. Materials* iii. 50 In many cases it is convenient to avoid drawing the complete crystal lattice extended over many unit cells, and merely to draw the unit cell itself. **1977** A. Hallam *Planet Earth* 114 All crystalline substances have lattices built of one of these types of unit cell. **1902** Bateson & Saunders *Rep. Evol. Comm. R. Soc.* I. 126 The purity of the germ-cells, and their inability to transmit both of the antagonistic characters, is the central fact proved by Mendel's work. We thus reach the conception of unit-characters existing in antagonistic pairs. Such characters we propose to call allelomorphs. **1903** *Biometrika* II. 286 Mendel was the first to systematically analyse the differential characters of a race or species into a series of unit-characters, each of which might..be inherited independently of the others. **1915** T. H. Morgan et al. *Mechanism of Mendelian Heredity* ix. 210 So much misunderstanding has arisen amongst geneticists themselves through the careless use of the term 'unit character' that the term deserves the disrepute into which it is falling. **1945** M. F. Glaessner *Princ. Micropalaeontol.* v. 79 The numerical values of morphological features (unit characters) plotted against numbers of specimens in which the progressive values occur, tend to arrange themselves in a regular curve. **1966** E. A. Carlson *Gene* ii. 13 The unit-character [of Bateson] combined the 'differentiating character' used by Mendel with the 'formative element' which he assumed to represent it in the germ cell. **1921** *Conquest* May 291/2 Houses built on the 'Unit' construction system... The concrete blocks are made of a standard size, the dimensions of windows and door openings being made multiples of the block size. **1959** *Motor Manual* (ed. 36) v. 3 The body now forms the main structure of the car... This form of construction is now known by a variety of names, including 'integral construction', 'unit construction' and 'chassisless construction'. **1964** *McCall's Sewing* ii. 33/1 *Unit construction*, organisation of sewing procedure so that an entire garment section is completed before it is joined to another. **1914** E. H. Jones *Unit Construction Costs from New Smelter* 1498 These unit costs..represent delays in material shipments.., delayed plans,..labor troubles, [etc.]. **1962** *Listener* 17 May 835/1 Wages and unit costs rise faster than ever. **1978** J. Kellock *Elements of Accounting* iii. 66 The stock valuation..is calculated by taking a physical stock count of the stock on hand at the end of the period and multiplying each item by the appropriate unit of cost... Unit cost is the cost of purchasing or manufacturing identifiable units of stock. **1911** Unit factor [see *gene]. **1926** J. S. Huxley *Ess. Pop. Sci.* 9 Inheritance takes place by means of separable units, generally known as unit-factors or genes. **1966** E. A. Carlson *Gene* iv. 26 When unit-character was changed to 'unit-factor' or to 'factor' alone, Castle no longer dissociated the transmitting agent from its effect on a character. **1965** M. Naylor *Your Money* 87 One great advantage of unit trusts is that unit-holders can buy or sell at any time, and get the 'true' value of their investment. **1969** *Daily Tel.* 8 Feb. 6/3 A unit trust management pays capital gains tax at 30 p.c. for either long- or short-term gains, irrespective of the tax position of the individual unitholder. **1969** *Times* 30 Apr. 28/3 Nearly every time we open the paper we read of the attractions of Unit Trusts and Unit-linked life assurance policies. **1979** F. E. Perry *Dict. Banking* 258/2 *Unit-linked policy*, a type of life assurance policy where a part of the premium is invested on behalf of the assured in a unit trust. **1939** *Steel* 12 June 54/1 (*caption*) Unit load of four edgewise-wound copper coils on pallet handled by fork truck. **1945** D. L. Beattie *Unit Load Materials Handling* I. 9 Once the unit load is established for a material, there is every reason to expect that this unit load may be standardized. **1970** *Times* 2 June (Container Suppl.) p. i/1 The British Transport Docks Board has a nationwide network of nine well equipped ports, providing some of the most advanced facilities for unit-load handling. **1862** Unit-matrix [see *premultiplication]. **1972** M. Kline *Math. Thought* xxxiii. 807 The product of a matrix and its inverse is the unit matrix, denoted by *I*. **1959** J. D. Robertson in E. M. Crook *Structure & Function Subcellular Components* (Biochem. Soc. Symposium XVI) 33 Perhaps the gap substance or the character of the unit membrane surfaces here is different. **1970** Ambrose & Easty *Cell Biol.* v. 173 The chloroplast, like all plastids, is bounded by a double unit membrane. **1934** Webster, Unit price. **1953** [see *field *sb.* 15 f]. **1977** P. Way *Super-Celeste* i. 45 Whoever sold a plane here would sell it to NATO through the 1990s. Sell here and the unit price would come down. **1970** *Wall St. Jrnl.* 17 June 40/4 Mr. Alldredge..told the meeting that 'unit pricing', or the marking of all packaged commodities with the price per unit weight, 'would be frighteningly expensive'. **1971** *Guardian* 3 June 2/6 Unit pricing, a new system under which large supermarkets have to indicate the cost of food items by measure, completed its first day here [*sc.* in New York]. **1967** *Times Rev. Industry* Apr. 47/2 Unit trains working on the principles now applied in the Great Lakes coal trade would discharge coal through ground hoppers without uncoupling. **1979** *Sci. Amer.* Jan. 29/1 (*caption*) Coal-carrying 'unit' trains have been developed to move coal expeditiously at low cost, usually between one mine and one customer, which is most often an electric utility. The trains shuttle back and forth without being uncoupled, acting much like a conveyor belt. **1936** *Economist* 18 Apr. 135/2 Three new trusts with different degrees of flexibility have recently appeared, which extend the activities of the unit trust movement into new fields. **1958** *Spectator* 18 July 108/1 All unit trusts have this much in common: investments..are deposited with a bank or insurance company, acting as trustee, who issues participation certificates (called units) in exchange. **1980** *Times* 5 Jan. 18 Most of the unit trusts managed not to lose too much money for unit holders last year.

unitard (yū·nitɑːd). orig. *U.S.* Also **Unitard, unitards.** [f. Uni- + *leo)tard.] A tight-fitting one-piece garment of stretchable fabric which covers the body from neck to feet, worn by gymnasts, dancers, and as a fashion garment. (Formerly a proprietary name in the U.S.) Cf. *cat-suit* s.v. *cat *sb.*[1] 18.

1961 *Official Gaz.* (U.S. Patent Office) 5 Dec. TM15/1 Danskin Inc., New York... Unitard. For one piece form-fitting integral neck-to-ankle..garment, with sleeves, for gymnastics, and dance use. **1978** *Newsweek* 13 Feb. 68/3 Danskin now offers 75 styles for men, women and children, including..a one-piece neck-to-toe 'Unitard'. **1978** *Washington Post* 11 Dec. B8/2 Stan Fowler..had cut, dyed and sewn together the pieces of his 'milliskin unitard' to get the Spiderman look of bright blue and red from head to toe. **1979** *N.Y. Times* 2 Feb. C16 One woman, dressed in unitards and a wide gold sash, bounces dull-eyed in the center of the rooms. **1984** *Times* 14 Feb. 9/2 Unitards—one-piece suits with built-in leg interest like stripey panels at the calf.

Unitarian, *sb.* and *a.* Add: **A.** *sb.* **2. c.** (Earlier example.)

1832 *Ann. Reg. 1831 Hist.* xv. 464/2 The Unitarians were dispossessed of the government of that province [*sc.* Entre-rios, Argentina], and the preponderance of Buenos Ayres restored.

d. A critic who ascribes the *Iliad* and the *Odyssey* to the same author. Opp. *separatist *sb.* 1 f. Cf. Chorizontes *sb. pl.*

1959 *Times Lit. Suppl.* 13 Mar. 138/4 Any Unitarian must depend very largely on demonstrating some recognizable pattern or design in the Homeric poems as evidence of single authorship. **1976** [see *separatist *sb.* 1 f].

B. *adj.* **2. d.** Applied to the theory that the *Iliad* and the *Odyssey* are the work of a single person. Cf. *Homeric question* s.v. Homeric *a.*, and prec. sense.

1865 M. Pattison in *North British Rev.* June 277 Even on the more special question of the origin of the Homeric poems,..we may safely say that no scholar will again find himself able to embrace the unitarian hypothesis.

unitary, *a.* Add: **4. d.** *Math.* and *Physics.* Applied to mathematical entities that in some specific way are described by or related to a *unitary matrix*, one which when multiplied by the transpose of its complex conjugate gives the unit matrix; *unitary group*, the group of all square unitary matrices of a given size; *unitary symmetry*, the symmetry of a unimodular unitary group as used to relate the properties of different sub-atomic particles.

1908 H. Hilton *Introd. Theory Groups Finite Order* iii. 16 The substitution *A* is called..unitary if $A\bar{A}' = 1$. **1935** P. A. M. Dirac *Princ. Quantum Mech.* (ed. 2) v. 111 We can now see that a unitary transformation transforms observables into observables. **1937** *Physical Rev.* LI. 109/2 The representations of the four-dimensional unitary group will characterize the multiplet systems. **1941** Birkhoff & MacLane *Survey Mod. Algebra* ix. 255 One may adopt the properties of linearity, skew-symmetry, and positiveness as the postulates for an inner product.. in an abstract vector space over the complex numbers; the space is then called a unitary space. *Ibid.*, A linear transformation *T* of the space is unitary if it preserves lengths $|\xi T| = |\xi|$. **1961** M. Gell-Mann in Gell-Mann & Ne'eman *Eightfold Way* (1964) i. 12 We attempt..to treat the eight known baryons as a supermultiplet, degenerate in the limit of a certain symmetry but split into isotopic spin multiplets by a symmetry-breaking term... The symmetry is called unitary symmetry and corresponds to the 'unitary group' in three dimensions in the same way that charge independence corresponds to the 'unitary group' in two dimensions. **1969** [see *Lie]. **1975** *Physics Bull.* Apr. 176/2 Strong interactions among nucleons are invariant under a group of unitary symmetry transformation which changes protons into neutrons and vice versa—the group SU(2). **1979** Cheng & O'Neill *Elementary Particle Physics* xiii. 275 The mathematical groups on which elementary particle physicists have concentrated most of their attention are..continuous groups described by matrices *U* that are unitary: $U^{\dagger}U = 1$.

6. Special collocations: *unitary taxation* (U.S.), a system of taxation by which a company or business is taxed on a proportion of its worldwide earnings, and not just on those made within the jurisdiction of the taxation authority (i.e. a State government); also *unitary tax*.

1977 *Washington Post* 14 Aug. A8/4 Brown is moving to alleviate concerns of multinational companies over the state's 'unitary tax'. **1979** *Economist* 7 July 91/2 Unitary taxation (purists call it combined or consolidated income reporting)..hits a company not on profits made in a given state but on a percentage of the parent's total (multi-state or world-wide) income. **1984** *Miami Herald* 6 Apr. 22A/3 When the governor crawfishes out of his ill-advised unitary tax (his great tax-reform promise), the greedy ones might try to increase property taxes again.

Hence **u·nitarily** *adv.*, in a unitary manner; **unita·rity**, the property of being unitary.

1932 *Amer. Jrnl. Math.* LIV. 149 Similar unitary matrices are..always unitarily equivalent. **1959** *Nuovo Cimento* XIII. 354 The unitarity of the *S*-matrix implies that it can be written in terms of a hermitian matrix *A* in the form *S* = [etc.]. **1969** *Nature* 24 May 720/1 SU2 and SU3..are simple unitary symmetries in which the unitarity ensures that a set of possibilities has unit probability. **1979** J. C. Polkinghorne *Particle Play* vi. 88 S-matrix theory played a valuable role in highlighting certain general properties (unitarity, crossing, analyticity) which are important aspects of relativistic quantum mechanics.

united, *ppl. a.* Add: **4. a.** *United Empire Loyalist*: see Loyalist; *United Front*, a common alliance of political groups; *spec.* in Communism: (*a*) = *Popular Front; (*b*) in Chinese communism, an alliance with the Kuomintang; subsequently, a coalition of several parties in a Communist government; also *transf.*

1934 A. Werth *France in Ferment* xiii. 277 The rank and file of the United Front and of Bergery's Front Commun are merely unhappy and disgruntled people. **1935** B. Russell *Relig. & Sci.* ii. 42 The wars of religion made a 'united front' desirable. **1937** E. Snow *Red Star over China* iii. iii. 101 The building up of a United Front, such as has been advocated by the Communist Party ever since 1932. **1943** J. T. Pratt *War & Politics in China* xv. 264 Ch'iang Kai Shek..sternly rejected the overtures of the Shensi communists who naively proposed to enter the united front as the equal allies of the Kuomintang. **1954** *Round Table* Dec. 46 United Front leaders in East Bengal. **1958** J. Cannan *And be Villain* i. 6 That blasted Primrose will have arrived..and the old witch herself will be there. ..I'll have a united front to cope with. **1971** J. J. Taylor in D. J. Dwyer *China Now* (1974) xxii. 412 Mao's insistence on the development of an armed capability..is a reflection of the history and the experience of the Chinese Communist Party, most notably the failure in 1927 of the First United Front with the KMT and the marked Communist success with the Second United Front between 1937 and 1945. **1980** S. J. Burki *Pakistan under Bhutto* ii. 22 The Muslim League was squarely beaten in Bengal by the United Front.

b. United Kingdom: (after the formation of the Irish Free State in 1921) of Great Britain and Northern Ireland.

d. United Nations: in the war of 1939–45, the Allied nations who united against the Axis powers; hence, an international peace-seeking organization of these and many other States, founded by charter in 1945 (in full, *United Nations Organization*), with a permanent headquarters in New York; abbrev. *U.N.* s.v. *U 4 a; cf. *League of Nations; *Security Council* s.v. *security 12 e; *trusteeship 2 b.

1942 *Daily Tel.* 28 Jan. 3/3 But at any rate it will be long enough for Japan to inflict..losses upon all of the United Nations who have..possessions in the Far East. **1942** H. A. Wallace in *N.Y. Times* 9 Nov. 19/7 The first article in the international law of the future is undoubtedly the United Nations' Charter. **1944** [see *Security Council* s.v. *security 12 e]. **1946** A. Boyd (*title*) The United Nations Organisation handbook. **1953** R. Niebuhr *Christian Realism & Polit. Probl.* (1954) ii. 25 The necessarily minimal constitutional structure which we have embodied in the United Nations. **1958** *Times* 7 Aug. 7/5 It emphasizes..the case for creating a permanent United Nations police force, including an increased number of United Nations observers. **1974** P. Gore-Booth *With Great Truth & Respect* 141 Mrs Eleanor Roosevelt came to propose that the organization be called 'The United Nations'... I put forward a motion to the effect that we accept Mrs Roosevelt's proposal subject to a committee of jurists being satisfied that the term 'United Nations' presented no legal difficulty. **1980** *Jrnl. R. Soc. Arts* July 501/2 The *inter-governmental* component of world conservation is represented by the United Nations Environment Programme (UNEP).

United States. 1. b. (Earlier examples.)

1776 *Jrnls. Continental Congress* (1906) VI. 865 Resolved, that the inhabitants of Canada, captivated by the United States..be released and sent home.

attrib. **1819** G. Flagg *Let.* 12 June in *Trans. Illinois State Hist. Soc. 1910* (1912) XV. 165 They settle on united States land.

Uniterm (yū·nitəɹm). *Library Science.* Also † **unit term.** [f. Uni- 2 or Unit *sb.* (and *a.*) + Term *sb.*] The name for a system of indexing whereby each of a series of documents is accessible through an alphabetical index of subject headings; a keyword which forms one of these subject headings.

1952 M. Taube in *Amer. Documentation* III. 213/2 The basic ideas of unit terms as a substitute for standard indexing for subject headings and logical combination and order as a substitute for..alphabetic cross-reference structures. **1953** —— et al. *Studies in Compar. Indexing* I. 5 We have used the name 'coordinate indexing' for this general method and the more specific name 'Uniterm System' to designate a particular manual application of coordinate indexing. **1961** T. Landau *Encycl. Librarianship* (ed. 2) 100/1 Co-ordinate indexing..is based on the conception of the Uniterm... In the Uniterm system each book..or other item is numbered as it is received and.. it is possible to gain an approximate idea of the date of any currently-published item from its serial number. The title, salient contents, etc.,..are then analysed into fundamental terms usually of one word each. These constitute the Uniterms. **1976** *Gloss. Documentation Terms* (*B.S.I.*) 70 *Uniterm*, originally a single word selected from, and characterizing a part of the subject matter of, a document, for use in a co-ordinate indexing system. Now loosely used as a synonym for keyword or descriptor.

unitiza·tion. [f. next + -ation.] **1.** The joint development of a petroleum source which straddles territory controlled by several companies.

1930 *Handbk. Unitization of Oil Pools* (Mid-Continent Oil & Gas Assoc.) i. 15 The term 'Unitization' refers to the practice of unifying the ownership and control of an actual or propective oil or gas pool by the issuance or assignment of units or undivided interests in the entire area with provision for development and operation by an agent, trustee or committee representing all holders of undivided interests therein. **1938** D. Hager *Practical Oil Geol.* (ed. 5) ix. 263 The ideal is for one oil concern to own a whole field and to unitize the leases so that property owners are allowed a royalty on all the oil produced in proportion to their property holdings. *Ibid.*, Unitization as an ideal is fine for the oil producer. **1952** *South Western Reporter* (U.S.) CCXLIX. 917/1 Respondents suggest that the conclusion we have reached will discourage the making of unitization agreements. **1977** *Internat. & Compar. Law Q.* XXVI. 353 Discussions are already under way between Norway and the United Kingdom on the unitisation of the Statfjord oil and gas field.

2. The packaging of cargo into unit loads (see *unit *sb.* (and *a.*) 3 c); = *palletization.

1953 *Times* 20 Jan. 2/5 Addresses will be given on.. 'Packaging and air freight', and 'Packaging and unitization'. **1967** D. Wilson *Use of Expendable Pallets* 1 Since most modern handling systems of unit loads are based around the fork-lift truck there has to be a common denominator of any method of unitisation i.e. that it is capable of being lifted and moved by fork-lift truck. **1981** E. Corlett *Revolution Merchant Shipping* 12/1 Militating against the spread of container unitisation was the lack of infra-structure.

3. Conversion of an investment trust to a unit trust (see *unit *sb.* (and *a.*) 3 c).

1974 *Daily Tel.* 10 Aug. 17/4 The cost of unitisation 'would be high'. **1982** *Observer* 7 Feb. 20/1 Fleming.. may well find that unitisation cannot be avoided in respect of some of the trusts.

unitize, *v.* Delete *rare* and add: **1.** (Later examples.)

1939 D. Hager *Fund. Petroleum Industry* ix. 201 The new drilling outfits are unitized, i.e., the various sections are mounted on single steel frames which are enclosed in steel cases to protect the workers from the machinery. **1962** *Engineering* 21 Sept. 369 As much as possible of each engine has been 'unitized'.

2. *techn.* In the senses of: **a.** *unitization 1.

1938 D. Hager *Pract. Oil Geol.* (ed. 5) ix. 263 The ideal is for one oil concern to own a whole field and to unitize the leases.

b. *unitization 2.

1962 [see *containerize *v.*]. **1968** *Globe & Mail* (Toronto) 13 Feb. B1/8 The parcel was not drilled, but was unitized into one of the Rainbow pools and is producing revenue pro-rated to the company's share of the pool's reserves. **1973** (*title*) Packing for profit 1: the economic advantages of unitising break-bulk cargo.

c. *unitization 3. Also *intr.* or *absol.*

1978 *Daily Tel.* 4 Feb. 21/1 With the current average discount on investment trust shares running at around 30 p.c. there is considerable pressure from the private shareholder to unitise the trusts, which would mean a payout at the full value of the underlying investments. **1982** *Sunday Times* 7 Feb. 54/1 Robert Fleming..promised to visit unitising seriously.

unitized *ppl. a.* (later examples).

1947 *Sun* (Baltimore) 23 Aug. 7 You must see the Nash '600' to realize how far into the future this big car takes you..with..girder-strong unitized body and frame. **1950** *Nucleonics* May 15/2 The fitting of unitized furniture into the laboratory is a critical consideration which must be applied to the dimensioning of all of the rooms. **1961** *Times* 22 Feb. 11/6 In the United States mechanized and 'unitized' general cargo handling is racing ahead. **1964** *Economist* 26 Sept. 1243/1 The roads have..introduced.. unitised trains made up of wagons carrying one product to one customer. **1970** R. P. Loveland *Photomicrography* I. iii. 121 Unitized construction allows change of body tube between binocular and monocular for photomicrography. **1978** *N.Y. Times* 29 Mar. D10/5 The Institute of Mental Health, a unitized psychiatric hospital, requires a clinical psychologist PhD.

Univ (yū·niv), colloq. abbrev. of University *sb.* 1; *spec.* University College (Oxford, etc.) Cf. *uni.

1896 F. W. Maitland *Let.* 6 Dec. (1965) 153 We have several good MSS at the Univ. Lib. **1903** Farmer & Henley *Slang* VII. 256/1 *Univ, subs.* (Oxford University), University College. **1950** M. Marples *University Slang* 131 *Oxford colleges... University*: always *Univ* nowadays, but apparently *Varsity* during the second half of the last century.

univalent, *a.* Add: **1.** Now usu. with pronunc. (yūni,vēⁱ·lěnt).

2. *Cytology.* (yūni·vălěnt). [ad. mod.L. *univalens* (introduced in Ger. by O. Hertwig 1890, in *Arch. f. mikrosk. Anat.* XXXVI. 6).] Of a chromosome: remaining unpaired during meiosis. Cf. *monovalent *a.* 3.

1898 *Zool. Jahrb.* (Abt. für Anat.) XII. 79 The chromosomes of the 1st reduction division are univalent, when they occur in the normal number. **1916** *Jrnl. Morphol.* XXVII. 226, I believe he [*sc.* Haecker] is wrong in thinking that the 'univalent' chromosomes making up these 'bivalents' are to be considered as members of homologous chromosome pairs. **1971** *Nature* 19 Feb. 570/2 Many authors have reported that the behaviour of univalent chromosomes at meiosis is irregular. **1981** *Jrnl. Cell Biol.* LXXXVIII. 281 During meiosis I in males of the mole cricket *Neocurtilla (Gryllotalpa) hexadactyla*, the univalent X_1 chromosome and the heteromorphic X_2Y chromosome pair segregate nonrandomly.

3. *Immunol.* = *monovalent *a.* 2 b.

1939 *Bacteriol. Rev.* III. 76 If Hooker and Boyd now believe antibody to be univalent they must abandon the entire basis for these and other of their calculations. **1940** *Jrnl. Exper. Med.* LXXI. 271 Antibody is referred to as low grade, incomplete, imperfect, or 'univalent' in instances in which it is incapable by itself of precipitating with added antigen. **1977** M. W. Steward in Glynn & Steward *Immunochemistry* vii. 245 There are several reports which show the reduction in neutralization of both animal viruses..and bacteriophages..when univalent antibodies have been used.

B. *sb. Cytology.* (yūni·vălěnt). A univalent chromosome.

1912 *Jrnl. Exper. Zool.* XIII. 350 In the first division the X- and Y-chromosomes divide as separate univalents. **1921** *Ann. Bot.* XXXV. 173 These chromosomes were of two types, as revealed during meiosis, fourteen being bivalents and twenty-one univalents. **1971** *Nature* 19 Feb. 570/2 In the triploid species *Leucopogon juniperinus* univalents are close to the poles at metaphase, but..they are not in the same plane as the spindle on which the bivalents are positioned.

universal, *a.* (*adv.*) and *sb.* Add: **A.** *adj.* **9. b.** Also *Universal Aunts*, the name of a company incorporated in 1922 and based in London, which provides domestic assistance to its clients through a staff of professional helpers; hence *Universal Aunt*, a member of the organization; usually *transf.* Cf. *aunt 1 b. Similarly *Universal Uncle*.

1922 *Certificate of Incorporation No. 185,178* (Department of Trade) 20 Oct., I hereby certify that Universal Aunts, Limited is this day incorporated under the Companies Acts..and that the Company is Limited... Registrar of Joint Stock Companies. **1923** *Westm. Gaz.* 10 Jan. 7/6 Associations such as 'Universal Aunts' and 'Useful Women' who supply workers for..social work. **1929** M. Allingham *Mystery Mile* iii. 38 He's really a sort of 'Universal Aunt', isn't he? 'Your adventures undertaken for a small fee.' **1931** —— *Look to Lady* iii. 42, I am..a sort of universal uncle, a policeman's friend and master-crook's factotum. **1937** A. THIRKELL *Summer Half* viii. 229 The universal uncle went down to dinner. **1961** *Listener* 12 Oct. 576/1 His role of cultural Universal Uncle. **1978** M. DICKENS *Open Book* iv. 33 There was a domestic agency in Knightsbridge called Universal Aunts—now in Chelsea—which was famous for doing things that real aunts ought to be doing, like meeting small boys from India at the boat train and taking them across London to their train for school.

c. Also *universal decimal classification*, a form of decimal library classification (see *DECIMAL *a.* 1 a).

1930 [see *DECIMAL *a.* 1 a]. **1949** *College & Research Libraries* Oct. 333 The Universal Decimal Classification (U.D.C.). This last was the name given to the 'Brussels expansion' of the *Decimal Classification and Relative Index* of Melvil Dewey. **1958** *B.S.I. News* Sept. 12/1 The B.S.I., with the support of ASLIB and the Library Association, is arranging a series of one-day discussions on universal decimal classification.

14. universal donor *Med.*, a person whose blood is group O (so called because before the discovery of other blood group systems group O blood was thought to be compatible with that of any individual); **Universal Product Code** *N. Amer.* (see quot. 1979); **Universal Provider,** the name of a well-known general store formerly trading in London; freq. with small initials and *transf.*; **universal quantifier** *Logic* [tr. G. *allgemeiner quantificator* (Łukasiewicz & Tarski 1930, in *Sprawozdania z Posiedzeń Towarzystwa naukowego Warszawskiego* (Wydział III) XXIII. 44)], a quantifier referring to all the members of a universe or class; **universal set** *Logic* and *Math.* = UNIVERSE 2 d in Dict. and Suppl.; **universal time,** Greenwich time calculated from midnight at the Greenwich meridian (rather than from noon, as formerly).

1922 G. KEYNES *Blood Transfusion* iv. 72 Individuals of Groups I and IV have therefore been named 'universal recipients' and 'universal donors' respectively. **1976** EDINGTON & GILLES *Path. in Tropics* (ed. 2) 480 Universal donor group O blood should not therefore be employed for transfusing A or B recipients without prior investigation. **1974** *Consumer Reports* (U.S.) May 364/2 A computer..knows the package code (the grocery industry has agreed on a universal product code). **1979** *Hammond Almanac 1980* 761/2 *Universal Product Code*, a pattern of lines and numbers by which information about a product may be encoded for automatic scanning by a device..that records its price for charging the consumer as well as its stock numbers, inventory, etc. **1884** *List of Subscribers* (London & Globe Telephone Co.), *Whiteley, W.*, Universal Provider, Westbourne Grove, W. **1903** BEERBOHM *Around Theatres* (1924) I. 461 As a curate he has to offer that consolation of which he is universal provider. **1953** *Guardian* 11 Sept. 6/5 To our children we will always be a kind of Universal Provider, vague of face but soft of bosom. **1962** *Sunday Express* 23 Dec. 2/4 The world-famous 'Universal Provider'. Anything from a flea to an elephant..Whiteley boasted he could provide. [**1845** *Encycl. Metrop.* I. 207/1 When the subject of a Proposition is a common Term, the universal signs ('all, no, every') are used.] **1936** *Amer. Jrnl. Math.* LVIII. 353 Then..$(x)P$ and $(\exists x)P$ are propositions of elementary number theory, where (x) and $(\exists x)$ are respectively the universal and existential quantifiers. **1940,** etc. [see *QUANTIFIER 1 a]. **1961** J. E. WHITESITT *Boolean Algebra* iii. 60 $\forall x$ is called the universal quantifier of the variable x and is usually read 'for all x' or 'for every x'. **1980** E. P. LYNCH *Applied Symbolic Logic* i. 11 The universal quantifiers are 'all', 'for every', 'for all', and so on. [**1910** WHITEHEAD & RUSSELL *Principia Mathematica* I. i. 30 The class determined by a function which is always true is called the universal class, and is represented by V.] **1959** Universal set [see *solution set* s.v. *SOLUTION *sb.* 12]. **1975** I. STEWART *Concepts Mod. Math.* iv. 57 In any particular problem, the sets one is concerned with often lie inside some reasonably small universal set. **1882** *Monthly Notices R. Astron. Soc.* XLII. 205 (*heading*) Universal time and the selection of a prime meridian. *Ibid.*, The American Meteorological Society further considered it desirable that in the future a universal time reckoned from the meridian 180° from that of Greenwich should be generally introduced. **1969** *Times* 24 June 4/7 The object rose above the eastern horizon at 2.49 a.m., universal time.

B. *sb.* **5.** An artificial language invented for universal use by H. Molenaar; also known as *PAN-ROMAN. Cf. sense 3 c of the adj.

1907, etc. [see *PAN-ROMAN, PANROMAN]. **1928** O. JESPERSEN *International Lang.* 40 Among numerous systems of the same type, but not worked out to the same extent as Neutral, I shall here mention only H. Molenaar's *Universal* (1906). **1947** [see *NEUTRAL *sb.* 5].

6. *Linguistics.* Any of the fundamental rules or features proposed as universal attributes of natural languages (see quots.).

1948 B. W. & E. G. AGINSKY in *Word* IV. 109 What are the universals of language?.. All languages employ sound sequences in which may be discerned a limited number of recurring types of speech-sound segments. These..are meaningless.., but enter into the meaningful units of form, the morphemes. All languages employ such morphemes in sequences. **1964** KATZ & POSTAL *Integrated Theory of Linguistic Descriptions* 160 A formal universal is a specification of the form of a statement in a linguistic description, while a substantive universal is a concept or set of concepts out of which particular statements in a linguistic description are constructed. **1965** N. CHOMSKY *Aspects of Theory of Syntax* i. 28 The study of linguistic universals is the study of the properties of any generative grammar for a natural language. *Ibid.*, It is useful to classify linguistic universals as *formal* or *substantive*. A theory of substantive universals claims that items of a particular kind in any language must be drawn from a fixed class of items. **1972** HARTMANN & STORK *Dict. Lang. & Linguistics* 245/2 Examples of universals are the conventional character of language.., the duality of transmission and reception, the presence of names and deictic elements. A distinction is sometimes made between *substantive universals*, i.e. features of sound substance such as the phonological elements..and *formal universals* which are made explicit by the linguist in the form of grammatical rules. **1973** *Language* XL. 178 It seems to be a language universal that productive inflectional morphemes are not only very short, but also employ a reduced inventory of phonemes.

universalism, *a.* Add: Also *spec.* = UNIVERSALISTIC *a.* 1. (Earlier examples.)

1837 W. JENKINS *Ohio Gazetteer* 357 It has..three houses for public worship (methodist, presbyterian, and universalian). **1852** J. REYNOLDS *Hist. Illinois* 327 He is one of the Universalian Baptists.

universalism. Add: **3.** (Earlier example.) Also *spec.* in *Sociol.* and *Econ.*, contrasted with *PARTICULARISM 5 b and *REGIONALISM 1.

1835 *Leigh Hunt's London Jrnl.* 11 July 221/1 What (if we might take the liberty to coin a word) we would call the universalism of the Homeric poetry. **1939** T. PARSONS in *Social Forces* May 462/2 The fact that the central focus of the professional rôle lies in a technical competence gives a very great importance to universalism in the institutional pattern governing it. **1947** —— *Weber's Theory Social & Econ. Organization* 72 Ethical universalism, the insistence on treatment of all men by the same generalized, impersonal standards. **1955** *Bull. Atomic Sci.* Apr. 142 The humanitarian theme of the two preceding centuries certainly persisted, but universalism yielded step by step to national particularism.

universalist, *sb.* Add: **1. b.** *transf.* One who believes in the brotherhood of all men in a manner not subject to national allegiances.

1944 [see *REGIONALIST]. **1952** V. GOLLANCZ *My Dear Timothy* xii. 110 A universalist is a person for whom nations don't exist, only persons. **1955** *Times* 25 Aug. 7/2 It seemed unfair to call him an expatriate, for he was a true universalist. It is as a man who loves his fellow men..that Mr. MacDonald has succeeded in being a one-man civilizing factor in this territory.

u:niversali·zable, *a.* Chiefly *Philos.* [f. UNIVERSALIZE *v.* + -ABLE.] That can be made or rendered universal; capable of universal application.

1952 A. E. DUNCAN-JONES *Butler's Moral Philos.* viii. 171 In order that he shall be said to make a moral judgement, his attitude must be 'universalisable'. **1955** *Proc. Aristotelian Soc.* LV. 170 If too few details are included in the maxims, it will be difficult to find *any* that will be universalisable at all. **1977** P. BAELZ *Ethics & Belief* ii. 18 Reasons are impersonal, or inter-personal. They are logically impartial, or universalizable. **1982** *Times Lit. Suppl.* 24 Dec. 1423/4 That a moral imperative should be universalizable seems to be at the heart of what we understand when we understand it as a *moral* imperative.

Also **unive:rsalizabi·lity; u:niversali·zably** *adv.*

1952 A. E. DUNCAN-JONES *Butler's Moral Philos.* viii. 173 What we are calling the universalisability of his attitude consists in his being disposed..to respond in an equivalent way to people and situations of a given kind, should he come to consider them. **1954** W. D. ROSS *Kant's Theory of Ethics* 33 But the man who tells the lie may well retort to Kant 'Why should the test of universalizability be applied to my act regarded in this very abstract way, simply as a lie?' **1963** R. M. HARE *Freedom & Reason* vi. 91 This argument would break down if 'ought' were not being used both universalizably and prescriptively. **1982** *Times Lit. Suppl.* 2 July 713/1 'Ought'..commits one to universalizability, in the sense that if I say you ought to do *A*, I implicitly affirm that everyone ought to do *A* in identical circumstances.

universe. Add: **2. d.** *universe of discourse*: also *absol.* For def. read: the totality of entities under consideration; all those that the terms of a proposition may refer to. Also (as *universe*) in *Statistics*, = *POPULATION[2] 2 d. (Earlier and later examples.)

1849 A. DE MORGAN in *Trans. Cambridge Philos. Soc.* VIII. 380 By not dwelling upon this power of making what we may properly (inventing a new technical name) call the universe of a proposition, or of a name, matter of express definition, all rules remaining the same, writers on logic deprive themselves of much useful illustrations. *Ibid.*, Let the universe in question be 'man': then *Briton* and *alien* are simple contraries. **1898** A. N. WHITEHEAD *Treat. Universal Algebra* I. II. v. 110 If we extend the Universe of self-evident propositions either by some natural or conventional definition, we may extend the conception of conversion. **1911** G. U. YULE *Introd. Theory Statistics* ii. 17 For actual work on any given subject, no term is required to denote the material to which the work is so confined... But for theoretical purposes some term is almost essential to avoid circumlocution. The expression the *universe of discourse*, or simply the *universe*, used in this sense by writers on logic, may be adopted. **1939** A. E. TRELOAR *Elements Statistical Reasoning* i. 8 Such a type of selective sampling from this universe is wholly impossible. **1967** G. WILLS in Wills & Yearsley *Handbk. Management Technol.* 191 Numbers of calls made by sales representatives is a meaningless item of statistics unless it can be related to..the total universe of outlets which can handle such a product. **1972** *Science* 23 June 1306/2 The universe of discourse is severely restricted in this jargon. **1975** *Brit. Jrnl. Sociol.* XXVI. 37 The universe from which the sample was drawn was all Royal Navy officers stationed in England.

university, *sb.* Add: **I. 1. a.** Const. without article: *at* (or *to*) *university*, etc.

1959 *Listener* 22 Jan. 153/2 Is the son of a miner working-class, suppose he has gone to university. *Ibid.* 5 Mar. 405/2 At school or at university. **1968** *New Society* 22 Aug. 266/2 'He's at university' (very widely used) is certainly non-U.

b. Also in phr. *the university of life*, the experiences of life, considered as a means of instruction. Cf. *the school of hard knocks* s.v. *SCHOOL *sb.*[1] 4 b.

1959 A. GLYN *I can take it All* i. 12 A revolting cliché like 'educated in the University of Life'. **1972** [see *LIFE *sb.* 12 d]. **1978** P. HILL *Enthusiast* iii. 25 Bob..had the chance to educate him in the real world of people, in the university of life.

c. *University of the Air*: † (*a*) *Aeronaut.* (see quot. 1931); (*b*) an organization which provides a course of (higher) education partly through radio and television broadcasts; *spec.* an early name for the Open University (see *OPEN *a.* 22 c).

1931 *Civil & Milit. Gazette* (Lahore) 4 Nov. 2/3 To meet the demand for trained and competent personnel..the College of Aeronautical Engineering has been formed—the University of the Air. **1959** *Twentieth Cent.* Nov. 369 Any government that was determined could give us a University of the Air tomorrow. **1963** *Glasgow Herald* 9 Sept. 1/1 Mr Wilson..suggested the broadcasting time for the 'university of the air' could be obtained by allocation of the fourth television channel... There could also be appropriate radio facilities. **1969** *Radio Times* 27 Nov. 12 Originally named 'the University of the Air', the Open University offers an exciting new opportunity for adults throughout the country to study for degree qualifications through the media of integrated television, radio and specially-designed correspondence courses. **1984** *Listener* 10 May 7/2 When the idea of a university of the air was first floated, sceptics abounded.

III. 6. a. *university campus, education* (earlier and later examples), *entrance, grant, library* (earlier and later examples), *oath, town* (earlier example); *university-level* adj.

1623 W. L'ISLE *Sax. Treat. conc. Old & New Test.* f. e 3, I meane ere long to let the world know what is more remaining; as more I have seene both in our Universitie Libraries, and that of Sir Robert Cotton. **1721** SWIFT *Let. to Young Gentleman* 26 You cannot but have already observed, what a violent Run there is among too many weak People against University Education. **1823** J. S. MILL in *Morning Chron.* 8 Feb. 3/1 The violation of the University oath, in every case where its observance interferes in the slightest degree with the convenience of the swearer, is a complete proof that the ceremony of swearing affords no security whatever for veracity in any other case. **1857** C. M. YONGE *Dynevor Terrace* I. v. 68 Fitzjocelyn was twenty-one, and had nearly finished his university education. **1872** O. W. HOLMES *Poet at Breakfast-Table* 23 The soil of the University town is divided into patches of sandy and of clayey ground. **1919** *Treasury Minute* 14 July in *Rep. University Grants Comm.* 2 in *Parl. Papers* (1921) XI. 362 The Chancellor of the Exchequer states..that he proposes to appoint a Standing Committee..to enquire into the financial needs of University Education... He proposes that the Committee should be known as 'The University Grants Committee'. **1939** University campus [see *CAMPUS]. **1957** *Encycl. Brit.* VIII. 941/2 The relationship between the G.C.E. and university entrance qualifications had in the early 1950s reached only a temporary definition. **1962** E. SNOW *Other Side of River* (1963) xxx. 226 Among full-term university-level students 283,000 were engineers. **1974** N. FREELING *Dressing of Diamond* 149 A university education served this much purpose..that emotional problems always got placed at the level of intellectual argument. **1982** H. R. LANE tr. *M. Vargas Llosa's Aunt Julia & Scriptwriter* xv. 266, I had a sudden inspiration and headed..for the university campus. **1982** 'J. ROSS' *Death's Head* xiii. 75 Mrs Knostig's work is financed by a university grant. **1983** *Chron. Higher Educ.* 19 Oct. 1 More and more university libraries are charging fees for interlibrary loans.

b. *university student.*

1914 G. B. SHAW *Misalliance* p. lxv, An office boy of fifteen is often more of a man than a university student of twenty. **1981** A. EDWARDS *Sonya* iii. 45 Putting his school in the hands of a young university student who had become his assistant.

c. *university don, professor, staff, teacher.*

1907 G. B. SHAW *Major Barbara* II. 236 This love of the common people may please an earl's granddaughter and a university professor. *Ibid.* III. 277 How can you succeed in business when you are willing to pay all that money to a University don who is obviously not worth a junior clerk's wages! **1948** M. LASKI *Tory Heaven* iv. 54 The White Paper analysing the origins and opinions of University staffs appalled the whole nation. **1954** M. BERESFORD *Lost Villages* viii. 266, I went north in April 1948 to become a University teacher. **1971** HALSEY & TROW *Brit. Academics* xv. 413 We see the results in their university teacher children. **1977** *Times* 19 Sept. 3/4, 10,000 more students..with a reduction in the unit cost per student..is effectively increasing university dons' teaching loads. **1977** M. KENYON *Rapist* iv. 42 Miss Hitchcock, a university professor, arrived in Ireland only yesterday.

d. *university-educated* adj.; also with vbl. sbs., as *university teaching*.

1923 R. MACAULAY *Told by Idiot* I. 44 No creature was ever more solemn, more earnest,..than the university-educated young female of the eighties. **1962** C. L. BARBER in F. Behre *Contrib. Eng. Syntax* 21 Those countries where a great deal of university-teaching is carried out in English. **1981** J. HALKIN *Fatal Odds* iii. 49 Well-heeled families, university-educated.

7. university college = COLLEGE *sb.* 4 d, *spec.* one which is not or was not empowered to grant degrees (see also quot. 1981); **university member**, a member of the House of Commons representing a university or a group of universities (university seats were abolished in Britain in 1948).

1838, etc. [see COLLEGE *sb.* 4 d]. **1954** *Times* 1 July 9/6 University College of North Staffordshire..is the only university college empowered to grant degrees. **1981** D. ROWNTREE *Dict. Educ.* 335 *University colleges.* 1. The name formerly given to the UK civic universities which, when first set up, did not have the power to grant their own degrees and usually granted those of London University instead. The last such (Leicester) became autonomous in 1957. 2. In addition, Oxford, Cambridge, Durham and London each has a college named University College, and it is also the name of the independent university at Buckingham. **1867** *Hansard Commons* 18 June 29, I share the opinion of my hon. Friend the Member for Birmingham, that we are already overstocked with University Members. **1949** A. P. HERBERT in *Punch* 27 Apr. 453/3 Mr. Haddock, by the way, complains rather bitterly that the University Members are being flung out of Parliament in the sacred name of 'One-Man-One-Vote'. **1979** J. ADAM SMITH *John Buchan & his World* 80 Buchan was delighted, especially because a university member could sit fairly loose to party.

univoca·lity. [f. UNIVOCAL *a.* + -ITY.] The state or condition of being univocal (sense 1 b).

1934 *Theology* XXIX. 342 The Scotists, for whom analogy of being gives way to univocality of being. **1959** *Analysis* XX. 7 Calling them by one name because of three features that they all lack (predicative meaning, ascriptive force, and univocality). **1977** E. VON GLASERSFELD in D. M. Rumbaugh *Language Learning by Chimpanzee* v. 125 It is unlikely that this univocality will be preserved when more correlators and conceptual lexigram classes are added.

unjust, *a.* **1. b.** (Further examples, in *unjust enrichment*.)

1942 *Law Rep.* 4 July 135 It is clear that any civilised system of law is bound to provide remedies for cases of what has been called unjust enrichment or unjust benefit, that is, to prevent a man from retaining the money of.. another which it is against conscience that he should keep. **1962** A. TURNER *Law of Trade Secrets* IV. iv. 346 The term 'unjust enrichment' refers to the use to which a disclosure is put. **1973** *N.Y. Law Jrnl.* 24 July 12/3 The defendants ..have counterclaimed for $7,500, in damages for unjust enrichment.

unjustified, *ppl. a.* Add: **3. b.** With type not adjusted to fill up the line or produce an even margin.

1961 WEBSTER, *Unjustified*,..of a line of type: not adjusted properly to fill the measure. **1963** *Times* 6 Mar. 9/6 The *Oklahoma City Times* published its regular editions today with type set entirely by computer... 'Unjustified' perforated tape, such as might be made by a reporter working on a special tape-producing typewriter, is fed into the computer, which cuts a perforated tape. **1971** *Sci. Amer.* Aug. 116/2 This 300-page book, with.. its text in unjustified typescript, indexes the work of the center. **1980** C. BURKE *Printing Poetry* iii. 32 Some.. of the problems in a prose setting can be obviated by setting it 'ragged right', that is by leaving the right-hand margin unjustified.

unk (ʊŋk), *sb.* Also **unkie, unky.** Colloq. or nursery abbrevs. of UNCLE *sb.*

1907 A. BENNETT *Grim Smile of Five Towns* 21 'You carry me down-stairs, unky?' the little nephew suggested. **1957** W. FAULKNER *Town* iii. 65 'We need a grindstone,' Gowan said. 'Unk Noon,' Top said. 'We'll take the gun like we're going rabbit hunting,' Gowan said. So they did: As far as Uncle Noon Gatewood's blacksmith shop on the edge of town. **1959** N. MARSH *False Scent* (1960) ii. 50 It's so hard to explain, Unky. **1971** A. DIMENT *Think Inc.* ii. 19 Didn't you realise you should come home ..and tell Unkie Rupert all about it? **1977** C. MCCULLOUGH *Thorn Birds* xvii. 408 There's been tons of male influence for your children with the Unks around.

unkingdomed, *ppl. a.* (Later example.)

1917 J. B. CABELL *Cream of Jest* (1923) xix. 109 The Stuarts or the Valois or the Cæsars, or other dynasties long since unkingdomed.

unki·nk, *v.* [UN-² 3, 7.] **a.** *trans.* To take the kinks out of, to smooth, to straighten. **b.** *intr.* To lose the kinks, become straight. Also *fig.*

1891 KIPLING & BALESTIER in *Cent. Mag.* Dec. 193/1 Tarvin got himself out of the cart, unfolding his long stiffened legs..and unkinking his muscles one by one. **1947** *Daily Progress* (Charlottesville, Va.) 20 Mar. 8 Designed to un-kink highways. **1947** J. STEINBECK *Wayward Bus* ii. 18 Unkinking the cable behind him on the ground. **1972** C. SHORT *Blue-Eyed Boy* viii. 82 Gradually my soul began to unkink. **1980** J. MCNEIL *Spy Game* xiv. 138 The road unkinked and far ahead Corrigan was hopping past a goods van.

unknowing, *vbl. sb.* For † read 'revived in mod. use, esp. in phr. *cloud of unknowing* (after quot. *a* 1400)' and add later examples.

a **1400** (*title*) Þe clowde of vnknowyng. **1629** A. BAKER *Commentary on Cloud* (1924) II. iii. 355 This cloud of unknowing..is but the self-same knowledge and sight of God which I and others do usually term the light, sight and knowledge that we have by our faith. **1911** E. UNDERHILL *Mysticism* II. vii. 415 Reason finds itself, in a very actual sense, 'in the dark'—immersed in the Cloud of Unknowing. **1939** T. S. ELIOT *Family Reunion* II. ii. 110 Accident is design And design is accident In a cloud of unknowing. **1957** *Oxf. Dict. Christian Church* 402/2 This [progressive deification of man] is to be obtained by a process of 'unknowing', in which the soul leaves behind the perceptions of the senses as well as the reasoning of the intellect. **1976** H. MONTEFIORE in *Christian Believing* 154 Even in granting as much as this to doctrine and dogma, I have to enter into the cloud of unknowing and assert the Church's apophatic tradition. **1984** *Daily Tel.* 9 Feb. 16/5 This is one of those incidents which cloud the mind with mystery, forming, as we brood on it, a positive cloud of unknowing. **1984** *Sunday Tel.* 8 July 18/4 Ideally, the fearful void of unknowing should be filled by the ballast of faith.

unknow·ledgeable, *a.* [UN-¹ 7 b.] **1.** Unknowable. *rare.*

1920 C. M. GRIEVE in *Northern Numbers* 69 The barrier ..Lifts sheerly..To the unknowledgeable skies. **1926** W. DE LA MARE *Connoisseur* 303 Such facts were strange, and, as you might say almost unknowledgeable.

2. Not knowledgeable; uninformed.

1969 *Islander* (Victoria, B.C.) 9 Nov. 7/2 Many unknowledgeable people find their way into the mountains. **1974** H. L. FOSTER *Ribbin', Jivin', & Playin' Dozens* iv. 128 By using the inversion process blacks were able to take advantage of the unknowledgeable white opponents.

unknown, *ppl. a.*¹ and *sb.* Add: **A.** *adj.* **1. b.** (Further examples of *unknown God*: see quot. 1526 in Dict.) *unknown soldier* or *warrior*, an unidentified soldier whose tomb symbolizes that of all those killed in battle.

1607 E. TOPSELL *Four-footed Beasts* 96 The Arabians sacrifice a camell to the vnknowne god. *c* **1848** M. M. SHERWOOD *Last Days of Boosy* (ed. 2) 152 The child.. addressed the fearful name..as I had taught him to do to the to him unknown God who made the heavens. **1920** *Times* 11 Nov. 14/1 The Unknown Warrior..was brought to London by night... He lay..awaiting burial today in the Abbey among the greatest of his race. *Ibid.* 12 Nov. 13/1 The body of the Unknown Warrior..was buried in Westminster Abbey yesterday, the King being chief mourner. **1942** E. WAUGH *Put out More Flags* i. 36 Rupert Brooke, Old Bill, the Unknown Soldier—thus three fond women saw him. **1947** E. M. FORSTER in *Harper's Mag.* July 9/2, I add the proviso 'if all goes well' because success lies on the knees of an unknown God. **1970** *Times* 3 June 5/6 Princess Margaret drove today to Mount Avala to lay a wreath of red poppies on the tomb of the unknown soldier. **1980** I. MURDOCH *Nuns & Soldiers* i. 42 The soldiers at the Unknown Warrior's grave in Warsaw.

c. *unknown quantity* (examples of *fig.* use).

1865 W. BAGEHOT in *Fortn. Rev.* 15 May 21 The first election of Mr. Lincoln..was government by an unknown quantity. **1883** [see QUANTITY 12]. **1951** *Sport* 30 Mar.–5 Apr. 6/3 Mel Ford, the Aberavon prop who gets a 'cap' is an unknown quantity in the North. **1973** *Times* 16 Apr. 14/2 Unless some formula is found for substantial alternative investments for Arab oil money it will continue to be an unknown quantity on the world money market.

B. *sb.* **2. b.** More widely, an unknown thing; an unknown factor (merging with *fig.* use of sense 3).

1878 E. DICKINSON *Poems* (1955) III. 849 Let my first Knowing be of thee With morning's warming Light—And my first Fearing, lest Unknowns Engulph thee in the night. **1947** H. S. SHELTON in Dewar & Shelton *Is Evolution Proved?* xi. 319 We cannot, therefore, correlate all these unknowns and say what variations result from what changes. **1948** R. SPILLER et al. *Literary Hist. U.S.* 1159 Sensitivity to spiritual unknowns. **1964** M. GOWING *Britain & Atomic Energy 1939–1945* i. 36 He acknowledged the unknowns in the situation.

unknownst. (Earlier example.)

1805 E. CAVANAGH *Let.* 4 Oct. in Londonderry & Hyde *Russ. Jrnls. M. & C. Wilmot* (1934) II. 185 An Army, God knows, might live *unknownst* in the House!

u·nk-unks, *sb. pl. U.S. slang.* [duplication of the first three letters of the word *unknown* + *pl.* ending *-s.*] A condition resulting from fear of or apprehension about the unknown; unknown factors.

1970 *Time* 9 Mar. 63 Lately the industry has suffered a succession of blows:..As a result, aerospacemen have come down with a severe case of what they call the 'unk-unks'—the 'unknown unknowns'. **1970** *Guardian Weekly* 1 Aug. 24 'Unk Unks'..are the villains favoured by Lockheed to explain the extraordinary series of financial disasters that has led it to the verge of bankruptcy.

unky: see *UNK *sb.*

unlabelled, *ppl. a.* Add: Also **unlabeled.** (Examples in *Biol.* and *Chem.*: cf. *LABELLED *a.* d.)

1935 [see *LABEL *v.* 2]. **1981** *Jrnl. Gen. Microbiol.* CXXVI. 97 Catechol methyltransferase..was localized immunocytochemically in the yeast *Candida tropicalis* by the unlabelled antibody enzyme method.

unladen, *ppl. a.* (Later examples, of the weight of a vehicle.)

1930 *Road Traffic Act* 20 *Geo. V* 24 in *Parl. Papers 1929–30* IV. 140 The weight unladen of any vehicle shall be taken to be the weight of the vehicle..exclusive of the weight of water, fuel or accumulators used for the purpose of propulsion. **1959** *Motor Manual* (ed. 36) xiii. 270 'Unladen weight' is open to all sorts of interpretation and may bear little relation to what the caravan weighs when it eventually comes to the customer.

unlaid, *ppl. a.* and *sb.* Add: **1. d.** Of a woman with whom no one has had, or a particular person has not had, sexual intercourse. *slang.*

1962 'E. MCBAIN' *Like Love* (1964) iv. 56 What it all meant was: 1. Gaspipe. 2. Sober. 3. Unlaid. **1977** *Sunday Times* 27 Mar. 42/2 A thousand places visited and not absorbed, a thousand paperbacks unread, a thousand unlaid airhostesses.

un-Latin, *a.* Restrict † *Obs.*⁻¹ to sense in Dict. and add: **b.** Not true to the character of the Latin language or of Latins.

1846 [see UN-GREEK *a.*] **1858** J. A. SYMONDS *Let.* 28 Nov. (1967) I. 173 After the Greek paper came..Latin prose from [Sir Francis] Bacon—a queer and Un Latin piece. **1932** *Times Lit. Suppl.* 21 Jan. 37/3 In one of these [Catalan] poems he writes:..'I know not what thou wouldst say to me..': certainly an un-Latin vagueness.

unlawyer-like, *a.* (Earlier example.)

1869 TAYLOR & DUBOURG *New Men & Old Acres* III. 53 Everything hurried through in the most unlawyer-like manner.

unleached, *ppl. a.* (Earlier example.)

1804 in J. Roberts *Penn. Farmer* 111 Are leeched or unleeched ashes most beneficial as manure?

unleaded, *ppl. a.* Add: **3.** Of petrol, etc.: without added lead. Also *ellipt.*

1965 *Oil & Gas Jrnl.* 20 Dec. 26/1 The industry association will make a study next year of the cost of producing unleaded gasoline. **1970** *Daily Tel.* 14 Oct. 11/8 While a change to unleaded petrol reduces exhaust emission and engine deposits..it necessitates a reduction in the compression ratios to cope with lower octane fuels. **1981** J. D. MACDONALD *Free Fall in Crimson* iv. 38 He pulled up to the pump... He took six and four-tenths gallons of unleaded, which came to eight sixty-four.

unleave, *v.* Add: **b.** *intr.* To lose or shed leaves. *rare.*

1880 G. M. HOPKINS *Poems* (1967) 88 Margaret, are you grieving Over Goldengrove unleaving?

unless, *prep. phr.*, etc. Add: **2. c.** (Examples in *unless and until.*)

1937 D. JONES in *Le Maître Phonétique* Apr.–June (Suppl.), We should as a rule stick to that pronunciation unless and until we find another native whose speech we have reason to think is more characteristic. **1956** A. WILSON *Anglo-Saxon Attitudes* II. ii. 335 Mother and son had both arrived with the fixed determination of not leaving unless and until either of the two women..should have paid handsomely to secure their departure. **1983** *Times* 1 Feb. 15/1 Unless and until the government also proposes the abolition..of the GLC, the savings in public money are likely to be minimal.

unliberated, *ppl. a.* (Examples corresponding to *LIBERATE *v.* d.)

1970 *Time* 31 Aug. 18 Unliberated honorifics like 'Mrs.' and 'Miss' are replaced by the noncommittal 'Ms.'. **1971** S. BERMAN *Underground Guide to College of your Choice* 144 Most chicks are still unliberated and the virginity index is still quite high. **1975** *Listener* 9 Oct. 486/4 Ann is..the unliberated woman striving for acceptance in a permissive world. **1981** J. SUTHERLAND *Bestsellers* vii. 85 The unliberated condition of woman—incarcerated, flagellated, degraded, violated—was celebrated time and again.

unlimited, *ppl. a.* Add: **4.** Of a hydroplane: having no limit placed on its engine capacity. Also *absol.* as *sb. U.S.*

[**1953** W. A. SHRADER *Fifty Yrs. of Flight* 54 Fifth Annual All-American Air Races are held at Miami, Fla. In the free-for-all unlimited engine displacement race, James Wedell is the winner.] **1956** *Rudder* Apr. 40/2 A dozen open regattas for unlimited inboard hydroplanes have been scheduled. **1959** *Yearbk. Amer. Power Boat Assoc.* 165 Unlimited Hydroplanes shall be designated by the prefix letter 'U'. **1962** *New Yorker* 29 Sept. 102/2 The sleek-shaped unlimiteds, gaily painted like some archaic 'flying circus'. **1972** *Collier's Encycl. Year Bk. 1971* 521 Unlimiteds, those manta-ray shaped thunderboats that have over 200 mph on straightaways. **1976** *World Bk. Year Bk.* 218 The national championship series for unlimited hydroplanes consisted of 10 races with $350,000 in purses.

unlingui·stic, *a.* [f. UN-¹ 7 a + LINGUISTIC *a.*] Not related to linguistics.

1960 [see *STANCE *sb.*² 1 e]. **1962** Y. OLSSON in F. Behre *Contrib. Eng. Syntax* 98 Unlinguistic speculations.

unlisted, *ppl. a.* Add: **2.** *spec.* **a.** *Stock Exchange.* Formerly designating securities not dealt in on the Stock Exchange; also (*N. Amer.*), those sold over the counter (see *OVER THE COUNTER *adv.* (*a.*) b); now in *unlisted securities market*, a market for securities in small companies admitted for trading on the Stock Exchange but not bound to comply with the rules for listed securities.

1905 [in Dict.]. **1921, 1929** [see *OVER THE COUNTER *adv.* (*a.*)]. **1979** *Times* 13 Dec. 17/5 A new Unlisted Securities Market (USM) has been proposed which will provide a half way house between a private company and an official listing. **1983** *Sunday Tel.* 10 Apr. 22/6 The Unlisted Securities Market (U.S.M.) is now an established part of The Stock Exchange London.

b. Of a telephone (number): = *EX-DIRECTORY *a.* Chiefly *U.S.*

1937 R. CHANDLER in *Dime Detective Mag.* Nov. 48/2 Willie Peters..did a sideline selling unlisted telephone numbers bribed from maids and chauffeurs. **1942** E. S. GARDNER *Case of Careless Kitten* xiv. 137 Mason's unlisted telephone was ringing as he opened the door of his apartment. **1974** 'J. LE CARRÉ' *Tinker Tailor Soldier Spy* xi. 84 A belly-ache from Admin..about the misuse of unlisted Circus telephones for private calls. **1980** G. V. HIGGINS *Kennedy for Defense* v. 48 Gretchen doesn't give out the unlisted number. If I had a call, it was from somebody important.

unliterary, *a.* Add: Hence **unli·terariness.**

1961 C. S. LEWIS *Experiment in Criticism* viii. 76 His very unliterariness saves him from confusing the two [*sc.* art and knowledge].

unliterate, *a.* Add: **b.** Unliterary; not interested in reading or literature. Also *absol.*

1950 M. MEAD *Male & Female* xiii. 271 The Gesell norms used by the reading mother or the neighbourhood gossip of the unliterate. **1960** *Guardian* 13 June 5/2 The innumerate humanist and the unliterate scientist were equally inadequate.

unliv(e)able, *a.* **2.** (Earlier example.)

1834 M. EDGEWORTH *Tour in Connemara* (1950) i. 43 The want of window curtains..gave the whole an unfinished unlivable appearance.

unlived, *ppl. a.*[2] Add: **b.** [UN-[1] 8 c.] With *-in.* Appearing to be uninhabited; unused by the inhabitants.

1931 H. NICOLSON *Diary* 28 Jan. (1966) 67 The room has an unlived-in appearance. **1943** D. WELCH *Jrnl.* 15 June (1952) 74 There is the feeling about the whole place of utter solitude, stealth, the ghostly, unlived-in, fascinating feeling of week-end houses. **1975** *New Yorker* 29 Dec. 22/1 Any room..has an unlived-in corner. **1979** J. GARDNER *Nostradamus Traitor* xxiii. 95 The vestibule led to the main room, large and uninviting... The place looked unlived-in.

unliving, *ppl. a.* Add: Hence **unli·vingness.**

1914 D. H. LAWRENCE *Prussian Officer* 80 The sick man lay as if dead... Miss Louisa was heavy-hearted under the load of unlivingness. **1928** [see *rubber-necked* s.v. *RUBBER *sb.*[1] 13 c].

unload, *v.* Add: **1. b.** (Later examples.) Also with *on.*

1887 B. HARTE *Millionaire & Devil's Ford* 158 He might unload his gossip because Mamie wouldn't have him. **1904** *Minneapolis Times* 28 June 6 Dr. Dowie has landed in New York and unloaded an interview in praise of President Roosevelt. **1976** J. I. M. STEWART *Memorial Service* v. 66 This was probably why he unloaded on me these useless gobbets of information. **1978** 'S. WOODS' *Exit Murderer* 160 If we succeed in identifying Mr. X I shall unload the whole thing on them [*sc.* the police].

2. a. (Later *fig.* examples.) *esp.* To confide in someone, to divulge information, etc. Also with *on.*

1904 W. H. SMITH *Promoters* i. 8 I'm so full of it that I shall burst if I don't unload. **1972** 'J. GODEY' *Three Worlds of Johnny Handsome* (1973) ii. 27 If you get along with your cell partner, you usually unload. I did the same with him. **1978** 'D. KYLE' *Black Camelot* xii. 185 'What's the problem with this German? Why won't he unload?'.. 'He thinks once he comes through..we'll knock him off because he knows too much.' **1984** *Miami Herald* 30 Mar. 3 B/1 Your letter exhibits a great deal of bottled rage. I strongly suggest that you unload on a counselor.

6. a. (Earlier example.)

1870 J. K. MEDBERY *Men & Mysteries Wall St.* 138 To unload, is to sell out a stock which has been carried for some time.

b. *transf.* To sell or dispose of (anything); to get rid of by sale; *esp.* to dispose profitably of something that is unwanted or that constitutes an embarrassment. Also with *on.*

1884 *Boston Jrnl.* 15 Mar. 2/3 There is a flavor of reviving an excitement in order to unload oil lands. **1901** MERWIN & WEBSTER *Calumet 'K'* ii. 30 They're going to make a mighty good try at unloading it on him and making him pay for it. **1929** D. HAMMETT *Dain Curse* v. 40 That dinge of yours—Rhino Tingley—was picked up in a hock shop last night trying to unload some jewelry. **1946** *Time* 25 Mar. 82/3 Many a landlord..has already unloaded a building, at a fat price, on his tenants. **1976** 'M. DELVING' *China Expert* v. 56 Tashjian..had only the day before unloaded an extremely dubious Han tomb figurine on an unsuspecting dealer.

c. To get rid of (a person).

1973 E.-J. BAHR *Nice Neighbourhood* xiii. 139 John wasn't about to be any problem when she had everything set up and wanted to unload him. **1982** C. WATSON *Whatever's been going on at Mumblesby?* xvi. 150 Cork-Bradden's main object was to 'unload' the woman on to me, in order to placate his wife.

unlogical, *a.* Add: Also, not involving logic. Hence **unlo·gically** *adv.*

1897 W. M. URBAN *Hist. Princ. Suff. Reason* iv. 45 Sufficient Reason he speaks of as a metalogical truth.. which functions unlogically in space, time, causality and motivation. **1922** tr. *Wittgenstein's Tractatus* 43 We cannot think anything unlogical, for otherwise we should have to think unlogically.

unlo·nely, *a.* [UN-[1] 7 a.] Not lonely. Also *absol.*

1952 J. STEINBECK *East of Eden* 396 The poison of loneliness and the gnawing envy of the unlonely. **1967** H. W. SUTHERLAND *Magnie* iv. 63 A man should sleep with his wife in winter. It's warm—unlonely. **1971** P. SCOTT *Towers of Silence* III. iv. 197, I am not unlonely.

unluck. (Earlier example.)

1795 E. WYNNE *Diary* 16 Jan. (1937) II. ii. 12 This feast has great many misfortunes we have every day more unluck.

unmade, *ppl. a.* **3. b.** (Later examples with *up.*)

1936 D. POWELL *Turn, Magic Wheel* II. 133 Their decently un-made-up little wives. **1960** *News Chron.* 12 Oct. 3/2 Her unmade-up face smiling. **1971** J. TURNER *Stone Dormitory* vi. 63 He went on along the unmade-up road. **1978** R. HILL *Pinch of Snuff* iv. 42 He was roused from the unmade-up spare bed by Ellie pulling his hair.

unmaid, *v.* (Later example.)

1922 JOYCE *Ulysses* 386 She was there unmaided.

unmakable, *a.* (Later examples.)

1939 W. FORTESCUE *There's Rosemary* l. 282 The designer had drawn a lovely but unmakeable model which had only one side. **1974** E. BRAWLEY *Rap* (1975) I. xi. 183 He knew escape was impossible, an unmakable caper. **1979** *Country Life* 4 Oct. 1127/2 Seven No Trumps was unmakeable.

unman, *v.* Add: Hence also **unma·nningly** *adv.*

1947 DYLAN THOMAS in *Horizon* Dec. 302 For who unmanningly haunts the mountain ravened eaves.

unmanned, *ppl. a.*[1] **1.** (Examples relating to aviation, space travel, etc.)

1906 *Nature* 8 Nov. 35/2 The machines he made and launched were all 'unmanned'. **1907** *Ibid.* 4 Apr. 538/2 During the course of the last few years very rapid strides have been made in investigating the upper air by means of manned and unmanned balloons. **1946** *Congressional Digest* May 154/2 'Drone' aircraft—they are unmanned, radio controlled. **1954** *Economist* 11 Sept. 3/2 The manned fighter is surrendering some of its duties to wingless, almost tailless, unmanned missiles. **1962** F. I. ORDWAY et al. *Basic Astronautics* xiii. 552 Unmanned satellites and guided missiles. **1969** *Listener* 20 Feb. 232/2 The pictures you brought back from the Moon were not as good as those taken on an unmanned flight. **1972** *Guardian* 22 Feb. 2/4 The unmanned Soviet moon probe Luna 20 made a soft landing on the moon's surface last night. **1977** *R.A.F. News* 11–24 May 3/4 The RAF was watching the developments concerning Cruise missiles and other unmanned systems... If unmanned vehicles could be developed to take on some of the roles of air power this would be welcomed.

unmarked, *ppl. a.* Add: **1. a.** Add to def.: having no distinguishing or identificatory mark. (Further examples.)

1936 M. MITCHELL *Gone with Wind* xxx. 502 The thousands in unmarked graves who would never come home. **1960** 'E. MCBAIN' *Give Boys Great Big Hand* (1962) v. 42 The unmarked police sedan pulled to the curb. **1967** L. HUGHES *Panther & Lash* 65 They buried Lumumba In an unmarked grave. But he needs no marker—For air is his grave. **1975** *New Yorker* 2 June 101/1 The two patrolmen had driven in their unmarked car to the west end of the Mercer Island Floating Bridge. **1979** C. MCCARRY *Better Angels* III. iii. 208 He had flown in from Paris..in his own unmarked plane.

b. (Earlier example.)

1791 F. BURNEY *Jrnl.* Dec. (1972) I. 103 Our visit to Mrs. Montagu turned out very unmarked; I met my good Mrs. & Miss ord, & a little chat with them was all my entertainment.

c. Of a linguistic construction, form, etc.: not marked (see *MARKED *ppl. a.* 1 c).

1933, etc. [see *MARKED *ppl. a.* 1 c]. **1964** C. BARBER *Present-Day Eng.* iv. 105 *Author*..can be used of both men and women; this is called the *unmarked* member of the pair [*author: authoress*]. **1978** *Sci. Amer.* Nov. 95/1 In the case of 'wide' and 'narrow', 'wide' is the unmarked word: asking 'How wide is the road?' does not suggest that the road is wide, but asking 'How narrow is the road?' does suggest that the road is narrow. **1980** *Amer. Speech* LV. 88 Features of an unmarked register may be imported into a marked one, but not vice versa.

unmarried, *ppl. a.* **1.** (Further examples, of parents.)

1834 *Rep. Poor Laws* 196 in *Parl. Papers* XXVII. 200 An unmarried mother has voluntarily placed herself in the situation of a widow. **1933** D. C. E. PEEL *Life's Enchanted Cup* i. 9 People did not look upon unmarried mothers with so lenient an eye as they came to do during the war. **1965** HALL & HOWES *Church in Social Work* ii. 50 Unmarried fathers and 'other men in moral difficulty'. **1972** *Guardian* 15 Nov. 9/1 One [letter] suggests that if unmarried mums were only encouraged to keep their babies, this sort of thing couldn't happen. **1983** J. GARDNER *Elephants in Attic* iv. 29 In the thirties unmarried mums were not the 'in' thing.

2. (Later examples, of parenthood.)

1930 R. LEHMANN *Note in Music* IV. 157 He carried on the splendid tradition of unmarried fatherhood. **1962** *Sunday Express* 30 Dec. 19/5 The problems of unmarried motherhood. **1980** C. FREMLIN *With No Crying* i. 6 Friends..passionately defending her right to unmarried motherhood.

unmechanized, *ppl. a.* (Later examples.)

a **1930** D. H. LAWRENCE *Last Poems* (1932) 180 But oh, men, men still unmechanised,..what are you going to do, entangled among all the engines? **1937** B. H. L. HART *Europe in Arms* xxii. 296 The enemy is not only taken unaware but is himself unmechanized. **1973** R. LANE FOX *Alexander the Great* iv. 79 An agricultural and unmechanized world.

unmeditative, *a.* (Earlier example.)

1831 *Examiner* 12 June 370/1 The inert, unobserving unmeditative mass.

unmentionability. Add: **b.** The fact of (some things') being unmentionable.

1909 G. B. SHAW in *Three Plays by Brieux* (1911) p. xv, Their imitators assumed that unmentionability was an end in itself. *c* **1925** D. H. LAWRENCE *Virgin & Gipsy* (1930) i. 12 The children were brought up in this atmosphere of cunning self-sanctification and of unmentionability.

unmentionable, *a.* and *sb.* Add: **b.** (Earlier example.) Also, underpants, and (chiefly *joc.*) underwear, esp. women's.

1823 *London Mag.* Oct. 433/2 Liston, in a pair of *unmentionables* coming half-way down his legs. **1910** O. JOHNSON *Varmint* 221 Each [boy] was required to don upper and lower unmentionables. **1930** *Amer. Speech* V. 497 Silk nighties, panties, and undies in general..these articles were consistently grouped in the common speech as 'unmentionables'. **1972** *Daily News-Miner* (Fairbanks, Alaska) 3 Nov. 1/7 The Russians..'d buy up perfume, wrist watches and ladies' unmentionables. **1974** *Times* 5 Jan. 10/6 Fear of being ambulanced away to a place where nurses will..snigger at your frayed unmentionables.

c. *sb.* A person or thing not to be mentioned (by name). Chiefly *pl.*

1928 *Public Opinion* 8 June 547/3 If you pinched a penny of his pay you passed beyond the pale, you became an unmentionable, you ceased to be a comrade. **1939** F. THOMPSON *Lark Rise* iii. 51 Those parts of the human body then known as 'the unmentionables'. **1975** *Nature* 17 Jan. 149/3 The lowest grade, dirty, wet mixtures of plastic, paper and other organic unmentionables could at least provide heat, if distilled in a pyrolysis plant set up on a wasteplex site. **1976** *Sat. Rev.* (U.S.) 30 Oct. 24/2 *Feijoada*, a Brazilian mix of rice, beans, and pork unmentionables. **1981** *Times* 6 Mar. 6/5 Already the unmentionables have been mentioned and the unpublishables published in the main..weeklies. **1982** 'P. LORAINE' *Sea-Change* III. vii. 168 The whole plan was based upon unmentionables.

unmet, *ppl. a.*[1] (Examples corresponding to MEET *v.* 7.)

1962 *Guardian* 13 July 10/4 Housing needs often make unmet demands. **1969** *Listener* 6 Feb. 172/3 There remains a massive unmet need for advice and aid from legally trained people. **1980** *Times Lit. Suppl.* 6 June 652/2 The particular need of the rapidly growing sectors, unmet by the traditional capital market, was to be of significance.

unmetaphorical, *a.* Add: (Earlier example.)

1746 J. WESLEY *Let.* 25 June (1982) II. 199 In as plain and unmetaphorical words as the nature of the thing would bear.

Hence **unmetapho·rically** *adv.*

1829 G. GRIFFIN *Collegians* II. xxiv. 193 Sitting down to her, unmetaphorically, bitter draught with the meekest resignation. **1932** H. H. PRICE *Perception* i. 13 This assumption when openly and unmetaphorically stated, is.. extraordinary. **1963** R. M. HARE *Freedom & Reason* xi. 210 Prepositions expressed in terms of them [*sc.* metaphors] are, when put unmetaphorically, true.

unme·tered, (*ppl.*) *a.* [UN-[1] 8, 9.] Not measured by means of a meter; not provided with a meter.

1909 in WEBSTER. **1967** *Guardian* 13 Sept. 8/3 It is quite untrue that airport taxis are unmetered... The tariff is clearly displayed inside the cab on the taximeter. **1977** C. BRANDRETH *Parking Law* 57 Any unmetered spaces are provided for loading and unloading and picking up and setting down passengers. **1980** *Blair & Ketchum's Country Jrnl.* Oct. 111/2 A 1975 report on metropolitan area water usage and 'unmetered water'—quantities leaked, used to flush mains or extinguish fires, or consumed free by public facilities.

unmi·ssable, *a.* [UN-[1] 7 b.] That cannot or should not be missed.

1934 in WEBSTER. **1972** *Guardian* 18 Mar. 10/2 Radio 4's unmissable 'Word in Edgeways'. **1978** *Times* 28 Aug. 8/8 William Randolph Hearst's fairy castle..is an unmissable monument to random acquisitiveness. **1980** *Daily Tel.* 23 Aug. 10 One act in the 'unmissable' category at the Edinburgh festival must surely be the Prvimaj Pirot Workers Culture Art Band from..Yugoslavia. **1983** *Observer* (Colour Suppl.) 13 Mar. 32/3 One unmissable part of her daily routine.

unmistakable, *a.* Add: Hence also **u:nmistakabi·lity.**

1923 J. M. MURRY *Pencillings* 13 It matters only if another writer should arise who..will take advantage of some of Henry James's explorations and use them in order to increase his own unmistakability. **1972** *Daily Tel.* (Colour Suppl.) 19 May 41/3 One thing all [these villages] possess, and Torremolinos-rampant does not, is unmistakeability.

unmix, *v.* Add: **a.** (Later example of *trans.* use.)
1973 *Sci. Amer.* Apr. 115/2 That is why it is easy to mix cream into a cup of coffee but difficult to unmix the two.
b. *intr.*
1968 *Physical Rev. Lett.* XX. 318/1 These particles will phase 'unmix' causing the appearance of a third wave, 'the echo'. **1971** I. G. Gass et al. *Understanding Earth* i. 18/1 A high temperature feldspar..frequently 'unmixes' if cooled slowly to form a crystal composed of discrete blebs or laminae of two compositionally different feldspars. **1980** *Phil. Mag.* A. XLI. 637 For situations in which a true thermodynamic equilibrium can be attained, the equilibrating species unmix, producing a heterogeneous composition.

unmi·xing, *vbl. sb.* [Un-[2] 8.] The process by which the components of a mixture separate.
1929 *Amer. Mineralogist* XIV. 235 Pentlandite is supposed to be one of the components of the 'unmixing' of a solid solution of (Fe, Ni)S. **1934** *Proc. Nat. Acad. Sci.* XX. 452 This is evidently the reason for unmixing of a solid solution (in mineralogical parlance) or the formation of a segregate phase (in metallographic parlance). **1950** [see *solvus]. **1974** *Nature* 9 Aug. 480/1 To avoid any appreciable unmixing occurring on cooling, the sample was rapidly removed from the hot furnace into a water-cooled brass jacket.

unmodish, *a.* Delete † *Obs.* and add later example.
a **1974** R. Crossman *Diaries* (1977) III. 225 Of all the places which are not exactly with-it that dreary part of South London is the worst, brand new and yet unpopular and unmodish.

unmollified, *ppl. a.* (Later examples.)
1934 W. S. Churchill *Marlborough* II. xxiv. 531 Slangenberg, unmollified, objected even to receiving the order of his own Government from the Commander-in-Chief under whom he was to serve. **1968** *Punch* 12 June 853/1 Animals not allowed, said the hatchet manageress. Good God, woman, this is our last night in England. She was unmollified.

unmortal, *a.* Delete † and add later example.
1935 Dylan Thomas in *New Verse* Aug.–Sept. 2 My man of leaves and the bronze root, mortal, unmortal.

unmould, *v.* Add: **1. b.** (Further examples.) Also *absol.*
1971 *Daily Tel.* 15 July 15/2 The no-cooking puddings.. can await your pleasure in the freezer..; but do remember not to unmould them until the moment of service. **1972** *Ibid.* 28 Dec. 11/3 Unmould, and dust with sifted icing sugar and serve with orange sauce. **1977** *Lancashire Life* Mar. 111/2 Pour into a suitable mould and chill or leave to set. Unmould onto lettuce leaves and serve with mayonnaise. **1982** L. Chamberlain *Food & Cooking of Russia* (1983) 265 Refrigerate for a few hours. Unmould on to a serving plate.

unmoving, *ppl. a.* **2.** Delete *rare*$^{-1}$ and add later example.
1971 S. Hill *Strange Meeting* 188 We have had a pep talk from the Brigadier, and last week, a pep letter came round to all officers and N.C.O.'s—entirely unmoving.

unmusicality. (See small-type note s.v. Unmusical *a.*) (Examples.)
1946 *Penguin Music Mag.* Dec. 14 Our vaunted choral singing is really the proof of our fundamental unmusicality, because any amateur can sing in a chorus. **1963** *Times* 17 May 18/6 Beethoven (whom to admit disliking is still tantamount to an admission of unmusicality). **1984** *Listener* 12 Jan. 28/3 Their unmusicality demands public exposure.

unmusicalness. (Later examples.)
1873 C. M. Yonge *Pillars of House* I. x. 201 Geraldine resembled Fulbert in unmusicalness. **1922** *Daily Mail* 10 Nov. 7 She had been painfully struck by..'the unmusicalness' of the bells of public clocks.

unnerve, *v.* Add: Hence also **unne·rvingly** *adv.*
1962 I. Murdoch *Unofficial Rose* xxxiii. 313 There was something unfocussed, something a little unnervingly fragmentary, in his present apprehension of Lindsay. **1976** T. Heald *Let Sleeping Dogs Die* i. 10 Parkinson had been unnervingly friendly.

unneutral, *a.* (Later examples.)
1895 T. A. Walker *Man. Public Internat. Law* iv. ii. 165 A neutral Government is in general responsible in respect of the unneutral employment of its territories and territorial waters. **1949** W. S. Churchill *2nd World War* II. ii. xx. 358 The transfer to Great Britain of fifty American warships was a decidedly unneutral act by the United States. *a* **1974** R. Crossman *Diaries* (1976) II. 366 Most of the gains we made by the July measures would have been upset by an unneutral policy.

unnoticeably, *adv.* (Earlier example.)
1872 Geo. Eliot *Middlem.* IV. viii. lxxx. 285 She would make as quietly and unnoticeably as possible her second attempt to see and save Rosamond.

unobservable, *a.* Add: **3.** *sb. pl.* Things which cannot be observed.
1944 *Mind* LIII. 227 It is not at all certain that there are not highly respected scientific hypotheses which allege the existence of unobservables. **1980** *Times Lit. Suppl.* 17 Oct. 1181/2 The logical positivists held that for a sentence to be meaningful it must be capable of experiential verification. In consequence they had a central problem with discourse about unobservables... Their standard line of solution was some kind of definitional reduction of unobservables to observables.
Hence **u:nobservabi·lity.**
1944 *Mind* LIII. 224 The positivist principle..does not tell us anything at all about the observability or unobservability of the facts stated in P. **1979** *Amer. Pol. Sci. Rev.* Mar. 164/2 Unobservability is one reason..for the relative unfamiliarity of political things.

unobtainable, *a.* (Examples in *Teleph.*)
1930 [see *number *sb.* 4 f]. **1961** E. Waugh *Unconditional Surrender* ii. iv. 96 When they tried to ring him up they were told the number was 'unobtainable'. **1968** P. Geddes *High Game* v. 58 He..retreated to telephone. .. A misconnection to Guildford, two unobtainable signals and nine minutes later he had finally made it. **1976** 'K. Royce' *Bastillo* vi. 82 He..rang Todashi... He got the unobtainable tone.

unoccupied, *a.* Add: **3. c.** *spec.* Designating that part of France not held under German military occupation during the war of 1939–45. Cf. *occupied *ppl. a.*
1940 *New Statesman* 19 Oct. 380 A Jewish friend (who recently returned from unoccupied France to his home in Paris) told me that he liked the English immensely. **1942** Mrs. Belloc Lowndes *Let.* 3 July (1971) 230, I hear dreadful accounts of France—all old people and delicate people, are dying—especially..in the unoccupied districts. **1978** A. Price *'44 Vintage* xviii. 210 A chateau south of the Loire..in the Vichy zone of unoccupied France.

unofficial, *a.* and *sb.* Add: **1.** *unofficial strike*: one not endorsed by the relevant union.
1946 'G. Orwell' in *Partisan Rev.* Summer 321 There is resentment against long hours and bad working conditions, which has shown itself in a series of 'unofficial' strikes. **1955** *Times* 24 June 4/3 The Minister of Labour could not deal with unofficial strikes in the normal way. That was a matter for the union concerned to re-establish its authority over its own members. **1972** *Guardian* 24 Nov. 10/1 Lower-paid hospital workers are resorting to a series of unofficial strikes.
2. a. spec. *unofficial member* = *private member* s.v. Private *a.* 2 c.
1879 *Tablet* 31 May 709/1 An unofficial member. **1893** Erskine May *Law of Parl.* (ed. 10) viii. 245 The relative precedence of government business, and business in charge of unofficial members,..is prescribed by the standing orders. **1970** A. P. Herbert *In Dark* iii. 74 There spoke, besides two long-suffering Ministers, 14 private (or 'unofficial') members—12 against and 2 in favour.

unoperated, *ppl. a.* Add: In *Med.*, not having been operated on.
1932 J. S. Huxley *Probl. Relative Growth* iv. iv. 126 The effect of regeneration on the normal growth of neighbouring unoperated structures. **1975** *Year Bk. Ear, Nose & Throat* 119 Increased uptake in the unoperated ear.

unordered, *ppl. a.*[1] Add: **2. b.** *Linguistics.* Of rules: not requiring to be applied in a particular order.
1968 *Language* XLIV. 696 Unordered disjunctive sets [of rules] are abbreviated by variables. **1970** *Canadian Jrnl. Linguistics* XV. 97 These rules are considered unordered; the initial numbers are inserted merely for reference. **1979** *Trans. Philol. Soc.* 106 The type of phonological theory which allows the maximum simultaneity of application of rules is the so-called 'unordered rule hypothesis'.

unoriginal, *a.* and *sb.* Add: Hence **unori·ginally** *adv.*
1934 in Webster. **1963** V. Nabokov *Gift* v. 297 'And so I'll never see him again,' he told himself, unoriginally. **1964** *Archivum Linguisticum* XVI. 15 Several handbooks discuss our problem either too cursorily or too unoriginally to invite analysis.

unorthodox, *a.* Add: Hence **uno·rthodoxly** *adv.*
1934 in Webster. **1969** *Daily Tel.* 25 Apr. 21/3 Everything seemed to be right, both in this unorthodoxly proportioned work itself and in the expounding of it. **1977** A. Wilson *Strange Ride R. Kipling* vi. 285 The loves in the village world..are enjoyed precariously and unorthodoxly.

unostentatiousness. (Contextual example.)
1901 *Chambers's Jrnl.* Apr. 234/2 A pattern of unostentatiousness.

unpack, *v.* Add: **2. a.** *fig.* (Later examples.)
1966 *Philosophy* XLI. 30 If we unpack what is meant by 'positive morality' we come down to the opinions of individual people. **1979** A. R. Peacocke *Creation & World of Sci.* i. 39 The theological enterprise has always involved much unpacking and elaborating of this image.
5. *Computers.* To convert (an item of stored data) *into* two or more separate items; to retrieve data from (a record). Cf. *pack *v.*[1] 3 g.
1954 *Computers & Automation* Dec. 22/2 Unpack, to separate packed items of information each into a separate machine word. **1959**, etc. [see *pack *v.* 3 g]. **1960** Gregory & Van Horn *Automatic Data-Processing Systems* iii. 104 The 13 instructions given above..are required to unpack each meter-reading card and set up the quantity for bill calculation. **1972** *Computer Jrnl.* XV. 199/1 A stream..might be formed by one stream function which unpacks words into bytes.

unpacker. (Earlier example.)
1768 J. Wedgwood *Let.* 13 June (1965) 64 He writes a good Hand, and will be more useful in that Respect than as an unpacker.

unpalatable, *a.* Add: Hence also **u:npalatabi·lity.**
1934 in Webster. **1974** *Nature* 25 Jan. 170/1 The potential unpalatability of a current policy designed to affect the demographic situation in the next century. **1981** *Birds* Summer 37/2 Inedible insects advertise their unpalatability by wearing warning colours—usually black and yellow or black and red.

unpapered, *ppl. a.* (Earlier contextual example.)
1805 F. Burney *Let.* 29 May (1975) VI. 517 It is unfurnished, indeed, unpapered, & every way unfinished.

unpatterned, *ppl. a.* Add: **3.** Not formed or cast into a pattern.
1949 M. Mead *Male & Female* ix. 190 Man, the heir of tradition, provides for women and children. We have no indication that man..unpatterned by social learning, would do anything of the sort. **1960** T. McLean *Kings of Rugby* xi. 192 Too much unpatterned play. **1977** *Sci. Amer.* Jan. 117/1 Consider an analogous isomorphism exhibited by a sequence of unpatterned digits such as pi.

unpeg, *v.* Add: (Later examples.) Also *fig.* Hence **unpe·gging** *vbl. sb.*
1923 J. M. Keynes *Tract on Monetary Reform* 121 The present situation..did not begin until after the 'unpegging' of the leading exchanges in 1919. **1975** 'M. Yorke' *Small Hours* i. 14 A young woman came to unpeg them [*sc.* the clothes]. **1977** *Guardian Weekly* 7 Aug. 10/1 Unpegging sterling from the US dollar is a thoroughly sensible move. **1977** *Times* 29 Oct. 19/4 The Israel pound fell sharply as it was unpegged from its official rate of 10 to the dollar. **1981** *Times* 21 Jan. 11/4 They chat as they unpeg the washing.

u·npeople, *sb.* [Un-[1] 12.] **a.** People excluded from 'the people' as understood politically. **b.** Unpersons.
1962 E. Snow *Other Side of River* (1963) l. 380 There is less mystery in China today than in most Communist countries about what both people and 'unpeople' find unbearable. **1968** *Guardian* 28 Nov. 11/2 (*heading*) Czech unpeople down on the farm. **1970** *Guardian Weekly* 21 Mar. 6 People on foot on a hot road..walking from nowhere to nowhere... Tired people. Unpeople. **1975** P. Lively *Going Back* vii. 88 Who are those people the Greeks knew about—the ones who wander around the Styx? The unburied dead: grey, unpeople. I am one of them. **1975** Ld. Hailsham *Door wherein I Went* vi. 28 Communists teach that there was no such person as Jesus at all... He is the unperson to end all unpeople.

u·nperson. [Un-[1] 12: introduced by 'George Orwell'.] A person who, usu. for political misdemeanour, is deemed not to have existed and whose name is removed from all public records. In extended use, a person whose existence or achievement is officially denied or disregarded; a person of no political or social importance.
1949 'G. Orwell' *Nineteen Eighty-Four* ii. 159 Syme was not only dead, he was abolished, an *unperson.* **1954** *Economist* 18 Sept. 883/2 Beria is already an 'unperson', the record of his career 'unfacts'. **1961** *Guardian* 28 Apr. 8/5 The concentration camp was a factory for processing people into un-persons. **1962** *Listener* 15 Feb. 308/1 From the Soviet point of view they are 'unpersons', ignored or slandered in Soviet travesties of literary history. **1969** H. E. Salisbury *Siege of Leningrad* i. iii. 24 Berezhkov omits any mention of Dekanozov's name or of the Dekanozov-Weizsäcker meeting. Because of his execution in 1953 Dekanozov apparently has become an unperson. **1981** P. Dickinson *Seventh Raven* xi. 151 You've got absolutely nothing to do..in hospitals... Places like that tend to turn you into a kind of unperson. **1983** *Listener* 16 June 4/1 He omitted the then Foreign Secretary, Francis Pym, who seemed even then to have become an unperson.
Hence **unpe·rson** *v.* to make into an unperson (usu. in *pa. pple.*); **unpe·rsoning** *vbl. sb.* Also *transf.*
1966 Page & Burg in *Soviet Stud.* XVIII. 96 (*title*) Unpersoned: the fall of Nikita Sergeyevitch Khrushchev. **1973** *Listener* 4 Jan. 8/2 On television... The addition of a face..turns the newsreader into a person, but the job then requires him to unperson himself. **1976** *Times Lit. Suppl.* 13 Feb. 156/3 The unpersoning process [in Czechoslovakia] had gathered momentum and many of the notables of 1968–69 were being rapidly transmogrified into the nobodies of the 1970s. **1977** *Listener* 16 June 790/2 One of them dead and the other efficiently unpersoned and confined to a political asylum. **1983** *Daily Tel.* 12 Mar. 14/2 In 1956, Bob..brought in Hamilton.. as editorial director... But in the new edition it looks as if all the work was done by his successor, Harold Harris. 'It is no trivial matter to be "unpersonned",' says Hamilton.

unperturbed, *ppl. a.* (Examples in *Physics*: cf. *PERTURBED *ppl. a.* 2.)
1937 [see *PERTURBED *ppl. a.* 2]. **1967** MARGERISON & EAST *Introd. Polymer Chem.* ii. 67 A 'poor' solvent, on the other hand, is one in which the polymer dimensions approach those of the unperturbed configuration. **1974** G. REECE tr. *Hund's Hist. Quantum Theory* xiv. 184 The function ψ^{0} is a solution of the 'unperturbed' problem $H^{(0)}$.

unphysiological, *a.* Add: Also **unphysiolo·gic** *a.* (chiefly *U.S.*); **unphysiolo·gically** *adv.*
1934 WEBSTER, *Unphysiologic.* **1948** *Endocrinology* XLIII. 118 The amount of food consumed..was unphysiologically large in most instances. **1969** *Obstetrics & Gynecol.* XXXIII. 419/1 It is unphysiologic for newlywed apareunia. **1970** *Nature* 17 Oct. 210/1 The significance of this effect *in vivo* may be limited, for it takes place *in vitro* only at unphysiologically high levels of glucose.

unpick, *v.* **2.** (Earlier contextual example.)
1808 JANE AUSTEN *Let.* 7 Oct. (1932) I. 217 Your gown shall be unpicked.

unpicturesquely, *adv.* (Earlier example.)
1841 in H. H. Wilson *Trav. W. Moorcroft & G. Trebeck* I. i. 39 Bilaspur is not unpicturesquely situated.

unpin, *v.* Add: **5.** *trans. Chess.* To release (a piece that has been pinned). Hence **unpi·nning** *vbl. sb.*
1878 S. LOYD *Chess Strategy* 145 The key unpins the Black Queen. **1906** A. C. WHITE *Tours de Force* p. xxxvii, The more general tasks can be grouped under several heads: checking, sacrificing, pinning and unpinning, [etc.]. **1967** V. NABOKOV *Speak, Memory* (rev. ed.) xiv. 289 Themes in chess..are such devices as forelaying, withdrawing, pinning, unpinning and so forth.

u·npin, *sb. Chess.* [f. the vb.] The action or fact of releasing a piece that has been pinned.
1922 HUME & WHITE *Good Compan. Two Mover* 187 There are six unpins, five of which are direct..while the sixth is an Interference Unpin. **1928** [see *half-pin* s.v. *HALF II. i].

un-pin-dow·nable, *a.* [UN-[1] 7 b (*b*) + *PIN *v.*[1] 6 c.] That cannot be pinned down or defined.
1966 *Punch* 14 Feb. 249/2 Of all the great detectives he has the most un-pindownable character. **1973** *Guardian* 28 June 14/6 Harold Pinter is..our most tangible and un-pin-downable playwright.

unpinned, *ppl. a.* Add: **a.** (Later examples.)
1776 F. BURNEY *Diary* 6 Apr. (1889) II. 139 Two of her curls came quite unpinned, and fell lank, on one of her shoulders. **1821** M. EDGEWORTH *Let.* 27 Nov. (1971) 281 An end of her frill was unpinned.
b. Of a grenade: having had the pin (*PIN *sb.*[1] 1 n) removed.
1974 P. DICKINSON *Poison Oracle* vi. 159 The Jap pilot who brought the plane down..on to an inadequate runway with an assassin sitting beside him holding an unpinned grenade.

unpiteous, *a.* Restrict † *Obs.* to sense 1 in Dict. and add: **2.** (Later example.)
1954 W. FAULKNER *Fable* 289 In our country, in our hard and unpiteous mountains, people used..children as people in lands savage with dangerous animals used guns and bullets: to defend, preserve themselves.

unplayable, *a.* Add: Hence **unplay·ably** *adv.*
1955 *Times* 6 June 3/1 Before luncheon the occasional ball turned and lifted nastily, and the one that accounted for May did so almost unplayably. **1978** *Daily Tel.* 21 Feb. 13/6 Next the unplayably simple A flat, made to sound telling and enigmatic at the same time, a great success.

unpleasable, *a.* (Later example.)
1951 A. L. ROWSE *English Past* 24 The two sons were growing up not much to the liking of their virtuous, unpleasable mother.

unpleasantness. Add: **b.** *the late unpleasantness* (U.S.), the American Civil War; also *transf.*
1868 D. R. LOCKE *Ekkoes from Kentucky* 23 (Th.), That cuss cum back here, doorin' the late onpleasantniss, kernel of a rigiment. **1872** *Harper's Mag.* Feb. 479/1 During our 'late unpleasantness' a convalescent hospital was established..in Nashville. **1903** *N.Y. Times* 19 Sept. 3 The only soldier to be killed from Orange during the late unpleasantness with the Filipinos. **1930** S. HENRY *Conquering Great Amer. Plains* 33 When 'the late unpleasantness' terminated, the Texan drover lacked a satisfactory market. **1948** *Amer. Jrnl. Nursing* Dec. 770/2 Among the stamps of particular interest to nurses to come out of the 'late unpleasantness', are a Hungarian Red Cross series,..and a German child welfare series. **1981** *Times* 25 Aug. 7/1 The British and the Germans.. were all of that older generation which well remembers the late unpleasantness between our two countries.

unpleasure. Add: **a.** (Earlier example.)
1792 F. BURNEY *Jrnl.* Jan. (1972) I. 111, I told him, very truly, of the pleasure with which I had re-entered his Roof—but I [write] the *un*pleasures that followed!
b. *Psychoanal.* [tr. G. *unlust.*] The sense of inner pain, discomfort, or anxiety which results from the blocking of an instinctual impulse by the ego and is the opposite of the affect of pleasure.
1919 A. WOHLGEMUTH in *Brit. Jrnl. Psychol.* Monogr. Suppl. VI. i. 1 The affective elements are Pleasure-Unpleasure. **1925** I. A. RICHARDS *Princ. Lit. Crit.* xii. 95 Unpleasure being frustrated, chaotic, mal-successful activity. **1949** KOESTLER *Insight & Outlook* xv. 208 The nervous processes which determine the pleasure-unpleasure tone of emotional experience. **1974** *Nature* 11 Oct. 500/2 The monkeys' 'interest' overrode—so long as it lasted—their 'unpleasure'.

unplucked, *ppl. a.* (Examples of eyebrows.)
1959 'E. PETERS' *Death Mask* i. 8 Her brows were still high, shapely, and unplucked. **1974** *Times* 26 Oct. 8/8 Her chalk-white complexion, emerald, Kohl-rimmed eyes with unplucked eyebrows.

unplug, *v.* (Examples of an electrical appliance: opp. *PLUG *v.* 1 e.)
1942 *Tee Emm* (Air Ministry) II. 141 Nothing is more annoying than to find..one glove [of an electrically-heated flying suit] unplugging itself every time you move your arm. **1969** A. GLYN *Dragon Variation* vi. 184 Mr. Jackson unplugged the television and turned out the lights.

unpolicied, *ppl. a.* (Later example.)
1947 AUDEN *Nones* (1952) 64 The unamerican survivor Hears angels drinking fruit-juice with their wives Or making money in an open Unpolicied air.

unpolitic, *a.* (Later example.)
1978 J. UPDIKE *Coup* (1979) i. 20 The unpolitic loyalty of the fearful.

unpolitical, *a.* Add: Hence **unpoli·tically** *adv.*
1930 E. SITWELL *Alexander Pope* v. 63 The young and un-politically-minded Pope. **1962** *Times* 5 Dec. 17/6 It [*sc.* a film] is unpolitically concerned with people.

unpompous, *a.* (Later examples.)
1928 *Daily Express* 8 May 5 This is an unpompous age, and the tendency to poke fun at that ancient spectacle, grand opera,..does not decrease. **1946** D. WELCH *Jrnl.* 9 Apr. (1952) 197 He quickly dropped the 'sir' when he was sitting beside me... This I knew was a compliment in some way. I suppose I interpreted it as a tribute to an unpompous or young appearance. **1959** J. OSBORNE *World of Paul Slickey* I. iii. 29 We can safely say in a not unpompous way, blind Them with words! **1978** *Even. Standard* 29 Sept. 20/5 At yesterday's function Sir Peter read a neat, unpompous little speech.

unpornogra·phic, *a.* [UN-[1] 7 a.] Not pornographic.
1938 *New Statesman & Nation* 23 July 156/2 This admirable and totally unpornographic novel. **1943** D. WELCH *Jrnl.* 20 Apr. (1952) 61 As Bernard Shaw said to me when we were all called to give evidence over the *Well of Loneliness* fuss, 'Here I am, asked to say something about this pathetic book, and I don't know what to do, because I know it's serious, unpornographic, but it's so bad as literature.' **1968** *Punch* 5 June 829/1 The story is not only quite unpornographic, it is also very funny.

unpowdered, *ppl. a.* Add: **3.** Not wearing face-powder; without face-powder.
1917 J. F. MACDONALD *Two Towns—One City* III. ii. 210 Flushed, and dishevelled, and unpowdered Fifine becomes. **1921** W. DE LA MARE *Mem. Midget* xli. 276 Her clear, unpowdered skin had the faint sheen of a rose. **1956** 'C. BLACKSTOCK' *Dewey Death* iii. 59 The fair hair was falling over her face; her skin was blotched and unpowdered. **1974** J. MANN *Sticking Place* v. 88 Look at her now, shabby, unpowdered.

unpracticalness. (Earlier example.)
1843 J. S. MILL *Let.* in *Wks.* (1963) XIII. 579 The chief fault seems to me that of entire unpracticalness.

unprayable, *a.* Add: **2.** That cannot be uttered as a prayer. *rare.*
1941 T. S. ELIOT *Dry Salvages* ii. 9 The prayer of the bone on the beach, the unprayable Prayer at the calamitous annunciation.

unpredictable, *a.* Add: Hence **u:npredictabi·lity.**
1920 S. ALEXANDER *Space, Time, & Deity* II. 324 Unpredictability is not limited to human determinism. **1955** *Bull. Atomic Sci.* Mar. 87/1 Their freedom imparts an unpredictability to historic events. **1977** J. L. HARPER *Population Biol. Plants* 769 Organisms in nature live in environments that contain rhythms and unpredictabilities, patterns and noise.

unpressed, *ppl. a.* **1.** (Examples corresponding to *PRESS *v.*[1] 4 a.)
1932 W. FAULKNER *Light in Aug.* xix. 419 A tall, loosejointed man with a constant cob pipe,..wearing always loose and unpressed dark gray clothes. **1968** J. IRONSIDE *Fashion Alphabet* 96 Soft pleats with edges rounded and left unpressed. **1974** J. FLINT *Cecil Rhodes* (1976) ii. 19 Rhodes was notable for the shabbiness of his unpressed suits. **1977** *Lancashire Life* Nov. 115/3 (*caption*) A dress with an intricately seamed bodice falling into unpressed pleats.

unpretty, *a.* Add: Hence **unpre·ttily** *adv.*
1929 W. FAULKNER *Sartoris* II. vi. 157 She mouthed her food unprettily. **1982** R. BARNARD *Death & Princess* xiv. 141 The Princess Helena pouted unprettily.

unpriceable, *a.* Add: **b.** That cannot be priced.
1951 P. LARKIN *XX Poems*, And to hear how the past is past and the future neuter Might knock my darling off her unpriceable pivot.

unprinceliness. (Earlier example.)
1855 G. H. LEWES *Life & Wks. Goethe* I. IV. i. 310 The princely unprinceliness of selling to the Jews a diamond ring.

unprintable, *a.* and *sb.* Add: Hence **unpri·ntably** *adv.*
1934 in WEBSTER. **1940** E. HEMINGWAY *For whom Bell Tolls* iii. 44 Go then unprintably to the campfire with thy obscene dynamite. **1965** D. FRANCIS *Odds Against* xi. 153 Jones-boy unprintably told Chico where he could find his coffee. **1977** *Gay News* 7–20 Apr. 23/2 It's infuriating trying to write about Anger because so much is unprintably scandalous.

unproblematic, *a.* (Later examples.)
1944 C. G. MYRDAL et al. *Amer. Dilemma* II. 1032 The system of mores, conceived of as a homogeneous, unproblematic, fairly static, social entity. **1981** *Word 1980* XXXI. 196 Something that was not possible within the tonetic stress marks theory proves relatively unproblematic for the configurational model. **1984** *Listener* 19 Apr. 16/2 Nor is there any unproblematic external standard with which to compare competing paradigms.

unprocessed, *ppl. a.* (Later examples, corresponding to PROCESS *v.*[1] 3.)
1959 *Times* 6 Mar. 11/7 The United States..want the unprocessed raw materials. **1962** E. SNOW *Other Side of River* (1963) lxxix. 607 In Peking I had been assured that I would be permitted to take out unprocessed film. **1974** *Brit. Med. Jrnl.* 19 Jan. 109/2 Unprocessed bran is an ideal additive to the diet in such cases.

unprofessional, *a.* and *sb.* Add: Hence **unprofe·ssionalism.**
1934 in WEBSTER. **1955** A. L. ROWSE *Expansion Elizabethan England* 382 The clue to English ill-success was, as usual, amateurishness, unprofessionalism, in the beginning. **1977** *Time* 28 Feb. 22/1 The Carter Administration was still marred in some areas by confusion and unprofessionalism; the staff work was sometimes shoddy and key memos poorly prepared.

unprotestant, *a.* (Earlier example.)
1839 J. S. MILL in *Westm. Rev.* Apr. 504 The unprotestant and unchristian doctrines..which are extensively professed.

unpublishable, *a.* Add: Also as *sb.*
1981 [see *UNMENTIONABLE *a.* and *sb.* c].

unpublished, *ppl. a.* Add: **1. b.** Of an author: having had no writings published.
1934 R. MACAULAY *Milton* 26 A severe judgment on a writer already so fruitful, though as yet unpublished. **1976** *Scotsman* 20 Nov. (Weekend Suppl.) 3/8 (Advt.), This second anthology of new poems..includes work by.. other established poets as well as by very talented but previously unpublished poets.

unpunctuality. (Earlier example.)
1814 JANE AUSTEN *Mansfield Park* II. iv. 84 Their remoteness and unpunctuality, or their exorbitant charges.

unpunctuated, *ppl. a.* (Earlier example.)
1860 W. JAMES *Let.* 12 Aug. in R. B. Perry *Thought & Character W. James* (1935) I. 196 Alice must be locked up alone..to write a letter, unassisted, uncorrected and unpunctuated, to her loving brothers.

unquakerlike, *a.* (Earlier example.)
1832 F. TROLLOPE *Domestic Manners of Americans* II. xxx. 154, I overheard many unquakerlike jokes.

unqualifiedly, *adv.* (Earlier example.)
1861 MILL *Repr. Govt.* iii. 57 On the question of strikes ..it is doubtful if there is so much as one among the leading members of either House, who is not firmly convinced that the reason of the matter is unqualifiedly on the side of the masters.

unquick, *a.* **2.** (Later example.)
1925 D. H. LAWRENCE *Refl. Death Porcupine* 111 The novel..can't exist without being 'quick'. The ordinary unquick novel, even if it be a best seller, disappears into absolute nothingness.

u·nquote, *v.* [UN-[2] 3.] *intr.* Used as a formula in dictation, etc.: terminate the quotation. See *QUOTE *v.* 4 c.
1935 E. E. CUMMINGS *Let.* Mar. (1969) 139 But he said that if I'd hold up publication of No Thanks for 15 days he'd kill unquote a page of Aiken. **1935**, etc. [see *QUOTE *v.* 4 c]. **1969** *New Yorker* 11 Oct. 48/2 Then Mr. Tanks announced the last downtown stop. He said, 'Madison Square Garden, Penn Station..et cetera, et cetera, et cetera, unquote'.

unquoted, *ppl. a.* (Later examples: cf. QUOTE *v.* 7.)
1969 *Times* 2 May 31/6 Cranfields is an unquoted public company in flour milling and baking. **1977** JOHNS & GREENFIELD *Dymond's Capital Transfer Tax* iii. 54 (*heading*) Condition (4) Sale of unquoted shares or debentures.

unra·ced, *ppl. a.*³ [UN-¹ 8 + RACE *v.*¹] That has not taken part in a race.

1955 *Motor* 26 Jan. 57/1, 2-seater sports, one owner, pale green, unraced, £975. **1963** *Times* 21 May 3/6 Lord Derby's brown gelding, Robinson Crusoe, unraced as a two-year-old but winner of two races at Newmarket this season, gave a first rate display of stamina and gameness at Leicester yesterday. **1976** *Horse & Hound* 3 Dec. 9/4 Miles Away was bought by the combination at the Ballsbridge November Sales for 10,000 guineas, a record price in Ireland for an unraced gelding of his age.

unracy, *a.* (Earlier example.)

1847 *Dublin Rev.* Sept. 228 The style..is seldom chargeable with the defects of unracy or unidiomatic phraseology, commonly objected to Johnson's.

unrailed, *ppl. a.* (Earlier contextual examples.)

1842 *Rep. Comm. Children's Employment* 384 in *Parl. Papers* XVI. 1 Women and children employed to carry coal on their backs in unrailed roads. **1891** KIPLING & BALESTIER in *Century Mag.* Nov. 35/1 The unrailed bridge that crossed the irrigating-ditch.

unrea·cted, *ppl. a. Chem.* [UN-¹ 8.] Not having undergone reaction.

1950 *Jrnl. Amer. Chem. Soc.* LXXII. 10/1 If the recovered unreacted bismuth compound is considered, the yield..was 62·4%. **1977** A. HALLAM *Planet Earth* 33/3 After neutralizing or evaporating off any unreacted acid, the resulting rock solution is then sprayed into a hot flame.

unrea·ctive, *a. Chem.* [UN-¹ 7 a.] Not reactive (*REACTIVE *a.* 5 a).

1934 in WEBSTER. **1946** *Nature* 28 Sept. 437/1 In this substance..the Cl atoms are unreactive. **1965** PHILLIPS & WILLIAMS *Inorg. Chem.* I. x. 348 Molecules with very high dissociation energies such as C_2, N_2, and O_2 would be expected to be unreactive, while Li_2, Be_2, and F_2, with very low dissociation energies, would be reactive. **1978** *Jrnl. Physical Chem.* LXXXII. 2554/1 The zwitterion is relatively unreactive.

Hence **unreacti·vity.**

1946 *Nature* 14 Sept. 383/1 This chemical unreactivity of the fluorine atom of the FCH_2-group is shared by many of the compounds mentioned in this communication. **1978** *Jrnl. Physical Chem.* LXXXII. 2549 The unreactivity of glycine-like, α-amino acid zwitterions does not appear to be due to rate-limiting ring closure.

unreadable, *a.* Add: Hence also **unrea·dably** *adv.*; **unreadableness** (earlier example).

1780 F. BURNEY *Diary & Lett.* (1842) I. VII. 316 In the evening we had Mrs. Lambert, who brought us a tale, called 'Edwy and Edilda', by the sentimental Mr. W—, and unreadably soft, and tender, and senseless is it. **1838** J. S. MILL in *Westm. Rev.* Aug. 506 He could stop nowhere short of utter unreadableness. *a* **1974** R. CROSSMAN *Diaries* (1975) I. 564 She may be right that if you want to impress people you must make things unreadably long.

unre·alist, *sb.* and *a.* [UN-¹ 12, 7 a.] **A.** *sb.* One who is not a realist. **B.** *adj.* Not realistic or realist.

1934 WEBSTER, Unrealist, *n.* **1936** E. GILL *Let.* 10 Oct. (1947) 367 It is unrealist to write..saying 'art is a way of life..that should govern all we do and make, not to say think'. **1938** A. L. ROWSE in *Pol. Q.* Jan.–Mar. 24 The hopeless doctrinaires,..the chronic unrealists, who are the despair of the [Labour] Party. **1958** S. SPENDER *Engaged in Writing* 67 They, with their fairy stories,..are the unrealists. **1973** *Screen* Spring/Summer 40 Certain types of cinema (modern, realist, 'un-realist'. [etc.]). *Ibid.* 48 Films which are deliberately 'un-realist' (legends, fairy stories, films of the *phantastique* genre, etc.).

unrealistic, *a.* Add: Hence **unreali·stically** *adv.*

1961 *Listener* 16 Nov. 797/2 Our critics often use their weapons unrealistically, and unhistorically. **1977** *Times Lit. Suppl.* 20 May 610/3 He kidded him for making American life unrealistically grim.

unrecallable, *a.* (Later example.)

1930 W. DE LA MARE *On the Edge* 293 Not that she had ever confessed this in so many raw unrecallable words.

unreconstructed, *ppl. a.* Add: *spec.* (orig. *U.S.*) not reconciled to the outcome of the American Civil War; hence *gen.* not reconciled or converted to the current political orthodoxy; unreformed; die-hard. (Earlier and later examples.)

1867 *Harper's Weekly* 9 Nov. 707/2 The Democratic candidates in Maryland are..of the 'unreconstructed' kind. *a* **1936** KIPLING *Something of Myself* (1937) vii. 195 There came..with her married daughter the widow of a Confederate Cavalry leader; both of them were what you might call 'unreconstructed' rebels. **1944** *Univ. of Chicago Mag.* May 6 The young are in increasing numbers, not only in Oklahoma but in much of the vast inland region of our republic, moving to the cities, leaving the unreconstructed small towns to their elders and to decay. **1946** J. FLANNER in *New Yorker* 9 Mar. 80/1 Nuremberg defense counsel have just offered..an absolutely first-rate demonstration of the still unreconstructed prewar German mind. **1949** B. A. BOTKIN *Treas. S. Folklore* I. i. 4 As the type and symbol of the 'unreconstructed Southerner', Donald Davidson selects 'Cousin Roderick', an idealized Middle Georgia country gentleman, who combines the 'bearing of an English squire' with the 'frontier heartiness' of A. B. Longstreet's *Georgia Scenes.* What principally distinguishes Cousin Roderick from 'Brother Jonathan' (the Vermont 'unreconstructed Yankee' who resembles the Georgian in so many ways)..is the fact that he does not work with his own hands. **1962** A. SAMPSON *Anat. of Britain* XXX. 480 He and his board have reacted..to revelations about their monopoly, with the old-fashioned sang-froid of unreconstructed businessmen. **1968** *Economist* 6 Jan. 34/3 The trial had an even greater impact because of the blunt rebukes hurled at the defendants by Judge Harold Cox, once considered one of the more unreconstructed judges in the South. **1972** R. PLANT in Cox & Dyson *20th-Cent. Mind* II. iv. 91 The major opposition to Roosevelt's New Deal policies in fact came from these unreconstructed *laissez-faire* liberals who failed to realize that planning was necessary in order to make individual freedom a *real* possibility for the masses. **1973** [see *RECONSTRUCTED *ppl. a.* b]. **1979** *Guardian* 2 Oct. 10/2 A further entrenchment of unreconstructed union power. **1981** 'A. CROSS' *Death in Faculty* i. 12 The place is pretty much unreconstructed..an ancient bathroom complete with mahogany bathtub.

unreduced, *ppl. a.* Add: **7.** *Phonetics.* Of a vowel sound or other phonetic element: not reduced (see *REDUCED *ppl. a.* 6 b).

1953 K. JACKSON *Lang. & Hist. Early Brit.* 658 Unreduced forms are almost never found in Welsh. **1964** E. BLANCQUAERT in D. Abercrombie et al. *Daniel Jones* 300 English weakened syllables are pronounced unreduced.

unreflectingly, *adv.* (Earlier examples.)

1696 J. SERGEANT *Method to Sci.* II. ii. 131 The Former comes by Experience Unreflectingly; the Later is attain'd by Study and Reflexion. **1854** A. G. HENDERSON tr. *Cousin's Philos. of Kant* p. lx, Thou wouldst not unreflectingly confer it upon the first comer.

unrelatable, *a.* (Later examples.)

1963 BRUNER & OLVER in J. S. Bruner *Beyond Information Given* (1974) xx. 361 The lists proceed from near to far items, from easily associated to almost unrelatable elements. **1968** *Listener* 1 Aug. 147/3 The relative pronoun hangs in the air, unrelatable to anything in particular.

unreleased, *ppl. a.* (Later examples.)

1960 *Lang. & Speech* III. 109 (*heading*) On the perception of unreleased voiceless plosives in English. **1982** *Times* 13 Feb. 6/1 This successful, though unreleased, movie.

unremaining, *ppl. a.* (Later example.)

1936 A. E. HOUSMAN *More Poems* 63 Here the child comes to found His unremaining mound.

unremember, *v.* (Later example.)

1983 *Spectator* 16 Apr. 22/2 We cannot unremember Auschwitz.

unremunerated, *ppl. a.* (Examples.)

1895 J. WILLIAMS *Briefless Ballads* 51 We mourn in unremunerated pain Those brave old days. **1945** A. L. ROWSE *West-Country Stories* 3 His services were unremunerated.

unrenewable, *a.* (Later example.)

1977 *Church Times* 25 Feb. 7/2 Its chronic prodigality in the use of unrenewable fossil fuels.

unrepair. (Earlier example.)

1843 THACKERAY *Irish Sk.-Bk.* II. xii. 225 A dismal state of unrepair.

unrepresentative, *a.* Add: Hence **unrepresentativeness.**

1958 A. TOYNBEE *East to West* 221 This unrepresentativeness of the capital is one of its generic defects. **1980** BUTLER & PINTO-DUSCHINSKY in Z. Layton-Henry *Conservative Party Politics* viii. 198 Does Conservative unrepresentativeness harm the party in other ways?

unreprodu·ctive, *a.* [UN-¹ 7.] Not reproductive.

1930 W. K. HANCOCK *Australia* viii. 161 Informed opinion was ready to welcome the report of the British Economic Mission (January 1929), which warned Australia that unreproductive developmental expenditure was imposing 'a heavy burden on the general community.' **1968** P. SCOTT *Day of Scorpion* (1973) II. ii. 330 Hers were the menstrual flows of a virgin, sour little seepages such as Barbie Batchelor had presumably sustained for a good thirty years of her unreproductive life.

unrepulsive, *a.* (Later example.)

1946 D. WELCH *Jrnl.* 12 Jan. (1952) 185 The person who built this church was unclogged with 'book-learning' and so his church is unrepulsive and almost pretty and good.

unresponsible, *a.* Add: Hence also **u:nresponsibi·lity.**

1935 E. HEMINGWAY *Green Hills of Africa* xii. 235, I..settled, happily, with the darkness into the unresponsibility of victory; only emerging to direct M'Cola in where to cut.

unrested, *ppl. a.*¹ **b.** (Later examples.)

1940 N. LAST *Diary* 22 Oct. in *Nella Last's War* (1983) iii. 81, I got up, tired and unrested, after a very broken night. **1981** D. BOGGIS *Time to Betray* xvii. 94 Nigel lay sleepily, unrested, worried.

unrip, *v.* **3. b.** For † read 'Now *rare*' and add later example.

1928 BARRIE *Peter Pan* II, in *Plays* 42 Unrip your plan, Captain.

unrope, *v.* Add: Also *absol.* for *refl.* in *Mountaineering.*

1902 G. BELL *Let.* 3 Aug. (1927) I. vii. 146 About 6 we got to where we could unrope—having been 48 hours on the rope. **1957** J. MASTERS *Far, Far the Mountain Peak* 67 She began to unrope, and a moment later the second *cordée* had joined them.

unsacerdotal, *a.* (Earlier example.)

1844 J. S. MILL in *Edin. Rev.* LXXIX. 33 The Papacy could..indulge within certain limits their [*sc.* the Franciscans'] most unsacerdotal preference of grace to the law.

unsa·ckable, *a.* [UN-¹ 7 b.] Not sackable.

1980 *Daily Tel.* 14 Feb. 14/8 It is a fair description of the real world of unsackable functionaries whom not God nor Sir Derek Rayner nor TNT will remove. **1984** *Listener* 12 July 17/2 The system introduced in the 1940s ..made the men who handled the catches in the registered fishing ports unsackable.

unsaddling, *vbl. sb.* (Further *attrib.* examples.)

1951 *People* 3 June 7/5 Horses shied; off scampered the rabbit to the unsaddling enclosure. **1972** D. FRANCIS *Smokescreen* iv. 51 We walked down from the stands and over towards the unsaddling enclosures.

unsafe, *a.* Add: **2. c.** *unsafe period*, the part of the menstrual cycle during which conception is most likely.

1961 G. GREENE *Burnt-Out Case* III. i. 82 He sometimes allowed her to be alone during her monthly or unsafe periods. **1969** *Times* 20 Nov. 3/3 The Roman Catholic Church has revised its ideas about the..'unsafe period' and now makes it four days around the mid-point of the female cycle.

unsalt, *a.* (Later example.)

1935 E. BOWEN *House in Paris* II. ix. 143 Here the sea air was washed unsalt by the rain.

unsalubrious, *a.* (Later examples.)

1951 M. MCLUHAN *Mech. Bride* (1967) 118/2 Nobody can do much about changing the noisy and unsalubrious character of the big cities in which most of us live and work. **1971** *Daily Tel.* 13 Dec. 7/8 There have been demonstrations in several [French] jails recently against unsalubrious conditions.

unsa·turate. *Chem.* [UN-¹ 12.] Any unsaturated compound, esp. an unsaturated fat or fatty acid. Cf. *polyunsaturate* sb. s.v. *POLYUNSATURATED *a.*

1934 *World Petroleum* Apr. 123/2 Whereas straight run fuel contained less than two percent unsaturates, cracked gasoline contained from 10 to 40 percent unsaturated compounds. **1959** LOGAN & MAGGIOLO in E. S. Pattison *Industr. Fatty Acids* v. 41 These unsaturates can be cleaved to produce monobasic and dibasic acids and their derivatives. **1974** *Radiation Res.* LIX. 109 When these substances undergo moderately rapid reaction the surface temperature of the unsaturate is considerably higher than 77°K.

unsaturated, *ppl. a.* (Examples corresponding to *SATURATED *ppl. a.* 3 b.)

1866 *Notices Proc. R. Inst. Gt. Brit.* IV. 417 The two nitrogen arms which are left exposed sufficiently indicate that two attraction units remain unsaturated. **1872** *Phil. Mag.* XLIII. 259 A radical..is a portion of a molecule, a group of atoms, the affinities of which do not wholly saturate one another, the radical being uni-, bi-, tri-, quadri-, &c. valent, according as 1, 2, 3, 4, .. affinities are left unsaturated. **1916** *Jrnl. Amer. Chem. Soc.* XXXVIII. 778 It has been generally assumed that what is known as a bivalent element must be tied by two bonds to another element or elements, or remain with an 'unsaturated valence'. **1951** I. L. FINAR *Org. Chem.* iv. 67 The acetylenes are unsaturated hydrocarbons that contain one triple bond. **1982** J. E. FERNANDEZ *Org. Chem.* v. 89 The alkenes are unsaturated: that is they contain fewer hydrogen atoms than the alkanes.

unsaturation. Add: *Chem.* The condition of a compound, esp. an organic one, of having one or more multiple bonds in its molecule. Cf. SATURATION 3 a in Dict. and Suppl. (Further examples.)

1932 I. D. GARARD *Introd. Org. Chem.* v. 59 The cause, or explanation, of the unsaturation is not the same in all instances. **1964** N. G. CLARK *Mod. Org. Chem.* vii. 115 Chemical reagents attack the site of unsaturation but this occurs less readily than in the case of the related olefins. **1975** *Sci. Amer.* Mar. 78/3 The greater the unsaturation in a fat or a wax, that is, the greater the number of double bonds, the more likely it is that the substance will be liquid at low temperatures.

unscalped, *ppl. a.* (Earlier example.)

1726 C. LYMAN in S. Penhallow *Hist. Wars New-England* 22 We found seven dead upon the spot: Six of whom we scalpt, and left the other unscalpt.

unscattered, *ppl. a.* (Later examples.)

1941 in M. Gowing *Britain & Atomic Energy 1939–45* (1964) 400 The 'elastically' scattered neutrons are deviated only through small angles by the collisions and to a final approximation may be treated as unscattered. **1966** D. G. BRANDON *Mod. Techniques Metallogr.* 48 The thickness of film that will reduce the unscattered transmitted intensity to $1/e$ of its original value is given by $t = 20V/\rho$.

unscented, *a.* (Later examples.)
1884 *Girl's Own Paper* 26 Jan. 271/3 Employ a mild, unscented soap at night. **1914** [see *SAPELE]. **1979** C. McCARRY *Better Angels* I. x. 92 Philindros was odourless; he..used an unscented soap.

unsceptre, *v.* (Later example.)
1897 F. THOMPSON *New Poems* 110 Unsceptre thee of state and place!

unscra·mble, *v.* [UN-² 3.] **1.** *trans.* To reverse the process of scrambling (eggs). Also in *fig.* contexts.
This would appear to be the earlier sense though pre-1926 printed evidence has not been found.
1926 R. H. TAWNEY *Relig. & Rise of Capitalism* ii. 88 But the discovery of the sage who observed that it is not possible to unscramble eggs had already been made. **1928** C. SANDBURG *Good Morning, America* 18 Can you unscramble eggs?..J. Pierpont Morgan's query as to court decrees dissolving an inevitable industrial combination. **1969** *P.E.N.* IX. 46 She quoted, as an example, 'Mr. Enoch Powell called last night for the denationalisation of all State-owned industries and explained exactly how to unscramble the eggs.' **1980** J. WAINWRIGHT *Tainted Man* 131 You demanded retribution..*your* law..unscrambles all eggs.

2. To put into or restore to order; to disentangle; to make sense of (something) confused; to extricate from (or *from*) a state of confusion or muddle; to separate into constituent parts; to 'dismantle' (an organization or system); *spec.* to restore (a signal) by applying the reverse of the process previously used to scramble it; to render intelligible in this way.
1923 WODEHOUSE *Inimitable Jeeves* x. 104, I collapsed on to the settee and rather lost interest in things for the moment. When I had unscrambled myself I found that Jeeves and the child had retired. **1927** [see *SCRAMBLE *v.* 3 c]. **1952** *Times* 17 Nov. 6/1 The Government propose to 'unscramble' nationalized road haulage service. **1955** [see *SCRAMBLE *v.* 3 c]. **1956** *Archivum Linguisticum* VIII. 153 Since Trubetzkoy's untimely death the task of unscrambling them [*sc.* phonology and phonemics] has been pursued with wearisome halts. **1956** AUDEN & KALLMAN *Magic Flute* (1957) 116 So english, remodel Our lines as you please, Unscramble the drama and jumble the keys. **1958** *Times* 19 Aug. 9/2 Very broadly the intention seems to be to 'unscramble' from the French legislature those territories which wish to become federated. **1959** *Daily Tel.* 6 Mar. 14/3 By putting money in a box attached to a set the viewer automatically 'unscrambles' the transmission. **1963** *Ibid.* 10 Jan. 1/8 The process of 'unscrambling' Northern Rhodesia..will take very much longer. **1973** 'I. DRUMMOND' *Jaws of Watchdog* ii. 31 The message was unscrambled by a radio on a fast, low-profile motor-yacht. **1974** *Listener* 9 May 597/1 When the Conservatives returned to office in 1951 they didn't unscramble the National Health Service. **1978** R. LUDLUM *Holcroft Covenant* xxxvi. 420 You should bring him instead a potion to unscramble his doddering brains. **1981** *Sunday Express* (Colour Suppl.) 12 July 33/4 Only those who pay the extra rental are provided with a device to unscramble the film signals. **1983** *Listener* 18 Aug. 8/1 It was often more fruitful than trying to unscramble what he was actually saying.

Hence **unscra·mbled** *ppl. a.*; **unscra·mbling** *vbl. sb.*
1955 J. G. DAVIS *Dict. Dairying* (ed. 2) 993 (*caption*) Unscrambling machine. **1958** *Listener* 25 Sept. 463/2 The unscrambling attachments to the receiving sets. **1959** *Times Lit. Suppl.* 16 Jan. 30/3 To be brought up short on page 78 by a sentence scrambled by the printer almost beyond unscrambling. **1959** *Daily Tel.* 6 Mar. 14/3 In another method, the 'unscrambling' is done by dialling, as on a telephone. **1959** *Times* 11 June 5/7 The transparency of the texture and the clean, fresh sounds of unscrambled timbres. **1964** L. DEIGHTON *Funeral in Berlin* xxx. 156 There was a din of unscrambled noise before Charlotte Street switched the scrambler into the circuit.

unscra·mbler. [f. prec. + -ER¹.] A device for unscrambling scrambled messages or signals.
1968 A. B. CARLSON *Communication Systems* v. 218 The system shown..is a simplified speech scrambler... Show that an identical system will suffice as an unscrambler. **1976** 'A. HALL' *Kobra Manifesto* vi. 80 We began reading the signals as they came off the integral unscrambler. **1979** *Maclean's Mag.* 26 Mar. 59/1 Methods range from such simple expedients as wrapping antennas with aluminum foil to black-market sales of 'unscramblers' that decode signals.

unscreened, (*ppl.*) *a.* Add: **2. b.** Not investigated or checked for security: see *SCREEN *v.* 4 c.
1970 R. CLAPPERTON *Victims Unknown* xi. 101, I have been severely criticised..for authorising the employment on intelligence work of an unscreened individual. **1979** H. KISSINGER *White House Years* xix. 748 The beady eye of Secret Service agents Ready and McLeod, who were not about to leave me to the mercy of unscreened foreigners.

unseasonableness. a. (Later examples.)
1853 C. M. YONGE *Heir of Redclyffe* II. i. 2 Mrs. Ashford put the matter off for the present by the unseasonableness of the weather. **1971** *Daily Tel.* 3 July 9/1 Summer..is the season when unseasonableness becomes most glaring and least sufferable.

unsectarianize, *v.* (Earlier example.)
1832 J. S. MILL *Let.* 17 Sept. in *Wks.* (1963) XII. 118 The editor & his writers..are but Unitarians & liberals, unsectarianized.

unsedentary, *a.* (Later example.)
1915 W. B. YEATS *Tribute to Thomas Davis* (1947) 15 A gallant unsedentary man.

unseeming, *ppl. a.* Restrict † *Obs.* to sense in Dict. and add: **2.** Unapparent. *rare.*
1923 D. H. LAWRENCE *Birds, Beasts & Flowers* 174 The elephants ponderously, with unseeming swiftness, galloped uphill in the night.

unselfconsciously, *adv.* (See small-type note s.v. UNSELFCONSCIOUS *a.*) (Examples.)
1921 H. CRANE *Let.* 26 Nov. (1952) 72, I..carry these encumbrances..deftly and un-selfconsciously. **1958** P. WINCH *Idea of Social Sci.* IV. iv. 102 Science..applies its criteria unselfconsciously. **1977** P. STREVENS *New Orientations Teaching of Eng.* ii. 17 Young children (say, age 6–13)..tend to learn easily and unselfconsciously.

unse·llable, *a.* [UN-¹ 7 b.] Lacking a buyer; that no one wants to buy.
1975 *Daily Tel.* 22 Oct. 16 The Wardle farm was derelict and regarded as unsellable before the family..bought it two years ago. **1981** *Times Lit. Suppl.* 18 Sept. 1061/1 New ways of getting the johns to spend their money on previously unsellable old tat.

unsensational, *a.* (Earlier example.)
1854 GEO. ELIOT tr. *Feuerbach's Essence Christianity* xxii. 213 God sees..all objects of sense in an unsensational manner.

unsentimental, *a.* (Earlier example.)
1752 H. WALPOLE *Let.* 23 June (1974) XXXVII. 340 He..was even so unsentimental as to talk, of desiring to make her happy.

unseriousness. (Later examples.)
1973 I. ROBINSON *Survival of English* ii. 62, I am not discussing in this book the gross popular examples of breakdown or coarsening..nor shall I more than mention the increasing unseriousness of the denominational press. **1978** *Detroit Free Press* 5 Mar. B 9/1 Aliette works so hard she brooks no unseriousness.

unsex, *v.* Add: Also *fig.*
1955 AUDEN *Shield of Achilles* i. 27 A day that meekly takes The potter's cuff, a gravel that as concrete Will unsex any space which it encloses.

unshadow, *v.* (Further examples.)
1895 A. MACHEN *Three Impostors* 93, I, too, burned with the lust of the chase, not pausing to consider that I knew not what we were to unshadow. **1926** D. H. LAWRENCE *David* xv. 121 Is my heart fireless..? Kindler! it shall not be so! My heart shall shine to Thee, yea, unshadow itself. **1953** A. CLARKE *Moment Next to Nothing* II. 41 All that men think of would be immaterial Could they but watch these women shadowing, Unshadowing themselves.

unshakeable, *a.* Add: Hence also **u:nshak(e)abi·lity.**
1907 W. JAMES in *Philos. Rev.* Jan. 9 The result claimed [from yoga, etc.]..is strength of character, personal power, unshakability of soul. **1952** GERTH & MARTINDALE tr. *Weber's Ancient Judaism* xv. 387 The complete unshakability of its communities by the foreign environment from which they segregated themselves.

unsharp, *a.* Add: Hence **unsha·rpness.**
1961 in WEBSTER. **1967** E. CHAMBERS *Photolitho-Offset* xi. 161 Normal action of the diffusing stop, when all the small apertures are clear, results in a moderate degree of unsharpness. **1977** J. HEDGECOE *Photographer's Handbk.* 314/2 Overall unsharpness can be caused by gross misfocus.

unshi·rted, *a. U.S. slang.* [UN-¹ 9.] In phr. *unshirted hell*, serious trouble; 'a bad time'.
1932 *Sun* (Baltimore) 6 Jan. 10/3 When he proposed certain policies on prohibition..he was given what is known in rural districts hereabouts as 'unshirted hell'. **1954** F. P. KEYES *Royal Box* v. 67 She and his playboy son are going to fall for each other and then there will be unshirted hell. **1979** H. KISSINGER *White House Years* xxi. 897 I've been catching unshirted hell every half-hour from the President who says we're not tough enough.

unshook. (Later example.)
1893 KIPLING *Many Inventions* p. ix, May I look with heart unshook On blow brought home or missed.

unshrinkable, *a.* Add: Hence **u:nshrinkabi·lity.**
1934 in WEBSTER. **1946** *Nature* 5 Oct. 476/2 A high degree of unshrinkability is obtained with 10 per cent of polymer within the fibres. **1963** A. J. HALL *Textile Sci.* v. 249 This treatment is continued until almost complete unshrinkability is obtained.

unsight, *v.* Add: **3.** *trans.* Of a participant in a game: to deprive (another player or an official) of a clear view. Freq. in *pa. pple.*
1923 *Daily Mail* 15 Jan. 11 The referee..was unsighted and so, apparently, was the linesman to whom he appealed. **1928** *Daily Express* 8 June 17/2 Gibbons..would have been caught by slip if the wicketkeeper had not unsighted that fieldsman. **1951** *Sport* 30 Mar.–5 Apr. 10/2, I felt sorry for Hendon's goalkeeper, Reg Ivey, who was unsighted both times and had hitherto played a very sound game! **1972** *Times* 3 Mar. 7/2 Mr Kelly was travelling some two to three lengths behind Mr Smith and inevitably that unsighted him for a reasonable distance in front of Mr Smith. **1976** *Alyn & Deeside Observer* 10 Dec. 3/2 It was afterwards revealed that the umpire had been unsighted and had not seen the ball hit by a Chester player in the circle.

4. To make unseen. *nonce.*
1914 HARDY *Satires of Circumstance* 17 Nor God nor Daemon can undo the done, Unsight the seen.

unsi·gned, *a. Math.* [UN-¹ 9.] Of a number: without a plus or minus sign, or a bit representing this.
1953 *Electronic Engin.* Jan. 6/1 One advantage possessed by the complement notation for signed numbers is that the processes of addition and subtraction can be carried out by exactly the same methods on signed and unsigned numbers. **1970** O. DOPPING *Computers & Data Processing* xvii. 273 The 'compare' instruction can hardly be used for numerical information except when it is certain that all the keys are unsigned, that all keys have a plus sign, or that all keys have a minus sign. **1979** *Sci. Amer.* June 18/2 The problem asks whether for different values of *n* it is possible to pair each number in one subset with a number in the other so that the 2*n* sums and absolute, or unsigned, differences of the numbers in each pair are all distinct.

unsilenced, *ppl. a.* (Later examples: cf. *SILENCED *ppl. a.* b.)
1923 *Autocar* 7 Dec. 1151/2 Unsilenced engines. **1971** *Daily Tel.* (Colour Suppl.) 12 Nov. 21/4 A motor-bike of approximately six litres, unsilenced. **1981** M. KENYON *Zigzag* xxv. 171 Kelly's new unsilenced gun was shaping up..effectively.

unsi·mplify, *v.* [UN-² 3.] *trans.* To make less simple; to state in a more complex form.
1858 F. W. FABER *Foot of Cross* iv. 219 Why should she..unsimplify her worship, by disuniting in thought what God had united. **1960** R. A. KNOX *Occas. Sermons* xx. 94 We try to simplify modern politics, by making them all black and white, all heroes and villains; and in doing that we only unsimplify ourselves. **1975** *Sci. Amer.* Oct. 100/1 (Advt.), To understand, then, why there is a controversy, it is necessary to unsimplify the issue.

unska·ted, *ppl. a. rare.* [UN-¹ 8.] Not skated on.
1936 DYLAN THOMAS *Twenty-Five Poems* 19 December's pools..Lie this fifth month unskated.

unskin, *v.* (Later example.)
1935 T. S. ELIOT *Murder in Cathedral* i. 20 And our hearts are torn from us, our brains unskinned like the layers of an onion.

unsmoothed, *ppl. a.* Add: **b.** Of data, etc. (cf. *SMOOTH *v.* 1 e). **c.** Of a voltage: with any ripple left in.
1945 *16th Census: Population: Diff. Fertility: Women by Children under 5* (U.S. Bureau of Census) 2/2 An indication of the effect of inaccuracy in reported ages of women on the fertility statistics is given by a comparison of the unsmoothed figures with the smoothed figures. **1957** *Practical Wireless* XXXIII. 557/1 The frequency of the mains input is 50 c.p.s. and the output 'unsmoothed' H.T. has a 100 c.p.s. ripple. **1981** *Jrnl. Geophysical Res.* LXXXVI. 8002/1 The relative velocities are computed from the unsmoothed data.

unsnarl, *v. intr.* (Earlier example.)
1844 'J. SLICK' *High Life N.Y.* II. xxviii. 167 All on 'em seemed kinder tangled up and trying to unsnarl all over the floor.

unsneck, *v.* Add: (Later examples.) Also *intr.*
Apparently now not restricted to *north.* and *Sc.*
1932 L. G. GIBBON *Sunset Song* i. 77 She unsnecked the door of the kirkyard wall, passing through to the Manse. **1948** A. JOBSON *This Suffolk* iii. 50 A little wicket gate ..snecks and unsnecks, to let one in or out. **1967** 'G. NORTH' *Sergeant Cluff & Day of Reckoning* xv. 139 Mole ..unsnecked the door of the bedroom.

unsni·b, *v.* [UN-² 3.] *trans.* To unfasten (a catch); to unlatch.
1904 GLEGG & DUNCAN *Law Reparation Scotl.* (ed. 2) ii. 39 When he unsnibs the window to clean it. **1966** J. MCCLENAGHAN *Moving Target* xiv. 148 He unsnibbed the chain which held the dogs together, and..they slipped away. **1980** R. HILL *Spy's Wife* xxiii. 178 She snibbed her bedroom door, but after a few seconds in bed got up and unsnibbed it.

unsociably, *adv.* (Later examples.)
1977 *Gramophone* June 117/2 Such indiscretions apart, and the inevitable rash of black sheep playing music at unsociably high volumes..the show had much to offer the keen visitor. **1981** A. FRASER *Splash of Red* xiii. 145 She had once been prepared to toil unsociably for the whole of August.

unsocial, *a.* Add: **b.** *unsocial hours*, socially inconvenient working hours.
1973 *Times* 4 Dec. 1/1 A proposed unsocial hours payment in recognition of the odd times of the day and night that a [train] driver has to report for duty. **1976** *Evening Post* (Nottingham) 17 Dec. 15/7 (Advt.), Waiter-waitress required for Lenton Hall of Residence... Good holidays and unsocial hours payment for week-end work. **1982** *Economist* 13 Nov. 50/1 If the government is to avoid the annual pay squabble with the nurses the new review body should first establish realistic pay scales..taking into

account the unsocial hours. **1984** *Brit. Med. Jrnl.* 21 July 145/2 The unsocial hours during which most emergency operating is done has meant that much of it has been unsupervised.

unsocialism. Add: **b.** An absence of socialism. *rare.*

1889 G. B. Shaw *Fabian Ess. Socialism* 4 The gambling spirit urges man to..secure some acres of her [*sc.* Stepmother Earth]... This is Private Property or Unsocialism.

unso·cialist, *sb.* and *a.* [Un-[1] 12, 7.] **A.** *sb.* One who is not a socialist. **B.** *adj.* Not socialist.

1892 G. B. Shaw *Fabian Soc.* 6 Socialist statesmanship must..consist largely of taking advantage of the party dissensions between the Unsocialists. **1893** —— *Impossibilities of Anarchism* 4 It was bad enough to have to contend with the conservative forces of the modern unsocialist State. **1935** N. Mitchison *We have been Warned* iv. 423 She'd been afraid..in strange, unsocialist towns. **1967** *Spectator* 28 July 103/3 To an unsocialist, socialism is as unmoral as it is fatuous. Suez revealed the extent to which the Conservative party has given up the idea of an unsocialist morality. **1979** *Guardian* 9 Oct. 4/8 You can't..let this community be destroyed. It's un-Christian, let alone unsocialist.

unsolvable, *a.* Add: Hence also **u:nsolvabi·lity.**

1947 *Jrnl. Symbolic Logic* XII. 7 They become decision problems of recursively enumerable sets of positive integers of the same degree of unsolvability as the complete set *K*. **1979** *Sci. Amer.* May 131/1 One approach for circumventing unsolvability is to limit the kinds of statements given to the computer.

unsophistically, *adv.* (Later example.)

1890 W. James *Princ. Psychol.* I. xiii. 500 A formulation of the facts which offers itself so naturally and unsophistically.

unspan, *v.* (Later example.)

1914 T. A. Baggs *Back from Front* xxiv. 120 They unspanned in a neighbouring field and invited me to supper.

unspeakableness. (Later example.)

1963 B. Friedan *Feminine Mystique* viii. 182 After the loneliness of war and the unspeakableness of the bomb,.. women as well as men sought the comforting reality of home and children.

unspeaking, *ppl. a.* (Later example.)

1935 E. Bowen *House in Paris* ii. iv. 129 Karen herself had more than once been the victim of that unspeaking smile.

unspiked, *ppl. a.* (Further examples: cf. *spiked *a.*[2] 3 a, b.)

1969 *Lithos* II. 138 Unspiked measurements of Sr^{87}/Sr^{86} and Sr^{88}/Sr^{86} were made for all other samples. **1980** *Nature* 31 Jan. 438/2 Completely separate sets of equipment were used for spiked and unspiked sample solutions, thus eliminating the possibility of cross-contamination.

unspoilableness. (Earlier example.)

1873 C. M. Yonge *Pillars of House* I. xi. 232 Geraldine thought it was a great proof of his unspoilableness.

unspoilt, *ppl. a.* (Further examples, of the environment.)

1925 C. Connolly *Let.* 8 Apr. in *Romantic Friendship* (1975) 68, I hope to see some good unspoilt villages. **1939** *Country Life* 11 Feb. p. v (Advt.), 3 miles south of Dorking in beautiful unspoilt country, with lovely views. **1968** T. Wolfe *Electric Kool-Aid Acid Test* v. 59 Kesey wasn't primarily an outdoorsman. He wasn't that crazy about unspoilt Nature.

unspoo·l, *v.* [Un-[2] 3.] *trans.* To unwind (thread, tape, etc.) from a spool; *spec.* in *Cinematogr.*, to project (a film); also *intr.* of the thread, etc., or the film shown. Also *fig.*

1940 *Amer. Speech* XV. 205/1 *Unspool*, to project a film. **1961** S. Plath in *London Mag.* Aug. 8 The heath grass glitters and the spindling rivulets Unspool and spend themselves. **1962** A. Nisbett *Technique Sound Studio* 271 *Spill*,..to unspool a quantity of tape by accident. **1973** *Listener* 22 Feb. 254/2 The new play..unspools inside Christopher's head. **1980** *Times* 10 Oct. 14/1 A noisy adventure film..opened (or unspooled as local jargon has it) in Delhi.

unsporting, *ppl. a.* Add: Hence **unspo·rtingly** *adv.*, **unspo·rtingness.**

1932 R. Campbell *Taurine Provence* 17 The 'unsportingness' of hunting an animal in an enclosure. *a* **1974** R. Crossman *Diaries* (1976) II. 222, I was now in the dock for unsportingly challenging the rules when I'd lost a round in the parliamentary game. **1978** R. V. Jones *Most Secret War* xxv. 217 The Joint Intelligence Committee decided, very unsportingly, I thought, to hold back Colvin's account while they invited Ewen Montague..to write an officially approved account.

unspringy, *a.* (Later example.)

1936 *Scrutiny* IV. 398 The new verse moves line by line, the characteristic single line having..an evenly distributed weight—a settled, quite unspringy balance.

unspru·ng, *ppl. a.*[2] [Un-[1] 8 b + *sprung *ppl. a.*[2]] Not provided with a spring or springs. Of a (dance-)floor: not constructed so as to be resilient.

1928 C. F. S. Gamble *Story N. Sea Air Station* i. 32 The floats of seaplanes were practically unsprung. **1939** M. Allingham *Mr Campion & Others* i. viii. 171 A small unsprung dance-floor. **1973** R. Perry *Ticket to Ride* xii. 162 Both bunks boasted a mattress of sorts, thin and unsprung.

unsqueamish, *a.* Add: Hence **unsquea·mishly** *adv.*; **unsquea·mishness.**

1922 F. L. Lucas *Seneca & Elizabethan Tragedy* iv. 97 With Tudor unsqueamishness the audience then proceeded to watch Tereus dining off his son's flesh. **1959** *Times* 24 Jan. 7/7 The Calvinism that Burns satirized..was unsqueamishly aware of man's carnal nature. **1970** *Daily Tel.* 6 Feb. 17 The nurses are..tireless. All the virtues of the Victorian heroine are there, with unsqueamishness added for good measure. **1976** *National Observer* (U.S.) 27 Mar. 19/2 Vidal's fiction is true to the spirit of 1876, an age that was unsqueamishly exploitive and loved the grand scale.

unstable, *a.* Add: **3. c.** *Physics.* (Cf. *stable *a.* 3 d.)

1904 F. Soddy *Radio-Activity* viii. 123 Our knowledge of unstable atoms is necessarily limited. *Ibid.* 124 Radioactivity..has thus introduced us to a whole series of new unstable elements. **1924** O. Lodge *Atoms & Rays* ii. 33 The possibility of building up still more complex, and probably still more unstable, elements..remains a subject for future discovery. **1981** C. E. Swartz *Phenomenal Physics* xxxiii. 715 Most elements exist naturally as a mixture of several isotopes... The diagram shows all of the stable isotopes, and many of the unstable ones.

unstained, *ppl. a.* **1.** (Further examples.)

1918 *Heal & Son Catal.: Cottage Furnit.* 3 This furniture is left quite plain, unstained and unpolished. **1936** 'N. Blake' *Thou Shell of Death* ii. 27 A cream-washed bedroom, furnished..with unstained oak.

Unstan (ʊ·nstăn). The name of the site of a chambered tomb on Mainland, Orkney, used *attrib.* to denote a type of early neolithic pottery originally found on that site.

1932 *Proc. Prehistoric Soc.* VII. 64 The hatched and shaded Triangle motif occurs on the Unstan bowls. **1954** S. Piggott *Neolithic Cultures* viii. 248 The bulk of the pottery..can best be classed as Unstan ware from the thirty or so vessels found in that tomb. **1978** *Times* 27 May 3/3 One post-hole also yielded shreds of 'Unstan' pottery, characteristic of the early Neolithic period of the Orkney Islands.

unstarred, *ppl. a.* Add: *spec.* of a Parliamentary question: denoting that a written reply is required.

1902 *Hansard Commons* 18 June 958 To ask the First Lord of the Treasury if arrangements can be made by which the answer to an unstarred Question shall be communicated to the Member asking the Question within an hour after the sitting of the House on the day..the Question is asked. **1919** Ld. Curzon in *Hansard Lords* 11 Mar. 633 His alternative, I think, was this—that one is to assume that a Question in future, starred or unstarred, is a Question only. **1978** T. Willis *Buckingham Palace Connection* i. 10 Prayers had been said, and the business of the afternoon began, as usual, with a series of four Unstarred Questions.

unstayable, *a.* (Later examples.)

1940 G. Greene *Power & Glory* ii. i. 113 It had been set up in a minute clearing by a small farmer the forest must have driven out,.. an unstayable natural force which he couldn't defeat with his machete. **1980** D. K. Cameron *Willie Gavin* xviii. 177 He had risen on the unstayable tide of his master's success.

unstick, *v.* Add: **2.** *Aeronaut. intr.* (occas. *refl.*). To take off (*from* the surface of the ground, water, etc.).

1912 *Aero* May 134/1 It attains a high speed when running awash and 'unsticks' (*decoller*) very easily. **1913** *Flight* 19 Apr. 432/1 A head wind helps them materially to 'unstick' themselves from the water. **1913** *Captain* Sept. 1074/2 It is necessary to design the floats with the greatest care, so that they may 'unstick', or leave the water easily. **1926** *Chambers's Jrnl.* Sept. 581/2 It needs almost as long a run as the ordinary aeroplane to 'unstick'. **1964** G. Lyall *Most Dangerous Game* xix. 152 When she unstuck from the water..we went away low. **1977** J. Gardner *Werewolf Trace* i. 15 The British Airways Trident unstuck from the cold stressed-concrete.

Hence **unsti·cking** *vbl. sb.*

1926 'N. Shute' *Marazan* vi. 206, I took the whole length of the aerodrome to get off. It was some time since I had flown a Thirty-four, and unsticking was never her strong point at the best of times.

u·nstick, *sb. Aeronaut.* [f. the vb.] The moment of take-off. Also *attrib.*

1935 C. G. Burge *Encycl. Aviation* 606 *Unstick*, the moment during the take-off when an aerodyne definitely leaves either the ground (or a solid platform) or water. **1936** *Jrnl. R. Aeronaut. Soc.* XL. 519 Stalling to the extent of losing two-thirds of the static thrust, while it increases the 'unstick' time due to reduced acceleration, has only a small effect on the length of the take-off run. **1966** D. Francis *Flying Finish* xii. 154 Inside the windowless lavatory compartment it was impossible to tell the exact moment of unstick, but the subsequent climb held me close anyway against the wall, as I faced the tail. **1969** K. Munson *Pioneer Aircraft 1903–14* 154/2 The 1904 multiplane had an 'unstick' speed of some 34 m.p.h... and was tested at Streatham, but apparently made no flights of significant length.

unstoppable, *a.* Add: Hence **u:nstoppabi·lity**; **unsto·ppably** *adv.*

1961 Webster, Unstoppably. **1966** D. F. Jones *Colossus* i. 13 There is no way of walking back. The whole point is the Project's unstoppability. **1975** K. P. Barr in Barr & Line *Ess. Information & Libraries* iii. 40 He had..the entire programme in his head from the start and moved firmly and unstoppably towards its completion. **1980** R. Adams *Girl in Swing* xii. 125 He was generous to the point of embarrassment, having..a kind of baffling unstoppability when it came to paying restaurant bills. **1984** *Times* 11 Aug. 19/8 An audience of adults and children chattered unstoppably.

unstrea·m, *v. Educ.* [Un-[2] 3 + *stream *v.* 14: cf. *unstreamed* s.v. *un-[1] 8 a (a).] *trans.* In a school, to end the practice of streaming different abilities; to fail to stream in this way. Also *absol.*

1961 *Listener* 12 Oct. 565/3 Primary headmasters who have unstreamed their schools report that they have been able to raise the standard of work of the school as a whole. **1969** *Guardian* 29 Sept. 12/2 As a head, when a majority of the staff wanted it, he unstreamed a school. **1971** *Daily Tel.* (Colour Suppl.) 2 Apr. 18 (*caption*) You can't unstream—as the Swedes have done—and still hang on to classroom discipline.

Hence **unstrea·ming** *vbl. sb.*

1964 *Listener* 3 Dec. 904/1 Teachers..oppose unstreaming because they think it would threaten the interests of the 'A' stream. **1972** *Guardian* 9 June 9/5 Unstreaming, or teaching children in mixed ability groups.

u·nstress, *sb. Phonetics.* [Un-[1] 12.] Absence of stress; the pronunciation of a syllable, etc., without stress.

1945 E. K. Chambers *Eng. Lit. at Close of Middle Ages* i. 61 In this play aureate language..is exaggerated, almost to the point of burlesque, and is accompanied by anapaestic unstress, but not alliteration. **1953** C. E. Bazell *Linguistic Form* iii. 30 In the case of phonemic oppositions, the most striking case of a contradiction between the criteria of freedom of distribution and frequency would be the opposition of stress and unstress. **1970** B. M. H. Strang *Hist. Eng.* vi. 341 Hesitation between the spellings *u* and *o* in unstress does not indicate a sound midway between the two phonemes.

unstressed, *ppl. a.* (Further examples.)

1927 W. Deeping *Kitty* ix. 118 There seemed to be comfort for him in those fields... So peaceful and unstressed. **1946** P. Bottome *Lifeline* ii. 17 The peasants..unstressed, simple people.

unstring, *v.* Add: **3. c.** *intr.* Of the nerves: to be released from tension, to become lax.

1906 Hardy *Dynasts* ii. vi. v. 308 My nerves unstring, my friends, my flesh grows weak. **1972** D. Bloodworth *Any Number can Play* xv. 130 He systematically slackened his body and mind..feeling the knots twitch loose, the nerves unstring.

unstu·ck, *ppl. a.* [Un-[1] 8 b.] **a.** *to come unstuck*: see *come *v.* 24 d. **b.** *to get, come,* etc., *unstuck* (Aeronaut.), to get into the air, to take off: cf. *unstick *v.* 2.

1913 A. E. Berriman *Aviation* xvi. 157 It is not easy to acquire a proper flight-speed while trying to rise from the water, and it is only with considerable difficulty that pilots are able to get some machines 'unstuck'. **1920** *Flight* 17 June 639/2 The machine had a very low landing-speed, got 'unstuck' after a very short run, and was very easy to fly. **1934** *Ibid.* 8 Feb. 121/2 No one seeing her for the first time would have expected her to come unstuck so quickly as she did. **1958** 'N. Shute' *Rainbow & Rose* viii. 295 We came unstuck at the fourth flare. **1979** *Truck & Bus Transportation* Apr. 16/3 With the motors running at high pitch, the end of the asphalt loomed up very quickly and with a deft flick of the wrist by the 'skipper' the aircraft became 'unstuck' just in time.

unsubstantially, *adv.* (Later examples.)

1890 W. H. Dawson *Unearned Increment* vii. 84 It matters not to the speculator how unsubstantially his houses are built. **1972** P. D. James *Unsuitable Job* iii. 96 The sitting-room was elegantly but unsubstantially furnished.

unsubtle, *a.* (Later examples.)

1942 A. L. Rowse *Cornish Childhood* ii. 29 My father.. was a man of simple texture, upright, hard-working..but he was uneducated, unintrospective, unsubtle. **1978** R. Nixon *Mem.* 526 The Soviets moved troops to the Chinese border in an unsubtle attempt to tie up Chinese forces and prevent them from going to the aid of Pakistan.

Hence **unsu·btly** *adv.*

1934 in Webster. **1959** *Times* 24 Oct. 9/1 French vowels fall unsubtly from her lips. **1976** *Daily Tel.* 8 July 16 Anyone who goes around announcing, or unsubtly implying, that he is so terribly tough, aggressive and exciting is unlikely to be any of those things.

unsupportable, *a.* **3.** (Later examples.)

1904 A. H. Sayce *Monument Facts & Higher Critical Fancies* (ed. 2) i. 18 The unsupported and unsupportable assumptions of the modern scholar. **1984** *Times* 6 June 5/3 The present overregulated system of air transport was quite unsupportable.

unsurprising, *ppl. a.* (Later examples.)

1927 *New Republic* 12 Oct. 219/1 The unsurprising result is a sermon of the first class, and a novel of the third.

1975 *Listener* 18 Dec. 819/1 Adaptations of Dickens's works..are meant to make you feel good. This is unsurprising, as..it could be argued that this is exactly how Dickens intends you to feel.

Hence **unsurpri·singly** *adv.*

1961 in WEBSTER. **1972** *Bankers Mag.* (Boston, Mass.) Winter 73/1 Unsurprisingly, no agency has ever approved any proposal that would reduce its own supervisory role. **1979** *Field* 28 Nov. 1417/2 The passage concluded unsurprisingly.

unswayable, *a.* (Later examples.)

a **1945** E. R. EDDISON *Mezentian Gate* (1958) i. 5 He was..hard-necked and unswayable in policy. **1979** *United States 1980/81* (Penguin Travel Guides) 84 Bostonians..have the Irish tradition of impassioned and unswayable conviction.

unsweetened, *ppl. a.* Add: Also *ellipt.* as *sb.*, unsweetened gin. ? *Obs.*

1886 GREEN & HALL *Jack in Box* (Brit. Libr. MS. LCP 53369 Q) f. 37, And if to hint sir, I might be so bold. *Jack.* Unsweetened with a little water cold. **1890** BARRÈRE & LELAND *Dict. Slang* II. 390/1 Those who are partial to the *unsweetened* or 'Old Tom'.—*Bird o' Freedom.* **1910** WODEHOUSE *Psmith in City* xii. 100 The messengers were..endeavouring to restore their nerve with about sixpenn'orth of the beverage known as 'unsweetened'.

unswept, *ppl. a.* Add: **b.** Of the wing of an aircraft: not swept-back (see *SWEPT *ppl. a.* 3), not having sweepback or sweep-forward (see *SWEEP- 3).

1946 *Jrnl. Brit. Interplanetary Soc.* VI. 95 The application of sweep-back to wing shapes implies a swept V-shaped wing, in which the centre section is effectively unswept. **1977** *R.A.F. News* 11–24 May 6 (Advt.), Wingspan: 63 ft. unswept.

unsyllabic, *a.* (Further examples.)

1932 W. L. GRAFF *Language & Languages* 56 The sound that possesses the highest degree of sonority in a syllable is called syllabic or sonant, the others are unsyllabic or con-sonant. **1964** H. KURATH in D. Abercrombie et al. *Daniel Jones* 146 There is no difference in the system of consonants, except that unsyllabic |ə̯|..appears only in dialects that lack postvocalic |r|. **1970** *Publ. Amer. Dial. Soc. 1968* L. 6 The unsyllabic phone [ə̯]..will here be treated as the semi-vowel /ə̯/.

unsympathetic, *a.* (Examples corresponding to *SYMPATHETIC *a.* 2 b.)

1937 L. MACNEICE in *Ess. & Stud.* XXII. 145, I have recently been to an exhibition of nineteenth-century French painting and was surprised to find it so unsympathetic. **1946** *Ann. Reg. 1945* 438 Dreiser was a most unsympathetic personality, yet during the 1920's he was regarded as probably the most impressive figure in American literature since Walt Whitman. **1968** B. FOSTER *Changing Eng. Lang.* ii. 75 *Sympathetic* and *unsympathetic* have latterly taken on an extra meaning in imitation of French idiom (or possibly also Spanish), where *sympathique* means 'likable'. **1981** *Daily Tel.* 12 Feb. 16/6 An insidious invasion, unfamiliar, unsympathetic, alien.

unsystematized, *ppl. a.* (Earlier example.)

1832 F. BURNEY *Mem. Dr. Burney* III. 323 His internal resources were too diffuse and unsystematized.

unta·ck, *v.*² [UN-² 4 + *TACK *sb.*⁷ b, *v.*⁵] *trans.* To remove the saddle and bridle from (a horse). Also *absol.*

1962 W. FAULKNER *Reivers* viii. 185 We went back to the barn and untacked and Lycurgus brought a bucket and a rag and Lycurgus washed him down..before stabling and feeding him. **1977** F. PARRISH *Fire in Barley* iv. 40 Would you like me to untack her?..Take off the saddle and bridle?

untalented, *a.* (Later example.)

1981 *London Rev. Bks.* 19 Nov.–2 Dec. 16 Wittgenstein..was impatient with untalented or lazy pupils.

untalked, *ppl. a.* (Later examples.)

1807 E. WEETON *Let.* 3 Dec. (1969) I. 53 She has for a long time been untalked of. **1926** G. BELL *Let.* 25 Jan. (1927) II. xxvi. 745 We seem to have left such a lot of things untalked about.

untarnishable, *a.* (Earlier example.)

1887 in A. Adburgham *Shops & Shopping* (1964) vii. 77 A thread of untarnishable gold or silver interwoven with the worsted.

untelling, *ppl. a.* Add: Also *U.S. dial.* **1.** Delete † *Obs.* and add further examples.

1834 *Chambers's Edin. Jrnl.* 28 June 170/1 It being untelling the number of lodgers who used to elope without coming to a settlement. **1925** E. C. SMITH *Mang Howes* 1 The road was thrang wui droves o nout—aa keinds, untellin. **1951** H. GILES *Harbin's Ridge* iii. 18 It's untelling the times me and Faleecy John have walked the snake-back of that barnyard fence.

2. (Further example.)

1941 *Sat. Even. Post* 10 May 36/2 A man's notions are untelling.

unte·nse, *v.* [UN-² 3, 7.] *trans.* and *intr.* To render or become less tense or rigid; to relax.

1970 N. FLEMING *Czech Point* i. 7, I hooked my ski-sticks on to the T-bar and with some difficulty untensed my leg muscles. **1970** E. TIDYMAN *Shaft* (1971) i. 10 Anderozzi untensed: Shaft wasn't going to run. **1976** A. J. RUSSELL *Pour Hemlock* vii. 72 She untensed and started walking again. **1978** *Times Lit. Suppl.* 1 Dec. 1406/4 The triplets helped Tomlinson to un-tense his diction.

‖ **untergang** (u·ntəɹgaŋ). [Ger., = decline, downfall.] An irreversible decline, esp. leading to the destruction of culture or civilization.

1938 L. MACNEICE *I crossed Minch* ix. 133 The Untergang, the collapse of civilisation. **1962** *Listener* 12 July 51/2 There were times when Zarathustra—and, I believe, Nietzsche himself—longed for the *Untergang*, the going down, the descent, among the many, for the many, into death. **1965** *New Statesman* 30 July 166/1 The rooms and houses seemed on a depressingly small scale for a civilisation which it had always pleased me to think of as suffering the disease of gigantism which afflicts societies in full *untergang.*

‖ **untermensch** (u·ntəɹmenʃ). Pl. **-menschen.** [Ger.] Esp. with reference to the Nazi régime (1933–45): a racially inferior person, a sub-human person. Cf. ÜBERMENSCH.

1964 *Punch* 13 May 723/1 A Negro American..is a benighted *Untermensch.* **1966** *Sat. Rev.* (U.S.) 26 Mar. 34 To the Germans, Lithuanians were *Untermenschen*, a second-class people to be exploited and, when politically expedient, enslaved. **1974** A. GODDARD *Vienna Pursuit* II. 60 The Jews were shown to be people beyond the pale—*untermenschen* who had murdered Christ. **1981** R. BARNARD *Sheer Torture* xii. 132 Maria-Luisa had been shouting insults... Comes from the gutter. Scum. *Untermensch.*

‖ **unteroffizier** (u·ntərɒfitsīᵊ·ɹ). *Mil.* [Ger.] A German non-commissioned officer.

1917 T. E. LAWRENCE *Let.* 10 July (1938) 228 We entered Akaba..with 600 prisoners, about 20 officers, and a German unteroffizier. **1942** *Order of Battle of German Army* (U.S. War Dept. General Staff) 33 *Hauptgefreiter*, no equivalent grade... *Unteroffizier*, Corporal. **1980** R. BUTLER *Blood-Red Sun at Noon* (1981) I. i. 22 *Unteroffizier* Neumann was..shot down.

untha·nking, *ppl. a.* [UN-¹ 10.] Not giving thanks (for something); ungrateful.

1902 KIPLING *Five Nations* (1903) 138 Arid, aloof, incurious, unthinking, unthanking, gelt. **1932** CHESTERTON *Chaucer* i. 36 We may sometimes be unthinking about it; unthinking and especially unthanking.

u·nthink, *sb.* [UN-¹ 12.] Passive acceptance; failure to use logical reasoning.

1958 *Spectator* 14 Nov. 641/2. Mr. Wechsler..got on his feet rampaging against 'latrine prose' and the tedious doctrine of 'un-think'. **1961** *Guardian* 9 June 11/6 The undiscriminating unthink of the new middle class. **1974** P. GORE-BOOTH *With Great Truth & Respect* 421 And let us not talk of a 'Lost Empire'; that is a piece of 'unthink' which implies that, if only we had been cleverer, Australia would still have been governed from London.

unthought, *ppl. a.* Add: **1. b.** Also with *out.* (Cf. THINK *v.*² 15.)

1919 M. K. BRADBY *Psycho-Anal. & its Place in Life* x. 12 An unthought-out attitude is shown and resulting unhappiness. **1933** W. E. ORCHARD *From Faith to Faith* vi. 80 It may..reveal to those who cling to a merely traditional and un-thought-out orthodoxy what it is that often inspires such liberalism. **1978** R. LUDLUM *Holcroft Covenant* xiv. 163 There were canvases with bold dashes of color and heavy, un-thought-out lines.

unthriftiness. 2. Delete *Obs. rare* and add later examples.

1950 *N.Z. Jrnl. Agric.* Apr. 327/1 At the first sign of unthriftiness calves should be drenched with phenothiazine. **1955** W. W. DENLINGER *Complete Boston* 83 Much of the unthriftiness and langor that are charged to worms are caused by other diseases. **1973** *Country Life* 7 June 1660/1 If the calves are under stress..unthriftiness or mortality will follow.

unthrown, *ppl. a.* (Examples corresponding to *THROW *v.* 32 d.)

1959 G. GREENE *Complaisant Lover* I. i. 4 *Victor* (*quite unthrown*). Take him any way. **1977** C. WOOD *James Bond, Spy who loved Me* xiv. 128 Bond tried to appear unthrown.

until, *conj.* For examples of *unless and until* see *UNLESS *prep. phr.*, etc. 4 c.

untipped, *ppl. a.*¹ Add: **2.** *spec.* Of a cigarette: without a filter tip. Also *absol.*

1968 *Times* 15 Nov. 8/8 More men than women smoke heavily, inhale deeply and prefer untipped cigarettes. **1969** J. ELLIOT *Duel* I. iii. 67 'Smoke?'..We both took untipped and she lit them. **1973** H. GILBERT *Hotels with Empty Rooms* xiii. 111 The smoke from a hundred untipped Gitanes lay low in the air.

u:ntouchabi·lity. [f. UNTOUCHABLE *a.*: see -ILITY.] The quality or state of being untouchable; the condition or status of an untouchable; the social practice of having a class or caste of untouchables. Also *transf.*

1919 F. B. FISHER *India's Silent Revolution* v. 110 The depressed classes are now holding Untouchability Conferences at frequent intervals. **1928** *Speeches Maharaja of Baroda* 244 The question of untouchability was particularly Hindu. **1929** *Nineteenth Cent.* Dec. 763 His own system..tends to perpetuate such cruel social abuses as untouchability and child marriage. **1952** A. R. RADCLIFFE-BROWN *Structure & Function in Primitive Society* vii. 138 An extreme sanctity or untouchability attached to a chief born of a brother and sister who were themselves children of a brother and sister. **1958** *Times* 9 Sept. 9/6 The origin of untouchability in Japan is not clear. **1978** L. HEREN *Growing up on The Times* ii. 44 Untouchability, surely the greatest injustice in the history of mankind. **1979** J. WAINWRIGHT *Tension* xvii. 59 She has a perpetual air of untouchability about her. **1982** *Times* 24 June 3 Among the first generation [of Asians], untouchability is practised..in Britain... The Hindus of Southall have a separate temple for their untouchables.

untouchable, *a.* Add: **3.** (Examples referring to social outcasts.) Also *transf.*

1909 *Indian Spectator* 23 Oct. 843/2 Persons in mourning are..considered to be defiled and untouchable for some days. **1910** *Times* 29 July 5/6 In non-essentials Brahmanism soon found it expedient to relax the rigour of caste obligations, as for instance to..travel even in their own country in railways..without incurring the pollution of bodily contact with the 'untouchable' castes. **1943** G. MUFF *Let.* in *Times* 8 July 5/5 There was a gulf between the public school and the elementary school—a caste system; when all the while we knew the child of the worker was neither 'untouchable' nor belonged to a depressed class. **1963** T. & P. MORRIS *Pentonville* ii. 27 The work of the general work cleaners is of 'untouchable' status and is frequently given to the Maltese and 'blacks' for this reason. **1979** A. BRINK *Dry White Season* III. vii. 237 He is untouchable, protected by the entire bulwark of his formidable system.

Hence **untou·chableness,** the state or condition of being untouchable.

1909 *Times of India* (Mail ed.) 23 Oct. 19/3 The Hon. Mr. Ghokale..thought if only the untouchableness went, it would be a comparatively easy matter to help these classes. **1916** *Indian Review* Feb., in M. K. Gandhi *Coll. Works* (1964) XIII. 232 This miserable, wretched, enslaving spirit of 'untouchableness'. **1970** *Daily Tel.* 7 Feb. 9/6 It [*sc.* Verdi's 'Macbeth']..had to overcome our strong proprietorial feelings about the untouchableness of Shakespeare.

untou·chable, *sb.* [f. the adj.] A Hindu of a hereditary low caste, contact with whom was regarded as defiling members of higher castes. Also *transf.* and *fig.* Cf. *HARIJAN.

Use of the term, and the social restrictions which accompany it, were declared illegal in the constitution adopted by the Constituent Assembly of India in 1949 and of Pakistan in 1953.

1909 *Indian Spectator* 23 Oct. 843/2 Our untouchables were not clean. **1911** *Times* 2 Feb. 5/5 When it is remembered in what manner the lower classes are treated in daily life it may appear strange that the higher castes should be so..alarmed at the prospect of the untouchables ceasing to be regarded as Hindus. **1920** *Asiatic Review* XVI. 172 The term 'untouchable', as a name for the 'depressed classes', or 'outcastes', is a revival of the most ancient designation of these people. **1926** [mentioned in Dict. s.v. UNTOUCHABLE *a.* 3]. **1928** *Daily Express* 22 May 10/2 Those in Whitehall may go on thinking there is something extremely meritorious in treating Russia as a diplomatic untouchable. **1931**, etc. [see *HARIJAN]. **1960, 1969** [see *ETA, ETA³]. **1975** *Guardian* 27 Jan. 5 Five hundred Untouchables—low caste Indians—marched on Downing Street yesterday. **1978** N. J. CRISP *London Deal* vi. 104 'Well, I've become a non-copper.' 'You mean you've been suspended?'..'A modern untouchable.' **1981** G. PRIESTLAND *Priestland's Progress* vi. 93 The Indian untouchable who becomes a Christian often has to pay a heavy price for his liberation.

untouched, *ppl. a.* Add: Hence **untou·chedness.**

1889 KIPLING *From Sea to Sea* (1899) I. xviii. 145 The utter untouchedness of the town was one-half the charm.

untrilled, *ppl. a.* (Earlier example.)

1866 *Jrnl. Amer. Oriental Soc.* VIII. 342 The production of this untrilled *r* may be carried as far back in the mouth as we choose.

untuned, *ppl. a.* Add: **3.** Of an electronic device: not tuned to any one frequency; able to deal with signals of a wide range of frequencies. Also *transf.*

1905 *Electrician* Mar. 822/1 A forest would have great influence in impeding if not in staying altogether the transmission of signals over its surface, more especially in an untuned system. **1962** SIMPSON & RICHARDS *Physical Princ. Junction Transistors* vii. 136 Small-signal operation in the region beyond cutoff is usually confined to two types of amplifier: 1. The tuned band-pass type... 2. The untuned wide-band or video amplifier. **1978** G. SIMS *Rex Mundi* vii. 47 The disorganisation..extended even to the absence of..canned *bouzouki* music. Instead there was the untuned blare of a radio station.

unty·pable, *a. Med.* and *Biol.* [UN-¹ 7 b.] That cannot be assigned to a specific type.

1950 *Britannica Bk. of Year* 682/2 Untypable. **1961** *Lancet* 22 July 173/2 Both strains [of Staphylococci] were untypable. **1977** *Ibid.* 14 May 1047/1 The isolate derived from the mincer was of serotype 1, and that from the butter beans was untypable.

‖ **unum necessarium** (ū·nŏm nesĕsēᵊ·riŏm). [mod.L., ad. Vulgate *unum est necessarium* one thing is necessary (Luke x. 42).] The one, or the only, necessary thing; the essential element.

1931 H. H. HENSON *Let.* 21 Oct. (1950) 63 So long as episcopacy is looked upon as the *unum necessarium* of a

Christian Church, I am sure that no reunion with the presbyterian and congregational churches is possible. **1937** *Times Lit. Suppl.* 15 May 379/1 Mr. Wilkins has the *unum necessarium* of a storyteller in this kind. **1938** W. S. CHURCHILL *Marlborough* IV. xxxi. 522 His exclusion was, he said, the *unum necessarium.*

unuseful, *a.* (Later examples.)
1977 *Western Morning News* 1 Sept. 8/1 A correspondent in Derriford, Plymouth, says he finds it is the unnecessary or 'unuseful' noises which annoy him most. **1982** *N. & Q.* Aug. 357/2 The transference of the term to English literature is unuseful. **1984** *Ibid.* June 259/1 The concatenation of Rolle, Langland and Wycliffe is decidedly unuseful.

unutterable, *a.* **2. b.** (Earlier example.)
1849 *Jrnl. Amer. Oriental Soc.* I. 423 The endless, and to a European, unutterable jargons of the other class.

unvenom, *v.* (Later example.)
1906 F. THOMPSON in *Dublin Rev.* Apr. 381 You did, with thrift of holy gain, Unvenoming the sting of pain, Hive its sharp heather-honey.

unvizard, *v.* Add: Also *absol.* for *refl.* (Later example.)
1911 H. G. WELLS *New Machiavelli* IV. i. 388 People who unvizard to talk more easily at a masked ball.

unvocalized, *ppl. a.* (Earlier example.)
1855 C. R. LEPSIUS *Stand. Alphabet* 39, *h* belongs, therefore, to the unvocalised strong fricatives.

unwaged, *ppl. a.* Add to def.: not receiving a wage, out of work. Also *absol.* (Later examples.)
1971 DALLA COSTA & JAMES in *Power of Women* (1975) 33 (*heading*) The productivity of wage slavery based on unwaged slavery. **1981** *Evening Mail* (Birmingham) 30 Apr. 22/2 (Advt.), Women's Theatre Group presents their new play on Nuclear Power, Breaking Through, at Small Heath Community School... £1·50 waged, £1 unwaged. **1982** *Libr. Assoc. Rec.* (Vacancies Suppl.) 30 Nov. p. cxlviii, The cost will be £2 per line for waged persons or £1 per line for those who are unwaged. **1982** *Guardian* 24 Feb. 10/4 They're supposed to do unwaged work for their whole lives.

unwalkable, *a.* Add: **c.** Unfit for walking on.
1976 *N.Y. Times Mag.* 12 Sept. 85/2 The top step is 2 feet high and unwalkable. **1981** *New Scientist* 16 July 141 A nasty mixture of coal slurry and raw sewage makes the sand unwalkable. **1982** *London Rev. Bks.* IV. xxiv. 8/3 These proud owners of this awful model house, tripping around on an artistic but farcically unwalkable pattern of paving-stones.., conduct themselves with a sober sense of import and duty.

unwanted, *ppl. a.* Add: Also *absol.* as *sb.*
1932 *New Statesman* 10 Sept. 284/2 We don't take no notice although she did 'ave a little Unwanted. **1949** *Here & Now* (N.Z.) Oct. 18/1 The new freedom has to be weighed against the risk of rearing a generation of unwanteds, filled with..hostility. **1976** *Daily Record* (Glasgow) 4 Dec. 31/5 The problem is not peculiar to Saints... Bigger teams heave out unwanteds, their feet not touching the ground.

unware, *a.* **2. a.** *ellipt.* (Later example.)
1866 HARDY *Wessex Poems* (1898) 10, I lived unware, uncaring all that lay locked in that Universe taciturn and drear.

unwashed, *ppl. a.* **2. b.** (Earlier examples with and without *great.*)
1830 LYTTON *Paul Clifford* I. p. xix, He is certainly a man who bathes and 'lives cleanly', (two especial charges preferred against him by Messrs. the Great Unwashed). **1840** *Tipperary Constitution* 21 Aug. 2/3 The learned gentleman then briefly addressed the few *unwashed*, who were attracted to the scene.
unwashedness (earlier example).
1890 W. BOOTH *In Darkest England* II. ii. 106 You can have a thorough wash-up at last, after all these days of unwashedness.

unwatering, *vbl. sb.* (Later examples.)
1909 R. H. RICHARDS *Text-bk. Ore Dressing* XV. 452 Unwatering devices are used to diminish the water carried by sand, or the sand carried by water. **1935** *Economist* 21 Dec. 1283/2 Their consulting engineer on the spot estimated that the unwatering of the old mine should commence about the beginning of February. **1976** *Northern Miner* (Toronto) 19 Aug. 13/3 Stage 1 included.. unwatering, sampling and surface and underground drilling.

unwed, *ppl. a.* (Later examples, of parents.)
1967 E. S. GARDNER *Case of Queenly Contestant* (1973) viii. 103, I would keep on working as long as I was able. Then I would go to a home for unwed mothers and have my child. **1981** R. MCCLURE *Coram's Children* x. 124 In 1764 forty-nine children were reclaimed by their parents, often unwed mothers.

unweighted, *ppl. a.* (Examples corresponding to WEIGHTED *ppl. a.* 2c in Dict. and Suppl.)
1927 BOWLEY & STAMP *National Income 1924* 23 The unweighted average is obtained by adding up the percentages and dividing by the number of them. **1966** *Rep. Comm. Inquiry Univ. Oxf.* II. 260 (*heading*) Student/staff ratios (unweighted) for certain universities. **1977** *Econ. & Social Rev.* (Dublin) VIII. 146 In cases where an unweighted regression applied to all twenty-six Irish counties would yield inefficient estimates, re-estimating the equation with Dublin omitted is in practice equivalent to applying a full correction for heteroscedasticity.

unwelcome, *sb.* Add: **2.** Lack of welcome; a cold reception. *rare.*
1912 D. H. LAWRENCE *Trespasser* i. 2 A stranger..was assured of his unwelcome.

unwell, *a.* **b.** (Later examples.)
1934 J. RHYS *Voyage in Dark* I. vi. 78 When I was unwell for the first time it was she who explained to me, so that it seemed quite all right. **1964** E. BOWEN *Little Girls* II. iii. 96 Miss Kinmate, herself *unwell* today, had not the slightest intention of going in.

unwhipped, *ppl. a.* Add: **3.** Not directed by the interests of a political party; not subject to a party whip.
1959 *Manch. Guardian* 11 Aug. 6/4 The argument for the independent 'unwhipped' councillor. **1971** HINDELL & SIMMS *Abortion Law Reformed* xi. 233 It might..turn out that members would cast their ballots to some extent along party lines, even though unwhipped. **1979** *Guardian* 6 July 26/2 The plan is for an unwhipped vote on a motion covering the principle of the return of the death penalty.

unwhitewashed, *ppl. a.* (Earlier and later examples.)
1797 J. C. DAVIE *Let.* July in *Lett. from Paraguay* (1805) 118, I would have had the whole house..left unwhitewashed. **1909** M. B. SAUNDERS *Litany Lane* III. xx. 188 It is to be feared that in her suppressed excitement she betrayed the unwhitewashed Hilda.

unwifed, *ppl. a.* For **1840** read **1834.**

unwind, *v.*[1] Add: **1. c.** *fig.* Add: *esp.* To relieve from tension or anxiety, to cause to relax. (Later examples.)
1958 B. MALAMUD in *Partisan Rev.* Spring 180 He managed to unwind himself and relax. **1975** 'W. HAGGARD' *Scorpion Tail* ix. 131 They sat down..the almost neat whisky unwound her.
3. *fig. esp.* To obtain relief from tension or anxiety; to relax. (Later examples.)
1938 D. BAKER *Young Man with Horn* IV. vii. 276 He was tired... If he'd ever unwound and relaxed, it would have been all over, he couldn't have lifted a finger. **1958** *Radio Times* 3 Oct. 34/1 (Advt.), After interviews Edana finds she can 'unwind' with 'Aspro' and a cup of tea. **1982** M. RUSSELL *Rainblast* iii. 14 He loved the solitude... Helped him unwind.
unwinding *vbl. sb.* (further examples).
1933 H. G. WELLS *Bulpington of Blup* ix. 398 He began ..to play with himself that tedious parlour game known as 'unwinding'. **1971** D. CLARK *Sick to Death* ii. 23 The unwinding part of the day when most people like to take their ease. **1977** A. MORICE *Scared to Death* xiv. 94 There is something anti-climactic about going straight home.. when the curtain comes down and it is quite pleasant to indulge in some gentle unwinding.

unwinnable, *a.* Delete Chiefly *Sc.* and add later examples.
1972 D. HALBERSTAM *Best & Brightest* 495 The war was unwinnable, or at least it was for a civilized government. **1975** F. BRESLER *You & Law* 148 What would make the case absolutely unwinnable would be if the tenant was also coloured. **1980** *Daily Mail* 24 Dec. 15/5 The fifth year of his unwinnable Vietnam-style war.

unwinter, *v.* **1.** (Later *intr.* example.)
1944 L. MUMFORD *Condition of Man* iv. 108 Spring was coming to Western Europe: the darkness and cold were almost over. But it did not unwinter suddenly.

unwished, *ppl. a.* **2.** (Later examples.)
1918 *Glasgow Herald* 21 July 4/2 An echo—modified..by reinforcements of sound at one point or an unwished for diminuendo at another. **1959** 'O. MILLS' *Stairway to Murder* v. 49 Her collection of unwished-for guests.

unwishing, *ppl. a.* (Later example.)
1951 S. SPENDER *World within World* iii. 120 When he even no longer feels desire, he can in an idle, abstract and unwishing kind of way prove to himself..that the hidden life of forbidden wishes exists.

unwomanliness. (Earlier example.)
1854 H. JAMES *Let.* in R. B. Perry *Thought & Character W. James* (1935) I. 135 The machinery by which it works is lying, theft, fraud and every species of unmanliness and unwomanliness.

unworkable, *a.* Add: Hence also **unwo·rkably** *adv.*
1927 C. HOLLIS *Amer. Heresy* 164 A plan, unworkably complicated. **1972** W. A. PANTIN *Oxford Life* iii. 25 As late as 1850 some people thought that a Congregation which might amount to over 100 would be unworkably large.

unworldliness. (Earlier example.)
1803 D. WORDSWORTH *Jrnl.* 28 Aug. (1941) I. 286 That visionariness which results from a communion with the unworldliness of nature.

unwrapped, *ppl. a.* Delete *rare*$^{-0}$ and add contextual examples.
1921 *Daily Colonist* (Victoria) 20 Mar. 8/1 Why buy soap in packages when you can buy it cheaper 'unwrapped'? **1968** D. E. ALLEN *British Tastes* iii. 77 Bread, being brought to the door and made more by small local bakers, tends to be unwrapped (and, of course, unsliced) more frequently than elsewhere. **1978** A. NEAVE *Nuremberg* vii. 78 He handed over to Andrus and myself odd little packets of food and three bars of unwrapped chocolate for analysis.

unzi·p, *v.* [UN-[2] 3, 7: cf. next.] **1.** *trans.* To unfasten the zip of; to unfasten (a zip). Also *transf.* and *fig.*
1939 L. MACNEICE *Autumn Jrnl.* iii. 18, I shall..make the world my sofa, Unzip the women and insult the meek. **1951** G. FRANKAU *Oliver Trenton* xvi. 138 Sancha..unzipped her skirt. **1959** *Encounter* Aug. 75/2 When his lips are sealed, not even a loving wife can unzip them. **1972** R. QUILTY *Tenth Session* I. 140 Shirley..emerged with a brace of glistening Carlsbergs... She tossed one over and perched again to unzip her can. **1976** 'D. FLETCHER' *Don't whistle 'Macbeth'* 156 Unzip me, please? **1979** R. JAFFE *Class Reunion* I. xi. 105 She reached for the zipper of her skirt and unzipped it.
2. *intr.* To unfasten by means of a zip. Also *fig.*
1971 *Daily Tel.* 11 Oct 11 (Advt.), A double bed that simply unzips into two singles when preferred. **1979** D. ATTENBOROUGH *Life on Earth* i. 19 DNA..is shaped like two intertwined helices. During cell division, these unzip, splitting the molecule.

unzi·pped, *ppl. a.* [UN-[1] 8; partly also f. prec.] With the zip unfastened; not zipped up. Also *fig.*
1951 N. BLAKISTON *Canon James* 69 He could not turn his eyes away from its nakedness, its shameless unzipped modernity. **1971** 'M. UNDERWOOD' *Trout in Milk* ix. 105 A pair of unzipped trousers. **1978** J. GARDNER *Dancing Dodo* xxvii. 218 The men wore protective silver coveralls, unzipped and with the hoods down. **1980** J. MCCLURE *Blood of Englishman* v. 46 He lay unzipped from pubic arch to jaw bone.

unzi·pper, *v.* [UN-[2] 3: cf. next.] *trans.* = *UNZIP *v.* 1.
1961 in WEBSTER. **1977** J. CHEEVER *Falconer* 202 He unzippered the sack.

unzi·ppered, *ppl. a.* [UN-[1] 8; partly also f. prec.] = *UNZIPPED *ppl. a.*
1953 *Manch. Guardian Weekly* 20 Aug. 7/1 He had on linen slacks, a polo shirt, and an unzippered linen coat. **1960** M. K. JOSEPH *I'll soldier no More* 291 Reaching inside his unzippered windcheater.

‖ **uomo universale** (ŭwō·mo ūnĭvɛɹsā·le). Pl. **uomini universali.** [It., = universal man.] A man who excels in the major fields of learning and action. Cf. *Renaissance man* s.v. *RENAISSANCE 1 d.
1963 *Times* 28 May 10/7 The newspaper poses the question who is to replace this *uomo universale,* with his good and bad traits. **1979** *Guardian* 16 May 12/6 Time was when the prestigitating [*sic*] Uomo Universale was considered a pillar of any civilised society. **1983** *Punch* 4 May 28/2 Some others, by comparison, are positive *uomini universali.*

up, *sb.* Add: **2. d.** A state of mental stimulation or excitement. Cf. *HIGH *sb.* 1 h. *U.S. colloq.*
1966 ROTE & WINTER *Lang. Pro Football* III. 144/1 *Up*,..state of being emotionally prepared for a game. **1979** *N.Y. Times* 1 Apr. 9/2 Young women want to be with it. The shapes in your ad are all sleek and slim and they come in colors you can get an up from.
e. Phr. *in two ups*: see *TWO *sb.* 2 g.
3. (Earlier example.)
1849 F. B. HEAD *Stokers & Pokers* ix. 82 Her daughter ..listens for the rumbling of 'the 3½ A.M. goods up'.
4. Colloq. phr. *on the up-and-up.* **a.** Honest(ly), straightforward(ly), 'on the level'. orig. and chiefly *U.S.*
1863 *Humboldt Reg.* (Unionville, Nevada) 4 July 2/1 Now that would be business, on the dead up-and-up. **1929** D. HAMMETT *Red Harvest* vii. 71 He phoned the old man's residence to find out if the check was on the up-and-up. **1932** WODEHOUSE *Hot Water* i. 20, I kept telling her the whole thing had been strictly on the up-and-up, but she wouldn't listen. **1952** M. ALLINGHAM *Tiger in Smoke* iii. 65 They've *got* to be on the up-and-up, see? **1974** P. DE VRIES *Glory of Hummingbird* xiii. 200 Thus I ended..on the up-and-up. I had restored some honesty to..a thoroughly shady enterprise.
b. Steadily rising, improving, or increasing; prospering, successful.
1930 *Sun* (Baltimore) 18 Aug. 6/1 From now on, we are led to believe, law and order will be on the up and up, as the current phrase is. **1937** G. HEYER *They found him Dead* xiii. 265 He certainly wasn't on the up-and-up when I knew him. He was picking up a living doing odd jobs for any firm that would use him. **1959** *Encounter* Oct. 25/2 Private travel is on the up and up. **1971** *Farmer & Stockbreeder* 23 Feb. 10 (*heading*) Drainage work on the up and up. Drainage work completed in England and Wales during the coming year is likely to reach an all-time high.
5. In Winchester College Football, a forward.
1869 *Wykehamist* Oct. 6/1 J. W. Barry, a good and persevering 'up'. **1900** R. T. WARNER *Winchester* ix. 142 It begins with a 'hot' or scrimmage, in which all the 'ups' take part. **1975** *Oxf. Compan. Sports & Games* 397/2 In the 15-a-side—XV—game, a team is composed of eight 'ups', four 'hotwatchers', and three 'behinds' or 'kicks'.
6. *U.S. slang.* A prospective customer.

1942 BERREY & VAN DEN BARK *Amer. Thes. Slang* § 542/21 *Forward, front, up*, a prospective customer in a store. **1949** *N.Y. Times* 1 May 62 The hottest salesman who ever turned a looker into an up. **1977** *Drive* Sept.–Oct. 112/1 You go to buy a car, offering your Old Faithful in part-exchange... In New York, you would be the up. 'I'm sitting at my desk. The guy comes through the door, so I gotta get up. See?'

7. = *UPPER *sb.*[2] Freq. in *pl. slang.*

1969 R. JAFFE *Fame Game* xi. 164 Bonnie had taken a pill, one of the little cache of Ups Bonnie got from the queens in the gay bars. **1972** M. PEREIRA *Singing Millionaire* iii. 31 'Meth', he said,..'not meths. Methedrine. Speed. Up. Chrystal. Crank.' **1978** P. G. WINSLOW *Coppergold* 172 'She did take pills, ups, if you get me.' Capricorn understood her to mean amphetamines.

up, *a.* Add: **3. a.** (Later examples.)

1910 H. G. WELLS *Hist. Mr Polly* iv. 107 Mr. Johnson, at large: '*Ain't* the beer up! It's the 'eated room.' **1934** S. BECKETT *More Pricks than Kicks* 12 Their bottled stout was particularly excellent and well up.

4. b. Of a lift, escalator, etc.: ascending, moving upwards, carrying persons to a higher floor. Also applied to the button which operates or summons this.

1948 G. V. GALWEY *Lift & Drop* v. 124 Lord Swale.. was usually the sole first occupant of the 'up' lift. **1967** 'M. CARREL' *Dark Edge of Violence* v. 42 The man then slammed the gate and punched the 'Up' button. **1976** J. WAINWRIGHT *Bastard* i. 16 He fell down the escalator. The 'up' escalator.

5. In a state of emotional or nervous stimulation, either naturally or as a result of taking drugs; excited, elated; at a peak of performance. Cf. *HIGH *a.* 16 c. *colloq.*

1942 [see *SNOW *v.* 7]. **1964** H. SELBY *Last Exit to Brooklyn* 49 Waiting for the time to fly, as it does when you're up on bennie. **1972** *Times* 31 May 7/6 She is playing lovely tennis. In the language of the game, she is really 'up' for this one. **1975** W. SAFIRE *Before Fall* I. v. 55 He's too 'up' to sleep—can you sit around with him until he runs out of gas? **1981** *Gossip* (Holiday Special) 10/2 He was very up about his job (in the CBS studio mailroom) and people in general.

6. *Particle Physics.* Applied to a quark carrying a flavour with a charge of +2/3; symbol *u* (*U 4 a). [An arbitrary choice of word, which appeared in print later than the symbol for the up quark.]

1975 *Sci. Amer.* Oct. 41/3 Gell-Mann designated the three quarks *u*, *d* and *s*, for the arbitrary labels 'up', 'down' and 'sideways'. **1977** *McGraw-Hill Yearbk. Sci. & Technol.* 208/1 The common baryons, the proton and the neutron, are composed of only up (*u*) and down (*d*) quarks (proton = *uud*, neutron = *udd*). **1978** *Nature* 2 Feb. 406/3 The best known meson is the pion (π) which is a combination of an up and a down quark. **1982** *Sci. Amer.* Nov. 134/1 Charm, like up, down and strange, is a quark flavor.

up, *v.* Add: **I. 4*. a.** *Cards.* To raise (a bid, stake, etc.). Cf. *RAISE *v.*[1] 32 a. Also *transf.* Chiefly *U.S.*

1915 *Munsey's Mag.* Apr. 488/1 I'd 'a' upped it till the hot place froze over! *Ibid.* 489/1 I'll up that! the old man was saying. **1942** BERREY & VAN DEN BARK *Amer. Thes. Slang* § 746/3 *Raise*, go (it) one (*or* more) better, hike, press, up. **1984** *Listener* 3 May 16/1 Some competitors see it as his way of upping the ante.

b. To increase or raise (prices, production, mechanical power, etc.). *colloq.* (orig. *U.S.*).

1934 *Amer. Speech* IX. 76/1 In Birmingham on September 17, Dr. Sterling J. Foster..warned his hearers that 'if a certain fatal mistake is made, taxes will be upped on every house in the city'. **1943** *Sun* (Baltimore) 1 Dec. 9/3 (*heading*) Shot of water ups engine power. **1953** W. BURROUGHS *Junkie* xi. 116 You can only buy P.G. so often, or the druggist gets wise. Then he packs in, or ups the price. **1957** WODEHOUSE *Over Seventy* viii. 94 These negotiations are better left to one's agent. I have instructed mine to arrange for a flat payment of ten guineas, to be upped, of course, if they want to know what I had for dinner at that amusing château in the wine country. **1969** *Daily Tel.* 16 Apr. 23/2 This 28 per cent. increase now ups the annual bill of the trade from £36 million to about £47 million. *a* **1974** R. CROSSMAN *Diaries* (1975) I. 108 I'd talked this over with the Dame before lunch and cautiously suggested that we should make our target 135,000 houses... Harold immediately upped me to 150,000. **1978** G. A. SHEEHAN *Running & Being* x. 135 Athletes upped their practice time fivefold.

c. To promote in rank. *colloq.*

1945 H. BROWN *Artie Greengroin* 182 Someday that mess sergeant is going to fill the Spam full of arsenic and knock off the whole company for a laugh. The day he does that they'll probably up him to tech. **1970** G. F. NEWMAN *Sir, You Bastard* iii. 111 Both the detectives' names and ranks were correct; neither was upped to DCS. *a* **1974** R. CROSSMAN *Diaries* (1975) I. 609 Harold Wilson breezed up and said 'Meet your new Lord President.'..They were astonished that Harold had upped me into the stratosphere.

d. To improve, to 'boost'. *colloq.*

1968 *Globe & Mail* (Toronto) 17 Feb. 28 You can up your morale all so easily. **1976** *Daily Express* 29 June 5/4, I did make a perfunctory attempt to up my image by purchasing chic glasses.

II. 5. b. (*b*) (Later examples.)

1935 E. E. CUMMINGS *Let.* 31 Jan. (1969) 135 And he ups and hands Am [*Eimi*] such a boost as would knock Karl Marx's whiskers out of Benjamin G. Woozeythought's cabinet d'aisance. **1958** 'A. GILBERT' *Death against Clock* 81 So you upped and fled. **1961** O. NASH *Coll. Verse* 33 One of these days not too remote I'll probably up and cut your throat. **1973** *Black World* Jan. 62/1 It did no good. I upped and died. **1979** J. RATHBONE *Joseph* I. i. 20 As soon as we could we upped and fled.

up, *adv.*[1] Add: **III. 26. up to—. e.** Bridge. *to lead up to*: to lead in a manner which allows (a particular card or suit) to be played from the third or fourth hand. Also after the sb.

1911 L. LEIGH *Blue Bk. Bridge & Auction* iii. 97 In a trump deal, if the lead has been a low card the suit cannot be more than moderately strong, and the third hand.. may lead up to a weak holding in Dummy's hand. **1927** L. HATTERSLEY *Auction & Contract Bridge Clarified* xxv. 251 The Queen should *never* be led up to the Ace with the vain idea of making a finesse. **1950** G. S. COFFIN *Learn Bridge* iv. 26 He must lead a ◇ away from his king up to dummy's ace-queen. **1964** R. L. FREY *Official Encycl. Bridge* 655/2 The old maxim recommending a lead 'up to weakness' is valid but not very helpful. **1973** REESE & DORMER *Compl. Bk. Bridge* xvii. 223 He leads up to and not away from dummy's high cards.

26*. up until—. = *up to—*, sense 26 c (*c*). Cf. *up till—*, sense 25.

1938 *Tablet* 28 May 698/2 Up until the time when *Mit Brennender Sorge* and the associated Encyclicals appeared, there was indeed some reason for believing that the idea of Catholic Action was to be interpreted more or less in such a manner. **1971** *Sci. Amer.* Oct. 118/3 Up until the past few years all the pictures we saw of that world.. seemed less photographic, for all their authenticity, than maplike.

29*. *ellipt.* for *up with—* (sense 30 e). *colloq.*

1937 S. BECKETT in A. Chisholm *Nancy Cunard* (1979) xxiii. 241 Up the Republic! *a* **1966** 'M. NA GOPALEEN' *Best of Myles* (1968) 330 'Up the Prince of Wales' or something, I suppose. **1980** M. MCMULLEN *My Cousin Death* (1981) xi. 131 Conor's taken him off... Up Conor, I say.

up, *adv.*[2] Add: **I. 3. e.** Of a woman's hair: worn tied or pinned on top of or at the back of the head, not hanging down; *spec.* as an indication of entry into adult society.

1911 BEERBOHM *Zuleika D.* xiv. 207 Her hair, tied back at the nape of her neck, would very soon be 'up'. *a* **1976** A. CHRISTIE *Autobiogr.* (1977) IV. i. 166, I was now ready to 'come out'. My hair was 'up', which at that period meant..large knots of curls high up on the head.

6. d. *Baseball.* At bat.

[**1862** *N.Y. Sunday Mercury* 13 July 6/1 Crane came up to open the inning.] **1896** *Sun* (N.Y.) 13 May 4/1 At th beginning of the tenth inning the score was a tie. Van Haltren was the first New Yorker up. **1909** R. H. BARBER *Double Play* xvii. 208 The fourth man up chose a ball to his liking and sliced it down the first-base line. **1942** P. GALLICO *Lou Gehrig* viii. 97 Koenig was up next, a precision machine at getting a man along to second with hit or sacrifice. **1976** E. BLACKWELL in *Baseball between Lines* 52 They got a man in scoring position with two out and Buddy Kerr up.

7. d. In various colloq. phrases: *up and about, around*, active, moving about, esp. of a person who has been ill, no longer in bed; *up and doing*, busy and active.

1817 H. GRANVILLE *Let.* in B. Askwith *Piety & Wit* (1982) vii. 103 We are all much better for her presence—it says 'up and doing', she looks so reviving. **1893** 'MARK TWAIN' in *Century Mag.* Dec. 234/2 She was up and around the same day. **1901** Up and doing [see sense 19 in Dict.]. **1909** *Dialect Notes* III. 385 *Up and about*,..used in expressing moderate health. **1927** G. HUNTING *Vicarion* xxi. 350 It required another week for him to get up and about. **1946** K. TENNANT *Lost Haven* (1947) 3 Steamy rains wash..from men's minds all desire to be up and doing. **1978** *Lancashire Life* Sept. 88/2 It was not unusual to hear her up and about in the middle of the night, checking on a seriously ill patient.

8. e. Cf. sense 15* below.

f. Of a foxhound or a follower of the hunt: keeping pace with the fox; present at its death.

1839 'HARKAWAY' *Jrnl.* 4 Jan. in E. A. Pease *Cleveland Hounds* (1887) iii. 63 Sly Reynard ran down the lane a field's length, and then took the fields. This gave the leaders a sob and the second-raters time to get up. **1889** F. MASON *Flowers of Hunt* 199 Ride as they might, the pace was so great that only a select few were on anything like terms with the hounds. 'Only eight of us up!' remarked Tom Chirpington. **1908** *Punch* 8 Apr. 267/1 Biggest ole dog-fox what ever I see!..Nobody up but the Master an' me! **1972** *Daily Tel.* 21 Nov. 19 On the second occasion the pack accounted for a brace of foxes, but the Princess's party was not up at either kill.

II. 10. c. Also *fig.*

1922 JOYCE *Ulysses* 295 Bob's a queer chap when the porter's up in him.

11. d. Delete 'Chiefly with *what*'. Also, amiss, wrong. (Earlier example.)

1838 MRS. GASKELL *Let.* 19 Aug. (1966) 37, I did not mention a word to Lucy but she must have guessed something was 'up'.

e. Of food, drink, etc.: ready, served; freq. (*tea up!*, etc.) as an indication that something is ready to be served, eaten, or drunk. *colloq.*

1941 J. SMILEY *Hash House Lingo* 55 *Up.* This is usually added to another as 'coffee up' 'waitress up' or 'bread up' and designates the want or approach of a person or thing. **1950** 'D. DIVINE' *King of Fassarai* xxi. 177 They heard her voice, 'Chow up!' **1972** J. PORTER *Meddler & her Murder* xi. 138 Grub's up!.. Them as wants forks can fetch 'em! **1981** J. WAINWRIGHT *All on Summer's Day* 14 'Tea up.' Wooley..carrying a steaming pot.

12. f. (Earlier example.)

1829 P. EGAN *Boxiana* 2nd Ser. II. 243 When time was called, it was 'all up' with Bob, and Jem was declared the winner.

13. b. Also (in *Computing*), in working condition. Freq. in phr. *up and running*. Cf. *UP TIME.

1978 *Computing* 9 Feb. 1/1 British Steel's giant private packet-switched network is up—and running successfully. **1978** *Nature* 24 Aug. 746/1 The host computer had just broken down, forcing a delay until it could be brought up again. **1983** *Austral. Personal Computer* IV. 106/3 A lot of other facilities need to be available to make a complete up-and-running software package.

III. 15. up against—. (Earlier example.)

1896 ADE *Artie* i. 7, I saw I was up against it.

15*. up at—, attending (a specified college or university). Cf. sense 8 e in Dict.

1873 TROLLOPE *Lady Anna* (1874) I. viii. 96 The grand idea that young Jack Bluestone, who was up at Brasenose, should marry the Lady Anna. **1926** J. BUCHAN *Dancing Floor* I. i. 11 It's old Milburne. He's up at Magdalen with me.

15. up for—. a.** Liable to, having to submit to, due to receive; under consideration for, having been proposed for.

1918 L. E. RUGGLES *Navy Explained* 52 Down for a shoot,..or up for a shot are all the same. It means that a man has been placed on the report and will have to appear at the mast before the captain. **1921** [in Dict., sense 14 b]. *a* **1936** KIPLING *Something of Myself* (1937) ii. 29 The Prefects.. were all of the 'Army Class' up for the Sandhurst or Woolwich Preliminary. **1979** A. SCHOLEFIELD *Point of Honour* 34 She said he was up for a medal... And a few weeks later there was the announcement of the VC.

b. *up for grabs*: see *GRAB *sb.*[2] 1 b.

17. up to—. d. (Earlier example.) orig. *U.S.*

1896 ADE *Artie* ii. 11 Up to me—see!

e. In phr. *to be up to* (a master), to be tutored by (him). *Public school colloq.* (chiefly *Eton College*).

1874 C. M. YONGE *Life J. C. Patteson* I. ii. 19 The lower remove of the fourth form..was then 'up to' the Rev. Charles Old Goodford, *i.e.* that was he who taught the division so called in school. **1910** A. HUXLEY *Let.* 15 Feb. (1969) 33 This half we are all up to that ignorant creature Heygate. I have successfully proved his ignorance. **1927** H. E. WORTHAM *Oscar Browning* vii. 99 Curzon was subsequently 'up to him'. **1977** A. J. AYER *Part of my Life* ii. 36 In the official language of the school..to be in a master's division was to be up to him.

IV. 19. Also *up-and-at-'em.*

1909 O. H. BALL *Their Oxford Year* 193 It was always the up-and-at-'em aspect of things that appealed to him. **1933** DYLAN THOMAS *Let.* 25 Dec. (1966) 82 You like the ..'up-&-at 'em'..shoutings of Mr. Kipling.

up, *prep.*[2] Add: **I. 1. c.** (Earlier and later examples.) *local.*

1774 P. V. FITHIAN *Jrnl.* 16 July (1900) 209 She then retired up chamber. **1893** S. HALE *Let.* 22 May (1919) 282 Louise..is now carrying some new pails up garret.

d. *vulgar.* Of a man: having sexual intercourse with.

1937 PARTRIDGE *Dict. Slang* 926/2 *Up*,..in coïtion with (a woman): low: late (? mid-) C. 19–20. **1973** 'J. PATRICK' *Glasgow Gang Observed* xii. 108 We've aw been up her. **1977** C. WATSON *One Man's Meat* viii. 74 The younger man said to the older: 'I'd rather be up her than up in Newcastle.'

3. b. *up yours*, an exclamation of contemptuous rejection, often used *imp.* (and accompanied by an impolite gesture) [shortened f. *up your arse* (or a similar expression): cf. *SHOVE *v.* 10 e]. *coarse slang.*

1956 'E. MCBAIN' *Cop Hater* ii. 18 'How's the graft these days?'..'Up yours,' Carella answered drily. **1969** B. MALAMUD *Pictures of Fidelman* vi. 208 Fidelman blew a..green horse for Beppo..'Up yours,' said the glass blower. **1970** A. TOFFLER *Future Shock* viii. 154 The upraised finger—the 'up yours' gesture—appears to be gaining greater respectability. **1975** J. SYMONS *Three Pipe Problem* xviii. 208 She made a V sign at the audience, said distinctly 'Up yours'. **1978** J. HYAMS *Pool* xi. 168 'Up yours, Richie Lesser,' Freda said without malice. 'I'm smarter than you are any day.'

II. 6. a. (Earlier example of *up the stage.*)

1795 T. WILKINSON *Wandering Patentee* III. 244 She turned quite round up the stage, (though not in character) as much as to say, kiss—.

b. *U.S.* Up in (the), up at. Cf. sense 1 c.

1845 S. JUDD *Margaret* II. ix. 344 You will find..in the bottom of my chest, up garret, five dollars and a quarter. **1862** M. D. COLT *Went to Kansas* 274 My nephew is.. teaching among the Indians up Lake Superior. **1884** 'MARK TWAIN' *Huck. Finn* xxvi. 237 Up garret was a little cubby with a pallet in it. **1923** R. FROST *Two Witches in New Hampshire* 66 Then we asked was there anything Up attic that we'd ever want again.

c. Up at. *colloq.* and *dial.*

1960 M. SPARK *Ballad Peckham Rye* vi. 122 Collie Gould up the Elephant with young Leslie. **1967** J. BURKE *Till Death us do Part* xi. 165 'Where you been? That's what I want to know.' 'Up the pictures.' **1975** A. DRUMMOND *Thames Jrnls. Vicesimus Lush* 23 Vicesimus Lush..was living in a cottage near the Hape mine—'up the Hape' in the local speech.

up-, *prefix.* Add: **I. 2. a.** *upclimb, -cry* (later example), *-curve* (examples), *-draw, -flutter, -haul* (examples), *-reach, -shine.*

1920 *Blackw. Mag.* July 69/2 The lonely halts of the

long upclimb. **1929** O. F. DUDLEY *Masterful Monk* viii. 88 There would undoubtedly be an upcry from Rome. **1928** *Nation* 27 June p. iii/3 Our circulation is on the up-curve. **1950** FRASER & THOMSON *Honest Bread* vii. 64 The upcurve in public drinking. **1912** J. LONDON *Son of Sun* I. ii. 23 Grief, with a quick updraw of his knees to the other's chest, broke the grip and forced him down. **1929** D. H. LAWRENCE *Pansies* 35 And then the geese scuttled in..and round the ring they went..then doubled, and back, with a funny up-flutter of wings. **1981** *Sunday Express Mag.* 14 June 24 (*caption*) Uphaul line with knots, used to pull sail up from water. **1984** *Times* 25 Aug. 11/2 Taking all the weight on my legs I eased the sail out of the water using the uphaul and paused for it to drain. **1926** D. H. LAWRENCE *David* xiii. 100 So the upreach of his love fails him. **1934** F. SCOTT FITZGERALD *Tender is Night* II. iv. 176 The upshine of a street-lamp.

b. *up-road* (examples).

1938 X. HERBERT *Capricornia* (1939) xiii. 185 Up-road guests may come by special train..at excursion rates. **1984** *Times* 18 July 19/2 'Footsie' started on the uproad.

III. 4. b. upspi·n *trans.*; **upbu·bble** *intr.*

1865 E. CASWALL *May Pageant* ii. 25 Close to where St. Oswy's ancient well Up-bubbles from its arch'd and mossy cell. **1954** L. MACNEICE *Autumn Sequel* xxvi. 160 Wells of words Upbubble. **1925** E. BLUNDEN *English Poems* 27 The darkening room by use well knows Each thread of life that these upspin.

5. (*b*) **upbrushed, -starched, -stiffed.**

1894 W. J. LOCKE *At Gate of Samaria* (1895) viii. 87 A shapely neck, on which clustered coquettishly a few tiny madcap curls below the smooth, upbrushed, fair hair. **1968** *Guardian* 24 July 7/1 He was responsible for the 'up-brushed' coiffures. **1922** Upstarched [see *SAMBO]. **1922** JOYCE *Ulysses* 39 In a Greek watercloset he breathed his last:..stalled upon his throne, with upstiffed omophorion, with clotted hinderparts.

7. (*b*) **up-pouring.**

1918 W. STEVENS in *Others* Dec. 9 A deep up-pouring from some saltier well Within me, bursts its watery syllable.

-up, *suffix*. The adverb UP appended to vbs. (sbs., etc.) as a suffix forming substantival or adjectival compounds (usu. derived from a simple vbl. phr.: see UP *adv.*[1] II), implying an instance or spell of an activity, an abundance or abuse of something, characterized by the action of the specified vb., etc. Such combinations are typically disyllabic and stressed on the first element: e.g. *balls-, beer-, booze-, brush-, foul-, fuck-, mop-, nosh-, show-, sign-up*, see at main element in Suppl.; *blow-, break-, build-, call-, clean-, close-, cock-, cover-, dust-, flare-, hold-, jam-, knees-, lay-, link-, make-, mark-, mock-, muck-, mug-, pick-, pile-, pin-, press-, pull-, punch-, push-, round-, run-, set-, shape-, smash-, speed-, stack-, stand-, stick-, tip-, tune-, walk-, warm-up*, see as main entries in Suppl.

up-along, *adv. dial.* Along in a particular or specified direction; in the world at large; in or towards a larger community outside an isolated region. Freq. in Cornish speech: up North, uphill. Also as *sb.*

a **1552** J. LELAND *Itinerary* (1721) IV. 89 The Beauty of Bermingham..is one Street going up alonge almost from the left Ripe [= bank] of the Brooke. **1905** E. PHILLPOTTS *Secret Woman* III. ii. 249 'I wish I had the mastery of the Word that man hath.' 'Very fine,' said Mr. Tapp, 'but I hate fog—whether 'tis up-along or in church. The man goeth in a mist, an' his landmarks fail him.' **1908** K. GRAHAME *Wind in Willows* ix. 199 'Nice little farm,' replied the wayfarer briefly. 'Upalong in that direction'—he nodded northwards. **1913** H. S. WALPOLE *Fortitude* I. iv. 45 Well, 'ere's the end of yer as yer are... Up along they'll change yer. **1959** *Coast to Coast 1959–60* 136 Wish she'd stop going then. Where we heading? Up-a-long or down-a-long? **1963** C. BERRY *Portrait of Cornwall* (1984) iii. 54 'Coming up-along, are 'ee?' asks a West Cornwall man of his friend at the foot of the hilly street. **1966** J. AIKEN *Trouble with Product X* vii. 128, I said as how you'm taking Miss Whatname upalong to hospital. **1972** *Even. Telegram* (St John's, Newfoundland) 29 June 3/1 If you have some of your people down from upalong, keep a modest bearing and don't go boasting. They may say, in their curious mainland accents: 'Waal, gee! Will ya look at all those birds. Why, this is incredible!'

‖ **Upanayana** (*upanā·yănă*). Also **Upanayan, Upanayanam.** [a. Skr. *upanayana*, f. *upa* towards + *nayana* leading, bringing (f. *nī* to lead).] An initiation ceremony, one of the rites undergone by Hindu Brahman boys between the ages of eight and sixteen.

1817 tr. *Dubois' Descr. People of India* II. i. 92 The children of Brahmans are invested with the Cord when they come to the age of seven or nine years... The ceremony..is called *Upanayana*, or, *the Introduction to the Sciences*. *Ibid.*, I had some difficulty in bringing myself to detail the whole of this ceremony of the Upanayana, it is so filled with minute and trifling superstition. **1877** J. N. WILSON *Indian Caste* I. v. 188 The *Upanayana* (or sacrificial endowment with the string) of a Bráhman should take place in his seventh year. **1919** S. CAVE *Redemption Hindu & Christian* iv. 97 The three higher castes alone can perform the *upanayana* ceremony, they alone can qualify themselves for the study of the Veda. **1935** L. S. S. O'MALLEY *Pop. Hinduism* iv. 112 For the twice-born castes the most essential is the *upanayan* or investiture with the sacred thread, which takes place in a boy's eighth, eleventh or twelfth year according to his caste. **1950** M. K. GANDHI *Hindu Dharma* lv. 91 The *upanayanam* ceremony, though I have discarded it myself, it has..a deep meaning. The sacred thread is a sign of new birth, a regeneration. **1971** *Illustr. Weekly India* 4 Apr. 11/1 Among all the sixteen *sanskars*, the *upanayana* is the most important. It signifies the practice of making over a boy to a learned religious teacher for education.

up-anchor, *v.* (Earlier example.)

1889 'MARK TWAIN' *Connecticut Yankee* xi. 137, I was all complete and ready to up anchor and get to sea.

up-and-co·ming, *a.* [UP *adv.*[2] 19.] **a.** *U.S.* Active, alert, wide-awake, energetic.

1889 *Harper's Mag.* Dec. 146/2 Can't you hear just how up an' comin' it was? **1901** [see UP *adv.*[2] 19]. **1926** F. N. HART *Bellamy Trial* i. 10 Redfield's pretty up and coming for a place of its size. **1946** R. LEHMANN *Gipsy's Baby* 59 They are of course admitting the blond curls of my brother; perhaps the juicy, up and coming appearance of all the four. Jolly-looking family. **1954** WODEHOUSE *Jeeves & Feudal Spirit* ii. 20 His attitude towards me had been that of an official at Borstal told off to keep an eye on a more than ordinarily up-and-coming juvenile delinquent.

b. Promising, making progress, beginning to achieve success. orig. *U.S.*

1926 R. HUGHES in *Hearst's Internat.* Feb. 44/1 The up-and-coming young prize-fighter 'Curly' Boyle. **1950** G. HACKFORTH-JONES *Worst Enemy* i. 19 Next to Meriton I would have placed Peters (on his reports) as a most up-and-coming youngster. **1959** 'R. SIMONS' *Houseboat Killings* vi. 67 'He's one of our up-and-coming young men.' 'Oh. So he is a successful artist?' **1977** B. PYM *Quartet in Autumn* xviii. 161 Their fashionable little house in that up-and-coming district by the common.

Hence **up-and-co·mer,** an up-and-coming person; **up-and-co·mingness.**

1890 Up-and-comingness [see UP *adv.*[2] 19]. **1944** *Gen* 9 Sept. 24/2 I've named only a few of the up-and-comers. **1968** T. STOPPARD *Real Inspector Hound* (1970) 40 Ah—yes—well, I like to give young up and comers the benefit of my—er—of course, she lacks technique as yet—. **1982** 'W. HAGGARD' *Mischief-Makers* vi. 77 He's one of their up-and-comers.

up and down, *adv., prep., a.,* and *sb.* Add: **A.** *adv.* **1. a.** (Later *fig.* example.)

1974 M. BIRMINGHAM *You can help Me* iv. 106 Robin had been exceptionally quiet at lunch... He usually showed off in front of visitors. Still, he did go up and down.

c. Delete †*Obs.* and add later example. Now also often in sense 'of varying quality'.

1945 C. S. LEWIS *Let.* 28 May (1966) 207 Mrs. Moore is up and down; very liable..to fits of bad jealousy.

7. (Earlier example.)

1854 'O. OPTIC' *In Doors & Out* 29, I told her, up and down, that she was not what she used to be when she lived with you.

C. *adj.* **3. b.** Also, of a person: subject to alternating or changing moods.

1960 I. CROSS *Backward Sex* 125 She had always been an up-and-down sort of person, depressed one minute and elated the next.

D. *sb.* **II. 6.** A rapid or cursory survey or perusal; the 'once-over'. *rare.*

1923 WODEHOUSE *Inimitable Jeeves* x. 102 'Read this letter.' He gave it the up-and-down.

up-and-do·wner. *slang.* Also **up-and-a-downer, upper and downer.** An up-and-down fight or argument (UP AND DOWN *a.* 5 a); a violent quarrel.

1927 *Daily Tel.* 6 Sept. 7/7 My daughter's young man wants to be king of the castle,..and the trouble is that the missus thinks more of him than she does of me. We has a bit of an up-and-a-downer last night, and he has the cheek to fetch a policeman. **1932** P. MACDONALD *Rope to Spare* xii. 174, I 'appened to hear them in a proper up-and-downer. **1955** M. GILBERT *Sky High* v. 71 Regular upper-and-downer you seemed to be having with Miss Palling. **1978** D. WILLIAMS *Treasure up in Smoke* viii. 73 I've just had the most glorious up-and-downer with my brother.

up-and-o·ver, *a.* [UP *adv.*[1] + OVER *adv.*] Denoting a type of garage door which opens by moving horizontally as it is raised.

1959 *Motor Manual* (ed. 36) ix. 221 Up-and-over doors, which are counterbalanced and swing away into the roof space..are gaining popularity. **1968** P. MARLOWE *Hire me a Hearse* xii. 169 The garage up-and-over door..had a tendency to rattle on its pulleys. **1979** J. COOPER *Class* xi. 197 The Weybridged house has..an up-and-over garage door.

up and u·nder. *Rugby Football.* [f. UP *adv.*[1] + UNDER *adv.*] A high kick intended to give the kicker and some other members of his team time to reach the point where the ball will come down. Also *up-and-under kick*.

[**1949** D. M. DAVIN *Roads from Home* ii. 28 'Up and under,' their captain cried and Star forwards..raced ahead to be under it when it fell.] **1960** V. JENKINS *Lions down Under* 208 An early tackle when he followed through after kicking an up-and-under. **1960** *Times* 18 Nov. 22/2 Oxford regained the lead from a high up-and-under kick. **1979** J. P. R. WILLIAMS *JPR* i. 32 Up on Lock's Common the wind is at its strongest; this is where dad chose for his barrage of up and unders for us all to catch.

Upanisha·dic, *a.* Also **Upaniṣadic, Upnishadic.** [f. UPANISHAD + -IC.] Of or pertaining to the Upanishads.

1921 M. A. BUCH *Philos. Shankara* 1 All the main ideas of Shankara's theory are anticipated by the Upnishadic seers. **1927** BELVALKAR & RANADE *Hist. Indian Philos.* II. vii. 242 (*heading*) A critical exposition of Upanishadic texts. **1937** *Mind* XLVI. 407 Witness his cogent criticism of Zeller and Burnet on Parmenides and his comments on the Upaniṣadic theories of self-consciousness. **1954** A. L. BASHAM *Wonder that was India* vii. 332 The great Śaṅkara himself..maintained the rigid Upaniṣadic doctrine of salvation by knowledge. **1964** *Language* XL. 112 A series of studies of Vedic and Upanishadic problems of interpretation..preluded his inheritance of Bloomfield's projected Vedic variants.

upa·rch, *v. Geol.* [f. UP- 4.] *trans.* To raise (strata, etc.) to form a broad dome or anticline. Hence **upa·rching** *vbl. sb.*, the raising of strata into an anticlinal form; the structure so produced.

1877 G. K. GILBERT *Rep. Geol. Henry Mountains* iv. 95 So soon as the lava can uparch the strata it does so, and the sheet becomes a laccolite. **1911** *Ann. Assoc. Amer. Geographers* I. 43 The present form and altitude of the range is therefore not due to the monoclinal displacement of the compound mass..but to the broad and simple up-arching of a much later date. **1954** *Jrnl. Glaciol.* II. 420 In a small quarry ..I again photographed up-arching of granite. **1970** R. J. SMALL *Study of Landforms* iii. 94 The strong tensional forces arising from uparching produce structural weaknesses..at the crest of an anticline. **1979** *Prof. Papers U.S. Geol. Survey* No. 1127. 1/1 A regional north-south compression..uparched several east-trending anticlines in central Washington.

upbeat, *sb.* Add: **2.** (Examples with reference to Old English poetry.)

1942 J. C. POPE *Rhythm of Beowulf* 49 Anacrusis derives its effect..from being placed in the up-beat or arsis. **1948** S. O. ANDREW *Postscript on Beowulf* 120 Anacrusis is an introductory unstressed up-beat.

3. *fig.* An optimistic or positive mood, development, etc.; a pleasant occurrence.

1950 C. MCCULLERS in *Theatre Arts* Apr. 28/1 The publisher says this character must not die and the book should end on an 'up beat'. **1955** *N.Y. Times Mag.* 1 May 28 (*heading*) Upbeat for modern dance. **1969** H. WAUGH *Young Prey* xiii. 118 Breakfast with a pretty airlines hostess..was Frank Sessions' only upbeat of the morning. **1976** *National Observer* (U.S.) 31 July 17/6, I don't think he's going to end tragically—he's in the classic sense a comic character, on the upbeat rather than the down.

upbeat, *a.* [f. the sb.] *colloq.* (orig. and chiefly *U.S.*). Cheerful, happy; hopeful, optimistic, positive; lively, vigorous.

1947 *N.Y. Herald-Tribune* (U.S.) 26 Sept. 16 (*heading*) Dizzy Gillespie, Yardbird Parker, Thelonius Monk get nod in up-beat set. **1952** *Variety* 2 Jan. 5, '51 was 'Up-beat' but '52 looms as 'Challenge Year'. **1961** *John o'London's* 25 May 591/3 Diana Sands as Beneatha brings a much-needed touch of up-beat comedy. **1965** *Punch* 25 Aug. 275/2 Like Queen Victoria I am inordinately cheered up by the delivery of pieces of upbeat information, not merely about my own luck, but about others, even. **1977** C. MCFADDEN *Serial* (1978) xxvi. 58/2 I'm feeling a lot more upbeat about Gregor now. **1984** *Times* 27 Mar. 10/2 (*heading*) Upbeat mood as Hongkong talks start again.

u·pbound, *a.* and *adv.* *U.S.* [UP *prep.*[2] 2.] Going upstream.

1884 'MARK TWAIN' *Huck. Finn* xii. 99 We watched the ..up-bound steamboats fight the big river in the middle. **1976** *Advance News* (Ogdensburg, N.Y.) 18 July 9/1 The Britannia, Royal Yacht of Queen Elizabeth II and Prince Philip of England, is due to transit the Dwight D. Eisenhower Locks upbound on the St. Lawrence Seaway.

upbrushed, -bubble: see *UP- 5, 4 b.

u·p-card. *U.S.* [UP *a.*] In various card games: a card turned face up on the table; a turn-up (TURN-UP *sb.* 3 a).

1938 WOOD & GODDARD *Compl. Bk. Games* 223 The next card, called the up-card, is faced up beside the undealt cards, or stock. **1951** *Amer. Speech* XXVI. 102/1 *Up cards*, cards that are dealt face up in stud [poker]. **1964** *Life* 27 Mar. 80 Charts at top tell player how to play his hand, depending on the dealer's up card. **1974** J. SCARNE *New Compl. Guide to Gambling* 375 This example should make it clear to the reader why Black Jack experts attach so much importance to the dealer's upcard.

up-cha·nnel, *adv.* and *a.* [UP *prep.*[2] 2.] (Moving, leading, etc.) towards the upper end of a channel.

1893 KIPLING *Seven Seas* (1896) 4 Go, get you gone up-Channel with the sea-crust on your plates. **1898** [in Dict. s.v. UP *prep.*[2] 2]. **1925** BELLOC *Cruise of 'Nona'* 135 Anyone going up-Channel makes for the lighthouse..for this shortens an up-Channel course. **1936** E. G. BOWEN in H. C. Darby *Hist. Geogr. Eng.* i. 24 The up-Channel shift of the important trade routes. **1954** —— *Settlement Celtic Saints in Wales* ii. 45 Llanilltud..and Nant Carban ..are..conveniently well up-Channel to provide an easy crossing.

upchuck (*ʌ*·ptʃʌk), *v. U.S. slang.* [Up *adv.*[1]: cf. *to throw up* s.v. Throw *v.*[1] 48 b.] *intr.* To vomit. Also *trans.*

1960 Wentworth & Flexner *Dict. Amer. Slang* 561/2 *Up-chuck, upchuck,* v.i., v.t. to vomit. Since c 1925... Considered a smart and sophisticated term c 1935, esp. when applied to sickness that had been induced by over-drinking. **1967** 'T. Wells' *What should you know of Dying?* i. 19 Anyway, Natalie had to upchuck, it's that kind of bug. **1975** P. de Vries *Glory of Hummingbird* ii. 21 'Did I ever tell you about the time I got sick in Miss Haley's dancing class?'..He..had quite copiously up-chucked. **1981** 'A. Cross' *Death in Faculty* i. 9 She up-chucked it..onto the bedroom floor.

u·pcoast, *adv.* [Up *prep.*[2]] Situated or travelling further up the coast.

1909 J. Masefield *Multitude & Solitude* xii. 296 He lay in his bunk in a cabin.., on his way up-coast. **1931** H. T. Concannon *St. Patrick* 241 Muirchu writes of the Saint as having sailed up-coast. **1974** W. R. Hunt *North of 53* i. 5 St Michael, just upcoast from the Yukon River delta.

upcoming, *ppl. a.* Add: **b.** That is about to happen, etc., forthcoming. Chiefly *U.S.*

1959 A. Huxley *Let.* 3 Sept. (1969) 878, I am working like mad..on my lectures for the upcoming semester. **1967** Mrs. L. B. Johnson *White House Diary* 5 June (1970) 521 Today it was work on the speeches for the upcoming trip to New England. **1971** *Publishers' Weekly* 1 Nov. 18/1 Booth and Haley did their upcoming books no harm. **1973** *Express* (Trinidad & Tobago) 27 Apr. 31/3 The up-coming contest is open to all karate associations. **1982** T. Barling *Terminate with Prejudice* iv. v. 104 An upcoming visit by a member of the Soviet Politburo. **1984** *Daily Tel.* 25 Feb. 17 No change in the law was required, the existing statute was merely being clarified and there was no need to insert a special clause in the upcoming Finance Bill.

up-conve·rter. Chiefly *Electr.* [Up- 8.] A device for converting a signal to a higher frequency. So **up-conve·rsion**; also **up-conve·rt** *v. trans.*, **up-conve·rted** *ppl. a.*

1958 *Bell Syst. Technical Jrnl.* XXXVII. 989 (*heading*) Gain and noise figure of a variable-capacitance up-converter. *Ibid.*, In up-conversion (modulation) a power gain results, with the power added to the input signal being supplied by the beat oscillator. In down-conversion a power loss results. **1968** *Microwave Jrnl.* Aug. 52/2 The 12·4 GHz signal from the frequency up-converter is first down-converted to 160 MHz..then upconverted to 12·4 GHz in a single frequency parametric upconverter. **1970** *New Yorker* 11 Apr. 34 A laser beam can be used to upconvert infrared light to visible light. **1972** *Physics Bull.* Jan. 18/2 Since the upconverted radiation now has a wavelength close to both the helium-neon and krypton (0·605 μm) wavelengths, an accurate interferometric comparison is much easier to perform than with the 9·3 μm line directly. **1972** Upconverter [see *parametric *a.*[1] b]. **1975** D. G. Fink *Electronics Engineers' Handbk.* xiv. 72 There is a distinct advantage to up-conversion; image rejection is easily achievable by a simple low-pass filter. **1976** *Which?* Nov. 262/3 UHF signals received at the aerial are sometimes translated to VHF or even lower frequencies (HF). These VHF (or HF) signals can't be plugged directly into a UHF TV... They need either a box (called an up-converter) to turn them back into UHF signals, or a specially modified TV. **1983** E. Trundle *Beginner's Guide Videocassette Recorders* v. 91 The up-conversion process during replay involves a heterodyne system.

up-country, *sb.*, *a.*, and *adv.* Add: **1.** *sb.* **b.** (*b*) (Earlier examples.)

1817 M. L. Weems *Let.* in *M. L. Weems: Works & Ways* (1929) III. 176, I have a number due in the up country. **1835** J. H. Ingraham *South-West* I. xxiii. 248 In the cabin are the merchants and planters of the 'up country'.

2. *adj.* (Earlier and later examples.) Also, situated in, etc., a part of the country away from any town. (Now rare in the U.K.)

In this sense and as *adv.* sometimes implying 'higher in altitude'.

1810 M. L. Weems *Let.* in *M. L. Weems: Works & Ways* (1929) III. 27 Not thinking the little up-country post offices safe in matters of money [etc.]. **1831** *Canton Miscell.* V. 321 Up-country stations in India. **1859** F. Fuller *Five Years' Residence N.Z.* xi. 233 The up-country tracks were not then marked out. **1911** C. E. W. Bean *'Dreadnought' of Darling* xx. 193 The fact that each of seven station hands *could* agree to put in £70 may throw some light upon the conditions amongst upcountry workers in Australia. **1911** W. H. Koebel *In Maoriland Bush* xxii. 284 Homely little upcountry race meetings. **1923** [see *station *sb.* 13 d]. **1929** K. S. Prichard *Coonardoo* xvi. 162 Poor degraded wretches,..drifting about the up-country towns and settlements along the coast. **1962** J. Frame *Edge of Alphabet* xviii. 102 How I would have liked to..live in an upcountry house whose tall windows faced the mountains. **1965** B. Wannan *Fair Go, Spinner* iv. 131 The Drongo once got a job on an up-country farm. **1970** *Kenya Farmer* Feb. 9/1 One of the greatest pleasures that Kenya can offer—a weekend on an 'up country' farm. **1977** *Church Times* 29 July 6/3 A BCMS missionary nurse in upcountry Uganda. **1981** *Times* 2 Feb. 16/7 He was the first Kandyan (upcountry) Sinhalese Buddhist to be appointed Governor-General, his predecessor having been a low country Sinhalese Christian.

3. *adv.* (Later examples.) Also, away from any town, remote.

1866 M. A. Barker *Station Life N.Z.* (1870) vi. 37, I had danced with a young gentleman whose station was a long way 'up country'. **1891** G. Chamier *Philosopher Dick* I. ii. 43 Here, up country, we have mostly a moving population of tramps, topers and outcasts. **1911** E. M. Clowes *On Wallaby* iv. 86 Up-country the sundowner, or *bona fide* worker in search for a job, will find 'tucker' for the asking at any farm or station. **1911** W. H. Koebel *In Maoriland Bush* xiii. 183 Nature is a staunch friend to this obsolete atmosphere. Nowhere, perhaps, does it come to its aid with greater fervour than in New Zealand, up-country. **1962** J. Frame *Edge of Alphabet* i. 14 As if his head were a secret gully somewhere up-country. **1962** *Housewife* (Ceylon) Apr. 10 Children's woollen clothes very moderately priced and ideal for wear, both up-country and abroad. **1971** *Inside Kenya Today* Mar. 48/1 Farmers..can grow a variety of crops—just as much as their counterparts up-country could. **1980** *Word 1979* XXX. 167 Transportation problems, levels of literacy, as well as economic factors, tend to restrict the diffusion of the newspapers up-country.

u·pcurrent, *sb.* [Up- 2.] A rising current of air.

1909 F. W. Lanchester in *Flight* 22 May 296/1 When a plane falls normally through a vertical path, there is set up around the edges an up-current of air. **1921** *Flight* 8 Sept. 604/1 This map brings out very clearly..the manner in which Klemperer followed the valleys and took advantage of the gusts, up-currents, etc., which were caused by the nature of the country. **1931** *Air Ann. Brit. Empire* 30 The most elementary form of up-currents are caused by the deflection of winds over hills..necessary for soaring flight. **1953** N. Tinbergen *Herring Gull's World* iv. 39 The influence of the upcurrent on their flight is seen most impressively when..one forces the gulls to make a detour out over the beach. **1979** B. L. C. Johnson *Pakistan* iv. 55/1 It limits the scope for upcurrents in the surface monsoon air stream to rise very high.

u·p-cut. *Engin.* [Up- 2.] A cut made by a cutter rotating so that the teeth are moving upwards when cutting; so *up-cut milling.*

1934 Webster, Upcut. **1950** J. A. Oates in A. W. Judge *Machine Tools & Operations* III. ii. 113 Down-cut milling produces a dull surface, in contrast to the bright and polished type resulting from ordinary up-cut milling. **1964** S. Crawford *Basic Engin. Processes* vi. 166 The normal or conventional method of milling is known as up-cut milling. **1973** J. G. Tweeddale *Materials Technol.* II. vi. 146 Figure 6.4 c shows an 'upcut'.

upda·table, *a.* [f. next + -able.] That may be updated.

1976 *Business Week* 5 Apr. 44/2 Eastman Kodak Corp. and Xerox Corp. are experimenting with nonsilver imaging and updatable microfiche. **1977** *Financial Times* 19 May 17/1 GEC have developed a magnetic card which looks much like existing credit cards, but carries updatable information which frees banks from their present large central accounting systems.

upda·te, *v.* orig. *U.S.* [Up- 4; cf. Up to date, up-to-date *adv. phr.*] *trans.* **a.** To bring (information, esp. written material or material recorded in some other form) up to date.

1948 *Time* 11 Oct. 22/1 [The speech] had been corrected and updated after last-minute teletype reports from.. Paris. **1959** *Times Lit. Suppl.* 20 Mar. 155/2 He would streamline the production, add a chorus of dancing girls, update the lyrics, and upjazz the music. **1962** C. Walsh *From Utopia to Nightmare* 12 All current allusions have been 'updated' (as of early 1962). **1979** *Ottawa Law Rev.* XI. 815 The entry for 'Hudson's Bay Company' needs to be updated.

b. To supply (a person) with the most recent information; to bring (a person) up to date.

1952 *N.Y. Herald-Tribune* 14 Mar. 21/2 He updated me on a couple of gimmicks. **1970** J. Earl *Tuners & Amplifiers* 7 The book will have appeal, too, to the older hand, allowing him to become quickly updated without the task of researching into piles of technical literature. **1975** *Sunday Times* 16 Nov. 44/4 No doubt I'll update myself in a few weeks and emerge as a real Seventies mum.

c. Of equipment, processes, etc.

1959 *Listener* 4 June 998/1 This prescience has now been 'up-dated', as they say, by reference to nuclear warfare. **1970** *Islander* (Victoria, B.C.) 8 Feb. 7/2 Despite ..updating the equipment to include new freezing facilities..this [whaling] venture also folded. **1977** *N.Y. Rev. Bks.* 13 Oct. 45/1 To update the 'dirty test tube' analogy, the effects of the contaminants have been estimated and found to be minor. **1984** *Daily Mail* 1 Dec. 14/1 (Advt.) This way, you can update your equipment whenever you want.

Also **upda·ted** *ppl. a.*; **upda·ting** *vbl. sb.*

Quot. 1910 is an isolated early British example.

1910 Hardy *Satires of Circumstance* (1914) 222 Your up-dated modern page. **1954** *Newsweek* 27 Sept. 58/1 The new research center is an updated transplant of the National Bureau of Standards world-wide radio investigations formerly based in Washington. **1959** *Spectator* 31 July 134/2 Despite the up-dating and jazzy typographical treatment, one fairly quickly perceives an enduring pattern of traditional attitudes. **1974** Adby & Dempster *Introd. Optimization Methods* iv. 96 Round-off errors in the computations of the up-dating process can lead to non-positive definitive S_k and divergence. **1978** *Jrnl. R. Soc. Arts* CXXVI. 672/1 The plan adopted is said to be a revised and updated version of an outline plan for the development of the economy produced in 1975.

u·pdate, *sb.* orig. *U.S.* [f. the vb.] **1.** New information received or supplied; an updated version of something. Also, an account or report of the present state of affairs. *colloq.*

1967 *Britannica Bk. of Year* (U.S.) 804/3 *Update*, current information for use by a computer in order to make the calculations necessary for achieving a particular goal. **1970** N. Armstrong et al. *First on Moon* v. 116 When you're ready to copy..I've got a couple of small flight plan updates. **1975** B. Garfield *Hopscotch* ix. 92 Thanks for the update. Keep on it. **1976** *Physics Bull.* July 313/2 Quarterly updates are available for each course. **1977** H. Greene *FSO-1* xiii. 119 One of his people will..give you a full update on related problems. **1983** *Brit. Med. Jrnl.* 6 Aug. 417/1 The editors of *Harrison's Principles of Internal Medicine* have bridged the gap between the 9th and 10th editions with a series of updates. **1984** *Miami Herald* 6 Apr. 11D/1 An embarrassing update of the 1960s comedy filmed on Fort Lauderdale Beach. **1985** *Times* 5 Jan. 17/7 The new album is a high-grade Motown update, funky, sleek and packed with potential hits.

2. The action or result of updating; the supplying of new information, data, etc. Freq. in *Computers.*

1968 *Amer. Documentation* Jan. 75/1 Thus, interrogations, extractions and updates can be based upon items or subitems, but not upon units smaller than these. **1972** *Computer Jrnl.* XV. 191/2 The effect, of course, is to put the clock back to the time of the last dump and all updates made since then must be repeated. **1976** *Gramophone* Aug. 353/3 Such 'updates' as they are called, involve switching individual tracks of the tape from the 'read' to the 'write' mode. **1982** *ICL News* No. 96. 5/1 A pre-Conference session..was followed by an overall update and presentations on latest versions of data management software.

3. *attrib.*

1969 *Sunday Times* 13 July 13/2 *Update pad*, information on spacecraft attitudes, and other data, transmitted to the crew in standard format. **1972** *Computers & Humanities* VII. 127 Working with this printout, the editor prepares data for the update module in which insignificant variants are deleted and citations added. **1983** *Word Ways* Nov. 197 It..is supplemented by update lists which the computer automatically generates.

up-dip, *a.* and *adv. Geol.* [f. Up *prep.*[2] + Dip *sb.*] **A.** *adj.* (Stressed *u·p-dip.*) Situated or occurring in a direction upwards along the dip. **B.** *adv.* (Stressed *up-di·p.*) In an up-dip direction.

1916 F. H. Lahee *Field Geol.* viii. 191 When a fault is approximately parallel to the strike of the strata, the block on the side of the fault toward which the dip of the beds is measured may be termed the down-dip block, and the other one is the up-dip block. **1957** G. E. Hutchinson *Treat. Limnol.* I. i. 156 The bays originated as artesian springs, which tended to migrate inland up-dip. **1965** [see *lenticularity]. **1974** R. D. Grace in P. L. Moore et al. *Drilling Practices Manual* xiii. 329 It predicts up-dip deviation when drilling into softer rock.

up-do (*ʌ*·pdū). *colloq.* (orig. *U.S.*). Also **updo.** [f. Up *adv.*[1] + Do *sb.*[1] 2, after *hair-do.*] A style of dressing women's hair by sweeping it up and securing it away from the face and neck.

1938 *Sun* (Baltimore) 29 Nov. 9/4 The 'up-do' hair style does not click with De Paul University men students... The 'up-do' probably will go back down after movie stars get tired of it. **1966** J. S. Cox *Illustr. Dict. Hairdressing & Wigmaking* 157/1 *Up-do*, a hair style dressed away from the forehead and neckline. Updo: American Spelling. **1984** *Daily Tel.* 3 Sept. 13/5 She has not appeared to be wearing anything in her hair. If Miss Resnik returns to space a second time, Mr Menchaca said he would consider putting in 'braids or an up-do'.

updo·ming, *vbl. sb. Geol.* [Up- 7.] The upward expansion of a rock mass into a dome shape.

1964 *Bull. Vermont Geol. Survey* No. 23. 7 Updoming was the deforming mechanism of the anticlinorium. **1977** A. Hallam *Planet Earth* 78/3 The heating of the rocks beneath the rift zone causes expansion, and this accounts ..for the updoming.

updraught. Restrict † *Obs. rare* to sense in Dict. and add: **2.** Also (chiefly *U.S.*) **updraft.** [Draught *sb.* 24.] An upward-moving current of air. Cf. Down-draught 1. Also *fig.*

1909 *Daily Graphic* 26 July 10/1 While the planes are fighting against the wind their area will be comparatively small, but when floating on an up-draught they will be expanded as a fan expands. **1935** C. Day Lewis *Time to Dance* 31 Some aimed at a small objective but the fierce updraught of their spirit Forced them to the stars. **1953** N. Tinbergen *Herring Gull's World* iv. 28 A north wind caused an updraught, which enabled the birds to hang motionless in the air for many minutes. **1954** R. J. Schwartz *Dict. Business & Industry* 533 Updraft. *a* **1963** S. Plath *Crossing Water* (1971) 38 A sheet of newsprint on the fire Levitating a numb minute in the updraft. **1983** D. Boggis *Woman they sent to FIGHT* iv. 28 Brakes off, undercarriage down..*Slam* through the updraught off the spinney.

updry, *v.* (Later *poet.* example.)

1889 F. Thompson in *Merry England* Sept. 306 Till Time, the hidden root of change, updries, Are Birth and Death inseparable on earth.

up-end, *v.* Add: **1.** Also *fig.*

1970 G. Greer *Female Eunuch* 37 By growing their hair they managed to up-end some strange presupposition about its sexual significance.

2. *spec.* of waterfowl: to dip the head below water and raise the tail into the air, when searching for food in shallow water. (Later examples.)

1927 E. SANDARS *Bird Bk. for Pocket* II. 126 [Brent Geese] sometimes when feeding at high tide, up-end like Ducks. **1954** A. W. P. ROBERTSON *Bird Pageant* i. 20 Avocets..often when water-borne..up-end like ducks. **1957** R. A. H. COOMBES in D. A. Bannerman *Birds Brit. Isles* VI. 266, I never saw them 'upending' in the shallows as the other geese were fond of doing. **1981** *Birds* Summer 47/2 An up-ending mallard is a feeding mallard, but this, our commonest duck, is as adaptable in its feeding technique as it is in its choice of food.

upfield, *adv.* and *a.* **A.** *adv.* (Stressed *upfie·ld.*) [UP *prep.*²] **1.** *Football*, etc. In or towards the end of the field nearest the goal which the team is attacking.

1951 *Sport* 27 Apr.–3 May 8/1 The wee Scot whipped the ball upfield to the late Jack Lambert before Huddersfield had organised their ranks. **1960** *Times* 29 Feb. 3/3 France worked their way upfield again. **1976** *Evening Advertiser* (Swindon) 31 Dec. 19/4 He would not stay upfield wide on the wing and was coming back too deep.

2. *Chem.* and *Physics.* In a direction corresponding to greater field strength.

1965 *Jrnl. Chem. Physics* XLII. 636/2 The $^{205}Tl^{+}$ resonance is shifted upfield by a very large amount. **1976** *Nature* 29 July 424/3 The statement..makes the dangerous assumption that no aromatic protons are shifted upfield or downfield out of this region by local ring current effects.

B. *adj.* (Stressed *u·pfield.*) **1.** *Football*, etc. Directed into or occurring in a part of the field near(er) the goal attacked.

1960 *Times* 18 Nov. 22/2 Long upfield kicks by stand-off Evans. *Ibid.* 6 Dec. 18/3 Upfield support of forwards by the backs. **1983** *N.Y. Times* 30 Jan. v. 8/6 Manley is the upfield pass rusher.

2. *Chem. & Physics.* Situated or occurring in the direction of greater field strength.

1967 *Inorg. Chem.* VI. 1133/2 Increased metal to ligand π bonding produces an upfield coordination chemical shift. **1979** *Macromolecules* XII. 763/1 These spectra show an upfield peak separated from a smaller peak, $2{\cdot}36 \pm 0{\cdot}1$ downfield.

upfloor. Add: (Later archaizing example in sense 'an upper floor').

1922 JOYCE *Ulysses* 381 Sir Leopold heard on the upfloor cry on high and he wondered what cry that it was whether of child or woman.

upfront, *adv.* and *a. colloq.* (orig. *U.S.*). Also **up-front, up front.** [f. UP *adv.*¹, *adv.*² + FRONT *sb.*] **A.** *adv.* **a.** At the front, in front.

1937 [see *LATCH *v.*¹ 1]. **1954** A. FULLERTON *Bury Past* I. i. 9 In their sealed compartment up front the sound came thinly. **1968** *Listener* 25 July 107/2 'Get your parachutes on.' He added reluctantly: 'We're having a little trouble up front and you may have to jump.' **1976** *Sunday Post* (Glasgow) 26 Dec., Alloa just deserved their success because they were a bit sharper up front.

b. *transf.* Of payments: in advance; initially. Also openly, frankly.

1972 *Britannica Bk. of Year* (U.S.) 733/3 *Up front, adv.*, in advance (actors demanding $1 million *up front*). **1980** *Maledicta* III. II. 238 That is much like the 'frank' people these days who confess their inadequacies or even villainies *up front* and then are shocked when you do not cancel those things out as exculpated by admission. **1982** S. WILSON *Dealer's Wheels* xiv. 135 'How much cash did you have in mind?' 'Five thousand, up front.' 'I beg your pardon?' 'In advance.'

B. *adj.* That is in the forefront; honest, open, frank; (of money) paid in advance. **a.** *attrib.*

1967 *Time* 29 Dec. 24/2 What the up-front struggle really amounts to is an angry, private little war between two people. **1975** *New Yorker* 20 Jan. 31/1, I'd like to suggest that we get most of the people involved below the line, so we won't need much of that scarce up-front bread. **1977** *Bulletin* (Sydney) 22 Jan. 88/1 Lunch with local film people who want to buy film rights... They chat about 'up-front money' and consider whether Robert Altman or Werner Herzog would do the better job. **1980** *Fortune* 24 Mar. 70/2 The up-front problem in the division today is that it does not garner deposits. **1982** *Chicago Sun-Times* 14 Oct. 100/1 'We've never had a budget to market these properties before,' he said. 'This time we have $250,000–$300,000 in upfront money.' **1985** *Broadcast* 11 Jan. 7/1 As well as the up-front money from RAI on these two documentaries RAI Channel 1 will also be taking up to 100 hours of natural history and scientific documentaries from Horizon..and QED.

b. *predic.*

1970 J. LENNON in J. Wenner *Lennon Remembers* (1972) 67 That game of 'Well, I'm going to be up-front because..a few people said she'd got a lousy name in New York.' **1973** D. LANG *Freaks* 119 You might as well live in a totalitarian state that's up front with it, at least. **1978** M. PUZO *Fools Die* xxiii. 258 He would..make them understand in a nice way that he would trade space for a piece of ass. He was that upfront about it. **1980** *Washington Star* 2 July C2 Sirois was totally 'up front', O'Malley said, in his efforts to inform and ask for help from the Caps.

u·pgiven, *ppl. a. poet. nonce-use.* [UP- 5.] Surrendered, resigned. Cf. GHOST *sb.* 1.

1947 DYLAN THOMAS *In Country Sleep* in *Horizon* Dec. 304 The upgiven ghost Of the dingle torn to singing.

u·pglide. *Phonol.* [UP- 2 a: see next and GLIDE *sb.* 4.] An upward glide.

1930 [see *DOWN-GLIDE]. **1957** *Publ. Amer. Dial. Soc.* XXVIII. 115 Normally *or* marks the division between rise and fall, itself occurring at the end of the upglide. **1972** W. LABOV *Language in Inner City* i. 9 In New York and other northern cities,..the back upglide of *ball* and *hawk*, so characteristic of many southern areas, is rarely heard.

u·pgliding, *ppl. a. Phonol.* [UP- 6 b: see prec.] Gliding towards a high(er) vowel.

1933 O. JESPERSEN *Essentials Eng. Gram.* iv. 42 The *r*, or the resulting vowel [ə], also prevents the formation of the up-gliding diphthong [ou] in words like *oar*, *board*, [etc.]. **1948**, **1962** [see *INGLIDING *ppl. a.*]. **1970** *Publ. Amer. Dial. Soc.* 1968 L. 19 An upgliding diphthong occurs sporadically. **1981** *Amer. Speech* 1977 LII. 203 Variants listed as deviating from his constructed general pattern of simple, upgliding, and ingliding vowels.

upgra·dable, *a.* Also **upgradeable.** [f. *UPGRADE *v.* + -ABLE.] Capable of being upgraded or raised to a higher standard; *spec.* in *Computers*, applied to (the storage size of) a system. Hence **upgradabi·lity.**

1974 *Physics Bull.* Dec. 568/1 (Advt.), ND 100 has a completely solid state memory with 1K, 2K, or 4K memory capacity (field upgradeable). **1982** *Which Computer?* June 44/3 The ease of software upgradability certainly makes it attractive. **1983** *Daily Tel.* 14 June 6 (Advt.), The Exxon 8431 System features an advanced central controller with upgradeable storage up to 320 MB. **1985** *Personal Computer World* Feb. 42/2 (Advt.), Works equally well on 5¼″, 3½″, or 3″ disks, with upgradability built-in from 100K to 2.6 Mbyte.

up-grade, *sb.* and *adv.* Add: **1. a.** (Earlier example.)

1873 J. H. BEADLE *Undevel. West* xv. 257 Forty miles of staging over boulder and rocky up-grade.

2. *on the upgrade* (*fig.*) (later examples). Also, improving.

1914 A. BENNETT *Price of Love* vi. 110 'Auntie still on the up-grade?' he inquired... He guessed..that Mrs. Maldon must be still better. **1926** *Ladies' Home Jrnl.* Oct. 143 Monty's been the hardest child we've had to handle,.. but I believe he's on the upgrade. **1951** 'J. TEY' *Daughter of Time* iv. 55 Don't you worry. I'm on the up-grade. Even my temper has improved. **1972** *Daily Tel.* 21 Jan. 1/2 Various indices..show that the economy is now firmly on the upgrade.

3. [f. the vb.] An upgraded version. Also, an upgrading to a higher standard (chiefly, in *Computers*, to a larger and more powerful system).

1980 *Nature* 17 Apr. 599/1 The upgrade of this facility, PBFA-II, will deliver 3.5 MJ at 100 TW and will be available for experiments in 1986. **1982** *Which Computer?* June 55/2 They can reach down to the more sophisticated microcomputer user, holding out the possibility of an upgrade to a larger machine. **1983** *What's New in Computing* Jan. 30 (Advt.), PT7/s powerful local processing..allows simpler planning of mainframe upgrades.

upgra·de, *v.* Also **up-grade.** [f. UP- 4: cf. the sb.] **1.** *trans.* To increase the grade or status of (a job); to raise (an employee) to a higher grade or rank. Also *fig.*

1920 [implied at *UPGRADING *vbl. sb.*]. **1928** *Daily Express* 5 Mar. 3/5 His job..has become so important that the post is being 'up-graded'. **1942** *Tee Emm* (Air Ministry) II. 130 In future they are going to be upgraded [from angels] to archangels. **1955** [see *DOWN-GRADE *v.*]. **1976** *National Observer* (U.S.) 20 Nov. 14/2 The commission agreed to upgrade controllers at 32 facilities, but fewer controllers would be promoted than the union demands. **1985** *Contact* (Pre-School Playgroups Assoc.) Feb. 23/1 Teachers who underestimate the richness of children's homes decide to upgrade the children's language skills.

2. a. To raise (something, esp. equipment or facilities) from one grade to another; to improve or enhance physically.

1935 [implied at *UPGRADED *ppl. a.*]. **1955** M. REIFER *Dict. New Words* 217/2 *Upgrade*, to improve the grade of a product. **1959** *Globe & Mail* (Toronto) 17 July 13/3 If Canada were to maintain and extend its capabilities in this field, it was necessary that its effective weapons be continuously upgraded. **1964** G. L. COHEN *What's Wrong with Hospitals?* vii. 143 These old places are really quite comfortable, you know; they've been up-graded out of all recognition. **1971** *Daily Tel.* 13 Sept. 10/6 The money.. would be spent on financing sewerage schemes and upgrading existing effluent treatment facilities. **1976** A. HOPE *Hi-fi Handbk.* 14 If you wish to up-grade a music centre, you can only throw it out and replace it with a better one. **1979** 'J. LE CARRÉ' *Smiley's People* xvii. 211 He booked a first-class seat and said he would upgrade his economy ticket on arrival at the airport.

b. More generally, to raise to a higher level; to improve.

1959 G. D. MITCHELL *Sociol.* 120 Generally it was found that women were more likely than men to up-grade themselves. **1962** M. MCLUHAN *Gutenberg Galaxy* 43 For until men have up-graded the visual component communities know only a tribal structure. **1977** *New Yorker* 24 Oct. 79/2 They have upgraded their criminal expertise by watching such programs as..'Kojak'. **1983** *Times* 29 Oct. 16/4 A lunch in the City..led to one broker upgrading his forecast for the year.

c. *absol.* or *intr.* (for *refl.*).

1950 *Sun* (Baltimore) 2 Oct. 9/1 Movers say that the bulk of families moving are 'upgrading'. By that they mean that they are occupying new apartments renting for much more than they have been paying. **1967** *Boston Sunday Globe* 23 Apr. B41/5 The head of a family..wants to upgrade—and usually does. **1970** J. EARL *Tuners & Amplifiers* iii. 60 This may differ slightly if we already possess some items of equipment and merely wish..to upgrade by changing a particular item..for an equivalent of improved quality.

Hence **upgra·ded** *ppl. a.*; **upgra·ding** *vbl. sb.*

1920 *Glasgow Herald* 19 Aug. 8/3 The government proposals for..the upgrading of the unskilled labourers.. were rejected by the operatives. **1935** *Times* 1 Oct. 4/4 The rates on the upgraded stretch and the 1 in 22½ Dashwood Hill were 15 and 50 and 30 and 44 m.p.h. **1938** *Encycl. Brit. Bk. of Year* 214/1 The Burnham Committee ..dealt with the up-grading and down-grading of Elementary Schools for the assessment of Head Teachers' salaries. **1959** *Times Lit. Suppl.* 9 Oct. 579/1 The danger of 'escalation'—the upgrading of the size of the weapons in reply to the apparent use by the enemy of bigger types. **1976** P. R. WHITE *Planning for Public Transport* viii. 186 A preliminary study suggests that investment in an upgraded rail link may provide net benefits as high as for a parallel road scheme.

uphaliday. 1. c. See next.

Up-Helly-Aa (ʌ:pˌheliˌā·). Also **-A'.** [See UPHALIDAY.] (A revival of) a traditional midwinter fire-festival held at Lerwick in the Shetland Islands (see quots.).

1872 *Saturday Herald & Shetland Gaz.* (Kirkwall) 10 Feb. 1/3 Monday night was what is here [*sc.* in Lerwick] called 'Up-haly a', and the youths here indulged in their savage sports of tar-barrel burning. **1901** *Shetland News* 5 Jan., The principal Festival of the season to Lerwegians, namely 'Up-helly A',..is now celebrated with.. Norse galleys, torch-light processions, and guizing galore. **1934** W. MOFFAT *Shetland* 129 Up-Helly-Aa night was the twenty-fourth night of the Helli or Holy Days, and that period of feasting, drinking, singing and rejoicing concluded with a great flare-up on Up-Helly-Aa night. **1948** C. E. MITCHELL *Up-Helly-Aa* 2 Up-Helly-Aa is the final day of the Jola Bød or Yule Period which commenced on the fifth day of January, old style, and ended twenty-four days later in a climax of revelry. **1955** *Shetland Times* 28 Jan., When a man is elected to the Up-Helly-A' Committee he can expect to become Guizer Jarl according to his seniority. **1972** *Guardian* 15 Jan. 14/5 The fire festival of Up-Helly-A in the Shetlands, which celebrates the passing of midwinter with..torchlight processions..and a lifesize longboat that goes up in flames.

upholding, *ppl. a.* Add: Hence **upho·ldingly** *adv.* (nonce poet. formation).

1934 KIPLING *Non nobis Domine* in *Verse* (1940) 512 O Power by whom we live—Creator, Judge and Friend, Upholdingly forgive.

upholster, *v.* Add: **2. b.** *fig.* Also, to provide with (fine or smart) clothes, to dress. (Earlier example.) Cf. *UPHOLSTERED *ppl. a.*

1873 'MARK TWAIN' *Gilded Age* xxxiii. 300 It had cost something to upholster those women.

upholstered, *ppl. a.* Add: *fig.* and *transf.* Also, of persons (*euphemistically*): (well-)-dressed; plump, stocky. See also *WELL-UPHOLSTERED *ppl. a.*

1924 WODEHOUSE *Leave it to Psmith* iii. 60 This sumptuously upholstered young woman. **1929** D. H. LAWRENCE *Pansies* 31 The upholstered dead that sit in deep arm-chairs. **1958** S. J. PERELMAN *Most of S. J. Perelman* 21 Where are those big, jolly, upholstered girls one used to see? **1976** R. LEHMANN *Sea-Grape Tree* 6 British travellers..stoutly upholstered middle-aged couples from the Midlands.

up Jenkins (ʌp dʒe·ŋkinz). [f. UP *adv.*¹ + the surname *Jenkins*.] The name of a parlour game resembling tip-it.

1889 K. GREENAWAY *Bk. Games* 25 *Up Jenkins.* The company divide into two parties and sit round a table. One party then puts their hands under the table and a shilling or other small article is placed in one of the palms. The other side then calls out: 'Up Jenkins!' and the players whose side has the shilling concealed must all place their closed hands on the table. The opposite side must then guess in which hand the shilling is concealed. **1916** D. H. LAWRENCE *Twilight in Italy* 193 Afterwards we played 'Up, Jenkins'. **1928** E. WAUGH *Decline & Fall* III. iv. 255 'I must ask you both to put your hands on the table in front of you,' said the warden. 'Like Up Jenkins,' said Margot faintly. **1933** S. JAMESON *Day Off* 83 They played Up Jenkins, in which a button is passed frenziedly from hand to hand. **1946** L. P. HARTLEY *Sixth Heaven* viii. 164 They..pressed their hands on the table as if for 'Up Jenkins'. **1951** S. SPENDER *World within World* iii. 144 Sometimes he would play childish games such as 'Up Jenkins'. **1981** P. THEROUX *Mosquito Coast* xvi. 212 We played Up Jenkins on the Gallery floor.

uplift, *sb.* Add: **3.** The support or lift gained from a garment that raises part of the body, esp. the bust; the (part of the) garment which achieves this.

1929 *Radio Times* 8 Nov. 435/3 A supporting stocking. .. Its gentle uplift massaging action has a beneficial effect upon the varicose veins. **1934** *Times* 22 June 17/6 The skirt covers neatly fitting trunks and clings closely to the figure; the top has a knitted uplift. **1955** J. P. DONLEAVY *Ginger Man* xxv. 297 Bras the uplift of which will put a new lust into the hearts of these citizens. **1957** *Daily Mail* 25 Oct. 10/4 When the vulgarity of too much uplift, too much emphasis on the female form finally overwhelmed us Dior sensed it before we did. **1959** *Housewife* June 22 The bra that gives a natural uplift.

4. An increase (in prices, wages, etc.).

1949 *Times* 26 Oct. 5/5 The whole conception of uplift.. assumes that the manufacturer of consumer goods has..

two prices, one for sales to the wholesaler and one for direct sale to the retailer. **1952** *Sunday Express* 15 Nov., These appliances are given an uplift of 100% between the maker and the public. **1955** *Canadian Tax Jrnl.* III. 99 If the price of the transaction differed [from normal]..an uplift would be applied to the actual sale price to determine price for tax purposes. **1962** E. GODFREY *Retail Selling & Organization* xv. 158 If goods normally purchased through a wholesaler are bought at a lower price direct from a manufacturer, they may be subject to uplift. **1979** *Daily Tel.* 1 Dec. 21 The Ford agreement.. consists of a 20·5 p.c. uplift in wages plus an extra 1 p.c. to cover an increase in the supplementary payment.

5. *attrib.* **a.** In sense 2.

1915 *Sphere* 23 Jan. 110/2, I find in an American paper a scornful reference to one of the 'uplift' magazines. **1930** J. BUCHAN *Castle Gay* ii. 32 Thomas was beginning to be much in request by uplift societies. **1940** R. S. LAMBERT *Ariel & all his Quality* ii. 50 The 'uplift' experiment..fell between..the professors of adult education..and the broadcasting experts. **1977** P. JOHNSON *Enemies of Society* ix. 122 Schneider and Dornbusch identified four common characteristics in the religion idealized in these uplift books: activism, optimism, individualism and pragmatism.

b. uplift bra(ssière), a brassière that provides uplift (sense 3 above).

1932 *Week-End Rev.* 1 Oct. 373/1 An 'up-lift' brassière would make you look rounder, of course. **1949** M. MEAD *Male & Female* iv. 80 Far enough removed from the uplift bras and the way Grandfather looks when Granddaughter wears one of them. **1957** J. D. MACDONALD *Executioners* (1959) vii. 134 She wore nothing under pants and blouse except an uplift bra. **1977** E. J. TRIMMER et al. *Visual Dict. Sex* (1978) iv. 51 The flavour of that era of uplift bras and pencil-skirts is still nostalgically preserved.

uplift, *v.* Add: **3. b.** More generally, to collect or pick up (something other than money); *spec.* of a bus: to take up (passengers). Chiefly *Sc.*

1961 *Alexander's (Midland) Bus Timetable, Falkirk* 171 Only passengers who are travelling beyond Milngavie Cross will be uplifted between Glasgow (Buchanan Street) and Milngavie Cross. **1967** E. RUDINGER *Wills & Probate* 109 The court is asked to confirm that the executors who have sworn the inventory are the persons entitled to uplift and administer the various items of estate listed in the inventory. **1968** 'S. JAY' *Sleepers can Kill* xvii. 175 Somebody..has left a message for Felson. The objective is to uplift the message without being detected. **1976** *Buses* XXVII. 421 Near-empty SBG buses, none allowed to uplift potential passengers, glide into town. **1982** G. HAMMOND *Game* xii. 129 The letter was waiting at the airport for him. I checked up yesterday, and the letter was uplifted.

4. b. = RAISE *v.*[1] 32. Cf. sense *4 of the sb.

1962 E. GODFREY *Retail Selling & Organization* xv. 158 The Inland Revenue Department uplifts the price to what the goods would have cost had they been purchased through a wholesaler. **1971** *Timber Trades Jrnl.* 14 Aug. 45/2 Devaluation of sterling..technically should have had the effect of uplifting import prices by 16·7%.

uplifter. Add: **3.** *N. Amer.* One engaged in social reform; a 'do-gooder'.

1923 [see *DO-GOOD]. **1935** S. LEWIS *It can't happen Here* xvii. 191 Social workers, both amateurs and long-trained professional uplifters. **1971** J. H. GRAY *Red Lights on Prairies* iv. 97 As the publisher of the paper explained when uplifters complained..it was no part of the responsibility of a newspaper to police the morals of its tenants.

upli·ftment. Chiefly *Black* and *Indian English.* [f. UPLIFT *v.* + -MENT: see UP- 2.] The action or process of improving or raising to a new standard; *spec.* amelioration of economic or social conditions; the result of this.

1926 *Brit. Weekly* 15 Apr. 46/3 Native women of the educated class might be potent influences in the upliftment and betterment of their people. **1973** *Caribbean Contact* Feb. 11/3 A company of West Indians formed for the economic upliftment of the people of the region. **1976** *Nigerian Chron.* 18 Aug. 12/2 Mr Onette congratulated the people of Osomba..for their initiative towards educational up-liftment in their community. **1979** P. NIHALANI et al. *Indian & Brit. Eng.* I. 187 The upliftment of the rural areas should be a top priority for the government. **1984** *Times* 25 Aug. 5/2 His immediate priorities would be the economic and educational upliftment of his people.

u·plight. [UP- 2.] = next.

1982 *Program 1982/83* (Erco trade catal.) 56 Up-lights are the free-standing version of downlights. They illuminate the ceiling. **1983** *Homes & Gardens* Mar. 92/2 We decided to have uplights to cast light on to the fabric.

u·plighter. [UP- 2.] A light placed or designed to throw illumination upward.

1969 *Queen* 17–30 Sept. 96/2 Rotaflex uplighters in plain black cans, shining on, say, a picture. **1974** *Habitat Catal.* 116/1 Uplighter..to stand on the floor or a low table to light a strategically placed plant or shapely object. **1978** J. KRANTZ *Scruples* iii. 67 He installed three ten-foot-tall Kentia palms he got wholesale at Kind's, lit them from underneath with uplighters. **1983** *Homes & Gardens* Nov. 137 Best lighting for watching television comes from an uplighter placed behind the set; it cuts down glare and avoids reflections on the screen.

u·plink. [UP- 2.] A communication link for transmissions from the earth to a satellite, weather balloon, etc. Freq. *attrib.*

1968 W. M. GRIGGS *AMSS Prototype Radiosonde* (Rep. AD-680-409) 4 The radiosonde is designed to perform two functions... As a transponder, it must receive the uplink range tones. **1975** *Sci. Amer.* June 127/1 Since its launch in late 1972 it has offered a repeater service open to all, with an uplink at two meters and a downlink at 10. **1982** *New Scientist* 9 Sept. 682/1 These 'uplink' signals are at frequencies between 5·9 and 6·4 gigahertz.

uplook, *sb.* (Earlier example.)

1836 T. POWER *Impressions of Amer.* II. 235 The Virginian, tall of stature,..with an open up-look.

Upmann (*ʊ*·pmăn). The proprietary name of a make of (Havana) cigar.

[**1878** *Trade Marks Jrnl.* 16 Jan. 59 H. Upmann... Henry Upmann and William Rocholl, trading as H. Upmann and Co., Havana, Cuba; cigar manufacturers. Manufactured tobacco, cigars. **1912** *Official Gaz.* (U.S. Patent Office) 15 Oct. 770/1 H. Upmann & Co., Habana, Cuba... Cigars.] **1969** N. FREELING *Tsing-Boum* xxi. 148 He..had a cigar going, an Upmann that could have been made of tightly-rolled hundred-franc notes. **1979** A. SCHOLEFIELD *Point of Honour* 142 He was dispensing Upmanns from a humidor.

u·pmanship. *colloq.* = *one-upmanship* s.v. *ONE *numeral a., pron.*, etc. 29* c.

1962 *Spectator* 23 Nov. 837/2 (Advt.), Upmanship is the art of being one up on all the others. **1967** *Ibid.* 25 Aug. 212/2 He obviously thought I was trying upmanship on him before that word had been invented. **1976** *Casper* (Wyoming) *Star-Tribune* 29 June 19/1 (*caption*) Hospital upmanship: My Doc' is better'n yours! **1980** *Brit. Med. Jrnl.* 6 Sept. 666/1 In a moment of inspired upmanship this young moonlighting casualty officer had quietly dropped the word that he was a famous specialist in exotic diseases.

u·p-market, *a.* and *adv.* [UP *prep.*[2]] **A.** *adj.* **1.** Of merchandise, etc.: characteristic of or designed for the more expensive end of the market; superior, expensive, 'quality'.

1972 *Times* 28 June 14/4 Glass has still, apparently, a more up-market image than plastic. **1974** *Daily Tel.* 17 Sept. 6 An 'up-market' £1,950 version of the Austin Allegro, hand-finished by the Vanden Plas coachbuilders. **1976** *Daily Mail* (Hull) 30 Sept. 18/3 Sarila Kitchens are the ultimate in luxury and design. Naturally, they are also up-market in price. **1980** *National Times* (Austral.) 24 Aug. 4/3 Franchised lines, apart from the usual T-shirts, badges, posters and dolls run up to a range of $200 couturier ensembles and an upmarket line of cosmetics.

2. *transf.* and *fig.*

1976 *Listener* 6 May 584/1, I cannot allow other people to have all the most up-market remarks. **1979** *Early Music* Jan. Suppl. 13/3 Trust House Forte's up-market evenings..are presenting several early music groups in 1979. **1981** *Times Lit. Suppl.* 30 Jan. 117/5 Linguistic shamanism is respected, for there have been some distinguished practitioners. Sir Ernest Gowers was an up-market shaman. So was H. W. Fowler.

B. *adv.* Towards the more expensive end of the market. Also *transf.* and *fig.*

1975 *Daily Tel.* 12 Apr. 12/4 Lyons-Tetley go up-market a bit with their Red Label and Orange Label [tea]. **1978** *South China Morning Post* 24 Nov. 14/7 Protectionism will increase in European Common Market countries so that Hongkong will have to diversify upmarket. **1980** *Times Lit. Suppl.* 24 Oct. 1206/2 Even the secessionist New English Art Club moved up-market to become a nursery for the Academy, with its paintings of..the pleasing and the picturesque. **1983** *Daily Tel.* 14 Mar. 11/8 Slightly upmarket of the rest of the channel's evening fare, *Omnibus* (BBC-1) has settled for an Everyman figure.. as presenter. **1984** W. GOLDING *Paper Men* xi. 125 To contemplate the nature of predestinate insects or, moving up-market, Lobsters and crabs.

Also as *v. trans.*, to raise the standing of (a product) in the market, esp. by advertisement or actual improvement. Hence **up-ma·rketing** vbl. sb.

1972 *Times* 25 Aug. 7 Mathew Clark wants to upmarket Noilly Dry French, plugging heavily the drink's provenance compared with that of Italian Martini and Cinzano. **1975** *Listener* 4 Dec. 735/3 Leyland..decided the group's future lay in..improving its cars and charging more for them... It would take a lot of up-marketing to keep it [*sc.* Leyland] at even half its present size. **1977** *Daily Mirror* 21 Mar. 12/2 The British Sausage Bureau, in short, is trying to up-market its succulent product. **1980** *Times Lit. Suppl.* 19 Sept. 1030/4 In 1819 Harris, now joined by his son, sensed the way trade was going and boldly up-marketed his nursery books still further.

upon, *adv.* Add: **1. b.** (Later examples after biblical use: see quot. 1611.) Cf. CLOTHE *v.* 9.

1895 L. JOHNSON *Poems* 34 Old ramparts, gray and stern; But comely clothed upon With wealth of moss and fern. **1930** *Month* Mar. 230 Ancient stones, like Ezekiel's dry bones, need to be clothed upon.

u·p-patient. [UP *a.*; Cf. UP *adv.*[2] 7 a.] An in-patient in hospital no longer confined to bed.

1952 'R. GORDON' *Doctor in House* xi. 119 Two up-patients, dressing-gowned old gentlemen. **1959** *Manch. Guardian* 19 Aug. 5/6 Topham is an up-patient... We started him with a couple of hours up each morning. **1976** J. GRENFELL *Joyce Grenfell requests Pleasure* (1977) xi. 163 Up-patients sat on the grass on grey army blankets.

upper, *sb.* Add: **1. a.** (Earlier example.)

1789 G. PARKER *Life's Painter of Variegated Characters* v. 36 If the top and leg of a jack-boot were joined to a dog-skin upper and a buff sole.

c. (Further examples.) Formerly in fig. phr. *to walk* (etc.) *on one's uppers.* Also *down on one's uppers.*

1886 *Lantern* 8 Sept. 4/3 The Royal Street actors who are walking on their uppers, must mourn..when they.. hear of some of the boys spending 200 a week yachting. **1895** ROBERTS & MORTON *Adv. Arthur Roberts* xi. 143, I know two actors who were left, as the term goes, 'on their uppers', in a town in the heart of the Midlands. **1899** 'J. FLYNT' *Tramping with Tramps* I. v. 117 I's been a moocher, an' now I's shatin' on me uppers. **1903** *Judy* 9 Dec. 577/1 'What would you do if you were in my shoes?' 'Eh? Oh, then I should be fairly down on my uppers.' **1918** *Blackw. Mag.* May 602/2 We are pretty well down on our uppers as regards transport. **1985** D. WILLIAMS *Wedding Treasure* ii. 31 My guess is the swine's on his uppers... He's going for the ten thousand a year.

2. b. *ellipt.* for upper deck, storey, berth, etc.

1938 'GIRALDUS' *Merry Matloe Again* 179 Just sit down opposite the hatch and contemplate your new shipmates as, one by one, they troop on the 'upper'. **1955** F. O'CONNOR *Wise Blood* i. 17 The man in the station..had sold him a berth..an upper one... A sign said to get the porter to let you into the uppers. **1968** *Globe & Mail* (Toronto) 13 Feb. 30/6 (Advt.), Well located duplex with extra large upper. **1969** *Down Beat* 17 Apr. 16/1 Two chartered sleeping cars carried the men across the United States like royalty—and nobody ever had to take an upper.

4. a. *Public school slang.* A pupil of the upper school.

1929 J. BUCHAN *Courts of Morning* II. viii. 379 The Eton Beagles in the fields beyond Slough, and himself and Lariarty, both newly become uppers, struggling desperately to keep up with the field. **1937** [see *PI-JAW *sb.*].

b. *colloq.* An upper-class person.

1955 T. H. PEAR *Eng. Social Differences* iii. 90 While many people use 'person' indiscriminately, some 'uppers' employ it chiefly in a derogatory sense. **1967** [see *LOWER *a.* (*sb.*) 3 a]. **1968** *Economist* 27 Apr. p. v/1 The genuine uppers' genuine feeling of superiority.

u·pper, *sb.*[2] *slang* (orig. *U.S.*). [f. UP *v.* + -ER[1]; cf. *UP *a.* 5.] **1.** A drug (esp. an amphetamine) which has a stimulant or euphoric effect, often in the form of a pill.

1968 *Current Slang* (Univ. S. Dakota) Fall 50 *Upper*, type of drug that makes you feel active. Amphetamine is a commonly used stimulant of this kind. **1969** FABIAN & BYRNE *Groupie* (1970) xix. 133, I wasn't used to so many uppers all at once. **1976** 'R. ROSTAND' *D'Artagnan Signature* vii. 45 The trained-down leanness..likely came from epsom salts and uppers. **1981** 'D. SHANNON' *Murder most Strange* ii. 52, I want all your pills, man, all the uppers and downers you got.

2. *transf.* and *fig.*

1973 *Time* 1 Jan. K2 It certainly is a relief to know that State 2 is an upper; but by that time, who cares? **1976** *National Observer* (U.S.) 27 Nov. II. 22/3 Shorty's alchemy with rum and other potions produces something called a Goombay Smash that is a definite upper. **1977** *Time* 18 Apr. 45/2 Singing is a real upper. It makes me feel dizzy and energetic.

upper, *a.* Add: **I. 3. a.** *fig.* Also in phr. (*crushed*, etc.) *between the upper and the nether millstones*, between two irreconcilable opposing forces.

1902 G. B. SHAW *Mrs Warren's Profession* Pref. p. xxi, Thus am I crushed between the upper millstone of Mr Redford, who thinks me a libertine, and the nether popular critic, who thinks me a prude. **1921** L. STRACHEY *Queen Victoria* v. 167 His position, crushed between the upper and the nether millstones, grew positively unbearable. **1948** F. R. COWELL *Cicero & Roman Republic* vii. 131 [A] Consul..was a link between Senate and People, responsible to both, an unenviable situation between an upper and a nether millstone. **1950** A. BRYANT *Age of Elegance* ii. 40 Not only were the French Armies of Portugal and the North..marching to the fortress's relief, but Soult and Joseph with 60,000 men were threatening Madrid from Valencia. The British were in danger of being crushed between the upper and nether millstones.

7. *upper cut* (earlier example); also in *Cricket*, a cut that sends the ball up (*obs.* exc. *humorously*).

1842 *Spirit of Times* 17 Sept. 339/2 Giving him a sharp upper cut as he fell. **1865** *F. Lillywhite's Guide to Cricketers* 128 [He] has..made some good scores this year, his 'upper cut' being particularly effective. **1872** *Baily's Mag.* June 44 Smith's plucky innings was considerably helped by hits known as 'upper cuts'. **1955** A. ROSS *Australia 55* 133 Two upper-cuts sent second and third slip on futile chases to the boundary.

II. 8. a. (Further examples, of domestic servants.) Cf. *UPSTAIRS *a.* c.

1776 J. WOODFORDE *Diary* 3 June (1924) I. 182 One of them is to be an upper servant and she lived very lately with Mr. Howes. **1783** *Ibid.* 24 Mar. (1924) II. 65 Betty, my Upper Maid stayed at home being Washing Week. *a* **1817** JANE AUSTEN *Persuasion* (1818) III. vi. 102 Her upper-housemaid and laundry-maid. **1872** [see *QUAVER *v.* 3 b]. **1958** R. WILLIAMS *Culture & Society* III. 329 That kind of confidence which will enable the upper servants to supervise and direct the lower servants.

b. *Comb.* (Predic. examples of *upper class.*) Also used to indicate finer gradations in the social scale, as *upper-lower, -middle, -upper, -working* (class); see also *UPPER-MIDDLE-

CLASS *a.* and *sb.* as main entry. Also *upper bourgeois.*

1907 M. BERENSON *Let.* 6 Mar. (1983) 139 So you aren't a 'County Family'..'not knowing yet' whether you're Upper Middle or only Middle. **1938** E. BOWEN *Death of Heart* III. vi. 420 Oh, shut up, darling... Don't be so upper class. **1940** HARRISSON & MADGE *War begins at Home* v. 103 The response was best from the upper and middle classes; whilst the upper-working or artisan class supplied its quota. **1955** T. H. PEAR *Eng. Social Differences* iii. 88 Radio-copies of lower-middle, upper-lower and middle-lower speech. **1955** *Caribbean Quarterly* IV. II. 109 The 'upper-upper' French Creoles who number under 200 consider all the rest to be of mixed ancestry. **1964** T. B. BOTTOMORE *Elites & Society* iv. 82 The postwar reforms of recruitment to the French higher civil service ..have changed the ethos of education for the administrative elite—have made it more 'managerial' and less 'upper class'. **1964** C. BARBER *Ling. Change Present-Day Eng.* ii. 18 The general pattern of usage is as follows: *pudding* (upper and upper-middle), *sweet* (middle), [etc.]. **1967** M. ARGYLE *Psychol. Interpersonal Behaviour* iv. 83 A development in the British class system during the 1950s was the emergence of an upper working class. **1970** P. DICKINSON *Seals* vi. 123 The harryings of ninety sets of upper-bourgeois parents. **1974** H. WAUGH *Parrish for Defence* (1975) xxxix. 182 You're closer to where it's at if you're only upper middle class than if you're upper upper.

absol. (Later example.)

1967 N. FREELING *Strike out where not Applicable* 74 She was too much upper to say cheers.

c. *upper-bracket* adj., belonging to or characteristic of the higher section of a (social) scale; upper-class, wealthy, influential; cf. (*income*) *bracket* s.v. *BRACKET *sb.* 5 c; also *upper-income* adj.

[**1943** Upper bracket: see *BRACKET *sb.* 5 c.] **1945** S. LEWIS *Cass Timberlane* 157, I go there all the time, to shave the upper-bracket crooks when they got too big a hang-over to walk. **1957** O. NASH *You can't get there from Here* 130 And, should upper-bracket dreamers wake, Squab o' Neptune, and Plankton Steak. **1960** N. MITFORD *Don't tell Alfred* ix. 98 He's all set for the upper-income group—tax free of course. **1973** J. ROSSITER *Manipulators* xiv. 138 Luckhurst's overcoat and suit had been expensively tailored, the watch on his wrist an upper-bracket Rolex. **1978** *Detroit Free Press* 16 Apr. 8A/1 The migration of middle and upper-income whites out of the central cities has become a headlong flight.

9. b. With an ordinal number, designating: (*a*) the senior division of a class or form at school, as *Upper Sixth* (*form*), etc.; (*b*) the upper division of a second-class honours degree.

1856 C. M. YONGE *Daisy Chain* I. ix. 90 They are a low, ungentlemanly lot just now, about sixth and upper fifth form. **1858** J. A. SYMONDS *Let.* 6 June (1967) I. 145 Bosanquet is an Upper Sixth Boy and nearly a Monitor. **1905** R. BROOKE *Lett.* (1968) 29, I decided that Swinburne would be a great aesthetic blessing to the starved Upper Sixth. **1935** C. ISHERWOOD *Mr. Norris changes Trains* i. 7 An incident..To do with the upper fourth form classroom. **1981** E. NORTH *Dames* ii. 24 The form previously called Middle Five B would now be known as Upper Fifth. **1982** *Oxford Times* 25 June 11/3 He decided he wanted to see America, after graduating at Oxford with an Upper Second in Geography.

III. 11*. **upper air** = **upper atmosphere*; **upper atmosphere,** the upper part of the earth's atmosphere; now *spec.* that above the troposphere; **upper berth** *U.S.*, the higher of two bunks set one above the other, usu. in a boat, sleeping-car, etc.; **upper circle,** the tier of seats above the dress circle in a theatre; cf. CIRCLE *sb.* 11 b; **upperclassman** *U.S.*, a junior or senior student in school or college (as opp. FRESHMAN).

[**1877** *Q. Jrnl. Meteorol. Soc.* III. 447 It would not.. do to imagine that every cloud in the rear of another cloud was cirrus, and yet it might be a distinct upper air current.] **1895** *Ibid.* XXI. 182 The scheme of exploring the upper air by means of small balloons was first proposed by Geheimrat A. Meydenbaur. **1957** *Encycl. Brit.* XXII. 883B/1 In meteorology the exploration of the upper air, using instruments carried by balloons, kites or aircraft, is an important part of observational technique. **1979** G. B. NAVARRA *Atmosphere, Weather & Climate* x. 357 Aircraft provide a highly mobile way of gathering data in the upper air. **1895** *Q. Jrnl. R. Meteorol. Soc.* XXI. 182 The Upper Atmosphere.—On July 7th, 1894, Dr. Assmann set free at Charlottenburg a balloon, equipped with self-registering apparatus for the determination of meteorological data in the higher regions of the atmosphere. **1933** *Discovery* Dec. 359/2 There is a monthly sequence of intense magnetic activity when wireless waves are absorbed and not reflected by the upper atmosphere. **1976** *Physics Bull.* Dec. 554/2 The author looks at the earth's upper atmosphere, taking the tropopause as its lower boundary. **1894** F. M. CRAWFORD upper berth. **1917** J. HUSBAND *Story of Pullman Car* 29 The upper berth might be closed in the day time and also serve as a receptacle for bedding. **1829** *Harlequin* 20 June 46 The upper circle and lower gallery were reserved for company to view the entertainment. **1889** *Theatre* May 292 The house consists of four tiers, pit and stalls, dress circle, upper circle, and gallery. **1926** A. CONAN DOYLE in *Liberty* 18 Dec. 9/1 Amberley..had taken two upper-circle seats at the Haymarket Theater. **1871** L. H. BAGG *4 Years at Yale* 70 Only a few upper-class men will be found there. **1897** [in Dict., sense 9]. **1933** F. SCOTT FITZGERALD *Let.* 26 June (1964) 502 Insofar as upperclassmen are concerned I saw a rather depressed runt at the Yale game. **1978** J. IRVING *World according to Garp* ii. 48 He befriended Garp in a very decent fashion while he was an upperclassman at Steering and Garp was just starting out.

III. 12. upper crust. c. (Earlier example of sense 'a hat'.)

1829 P. EGAN *Boxiana* 2nd Ser. II. 461 Ward.. threw his upper-crust into the ring.

e. For 'Chiefly *U.S. colloq.* (also *attrib.*)' read: *colloq.* (orig. *U.S.*). Freq. *attrib.* or as *adj.* (Further examples.)

1863 G. DU MAURIER *Let.* May in *Young G. du Maurier* (1951) 204 All Millais' [paintings] are upper crust. **1878** W. S. GILBERT *H.M.S. Pinafore* II. 31 Two tender babes I nussed: One was of low condition, The other, upper crust, A regular patrician. **1957** *New Statesman* 19 Oct. 1/2 Views which are commonplace in upper-crust circles. **1966** D. FRANCIS *Flying Finish* vii. 82 One particular horse from an upper crust stud. **1973** M. AMIS *Rachel Papers* 116, I stalked up to the door and rapped, with an upper-crust rap, on the knocker.

f. Hence **upper-crusty** *a.*, aristocratic, (socially) superior.

1977 *Time* 26 Dec. 1/1 The politicians' wives, looking upper-crusty. **1980** *TWA Ambassador* Oct. 77/3 We lived in Garden City, the upper-crusty part.

13*. upper dog. [After UNDERDOG.] The victorious party in a contest; the one who has the upper hand or a position of superiority. Cf. *OVERDOG. *rare.*

1903 G. BOWLES in *Parl. Debates* 18 Feb. 224 If it came to a question of force, we should always be the 'upper dog' in Persia. **1940** 'G. ORWELL' *Inside Whale* 82 One has got to change sides when the underdog becomes an upperdog. **1971** *Daily Progress* (Charlottesville, Va.) 30 Mar. 4/2, I am for the upperdog—the achiever, the succeeder.

18. upper ten. a. (*b*) (Earlier example.)

1846 A. J. H. DUGANNE *Daguerreotype Miniature* 20 Major Peyton Florence was held in great reverence by the 'upper ten'.

b. upper-tendom (earlier example).

1848 F. A. BUCK *Yankee Trader in Gold Rush* (1930) 13, I suppose you and those other families left out constitute an *Upper Ten-dom*, in the place.

upper-middlebrow, *sb.* (*a.*) [UPPER *a.* 8 b.] One whose cultural interests lie between those of the middlebrow and those of the highbrow. Also *attrib.* or as *adj.*

1956 R. CONQUEST *New Lines* p. xiv, A sort of upper-middle-brow equivalent of the horror-comic. **1959** *Economist* 28 Feb. 787/1 Magazines for upper middle-brows. **1974** *Country Life* 14 Mar. 588/2 The middle to-upper-middle brow range that Chichester programmes now generally encompass. **1977** *Listener* 11 Aug. 170/1 In *Life* magazine, nearly 30 years ago, an American critic said: What culture and civilized living we have today is provided by the interaction of..the aesthetic radical highbrow and the somewhat more conservative upper-middlebrows.

upper-middle-class, *a.* and *sb.* [UPPER *a.* 8 b.] **A.** *adj.* Of, pertaining to, or characterized by the class of polite society next below the upper class.

1872 *Times* 26 Dec. 5/4 Upper and upper middle-class society is represented in all its grades. **1906** GALSWORTHY *Man of Property* I. i. 3 Those privileged to be present at a family festival of the Forsytes have seen..an upper middle-class family in full plumage. **1949** W. L. WARNER in M. Fortes *Social Structure* 4 Excerpts from the Total Configuration of an upper-middle-class doctor illustrate how this technique is used. **1967** M. ARGYLE *Psychol. Interpersonal Behaviour* iv. 80 English upper-middle-class speech includes considerable understatement; a person who fails to follow this convention is regarded as boastful. **1982** 'W. HAGGARD' *Mischief-Makers* ii. 20 Willy's skin was the colour of coal... He thought of himself as an upper-middle-class Englishman.

B. *sb.* **1.** Usu. unhyphened. This class itself, or its members.

c **1885** M. DARWIN *Let.* in G. Raverat *Period Piece* (1952) vi. 98 The upper middle class think they are acting rightly by over-protecting their daughters. **1891** [see MIDDLE CLASS *sb.*]. **1903** G. GISSING *Private Papers H. Ryecroft* 210 A lad whose education ranks him with the upper middle class. **1923** A. BENNETT *Riceyman Steps* I. ii. 5 He had the air neither of a bookman nor of a member of the upper-middle class. **1955** H. ROTH *Sleeper* xii. 99 Stamford, Connecticut, is a typical transplanting ground of the upper middle class. **1965** R. WILLIAMS in *Tribune* 5 Mar. 1/5 The English upper-middle class.

2. *ellipt.* as *upper-middle*, a member of the upper middle class. Usu. in *pl.*

1955 [see *middle-middle* s.v. *MIDDLE *a.* 6]. **1967** *Economist* 18 Feb. 607/2 In Birmingham, Manchester, Liverpool, the upper-middles do not choose to live in the city. **1978** R. WESTALL *Devil on Road* xv. 111 When my parents quarrel, they..fight in hoarse whispers. But like a lot of upper-middles..Derek and Susan let it all hang out.

Upper Vo·ltan, *a.* and *sb.* [f. *Upper Volta* (see def.) + -AN: cf. UPPER *a.* 1.] **A.** *adj.* Of or pertaining to Upper Volta, an inland republic in West Africa (a former French colony whose independence was recognized in 1960, now called Burkina). **B.** *sb.* A native or inhabitant of Upper Volta. Cf. *VOLTAIC *sb.* and *a.*[2]

1972 *N.Y. Times* 28 Nov. 2/4 Horsemen from the Upper Voltan fringes of the Sahara called out, 'Pa! Pa! Pompidou!' **1975** *Congress. Q.: Editorial Research Rep.* (Daily Service) 7 May, For many Upper Voltans the real villain of the piece is not Mali but France. **1976** *Facts on File* 17 Apr. 269/3 Upper Voltan trade unions had welcomed the formation of the new government. **1983** *Times* 25 Jan. 6/1 There are more than 500,000 immigrants from Niger, as well as..Togolese, Beninese, Upper Voltans and Chadians.

uppie (*ʌ*·pi). *slang.* [-Y[6], -IE.] = *UPPER *sb.*[2]

1966 *Sunday Times* (Colour Suppl.) 13 Feb. 35/4 *Uppies and downies*, pep pills and tranquillisers. **1975** J. F. BURKE *Death Trick* (1976) ii. 22 There's nothing in the box but a few uppies. I haven't got a regular prescription.

u·ppishly, *adv.* [f. UPPISH *a.* + -LY[2].] **a.** *Cricket.* Of the ball, etc.: in a slightly upward direction, esp. so as to give some chance of a catch.

1904 P. F. WARNER *How we recovered Ashes* 109 Just after he had passed his hundred, he sent one uppishly through the slips. **1955** A. ROSS *Australia 55* 137 Hutton ..then turned Archer a shade uppishly through the short-legs. **1963** *Times* 11 Jan. 10/6 Guest..drew one false stroke out of Dexter which went uppishly past gully.

b. In an uppish (sense 2 d) manner.

1911 G. B. SHAW *Blanco Posnet* Pref. 307 The majority of the Committee began by taking its work uppishly and carelessly. **1960** M. SPARK *Ballad Peckham Rye* vii. 141 'Miss Merle Coverdale, one of my unofficial helpers,' Dougal said uppishly. **1981** *Times Lit. Suppl.* 26 June 727/2 Rowland Lacy, wooer of the uppishly poised Rose.

uppity (*ʌ*·pĭti), *a. colloq.* (orig. and chiefly *U.S.*). [f. UP *adv.*[1] + *-it-* + -Y[1]: cf. *BIGGITY *a.*] Above oneself, self-important, 'jumped-up'; arrogant, haughty, pert, putting on airs. Cf. UPPISH *a.* 2 d. **a.** *attrib.*

1880 J. C. HARRIS *Uncle Remus* 86 Hit wuz wunner deze yer uppity little Jack Sparrers, I speck. **1933** *Times Lit. Suppl.* 9 Nov. 776/2 Grammy is living contentedly enough with an 'uppity' young creature named Penny. **1952** F. L. ALLEN *Big Change* II. viii. 130 The effect of the automobile revolution was especially noticeable in the South, where one began to hear whites complaining about 'uppity niggers' on the highways, where there was no Jim Crow. **1982** B. CHATWIN *On Black Hill* v. 28 He had a head for figures and a method for dealing with 'uppity' tenants.

b. *predic.*

1932 *Sun* (Baltimore) 23 Aug. 6/2 [She] could have plenty o' friends. The trouble with her is she thinks folks too common to bother with unless they're too uppity to bother with her. **1947** 'N. SHUTE' *Chequer Board* 68 They've been here alone too long, and they've got uppity. **1955** F. O'CONNOR *Wise Blood* v. 89, I reckon you ain't as uppity as you was last night. **1966** D. BAGLEY *Wyatt's Hurricane* i. 27 The Navy is trying to build up Cap Sarrat as a substitute for Guantanamo in case Castro gets uppity and takes it from them. **1973** P. WHITE *Eye of Storm* viii. 381, I came prepared to rough it... It's Dorothy who grows uppity if all the cons aren't mod.

Hence **u·ppitiness,** the quality of being 'uppity'; an instance of this.

1935 H. L. DAVIS *Honey in Horn* x. 145 Clay's bravery and uppitiness had done nothing. **1966** *Listener* 27 Oct. 622/1 She had decided that Joyce was 'pretentious' and 'under-bred'... But who was Virginia Woolf to talk (in this purely literary sense) of 'uppitiness'? **1975** *Ibid.* 9 Oct. 479/1 Few delegates seemed versed in *Private Eye* nomenclature and would, anyway, disapprove of such uppityness. **1982** R. BARNARD *Death & Princess* ii. 17 Joe may appreciate my couthness..but he can sniff out uppitiness.

up-pouring: see *UP- 7 (*b*).

u·p-push. *rare.* [UP- 2.] A pushing upwards.

1910 J. W. GREENE *Clin. Course Dental Prosthesis* 46 There is now a little general up-push all along the yielding line. **1940** *Sun* (Baltimore) 5 Apr. 23/1 (*heading*) Rails continue up-push in bonds. **1960** R. W. MARKS *Dymaxion World B. Fuller* 28/1 If such a man took the proper headlong attitude, with respect to air resistance, the amount of up-push required to keep him plummeting forward should be no more than that supplied by his leg muscles to give him his initial altitude.

upraised, *ppl. a.* Add: **2.** Of the eyes: (earlier examples).

1707 E. SETTLE *Siege of Troy* I. ii. 9 Hail, beauteous goddess, all divine, Our up-rais'd eyes and hearts all thine. **1817** COLERIDGE *Biog. Lit.* II. xxiv. 309 The upraised Eye views only the starry Heaven.

upraising, *vbl. sb.* (Later examples.)

1926 *Daily Colonist* (Victoria, B.C.) 19 Jan. 17/4 The upraising going on in the underground working is progressing very satisfactorily. **1936** BELLOC *Battle Ground* xi. 225 Some said he was Elias, come back to the upraising of men.

upra·te, *v.* [UP- 4.] *trans.* To raise to a higher standard, to upgrade; *spec.* to improve the performance of (a mechanical device or process); to increase the value of (a commodity, grant, etc.).

1965 *National Observer* (U.S.) 8 Feb. 15/1 The first stage of the Saturn 1-B is similar..except that its engines have been uprated to produce more power. **1968** *Listener* 1 Aug. 159/1 At a time when petrol prices were rather unstable, Esso uprated their Extra..to super or five-star grade. *a* **1974** R. CROSSMAN *Diaries* (1976) II. 372 Every two years we up-rate pensions in order to see that they don't lose their purchasing power. **1980** 'D. RUTHERFORD' *Turbo* ii. 29 The [car] springs had been uprated to carry the extra weight. **1984** *Daily Tel.* 25 Jan. 17/4 Government plans to uprate early leavers' pensions by up to 5 p.c.

Hence **upra·ted** *ppl. a.*, **upra·ting** *vbl. sb.* and *ppl. a.*

1967 *Jane's Surface Skimmer Systems 1967–68* 116/2 More recent models are fitted with the uprated..version of this marine diesel. **1968** *Listener* 1 Aug. 159/1 The recent mass switch to five-star petrol may..be partly due to the uprating of Extra. *a* **1974** R. CROSSMAN *Diaries* (1976) II. 372, I can tell you we should now expect a pension up-rating Bill to be published within the next fortnight. **1981** *Sunday Express* (Colour Suppl.) 14 June 21 An uprated sports suspension makes sure that all this extra power is kept under control.

‖ **uprava** (*u*prā·vă). [Russ., = authority.] In Imperial Russia: the executive board of a municipal council.

1870, 1886 [see ***DUMA**]. **1918** G. A. BIRKETT in R. Beazley et al. *Russia* III. iii. 432 Thirty-four provinces of European Russia..received self-government under the law of 1864. Each district had its own zémstvo council, which elected an executive board (*upráva*) sitting constantly and reporting to the annual meeting of the council. **1954** G. VERNADSKY *Hist. Russia* (ed. 4) x. 221 The representatives elected a board known as the *uprava* for a term of three years. **1967** H. SETON-WATSON *Russ. Empire 1801–1917* xi. 385 Every city was to have a municipal council..and they elected from their number an executive board (*uprava*).

upre·nd, *v. rare.* [UP- 4.] *trans.* To pull or tear up; to uproot.

1911 CHESTERTON *Ballad White Horse* I. 9 Earthquake swallowing earthquake Uprent the Wessex tree. **1932** *Sphere* 10 Dec. 435/1 (*caption*) A 130+ m.p.h. gale.. uprent the expedition's wireless mast.

upright, *sb.* Add: **3. b.** Also *spec.* in *Football*, a goalpost (as opp. to the crossbar).

1910 *Glasgow Herald* 14 Feb. 12/6 Barr..had little difficulty in placing the ball between the uprights. **1927** W. E. COLLINSON *Contemp. Eng.* 24 There were all the 'Kennings' in the sporting columns... Sphere for football, the uprights or sticks for the goalposts. **1951** *Sport* 27 Apr.–3 May 4/1 Bill rapped the upright with a penalty-kick. **1954** J. B. G. THOMAS *On Tour* 72 Morkel hit an upright with his conversion attempt. **1977** *Irish Press* 29 Sept. 18/2 Mick Lawlor's 24th minute left-footed drive.. hit the bottom part of the upright and rebounded into play.

f. *Basketry.* A plane used for shaving skeins to a required width.

1842 *Encycl. Brit.* IV. 429/1 In order to bring the split into a shape still more regular, it is passed through another implement called an upright, consisting of a flat piece of steel, each end of which is fashioned into a cutting edge. **1907** *Jrnl. Soc. Arts* 11 Jan. 190/1 For finer work the rod is split into three or more skeins by a cleaver; the splits are then successively drawn through a shave to remove the central pith and through an upright to render them uniform in width. **1929** A. G. KNOCK *Fine Willow Basketry* 37 For most skein work the skeins can be used after being shaved, but for..extra fine skein work of other kinds they are made uniform in width and as narrow as required by being drawn through the upright. **1961** L. G. ALLBON *Basic Basketry* iii. 18 Two specialized planes complete the process. The shave skims away the pith and renders the skein of even thickness; the upright straightens up the sides of the skein to an even width. **1981** T. W. BAGSHAWE *Basket Making in Bedfordshire* 16 (*caption*) Uprights for shaving to uniform width.

g. In a crossword puzzle, one of the clues whose solution is to be entered vertically in the frame.

1917 M. T. HAINSSELIN *Grand Fleet Days* xv. 96 How far have you got? Only as far as the 'uprights'—Belgium and Berlin. **1967** *Sci. Amer.* Sept. 268/2 The first stanza gives clues for two words, called the uprights, that are spelled vertically by the initial and final letters of the words to which clues are given by the numbered stanzas.

up-river, *a.* Add: orig. *U.S.* **1. a.** (Earlier examples.)

1774 I. LITCHFIELD *Jrnl.* 19 Apr. in W. J. Litchfield *Litchfield Family in Amer.* (1906) I. 334, I..ordered them to meet at upriver meeting house by the Sun an hour high Compleat in arms with 4 Days provision. **1857** *Trans. Mich. Agric. Soc.* VIII. 732 Charming villages are also rapidly springing into existence along the up river bank of the Grand River in this country.

b. (Earlier examples.)

1836 *Southern Lit. Messenger* II. 698/1, I had never imagined that any thing half so grand..awaited us on our up-river jaunt. **1857** W. CHANDLESS *Visit to Salt Lake* I. i. 1, I passed a few days there, waiting for an up-river boat.

up-ri·ver, *adv.* [UP *prep.*[2] 2.] Towards or in the direction of the source of a river.

1848 THOREAU in *Union Mag.* Nov. 220/2 Only a few axe-men have gone 'up river' into the howling wilderness which feeds it. **1887** *Harper's Mag.* Apr. 667/1 Logs were usually cut and hauled in summer-time to the banks of streams, often a long distance 'up-river'. **1929** BELLOC *Joan of Arc* ii. 38 He had been all day up-river in the marshes shooting quail. **1981** M. NABB *Death of Englishman* I. i. 25 Upriver the ghost of the Ponte Vecchio.. was straddling nothing.

uproarious, *a.* **2.** (Earlier example.)

1818 LADY GRANVILLE *Let.* 12 Aug. (1894) I. 135 We arrived here to dinner and found Hart in uproarious spirits.

uproll, *sb. rare.* [UP-2.] A rolling movement upwards.

a **1885** G. M. HOPKINS *Poems* (1967) 192 Moist..With the uproll and the downcarol of day and night delivering Water. **1984** A. PRICE *Sion Crossing* v. 83 David must have been..not quite senior enough to have sighted the gun and pulled the lanyard on the uproll—?

uproo·tedness. [f. UPROOTED *ppl. a.* + -NESS.] The state of being uprooted; a condition of severance from one's natural origins. Chiefly *fig.*

1927 J. LAVRIN *Russ. Lit.* v. 29 The negative features of a romantic type: uprootedness, fear and hatred of reality. **1954** KOESTLER *Invisible Writing* xxii. 247 What a refugee craves most is relief from his permanent feeling of uprootedness. **1974** O. COOK *Eng. Country House* i. 7 The contrast..between our uprootedness and the continuity and stability of the life led in the great mansion.

uprush, *sb.* (Earlier example.)

1871 BROWNING *Balaustion's Adventure* 31 In the fire-flash of the appalling sword, the uprush and the outburst.

upsaddle, *v.* (Earlier example.)

1838 in W. B. Boyce *Notes S. Afr. Affairs* vi. 148 Dingaan..inveigled them within an enclosure..just as they were up-saddling to depart, and massacred..every living soul of them.

‖ **upsara** (*ʊ*·psʊrā). *Indian Mythol.* Also **apsaras.** [Hindi *apsarā*, f. Skr. *apsarās.*] A celestial nymph, one of the wives of the Gandharvas (heavenly minstrels).

[**1846** J. T. THOMPSON *Dict. Hindee & Eng.* 17/2 *Ŭpsura*.., a female dancer or courtezan in *Swurg*, the hindoo paradise.] **1865** [see *Vedaic* adj. s.v. VEDA]. **1879** J. DOWSON *Class. Dict. Hindu Mythol. & Relig.* 20 The Apsarases..are fairylike beings... They are the rewards in Indra's paradise held out to heroes who fall in battle. **1892** KIPLING *Barrack-Room Ballads* 105 Above the dark *Upsaras* flew, beneath us plashed the blood. **1932** F. M. ATKINSON tr. H. de Wilman-Grabowska in J. Hackin et al. *Asiatic Mythol.* 113 The Apsarases are the recognized courtesans of the sky. **1968** B. WALKER *Hindu World* II. 143 In Hindu mythology the celestial nymph or *apsarā* (ap-sara, wet-flow) is a personification of the mists or clouds in the form of a beauteous damsel.

u·pscale, *a. U.S.* [UP *prep.*[2]] At the higher end of a (social) scale; superior, of a high quality; 'up-market'.

[**1945** *Newsweek* 2 Apr. 68/2 The Mullikin selling method, which he called 'upscaling', aimed to build up the idea that prefabricated houses were rich-looking, comfortable and permanent.] **1966** *One Hundred Basic Media Terms Defined* (Batten, Barton, Durstine & Osgood Inc. Media Dept.) 15 Downscale is a term used to describe a market or audience with above-average representation at the lower end of the socio-economic scale. Its opposite is 'upscale'. **1975** *New Yorker* 1 Dec. 44/1 A lot of advertising people don't think jazz fans have that all-important rage to consume. They don't think the jazz audience is 'up-scale' enough. **1977** P. STREVENS *New Orientations Teaching of English* xiii. 163 The *up-scale* lab has all typical facilities, plus full remote control of each student machine. **1983** *Chicago Sun-Times* 24 Nov. 110 '20-20' generally finishes behind 'Hill Street', whose up-scale audience it shares. **1984** *Christian Science Monitor* 2 Mar. 10/4 He cites Chi-Chi's Mexican restaurants as appealing to customers who want a bit more upscale atmosphere.

upset, *sb.* Add: **I. 3. c.** *Basketry.* Usu. **upsett.** The first section of waling, which sets the stakes firmly in place.

1907 T. OKEY in *Jrnl. Soc. Arts* 11 Jan. 191 (*caption*) It will be seen that the bye-stakes are merely inserted in the upsett. **1946** N. WYMER *Eng. Country Crafts* vii. 73 He then lets in the stiff 'uprights' and fastens them securely by working in several willows together to form the 'upset'. **1977** B. MAYNARD *Basketry* 19/2 You may like to start the upsett with one round of 4-rod wale.

upset, *v.* Add: **I. 1. e.** Usu. **upsett.** (Pa. t. and pa. ppl. also **upsetted.**) (*a*) To bend upwards (a stake) plaited into the base of a basket to form part of the frame for the side; (*b*) to form the 'upset' of (a basket); also *absol.*

1875 *Encycl. Brit.* III. 423/1 Osiers..are forced or 'scallumed', between the rods of the bottom from the edge towards the centre, and are turned up, 'upset', in the direction of the sides. **1907** T. OKEY in *Jrnl. Soc. Arts* 11 Jan. 190/2 If a foot is needed it is now put on by inserting the tops cut off from the stakes alongside the upsetted stakes. **1912** —— *Art of Basket-Making* vi. 33 Very coarse work..is upsetted with a pair instead of a wale. **1945** H. J. MASSINGHAM *Wisdom of Fields* v. 94 My basketer..after 'scalluming' the foreign rods..proceeded to wale up the sides, 'upsetting' as it is called, that is to say, building up the frame. **1977** B. MAYNARD *Basketry* 19/2 Stake up with the 40 side stakes, nip them at the edge of the base and tie them together tightly at the top. ..Upsett with six rounds of waling with No. 6 cane keeping the sides quite vertical.

upset, *pa. pple.* and *ppl. a.* Add: **4.** Physically disordered: said esp. of the stomach.

1973 C. LEACH *Send-Off* iii. 26 All you get is a burned back and an upset tummy. **1980** J. GARDNER *Garden of Weapons* III. iii. 249 Hoffer had sent him back because of his upset stomach.

upse·ttable, *a.* [f. UPSET *v.* + -ABLE.] Capable of being upset.

1930 R. C. HUTCHINSON *Thou Last Devil* xii. 167 He was, of course, in an upsettable mood. **1958** J. CANNAN *And be a Villain* vi. 145 'Hugh is..the most upsettable.' 'Couldn't agree more,' said Laura, 'thirteen's too young for funerals.' **1973** J. ELSOM *Erotic Theatre* iii. 53 In the dialogue, he tiptoes around the subject with the clumsy concern of Bertie Wooster, surrounded by upsettable coffee tables.

upsetting, *vbl. sb.* Add: **1. g.** *Basketry.* = ***UPSET** *sb.* 3 c; the formation of this.

1924 C. CRAMPTON *Canework* 13 *Upsetting*, the three or four rows [of weaving] worked at the commencement of the side..to 'set' the stakes in order. **1937** A. H. CRAMPTON *Raffia Wk. & Basketry* II. ii. 44 The first row of upsetting is worked with four canes, each passing in front of three stakes and behind one. **1953** A. G. KNOCK *Willow Basket-Wk.* 20 The number of rounds of waling forming the upsetting should, in fine basket-work, never be less than two, and seldom less than three. **1964** H. HODGES *Artifacts* x. 146 Waling was frequently used at the base of baskets in order to hold the upright stakes securely..in which case it is..referred to as upsetting.

upse·ttingly, *adv.* [f. UPSETTING *ppl. a.* + -LY[2].] In an upsetting manner; distressingly.

1926 'L. MALET' *Dogs of Want* vi. 155 Barbara Heritage's graceful silhouette had, somehow, become interchangeable with that of the Margate peroxide blonde of ten years back. Most upsettingly, but, also, most unjustifiably so. **1981** *Washington Post* 26 Apr. H9/1 To traditionalists it is upsettingly disheveled chaos.

upse·ttingness. [f. as prec. + -NESS.] The quality of being upsetting or disturbing.

1922 *Glasgow Herald* 23 Feb. 6/8, I have heard an old man speak with asperity of the 'upsettingness' of one who had adopted 'Mac', which his father had not used. **1949** G. RYLE *Concept of Mind* iv. 93 The degrees of upsettingness..are ordinarily characterised as degrees of violence. **1977** 'M. INNES' *Honeybath's Haven* xviii. 167 He had taken the reason to have been simply the general upsettingness of Melissa's turning up on them in that restaurant in Rome.

u·pshift, *sb.* Chiefly *U.S.* [UP- 2.] A movement upwards (esp. in various devices); *spec.* a change to a higher gear in a motor vehicle.

1839 [see UP- 2]. **1951** W. K. TOBOLDT et al. *Automatic Transmissions* iv. 129 The point of upshift from second to third and from third to fourth is excessively high. **1967** D. G. HAYS *Introd. Computational Linguistics* iv. 65 In standard paper-tape machines, a single capital letter is represented by three frames of tape, one for *upshift*, one for the character, and one for *downshift*. **1978** L. PRYOR *Viper* (1979) ix. 175, I missed one upshift and smashed gears.

u·pshift, *v.* Chiefly *U.S.* [UP- 4.] *intr.* To change into higher gear in a motor vehicle. Also used of the gear itself. Cf. ***SHIFT** *v.* 12 e. Hence **u·pshifting** *vbl. sb.*

1956 W. H. CROUSE *Automotive Mechanics* (ed. 3) xxiv. 513/2 If the brake band is released and at the same time the clutch is applied, the planetary set upshifts or goes into direct drive. *Ibid.* 515/2 Upshifting is controlled by both throttle opening and car speed. **1979** *Truck & Bus Transportation* 31 July 25/2 The flexibility..covers up an out-of-sequence ratio gap between 3rd and 4th gears. It is not at all apparent when upshifting..but it is noticeable when changing down.

upshoot, *sb.* **2.** (Earlier example.)

1850 W. HOWITT *Year-Bk. of Country* iv. 172 His oaks and elms in his park..what are they but the towering upshoots of his prejudices?

upsidaisy, *int.* Add: Also **ups-a-daisy, upsy daisy,** etc. (Later examples.)

1912 J. SANDILANDS *Western Canad. Dict. & Phrase-Bk.*, *Ups-a-daisy*, the tender words of the fond father when engaged in baby-jumping. **1934** D. L. SAYERS *Nine Tailors* I. ii. 61 Hoops-a-daisy, over she goes! **1940** *Horizon* Mar. 204 Come on, sonny, that's the way! Upsy-daisy! **1948** 'P. QUENTIN' *Run to Death* xx. 153 'Upsy daisy.' I picked her up, swung round and dumped her in the bath-tub. **1969** 'I. DRUMMOND' *Man with Tiny Head* vii. 92 'Upsidaisy,' said Jenny. 'No time to waste.' **1984** *New Yorker* 13 Feb. 125/1 The Great Rudner is.. given the most labyrinthine acrobatic choreography—a tortuous series of slithers, blind leaps, upsy-daisy lifts, and ass-over-heels floorwork.

Hence *ellipt.* as **u·psa** (and varr.) *int.*

1922 JOYCE *Ulysses* 491 Hoopsa! Don't fall upstairs. **1928** E. M. FORSTER *Life to Come* (1972) 141 'Upsa! Take care!' 'Upsa!' were some drops of brandy, which Conway had spilt.

upside. Add: **4.** *Comm.* An upward movement of share prices, etc.; also = **upside potential*. Also as *adj.*, esp. *upside potential*, the possibility of (gain from) such a rise in value.

1961 in WEBSTER. **1969** *Punch* 5 Feb. 206/1 The share price..needs to improve by only 50 per cent... Likewise, your original upside potential would be considerably higher. **1977** R. E. MEGILL *Introd. Risk Analysis* xvi. 175 Most parameters have up-side and down-side possibilities in addition to a most probable value. **1983** *Sunday Tel.* 27 Feb. 20/7 The share price..is vulnerable to even the most modest of bear rumour and..the downside substantially exceeds the upside. **1983** *Observer* 29 May 19/1

Could Pilkington Brothers..be poised to meet that dream investment criterion—downside risk low; upside potential high? **1984** *Times* 18 June 17/3 The upside should again be approximate yield parity with the equity market.

5. Quasi-*adv.* (or *prep.*). *upside* (one's) *head, knot,* (of a blow) on the head; esp. *to go upside* (someone's) *head,* etc., to strike on the head; to attack or fight. Chiefly *U.S. Blacks'*.

1970 H. E. Roberts *Third Ear* 14/2 *Upside one's head,* to fight someone. **1971** *Black Scholar* Apr.–May 35/2 This is until a white cop comes up and go upside your knot. **1973** E. Bullins *Theme is Blackness* 6 The TV slap of a pigstick upside some sister's head in front of an Alabama courthouse. **1976** *New Yorker* 8 Mar. 33/3 There is a further penalty of a hit upside the head for stiffing the toll collector. **1978** J. Wambaugh *Black Marble* iv. 28 When I busted her old man that time he went upside her head with a meat mallet.

upsilon. Add: **3.** *Particle Physics.* A meson with a mass of about 9·4 GeV that is thought to consist of a *b* quark and its antiquark; also *upsilon particle.* Freq. designated by *Υ*.

[**1976** *Daily Tel.* 7 Feb. 10/4 Upsilon was discovered by a team of scientists from Columbia University, New York, the Fermi Laboratory and the State University of New York. **1976** D. C. Hom et al. in *Physical Rev. Lett.* 24 May 1239/2 We suggest the name *Υ* (upsilon) be given either to the resonance at 6 GeV if confirmed or to the onset of high-mass dilepton physics.] **1977** S. W. Herb et al. in *Ibid.* 1 Aug. 255/2 Following ref. 1 [*sc. prec. quot.*], a reasonable designation for this enhancement is *Υ*(9·5). **1979** *Nature* 7 June 482/2 The more recently discovered upsilon T [? *read Υ*]..should provide an even better system for investigating QCD effects as the coupling strength for that very massive quark system is even smaller. **1980** *TWA Ambassador* Oct. 61/3 Dr. Charles had told me about Truth and Beauty—that is, the quarks given those names—and the discovery in 1977 of the upsilon particle, which seems to be a meson consisting of a beauty quark and a beauty antiquark.

u·pslope, *sb., a.,* and *adv.* [Up *prep.*^{2}] **A.** *sb.* An upward slope; rising ground.

1920 D. H. Lawrence *Lost Girl* v. 63 The eye would instinctively wander..to the long upslope opposite. **1929** —— *Escaped Cock* ii. 58 Inland, the steep grooved upslope was dark, to the long wavering outline of the crest against the translucent sky. **1973** *Times* 6 Mar. 2/7 He walked up the main up-slope for a closer inspection. **1977** *New Yorker* 8 Aug. 55/2 The ball, after landing on the upslope to the green, hopped through the opening between the two front bunkers and curled directly toward the pin.

B. *adj.* Caused by, occurring, or acting upon an upward slope; esp. as *upslope fog* (see quot. 1956).

1941 [see *advection]. **1956** J. C. Swayne *Conc. Gloss. Geogr. Terms* 146 *Upslope fog,* fog formed when moist air blows over hilly ground and is cooled adiabatically until its dew point is reached and condensation takes place. **1970** R. J. Small *Study of Landforms* vi. 215 Upslope factors are considered to be of virtually no importance in Penck's theory. **1973** *Nature* 9 Feb. 394/1 If the grain size were halved instead of doubled the upslope fluid drag on each grain would be reduced to a quarter.

C. *adv.* At or towards a higher point on a slope.

1956 A. G. Garnett in D. L. Linton *Sheffield* 53 Temperatures in the bottom of Edale..are..colder than at points only a few hundred feet up-slope. **1970** R. J. Small *Study of Landforms* vi. 214 In time an almost infinite number of new units, each of gentler gradient than the next unit above it, will be formed at the foot of the slope and undergo migration upslope. **1979** *Sci. Amer.* July 110/1 Walcott returned to the spot the following year to search upslope for the shale stratum that had been the source of his fallen rock.

upspin: see *up- 4 b.

upstage, *adv., a.* (and *sb.*). [Up *prep.*^{2} 6.] **A.** *adv.* (Stressed **upsta·ge.**) At or in the direction of the back of the stage; on that part of the stage furthest from the audience. Also *fig.*

1870 O. Logan *Before Footlights & Behind Scenes* xxxv. 500 And in one minute..has been convulsed with laughter at a side-speech given 'up stage' and as a sort of sequel to the sentiment delivered to the audience. **1923** J. Agate *At Half-Past Eight* 209 You remember how Marcus and Mercia..with the lions roaring up-stage, kept a steadfast face to their admirers. **1938** C. Mackenzie *Windsor Tapestry* xx. 418 At this point the dapper figure of Mr Anthony Eden crosses upstage. **1946** A. Clarke *Second Kiss* 11 Columbine enters, right, upstage, hesitant, and as if in fear. **1967** T. Stoppard *Rosencrantz & Guildenstern are Dead* i. 23 Rosencrantz and Guildenstern occupy the two downstage corners looking upstage. **1976** *Listener* 1 Apr. 404/2 The Wallace family felt able to emerge from its bailiff-proof bolt-hole in SE4, and move upstage a bit to Clarence Gate Gardens, by Baker Street.

B. *adj.* (Stressed *u·pstage.*) **1.** Superior or aloof in manner; 'stuck-up'. Chiefly of persons.

1918 F. Hunt *Blown in by Draft* 287 As doggy as the military police, as upstage as the Engineers..the Field Signal Battalion has the additional point of being of strangest birth. **1927** *Sunday Express* 8 May 10 Although Costello..had definite ideas..in connection with his art, as he took pictures seriously, he was never in the least bit 'up stage' with us youngsters. **1938** *Sun* (Baltimore) 3 Oct. 8/3 Even without 'Cotton Ed's' upstage behavior, this plea would have been unimpressive. **1947** N. Marsh *Final Curtain* xii. 188 All upstage and county! **1966** 'J. Hackston' *Father clears Out* 84 He was a little patronizing to me, upstage in his bearing.

2. That is situated or occurs at or towards the rear of the stage. Also as *sb.*, the back of the stage, furthest from the audience.

1933 P. Godfrey *Back-Stage* i. 14 The up-stage O.P. flood. **1959** [see *dither *v.* 1]. **1974** F. Warner *Meeting Ends* i. viii. 30 Hanging on upstage side of pump..are a brightly coloured towel and a black shawl.

upsta·ge, *v.* [f. the adv.] **1.** *trans. Theatr.* To move upstage of (another actor), forcing him to face away from the audience; to divert attention from (a fellow performer) to oneself, to 'steal the scene' from.

1933 [implied in *upstager, *upstaging *vbl. sb.*]. **1958** B. Nichols *Sweet & Twenties* 200 Miss Tempest always 'upstaged' her—..she slowly pushed her chair to the rear so that..Miss X was obliged to turn away from the audience. **1958** *New Statesman* 6 Sept. 302/2 So if Strether's 'tragedy' seems..rather trivial, that is partly because the hero has been upstaged by the backdrop. **1972** *Islander* (Victoria, B.C.) 18 June 6/3 While Gracie was singing her famous aspidistra song, a stray dog wandered onto the stage and upstaged her. **1976** *Early Music* Oct. 400/1, I would hesitate before *telling* an Aeneas that he is being literally upstaged during his climactic high F.

2. *fig.* To put (a person, etc.) at a disadvantage; to outshine. Also, to treat in a haughty or snobbish manner. *colloq.*

1921 H. C. Witwer *Leather Pushers* x. 268 Nada Nice has upstaged the Kid..at your orders. **1946** 'Brahms' & 'Simon' *Trottie True* v. 103 The Duchess stood there exerting her personality to its most ducal extent... 'Blast,' said Trottie under her breath. 'Upstaged.' **1967** *Daily Tel.* 10 Apr. 10/6 My sister..didn't get on with the other debs—she was more beatnik. They were rude and kept up-staging her. **1974** 'R. Tate' *Birds of Bloodied Feather* iii. 57 It was the only occasion in Edward's life that he had been upstaged by his younger brother.

So **upsta·ger; upsta·ging** *vbl. sb.* and *ppl. a.*

1933 P. Godfrey *Back-Stage* iii. 40 With the chronic up-stager the only remedy for the other actors is to withhold their speech until they have deliberately taken up a position favourable to themselves. *Ibid.*, 'Crowding' and 'up-staging' are tricks of the selfish actor..'Up-staging' is to take up a position nearer to the back of the scene than the other players. This forces them to turn three-quarter-back to the audience when speaking to the up-stage actor. **1968** M. Woodhouse *Rock Baby* v. 46 I'd been running a bright, upstaging little war with Driver and McKellar and patting myself on the back. **1982** P. Lovesey *False Inspector Dew* ii. iii. 29 With her dramatic training, she knew all about up-staging.

upstairs, *adv., sb.,* and *a.* Add: **A.** *adv.* **1. c.** (*a*) *Parliament.* In phr. *to send* (*a bill*) *upstairs,* to refer (a bill) for its committee stage from the floor of the House to a standing committee. Cf. Commit *v.* 4.

1835 *Mirror of Parl.* 17 June 1399/2, I rise to suggest, that if this Bill requires mature deliberation with respect to its details, it should be referred to a Committee upstairs, and not to the Registration Committee. **1907** *Hansard Commons* 11 Apr. 419 Was it the intention of the Government that such a Bill as the Army Bill should go upstairs? **1931** *Economist* 31 Jan. 215/2 In spite of the Government's majority, it is clear that the Bill will emerge from Committee in a very different form from the one in which it is sent upstairs. **1959** *Daily Tel.* 13 Nov. 13/3 For detailed consideration, the Bill will be sent to a Committee 'upstairs', consisting of about 45 M.P.s. **1975** J. P. Morgan *House of Lords & Labour Govt.* ii. 54 All Public Bills usually have their Committee Stage in the Lords on the Floor of the House... In response to the pressure of legislation in 1968 the Lords tried the experiment of taking some Bills 'upstairs' for their Committee Stage.

(*b*) Hence more generally, (i) to a more influential position (sometimes *ironical*); (ii) to a higher authority (of a matter referred for judgement). *colloq.*

1965 [see *plenum 2]. **1977** D. Bagley *Enemy* xi. 75 I'll have to push it upstairs for a ruling. **1978** S. Brill *Teamsters* vii. 289 The Pressers get him another job with the Joint Council or the statewide union. You know, he gets thrown upstairs.

d. *Aeronaut.* Up in or into the air. In phr. *to go* (*climb,* etc.) *upstairs,* to become airborne. *colloq.*

1908 *Punch* 10 June 429/2 Climbing upstairs over Richmond Park [in a balloon] in search of conducive current. **1919** C. P. Thompson *Cocktails* 250 We hauled the plane from the trees where she had been pushed out of sight..and..went upstairs at speed.

2. c. as *sb.* (Earlier example.)

1872 E. Eggleston *End of World* i. 19 They say, he has all up-stairs full of books.

d. *Aeronaut.* In the air; in flight; aloft. *colloq.*

1918 H. A. Bruno *Flying Yankee* v. 77 Cold as the devil upstairs. *Ibid.* xii. 193 'Upstairs' a stiff breeze was blowing. **1934** V. M. Yeates *Winged Victory* ii. v. 232 There won't be any Huns about upstairs [on] a day like this. **1940** N. Monks *Squadrons Up!* 252 Dashing about 'upstairs' in stratospherical aloofness. **1967** W. Lord *Incredible Victory* 94 By 5:30 the weather was clearing 'upstairs'. **1981** I. St. James *Balfour Conspiracy* v. 138 The R.A.F. are upstairs now..at about seventy thousand feet.

e. Mentally, 'in the head'. Chiefly in phrases indicating weak (or abundant, etc.) mental capacity. *slang.*

1932 J. Farrell *Young Lonigan* i. 44 Aw, she's all vacant upstairs. **1945** A. Kober *Parm Me* 179 '*Meshugeh* upstairs!' Jennie laughed and drummed on her forehead. **1952** G. W. Brace *Spire* xxvii. 322 He just ain't right upstairs. **1962** A. Huxley *Island* xi. 184 'One may be very stupid upstairs.' She patted the top of her head. **1974** P. De Vries *Glory of Hummingbird* (1975) v. 63 Assurances that my progress here would be well lubricated by my having 'plenty upstairs'.

f. *the Man Upstairs,* euphem. and slang for 'God'. Cf. *up there 1. *U.S.*

1961 J. Heller *Catch-22* xviii. 184 'When you talk to the man upstairs,' he said, 'I want you to tell Him something for me.' **1971** *Guardian* 8 Oct. 9/4 Everything that's happened to me has been very much because of the Man Upstairs. **1976** H. Kemelman *Wednesday Rabbi got Wet* xix. 120 I'd just lost my wife, see. I guess the Man Upstairs wanted her.

B. *adj.* **1. c.** *fig.* Of, pertaining to, or characteristic of life 'above stairs' (i.e. in the private rooms of a household, as opp. to the servants' quarters) (chiefly *Hist.*); refined, genteel, privileged. Freq. in phr. *upstairs-downstairs* adj., denoting the social contrast between employer and domestic servant.

1942 'M. Innes' *Daffodil Affair* i. ii. 13 Almost might she be said, in upstairs language, to be receiving. [**1971** *TV Times* 9 Oct. 6/2 A six-part series, *Upstairs, Downstairs* (or Secrets of an Edwardian Household), starting Sunday, lovingly, critically examines life at that time through one family.] **1974** D. Francis *Knock Down* i. 6 To one side of the sale ring, and built to a specification as Upstairs as the wooden circle was Downstairs, was a magnificent turn of the century stable yard. **1975** *New Society* 6 Nov. 305/2 Our system is too monolithic, based as it is on an upstairs–downstairs view of music. Upstairs people choose the classics on Radio Three... Downstairs, people listen to pop. **1978** G. Mitchell *Mingled with Venom* i. 4 She had been taken on as kitchen-maid... She was..a ready learner of upstairs speech and manners. **1980** E. Behr *Getting Even* i. 18 The lady in black with white lace cap and apron, a real upstairs-downstairs figure.

upstand, *sb.* Add: *spec.* a turned-up edge of any flat surface or sheeting, esp. in a roof space where it meets the wall; also *attrib.* (see quot. 1963).

1955 *Archit. Rev.* CXVII. 283/3 It [*sc.* a roof tile]..is readily adapted to different plan shapes having an easy repertoire of trimming details at eaves, verges and upstands. **1956** *Ibid.* CXX. 10 The steel box frames forming the turbine-house rooflights make a self-contained rigid frame with sliding joints supported on concrete upstand curbs from the main roof. **1963** *Gloss. Building Terms* (*B.S.I.*) 16 *Upstand beam,* a beam projecting above an adjoining slab. **1974** W. E. Kelsey *Building Construction* viii. 141 It [*sc.* a damp-proof course] is best placed where the upstand or skirting of the roof covering is turned into a mortar joint. **1983** *Ideal Home* June 69 An upstand at the back of the worktop will make it easier to clean and more hygienic—no crumbs or food waste can get trapped in the gap at the back.

upstarched: see *up- 5 (*b*).

upstart, *sb.* **2. a.** For † *Obs.*$^{-1}$ read 'Now only in sense *2 c' and add later *poet.* example.

1923 [see *round-barred* s.v. *round *a.* 16 a].

c. *Gymnastics.* On the horizontal, parallel, or asymmetric bars: a series of movements by which the gymnast swings to a position with the body supported by the arms above the bar, esp. at the start of a routine.

1909 A. Moss *Horizontal Bar Exercises* 22 *Upstart.* Stand about three feet from the bar, then jump and catch it..force the legs well to the front with a swing, and bring them to the bar. Kick them outwards and downwards; at the same time pull, so that you rise above the bar. **1931** E. Linklater *Juan in Amer.* iii. v. 246 Saturdays were more strenuously occupied with up-starts, long arm balancing, vaulting, and similar exercises. **1956** Kunzle & Thomas *Freestanding* v. 58 *Agility.* This group of movements includes the upstarts, headspring and hand-spring. **1972** P. Prestidge *Women's Gymnastics for Performer & Coach* viii. 55 The upstart..is one of the most important movements for the gymnast to master, for a complete routine cannot be composed without upstarts.

u·pstate, *adv., a.,* and *sb.* orig. and chiefly *U.S.* Also **up-State, up State,** etc. **A.** *adv.* **1.** (See Up *prep.*^{2} 6.) (Later examples.)

1938 J. Daniels *Southerner discovers South* 247, I heard about it upstate. **1958** *Economist* 8 Nov. 504/2 Confident..that he would do well in the city.., Mr Harriman had concentrated his efforts upstate. **1977** *New Yorker* 5 Sept. 29/3 He was coming upstate Friday, and staying for the weekend. **1985** *Village Voice* (N.Y.) 8 Jan. 3/1 At that time, the remaining six projects located upstate with 175 beds will be under construction.

2. *U.S. slang.* In prison.

1934 T. V. Wilder *Heaven's my Destination* 23 You get the strait-jacket..upstate. **1977** 'E. McBain' *Long Time no See* xi. 177 She got married while I was upstate doing time.

B. *adj.* Of, pertaining to, or characteristic of, an area upstate; situated upstate, rural;

also, designating part of a State remote (esp. north) from a large city, as *upstate New York.*

1901, 1904 [see UP *prep.*[2] 6]. **1935** *Amer. Speech* X. 107 Pronunciation in upstate New York... Upstate speech has been studied..by three previous investigators. **1949** *Southern Weekly* 16 Nov. 3/2 This is the figure with complete returns from Greater New York and 19 up-State districts missing. **1969** *Wall St. Jrnl.* 30 Sept. 28/3 Five days at an upstate New York county fair. **1978** J. UPDIKE *Coup* vi. 219 Not a metropolis, but a small industrial city, of the type you call..upstate. **1983** 'W. HAGGARD' *Heirloom* i. 6 He had taken her back to up-State New York.

C. *ellipt.* or as *sb.* An upstate region; a rural area.

1965 *Economist* 23 Jan. 323/1 It was the Democrats from 'upstate' (outside the city) who swung behind Mr Kennedy at once. **1972** *Village Voice* (N.Y.) 1 June 78/2 The Liberal Socialists, who came down every week from upstate for meetings. **1974** *Progress* (Easley, S. Carolina) 24 Apr. 11. 8/4 Many of us in the upstate do not appreciate the value of the Tidelands..to our environment.

Hence **u·pstater**, one who lives or comes from upstate.

1944 E. A. HOLTON *Yankees were like This* xvii. 202 The Cape Codder and the Up-Stater are blood brothers with only the difference in the backdrops of sea or mountain. **1965** *Economist* 23 Jan. 323/1 Now, around the figure of Senator Kennedy,..the upstaters have begun to develop some strength. **1975** *New Yorker* 10 Feb. 106/3 In a move to put upstaters' minds at ease about one thing, Carey..assured them, 'The capital of this state is not New York City or elsewhere.'

up stick(s: see STICK *sb.*[1] 7 in Dict. and Suppl., and UP *adv.*[1] 29.

upstiffed: see *UP- 5.

up-stream, *adv.* and *a.* Add: **A.** *adv.* **2.** In the oil and gas industries: at or towards the source of production; *spec.* at a stage in the process of extraction and production before the raw material is ready to be refined.

1973 *Auckland Star* 10 Feb. 18 The most natural way the oil producers can spend their vast wealth..is in developing the industry itself. Huge investment is needed 'upstream'. **1983** *Business Week* 21 Feb. 61/1 KPC has not neglected foreign activities upstream. It wants to expand exploration in the U.S.

B. *adj.* **4.** Relating to the stages in the production of oil and gas before the raw material is ready for refining.

1965 WILLIAMS & MEYERS *Oil & Gas Terms* (ed. 2) 429 Gathering activities are..ended when gas reaches a central point... Facilities used before this point of demarcation are upstream facilities. **1981** *Times* 3 Apr. 17/1 Upstream activities..are overshadowed by the comfortable world supply position while downstream, weak demand is making it more difficult to recoup rising operating costs.

u·pstreet, *adv. colloq.* and *dial.* [UP *prep.*[2] 5.] Up or along the street; in, into, or towards the higher part of a town, etc.

1828, etc. [see *DOWN-STREET *adv.* (*a.*)]. **1933** [see *PIE *sb.*[2] 4 a].

up-stroke. Add: Also **upstroke. 4.** *Physiol.* The part of a nerve impulse when the action potential is becoming more positive.

1974 *Nature* 4 Jan. 69/2 The upstroke of the action potential is considered the result of a Hodgkin cycle. **1979** *Sci. Amer.* Sept. 65/2 The depolarizing upstroke of the action potential is produced mainly by the inflow of sodium ions into the terminal.

u·psurge. [UP- 2.] **1.** A sudden rise or increase of feeling.

1928 *Catholic Times* 11 May 11/5 His books are an upsurge of primitive passion. **1944** D. WELCH *Jrnl.* 20 June (1973) 123, I remember..saying, 'That's a wonderful poem,' and his vital upsurge of agreement. **1958** *Times* 28 June 9/3 There has been a great upsurge of interest in recent years in regal pelargoniums. **1971** *Times* 22 Feb. (Canada Suppl.) p. vii/2 More recently there has been a noisy upsurge of English-Canadian nationalism in Toronto.

2. An uprising, an insurrection.

1930 *Aberdeen Press & Jrnl.* 4 Feb. 7/5 The beginnings of a widespread revolutionary upsurge..are visualised in a proclamation issued by the Red International. **1937** E. LYONS *Assignment in Utopia* (1938) II. ii. 68 The Chinese heritage asserted itself. [Eugene] Chen traveled to the land of his forebears and, without knowing its language, became a leader in the revolutionary upsurge. **1963** *Ann. Reg. 1962* 291 Political machinery for collective leadership to guarantee the revolutionary upsurge.

3. A sharp rise in economic activity, demand, prices, etc.

1935 *Sun* (Baltimore) 22 Apr. 8/2 A sharp upsurge in the postal receipts at Denver. **1955** *Times* 14 July 13/1 It was hardly to be expected that the paint industry could fail to share in the general upsurge of industrial activity over the past 18 months. **1962** *Listener* 7 June 980/2 The speediest possible upsurge in the production of meat and milk. **1974** *Guardian* 25 Jan. 14/1 An upsurge in exports this year has boosted the national output by 6·9 per cent. **1985** *Times* 8 Jan. 17/2 Distillers Co...was another to fail to join the upsurge.

4. A rapid growth in number or size.

1955 A. L. ROWSE *Expansion of Elizabethan Eng.* 161 The sudden upsurge..is witnessed precisely by Hakluyt. **1974** *Sunday Post* (Glasgow) 31 Mar. 9/1 In this year of strife there's been an upsurge of Scots wanting to emigrate.

5. *lit.* A surging upwards.

1969 *Daily Tel.* 5 Feb. 1/8 There was such an upsurge of gas that 14 surplus workmen were evacuated by helicopter. But then the safety valve clicked in.

upsu·rgence. [f. prec. + -ENCE, after *resurgence*, etc.] = *UPSURGE.

1934 in WEBSTER. **1945** *Sun* (Baltimore) 5 Feb. 40/2 Mr. Harry L. Hopkins' view of what is needed to keep the Germans and Japanese from new upsurgences is certainly not a frivolous one. **1958** *Church Times* 22 Aug. 3/4 He emphasized the great dangers of the upsurgence of non-Christian religions in the Eastern world—particularly Buddhism. **1971** I. G. GASS et al. *Understanding Earth* xii. 160/1, I have mentioned the possible effect of plant upsurgence during the Carboniferous.

u·psweep. [UP- 2.] **1.** An upward movement in a long, sweeping curve; a raising or lifting up. Also *fig.*

1898 W. J. LOCKE *Idols* xx. 285 'Who knows?' said Minna, with an insolent upsweep of her lazy lashes. **1954** M. OLIVER *Failing Wine* xxvii. 100 But what are we to say of the upsweep of the moral curve? **1976** *Daily Tel.* 2 Aug. 10 As a result I believe we would see an upsweep in the morale of the whole country.

b. *spec.* An upswept hair-style.

1946 'P. QUENTIN' *Puzzle for Fiends* (1947) xxi. 151 She moved out of the room..absently patting the stray hairs of her upsweep. **1978** J. UPDIKE *Coup* iii. 105 The trim Dacron skirt and jacket, with secretarial upsweep and..dearth of bangles.

upswept, *a.* (In Dict., UP- 5(*b*).) Add: **2.** Applied to (a style of) hair brushed up and fastened at the top of the head; = *swept-up* s.v. *SWEPT *ppl. a.* 1.

1938 *Vogue* 15 June 34 Those toy-size doll hats..on many French heads already—and what a fine solution they are to up-swept hair. **1939** M. B. PICKEN *Lang. Fashion* 160/3 *Up-swept*, term applied to style of hairdress with smooth, high-swept back and small curls on top of head. **1946** 'P. QUENTIN' *Puzzle for Fiends* (1947) xvii. 119 Her rakish upswept hair-do. **1959** *News Chron.* 12 Aug. 3/6 Two oval faces, with smooth up-swept hair. **1976** J. GRENFELL *Joyce Grenfell requests Pleasure* xiii. 182 Lynn showed me how to achieve a fold at the back of my up-swept hair. **1981** A. LURIE *Lang. Clothes* iii. 72/1 Her upswept hairdo, puffed out over pads of wire and horsehair.

3. More generally, having an upward sweep, curved upwards.

1960 *News Chron.* 16 Sept. 1/7 The woman the police are seeking..wears glasses with blue upswept frames. **1961** *Shropshire Mag.* Apr. 43/1 (Advt.), New spectacle frames... Two-tone 17/–; Upswept 20/–. **1961** WEBSTER s.v., Upswept rear fenders. **1984** *Washington Post* 9 July C7/1 There he is, with his striped pantaloons and upswept conquistador hat.

u·pswing. [UP- 2.] **1.** *Golf.* = *back-swing* s.v. *BACK- A. 11. *rare.*

1922 WODEHOUSE *Clicking of Cuthbert* vi. 145 His upswing was shaky, and he swayed back perceptibly.

2. a. *Econ.* An upward movement or trend in economic conditions; a (period of) improvement in trading activity. Freq. in advb. phr. *on the upswing.*

1934 *Sun* (Baltimore) 20 Oct. 1/2 Reflecting a sharp upswing in retail trade throughout the country, data on current employment and pay roll trends were made public today. **1946** [see *DOWN-SWING]. **1953** *Times* 31 Oct. 1/11 They do not..reflect the vigorous upswing in the industrial output this year, as revealed by the monthly Treasury indices. **1967** *N.Y. Herald Tribune* (Internat. ed.) 11–12 Feb. 7/7 (*heading*) Market closes on upswing; color TV comes into demand. **1973** 'R. MACLEOD' *Burial in Portugal* iv. 90 When he'd bought in, Consolidated had already been shading at 130 and Maltsters had been on the upswing at 146. **1983** *Daily Tel.* 20 Oct. 21/2 The latest batch of cyclical indicators suggest that the upswing in the economy will continue well into 1984.

b. *transf.* and *fig.*

1947 *Ann. Rev. Microbiol.* I. 351 The seasonal upswings of influenza A or B are much less uniform in time than those of other diseases such as diphtheria, measles, or chickenpox. **1951** *Sunday Pictorial* 21 Jan. 12/5 There is a general upswing in your affairs. **1963** 'E. MCBAIN' *Ten Plus One* (1964) ii. 27 Gang violence..seemed to enjoy an upswing during the summer months. **1976** A. CASSORLA *Skateboarder's Bible* 13 The Sport was once again on the up-swing.

uptake, *sb.* **1.** Delete '(and still chiefly)' and add: *quick* (*slow*, etc.) *in the uptake* (later examples). Also with *at the uptake* (later examples), and now most commonly *on the uptake.*

1911 E. M. CLOWES *On Wallaby* vi. 162 They..are not so 'smart', so quick in the up-take, as themselves. **1927** H. A. VACHELL *Dew of Sea* 259 For a moment the chieftain was puzzled. But he was fairly quick at the up-take, replying after a pause. **1931** D. L. SAYERS *Five Red Herrings* viii. 92 A good girl..but slow in the uptake. **1940** R. S. LAMBERT *Ariel & all his Quality* viii. 190 No one was 'quicker on the uptake'; no one responded quicker to a nod or a wink. **1949** *Here & Now* (N.Z.) Oct. 13/1 An energetic, likeable, cockily pugnacious figure, but slow, almost Neanderthally slow, on the uptake. **1957** H. NICOLSON *Journey to Java* vi. 106 Being quick at the uptake, he then realized that the flat had been visited by house-breakers. **1980** K. CROSSLEY-HOLLAND *Norse Myths* p. xxvi, He was..a bit slow in the uptake, but immensely strong and dependable.

5. Absorption or incorporation by a living system. Also *transf.*

1931 W. O. JAMES *Introd. Plant Physiol.* vi. 156 (*heading*) The uptake of water. **1956** *Nature* 28 Jan. 192/1 The uptake of potassium ions by disks of red beet root tissue. **1971** *Country Life* 8 July 119/1 Between 1968 and 1975 the textile industry's uptake of wool would fall by 23 per cent. **1974** [see *photoscan* s.v. *PHOTO- 2].

up te·mpo, *a.*, (*adv.*) *Mus.* [UP *a.*] Of music, etc.: characterized by or played at a fast tempo.

1948 *Down Beat* 19 May 13 'Sleeps' is an up tempo thing by Norvo. **1958** A. MORGAN in P. Gammond *Decca Bk. Jazz* xii. 139 None..has achieved the same degree of tension.., a feeling which is more obvious in such up-tempo excursions as *Cherokee*. **1961** *Down Beat* 19 Jan. 31 'Sesame', in particular, is swift-moving and taken up-tempo. **1968** *Times* 22 Nov. 9/3 The flip side of Hey Jude was an up-tempo song called Revolution. **1976** *New Musical Express* 17 Apr. 19/6 It's uptempo with a rather slight melody.

u·pter, *predic. adj. Austral. slang.* Also **upta.** [A corruption of *up to putty* (see *PUTTY *sb.* 3 b), or some similar phr.] Bad or worthless; no good.

1919 W. H. DOWNING *Digger Dialects* 52 *Up to putty*, bad; useless; ineffectual. *Upter*, a corruption of 'up to putty'. **1949** J. CLEARY *You can't see round Corners* xxvi. 169 'How are you going?' 'Upta. I've lost on every race so far.' **1953** 'CADDIE' *Sydney Barmaid* xxxviii. 219 Dadda made some derogatory remark about the tucker. 'If it's upter why don't you 'ave a go?'

up there, *adv. phr.* [UP *adv.*[2]] **1.** Above the earth; in heaven; *spec.* with reference to God. Cf. ABOVE *adv.* 1 b.

1938 M. MUGGERIDGE *In Valley of this Restless Mind* xvi. 145 Don't imagine..that the old gentleman up there is going to interfere... He doesn't exist. **1969** P. THEROUX *Murder in Mount Holly* iii. 44 You had to..really believe in that Big Man Up There. **1977** J. MCVEAN *Bloodspoor* xx. 260 Sometimes I almost get to feel someone up there must be pitching for us.

2. Up on a level *with* (something else highly rated). *colloq.*

1970 *Globe & Mail* (Toronto) 25 Sept. 6/1 The Post Office, which among things to have, rates right up there with athlete's foot. **1977** *Gay News* 7–20 Apr. 32/1 It is necessary to her kind of survival not to make an impression, either as an award-laden superstar (up there with Streisand..and Fonda) or even as an actress.

upthrust, *sb.* Add: **1. b.** The upward force that a liquid exerts on a body in it.

1916 ALLEN & MOORE *Text-bk. Pract. Physics* 54 The resultant supporting force may be termed the upthrust. **1982** J. J. WELLINGTON *Physics for All* vii. 46 A heavy ship needs a very large upthrust on it to make it float.

2. An upthrust body of rock or the accompanying fault.

1942 M. P. BILLINGS *Structural Geol.* viii. 154 Upthrusts are high angle faults along which the relatively uplifted block has been the active element. **1977** G. SCOTT *Hot Pursuit* viii. 75 Mountains run the whole length of the North Island of New Zealand, great upthrusts of greywacke and jointed sandstone. **1982** T. HILLERMAN *Dark Wind* (1983) viii. 46 The plane..had struck an upthrust of basalt which jutted from the floor of the wash.

upthru·sting, *vbl. sb.* [UP- 7.]

1924 A. GEIKIE *Long Life's Work* vii. 229 He was greatly interested in the proofs of the stupendous upthrusting of the strata. **1931** J. S. HUXLEY *What dare I Think?* vi. 183 This generation's multifarious upthrustings of the religious spirit. **1984** W. GARNER *Rats' Alley* xi. 235 Antequera, an upthrusting of castle, belfries and white walls.

upthru·sting, *ppl. a.* [UP- 6.]

1951 A. L. ROWSE *England of Elizabeth* 314 Monastic buildings that could be made into comfortable country houses for up-thrusting families. **1958** T. EDWARDS *Worlds Apart* x. 205 Upthrusting granite crags polished by sun and wind.

u·p-tick. Chiefly *U.S.* [UP-2.] An upward trend; an increase in rate.

1970 *Time* 27 Apr. 84/1 The Government reported upticks in three key indicators. **1975** *Newsweek* 10 Feb. 30/1 A modest uptick would begin around the end of the year, and..produce real growth of 4.8 per cent. **1977** *Time* 18 July 44/3 Less cheering was an uptick in the unemployment rate. **1982** *Times* 20 May 17/8 A further up-tick in interest rates offers little encouragement to London's bulls.

upti·ght, *a. colloq.* and *slang.* (orig. *U.S.*). [UP- 3.] **1. a.** Of a person: in a state of nervous tension or anxiety; inhibited, worried, 'on edge'; angry, 'worked up' (*about* something).

Quot. 1934 is an isolated early example.

1934 J. M. CAIN *Postman always rings Twice* xvi. 190 I'm getting up tight now, and I've been thinking about Cora. Do you think she knows I didn't do it? **1966** *Sunday Times* (Colour Suppl.) 13 Feb. 35/4 *Up tight*, tense. **1968** *Mad* LXXVII. 30 'Uptight' means, like, a bad scene. It's when you're hung up, or wigged out, or you can't make it. We all get 'uptight' once in a while. **1969** C. YOUNG *Todd Dossier* 38 He looked worried. Really worried. As the kids say, he was up-tight. **1973** E.

CALDWELL *Annette* (1974) VI. ii. 137 I'd guess you'd gotten so uptight from being denied motherhood that you were ready to leave home. **1975** D. LODGE *Changing Places* ii. 83 You're feeling all cold and uptight and wishing you hadn't come. **1977** M. EDELMAN *Political Lang.* v. 90 To the uptight policeman everyone is a potential offender. **1981** P. P. READ *Villa Golitsyn* II. iv. 112, I was afraid you might be a little uptight about that sort of thing.

b. *fig.* Characteristically formal in manner or style; correct, strait-laced.

1969 *Manch. Guardian Weekly* 28 Aug. 18 Who would have thought that an uptight institution like the august Oxford University Press would have done a thing like this? Here is a..spirited and spiritous piece of autobiography..served up as a book. **1970** E. M. BRECHER *Sex Researchers* ix. 253 They tended to swing in the same socially correct, formal, 'up-tight' style they followed in their other activities. **1976** *Chatelaine* (Montreal) Jan. 73/3 In the morning, the apartment looked curiously uptight to Meredith.

2. In approbation: that reaches the desired standard; excellent, fine.

1962 *Down Beat* Aug. 20/2 *Jazz* Gene Ammons *Up Tight!* **1966** [see *OUT-OF-SIGHT *adj. phr.* (*sb.*) 2]. **1969** *Courier-Mail* (Brisbane) 31 May 11/7 Disc jockeys..talk in a kind of sub-English..as in 'All right baby sock-it-to-me it's allright uptight yeah.'

3. Short or out of money; 'broke'.

1967 *Time* 6 Jan. 18/3 'Up tight' can mean anxious, emotionally involved or broke. **1968** *Esquire* Apr. 160/3 The expression 'uptight', which meant being in financial straits, appeared on the soul scene in the general vicinity of 1953.

Hence **upti·ghtness.**

1969 FABIAN & BYRNE *Groupie* vi. 46 The paranoia and savage uptightness which comes from three such guys living on top of each other and attempting to lead very together type lives while being stoned most of the time. **1974** A. LASKI *Night Music* 95 It hadn't made him any looser..that rigid uptightness was still in him. **1976** *New Yorker* 8 Mar. 57/3 In [*The Entertainer*]..Archie contrasted the uptightness of the British who don't make 'a fuss' with a fat black woman he once heard in America who sang 'her heart out to the whole world'.

u·ptime. *Computers.* [UP *adv.*[2]] Time when a computer or similar device is 'up' or able to function. Cf. *UP *adv.*[2] 13 b.

1958 *Communications Assoc. Computing Machinery* June 23 Uptime is based on productive time vs scheduled time. **1970** *IEEE Trans. Reliability* XIX. 24/1 Expressions are given in the literature for the availability, mean-time-between-failures, mean uptime, and mean downtime for systems consisting of a number of identical modules in redundancy. **1982** *What's New in Computing* Nov. 5/4 The document transport system has been designed for maximum reliability and uptime.

up to date, up-to-date, *adv. phr.* and *a.* Add: **up-to-da·tedness; up-to-da·tely** *adv.* (Both *rare*[−1].)

1928 *Daily Express* 23 Mar. 5/4 Furnish and equip her studio charmingly..and above all up-to-dately. **1931** A. HUXLEY *Music at Night* IV. 224 The public is taught that up-to-datedness is one of the first duties of man.

up top, *adv. phr.* [UP *adv.*[2]] **1.** *Mil. slang.* **a.** Above decks. **b.** Of an aircraft: in the sky.

1917 'TAFFRAIL' *Off Shore* 36 'Up top there!' bellowed James... 'Help!' James shouted. **1934** V. M. YEATES *Winged Victory* I. xix. 154 Then he saw the Fokkers. Where were the people up top? **1942** G. HACKFORTH-JONES *One-One-One* ix. 88 'What's going on up top?' he asked after he had received the Commander's message.

2. *fig.* In a position of authority or influence.

1967 WODEHOUSE *Company for Henry* iv. 66 It doesn't do any harm if she lends a hand herself. Can't leave everything to the men up top. **1979** *N.Y. Times Mag.* 30 Sept. 33/1 Sonny had friends up top in all these places—people he'd take to race-track junkets, or to theater outings.

up to the mi·nute, *adv.* (and *adj.*) *phr.* [UP *adv.*[1]] Right up to the present time; in the latest fashion (see *MINUTE *sb.*[1] 1 b). Chiefly *attrib.* or as *adj. phr.* (hyphened), as up to date as possible; completely modern; most recently available. Similarly *up-to-the-moment, -second* adj. phrs.

1909 R. A. WASON *Happy Hawkins* xxvii. 322 They had stopped for over a month with his friends in England, an' was posted up to the minute. **1922** S. LEWIS *Babbitt* vi. 69 Babbitt, the..efficient, up-to-the-minute and otherwise perfected modern. **1933** J. B. PRIESTLEY *Wonder Hero* v. 185 A very bright, up-to-the-minute sort of room. **1937** [see *MINUTE *sb.*[1] 1 b]. **1938** *Times* 3 May 13/2 Feminine dress, new and old, is here displayed—up-to-the-moment gowns of British design. **1950** 'S. RANSOME' *Deadly Miss Ashley* iv. 44 Her black hair-do was smartly plain to set off her up-to-the-minute face. **1956** [see *MINUTE *sb.*[1] 1 b]. **1967** *N.Y. Daily News* 13 Oct. 17 Dr. Frank Field..brings you up-to-the-second weather reports. **1979** A. HAILEY *Overload* I. i. 6 This place with its up-to-the-second information. **1980** *Radio Times* 25 Nov.–5 Dec. 102/3 It's important to look up-to-the-minute, but clothes are too costly to be bought for just one appearance. **1985** *Broadcast* 11 Jan. 19/3 A lot of what you see about Poland is the latest up-to-the-minute riot or government move. There's very little that is reflective.

Hence **up-to-the-mi·nutely** *adv.*; **up-to-the-mi·nuteness.**

1940 D. A. LORD *Our Lady in Modern World* iii. 141 They proclaim their up-to-the-minuteness. **1959** *Listener* 2 Apr. 600/1 The heart of his ambition was to be..as smartly and up-to-the-minutely American as possible.

u·p-to-then, *adv. phr.* [UP *adv.*[1]] Before a given point in time; until then.

1959 P. BULL *I know Face* ix. 152, I did get my revenge by calling him Audrey instead of Aubrey, in the up-to-then famous dinner-table scene. **1976** *Brit. Jrnl. Sociol.* XXVII. 345 [National liberation struggles] in fact shook the up-to-then facile dominance of the developmentalists in the academy.

up-town, *adv.* and *a.* Add: **1.** *adv.* (Earlier examples.)

1802 J. COWLES *Diary* 8 Apr. (1931) 65 Mama went uptown today. **1839** C. F. BRIGGS *Harry Franco* I. xiii. 96 The rain was pattering against the windows, and the house was far uptown.

3. as *sb.* The higher or upper part of a town or city, *spec.* the residential or more prosperous area. *U.S.*

1946 R. BLESH *Shining Trumpets* vii. 160 New Orleans' downtown is the old quarter north of Canal Street. Uptown is the district around the nucleus of the American Quarter. **1975** J. GORES *Hammett* vii. 50 The frisk..was for show, to impress high-rollers from uptown out for a night of slumming.

Hence **u·ptowner,** a person from 'uptown'.

1924 [see *HIGH-HAT *v.*]. **1981** P. MALLORY *Killing Matter* xii. 129 The area had..its own rough charm, but it was as remote as Mozambique..to your educated Uptowner.

u·ptrend. Chiefly *U.S.* [UP- 2.] An upward tendency; *spec.* in *Econ.*, a rise in value over a period of time.

1926 *Daily Colonist* (Victoria, B.C.) 23 Jan. 17/3 A fair demand at the opening of the [stock market] session influenced a temporary up-trend. **1934** *Sun* (Baltimore) 1 Dec. 17/1 The mercantile agency finds the irregular increases in factory operations..have been 'transferred into a steady uptrend'. **1961** *Times* 29 Nov. 11/5 The uptrend is of less significance. **1979** *Arizona Daily Star* 5 Aug. D 1/2 Schrikker's charts show both the U.S. dollar and the pound sterling in important uptrends. **1984** *Times* 23 Nov. 19/5 AGB Research went back on an uptrend as market men heard whispers of good news from America.

up·trunk. *nonce-wd.* [UP- 2.] Punning reference to a brass musical instrument and the trunk of an elephant.

1922 JOYCE *Ulysses* 280 Tuning up... That's music too. Brasses braying asses through uptrunks.

upturn, *sb.* Add: **1. b.** A portion of the material of a garment turned up, e.g. at the end of a leg. *rare.*

1923 *Daily Mail* 11 Aug. 1 (Advt.), Shorts have good upturns for lengthening. **1926** *Minister's Rep. of Fashion for Gentlemen* Feb. 8/2 Trousers for wear with morning coats and dressy lounges are, of course, finished with plain bottoms, but for general wear the permanent up-turn still holds the field.

3. An improvement or upward turn, esp. in economic conditions; a rise in rate or value.

1930 *Daily Express* 6 Sept. 2/6 The turnover..remained light, the upturn reflecting an extreme scarcity of sellers rather than any considerable number of buyers. **1932** *Sun* (Baltimore) 5 Nov. 14/7 Helping to hoist wheat prices were upturns in securities and cotton. **1940** [see *DOWN-TURN *sb.*] **1944** [see *split-up* s.v. *SPLIT-]. **1958** *Spectator* 13 June 783/2 There will be no quick upturn in the economy. **1971** LD. ROBBINS *Against Inflation* (1979) x. 51 Certainly I think that the measures which the Chancellor of the Exchequer and the Government have taken could produce..some upturn, provided that confidence is restored. **1981** *Daily Tel.* 9 July 1/6 It is less sanguine about an imminent upturn in the economy.

4. *Linguistics.* A rise in pitch.

1964 [see *DOWN-TURN, DOWNTURN *sb.*]. **1967** D. STEIBLE *Conc. Handbk. Linguistics* 132 *Upturn*, a term designating a rise in pitch, most noticeable as the terminal rise on the last syllable of an interrogative construction.

upupa (upū·pă). Now *rare* exc. as the name of a genus. [L.] = HOOPOE.

1601, etc. [see HOOP *sb.*[3] 1]. **1677** [see HOOPING *ppl. a.*[2]]. **1688** [see HOOPOE]. **1922** JOYCE *Ulysses* 407 Agendath is a waste land, a home of screechowls and the sandblind upupa. [**1979** P. MATTHIESSEN *Snow Leopard* i. 53 Then the first ray of sun in days strikes the harlequin feathers of a hoopoe, and I smile. Like many of the foothill birds, *Upupa* is a bird of Africa, but I saw one much more recently—last month, in fact—in the mountains of Umbria, in Italy.]

u·pvaluation. *Econ.* [UP- 2.] A revaluation upwards, esp. of one currency in relation to others on a common standard.

1953 *N.Y. Times* 12 Jan. 26/3 Why suppose that the situation would be bettered by a new up-valuation of gold, with its invitation to a new round of inflation? **1958** *Spectator* 18 July 92/1 The disruptive rumours of an up-valuation of the German mark have disappeared. **1962** *Punch* 28 Mar. 508/1 The upvaluation of the guilder.. must have had some effect. **1976** *Economist* 10 Apr. 18/1 The French have taken the franc out of the snake, and the weedy reptile that remains may soon be killed by an overdue upvaluation of the German mark.

Hence (as a back-formation) **u·pvalue** *v. trans.*, to raise the value of (a currency, etc.) on a scale.

1968 *Guardian* 23 Nov. 8/1 The refusal of the Germans to upvalue their D-mark. **1974** *Times* 9 Mar. 15/7 Sterling could have been upvalued and inflation reduced.

upwa·ft, *v. poet. rare.* (UP- 4.) *trans.*

1757 [see *upwafting* s.v. UP- 6 (*b*)]. **1944** BLUNDEN *Shells by Stream* 20 The winds up-waft The smoke of an enchanter's fire.

upward, *adv.*, *prep.*, *a.*, and *sb.* Add: **A.** *adv.* **I. 1. e.** Sociol. *upward mobility*, movement from a lower to a higher social level. Hence *upward-mobile* adj. phr., possessing upward mobility.

1949 *Amer. Jrnl. Sociol.* LIV. 519/2 These children were learning attitudes and habits leading to upward social mobility. **1964** GOULD & KOLB *Dict. Soc. Sci.* 434/2 A change in social class position..is called vertical mobility, with the sub-classes of upward mobility and downward mobility. *Ibid.* 604/2 A hungry rat may be rewarded by food, an upward-mobile person by a symbol of prestige. **1969** J. & S. BARATZ in T. Kochman *Rappin' & Stylin' Out* (1973) 14 The price of integration for the upward-mobile black man has been continuous tension and anxiety. **1978** J. UPDIKE *Coup* (1979) vii. 259 Her hard-packed determination to achieve, with her husband Bud, upward mobility.

6. Comb. *upward-climbing, -curving; up-ward-parted.*

1920 KIPLING in Kipling & Graves tr. *Horace's Odes* v. 17 For fierce she-Britons, apt to smite Their upward-climbing sisters down. **1963** *Times Lit. Suppl.* 8 Mar. 168/3 Upward-climbing iambics. **1922** JOYCE *Ulysses* 24 He walked along the upwardcurving path. **1865** G. M. HOPKINS *Poems* (1967) 151 A brush of trees Rounded it, thinning skywards by degrees, With parallel shafts,—as upward-parted ashes.

10. *upward compatibility*, the property of computer software and hardware by virtue of which software written for a less capable machine can be used on a more capable one; so *upward-compatible* adj. phr., exhibiting upward compatibility.

1964 *Computer Bull.* June 44/2 The IBM SYSTEM/360 is available in six models... IBM is developing an additional, very high performance system to be upward-compatible with these models. **1965** *Ibid.* June 20/1 In addition to upward compatibility the Compatibles/100 offer users the protection of a more complete range of software. **1976** *Aviation Week* 6 Sept. 155/1 All software in the series is upward-compatible. **1979** *Business Week* (Industr. Ed.) 27 Aug. 83 The new system is aimed at providing the current users of GSD's systems with a more powerful, upward-compatible system. **1982** *Computerworld* 15 Mar. 4/1 The system is upward-compatible with both the Harris 1600 and Harris 9200 series processors. **1983** *Australian Personal Computer* Oct. 49/2 There are..rumours that IBM will soon release an in-house developed DOS..which will be more upward compatible to IBM disk operating systems. **1983** *Pop. Computing* Nov. 15 Instruction sets for the microprocessors are 'upward compatible', that is, a program written for the original Z80 will also work on the faster Z80A, Z80B, or Z80H, but the reverse is not necessarily true. **1984** *Computerworld* 16 Apr. 47 Version 4.0 provides full upward compatibility for Template Version 3.0 applications programs.

upwardly, *adv.* Add: **2.** special collocations: *upwardly compatible* adj. phr. *upward-compatible* adj. phr. s.v. *UPWARD *adv.* 10; *upwardly mobile* adj. phr. = *upward-mobile* adj. phr. s.v. *UPWARD *adv.* 1 e.

1981 *Electronics* 24 Mar. 8 In 1976 J. L. Wagener suggested 'structured Fortran—an evolution of standard Fortran' as an extended upwardly compatible compiler. **1984** *Austral. Micro Computerworld* Feb. 28/1 Macintosh is the bottom-end system of the Apple 32 Supermicro family comprising Macintosh, a bridge product, Lisa II, Lisa II/5 and Lisa II/10. These machines are upwardly compatible. **1964** *Sunday Times* 23 Aug. 10/2 The barriers within that structure..can be crossed by upwardly-mobile Jews. **1967** A. LURIE *Imaginary Friends* vi. 68 Suppose she were to..marry some upwardly mobile local boy. **1973** *Publishers Weekly* 3 Sept. 50/2 Son of upwardly mobile parents, his youth has been a series of movings—from apartment to ever better apartment. **1981** *Times* 22 May 14/2 The Liberal voter.., the upwardly mobile, ex-working-class malcontent. **1984** *New Yorker* 13 Feb. 39/1 A purely personal prejudice, this, and not to be taken seriously by upwardly mobile executives.

u·pwarp. *Geol.* [UP- 2.] A gentle, extensive elevation of part of the earth's surface. Hence **upwa·rping** *vbl. sb.*, the raising of part of the earth's surface to form an upwarp.

1917 *Prof. Papers U.S. Geol. Survey* No. 93. 109/1 Synclines and anticlines, both broad and narrow, sharply delineated monoclines, and domical upwarps follow one another in succession. **1952** *Geol. Mag.* LXXXIX. 130 Three domal upwarps are superimposed on the simple anticlinal structure. **1954** W. D. THORNBURY *Princ. Geomorphol.* ix. 223 Intermittent upwarping took place, but there were periods of relative stillstand which are marked by erosional surfaces and terraces. **1974** *Nature* 23 Aug. 684/1 Owing to large scale Plio-Pleistocene upwarpings of the South African coastal margins, many rivers show substantially steeper gradients along their lower courses than in higher reaches. **1977** A. HALLAM *Planet Earth* 78/2 An important feature of rift valleys is that they follow the crests of long, low upwarps of the Earth's crust.

u·pwash. [UP- 2.] **1.** A wash of a wave up a beach. *rare*⁻¹.

1923 D. H. LAWRENCE *Kangaroo* v. 93 Then suddenly he saw Jack running across the sand in a bathing suit, and entering the shallow rim of a long, swift upwash.

2. *Aeronaut.* The upward deflection of an airstream by an aerofoil. Cf. *DOWNWASH.

1936 *Aircraft Engin.* VIII. 251/3 With highly tapered wings there is an upwash at the wing tip. **1974** *Sci. Amer.* Mar. 79/2 The flow field in the vortex wake can be viewed as an induced upwash at the outer edge. **1979** *Nature* 20/27 Dec. 778/2 Beyond the wing there is an upwash, which is very intense near the wingtip.

upwe·ll, *v.* [UP- 4.] *intr.* To well up; *spec.* of liquid, esp. seawater: to surge upwards. Also *fig.*

1885 [in Dict. s.v. UP- 4 b]. **1886** *National Rev.* Apr. 229 As when, up-welling from his fountain deeps, The Infant River leaves his native snows. **1913** R. KANE *Good Friday to Easter Sunday* 29 A fresh warm tear..is born,..silently upwelling. **1938** *Nature* 29 Oct. 778/1 Atlantic water..is rich in phosphate because it contains water that has upwelled at the edge of the continental shelf. **1973** C. SAGAN *Cosmic Connection* xvi. 115 Hot molten rock, called lava, upwells through tubes in the upper layers of the Earth. **1979** *Nature* 8 Feb. 470/2 Most meltwater from icebergs may spread laterally rather than upwell along the sides.

upwe·lled, *ppl. a.* (UP- 5; cf. prec.)

1938 *Jrnl. Marine Res.* I. 161 The upwelled water will in turn be carried away from the coast. **1957** G. E. HUTCHINSON *Treat. Limnol.* I. v. 280 Recently upwelled water rich in plankton. **1970** *Sci. Amer.* Feb. 32/3 The upwelled strips of basalt are distinguishable from one another by differences in the direction of their magnetic polarity.

upwe·lling, *ppl. a.* (Later examples in *spec.* sense of the vb.)

1936 *Discovery* Aug. 259/1 The cold up-welling polar waters. **1964** *Oceanogr. & Marine Biol.* II. 348 The muscle band..may act as a reflector for upwelling luminescence.

upwe·lling, *vbl. sb.* [UP- 7.] **1.** *gen.* A welling upwards.

1868 J. H. NEWMAN *Verses on Various Occasions* 309 The fresh upwelling of thy tranquil spirit. **1896** MRS. H. WARD *Sir G. Tressady* II. xx. 462 Strange up-wellings of feelings long trampled on and suppressed. **1976** J. WHEELER-BENNETT *Friends, Enemies & Sovereigns* v. 164 Truman derived his own keen perception from within himself, through an upwelling of his own inner consciousness.

2. *spec.* The rising of water from the depths of the ocean, often bringing with it a renewed source of nutrients; also, the water thus risen.

1912 *Internat. Rev. der gesamt. Hydrobiol. und Hydrographie* V. 250 Holway..attributed the cold surface water to an upwelling of bottom water. **1922** W. G. KENDREW *Climates of Continents* 11 This is a cool current ..partly owing to the upwelling of cold water along the coast. **1963** G. L. PICKARD *Descriptive Physical Oceanogr.* iv. 39 Upwelling is important in replenishing the surface layers. **1967** *Oceanogr. & Marine Biol.* V. 57 This gives rise along the south coast of New Guinea to a violent upwelling whose existence is evident only during this month. **1973** *Sci. Amer.* June 22/3 The concentration of nutrients in the Peru upwelling is many times greater than that in the open ocean.

up-wind, *adv.* Add: **B.** *adj.* Occurring in a direction against the wind.

1942 *Tee Emm* (Air Ministry) II. 95 The aircraft should always be ditched on the upwind slope of the swell. **1943** [see *PRANG *v.* 2]. **1980** *Yachts & Yachting* 29 Feb. 651/1 For upwind work, we chose to use a Navik vane.

upwi·ng, *v. poet. rare.* [UP- 4.] *intr.* To soar or fly up; to rise. Occas. *trans.*, to fly above.

1885 *Nineteenth Cent.* Aug. 262 Anon with joy it singeth, Vie with the lark it will, And praising God upwingeth Full many a holy hill. **1927** K. MACLEOD *Road to Isles* 212 Gold the morn at dawn upwingeth. **1964** H. E. G. ROPE *Dream Holiday* 10 Amid the kindled altar lights upwings The voice of many martyrs she hath slain.

upya (ʊ·pyă), *int. slang* (chiefly *Austral.*). Also **upyer.** [Corruption of *up you*: see UP *prep.*² 3 b.] (See quots.)

1941 BAKER *Dict. Austral. Slang* 79 *Upya!*, a contemptuous ejaculation. **1955** D. NILAND *Shiralee* 101 No, he said, I won't truckle to you. Upya for the rent. **1966** 'L. LANE' *ABZ of Scouse* II. 112 *Upyer!*, a term of defiance and/or contempt, but often made jocularly.

ur-, *prefix.* Delete 'and occurring in a few terms' and add further examples. See also *URHEIMAT, *URSCHLEIM, *URSPRACHE, *URTEXT.

1926 A. MØLLER tr. *Pedersen's Israel* I. I. 245 The word *shēm* is found in all Semitic languages and belongs to the absolutely certain ur-semitic components. **1927** A. H. MCNEILE *Introd. to Study of New Testament* iii. 50 It was an *Ur-Evangelium*, a primitive written Gospel, some say in Hebrew, some in Aramaic, on which our Gospels were based. **1937** O. JESPERSEN *Analytic Syntax* 142 Some well-known students of language who even call this [*sc.* 'S is P'] the 'urform' of sentences. **1943** V. NABOKOV in *Atlantic Monthly* May 69/2 The dreadful vulgarity, the Ur-Hitlerism of those ludicrous but vicious organisations. **1947** AUDEN *Age of Anxiety* (1948) ii. 46 For Long-Ago has been Ever-After since Ur-Papa gave The Primal Yawn that expressed all things. **1949** F. FERGUSSON *Idea of Theater* i. 26 An enactment of the Ur-Myth of the year-god. **1950** *Psychiatry* XIII. 168/2 The concept of ur-language and ur-symbolism is of particular importance in Freud's thought. **1964** C. S. LEWIS *Discarded Image* iv. 54 Plato's ur-Freudian doctrine of the dream as the expression of a submerged wish. **1966** *Punch* 9 Nov. 718/2 Above is Leonardo da Vinci's design for an ur-tank. **1971** *Astrophysics & Space Sci.* X. 363 (*heading*) Orientation of galaxies and a magnetic 'urfield'. **1977** *Listener* 31 Mar. 416/1 The importance of the folk example which he [*sc.* Bartók] argued to be one of the ur-sources of music. **1979** *Ibid.* 14 June 831/1 Sir Nikolaus Pevsner's ur-history, *Pioneers of Modern Design.* **1983** *Sunday Tel.* 13 Mar. 14/6 Russell Hoban is an ur-novelist, a maverick voice that is like no other.

uracil (yūᵊ·răsil). *Biochem.* [a. G. *uracil* (R. Behrend 1885, in *Ann. d. Chemie* CCXXIX. 11), of unknown origin (perh. f. Eng. UR(EA + G. *ac-etsäure* acetic acid + *-il*).] A pyrimidine base, $C_4H_4N_2O_2$, which is a constituent of RNA.

1890 ROSCOE & SCHORLEMMER *Treat. Chem.* (ed. 2) III. 387 Behrend has succeeded in preparing..compounds, which are derivatives of a hypothetical substance, to which he has given the name uracil. **1907** *Jrnl. Biol. Chem.* III. 187 The uracil dissolved completely on warming. **1944** [see *OROTIC *a.*]. **1959** *Times* 12 June 15/7 It has been calculated..that a thousand-unit polynucleotide chain consisting of a coded repeat of only four different components—adenine, guanine, cytosine, and uracil—in the same ratio as exists in tobacco mosaic virus nucleic acid could form about 10^{67} different arrangements. **1975** *Sci. Amer.* May 25/2 Poliovirus RNA is a single chain of about 7,500..nucleotides, each of which consists of a ribose sugar component and one of four organic bases: adenine, uracil, guanine and cytosine.

Ural¹. b. (Earlier examples.)

1853 C. BUNSEN *Let.* 2 Aug. in Max Müller *Chips* (1873) III. 482 Therefore, for Turanian = Ural-Altaic, or the north-eastern branch. **1854** —— *Outl. Philos. Universal Hist.* I. 291 In the Ural-Altaic languages..we have *one* declension and *one* conjugation, and only a very small number of irregular forms.

uralborite (yūᵊrălbōᵊ·rəit). *Min.* [ad. Russ. *uralborit* (S. V. Malinko 1961, in *Zap. Vsesoyuznogo Min. Obshchestva* XC. 673), f. the name of the *Ural* Mountains: see -ITE¹.] A basic calcium borate, CaB_2O_4, occurring as colourless monoclinic crystals.

1962 *Amer. Mineralogist* XLVII. 1482 Uralborite occurs in radiating-fibrous aggregates of columnar crystals up to 0·5–0·7 cm. **1971** [see *NIFONTOVITE]. **1977** *Soviet Physics—Doklady* XXII. 279/1 The most interesting feature of uralborite is the $[B_4O_4(OH)_8]^{4-}$ 'island' groups ..which are overlapped by the Ca deltadodecahedra forming a three-dimensional cationic skeleton.

urali. (Earlier example.)

1843 MILL *Logic* I. III. vii. 446 If we knew nothing of the Indian arrows but their fatal effect, accident alone could turn our attention to experiments on the urali.

Uralic, *a.* Add: Also as *sb.*, esp. a sub-family of the Ural-Altaic family of languages.

1959 [see *OSTYAK]. **1963** E. A. SEEMAN in *Current Trends in Linguistics* I. 392 (*heading*) Uralic. **1972** [see *OSTYAK]. **1975** G. F. CUSHING tr. *Hajdú's Finno-Ugrian Lang. & Peoples* I. 32 Finno-Ugrian and Samoyed are themselves descendants of a common language called Uralic.

Uralite² (yūᵊ·rălәit). [Etym. unknown.] A proprietary name for an asbestos-based building material.

1899 *Trade Marks Jrnl.* 30 Aug. 1050 *Uralite*... Compounds of asbestos and silica, being manufactures for building and decoration. The British Uralite Company, Limited,..London; manufacturers. **1902** *Chambers's Jrnl.* Nov. 748/1 A demonstration was recently given at the factory at Higham, Kent, of a fireproof material called uralite... Its principal ingredient is asbestos, which is combined with chalk, water-glass and other materials. **1967** 'M. HUNTER' *Cambridgeshire Disaster* v. 33 Prefabricated Uralite billets. **1978** J. MATSON *Dear Osborne* xxi. 133 The buildings..were prefabricated in sections clad with a material called Uralite.

uralitization (yūᵊ:rălitәizēⁱ·ʃәn). *Petrol.* [f. URALITE + -IZATION.] The alteration of a pyroxene, esp. augite, to form an amphibole, esp. actinolite. Hence **u·ralitized** *ppl. a.*

1888 J. P. IDDINGS tr. *Rosenbusch's Microsc. Physiogr. Rock-Making Minerals* 241 The alteration of augite into a hornblende mineral, uralitization, is very common. **1909** *Q. Jrnl. Geol. Soc.* LXV. 378 The uralitized pyroxenes ..have not been transformed into true nephrite. **1954** H. WILLIAMS et al. *Petrography* vi. 112 Also to be ascribed to deuteric action is the widespread uralitization of the augite seen in many monzonites. **1970** *Nature* 23 May 692/1 The rocks..retain much of their original structure and texture, the basalts being uralitized or chloritized.

Uralo-. Add: *Uralo-Altaic* (earlier example).

1877 A. H. KEANE tr. *Hovelacque's Sci. of Lang.* vi. 308 In Central Asia other Uralo-Altaïc [*sic*] tribes have.. adopted Persian.

Uranian, *a.*¹ Add: **1. c.** Homosexual (from the reference to Aphrodite in Plato's *Symposium*). Cf. *URANISM, *URNING.

1893 J. A. SYMONDS in *Spirit Lamp* III. II. 29 Thou standest on this craggy cove, Live image of Uranian Love. **1898** O. WILDE *Let.* c 18 Feb. (1962) 705 To have altered my life would have been to have admitted that Uranian love is ignoble. **1914** E. CARPENTER *Intermediate Types among Primitive Folk* 11 Inversion in some form was regarded as a necessary part of social life, and the Uranian man accorded a certain meed of honour. **1975** P. FUSSELL *Gt. War & Mod. Memory* viii. 294 The effect of the revision is to efface indications of the poem's Uranian leanings, to replace the pretty of 1913 with the nasty of 1917.

B. *sb.*² A homosexual.

c **1908** 'X. MAYNE' *Intersexes* vii. 173 An appreciable influence in developing early Uranism is the fact that the tutor..may be an Uranian of pederastic inclinations. **1909** E. CARPENTER *Intermediate Sex* i. 13 One may safely say that the defect of the male Uranian, or Urning, is *not* sensuality—but rather *sentimentality.* **1947** E. RICKWORD *Coll. Poems* 58 When blessed parthenogenesis arrives and he-uranians can turn honest wives. **1975** P. FUSSELL *Gt. War & Mod. Memory* viii. 283 A less respectable.. tradition of homoeroticism was that of the so-called Uranians, a body of enthusiastic pedophils.

uraniferous (yūᵊrăni·fĕrәs), *a.* [f. URAN- + -IFEROUS.] Containing or yielding uranium.

1912 [see *BETAFITE]. **1957** G. E. HUTCHINSON *Treat. Limnol.* I. xv. 831 Judson and Osmond..have recorded.. much higher values from ground waters in uraniferous localities. **1977** A. HALLAM *Planet Earth* 149 In zones where water has percolated down through uraniferous deposits, torbernite..may occur.

uranism (yūᵊ·răniz'm). *rare.* [ad. G. *uranismus*, f. L. *Urania*, ad. Gr. Οὐρανία, an epithet of Aphrodite: see URANIA, -ISM.] Homosexuality. Hence **u·ranist**, a homosexual. Cf. *URANIAN *a.*¹ 1 c, *sb.*², *URNING.

1895 *Jrnl. Compar. Neurol.* V. 33 The education of congenital inverts (or uranists, to employ a word invented by a famous invert) has not yet been undertaken. *Ibid.* 34 The causes of uranism..are probably as mysterious as those of the difference of sex. **1899** [see MASOCHISM]. *c* **1908** [see *URANIAN *sb.*²].

uranium. Add: **1.** Now important as fissile material in nuclear reactors and atomic bombs. Also with following (arabic) numeral, denoting the mass number of the isotope concerned; and with following (usu. Roman) numeral or capital letter denoting an isotope of uranium or one formed by the decay of uranium.

uranium I, uranium 238; *uranium II*, uranium 234; *uranium X* or X_1, thorium 234 (the decay product of uranium I); *uranium* X_2, metastable protactinium 234 (the decay product of uranium X_1); *uranium Y*, thorium 231 (a decay product of uranium 235); *uranium Z*, protactinium 234 in its ground state.

[**1900** W. CROOKES in *Proc. R. Soc.* LXVI. 418 The new body must have a name. Until it is more tractable I will call it provisionally UrX—the unknown substance in uranium.] **1903** *Phil. Mag.* V. 442 It was shown in 1900 by Sir William Crookes (*Proc. Roy. Soc.*, 1900, vol. lxvi. p. 409) that the activity of uranium to a photographic plate is caused by the presence of a minute amount of a foreign substance to which he gave the name Uranium X. **1911** G. N. ANTONOFF in *Ibid.* XXII. 425 The period of the new product deduced from the curve is 1·5 days... It is proposed to call the new product uranium Y (UrY). **1912** GEIGER & NUTTALL in *Ibid.* XXIII. 444 It enables us to calculate the period of ionium and of the second product in uranium (uranium II.) with greater certainty than has hitherto been possible. Uranium I. therefore.. emits α particles of range 2·5 cm. in air..and is followed by another α-ray product, uranium II., which..emits α particles of range 2·9 cm. **1950** tr. *Hahn's New Atoms* 109 The element 93 remains in bulk in solution—free from uranium, uranium X and the fission products. **1950** GLASSTONE *Sourcebk. Atomic Energy* xiv. 401/2 The non-fissionable uranium-238..constitutes over 99·2 per cent of ordinary uranium. **1960** W. T. L. NEAL in J. C. Collins *Radioactive Wastes* ii. 25 Reactors are operated for three purposes—for fuel production (e.g. production of plutonium-239 from uranium-238, or uranium-233 from thorium-232), for power production and for research. **1962** *Newnes Conc. Encycl. Nucl. Energy* 659/1 Uranium II, U^{234}, is a decay product of natural uranium, being formed by beta decay of uranium X_2 and uranium Z.

b. *uranium fission, fuel*; **uranium bomb**, an atomic bomb in which uranium is the fissile material; **uranium hexafluoride**, a whitish crystalline hygroscopic compound, UF_6, which sublimes at 56°C and is the form in which uranium isotopes are separated by gaseous diffusion; **uranium lead,** (*a*) the isotope lead 206, = *radium G* s.v. *RADIUM 1 b; (*b*) used *attrib.* (with hyphen) to designate a method of isotopic dating, and the results obtained with it, based upon measurement of the relative amounts in rock of uranium 238 and 235 and of their ultimate decay products lead 206 and 207; **uranium series,** the series of isotopes produced by the radioactive decay of uranium 238, each member resulting from the decay of the previous one.

1941 in M. Gowing *Britain & Atomic Energy 1939–1945* (1964) 394 We have now reached the conclusion that it will be possible to make an effective uranium bomb..which would be equivalent as regards destructive effect to 1,800 tons of T.N.T. **1955** *Times* 14 June 6/5 Information appears to be coming to light here which confirms that the so-called hydrogen bomb exploded at Bikini last year was a uranium bomb involving a triple process of fission-fusion-fission. **1964** M. Gowing *Britain & Atomic Energy 1939–45* i. 38 As war began there was much speculation about Hitler's supposed 'secret weapon' and..the uranium bomb was among the candidates for this title. **1942** Pollard & Davidson *Applied Nucl. Physics* x. 187 The answer lies in the discovery of uranium fission by Hahn and Strassman. **1955** J. Lindhard in W. Pauli *Niels Bohr* 193 Through the discovery of uranium fission it became possible to investigate the penetration of highly charged nuclear fragments. **1956** A. H. Compton *Atomic Quest* 321 Uranium fuel must compete economically with such energy sources as coal. **1899** *Collective Index Trans. & Abstr. Chem. Soc. 1873–1882* 629/1 Uranium *hexafluoride*. **1941** in M. Gowing *Britain & Atomic Energy 1939–45* (1964) 395 Work on a fairly large scale is needed to develop the chemical side for the production in bulk of uranium hexafluoride, the gaseous compound we propose to use [for the manufacture of ^{235}U]. **1971** Uranium hexafluoride [see *hex]. **1984** *Times* 27 Aug. 1/6 The ship's owners identified the material as uranium hexafluoride, a radioactive gas. **1914** *Phil. Mag.* XXVIII. 825 The equation for the complete disintegration of uranium is U→8He+Radium G (uranium lead). **1955** [see *thorium lead* s.v. *thorium 2]. **1955** *Bull. Geol. Soc. Amer.* LXVI. 1141/1 (*heading*) Uranium-lead age of the granite. **1977** A. Hallam *Planet Earth* 184/2 Isotopic age measurements by the uranium-lead and rubidium-strontium methods on most meteorites have yielded a solidification age close to 4600 million years. **1909** *Chem. News* 26 Mar. 146/2 (*heading*) A new radio-active product of the uranium series. **1973** Uranium series [see *thorium series* s.v. *thorium 2].

Uranus. Add pronunc. (yurēˈnɒ̆s). For 'one' read 'two'.

Urartian (urăˑɹtiăn), *sb.* and *a.* Also **Urartæan, Urartean.** [f. the name of *Urart(u*, an ancient kingdom in eastern Asia Minor + -ian.] **a.** = *Khaldian b. **b.** A native or inhabitant of Urartu.

1934 Webster, Urartaean *a.* and *n.* **1939** [see *Khaldian]. **1939** A. Toynbee *Study of Hist.* VI. 62 Rediscovered language..Sumerian, Akkadian, Elamite, Urartian,..and so on. **1950** H. L. Lorimer *Homer & Monuments* v. 176 Though the early history of the Urartians is obscure, they are believed to have come eastward to Lake Van from Anatolia. **1964** G. Roux *Ancient Iraq* xiv. 192 Their language [*sc.* that of the Hurrians].. is neither Semitic nor Indo-European, but belongs to the vague so-called 'Asianic' group, its nearest relative being Urartian, the language spoken in the country of Urarṭu (Armenia) in the first millennium B.C. **1965** J. Puhvel *Evidence for Laryngeals* 84 The Urartean *Kulḫai* may correspond to the later city of *Κολχίς* in Armenia. **1972** W. B. Lockwood *Panorama Indo-Europ. Lang.* 175 The I[ndo-E[uropean] immigrants imposed their language on both Hurrians and Urartians and doubtless the non-IE people are ultimately responsible for many of the peculiar and unexplained features of Armenian. *Ibid.* 263, Hurrian is a non-IE language which has affinities with Urartian, the language of the kingdom of Urartu ('Ararat'), centred on the area between the lakes Van, Urmia and Sevan. **1977** *Antiquaries Jrnl.* LVII. 264 The Copenhagen cauldron can be regarded as Greek work of Urartian inspiration in the eighth or seventh centuries B.C.

urban, *a.* and *sb.* Add: **A.** *adj.* **3.** Special collocations: *urban blight*, the gradual unfolding or existence of slum areas, waste land, ghettos, etc., within a city or town (cf. *blight *sb.* 4 b); *urban district*: see District *sb.* 3 b; *urban district council*, the local council of an urban district; abbrev. **U.D.C.*; *urban guerrilla*, a guerrilla operating in cities or towns and involved in kidnapping, etc.; also *attrib.*; *urban guerrilla warfare*, irregular kidnapping, bombing, etc., by urban guerrillas; *urban renewal* (orig. *U.S.*), the clearance and redevelopment of slum areas, waste land, ghettos, etc., within a city or town; also *attrib.* and *fig.*; *urban–rural* adj., of or pertaining to both town and country; *urban sprawl*, the uncontrolled expansion of urban areas; *urban village*, a small self-contained district or community within a city or town (= *village *sb.* 1 e); so *urban villager*, an inhabitant of an urban village.

1938 M. L. Walker (*title*) Urban blight and slums. **1975** M. Bradbury *History Man* i. 14 A real town of urban blight and renewal, social tensions, discrimination. **1894** Urban district council [see sense A. 1b]. **1973** *Whitaker's Almanack 1974* 617/2 Urban district councils are also highway authorities. **1967** G. Jackson *Let.* 31 Jan. in *Soledad Brother* (1971) 106, I have made inroads into political economy..and when I can get hold of them some of the works on urban guerrilla warfare. **1972** *Guardian* 17 Jan. 11/2 The army..is claiming only that it has the measure of the urban guerrilla in Belfast. **1979** G. Seymour *Red Fox* iii. 44 The threat..posed by the rash of urban guerrilla groups. **1955** *Statutes at Large U.S.A.* LXVIII. 1. 622 The heading of title I of the Housing Act of 1949..is hereby amended to read Title I—Slum Clearance and Urban Renewal. *Ibid.*, A fund..known as the 'Urban Renewal Fund', shall be available for advances, loans and capital grants to local agencies for urban renewal projects. **1961** E. A. Powdrill *Vocab. Land Planning* iii. 55 'Urban renewal' can be defined as a generic expression or term which comprises the elements of redevelopment (demolition and rebuilding), rehabilitation (repairing, altering and remodelling), and conservation (the preservation of buildings or groups of buildings). **1966** H. Nielsen *After Midnight* (1967) iv. 61 He heads some extremist group... Sort of an urban renewal project of the Ku Klux Klan. **1977** D. M. Smith *Human Geogr.* v. 104 Some change such as urban renewal or the construction of a new hospital has the capacity to shift the welfare frontier. **1984** *Times* 24 Apr. 13/4 Our delegation visited and discussed urban renewal. **1953** A. E. Smailes *Geogr. of Towns* ii. 33 There is no longer either socially or physically a simple clear-cut dichotomy of town and country; rather it is an urban-rural continuum. **1970** R. Stavenhagen in I. L. Horowitz *Masses in Lat. Amer.* vii. 256 There may be those who see in this situation only an ecologic relation, an 'urban-rural' conflict. **1958** *Listener* 25 Sept. 448/2 The result is a disturbing incidence of crime, juvenile delinquency, road accidents, congestion, urban sprawl, ignorance, and ugliness. **1979** *Monitor* (McAllen, Texas) 8 July 8D/3 Houston's urban sprawl is greater than that of Los Angeles. **1962** H. J. Gans *Urban Villagers* i. 4 The West End was an urban village, located next to Boston's original and once largest skid row area, Scollay Square. **1974** *Times* 15 Apr. 2/4 A device to create an 'urban village' in a predominantly middle-class area. **1962** H. J. Gans (*title*) Urban villagers.

B. *sb.* **2.** = *urban district council* (see sense A. 3 above). *rare.*

1952 M. Laski *Village* ii. 40 'What do you think of this proposal to bring us under Walbridge Urban?'..'Well, I suppose it might mean some street lighting.'

urbanism. (In Dict. s.v. Urban *a.* and *sb.*) Add: Also, town-planning; town-life; urbanization.

1929 *Times* 16 July 17/6 In all the opening speeches.. the newly coined word 'urbanism' was prominent. It denotes town-planning, [etc.]. **1934** A. Huxley *Beyond Mexique Bay* 258 Many primitive virtues are obviously incompatible with urbanism and industrialism. **1952** Gerth & Martindale in *Weber's Anc. Judaism* p. xviii, Weber saw the civic society of Palestine as a variation of ancient Mediterranean urbanism. **1977** *Ecologist* VII. 52/3 The dynamic of urbanism as we know it makes inevitable the syndrome of violence, alienation, high crime rates and delinquency that we associate with our cities. **1980** *Times Lit. Suppl.* 26 Sept. 1061/5 The discussion of the Capitol's urbanism and topography.

Urbanist[1]. Add: **1.** Also *attrib.*

1926 S. F. Smith *Great Schism of West* 22 To say..that the urbanist succession was valid is by no means the same as [etc.].

u·rbanist[2]. [f. Urban *a.* and *sb.* + -ist.] A specialist in or advocate of town-planning.

1930 *Times Lit. Suppl.* 11 Sept. 708/4 To do so would be to entrust the fate of a city to the technical urbanist. **1964** *Economist* 5 Sept. 917/1 The 'urbanists' fight for more railways to revive the city's heart. **1979** *Jrnl. R. Soc. Arts* Nov. 776/1 The Urbanist's rôle is to design fragments of the city which reflect the culture and ideals of these groups while contrasting them with other orders —pragmatic or architectural.

Hence **urbani·stic** *a.*, **urbani·stically** *adv.*

1959 *Listener* 12 Feb. 289/1 Though he [*sc.* Le Corbusier] has derived so much from the study of the city, his own urbanistic achievements are scarcely to be considered to rank alongside his architectural ones. **1975** *Times Lit. Suppl.* 13 June 660/2 Urbanistically, there is no Middle America. **1983** *Listener* 21 Apr. 7/3 An international competition was held for an urbanistic plan for the Sassi.

urbanite (ɒ̄·ɹbănəit). [f. Urban *a.* and *sb.* + -ite[1].] A dweller in a city or town.

1897 *Advance* (Chicago) 29 Apr. 542/1 They will capture streets.., will say to urbanites and suburbanites, 'Stand and deliver.' **1927** *Irish Rosary* July 508 All comes from splendid organizing, bringing peasants, villagers, townsmen and urbanites to meet..and work with bishops, priests, university men. **1960** *Twentieth Cent.* Apr. 347 The urbanite's usual excessive enthusiasm for the beauties of nature. **1979** *Church Times* 29 June 10, I was..only doing what hundred of thousands of other Londoners do every day, as do urbanites in other big cities.

urbanize, *v.* Add: **3.** To accustom to life in a city or town. Chiefly as *pa. pple.* and *ppl. a.*

1948 *Rep. Native Laws Commission 1946–48* (Dept. Native Affairs, S. Afr.) 19/1 There are large numbers of Natives in a transitional state, who are partly urbanised but have not yet broken their ties with the Reserves. **1963** *Daily Tel.* 18 Jan. 15/3 Robins are becoming more 'urbanised'..and will now take crumbs from the hand at the cafeteria. **1969** *Ibid.* 9 Sept. 13/2 The 'good old Mother Earth' myth..can turn the most urbanised of people into horticultural maniacs. **1974** *Times* 22 Apr. 7/3 What about the eight million urbanized blacks living in white cities?

urbanology (ɒ̄ɹbănǫ·lŏdʒi). [f. Urban *a.* and *sb.* + -ology.] The study of cities or towns and their problems. So **urbano·logist.**

1967 *Time* 28 July 11 The 'urbanologist' aspires to be a student of the entire city,..whose concerns go beyond brick and mortar to budgets and laws, souls and sensibilities. Just as the word urbanology is a cross between Latin and Greek, the science..is a mélange of disciplines. **1972** *Daily Colonist* (Victoria, B.C.) 27 Apr. 33/1 The solution as some urbanologists see it is to come up with a new concept in automotive packaging. **1972** *New Yorker* 16 Sept. 124/2 A landscape that transcends all the nickel-and-diming defeats of our urbanology. **1975** M. Bradbury *History Man* iii. 51 The local council, now impressed with Howard's urbanology, have accepted this scheme;..the surviving houses in the terrace will ultimately be restored.

urbicide (ɒ̄·ɹbisəid). [f. L. *urbis, urbs* a city + -cide 2.] The destruction of a city or its character.

1966 *Harper's Mag.* May 94/1 This fearful instrument of urbicide will be not only the tallest, but unquestionably one of the ugliest buildings in the world. **1972** *N.Y. Times* 15 Oct. iv. 14 It does no good to speculate at what point real estate becomes art, or history, or a talisman of place. When it does, it enters the public domain. To destroy it is an act of urbicide.

urbiculture (ɒ̄·ɹbikɒltiŭɹ). [f. L. *urbis, urbs* a city + Culture *sb.*] **a.** The development of cities and towns and urban life; the cultivation of urban interests. **b.** = *rurbanization* s.v. *rurban *a.*

1954 *Daily Progress* (Charlottesville, Va.) 26 July 16/1 A bill introduced by Rep. J. Arthur Younger..to create a U.S. Department of Urbiculture. **1959** [see *rurbanization].

Hence **u:rbicu·lturist.**

1977 *Sat. Rev.* (U.S.) 23 July 48/1 The urbiculturists—give a multimillion-dollar skyscraping enclave or two—move now not to knock down and build anew, but to make over or, to use today's mot juste, to recycle.

‖ **urbi et orbi** (ɒ̄·ɹbi et ǭ·ɹbi), *adv. phr.* [L.] Of papal proclamations, blessings, etc.: to the city (of Rome) and to the world. Also *transf.*, for general information or acceptance; to everyone.

1867 *Chambers's Encycl.* IX. 671/2 *Urbi et Orbi*.., a form used in the publication of papal bulls, for the purpose of signifying their formal promulgation to the entire Catholic world, as well as to the city of Rome. **1876** Mrs. Tait tr. *Klaczko's Two Chancellors* viii. 268 These were the expressions contained in an official document of incontrovertible authority, a diplomatic manifesto which announced *urbi et orbi* the lofty thoughts of the Imperial Government of France. **1889** M. S. Van de Velde *Cosmopolitan Recoll.* II. v. 165 The Conclave met; the election of Camerlingo Pecci was foreseen, it was voted without opposition, and at one p.m., March 3rd, announced *urbi et orbi* from the *loggia* of St. Peter. **1907** G. W. E. Russell *Pocketful of Sixpences* 21 On the eve of the General Election of 1880 she [*sc.* Lady Burdett-Coutts] issued a proclamation, *urbi et orbi*, enforcing the need for a 'strong government'. **1924** J. O. Field *Uncensored Recoll.* xiii. 239 The great pose of Morès..was a deep-rooted hatred of England, to which sentiment he was always giving very loud and dramatic utterance, *urbi et orbi*. **1958** *Listener* 27 Nov. 861/1 The familiar figure dressed in white..giving his benediction *urbi et orbi* from the loggia of St. Peter's. **1961** *Times* 7 Jan. 9/3 The voice of the poet addressing himself *urbi et orbi*. **1973** M. Bence-Jones *Palaces of Raj* v. 105 One of the nobles, whose bard would, every two hours of the night, proclaim *urbi et orbi*..his titles and honours. **1980** *Times* 27 Dec. 3/6 The Pope's traditional Christmas homily *Urbi et Orbi* (to the city and the world).

Urbino (ɒɹbī·no). Name of a city in the province of Le Marche, Italy, and of a former duchy, used *attrib.* to designate (items of) majolica made there from the fifteenth to the seventeenth centuries.

1881 C. C. Harrison *Woman's Handiwork* ii. 104 An Urbino drug-pot, or a Delft plaque. **1883** J. W. Mollett *Illustr. Dict. Art & Archæol.* 331/1 *Urbino ware*, made at Urbino, under the patronage of its Duke. **1924** Rackham & Read *Eng. Pottery* iv. 47 Another class of Italian motives is the strange brood of caryatids, sphinxes, winged beasts, dragons, and semi-monstrous birds... The seed of this kindred may have come in some cases from some piece of Urbino maiolica. **1940** *Burlington Mag.* Aug. 64/2 A large Urbino dish in the Musée de Cluny. **1952** B. Rackham *Italian Maiolica* v. 24 A dish at Cambridge..interesting as an example of Urbino ware with lustre enrichment added by Maestro Giorgio at Gubbio—is now considered to be the work of the son. **1973** *Times* 3 Nov. 2/2 The sale also contained an Urbino majolica dish painted with the murder of Amphiarus by Francesco Xanto.

urchin. Add: **8. urchin cut**, a short style of haircut for women; also as *ppl. adj.*, and *urchin hair-cut.*

1951 [see *cut *sb.*[2] 16 a]. **1958** 'E. Dundy' *Dud Avocado* i. vii. 132 A lot of rather gorgeous..girls floating around with urchin hair-cuts. **1958** *Woman's Own* 4 June 9/1 She was long-limbed, slender, her shining hair urchin-cut. **1958** *Woman* 11 Oct. 32/3 She was small and boyish, with urchin-cut hair. **1979** N. Freeling *Widow* v. 26 A small girl with an urchin face and an urchin-cut.

urea. Add: Delete ‖. Also with pronunc. (yurī·ă).

1. b. A urea-formaldehyde plastic or resin.

1935 *Economist* 7 Dec. 1142/2 Phenolic plastics are used for various mouldings, urea is translucent plastic. **1961** H. R. Symonds *Source Bk. New Plastics* II. ii. 32 A new urea especially prepared for the bonding of particle board. **1969** L. K. Arnold *Introd. Plastics* vi. 83 The ureas are somewhat more expensive [than the phenolics] but have the advantage of being available in a wide range of light colors.

2. urea-formaldehyde, used *attrib.* and *absol.* to designate plastics, resins, etc., made by condensation of urea with formaldehyde;

urea resin, a synthetic resin derived from urea; a urea-formaldehyde resin.

1928 *Brit. Patent 291,473* 3/2 When using urea-formaldehyde resins, alkaline catalysts may be used to obtain the intermediate condensation product. **1933** [see *phenol-formaldehyde* s.v. *PHENOL c]. **1976** *Milton Keynes Express* 9 July 14/4 The majority of houses have cavity walls and these can be insulated by filling the cavity with..a foaming resin called urea formaldehyde. **1984** *Christian Science Monitor* 2 Mar. 23/1 The safety of urea-formaldehyde insulation..has been a subject of debate for years. **1937** R. S. MORRELL et al. *Synthetic Resins* ii. 52 Tootal, Broadhurst, Lee Company Limited have patented the use of urea resins to prevent the crushing of cellulosic fabrics. **1975** M. P. STEVENS *Polymer Chem.* xii. 329 Decorative interior plywood is normally glued with urea resin because the dark-colored phenolic resins can stain the veneer.

ureaplasma (yūᵊrĭ,ăplæ·zmă). *Biol.* Pl. **-plasmas.** [f. UREA + PLASMA.] A micro-organism of the genus *Ureaplasma*, formerly included within the genus *Mycoplasma* (cf. *MYCOPLASMA), which is characterized by the ability to metabolize urea.

[**1974** M. C. SHEPARD et al. in *Internat. Jrnl. Syst. Bacteriol.* XXIV. 160 It is reasonable to propose establishing a new, separate genus in the family *Mycoplasmataceae* in which to classify the T mycoplasmas isolated from man and lower animals. The name *Ureaplasma* is proposed for this new genus, which at present contains a single human species.] **1975** *Jrnl. Med. Microbiol.* VIII. 528 Mouse mastitis is suggested as being a suitable small animal model for studying ureaplasma infections. **1981** *Annales de Microbiol.* CXXXII. B. 172 Ureaplasmas were isolated first from the human genito-urinary tract.

urease (yūᵊ·rĭ,ēⁱz). *Biochem.* [f. URE(A + *-ASE.] An enzyme produced in bacteria and certain plants which converts urea into carbon dioxide and ammonia.

1892 *Jrnl. R. Microsc. Soc.* 515 M. P. Miquel describes a new diastase which according to the nomenclature of Duclaux is called urease. **1926** *Jrnl. Biol. Chem.* LXIX. 437 The jack bean appears to contain a very large amount of urease. **1967** M. E. HALE *Biol. Lichens* iv. 58 These lichens often contain urease enzyme systems. **1982** T. I. DIAMONDSTONE in T. M. Devlin *Textbk. Biochem.* xi. 544 The source of this ammonia is urea, which, being freely diffusible, finds its way into the large intestine, where it is acted upon by bacterial urease.

Urecholine (yūᵊrĭkōᵘ·līn, -in). *Pharm.* Also **ure-**. [f. URE(A + *CHOLINE.] A proprietary term in the U.S. for the preparation of carbaminoyl-β-methyl choline chloride, $C_7H_{17}ClN_2O_2$, a quaternary ammonium compound used as a parasympathomimetic agent to stimulate bowel or bladder muscle activity.

1941 *Official Gaz.* (U.S. Patent Office) 29 Apr. 1104/2 Merck & Co., Inc....*Urecholine* for medicinal preparation for the treatment of disorders of the peripheral circulatory system and for stimulation of the para-sympathetic nervous system. **1954** S. DUKE-ELDER *Parsons' Dis. Eye* (ed. 12) v. 70 Two drugs are sometimes employed which combine the direct and indirect methods of stimulation—doryl..and urecholine (carbaminoyl-β-methyl-choline chloride). **1961** A. GOTH *Med. Pharmacol.* iv. 51 Bethanechol (Urecholine) and methacholine (Mecholyl) have many of the actions of acetylcholine on glands. **1981** GERALD & O'BANNON *Nursing Pharmacol. & Therapeutics* vii. 64/2 Bethanechol (Urecholine), possessing relatively specific effects on the smooth muscle of the gastrointestinal tract and urinary bladder, is clinically employed to restore parasympathetic tone and relieve postoperative abdominal distention and urinary retention.

uredinium (yūᵊridi·niǒm). *Bot.* Pl. **-inia.** [f. L. *ūrēdin-, ūrēdo* UREDO + *-ium*.] A cluster or sorus of uredospores and the hyphæ which bear them. So **uredi·nial, uredi·noid** *adjs.*

1900 B. D. JACKSON *Gloss. Bot. Terms* 283/1 Uredinial. **1905** J. C. ARTHUR in *Bot. Gaz.* XXXIX. 221 For the sorus of the second spore-stage,..I propose *uredinium*..; derivatives *uredinial, urediniospore* or if preferred *uredospore*, etc. **1916** *Mycologia* VIII. 182 Since the development of the uredinial stage is supposed to be subepidermal as a rule, this deviation seems worthy of note. **1929** J. C. ARTHUR et al. *Plant Rusts* i. 13 Less easily recognized as aecia, with spores borne singly on pedicels and usually without peridia or paraphyses, are the stylosporic or uredinoid aecia. **1970** J. WEBSTER *Introd. Fungi* II. iv. 375 Rusts with uredinoid aecia. **1974** G. W. BURNS *Plant Kingdom* ix. 168 (*caption*) Diagrammatic section through a uredinium. *Ibid.* 169 The uredinia begin their development beneath the epidermis of the host. **1982** HIRATSUKA & SATO in Scott & Chakravorty *Rust Fungi* i. 12 The uredinial state is the most destructive spore state of such rusts as wheat stem rust..and poplar leaf rust.

uredium (yurī·diǒm). *Bot.* Pl. **uredia.** [mod.L., f. UREDO.] = *UREDINIUM. Hence **ure·dial** *a.*

1937 *Nature* 8 May 800/2 Forty-four days after the inoculation was made, we observed small uredia on the upper surface of several of the pustules. **1937** Uredial [see *ÆCIUM]. **1949** B. B. MUNDKUR *Fungi & Plant Dis.* vii. 155 Towards the end of the growing season the formation of uredia ceases and teliospores begin to appear. **1967** *Trans. Brit. Mycol. Soc.* L. 192 Aecia usually result from a fertilization process..but they may also originate from aeciospores and, thus, can be a repeating spore form (uredial aecia as in *Cronartium* and *Coleosporium*). **1970** J. WEBSTER *Introd. Fungi* II. iv. 369 A single uredium may contain from 50,000 to 400,000 spores.

uredosorus (yurīdosōᵊ·rǒs). *Bot.* Pl. **-sori.** [f. UREDO + SORUS¹.] = *UREDINIUM.

1905 *Bot. Gaz.* XXXIX. 221 The structure which arises from a single, fertile hyphal mass, or hymenium, either with or without a peridium, now usually called spermogonium, aecidium, uredosorus, teleutosorus, or kindred names. **1930** *N.Z. Jrnl. Sci. & Technol.* XII. 126 The term 'uredosorus' is applied to sori in which the spores are borne singly on distinct pedicels. **1973** *Nature* 17 Aug. 463/1 The majority of plants in the plot were infected, some severely (500-2,000 uredosori per plant).

uredospore. Add: Also **uredi·niospore** [cf. *UREDINIUM], **ure·diospore,** in the same sense.

1905 Urediniospore [see *UREDINIUM]. **1937** *Nature* 8 May 801/1 The urediospores germinate normally and readily infect wheat seedlings. **1970** J. WEBSTER *Introd. Fungi* II. iv. 368 The urediospores [*ed.* 2 (1980): urediniospores] are detached by wind and blown to fresh wheat leaves upon which they germinate. **1978** *Bio Systems* X. 32/1 The first method..has been seen only in two related species of *Uromyces*, although it is the standard means of urediniospore separation as far back as the fern rusts.

ureilite (yūᵊrĭ,ĭləit). *Geol.* [ad. Russ. *ureĭlit* (Erofeev & Lachinov 1888, in *Zhurnal Russ. fiziko-khim. Obshchestva pri Imper. St. Petersburgsk. Univ.* XX. 213), f. the name of Novo-*Ureĭ*, a village near Penza, in the vicinity of which a meteorite belonging to this class fell.] Any of a group of calcium-poor achondrite meteorites that consist mainly of olivine and pigeonite.

[**1889** *Jrnl. Chem. Soc.* LVI. 225 The authors find, after comparison with known classes of aerolites, that the meteorite described above differs from all of them in many points, and propose to name this form ureïlithe.] **1916** *Mineral Mag.* XVIII. 38 The ureilites consist of a coarsely crystalline aggregate of olivine and monoclinic pyroxene cemented together by a film of nickel-iron and carbonaceous matter. **1962** B. MASON *Meteorites* 111 The ureilites form a unique group of three meteorites, quite distinct from all other achondrites. **1971** I. G. GASS et al. *Understanding Earth* viii. 116/1 The presence of diamond in the small group of ureilites appears to be due to extraterrestrial shock effects.

ureotelic (yūᵊrĭ,ote·lik), *a.* *Biochem.* [ad. It. *ureotelico* (A. Clementi 1916, in *Atti della R. Accad. dei Lincei: Rendiconti* XXV. I. 366), f. *ureo-* UREO- + Gr. τελικός final.] Of an animal or its metabolism: producing nitrogenous waste chiefly in the form of urea.

1924 [see *URICOTELIC *a.*]. **1972** M. S. GARDINER *Biol. Invertebrates* xiii. 500 Animals are conveniently classified as ammonotelic, ureotelic, or uricotelic.

uretero-. Add: **ureterocele** [Gr. κήλη tumour, rupture], an outward protrusion of the wall of a ureter; **uretero·graphy**, radiography of the ureters; **ureterosigmoido·stomy** [*-STOMY], the operation of implanting the ureters into the sigmoid flexure of the colon.

1913 *Interstate Med. Jrnl.* XX. 346 On close observation of the right ureter orifice..during urinary excretion, a considerable cystic dilation was noticed and the condition was diagnosed as a ureterocele. **1976** *Lancet* 11 Dec. 1302/1, I would have appreciated more information about those boys with radiological abnormalities who did not undergo surgery, the one with a right ureterocele,..and the 8-year-old with grade-III reflux. **1912** STEDMAN *Med. Dict.* (ed. 2) 961/2 Ureterography. **1926** YOUNG & DAVIS *Young's Pract. Urol.* II. xiii. 241 Ureterography.—The contour of the ureter may be shown by filling it with various shadowgraphic media and taking the *x*-ray film or plate in the same manner as described for pyelography. **1977** *Proc. R. Soc. Med.* LXX. 187/1 Mr Hendry..has described the methods by which today an accurate and precise diagnosis may be made by early high-dose urography and ureterography. **1934** WEBSTER, Ureterosigmoidostomy. **1940** A. I. DODSON *Urol. Surg.* xxxix. 600 If this fails, muscle transplants or ureterosigmoidostomy should be done, depending upon the extent of the deformity. **1977** *Proc. R. Soc. Med.* LXX. 536/2, 2 teenage girls with bladder exstrophy and previous bilateral ureterosigmoidostomy performed in childhood.

urethane. Add: Now usu. with pronunc. (yūᵊ·rĭþēⁱn). [Coined by J. B. A. Dumas 1833, in *Ann. d. Chim. et Physique* LIV. 236.] **1. b.** Any ester of carbamic acid. **c.** By extension, any compound which includes the group —NH·CO·O— in the molecule.

1856 *Jrnl. Chem. Soc.* VIII. 276 Butylic urethane.. forms beautiful nacreous scales. **1876** *Encycl. Brit.* V. 578/1 The neutral ethereal salts of carbamic acid are known as urethanes. **1926** *Jrnl. Amer. Chem. Soc.* XLVIII. 2176 It was decided..to prepare the mono- and dicarbethoxy-guanidines... The compounds may be regarded as urethans. **1954** C. H. FISHER et al. in G. S. Whitby *Synthetic Rubber* xxv. 926 The diisocyanate reacts with the terminal hydroxyls of the polyester, forming urethane linkages. **1968** R. O. C. NORMAN *Princ. Org. Synthesis* xiv. 447 The isocyanate is converted into an amine or a urethane. **1976** A. L. TERNAY *Contemporary Org. Chem.* xxii. 688 Urethanes have high melting points, making them useful as derivatives of phenols.

2. = *POLYURETHANE; also *attrib.* and *fig.*

1956 [see *PROCESSABLE *a.*]. **1969** *Jane's Freight Containers 1968–69* 463/2 Construction: Aluminium extrusion and sheet,..urethane foam, laminated wood. **1971** *Cabinet Maker & Retail Furnisher* 1 Oct. 14/2 Children's stools made of ICI's new solid urethane plastic are being supplied to infant and primary schools. **1976** A. CASSORLA *Skateboarder's Bible* 9 The past can be shrouded by the translucent urethane gauze of the present. **1979** *Arizona Daily Star* 8 Apr. A3/3 (Advt.), Madly flattering sandals of soft kid urethane, with flexible, easy going soles.

urethro-. Add: **urethro·graphy**, radiography of the urethra.

1933 R. M. LECOMTE *Man. Urol.* i. 38 Urethrography. This is done by filling the urethra with a radiopaque solution and taking an x-ray film. **1974** J. D. MAYNARD in R. M. Kirk et al. *Surgery* viii. 157/1 Urethrography. Micturating cystograms do not produce satisfactory radiographs of the urethra.

Urfirnis (ūᵊ·ɹfɔ̄ɹnis). [Ger., f. *ur-* UR- + *firnis* varnish, veneer.] A form of early Greek pottery (see quots.).

1912 WACE & THOMPSON *Prehist. Thessaly* ii. 21 Urfirnis Ware..was first found..at Orchomenos... The whole vase is covered with a thin semi-lustrous wash which varies in colour from red-brown to..black... The Orchomenos Urfirnis naturally occupies a middle position between the Tirynthian and that from Lianokladhi. **1928** PEAKE & FLEURE *Steppe & Sown* x. 126 Into this mixed population [around Corinth] came the Cycladic traders with their characteristic *Urfirnis*, or primitive glazed pottery. **1939** J. D. S. PENDLEBURY *Archaeol. Crete* ii. 75 The pottery, peculiar to Vasilike, is a highly specialized form of 'Urfirnis' ware—the pottery covered with a lustrous black or brown wash—which develops in Greece and the Islands, no doubt with an ultimate Anatolian origin. **1957** V. G. CHILDE *Dawn Europ. Civilization* (ed. 6) v. 65 Besides self-coloured wares a light fabric was made and covered all over with shiny brown or black paint. This ware, termed 'neolithic urfirnis', looks like an attempt to reproduce the appearance of black burnished ware in kiln-fired vases, but is said to begin in Middle Neolithic times in Corinthia. **1970** BRAY & TRUMP *Dict. Archaeol.* 245/2 *Urfirnis*, a characteristic ware of the Early Helladic II period of Greece. It has a buff fabric decorated partly or all over with a dark lustrous slip, often loosely called a glaze.

urgency. Add: **I. 1. b.** (Earlier example.)

1881 E. W. HAMILTON *Diary* 14 Mar. (1972) I. 116 In consequence of these tactics on the part of the Tories, the Government of course failed this afternoon to get the necessary majority to vote urgency.

III. 9. (Earlier example.)

1881 E. W. HAMILTON *Diary* 14 Mar. (1972) I. 116 Another piece of news which took one by surprise was Sir S. Northcote's manifesto deprecating resort to the urgency rules of which Mr. Gladstone had given notice for supply this evening.

urger. Add: **1. b.** A man who obtains money illegally or discreditably, esp. as a tipster at a racecourse. *Austral. slang.*

1919 V. MARSHALL *World of Living Dead* 69 The truly light-fingered gentry, the racecourse urger (tip slinger), the magsman..never hesitate to express their contempt for the more roughly inclined of the profession. **1934** *Bulletin* (Sydney) 21 Mar. 40/3 He was a tout or an urger, I gathered. 'Mixed up in racecourses,' was the way she put it. **1960** A. KIMMINS *Lugs O'Leary* v. 74 'An urger,' explained Lugs patiently, 'is a man who looks around for suckers like you and tips each one a different horse. Someone's *got* to win.'

urgingly, *adv.* (In Dict. s.v. URGING *ppl. a.*) (Earlier example.)

c **1882** 'MARK TWAIN' *Speeches* (1923) 104, I say it beseechingly, urgingly.

‖ **Urheimat** (ūᵊ·rhəimāt). [Ger., f. *ur-* UR- + *heimat* home, homeland.] The place of origin of a people or of a language.

1934 PRIEBSCH & COLLINSON *German Lang.* i. 17 The 'cradle' or primeval home (*Urheimat*) of the Indo-Europeans and their physical characteristics are still matters of controversy. **1950** J. R. FIRTH *Papers in Linguistics 1934–51* (1957) xiv. 178 The more romantic theorists who enjoy Indo-European fantasies and from *Ursprache* go on to speculate on the *Urvolk* and the *Urheimat*. **1976** D. R. SNOW in W. Cowan *Papers 7th Algonquian Conf.* 339 (*heading*) Archaeological implications of the Proto-Algonquian Urheimat.

Uriah Heep (yurəi·ă hīp). The name of a character in Dickens's *David Copperfield* (1850) used allusively for a man who is hypocritically humble. Also *attrib.* Hence **Uriah Heepish** *a.*, reminiscent of Uriah Heep.

1876 [see *ANANIAS]. **1915** J. WEBSTER *Dear Enemy* 77 The Uriah Heepish attitude toward trustees that characterized Mrs. Lippett's manners. **1947** I. BROWN *Say the Word* 106 Uriah Heepish creatures. **1974** *Listener* 4 Apr. 438/1 'If I may—' often issues from the lips of the Uriah Heeps. **1976** A. J. RUSSELL *Pair Hemlock* v. 57 A Uriah Heep kind of guy named Logan.

urial, now the usual spelling of OORIAL, *Ovis orientalis*.

1903 [mentioned s.v. OORIAL]. **1912** R. LYDEKKER *Sheep & its Cousins* xiii. 263 The range of the urial is very wide. **1950** T. LONGSTAFF *This my Voyage* ix. 180 We were astonished to see a herd of urial. **1977** G. B. SCHALLER *Mountain Monarchs* ix. 227 Urial ewes, as well as urial lambs, differed from the others in being almost passive.

uricase (yūᵊ·rikēⁱz). *Biochem.* [a. F. *uricase* (Battelli & Stern 1909, in *Compt. Rend. des*

Séances & Mem. de la Soc. de Biol. LXVI. 412): see URIC *a.* and *-ASE.] An enzyme which promotes the conversion of uric acid into allantoin and is found in certain insects and most mammals other than primates.

1910 *Jrnl. Biol. Chem.* VII. 172 If we limit the use of this term..to the oxidizing enzyme which produces allantoin and CO_2 from uric acid, and appreciate there may possibly exist other enzymes which destroy uric acid.., we find that either the kidney or the liver of every animal investigated, except man..possesses uricase. **1934** *Times Lit. Suppl.* 19 Apr. 286/1 The preparation of soluble uricase from ox kidney. **1956** *Nature* 31 Mar. 622/2 It was also possible to demonstrate the presence of the uricase enzyme in those fungi. **1977** D. E. METZLER *Biochem.* xiv. 883/2 Injection of the uric acid-hydrolyzing enzyme uricase has been tested experimentally.

uricosuric (yūᵊrikosūᵊ·rik), *a. Med.* [f. URIC *a.* + -O + *-s-* + URIC *a.*] Causing or characterized by an increased excretion of uric acid or urate in the urine.

1948 *Amer. Jrnl. Med.* IV. 774/1 This effect is similar to that produced by other drugs..all of which produce a simultaneous increase in minute excretion of urate and a decrease in plasma urate concentration. This pattern of pharmacologic actions has been termed the 'uricosuric effect'. **1961** *Lancet* 19 Aug. 430/2 All phosphate levels were estimated before starting, or at least one month after finishing, uricosuric therapy. **1974** M. C. GERALD *Pharmacol.* xiv. 269 High doses of aspirin, about 5 g, have a uricosuric action. **1980** *Brit. Med. Jrnl.* 17 May 1212 An orally active diuretic with uricosuric properties.

uricotelic (yūᵊrikote·lik), *a. Biochem.* [ad. It. *uricotelico* (A. Clementi 1916, in *Atti della R. Accad. dei Lincei: Rendiconti* XXV. I. 366), f. *urico* URIC *a.* + Gr. τελικός final.] Of an animal or its metabolism: producing nitrogenous waste chiefly in the form of uric acid or urates, as in certain insects, birds, and reptiles, rather than urea.

1924 *Proc. R. Soc.* B. XCVII. 227 Clementi enunciated the doctrine that arginase is present in the livers of all those animals which have what he calls a 'ureotelic' metabolism—a metabolism, that is, in which urea is the final product of protein degradation—and absent from the livers of those in which protein metabolism is 'uricotelic'—ending in uric acid. **1934** *Biochem. Jrnl.* XXVIII. 1390 The uricotelic character of the metabolism of this gastropod is supported by new *in vitro* experiments. **1954** *New Biol.* XVII. 45 The uricotelic nitrogen metabolism of insects..is economical of water since uric acid can be excreted without much water loss. **1979** *Jrnl. Compar. Physiol.* CXXXIII. 211/2 Xeric adapted arboreal frogs of at least two genera..excrete nitrogen predominantly in the form of urate (uric acid), in proportions and amounts similar to uricotelic reptiles.

uridine (yūᵊridīn). *Biochem.* [ad. G. *uridin* (Levene & Jacobs 1910, in *Ber. d. Deut. Chem. Ges.* XLIII. 3152), f. *ur-acil* *URACIL: see *-IDINE.] A pyrimidine nucleoside, $C_5H_9O_4{\cdot}C_4H_3N_2O_2$, in which the base is uracil and the sugar ribose, and which is a constituent of RNA and various intermediates in cell metabolism.

1911 *Jrnl. Chem. Soc.* C. I. 96 Nitrous acid effects the quantitative elimination of the amino-group from cytidine, and uridine is obtained. **1946** [see *NUCLEOSIDE]. **1970** R. W. MCGILVERY *Biochemistry* xx. 477 Uridine triphosphate can be used for nucleic acid synthesis or in the formation of metabolic intermediates such as uridine diphosphate glucose. **1976** *Sci. Amer.* Feb. 33/2 RNA..differs from DNA in that all the thymidine units are replaced by uridine.

uridylic (yūᵊrĭdi·lik), *a. Biochem.* [f. prec. + -YL + -IC.] *uridylic acid*: the phosphoric acid ester, $C_5H_8O_3(PH_2O_4){\cdot}C_4H_3N_2O_2$, of uridine, one of the four nucleotides present in RNA.

1933 *Jrnl. Biol. Chem.* CI. 529 Cytidine is readily transformed into uridine, having properties identical with those of the uridine from uridylic acid. **1946** [see *NUCLEOSIDE]. **1975** *Sci. Amer.* May 25/2 There are four kinds of nucleotide, named for their bases: adenylic acid, uridylic acid, guanylic acid and cytidylic acid, better known as *A, U, G* and *C*.

urinalysis. Delete *U.S.* and add further examples.

1971 *Nature* 12 Mar. 113/1 All subjects had a routine physical check-up, including complete blood counts, urinalysis, chest X-ray, [etc.]. **1980** *Daily Tel.* 15 Oct. 19/6 A post-fight urinalysis showed the presence in Ali of opiates and the drug Phenothiazine.

urine, *sb.*[1] Add: **3.** *urine-sodden* adj.

1912 *Man. Elem. Milit. Hygiene* (War Office) x. 62 The front of the latrine rapidly becomes a urine-sodden quagmire. **1944** *Public Health* LVII. 137/1 Nauseating odours assail one's nostrils on entry, and the source is usually located in some urine-sodden faecal-stained mattress in an upstairs room.

urine·tte. [pseudo-Fr., f. URIN(E *sb.*[1] + -ETTE.] (See quot. 1967.)

1954 J. PUDNEY *Smallest Room* 35 The 'urinettes' have always been there. **1967** *Gloss. Sanitation Terms* (*B.S.I.*) 58 *Urinette*, a urinal like an elongated W.C. pan, for female use.

‖ **urinoir** (ürinwār). [Fr.] A public urinal.

1955 G. GREENE *Quiet American* II. iii. 147 The old women gossiped as they had always done, squatting on the floor outside the urinoir. **1962** *Spectator* 16 Nov. 770 A wrought iron urinoir in Holborn.

Urkey (ɔ̄·ɹki). [Origin unknown.] A local name of a children's game (see quot.). Also, the person who is 'it' in this game. As *v. trans.*, to defeat in this game. Cf. *LERKY.

1938 E. THOMAS *Childhood E. Thomas* iii. 53 The best game was an evening one, called Urkey. One boy who was Urkey stood still by a tin can while the others hid. When a shout told that they had found a hiding place he went in search of them. His object was to see one and run home to the can, crying 'I Urkey Johnny Williams.'

urlar (ūᵊ·ɹlăɹ). [Gael.] (See quots.)

1889 *Cent. Dict.* s.v. *Pibroch*, It consists of a ground-theme or air called the *urlar*, followed by several variations,..the whole concluding with a quick movement called the *creanduich*. **1900** C. S. THOMASON *Ceol Mor* 5 The Ground or *Urlar*, which corresponds to the *Thema* or Theme of ordinary modern music. **1925** J. P. GRANT *Piobaireachd* 27 All that appears is the Urlar and a Doubling. The first and third lines of the Urlar correspond with Angus Mackay's MS. **1962** A. MACLEOD *Eighth Seal* iv. 44 Flora had been working out the *urlar*, the groundwork or theme of her pibroch. **1977** *Meanjin* (Austral.) XXXVI. I. 80 *Urlar* and *Siubhal*..are respectively the 'ground' and 'variations' in classical pipe music.

urn, *sb.* Add: **7. urnfield,** a cemetery of individual cremation graves with remains in pottery urns, *esp.* as used by North European peoples from *c* 1200 B.C. onwards; also *attrib.*, esp. designating peoples using this rite or their cultures.

1889 [see URN *sb.* 7]. **1928** V. G. CHILDE in *Antiquity* II. 37 On the continent as in Britain the later phases of the Bronze Age are marked by the spread of large cremation cemeteries generally termed urnfields. One of the several groups of urnfield cultures in Central Europe occupies such a pre-eminent position that it may even claim to be the parent of all the rest. It is known as the Lausitz or Lusatian culture. **1958** T. G. E. POWELL *Celts* 38 The dead were generally cremated, and the broken bones placed in an urn for burial in a flat cemetery. Many of these cemeteries..have been called urnfields so that the descriptive labels 'Urnfield Period' and 'Urnfield Culture' have come into use. **1968** A. POWELL *Military Philosophers* iv. 177, I walked up the road.., leaving them [*sc.* Welshmen] to move eastward towards the urnfields of their Bronze Age home. **1979** B. CUNLIFFE *Celtic World* 15/1 This period, generally referred to..as the Urnfield period, is typified by the appearance of large cremation cemeteries, the ashes of the dead interred in urns. The tradition took form in Hungary sometime in the thirteenth century B.C. and was rapidly adopted further west.

urning (ɔ̄·ɹniŋ). Now *rare*. Also **Urning.** [a. Ger., coined by K. H. Ulrichs ('Numa Numantius') in 1864.] A homosexual. Cf. *URANIAN *a.*[1] I c, *sb.*[2], *URANISM.

1883 *Jrnl. Nervous & Mental Dis.* Apr. 200 For himself and fellow-Urnings there was nothing left but this unnatural love. **1892** C. G. CHADDOCK tr. *Krafft-Ebing's Psychopathia Sexualis* 255 The urning loves and deifies the male object of his affections. **1896** J. A. SYMONDS *Probl. Mod. Ethics* vii. 91 Man, Woman, and Urning—the third being either a male or a female in whom we observe a real and inborn, not an acquired or a spurious inversion of appetite. **1909** E. CARPENTER *Intermediate Sex* (ed. 2) 135 According to the information of De Joux.. the number of Urnings in all Europe is about five millions.

uro-[1]. Add: **urodyna·mics,** the branch of medicine concerned with the containment and flow of urine in the body; hence **urodyna·mic** *a.*; **urolithi·asis,** lithiasis in the bladder or urinary tract; **urothe·lium** [EPI)THELIUM], the epithelium of the urinary tract, esp. the bladder; hence **urothe·lial** *a.*; **urotro·pine** (-pīn), † **-in** [ad. G. *urotropin* (A. Nicolaier 1895, in *Deut. med. Wochenschr.* 22 Aug. 541/1): see *-TROPIC, -INE[5]] = *hexamethylenetetramine* s.v. *HEXA-.

1963 *Jrnl. Urol.* XC. 730/2 Practical application of electromanometric urodynamic studies depends upon additional information. **1981** *Brit. Med. Jrnl.* 23 May 1706/3 The clinical and urodynamic evaluation of incontinence in elderly patients. **1954** D. M. DAVIS in *Ann. Surg.* CXL. 839 (*heading*) The hydrodynamics of the upper urinary tract (urodynamics). **1977** *Lancet* 13 Aug. 335/2 The past decade has witnessed an enormous step forward in our knowledge and understanding of the mechanisms involved in incontinence in women and consequently of the principles of management. The new science that has evolved is that of urodynamics. **1865** W. ROBERTS *Pract. Treat. Urinary & Renal Dis.* II. iii. 209 (*heading*) Gravel and calculus. (Urolithiasis.) **1926** YOUNG & DAVIS *Young's Pract. Urol.* I. vi. 388 Urolithiasis is one of the four important and serious conditions causing hematuria. **1966** *Lancet* 31 Dec. 1455/2 The prevalence of urolithiasis in Arad was lower than in the Beersheba settlers, and the urinary output was higher. **1977** *Ibid.* 26 Mar. 684/2 Close similarities between Balkan nephropathy and urothelial tumours with respect to geographical clustering, age, and sex. **1954** P. A. NARATH in M. Campbell *Urology* I. I. iii. 88 Absorption is accomplished by the urothelium which lines the tract. **1977** *Proc. R. Soc. Med.* LXX. 413/2 In patients with bacterial infections of the lower urinary tract it is possible that small amounts of nitrosamines may be produced which could initiate neoplastic or preneoplastic changes in the urothelium. **1895** *Amer. Practitioner & News* XX. 486 The name urotropin was applied to hexamethylenetetramin owing to the changes which its administration brought about in the urine. **1897** *Lippincott's Med. Dict.* 1097/2 Urotropine. **1898** *Therapist* VIII. 115/1 (*heading*) Administration of urotropine and its effects upon the urine. **1940** [see *hexamethylenetetramine* s.v. *HEXA-]. **1967** J. A. SIMMONS et al. in H. S. Pieser *Crystal Growth* (Jrnl. Physics & Chem. Solids Suppl.) 270/1 In the cases of urotropine and arsenolite the growth forms change when the crystal starts with disturbed growth.

urobilin. Add: [Coined as G. *urobilin* by M. Jaffe 1869, in *Arch. f. Path. Anat. & Physiol.* XLVII. 406.]

urobilinogen (yūᵊrobəili·nŏdʒĕn). *Biochem.* [f. prec. + *-OGEN.] Any of a group of colourless tetrapyrrole compounds produced by the reduction of bilirubin, esp. by bacterial action in the gut, and forming urobilin upon subsequent oxidation.

1893 A. EICHHOLZ in *Jrnl. Physiol.* XIV. 331 Reserving the name urochromogen for the body isolated from urine, one may perhaps adopt the name urobilinogen for this artificial product. **1947** *Radiology* XLIX. 303/2 This excessive destruction of red cells is also indicated by a maintained increase in excretion of fecal urobilinogen and urinary bilirubin. **1974** R. M. KIRK et al. *Surgery* vi. 97 Jaundice... The kidneys excrete conjugated bilirubin.. and urobilinogen..so that the urine is dark.

uroboros (yūᵊrobǫ·rŏs). Also **ouroboros, uroborus.** [ad. Gr. οὐροβόρος, also οὐρη-, devouring its tail (freq. connected with δράκων).] The symbol, usu. in the form of a circle, of a snake (or dragon) eating its tail.

1940 H. G. BAYNES *Mythol. of Soul* vi. 221 Thus the *uroborus* symbol represents our psychic continuity with the immemorial past. *Ibid.*, Geber, or Jabir, the most famous of the Arabian alchemists, who lived in Kufa about A.D. 776, used the *uroborus* to represent a closed system or magic ring, denoting the idea of an eternal process. **1953** R. F. C. HULL tr. *Jung's Psychol. & Alchemy* in *Coll. Wks.* XII. III. v. 357 The alchemical parallel.. is the double nature of Mercurius, which shows itself most clearly in the Uroboros, the dragon that devours, fertilizes, begets, and slays itself and brings itself to life again. **1957** N. FRYE *Anat. Criticism* 157 Alchemical symbolism takes the ouroborus and the hermaphrodite..in this redemptive context. **1975** HUGHES & BRECHT *Vicious Circles & Infinity* Fig. 11 The ouroboros, the snake with his tail in his mouth, is the prototype of the vicious circle. ..The 'Endless Snake' depicts an ouroboros who has become one with himself. It has fallen into the mathematical sign for infinity.

urochloralic (yūᵊ:rokloᵊræ·lik), *a. Biochem.* [tr. G. *uro-chloralsäure* urochloralic acid (von Mering & Musculus 1875, in *Ber. d. Deut. Chem. Ges.* VIII. 666), f. URO-[1]: see *chloralic* adj. s.v. CHLORAL.] *urochloralic acid*: a metabolite formed in the body after chloral has been administered (see quot. 1977).

1875 *Jrnl. Chem. Soc.* XXVIII. 1040 The authors propose to give it the provisional name of urochloralic acid. **1882,** etc. [see *GLYCURONIC *a.*]. **1931** *Chem. Abstr.* XXV. 349 (*heading*) The pharmacology of urochloralic acid with special regard to the diuretic action of the sodium salt of this acid. **1977** *Martindale's Extra Pharmacopoeia* (ed. 27) 753/2 Chloral hydrate is..excreted slowly in the urine as trichloroethanol and its glucuronide (urochloralic acid).

urodæum, -eum. (yūᵊrodī·ɒ̆m). *Zool.* Pl. **-æa, -ea.** [mod.L., irreg. f. URO-[1] + Gr. ὁδαῖος on or by the way.] The part of the cloaca into which the urinary ducts open.

1888 H. GADOW in *Phil. Trans. R. Soc.* B. CLXXVIII. 28, I propose to designate the typical urino-genital and fæcal chambers the Urodæum and Coprodæum in accordance with Professor E. Ray Lankester's terms Stomodæum and Proctodæum. **1897** PARKER & HASWELL *Text-bk. Zool.* II. xiii. 368 The cloaca is a large chamber divided into three compartments, the coprodæum.., the urodæum.., and the proctodæum. **1959** W. ANDREW *Textbk. Compar. Histol.* xi. 444 Urine formed in the kidney is concentrated in the cloacal chambers (urodeum and coprodeum) where water is absorbed through the walls. **1975** *Nature* 17 Jan. 217/2 At the other end, the proctodeum opens into urodeum leading to the coprodeum.

urogastrone (yūᵊrogæ·strōᵘn). *Biochem.* [f. URO-[1] + GASTR(IC *a.* + -ONE; cf. *enterogastrone* s.v. *ENTERO-.] Any of a number of closely related humoral agents in mammalian urine which retard gastric secretion and motor activity.

1940 J. S. GRAY et al. in *Proc. Soc. Exper. Biol. & Med.* XLIII. 228 Until such time as the gastric inhibitory factor is definitely identified, we propose to call it urogastrone. **1946** *Nature* 31 Aug. 305/1 (*heading*) Urease in the gastric mucosa and its increase after a meat diet, soya bean flour diet or urogastrone injections. **1966** WRIGHT & SYMMERS *Systemic Path.* I. xiv. 494/1 Extracts of normal urine contain a substance, urogastrone, that inhibits the action of pepsin and hydrochloric acid. **1975** *Nature* 25 Sept. 325/1 The two urogastrones were shown to be water-soluble polypeptides of relatively low molecular weight and the difference between them could be shown by various physical techniques including acrylamide gel electrophoresis.

urography (yurǫ·grăfi). *Med.* [f. URO-[1] + -GRAPHY.] Radiography of the urinary tract.
1925 W. F. BRAASCH in *Jrnl. Urol.* XIV. 631 The present widespread employment of urography as an aid in the diagnosis of surgical conditions affecting the urinary tract merits careful consideration. **1962** *Lancet* 19 May 1049/1 Excretory urography showed that both kidneys were functioning well. **1977** *Proc. R. Soc. Med.* LXX. 187/1 An accurate and precise diagnosis may be made by early high-dose urography and bulb ureterography.

Hence **urogra·phic** *a.*; also **u·rogram**, a radiogram of the urinary tract.
1925 W. F. BRAASCH in *Jrnl. Urol.* XIV. 632 The personal equation may be a large factor in interpreting the urogram. *Ibid.* 634 That it is often the cause of obscure abdominal pain..is not borne out by pathologic, urographic or clinical evidence. **1940** P. S. PELOUZE *Office Urol.* xii. 520 Every patient in whom a movable kidney is felt or suspected should be subjected to urographic study. **1980** *Nature* 17 Apr. 619/1 The success of transplantation and the cross-sectional area of the kidneys were demonstrated on excretory urograms.

urokinase. (yūᵊrokəi·nēⁱz). *Biochem.* and *Pharm.* [f. URO-[1] + *KINASE.] An enzyme which catalyses the conversion of plasminogen to plasmin and is used in the treatment of blood clots.
1952 G. W. SOBEL et al. in *Amer. Jrnl. Physiol.* CLXXI. 768/2 Normal human and dog urine contains..a potent activator of profibrinolysin (plasminogen). The activator ..we have designated urokinase. **1977** *Daily Colonist* (Victoria, B.C.) 23 Oct. 10/5 Urokinase is used in the treatment of blood clots and scientists said it has the potential of preventing 50,000 deaths per year in the United States alone. **1983** DAVIES & MCNICOL in *Oxf. Textbk. Med.* II. xix. 132/2 Urokinase is produced naturally by cells in the kidney and is present in human urine, probably to aid maintenance of ureteric patency.

urolagnia (yūᵊrolæ·gniă). *Psychol.* [f. URO-[1] + Gr. λαγνεία, act of coition, lust.] Sexual pleasure derived from urination. Hence **urola·gnic** *a.*
1906 H. ELLIS *Stud. Psychol. Sex* V. iii. 47 These [functions] are sometimes termed the scatalogical group, with the two subdivisions of urolagnia and coprolagnia. *Ibid.* 62 So far we have been concerned with the urolagnic.. variety of scatalogical symbolism. **1940** HINSIE & SHATZKY *Psychiatric Dict.* 545/1 *Urolagnia*.., pleasure connected with urine... Some individuals gain gratification in watching others urinate. **1980** *Spectator* 5 July 20 Was it his mother's fault that he suffered from urolagnia?

uronic (yurǫ·nik), *a. Chem.* [f. URO-[1] + *-n-* + -IC 1 b, or f. *GLYC)URONIC *a.*] *uronic acid*: any derivative of a monosaccharide in which the —CH_2OH group has been oxidized to a —COOH group.
1925 D. R. NANJI et al. in *Jrnl. Soc. Chem. Industry* 253 T/2 Lactose oxidised by bromine in presence of calcium carbonate yields a dicarboxylic acid from which galacturonic acid can be obtained on hydrolysis, whilst sucrose under similar treatment yields glycuronic acid. We shall refer to these compounds as 'uronic' acids. **1946** *Nature* 24 Aug. 271/1 The viscosity of solutions containing the 'recovered' sodium alginate is..higher..than that of solutions of salts of low molecular uronic acids. **1982** N. B. SCHWARTZ in T. M. Devlin *Textbk. Biochem.* viii. 430 The long heteropolysaccharide chains are made up largely of disaccharide repeating units, in which one sugar is a hexosamine and the other a uronic acid.

uropod (yūᵊ·ropǫd). *Zool.* [f. URO-[2] + Gr. πούς, ποδ- foot.] Orig., any abdominal appendage of a crustacean; now *spec.* each of the sixth and last pair of abdominal appendages of malacostracan crustacea, which together form part of the tail fan in lobsters.
[**1884** A. SEDGWICK tr. *Claus's Elem. Text-bk. Zool.* x. 454 The three posterior pairs of abdominal feet (uropoda) are well developed and often much elongated.] **1893** T. R. R. STEBBING *Crustacea* iv. 46 In Amphipoda the fourth and fifth pairs [of abdominal appendages] are more or less adapted for springing, and bear the name of uropods, or tail-feet. This name is also given to the appendages of the twentieth segment whenever they are present. **1933** R. H. WOLCOTT *Animal Biol.* xlii. 251 The appendages of the last abdominal segment [of the crayfish] are broad and flat and are called uropods. **1974** *Encycl. Brit. Macropædia* V. 547/1 In hermit crabs the uropods are modified into structures that help to hold the abdomen of the crab in the gastropod shell in which it lives.

uroporphyrin (yūᵊropǭ·ɹfirin). *Biochem.* [ad. G. *urinporphyrin* (H. Fischer 1915, in *Zeitschr. f. physiol. Chem.* XCV. 34): see URO-[1] and *PORPHYRIN.] Any of a group of porphyrins, occurring esp. in the urine during certain types of porphyria, in which each of the pyrrole rings has one acetate and one propionate side chain.
[**1915** *Chem. Abstr.* IX. 2884 Methyl ester..prepd. by the action of MeOH-HCl upon urinoporphyrin.] **1924** *Ibid.* XVIII. 2720 For uroporphyrin and coproporphyrin ..the spectra are now shown to be quite distinct. **1939**, etc. [see *PORPHOBILINOGEN]. **1955** [see next]. **1958** *New Biol.* XXV. 75 The African plantain-eaters [*sc.* a family of birds]..are unique in possessing two uroporphyrin pigments, green turacoverdin and the turacin. **1978** A. R. BATTERSBY in Porter & Fitzsimons *Further Perspectives Org. Chem.* (CIBA Symp. No. 53) 37 M. Thompson mixed the protiomethyl ester of uroporphyrin-II with the corresponding deuteriomethyl ester.

uroporphyrinogen (yūᵊ:ropǭɹfiri·nǒdʒĕn). *Biochem.* [a. G. *uroporphyrinogen* (Fischer & Zerweck 1924, in *Zeitschr. f. physiol. Chem.* CXXXVIII. 242): see prec. and *-OGEN.] Any porphyrinogen in which the pyrrole rings have side chains as in a uroporphyrin.
1924 *Chem. Abstr.* XVIII. 3063 (*heading*) Uroporphyrinogen heptamethyl ester and a new conversion of uro- into coproporphyrin. **1955** *Science* 17 June 878/2 Uroporphyrins and very small amounts of coproporphyrins have been recovered after incubation of uroporphyrinogen I or III..with *Chlorella* preparations. **1982** T. M. DEVLIN *Textbk. Biochem.* xxii. 1077/1 This enzyme acts on the side chains of the uroporphyrinogens to form the coproporphyrinogens.

uropygium. (Earlier example.)
1771 G. WHITE *Let.* in *Selborne* (1789) xxxv. 92 The trains of those magnificent birds [*sc.* peacocks]..growing not from their *uropygium*, but all up their backs.

urs (ūᵊɹs). Also **'urs, Urs.** [a. Arab. *'urs*, lit. 'marriage ceremony'.] A ceremony celebrating the anniversary of the death of a Muslim saint. Also *attrib.*
1839 T. J. NEWBOLD *Straits of Malacca* I. v. 252 There is no particular day..on which they congregate to perform the Urs, or pilgrimage. **1885** T. P. HUGHES *Dict. Islam* 655/2 *'Urs*.., the ceremonies observed at the anniversary of the death of any celebrated saint or *murshid*. **1974** *Encycl. Brit. Macropædia* IX. 920/1 The Muslim masses also celebrate the death anniversaries of various saints in a ceremony called *'urs* (literally, 'nuptial ceremony'). The saints, far from dying, are believed to reach the zenith of their spiritual life on this occasion. **1975** *Bangladesh Observer* 18 July 8/1 Five hundred Muslims from Bangladesh and 150 from Pakistan were among about one lakh devouts who attended the urs. **1979** *Morning News* (Karachi) 24 May 3/4 An exquisite silver embroidered velvet green 'Chadar'..will be flown..from Lahore for laying at the Mazar of Hazrat Khwaja Moeenuddin Chishti during the Urs celebrations starting at Ajmer Sharif from May 28.

‖ **Urschleim** (ūə·rʃləim). [Ger., f. *ur-* UR- + *schleim* slime.] In early biology, the original form of life; protoplasm.
1921 G. B. SHAW *Back to Methuselah* p. xxix, Lorenz Oken..defined the original substance from which all forms of life have developed as protoplasm, or, as he called it, primitive slime (*Urschleim*). **1958** *Times Lit. Suppl.* 15 Aug. 454/4 When first it was investigated a belief arose in a plain of *Urschleim* on the ocean bed, a protoplasmic half-living matter, in which the process of creation was still at work.

ursid (ɒ̄·ɹsid), *a.* and *sb.* [a. mod.L. family name *Ursidæ*, f. L. *ŭrsus* bear, adopted as a generic name by Linnæus (*Systema Naturæ* (1735)): see -ID[3].] **A.** *adj.* Of, pertaining, or belonging to the family Ursidæ. **B.** *sb.* A mammal of this family.
1921, 1973 [see *PROCYONID *sb.* and *a.*]. **1976** *Nature* 22 Apr. 700/1 They have revealed..the ursid nature of the giant panda. **1979** *Ibid.* 12 July 138/1 Groups thus added to the Sahabi faunal assemblage include primates, ursids, [etc.].

ursinia (ɒ̄ɹsi·niă). [mod.L. (J. Gaertner *De Fructibus et Seminibus Plantarum* (1791) II. 462), f. the name of John *Ursinus* (1608–66), German botanist + -IA[1].] An annual or perennial aromatic herb of the genus of this name, belonging to the family Compositæ, native to South Africa, and bearing orange, yellow, or white flowers.
1928 *Gardeners' Chron.* 7 July 9/1 This Ursinia remains open until dark. **1959** *Listener* 26 Mar. 572/1 For the cool greenhouse ursinias make lovely pot plants. **1976** *Hortus Third* (L. H. Bailey Hortorium) 1140/1 The annual ursinias of the flower garden are grown from seeds planted indoors or directly in the open.

‖ **Ursprache** (ūᵊ·ɹʃprāχə). Also **ursprache.** Pl. **-en.** [Ger., f. *ur-* UR- + *sprache* speech: see note s.v. UR-.] = *PROTO-LANGUAGE.
1908 T. G. TUCKER *Introd. Nat. Hist. Lang.* ix. 163 The Semitic Ursprache (or common parent). **1922** O. JESPERSEN *Language* iii. 85 The basis of the whole was not an artificially constructed nebulous *ursprache*, but the familiar forms and words of an historical language. **1937** *Science & Society* I. 158 The term 'Indo-European school' is..applied..to all scholars using the general methods employed in the study of these languages (for instance, the building of *Ursprachen* on the basis of detailed comparisons in surviving languages). **1950** [see *URHEIMAT]. **1964** R. H. ROBINS *Gen. Linguistics* viii. 319 The 'starred forms'..give reasons for assuming the existence of an earlier relatively unitary stage of I[ndo]-E[uropean] (or any other family established in this way), the so-called Ursprache, or parent language; but they do not constitute it, or represent word forms in it or any other language. The evidence for the earlier existence of an Ursprache is not the same as bits of the Ursprache itself. *a* **1975** A. TOYNBEE *Greeks & their Heritages* (1981) 122 Greek, Latin and Sanskrit..are all close enough in structure to their common progenitor, the *Ursprache*, to have retained the *Ursprache*'s principal characteristic.

‖ **Urtext** (ūᵊ·ɹtekst). Also **urtext.** [Ger., f. *ur-* UR- + *text* TEXT *sb.*[1]] An original text; the earliest version. Also *attrib.* or as *adj.*
1932 *Times Lit. Suppl.* 14 July 511/3 In these volumes ..we have the nearest thing possible in Chopin's case to an *Urtext*. **1959** *Cambr. Rev.* 6 June 598/2 Authoritative editions allegedly based on urtexts. **1963** S. WEINTRAUB *Private Shaw & Public Shaw* iv. 119 The earlier version still retains advocates, because of its more complete, ur-text quality, and the comfortable feeling that no Procrustean games were played with its vocabulary and sentence structure. **1974** *Early Music* Oct. 259/1 The edition is *urtext*, with prefatory staves, showing the original clefs and signatures. **1982** *Times* 2 Apr. 14/2 An *urtext* edition of the 21 Schubert piano sonatas. **1983** *London Rev. Bks* 7–20 July 21/4 Elaborate versions often point back to the gospel of Mark as a kind of cryptic *Urtext*.

urucuri. (Earlier example.)
1860 [see *INAJÁ].

Uruguayan (yūᵊrŭgwəi·ăn, ūᵊr-, -gwēⁱ-), *a.* and *sb.* [f. *Uruguay*, the name of a republic in eastern S. America + -AN.] **A.** *adj.* Of or belonging to Uruguay or its inhabitants; produced in or characteristic of Uruguay. **B.** *sb.* A native or inhabitant of Uruguay.
1869 *Jrnl. R. Geogr. Soc.* XXXIX. 340 A piece of solid gold weighing over 1 lb..has been taken out of the quartz on the surface, and is in the hands of the Uruguayan minister of war. **1889** *Cent. Dict.*, *Uruguayan*..*a.* and *n.* **1912** *20th Cent. Impr. of Uruguay* 225/2 The Uruguayan soil contains the necessary chemical components for the general run of agricultural farming. **1923** R. SETON *Memories Many Years* 113 There I met the Uruguayan idling about. **1972** *Daily Tel.* 11 Apr. 13/8 While duelling is perfectly within Uruguayan law, there are one or two ways in which the authorities seek to discourage it. **1976** *Nature* 22 July 243/2 The Uruguayans in their zeal to stamp out the Tupamaro guerillas seem to have 'processed' an extraordinarily large proportion of the population.

Uruk (u·rŭk). The Sumerian name of an ancient city in southern Iraq (mod. Warka), used *attrib.* in *Uruk period* to designate a phase in Sumerian-Akkadian culture.
1932 *Antiquity* VI. 198 The Jemdet Nasr culture is preceded at Uruk (Warka)..by an older urban civilization in which writing was being developed, that is termed the URUK I culture. *Ibid.* 522 (Index), Uruk culture. **1934** V. G. CHILDE *New Light Most Anc. East* vi. 146 The next phase is..best known as a result of the excavations so meticulously conducted and so promptly published by the Germans at Erech. It is accordingly designated the Uruk period (Uruk is just the Babylonian form of the Hebrew Erech). **1947** D. DIRINGER *Alphabet* i. 41 The earliest extant written cuneiform documents, consisting of over one thousand tablets and fragments, discovered mainly at Uruk or Warka, the Biblical Erech, and belonging to the 'Uruk Period' of the Mesopotamian pre-dynastic period, are couched in a crude pictographic script and probably Sumerian language. **1958** L. COTTRELL *Anvil of Civilisation* vii. 94 Phase Two, the so-called 'Uruk' period, [was discovered] by the Germans at Warka.

‖ **urushi** (urū·ʃi). Also 8 **urusi.** [Jap.] The Japanese lacquer tree, *Rhus verniciflua*; also, Japan lacquer, used for coating Japan ware.
1727 [see *Japan varnish (tree)*]. **1881** *Encycl. Brit.* XIII. 590/2 The varnish tree is of several kinds, and the *Urushi* tree growing in Japan..supplies, it is said, a finer gum than any other of the same species. **1909** *Cent. Dict.* Suppl., *Urushi*,..Japanese lacquer; varnish. **1965** W. SWAAN *Jap. Lantern* x. 120 Lacquer is made from the sap of the *urushi* or lac tree. **1983** *New Scientist* 21 Apr. 149/1 Far Eastern lacquer, or *urushi*, is a poisonous exudate from the stems of the lacquer tree, or varnish sumach.., which can be tapped like those of rubber trees.

urushiol (ŭrū·ʃiǫl). *Chem.* [f. Jap. *urushi* (see prec.) + -OL.] An oily phenolic liquid causing skin irritation which is present in various plants and is the main constituent of the lacquer obtained from the Japanese lacquer tree.
1908 *Chem. Abstr.* II. 2307 According to the author [*sc.* K. Miyama] the main constituent of the lac is a polyhydrophenol with unsaturated radicles in the side chains, the name Urushiol is proposed for it. **1945** *Jrnl. Amer. Med. Assoc.* 7 Apr. 920/2 It is highly probable that urushiol is the irritant common to ivy, sumac and the lac trees. **1974** J. E. UNDERHILL *Wild Berries Pacific Northwest* 95 Sumach is closely related to Poison Ivy.. and Poison Sumach... It lacks the poisonous oil, urushiol, that makes them such a hazard.

us, *pers.* and *refl. pron.* Add: **I. 1. c.** *one of us*: see *ONE *numeral a., pron.*, etc. B. 15 b.

f. Persons like ourselves; ordinary citizens, as opp. to those in authority.
1948 *Observer* 17 Oct. 5/2 The 'whistle stops'..break down the difference between 'them' and 'us'. **1957**, etc. [see *THEM *pers. pron.* 1 e]. **1962**, etc. [see *THEM *pers. pron.* 3 c]. **1984** *Times Lit. Suppl.* 26 Oct. 1206/1 The Chinese awareness of 'us and them' is intense, pervasive and hard to break down.

2. b. For † Obs. read *'Obs. exc. dial.'* and add later examples.

1861 O. W. NORTON *Army Lett.* (1903) 35 We..then took possession of a stack of wheat and made us good beds and slept well. **1907** S. E. WHITE *Arizona Nights* x. 166 We got us timbers, and made a scow. **1928** 'M. CHAPMAN' *Happy Mountain* 42 We'll make us a heap o' cash money. **1942** *Sat. Even. Post* 22 Aug. 42/3 Le's go and wake us up a preacher.

5. d. Also as *adj.*, suited to or representative of our tastes, personality, etc.; appropriate for us. Usu. *predic.*

1940 M. DICKENS *Mariana* viii. 312 'How could you know I'd like something like this?'..'It just looked absolutely us, somehow.'

usage, *sb.* Add: **10.** *attrib.*, as (sense 8) *usage guide, label, labelling.*

1972 R. D. WALSHE in G. W. Turner *Good Austral. Eng.* xi. 241 There is a need for up-dating. This is true of most of the 'usage guides' which editorial offices and printeries use in order to impose a consistency of style. **1980** *Amer. Speech* LV. 134 Readers of these usage guides too often take them as gospel truth. **1967** F. CHRISTENSEN in P. B. Gove *Role of Dict.* 24/2 The new dictionary has dropped the usage label *colloq.*..altogether. **1981** *Dictionaries* II.–III. 75 Usage-label treatment is just as important to the composition student as treatment of synonyms. **1977** *Computers & Humanities* XI. 89/2 In this kind of usage labeling, 'label' is not to be taken literally. **1982** *Papers Dict. Soc. N. Amer. 1977* 66 The first of these anxieties gives weight to the need for rather particular status-labelling—and this term (used in Webster's) also seems..preferable to 'usage-labelling'.

Usbeck, Usbeg, etc., varr. *UZBEK.

use, *sb.* Add: **IV. 17.** (Examples of *for the use of* with the obj. of *of* preposed.)

1959 [see *MALLABY-DEELEY]. **1971** D. FRANCIS *Bonecrack* iv. 44 There was..an armchair of sorts, visitors for the use of.

21. b. (Earlier example.)

1872 *Harper's Mag.* June 158/2 He was an obstinate fellow..and moreover, he 'had no use for' the defendant any way.

V. 22. use immunity *U.S. Law* (see quot. 1972); **use-life,** useful life.

1972 *New Yorker* 25 Mar. 86/3 The suggested revision, known as 'use immunity', would prevent anyone who was compelled to testify from being prosecuted on the basis of that testimony. **1976** *Ibid.* 19 Apr. 42/3 Under use-immunity law, however, people who were compelled to testify could later be prosecuted as long as the government did not base its case against them directly or indirectly, on their own testimony. **1950** *Chambers's Jrnl.* Mar. 191/2 It is now reported that the magnesium type of dry-cell has a 'use-life' of about thirty hours. **1972** *Computers & Humanities* VII. 87 Interactive systems on today's scale are very recent; for the program designer there are obstacles of rapid change, little standardization, and relatively high development expenses in relation to the probable use-life of the programs.

use, *v.* Add: **II. 11.** (Further examples.) Now *esp.*, to take or consume (an alcoholic drink, a narcotic drug) regularly or habitually.

1902 KIPLING *Traffics & Discoveries* (1904) 15, I don't use rum as a rule, but I did then, because I needed it. **1906** W. CHURCHILL *Coniston* I. ix. 104 Unlike Jethro, he 'used' tobacco. **1921** J. BUCHAN *Path of King* xiv. 276 It's curious that a man who don't use tobacco or whisky should be such mighty good company. **1929** D. HAMMETT *Dain Curse* xiv. 149 He..picked up the morphine paper... 'What do you suppose this is doing here?' he asked. 'She uses it.' **1942** J. D. CARR *Seat of Scornful* iv. 43 'Not that I've got any objections to 'em,' Mr. Morell assured him, alluding to the tobacco and the spirits. 'Just don't use 'em.' **1962** H. BURN *Drugs, Med. & Man* x. 106 The best known drugs of addiction are morphine, heroin and cocaine. Somewhat less well known are cannabis..and pethidine. These are the main drugs, other than alcohol, which are used by addicts. **1982** J. WAINWRIGHT *Anatomy of Riot* 31 Okay, a little hash here an' there. He sold it. Maybe he used it. Okay, he used it.

14*. *to be able to use*, to be in need of, to be in a position to benefit from, to want. *colloq.*

1956 'N. SHUTE' *Beyond Black Stump* viii. 217 But I could use a river, and the sight of snow on a mountain. **1958** V. SCOTT *Savage Affair* ix. 152 Listen..they said they might see their way to an advance. Two-fifty apiece. You could use two hundred and fifty dollars, couldn't you? **1961** R. GODDEN *China Court* 258 'I could use a gin,' said Bella. **1976** *Ulverston* (Cumbria) *News* 3 Dec. 1/6 The tarn is the most beautiful part of the village and The Landings can use some cleaning up. **1977** *Oxford Diocesan Mag.* July 18/1 We could have used more time to explore this avenue.

V. 20. Add to note: and *colloq.* in *did* (*not*) *use* (or *used*) *to*; see also *USEN'T, *USETER. (Further examples.) *used to could*: see *CAN *v.*[1] A. 7.

1857 C. M. YONGE in *Monthly Packet* Jan. 34 'Things didn't use to be so stupid when Ned was there!' sobbed Gilbert. **1873** —— *Pillars of House* II. xvi. 105 Did Alda use to be nice, or is it love? **1925** S. LEWIS *Arrowsmith* xviii. 192 Didn't we used to have fun. **1927** E. HEMINGWAY *Men without Women* 154 He certainly did used to make the fellows he fought hate boxing. **1935** E. FARJEON *Nursery in Nineties* III. i. 124 Mama, did you use to be a flirt? **1963** V. NABOKOV *Gift* ii. 117 And now I continually ask myself what did he use to think about in the solitary night. **1974** *Radio Times* 28 Feb. 25, I suppose I did use to be a prophet of doom. **1983** *Listener* 10 Feb. 31 (*heading*) Adrenalin sports are big. TV didn't used to be one.

24. To take drugs. *slang.*

1953 W. BURROUGHS *Junkie* (1964) x. 104 The reason it is practically impossible to stop using and cure yourself is that the sickness lasts five to eight days. Twelve hours of it would be easy, twenty-four possible, but five to eight days is too long. **1960** C. COOPER *Scene* 15 Why don't you bust a cap with me? It's choice. I used this morning and I'm still nice. **1962** 'K. ORVIS' *Damned & Destroyed* xi. 71 Almost twenty-four hours..since I've had a fix... Are you the only one?..You forget I use, too.

used, *ppl. a.* Add: **I. 1. b.** *spec.* (*a*) (esp. of a vehicle) = SECOND HAND, SECOND-HAND B. 2; also in hyphenated attrib. phr.; (*b*) of paper currency: not in mint condition.

1931 *Punch* 3 June 589/2 It seems there is little demand nowadays for used cars. People find they can get all the walking exercise they need without buying a second-hand car. **1932** L. N. WRIGHT *Links of Old Family Tree* x. 184 She was tempted to go into the business of dealing in used furniture. **1938** [see *REPOSSESSION 1]. **1955** F. O'CONNOR *Wise Blood* iv. 67 By six-thirty, he was down town, looking for used-car lots. **1960** I. JEFFERIES *Dignity & Purity* i. 12 He gave me five hundred quid in used ones. **1966** J. B. PRIESTLEY *Salt is Leaving* i. 12 Albert is doing quite nicely in the used-car business. **1970** 'D. HALLIDAY' *Dolly & Cookie Bird* vii. 109 Nine thousand used dollar bills.

II. 5. (Earlier example.)

1839 H. MCLEOD *Let.* 18 Jan. in *Papers M. B. Lamar* (1922) II. 423, I will come down in a few days with Genl Rusk, but I am really so 'used up' now, that I cannot undergo the fatigue.

u·sed-to-be, *sb. U.S.* [cf. USE *v.* 20 *Comb.*] A person whose time of popularity or efficiency is past; also = *EX *sb.*[1]

1853 [see *HAS-BEEN *sb.*]. **1911** [see *never-was* s.v. *NEVER *adv.* 8]. **1942** L. HUGHES *Shakespeare in Harlem* 50, I want to tell you 'bout that woman, My used-to-be—She was de meanest woman I ever did see.

useful, *a.* and *sb.* Add: **1. c.** Applied to an odd-job man. *Austral. colloq.*

1866 R. HENNING *Let.* 16 May (1966) 219 There are three men employed about the place [*sc.* a logging business]. The bullock-driver, the punt-man and a 'generally useful' man. **1900** H. LAWSON *Middleton's Peter* in *Stories* (1964) 1st Ser. 293 There were two rooms..attached to the stables. One was occupied by a man who was 'generally useful'.

2. c. *useful load* (Aeronaut.), the difference between the maximum permitted weight of an aircraft and its weight when empty, including cargo, passengers, crew, fuel and (with some writers) fixed equipment such as radios also; similarly *useful weight.*

1909 A. BERGET *Conquest of Air* II. iv. 205 A 'useful weight' in the form of fuel and oil to the extent of 80 kilogrammes. **1914** *Sphere* 7 Mar. 298/2 The most remarkable of the new aeroplanes is the Sikorsky... It can carry a useful load of over a ton. **1978** D. B. THURSTON *Design for Flying* ix. 112 If the airplane is intended for the ..private market, thin skin could be used and the weight saved converted to useful load.

d. Of a performer or performance: reasonably effective, fairly successful.

1955 *Amer. Speech* XXX. 23 A horse with a seemingly excellent racing background will be described as good; and a horse the record of which..would seem good will be described as useful. **1959** *Listener* 23 July 129/1 He.. played a useful game of cricket..with a local league side. **1971** N. STACEY *Who Cares?* i. 19, I had been a useful school sportsman and got into the first eleven at most sports at Dartmouth.

e. Of a woman's dress; practical, unostentatious; suitable for a variety of occasions.

1963 *Observer* 3 Nov. 33/1 In the dress trade, 'a useful little dress' means one with no distinguishing characteristics; 'romantic' means 'cleft to the waist'. **1968** M. JONES *Survivor* i. 22 The dinner was arranged... She had dressed with restraint in a 'useful' black dress.

B. *sb.* **1.** See sense 2 b in Dict.

2. An odd-job person. *Austral. colloq.*

1898 A. JOYCE *Homestead Hist.* (1969) 41 Our friends had met with a trained carpenter in town, whom with his wife they had hired for £20 a year, the man as general useful,..and his wife as cook. **1935** K. TENNANT *Tiburon* 37 Roman stepped out of the room next to the laundry of O'Brien's Hotel, where he was barman, yardman and general useful. *a* **1963** J. FOUNTAIN in 'B. James' *Austral. Short Stories* (1963) 277 Every boy..knew the..circumstances of..Maggie's affair with the useful from the hotel.

usen't, colloq. shortening of *used not.*

c **1863** T. TAYLOR in M. R. Booth *Eng. Plays of 19th Cent.* (1969) II. 96, I usen't to mind unkind looks and words much once. **1907** G. B. SHAW *Major Barbara* III. 255 That is a new accomplishment of Andrew's, by the way. He usent to drink. **1929** 'H. H. RICHARDSON' *Ultima Thule* III. v. 279 Usen't Richard to say that it was etiquette in the profession to treat a patient's relatives.. as so many cretins?

user[1]. Add: **1. a.** *spec.* A person or organization that makes use of a computer. Freq. *attrib.* and *Comb.* (cf. sense 5 below).

1967 [see *user-assigned* adj., sense 5 below]. **1973** C. W. GEAR *Introd. Computer Sci.* iv. 151 The software makes it possible for a user to prepare procedures and have them executed by the computer with a minimum of effort. **1984** *Which Micro?* Dec. 8/1 Micro breakdown..drives users to despair.

b. A person who takes narcotic, etc., drugs. orig. *U.S.*

1935 A. J. POLLOCK *Underworld Speaks* 129/2 *User*, a person addicted to any of the poisonous habit forming drugs; a hop-head; dope fiend. **1953** W. BURROUGHS *Junkie* (1964) vi. 58 The owner knew Tony had been a user and had told him to stay off the stuff or get another job. **1969** *Guardian* 3 Dec. 9/1 She was taking six grains of heroin a day... She had been a user for about six months. **1975** H. WHITE *Raincoast Chron.* (1976) 144/2 There had always been users around in the shadowy back streets. **1983** *Easyriders* Feb. 111/4 Harley man, 29 ..seeks lady 5′7″ or under for friend, lover, and partner... No boozers or heavy users.

5. *attrib.* and *Comb.*, as *user benefit, charge, cost, fee, group*; *user-assigned, -supplied* adjs.; *user-processing*; **user-definable** *a. Computers*, having a function or meaning that can be specified and varied by a user; so **user-defined** *a.*; **user-friendly** *a. Computers*, easy to use; designed with the needs of users in mind; also *transf.*; hence **user-friendliness**; **user interface**, the means by which a person is enabled to use a computer; **user-orientated, -oriented** *adjs.*, designed with the user's convenience given priority; **user-programmable** *a. Computers*, capable of being programmed or assigned a function by the user.

1967 COX & GROSE *Organization & Handling Bibl. Rec. by Compuer* 84 The valves DCN, DATE, DAY, etc. are the user-assigned names for the bibliographic data fields. **1972** *Computers & Humanities* VI. 303 We will study the cost-effectiveness of stripping away various features.. with least prejudice to user-benefit. **1945** *Sun* (Baltimore) 29 Sept. 3/2 John J. Pelley, president of the Association of American Railroads, urged..that 'user charges' be levied against highway, waterway and airway carriers. **1976** *Times* 29 Nov. 12/2 It is possible to raise only one cheer for user charges as a means of avoiding the dilemma of cutting public services or increasing taxes. **1936** J. M. KEYNES *Gen. Theory Employment* vi. 70 We have defined the user cost as the reduction in the value of the equipment due to using it as compared with not using it. **1969** D. C. HAGUE *Managerial Economics* (1971) II. v. 103 The cost of servicing and repairs is part of what economists call 'user cost', the cost of using the car (or any other asset) instead of leaving it idle. **1972** *IBM Technical Disclosure Bull.* XIV. 3553 (*heading*) Representation of tree data structures as matrices suitable for user-definable traversing. **1983** *MicroComputer Printout* Sept. 69/1 A programmable character set (also called user-definable) may let you design your own characters—mathematical symbols, or foreign alphabets. **1985** *Personal Computer World* Feb. 133/1 The number of user-definable characters that you can enter at the Model 4 Keyboard in this way is limited to 20. **1968** *Simulation* XI. 304/2 User-defined functions. **1984** *Which?* July 302/1 In rating graphics..we looked at..the range of graphics features provided with the computer-graphics characters, ..sprites,..user-defined graphics (shapes you can set up yourself) and so on. **1984** *Personal Software* Winter 26/2 The program will allow you to have up to fifty user defined commands. **1980** *Tucson* (Arizona) *Star* 4 Mar., He sees no reason why 'user fees'..should not be charged for libraries. **1984** *Gainesville* (Florida) *Sun* 28 Mar. 12A/5 It is clear that (Proposition 1) fails to allow for increased demand on government-owned utilities and other user-fee services resulting from population increases and other causes. **1979** *Interfaces* May 72 User friendliness is a term coined by Harlan Crowder to represent the inherent ease (or lack of ease) which is encountered when running a computer system. **1982** *Daily Tel.* 7 Dec. 2 (Advt.), The system has been very well received—a credit to the HP 3000's user-friendliness. **1977** BIRSS & YEH *Set Theoretic Data Structures* (*STDS*) 31 STDS-I does not provide the user with a sufficiently 'user-friendly' interface to allow noncomputer scientists to easily work with a data base. **1982** *New Scientist* 30 Sept. 931/1 The program it works from is 'user-friendly' insofar as the commands are based on initials such as CV for 'centre vertically' and FD for 'forms design'. **1984** *Which Micro?* Dec. 3 (Advt.), Every computer manufacturer now claims its products are 'user friendly'. **1984** *Listener* 13 Dec. 38/1 No TV show (not even the news) could close without reference to this user-friendly family of dolls. **1972** *Accountant* 26 Oct. 518/2 To satisfy the information needs of entrepreneurs, investors, and other outside user-groups is to guarantee a full and active future for the accountant. **1983** *Lebende Sprachen* XXVIII. 48/1 Language mediators represent one of the largest user groups of terminology. **1968** *Proc. Internat. Fed. Information Processing* (1969) I. II. 570 Three levels of user interface are defined for the information retrieval language. **1983** *Byte* Feb. 36/1 The company's first task was to devise a new user interface—that is, a new and better way for humans to interact with the computer. **1985** *Personal Computer World* Feb. 137/2 The operating system, GSX and GEM Services bind together to form the programmer interface, but they do not provide the user interface directly. **1969** *Computer Aided Design* Winter 5/2 The plea for more languages..which are specific to particular problems, and in this sense 'user-orientated'. **1978** *Hi-Fi News* Sept. 218 (Advt.), There's a low distortion equaliser, tape duplication switch..plus a host of user-orientated features. **1964** *Communications Assoc. Computing Machinery* VII. 290/1 (*heading*) An experiment in a user-oriented computer system. **1979** *Dictionaries* I. 110 User-oriented service programs..could put the student in immediate contact with a wealth of lexicographic information. **1958** *Newnes Compl. Amat. Photogr.* 283 Kodak Ltd. propose eventually to market processing kits..for the user-processing of Kodacolor Film. **1976** *Scientific & Technical Aerospace Rep.* XIV. XXII. 2927/1 To fulfil all desired capabilities, a user programmable communication device is required. **1983** *What's New in Computing* Jan. 60/1 The full alphanumeric and function key keypad..includes..eight user-programmable keys. **1969** *Computers & Humanities* III. 130 It contains the ability to perform, *inter alia*, the following tasks:... Generate reports of extracted data according to user-supplied format.

useter (yū·stəɹ). Also **useta, uster.** Repr. an informal or uneducated pronunc. of *used to* (see USE *v.* 20 in Dict. and Suppl.).

1890 *Dialect Notes* I. 69 When it rains and wets our old rooster, He don't look like he useter. **1898** J. D. BRAYSHAW *Slum Silhouettes* 215 I've just seed Liz Dukeson,.. her that Cocky uster cart abaht. **1921** E. O'NEILL *Emperor Jones* v. 185 Is you sellin' me like dey uster befo' de war? **1935** in Z. N. Hurston *Mules & Men* (1970) I. viii. 172 Naw, dat's Uncle Yistiddy, he's a useter-be! **1937** D. L. SAYERS *Busman's Honeymoon* i. 57 You mind the little cottage down by the river..where old Blunt useter live? **1952** M. STEEN *Phoenix Rising* vi. 134 Dey say she gone to Harlem... Useta teach school. **1978** L. BLOCK *Burglar in Closet* (1980) i. 8, I useta beg her to keep some of that stuff in a safe-deposit box. **1982** A. TAYLOR *Caroline Minuscule* x. 79 'He said it'd be all right for me to doss down here... He useter—' 'Liar. He couldn't have done.'

ush, *v.*[2] **2.** (Earlier example.)

1890 *Harper's Mag.* Dec. 160/2 The six gentlemanly cow-boys..swore that whoever should prove to be the lucky man, the others would ush for him at the ceremony.

ushabti (uʃæ·bti). *Egyptology.* Also **ushebte, ushebti.** Pl. **ushabtis, -iu.** [a. Egyptian *wšbty* answerer.] A figurine of a deceased person, made of faience, stone, wood, etc., and placed in an ancient Egyptian tomb to act as a substitute for the dead person in any work he might be called upon to do in the afterlife. Also *ushabti-figure.* See also *SHABTI, *SHAWABTI.

1885 E. A. W. BUDGE *Dwellers on Nile* viii. 164 The figures placed with the dead were called *ushabtiu*, and were inscribed with the name of the deceased and the sixth chapter of the Book of the Dead. **1894** H. M. TIRARD tr. *Erman's Life in Anc. Egypt* xiii. 317 Besides these models of servants and of sailors which replaced the earthly domestics of the departed, there were many other figures of a different kind... These are the so-called funerary statuettes, or as they are termed in Egyptian the Ushebte, *i.e.* the *answerers.* **1910** *Encycl. Brit.* V. 709/1 This polychrome faience was also now [*sc.* in the Eighteenth Dynasty] used for the *ushabti* figures which were placed in the tombs; hitherto they had been made exclusively of stone or wood..the plain blue and black of the ordinary vases was adopted. The *ushabtis* of King Seti I...are fine specimens of this type. **1925** *Glasgow Herald* 27 July 8 The ushabtiu figures..were deposited either in the coffin itself or near to it. **1933** A. W. SHORTER *Everyday Life in Anc. Egypt* viii. 175 The actual meaning of the word *ushabti* is not known for certain, one explanation being that the word is derived from the verb *usheb* 'to answer', and therefore means 'answerer'—i.e. one who comes at the summons of the deceased. *Ibid.* 176 The *ushabti*..represents the deceased himself in mummy form... The *ushabti*-figures of the Eighteenth Dynasty.. are made of wood or stone... The manufacture of faïence *ushabtiu*, however,..became popular. **1957** L. DURRELL *Justine* I. 57 The air was all at once full of..tear-bottles, Ushabti, and Sèvres. **1961** A. H. GARDINER *Egypt of Pharaohs* iii. 32 The tombs of the well-to-do often yield hundreds of small statuettes mostly of faience or wood now generally known by their later name of *Ushabti* figures or 'answerers'..; the earlier writing Shawabti is of doubtful meaning. **1979** H. EVANS *Mystery of Pyramids* ii. 62/2 To make this everlasting life as comfortable as possible, the spirit called upon the magical aids and implements provided in its earthly tomb. These facilities even included model figures, *ushabtis*, that could act as substitutes if the gods called for workers in the fields.

Ushak (u·ʃak). [ad. Turk. *Uşak.*] Also **Ouchak, Oushak.** The name of a town in W. Turkey used *attrib.* or *ellipt.* to denote a type of antique rug made there.

1901 J. K. MUMFORD *Oriental Rugs* iv. 35 For rugs of the heavier quality, such as the ponderous Oushaks and Anatolians, the sheep of the Asia Minor plains produce a wool that is adequate in length, and..soft to the touch. **1905** M. C. RIPLEY *Oriental Rug Bk.* xv. 115 In Turkish carpets of large size many styles are grouped under the trade name 'Ouchak' in which modern methods are observable. **1922** KENDRICK & TATTERSALL *Hand-Woven Carpets, Oriental & European* I. II. i. 100 The carpets of Asia Minor, of the kind called Ushak, which date from the fifteenth to the seventeenth centuries, are invariably woven with the Ghiordes knot. **1931** A. U. DILLEY *Oriental Rugs & Carpets* Pl. 45 (*caption*) Ushak prayer rug, late sixteenth.century. **1952** B. MIALL tr. *Jacoby's How to know Oriental Carpets & Rugs* 106 From the very first the Ouchaks differed very perceptibly, in colour and design, from the Persian carpets. **1975** 'E. LATHEN' *By Hook or by Crook* xvi. 152 We should list some of our best rugs... Or just mention the Ushak. **1977** *Times* 12 Feb. 14/6 (*heading*) Rare Ushak carpet is sold for £42,000. **1984** *Times* 1 June 12 (*caption*) Charles Sternberg with the large Ushak (or Mahal) for which he paid £48,600.

usher, *v.* Add: **1. d.** Also, to act as an usher in a cinema. *U.S.*

1973 *Publishers Weekly* 27 Aug. 243/1 A 13-year-old boy who ushers in a movie house. **1980** M. GORDON *Company of Women* (1981) I. i. 26 It was teen-agers who flocked to see that kind of movie. Mary Rose had to usher at those movies now.

usherette. [f. USHER *sb.* + -ETTE.] A female usher in a cinema or theatre.

1925 *College Humor* Aug. 66/2 The obese usherette in the toney movie house who has to wear a different fancy dress costume every week. **1926** *Bulletin* 27 Feb. 2 Thirty beautiful girls..will receive visitors to..the Plaza, at its opening on Tuesday. They will be called 'usherettes'. **1948** *Times* 24 Feb. 7/4 Will the usherette hush the little fellow crying in the stalls. **1960** M. SPARK *Ballad Peckham Rye* vii. 136 She's an usherette at the Regal from six-thirty to ten-thirty. **1980** R. BUTLER *Blood-Red Sun at Noon* (1981) II. i. 129 Nothing in her career as theatre usherette, conjuror's assistant and night-club hostess had prepared her for this kind of life.

ushership. 2. (Earlier example.)

1788 W. COWPER *Let.* 30 Nov. (1982) III. 233, I was under his ushership at Westminster.

usitative, *a.* For *rare*[−1] read *rare* and add later example.

1939 [see *CONSUETUDINAL *a.* and *sb.*].

usnea. (Earlier *attrib.* example.)

1854 THOREAU *Walden* 137 The single spruce stands hung with usnea lichens.

u-s-ness. [-NESS.] The fact of being or feeling united in mind, feeling, or purpose; the fact of forming a unity.

1927 *Glasgow Herald* 7 Mar. 6 In a magazine story... 'It's Us-ness that makes love,' the heroine of the tale is made to say to the hero, 'it's being two of you together against the world.' **1958** *Listener* 27 Nov. 874/1 One of the dangers of 'The Method' is that it tends to reduce everything to us-ness, if I may so put it. **1966** P. J. KAVANAGH *Perfect Stranger* vii. 77 There was a pleasant feeling of 'us-ness' in the unit. Were the prisoners 'us' or had they comfortably become 'them'? **1976** *Christian* III. 167 This has the effect of buttressing and reinforcing the me-ness of me (insistently individual) as part of the intensified us-ness of us (compellingly corporate).

‖ **usque ad nauseam** (ʊ·skwe æd n·ǭziæm). Also **ad nauseum usque.** [L., = 'right up to sickness'.] = *AD NAUSEAM.

1616, 1693 Ad nauseam usque [see *AD NAUSEAM]. **1819** T. MOORE *Tom Crib's Memorial* p. xxxi, That person has already been exhibited, perhaps, 'usque *ad nauseam*',. before the Public.

ussingite (ʊ·siŋəit). *Min.* [ad. Da. *ussingit* (O. B. Bøggild 1913, in *Meddelelser om Grønland* (1914) LI. 103), f. the name of N. V. *Ussing* (1864–1911), Danish mineralogist: see -ITE[1].] A triclinic basic sodium aluminosilicate, $Na_2AlSi_3O_8OH$, found as reddish-violet crystals.

1914 *Chem. Abstr.* VIII. 3170 (*heading*) Ussingite, a new mineral from Kangerdluarsuk, Greenland. **1975** *Jrnl. Geol.* LXXXIII. 763/1 In both localities, ussingite is late-stage in character, occurring as a pegmatitic mineral in Lovozero [in the Kola Peninsula, USSR].., and as a hydrothermal vein mineral, in the Ilimaussaq intrusion [in Greenland].

ustad (u·stād). Also **Ustad.** [Pers., Urdu.] A master, esp. of music.

1903 M. A. STEIN *Sand-Buried Ruins Khotan* viii 125 The few 'ustads' (masters) who cared to attend to my orders. **1967** V. MEHTA *Portrait of India* 40 He is Hindustani music's unrivalled *ustad* (Urdu for 'master'). Actually, '*ustad*' is a sort of Muslim counterpart of '*guru*'. **1971** *Femina* (Bombay) 16 Apr. 8/3 She was able to become the pupil of the well-known Ustad Atah Khan of Patiala.

Ustashi (ustā·ʃi), *sb. pl.* (also taken as *sing.* with pl. *-s*). Also **-chi, -ci, -sha, -ša, -še, -si.** [a. Serbo-Croatian *Ustaše* pl., *Ustaša* sing., insurgent rebel.] (Members of) a party and separist movement of Croatians; the soldiers and supporters of the autonomous Croatian régime between 1941 and 1944: as *sing.*, a member or supporter of the Croatian separatist movement. Also *attrib.*

1932 *Times* 8 Oct. 11/6 The Ustasi move in small groups from village to village and organize their adherents, train them in shooting, and disappear as suddenly as they came. **1943** C. HOLLINGWORTH *German just behind Me* xiii. 258 There are also the terrorist societies such as the Croat *Ustashi.* **1946** A. M. HYAMSON *Dict. Internat. Affairs* 334 *Ustaci, The,* the party of Croatian Fascists who, under Pavelitch and subject to the overriding veto of Germany and Italy, governed Croatia after its conquest in 1941 by Germany. **1949** KOESTLER *Promise & Fulfilment* II. i. 217 The Arab troops in this region were..reinforced by.. Croat Ustachis. **1949** F. MACLEAN *Eastern Approaches* III. iii. 334 The independent State of Croatia..was a kingdom, but its King, the Italian Duke of Spoleto, had wisely omitted to take up his appointment and power was in the hands of Ante Pavelić and his Ustaše, supported by the Wehrmacht. *Ibid.,* Orthodox churches were..burned down with the screaming congregation inside them (an Ustaše speciality, this). **1961** E. WAUGH *Unconditional Surrender* III. i. 210 There are five or six divisions of Cetnics and Ustachi..the Serb and Croat Quislings. **1972** *Guardian* 28 Jan. 11/2 If Ustashi activists..planted a bomb on board the Yugoslav airliner..it will be their biggest outrage since the war. **1973** *Nation Rev.* (Melbourne) 24–30 Aug. 1405/1 Frequent statements that the Ustasha exists in Australia and that the croatian community..condones terrorist acts. **1976** *New Yorker* 22 Mar. 64/2 Two Croatian nationalists—members of Ustaša, the party that ran an 'autonomous' Croatian state for the Nazis during the Second World War, killed hundreds of thousands of other Yugoslavs, and operates now as a secret terrorist society—tortured and then murdered the Yugoslav ambassador to Sweden. **1976** J. COLVILLE *Footprints in Time* xxxvii. 213 The fanatic Croat Ustasi. **1978** 'G. VAUGHAN' *Belgrade Drop* vii. 46 The caves where the Ustaše, the Croat fascists whose fanaticism in Hitler's cause had rivalled that of the SS, had butchered the Partisans. **1980** *Listener* 28 Feb. 265/3 The Ustashas were Croat Fascist collaborators.

usual, *a.* Add: **3.** Freq. in *usual channels* [CHANNEL *sb.*[1] 8]; *usual office(s*: see *OFFICE *sb.* 9 b.

1905 *Hansard Commons* 16 May 500 In reply to the Question of the hon. Member for Waterford, I have to ask him to communicate with my right hon. friend near me through the usual channels. **1946** *Erskine May's Law of Parl.* (ed. 14) xii. 245 The Government Chief Whip.. together with the Chief Whips of the other parties, constitutes what is known as the 'usual channels', through which communications pass as to business arrangements and other matters which concern the convenience of Members as a whole. **1975** J. P. MORGAN *House of Lords & Labour Govt.* viii. 213 The usual channels had collapsed and, in the absence of the customary arrangements, the Government could only hope that they might limit discussion by imposing a guillotine.

uszza, ussza (ʊ·ză), *int.* [App. a mere exclamation, but cf. HUZZA *int.*] A shout of anger or effort.

1913 D. H. LAWRENCE *Sons & Lovers* ii. 30 As he sat on his heels, or kneeled, giving hard blows with his pick, 'Uszza-uszza!' he went. **1914** —— *Widowing of Mrs. Holroyd* II. 36 Let me smash that bloody door in. Come out—come out—ussza!

‖ **uta** (yū·ta). [Jap., poem, song, f. *utau* to sing.] A Japanese poem; *spec.* = *TANKA[2].

1855 R. HILDRETH *Japan* xxxiv. 335 He found out certain words which he brought together into an *Uta*, or verse. **1897** *Japan Times* 23 Mar. 2/6 The collection of the *uta* of the old school being a riddle to the ordinary reading public. **1911** *Encycl. Brit.* XV. 169/1 Such couplets [which admitted Chinese words] were called *shi* to distinguish them from the pure Japanese *uta* or *tanka.*

Ute (yūt), *sb.*[1] and *a.* Also 9 **Eutaw, Utaw,** etc. [Shortening of *Utah*, a. Sp. *Yuta* an unidentified Indian language.] **A.** *sb.* **a.** A Shoshonean Indian people inhabiting parts of Colorado, Utah, and New Mexico; a member of this people. **b.** The language of this people. **B.** *adj.* Of or pertaining to the Ute or their language.

1826 in D. M. Frost *Notes on General Ashley* (1960) App. B. 136 The Eutaws and Flatheads..express a great wish that the Americans should visit them frequently. **1846** G. R. GIBSON *Jrnl.* 13 Oct. in *S.W. Hist. Ser.* (1935) III. 252 About fifty Ute Indians came in and held a council with Colonel Doniphan. **1846** M. B. EDWARDS *Jrnl.* 2 Nov. in *Ibid.* (1936) IV. 212 Major Gilpin..made a long and arduous journey through the country of the Ute and Navajo. **1885** D. G. BRINTON in *Pennsylvania Mag.* Apr. 30 The simple form of the verb may convey three different ideas, as in Ute, where the word for 'he seizes' means also 'the seizer'. **1907** *Univ. Calif. Publ. Amer. Archaeol. & Ethnol.* IV. III. 67 The Ute vocabulary was obtained, also in 1900, among the Uintah Ute. **1933** [see *PAIUTE *sb.* b]. **1958** L. C. PRITCHETT *Cabin at Medicine Springs* (1959) xxii. 199 Tha's talk of herdin' all the Utes out of Colorado. **1973** A. H. WHITEFORD *N. Amer. Indian Arts* 93 Plains lazy-stitch sewing is characteristic of the work of..the Ute of the Plateau. **1979** C. MCCARRY *Better Angels* III. iii. 180 Woolen socks, hand-knitted by Ute women.

ute (yūt), *sb.*[2] Colloq. (chiefly *Austral.* and *N.Z.*) abbrev. of *UTILITY 4 b.

1943 HUNT & PRINGLE *Service Slang* 68 *Ute,* short for Utility truck, a light van used by the Army. **1951** E. LAMBERT *Twenty Thousand Thieves* 178 He gets pissed one night, pinches a ute from the transport lines. **1961** J. DANVERS *The Living Come First* i. 17 I'd like you to take the ute and drive in to Alice. The wire we ordered has arrived. **1971** *N.Z. Listener* 8 Nov. 15/5 Wind whipped at the ute and rocked it on the road's sharp corners. **1981** *National Times* (Austral.) 25–31 Jan. 23/4 We used to help load Teddy into the back of the ute. **1984** *NZ Farmer* 12 Apr. 39/1 Now Nissan has followed it with a tough new 4 × 4 ute, known at this stage just as the 720.

utile (yū·tĭli), *sb.* [a. the specific epithet of the tree's Latin name: see UTILE *a.*] The timber of a large West African forest tree, *Entandrophragma utile,* of the family Meliaceæ; also, the tree itself.

1956 *Handbk. of Hardwoods* (Forest Prod. Res. Lab.) 228 Utile reaches a height of 150 ft or more. *Ibid.,* In structure and general appearance utile resembles the closely allied sapele..and is somewhat more open in texture. **1970** *Timber Trades Jrnl.* 21 Mar. 54/1 There are now signs of weaker prices for utile. **1980** *Yachts & Yachting* 29 Feb. 680/2 As nice a piece of red utile as you'll see this side of a stereo cabinet.

Utilidor (yuti·lĭdǭɹ). *Canad.* Also **u-.** [f. UTILITY *sb.* + *-dor* ad. Gr. δῶρον gift. For the formation cf. CUSPIDOR, *HUMIDOR, and THERMIDOR.] The proprietary name of a system of enclosed conduits used esp. for carrying water and sewerage in regions of permafrost.

1957 *Maclean's Mag.* 14 Sept. 92/2 At many outposts such as Churchill, Norman Wells and Frobisher ingenious insulated conduit boxes called 'utilidors' are used to convey water, sewage and heating pipes to their destinations. The idea is that the warmth from the heating pipes is just enough to keep the other two pipes from freezing. **1969** *Official Gaz.* (U.S. Patent Office) 15 Apr. TM 112 Ric-Wil, Incorporated, Barberton, Ohio. Filed June 12, 1967. *Utilidor.* For prefabricated conduits used in underground services... First use at least as early as Apr. 30, 1950. **1977** *Islander* (Victoria, B.C.) 21 Aug. 14/3 Each year one expects to pay $5000 for utilities hooked to each house by the famous utilidor.

utility, *sb.* Add: **1. d.** The intrinsic property of anything that leads an individual to choose it rather than something else; in game theory, that which a player seeks to maximize in any situation where there is a choice; the value of this, as (actually or notionally) estimated numerically.

1881 F. Y. EDGEWORTH *Math. Psychics* p. vi, It is argued from mathematical considerations that the basis of arbitration between contractors is the greatest possible utility of all concerned. **1934** *Economica* Feb. 53 Suppose ..that we have a utility function given; that is to say, we know, for the individual in question, how much utility he would derive from any given set of quantities of the goods on the market. **1944** VON NEUMANN & MORGENSTERN *Theory of Games* i. 16 We feel..that one part of our assumptions at least—that of treating utilities as numerically measurable quantities—is not quite as radical as is often assumed in the literature. **1948** *Jrnl. Polit. Econ.* LVI. 280/1 Choices among riskless alternatives are explained in terms of maximization of utility: individuals are supposed to choose as they would if they attributed some common quantitative characteristic—designated utility—to various goods and then selected the combination of goods that yielded the largest total amount of this common characteristic. **1960** A. RAPOPORT *Fights, Games, & Debates* iv. 64 The more he worked, the more he would get and so the more utility would accrue to him on that account. The more he worked, however, the more tired he would get and the more *negative* utility would accrue to him on that account. **1965** *Papers Regional Sci. Assoc.* XV. 162 The individual will tend to locate himself at a place whose characteristics possess or promise a relatively higher level of utility than in other places which are conspicuous to him. **1968** G. OWEN *Game Theory* vi. 133 This cannot be determined simply by measuring the increase and decrease of utility which this action causes to the two individuals, for..the units of utility scales are arbitrary and thus cannot be used for interpersonal comparisons. **1973** *Proc. R. Soc.* B. CLXXXIV. 421 In such a calculus [of medicine] it is necessary to assume that it is possible to attach a measure of worth or value to any state of health, and for this measure we use the word utility. **1980** A. J. JONES *Game Theory* iv. 178 If you assign a utility of −50 to the loss of $10, then it will not pay you to engage in this gamble if your utility for a gain of $20 is less than 75. *Ibid.* 180 One alternative possesses a larger utility than another because it is preferred, not the other way round.

3. c. *public utility*: see *PUBLIC *a.* 2 i. Also simply *utility*. Also, a company providing such a service or supply. In *pl.* also shares in such a company. chiefly *N. Amer.*

1930 *Daily Express* 6 Sept. 2/6 Utilities joined in the forward movement, which gathered considerable momentum in the final dealings, and the closing was strong. **1935** *Economist* 26 Jan. 195/1 Steel shares were merely steady, but utilities were inclined to take fresh heart... Mayor La Guardia indeed turned his attention this week from power utilities to the transit companies. **1936** L. C. DOUGLAS *White Banners* iii. 46 It was a new..sensation to be free of bill-collectors... You would have thought him another person than the..apologizer..who had abased himself before..the credit departments of the stores and the utilities. **1942** *Sun* (Baltimore) 7 Mar. 20 Additional housing..within the limits of existing utilities..is immediately desirable. **1957** [see *DOW-JONES]. **1968** *Globe & Mail* (Toronto) 17 Feb. 5/1 Toronto Hydro's request for a 700-foot smokestack on the..steam heating utility. **1974** *N.Y. Times* 8 Dec. IV. 3/1 American Electric Power Co., the nation's largest privately owned utility.

4. a. Also, the activity of a utility actor, the taking of any small part.

1803 T. WILKINSON *Let.* in A. Mathews *Mem. C. Mathews* (1838) I. xvii. 359, I take it for granted in very full plays you will..not object to pantomine utility, being a lord mayor, a witch, &c. **1846** G. A. A'BECKETT *Quizziology of Brit. Drama* 10 The heavy man, who is paid thirty shillings a week for doing the 'respectable utility'.

b. A utility vehicle (see sense 5 c (a) below). chiefly *Austral.* and *N.Z.*

1944 *Coast to Coast 1943* 162 They walked..to where a fairly new utility was parked with one or two other cars and an old truck. **1949** *Automobile & Carriage Builders' Jrnl.* Nov. 34 (*caption*) Two views of an Alvis Fourteen utility. **1960** *Guardian* 28 Dec. 2/3, I bought a 1949 Jowett Bradford utility two years ago. **1961** D. STUART *Driven* iv. 40 He had come to the well in the utility and found the footmen washing their clothes. **1968** K. WEATHERLY *Roo Shooter* 101 As he passed the bore he noticed a very battered looking utility parked there. **1971** *N.Z. Listener* 8 Nov. 15/5 He got in the utility by Honi, who waited with the motor running. **1984** *Auckland Star* 2 Mar. A3/7 A 54-year-old Southland man..died in a four-wheel drive utility accident.

c. A utility suit (see sense 5 c (c) below).

1945 J. B. PRIESTLEY *Three Men in New Suits* ii. 12 His clothes were rather like yours. He must have been dressed in his best Utility. **1957** J. BRAINE *Room at Top* xviii. 164 The suit was my demob Utility.

d. *Computers.* Short for *utility program* (see sense 5 a below).

1972 *Computers & Humanities* VI. 277 There are..a number of natural-language utilities available, but often they do not fit exactly the user's research design. **1983** *Daily Tel.* 30 Apr. 25/3 Commodore..has now produced a utility, called 'SIMONS BASIC' which is both delightful and infuriating to use.

e. Short for *utility room* (see sense 5 a below).

1976 *Field* 18 Nov. 948 (Advt.), Drawing room, dining room, study, cloakroom, kitchen, utility, etc.

5. a. *utility value*; (sense *3 c) *utility bill, company, executive, pole, wire*; **utility area,** a part of a house set aside for general use rather than for habitation; **utility curve,** a graph of a utility function; **utility function,** a mathematical function which ranks alternatives according to their utility to an individual; **utility man,** (*a*) (earlier example); **utility program, routine** *Computers*, one for carrying out routine tasks associated with the use of a computer; **utility room,** a room set aside for domestic appliances such as a boiler for a central heating system, a washing machine, etc., and for the storage of other equipment; **utility routine**: see *utility program* above.

1969 'E. LATHEN' *Murder to Go* (1970) xiv. 135 The new Hedstrom house..consisted of one spacious common room and assorted bedrooms, serviced by tiny utility areas. **1978** *Morecambe Guardian* 14 Mar. 24/2 (Advt.), Accommodation comprises: entrance hall, lounge, dining room, kitchen, 2 bedrooms, bathroom/WC. Utility area. **1976** *National Observer* (U.S.) 24 Jan. 13/3 Warmer-than-usual weather has reduced the schools' projected utility bills. **1984** *New Yorker* 30 Jan. 48/1 Whether it's utility bills or telephone bills or taxes or health costs or heating costs, it seems that the cost of the average family raising their family is going up. **1926** *Daily Colonist* (Victoria, B.C.) 1 Jan. 18/3 The progress and prosperity of a community naturally is reflected in the fortunes of the utility companies whose duty it is to supply such essentials as light, water, power, [etc.]. **1980** *Amer. Speech* LV. 54 Presumably, the utility companies..specify certain hours of the day as the peak hours. **1948** *Jrnl. Pol. Econ.* LVI. 297/1 A single prize will be the optimum..if..every chord from the utility curve at the current income to the utility of a higher income is everywhere above the utility curve. **1969** Utility curve [see *INDIFFERENCE 8]. **1931** F. L. ALLEN *Only Yesterday* iii. 59 Book-censors, Jew-haters, Negro-haters, landlords, manufacturers, utility executives, upholders of every sort of cause,..all wrapped themselves in Old Glory and the mantle of the Founding Fathers. **1979** *Time* 8 Jan. 39/1 Says a utility executive in Iowa: 'People have been had too many times.' **1934** Utility function [see sense 1 d above]. **1977** *Dædalus* Fall 84 Models now start from mathematical representations of personal choice (utility functions) where work and leisure stand in the 'correct' relationship to each other and where mathematics imposes a 'correct' income and substitution effect. **1849** *Theatrical Mirror* 1 Oct. 37/1 He is a great friend of the utility-man's. **1961** in *Webster*, His car sideswiped a utility pole. **1973** *Advocate-News* (Barbados) 15 Feb. 4/2 The car fell into a three-foot gully and came to rest against a utility pole which kept it from overturning. **1964** T. W. MCRAE *Impact of Computers on Accounting* i. 24 Utility programmes have been devised for the same reason as the autocodes. **1980** S. HOCKEY *Guide Computer Applications in Humanities* ii. 29 Most computer centres have a utility program which makes copies of magnetic tapes. **1953** C. ARMSTRONG *Catch-as-catch-Can* xviii. 153 They were in a small lumber room, utility room, the Californian equivalent of a cellar. **1959** *Housewife* Oct. 69/1 The utility room is fitted with a sink and drainer and also houses the fuel store and gas boiler. **1964** G. L. COHEN *What's Wrong with Hospitals?* vi. 115 A partial answer comes from North America, where the treatment and utility rooms are increasingly made up of movable partitions. **1978** *Cornish Guardian* 27 Apr. 14/7 (Advt.), The accommodation comprises..rear hallway, wash house/utility room, [etc.]. **1962** Utility routine [see *HOUSEKEEPING *sb.* 5]. **1980** M. S. WU *Introd. Computer Data Processing with BASIC* ix. 188 If an installation frequently receives data from various locations on small reels of magnetic tape, a utility routine may be written to combine the data from the short reels onto one large reel of tape prior to processing. **1926** A. E. TAYLOR *Plato* xvi. 431 Our question is not what 'art' has the.. greatest utility-value, but simply which sets up the most severe standard of truth and accuracy. **1974** B. PEARCE tr. *Amin's Accumulation on World Scale* I. i. 64 It is impossible to 'measure' statistically the advantage (or disadvantage) that the underdeveloped countries derive from international exchange, whether one looks at the matter from the angle of labor value or from that of utility value. **1968** *Listener* 22 Aug. 235/1 Ugly poles carrying utility wires. **1973** *Sunday Advocate-News* (Barbados) 25 Feb. 18/6 We experience a lot of damage done to roofs by overhanging trees over-hanging verandahs and low-hanging utility wires.

c. Intended for use; generally useful; (passing into) merely functional; *spec.*: (*a*) of a motor vehicle: designed for carrying both passengers and goods; (*b*) of a player in a team game: able to play competently in more than one position; (*c*) during and in the aftermath of the war of 1939–45, designating clothes and household goods made in a standardized form in accordance with an official allowance of materials (cf. *AUSTERITY 4 b).

1895 *Montgomery Ward Catal.* Spring & Summer 585/1 Combination Barrel and Utility Cart... Cart will pick up barrel or body in a moment. **1908** Utility vehicle [see sense 5 b]. **1911** Utility man [see def. s.v. *utility man* (b)]. **1911** *Daily Colonist* (Victoria, B.C.) 25 Apr. 20/2 (Advt.), 1000 Yards Utility Cloth, fast colors..Per yard, 20¢. **1920** *Car* 3 Nov. 225/1 No greater mistake could be made than in the assumption that America's resources are limited to the production of 'utility' motor vehicles. **1942** *Daily Express* 24 Mar. 4/1 (*caption*) Frankly, Meadows, can you see *me* in a utility suit? **1943** *Ann. Reg. 1942* 32 Exempting so-called 'utility' cloth and clothing and boots and shoes from purchase tax. **1943** *Archit. Rev.* XCIII. 3 An exhibition has recently been held of utility furniture and utility pottery. **1944** F. CLUNE *Red Heart* 11 A utility truck stood at the edge of the landing-ground. **1947** *Jane's Fighting Ships 1946–47* 57 *Savage* and ships of 5 later groups have been described officially as a 'utility' type. **1948** *Observer* 8 Feb. 5/3 The dental profession.. will..refuse to enter a service which..will lower the present high standard of dental treatment to a utility level. **1949** *Automobile & Carriage Builders' Jrnl.* Nov. 49/1 The utility car, estate wagon or shooting brake has been standardized by some motor manufacturers. **1950** *RAC Guide & Handbk. 1950–51* 52 The utility vehicle, shooting brake, or station wagon is not a class of vehicle known as such to the law. **1952** M. LASKI *Village* i. 14 Mrs. Wilson made the tea and then they both sat down on their camp-beds and sipped it out of thick white Utility cups. **1959** W. GOLDING *Free Fall* iv. 100 No, madam, I'm sorry, we don't supply them at that price. This is a utility model. **1963** *Daily Tel.* 13 Nov. 25 (*heading*) 'Utility' state opening without the Queen..Peers and M.P.s in ordinary dress. **1970** *Times* 2 Nov. 14/8 They would be the centres, with Davies (a centre last year) on the right wing and Linnecar, a utility player, on the left. **1971** *E. Afr. Standard* (Nairobi) 10 Apr. 2/2 Kadir, an intelligent utility half-back. **1974** *Country Life* 26 Sept. 828 Utility clothes, furniture and household goods..were the wartime government's solution. **1976** *National Observer* (U.S.) 16 Oct., Pickup trucks and four-wheel-drive utility vehicles have jumped in popularity in the West and may bid for a national status rivaling the van's. **1978** *Early Music* Oct. 587/2 The selection of illustrations ..ranges from fine illuminated manuscripts to simple 'utility' articles. **1984** *NZ Rugby News* 9 May 2/2 Utility Laurie Holmes has shifted to Sydney.

utilization. Add: **2.** *Comb.*, as **utilization factor,** the proportion of a given resource which is being used or is available for use.

1921 A. P. TROTTER *Elem. Illumination Engin.* viii. 81 The ratio of the flux of light which reaches the working plane, whether directly or by reflection, to the whole flux of light from a lamp, is called the utilization factor, or coefficient of utilization. **1982** *IEEE Jrnl. Solid-State Circuits* XVII. 671/1 A gate utilization factor of ~95 percent has been achieved in programming the gate array.

‖ **uti possidetis** (yū·tai pǫsidī·tis). [late L., = as you possess, f. *utī* (*ut* conj.) + *possidētis* 2nd pers. pl. of *possidēre* to possess.] (See quot. 1980.)

1681 [see INTERDICT *sb.* 2 a]. **1763** J. BELL *Trav. from St. Petersburg* I. II. vi. 307 All matters were soon accommodated..on the footing of *uti possidetis*; i.e. each of the parties [*sc.* Russia and China] retaining the people and territories that then belonged to them. **1780** BURKE *Let. Affairs Ireland* 20 The six resolutions were to be considered as a sort of *uti possidetis*. **1823** BYRON *Don Juan* x. xlv. 75 A sort of treaty or negotiation, Between the British cabinet and Russian,..Something about the Baltic's navigation, Hides, train-oil, tallow, and the rights of Thetis, Which Britons deem their 'uti possidetis'. **1905** *Cambr. Mod. Hist.* (1907) III. xxi. 709 In 1593 a truce had been arranged on the *uti possidetis* basis. **1934** A. TOYNBEE *Study Hist.* I. 381 He made peace..on a basis of *uti possidetis*. **1980** *Oxf. Compan. Law* 1269/1 *Uti possidetis*, in the Roman law, an interdict whereby the colourable possession of real property by a *bona fide* possessor was continued until the rights of parties were finally determined. The phrase is sometimes referred to as a principle under which property not expressly provided for in a treaty terminating hostilities is to remain in the hands of the party who happened to have possession of it when hostilities ended.

Uto-Aztecan (yū:to,æzte·kăn), *sb.* and *a.* Also **Uto-Aztekan, Utaztekan.** [f. *UTE *sb*[1] and *a.* + -O + *Aztecan* adj. s.v. *AZTEC *sb.* and *a.*] **A.** *sb.* A family of languages spoken in central America and western North America. **B.** *adj.* Of or pertaining to this language family.

1891 D. G. BRINTON *Amer. Race* 44 Different bands of the same linguistic stock were found, some on the highest, others on the lowest stages of development, as is strikingly exemplified in the Uto-Aztecan family. *Ibid.* III. i. 118 Of all the stocks on the North American Continent, that which I call the *Uto-Aztecan* merits the closest study. **1913** E. SAPIR in *Jrnl. de la Société des Américanistes de Paris* X. II. 384 Southern Paiute has developed a number of secondary forms of the original Uto-Aztekan vowels and consonants. *Ibid.* 422 In..Ute-Chemehuevi pre-nominal elements occur as suffixes..not prefixes, as ordinarily in Uto-Aztekan. **1935** *Amer. Anthropologist* XXXVII. 608 Are there any traits that distinguish 'Shoshonean' from the rest of Uto-Aztecan? If there are, I do not know what they are. **1937** J. R. FIRTH *Tongues of Men* vii. 93 The Uto-Aztekan group of related languages, spoken by the Indians of Utah, Arizona, California, and Mexico. **1968** *Occas. Papers Idaho State Mus.* XXII, (*title*) Utaztekan prehistory. **1979** I. DAVIS in Campbell & Mithun *Lang. Native Amer.* 409 The differences between Uto-Aztecan and Kiowa-Tanoan both in phonology ..and grammar are striking.

Also **U·to-Aztec** *a.* and *sb.*

1932 W. L. GRAFF *Lang.* xi. 430 The Uto-Aztec group comprises the three branches of Shoshonean, Pima-Sonoran, and Nahuatl. **1956** J. WHATMOUGH *Lang.* (Map facing p. 22) Uto-Aztec.

Utopianize, *v.* Add: **2.** *intr.* = *Utopia-ize* vb. s.v. Utopia.

1905 H. G. Wells *Mod. Utopia* ii. 62, I pass..from Utopianising altogether, to ask the question that.. Schopenhauer failed completely to answer. **1911** —— *New Machiavelli* i. iv. 141 We planned, half in earnest and half Utopianizing, a League of Social Service.

utopiate (yutōᵘ·piĕⁱt). [Blend of Utopia and Opiate *sb.*] A drug which induces fantasies of a utopian existence; a euphoriant.

1964 R. Blum *(title)* Utopiates: the use and users of LSD 25. *Ibid.* xiv. 292 The movement promises much—a return to paradise, a Utopia of the inner life—and so LSD-25 becomes, if one may be allowed a neologism, a 'Utopiate'. **1983** *Guardian* 11 Aug. 18/3 The typical recruit for drug addiction is the young, weak, inadequate person for whom the drug is a 'utopiate', an escape from the problems of reality.

utriculoplasty. (yutri·kiŭloplæsti). *Surg.* [f. Utricul(us² + -o + -plasty.] An operation to reduce the size of the uterus by removing part of the uterine wall.

1910 *Practitioner* June 788 The operation of utriculoplasty as carried out by Howard Kelly. **1911** V. Bonney in *Proc. R. Soc. Med.* IV. (Obstetr. & Gynecol. Sect.) 272, I have ventured to apply to it the term 'utriculoplasty' as best describing its object. **1974** Passmore & Robson *Compan. Med. Stud.* III. xxviii. 68/2 Plastic repair of a bicornuate uterus (utriculoplasty) may be indicated in cases of recurrent abortion.

‖ **ut supra** (ut sⁱū·prā). [L., f. *ut* as + *suprā* Supra *adv.*, (*a.*), *prep.*] As previously, as before (in a book or writing), as above. Also shortened **ut sup.**

c **1450** in J. Stainer *Early Bodl. Music Sacred & Secular Songs* (1901) I. no. lxii, Chorus. vt supra What tydynges. **1520** R. Elyot in T. Elyot *Governour* (1880) I. 310 And the prest vid to synge ut supra. **1526** [see Supra 1]. **1651** T. Ireland *Abridgment Rep. Sir J. Dyer* 202 The going at large *ut supra*, is not an escape. **1668** [see Supra 1]. **1875** Paley & Sandys *Select Private Orations Desmosthenes* I. 164/1 He let the arbitrators give judgment against him by default (compare Mid. *ut sup.*) and then moved for a new trial. **1959** E. Pound *Thrones* xcviii. 43 That the books you read shall be Cheng King Ut supra.

utter, *a.* Add: **4. f.** As a trivial emphasizer.

1898 G. B. Shaw *You never can Tell* iv. 308 Certainly not. It's utter bosh. Nothing can be in better taste. **1914** —— *Misalliance* 33 You are the only really clever..man I know who has given himself away to me by making an utter fool of himself with me. **1930** N. Coward *Private Lives* iii. 78 You're talking utter nonsense! **1956** *Times* 3 Jan. 3/6 Professor Richard van der Riet Woolley, the newly appointed Astronomer Royal, said..that the prospect of interplanetary travel was 'utter bilge'.

utter, *v.*¹ **2. c.** For † *Obs.* read 'Now *arch. rare*' and add later example.

1977 'M. Innes' *Honeybath's Haven* iv. 37 He..placed on the seat beside him his hat, his gloves, and the handsomely illustrated brochure uttered by the proprietors of Hanwell Court to their prospective clients (or inmates).

utterance¹. Add: **I. 5.** Freq. in *Linguistics*, spoken or written words forming the complete expression of a thought. (Used with varying degrees of technicality.)

1932 A. H. Gardiner *Theory of Speech & Lang.* iv. 206 Under the term 'utterance' writing must be included. **1951** Z. S. Harris *Methods in Structural Linguistics* ii. 14 An utterance is any stretch of talk, by one person, before and after which there is silence on the part of the person. The utterance is, in general, not identical with the 'sentence'. **1955** J. L. Austin *How to do Things with Words* (1962) v. 61 Written utterances are not tethered to their origin in the way spoken ones are. **1964** M. A. K. Halliday et al. *Linguistic Sci.* iv. 95 The utterance, the smallest institutional unit of language activity. **1966** Y. Bar-Hillel in *Automatic Transl. of Lang.* (NATO Summer School, Venice, 1962) 17, I have already suggested..to distinguish artificially between them *qua* technical terms and use 'utterance' for observational entities and 'sentence' for theoretical ones.

III. 7. *attrib.* and *Comb.*, as *utterance-type*; *utterance-final, -initial, -interior, -medial* adjs.; *utterance-finally* adv.

1953 C. E. Bazell *Linguistic Form* 5 The most common English utterance-type. **1957** in *Amer. Speech* 1972 (1975) XLVII. 229 Even assuming there may be for some speakers certain contrasts in utterance-interior positions which might require both /č/ and /tš/ in the inventory, surely there are no such contrasts in utterance-initial and utterance-final sequences. **1964** W. Jassem in D. Abercrombie et al. *Daniel Jones* 346 Voiced stops do not occur utterance-finally in Polish. **1970** *Language* XLVI. 80 Even in his speech the laryngeal is lost in utterance-medial positions. *Ibid.* 82 For the nasal consonants, the variant which occurs in utterance-initial syllable onset before nasal vowels is taken to be basic. **1977** *Ibid.* LIII. 318 The optional utterance-final particle *-o* may be added to both imperatives and vocatives. **1978** C. Hookway in Hookway & Pettit *Action & Interpretation* 32 The notion of utterance type is itself translational, as Wallace puts it.

utu. (Earlier example.)

1828 in W. Colenso *Papers* (typescript) III. 18 Until another chief has been killed as an utu or payment.

uvala (ū·vălă). *Physical Geogr.* Also **ouvala.** [a. Serbo-Croat *uvala* hollow, depression.] A depression in the ground surface occurring in karstic regions (see quots.).

1902 *Geogr. Jrnl.* XX. 429 Dr. Cvijić's researches have led him to consider the uvala (Karstmulde) as an intermediate form between doline and polye. The uvala is a large, broad sinking in the karst with uneven floor, formed by the breaking down of the wall between a series of dolines. **1921** *Geogr. Rev.* XI. 600 As time goes on, the divisions between neighboring dolines are broken down; and larger depressions, called 'uvalas' or 'ouvalas', are created. **1922** *Geol. Mag.* XIX. 401 Several of the smaller ..poljes of Southern Herzegovina..appear to result from the collapse of underground watercourses. To such depressions it would perhaps be better to restrict the use of the local Bosnian term 'uvalas'. **1954** W. D. Thornbury *Princ. Geomorphol.* xiii. 323 The Bosnian term uvala is most commonly applied to the larger depressions resulting from the collapse of extensive roof sections over underground watercourses. What have been designated above as compound sinkholes are sometimes called uvalas, but this usage of the term does not seem justified. **1970** R. J. Small *Study of Landforms* iv. 152 In many areas closely adjoining sotchs have amalgamated, through lateral extension, to give larger depressions comparable with the 'uvalas' of the Karst proper.

uveoparotid (yū·viopărǫtid) *a. Med.* [f. Uve(a + -o + Parotid *a.* and *sb.*] Affecting or involving the uvea and the parotid gland. So **u·veoparoti·tis,** inflammation of the uvea and the parotid.

1917 *Brit. Jrnl. Ophthalmol.* I. 619 He came to the conclusion that..uveo-parotid fever is nothing more than atypical mumps. *Ibid.* 620 The case for mumps as the sole cause for uveo-parotitis is as yet, 'not proven'. **1961** *Lancet* 16 Sept. 614/1 In 5 out of 13 patients who have uveoparotitis the pulmonary disease..has led to severe fibrosis. **1967** [see *lymphogranuloma]. **1974** Passmore & Robson *Compan. Med. Stud.* III. xv. 1/1 A generation ago textbooks gave accounts of Hutchinson's disease, Besnier's disease, Boeck's disease, lupus pernio and uveoparotid fever... All these conditions..are different expressions of the disorder now known as sarcoidosis. **1975** *Brit. Med. Jrnl.* 27 Dec. 731/2 Two middle-aged sisters, living separately, developed sarcoidosis with bilateral uveoparotitis and cranial palsies within six months of each other.

uxorilocal (ɒ:ksorilōᵘ·kăl), *a. Anthrop.* [f. L. *uxōri-us* (f. *ūxor* wife) + Local *a.*] Applied to or denoting residence after marriage in the area of the wife's home or community. Cf. *matrilocal *a.*; *residence *sb.*¹ 1 d; *virilocal *a.*

1936 R. Firth *We, the Tikopia* xvi. 596 The greater tendency to uxorilocal settlement at marriage. **1948** L. Adam in *Man* Jan. 12/2 The adjectives 'patrilocal' and 'matrilocal' do not fulfil these requirements [of accuracy and clarity]... I therefore propose adoption of the adjectives 'virilocal' and 'uxorilocal' to indicate whether a married couple shares the domicile with the family of the husband or of the wife. **1958** *Man* Apr. 69/1 Marriages are about equally virilocal and uxorilocal. **1974** A. P. Wolf *Relig. & Ritual in Chinese Soc.* 156 When a family has no sons who survive to marry, they ordinarily must arrange an uxorilocal marriage for a daughter or an adopted daughter.

Hence **u:xorilo·cally** *adv.*

1963 *Brit. Jrnl. Sociol.* XIV. 24 So that now you may read about individual couples 'marrying avunculocally' or 'living uxorilocally'. This seems to me an abuse of terminology. **1974** A. P. Wolf *Relig. & Ritual in Chinese Soc.* 148 From her father's point of view, a daughter is an outsider. She can achieve the right to a place on his altar only by marrying a man who agrees to reside uxorilocally.

Uzbek (u·zbek, ɒ·z-). Also formerly **Usbeck, Usbeg, Uzbeg,** and other varr. [Russ.] One of a Turkic people of central Asia, forming the basic population of the Uzbek SSR (Uzbekistan), and also living in Afghanistan; the language of this people. Also *attrib.* or as *adj.*

1616 T. Roe *Let.* 17 Jan. in *Embassy to Court of Gt. Mogul* (1899) II. 113 The King..intendeth the conquest of the Vzbiques, a Nation between Smarchand and him. **1715** J. Stevens *Hist. Persia* xxii. 221 To make war on the Usbecks. **1788** Gibbon *Decl. & F.* VI. lxiv. 292 A descendant of Zingis, who reigned over the Usbeks of Charasm, or Carizme. **1834** A. Burnes *Bokhara* I. viii. 262 We now found ourselves among the Uzbeks. **1841** J. Wood *Personal Narr. Journey to River Oxus* xiv. 215 Murad Beg, the head of this Uzbek state. **1876** E. Schuyler *Turkistan* I. iii. 106 The Uzbeks are the descendants of the Turkish tribes who..migrated to this part of Asia [*sc.* Tashkent], both before and since the time of Tchinghiz Khan. **1889** G. N. Curzon *Russia in Central Asia* vi. 153 The huge sheepskin bonnets..disappeared in favour of the capacious white turban of the Uzbeg or the Tajik. **1891** A. Constable tr. *Bernier's Trav. in Mogul Empire* 120 There are probably no people more narrow-minded, sordid or uncleanly, than the Usbec Tartars. **1900** 'Odysseus' *Turkey in Europe* iii. 101 Uzbek also is not strictly a linguistic name, but political, and denotes the Turks who are, or were, the ruling faction in the Khanates of Khiva, Bokhara, and Kokand. **1927** *Glasgow Herald* 15 Aug. 13 Agitation has been set on foot among the Uzbek people, on the southern banks of the Oxus, who now demand affiliation with their Soviet kinsmen across the river. **1929** [see *Jagatai]. **1933** L. Bloomfield *Language* iv. 68 The Turkish..family of languages ..Turkish, Tartar, Kirgiz, Uzbeg, Azerbaijani. **1957** H. Bower *Short Guide Soviet Life* 7 Constituent Republics (SSR) are with capitals in parenthesis..Turkmen SSR (Ashkhabad) Uzbek SSR (Tashkent) Tadzhik [etc.]. **1961** [see *Iranize* vb. s.v. *Iranian *sb.* 2]. **1964** G. Wheeler *Mod. Hist. Soviet Central Asia* ix. 212 Firqat (1858–1909) ..did the first translation of a Russian classic—Tolstoy's *What Men Live By*—into Chagatay, or old Uzbek, as it is now called, in 1877. **1974** T. P. Whitney tr. *Solzhenitsyn's Gulag Archipelago* I. i. ii. 59 On the Volga Canal construction site newspapers were published in four national languages: Tatar, Turkish, Uzbek, and Kazakh. **1976** *Times* 3 Nov. 16/5 A dark-haired agronomist from an Uzbek collective farm.

Uzi (ū·zi). Also (*erron.*) **Uzzi.** The name of Uziel Gal, Israeli army officer, used *attrib.* or *absol.* to designate an Israeli type of sub-machine gun designed by him.

1959 E. O'Ballance *Sinai Campaign* ii. 73 The personal small arms of the man was either the Mauser rifle or the Uzi sub-machine-gun. *Ibid.*, The Uzi is one of the finest guns of this type I have ever handled. **1966** L. Davidson *Long Way to Shiloh* xi. 156 Too many men and too many Uzzis which were much too easy to fire. **1971** *Scope* (S. Afr.) 19 Mar. 17/2 A loaded Uzzi sub-machine-gun..is always within reach. *Ibid.* 22/1 The Uzzi..fires a clip of 9 mm bullets in double-quick time and is accurate up to 100 metres. **1976** G. Seymour *Glory Boys* viii. 94 Two other young men, both of whom had been issued with licences..to carry Uzi sub-machine-guns. **1981** C. R. Lajeunesse *Dead Man Running* lxii. 177 Cyril was cut in two by bullets from Weasel's Uzi.

V

V. Add: **I. 2. a.** (Further examples.) Cf. VEE I.

a **1917** W. De Morgan *Old Madhouse* (1919) ii. 14 Until you've seen her in a low neck, or at least a V, you really can't tell. **1930** *Sat. Even. Post* 13 Dec. 11/3 Midway, the range was cleft from summit to base by a V more than 2000 feet deep. **1958** E. Birney *Turvey* vii. 78 The V of Ashanti spears above the fireplace. **1985** J. Melville *Death Ceremony* xxi. 156 A pulsing at her throat above the V of her delicate silk under-kimono.

b. *V-blouse, body, -formation, -front, girder, hut* (earlier example); **V aerial, antenna,** an aerial in which the conductors form a large horizontal V that transmits principally along its axis; **V-belt,** a belt which is V-shaped in cross-section in order to give better traction on a pulley; **V-block,** a metal block with a V-shaped recess cut in it to hold a cylindrical object while it is being worked on; **V-eight,** an internal combustion engine with eight cylinders arranged in two rows of four at an angle to each other, forming a V-shaped cross-section; freq. *attrib.* and written **V-8;** also, a motor vehicle with such an engine; so **V engine; V-neck,** a garment neckline in the shape of a V; freq. *attrib.*; also *absol.*, a garment, as a pullover etc., with a V-shaped neckline; **V-thread,** a screw thread which is V-shaped in profile. Cf. *VEE 2.

1961 *Amat. Radio Handbk.* (ed. 3) xiii. 385/2 The V aerial produces one major beam along its axis, together with a rather complex pattern of minor lobes. [**1931** *Proc. IRE* XIX. 1822 Fig. 41 is a polar diagram showing the power distribution for a *V* wire, having sides equal to one wave, in the plane of the wires.] **1932** *Ibid.* XX. 1033 These [curves] were taken during the process of adjustment of a V antenna system in which both antenna and reflector units each consisted of 2 V wires one above the other. **1959** K. Henney *Radio Engin. Handbk.* (ed. 5) xx. 60 V antennas are arranged to utilize this main lobe from all wires of the system. **1911** C. S. Lake *Motor Cyclist's Handbk.* viii. 116 The most common form of transmission on a motor cycle is that of a 'V' belt. **1973** A. Parrish *Mech. Engineer's Ref. Bk.* xiii. 7 One of the problems associated with V belts..is the variation in velocity ratio which occurs from time to time. **1901** *Shop & Foundry Pract.* (Colliery Engineer Co.) II. §10.45 Cylindrical parts are usually supported on V blocks. **1971** B. Scharf *Engin. & its Lang.* viii. 54 V-blocks are usually made in pairs so that they can support a long tube. **1915** *Contemp. Rev.* Sept. 370 Quaker maidens now wear tucks or V-blouses or anything else that is the fashion. **1885** 'Mrs. Alexander' *Valerie's Fate* iv. 69 That black satin and lace costume..with the clear sleeves and a V body. **1930** *Autocar* 2 May 841/2 It is said..that the V eight.. is superior as regards compactness of build. **1936** *Motor Man.* (ed. 29) ii. 40 The V-eight engine comprises two blocks, each containing four cylinders, which are set at right angles on a single crankcase. **1942** G. R. Gilbert in D. M. Davin *N.Z. Short Stories* (1953) 252 Lena would giggle and look pleased as though she had Prince Charming waiting in a V8 outside the kitchen door. **1959** I. Jefferies *Thirteen Days* x. 162 A V-8 pick-up was parked, with a pair of Haganah in the back. **1963** Bird & Hutton-Stott *Veteran Motor Car* 57 Often claimed to be the first V-eight to be marketed. **1982** *Times Lit. Suppl.* 5 Mar. 249/4 The comparison between the purist Bugatti engine..and an American V-8 engine of thirty years later. **1924** *Motor Man.* (ed. 25) i. 19 An eight-cylinder V engine. **1967** *Economist* 29 July 425/3 Berliet has a range of v-engines due to appear soon. **1949** Koestler *Insight & Outlook* xi. 163 The V-formation of migrating geese. **1974** 'J. Graham' *Bloody Passage* i. 10 A flight of Brent geese drifted across the sky..in a v formation. **1895** *Montgomery Ward Catal.* Spring & Summer 92/1 Men's Rutland V front collars. **1919** *Brit. Manufacturer* Nov. 24/1 The output of 'T', 'V', and lattice girders of all gauges. **1851** *Lyttelton* (N.Z.) *Times* 1 Feb. 3 One V hut was blown away. **1910–11** *T. Eaton & Co. Catal.* Fall & Winter 20/1 Women's coat sweater... The V-neck and fronts have wide, plain knitted border. **1921** [see *house-dress* s.v. *HOUSE *sb.*[1] 19]. **1949** O. Nash *Versus* 62 They lose their rubbers and store their V-necks. **1970** T. Lewis *Jack's Return Home* 127 He had on a white shirt.., a bottle green V-neck, twill trousers. **1978** *Detroit Free Press* 5 Mar 30 (Advt.), T-shirts or V-neck shirts. *a* **1877** Knight *Dict. Mech.* III. 2061/2 (*caption*) V-thread. **1887** [in Dict.]. **1939** [see *square thread* s.v. *SQUARE *a.* 14 a]. **1971** B. Scharf *Engin. & its Lang.* xi. 101 A distinction is also made between V-threads and square threads, according to their cross-section.

c. *V-shaped* adj. (further examples); *spec.* designating or pertaining to a valley having such a cross-section, esp. when contrasted with a U-shaped valley; also in *Comb.* with other adjs., ppl. adjs., and sbs., as *V-cut, -fronted, -like, -necked, -type, -winged* adjs. Cf. *VEE 2.

1912 S. Ford *Shorty McCabe's Odd Numbers* 107 Maybe Cornelia will have some plans of her own, thinks I, as I gets into my silk faced dinner jacket and V-cut vest. **1977** H. Kaplan *Damascus Cover* iv. 36 She wore a V-cut peasant blouse. **1927** *Blackw. Mag.* Jan. 76/1 They stamp the snow from their V-fronted high-heeled jackboots. **1929** E. Linklater *Poet's Pub* xxiv. 258 A cattle-track.., branching V-like off the road. **1971** V-necked [see *SIGNATURE *sb.* 4 b]. **1894** V-shaped [see *U-shaped* s.v. *U 2 a]. **1907** *Bull. Geol. Soc. Amer.* XVIII. 355 Downstream from the glacial region the valley ceases to be U-shaped. It becomes narrow and V-shaped, and the terraces die out. **1937** [see *HYPSOGRAPH]. **1970** R. J. Small *Study of Landforms* i. 6 On the resultant maps..the forms of valley floors (whether V-shaped, rounded, or flat-bottomed)..[are] shown. **1967** *Technology Week* 20 Feb. 35/1 The 'V' type antenna is used because it can be designed to give good performance even if distorted. **1876** G. M. Hopkins *Poems* (1967) 178 Through the velvety wind V-winged..To the nest's nook I balance and buoy.

d. as *v. intr.* Of geese: to fly forming the shape of a horizontal V. Cf. *V-formation*, sense 2 b above and V 2 a (quot. 1894).

1907 *Canad. Mag.* XXIX. 21/1 Then across his senses came the nearing doom—the honk, honk of wild geese V-ing their way along the shadow trail of the night sky. **1970** R. Lowell *Notebk.* 245 The usual autumn Flight of Canada geese V above it, moonborne. **1972** J. Gores *Dead Skip* ii. 14 Another batch of kids..their cries as full of spring as geese V-ing north.

3. *V-agent*, any of a group of organophosphorus nerve gases having anticholinesterase activity; *VX*, a type of V-agent, O-ethyl *S*-2-diisopropylaminoethyl methylphosphonothiolate.

1964 Kirk & Othmer *Encycl. Chem. Technol.* (ed. 2) IV. 874 Aerosolized V agents also are quite lethal by inhalation. **1975** *Nature* 10 Jan. 82/3 The nerve gas codenamed VX is the most toxic of a family of V-agents produced by British chemical warfare scientists since World War Two. **1966** *New Statesman* 16 Dec. 900/1 The Americans..have also produced less volatile gases called V agents, particularly a liquid called VX. **1980** *Sci. Amer.* Apr. 36/1 Some 5,000 tons of VX were made between 1961 and 1967.

III. 5. a. vs., *versus*.

1889 in *Cent. Dict.* **1949** E. Pound *Pisan Cantos* lxxix. 74 Kumasaka vs/ vulgarity. **1967** *Boston Sunday Herald* 26 Mar. vi. 4/7 It has developed a way of seeing Europe that seems the perfect answer to the group vs. non-group argument. **1970** *Jrnl. Gen. Psychol.* LXXXIII. 133 Conditions..are optimal for divergent *vs.* convergent tasks.

b. v = very (earlier examples); V, victory, *spec.* used as the symbol of allied victory in the war of 1939–45 (cf. *V-Day* below; *VE, *VJ, *V-SIGN); V, v, volt; VA (*U.S.*), Veterans' Administration; V.A., Vice-Admiral; V.A., visual acuity; V.A.D., (a member of a) Voluntary Aid Detachment; V. and A., Victoria and Albert Museum; VASCAR, Vascar, visual average speed computer and recorder; V-bomber (see quot. 1955); V.C., Vice-Chancellor; V.C., Victoria Cross (earlier example); also, a holder of the Victoria Cross; VC (orig. and chiefly *U.S.*) = *Viet Cong *sb.* and *a.*; V.C.H., Victoria County History (or Histories); V.C.O., Viceroy's Commissioned Officer; VCR, videocassette recorder; V.D., v.d., venereal disease; freq. *attrib.*; V.D., Volunteer Decoration (formerly awarded in the Territorial Army or the Royal Naval Volunteer Reserve); V-Day, V-day, V Day, Victory Day, used variously with reference to allied victory in the war of 1939–45 (cf. *VE-day* s.v. *VE; *VJ-day* s.v. *VJ); also *transf.* and *fig.*; VDT, video (or visual) display terminal; VDU, vdu, visual (or video) display unit; V.F. (*R.C.Ch.*) = *vicar foran(e)* s.v. Vicar 4 c; V.F.A. (*Austral.*), Victorian Football Association; V.F.L. (*Austral.*), Victorian Football League; V.F.R., visual flight rules; VFW (*U.S.*), Veterans of Foreign Wars; V.G. = Vicar general (sense 2); VHD, video high density (system); VHF, vhf, very high frequency: applied to radio waves with a frequency between 30 and 300 MHz; VHS, Video Home System; VIP, vasoactive intestinal (poly)peptide; VISTA, Volunteers in Service to America; VLA (*Astron.*), very large array (system of radio telescopes in the U.S.); VLBI (*Astron.*), very long baseline interferometry (method of measuring signals from a radio astronomical source); VLCC, very large crude (oil) carrier; VLDL (*Biochem.*), very low-density lipoprotein; VLF, very low frequency: applied to radio waves with a frequency between 10 and 30 kHz; V.L.R., very long range; VLSI (*Electronics*), very large scale integration (*or* integrated); V-Mail (*U.S.*), victory mail (see quot. 1966); VOA, Voice of America; VOR, VHF omnirange (cf. *omnirange* s.v. *OMNI-); VP, verb phrase (in Transformational Grammar); V.P., Vice-President (examples); V.P.P. (*India*), value payable post (see quot. 1975); V.S., veterinary surgeon (example); V.S.O., Voluntary Service Overseas; a member of the organization thus called; V.S.O.P., very special old pale (brandy); V-STOL, V/STOL, VSTOL, vertical and short take-off and landing; VTO(L), vertical take-off (and landing); VTR, video tape recorder; VU, vu (*Electronics*) [prob. abbrev. of *volume unit*: cf. quots. for this s.v. *VOLUME 10 c, where it is implied to be so], a unit in which some types of volume indicator are calibrated, a sine wave with a power of 1 mW being assigned the reference value of 0 VU (see quot. 1940 and cf. *volume indicator* s.v. *VOLUME 10 c); freq. *attrib.*, esp. in *VU meter*, any volume indicator employing the VU scale. See also (as main entries) *VAT, *VE, *VEEJAY, *V.I.P., *VJ, *V-SIGN.

1863 *Q. Rev.* Jan. 159 It is said also, that the prisoners have been known to make an example of a warden who was not in their opinion sufficiently liberal with his V.G.'s ('Very Good,' as marked in the accounts). **1891** W. S. Churchill *Let.* 1 Jan. in R. S. Churchill *Winston S. Churchill* (1967) I. Compan. i. v. 219 V-happy V. well. **1941** C. Milburn *Diary* 20 July (1979) 104 The V campaign (. . . —) was launched by Mr Churchill today. V for victory, the opening notes of Beethoven's V (fifth) symphony. **1973** D. Westheimer *Going Public* iv. 67 She raised her hand in a peace sign... He realized it was not the peace sign at all. To those of the old woman's generation it was V for Victory. **1889** W. P. Maycock *Pract. Electr. Notes & Definitions* ii. 23 Comparison of various E.M.F.s... Continuous dynamo = 10V to 500V. **1943** C. L. Boltz *Basic Radio* x. 166 Mains valves..can be operated with 200V, 300V, and even 400V on the anode. **1966** *Wireless World* July (Advt. section) 83 Power pack kits. Fully smoothed output 250 v. 60 mA. H.T. and L.T. 6·3 v. 1·5 amps. **1945** *Newsweek* 16 Apr. 40/2 Last week.. unfavourable publicity hit the VA. **1976** N. Thornburg *Cutter & Bone* xii. 275 He spent a long time with the shrinks in VA hospitals. **1794** R. F. Greville *Diary* 23 Aug. (1930) 300 We near'd the *Minotaur*, on which V.A. McBride took that Opportunity of hoisting out His barge. **1915** W. S. Churchill 23 Jan. in M. Gilbert *Winston S. Churchill* (1972) III. Compan. i. 444 In the absence of Adl Carden, Adl de Robeck will have a temporary rank of V.A. **1932** *Optician* LXXXIII. 398/2 No effect on the peripheral V.A. of one half of an eye was noted when the other half was illuminated. **1982** M. Urvoy et al. in François & Maione *Paediatric Ophthalmol.* 399/2 For a subjective measurement of V.A., we have four groups of tests. **1915** G. Bell *Let.* 10 Feb. (1927) I. xiv. 359 She is a V.A.D. part of a detachment which is going up as orderlies to the Cross Hospital at G.H.Q. **1916** *Lancet* 18 Mar. 651/1 Whether he had received any complaints from the V.A.D. hospitals as to the strict nature of the regulations governing the movements of convalescent wounded. **1980** 'M. Yorke' *Scent of Fear* x. 85 In that earlier war she had become a VAD nurse. **1937** Partridge *Dict. Slang* 929/1 *V. and A., the*..The Victoria and Albert Museum: museum-world coll.; late C. 19–20. **1958** *Listener* 28 Aug. 317/1 At the V. and A. both the Morris dining-room and the magnificent Poynter grill room..have gone. **1977** J. Aiken *Last Movement* vi. 115 He sold them [*sc.* pictures] all to the V & A. **1966** *N.Y. Times* 1 Oct. 39/5 Trademarked Vascar, the instrument divides the time a car takes by the distance it travels, and shows the answer in miles an hour. **1967** *Traffic Digest & Rev.* May 3/2 VASCAR is a device which allows an operator by measuring quantities of distance and time to compute the speed of vehicles on a highway. The chief advantage of VASCAR, according to its inventor, Arthur N. Marshall of Richmond, Virginia, is that the officer in a car equipped with VASCAR can maintain regular patrol and still clock the speed of other vehicles on the road. **1973** *Times* 13 Aug. 4/3 Essex police are..to introduce a new speed detection device. Known as VASCAR—visual average speed computer and recorder—it has been tested in the country for two years. **1983** *Times* 24 Feb. 3/8 He had decided to make a Vascar speed check with the equipment fitted in his vehicle, which meant choosing two fixed features on the road—this case a large tree and a bridge. **1955** *Britannica Bk. of Year* 489/2 Concentration on air-power was reflected in terms like *V-Bomber* (the initial referring to the types, Victor, Vulcan and Valiant). **1958** *Spectator* 10 Jan. 59/1 This weapon is the natural armament of the 'V' bombers. **1975** in R. Crossman *Diaries* I. 57 Mr Wilson proposed to replace the M.L.F. with an Atlantic nuclear force, which would include American Polaris submarines, British V-bombers, 'some kind of mixed-manned, jointly owned elements' and the British Polaris submarine that Labour was not going to scrap after all. **1715** in Bodleian MS. Ballard 49 f. 154, We the V.C. & Heads of Houses & Professors think it incumbent on Us to make this publick Declaration of our Utmost Abhorrence & Detestation of Such Offences. **1866** *Law Rep.*

(Chancery Appeal Cases) I. 66 V.C. *Wood* held that the Plaintiff's having come to the nuisance did not disentitle him to equitable relief. **1883** J. A. H. MURRAY *Let.* 8 Nov. in K. M. E. Murray *Caught in Web of Words* (1977) xii. 227 The V.C. had to rush off in a cab. **1953** M. DAVIDSON *Medicine in Oxford* ii. 26 It seems not unlikely that the latter may have consulted the V.-C. about Francis's migration. **1971** *Rayden's Pract. & Law of Divorce* (ed. 11) I. iii. 43 Sir Richard Kindersley V.-C., nevertheless said [etc.]. **1859** A. THACKERAY *Let.* in H. Ritchie *Lett. A. T. Ritchie* (1924) v. 111 Papa gave us a letter to read ..from Edward Thackeray's colonel recommending him for a V.C. **1929** *Daily Express* 7 Nov. 13/5 Mr. Thomas Dinesen, the Danish V.C., and the only foreigner to win the decoration, arrived at Liverpool-street Station. **1964** *N.Y. Times* 16 Sept. 4 V.C.—They are of course the Vietcong, the enemy. But when a private displeases his sergeant, he may hear 'you knucklehead V.C.!' **1965** *Punch* 11 Aug. 214/1 Some of them [*sc.* GIs] responded to a professional sergeant's claim that they were..eager to get to grips with the 'VCs', as the Viet Cong are now known in the trade. **1968** *Listener* 23 May 656/3, I felt rather anxious that the patrol might have disappeared and left me in the empty suburb with Mr Van and the VC snipers. **1977** *N.Y. Rev. Bks.* 23 June 6/3 A nineteen-year-old Marine is discovered cutting the ears off a dead VC. **1931** *Times Lit. Suppl.* 10 Sept. 683/1 Thornton Riseborough, according to the V.C.H., appears always with a double title after the twelfth century. **1965** *Listener* 8 Apr. 531/3 The V.C.H., as it is known to all its users, is a great work of reference, but it is unreadable. **1945** C. J. AUCHINLECK *Let.* 24 Nov. in Mansergh & Moon *Transfer of Power* (1976) VI. 531 Officers, V.C.O.s, and I.O.R.s who became officers in the I.N.A. **1977** 'D. MACNEIL' *Wolf in Fold* ii. 15 The acting squadron commander's a VCO—a *risaldar* named Jalala Khan. **1971** *New Scientist* 26 Aug. 469/1 So that the television does not have to be adapted to take the recorder, the VCR is put between the TV and its aerial. **1983** *Listener* 12 May 3/1 VCRs whirred away as people took advantage of watching the latest movies. **1984** *What Video?* Aug. 5/4 The cassette is totally incompatible with British VCRs and TV sets. **1920** *Ann. Rep. Chief Med. Officer, Ministry of Health* II. iii. (*caption facing* p. 163), V.D. clinic. Suggested plan of arrangement of a..hut. **1920** F. FOX *G.H.Q.* vi. 87, I do not know where the idea sprang from that v.d. was very common in the Army. **1962** E. SNOW *Other Side of River* (1963) xxxv. 262, I didn't spend my old man's money learning to become a V.D. quack for a gangster society. **1978** 'L. BLACK' *Foursome* ii. 15, I don't do it for money—only with men I like the look of. And I haven't got VD. **1901** T. F. FREMANTLE *Bk. of Rifle* p. v, The Hon. T. F. Fremantle, V.D. **1946** *Jrnl. R. United Service Institution* XCI. 129 Captain C. A. R. Shillington, V.D., R.N.V.R. **1941** *Newsweek* 28 July 22/3 Encouraged by the success [of the V propaganda campaign], Britain proclaimed July 20 as 'V Day'. **1942** *Time* 16 Mar. 11/1 We at Hercules are eager to learn of any new material, process, or equipment..which can enable us to create more employment after V-Day. **1945** *Times* 5 Apr. 5/2 To-day the battle still rages with loss and peril in Europe. On V Day it will still go on over great stretches of land and water in the Far East. **1949** KOESTLER *Promise & Fulfilment* I. xiii. 146 It was Jewry's V-day—the first since the time of the Maccabeans. **1967** A. CHRISTIE *Endless Night* xxiii. 211 'Well,' said Greta with a deep satisfied sigh, 'we've made it.' 'V-Day all right,' I said. **1975** *Nature* 16 Oct. 557/1 If reporters can operate typewriters with the accuracy necessary for an OCR reader they can probably operate keyboards producing punched tape for the computer or sophisticated visual display terminals (VDTs) on-line to the computer. **1979** *Globe & Mail* (Toronto) 20 Feb. 9/1 Mr. Brown described himself as not very mechanically minded, but said he has worked hard to become knowledgeable about the video display terminals—known as VDTs. **1982** A. CLEMENTS *Microcomputer Design & Construction* ii. 236 The main output device..of many microprocessor systems is the video display terminal (VDT). **1968** *Brit. Med. Bull.* XXIV. 192/2 The data-terminal..may consist of a 'video display unit' (VDU), in effect the combination of a television-like display tube with a keyboard. **1970** *Computer Management* Nov. 52 (*caption*) Entering data via the keyboard of the VDU. **1976** *Liverpool Echo* 24 Nov. (Advt.), Hardware consists of an ICI 1900 mainframe linked to mini-computers with disc storage, local printers and VDUs. **1982** *What's New in Computing* Nov. 5/3 Because the entire unit is stalk mounted, the vdu angle can be adjusted for best visibility. **1985** *Personal Computer World* Feb. 195/2 Designs published to date have concentrated on putting the intelligence in the node controller which then allows operation of the system through an ordinary VDU. *a* **1912** W. T. ROGERS *Dict. Abbrev.* (1913) 197/1 V.F., Vicar Forane. **1922** JOYCE *Ulysses* 312 The rev. John Lavery, V.F. **1936** *Age* (Melbourne) 1 May 7/8 (*heading*) V.F.A. Seconds. **1969** *Melbourne Truth* 12 July 24/1 Dandenong and Preston meet in the most tension packed VFA game of the season. **1936** *Age* (Melbourne) 1 May 7 (*heading*) V.F.L. Season opens on Saturday. **1969** *Melbourne Truth* 12 July 2/6 The new kicking out-of-bounds rule introduced by the VFL this season. **1949** *Jrnl. R. Aeronaut. Soc.* LIII. 967/2 Under V.F.R. (Visual Flight Rules) it appears that communication takes place between the ground and the aircraft for an aggregate time of about 60 seconds. **1974** L. DEIGHTON *Spy Story* xv. 146 This aircraft's electronics were primitive. Flying V.F.R. meant he'd have to put it down before dark. **1981** *Pilot* Jan. 13/1 A special VFR clearance. **1920** *Foreign Service Mag.* Dec. 12/1 The V.F.W. is an organization for service. That is the purpose of its existence. **1977** C. MCFADDEN *Serial* (1978) xlviii. 103/2 You're gonna get all those calls again from people who want you to sing 'God Bless America' at VFW conventions. **1871** *Tablet* 14 Oct. 502/1 Very Rev. Dr. O'Shea, P.P., V.G. **1922** JOYCE *Ulysses* 312 The rt rev. Mgr M'Manus, V.G. **1980** *New Scientist* 13 Nov. 442 In the US, VHD will face stiff competition from Philips's laser-reading (VLP) system. **1984** *What Video?* Aug. 11/1 The juke boxes use Thorn EMI VHD disc players and discs (not available for the home). **1932** *Admiralty Handbk. Wireless Telegr. 1931* p. ii, The range of frequencies of the æther waves used in wireless communication is now subdivided as follows:.. Above 30,000 kc./s... Very high Frequencies (V.H.F.). **1951** 'N. SHUTE' *Round Bend* ii. 50 A small V.H.F. radio set. **1955** *Times* 29 July 5/4 The present system of amplitude modulation in the v.h.f. maritime services should be changed to one of frequency modulation. **1956** *B.B.C. Handbk. 1957* 134 The introduction of very high frequency transmissions, with frequency modulation (VHF/FM) in several parts of the country, was the major development of the year in sound broadcasting. **1974** HARVEY & BOHLMAN *Stereo F.M. Radio Handbk.* ii. 9 Also, at v.h.f., there was sufficient bandwidth available for hi-fi quality. **1982** *Daily Tel.* 30 July 3/5 (Advt.), Simple to use VHS recorder with 10-day timer. **1984** *What Video?* Aug. 10/2 SKC..is also launching a range of high grade cassettes in standard lengths in VHS and Beta formats. **1972** *Bioorganic Chem.* II. 30 (*heading*) Synthesis of the vasoactive intestinal peptide (VIP). *Ibid.* 87 Information on partial sequences of VIP became available recently. **1983** R. G. LONG et al. in *Oxf. Textbk. Med.* I. xii. 50/1 VIP secretion has been demonstrated after direct neural stimulation. **1964** *Amer. Forests* Oct. 13/1 The act provides for establishment of the Volunteers In Service To America (VISTA)—a sort of domestic peace corps. **1980** *New Age* (U.S.) Oct. 42/2 NOFA..sponsored VISTA workers to help set up farmers' markets in New Hampshire and Vermont. **1974** VLA [see *OPTICAL *a.* 2 a]. **1978** PASACHOFF & KUTNER *University Astron.* xxvi. 669 When fully operational..the VLA will make pictures of a field of view a few minutes of arc across, with resolutions comparable to the 1 arc sec of optical observations from large telescopes, in about 10 hours. **1969** *Sci. Jrnl.* Aug. 63/2 This interferometer system which is called the very long baseline interferometer (VLBI) is unusual in that there is no connection between the receiving elements. **1982** *Sci. Amer.* May 85/3 The VLBI maps now being made are as good as the maps made with linked telescopes 10 years ago. **1968** *Punch* 24 Apr. 612/3 The introduction of VLCCs (very large crude carriers, supertankers of up to 200,000 tons) will cut transport costs dramatically. **1974** *Nature* 19 Jan. 196/1 In December 1969 three VLCCs had serious explosions in one of their centre tanks during tank cleaning. **1975** *Times* 30 June 16/5 Tanker rates continued to increase..as Very Large Crude Carrier (VLCC) premiums moved up. **1977** *Time* 21 Nov. 40/1 Among the largest and lightest of these globules are the very-low-density lipoproteins (VLDL). **1938** *Admiralty Handbk. Wireless Telegr. 1938* I. (Nomenclature of Waves), On the basis of a recent C.C.I.R. recommendation, promulgated in French; a suitable nomenclature, likely soon to be accepted internationally, may be given in English as follows:— Below 30 kc/s...Very Low Frequencies (V.L./F.). **1962** L. DEIGHTON *Ipcress File* xx. 136 There was a V.L.F. (very low frequency) radio wave-length and a compass bearing. **1983** *New Scientist* 13 Jan. 93/1 Scientists in California have discovered that the Earth's magnetic field can act as a giant neutral amplifier for very low-frequency (VLF) radio waves. **1943** W. S. CHURCHILL in *Hansard Commons* 8 June 566 We took the measures which have thrown the long-range aircraft—the very long-range aircraft—the V.L.R., as they are called—, effectively in to the anti U-boat struggle. **1946** *Happy Landings* July 7/3 In April, 1945 [he] became A.O.A., Tiger Force (V.L.R.), Bomber Force for the bombing of Japan. **1978** *World Book Year Bk.* 309/1 In 1977..the semiconductor segment of the industry was virtually on the threshold of a new frontier—very large scale integration (VLSI). **1979** W. J. CAELLI *Microcomputer Revolution* p. xvii, VLSI—Very Large Scale Integration. This term flows on from the LSI designation and refers to component densities of well over 1000 components. **1983** *Listener* 25 Aug. 25/2 The amount of VLSI (Very Large Scale Integrated) circuitry needed to enable them to sync Autocue clichés with corny visuals is as great as that employed in the space shuttle. **1984** *Ann. Rep. Racol Electronics PLC* 6/1 The collaborative development of a microelectronic very large scale integrated (VLSI) process. *Ibid.* 7/1 The design of VLSI chips. **1942** *N.Y. Times* 13 June 17/6 The new V-Mail for United States overseas forces, patterned after the British microfilm postal system, was started when letters were delivered to President Roosevelt today. **1943** R. VANCE *They made me a Leatherneck* 44 'George never lets up on V mail to that female,' Weber observed. **1966** *Sunday Times* (Colour Suppl.) 4 Dec. 73/4 [GI jargon.] *V-Mail*, letters to or from home, reproduced photographically to conserve shipping space. **1949** *Bull. U.S. Dept. of State* 27 Mar. 396/2 The second part [of a broadcast] originating in the VOA offices in New York, will include news. **1975** *New Yorker* 26 May 28/3 The basic problem is that V.O.A. has been placed at the intersection of journalism and diplomacy: the practice of one of these disciplines negates the practice of the other. **1955** *Times* 17 Aug. 6/4 There was controversy earlier this year over how soon—if at all—Tacan should replace VOR/DME..as the standard air navigation system in the United States for civil as well as military aircraft. **1982** T. BEATTIE *Diamonds* xviii. 157 'Could you confirm your VOR is monitoring?' 'Freetown roger... The VOR is unserviceable.' **1972** HARTMANN & STORK *Dict. Lang. & Linguistics* 249/1 In transformational-generative grammar, the verb phrase is that constituent of a sentence which contains the predicate (or complement or adjunct). .. The abbreviation VP is used in phrase structure rules. **1976** *Word 1971* XXVII. 248 The main verb or an auxiliary verb, if there is one, is placed in the final position of a verb phrase in German deep structure while it occupies the initial position of a VP in surface structure. **1887** *Irish Times* 30 Nov. 5/3 Sir Andrew Hart, V.P., T.C.D. **1925** C. S. LEWIS *Let.* 14 Aug. (1966) 103 When the V.P. [of Magdalen College, Oxford] laid a red cushion at his feet I realized..that this was going to be a kneeling affair. **1978** M. PUZO *Fools Die* xxxvii. 310 With his bosses, like the VP in charge of production at Wartberg's Tri-Culture International Studios,..he was much more frank, more human. **1888** KIPLING *Barrack-Room Ballads* (1892) 112 How he met with his fate and the V.P.P. **1975** C. ALLEN *Plain Tales from Raj* viii. 93 With VPP or Value Payable Post, you paid the postman the value of the goods in the parcel. **1952** A. M. SULLIVAN *Last Serjeant* xiii. 139 The ancient claimant to the degree of V.S. was a little more learned but often a little less skilful than the country cow doctor. **1960** *Voluntary Service Overseas* 4 Volunteers give their service free... This leaves V.S.O. with the task of raising funds to cover the cost of travel and insurance. **1962** *Times Lit. Suppl.* 28 Dec. 1007/3 Mrs. Dickson's husband was largely responsible for initiating the scheme, known as Voluntary Service Overseas (VSO). **1965** *Listener* 7 Jan. 21/2 He was the first British V.S.O. to come to Libya. **1967** *Guardian* 30 May 5/5 The conflict came to a head shortly before my VSO year came to an end. **1980** *Jrnl. R. Soc. Arts* Jan. 111/1 She has a VSO working with her and six or seven dedicated staff. **1981** E. NORTH *Dames* xiii. 256 Your children will..work for V.S.O. and Amnesty International. **1907** *Yesterday's Shopping* (1969) 99/2 J. and F. Martell's..V.S.O.P.—108/0. **1951** R. POSTGATE *Plain Man's Guide to Wine* ix. 125 Five Stars should indicate a good brandy; higher-up the various firms have their own indications: X.O., V.S.O.P., Cordon bleu, and so forth. **1982** M. O'DONNELL *Devil's Prison* II. i. 88 The waiters had left them alone with a jug of coffee and a bottle of VSOP. **1960** *Aeroplane* XCVIII. 234/1 In the United States, NASA applies the STOL appelation to any fixed-wing type capable of operating from a 500-ft. strip surrounded by 50-ft. obstacles. This is sufficiently drastic, however, to eliminate all but a handful of experimental aircraft, which may more accurately be described as V-STOL (very short take-off, etc.) types. **1961** *New Scientist* 23 Feb. 462/2 Construction of economical V/STOL aircraft.. is..a much more urgent and profitable line of development than supersonic aircraft will ever be. **1977** *R.A.F. News* 30 Mar.–12 Apr. 13/2 The future of military VSTOL would seem to be assured in a maritime context. **1954** *Aviation Week* 26 Apr. 30/2 New approaches to the problems of developing vertical-rising aircraft are being explored... NACA has been doing basic research in the VTO field for more than a decade. **1955** *Sci. Amer.* Apr. 106/3 V.T.O. aircraft (vertical take-off) are being developed vigorously in both England and the U.S. **1963** *Ann. Reg. 1962* 390 Bristol-Siddeley had produced a prototype supersonic VTO fighter. **1955** *Wall St. Jrnl.* 4 Feb. 3/4 Bell Aircraft Corp. announced it has built and flown the first jet-propelled vertical rising airplane which takes off and lands without needing a runway. The test VTOL (vertical take-off and landing) airplane weighs about 2,000 pounds, is 21 feet long, has a wing span of 26 feet, and carries only the pilot. **1958** *Times* 1 Mar. 7/3 V.T.O.L. designs are as yet in their infancy. **1979** N. SLATER *Falcon* i. 24 The basic [plane] design owed much to the VTOL Harrier. **1954** *Britannica Bk. of Year* 638/1 VTR (video tape recorder). **1968** *Globe & Mail* (Toronto) 17 Feb. 51 (Advt.), Minimum of two years experience preferably in colour telecine and Ampex VTR. **1982** J. GARDNER *For Special Services* xii. 109 Each [cabin] had a large sitting room with television, stereo and VTR. **1940** H. A. CHINN et al. in *Proc. IRE* XXVIII. 14/2 It was thought..that there would be less confusion in adopting the new standards if a new name were coined for expressing the measurements. The term selected is 'vu', the number of vu being numerically the same as the number of decibels above or below the new reference-volume level. **1944** *Ibid.* XXXII. 601/1 A key located to the left of the VU meter should be used. **1959** K. HENNEY *Radio Engin. Handbk.* (ed. 5) xiii. 19 The A scale emphasizes the VU markings and has an inconspicuous voltage scale. **1976** *Canad. Jrnl. Linguistics* Spring 70 The speaker made every attempt to maintain equal intensity across syllables by monitoring his output on a VU meter.

d. Of German words: V, *Vergeltungswaffe*, 'reprisal weapon'; used to denote German missiles of the war of 1939–45, as *V-1* = *flying bomb* s.v. *FLYING *vbl. sb.* 3; hence *V-bomb*; *V-2*, a type of rocket bomb; hence *V-weapons*; VW, Volkswagen.

1944 *Times* 30 June 3/5 For two weeks London has now been subjected to ceaseless bombardment by the German weapon V1. **1944** *Life* 21 Aug. 17/1 It seems probable..that the V-2, successor to the V-1 robot bomb, will be a heavy rocket. **1944** *Evening Sun* (Baltimore) 13 Sept. 1/6 The Germans, after toning down their 'V' weapons threat for a few days, are now making new threats. **1944** *Sun* (Baltimore) 20 Nov. 3/4 Lord Vansittart found no substance in objections that German V-bombs debar a Big Three meeting in Britain. **1952** M. ALLINGHAM *Tiger in Smoke* ii. 43 Night. V2 time... Remember V2's?.. Suddenly, no warning, no whistle, wallop! **1962** F. I. ORDWAY et al. *Basic Astronautics* ii. 23 The modern space carrier vehicle is a direct descendant of the V2 guided missile developed by the German army during World War II. **1978** D. KYLE *Black Camelot* x. 156 Hitler remains confident he can win the war... The V-weapons, I suppose. **1982** T. FITZGIBBON *With Love* II. viii. 155 After D-Day, 6 June 1944, a new horror arrived..the pilotless flying bombs, called V1s and known..as 'doodlebugs'... In September..the first rockets (V2s) reached London. **1958** S. ABBEY *Bk. of Volkswagen* v. 45 It is possible to improve the performance of the VW by a standardized engine tuning process... The VW owner is saved the cost of several accessories which are desirable. **1962** A. LURIE *Love & Friendship* vii. 135 Maybe it's just the fellow feeling of his Volkswagen for my Renault; he would be equally helpless if the VW broke down. **1977** C. MCFADDEN *Serial* (1978) iii. 13/1 She..extricated Kat Vonnegut..from the rear of her VW bus.

e. Of French words: V.D.Q.S., *vin délimité de qualité supérieure*, a wine of superior quality from amongst the wines of a limited area.

1962 *Wine Mag.* Sept.–Oct. 253/2 Next in order of quality are the V.D.Q.S. wines, or, to give them their full title, the *Vins Delimités de Qualité Supérieure*. **1966** P. V. PRICE *France: Food & Wine Guide* 135 Below the A.C. wines come those marked V.D.Q.S.— *vins délimités de qualité supérieure*. **1974** *Times* 2 Dec. (Suppl.) p. ii/1 The VDQS stamp..[is] a stamp of quality awarded by the French Government. VDQS stands for 'Vins Délimités de Qualité Supérieure'.

IV. Symbolic uses.

6. *Particle Physics.* V is used to designate the heavy unstable particles that produce characteristic V-shaped tracks when they decay (*V-events*), now identified as hyperons and kaons. *Obs.* exc. *hist.*

1950 P. M. S. BLACKETT *Let.* 12 July (MS.), We have been discussing here the question of nomenclature and I would like to ask your views about the following suggestion. This is that we should call the special type of track that you and we have observed v-tracks and the particle or particles which make them v-particles. The advantage of this seems to be that the letter v is reasonably unallocated and that the name has strong mnemonic values as, in fact, the tracks are v shaped. **1951** *Nature* 31 Mar. 503/1 Six charged *V*-tracks are due to the decay of new unstable particles. *Ibid.* 503/2 Two schemes are suggested to explain the photographs: $V^\circ \to p^+ + \pi^- \ldots; V^\circ \to \pi^+ + \pi^-$. **1952** *Sci. Amer.* Jan. 26/2 The V-particles appear to be somewhat more massive than a proton or neutron, because in some instances a proton is a decay product. **1968** M. S. LIVINGSTON *Particle Physics* v. 98 If an incident neutral particle has an interaction leading to two charged particles, the vertex of the V event shows the location, and the balance of transverse momenta identifies the incoming direction of the neutral particle. **1974** FRAUENFELDER & HENLEY *Subatomic Physics* vii. 170 By about 1952, many *V* events had been seen, and a mystery had developed: the *V* particles were produced copiously but decayed very slowly.

Vaad Leumi (vā·ād lə͵umī·). [Heb. *wa'ad* committee + *lə'ummī* national.] A national committee of Palestine Jews, serving as their official representative during the period of the British Mandate from 1920 to 1948.

The form *Vaad Haleumi* in the 1926 example includes the definite article.

1926 *Zionist Rev.* Feb. 127/2 The Second Jewish National Assembly appoints a Vaad Haleumi composed of 38 members. **1932** *Palestine Post* 4 Dec. 1/2 Mr I. Ben Zevi, a member of the Vaad Leumi Executive. **1941** *Contemp. Jewish Rec.* IV. 428/2 The threat of Nazi occupation caused the Agency Executive..to ratify an agreement between the Vaad Leumi and the Right bloc. **1949** KOESTLER *Promise & Fulfilment* I. xv. 169 On March 1 the *Vaad Leumi* met in Tel Aviv. **1963** *Times* 24 Apr. 16/1 He later became one of the founders of the General Council for Palestine Jews (*Vaad Leumi*), the executive body of the Jewish community, and served as chairman or president from 1931 until it was dissolved with the establishment of the State of Israel. **1971** *Encycl. Judaica* XVI. 49 The Va'ad Le'ummi represented the *yishuv* in its relations with the Mandatory government and the Arab leaders and dealt with internal matters (such as the school system) which were delegated to it by the Zionist Executive.

vaalhaai (fā·lhai). *S. Afr.* Also **Vaalhai.** [Afrikaans, f. Du. *vaal* pale + *haai* shark.] A local name for the tope, *Galeorhinus galeus*; = TOPE *sb.*² Also *attrib.*

1947 K. H. BARNARD *Pict. Guide S. Afr. Fishes* 10 Tope; Vaal-haai... This medium-sized (6 feet) cosmopolitan shark has recently become of considerable economic importance in South Africa for the extraction of vitamins from its liver-oil. **1949** *Cape Times* 24 Sept. 1/6 Any person capturing a Vaalhaai shark shall land it in a whole state. **1958** *Cape Argus* 14 June 13/4 The vaalhaai.. grows to about 6 ft. and is harmless to man. **1973** *Stand. Encycl. S. Afr.* IX. 603/2 In South Africa that [*sc.* the liver] of the liver-oil shark *Galeorhinus* (vaalhaai) is especially rich, and from 1940 to 1955 this species was specially hunted for it.

‖ **vaaljapie** (fā·lyāpi). *S. Afr.* Also **Vaal Japie.** [Afrikaans, lit. 'tawny Jake', f. as prec. + *japie* dim. of the name *Jaap* f. *Jakob.*] Rough young wine, inferior wine.

1945 *Cape Times* 21 May, What I say is 'Come quick, go quick,' and Vaal Japie is my best friend. **1949** L. G. GREEN *Land of Afternoon* 59 Young wine, not matured but about six months old, is known as Vaaljapie... It takes its name from its tawny colour though some varieties are red. **1958** *Cape Times* 29 Nov. 1/5 Some woodcutters..made him drunk on *vaaljapie* and called the police while he was asleep. **1968** D. J. OPPERMAN *Spirit of Vine* 242 Brandy and vaaljapie have always had an irresistible attraction for these people. **1975** *Stand. Encycl. S. Afr.* XI. 464/2 The wine ration given by farmers to their labourers..is referred to as 'boys' wine', or 'vaaljapie'.

‖ **Vaalpens** (fā·lpens). *S. Afr.* Pl. **-pens, pense(n).** Also with small initial in attrib. use. [Afrikaans, f. as prec. + *pens* paunch, belly.] **a.** A name for a member of the Ba-Kalahari tribe. **b.** *colloq.* A nickname for a Transvaler.

1871 J. MACKENZIE *Ten Years North of Orange River* iii. 53 Their fellow-countrymen to the south..sometimes call them 'Vaalpensen', which is the Dutch for Bakalahari, the ill-favoured and lean vassals of the Bechuanas. **1899** *Eastern Province Herald* (Port Elizabeth) 6 Dec. 3/4 A South African Dutchman writes us a somewhat bitter letter... He writes as a Dutch Afrikander, a Vaalpens in fact. **1900** A. H. KEANE *Boer States* iii. 32 Here [in the Bosch Veld] is also the true home of the Vaalpens, most degraded of all the South African aborigines. **1916** *Eastern Province Herald* (Port Elizabeth) 28 Sept. 3 The Vaalpens reported that one of our oxen had been mauled. .. We saddled up and with three Vaalpens soon found where the lion had caught the ox. **1934** *Star* (Johannesburg) 1 May 13/1 For the past 50 years and more Free Staters have been known among Dutch-speaking South Africans as Blikore (tin ears) and Transvaalers as Vaalpense, the latter so called after a certain native tribe of that name who lived in the Transvaal. *a* **1936** E. MARAIS *Soul of Ape* (1969) iii. 92 Here in Waterberg..a case of 'homing' in a descendant of the so-called 'vaalpens pygmies' that at one time inhabited the Bushveld of the northern Transvaal. **1970** *Personality* Competition, The 'Vaalpens' are very scarce in South Africa nowadays.

‖ **va banque** (va baṅk). *Gambling.* [Fr., lit. 'go bank'.] In baccarat and chemin-de-fer, a bet against the whole of the banker's stake. (In quots., *fig.*) Cf. *BANCO *int.*

1946 A. J. P. TAYLOR *Course of German Hist.* ii. 38 Both dynasties desired the defeat of Napoleon; but the Hohenzollerns, having nothing more to lose, were ready to bid *va banque*—the Habsburgs were not. **1966** *Economist* 12 Nov. 683/3 Disraeli..was an adventurer who played the great game *va banque* with a courage and effrontery that commanded, perhaps even deserved, success.

vac², colloq. abbrev. of *VACUUM *v.*

1942 N. LAST *Diary* 23 July in *Nella Last's War* (1981) vii. 212, I hurried home to bake my bread, vac the dining-room and dust. **1970** J. WAINWRIGHT *Prynter's Devil* iii. 50 Vac the room first, kiddo. Then start the repaint job. **1971** *Guardian* 26 Nov. 11/5 Little ladies in nylon overalls were noisily vaccing the deep red carpet. **1981** J. WAINWRIGHT *Urge for Justice* II. i. 100 My cleaning lady..vacs and polishes around.

vac³, colloq. abbrev. of *vacuum cleaner* s.v. VACUUM 4.

1974 P. WRIGHT *Lang. Brit. Industry* xvii. 164 The brave new indoor world of *vacs, mixers, mincers* and all the rest. **1976** *Star* (Sheffield) 20 Nov. (Advt.), Cash paid for Washers, Vacs and Fridges in good condition. **1979** *Arizona Daily Star* 1 Apr. (Advt. Suppl.), Wards has jiffy vacs priced low as 22.88.

vac, abbrev. VACANT *a.*: see *sit(s) vac* s.v. *SIT *sb.*²

vacance. Add: **5.** *poet. nonce-use.* A rendering of Fr. *absence* in the original.

1930 T. S. ELIOT tr. *St.-J. Perse's Anabasis* viii. 53 To the scale of our hearts was such vacance completed!

vacancy. Add: **II. 6. c.** A vacant room in a hotel, guest-house, etc. Usu. *attrib.* as *vacancy sign*, a signboard advertising available accommodation, or in *pl.*

1953 'R. MACDONALD' *Gone Girl* in *Lew Archer, Private Investigator* (1977) 24 The first motel I came to..was decorated with a vacancy sign. **1970** R. H. GREENAN *Nightmare* iv. 15 The place..is a bit sleazy... There's a vacancy sign out. **1972** *Guardian* 17 May 12/3 Hotels are replacing the 'Vacancy' signs with hoardings saying 'For Sale'. **1973** *Value Added Tax Tribunals Rep.* I. 165 Students have at their choice, provided vacancies are available, three types of accommodation. **1982** M. BABSON *Death beside Seaside* xiii. 111 Most of the trippers will be leaving this afternoon. There'll be plenty of vacancies.

III. 9. c. *Cryst.* A defect in a crystal lattice consisting of the absence of an atom or ion from a position where there should be one.

1951 *Physical Rev.* LXXXII. 551/1 The experiments described below seem to be the most direct evidence, to date, that diffusion in close-packed metals occurs, predominantly, through the movement of vacancies. **1958** [see *SCHOTTKY 2]. **1967** A. H. COTTRELL *Introd. Metallurgy* xx. 365 The quench..produces a supersaturated solution of vacancies and..these vacancies agglomerate to form dislocation rings or other defects which harden the metal by acting as obstacles to gliding dislocations. **1971** *New Scientist* 25 Mar. 664/2 The interstitial migrates by jumping from one site to another, while the vacancy migrates as a result of a neighbouring atom jumping into the vacant hole. **1974** *Encycl. Brit. Macropædia* V. 334/1 Theoretical considerations require that all crystals have vacancies except at absolute zero temperature.

vacant, *a.* Add: **7. a.** *vacant-eyed, -minded* (earlier example), *-seeming* adjs.

1836 POE in *Southern Lit. Messenger* Apr. 339/2 Not a broad, forced, loud vacant-minded joke, but a quiet, pungent, sly, laughter-moving conceit. **1922** D. H. LAWRENCE *Aaron's Rod* xiii. 186 It was a large, vacant-seeming, Empire sort of drawing-room. **1936** L. H. MYERS *Strange Glory* II. ix. 150 A boy of about ten.., ill-nourished and vacant-eyed. **1965** J. A. MICHENER *Source* (1966) 59 From the shores of Morocco..came frightened, dirty, pathetic Jews, illiterate, often crippled with disease and vacant-eyed.

b. In phr. *vacant possession*, with reference to premises (esp. those offered for sale): available for occupation by the purchaser, not occupied by the vendor or a tenant or tenants.

The legal interpretation of the term can be modified in certain circumstances by agreement between the vendor and the purchaser.

1825 H. ROSCOE *Treat. Law of Actions relating to Real Property* I. 546 Ejectment cannot be maintained, as on a vacant possession, where there is any thing left by the tenant on the premises, however trifling. **1883** *Wharton's Law-Lexicon* (ed. 7) 287/1 In case of vacant possession the writ may be served by posting a copy on some conspicuous part of the property. **1927** *Daily Tel.* 24 May 4/7 Vacant possession at Michaelmas will be given of the Manor Farm, 428 acres, at Oxwick. **1946** *Law Rep.* (King's Bench) 264 A vendor who leaves chattels of his own on property sold by him to an extent depriving the purchaser of the physical enjoyment of part of the property has failed to give vacant possession. **1973** *Country Life* 15 Mar. 713/1 The average price of vacant-possession farms in England is £273 an acre. **1976** *Morecambe Guardian* 7 Dec. 28/1 (Advt.), Three bedroom semi-detached house with vacant possession.

vacate, *v.* Add: **1. b.** (Later example.)

1895 'MARK TWAIN' in *N. Amer. Rev.* July 3 In the 'Deerslayer' tale this rule is vacated.

4. c. (Earlier example.)

1836 *Knickerbocker* VII. 15 Ned and I were vacating.. at his father's charming residence.

vacating (vǎkē̆i·tiŋ), *ppl. a.* [f. VACATE *v.* + -ING².] That is retiring from office, etc.

1921 *Act* 11 & 12 *Geo. V* c. 21 Sched. 1. 6 Where the unexpired portion of the term of office of the vacating member is less than one year. **1981** *N.Y. Times* 18 Jan. XI. 20 Mrs. Kennelly suggested that the leader of the Senate or the House from the party of the vacating member be able to appoint a substitute legislator.

vacation, *sb.* Add: **III. 9.** (Earlier example.)

1860 *Players* 14 Apr. 121 Since Mr Kean's vacation of the Princess's, Miss Murray has joined the present company at the St. James's Theatre.

IV. 10. *Comb.*, as **vacation home** *U.S.*, a house used by the owner for holidays or at weekends (cf. *holiday home* (*b*) s.v. *HOLIDAY *sb.* 4 a); **vacation job,** paid employment for a student during vacation from a university, polytechnic, etc.; **vacation-land** *U.S.*, an area attracting holiday-makers.

1969 'E. LATHEN' *When in Greece* xiii. 146 The whole area is honeycombed with vacation homes. **1978** D. WILLIAMS *Treasure up in Smoke* iv. 40 A big-spending visitor who maintained a vacation home. **1971** *Guardian* 23 July 6/7, 24,400 students registered for vacation jobs. **1977** D. JAMES *Spy at Evening* x. 68, I had..managed to get a vacation job as reserve stoker in a block of flats. **1927** *Scribner's Mag.* Apr. 100 The glories of Yellowstone Park take on new meaning this year with our discovery of Gallatin Gateway! It is the great sensation of vacation-land. **1977** *Chicago Tribune* 2 Oct. IV. 18/1 The region is a vacationland of great variety. There are spas, county fairs, antiques and crafts shows, [etc.].

vacationer, (*a*) for *U.S.* read orig. *U.S.* and add later examples; **vaca·tioning** *ppl. a.* and *vbl. sb.* (*U.S.*).

1926 *Scribner's Mag.* Aug. 7/2 Advice to vacationing young folks: In the dog days, don't be too Sirius. **1961** *Times* 28 Nov. 13/7 The organized and the individual vacationers. **1967** *Idle Moments* (Austral.) Sept. 27/3 The vacationer's body also will have reduced metabolic needs which may take two or three weeks for adjustment. **1976** *National Observer* (U.S.) 24 Jan. 8/2 (Advt.), *Off-the-Beaten Path* names the really low cost Florida retirement and vacationing towns. **1978** *Detroit Free Press* 16 Apr. (Parade Suppl.) 13/1 Increasingly, vacationing Americans are taking to the woods, mountains, deserts and seashores.

vaccinate, *v.* **1. b.** For 'virus' read 'vaccine'. (Earlier and later examples.)

1882 E. KLEIN in *11th Ann. Rep. Local Govt. Board* in *Parl. Papers* (C. 3337. 1) XXX. II. 509 In Pasteur's case the sheep inoculated with such bacilli..are not killed by anthrax, but 'vaccinated', and protected. **1955** [see *POLIO 1]. **1983** *Oxford Times* 3 June 18/2 Women are being urged to check that they have been vaccinated against German measles after a serious outbreak of the disease.

vaccination. 1. b. Substitute for def.: The inoculation of an individual with any vaccine in order to induce or increase immunity. (Further examples.) [The use of the term for diseases other than small-pox is due to Pasteur (*Trans. 7th Session Internat. Med. Congr.* (1881) I. 90).]

1896 *Lancet* 19 Sept. 809/2 These anti-cholera inoculations have served as a pattern for the typhoid vaccinations. **1955** *Sci. Amer.* Apr. 44/3 Tests show that antibody persists for an appreciable time after vaccination with the killed-virus vaccine. **1978** T. R. BOWRY *Immunol. Simplified* iv. 14 Cholera vaccination is still required for travel to a few countries.

2. *vaccination mark.*

1899 A. E. HOUSMAN in *Univ. College Gaz.* 22 Mar. 34/2 Vain his laced boots, and vain his eyebrow dark, And vain, ah! vain, his vaccination mark. **1914** D. H. LAWRENCE *Widowing of Mrs. Holroyd* III. 92 And such arms on 'im! Look at the vaccination marks, Lizzie. **1983** *N.Y. Times* 20 Mar. 13/1 Her face was as powdered and pitted as the vaccination mark on her arm.

vaccine, *sb.* **2. b.** Substitute for def.: A preparation of the causative organism or substance of a disease (or its products) that has been specially treated for use in vaccination (see also quot. 1983). (Earlier and later examples.)

1882 E. KLEIN in *11th Ann. Rep. Local Govt. Board* in *Parl. Papers* (C. 3337. 1) XXX. II. 509, I have not yet succeeded in discovering the method employed by M. Pasteur..for the production of 'vaccine' protective against anthrax. **1892** *Brit. Med. Jrnl.* 28 May 1157/2 M. Pasteur has for some years directed his attention to the treatment of epilepsy by antirabic vaccine. **1911** *Lancet* 16 Sept. 814/1 The treatment of hay fever by hypodermic inoculations of pollen vaccine. **1931** W. T. VAUGHAN *Allergy & Appl. Immunol.* xxix. 328 While the use of immune sera has not been successful in the treatment of typhoid fever, the vaccine has more than demonstrated its efficiency as a preventive. **1962** J. H. BURN *Drugs, Med. & Man* xii. 132 Evidence concerning the value of whooping-cough vaccine to protect children against whooping-cough. **1980** D. J. RAPP *Allergies & your Family* xiii. 220 Measles vaccine should be avoided by children who are receiving steroids. **1983** *Sci. Amer.* Feb. 48/2 There has been increasing interest in the preparation of synthetic vaccines, which is to say vaccines containing not intact viruses but merely peptides..that have been constructed in the laboratory to mimic a very small region of the virus's outer coat.

3. Special Combs.: **vaccine-damaged** *a.*, harmed, esp. seriously, as a result of being vaccinated; also *absol.*; **vaccine therapy,** (G. B. Shaw) **vaccinetherapy,** treatment of a disease with an appropriate vaccine.

1976 *S. Wales Echo* 22 Nov. 8/8 As a parent of a vaccine-damaged daughter who is classed as severely subnormal I can say every word Mr. Peter Ellershaw wrote was true. **1980** *Times* 15 Jan. 4/1 (*heading*) New campaign to win state help for the vaccine-damaged. **1907** *Jrnl. Infectious Dis.* IV. 313 (*heading*) The opsonic index and vaccine therapy of pseudodiphtheric otitis. **1911** G. B. SHAW *Doctor's Dilemma* p. lxxxviii, The theory and practice of securing immunization from bacterial diseases by the inoculation of 'vaccines' made of their own bacteria: a practice incorrectly called vaccinetherapy (there is nothing vaccine about it). **1974** *Mycopathologia et Mycol. Applicata* LIII. 25 (*heading*) Pompholyx of the hands and feet. Its etiology, pathogenesis and specific vaccine therapy.

vaccinee. Delete *rare* and add later examples.

1970 *Nature* 24 Oct. 307/1 Some of the vaccinees might unknowingly be pregnant. **1977** *Lancet* 20 Aug. 400/1 First results were obtained from 20 sera of vaccinees.

‖ **vacherin** (vaʃ'ræn). [Fr.] **a.** A kind of cheese (see quot. 1936). **b.** A confection of meringue and whipped cream.

1936 A. L. SIMON *Catechism concerning Cheeses* 44 *Vacherin.* A French Savoy and Swiss cheese made during the winter. **1960** E. DAVID *French Provincial Cooking* 34 We were then beguiled into eating a sweet called a *Vacherin glacé*. This turned out to be..ice-cream, glacé fruits, frozen whipped cream, and meringue. **1965** A. ROUDYBUSH *Season for Death* (1966) xxiii. 133 An impromptu supper of..venison baked in wine and great vacherin meringues was served. **1969** R. & D. DE SOLA *Dict. Cooking* 231/1 *Vacherin*, Swedish cheese used as a spread, creamy and aromatic. **1979** *N.Y. Times* 18 May C14/4 A vacherin of nutted meringue layers with whipped cream and strawberries.

vacky (væ·ki). *colloq. abbrev.* Also **vaccy, vakky.** [f. *EVACUEE: cf. -Y[6].] An evacuee, *esp.* a child evacuated from the city to the country esp. at the beginning of the 1939–45 war.

1940 *John o' London's Weekly* 3 May 147/1 These little vackies and their country friends. **1940** J. CARY *Charley is my Darling* ii. 16 There are only eight vackies in the place. **1949** E. COXHEAD *Wind in West* iii. 66, I was a vakky. My home's in Clapham really, but our school was sent to Bedfordshire. **1962** M. DUFFY *That's how it Was* viii. 71 The Wortbridgers distrusted the vaccies with their quick ways and sharp, pinched faces. **1979** *Bookseller* 25 Aug. 832/2 A 'must' book for all ex-'vaccies, and their parents, and their children. **1982** J. AIKEN *Whisper in Night* 151 The Welsh landscape had changed..since he was a Vakky, sent here for safety from the Birmingham bombs.

vacuolating (væ·kiu,ǒlēˈtiŋ), *ppl. a. Med.* [Back-formation from VACUOLATION: see -ING[2].] *vacuolating agent* or *virus*: a papovavirus, orig. obtained from rhesus monkey kidney tissue, which is capable of causing tumours in animals and animal tissue cultures; also called *SV 40* (cf. *SV* s.v. *S 4 a); also, a virus related to this.

1960 SWEET & HILLEMAN in *Proc. Soc. Exper. Biol. & Med.* CV. 420/1 This agent has been called the 'vacuolating virus' by us because of the prominent cytoplasmic vacuolation seen in infected cell cultures... The discovery of this new virus, the vacuolating agent, represents the detection..of a hitherto 'non-detectable' simian virus of monkey renal cultures. **1965** *Listener* 11 Mar. 369/2 A remarkable situation is also presented by..vacuolating virus or simian virus 40. This virus..was accidentally given to millions of human subjects with early batches of polio vaccine. **1977** *Jrnl. Virology* XXI. 179/1 Papovaviruses of the simian virus 40 (SV 40)-polyoma subgroup ..occur in the mouse.., the rabbit (rabbit kidney vacuolating virus [RKV]), [etc.].

vacuolized (væ·kiu,ǒləizd), *ppl. a.* [f. VACUOLE + -IZE + -ED[1].] = VACUOLATED *ppl. a.*

1910 *Ann. Bot.* XXIV. 733 These bands and masses may be homogeneous or vacuolized. **1961** *Lancet* 2 Sept. 525/2 The cells were enlarged and their cytoplasm was vacuolised.

vacuome (væ·kiu,ōᵘm). *Cytology.* [a. F. *vacuome*, f. L. *vacu-us* empty: see *-OME.] The vacuoles of a cell collectively (see quot. 1976).

1926 [see *PLASTIDOME]. **1936** *Nature* 20 May 914/2 The vacuome and chondriome systems can be distinguished by their behaviour to vital stains. **1947** *Ann. Rev. Microbiol.* I. 9 In the dinoflagellate, *Polykrikos schwartzi*, ..mitochondria, Golgi material, vacuome, fat globules and glycogen have been described. **1959** W. ANDREW *Textbk. Compar. Histol.* v. 146 As it [*sc.* the food particle] approaches the vacuome (Golgi substance), particles from this structure are attracted to its surface. **1960** L. PICKEN *Organization of Cells* vi. 235 According to a theory elaborated by Parat and Painlevé..all cells contain two systems, unrelated though of profound importance in cell economy: the chondriome—a lipoidal 'phase' manifested as isolated mitochondrial networks; and the vacuome—a dispersed phase of aqueous droplets staining with neutral red, to be equated with the Golgi apparatus. **1976** R. RIEGER et al. *Gloss. Genetics & Cytogenetics* (ed. 4) 564 *Vacuome*, originally, a system comprising a variety of inclusions of plant cells, from the highly hydrated tonoplast to the dense aleuron granules, all with the common ability to stain vitally with neutral red. Today, all the membrane-bounded spaces of the cell with the exception of the mitochondria and the plastids which make up the chondriome..and the plastome respectively. **1981** *Jrnl. Ultrastructure Res.* LXXVI. 317 Multivesicular bodies seen in section of the unicellular green alga *Scenedesmus obtusiusculus* are profiles of a continuous cisternum, the vacuome.

vacuum. Delete ‖ and add: **2. c.** *ellipt.* for *vacuum cleaner*, sense 4 below. *colloq.* (orig. *U.S.*).

1910 *Judge* 9 Apr. 8/2 A vacuum was the only thing she could be trusted to handle with safety. **1922** *Hotel World* 25 Mar. 14/1, I have three vacuums going all day. **1960** *Farmer & Stockbreeder* 8 Mar. (Suppl.) 10/1 Is it better to have a *powerful* or a *handy* cleaner? That has always been a problem when choosing a 'vacuum'. **1977** *New Yorker* 24 Oct. 88/3 Green Haven's dep [*sc.* deputy superintendent] of administration was preoccupied with the size of the wet-dry vacuums being used to clean the prison kitchen.

4. *vacuum-jacketed* adj.; **vacuum activity** (see quot. 1981); **vacuum aspiration,** a method of induced abortion in which the contents of the uterus are removed by suction through a tube passed into it via the vagina; **vacuum bottle** = *vacuum flask* below; **vacuum chamber,** a chamber designed to be emptied of air; **vacuum cleaner,** an electrical appliance for removing dust (from carpets and other flooring, soft furnishings, etc.) by suction; also *transf.* and *fig.*; hence (as a back-formation) **vacuum-clean** *v. trans.*, = *VACUUM *v.*; so **vacuum-cleaning** *vbl. sb.*; **vacuum deposition,** deposition of a substance by allowing it to condense from the vapour in what is otherwise a vacuum; so **vacuum-deposit** *v. trans.*, **-deposited** *ppl. a.*; **vacuum extraction** *Obstetr.*, the application of suction to a baby's head to assist its birth; so **vacuum extractor,** a cup-shaped appliance for achieving this; **vacuum-fitted** *a.*, of a railway car: furnished with a vacuum brake; **vacuum flask,** a vessel with a double wall enclosing a vacuum so that liquid in the inner receptacle retains its temperature (cf. THERMOS in Dict. and Suppl.); also *transf.* in *attrib.* use; **vacuum fluctuation** *Physics*, a fluctuation in field strength in a nominally field-free vacuum, occurring in consequence of the quantization of any radiation field; **vacuum forming,** a type of thermoforming in which a vacuum is used to draw the plastic into the mould (see quot. 1974); **vacuum grease,** a grease which because of its low vapour pressure is suitable for sealing joints in a vacuum apparatus; **vacuum packaging,** (*a*) = *vacuum-packing* vbl. sb. s.v. *VACUUM-PACK *v.*; (*b*) the vacuumized container used in vacuum-packing; **vacuum polarization** *Physics*, the spontaneous appearance and disappearance of electron–positron pairs in a vacuum; **vacuum pump,** a pump for evacuating a container of air or other gas; (examples); **vacuum-tight** *a.* = AIR-TIGHT *a.*; **vacuum wax** = *vacuum grease* above.

1953 N. TINBERGEN *Herring Gull's World* iv. 35 It is possible..this was just a kind of 'vacuum activity' due to the accumulation of the urge to paddle. **1981** *Oxf. Compan. Anim. Behaviour* 579/1 Vacuum activities occur in the apparent absence of the external stimuli that normally elicit the activity. **1967** *Obstetrics & Gynecol.* XXX. 28 (*heading*) A critical view of vacuum aspiration: a new method for the termination of pregnancy. **1974** PASSMORE & ROBSON *Compan. Med. Stud.* III. xlii. 7/2 Before the 12th week it is customary and simplest to evacuate the uterus via the vagina by vacuum aspiration. **1978** F. WELDON *Praxis* ii. 13 If by mistake they fall pregnant, they abort by vacuum aspiration. **1910** *Chambers's Jrnl.* June 413/2 The vacuum-bottle has entered so extensively into the domestic circle as to become regarded almost as indispensable. **1976** *Daily Colonist* (Victoria, B.C.) 6 Mar. 19/5 Use lunch buckets or vacuum bottles to keep foods hot or cold. *a* **1877** KNIGHT *Dict. Mech.* III. 2687/2 Huffer..claims the use of exhaust steam from an engine to condense in a vacuum-chamber, and so raise water to turn a wheel. **1971** *Materials & Technol.* II. v. 230 A certain amount of water is evaporated from the clay as it passes through the vacuum chamber. **1912** *Sci. Amer.* 22 Nov. 442/2 (*caption*) Vacuum-cleaning an automobile. The exhaust gases of the motor create the suction. **1924** KIPLING *Debits & Credits* (1926) 149 The organ-bench, whose purple velvet cushion was being vacuum-cleaned on the floor below. **1956** *Good Housek. Home Encycl.* (ed. 4) 316/2 Wickerwork..requires to be brushed or vacuum-cleaned regularly. **1973** *Physics Bull.* Feb. 110/3 These..could then be scraped and vacuum cleaned from the carpet. **1977** J. R. L. ANDERSON *Death in City* i. 10 A team..did the rooms,..vacuum-cleaning floors. **1983** *Daily Tel.* 8 Apr. 16/3 Soviet spies are vacuum cleaning the West for its industrial and scientific secrets. **1903** Vacuum cleaner [in Dict.]. **1907** *Yesterday's Shopping* (1969) 113/1 The 'Witch' Dust Extractor is a vacuum cleaner suitable alike for carpets, upholstery, clothing, &c. **1962** A. LURIE *Love & Friendship* i. 12 She..did not hear the noise of the vacuum cleaner sucking its way up the stair carpeting. **1972** *World Bk. Sci. Ann. 1971* 342 The vacuum cleaner is actually a hydraulic pump designed to lift as much as 400 tons of material from the sea floor daily. **1976** *Times* 1 Mar. 13/3 The conservation of fish stocks.. in the face of over-developed world fishing fleets and 'vacuum cleaner' techniques of fishing. **1902** *Let.* 20 Oct. in *Goblin Story* (Goblin Ltd.) (1969) 9, I have submitted the subject of the Vacuum Cleaning Company's operations to the King. **1916** J. WEBSTER *Dear Enemy* 71 'Well?' said she, her tone implying that I was a vacuum-cleaning agent. **1939** *Country Life* 11 Feb. p. vi (Advt.), Vacuum cleaning plant. **1946** *Nature* 14 Dec. 862/1 Mollwo reported on the density of vacuum-deposited salt layers. **1960** *McGraw-Hill Encycl. Sci. & Technol.* X. 596/2 Fabrication of printed resistors by vacuum deposition is an expensive process and there has been no general application of this technique except for precision resistive elements. **1982** *Jrnl. Colloid & Interface Sci.* XC. 335 When certain materials such as Se or Sn are vacuum-deposited onto heated polymers under appropriate conditions, a most unusual structure can form. *Ibid.* 337/1 The structure of the monolayer assemblies formed by vacuum deposition is almost independent of the deposition rate. *Ibid.*, The vacuum deposited structure is little altered if the system pressure during deposition is allowed to rise. **1961** *Lancet* 22 July 189/2 They concluded that vacuum extraction does not distress the fœtus. **1975** I. ILLICH *Med. Nemesis* vii. 120 The vacuum extraction method has rendered the interruption of pregnancies safe, cheap and simple. **1954** T. MALMSTRÖM in *Acta Obstetrica et Gynecologica Scandinavica* XXXIII. Suppl. No. 4. 5 The vacuum extractor ad modum Dr Malmstrom is constructed and manufactured in co-operation with R. Soderberg & Co, Gothenburg, Sweden. **1960** *Proc. R. Soc. Med.* LIII. 749/1 The vacuum extractor consists of a flattened round metal cup with bulging sides. **1980** S. KITZINGER *Pregnancy & Childbirth* 260 Sometimes a vacuum extractor, or ventouse, is used instead of forceps. **1937** Vacuum-fitted [see *passenger train* s.v. *PASSENGER 7 a]. **1968** *Listener* 15 Aug. 210/1 We..have a brake which is known as the vacuum brake, and our wagons are known as vacuum-fitted. **1917** *Harrods Gen. Catal.* 946/3 The 'Icy-Hot' Vacuum Flasks, improved designs, will keep liquids hot for 24 hours or cold for 3 days. **1926** *Daily Colonist* (Victoria, B.C.) 20 Jan. 5/1 This vacuum flask will keep things hot for you indefinitely. **1958** *New Statesman* 23 Aug. 214/2 Investigation in person will clearly have to wait until travellers are provided with armour-plated vacuum-flask suits. **1978** M. BABSON *Tightrope for Three* vi. 39 She..filled the kettle..and..the vacuum flask as well. **1955** L. ROSENFELD in W. Pauli *Niels Bohr* 88 The 'vacuum' fluctuations of the field variables. **1973** *Nature* 14 Dec. 397/1 The laws of physics place no limit on the scale of vacuum fluctuations. The duration is of course subject to the restriction $\Delta E \Delta t \sim h$. **1979** J. C. POLKINGHORNE *Particle Play* v. 74 Buffeted by vacuum fluctuations the elementary particle has a pretty rocky ride. This is the origin of the infinities which people found when they first tried to calculate with quantum field theories. **1946** J. SASSO *Plastics Handbk. for Product Engineers* v. 308 In the vacuum-forming process the plastic sheet is heated to approximately 250F. **1974** *Encycl. Brit. Macropædia* XIV. 521/1 In simple vacuum forming, the plastic sheet is clamped over an airtight box, from which air is exhausted, rapidly drawing the heated plastic down on a 'former' within the box, thus reproducing its shape. **1946** *Jrnl. R. Aeronaut. Soc.* L. 393 Connection to the vacuum system is made by a ground metal joint sealed with vacuum grease. **1977** *Vacuum* XXVII. 431/1 There are three factors involved in choosing a vacuum grease—cost, convenience, and its effect on the vacuum system. **1946** *Nature* 20 July 105/1 The best way to carry methane on motor-vehicles is as a liquid in vacuum-jacketed tanks. **1970** *Sci. Jrnl.* Aug. 82/3 The 'lagged storage tank' for LNG would need to be vacuum jacketed. **1954** L. C. BARAIL *Packaging Engineering* xx. 249 The cans filled with the whole products are then sealed by means of vacuum machines, a process known as vacuum packaging. **1982** R. MANHEIM tr. *Grass's Headbirths* iv. 65 The cut in the vacuum packaging could be patched up. [**1935** *Physical Rev.* XLVIII. 55/2 The existence of [such] an induced charge corresponds to a polarization of the vacuum.] **1951** *Ibid.* LXXXI. 664/1 We shall illustrate this assertion by applying such a gauge invariant method to treat several aspects of the problem of vacuum polarization by a prescribed electromagnetic field. **1979** CHENG & O'NEILL *Elementary Particle Physics* iii. 82 The two dominant processes that modify the electron's interaction with the proton.., resulting in the Lamb shift, are the vertex correction and vacuum polarization. **1882** *Chem. News* 27 Oct. 192/1 In the machine in question the refrigeration is effected simply by the evaporation of water under a special vacuum-pump. **1979** J. MATLEY *Fluid Movers* v. 267/1 A good seal between the inlet and outlet sides is essential in all mechanical vacuum pumps. **1927** *Brit. Jrnl. Radiol.* XXIII. 143 The glass is directly sealed to a chromium-iron alloy which is perfectly vacuum-tight. **1946** *Nature* 23 Nov. 756/2 Vacuum-tight seals through hard glass with bare tungsten wire are difficult to make. **1964** M. GOWING *Britain & Atomic Energy 1939–1945* viii. 219 New techniques had to be developed for ensuring that the machinery was..exceptionally vacuum-tight. **1926** J. H. SMITH tr. *L. Dunoyer's Vacuum Practice* iii. 142 Vacuum waxes. Golaz wax has been in use since Regnault's time. **1971** *Sci. Amer.* Aug. 108/1 The joint was sealed with Apiezon W-100 vacuum wax.

vacuum (væ·kiu,ǒm), *v. colloq.* (orig. *U.S.*). [f. the sb.] *trans.* To clean (a room, carpet, etc.), or to remove (dust, etc.) with a vacuum cleaner. Also *fig.* and *absol.* Occas. *intr.* for *pass.*

1922 *Hotel World* 25 Mar. 14/1, I have every room in the hotel vacuumed every week, furniture and all. **1934** in WEBSTER. **1950** *Sun* (Baltimore) 28 Apr. 36/7 Apparently electrocuted when she stepped on a metal furnace grating while vacuuming the floor. **1959** *Times* 11 Feb. 12/6 Why could not..the whole establishment be dusted one day, vacuumed another, and so on? **1961** *Time* (Atlantic ed.) 20 Jan. 17 Her retentive mind vacuums odd details from the newspapers. **1967** D. FRANCIS *Blood Sport* xv. 179 'He says the whole place is *covered* in flour.'..'It'll vacuum quite easily, won't it?' **1974** J. IRVING *158-Pound Marriage* (1980) ix. 203 Together we vacuumed fragments from every crevice. **1978** M. DICKENS *Open Bk.* xv. 141 In the living room, the carpet was so old, it came up in dusty shreds if you vacuumed. **1980** *Daily Tel.* 6 Feb. 18 Toads are hungry creatures: no-one better to vacuum a garden of slugs and other pests. **1985** *Listener* 21 Mar. 25/2 'Syd'..watered his milk, left fat on his lamb chops, and vacuumed when he was listening to symphonies on the radio.

Hence **va·cuuming** *vbl. sb.*

1953 L. KUPER *Living in Towns* ii. 16, I try to do my vacuuming quickly. **1972** J. PORTER *Meddler & her Murder* xii. 160 The lounge could do with the usual dusting and vacuuming. **1979** *Tucson Mag.* Apr. 62/3 One owner..has worked out his own vacuuming routine over the years. **1984** A. BROOKNER *Hotel du Lac* i. 14 After ten o'clock..all household noises had to be silenced; no vacuuming was heard.

vacuumize (væ·kiu̯,ŭmaiz), *v.* [f. VACUUM + -IZE.] *trans.* To create a vacuum in (something); to seal (a container) from which air has been artificially withdrawn. Hence **va·cuumized** *ppl. a.*; so **va·cuumizing** *vbl. sb.*

1909 *Chambers's Jrnl.* July 478/1 Vacuumising is effected by means of a hand-wheel, or the machine can be worked by power if desired. **1939** R. S. LYONS *Wonders of Modern Industry* xi. 131 To preserve the cigarettes in fresh condition, each tin has a vacuum created inside it before being sealed. The method of vacuumizing is as ingenious as it is simple. *Ibid.* 132 It sometimes happens that some of the tins are not quite vacuumized. **1942** *N.Y. Times* 13 Feb. 18/5 The glass industry 'has always had equipment for vacuumized products'. **1980** *Cement & Concrete Res.* X. 853 The press-method of concrete compaction with simultaneous vacuumizing makes it possible to add an increased volume of mix water to concrete mix. **1983** *Mod. Metals* Jan. 66/1 Made of either tinplate or tin free steel, the TAB-E end can be applied to vacuumized, pressurized or still-filled cans.

va·cuum-pack, *v.* [f. VACUUM + PACK *v.*[1]] *trans.* To pack (something) in an air-tight container from which the air has been withdrawn; to pack (such a container).

1951 *Good Housek. Home Encycl.* 416/2 Coffee that is both freshly ground and freshly roasted (or vacuum-packed). **1954** L. C. BARAIL *Packaging Engineering* xx. 249 Whether the cars have been sealed after exhausting or vacuum packed without being exhausted, they have to be processed in order to destroy microorganisms.

Hence **va·cuum-packed** *ppl. a.*; also *fig.*; **va·cuum-packing** *vbl. sb.*

1955 *Hebrew Union College Annual* XXVI. 108 No longer can we assume that Greece is the hermetically sealed Olympian miracle, any more than we can consider Israel the vacuum-packed miracle from Sinai. **1960** *Farmer & Stockbreeder* 19 Jan. (Suppl.) 41/3 The final processing involves..draining, swabbing and then vacuum-packing in transparent film bags. **1962** *Spectator* 4 May 602/3, I was at a testing of vacuum-packed bacon. Vacuum-packing is likely to spread, because it is so convenient for the handlers. **1975** *Times* 18 Feb. 13/2 The vacuum-packed fine arts sector. **1984** *Listener* 5 Apr. 10/2 The girl said it came vacuum-packed.

vacuum tube. 1. An evacuated tube or pipe, esp. one along which vehicles or other objects can be propelled by allowing air to enter behind them.

1784 in *Pall Mall Mag.* (1896) Aug. 586 Grand Vacuum Tube Company. Direct to Bengal. **1846** *Patent Jrnl.* 4 July 90/1 Fig. 1 is a ..section of a railway carriage and traction tube. Fig. 2 is a cross section..showing the communication between the carriage and the piston. The traction or vacuum tube..is the same as generally used. **1920** D. H. LAWRENCE *Touch & Go* 7 A system of vacuum tubes for whooshing Bradburys about from one to the other. **1972** *Daily Tel.* 30 Dec. 6/5 The explanation, it is believed, is that while it was being scooped up it became mixed with the dark grey soil usually found on the Moon. It could not have changed as a result of exposure to the Earth's atmosphere, because it is stored in vacuum tubes. **1973** *Times* 15 Oct. 6/3 High-speed surface systems should be studied as an alternative to air travel, including advanced systems such as the gravity vacuum tube, which would give high speeds for amazingly low energy consumption. **1974** [see *people mover* s.v. *PEOPLE *sb.* 8].

2. An evacuated tube (sense *2 g) (orig. a glass cylinder); *spec.* one used as a thermionic valve.

1859 *Phil. Trans. R. Soc.* CXLVIII. 15 The direct discharge is that which is visible when taken from two wires hermetically sealed in a vacuum tube. **1880** *Rep. Brit. Assoc. Adv. Sci. 1880* 260 The band-spectrum of nitrogen... It was first observed by Plücker (1858) in a vacuum tube. **1901** *Engineer* 17 May 507/2 One of the most interesting exhibits was a number of electric vacuum-tube lamps. **1915** W. H. ECCLES *Wireless Telegr. & Teleph.* 376 A. Langmuir has applied his vacuum tube with third electrode (the 'pliotron') in a manner different from those just described. **1923** *Electr. Communication* II. 157/2 No single advance has contributed so largely to change our whole picture of art as the advent of the thermionic valve or vacuum tube as it is designated in America. **1931** MOYER & WOSTREL *Radio Handbk.* vi. 317 The increased use of vacuum tubes for other than radio services has made it necessary to design vacuum tubes which will be suitable for handling much larger currents. **1957** K. R. SPANGENBERG *Fund. Electron Devices* xi. 235 The transistor is, like the vacuum tube, a device that owes its amplifying characteristics to electric-field control of current within the device. **1972** *Sci. Amer.* June 52/2 It produces a television-like image without the cumbersome vacuum tube, electron beam and high voltage required by conventional television systems.

attrib. **1923** *Electr. Communication* II. 157/2 The vacuum tube telephone repeater has made possible telephonic transmissions over practically unlimited distances. **1929** K. HENNEY *Princ. Radio* xiv. 343 Such vacuum tube voltmeters are useful at all audio and nearly all radio frequencies, and can be made to read d.-c. voltages. **1950** [see *INSTRUMENT *sb.* 2].

vade-mecum. Add: Now usu. with pronunc. (vā·de mē̆ⁱ·kŏm). Also as one word. **1.** Also, a handbook or guidebook. (Further examples.)

1927 *New Republic* 12 Oct. 216/1 His little book, indeed, is a religious document, and might well serve as a *vade mecum* for all those disillusioned moderns who think that, because they cannot have all, they must be content to accept nothing. **1963** *Times* 2 May 15/3 In 1935, someone *did* collect James's prefaces together into what *has* become a vade-mecum for practitioners ('required reading' for students). **1977** *Amer. N. & Q.* XV. 108/1 From the standpoint of the non-expert buyer.., it is a singularly useful and dependable vademecum. **1983** *Archæology* Jan.–Feb. 72 This is the book that all of us have been looking for: a reasonably complete vade mecum to every worthwhile site in mesoamerica.

2. (Later example.)

1966 C. MACKENZIE *Paper Lives* iv. 55 A fellow Jacobean called Horner had won £77 in what are called the Pools and this sum was being used as the financial *vade mecum* for their escapade.

vadose (veⁱ·dōᵘs, -z), *a. Physical Geogr.* [f. L. *vadōs-us*, f. *vadum* shallow piece of water: see -OSE[1].] Of, pertaining to, or designating underground water occurring above the water-table. Cf. PHREATIC *a.* in Dict. and Suppl.

1894 F. POSEPNY in *Trans. Amer. Inst. Mining Engineers* XXIII. 213 For that part of the subterranean circulation, bounded by the water-level, and called the vadose or shallow underground circulation, the law of a descending movement holds good. **1909** [see *PHREATIC *a.* 2]. **1954** [see *PHREATIC *a.*]. **1973** *Sci. Amer.* Apr. 48/2 Of the total amount of underground water, vadose water (water present in soils) accounts for only ·066 × 10[16] cubic meters. **1977** A. HALLAM *Planet Earth* 108 (*caption*) Vadose cave formed by the waters of the Quashies River, Jamaica.

væ (vai). Restrict *Obs.* to sense in Dict. and add: **2.** *væ victis* [LIVY *Hist.* V. xlviii. 9]. **a.** *int.* Woe to the vanquished. **b.** *sb. phr.* The humiliation of the vanquished by their conquerors; the phrase as a maxim or utterance.

1612 J. SELDEN in Drayton *Poly-Olbion* viii. 124 Whence, vpun a murmuring complaint among the Romanes, crying væ victis, came that to be as prouerbe applied to the conquered. **1792** BURKE *Let.* 3 Jan. in M. Arnold *Lett., Speeches & Tracts on Irish Affairs* (1881) 259, I cannot say *væ victis*, and then throw the sword into the scale. **1819** SCOTT *Ivanhoe* I. ii. 39 The *vae victis*, or severities imposed upon the vanquished. **1856** M. BERNARD in *Oxford Ess.* II. ii. 90 The stonecutter has laboured to produce a vigorous representation of the *vae victis*—of triumphant pride and abject humiliation. **1904** G. K. FORTESCUE in *Cambr. Mod. Hist.* (1907) VIII. xvi. 512 *Vae victis* was one of the few unchanging revolutionary maxims. **1936** J. NEHRU *Autobiogr.* l. 401 *Vae victis* seems to run like a thread through these utterances. **1944** S. BELLOW *Dangling Man* 112 Life is hard. *Vae victis!* The wretched must suffer.

vaesite (vē̆ⁱ·zəit). *Min.* [f. the name of J. F. *Vaes*, 20th-c. mineralogist in the Belgian Congo + -ITE[1].] A mineral of the pyrite group, ideally nickel sulphide, NiS_2, found as grey isometric crystals.

1945 P. F. KERR in *Amer. Mineralogist* XXX. 483 Material approaching NiS_2 in composition and having a pyrite type of lattice has been found in the Kasompi mine of the Belgian Congo. This mineral is tentatively called vaesite. **1962** W. A. DEER et al. *Rock-Forming Minerals* V. 132 They suggest that many of the natural bravoites are actually vaesite solid solutions or two phase mixtures of nickel-rich pyrite and iron-rich vaesite. **1978** *Mineral. Abstr.* XXIX. 80/2 The first occurrence of vaesite in Japan is described from the Kuroko-type deposits of the Kosaka mine... It contains small amounts of Fe, Cu, and Co.

‖ **va-et-vient** (va *e* vʸæ̃). [Fr., lit. 'goes-and-comes'.] Coming and going, toing and froing; commerce, exchange; bandying (of argument).

1919 R. FRY *Let.* 3 Nov. (1972) II. 465 There is..a considerable *va et vient* of Paris artists. **1933** G. ARTHUR *Septuagenarian's Scrap Book* 18 For a large percentage of women life, day in day out, is a happy *va-et-vient*, sometimes rich in excellent results of practical value, sometimes only resolving itself into a flutter of delicious nothings. **1959** C. SPRY *Favourite Flowers* iii. 28 Looking back over the quite gentle *va-et-vient* of this argument I know that really we are in agreement. **1966** *Guardian* 19 Mar. 7/4 All the well-intentioned wordy *va-et-vient* about Capote's book. **1978** *N.Y. Rev. Bks.* 23 Feb. 8/3 In one university which has an art school, a history of art department, and a school of architecture and planning within five hundred yards of one another, the influence of one upon the other, or even the *va et vient* among the three, is virtually nonexistent. **1981** *Times Lit. Suppl.* 22 May 563/2 His whole teasing *va-et-vient* between the past and the present, at one moment restricting himself to 'period' viewpoint.., at the next speaking as from the 1970s.

vag, *Austral.* and *N. Amer. slang* abbrev. of **a.** VAGRANT *sb.* **b.** VAGRANCY. Phr. *on the vag*, on a charge of vagrancy.

1859 G. W. MATSELL *Vocabulum* 94 *Vag.* Vagrant. 'Done on the vag', committed for vagrancy. **1868** *Daily Territorial Enterprise* (Virginia City, Nevada) 1 Feb. 3/1 The authorities have a big crowd of 'vags' spotted, and are determined to make them travel. **1877** T. E. ARGLES *Pilgrim* ii. 21 She had got three months 'on the vag' for making a sleeping place of a prominent doorstep. **1919** [see *HUM *sb.*[2] 2]. **1931** 'D. STIFF' *Milk & Honey Route* 189 He's pulled for a vag, his excuse won't do. 'Thirty days,' said the judge. **1959** K. S. PRICHARD *N'Goola* 148 Was you on the game, love? Or did they get you on the vag? **1963** H. GARNER in R. Weaver *Canad. Short Stories* (1968) 2nd Ser. 41 Who would listen to a harvest stiff in the middle of the tobacco country? I'd end up on the wrong end of a vag charge myself. **1965** X. HERBERT *Larger than Life* 40 'We got a prisoner, eh?' The servant grunted. 'Just a vag.' **1976** 'TREVANIAN' *Main* (1977) vi. 122 Either we go right now..or you start ten days of a vag charge.

vag (væg), *v. Austral.* and *N. Amer. slang.* [f. prec.] *trans.* To charge with vagrancy.

1876 L. HEARN in *Cincinnati Commercial* 27 Aug. 6/3 If you keep on this way, Dolly,..I'll 'vag' you. **1908** W. G. DAVENPORT *Butte & Montana* 46 If the Kalispel police had done their duty she would have been 'vagged' years ago. **1930** *Bulletin* (Sydney) 9 July 28 We can't have the public's mind polluted by abusive language. You're vagged. **1953** K. TENNANT *Joyful Condemned* xxi. 203 If you have no visible means of support you can be vagged. **1975** B. GARFIELD *Death Sentence* v. 31 The cops go right on vagging prostitutes and shaking down storekeepers.

vagabond, *sb.* Add: **3.** In full *vagabond hat*, = SLOUCH HAT.

1927 *Daily Express* 7 Mar. 3/4 The two greatest millinery successes of modern times, the cloche and the vagabond. **1939** R. CHANDLER *Big Sleep* vi. 38 A small slim woman in a vagabond hat. **1952** C. W. CUNNINGTON *English Women's Clothing* vii. 256 'The vagabond' felt hat, slouched over one eye.

Vagabondia (vægăbǫ·ndiă). *U.S. joc.* [f. VAGABOND *sb.* + -IA[1].] The realm or world of vagabonds.

1894 CARMAN & HOVEY (*title*) Songs from Vagabondia. **1908** W. STEVENS *Let.* 7 Dec. (1967) 111 And white gloves—and a proud air, the like of which was never before in Vagabondia. **1931** 'D. STIFF' *Milk & Honey Route* i. 16 You should not make the mistake of confusing Hobohemia with Vagabondia. The latter is a more ancient and less alluring realm of the Old World.

vagabonding, *vbl. sb.* (In Dict. s.v. VAGABOND *v.*) (Later example.)

1925 H. L. FOSTER *Trop. Tramp with Tourists* 148 In years of vagabonding about the far corners of the earth.. I have never seen [etc.].

vagabondish, *a.* **1.** (Earlier example.)

1805 C. WILMOT *Let.* 4 Aug. in Londonderry & Hyde *Russ. Jrnls.* (1934) II. 165 His appearance was rather *Vagabondish* at the first glimpse.

vagabondizing, *vbl. sb.* (Earlier example.)

1755 C. CHARKE *Life* 223 The Aversion I had conceived for Vagabondizing..and the good Nature of my Friends in Chepstow put it strongly in my Head to settle there.

vagal, *a.* Add: Hence **va·gally** *adv.*, by, or by means of, the vagus.

1951 *Gastroenterology* XIX. 263 In dogs with vagally innervated or vagally denervated gastric pouches intravenous injections of Banthine..and of atropine..almost completely inhibited the secretion of hydrochloric acid. **1961** *Lancet* 26 Aug. 475/1 Unconsciousness can follow irritation of vagally innervated viscera. **1978** *Nature* 28 Sept. 323/2 Vagally induced release of Ach.

vagancy. Delete † *Obs.* and add later example.

1945 A. J. MACDONALD *Episcopi Vagantes in Church Hist.* 8 The sentence of deprivation, which was intended as a means of checking episcopal vagancy, in effect only made it worse, by causing the offender to pass from being an occasional vagans into a condition of permanent vagancy.

‖ **vagantes** (vāgæ·ntīz), *sb. pl.* [L. pres. pple. of *vagārī* to wander.] The scholar monks who travelled about Europe in the Middle Ages. Occas. in sing. form *vagans*.

1927 H. WADDELL *Wandering Scholars* p. v, The historical interest of the *Vagantes* as one of the earliest disintegrating forces in the mediaeval church has been left on one side. **1945** [see *VAGANCY]. **1946** *Scrutiny* Dec. 90 Carols, nursery rhymes and the songs of the vagantes. **1973** M. BLACKETT *Mark of Maker* viii. 79 Helen began serious work on selection and translation of the lyrics of her 'vagantes'. **1982** F. CORRIGAN in H. Waddell *Songs* *of Wandering Scholars* 9 Her research brought her face to face with *vagantes*, wandering scholars, from the very dawn of Christianity.

vagary, *sb.* Add: Now freq. with pronunc. (vēi·gări). **1. c.** An irregular course or distribution.

1923 *World's Work* May 566/1 Huster's attention was arrested by the uniformity in the course and distribution of nerves in comparison with the vagary of blood-vessels.

vagile (væ·-, vēi·dʒəil), *a. Biol.* [ad. G. *vagil*, f. L. *vag-us* wandering, straying.] Of an organism or group of organisms: having the ability to disperse or be dispersed in a given environment. Hence **vagi·lity** (also *fig.*).

1903 *Amer. Geologist* XXXI. 214 Their recent descendants find it..advantageous..to prey upon the much richer fauna of the vagile benthos. **1937** Allee & Schmidt tr. *Hesse's Ecol. Animal Geogr.* vi. 76 The power of dispersal of an animal species may be summed up as its 'vagility'. The less the vagility of a species, the less it is able to overcome barriers..and hence the more numerous the opportunities for independent variation. **1967** *Oceanogr. & Marine Biol.* V. 478 Many small vagile species swim in the water washing the algae. **1979** E. A. & L. D. Bloom *Satire's Persuasive Voice* vi. 269 Eighteenth-century satire registers a widening discontent with the collapse of native culture and, conversely, a search for its own kind of moral vagility. **1981** *Science* 12 June 1291/2 Taxa with small N_e [*sc.* effective population size] due to low vagility..are expected to experience rapid..speciation rates.

vagina. Add: **1. c.** *vagina dentata* (Anthrop. and Psychol.). [L. *dentata* adj., having teeth, toothed], the motif or theme of a vagina equipped with teeth which occurs in myth, folklore, and fantasy, and is said to symbolize fear of castration, the dangers of sexual intercourse, of birth or rebirth, etc.

1908 R. H. Lowie in *Jrnl. Amer. Folklore* XXI. 108 Its variants in North America are innumerable; the most important being the crushing entrance to heaven, snapping doors,..and the vagina dentata. **1926** J. I. Suttie tr. *Ferenczi's Further Contributions Psycho-Anal.* xxxii. 279 Anxiety in regard to the mother's vagina (vagina dentata=birth anxiety). **1932** *Jrnl. R. Anthrop. Inst.* LXII. 219 There is in fact one fear, the neurotic dread of sexual intercourse, which is symbolized in the same manner as *vagina dentata* by many people in many countries. **1950** [see *Beast *sb.* 4 b]. **1958** W. R. Trask tr. *Eliade's Birth & Rebirth* iii. 51 The return [to the womb] implies the risk of being torn to pieces in the monster's jaws (or in the vagina dentata of Mother Earth). **1976** *Listener* 26 Feb. 249/3 *Vagina dentata*, that prototype male nightmare which..always seems to crop up more often in books than real life. **1983** *Observer* 5 June 32/3 The heroes fight against being fed into the all-consuming mouth..of a nightmarish gigantic vagina dentata.

vaginal, *a.* Add: **2.** *vaginal smear*: see *Smear *sb.* 3 b.

Hence **vagi·nally** *adv.*, via the vagina; in the vagina.

1929 *Amer. Jrnl. Obstetr. & Gynecol.* XVIII. 245 We are very slow to examine primiparae vaginally. **1966** Masters & Johnson *Human Sexual Response* ix. 137 A subjective awareness of tachycardia described frequently as feeling the heartbeat vaginally. **1979** *Nature* 6 Sept. 15/1 The new compounds seem to produce fewer gastrointestinal side effects and can be given intramuscularly, vaginally or orally. **1982** 'D. Shannon' *Motive on Record* iii. 53 She'd been raped vaginally and anally.

vaginismus. Add after 'vagina': in response to physical contact or pressure. (Further examples.)

1936 W. Shaw *Textbk. Gynæcol.* xi. 234 Typical cases of vaginismus always have a psychical basis. **1974** Passmore & Robson *Compan. Med. Stud.* III. xxxv. 35/1 Frigidity..also includes the symptoms of those women in whom spasm of the perineal muscles (vaginismus) make the [sexual] act painful..or impossible. **1984** *Listener* 8 Mar. 34/4 Dr Stanley gives some candid advice on premature ejaculation and vaginismus, the involuntary muscular spasm of the outer third of the vagina which prevents penetration.

vagitus (vădʒəi·tŏs). [L., f. *vāgīre* to utter cries of distress, to wail.] A cry or wail; *spec.* that of a new-born child.

1652 N. Culverwel *White Stone* in *Elegant Discourse Light of Nature* ii. 119 Thou hast not yet the strength a well grown Christian; well, but is there the *vagitus* of an Infant? **1825** R. Hooper *Lexicon Medicum* (ed. 5) 1237/1 *Vagitus*, the cry of young children; also the distressing cry of persons under surgical operations. **1921** *19th Cent.* July 28 The various inspired articles..hardly went beyond the vagitus, the earliest cry of the new-born method. **1938** S. Beckett *Murphy* v. 71 To go back no further than the vagitus, it had not been the proper A of international concert pitch,..but the double flat of this. **1957** V. Nabokov *Pnin* ii. 47 He actually seemed to forehear the babe's vagitus. **1977** A. Sheridan tr. *J. Lacan's Écrits* iii. 31 My speech was to be nothing more than a *vagitus*, an infantile cry.

vago-. Add: **vago·tomy** *Surg.* [-tomy], an operation in which the vagus nerve is cut, either as a research technique or as a means of reducing the rate of gastric secretion; hence **vago·tomized** *ppl. a.*

1906 J. R. Murlin tr. *R. Tigenstedt's Text-bk. Human Physiol.* vi. 190 The hearts of dogs which had survived bilateral vagotomy for several months presented no anatomical changes whatsoever. **1948** *Gastroenterology* X. 415 He then produced ulcers in the vagotomized animals. **1955** W. Gaddis *Recognitions* i. v. 180 You ought to go back to analysis. Or have a vagotomy. **1974** R. M. Kirk et al. *Surgery* vi. 79 Alternatively, the available gastric acid may be reduced by performing partial gastrectomy, or vagotomy and a drainage procedure if fibrous scarring has made the oesophagus too short to restore the cardia to the abdomen. **1975** *Nature* 20 Nov. 227/1 In response to isoprenaline, vagotomised rats also failed to drink normally.

vagotonia (vēigotōu·niă). *Physiol.* Also anglicized as **vagotony** (vēi-, văgǫ·tŏni). [f. Vago- + *-tonia.] The state or condition in which there is increased influence of the autonomic nervous system and increased excitability of the vagus nerve. Also **vagoto·nus**, in the same sense.

1916, etc. [see *Sympathicotonia]. **1929** A. Kuntz *Autonomic Nervous System* xviii. 432 The clinical conception of vagotonia and sympatheticotonia was first formulated by Eppinger and Hess in 1909... They assumed that clinical cases exhibiting a functional imbalance between the sympathetic and parasympathetic nerves could be classified as vagotonic or sympatheticotonic. **1977** *Lancet* 12 Nov. 1027/2 Beta-blockers..are probably unable to turn the situation so far towards parasympathicotony (vagotony) that more profuse lachrymation would be resumed. **1981** *Acta Astronautica* VIII. 798 Numerous disorders have been related to vagotonia.

Hence **vagoto·nic** *a.*, displaying or promoting vagotonia.

1929 [see above]. **1977** *Proc. R. Soc. Med.* LXX. 159/1, I consider it dangerous to use a widespread sympathetic block..combined with halothane (with its vagotonic action and myocardial depressant effect).

vagrance. (Later U.S. example.)

1951 W. Faulkner *Requiem for Nun* iii. i. 266 Of course, the other niggers would just be in and out over Saturday and Sunday night for fighting or gambling or vagrance or drunk.

vague, *a.* Add: **3. a.** Used in superl. with ellipsis of *idea, notion.* Cf. *Faint *sb.* 5 d.

1968 N. Marsh *Clutch of Constables* viii. 201 'Have you seen this particular photograph, Mr Pollock?'.. 'Haven't the vaguest.' **1981** D. Uhnak *False Witness* (1982) xi. 94 'Any particular place your customers go on Tuesday nights?' 'I haven't the vaguest.'

7*. *Comb.*, as *vague-looking* adj.

1904 W. H. Hudson *Green Mansions* vi. 82 How different she seemed now; the brilliant face grown so pallid and vague-looking! **1948** Wyndham Lewis *Let.* 25 Oct. (1963) 469 This super-dream..is I imagine too vague-looking to be practical.

‖ **vague** (vāg), *sb.*[3] [Fr., lit. 'wave'.] A movement, trend, vogue. Cf. *Nouvelle vague.

1962 *John o' London's* 19 Apr. 371/3 Here is one requisite which must be regarded as essential in any new *vague*. It must not, whatever else it is, be vague. **1970** R. Lowell *Notebk.* 219 The *vague*, the vogue, what do they tell the critic? **1974** *Times Lit. Suppl.* 20 Dec. 1439/4 He has beautifully caught the old Hungarian *vague* of British cinema under Alexander Korda... The Hungarian *vague* also swept on to the Denham studio floor such interesting flotsam as Gabriel Pascal.

vague, *v.*[1] **a.** γ. (Later example.)

1874 L. Troubridge *Life amongst Troubridges* (1966) 88 We vagued about until tea-time.

vagulate (vēi·giŭlēit), *v. rare.* [Fanciful formation f. L. *vagul(us* nonce dim. of *vagus* wandering + -ate[3]; perh. influenced by Undulate *v.*] *intr.* To wander in a vague manner; to waver.

Only in the writings of Virginia Woolf.

1918 V. Woolf *Diary* 3 Nov. (1977) I. 213 Emphie vagulates in & out of the room. **1921** *Ibid.* 6 Mar. (1978) II. 97 All is too soft & emotional. Now for writing or anything I believe you must be able to screw up into a ball & pelt straight in people's faces. They vagulate & dissipate. **1930** —— *Let.* 27 June (1982) IV. 182 Poor dear Angus vagulating like some pale anemone in a cranny.

vagulous (vēi·giŭləs), *a. nonce-wd.* [f. L. *vagulus*: see prec.] Wayward, vague, wavering.

1919 V. Woolf *Diary* 12 July (1977) I. 291, I like Forster very much, though I find him whimsical & vagulous to an extent that frightens me with my own clumsiness and definiteness.

‖ **vahana** (vā·hana). Also **vahan.** [Skr. *vāhana*, lit. 'conveyance', f. *vah-* to carry, transport.] In Indian mythology, the mount or vehicle of a god.

1810 E. Moor *Hindu Pantheon* 16 Lacshmi..is with him [*sc.* Vishnu] on his *vahan*, or vehicle, Garuda. **1879** J. Dowson *Class. Dict. Hindu Mythology* 330 *Vāhana*. 'A vehicle'. Most of the gods are represented as having animals as their vāhanas. **1891** J. L. Kipling *Beast & Man* vi. 122 The bull receives high honours as the vâhan or steed of Shiva. **1971** *Illustr. Weekly India* 11 Apr. 11/1 (*caption*) Return of the procession after lustral rites of a Jina, with the gods and goddesses on their *vahanas*.

vahine (vāhī·ne). Also **vahini.** [Tahitian.] A Tahitian woman or wife. Cf. *Wahine.

1950 F. H. Lyon tr. *Heyerdahl's Kon-Tiki Exped.* viii. 217 They had a lively and spirited leading singer in a luxuriantly fat *vahine*. **1960** H. E. Bates *Aspidistra in Babylon* 187 Better take a *vahini*..and settle down. *Ibid.* 227, I will build a house and live like your *vahine*. It cost nothing. I'll be your *vahine* and work for you. I'll work for you and you can love me. **1980** *London Mag.* July 24 The village of Mataiea, where Gauguin..lived..with his beloved *vahine* Teha'amana.

Vai (vəi). Also **Vei,** 9 **Vy.** [ad. a native name.] (A member of) a people of the southern coasts of Liberia and Sierra Leone; also, their language. Also *attrib.* or as *adj.*

1845 *Encycl. Metrop.* XX. 18/1 The Country near Cape Mount was anciently inhabited by the Vaï, or Faï, and Pwi Tribes. *Ibid.* 18/2 The Vaï, or Veï, were not reduced without difficulty. **1849** S. W. Koelle (*title*) Narrative of an expedition into the Vy country of West Africa. *Ibid.* 9 The Vei language is very simple, harmonious, with scarcely any grammatical inflexions, rich in vowels. **1854** —— *Outl. Gram. Vei Lang.* p. iv, If we compare the dialects spoken by the Manis and the Veis, we discover a difference which can scarcely have arisen in less than a couple of centuries. **1923** A. L. Kroeber *Anthropol.* ix. 225 All the values of his signs were syllabic. The same holds of the West African Vei writing invented in the nineteenth century by a native. He..fell back on syllabic signs even though this necessitated two hundred different characters. **1932** W. L. Graff *Language & Languages* xi. 434 Of some 435 Sudanese languages..only five or six are written. These are Vai, of the Nigero-Senegalese group,.. [etc.]. **1936** G. Greene *Journey without Maps* ii. i. 99 Mr. Reeves was a Vai, a Mahommedan. **1949** L. D. Turner *Africanisms in Gullah Dial.* i. 14 The Vai word for 'fat' is..lit. 'mouth full'. **1957** M. Banton *W. Afr. City* vii. 127 Vai territory in Sierra Leone amounts only to some twenty-five square miles on the coastline next to the Liberian frontier. There are hardly any Vai in the colony. **1965** *Sierra Leone Lang. Rev.* (*Afr. Lang. Rev.*) IV. 81 The derivations listed for these 85 terms are *prima facie* astonishing, for 63 are Mende and 21 are Vai. **1974** J. R. Baker *Race* xxi. 411 The Mende tribe (a subdivision, like the Vai, of the Mandingo group of tribes). **1979** *Africa* XLIX. 92 The Vai script is so famous that it is surprising to realize that the language is spoken by, at most, 40,000 people. **1983** *Word* XXXIV. 136 Reading and writing Vai script was associated with certain specific skills.

Vaisākha, var. *Vesak.

‖ **Vaishnava** (vəi·ʃnavă). [a. Skr. *vaiṣṇavá* relating, belonging, or sacred to Vishnu; a worshipper or follower of Vishnu.] **A.** *sb.* A member of one of the three great divisions of modern Hinduism, exclusively devoted to the worship of the god Vishnu as the Supreme Being. **B.** *adj.* Of or pertaining to this division of Hinduism.

1845 [see *Sakta]. **1876** [see *Saiva *sb.* and *a.*]. **1882** [see Vedism]. **1903** *Times* 2 May 16/2 The 'holy basil' is ..planted before every Vaishnava house, and every Vaishnava wears necklaces, or armlets, and carries a rosary, made up of sections of its stalks or roots. **1944** E. Thompson *Robert Bridges* xi. 95 They both thought it worthless and in bad taste, as Rabindranath Tagore considered Bengali Vaishnava erotic mystical verse. **1968** *Jrnl. Mus. Acad. Madras* XXXIX. 61 To the Vaishnava devotees all over India Sri Krishna has been the Godhead for meditation.

Hence **Vai·s(h)navism** = Vishnuism; **Vai·s(h)navite** *a.*, of or pertaining to Vaishnavas or Vishnuism.

1877 [see *S(h)aivism* s.v. *Saiva *sb.* and *a.*]. **1919** N. Macnicol *Psalms of Maratha Saints* 5 There are one hundred and eight *tulsi* beads on the rosary worn by the Vaisnavite devotee. **1934** *Nature* 5 May 680/2 The ingrained love of life disclosed by the religions of Saktism and Vaisnavism among the Bengalis, comparable to that found among the Aryans, is a racial psychological trait to be associated with the brachycephalic Bengali castes. **1956** [see *S(h)aivism* s.v. *Saiva *sb.* and *a.*]. **1967** Singha & Massey *Indian Dances* i. 35 Of the Vaishnavite temples those at Belur and Halebid have an important significance. **1969** *Indo-Asian Culture* Oct. 70 Both Saivism and Vaishnavism were popular in Srihatta and the neighbouring region during the late Gupta and medieval times.

vaisya. Add: Also **vaish(y)a.** (Later examples.)

1920 H. G. Wells *Outl. Hist.* I. xx. 159/1 The four main castes seem to have been:..The Vaisya—herdsmen, merchants, money lenders, and land-owners. **1956** R. Pieris *Sinhalese Social Organization* v. i. 170 The existence among the Sinhalese of a system akin to the classical Hindu four-fold scheme—priestly *brahmins*, *kshatriyas* or warriors, the pastoral *vaisyas*, and the lowly *sūdras*.. is attested in the survival in Ceylon of the place-name 'brahmin village'. **1958** *Spectator* 17 Jan. 70/3 Brahmins, Kshattriyas, Vaishas and Sudras. **1971** *Illustr. Weekly India* 11 Apr. 11/1 Rishabhadeva also classified the people according to their occupations, the kshatriyas who were warriors, the vaisyas who were traders, and the sudras who made their living by manual labour. **1971** K. Kent in C. Bonington *Annapurna South Face* 309 *Vaishya*, common man or merchant.

‖ **vajra** (va·dʒră). [a. Skr. *vájra*.] In Hinduism and Buddhism, a thunderbolt or mythical weapon esp. one wielded by the god Indra.

1788 *Asiatick Researches* I. 241 His weapon, *Vajra*, or the thunderbolt. **1854** A. Cunningham *Ladák* xiii. 371,

I should suppose that they pay especial reverence to the holy *Dorje* (*Vajra*, or thunderbolt) which descended through the air, and fell at Sera in Tibet. **1897** H. K. Beauchamp tr. *Dubois's Hindu Manners* II. iii. v. 638 Indra's vehicle is an elephant, and his weapon the *vajra*, a kind of sharp knife. **1980** *Catal. Fine Chinese Ceramics* (Sotheby, Hong Kong) 134 Painted with a triple band of Tibetan characters on the underside.., and with a cruciform double *vajra* tied with curling ribbons knotted under a central roundel on the interior. *Ibid.*, For the fifteenth century origin of the double *vajra* design compare the Chenghua dish in the British Museum.

vakeel, vakil. 2. (Earlier examples.)
1776 N. B. Halhed tr. *Code Gentoo Laws* iii. 105 (*heading*) Of appointing a Vakeel (or Attorney). **1850** *Directions Revenue Officers N.-W. Provinces* 230 He is allowed the assistance of the ablest Vakeel or pleader in the Court.

vakky, var. *vacky.

vakoof, vakuf, varr. *wakf, waqf.
1860 *Papers relating to Admin. Affairs in Turkey* 37 in *Parl. Papers* (1861) LXVII. 599 'Vakoof' property, which only descends..in a direct line. **1889** G. N. Curzon *Russia in Central Asia* vii. 243 It has since been suggested that a Russian class should be added compulsorily to the latter, which are already richly endowed by the *Vakufs* of deceased benefactors. **1928** *Daily Tel.* 28 Aug. 10/4 The Soviet Government has resolved to confiscate in Turkestan all landed property belonging to mosques (vakoofs).

valance, *sb.*[1] Add: **3. c.** A protective panel extending below the basic chassis construction of a vehicle.
1933 Auden in *Rev. Eng. Stud.* (1978) Aug. 305 A four-door sporting coupé..valances and wings in black. **1937** *Times* 11 Dec. 4/7 Here also..are..the coil on the wing valance, and the electric petrol pump on the dash. **1972** *Daily Tel.* (Colour Suppl.) 13 Oct. 27 His car incorporates a valance to hide mechanical parts underneath the body. **1979** *International Railway Jrnl.* Dec. 51/3 Underframe members are enclosed by the addition of extra panels at the front and deeper valances along the sides.

Valanginian (vælăndʒi·niăn), *a. Geol.* Also † **Valenginian.** [ad. F. *valanginien* (E. Desor 1853, in *Bull. de la Soc. des Sci. Naturelles de Neuchâtel* III. 177), f. the name of the Château de *Valangin*, near Neuchâtel, Switzerland, in the vicinity of which are exposures of this series.] Of, pertaining to, or designating a stratigraphical stage, a division of the Neocomian, which forms part of the Lower Cretaceous. Also *absol.*
1885 A. Geikie *Text-bk. Geol.* (ed. 2) vi. 836 Valenginian—a group of limestones and marls. **1903** *Ibid.* (ed. 4) II. vi. 1197 The lowest dark marl..indicates the emersion of these rocks at the close of the Jurassic period, and may represent the Valanginian stage. **1944** *Bull. Amer. Soc. Petroleum Geologists* XXVIII. 1141 The lower member consists of..limestone and contains Valanginian ammonites. **1973** *Nature* 23 Nov. 211/2 The age of the oldest magnetic lineations..is also coincident with the marine transgressions of southern Africa..and southern Argentina during the Upper Valanginian. **1978** *Ibid.* 13 July 133/1 The fault activity of this tectonic phase lasted into Valanginian times.

Valdepeñas (vældėpe·nyăs, ‖ valdepe·nyas). Also **Val de Peñas, Valdepenas, Val de Penas.** [The name of a district of south central Spain.] A wine produced in this district.
1832 [see *bota 1]. **1833** C. Redding *Hist. Mod. Wines* vi. 181 The province of La Mancha is chiefly a wine district, and there the justly celebrated wine called Val de Peñas is made... It is grown upon a rocky or stony soil, as *Val de Peñas*, or 'Valley of Stones', indicates. **1845** R. Ford *Hand-bk. Spain* I. ii. 309/1 *Valdepeñas* is *the* wine of Madrid..rich, fruity. **1931** S. Jameson *Richer Dust* v. 132 A red wine, clean, dry, strong, called Val de Penas, which they bought in La Mancha. **1963** L. Deighton *Horse under Water* li. 216 In the tiny *tasoa* the marble-tops were covered in glasses of Valdepenas. **1974** *Times* 31 Aug. 9/1 Valdepeñas wines do not at all resemble the better-known Riojas.

vale, *sb.*[1] **2. b.** (Later examples.)
1911 G. B. Shaw *Shewing-Up of Blanco Posnet* 405, I thought I was a man and not a snivelling canting.. apprentice angel serving his time in a vale of tears. **1963** *Times Lit. Suppl.* 22 Feb. 130/3 It looks..to heaven, but with no vale-of-tears morality. **1977** D. E. Westlake *Enough* i. 22, I was about as safe as anybody ever is in this vale of tears.

valedictorily, *adv.* (In Dict. s.v. Valedictory *a.* and *sb.*) For *rare*$^{-1}$ read *rare* and add further example.
1925 F. M. Ford *No More Parades* ii. 64 He added valedictorily to Tietjens, 'I'd better..put this draft.. twenty in a tent.'..Tietjens and the colonel began to push men out of their way, going towards the door.

valedictory, *sb.* **1.** (Earlier example.)
1779 *New-Jersey Gaz.* (Trenton) 13 Oct. 1/1 The six young undergraduates pronounced orations; John Woodford the Salutatory in Latin and Stephen Renselaer the Valedictory in English.

valence[2]**.** Add: **3.** [ad. G. *valenz* (H. Wichelhaus 1868, in *Ann. d. Chem.* Suppl. VI. 257), f. *quantivalenz* (A. W. Hofmann 1865).] (Further examples.)
1965 Phillips & Williams *Inorg. Chem.* I. iv. 102 In the transition series a great number of valences are observed. **1972** [see *solarization 1 d].

4. *Psychol.* Emotional force or significance, *spec.* the feeling of attraction or repulsion with which an individual invests an object or event (see quot. 1935).
1917 C. R. Payne tr. *Pfister's Psychoanal. Meth.* xi. 269 They are all representations of the cottage itself and more exactly the embodiment of inhibited endeavours of high valence, the so-called libido-symbols. **1935** Adams & Zener tr. *Lewin's Dynamic Theory of Personality* ii. 51 A certain object or event..is experienced as an attraction (or repulsion)... We shall say of such objects that they possess a '*valence*'. *Ibid.* iii. 81 The positive valences (+), those effecting approach; and the negative(−), or those producing withdrawal or retreat. **1952** W. Sprott *Social Psychol.* ii. 30 The piece of chocolate is said to have 'positive valence' for the child and exercises an attractive force. *Ibid.*, A threat of punishment, and a 'negative valence' is added which alters the dynamic character of the 'field'. **1967** M. M. Glatt et al. *Drug Scene* vi. 79 His positive valences are toward the use of drugs. **1976** S. Larsen *Shaman's Doorway* iii. 132 Its [*sc.* the religious archetype's] powerful valence is attracted to any life activity or belief which assumes a central role for an individual.

5. *attrib.* and *Comb.*, **valence band,** the energy band (range of possible energies) that contains the valence electrons in a solid and is the highest filled or partly filled band; **valence bond,** orig., a chemical bond thought of in terms of atomic valencies; in mod. use, one described in terms of individual valence electrons rather than molecular orbitals; freq. *attrib.*; **valence electron** [tr. G. *valenzelektron* (J. Stark 1908, in *Physik. Zeitschr.* IX. 85/1)], any of the electrons of an atom that are involved when it forms a bond with another atom, viz. those in the outer shell; **valence shell,** the outer shell (*shell *sb.* 19 b) of an atom, incompleteness of which is responsible for its valency.
1956 L. P. Hunter *Handbk. Semiconductor Electronics* ii. 7 At an intermediate temperature, therefore, the donor levels will be completely ionized..while the valence band remains practically filled. **1982** J. E. Uffenbeck *Introd. Electronics* i. 7 We can think of the valence band as containing all electrons still held by their parent atoms, while the conduction band contains all *free* electrons. **1913** *Jrnl. Amer. Chem. Soc.* XXXV. 1443 This view leads to the grouping of substances into two general classes, according as the valence bonds are chiefly polar or non-polar in nature. **1931** *Physical Rev.* XXXVII. 481 This is a homopolar valence bond, and the two electrons forming such a bond are inactive in forming further bonds, just as if they were in closed shells within a single atom. **1965** [see *molecular orbital* s.v. *molecular *a.* 5]. **1978** P. W. Atkins *Physical Chem.* xv. 493 Just as in m.o. theory, the strength of the bond according to valence-bond theory can be traced in large part to the effects of the accumulation of electron density in the bonding region between the two nuclei. **1923** Kramers & Holst *Atom & Bohr Theory of its Structure* vii. 206 The last group [of electrons] is naturally of a very different nature from the first; they are 'valence electrons'. **1974** D. M. Adams *Inorganic Solids* i. 3 Three factors were considered as fundamental in alloy structures: (*a*) size of the atoms; (*b*) their relative electronegativities; (*c*) the valence-electron concentration. **1923** G. N. Lewis *Valency* iv. 57 The valence shell of a free (uncombined) atom never contains more than eight electrons. **1972** R. A. Jackson *Mechanism* v. 99 Boron compounds are unusual (in relation to most organic compounds) in having an empty valence-shell orbital.

valencia. 2. (Earlier example.)
1838 *Actors by Daylight* I. 8/2 (Advt.), Shawls, Valencias, Silks, and Figured Velvets of the choicest patterns, for Waistcoats.

Valencian, *sb.* and *a.* Add: **A.** *sb.* (Later examples.) Also, the language of Valencia.
1933 *Morning Post* 11 July 13/3 That same language, which is called Provençal, Limousin, Catalan, Valencian, or Mallorquin, according to the place..the langue d'oc. **1937** F. Borkenau *Spanish Cockpit* iii. 232 The anxious question 'Will they come back to-night?' remained and racked the nerves of the Valencians. **1956** J. Brodrick *St Ignatius Loyola* ix. 242 Juan de la Peña.., like Vives, was a Valencian. **1967** *Westm. Cathedral Chron.* May 70/1 Valencian is a dialect of Catalan, but not so widely spoken.

B. *adj.* (Earlier example used of the language, and later examples.)
1845 R. Ford *Hand-bk. Spain* I. i. 69 It is called *Michi Michi*, from the Valencian *Mits e Mits*, 'half and half'. **1937** F. Borkenau *Spanish Cockpit* ii. 116 In Valencia there is a regional movement too, claiming..equality of rights for the Valencian dialect with the Castilian language. **1970** R. A. H. Robinson *Origins of Franco's Spain* ii. 81 Members were busy drawing up a statute of autonomy for the Valencian region. **1976** 'D. Halliday' *Dolly & the Nanny Bird* xii. 155 A Tam lorry full of Valencian oranges passed by a grove of citrus trees.

valency. Add: **3. a, b.** (Earlier examples.)
1869 *English Mechanic* 19 Nov. 222/1 The Molecule..is therefore a body in which all the attractions or valencies are satisfied, leaving the combined atoms to act as a whole from one centre. *Ibid.* 222/2 Any typical atom in any molecule may be replaced by another atom of similar valency, without altering the arrangement of the molecule.

5. *attrib.* and *Comb.*, **valency electron** *Physics* = *valence electron* s.v. *valence[2] 5.
1908 *Jrnl. Chem. Soc.* XCIV. ii. 138 Two types of electrons are distinguished: the one type, arranged in the form of a ring, represents the positive electricity of the atom, and the second type consists of electrons which neutralise the positive charge of the ring and are separated from the atom when ionisation takes place, these being termed the valency electrons. **1973** J. G. Tweeddale *Materials Technol.* I. iv. 97 Metals tend to be good conductors of heat primarily because there is sharing of valency electrons..and so electron transfer is easy.

‖ **valenki** (vā·lĕnki), *sb. pl.* Also **valinki, -ky.** [Russ., pl. of *valenok* felt boot.] Felt boots of a type worn by Russians.
1943 E. M. Almedingen *Frossia* v. 201 Maria Nikolævna sat shivering,..her feet thrust into 'valenky' with many holes in them. **1951** 'A. Garve' *Murder in Moscow* xiii. 120, I must have appeared indigenous enough in my fur hat and *shuba* and felt *valinki*. **1969** P. Chavchavadze tr. *Alliluyeva's Only One Year* 247 All of them had to get used to Russian frosts, to valenki (knee-high felt boots) and fur caps—poor unhappy birds of passage. **1975** *Country Life* 30 Oct. 1194/2 Turkish-style 'Valenki' embroidered apres ski boot £29·95. **1981** M. C. Smith *Gorky Park* i. viii. 107 The girl..dressed in..the kind of felt boots called *valenki*.

-valent. [ad. L. *valent-em*, pres. pple. of *valēre* to be worth.] A formative element occurring in a few words of general currency, as *equivalent, prevalent* (directly f. L.), *ambivalent*, and in various scientific contexts, being used with prefixes denoting number: (*a*) in Chem. (usu. with pronunc. (-vēi·lĕnt)) forming adjs. denoting 'having a valency of the specified number' (Valency 3); also used in an analogous sense in Immunol. (cf. *multivalent *a.* b); also with arabic number prefixed; (*b*) in Cytology (usu. with pronunc. (-·vălĕnt)) forming adjs. and sbs. denoting '(a meiotic structure) composed of the specified number of chromosomes' (cf. *multivalent *a.* and *sb.*, *quadrivalent *a.* and *sb.*, *trivalent *a.* and *sb.*).
This suffix was first used in its Chem. sense by L. Meyer 1864, in *Mod. Theorien d. Chem.* 67.
1977 *Lancet* 25 June 1338/2 A double-blind controlled trial of a 14-valent pneumococcal polysaccharide vaccine was carried out.

Valentian (vălе·ntiăn), *a. Geol.* [f. *Valentia*, name of a Roman province in S. Scotland + -an.] Designating or pertaining to the earliest stratigraphical division of the Silurian in Britain, preceding the Wenlockian. Also *absol.*
1879 C. Lapworth in *Ann. & Mag. Nat. Hist.* III. (table facing p. 455), Silurian system... Lower division (Valentian). **1880** —— in *Ibid.* V. 47 In the south of Scotland (*Valentia*)..three subformations are recognizable... Until geologists are willing to include the Tarannon in the Llandovery it will..be best to speak of this great Scottish formation and its equivalents as the Valentian formation, its three divisions, Lower, Middle, and Upper, representing respectively the Lower Llandovery, Upper Llandovery, and Tarannon of Wales and Siluria. **1921** *Q. Jrnl. Geol. Soc.* LXXVII. 158 Some assistance in this comparison is afforded by the Valentian rocks of the Lake District. **1946** [see *Ludlovian *a.*]. **1974** *Encycl. Brit. Macropædia* XVI. 774/2 The oldest interval, the Llandoverian (or Valentian), saw the beginning of a sharp distinction between basin graptolitic shale facies and calcareous..shelf facies.

valentine, *sb.* Add: **3. b.** For † read '*Obs.* exc. *U.S.*' and add later examples.
1962 A. Lurie *Love & Friendship* ix. 167 More flowers... On the tables, on the mantelpiece, on the bookcases... All red and white, and of course it was February 14th... Would Will himself see that the whole party was a valentine for him? **1965** [see *peanut brittle* s.v. *peanut b].

4*. (With capital initial.) A British type of heavy tank, much used during the war of 1939–45. (So called because production was reputedly approved on 14 Feb. 1938.)
1941 *Times* 7 July 2/2 Details have now been released by the Ministry of Supply of a new British tank, officially designated as the Mark III, but now to be known as Valentine. It is a 16-ton heavy infantry tank. **1959** *Chambers's Encycl.* XIII. 451/1 Two cruiser types were in production... The Mark I (A.9) was modified..; this modified type was known as the Mark II (A.10); from it was developed the Valentine. **1960** C. Barnett *Desert Generals* v. iii. 212 Of ninety-seven Valentines, eleven returned. **1979** D. Crow *Tanks of World War II* iii. 45/1 Infantry Tank Mark III, the Valentine, was produced in far greater numbers than any other British tank. The first Valentine, built by Vickers-Armstrongs..came off the production line in May 1940.

5. *valentine card*; **Valentine (infantry) tank** = sense 4* above.
1959 I. & P. Opie *Lore & Lang. Schoolch.* xii. 236 Valentine cards are definitely in fashion again. **1977** *Times* 1 Feb. 8/5 Make your own Valentine card. **1943** W. S. Churchill *End of Beginning* 140 It would be wrong ..to write off as useless..the Valentine tanks. **1944**

Return to Attack (Army Board, N.Z.) 16/2 A squadron of Valentine infantry tanks..was sent to join them.

Valentino (vælĕntī·no). [The name of Rudolph *Valentino* (Rodolfo Guglielmi di Valentino, 1895–1926), Italian-born American film actor, particularly noted for being adored by women.] **1.** †**a.** A gigolo. *Obs.* **b.** A man having the sort of romantic good looks associated with Rudolph Valentino.

1927 *Dialect Notes* V. 466 *Valentino*, n., a handsome man kept by an oldish woman. **1930** A. P. Herbert *Water Gipsies* ii. 12 No one could call you a Valentino, not for emotion, could they? **1961** J. H. Griffin *Black like Me* 34 You have to..have your hair all slicked out and look like a Valentino. **1967** *Listener* 20 July 82/3 You expect a Rudolph Valentino? **1974** V. Gielgud *In Such a Night* iv. 38 Her current leading man..frequently referred to as 'the contemporary Valentino'.

2. Used *attrib.* or as *adj.* to designate looks, actions, etc., associated with Rudolph Valentino.

1934 F. Stark *Valleys of Assassins* ii. 69 A young man with Rudolf Valentino looks. **1967** A. Wilson *No Laughing Matter* iii. i. 206 His short black Valentino side whiskers. **1979** J. Drummond *I saw him Die* ix. 87, I saw Crozier..take her hand; very tender, very Valentino. **1981** P. Dickinson *Seventh Raven* iv. 47 That colossally handsome Valentino chappie.

valet, *sb.* Add: **3. b.** *valet service*; **valet parking** *N. Amer.*, a service provided at a restaurant, etc., in which an attendant parks patrons' motor vehicles; hence (as back-formation) **valet-park** *v.*

1983 C. Hyde *Tenth Flight* ix. 87 They valet-parked the Triumph and they made the flight with ten minutes to spare. **1960** *Britannica Bk. of Year* 558/1 *Valet parking* ..referred to a system in which an attendant was responsible for parking the car. **1976** *Globe & Mail* (Toronto) 8 Nov. 16/7 A swish little marquee blinks out an offer of valet parking. **1984** *Tampa* (Florida) *Tribune* 5 Apr. 3D/5 Reservations are due for the Scholarship Night at Tampa Jai-Alai Fronton... Valet parking is available. **1939** R. Stout *Some buried Caesar* xvi. 233 You should have put on some old clothes. The valet service here is terrible. **1981** D. Boggis *Time to Betray* i. 9 Rousselot wore a different pair of expensive slacks, with the abandon of a man used to valet service.

valet, *v.* Add: **b.** To look after (clothes, etc.).

1931, 1951 [see *valeting *vbl. sb.*].

c. To clean (a motor vehicle).

1972 *Drive* Spring 147/1 It's not difficult to imagine an owner confining his chauffeur to valeting the car, while he hogs the driving. **1976** *Star* (Sheffield) 20 Nov. (Advt.), Young Man wanted..to serve petrol, valet cars, take forecourt enquiries.

valeting *vbl. sb.* (further examples).

1931 *Times* 16 Mar. 1/3 (Advt.), *Clothes valeting*... They will stand years of hard wear if you send them to us to be *turned*. **1951** *Good Housek. Home Encycl.* 296/1 Careful valeting lengthens the life of clothes. **1976** *Drive* Jan.–Feb. 11/2 The eight suggestions that, in order of importance, would contribute most to the economical running and upkeep of the average family car were: 1 regular servicing;..5 regular valeting.

valeta, var. *veleta.

validate, *v.* Add: **2. b.** To examine for incorrectness or bias; to confirm or check the correctness of.

1957 Kendall & Buckland *Dict. Statistical Terms* 309 A sample of human beings is partly validated by comparing, *inter alia*, its sex and age constitution with the known figures for the population from which it was chosen. **1963** Laden & Gildersleeve *System Design for Computer Applications* iii. 33 Because of this power of the control total to validate individual fields of data, the control total approach to the validation of a field is sometimes chosen in preference to performing some type of validation check on each field as it comes up. **1967** *Oxford Computer Explained* 20 Run 1. Reads the paper-tape Input, validates it (reporting any errors) and converts suitable records to magnetic tape. **1967** D. Wilson in Wills & Yearsley *Handbk. Management Technol.* 44 Figure 3.1 outlines the basic steps for validating (editing), processing.., and recording the output. **1979** *Sci. Amer.* Feb. 58/2 With this unique record it should be possible to construct (and validate) new, highly realistic models of atmospheric circulation. **1980** C. S. French *Computer Sci.* xxxi. 269 The transaction tape is already validated and sequenced in the order of the master file.

validated *ppl. a.* (further examples).

1965 A. G. Favret *Introd. Digital Computer Applications* xii. 184 Both the master file and the validated transactions are stored on magnetic tape reels and used as input. **1965** P. Caws *Philos. of Sci.* xxvi. 193 A validated theory requires statements which are both significant and true.

validation. Add: (Further examples.)

1957 Kendall & Buckland *Dict. Statistical Terms* 309 *Validation*, a procedure which provides, by reference to independent sources, evidence that an inquiry is free from bias or otherwise conforms to its declared purpose. In statistics it is usually applied to a sample investigation with the object of showing that the sample is reasonably representative. **1967** D. Wilson in Wills & Yearsley *Handbk. Management Technol.* 44 In commercial applications the first step is normally the validation of the input data. **1967** *Oxford Computer Explained* 13 After validation, the records are converted to magnetic tape. **1980** C. S. French *Computer Sci.* xvii. 91 When data is first input to the computer, different checks can be applied to prevent errors going forward for processing. For this reason, the first computer run is often referred to as *validation* or *data vet.*

b. *attrib.*

1965 A. G. Favret *Introd. Digital Computer Applications* xii. 184 The 'A' type transactions are processed daily through a validation run on the computer which checks for completeness and, to some extent, for the correctness of the data. **1967** *Oxford Computer Explained* 8 All programs, except a special general purpose validation routine, would be written in Cobol. **1969** *Computers & Humanities* III. 130 Validation criteria contain limits the user places on specific items. **1973** *Jrnl. Genetic Psychol.* CXXIII. 11 A validation study..had found that among others, the IE test was correlated (negatively) with the ACL self-confidence scale. **1979** *Sci. Amer.* Sept. 99/2 All keyed entries are subjected to validation procedures, so errors are caught and corrected on the spot.

validator (væ·lideⁱtǫɹ). [f. Validate *v.* + -or 2.] One who or that which confirms the validity of something. Also *attrib.*

1951 R. Firth *Elem. Soc. Organ.* vii. 245 The prophet, the mystic, the spirit-medium are valuable interpreters and validators of religious belief. **1971** *Engineering* Apr. 31/1 Diagram showing the component parts of the coin validator mechanism. **1978** *Washington Post* 13 Jan. B2/5 The piece of equipment that accepts bills, called a validator, doesn't like cold weather. **1980** *Observer* 16 Mar. 22/7 The key is not a security device and that is that. It's a validator, to make sure that somebody hasn't made a typing error in sending the message.

validity. Add: **6.** *attrib.* and *Comb.*, **validity check** *Computers*, a check that data items conform to coding requirements; so **validity checking.**

1957 *Control Engin.* May 113/2 The double entry system of book-keeping is another example of coding the work so that a validity check is readily available. **1982** *What's New in Computing* Nov. 61/1 The validity checks include field length, ranges, check digit verification and table look-up. **1960** *Communications Assoc. Computing Machinery* III. 418 (*heading*) Combining algol statement analysis with validity checking.

valine (vēⁱ·līn). *Biochem.* [ad. G. *valin* (E. Fischer 1906, in *Ber. d. Deut. Chem. Ges.* XXXIX. 2321), f. G. *valerian-säure* valerianic acid (see Valerianic *a.*): see -ine⁵.] An amino-acid that is an essential nutrient for vertebrates and a general constituent of proteins; α-aminoisovaleric acid, $(CH_3)_2$-$CHCH(NH_2)COOH$.

1907 *Chem. Abstr.* I. 2566 Valine on heating yielded the anhydride. **1962** [see *isoleucine]. **1982** T. I. Diamondstone in T. M. Devlin *Textbk. Biochem.* xii. 604/1 The diagnosis of a defect in the transamination of valine to α-ketoisovaleric acid was suspected.

valinomycin (væ·linoməi·sin). *Pharm.* [a. G. *valinomycin* (Brockmann & Schmidt-Kastner 1955, in *Ber. d. Deut. Chem. Ges.* LXXXIII. 57), f. *valin* *valine (a product of its hydrolysis): see *-mycin.] A dodecapeptide obtained from the fungus *Streptomyces fulvissimus*, which has antibiotic activity against Gram-positive bacteria and is used experimentally.

1955 *Chem. Abstr.* XLIX. 16068 *Streptomyces fulvissimus* grown in a medium..gave 2·3g. of dry mycelium (I) per l. It..gave an oil, which on cooling deposited valinomycin. **1969** *New Scientist* 31 July 225/1 Valinomycin is lethal to cells because it makes the membranes of mitochondria permeable to ions, particularly potassium, and stops them making energy available to all the other processes in the cell. **1979** *Sci. Amer.* Sept. 77/3 To prove that the gradient existed between the mitochondria and the surrounding cytoplasm the investigators added the drug valinomycin, which increases the rate of cell respiration and establishes an equilibrium in the concentration of potassium ions on both sides of the mitochondrial membrane.

Valium (væ·liɒm). *Pharm.* Also **valium.** [Etym. uncertain.] A proprietary name for the drug diazepam, $C_{16}H_{13}N_2OCl$, used esp. as an anti-anxiety agent, hypnotic, and muscle relaxant given orally or by injection; a tablet of this.

1961 *Official Gaz.* (U.S. Patent Office) 10 Oct. TM 50/1 Hoffmann-La Roche Inc., Nutley, N.J... *Valium* for psychotherapeutic agent. **1962** *Trade Marks Jrnl.* 10 Jan. 32/2 *Valium*... All goods included in Class 5. Roche Products Limited,..Welwyn Garden City, Hertfordshire; manufacturers. **1972** *Guardian* 18 Sept. 14/5 She had taken an overdose of Valium after getting drunk the night before. **1976** C. Blackwood *Stepdaughter* i. 59, I have been swallowing fistfuls of valium to try to calm myself. **1979** N. Mailer *Executioner's Song* (1980) i. xx. 342 Even with two Valiums to mellow her out, she felt crazy inside every time she thought about Barrett selling her car, so kept waiting for the Valium to take effect, but they didn't.

Hence **Va·liumed** *ppl. a.*, affected by taking Valium.

1973 M. Amis *Rachel Papers* 21 My Valium-ed mother fluttered between them on the sofa. **1978** 'P. Mann' *Steal Big* ii. 16, I spent about a year this way..Valiumed out of my skull for ten terrible days.

Valkyrian, *a.* Delete *rare*⁻¹ and add later examples. Also **Valkyriean.**

1937 J. W. Day *Sporting Adv.* 250 They came baying, like Valkyriean hounds, the skeins of brent. **1938** —— *Dog in Sport* xix. 266 On the hillside, far beyond the wood ..he lifted like a Valkyrian shadow against the clear horizon of a mountainside that had seen his kind since the birth of history. **1977** D. Williams *Treasure by Degrees* iii. 31 She opened her arms wide..in a Valkyrian gesture. **1981** J. M. Brinnin *Beau Voyage* (1982) 173/2 German ships..would become..galleries of an aspiration so Valkyrian that one would think only megalomaniacs might dally there.

valleriite (vǎlīᵊ·riˌəit). *Min.* [ad. Sw. *valleriit* (C. W. Blomstrand 1870, in *Öfversigt af K. Vetensk.-Akad. Förhandlingar* XXVII. 19), f. the name of J. G. Vallerius (1683–1742), Swedish mineralogist: see -ite¹.] A hexagonal basic sulphide of iron, copper, magnesium, and aluminium found in high-temperature copper and iron deposits as minute cream or yellowish crystals.

1875 E. S. Dana *Dana's Syst. Min.* (ed. 5) App. II. 58 Valleriite... Massive, without a trace of crystalline texture. **1976** *Contrib. Mineral. & Petrol.* LV. 265 Chromian valleriite occurs as a replacement product of chrome spinel in the Nepean and Perseverance nickel-iron ore sulphide deposits of Western Australia.

valley, *sb.* Add: **3. b.** *spec.* A region of a graph which is shaped like a valley, or a set of low values of a varying quantity which would form such a region if plotted as a graph.

1935 [see *high frequency 1 b]. **1959** *Daily Tel.* 11 Dec. 1/1 A prompt decision by the Government is urged, that the age can be compulsorily raised in one of the three 'valley' years between 'bulges' in the number of children, 1966, 1967 and 1968. **1968** F. B. Morinigo *tr. von Buttlar's Nucl. Physics* xiii. 103 Nuclei that can decay in two ways..are always odd-odd nuclei and lie near the bottom of the valley of stability. **1973** *Physics Bull.* Apr. 239/1 The spectrometer is claimed to provide..high resolution analysis. Its resolution is more than 10,000 with a 10% valley. **1974** Adby & Dempster *Introd. Optimization Methods* i. 16 Long curved narrow valleys are especially troublesome to simpler optimization procedures.

7. *valley-bottom* (earlier example), *-dweller*, *-mist*, *-mouth*, *-tomb*, *-wall*; *valley-wards* adv.; **valley fever** *U.S.* = *coccidioidomycosis; **Valley Girl** *U.S.*, a teenage girl from San Fernando Valley in southern California; also = *Valleyspeak* below; also *attrib.*; **Valleyspeak** *U.S.*, a form of slang originating among teenage girls in San Fernando Valley in southern California; **valley tan** *U.S. local*, a kind of whisky produced in Salt Lake Valley, Utah; **valley train** *Physical Geogr.*, a deposit of glacial outwash along a valley bottom.

1863 B. Taylor *Hannah Thurston* xxix. 373 The elms.. had grown up since the valley-bottom was cleared. **1927** Peake & Fleure *Peasants & Potters* iii. 37 It [*sc.* the wild ass] was certainly tamed by the Libyans..from whom it reached the valley-dwellers not long after 4000 B.C. [**1937** *Jrnl. Amer. Med. Assoc.* 3 July 66/1 The disease is often diagnosed as erythema nodosum and is popularly known as 'San Joaquin Valley fever' or desert fever.] **1938** *Ibid.* 8 Oct. 1362/2 It has been found that a symptom complex like that of the first of these patients is common in the San Joaquin Valley; so common, in fact, that it is popularly known as 'valley fever' or 'desert fever'. **1979** *Tucson* (Arizona) *Citizen* 20 Sept. 1D/3 He's already a full-fledged Arizonan because Homero is recovering from a bout with valley fever. **1982** *Guardian* 26 Oct. 8/7 The Valley Girl, well-heeled with time on her hands, suburban and middle-class, is, first and foremost, a consumer. **1982** *Time* 8 Nov. 91/1 Where is the next generation of slang to come from? Not from Valley Girl, the argot made famous lately by singer Frank Zappa and his daughter. **1983** *N.Y. Times Mag.* 21 Aug. 11/1 The Brooklyn accent,.. even California valley-girl slang—these are as much part of our linguistic heritage as computer jargon,.. and words ending in *gate.* **1984** *Daily Mail* 20 Oct. 12/1 But the stilettoed, 10th-grade, 'Valley Girls', who stalk the West Coast Galleries..have been replaced by the Mall Girls. **1930** Blunden *Summer's Fancy* 35 Groves crouched in the deep Of valley-mist. **1923** D. H. Lawrence *Birds, Beasts & Flowers* 188 The trees of the Lobo dark valley-mouth. **1983** *Washington Post Mag.* 23 Jan. 8 'The creative act that doesn't respond to some kind of social need isn't going to be picked up.' Clearly Valley-speak struck a responsive chord. **1860** *Mountaineer* (Salt Lake City, Utah) 16 June 169/3 Which food do you prefer, rum, mixed drinks or Valley Tan? **1942** *Oregon Hist. Q.* Dec. 339 Only among his cronies could he crack a quart of valley tan..with any freedom. **1930** Blunden *Poems* 290 Cause not our very joy to go Among old valley-tombs of flesh and blood and years. **1882** *Ann. Rep. State Geologist 1881* (Geol. Survey New Jersey) 96 The drift thus deposited in a valley has sometimes been called a valley train of sand and gravel. **1954** W. D. Thornbury *Princ. Geomorphol.* xv. 377 Study of the valley trains extending down from the Alps led Penck and Brückner to a recognition of four stages of glaciation. **1974** *Encycl. Brit. Micropædia* VII. 636/3 When confined within valley walls, the outwash deposit is known as a valley train. **1931** H. Crane *Let.* 21 Sept. (1965) 381 With the high valley walls in the Wizard's circle. **1974** Valley wall [see *valley train* above]. **1880** 'Mark Twain' *Tramp Abroad* xxxv. 387 He went swinging along valleywards again. **1962** H. R. Loyn *Anglo-Saxon England* i. 10 Native inhabitants..survived and came to terms, attracted valleywards by force or by superior agricultural technique.

valley, obs. var. VLEI in Dict. and Suppl.

Vallombrosan (vælǭmbrǭᵘ·săn), *a.* and *sb.* [f. *Vallombrosa* near Florence, Italy + -AN.] **A.** *adj.* Of or pertaining to Vallombrosa; *spec.* designating a Benedictine congregation established there in the eleventh century by Giovanni Gualberto. **B.** *sb.* A monk of this congregation.

1851 E. B. BROWNING *Casa Guidi Windows* I. xxix. 77 The Vallombrosan brooks were strewn as thick. **1884** A. J. C. HARE *Cities Central Italy* I. xi. 297 The habit of the Vallombrosans was light grey, but the late monks wore a black cloak and a large hat when abroad. **1901** M. CARMICHAEL *In Tuscany* 141 They were succeeded in 1793 by monks of the Vallombrosan Congregation of Benedictines. **1922** JOYCE *Ulysses* 332 The monks of Benedict of Spoleto, Carthusians and Camaldolesi,.. Oratorians and Vallombrosans.

valorization. Delete *U.S.* and add: Also *gen.*, evaluation, giving validity to, making valid. (Later examples.)

1957 *Times* 28 Dec. 10/1 The announcement of a retention and valorization scheme by the Brazilian authorities in the spring touched off the rise in prices [of cocoa]. **1975** J. DE BRES tr. *Mandel's Late Capitalism* 9 The first four chapters..deal..with..the connection between the development of capitalist technology and the valorization of capital itself. **1975** *Times Lit. Suppl.* 22 Aug. 942/1 The new structuralist model, with its valorization of the synchronic system over the older historical, genetic, diachronic modes of understanding. **1980** J. P. FARRELL *Revolution as Tragedy* v. 247 A Victorian protest against the Romantic valorizations of tragedy that announce themselves in the works of Scott, Byron, and Carlyle.

valorize (væ·lǫ̆rəiz), *v.* [f. VALOR + -IZE.] *trans.* To raise or stabilize the value of (a commodity, etc.) by a centrally organized scheme; *gen.* to evaluate, to make valid. Hence **va·lorized** *ppl. a.*

1921 *Contemp. Rev.* July 53 It attempted both to regulate the output and to stabilise and to 'valorise' the prices. **1934** C. LAMBERT *Music Ho!* II. 79 Artists..have valorized the dream. **1976** T. EAGLETON *Crit. & Ideology* v. 164 Criticism becomes a mutually supportive dialogue between two highly valorised subjects: the valuable text and the valuable reader. **1976** *Daily Tel.* 1 Nov. 16 Merely 'valorising' specific duties..to recoup inflation since April would bring in £250 million. **1978** *Dædalus* Summer 48 The *Emile* and the *Contrat social* provide the explanation of the positively valorized concepts (virtue, morals, patriotism). **1984** *Christian Science Monitor* 2 Mar. B8/4 He has actually managed to suggest that the mire and blood, the 'refuse' of the embittered heart, is valorized by the poetic artifacts created from it.

valorousness. (In Dict. s.v. VALOROUS *a.*) For *rare* $^{-0}$ read *rare* and add examples.

1920 G. SANTAYANA *Character & Opinion in U.S.A.* vii. 214 Their valorousness and morality consist in their indomitable egotism. **1922** E. R. EDDISON *Worm* xxvii. 346 The Demons..by their strength and valorousness set free the Lord Goldry Bluszco.

valpack (væ·lpæk). *U.S.* Orig. (a proprietary name) **Val-A-Pak.** Also **valpac, valpak,** etc. [perh. f. elements of VALISE, PACK *sb.*[1], etc.] A type of soft zip-up travel bag.

1934 *Official Gaz.* (U.S. Patent Office) 30 Oct. 1005/2 Val-A-Pak. For Hand Bags. **1935** *Esquire* Dec. 212/1 (Advt.), Val-A-Pak hangs flat against the wall of a stateroom berth or closet. *Ibid.*, By the exclusive Val-A-Pak construction, the bag whether flat or folded for carrying, always conforms to its contents. **1946** J. P. MARQUAND *B.F.'s Daughter* ix. 111 Later in his room at the Bachelor Officers' Quarters he opened his valpack and took out a packet of letter paper. **1966** E. WEST *Night is Time for Listening* ii. 45 He hung out his Valpak, removed his overcoat, and lit a cigarette. **1967** *Sat. Rev.* (U.S.) 22 Apr. 52/2 Experienced travelers in 1947 favoured the Valpack to carry clothes. It was like an Army kitbag and zipped up. **1977** E. LEONARD *Hunted* (1978) ix. 86 He threw extra clothes into a valpac.

Valpolicella (vælpǫlitʃe·lă). Also earlier **Val Policella.** The name of a valley in the western Veneto, Italy, used to designate the red or rosé wine made there.

1903 N. NEWNHAM-DAVIS *Gourmet's Guide to Europe* ix. 164 A bottle of Val Policella is exactly suited to this kind of repast. **1935** SCHOONMAKER & MARVEL *Compl. Wine Bk.* v. 130 Of the Veronese wines, the red Valpolicella is decidedly the best. **1950** E. HEMINGWAY *Across River* xii. 103 What about a fiasco of Valpolicella? **1970** A. SILLITOE *Start in Life* vi. 294 Glasses of Valpolicella not yet touched. **1979** C. CURZON *Leaven of Malice* xi. 126 *Tournedos Rossini* with salad and a reasonable Valpolicella.

valproic (vælprǭᵘ·ik), *a. Pharm.* [f. VAL(ERIC *a.* + PRO(PYL + -IC.] 2-Propylpentanoic acid, $C_8H_{15}OOH$, a branched-chain fatty acid; also, a salt of this. Hence **valpro·ate,** a salt of this acid, esp. the sodium salt, an anticonvulsant drug given orally in cases of epilepsy.

1972 *Approved Names* (Brit. Pharmacopœia Commission) Suppl. IV. 6 Valproic acid. **1974** *Brit. Med. Jrnl.* 15 June 584/1 The anticonvulsant effects of sodium dipropylacetate (sodium valproate) were first reported in France. **1977** *Lancet* 22 Oct. 860/1 The antiepileptic activity of valproic acid (dipropylacetic acid) was recognized serendipitously when the agent was administered to animals as a vehicle for a series of test compounds. **1983** F. E. DREIFUSS in Pedley & Meldrum *Rec. Adv. in Epilepsy* I. iii. 35 Clinical experience with Valproate extends over nearly 20 years. *Ibid.*, The term Valproate is used here to refer both to valproic acid and its salts (sodium or magnesium).

Valsalva (vælsæ·lvă). *Med.* The name of Antonio M. *Valsalva* (1666–1723), Italian anatomist, used *attrib.*, in the possessive, and *absol.* to designate the action, described by him, in which an attempt is made to exhale air while the nostrils and mouth, or the glottis, are closed, so as to increase pressure in the middle ear and the chest.

1886 *Buck's Handbk. Med. Sci.* II. 577/2 To insure a proper performance of this (Valsalva's) method of inflation, it is merely requisite that the patient shall make a strong expiratory effort while holding both his mouth and his nose firmly closed. **1893** H. RICHARDS in C. H. Burnett *Syst. Dis. Ear, Nose, & Throat* I. I. 112 The patient is the operator of the Valsalva inflation. **1913** *Jrnl. Physiol.* XLVI. 186 The radial artery was released and the first rise of the Valsalva experiment was resumed. *Ibid.*, In Fig. 5 is shown another tracing of occlusion of the aberrant radial artery during Valsalva. *Ibid.* 187 The first rise in the sphygmographic curve in Valsalva's experiment is due to increased blood-pressure with increase of the calibre of the artery. **1943** *Bull. Hist. Med.* XIV. 313 Only the historian can fully realize the relative unfruitfulness of the vast amount of experimentation and of study devoted to the Valsalva. **1972** *Sci. Amer.* Feb. 85/2 In attempting to stop the heart the yogis usually performed what is called the Valsalva maneuver. **1977** *Lancet* 28 May 1140/1 In shallow diving an over-forceful Valsalva manœuvre may give rise to neuro-sensory hearing loss, with or without vertigo.

Valspeak (væ·lspīk). *U.S.* [f. VAL(LEY *sb.* + *-SPEAK.] = *Valleyspeak* s.v. *VALLEY *sb.* 7.

1982 *People Mag.* 13 Sept. 90/2 On the record, in pure, uncut Valspeak, Moon laments in bubbly staccato that, 'Like my mother like makes me do the dishes. It's like so *gross*.' **1982** *Guardian* 26 Oct. 8/4 Valspeak is the latest teentalk craze to surface in the real world.

valuation. Add: **1.** *attrib.* Also *valuation office, officer.*

1905 G. B. SHAW *Let.* 3 Jan. (1972) II. 503 A high official in the Valuation Office. **1925** *Act* 15 & 16 *Geo. V* c. 90 § 55(1) It shall be lawful for rating authorities, assessment committees, and county valuation committees to appoint for the purposes of this Act such rating officers, valuation officers and other officers as they think fit. **1976** *Evening Post* (Nottingham) 14 Dec. 4/7 A spokesman for the Inland Revenue said it was customary for the valuation officers to try to reach agreement with the ratepayers. **1978** *Ryde's Rating Cases* (1979) XXI. 143 He had stated that on evidence now to hand the valuation office erred in some cases in not projecting forward the 1967/1969 rents.

valuative, *a.* Delete † *Obs.*$^{-1}$ and add later examples.

1946 [see *APPRAISIVE *a.*]. **1958** *Listener* 12 June 983/1 Valuative disputes arise both about what is to be passed on [by education] and about the manner of passing it on.

value, *sb.* Add: **I. 1.** In phr. *value for money* (freq. *attrib.*).

[**1806:** see Dict.]. **1902** W. S. CHURCHILL in R. S. Churchill *Winston S. Churchill* (1969) II. Compan. I. 132 The first limitation is therefore the restriction of a committee on estimates to the 'merit' or 'value for money' aspect of expenditure. **1929** *Radio Times* 8 Nov. 444/3 Lissen are famed for the keen value-for-money of every component. **1951** [see *PROMOTION 1 e]. **1976** *Jrnl. R. Soc. Arts* CXXIV. 509/2 Every natural salesman knows that the true test of marketability is the subtle ratio between specification and price which even after years of anxious thought Consumers' Association can still only call 'value for money' and can still only nominate and not measure. **1977** *Management Today* July 72/2 Both in extroversion and value-for-money terms, the XJS retains the edge. **1984** *Times* 30 Apr. 25/3 The marketing manager will be impressed by an easy-to-handle, value-for-money approach.

2. c. *good value* (colloq.), entertaining, worth keeping company with, worth seeing, etc.

1930 R. LEHMANN *Note in Music* III. 102, I rather like her... She might be good value, given a chance. **1934** R. KNOX *Still Dead* vii. 91 Lisbon..is really pretty good value, coming into the harbour especially. **1937** AUDEN & MACNEICE *Lett. from Iceland* xii. 161 The geyser was better value, it went off. **1961** J. B. PRIESTLEY *Saturn over Water* vii. 104 Her eyes shone with excitement. Either the Garlettas were exceptionally good value or she was longing to get out of this house. **1979** 'S. WOODS' *This Fatal Writ* 34 If it weren't for the chap's confounded habit of asking questions, he would be finding his client rather good value..because of the refreshingly casual way in which he treated..a very serious charge.

d. *value added* (Econ.), the amount by which the value of an article is increased at each stage of its production by the firm or firms producing it, exclusive of the cost of materials and bought-in parts and services; also *attrib.*, esp. in *value added tax* [cf. G. *mehrwertsteuer*], a tax levied on the value added to an article or the raw material forming it at each stage during its production or distribution.

1935 *Social Research* II. 161 We may call the value added tax a 'refined sales tax'. *Ibid.*, A tax which chooses as its basis of assessment the sales after deduction of all expenses for raw material and for repair or replacement of equipment, that is, a tax on the 'value added by manufacture'. **1940** *Jrnl. Polit. Econ.* XLVIII. 652 A rather imperfect form of a value-added tax was incorporated by Mr. Arthur L. Johnson in his revised old age pension bill in 1939. **1951** P. A. SAMUELSON *Economics* (ed. 2) xi. 236 If we insist upon decomposing the 10 cents of final product represented by the bread into the contributions of the different stages of production, we can always do so by concentrating on the so-called 'value-added' at each stage of production. **1957** J. F. DUE *Sales Taxation* vii. 125 The basic intent of a value-added tax is to tax each firm on the sum of the value which it has added in the manufacturing and distribution process. **1962** *Economist* 3 Mar. 827/1 The French system of a value-added tax—that is to say, a tax on net sales, or total sales less the cost of bought-in materials and components. **1967** *Ibid.* 21 Jan. 243/2 The aids must..bring in industries with rapid growth rates and a high value-added element. **1977** M. WALKER *National Front* vi. 142 A Government in mid-term (which had moreover introduced the unpopular Value Added Tax the previous month).

6. In *Philos.* and *Social Sciences*, regarded esp. in relation to an individual or group; *gen.* in *pl.*, the principles or standards of a person or society, the personal or societal judgement of what is valuable and important in life.

1902 J. M. BALDWIN *Dict. Philos. & Psychol.* II. 823/2 Since value is a function of desire or judgment, expressing a relation between subject and object. **1918** THOMAS & ZNANIECKI *Polish Peasant* I. 21 By a social value we understand any datum having an empirical content accessible to the members of some social group and a meaning with regard to which it is or may be an object of activity. *Ibid.* 33 Sociology..has this in common with social psychology: that the values which it studies draw all their reality, all their power to influence human life, from the social attitudes which are expressed or supposedly expressed in them. **1921** *Times Lit. Suppl.* 3 Nov. 705/4 In the effort, again, to give his characters and scenes the vivid impression of reality, the novelist, whether voluntarily or not, cannot avoid revealing not merely his powers of mind and imagination, but his spiritual and philosophical bias, his views of society, of religion, his 'values'. **1933** *Economica* XIII. 30 Like all human action social behaviour is determined..in accordance with standards of value or through conscious belief in standards assigning intrinsic value to certain types of behaviour. **1938** E. BOWEN *Death of Heart* III. iv. 394 You've got a completely lunatic set of values. **1950** I. BERLIN in *Foreign Affairs* XXVIII. 382 Crumbling values and the dissolution of the fixed standards and landmarks of our civilization. **1955** *Times* 10 May 8/3 Restoring to Germany the basic values of democratic civilization. **1958** *Listener* 9 Oct. 548/1 The reason..lies, I believe, in the structure of Arab society..and in its economic values. **1964** GOULD & KOLB *Dict. Soc. Sci.* 744/1 Social scientists for the most part..have confined their attention to values..as empirical variables in social life whose *scientific* importance is not so much dependent on their validity and correctness as..upon the fact that they are believed..by those who hold them. **1970** N. CHOMSKY *At War with Asia* vi. 299 By their willingness to die, the Asian hordes..exploit our basic weakness—our Christian values which make us reluctant to bear the burden of genocide, the final conclusion of our strategic logic.

attrib. (Further examples.)

1910 *Mind* XIX. 227 Our æsthetic, ethical and directly sensational judgments are all expressions of the fundamental value-attitude in specifically different relations. **1936** *Mind* XLV. 289 A will to maintain the society in spite of one's dissatisfaction with certain elements in its total value-pattern. **1949** G. BATESON in M. Fortes *Soc. Structure* 49 Of these differences between von Neumannian and human systems, only the differences in value scales.. concern us here. *a* **1952** H. READ *Anarchy & Order* (1954) 195, I am going to assume..that 'good' and other ethical value-terms have only an emotive meaning. **1952** *Mind* LXI. 290 Attempts to construct various value-hierarchies. **1952** R. M. HARE *Lang. Morals* i. 8 'Bad' is a value-word, and therefore prescriptive. **1954** W. K. HANCOCK *Country & Calling* vi. 173 Myrdal saw only one remedy for it—to state explicitly the value-premises of his exploration so that writer and reader alike would always be able to distinguish the discussion of *is* from the discussion of *ought*. **1964** A. EDEL in I. L. Horowitz *New Sociol.* 220 Some value-attitudes..are ushered into the inner sanctum of science. **1977** A. GIDDENS *Stud. in Social & Polit. Theory* i. 91 The initial statement conceals a value premise. *Ibid.* 94 Ultimate values..involved in both the value hierarchies of individual actors, and those of overall cultures. **1970** S. L. BARRACLOUGH in I. L. Horowitz *Masses in Lat. Amer.* iv. 123 The principal 'causes' of the agrarian problem are to be found in the population explosion,..and changing value patterns. **1977** BULLOCK & STALLYBRASS *Fontana Dict. Mod. Thought* 47/2 Any field of human discourse in which the general value-terms 'good' and 'ought' figure falls within the range of axiology. **1977** P. HOWARD *New Words for Old* xliii. 117 (*heading*) Value Words... The change from description to evaluation is one of the most potent agents for decaying meanings.

f. The quality of a thing considered in respect of its power and validity for a specified purpose or effect.

1906, etc. [see *news value* s.v. *NEWS *sb.* (*pl.*) 6 b]. **1933,** etc. [see *nuisance value* s.v. *NUISANCE 3]. **1935** A. P. HERBERT *What a Word!* 8 To-day, instead of 'fun', we learn to speak of 'entertainment-value'. **1937,** etc. [see *ENTERTAINMENT 13]. **1962** C. WINSTON *Hours Together* vi. 129 In a decade..all this would also be a joke, and the names of these neighbourhoods..would have the same comedy value as the names he had grown up with. **1966** H. MOORE *On Sculpture* 167 These small figures, seen so much bigger, take on an extra importance and impressiveness, and are a proof that size itself has an emotional value. **1978** K. HUDSON *Jargon of Professions* 1 The solidarity-value of such nonsense-language certainly should not be underestimated. **1979** J. RABAN *Arabia through Looking Glass* v. 196 It's a synthetic soil-substitute, better than real soil by far. Its nutritional value's *much* higher.

8. Special Combs.: **value analysis,** the systematic and critical assessment by an organization of design and costs in relation to realized value; also *transf.*; **value analyst,** one who undertakes a value analysis; **value calling** *Bridge,* a system of estimating bids which takes into account the scoring values of the suits; **value engineering,** the modification of designs and systems according to value analysis; **value-free** *a.*, free from criteria imposed by subjective values or standards; purely objective; = **value-neutral*; hence *value-freedom*; **value-judgement** [cf. G. *werturteil*], a judgement predicating merit or demerit of its subject; **value-laden** *ppl. a.* = **value-loaded* ppl. adj.; hence *value-ladenness*; **value-loaded** *ppl. a.*, weighted or biased in favour of certain values; **value-neutral** *a.*, involving no value judgements, neutral with respect to (personal or group) values; **value-orientation,** the direction given to a person's attitudes and thinking by their beliefs or standards; so *value-oriented ppl. a.*; **value-system,** any set of connected or independent values; **value theory,** (*a*) *Pol. Econ.*, the (Marxist) labour theory of value; (*b*) *Philos.*, axiology.

1955 K. E. BOULDING *Econ. Anal.* (ed. 3) xxxiii. 714 We can, therefore, perform something with the tools of economic analysis which might be called 'value analysis', and which should be of use in clarifying the choices involved in economic policy. **1963** *Engineering* 9 Aug. 162/1 When good engineering, manufacturing and purchasing practices are supplemented by value analysis, the cost of a product..can be reduced by up to 25 per cent. **1977** R. HOLLAND *Self & Social Context* i. 12 It will be necessary to apply sociological techniques of value analysis in order to reach a full understanding of the theories. **1969** J. ARGENTI *Managem. Techniques* 265 Some companies establish permanent teams under a Value Analyst. **1927** *Daily Express* 8 Nov. 1/5 We do not consider that there is any general desire for the adoption of majority calling in place of value calling. **1959** *Ship & Boat Builder* Oct. 349 (*heading*) Can value engineering cut costs? **1962** *Engineering* 19 Oct. 515 Value engineering is a well-established technique in the USA... They define it as 'the systematic application of techniques and principles which aim at cutting production costs'. **1973** *Lebende Sprachen* XVIII. 73/1 *Value engineering* is a technique for reducing total cost while maintaining or improving the overall usefulness of the product or service. **1949** J. A. PASSMORE in Feigl & Brodbeck *Readings in Philos. of Sci.* (1953) 674 (*heading*) Can the social sciences be value-free? **1979** *Nature* 19 July 185/1 Science and technology are not neutral or value-free but are instruments of power, and that means political power. **1984** *Times Educ. Suppl.* 30 Nov. 3/2 Europe Singh, a maths teacher..believes maths and the sciences have wrongly been considered to be neutral and value-free. **1959** P. RIEFF *Freud* viii. 299 Scientific energies, by the facile transformation of the objectivity necessary to science into..'value-freedom', are easily enlisted to the aims of society, whatever these may be. **1892** J. ORR in *Thinker* II. 146 Two kinds of knowledge are distinguished by Ritschl—the one, religious knowledge which moves solely in the region of what he calls worth or value-judgments. **1899** [see sense 6 *attrib.*]. **1941** J. S. HUXLEY *Uniqueness of Man* xi. 229 Even in natural science, regarded as pure knowledge, one value-judgment is implicit—*belief in the value of truth.* **1961** *Listener* 30 Nov. 912/1 The decision depends on what may ..be called policy considerations; that is, where the court has to make a value judgment. **1975** *Amer. N. & Q.* XIV. 53/2 Robert Frost's penchant for 'the fact' (as in 'Mowing') provides a useful measuring stick for determining the worth of value judgments about him. **1980** *Times Lit. Suppl.* 3 Oct. 1085/2 The method adopted here is a detailed interpretative analysis of poetic language and structure, liberally sprinkled with value-judgments. **1971** *Ibid.* 13 Aug. 958/4 For them, even the internal content of science is value-laden, and to some extent ideologically determined. **1977** *Jrnl. Politics* XXXIX. 24 The growing acceptance of the thesis that political science is necessarily a value-laden discipline. **1978** M. HESSE in Hookway & Pettit *Action & Interpretation* 8 A distinction between two sorts of 'value-ladenness' in social science. **1951** D. RIESMAN *Individualism Reconsidered* (1955) 33 Obviously, the very term 'masses' is heavily value-loaded. **1974** tr. *Wertheim's Evolution & Revolution* 35 To state that a given situation shows 'progress' or 'evolution'..in relation to another situation implies the use of value-loaded criteria. **1946** GERTH & MILLS tr. M. Weber in *From Max Weber* (1947) ix. 247 Even a pirate genius may exercise a 'charismatic' domination, in the value-neutral sense intended here. **1979** *Dædalus* Winter 55 'Excellence' is not a value-neutral concept. **1951** G. W. ALLPORT in Parsons & Shils *Toward Gen. Theory Action* iv. i. 365 Prejudice is manifestly a value-orientation. **1968** W. E. LAMBERT et al. in J. A. Fishman *Readings Sociol. of Lang.* 488 In general, value orientations do not play an important role in predicting who will or will not do well in French. **1980** N. ABERCROMBIE et al. *Dominant Ideology Thesis* ii. 48 System integration is defined in terms of the processes whereby value-orientation patterns are institutionalised at the social level via the mechanism of social roles with the effect of organising the behaviour of adult members of society. **1962** N. J. SMELSER *Theory Collective Behav.* iii. 49 Behind a vast array of religious and political value-oriented movements lie the same kinds of strain. **1977** *Bull. Amer. Acad. Arts & Sci.* Oct. 16 It is at this point that value-oriented parameters for assessing progress become necessary. **1936** *Mind* XLV. 288 Persons who are not *Buerger* (citizens)..like the Jews in Nazi Germany, or the bulk of the Bantu in the Union of South Africa. For such as these, the relation to the value-system embodied in the state is of the most tenuous and indirect kind. **1969** *Listener* 3 July 3/1 Two American sociologists examined the value system of a small rural town in the American Mid-West. **1980** *Jrnl. R. Soc. Arts* June 416/2 A society in which there are overlapping different value systems which create different structures. **1887** G. B. SHAW *Let.* 17 May (1965) I. 169 Socialism does not stand or fall by the Value Theory. **1941** *Mind* L. 198 The contributions to aesthetics, value-theory, theology and Spinozistic lore have all..been published before. **1966** S. BEER *Decision & Control* x. 221 We are now in the field of value theory, the subject which attempts to bring managerial value judgments within the compass of decision theory. **1979** D. MCLELLAN *Marxism after Marx* xxiii. 309 There has been a vigorous and sophisticated defence of traditional Marxian value theory.

valued, *ppl. a.* **2.** (Later example.)

1913 R. H. GRETTON *Mod. Hist. Eng. People* I. ii. 52 Rents were refused above the 'valued rent' scale.

valuta (vălⁱū·tă). Pl. **valute, valuten.** [(G. a.) It *valuta*:– late L. **valuta*, use as sb. of fem. pa. pple. of L. *valēre* to be worth.] Foreign currency; a monetary standard, the currency constituting an acceptable medium of exchange, the valuation constituting an acceptable rate of exchange. Also *attrib.*, *transf.*, and *fig.*

1893 R. BITHELL *Counting-House Dict.* (rev. ed.) 314 *Valuta*, Russian paper money. **1921** *Glasgow Herald* 28 Oct. 11 The speculation in valute and devisen has become ..ridiculous, as the great boom on the Berlin exchange proves. **1924** LUCAS & BONAR tr. *Knapp's State Theory of Money* 106 Everywhere there is a valuta or standard money. *Ibid.* 165 If there is more than one kind of money in the country, the value in valuta money is always meant. *c* **1939** E. BENN *Diary* in *Happier Days* (1949) xiv. 171 He doubted if the *valuten* could be found to send the Führer to England. **1954** E. H. CARR *Interregnum* i. 29 A general decree was issued 'On Valuta Operations'... It confined transactions in foreign valuta to the Exchanges. **1964** S. BELLOW *Herzog* 143 A mob broke into his house.. looking for *valuta*. **1967** *Economist* 19 Aug. p. xxix/1 Russia is still the chief importer of Skoda products, but the emphasis is gradually shifting to the West and other areas. A nominal level of *valuten* income is now set. **1972** M. MUGGERIDGE *Chron. Wasted Time* I. v. 252 All were deeply moved;..as, indeed, was I, despite my valuta origins and prospects. **1979** F. E. PERRY *Dict. Banking* 262/1 *Valuta*, rate of exchange, value, currency; entries in bank books which fix charges to be made or interest charges due, such as the determination of opening and closing dates for the relative periods.

valva (væ·lvă). *Ent.* [L.: see VALVE *sb.*¹] = VALVE *sb.*¹ 2 b, *c.

1802 W. KIRBY *Monographia Apum Angliæ* I. 110 *Valvæ*. These have been frequently noticed. Swammerdam calls them *appendages of the sting.* **1826** [see VALVE *sb.*¹ 2 b]. **1924** *Ann. Entomol. Soc. Amer.* XVII. 276 The term valvæ or valves was used to denote the two lateral outer appendages. **1975** *Entomologist's Gaz.* XXVI. 198 There is in my material a further specimen..showing some variation in the valva.

valvar, *a.* Delete *rare* and add later examples. In *Med.* = VALVULAR *a.* 3.

1895 *Jrnl. R. Microsc. Soc.* 669 Dr. O. Müller proposes a new terminology for diatoms... The plane which passes through the apical and the transapical axes is the valvar plane. **1946** *Nature* 26 Oct. 588/1 Division took place along the longitudinal axis in what would have been the valvar plane. **1955** *Guy's Hospital Rep.* CIV. 372 Kirklin *et al.*..have also drawn attention..to this association between valvar and infundibular stenosis. **1977** *Amer. Heart Jrnl.* XCIII. 461/1 Mitral regurgitation or other mitral valvar abnormality has been reported in four other cases. **1980** *Plant Systematics & Evolution* CXXXV. 266 (*caption*) Region of the intercalary bands seen parallel to the valvar plane.

valve, *sb.*¹ Add: **I. 2. c.** *Ent.* = *VALVULA 2.

1802 W. KIRBY *Monographia Apum Angliæ* I. 110 Linneus, in his character of *Ichneumon*, calls them the valves of the vagina of the aculeus. They are the covers of the genuine vagina. **1919** *Ann. Entomol. Soc. Amer.* XII. 277 The sternal region of segment nine is shifted.., thus bringing the bases of the dorsal and inner valvulæ into the same transverse plane with those of the ventral valves. **1969** R. F. CHAPMAN *Insects* xvii. 325 If the insect oviposits in plant or animal tissue the valves are sclerotised and lanceolate.

d. *Ent.* A clasper of a male butterfly.

1864 *Trans. Linn. Soc.* XXV. 35 There remain therefore only the characters of the perfect insect, the most important of which are the anal valves in the male. These.. are furnished with projecting points or spines..which serve to attach the male more firmly to the female *in copulâ*. **1883** *Ibid.: Zool.* II. 332 *C. Eubule* has a very curious valve, armed as elaborately, and as singularly, as that of many a *Papilio*. **1964** R. M. & J. W. FOX *Introd. Compar. Entomol.* iii. 109 Other orders with periphallic claspers (harpes, harpagones, valves, etc.) form them from the coxae and exite styli of the appendages of at least the ninth segment.

3. c. Each of the two siliceous cell walls of a diatom, similar in shape but slightly different in size, with one overlapping the other.

1852 A. PRITCHARD *Hist. Infusorial Animalcules* (rev. ed.) III. 295 Siliceous valves are deposited *exterior* to a cell-membrane. **1857** [see sense 3 b in Dict.]. **1898** H. C. PORTER tr. *Strasburger's Text-bk. Bot.* II. i. 313 Both valves are so strongly impregnated with silica, that, even when subjected to intense heat, they remain as a siliceous skeleton, retaining the original form and markings of the cell walls. **1973** R. G. KRUEGER et al. *Introd. Microbiol.* iii. 125/1 The newer valve of any diatom is invariably the smaller valve, because it is constructed within the confines of the older valve.

II. 6. a. *fig.* (Later examples.)

1930 AUDEN *Poems* 56 No chattering valves of laughter emphasized..the sessile hush. **1933** E. O'NEILL *Ah, Wilderness!* IV. i. 116 Seizes this as an escape valve—turns and fixes his youngest son with a stern forbidding eye.

b. *Electronics.* = *thermionic valve* s.v. *THERMIONIC *a.*

1905 J. A. FLEMING in *Proc. R. Soc.* LXXIV. 478 We have in this vacuum valve and associated mirror galvanometer a means of detecting feeble alternating electric currents or oscillations. *Ibid.* 479 This arrangement of a differential galvanometer and two valves transforms.. more of the alternating oscillation into direct current than when one valve alone is used. **1924** GIBSON & COLE *Wireless of To-Day* xxiv. 307 Monster valves have now been manufactured absorbing as much as 100 kw. each, and in consequence of the tremendous heat generated, the electrodes are specially constructed permitting water to circulate within for cooling purposes. **1928** *Electr. Communication* VI. 241/2 The high-power amplifying tubes, which over here [*sc.* in Britain] we call 'valves'. **1943** C. L. BOLTZ *Basic Radio* x. 165 All battery-fed radio apparatus utilizes directly-heated valves, which need 2V on the filament. **1968** M. GUYBON tr. *Solzhenitsyn's First Circle* lxxv. 476 He was a radio engineer by training, and hadn't a box containing two valves been found during the search of his flat?

c. *Chess.* (See quot. 1930.)

1930 WHITE & HUME *Valves & Bi-Valves* 7 In chess problem terminology, the designation of a Valve has been given to any move which simultaneously opens one line while it closes another. In a broad sense, Valves include a large domain with many varied combinations of themes. There is a much narrower application of the term: Valve, and that is the particular case where not only is the move made by Black, but both of the lines affected are also Black. **1936** P. W. SERGEANT tr. *Znosko-Borovsky's Art of Chess Combination* II. v. 62 In the interception of lines one closes lines to the adversary at critical points, while here one opens lines to one's own pieces. The skilled hand deals with the valves on this side and on that.

7. a. *valve line, stem*; also used to designate brass instruments whose range is increased by the addition of valves, as *valve horn, trombone* (so *trombonist*), *trumpet*; in sense *6 b, esp. designating apparatus employing valves, as *valve circuit, detector, heater, -holder, oscillator, receiver, set, voltmeter.*

1915 HAWKHEAD & DOWSETT *Handbk. Wireless Telegraphists* 119 If an E.M.F. be applied to the valve circuit a more sensitive condition is obtained. **1934** *Times Rev. 1933* 1 Jan. p. ix/4 The Wireless Exhibition at Olympia illustrated the exceptional advances made during the year in valve and valve-circuit technique. **1915** HAWKHEAD & DOWSETT *Handbk. Wireless Telegraphists* 120 The valve detector is used with various circuits. **1929** *Radio Times* 8 Nov. 443/3 Get the necessary output from a Regentone mains unit for A.C. valve heaters. **1960** *Practical Wireless* XXXVI. 326/2 Commence wiring the valve heaters by taking a tightly twisted pair of insulated wires from V1 to V2. **1922** *Wireless World* 4 Mar. 748/1 The base..carries the valve holder. **1960** *Practical Wireless* XXXVI. 392/2 Positions for the valve holders can be marked out from the measurements indicated in Fig. 2. **1877** Valve horn [see *valve trumpet* below]. **1938** *Oxf. Compan. Mus.* 439/2 The valve horn has the immense advantage of..a chromatic series, for three valves add instantaneously to the air column a length corresponding respectively to a semitone, two semitones, and three semitones. **1959** *Listener* 4 June 1001/3 The more limpid yet penetrating tone of the narrower-bored French valve-horn. **1977** *Early Music* Apr. 221/2 Scores of the valve horn era. **1871** *Leisure Hour* 8 Apr. 222/2 The balloon had been gyrating, and the valve-line become twisted. **1963** [see *rip line* s.v. *RIP *sb.*⁴ 5]. **1969** *Gloss. Aeronaut. & Astronaut. Terms (B.S.I.)* VII. 8 *Valve line*, a cord for the operation of a valve. **1935** *Discovery* Aug. 226/1 In some forms of valve oscillator, the high-tension supply is such that only half of the wave of the a.c. feed mains is rectified. **1913** *Wireless World* Nov. 478/1 A valve receiver of rather longer range than usual is used. **1929** *Radio Times* 8 Nov. 437/1 This popular Loud Speaker unit..gives..perfect results with any valve Receiver. *Ibid.* 397/1 Her nursery..is wired for broadcasting and..her movements or cries are now heard loud in the sitting-room..where our valve set is placed. **1981** S. BRIGGS *Those Radio Times* i. 28/2 By 1926..the valve set playing through loudspeakers replaced the simple crystal set. **1888** *Lockwood's Dict. Mech. Engin.* 397 *Valve stem*, a valve spindle or rod. **1889** J. M. WHITHAM *Steam-Engine Design* iv. 98 If the valve.. is long, the weight, friction, and diameter of the valve-stem are increased. **1970** K. BALL *Fiat 600, 600D Autobook* i. 13/1 Valve stems, once bent, cannot be straightened satisfactorily. **1883** O. COON *Harmony & Instrumentation* xxvi. 73 The valve Trombone is often substituted for the one with a slide. **1979** *Jazz Jrnl.* XXXII. 11/1 (*caption*) Thad Jones on valve trombone. **1946** R. BLESH *Shining Trumpets* (1949) xii. 263 The valve trombonist Brad Gowans. **1877** E. PROUT *Instrumentation* v. 81 The valve-trumpet..possesses, like the valve-horn, a complete chromatic scale. **1979** *Oxf. Junior Compan. Music* 331/4 The trumpet now in everyday orchestral use is the *valve trumpet*. That is to say, it has extra lengths of tubing coiled alongside its main tube, and these can be brought into action by pressing down a 'valve'. **1925** Valve voltmeter [see *slide-back* s.v. *SLIDE- c].

c. valve head *Mech.*, the part of a lift valve that is lifted off the valve aperture to open the valve; **valve train** *Mech.*, in an internal-combustion engine, the gearing and linkages by which the crankshaft is caused to open and close a valve at the proper time.

1904 A. B. F. YOUNG *Compl. Motorist* (ed. 2) iv. 91 The valve-head is provided with a slot for the insertion of a tool for grinding purposes. **1971** B. SCHARF *Engin. & its Lang.* xii. 176 One also differentiates between ordinary, high lift and full lift safety and relief valves according to the distance by which the valve head is automatically raised. **1955** W. H. CROUSE *Automotive Engines* vii. 222 The L-head engine uses a relatively simple valve train, or valve mechanism. **1981** *Pop. Hot Rodding* Feb. 31/1 A Sig Erson camshaft actuates the mildly worked valve-train, composed of Crane valve-springs, steel retainers, and TRW chrome-moly pushrods.

valve, *v.* For *rare* read '*rare* exc. in ballooning, etc.' and add: **1.** Also *fig.*

1960 R. W. MARKS *Dymaxion World B. Fuller* 11/1 The harnessing factor—the activity which 'valves' the mass-energy of the universe to human advantage—is inventive wisdom born of intuition and experience and put to use in a global industrial complex.

2. (Further examples in ballooning.)

1936 *Nat. Geogr. Mag.* LXIX. 71 Andy valved, and valved again and again! **1963** A. SMITH *Throw out Two Hands* v. 63 You valve a little. You start coming down.

3. *trans.* To discharge gas from (an airship or balloon) by opening a valve; to discharge, or let *off*, (gas) thus.

1925 *Sci. Amer.* Nov. 301/3 She was swept rapidly upwards..Commander Lansdowne valved her freely, pointed her nose down with engines running, and she came down with..rapidity. **1928** *Engineering* 3 Aug. 141/3 As an airship uses up its fuel, it is necessary to reduce the lift, and hitherto this has been done by simply 'valving' off some of the hydrogen used for inflation. **1928** *Daily Tel.* 18 Sept. 9/6 The extra lifting effect of the expanding gas cannot be counteracted by allowing the gas to escape, or in other words by valving the gas. **1936** *Nat. Geogr. Mag.* LXIX. 71 He opened the valves for..another half-minute interval (which is a very long time for a balloon to be valved at low altitude).

valved, *a.* Add: **2.** (Further examples.) Also *fig.*

1856 M. C. CLARKE tr. *Berlioz's Treatise Mod. Instrumentation* (1858) 146/2 *Valved trumpets*,—called so on account of a movable valve similar to that of the trombone, and which is moved by the right hand,—are adapted to produce the truest intervals. **1923** D. H. LAWRENCE *Birds, Beasts & Flowers* 26 To me, all faces are dark, All lips are dusky and valved. **1927** *Bull. U.S. Nat. Museum* No. 136. 51 A valved trumpet marked 'alto B flat'... It has three rotary valves. **1970** J. EARL *Tuners & Amplifiers* 7 This book is concerned essentially with transistored equipment, for the days of the valved amplifiers and tuners have now gone for ever.

valvifer (væ·lvifəɪ). *Ent.* [f. L. *valva* VALVE *sb.*[1] + -I- + L. *-fer* (see -FEROUS).] In some insects, a modified coxa on each of the eighth and ninth abdominal segments that forms a basal plate of the ovipositor and bears a valvula.

1917 G. C. CRAMPTON in *Jrnl. N.Y. Entomol. Soc.* XXV. 236 Basal sclerite of valvula of ovipositor (Valvifer). **1935** R. E. SNODGRASS *Princ. Insect Morphol.* xix. 611 The basal apparatus consists essentially of two pairs of lobes or plates, the first and second valvifers..which support the ovipositor shaft by the bases of the valvulae. **1981** *Animal Behaviour* XXIX. 299/1 The valvifers at its base could be seen to be moving rhythmically back and forth.

valving (væ·lviŋ), *vbl. sb.* [f. VALVE *sb.*[1] + -ING[1].] **a.** A system or arrangement of valves; valves collectively. **b.** Opening and shutting in the manner of a valve; valve-like operation.

1948 *Chem. Industries* Feb. 222/1 (*heading*) Valving CC's. **1957** *Petroleum Engineer* Oct. c. 66 (*heading*) Valving critical in elaborate distribution system. **1968** *Jrnl. Dental Res.* XLVII. 1013/2 Physiologic and temporal features of oral and palatopharyngeal valving were correlated with velocity and volume of oral-nasal flow, and intraoral air pressure. **1973** *Sci. Amer.* Dec. 143/1 [A giraffe's] elevated brain is supplied with oxygen by blood vessels that manage a lot of valving and pumping. **1978** *Ibid.* May 38/1 The valving [of the Newcomen steam engine] was automatic from a very early stage. **1981** *Jrnl. Air Pollution Control Assoc.* XXXI. 377 Thermal mass flowmeters, with microprocessor controlled flow and automatic valving, supply variable levels of concentrated odorant and clean dilution air to a static mixing device.

valvotomy (vælvǫ·tǒmi). *Surg.* [f. VALVE *sb.*[1] + -O + -TOMY.] An operation in which an incision is made into a valve, esp. of the heart.

1903 *N.Y. Med. Jrnl.* LXXVIII. 296/2 The rectitis should be recognized by the general practitioner, that the rectum may be so treated that absorption of the exudate may result rather than the formation of an organized deposit rendering rigid the rectal valve—thus may valvotomy be made unnecessary. **1912** *Proctologist* VII. 155 Valvotomy is a justifiable operation, as it frequently relieves obstipation and constipation. **1962** *Lancet* 8 Dec. 1195/2, 7 days later aortic valvotomy was successfully performed. **1980** *Brit. Med. Jrnl.* 23 Feb. 563/2 We would like to plead for the continued use of closed valvotomy, notably in third world countries where large numbers of patients with mitral stenosis could overwhelm the relatively small number of surgical units equipped for open heart surgery.

valvula. Add: **2.** *Ent.* An elongated blade-like process attached to the coxa on the eighth or ninth abdominal segments of some insects and forming part of the ovipositor; = *VALVE *sb.*[1] 2 c.

1917, 1935 [see *VALVIFER]. **1964** R. M. & J. W. FOX *Introd. Compar. Entomol.* iii. 106 The ovipositor is present in its fully developed form, with three pairs of valvulae, in Phasmida, Grylloblatodea, Dictyoptera, Odonata and Corrodentia. **1978** H. V. DALY et al. *Introd. Insect Biol. & Diversity* ii. 36/2 Eggs issue from the genital opening.., pass down a channel formed by the valvulae, and are deposited in the ovipositional medium.

valvulotomy (vælviūlǫ·tǒmi). *Surg.* [f. VALVUL(E + -O + -TOMY.] = *VALVOTOMY.

1916 J. F. BINNIE *Operative Surg.* (ed. 7) II. xxxi. 332 Such operations may be named internal valvulotomy. **1951** *Lancet* 21 Apr. 896/2 Valvulotomy for mitral stenosis. **1970** *New Yorker* 21 Nov. 68/2 Any two-bit surgeon who can do a valvulotomy can have a patient in this unit.

vamose, vamoose, *v.* Restrict *U.S.* to sense 2 and add: Now usu. *vamoose.* **1.** (Earlier U.S. and further examples.)

[**1827** W. CLARKE *Every Night Bk.* 30 They have done more foolish things in their day—but vamos.] **1834** *Knickerbocker* IV. 455 Be off, you good-for-nothing rascals—*vamos!* **1892** STEVENSON & OSBOURNE *Wrecker* xvi. 254 Well, of course he can vamoose with the entire speculation, if he chooses. **1936** F. CLUNE *Roaming round Darling* ix. 82 The river was going downhill, and the country growing more and more similar in appearance to the Lachlan, before it vamoosed in the marshes. **1958** 'J. REEVES' *Mulbridge Manor* xii. 155 'See anyone?' asked Winston. 'Not a soul. Whoever it was has vamoosed.'

2. (Earlier example.)

1847 'M'C' *Let.* 2 Apr. in *Rough & Ready Ann.* (1848) 245 On the morning after I wrote the letter to father.. they..stacked their arms and colors, and 'vamossed the ranch'.

Hence **vamo(o)·sing** *vbl. sb.*

1862 J. R. LOWELL *Biglow Papers* 2nd ser. v. 75 Or, when the vamosin' come, ever to find [etc.].

vamp (væmp), *sb.*[3] *U.S. slang.* [Origin unknown.] A volunteer fireman.

1877 *Fireman's Jrnl.* I. 15/1 Our old friend..seems to have the run of the old vamps. **1942** BERREY & VAN DEN BARK *Amer. Thes. Slang* § 850/2 *Vamp*, a volunteer fireman.

vamp (væmp), *sb.*[4] [Abbrev. of VAMPIRE *sb.*] A woman who intentionally attracts and exploits men; an adventuress; a Jezebel; freq. as a stock character in plays and films.

a **1911** CHESTERTON *Lunacy & Letters* (1958) xxxvi. 178 Thackeray took it for granted that Mary Stuart was a vamp. **1918** *N.Y. Times* 15 July 9 Enid Bennett In a New 'Vamp' Story... 'The Vamp'..is a pleasing light comedy..in which Enid Bennett..appears as Nancy; an ingenuous wardroom girl at a musical comedy theatre where she hears sophisticated chorus girls tell how the female of the species may make the male buy her dinners and diamond bracelets by 'vamping' him... So Nancy, taking a tip from the chorus girls, 'vamps' him—and the wedding is a quick result. **1930** G. B. SHAW *Wks.* VII. 156 Ask yourself whether, if the lot in life therein described were your lot in life, you would not rather be a jewelled Vamp. **1973** *Times* 22 Dec. 9/2 Exotic red flowers like the lips of vamps. **1976** H. R. F. KEATING *Filmi, Filmi, Inspector Ghote* v. 44 She was..playing the Vamp in a film.

vamp (væmp), *v.*[3] [f. *VAMP *sb.*[4]] **1.** *intr.* To behave seductively; to act as a vamp, to be a vamp. *rare.*

1904 ADE *True Bills* 60 Any time that he fills in from eight o'clock to Midnight he certainly has to do some Vamping. **1922** *Observer* 1 Oct. 5/4 Trollope's Signora Neroni certainly never vamped.

2. *trans.* To act as a vamp towards; to attract and exploit (a man, occas. a woman).

1918 [see *VAMP *sb.*[4]]. **1927** *Observer* 20 Mar. 15/3 Her friend, Violet Usher..shamelessly vamped Randall, and he felt obliged to marry her. **1939** L. M. MONTGOMERY *Anne of Ingleside* xxv. 166 Don't try to vamp me, woman. I've paid you all the compliments I'm going to. **1973** T. PYNCHON *Gravity's Rainbow* II. 245 Eager young chaps with patent-leather hair rush about trying to vamp the ladies. **1979** D. ANTHONY *Long Hard Cure* xix. 150 Gavin's secret girl, who vamped him on the nights those four women were assaulted.

va·mping, *vbl. sb.*[2] [f. *VAMP *v.*[3] + -ING[1].] Seductive behaviour; acting as a vamp.

1904 [see *VAMP *v.*[3] 1]. **1918** *N.Y. Times* 15 July 9 Nancy tries her 'vamping' tactics on him and he confesses his crime.

vampire, *sb.* Add: **2.** *spec.* = *VAMP *sb.*[4] (Further examples.)

1903 G. B. SHAW *Man & Superman* IV. 170 You lie, you vampire, you lie. **1918** *National Police Gaz.* (U.S.) 20 Apr. 4 (*caption*) Theda Bara... Vampire of the Screen. **1919** *Honey Pot* I. 42 Miss Maitland was a 'vampire' of an entirely new type. **1920** C. D. FOX *Who's Who on Screen* 301 Louise Glaum, who is credited with having given to the screen one of the most perfect vampire characterizations, was born near Baltimore. *a* **1953** E. O'NEILL *Long Day's Journey into Night* (1956) IV. 165 Made whores fascinating vampires instead of poor, stupid, diseased slobs they really are. **1968** *Word Study* Dec. 4/2 A vampire is a woman who uses sex to facilitate the acquisition of money or other signs of wealth. **1978** LD. BIRKENHEAD *Rudyard Kipling* vii. 99 A grim but authentic picture.. of callow subalterns trotting beside the rickshaw wheels of faded provincial vampires.

5. *vampire-winged* adj.; **vampire trap** (earlier example).

1846 S. F. SMITH *Theatr. Apprenticeship* viii. 63 Down I went through the trap-door (it was what actors call a Vampire trap) before any one was aware of my intentions. **1831** POE *Poems* 64 Some tomb, which oft hath flung into black And vampyre-winged pannels back.

Hence **va·mpiredom,** the state of being a vampire (sense 1); the acts of a vampire; **vampiric** *a.* (earlier and later examples); **va·mpirine** *a.* = VAMPIRIC *a.*; **vampirish** *a.* (further examples).

1933 *Times Lit. Suppl.* 28 Sept. 653/3 The more obvious literary possibilities of vampiredom were thoroughly explored and exploited nearly forty years ago. **1972** *Daily Tel.* (Colour Suppl.) 12 May 56 There before the horrified gaze of the living was all the evidence of vampiredom—twisted position, torn shroud and blood. **1853** D. G. ROSSETTI *Let.* 17 Apr. (1965) I. 136 Such are the vampyric notions of reciprocity. **1963** *Listener* 24 Jan. 165/2 She [*sc.* Marilyn Monroe] had all the physical equipment of the vamp, but the spirit of the girl next door... Marilyn was never truly vampiric on the screen, and she was never a 'taker' in life. **1914** in D. McCarthy *Drama* (1940) 129 This is too much for Vanya; he explodes at the old vampirine humbug, and..dashes from the room. **1946** BLUNDEN *Shelley* x. 135 Byron began and dropped a thriller which was becoming vampirine. **1929** *Sunday Dispatch* 13 Jan. 1/2 Among my own friends my reputation is notoriously the reverse of vampirish, money means nothing to me. **1944** R. LEHMANN *Ballad & Source* v. viii. 300 Mother fastened vampirish eyes on her. **1981** N. TUCKER *Child & Book* vii. 198 Religious references.. to the Virgin Mary behaving in a way that is distinctly vampirish have been glossed over.

vampish (væ·mpiʃ), *a.* [f. *VAMP *sb.*[4] + -ISH[1].] Suggestive or characteristic of a vamp. Hence **va·mpishness.**

1922 S. FORD *Trilby May crashes In* iv. 60, I have got something more over the footlights than just my ankles and a few vampish hip motions. **1922** *Observer* 1 Oct. 5/4 'The Vavasour' in 'Strathmore'..out of pure vampishness makes a conquest of the hero. **1928** *Ibid.* 15 July 12/4 Not international 'stars' of vampish wiles, but hundreds of Miss Betty Balfours should be sought and cherished. **1971** *Petticoat* 24 July 24/3 At last a girl who admits that she would like to look vampish and look a 'tramp' or 'tart'. **1972** J. WILSON *Hide & Seek* ii. 36 Her crêpe dress, low-cut and forties style, very vampish and sexy. **1977** *Time* 14 Mar. 32/1 That vampish young lady in black hardly looks like the type to drive a race car or ride a bucking bronco.

vampy (væ·mpi), *a.* [f. *VAMP *sb.*[4] + -Y[1].] That is a vamp; vampish. So **va·mpiness.**

1928 *Sunday Express* 29 July 4 The varnished vampiness of Greto Garbo. **1949** *Richmond* (Va.) *Times-Dispatch* 7 Oct. 10 Barbara Stanwyck has come up with the statement that the vampy, predatory female makes a good wife. **1977** *Spare Rib* July 49/1 You see a lot of stilettoes, tights, revealing things, black vampy make-up.

van, *sb.*[3] Add: **1. a.** Now usu. motorized.

b. Also *police van*: see *POLICE *sb.* 6. Also, a light covered vehicle employed to carry passengers.

1973, etc. [see *van pool*, etc., below]. **1979** *N.Y. Rev. Bks.* 25 Oct. 7 (Advt.), Every morning, 1,441 Gulf employees who used to drive their own cars to work now make the trip in vans.

c. A gypsy caravan or one used by a showman; a holiday-maker's caravan; a camper.

1858 DICKENS *Going into Society* in *Househ. Words* Extra Christmas No., 7 Dec. 22/1 The House was so dismal arterwards, that I giv it up, and took to the Wan again. **1876** C. M. YONGE *Three Brides* II. v. 107 He was born in one of they vans, and hadn't never been to school. **1926** KIPLING *Debits & Credits* 237 You can stand at your door and mock when the gipsy-vans come through. **1952** *Motor Manual* (ed. 34) xiii. 244 The owner who wants to tow his caravan from home to some pleasant site where he can leave the van during the summer months. **1972** *Guardian* 5 Feb. 14 The trailer tent..[is] easier to tow than a full-scale trailer 'van. **1976** *Kingston* (Ontario) *Whig-Standard* 4 Aug. 25/4 In California travelling in his own van. **1979** *Observer* 15 July 2/5 Australians who fly in and buy a van to take them round Britain are finding they have to omit the extremities from their itinerary. **1980** R. HILL *Killing Kindness* vii. 62 Dave Lee had gone off in his van.

2. (Earlier example.)

1854 DICKENS *Hard Times* II. i. 143 Very heavy train and vast quantity of it [*sc.* luggage] in the van.

3. *van-guard*; **van pool** *U.S.*, a group of workers sharing a van provided by their employer to transport them to work; so *van-pooler, -pooling.*

1921 *Dict. Occup. Terms* (1927) § 723 *Van guard*.. travels with and guards contents of mail vans. **1931** *Daily Express* 22 Sept. 7/3 A vanguard..was accused of being concerned with another man..in stealing a motor-car. **1973** *Sunday Bull.* (Philadelphia) 7 Oct. (Parade Suppl.) 14/2 (*heading*) Van pooling. *Ibid.*, The 3M Company in St. Paul, Minn., bought six 12-passenger vans and assigned them to workers to form 'van pools'... Van pool driver-coordinators receive free rides and can use the van during off-duty hours. **1974** *Woman's Day* (N.Y.) Oct. 138/2 Van pools are working so well at Minnesota Mining and Manufacturing's huge complex..that the company now has fifty-seven company-owned vans. **1976** *National Observer* (U.S.) 16 Oct., Van pooling is a new commuting style looking for a permanent place in transportation between private cars and mass-transit facilities. **1983** *Mass Transit* (U.S.) Apr. 24/1 The average vanpooler saves about 400 miles of driving and 25 gallons of gas a month.

van (væn), *sb.*[5] *Lawn Tennis.* Abbrev. of VANTAGE *sb.* 6.

1927 in W. E. Collinson *Contemporary Eng.* 36. **1960** N. HILLIARD *Maori Girl* 47 They counted in lawn-tennis style with vans and loves. **1977** *Fremdsprachen* XXI. 125 Van in, van out: my van, your van.

vanadian (vănēɪ·diăn), *a. Min.* [f. VANAD(IUM + *-IAN.] Of a mineral: having a (usu. small) proportion of a constituent element replaced by vanadium.

1930 W. T. SCHALLER in *Amer. Mineralogist* XV. 572 Vanadium—vanadian. **1951** C. PALACHE et al. *Dana's Syst. Min.* (ed. 7) II. 1084 The so-called eosite from Leadhills, Scotland, apparently is a highly vanadian wulfenite.

vanadiate. (Earlier example.)

1833 *Rep. Brit. Assoc. Adv. Sci. 1832–3* 470 Vanadiate of lead.

vanadic. Add: (Earlier example.] Now *Obs.*

1833 *Rep. Brit. Assoc. Adv. Sci. 1832–3* 469 Vanadic acid..in the state of powder is yellow.

vanadium. (Earlier example.)

1833 *Rep. Brit. Assoc. Adv. Sci. 1832–3* 468 Vanadium ..was discovered by Sefström towards the end of 1830, in the iron from the forges of Eckersholm in Sweden.

vanadous, substitute for entry in Dict.:
vanadous (væ·nădɒs), *a. Chem.* [f. VANAD(IUM + -OUS.] Of or containing vanadium, *spec.* in an oxidation state of +2.

1850 H. WATTS tr. *Gmelin's Hand-bk. Chem.* IV. 90 (*heading*) Bisulphide of vanadium.—Vanadous sulphide. **1858** [in Dict.]. **1887** C. M. TIDY *Handbk. Mod. Chem.* (ed. 2) xvii. 504 Preparation [of Vanadium].—By heating vanadous chloride (VCl_3) in a current of dry hydrogen, air and moisture being excluded. **1927** *Amer. Mineralogist* XII. 236 There may also be assumed to be present..:..a vanadous acmite, $Na_2O{\cdot}V_2O_3{\cdot}4SiO_2$. **1954** *Thorpe's Dict. Appl. Chem.* (ed. 4) XI. 833/1 Vanadous Oxide, VO, has not been prepared pure. **1962** H. L. KERN et al. in A. Pirie *Lens Metabolism Rel. Cataract* 386 The tubes were.. gassed with N_2—CO_2 (95:5) from which the oxygen had been removed by passage through vanadous sulphate. **1980** *Jrnl. Amer. Chem. Soc.* CII. 3035/1 The change from a d^4 (chromous) to a d^3 (vanadous) ion results in a profound change in the stoichiometry.

Van Allen (væn æ·lĕn). Also (*erron.*) **van Allen.** The name of James A. *Van Allen* (b. 1914), U.S. physicist, used *attrib.* to designate each of two regions reported by him in 1958, partly surrounding the earth at heights of several thousand kilometres and containing intense radiation and many high-energy charged particles trapped by the earth's magnetic field; also applied to similar regions around other planets.

1959 *Nature* 8 Aug. 439 (*heading*) The upper boundary of the Van Allen radiation belts. **1965** *Wireless World* Sept. 447/1 This [sensitivity to radiation damage] limits the application of junction detectors in reactor instrumentation and in the van Allen belts. **1971** *Nature* 28 May 217/2 The circular polarization of about one per cent which is emitted by the planet Jupiter indicates the presence of a field of 0·4 gauss in its van Allen belts. **1974** *Times Lit. Suppl.* 13 Sept. 968/2 It girds us Transparently like the Van Allen Belt, Simply like the tie-belt of a mac. **1983** *New Scientist* 13 Jan. 93/2 They penetrated the Van Allen radiation belt (which is contained by the Earth's magnetic field) and loosened showers of electrons.

vanaspati (vănɒ·spăti). [Skr. *vánas-páti*, lord of the wood, forest tree.] A vegetable ghee used in India. Also *attrib.*

1949 *Food Manufacture* XXIV. 500/2 On account of the shortage of butterfat in India, the consumption of hydrogenated oils, known locally as *vanaspatis*, has recently been greatly increased. **1969** *National Herald* (New Delhi) 29 July 9/3 Oils and seeds sought lower levels following fears of nationalization of the vanaspati industry. **1973** *Indian Express* (Bombay) 29 Oct. 4/5 Several temples used vanaspati instead of ghee to keep the lamps before the deities burning. **1979** *Eastern Economist* 14 Sept. 534/1 Ensuring price stability as well as availability of vanaspati.

Vanbrughian (vænbrū·iăn), *a.* [f. the name of Sir John *Vanbrugh* (or *Vanburgh*) (see below) + -IAN.] Of, pertaining to, or characteristic of the architecture, landscaping, or plays of Sir John Vanbrugh (1664–1726). Also *ellipt.* as *sb.*, Vanbrughian style.

1947 J. LEES-MILNE *Diary* 3 July (1983) 178 The windows tame Vanbrughian. **1972** *Country Life* 5 Oct. 812 The heavy Doric frieze and Vanbrughian chimneypiece. **1979** *Garden* (Victoria & Albert Mus.) 63/2 Early in the twentieth century there was..a Vanbrughian [garden] mode. **1980** *Country Life* 17 July 243/2 A tale that is.. gorgeous, pyrotechnic, Vanbrughian.

vancomycin (væŋkomai·sin). *Pharm.* [f. *vanco-*, of unkn. origin + *-MYCIN.] A glycopeptide antibiotic produced by the actinomycete *Streptomyces orientalis* and active against most Gram-positive bacteria.

1956 M. H. MCCORMICK et al. in *Antibiotics Ann. 1955–6* 606 A new antimicrobial agent, vancomycin, has been isolated..from strains of *Streptomyces orientalis*, n. sp. **1974** R. M. KIRK et al. *Surgery* ii. 29/1 Vancomycin is effective against some penicillin-resistant staphylococci but is too toxic for routine use. **1982** *Brit. Med. Jrnl.* 22 May 1508/2 In the past few years..vancomycin has re-emerged as a valuable antibiotic in three clinical settings: endocarditis, multiresistant staphylococcal infections, and as the first-line treatment of pseudomembranous colitis.

Vandal, *sb.* Add: (With small initial.) **2. b.** *attrib.* and *Comb.*, as *vandal-proof*, *-resistant* adjs.

1971 H. PACY *Road Accidents* iv. 115 A vandalproof phone, consisting of a loudspeaker and microphone sheltered behind heavy steel grids. **1977** *Linlithgowshire Jrnl. & Gaz.* 15 Apr. 3/5 We have tried to make the hall vandal-proof by introducing a number of safeguards. **1977** C. BRANDRETH *Parking Law* 50 Boston (Mass.)..have vandal-resistant meters, the coins encased in a heavy iron box.

vandalistic, *a.* Add: Hence **vandali·stically** *adv.*

1922 *Weekly Dispatch* 10 Dec. 7 Drew a picture of Spion Kop, of myself,..and others of the party on the table-cloth... One of the party began vandalistically to cut the square out of the cloth. **1970** J. STEER *Conc. Hist. Venetian Painting* v. 134 The *Presentation of the Virgin* [by Titian]..still hangs in the position for which it was designed, although a hole has been vandalistically cut in the left-hand side to make room for an extra door. **1980** *Times* 30 Aug. 10/3 Customers who behave so inconsiderately, not to say vandalistically.

vandalization. Add: Also, an act of vandalism.

1984 *Times* 16 June 18/8 We know one couple who finally gave in to silent local pressure to move out (five break-ins..two vandalizations).

vandalize, *v.* Add: (Later examples.)

1905 *Chambers's Jrnl.* Dec. 17/1 A very remarkable church, spoilt and vandalised by the introduction of galleries and deal pews. **1968** *Wall Street Jrnl.* 19 Feb. 1/1 These militants roamed the campus, vandalizing the bookstore and a dining hall and terrorizing students. **1971** J. WAINWRIGHT *Last Buccaneer* I. 48 He had to run more than a mile before he could find a kiosk which had not been vandalised. **1978** *Daily Tel.* 17 Aug. 2/8 Newcastle..is to incur even heavier expenditure by importing more costly American [parking] meters said to be harder to vandalise.

Hence **va·ndalized** *ppl. a.*, **va·ndalizing** *vbl. sb.*

1971 *Oxford Times* 13 Aug. 5/7 In a two-week campaign they restored 21 vandalised kiosks to working order. **1979** U. CURTISS *Menace Within* xvi. 169 Inquiries..in connection with the vandalizing of a local school. **1984** *Times* 8 Oct. 14/3 In Minster Court, Liverpool, buyers rushed for well landscaped flats in what had been a vandalized estate.

van de Graaff (væn də grɑf). Also **Van de Graaff.** The name of R. J. *van de Graaff* (1901–67), U.S. physicist, used *attrib.* and *absol.* to designate a machine devised by him for generating electrostatic charge by means of a vertical endless belt which collects charge at its lower end from needle points connected to a voltage source and carries it to similar points at the top connected to the inside of a metal dome, whose potential is thereby increased; also a particle accelerator based on this machine.

1934 *Rev. Sci. Instruments* V. 18/1 The paper discusses the design and construction of a Van de Graaff electrostatic generator capable of an output of 500 microamperes and more than a million volts. **1961** G. R. CHOPPIN *Exper. Nuclear Chem.* xii. 193 Positive ions..are obtainable in cyclotrons as well as Van de Graaff and linear accelerators. **1973** *Physics Bull.* Dec. 722/1 Both tandem van de Graaffs and cyclotrons currently accelerate a variety of high quality beams. **1980** J. W. HILL *Intermediate Physics* xviii. 172 Two metal plates about 5–7 cm apart are..connected to..earth and the dome of a Van de Graaff generator.

vandendriesscheite (vændĕndrī·ʃ(ə)ait). *Min.* [a. F. *vandendriesscheite* (J. F. Vaes 1947, in *Ann. de la Soc. géol. de Belgique: Bull.* LXX. 217), f. the name of A. *Vandendriessche* (1914–40), Belgian mineralogist: see -ITE[1].] A hydrated oxide of lead and hexavalent uranium, $PbU_7O_{22}.12H_2O$, found as orange orthorhombic crystals.

1947 *Mineral. Abstr.* X. 146 Vandendriesscheite,.. pseudo-hexagonal barrel-shaped crystals, perfect cleavage. **1971** *Ibid.* XXII. 158/2 Among the secondary V- and Th-minerals occurring in the uraninite-bearing pegmatite at Einerkilen [in Norway], the following have been identified..: thorogummite, vandendriesscheite, [etc.].

Vanderbilt (væ·ndəɹbilt). [Name of Cornelius *Vanderbilt* (1794–1877), U.S. railway magnate, and his descendants.] One who resembles a member of the Vanderbilt family in being exceptionally rich; a millionaire. So **Va·nderbilter.**

1885, 1910 [see *ROTHSCHILD I]. **1975** M. AMIS *Dead Babies* xv. 73 So then of course some Vanderbilters get along from Nashville and Skip starts to hang out with them.

Van der Hum (væn dəɹ hɒ·m). Also **Vanderhum,** † **vanrhum.** [perh. a personal name.] A South African brandy-based liqueur made with nartjies.

1861 *Let.* 14 Oct. in *Cape Monthly Mag.* (1870) Oct. 225 Mrs M...has even promised to show me how to brew liqueurs, and distil 'vanrhum',—the latter a most aromatic and powerful *elixir vitæ*. **1893** KIPLING *Many Inventions* 330 Judson's best Vanderhum, which is Cape brandy ten years in the bottle, flavoured with orange-peel and spices. **1913** D. FAIRBRIDGE *That which hath Been* xxi. 240 If you want a *zoopje* there is Van der Hum on the table yonder and a bottle of old dop. **1949** A. WILSON *Wrong Set* 41 Wait..till he tasted the Van Der Hum after the meal, then he would see what the Union could do. **1966** [see *NARTJIE]. **1978** K. BONFIGLIOLI *All Tea in China* xi. 141 A black, fat-bellied bottle of something called 'Van Der Hums' which he had prudently laid in at the Cape.

van der Waals (væn dəɹ vā·ls). *Physics.* Also **Van der Waals.** The name of Johannes *van der Waals* (1837–1923), Dutch physicist, used *attrib.* and in the possessive to designate (*a*) an equation of state of a gas (proposed by him in 1873) that allows for intermolecular attraction and finite molecular size, viz. $(p + a/V^2)(V - b) = RT$ (where p is the pressure, V the volume, R the gas constant, T the absolute temperature, and a and b are constants); (*b*) short-range attractive forces between uncharged molecules arising from interaction between (actual or induced) electric dipole moments; so *van der Waals attraction*, etc.

1895 C. S. PALMER tr. *Nernst's Theoret. Chem.* II. ii. 186 The equation assumes the form $(p+a/v^2)(v-b) = RT$. This is van der Waals' equation of condition. **1923** *Jrnl. Chem. Soc.* CXXIII. 3403 At the critical point in particular, Van der Waals's equation predicts that pv will be $2\frac{2}{3}$ times as great as the value given by the simple law of Boyle. **1930** *Engineering* 5 Dec. 700/3 There were, further, different types of cohesion forces. (1) Van der Waals cohesion. **1964** J. W. LINNETT *Electronic Struct. Molecules* ii. 28 No chemical bond is formed and, except for a weak van der Waals (polarization) attraction at large distances, the two atoms repel one another. **1965** P. CAWS *Philos. of Sci.* xxii. 166 The gas law..is hopelessly inadequate in most cases, and has to be replaced by Van der Waals' equation..which is itself only approximately valid. **1979** *Sci. Amer.* Dec. 145/1 If the sauce is kept cool, the colloidal particles are unlikely to touch one another with a frequency that would allow the van der Waals forces to make them coalesce into pools of butter.

Vandyke, *sb.* Add: Also **Van Dyke.** **5*.** = *Vandyke beard.*

1909 in WEBSTER. **1933** H. ALLEN *Anthony Adverse* III. VIII. lix. 949 A carefully trained moustache and a vandyke turning white contrived to be at once distinguished and benign. **1951** E. PAUL *Springtime in Paris* xi. 204 The 'Zazous' quarter surpasses even Oberammergau, as far as beards are concerned... The hearties have stiff whiskers, and some of the Central and South American boys sport silken Van Dykes. **1974** P. DE VRIES *Glory of Hummingbird* xvi. 252 A false mustache and Vandyke..completed the transformation. **1982** S. B. FLEXNER *Listening to Amer.* 65 The first group mainly wore short *Imperials* or waxed and pomaded *Van Dykes*.

Hence **Van Dy·ckian,** pertaining to or characteristic of the paintings of Vandyke.

1942 *Burlington Mag.* Feb. 43/2 The stage effects of court painting in the Van Dyckian vein. **1979** *N. & Q.* Feb. 71/2 The pose..is pure convention: a Van Dyckian cliché lifted from Van Dyck's etching of Pieter Brueghel the Younger.

vanette (væne·t). [f. VAN *sb.*[3] + -ETTE.] A small van.

1921 *Glasgow Herald* 23 July 8 A company..were sent out from Jandola, followed..by Lewis guns in vanettes and an armoured motor car. **1957** V. W. TURNER *Schism & Continuity in Afr. Society* v. 147 Once Mukanza was in my vanette he was my responsibility and no longer that of the village members.

Van Gelder (væn ge·ldəɹ). The name of a Dutch paper-maker, used *attrib.* and *absol.* to designate a fine handmade paper with deckle edges.

1892 in G. Meredith *Jump to Glory Jane* 2 This edition is limited to an issue of 1,000 copies..and a special issue of 100 copies on Van Gelder paper. **1928** S. J. LOOKER *Booklover's Catal.* Jan. 6 Long Ago, First American Edition,..one of 925 copies on Van Gelder paper. **1934** H.

HILER *Notes Technique Painting* iii. 224 Some good papers for practical working are cartridge, Whatman,.. Van Gelder, [etc.]. **1960** G. A. GLAISTER *Gloss. Bk.* 429/2 *Van Gelder*, one of the most famous of all hand-made papers, produced for a century or more in Holland and said to contain 100% rag. It is used by artists and publishers of fine editions. **1974** *Country Life* 17 Jan. 75/1 The..tragic etching of 1904, *Le Repas Frugal* on van Gelder paper.

vanguard. Add: **1. c.** In *Communism*, the elite party cadre which, according to Lenin, would be used to organize the masses as a revolutionary force and to give effect to communist planning.

1928 E. & C. PAUL tr. *Stalin's Leninism* I. 95 As far back as 1902, foreseeing the special role of our Party, he [*sc.* Lenin] thought it necessary to point out that: Only a party guided by an advanced theory can act as vanguard in the fight. **1941** tr. *Lenin's One Step Forward* 85 The stronger our Party organizations..the richer..will be the influence of the Party on the elements of the working class *masses*..guided by it. After all, the Party, as the vanguard of the working class, must not be confused with the entire class. **1952** P. SELZNICK *Organizational Weapon* 10 Only the vanguard is exposed to a full statement of communist aims and methods. **1973** C. D. KERNIG *Marxism, Communism & Western Soc.* VIII. 270/1 The vanguard proves itself both in and after the victorious proletarian revolution by taking over the leadership in all spheres of life.

d. The name of a political party in Northern Ireland, representing a secession from Ulster Unionism. Freq. *attrib.*

1972 *Times* 14 Feb. 2/4 A crowd of 1,500 attended a rally called by Mr William Craig, MP for Larne, who has founded what he calls the Vanguard Movement. *Ibid.* 13 Mar. 1/4 When it began three months ago, Vanguard was described by one Government minister as a 'comic opera'. **1973** *Times* 31 Mar. 1/2 Mr William Craig... chose the steps of Stormont to announce the formation of the Vanguard Unionist Progressive Party. **1975** BUTLER & SLOMAN *Brit. Political Facts* (ed. 4) xvi. 354 On June 28, 1973 the..Assembly was elected; its composition was 22 Ulster Unionist..15 Loyalist Coalition (7 Vanguard.. 8 Democratic Unionist), [etc.]. **1982** M. WALLACE *Brit. Govt. in Northern Ireland* vii. 133 The Vanguard Unionists had decided in November 1977 to return to the official Unionist Party, while remaining a 'movement'.

attrib. (Further examples: cf. *AVANT-GARDE 2.)

1958 *Times* 9 Sept. 5/1 But it was not the pretentious nonsense that so often passes for 'vanguard' culture. **1977** *Guardian Weekly* 16 Oct. 19/3 One prominent vanguard dealer in London..had only sold one single work so far this year. **1980** *Listener* 13 Nov. 648/3 Today, vanguard art seems to have lost its 'political' role.

Hence **va·nguardism**, the quality of being in the vanguard of a political, cultural, or artistic movement (cf. *AVANT-GARDISM); **va·nguardist**, a person in the vanguard of a political, cultural, or artistic movement; also *attrib.* or as *adj.*; (cf. *AVANT-GARDIST(E)).

1934 WEBSTER, Vangdguardist. **1952** P. SELZNICK *Organizational Weapon* ii. 91 (*heading*) Vanguardism in semicolonial areas. **1964** *Spectator* 15 May 664/1 It is not true that this complex personality comes out of the same box as Rauschenberg. That vanguardist exclaims, 'Hell, what a marvellous universe.' **1971** *New Yorker* 16 Oct. 148/2 The integration of art and non-art is the essence of twentieth-century vanguardism in art. **1976** *Ibid.* 12 Jan. 22/1 Just being there must make the average armchair nihilist want to argue with his fellow-man over the merits of anarcho-syndicalism, vanguardism, and radical conformism. **1976** *Spare Rib* Nov. 21/1 After wading through some vanguardist rhetoric, and an informal discussion.. things became even more complicated. **1981** *Times Lit. Suppl.* 24 Apr. 465 (*heading*) From vanguardism to fascism.

vanilla. Add: **3. c.** A vanilla ice cream.

1955 T. STERLING *Evil of Day* viii. 84 You should go to Schrafft's for a plain vanilla with marshmallow sauce. **1970** *Guardian* 13 July 9/3 They'll have a vanilla, our Ethel, ta.

4. *vanilla ice cream*; *vanilla-flavoured*, *-sweet* adjs.; **vanilla slice**, an oblong pastry containing custard flavoured with vanilla and usu. iced.

1972 *Harrods Christmas Catal.* 59/4 French marrons in vanilla flavoured syrup. **1974** L. DEIGHTON *Spy Story* xix. 207 That big vanilla-flavoured ice-cream sundae. **1904** Vanilla ice cream [see *SUNDAE]. **1911** [see **Neapolitan ice*]. **1974** *Times* 6 Apr. 12/5 Serve the oranges very cold with vanilla ice cream. **1930** *Radiation Cookery Book* (ed. 12) vii. 119 Vanilla Slices. *Ingredients*—½ lb. puff paste. A few drops vanilla, ½ pint thick custard... When the pastry is cool, spread the custard on one strip and put the second strip over the top; cover with icing, and cut with a sharp knife in strips about 2 inches wide. **1979** *This England* Winter 19/1 I've brought you one of your favourite vanilla slices as well! **1940** L. MACNEICE *Plant & Phantom* (1941) 59 All her vanilla-sweet forgotten vaudeville nights.

b. Passing into *adj.*: vanilla-coloured, vanilla-flavoured. (Not clearly distinguishable from some of the quots. in sense 4 a.)

1946 A. CHRISTIE *Come, tell me how you Live* viii. 133 A vanilla soufflé, for a wonder, goes right. **1962** Vanilla soda [see *SODA[1] 4 b]. **1980** H. ENGEL *Suicide Murders* xviii. 121, I ordered a vanilla marshmallow sundae and a vanilla milkshake. **1982** M. RUSSELL *All Part of Service* iii. 23 A box of vanilla fudge. **1984** *Guardian* 5 Oct. 17/8 Old-fashioned vanilla sundae with hot fudge sauce.

vanillyl (væ·nilil). *Chem.* and *Biochem.* [f. VANILL(IC *a.*, -IN + -YL.] The radical, $OCH_3C_6H_3(OH)CH<$, derived from vanillin; *vanillylmandelic acid* [MANDELIC *a.*], the end-product of the metabolism of adrenaline and noradrenaline, measured to test for certain tumours; 4-hydroxy-3-methoxymandelic acid, $OCH_3C_6H_3(OH)CH(OH)COOH$.

1876 *Jrnl. Chem. Soc.* XXIX. 76 This body, which is still under investigation, is vanillyl alcohol. **1932** *Jrnl. Pharmacol. & Exper. Therapeutics* XLV. 165 The salts of vanillyl-ethylamine and methylamine were found to be quite soluble. [**1957** ARMSTRONG & MCMILLAN in *Pharmacol. Rev.* XI. 395 Because of the cumbersome nature of the proper name for this compound..the trivial name 'vanilmandelic acid' is proposed, and the abbreviation 'VMA'.] **1961** *Clin. Chem.* VII. 257 The determination of 3-methoxy-4-hydroxymandelic acid, also called vanillylmandelic acid (VMA), in urine has recently come into use as a confirmatory test for pleochromocytoma. **1979** *Nature* 1 Mar. 41/2 Many oxidative degradations have also been carried out to break coal down into simpler species; however, isolation and identification of *p*-hydroxyl (IV), vanillyl (V), and syringyl (VI) groups, which are characteristic lignin oxidation products, have not yet been confirmed. **1979** *Jrnl. R. Soc. Med.* LXXII. 533 Twenty-four hour urinary vanillylmandelic acid (VMA) estimations were within normal limits.

vanish, *sb.* **1.** (Later example.)

1872 'MARK TWAIN' *Roughing It* iii. 33 He..left for San Francisco at a speed which can only be described as a flash and a vanish.

vanish, *v.* **4.** Delete 'Now *rare*' and add later examples, chiefly with reference to conjuring.

1934 H. G. WELLS *Exper. Autobiogr.* I. v. 264 Lenin conjured government by mass-democracy out of sight, 'vanished' it as conjurors say, by his reorganization of the Communist Party. **1949** [see *DISAPPEAR *v.* 3]. **1981** *Daily Tel.* 4 Jan. 6/8 Thurston..could make a girl disappear from a cage suspended in mid-air, or vanish a girl playing a piano (and the piano).

vanishing, *vbl. sb.* Add: **2.** *vanishing point*: also *fig.*

1913 *Times* 7 Aug. 8/2 The danger of operation, *gas* operation, is retreating to a vanishing point. **1963** *Lancet* 12 Jan. 96/2 Routine application of this test reduces to vanishing-point the mortality from air embolism during neurosurgery in the sitting position.

3. *vanishing act, trick.*

1923 H. C. BAILEY *Mr. Fortune's Practice* vi. 160 She goes off walking at night with nothing but what she stood up in. If you ask me to believe she meant to do the vanishing act..I can't see how it's likely. **1981** P. MALLORY *Killing Matter* vii. 79 He's chosen to pull a vanishing act just when the painting is lifted. **1973** G. SIMS *Hunters Point* xviii. 174 At the end of the path Jaeckel disappeared and it was Buchanan's turn to stop, momentarily at a loss..mystified by the vanishing trick.

vanishing, *ppl. a.* Add: **3.** *vanishing cream*, a cosmetic cream that is readily absorbed by the skin; also *fig.*

1916 *Daily Colonist* (Victoria, B.C.) 11 July 14/5 (Advt.), Pond's Vanishing Cream. **1923** W. A. POUCHER *Perfumes & Cosmetics* III. vi. 390 *Vanishing Creams*.. consist of stearic acid, partially saponified with alkali, the bulk of the fatty acid being emulsified by the soap thus formed. *a* **1951** in M. McLuhan *Mech. Bride* (1967) 47/2 It's like your wife's vanishing cream—not greasy or sticky. **1981** E. AMBLER *Care of Time* ix. 149 If his luck holds, he's getting the defectors' vanishing-cream treatment..somewhere in North America.

‖ **vanitas** (væ·nitās). [L., lit. 'vanity, emptiness'.] **1.** *vanitas vanitatum* (from the Vulgate transl. of Eccles. i. 2): vanity of vanities, an exclamation of disillusionment or pessimism; futility.

1565 J. JEWEL *Replie unto M. Hardinges Answeare* iii. 164 This labour may well be called *Vanitas vanitatum*. **1848** THACKERAY *Vanity Fair* lxvii. 624 Ah! *Vanitas Vanitatum!* Which of us is happy in this world? Which of us has his desire? or, having it, is satisfied? **1910** CHESTERTON *G. B. Shaw* 105 In Shakespeare he saw nothing but profligate pessimism, the *vanitas vanitatum* of a disappointed voluptuary. **1978** H. SHAW in *Islands* (N.Z.) Aug. 105 Ah *Vanitas! Vanitatum!* All had been so totally suppressed, yet..I *had* sensed certain emanations.

2. (Usu. with capital initial.) Used *attrib.* and *absol.* of a 17th-century Dutch genre of still-life painting that incorporated symbols of mortality or mutability.

1909 M. L. CLARKE tr. *Bode's Great Masters Dutch & Flem. Painting* 241 The artist [*sc.* J. Davidsz. de Heem] became a follower of the peculiar art movement of the older Leyden still-life painters, as several pictures of a 'Vanitas' show. *Ibid.* 239 The 'Vanitas' presentments required a monochrome treatment. **1942** *Burlington Mag.* Dec. 293/1 Paul..was a painter of some consequence, as shown for instance by his *Vanitas* still-life at Berlin (1636). **1947** BERGSTRÖM & TAYLOR tr. *Bergström's Dutch Still-Life Painting 17th Cent.* iv. 154 On account of its literary symbolism, often rather elaborate, the *Vanitas* occupies a special place among the forms of Dutch still-life painting. **1963** E. H. GOMBRICH *Meditations on Hobby Horse* 104 Is the spread of the genre [*sc.* still life] due to the religious appeal of the *vanitas* motif? *Ibid.*, Any painted still life is *ipso facto* also a *vanitas*. **1980** *Times* 13 Aug. 14/3 A painting by Frans Hals, 'Young Man Holding a Skull'..is a *vanitas*, a reminder of human vanity.

Vanitory (væ·nitǒri). orig. *U.S.* Also **vanitory.** [f. VANIT(Y + -ORY[1].] A proprietary name for a vanity unit.

1951 *Official Gaz.* (U.S. Patent Office) 13 Mar. 355/1 *Vanitory.* For combination dressing table–lavatory unit. **1958** *Trade Marks Jrnl.* 16 July 720/2 *Vanitory.* All goods included in class 11... 22nd November 1957. **1960** *Spectator* 26 Feb. 300 Bathing-dressing-rooms, complete with vanitories. **1961** *Ibid.* 10 Mar. 345 The appearance of Vanitory units in the ballroom as well as the bedroom for which they were designed. **1972** *House & Garden* Dec.–Jan. 82/1 One of the bathrooms..with built in vanitory unit. **1984** *Sunday Tel.* (Colour Suppl.) 29 Apr. 40/4 A roll-out bidet which, when not in use, is neatly concealed in a vanitory unit beneath the basin.

vanitous (væ·nĭtəs), *a. rare.* [f. VANITY + -OUS or ad. F. *vaniteux*.] = VAIN *a.* 4.

1900 G. MEREDITH *Let.* 12 July (1970) III. 1351 An accurate perception of foibles in those whom we love..is only a vindication of our intellect—the seeing in what way our hero or friend or beloved is a little vanitous and pretentious. **1905** *Ibid.* 30 July 1536 French criticism.. instructs without wounding any but the vanitous person. **1930** *Musical Times* 1 Mar. 210/2 It is only the very young, or the very vanitous, who think of making a world of themselves.

Hence **va·nitously** *adv.*

1939 V. WOOLF *Diary* 3 Mar. (1984) V. 207, I was pleased, vanitously, to find that Inez thinks me a poet-novelist.

vanity. Add: **4. b.** (Later example.)

1894 'MARK TWAIN' in *Century Mag.* June 236/1 The claim that the knife had been stolen was a vanity and a fraud.

5*. *N. Amer.* **a.** = *vanity table* (see sense 6 below). **b.** = *vanity unit* (sense 6 below).

(*a*) **1937** 'E. QUEEN' *Door Between* xiv. 148 She sat down before the vanity to cold-cream her face. **1967** 'V. SILLER' *Biltmore Call* 124 Her make-up and perfume bottles and jars were still on a kidney-shaped vanity.

(*b*) **1967** *Boston Sunday Herald* 26 Mar. (Advt.), Classic elegance for your bathroom is yours with this 30 × 20-in. vanity... Vitreous china top and bowl. **1977** *Chicago Tribune* 2 Oct. XII. 8/2 (Advt.), Ceramic tile baths and vanities. **1984** *Tampa* (Florida) *Tribune* 5 Apr. (Sears Suppl.) 9/3 Start your bath remodeling with this lovely vanity.

6. *vanity-bait*; **vanity bag** (examples); **vanity basin**, a wash-basin for a vanity unit; **vanity box** (examples); **vanity case** (examples); **vanity mirror,** (*a*) a small make-up mirror, *esp.* as a fitting in a motor vehicle; (*b*) a dressing-table mirror; **vanity number plate,** *U.S.* **vanity plate** (see quot. 1967); **vanity press, publisher** orig. *U.S.*, a publisher who publishes only at the author's expense; so *vanity publishing*; **vanity set,** (*a*) a set of cosmetics or toiletries; (*b*) *U.S.*, a matching bath and vanity unit; **vanity table,** a dressing-table; **vanity unit,** a unit comprising a wash-basin set into a fixed dressing-table.

1907 *Yesterday's Shopping* (1969) 404/1 The Vanity Bag. Containing on one side mirror, separate pocket for powder..with puff,..gusset pockets..for gold on other side, pocket for cards, papers, &c. **1946** K. TENNANT *Lost Haven* (1947) xviii. 295 The silver-beaded white vanity-bag that carried her money, her lipstick, her handkerchief. **1974** J. CLEARY *Peter's Pence* iii. 78 The note..had said she was spending the night with Fergus... She had taken a small vanity bag and slipped out of the apartment. **1816** JANE AUSTEN *Emma* II. xiv. 278, I should never have expected you to be lending your sanction to such vanity-baits for poor young ladies. **1972** *House & Garden* Dec.–Jan. 84/3 'Luxe' vanity basin..£11.25. **1912** G. R. CHESTER *Five Thousand an Hour* ii. 10 She carried her own vanity box. **1978** N. MARSH *Grave Mistake* iv. 136 A vanity box..lay on the table. **1913** S. STORY *Spirit of Paris* 52 The exquisite *femme du monde*..has a final glance at herself, 'vanity case' in hand. **1957** *Practical Wireless* XXXIII. 531/1 The Sky Casket by Every Ready ..is of the vanity-case type—no controls or other external components being visible. **1979** M. MCCARTHY *Cannibals & Missionaries* xi. 323 He had slipped a folded plan of the house..into Eloise's vanity case, under her powder-puff, camouflaged by a thick layer of face-powder. **1959** *Observer* 1 Mar. 21/5 Visors with vanity mirror are flush fitting. **1966** T. PYNCHON *Crying of Lot 49* i. 16 A half hour in front of her vanity mirror. **1971** 'D. HALLIDAY' *Dolly & Doctor Bird* viii. 100 The vanity mirror..was surrounded by fourteen ormulu makeup lamps. **1983** *Listener* 27 Oct. 25/2 (Advt.), Such thoughtful touches as an illuminated vanity mirror..and seat back map pockets are all standard. **1983** *Daily Tel.* 10 Oct. 13/4 They will sell you a personalised or 'vanity' number plate for as little as ten dollars. **1967** *Britannica Bk. of Year* (U.S.) 804/3 *Vanity plate,* an automobile license plate bearing distinctive letters, numbers, or a combination of these and usually available at extra cost. **1974** 'D. SHANNON' *Crime File* (1975) xi. 194 The drivers who wanted to pay extra.. could buy the vanity plates. **1969** C. ARMSTRONG *Seven Seats to Moon* vi. 61 Are you planning to pay that Vanity Press to publish your father's book? **1976** *N.Y. Times Bk. Rev.* 7 Mar. 12/2, I read this book with the kind of horrified fascination with which one reads vanity press confessions. **1922** HOLLIDAY & VAN RENSSELAER *Business of Writing* 138 Numerous devices are employed by the 'vanity publisher' to lead the innocent author on toward becoming famous in his own eyes and those of his friends. **1978** *Amer. N. & Q.* Nov. 45/2 There are all sorts of literary histories, ranging from the pathetic things by which vanity publishers con local authors into expenditures far beyond their means, up to the CHEL and comparable works. **1984** H. SPURLING *Secrets of Woman's*

Heart 19 Ivy placed *Pastors and Masters*..with a small firm of 'vanity' publishers called Heath Cranton in Fleet Lane, paying for publication herself. **1960** G. A. Glaister *Gloss. Bk.* 429/2 *Vanity publishing*, publishing on behalf of and at the expense of an author who pays for the production and often for the marketing of his book. **1981** V. Glendinning *Edith Sitwell* iii. 45 She had emerged from vanity publishing to the real thing... 'I have found a publisher.' **1930** A. P. Herbert *Water Gipsies* xix. 285 She lightly powdered her face. Lily had..given her a 'vanity set'. **1970** *Washington Post* 30 Sept. B11/6 (Advt.), New tub. Toilet and vanity set. **1979** D. Cook *Winter Doves* ii. i. 45 He had packed dolls' Vanity Sets into boxes. **1936** L. C. Douglas *White Banners* i. 9 The mirror of the vanity table. **1954** W. Tucker *Wild Talent* (1955) xiv. 183 A vanity table likewise revealed occupied drawers. **1980** L. Birnbach et al. *Official Preppy Handbk.* 191/2 Women's locker rooms often boast vanity tables with combs and face powder. **1973** Vanity unit [see *limed *ppl. a.* 2 b]. **1983** *Sunday Tel.* 21 Aug. 31/4 The property has modern conveniences, including..fitted kitchen, bathroom with vanity unit and plenty of power points throughout.

vanner[2]. Add: **2.** *N. Amer.* An owner or operator of a van, *esp.* one who uses the van for recreation.

1973 *Hot Rod* Nov. 71/3 Hot Rod editor Terry Cook and art director Jervis Hill indulged their..fantasies by forming vans into what may be the largest "Keep on Truckin'" ever created. The vanners were willing to help. **1976** *National Observer* (U.S.) 10 Apr. 15/1 Vanners.. converge on campgrounds and recreational areas every week end for van fetes all over the country. **1976** *Kingston* (Ontario) *Whig-Standard* 4 Aug. 25/3 Coming up for vanners in the area, are a few special events.

Vannetais (va·nte, ‖ vantę), *sb.* and *a.* [Fr., f. *Vannes* (see below).] (Designating) a dialect of Breton spoken in the region of Vannes in Brittany.

1953 K. H. Jackson *Lang. & Hist. in Early Britain* ii. xiv. 301 He argues that the change to *-ec* took place also in Vannetais. **1967** —— *Historical Phonol. of Breton* ii. i. 18 The Vannetais dialect coincides on the whole quite closely on the west with the diocesan boundary in the valley of the Ellé, as far north at least as near le Faouet. **1977** *Word* 1972 XXVIII. 14 The mixed character of the Vannetais dialect of Breton is explainable by the profound influence of these early Romance dialects. *Ibid.* 19 The area now occupied by Vannetais had less chance of retaining Gaulish than did the northwestern part of Brittany.

Vannic (væ·nik). [f. *Van*, the name of a town on the site of an ancient centre of Armenian civilization + -ic.] = *Khaldian b. Also as *adj.* Cf. *Urartian *sb.* and *a.*

1882 *Jrnl. R. Asiatic Soc.* 14 July 380 The Vannic inscriptions were noticed by Sir H. Rawlinson. **1888** A. H. Sayce *Hittites* vii. 134 The language of Ararat itself, the so-called Vannic, may belong to the same family of speech. **1897** W. H. Ward in H. von Hilprecht *Rec. Res. in Bible Lands* 172 We judge that the land of the Hittites, invaded by these Vannic kings, stretched along the upper course of the Euphrates. **1908**, etc. [see *Khaldian]. **1974** *Encycl. Brit. Macropædia* I. 832/2 The terms Chaldean and Vannic have also been used as designations for Urartian during earlier stages of research. **1977** C. F. & F. M. Voegelin *Classification & Index World's Lang.* 162 Vannic Haldean... Formerly spoken in the Mount Ararat region near Lake Van.

vanrhum, obs. var. *Van der Hum.

Vansittartism (vænsi·ta:tiz'm). [f. the name of Robert Gilbert *Vansittart* (1881–1957), English diplomat + -ism.] The foreign policy advocated by Sir Robert (later Lord) Vansittart, *spec.* with regard to the demilitarization of Germany. Also *transf.*

1941 *Economist* 27 Dec. 778/2 It is against this background that the futility of both Vansittartism and appeasement can best be judged. **1944** D. J. Enright in *Scrutiny* Spring 103 It is a fine thing to see their books published at a time when, among the circles of the learned, a kind of Vansittartism is beginning to pervade the sphere of culture. **1967** R. C. D. Jasper *George Bell* xiv. 261 Bell..had good cause to suspect that the Government had determined upon a policy of treating all Germans alike whether they were Nazis or not... And it was with 'Vansittartism' in mind that he wrote a letter to *The Sunday Times* on 20 January 1941. **1978** N. Rose *Vansittart* xii. 260 A prolonged occupation by the allied forces; the complete destruction of the German army; drastic control of German heavy industry; the total disarmament of Germany; and the re-education of the German people. This was the essence of Vansittartism.

So **Vansi·ttartite**, a supporter of the policy of Vansittart; also *attrib.* or as *adj.*

1942 *New Statesman* 7 Mar. 166/3 Those who were once appeasers and then Vansittartites. **1973** R. W. Clark *Einstein* xxi. 567 His..refusal to budge from an almost Vansittartite approach to Germany.

vantage, *sb.* Add: **3.** Also, a vantage-point.

1908 L. M. Montgomery *Anne of Green Gables* ii. 31 It was already quite dark, but not so dark that Mrs Rachel could not see them from her window vantage. **1969** M. Bragg *Hired Man* viii. 83 There were halloes every few minutes and the men themselves became hunters, climbing the heights in anticipation of a vantage which would give them a total view and enable them to race down when the kill was near.

6. (Further example.)

1904 J. P. Paret *Lawn Tennis* 352 *Vantage-in* (or vantage server). A term used to indicate that the server has won the 'vantage' point (opposite of 'vantage-out'). *Vantage-out* (or vantage striker) [etc.].

7. (sense 3) *vantage-nook.*

1930 Blunden *Summer's Fancy* 30 The many vantage-nooks That nature sets about the wooing weald.

van't Hoff (vænt hǭ·f). *Chem.* Also **Van't Höff.** The name of J. H. *van't Hoff* (1852–1911), Dutch chemist, used *attrib.* and in the possessive to designate rules or hypotheses put forward by him with reference to: **a.** Stereochemical properties of molecules.

1888 *Jrnl. Chem. Soc.* LIV. 597 (*heading*) Investigation of the second Van't Hoff hypothesis. **1979** A. Beknazarov tr. *Potapov's Stereochemistry* iv. 221 In the early thirties of our century there appeared data contradicting the van't Hoff second postulate—the assumption of free rotation about single bonds.

b. The osmotic pressure of solutes in solution.

1890 *Jrnl. Chem. Soc.* LVIII. 845 (*heading*) Deductions from Van't Hoff's theory. *Ibid.* 846 The author..discusses the determination of the value of *i* for solids in solution from Van't Hoff's equation. **1926** [see *lyotropic *a.* 1]. **1978** P. W. Atkins *Physical Chem.* viii. 223 The equation simplifies into the van't Hoff equation: $\Pi V = n_B RT$. The van't Hoff equation is very suggestive of the ideal gas equation.

c. The thermodynamics of chemical reactions.

1909 H. J. H. Fenton *Outl. Chem.* I. xiii. 159 Van't Hoff's 'principle of mobile equilibrium' is an application of this rule [of le Chatelier] to the case in which the imposed constraint is an alteration of temperature. **1923** *Chem. Abstr.* XVII. 2211 This [calculation] is offered as a kinetic explanation of van't Hoff's rule that for a temp. rise of 10° the speed of a reaction is doubled. **1978** P. W. Atkins *Physical Chem.* ix. 262 This [*sc.* the Gibbs–Helmholtz equation] immediately implies the van't Hoff equation.

¶ In Du. (rarely in Eng.) written *van 't Hoff.*

vanthoffite (vænthǭ·fəit). *Min.* [ad. G. *vanthoffit* (K. Kubierschky 1902, in *Sitzungsber. d. Preuss. Akad. d. Wissensch. zu Berlin* XXI. 407), f. the name of J. H. *van't Hoff, who first synthesized the compound: see -ite[1].] A sulphate of sodium and magnesium, $Na_6Mg(SO_4)_4$, found as colourless, grey, or pale yellow monoclinic crystals that are transparent with a vitreous lustre and occur esp. in oceanic salt deposits.

1902 *Jrnl. Chem. Soc.* LXXXII. ii. 406 The following salts are present in the mixture:..$3Na_2SO_4$, $MgSO_4$, to which the name *vanthoffite* is given. **1966** *Prof. Papers U.S. Geol. Survey* No. 550-b. 125/1 The halite rock in which the double sulfate minerals occur is medium to coarse grained... Loewite, vanthoffite, bloedite, and leonite are constituents of the ore zones.

Vanuatuan (vænwatū·an), *a.* [f. *Vanuatu* + -an.] Of or pertaining to the Vanuatu Republic (formerly the Condominium of the New Hebrides) or any of its constituent islands.

1980 *Sunday Times* 24 Aug. 1/1 Two British soldiers of the joint military force withdrawn from the rebel Vanuatuan island of Espiritu Santo on Monday have been charged with looting. **1983** *Defense & Foreign Affairs Weekly* 28 Mar. 4 Within an hour of hoisting its flag, the Vanuatuan naval ship was being 'peaceably escorted' out of the area.

vaporetto (væpore·to). Pl. **-etti, -ettos.** [It., dim. *vapore* f. L. *vapor* steam.] In Venice, a canal motor-boat (orig. steamboat), used as a form of public transport.

1926 C. Beaton *Diary* 25 Aug. in *Wandering Years* (1961) v. 121 We set off blindly, taking the *vaporetto.* **1941** W. Graham *Night Journey* v. 62, I can catch a vaporetto from the Quay. **1956** R. Macaulay *Towers of Trebizond* xxiv. 278, I remember it when there was nothing on the canals but gondolas, none of those horrid steamers and vaporetti. **1963** *Economist* 6 Apr. 37/1 The tourists.. prefer the speed of the municipally-owned vaporettos to the romance of the older hand-driven craft [*sc.* gondolas]. **1977** *Time* 28 Nov. 30/3 Other names..soon became household words at the staid Café Florian, on every *vaporetto* water bus and in the intellectual salons of the Salute island. **1984** *New Yorker* 23 Apr. 92/3 As soon as I got off the *vaporetto*, I felt that this was where I should be.

vapour, *sb.* Add: **1.** (Further examples. Cf. next sense.)

1845 *Encycl. Metrop.* IV. 246/2 Comparing a given space filled with gas, and another saturated with vapour, at a given temperature; if we suppose that space to be diminished, the gas will be compressed..but the vapour will be partly condensed. **1863** E. Atkinson tr. *Ganot's Elem. Treat. Physics* iv. i. 93 Heat..converts liquids.. into the aeriform state in which they obey all the laws of gases. This aeriform state of liquids is known by the name of *vapour*, while gases are bodies which, under ordinary temperature and pressure, remain in the aeriform state.

2. (Further examples.) In mod. scientific use, a fluid that fills a space like a gas but, being below its critical temperature, can be liquefied by pressure alone.

1823 Faraday in *Q. Jrnl. Sci., Lit., & Arts* XVI. 237 Now that we know the pressure of the vapour of chlorine, there can be no doubt that the following passage describes a true liquefaction of that gas. *Ibid.* 239 During the condensation of the gas in this manner, a liquid has been observed to deposit from it. It is not, however, a result of the liquefaction of the gas, but the deposition of a vapour (using the terms gas and vapour in their common acceptation) from it, and when taken out of the vessel it remains liquid at common temperatures and pressures. **1823** H. Davy in *Phil. Trans. R. Soc.* CXIII. 165 The compression [of gases] resulting from their slow generation in close vessels..may be easily assisted by artificial cold in cases where gases approach near to that point of compression and temperature at which they become vapours. **1883** E. Atkinson tr. *Ganot's Elem. Treat. Physics* (ed. 11) vi. v. 312 A vapour may be defined as being a gas at any temperature below its critical point. Hence a vapour can be converted into a liquid by pressure alone, and can therefore exist in the pressure of its own liquid, while a gas requires cooling as well as pressure to convert it into a liquid. **1979** T. B. Akrill et al. *Physics* xi. 141/1 It is *conventional* to use the term *vapour* to describe a gas which is at a temperature below the critical temperature for that substance, but there is no obvious difference between a vapour just below T_c..and a gas just above T_c.

4. For † *Obs.* read 'Now *rare*'. (Later examples.)

1841 J. Romilly *Diary* 16 Apr. (1967) 214 Ray.. reminded me I had said I w[d] give a Guinea when the Peterhouse wall was replaced by an iron-rail:—this work is now going on:—I had forgotten this vapour; but produced the Guinea. **1940** W. B. Yeats *If I were Four-&-Twenty* iv. 8 Men whose lives had been changed by Balzac, perhaps because he cleared them of Utopian vapours.

5. a. *vapour-capacity, -phase, -pipe*; **vapour lock,** an interruption in the flow of a liquid through a pipe as a result of its vaporization; **vapour pressure,** the pressure exerted by a vapour; **vapour-proof** *a.*, impervious to vapour; **vapour tension** = *vapour pressure* above; **vapour trail,** a visible trail of condensed water vapour in the sky, in the wake of an aircraft; also *fig.*

1922 W. G. Kendrew *Climates of Continents* 215 The sea is then coolest relatively to the land, so that the vapour-capacity of air blowing from the sea is increased over the land. **1930** *S.A.E. Jrnl.* XXVII. 93/1 The more volatile a fuel, the greater will be the tendency to boil in the fuel-feed system as the engine warms up. If the fuel boils, then interruptions of flow due to vapour lock may be expected. **1951** O. Berthoud tr. *P. Clostermann's Big Show* 39 My jettison-tank gave out—probably a vapour-lock in the feed pipes. **1974** *Times* 22 Mar. 15/4 Filter King is said..to prevent carburettor flooding..and to prevent vapour 'lock'. **1946** *Nature* 19 Oct. 562/1 A process has been developed for the preparation of motor fuel and other petroleum products by a method based on vapour-phase cracking of the vegetable oils contained in seeds. **1964** N. G. Clark *Mod. Organic Chem.* xxv. 515 The vapour-phase nitration of propane. **1913** V. B. Lewes *Oil Fuel* 79 A horizontal cylindrical boiler with a dome from which a broad vapour-pipe leads the distilling vapours to the condensers. **1875** *Encycl. Brit.* III. 385/2 As regards the atmosphere, evaporation [of water] goes on until the maximum vapour pressure for the temperature has been attained, at which point the air is said to be saturated. **1978** P. W. Atkins *Physical Chem.* vii. 175 The vapour pressure of water at 100°C is 1 atm. **1946** *Sun* (Baltimore) 17 May 13/3 About a foot of earth was scraped away from the site and a layer of vapor-proof material placed on the ground. **1963** *Engineering* 16 Aug. 205/1 A heat resisting gasket..is fitted..to render the unit vapourproof and weatherproof. **1981** *Oil & Gas Jrnl.* 20 Apr. 167/2 The recorder case is made of die cast aluminum, and it's vapor-proof. [**1845** *Phil. Trans. R. Soc.* CXXXV. 169 Cyanogen..yielded on different occasions results of vaporous tension differing much from each other.] **1864** Vapour tension [in Dict.]. **1933** W. Lindgren *Mineral Deposits* (ed. 4) x. 116 Sudden separation of the gaseous phase will take place..only if the vapor tension of the solutions is greater than the external pressure. **1941** *Picture Post* 3 May 23/1 The vapour trails are left by the R.A.F. fighters weaving in and out of the German formation. **1948** L. Durrell *Let.* in *Spirit of Place* (1969) 98 Vapour-trails of cows on the pampas, desolation. **1977** W. McIlvanney *Laidlaw* xxvi. 115 The vapour trails left by interrupted conversations. **1979** C. Priest *Infinite Summer* 18 There, high in the blue, were several curling white vapour-trails, but no other sign of the German bombers.

b. *vapour-turbanned.*

1892 W. B. Yeats *Countess Kathleen* 125 Under that cold and vapour-turbanned steep.

vapouring, *vbl. sb.* **3.** (Earlier examples.)

1866 'Mark Twain' *Lett. from Hawaii* (1967) 118 All the good sound sense or point there was in his vaporings could have been boiled down into half a page of foolscap. *Ibid.* 242 The creature has got no sense, but his vaporings sound strangely plausible sometimes.

vaquero. Add: Also **vacero. 1.** (Earlier examples.)

1826 in E. C. Barker *Austin Papers* (1924) 1483 D[n] Luciano..rarely has communication with any one, except his Vaceros Comes to *Town* to *Hug* his Frigoña, once a month. **1831** F. W. Beechey *Narr. Voy. Pacific* II. 40 Intrusting their baggage to the care of two vaqueros (Indian cattle drivers) who were to accompany them.

var (vāɹ). *Canad.* Also **varr.** [dial. var. of Fir.] The balsam fir, *Abies balsamea.*

1793 P. Campbell *Trav. N. Amer.* 57 The men set to work, and..cut the crops of a species of ever green wood, which they call *varr* [in New Brunswick]. **1842** R. H. Bonnycastle *Newfoundland* II. 266 The bark of the.. var..was taken off. **1907** J. G. Millais *Newfoundland* iv. 99 Trees standing clear against a brown mass of tall 'vars' and spruces. **1959** *Atlantic Advocate* Jan. 74 In the feel of drawknife in wood, smoothing a shingle out of straight-grained var, there was something that smoothed the mind. **1982** *Evening Telegram* (St. John's, Newfoundland) 8 Feb. 24 Many an axe is biting into a piece of crooked var.

vara. Add: **2.** *Bullfighting.* A long spiked lance used by a picador.

1932 E. Hemingway *Death in Afternoon* i. 6 The picador can perform his mission with the spiked pole, or vara. **1934** R. Campbell *Broken Record* 83 Trident, vara, and lance. **1967** McCormick & Mascareñas *Compl. Aficionado* i. 20 It [*sc.* tercio] is used both of the entire *lidia* ('bull fight'..), which is said to be divided into the tercio of the *vara* (from the picador's long pole tipped by the pic), of the banderillas; and the faena. **1968** [see *morillo].

varactor (văræ·ktəɹ). *Electronics.* [f. *var-(iable re)actor.*] A reverse-biased *p–n* junction whose capacitance depends on the bias voltage in a definite way. Also called *varactor diode.*

1959 Pfann & Garrett in *Proc. IRE* XLVII. 2011/1 (*heading*) Semiconductor varactors using surface space-charge layers. **1965** *Wireless World* July 62 (Advt.), Elimination of manual tuning by a unique self-tuning system (using servo controlled varactor diodes). **1975** *Physics Bull.* Sept. 401/1 Varactor diodes are extensively used in voltage-variable tuning applications, such as in modern solid-state radio and television circuits. **1979** A. Bar-Lev *Semiconductors & Electronic Devices* xvii. 325 Varactors are also used for frequency multiplication or harmonic power generation in the microwave range.

varanus (væ·rănəs). [mod.L. (B. Merrem *Tentamen Systematis Amphibiorum* (1820) 58): see Varan.] = Varan. Cf. *goanna, *iguana 2, Monitor *sb.* 5 in Dict. and Suppl.

1934 A. Russell *Tramp-Royal in Wild Austral.* viii. 60 What should come scuttling across the track but a big varanus liazrd. **1953** A. Smith *Blind White Fish in Persia* vi. 99 A Varanus in fact, a type of lizard, but it had the appearance of a Rhinegold dragon.

vardo. Delete † *Obs.* and add: Also **varda.** [Romany.] Now *spec.* a gypsy caravan.

1934 P. Allingham *Cheapjack* vi. 59 As me brother David pointed out to me in the vardo afterwards, this 'ere finger called me a bastard—and he was right. **1940** [see *Reading 3]. **1977** *New Society* 29 Sept. 643/2 You know what a varda is. It's one of those painted wagons, drawn by horses, that gypsies donate to folk museums. **1980** R. Hill *Killing Kindness* xxvi. 263 Don't forget I'm pure bred Romany... To end my days sitting on the *vardo* steps puffing away at an old pipe. **1982** *Times* 30 Apr. 10/3 This 'ere Gorse Hill..was always too tiring for an 'orse after pullin' a *varda*..10 or 12 mles.

vargueño (vāɹgē¹·nyo). [ad. Sp. *bargueño, vargueño* adj., of Bargas, a village near Toledo, the former place of manufacture.] A kind of cabinet made in Spain in the 16th and 17th centuries, with numerous small compartments and drawers behind a fall front which opens out to form a writing surface.

1911 E. Foley *Bk. Decorative Furnit.* I. 159 Prominent amid the Hispano-Moresque decorative woodwork probably made by these Moorish craftsmen is the vargueño: a box with a door in front, evolved from the chest or hucha, and mounted on a stand. *Ibid.* 160 It has been reasonably conjectured that the vargueño cabinet took its title from the small town of Vargas, near Toledo. **1923** G. L. Hunter *Decorative Furnit.* ix. 265 The most distinctive piece of Spanish furniture is the vargueño. Like the two-story cabinets or highboys of other countries, it was a development from the chest. **1960** H. Hayward *Antique Coll.* 24/2 *Bargueño* or *vargueño*, Spanish cabinet with fall-front enclosing drawers and often mounted on a stand. **1975** *Oxf. Compan. Decorative Arts* 809/2 The most typical *vargueños* are in the Mudejar style... In 1568 the guilds of Mexico required a cabinet-maker to be able to make a *vargueño*..as a condition of qualification.

vari- (vēᵊ·ri), comb. form of Variable *a.* (in some words infl. by Variation or Various *a.*).

variable, *a.* and *sb.* Add: **A.** *adj.* **6. d.** *variable cost* (see quot. 1974).

1953 [see *prime cost* s.v. *prime *a.* 9 a]. **1967** A. Battersby *Network Analysis* (ed. 2) xii. 200 There are other cases which more closely resemble the variable-cost control, as when the number of men allocated to a job is variable and governs duration. **1969** D. C. Hague *Managerial Economics* i. 15 The remainder of total cost is made up of those costs that do vary with output—with what are therefore known as variable costs. **1974** *Terminol. Managem. & Financial Accountancy* (Inst. Cost & Managem. Accounts) 24 *Variable cost,* a cost which, in the aggregate, tends to vary in direct proportion to change in the volume of output or turnover.

9. Special collocations. **a.** In *attrib.* use, as *variable-area, -length, -reluctance, -speed.*

1920 *Flight* XII. 5/1 Variable area or variable camber wings—or other means for reducing the landing speed of a machine. **1957** Manvell & Huntley *Technique Film Music* iii. 171 This optical wedge is caused to oscillate over a light slit by the motion of the pendulums, producing a variable-area type of sound-track. **1959** E. M. McCormick *Digital Computer Primer* viii. 119 These difficulties are avoided in many business computers by organizing the storage to accommodate variable-length records. **1970** *Computers & Humanities* IV. 327 The data fields of the customer's data base in variable-length capability. **1980** C. S. French *Computer Sci.* xi. 60 Variable length records mean difficulties for the programmer but better utilisation of storage. **1959** W. S. Sharps *Dict. Cinematogr.* 138/1 A variable-reluctance microphone is a microphone which depends for its operation on variations in the reluctance of a magnetic circuit. **1875** Variable-speed [in Dict., sense 7 a]. **1978** P. Griffiths *Conc. Hist. Mod. Music* viii. 116 Cage went further and created..his *Imaginary Landscape no. 1,* in which musicians have to perform with frequency recordings on variable-speed turntables. **1984** B. Francis *AA Car Duffer's Guide* 67/2 A variable-speed fan is provided to boost the air-flow throughout the car's interior at low speeds.

b. *variable geometry,* a configuration of component parts that can be varied; *spec.* in *Aeronaut.* = *variable sweep* below; freq. *attrib.*; *variable-mu* adj. (Electronics), (of a valve) having an amplification factor that can be varied; *variable-pitch* adj., of or pertaining to † (*a*) a propeller in which the blades are shaped so that the pitch varies along their length (see quot. 1912) (*obs.*); (*b*) a propeller, fan, etc., in which the angle of the blades with respect to the direction of air flow can be adjusted, esp. while they are in motion; *variable sweep* (Aeronaut.), sweep (sense *14*) that can be varied during flight according to requirements; usu. *attrib.*

1957 *Jrnl. Brit. Interplanetary Soc.* XVI. 166 The design characteristics of such gliders may include..variable geometry lifting surfaces, to be very thin at high speeds and to have good lift properties at landing. **1963** *Times* 10 June 10/1 He believed that variable geometry would give a better aircraft. **1969** *Sci. Jrnl.* Apr. 48/1 The wing surface [of a bat's wing] is an elastic membrane of skin stretched between the four long fingers, with at least 11 movable joints in each wing. This very variable geometry permits a high degree of manoeuvrability and control. **1970** *New Scientist* 30 July 236 (*caption*) These drawings show the variable geometry of the air intake on the Olympus 593-3B engine. **1977** P. Way *Super-Celeste* 39 The rival to the Super-Celeste, the variable geometry wing F-24, was airborne again. **1930** Ballantine & Snow in *Proc. IRE* XVIII. 2102 (*heading*) Reduction of distortion and cross-talk in radio receivers by means of variable-mu tetrodes. **1962** [see *mu 2]. **1971** E. N. Lurch *Fundamentals of Electronics* (ed. 2) v. 143 The tube employing this special grid is termed cutoff, supercontrol, or variable-mu. **1912** Ledeboer & Hubbard tr. *Duchêne's Mech. of Aeroplane* vii. 197 M. Drzewiecki, with the idea of getting the maximum efficiency out of every part of the propeller, varies the pitch at each point so that the actual angle of incidence is everywhere the optimum angle. Propellers of this kind are known as variable-pitch propellers, and are consequently no longer true screws. **1918** W. H. Berry *Aircraft in War & Commerce* vii. 91 Worked in combination with a variable pitch propeller the gearbox would allow the pilot a range in power and speed. **1919** H. Shaw *Text-bk. Aeronaut.* xi. 147 In the variable pitch type, the blade angle is varied continuously from the hub outwards in such a way that the slip column of air is forced backwards with a velocity which is uniform throughout. **1952** [see *static thrust* s.v. *static *a.* 7]. **1971** *Daily Tel.* 4 Nov. 3 (Advt.), Variable pitch engine cooling fan. Large range to fit most popular cars. **1974** *Encycl. Brit. Micropædia* I. 375/1 Additional features have been engineered into variable-pitch propellers; first, the ability to feather..a propeller on an engine stopped in flight. **1954** *Economist* 11 Sept. 12/3 *Variable sweep.* After take-off with wings only partially swept, means are provided to sweep them back more sharply in flight. Strictly experimental. **1965** *New Scientist* 22 Apr. 217/1 The development of the variable-sweep wing in collaboration with the French might lead to a load-carrier of outstanding performance. **1966** *Economist* 22 Jan. 330/1 Massive, variable-sweep aircraft whose wings pivot around stanchions as thick as tree-trunks. **1978** D. Küchemann *Aerodynamic Design of Aircraft* iv. 120 E. von Holst flew models with various arrangements of variable sweep.

B. *sb.* **1. b.** *Computers.* A data item that can take on more than one value during or between programs and is stored in a particular designated area of memory; the area of memory itself; (also *variable name*) the name referring to such an item or location.

1837 C. Babbage in B. Randell *Origins Digital Computers* (1973) 23 The number of variables which can be contained within the store will depend on the length of the rack. **1843** *Scientific Mem.* III. 666 We have..written Variable with a capital letter when we use the word to signify a *column of the engine,* and variable with a small letter when we mean the *variable of a formula.* **1957** [see *subscript *sb.* 2 b]. **1967** Beckett & Hurt *Numerical Calculations & Algorithms* i. 23 Variable names are usually limited in length because they must be coded as numbers and space is required to store these numbers... The number of characters used to define a variable is arbitrary, provided that it does not exceed a given maximum. **1972** Bergman & Bruckner *Introd. Computers & Computer Programming* ix. 288 [In FORTRAN] the data locations are divided into constants and variables... Variables are locations into which we may read numbers or place (store) numbers at execution time. **1975** H. Katzan *Introd. Computer Sci.* v. 108 The names hours, rate, and pay are variables... A variable is an identifier that names a data item. **1979** *Sci. Amer.* Dec. 85/1 In programming languages a variable is not an item of data but a label for a location in the memory of the computer. The value of a variable at any moment is the information currently stored there. **1981** W. S. Davis *Computers & Business Information Processing* xiii. 234 A FORTRAN variable consists of from one to six letters or digits, the first of which must be a letter. **1982** Cooper & Clancy *Oh! Pascal!* i. 10 The variables that computers use are like the memory keys of hand calculators—they store values... Variables can hold different types of values, including integers.., characters.., or even logical values.

c. *Logic.* A symbol whose exact meaning or referend is unspecified, though the range of possible meanings usually is.

1910 Whitehead & Russell *Principia Mathematica* I. i. 4 In mathematical logic, any symbol whose meaning is not determinate is called a variable. *Ibid.,* If a statement is made about 'Mr A and Mr B', 'Mr A' and 'Mr B' are variables whose values are confined to men. **1937,** etc. [see *open *a.* (*adv.*) 11 j]. **1939** *Jrnl. Philos.* XXXVI. 702 Whereas the singular existence statement calls the alleged existent by name, e.g., 'Pegasus', the general existence statement does not; the reference is made rather by a variable '*x*', the logistical analogue of a pronoun 'which', 'something which'. **1954** A. J. Ayer *Philos. Ess.* ix. 216 The range of our ontological commitments may..be reduced by our ability to recast some of our existential statements in such a way that variables which take a certain type of value disappear from them. **1969** Feys & Fitch *Dict. Symbols Math. Logic* 6 In interpreting a formalized language it is usual to specify the respective ranges of the various variables of the language. **1978** S. Haack *Philos. Logics* iv. 39 In general, prefixing a quantifier binding one of its free variables to an open sentence with *n* free variables yields an open sentence with *n*−1 free variables.

Variac (vēᵊ·riæk). *Electr.* [f. Vari(able *a.* + *-ac,* perh. repr. *a.c.,* alternating current.] A proprietary name for a type of autotransformer in which the ratio of the input and output voltages can be varied.

1933 *Official Gaz.* (U.S. Patent Office) 26 Dec. 874/2 General Radio Company, Cambridge, Mass... *Variac* for transformers. **1938** *Trade Marks Jrnl.* 16 Feb. 188/2 *Variac*... Electrical transformers (not being machines). General Radio Company.., Cambridge, State of Massachusetts. **1943** *Electronic Engin.* XV. 516/3 The movement of the sliding contact on the Variac is effected by a small reversible motor. **1945** [see *interlock *sb.* 2 b]. **1983** *Sci. Amer.* Feb. 118/3, I plugged the immersion heater into a Variac so that I could experiment with the rate at which heat was released in the water.

‖ **varia lectio** (vēᵊ·ria le·ktio). Pl. **variae lectiones.** [L., fem. of *var-ius* Various *a.* + *lectio* reading: cf. Lection.] = *various reading* s.v. Various *a.* 8 d.

1652 N. Culverwel *Light of Nature* x. 81 'Tis some accurate piece that passes so many Criticks..without any *Variæ lectiones.* **1871** [see Q=*Quarto* 2 s.v. *Q II. 2 a]. **1969** R. Renehan *Greek Textual Crit.* 91 Some MSS have a *varia lectio* διακοιρανέοντα. **1980** *Times* 24 May 14/1 *The Book Collector*..is the place to read..about incunabula and..*variae lectiones.*

variance. Add: **I. 3. d.** *U.S. Law.* An official dispensation from a building regulation.

1925 *New Hampshire Public Laws* xlii. 191 To authorize upon appeal in specific cases such variance from the terms of the ordinance as will not be contrary to the public interest. **1938** *Atlantic Reporter* CC. 521 A literal enforcement of the ordinance may be disregarded to permit a variance, while conditions for an exception must be found in the ordinance and may not be varied. **1973** *N.Y. Law Jrnl.* 19 July 13/7 Judgment is granted in favor of the petitioner..directing the issuance of a variance for the installation of a second kitchen in the premises. **1977** *Sat. Rev.* (U.S.) 3 Sept. 47/3 The only hotel on the island [*sc.* Bermuda] ever given a variance to be built on a hilltop. The permission took 12 years to get.

e. *Econ.* The difference between actual and expected costs, profits, output, etc., in a statistical analysis.

1964 *Times Rev. Industry* Apr. 8/2 An expression of the variation between standard cost and actual achieved cost is called 'variance'. In 1951 under manual control the variance was 31.6 per cent. **1967** D. Goch in Wills & Yearsley *Handbk. Managem. Technol.* 145 The following example will illustrate the application of this method of variance analysis to an imaginary product. **1974** *Terminol. Managem. & Financial Accountancy* (Inst. Cost & Managem. Accountants) 13 *Variance analysis,* that part of variance accounting..which relates to the analysis into constituent parts of variances between planned and actual performance. **1978** *Accountants' Rec.* Dec. 15/1 Causal factors of the sales variance have been established by analysis... Sales variance analysis..provides data enabling management to reconsider its marketing philosophies.

4*. *Statistics.* The mean of the squares of the deviations of a set of quantities; the square of the standard deviation.

1918 R. A. Fisher in *Trans. R. Soc. Edin.* LII. 399 It is..desirable in analysing the causes of variability to deal with the square of the standard deviation as the measure of variability. We shall term this quantity the Variance. **1948** *New Biol.* IV. 34 Measurements of the resting blood pressure of a group of fifty young men... We compute the mean blood pressure and the variance of the observed values, the variance being a measure of scatter of values around the mean. **1970** *Nature* 25 July

376/2 Analysis of variance gave highly significant population and fertilizer effects. **1977** R. E. MEGILL *Introd. Risk Analysis* iii. 23 Because all values are squared in the variance the standard deviation is larger than the mean deviation.

variant, *sb.* Add: **1. b.** Also *spec.* a textual variation in two or more copies of a printed work (not necessarily implying reimpression).

1927 R. B. MCKERROW *Introd. Bibliogr.* II. vi. 208 Besides these added lines, *The Devil's Charter* exhibits a very large number of striking variants in different copies, some being mere corrections of literal errors, others important alterations in wording. **1953** C. HINMAN in *Shakespeare Q.* IV. 280, I have been able to construct an instrument which..has enabled me to collate well over a hundred folio pages a day for some months... Taking reasonable care, the investigator can hardly fail to note any variant, however minute, in two copies of the page being examined. **1972** P. GASKELL *New Introd. Bibliogr.* 357 Warner Barnes..machine-collated an average of six copies of each of his author's eighteen primary editions... In ten of them he found possible evidence of concealed.. reimpressions; in another four, variant states of the type not indicating reimpression... Most of the variants shown up by the machine were trivial.

variate (vēᵊ·riăt), *sb. Statistics.* [f. as VARIATE *a.*] † **a.** The value of an attribute common to a number of individuals in any one instance; an observed value of a variate (sense *b). *Obs.*

1899 C. B. DAVENPORT *Statistical Methods* i. 1 A variate is a single magnitude-determination of a character... Integral variates are magnitude-determinations of characters which from their nature are expressed in integers. Such magnitudes are determined by counting; *e.g.*, the number of teeth in a porpoise. **1906** R. H. LOCK *Rec. Progress Study of Variation* iv. 90 A variate is one of the separate numerical values from which a curve of variability can be constructed; the biometrician usually deals with some such number as 1,000 variates.

b. A quantity or attribute having a numerical value for each member of a population; *esp.* one for which the values occur according to a frequency distribution.

1909 *Biometrika* VII. 97 We have, σ_1 and σ_2 being the standard deviations of the two variates and r their correlation, $\bar{p} = r\sigma_1/\sigma_2\bar{q}$. **1925** R. A. FISHER *Statistical Methods for Res. Workers* i. 5 The variable quantity, such as the number of children, is called the variate, and the frequency distribution specifies how frequently the variate takes each of its possible values. **1952** *Sci. News* XXIV. 109 The histogram gives the frequency with which the weight, a variate, takes values in a certain range in the sample. **1968** [see *RANDOM *a.* 1 b]. **1971** *Brit. Med. Bull.* XXVII. 2/1 Epidemiology also has a contribution to make..to the study of attributes (or variates, as some call them) such as intelligence..and blood pressure.

variation. Add: **II. 8. b.** (Further examples.)

1810 R. WOODHOUSE *Treat. Isoperimetrical Probl.* ii. 23 If problems involving merely one property, the maximum, require the variation of two, and those involving two properties, the variation of three elements [etc.]. **1847** *Cambr. & Dublin Math. Jrnl.* I. 264 We have, in this case, by Lagrange's theory of the variation of the arbitrary constants, the formulæ $da/dt =$ [etc.]. **1918** H. C. PLUMMER *Introd. Treat. Dynamical Astron.* xii. 134 This is the foundation of Lagrange's method of the variation of arbitrary constants. **1966** H. POLLARD *Math. Introd. Celestial Mech.* iv. 91 We shall begin with the undisturbed system $\ddot{x}_1 = -x_2$, $\ddot{x}_2 = k^2x_1$, and apply the method of variation of parameters.

e. The difference between the values of a function at either end of a subinterval; the sum of such differences for all the non-overlapping subintervals into which a given interval is divided; the upper bound (if any) of this sum when all possible modes of subdividing the interval are considered.

1905 J. PIERPONT *Lect. Theory Functions Real Variables* I. xii. 349 An important class of limited integrable functions is formed by functions with limited variation. **1911** *Q. Jrnl. Pure & Appl. Math.* XLII. 57 Although in forming the positive (negative) variation over (a, b) we considered all possible sets of non-overlapping intervals, we may without loss of generality confine ourselves to sets consisting of a finite number of intervals only. **1946** H. & B. S. JEFFREYS *Methods Math. Physics* i. 23 The total variation is of interest since it is related to the condition for existence of a Stieltjes integral..and to the determination of the total length of a curve. **1971** E. R. PHILLIPS *Introd. Anal. & Integration Theory* ix. 251 Let us assume that the set of nonnegative variations..is bounded from above.

III. 13. b. *variation*, the amount by which some quantity changes in value, or the addition made to the quantity; *esp.* the change in a function when there is a small change in the variables or constituent functions of the function.

In the calculus of variations the function concerned is usu. an integral, and the aim is to find what relation between the variables in the integrand makes the integral a maximum or a minimum.

1810 R. WOODHOUSE *Treat. Isoperimetrical Probl.* iii. 45 The general form of these equations is, $P.bg - Q.ci + R.d\theta$, $d\theta$ being a variation of the ordinate similar to the variations bg and ci. **1814** J. TOPLIS tr. *Laplace's Treat. Analytical Mech.* ii. 46 Of all the curves along which a moving body, subjected to the forces P, Q, and R, can pass from one given point to another given point, it will describe that in which the variation of the integral $\int vds$ is nothing, and in which, consequently this integral is a minimum. **1834** [see *LEAST *a.* 1 e]. **1845** *Encycl. Metrop.* II. 209 To obtain the variation of a function of y we must write $y + \delta y$ for y, and having expanded the new function according to the powers of δy, subtract from it the original function, and the first term of the difference will be the variation required. **1934** W. V. HOUSTON *Princ. Math. Physics* v. 56 The variation of the integral is defined as its value when α has the infinitesimal value $\delta\alpha$, minus its value when α is zero. **1972** M. KLINE *Math. Thought* xxiv. 578 By equating the variation of the integral to zero and by using a crude limiting process to transform the resulting difference equation, he obtained the differential equation which must be satisfied by the minimizing arc.

14. b. *elegant variation*: in writing, the stylistic fault of studiedly avoiding repetition by using different words for the same thing. Also *transf.* and in ironic use.

1906 H. W. & F. G. FOWLER *King's English* iii. 178 The locking of arms is..only an elegant variation for clinging. **1926** H. W. FOWLER *Mod. Eng. Usage* 131/1 It is the second-rate writers..that are chiefly open to the allurements of elegant variation. **1947** PARTRIDGE *Usage & Abusage* 16/1 Mr Herd then picks on the device known as 'elegant variation'. 'If,' he says, 'the mayor has been mentioned, he makes further appearance as 'the civic chief', 'the leader of our official life'..and so on.' **1981** *Guardian Weekly* 5 July 21 Most of the costumes are.. elegant variations on dancers' practice dress. **1982** *Washington Post* 7 May D2/6 ... rarely occurs less than twice per page, and often as many as five, with a 'f---' or two stuck in for elegant variation.

c. *Ballet.* A solo dance.

1912 *Dancing Times* Aug. 420/2 [Grahn's] career was interrupted by an accident while rehearsing a *variation* which she was to perform at [a] benefit. **1948** *Ballet Ann.* II. 49 She attacks the formidable difficulties of the variation and adagio with an ease and confidence. **1980** 'M. FONTEYN' *Magic of Dance* 65 He makes the preparation for his 'variation', or solo, with utmost care and accuracy.

15. variation method *Physics*, a method for finding an approximate solution to Schrödinger's equation by varying the trial solutions to find which gives the lowest value for the energy and is therefore closest to the true solution; **variation order**, an order authorizing a change in an original order or contract (see quots.); **variation principle** *Physics*, the principle (employed in the variation method) that the energy corresponding to an arbitrary wave function cannot be less than the actual lowest energy of the system under consideration.

1935 PAULING & WILSON *Introd. Quantum Mech.* vii. 182 The variation method is..very frequently used to obtain approximate wave functions as well as approximate energy values. **1960** [see *quantum-chemical* adj. s.v. *QUANTUM 7 a]. **1974** P. W. ATKINS *Quanta* 96/2 With these approximations in hand the variation method is applied to determine the best linear combination of atomic π-orbitals to describe the structure of the molecule. **1940** *Chambers's Techn. Dict.* 886 *Variation order*,..a document giving authority for some alteration in work being done under contract. **1975** E. B. CEADEL in Barr & Line *Essays on Information & Libraries* iv. 58 Where a change is made in the contract arrangements, it is listed by the architect as a *variation order*, which is subsequently costed by the quantity surveyors. **1977** *Daily Tel.* 19 Nov. 3/2 An order was prepared..requiring him to leave by Nov. 17... The Home Secretary..had considered whether, instead of issuing a 'variation order', he should proceed under another provision of the Immigration Act 1971 with a view to deportation. **1923** Variation principle [see *quantum condition* s.v. *QUANTUM 7 a]. **1975** H. F. HAMEKA *Quantum Theory Chem. Bond* i. 28 We shall discuss the two methods of approximation that are most widely used in quantum chemistry, namely the variation principle and perturbation theory.

variational, *a.* Add: *spec.* with reference to VARIATION 13 b in Dict. and Suppl.

1897 *Acta Math.* XXI. 99 His substitution of the Variational Curve for the ellipse as the intermediate orbit is..of primary importance in the Lunar Theory. **1937** E. C. KEMBLE *Fund. Princ. Quantum Mech.* iv. 130 Let J denote the integral $J[y, \lambda]$... Let δy denote the first variation in $y(x)$... Let it be required to find a function $y(x)$ and a corresponding value for the parameter λ which satisfy the variational equation $\delta J = 0$. **1957** L. FOX *Numerical Solution Two-Point Boundary Probl.* viii. 259 With a single second-order equation we were able to fix both y_0 and y_1, so that y_n was a function only of λ, and by solving a variational equation for $\partial y/\partial\lambda$ we were able to alter λ systematically until a solution was obtained. **1962** C. S. OGILVY *Tomorrow's Math* ix. 125 Questions asking what shape, what path, or what form will yield a minimal or optimal result are known as variational problems. **1971** *Physics Bull.* Jan. 17/1 We introduce a trial wave-function ψ containing as many variational parameters as we feel to be necessary or sufficient, and then choose the values of these parameters in such a way that the Rayleigh ratio..shall be stationary.

variationist. Add: **1. b.** One who practises variation or introduces variety in anything.

1926 H. W. FOWLER *Mod. Eng. Usage* 132/1 The writers are confirmed variationists. **1928** J. Y. T. GREIG *Breaking Priscian's Head* 66 Mr Fowler..pokes fun at the 'elegant variationist'. **1981** *N.Y. Times* 25 Jan. II. 25/4 Johns is by nature a variationist—someone who hates to let a good idea go while there is still something that can be done with it. *Ibid.* 2 Oct. C28/6 It works wonderfully well in terms of Mr. Judd's skill as a variationist. Every one of the 10 sections of the work has the same basic set of themes.

2. One who studies variations in usage among different speakers of the same language.

1975 *Amer. Speech 1973* XLVIII. 37 What variationists have discovered is the extraordinary stylistic and sociological importance of such variation, and the apparently remarkable consistency with which the frequency of a given alternant is patterned throughout society and throughout an individual's stylistic repertoire. **1978** *Archivum Linguisticum* IX. 48 Committed variationists.. seem to disagree on how variation is to be incorporated into the grammar of a language. **1983** *Canadian Jrnl. Linguistics* XXVIII. 1. 82 It is not, however, a problem for the variationists, but for those who would arbitrarily reduce linguistics to a branch of cognitive psychology.

variceal (værisī·ăl), *a. Med.* [f. L. *varic-*, VARIX + -AL; *-eal* after *corneal, laryngeal*, etc.] Of, pertaining to, or involving a varix.

[**1947** *Jrnl. Amer. Med. Assoc.* 8 Nov. 630/1 (*heading*) Intraesophageal venous tamponage. Its use in a case of varical hemorrhage from the esophagus.] **1961** POSTLETHWAIT & SEALY *Surg. Esophagus* xii. 392/1 Others.. later used tamponade for control of variceal hemorrhage. **1981** *Brit. Med. Jrnl.* 17 Jan. 189/2 Haemorrhage from varices around an artificial intestinal stoma..is well documented... Variceal haemorrhage from a colostomy has been less frequently reported.

varicocelectomy (væ:rikosīle·ktŏmi). *Surg.* [f. VARICOCEL(E + *-ECTOMY.] An operation to remove a varicocele.

1894 GOULD *Med. Dict.* 1590/1 *Varicocelectomy*.., excision of a varicocele. **1950** A. I. DODSON *Urol. Surg.* (ed. 2) xliv. 719 (*heading*) Inguinal varicocelectomy. **1980** S. J. SILBER *How to get Pregnant* (1981) v 149 The first successful case of restoration of fertility after varicocelectomy.

varicap (vēᵊ·rikæp). *Electronics.* [f. *vari(able cap(acitance.*] = *VARACTOR.

1967 AEGERTER & HABIAN in *IEEE Trans. Broadcast & Television Receivers* Nov. 103/1 A varicap is a variable capacitance diode. **1975** G. J. KING *Audio Handbk.* iv. 98 Tuner-amplifiers in which varicaps are employed for tuning must also feature supply regulation. **1981** J. C. SPROTT *Introd. Mod. Electronics* vi. 137 A typical varicap has a capacitance that varies over about a factor of 10 in the picofarad range.

variegated, *ppl. a.* **1. c.** (Earlier example.)

1818 M. EDGEWORTH *Let.* 4 Oct. (1971) 107 All the varieties of trees and shrubs..he has now revealed to view—The tulip tree and acacia and variegated oak and.. the variegated rhododendron.

varietal, *a.* Add: **1.** Similarly in *Min.* with reference to minerals.

1933 [see *ŒLLACHERITE]. **1966** [see *CASWELLITE].

2. Of wine: made predominantly from a single variety of grape; also, of or pertaining to the vine or grape of a particular variety. orig. *U.S.*

1941 SCHOONMAKER & MARVEL *Amer. Wines* xi. 260 The expense of..certification could be borne by a small per-gallon tax levied upon varietal wine. *Ibid.*, Until it [*sc.* identification of the grape varieties grown in America] has been accomplished, a system of honest varietal labeling is virtually unattainable. **1955** J. STORM *Invitation to Wines* 72 The success of varietal wines in California has nfluenced some Eastern vintners. **1968** *Amer. Speech 1967* XLII. 80 Varietal types of wines. **1973** *Bulletin* (Sydney) 25 Aug. 7/2 (Advt.), An aromatic wine..with varietal flavour. **1979** A. HAILEY *Overload* III. v. 214 Among other things, Nim Goldman was a wine buff. He had a keen nose and palate and especially liked varietal wines from the Napa Valley. **1981** *Times* 2 Mar. 12/6 Limousin oak casks..contributed another complex dimension to its distinct varietal personality.

B. as *sb.* A wine made from a single variety of grape. orig. *U.S.*

1955 J. STORM *Invitation to Wines* 72 The wines labeled according to the name of the chief informing grape are called varietals. **1977** H. FAST *Immigrants* IV. 254 There is no need for you to try to produce a varietal, which simply means a wine produced out of a single variety of grape. **1977** *Times* 15 Nov. (Italian Wine Suppl.) p. iii/3 Lambrusco, the famous wine of Modena..is a varietal, the Lambrusco being the grape from which it is vinified. **1979** *Tucson* (Arizona) *Citizen* 28 Apr. (Weekender Mag.) 7/2 A 1977 Emerald Riesling..displayed a high acidity that may be typical of the varietal.

varietally *adv.* (later example).

1942 M. F. MABON *ABC of America's Wines* ii. 13 The majority of varietally named wines happen to be blends.

varietist (vărəi·ĕtist), *sb.* [f. VARIET(Y + -IST.] One who chooses variety, esp. in the satisfaction of (sexual) desires; also *attrib.* or as *adj.* Hence **vari·etism,** the practice or result of such choices.

1911 G. B. SHAW *Getting Married* Pref. 153 The reassurance that man is not promiscuous in his fancies must not blind us to the fact that he is (to use the word coined by certain American writers to describe themselves) something of a Varietist. **1925** T. DREISER *Amer. Tragedy* I. I. xiii. 101 So captivated was he by this savor of sensuality and varietism that was about her. **1968** *Ann. Amer. Acad. Pol. & Social Sci.* July 65/2 Some sexual varietists..believe that they *need* plural sex-love affairs. *Ibid.*, Such individuals manage to have their varietist inclinations fulfilled. *Ibid.* (*heading*) Sexual varietism. **1977** *N.Y. Rev. Bks.* 15 Sept. 26/2 'Free love' never meant libertinism..but quite simply that there should be no coercion in sexual relationships... There were 'exclusivists' and 'varietists'.

variety. Add: **8.** Also, this species of entertainment, including its presentation on radio and television. (Earlier and later examples.)

1904 [see *LEGIT., LEGIT]. **1929** *Illustr. London News* 13 Apr. 609/1 (*caption*) Broadcasting variety from 2LO. **1967** *Stage* 2 Mar. 3/4 Variety makes a comeback to Edinburgh on Monday. **1977** J. FLEMING *Every Inch* III. v. 134 He realized..that variety was not..on the way out. It was..very much alive.

9. a. For *U.S.* read *N. Amer.* and add earlier U.S. and later Canad. examples.

1768 *Boston Even.-Post* 21 Nov. 3/3 Just imported in the Bristol Packet..and to be Sold by William Jackson At his Variety Store,..Nails, Brads, and Tacks of all sorts. **1790** *Columbian Sentinel* (Boston) 15 Sept. 4/2 To be sold, at J. Brazer's Variety-store,..Holland Gin, of the best kind, in cases. **1965** H. HOOD in R. Weaver *Canad. Short Stories* (1968) 2nd Ser. 218 We proceeded to the general store, grocery store, variety store, butcher shop, what would you call it? **1975** *Weekend Mag.* (Montreal) 1 Nov. 25/1 Variety store owners just grin and bear the hockey card mania.

b. (Earlier and further examples.)

1868 *Oregon State Jrnl.* 17 Oct. 3/1 Variety Troupe.—This troupe gave an entertainment in the Court House. **1878** *Appleton's Jrnl.* XIX. 36/2 A 'music-hall', a place of entertainment like that which we call a 'variety theatre' in America. **1882** [see *advance agent* s.v. *ADVANCE *sb.* V]. **1895** STUART & PARK (*title*) The variety stage. **1926** G. B. SHAW *Transl. & Tomfooleries* 232 This is not a serious play: it is what is called a Variety Turn for two musicians. **1967** *Stage* 2 Mar. 3/4 A new variety-revue opens at the Palladium Theatre. **1982** C. CASTLE *Folies Bergère* ii. 60 Provincial English variety theatres before World War Two.

varifocal (vēᵊrifōᵘ·kăl), *a.* [f. *VARI- + FOCAL *a.*] **a.** Having a focal length that can be varied.

1945 *Jrnl. Soc. Motion Picture Engineers* XLV. 466 A new positive Vari-Focal view-finder for motion picture cameras. **1962** *Jrnl. Optical Soc. Amer.* LII. 353/2 The two-lens varifocal system consists of a single movable component placed behind a fixed component. **1967** *Appl. Optics* VI. 1085 (*heading*) Stereoscopic display using rapid varifocal mirror oscillations. **1979** *Ibid.* XVIII. 5/1 We have used a varifocal lens to compensate for changes in refractive index of lens elements with wavelengths from 190 nm to 600 nm.

b. *Ophthalm.* = *omnifocal* adj. s.v. *OMNI-. Also *ellipt.*

1975 L. S. SASIENI *Princ. & Pract. Optical Dispensing & Fitting* (ed. 3) xii. 373 Varifocal lenses have two areas of specified powers, for distance and reading, and an intermediate region in which the power gradually changes, from one to the other. **1982** *Ophthalmic & Physiol. Optics* II. 75 (*heading*) Theoretical aspects of concentric varifocal lenses. *Ibid.*, Substantial amounts of unwanted astigmatism in the transition zone are intrinsic to the design and to other forms of concentric varifocal.

varihued (vēᵊ·rihiūd), *a.* [f. HUED *ppl. a.*, after *varicoloured.*] = VARI-COLOURED, VARICOLOURED *a.*

1921 *Nat. Geogr. Mag.* Sept. 274 The varihued deposits resemble brilliant mosaics. **1950** *John o'London's Weekly* 7 July 435/1 Queer fish of another sort..make his book an aquarium of vari-hued specimens.

varimax (vēᵊ·rimæks). *Statistics.* [f. VARI(ANCE + MAX(IMUM.] A method of factor analysis in which uncorrelated factors are sought by a rotation (*ROTATION 1 d) that maximizes the variance of the factor loadings. Usu. *attrib.*

1956 H. F. KAISER (title of thesis, Univ. of California) The varimax method of factor analysis. **1958** —— in *Psychometrika* XXIII. 187 Dr. John Caffrey suggested the name varimax. **1969** *Language* XLV. 89 The purpose of the varimax rotation was to focus these indices on possible natural groupings of the words according to their positional characteristics. **1974** R. L. GORSUCH *Factor Analysis* x. 193 Varimax is available on virtually every computer which has any programs for factor analysis. **1977** M. MAC GRÉIL *Prejudice & Tolerance in Ireland* xv. 467 Factor No. 3 'Republican Political'..: The high varimax loadings of the four categories which constitute this cluster is akin to that of the racial cluster in Factor 1.

vario-coupler (vēᵊ·rioknplǝɹ). *Electr.* ? *Obs.* Also **variocoupler.** [f. *VARI- + -O + COUPLER.] A device, consisting of two unconnected coils, one inside the other, whose relative position can be varied to vary the mutual inductance between two circuits.

1922–3 *T. Eaton & Co. Catal.* Fall & Winter 401/4 Variocouplers, built up on black fibre cylinder, with taps, fitted with lugs. **1925** P. J. RISDON *Crystal Receivers & Circuits* ii. 21 A vario-coupler..is a sort of combination of a variometer and an ordinary tapped tuning inductance. **1937** *Discovery* Feb. 54/2 (*in figure*) Vario-coupler.

variometer (vēᵊriǫ·mĭtǝɹ). [f. *VARI- + -OMETER.] **1.** An instrument for measuring variations in the intensity of the earth's magnetic field.

1889 in *Cent. Dict.* **1916** *Proc. R. Soc.* A. XCII. 321 There can be no question of the enormous simplification of the field work which such a portable variometer produces. **1972** *Nature Physical Sci.* 25 Dec. 184/2 Telluric recording equipment was operated in conjunction with a magnetic variometer array.

2. *Electr.* (*a*) An inductor (*INDUCTOR 3 d) whose total inductance can be varied by altering the relative position of two coaxial coils connected in series, and can thus be used to tune a circuit. (*b*) A device achieving a similar function by means of permeability tuning.

1908 C. C. F. MONCKTON *Radio-Telegr.* xv. 255 The antenna and the receiving circuit are tuned to the incoming oscillations by means of the variometer. **1921** *Wireless World* IX. 6/1 For amateur use the variometer has the advantage that it is cheap compared with a variable condenser. **1926** 'R. KEVERNE' *Carteret's Cure* vii. 168 Mr. Pell turned to the listening set and picked up the head-phones while his fingers played deftly with the variometer. **1959** K. HENNEY *Radio Engin. Handbk.* (ed. 5) iii. 14 Another form [of variable inductor], which is rather bulky..and now little used, is the variometer... Much more common is the variation of inductance through the variation of the permeability of the core. **1977** *Elektor* Mar. 22/1 The variometer is an updated version of the old permeability tuners.

3. An instrument for indicating the rate of climb or descent of an aircraft.

1924 *Sci. Amer.* Feb. 83/2 Air speed indicator... Turn indicator... Variometer. **1930** STARTUP & KINNEAR tr. *Stamer & Lippisch's Gliding & Sail-Planing* x. 111 An instrument called a variometer exists for the purpose of indicating ascent and descent and is much used in balloons. **1969** *Daily Tel.* (Colour Suppl.) 21 Nov. 64/2 A variometer can confuse you; you might be going down in a rising thermal, so it's no good just knowing how you are doing relative to the air you're in. **1973** *Q. Jrnl. Meteorol. Soc.* XCIX. 768 Height changes give a check on the calibration of the variometer.

variorum. Delete ‖ and add: **1. c.** (Earlier examples.) Also applied to a single reading.

1850 *N. & Q.* 19 Oct. 325 A very curious variorum reading. **1873** (*title*) Osorio. A tragedy as originally written in 1797 by Samuel Taylor Coleridge. Now first printed from a copy recently discovered by the publisher with the variorum readings of 'Remorse' and a monograph on the history of the play in its earlier and later form by the author of 'Tennysoniana'.

d. Used, chiefly *attrib.*, to denote an edition, usu. of an author's complete works, containing variant readings from manuscripts or earlier editions.

This use is deplored by some scholars.

1955 *Times* 11 June 9/3 How delighted he [*sc.* Johnson] would have been to have known of the Yale University project for a really complete variorum edition of his works. **1957** (*title*) The variorum edition of the poems of W. B. Yeats. **1964** *Times Lit. Suppl.* 29 Oct. 979/4 The variorum edition of Emily Dickinson..(meaning, it appears, an edition containing variant readings). The..use of the term is incorrect. **1980** *N.Y. Times* 26 July II. 22 The book, a variorum, records every usable fact and opinion about the play—every significant textual variant, every influential interpretation, [etc.]. **1983** P. G. RUGGIERS in Beadle & Griffiths *St. John's College Cambridge MS. L.1.* p. xiii, Having then presented these two essential manuscripts, consideration was given by the Variorum editors [*sc.* the editors of the Variorum Chaucer] to providing other materials essential to the understanding of an evolving Chaucer text.

2. (Later examples.) *Sc.*

1876 J. SMITH *Archie & Bess* 95 It's a lang time since I heard ye sing't and it'll aye be a variorum. **1901** R. TROTTER *Galloway Gossip* 11 They widna let the Paraphrases be sung in the kirk, or tunes wi' variorum about them. **1930** in *Sc. Nat. Dict.* (1974) IX. 520/2 A'm guid at readin' write gin it has nane o' your variorums and whirligigs.

variphone (vēᵊ·rĭfōᵘn). *Linguistics.* [f. *VARI- + PHONE *sb.*[1]] One of two or more sounds used interchangeably by the same speaker in the same phonetic context.

1932 D. JONES in E. P. Hamp et al. *Readings in Linguistics II* (1966) 32 Variphones are found in some varieties of German, where *p* and *b*, ʃ and ʒ, and other corresponding voiced and voiceless consonants are apparently used indifferently. **1934** YUEN-REN CHAO in M. Joos *Readings in Linguistics I* (1966) (ed. 4) 39/2 Bloomfield makes no explicit mention of free phonemes or variphones. *Ibid.*, Variphones are also phonemes, except that the choice of the exact shade of the sound used is determined by psychological and physiological factors other than those of phonetic environment. **1950** D. JONES *Phoneme* xxviii. 206 ŋg and ŋ form a variphone in the speech of Midland districts of England.

Variscan (vări·skăn), *a. Geol.* [f. L. *Varisc-ī* (see quot. 1906[1]) + -AN, after G. *variscisch* (E. Suess *Antlitz der Erde* (1888) II. III. ii. 131).] Of, pertaining to, or designating a mountain system that formerly extended from southern Ireland and Britain through central France and Germany to southern Poland, or the orogeny that gave rise to it during late Palæozoic time.

1906 H. B. C. & W. J. SOLLAS tr. *Suess's Face of Earth* II. III. ii. 111 It is thus fitting that the name of this range, which includes most of the German horsts, should be borrowed from the land of the Varisci or the Vogtland; and we shall name it therefore the Variscan range, from the Latin name of Hof in Bavaria (*Curia Variscorum*). **1908** *Ibid.* III. IV. viii. 346 The Carnic mountains are a chain.. and of Variscan age. **1956** W. EDWARDS in D. L. Linton *Sheffield* i. 22 Earth-movements of the Variscan orogeny were already in action during deposition of the Lower Carboniferous. **1969** BENNISON & WRIGHT *Geol. Hist. Brit. Isles* xi. 255 The building of the Variscan mountain chains profoundly affected the geography of Europe, both in the distribution of land and sea and climatically. **1974** *Encycl. Brit. Macropædia* VI. 14/1 The European geosyncline is called the Variscan.

variscite (væ·risǝit, variskǝit). *Min.* [ad. G. *variscit* (A. Breithaupt 1837, in *Jrnl. f. prakt. Chem.* X. 506), f. med.L. *Varisc-ia*, name of the Vogtland district of E. Germany where the mineral was first found: see -ITE[1].] An orthorhombic hydrated aluminium phosphate, $AlPO_4.2H_2O$, which is dimorphous with metavariscite and occurs usu. as green or colourless, translucent or transparent, fine-grained masses, crusts, and nodules.

1850 D. T. ANSTED *Elem. Course Geol., Mineralogy* ix. 187 Variscite is also a phosphate of alumina, of a green colour. **1912** *Proc. U.S. Nat. Museum* XLI. 415 The variscite and variscite-matrix from this locality would yield very beautiful gems for the so-called barbaric jewelry. **1964, 1975** [see *REDONDITE]. **1979** *Arizona Highways* Apr. 40/1, I did a series of shields with variscite, which is a dark stone that has some turquoise in it.

vari-sized (vēᵊ·ri,sǝizd), *a. rare.* [f. SIZED *ppl. a.*[1] 1 b, after *varicoloured*, etc.] Of various or different sizes.

1936 F. CLUNE *Roaming round Darling* xxi. 208 Beneath..were nineteen dogs... All were vari-coloured, vari-bred, vari-sized and -shaped. **1940** W. FAULKNER *Hamlet* IV. i. 243 Vari-sized and -coloured tatters torn at random from large billboards.

varistor (vēᵊri·stǝɹ). *Electr.* [f. VAR(IABLE *a.* + *RES)ISTOR.] A semiconductor diode whose resistance varies non-linearly with the applied voltage.

1937 *Bell Telephone Q.* Apr. 114 A varistor is a device, for example a copper oxide rectifier, whose resistance varies with the applied voltage. **1957** *Electronic Engin.* XXIX. 386/1 Varistors exhibit a practical resistance variation of several decades over their normal rated working range of current or voltage. **1978** *Sci. Amer.* Mar. 59/1 The compensation is termed equalization and is achieved by adding two varistors, or variable resistors, to the speech network.

Varityper (vēᵊ·rĭtǝipǝɹ). orig. and chiefly *U.S.* Also **Vari-typer, varityper.** [f. *VARI- + TYPER.] The proprietary name of a kind of typewriter that has interchangeable type faces. Also, a kind of type-composing machine with similar operation.

1928 *Official Gaz.* (U.S. Patent Office) 16 Oct. 494/1 *Varityper.* For typewriter machines. **1931** *Times Lit. Suppl.* 1 Oct. 760/4 Latest Hammond (Varityper) Typewriter... Turn knob and you get another type shuttle—italics, smaller letters or accented, or Greek, each with close or open spacing. **1948** *Economist* 13 Nov. 781/1 The varityper..has kept the Chicago newspapers going through a compositors' strike. **1956** *Trade Marks Jrnl.* 11 Jan. 27/1 *Vari-typer*... Type composing machines for office use and parts thereof... Ralph C. Coxhead Corporation,..Newark, State of New Jersey, United States of America; manufacturers. **1959** *Oxf. Univ. Gaz.* 3 Dec. 369/2 New 'Vari-typer' composition service with small-offset-litho reproduction. **1977** *San Antonio* (Texas) *Express News* 30 Oct. 5E/4 She designed the layout, typeset it at home on an old varityper and made the negatives for the printer.

Hence **Va·ri-type** *v. trans.*; **Va·rityping** *vbl. sb.*

1955 H. QUASTLER *Information Theory in Psychol.* p. iv, 'Information Theory in Psychology' was Vari-typed by Diane Folk, Stenographic Bureau, University of Illinois. **1960** *World's Press News* 30 Dec. 15 Varityping plus photo litho printing results in lower cost and faster delivery for brochures, handbooks, leaflets, catalogues.

varlamoffite (vāɹlămǫ·fǝit). *Min.* [a. F. *varlamoffite* (H. Buttgenbach *Les Minéraux de Belgique et du Congo Belge* (1947) 182), f. the name of N. *Varlamoff*, mining engineer who found the mineral: see -ITE[1].] A yellowish cryptocrystalline powdery material, perhaps $(Sn,Fe)(O,OH)_2$, that is related to or perhaps identical with cassiterite.

1948 *Mineral. Abstr.* X. 354 A new mineral varlamoffite, H_2SnO_3, as yellow earthy material mixed with grains of cassiterite from Kalima, Belgian Congo, is here included for the first time. **1970** *Mineral. Mag.* XXXVII. 626 Most of the reported occurrences of varlamoffite show a strong spatial association with stannite, and most workers have concluded that it is a secondary mineral resulting from the attack of meteoric waters on stannite.

varment, varmint, *sb.*[1] and *a.*[1] Add: **1. a, b.** Also **varmit.**

1856 *Porter's Spirit of Times* 20 Sept. 38/2 Why, massa, dat 'tarnal varmit hab fooled me bad. **1974** *Evening Herald* (Rock Hill, S. Carolina) 18 Apr. 13/3 She didn't care if my face was black. She didn't treat me like no varmit or nothing.

Hence **va·rminty** *a. colloq.*, suggestive of or resembling a varmint; sharp, cunning.

1907 A. Conan Doyle *Thr. Magic Door* ii. 34 Louis, thin, ascetic, varminty. **1922** R. Leighton *Compl. Bk. Dog* xvii. 261 The General Appearance of the West Highland White Terrier is that of a small, game, hardy-looking terrier..with a 'varminty' appearance. **1962** R. H. Smythe *Anat. Dog Breeding* 52 The 'varminty' eye of a Fox Terrier.

‖**varna** (vā·ɹnă, vʊ·rnă). [Skr. *varṇa*, colour, appearance.] Any one of the four early castes or social classes of Hindu society (see Caste 2 a); the system or basis of this division.

1838 *Penny Cycl.* XII. 230/1 The division of Hindus into ..castes..existed from the earliest times. In Sanskrit they are called *varnas*, that is, 'colours'. **1876** *Encycl. Brit.* IV. 203/1 The idea of caste is expressed by the Sanskrit term *varna*, originally denoting 'colour', thereby implying differences of complexion between the several classes. **1931** [see *jat[2]]. **1959** *Times Lit. Suppl.* 1 May 262/5 Viewing the *varna* system of ancient India through rose-tinted spectacles. **1974** *Encycl. Brit. Macropædia* IX. 347/2 The traditional view that *varna* reflected the organization of Indian society has recently been questioned; it has been suggested that..the concept of *jāti* is more central to caste functioning than *varṇa*, which may be the theoretical rationalization. **1977** M. & J. Stutley *Dict. Hinduism* 323 *Varṇa*. The word is generally used to denote colour, but its primary meaning, derived from the root vṛ is 'screen, veil, covering, external appearance', and hence colour is only one of the many aspects of the term.

varnish, *sb.*[1] Add: **1. f.** A resinous deposit formed in engines by the oxidation of fuel and lubricating oils.

1948 A. P. Fraas *Combustion Engine* viii. 241 The resins may deposit with the sludge or may form thin adherent coatings on engine parts. In the latter case the coatings are called varnish or lacquer because of their appearance. **1967** *Boston Sunday Herald* 26 Mar. I. 1/2 Don't be fooled by slow cranking because 'varnish' on the pistons will cause so much drag that a hot engine may resist cranking until it cools. **1981** *Pop. Hot Rodding* Feb. 84/1 Oxidation produces new compounds, loosely termed sludge, varnish and acid, which are detrimental to the lubrication system.

5. *varnish remover*; *varnish-like* adj.

1916 *Nature* 25 May 269/2 Boiled linseed oil on exposure to the air is converted by oxidation into a hard varnish-like product. **1965** Finer & Savage *Sel. Lett. J. Wedgwood* 13 The ancient red-figure vases were decorated by reserving the figures on a red pottery ground, surrounding them with a black varnishlike slip. **1965** P. D. Samman *Nails in Disease* ix. 83 Nail varnish and varnish removers and excess manicuring may be of some importance aetiologically. **1973** C. Williams *Man on Leash* ix. 131 That crap they shot into my arm. Battery solution or varnish remover.

varnish, *v.* **1.** (Later *absol.* example.)

a **1817** Jane Austen *Persuasion* (1818) III. xi. 234 He drew, he varnished, he carpentered.

varnishing, *vbl. sb.* Add: **1. b.** = *vernissage. Cf. *varnishing day*, sense 3 in Dict.

1951 N. Mitford *Blessing* ii. iv. 188, I was to go round at six, take her to a varnishing, and then dine with her. **1971** R. A. Carter *Manhattan Primitive* vii. 63 Thatcher preferred the French word for openings; 'varnishings' were what they usually turned out to be.

varoom (vărū·m), var. *vroom.

Varroa (væ·roă). *Ent.* Also **varroa.** [mod.L., coined in Ger. (A. C. Oudemans 1904, in *Entomol. Ber.* (Amsterdam) XVIII. 161), f. the name of Marcus Terentius *Varro* (116–27 BC), Roman scholar.] A small mite, *Varroa jacobsoni*, which is a fatal parasite of the honeybee in the Far East and has spread to other parts in modern times; infection with this mite.

1974 *Jrnl. Washington Acad. Sci.* LXIV. 10/2 '*Varroa* disease' of the honey bee. **1978** *Bee World* LIX. 165 Bees imported from Japan brought *Varroa* to Paraguay. **1979** *Guardian* 26 July 1/4 The barely visible varroa began infesting Russian honey-bees in 1964 and since then it has flourished dramatically. **1984** L. A. Stephens-Potter *Beekeeper's Man.* x. 111/2 In countries where varroa is present it has spread with alarming rapidity and caused enormous losses of bee colonies. **1984** *Times* 11 Oct. 3/2 At the queen examination centre..Ministry of Agriculture scientists make sure she is free of Varroa.

Varsity. Add: **a.** (Earlier and further examples.) Now (in the U.K.) somewhat *joc.* exc. in *varsity match*, a sporting contest, esp. the annual Rugby football match between the universities of Oxford and Cambridge.

1863 *Baily's Mag.* Jan. 360, I had conjured up all the most extravagant and erroneous ideas as to my 'Varsity career'. **1885** A. Edwardes *Girton Girl* III. xvi. 291, I'm darned..if it be'ant my Varsity man, after all! **1908** E. H. W. Meyerstein *Let.* 21 Oct. (1959) 33 It seems to me that the real attractions of varsity life are reserved for the sportsman and the loafer. **1921** *Granta* 30 Nov. 146/1 What would you do if in the 'Varsity match just as you were off, on a clear half-way run down the field somebody ripped your shorts off? **1927** C. Connolly *Let.* 25 Jan. in *Romantic Friendship* (1975) 228 O blessed chastity (rare at the varsity). **1967** F. Sargeson *Hangover* iii. 19 And that damn cleaning man across from the varsity. **1979** *Times* 6 Dec. 4 (*heading*) The varsity match. **1982** *Guardian Weekly* 27 June 23 [He] would become the first university Blue to miss the Varsity match because he will be playing [cricket] for England. *Ibid.* 19 Dec. 23 Cambridge won 20-13, but on the next day Oxford had some revenge in winning the soccer varsity match at Wembley 4–2. **1983** *Metro* (Auckland) Feb. 13/4 Instead he went to varsity with the ambition of taking a science degree.

b. *U.S.* Applied *attrib.* to sporting events, teams, etc., at or of a university or college. Occas. *absol.*, a college team. (See also quot. 1930.)

1891 *Outing* Dec. 241/1 The 'varsity captain whistled a lively air. **1898** *Ibid.* June 305/1 The..excitement generally attendant upon..trips by 'varsity nines. **1902** L. L. Bell *Hope Loring* (1908) 79 Being on the 'Varsity football team. **1928** E. O'Neill *Strange Interlude* viii. 278 It's Gordon's last race, his last appearance on a 'varsity. **1930** *Amer. Speech* V. 243 *Varsity*..is applied always to a student team, as in athletics or debate, not to an institution. **1973** R. Ludlum *Matlock Paper* iv. 32 The coach of varsity soccer. **1978** *Nature* 29 June 794/1 In the intercollegiate ('varsity') sports, which play a large role in American colleges, Conant replaced an autonomous body led by the alumni association, which is the norm in American universities and is the source of athletic scholarships, by a departmental structure administered by a faculty committee. **1978** *New Yorker* 9 Oct. 184/3 The Harvard varsity..came up a winner 10-0, against Massachusetts. **1979** *Tucson* (Arizona) *Citizen* 20 Sept. 1D/4 He went on to stardom at Niles McKinley High School... McKinley had a 21-6-1 record in Sammy's three years of varsity football. **1980** *N.Y. Times* 1 June xxiii. 12/3 Classic Yale-Harvard Regatta in New London... The four-mile varsity race..will be rowed on the Thames River.

Varsovian, *a.* Add: (Earlier example of spelling *Warsovian.*) Also as *sb.*, a native or inhabitant of Warsaw.

1764 H. Grenville *Let.* 10 Mar. in *Desp. & Corr. 2nd Earl of Buckinghamshire 1762–5* (1902) II. 153 The apprehensions of your Warsovian correspondent appear but too well founded. **1959** *Listener* 17 Dec. 1071/2 The Palace of Culture is intensely disliked and resented by the Varsovians. **1978** M. Tripp *Wife-Smuggler* i. 16 One of the best restaurants..where Varsovians go when they wish to treat..distinguished guests.

vartabed (vā·ɹtăbed). Also **vardapet, vartabad, vartapet,** etc. [Armenian.] A member of an order of clergy in the Armenian church (see quot. 1847).

1718 J. Ozell tr. *Pitton de Tournefort's Voy. Levant* II. viii. 303 These Vertabiets, who make such a noise among the Armenians, are not in reality great Doctors. **1841** L. Coleman *Christian Antiq.* xxiii. 470 The vartabeds live not among the people, but in convents. **1847** J. Wilson *Lands Bible* II. 482 The monkish clergy are denominated Vartabads or Doctors, and it is their peculiar office to teach and preach. **1875** *Encycl. Brit.* II. 549/2 The vartabed, or doctor of theology..has frequently charge of a diocese, with episcopal functions. **1923** *Blackw. Mag.* Aug. 252/1 The Patriarch and an Armenian *vartabed*..are pushed inside. **1957** *Oxf. Dict. Christian Church* 87/1 Bishops..are usually chosen from among the vardapets. **1964** [see *rasophore]. **1982** *Encycl. Brit. Macropædia* VI. 140 Another class of priests is represented by the vartabeds, or doctors, who must remain unmarried.

varus[2]. (Earlier example.)

1756 [see *ephelis].

varve (vāɹv). [ad. Sw. *varv* layer, turn.] A pair of thin layers of clay and silt of contrasting colour and texture which represents the deposit of a single year (summer and winter) in still water at some time in the past (usu. in a lake formed by a retreating ice-sheet); they have been used to establish a chronology of the late glacial and post-glacial period. Also *attrib.* and *Comb.* Hence **varved** (vāɹvd) *a.*, characterized by such layers.

[**1887** *Encycl. Brit.* XXII. 740/1 The glacial clay consists generally of..darker and lighter coloured layers, which give it a striped appearance, for which reason it has often been called *hvarfvig lera* (striped clay).] **1912** G. De Geer in *Compt. Rend. XI Session Congrès Géol. Internat.* 253 The Swedish word *varv*, subst. (old spelling: hvarf), means as well a circle as a periodical iteration of layers. An international term for the last sense being wanted it seems suitable to use the transcription *varve*, pl. *-s*, in Engl. and Fr. **1929** C. R. Longwell *Pirsson's Textbk. Geol.* (ed. 3) I. v. 126 Lake Deposits.—Remarkably banded clays have been formed in patches within the glaciated regions... The Swedish geologists call them varved clays. **1936** *Times Lit. Suppl.* 9 May 392/2 Varve-variation in its general features is a function of solar radiation. **1948** *Bull. Geol. Soc. Amer.* LIX. 646 In this basin (Fossil, Wyo.) hundreds of thousands of beautifully preserved fish are entombed in the varved sediments. **1953** *Antiquity* XXVII. 35 What we most need now, apart from archaeology, is a study of the post-glacial climatic fluctuations in the Tigris and Euphrates valleys. Here the techniques of Western Europe, such as pollen analysis and varve-counting, seem unlikely to be of any use. **1957** G. E. Hutchinson *Treat. Limnology* I. i. 8 The dating of the events, based primarily on the varve chronology, is in fair accord with the radiocarbon chronology. **1974** *Nature* 15 Nov. 182/1 The thickness of the varves..provide [*sic*] a guide to the year-by-year changes in mean climate; but that is at best a crude measure.

vary, *sb.* (Later example.)

1929 R. Bridges *Testament of Beauty* i. 26 We should not in the field of Reason look to find less vary and veer than elsewhere in the flux of Life.

vas. Add: **1. a.** *vas deferens* (pl. *vasa deferentia*) [L. *dēferens*, pres. pple. of *dēferre* (see Deferent *a.*[1] and *sb.*)], a fibromuscular tube which carries spermatozoa from the epididymis at ejaculation, in man joining the duct from the seminal vesicle at the prostate gland to form the ejaculatory duct.

1578 J. Banister *Hist. Man* vi. 87 (*marginal note*) Why these ij. are called Vasa deferentia. **1713** W. Cheselden *Anat. of Humane Body* iv. i. 163 On the upper part of the Testicles, are hard Bodies call'd Epididymi; which are evidently the beginnings of the Vasa Deferentia. **1849–52** R. B. Todd *Cycl. Anat. & Physiol.* IV. 981/1 The vas deferens is round and indurated,—harder than any other excretory duct in the body, by which character it is easily distinguished, when handled, from the other parts constituting the spermatic cord. **1975** *Nature* 9 Oct. 488/1 For collection of spermatozoa, the vasa deferentia were excised aseptically from adult Wistar strain rats.

VASCAR, Vascar: see *V III. 5 b.

vascular, *a.* Add: **1. e.** *vascular wilt disease*): wilt disease involving the vascular system of a plant; *spec.* = *Panama disease* s.v. *Panama.

1946 *Nature* 16 Nov. 712 The presence of a vascular wilt disease of the oil palm. **1951** *New Biol.* XI. 76 Vascular Wilt Disease..of bananas in the Old World made its appearance in Central America towards the end of the nineteenth century. **1972** [see *Panama disease* s.v. *Panama].

vasculature (væ·skiŭlătiuɹ). *Anat.* [f. L. *vāscul-āris* Vascular *a.* + *-ature*, after *musculature.*] The vascular system and its arrangement in the body or a part.

1934 in Webster. **1942** F. A. Mettler *Neuroanatomy* x. 194 Concerning the vasculature within the vertebral canal. **1962** *Lancet* 22 Dec. 1327/1 Burton has shown that a critical opening and a critical closing pressure are peculiar also to the intrarenal vasculature. **1975** *Nature* 18 Sept. 224/1 The vasculature of regenerating limbs of the newt..was investigated.

vasculitis (væskiŭləi·tis). *Path.* Pl. **vasculitides** (-əi·tidīz), **vasculitises.** [f. L. *vāscul-um*, dim. of *vās* Vas + -itis.] An inflammatory reaction in a blood vessel; any of various conditions characterized by such reactions.

1900 in Dorland *Med. Dict.* **1945** *Jrnl. Amer. Med. Assoc.* 2 June 337/1 We believe that some of these cases could more properly be grouped with cases of nodular vasculitis. **1976** *Proc. R. Soc. Med.* LXIX. 927/1 The vasculitis and other non-articular manifestations of rheumatoid disease are distinctly uncommon in this age group. **1983** Byron & Hughes in *Oxf. Textbk. Med.* II. xvi. 36/2 For clinical purposes, the vasculitides can be divided into those with skin lesions and those without.

Hence **vasculi·tic** *a.*, of the nature of, or characteristic of, vasculitis.

1971 *Clin. & Exper. Immunol.* IX. 754 Endothelial changes seem to be an important component of a number of vasculitic disorders. **1980** *Jrnl. R. Soc. Med.* LXXIII. 208 His rheumatoid disease became more active and vasculitic lesions appeared once again on his fingertips. **1983** T. J. Ryan in *Oxf. Textbk. Med.* II. xx. 63/2 There have been a number of more recently described vasculitic syndromes in which urticaria is the only skin manifestation.

vasculotoxic (væskiŭlotǫ·ksik), *a.* *Physiol.* [f. as prec. + -o + Toxic *a.*] Affecting the vessels of the body adversely. Hence **va:sculotoxi·city.**

1957 *Dorland's Med. Dict.* (ed. 23), Vasculotoxic. **1962** *Endocrinology* LXXI. 505/1 The vasculotoxic and nephrotoxic effects of renin. **1973** *Nature* 30 Mar. 334/2 The vasculotoxicity of renin is also suggested by its presence in excessive amounts in human malignant and renovascular hypertension. **1977** *Lancet* 8 Jan. 83/2 There is as yet little information on the relation of blood-levels to nephrotoxic or vasculotoxic potential.

vasculum. Add: Pl. **-a, -ums. 2.** (Earlier examples.)

1782 J. Lightfoot *Let.* 11 July in W. H. Curtis *William Curtis* (1941) 59, I am extremely obliged to you for the contents of your Botanic *Vasculum.* **1818** G. Graves *Naturalist's Pocket-bk.* 295 These [specimens] must be gathered on a dry day, and placed in a common tin vasculum or pocket herborising Box. **1839** J. D. Hooker *Jrnl.* in L. Huxley *Life J. D. Hooker* (1918) I. 47 Two Botanising vascula.

vase. Add: **3.** *vase-maker*: quot. 1894 should be cited as '**1770** J. Wedgwood *Let.* 19 May (1965) 92'; **vase carpet,** an oriental (esp. Persian) carpet with a pattern incorporating a stylized vase of flowers.

1915 *Guide to Collection of Carpets* (Victoria & Albert Mus.) i. 27 Another type of pattern, in which animal and bird life are entirely absent, has given rise in Germany to the name 'vase-carpets'. **1983** *Eastern Carpet* (Hayward Gallery Catal.) 31/2 Another group of Persian carpets with beautiful floral designs are the so-called vase carpets, believed to have been made in the Kerman area.

vasectomized, *ppl. a.* Add: Also, having undergone ligation of one or (usually) both *vasa differentia*. So **vase·ctomize** *v. trans.*

1923 *Physiol. Rev.* III. 342 If..the female rat undergoes a sterile coition with a vasectomized male the corpus luteum persists for a longer period. **1970** *Nature* 11 Apr. 162/2 Spontaneously ovulating females were mated with vasectomized males of strain A, whose sterility had been checked repeatedly. **1977** *Spare Rib* June 31/1 Male, 31, healthy wealthy and dull, seeks girlfriend. Vasectomised. Ideal pet for liberated woman. **1980** *Aggressive Behavior* VI. 218 All six adult males were vasectomized by double ligature of the vas deferens four months before the first copulation was seen in November. **1982** *Times* 6 Dec. 6/8 One man said the number three song on the Thai hit parade 'I'm vasectomized' had 'inspired him [to have a vasectomy].

vasectomy. Add: Also, ligation of one or (more commonly) both *vasa deferentia*, usu. performed to render the subject infertile.

1897 *Lancet* 11 Sept. 658/1 A case of double vasectomy. **1900** [see VAS 1 a]. **1923** *Physiol. Rev.* III. 339 Pregnancy is prevented through coition being made sterile..by submitting the male to vasectomy. **1970** *Daily Tel.* 2 May 1/4 Vasectomy has recently become much more usual among men as a method of family planning. **1972** [see *SEMEN 2]. **1979** *Toronto Star* 15 May E7/3 Commercial sperm banks in several major U.S. cities have reported growing numbers of donors, particularly..men who choose to store their sperm before undergoing vasectomies. **1985** *Times* 8 Mar. 10/7 A shipyard mechanic who had a vasectomy last autumn said yesterday he was 'lucky' after learning his wife is pregnant with sextuplets.

Vaseline, *sb.* Add: Also **vaseline.** (Further examples.)

Vaseline is still (1984) a proprietary term.

1897, etc. [see *petroleum jelly*]. **1924,** etc. [see *PROPRIETARY *a.* 1 a]. **1927** *Trade Marks Jrnl.* 3 Aug. 1383/2 Vaseline 479,707. Petroleum Jelly and Disinfectant Soap for Veterinary use. Chesebrough Manufacturing Company Consolidated... 11th April 1927. **1930** A. HUXLEY *Brief Candles* 13 Hearts of putty, hearts of vaseline. **1965** [see *soft ground* s.v. *SOFT *a.* 27]. **1974** *Cleveland* (Ohio) *Plain Dealer* 26 Oct. 4-D/1 Walter Youngblood, one of his trainers, is smearing Vaseline on his face, torso, arms and legs. **1976** BOTHAM & DONNELLY *Valentino* xiv. 107 Vaseline, and other hair-care applications, would experience a significant sales-boost. **1978** J. IRVING *World according to Garp* xix. 410 The Vaseline made his ear slippery.

b. The greenish-yellow colour of Vaseline as used in the manufacture of glass; glassware of this colour.

1966 J. LAVER *Victoriana* 168 The Victorians used a wide variety of colour in their glass—Bristol Blue..and the yellowy-green known as Vaseline. **1973** *Washington Post* 13 Jan. F1/7 (Advt.), Old glassware, Red Mark Prussia, Ruby, Vaseline, [etc.]. **1975** *Daily Colonist* (Victoria, B.C.) 26 Oct. 30/8 Vaseline is a greenish yellow glassware resembling its namesake. It dates from 1870 to the present day. **1980** *Times* 1 Nov. 24/7 Its shade is made of vaseline glass—a turn of the century technique which Christopher Wray has reintroduced.

Hence as *v. trans.*, to treat with Vaseline; **va·selined** *ppl. a.*; **va·selining** *vbl. sb.*

1921 *Librarian* Nov. 74 The combination of vaselining and varnishing is the best thing for the text books. **1934** V. M. YEATES *Winged Victory* II. ix. 262 His neck was still sore with all yesterday's twisting to watch his tail. He ought to have vaselined it last night. **1938** F. CHESTER *Shot Full* xii. 114 A coloured man, his hair..vaselined to stick up. **1942** R. W. RAVEN *Surg. Care* xviii. 138 A piece of vaselined-gauze should be placed lightly over the colostomy. **1965** 'MALCOLM X' *Autobiogr.* iii. 55 He draped the towel around my shoulders, over my rubber apron, and began again vaselining my hair. **1977** *Rolling Stone* 16 June 39/1 Vaselined hair and a semidignified zoot suit. **1983** *Times* 21 Apr. 14/6 'Have you Vaselined your nipples?' asked a solicitor from Peckham.

vaso-. Add: **vasoconstri·cting, -dila·ting** *ppl. adjs.*, **-dila·tion; vasoliga·tion** *Surg.*, ligation of a vessel, esp. of the vasa deferentia; **va·sospasm** a sudden constriction of a blood vessel, resulting in reduced flow; hence **vasospa·stic** *a.*; **vasova·gal** *a.*, involving the vagus nerve and the vascular system: applied to an attack (often the result of emotional stress) in which there is a slowing of the pulse and a fall in blood pressure, causing pallor, fainting, sweating, and nausea; **va:sovaso·stomy** *Surg.* [*-STOMY], an operation to reverse a vasectomy by rejoining the cut ends of the *vasa deferentia*.

1925 *Proc. R. Soc.* B. XCVII. 325 The toxic and vasoconstricting action..has not been confronted by us provided we make use of freshly defibrinated blood. **1975** *Daily Colonist* (Victoria, B.C.) 16 July 2/3 One of the vasoconstricting drugs..can be helpful. **1956** *Nature* 18 Feb. 340/1 The well-known vasodilating effect of an increased concentration of carbon dioxide. **1962** in L. Kudrow *Cluster Headache* i. 9 Vasodilating headache: a suggestive classification. **1977** *Lancet* 30 July 231/1 A drug such as isoprenaline with a cardiac stimulant and peripheral vasodilating action can improve tissue perfusion. **1908** *Practitioner* Aug. 348 The tourniquet is then released, the affected members then become bright red, owing to a sudden vasodilation. **1974** M. C. GERALD *Pharmacol.* vi. 111 Beta-receptor activation causes a widening of small blood vessels (vasodilation). **1926** W. N. BERKELEY *Princ. & Pract. Endocrine Med.* ix. 299 Vasectomy or vasoligation in old men is said..to cause atrophy of the sperm mechanism of the testis. **1932** C. R. MOORE in E. Allen *Sex & Internal Secretions* vii. 314 There is no acceptable evidence that vasectomy or vasoligation has any rejuvenating effect. **1973** *Washington Post* 13 Jan. A-8/4 The experiments involved the use of the vasectomy technique, or a closely related one called 'vasoligation', to close off the two tiny ducts that carry the male spermatozoa. **1902** *Buck's Handbk. Med. Sci.* (rev. ed.) V. 74/1 Sedation of maniacal excitement and relaxation of vasospasm in melancholic stupor are better accomplished by warm than cold baths. **1977** *Lancet* 14 May 1039/2 Workers with vibrating hand tools, such as pneumatic drills and chain saws, are at risk of episodic vasospasm, particularly when the vibration is associated with cold exposure. **1932** *Glasgow Med. Jrnl.* CXVIII. 146 Promising results have been obtained in certain cases of scleroderma in which a vasospastic element is present. **1980** *Brit. Med. Jrnl.* 18 Oct. 1033/2 The results..indicate that prostaglandin E_1 given by central venous infusion is a safe and effective method of treating severe vasospastic disease. **1907** W. R. GOWERS *Border-Land of Epilepsy* ii. 18 When the vaso-motor spasm preponderates, the case may seem to differ from the type more than it really does. Such cases may be termed 'vaso-vagal'. **1974** R. M. KIRK et al. *Surgery* iii. 41/2 Vasovagal..shock, and fainting caused by an emotional crisis, produce marked dilation of vessels in the muscles, reducing circulatory blood volume. **1976** *Nature* 27 May 334/2 Some had a frank vasovagal reaction with yawning, bradycardia and pallor and could not continue the test procedure. **1949** *New Gould Med. Dict.* 1119/1 Vasovasostomy. **1957** *Jrnl. Urol.* LXXVIII. 79 For this study vasovasostomy, rather than epididymovasostomy was chosen. **1982** *Jrnl. Andrology* III. 21/2 Seven patients undergoing vasovasostomy for reversal of male sterility secondary to vasectomy.

vaso,a·ctive, *a. Physiol.* [f. prec. + ACTIVE *a.*] Affecting the physiological state of blood vessels, esp. their calibre; *vasoactive intestinal (poly)peptide*, a polypeptide 28 amino-acids long which is a neurotransmitter found esp. in the brain and gastrointestinal tract; abbrev. *VIP*.

1958 *Brit. Jrnl. Pharmacol.* XIII. 113 *(heading)* Vasoactive substances in the nasal mucosa. **1962** *Times* 17 May 14/4 New Appointments... M. R. Lee, M. A. (Oxon)..to investigate the control of the generation of vasoactive polypeptides in the blood, at the..Radcliffe Infirmary, Oxford. **1970** *Nature* 28 Feb. 864/2 If the liver is normally the main site for inactivating this vasoactive intestinal peptide, its failure of destruction when liver function is seriously impaired..could account for.. peripheral vasodilatation. **1972** [see *VIP* s.v. *V 5 b]. **1976** *Nature* 22 Jan. 224/1 Release..of vasoactive lymphokines, such as prostaglandins,..might not necessarily leave a morphological trace.

Hence **vasoacti·vity**, vasoactive power.

1968 *Experientia* XXIV. 1126/1 These results have been interpreted as evidence that plasma has..intrinsic vasoactivity. **1982** *Amer. Jrnl. Path.* CVII. 289/2 When such lesions were induced in sheep and the lymph plasma draining the stimulated nodes was assayed for vasoactivity, a hyperemia-inducing activity was indeed found to be present.

vasopre·ssin. *Physiol.* [f. as next + -IN[1].] A polypeptide hormone present in the neurohypophysis of mammals which controls the retention of water in the kidneys and when given in large quantities raises the blood pressure by vasoconstriction.

1928 [see *OXYTOCIN]. **1951** A. GROLLMAN *Pharmacol. & Therapeutics* xxvi. 553 Vasopressin is also used in the form of a tannate... A single injection of this preparation every 24 to 48 hours may adequately control the polyuria and polydipsia of patients with diabetes insipidus. **1965** LEE & KNOWLES *Animal Hormones* ii. 29 The basic action of one of the two hormones, vasopressin or an analogous substance, is apparently the same in all terrestrial vertebrates, namely the maintenance of the osmotic tension of the extracellular fluid, and indirectly that of the intracellular fluid. **1976** SMYTHIES & CORBETT *Psychiatry* vii. 115 After surgery vasopressin secretion induced by stress makes it impossible to dilute urine. **1981** *Sci. Amer.* Oct. 114/1 Vasopressin, a peptide hormone, turns out to be also a neurotransmitter: nerve cells in the hypothalamus, a part of the brain, rely on vasopressin to signal other nerve cells in the brain.

va·sopressor, *a.* and *sb. Pharm.* [f. VASO- + PRESSOR.] **A.** *adj.* Causing the constriction of blood vessels. **B.** *sb.* A drug with this effect.

1928 *Proc. Soc. Exper. Biol. & Med.* XXVI. 243 Recently Kamm [et al.]..separated from pituitary extracts what they believe to be nearly pure vasopressor and oxytocic hormones. **1964** *Brit. Jrnl. Oral Surg.* II. 131 The conditions under which these experiments have been carried out are..far removed from clinical situations since large amounts of vasopressor were used. **1966** WRIGHT & SYMMERS *Systemic Path.* II. xxix. 1034/1 It has not yet been demonstrated that the vasopressor action of the hormone is of any importance in the normal human. **1975** *Amer. Heart Jrnl.* XC. 233/2 Vasopressors and inotropic drugs were discontinued and cardiopulmonary bypass support was ultimately discontinued. **1977** *Proc. R. Soc. Med.* LXX. 157/1 Vasopressor drugs were very seldom used and then only in an emergency.

vassalled, *ppl. a.* (In Dict. s.v. VASSAL *v.*) (Later example.)

1933 W. FAULKNER *Green Bough* 63 Thrall to the vassalled garrison that keep Thy soft unguarded breast's white citadel.

vassaldom. For *rare*[−1] read *rare* and add later example.

1965 J. A. MICHENER *Source* (1966) 224 In the end Moab had been reduced to a kind of vassaldom.

vastidity. Delete † *Obs.* and add later examples.

1929 R. BRIDGES *Testament of Beauty* IV. 190 The spiritual idea of Friendship, the huge vastidity of its essence. **1931** C. WILLIAMS *Many Dimensions* xvii. 260 In the foreground of that vastidity, he saw rising the Types of the Stone. **1962** W. NOWOTTNY *Lang. Poets Use* iv. 83 The sense of vastidity of meaning in the sonnet derives from these many transformations of old into new.

‖ **vastrap** (fa·strap). Also † **vast-trap.** [Afrikaans, f. *vas* firm(ly), (Du. *vast*) + *trap* step, stand.] A quick South African folk dance; the music for this dance.

1913 *East London* (S. Afr.) *Dispatch* 3 Jan. 5 The *vast-trap* was performed by a number of nondescript characters who provided much amusement by their antics. **1926** O. SCHREINER *From Man to Man* 360 Then she paused and began a reel. 'This is the "vastrap",' she said... 'It's what the Hottentots dance.' **1944** M. DE B. NESBITT *Road to Avalon* xiv. 114 The band is playing a lively 'vastrap'. **1957** *Cape Times* 17 Jan. 7/1 Rock and roll has affiliations with our own vastraps and tiekiedraais to which Coloured bands used to thrum the beat. **1970** L. G. GREEN *Giant in Hiding* xi. 105 You remember the candle light, the *vastrap* music.

vat, *sb.* Add: **5. vat colour** = **vat dye*; **vat dye, dyestuff**, a water-insoluble dye that is applied in a reducing bath that converts it to a soluble leuco-form with affinity for the fibre, the colour being obtained upon subsequent oxidation; so **vat-dyed** *a.*; **vat dyeing** *vbl. sb.*

1912 L. A. OLNEY in A. Rogers *Industr. Chem.* xxxviii. 768 The reduction vat colors have come into great prominence during recent years owing to their great resistance to practically all of the color destroying agencies. **1947** KIRK & OTHMER *Encycl. Chem. Technol.* I. 968 With respect to all-around tinctorial and fastness properties, vat colors have no peer in any class of dyes. **1903** C. SALTER tr. *G. von Georgievics's Chem. Dye-Stuffs* 4 Vat Dyes..have no affinity for textile fibres, and can only be fixed thereon by reduction or subsequent oxidation. **1981** H. GUTJAHR in L. W. C. Miles *Textile Printing* v. 159 Vat dyes provide a wide range of colours of good all-round fastness properties, but great care, or specialized equipment, is required for their successful use. **1946** M. R. FOX *Vat Dyestuffs & Vat Dyeing* iv. 55 *(heading)* Fastness tests for vat-dyed wool and silk. **1960** *Farmer & Stockbreeder* 22 Mar. (Suppl.) 11/2 These vat-dyed, colour-fast, 48in wide cotton furnishing materials, are identically patterned on both sides. **1912** L. A. OLNEY in A. Rogers *Industr. Chem.* xxxviii. 756 The alkaline bath of indigo white is commonly called an indigo vat, and this process of coloring is usually spoken of as vat dyeing. **1946** M. R. FOX *(title)* Vat dyestuffs and vat dyeing. **1914** F. W. ATACK tr. *Wahl's Manuf. Organic Dyestuffs* xix. 220 For a long time the vat-dyestuffs were limited to Indigo, its derivatives, and the Indophenols. **1973** *Materials & Technol.* VI. vii. 488 Nylon shows very little affinity for the vat dyestuffs.

VAT (vī,ē¹,tī·, væt), also **vat,** abbrev. of *value added tax* s.v. *VALUE *sb.* 2 d. Cf. TVA s.v. *T 6 a.

1966 *Economist* 29 Oct. 432/2 This may be true of the conventional VAT. **1971** *Guardian* 29 Sept. 5/3 The substitution of VAT (value added tax) for purchase tax and SET in June 1973. **1978** *Hi-Fi News* Sept. 204 (Advt.), All prices include vat at 12½%.

Hence **VA·T-, va·table** *a. colloq.*, liable to VAT; **VA·Tman** *colloq.*, a Customs and Excise officer who deals with VAT.

1973 *Times* 31 Oct. 14/8 A glance at how Alice is faring will show how plays themselves are affected. At present she and her like are VAT-able and non VAT-able according to circumstances. **1976** *Daily Tel.* 4 Nov. 21 The last [*sc.* higher indirect taxes] would put up the cost of living but, to a large extent, the extra cost of vatable items..is voluntary. **1977** T. HEALD *Just Desserts* ii. 30 Those absolute fiends from the Inland Revenue or..the dreaded VATmen. **1979** *Accountancy Age* 16 Feb. 7/1 *(heading)* Convincing fanciful VATmen you don't have the goods. **1984** *Listener* 11 Oct. 42/1 The income-tax inspector knows as little about it as the VAT-man.

vaterite (vā·tĕrəit, f-). *Min.* [ad. G. *vaterit* (W. Meigen 1911, in *Verhandl. d. Ges. deutsch. Naturforscher und Ärzte* LXXXII. II. I. 124), f. the name of H. A. *Vater* (1859–1930), German mineralogist and geologist: see -ITE[1].] A relatively rare, metastable form of calcium carbonate, $CaCO_3$, that is polymorphous with calcite and aragonite and crystallizes in the hexagonal system.

1913 *Mineral. Mag.* XVI. 374 Vaterite... Vater's third modification of calcium carbonate prepared artificially in the form of minute spherules. **1962** *Acta Chirurg. Scand.* CXXIV. 324/1 X-ray crystallographic studies have shown that the three crystalline forms of calcium carbonate, namely vaterite, aragonite and calcite, can all occur in concretions from the pancreas, biliary- and urinary tract. **1975** *Science* 25 Apr. 363 The spicules of the common tropical ascidian, *Herdmania momus*, are mineralized with vaterite.

‖ **Vaterland** (fā·təɹlant). [Ger., = fatherland.] A German's fatherland.

1852 C. LEVER *Daltons* I. xxii. 184 Hansel was the kind, quaint emblem of his own dreamy 'Vaterland'. **1894** G. DU MAURIER *Trilby* I. II. 111 The buttercups and daisies of the Vaterland! **1950** *New Yorker* 26 Aug. 70/2 Germans whose every act and thought was directed.. toward the enhancement of the *Vaterland*. **1977** N.

Freeling *Gadget* iv. 151 A stone slab had carved upon it the..names of the village boys dead for the Vaterland in '14–'18.

Vatican. Add: **2. a.** *Vatican Council*: now also, the Second Vatican Council (1962–5), also called Vatican II, which is noted for the introduction of the vernacular for the Mass and other reforms.

1961 *Times* 12 Dec. 6/3 On Christmas Day the Pope is to issue his Bull summoning the second Vatican Council. **1963** E. Schillebeeckx in *Life of Spirit* June 504 Is it possible at this stage to surmise what the outcome of Vatican II is going to be? Yes, in principle it is. The majority have expressed themselves in favour of a different approach. **1969** A. Richardson *Dict. Christian Theol.* 354/2 Vatican II..teaches that bishops possess, by virtue of their consecration, 'the fullness of the priesthood', including the threefold role of sanctifying, teaching and governing. **1976** *Jrnl. R. Soc. Arts* Mar. 164/1 The Second Vatican Council may well have an understanding of the Sack of Rome and the Council of Trent which was denied to writers in the earlier part of this century. **1979** D. Gageby in J. J. Lee *Ireland 1945–70* 132 John Horgan, now a member of the Dáil, writing about Vatican II and the ecclesiastical changes. **1983** *Times* 16 May 12/6 The Protestant Ethic..is definitely out of fashion, theologically. Today, they all quote Temple, or Vatican II.

b. Special Combs.: **Vatican City** (or **State**), the temporal state established by the Lateran Treaty of 1929, comprising the area immediately surrounding the Vatican Palace in Rome and headed by the Pope; **Vatican roulette** *colloq.*, the rhythm method of birth control, as permitted by the Roman Catholic Church.

1929 *Times* 8 Feb. 14/1 The new Papal State, which is to be known as the 'Vatican State' or as the 'Vatican City', will be confined to a small extent of territory in the neighbourhood of the Vatican. **1974** *Encycl. Brit. Macropædia* XIX. 36/1 The Vatican City is in all ways independent from Italy. **1962** *Western Folklore* Jan. 34 Vatican roulette—the rhythm system of birth control. **1965** D. Lodge *British Museum is falling Down* 172 That's another thing against the safe method there are so many things that can affect ovulation... No wonder they called it Vatican Roulette. **1977** H. G. Burger in B. Bernardi *Concept & Dynamics of Culture* 458 When Roman Catholicism permitted only the 'rhythm method' of birth control, sometimes satirized for its ineffectiveness as 'Vatican roulette', the Toronto archbishop authorized birth control pills.

Vaticanology (væ:tikănǫ·lŏdʒi). *colloq.* [f. Vatican + -ology.] The study of the history, or analysis of the policies, of the Vatican. So **Va:ticano·logist.**

1975 *Guardian Weekly* 14 Dec. 27 His publishers describe him as 'a leading Vaticanologist', and he does appear to know more than most people about the Curia. **1976** *Times Lit. Suppl.* 13 Aug. 1018/4 It is..several generations since Chesterton's sallies delighted the devout, and Vaticanology has few students in non-Catholic countries. **1979** M. Craig *Man from Far Country* xv. 173 Father F.X. Murphy, a renowned Vaticanologist. **1982** *Times Lit. Suppl.* 12 Feb. 154/1 It is high time that Vaticanology was recognized as a serious field of historical inquiry. **1984** D. Yallop *In God's Name* 62 If the 111 cardinals were as perplexed as the Vaticanologists then the Church was in for a long, confusing Conclave.

vaticinatory (vătisinē̆ⁱ·tŏri), *a.* Delete *rare*$^{-1}$ and add further examples.

1895 *Starting Price* 23 Mar. 3/3 To test the vaticinatory skill of professional and amateur prophets, we offer a prize of £10 for a tipping contest. **1930** Wyndham Lewis *Apes of God* xii. vii. 483 There was, as well as a great vaticinatory verve, a certain boastfulness about this Fascist. **1980** V. Cunningham *Penguin Bk. Spanish Civil War Verse* 38 Cornford is blamed for not being vaticinatory enough about these 'political surrealists' who couldn't wait for the revolution.

Vatinian, *a.* For † *Obs.* read 'Now *rare*' and add later example.

1927 T. Wilder *Bridge of San Luis Rey* ii. 62 The Archbishop of Lima..hated her, with what he called a Vatinian hate and counted the cessation of her visits among the compensations for dying.

vatje (fa·kʸi). *S. Afr.* Also **fadje, fagie, fatje, fikey, vaatjie, vaitje.** [ad. Afrikaans *vaatjie*, dim. of *vat* water-carrier (see Fat *sb.*[1]).] A small cask or barrel for carrying water or wine; a soldier's canteen.

1850 R. G. Cumming *Five Years Hunter's Life S. Afr.* i. 7/1 The..general stores which I carried with me were as follows:..2 large 'fagie' or water-casks, [etc.]. **1871** J. McKay *Reminisc. Last Kafir War* ii. 8 The soldier acts as the beast of burden, having been supplied with a large wooden vessel, by soldiers called 'fadje', or keg, capable of holding about half a gallon; and in this he had to carry with him what water he thought necessary. **1871** J. Mackenzie *Ten Yrs. North of Orange River* vii. 115 Khosimore jealously guarded his 'vatjes', or water-vessels. **1891** E. Glanville *Fossicker* xix. 166 One of the three rose up..took a final pull at the water 'fikey', and stretched himself on the bare ground. **1909** *Chambers's Jrnl.* Dec. 28/1 Some Congo brandy and a *vatje* of water. **1951** L. G. Green *Fully Many a Glorious Morning* xviii. 234 We gave up part of a *vaatjie* of red wine and soaked it and then roasted it in front of a huge fire. **1970** in *Voorloper* (1976) 833 The coloured people buy their wine in a vaatjie for celebrations.

VATman: see *VAT.

vauclusian (vǫklū·ziăn), *a. Physical Geogr.* Also **Vauclusian.** [f. the name of the Fontaine de *Vaucluse* in S. France: see -ian.] Applied to a type of spring, often large, occurring in karstic regions, in which the water is forced out under artesian pressure.

1937 Wooldridge & Morgan *Physical Basis Geogr.* xix. 294 Cheddar Gorge..and the spectacular Wookey Hole with its 'Vauclusian spring', show true karstic features. **1977** A. Hallam *Planet Earth* 82/3 There are two main types of karst spring, one where the water issues by means of free flow, the other where the water issues under forced or artesian flow: the latter type is sometimes known as a vauclusian spring. **1980** J. C. Schmid tr. *A. Bögli's Karst Hydrol.* ix. 124 In a genuine vauclusian spring the water course runs upwards through the rock.

vaude (vǭd, vōᵘd). *N. Amer. colloq.* Also **vaud.** [Abbrev. of Vaudeville.] Vaudeville (sense 2); a vaudeville theatre. Also *attrib.*

1933 *Ladies' Home Jrnl.* Mar. 21/3 He was wearing a cap with purple and green in it and the loudest checked suit I have ever seen on anybody outside of a vaud. **1951** Green & Laurie (*title*) Show biz, from vaude to video. **1975** R. Davies *World of Wonders* (1977) i. viii. 105 A rabble of acts..which played for rotten pay in the worst vaude houses.

vaudeville. Delete ‖ and add: Now freq., esp. *U.S.*, with pronunc. (vǭ·dvil, vǭ·dəvil). **2.** (Earlier and further examples.) Now in frequent use in the U.S. to designate variety theatre (Variety 9 b) or music hall.

1827 T. Dibdin *Reminiscences* I. xii. 268, I also had the honour..of being selected by her Royal Highness the Princess Elizabeth to write a sort of *vaudeville* farce. *c* **1831** J. H. Reynolds in J. R. Planché *Recollections & Reflections* (1872) I. xii. 181 And lure for you the light Vaudeville from France. **1911** G. B. Shaw in *Daily Graphic* 2 Dec. 4/3 There are vaudeville theatres in America and variety theatres in England. **1917** *Lit. Digest* 25 Aug. 28/2 The phrase 'Jaz her up' is a common one to-day in vaudeville and on the circus lot. When a vaudeville act needs ginger the cry from the advisers in the wings is 'put in jaz'. **1940** R. Chandler *Farewell, my Lovely* v. 30 You would find them in tank town vaudeville acts..in the cheap burlesque houses. **1967** *Stage* 2 Mar. 4/1 The merging of vaudeville and tombola as a major February attraction at Blackpool last week succeeded. **1976** *New Yorker* 8 Mar. 57/1 The play is a lewd, tragic vaudeville about the life of a bankrupt pursued by creditors. **1976** J. Crosby *Nightfall* xxxiii. 197 You're a fifth-rate vaudeville actor. **1982** *Verbatim* Autumn 23/2 The subject is given light-hearted treatment, as though this jargon were little more than food for variety turns (i.e., vaudeville acts).

vaudevillain (vōᵘ·d(ə)vilăn, vǭ·d-). *U.S. colloq.* ? *Obs.* [f. Vaudeville, after Villain *sb.*] = *vaudevillian *sb.*

1909 *Sat. Even. Post* 5 June 17/2 One thrifty vaudevillain made sixty-five weeks one season in this way. **1916** J. K. Bangs *From Pillar to Post* xvi. 326 The major was a great believer in the value of Author's Readings by what he used to call 'running mates'—teams, as the vaudevillains have it.

vaudevillian (vǭd-, vōᵘd(ə)vi·liăn), *sb.* and *a.* orig. and chiefly *U.S.* Also **-ean.** [f. Vaudeville + -ian.] **A.** *sb.* A performer in vaudeville. **B.** *adj.* Of or pertaining to vaudeville.

1913 *Technical World Mag.* Mar. 19 'That's great!' cried one of the 'vaudevillians', clapping his hands appreciatively. **1924** *Sat. Even. Post* 4 Oct. 70/2 Give them to some small-time vaudevillian to repeat. **1930** *Punch* 8 Oct. 415 The modish songs..serve pleasantly to exercise the vaudevillean gifts of Mr. Coward and Miss Lawrence. **1961** *John o' London's* 5 Oct. 373/1 The elder Glasses were vaudevillians (music-hall artists). **1962** J. D. Salinger *Franny & Zooey* 120 The children's father, a former international vaudevillian. **1975** *Times* 2 Aug. 12/1 (*heading*) Behind the vaudevillian smoke-screen. **1980** *Redbook* Oct. 213/3 Later, years later, he was to win an Academy award playing an old vaudevillian in *The Sunshine Boys*. **1985** *Listener* 23 May 37/1, I don't just mean old vaudevillians like George Burns.

vaudevillist. (Earlier example.)

1839 [see *stenographist].

vaudoux. Add: Also **vaudo.**

1862 J. Le Grand *Jrnl.* 20 Dec. (1911) 57 Heard today of the existence of a negro society here called the 'vaudo' (I believe).

vault, *v.*[2] Add: **3.** *trans.* To cause to rise *to* or *into* a considerably higher position or situation.

1976 *National Observer* (U.S.) 31 July 1/2 Nadia Comaneci's electrifying gymnastics performances vaulted her from obscurity to world-wide renown. **1977** *Detroit Free Press* 11 Dec. 2-D/2 Severiano Ballesteros of Spain shot a three-under-par 69 Saturday and vaulted his team into a three-stroke lead over Canada after 54 holes of the 25th World Cup Golf Championship Saturday.

vauntingness. For *Obs.*$^{-0}$ read *rare* and add example.

1955 E. Bowen *World of Love* v. 83 If she chose to make history out of her vicissitudes, that was really from vauntingness—nothing beat her.

vauntless (vǭ·ntlės), *a. nonce-wd.* [f. Vaunt *sb.* + -less.] Not bragging or boasting.

c **1879** G. M. Hopkins *Poems* (1967) 82 Tongue true, vaunt- and tauntless.

Vauxhall. Add: **b. Vauxhall lamp, light,** an ornamental glass lantern designed to hold a candle and used for outdoor illumination.

1907 *Yesterday's Shopping* (1969) 258/2 Garden or Vauxhall lamps. For illuminations, &c. Diamond moulding, size 2¼ in. by 3½ in... Wired ready for hanging. **1974** *Country Life* 17 Oct. 1075/3 A pleasure ground..at Tollard Royal..in late Victorian and Edwardian times... The Gardens were illuminated with thousands of Vauxhall lights.

2. Used *attrib.* and *absol.* to designate antique plate glass resembling that made at the Vauxhall Glassworks from *c* 1663 to the end of the 18th cent.

1830 W. Dawson in W. H. Bowles *Hist. Vauxhall & Ratcliff Glass Houses* (1926) 58 Edward Dawson of the Glass House Vauxhall who died Jan. 12 1755 made some great improvements which enabled John Dawson his son to produce those brilliant glasses still distinguished as 'Vauxhall plates'. **1900** *Archit. Rev.* June p. xxii, The mirror has a flat bevel, after the manner of the old Vauxhall plates. **1926** W. H. Bowles *Hist. Vauxhall & Ratcliff Glass Houses* iii. 19 To this day all mirrors made in this country between 1670 and 1750 are styled by dealers 'Vauxhall'. **1972** *Country Life* 27 Jan. (Suppl.) 24/1 (Advt.), Queen Anne walnut bureau-bookcase.. retaining original Vauxhall mirror door. **1975** *Oxf. Compan. Decorative Arts* 571/1 In 1663 the second Duke of Buckingham established a plate-glass manufactory at Vauxhall, of which the products have become legendary. The term 'Vauxhall glass' has for long been used to describe any old-looking mirror although no existing example can be traced with certainty to that source. **1977** *Times* 20 Aug. 8/5 English merchants began to export Vauxhall glass..to China.

vauxite (vǭ·ksəit). *Min.* [f. the name of George *Vaux* (1863–1927), U.S. mineral collector + -ite[1].] A secondary mineral that is a hydrated basic phosphate of aluminium and ferrous iron, $Fe^{2+}{}_2Al_2(PO_4)_2(OH)_2.6H_2O$, and occurs as blue, transparent triclinic crystals, usu. in association with paravauxite and wavellite.

1922, 1944 [see *paravauxite* s.v. *para-[1] 2 c]. **1974** *Amer. Mineralogist* LIX. 843 Montgomeryite, $Ca_4Mg(H_2O)_{12}[Al_4(OH)_4(PO_4)_6]$,..possesses chains of corner-linked Al–O octahedra which are topologically and geometrically equivalent to the chains in vauxite.

väyrynenite (vē̦irī·nėnəit). *Min.* [ad. G. *väyrynenit* (Volborth & Stradner 1954, in *Anz. Math.-Naturwiss. Kl. Österr. Akad. Wissensch.* XCI. 21), f. the name of H. *Väyrynen*, 20th-c. Finnish mineralogist: see -ite[1].] A phosphate and fluoride of beryllium and manganese, $BeMnPO_4(OH,F)$, found as red transparent monoclinic crystals.

1954 *Chem. Abstr.* XLVIII. 4380 Optical data of väyrynenite are presented. **1977** *Mineral. Abstr.* XXVIII. 207/2 Crystals acquired in a bazaar in Chitral, Pakistan, have been identified as väyrynenite.

VE (vī̦,ī·). [f. the initial letters of *V*ictory in *E*urope.] Used *attrib.* and *absol.* to denote the victory of the Allied forces over those of Germany during the second World War; esp. as *VE-day*, designating the date of Germany's surrender, 8 May 1945.

1944 *Washington Post* 10 Sept. 3/1 James F. Byrne, director of War Mobilization, found a new designation for the two victory days... Last night he referred to the date of Germany's impending surrender as V-E (victory in Europe) Day, and the day of Japan's defeat as V-J (Victory over Japan) Day. **1945** *Daily Mirror* 8 May 1/2 Today is VE-Day—the day for which the British people have fought and endured five years, eight months and four days of war. **1956** A. H. Compton *Atomic Quest* iv. 273 At Yalta,..President Roosevelt endeavored..to obtain Stalin's commitment to enter the war against Japan. Eventually Stalin agreed to do so within three months after V-E day. **1974** P. Lively *House in Norham Gardens* x. 130 Mrs Hedges..talked about..D-day and VE night. **1977** *Wandsworth Borough News* 16 Sept. 12/4 The jubilee street parties are reminiscent of those marvellous V.E. and V.J. celebrations, when pianos were pulled on to the streets and everyone—strangers or not—were welcomed. **1978** R. V. Jones *Most Secret War* xxxvi. 312 Some months after V-E Day he was arrested in the American Zone of Germany.

veal, *sb.*[1] Add: **3. a.** *veal and ham pie* (earlier examples), *veal cutlet* (earlier examples).

1728 E. Smith *Compl. Housewife* (ed. 2) 41 (*heading*) To make veal cutlets. **1811** Jane Austen *Sense & Sens.* II. iv. 53 Preferring salmon to cod, or boiled fowls to veal cutlets. **1848** Thackeray *Pendennis* (1849) I. v. 49 That girl, sir, makes the best veal and ham pie in England. **1861** Mrs. Beeton *Bk. Househ. Managem.* 942 *Saturday.* 1. Rump-steaks, broiled, and oyster sauce, mashed potatoes; veal-and-ham pie.

b. veal calf, (*a*) (later examples); **veal**

parmigiana [It. *parmigiano* Parmesan cheese], a dish of small escalopes of veal and cheese; **veal piccata,** a dish of small escalopes of veal.

1946 F. H. Garner *Brit. Dairying* xi. 228 Veal calves demand much milk when being reared. **1981** *Times* 25 July 3/2 Veal calves are penned in tight crates on liquid feeds throughout their lives. **1963** R. Carrier *Gt. Dishes of World* ix. 161 Veal parmigiana. **1972** [see *linguine]. **1983** C. McCarry *Last Supper* iv. i. 184 He..ordered veal parmigiana..crusty veal with its rubbery slab of strange white cheese covered with tomato sauce. **1973** Veal piccata [see *prime *a.* 4 a]. **1982** J. D. MacDonald *Cinnamon Skin* xvii. 172 The veal piccata..went well with the Valpolicella.

vealer. (In Dict. s.v. Veal *sb.*[1]) Delete *U.S.* and add examples.

1931 *Daily News-Journal* (Murfreesboro, Tennessee) 17 Apr. 4/1 Better grade vealers around 50c higher. **1977** *West Briton* 25 Aug. 11/1 Calves—vealers to £26. **1984** *Grass Roots* (N.Z.) Feb. 13/1 We have been developing a thriving vealer mini project on 25 acres at Neerim South in West Gippsland, Victoria.

veatchite (vī·tʃəit). *Min.* [See quot. 1938 and -ite[1].] Any of three polymorphs of a hydrous strontium borate, $Sr_2[B_5O_8(OH)]_2 \cdot B(OH)_3 . H_2O$, of which two (*veatchite* and *p-veatchite*) are monoclinic and one (*veatchite-A*) is triclinic.

1938 G. Switzer in *Amer. Mineralogist* XXIII. 411 It seems fitting to name this new borate veatchite after Dr. John A. Veatch, who was the first to detect the presence of borates in the mineral waters of California, on January 8, 1856. **1960** *Mineral. Mag.* XXXII. 500 A mineral from the Permian lower evaporite bed of the Eskdale No. 2 boring in Yorkshire... Single-crystal X-ray work now proves that this mineral is *p*-veatchite. **1979** *Amer. Mineralogist* LXIV. 362 A third modification of veatchite occurs in Emet colemanite deposit, Kütahya, Turkey, as white cauliflower-shaped nodules associated with colemanite, hydroboracite, realgar, orpiment and montmorillonite. The new mineral is triclinic... Crystals are transparent, colorless... The new modification is named veatchite-A.

veber, obs. var. Weber[1] in Dict. and Suppl.

Veblenian (vĕblī·niăn), *a.* and *sb.* [f. the name *Veblen* + -ian.] **A.** *adj.* Of or pertaining to the work of Thorstein Veblen (1857–1929), U.S. economist and social scientist, esp. the ideas (as of conspicuous consumption) expounded in his book *Theory of the Leisure Class* (1899). **B.** *sb.* One who supports or advocates Veblenian ideas.

1931 *Encycl. Social Sci.* V. 388/2 The Veblenian terminology of American institutionalism. **1953** D. Riesman *Thorstein Veblen* viii. 180 Those high-income people..who buy..with a Veblenian ascetic eye on their own motivations. **1968** *Internat. Encycl. Social Sci.* IV. 462/2 Economists working in the Veblenian tradition. **1973** *Hist. Political Econ.* V. 449 (*heading*) Hoxie's economics in retrospect: the making and unmaking of a Veblenian. **1982** *Jrnl. Econ. Issues* XVI. 757 The Veblenian dichotomy is the central analytical tool of institutional economists in the Veblen–Ayres tradition. **1982** J. D. MacDonald *Cinnamon Skin* xix. 210 Veblen died in 1929 at the age of seventy-two... I have never been a Veblenian myself.

vecchio (ve·ki,o). For *Obs.* read *rare* and add later examples.

1938 E. Hemingway *Fifth Column* 273 'Three marsalas,' said the young gentleman to the girl behind the pastry counter. 'Two, you mean?' she asked. 'No,' he said, 'One for a vecchio.' **1944** G. B. Shaw *Let.* 4 Dec. in *To a Young Actress* (1960) 180, I am a vecchio, nearly eightyeight and a half.

Vectian (ve·ktiăn), *a. Geol.* [f. L. *Vect-is*, name of the Isle of Wight + -ian.] Of or pertaining to the Isle of Wight or the Lower Greensand strata exposed there; *spec.* (see quot. 1961).

[**1845** W. H. Fitton in *Q. Jrnl. Geol. Soc.* I. 189 If hereafter a change [from Lower Green Sand] be thought desirable, he [*sc.* the author] conceives that the new denomination should be taken from the *Isle of Wight*..; and if such a case should arise, he suggests the name of *Vectine* for the strata now called Lower Green Sand, from the ancient name of that island,—*Insula Vectis* of the Romans.] **1885** A. J. Jukes-Browne in *Geol. Mag.* Decade III. ii. 298 The Lower Greensand can be studied so well in the Isle of Wight..that no name can be more appropriate than *Vectian*; and I regard the introduction of a new name as preferable to the adoption of the French names *Aptien* and *Urgonien*. **1922** [see *Selbornian *a.* 2]. **1961** *Palaeontology* III. 502 The Vectian Province comprises the Isle of Wight and a small part of the Dorset mainland where a strip of Lower Greensand extends westwards from Swanage to Lulworth Cove. **1969** Bennison & Wright *Geol. Hist. Brit. Isles* xiv. 323 In this Vectian Province the Lower Greensand becomes attenuated westwards at a more rapid rate than the Wealden (Neocomian) Beds.

vector, *sb.* Add: **2. a.** (Earlier and further examples.) *axial vector* = *pseudovector *sb.*; *polar vector*, a vector which changes sign when the signs of all its components are changed.

1846 W. R. Hamilton in *Phil. Mag.* XXIX. 27 The algebraically imaginary part, being geometrically constructed by a straight line, or radius vector, which has, in general, for each determined quaternion, a determined length and determined direction in space, may be called the vector part, or simply the vector of the quaternion. **1873** J. C. Maxwell *Treat. Electr. & Magn.* I. 9 A Vector, or Directed Quantity, requires for its definition three numerical specifications, and these may most simply be understood as having reference to the directions of the coordinate axes. **1903** *Nature* 22 Oct. 610/1 This algebra.. does not discriminate between 'polar' vectors, *e.g.* forces and 'axial' vectors, *e.g.* couples. **1968** M. S. Livingston *Particle Physics* v. 101 Angular momentum is an axial vector quantity, unlike linear momentum which is a polar vector.

b. An ordered set of two or more numbers (interpretable as the co-ordinates of a point); a matrix with one row or one column; also, any element of a vector space.

[**1873:** see prec. sense. **1881** J. W. Gibbs *Sci. Papers* (1906) II. 17 The numerical description of a vector requires three numbers.] **1922** J. B. Shaw *Vector Calculus* i. 6 A vector is usually designated by a triple as (x, y, z), and usually such triple is called a vector. **1938** R. A. Frazer et al. *Elem. Matrices* i. 2 A row matrix is often called..a vector of the first kind..; while a column matrix is referred to as a vector of the second kind. **1940** D. E. Littlewood *Theory Group Characters* i. 5 A square matrix..of order n^2 may be regarded as composed of n column vectors. **1961** *Communications Assoc. Computing Machinery* IV. 424/2 The analysis of a program into phases and sequences is accomplished by associating with each sequence a vector of ones and zeros. **1965** Patterson & Rutherford *Elem. Abstr. Algebra* v. 155 The polynomial ring $P(F)$ is a vector space over the same field F... The polynomials are in this case the vectors of this vector space. **1976** *Biometrika* LXIII. 438 Given N_0, the vector $(n_1, \ldots, n_{X_0})$ will have a multinomial distribution with N_0 trials. **1981** N. Rau *Matrices & Math. Programming* i. 16 Up to this point, vectors have been considered simply as a special case of matrices... For the rest of this book..'vector' will always be used to mean column vector.

c. *Aeronaut.* A course to be taken by an aircraft, or steered by a pilot.

1941 D. Masters *So Few* xxx. 333 'I've got to get a Hun tonight. I'll give you a bottle of champagne if you put me on to one.'..'All right, ..I'll give you a vector.' **1951** O. Berthoud tr. *Clostermann's Big Show* 102, I am climbing flat out on vector 095. **1978** R. V. Jones *Most Secret War* xxi. 177 The ground station ordered an aircraft to steer a course of 270° (i.e. due west) presumably because it was east of the beam, and this was the vector required to bring it to the right point to start its bombing run.

d. *Computers.* A sequence of consecutive locations in memory; a series of items occupying such a sequence and identified within it by means of one subscript; *spec.* one serving as the address to which a program must jump when interrupted, and supplied by the source of the interruption.

1961 *Communications Assoc. Computing Machinery* IV. 61/1 Since it is often necessary to refer to memory addresses and the contents of memory cells in this discussion, the almost-legitimate device of the 'Memory vector' will be used. This is done by assuming the entire memory of the machine in question to constitute a single one-dimensional vector, named 'Memory'. **1962** E. W. Dijkstra *Primer of ALGOL 60 Programming* 37 The simplest example of such an array is a vector, i.e. a sequence of subscripted variables. **1967** D. G. Hays *Introd. Computational Linguistics* ii. 26 When the program stops, the J-th column of the matrix F has been copied into the vector G. **1967** P. A. Stark *Digital Computer Programming* xiv. 255 After checking the transfer vector to see that the subroutine name is there, the loader goes back into the mainline program and fixes the linkage so that the mainline program jumps into the transfer vector. **1975** R. H. Eckhouse *Minicomputer Systems* vi. 186 The new contents of the PC [*sc.* program counter] and the PS [*sc.* processor status] are loaded from two preassigned consecutive memory locations called an interrupt vector... The contents of these vectors are determined by the programmer. **1982** *Economist* 3 Apr. 128/3 Individual units of data (ie, binary numbers) are stored in the computer's memory in long lists called vectors. **1982** R. A. Sparkes *Microcomputers in Sci. Teaching* v. 199 A test must be included into the routine to ascertain if the user wants to return to normal working. If so, the ISR [*sc.* interrupt service routine] vector is changed back to 58926 and the extra routine is by-passed. **1984** *Personal Software* Winter 89/3 During loading, a message is displayed on the screen and the keyboard and screen vectors are changed to effect automatic program execution.

3. a. *Med.* and *Biol.* A person, animal, or plant which carries a pathogenic agent and acts as a potential source of infection for members of another species. Also *transf.* Cf. *carrier 1 l (i).

1922 [see *Arthropoda, arthropod]. **1944** *Nature* 5 Aug. 167/2 Regular transmission of viruses by the egg of the host plant (the insect vector does not concern us unless it suffers) probably does not occur. **1963** R. Carson *Silent Spring* xvi. 220 An even more serious problem concerns the vector of yellow fever. **1972** *Lancet* 17 June 1338/2 The stethoscope is yet another vector of pathogenic organisms. **1974** Passmore & Robson *Compan. Med. Stud.* III. xii. 64/2 The spread of each of the insect-borne diseases depends on a complicated chain of events involving..a reservoir of infection which may be either in man or in other animals,..the insect vector and..a susceptible human population. **1976** *Dumfries & Galloway Standard* 25 Dec. 8/6 A small boy recovered after being bitten by a rabid bat, it being thought that the disease had been modified by passage through this unusual vector.

b. *Genetics.* A bacteriophage which transfers genetic material from one bacterium to another; also, a phage or plasmid used to transfer extraneous DNA into a cell.

1958 *Abstr. 7th Internat. Congr. Microbiol.* 53 The modified phage particle so produced has been identified as the transducing vector. **1968** W. Hayes *Genetics of Bacteria & their Viruses* (ed. 2) xvii. 478 Some other temperate phages..can act as vectors for the transfer, to recipient bacteria, of virtually any region of the host chromosome. **1976** *Proc. Nat. Acad. Sci.* LXXIII. 2838/1 Gene transfer between two closely related mouse cell lines has been carried out, using as the vector a cell-free preparation of metaphase chromosomes and nuclei. **1982** T. M. Devlin *Textbk. Biochem.* xx. 986/2 The methodology involves obtaining the DNA of the desired gene; placing the DNA into a vector or vehicle capable of transporting the gene and maintaining it inside an *E. coli* cell;..and determining whether the gene is functional in *E. coli*. **1983** *Sci. Amer.* Jan. 58/2 Plasmids are routinely used as vectors for introducing foreign DNA into bacteria. **1985** Old & Primrose *Princ. Gene Recombination* (ed. 3) 222 This may have the additional property of being a shuttle vector, capable of stable replication in *E. coli* and *A. tumefaciens*.

4. *transf.* and *fig.*

1926 *Spectator* 30 Oct. 735/1 Even if there was a listener-in within the narrow vector of the vibrations, he could not hope to receive the messages at the rate at which they will be sent. **1954** W. Faulkner *Fable* 82 He identified himself, naming his battalion and its vector. **1957** L. Durrell *Bitter Lemons* 37 But I was on a different vector, hunting for other qualities which might make residence tolerable, or might isolate me from my fellows. **1976** *Listener* 15 Apr. 466/1 Once, a long vector of geese flew over. **1977** A. Hecht in *Oxf. Bk. Contemp. Verse* (1980) 173 The athlete's dancing vector, the spirit's need, And muscle's cleanly diction. **1979** *UCT Studies in English* (Univ. Cape Town) Sept. 39 Antithesis is, of course, the chief trope of the rape genre, not only in respect of the obvious contrasts drawn between the heroine's purity and her shame, but also with regard to the vectors of these states—contrastive images of light and dark.

5. a. In the sense 'of the nature of a (mathematical) vector, representable by a vector'; also as *adj.*

1846 [see sense 2 a above]. **1873** J. C. Maxwell *Treat. Electricity & Magn.* I. 9 A vector quantity has direction as well as magnitude, and is such that a reversal of its direction reverses its sign. **1880** [in Dict., sense 2]. **1881** J. W. Gibbs *Sci. Papers* (1906) II. 37 Maxwell has called $-\nabla . \nabla u$ the concentration of u, whether u is scalar or vector. **1962** Corson & Lorrain *Introd. Electromagnetic Fields & Waves* i. 1 Wind velocity, gravitational force, and electric field intensity are examples of..vector quantities. **1975** *Nature* 18 Sept. 191/1 β-decay within isospin multiplets of $J^{\pi} = 0^+$ is pure vector because there is no nuclear spin to flip.

b. In the sense 'involving (mathematical) vectors', as *vector addition, algebra, analysis, calculus, method*, etc.

1873 Kelland & Tait *Introd. Quaternions* iii. 32 (*heading*) Vector multiplication and division. **1881** A. S. Hardy *Elem. Quaternions* i. 3 The operation of vector addition is commutative. **1881** J. W. Gibbs *Sci. Papers* (1906) II. 17 An algebra or analytical method in which a single letter or other expression is used to specify a vector may be called a vector algebra or vector analysis. **1897** [in Dict., sense 2]. **1904** *Rep. Brit. Assoc. Adv. Sci. 1903* 53, I cannot help thinking that he would have used vector methods throughout if he had found ready to hand a vector analysis instead of a theory of quaternions. **1955** A. Huxley *Genius & Goddess* 38 The great man would get bored and quietly fade away, leaving me to solve Timmy's problem by some method a little simpler than vector analysis. **1964** J. W. Linnett *Electronic Struct. Molecules* i. 7 The resultant angular momentum is, therefore, by vector addition..$\sqrt{2}h/2\pi$. **1968** E. T. Copson *Metric Spaces* ix. 138 This is ordinary vector algebra without scalar and vector products. **1969** *Jane's Freight Containers 1968–69* 147/2 It has been assumed..that the vector sum (the actual value of the lashing tension) will not exceed 30 400 kgf. **1972** M. Kline *Math. Thought* xxxii. 786 By Maxwell's time a great deal of vector analysis was created by treating the scalar and vector parts of quaternions separately. **1973** H. M. Schey *Div, Grad, Curl, & All That* i. 1 Much of vector calculus was invented for use in electromagnetic theory and is ideally suited to it. **1982** *Sci. Amer.* Jan. 117/3 For any operation that can be applied to a single operand (such as the extraction of the square root) there is a corresponding vector operation that consists of applying the same operation to every element of a vector.

c. *Particle Physics.* Used *attrib.* to designate particles with a spin of 1; *vector boson*, esp. any of a group of three heavy bosons (the $W^{\pm}$ and Z^0, qq.v. in Suppl.) thought to exist as mediators of the weak interaction. [See quot. 1961.]

1942 *Physical Rev.* LXII. 403 The β-matrices in the vector meson theory can be reduced to the simpler ζ-matrices and S matrices (spin matrices). **1949** *Ibid.* LXXVI. 784/1 The exchange of two charged vector mesons. **1959** *Bull. de l'Acad. Polonaise des Sci.: Série des Sci. Math.* VII. 729 Recently a hypothesis of a charged vector boson, which would mediate in weak interactions, was much discussed. **1968** M. S. Livingston *Particle Physics* xii. 218 The agency of this weak force is presumed to be a vector boson. **1975** *Nature* 3 Apr. 387/2 In a simple SU(4) scheme there is an obvious place for one ψ particle, in the same multiplet as the well established vector mesons ρ, ω and ϕ. **1976** *Sci. Amer.* Jan. 46/1 They are called vector bosons because the quantum-mechanical equation that describes particles with a spin of 1 takes the form of a four-dimensional vector. **1978** *Nature* 12 Oct. 483/1 These fermions interact through vector particles: the photon, charged and neutral massive vector bosons, and gluons which are responsible for the electromagnetic, weak and strong interactions, respectively. **1983** *Ibid.* 27 Jan. 285 Physicists in Geneva have discovered the intermediate vector boson.

d. Special Combs.: **vector address** *Computers*, an address specified by an interrupt vector (see sense 2 d above); **vector-borne** *a.*, (of a disease or pathogen) transmitted or carried by a vector (sense 3 a above); **vector field**, a field defined at each point by a vector quantity; a map from a space to a space of two or more dimensions; **vector function**, a function whose value is a vector quantity; **vector potential**, a potential function that is a vector function (see *POTENTIAL *sb.* 4 a); **vector product**, a vector function of two vectors, (a_1, a_2, a_3) of length *a* and (b_1, b_2, b_3) of length *b*, equal to $(a_2b_3-a_3b_2,\ a_3b_1-a_1b_3,\ a_1b_2-a_2b_1)$, representing a vector perpendicular to them both and of magnitude $ab \sin\theta$ (where θ is the angle between them); **vector space**, a group whose elements can be combined with each other and with the elements of a scalar field in the way that vectors can, addition within the group being commutative and associative and multiplication by a scalar being distributive and associative; **vector triple product**, a vector function of three three-vectors equal to the vector product of one of them with the vector product of the other two, i.e. $\mathbf{a}\times(\mathbf{b}\times\mathbf{c})$.

1975 R. H. ECKHOUSE *Minicomputer Systems* vi. 189 The various vector addresses and priority levels for the teletype, high-speed reader/punch, and clock on the PDP-11 are as follows. **1982** R. A. SPARKES *Microcomputers in Sci. Teaching* v. 199 All we have to do is to change the vector address and the ISR [*sc.* interrupt service routine] will start by executing our routine instead. **1956** *Nature* 25 Feb. 367/1 With its further expansion..the designation of the East African Malaria Unit has been changed to the East African Institute of Malaria and Vector-Borne Diseases. **1963** *Lancet* 12 Jan. 109/2 This tumour..might be due to a vector-borne virus. **1971** P. C. C. GARNHAM *Progress in Parasitol.* i. 3 In order to prevent too wide a diffusion of parasitology it is useful to impose some sort of restriction, and this perhaps can best be done by adding to the classical subjects of protozoology and helminthology, only vector-borne infections of other types. **1922** J. B. SHAW *Vector Calculus* iii. 26 A vector field is a system of vectors each associated with a point of space, or a point of a surface, or a point of a line or curve. **1932** [see *scalar field* s.v. *SCALAR *sb.* 2]. **1976** *Physics Bull.* Sept. 387/3 The vector fields that are particularly relevant to cosmology are those representing the motion of particles and electric charges. **1873** J. C. MAXWELL *Treat. Electr. & Magn.* I. 10 Quantities of this class require *nine* numerical specifications. They are expressed in the language of Quaternions by linear and vector functions of a vector. **1971** [see *POTENTIAL *sb.* 4 a]. **1972** M. KLINE *Math. Thought* xxxii. 786 Maxwell noted..that the curl of a gradient of a scalar function and the divergence of the curl of a vector function are always zero. **1873**, etc. Vector-potential [see *POTENTIAL *sb.* 4 a]. **1881** [in Dict.]. **1962** CORSON & LORRAIN *Introd. Electromagn. Fields* v. 186 We shall now show that the magnetic induction **B** is related to a certain quantity **A** through the equation $\mathbf{B}=\nabla\times\mathbf{A}$, where the vector **A** is called..the vector potential. **1878** Vector product [in Dict.]. **1901** [see *scalar triple product* s.v. *SCALAR *sb.* 2]. **1965** [see *outer product* s.v. *OUTER *a.* 3]. **1972** A. G. HOWSON *Handbk. Terms Algebra & Anal.* xxxiv. 169 Given two vectors **a**.., **b**..we define their vector product (cross product or outer product) denoted by $\mathbf{a}\times\mathbf{b}$ (or $\mathbf{a}\wedge\mathbf{b}$). **1937** A. A. ALBERT *Mod. Higher Algebra* 319/2 (Index), Vector space; *see* Linear set. **1965** [see sense 2 b above]. **1970** *Nature* 19 Dec. 1234/2 A vector space is built up linearly by means of 'scalar' multipliers from a number field. **1972** A. G. HOWSON *Handbk. Terms Algebra & Analysis* viii. 39 Homomorphisms of vector spaces..preserve linear combinations of the type $\lambda_1a_1+\lambda_2a_2+\ldots+\lambda_na_n$. **1901** GIBBS & WILSON *Vector Analysis* ii. 72 The vector triple product may be used to express that component of a vector **B** which is perpendicular to a given vector **A**. **1964** Vector triple product [see *scalar triple product* s.v. *SCALAR *sb.* 2].

vector (ve·ktəɹ), *v.* [f. the sb.] *trans.* **a.** To direct (an aircraft) on its course or towards a target.

1945 *Radar* 34 If the pilot had to ditch, the radar set spotted where he went down, vectoring out to that exact spot the air-sea rescue planes. **1958** *Daily Mail* 24 Oct. 9/2 If the pilot of a military aircraft wants to cross one of the ten-mile-wide airways radiating from the big airports ..he can be 'vectored' across by R.A.F. radar. **1976** B. JACKSON *Flameout* i. 20 He'd been first officer of a DC-8 vectored over Newark when a Constellation had collided with the jet.

b. *gen.* To direct, esp. towards a destination; to change the direction of.

1966 *New Scientist* 27 Jan. 213/3 A flexible cup to hold a rocket's nozzle and so allow it to be vectored or swung for steering purposes. **1978** K. AMIS *Jake's Thing* ii. 20 This time Brenda's tone was warm but the warmth was firmly vectored on her friend. **1979** KRAFT & TOY *Mini/Microcomputer Hardware Design* viii. 391 The address found..vectors the processor to the appropriate device service routine. **1983** *Your Computer* Aug. 21/2 Version 1.2 contains several new features, such as the ability to vector output to one of a number of outputs.

Hence **ve·ctored** *ppl. a.*; *vectored thrust*, thrust that can be varied in direction.

1960 *Aeroplane* XCVIII. 261/1 The Ryan VZ-3RY Vertiplane 'vectored-slipstream' VTOL research aircraft was destroyed early this month during a test flight. **1962** *Flight International* LXXXI. 234/1 The future will undoubtedly see larger, heavier and more complex VTOL aircraft using the principle of 'vectored thrust'. **1973** *Black World* May 6/2 Our scholars and leaders and common people must have vectored minds if we are to prevail. This means we must actively seek stabilizing forces. **1982** *Daily Tel.* 15 June 3/1 He knew of no occasion in which a Harrier had found it necessary to use the special jump-jet tactic of using vectored thrust..to hop out of the way of an attacking aircraft.

vectorca·rdiogram. *Med.* [f. VECTOR *sb.* + *cardiogram* s.v. *CARDIO-.] An electrocardiogram (usu. a photograph of an oscilloscope display) that represents the directions as well as the magnitudes of electric currents in the heart.

1938 WILSON & JOHNSTON in *Amer. Heart Jrnl.* XVI. 15 In 1920 Mann..constructed a number of curves of this kind and called them monocardiograms. Granting the priority of this name, we prefer to call them vectorcardiograms in order to emphasize the true nature of the difference..between them and ordinary electrocardiographic curves, which are scalar functions of the time.

Hence **ve:ctorcardio·graphy**, the practice or technique of obtaining and interpreting vectorcardiograms.

1946 *Brit. Heart Jrnl.* VIII. 160 (*heading*) Possible application to vector-cardiography. **1976** *Lancet* 18 Dec. 1339/1 A parallel science of vectorcardiography grew up in specialist centres, in which cardiac currents were studied on oscilloscopes in more than one dimension at a time and with leads and electrodes appropriate to three orthogonal or right-angled axes.

vectored (ve·ktəɹd), *a.* *Computers.* [f. VECTOR *sb.* + -ED[2].] Of a facility for interrupting a program: supplying the address to which the program must jump when it is interrupted.

1976 M. HEALEY *Minicomputers & Microprocessors* iv. 136 The obvious advantage of vectored interrupts is the low time that exists between an interrupt being accepted and the specific service routine commencing. **1979** *Sci. Amer.* July 1/2 (Advt.), The new Series Sixteen stands out for state-of-the-art technology as well:..no fewer than 255 vectored interrupts and battery backup for memory retention during power failures. **1982** A. CLEMENTS *Microcomputer Design & Construction* vi. 170 Motorola have introduced a hardware device giving the 6800 a vectored interrupt facility.

vectorial, *a.* Add: **3.** *Path.* Of or pertaining to the ability to act as a vector of a disease.

1964 *Bull. World Health Organization* XXXI. 71 In malaria eradication the residual insecticide exerts upon the mosquito's vectorial capacity a direct insecticidal impact. **1981** *Trop. Med. & Hygiene News* Feb. 24 The vectorial capacity (i.e., the risk of transmission of the parasite) was found to be about 1000 times the critical value required for the maintenance of endemic malaria.

Hence **vecto·rially** *adv.*, as a vector or vectors.

1895 *Phil. Trans. R. Soc.* A. CLXXXVI. 706 The integral of this rotation taken (vectorially) throughout a small volume including the initial and final positions of the electron is equal to the strength of the electron multiplied by its linear displacement. **1909** BEDELL & PIERCE *Direct & Alternating Current Man.* vi. 201 Currents,..when of different phases, are added vectorially to obtain the resultant current. **1947** *Proc. Physical Soc.* LIX. 24 If the remaining admittance is plotted vectorially, a circle of diameter $1/(S+Si)$ is obtained. **1978** *Sci. Amer.* May 126/2 The point will have two components of apparent motion. .. The components add vectorially, and the point appears to move diagonally rather than either horizontally or vertically.

vectoring (ve·ktəriŋ), *vbl. sb.* [f. VECTOR *sb.*, *VECTOR *v.* + -ING[1].] **1.** The action of *VECTOR *v.*

1956 W. A. HEFLIN *U.S. Air Force Dict.* 553/1 Vectoring is usually done from the ground, or from a mother aircraft.

2. *Computers.* The provision or use of interrupt vectors.

1977 E. E. KLINGMAN *Microprocessor Systems Design* xii. 352 These [lines] are for 'cascading' several 8214s if more than eight interrupting devices need vectoring. **1979** *Personal Computer World* Nov. 84/4 Software vectoring of interrupts to allow more than one interrupt driven peripheral at a time, and also multi-programming.

vectorscope (ve·ktərskōᵘp). *Electronics.* [f. VECTOR *sb.* + -SCOPE.] A type of oscilloscope used to analyse colour television signals (see quot. 1957).

1957 SMITH & MATLEY in *Electronic & Radio Engineer* XXXIV. 198/1 The vectorscope..has been designed to display the chrominance component of the colour television signal as a pattern of vectors. **1979** A. A. LIFF *Colour & Black & White Television Theory & Servicing* xviii. 652 Some manufacturers recommend the vectorscope for the alignment of the bandpass amplifier tuned circuits.

vedalia (vĭdēⁱ·liă). *Ent.* Also **Vedalia.** [mod.L. (E. Mulsant 1850, in *Ann. de la Soc. d'Agric. de Lyon* II. 901), of unkn. etym.] The ladybird *Rodolia cardinalis* (formerly included in the genus *Vedalia*), which is native to Australia but has been imported into California and elsewhere to control scale insects.

1889 *Insect Life* II. 112 The Vedolia [*sic*] has multiplied in numbers and spread. **1935** H. T. FERNALD *Applied Entomol.* (ed. 3) xxvi. 222 In Australia it [*sc.* the cottony cushion scale] had an enemy known as the Vedalia. **1964** *Discovery* Oct. 62/3 The vedalia ladybird..in less than a year had brought about the virtual elimination of the cottony cushion scale. **1973** P. A. COLINVAUX *Introd. Ecol.* xxix. 410 All stages of the vedalia beetle were carnivorous.

Vedanta. (Earlier example.)

1788 *Asiatick Researches* I. 223 The word *máyá*, or *delusion*, has a more subtile and recondite sense in the *Védánta* philosophy.

Veddoid (ve·doid), *sb.* and *a.* *Physical Anthrop.* [f. VEDD(A + -OID.] **A.** *adj.* Belonging or pertaining to a racial group of uncertain status typified by the Veddas of Sri Lanka, characterized by dark skins, short stature, and wavy hair, and occurring chiefly in parts of southern Asia. **B.** *sb.* A member of this group.

1948 A. L. KROEBER *Anthropology* (ed. 2) iv. 139 The Veddoids are almost invariably culturally retarded hill or jungle people who evidently represent an old stratum of population pushed back by Caucasians or Mongoloids, or almost absorbed by them. **1956** *Nature* 7 Jan. 41/2 The sickle cell trait was found to be present in a number of Veddoid communities of southern India. **1963** S. COLE *Races of Man* vii. 85 The Veddoids are short, average stature 157 c.m., skin colour is chocolate brown, hair very wavy or curly. **1974** *Encycl. Brit. Macropædia* XIX. 1081/1 Non-Mediterranean Veddoids (Australoids) are found as minorities [in Southern Yemen]. *Ibid.*, The original islanders [of Socotra in the Arabian Sea], forming about half the population, are Veddoid. **1977** G. CLARK *World Prehist.* (ed. 3) vi. 260 Low-headed people [in the Indian sub-continent] with retreating foreheads, pronounced supraorbital ridges and relatively broad noses with depressed roots appear to be related to a Veddoid-Australoid stock of indigenous character.

veddy (ve·di), repr. a childish, affected, or (*U.S.*) British pronunc. of *very.* Freq. *joc.*

1859 E. EDEN *Semi-Detached House* xix. 257 Charlie would gravely say, 'Yes, veddy true, pooty Rachel.' **1938** *Amer. Speech* XIII. 157/2 For jocularity, newspaper writers..now sometimes write *veddy* for 'very'. **1960** L. KAUFFMANN *Waldo* i. 14 Elegant and veddy sophisticated and all that sort of thing. But wastrels. **1967** J. P. CARSTAIRS *No Thanks for Shroud* ii. 17 'Is that British?' '*Veddy*,' I grinned. **1975** *Publishers Weekly* 24 Feb. 114/1 Note humorous anachronism as Dylan's fish-girl pours him tea from a bone china teapot—veddy British!

vedette. Add: **2.** More widely, any motor launch. Also *ellipt.*

1977 E. W. MIDDLETON *Lifeboats of World* v. 178, 90 fast vedettes. **1982** H. A. WILLIAMS *Some Day I'll find You* I. viii. 23 If it was low tide the passengers had to land in *vedettes*.

3. With pronunc. (vəde·t). A stage or film star.

1963 *Listener* 28 Mar. 572/2 The 'pop' singers' predecessors were the music-hall vedettes, among them Marie Lloyd and Maurice Chevalier, who..lit up the souls of their audiences with wit and innuendo. **1980** L. ST. CLAIR *Obsessions* viii. 150 At the sight of..the Hollywood *vedette*, the maitre d'..escorted his guests to the window table.

Vedic, *a.* and *sb.* (Earlier examples.)

1848 *Rep. Brit. Assoc. Adv. Sci. 1847* 321 It may be observed that in the Vedic hymns..some dialectic differences and many grammatical discrepancies occur. **1853** *Jrnl. Amer. Oriental Soc.* III. 297 In many of the points in which Vedic and Sanskrit disagree, the former strikingly approaches its next neighbors to the westward, the language of the Avesta [etc.].

‖ **veduta** (vedū·ta). Pl. **vedute; vedutas.** [a. It. *veduta* a view, f. *vedere* to see.] A realistic, detailed picture of a town scene with buildings of interest, esp. one belonging to the genre represented by eighteenth-century Italian artists such as Canaletto, Guardi, and Piranesi; *veduta ideata* (pl. *vedute ideate*), a picture in this style but showing an imaginary scene, esp. one by Pannini.

1906 *Studio* (Special Summer No.) A. p. iii, Rudolf [von Alt] was the leader of the Viennese 'Veduta' painting, the true biographer of Vienna. **1934** *Burlington Mag.* Aug. 71/2 Topographical exactitude and the precision of linear perspective—the two essential elements of an ideal *veduta*. **1944** *Ibid.* Sept. 216/2 Little *vedutas* of the Swedish countryside. **1959** *Listener* 25 June 1118/1 Such *vedute ideate* were..a regular branch of Italian landscape painting since the latter part of the seventeenth century. **1961** *Guardian* 16 Nov. 7/7 The boom in Venetian *vedute* by Guardi in 1948. **1967** G. SIMS *Last Best Friend* xix. 180 There was an eighteenth-century Venetian Veduta painting. **1970** *Oxf. Compan. Art* 199/1 Canaletto..enlarged his repertory to include subjects from the Venetian mainland ..and *vedute ideate* or imaginary landscapes. **1978** *New York* 3 Apr. 64/2 Instead it dwells on the fresh spring light and dank shade falling over ordinary buildings, with a sparseness, accuracy, and austere gaiety that suggest Canaletto's *vedute* of London.

Hence **veduti·sta** (pl. **-i, -e**), a painter of *vedute*.

1962 R. G. Haggar *Dict. Art Terms* 355/1 The most notable *vedutisti*..were Pannini and Piranesi..and Canaletto and Guardi. **1967** C. Rougvie *When Johnny Died* ii. 55 *Vedute*..are..paintings of Venice..both Canaletto and Guardi were *vedutiste* (sic).

vee. Add: **1.** The name of the letter V, used to denote things having or arranged in this shape. (Examples.)

1933 *Jrnl. R. Aeronaut. Soc.* XXXVII. 845 This..can easily be achieved by making the vee of the hull sufficiently deep. **1939** *War Illustr.* 29 Dec. 538/2 A Squadron of fighters or bombers will fly in a 'vee' with three Flights of three machines each. **1950** B. Pym *Some Tame Gazelle* i. 9, I must have something to cover up the neck of my green frock. Perhaps it would have been better if I hadn't tried to alter it to a Vee. **1965** G. McInnes *Road to Gundagai* xiii. 222 A tall man with..a shock of receding curly hair in a Vee. **1970** *Commercial Motor* 25 Sept. 97 The trend in diesel engine development in this country is now clearly towards vees and/or turbocharging. **1977** 'E. Crispin' *Glimpses of Moon* vi. 93 At some stage she stood in the vee with her back to the parapet..and lost her balance and went headlong.

2. *attrib.* and *Comb.*, as *vee aerial, antenna, belt, block, formation, joint, neck(line), thread; vee-necked, -shaped* adjs.; **vee engine,** an engine with two lines of cylinders inclined so as to form a V. Cf. *V 2 b.

1939 *Amat. Radio Handbk.* 158/2 Such an arrangement ..is known as the RCA Vee aerial. **1950** A. L. Albert *Electr. Communication* (ed. 3) xii. 481 (*caption*) The non-resonant Vee antenna is composed of two wires several wavelengths long, and connected to ground through terminating resistors. **1981** R. S. Elliott *Antenna Theory & Design* ix. 436 The Vee antenna..is a simplification of the rhombic, with legs 3 and 4 removed. **1937** *Motor Catal.* (E. London Rubber Co. Ltd.) 39/2 A range of twelve Romac New-Vee Fan Belts will fit 194 popular cars. **1971** *Power Farming* Mar. 44/2 Machines..lift the root by gripping the leafy top growth of the plant between a pair of..rubber vee-belts. **1893** J. G. Horner *Princ. Fitting* v. 64 The vee blocks are employed chiefly for supporting shafts and circular spindle-like work generally. **1975** Bram & Downs *Manuf. Technol.* i. 27 Place the component in a suitable vee-block and slowly rotate it about the diameter to be checked. **1957** J. M. Bruce *Brit. Aeroplanes 1914–18* 213 It was one of the first aeroplanes to have the then-new Rolls-Royce Condor twelve-cylinder vee engine. **1972** *Practical Motorist* Oct. 70/1 Vee engines have a non-return valve for the crankcase emission control system in the offside rocker cover. **1960** *Times Rev. Industry* Nov. 18/1 Cylinders in Vee formation. **1964** S. Crawford *Basic Engin. Processes* iii. 93 Fig 17(a) shows the single vee-joint suitable for plates up to ⅜ inch in thickness. **1970** *Islander* (Victoria, B.C.) 15 Feb. 15/4 The original interior finish has been retained. The walls of pine 'Vee' joint; pews, chancel and rails of Douglas fir have darkened and mellowed with age. **1970** *Times* 24 Mar. 9/4 They are all of the same shape, vee neck front. **1973** *Guardian* 10 Apr. 13/2 Checked vee-necked dress with contrast ribbing. **1949** *Sun* (Baltimore) 24 Mar. 8 (Advt.), Elongated vee neckline, especially becoming to the larger woman! **1959** *Listener* 31 Dec. 1157/2 Conditions began to take a happy turn..but, very unfortunately, they never became perfectly vee-shaped. **1964** S. Crawford *Basic Engin. Processes* i. 36 The vee-shaped groves are accurately ground parallel and square with the outside faces. **1914** E. Pull *Mod. Workshop Pract.* xii. 229 (*heading*) Vee threads. **1975** Bram & Downs *Manuf. Technol.* iv. 120 The buttress thread combines the anti-friction advantages of the square thread with the strength of the vee thread.

Hence **veed** *a.*, V-shaped.

1934 *Times* 23 Oct. 7/4 The radiator is in a case which has a Vee'd dummy honeycomb front. **1938** *Times* 9 Aug. 8/7 A movable section—in front of the driver—in a sloping, divided, veed screen. **1972** C. Mudie *Motor Boats & Boating* 144 Outwardly the racing boats have developed from a heterogeneous collection towards a clean, fine lined, deep Veed fleet.

veeboer (fī·būᵊɹ). *S. Afr.* Also as two words and with capital initial(s). Pl. **-boer, -boere, -boers.** [Afrikaans, f. *vee* cattle, livestock (f. Du. *vee*: see Fee *sb.*¹) + Boer.] A livestock farmer.

1824 *S. Afr. Jrnl.* I. 29 Poor Gert Schepers, a Vee Boer of the Cradock District, was less fortunate in an encounter with a South African lion. **1912** *Agric. Jrnl. Union of S. Afr.* July 61 These plants were known to the veeboer or schaapboer as the cause of the troubles they produce long before any scientific investigation of their properties had been made. **1944** J. Mockford *Here are S. Africans* iv. 39 Here the free burghers, the vee-Boers, rapidly acquired qualities unknown to the more sedate residents of Table Valley. **1954** H. Gibbs *Background to Bitterness* i. i. 25 Most free men at the Cape wanted to become a *veeboer*, cattle-farmer. **1965** M. G. Atmore *Cape Furniture* iii. 56 Thus arose the 'veeboere', each tenant on some 6,000 acres of cattle ranching country.

veejay (vīdʒēⁱ·). Also **vee-jay, VJ.** *slang* (chiefly *U.S.*). [Pronunc. of the initial letters of *video jockey*, after D.J. s.v. *D III. 3; cf. *dee-jay, dee-jay.] One who presents a programme of (popular music) video recordings, esp. on television.

1982 *N.Y. Times* 4 July iii. 17/1 The image..flashes.. to a loft studio where a video jockey—or 'veejay', a cross between a disc jockey and a TV emcee—announces what has just been played on MTV. **1983** *Amer. Way* June 170/1 VJs, or video jockeys, at MTV's studio cue up as many as 13 videos an hour. **1984** *Sunday Tel.* (Colour Suppl.) 29 Jan. 16 (*caption*) Mike Read and colleagues— today's disc jockeys will be tomorrow's 'veejays'.

veena, var. Vina in Dict. and Suppl.

veep (vīp). *U.S. colloq.* Also **Veep.** [f. the initials *V.P.* (vīpī); cf. *jeep *sb.*] A vice-president.

1949 *News-Age-Herald* (Birmingham, Alabama) 12 June D-24 (*heading*) 'Veep' Barkley's name now often tied with some eligible widow's. **1952** *N.Y. Times* 19 June 25/1 (*heading*) Woman 'veep' urged. **1961** *Manila Times* 12 Sept. 1 (*heading*) Veep offers self as rice czar. **1977** *Time* 17 Oct. 14/1 Kremlinologists have been speculating about who might be named to the newly created post of Vice President. A Veep was needed to take over the fatiguing ceremonial functions of the presidency. **1983** *Fortune* 28 Nov. 152/3 His Makati business club constituents would be happy to nominate E.Z. for veep.

veery. For *Turdus* read *Hylocichla* and add earlier example.

1838 Thoreau *Jrnl.* in *Writings* (1906) VII. 70 Sometimes I hear the veery's silver clarion.

veg (vedʒ). Pl. **veg, veges.** Colloq. abbrev. of *vegetable* (in quot. 1898, of *vegetarian* (restaurant)). Cf. *vegie.

1898 A. Bennett *Man from North* xi. 95 You know Miss Roberts at the veg—red-haired tart. **1918** G. Frankau *One of Them* xxviii. 219 Clerk of the Court, begone to veg. and joint! **1940** Wodehouse *Quick Service* ii. 21 Have a custard apple? It's on the house. The fruit and veg. department has just given of its plenty. **1946** Koestler *Thieves in Night* 115 She had come in straight from the veg-garden. **1960** A. Wesker *I'm talking about Jerusalem* i. 26 Good garden here. Grow your own veges. **1974** J. Aiken *Midnight is a Place* v. 146 A crudely painted sign that said *Veg Soup Half-Penny Per Cup*. **1983** *Truck & Bus Transportation* June 81/3 We'll heat a can of veges. **1984** *Economist* 3 Nov. 18/1 Treasury officials paying for their meat and two veg are rightly suspicious.

vegan (vī·găn, *U.S.* ve·dʒăn). [f. Veg(etable *sb.* + -an.]

1. A person who on principle abstains from all food of animal origin; a strict vegetarian.

1944 D. Watson in *Vegan News* Nov. 2 'Vegetarian' and 'Fruitarian' are already associated with societies that allow the 'fruits' of cows and fowls, therefore..we must make a new and appropriate word... I have used the title 'The Vegan News'. Should we adopt this, our diet will soon become known as the *vegan* diet, and we should aspire to the rank of *vegans*. **1945** *Ibid.* Feb. 3 Two members have asked how 'Vegan' is pronounced. Veegan, not Veejan. **1955** *Irish Press* 29 Nov. 618 A true-blue Vegan, I'm assured,..will even exclude from his or her diet, milk and..honey. **1965** *New Scientist* 20 May 526/3 Vitamin B_{12}..is found almost exclusively in animal foods, so that strict vegetarians (like vegans) may go short unless they take special precautions to ensure a supply. **1977** J. F. Fixx *Compl. Bk. Running* xiv. 170 There are..three kinds of vegetarians: the 100 percent vegetarian, sometimes called a vegan; the lacto-vegetarian..; and the lacto-ovo-vegetarian. **1979** J. I. M. Stewart *Our England* 177 Robin had discovered the duty of being a vegetarian. Indeed, he had become a vegan, and that seemed to mean that he could eat virtually nothing at all. **1985** *Times* 1 Feb. 12/2 'Beanmilk: milk that's never even seen a cow' is to vegans, who deplore exploitation of animals and eat nothing derived from them, a highly desirable commodity.

2. *attrib.* or as *adj.*

1944 [see sense 1 above]. **1945** *Vegetarian Messenger* XLII. 163 Following the articles and correspondence regarding the use of dairy products..in *The Vegetarian Messenger* last year, a number of our members who do not use animal products of any kind formed themselves into a group which has since adopted the title of 'The Vegan Society'. **1951** *News Chron.* 13 Dec. 3 A true vegetarian or vegan diet may not be nutritionally adequate, said Dr. Hill. **1973** *Listener* 8 Feb. 178/1 The good ecological life: no car, vegan cooking, and a mangle technology in a tumbledown cottage. **1978** *Peace News* 25 Aug. 18/3 A group of people from a 1750 acre vegan farming community in Tennessee..are coming to visit Britain in late September or early October. **1984** *Listener* 9 Aug. 17/2 The facts that CIWF is able to marshal must drive many who read its literature to a vegan diet.

Hence **ve·ganism,** the beliefs or practice of vegans; abstention from all food of animal origin.

1944 *Vegan News* May 1 Veganism is the practice of living on fruits, nuts, vegetables, grains, and other wholesome non-animal products. **1972** *New Scientist* 4 May 297/2 Universal vegetarianism would..tend to disrupt organic farming and the organic cycle—soil, plant, animal, man. It would also, if logically carried on as in Veganism, abolish milk and eggs. **1977** S. R. L. Clark *Moral Status of Animals* ix. 185 Veganism is a better project than lacto-vegetarianism, though we may in the end be able to take *some* milk from our kin without injustice.

Veganin (ve·dʒănin). Also **veganin.** *Pharm.* A proprietary preparation of aspirin, paracetamol, and codeine phosphate used as an analgesic.

1926 *Trade Marks Jrnl.* 23 June 1442 *Veganin*... Chemical substances prepared for use in medicine and pharmacy. Gödecke & Co., Chemische Fabrik Aktien Gesellschaft..Berlin-Charlottenburg, Germany; manufacturers. **1943** S. Ertz *Anger in Sky* iv. 98 Take an aspirin, take two, take three. Take veganin. Take anything. **1951** G. Greene *End of Affair* iii. vii. 141 'I've got a bad headache, that's all.'..'I'll get you some veganin.' **1979** G. Watson *Black Jack* i. 9 There was a stock of Veganin in the house.

vegeculture (ve·dʒĭkɒltiŭɹ). [f. Vege(table *sb.* + Culture *sb.*] The cultivation of vegetables. Hence **vegecu·ltural** *a.*

1917 H. A. Day (*title*) Vegeculture: how to grow vegetables, salads, and herbs. **1962** J. D. Clark in Braidwood & Willey *Courses toward Urban Life* 23 The distribution of the bored stone in central and south-central Africa suggests that it may also sometimes accompany a vegecultural,..even an incipient agricultural, level of economy during later stone age times. **1964** S. Cole *Prehist. E. Afr.* x. 275 Only after the introduction of ironworking do we find evidence of food production... This does not mean that some form of vegeculture did not exist—perhaps based mainly on plants with edible roots or tubers. **1977** G. Clark *World Prehist.* (ed. 3) v. 226 It looks as if there was a greater emphasis on vegetable food and even as if some form of vegeculture may have been practised.

vegetable, *sb.* Add: **2*.** *fig.* A person who leads an uneventful or monotonous life, without intellectual or social activity; also, one reduced by illness to little more than a physical body. Cf. Vegetable *a.* 5.

1921 G. B. Shaw *Back to Methuselah* i. 26 What use is this thousand years of life to you, you old vegetable? **1933** A. Huxley *Let.* 9 Oct. (1969) 373, I was so glad to hear from Norah that you were going on as well as cd be expected. It will be a weary business for a bit,.. sitting still and being a vegetable. **1953** *Chicago Daily Sun-Times* 29 Dec. 40/5 It should not be inferred that Rocky is a vegetable, incapable of thinking for himself. **1961** J. Dawson *Ha-Ha* iii. 48 I'm going to go on working... Tony says he would hate a wife who was just a vegetable. **1976** Smythies & Corbett *Psychiatry* vii. 123 Eventually they become bedridden and incontinent 'vegetables'. **1980** B. Castle *Castle Diaries* 242, I hope and pray she will die with dignity and not be reduced by a stroke into a vegetable.

3. a. *vegetable dish* (earlier example), *garden* (earlier example), *juice, oil, patch, rack.*

1820 D. Wordsworth *Jrnl.* 20 July (1941) II. 39 A level bottomed oval vessel like the foundations of our vegetable dishes. **1887** *Outing* X. 12/1 Back of its hacienda is a fine orchard and vegetable garden. **1907** *Yesterday's Shopping* (1969) p. lxi/5 (Index), Vegetable racks. **1921** *Daily Colonist* (Victoria, B.C.) 20 Mar. 17/1 The born gardener is still looking ahead in the Fall when other people store their tools and never do a hand's turn in the vegetable patch until the Spring urge comes upon them again. **1926** *Ibid.* 16 Jan. 15/3 Listed in the..general cargo..is a large quantity of vegetable oil in bulk. **1975** P. G. Winslow *Death of Angel* ii. 65 Vegetable juice and soya beans. **1977** *Times* 6 May 13/4 EEC imports of vegetable oils and oil-cakes. **1978** G. Mitchell *Mingled with Venom* x. 102 The poison roots were never in your vegetable rack. **1979** J. D. MacDonald *Green Ripper* (1980) i. 15 One of her vegetable juice cocktails. **1979** A. Clarke *Poisoned Web* x. 77 She was down..in the vegetable patch..staring at the runner-beans.

vegetable, *a.* Add: **7.** *vegetable fat, oil,* fat or oil obtained or manufactured from plants; *vegetable lard,* a solid cooking fat prepared from vegetable products; *vegetable spaghetti,* a variety of vegetable marrow bearing fruits whose flesh resembles spaghetti in appearance; also, the fruit itself or its flesh; *vegetable sponge* = *dishcloth gourd* s.v. *dish-cloth 2.

1797 *Encycl. Brit.* XIII. 192/1 Vegetable oils are obtained by expression, infusion, and distillation. **1884** *Ibid.* XVII. 741/1 The ordinary method for separating vegetable oils and fats from the nuts, seeds, &c., of which they form constituent parts is by pressure. **1889** *Cent. Dict.* s.v. *Sponge-gourd,* The netted fiber from the interior of the fruit is used for washing and other purposes, hence called vegetable sponge. **1894** C. R. A. Wright *Animal & Vegetable Fixed Oils* xiv. 305 Amongst the Hindoos and others whose religious beliefs preclude the use of animal fats..a large sale now exists for purely vegetable fats of buttery consistence (vegetable lard). **1918** C. A. Mitchell *Edible Oils & Fats* iii. 33 Coconut oil is treated with alcohol and animal charcoal and the resulting product, which is practically tasteless, is sold as 'vegetable lard'. **1956** Vegetable fat [see *nordihydroguaiaretic acid* s.v. *nor-]. **1967** *Ann. Reg. 1966* 166 The long-delayed common market regulations for sugar, vegetable fats and oils, and fruit and vegetables. **1973** *Times* 2 Nov. 22/8 If vegetable spaghetti is as tasteless as marrow, which I believe it is, no self-respecting British housewife would buy it at any price. **1978** J. U. Crockett *Vegetables & Fruits* v. 109 There are also several unusual kinds [of marrow], including the vegetable spaghetti, with bright yellow, 20 cm (8 in.) marrows, which, when cooked, spill out their flesh like spaghetti. **1978** R. Whitlock *Growing Unusual Vegetables* 50/2 The vegetable spaghetti plant is of the trailing type, not bush, so allow room for it to ramble. **1984** *Gardening from 'Which?'* Mar. 75/1 The loofah's other common names of vegetable sponge or dish cloth gourd give a clue to its true identity.

vegetal, *a.* Add: **4.** *vegetal pole* (Embryology), the lower pole of an ovum or a young embryo, which divides more slowly than the upper (animal) pole and in telolecithal ova contains most of the yolk. Cf. *animal pole* s.v. *animal C. 1.

1914 W. E. Kellicott *Textbk. Gen. Embryol.* iii. 92

The vegetal pole is frequently occupied largely by the relatively inert food substance, the materials in general related with the vegetative organs of the developing embryo. **1926** JORDAN & KINDRED *Textbk. Embryol.* v. 32 When the yolk is more abundant,..it tends to segregate at one pole, thus determining a yolk-free pole, the animal pole, and a yolk-laden pole, the vegetal pole. **1947** L. B. AREY *Devel. Anat.* (ed. 5) ii. 31 At the other end of the polar axis is the vegetal pole. Its territory tends to be more sluggish and is concerned with the development of nutrient organs. Cytoplasmic components..are often disposed in a polarized or stratified way. This is well illustrated in telolecithal eggs, whose animal pole is more protoplasmic and whose vegetal pole is more yolk-laden. **1978** *Nature* 16 Mar. 255/1 (*caption*) Injection was aimed at the vegetal pole.

vegetarian, *sb.* Add: **1. a.** (Earlier example.)
1839 F. A. KEMBLE *Jrnl. Residence on Georgian Plantation* (1863) 251 If I had had to be my own cook, I should inevitably become a vegetarian.

vegetarianism. (Earlier examples.)
1851 DUNGLISON *Dict. Med. Sci.* (ed. 8) 896/2 *Vegetarianism*,..a modern term, employed to designate the view that man..ought to subsist on the direct productions of the vegetable kingdom and totally abstain from flesh and blood. **1852** *Punch* 7 Aug. 68/1 Vegetarianism is evidently progressing.

vegetation. Add: **I. 4.** (Earlier example.)
1760 M. W. MONTAGU *Let.* 25 Oct. (1967) III. 245, I am not surpriz'd at the long Vegetation of the D[uche]sse of Argyle.

II. 6. c. Used *attrib.* with reference to the death and regeneration of plant life and the alternation of the seasons as symbolized or represented in religious or cultic beliefs and rituals.
1914 J. G. FRAZER *Golden Bough: Adonis Attis Osiris* (ed. 3) II. III. vii. 126 Professor Ed. Meyer also formerly regarded Osiris as a sun-god; he now interprets him as a great vegetation god. **1918** in Gray & Moore *Mythol. All Races* XI. 25 Here there seems to be indication of a vegetation cult. *Ibid.* 75 Closely connected with the earth goddesses are their children, the vegetation-deities. **1922** T. S. ELIOT *Waste Land* 53 Anyone who is acquainted with these works will immediately recognize in the poem certain references to vegetation ceremonies. **1967** *Listener* 6 Apr. 471/3 It [*sc.* the Easter holiday] should have been all outside broadcasts of drunken baroque processions.., villages abusing each other's religious banners.., vegetation ceremonies still describable in pace-egging and mummers' plays.

Hence **vegeta·tional** *a.*
1926 *Spectator* 4 Sept. 354/2 The dark areas observable on the surface of Mars are vegetational regions. **1958** *New Biol.* XXVI. 32 These communities..are prevented, by haymaking and the grazing of sheep, cattle, and rabbits, from entering the normal phases of vegetational succession. **1977** J. L. HARPER *Population Biol. Plants* iv. 95 The buried seed population of mature or climax communities generally contains a living..record of the past vegetational history of the succession.

vegetative, *a.* Add: **1. d.** *vegetative pole* (Embryology) = *vegetal pole* s.v. *VEGETAL *a.* 4.
1892 E. L. MARK tr. *O. Hertwig's Text-bk. Embryol.* i. 11 The dissimilar poles are distinguished:..the under, heavier and richer in yolk, as the vegetative pole. **1909** [in Dict.]. **1946** B. M. PATTEN *Human Embryol.* iv. 60 In mammals, as is the case with surprising uniformity throughout the animal kindom, the mitotic spindle of the first cleavage division forms at right angles to an imaginary axis passing through the ovum from animal to vegetative pole. **1958** —— *Foundations Embryol.* ii. 52 The region opposite the animal pole is called the vegetative, or vegetal, pole because while material for growth is drawn from this region, it remains itself relatively less active.

e. *Biol.* Pertaining to or being a stage in the replication of a virus at which non-infective viral components are synthesized and assembled within the host cell prior to its lysis.
1953 M. DELBRÜCK in *Cold Spring Harbor Symp. Quantitative Biol.* XVIII. 1/1 One new feature is the recognition that the infecting virus undergoes an essential change before it multiplies. The multiplying form is here called the vegetative phase, in analogy to the use of the word 'vegetative' in the bacteriology of sporulating bacteria. **1967** K. M. SMITH *Insect Virol.* viii. 147 Whenever it has been shown that viruses of animals or higher plants go through cycles as described for bacteriophages, the terms provirus, vegetative virus and infective virus are appropriate for the corresponding stages. **1973** [see *PROPHAGE]. **1982** FRAENKEL-CONRAT & KIMBALL *Virology* i. 11 The relative simplicity of extracellular viruses, termed the dormant phase, and the complexity of their interaction with host cell components leading to their replication, termed the vegetative phase, have placed viruses among the most useful tools in the study of all phenomena related to replication, information transfer, mutation, and many other aspects of molecular biology.

6. b. (Further examples.)
1969 *Sci. Jrnl.* Feb. 11/3 Two other patients..had flat EEG readings for prolonged periods, but subsequently recovered, although they remained 'vegetative'. **1972** *Lancet* 1 Apr. 734/1 Patients with severe brain damage due to trauma..may now survive indefinitely... Such patients are best described as in a persistent vegetative state. **1976** *National Observer* (U.S.) 19 June 2 (*caption*) Their comatose daughter..has been in what doctors call a 'vegetative state' for 14 months... The Quinlans last March won court permission to turn off Karen's life-sustaining devices. **1982** *Brit. Med. Jrnl.* 20 Oct. 1022/2 The term 'persistent vegetative state' was suggested in 1972 to describe those patients with irreversible brain damage..who on recovery from deep coma pass into a state of seeming wakefulness and reflex responsiveness but do not return to a cognitive sapient state.

vegie (ve·dʒi). Also **veggie.** Colloq. abbrev. of *vegetable.* Usu. *pl.* Cf. *VEG.
1955 C. BROWN *Lost Girls* xii. 132, I did get a job for myself, selling vegies at a stall in the market. **1966** [see *KINDY]. **1973** *Philadelphia Inquirer* (Today Suppl.) 14 Oct. 8/3 Sushi rice (rice and vegies wrapped in seaweed). **1976** *New Yorker* 8 Mar. 28/3 They wash and chop veggies and hand them out at the right time to the right people. **1983** *Chicago Sun-Times* 27 Aug. (Guide) 83 Also included, a fresh veggie and..a carafe of one of eight wines of your choice. **1984** *Grass Roots* (N.Z.) Feb. 8/2 The vegie gardens are fenced.

Vegliote (velyo·t). Also **Vegliot, Veliote.** [f. *Veglia* + -OTE.] An extinct dialect of Dalmatian, formerly spoken on the island of Veglia (now called Krk) off the Dalmatian coast of Yugoslavia.
1910 *Encycl. Brit.* XIV. 891/2 The Vegliote dialect is the last remnant of a language which some long time ago extended..along the Dalmatian coast. **1933** Veliote [see *DALMATIAN *a.* and *sb.* 2]. **1960** W. D. ELCOCK *Romance Lang.* i. 163 Lat. *mensa*, attested as *mesa*..is also found in Rheto-Romance..and in Vegliote (*maisa*). **1974** *Encycl. Brit. Macropædia* XV. 1038/1 Romanian, Vegliot, Spanish, and perhaps Rhaetian show similar developments in all accented syllables. **1984** *Trans. Philol. Soc.* 20 Vegliot is a 'dead' language once spoken on the island of Veglia (Krk) off the Jugoslav coast.

vehicle, *sb.* Add: **I. 3. d.** In a metaphor, the literal meaning of the word or words used metaphorically, as distinct from the subject of the metaphor; the image or idea whose association with the subject constitutes the metaphor. Opp. *TENOR *sb.* 1 d.
1936, etc. [see *TENOR *sb.* 1 d]. **1957** S. ULLMANN *Style in French Novel* vi. 214 It is an essential feature of a metaphor that there must be a certain distance between tenor and vehicle. Their similarity must be accompanied by a feeling of disparity. **1977** *Studies in Eng. Lit.: Eng. Number* (Tokyo) 36 In this metaphor, the tenor and vehicle are not expected to fit each other perfectly.

II. 7. a. (Further examples.)
1947 *N.Y. Times* 20 Mar. 3/1 The statement 'there is no defense against the atomic bomb'..assumes that this bomb is being carried by a vehicle at a velocity well in the supersonic range. *Ibid.*, V-2 type vehicles. **1973** *Sci. Amer.* Feb. 72/3 [They] mounted sensitive probes on a vehicle towed horizontally behind a ship. **1982** *Nature* 27 May 254/1 Vehicles carrying people, whether ships or aircraft, moving in an environment in which radar detection at long range is technically straightforward, have become exceedingly vulnerable to attack.

b. A space rocket, in relation to its (actual or intended) payload.
1959 *Daily Tel.* 13 Mar. 15/6 Black Knight is entirely a research vehicle and will never be manufactured into a weapon. **1967** *Technology Week* 20 Feb. 36/1 A satellite launched into an eight-hour orbit by an *Atlas-Agena* vehicle. **1983** *Chicago Sun-Times* 13 July 17 Last week, the Soviets proposed a sub-ceiling of 1,100 on MIRVed missiles and bombers within the over-all ceiling of 1,800 strategic nuclear delivery vehicles.

8. *fig.* A song, play, film, etc., that is intended or serves to display the actor (or performing artist) to the best advantage.
1863 *Illustrated Times* 15 Aug. 103/3 Then came..Lady Gifford's quasi-comedy of '*Finesse*', which..simply served as a vehicle for some of Mr. Buckstone's practical drolleries and preposterous costumes. **1868** in P. Bailey *Leisure & Class in Victorian Society* (1978) vii. 152 A good song must be written, not for its own sake, but for that of the singer... It must simply be a vehicle. **1922** *N.Y. Times* 16 Oct. 20/2 Charles Ray is back on Broadway—his vehicle being 'A Tailor Made Man', and his stopping place for a week the Strand Theatre. **1928** MRS. P. CAMPBELL *Let.* 19 Jan. in *B. Shaw & Mrs. Campbell* (1952) 264, I only saw it as a commonplace, ordinary and good sort of working vehicle, or whatever the right word or expression is for that kind of play. **1955** *Times* 16 Aug. 5/4 It might be as well to rule out at the beginning the 'vehicle' especially created to exploit the talents and personality of the individual actor. **1966** *Listener* 27 Jan. 131/1 If at the start of his career an actor can somehow gain acceptance from the critics, it is possible for him to go on and give a series of inadequate performances in low-calibre vehicles and still emerge with reputation intact. **1981** *Times* 2 July 10/6 Star names and vast budgets ..wedded to a limp vehicle, can destine a feature to oblivion.

9. *Comb.*, as *vehicle-park*; *vehicle-actuated* adj.; **vehicle-mile,** a distance of one mile travelled by one vehicle, used as a statistical unit; **vehicle mine,** a land-mine designed to destroy vehicles.
1937 *Times* 13 Apr. p. viii/1 With the wide adoption of electromatic vehicle-actuated traffic lights of recent years, complaints of unnecessary delay at signal-controlled crossings have been much dispelled. **1967** *Gloss. Highway Engin. Terms* (*B.S.I.*) 62 *Vehicle actuated traffic signals*, traffic signalling equipment in which the duration of the red and green signals and the time of the cycle vary in relation to the traffic flow into and through the controlled area. It is actuated by the traffic. **1964** *Times Rev. Industry* Feb. 36/2 The statistics of vehicle-miles travelled ..show that usage of light vans has, in fact, been steadily increasing faster than road transport in general. **1976** *New Yorker* 16 Feb. 68/2 About eighty per cent of highway use (measured in vehicle-miles) is auto travel. *a* **1944** K. DOUGLAS *Alamein to Zem Zem* (1946) xiv. 82 The verges of gaps in the road were mined with anti-personnel and vehicle mines. **1972** *Times* 27 Dec. 6/2 There had been almost no interference with road building, apart from the odd vehicle mine. **1940** Vehicle park [see *gun-park* s.v. *GUN *sb.* 14 a]. **1976** *Cumberland News* 3 Dec. 11/6 (Advt.), Training hall and use of adjacent site as vehicle park at Parkhill Road, Kingstown, Carlisle.

Vei, var. *VAI.

veil, *sb.*[1] **8.** (Example.)
1857 *Quinland* I. xiii. 186 Aunt Hepsa says he was born with a veil over his face, and says he can see things that we must not inquire about.

veilleuse. Now usu. a night-light; also, a small, decorative, bedside food-warmer, usu. burning oil in a wick and made of pottery or porcelain so as to let out some light. (Further examples.)
1897 *Private Life of Queen* xv. 122 The Queen betakes herself to bed... The signal comes for extinguishing all the lights but the *veilleuse*. **1955** *Apollo* LXI. 35/1 The *veilleuse* of pottery or porcelain is..a hollow pedestal on which sits either a covered warming bowl..or a teapot. **1961** *Times* 2 Sept. 9/6 One was the earthenware bedside food warmer. Some collectors know these companionable little sets as *veilleuses*. **1969** E. H. PINTO *Treen* 124/2 The oddest material for making *veilleuses* was probably wood and the fact that so few have survived is doubtless ..because of their inflammability. **1983** *Thames & Hudson Catal.* July–Dec. 31 The *veilleuse*, intended as a food or tea warmer for bedroom use..consists of..a supporting hollow pedestal, a small burner (*godet*) and a covered bowl or..teapot.

vein, *sb.* Add: **IV. 15. c. vein-gold,** gold occurring in a vein or veins.
1848 W. COLTON *Jrnl.* 6 Nov. in *Three Years Calif.* (1850) xxiii. 312 Vein-gold in these rocks is as uncertain and capricious as lightning. **1956** G. TAYLOR *Silver* i. 2 The bankets of Witwatersrand, in which vein-gold and alluvial deposits are mixed. **1979** *Econ. Geol.* LXXIV. 1420 (*heading*) Fluid inclusion and geochemical studies of vein gold deposits.

d. In sense 3 b, as **vein-banding,** a symptom of some virus diseases of plants, characterized by a change of colour along the main veins of leaves; freq. *attrib.*
1930 *Bull. Kentucky Agric. Exper. Station* No. 309. 481 Veinbanding is a common disease of tobacco in locations where potatoes have been grown. **1957** *Phytopathology* XLVII. 139 (*heading*) Effects of insecticides and physical barriers on field spread of pepper veinbanding mosaic virus. **1979** *Jrnl. Horticultural Sci.* LIV. 23/1 Gooseberry vein banding virus..is aphid transmitted..and, although it is widespread in Europe.., little is known of its economic importance.

veining, *vbl. sb.* **1. b.** (Earlier example.)
c **1840** [see *SEEDING *vbl. sb.* 3*].

veinlet. Add: **c.** *spec.* in *Geol.* Cf. VEIN *sb.* 7.
1927 [see *IANTHINITE]. **1955** [see *KUTNAHORITE]. **1974** *Encycl. Brit. Micropædia* IX. 699/1 Sussexite occurs as hydrothermal fibrous veinlets in the U.S. at Franklin, N.J.

veitchberry (vī·tʃberi). [f. *Veitch*, surname of a family of nurserymen + BERRY *sb.*[1]] A hybrid bramble produced in 1925 by crossing a raspberry and a blackberry; the fruit of this, resembling a large reddish blackberry.
1925 *Daily News* 26 Aug. 3/2 One of the novelties at the Royal Horticultural Society's Show, in Vincent-square, W., held yesterday, is the veitchberry—produced from a blackberry and a raspberry. *Ibid.* (*caption*) The veitchberry compared with the size of a halfpenny. **1956** *Good Housek. Home Encycl.* (ed. 4) 118/1 Plant..veitchberries and wineberries 6 feet apart. **1980** *Amat. Gardening* 25 Oct. 20/1 Other hybrid berries..include the boysenberry, with large fruits but darker than a Loganberry, the Veitchberry and the Youngberry.

velar, *a.* Add: Hence **vela·rity,** velar quality.
1952 *Archivum Linguisticum* IV. 72 The apostrophe after *n* and *g* indicates velarity. **1964** [see *alveolarity* s.v. *ALVEOLAR *a.* and *sb*].

velaric (vĭlæ·rik), *a. Phonetics.* [f. VELAR *a.* + -IC.] Produced or characterized by a velar articulation, in which there is total or partial closure between the back of the tongue and the velum.
1934 in WEBSTER. **1938** D. M. BEACH *Phonetics of Hottentot Lang.* vi. 74 A..bilabial implosive may be made by closing the lips together, raising the back of the tongue to touch the velum, and then producing a partial vacuum between the lips & the velum by lowering the front of the tongue... This bilabial implosive may be termed a bilabial velaric click. **1959** [see *GLOTTALIC *a.*].

velarization (vīlărəizē·ʃən). *Phonetics.* [f. VELAR *a.* + -IZATION.] A (normally secondary) articulation of a consonant, in which the back of the tongue is raised to or towards the velum; also, in some languages, applied to the articulation of some vowels.

1915 G. Noël-Armfield *Gen. Phonetics* xvii. 102 If it be found necessary to indicate velarisation in a script it may be done by placing a small *u* over the usual symbol. **1936** *Language* XII. 17 A further example is the velarization of the nasal consonant of Spanish *Cinco* [θiŋko], which is still felt to be a member of the *n* phoneme. **1962** A. C. Gimson *Introd. Pronunc. Eng.* iv. 30 In the so-called 'dark' [ł]..there is an essential raising of the back of the tongue towards the velum (velarization). **1975** I. R. Macpherson *Spanish Phonology* vi. 43 When *a* precedes a velar consonant, the semivowel *w*, or a velar vowel, it is..attracted towards the point of articulation of the following sound and may become slightly velarized. The diacritical sign – can be placed under the vowel to indicate a degree of velarization. **1976** *Archivum Linguisticum* VII. 93 These [Rhenish] dialects further have velarization of final [n] in, for example, [wiŋ'] *Wein*, [bruŋ'] *braun*.

So **ve·larize** *v. trans.* (*rare*), (*a*) to prescribe velarization for; (*b*) to produce by velarization; **ve·larized** *ppl. a.*

1915 G. Noël-Armfield *Gen. Phonetics* xvii. 102 Similarly there are consonants, otherwise normal, in the production of which the back of the tongue is raised to the *u* position. These are known as velarised sounds. *Ibid.*, [*Note*] Confusion should not be made between velarised and velar consonants. n^u is quite different from ŋ. The Arabic emphatics are velarised consonants. **1939** L. H. Gray *Found. Lang.* iii. 57 There are..many modifications of consonants, such as palatalised (e.g., Irish *te*..'hot'..); velarized or pharyngalized (e.g. the final sound of English *little, feel*). **1960** D. De Camp in Le Page & De Camp *Jamaican Creole* II. 137 Postvocal /l/ is so strongly velarized that such pairs as /fuul/ *fool* and /fuo/ *foe* are acoustically very similar. **1977** *Word 1972* XXVIII. 173 The rule which velarizes an alveolar consonant must precede the one which reduces prestress syllables. **1980** A. Alpers *Life K. Mansfield* 12 His sisters ..often called him 'Bogie', or 'Bogey' (which perhaps was velarised from 'Boy').

velation. For *rare*$^{-0}$ read *rare*$^{-1}$ and add: **a.** (Example.)

1922 Joyce *Ulysses* 719 The visible signs of post-satisfaction? A silent contemplation: a tentative velation.

Velcro (ve·lkro). Also **velcro.** [f. F. *vel*(*ours cro*)*ché* hooked velvet.] A proprietary name for a fabric made in narrow strips for use as a fastener, one strip having tiny loops and the other hooks so that they can be fastened or unfastened simply by pressing together or pulling apart.

1960 *Trade Marks Jrnl.* 30 Nov. 1521/1 Velcro... Narrow fabrics in imitation of velvet being textile smallwares for use as fasteners or fastenings for clothing. **1961** *Practitioner* July 113 We have been experimenting for some time with the new Bri-nylon fastener, 'velcro', using it particularly for patients who have difficulty in doing up buttons, trousers and belts. **1968** *Guardian* 9 May 9/4 False ringlets on a Velcro band. **1971** 'A. York' *Infiltrator* vii. 96 They had dressed him in a blue sleepcoat, which..was secured up the front by a strip of velcro. **1979** P. L. G. Bateman *Household Pests* ii. 76 Fly screening of windows..is fairly easy with flexible plastic flyscreens which use Velcro to fasten them to the window frames. **1982** *Habitat Catal. 1982/83* 14/1 The roll overarm cushions, filled with polyester, can be held in place with velcro, if required.

Hence **Ve·lcroed, ve·lcroed** *a.* (or pa. pple. of *Velcro* vb.), provided with Velcro; attached by Velcro.

1972 O. Sela *Bearer Plot* xxiv. 152 He..pulled the carpet. 'Note the velcroed edge... Just put it back and it sticks.' **1981** J. D. MacDonald *Free Fall in Crimson* xviii. 204 By early June I was walking... I worked with the weight Velcroed around my ankle every evening. **1983** *Washington Post* 13 Feb. c-3/3 You put a hand out to stop yourself..and bump all those Velcroed things off the wall.

veldt, veld. Add: The spelling *veld* is now the only permissible form in S. Africa and the more usual form in other varieties of English. **1.** (Earlier examples.)

1785, 1801 [see next sense]. **1835** A. Steedman *Wanderings S. Afr.* I. ii. i. 92 Here for the first time we bivouacked in what is called the *Veld*.

2. a. (Earlier and further examples.)

1785 G. Forster tr. *Sparrman's Voy. Cape of Good Hope* II. xiv. 144 The *land-drost* has appointed one of the farmers, with the title of *veld-corporal*, to command in these wars. **1801** J. Barrow *Trav. S. Afr.* I. 378 Louw, the Veld Commandant, readily offered his services. **1946** R. Campbell *Talking Bronco* 66 With veld-flowers as an afterthought. **1959** *Cape Times* 18 July 2/5 The veld flowers should be excellent this year.

b. veld-cornet (earlier example); **veld-craft,** skill in matters pertaining to survival on the veld; **veld-kost**: also **-kos** (later examples).

1802 G. M. Theal *Rec. Cape Colony* (1899) IV. 324, I have the honor to add the original report of the Veld Cornet Nicholaus Johannes Roets, sent to me with those Hottentots. **1905** D. Blackburn *R. Hartley, Prospector* 205 He associated with greedy, scheming directors, who were ignorant of veld-craft. **1910** J. Buchan *Prester John* xiv. 232 The veld-craft I had mastered had taught me a few things. **1980** *Country Life* 9 Oct. 1258/1 Olive Schreiner..possessed considerable veldt-craft and also the power of minute observation. **1948** *Cape Argus* (Mag. Section) 23 Oct. 1/7 The summer rains of 1915 had revived the fountains and veldkos was abundant. In a drought year he could not have survived. **1961** *Africa* XXXI. 231 When !U had a baby, her sister, Di!ai, gathered veldkos for her for five days.

veldt-shoe. Add: Also **vel(d)skoen** (fe·l(t)-skun), pl. **-skoen, -skoene, -skoens.** Now, a heavy boot or shoe for outdoor work. (Further examples.)

The most common forms in S. Afr. English are *veldskoen* and *velskoen* (pl. *-s* or *-e*) but the anglicized form *veld-shoe* is occasionally used.

1892 *Journal* (Grahamstown) 11 July 3 (Advt.) Colonial-made 'Star' Standard screw veldschoens and boots. **1919** *Manch. Guardian* 10 Dec. 4 (Advt.), I believe this is the latest development of the Lotus welted-veldtschoen. **1939** S. Cloete *Watch for Dawn* xxii. 312 He made a new belt, new velskoen. **1942** 'B. Knight' *Sun climbs Slowly* ii. 12 The life in Pretoria is very simple..to be called 'Lotta' and wear print frocks and *veldskoen*. **1945** *Cape Times* 29 Oct. 1/3 He was wearing..grey flannel trousers, a white silk shirt and velskoene. **1962** L. Deighton *Ipcress File* xxxii. 207, I put on Irish tweed with Veldtshoen, cotton shirt, and wool tie. **1969** J. Selby *Boer War* i. 34 They wore wide-brimmed felt hats and soft veldschoen on their feet. **1972** *Stand. Encycl. S. Afr.* XI. 545/1 By the end of the 1960s..the veld-shoe industry..declined because antiquated machinery.. proved too much of a handicap. **1974** N. Gordimer *Conservationist* 215 Alina..finds a pair of veldskoen in the house and brings them. **1977** *Listener* 3 Mar. 279/4 (Advt.), Veldtschoën... Virtually waterproof... Double leather soles..£21.50.

veleta (vělī·tă). Also **valeta.** [f. Sp. *veleta* weathervane.] A ballroom round dance for couples in triple time, originating in England in 1900.

1900 A. Morris (*sheet-music title*) Veleta. **1911** D. H. Lawrence *White Peacock* i. viii. 148 She made me take her through a valeta, a minuet, a mazurka, and she danced elegantly. **1936** 'R. Hyde' *Passport to Hell* 84 The pre-war dances—..the Maxina, the Valeta. **1966** [see *Gay Gordons* s.v. *gay *a.* 9]. **1974** D. Smith *Look back with Love* xii. 113 Most of the evening was taken up with waltzes, barn dances and veletas. **1978** S. Sherlock in D. Abse *My Medical School* 105 We danced the Veleta, the Gay Gordons, the Dashing White Sergeant.

velic (vī·lik), *sb.* and *a. Phonetics.* [f. Vel(um + -ic.] **A.** *sb.* (See quot. 1943.) **B.** *adj.* Pertaining to or involving the velic or its movement.

1943 K. L. Pike *Phonetics* iv. 58 The upper part of the soft palate facing the nasopharynx is the velic (so called in this discussion to distinguish it from the velum, which represents the lower side toward the mouth); the closure of the nasal passage is therefore a velic closure (in contrast to velar closure, when the tongue touches the soft palate). **1971** Chin-Wu Kim in W. O. Dingwall *Survey Linguistic Sci.* 34 At time 4, the lip rounding for [u] and [w] is superimposed on [k]; at time 5, their velic quality underlies [l]. **1975** *Amer. Speech 1972* XLVII. 244 *Pin* and *bin* are the same at the end and in the middle and *partly* the same at the beginning: for both, the lips are closed and the velic is closed. **1981** *Canad. Jrnl. Linguistics* Spring 81 The key features involved are velic closure (for nasalization), apical closure (for stops, fricatives, liquids), and vocal cord vibration (voicing).

Velikovskianism (velikǫ·vskiăniz'm). [f. the name *Velikovsky* + -ian + -ism.] The (controversial) theories of cosmology and history propounded by Immanuel Velikovsky (1895–1979), Russian-born psychologist, based on the hypothesis that other planets have approached close to the Earth in historical times. Also **Veliko·vskyism,** in the same sense. So **Veliko·vskian** *a.*, of or pertaining to Velikovskianism; **Veliko·vskyite,** an adherent of Velikovskianism.

1972 P. Moore *Can you speak Venusian?* vi. 61 Therefore, say the anti-Velikovskyites, it is rather difficult to see how a comet could change into a planet. *Ibid.* 62 Neither of these gentlemen accepted Velikovskyism hook, line and sinker. **1974** *Science* 15 Mar. 1061/1 The earliest known examples of writing..contain references to regular appearances of Venus in the sky 1500 years before its Velikovskian brushes with Earth. **1978** *Ibid.* 20 Jan. 288/2 A platform to square off pro- and anti-Velikovskyites. *Ibid.*, In a succinct foreword Isaac Asimov discusses the human psychology of Velikovskianism. **1979** *N.Y. Rev. Bks.* 25 Oct. 52/2 Professor Rose, an intrepid contributor to Velikovskian publications, is right on one count. *Ibid.* 52/3, I suppose it is too much to expect the Buffalo philosopher, when he teaches his next course on Velikovskianism, to let his students know some of the overwhelming evidence against such hoary balderdash.

vellumy, *a.* (In Dict. s.v. Vellum.) (Example.)

1925 H. A. Maddox *What Stationer & Printer ought to know about Paper* (ed. 3) i. 14 There are smooth vellums which derive their title from..a vellumy thickness and clarity of appearance.

velly (ve·li). A representation of a Chinese pronunc. of 'very'; also used *joc.*

1898 *Applause Reciter* 16 Ole man talkee, 'No can walk, Bimeby lain come, velly dine; Have got water, velly wide!' **1937** D. & H. Teilhet *Feather Cloak Murders* ii. 48 The Chinese woman rushed to him. 'You neahlly killed... Velly neahlly killed.' **1948** L. Durrell *Spirit of Place* (1969) 98 Shakespear him velly fine big-speak sing song man. **1970** J. Lees-Milne *Another Self* iii. 47 Poor Janie still loves her little cousin velly, velly much. **1974** N. Bentley *Inside Information* xiii. 135 Velly good, sir.' Cheng bowed.

velocimeter. Add: **veloci·metry,** the measurement of speed, esp. speed of flow, by special techniques.

1969 *IEEE Trans. Aerospace & Electronic Systems* V. 687/1 (*heading*) Fundamentals of holographic velocimetry. **1978** *Sci. Amer.* Aug. 30/3 Swedish and Japanese workers have been testing laser velocimetry, a technique that utilizes the reflection of light from small particles in the flow to determine the magnitude and direction of the circulatory patterns. **1980** *Recent Adv. Surg.* X. 84 The first to apply the technique of Doppler ultrasound velocimetry to the detection of pulsatile arterial flow in the digital vessels.

velocipede. 1. (Earlier example.)

1818 W. Sewall *Diary* 19 June (1930) 53/2 Then I went to the circus and rode on the velocipede, which is a new machine.

velocity. Add: **1. c.** In scientific use, speed together with the direction of travel, as a vector quantity.

1847 *Proc. R. Irish Acad.* III. 345 We may always imagine a succession of straight lines, or vectors, to be drawn from some one point, as from a common origin, in such a manner as to represent, by their directions and lengths, the varying directions and degrees (or quantities) of the velocity of the moving point. **1873** J. C. Maxwell *Treat. Electr. & Magn.* I. 9 The velocity of a body, its momentum,..an electric current,..are instances of vector quantities. **1883** *Encycl. Brit.* XV. 680/1 We are concerned only with what we may call the 'speed' of the motion. (We purposely avoid the use of the term 'velocity' here, because it properly includes direction as well as speed.) **1963** A. F. Abbott *Ordinary Level Physics* v. 50 In ordinary conversation the word 'velocity' is often used in place of speed. In science, however, it is important to distinguish between these two terms.

2. b. *Econ.* The rate at which notes and coins change hands; the rate of spending in an economy.

1909 I. Fisher in *Jrnl. R. Statistical Soc.* LXXII. 618 When we know statistically the velocity of circulation of money we shall be in a position to study inductively the 'quality theory' of money. **1911** —— *Purchasing Power of Money* ii. 17 Velocity of circulation, or rapidity of turnover, is simply the quotient obtained by dividing the total money payments for goods in the course of a year by the average amount of money in circulation by which these payments are effected. **1930** J. M. Keynes *Treat. Money* II. xxiv. 20 The expression 'velocity (or rapidity) of circulation' first came into use before the development of the cheque system... The 'velocity' measured the average frequency with which a loan (or a bank-note) changed hands. **1957** *Economist* 19 Oct. 209/1 The note issue is a good indicator because the velocity of notes, unlike that of deposits, is fairly steady. **1982** *Chase Economic Observer* Jan.–Feb. 3/1 Velocity, the rate of turnover of money, is typically measured as the ratio of GNP to the narrowly defined money stock.

3. velocity head [Head *sb.* 17], the velocity pressure of a fluid expressed in terms of the height from which the fluid would have to fall to attain the velocity exerting this pressure; **velocity microphone,** a microphone whose diaphragm is freely exposed to the air on both sides and so responds to the particle velocity within a sound wave rather than its pressure; **velocity potential** [tr. G. *geschwindigkeitspotential* (H. von Helmholtz 1858, in *Jrnl. für die reine u. angewandte Math.* LV. 25)], a scalar function of position such that its space derivatives at any point are the components of the fluid velocity at that point; **velocity pressure,** that part of the total pressure exerted by a fluid which is due to the velocity it possesses.

[**1881** *Encycl. Brit.* XII. 462/2, $v^2/2g$ may be termed the head due to the velocity *v.*] **1884** A. Daniell *Text Bk. Princ. Physics* xi. 276 We may say that the velocity-head and the pressure-head are together equal to the total head. **1937** O'Brien & Hickox *Appl. Fluid Mech.* ix. 271 The true velocity head to be used in Bernoulli's equation is the average kinetic energy per unit weight of water flowing. **1979** A. L. Lydersen *Fluid Flow & Heat Transfer* i. 5 (*caption*) Pressure head ($p/\rho g$) and velocity head ($V^2/2g$) for frictionless flow from point 1 to point 2. **1931** H. F. Olson in *Jrnl. Soc. Motion Picture Engineers* XVI. 695 The ribbon microphone..can therefore very appropriately be termed a 'velocity microphone'. **1951** A. Sheingold *Fund. Radio Communications* xiii. 281 Velocity microphones may be designed to be unidirectional in their response. **1978** V. Capel *Microphones in Action* ii. 19 The polar diagram of a velocity microphone is different from anything we have discussed so far. **1867** P. G. Tait tr. Helmholtz in *Phil. Mag.* XXXIII. 485 In integrating the hydrodynamical equations, the assumption has been made that the components of the velocity of each element of the fluid in three directions at right angles to each other are the differential coefficients, with reference to the coordinates, of a definite function which we shall call the velocity-potential. **1907** F. W. Lanchester *Aerodynamics* iii. 91 Fluid in irrotational motion has a velocity potential. **1937** [see *stream function* s.v. *stream *sb.* 9 c]. **1980** Bober & Kenyon *Fluid Mech.* ix. 417 The velocity potential, Φ, or the stream function, Ψ, are often introduced into fluid-flow problems because they frequently reduce the difficulty in obtaining a solution to a particular problem. **1904** *Proc. Inst. Mech. Engin.* Feb. 298 They used dry, clean air, and therefore it was possible to keep the Pitot tube extremely small, and to measure the static pressure in the close neighbourhood of the point at which the velocity pressure was measured.

1959 N. C. HARRIS *Mod. Air Conditioning* xv. 293 Velocity pressure is best measured by a Pitot tube combined with a draft gage which reads in inches of water. **1969** *Oceanology* IX. 585 The instrument is based on the measurement of the velocity pressure created by the wind.

velodrome. (Further examples.)

1973 *Trinidad Guardian* 1 Feb. 18/9 Neither the all-weather athletic track nor the cycling velodrome will be trampled upon at Carnival time. **1975** *Daily Colonist* (Victoria, B.C.) 22 Aug. 19/6 Taillibert designed the 70,000-seat stadium, velodrome, an underpass..and the competition swimming pool.

velodyne (ve·lo-, vī·lodəin). *Electr.* [f. L. *vēlo-x* swift + Gr. δύν-αμις force.] A device in which the output of a tachogenerator is fed back so as to keep the rotational speed of a shaft proportional to an applied voltage.

1947 CROWTHER & WHIDDINGTON *Science at War* 83 The Velodyne..is an electro-magnetic system that integrates the resultant of several motions. **1952** *Electronic Engin.* XXIV. 382 An electro-mechanical differential analyser, employing velodynes. **1972** *Internat. Jrnl. Control* XVI. 37 The amplified output is fed to the split field of the velodyne motor, the armature of which is supplied from a constant current source.

velometer (velǫ·mĭtəɹ). [Irreg. f. VELO(CITY + -METER or by contraction of VELOCIMETER.] † **1.** A kind of governor for a marine steam engine. *Obs.*

1878 *Engineer* 13 Sept. 190/1 A marine governor or anti-racer... The..'Velometer'..has got into use entirely by force of its own merits.

2. An instrument for measuring the speed of air, or of an aircraft through the air.

1914 *Flight* 24 Jan. 82/2 The velometer..balances a pressure due to the speed through the air against the apparent weight of a column of liquid. **1939** *Jrnl. R. Aeronaut. Soc.* XLIII. 931 The design and application in mines of a spring-controlled vane-type air flow meter known as the Velometer. **1974** *IEEE Trans. Instrumentation & Measurement* XXIII. 203/1 A sonic velometer uses the passage of sound waves through air to determine the air velocity.

velours. 2. a, b. (Earlier examples.)

1794 A. YOUNG *Trav. France* (ed. 2) I. xix. 550 Rouen. ..At present, the velours and *cotton toiles* are the most flourishing. The fabrics spread over all the country... They have also some woollens. **1805** T. FREMANTLE *Let.* 19 Nov. in *Wynne Diaries* (1940) III. vi. 234 Mistress Tittler with a black Velour pelisse. **1822** M. EDGEWORTH *Let.* 24 Feb. (1971) 357 My sage-colored French velours simulé pelisse and Fanny and Harriets purple ditto are quite the thing for carriage visits.

‖ **velouté** (vəlute). *Cookery.* [Fr., = velvety.] In full *velouté sauce.* A white sauce made with chicken or veal stock.

1830 [see *RAVIGOTE]. **1835** E. A. POE in *Southern Lit. Messenger* May 516/1 He mentioned..Muriton of red tongue and Cauliflowers with *Velouté* sauce. **1868**, etc. [see *ALLEMANDE *sb.* 3]. **1936** LUCAS & HUME *Au Petit Cordon Bleu* 71 Have ready ½ pint of *velouté* sauce. **1948**, **1961** [see *SUPRÊME *sb.* (*a.*) 1]. **1973** *Times* 6 Dec. 9/6 The vegetable and fish chefs will have made up *velouté* sauce, lobster sauce and a little bechamel sauce.

veltheimia (velthəi·miă). [mod.L. (J. G. Gleditsch 1769, in *Nouveaux Mém. Acad. R. Sci. Berlin* 66), f. the name of August Ferdinand, Graf von *Veltheim* (1741–1801), German patron of botany + -IA[1].] A bulbous plant of the genus of this name, belonging to the family Liliaceæ, native to South Africa, and bearing thick, oblong leaves and spikes of pink, red, or yellow flowers.

1808 *Curtis's Bot. Mag.* XXVII. 1091 (*heading*) Glaucous-leaved veltheimia. **1946** M. FREE *All about House Plants* facing p. 240 (*caption*) Veltheimia, a dependable winter-flowering bulb with glossy green foliage. **1980** *Flower & Garden Mag.* Sept. 24 The remarkable veltheimia deserves more attention as a houseplant.

velvet, *sb.* Add: **I. 1. c.** *to tip the velvet* (example).

1821 P. EGAN *Real Life in London* I. ix. 182 And when that they had sluiced their gobs With striving to excel wit, The lads began to hang their nobs, And tip their frows the velvet.

d. (Earlier example.)

1749 J. CLELAND *Mem. Woman Pleasure* II. 114 The deceiving him became so easy, that it was perfect playing upon velvet.

f. Gain, profit, winnings; *to the velvet,* to the good. *slang.*

1901 S. E. WHITE *Westerners* xxiii. 228 They's a good many ton of ore in four hundred foot of shaft.'..'Let that go for now... We can call that 'velvet'.' **1908** K. MCGAFFEY *Sorrows of Show Girl* 240 Before the whistle blew for dinner I was several hundred to the velvet. **1912** F. IRWIN *Fine Points Auction Bridge* 56 Do your doubling early in the rubber (so as to pile up 'velvet' for yourself). **1940** WODEHOUSE *Eggs, Beans & Crumpets* 138 It would be money for jam... Just so much velvet. **1942** *Amer. Speech* XVII. 93/2, I have been taking in plenty of velvet these days working the Fair. **1951** E. PAUL *Springtime in Paris* ii. 38 A good French mechanic..would have to work two and one half days to earn 2,430 francs, which on account of taxes..would not be all velvet.

g. A velvet dress.

1851 E. RUSKIN *Let.* 6 Nov. in M. Lutyens *Effie in Venice* (1965) II. 212, I had on my black velvet because it was mourning. **1944** R. LEHMANN *Ballad & Source* v. v. 222 We stood revealed in our long-sleeved velvets—Jess's sapphire blue, mine claret-coloured. **1963** N. STREATFEILD *Vicarage Family* ii. 16 Isobel's velvet was of a pale green with a very full skirt.

II. 4. c. *velvet-blue, -brown, -green, -red.*

1924 'J. SUTHERLAND' *Circle of Stars* iv. 26 She looked up sharply to see herself in the mirror, a rather pale face.. and dusky velvet-brown eyes. *Ibid.* ix. 95 Overhead the sky is deep velvet-blue all a-fire with stars. **1952** A. G. L. HELLYER *Sanders' Encycl. Gardening* (ed. 22) 31 *Sanderianus*, large, velvet-green with copper-red veins. **1976** *Flintshire Leader* 10 Dec. 27/1 (Advt.), New Fords for immediate delivery... Granada 2000GL, Velvet Red.

5. *velvet-coated.*

1881 O. WILDE *Poems* 74 After yon velvet-coated deer the virgin maid will ride. **1926** M. LEINSTER *Dew on Leaf* II. vi. 227 Your pretty face can charm of itself,..as a pale rose standing still lures the velvet-coated bee.

7. velvet carpet, a cut-pile carpet similar to Wilton; **velvet glove,** an appearance of suavity and gentleness of manner, esp. one that masks determination or inflexibility (cf. *iron hand* s.v. *IRON *a.* 3 c); also *attrib.* (with hyphen); **velvet-painting** (earlier example); **velvet sauce** = *VELOUTÉ.

1860 GEO. ELIOT *Mill on Floss* II. IV. iii. 188 Good society has its claret and its velvet carpets. **1908** L. M. MONTGOMERY *Anne of Green Gables* xxix. 325 'Velvet carpet,' sighed Anne luxuriously, '*and* silk curtains!' **1979** A. S. GARSTEIN *How-To Handbk. Carpets* ii. 15 At first velvet carpets were woven of solid colors in pile heights ranging from closely woven low pile to longer 'plush' fabrics. **1850**, etc. Velvet glove [see *IRON *a.* 3 c]. **1946** W. S. MAUGHAM *Then & Now* xxii. 125 The velvet glove was off and the mailed fist was bared. **1969** S. HYLAND *Top Bloody Secret* II. 202 Concentrated velvet-glove charm. **1973** 'M. INNES' *Appleby's Answer* iv. 41 Blackmail..of the very most genteel and velvet-glove sort. **1809** *Charges against H.R.H. Duke of York* 386/1 Did he ever instruct you in velvet-painting? **1893** T. F. GARRETT *Encycl. Pract. Cookery* II. 398/2 Velvet sauce (Velouté). **1952** E. WHITE *Good Eng. Food* IV. i. 171 Aspic Cream. Take ½ pint of liquid aspic jelly and mix it with ½ pint of velvet sauce.., ¼ pint thick cream and four sheets of gelatine.

b. velvet ant (examples); also, a parasitic wasp of the family Mutillidæ, having a velvety appearance.

1748 M. CATESBY *Nat. Hist. Carolina* App. 13 The Velvet Ant... The whole body and head resembled crimson velvet. **1842** T. W. HARRIS *Insects Injurious to Vegetation* 14 Stinging velvet-ants..are predaceous in their habits. **1932** E. STEP *Bees, Wasps, Ants Brit. Isles* 57 The Velvet-ants are not Ants: the name is only a courtesy title given when..the wingless female..was a more familiar object than the winged male. **1968** T. WOLFE *Electric Kool-Aid Acid Test* xxi. 305 He can *feel* ..every verruga fly, velvet ant, murine fleas and crabs. **1975** *Sci. Amer.* Dec. 115/1 The natural enemies of *Bembix* include mutillid wasps (sometimes called velvet ants).

velvet, *v.* Add: **2.** Also *fig.*

1959 R. GRAVES *Coll. Poems* 96 We velveted our love with fantasy Down a long vista-row of Christmas trees.

velveteen. Add: **1. c.** A dress of velveteen.

1873 *Young Englishwoman* Aug. 414/1 Would a black velveteen be suitable for the autumn? **1932** 'E. M. DELAFIELD' *Thank Heaven Fasting* II. i. 156 Run upstairs and put on the green velveteen. It suits you.

velvetiness. Add: Also *fig.*

1906 GALSWORTHY *Man of Property* II. iv. 167 The peculiar exasperation, velvetiness, and mockery, of which Bosinney's manner had been composed.

Venda (ve·nda), *sb.* and *a.* [An African word; since 1973 the name of a self-governing Bantu homeland in north Transvaal.] **A.** *sb.* **a.** (A member of) a Bantu people inhabiting the north-eastern Transvaal and southern Zimbabwe. **b.** The language of this people. **B.** *adj.* Of or pertaining to this people or their language.

[**1905** *Jrnl. Anthropol. Inst.* XXXV. 365 That part of the Bantu race of which I have to treat in this paper calls itself *Bawenda*, that is to say, people of Wenda, or inhabitants of Wenda.] **1908** *Jrnl. Afr. Society* VII. 412 Venda. Spoken by the Bavenda in North Transvaal. **1912** H. A. JUNOD *Life S. Afr. Tribe* I. i. 18 We find colonies of emigrated Thonga in many parts of the Transvaal. The largest is in the Spelonken district... There they are called *Magwamba* by the Venda and Bvesha who possessed the country before them. *Ibid.* II. VI. i. 327 There is a third tradition relating to the first man, but it has.. been borrowed from the Venda or Pedi tribes. **1921** *S. Afr. Jrnl. Sci.* Apr. 208 All these Venda clans (and the Malemba also) speak of their mountain. **1931** H. A. STAYT *BaVenda* p. xi, These boys..were familiar with the whole country and understood the different Venda dialects. **1937** [see *INKOSI]. **1950** I. SCHAPERA in Radcliffe-Brown & Forde *Afr. Syst. Kinship & Marriage* 144 Paternal aunts..do not command anything like the great authority they are said to possess among the Venda. **1977** *Times* 23 Nov. 20/8 We are oppressed..not as Zulus, Xhosas, Vendas or Indians. We are oppressed because we are black. **1979** J. DRUMMOND *I saw him Die* vii. 74 She began talking in some dialect I didn't understand—Venda, perhaps. **1979** *Guardian Weekly* 12 Aug. 6/3 In last year's general election, Chief Mphephu's ruling Venda National Party was decisively defeated by the Opposition Venda Independence Party.

‖ **vendange** (vandãʒ). Also † 8 **vandange.** [Fr.: see VENDAGE.] In France, the annual grape harvest, the vintage (sense 2).

1766 SMOLLETT *Trav.* I. viii. 133 The mountains of Burgundy are covered with vines... The *vandange* was but just begun, and the people were employed in gathering the grapes. **1852** MRS. E. TWISLETON *Let.* 9 Oct. (1928) iv. 56 The *vendange* for the year is over, but the crop is not good and..they say none of the best wines will be made from it. **1893** SOMERVILLE & 'ROSS' *In Vine Country* viii. 147 Of course we left vowing to return for the *vendange* next year. **1944** W. FORTESCUE *Mountain Madness* xi. 83 And when the *jasmin* harvest was over, there was the *vendange*, my grapes to be picked and made into wine. **1969** B. WEIL *Dossier IX* xxiii. 180 It's a good time to go south. The *vendange* is just starting. **1972** *Daily Tel.* 8 Apr. 14/7 Last year's *vendange*.

Hence **vendangeur,** a grape-picker.

1893 SOMERVILLE & 'ROSS' *In Vine Country* v. 91 We had to drive for some distance before we saw the first group of *vendangeurs*, standing waist-deep in the vines, snipping off the bunches and putting them into square wooden baskets. **1971** *Country Life* 2 Dec. 1501/3 The carver of a misericord in Ely cathedral certainly knew what was what when he displayed an Ely *vendangeur* of 1340 or thereabouts.

‖ **Vendémiaire** (vandemiɛr). [Fr., f. L. *vindēmia* vintage.] The first month of the French republican calendar, introduced in 1793, extending from Sept. 22 to Oct. 21.

1799 *Times* 1 June 3/1 In the month of last Vendemiaire. **1910** B. MIALL tr. *Aulard's French Revolution* III. vi. 267 An important measure of police law..was not presented and voted until the 6th and 7th of *Vendémiaire* of the year IV. **1923** S. MATTHEWS *French Revolution* xx. 293 Bonaparte..with the true adventurer's instinct accepted the command (Vendémiaire 13). **1981** *Encounter* Dec. 31/1 *Vendémiaire* could be joyfully evoked..by those who had not the first idea of the process of wine-making.

‖ **vendemmia** (vende·mia). [It.] The Italian grape-harvest or vintage. Cf. *VENDANGE, *VENDIMIA.

1826 M. KELLY *Reminisc.* I. 179, I..was delighted by the appearance of the elegant villas.., belonging to noble Venetians, who, during the theatrical season, pass their vendemmias there. **1871** C. M. YONGE *Little Lucy's Wonderful Globe* iii. 21 Ah, ah! 'tis the *vendemmia*! all may eat grapes. **1926** D. H. LAWRENCE *Let.* 17 Oct. (1962) II. 942 The peasants finished the *vendemmia* two days after we got here—but the wine is still to be made. **1978** J. PEARSON *Façades* xxviii. 473 The vineyards had yielded a record crop in the *vendemmia* that year.

‖ **vendeuse** (vandöz). [Fr.] A saleswoman; *spec.* one employed in a fashion house.

1913 E. WHARTON *Custom of Country* xiii. 181 Slender *vendeuses* floating by in a mist of opopanax. **1936** 'R. WEST' *Thinking Reed* ii. 61 This girl had been a *vendeuse* with a great French couturier. **1957** M. SHARP *Eye of Love* iii. 37 In the show-room Miss Molyneux, vendeuse and model, and Miss Harris, who fitted, were as usual discussing the private lives of film-stars. **1976** *Times Lit. Suppl.* 3 Sept. 1074/5 Went into a smart milliners and asked the *vendeuse* to 'show me a hat for an ugly middle-aged woman whose husband no longer loves her'.

‖ **vendimia** (vendi·mia). [Sp., = vintage.] The Spanish grape harvest; also, the festival celebrating the end of the vintage. Cf. *VENDANGE, *VENDEMMIA.

1965 *Listener* 30 Sept. 495/3 The vendimia or harvest festival at Jerez..is a time of gaiety and laughter. **1975** *Harpers & Queen* May 50/2 The well-known 'vendimias' or wine harvest cavalcades. **1978** *Times* 21 Nov. 12/2 The crowning of the queen of the *vendimia* or wine harvest. **1979** *Country Life* 25 Oct. 1392/2 (*caption*) Last month's ceremony was the 32nd Vendimia to be celebrated in Jerez de la Frontera.

vending, *vbl. sb.* Add: **2.** Special Comb.: **vending machine,** a slot machine from which comestibles or other small goods may be obtained.

1895 *Funk's Stand. Dict.*, *Vending-machine*, a machine having a mechanism, controlled by the dropping of a coin into a slot, for delivering any small article with which it has been charged, as a slot machine for selling chewing-gum. **1947** J. C. RICH *Materials & Methods of Sculpture* i. 15 A medium to low relief is used for coins, with a raised rim about the edge of the coin to protect the relief from such wearing factors as vending machines, turnstiles, and stacking. **1980** *Times* 13 Nov. 4/8 The tea trolley is being wheeled back into offices and the anonymous vending machine, the butt of many jokes..is on the way out.

Venedotian, *a.* (Further example.)

1877 J. RHYS *Lect. Welsh Philol.* iv. 145 Here also may be mentioned..the Venedotian versions of the Laws of Wales, which Aneurin Owen found to be in manuscripts of the 12th century.

veneer, *sb.* Add: **4*.** *Dentistry.* = *veneer crown* in sense 5 below.

1930 G. M. HOLLENBACK in I. G. Nicholls *Prosthetic Dentistry* xlii. 653 It..does not provide as good retention, nor as good support for the abutment tooth as a partial veneer. **1965** L. A. WEINBERG *Atlas Crown & Bridge Prosthodontics* xii. 232/1 Plastic veneers or porcelain jacket restorations should be tried in the mouth before final finishing. **1975** D. STANANOUGHT *Laboratory Procedures Inlays, Crowns & Bridges* ii. 22 Full veneers may be constructed entirely in metal, or in a combination of metal with either acrylic resin or porcelain on the labial surface.

5. veneer crown *Dentistry*, a crown in which the restoration is placed over the prepared surface of a natural crown.

1927 *Dental Cosmos* LXIX. 951 The next application [of porcelain to dental restoration]..was the so-called porcelain veneer crown which was the progenitor of the present highly perfected porcelain-jacket crown. **1954** J. E. EWING *Fixed Partial Prosthesis* xi. 61 The three-quarter partial veneer crown is primarily concerned with esthetics, for which function it owes its origin. **1975** D. STANANOUGHT *Laboratory Procedures Inlays, Crowns & Bridges* ii. 21 The restoration..may be a full veneer crown (shell crown) with the restoration covering the whole of the crown, or a partial veneer crown (three-quarter crown) with the labial or buccal surface of the crown excluded from the restoration.

venepuncture (ve·ni-, vī·nipʊːŋktiŭɹ). *Med.* Also **veni-**. [f. L. *vēna* VEIN *sb.* + PUNCTURE *sb.*] Puncture of a vein, esp. with a hypodermic needle to withdraw blood or for intravenous injection.

1923 *Jrnl. Biol. Chem.* LVI. 106 Blood was drawn by venepuncture from a normal man. **1935** WHITBY & BRITTON *Disorders of Blood* xxiv. 475 Blood is obtained by venipuncture without using a tourniquet. **1957** W. MARTIN in R. K. Merton *Student-Physician* 196 Being able to do a venipuncture without difficulty. **1974** F. ELLIS in R. M. Kirk et al. *Surgery* viii. 172/1 A period of six weeks is necessary before the veins are sufficiently dilated to be used for regular venepuncture. **1979** *Arizona Daily Star* 5 Aug. (Advt. section) 3/4 Venipuncture hospital experience preferred.

veneratingly, (ve·nĕrĕ^i^tiŋli), *adv. rare*⁻¹. [f. VENERATING *ppl. a.* + -LY².] In a reverential manner.

c **1925** V. WOOLF in *Mrs Dalloway's Party* (1973) 68 She and Bertram sat down on deck chairs, she looked at the house veneratingly, enthusiastically.

venereal, *a.* and *sb.* Add: **2. d.** *sb.* A person with venereal disease.

1788 W. BLIGH in R. M. Bowker *Mutiny!!* (1978) vi. 266 Three Venereals in the List. **1933** *Sun* (Baltimore) 23 Feb. 8/3 A veneral draws $257.50 a month, or more than a man blinded by an enemy shell.

venereally (vĭnī^ə^·rĭăli), *adv.* [f. VENEREAL *a.* + -LY².] **a.** By sexual intercourse. **b.** With venereal disease. *rare.*

1945 [see *BEJEL]. **1973** *Sci. Amer.* Apr. 119/2 His [*sc.* Linnæus's] chief practice was among the venereally ill young rakes of Stockholm. **1978** *Nature* 28 Sept. 334/2 Genital warts..are benign tumours which are mostly venereally transmitted.

venereology. Add: (Examples.) Hence **venereolo·gical** *a.*; **venereo·logist**, an expert or specialist in venereology.

1894 GOULD *Dict. Med.* 1595/2 Venereology. **1934** WEBSTER, Venereologist. **1944** *Jrnl. R. Army Med. Corps* LXXXIII. 102 Non-gonococcal urethritis..is worrying many venereologists nowadays. **1946** *Nature* 17 Aug. 242/2 (*heading*) Adviser in venereology to the War Office. **1961** *Lancet* 29 July 246/2 Their study..included others admitted to non-venereological departments. **1970** *Daily Tel.* 25 Sept. 6/8 Permissive doctors..were condemned yesterday by Dr Ambrose King, consulting venereologist to the London Hospital. **1972** *Lancet* 10 June 1295/1 He could not see why venereology should be considered a specialty in its own right. **1979** D. BARLOW *Sexually Transmitted Diseases* iii. 29 This is the only country in the EEC..that recognizes venereology as a distinct specialty. **1982** *Acta Dermato-Venereologica* LXII. 367/2 Every patient with a finding or history of Pediculosis pubis should be offered a venereological examination including test for both gonorrhea and syphilis.

venerous, *a.* Restrict † *Obs.* to senses 1 and 3 and add: **2.** (Later example.) Now *rare.*

1968 W. D. JORDAN *White over Black* i. 33 Long before the first English contact with West Africa, the inhabitants of virtually the entire continent stood confirmed in European literature as lustful and venerous.

venesector. Delete *rare*⁻¹ and add further examples. In mod. use, one who takes blood samples as a profession; a phlebotomist.

1976 *Nursing Times* 17 June A53/3 (Advt.), Venesector required to take blood samples from patients for Pathology Department. **1977** *Lancet* 5 Nov. 969/2 The use of a technician rather than a medically qualified venesector is economical and reduces the need to involve the family doctor in the somewhat troublesome, repetitive, and perhaps tedious routine of taking, packaging, and posting, blood-samples.

Venetian, *sb.* and *a.* Add: **A.** *sb.* **1. b.** The dialect of Italian spoken by the inhabitants of Venice.

1598 [see *LOMBARD *sb.*¹ 1 c]. **1642** [see *ROMAN *sb.*¹ 3 c]. **1852** E. RUSKIN *Let.* 27 June in M. Lutyens *Effie in Venice* (1965) II. 328 You may imagine how I am put to it sometimes when three or four people question me at once in Venetian. **1901** M. CARMICHAEL *In Tuscany* 99 Had Dante..written in Venetian..there would have been two classical languages in Italy today. **1921** R. L. GALES *Old-World Essays* 140 It is strange to think of these careless people, all talking Venetian in the clear Paduan air four hundred years ago. **1980** *Listener* 23 Oct. 528/2 Catalan..is to Castilian Spanish what Venetian is to Italian.

B. *adj.* **1.** Also, of or pertaining to the ancient Veneti of Gaul or Venetia. *rare.*

1866 W. P. DICKSON tr. *Mommsen's Hist. Rome* IV. v. vii. 252 The legions expended their time and strength in the sieges of the Venetian towns. *Ibid.* 253 Caesar caused ..the people of the Venetian canton to the last man to be sold into slavery. **1897** *Archæol. Jrnl.* LIV. 393 Through the Venetian traders the beautiful southern designs..on the golden and bronze ornaments in Ireland might..have been introduced.

2. *Venetian blue*, a turquoise or cobalt blue; *Venetian-Gothic* adj. (earlier example); also *absol.* as *sb.*; *Venetian raised (point) lace*, a point lace in which all outlines are in relief; = *punto a rilievo* s.v. *PUNTO¹ 7; also *Venetian (raised) point* (cf. *Venice point* s.v. VENICE 1).

c **1840** LADY WILTON *Art of Needlework* vii. 75 A rich robe of Venetian blue embroidered with golden eagles. **1947** J. H. BUSTANOBY *Princ. Color* 12/2 *Cobalt blue*, similar brands: Cobalt ultramarine, Hungary blue,.. Venetian blue. **1976** *Milton Keynes Express* 18 June 40/4 (Advt.), New Kitten Estate. Venetian blue. **1849** E. RUSKIN *Let.* 3 Dec. in M. Lutyens *Effie in Venice* (1965) I. 81 We..looked over several Palaces... The outsides are splendid Venetian Gothic. **1933** J. BETJEMAN *Ghastly Good Taste* vii. 116 The red brick Flemish revival of Brondesbury and the Venetian Gothic of Kew. **1980** J. LEES-MILNE *Harold Nicolson* I. ix. 170 They went up the Canal in a gondola, arguing about Venetian-Gothic. **1872** F. B. PALLISER *Notes Hist. Lace* 27 Finest raised Venetian point. **1882** CAULFIELD & SAWARD *Dict. Needlework* 513/1 The raised Venetian Points were not worked before 1600. *Ibid.*, The Venetian Raised Points are extremely rich and varied. **1960** H. HAYWARD *Antique Coll.* 295/1 *Venetian raised point lace*, needlepoint. **1974** [see *PUNTO¹ 7].

Hence **Vene·tianly,** *adv.*

1851 H. MELVILLE *Moby Dick* II. xii. 91 Through all the wide contrasting scenery..flows one continual stream of Venetianly corrupt and often lawless life. **1965** *Guardian* 3 Apr. 7/5 If you want to eat well and Venetianly in Venice..go to the best restaurants.

Venetic, *a.* Add: Also, of or pertaining to the language of the Veneti.

1922 *Jrnl. Anthropol. Inst.* XXV. 214 Indiscriminate combinations of letters from the Venetic alphabet. **1949** M. S. BEELER *Venetic Lang.* 4 That the Venetic alphabet in particular is in fact derived from the Etruscan is now certain.

B. as *sb.* The language of the ancient Veneti.

1904 [see *ETEOCRETAN *a.* and *sb.*]. **1932** [see *MESSAPIAN *sb.* and *a.*]. **1977** [see *RHAETIC *sb.*].

Venezuelan, *a.* and *sb.* **a, b.** (Earlier examples.)

1820 *Ann. Reg. 1819* 242/1 On every point the efforts of the Venezuelans were crowned with success. *Ibid.* 242/2 The Venezuelan fleet.

venial, *sb.* For † *Obs.* read 'Now *rare*' and add later example.

1969 J. D. CRICHTON in J. Fitzsimons *Penance* ii. 32 One thing that the present system inhibits, with..its neat parcels of 'mortals' and 'venials'—the sin-grid, in fact—is the expression of the diffused feeling of sinfulness.

Venice. Add: **1.** *Venice lace, point* (earlier example); *Venice soap* (earlier examples).

1865 F. B. PALLISER *Hist. Lace* iv. 45 It is not, however, till the reign of Elizabeth, that Italian cutworks and Venice lace came into general use. **1929** *Oxford Poetry* 3 Every fallen shadow weaves Venice lace for kindly aunts. **1974** *Times-Picayune* (New Orleans) 15 Aug. v. 6/1 A flounce capelet edged in venice lace. **1865** F. B. PALLISER *Hist. Lace* iv. 47 This is our Rose (raised) Venice point, the Gros Point de Venise, the Punto a rilievo, so highly prized and so extensively used for albs, collerettes..and costly decoration. **1673** J. RAY *Observations Journey Low-Countries* 202 *Venice-Sope*..is very like and nothing inferiour to *Castile-Sope*. It is made of the best Oil Olive. **1792** J. WOODFORDE *Diary* 26 July (1927) III. 364 At D[itt]o. for Venice Soap 1. 0.

venidium (veni·diŏm). [mod.L. (C. F. Lessing 1831, in *Linnæa* VI. 91), f. L. *vēna* vein, in allusion to the ribbed achenes of some species.] An annual or perennial herb of the genus *Venidium*, belonging to the family Compositæ, native to South Africa, and bearing cream or yellow flowers.

1937 R. HAY *Annuals* 230 Venidiums prefer a light soil. **1962** [see *CLEOME]. **1976** *Hortus Third* (L. H. Bailey Hortorium) 1147/2 Venidiums are usually treated as annuals in the garden.

venison. Add: **4. b.** *venison ham, pâté, steak.*

1772 B. ROMANS *Jrnl.* 16 Jan. in *Nat. Hist. Florida* (1775) 331, I purchased some bear, bacon and venison hams of them. **1788** M. CUTLER *Jrnl.* 7 Sept. (1888) I. 419 Dined..on venison steak and squirrel pie; very good dinner. **1833** J. HALL *Harp's Head* 214 A little further up were venison steaks, then fried ham. **1860** E. J. LEWIS *Jrnl.* 26 May in *Colorado Mag.* (1937) XIV. 219 Bought some venison ham for a dollar. **1975** *Harpers & Queen* May 68/2 The chef makes the most delicious venison paté. **1980** J. WAINWRIGHT *Man of Law* xliv. 205 Venison pâté sandwiches and watered-down whisky. **1980** C. & T. CONRAN *Cook Bk.* II. 248/1 Charcoal grilled venison. 1 venison steak from the leg or loin, weighing 2–3 lb.

Venizelist (venizē^i^·list), *a.* and *sb.* [f. the name of the Greek statesman Eleuthérios *Venizélos* (1864–1936) + -IST.] **A.** *adj.* Of, pertaining to, or supporting Venizélos or his political policies.

1915 *Times* 12 June 5/3 The Venizelist Press, in discussing the Government electoral programme, observes that the promised reforms are almost the same as those brought forward by M. Venizelos. **1916** *Morning Post* 25 Apr. 6/5 (*heading*) Repressing a Venizelist ovation. **1920** *Glasgow Herald* 4 May 7 Even the so-called Venizelist Divisions were nothing more than a collection of supers. **1931** *Times Lit. Suppl.* 19 Mar. 218/2 He confesses that..he was blown about by every wind of doctrine—now Venizelist, now Royalist. **1946** R. CAPELL *Simiomata* II. 61 There were senior officers of integrity, old Venizelist colonels like Tsamákos and Matsoukos in Thessaly. **1972** D. DAKIN *Unification of Greece* xvi. 238 The majority of the government was moderate Venizelist. **1980** J. LEES-MILNE *Harold Nicolson* I. vi. 84 Harold..was..put to work on.. the supply of stores to the Venizelist forces in Egypt.

B. *sb.* A supporter or adherent of Venizélos or his political policies.

1915 *Times* 15 June 5/3 The processions formed by the Venizelists became so numerous that several attempts were made by the cavalry to disperse them. **1920** V. J. SELIGMAN *Victory of Venizelos* 8 The views..of leading 'Venizelists' and 'Constantinians'. **1946** R. CAPELL *Simiomata* III. 127 There used to be furious feeling between Venizelists and monarchists. **1981** *Times Lit. Suppl.* 22 May 584/3 Is it not a little unfair to say that there have been no distinguished Cretans apart from King Midas and El Greco? The verdict will not please the Venizelists.

Hence **Venize·lism.**

1931 C. MACKENZIE *First Athenian Memories* xv. 380 This result was not gained merely by abstentions in the Islands and the new territories where Venizelism was naturally predominant.

Venn diagram (ven). [Named after its inventor, John *Venn* (1834–1923), English logician.] A group of circles that may or may not intersect according as the logical sets they represent have or have not elements in common.

[**1884** J. N. KEYNES *Stud. & Exerc. Formal Logic* III. v. 207 The application of Mr Venn's diagrammatic scheme to syllogistic reasonings. **1894** *Ibid.* (ed. 3) III. iv. 298 Syllogisms in *Barbara* and *Camestres* may be taken in order to show how Dr Venn's diagrams can be used.] **1918** C. I. LEWIS *Survey Symbolic Logic* i. 77 This method resembles nothing so much as solution by means of the Venn diagrams. **1952** W. V. QUINE *Methods of Logic* 70 Whiteness of a region in a Venn diagram means nothing but lack of information. **1970** O. DOPPING *Computers & Data Processing* i. 28 By means of Venn diagrams..set theoretic operations such as intersection can be shown in geometrical form. **1977** J. L. HARPER *Population Biol. Plants* xxiii. 725 These results are interpreted as a Venn diagram in Fig. 23/11a to show presumed niche relationships between the groups of species.

veno- (vīno), Comb. form of L. *vēna* VEIN *sb.*, employed in terms relating to the vascular system, as **venocly·sis** [Gr. κλύσις drenching], the introduction of liquid into the circulation by an intravenous drip; **venoconstri·ction,** constriction of a vein; **veno-occlu·sive** *a.*, characterized by occlusion of veins: applied esp. to a tropical disease in which this is the chief pathological feature; **ve·nospasm,** sudden, transient contraction of a vein; **veno-sta·sis,** a reduction (induced or spontaneous) in the flow of venous blood from a part of the body.

[**1910** M. F. DONAHOE *Man. of Nursing* ix. 166 In preparing for a veneclysis the nurse should take as much care as for an abdominal operation.] **1926** *Texas State Jrnl. Med.* XXI. 664/2, I regard the main indications for venoclysis as being any form of grave collapse, grave toxemia, prolonged shock, or serious dehydration from any cause. **1961** *Lancet* 2 Sept. 538/2 Some such device is essential for venoclysis in infancy. **1937** K. J. FRANKLIN *Monograph on Veins* x. 127 Perfusion of the corpus striatum with hot and cold fluids resulted in superficial venodilation and venoconstriction respectively. **1977** *Proc. Soc. Med.* LXX. 691/2 Blood samples were taken without venoconstriction at 13:00 and 14:00. **1954** G. BRAS et al. in *Arch. Path.* LVII. 285 (*heading*) Veno-occlusive disease of liver with nonportal type of cirrhosis, occurring in Jamaica. **1969** EDINGTON & GILLES *Path. in Tropics* xi. 489 It is now generally accepted that veno-occlusive disease in the West Indies is due to ingestion of 'bush tea' containing the alkaloids of *C*[*rotolaria*] *fulva*. **1950** P. WOOD *Dis. Heart & Circulation* i. 13 Venospasm is avoided by proper skin anæsthesia, and by choosing a catheter that is not too large for the vein. **1977** *Lancet* 1 Jan. 29/2 The damage is caused by pulmonary venospasm (occurring as the shock is relieved). **1931** R. J. E. SCOTT *Gould's Med. Dict.* (ed. 3), Venostasis. **1965** *Thrombosis & Diathesis Hæmorrhagica* XIV. 501 Venostasis was induced by means of a sphygmomanometric cuff (systolic pressure diminished by 20 mmHg). **1976** *Lancet* 11 Dec. 1265/2 Despite the presence of venostasis in the legs, intermittent compression of the arms during and after surgery reduced the incidence of deep venous thrombosis..in the legs to half that in control patients.

venography (vĕnǫ·-, vīnǫ·grăfi). *Med.* [f. *VENO- + -GRAPHY.] Radiography of a vein after injection of a contrast medium.

1935 *Arch. Surg.* XXXI. 272 Venography..showed an obstruction in the axillary vein distal to the first rib. **1980** *Brit. Med. Jrnl.* 18 Oct. 1039/1 No arteriovenous malformation was detected by venography or arteriography.

Hence **venogra·phic, -ical** *adjs.*; **venogra·phically** *adv.*; also **ve·nogram,** a radiogram of a vein.

1935 *Arch. Surg.* XXXI. 272 A venogram made with a stabilized solution of thorium dioxide on the third day after admission showed a point of obstruction in the axillary vein distal to the first rib. **1940** *Surg., Gynecol. & Obstetr.* LXXI. 701/1 Venographic studies were carried out. **1940** *Acta Chir. Scand.* Suppl. LXI. 22 The venographical method has proved to be a very valuable diagnostic aid in manifest and suspect..thrombosis. **1940** Venographically [see *thromboembolic* adj. s.v. *THROMBO-]. **1972** *Science* 16 June 1236/3 A considerable advantage of these images [produced by ultrasonic Doppler technique] is that they look like present-day arteriograms and venograms. **1978** *Lancet* 12 Aug. 331/2 Limbs with chronic venous insufficiency which had no venographically detected thrombosis. **1980** *Ibid.* 16 Feb. 332/2 We found venographic evidence of compression of popliteal veins by such a cyst in only 1 case.

vent, *sb.*² Add: **I. 2. c.** *full vent,* advb. phr., at full pitch; to the utmost of one's capacity.

1927 D. H. LAWRENCE *Mornings in Mexico* 11 It is so unlike him, to be whistling full vent, when any of us is around.

II. 10. f. = *PORT *sb.*³ 4 d.

1940 *Electronics* Mar. 54/2 The vent should be located near the speaker... The vent areas need not necessarily be circular. **1975** G. J. KING *Audio Handbk.* vi. 143 (*caption*) Inside of Rectavox Omni Mk II loudspeaker system, showing the bass and treble units, the tube extension from the vent and the frequency divider network at the bottom.

vent, *sb.*⁴ Theatr. slang abbrev. of VENTRILOQUIST.

1893 R. GANTHONY *Practical Ventriloquism* iii. 89 The Vent: does not suffer provided he makes capital out of unforeseen interruptions. **1945** L. LANE *How to become Comedian* xiv. 116 When an imaginary character answers from the roof the 'vent' looks upwards. **1976** *National Observer* (U.S.) 4 Sept. 6/3 We've got magicians here... We've got jugglers, mentalists, clowns, and vents.

vent, *v.*² **I. 1. a.** Delete † *Obs.* and add later examples. Also, to empty (a confined space) of gas in this manner.

1947 J. C. RICH *Materials & Methods of Sculpture* xi. 355 Molds may be vented to permit the ready escape of air from undercuts. **1969** *Times* 23 May 1/2, To close their hatch, the pressure in the tunnel had to be lowered. 'I am not able to vent the tunnel,' Commander John Young reported at 6.15 p.m...last night. **1978** *Daily Tel.* 18 Aug. 30/6 The balloon's crew were then able to..fall into the most likely airstream by..venting the balloon—letting out the helium and allowing it to drop.

2. a. Delete † *Obs.* and add later examples. Freq. *pass.*

1962 F. I. ORDWAY et al. *Basic Astronautics* v. 197 After arrival on the moon the fluid is vented. **1969** *Daily Mail* 15 Jan. 5/4 The rocket..vented quite a lot of fuel overboard and the fuel formed millions of ice particles. **1980** *Nature* 29 May 278/3 A total of 10 millicuries of krypton-85 was vented to the atmosphere during the procedure and the engineers received a whole body radiation dose of 10 to 15 mrem. **1983** *Sci. Amer.* Apr. 80/1 The pilot vented the ballast tanks, surrounding *Alvin* with a column of bubbles.

II. 11. Delete 'Now *rare*' and add later examples. Also used of a force causing an outlet to be made.

1966 *Economist* 19 Feb. 686/3 Some of these test explosions 'vent' through the earth's surface and thus contaminate the atmosphere. **1970** *Times* 15 Apr. 1/7 The particles have diminished greatly—almost ceased now, which indicates maybe what was venting has almost stopped. **1980** *Courier-Mail* (Brisbane) 27 Nov. 31/4 Fuel was venting from the tanks. The loss was so great that it was doubted that they would make it to an airfield.

vented, *ppl. a.* **b.** (Later example.)

1977 *Sci. Amer.* Apr. 27/2 Fortunately the vented gas did not ignite.

vented (ve·ntėd), *a.* [f. VENT *sb.*² + -ED².] Equipped with vents or apertures. Cf. *PORTED *a.*¹ 2.

1940 *Electronics* Mar. 34/1 The vented speaker enclosure uses a conventional cone type dynamic speaker mounted in a box lined with sound absorbent material. **1957** *IRE Trans. on Audio* V. 38/2 The vented enclosure allows the hf speaker to be mounted with its centroid to lie on the same point as that of the lf speaker. **1975** [see *PORTED *a.*¹ 2].

venter¹. Add: **I. 3*.** *Bot.* The enlarged, basal part of an archegonium, where the egg cells develop.

1887 BALFOUR & GARNSEY tr. *K. Goebel's Outl. Classification & Special Morphol. Plants* 175 The archegonium when fully formed consists of a thick and rather long stalk, a roundish-ovoid venter resting on the stalk, and above it a long slender neck usually twisted on its axis. **1938** G. M. SMITH *Cryptogamic Bot.* II. ii. 17 The mature venter is therefore 12 to 20 cells in perimeter instead of six cells as in the neck. **1978** T. L. HUFFORD *Botany* vii. 177 The archegonia are frequently long stalked with an only slightly enlarged venter (egg chamber) and an elongated neck.

ventifact (ve·ntifækt). [f. L. *vent-us* WIND *sb.*¹ + -I- + *fact-us,* pa. pple. of *facere* to make.] A faceted stone shaped or altered by wind-blown sand.

1911 J. W. EVANS in *Geol. Mag.* Decade V. VIII. 335 If a general expression be required for any wind-shaped stone, we might speak of a 'ventifact', on the analogy of artifact, sometimes spelt 'artefact',..and of 'ventiduct', which has been employed in architecture. **1935** *Times* 28 Jan. 15/4 Dr. Spencer brought back many fine examples of wind-worn rock and ventifacts for further study. **1944** [see *DREIKANTER.] **1949** K. P. OAKLEY *Man the Tool-Maker* ii. 10 Stones splintered by fire, or faceted by sandstorms (ventifacts or dreikanters) are occasionally mistaken for the work of man. **1970** [see *DREIKANTER].

ventilate, *v.* Add: **I. 5. a.** Now *Obs.*

c. *trans.* To supply air to (the lungs); to supply air, esp. artificially, to the lungs of; also *transf.*

1919 FLACK & HILL *Textbk. Physiol.* xxxii. 288 It is only when the lungs are well ventilated that the parts most remote from these surfaces of direct expansion are brought properly into action. **1946** J. F. FULTON *Howell's Textbk. Physiol.* (ed. 15) xxxix. 871 Under normal rest conditions..5·6 litres of air..are available to ventilate the alveoli. **1971** *Nature* 21 May 181/1 When necessary the lungs were ventilated mechanically with a Palmer respiration pump. **1975** *Ibid.* 23 Oct. 674/1 Animals were artificially ventilated with a mixture of N_2O–O_2–CO_2. **1978** *Sci. Amer.* Aug. 95/2 Heating the hypothalamus caused the fish to ventilate its gills faster. **1979** *Daily Tel.* 6 Nov. 3/6 All they had in fact when the plug was pulled was a corpse being ventilated by a machine.

8. c. *slang.* To shoot (someone or something) with a gun, usu. to kill. Also of a bullet: to make a hole in (something).

1875 C. B. LEWIS *Quad's Odds* 473 Some of our folks cleaned up their revolvers..hoping to get a shot at McGrady and to ventilate the mule. **1917** [see *COCKPIT 3 c]. **1948** 'R. MACDONALD' in H. Q. Masur *Murder Most Foul* (1973) 103 'A man was shot in one of his rooms.'..'Who was it got himself ventilated?' **1979** C. EGLETON *Backfire* ix. 98 You'd just better pray he doesn't kill somebody..because he's talking about ventilating people.

ventilated, *ppl. a.* Add: Also, supplied with continual fresh air.

1951 D. W. RICHARDS in Cecil & Loeb *Textbk. Med.* (ed. 8) 844/1 The trapping of air in poorly ventilated air spaces, on repeated deep breathing, is shown by a step-wise rise in the spirogram. **1975** *Anaesthesia & Intensive Care* III. 237 (*heading*) A simple clinical method of quantitating the effects of chest physiotherapy in mechanically ventilated patients. **1980** *Daily Tel.* 3 Nov. 16 A substantial sample has..accrued from the innumerable ventilated patients who have not become organ donors.

ventilation. Add: **I. 3. a.** Now *Obs.*

b. The supply of fresh air or oxygen to the lungs (or gills), by the process of breathing or artificially.

1891 A. D. WALLER *Introd. Human Physiol.* iv. 136 The bronchus being blocked a portion of the lung is cut off from ventilation. **1919** FLACK & HILL *Textbk. Physiol.* xxxii. 284 To facilitate gaseous interchange, the process of breathing or ventilation of the lungs takes place. **1951** E. A. STEAD in Cecil & Loeb *Textbk. Med.* (ed. 8) 1052/2 In cardiac failure the increased ventilation..is produced by the reflex stimulation of respiration from the congested lungs and great vessels. **1974** *Nature* 19 Apr. 631/1 Where the patient is being kept 'alive' artificially by ventilation the doctor..must decide when the brain has died and when the ventilator has passed the point at which it will invoke any involuntary response in the patient. **1978** *Sci. Amer.* Aug. 95/2 The fish could..wait until an oxygen deficit occurs and then respond by increasing its gill ventilation.

4. c. *ventilation duct.*

1937 *Discovery* Nov. 345/1 The original roof of the Saxon chapel was almost certainly of wood, probably with ventilation ducts or cowls of a shape which may have suggested to the 16th century builders their idea for the dormer roof lights. **1964** *Listener* 12 Nov. 751/2 The claim to carry a ventilation duct across another's property was just as novel as the claim to protection against the weather.

ventilator. Add: **1. b.** (Earlier example.)

1822 M. EDGEWORTH *Let.* 9 Mar. (1971) 369 We went one night to the House of Commons—to the Ventilator.

e. *Med.* = *RESPIRATOR 3.

1961 I. W. B. GRANT in D. Dunlop et al. *Textbk. Med. Treatment* (ed. 8) 945 The patient retains fairly powerful respiratory movements and may have difficulty in synchronizing with any ventilator which is not triggered by his own inspiratory efforts. **1976** *Lancet* 13 Nov. 1069/1 It has become commonplace for hospitals to have deeply comatose and unresponsive patients with severe brain damage who are maintained on artificial respiration by means of mechanical ventilators. **1982** *Times* 10 June 7/2 Mr Argov was taken off his ventilator for two hours yesterday, although he remained unconscious.

ventilatory, *a.* Restrict *rare*⁻¹ to sense in Dict. and add: **2.** Of, pertaining to, or serving for ventilation of the lungs.

1946 J. F. FULTON *Howell's Textbk. Physiol.* (ed. 15) xxxix. 871 The maximum voluntary ventilatory rate is a useful index of the capabilities of an individual for doing work. **1963** J. B. HICKAM in Beeson & McDermott *Cecil-Loeb Textbk. Med.* (ed. 11) 524/1 Pulmonary tests are awkward to group according to particular kinds of function because they frequently overlap categories. A common and useful procedure is to divide them into tests of ventilatory and respiratory function. 'Ventilatory function' refers to lung volumes and the process of moving gas in and out of the lungs from ambient air to alveolar wall. 'Respiratory function' refers to the transfer of gas between alveoli and blood. **1980** *Daily Tel.* 16 Oct. 20 There is a time in the management of patients with severe brain damage..when the decision as to continue or not with ventilatory support is made.

venting, *vbl. sb.*¹ Add: **I. 1. a.** *spec.* The emission into the atmosphere of radioactive dust and debris from an underground nuclear explosion.

1963 *Wall St. Jrnl.* 27 Sept. 1/1 More unsettling, however, is the possibility that ventings of underground blasts have been adding undetected amounts of radioactive iodine to milk. **1971** *Nature* 30 July 291/3 One fear..is that if massive venting does occur..radioactive fallout could be carried outside United States territory. **1980** *New Scientist* 3 July 4/1 The venting of radioactive krypton-85 from the crippled reactor at Three Mile Island..began at 8 am last Saturday.

venting, *ppl. a.* Restrict † *Obs.*⁻¹ to sense in Dict. and add: **2.** Of gas: that finds escape by the action of venting.

1974 *Physics Bull.* June 253/1 An air filter cartridge for dehydration of the venting gas.

‖**Ventôse** (vaṅtōᵘz), *sb.*² [Fr., ad. L. *ventōsus*: see VENTOSE *a.*] The sixth month of the French republican calendar, introduced in 1793, extending from 19 Feb. to 20 Mar.

1802 C. WILMOT *Let.* 13 Mar. in *Irish Peer* (1920) 50 (*heading*) 13 March, 1802. 22 Ventose. **1910** *Encycl. Brit.* XI. 171/1 The winter months were Nivôse, the snowy, Pluviôse, the rainy, and Ventôse, the windy month. **1943** J. M. THOMPSON *French Revolution* xxiv. 463 The attempt, shown in the *maximum* decree of February 21st [1794] and the so-called 'Laws of Ventôse'..to conciliate the working-class support. **1981** *Encounter* Dec. 41/2 The Year III... Ventôse this time witnessed a sudden and massive thaw.

‖ **ventre à terre** (vaṅtr a tẽr) *adv. phr.* [Fr., lit. 'belly to the ground'.] **a.** In the posture assumed (esp. in sporting prints) by a horse at full gallop; hence at full speed, 'all out'. Also *attrib.*

1847 THACKERAY *Van. Fair* (1848) iii. 476, I instantly called for the carriage, and..drove *ventre à terre* to Nathan's. **1867** 'OUIDA' *Under Two Flags* I. xiii. 302 You know what the Arabs are... They..pick up their sabre from the ground, while their horse is galloping *ventre à terre.* **1918** G. B. SHAW in F. Harris *Oscar Wilde* II. 28 To be called on to gallop ventre à terre to Erith. **1947** J. STEVENSON-HAMILTON *Wild Life S. Afr.* xxii. 170 He [*sc.* a charging lion] goes not in a series of bounds, but at a *ventre à terre* gallop, and incredibly fast. **1974** *Country Life* 2 May 1059/1 His personal progression from the 19th-century *ventre à terre* animal motion—*à la* Herring and Pollard—to the transverse and rotatory images. **1977** 'E. CRISPIN' *Glimpses of Moon* xi. 223 Man and horse.. went on to gallop almost *ventre à terre* in the direction of the hedge.

b. Lying on one's stomach, prone.

1960 *Times* 18 July 15/4 Down at the firing point they formed a line *ventre à terre.* **1968** *Economist* 27 Jan. 4/3 The Cresta, which is run by the St. Moritz Toboggan Club, on which the rider uses a skeleton, or the bob run in which the bobsleigh crew descend either *ventre à terre* or sitting up.

ventriculitis (ventrikiŭləi·tis). *Path.* [f. L. *ventricul-us* VENTRICLE + -ITIS.] Inflammation of the lining of the ventricles of the brain.

1926 in R. J. E. SCOTT *Gould's Med. Dict.* **1946** *Med. Jrnl. Australia* 13 Apr. 513/1 A case of staphylococcal ventriculitis. **1967** *Brit. Med. Jrnl.* 27 May 542/2 Three babies with meningitis and ventriculitis were successfully treated with gentamicin. **1977** *Proc. R. Soc. Med.* LXX. 234/1 A considerable percentage will survive ventriculitis from an infected back.

ventriculo- (ventri·kiŭlo), Comb. form of L. *ventricul-us* VENTRICLE, occurring in various words in *Anat.*, as **ventri:culoa·trial** *a.*, involving or connecting a ventricle (usu. of the brain) and the atrium of the heart; **ventri:culoperitone·al** *a.*, involving or connecting a ventricle of the brain and the peritoneum.

1959 *Amer. Jrnl. Dis. Children* XCVIII. 467/2 (*heading*) Clinical observations on twenty hydrocephalic children subjected to ventriculoatrial shunt. **1962** *Lancet* 12 May 991/1 The experiments with the rubber slings designed to reduce ventriculoatrial reflux were not consistent. **1977** *Proc. R. Soc. Med.* LXX. 235/2 The ventriculo-atrial shunt is the most physiological, and in spite of its drawbacks I prefer it to ventriculopleural or ventriculoperitoneal drainage except in special circumstances. **1913** *Ann. Surg.* LVII. 468 Ventriculoperitoneal drainage. In 1905, Kausch performed this operation by uniting the lateral ventricle with the peritoneal cavity by means of a small rubber tube, placed subcutaneously. **1977** *Lancet* 30 Apr. 951/1 A ventriculoperitoneal shunt was inserted for relief of the hydrocephalus.

ventriculography (ventrikiŭlǫ·grăfi). *Med.* [f. *VENTRICULO- + -GRAPHY.] Radiography of the brain with the cerebral fluid of the ventricles replaced by air or some other contrast medium. Hence **ventri:culogra·phic** *a.*; also **ventri·culogram,** a radiogram of the ventricles of the brain.

1918 W. E. Dandy in *Ann. Surg.* LXVIII. 5 (*heading*) Ventriculography following the injection of air into the cerebral ventricles. *Ibid.* 7 Owing to the lighter weight of air, the ventriculogram represents the ventricle farthest from the X-ray plate. **1932** *Amer. Jrnl. Roentgenol.* XXVII. 660/1 The size of the lateral ventricle, and the patency of the foramen of Munro, can be determined readily during this particular part of the ventriculographic procedure. **1936** *Brit. Med. Jrnl.* 28 Mar. 661/2 The usual procedure..was to make a ventriculogram first thing in the morning, and start operating two or three hours later. **1947** *Radiology* XLVIII. 59/1 Ventriculography..showed the posterior portions of both lateral ventricles to be dilated and revealed similar enlargement of the temporal horns. **1974** C. B. T. Adams in R. M. Kirk et al. *Surgery* xiv. 273/2 Often, the brain plugs the fracture and a rise of intranasal pressure by nose blowing forces the air into the brain, an aerocele, and, occasionally, into the ventricle, producing a ventriculogram on X-ray. **1978** *Science* 24 Feb. 854/1 Asymmetries in the size of the left and right lateral ventricles [of the brain] can..be demonstrated..by injecting air into the ventricles during pneumoencephalography and ventriculography.

ventriloquial, *a.* **2.** (Earlier example.)

1818 in A. Mathews *Mem. Charles Mathews* (1838) II. 452 So well did he by his ventriloquial power imitate the voice of a child, without any movement of the natural organs of speech.

ventripotent, *a.* Add: Hence **ventri·potenee** *rare.*

1922 [see *ovablastic *a.*].

ventro-. Add: **ventrome·dial** *a.*, both ventral and medial; situated towards the median line and the ventral or anterior surface; hence **ventrome·dially** *adv.*, in a ventromedial direction.

1908 H. E. Santee *Anat. Brain & Spinal Cord* vi. 340 Only the ventro-medial group is present above the sixth cervical segment. **1942** F. A. Mettler *Neuroanatomy* x. 199 Ventromedial to these small cells and encapsulated by them, is a round collection of cells of varying size. **1974** D. & M. Webster *Compar. Vertebr. Morphol.* v. 99 In Crocodilia the girdle is primarily endochondral with a large dorsal scapula and a ventromedial procoracoid. **1960** J. D. Boyd in G. H. Bourne *Struct. & Function Muscle* I. iii. 68 These mesenchymal cells migrate ventromedially round the notochord. **1978** *Nature* 31 Aug. 871/1 The bristles on the wing margin..send similar short, dense projections ventromedially. **1984** *Brit. Med. Jrnl.* 25 Aug. 455/1 Patients with hyperthalamic defects—especially in the ventromedial-arcuate region, which has been implicated in GH regulation—may show raised plasma immunoreactive GRF concentrations.

venture, *sb.* Add: **10. b.** Special Comb.: **venture capital** = *risk capital* s.v. *risk *sb.* 3; hence **venture capitalist; Venture Scout,** a male or (since 1976) female member of that section of the Scout Association for those between 16 and 20 years of age (cf. *rover scout* s.v. *rover[1] 3 d); hence **Venture Scouting.**

1943 M. A. Shattuck in *Addresses at Membership Forum* (Nat. Assoc. Investment Companies) 22 Industry during the last decade has not only lacked venture capital for new enterprises; it has also lacked venture capital for established concerns. **1971** *Financial Mail* (Johannesburg) 26 Feb. 681/1 These are some of the..successes which have brought just about every major US institution into the venture capital arena. *Ibid.* 681/2 Some venture capitalists insist on a majority equity stake. **1981** *Sci. Digest* Aug. 118/1 Venture capital, the money that bankrolls people with an innovative product, dried up in 1969. **1966** Venture scout [see *rover[1] 3 d]. **1978** *Broadcast* 27 Mar. 20/3 With many young men of 20 Venture Scouts..'Boy' Scout is hardly an accurate description for a large part of our membership. **1982** *Scouting* Sept. 582/1 This is the year the Venture Scout Section celebrates its fifteenth birthday. *Ibid.* 582/2 (*caption*) Female Venture Scouts have played an important part in the Section since 1976. **1967** *Venture Scouting* (Scout Assoc.) xv. 168 Venture Scouting is not always cheap; it isn't easy to get the right kind of gear. **1983** *Times* 23 Aug. 2/5 Venture Scouting has increased from a membership of 30,000 in 1979 to more than 36,000 this year... Girls..make up about 20 per cent of overall numbers.

Venturi (ventiṻ·ri). Also **venturi.** The name of G. B. *Venturi* (1746–1822), Italian physicist, used: **a.** *attrib.* to designate a short constriction in a tube between two longer tapered portions that are usu. of unequal length but terminate with the same diameter, so that there is a drop in pressure in a fluid flowing through the constriction which may be used to determine the rate of flow or used as a source of suction; also devices having this form and the effect involved.

1887 C. Herschel in *Trans. Amer. Soc. Civil Engineers* XVII. 231 Bourdon's anemometer is founded upon the property of a Venturi tube to exercise a sucking action. *Ibid.* 232 Then came the Bourdon anemometer..and now the instrument herein described, the Venturi Water Meter. *Ibid.* 239 The actual operations of the Venturi meter as applied to a water-pipe in ordinary service. **1894** W. K. Burton *Water Supply of Towns* 285 The 'Venturi tube', which has long been used as a means of roughly estimating the velocity of air-currents, has recently been used as a water-meter. **1917** *Jrnl. Agric. Res.* IX. 115 Preliminary experiments on a new type of device, called the 'Venturi flume', for measuring water in open channels. **1930** *Engineering* 24 Jan. 97/1 Each branch has a Venturi section for measurement of flow. **1931** *Handbk. Aeronautics* (R. Aeronaut. Soc.) viii. 515 Venturi anemometer heads use a venturi for producing a suction in order to increase the pressure difference obtainable with a pitot static tube. **1937** *Times* 4 Oct. 23/4 Provision against freezing and against blocking by ice and snow must be made in carburettors, venturi tubes, and the vents of fuel and oil tanks in new passenger aircraft. **1951** *Industr. & Engin. Chem.* June 1325/1 Deposition of a spray on the walls must be considered in the design and operation of several types of industrial equipment, including Venturi scrubbers and atomizers, combustion chambers in which liquid fuels are burned, and spray dryers. **1971** J. W. Ireland *Mechanics of Fluids* ix. 340 A venturi-flume is to be installed in a channel conveying water with the object of raising the level of the water upstream. **1973** *Times* 12 Feb. (Anchor Project Suppl.) p. ii/6 Collection of exhaust gases from the BOS vessels will be by the OG suppressed combustion system, and their cleaning by a two-stage venturi scrubber system. **1974** *Sci. Amer.* Feb. 100/3 The venturi effect in the narrow spaces between buildings can increase the velocity of the wind. **1977** *Lancet* 24 Sept. 641/1 We describe a method of pooling the contents of several packs by means of a simple vacuum box worked from an ordinary water tap and a Venturi pump.

b. *absol.*

1887 C. Herschel in *Trans. Amer. Soc. Civil Engineers* XVII. 239 The water was passing through the Venturi with similar velocities. **1921** *Sci. Amer.* 15 Oct. 275/1 An idea of the shape of the venturi becomes obvious by comparing it with an old-fashioned blunderbuss. **1942** G. Casey in Murdoch & Drake-Brockman *Austral. Short Stories* (1951) 361 Venturis down below [in a mine] and water everywhere to keep the dust down. **1952** *Archit. Rev.* CXI. 138/2 A drip-proof high efficiency burner with fixed venturi, providing flame stability at low consumptions. **1976** K. Thackeray *Crownbird* ii. 36 The wind played strange tricks, the entrance acting as a venturi with gusts swirling in great spirals.

venue. Add: **5. e.** *Theatr.* The site of a theatrical performance, *spec.* one used by touring companies.

1967 *Stage* 2 Mar. 21/4 (Advt.), Clubland Promotions urgently require first-class artists..for venues in South and West Wales. **1980** *Times* 25 Nov. 6/4 Cologne Opera and San Francisco Ballet have both inspected the theatre and are considering it as a venue. **1984** *Times* 8 Mar. 4/2 The largest computerized box office system in Britain, which will link every main venue in the city. Instant ticket printing means that venues can put on performances at short notice.

Venus[1]. Add: **I. 1. e.** *Archæol.* A palæolithic female figurine distinguished by exaggerated breasts, belly, and buttocks. Cf. *steatopyga.

1912 R. Munro *Palæolithic Man* x. 239 Laugerie Basse has supplied a fragment of bone with a pregnant woman and reindeer engraved on it..; the Venus..a headless statuette carved in ivory. **1920** H. C. Bailey *Call Mr. Fortune* 191 'My new palæolithic Venus.' 'You left her in the library.... There are not many men..who have a Hottentot Venus to lose.' **1937** Auden & MacNeice *Lett. from Iceland* xvii. 245 We leave to that poor soul A. M. Ludovici the Venus of Willendorf. **1958** *Times Lit. Suppl.* 11 Apr. 198/4 One archaeologist's interpretation of palaeolithic figurines or 'Venuses' as 'the characteristic products of unregenerated male imagination'. **1979** Mills & Mansfield *Genuine Article* ii. 34 The Venus figurine[s]..date from around 25,000 to 22,000 B.C... One of the most celebrated is the 'Venus of Willendorf' from Austria.

Venusberg (vī·nŭsbę̄ɪg, ‖vē·nŭsbęrk). [Ger., lit. 'mountain of Venus'.] The court of Venus, in German legend and esp. in Wagner's *Tristan* found in a grotto on the Hörselberg mountain; hence in *transf.* use, any environment whose primary characteristic is sensual pleasure.

1855 [see *saga[1] 2]. **1890** G. B. Shaw *How to become Mus. Critic* (1960) 192 Not even a visit from the ghost of Sterndale Bennett could have waved him back from the Venusberg then. **1925** H. Crane *Let.* 28 Feb. (1965) 199 A perfect Venusberg of flowers and shrubbery. **1934** H. G. Wells *Exper. Autobiogr.* I. iii. 107 Bowkett had his own secret incidental twilight Venusberg. **1962** *Guardian* 15 Nov. 9/3 We had wonderful plans for Windsor. It was to have been an expense account Venusberg. **1981** M. J. Benkovitz *Aubrey Beardsley* iv. 110 Beardsley depicted..[a] more violent encounter between satyrs and the residents of the Venusberg.

Hence **Venusbe·rgian** *a.*

1896 G. B. Shaw *Let.* 19 Feb. (1965) I. 602 A Venusbergian Asta is too much. **1977** *Gramophone* Dec. 1087/1 Those whining Wagnerian tubas in 'Mars' are matched by the almost Venusbergian sensuousness of 'Venus' here.

Venusian (vėniū̆·siăn), *a.*[1] *rare.* [f. L. *Venusia* (see below) + -an.] Of or pertaining to Venusia, an ancient town in southern Italy, and birthplace of the poet Horace; hence used allusively.

1616 B. Jonson *Poetaster* in *Workes* 310 And to his steps my Genius inclines, Lucanian, or Apulian, I not whether; For the Venusian colonie plowes either. **1875** F. Arnold *Our Bishops & Deans* I. v. 289 But the Venusian adage is true how the generous wine evermore retains the early flavour which was accidentally imparted to it.

Venusian (vėniū̆·siăn), *sb.* and *a*[2]. [f. Venus[1] II + -ian.] **A.** *sb.* **1.** *Science Fiction.* A supposed inhabitant of the planet Venus; also, the language spoken by such a being.

1874 A. Blair *Ann. 29th Cent.* III. iii. 56, I suspected from the circumstances the frames of the Venusians were so constituted that sustenance was superfluous. **1897** J. Munro *Trip to Venus* ix. 173 'The good of it?' rejoined the Venusian; 'it is beautiful, and gives us pleasure.' **1927** *Spectator* 24 Dec. 1127/1 It is the Venusians who record the Last Judgment. **1955** W. Girvan *Flying Saucers & Common Sense* i. 15, I do not think it is because of a desire that I should be visited by Martians or Venusians. **1972** P. Moore *Can You Speak Venusian?* xvi. 167 He is fluent in Venusian, Plutonian and Krügerian. **1977** *N.Y. Rev. Bks.* 12 May 36/4 There are several stories which insist on the..general nastiness of human beings, who thus take on the..role which used to be assigned to Martians and Venusians and the like in Fifties science fiction.

2. *Astrol.* A person born under the sign of Venus and thus supposedly subject to the influence of the planet. *rare.*

a **1963** L. MacNeice *Astrol.* (1964) ii. 55 But the sensuality of the *Kalendar* Venusians is not of the violent 'dark god' type.

B. *adj.* **1.** Of, pertaining to, or characteristic of the planet Venus or its supposed inhabitants.

1874 A. Blair *Ann. 29th Cent.* III. iii. 58 At the first glimpse I received of Venusian waters, my admiration was taken by storm. *Ibid.*, I now commenced the acquisition of the Venusian language. **1934** *Jrnl. Brit. Interplanetary Soc.* II. 4 It cannot be over-emphasised that Venusian life cannot be other *than* Venusian. **1956** C. Simak *Time & Again* ix. 42 Earth news..was followed by Martian news, by Venusian news, by the column from the asteroids. **1968** *Times* 12 Oct. 18/6 Further reason for doubting the radius of Venus..has emerged from a computer simulation of the Venusian atmosphere. **1982** *Austin* (Texas) *Amer.-Statesman* 28 Feb. A-17/1 The first [space probe]..is expected to drop through thick Venusian clouds.

2. *Astrol.* Designating or pertaining to the movement or influence of the planet Venus. *rare.*

1913 'Sepharial' *Kabala of Numbers* II. xii. 189 Suppose..that a child is born when the influence of Venus is predominant, and the local mode of etheric vibration is what may be termed Venusian. **1924** C. E. O. Carter *Conc. Encycl. Psychol. Astrol.* 30 Attractiveness is an essentially Venusian quality. *Ibid.* 81 In the horoscopes of poets and painters we see the faculty of artistic imagination denoted by the mixture of Lunar, Mercurial, and Venusian action.

Vepsian (ve·psiăn). Also **Veps, Vepsic, Vesp, Wepsian,** etc. [f. Russ. *Vépsi* + -an, -ian.] **a.** (A member of) a Finnish people dwelling in the region of Lake Onega, now in the north-west of the U.S.S.R. **b.** The Finno-Ugric language spoken by this people. Also *attrib.* or as *adj.*

1859 R. G. Latham *Descr. Ethnol.* I. xix. 409 *Tshud..* is a word which the Slavonians of Novgorod applied to the Non-slavonic populations with which they came in contact. We shall see its import more clearly after a notice of the Vod, and the Vesp. **1863** —— *Nationalities of Europe* I. xvi. 162 Of the Vesp dialect, *eo nomine*, I have seen no specimens. **1877** A. H. Keane tr. *Hovelacque's Sci. of Lang.* iv. 91 With the Suomi are grouped..the *Chudic* [language], situated in a very scattered district south of Lake Onega; the *Wepsic*, which is northern Chudic, [etc.]. **1878** *Encycl. Brit.* VIII. 700/1 Finnic or Ugrian represented by..Finnish proper..Karelian..Tchudic..Vepsic. **1879** *Ibid.* IX. 219 The Chudic, a Slav term..now restricted to the Veps or northern Chud and the Votic or southern Chud, dwelling..round the shores of Lake Onega. **1921** [see *Ludian]. **1933** L. Bloomfield *Language* iv. 68 The other languages of the Baltic branch [of the Finnish-Lapponic languages], Carelian, Olonetsian, Ludian, Vepsian, Livonian, Ingrian, and Votian, are far smaller, and some of them are near extinction. **1933** *Amer. Anthropologist* XXXV. 309 The Leningrad section studied the Finnish tribes, the Vesps, the Izhors, and some purely Russian peoples. **1955**, etc. [see *Ludian]. **1964** *Language* XL. 98 The Veps, Votic, and Estonian cognates. **1977** *Ibid.* LIII. 477 Since the boundaries of the European continent make up the geographical framework of H's analysis, he includes such little-known languages as Votyak, Cheremis, and Vepsian (Uralic), and Bashkir, Karaim, and Kalmyk (Altaic).

‖ **vera causa** (vē·ră kɑu·ză). *Philos.* [L., lit. 'real cause'.] A true cause which brings about an effect as a minimum independent agency.

[**1687** I. Newton *Philosophiae Naturalis Princ. Math.* III. 402 Causas rerum naturalium non plures admitti debere, quam quæ & vera [*sic*] sint & earum Phænomenis explicandis sufficiunt.] **1831** J. F. W. Herschel *Prelim. Discourse* II. vi. 144 To such causes Newton has applied the term *veræ causæ*; that is, causes recognized as having a real existence in nature, and not being mere hypotheses or figments of the mind. **1865** Mill *Exam. Hamilton's Philos.* xxiv. 469 By *verae causae* Newton meant agencies the existence of which was otherwise authenticated. **1890** W. James *Princ. Psychol.* I. ii. 67 Inhibition is a *vera causa*, of that there can be no doubt. **1927** B. Russell *Analysis of Matter* ii. 19 In Newton, 'force' plays a great part, and there seems no doubt that he regarded it as a *vera causa*. **1942** R. G. Collingwood *New Leviathan* xxxiii. 279 Stupidity, I reply, is not a *vera causa*. If he thought that, I want to know why; and to say 'because he was stupid' is not an answer. **1977** *Brit. Jrnl. Hist. Sci.* X. 238 Darwin's commitment to the *vera causa*—or 'true cause'—principle.

‖ **vera copula** (vē·ră kǫ·piŭlă). *Law.* [L., lit. 'true union'.] Sexual intercourse; coitus requiring erection and penetration but not necessarily the power of conception.

1845 J. E. P. ROBERTSON *Rep. Cases Argued & Determined in Ecclesiastical Courts at Doctors' Commons* I. I. 299 If there be a reasonable probability that the lady can be made capable of a *vera copula*—of the natural sort of coitus, though without power of conception, I cannot pronounce this marriage void. **1945** *Times Law Rep.* LXI. 526/2 It is well established that there must be what Dr. Lushington referred to as *vera copula.* **1961** *Times* 30 June 5/4 The question was whether the fact that the wife would have an artificial vagina would prevent sexual intercourse achieved by such means from constituting, in law, *vera copula.* **1971** *Rayden on Divorce* (ed. 11) I. vi. 156 Sexual intercourse or consummation is sometimes referred to as *vera copula.*

veranda, verandah. Add: **1. c.** (Later N.Z. examples, esp. one built over the pavement outside business premises.)

1940 F. SARGESON *Man & Wife* (1944) 45 The house is a very old house. Once it was a grocer's shop..but.. the old man couldn't get another shopkeeper to take it. So he had the verandah roof pulled down, and the front altered. **1959** M. SHADBOLT *New Zealanders* 80 An untidy collection of bicycles and boys in the shade of a shop verandah.

2. *veranda-chair.*

1902 *Chambers's Jrnl.* 14 June 437/2 Miss Tresscott.. sought to show her disapproval..by turning her veranda-chair with its back to the gay scene. **1973** *Advocate-News* (Barbados) 17 Feb. 12/6 (Advt.), Household furniture... It includes:—Verandah chairs.

verapamil (vĕræ·pămil). *Pharm.* [f. V(AL)ER(ONITR)IL(E with inserted *-apam-* (of unkn. origin).] A drug, $C_{27}H_{38}N_2O_4$, that is given orally and intravenously (usu. as the hydrochloride) in the treatment of angina pectoris and cardiac arrhythmias.

1967 *Lancet* 5 Aug. 310/2 The effect of verapamil..on tachycardia was studied in 6 healthy male volunteers. **1983** R. BALCON in *Oxf. Textbk. Med.* II. XIII. 171/1 Nifedipine and verapamil are the two calcium antagonistic agents..widely used in the treatment of angina pectoris.

veratr-. Add: **vera·tridine** [*-IDINE], an alkaloid ester, $C_{36}H_{51}NO_{11}$, present in veratrum and sabadilla and having anti-hypertensive properties, but now used chiefly for experimental purposes.

1907 *Brit. Pharmaceut. Codex* 242 Cevadine is accompanied in cevadilla seeds by the alkaloids veratridine.. and sabatrine. **1935** *Jrnl. Chem. Soc.* 123 On hydrolysis, veratridine gave veratric acid and..cevine. **1954** O. KRAYER in V. A. Drill *Pharmacol. in Med.* XXXIII. 8/2 The monoester veratridine is of no clinical use because it has an inadequate therapeutic range and its duration of action is too short. **1976** *Nature* 25 Mar. 337/2 The effects of veratridine, an alkaloid well known for its ability to increase Na^+ permeability in nerve cells, were examined. **1976** [see *SABADINE].

verb. Add: **1. b.** *verb-complement, -form, -phrase, -stem* (earlier example), *-tense*; *verb-centered, -like* adjs.; also in combinations (freq. *attrib.*) with the sense 'verb and —', as *verb-adverb, object.*

1887 SOUTHWORTH & GODDARD *Our Lang.* II. iv. 35 A verb-phrase is a group of words used as a single word. **1888** B. H. KENNEDY *Rev. Lat. Primer* 94 Verbs..in which the Verb-Stem was formed by a so-called Thematic vowel added to the root. **1912** A. D. SHEFFIELD *Gram. & Thinking* vi. 92 These classes we can then subdivide, thus... Auxiliaries, forming 'verb phrases' (*is white, may go*) [etc.]. **1924** H. E. PALMER *Gram. Spoken Eng.* 121 The Anomalous Finites are the only verb-forms which may be shifted to front-position. **1933** *Amer. Speech* VIII. IV. 7/1 The verb-adverb combination *make up* was capable of expressing at least fourteen different meanings. **1935** Verb-like [see *noun-like* adj. s.v. *NOUN 1 c]. **1935** T. HUDSON-WILLIAMS *Short Introd. Stud. Compar. Gram.* 6 The personal endings of a verb-tense or the case-endings of a noun serve all practical purposes. **1957** *Publ. Amer. Dial. Soc.* XXVIII. 132 If the IW appears with no accompanying verb-complement..the contrast..is suspended. **1962** C. L. BARBER in F. Behre *Contrib. Eng. Syntax* 21, I shall use traditional terminology..in the discussion of verb-tenses and of subordinate clauses. **1963** F. T. VISSER *Hist. Syntax* iv. 356 The verb-object relation..is always easily recognisable when the complement is in an unequivocal genitive case. **1964** R. H. ROBINS *Gen. Linguistics* 331 Abaza, a Caucasian language, has been cited as an extreme case of a verb-centred language. **1965** N. CHOMSKY *Aspects of Theory of Syntax* ii. 64 The grammatical relation Verb-Object holds of the pair (*frighten, the boy*). *Ibid.* 105 'Unspecified—subject is working at this job quite seriously', where 'at this job' is a Verb-Complement. **1965** *English Studies* XLVI. 76 The statements about the correlations between verb-forms and contextual factors. **1966** *Ibid.* XLVII. 56 The problem of the verb-adverb combination (e.g. he *takes off* his hat). **1974** *Amer. Speech 1970* XLV. 266 Not only does he place himself in the mainstream of..the verb-centred approach.., but he also clearly anticipates the drift towards..the verb-centered generative semantics of..Chafe. **1977** *Dædalus* Fall 118 It might have a rule that rewrites sentence as Noun Phrase followed by Verb Phrase. **1978** *Language* LIV. 118 When we consider the range of verb-like elements, the explanation in terms of proximity becomes more interesting.

verbal, *a.* and *sb.* **A.** *adj.* **1. b.** For † *Obs.* read *rare* and add later example. Also, ready to use words; articulate.

1976 *National Observer* (U.S.) 12 June 15/2 It's made a difference... She's more confident and verbal.

2. e. *verbal diarrhœa* (*colloq.*), a tendency to talk too much; extreme verbosity. Cf. DIARRHŒA 2.

1823 *London Mag.* Sept. 281/1 All our modern tragedists indulge in..the talking-principle... A verbal diarrhoea is the epidemic disease which afflicts the whole tribe. **1938** N. MARSH *Death in White Tie* xiii. 146 Her chief complaint is..acute verbal diarrhoea. **1981** N. J. CRISP *Festival* vi. 142 This fathead suffers from verbal diarrhoea.

f. *verbal conditioning* (Psychol.), the reinforcing of certain verbal responses with the object of establishing the use of particular words or ways of speaking.

1954 *Jrnl. Exper. Psychol.* XLVIII. 355 (*title*) Influence of awareness of reinforcement on verbal conditioning. **1967** M. ARGYLE *Psychol. Interpersonal Behaviour* vii. 131 People may embark on all kinds of self-improvement,.. including the modification of styles of interaction as in operant verbal conditioning. **1971** *Jrnl. Gen. Psychol.* Apr. 267 Verb impression value..was an important variable influencing response tendencies in verbal-conditioning and sentence-making tasks. **1979** J. P. HOUSTON et al. *Invitation to Psychol.* v. 177 Verbal conditioning is another example of reward training in which a particular response is rewarded if it occurs.

7. Forming compound adjs. with the sense 'verbal and —', as *verbal-acoustic, -metrical, -visual*, etc.

1901 E. B. TITCHENER *Exper. Psychol.* I. xii. 393 The verbal-motor type stands, in the author's experience, next in order of frequency to the visual. **1911** S. S. COLVIN *Learning Processes* vii. 107 If I recall the name as written or printed on a page, I have a verbal-visual image; if I recall the name as spoken by some one, I have a verbal-acoustic image; if I recall the name in terms of the movements of my throat in speaking, I have a verbal-motor image. **1948** L. SPITZER *Linguistics & Lit. Hist.* 201 The verbal-metrical scheme of the strophe. **1972** R. E. ORNSTEIN *Psychol. of Consciousness* ii. 39 The scientist, the writer, the mathematician are examples of the culturally 'dominant' verbal-rational mode. *Ibid.* x. 225 Modern Science is primarily verbal-logical.

B. *sb.* **3.** *Gram.* A word or group of words performing the function of a verb.

1935 [see *PARTICLE *sb.* 3]. **1965** *Amer. Speech* XL. 206 Adverbials which serve purely as modifiers of sentences and verbals. **1978** *Language* LIV. 88 Some support for the status of the items listed as verbals is that they are considered predicates in generative-semantic treatments of syntax.

4. *colloq.* A verbal statement, *spec.* a damaging admission, alleged to have been made by a suspected criminal and offered in evidence against him at a trial. Freq. *pl.*

1963 *Times* 22 Feb. 6/5 Who will believe you after I said I wasn't going to make a verbal? **1974** 'M. UNDERWOOD' *Pinch of Snuff* xxi. 171 'Have a look through the police evidence.'..'At least, they haven't put in any verbals.' **1980** *Daily Mirror* 24 June 19 Opponents of 'verbals' (alleged admissions of arrested persons to police which are not signed but are admitted in evidence) could see the meeting as a chance to further their campaign.

5. *slang.* Insult or abuse. Esp. in phr. *to give* (someone) *the verbal* and var.

1973 *Time Out* 2–8 Mar. 13/2 We faced them, and gave them a load of verbal across the street. **1977** *Times Educ. Suppl.* 21 Oct. 43/2 Insulting and humiliating rivals—'giving them the verbal'. **1982** *Observer* 10 Oct. 40/7 Each 'ball' consisted of a distinctly lethargic head-high bouncer.., followed by a rousing collection of verbals (money will be paid to lip-reading viewers for translation).

verbal, *v. colloq.* [f. *VERBAL *sb.* 4.] *trans.* To attribute a damaging statement to (an accused or suspected person). Also const. *up.*

1963 *Times* 22 Feb. 6/5 Those chaps were about and they won't be able to verbal me. **1970** P. LAURIE *Scotland Yard* vi. 146 The aggravation of it. He verbals up my villain and then says he'll let him off. **1973** *Courier-Mail* (Brisbane) 17 Oct. 10/4 Finch has claimed that detectives 'verballed' him—fabricated a confession to arrest him. **1981** C. ROSS *Scaffold* 145 'He's made no statement yet either.' 'But you verballed him?'..The police officer said nothing.

Hence **ve·rballing** *vbl. sb.*

1973 *Observer* 11 Nov. 15/2 'Verballing'—putting damaging remarks or 'verbals' into suspects' mouths—has existed as long as detectives have been dealing with criminals. **1977** 'C. AIRD' *Parting Breath* iv. 47 It wasn't, the policeman consoled himself, really and truly verballing. Verballing was putting words into a man's mouth—and statement.

verbalistic (vɜ̄ɹbăli·stik), *a.* [f. VERBALIST + -IC.] Of, pertaining to, or characterized by verbalism.

1934 *Mind* XLIII. 409 (*title*) Verbalistic tendencies. **1953** H. H. PRICE *Thinking & Exper.* viii. 237 It is no sillier than the purely Verbalistic theory which is at present fashionable. **1975** *Amer. Speech 1969* XLIV. 128 We live in a highly verbalistic culture.

Hence **verbali·stically** *adv.*

1934 *Mind* XLIII. 411 To do full justice to a speaker's intended meaning..instead of verbalistically insisting that he 'must' mean exactly what he *says.* **1940** *Theology* XL. 426 Pose the question thus verbalistically, and at once one suggests the method of lexicographical analysis.

verbality. Add: **1.** (Later example.)

1877 W. R. ALGER *Life Edwin Forrest* II. xxii. 767 He was no starveling fed on verbality and ceremony, no pigmy imitator or empty conformist.

2. (Later examples.)

1899 W. JAMES *Talks to Teachers* 257 We are stuffed with abstract conceptions, and glib with verbalities and verbosities. **1935** B. MALINOWSKI *Coral Gardens & their Magic* II. VI. vi. 246 The fact that the community are aware of the spell and know its wording is the most important clue to the appreciation of the verbalities of magic.

verbalizable (vɜ̄·ɹbăləi·zăb'l), *a.* [f. VERBALIZ(E *v.* + -ABLE.] Capable of being expressed in words; able to be verbalized. Hence **ve:rbalizabi·lity.**

1951 C. KLUCKHOHN et al. in Parsons & Shils *Toward Gen. Theory of Action* IV. ii. 397 'Verbalizable' is not to be equated with 'clearly and habitually verbalized'. The actor's values are often..incompletely..verbalized by him. But implicit values remain 'conceptions'..which can be put into words by the observer... Verbalizability is a necessary test of value. **1981** *N.Y. Times Mag.* 24 May 10/4 The path was cleared for the substitution of the verbalizable 'or' by the unspeakable '/' in the legalistic term 'and/or'.

verbalization. Add: **2.** A verbal expression or statement.

1951 C. KLUCKHOHN et al. in Parsons & Shils *Toward Gen. Theory of Action* IV. ii. 398 Implicit values will be manifested only in behavior and through verbalizations that do not directly state the pertinent values. **1965** *Times Lit. Suppl.* 16 Sept. 812/1 Many of these potential multiple nouns will founder because..a more efficient verbalization is to hand. **1976** *Howard Jrnl.* XV. I. 17 The practitioner 'sees through' the client's verbalizations to a reality that lies behind them.

verbalizer (vɜ̄·ɹbăləizəɹ). [f. VERBALIZE *v.* + -ER[1].] One who registers stimuli or thoughts mentally in verbal terms rather than through the senses (cf. VISUALIZER); one who verbalizes.

1937 *Brit. Jrnl. Psychol.* Jan. 278 The meaning of many a word may be more clear-cut to a visualizer, because accompanied by a visual image, than to a verbalizer. **1952** *Ibid.* May 122 It would..be expected that the better verbalizers would be the better learners. **1975** C. L. BURT *ESP & Psychol.* 7 A verbalizer who (like myself) may be almost devoid of visual or other kinaesthetic imagery, tends rather to think in terms of abstractions and for him material and mechanical structures lose much of their theoretical importance. **1980** *Times Lit. Suppl,* 15 Feb. 173/2 In Ireland what a man said was deemed more important than what he did. The tradition of verbalizer is old and deep..and sprang from the imperative to keep the old cultural matrix alive.

verbicide[2]. Add: Hence **ve·rbicidal** *a.*, tending or liable to destroy the sense or value of a word.

1978 *Forum on Med.* Apr. 85/1 Other verbicidal entertainers who were school dropouts have also received 'honorary' degrees. **1985** *Times* 27 Mar. 12/8 The verbicidal impulses of Pentagonese.

verbid (vɜ̄·ɹbid). [f. VERB + -ID[1].] *Gram.* A word, as an infinitive, gerund or participle, which has some verbal characteristics but lacks the power of forming sentences. Also *attrib.* and in *Comb.*

1914 O. JESPERSEN *Mod. Eng. Gram.* II. 7 We shall.. restrict the name of verb to those forms that have the eminently verbal power of forming sentences, and..apply the name of verbid to participles and infinitives. **1940** BRYANT & AIKEN *Psychol. of Eng.* 23 Such a unit [*sc.* John having called the dog] is called a verbid clause, because *having called* is not a full verb. **1966** R. L. ALLEN *Verb System Present-Day Amer. Eng.* 136 Of the 4800 verb and verbid-clusters included in the corpus, 1191.. are clusters with some form of BE as the verb.

verbigeration. (In Dict. s.v. VERBIGERATE *v.*) (Earlier example.)

1886 *Jrnl. Nerv. Dis.* XIII. 699 Some emotion, at variance with his 'verbigeration'.

verbo-. (Examples of *verbomania.*)

1923 OGDEN & RICHARDS *Meaning of Meaning* ii. 89 A veritable orgy of verbomania. **1977** J. GARVIN in D. Ó Muirithe *Eng. Lang. in Ireland* 112 *Finnegans Wake* abounds in Anglo-Irish idiom..but it is subsumed into.. 'slanguage' which leaves the book adrift in a polyglottic sea of verbomania.

‖ **verboten** (feɹbō·tĕn), *a.* [Ger.] Forbidden; not allowed.

1912 R. BROOKE *Old Vicarage, Grantchester* (1916) 8 Meads towards Haslingfield and Coton Where *das Betreten*'s not *verboten.* **1916** J. BUCHAN *Greenmantle* v. 63, I got very bored, for I had nothing to read and my pipe was *verboten.* **1949** E. BENN *Happier Days* xviii. 217 The unfortunate German, bred and trained from childhood to understand that everything is *verboten* unless specifically permitted. **1968** FINCH & CAIN in J. Marmor *Mod. Psychoanal.* xvii. 446 The obviously important but almost verboten subject of the implicit structure of rewards. **1979** R. MUTCH *Gemstone* viii. 94 She was *verboten,* strictly off limits.

‖ **verbum sap.** Add: Also **verb sap.**

1841 E. BRONTË in *Brontës: Lives, Friendships & Corr.* (1932) I. x. 238, I have just made a new regularity paper!

and I mean *verb sap* to do great things. **1889** E. DOWSON *Let.* 9 Nov. (1967) 115 Mark that horse & when he runs next plump on him with all your available capital. Verb Sap. This tip I may add doesn't come from Museum Mansions but from a man who spotted Primrose Day for the C'wtch. **1976** J. I. M. STEWART *Young Pattullo* ii. 40 Mind your Ps and Qs, if I were you. *Verb. sap.*—eh?

verd. Restrict † *Obs.* to senses in Dict. and add: **1. b.** *poet.* The colour green. *rare.*
1915 G. C. M. BIRDWOOD *Sva* 59 The whole paradisaical scene shining in the setting sun with the transcendent resplendence of its various verds and shimmering gold. **1929** S. LESLIE *Anglo-Catholic* ix. 110 The pavement was tesselated purple and verd. Great tapestries hung between pillars.

‖ **verdelho** (vɛ̄ɹde·lyu). [Pg.] A prolific vine yielding a white grape orig. grown in Madeira and now found in Portugal, Sicily, Australia, and South Africa; also, a medium white Madeira wine made from this grape.
1824 A. HENDERSON *Hist. Anc. & Mod. Wines* viii. 249 Among the various species of grapes cultivated, those called *verdelho, negra*..and *sercial*, yield the best wines. **1883** *Encycl. Brit.* XV. 178/1 The wine usually termed Madeira..is made from a mixture of black and white grapes, which are also made separately into wines called Tinto and Verdelho. **1926** P. M. SHAND *Bk. Wine* iii. 41 Two thirds of the vines grown on the island are of the celebrated Verdelho species. **1935** A. L. SIMON *Dict. Wine* 249 *Verdelho*, one of the white fortified wines of Madeira, which used to be made with the Verdelho grape, now all but extinct. **1959** W. JAMES *Word-bk. Wine* 195 *Verdelho*, a white grape which gives its name to a sweet dessert type of madeira, though the vine is not grown on the island to any great extent. **1980** *Times* 27 Nov. 20/4 The two drier styles of wine, Sercial and Verdelho.

Verdian (vē·ɹdiăn), *a.* and *sb.* [f. the name of Giuseppe *Verdi* (1813–1901), Italian composer + -AN.] **A.** *adj.* Of, pertaining to, or characteristic of Verdi or his music. **B.** *sb.* An admirer of Verdi; a (skilled) exponent of his music.
1947 A. EINSTEIN *Mus. Romantic Era* xvi. 284 One should not think that *Otello*..became..a drama with music. It remained Italian opera, Verdian opera, which preserves almost completely its connection with the composer's earlier work. **1962** *Listener* 21 June 1091/2 An opera in a broad Verdian style brought up to date. **1976** *Gramophone* Aug. 334/1 Bergonzi is much the more stylistically correct Verdian. **1977** *Times* 20 Dec. 10/5 The Verdians cannot get out of it by saying that Beethoven was the greater genius. Of course he was. **1978** *Times* 10 Oct. 9/4 A noted Verdian and a remarkable Violetta.. Miss Sass was perhaps ill-advised to begin her first London recital with Schumann. **1980** *Daily Tel.* 4 June 15/2 [Its] moral and imaginative qualities..have always endeared it to dedicated Verdians. *Ibid.* 15/4 His direction growing in authentically Verdian conviction.

‖ **Verdicchio** (vɛɹdi·kio). [It.] A white grape grown in the Marche region of Italy; also, the dry white wine made from this grape.
1940 H. J. GROSSMAN *Guide to Wines* vi. 80 Not many great wines are grown in this region, but two demand attention: a fine white, light wine—the Verdicchio di Jesi [etc.]. **1954** E. DAVID *Italian Food* 310 The white wines of the Castelli di Iesi, in the Marche, produced from Verdicchio grapes, and called usually by that name, are pleasant and refreshing to drink on the spot. **1967** F. SCHOONMAKER *Encycl. Wine* 305 *Verdicchio*, superior Italian white wine grape; also its wine. **1978** 'A. STUART' *Vicious Circles* 109, I ordered an ice-cold bottle of Verdicchio.

verdict, *sb.* Add: **1. c.** *open verdict*, a verdict of a coroner's jury affirming the commission of a crime (but not specifying the criminal), or the occurrence of a suspicious but unexplained death.
1769 [in Dict.]. **1864** DICKENS *Mut. Fr.* (1865) I. I. iii. 18 Inquest to-morrow, and no doubt open verdict. **1977** 'M. INNES' *Honeybath's Haven* xiii. 123 His jury..will bring in what is called an open verdict.

verdictive (vɜ̄·ɹdiktiv). *rare.* [f. VERDICT *sb.* + -IVE.] An utterance which consists in the delivering of a verdict. Also *attrib.* or as *adj.*
1955 J. L. AUSTIN *How to do Things with Words* (1962) xii. 150, I call these classes of utterance..by the following more-or-less rebarbative names:..Verdictives..Exercitives [etc.]. *Ibid.* 152 A verdictive is a judicial as distinct from legislative or executive acts... Verdictives have obvious connexions with truth and falsity. *Ibid.* 160 We may dispute as to whether these [expositives] are not verdictive, exercitive, behabitive, or commissive acts as well. **1975** *Language* LI. 106 Examples of performatives assuming the agent-authority are verdictives..such as *acquit, convict, find* etc. (mostly judicial).

verdin (vɜ̄·ɹdin). Also **Verdin.** [a. F. *verdin* yellow-hammer.] A small grey tit with a yellow head, *Auriparus flaviceps*, found in south-western North America.
1881 *Amer. Naturalist* XV. 217 Another minute species of the titmouse family, the verdin or yellow-headed titmouse. **1903** *Atlantic Monthly* July 103 The same fretful verdin was talking about something with the old emphatic monotony. **1939** G. B. PICKWELL *Deserts* 139/2 This is the voice of the Verdin, a true bird of the desert. **1974** L. GOMBRICH tr. *von Frisch's Animal Archit.* (1975) 211 The verdin barricades its nest with thorns.

verdite[2] (vɜ̄·ɹdəit). [f. *verd-* (as in VERDURE) + -ITE[1].] A green ornamental rock from South Africa.
1908 *Mineral Industry* XVI. 810 During 1907 there was found on the south bank of the North Kaap river, in South Africa,..another..stone that has the deep green color of..chromiferous syenite... It has a hardness of about three, and is susceptible of a high polish; the color is a rich chrome green and the stone contains a chrome-muscovite and some argillaceous material... The stone is obtained in blocks weighing one ton or more... The name verdite has been suggested for it. **1916** *Chambers's Jrnl.* Apr. 272/2 Articles of jewellery and ornaments are made of verdite. **1935** *Archit. Rev.* LXXVIII. 104/1 In the Midland Headquarters in the City, it is said that each of the Verdite pilasters..cost a Thousand pounds, and there are a considerable number of them. **1979** HURLBUT & SWITZER *Gemology* xiii. 143/1 Verdite is a green rock consisting of fuchsite (a chrome mica), and clayey mica.

‖ **verdomde** (fəɹdǫ·mdə), *a.* *S. Afr. slang.* Also **verdoemde, verdomd.** [Afrikaans, ad. Du. *verdoemd.*] Damned, infernal.
1850 R. G. CUMMING *Five Years Hunter's Life S. Afr.* ix. 53/1, I overheard him remark to three other gruff-looking Boers who stood beside him that I was 'a verdomd Englishman'. **1878** T. J. LUCAS *Camp Life & Sport S. Afr.* 232 Ah, you verdomde beast! **1909** R. DEHAN *Dop Doctor* 90 He was no Baas of mine the verdoemde rooinek! **1913** D. FAIRBRIDGE *That which hath Been* 125 This verdoemde Governor is obstinate on this point. **1926** E. LEWIS *Mantis* I. iv. 80 Why, even with Government helping you not to make a goat of yourself farming's a *verdomde* lottery, believe me. **1964** A. TREW *Smoke Island* vi. 106 Pride wouldn't allow him to claim that achievement for his people now, and this *verdomde* native knew it.

verdure. I. 3. Delete † *Obs.* and add later *Hist.* examples.
1934 *Burlington Mag.* Feb. 65/2 The work of the oldest tapestry factory in England... A 'verdure', a type very popular with Worcestershire weavers. **1977** *Anc. Tapestries from Belgium* (Nat. Arts Centre, Ottawa) 77 Oudenarde was famous for its 'verdures' (tapestries representing trees or foliage).

Verel (vīᵊ·rĕl). orig. *U.S.* The proprietary name of a synthetic acrylic fibre.
1956 *Official Gaz.* (U.S. Patent Office) 2 Oct. TM3 *Verel*, for synthetic staple fiber. **1956** *Trade Marks Jrnl.* 24 Oct. 1050/2 Verel B755,848. Raw or partly prepared synthetic textile fibres. Eastman Kodak Company..343, State Street, Rochester, State of New York, United States.. Manufacturers. **1956** *America's Textile Reporter* 22 Mar. 13/2 Processing and ironing temperatures should be held to a maximum 300 degrees Fahrenheit when 100 per cent 'Verel' fabrics are being handled. **1959** A. J. HALL *Stand. Handbk. Textiles* (ed. 5) i. 73 Verel fibres are more hydrophile than usual for synthetic fibres. **1963** —— *Textile Sci.* ii. 87 This [acrylic] group includes all those fibres made from polymers consisting wholly or partly of acrylonitrile, and important members are..Courtelle, Verel, Zefran, etc. **1978** P. G. TORTORA *Understanding Textiles* ix. 134 For many years only two modacrylic fibers were made commercially: Dynel..and Verel.

‖ **Verfremdungseffekt** (feɹfre·mduŋs,efe·kt). [Ger.: see *ALIENATION 1 d.] = *alienation effect* s.v. *ALIENATION 1 d. Similarly **Verfremdung**, distancing, alienation (occas. in sense of *ALIENATION 1 c).
1945 *Kenyon Rev.* VII. 470 The distancing ('Verfremdung') which Brecht desires is complemented by his concreteness which makes any escape from the reality demonstrated upon the stage impossible. **1951** *World Rev.* Jan. 67/2 Brecht generally sticks closely and with success to his technique of alienation (*Verfremdungseffekt*, he calls it). **1959** *New Statesman* 28 Mar. 442/2 His famous principle of *Verfremdung*, for example: of the distancing of the actor from his part, of breaking that theatrical illusion which mesmerises the audience into a witless passivity. **1960** J. BAYLEY *Characters of Love* iii. 145 We are to feel nothing but alienation, a Brechtian *Verfremdungseffekt*. **1980** *Times Lit. Suppl.* 17 Oct. 1172/5 Rylance Waters.. provides a brilliant *Verfremdungseffekt*. **1981** F. INGLIS *Promise of Happiness* iii. 86 If, with Marx, we are to speak of *Verfremdung*, estrangement or alienation, as the most destructive and wounding experience of labour under capitalism.

verge, *sb.*[1] **I. 1. a.** Delete † *Obs.*[−1] and add later example.
1887 [see *FELLATIO].
7. c. *verge watch* (later examples).
1963 *Times* 6 Feb. 12/4 An anonymous purchaser gave 290gns. for a seventeenth-century verge watch by John Drake. **1977** *Cleethorpes News* 6 May 22/4 (Advt.), Clocks, silver watches, verge watches.
IV. 16. b. Also, an unpaved strip of land, usu. planted with grass, separating a pedestrian pavement from a road; a (grass-covered) edging to a road. Cf. *grass verge* s.v. *GRASS *sb.*[1] 13.
1953 H. E. BATES *Nature of Love* 16 She had just time to pull the pram into the verge before Parker went past her and the Ford, bouncing, hit the snake fence thirty yards beyond. **1955** *Times* 9 July 7/5 If there were three lanes the slow traffic would be far more inclined to keep within their lane nearer the verge and allow faster vehicles to pass. **1972** *Human World* Nov. 29 The other passengers ..crowded towards the windows. The excitement was caused by a small tribe of gypsies encamped on the verge. **1979** J. GRIMOND *Memoirs* vii. 108 Before the stupid and expensive cutting of the verges the roadsides were thick with clover and cow-parsley.

verge, *v.*[3] [Back-formation f. VERGER[2] 1.] *intr.* To act as a verger; to be a verger. Hence **ve·rging** *vbl. sb.*
1900 W. How *Lighter Moments* 54 He werges up one side of the church and I werges up the other. **1926** *Punch* 13 Oct. 400/2, I verges up the centre aisle; he verges up the sides. **1927** H. V. MORTON *In Search of England* i. 14 The profession of verging appears to induce mousey manners. **1976** *Church Times* 29 Oct. 18/4 (Advt.), A Christian couple required by St. Paul's Church, Slough. Lady to do cleaning, gent for verging at weekends.

verge-board. (Earlier example.)
1827 T. F. HUNT *Designs for Parsonage Houses* 5 Ornamental barge-boards... [*Note*] By some called *verge*-boards.

vergée (vē·rʒe). [Anglo-Norman, f. F. *terre vergée* measured land.] In the Channel Islands, a superficial measure of land, varying between Jersey and Guernsey (see quot. 1971).
In quot. 1915, in Flanders.
1834 H. D. INGLIS *Channel Islands* I. ix. 180 Rent in the neighbourhood of St. Helier is as high as from £3 to £4 per vergée... Two vergées and one quarter, make an English acre. **1858** F. F. DALLY *Channel Islands* v. iv. 235 The Guernsey vergée is forty perches, and two vergées and a half are rather more than the English acre. **1915** *Contemp. Rev.* July 107, 400 *vergées* (about one acre and a half), were kept under cultivation. **1971** *Nat. Geogr. Mag.* May 722/2, I do 50 *vergées* of potatoes a year... The vergée, an old Norman measure, is still the legal land unit of the Channel Islands. On Jersey, two-and-a-quarter vergées make one English acre, but Guernsey disagrees, and counts two-and-a-half to the acre. **1977** *Jersey Even. Post* 26 July 11/2 The IDC would like to transfer 1½ vergées of land at the corner of Rouge Bouillon and Roussel Street.

vergence (vɜ̄·ɹdʒĕns). [f. VERGE *v.*[2] + -ENCE.] **1.** *Ophthalm.* The simultaneous movement of both eyes towards or away from one another, as when they focus on a point that is nearer or farther away.
1902 E. C. ELLETT in *Jrnl. Amer. Med. Assoc.* 18 Oct. 969/2, I would suggest as a temporary table at least, a sort of composite arrangement, as follows: Movements of the visual axis... Associated disjunctive movements (vergences)..convergence.. supervergence. **1940** F. B. CHAVASSE in Ridley & Sorsby *Mod. Trends Ophthalmol.* xxvi. 280 By growth, extension, and refinement of this reflex is developed the proper vergence (notably convergence) of the eyes upon (say) the prey. **1979** *Sci. Amer.* Jan. 88/1 Abrupt target jumps generate two types of eye movements: slow, smooth vergence eye movements..and sharp, rapid saccadic eye movements.
2. *Geol.* [ad. G. *vergenz* (H. Stille 1930, in *Nachrichten von d. Ges. d. Wissensch. zu Göttingen, Math.-Physik. Klasse* III. 380).] The direction in which a fold is inclined or overturned.
1960 *Trans. Edin. Geol. Soc.* XVIII. 51 Isoclinal recumbent folds with an average trend ENE-WSW; vergence SSE to NNW. [*Note*] The authors use the term 'vergence'..to indicate the direction of overturning of folds. **1978** *Nature* 7 Dec. 604/1 At the northern apex of the Tyrrhenian Sea, two mountain chains face each other displaying opposite vergence: the Corsican alpine chain and the Northern Apennines.

verglas (vē·ɪglā). Also (formerly) **ver-glas, ver glas.** [Fr., f. *verre* VERRE + *glas* (mod.F. *glace*) ice: see GLACE *sb.*[1]] = *silver thaw* s.v. SILVER *sb.* and *a.* 21.
1808 H. GRAY *Lett. from Canada* (1809) 301 During the thaw, a very extraordinary effect is produced, sometimes, on the trees. The Canadians call it a *ver-glas*. **1863** E. H. WALSHE *Cedar Creek* 310 Perhaps you could tell me the cause of the *ver glas*? What makes that thin incrustation of ice over the trunk and every twig? **1886** G. MEREDITH *Let.* 26 Dec. (1970) II. 844, I dread the many possible things from verglas to bronchitis. **1925** N. E. ODELL in E. F. Norton *Fight for Everest: 1924* III. iii. 310 A considerable snowfall will in spring and summer have evaporated into thin air in a few hours without any visible melting. Consequently, and fortunately, 'verglas' does not exist. **1950** tr. *Mountaineering Handbk.* (Assoc. Brit. Members Swiss Alpine Club) vi. 69 Verglas, which is the result of a frozen trickle of water or rainwater, and which covers the rocks like a sheet of glass, is no less dangerous. **1972** D. HASTON *In High Places* i. 12 Verglas can also be very difficult. This is a thin veneer that forms on rock, caused by the thawing and re-freezing of running water or drips.

veridian (vĭri·diăn), var. VIRIDIAN *sb.* and *a.*
1902 R. FRY *Let.* 13 Oct. (1972) I. 197 The trees [are] strawy green, the glass almost veridian. **1950** M. PEAKE *Gormenghast* lxiii. 355 The waters became stained with evergreen from the softest olive to veridian. **1974** R. RENDELL *Face of Trespass* viii. 70 A new name..in veridian neon, stuck up above the portico.

veridically, *adv.* (Earlier example.)
1832 F. BURNEY *Mem. Dr. Burney* II. 179 Next to Shakespeare himself, Pope draws human characters the most veridically, perhaps, of any poetic delineator.

veridi·city. [f. VERI(DICAL *a.* + -ICITY.] Veridicality.

1937 *Theology* XXXIV. 284 The veridicity of psychic phenomena. **1942** *Mind* LI. 67 The Pragmatist holds that what works is true. If the arguments of this paper were wrong, that would probably be about the best status one could find for the veridicity of memory. **1977** *N.Y. Rev. Bks.* 29 Sept. 21/3 There are various reasons, particular and general, why this example of tampering with what Mr. Stewart likes to call 'veridicity' is important.

verifiability. Add: **a.** (Earlier example.)

a **1881** A. BARRATT *Physical Metempiric* (1883) p. xxv, I cannot believe that the test of sensible verifiability will ever satisfy the higher longings..of humanity.

b. *Philos.* The fact of being capable of verification (sense *3 c). Freq. *attrib.*

1936 A. J. AYER *Lang., Truth & Logic* i. 31 Every empirical hypothesis must be relevant to some actual, or possible, experience, so that a statement which is not relevant to any experience is not an empirical hypothesis, and accordingly has no factual content. But this is precisely what the principle of verifiability asserts. **1936** M. SCHLICK *Gesammelte Aufsätze* (1938) xiv. 348 When we speak of verifiability we mean logical possibility of verification. **1939** I. BERLIN in *Proc. Aristotelian Soc.* XXXIX. 225 The thesis which I shall try to establish is that the principle of verifiability or verification after playing a decisive rôle in the history of modern philosophy ..leads to wholly untenable consequences. **1951** H. REICHENBACH in Feigl & Brodbeck *Readings Philos. of Sci.* (1953) 93 The verifiability theory of meaning lays down rules for the construction of meaningful expressions. **1967** *Encycl. Philos.* VIII. 241/1 We shall understand the verifiability principle as claiming that the cognitive meaning..of a sentence is to be determined by reference to the verifiability..of the statement expressed by the sentence.

verification. Add: **3. c.** *Philos.* The action or process of verifying a proposition or sentence through empirical experience (associated esp. with logical positivism). Freq. *attrib.*, esp. as *verification principle.*

1932 M. SCHLICK *Gesammelte Aufsätze* (1938) viii. 181 The meaning of a proposition is the method of its verification. **1934** C. I. LEWIS in *Philos. Rev.* XLIII. 131 Suppose it maintained that no issue is meaningful unless it can be put to the test of decisive verification. **1936** A. J. AYER *Lang., Truth & Logic* 12, I adopt what may be called a modified verification principle. **1937** *Mind* XLVI. 348, I should have thought the first duty of any advocate of a verification theory of meaning would be to inquire how his theory itself was to be verified. **1956** J. O. URMSON *Philos. Anal.* vii. 107 The verification principle is not essentially a very novel or obscure doctrine except in its traditional formulation. This formulation is that the meaning of a statement is the method of its verification. **1963** W. H. WALSH *Metaphysics* i. 15 Logical Positivists.. sought to fashion, in their celebrated Verification Principle of Meaning, a weapon which would destroy metaphysics once and for all. **1977** A. GIDDENS *Stud. in Social & Polit. Theory* i. 45 What came to be called the 'Verification Principle' went through numerous versions, as the inadequacy of Schlick's original formulation..became very rapidly apparent.

d. *spec.* (see quot. 1972).

1953 *Ann. Reg. 1952* 145 This plan provides for the discussion of the regulation of all armaments..and of their disclosure and verification by two committees. **1962** *Listener* 1 Nov. 720/1 Mr Khruschev says he agrees to order dismantling of missile sites in Cuba under U.N. verification. **1972** *Dict. Milit. Terms* (U.S. Dept. Defense) 316/1 *Verification*.., in arms control, any action, including inspection, detection, and identification, taken to ascertain compliance with agreed measures.

4. (Earlier example.)

1789 A. YOUNG *Jrnl.* 8 June in *Trav. France* (1792) I. 103 If..by the verification of their powers in one chamber, they shall once come together, the popular party hope that there will remain, no power afterwards to separate.

verifica·tionism. [f. VERIFICATION + -ISM.] The philosophical doctrine or principles associated with verification (sense *3 c).

1939 I. BERLIN in *Proc. Aristotelian Soc.* XXXIX. 226 It will tend to show that historical connexion between phenomenalism and 'verificationism' is not a logical one, and that the failure of the latter does not necessarily invalidate the former. **1943** *Mind* LII. 98 Full-blooded verificationism..has now commonly been abandoned in favour of what might be called methodological verificationism. **1965** [see *OPERATIONALISM].

verifica·tionist, *a.* and *sb.* [f. VERIFICATION + -IST.] **A.** *adj.* Of, pertaining to, or supporting verificationism. **B.** *sb.* An adherent or supporter of verificationism.

1940 *Mind* XLIX. 456 He [*sc.* Eddington] is as empirically 'verificationist' as any Logical Positivist. **1941** *Mind* L. 163 Most verificationists contend that realism is meaningless. **1952** R. M. HARE *Lang. Morals* i. 8 The so-called 'verificationist' theory of meaning. **1956** J. O. URMSON *Philos. Anal.* xi. 169 If..the verificationist takes the line that the verification principle is a rule of language for the use of the word 'meaningful'..it is a hard saying. **1980** *Times Lit. Suppl.* 17 Oct. 1181/5 How far such verificationist arguments are sound..depends on questions of meaning.

verifier. Add: **1. b.** That which verifies.

1845 J. S. MILL in *Edin. Rev.* LXXXII. 384 In the philosophy of society,..we look upon history as an indispensable test and verifier of all doctrines and creeds. **1944** *Mind* LIII. 341 If I say 'you are hot', this sentence expresses my belief.., and if you are hot, it indicates your state... Your hotness can be called the 'verifier' of my sentence. **1959** B. RUSSELL *My Philos. Devel.* xv. 185, I call the fact which makes the statement true its 'verifier'.

2. b. A keyboard device for checking whether a card or paper tape is correctly punched by indicating any discrepancy when it is inserted and the data on it keyed a second time.

1940 W. J. ECKERT *Punched Card Methods* 9 The mechanical verifier is used to check the punching of the initial data on the cards. **1949** [see *INTERPRETER 5 a]. **1956** G. A. MONTGOMERIE *Digital Calculating Machines* viii. 154 More complicated electrically driven verifiers are available and in some makes they resemble the electrically driven punches. **1978** J. KELLOCK *Elements of Accounting* xii. 214 After the information has been punched on to the cards, the cards are verified on a machine known as a verifier.

verifying, *vbl. sb.* Add: (Later examples.) Cf. prec. 2 b.

1932 *Monthly Notices R. Astron. Soc.* XCII. 700 In commercial practice punching is usually verified by a special verifying punch. **1954, 1965** [see *keypunching* vbl. sb. sv. *KEYPUNCH *v.*]. **1968** *Brit. Med. Bull.* XXIV. 207/1 Four-fifths of the costs of linking a record by computer arise in preparation of the data—i.e., abstraction, classification and coding, card or tape punching and verifying. **1973** F. R. CRAWFORD *Business Systems with Punched Card Data Processing* v. 89 Proper design of documents and card forms is essential for accurate, efficient card punching and verifying.

verisimilous, *a.* For † *Obs.* read 'Now *rare*' and add later example.

1958 *New Scientist* 23 Oct. 1119/2 Narratives which, although verisimilous to a degree, are shot through and through with the credulous and superstitious outlook of the seventeenth century.

‖ **verismo** (veri·zmo). [It.] Realism or naturalism in the arts; esp. with reference to Italian opera of the late 19th century. Freq. *attrib.* Cf. VERISM.

1908 R. DUNSTAN *Cyclopædic Dict. Music* 435/1 *Verismo*, truth, naturalism. **1919** G. KOBBÉ *Compl. Opera Bk.* 91 What is true of 'Aida', is equally applicable to the whole School of Italian *versimo* [sic] that came after Verdi—Mascagni, Leoncavallo, Puccini. **1940** *Scrutiny* IX. 51 If the opera is too realistic it may be boring... The *verismo* of the latterday Wagnerians cannot escape this charge. **1954** *N.Y. Times* 28 Dec. (Late City Ed.) 21/1 Gian-Carlo Menotti's 'The Saint of Bleecker Street'..is Italian 'verismo' opera. **1970** R. LOWELL *Notebk.* 224 *Verismo* is no *vehicle* for Death. **1976** *Times* 23 Jan. 14/8 The movement towards *verismo* in film and theatre. **1978** LD. DROGHEDA *Double Harness* xxi. 289 Unfortunately Colin Anderson himself took against what he dismissed somewhat derisorily as Franco's *verismo* method. **1983** *Observer* 29 May 33/2 Kiri Te Kanawa, happily back on Mozartian territory after her unhappy excursion into *verismo.*

veritableness. Delete *rare*$^{-1}$ and add later examples.

1890 W. JAMES *Princ. Psychol.* I. vii. 189 But the psychologist must not only *have* his mental states in their absolute veritableness, he must report them and write about them. **1926** R. CLEMENTS *Stately Southerner* 142 Whatsoever shape the apparition may have taken, a belief in its veritableness has persisted from of old.

‖ **vérité** (verite). [Fr., = truth.] Realism or naturalism, esp. in cinema, radio, and television; documentary method. Also *attrib.* and in *Comb.* Cf. *CINÉMA-VÉRITÉ; VERISM.

1966 *Listener* 15 Dec. 880/2 There is an advanced cinema, a cinema of *vérité* which is rightly admired by intellectuals. **1976** *Ibid.* 23 & 30 Dec. 841/1 Jack Gold's early vérité-style account of an industrial dispute. **1978** *Broadcast's Programme Edin. TV Festival* 10/2 The film was heavily criticised..[as] impressionistic, partial..an indication of the problematic nature of verite's claim to be..untainted evidence. *Ibid.*, Verite film brings to the screen the pathetic death of a drowned boy. **1979** *Daily Tel.* 7 Dec. 17/3 The method of 'radio vérité' reporting, with victims telling their own emotional stories and the guilty parties often getting quite annoyed, make [*sic*] compulsive listening. **1984** *Listener* 1 Mar. 32/1 What is over-the-top in a vérité film may be just what is required in sit-com.

verkramp (fɛ̞ɹkra·mp), *predic. a.* *S. Afr.* Also **verkrampte** when used *attrib.* [Afrikaans, lit. 'narrow, cramped'.] Narrow or reactionary in political, religious, social, etc., matters.

1968 *Green Bay Tree* 29 June p. xlv, The most *verkrampte* Nationalist politicians are frightened of liberal foreign propaganda appearing on their screens. **1969** *Sunday Times* (Johannesburg) 24 Aug., On a very strict, narrow interpretation, my guess is that most Nationalists are verkramp. **1971** *Ibid.* 11 Apr. 3 Mr. — is verkramp. He can make what threats he likes, I'll keep on wearing split skirts. **1973** *Deb. Senate S. Afr.* 17 May 2790 A Sunday paper fairly recently referred to certain members of the United Party as a 'verkrampte mafia'. This was not defamatory. **1974** *Argus* (Cape Town) 2 Aug. 3/2 It is believed that conservative resistance to more enlightened policies has been significantly reduced and that verkrampte views will in future meet with little sympathy. **1974** *Rand Daily Mail* 30 Nov. 1/1 This reasoning has now become an excellent excuse for talking verlig and acting verkramp. **1977** *Time* 31 Oct. 19/3 The Cabinet was clearly aware of charges by the *verkrampte* (conservative) wing of the Nationalist Party that the government's power and authority were eroding in the face of protests by urban blacks. **1981** *Observer* 5 Apr. 11/7 Like most black African Muslims, Edvis favours a liberal interpretation of the Koran, being *verligte* rather than *verkrampte* in that regard. Very wisely he likes to drink Pinot Noir from California.

Hence (the *attrib.* form **verkrampte**) as *sb.* A person with rigidly traditional views, esp. as regards apartheid and the preservation of white supremacy. Cf. *VERLIG *a.*

At first applied only to politicians but now extended to any person holding narrow-minded or ultra-conservative views on social, religious, etc., matters.

1967 *Race Relations News* Sept. 7/4 The verligtes–verkramptes controversy must have raised in many minds the hope of a change of outlook in influential South African circles. **1968** *Economist* 17 Aug. 32/2 The real object was to strengthen Mr Vorster in the ideological dispute that has arisen within his party in recent months between the *verligte* ('enlightened') wing and the *verkramptes* (that is, literally, the cramped ones). **1969** *Times* 18 Sept. 9/1 The Army and its political directors have come in for much criticism..from Unionist *verkramptes*, for apparent irresolution in bringing down the barricades. **1971** *Leader* (Durban) 7 May 6/5 With a so-called outward-looking policy, the Government is beginning to see things in better light. It has shaken itself of some of the old die-hard Calvinistic verkramptes and is able to look at the world at large a little verlig. **1979** *Economist* 8 Sept. 59/3 Now Transvaal *verkramptes* (Conservatives) are saying he exploited Muldergate to destroy their leaders.

Verlainesque (vɛ̞ɹlēⁱne·sk), *a.* [f. the name *Verlaine* (see below) + -ESQUE.] Of, pertaining to, or characteristic of the French poet Paul Verlaine (1844–96), or his works.

1891 E. DOWSON *Let.* 20 Mar. (1967) 189 Its an attempt at mere sound verse..a vague, Verlainesque emotion. **1915** WYNDHAM LEWIS *Lett.* (1963) 68 He told me he had written a lot of filthy sexual verse... He described it as Verlainesque, damn his shifty little eyes.

verlig (fɛ̞ɹli·χ), *predic. a.* *S. Afr.* Also **verligte** when used *attrib.* [Afrikaans, = enlightened.] Regarded as progressive or enlightened, in political, religious, social, etc., matters. Cf. *VERKRAMP *a.*

1968 [see *VERKRAMPTE *sb.*]. **1969** *Sunday Times* (Johannesburg) 24 Aug. 25 The odd thing about the whole affair is that the word 'verlig' should become an embarrassment to the Nationalists... There must be few countries where it is an insult to be called 'enlightened'. **1969** *Rand Daily Mail* 25 Sept. 17/3 Verlig long before it was comparatively easy to be so, he condemned arrogant racialism or nationalism wherever he found it. **1970** *Times* 19 Aug. 8/4 It is not just non-aligned countries such as Tanzania, Zambia or Yugoslavia, which are benefiting from the new spirit of goodwill emanating from Peking. China's *verligte* policies have even percolated as far as London. **1971** [see *VERKRAMPTE *sb.*]. **1974** *Argus* (Cape Town) 2 Aug. 3/2 The United Party is believed to have irrevocably committed itself to a more boldly verligte political stance. **1974** [see *VERKRAMP *a.*] **1977** *Cape Times* 10 Oct. 3/4 The vast majority of Nationalist voters are a lot more verlig than they think and support the need for change in South Africa. **1981** *Guardian* 14 Dec. 6/5 The Verligte or enlightened faction of his party.

Hence (the *attrib.* form **verligte**) as *sb.* A person regarded as progressive or enlightened in politics, esp. with regard to the future of apartheid. In extended use, one who is enlightened or broadminded in other matters.

1967 [see *VERKRAMPTE *sb.*]. **1969** *Guardian Weekly* 24 July 14 If the *verkramptes* of Louis Stoffberg and Dr Herzog win the day, against Mr Vorster's *verligtes* and their good neighbour policy towards black Africa, it will be a useful gain for Peking. **1970** *News/Check* 29 May 9 People who later on were to become known as verligtes sided with Silbersteins; the verkramptes summed up the book as sinful. **1976** *Times* 26 June 5/4 The increasingly vocal Verligtes in the universities. **1980** *Economist* 21 June (S. Afr. Suppl.) 6/1 To the more radical verligtes who make up his praetorian guard, a sort of strategy is clear.

vermiculite. Add: **1. c.** Flakes of this mineral used as a moisture-holding medium for plant growth or as a protective covering for the storage of bulbs or tubers.

1950 *Los Angeles Times Home Mag.* 12 Feb. 38/3 Vermiculite is one of the finest storage materials for bulbs, tubers and corms as it insulates them from sudden temperature changes. **1981** *Farmstead Mag.* Winter 71/1 All that is necessary for this March project is a few waterproof trays, fiber or wooden slats, vermiculite for seed germination, and soilless mix such as 'Promix' for filling the flats. **1983** *Which?* Sept. 398/3 Wash off as much soil as possible, then stand the tubers, stem-down, in a dry, frost-free place..before..storing in boxes of dry peat or vermiculite.

vermigrade (vɜ̄·ɹmigrēⁱd), *a.* *rare*$^{-1}$. [f. VERMI- + *-GRADE.] Proceeding in a worm-like manner. (In context *fig.*)

1938 S. BECKETT *Murphy* viii. 134 Celia was in a state indeed, trembling and ashen. The footsteps overhead had become part and parcel of her afternoon, with the rocking-chair and the vermigrade wane of light. An Ægean nightfall suddenly in Brewery Road could not have upset her more than this failure of the steps.

vermilionize, *v.* For *rare*⁻¹ read *rare* and add later *fig.* example.

1924 W. J. Locke *Coming of Amos* iv. 43 If I had found myself at five-and-twenty with fifty thousand pounds lying at the bank, verily, I believe, I should have vermilionized the cosmos.

vermin, *sb.* (and *a.*). Add: **5. b.** *vermin-proof* adj. **c.** *vermin-eaten, -like* (later example) adjs.

1837 Dickens *Let.* 7 Sept. (1965) I. 304 If the *Pickwick* has been the means of putting a few shillings in the vermin-eaten pockets of so miserable a creature, [etc.]. **1931** R. Campbell *Georgiad* i. 16 So many poets..sigh to share their [*sc.* gypsies'] vermin-eaten ways. **1914** Joyce *Dubliners* 86 A horde of grimy children populated the street... He picked his way deftly through all that minute vermin-like life. **1937** *Discovery* Dec. 388/1 Vermin-, rot- and fire-proof. **1982** M. Young *Elmhirsts of Dartington* iv. 81 A vermin-proof rice store.

verminous, *a.* Add: **4. c.** *verminous bronchitis* = *hoose, hooze *sb.*

1925 [see *parasitic *a.* 5]. **1970** W. H. Parker *Health & Dis. in Farm Animals* xx. 268 This is the first sign of the disease known as Husk, or Verminous Bronchitis.

verminicide (vəɹmi·nisəid). [f. Vermin *sb.* + -cide[1].] A preparation for killing vermin.

1925 *Blackw. Mag.* Sept. 313/2 During the summer verminicide became a necessary item in the 'bazar'. **1965** N. H. Johnson *Compl. Bk. Dogs* (1968) xii. 387 Detergents and verminicides, as well as sleeping and reducing pills, are equally dangerous.

Vermont (vəɹmǫ·nt). The name of one of the north-eastern states of the United States of America, used *attrib.* in *Vermont merino*, a sheep belonging to a breed developed there.

1891 R. Wallace *Rural Econ. Austral. & N.Z.* xxvii. 359 The Vermont Merino..is one of the most perfect as regards good covering and density of fleece. **1957** *New Biol.* XXII. 92 Vermont merinos were imported into Australia from the United States in the 1880s. These sheep had wrinkly skins, and many that crossed the Pacific by 1890 presented a concertina-like appearance.

† **Vermonteer.** *Obs.* [f. prec. + -eer.] = next.

1778 *15th Rep. R. Comm. Hist. MSS.* App. 396 in *Parl. Papers 1897* (C. 8551) LI.1 We may hence learn that we are not to flatter ourselves with the hope of winning over the Vermonteers to the Crown side. **1801** *Hist. Rev. & Directory N. Amer.* II. 346 Great numbers of the Vermonteers bring their produce here.

Vermonter (vəɹmǫ·ntəɹ). [f. as prec. + -er[1].] A native or inhabitant of the State of Vermont.

1787 A. Hamilton *Works* (1886) VII. 6 The peace found the Vermonters in a state of actual independence. **1851** H. Melville *Moby Dick* I. vi. 51 There weekly arrive in this town [*sc.* New Bedford] scores of green Vermonters. **1961** W. Vaughan-Thomas *Anzio* v. 67 Its tough, stocky commander, General Ernie Harmon, was a Vermonter. **1979** *United States 1980/81* (Penguin Travel Guides) 662 For Vermonters maple sugaring time is a celebration of spring. **1984** *Sci. Amer.* May 22/3 [So] wrote Vermonter Zerah Colburn in 1833.

Vermontese (vəɹmǫntī·z), *sb.* and *a.* Also † **Vermonteze.** [f. as prec. + -ese.] **A.** *sb.* = prec. Also *collect.* **B.** *adj.* Of or belonging to Vermont.

1783 *Polite Traveller* 100 The persons, manners, and customs, of the Vermontese, are nearly the same with those provinces from whom they emigrated. **1798** I. Allen *Nat. & Pol. Hist. Vermont* 280 Our Vermontese house-wives are not a little vain of their knowledge in making home-made wines. **1804** T. G. Fessenden *Orig. Poems* 123 Hamilton was an impudent Vermonteze. **1845** *Knickerbocker* XXVI. 583 We should be pleased to hear these lines applauded by the Vermontese. **1851** *San Francisco Picayune* 20 Sept. 2/4 On a late visit to an ancient Vermontese lady, he was asked, 'Did you see Professor Webster hung?'

Vermoral (vɜ̄·ɹmorăl). Also **-el.** [Said to be the name of V. *Vermorel*, French manufacturer.] A type of sprayer used in the war of 1914–18 to produce a fine spray of water that would absorb residual poison gas.

1916 'H. Rae' *Maple Leaves* 264 'A vermoral sprayer is a new form of frightfulness for spraying the front-line trench.' 'What with? Liquid fire?'..'No, liquid water.' 'For the flies?' 'No, for the gas.' **1929** R. Graves *Good-Bye to all That* xv. 204 Vermorel-sprayers had cleared out most of the gas, but we still had to wear our masks. **1930** Blunden *De Bello Germanico* iii. 30 A 'Vermoral Sprayer' for nullifying gas.

vermouth. Add: **c.** *vermouth-cassis*: see *cassis.

vernaccia (vəɹna·tʃa). [It.: see Vernage.] A wine (usu. white) produced in the San Gimignano area of Italy and in Sardinia; also, the grape from which it is made.

1824 A. Henderson *Hist. Anc. & Mod. Wines* ii. vi. 237 Another source of error arises from the circumstance of several of the best Tuscan wines receiving their appellations from the grapes which yield them, as, for example,.. the *Vernaccia*, &c; and as these names are not confined to Tuscany, but are common to the growths of other parts of Italy, the difficulty of distinguishing them is..further increased. **1833** C. Redding *Hist. Mod. Wines* ix. 241 Their sweet wines the Italians call *Abbocati*... Of the former kind are the Moscatello, Aleatico, and Vernaccia, a white wine, of considerable note among the writers of Italy. **1929** P. M. Shand *Bk. of Other Wines* 85 The vines grown are—*red*: Chiavennasca.., Vernaccia, [etc.]. **1966** C. Ray *Wines of Italy* ix. 95 Vernaccia di Serrapetrona, sweetish sparkling red wine made from the Vernaccia Rossa grape, and interesting to those who are interested in sparkling sweet red wines. **1973** *Times* 31 Jan. (Mediterranean Suppl.) p. ii/4 Pecorino sheep cheese and vernaccia wine have enjoyed steady, if limited, markets outside the island. **1975** *Times* 14 Apr. (Ital. Wines Suppl.) p. iii/4 A..dry golden vernaccia, from..San Gimignano (not to be confused with that potent vernaccia in Sardinia).. is dry enough to accompany fish.

vernacular, *a.* and *sb.* Add: **A.** *adj.* **6.** *spec.* in *vernacular architecture*, architecture concerned with ordinary domestic and functional buildings rather than the essentially monumental.

1857 G. G. Scott *Remarks Secular & Domestic Archit.* p. ix, I want to call attention to the meanness of our vernacular architecture, and to the very partial success which has hitherto attended the attempts at its improvement. **1939** *Country Life* 11 Feb. 154/2 It is as delightful an example as one could find of Georgian vernacular architecture. **1976** [see *spinning *vbl. sb.* 7 c]. **1977** *Dædalus* Summer 3 The studies of so-called vernacular architecture (like barns) no longer seem eccentric in an atmosphere in which architecture can be defined not in terms of monuments but as any changes at all that man makes in his environment.

B. *sb.* **1. a.** Also, the informal, colloquial, or distinctive speech of a people or a group. Cf. sense 1 b below.

1925 F. N. Scott in *McNaught's Monthly Mag.* May 144 (*heading*) English and American vernacular. **1930** G. B. Shaw *Admirable Bashville* 89 With the advent of compulsory education sixty years ago,..newspapers and plays alike soon came to be written by illiterate masters of the vernacular. **1984** *Gainesville* (Florida) *Sun* 28 Mar. 7B/2 Observe feminist vernacular: Call it a 'personhole cover'.

b. (Later example with reference to colloquial speech.) Cf. sense 1 a above.

1975 L. Gillen *Return to Deepwater* iv. 62 In the vernacular,..I couldn't care less what you do.

4. A vernacular style of building. Cf. sense A. 6 above.

1910 *Encycl. Brit.* II. 436/1 The culture of the 'Queen Anne' type of architecture..presented a simple vernacular of construction and detail. **1967** *Listener* 7 Sept. 292/3 What was normally North American about these houses..was their general internal planning..an open-plan vernacular that still works well today. **1977** M. Girouard *Sweetness & Light* ii. 25 They came back to London to design buildings in which Gothic merged into farmhouse vernacular.

verna·cularist. [f. Vernacular *a.* and *sb.* + -ist.] **1.** An advocate of the use of a regional mode of speech; a speaker or writer in a regional or demotic idiom.

1867 [see *Anglicist 1]. **1926** *Glasgow Herald* 27 July 10 There was ample material..in the industrial struggle with which Clydeside was so familiar, which in the hands of a Vernacularist of genius could produce a play so striking as 'Strife'. **1974** *Sat. Rev. World* (U.S.) 4 Dec. 46/2 Creosote bush, which the Spaniards called *hedonillo* but the American vernacularists termed 'little stinker'.

2. *R.C.Ch.* An advocate of the use of the vernacular in the liturgy. Also *attrib.* or as *adj.*

1956 *Catholic Herald* 9 Mar. 2/4 Was St. Thomas a Vernacularist? **1982** *Observer* 25 Apr. 30/3 Mr St John-Stevas's Latin is not good.., but that is a venial sin in these vernacularist days.

vernacularity. 1. (Later examples.)

1904 'O. Henry' in *N.Y. World Mag.* 25 Dec. 2/6 Remsen touched his cap..and took refuge in vernacularity. **1943** Entwistle & Gillet *Lit. of Eng.* iv. 41 He [*sc.* John Lyly] cultivated..unexpected vernacularity amid refined 'conceits'.

vernalization (vɜ̄:ɹnăləizēi·ʃən). [f. Vernal *a.* + -ization, as tr. Russ. *yarovizátsiya.*] The technique of exposing seeds, young plants, etc., to low temperatures in order to hasten subsequent flowering; also, the natural process induced by cold weather which this technique imitates. Also *transf.* and *fig.*

1933, 1934 [see *jarovization]. **1957** V. Nabokov *Pnin* ii. 47 The vernalization of the visas, and the preparations [for going to America]. **1971** E. O. Wilson *Insect Societies* viii. 154/1 The vernalization (chilling) effect that renders *Myrmica* and *Formica* brood queen-potent can be interpreted as a token stimulus. **1974** A. J. Huxley *Plant & Planet* x. 100 In beet..the rosette normally made in the first year..requires winter chilling for flowering the following summer. This winter chilling is called vernalization. *Ibid.* xxvii. 315 Vernalization consists..in giving the seed to be sown in spring a cold period..with a small amount of water.

Hence (by back-formation) **ve·rnalize** *v. trans.*, to treat or affect (seeds, etc.) in this way; **ve·rnalized** *ppl. a.* (in quots. *transf.*), **ve·rnalizing** *vbl. sb.*

1933 Whyte & Hudson in *Bull. Imperial Bureau Plant Genetics* No. 9. 8 (*heading*) Technique for vernalizing long-day plants. **1946** *Nature* 5 Oct. 485/2 The time taken for development to have begun in all the vernalized [sponge] gemmules..is less than in December. **1947** *Ibid.* 4 Jan. 32/1 This [*sc.* premature flowering] may be due.. to a vernalizing effect on the..germinated seed..of naturally experienced low soil..temperatures in early spring. **1971** E. O. Wilson *Insect Societies* viii. 150/1 It is from some of these vernalized larvae that the yearly crop of queens is matured in the spring. **1976** *Sci. Amer.* Sept. 99/3 The crop flowers and produces grain in the spring after being vernalized, or induced to flower, by the low temperatures in winter.

vernation. 2. (Later example of extended use.)

1929 S. Leslie *Anglo-Catholic* x. 121 In the vernation of the year Edward felt the old desire for the earth, a renewed longing to labour and drive the plough.

Verné (vę·rne). Also **Verneh.** [Origin unknown.] **a.** A Caucasian pileless rug or kilim. **b.** An Anatolian brocaded rug. In full *Verné kilim, rug*, etc.

1922 Kendrick & Tattersall *Hand-Woven Carpets* I. iv. 165 Thin and soft Kilims made in the neighbourhood of Shusha are known in the trade by the name of *Verné*. *Ibid.* II. Pl. 143 (*caption*) Verné Kilim carpet. **1931** A. U. Dilley *Oriental Rugs & Carpets* Pl. 53 (*caption*) Verné animal and bird khilim. **1973** *Country Life* 29 Nov. 1823 Verné rug 7′1″ × 5′6″..Armenia circa 1900. **1975** *Times* 13 June 3/1 An unusual feature of the sale was the presence of two antique Verneh rugs. **1981** I. Bennett *Oriental Rugs* I. 364/2 There are several varieties of so-called bird verneh rugs.

Vernean (vɜ̄·ɹniăn), *a.* Also **Vernian.** [f. the name of Jules *Verne* (1828–1905), French author: see -an, -ian.] Of, pertaining to, or characteristic of the science fiction of Jules Verne. Also **Jules Vernean.**

1960 K. Amis *New Maps of Hell* (1961) i. 37 The book closes with a straightforward Vernean sermon on the dangers of scientific progress considered as an embodiment of human arrogance. **1964** *Listener* 12 Nov. 743/2 The conquest of space no longer strikes us as Wellsian or Jules Vernian. **1980** *Time* 1 Dec. 60/2 Visionaries like Jules Verne were suggesting a better way. A bullet-shaped vehicle..could be propelled far faster by using powerful electromagnetic fields. Now, as a result of lab work in the U.S. and abroad, the Vernean scheme shows promise of becoming a practical reality.

Verner's law: see Law *sb.*[1] 17 c.

Verneuil (vęrnö·y). The name of A. V. L. *Verneuil* (1856–1913), French chemist, used *attrib.* with reference to a technique invented by him for producing artificial rubies.

1912 *Chem. Abstr.* VI. 55 A description of the Verneuil method of preparing artificial rubies. **1951** Kirk & Othmer *Encycl. Chem. Technol.* VII. 163 A typical Verneuil crystal-growth apparatus is shown schematically in Figure 2. **1979** Mills & Mansfield *Genuine Article* vii. 116 The little bubble which you often see in a Verneuil synthetic.

vernier. Add: **3.** *Astronautics.* Used *attrib.* and *absol.* to designate a small auxiliary rocket engine for effecting minor changes in the velocity or attitude of a spacecraft.

1958 *Observer* 12 Oct. 1/2 Eight small 'vernier', or guidance rockets,..had been fitted to Pioneer. Any or all of these could be fired from the earth to make any necessary correction in the final phase of the flight. **1960** *Aeroplane* XCVIII. 562/1 In its nose would be a third stage employing low-thrust 'vernier' rocket motors. **1968** A. C. Clarke *2001* xxxv. 184 The main thrust died and only the verniers continued to nudge *Discovery* gently into orbit. **1968** *Sci. Jrnl.* Nov. 76/2 The rocket..had no fewer than 20 main thrust chambers and 12 swivelling verniers—small motors for fine control of speed and direction. **1979** J. W. Cornelisse *Rocket Propulsion & Spaceflight Dynamics* x. 212 A third method to ensure ignition after coasting is the use of small (Vernier) rockets, which give the vehicle a sufficiently large acceleration to position the propellant at the sump.

vernis martin (vęrni· mārtæ·ṅ). Also **vernis Martin, Vernis Martin,** and hyphenated. [Fr., f. *vernis* varnish + *Martin* (see below).] A lacquer or varnish used in the eighteenth century by the French brothers Étienne, Guillaume, Julien, and Robert Martin and their contemporaries on a range of furniture, ornaments, etc., to imitate oriental lacquer. Also *fig.*

1877 C. Schreiber *Jrnl.* (1911) II. 18 Some curious boards for the game of Loto [*sic*], done in Vernis Martin. **1883** J. W. Mollett *Illustr. Dict. Art & Archæol.* 337/1 *Vernis-Martin work*, a Japanese style of painting and enamelling on furniture, carriages, and small objects. **1899** R. Whiteing *No. 5 John St.* xvi. 163 That polish of the world which is not exactly vernis-Martin for transparency. **1911** Louisa of Tuscany *My Own Story* vi. 87 It was a magnificent historical vehicle painted in vernis Martin. **1942** *Burlington Mag.* Apr. 104/2 A fine collection of small boxes—vernis martin, ivory, etc.,..will be sold in May. **1963** *Times Lit. Suppl.* 15 Mar. 192/4 A fine example of a 'Vernis Martin' binding of *c.* 1800. **1978** *Country Life* 8 June (Suppl.) 97/3 French vernis martin snuff-box, c. 1780.

‖ **vernissage** (vɛrnisāʒ). Also **Vernissage.** [Fr.] A day before the exhibition of paintings on which exhibitors may retouch and varnish their pictures already hung. Now usu. denoting a private view of paintings before public exhibition. Cf. *VARNISHING *vbl. sb.* 1 b.

1912 *Queen* 20 Apr. 643/2 The Salon Nationale des Beaux Arts. The vernissage was on Saturday, and was marked by the usual miscellaneous crowd of French people and foreigners. **1920** R. FRY *Let.* 28 Sept. (1972) II. 491 My landscape is accepted all right at the Autumn Salon... I went to..give it some *vernis à retoucher* at the *Vernissage.* **1930** *Observer* 26 Jan. 10 The Indépendants have once more occupied the Grand Palais... The crowd at the vernissage did not seem to be moving so fast. **1958** *Spectator* 11 July 56/2 Artists were excluded from the *vernissage* of the twenty-ninth *Biennale* at Venice. **1961** *Times* 18 Mar. 3/7 At the height of the season art critics in Paris receive an average of 20 vernissage invitations each week. **1967** *Times* 3 May 9/7, I found myself completely at sea at the 'vernissage' of an exhibition of paintings..at one of London's..art galleries. **1979** M. SOAMES *Clementine Churchill* ii. 23 Mlle Henri had procured tickets for a *Vernissage.*

vernix. Restrict ‖ and *Obs. rare* to sense in Dict. and add: **2.** *Med.* In full, *vernix caseosa* [mod.L. *caseōsus*, f. L. *caseus* cheese]. A greasy deposit covering the skin of a baby at birth.

1846 DUNGLISON *Dict. Med. Sci.* (ed. 6) 785/1 Vernix caseosa. **1882** W. T. LUSK *Sci. & Art of Midwifery* iii. 75 In the fifth month the surface of the fetal body is covered by the *vernix caseosa*, a whitish substance composed of.. surface epithelium, down, and the products of the sebacious glands. **1956** *Nature* 18 Feb. 330/1 The specimens [of amniotic fluid] were centrifuged and the vernix and supernatant fluid removed. **1978** *Jrnl. R. Soc. Med.* LXXI. 212 Copious vernix caseosa is often present. **1980** *Brit. Med. Jrnl.* 25 Oct. 1138/1 With difficulty but determination she gave birth to an enormous child coated in so much vernix that it seemed to wear a cream cheese pack.

Veronese, *sb.* Add: **1.** (Examples in *sing.*)

1673 J. RAY *Observations Journey Low-Countries* 220 The Antiquities of Verona written by Torellus Saraina a Veronese. **1967** *Guardian* 10 May 7/2 A Veronese himself, Professor Forlati came to Venice in 1912.

veronica[2]. Add: **2.** In *Bullfighting*, a movement typical of the first tercio in which the matador swings the cape in a slow circle round himself in order to persuade the charging bull to follow the movement of the cape. Also *fig.*

1926 E. HEMINGWAY *Sun also Rises* xviii. 217 The bull wanted it again, and Romero's cape filled again... He made four veronicas like that, and finished with a half veronica that turned his back on the bull. **1936** R. CAMPBELL *Mithraic Emblems* 18 Enemy of my inward night..whose arm against the Bull designs The red veronicas of light. **1957** A. MACNAB *Bulls of Iberia* vi. 57 In two-handed passes, the cape is held on either side of the collar. The fundamental pass is the *verónica*... The name *verónica* is derived from the attitude of the man holding the cape out in his two hands, which resembles that in which St. Veronica is depicted holding out the towel to Our Lord on the way to Calvary. **1976** *Listener* 29 Apr. 541/1 The oldest of old-time waltzes, the couples dancing a mile apart, the women—executing neat veronicas with the men in swallow-tails—got up like Christmas paper bells.

‖ **veronique** (verǫnik). [Fr.] **1.** *Cookery.* (Usu. in form *Véronique.*) Applied to dishes (esp. of fish or chicken) prepared or garnished with grapes.

1907 G. A. ESCOFFIER *Guide Mod. Cookery* 302 *Filets de soles Véronique.* Raise the fillets of a fine sole. **1940** A. L. SIMON *Conc. Encycl. Gastron.* II. 103/2 *Véronique*, stuffed fillets of sole, rolled and poached, garnished with one muscat grape upon each fillet and muscat grapes round the dish. **1958** B. PYM *Glass of Blessings* iii. 38 He was even now preparing them a delicious sole véronique. **1960**, etc. [see *SOLE *sb.*[2] 1 c] **1963** A. SIMON *Guide Good Food & Wines* 379 Véronique, stuffed fillets of sole, rolled and poached, garnished with one muscat grape upon each fillet and muscat grapes round the dish. **1979** *United States 1980/81* (Penguin Travel Guides) 298 The menu is imaginative,..—trout Véronique (poached and topped with green grapes and hollandaise sauce).

2. = prec.

1931 R. CAMPBELL *Georgiad* II. 32 My passes brought the colour to his cheeks, The loudest he to cheer my veroniques. **1932** —— *Taurine Provence* iii. 72 A heroic series of repeated veroniques against a bull of *grande vaillance.*

‖ **verre églomisé** (vɛ̄r' eglomize). [Fr., f. *verre* (see VERRE) + *ÉGLOMISÉ *a.* and *sb.*] Glass decorated with a layer of engraved gold (see quots. 1971, 1977).

1907 E. DILLON *Glass* viii. 140 The variety of painted glass known in later times as *verre églomisé*. **1933** *Connoisseur* XCII. 372/2 The term '*verre églomisé*'..has for long been applied to this work, in common with the art of painting under glass. **1941** *Burlington Mag.* Feb. 59/1 The cabinet illustrated..and a pair of looking-glasses, with glass borders ornamented with *verre églomisé* decoration in scarlet and gold..were brought from Spain five or six years ago. **1967** [see *ÉGLOMISÉ]. **1971** *Country Life* 15 July 150/2 He was a native of Amsterdam and worked in *verre églomisé*—that is gold and silver leaf laid under glass and engraved with a pointed tool. It is a very ancient technique going back to Roman times, but its customary name is derived from that of a well-known 18th-century picture-frame maker named Glomy who employed the method extensively. **1977** FLEMING & HONOUR *Penguin Dict. Decorative Arts* 826/2 *Verre églomisé*, glass decorated on the back by unfired painting or, usually, by gilding... The painting or gilding is protected by another sheet of glass or by a coat of varnish or a layer of metal foil.

Verrocchiesque (verǫkie·sk), *a.* [f. the name of Andrea del *Verrocchio*, a Florentine painter and sculptor (1435–88 + -ESQUE.] Suggestive of or resembling in subject or style the works of Verrocchio. Also **Verro·cchian** *a.* [-IAN].

1902 R. FRY *Let.* 23 Jan. (1972) I. 188 He went on to Verrochian and Botticellian ideas as the *Archangel and Virgin Enthroned* suggest. **1933** *Burlington Mag.* Mar. 140/1 The whole technique is closest to the most Verrocchiesque of all Leonardo's drawings. **1942** *Ibid.* Oct. 243/2 This panel has been attributed to Verrocchio; and ..we must expect to find in it pronouncedly Verrocchiesque features.

verruga. Delete ‖ and substitute for def.: The second, chronic stage of an infection by the bacterium *Bartonella bacilliformis*, characterized by wart-like skin lesions: see *OROYA FEVER. Also *verruga peruana*, *peruviana* [Sp. *peruana* Peruvian; *peruviana*, mod.L. rendering of this]. (Earlier and later examples.)

[**1825** W. B. STEVENSON *Hist. & Descr. Narr. Twenty Years' Residence in S. Amer.* I. xiv. 347 *Berrugas*, warts of a peculiar kind, are common in some of the valleys of the coast [of Peru].] **1873** T. J. HUTCHINSON *Two Years in Peru* II. xx. 58 He was getting through an attack of that dreadful disease, the verrugas, and appeared but the shadow of a man. **1949**, etc. [see *OROYA FEVER]. **1961** R. D. BAKER *Essent. Path.* ix. 190 Bartonellosis is a peculiar disease which occurs in Peru and is characterized by Oroya fever and verruga peruviana. **1968** T. WOLFE *Electric Kool-Aid Acid Test* xxi. 305 He can *feel*.. every verruga fly, velvet ant, murine fleas and crabs.

Versailles (vēᵊɹsai·). The name of a hunting lodge to the south-west of Paris built by Louis XIII and enlarged into a palace by Louis XIV in the 17th century, used to denote: **1.** *transf.* A building of similar style or splendour. Also *fig.*

1749 J. CLELAND *Mem. Woman Pleasure* I. 134 But had it been a dungeon..his presence would have made it a little Versailles. **1899** KIPLING *From Sea to Sea* I. xvii. 159 Jeypore Palace may be called the Versailles of India. **1959** M. CROSLAND tr. *J. Rovan's Germany* 140 Potsdam, the Prussian Versailles. **1968** *N.Y. City* (Michelin Tire Corp.) 47 The Hotel Pierre..a sort of '40-story Versailles'. **1977** 'R. PLAYER' *Month of Mangled Models* vii. 125 It was Jules Goncourt who had called the whole house the Versailles of Whoredom.

2. The site of the peace conference held there at the conclusion of the 1914–18 war which gave its name to the treaty signed there in 1919. Also *transf.*

1928 J. BUCHAN *Runagates Club* x. 273 The soldiers.. would have made a cleaner and fairer job of it than the kind of circus that appeared at Versailles. **1936** G. B. SHAW *Millionairess* 117 There remained the clauses of the Versailles Treaty by which Germany was to be kept in a condition of permanent, decisive, and humiliating military inferiority to the other Powers. **1967** *Sat. Rev.* (U.S.) 8 Apr. 16/3 Most German politicians..ominously refer to this treaty as another 'Versailles'. **1971** *Guardian* 5 Aug. 10/4 In 1936..the Guardian was busily condemning the Versailles terms. **1981** J. WAINWRIGHT *Urge for Justice* I. ix. 59 Versailles is being repaid...Hitler..is putting greatness back into Germany.

versal, *sb.* Restrict † *Obs. rare* to sense in Dict. and add: **2.** A special style of ornate capital letter used at the beginning of a verse or paragraph, etc., esp. in an illuminated manuscript; in modern calligraphy applied to capitals built up by inking between pen strokes and having serifs in the form of long, thin, straight lines. Freq. *attrib.* as *adj.*

1895 E. F. STRANGE *Alphabets* ix. 257 (*caption*) Versal letters. *Ibid.* 258 The versal is [a letter]..at the beginning of a chapter or section thereof. **1906** E. JOHNSTON *Writing & Illuminating* vii. 114 The earlier Versals had very simple and beautiful pen shapes... After the fourteenth century they were often..overdone with ornament. *Ibid.* xii. 205 In twelfth-century MSS. long delicate flourishes are commonly found, in red, blue, or green—matching the colours of the Versals. **1912** A. W. POLLARD *Fine Books* vi. 84 The small red letters at the beginning of each verse of a psalm, sometimes called versals. **1979** T. GOURDIE *Calligraphic Styles* 53 Versal Capitals are a pen-built form of the 'Trajan Roman' and are normally used to begin verses and chapters but may also be used to make impressive panels of lettering. **1981** D. MAHONEY *Craft of Calligraphy* 90 A versal letter is built up with a definite number of pen strokes. *Ibid.* 93 The stem width is the same in Versals of varying height.

versatile, *a.* Add: **1. c.** Both heterosexual and homosexual. *slang.*

1959 [see *BENT *ppl. a.* 5 c]. **1960** M. SPARK *Ballad Peckham Rye* iii. 32 Dougal was probably pansy. 'I don't think so... He's got a girl somewhere.' 'Might be versatile.'

‖ **vers de société** (vɛ̄r də sosiete). [Fr., lit. 'verse of society'.] Verse that treats of topics provided by polite society in a light, often witty style.

1796 I. D'ISRAELI *Miscellanies* 149 This species of poetry can only exist in an age when refinement is introduced into literature, as well as into everything else. We must, therefore, look for it..among a people the most refined among it's [*sic*] neighbours... It has been significantly called '*Vers de Societé*'. **1817** G. CRABBE *Jrnl.* 11 July in *Poet Wks.* (1834) I. 248 His poetry [is] far beyond that implied in the character of *Vers de Société.* **1867** F. LOCKER-LAMPSON *Lyra Elegantiarum* 9 Smoothly written *vers de société*, where a boudoir decorum is, or ought always to be, preserved; where sentiment never surges into passion, and where humour never overflows into boisterous merriment. **1934** T. S. ELIOT *Elizabethan Ess.* 35, I am used to..being informed that something which I meant seriously is *vers de société.* **1976** *Times* 26 Jan. 7/5 Quirky *vers de société*..by Ogden Nash.

‖ **vers d'occasion** (vɛ̄r dokazyoṅ). [Fr.] Light verse written for a special occasion (see OCCASIONAL *a.* 2 b in Dict. and Suppl.).

1867 F. LOCKER-LAMPSON *Lyra Elegantiarum* 11 *Vers de société* and *vers d'occasion* should be short, elegant, refined, and fanciful. **1933** *N. & Q.* 26 Aug. 143/1 Many of his pieces are somewhat unskilful *vers d'occasion.* **1946** R. LEHMANN *Gipsy's Baby* 71 She was a great one for *vers d'occasion.* Upon my birthday..I received..a pale pink scalloped gilt-edged card inscribed..in a frame of hand-painted roses. **1960** *20th Cent.* Sept. 276 The *vers d'occasion* includes some limericks and clerihews. **1982** B. ASKWITH *Piety & Wit* vii. 112 The bons mots, the puns, the vers d'occasion, travel badly in time.

verse, *sb.* Add: **1.** (Examples with reference to Old English poetry.)

1715 E. ELSTOB *Rudiments Gram. Eng.-Saxon Tongue* 68 The Saxon Verses consist of three, four, five, six, seven, eight, or more syllables. **1883** H. M. KENNEDY tr. *Ten Brink's Hist. Eng. Lit.* I. 22 The sentence rarely closes with the ending of the verse. **1938** A. CAMPBELL *Battle of Brunanburh* 16 Sievers showed once and for all the combinations of accentual elements, which might be used to build a verse. **1958** A. J. BLISS *Metre of Beowulf* 1 The term 'verse' is here used instead of the more cumbrous 'half-line' or 'hemistich'.

5. c. That part of a modern popular song which leads into the chorus, or separates one chorus from another. Cf. *CHORUS *sb.* 6 c.

1927 *Melody Maker* Aug. 782/2 The verse is then taken 'hot' by the trumpet, who gives a fine example of what modern 'hot' playing..should be. **1929, 1935** [see *CHORUS *sb.* 6 c]. **1966** *Melody Maker* 7 May 13/1 Wonder charges through the verse and builds up into the repetitious chorus.

8. a. *verse-beat*, *-end*, *-form*, *-line*, *-pair*, *-rhythm*, *-unit.*

1943 E. SITWELL *Poet's Notebk.* xxviii. 134 The verse-beat is *not* very strong in this passage. **1930** T. SASAKI *On Lang. R. Bridges' Poetry* I. v. 24 The fully strong stress at the verse-end. **1887** G. M. HOPKINS *Let.* 20 Oct. (1956) 381 The style of prose is a positive thing and not the absence of verse-forms. **1906** G. P. KRAPP *Andreas* p. xlvi, The distinctively epic verse-form. **1966** *English Studies* XLVII. 97 In a difficult and restrictive verse-form, one might expect the poet to resort to the use of convenient whole-line units more..often. **1927** D. H. LAWRENCE *Mornings in Mexico* 66 He had written the thing [*sc.* a love-poem] straight ahead, without verse-lines or capitals. **1953** *Speculum* XXVIII. 449 The recurrence of verses and verse-pairs in Anglo-Saxon poetry. **1930** T. SASAKI *On Lang. R. Bridges' Poetry* I. v. 21 Lines in verse.. form units of verse-rhythm intermediate between a 'foot' and a 'stanza'. **1942** J. C. POPE *Rhythm of Beowulf* 22 In no case is it necessary to pass beyond the limits of accentual adjustment that verse-rhythm everywhere allows. **1948** *Mod. Philology* XLVI. 77 When the character of the dipody, or verse unit, is examined, the first impression is one of extreme variation. **1966** *English Studies* XLVII. 96 The verse-unit, the half-line, was quite short.

b. *verse drama*, *epistle*, *epitaph*, *letter*, *play.*

1925 R. GRAVES *Welchman's Hose* 31 Then the first draft of a verse-epitaph. **1931** *Times Lit. Suppl.* 5 Nov. 850/2 It might be inferred certainly from the verse-epistles [of Burns] alone: not quite so certainly from the prose letters alone. **1952** T. S. ELIOT *Film of 'Murder in the Cathedral'* 7 *Murder in the Cathedral* is, I believe, the first contemporary verse play to be adapted to the screen. **1962** *Times* 14 Aug. 11/1 Jean Cocteau's verse-drama *Renaud et Armide.* **1963** M. H. ABRAMS in N. Frye *Romanticism Reconsidered* 37 In a verse-letter of 1800 Blane identified the crucial influences in his spiritual history as a series beginning with Milton.

c. *verse-painting*, *-reading* (later example), *-speaking* ppl. adj. and vbl. sb., *-writing* (earlier example).

1942 BLUNDEN *Romantic Poetry & Fine Arts* 19 A single touch of his originality in the 'Ancient Mariner' holds the secret of his verse-painting. **1938** L. MACNEICE *Mod. Poetry* ii. 41 This [*sc.* the *Golden Treasury*] was my chief verse-reading for two years. **1933** *Amer. Speech* VIII. IV. 39/2 Outside of the school there may be a place for verse-speaking choirs. **1980** *Times* 5 Sept. 11/7 His verse-speaking consists of a heavy lurch from beat to beat. **1755** M. BARBER in Colman & Thornton *Poems by Eminent Ladies* I. 23 There's nothing I dread, like a verse-writing wife.

verseless, *a.* (Later examples.)

c **1873** G. M. HOPKINS *Note-bks. & Papers* (1937) 221 Where verse ends and prose (or verseless composition) begins. **1975** *Gramophone* May 2020/3 The rapid succession of verseless office antiphons..gave me a slight feeling of dizziness because of their varying pitches.

Versene (vɜ̄·ɹsīn). Also **versene.** A proprietary name for a preparation containing ethylenediamine tetra-acetic acid (q.v. s.v. *ETHYLENE 2) or a similar chelating agent.

1944 *Official Gaz.* (U.S. Patent Office) 29 Aug. 734/2 The Martin-Dennis Company, Newark, N.J... *Versene* for water softening agents in powdered and liquid form with or without detergents. **1951** *Trade Marks Jrnl.* 14 Nov. 1040/2 *Versene*... Chemical products used in industry. Bersworth Chemical Company,..Framingham,.. Massachusetts, United States of America; manufacturers. **1952** *Nature* 19 July 119/2 Although versene protects the enzyme systems from the inactivation caused by the incubation, it does not reverse such inactivation. **1980** *Bull. Environmental Contamination & Toxicol.* XXIV. 543 (*heading*) Acute fish toxicity of the Versene family of chelating agents.

versicler. For *rare*[−1] read *rare.* (Earlier example.)

1860 G. Meredith *Let.* ? Aug. (1970) I. 61 But do. pray, exclude some of your present versiclers.

versificatory, *a.* For † *Obs.*[−0] read *rare.* (Example.)

1963 V. Nabokov *Gift* iii. 146 It was then also that my versificatory illness began.

versine (vɜ̄·ɹsəin). [Expansion of Versin after Sine[2].] = *versed sine* a s.v. Versed *a.* 1 a.

1943 R. A. Hamnett *Brit. Railway Track* ix. 273 To obtain the versine of a turnout curve on a chord joining the switch heel and the intersection point of the crossing, (G−H) must be substituted for 'G'. **1958** Clark & Clendinning *Plane & Geodetic Surveying* (ed. 5) I. 634 (*heading*) 'Versine' method of establishing intermediate points on the Euler spiral transition curve. **1976** J. B. Garner et al. *Surveying* 278 Versines are used to compute slope corrections.

version. Add: Also with pronunc. (və·ɹʒən).

‖ **vers libre** (vɛ̄r lībr). Pl. **vers libres.** [Fr., free verse.] Poetic writing in which the traditional rules of prosody, esp. those of metre and rhyme, are disregarded in favour of variable rhythms and line lengths; a composition in this style; = *free verse* s.v. *FREE *a.* D. 2.

1902 *Encycl. Brit.* XXVIII. 497/2 M. Viélé-Griffin..and M. Gustave Kahn..gave us *vers libres* which, but for their typographical arrangement, are indistinguishable from prose. **1912** *Poetry* I. ii. 65 Mr. Richard Aldington is a young English poet, one of the 'Imagistes', a group of ardent Hellenists who are pursuing interesting experiments in *vers libre.* **1920** *Glasgow Herald* 8 July 4/2 Mr. Bunker..is most interesting in his vers-libres; unfortunately they are not poetry, though happily free of the pretentiousness of most vers-librists. **1928** T. S. Eliot in E. Pound *Sel. Poems* p. viii, I remarked some years ago, in speaking of *vers libre,* that 'no *vers* is *libre* for the man who wants to do a good job'. The term, which fifty years ago had an exact meaning, in relation to the French alexandrine, now means too much to mean anything at all. **1937** W. Inge *Modernism in Lit.* 13, I have no doubt that cubism and futurism and most of *vers libre* will soon pass into limbo. **1955** C. Carrington *Rudyard Kipling* xiv. 352 Kipling..experimented in almost every conventional verse-form, and wrote remarkably successful *vers libres.* **1978** *Times Lit. Suppl.* 1 Dec. 1406/3 His was.. a phrased rather than a cadenced poetry. His rhythmic strategy meant that he retained the option of vers libre, the thematic resources of dream, and the technical resources of modernism.

Hence **vers-li·brist(e** (also **-libre-ist** and as one word without hyphen), a writer of *vers libre.*

1916 *Independent* LXXXVIII. 104/3 If the public can be convinced that the vers libristes have something to say worth attention, it will have more sympathy. **1926** *British Weekly* 21 Jan. 395/2 Vers-libre-ists are in poetry very much what the futurists were in art, rebels against the established order. **1957** *Archivum Linguisticum* IX. 142 Certain *vers-libristes* of the Symbolist movement. **1969** J. Gross *Rise & Fall Man of Lett.* viii. 229 By 1911 Ezra Pound was a regular contributor, the verslibrists were arguing their case, Imagism was already in the air. **1981** *N. & Q.* Dec. 571/2 Whether one should see in the experiments of modern vers-libristes a fusion of the two systems..must remain a matter for individual response.

‖ **Versöhnung** (fɛɹzö·nuŋ). [Ger., conciliation, propitiation.] A reconciliation of opposites.

1867 J. A. Symonds *Let.* 22 Aug. (1967) I. 750 The truest *Versöhnung* in art I know is to be found in Beethoven's C Minor Symphony. There he first posits all the contradiction of passions, aspirations, and sorrows, then combines them..so transfiguring them that the termination is triumph; the victory and majesty of the soul are wrought out of its defeats and humiliations. **1976** G. Talbot *Permission to Speak* viii. 106 It was a jarring note in an evening of festive international *versöhnung.*

‖ **Verstandesmensch** (fɛɹʃta·ndĕsmenʃ). Pl. **-menschen.** [Ger.] A matter-of-fact person; a realist.

1879 W. James *Coll. Ess. & Rev.* (1920) 133 Such also is the attitude of all hard-minded analysts and *Verstandesmenschen.* **1938** *Mind* XLVII. 528 He rejects as an unhistorical caricature the view of Kant as a cold *Verstandesmensch.*

‖ **Verstehen** (fɛɹʃtē·ən). *Social Sci.* Also **ver-.** [Ger., comprehension.] The use of empathy to understand human action and behaviour, as a method of interpreting historical and sociological phenomena. Also **verste·hende** (fem. pres. pple. of *verstehen* comprehend) *a.*, employing *Verstehen.*

1933 *Economica* XIII. 31 In this sense *verstehende* sociology is rationalistic. **1934** *Psychol. Bull.* XXXI. 298 Ch. Bühler makes use of *Verstehen* as well as statistics in her analysis of life histories. **1937** T. Parsons *Structure Social Action* xvi. 583 This is the first appearance in Weber's methodology of the fundamentally important concept of *Verstehen.* **1948** T. Abel in Feigl & Brodbeck *Readings in Philos. of Sci.* (1953) 682 The characteristic feature of the operation of *Verstehen* is the postulation of an intervening process 'located' inside the human organism, by means of which we recognize an observed.. connection as relevant. **1974** R. D. Jessop *Traditionalism, Conservatism & Brit. Political Culture* i. 18 A pure *verstehende* technique which treats action as the logical concomitant of the actor's ideas, motives, reasons, and beliefs. **1979** *Internat. Jrnl. Sociol. of Law* VII. 327 Problems of *verstehen* sociology—that the analysis should have some regard to the meanings that the actors give to their actions.

vert (vɜ̄ɹt), *a.*[2] *poet. nonce-wd.* [Cf. Vert *v.*[1]] Turning.

1947 Auden *Age of Anxiety* (1948) ii. 49 O Primal Age When we danced deisal, our dream-wishes Vert and volant.

vertex. Add: **1. d.** *Math.* A junction of two or more lines in a network or graph (Graph *sb.*[1] 1 in Dict. and Suppl.); = *NODE *sb.* 7 b.

1931 *Proc. Nat. Acad. Sci.* XVII. 125 A graph *G* is composed of two sets of symbols: vertices, *a, b, . . ., f,* and arcs, α(*ab*).., β(*ac*), . . ., δ(*ef*). **1942** G. T. Whyburn *Analytic Topol.* x. 182 Such a decomposition of a graph *A* into vertices and edges is called a subdivision of *A.* **1975** I. Stewart *Concepts Mod. Math.* xi. 160 A network has two main parts: (i) a set *N*, whose elements are called nodes or vertices, (ii) a way of specifying when two vertices are joined together. **1979** *Sci. Amer.* May 98/3 Alpha-actinin was localized primarily at the vertexes of the network and tropomyosin was localized along the short fibers connecting the vertexes.

3. a. *vertex presentation,* a presentation (Presentation 8 b) in which the vertex of the fœtus lies nearest to the cervix as labour begins.

1841 F. H. Ramsbotham *Princ. & Pract. Obstetr. Med.* 135 (*heading*) Comparative frequency of the various modes of vertex presentation. **1899** [in Dict.]. **1974** *Encycl. Brit. Micropædia* VIII. 195/2 In vertex presentations the head of the fetus most commonly faces to the right and slightly to the rear. This position is said to be the most usual one, because the fetus is thus best accommodated to the shape of the uterus.

vertical, *a.* and *sb.* Add: **A.** *adj.* **3. d*.** *Mus.* Involving, pertaining to, or directed at the relationship between notes sounded simultaneously, rather than the pattern of successive notes; harmonic or chordal rather than melodic.

1889 *Cent. Dict., Vertical composition,* musical composition in which the chief attention is put on the harmonic structure of the successive chords. **1928** *Grove's Dict. Mus.* (ed. 3) V. 164/1 Later events have made it almost superfluous to discuss..his [*sc.* R. Strauss's] theories of 'vertical hearing'. **1942,** etc. [see *HORIZONTAL *a.* (*sb.*) 4]. **1946** A. Bliss in A. L. Bacharach *Brit. Mus. of our Time* xi. 156 As in all his music, one must concentrate on horizontal as well as vertical listening so as to savour the beauty and interest of the inner parts.

e. *vertical breeze* = *BREEZE *sb.*[2] 3 b; *vertical cut,* motion of a recording stylus up and down, rather than from side to side; also *attrib.*; cf. *hill and dale* s.v. *HILL *sb.* 1 b; opp. *lateral cut* s.v. *LATERAL *a.* 3 j; *vertical file, filing*; *vertical gust* = *vertical breeze* above; *vertical interval,* the vertical distance between the heights represented by adjacent contours on a map; *vertical man,* a living man, one standing upright (as opposed to a recumbent or dead one); *vertical recording,* magnetic recording in which the direction of magnetization is at right angles to the plane of the recording medium. Also in collocations used *attrib.*, as *vertical-shaft, -spindle, -take-off.*

1925 Fraser & Gibbons *Soldier & Sailor Words* 296 *To suffer from a vertical breeze* (also *vertical gust*), to be nervous. **1934** D. L. Sayers *Nine Tailors* iii. 279 He got a vertical breeze up. **1965** J. R. Hetherington *Selina's Aunt* 59 The term 'vertical breeze' was co-temporary [with 'wind up'], and may have been either the originating phrase or a further refinement. **1935** J. Mills *Fugue in Cycles & Bels* (1936) xi. 145 Vertical-cut phonograph discs of the most recent type can record from 40 to 9000 cycles. **1975** [see *LATERAL *a.* 3 j]. **1977** *Gramophone* Apr. 1522/1 Every one of these hill-and-dale vertical-cut labels had given place to lateral-cut issues under the same mark by that year [*sc.* 1920]. **1906** *Library Jrnl.* XXXI. 13 A newspaper man..goes to the vertical file, picks out a handful of articles on the subject. **1909** *Independent* (N.Y.) 18 Nov. 1126/1 An assistant..deposits the article in an oblong vertical filing-envelope, ten by eleven inches. **1917** *Daily Mail* 19 July 4/5 Stalled his 'bus and pancaked thirty feet...crashed completely...put a vertical gust up me. **1925** Vertical gust [see *vertical breeze* above]. **1885** G. W. Usill in H. S. Marrett *Pract. Treat. Land & Engin. Surveying* (ed. 4) 320 In this way a table may be calculated showing the horizontal equivalents for the required vertical interval at each degree of slope up to about 30°. **1969** G. C. Dickinson *Maps & Air Photographs* iv. 62 Although contours are widely understood several aspects of their significance are not always fully appreciated. For example their effectiveness in representing terrain is closely controlled by the vertical interval. **1930** Auden *Poems* 2 Let us honour if we can The vertical man Though we value none But the horizontal one. **1961** *Guardian* 16 Feb. 10/5 He was..a 'vertical man', and that in an age when intellectuals have been found flat on their faces. **1975** G. Howell *In Vogue* 61 T. S. Eliot was one vertical man who was honoured..by contemporary writers. **1982** *Sci. Amer.* July 71/3 A number of companies in the U.S., Europe and Japan are working on high-density memory systems based on vertical recording. **1983** *Austral. Microcomputer Mag.* Aug. 67/1 It has announced prototypes of vertical-recording technology disk drives. **1940** *Chambers's Techn. Dict.* 891/2 Vertical shaft alternator. **1967** Vertical-shaft [see *PLANETARY *a.* 1 f]. **1935** *Discovery* May 143/1 Vertical spindle pump. **1964** S. Crawford *Basic Engin. Processes* vii. 190 Vertical-spindle machine employing the face of a cup or segmental wheel. **1935** *Jrnl. R. Aeronaut. Soc.* XXXIX. 1137 So that probably on any day one could actually hover in an autogiro; and they knew also that with the machine which had been illustrated they could achieve vertical take-off as well. **1960** *Daily Tel.* 26 Apr. 1 Britain, France and West Germany are to co-operate in developing a supersonic, vertical-take-off military aircraft. **1972** *Guardian* 28 June 1/2 The fourth of the RAF's vertical take-off Harriers to crash in the past few weeks came down yesterday at Düsseldorf.

7. Of or pertaining to the different levels of a hierarchy or progression. **a.** Extending over or involving successive stages in the production of a particular class of goods. Opp. *HORIZONTAL *a.* (*sb.*) 3 b.

1920 *Westm. Gaz.* 2 Dec. 6/1 The vertical Trusts constructed by Stumm, Thyssen and the other raw-material magnates. **1927** *Daily Tel.* 11 Oct. 15/4 He had created what is technically called a vertical combination, embracing every stage of the soap industry. **1959** *Listener* 5 Nov. 768/2 The existing vertical firms have been operating in a market dominated by the factors created by horizontal trading and few indeed have controlled their price policies by vertical statistics and vertical objectives. **1960** [see *AGRIBUSINESS]. **1962** R. B. Fuller *Epic Poem on Industrialization* 27 A corporation gun nuzzling trick;..precipitating vertical merger. **1967, 1968** [see *HORIZONTAL *a.* (*sb.*) 3 b]. **1975** *N.Y. Times Mag.* 3 Oct. 15 Proponents of the effort call it vertical divestiture, by which they mean forcing the largest oil companies to pick one activity—production or refining or transportation/marketing—and sell off the other parts of the action. **1975** J. De Bres tr. *Mandel's Late Capitalism* xii. 384 The process of centralization can only find expression in a growing centralization of capital, among other things, in the form of vertical integration of big companies.

b. Involving differences or changes of level as in social class, income group, or the like.

1927 P. A. Sorokin *Social Mobility* vii. 133 There are two principal types of social mobility, horizontal and vertical. **1931,** etc. [see *HORIZONTAL *a.* (*sb.*) 3 c]. **1976** F. Zweig *New Acquisitive Society* i. v. 52 The shedding of middle-class values and style of life in the younger generation..is of much deeper significance, transcending the confines of vertical mobility.

c. *vertical union,* a trade union which draws its members from a particular industry without regard to their individual crafts; *vertical market,* one comprising all the potential purchasers in a particular occupation or industry.

1933 *Sun* (Baltimore) 1 Sept. 2/1 This means a vertical union in each industry, free of domination or control either by employers or outside labor leaders. **1937, 1950** Vertical union [see *HORIZONTAL *a.* (*sb.*) 3 d]. **1978** *Business Week* (Industr. Ed.) 17 July 36G H-P's role has been primarily as a systems company emphasizing vertical markets needing a wide variety of supporting electronics. **1983** *Austral. Microcomputer Mag.* Aug. 16/3 HiSoft believes there is a big need for vertical market software, in which a common shell is modified to suit individual needs. **1984** *Sydney Morning Herald* 10 Nov. 6/1 (Advt.), They are presently expanding into a new and highly promising vertical market and offer a Sales Management Opportunity. **1985** *Which Computer?* Apr. 45/1 This means that BOS is one of the richest potential sources of vertical market software written in the UK for the UK market.

d. *vertical proliferation* (see quots.).

1966 *Economist* 22 Oct. 350/2 Like other near-nuclear nations, they are unwilling to promise to stay out of the club unless its members will promise to halt what Canada's foreign minister has called their 'vertical proliferation'; that is, promise to stop testing, producing and piling up nuclear arms. **1980** *Sci. Amer.* July 31/2 In the circumstances what can be done to curb both 'vertical' proliferation (the increase in the numbers and kinds of nuclear weapons in the hands of the nuclear-weapons states) and 'horizontal' proliferation (the further spread of nuclear weapons to nations that do not already have them)?

e. *vertical thinking,* deductive reasoning; opp. *lateral thinking* s.v. *LATERAL *a.* 1 b.

1966, 1967 [see *LATERAL *a.* 1 b]. **1970** G. Greer *Female Eunuch* 108 The take-over by computers of much vertical thinking has placed more and more emphasis on the creative propensities of human thought.

8. Pertaining to or being an aerial photograph taken looking vertically downwards.

1925 Jones & Griffiths *Aerial Surveying by Rapid Methods* ii. 8 Such a procedure will..be necessary when mapping any large area, whether the work be done by 'vertical' or 'oblique' photographs. **1932** *Jrnl. R. Aeronaut. Soc.* XXXVI. 503 The first field operation is the vertical photography along strips about thirty miles apart. *Ibid.*, As soon as each vertical flight was completed the films were developed. **1974** P. R. WOLF *Elem. Photogrammetry* vi. 117 Relief displacement often causes straight roads, fence lines, etc., on rolling ground to appear crooked on a vertical photograph. **1983** J. C. MCCORMACK *Surveying Fund.* xxii. 404 The oblique view is more easily understood by the public than is the plan view contained in vertical aerial photographs.

B. *sb.* **2. d.** *Austral. Opal-Mining.* (See quots.)

1934 *Geol. Survey, Mineral Resources* (New South Wales Dept. Mines) No. 36. 116 The mineral is found also in vertical or sub-vertical joints and cracks..known locally as 'verticals'. **1967** I. L. IDRIESS *Opals & Sapphires* 48 A vertical seam cuts in: that is, a seam running downward from the roof..which in general we used to call a 'vertical'.

5. A vertical aerial photograph (see sense A. 8 above).

1925 JONES & GRIFFITHS *Aerial Surveying by Rapid Methods* vi. 69 These [oblique photographs] provide valuable information about the nature of the ground which eventually is to be mapped by verticals. **1954** W. D. THORNBURY *Princ. Geomorphol.* xxi. 535 Verticals are more widely used than obliques in geologic field work. **1976** J. B. GARNER et al. *Surveying* xiii. 233 If it is required to photograph a long strip of land, many photographs will be required. Each photograph should be a good vertical.

ve·rticalize, *v.* [f. VERTICAL *a.* + -IZE.] *trans.* and *absol.* To render vertical, in any sense. Hence **ve·rticalized, ve·rticalizing** *ppl. adjs.*

1959 *Times Rev. Industry* Dec. 6/3 The..Fair..was one of the first..trade fairs to verticalize by organising..specialised events during..a year, rather than staging one general fair. **1964** M. CRITCHLEY *Developmental Dyslexia* ix. 59 There is a tendency for the child to convert figures, especially those that are verticalised and closed, into a man by drawing a face within the enclosure. **1965** *Economist* 2 Jan. 54/2 The three or four main 'verticalising' companies will have less to feed their appetites and more time to digest what they have. **1982** *Christian Sci. Monitor* 21 Sept. B2/2 As a matter of corporate policy, Hewlett-Packard divisions are 'verticalized', each one functioning as a small company on its own.

Hence **ve:rticaliza·tion**, the action or result of verticalizing.

1962 G. PERLE *Serial Composition & Atonality* iii. 42 Verticalization..represents a fundamental concept of atonal composition—that any group of notes which is statable in horizontal succession is also statable as a simultaneity.., a concept sometimes designated by the rather questionable term, 'vertical melody'. **1964** M. CRITCHLEY *Developmental Dyslexia* ix. 59 There is some disorientation of the background, usually by rotation of mobile figures, or by 'verticalisation'. **1965** *Economist* 19 June 1439/3 Courtaulds being particularly weak in weaving so that effective verticalisation ends at the yarn stage. **1970** *Daily Tel.* 10 Jan. 7/7 He does renounce..that festering sore of serialism, the automatic verticalisation of melodies. **1979** *Nature* 15 Mar. 226/1 The late alkaline rocks in the ring-complexes may be related to verticalisation of the Benioff plane accompanied by a diapiric rise of mantle material. **1984** *Christian Sci. Monitor* 7 Feb. 39/2, I praised Masotti's movement of his necktie from his stomach to his pocket and its slight verticalization.

vertically, *adv.* Add: **1. a.** (Examples in *Mus.* Cf. *VERTICAL *a.* 3 d*.)

1934 *Hound & Horn* July–Sept. 596 He..feels that he is tired of exploiting the folk tune, horizontally, vertically, atonally, seriously, or comically. **1954** *Grove's Dict. Mus.* (ed. 5) VIII. 126/2 Pre-war controversy as to the justification of programme music and 'hearing vertically' began to have no more than antiquarian interest. **1969** *Listener* 26 June 905/1 Strauss's counterpoint tends to be the result of thinking 'vertically', against strongly defined chord-progressions.

2. Throughout the different levels of a hierarchical system.

1933 *Sun* (Baltimore) 2 Sept. 2/1 With an industry organized vertically, the logical labor organization is vertical. **1958** *Listener* 9 Oct. 547/2 Differences throughout the Arab sectors run both vertically and horizontally: between religious sects, social strata, settlers and nomads. **1962** *Economist* 27 Oct. 393/1 The industry should..be concentrated into fewer, vertically-integrated firms. **1974** J. WHITE tr. *Poulantzas's Fascism & Dictatorship* III. ii. 95 The big stores competed for growth as they were vertically integrated into the industrial trusts.

verticillium (vɜːtisi·liɒm). *Bot.* [mod.L. (C. G. Nees von Esenbeck *Das System der Pilze und Schwämme* (1816) 56), f. VERTICILL(US + -IUM.] A hyphomycete fungus of the genus of this name, some species of which cause plant disease; *verticillium wilt*, wilt caused by this fungus, affecting many flowers, vegetables, and fruit bushes.

1916 *Sci. Proc. R. Dublin Soc.* XV. 63 (*heading*) The Verticillium wilt of the potato. **1931**, etc. [see *hadromycosis* s.v. *HADROME]. **1951** *Sci. News* XXI. 110 Verticillium wilt of hops..has been a serious disease in Great Britain since 1932. **1971** *Country Life* 18 Feb. 381/1 So serious have they [*sc.* chrysanthemum diseases] become (two caused by viruses and one by a verticillium, in particular) that the future popularity of this florist's flower is said to be in danger. **1978** *Sci. Amer.* Aug. 68/3 In California..plantings [of tomato] are mainly limited to cultivars that resist the wilt caused by fusarium and verticillium fungi.

vertisol (vɜ̄·ɹtisɒl). *Soil Sci.* Also **Vertisol.** [f. VERTI(CAL *a.* + *-SOL.] A clayey soil with little organic matter found in regions having distinct wet and dry seasons, characterized by deep, wide cracks when dry and an uneven surface owing to the swelling and shrinking of the clay.

1960 *Soil Classification: 7th Approximation* (U.S. Dept. Agric.) ix. 124/1 The central concept of Vertisols is one of soils that crack widely, and that often remoisten from water that runs into the cracks rather than from water that percolates through the soil. **1970** *Nature* 2 May 429/1 Dark, cracking tropical clays, that is, vertisols, are characteristic of..the restricted clay plugs and backswamps of the Omo Floodplain [in Ethiopia]. **1981** *Jrnl. Soil Sci. Soc. Amer.* XLV. 668/1 In Vertisols, because of swelling and shrinking, bulk density of the soil is dependent on moisture content.

very, *adv.* Add: **2. a.** (Further examples.) *very difficult, severe*: two of the categories used in classifying rock climbs; also *absol.*; *very high* and *low frequency* (Telecommunications): see VHF, VLF s.v. *V 5 b; freq. *attrib.*

1920 *Radio Rev.* Sept. 579 (*heading*) Circuit for producing very high frequencies. **1938**, etc. [see VLF s.v. *V 5 b]. **1951**, etc. [see *SEVERE *a.* 9 b]. **1958** *Economist* 26 July 271 With very high frequency radio broadcasting..providing almost perfect reception, the collector of classical music..can make high fidelity recordings..on a £2 tape. **1967** *Electronics* 6 Mar. 68/2 Navy project officers expect a go-ahead..on construction of a worldwide very-low-frequency Omega navigation system. **1969** 'A. GARVE' *Ascent of D. 13* ii. 35 I've been climbing ever since I was a kid... I've done more Very Severes than I can remember. **1972** *McGraw-Hill Yearbk. Sci. & Technol.* 229/2 Some of the techniques developed for determining the geodetic coordinates for land use..can be applied at sea... In addition, the very-long-baseline interferometry (VLBI) technique is potentially applicable. **1974** *Encycl. Brit. Macropædia* XV. 425/1 The variation of carrier frequency is known as the frequency deviation, and for very-high-frequency broadcasting it can reach ±75 kilohertz. **1976** *Time* 24 May 64/3 The Japanese government..has declared the development of Very Large Scale Integrations—the technical heart of the next generation of computers—a 'national project'. **1978** PASACHOFF & KUTNER *University Astron.* xxvi. 667 With this ability, astronomers can make up an interferometer of two or more dishes very far apart, even thousands of kilometers. This technique is called very-long-baseline interferometry. **1982** *Times* 14 Jan. (Information Technol. Suppl.) p. v/4 Very large-scale integration (VLSI)... VLSI puts as many as 100,000 components on a chip.

e. Qualifying a sb. or proper name used adjectively (for emphasis).

1937 [see *PREDICATIVAL *a.*]. **1968** *Listener* 21 Mar. 389/3 The total effect is very Kirov: it has more in common with the Leningrad *Cinderella*..than with ours. **1978** *Hot Car* July 87/5 *Scallops*, a very fifties paint idea, consisting of a long U-shaped design, the ends of which taper off to points.

4. *veryvery* (as one word).

1969 A. LURIE *Real People* 16 Croquet's become very-very intense this year. **1977** *Transatlantic Rev.* LX. 68 You have a very nice face... And were very very nice to me.

Very[2] (ve·ri, vɪ̄ᵊ·ri). Also (*erron.*) **Verey, Vérey.** The name of Edward W. *Very* (1847–1910), U.S. naval officer, used *attrib.* with reference to a coloured pyrotechnic flare projected from a special pistol for signalling or temporarily illuminating an area; as *Very light, pistol*, etc.

1907 *Jrnl. Mil. Service Inst. U.S.* XLI. 368 In connection with night signaling it may be well here to mention the Very system,..found serviceable in sea-coast signaling. **1915** D. O. BARNETT *Let.* 17 Mar. 95 When the 'Very' pistol came, I fired a rocket. **1917** R. NICHOLS in E. B. Osborn *Nurse in Arms* 49 Before he was aware The 'Verey' light had risen..on the air It hung glistering. **1920** *Blackw. Mag.* June 747/2 Very flares were continually being fired into the air to light up dark corners. **1928** BLUNDEN *Undertones of War* ii. 16 Another officer..showed me..how to fire a flare... He had with him a cumbrous brass gun, called a duck-gun; from this he fired a Vérey cartridge. **1930** C. R. SAMSON *Fights & Flights* 177 My sole equipment consisted of an electric torch..and a Verey-light pistol. **1959** *Chambers's Encycl.* XI. 390/1 The Very pistol, a short-barrelled smooth-bore weapon of 1-in. or 1½in.-calibre, firing a cartridge which is in effect a short roman candle throwing up a single star, is the most generally used pyrotechnic signal. **1976** 'A. YORK' *Dark Passage* xiii. 162 He..found a Very pistol..and fired. The glowing orange ball arced over his head, and then hung, perhaps a hundred feet above the yacht. **1981** J. B. HILTON *Playground of Death* ii. 15 What we were really playing at was War... A Roman candle..was a Very light.

Vesak (ve·sāk). Also **Wesak; Vai-, Ve-, Visākha.** [Skr. *vaiśākhá*, name of a month, f. *vi-sākhā* branched, (also) the name of a constellation, f. *vi* apart + *śākhā* branch.] An important Buddhist festival commemorating the birth, enlightenment, and death of the Buddha, observed on the day of the full moon in the month Visākha (April–May).

1927 E. J. THOMAS *Life of Buddha* iii. 34 In 1922 the Feast of Wesak (Visākha) in Ceylon was at full moon on May 10. **1961** R. A. GARD *Buddhism* iv. 156 Doctrinally speaking, there is the practice of venerating the Buddha..especially the Vesākha/Vaiśākha-puja (often called 'Wesak' in South and Southeast Asia). **1965** *Festival Malaysia 1965: Calendar of Events* 9/3 May 15—Wesak Day: Celebration of Lord Buddha's Birthday. **1971** *Carry Singapore in your Pocket* (Singapore Tourist Promotion Board) (ed. 3) 38 May 9. Vesak Day. Celebration of Lord Buddha's birth, death and enlightenment. **1978** C. HUMPHREYS *Both Sides of Circle* x. 109 The Buddhist Society too carried on. *Wesak*, the annual equivalent of Christmas Day, was held in May as usual. **1978** *Oxford Diocesan Mag.* Aug. 20/3 It is instructive to know what our Jewish neighbours are doing and why at, for example, Yom Kippur, or our Buddihst friends at Vesakha or the Moslems at Meelad al Nabi.

vesicant, *sb.* Add: Also, a vesicant substance for use in warfare.

1923 *Biochem. Jrnl.* XVII. 275 We are trying to find what common factor..underlies the effect of the mustard gas group of vesicants. **1936** A. HUXLEY *Olive Tree* 87 To go and throw thermite, high explosives and vesicants upon the inhabitants of neighbouring countries. **1936** [see *blister gas* s.v. *BLISTER *sb.* 4]. **1944, 1964** [see B.A.L. s.v. *B III]. **1974** M. C. GERALD *Pharmacol.* vii. 137 Lewisite is an arsenic-containing vesicant capable of producing immediate pain.

vesico-. Add: Also occas. used for VESICULO-. **ve:sicopu·stular** *a.* = *vesiculo-pustular* adj. s.v. *VESICULO-; **ve:sico-ure·teral, -urete·ric** *adjs.*, of or pertaining to the bladder and the ureters; *spec.* applied to a flow of urine from the former back into the latter.

1902 H. W. STELWAGON *Treat. Dis. Skin* 63 The lesions often do not become strictly purulent, but are of a sero-purulent character, forming vesicopustules, and when such a feature is a predominant one, the eruption is usually designated vesicopustular. **1951** WHITBY & HYNES *Med. Bacteriol.* (ed. 5) xxiv. 393 The viruses of this group..characteristically produce a vesico-pustular eruption. **1906** DORLAND *Med. Dict.* (ed. 4) 815/1 Vesico-ureteral. **1951** M. CAMPBELL *Clin. Pediatric Urol.* i. 67 Vesico-ureteral reflux also results from obstructions of the lower urinary tract. **1982** *Jrnl. Urol.* CXXVIII. 774/1 Vesicoureteral reflux is a common abnormality occurring in children and a major cause of renal failure in early adult life. **1965** *Brit. Jrnl. Urol.* XXXVII. 531 Vesico-ureteric reflux may follow operations on the vesico-ureteric junction. **1977** *Proc. R. Soc. Med.* LXX. 149/2 This finding is not necessarily applicable to children with symptomless infection even though infection in these children is accompanied by vesicoureteric reflux in 23% of cases.

vesicularity (vĭsikiŭlæ·riti). [f. VESICULAR *a.* + -ITY.] Vesicular condition.

1908 *Mineral. Mag.* XV. 129 The first results..were usually increased vesicularity in the quartz and assumption by much of it of the idiomorphic condition. **1978** *Nature* 20 July 218/1 Vesicularity of seafloor basalt, when plotted against depth of eruption, defines a family of three curves.

vesiculate, *v.* Add: **2.** (Examples.)

1966 *Earth-Sci. Rev.* I. 158 A gas-charged lava flow..might vesiculate so violently at and near its surface that it would form glass and pumice fragments. **1971** *Nature* 31 Dec. 539/1 Pulsations of ejected molten lava vesiculated and disintegrated passing immediately into the grey ash cloud. **1978** *Jrnl. Histochem. & Cytochem.* XXVI. 1 When a semisynthetic diet containing 1% orotic acid..is fed to rats, the endoplasmic reticulum..of hepatocytes vesiculates and lipoprotein..droplets accumulate within the vesicles.

Hence **vesi·culating** *ppl. a.*

1966 *Earth-Sci. Rev.* I. 158, 10 years later Iddings (1909)..omitted the vesiculating flow idea. **1971** *Nature* 31 Dec. 538/2 Blobs and droplets of expanded, molten, vesiculating magma are carried aloft with an expanding vapour. **1979** *Biochim. & Biophys. Acta* DL. 222 Electron microscopy of vesiculating cells shows physical continuity between cell plasma membrane and vesicle membrane. **1983** *Sci. Amer.* Nov. 148/3 Both pumice and ash are frothy glassy materials created by the chilling of vesiculating magma.

vesiculation. Add: Also *Geol.*

1914 R. A. DALY *Igneous Rocks & their Origin* xiii. 264 The basal assumption, that vesiculation occurs at great depth in a volcanic conduit, is..difficult to test. **1971** *Nature* 31 Dec. 538/2 Both articles describe the vesiculation of a magma in terms of the formation, motion and coalescence of bubbles.

vesiculo-. Add: **vesi:culo-bu·llous** *a.*, characterized by or involving both vesicles and bullæ; **vesi:culo-pu·stular** *a.*, characterized by or involving both vesicles and pustules.

1923 R. W. MACKENNA *Dis. Skin* xii. 250 In every well-marked case of Dermatitis herpetiformis it is the vesiculo-bullous lesion which predominates. **1980** *Brit. Med. Jrnl.* 18 Oct. 1041/2 Herpes gestationis (HG) is a severely itching, vesiculobullous skin affection. **1911** STEDMAN *Med. Dict.* 959/1 Vesiculopustular. **1946** *Nature* 27 July 119/1 A fully developed vesiculopustular reaction developed at the site of inoculation. **1973** *Ibid.* 16 Feb. 425/3 There was a prodromal illness of a few days' duration followed by a vesiculopustular rash which was peripheral in distribution.

Vespa (ve·spă). Also **vespa.** Pl. **Vespas,** ‖ **Vespe** (ve·spe). [It., lit. 'wasp, hornet'.] A proprietary name for an Italian make of motor scooter.

1950 *Trade Marks Jrnl.* 22 Mar. 270/2 *Vespa*... Motor Cycles. Piaggio & C. Societa Perazioni,..Genova, Italy:

manufacturers. **1956** A. Thorne *Baby & Battleship* i. 28 Those eternal bantam motor-bicycles, the little *Vespe* that the Italians love. **1958** J. Cannan *And be a Villain* vii. 164 It was one of the first of the motor scooters—before the Vespas. **1960** Auden *Homage to Clio* 80 This could be a reason why they take the silencers off their Vespas. **1965** D. Du Maurier *Flight of Falcon* v. 56 The young were everywhere, pouring out of lecture rooms, laughing, talking, getting on to vespas. **1983** 'D. Rutherford' *Stop at Nothing* iv. 76 A three-wheeler Vespa with a miniature van on the back.

vespasian (vespēi·ʒăn). [Anglicized form of next.] = next.

1938 I. Goldberg *Wonder of Words* 139 Vespasian. **1980** *Times* 27 Feb. 6/8 The City of Paris has decided to erect..three space age vespasians..new 'chalets of necessity'—as they are called.

‖ **vespasienne** (vespazi,e·n). [Fr. (19th cent.), shortening of *colonne vespasienne* Vespasian column, f. the name of Titus Flavius *Vespasianus*, Roman Emperor, 69–79, who introduced a tax on public lavatories.] A public lavatory in France.

1922 E. E. Cummings *Enormous Room* iii. 44 My first request was permission to visit the *vespasienne*. **1962** P. Brickhill *Deadline* x. 130 A pissoir, or, to give it its polite name, a vespasienne, after the emperor who was so solicitous of man's frailty. **1975** *Times* 4 Mar. 6/1 The vicissitudes of a village *vespasienne*.

vesper. Add: **4.** (Later examples.)

1874 O. W. Holmes *Poetical Wks.* (1892) I. 352 How blest to the toiler his hour of release When the vesper is heard With its whisper of peace! **1927** A. Clarke *Son of Learning* 18 *Brother*: I must ring the Vesper.

8. b. *vesper-born.*

1928 Blunden *Retreat* 50 O vesper-born, Stiff-necked I stand like that hewn knotty tree, As if heaven were my halo.

vesperal, *a.* **a.** (Later examples.)

1887 L. Johnson *Incense in Ireland* (1897) 60 Pensive and solitary old age finds Calm in the vesperal, mild air. **1951** V. Nabokov *Speak, Memory* iv. 47 The day would take hours to fade, and everything..would be kept in a state of infinite vesperal suspense.

ve·spering, *ppl. a. rare*$^{-1}$. [f. Vesper + -ing^2.] Flying westwards (towards sunset).

1914 Hardy *Year's Awakening* in *New Weekly* 21 Mar. 9 O vespering bird, how do you know?

vespertilian, *a.* Delete *rare*$^{-1}$ and add later examples.

1911 W. J. Locke *Glory of Clementina Wing* xxii. 277 As the studio was rigorously closed to him during the daylight hours his visits were vespertilian. **1955** R. Graves *Crowning Privilege* 222 The fiend..Flaunts vespertilian wing and cloven hoof.

vespertilionid, *a.* Add: Also as *sb.*, a bat of the family Vespertilionidæ.

1965 B. E. Freeman tr. *Vandel's Biospeleology* xxvii. 454 The ears of vespertilionids are immobile. **1976** *Nature* 15 Apr. 628/1 Within our sample alone, species are represented whose primary foods are..insects (the mormoopids, natalids, vespertilionids and molossids).

vessel, *sb.*^{1} Add: **4. c.** An airship or hovercraft.

1915 *Sphere* 3 Apr. 22/1 The long covering of the balloon seemed to have been broken. Some people were running beside the vessel. **1916** *Ibid.* 18 Mar. 293/1 As an airship rises it encounters air which has less supporting power, and ultimately..the vessel floats in equilibrium. **1957** I. Asimov *Naked Sun* ix. 93 Baley was in an air-borne vessel again, as he had been on that trip from New York to Washington. **1972** *Daily Tel.* 25 Apr. 1/4 British Rail's hovercraft Princess Anne made an emergency landing on a sandbank yesterday... The vessel was beached at Andressells, eight miles north of Boulogne.

vest, *sb.* Add: **3. b.** Now *N. Amer.* (Further examples.)

1925 F. Scott Fitzgerald *Great Gatsby* ix. 202 While he took off his coat and vest I told him all arrangements had been deferred. **1937** H. G. Wells *Brynhild* vii. 103 He was sitting without jacket or vest, looking neat and healthy in his shirt and black tie. **1968** *Globe & Mail* (Toronto) 17 Feb. 7/3 Hooking his thumbs in his vest, he answered questions in a calm, almost offhand manner. **1978** J. Irving *World according to Garp* ii. 37 Bodger.. tucked in his shirt, which was escaping ..from under his tight vest.

d*. A short, sleeveless jacket for a woman. *U.S.*

1909 in Webster. **1974** *Times-Picayune* (New Orleans) 14 Aug. iii. 1 (Advt.), Plaid vest, 18.00. **1978** *Detroit Free Press* 5 Mar. (Spring Fashion Suppl.) 11/1 Vests have never looked quite so fresh and right as they do this spring. They can be the perfect sleeveless jacket, topping all the softness.

d.** A singlet denoting membership of a representative athletics team.

1971 N. Stacey *Who Cares?* ii. 25 It was harder to get a Blue than an international vest.

e. vest-pocket: also *attrib.* as *adj.*: small enough to fit into a vest pocket, very small of its kind; also *fig.*; **vest-slip** = sense 3 b in Dict. and Suppl.

1848 *Sporting Life* 29 July 274/1 This vest pocket companion for cricketers. **1897** 'Mark Twain' *Following Equator* 629 Toy peaks, and a dainty little vest-pocket Matterhorn. **1912** *Brit. Jrnl. Photogr.* 5 July 525 The vest-pocket 'Tenax' camera. **1931** *Times* 16 Mar. 1/3 (Advt.), Unique vest-pocket treatment for catarrh. **1947** *Horizon* Apr. 152 Our provincial hotels with their vest-pocket electric fires. **1983** *Chicago Sun-Times* 9 July 15 Vest-pocket garden-parks provide relaxed places for people to interact with one another. **1984** *Newslet. Amer. Dial. Soc.* Sept. 23/1 He was responsible for..a series of popular vest-pocket dictionaries and reference books. **1920** *Punch* 9 June 456/2 My top-hat was on my head and my vest-slip was all right. **1922** Vest-slip [see *Oxford 1 b].

vest, *v.* **II. 6. b.** (Earlier example.)

1848 C. H. Hartshorne *Eng. Medieval Embroidery* 130 The sides [of the altar] must be covered or vested... Where the table stands away from the wall, the back must be vested likewise.

vested, *ppl. a.* Add: **1. c.** Of a suit: three-piece, having a waistcoat. Chiefly *N. Amer.*

1976 *Daily Colonist* (Victoria, B.C.) 6 Oct. 5/8 (Advt.), Save a great deal on a Tip Top vested suit. **1982** 'W. R. Duncan' *Queen's Messenger* viii. 74 Ross..nattily dressed as usual in his vested dark suit.

vestee. Restrict *rare* to sense in Dict. and add: **1.** Also *transf.*

1937 *Virginia Q. Rev.* XIII. 591 In a department of English, as in any other going business, the proprietary interest becomes vested, and in old and reputable departments the vestees have uniformly been gentlemen who have gone through the historical mill.

2. [f. Vest *sb.*] A vest (sense 3 a or *3 d) or dickey (sense 6). Chiefly *N. Amer.*

1904 *T. Eaton & Co. Catal.* Spring & Summer 87/3 Boys' Vestee Suits, three-piece style, with single-breasted vest. **1916** *Daily Colonist* (Victoria, B.C.) 7 July 14/5 (Advt.), Silk Crepe de Chine Waists..featuring the small button front and vestee effect outlined by French Veining. **1928** *Daily Express* 17 Aug. 4 (*heading*) Vestee and cuff set. **1943** *Sun* (Baltimore) 4 Feb. 17/2 The Chicago Cubs.. have worn sleeveless baseball shirts, or vestees, for the last three years. **1963** J. Mitford *Amer. Way of Death* iv. 56 The women's lingerie department of Practical Burial Footwear supplies a de-luxe package..of 'pantee, vestee' and nylon hose.

vestibular, *a.* Add: **a.** *spec.* Of or pertaining to the vestibule of the ear or its function as an organ of equilibrium. (Further examples.)

1902 D. J. Cunningham *Text-bk. Anat.* 482 Its fibres.. end in the nucleus of Deiters, the chief vestibular nucleus. **1923** *Physiol. Rev.* III. 209 (*heading*) The function of the vestibular apparatus. **1948** A. Brodal *Neurol. Anat.* vii. 213 The parts of the labyrinth generally assumed to be concerned with vestibular function..are..the saccule and the utricle, and the three semicircular canals. **1956** A. C. Guyton *Textbk. Med. Physiol.* xlvi. 575/1 Equilibrium is controlled especially by the vestibular apparatus. **1962** V. Grissom in *Into Orbit* 80 The doctors call this sensation 'vestibular nystagmus', and it is an uncontrollable movement of the eyeballs which occurs when the balance mechanism in your body gets all messed up from the twisting and tumbling. **1983** *Oxf. Textbk. Med.* II. xxv. 29/2 Either the cochlear or the vestibular fibres of the eighth nerve may be damaged within the brainstem, although vestibular symptoms are appreciably more common from this cause.

vestibulo- (vesti·biŭlo), comb. form of L. *vestibul-um* Vestibule *sb.*, used chiefly with reference to the vestibule of the ear, as **vesti:bulo-au·ditory** *a.*, involving the vestibules and hearing; **vesti:bulocerebe·llar** *a.*, applied to nerves running from the vestibular nucleus of the brain to the cerebellum; **vesti:bulocochle·ar** *a.*, designating or pertaining to the vestibular and cochlear nerves jointly; **vesti:bulo-o·cular** *a.*, involving both the vestibular and the oculomotor nerves; **vesti:bulospi·nal** *a.*, applied to a tract of nerves in the spinal cord that originate in the vestibular nucleus of the brain. Also Vestibulotomy.

1945 *Arch. Ophthalmol.* XXXIII. 149/1 The vestibulo-auditory symptoms began abruptly with vertigo, tinnitus and deafness. **1980** *Medicine* (Baltimore) LIX. 426/1 Cogan syndrome..is a disease of young adults and consists of acute interstitial keratitis..with vestibuloauditory dysfunction. **1932** *Jrnl. Compar. Neurol.* LIV. 150 Vestibulocerebellar fibers. **1974** D. & M. Webster *Compar. Vertebr. Morphol.* xii. 292 The vestibulocerebellar tract runs from the vestibular nuclei in the brainstem through the restiform body to terminate in the cerebellar cortex. **1962** *Gray's Anat.* (ed. 33) 1141 The vestibulocochlear nerve appears in the groove between the pons and the medulla oblongata. **1974** *Encycl. Brit. Micropædia* III. 413/1 In nerve deafness, some defect in the sensory cells of the inner ear..or in the vestibulocochlear nerve prevents transmission of sound impulses from the inner ear to the auditory centre in the brain. **1982** *Audiology* XXI. 172 Streptomycin..passes into the fetus ..producing vestibulocochlear neural abnormalities. **1921** Tilney & Riley *Form & Function Central Nervous System* xxx. 532 Vestibulo-ocular associated reflex. This reflex is elicited by electrical, thermal and mechanical stimulation of the receptors in the vestibule of the internal ear. **1963** *Jrnl. Theoret. Biol.* IV. 215 The simplest description of this vestibulo-ocular reflex is to say that, if the head is rotated in one direction, the eyes tend to rotate, with respect to the head, in the opposite direction, and then come back to their undeviated position. **1979** *Sci. Amer.* Jan. 88/1 The two other major types of eye movements—the vestibulo-ocular movements, which maintain visual stability during head movements, and the smooth-pursuit eye movements, which follow a moving object such as a flying bird—do not appear..since neither of these types of movements is elicited by target jumps. **1899** L. F. Barker *Nervous System* lviii. 960 It would seem that this uncrossed descending vestibulo-spinal neurone system has been described by various authors under different names. **1948** A. Brodal *Neurological Anat.* v. 118 The most important descending connexion appears to be the vestibulo-spinal tract. **1983** *Brain Res.* CCLIX. 217/1 The vestibulospinal system has a complex organization both in aspects of its afferent connection and of its spinal projection.

vestigial, *a.* Add: **a.** (Earlier example.)

1877 *Gray's Anat.* (ed. 8) p. clxvi, The only remains of the Wolffian body in the complete condition of the female organs are two rudimentary or vestigial structures.

2. Telecommunications. *vestigial side band*, a side band which is partially attenuated (usu. at the higher frequencies) before transmission; freq. *attrib.*, with reference to a system in which one full side band and one vestigial side band are transmitted (with or without the carrier), esp. to improve the transmission of low-frequency components of the signal.

1940 D. G. Fink *Princ. Television Engin.* vii. 288 At the transmitter, the principal problem of vestigial side-band transmission (as the above-described system is called) is the design of a filter having the pass characteristics shown in Fig. 162. **1966** *McGraw-Hill Encycl. Sci. & Technol.* I. 352/1 In standard television broadcasting in the continental United States..the vestigial sideband has a bandwidth one-sixth that of a full sideband. **1979** A. A. Liff *Colour & Black & White Television Theory & Servicing* ii. 55 The FCC standards require that the lower sideband be transmitted in vestigial sideband form and that the upper sideband be transmitted in its entirety.

vestigium. b. (Later example.)

1970 H. Braun *Parish Churches* ix. 124 These [arches] are not, as might have been supposed, the remains of an earlier clearstory, but simply vestigia of the original windows of a pre-medieval nave.

vesting, *sb.* (Earlier example.)

1813 *Weekly Reg.* IV. 295/1 For the best and handsomest fancy vesting, of cotton..a premium of..forty dollars.

vesting, *vbl. sb.* **1.** (Later *attrib.* examples.)

1922 *Act* 12 & 13 *Geo. V* §188. 238 In relation to settled land, 'vesting deed' or 'vesting order' means the instrument whereby the land is conveyed or vested; 'vesting assent' means the instrument whereby a personal representative, after the death of a tenant for life..vests the land in the successor in title..; 'vesting instrument' means a vesting deed, assent or order. **1948** *Secretary* July 180 (*heading*) Vesting day, 1st April, 1948. **1950** *Engineering* 24 Mar. 318/3 It is difficult to forecast whether or not the iron and steel industry will..pass into State ownership on the vesting date, January 1, 1951. **1964** *Financial Times* 23 Mar. (Defence Suppl.) 14/5 With 'vesting day' only a few days off, staffs are still settling down. **1967** *Economist* 1 Apr. 21/2 For compulsory purchase, the commission may use a procedure called the 'vesting declaration' which virtually cuts out conveyancing, while granting a firm title. **1977** *Belfast Tel.* 19 Jan. 7/2 A vesting order for the land was signed on February 12 last. **1982** *Equity & Law Life Ann. Rep. 1981* 16 Vesting bonus of 30% of the total pension will be allotted to personal pension deferred annuities.

Vestinian (vesti·niăn), *sb.* and *a.* [f. L. *Vestīni* + -an.] **A.** *sb.* **a.** A member of an ancient Oscan people who lived in the Gran Sasso d'Italia area of Italy. **b.** The language of this people. **B.** *adj.* Of or pertaining to this people or their language.

1578, etc. [see *Marrucinian *sb.* and *a.*]. **1933, 1939** [see *Marsian *sb.* and *a.*]. **1966** M. S. Beeler in Birnbaum & Puhvel *Anc. Indo-European Dial.* 53 So far as I know no voice has..ever been raised to question the propriety of regarding these languages (and the minor dialects of the Paelignians, Marrucinians, Vestinians, and Volscians) as differentiated forms of a single common ancestor..here termed Oscan-Umbrian.

vestmental, *a.* For *rare*$^{-1}$ read *rare* and add later example.

1978 *New York* 3 Apr. 92/1 Hermitage prospers now on the commerce of those who pursue chic and never catch it... They occupy every table, tailored flannels and sharkskins seated beside superb little Bendel numbers—vestmental perfections without a stitch of art.

vestock (ve·stǫk). [Blend of Vest *sb.* and Stock *sb.*^{1}] A clerical stock that extends to the waist.

1975 *Rep. Patent Cases* 473 The..vestock..can be described as a sort of black bib, with a hard upstanding collar round at the front. **1981** *Oxf. Diocesan Mag.* May 24 (Advt.), Fine bespoke tailors and hosiers. Now stock clerical shirts, collars, stocks, vestocks, etc.

vestry^1. Add: **2. b.** In England the sole remaining power of the vestry is the election of churchwardens, its other ecclesiastical powers having been transferred to the parochial church council and the annual parochial church meeting; *select vestry* (*Obs.* exc. *Hist.*) (see quots, 1845, 1906).

1698 *MSS. House of Lords* (1905) III. 261 Dec. 9. Poor Relief (Select Vestries) Bill.—Draft of an Act for preventing the Poor's being cheated. **1845** *Encycl. Metrop.* XXIII. 486/2 In other Parishes,..the rate-payers place the powers intrusted to them in the hands of a small Body, chosen by them from their own number, called sometimes the Select Vestry, and sometimes the Guardians of the Poor. **1906** S. & B. WEBB *Parish & County* I. v. 173 The Close or..Select Vestry...consisted of a body of one or two dozen persons, or occasionally more, serving for life and filling vacancies among themselves by co-option. **1921** *Parochial Church Councils (Powers) Measure* 4 From the commencement of this Measure there shall be transferred to the Council of every parish—(i) All powers, duties and liabilities of the Vestry of such parish relating to the affairs of the Church, except as regard the election of churchwardens and sidesmen and as regards the administration of ecclesiastical charities. **1959** JOWITT *Dict. Eng. Law* II. 1610/1 The Select Vestries Bill is the title of a Bill always formally read a first time in the House of Lords at the beginning of a new session before the House proceeds to debate the king's or queen's speech, as an assertion of its independence.

vestryman. Add: Also *fig.*

1910 *Blackw. Mag.* Apr. 585/1 Mr. Shaw is the vestryman of dramatists. His work savours horribly of St. Pancras.

Vesuvius (vǐsiū·viŏs). [The name of a volcano near Naples (see VESUVIAN *a.* and *sb.*).] A great explosion of emotion; something or someone liable to sudden outbursts.

1845 POE in *Broadway Jrnl.* 6 Sept. 136/2 The poetical and critical world of England were, about six years ago, violently agitated (in spots) by the eruption of 'Festus', a vesuvius-cone at least—if not an..Ætna. **1886** G. MEREDITH *Let.* 9 June (1970) II. 815, I confess that a faint form of decent excuse for your conduct..would have partly appeased my natural indignation. I put it by among other things for the Day of my Vesuvius. **1929** D. H. LAWRENCE *Pansies* 130 The women are like little volcanoes... It is rather agitating, sleeping with a little Vesuvius.

veszelyite (ve·sĕlyəit, -lǐ,əit). *Min.* [ad. G. *veszelyit* (A. Schrauf 1874, in *Anzeiger d. Akad. d. Wissensch., Wien* XI. 136), f. the name of A. *Veszely*, Hungarian mining engineer: see -ITE[1].] A hydrated basic phosphate of copper and zinc,$(Cu,Zn)_3(PO_4)(OH)_3 \cdot 2H_2O$, occurring as aggregates of bluish monoclinic crystals.

1875 E. S. DANA *Dana's Syst. Min.* (ed. 5) App. II. 59 Veszelyite... In crystalline crusts on garnet-rock. **1920** *Nature* 1 July 569/2 Rare zinc-copper minerals from.. Northern Rhodesia... Still rarer are the copper-zinc minerals aurichalcite and veszelyite; the latter forms minute sky-blue monoclinic crystals.., and differs from the original material from Hungary in its colour and in containing little or no arsenic. **1977** *Mineral. Abstr.* XXVIII. 207/2 The veszelyite appears to have been formed in an oxidation zone by low-*T* hydrothermal processes.

vet, *sb.* Add: **2.** A doctor of medicine. *slang.*

1925 FRASER & GIBBONS *Soldier & Sailor Words* 296 *Vet, the*, medical officer. **1938** [see *pill shooter* s.v. *PILL *sb.*[2] 5]. **1965** M. SPARK *Mandelbaum Gate* v. 119 'The vet gone?' Gardnor said... 'You might have a relapse.' **1975** A. POWELL *Hearing Distant Harmonies* ii. 83 Saw my vet last week. Said he'd never inspected a fitter man of my age.

vet, *sb.*[2] N. Amer. abbrev. of VETERAN *sb.* in Dict. and Suppl.

1848 *Sporting Life* 17 June 190/2 The same remark may be applied to a much younger man than the above 'vets', whose Spring-like qualities seem to defy old winter. **1866** *Pictorial Bk.* 452/2 Colonel A..took it upon himself to chide the exasperated and unfortunate 'vet' for using such unchristianlike language. **1926** *Amer. Speech* I. 369/1 The [baseball] players are, as in the army, 'vets' or 'rookies' according to the length of time they have served. **1936** *Esquire* Sept. 159/2 'Jesse Lasky's Broadway Booneing' means that the vet producer is scouting plays and talent in N.Y. **1951** M. MCLUHAN *Mech. Bride* (1967) 144/2 The *Fortune* survey editors..were surprised to find nearly all the vets in favor of getting inside a *big* business. **1968** *Listener* 27 June 841/1 The scene is New York,..the academic 'host' is Columbia University, where a number of young Second World War vets..are making gestures at working for degrees. **1979** *Tucson* (Arizona) *Citizen* 20 Sept. 8c/1 When he talked to vets in other service organizations, he found a lot of them felt they owed something to the Veterans Administration too.

vet, *v.* Add: **3.** To examine carefully and critically for deficiencies or errors; *spec.* to investigate the suitability of (a person) for a post that requires loyalty and trustworthiness.

1904 KIPLING *Traffics & Discoveries* 270 These are our crowd... They've been vetted, an' we're putting 'em through their paces. **1924** H. A. VACHELL *Quinney's Adventures* 267 Shelagh 'vetted' Mr. Dolan's brogue, and passed it as sound enough for an Irish-American. **1925** E. F. NORTON *Fight for Everest: 1924* III. vi. 338 He should have all equipment..completely ready three or four months before shipment—only thus can everything be properly 'vetted' and criticized. **1938** G. ARTHUR *Not Worth Reading* viii. 110 The official in Pall Mall..who 'vetted' us..swallowed without a gulp some rather mendacious replies as to one's technical knowledge of the various parts of a Canadian boat. **1947** E. WAUGH *Let.* 29 May (1980) 251 The romantic castle was condemned by the architect I sent to vet it, as moribund. **1959** DUKE OF BEDFORD *Silver-Plated Spoon* vi. 128 We went through an awful period while Brownie was 'vetted' at a series of interviews with relations, each more embarrassing than the last. **1978** G. GREENE *Human Factor* II. i. 63 HQ had had her vetted.

veteran, *sb.* and *a.* Add: **A.** *sb.* **1. b.** Any ex-serviceman. Chiefly *N. Amer.*

Not always distinguishable from sense 1 a.

1798 W. DUNLAP *André* p. iv, The Author has gone near to offend the veterans of the American army who were present on the first night. **1838** *Southern Lit. Messenger* IV. 796 When the revolutionary pension-law was enacted, a majority of the war-worn veterans had travelled..beyond the reach of human reward. **1912** I. S. COBB *Back Home* 38 Saturday..was also Veterans' Day, when the old soldiers were the guests of honor of the management. **1931** *U.S. Laws & Statutes* XLVI. I. 1016 The President is authorized..to consolidate and coordinate any hospitals and executive and administrative bureaus..into an establishment to be known as the Veterans' Administration. **1946** *Sun* (Baltimore) 7 Oct. 2/5 The War Assets Administration ordered its surplus building materials pushed into the veterans housing program within 60 days. **1954** *Birmingham* (Alabama) *News* 11 Nov. 41/1 The Sheppard murder trial jury took a Veterans Day holiday today. **1974** C. RYAN *Bridge too Far* IV. x. 348 'It was the heaviest volume of fire I ever encountered,' recalls Sergeant Spencer Wurst, a 19-year-old veteran who had been with the 82nd since North Africa. **1979** G. F. NEWMAN *List* viii. 67 He was planning for Veteran's Day weekend. November 11 fell on a Monday this year. **1982** *Times* 13 Dec. 3/6 (*heading*) Falklands veteran killed at 22.

3. A veteran car.

1965 *Guardian* 6 Nov. 3/8 A 'Veteran' is any car made before December 31, 1904. **1968** [see *EDWARDIAN *a.* 3].

B. *adj.* **3. b.** Applied to cars made before a certain stipulated date (normally a vehicle not less than fifty years old). Also *transf.* (often coupled with *vintage*).

1933 A. G. MACDONELL *England, their England* xiii. 222 A three-mile clatter in the veteran car—'never can get the new car,' explained Mr. Fielding. **1958** M. KELLY *Christmas Egg* III. 107 An apartment..was devoted to the needs of those who..wished to play vintage and veteran records. **1959** *Listener* 29 Jan. 201/2 A veteran car is generally considered to be a pre-1917 model though a few extremely exclusive owners recognise only pre-1905 cars as qualifying for the title. **1961** J. SHELDON (*title*) Veteran and vintage motor cycles. **1965** L. HUNT (*title*) Veteran and vintage aircraft. **1980** *Times* 1 Nov. 14/2 Nineteen-thirty had seen the foundation of the Veteran Car Club of Great Britain.

veto, *sb.* Add: **2. a.** *liberum veto* [L. *liber* free], a power of veto possessed by every member of a legislative body, *spec.* that which existed under the later Polish monarchy. Also *transf.*

1792 W. COXE *Trav. Poland* I. I. v. 96 In all state-matters of the highest importance no resolution of the diet is valid, unless ratified by the unanimous assent of every nuntio; each of whom is able to suspend all proceedings by his exertion of the *Liberum Veto.* **1831** J. FLETCHER *Hist. Poland* iii. 89 It was in this King's reign [*sc.* 1648–68] that the *liberum veto*, or privilege of the deputies to stop all proceedings in the diet, by a simple dissent, first assumed the form of a legal custom. **1931** E. HOWELL *Mizh* (1979) x. 96 What he had in mind was the *liberum veto* which any young hot head could exercise by the use of his rifle. **1938** H. V. HODSON *Slump & Recovery* viii. 245 Her [*sc.* Bolivia's] *liberum veto* thus stood in the way of any increase of quota allowances. **1952–4** *Proc. Brit. Acad.* XXXVIII. 217 In Jan. 1831 the opposition of a single Cabinet Minister to the proposed grant to Queen Adelaide for an outfit, compelled the Cabinet to abandon it: an example of the *liberum veto.*

3. *veto-free, -proof* adjs.

1959 *Daily Tel.* 27 Apr. 10 The Prime Minister..proposed breaking the existing deadlock over a control system by a 'quota' plan limiting the number of veto-free inspections per year. **1972** *National Observer* (U.S.) 16 Sept. 2/5 The debt-limit extension, veto-proof because of its importance, could become a Christmas tree of Democratic proposals. **1973** *San Francisco Examiner* 20 Sept. 9/2 The American Federation of Teachers..reacted to the vote by calling for the election of a 'veto-proof Congress..no longer intimidated by the big stick of a Nixon veto'.

vetoism. (Earlier example.)

1815 D. O'CONNELL *Let.* 13 June (1972) II. 47 A priest suspected of Vetoism loses all his respect.

vetoist. (Earlier example.)

1815 *Dublin Evening Post* 19 Jan. 2 The Vetoists.. have been routed.

vetter (ve·təɹ). [f. VET *v.* + -ER[1].] One who vets people or things.

1972 *Daily Tel.* (Colour Suppl.) 9 June 7/3 One should be able to assume..that for the BBC's announcers and commentators, as well as for the authors, vetters and readers of scripts, literacy and oral propriety are automatic conditions of employment. **1982** *Listener* 16 Dec. 3/3 The Americans..are privately scathing about the failure of positive vetters to pick up an obvious security risk. **1984** *Daily Tel.* 1 Nov. 2/7 This follows recommendations by the Security Commission into the case of Geoffrey Prime, the spy, whose psychological flaws went undiscovered by security vetters.

ve·tting, *vbl. sb.* [f. VET *v.* + -ING[1].] The action or process of vetting a person or thing; *esp.* the investigation of a person's background and credentials to determine his loyalty or trustworthiness; *positive vetting*, vetting which includes a search for weaknesses of character or anything else that could render the subject vulnerable to exploitation.

1918 H. A. VACHELL *Some Happenings* iv. 42 Doctors were so ridiculously cocksure! All the same, he felt mildly interested in the vetting... Constitutionally he was as sound as a bell. **1927** *Observer* 17 July 13/1 The 'vetting' of applicants for loans would involve the State in an expenditure on itinerant investigators and inspectors. **1955** H. MACMILLAN in *Hansard Commons* 7 Nov. 1499 At the beginning of 1952, a regular system of positive vetting was introduced. This procedure entails detailed research into the whole background of the officer concerned. **1970** *Canadian Antiques Collector* July–Aug. 5/2, I was pleased to see that the vetting committee had done their work well. **1978** G. GREENE *Human Factor* I. iii. 38 Of course, he belongs to the slack vetting days, but I'd say he was clear. **1982** *Daily Tel.* 20 July 3/1 There are some 68,000 government posts currently requiring positive vetting. Civil servants of Under Secretary rank and above are automatic candidates.

‖ **veuve** (vöv). [Fr.] **1.** A widow; also prefixed as a title to the name.

1793 F. BURNEY *Jrnl.* 13 Apr. (1972) II. 77, I told him I should have the pleasure to present him to another sister—*la veuve!* **1868** C. M. YONGE *Chaplet of Pearls* I. xix. 258 He found her..with her hands in Veuve Laurent's flour. **1894** M. M. VERNEY *Mem. Verney Family* III. ix. 330 We hope Mrs. Aris *veuve* was treated to some of those lovely phrases for home consumption. **1922** E. E. CUMMINGS *Enormous Room* iii. 42 She must have been very pretty before she put on the black. Her friend is also a *veuve.* **1953** D. PARRY *Going up—going Down* v. viii. 252 It's quite a popular sport now, to drop in and cheer the Veuve Tyndale. **1977** T. HEALD *Just Desserts* viii. 190 In the hall were two men unmistakably French.. policemen..arguing..with la Veuve.

2. Veuve Clicquot (klīko), *erron.* **Cliquot,** the shortened form of a proprietary name for champagne produced by the firm of Veuve Clicquot-Ponsardin in Reims.

1898 W. J. LOCKE *Idols* xx. 278, I am glad that you prefer champagne *extra sec*... So many women go for Veuve Cliquot, when they can. **1906** GALSWORTHY *Man of Property* I. ii. 33 His pint of champagne was dry and bitter stuff, not like the Veuve Clicquots of old days. [**1926** *Trade Marks Jrnl.* 9 June 1355 Veuve Clicquot–Ponsardin... Champagne wines. Bertrand de Mun & Cie., successeurs de Veuve Clicquot-Ponsardin.., Reims, France; wine merchants.] **1964** [see *TAITTINGER]. **1968** *Guardian* 20 Sept. 11/4 A fine pink Veuve Clicquot, say, still remains a fine wine. **1979** P. ALEXANDER *Show me a Hero* xvi. 171 He came in from the other reception room with a bottle of Veuve Cliquot and two glasses on a tray.

‖ **vexata quæstio** (veksā·tă kwī·stio). [L.] = *vexed question* s.v. VEXED *ppl. a.* 4.

1813 *Edin. Rev.* Oct. 143 We do not mean to enter upon the *vexata quæstio* of the tones and delivery. **1838** J. S. MILL in *Westm. Rev.* XXXI. 393 The *vexata quæstio* of codification..has now passed into one of Practice. **1889** G. N. CURZON *Russia in Central Asia* ix. 368 This has long been a *vexata quæstio* of Central Asian politics. **1978** *Language* LIV. 425 For the vexata quaestio of the 'gorgia toscana', cf. most recently Izzo 1972.

vexedness. (In Dict. s.v. VEXED *ppl. a.*) For *rare*[−1] read *rare* and add later example.

1909 W. J. LOCKE *Septimus* xi. 160 Zora, regarding the egoist with mingled admiration and vexedness, could only say, 'Oh!'

vexillology (veksilǫ·lŏdʒi). [f. L. *vexill-um* flag + -OLOGY.] The study of flags.

1959 *Arab World* (N.Y.) Oct. 13/1 One of the most interesting phases of vexillology—the study of flags—is the important contribution to our heritage of flags by the Arab World. **1961** *Flag Bull.* Fall 7/2 Editors Grahl and Smith use 'vexillology' and its cognates, vexillologist, vexillological. **1966** *Occasional Newslet. to Librarians* Jan. 4 This unknown specialist has demonstrated his great knowledge of heraldry and vexillology. **1970** W. SMITH *Flag Bk. U.S.* i. 3 In 1965 the first International Congress of Vexillology was held in the Netherlands.

Hence **vexillolo·gical** *a.*; **vexillo·logist.**

1961 [see above]. **1963** *Recall* (Boston) Oct. 4 (*heading*) Travel notes and vexillological addendum. **1965** W. SMITH *Bibliogr. Flags of Foreign Nations* p. v, Its three principal activities have been the encouragement of contacts and exchanges of information between vexillologists around the world, the coordination of research efforts, and the building up of a library of books and other flag materials. **1971** *Daily Tel.* 19 Nov. 13/7 Between 60 and 70..historians, antiquaries, designers and students of heraldry are expected at an international vexillological congress. **1973** *Smithsonian* Dec. 50/2 Redividing the states would mean redesigning the flag. In vexillologist Whitney Smith's scheme, he retains the symbolism of 13. **1983** *Christian Science Monitor* 8 Apr. 20/1 Father Young is the official community vexillological custodian.

via, *sb.* Add: **2.** *esp.* One in Italy or one of the great Roman roads. Cf. WAY *sb.*[1] 1 c. (Earlier and later examples.)

1673 J. RAY *Observations Journey Low-Countries* 369 We departed from Rome and began our journey to Venice; riding along the Via Flaminia..which reaches as far as

Rimini. **1822** M. Wilmot *Jrnl.* 21–25 May in *More Lett.* (1935) 166 Cecilia Metella's Tomb..so well preserved amidst the many ruined tombs with which the old Via Appia abounds. **1851** E. B. Browning *Casa Guidi Windows* I. iv. 8 That winter-hour, in Via Larga, when Thou wert commanded to build up in snow Some marvel of thine art. **1929** Kipling *Limits & Renewals* (1932) 99 What was your best day's march on the Via Sebaste? **1973** G. Sims *Hunters Point* xix. 177 The frontier town of Menton..where the French Route Nationale joins the Italian Via Aurelia. **1984** A. Elliot *On Appian Way* 6 This poem represents a journey from Rome to Brindisi, more or less following the Via Appia.

b. *Via Crucis* (krū·tʃis) = *Way of the Cross* s.v. Way *sb.*[1] 4 g; also *fig.*, an extremely painful experience that has to be borne with fortitude; *Via Dolorosa* (dǫlǭrōᵘ·ză) [L. *dolōrōsus* Dolorous *a.*], the route in Jerusalem that Christ is believed to have followed from Pilate's judgement-hall to Calvary; also *fig.*, = fig. sense of prec.

1844 *Orthodox Jrnl.* 10 Aug. 100 Thirteen small altar pieces surround the arena [of the Colosseum], and Benedict XIV. introduced here the *Via Crucis*, or devotion to the passion, performed by a brotherhood of monks every Friday afternoon. **1878** R. L. Stevenson *Inland Voyage* 186 Fitly enough may the potentate bestride his charger, like a centurion in an old German print of the *Via Dolorosa*; but the toys should be put away in a box among some cotton, until..the children are abroad again. **1901** M. Carmichael *In Tuscany* 236 The loggia is 250 feet in length, on one side of it is a *Via Crucis* in bas-relief, on the other frescoes representing scenes from the life of the Saint. **1904** H. O. Sturgis *Belchamber* ii. 23 Each step in the *via dolorosa* of his existence was fated to be more awful than the last. **1910** C. E. Montague *Hind let Loose* xv. 290 Fay, with his feeble pity for all souls in trouble, winced to see this one..sneaking..down the same *via dolorosa.* **1923** G. M. Trevelyan *Manin & Venetian Revolution* iv. 68 Silvio Pellico, whose narrative of his own martyrdom was the guide-book of Italian patriots on their *via crucis.* **1944** *Horizon* July 71 Every human being makes the *via crucis* from innocence to experience. **1972** *Guardian* 30 Nov. 14/5 'Via Galactica' [*sc.* a play] turns out to be Peter Hall's Via Dolorosa. **1980** O. Manning *Sum of Things* xix. 154 In the Via Dolorosa a procession was advancing slowly over the spacious, creamy flagstones. **1982** 'M. Hebden' *Pel & Staghound* xvii. 191 The Lord never intended the Via Crucis to be travelled with ease, child. **1984** *Observer* 25 Nov. 9/2 Whatever might have happened to other 'wets' on their *via dolorosa* between 1979 and 1983, it was..hardly on the cards that Mrs Thatcher would simply drop Peter Walker.

3. *via media* (earlier and later examples).

1834 J. H. Newman *Via Media* (Tracts for the Times No. 38) sig. A3ᵛ, The glory of the English Church is, that it has taken the Via Media... It lies *between* the (so called) Reformers and the Romanists. **1936** E. Underhill *Worship* xv. 324 The *Via Media* eludes not only the extremes of Catholic and Protestant cultus, but also the heights and deeps of the spiritual life. **1978** *Christian* IV. 355 What the Chalcedonian definition attempted was a compromise, a *via media*, between conflicting interpretations of the union of the human and divine natures of Christ.

b. Theol. *via negativa*, the approach to God in which his nature is held so to transcend man's understanding that no positive statements can be made about it; the way to union with God in which the soul leaves behind the perceptions of the senses and the reasoning of the intellect; also *transf.*, a way of denial; so *via affirmativa*, the approach to God through positive statements about his nature.

1856 R. A. Vaughan *Hours with Mystics* I. iv. ii. 124 These two paths, the *Via Negativa* (or Apophatica) and the *Via Affirmativa* (or Cataphatica) constitute the foundation of his [*sc.* Dionysius's] mysticism. **1899** W. R. Inge *Christian Mysticism* iii. 114 When Luther had the courage to break with ecclesiastical tradition, the *via negativa* rapidly disappeared within the sphere of his influence. **1942** [see *isness]. **1956** G. Macleod *Only One Way Left* viii. 152 The Via Negativa: the way of interior denial. Unfortunately the Via Negativa cuts dead across the Emmaus Road. **1963** J. A. T. Robinson *Honest to God* v. 95 The *via negativa* underlay the whole medieval 'way of perfection'. **1974** *Encycl. Brit. Macropædia* IV. 549/2 He [*sc.* the pseudo-Dionysius] recognizes the partial validity of the positive approach (*via affirmativa*). **1977** *Times Lit. Suppl.* 21 Jan. 88/5 As regards the Revolution, M Meyer's work is an exercise in the *via negativa.*

via, *prep.* Add: **1.** (Examples of the sense 'by way of' referring to a specific person or thing.

1856 C. M. Yonge *Daisy Chain* II. xxii. 589 Ethel's misanthropy was happily conducted off *via* the Cocksmoor children. **1899** Kipling *Stalky & Co.* 56 Beetle.. overturned a student's lamp, which dripped, *via* King's papers..on to a Persian rug. **1931** R. Fry *Let.* 3 Mar. (1972) II. 654, I was ever so glad to hear, via Helen, of you. **1958** A. Sillitoe *Saturday Night & Sunday Morning* iv. 60 Arthur and his father walked via the scullery into the living-room. **1959** M. Gilbert *Blood & Judgement* xiii. 138 More..had come to the Police via the Lower Deck of the Royal Navy. **1981** G. Household *Summon Bright Water* iii. 149 He led me to talk of my interest in ancient economies and thus, via agriculture in the Forest of Dean, eased the way to my impressions of Broom Lodge.

2. By means of, with the aid of.

1930 in *Amer. Speech* VI. 122 Eastbay youth admits thefts via fish pole. **1972** M. Kaye *Lively Game of Death* (1974) vii. 41 Any deal..would have to be..concluded via contracts, attorneys, the whole *schmeer.* **1977** *Rep. Comm. Future of Broadcasting* iv. 30 It would in theory be possible to provide five more services with national coverage via satellite.

viability[1]**.** Add: In *transf.* use: now *esp.* feasibility; ability to continue or be continued; the state of being financially sustainable. (Further examples.)

1955 *Bull. Atomic Sci.* Mar. 81/1 Considerations of defense, in addition to mobilizing offensive strength, do not in the least imply softness or lack of viability. **1962** *Listener* 11 Oct. 549/1 They are a main factor in giving it [*sc.* the country] such economic viability as it possesses. **1971** *Nature* 19 Feb. 518/2 Mr Stein's apparently innocent bill to limit noise at New York airports..could be..a serious threat to the viability of Concorde. **1977** K. M. E. Murray *Caught in Web of Words* viii. 150 He also had some doubts about the viability of the work financially.

viable, *a.*[1] Add: **c.** In recent use *esp.* workable, practicable, esp. economically or financially. (Further examples.)

1955 *Scottish Jrnl. Theol.* VIII. 93 A viable faith in the twentieth century must be able to take into itself a certain scepticism and relativism with regard to all rational systems. **1958** 'A. Burgess' *Enemy in Blanket* xv. 174 It was time he..planted the seeds of a viable relationship between his wife and himself. **1958** *Economist* 8 Nov. 485/2 The plans must..be such as to make the farm 'viable or more viable'—i.e. capable..of yielding its occupier at least the income of a skilled agricultural worker. **1962** *Listener* 5 Apr. 605/2 The Russian nuclear capacity appears..to be..not capable of destroying anything like enough of the American potential for a Russian first strike to be a viable proposition. **1962** P. Gradon in Davis & Wrenn *Eng. & Medieval Stud.* 66 This simple explanation..is not viable for another group of texts to which I now wish to turn. **1971** H. Macmillan *Riding the Storm* iv. 146 It [*sc.* Jordan] was not in economic terms a viable state without British support. **1977** M. Wiles in J. Hick *Myth of God Incarnate* i. 3 They do not of themselves prove that the concept of a 'Christianity without incarnation' is a viable concept.

viaducted (vai·ădɒktėd), *a.* [f. Viaduct + -ed[2].] Provided with a viaduct.

Quot. 1963 is pa. pple. of a finite verb *viaduct.*

1963 *Engineering* 18 Jan. 80 The dual carriageway will be viaducted to link up with existing roads. **1981** J. Pearson *Kindness of Dr. Avicenna* xviii. 171 The *autostrada*..a marvel of tunnelled mountains, viaducted gorges.

‖ **viale** (viā·le). Pl. **viali.** [It.] A broad street in an Italian city.

1969 M. Gilbert *Etruscan Net* I. vii. 88 Broke..drove up the Viale, using dipped headlights. **1979** G. Watson *Black Jack* xxviii. 236, I..walked over to the window looking on the broad *viale* below. **1982** J. O'Faolain *Obedient Wife* ii. 39 They'd hang around the warm squares and *viali* in groups.

vialled, *a.* (In Dict. s.v. Vial *sb.*) (Later example.)

1906 Hardy *Dynasts* II. v. i. 188 The riskful blood of my previsioned line..To linger vialled in my veins alone.

viander[1]**. 4.** (Earlier example.)

1761 *London Gaz.* 17–21 Jan. 2/1 The Vyanders and Principal Inhabitants of the Borough of Newport.

viatic, *a.* For † *Obs.*⁻¹ read: *Obs. rare* exc. for revived *nonce-uses.*

1974 V. Nabokov *Look at Harlequins* (1975) iv. i. 156 Look at that strange fever rash of viatic tabulation in which I persevered. **1976** —— *Details of Sunset* 74, I love the process of settling into viatic quarters—the cool linen of the berth, the slow passage of the station's departing lights.

viatical, *a.* (Earlier and later examples in *Bot.*)

1847 H. C. Watson *Cybele Britannica* I. 66 Viatical. Plants of road-sides, rubbish heaps, and frequented places. **1932** G. C. Druce *Comital Flora Brit. Isles* 349 *A[grostis] verticillata...* Viatical. Germanic, Waysides, waste places.

vibe (vəib), *sb.* **1.** *pl.* Abbrev. of *vibraphone. *colloq.*

1940 *Swing* July 17 Lastly, some too-formal ensemble riffing with vibes. **1957** L. Feather *Bk. Jazz* xvi. 134 Adrian Rollini, known earlier as a bass saxophonist, had been concentrating on vibes since the early 1930s. **1962** J. Wain *Strike Father Dead* v. 211 He could play just as well with a group led by an alto and including vibes, clarinet..or even flute. **1977** *Rolling Stone* 24 Mar., He fell back on his musical training to support the family, playing trumpet and vibes in a succession of third-rate cabaret bands.

2. Abbrev. of *vibration 3 d. Usu. *pl. slang.*

1967 *Sunday Times* 1 Oct. 10 We're not getting the right vibes. **1970** J. Lennon in J. Wenner *Lennon Remembrance* (1973) 67 'You give off bad vibes.' That's what George said to her [*sc.* Yoko Ono] and we both sat through it, and I didn't hit him, I don't know why. **1972** *Daily Tel.* (Colour Suppl.) 1 Dec. 56/1 As I arrive they have finished rehearsing *Hair* in the lobby [of the Chateau Marmont, Los Angeles]... Will this diminish the place's vibes? **1976** *New Mus. Express* 31 July 16/1, I remember when I first saw The Grateful Dead... I didn't like them much but I felt that same vibe—something is happening. **1981** P. Carey *Bliss* iv. 151 Always give out a good vibe, never let them think you hate them. **1983** E. Rossiter *Lemon Garden* vi. 96 The damned thing's got bad vibes... Throw it in the lake.

Hence **vi·bist,** a player on the vibraphone.

1955 *Jazzbook 1955* 20 The musicianly sounds produced by vibist Milt Jackson and pianist Thelonius Mark. **1962** *Melody Maker* 21 July 7/1 The vibist's phrasing shows his early Gospel penchant. **1977** *Listener* 23 June 829/2 Drummer/vibist Cal Tjader.

vibraharp (vəi·brăhāɹp). [f. Harp *sb.*[1], after *vibraphone.] A vibraphone; orig., a proprietary name for a particular U.S. make of vibraphone.

1930 *Official Gaz.* (U.S. Patent Office) 15 Apr. 545/1 J. C. Deagan, Inc., Chicago, Ill. Filed Jan. 22, 1930. *Vibra-harp...* Claims use since Aug. 1, 1928. **1949** L. Feather *Inside Be-Bop* III. 88 Milton Jackson, vibraharp; b. Detroit, 1923. **1959** [see *electric guitar* s.v. *electric *a.* 2 b]. **1968** *Jazz Monthly* Jan. 25/2 The programme too is attractively old-fashioned..and the accompaniment, on most tracks by guitar, clarinet, vibraharp, organ and drums, discreet and musicianly. **1977** *Melody Maker* 26 Mar. 34/1 The history of the vibraphone (or vibraharp, as it's sometimes called) in jazz has been strictly delineated by its most famous exponents.

Hence **vi·braharpist,** a player on the vibraharp.

1943 *Metronome* Oct. 32/1 Darned if I can remember hearing ten vibraharpists in my life! **1966** *Melody Maker* 29 Jan. 8/6 Ayers is a vibraharpist. **1978** *Country Life* 5 Oct. 1003/3 Milt Jackson..the great vibraharpist.

Vibram (vəi·brăm). Also **vibram.** The proprietary name of a kind of moulded rubber sole used on climbing boots; also applied to a boot having this sole; so **Vibram-soled** adj. Also *absol.*

1950 tr. *Mountaineering Handbk.* (Assoc. Brit. Members Swiss Alpine Club) ii. 22 Later experience shows that boots with moulded rubber soles—'Vibrams'—are an advantage on rock climbs but are dangerous on greasy or iced rock. **1957** Clark & Pyatt *Mountaineering in Britain* xvi. 237 Vibrams, boots whose soles consisted of rubber moulded into the shape of conventional nails, were just becoming available in Britain when war broke out. **1963** 'G. Carr' *Lewker in Norway* iv. 76 The climbing breeches, thick stockings, and Vibram-soled boots he would wear. **1976** *Trade Marks Jrnl.* 24 Nov. 2470/1 *Vibram...* Soles, heels, heel-tips, cork-soles and intersoles for shoes. Vibram S.p.A..., Albizzate, Italy; manufacturers and merchants. **1979** C. McNeish *Youth Hostelling* ii. 15 I'm sure you can visualise the effect a hundred pairs of vibram-soles a day can have on a lino floor.

vibrant, *ppl. a.* Add: Hence **vi·brantly** *adv.*

1926 *Record Home & Mission Wk. United Free Church of Scotland* July 316/1 The Christian Church should make its protest vibrantly felt. **1976** *Gramophone* Mar. 1481/1 The warm, vibrantly sympathetic recording acoustic makes no little contribution.

vibraphone (vəi·brăfōᵘn). *Mus.* [f. Vibra(tion, Vibra(to, etc. + *-phone 1.] A percussion instrument consisting of a series of metal bars, arranged as in a xylophone, and characterized by the vibrato that can be given to the notes, an effect produced either by electrically rotated vanes in tube resonators under the bars or electronically.

1926 [see *marimbaphone]. **1929** *Melody Maker* Apr. 359/1 Lester takes a Vibraphone solo. **1934** S. R. Nelson *All about Jazz* ii. 51 The leading drummers..are expert on the xylophone and vibraphone. **1957** L. Feather *Bk. Jazz* xvi. 134 The vibraphone, like the xylophone, was an instrument long associated with novelty music. **1966** *Listener* 10 Mar. 364 The programme was completed by Stockhausen's *Refrain*, for piano, celesta, and vibraphone. **1978** P. Griffiths *Conc. Hist. Mod. Music* ix. 137 The vibraphone is used as a substitute for the gamelan while xylorimba and percussion suggest the influence of black African music.

Hence **vi·braphonist,** a player on the vibraphone.

1929 *Melody Maker* Dec. 1119/1 Amateur vibraphonists are requested not to attempt to copy it! **1978** *Detroit Free Press* 16 Apr. (Detroit Suppl.) 29/2 How else could he have known that Milt Jackson would become one of the world's greatest vibraphonists.

vibrated, *ppl. a.* Add: *spec.* Designating or pertaining to concrete which is being or has been compacted with a vibrator (*vibrator 1 b (*a*).

1930 *Concrete & Constructional Engin.* XXV. 686/1 The vibrated concrete acts like a liquid and the vibrator rises automatically. **1948** *Archit. Rev.* CIII. 148 The roof-covering is of pre-cast vibrated concrete slabs. **1976** *Derbyshire Times* (Peak ed.) 3 Sept. 10/6 (Advt.), Paving slabs... Remanufactured top quality vibrated plain and coloured paving in a range of sizes.

vibration. Add: **3. d.** Now, an intuitive signal about a person or thing; (*pl.*) atmosphere. Usu. *pl.*

In some instances more or less identical with the *fig.* use of sense 3 b.

1899 O. Wilde *Importance of being Earnest* I. 28 There is very little music in the name Jack, if any at all, indeed. It does not thrill. It produces absolutely no vibrations. **1901** *Chambers's Jrnl.* Apr. 263/1 There is a man in Denver, Thomas J. Shelton who is said to be making his £10,000 a year by selling what he calls 'vibrations'... Mr Shelton's 'vibrations'..he himself explains as being a special force of his inner consciousness, which can be sent through space to purchasers by his mere act of will; and claims for the 'vibrations' so sent a subtle power capable of influencing a man in any direction that may be desired. **1919** CONRAD *Arrow of Gold* IV. ii. 157 The Blunt atmosphere, the reinforced Blunt vibration stealing through the walls... Nothing to me, of course—the movements of Mme. Blunt, *mère*. *Ibid.* 164, I listened deferentially to the end yet with every nerve in my body tingling in hostile response to the Blunt vibration, which seemed to have got into my very hair. **1922** JOYCE *Ulysses* 497 You can rub shoulders with a Jesus, a Gautama, an Ingersoll. Are you all in this vibration? **1934** M. ALLINGHAM *Death of Ghost* i. 23 Other people's pictures in *his* studio—it's sacrilege, isn't it? The vibrations won't be right. **1956** R. M. LESTER *Towards Hereafter* ii. 36 When I had a sitting with a medium who was obviously on the same vibration as myself the results were first-class. **1957** J. KEROUAC *On Road* II. vi. 146 Something curiously unsympathetic and cold between them was really a form of humor by which they communicated their own set of subtle vibrations. **1968** T. WOLFE *Electric Kool-Aid Acid Test* ii. 20 Something's getting up tight, there's bad vibrations. **1971** J. MANDELKAU *Buttons* v. 62 William showed me upstairs to what was going to be my 'home' for the next few weeks and let me wander around the house bumping into people and picking up on the vibrations. **1977** MILLER & SWIFT *Words & Women* i. 4 Names do seem to give off vibrations of a sort. **1979** N. MAILER *Executioner's Song* II. ii. 525 Stupor on top of old woe was the sad vibration Dennis was getting from Maximum.

7. Comb. *vibration-proof* adj.; **vibration damper** = *DAMPER 4 c; *spec.* a device for counteracting torsional vibration in a crankshaft.

1932 *Motoring Encycl.* 183/1 Special forms of frictional clutch on the front end of the crankshaft to reduce engine vibration are dealt with under the heading Vibration Damper. **1936** *Gloss. Terms Electr. Engin.* (*B.S.I.*) 87 *Vibration-damper*, of an overhead line. A device attached to a conductor, and designed to suppress vibrations caused by the action of wind. **1952** *Chambers's Jrnl.* Jan. 64/1 Most of the risk of deterioration can be eliminated by using vibration-dampers under machinery. **1961** [see *DAMPER 4 c]. **1968** R. H. BACON *Car* v. 66 (*caption*) Crankshaft torsional vibration damper, fan belt pulley and camshaft drive. **1917** C. C. TURNER *Aircraft of To-Day* vii. 114 The compass..must be carried in a vibration-proof bed.

vibrational, *a.* Add: **c.** *Physics.* Involving or resulting from particular modes of vibration or oscillation of the atoms in a molecule.

1923 [see *isotope effect* s.v. *ISOTOPE 2]. **1946** *Nature* 26 Oct. 593/2 From an analysis of a suitable vibrational spectrum, it is usually possible to trace the vibrational-levels in the ground-state from $V=0$ to $V=c.$ 20. **1970** I. E. MCCARTHY *Nuclear Reactions* I. v. 109 The nuclear probability amplitude for the excitation of vibrational states is obtained from the quantum theory of harmonic vibrations. **1973** C. SAGAN *Cosmic Connection* iv. 27 There are vibrational transitions that occur when two atoms in a given molecule oscillate with respect to each other.

vibra·tionally, *adv.* [f. VIBRATIONAL *a.* + -LY[2].] By vibration; as regards vibrational motion.

1961 *New Scientist* 16 Mar. 687/1 Vibrationally assisted forming results in more uniform deformation [of metals]. **1964** [see *de-excite* vb. s.v. *DE-EXCITATION]. **1974** *Nature* 30 Aug. 714/1 The object may be a very massive star.. which is vibrationally unstable. **1979** *Sci. Amer.* May 104/2 The advent of the laser would seem to be a chemist's dream come true, enabling him in principle to selectively excite reactants—electronically, vibrationally or rotationally, as he wishes.

vibrationless, *a.* (Further examples.)

1925 *Motor* 15 Dec. (Advt. Suppl.) 44, Ansaldo. The beautiful Italian car... Vibrationless. Silent. Fast. **1964** W. L. GOODMAN *Hist. Woodworking Tools* 157 To make for quicker and vibrationless cutting, the flat gullets vary in size in groups of three or four. **1982** *Sci. Amer.* Nov. 9 (Advt.), The instrument must be of rugged construction and vibrationless, without the aggravating oscillations of long-tubed conventional telescopes.

vibra·toless, *a.* [-LESS.] Without vibrato.

1975 *Daily Tel.* 12 Aug. 9/7 The pure vibrato-less style of Munrow's singers took on a piercing beauty. **1983** *N.Y. Times* 19 Dec. C13/1 The soloists for the Bach.. sang in an even-toned, vibratoless style.

vibrator. Add: **1. b.** *spec.* (*a*) A device for compacting concrete by vibration before it has set. (*b*) A small electrically operated device for producing sexual stimulation.

1930 [see *VIBRATED *ppl. a.*]. **1950** *Archit. Rev.* CVII. 331/3 When vibration was first introduced the lack of proper equipment prevented its use except on very large contracts, but many types of vibrator are now on the market. **1981** MINDESS & YOUNG *Concrete* x. 289 External vibrators can be clamped to formwork, when the proper use of internal vibrators is not possible.

1953 A. C. KINSEY et al. *Sexual Behaviour in Human Female* v. 163 Douches, streams of running water, vibrators,..and still other methods were occasionally employed [in masturbation]. **1970** in G. Greer *Female Eunuch* 217 As vibrators have been mentioned, may I add that it need not be the penis-shaped battery model. **1979** *Brit. Med. Jrnl.* 13 Oct. 883/2 In a study in which patients used a vibrator to achieve orgasm, all the major tranquillisers were said to interfere with ejaculation. **1983** CAUTHERY & STANWAY *Compl. Bk. Love & Sex* xxxii. 386 The biggest-selling sex aid by far is the vibrator.

vibrio. 2. (Earlier examples.)

1850 *Proc. Acad. Nat. Sci. Philadelphia* IV. 228 With them were also found two species of Vibrio. *Ibid.*, Much higher confervæ..are endowed with inherent power of movement, not very unlike that of the Vibrio.

vibriocidal (vibriō^u^səi·dăl), *a. Med.* [f. VIBRIO + -CIDE + -AL.] Destructive to vibrios.

1962 *Jrnl. Immunol.* LXXXIX. 265/1 Complement is required for the vibriocidal effect. **1978** *Nature* 14 Dec. 709/1 Table 1 indicates a good correlation between protection to challenge and vibriocidal antibodies in the serum.

vibrionic, *a.* (Earlier example.)

1850 *Proc. Acad. Nat. Sci. Philadelphia* IV. 235 All the innumerable objects of living nature..from the vibrionic filament to the noble oak..are the result of a force in connection with an amorphous vesicle, the organic cell-wall, with the contained nucleus.

vibriosis (vibri͵ō^u^·sis). *Vet. Sci.* [f. VIBRIO + -OSIS.] Infection with, or a disease caused by, vibrios.

1951 W. N. PLASTRIDGE in *Univ. Pennsylvania Veterinary Extension Q.* 3 Apr. 62 Improved methods of diagnosis and the increase of brucellosis-free herds account for the present increase in the interest in vibriosis. **1951** —— et al. in *Jrnl. Amer. Veterinary Med. Assoc.* June 367 In consideration of the several clinical manifestations of *V. fetus* infection and the probable existence of infection ..in some animals in the absence of clinical evidence, the term 'vibriosis' is proposed to indicate *V. fetus* infection. **1960** R. A. RUNNELLS et al. *Princ. Veterinary Path.* xix. 560/2 In Western Australia vibriosis is reported to be the immediate cause of at least 75 per cent of the infertility in dairy cows. **1980** *Nature* 10 Apr. 566/2 Epizootics of the widespread fish disease vibriosis.

vibro-. Add: **vi·bro-massage,** massage with a special vibrator; **vibrota·ctile** *a.*, of, pertaining to, or involving the perception of vibration through touch.

1923 *Daily Mail* 10 Aug. 5/2 The owner-experts get their features in knots..and may be seen going off for vibro-massages in the evening. **1968** *Listener* 11 July 45/3 People who see nothing either comic or disturbing about our export eastwards of..vibro-massage, canned TV, [etc.]. [**1934** tr. R. H. Gault in *L'Année Psychologique* XXXIV. 2 Le sens tactile (ou comme je préfère.. dire, les 'sens vibro-tactiles').] **1934** R. H. GAULT in *Jrnl. Acoustical Soc. Amer.* V. 253/2 We may legitimately describe the results of our vibro-tactile experiments as evidences of hearing, even though we are assured that the ear is not involved. **1980** *Pflügers Arch. European Jrnl. Physiol.* CCCLXXXIV. 170/1 Vibrotactile stimuli above the tuning threshold of the nerve fibers can elicit a continuous afferent impulse volley without adaptation during some seconds.

vibrograph. (In Dict. s.v. VIBRO-.) Add: *spec.* An instrument for measuring or recording mechanical vibrations.

1904 [in Dict.]. **1946** [see *ACCELEROMETER]. **1965** *Economist* 25 Dec. 1434/1 It took them some time to work out the best way of getting the job done without causing too much damaging vibration in the [Abu Simbel] temples—vibrographs were installed to check that the danger level was not exceeded. **1970** *Soviet Jrnl. Optical Technol.* XXXVII. 456 A method is given..for the calculation of the amplitude-frequency and phase-frequency characteristics of a vibrograph for recording small angular vibrations.

Hence **vi·brogram,** a record produced by a vibrograph.

1932 *Jrnl. R. Aeronaut. Soc.* XXXVI. 209 Vibrograms were obtained showing the vibration of different parts of the fuselage at various frequencies. **1950** *Engineering* 21 Apr. 431/2 The principal parameters of a vibrogram from which its effect on a building can be estimated are the maximum amplitude and the average frequency of the vibration. **1975** *Soviet Appl. Mech.* XI. 445 (*heading*) Damping determination according to vibrograms of random oscillations in linear systems.

vibronic (vəibrǫ·nik), *a. Physics.* [f. VIBR(ATIONAL *a.* + *ELECTR)ONIC *a.*] Of or pertaining to electronic energy levels or transitions associated with the vibration of the constituent atoms of a molecule.

1941 R. S. MULLIKEN in *Physical Rev.* LIX. 880/2 The vibronic wave function ψ_{ev} is a function of the electronic and vibrational coordinates. **1966** G. HERZBERG *Molecular Spectra & Molecular Structure* i. 22 For half-integral spin we have two-valued vibronic species. **1976** *Nature* 22 Apr. 675/1 No vibronic structure has been detected in the absorption spectrum of the chromophore of rhodopsin.

Hence **vibro·nically** *adv.*

1966 D. H. WHIFFEN *Spectroscopy* xii. 160 Transitions which are permitted solely on this account are called vibronic transitions or may be said to be vibronically allowed. **1978** *Nature* 19 Jan. 236/2 The results indicate that the afterglow is due to an emission to S_0 of the monomer or to a vibronically similar ground state.

Vic[1] (vik), colloq. abbrev. of VICTORIA[2], used to denote the Royal Victoria Theatre, London (popularly known as the *Old Vic*).

1858 G. A. SALA *Twice round Clock* (1859) 269 There is a transpontine theatre, situated laterally towards the Waterloo Road... This is the Royal Victoria Theatre... It is popularly termed the 'Vic'. **1888** KIPLING *Soldiers Three* (1890) 55 'Ave you ever bin in the Pit hentrance o' the Vic. on a thick night? **1915** *Times* 3 Oct. 11/5 At the Royal Victoria Hall ('the Old Vic').. a Shakesperian season opened last night. **1951** *Oxf. Compan. Theatre* 582/1 In 1833 it [*sc.* the Coburg Theatre] was renamed the Victoria, from the fact that Princess (later Queen) Victoria visited it once. It soon became affectionately known as the Old Vic. **1972** W. GARNER *Ditto, Brother Rat!* iv. 32 The Vic bars get pretty hectic, especially with only one interval. **1976** *Vogue* 15 Mar. 15/3 So goodbye Old Vic, tiptoeing off into the wings of theatrical history.

vic[2] (vik). Used for *v* in telephone communications and in the oral transliteration of code messages. Hence also in *Mil.* use, a V-formation of aircraft.

1913 [see *PIP *sb.*[4]]. **1927** W. E. COLLINSON *Contemp. Eng.* 98 Other artillery terms which spread were..vick for V, also ack emma for a.m. [etc.]. **1940** *Flight* 28 Mar. 295 Spitfires staged some plain and fancy beat-ups..in formation (excellent vic and echelon). **1942** I. GLEED *Arise to Conquer* 12 We flew back as a squadron, four sections in vic. **1952** M. TRIPP *Faith is Windsock* iv. 61 The Squadron was leading today's raid, and E-Easy.. led the Squadron. To port and slightly behind Easy's vic was C-Charlie, also with a vic.

vicar. Add: **2. a.** Now also in the Church of England a priest who is a member (team vicar) of a team ministry (*TEAM *sb.* 11) under the leadership of a team rector.

1972 *Daily Tel.* 7 Aug. 10/5 Only the leader of the team, usually called 'Rector', is the beneficed freeholder incumbent inducted by the bishop. His colleagues ('vicars') are licensed by the bishop as members of the team. **1977** [see *RECTOR 3 a]. **1984** *Church Times* 27 Jan. 17/1 (Advt.), Vicar required... N. Birmingham Team Ministry, modern vicarage.

4. c. *vicar apostolical.*

1731 in O. Blundell *Catholic Highlands Scotland* (1917) II. 99 His Holiness..appoints him also Vicar Apostolical with singular powers. **1847** J. A. MANNING *Pius XI* I. 168 Differences broke out between the Vicar Apostolical and the Chilian government. **1849** [in Dict.].

vicarage. Add: **6. vicarage tea-party,** used as the type of something mild, innocuous, and uneventful.

1973 *Times* 11 Apr. 1/2 Mr Heath's appearances in the Commons are never vicarage tea parties. **1984** *Daily Tel.* 31 Jan. 12/5 He surveyed the smoking ruins of..a fine old Elizabethan rectory,..and said: 'It makes the Dissolution of the Monasteries look like a vicarage tea-party.' **1984** *Guardian* 6 June 10 Politicians..who fear that events are about to take a nasty turn, frequently say that what they are predicting will make D-Day (or the ravages of Genghis Khan..—every speaker will have his own comparison) look like a vicarage tea party.

vicariad (vikē^ə^·ri͵æd). *Ecol.* [f. as next + -AD.] = *VICARIANT *sb.*

1944 S. A. CAIN *Found. Plant Geogr.* xviii. 266 Most of the studies of vicariads have referred to species. **1960** N. POLUNIN *Introd. Plant Geogr.* vii. 202 True vicariads (which have arisen from a common stock) should be distinguished from false ones which have not this close genetic relationship... True vicariads..may be classified according to the manner of their separation from one another into (1) horizontal (geographical), (2) altitudinal (physiographic), (3) habitat (ecological), and (4) seasonal (..closely related forms differing in their times of development). **1972** D. M. MOORE in D. H. Valentine *Taxonomy, Phytogeogr. & Evolution* viii. 119 The aquatic *Littorella*, absent from North America, is effectively an amphitropical vicariad and certainly results from a much more recent migration.

vicariant (vikē^ə^·riănt), *sb.* and *a. Ecol.* [f. L. *vicāri-us* substitute (see VICAR) + -ANT[1], tr. G. *vic-*, *vikarirend*, pres. pple. of *vikarieren* (now *vikariieren*) † to substitute for: cf. *vic-*, *vikarirend spezies* in F. Unger *Ueber den Einfluss des Bodens auf die Vertheilung der Gewächse* (1836) III. 92; M. Wagner *Die Darwin'sche Theorie* (1868) in *Die Entstehung der Arten durch räumliche Sonderung* (1889) 56.] **A.** *sb.* A vicariant form of a plant or animal.

1952 L. CROIZAT *Man. Phytogeogr.* iv. 224 Cruciferae and Capparidaceae..could bear being characterized as vicariants. **1957** P. DANSEREAU *Biogeogr.* ii. 104 On the Nimba mountains of West Africa, Schell..has cited many mountain vicariants in genera of both rain-forest..and savana. **1979** CARDONA & CONTANDRIOPOULOS in D. Bramwell *Plants & Islands* viii. 155 In the *Genista acanthoclada* DC. group..the following subspecies are vicariants: *G. acanthoclada* ssp. *acanthoclada* (Greece and Aegean Islands), ssp. *echinus* (Spach) Vals. (S. Anatolia), [etc.].

B. *adj.* Being or involving varieties, species, communities, or the like that have evolved out of effective contact with one another from a common ancestral stock, esp. in habitats that are similar though separated.

1952 L. CROIZAT *Man. Phytogeogr.* vi. 355 This form in the end will split up into..vicariant species. **1957** P. DANSEREAU *Biogeogr.* i. 22 Vicariant varieties, subspecies, species, and genera may differ not only in leaf shape..but also in habitat requirements. **1957** A. MACFADYEN *Animal Ecol.* i. 8 The practical advantages include the possibility of using certain 'vicariant' species as 'indicator organisms'..for the detection..of certain types of habitat. **1972** D. BRAMWELL in D. H. Valentine

Taxonomy, Phytogeogr. & Evolution ix. 153 A high degree of vicariant evolution is to be expected in an archipelago such as the Canaries where..sets of ecological conditions are replicated from east to west on a series of islands with similar vegetation zones. **1982** *Sci. Amer.* July 33/2 Whether they are vicariant species, with common parents but evolved in place, or whether they first became distinct and then spread is unclear.

Hence **vica·riance**, the existence of vicariant forms; the separation or subdivision of a population by the appearance of a geographical barrier and subsequent differentiation.

1957 A. MACFADYEN *Animal Ecol.* xv. 223 It is also possible to use other criteria..such as frequency, dominance or even 'vicariance'. **1972** D. BRAMWELL in D. H. Valentine *Taxonomy, Phytogeogr. & Evolution* ix. 151 Adaptive radiation..is a positive process where genetical response to the stimulus of the environment is the main factor; but vicariance, that is divergent evolution in which geographical isolation has been a very important factor, is perhaps a more passive process where the interaction of genetic drift and weak selection result in the establishment of distinctive characters in populations which occupy essentially similar ecological habitats to their parents. **1979** *Nature* 15 Feb. 562/1 It is possible that the presence of hadrosaurs in Laurasia and Gondwanaland represents vicariance rather than dispersal; if so, hadrosaurs would be expected to occur on most continents. **1981** NELSON & PLATNICK *Systematics & Biogeogr.* i. 45 Speciation, at least in animals, usually involves a process of geographic isolation.., and occurs when a formerly continuous population is divided by the appearance of a barrier (a process called vicariance).

vicariism (vikē·ri,iz'm). *Ecol.* Also **vicarism.** [f. as *VICARIANT *sb.* and *a.* + -ISM, or ad. G. *vikarismus*.] = *vicariance* s.v. *VICARIANT *sb.* and *a.*

1939 *Bull. Misc. Information* (R. Botanic Gardens, Kew) v. 229 Vicarious species are particularly instructive to study. These are species inhabiting contiguous but not (or scarcely) overlapping areas. Vicarism may be altitudinal or geographical. **1944** S. A. CAIN *Found. Plant Geogr.* xviii. 265 The concept of vicariism is equally applicable to other than the specific category, i.e., to subspecies, sections, etc., and to communities. **1953** R. GOOD *Geogr. Flowering Plants* (ed. 2) xi. 212 Another particular kind of vicariism, which may be described as climatic, is illustrated..by the two littoral species *Ipomoea pes-caprae* and *Calystegia soldanella*. The former is almost or quite pan-tropical, but the latter is more or less pan-temperate and the two meet at the Kermadecs and elsewhere in similar latitudes. **1969** M. D. F. UDVARDY *Dynamic Zoogeogr.* iv. 192 The concept of vicarism is used widely..when comparing certain types of distributional areas. **1974** *Boissiera* XXIII. 296 The distribution patterns of the different chromosome races agree with certain main types of false vicariism.

vicarious, *a.* Add: **4. d.** Experienced imaginatively through another person or agency.

1929 R. S. & H. M. LYND *Middletown* xvii. 237 To Middletown adults, reading a book means overwhelmingly what story-telling means to primitive man—the vicarious entry into other, imagined kinds of living. **1948** E. WAUGH *Loved One* 31 He had lived his twenty-eight years at arm's length from violence, but he came of a generation which enjoys a vicarious intimacy with death. **1976** A. POWELL *Infants of Spring* ix. 146 My father, between spasms of grumbling about school bills, and occasional resistance to attitudes of mind inevitably acquired at Eton, had taken a fair amount of vicarious pleasure in my being there.

6. *Ecol.* Of two or more species, etc.: similar to one another and occurring without the other(s) in different areas; usu., = *VICARIANT *a.*

1932 FULLER & CONARD tr. *Braun-Blanquet's Plant Sociol.* vi. 160 Closely related species found upon lime and clay slates he [*sc.* Unger] called substitute or vicarious species. **1937** R. HESSE et al. *Ecol. Animal Geogr.* vi. 77 Transitional variation may be wanting at the boundary between the ranges of vicarious forms which are then considered specifically distinct. **1960** N. POLUNIN *Introd. Plant Geogr.* vii. 201 With higher groupings—and even families and whole communities may in a sense be vicarious—there is less reason to suppose that their mutual exclusiveness is due to competition. **1981** P. STOTT *Hist. Plant Geogr.* viii. 115 Vicarious evolution has been invoked..to explain the distribution [in the Canaries] of endemic species in *Centaurea* sect. *Cheirolophus* subsect. *Flaviflorae*.

vicariously, *adv.* Add: **3.** At second hand, at one remove. Cf. *VICARIOUS *a.* 4 d.

1925 F. SCOTT FITZGERALD *Gt. Gatsby* vii. 157 Jordan and I tried to go, but Tom and Gatsby insisted..that we remain—as though..it would be a privilege to partake vicariously of their emotions. **1957** L. DURRELL *Justine* II. 127 Those interminable monologues about a life which has long since receded, lost its vital momentum, only to live on vicariously in the labyrinths of memory. **1984** *N.Y. Times* 13 May VI. 70/2, I think the greatest moral pitfall is not that we witness too much bang bang, but that, for the most part, we perceive it vicariously.

vi·carish, *a.* [f. VICAR + -ISH[1].] Suitable for or characteristic of a vicar.

1938 *Times Lit. Suppl.* 26 Oct. 734/2 Two maids..an amiable vicar and his very vicarish wife and a certain Captain Carling complete the party. **1976** *New Society* 29 Jan. 206/3, I was also subject to frequent visits by vicars, who popped their heads round my door in a vicarish manner every so often. **1979** K. M. PEYTON *Marion's Angels* i. 2 'It doesn't *belong* to her,' they said. 'It belongs to God, and so does Marion.' A typical, vicarish remark, they said.

Vicat (vī·kā). *Engin.* The name of L. J. *Vicat* (1786–1861), French engineer, used *attrib.* with reference to an apparatus for measuring the consistency and setting time of Portland cement and other materials.

1904 C. F. MARSH *Reinforced Concrete* iii. 125 For this test the Vicat needle apparatus may be employed. **1910** *Brit. Standard Spec. for Portland Cement* (Engin. Standards Comm.) 10 The mixture shall be plastic when filled into the Vicat mould. **1956** J. N. ANDERSON *Appl. Dental Materials* xviii. 211 An alternative method of testing for initial set [of plaster] is to use the Vicat needle. **1979** I. SOROKA *Portland Cement Paste & Concrete* ii. 29 (*caption*) Vicat apparatus for determining the standard consistence and setting times of Portland cement.

vice, *sb.*[1] Add: **1. c.** *ellipt.* for *vice squad*, sense 8 b below. *slang.*

1967 C. DRUMMOND *Death at Furlong Post* iv. 42 From his days on Vice Reed remembered the large free-spenders. **1976** *New Society* 4 Mar. 481/2 A woman they know is a junkie... She proceeds to tell them how she got picked up by the 'vice' the night before.

8. a. Also *spec.* with reference to certain crimes, esp. organized prostitution, as *vice den, racket, trade*, etc. orig. *U.S.*

1903 *McClure's Mag.* Nov. 89 In New York, Croker has failed signally to maintain vice-bosses whom he appointed. **1915** *Sci. Amer.* 30 Jan. 98/3 The Puritan conception of life, like that of vice-crusaders, suffragettes, and most crusaders, scorns all trifling with its weighty realities. **1937** Vice society [see *strip-teasing* vbl. sb. s.v. *STRIP-TEASE]. **1938** F. D. SHARPE *Sharpe of Flying Squad* vii. 78 Lots of the other men in the vice racket..were pulled in and interviewed. **1952** *Manch. Guardian Weekly* 8 May 3 The relations of one of these with a Chicago vice-syndicate may be merely an unfair reflection on Governor Warren. **1962** *Spectator* 6 July 12/2 The vicelands of Notting Hill. **1971** *It* 2–16 June 1/1 (*heading*) Vice girls of Princedale Road—the shocking truth! **1975** J. GORES *Hammett* (1976) v. 37 In a vice raid..police..trailed a group of three boys..to the house of prostitution..and jailed the inmates of the..vice-den. **1976** *Billings* (Montana) *Gaz.* 30 June 4-A/1 Suppose that you..prevented vice officers from arresting a drug suspect. **1981** P. O'DONNELL *Xanadu Talisman* v. 100 His wife was..sold into the vice trade.

b. Special Comb.: **vice ring**, a group of people criminally involved in organized prostitution; **vice squad** [*SQUAD *sb.*[1] 4 c] orig. *U.S.*, a police unit concerned with the enforcement of laws relating to prostitution, drug abuse, illegal gambling, etc.

1938 F. D. SHARPE *Sharpe of Flying Squad* xi. 125, I don't think..they were..connected with any vice ring. **1981** C. SCOTT *Heavenly Witch* vi. 80 Men in charge of vice rings spread rumours that the converts were paid to testify. **1905** *N.Y. Times* 22 June 8/6 Six of Capt. Cottrell's Tenderloin detectives will report to Capt. Egger this noon for duty on the Vice Squad. **1939** *Daily Tel.* 18 Dec. 8/4 Scotland Yard's vice squad..has been instructed to give special attention to small clubs opened in Soho since the outbreak of war. **1978** L. HEREN *Growing up on The Times* v. 167 The vice squad might have had a beady eye on me, but I was glad to hold his hand.

vice, *sb.*[7] Add: Also prefixed by *Mr.* as a form of address to a vice-chairman or vice-president.

1894 G. DU MAURIER *Trilby* II. 102 A table..at one end of which sits Mr. Chairman..and at the other 'Mr. Vice'. **1916** M. DIVER *Desmond's Daughter* II. iii. 61 The President at the far end of the table had lifted his glass. 'Mr Vice—the Queen,' said he. **1976** T. JEAL *Until Colours Fade* xxxvii. 325 The president of the mess rose..and brought down his silver mallet. 'Mr Vice, the Queen,' that officer said, addressing the vice-president at the opposite end of the table.

vice-. Add: **a.** *vice-chief of staff, -editor, -lieutenant* (later example), *-minister.*

1943 W. S. CHURCHILL *End of Beginning* 69 The Chiefs of Staff Committee are assisted by a Vice-Chiefs of Staff Committee. **1978** R. V. JONES *Most Secret War* xlv. 458 The Vice-Chiefs of Staff..advised that the threat was over. **1976** *National Observer* (U.S.) 12 June 22/2 A fellow with the title of vice editor. **1963** *Times* 4 June 13/5 His native county of Lincolnshire, of which he was Vice-Lieutenant for many years. **1909** E. M. SATOW in *Cambr. Mod. Hist.* XI. xxviii. 865 Ōki of Hizen, and Itō, Inouyé and Yamagata of Chōshiu were retained as vice-Ministers. **1976** *Eastern Daily Press* (Norwich) 19 Nov. 1/5 The agreement was signed by Iran's vice-minister of war.

b. *vice-chair* (earlier example).

1839 DICKENS *Nickelby* xlviii. 475 A farewell-supper..at which Mr. Snittle Timberry would preside, while the honours of the vice chair would be sustained by the African [Sword-]Swallower.

c. *vice-preside* vb.

1889 G. B. SHAW *London Music in 1888–89* (1937) 94 You are patronized by the Lord Mayor, presided over by the Duke of Westminster, and vice-presided over and councilled by nearly five dozen illustrious persons.

‖ **vice anglais** (vīs aṅglę). [Fr., lit. 'English vice' (VICE *sb*[1].).] The vice to which the English are said to be particularly prone (esp. with reference to corporal punishment).

1942 [see *SELF-MEDICATION]. **1947** *Horizon* Nov. 269 No novelist in the last decade of the century could create a character who practised *le vice anglais* without attributing to him some of Swinburne's physical characteristics. **1950** E. H. W. MEYERSTEIN *Let.* 6 Jan. (1959) 369 You must remember that it is much more important socially for a boy to play for his public school in cricket..than to win a prize... It is a very queer trait and a modern psychologist might quite possibly link it up with sadism ('le vice Anglais'), success consisting in *hitting* something, though that 'something' be no more than a ball. **1962** *Times* 21 July 4/5 *Whack-O!*—a programme whose long life testifies, if nothing else, to the continued popularity of *le vice anglais.* **1976** F. MUIR *Frank Muir Book* 73 Flogging in public schools..has been given as the reason for so many..English gentlemen enjoying a little corporal punishment later in life, 'le vice Anglais'. **1983** *Daily Tel.* 5 Aug. 12/1 The true *vice anglais* is the hatred felt by a sub-section of the middle class for their own country and their desire to humiliate her.

vi·ce-champion. [f. VICE- + CHAMPION *sb.*[1] 4.] The runner-up in a sporting contest.

1981 *N.Y. Times* 5 July v. 7/1 Only 251 fans showed up..to see Sao Paulo, the vice champion of Brazilian professional teams, play in that city of eight million people. **1984** *Soviet Union* IX. 53 The men's team, vice-champion of Europe, has twice beaten the world champion Pakistan team.

vice-like, *a.*[2] (Earlier example.)

1835 E. A. POE in *Southern Lit. Messenger* June 570/1 Clutching with a vice-like grip the long-desired rim.

vice-president. Add: **vice-presidency, -presidential** (earlier examples).

1804 *Guardian of Freedom* (Frankfort, Kentucky) 28 July 2/3 He is charged with having been long intriguing for the vice presidency. **1854** T. H. BENTON 30 *Years' View* I. 45/1 Mr. Calhoun was the only substantive vice-presidential candidate before the people. **1884** G. W. CABLE *Dr. Sevier* xlvi. 341 With a presidential candidate on one side and his vice-presidential man Friday on the other.

viceregal, *a.* (Earlier example.)

1836 DISRAELI *Lett. of Runnymede* x. 86 Ascending at last even to the Viceregal throne of India.

vice-regent. Add: Hence **vice-re·gency.**

1930 BELLOC *Wolsey* ix. 243 He drafted a form of Vice-regency, a delegation of Papal power to himself.

vicereine. Add: Now usu. with pronunc. (vəi·srēⁱn).

vicey-versey, vicy-versy, (vəi·si vɔ̄·ɹsi), repr. colloq. or joc. pronunc. of VICE-VERSA *adv. phr.*

1858 J. R. LOWELL in *Atlantic Monthly* Aug. 371 How far from these unhappy days When all is vicy-versy! **1979** K. O'HARA *Searchers of Dead* ix. 102 Actors work on directors as well as vicey-versey.

Vichy. Add: **1.** (Earlier *ellipt.* example.)

1882 *Harvard Lampoon* 26 Jan. 87/2 Vichy and Seltzer possessed of limpidity.

2. Used to denote the government of France which operated from Vichy (1940–44) in collaboration with the Germans; freq. *attrib.* and in *Comb.* Also *transf.* and *fig.*

1941 [see *COLLABORATION 2]. **1942** 'G. ORWELL' in *Partisan Rev.* Mar.–Apr. 159 Both Vichy and the Germans have found it quite easy to keep a façade of 'French culture' in existence. **1942** 'M. HOME' *House of Shade* vi. 96 Vichy French territory had been entered at Bardai. **1949** KOESTLER *Promise & Fulfilment* I. vii. 76 When, in 1941, British troops invaded Vichy-held Syria, they needed a vanguard of Commandos. **1965** B. SWEET-ESCOTT *Baker Street Irregular* ii. 54 Efforts to start something in Morocco, then occupied by the Vichy French, had been a failure. **1966** G. GREENE *Comedians* I. iii. 69 During the war..I served in the Political Intelligence Department of the Foreign Office, supervising the style of our propaganda to Vichy territory. **1970** R. WINGATE *Lord Ismay* iv. 59 The German ability to use Vichy-controlled Syria as a route for her aircraft. **1979** P. WAY *Sunrise* xiv. 146 The jail..had been convent no. 787 of the Poor Clares under West Africa's Vichy régime. **1980** *Times* 27 May 4/2 He went on to claim there was a 'Vichy mentality' in parts of the Foreign Office. The Home Office was 'stuffed with reactionaries'. **1981** M. WARNER *Joan of Arc* xiii. 263 Maurras's adherence to both Vichy and Joan of Arc.

Hence **Vi·chyist**, a supporter of the Vichy government.

1943 *Rev. Foreign Press* (Foreign Office Research Dept.) 23 Aug. 105/1 (*heading*) 'Combat' and' Liberté' demand severe measures against all Vichyists. **1958** *Times* 3 Dec. 8/5 M. Soustelle was in charge of intelligence and espionage, first against occupying Germans and then against Vichyists and Communists.

Vichyite (vi·ʃi,əit), *sb.* and *a.* [f. VICHY + -ITE[1].] **A.** *sb.* = *Vichyist* s.v. *VICHY. **B.** *adj.* Supporting the Vichy government (see *VICHY 2). Also *fig.*

1943 *Ann. Reg. 1942* 287 Yesterday a 'Vichy-ite', collaborating with the Nazis..today a French patriot. **1945** *Times* 30 Oct. 3/4 Vichyite officials in Indo-China. **1968** [see *COLLABORATEUR 2]. **1978** *Times* 9 Jan. 8/5 Each school of thought has its own pet profile of 'Treasury Man', whether it be the Institute of Economic Affairs seeing in him the symptoms of chronic Keynesianism or the Tribune Group of left wing Labour MPs sniffing for 'Vichyite' collaborators with the International Monetary Fund. **1979** *N.Y. Rev. Bks.* 8 Feb. 14/4 A *collabo*, someone who picked the wrong side, a Theban Vichyite?

vichyssoise (viʃiswā·z). Also with capital initial and ¶ **vichycoise, vichysoisse.** [a. Fr., in full **crême vichyssoise glacée** iced cream (soup) of Vichy.] A soup made with potatoes, leeks, and cream, usu. served chilled; a bowl of this soup.

1939 *Vogue's Cookery Bk.* 7 Creme Vichycoise. This is a special favourite in iced soups. **1941** A. Escoffier *Escoffier Cook Bk.* 262 Vichysoisse, now called Crême Gauloise, is made by adding cream and chilling. **1943** I. S. Rombauer *Joy of Cooking* (ed. 3) 63/1 Vichyssoise (French potato soup)... Now called 'de Gaullesoise' in a New York restaurant. **1950** M. Miller *Sure Thing* 35 Tetrazzini..and two Vichyssoise to start out, large coffees, later. **1959** *News Chron.* 30 Oct. 3/4 It happened..at the Savoy Hotel. The diner tasted his chilled Vichyssoise soup. **1969** *New Yorker* 20 Sept. 163/1 Vichysoisse..is usually served very cold. **1982** J. Aiken *Whisper in Night* 100 The night had grown stiflingly oppressive and humid. 'The air is like Vichyssoise,' said my uncle.

Vici (vəi·səi). *N. Amer.* Also **vici.** [perh. a. L. *vīcī*, pa.t. of *vincere* to conquer.] The name of a chrome-tanned kid leather used for shoes and boots. Freq. *attrib.*, esp. as *Vici kid.*

Formerly a proprietary name in the U.S.

1888 *Shoe & Leather Reporter* 19 July 133/3 Robert H. Foerderer courts the smiles of fortune with a horseshoe enclosing the word 'vici'. **1891** *Official Gaz.* (U.S. Patent Office) 13 Oct. 128/2 Kid, goat, and similar light weight leathers... The word 'Vici'. **1904** 'O. Henry' in *Everybody's Mag.* Feb. 187/1 He was the color of vici kid, and his whiskers was like excelsior made out of mahogany wood. **1906** *Daily Colonist* (Victoria, B.C.) 6 Jan. 12/7 (Advt.), Men's Vici Kid Shoes. **1937** H. H. Kroll *I was Sharecropper* x. 193, I had a pair of vici kid shoes for two dollars and a half. **1946** *Harper's Mag.* Oct. 311/1 There.. would be Pa in his Sunday clothes and vici shoes. **1946** H. R. Quimby *Pacemakers of Progress* vi. 115 Dressing high boots were often made with tops of silk or thin kid..; the lower parts were of patent leather or vici kid in black, bronze, white, or a color.

vicinism (vi·siniz'm). *Biol.* [f. L. *vīcīn-us* (see Vicine *a.*) + -ism.] (See quots. 1905, 1959.) Hence **vi·cinist,** a form produced by vicinism.

1905 H. De Vries *Species & Varieties* 188 For this purpose I propose the word vicinism..as indicating the sporting of a variety under the influence of others in its vicinity. *Ibid.* 201 Of two hundred seeds one became a blue atavist, or rather vicinist, while all others remained true to the white type. **1929** *Hereditas* XIII. 188 The percentage of vicinism has been exactly determined for one *Tetrahit* line... The flower colour of this line..is recessive to the red flower colour of the line T–G. **1959** *N.Z. Timber Jrnl.* Feb. 58/2 Vicinism... The tendency to variation caused by natural crossing with related forms growing nearby.

vicious, *a.* Add: **II. 9.** *vicious circle.* **c.** *gen.* A situation in which action and reaction intensify each other; a self-perpetuating process of aggravation. Similarly *vicious spiral,* in which the ill-effects are cumulative. Cf. *spiral *sb.* 2 d.

1839 [in Dict., sense 9 a]. **1892** H. James *Notebks.* (1947) 130 The whole situation works in a kind of inevitable rotary way—in what would be called a vicious circle. **1929** [see *Dosto(y)evskian *a.*]. **1940** M. Nicholson *How Britain's Resources are Mobilized* (Oxf. Pamphlets on World Affairs No. 30) 24 The result, when supplies of goods are short, is to bid up prices, thus raising the cost of living, inspiring demands for increased wages and starting the 'vicious spiral' of inflation. **1958** *Spectator* 11 July 60/2 All stress disorder is subject to this vicious-spiral rule. **1965** *Listener* 11 Nov. 741/2 It is sometimes necessary to enact laws against racism as a first step towards breaking a vicious circle. **1975** *Times* 23 Aug. 1/5 This is a vicious spiral of..mounting prices and declining traffic volume. **1982** *Times* 26 Aug. 3/8 It is a vicious circle. The boats cannot be sure of selling their fish until the processors invest in the new plant to handle it, and the processors cannot risk their money until they are sure that the fleet has guaranteed fishing areas and catch quotas.

10. *vicious abstraction* (Philos.), the abstraction of one quality or term from a thing or concept at the expense of other qualities or terms of which it is also composed; hence *vicious abstractionism.*

1883 F. H. Bradley *Princ. Logic* 511 If we recognize these elements our unit is not solitary; if we ignore them we fall into vicious abstraction. **1909** W. James *Meaning of Truth* xiii. 249 Let me give the name of 'vicious abstractionism' to a way of using concepts which may be thus described. **1932** H. H. Price *Perception* vii. 173 To use the language of the Idealist tradition, they only seem to be mere acceptances through a 'vicious abstraction'.

Vickers (vi·kəɪz). The name of a manufacturing company, orig. *Vickers*, Ltd., used: **1. a.** *attrib.* With reference to any of a variety of products of the firm, esp. armaments, aircraft, etc. Occas. also in the possessive.

1913 *303-Inch Machine Guns* (Ordnance College: Field Artillery & Small Arms Branch) 62 (*heading*) Gun, Vickers', ·303-in., Light. **1917** A. G. Empey *Over Top* 313 Vickers gun. **1919** *Vickers News* 15 Oct. 7/2 Vickers engines are occasionally tested on some such oil as Texas. *Ibid.* 1 Nov. 25 (*caption*) A Vickers airship is also seen leaving Barrow with letters for Sheffield. *a* **1944** K. Douglas *Alamein to Zem Zem* (1946) xiii. 79 Our supporting infantry manned their Vickers M.G.s on the flanks. **1945** *Penguin New Writing* xxiv. 31 In front of me the man carrying the Vickers ammunition. ? **1949** B. W. A. Dixon *Aircraft* i. 14/1 The Vickers 'Vimy', a twin-engined bomber designed originally for the long-distance bombing of Berlin. **1953** C. A. Lindbergh *Spirit of St. Louis* ii. vi. 295 Alcock and Brown..got across the ocean in their twin-engined Vickers bomber. **1974** *Encycl. Brit. Macropædia* XIX. 688/2 The Maxim machine guns, later often known as Vickers weapons, were used throughout the world well into the 1960s.

b. *absol.* One of a series of machine-guns manufactured by the company and used in both World Wars, esp. the ·303 or Vickers Maxim.

1917 G. Frankau *City of Fear* 18 You know what it's like in a listening-post, The Very candles aflare, Their bullets smacking the sand-bags, our Vickers combing your hair. **1918** T. E. Lawrence *Lett.* (1938) 243 A frontal attack of eighteen men, two Vickers, and two large Hotchkiss. **1942** E. Waugh *Put out More Flags* iii. 195 Nigel was full of questions;..what was the difference between a Bren and a Vickers. **1946** R. Capell *Simiomata* i. 36 The caiques scattered with Brens and Vickers raking them.

2. *attrib.* With reference to a method of testing the hardness of a material (esp. metal) by measuring the indentation produced when a small diamond pyramid is applied to the surface under a specified load.

1926 *Automobile Engineer* XVI. 105/1 In designing the Vickers machine..an impression having a diameter equal to three-eighths that of the ball has been taken as ideal. **1930** *Engineering* 12 Sept. 318/2 The hardness of hardened steel was further raised from Vickers number 950 to 1,100 by this treatment. **1973** J. G. Tweeddale *Materials Technol.* I. iv. 77 The most standard form of test is the Vickers hardness system performed by pushing a standard square pyramid diamond indenter..into the surface of the material.

vicomte (vi·kont). [Fr.] A viscount. Similarly **vicomtesse** (vikonte·s), a viscountess.

c **1786** T. Blaikie *Diary of Scotch Gardener* (1931) 204 The Vicomtese de Pons..had a Park to Make. **1847** C. Brontë *Jane Eyre* I. xv. 286, I knew him for a young roué of a vicomte—a brainless and vicious youth. **1889** C. M. Yonge *Reputed Changeling* II. xxi. 71 The mother.. was too proud of him to miss any opportunity of exhibiting him to an experienced mother and grandmother like the vicomtesse. **1928** C. A. Nicholson *Hell & Duchess* v. 94 You can scarcely blame the vicomte for suggesting a change. **1968** R. Amberley *Incitement to Murder* iii. 77 His uncle and aunt will be staying in the vicomte's house. **1980** C. Watson *Bishop in Back Seat* (1981) xxviii. 157 There was a sometime film producer,..a French count,..a vicomtesse who wrote best-sellers.

Viconian (vikōᵘ·niăn), *a.* [f. the name of Giovanni Battista *Vico* (1668–1744), Neapolitan philosopher + -ian.] Designating the theories or doctrines of Vico, esp. those concerned with the historical development of culture and its cyclical or repetitive character.

1957 N. Frye *Anat. Crit.* i. 62 Joyce and his Viconian theory of history. **1967** *Listener* 23 Mar. 391/3 Implying that the work should properly be..bound in such a way as to have no first or last page, a very embodiment of Viconian circularity. **1976** T. Eagleton *Crit. & Ideology* iv. 157 Human societies are specific sectors of that cosmic process, determined by its unalterable laws, moving inexorably through their Viconian cycles.

victim, *sb.* Add: **4.** *victim-hero.*

1962 *John o' London's* 1 Mar. 211/3 Young Cordier.. isn't the perfect victim-hero. **1975** P. Fussell *Gt. War & Mod. Memory* i. 8 Air bombardment, which was supposed to shorten the war, prolonged it by inviting those who were its targets to cast themselves in the role of victim-heroes and thus stiffen their resolve. *Ibid.* vi. 220 Guy Crouchback, Waugh's victim-hero.

victimization. Add: **c.** *spec.* With reference to the imposition of penalties on trade union members who go on strike.

1923 *Westm. Gaz.* 23 Apr., The expression 'no victimisation' implied that a striker's place was not to be filled by an outsider. **1925** S. O'Casey *Juno & Paycock* i, in *Two Plays* 8 Why did they sack her? It was a clear case of victimization. **1957** *Listener* 26 Dec. 1057/1 Victimisation, that 'doubletalk' word of today, was then a vivid and frequent reality. **1961** *Daily Tel.* 16 Dec. 7/1 They will receive severance pay from the company and a share of a 'victimisation fund' to tide them over until they find other jobs. **1966** [see *Newspeak]. **1974** *Socialist Worker* 23 Nov. 1/3 From the miners' ballot to the strikes of bakers and journalists, to the victimisation strike at Intex in Manchester, the will to fight is there.

vi·ctimless, *a.* orig. and chiefly *U.S.* [f. Victim *sb.* + -less.] Applied to a crime in which there is no injured party. Hence occas. *transf.* of the offender.

1965 E. M. Schor *Crimes without Victims* 171 A comparison of the three situations analyzed in this book may provide some hints as to the factors determining the expansion of deviance in the victimless crime sphere. **1971** *Wall St. Jrnl.* 29 Mar. 1/1 We have to find ways to clear the courts of the endless stream of 'victimless crimes'... There are more important matters..than minor traffic offenses, loitering and drunkenness. **1976** *Australasian Express* 1 Oct. 4/3 Prostitutes are to be given a say in possible changes to laws covering victimless crimes in N.S.W. **1982** *Times* 1 Sept. 3/2 A large amount of victimless, but technical crime. **1983** *Sunday Tel.* 3 July 10/3 If we sent fewer trivial victimless offenders to prison, the numbers in custody could very easily be halved without detriment to public safety.

victimo·logy. [ad. F. *victimologie* (B. Mendelsohn 1956, in *Rev. Internat. de Criminol. et de Police Technique* Apr.-June 97/1), f. *victime* Victim *sb.*: see -logy.] The study of the victims of crime, esp. of the psychological effects on them of their experience. Hence **victimo·logist.**

1958 *New Statesman* 5 July 6/1 We ought to establish a new science of victimology with chairs at the universities, field workers studying the effects rather than the causes of crime, and a special department assessing the impact of sex-crime on women. **1964** *Economist* 1 Feb. 417/1 'Victimology', an unusual aspect of the sociology of murder. **1971** *Time* 5 July 46 Some victimologists contend that rape victims invite attack. **1978** *Practitioner* Feb. 301/1 Any one of these fields of study—stress, coping, captivity, victimology—is a springboard for analysing the particular plight of the victim of terrorism.

Victor Charlie (vi·ktǒɹ tʃā·ɹli). *U.S. Services' slang.* [f. the communications code-names for the initial letters of *Viet Cong*; cf. VC s.v. *V 5 b.] = *Charley, Charlie 8.

1966 *New Yorker* 18 June 135/2 He..was told about being shot out of a helicopter by Victor Charlie. **1968** *Saturday Night* (Toronto) Aug. 15 [Westmoreland's] men say they have to get them one 'Victor Charlie'. **1982** T. Barling *Terminate with Prejudice* ii. i. 48 Casualties.. was inordinately high. Victor Charlie had too much bushcraft and too much jungle to hide in.

Victoria[2]. Add: **1. b.** A sovereign minted in the reign of Queen Victoria.

1870 E. G. E. Ward *Jrnl.* 9 Nov. in D. P. Carew *Many Years, Many Girls* (1967) i. 35 Let a packet of the bright, solid, sell-milled 'Victorias' reach you, and see if you do not deem them 'golden angels'! **1958** [see *pecorino].

7. a. *Victoria sandwich,* a sponge cake consisting of two layers of sponge sandwiched together with a jam filling; also *Victoria sponge* (*sandwich*). (The ingredients and style of presentation have not always been the same since the mid-19th century.)

1861 Mrs. Beeton *Bk. Househ. Managem.* 751 Victoria sandwiches... Spread one half of the cake with a layer of nice preserve, place over it the other half. **1902** *Little Folks* LV. 448/2 Auntie Kate told her cook to make some cakes,..some little cakes,..and some Victoria sandwich. **1976** *Burnham-on-Sea Gaz.* 20 Apr., Victoria sandwich. **1934** *Woman's Jrnl. Home Cookery* 150 (*heading*) Victoria sponge with grated pineapple. **1951** *Good Housek. Home Encycl.* 701/2 *Victoria sponge sandwich,* a sponge made with fat, which enables it to keep moist longer than the fatless type. **1980** D. Clark *Poacher's Bag* v. 121 He.. was..handing round wedges of Victoria sponge.

b. *Victoria green.*

1890 in Webster. **1934** H. Hiler *Notes Technique Painting* ii. 117 *Victoria green,* a potter's pigment, introduced by William Burton, but unfortunately not current, though it is absolutely permanent. *a* **1977** *Harrison Mayer Ltd. Catal.* 38/1 Body slip and glaze stains..colour..Victoria Green.

Victorian, *a.*[2] and *sb.* Add: **A.** *adj.* **1.** (Earlier examples.)

1839 *Athenæum* 2 Nov. 825/1 Perhaps the Annean authors, though inferior to the Elizabethans, are, on a general summation of merits, no less superior to the latter-Georgian and Victorian. **1850** E. P. Hood *Age & its Architects* ii. 71 The Victorian Commonwealth is the most wonderful picture on the face of the earth.

2. *fig.* Resembling or typified by the attitudes supposedly characteristic of the Victorian era; prudish, strict; old-fashioned, out-dated.

1934 in Webster. **1950** G. B. Shaw *Farfetched Fables* 72 He was helping the movement against Victorian prudery in a very practical way as a nudist. **1965** M. Spark *Mandelbaum Gate* vi. 157 In an emergency, one can't be Victorian about things, you know. **1977** P. G. Winslow *Witch Hill Murder* ii. xvi. 217 He was becoming rather heavily paternal to Linda. A Victorian parent. **1977** *Time Out* 17–23 June 5/2 Elsewhere in the files is an even worse example of what workers described as 'Victorian industrial relations'.

3. Special collocations: *Victorian Gothic* adj., designating the style of architecture typical of the Gothic Revival (see *Gothic *a.* 1 d); freq. *absol.* as *sb.*; *Victorian-Italianate* adj., designating a style of architecture revived in the nineteenth century in imitation of that of the Italian Renaissance.

1910 H. G. Wells *New Machiavelli* (1911) i. iii. 59 A new church in the Victorian Gothic. **1934** T. E. Tallmadge *Story Eng. Archit.* (1935) viii. 256 This structure [*sc.* the Albert Memorial] typifies to the last degree the Victorian Gothic style. **1961** *Times* 18 May 16/6 This small jewel of Victorian-Gothic architecture. **1980** 'L. Black' *Eve of Wedding* ii. 14 A huge red-brick mansion on three floors, heavy Victorian Gothic, a massive door in the centre of the front façade, leaded windows. **1963** A. Lubbock *Austral. Roundabout* 97 The public buildings are mostly in Victorian-Italianate style, pillared and porticoed; painted white, or in Edinburgh-rock colours. **1982** S. Radley *Talent for Destruction* vi. 40 The Victorian Italianate tower of the town hall.

B. *sb.* **2. b.** *U.S.* A house built during the reign of Queen Victoria.

1959 *House Beautiful* June 100 (*heading*) The virtues of a Victorian. **1978** J. GORES *Gone, no Forwarding* (1979) ix. 56 The house was an old Victorian, a Queen Anne which had been converted into rental units.

Hence **Victo·rianist; Victorianize** *v.* (later examples); **Victo·rianized** *ppl. a.*

1940 *Burlington Mag.* Apr. 127/2 The church had been so thoroughly 'Victorianised' that the discovery was all the more unexpected. **1946** J. W. DAY *Harvest Adventure* ii. 27 The gatehouse of Butley..owes its renaissance from a Victorianized ruin to a lovely house, full of medieval grace, to Dr Montague Rendall. **1970** *Guardian* 1 Oct. 11/8 Gillian Avery is an eminent Victorianist. She has written..neo-Victorian children's books.., she has edited a series of Victorian revivals. **1974** *Times* 22 Apr. 14/3, I amused myself by guessing which fellow-passengers were members of the Victorian Society. The man opposite ..did not quite fit my vision of a Victorianist. **1976** I. MURDOCH *Henry & Cato* I. 47 The tall Victorianized sash windows, which also served as doors, reached down to the ground. **1979** *Guardian* 3 Sept. 2/5 The building is unusually well preserved because it was never Victorianised or modernised. **1982** *UCT Studies in English* (Univ. Cape Town) Oct. 68 Writing as a Classicist and Victorianist, Jenkyns shows the enormous extent to which Hellenism influenced the generations of Victorians between about 1832 and the First World War.

Victorian, *a.*³ Add: **B.** as *sb.* A native or inhabitant of Victoria.

1862 *Temple Bar* Sept. 286 The Victorians went pluckily in for their second innings. **1901** A. W. JOSE *Australasia* x. 152 They are men of Melbourne, Brisbane, or Adelaide rather than Victorians or Queenslanders. **1943** K. TENNANT *Ride on Stranger* v. 47 All in the carriage were staunch Victorians, and his scathing references to the climate of Sydney were greeted with approval. **1973** *Sun-Herald* (Sydney) 26 Aug. 28/2 It's 41 years since Phar Lap died, but he lives on with a new generation of Victorians.

Victoriana (viktō³riā·nă). [f. VICTORIAN *a.*²: see *-IANA.] **1.** Matters relating to the Victorian period; attitudes characteristic of that time.

1918 E. POUND in *Future* Oct. 265/1 For most of us, the odour of defunct Victoriana is so unpleasant..that we are content to leave the past where we find it. **1931** *Times Lit. Suppl.* 23 Apr. 326/2 This book—Victoriana. A symposium of Victorian Wisdom. **1960** *Time* 8 Jan. 13/5, I think Shakespearian production is bogged down in a mire of Victoriana in this country. **1961** *Guardian* 21 Apr. 6/3 She provides many interesting domestic details for students of Victoriana. **1977** *S. Wales Echo* 18 Jan., Mr. Litterick added: 'He was talking straight Victoriana. That statement is straight out of Queen Victoria's age—it is arrogance.'

2. Objects, as furniture, ornaments, etc., made in the Victorian period; also, buildings or architecture of that era.

1940 *Illustr. London News* 11 May 640 (*caption*) The latest vogue in 'Victoriana'. Glass paper-weights to be sold at Sotheby's. **1947** N. MARSH *Final Curtain* xiii. 197 The terrifying Victoriana within. **1958** *Listener* 12 June 973/1 Victoriana is now the fashion in furniture and house decoration. **1958, 1959** [see *BETJEMAN]. **1968** *Canad. Antiques Collector* July 20/1 Whether the taste be for pine, Sheraton mahogany, or Victoriana, a lovely bouquet can be arranged to enhance antiques. **1978** *Lancashire Life* Mar. 71/1 There was one notable omission—namely, that of the dear old Princes Theatre. This was, prior to modernisation in 1932, a perfect specimen of Victoriana.

Victorianism. (In Dict. s.v. VICTORIAN *a.*² and *sb.*) Add: Victorian attitudes or style; (an example of) that which is characteristic of the Victorian era. (Later examples.)

1913 CHESTERTON *Victorian Age in Lit.* iii. 196 The real revolts that broke up Victorianism at last. **1913** MRS. H. WARD *Coryston Family* xi. 216 A heavy gold setting, whereof the Early Victorianism cried aloud. **1942** J. LEES-MILNE *Jrnl.* 5 Feb. in *Ancestral Voices* (1975) 16 Others took the absurd view that this important house is once again pure Jacobean since the Victorianisms have been purged by the fire, which was the best thing that could have happened. **1974** M. TIPPETT *Moving into Aquarius* 37 The two ways forward out of Victorianism seem to be equally dispiriting. **1978** *Dædalus* Fall 72 He jettisoned much of what we think of as Victorianism, but not on the whole, the values of his family, school, and university.

Victo·rianly, *adv.* [f. VICTORIAN *a.*² + -LY².] In a Victorian manner or style; also, prudishly, formally.

1917 *Duke of Norfolk Notebk.* 112 In conventional rooms, furnished Victorianly. **1933** C. WILLIAMS *Shadows of Ecstasy* i. 22 The clothes were late Victorian; the whole picture was Victorianly idyllic. **1940** E. F. BENSON *Final Edition* xii. 249 No doubt this boom in promiscuity was partly due to reaction, for an undue reticence had been Victorianly observed about sexual instincts. **1967** A. WILSON *No Laughing Matter* III. 250 This..conventionally, almost Victorianly clad huge body.

victorine, *sb.*¹ (Earlier example.)

1848 GEO. ELIOT *Let.* 31 May (1954) I. 263 We do not find it too warm, however, for I have ever felt the want of my Victorine.

victor ludorum (vi·ktər lūdō³·rŏm). [L., = victor of the games.] The overall champion in a sports contest (usu. at a school or college); the championship itself. Also *transf.* and *fig.*

1901 J. H. GRAY in W. B. Thomas *Athletics* v. 103 The sack race was no longer a consolation race, for Mr. Thornton the *victor ludorum* is returned as the winner. **1926** H. M. ABRAHAMS *Athletics* xiii. 114 There is far too much of this *victor ludorum* and champion athlete business at all schools. **1950** [see *RUNNING *vbl. sb.* 2 e (*b*)]. **1963** A. HOWARD in Sissons & French *Age of Austerity* i. 30 Labour, as the electoral *victor ludorum*, was collecting its long-coveted trophies. **1966** *Listener* 28 July 144/1 Last week's *victor ludorum* was undoubtedly 'Rendezvous with Death'..the story of the sinking of the Lusitania. *Ibid.* 27 Oct. 617/1 Ian outshone..generations of Etonians.. being Victor Ludorum two years running, the only boy in living memory to win that honour. **1980** 'T. HINDE' *Sir Henry & Sons* xiii. 104 The school honour-board inscribed with the names of the winners of the Victor Ludorum.

victory, *sb.* Add: **5.** *victory ball, celebration, dance, night, parade*; **victory bond,** a bond issued by the Canadian and British governments during or immediately after the war of 1914–18; **victory garden,** a vegetable garden maintained to provide food in wartime (*spec.* in the war of 1939–45); **victory point** *Bridge*, a point scored in a championship representing a number of international match points in accordance with an agreed scale; **victory roll,** a rotational manœuvre about a longitudinal axis performed by an aircraft as a sign of triumph (cf. *ROLL *sb.*² 1 d); also *fig.*; **victory sign,** a signal made by holding up the hand with the palm outwards and the first two fingers spread apart to represent the letter V (for *victory*) to indicate triumph (cf. *V-SIGN 2 a); also = *V-SIGN 1 b.

1945 AUDEN *Coll. Poetry* 117 We were To go to a great banquet and a Victory Ball. **1952** M. LASKI *Village* ii. 42 To bedeck the village hall on the night of the Victory Ball. **1917** *Canad. Year Bk. 1916–17* 693 On November 12, 1917, preparations were completed for the issue of a fourth Canadian War Loan in the form of five, ten and twenty year 'Victory Bonds' in denominations as low as $50. **1919** *Times* 14 June 19/1 The provision for Victory Bonds being accepted at their face value as cash for payment of death duties. **1977** JOHNS & GREENFIELD *Dymond's Capital Transfer Tax* xvii. 346 Victory bonds were accepted only for tax chargeable on death. **1945** J. REITH *Diary* 4 May (1975) vii. 347, I am dreading the victory celebrations and have no sort of heart for them. **1978** CADOGAN & CRAIG *Women & Children First* vi. 131 When the war ends [Susan]..is..caught up in the spurious gaiety of the victory celebrations. **1921** A. NOYES *Sel. Verse* iii. 5 (*title*) A victory dance. **1976** *Billings* (Montana) *Sunday Gaz.* 27 June 1-D/1 The Sioux and the Arapaho have come to share in this victory dance with us. **1942** WYNDHAM LEWIS *Let.* 10 Sept. (1963) 336 Why doesn't she lie low..and work in her victory-garden? **1978** H. WOUK *War & Remembrance* i. 13 She had started a victory garden and seemed the merrier for it. **1952** M. LASKI *Village* ii. 41 The coloured electric lights that Mr. Waters had dug out for Victory night. **1977** *Time* 26 Sept. 17/2 The victory-night hoopla of Norway's Laborites was, however, a bit premature. **1931** F. L. ALLEN *Only Yesterday* i. 10 Every other city has its victory parade. **1982** WARNER & SANDILANDS *Women beyond Wire* xi. 179 The war in Europe became progressively less of an Axis victory parade. **1962** *Listener* 8 Nov. 786/3 In the second half Britain went further ahead and won the match 6–0 in victory points. **1972** *Daily Tel.* 21 June 14/5 Britain scored 42 victory points out of 60 during Monday's play in the World Bridge Olympiad. **1942** *Tee Emm* (Air Ministry) II. 58 On returning to his aerodrome he began a victory roll, got into a spin and failed to recover. **1971** A. PRICE *Alamut Ambush* vi. 73 There was no point in doing a victory roll, however. It might even be premature if he failed to handle Havergal with compassion. **1981** T. BARLING *Bikini Red North* xi. 241 The F15 Eagle.. passed overhead, turning in a victory roll. **1942** M. DICKENS *One Pair of Feet* vii. 132 Her bell rang, not once, but as if she were giving the Victory sign in Morse. **1959** M. STEEN *Woman in Back Seat* II. viii. 310 One gave the 'victory' sign. 'We've beaten 'em.' **1978** L. THOMAS *Ormerod's Landing* v. 100 They went quickly, only the idiotic boy turning around and giving the victory sign.

Victrola (viktrō^u·lă). Also **victrola.** [f. the name of the *Victor* Talking Machine Co. + *-OLA.] The proprietary name of a kind of gramophone.

1905 E. JOHNSON *Let.* 9 June in *Amer. Speech* (1961) XXXVI. 116 The word Victrola is similar to nothing I have ever heard of and seems to me to have a sound suggestive of music, and would in all probability be the best word to use. **1906** *Official Gaz.* (U.S. Patent Office) 9 Jan. 644/2 Victor Talking Machine Company... Filed Dec. 1, 1905. Victrola. **1906** *Trade Marks Jrnl.* 9 May 628 Victrola 279,292. Philosophical instruments, scientific instruments, and apparatus for useful purposes. **1916** 'J. WEBSTER' *Dear Enemy* 318 The children..had a lot of new records for the victrola. **1937** N. COWARD *Present Indicative* VI. 259 A tall Renaissance chair with a red velvet cushion under which lived an electric victrola. **1952** J. STEINBECK *East of Eden* 374 He bought a Victor victrola..and he went regularly to see what new records had come in. **1979** P. THEROUX *Old Patagonian Express* xvii. 259, I found an old phonograph. It was literally a Victrola, a 1904 Victor.

vicy-versy: see *VICEY-VERSEY, VICY-VERSY.

vide, aphetic form of DIVIDE *v.* Delete † *Obs.*⁻¹ and add: **1.** (Later example.) Now only U.S. Blacks'.

1935 Z. N. HURSTON *Mules & Men* 20 'Way after while when He ketch dat Jew, He's goin' to 'vide things up more ekal'.

2. as *int.* A set parliamentary cry for the division of the house into two groups voting on each side of a question for the purpose of counting. Cf. DIVIDE *v.* 10.

1893 *Harper's Mag.* Dec. 39/2 This is usually done by shouting 'Divide! divide!' or, as the word is generally pronounced, ''Vide! 'vide!' **1908** H. W. LUCY *Mem. Eight Parliaments* vi. 242 Opposite and around him was a crowd of hilarious gentlemen shouting ''Vide! 'vide! 'vide!' **1951** J. BIGGS-DAVISON *George Wyndham* xiv. 206 From the Conservative Back Benches came a shout of ''Vide! 'Vide!'

videnda, *sb. pl.* (Later examples.)

1790 J. BYNG *Torrington Diaries* (1954) 312 Thus is one often humbug'd by printed accounts of visionary videnda! **1964** AUDEN in *Listener* 1 Oct. 525/1 Windows averted from plausible videnda but admitting a light one could mend a watch by.

video (vi·diō), *sb.* [f. L. *vidē-re* to see + -o, after *AUDIO-.] **I.** *attrib.* **1.** Of or pertaining to (*a*) television, or (*b*) the visual element of television broadcasts or the signals representing it.

1935 [see *AUDIO- II]. **1937** *RCA Rev.* July 17 Another important consideration has to do with the difficulty of feeding and switching video circuits. **1944** *Jrnl. Television Soc.* IV. 69/2 Trap circuits are commonly used..to keep the sound carrier out of the video channel. **1945** J. BARZUN *Teacher in Amer.* xix. 280 The copywriter.. must be the same who was impelled to call television 'the video art'. **1949** *Proc. IRE* XXXVII. 289/2 Video Techniques. Notable progress was made in the comparatively new field of television recording on film. **1951** KOESTLER *Age of Longing* 194 An American video commentator. **1959** N. MAILER *Advts. for Myself* (1961) 157 A hippopotamus of a television-radio-and-phonograph cabinet with the blind monstrous snout of the video tube. **1967** *Boston Herald* 1 Apr. 1/1 News commentator Chet Huntley claimed Friday he had the support of his video partner, David Brinkley, and all but three of 40 NBC newscasters in his bid. **1979** *Daily Tel.* 17 Dec. 12/6 Such moments..were rare in Alick Rowe's *Two People* (ITV)... Video-drama remains uncertain about the love story.

2. Of or pertaining to video recording; **video art,** art in which a video recording is the medium; so **video artist.**

1955, etc. [see *video film*, etc., sense 8 below]. **1972** *Harper's Mag.* June 92 Few of these programs are going to win awards as video art. *Ibid.* 90 Russ Connor is now in charge of granting money through the New York State Council to independent video artists. **1973** *Art Internat.* Mar. 42/2 The video sculpture *De La*, which utilizes the machine constructed for shooting *La Région Centrale*, carries on a discourse on perception at the same time that it exists as a fascinating mechanical object. **1975** *N.Y. Times* 14 Apr. 33 Mr. Gillette..is one of a growing breed of video artists, for whom the TV screen has become an esthetic medium... They produce videotapes that take ingenious advantage of the technology. **1975** *New Yorker* 5 May 44/1 The video-art movement, which has been in high gear for more than three years now, can have come as a surprise to practically no one. **1976** *Broadcast* Dec. 20/1 In a video world he has still a film-stock contribution to make to the overall impression of the whole. **1977** C. MCFADDEN *Serial* (1978) iv. 14/2 He said he'd had amazing results just acting out his anger with his patients. He was also big on video feedback.., role-playing..and Japanese hot tubs. **1978** *Chicago* June 14/4 Channel 11 producer Tom Weinburg [is] a video artist and part-owner of the White Sox. **1979** *Daily Tel.* 15 Dec. 15/5 Home video equipment is giving the Mafia a foothold in Britain, with illegal distribution of pornography and pirated films... 'Videocrime' is growing so fast that it will be the Crime of the '80s. **1980** *Times* 25 Jan. (Audio Visual Rep.) p. ii/5 Video programmes are being used by the National Bus Company for training drivers. **1982** *Listener* 23 & 30 Dec. 10/3 If you don't like what broadcast television offers, then you can supplement the diet from the video shop. **1984** *What Video?* Aug. 6/2 The VR-3995 has four video heads for noise-free still frame and slow motion.

II. *absol.* or as *sb.* **3.** That which is displayed or to be displayed on a television screen or other cathode-ray tube; the signal corresponding to this.

1937 *Printers' Ink Monthly* May 45/2 *Video*, the sight channel in television, as opposed to audio, the sound channel. **1940** *Broadcasting* 1 June 32 Video seen 230 miles at sea. Clear steady images picked up during test. **1946** [see *DISPLAY *sb.* 1 c]. **1949** *Hollywood Q.* Winter 157 And pipe the finished output of these segments, both video and audio, instantaneously and simultaneously to the kinescope recorders. **1951** *Proc. IRE* XXXIX. 8/1 One cycle of video during active horizontal scanning represents one dark and one light picture element on a particular scanning line. **1960** J. L. BERNSTEIN *Video Tape Recording* p. vii, Directors, editors, cameramen, and others..would benefit if they could learn the processes involved in recording video on tape. **1964** *Times* 7 Feb. p. iv/3 Except for its width..video tape looks exactly like sound recording tape. But it records not only sound but a continuous picture—video—as well! **1976** *Aviation Week* 10 May 131/1 An IBM scan converter transforms radar video into a format suitable for presentation on the TV monitors. **1977** *Gramophone* Aug. 361/2, I see it as the precursor of the all-purpose high quality cassette recorder that will record both video and audio. **1979** W. C. BRANDENBURG *Introd. Television Servicing* ii. 4/2 Both the audio and video can be broadcasted from the same antenna. **1982** G. WHITE *Video Techniques* vi. 134 Sound is as important as the video and often more difficult to edit.

4. Television as a broadcasting medium. *U.S. colloq.*

1941 *Amer. Mercury* Nov. 581/2 Vidio,..television. **1946** *Time* 25 Feb. 72 NBC published a 55-page booklet, listing words & phrases commonly used in video. **1954** *Billboard* 13 Nov. 21 Most of the big name spinners have taken a fling in video during the last five years, but their survival-average has been low. **1979** *Boston Globe* 10 Apr. 32 Their play was flashed by video to an adjoining room where experts commented on it before a throng.

5. A video recorder; also, a VDU.

1958 *Observer* 26 Jan. 14/6 The Video is like a combined tape-recorder and cinema camera. It records your television appearance complete with sound track and can be played back at the touch of a switch. **1979** *Television & Home Video* Mar. 7/2 There's not a lot of point in owning a home video and using it to record the rubbish you might otherwise have missed. **1982** *Times* 7 May 17/5 Last year over 900,000 videos were rented or sold in Britain. **1983** *What's New in Computing* Jan. 5/1 The rest of the machine, the discs, the power supplies and the videos are all retained or upgraded and existing software can be run side by side with new software. **1984** S. Townsend *Growing Pains A. Mole* 190 We are the only family in our street who haven't got a video.

6. A video recording; videotape as a recording medium.

1968 *Observer* 14 Jan. 28/4 The days of the disc, in the pop world at least, are numbered. For soon will come the video. We will have the top 20 videos which you plug into your home video-machine. **1978** *Radio Times* 4–10 Mar. 4/2 We've got some video of a man he has already made contact with... We'll just have to cut in with that if necessary. **1981** *Church Times* 7 Aug. 5/3 They..went down to BBC television... Later he popped round to the school and showed them a video of themselves. **1983** *New Scientist* 3 Mar. 569/1 The BBC recognised early on that there was money to be made from selling archive programmes on video. **1984** *Melody Maker* 6 Oct. 3/1 Spandau Ballet have just returned from Hong Kong where they filmed the video for 'Highly Strung'.

7. The production or use of video recordings.

1970 *It* 9–24 Apr. 7 There are also groups of people exploiting video in any way they can think of. **1977** *N.Y. Rev. Bks.* 23 June 25/4 Made images move (cinema) and achieved their simultaneous recording and transmission (video). **1980** *Times* 31 Mar. 24/6 There are enough able practitioners around to demonstrate how effectively video, like any other artistic tool, can be used. **1980** C. MacCabe *Godard* 26 You envisaged a different kind of distribution: film and video as a handcraft industry. **1982** *Listener* 11 Feb. 34/3 The good news is that things in video could be worse. The bad news is that things in video will get worse.

III. 8. Special Combs. (see also *video-).

Most of the following are written as one word or two, with or without a hyphen, so that the distinction between them and words f. *video- is to some extent arbitrary.

video amplifier, an amplifier able to amplify the wide range of frequencies present in video signals and suited to delivering a signal to the picture tube of a television set; **video art, artist** (see sense 2 above); **video camera,** a camera for producing an electrical signal corresponding to a changing scene, suitable for feeding to a video recorder; **video display terminal** or **unit** = *visual display unit* s.v. *visual *a.* 6 e; abbrev. VDU s.v. *V 5 b; **video film,** orig., a cinematographic film of a television broadcast; now, a recording on a videocassette; **video frequency,** a frequency in the range employed for the video signal in television (viz. a few hertz to several million hertz), *esp.* one in the higher part of this range; freq. *attrib.*; **video game,** a game played by electronically manipulating images displayed on a television screen; **video map,** a map produced electronically on a radar screen to assist in navigation; so **video mapping; video nasty** *colloq.*, a horror video film; **video piracy,** the illegal production and sale of copies of commercial video films; so **video pirate; video-player,** a machine used in conjunction with a television for playing videocassettes; **video signal,** a signal that contains all the information required for producing the picture in television broadcasting; **video terminal** = *video display unit* above.

1937 *Electronics* Aug. 22/1 A video amplifier is one that is responsive to picture signals, and therefore, is an extremely good audio as well as a very wide band radio frequency amplifier. **1975** D. G. Fink *Electronics Engineers' Handbk.* xx. 55 Finally the video amplifier raises the signal to from 50 to 100 V to drive the picture tube. **1978** *Tucson Mag.* Dec. 28/1 Videocameras for home productions range from $300 to $1500. **1983** *New Scientist* 24 Mar. 793/1 It is neither easy nor ethical to perch with notebook or video camera over spontaneous scenes of human mating or aggression. **1976** *New Yorker* 1 Mar. 23/2 A V.D.T.; or Video Display Terminal, is a machine that combines a television screen with a typewriter keyboard and is connected to 'a gigantic network of computers'. **1983** *Boston Globe* 12 July 3/5 Video display terminals, or VDTs, have become commonplace in many offices. **1968** Video display unit [see VDU s.v. *V 5 b]. **1969** *Jane's Freight Containers 1968–69* 114/3 New video display units provide instantaneous information to answer inquiries from customers concerning the location of cars. **1983** *Engin. & Mining Jrnl.* May 99/1 Engineers have at their disposal newly developed hardware and software, with modern distributed control systems using computer interface and video display units. **1944** R. E. Lee *Television* ix. 182 Even with the financial savings of videofilm, television is the most expensive way of selling things that man has ever concocted. **1955** *Amer. Cinematographer* XXXVI. 365/1 Within a matter of minutes, this video film recording can be quick-processed and screened. **1978** *Washington Post* 29 Mar. D-2/5 The flight scheduled to carry the video film of Sunday's game 'did not take off' Monday night. **1983** *Daily Tel.* 10 June 2/3 Management brought in video films which were shown in updated form every few months to enable employees to know how the company was functioning. **1937** *Electronics* Aug. 23/2 There are several ways of designing an amplifier to give satisfactory response for video frequencies. **1956** Amos & Birkinshaw *Television Engin.* II. i. 28 The video-frequency signal generated by scanning such a scene has a uniform level which is interrupted by the sync signals. **1982** *Electronics* 6 Oct. 63 In development.. is a..generator for cathode-ray-tube applications offering an 80-MHz video frequency. **1973** *Business Week* 10 Nov. 212/1 The astonishing ability of the video game to lure quarters from the public and the electronic techniques used in its design are forcing major changes on the coin-operated game business. **1983** *Wall St. Jrnl.* 5 Jan. 1/2 Coleco's 1982 earnings 'appear to be well in excess of five times 1981 levels of $7.7 million,' the third-largest maker of video games said. **1961** *Aeroplane* CI. 74/2 All displays are capable of accepting video map information. **1982** *Radar-82* (IEE Conf. No. 216) 307/1 Producing a video map very much more accurate than the radar data is unnecessarily costly. **1954** *Sun* (Baltimore) 18 Mar. (B ed.) 20/4 Another of the new developments, 'video mapping', electronically reproduces an area map on the radar scope—showing terrain hazards, airport runways and radio flight paths. **1962** *Flight Internat.* LXXXI. 283/2 The range of synthetic displays to be added to the raw radar..will include video mapping. **1983** *Listener* 10 Feb. 4/1 The same children are sometimes known to see video 'nasties' or horror films screened later on. **1984** *Ibid.* 14 June 3/2 Unless one has seen a video nasty..it is difficult to imagine the depths of degradation to which certain producers are willing to sink. **1980** *Times* 2 Aug. 2/4 Audio and video piracy..usually involve the copying of a legitimate product such as videotaped film. **1983** *Daily Tel.* 20 June 17/2 Customs and Excise is claiming the right to see documents seized under a court order by a firm of London solicitors acting for the British Videogram Association in a video piracy case. **1982** *Ibid.* 17 Nov. 2/3 A video pirate was fined £500 yesterday by magistrates in Chepstow, Gwent, in a test case which could start a new clampdown on the illegal copies. **1983** *New Scientist* 3 Mar. 569/1 The deal is a blow to the video-pirates, who have cashed in by selling illegal copies. **1970** *Sci. Amer.* Dec. 37/1 (Advt.), The little cartridge simply drops into the videoplayer you will have attached to your set. **1972** *Listener* 8 June 775/3, I would guess that in about fifteen years most people would have a video-player of one sort or another in their homes. **1983** *N.Y. Times* 23 Apr. 48/4 The man..slipped a cassette into his video player... A comedian..popped into view on the television screen. **1937** J. C. Wilson *Television Engin.* ix. 346 Fig. 210..shows a triode valve having its grid biased approximately at zero volts, so that on receipt of positive video signals it runs into grid current and the video-signal voltage is dropped across the series grid resistance. **1937** [see *fade *v.*[1] 9 b]. **1957** Amos & Birkinshaw *Television Engin.* I. i. 17 The composite signal obtained by combining a picture with a synchronising signal is known as a video signal. **1976** A. Davis *Television* ii. 28 The main problem was the high speed at which the tape needed to run in order to accommodate the wider range of frequencies of video signals compared with audio signals. **1970** *Computer Management* Nov. 52/2 The key point in all video terminal applications, present or future, is the ease of handling and understanding information presented in a familiar form. **1983** *N.Y. Times* 28 Jan. 18/2 I.R.S. operators will still do the talking, but the computers will catalogue and display on video terminals all the taxpayers' facts, figures and prior promises.

video (vi·dio), *v.* [f. the sb.] **1.** *trans.* To make a video recording of.

1971 *Jrnl. Soc. Motion Picture Engineers & Television Engineers* LXXX. 414 *Video*, to dub by rerecording the video signal recovered from the tape being copied. **1984** *What Video?* Aug. 4/2 My work..is videoing anything to do with the emergency services (road accidents, fires etc.).

2. *U.S.* To televise. *rare.*

1973 E. Bullins *Theme is Blackness* 5 Colored people knew they were black, unique, separate and had a future. For paeans of Blackness were videoed throughout Black America.

video- (vi·dio), *video *sb.* used as a formative element (cf. *video 8), as in **videocasse·tte,** a cassette of videotape; freq. *attrib.*; **vi·deo-co:nference,** an arrangement in which television sets linked by telephone lines or the like are used to enable a group of people in different places to see and hear whichever of them is speaking at the time; hence **video-co·nferencing** *vbl. sb.*, telecommunication in the form of a videoconference; **vi·deo-disc,** a disc on which (moving or static) visual images have been recorded in non-representational form for subsequent reproduction on a television screen or the like; **vi·deophone,** a telephone incorporating a television screen on which the other person may be seen speaking; also as *v. trans.*; **vi·deoporn** *colloq.*, pornography on video film; **video-te·lephone** = *videophone* above.

1970 *Times* 26 Sept. 12/1 The video-cassette comprises a pre-recorded, pre-packaged programme of pictures and sound, designed to be 'played' on a television set with a converter. **1976** *Broadcast* 23 Aug. 8/1 The videocassette editor..is a small desk-top box..controlling two Sony video-cassette recorders. **1978** *Lancashire Life* Nov. 112/1 (Advt.), The Philips N1700 uses a 2½ hour video cassette no larger than the average paperback, and like an audio cassette the video cassette recordings can be played back whenever you like and as often as you like. **1982** M. Babson *Death beside Seaside* xv. 132 That's a video cassette recorder! Where did he get that? We couldn't afford that. **1977** *Communications: Technol. for Better Tomorrow* (Proc. 13th Ann. Internat. Conf. Communications) III. 75/1 An experimental videoconference link has been installed in France. **1983** *Times* 25 June 8/5 Whether a face-to-face meeting is in any sense 'better' than a videoconference is a different question. **1977** *Communications: Technol. for Better Tomorrow* (Proc. 13th Ann. Internat. Conf. Communications) III. 75/1 Characteristics concerning typical pictures in video-conferencing. **1983** *New Scientist* 7 Apr. 7/3 British Telecom has been running video conferencing studios for the past 12 years. **1967** *Ibid.* 2 Feb. 285/3 We shall soon have on the market the video-disc, about the size of a gramophone record and costing about 22 shillings. **1975** *Broadcast* 28 July 11/2 Consider the mind-boggling experience of a visit to your local bookstore to purchase a videodisc with perhaps 150 books on it—or maybe 54,000 slides of paintings. **1982** *New Scientist* 21 Oct. 150/1 Video discs are the video equivalent of the long-playing record. **1982** *Jrnl. R. Soc. Arts* Nov. 781/1 The floppy disc can hold the equivalent of 40 pages of the *Concise Oxford Dictionary*, but the video disc the whole of the *Encyclopaedia Britannica*. **1955** C. L. Moore in 'E. Crispin' *Best SF* 129 He..called Maltzer's apartment by videophone. *Ibid.* 131 Maltzer videophoned him. **1971** *New Scientist* 1 July 14/2 The West Germans have recently begun operating a 240-mile experimental videophone link. **1976** *TV Guide* (U.S.) 1 May, To reach other videophone outlets, the user merely dials the telephone. **1979** *Daily Tel.* 15 Dec. 15/5 The programme claimed that a 'videoporn' cassette of Linda Lovelace's 'Deep Throat'..was made in America with Mafia money. **1982** *Punch* 13 Jan. 83/2 Before videoporn and clockwork dildo moved inexorably in. **1964** M. McLuhan *Understanding Media* xxii. 233 The possibility of shopping by two-way TV, or video-telephone. **1978** *Jrnl. R. Soc. Arts* CXXVI. 270/2 The interview will remain the mainstay of any selection procedure: even if it is transferred to the video telephone.

videogram (vi·diogræm). [f. *video- + -gram.] **1.** An apparatus for making or reproducing video recordings. *rare.*

1963 *Times* 17 Aug. 4/2 A young Wolverhampton design consultant said today that he had invented a record player which reproduced vision as well as sound..Mr. Mason's videogram—as he has named it—could be on sale soon. **1972** *Guardian* 11 Apr. 15/2 They have ordered 60 cassette recorders—videograms is the coming word.

2. A prerecorded video recording; a commercial video film or disc.

1972 *Publishers Weekly* 10 Apr. 27/2 Mr. Geranton insisting on the distinction between a video copy of a previous work (say a film) and an original 'videogram'. **1976** [see *phonogram 2]. **1980** *Daily Tel.* 15 Oct. 18 The newly formed British Videogram Association..will put an end to people taping a film on one television channel while they watch football..on the other. **1982** R. Dean *Home Video* vi. 71 Videogram sales and rentals are now dominated by features, with 'adult' subjects.. running close behind. **1983** *Times* 29 Jan. 4/2 Owners and distributors of videograms (pre-recorded video cassettes and discs) are to be asked..to approve cinema-type certifications.

So **video·grapher,** one who makes videograms; **video·graphy,** the process or activity of making a video recording using a video camera; the use of such a camera.

1976 (*title of periodical*) Videography. **1980** *Daily Tel.* 18 June 17/2 Videography is what they are calling it and it will revolutionise home movies. Following hard on the sales of video recorders..comes the video camera. **1983** *N.Y. Times* 24 July II. 30/6 One more advantage that the cinematographer has over the videographer is in the amount of lighting required. Video requires a lot of light to get a good result. **1984** *What Video?* Aug. 40/1 Colour settings are especially important with underwater videography. **1985** *Audio Visual* Feb. 54/3 Although obviously intended for a primary audience of stills photographers, David Kilpatrick's..volume could just as easily serve as a guide to in-house videographers.

videophile (vi·diofəil), *a.* and *sb.* orig. *U.S.* [f. *video- + -phile.] **A.** *adj.* Of or pertaining to a videophile or videophiles. **B.** *sb.* One who is very keen on watching television or video recordings.

1978 *Washington Post* 2 July M-4/2 In time there will be a videophile subculture: it is evolving now, as members of the baby-boom generation come to realize that television has played the cultural role in their lives that the movies and radio played in their parents' lives. **1980** *Business Week* 7 July 77/1 Pioneer Electronic Corp...is betting that it can turn its large base of audiophiles into videophiles. It..recently set up a new subsidiary..to produce music for videodiscs. **1984** *New Yorker* 20 Feb. 42/1 Kodak's new system had a maximum recording time of ninety minutes—not enough for a football game. The product, he said, would have 'some appeal to the upscale videophile'.

video recording, *vbl. sb.* Also with hyphen and as one word. [f. *video *sb.* + Recording *vbl. sb.*] **1. a.** The process of making a cinematographic film of what appears on a television screen. **b.** The process of recording on videotape; videotaping.

1949 *Tele-Tech* May 31/3 The most obvious problem in designing a suitable photographic camera for video recording is that of reconciling the 30 frames per second rate of American television with the 24 frame per second rate which is standard in motion pictures. **1953** *Proc. IRE* XLI. 466/1 Work on video recording has not been restricted to film. Advances were made in the experimental recording of video information on tape. **1962** R. BRETZ *Techniques Television Production* (ed. 2) xxiii. 495 A standard sound-record head contacts the tape a half-second after the video recording has been done. **1983** *Nature* 23 June 651/3 These..combine the recovery of [sea-]bed samples with the photography and video-recording of marine life.

2. a. A film of a television broadcast. **b.** A recording on videotape.

1950 *Tele-Tech* Nov. 32 (*heading*) Video recordings improved by the use of continuous moving film. **1968** A. WHITNEY *Every Man has his Price* vii. 59 She nearly died when we showed that videorecording to her! **1978** P. MARSH et al. *Rules of Disorder* iv. 112 Oxford fans were shown..a video-recording which was made..during their game with Plymouth Argyle. **1984** *Guardian* 5 Oct. 2/3 The court heard a video recording of an interview given by Mr. Scargill to Channel 4.

So **vi·deorecord** *v. trans.*, to make a video recording of; **vi·deorecorded** *ppl. a.*; **video recorder,** an apparatus for making video recordings; *spec.* a form of tape recorder for recording television programmes from a signal inside the set.

1951 *Jrnl. Soc. Motion Picture & Television Engineers* LVI. 222 (*caption*) Video recorder. **1954** *Tele-Tech* May 129 To be..acceptable to television stations, the magnetic video recorder must be capable of handling color signals with similar fidelity. **1960** J. L. BERNSTEIN *Video Tape Recording* i. 1 The video recorder is able to provide immediate playback after a scene has been shot. **1961** *Britannica Bk. of Year* 537/1 Science also provided a term for a relatively new process with *video-record*, to record..in pictures rather than sound. **1972** *Daily Tel.* 22 Jan. 2/5 The disadvantages of having all schools broadcasts from ITV in the mornings (..many teachers may now videorecord them if they have the equipment). **1975** *Language for Life* (Dept. Educ. & Sci.) xxii. 322 Such activities would involve the play-back in school hours of video-recorded evening programmes. **1978** *Lancashire Life* Sept. 131/1 Now the video-recorder has arrived in the home. **1979** *Jrnl. R. Soc. Arts* Apr. 265/2 This teaching sequence is video-recorded by the use of a simple CCTV system. **1979** *Financial Rev.* (Sydney) 5 Oct. 23/1 A US District Court judge has ruled that the non-commercial use of home video recorders to record television broadcasts is lawful. **1983** L. DEIGHTON *Berlin Game* vi. 65 You should have heard George when the au pair dropped his wretched video recorder.

videotape (vi·diotēɪp), *sb.* Also as two words or hyphenated. [f. *VIDEO- + TAPE *sb.*[1]] **1. a.** Magnetic tape on which can be recorded moving visual images such as television programmes (as well as sound).

1953 *Wall St. Jrnl.* 2 Dec. 1/4 With further development of video tape techniques, numerous possibilities will open up. Small portable television cameras are already in wide use in industry, in stores, banks and schools. **1965** *Listener* 10 June 857/2 A course of television mathematics lectures is now being recorded. Where these are transmitted from videotape the lecturer will be in the room with the students. **1973** C. BONINGTON *Next Horizon* viii. 117 We'll record the climb on video-tape the day before it actually goes out on the air. **1980** B. W. ALDISS *Life in West* i. 15 Standing by the bookstall was a white board announcing that the television series had been captured on videotape and would be shown in its entirety over the four evenings of the conference. **1985** *Listener* 24 Jan. 37/1 Videotape soon became a vehicle for prerecorded films and music programmes.

b. A length of videotape, or the recording it carries.

1960 *Guardian* 7 May 1 Video-tapes and film versions of the ceremony were being flown all over the world. **1967** *New Scientist* 2 Feb. 285/3 Americans have been at great pains to discover whether students learn as much from televised lectures and video-tapes as they do from 'live' lectures. *a* **1974** R. CROSSMAN *Diaries* (1976) II. 135 They wanted a video-tape to be made of every word said in the House of Commons and the House of Lords. **1977** *Language* LIII. 883 Videotapes of the lectures have been broadcast nationally. **1984** *What Video?* Aug. 14/1 (Advt.), You can easily view a negative or positive film image on a TV screen and also record it on a video tape.

2. *attrib.* **a.**

1958 *Times* 24 July 5/2 The BBC's VERA which tape-records complete television shows, picture and sound combined, and the AMPEX and R.C.A. videotape machines which do the same job for the independent television contractors, will greatly facilitate the provision of such Press shows. **1963** J. N. HARRIS *Weird World Wes Beattie* (1964) viii. 90 Sometimes she was in New York, holding a can of toilet-bowl cleanser in front of a videotape camera. **1976** B. JACKSON *Flameout* iii. 40 A man hefting a videotape camera on his shoulder brushed past, focusing his camera for another long shot. **1977** *Times of Swaziland* 11 Feb. 5 (Advt.), Kosie Smith v's Victor Galindez—light heavy weight title fight—in our Video-Tape Shows starting 8.30 every night. **1978** *Broadcast* 13 Nov. 23/1 The Circle is presently involved in forming.. a video tape library. **1979** *Globe & Mail* (Toronto) 5 May 48/2 The [tennis] club has 24 courts,..videotape playback, ball machines and individual stroke analysis.

b. videotape recorder, a tape recorder that will record and replay videotape recordings; **videotape recording,** a recording on videotape; also, the making of such a recording.

1954 *Proc. IRE* XLII. 731/2 Video tape recorders were demonstrated. *Ibid.* 756/2 Experimental video tape recording systems were demonstrated. **1959** *Daily Tel.* 9 Mar. 13/2 Television has entered an era of video tape recording that will profoundly influence future development. **1959** *Listener* 19 Mar. 499/2 Some executives think that video-tape recordings will help them to beat the film menace. **1963** *Guardian* 11 Sept. 7/6 Increasingly the television camera and videotape recorder, an unwieldy picture development of the ordinary tape-recorder, are being used where once the cine camera stood alone. **1971** *New Scientist* 16 Sept. 633/1 Videotape recording (VTR) offers them a freedom which is impossible with film. **1978** *Tucson Mag.* Dec. 28/1 Since videotape recorders hit the scene, television addicts don't have to choose between two conflicting programs. **1980** *Brit. Med. Jrnl.* 29 Mar. 889/1 Before and during stimulation the patients were examined clinically; videotape recordings made of their movements; [etc.]. **1984** *Listener* 19 July 34/2 There is.. an enormous park of video-tape-recorders in Britain.

Hence **vi·deotape** *v. trans.*, to record on videotape; **vi·deotaped** *ppl. a.*, **vi·deotaping** *vbl. sb.*

1964 *Times* 7 Feb. (Advt. Suppl.) p. iv/3 Even an expert cannot tell the difference between live and videotaped programmes. **1970** R. PARKES *Death-Mask* xv. 186 An agonising interview had been video-taped at the television studios. **1977** J. D. DOUGLAS in Douglas & Johnson *Existential Sociol.* i. 10 This form of linguistic ethnomethodology imposed the further constraint that only those accounts that could be tape-recorded or videotaped could be studied. **1977** *Times* 29 June 7/6 The FBI had set up an antique shop..fitted with wiretaps and hidden videotaping equipment. **1979** *Time* 30 July 12 After the lesson Carter ran through the speech and watched a videotaped replay, then practiced again, until he and Rafshoon were satisfied. **1980** B. W. ALDISS *Life in West* i. 28, I see..that some ingenious person..has videotaped my television series.

videotex (vi·dioteks). Chiefly *U.S.* [f. *VIDEO- + TEX(T *sb.*[1]) = next.

1978 *Globe & Mail* (Toronto) 16 Aug. B2/2 The Federal Department of Communications has developed a two-way television system called Videotex that it claims is superior to rival British and French systems. **1980** R. WOOLFE *Videotex* i. 4 This book is about two-way, interactive videotex... One-way videotex..is referred to as teletext. Two-way videotex is called plain videotex. **1980** *Economist* 9 Aug. 71/1 America is proceeding equally slowly with a cousin of teletext, known as viewdata or videotex. **1981** *Sci. Amer.* Oct. E5/1 (Advt.), The Prestel videotex service has been operating for two years and is the largest information retrieval network in the world. **1983** *Amer. Banker* 8 June 8/1 The role banks will play in the emerging videotex field—a technology which permits consumers to access a variety of data bases and transaction services with a home terminal—has been much debated.

videotext (vi·diotekst). [f. *VIDEO- + TEXT *sb.*] Any information system in which a television is used to display alphanumeric information selected by the user; viewdata or teletext, esp. the former.

1980 *Times* 25 Jan. (Audio Visual Rep.) p. i/6 There is evidence of companies in Britain becoming increasingly aware of the importance of video communications through the viewdata services such as the Prestel system of the Post Office, and a wide variety of other forms of computer-generated videotexts. **1980** *New Scientist* 3 July 49/4 The British pioneered viewdata (now known as videotext according to international standards) with Prestel, but the Gallic Teletel is running hard to catch up. **1981** *Ibid.* 10 Dec. 721/1 The first big order for a public videotext system—in West Germany—has gone to IBM, not to British Telecom's Prestel. **1983** *Christian Sci. Monitor* 15 Apr. B-12/2 Cable television is just one of several emerging video technologies, which include videodisc, teletext, and videotext.

vidicon (vi·dikǫn). [f. *VID(EO- + *ICON(O-SCOPE.] A kind of small television camera tube in which the image is formed on a transparent electrode coated with photoconductive material, the video signal being obtained from the variation in the current flowing to or from this as it is scanned by a beam of (usu. low-speed) electrons.

1950 P. K. WEIMER et al. in *Electronics* May 72/1 The name 'vidicon' has been coined to distinguish these tubes from the photoemissive tubes. **1961** *Listener* 2 Nov. 726/3 A vidicon tube is also used in a small lightweight 'radio camera'. **1966** *McGraw-Hill Encycl. Sci. & Technol.* XIII. 465/2 Nearly all closed-circuit television cameras utilize a vidicon. **1978** *Nature* 5 Oct. 414/1 The UV vidicons, when properly erased and prepared for use, can be exposed for several hours on very weak planetary emissions. **1981** 'A. HALL' *Pekin Target* xvi. 158 These are hard copies of some stuff we took from high altitude with vidicon cameras.

vie, *sb.*[1] Restrict † *Obs.* to senses in Dict. and add pronunc. (vī). ‖ **3.** Used in a number of mod.Fr. phrases, as **vie de Bohème** (dә boˌem), a Bohemian way of life; also *attrib.*; **vie de château** (dә ʃato), the way of life of a large country house; aristocratic social life; **vie de luxe** (dә lüks), a life of luxury; **vie d'intérieur** (dæ̃nteryö̆r), private or domestic life; **vie en rose** (añ röz) [app. from a French song by Edith Piaf containing the line '*je vois la vie en rose*'], a life seen through rose-coloured spectacles; **(la) vie intérieure** (æ̃nteryö̆r), one's inner life, the life of the spirit; **(la) vie intime** (æ̃ntim), the intimate personal life of a person; **Vie Parisienne** (parizyen), Parisian life, the name of a popular French magazine; used *attrib.* to denote a characteristic quality of voluptuous appeal; **vie romancée** (romañse) [see *ROMANCÉ *ppl. a.*], a fictionalized biography.

1888 MRS. H. WARD *Robert Elsmere* I. I. vii. 174 That golden *vie de Bohème* which she alone apparently of all artists was destined never to know. **1957** 'P. QUENTIN' *Suspicious Circumstances* i. 5 Two days later I was installed in a suitably Vie de Bohème apartment looking out on the Luxembourg gardens. **1980** S. T. HAYMON *Death & Pregnant Virgin* ii. 12 Who could have prophesied that Paul Falkener, that personification of the *vie de Bohème*, would fall so completely under her spell? **1924** A. D. SEDGWICK *Little French Girl* I. vii. 61 Is there a *vie de château* in the neighbourhood? **1979** A. BUCHAN *Scrap Screen* i. 4 The denigrated sentiment of nostalgia.. feeds on reconstructions of the *vie de château*. **1920** 'K. MANSFIELD' *Let.* Nov. (1928) II. 81 You realize the vie de luxe they are living—the very table—sweets, liqueurs, lilies, pearls. **1929** O. SEAMAN *Interludes of Editor* 81 And, when in Town you take your meed, I'll mark the *vie de luxe* you lead. **1889** M. H. VAN DE VELDE *Cosmopolitan Recoll.* I. vii. 235 Under the roof that shelters them it appears to her [*sc.* the Queen of Italy] that there is no room for that happy *vie d'interieur* of which she is so honestly fond. **1933** G. ARTHUR *Septuagenarian's Scrap Bk.* 201 The *vie d'intérieur* makes far less appeal. Take a look at the English drawing-room..conspiring to give a delicious sense of the room being lived in, a sense which is wholly foreign to the French *salon*. **1957** O. NASH *You can't get there from Here* 45 He was wafted into a glamorous *vie en rose* of amorous ruses. **1974** M. CECIL *Heroines in Love* vi. 157 So many hopes had tumbled that magazine writers were reluctant to present an unending *vie en rose*. **1912** C. MACKENZIE *Carnival* xxvii. 299 Suffragism viewed in retrospect was shoddy embroidery for the *vie intérieure* of Jenny. **1977** A. FRASER in A. Thwaite *My Oxford* 175 If caught, alone and inexplicably loitering, it was conventional to snatch up a book of poetry (Donne was rather smart) and indicate sudden world-weariness, a preference for *la vie intérieure*. **1984** *Listener* 5 Apr. 23/1 A work in which the *vie intérieure* of the American and European bourgeoisie is brought out into the daylight. **1891** S. WEBB *Let.* 23 May (1978) I. 272 *La vie intime*—I want to talk to you about very frankly. **1939** *Times Lit. Suppl.* 7 Jan. 4/4 A novel with real characters, who, however, are not likely on that account to prosecute him for libel, despite his plain-spoken exposure of their *vie intime*. **1979** L. LERNER *Love & Marriage* p. x, Those social historians who believe that *la vie intime* has a history which can be studied. **1890** KIPLING *Abaft the Funnel* (1909) 287, I replied that all my French was confined to the Vie Parisienne [*sc.* the French weekly *La Vie Parisienne*] and translations of Zola's novels with illustrations. **1936** C. CONNOLLY *Rock Pool* iii. 57 She.. gave him long, soft Vie Parisienne glances. **1983** L. MACDONALD *Somme* viii. 78 The saucy *Vie Parisienne*, whose cut-out pictures enlivened the decor of almost every dugout on the Western Front. **1941** *New Yorker* 13 Dec. 34/1 'The Beloved Returns', last year's full-length *vie romancée* about Goethe, started as a short sketch. **1976** *Times Lit. Suppl.* 9 Jan. 39/5 In biographical matters we have *vie romancée*: 'if the question flashed through Schiller's mind, he must have dismissed it'.

Vienna. Add: **1. a. Vienna Circle** [tr. G. *Wiener Kreis*], the name given to a group of empiricist philosophers, scientists, and mathematicians active in Vienna from the 1920s to 1938 who were chiefly concerned with methods of verifying statements, the formalization of language, the unification of science, and the elimination of metaphysics (cf. *logical positivism* s.v. *LOGICAL *a.* 7); **Vienna coup** *Bridge*, the playing of the highest ranking card of a suit as a preparation for eventually forcing an opponent to discard winning cards; **Vienna cross** (earlier example); **Vienna sausage,** a small frankfurter made of pork, beef, or veal (cf. *wienerwurst* s.v. *WIENER *a.* 2); **Vienna Secession** = *SECESSION 3 d; **Vienna steak,** a flat rissole made of minced beef; **Vienna white** (earlier example).

1934 *Philos. Rev.* XLIII. 125 Last..one would mention the logical positivism of the Vienna Circle. **1956** J. O. URMSON *Philos. Anal.* vi. 100 The main attack on metaphysics as such came from philosophers whom we have not previously discussed, the Vienna Circle and their associates. **1973** B. MAGEE *Popper* i. 11 The fashion prevailing..for his generation there and then was the logical positivism of the Vienna Circle. **1933** *Sunday Times* 5 Feb. 5/1 The coup formerly only known as the 'Vienna Coup', but now, more appropriately, also termed the 'Squeeze'. **1959** REESE & DORMER *Bridge Player's Dict.* 248 In technical terms, the Vienna Coup consists of the play of the top-ranking card of a suit so that a card of lower rank will be correctly positioned as a one-card threat in an automatic squeeze. **1974** *Country Life* 5 Dec. 1811/3 This is the Vienna Coup, essential if a squeeze on East is planned. **1881** C. C. HARRISON *Woman's Handiwork* I. 23 Vienna cross stitch..consists of two stitches crossing each other.. exactly alike on both sides of the material. **1958** *Catal. County Stores, Taunton* June 4 Vienna Sausages—a tin 4/–. **1977** *New Yorker* 27 June 64/3 A modest but welcome food cache—cornmeal, canned vegetables, Vienna sausage. **1964** LAKE & MAILLARD *Dict. Mod. Painting* (ed. 3)

182/2 Between 1898 and 1903, he [*sc.* Klimt] was president of the Vienna Secession. **1971** *Guardian* 19 Jan. 8/2 There stands in angular rectitude at the Vienna Secession Exhibition at the Royal Academy—a clock..by Adolf Loos. **1900** A. N. WHYBROW *Day-by-Day Cookery Bk.* 97 Vienna steaks... Take 1½lbs. each of rather lean beef or veal, trim.., chop very finely, add..onion or shallot,.. and 2 well beaten eggs... Form into steaks and fry in butter. **1951** G. GREENE *End of Affair* II. iii. 71 Henry chose a Vienna steak... He..expected something like a Wiener Schnitzel. **1854** Vienna white [see *KREMS].

b. (Earlier example.)

1845 E. ACTON *Mod. Cookery* xx. 545 This dish is sometimes called in England a Vienna cake; and..also.. a *Gateaux de Bordeaux*.

c. Used *attrib.* and *absol.* to designate (items made of) a hard-paste porcelain, often richly decorated, manufactured at Vienna from 1719 to 1864.

1784 H. WALPOLE *Descr. Strawberry-Hill* 9 A tea-pot and bason, six handle cups and saucers, with bottles in black, of Vienna china. **1875** C. SCHREIBER *Jrnl.* 13 Feb. (1911) I. 352 A most interesting Vienna tea service. **1885** *Encycl. Brit.* XIX. 640/1 Vienna porcelain..is greyish in tint; its paintings are very poor, and it depends for its effect chiefly on gilt-moulded scroll-work. **1900** F. LITCHFIELD *Pott. & Porc.* vii. 307 A..more tawdry description of Vienna china has been placed on the market... This would seem to have damaged the sale of the better class of modern Vienna. **1976** *Times* 30 Mar. 19/3 £3,850.. for a Vienna teabowl and saucer decorated in schwarzlot and gold. **1980** *Radio Times* 27 Sept. 14 (Advt.), Pair of Vienna porcelain vases and covers... Dark blue and cream.

2. as *sb.* A Vienna sausage.

1963 M. LEVINSON *Taxi!* xi. 132 The modern Jewish taxi-driver..doesn't mind..a plate of ham with his viennas, the traditional Jewish 'hot dog'. **1971** *Sunday Times* (Colour Suppl.) 27 June 50/2 *Frankfurters and Viennas* are the world's best-known boiling sausages. Made from a mixture of pork and veal and well smoked. Reheat for 10 minutes.

Viennese, *sb.* and *a.* Add: **A.** *sb.* **b.** (Examples.)

1849 E. RUSKIN *Let.* 22 Dec. in M. Lutyens *Effie in Venice* (1965) I. 94 Hanoverian German I understand pretty well, but Viennese, which these officers speak, is very different. **1981** LD. HAREWOOD *Tongs & Bones* vi. 108 Marion..talked fluent German (or rather Viennese),.. rattling the guttural Viennese 'r' round her throat.

B. *adj.* **b.** Special collocations: **Viennese Secession** = *SECESSION 3 d; **Viennese waltz,** (a piece of music for) the form of waltz originating in Vienna, characterized by a romantic, nostalgic quality (see quots. 1980, 1983).

1906 *Studio* (Special No.) p. A. iv, When, on the 3rd of April, 1897, nineteen young artists came together, to found the Viennese 'Secession', they chose as their leader Rudolf von Alt. **1960** *Burlington Mag.* CII. 395/1 The Viennese Secession movement (of which Klimt was co-founder and..first president). **1915** GIBSON & MILES tr. *Gayda's Mod. Austria* xxxi. 293 These worthy citizens.. give a light,..almost healthy tone to the urban life of the Empire—like the melodies of Strauss's Viennese waltzes. **1920** G. GROSSMITH in A. M. Cree *Handbk. Ball-Room Dancing* 12 Later came tight skirts and slow 'Bostons'. Then divided skirts, the 'Viennese Waltz', 'Two-Step',.. 'Turkey-Trot' [etc.]. **1979** *Listener* 19 July 71/1 'Musique-Dance', the latter..segueing from Viennese waltzes..to 'oom-pah' drinking-songs. **1980** *New Grove Dict. Mus.* XX. 206/1 The Viennese Waltz compositions of the second half of the 19th century, especially when played with the slight anticipation of the second beat of a bar and the subtle use of rubato which are characteristics of the traditional Viennese performance, remain a popular feature of concerts. **1983** *New Oxf. Compan. Mus.* II. 1966/2 The Viennese waltz developed the characteristic of a slight anticipation of the second beat of the bar,.. which gives a delightful and distinctive lilt to the playing.

Vierendeel (vī·rəndeᵊl). *Engin.* The name of A. *Vierendeel*, Belgian engineer and architect, used *attrib.* with reference to a type of girder introduced by him in 1896 in which there are no diagonal members, overall rigidity of the structure being maintained by rigidity at the joints of the vertical and horizontal members.

1930 *Engineering* 20 June 790/1 The types of steel coaches usually dealt with..could be reduced to two, in one of which the sides of the body were used as girders of the Vierendeel type. **1947** *Archit. Rev.* CI. 84/1 A special system was employed, using two contiguous spaces together with the columns and beams of the two upper floors, the whole forming a Vierendeel frame. **1970** *Internat. Jrnl. Solids & Structures* VI. 353 (*heading*) The minimum weight design of Vierendeel frames.

Vierkleur (fiᵊ·ɹklǭɹ). [Afrikaans, f. Du. *vier* four + *kleur* colour.] The flag of the nineteenth-century Transvaal Republic (1857–77 and 1881–1900), distinguished by three horizontal stripes of red, white, and blue, and one vertical green stripe on the left-hand side. Also *attrib.*

1900 W. S. CHURCHILL in *Morning Post* 17 July 8/1 Someone..produced a Union Jack (made during imprisonment out of a Vierkleur). **1911** H. H. FYFE *S. Afr. To-day* 106 Yet in Cape Town shop-windows are exhibited cards lamenting the 'Vierkleur', the four-coloured flag of the Transvaal. **1929** D. REITZ *Commando* iii. 20 On the left of the track stood a large marquee over which floated the vier-kleur flag of the Transvaal, indicating General Joubert's headquarters.

Viet (vyet), *sb.* and *a.* Abbrev. of *VIETNAMESE *a.* and *sb.*

1958 J. BUTTINGER *Smaller Dragon* i. 29 These Viets were probably moving into southeast China and toward the Indochinese peninsula at some time between 500 and 300 B.C. **1967** *Freedomways* VII. 128 Viet brothers come give us a hand We fight for freedom We fight for land. **1979** *Daily Tel.* 19 Jan. 4/6 (*heading*) Five Khmer areas fight Viet troops. **1979** *Tucson* (Arizona) *Citizen* 20 Sept. 1E/1 (*heading*) Viets say Nixon plots with China.

‖ **vi et armis** (vī et ā·ɹmis), *adv. phr.* [L., lit. 'with force and arms'.] Violently, forcibly, by compulsion; *spec.* in *Law*, causing direct damage to person or property; also *attrib.* Cf. FORCE *sb.*[1] 5 c.

1618 W. FULBECKE *Parallel of Civil & Common Laws* I. 80 a This Writ will not lye, for it is *vi et armis*. **1703** in *Eng. Rep. King's Bench* (1909) XCII. 137 So a man shall have an action against another for riding over his ground, though it do him no damage; for it is an invasion of his property, and the other has no right to come there. And in these cases the action is brought vi et armis. **1762** SMOLLETT *Launcelot Greaves* I. IV. 101 He compelled, *vi & armis*, a rich farmer's son to marry the daughter of a cottager. **1819** KEATS *Let.* 31 July (1958) II. 134 If I had not put pen to paper since I saw you this would be to me a vi et armis taking up before the Judge. *a* **1846** B. R. HAYDON *Autobiogr.* (1927) III. xvii. 338, I looked astounded, but casting a glance round the table easily saw..I was to be set at that evening *vi et armis*. **1873** C. M. YONGE *Pillars of House* II. xix. 181 It was current in the nursery that he was a black man who expelled us *vi et armis*. **1941** W. A. PERCY *Lanterns on Levee* xv. 179 The squad kept marching; it marched now like Beatrice Lillie, *vi et armis*, clear through an unyielding detachment planted in front of it. **1957** R. F. V. HEUSTON *Salmond's Law of Torts* (ed. 12) i. 5 To walk peacefully across another man's land is a forcible injury and a trespass, no less than to break into his house *vi et armis*.

Viet Cong (vyet kǫ·ŋ), *sb.* and *a.* Also **Vietcong.** [Vietnamese, lit. = Vietnamese Communist.] **A.** *sb.* (A member of) the Communist guerilla force(s) active in Vietnam between 1954 and 1976. **B.** *adj.* Of or pertaining to (the members of) this movement.

1957 *Ann. Reg. 1956* 321 Though small groups of dissidents remained in the jungles they ceased to be a danger, and the Communist dissidents known as the Viet Cong were equally ineffective. **1961** *Times* 27 Sept. 13/7 At the base of the Vietcong hierarchy is the village 'cell'. **1964** *Asia Mag.* 7 June 6 The war prevails, and it will, until the Viet Cong is wiped out. **1967** *Observer* 30 Apr. 12 The little cream schoolhouse is essential to the American dream of what we are doing in Vietnam, and it is essential for the soldiers to believe that in *Vietcong* hamlets no schooling is permitted. **1981** B. GRANGER *Schism* (1982) viii. 78 The village headman was a Viet Cong.

Viet Minh (vyet mi·n). Also **Vietminh.** [f. *Việt*-Nam Dôc-Lâp Dông-*Minh*, Vietnamese Independence League.] A nationalist independence movement (1941–50) in French Indo-China; *loosely*, the movement succeeding this; a member of one of these movements. Also *attrib.*

1945 *Times* 14 Sept. 3/6 There seem to be only two parties of any significance at the moment—the Viet-min and the Communists. **1945** *Times* 16 Nov. 3/3 It is believed some effort may be made to come to a compromise with the Viet Minh 'Government' in Hanoi. **1962** E. SNOW *Other Side of River* (1963) lxxxv. 684 The free Vietnamese armed forces..were guerrilla groups led largely by the Vietnamese Independence League—Viet Minh, for short. **1968** R. WEST *Sk. from Vietnam* i. 21 The Vietminh, precursors of the Vietcong, employed assassination and terror. **1975** *New Yorker* 21 Apr. 133/1 The structure of the three basic committees is reminiscent of the old Vietminh organizations established in the South between 1946 and 1954.

Vietnamese (vyetnămī·z), *a.* and *sb.* Also **Viet Namese.** [f. *Vietnam* (see below) + -ESE.] **A.** *adj.* Of or pertaining to the S.E. Asian country of Vietnam (formed in 1945 by the union of the former French colonial provinces of Annam, Tongking, and Cochin-China, and between 1954 and 1976 divided into North and South Vietnam), its inhabitants, or their language.

1947 *Facts on File* Apr. 129 Yesterday French troops claimed that 3 Japanese officers were killed near Hanoi while leading Viet Namese troops. **1951** M. B. EMENEAU (*title*) Studies in Vietnamese (Annamese) grammar. **1951** *Vietnam: Old Nation—Young State* (U.N.), As a result the Vietnamese language developed considerably and was able to free itself entirely from Chinese influence. **1962** E. SNOW *Other Side of River* (1963) lxxxv. 685 Gracey refused to see Vietnamese leaders who wished to negotiate terms of cooperation for disarming the Japanese. **1969** *Listener* 12 June 814/3 Whenever I see the members of the village council, I say to them: 'I'm not here to teach you what to do. I'm not Vietnamese. I don't look like you. I don't even speak your own language. You've got to make your own decisions.' **1977** *Early Music* July 365/2 (*caption*) Trân Van Khe playing the Vietnamese fiddle. **1983** P. NIESEWAND *Scimitar* xi. 247 It was an excellent meal, starting with..Vietnamese spring rolls..and finally squirrel fish, a whole baked fish.

B. *sb.* **a.** A native, *collect.* the natives, of Vietnam. **b.** The language of this people, considered by some philologists to belong to the Mon-Khmer family.

1947 H. R. ISAACS *New Cycle in Asia* viii. 157 Matters came to a head in Hanoi on December 19, 1946, when clashes in that city resulted in generalized warfare... The French charged that the Vietnamese were the instigators of the outbreak. **1950** *Times* 25 Apr. 7/2 The new State of Viet Nam has to rely so much on foreign support that many patriotic Vietnamese hold back or join with the Communists. **1953** W. W. GAGE (*title*) Verb constructions in Vietnamese. **1965** *New Statesman* 30 Apr. 680/2 As a Vietnamese, I feel I have the right to express my resentment at the US air raids on Vietnam. **1972** M. SHEPPARD *Taman Indera* 3 The people whom we now know as Chinese, Thais, Khmers, Vietnamese and Malays. **1978** E. TIDYMAN *Table Stakes* II. i. 141 He..shouted a string of orders in Vietnamese.

Vietnamize (vye·tnămaiz), *v.* [f. *Vietnam* (see prec.) + -IZE.] *trans.* To give a Vietnamese character to; to make Vietnamese; to transfer to Vietnamese (esp. as opposed to American) influence or control. (This now *Hist.* only.)

1957 *Holiday* Aug. 119/1 Cholon's Chinese ebullience has definitely quieted down as a result of Diem's drive to 'Vietnamize' the Chinese. **1969** *Daily Tel.* 25 Oct. 5/3 It was learned..that America had handed over another base to South Vietnam. Two of the United States major port facilities, including the one in Saigon, were next on the list to be 'Vietnamised'. **1972** *Nature* 22 Sept. 185/2 Last week's statement..criticizes the policy of the United States in 'Vietnamizing' the war.

Hence **Vie:tnamiza·tion; Vie·tnamizing** *vbl. sb.*

1957 *Holiday* Aug. 119/3 When the new idea of 'Vietnamization' is being fostered in the country..it is not surprising the Vietnamese prefer to approach..foreigners with care and reticence. **1969** *Daily Tel.* 11 Oct. 18/1 The Vietnamisation of the war continued with the transfer of 80 United States Navy river patrol boats to the South Vietnamese Navy. *Ibid.* 18 Nov. 14/4 The price for 'Vietnamising' the war..is clearly a Vietnamising of the country's politics as well. **1972** F. FITZGERALD *Fire in Lake* xvi. 404 'Vietnamization', the ironic name for the slow withdrawal of American ground troops and the buildup of Vietnamese armed forces to fight an American-directed war in their stead. **1980** *Word 1979* XXX. 125 The Committee also identified such new problems as..the Vietnamization of foreign terms.

Vietnik (vye·tnik). orig. *U.S.* [f. *Viet*(*nam* + *-NIK after *beatnik*.] (A usu. pejorative term applied to) an active opponent of American military involvement in the war between North and South Vietnam. Also *attrib.* Cf. *PEACENIK.

1965 *Time* 22 Oct. 25A/1 A ragtag collection of unshaven and unscrubbed—they could be called Vietniks—turned out last weekend to promote the most popular new anti-cause. *Ibid.*, The Vietnik rallies—which also attracted some tweedy faculty members..—seemed to bear out a Senate Internal Security report issued last week. **1966** *Wall St. Jrnl.* 31 Mar. 18/2 If the Communists believe that draft-card-burners and other Vietniks represent majority American opinion, they are simply misinformed. **1969** *T.V. Times* (Brisbane) 4 June 6/1, I am opposed to the Vietniks who want us to get out... I saw too many twisted bodies of women and children, mutilated by the Vietcong. **1977** *Time* 18 Apr. 47/2 Sometimes the argument has sounded like a replay of old Vietnik protests.

‖ **vieux** (vyö), *a.* The Fr. word for 'old', used in various idiomatic phrases, as *vieux jeu* (ʒö) [lit. 'old game'], (something or someone) old-fashioned, hackneyed, outmoded, 'old hat'; *vieux marcheur* (marʃör) ['old campaigner', f. *Le Vieux Marcheur* (1909), a play by Henri Lavedon], an elderly womanizer; also *transf.*; *vieux port* (pǭr) ['old port'], the old harbour area of a modern French seaport; *vieux rose* (rōz) ['old rose'] = *OLD ROSE b.

[**1888** H. JAMES *Reverberator* II. iii. 57 His father.. didn't think it well painted... 'Poor dear papa, he only understands *le vieux jeu!*' **1891** M. S. VAN DE VELDE *French Fiction of Today* I. i. 7 Their contempt for what they call vieux jeu.] **1896** MRS. H. WARD *Sir George Tressady* II. xvi. 361 'Did you see the new piece at the Français?' He made a face. 'Not I! One couldn't be caught by such *vieux jeu* as that!' **1900** G. MURRAY *Let.* 30 July in G. B. Shaw *Coll. Lett.* (1972) II. 181 Cæsar..did not invent the sarcasm of calling the soldiers 'Citizens'. It was vieux jeu. **1918** R. FRY *Let.* 14 Oct. (1972) II. 435 We are *vieux jeu* and incorrigibly nineteenth century. **1955** *Times* 30 June 15/1 Are not dilatory bus drivers and conductors by now somewhat *vieux jeu*? **1972** M. GLENNY tr. *Solzhenitsyn's August 1914* lxii. 600 To indulge in arguments with hostile, half-baked youth struck him as *vieux jeu* and boring. **1975** *Harper's & Queen* June 128/3 Henri's parents are very French *vieux jeu*... My mother-in-law talks about Louis XV as though she *knew* him. **1920** G. B. SHAW *Shaw on Theatre* (1958) 133 All the young men are cads and cowards, all the old men *vieux marcheurs*. **1937** *Times Lit. Suppl.* 16 Jan. 39/1 Of all the vieux marcheurs in nature, the cock pheasant has almost the worst reputation. **1940** G. ARTHUR *Concerning Winston Spencer Churchill* 108 The immortal hero of Khartum—so ran an odious whisper—was addicted to the brandy bottle; Mr. Gladstone, so it was vulgarly suggested, pursued paths associated with a *vieux marcheur*. **1945** E. WAUGH *Brideshead Revisited* I. ii. 44 Those leprous façades in the vieux port at Marseille. **1957** 'P. QUENTIN' *Suspicious Circumstances* xvii. 198 The lights on all the boats moved in the Vieux Port. **1981** 'D. RUTHERFORD' *Porcupine Basin* i. 11 Be at the Café des Voyageurs in the *vieux port*... Take a table on the *terrasse*. **1890** *Girl's Own Paper* 11 Oct. 31/2, I should get your village dressmaker..to make you a *vieux rose* zephyr dress. **1916** *Daily Colonist* (Victoria, B.C.) 1 July 12/3 The colors include white..old rose, gold..vieux rose, mid-brown, [etc.]. **1941** E. BOWEN *Look at Roses* 55 Light blared on the *vieux rose* curtains.

view, *sb.* Add: **III. 16. c.** *on view* (earlier example).

1850 *Punch* 19 Oct. 164/1 The South Western Railway ..keeps a quantity of hissing, smoking, screaming engines always 'on view'.

18. b. *to take the long view*, to have regard for more than the present; to provide for the future.

1924 *Times Trade & Engin. Suppl.* 29 Nov. 247/2 Those who took the long view and ordered more than just to meet current needs are now reaping the benefit of such a policy.

c. *to take a poor view*: see *POOR *a.* (*sb.*) 5 f. Also (in same sense) *to take a dim view*.

1941 *Newsweek* 7 July 27/2 Take a dim view—disapprove. **1947** H. GRIEVE *Something in Country Air* 13 Mr Everard took a dim view of his youngest niece. **1977** *Daily News* (Perth, Austral.) 19 Jan. 6/3 Bukovsky said he took a dim view of the way the West was pursuing detente.

IV. 19. a. *view day* (later example).

1850 *Art Jrnl.* July 224 The rooms were crowded during the 'view' days with visitors.

b. *view-painter*, *-painting*; **view card**, a picture postcard showing a view; **view-finder** (earlier example); **view-phone**, a (proposed) device for enabling telephone users to see each other during a call; **viewsite**, a site (for a house or other building) with a view (sense 8 b).

1938 BLUNDEN *On Several Occasions*, Buying a view-card and a book. **1973** *Express* (Trinidad & Tobago) 17 Mar. 14/2 Hobbies—art, stamps and collecting viewcards. **1889** View-finder [see FINDER 3 d]. **1968** *Listener* 20 June 796/1 Flocks of academic view painters..used to set up their easels round the picturesque little harbour at St. Ives. **1971** *Country Life* 2 Sept. 536/3 Worcester's view-painters may fairly be compared with such fellow professionals. *Ibid.*, Topographical view-painting was not confined to fortunate Worcester, of course. **1982** *Nat. Gallery News* Feb. 1 Tourists visited Venice, wanting to take away reminders of the city they might not see again. The growing market must have encouraged both Canaletto and Guardi to turn to view painting. **1964** F. POHL *Alternating Currents* (1966) 38, I turned off the viewphone, got up and walked out. **1966** *New Scientist* 24 Nov. 440/3 A 'viewphone' service (which could enable telephone users, to see each other during a call). **1978** *Times* 3 Nov. 27/4 The Post Office itself has listed the main telecommunications services..envisaged for the years 1985 and 2000... By 1985 there will be..radiopaging, confravision.., viewphone. **1971** *Sunday Express* (Johannesburg) 28 Mar. 20/2 (Advt.), Each stand a spectacular viewsite! **1977** *Chicago Tribune* 2 Oct. (TV Week Suppl.) 4/1 (Advt.), This economical two-story home turns its back to the street (or takes beautiful advantage of a viewsite) to create an uncommon sense of privacy even in a busy urban setting.

view, *v.* Add: **1. d.** *absol.* To look over a property to assess its suitability for purchase or rent.

1914 'E. BRAMAH' *Max Carrados* 79 The place is to be let... We will go on to the agents and get a card to view. **1967** N. MARSH *Death at Dolphin* i. 9 We hold the keys. Were you wanting to view? **1971** G. SIMS *Deadhand* II. iii. 92 Is it the house? No good—you can't view without a docket.

2. e. To watch (television); to watch on television. Also *absol.*

1935 *Discovery* Sept. 277/2 The comfort and interest with which the [television] pictures may be viewed in a semi-darkened room. **1936** *Times* 3 Nov. 9/2, I should be unwilling to lay heavy odds against a resident in Hindhead viewing the Coronation procession. **1948** *Something Done* 15 A number of people might now be viewing without having bothered about taking out a licence. **1956** *B.B.C. Handbk. 1957* 104 Asking them what broadcasts they listened to or viewed 'yesterday'. **1958** *Listener* 25 Dec. 1090/1 They view on average for thirteen hours a week. **1966** C. MACKENZIE *Paper Lives* x. 145, I was anxious for Humphrey Mowart to explain to me the operation of the various knobs..of a television set so that I shall be in control of the machine when we are what they call viewing.

viewing *ppl. a.* (examples corresponding to *VIEW *v.* 2 e).

1958 *Spectator* 6 June 730/3 It was a great deal better than half a dozen others which the viewing public has taken to its heart. **1975** *Listener* 18 Sept. 368/1 NHK.. will continue..to give Japan's viewing public all of what it wants.

view·able, *a.* [f. VIEW *v.* + -ABLE.] **1.** That may be viewed, inspected, or looked over.

1909 in WEBSTER. **1924** E. POUND *Lett.* (1971) 189 No. The Studio is not viewable till I get back. **1959** *Historic Houses & Castles in Gt. Britain & Northern Ireland* 51 Adm. 2/–, Chd. 1/–. Gardens not viewable. **1976** *New Yorker* 1 Mar. 64/3 He said that three planeloads of bodies had arrived in Oakland—one, on Monday, of 'viewable' bodies and two, on Tuesday, of 'non-viewable' bodies.

2. *spec.* Of a television programme: capable of being viewed with pleasure or interest, worth watching.

1957 *Observer* 22 Dec. 8/6 B.B.C.'s Friday night documentary... This piece, though viewable, was often wildly unconvincing. **1971** *Daily Tel.* 21 Aug. 7 The secret of the endlessly viewable National Film Theatre series on television..seems to lie quite simply in its subjects. **1979** *Now!* 21–27 Sept. 90/2 To make it viewable, they'd have had to make it easier.

Hence **viewabi·lity.**

1958 *Observer* 5 Oct. 19/4 You could argue hard about the precise degree of depth and reality in Granada's *The Liberty Man*, but there was no doubt about its viewability. **1966** *Listener* 2 June 813/1 This fascinating teaser, which I would match against any recent television drama for sheer viewability. **1977** *New Yorker* 16 May 114/1 Nicklaus..carefully molded his holes for exceptional viewability.

viewdata (viū·dēⁱtă). orig. also **Viewdata.** [f. VIEW *v.* + *data*, pl. of DATUM.] A system enabling a user's television set to show alphanumeric information selected from a computer database, with a telephone line providing two-way communication with the computer.

1975 S. FEDIDA in *Communications Networks* 275 An experimental study of a computer-based information distribution and retrieval interactive medium, called VIEWDATA, has been carried out. **1975** *Times* 24 Sept. 2/8 The telephone and television set could be linked to provide a significant new type of home information service... Known as Viewdata, the proposed new service was demonstrated publicly for the first time yesterday. **1976** *Nat. Electronics Rev.* Jan.–Feb. 11/1 Unlike these specialist orientated services, Viewdata has been developed as an interactive information service for use by the general public. **1979** *Guardian* 24 Sept. 20/6 The Post Office tried to register the name Viewdata for its product but this was refused on the ground that it was too all-embracing a title. Then it chose Prestel—and led a campaign to get viewdata accepted internationally as the generic term for computerised public information systems. **1979** *Austral. Financial Rev.* 21 Dec. 19/3 A meeting of a viewdata technical standards group in the Netherlands..has provided a draft standard which includes both Prestel and the French Teletel system. **1981** [see *TELETEXT]. **1983** *Computerworld* 23 May ID-14/1 Telematics regards its entry as timely because of..the rise in such dissemination systems as viewdata and teletext. **1984** *N.Z. Farmer* 23 Feb. 16/1 Two Viewdata pilot trials are to be started in the North Island this year.

viewer. Add: **2. b.** One who watches television. Cf. *TELEVIEWER. Also *attrib.*

1935 *Times* 16 May 9/3 When television sets are as numerous as broadcast receivers it is possible that there may be a demand for some form of record..with which the viewer would be independent of wireless broadcasts. **1936** *Times* 3 Nov. 9/1 At Alexandra Palace yesterday, when the new television service of the B.B.C. was officially opened, the Postmaster-General and others had to address themselves not only to listeners, but to 'viewers'. Within a radius of some 25 miles, 'viewers' saw and heard a ceremony which the speakers rightly described as historic. *Ibid.*, There was a speech by Mr. R. C. Norman, chairman of the B.B.C. who was the first to use the word 'viewers' in its new meaning. **1946** *Electronic Engin.* XVIII. 276 The poor light at Wimbledon did not entirely account for television's failure to convey to viewers, comfortably seated at home, the breathless thrill [etc.]. **1955** *Britannica Bk. of Year* 489/2 *Viewer-Research* (an investigation into the relative popularity of programmes shown). **1957** *Listener* 5 Dec. 956/2 In football and boxing the viewer has an immense advantage over the spectator on the spot. **1961** A. WILSON *Old Men at Zoo* iii. 125 The viewer response so far is jolly encouraging. **1966** G. N. LEECH *Eng. in Advertising* v. 50 The [television advertising] copywriter..does not despise the triviality of real-life conversation. In fact by deviating from it he stands to lose credibility and viewer-involvement. **1971** G. CHARLES *Destiny Waltz* i. 11 'You're probably familiar with some of our feature programmes if you watch a lot.' 'Yes, I'm a viewer all right,' said Jimmy. 'I've no false snobbery about TV.' **1977** *Rep. Comm. Future of Broadcasting* i. 3 The first decision we took was to ask individual viewers and listeners for their opinions. **1985** *Broadcast* 11 Jan. 21/3 Failure to cover such events, it is felt, would reflect badly on broadcasters in the minds of viewers.

4. An optical device for looking at film transparencies or the like.

1936 [see *microfilm viewer* s.v. *MICROFILM *sb.* 2]. **1940** A. L. M. SOWERBY *Wall's Dict. Photogr.* (ed. 15) 19 The principle involved is exactly that of the 'viewers' now sold for looking at prints or small transparencies. **1958** *Woman's Own* 8 Oct. 58/3 The X-ray on the viewer. **1972** *Sci. Amer.* Jan. 65/1 When viewed through a stereoscopic viewer, the resulting image is truly three-dimensional. **1972** M. J. BOSSE *Incident at Naha* ii. 67, I wondered what Virgil would learn from the microfilm. He had taken it to the university library where he could use the viewers.

Hence **view·ership**, the viewers of a television programme collectively; the number of such viewers.

1954 *Sun* (Baltimore) 30 Apr. 16/3 The extent of viewership of the subcommittee hearings was far from excessive. **1957** *Economist* 24 Aug. 637/2 More reliable estimates of 'viewership'. **1964** D. SUSSKIND *Let.* 26 Mar. in G. Marx *Groucho Lett.* (1967) 223 Please keep watching 'Open End'... We need viewership very urgently. **1979** *Arizona Daily Star* 1 Apr. (Tucson T.V. Suppl.) 12/3 CBS.. restored 'The White Shadow' to its former Monday night time period, where it once again is drawing a big viewership.

viewing, *vbl. sb.* Add: *spec.* (*a*) (*U.S.*) The action of taking a last look at the body of a dead person before the funeral; a time during which visitors may so view a body; (*b*) the activity of watching television; an instance or period of this.

(*a*) **1944** *Casket & Sunnyside* Dec. 31/3 At least during the trying hours of the viewings we had individualized the setting. **1955** HABENSTEIN & LAMERS *Hist. Amer. Funeral Directing* xiii. 571 The viewing is controlled in some parts of the country by the funeral director to the extent that certain visiting hours are established. **1956** *Washington Post* 10 Feb. 33/7 In addition to the viewing the mass also will be open to all who choose to attend. **1963** J. MITFORD *Amer. Way of Death* vi. 95 Demonstrably flimsy and ridiculous as the justifications for universal embalming and 'viewing' may be, they have nonetheless proved very effective and so far have been safe from authoritative contradiction. **1968** H. WAUGH '*30' Manhattan East* (1969) 182 The funeral home in which Monica Glazzard's mortal remains were to be displayed was on Lexington Avenue..and the viewing was ..Friday night from 8 P.M.

(*b*) **1959** *20th Cent.* Nov. 335 After a year's viewing the newcomer to television does view rather less than at first. **1960** *Guardian* 22 July 4/6 Much of the output..[is] unsuitable for 'family viewing'. **1974** *Times* 28 Feb. 16/8 The material is largely composed of old favourites, but that is an irony of television..a second, even third, viewing is welcome.

attrib. (Further examples.)

1935 *Times* 15 May 13/2 A few weeks ago a similar viewing post was opened in Berlin. **1940** *Chambers's Techn. Dict.* 893/1 *Viewing room*, a small projection theatre in a studio, for viewing rushes and completed films during the process of editing. **1949** *Radio Times* 15 July 43/1 Automatically raised to viewing position by press button control. **1955** 'J. CHRISTOPHER' *Year of Comet* i. 5 He knew her viewing habits... She alternated between three channels. **1956** *B.B.C. Handbk. 1957* 104 It is of obvious interest and importance to the BBC to know how those of the television public who have a choice of programmes, divide their viewing time. **1959** *20th Cent.* Nov. 335 American viewing figures..are slightly higher than ours. **1961** G. MILLERSON *Telev. Production* iii. 32 Clearly, if we use any camera lens-angle other than the audience's viewing angle (around 12° to 20°), distortion will occur. **1969** J. ELLIOT *Duel* I. ii. 36 Cutting rooms and a tiny viewing theatre. **1972** 'H. CALVIN' *Take Two Popes* iii. 23 Ramon could see himself herded into the viewing area. **1973** *Listener* 23 Aug. 261/3 There's a BBC view that if we have a spare viewing-room ready for researchers, we are bad housekeepers. **1975** *Broadcast* 14 July 6/2 BBC viewing hours have also gone up..but the profile proportion has decreased. **1975** *Language for Life* (Dept. Educ. & Sci.) ii. 14 Nothing this Committee can say in isolation will change the viewing pattern of those evening hours which children spend in front of a set. **1975** M. KEYNON *Mr Big* xx. 188 At the terminal he watched from the viewing platform but..was not even certain he was looking at the correct aircraft.

view·port. [f. VIEW *sb.* + PORT *sb.*³] **1.** A window in a spacecraft or in the conning tower of an oil rig.

1957 T. STURGEON *Thunder & Roses* 174 You just don't look through viewports very often. **1976** *Offshore Engineer* Apr. 61/1 The forward 'sphere'..has eight round viewports: two above, one forward, two each side and below and forward.

2. *Computers.* A defined part of a VDU display, such as may be allocated to a particular category of information.

1973 NEWMAN & SPROULL *Princ. Interactive Computer Graphics* vii. 126 It is possible to clip several different pictures to different viewports and display them simultaneously on the screen. **1982** J. E. SCOTT *Introd. Interactive Computer Graphics* ix. 183 The graphics package provides a full range of two- and three-dimensional viewing transformations, including window selection, viewport assignment, and clipping.

viff (vif), *sb.* and *v.* Also **vif** and in capitals. *colloq.* [f. initial letters of *vector(ing) in forward flight.*] **A.** *sb.* 'Viffing'; the ability to 'viff'.

1972 *Flight* 28 Dec. 946 The one distinct and inherent advantage possessed by the Hawker Siddeley aeroplane.. is the ability to vector its thrust. The possibilities of VIFF (vectoring in forward flight) have been under examination for some time. **1981** F. K. MASON *Harrier* viii. 118 Initial investigations demonstrated that VIFF considerably enhanced the aircraft's potential in air combat.

B. *v. intr.* Of an aircraft: to change direction abruptly as a result of a change in the direction of thrust of its engine(s). So **vi·ffing** *vbl. sb.* and *ppl. a.*

1981 B. GUNSTON *Harrier* vi. 78 No matter how inferior the starting position, the viffing Harrier invariably won the engagement. **1982** *Times* 3 May 3/7 With the exception of the Russian Yakovlev Yak 36MP, it is the only high-speed aircraft in the world which can take off without the advantage of an airfield, fly backwards, and 'viff' (vector in forward flight)—that is 'stop' in mid-air and swerve acutely sideways. *Ibid.* 15 June 4/2 There had been few dogfights in the air and thus few opportunities for the Harriers to demonstrate their unique ability to vector-in-flight or 'vif', outmaneuvring the enemy planes. **1982** *New Scientist* 27 May 557/3 US Marine Corps pilots developed a technique known as 'viffing' with their Harriers. **1983** *Times Lit. Suppl.* 14 Oct. 1109/2 The VSTOL Harrier with its swivelable jets and ability to 'viff'.

Vigenere, Vigenère (viʒənɛ̄r). The name of Blaise de *Vigenère* (1523–96), French scholar and student of ciphers, used *absol.* and *attrib.*

with reference to a polyalphabetic cipher described by him (*Traité des Chiffres*, 1586).

1916 P. Hitt *Man. Solution Mil. Ciphers* vii. 51 The cipher disk method is practically the Vigenere cipher with reversed alphabets. **1943** [see *modularly *adv.*]. **1944** H. McCloy *Panic* 73 He tapped the cipher message... 'This is obviously a Vigenère, and all Vigenères can be broken.' **1957** *Encycl. Brit.* V. 929/2 The Confederate army used the Vigenère cipher—which the Federal army cryptanalysts are said to have solved every time a message in it was intercepted. **1961** Shulman & Weintraub *Gloss. Cryptogr.*, *Vigenere cipher*, a periodic substitution cipher originally employed with a 26 × 26 tableau and later converted into a slide with a normal clear alphabet over a normal cipher alphabet. **1963** H. S. M. Coxeter *W. W. R. Ball's Math. Recreations & Ess.* (rev. ed.) xiv. 400 If the different alphabets are related as in a Vigenère square, certain properties of symmetry can be used to advantage.

vigent (vəi·dʒĕnt), *a. rare.* [ad. L. *vigent-*, *vigens*, pres. pple. of *vigēre* to thrive.] Flourishing; vigorous; prosperous.

1590 W. Clever *Flower of Physicke* 4 Forthwith after these painefull defatigations, let naturall sweate and quiet sleepe, consolidat and refresh the body, to become more vigent, and the stomacke more sharpe. **1930** J. Wall *Durham Cathedral* iv. 183 Durham College..after several changes of fortune is now vigent as Trinity College.

viggerish, var. *vigorish.

vigil, *v.* (Later examples.)

1915 G. Frankau *Tid'apa* vii. 40 Two days and two nights has he vigiled—the doctor dozes and blinks. **1975** J. Montague *Slav Dance* 57 We vigil by the dying fire, talk stilled for once.

vigilance. Add: **1.** *committee of vigilance* (U.S.) = *vigilance committee.*

1837 H. Martineau *Society in Amer.* II. 139 He was brought to trial by the Committee of Vigilance; seven elders of the presbyterian church of Nashville being among his judges. **1857** J. W. Gihon *Geary & Kansas* 35 A committee of vigilance..was appointed, whose duty it was to observe and report all such persons [i.e. abolitionists].

vigilante. Add: **1.** For *U.S.* read orig. *U.S.* and add: (Earlier example.) Also *transf.* and *attrib.*

Now normally with pronunc. (vidʒilæ·nti).

1856 C. Nordhoff *Man-of-War Life* xv. 255 The second day after the expiration of their liberty, notice was given the *vigilantes*, ashore, that five dollars reward would be paid for every man of the crew rendered on board. **1890** N. P. Langford *Vigilante Days* I. xiv. 181 In the name of Vigilante justice [some men] committed crimes which..were wholly indefensible. **1918** G. Frankau *One of Them* xxiv. 185 Shall Muses condescend to gutter-trilling; Or Pegasus, whose tail the strap-hitched star tickles, Feed like a cow-hocked yellow Rosinante In Grecian mangers of a Vigilante? **1939** Joyce *Finnegans Wake* 78 What vigilantes and ridings then. **1948** *Daily Tel.* 22 May 3/6 The Advertising Association is asking 24 advertising clubs..to form a 'vigilantes' committee to report cases of advertising..of a doubtful..nature. **1959** *Times* 22 Oct. 8/2 An appeal by Nottingham 'vigilantes'—a group of businessmen—for an inquiry into the city's Labour-controlled administration has been rejected. **1980** *Sunday Times* 24 Aug. 2/3 But the critical officers say that if normal police cover is continually reduced..there is a danger..that could lead to highly undesirable vigilante activity. **1984** S. Townsend *Growing Pains A. Mole* 42, I offered to set up a vigilante group but my father said that anyone who has carried an old mattress 300 yards in the dark is not going to be put off dumping it by a gaggle of spotty schoolboys.

Hence **vigila·ntism** (orig. *U.S.*), the principles or activities of vigilantes or vigilance committees.

1937 *Sun* (Baltimore) 27 Sept. 2/7 A public investigation of 'vigilantism' in strike areas was announced today through the American League Against War and Fascism. **1942** W. Stegner *Mormon Country* 96 Perhaps even those incidents were purely unofficial and spontaneous acts of devout Mormons, the Mormon equivalent of lynch law and vigilantism. **1953** *Economist* 19 Sept. 775/3 In the United States, neither private vigilantism nor the government seems prepared to treat a favourable verdict as final. **1979** *Times* 6 Dec. 3/1 Africa was confronted, he said, with a choice between a system of collective security and a system of international vigilantism. **1985** *Listener* 10 Jan. 9/1 The one genuine, spontaneous popular institution in the West was vigilantism.

vigintennial (vəidʒinte·niăl), *a. rare.* [f. Viginti-, after Biennial *a.* and *sb.*, Triennial *a.* and *sb.*, etc.] Occurring once in twenty years.

1921 *Glasgow Herald* 29 Jan. 13/3 Their [*sc.* the planets'] vigintennial conjunction is due a few months hence.

vigintivirate. Delete † *Obs.* and add later examples.

1904 Tyrrell & Purser *Corr. Cicero* (ed. 3) I. 319/2 Cicero..represents Caesar as having been offended at his refusal to become a member of the vigintivirate. **1976** *Classical Q.* XXVI. 312 He was born in about A.D. 55, and..we might assign the *latus clavus* and a post in the vigintivirate to this reign.

vignette, *sb.* Add: **2. b.** A brief verbal description of a person, place, etc.; a short descriptive or evocative episode in a play, etc.

1880 E. Simcox *Diary* 28 Mar. in K. A. McKenzie *Edith Simcox & George Eliot* (1961) iii. 61, I have thought ..of writing a little book of 'Vignettes'. **1901** [see Thumbnail 2]. **1934** *Punch* 19 Dec. 698/1 Its writer gets and provides what entertainment she can from them—witness her amusing vignette of the unfortunate *Habibullah.* **1957** *Practical Wireless* XXXIII. 558/1 The play was supposed to evoke the Edwardian era in a series of tiny vignettes interspersed with 'instrumental effects'. **1958** *Times* 12 Aug. 10/3 Miss Maria Lapinska, as his [dancing] partner came nearest to touching the heart in a wartime *vignette* entitled *1940.* **1980** *Jrnl. R. Soc. Arts* Mar. 226/1 Let me quote one vignette.

4. (Earlier example.)

1790 *Loiterer* 2 Jan. 5 Three..volumes in duodecimo; which, with..a handsome vignette frontispiece, will cut a respectable figure.

vignette, *v.* Add: **2.** *Optics.* To modify so as to give rise to vignetting of an image.

1945 *Jrnl. Optical Soc. Amer.* XXXV. 499/1 Otherwise, light rays coming from those points of the light source farthest from the optical axis will not spread out over the entire striation field but will be vignetted by the condenser aperture. **1961** *Jrnl. Sci. Instruments* XXXVIII. 93/1 At the edge of the field of $\pm 3\frac{1}{2}°$, the meridial section of the aperture is vignetted to about 80% of its axial value. Over the vignetted aperture, both the meridian plane and secondary plane sections of the emergent wave front lie [etc.]. **1973** *Optical Engin.* XII. 20/2 At 1 mm diameter pinhole in 1·5 mm lead severely vignettes the field off-axis.

vignetted *ppl. a.* (further example).

1961 [see *vignette *v.* 2].

vignetting, *vbl. sb.* Add: **1.** (Earlier example.)

1842 E. A. Poe in *Graham's Mag.* Apr. 201/1 The peculiarities of the design, of the *vignetting* and of the frame.

2. *Optics.* A dimming or disappearance of an image at its edge as a result of the blocking of some off-axis rays during their passage through the optical system.

1930 L. B. W. Jolley et al. *Theory & Design Illuminating Engin. Equipment* xxix. 449 This vignetting effect may result in a reduction in the illumination towards the edges of the image even in the most carefully designed lenses. **1959** Born & Wolf *Princ. Optics* iv. 187 Designers sometimes rely on vignetting to obliterate undesirable off-axis aberrations. **1974** *Sci. Amer.* Mar. 112/1 The diameter of the mirrors..must be at least as large as the ruled area of the gratings to prevent vignetting..and the scattering of stray light into the image. **1978** *SLR Camera* Aug. 64/1 The negative had good contrast and no discernible vignetting. **1984** *What Video?* Aug. 40/3 An lie [etc.]. **1973** *Optical Engin.* XII. 20/2 A 1 mm diameter pinhole in 1·5 mm lead severely vignettes the field off-axis.

vignoble. Delete † *Obs. rare* and add later examples.

1928 Joyce *Let.* 27 May (1966) III. 178, I found that the oldest vignoble in all Provence is the Clos S. Patrice. **1978** *Country Life* 16 Nov. 1618/1 Jurançon was almost wiped out by the phylloxera... The *vignoble*..was in danger of complete disappearance.

vigogne. 2. (Earlier example.)

1873 *Young Englishwoman* Feb. 75/1 Polonaise..of deep marine blue vigogne, a black silk tunic, trimmed with black Llama lace.

vigonia. 1. b. (Earlier examples.)

1803 T. Jefferson *Let.* 23 Apr. in R. G. Thwaites *Orig. Jrnls. Lewis & Clark Exped.* (1904) VII. 217, I saw a robe of what they called the Peruvian sheep, and I took to be of the Lama or Vigogna. **1818** M. Edgeworth *Let.* 29 Oct. (1971) 130 There is no black *Vigonia*—the Vigonia wool will not take black dye. Tell me which you prefer the Merino or the Queens cloth.

vigorish (vi·gərıʃ). *U.S. slang.* Also **viggerish,** etc. [prob. f. Yiddish, ad. Russ. *vyigrysh* gain, winnings.] The percentage deducted by the organizers of a game from the winnings of a gambler. Also, the rate of interest upon a usurious loan. Also *transf.* and *fig.*

1912 A. H. Lewis *Apaches of N. York* 51 Stuss licks up ..a round full fifth of all the East side earns, and to viggresh should be given the black glory thereof. **1943** *N.Y. Times Mag.* 31 Oct. 2/4, I have heard the word 'viggerish' used for the cut the house takes in dice games. **1959** R. Condon *Manchurian Candidate* xv. 201 Eugénie Rose Cheyney..loved Marco. That fact gave Marco a large edge, tantamount to wiping out the house percentage in banker's craps. No matter what the action, that is a lot of vigorish to have going for anybody. **1959** L. Katcher *Big Bankroll* iv. 51 Today,..with pari-mutuel betting..the various states, the race tracks, the local communities, all scoop their percentage off the top of each bet. The state practices a new, and highly profitable, type of 'vigorish'. **1964** 'E. McBain' *Ax* vi. 119 'Was he taking a house vigorish?' 'Nope.' 'What do you mean? He wasn't taking a cut?.. Then why'd he risk having the game in his basement?' **1966** 'E. V. Cunningham' *Helen* viii. 98 Being a widower who lived alone in the Cattleman's Club, he also bore areputation for having no use for the vigorish. He was honest when he wanted to be honest, and he was afraid of no one. **1968** *National Observer* (U.S.) 12 Feb., Mr. and Mrs. K were paying interest rates—called 'vigorish' in the loan-shark business—of 25 per cent a week. **1978** *Film Rev. 1978–9* 13/1 The companies are not in any way stealing from the picture-makers. They have to have built-in vigorishes—or else they'd go broke. Who pays for the 21 million dollars lost on *The Sorcerer*? The Studio!

‖ **viguier** (vigye). [S. Fr. var. of *vicaire*: see Vicar.] **a.** *Hist.* A magistrate in pre-Revolutionary southern France. **b.** Each of two government officials in Andorra (see quot. 1983).

1744 M. W. Montagu *Let.* 12 June (1966) II. 331 We have a new Vice Legate... The Magistrate next to him in place is call'd the Viguier, who is chose every year by the Hotel de ville. **1898** H. L. Smith in H. Spender *Through High Pyrenees* III. iii. 291 The President of the French Republic nominates a viguier with an unlimited tenure of office, and the Bishop of Urgel nominates another, who must be an Andorran, and who holds office for three years. **1922** *Glasgow Herald* 24 July 5 The chief of these is the supreme judicial authority, though the Viguiers—in theory at least—are also the heads of the militia. **1983** *Whitaker's Almanack 1984* 793/1 The sovereignty of Andorra is vested in two 'Co-Princes', the President of the French Republic and the Spanish Bishop of Urgel... They are represented by Permanent Delegates of whom one is the French Prefect of the Pyrenees Orientales Department at Perpignan and the other is the Spanish Vicar-General of the Diocese of Urgel. They are in turn represented in Andorra la Vella by two resident 'Viguiers' .., who have joint responsibility for law and order and overall administration policy, together with judicial powers as members of the Supreme Court.

vihara (vĭhā·ră). Also † **vihar, vihare.** [Skr.] In Sri Lanka and India, a Buddhist temple or monastery.

1681 R. Knox *Ceylon* III. iii. 74 Their Temples are styled Vehars... Many of the Vehars are endowed and have Farms belonging to them. **1875** [see *chaitya]. **1901** Kipling *Kim* i. 8 There were..fragments of statues and slabs crowded with figures that had encrusted the brick walls of the Buddhist *stupas* and *viharas* of the North Country. **1913** L. Woolf *Village in Jungle* i. 12 Years ago..he had gone on a pilgrimage to the vihare at Medamahanuwara. **1930** J. Still *Jungle Tide* ix. 220 In the *vihara*, every Buddhist monk is a member of an order, a celibate by profession. **1956** R. Pieris *Sinhalese Social Organization* I. iv. 24 The *vihara*..villages..were exempt from their jurisdiction. **1978** C. Humphreys *Both Sides Circle* v. 56 In 1928 three monks were sent from Ceylon by the Anagarika to found the first Western *vihara* or monastery.

‖ **vihuela** (vĭhwē·la). [Sp.] An early Spanish stringed musical instrument; *spec.* one of two early types of guitar (more fully *vihuela de mano*) or viol (more fully *vihuela de arco*).

1832 *Amer. Railroad Jrnl.* I. 15/1 The music..consisted of several vihuèlas (a small kind of guitar). **1870** C. Engel *Descr. Catal. Musical Instruments S. Kensington Museum* 46 The *guitar* is evidently an importation from the East..In Spain it had formerly also the name of *vihuela*..and in England, at the time of Henry VIII. we find it occasionally called 'the Spanish viol'. **1910** *Encycl. Brit.* VII. 514/1 Spanish..vihuela de arco. Guitarra Latina or vihuela de mano. **1961** T. Dart in A. Baines *Musical Instruments* 184 One hybrid..made a great contribution to the development of European music. Its origins lie in Spain, home of the flat-backed *vihuela de mano*, the five- or later six-stringed guitar. This instrument was held and played much like the plectrum guitar of the present day; the cross-fertilization consisted in applying to it a playing technique..associated with..the fiddles... The result was the *vihuela de arco* ('bowed' vihuela), which was to become known..as the *viol.* **1968** *New Oxf. Hist. Music* IV. xi. 560 Ortiz deals with the viol (*vihuela*), for which he describes three kinds of playing. **1975** *Gramophone* Dec. 1002/1 An attractive collection of Spanish Renaissance *vihuela* music..excellently played (on the lute) by Konrad Ragnossnig, would prove enjoyable.

Hence **vihueli·sta,** a player of the vihuela.

1925 J. B. Trend (*title*) Luis Milan and the vihuelistas. **1978** *Early Music* Oct. 623/1 It is the largest book of the vihuelistas and is..the most complete and representative collection drawn from the rich and varied musical repertoire of mid-16th-century Spain.

‖ **vila** (vī·lă). Pl. **vilas, vile.** [Serbo-Croat and Slovenian.] In Slavonic mythology: a fairy, a nymph, a spirit. Cf. *wili, willi.

1827 J. Bowring *Servian Pop. Poetry* p. xxxvii, An omnipresent spirit—airy and fanciful—making its dwelling in solitudes..a being called the *Vila.* **1887** *Folk-Lore Jrnl.* V. 347 Whosoever has compared the northern elves with the Slavonic vilas..will see that they are of modern origin. **1911** *Encycl. Brit.* XXIV. 689/2 The [Serbian] peasants believe in charms and omens, in.. ghosts, the evil eye and *vile* or white-robed spirits of the earth, air, stream and mountain, with hoofs like a goat and henna-dyed nails and hair. **1922** D. H. Low *Kraljević's Ballads* iv. 21 In Serbian song Vilas are represented as jealous and capricious beings but on the whole not unfriendly to mankind. **1974** *Encycl. Brit. Macropædia* XVI. 876/1 Particularly feared are maidens who died before marriage and are believed to be addicted to the kidnapping of bridegrooms and babies... They are called ..*vile*..in Serbo-Croatia and Bulgaria.

vile, obs. var. *ville[3].

Vilene (vəi·līn). Also **vilene.** A proprietary name for backing or an interlining for clothing material, etc.

1954 *Trade Marks Jrnl.* 9 Feb. 159/2 *Vilene*... Lining and stiffening materials for clothing, all being textile piece goods;..The Viledon Company Limited, 15, New Street, Bishopsgate, London E.C.1.; merchants. **1960** *News Chron.* 10 Oct. 8/4 This [dress] is made in fine black wool, with a vilene-backed skirt. **1961** *Guardian* 24 Mar. 12/4 Putting a very fine netting of 'Vilene' between two layers of paper, and the resulting material handles like cloth. **1976** *Woman's Weekly* 6 Nov. 44/2 Cut hymn book from Vilene interlining and sew to right hand.

vi·llaed, *a.* [f. VILLA + -ED[2].] Covered with villas.

1791 A. SEWARD *Let.* 30 July (1811) II. xxix. 95 A pretty little lawn..admits the near hill, so magnificently villaed. **1937** G. GREENE *Nineteen Stories* (1947) 51, I had forgotten too the turning to the left up a steep, villaed hill.

villaette. Add: Also **villarette.** (Earlier example.)

1792 F. BURNEY *Jrnl.* 2 June (1972) I. 184 Mrs. & Miss ord & myself set off for Sudbury, near Harrow, where her very elegant Relation, Mr. Orde, has a villarette. The House is half old, half new, but well fitted up.

villafy, *v.* (Earlier example, in sense (b).)

1865 C. M. YONGE *Clever Woman of Family* I. vii. 156 My sister lives..at Little Worthy, the next parish... It has a railroad in it, and the cockneys have come down on it and 'villafied' it.

Villafranchian (vilăfræ·ŋkiăn), *a. Geol.* [ad. F. *villafranchien* (L. Pareto 1865, in *Bull. Soc. Géol. de France* XXII. 262), f. the name of *Villafranca* d'Asti in N. Italy, in the vicinity of which exposures of this series occur: see -IAN.] Of, pertaining to, or designating a stratigraphical stage in Europe variously assigned to the Upper Pliocene and the Lower Pleistocene (see quots.). Freq. *absol.*

1893 A. GEIKIE *Text-bk. Geol.* (ed. 3) 1016 (*table*) Villafranchian. **1955** G. G. WOODFORD tr. *M. Gignoux's Stratigraphic Geol.* x. 558 From the viewpoint of evolution of mammalian faunas, the Burdigalian..and Villafranchian mark important changes. **1972** *Gloss. Geol.* (Amer. Geol. Inst.) 778/2 *Villafranchian*, European stage: lower Pleistocene... It is the terrestrial equivalent (in France and Italy) of the marine Calabrian. Before 1948, it was used for the latest division of the Pliocene. **1973** *Nature* 15 June 391/2 Recent data have shown that the continental type Villafranchian is essentially late Pliocene (pre-Calabrian). **1974** *Encycl. Brit. Micropædia* X. 436/3 It is likely that the Villafranchian includes within it the Plio-Pleistocene boundary. *Ibid. Macropædia* XIV. 568/2 The Villafranchian fauna was..greatly modified by extinctions and new additions.

village, *sb.* Add: **1. e.** A small self-contained district or community within a city or town; *spec.* † (*a*) see sense 1 c in Dict.; (*b*) (with capital initial) = *GREENWICH VILLAGE.

1865 [see sense 1 c]. [**1924**: implied in *Greenwich Villager* s.v. *GREENWICH VILLAGE.] **1929** E. WILSON *I thought of Daisy* i. 16 Sue Borglum's pleasantry had been in the vein of the Village; Daisy's was in the taste of Broadway. **1931**, etc. [see *GREENWICH VILLAGE]. **1949** M. ALLINGHAM *More Work for Undertaker* xii. 156 London is made up of many villages. **1952** *N.Y. Times* 17 Aug. VIII–IX. 1W/5 (*caption*) Sketch of section of..cooperative multi-family for Holliswood, Queens, to be known as Hilltop Village. **1971** A. THORBURN *Planning Villages* iv. 24 The word 'village' has a pleasant and attractive connotation for most of us, sufficiently so for it to be borrowed by many estate agents regardless of the context, and to be applied to self-contained neighbourhoods in towns (e.g. at Banbury and Washington, Co. Durham). **1975** *Harper's & Queen* June 35/1 Hampstead—the loveliest of London's historical 'villages'. **1977** *Guardian Weekly* 25 Sept. 8/3 They call it a village but Skokie is geographically a middle-income suburb of Chicago with a population of 70,000. **1979** M. MCMULLEN *But Nellie was so Nice* I. iv. 23 She had grown up in the Village, on West Ninth Street between Fifth and Sixth.

4. a. (Further examples.)

1636 MASSINGER *Duke of Florence* II. iii. sig. E1, 'Tis a plaine Village Girle Sir, but obedient. **1803** G. COLMAN *John Bull* IV. ii. 46 One of the prettiest little village-churches you ever saw in your life. **1817** SCOTT *Rob Roy* I. v. 111 The domestic chaplain, the village doctor.. and my uncle. **1818** T. G. FESSENDEN *Ladies Monitor* 124 Learning should never pose a woman's head,.. Whose wealth and beauty sanction higher aims, Than those of village-school instructing aims. **1824** M. R. MITFORD *Our Village* I. 6 The village shop, like other village shops, multifarious as a bazaar; a repository for bread, shoes, tea, cheese..for every thing, in short. **1841** DICKENS *Barnaby Rudge* xxv. in *Master Humphrey's Clock* III. 74 They hurried through the village street. **1842** TENNYSON *Poems* II. 201 He is but a landscape-painter, And a village maiden she. **1843** *Cumberland Pacquet* 1 Aug. 3/1 His [*sc.* a raven's] masterpiece was his correct repetition of the Lord's prayer; which..would have done no discredit to many a village schoolmaster. **1847** C. BRONTË *Jane Eyre* III. v. 121 To be a village-schoolmistress, free and honest. **1852** DICKENS *Bleak Ho.* (1853) vii. 61 A dark-eyed, dark-haired, shy, village beauty comes in. **1852** THACKERAY *Esmond* I. ii. 58 The village people began to be reconciled presently to their lady. **1853** C. M. YONGE *Heir of Redclyffe* I. vi. 94 A village boy, whom he caught misusing a poor dog. **1854** —— *Heartsease* I. i. 2 A party of village children..gathering cowslips. **1855** MRS. GASKELL *North & South* I. ii. 27 Mr. Hale..was anxious for the village postman, whose summons to the household was a rap on the back-kitchen window-shutter. *Ibid.* II. xxi. 281 The house fronted the village green. **1859** GEO. ELIOT *Adam Bede* I. ii. 28 Mr Rann's leathern apron and subdued griminess can leave no one in any doubt that he is the village shoemaker. *Ibid.* II. xvii. 5 That village wedding..where an awkward bridegroom opens the dance with a high-shouldered, broad-faced bride. *Ibid.* xviii. 36 An experienced eye would have fixed on him at once as the village blacksmith. **1860** C. M. YONGE *Hopes & Fears* I. viii. 316 The apartment was not much behind that at the village inn at Hiltonbury. *Ibid.* II. xviii. 347 It was..interesting to observe his impression of the English village-life at Hiltonbury. **1861** —— *Young Step-Mother* v. 58 The pleasures to which he had been introducing Gilbert, were not merely..the rabbit-shooting and rat-hunting of the farm, nor even the village cricket-match. *c* **1873** C. RHODES *Let.* in J. Flint *Cecil Rhodes* (1974) ii. 24 Whether I become the village parson.. remains to be proved. **1873** W. D. HOWELLS *Chance Acquaintance* 38 Under the porch of the village store some desolate idlers..had clubbed their miserable leisure. **1890** W. BOOTH *In Darkest England* II. iii. 138 Every effort will be made to establish village industries, and I..hope..we may be able to restore some of the domestic occupations which steam has compelled us to confine to the great factories. **1891** J. L. KIPLING *Beast & Man in India* viii. 194 The village Elders stand before him with joined hands to learn his Lordship's commands. *Ibid.* xii. 316 The Eastern cat..is used in a frequently-quoted saying about doubtful matters. 'If the Punchayat (village council) says it's a cat, why, cat it is.' **1892** C. M. YONGE *Old Woman's Outlook* 167 The village shopkeeper, the maker of the 'vinosity' bread. **1894** KIPLING *Second Jungle Bk.* (1895) 34 As soon as the villagers saw the smoke in the deserted shrine, the village priest climbed up..to welcome the stranger. **1895** C. M. YONGE *Long Vacation* i. 5 An expedition to play the zither and sing at a village fête. **1907** G. B. SHAW *Major Barbara* 148, I myself have had a village idiot exhibited to me as something irresistibly funny. **1912** R. MARSH *Judith Lee* i. 10 Dickson was at my bedside..and Pierce, the village policeman. **1913** CHESTERTON *Victorian Age in Lit.* ii. 143 Hardy became a sort of village atheist brooding and blaspheming over the village idiot. **1915** J. BUCHAN *Salute to Adventurers* i. 9 She was presently driven out of the place by..the baillie, and the village dogs. **1920** 'O. DOUGLAS' *Penny Plain* xxv. 296 The village women, with little girls in clean pinafores clinging to their skirts. **1923** M. KENNEDY *Ladies of Lyndon* ii. 70 I'm afraid..that Modern Art wouldn't be quite suitable... It's only simple village folk, Mr. Ervine. *Ibid.* 96 The Village Room is quite two miles off. **1924** H. DE SÉLINCOURT *Cricket Match* i. 10 Down by the Village Room, where pictures are shown on Friday evenings..and into the village square again. *Ibid.* ii. 27 Best cricket going, village cricket. **1926** L. ELMHIRST in M. Yonge *Elmhirsts of Dartington* (1982) vi. 138 Like the village community of earlier times,..the school community..must engage in many practical enterprises. **1929** C. DAY LEWIS *Transitional Poem* II. 24 It is high time to renounce This village idiocy. **1930** K. BOYLE *Plagued by Nightingale* (1931) xi. 87 Tomorrow was the village *fête*. **1930** A. P. HERBERT *Water Gipsies* xxiii. 350 She went many times..to the Chiswick Church in the little old village street beside the river. **1932** L. GOLDING *Magnolia Street* I. vi. 107 He would put up at the village pub until the moment to pounce was due. **1933** A. THIRKELL *High Rising* i. 25 She had formed a habit of ordering groceries..on a gigantic scale, from the village store. **1939** L. BEMELMANS *Life Class* III. v. 246 From the railroad station came crates and boxes with materials from New York and Vienna; the village children's hair was full of excelsior as they helped unpack them. **1939** F. THOMPSON *Lark Rise* x. 186 'Everybody who was anything'..kept a maid..stud grooms' wives, village schoolmasters' wives. *Ibid.* xii. 225 The position of a village schoolmistress was a trying one socially. **1942** M. CABLE *Gobi Desert* 122 To buy the printed likeness of the kitchen god at a village fair. **1943** A. CHRISTIE *Moving Finger* vii. 82 Emily Barton..has a mental picture of men as..smoking cigars, and in the intervals dropping out to do a few seductions of village maidens. **1948** F. THOMPSON *Still glides Stream* ii. 18 At that time village houses had no numbers or names. **1949** D. SMITH *I capture Castle* i. 5 He does nothing but read detective novels from the village library. **1950** *New Yorker* 23 Sept. 66/3 A lively, exalted young novice.. was formerly a village schoolteacher. **1951** R. FIRTH *Elements of Social Organization* iv. 134 Such behaviour is a function of the social structure, with its emphasis on the village community and the kinship group. **1952** M. LASKI *Village* i. 12 The village boys and girls still danced sedately. *Ibid.* iii. 52 The village people..normally had their radios on all day. **1953** G. E. & K. R. FUSSELL *Eng. Countrywoman* iv. 123 Farmhouse and cottage furniture was made by the village carpenter. **1953** S. BEDFORD *Sudden View* I. x. 94 In France, village *curés*.. exact fees from their parishioners. **1954** A. SETON *Katherine* vii. 119 Celibacy might be asked of monk or friar but hardly from..a village parson. **1957** J. CARY in R. S. Surtees *Mr. Sponge's Sporting Tour* (1958) p. xi, The few hundred who..had been able to..travel farther than the county town or the village fair. **1957** 'M. M. KAYE' *Shadow of Moon* xxi. 309 He called upon the Kotwal—the village headman. **1960** J. R. ACKERLEY *We think the World of You* 40 The small blank eyes mooned stolidly at me..it was like being gaped at by the village idiot. **1967** A. CORDELL *Bright Cantonese* ii. 28 The village elders were waiting for me on the little airstrip at Hoon. **1969** R. BLYTHE *Akenfield* ii. 60 Texts in glass cases hang outside.. and can be read by passengers in the village bus, which just stops there. *Ibid.* iv. 89 When the village shopkeeper sends things to out-of-the-way cottages..he's going to charge.. something for the service. **1969** *Listener* 12 June 814/1 The village chief himself asked us to a dinner of dried deer and shrimp crackers. **1971** O. NORTON *Corpse-Bird Cries* i. 3 Most of the fishing would probably be done in the company of a village bobby. *Ibid.* v. 96 Such a simple life, isn't it, being a village copper? **1973** *Stornoway Gaz.* 13 Jan. 7/2 The annual general meeting of Portree Village Council was held in the Portree Hotel, at which there was a fairly large attendance. *a* **1974** R. CROSSMAN *Diaries* (1976) II. 157 Then we rushed him down to the village hall, which has been built by the energy of Len Edwards, our remarkable local inventor of laundry machinery. **1975** *Country Life* 9 Oct. (Suppl.) 26/1 (Advt.), Family house on village green. **1976** 'H. CARMICHAEL' *False Evidence* ii. 25 The cottage was set in restful countryside, a quarter of a mile from the village inn. **1976** P. R. WHITE *Planning for Public Transport* vii. 142 Local village shops may also substitute for day-to-day needs. **1978** P. VAN GREENAWAY *Man called Scavener* ii. 21 Unhonoured assignations with village beauties. **1978** J. PORTER *Dead Easy for Dover* ii. 25 We had the funeral on the Saturday... The village church was absolutely packed. **1978** 'J. MELVILLE' *Axwater* ii. 57 The village girls used to go there at the new moon and wish. Like a wishing well. **1979** 'S. KEMP' *Goodbye Pussy* x. 125 The village doctor..saw her once in a while for measles and mumps. **1980** G. SIMS in *Winter's Crimes 12* 149 The village Postmistress, who delighted in gossip. **1981** M. WARNER *Joan of Arc* i. 20 Women who..were ducked in village ponds to find out whether or not they were witches. **1981** E. CLARK *Send in Lions* xiii. 121 The village postman..had seen Kemp that morning. **1981** A. EDWARDS *Sonya* xi. 175 On Christmas Eve the village priests came to hold a vespers service. **1981** C. MILLER *Childhood in Scotland* 63 We wore heavy black boots made by the village shoemaker. **1983** *Times* (Saturday Suppl.) 29 Jan.–4 Feb. 4/4 (*caption*) Rekindling village life in Chelsea.

c. *village-based*, *-made* adjs.

1976 P. R. WHITE *Planning for Public Transport* vii. 140 In this situation the village-based independent may score over the larger operator. **1883** R. JEFFERIES *Nature near London* 221 Each village-made crook had an individuality, that of the blacksmith.

d. village college (see quot. 1981); **village constable,** (*a*) *Hist.*, in Papua, a local man through whom the orders of the Australian administration were transmitted; (*b*) a police constable stationed in a village; **village gossip,** (*a*) the idle talk of a village (see GOSSIP *sb.* 4); (*b*) a woman who gossips (see GOSSIP *sb.* 3); **village Hampden,** a person like John Hampden (1594–1643), one without means or influence who opposes a powerful local person or organization (in imitation of quot. 1751); **village pump,** a village's communal water pump; freq. used allusively (cf. *parish pump* s.v. *PARISH *sb.* 7 b).

1924 H. MORRIS (*title*) The village college. **1981** D. ROWNTREE *Dict. Educ.* 342 *Village colleges*, a UK scheme in community education initiated in rural Cambridgeshire in the 1930s, with a number of colleges each serving a village not only as a secondary school but also as a cultural and recreational centre for old and young alike out of school hours. The scheme was later adopted by several other largely-rural counties. **1924** 'R. DALY' *Outpost* xxvii. 259 'They say they will have no chief but the village-constable,' he said, 'and no sorcery except that of the white man.' **1943** F. THOMPSON *Candleford Green* vii. 115 The village constable was still regarded by many as a potential enemy. **1965** *Austral. Encycl.* VI. 468/1 In the period before World War II, for the carrying out of policy, Administrations to some extent relied on selected headmen (called luluais) in New Guinea and on village constables in Papua. **1981** B. KNOX *Killing in Antiques* viii. 166 The village constable got there in ten minutes flat then ran for his car radio. **1847** C. M. YONGE *Scenes & Characters* xvi. 201 Jane sought for amusement in village gossip. **1952** M. LASKI *Village* ix. 146 He'd tell her the village gossip. **1972** P. D. JAMES *Unsuitable Job for Woman* iv. 143 The confiding relish of a village gossip about to relate the latest scandal. **1751** GRAY *Elegy* 8 Some Village-Hampden that with dauntless Breast The little Tyrant of his Fields withstood. **1857** C. M. YONGE *Dynevor Terrace* I. i. 3 He stalked along like a village Hampden, muttering, 'The old tyrant shall see whether I'm to be trampled on!' **1957** D. PIPER *English Face* iv. 111 Many of Johnson's portraits have now lost their names..yet some of them no doubt were 'village Hampdens'. **1978** A. SANDERS *Victorian Historical Novel* i. 23 Reade is not mourning the silence of village Hampdens, for..he is aspiring to a history which is 'familiar rather than heroic'. **1925** V. WOOLF *Common Reader* 112 The talk of old women round the village pump. **1953** G. E. & K. R. FUSSELL *Eng. Countrywoman* vi. Plate 48 (*caption*) The village pump at Fressingfield, Suffolk: still used. **1955** G. GORER *Exploring Eng. Character* iv. 61 What a 20-year-old Hereford student calls 'the proverbial "village pump" attitude and conflicts' seems to bedevil the life of many. **1978** *Listener* 6 July 27/2 Officially, the village of Montaillou was subject to the bailiff of the local count of Foix... But Professor Ladurie is able to tell us about the exercise..of authority at the level of the village pump.

e. (With capital initial.) Of, pertaining to, or characteristic of Greenwich Village. *U.S.*

1950 T. STERLING *House without Door* iv. 41 She's not a Village artist... She was very wealthy once. **1979** M. MCMULLEN *But Nellie was so Nice* I. i. 7 He wore a sort of Village uniform—corduroys and a turtle-necked dark jersey.

village *v.* (*b*) to visit a village in a pastoral capacity.

1871 F. KILVERT *Diary* 24 Feb. (1977) 130 Villaging about to Mrs Jones at the Infant School, Jo Phillips and Margaret Griffith. **1981** 'M. INNES' *Lord Mullion's Secret* 27 The Vicar of Mullion, an old man given to antique usages, sometimes described himself as having been 'villaging'—by which he meant going round the cottagers and chatting them up.

villagiza·tion. [f. VILLAG(E *sb.* + -IZATION.] In Africa and Asia, concentration of population in villages; the transfer of control of land to villagers communally; in Tanzania, *spec.* = *UJAMAA. Cf. *BHOODAN.

1963 *Punch* 10 July 42/1 'Villagisation' is the word. **1965** P. FORDHAM *Geogr. African Affairs* iv. 85 Part of the security measures during the Mau Mau rebellion was the forcible 'villagization' of the Kikuyu and the consolidation of fragmented holdings. **1970** *Guardian Weekly* 22 Aug. 2 The majority of land-owners in more than 140,000 Indian villages have declared themselves in favour of Gramadan (gift of village),..which involves the principle of villagisation (as distinct from nationalisation) of land. **1980** *Sci. Amer.* Sept. 152/1 A campaign of 'villagization' was begun, and over the next several years a massive transfer of rural population was accomplished.

villain, *sb.* Add: **1. b.** *transf.* (Later example.)

1832 *Q. Rev.* Mar. 234 Perchance one hound in ten may throw his tongue as he goes to inform his comrades, as it were, that the villain is on before them.

d. Esp. in phr. *villain of the piece* (now usu. *transf.*).

1854 A. C. MOWATT *Autobiogr. Actress* vii. 133 Ayesha, *the villain of the piece*,..had received a great wrong. **1867** [in Dict.]. **1928** WODEHOUSE *Money for Nothing* ix. 200 I'm sure you're on the right track. This bird Twist is the villain of the piece. **1937** *Discovery* May 163/1 Fascism, in its ultra-national aspect, is the villain of the piece. **1978** P. SUTCLIFFE *Oxf. University Press* v. i. 173 Ernest Barker and others took on Nietzsche and Treitschke, who could be regarded as the ultimate villains of the piece.

e. A professional criminal. *slang.*

1960 [see *BOGY[1], BOGEY[1] 4]. **1963** L. DEIGHTON *Horse under Water* xxxi. 125 This villain is doing a nice Cabinet Minister's home. **1975** *Sunday Tel.* 7 Dec. 1/2 A flying squad officer said: 'As far as we know these are no ordinary villains. We believe they are Irish IRA.' **1977** L. MEYNELL *Hooky gets Wooden Spoon* xiii. 156 There'll be a getaway car..waiting close to the house with a villain in it... I don't like thieving villains.

villainous, *a.* **7.** *villainous-looking* adj. (earlier example).

1777 J. WOODFORDE *Diary* 22 July (1924) I. 209 The Hangman was an old Man and a most villainous looking Fellow indeed.

villamaninite (vilămæ·ninəit). *Min.* [f. *Villamanín*, name of the locality (north of León in NW. Spain) near which the mineral was found + -ITE[1].] A black isometric mineral, $(Cu,Ni,Co,Fe)S_2$, of the pyrite group.

1919 *Nature* 20 Nov. 326/1 Dr. W. R. Schoeller and A. R. Powell: Villamaninite, a new mineral. **1968** *Neues Jahrb. f. Mineral.: Monatshefte* 189 The conditions under which villamaninite formed must have been quite extreme. Investigations of Ni-Cu ores from Katanga, Carrol County in Maryland and So. Wisconsin..where low temperature mineralizations are supposed to have occurred, failed to produce a new villamaninite locality. **1977** *Mineral. Abstr.* XXVIII. 205/1 Villamaninite breaks down to α-NiS, carrollite $(CuCo_2S_4)$, and some Ni and Co sulphates at around 400°C.

‖ **villancico** (vilʸanþī·ko). *Mus.* [Sp.] A Spanish and Portuguese musical form (see quots.).

1822 J. B. WHITE *Lett. from Spain* ix. 327 The music.. was..used in a species of dramatic interludes in the vulgar tongue, which were sung, not acted, at certain intervals of the service. These pieces had the name of *Villancicos*, from *Villano*, a Clown, shepherds and shepherdesses being the interlocutors in these pastorals. **1849** G. TICKNOR *Hist. Spanish Lit.* I. xxiii. 440 The 'Villancicos' that follow—songs in the old Spanish measure with a refrain and occasionally short verses broken in—are more agreeable, and sometimes are not without merit. **1876** STAINER & BARRETT *Dict. Mus. Terms* 446/2 *Villancico* (*Sp.*), a species of song of two or more stanzas, each containing seven lines, belonging to the poetry of the 15th century, which, like the madrigal, is of an epigrammatic form—formerly very popular in Spain... Those motets which are sung during high mass on Christmas-eve are always called Villancicos. **1937** M. N. HAMILTON *Music in 18th Cent. Spain* 5 In Eslava there were references to *villancicos*, which during the eighteenth century seemed to be the routine accomplishment of every chapel master. **1959** *Collins' Mus. Encycl.* 701/1 *Villancico*... (1) A type of song..current in Spain in the late 15th and 16th cent. It is characterized by the fact that it begins with a refrain, which is subsequently repeated after each verse... (2) In the 17th and 18th cent. a cantata for soli and chorus with instrumental accompaniment, frequently on the subject of Christmas. (3) In modern Spanish a Christmas carol. **1968** *New Oxf. Hist. Mus.* IV. iv. 135 In earlier times courtly love had been a favourite theme for *villancicos*... In the later fifteenth century a more popular tone invaded *villancicos*... The increasing number of religious *villancicos* found in the sixteenth century points towards the transformation of the form in the seventeenth century into an extended sacred cantata. **1980** *Early Music Gaz.* Jan. 16/1 The three papers are:..Manuel Carlos de Brito on 'A little-known collection of Portuguese Baroque Villancicos and Romances'; [etc.].

Villanova (vilănōᵘ·vă). *Archæol.* The name of a hamlet near Bologna, Italy, where archæological finds were made, used *attrib.* to designate an Italian culture of the early Iron Age.

1901 W. RIDGEWAY *Early Age Greece* I. ii. 237 After the Terramare came the Early Iron Age, usually termed the Villanova period by the Italian archaeologists, from the discovery of a large number of its characteristic remains at Villanova near Bologna. **1910** *Encycl. Brit.* V. 721/2 The next period..is known as the 'Villanova' period,..or as the period of pit-tombs (*a pozzo*), from the form of the graves in which the pottery has been found.

Villanovan (vilănōᵘ·văn), *sb.* and *a. Archæol.* [f. prec. + -AN.] **A.** *sb.* An inhabitant of Italy during the Villanova period. **B.** *adj.* Of, pertaining to, or designating the Villanova period. Also *absol.*

1924 D. RANDALL-MACIVER *Villanovans & Early Etruscans* 3 In the fifth century the Villanovans disappear as a recognizable people, stifled no doubt..by the dominant Etruscans who had settled beside them. **1928** —— *Italy before Romans* v. 73 Villanovan helmets and girdles and Villanovan ossuaries..may be seen side by side with Hallstatt swords. *a* **1930** D. H. LAWRENCE *Etruscan Places* (1932) ii. 55 It seems as if the primitive inhabitants of this part of Italy always burned their dead, and then put the ashes in a jar, sometimes covering the jar with the dead man's helmet, sometimes with a shallow dish for a lid, and then laid the urn with its ashes in a little round grave like a little well. This is called the Villanovan way of burial, in the well-tomb. **1957** [see *ATESTINE *a.* and *sb.*]. **1974** *Encycl. Brit. Micropædia* X. 438/3 During the first quarter of the 7th century an Orientalizing civilization..was superimposed on the Villanovan in Tuscany. The northern Villanovans of the Po valley..continued to produce a geometric art..as late as the last quarter of the 6th century. **1980** *Times Lit. Suppl.* 17 Oct. 1179/4 The Iron Age possessors of the material culture (or cultural material) conventionally known as 'Villanovan' ought at least to have been mentioned.

villarette, var. VILLAETTE in Dict. and Suppl.

Villar y Villar (vī·lār *i* vī·lāɹ). [Sp., = Villar (a surname) and Villar.] The proprietary name of a Havana cigar.

1878 *Army & Navy Stores Price List* 60 Cigars and tobacco... Villar y Villar. Reina Victoria... 62/– per 100. **1903** W. STEVENS *Let.* 20 Oct. (1967) 68 But to-night I've been polite..have..puffed a Villar y Villar.

ville[3] (vil, vəil). *slang* (now *U.S.*). Also 9 **vile.** [a. F. *ville* town.] A town or village.

1837 L. C. BOYNTON *Jrnl.* 11 Sept. in *Proc. Amer. Antiquarian Soc.* (1933) XLIII. 336 Amherst [Mass.] is a very pleasant little ville, but still and inactive. **1859** HOTTEN *Dict. Slang* 114 *Ville*, or *vile*, a town or village,—pronounced *phial*, or *vial. French.* **1891** 'F. W. CAREW' *No. 747* xxxv. 416 We made a long round back to vile. **1939** JOYCE *Finnegans Wake* 130 The brick of the viled ville of Barnehulme. **1977** M. HERR *Dispatches* 10 Once we fanned over a little ville that had just been airstruck.

Ville[4] (vil). *slang.* Also **'Ville, (')ville.** [Abbrev.] *the Ville*, Pentonville Prison in Greater London.

1903 'No. 77' *Mark of Broad Arrow* ii. 35 Before the notorious bank forgers had been in 'The Ville' a single hour they were located in different wings of the prison, thus rendering personal contact with each other impossible. **1962** *John o' London's* 25 Jan. 82/3 Pentonville Prison is *the ville*. **1962** D. WARNER *Death of Bogey* iv. iii. 146 A stretch in the Ville or on the Moor. **1936** [see *fly-paper* s.v. *FLY *sb.*[1] 11]. **1967** C. DRUMMOND *Death at Furlong Post* xii. 152, I don't want to see your great face up against me in the 'ville for twenty years. **1972** L. HENDERSON *Cage until Tame* vi. 51 Yeah, that's right, he was in the 'Ville.

-ville (vil), *suffix. colloq.* [ad. F. *ville* town.] A terminal element appended to sbs. (which freq. have a pl. suff.) or adjs. to denote: (*a*) a fictitious place; (*b*) a particular quality suggested by the word to which it is appended.

In *U.S.* usage orig. as — *from —ville.*

1567 HARMAN *Caveat* (ed. 2) sig. G3, Rome vyle London. **1843** G. CRUIKSHANK *Comic Almanack* sig. F4ᵛ, Tripe & Trotter Depôt..Meatville. **1891** *N.Y. Sporting Times* 11 July 3/4 Then he was as frisky as a young colt and a slugger from Sluggersville. **1906** F. H. BURNETT *Shuttle* (1907) xxxviii. 384 That girl is a winner from Winnersville. I take off my hat to her. **1932** *Magnet* 17 Sept. 13/3 I'm telling you you're the biggest bonehead from Boneheadville. **1939** [see *route march* s.v. *ROUTE *sb.* 4]. **1956,** etc. [see *SQUARESVILLE]. **1959, 1961** [see *Cubesville* s.v. *CUBE *sb.*[1] 1 c]. **1961** [see *SQUARESVILLE]. **1962** P. MORTIMER *Pumpkin Eater* xiii. 118 Tiny bit boring, between you and me. Strict secrets of course. English Rose stuff. Deathville, as far as I'm concerned. **1964** [see *RELOCATE *v.* 2]. **1967** J. AITKIN *Young Meteors* i. 35 University? Man, that's just dragsville. **1972** *Publishers' Weekly* 2 Oct. 56/1 There are some who will simply not get the fun of it out there in mass-marketville. **1979** *National Times* (Austral.) 13 Oct. 5/2 But there is a mite more to leadership, even here in Mediaville [*sc.* Washington], than looking pretty and carrying a resonant baritone voice.

‖ **ville lumière** (vil lümyę̄r). [Fr., = town or city of light(s).] A brightly-lit city or town; an exciting modern city or town; *la Ville Lumière*, Paris.

1920 W. J. LOCKE *House of Baltazar* xiv. 166 London ceased to be a city of dreadful night. In his enthusiastic eyes it had almost become a *ville lumière*. **1922** A. M. HYAMSON *Dict. Eng. Phrases* 353/2 *Ville Lumière, La*, (Fr., the light-city; the city of lights): Paris. **1923** W. J. LOCKE *Moordius & Co.* vii. 94 We are but nursing the lamp of la Ville Lumière till better times. **1955** E. WAUGH *Officers & Gentlemen* 137 Cape Town at the extremity of two dark continents was a *ville lumière* such as Trimmer had sought in vain. **1980** *Listener* 25 Sept. 389/1 The Eiffel Tower..proclaimed *la ville lumière* to be the modernist capital.

villiaumite (vi·liǭməit). *Min.* [a. F. *villiaumite* (A. Lacroix 1908, in *Compt. Rend.* CXLVI. 215), f. *Villiaume*, name of a French explorer in whose collection the mineral was first identified: see -ITE[1].] Native sodium fluoride, NaF, occurring as red, pink, or orange transparent isometric crystals.

The symmetry is erron. described in quot. 1908

1908 *Jrnl. Chem. Soc.* XCIV. ii. 201 This new mineral, called villiaumite, is tetragonal and pseudo-cubic, with three perfect cleavages at right angles to one another. **1970** *Amer. Mineralogist* LV. 126 Thermodynamic calculations show that fluorite is to be expected as the common fluoride mineral in both silica-saturated and undersaturated igneous rocks; in calcium- and silica-poor assemblages villiaumite is favored, but in calcium-poor quartz-bearing rocks, cryolite will prevail.

villiform, *a.* (Earlier example.)

1846 [see *close-set* s.v.* CLOSE C 1 and 2].

‖ **villino** (vilī·no). Pl. **villini.** [It., dim. of *villa* VILLA.] A small (rural, suburban, or urban) house in Italy (in quot. 1935, in France).

?**1863** MRS. GASKELL *Let.* 16 July (1966) 708 The pleasure of our intercourse at the Villino Trollope. **1923** A. HUXLEY *Let.* 12 Nov. (1969) 223 They have a Città Giardino just outside to the north and the number of horrible little villini..is extraordinary **1935** E BOWEN *House in Paris* I. ii. 31 Though Mrs. Arbuthnot had not.. been lent the villino at Beaulieu, she had been lent a flat at Mentone. **1958** 'M. INNES' *Long Farewell* I. 14 Then let's go up to the *villino*. The view's just as good from there. **1980** *Times* 11 Oct. 10/7 One restaurant..occupies a former *villino* or small house with a garden.

Villonesque (viyonè·sk, vilone·sk), *a.* [f. the name of François *Villon* (1431–1480 or 1489), French poet + -ESQUE.] Characteristic of (the style of) Villon.

1932 E. RICKWORD tr. *Coulon's Poet Under Saturn* vi. 163 A name evocative of the cells, the Villonesque name of Pierre Duchâtelet. **1937** *Times Lit. Suppl.* 20 Mar. 222/1 The self-portrait..is of a somewhat Villonesque character. **1979** M. A. SCREECH *Rabelais* iii. 86 His Villonesque ricks against the university and church dignitaries.

‖ **villotta** (vilǫ·tă). Also **villota.** Pl. **villot(t)e.** [It.] A type of villanella, originating in northern Italy.

1876 STAINER & BARRETT *Dict. Mus. Terms* 446/2 *Villotte* (*It.*). The name given to the first secular pieces in harmony after the rules of counterpoint were fixed. **1926** C. GRAY in Gray & Heseltine *Carlo Gesualdo* I. 10 They would spend whole nights out in the bay [of Naples], singing *villotte*, and madrigals. **1942** *Bull. Amer. Musicological Soc.* Apr. 9 The period of the *villota* is dated back by Torrefranca..to the first half of the 15th century... The theory is founded..chiefly upon a group of eleven *villote*..now preserved in the Marciana in Venice. **1958** [see *CANZONETTA]. **1980** *Early Music* Jan. 104/2 The *Libro primo* contains a wide variety of text forms including the madrigal, villotta, canzone, and ballata-madrigal.

vim. (Earlier example.)

1843 *Yale Lit. Mag.* VIII. 406 He would have acted out his real nature with all the *vim* and pathos which heroes always manifest in like circumstances.

Vim[2] (vim). Also **vim.** [Cf. VIM in Dict.] The proprietary name of a brand of detergent. Hence **vim** *v. trans.*, to clean with Vim.

1894 *Trade Marks Jrnl.* 6 June 484/1 *Vim*... All goods included in Class 48. Lever Brothers, Limited, Port Sunlight, near Birkenhead; soap manufacturers. **1926** R. MACAULAY *Crewe Train* II. x. 179 Denham looked vaguely at the vim. 'For the sink,' her aunt explained. 'And I've got you a..brush. That's to scrub the vim in with.' 'Thank you very much,' said Denham, doubtfully; 'I don't know how much I shall vim the sink, though.' **1948** 'N. SHUTE' *No Highway* viii. 205 Shirley collected scrubbers and soap and Vim and a dustpan and brush. **1968** *Listener* 14 Mar. 359/1 The real battle, though, is with the Saturday-night dancers who put down French chalk to make the floor slippery. The badminton players retaliate—of old with Vim or a mixture of tea-leaves, sand and water. **1976** T. SHARPE *Wilt* ii. 11 She got the washing-up done..and the bath Vimmed.

‖ **vimana** (vī·mā·nă). *India.* [Skr.] **1.** The central tower enclosing the shrine in an Indian temple.

1863 *Chambers's Encycl.* V. 552/1 The temples consist of the temple or vimana, in front of which is the pillared porch or mantopa, [etc.]. **1891** J. FERGUSSON *Hist. Indian & Eastern Archit.* II. ii. 221 There is one other peculiarity common to both Jaina and Hindu architecture..It is the form of the towers or spires called Sikras, or Vimanas, which invariably surmount the cells in which the images are placed. **1913** L. D. BARNETT *Antiquities of India* x. 233 When for the Buddhist relic is substituted the image or emblem of a god, the apse is changed into a closed cella, with a door, and its place as the holy of holies in the structure is marked by a spire or *śikhara*, forming with the cellā a *vimāna*. **1969** *Hindu Weekly Mag.* (Madras) 3 Aug. p. ii/5 He made a bold departure by making the 'vimana', the tower over the sanctum sanctorum, dominate the entire scheme of temple construction.

2. *Mythol.* A heavenly chariot.

1946 S. KRAMRISCH *Hindu Temple* II. 344 Their bodies inflated by air race in gusts across the atmosphere, support the Vimānas, the chariots of the gods. **1979** W. H. CANAWAY *Solid Gold Buddha* xv. 106 I've heard of a *vimana*, a sky chariot. Have you ever thought of using one of those things in the show?

‖ **vin** (væ̃n). [Fr.] Wine: used in various French phrases. **1.** Followed by *de*, *d'*, etc., designating a wine of a particular classification, district, or method of manufacture, etc., as *vin de Graves*, *de liqueur*, etc.

1699 M. LISTER *Journey to Paris* 161 Those Wines thus in the Must are called..*Vin des Liqueurs.* **1777** P. THICKNESSE *Year's Journey* II. xxxvii. 38 Barren as the *Crau* appears to be, it..produces such excellent wine.. that it is called *Vin de Crau,* by way of pre-eminence. **1833** C. REDDING *Hist. Mod. Wines* iii. 51 What are called in France *vins du liqueur*, are those in which the saccharine principle has not entirely disappeared during the process of fermentation, and been changed into alcohol. **1842** BROWNING *Dram. Lyrics* 15/2 For council dinners made rare havock With Claret, Moselle, Vin-de-Grave, Hock. **1911** Vin du Glacier [see *FENDANT]. **1939** B. COLLIER *Catalan France* xii. 273 In the case of wines intended to be drunk as *apéritif* or dessert wines..[the colour] is usually that indicated by the terms '*vin d'or*' or '*doré*'. **1955** *Times* 5 Aug. 7/4 The agreement also foresees an increase in the export of French vins d'appellation to the value of 350M. francs. **1967** A. LICHINE *Dict. Wines* 543/2 *Vin de liqueur.* This French term has two meanings. 1. A very sweet wine, such as a rich Sauternes. 2. Wine of approximately 18% of alcohol caused by the addition of brandy and added to Champagne prior to shipment. **1968** R. AMBERLEY *Incitement to Murder* i. 18 The wine..was not an *appellation contrôlée*, or even a *vin de qualité supérieure*; it was..an unpretentious local wine.

2. With (*ppl.*) *adjs.*, describing or purporting to describe wines of a certain quality or prepared in a certain way.

1833 C. REDDING *Hist. Mod. Wines* v. 176 At Moulins they make a species called *vin fou*, or mad wine, or rather ..'drunkard's wine'. They fill a small, strong-bound cask, having no bung, with must; this they put into another cask, and plunge it into the vat, from which it is not withdrawn until the fermentation ceases. **1849** GEO. ELIOT *Let.* 22 Dec. (1954) I. 324 Dear Sara's letter is..not at all physicky—rather an agreeable draught of *vin sucré.* **1920** G. SAINTSBURY *Notes on Cellar-Bk.* xi. 162 *Vin brulé*, a very popular beverage in Old France, and a regular Christmas and New Year tradition in the Channel Islands. **1952** V. WILKINS *King Reluctant* I. vi. 94 It is at least drinkable—a *vin bourgeois.* **1958** A. L. SIMON *Dict. Wines* 161/2 *Vin chaud*, mulled wine. **1966** P. V. PRICE *France: Food & Wine Guide* II. 238 The '*vin fou*' of the Jura is made by bottling either white or rosé wine at the peak of its first fermentation. **1974** *Times* 10 Aug. 11/2 A white Corbières. Vin Vert. Montagne d'Alaric.

3. Special collocations. **vin compris** [lit. 'understood']: (phrase denoting) wine included in the price of a meal or other entertainment; **vin cuit** = *wine cuit* s.v. CUIT, CUTE; an aperitif wine; **vin de paille** [lit. 'of straw'] = *straw wine* s.v. STRAW *sb.*[1] 14 (see quots.); **vin de table** = *table wine* s.v. *TABLE *sb.* 22; cf. *TAFELWEIN; **vin d'honneur,** a wine formally offered in honour of a person or persons; the reception at which the wine is offered; **vin doux (naturel)** [lit. 'sweet (unfortified)'], a sweet aperitif wine; **vin du pays** [lit. 'of the country'], a local wine; also *transf.* and *fig.*; **vin gris** [lit. 'grey'], a rosé wine of eastern France; **vin jaune** [lit. 'yellow'], (see quot. 1966); **vin mousseux** [*MOUSSEUX], sparkling wine. See also *VIN BLANC, ORDINAIRE, ROSÉ, ROUGE below as main entries.

1889 KIPLING *From Sea to Sea* I. xii. 308 The *vin ordinaire* which is *compris*, is good. **1910** G. B. SHAW *Let.* ?16 Apr. (1972) II. 921 Further excitement is provided by the institution of *vin compris* at meals. **1967** *Observer* 14 May 28/3 Vin compris in Camden. 'Free wine tasting,' promised the notice. **1833** C. REDDING *Hist. Mod. Wines* vi. 193 Their [*sc.* the Spaniards'] boiled wines, or vins *cuits*, as the French call them, are mingled with other growths. **1962** *Times* 21 Dec. 10/7 The bottle of *vin cuit* or unfermented wine. **1833** C. REDDING *Hist. Mod. Wines* iii. 51 The wines called *vins de paille* are so denominated from the grapes being laid for several months upon straw before they are taken to the press. **1964** A. SICHEL *Penguin Bk. Wines* III. 159 *Vins de paille*, the second of the unusual white wines of the Jura, get their name from the straw mats on which the black Poulsard and Trousseau grapes are dried for several weeks before being pressed. **1972** *Country Life* 14 Dec. 1660/1 Nowadays the grapes are normally laid not on mats but on trays... To produce a litre of *vin de paille* takes about 12–15 kilos of grapes. **1948** A. WAUGH *Unclouded Summer* vii. 142 They had treated it as a *vin de table.* **1981** *New Yorker* 28 Dec. 49/1, I took a half-litre bottle of Sichel le Cellier, *vin de table, rouge.* **1920** *Punch* 30 June 512/1 The Prime Minister was celebrating the longest—and pretty nearly the hottest—day by a *vin d'honneur* at Boulogne. **1947** E. WAUGH *Scott-King's Mod. Europe* 25 Vin d'honneur offered to the delegates by the Municipality of Bellacita. **1978** *Broadcast* 6 Mar. 4/1 A *vin d'honneur* at Television Centre for TFI's news director. **1958** A. L. SIMON *Dict. Wines* 162/1 *Vin doux*, grape-juice before it ferments and becomes wine; also used for a 'sweet' wine. **1959** W. JAMES *Word-bk. Wine* 197 *Vins doux naturels,* The Frenchman's logic has strange lacunae;.. the unnatural and fortified sweet wines made in the south-east [*read:* south-west] corner of his own country he blandly calls 'natural sweet wines'. **1981** *Country Life* 23 July 261/3 That delectable Muscat wine, a *vin-doux-naturel.* **1777** P. THICKNESSE *Year's Journey* II. xlix. 138, I could not help treating him with a bottle of *vin de pais.* **1822** L. SIMOND *Switzerland* I. 34 A well-seasoned veal pie, a boeuf-a-la-mode, plenty of the best *vin du pays*, and even a dessert. **1935** *Times Lit. Suppl.* 18 July 459 A renewed zeal for the land of England, and, especially for the savour of its products, of its beef and cheese and fruit and *vin du pays* or cider. **1965** Vin du pays [see *PREMIER CRU]. **1833** C. REDDING *Hist. Mod. Wines* v. 176 A *vin gris*, a grey or rather brown wine, is made here [*sc.* at Gannat] by leaving the must to ferment for forty-eight hours. **1958** A. L. SIMON *Dict. Wines* 162/1 *Vin gris*, light red wine of Lorraine and Alsace, usually made of mixed black and white grapes. **1974** *Times* 18 May (Suppl.) p. i/4 The *vin gris* of the Jura. **1833** C. REDDING *Hist. Mod. Wines* iii. 51 The *mousseux* wines of Arbois are called *vins blanc de garde*, and when old, *vin jaune.* **1966** P. V. PRICE *France: Food & Wine Guide* II. 239 The two extraordinary wines of the Jura are the *vins jaunes* and *vins de paille... Vins jaunes* are made solely from the Sauvignon grape.. taste slightly like sherry, though..they are not fortified in any way. **1981** *Times* 12 Dec. 12/4 The odd Jura wine, Château Chalon..is a *vin jaune*..staying long in cask, wherein a *veil* forms on the surface. **1789** Vin mousseux [see *MOUSSEUX]. **1833** C. REDDING *Hist. Mod. Wines* ii. 30 Those wines which effervesce (*vins mousseux*) are impregnated deeply with carbonic acid gas. **1972** A. ROSS *London Assignment* 47, I..pulled the napkin off the foil-topped bottle. It was a vin mousseux, and not a very good one.

vina. Add: The predominant spelling is now **veena.** Also *attrib.* and *Comb.* (Earlier and further examples.)

1788 W. JONES in *Asiatick Researches* I. 265 His [*sc.* Nared's] invention of the Vínà, or Indian lute, is thus described. **1848** J. H. STOCQUELER *Oriental Interpreter* s.v., *Veena*, an instrument of the guitar kind, with seven metal strings. It is the most ancient musical instrument of the Hindoos, and in good hands is capable of yielding great melody and expression. **1891** [see *TAMBOURA b]. **1896** [see *SURBAHAR]. **1921** H. A. POPLEY *Music of India* vii. 104 The vīṇā has seven strings, four of which pass over the frets and constitute the main playing strings. **1945** R. K. NARAYAN *Eng. Teacher* v. 109 He hardly made any special sound or noise, but it was there all the time, a permanent background against which all his speech and gestures occurred, something like the melody of a veena string from which music arises and ends. **1964** S. MARCUSE *Mus. Instruments* 564/2 *Vinā*.., stringed instr. of ancient and modern India. In modern times the word has become a generic term for chordophones in S. India. **1969** R. SHANKAR *My Music* i. 34/2 The stringed instrument par excellence..is the *veena* (also spelled *vina*). **1972** P. HOLROYDE *Indian Mus.* 258 It has been said by Yajnavalkya, the ancient Indian writer and philosopher: 'He who knows the art of veena-playing and sruti shastra can attain God easily.'

vinaigrette. Add: **1. b.** Now *spec.* a dressing of oil and (wine) vinegar, sometimes with herbs (esp. tarragon), used esp. with salads and cold vegetables. In full *vinaigrette sauce* (also F. *sauce vinaigrette*). Also *vinaigrette dressing.*

[**1877** *Cassell's Dict. Cookery* 1091 *Vinaigrette, Sauce à la.* This is a sauce much used in Paris for cold viands.] **1880** M. PARLOA *Appledore Cook Bk.* (new ed.) 235 (*recipe*) Vinaigrette sauce. **1906** MRS. BEETON *Bk. Househ. Managem.* xxxv. 1112 *Vinaigrette sauce*..4 tablespoonfuls of salad-oil, 2 tablespoonfuls of tarragon vinegar, [etc.]. **1936** LUCAS & HUME *Au Petit Cordon Bleu* 136 *Sauce vinaigrette*..tarragon vinegar..lemon..shallot..garlic.. mixed herbs..parsley..salad oil [etc.]. **1959** *Listener* 24 Dec. 1135/1 Mushrooms cooked and tossed in vinaigrette dressing. **1974** N. FREELING *Dressing of Diamond* 7 Colette..made vinaigrette for the avocadoes. **1982** T. FITZGIBBON *With Love* ix. 163 Calf's head with vinaigrette sauce, a dish seldom seen today.

vinaya (vinaya·). *Buddhism.* [Skr., lit. 'leading (away)'.] The rules of conduct that regulate Buddhist monastic life. Also *attrib.*

1854 A. CUNNINGHAM *Ladák* xiii. 383 Vinaya, or 'Rules of Discipline'. **1881** RHYS DAVIDS & OLDENBERG (*title*) Vinaya texts. *Ibid.* p. xiii, Upâli is mentioned as the first among the custodians of the Vinaya. **1924** S. DUTT *Early Buddhist Monachism* i. 15 The Council of Vesali must be dated about the middle of the fourth century B.C., and the compilation of a complex codex of Vinaya rules not much earlier than that date. **1956** R. PIERIS *Sinhalese Social Organization* II. ix. 74 The monks themselves were prohibited by *vinaya* rules from performing these mundane duties. **1979** *Jrnl. Asian Studies* XXXVIII. 671 The *Vinaya*, or Code of Conduct.

‖ **vin blanc** (væ̃ blɑ̃). [Fr.] **1. a.** French white wine.

1792 A. YOUNG *Trav. France* I. 164 He gave me a bottle of excellent *vin blanc mouseux*, made in Auvergne. **1814** M. BIRKBECK *Journey through France* 29 Pouilly, [renowned] for its Vin Blanc. **1853** [see *GOFER]. **1917** A. G. EMPEY *Over Top* 313 *Vin blanc*, French white wine made from vinegar. They forgot the red ink. **1958** 'E. DUNDY' *Dud Avocado* I. ix. 157 The vin blanc break around eleven o'clock. **1974** *Country Life* 31 Jan. 183/2 An enormous amount..must be sold not as burgundy at all but as plain *vin rouge* or *vin blanc.*

b. *vin blanc cassis* [*CASSIS], (see quot. 1964).

1964 A. SICHEL *Penguin Bk. Wines* III. 173 A popular liqueur is made from blackcurrants..and is known as Cassis. Mixed with white wine, it is often used as an aperitif drink in France, called 'Vin Blanc Cassis'. **1982** 'R. GRAYSON' *Montmartre Murders* iv. 31 Gautier was sipping the vin blanc cassis which a waiter had brought him.

2. In various joc. and illiterate spellings. Cf. *PLONK *sb.*[2] Chiefly *Mil. slang.*

1919 J. BUCHAN *Mr. Standfast* viii. 162 A pint and a dram for me. This is better than vongblong and vongrooge ...in those estaminets. **1933** F. RICHARDS *Old Soldiers never Die* vii. 83 An elderly Frenchman from Armentières ..was soon selling beer and ving blong and doing a roaring trade. **1934** BLUNDEN *Choice or Chance* 31 In Pop. we banqueted no doubt On *vin-blong*, malaga-and-stout.

vinblastine (vinblæ·stīn). *Pharm.* [f. mod.L. *Vin-ca*, former generic name (see PERIWINKLE[1]) + *leuco*)*blast* s.v. LEUCO- + -INE[5].] A cytotoxic alkaloid, $C_{46}H_{58}N_4O_9$, obtained from the periwinkle *Catharanthus roseus* and administered intravenously (usu. as the sulphate) in the treatment of lymphomas and other cancers. Cf. *VINCRISTINE.

1962 M. R. KARON et al. in *Pediatrics* XXX. 791/1 Several alkaloids were subsequently isolated from the crude extract [of *Vinca rosea*], two of which, leurosine and vinblastine (formerly called vincaleukoblastine), markedly inhibited this tumour. **1974** *Nature* 15 Mar. 239/1 The alkaloids colchicine and vinblastine interfere with the assembly of microtubules, yet they also affect several properties of the surface membrane of animal cells. **1983** *Oxf. Textbk. Med.* II. XIX. 96/1 Vincristine..is preferable to vinblastine..in the treatment of leukaemia.

vinca[1] (vi·ŋkă). Also **Vinca.** [mod.L.: see PERIWINKLE[1].] = PERIWINKLE[1] 1; **vinca alkaloid,** any of several alkaloids (as vinblastine, vincristine) obtained from a periwinkle.

1868 D. THOMSON *Handy Bk. Flower-Garden* ix. 250 For forming permanent edgings to large beds, these Vincas are very effective. **1937** A. T. JOHNSON *Woodland Garden* vii. 70 The vincas as a tribe are either misused or not used at all. **1961** D. STUART *Driven* xvii. 170 There had been pride and delight in her eyes when first the oleanders she tended so carefully had bloomed, and all the outside of the camp was a blaze of vincas that same season. **1970** PASSMORE & ROBSON *Compan. Med. Stud.* II. xxix. 11/2 Effects peculiar to the vinca alkaloids..include paraesthesia (especially round the mouth), temporary mental depression, loss of deep tendon reflexes and more rarely headaches, psychoses and convulsions. **1978** R. B. SCOTT *Price's Textbk. Pract. Med.* (ed. 12) IV. 374/1 The vinca alkaloids vinblastine (VLB) and vincristine (VCR).. have a variety of toxic effects other than those on dividing cells.

Vinča[2] (vi·ntʃă). *Archæol.* The name of a village site near Belgrade, used *attrib.* to designate a central Balkan culture of the chalcolithic age. Also *absol.*

1925 V. G. CHILDE *Dawn European Civilization* 174 The sunken oval huts, the shoe-last celts, the rude clay idols..and the spirals and meanders decorating the vases suffice to attach Vinča I to the contemporary culture of Moravia. **1940** C. F. C. HAWKES *Prehist. Foundations Europe* iv. 93 The early Vinča pottery shows Anatolian tradition. *Ibid.* 94 Some twenty other settlements of the Vinča culture have been identified along the Serbian bank of the Danube. **1974** *Encycl. Brit. Macropædia* II. 613/1 The Vinča sequence is best documented at the eponymous site, situated..east of Belgrade, overlying the Starčevo levels excavated by the Yugoslav archæologist Miloje Vasić, intermittently from 1908 to 1932. Fine Vinča ceramic wares are burnished in orange or black and decorated with a shallow linear channeling. **1977** *Jrnl. R. Soc. Arts* CXXV. 486/1 The mask-like face certainly recalls the conventions of this period in south-east Europe, notably those of the Vinča culture, or Porodin.

Vincennes (væ̃sen). The name of a château in the town of *Vincennes* (now a suburb of Paris), used *attrib.* and *absol.* to designate porcelain produced there in the eighteenth cent., before the manufactory was transferred to Sèvres (see SÈVRES *a.*); also applied to colour characteristic of Vincennes porcelain.

1766 in F. A. Barrett *Worcester Porcelain* (1953) vi. 29 Great improvements in the Worcester manufactory of china... It is hardly surpassed by the Vincennes, and much cheaper. **1874** C. SCHREIBER *Jrnl.* 13 Aug. (1911) I. 276 A Vincennes cup all but unique. **1900** F. LITCHFIELD *Pottery & Porcelain* vii. 104 The pieces having rich grand colours in claret colour or crimson lake, and in rich deep Vincennes blue. **1925** W. W. WORSTER tr. *Hannover's Pottery & Porcelain* III. xiii. 279 In the biscuit figures and groups of Vincennes we find..traces of the growing neo-classical movement. **1949** W. B. HONEY *European Ceramic Art* I. 40 The incomparable Vincennes gilding, with its soft-looking delicately tooled surface. **1960** H. HAYWARD *Antique Coll.* 254/1 The earliest Vincennes..includes jardinières, jugs, ice-pails and trays of simple shape. **1978** *Times* 22 July 8/2 A massive white Vincennes pot-pourri vase.

Vincent[2] (vi·nsĕnt). *Path.* The name of J. H. *Vincent* (1862–1950), French medical scientist, used in the possessive to designate a painful ulcerative condition of the inside of the mouth or the throat associated with infection with fusiform bacteria and spirochætes (described by him in 1896); also a similar condition of the gums that is accompanied by foul breath and bleeding.

1904 *Lancet* 16 July 135/2 Vincent's angina is a form of pseudo-diphtheria which is associated with, and is probably due to, certain characteristic micro-organisms. **1918** Vincent's disease [see *trench mouth* s.v. *TRENCH *sb.* 9]. **1926** J. L. T. APPLETON *Bacterial Infection* xxiv. The condition..goes under a great variety of names, *e.g.*, 'trench mouth', Vincent's gingivitis or stomatitis and ulcero-membranous stomatitis. **1935** *Motion Picture* Nov. 3/2 (Advt.), Keep gum disorders—gingivitis, pyorrhea and Vincent's disease far in the background. **1959** J. BLISH *Case of Conscience* i. 11 He saw few of the mixed bacilli and spirochetes which would have indicated a case of ordinary..Vincent's angina—'trench mouth'. **1962** BLAKE & TROTT *Periodontology* xvii. 173 The interdental cratering which follows longstanding Vincent's infection leads to interdental stagnation. **1983** *Oxf. Textbk. Med.* I. XII. 21/2 Acute ulcerative gingivitis... At times there are shallow necrotic ulcers affecting the oropharyngeal mucosa which shows diffuse erythema; this has been referred to as Vincent's angina.

Vincentian, *a.*[1] Add: (Examples.) Also, of or pertaining to St. Vincent himself.

1896 W. J. FITZPATRICK *Mem. Fr. Healy* i. 10 The Vincentian Seminary, 34, Usher's Quay, Dublin. **1934** G. B. SHAW *Too True to be Good* 23 The latest rediscovery of the Vincentian principle has been made by Mr Ford, who has testified that if you want a staff of helpful persons..you must not give them either title, rank, or uniform. **1982** G. GREENE *Monsignor Quixote* I. v. 73 Marquez ..did little entertaining apart from an occasional father from the Vincentian monastery. **1984** *New Yorker* 9 Apr. 52/3 St. John's is a Vincentian school... The Vincentians are trained missionaries.

Vincentian (vinse·nʃăn), *sb.*[2] and *a.*[3] **A.** *sb.* A native or inhabitant of St. Vincent in the West Indies. **B.** *adj.* Of or pertaining to St. Vincent.

1933 *Vincentian* 4 Feb. 2/2 We have much pleasure in publishing in this issue the Report of the Installation of officers of the 'Vincentian Progressive Friendly Society'. *Ibid.*, Vincentians abroad are fondly thinking of home. **1944** *Minutes Legisl. Council St. Vincent 1943* 92 The parent..was to all intents and purposes a Vincentian—who in turn was also from Vincentian parents. **1950** *Caribbean Q.* II. II. 18 In *Saraband* the light skinned Vincentian wants to marry a dark girl. **1974** *Advocate-News* (Barbados) 21 Feb. 2/1 Vincentians have temporarily thrown off cares of the current fuel crisis. **1980** *Oxf. Diocesan Mag.* Oct. 8/1 At Wycombe some 15% or more of the population is of immigrant origin—Pakistani, Vincentian, Indian, Jamaican, Polish, Italian, Yugoslav.

vinchuca (vintʃu·kă). [Amer. Sp., f. Quechua *wihchuykuk.*] One of several blood-sucking triatomine bugs of Central and S. America, esp. *Triatoma infestans.*

1932 *Listener* 17 Aug. 227/1 The Vinchuca, a horrid looking beetle from half to an inch long..settles on its victims and draws their blood. **1971** P. C. C. GARNHAM *Progr. Parasitol.* ix. 189 In the opinion of Adler..Darwin contracted Chagas' Disease..when he landed on the coast of Argentina and was bitten by the 'vinchucas' (the triatomid bugs which convey the infection).

vincristine (vinkri·stīn). *Pharm.* [f. as *VINBLASTINE + *leuco*)*cristine* (former name of the drug), perh. f. *LEU(KAEMIA + *-ro-* + *CRIST(A + -INE[5].] A cytotoxic alkaloid, $C_{46}H_{56}N_4O_{10}$, obtained from the periwinkle *Catharanthus roseus* and administered intravenously (usu. as the sulphate) in the treatment of acute leukæmia and other cancers.

1962 M. R. KARON et al. in *Pediatrics* XXX. 791 (*heading*) A preliminary report on vincristine sulfate—a new active agent for the treatment of acute leukemia. **1977** *Lancet* 19 Feb. 433/1 Complete remission [of acute lymphocytic leukæmia] was achieved on a regimen of vincristine, prednisone, and daunomycin. **1983** [see *VINBLASTINE].

vindaloo (vindălū·). *Cookery.* Also **bindaloo.** [Prob. f. Pg. *vin d'alho* wine and garlic sauce, f. *vinho* *VINHO + *alho* garlic.] An Indian curry dish made with meat, fish, or poultry in a sauce of garlic, wine (or vinegar), spices, etc., served with rice.

1888 W. H. DAWE *Wife's Help to Indian Cookery* 65 Vindaloo or Bindaloo—A Portuguese Kárhí... The best Vindaloo is prepared in mustard-oil... Beef and pork, or duck can be made into this excellent curry. **1954** S. CHOWDHARY *Indian Cooking* 51 Chicken vindaloo is very tasty with peas putao and other vegetable dishes. **1972** R. HILL *Fairly Dangerous Thing* I. iv. 39 A mouthful of Vindaloo prawn. **1982** BARR & YORK *Official Sloane Ranger Handbk.* 27/1 His macho-masochisms decree that he must order the hottest—Vindaloo, Madras or even Bangalore Phal. **1985** *Listener* 14 Mar. 15/3 Water is suggested as one option for Chinese food (expensive bottled water, of course), Guinness for oysters and lager for chicken vindaloo.

vine, *sb.* Add: **I. 2. d.** A suit of clothes; *pl.*, clothing. *U.S. slang.*

1932 *Evening Sun* (Baltimore) 9 Dec. 31/5 *Vine*, a suit of clothes. **1959** *Esquire* Nov. 70 J *Vines*, clothes. **1964** L. HAIRSTON in J. H. Clarke *Harlem* 285, I..laid out my vine, a clean shirt and things on my bed. **1973** A. DUNDES *Mother Wit* 238 I'm going to lay a vine under the Jew's balls for a dime. **1975** *Amer. Speech 1972* XLVII. 152 Without your vines you're nothing but FBI [*sc.* Fat, Black, and Ignorant].

4. c. (Earlier examples.)

1708 E. COOK *Sot-Weed Factor* 19 When sturdy Oaks, and lofty Pines Were level'd with Musmillion Vines. **1831** W. C. BRYANT *Marion's Men* 9 We know its walls of thorny vines, its glades of reedy grass.

III. 8. c. *vine-clad* (earlier example).

1824 LADY BLESSINGTON *Jrnl.* May in E. Clay *Lady Blessington at Naples* (1979) 102 The vine-clad hills and fertile Campania.

9. vine moth (earlier example).

1840 J. & M. LOUDON tr. *Kollar's Treat. Insects* III. 172 This Vine Moth is not the only species of the family *Tortricidæ* which selects the vine for its food.

vinegar, *sb.* Add: **6. vinegar-fly,** a fruit-fly, *Drosophila melanogaster*; cf. *DROSOPHILA; **vinegar stick,** a sword or walking-stick with a vinaigrette (sense 3) fitted into the handle (now *Hist.*); also *transf.*

1902 L. O. HOWARD *Insect Bk.* 185 They are also called 'vinegar flies', from the fact that their..larvae are frequently found in canned fruits and pickles which have been imperfectly sealed. **1937** *Discovery* Sept. 282/2 There is a type of cockroach found in vinegar breweries, at least two kinds of vinegar fly, and..the vinegar eel. **1979** P. L. G. BATEMAN *Household Pests* II. 19 The tiny red-eyed fruit fly *Drosophila melanogaster*, is one of several species associated with fermenting liquids or rotting fruit. They are also known as wine flies, yeast flies or vinegar flies. **1935** A. J. POLLOCK *Underworld Speaks* 129/2 *Vinegar stick*, a stiletto; a long bladed knife; a sword. **1968** *Canadian Antiques Collector* Nov. 21/1 The forerunner of the vinaigrette was the vinegar stick, a walking stick with a hollow head for a vinegar-soaked sponge. **1979** 'J. GASH' *Grail Tree* vi. 60 You get them in all shapes, even as 'vinegar sticks', where the container is cleverly made into the handle of a sword or walking-stick.

vi·negared, *ppl. a.* [f. VINEGAR *v.* + -ED[1].] Treated or flavoured with vinegar.

1861 [see *SLAW]. **1892** A. CONAN DOYLE *Great Shadow* vi. 74 He set a dish of vinegared herrings before him. **1978** R. CONDON *Bandicoot* xiii. 54 And a little of the vinegared sparrows of Wakayama.

vinegarish, *a.* Add: Hence **vi·negarishly** *adv.* (In quots. *fig.*)

1890 'MARK TWAIN' in M. D. L. Landon *Kings of Platform & Pulpit* 354 My companion said vinegarishly, 'Well, well! What do you say now?' **1976** 'J. ROSS' *I know what it's like to Die* xviii. 122 'I never ever laid a finger on him. We were very good friends,' he said vinegarishly.

vinega(r)roon (vi:nĭgărū·n). *U.S.* Also **vinagron, vinegarone, vineg(e)rone.** [ad. Amer. Sp. *vinagrón*, f. Sp. *vinagre* VINEGAR *sb.* + (depreciatory) augmentative suffix *-ón.*] A large whip scorpion, *Mastigoproctus giganteus*, which is native to southern North America and Mexico, emits a secretion smelling like vinegar when alarmed, and is often wrongly believed to be venomous. Also *transf.*

1853 L. SITGREAVES *Rep. Exped. Zuñi & Colorado Rivers* 34 Frequently did I find in the road that disagreeable-looking object known to the Mexicans as the vinagron. **1889** *Cent. Dict.* 6758/3 Vinegerone..so called on account of the strong vinegar-like odor of an acid secretion noticeable when the creature is alarmed. **1914** *Blackw. Mag.* July 123/1 His late breaking-in, the lengthy vacation,..keep the 'vinegarone' in his [*sc.* a bronco's] composition. **1920** *Glasgow Herald* 8 July 4/2 His animal friends, the chief of whom seem to be vinegrones, some species of bug. **1948** *Pacific Discovery* Mar. 8/2 The vinegaroons, those queer, eight-legged devils of the desert night, raced at top speed in and out of the shadows to gather insect prey. **1978** *Sci. Amer.* Mar. 36/3 Here are.. the acetic-acid-secreting vinegarroons.

viner[3]. For *U.S.* read orig. *U.S.* and add: esp. one used to harvest peas. (Later examples.)

1949 *Nat. Geogr. Mag.* Sept. 331/2 'Viners' that thresh out the peas were working day and night. **1963** *Times* 14 Jan. 13/1 Pea haulm silage, made under cover direct from the viners, plays a major part in the winter feeding. **1981** *Southern Horticulture* (N.Z.) Spring 36/1 In the 1950s the chore of hand-picking peas was removed with the development of a viner, to which the cut plants were cut and carted. **1982** *East Anglian Daily Times* 20 Nov. 5 The largest harvester around—the Mather and Platt SB8000 pea viner, soon to be produced in Suffolk.

Vinerian (vəinī°·riăn), *a.* [f. the name of Charles *Viner* (1678–1756), English jurist.] *Vinerian Professor*, the holder of the chair of English Common Law endowed by Viner at the University of Oxford; so *Vinerian Professorship.* Also applied to other posts or studentships (and their holders) similarly endowed by Viner at Oxford, or to the fund administered for this purpose.

1759 (*public notice dated* 18 June), The Vinerian Professor gives this public Notice, that he proposes to begin his..Course of private Lectures. **1765** BLACKSTONE *Commentaries* I. (title-page), Vinerian Professor of Law. *a* **1777** S. FOOTE *Devil upon Two Sticks* (1778) I. 3 Had you toil'd thro' the laborious page of the Vinerian professor. **1810** *Oxf. Univ. Calendar* 34 (*heading*) Vinerian Professorship of Common Law. **1846** *Ibid.* 58 Vinerian Professorship of Common Law. Charles Viner, Esq by his will..left about 12,000l. to the Chancellor, Masters, and Scholars of the University of Oxford, to establish a Professorship,..of the Common Law. **1934** *Law Q. Rev.* L. 196 Sir William Blackstone, the first Vinerian Professor. **1954** *Wadham Coll. Gaz.* Trinity Term 124 Mr. Gotlieb came as a Rhodes Scholar from Manitoba to Christ Church and took a First Class in the B.C.L., also winning the Vinerian Scholarship. **1980** *Statutes, Decrees, & Regulations Univ. Oxf.* 111 Any surplus income of the Vinerian Fund which remains after paying the emoluments of the scholars shall be applied towards defraying the stipend of the Vinerian Professor of English Law.

vineyardist. (Earlier U.S. example.)

1848 *Rep. Comm. Patents 1847* (U.S.) 199 A French wine maker and vineyardist..from Kentucky.

vingerpol (fi·ŋəɹpǫl). *S. Afr.* Also **fingerpoll, -pole.** [Afrikaans, f. Du. *vinger* FINGER *sb.* + *pol* tuft tussock.] One of several African species of *Euphorbia* producing succulent branches which resemble fingers.

1875 J. NOBLE *Descr. Handbk. Cape Colony* 178 The 'vingerpol' is another succulent plant in use: it has great fleshy fingers growing out of a crown, a foot in diameter. **1883** C. HOBSON *Farm in Karoo* 196 'Another very curious plant, circle within circle of things like fingers.' 'That is just what is is called... "Finger-pole".' **1889** H. A. BRYDEN *Kloof & Karroo* 258 Spent and foundered oxen,..when fed with fingerpoll, regained vitality. **1932** WATT & BREJER-BRANDWIJK *Medicinal & Poisonous Plants Southern Afr.* 104 *Euphorbia esculenta* Marl., Vingerpol, a drought-resisting plant of the Karroo; must not be confused with *Euphorbia caput medusae*, also known as Vingerpol. The former is a valuable fodder, the latter poisonous. **1966** E. PALMER *Plains of Camdeboo* xvi. 260, I dreamed I was struggling with a giant Vingerpol that bounced solidly and fleshily upon me.

vingt-et-un, vingt-un. Add: **vingt-un** has become *Obs.* (Earlier example of *β.*)

1772 DUCHESS OF NORTHUMBERLAND *Diary* 7 June (1926) xxxiii. 186 We play'd..at Vingt et un till supper Time.

vingty (væ·nti). [-Y[6].] Slang abbrev. of prec.

1936 F. J. WHALEY *Trouble in College* viii. 129 Perhaps there was a game of poker or vingty on somewhere. **1946** M. DICKENS *Happy Prisoner* ii. 34, I asked her to come and play Vingty. **1954** N. BALCHIN *Last Recoll. my Uncle Charles* i. 16 As you see, a small school of vingty is in progress.

‖ **vinho** (vī·nʸŏ). [Pg., wine: cf. *VINO.] Portuguese wine. Used in various collocations, as *vinho branco*, white wine; *vinho corrente* = *vino corriente* s.v. *VINO 1 b; *vinho da casa*, house wine; *vinho de consumo*, cheap wine equivalent to *vin ordinaire*; *vinho tinto*, red wine; *vinho verde*, [lit. 'green wine'] young wine that is not allowed to mature.

1835 J. E. ALEXANDER *Sketches in Portugal* iii. 65 Some of the elders..went to a press in the wall and took from it a square bottle of vinho branco, with which they washed the dust from their throats in order that the chaunting might be more effective. *Ibid.* v. 112 In an outhouse were many pipes of 'vinho tinto'. **1955** M. MCCARTHY in *New Yorker* 5 Feb. 93/1 Hotel and boardinghouse keepers are required to serve a third of a litre of wine (the *vinho da casa*) with every lunch or dinner. **1958** K. AMIS *I like it Here* xii. 152 A few glasses of *vinho tinto*. **1962** 'D. WILSON' *Search for Geoffrey Goring* v. 118 Penny copied the men, drinking the white *vinho verde*. **1975** P. V. PRICE *Taste of Wine* v. 100/1 There are, however, some wines such as the *pétillant* and *vinhos verdes* ('green wines'), which have a natural 'liveliness' or inclination to sparkle. **1980** *Times* 27 Nov. 21/5 Outstanding wines include ..the Beiramar *vinho corrente*. **1980** *Times* 10 June (Portugal Suppl.) p. vi/2 Prices of *vinho de consumo* (vin ordinaire) rosé. *Ibid.*, The northern Minho district which produces vinho verde. **1985** *Times* 26 Mar. 20/2 Organized tours from London will take tourists..to other regions such as the Dão, with its red and white table wines, and the regions of the *vinhos verdes* or green wines.

vining (vəi·niŋ), *vbl. sb.* [f. VINE *v.* + -ING[1].] The separation of certain leguminous crop plants from their vines and pods; *vining pea*, a pea grown for mechanical vining.

1928 JONES & ROSA *Truck Crop Plants* xi. 215 The vines [of peas] are loaded onto racks and hauled to the cannery or a field vining station. **1944** *Sun* (Baltimore) 26 Apr. 5/5 Prisoners..will be employed in vining and husking operations and in handling the cans after processing. **1959** *Times* 7 Sept. 19/2 One large..herd is getting its sustenance mainly from kale and vining pea silage. **1968** *Times* 16 Dec. 7/3 Peas for vining and threshing. **1975** LOCKHART & WISEMAN *Introd. Crop Husbandry* (ed. 3) iv. 147 Vining and pulling peas are not so dependent on dry weather at harvest.

vink (fiŋk). *S. Afr.* [a. Afrikaans.] Var. *FINK *sb.*[1]

1834 [see *FINK *sb.*[1]]. **1913** D. FAIRBRIDGE *That which hath Been* 30 Yellow vinks shrieked and jabbered on their hanging nests. **1925** *Centenary Bk. S. Afr. Verse* 235 The bird referred to in the text..is evidently a weaver-bird, locally known as Vink. **1958** *Cape Times* 15 July 8/8 Vinks feed on many kinds of tiny parasites and insects.

vino. [Sp. and It., wine; cf. *VIN.] **I.** Non-naturalized forms. (vī·nŏ). **1.** With various adjs. designating the quality, origin, etc., of a wine: **a.** *vino blanco* [Sp. = white], *dolce* [It. = sweet], *dulce* [Sp. = sweet], *fino* [Sp. = quality], *locale* [It. = local], *rosso* [It. = red], *secco* [It. = dry], *tinto* [Sp. = red] (cf. TINTO *sb.*[1] in Dict. and Suppl.).

1673 J. RAY *Observations Journey Low-Countries* 487 We left Cordova... This day we first met with red wine again which they call *Vino tinto*. **1846** R. FORD *Gatherings from Spain* xiv. 155 This *amontillado*..is very scarce, since out of a hundred butts of *vino fino*, not more than five will possess its properties. **1901** F. W. MAITLAND *Let.* 23 Feb. (1965) 224 When Carnival came, our cook took herself off to spend her wages in *vino tinto*. **1902** BELLOC

Path to Rome 317, I bought a bottle of a new kind of sweet wine called 'Vino Dolce'. **1911** *Encycl. Brit.* XXVIII. 725/2 Malaga is a sweet wine... It is generally.. a blend made from *vino dulce* and *vino secco*, together with varying quantities of *vino maestro, vino tierno, arope* and *color.* **1949** E. Pound *Pisan Cantos* lxxvi. 47 Ex rum-runner (the rum being vino rosso). **1950** E. Hemingway *Across River & into Trees* xxxvii. 226 A bottle of that *vino secco*, from Vesuvius, for the small soles. **1963** *House & Garden* Jan. 56/2 In little inns..you get a *vino locale* from the carafe. **1977** C. McCarry *Secret Lovers* xvi. 222 Mushrooms in one place..gazpacho in another..*vino tinto* in all. **1981** A. Fraser *Splash of Red* iv. 44 There's some lovely chilled *vino blanco* in the fridge.

b. Special collocations. **vino corriente** [Sp., lit. 'common, ordinary'] cheap wine equivalent to *vin ordinaire*; **vino cotto** [It., lit. 'cooked'], (see quot. 1965); cf. *vin cuit* s.v. *vin; **vino crudo** [It., lit. 'raw'], wine in its natural state, not boiled (cf. prec.); **vino de color** [Sp.], a rich sweet wine, used in the blending of sherry and other fortified wines; **vino de pasto** [Sp.], (see quot. 1965); **vino maestro** [Sp., lit.[4] 'master'], (see quots.); **vino nero** [It., lit. 'black'], dark red wine; **vino santo** [It., lit. 'holy'], a sweet white dessert wine; = *vinsanto; **vino tierno** [Sp., lit. 'tender'], (see quots.).

1932 E. Hemingway *Death in Afternoon* 338 *Vino corriente* is *vin ordinaire.* **1978** *Times* 21 Nov. 11/1 A humble *vino corriente.* **1673** J. Ray *Observations Journey Low-Countries* 387 The boil'd wine, which they call *Vin Cotto*, seemed to us much stronger than the wine unboil'd, which they call *Vin Crudo.* **1851** C. Redding *Hist. Mod. Wines* (ed. 3) vii. 209 Their boiled wine, the Italian *Vino Cotto*, or *vin cuit*, as the French call it, is mingled with other growths, as well as with sherries, for the sake of deepening colour or improving flavour. **1965** O. A. Mendelsohn *Dict. Drink & Drinking* 356 *Vino cotto*, Italian name of must..concentrated to a syrup by evaporation (boiling) and used for sweetening Marsala.. and similar fortified dessert wines. **1673** Vino crudo [see *vino cotto* above]. **1833** C. Redding *Hist. Mod. Wines* ix. 241 At Bologna they boil most of their wines, which are then called *vino cotto*, the unboiled they call *vino crudo.* **1851** *Ibid.* (ed. 3) 205 All sherry wine is by nature of a pale colour, the darker shades are conferred by age, or by *vino de color*, or boiled wine. **1966** H. W. Yoxall *Fashion of Life* xxv. 239 P.X., the *vino de color*.., so sweet and heavy as to taste more like a liqueur than a wine. *c* **1870** in H. W. Allen *Number 3 St. James's St.* (1950) 184/1 *Sherry..Vino de pasto*—56/–. **1902** A. Bennett *Grand Babylon Hotel* xxii. 251 The dry sherries of Spain..Manzanilla, and Amontillado, and Vino de Pasto. **1965** O. A. Mendelsohn *Dict. Drink & Drinking* 357 *Vino de pasto*, this Spanish term, literally 'pasture wine', is variable in meaning. It can stand for a family wine, one for everyday use... But it is also used by English wine merchants for a mediocre kind of sherry, pale and not too dry. **1977** J. B. Hilton *Dead-Nettle* x. 85 For strong drink he had laid in..an octavo cask of Vino de Pasto. **1911** *Encycl. Brit.* XXVIII. 725/2 The *vino maestro* consists of a must which has only fermented to a slight degree and which has been 'killed' by the addition of about 17% of alcohol. **1965** O. A. Mendelsohn *Dict. Drink & Drinking* 357 *Vino maestro*, Spanish name of the extra sweet and alcoholic wines used to top up the lesser breeds. Especially used in compounding malaga. **1968** *Listener* 29 Feb. 268/1 When the *vino nero* flows in village bars, songs are sung about Mesina (as they were about the late Sicilian bandit, Salvatore Guiliano). **1686** G. Burnet *Some Lett.* 122 There is near the Lake of Guarda a very extraordinary Wine which they call *Vino Santo*, which drinks like the best sort of Canary, it is not made till Christmas, and from thence it carries the name of Holy Wine. **1833** C. Redding *Hist. Mod. Wines* ix. 241 On the shores of the Lake of Garda they make a sweet wine..of prime quality, called Vino Santo. **1981** B. Healey *Week of Scorpion* v. 81 Their *Vino Santo*, the traditional Tuscan wine of hospitality. **1911** *Encycl. Brit.* XXVIII. 725/2 The *vino tierno* is made by mashing raisins..with water..pressing, and then adding alcohol..to the must. **1965** O. A. Mendelsohn *Dict. Drink & Drinking* 357 *Vino tierno*, Spanish wine made from partially dried grapes. Used in compounding malaga.

2. Also *bino.* An alcoholic liquor distilled from nipa-palm sap, drunk in the Philippines.

1901 *Army & Navy Jrnl.* 7 Dec. 341/3 The native drinks, ordinarily known as 'vino', manufactured in these islands, contain in a large amount the poisonous principle contained in wood alcohol. **1903** *Census of Philippine Islands* (1905) IV. 119 *Nipa* or *sasá* (*Nipa fructicans*) is a species of palm..from the sap or *tuba*..a liquor known as nipa wine, *vino*, or *bino*, is extensively distilled. **1964** J. M. Garvan *Negritos of Philippines* vii. 90 The young fellow hies off and finds a present for his future father-in-law. A very acceptable form is a large bottle of Filipino *vino.*

II. Naturalized forms. (vī·nōᵘ). **3.** Also **veeno.** Wine, esp. of an inferior kind. *slang.*

1919 W. H. Downing *Digger Dial.* 56 *Vino*, wine. **1935** L. Durrell *Spirit of Place* (1969) 31, I bear up very well under the stacks of local vino I am forced to consume. **1942** Berrey & Van den Bark *Amer. Thes. Slang* §100/14 *Wine*,..veeno, vino, wino. **1962** R. Jeffries *Exhibit No. 13* v. 50 We'd better use up the red vino. **1976** P. Cave *High Flying Birds* i. 7, I was far too stoned to take much notice of Lloyd's vino-inspired ramblings.

‖**vin ordinaire** (væ̃n ǫrdinę̄r). [Fr.; cf. *vin and *ordinaire *sb.*] Simple French wine for everyday use.

1820 *Edin. Rev.* XXXIII. 344 And why should as large a duty be levied from the *vins ordinaires*, as from those of the first quality? **1852** E. Twisleton *Let.* 9 Oct. (1928) iv. 56 You would laugh..if you saw me imbibing the Vin Ordinaire here! **1893** Somerville & 'Ross' *Vine Country* viii. 159 A long array of dark-haired, white-coifed women and girls were to be seen.. finishing their jugs of *vin ordinaire.* **1926** A. Huxley *Essays New & Old* 17 The red wines of Carthage are really delicious, and even the smallest of *vins ordinaires* are very drinkable. **1955** E. Pound *Classic Anthol.* ii. 133 Our wine but vin ordinaire, We share spare Food but with jollity. **1975** *Woman's Jrnl.* Sept. 73/3 We drank a good *vin ordinaire* out of unlabelled bottles.

‖**vin rosé** (væ̃n roze). [Fr., f. as *vin + *rosé *a.*] = *rosé *sb.*

1931 E. Waugh *Remote People* 138 We dined on the roof; a delicious dinner; iced *vin-rosé.* **1958** A. L. Simon *Dict. Wines* 162/1 *Vin rosé* (1) a pink wine made from very ripe black grapes, the skins of which are not allowed to ferment with the wine, so that they only impart to it a pink tinge instead of a dark red colour; (2) A pink wine made from black and white grapes mixed in the pressing; (3) A white wine coloured with cochineal to the degree of pink required. **1981** P. Inchbald *Tondo for Short* xvi. 174 Bread and cheese, a salad, a bowl of fruit, a litre bottle of vin rosé.

‖**vin rouge** (væ̃n rūʒ). [Fr., f. as *vin + Rouge *a.*] **a.** French red wine; = *rouge *sb.*[1] 6.

1917 A. G. Empey *Over Top* 313 *Vin rouge*, French red wine made from vinegar and red ink. **1922** E. E. Cummings *Enormous Room* vii. 169 A good deal of color in his cheeks and a good deal of vin rouge in his guts. **1931** E. Linklater *Juan in America* ii. iv. 79 Rumors of a Chianti racket or a corner in *vin rouge* are obviously premature. **1960** *Guardian* 31 Dec. 5/3 The working [French] man drinks..at each meal..a litre of vin rouge ordinaire. **1980** L. St. Clair *Obsessions* iv. 105 A bottle of *vin rouge* and two glasses.

b. In joc. or illit. spelling. Cf. *vin blanc 2. (In quot., *Mil. slang.*)

1919 [see *vin blanc 2].

‖**vinsanto** (vinsa·nto). [It.] = *vino santo* s.v. *vino 1 b.

1965 A. Sichel *Penguin Bk. Wines* iii. 203 Although made all over Italy where fine-quality sweet wine can be made from dried grapes, the true Vin Santo Toscano should be made from grapes that have been left on the vine to dry... Fine Vin Santo is also made from grapes picked at the normal time in October and allowed to dry until January or February and then crushed. **1973** *Country Life* 28 June 1919/3 The sweet dessert Vin Santo, made from dried grapes..is made quite widely in Italy. **1981** M. Nabb *Death of Englishman* i. i. 16 The Marshal drank half a litre of red every day..and a drop of *vinsanto* on Sundays.

‖**vinta** (vī·nta). [ad. Bisaya *binta.*] A kind of canoe used by the Moros in the Philippine Islands.

1900 F. H. Sawyer *Inhabitants of Philippines* xxxviii. 362 These vessels rendered good service, and to some extent checked the incursions of the pirates, but they had not the speed to follow up the fast-rowing *vintas* of the Moros, which could always escape from them unless caught in narrow waters. **1906** *Soldier Slang* in C. McGovern *Sarjint Larry an' Frinds, Parao*, a native canoe or row boat, usually a single hollowed-out log; propelled by one or two rude oars, with a paddle for a rudder. *Ibid.*, *Vinta*, same as 'Parao'. **1946** G. Stimpson *Bk. about Thousand Things* 47 Their *vintas*, fishing boats hewn from single long logs, were marvels of workmanship and efficiency. **1979** P. Driscoll *Pangolin* xvi. 127 The long, slender *vintas* of the Muslim fishermen lay at anchor.

vintage, *sb.* Add: **2*.** *transf.* and *fig.* **a.** The date or period when a person was born or flourished.

1883 *Sunday Mercury* (N.Y.) 23 Sept. 6/4 'I want to sue a man for breach of promise,' said a maiden of the vintage of 1842, coming into a lawyer's office. **1931** F. L. Allen *Only Yesterday* vi. 129 Harding had no sooner arrived at the White House than a swarm of practical politicians of the McKinley-Foraker vintage reappeared in Washington. **1945** A. L. Rowse *West-Country Stories* 2 He was..a benevolent pluralist of a rich vintage. **1967** M. Argyle *Psychol. Interpersonal Behaviour* iv. 79 In many cases the hero has a well-defined style of social behaviour—compare..the cowboy of 1890 vintage.

b. Hence, the date or period at which a thing was made or produced.

1929 R. S. & H. M. Lynd *Middletown* xiv. 199 Examination questions of the two periods indicate so little change in method and emphasis in teaching that it is almost impossible simply by reading a history examination to tell whether it is of 1890 or 1924 vintage. **1939** E. S. Gardner *D.A. draws Circle* vii. 105 Mrs Fermal drove up in a rattling car of ancient vintage. **1946** E. O'Neill *Iceman Cometh* (1947) i. 11 His pointed tan buttoned shoes, faded pink shirt and bright tie belong to the same vintage. **1972** J. Rossiter *Rope for General Dietz* iii. 31 Her accent was a creamy 1969-vintage Roedean.

3. b. *vintage chart, year* (in quots. *fig.*).

1933 T. E. Lawrence *Let.* 1 Aug. (1938) 773 Rather a vintage year, for books. **1964** A. Launay *Caviare & After* xv. 104 If you arm yourself with a vintage chart—easily obtainable from most wine merchants—you can learn the best years for the best wines. **1973** *Country Life* 15 Nov. 1542/3 Characteristic and impish Lowry of a fine vintage year 1960. **1985** *Times* 1 May 23/5 Britain's offshore oil and gas industry achieved a vintage year in 1984.

c. *transf.* Denoting an old style or model of something, esp. a vehicle; **vintage car,** a motor car made between 1905 (or 1917) and 1930; cf. *veteran car* s.v. *veteran *sb.* 3.

1928 M. Arlen *Lily Christine* ii. 23 You should see mine in London—a vintage Buick. **1933** *Sat. Even. Post* 13 May 4/2 Alfred P. Sloan tries out a vintage model automobile. **1950** T. Guthrie in *Plays of Year 1949–50* III. 569 Goes on working at her vintage telephone. **1958** *Listener* 21 Aug. 261/2 The details of a vintage aircraft or an early locomotive. **1965** *Guardian* 6 Nov. 3/8 A 'veteran' is any car made before December 31, 1904. From January 1, 1905 to December 31, 1910, the definition..is 'Edwardian', and from then to December 31, 1930, cars are classified as 'Vintage'. **1979** J. Leasor *Love & Land Beyond* iii. 32 The familiar vintage car smell of hot oil and old metal and carnauba wax polish. **1985** *New Yorker* 27 May 31/1 A debonair gentleman..wearing a vintage tweed jacket.

d. Characteristic of the best period of a person's work, etc.; classic.

1939 *Country Life* 11 Feb. 147/1 With a few minor reservations, this [play] may be recommended as vintage Coward. **1959** R. Gant *World in Jug* 7 My name is Larry Alden and maybe you'll only know it if you have a long memory or a stack of vintage jazz records. **1972** *Guardian* 25 Jan. 9/3 It was pure vintage Deauville to the background of Henry Hall type music. **1977** D. Mackenzie *Raven & Kamikaze* i. 20 The Pole's..tone was compassionate. 'She is in love with me.' This was vintage Zaleski. 'Of course.' said Raven.

vintage, *v.* **1.** (Later examples.)

1893 Somerville & 'Ross' *Vine Country* viii. 153 A little, incredibly bowed woman, who had been vintaging here at Quinault for the last eighty years. **1923** F. Stark *Let.* 16 Sept. (1974) I. 77 The people here are vintaging... All the country from Cette to this place is vine. **1975** P. V. Price *Taste of Wine* v. 94/2 In many vintages, such as 1964, they can make wines quite different from those of the Medoc, because being further south they vintage a little earlier.

vinyl. Add: Also with pronunc. (vəi·nəil).

1. Substitute for def.: The organic radical or group $CH_2{=}CH$—, which is equivalent to a molecule of ethylene with one hydrogen atom removed. Usu. *attrib.*

2. a. = *polyvinyl b. Freq. *attrib.*

1939 *Nature* 13 May 787/2 Resins more recently developed, such as vinyl and polystyrene, are slowly making headway. **1951** R. Mayer *Artist's Hand-bk. Materials & Techniques* iii. 152 The most promising synthetic varieties [of resin] at present are the alkyd, acrylic, and vinyl types. **1957** *Times* 18 Nov. 11/2 An unbreakable doll of vinyl, a glamorous young lady with elegant nylon-clad legs, costing 9 guineas. **1962** *B.B.C. Handbk.* 204 L.P. vinyl records giving basic pronunciation rules. **1969** J. H. Stickelmeyer in W. R. R. Park *Plastics Film Technol.* i. 7 Development of shrink wrapping techniques ..has brightened the future for vinyls. **1976** P. Lively *Stitch in Time* viii. 98 There is paint that is non-drip and paint that is vinyl or emulsion and paint that is specially good for this, that or the other. **1982** *Sci. Amer.* July 54/1 Most synthetic organic materials such as vinyl or polyethylene are electrically insulating.

b. *spec.* a covering material or fabric made of or containing polyvinyl.

1959 *House & Garden* July 11/2 (Advt.), Dining-chairs upholstered in washable vinyl. **1970** *Interior Design* Dec. 753/3 The walls are papered with a pale grey vinyl. **1978** S. Brill *Teamsters* vii. 263 The inside of the tractor ..was lined along the doors, the seats, and the dashboard in brown vinyl.

c. As the material of which gramophone records are made (so *piece of vinyl*). Also, a record. *colloq.*

1976 *New Musical Express* 31 July 27/1 A trio of knock out vinyl magnum opi, the like of which are not often to be heard on our sound systems. **1976** *Zigzag* Apr. 26/1 This is as depressing a piece of vinyl as I've listened to in many a full moon. **1977** *Ripped & Torn* vi. 6/2, I had rushed home, clutching this piece of shiny vinyl to my chest. **1980** *Musicians Only* 26 Apr. 12/3 He can continually judge the results on vinyl. **1984** *Sounds* 1 Dec. 24/2 When that song..was released at the beginning of this month as the band's first single, the Immaculate Fools proved they could cut it equally well on vinyl.

3. *attrib.* and *Comb.*, as (sense *2), *vinyl-coated, -covered, -faced, -surfaced* adjs.; (sense 1) **vinyl acetate,** a colourless liquid ester, $CH_2CH{\cdot}O{\cdot}CO{\cdot}CH_3$, used in the production of polyvinyl acetate and other commercially important polymers; **vinyl chloride,** a colourless toxic gas, CH_2CHCl, used in the production of polyvinyl chloride and other commercially important polymers; **vinyl resin,** any resin (*resin *sb.* 2*) that is composed of polyvinyl compounds.

[**1902** *Jrnl. Chem. Soc.* LXXXII. i. 256 Sodium vinylacetate is much less soluble in alcohol than sodium crotonate.] **1915** *Chem. Abstr.* IX. 2156 By acting with chem. rays on vinyl esters (vinyl acetate or vinyl chloracetate) solid masses are obtained..which..serve as a substitute for celluloid and like substances. **1974** *Encycl. Brit. Micropædia* VIII. 104/2 In addition to its conversion to polyvinyl acetate, vinyl acetate undergoes similar reactions with many other compounds. **1872** *Jrnl. Chem. Soc.* XXV. 891 Vinyl chloride undergoes a change by the action of sunlight, producing an isomeride. **1933** [see *polyvinyl chloride* s.v. *polyvinyl a]. **1978** *N.Y. Times* 30 Mar. A15/1 Fifty of the train's 116 cars left the tracks.. and a tanker loaded with highly toxic vinyl chloride exploded soon afterward. **1967** *Jane's Surface Skimmer Systems 1967–68* 47/1 The structure is decked in vinyl-coated nylon fabric, which is also used for the skirt. **1970**

A. Ross *Manchester Thing* 148 Two vinyl-covered kitchen chairs. **1977** 'E. Crispin' *Glimpses of Moon* i. 11 The furniture was all modern, from the oak counter..to the green glass-topped tables and the matching vinyl-covered chairs. **1960** *Times* 29 Nov. 2/4 Felt-backed vinyl-faced ..flooring. **1934** W. Davis *Adv. of Sci.* xiii. 141 The great versatility of the vinyl resins was strikingly demonstrated in a house which the Carbide and Carbon Chemicals Corporation erected. **1942** Gettens & Stout *Painting Materials* 3 Chemically, they [*sc.* polyacrylic resins] are closely related to the vinyl resins. **1943** *Electronic Engin.* XVI. 216/3 The variation of dielectric properties with plasticiser content is examined for the vinyl resins. **1983** *Which?* Oct. 453/1 These are water-thinned paints usually based on vinyl resins. **1978** *Morecambe Guardian* 14 Mar. 6/6 Washable gloss paint and vinyl-surfaced wall coverings are immensely childproof.

vinylidene (vəini·lidīn, vəinəi·lidīn). *Chem.* [f. Vinyl + *-idene.] The bivalent radical $CH_2{=}C{<}$; freq. *attrib.* Cf. *polyvinylidene.

1898 *Jrnl. Chem. Soc.* LXXIV. i. 188 Acetic anhydride converts it first into oxanilide, and subsequently into vinylidene oxanilide. **1940** [see *Saran]. **1980** *Chem. in Brit.* XVI. 473/1 Vinylidene, indole or leuco crystal violet are used as the colour formers.., and carbon tetrabromide or iodoform as the activator.

Vinylite (vəi·niləit, -əil-). Also **vinylite.** [f. Vinyl + -ite[1].] A proprietary name for a vinyl resin used esp. in the manufacture of gramophone records.

1929 *Official Gaz.* (U.S. Patent Office) 28 May 852/2 Carbide & Carbon Chemicals Corporation, New York... *Vinylite* for artificial resins in powder form or in form of plates or sheets and molding mixtures containing such resins. **1929** *Trade Marks Jrnl.* 25 Sept. 1635/2 *Vinylite*... Synthetic resin sold in slabs, sheets, bars and tubes for industrial purposes and moulding materials made of synthetic resin. Carbide and Carbon Chemicals Corporation .., New York. **1936** [see *Plexiglas]. **1956** A. Huxley *Adonis & Alphabet* 123 We must depend on the vinylite record and the slow-speed phonograph for any large-scale revival of spoken literature. **1974** *Encycl. Brit. Macropædia* XVII. 53/2 In 1948, fine-groove records of clear Vinylite were introduced by two different manufacturers. **1977** *Gramophone* May 1762/3 The ace up the CBS sleeve, which really made the LP viable, was the changeover from noisy, abrasive, brittle shellac to quiet, soft, unbreakable vinylite for the new disc material.

vinylogous (vəini·lŏgəs), *a. Chem.* [f. Vinyl + -logue + -ous (or directly after *analogous*).] Of, pertaining to, or being compounds that have the same molecular structure except for one or more —CH:CH— groups. Hence **vi·nylogue** (U.S. **-log**), a vinylogous compound; **viny·logy**, the relationships between vinylogous compounds.

1935 R. C. Fuson in *Chem. Rev.* XVI. 2 It is proposed to term such a group of compounds a vinylogous series. The members of a vinylogous series will then be vinylogs of one another. *Ibid.*, In this series the operation of the principle of vinylogy may be illustrated by a comparison of the esters of saturated fatty acids with their vinylogs, the α, β-unsaturated esters. **1966** *McGraw-Hill Encycl. Sci. & Technol.* XIV. 326/2 The principle of vinylogy may be used to explain why *o*- and *p*-nitrochlorobenzene are readily hydrolyzed to the corresponding nitrophenols, whereas the meta isomer is not. **1977** *Nature* 14 Apr. 660/2 The reaction (21)→(22) is not, as stated, a vinylogous Norrish type I reaction. **1978** A. J. Birch in Porter & Fitzsimmons *Further Perspectives Organic Chem.* 15 The decarboxylation needs only very mild conditions, a fact which suggests intervention of a β-keto acid or a vinylogue during the processes.

Vinylon (vəi·nilǫn). Also **vinylon.** [f. Vinyl + *-on* (perh. after *nylon).] Any of a class of synthetic fibres made from polyvinyl alcohol treated with formaldehyde which are used esp. in the manufacture of water-resistant fabrics.

1952 *Chem. Abstr.* XLVI. 1260 (*heading*) Pilot-plant manufacture of the synthetic fiber 'Vinylon'. **1955** Kirk & Othmer *Encycl. Chem. Technol.* XIV. 718 Fibers of polyvinyl alcohol, spun from water solution and treated with formaldehyde, as developed in Japan (Vinylon,.. [etc.]), have good strength, abrasion resistance, and heat retention. **1965** *Economist* 23 Jan. 362/3 The plant will produce 50 tons of vinylon a day. **1975** *Textile Res. Jrnl.* XLV. 591/1 Tetoron is a polyester containing a benzene ring; Vinylon has no benzene ring.

Vinyon (vi·nyǫn). [f. Viny(l + *-on*, after *rayon, cotton*]. Any of several synthetic fibres which are copolymers of vinyl chloride with other vinyl compounds.

1938 *Newsweek* 14 Nov. 10/2 An important company's chemists are experimenting with another silk-like yarn called 'Vinyon', for making hosiery, to rival du Pont's new 'nylon'. **1954** Kirk & Othmer *Encycl. Chem. Technol.* XIII. 831 The low softening point made later Vinyon fibers suitable for the production of sculptured carpet fabrics, nonwoven fabrics, paper, felts, and other such specialized products... However, inability to withstand boiling water permanently relegated Vinyon fiber to specialized uses. **1965** A. J. Hall *Standard Handbk. Textiles* (ed. 6) i. 61 The original Vinyon having a low softening temperature has now been almost completely replaced by Vinyon N and dynel, especially for textile purposes. **1975** J. Labarthe *Elem. Textiles* iv. 177 Vinyon fibers are made by three manufacturers in the United States at the present time.

viol, *sb.*[1] Add: **4.** *viol-string* (earlier example.)

1849 D. G. Rossetti *Let.* 8 Oct. (1965) I. 71 The hand trails weak upon the viol-string That sobs.

viola[2]. Add: **2. a.** Also *viola da gambist* = **viol da gambist.*

1977 *Early Music* Apr. 274 For viola da gambists there will be individual tuition.

4. With other distinguishing terms: **viola bastarda** = *lyra viol* s.v. Lyra 5; **viola da braccio** [lit. 'of the arm'], any member of the violin family, as opposed to a *viol da gamba*; *spec.* an alto violin, a viola; **viola pomposa,** an 18th-cent. viola with an additional string.

1724 Viola bastarda [see Viol *sb.*[1] 2 a]. **1980** *Early Music* Apr. 250 (Advt.), The *viola bastarda* style of playing was a highly developed idiom that involved frequent changes of register. **1864** Sandys & Forster *Hist. Violin* viii. 97 Vincentio Galilei, the father of the great astronomer, was an able writer on music, and in 1582 names the viola da braccio, which he says was called the lira not many years previously, the viola da gamba, and the violono, but not the violino. **1976** D. Munrow *Instruments Middle Ages & Renaissance* 90/1 The name *viola da braccio*, which first occurs in 1543, was first used as a generic term like the older *viola*, but gradually came to refer to the members of the new violin family. **1864** Sandys & Forster *Hist. Violin* xii. 164 John Sebastian Bach introduced an instrument he called the viola pomposa, in consequence..of the heavy style of violoncello performers in his time. **1954** Grove *Dict. Mus.* VIII. 810/1 Sanford Terry has shown that Bach's 'viola pomposa' was really the violoncello piccolo. **1976** *Gramophone* Apr. 1607/2 The viola pomposa a cross between cello and a big Tertis-style viola, with a splendidly rounded sound.

violable, *a.* Add: **violabi·lity** [-ity], the condition of being violable; cf. Inviolability; *rare.*

1926 *Glasgow Herald* 1 Apr. 8/4 The suggestion..raises the whole question of the violability of contracts.

violarite (vəiǒlā·rəit). *Min.* [f. L. *violār-is* of violet + -ite[1].] A rare isometric sulphide of nickel and iron, Ni_2FeS_4, occurring in massive form with a violet-grey colour and a metallic lustre.

1924 Lindgren & Davy in *Econ. Geol.* XIX. 318 It has been shown that the 'polydymite' from Vermilion, Ontario and Key West, Nevada, is not identical with polydymite... It might conveniently be designated as violarite. **1981** *Process Mineralogy* (Amer. Inst. Mining Engineers) 226 The close association of smythite with pentlandite indicates that its nickel content is derived from nickel liberated during the alteration of pentlandite to violarite.

violate, *v.* Add: **8.** To accuse or find (a prisoner on parole) guilty of violating the conditions of parole. *U.S. slang.*

1971 E. E. Landy *Underground Dict.* 193 *Violate*,.. be returned to prison for a parole violation—eg. *I was violated.* **1973** J. Mitford *Amer. Prison Business* (1974) xii. 222 If the parolee is 'violated' by his agent (this curious solecism is used, without any sense of irony, by everyone in Corrections, from the parole board to the convict), he is back to Square One. **1974** E. Brawley *Rap* (1975) x. 133 My parole officer violated me on another phony beef and I wound up in the Joint again. **1978** H. B. Franklin *Victim as Criminal & Artist* v. 191 Living outside Los Angeles, with life going reasonably well, Braly suddenly found himself with a zealous new parole officer, who threatened to violate him for driving a car, for having a woman spend the night in his apartment, or for writing anything he disapproved of.

violation. Add: **1. b.** Now freq. in the U.S., esp. = an infringement of the law; an infringement of the rules in some sports.

1961 in Webster. **1973** E. Caldwell *Annette* (1974) vii. i. 155 Jack immediately began complaining that the police had no right to follow him and charge him with a traffic violation when he was certain he had not driven through any stop signs or red lights and had been careful to stay under the speed limit. **1976** *Honolulu Star-Bull.* 21 Dec. h-2/1, I only hope Big Brother can take as hard a line against those who transferred out of the VH program should they be equally as guilty of violations. **1982** L. Block *Eight Million Ways to Die* (1983) iv. 47, I couldn't recall the last time I'd seen a cop ticket anyone for a moving violation.

violative, *a.* Delete quot. *a* 1797 (properly dated 1874).

violaxanthin (vəi:ǒlăzæ·nþin). *Biochem.* [a. G. *viola-xanthin* (Kuhn & Winterstein 1931, in *Ber. d. Deut. Chem. Ges.* LXIV. 327): see Viola[1] and Xanthin.] A xanthophyll, $C_{40}H_{56}O_4$, occurring as a yellow pigment in daffodils and some other plants.

1931 *Chem. Abstr.* XXV. 3351 The petals of the yellow pansy contain..a pigment wax which can be extd. with petroleum ether and on sapon. yields a well-crystd. xanthophyll, viola-xanthin. **1965** [see *lycopin]. **1978** *Nature* 13 July 160/2 The photosynthetic pigments found in [the green alga] *C*[*odium*] *fragile* (β-carotene, zeaxanthin,..violaxanthin,..and chlorophyll b).

viol da gamba. Add: Hence **viol da gambist,** one who plays the *viol da gamba*; a viola da gambist.

1915 E. S. J. Van der Straeten *Hist. Violoncello* iii. 32 The next viol da gambist whose name has been handed down to posterity is Vincenzo Galilei... He was the father of Galileo Galilei and an excellent lutenist, gambist, composer and a very learned master of musical theory.

violence, *sb.* Add: **1. d.** Now used in political contexts with varying degrees of appropriateness.

1972 *Science* 23 June 1300/3 It is interesting that 58 percent of American men think that burning a draft card is violence, in and of itself; 38 percent think student protest is violence; and 22 percent feel sit-ins are violence. Clearly, many Americans consider acts of dissent, per se, to be violent. *Ibid.* 1301/1 Only 35 percent of American men define 'police shooting looters' as violence and only 56 percent define 'police beating students' in this manner. **1984** *Times* 2 July 1/8 Mr Scargill..said: '..My facts show to me..that the people guilty of intimidation and violence in this dispute have been the police.' **1984** *Daily Telegraph* 5 Oct. 20/2 [At the Labour Party Conference] Much violence was done to the word violence, which it appears can be used to describe almost anything you do not care for.

violent, *sb.* Add: Revived in recent use. Also in *Comb.*

1978 *Jrnl. Communication* XXVIII. 180 The number of roles in which characters were the perpetrators of violence (violents), its victims, or both. *Ibid.* 187 The violent–victim ratio ranged from −1.40 in 1973 to −1.06 in 1977, suggesting persistently negative but perhaps decreasing risks of general victimization. **1983** J. Scott *All Pretty People* ii. 12 The psychiatric wards are filled with violents, and they release them every day.

violer. (Later examples in form *violar.*)

1797 *Encycl. Brit.* XII. 491/2 At this period *violars*, or performers on the vielle or viol,..abounded all over Europe. **1801** Busby *Dict. Mus.* s.v., *Violars*, certain practical musicians much encouraged in Provence during the twelfth century; and so named because they performed on the vielle and viol. **1931** M. Baring *In End is my Beginning* iv. 50 Her son was given..a band of four violars.

violet, *sb.*[1] Add: **4. b.** The scent of violets, esp. as used in cosmetics.

a **1850** in A. Davis *Package & Print* (1967) Pl. 8 Essence of Millefleur, Bouquet, Marechalle, Resida [*sic*], Violet, Tubereuse. **1890–1** *T. Eaton & Co. Catal.* Fall & Winter 42/2 Perfumes..white violet, Italian violet,..satchet powder,..violet. **1898** [see *lilac 2 c]. **1928–9** *Army & Navy Stores Catal.* 496/3 Natural Flower Perfumes.. Muguet, Rose, Violet. **1982** *Christian Science Monitor* 26 Nov. b8/3, I stocked up on Roger & Gallet hand soaps in violet and sandalwood.

4*. An onion; in *pl.* spring onions, sage and onions. *slang.*

In many dicts. of slang but no contextual examples found.

1890 Barrère & Leland *Dict. Slang* II. 397/1 *Violets* (common), an euphemism for sage and onions. **1903** Farmer & Henley *Slang* VII. 277/1 *Violet* (or *garden-violet*),..1. An onion: spec. in *pl.* = spring onions used as a salad. Also (2) in pl. = sage-and-onion stuffing. **1929** M. A. Gill *Underworld Slang*, *Violets*, onions. **1946** J. Irving *Royal Navalese* 182 *Violets*, spring onions.

5. b. *violet-adorned, -dewy, -rippling.*

1953 C. Day Lewis *Italian Visit* iii. 37 Violet-adorned beauties. **1932** Blunden *Halfway House* 73 All fresh and violet-dewy. **1949** —— *After Bombing* 29 And some have sung though never seen Melodious, voiceful, violet-rippling, blushful Hippocrene.

6. violet cream, (*a*) a violet-scented cosmetic cream; (*b*) a violet-flavoured confection; **violet powder** (earlier example); **violet tea,** an infusion made from dried violet flowers.

1912 J. Webster *Daddy-Long-Legs* 203, I started down town to-day to buy..a jar of violet cream and a cake of Castile soap. **1965** A. Christie *At Bertram's Hotel* xxi. 194 They were lovely chocolates... There were some violet creams. That's the sort of chocolate that has a crystallised violet on top. **1856** Dickens *Little Dorrit* (1857) ii. ii. 338 She mended her complexion with violet powder. **1853** Mrs. Gaskell *Ruth* III. iii. 115 She.. brought her up a cup of soothing violet-tea. **1904** *Cassell's New Dict. Cookery* xviii. 1033/1 *Violet tea*, this is a soothing beverage for persons suffering from bronchitis and similar affections.

violet, *a.* Add: **2. b. violet-green swallow,** a dark-coloured swallow with white patches, *Tachycineta thalassina*, found in western North America.

1858 S. Baird *Birds Pacific Rail Road* 311 Violet-Green Swallow..Rocky Mountains to Pacific. **1972** L. Hancock *Sleeping Bag* viii. 205 A pair of violet-green swallows built a nest..above our bedroom window.

d. *violet ray*: (*a*) a ray of violet light; (*b*) a ray of ultra-violet light. Also *attrib.* Now *rare.*

1803 *Jrnl. Nat. Philos.* V. 255 He placed muriate of silver without the solar spectrum and next to the violet rays. This oxide became blackened in a short time, it became still deeper in the violet rays, still more in the blue, and so on. **1903** *Sci. Amer.* 20 June 473/1 The so-called 'violet ray', which is now so common in literature, should be dropped, and 'blue ray' should be substituted in its place. **1925** A. Bennett *Jrnl.* 7 Feb. (1933) III. 74 He went to lie down under the light of his violet-ray lamp (equivalent of sunlight or some such thing) over his bed.

1929 *Proc. IRE* XVII. 1388 The real difficulty lies in the modernization of household equipment such as electric fans..and violet ray machines. All of these must be designed with elimination of radio interference in mind. **1933** *Amer. Speech* VIII. II. 55/2 *Nature-ray*, all right, or O.K., as in the phrase, *I'm feeling nature-ray*. It evidently is based on violet rays. **1966** J. S. Cox *Illustr. Dict. Hairdressing & Wigmaking* 79/2 *High frequency*, an electric current of high voltage and very low amperage, used in scalp treatment. Also called Violet Ray because of the violet light produced in the glass applicator.

4. Special collocation: *violet shift* (Astr.), displacement of spectral lines towards the violet end of the spectrum; decrease in the wavelength of electromagnetic radiation; usu. called a *blue shift*; cf. *RED SHIFT *sb.*

1959 *Listener* 3 Dec. 971/1 The spectroscope will reveal a violet shift for one component, and a red shift for the other, according to the familiar Doppler principle. **1977** J. NARLIKAR *Struct. Universe* iii. 76 Hence negative *z* is interpreted as 'blue-shift' or 'violet-shift'.

‖ **violetta** (vi͵ole·tă). Pl. **violette.** [It.] **1.** = VIOLET *sb.*[2] and VIOLETTE.

1740 J. GRASSINEAU *Mus. Dict.* 327 *Violetta*, or little viol, is in reality, our triple Viol. **1876** STAINER & BARRETT *Dict. Mus. Terms* 447/2 *Violetta*, a little viol. **1979** *Early Music* Jan. 137/3 Kolneder also points out that even violins, violas and *violette* are regularly written in the bass clef in the lower octave.

2. *violetta marina* (see quots.); cf. *viol d'amore* s.v. VIOL *sb.*[1] 2 b.

1801 BUSBY *Dict. Mus., Violetta Marina*, a stringed instrument not now in use. Supposed to have been similar in shape and tone to the *Viol d'Amour*. It was first introduced in England by Signior Castrucci in the year 1732. **1889** GROVE *Dict. Mus.* IV. 267/2 *Violetta marina*, a name found occasionally in the scores of Handel and his contemporaries, probably to designate the Viola d'Amore. **1963** *Listener* 21 Feb. 354/1 The use of the violetta marina in *Orlando*.

‖ **violette de Parme** (vi͵olet dᵊ parm). [Fr.] = *Parma violet* (*b*), (*c*) s.v. *PARMA[1].

1904 E. NESBIT *Phoenix & Carpet* xii. 232 A little scent sachet labelled 'Violettes de Parme'. **1913** 'SAKI' *When William Came* (1914) xiv. 243 All the hangings, *violette de Parme*, all the furniture, rosewood. *c* **1938** *Fortnum & Mason Price List* 55/1 Violette de Parme Toilet [soap]. **1968** M. KAY *Masha* xxv. 252 She..left, the smell of *Violette de Parme* perfume trailing behind her.

violin, *sb.* Add: **1. c.** Similarly, *to play second violin*, to take the subordinate part. *rare.*

1902 G. B. SHAW *Let.* 20 May (1972) II. 273, I dont see Janet playing a silly second moral violin like Judith.

4. *violin concerto, sonata, -stand; violin-player* (earlier examples), *-playing*; **violin spider** [see quot. 1969[2]], a small brown and orange spider, *Loxosceles læta*, whose bite can be fatal to man and which is chiefly found in South America.

1889 GROVE *Dict. Mus.* IV. 293/2 Mozart in his younger years was hardly less great as a violinist than a piano-player, and his Violin Concertos,..are the most valuable compositions in that form. **1934** Violin concerto [see *pianoforte concerto* s.v. *PIANOFORTE b]. **1797** *Encycl. Brit.* XII. 493 The most celebrated violin players of Italy..have been Farina, M. Angelo Rossi, [etc.]. **1814** JANE AUSTEN *Mansfield Park* I. xii. 243 The late acquisition of a violin player in the servants' hall. **1815** J. MAYNE *Jrnl.* 23 Jan. (1909) x. 250 The Romans have no idea of what good violin playing is. **1976** Y. MENUHIN in D. Villiers *Next Year in Jerusalem* 335 The technical points of violin-playing common to the Jew and the gypsy. **1889** GROVE *Dict. Mus.* IV. 288/2 Towards..1630, we find the first compositions containing rudimentally the form of the classical Violin Sonata. **1969** *Daily Colonist* (Victoria, B.C.) 8 June 14/1 War on a colony of deadly South American violin spiders in Sierra Madre Memorial Park was intensified Saturday when the city of Sierra Madre called a commercial exterminator into the battle. **1969** *Pest Control* Oct. 54/2 The violin spider is so named because in most instances it has the discernible shape of a violin on its head. The handle of the violin points toward the abdomen. **1979** *Daily Tel.* 15 Dec. 15/3 Hundreds of thousands of poisonous violin spiders, whose bite can be lethal and for which there is no known antidote, have invaded Johannesburg. **1915** D. H. LAWRENCE *Rainbow* iii. 80 A drawing-room..with a piano and a violin-stand.

Hence **violi·nic** (*rare*), **violini·stic** *adjs.*; **violini·stically** *adv.*

1776 J. HAWKINS *Gen. His. Sci. & Pract. Mus.* III. IV. i. 431 The Violini piccoli alla Francese must in often spoiling the phrasing and making violinistic rather than musical effects. **1963** V. NABOKOV *Gift* iv. 231 He had no real understanding of the real, violinic essence of the anapaest. **1976** Y. MENUHIN *Unfinished Journey* (1977) 376 Violinistically I can point to an understanding of my instrument which has grown day by day, year by year. **1978** *Gramophone* Aug. 348/3 The violinistic 'treatments' applied to every phrase are at first startling because people don't dare to play like this any more.

‖ **violino piccolo** (vi͵ŏlī·no pi·kŏlo). [It.; cf. PICCOLO.] A small variety of violin.

1776 J. HAWKINS *Gen. Hist. Sci. & Pract. Mus.* III. IV. i. 431 The Violini piccoli alla Francese must in strictness signify small violins; and of these there are none now known but that contemptible instrument called the Kit. **1889** GROVE *Dict. Mus.* IV. 813/1 *Violino piccolo*, a violin of small size, but of the ordinary parts and proportions, differing in this respect from the pochette or kit. **1961** *Times* 24 July 7/6 Mr. Carl Pini had taken the trouble to use a *violino piccolo* for the performance. **1979** *Early Music* Jan. 3 The instruments..include..violino piccolo (with its characteristically scalloped outline) theorbo-lute, and bass viol.

violist. Add: Also, a player on the viola.

1977 *Gramophone* Nov. 860/2, I prefer some details of phrasing and the greater warmth of the old Tchaikovsky Quartet which has Rudolf Barshai as violist. **1978** *Oxford Times* 3 Feb. 14 The splendid viola part reminds one of the fact that the composer was a violist.

viologen (vəi͵ōᵘ·lŏdʒĕn). *Chem.* [f. VIOL(ET *sb.*[1] + -O + -GEN.] Any of several salts of the 1,1′-dialkyl-4,4′-bipyridylium ion, (—$C_5H_4\dot{N}$.-R)$_2$, which are used as redox indicators.

1933 MICHAELIS & HILL in *Jrnl. Gen. Physiol.* XVI. 859 The new indicators will be designated as viologens... They differ from other indicators in several respects; in the first place, the color is exhibited by the reduced form, whereas usually the oxidized form is the colored one. **1964** J. W. LINNETT *Electronic Struct. Molecules* vii. 109 The viologens..can be formed by reducing γγ′-dipyridyl, or its derivatives, with zinc dust. **1980** *Nature* 27 Nov. 321/1 Methyl viologen (paraquat)..acts as electron carrier. **1984** *New Scientist* 17 May 23/1 New electrochromic displays (ECDs) based on viologens—close relatives of.. paraquat that turn purple when electrochemically reduced—look set for commercialisation.

violoncello. Add: **1. b.** A player on the violoncello. Cf. VIOLIN *sb.* 2.

1861 GEO. ELIOT *Let.* 6 Oct. (1954) III. 456 We have our violoncello, who is full of sensibility.

3. *violoncello player* (earlier example); ‖ **violoncello piccolo,** a small variety of violoncello; cf. *VIOLINO PICCOLO.

1788 J. WOODFORDE *Diary* 12 Sept. (1927) III. 46 There is not perhaps a better Violencello [*sic*] player in the Kingdom. **1889** GROVE *Dict. Mus.* IV. 813/1 *Violoncello piccolo*, a violoncello of the ordinary pitch, but of smaller size and having thinner strings. **1959** *Collins Mus. Encycl.* 706/1 *Violoncello piccolo*,..a small-sized cello for which Bach wrote obbligato parts in 9 of his cantatas. **1977** *Gramophone* Oct. 672/1 It falls short in the provision of a cello rather than Bach's own stipulation of a violoncello piccolo.

‖ **violon d'Ingres** (vi͵olon dæ̃ŋgr'). [Fr., lit. 'Ingres' violin'; cf. *INGRES.] An occasional pastime, an activity other than that for which one is well-known or at which one excels.

[**1931** *Larousse du XXe Siècle* IV. 68/1 *Violon d'Ingres.* Une légende, assez suspecte, prétend que le peintre Ingres était plus fier de son jeu sur le violon, jeu qui était fort ordinaire, que de sa peinture, qui l'avait rendu illustre. **1964** ROBERT *Dict. Langue Française* VI. 1004/1 *Violon d'Ingres*, le fait, pour un artiste, de pratiquer un art qui n'est pas le sien (le peintre Ingres aurait excellé au violon).] **1963** E. HYAMS *New Statesmanship* 255 President Eisenhower's *violon d'Ingres* being golf, it fell to.. John Foster Dulles to follow N. S. Kruschev into the pages of the *New Statesman.* **1968** J. M. WHITE *Nightclimber* v. 31 Fame, if we achieve it, is thrust upon us for a minor attribute that we rather despise. For example..Ingres.. preferred to play his violin—badly—to visitors..instead of showing them his pictures. Night-climbing was my *violon d'Ingres.* **1973** *Listener* 13 Sept. 345/2, I suspect that music was no more than Rousseau's *violon d'Ingres*.. and that the composition of *The Village Soothsayer* was a happy fluke.

viomycin (vəi͵oməi·sin). *Pharm.* [f. *vio-*, of unkn. origin + *-MYCIN.] A bacteriostatic antibiotic, $C_{25}H_{43}N_{13}O_{10}$, produced by several species of bacterium which has been given as an alternative drug in the treatment of tuberculosis, usu. by intramuscular injection of the sulphate.

1950 *Sun* (Baltimore) 22 Apr. 15/1 The company [*sc.* Chas. Pfizer & Co.] just announced a new anti-biotic drug called viomycin, hoped to be effective in the treatment of tuberculosis. **1983** *Oxf. Textbk. Med.* I. v. 254/2 Kanamycin, capreomycin, and viomycin are aminoglycosides which can be used as alternatives to the more potent streptomycin in patients hypersensitive to streptomycin or who are infected with strains resistant to first-line drugs.

viosterol (vəi͵ostīᵊ·rǫl). *Biochem.* [f. *ULTRA)VIO(LET *a.* and *sb.* + *-STEROL.] Calciferol (vitamin D_2) obtained by the irradiation of ergosterol with ultraviolet light.

1929 *Jrnl. Amer. Med. Assoc.* 31 Aug. 693/1 The Council [on Pharmacy and Chemistry] has adopted the term viosterol to designate irradiated ergosterol. **1933** *Discovery* May 160/1 The daily dose of yeast milk required for the prevention of rickets is approximately 24 ounces (120 rat units) of cod liver oil, 3 teaspoonful (200 rat units) and of viosterol 10 drops (800 units). **1971** A. A. MICHELE *You don't have to Ache* vii. 162 Today rickets is rare. Vitamin D and viosterol have done much to eliminate the disease.

V.I.P., VIP. 1. a. An abbrev. f. the initial letters of 'very important person', esp. a high-ranking guest. Freq. *Mil. slang* in early use.

1933 C. MACKENZIE *Water on Brain* viii. 111 'At the moment he has a V.I.P. with him'... Miss Glidden seemed to divine his perplexity, for..she turned round and whispered through a pursed up mouth, 'Very Important Personage'. **1945** *Daily Mirror* 11 Aug. 5/4 Then they started pouring buckets of water on the crowds below.. until a very important person happened along. The VIP got a bucketful all to himself... The VIP was a brigadier. **1946** E. WAUGH *Diary* 31 Mar. (1976) vi. 645, I found I had been categorized VIP—Very Important Person. It seemed odd to be asked 'Are you a VIP?' **1953** J. PUDNEY *Ring for Luck* 19 A sophisticated traveller, something of a V.I.P., expecting to be met and seen off wherever he went. **1964** MRS. L. B. JOHNSON *White House Diary* 24 Mar. (1970) 98 There were about three hundred people in front of the platform—VIP's from Huntsville. **1980** J. DITTON *Copley's Hunch* III. 221 For their own safety—as with all VIPs—their going had to be kept secret.

b. Spelt *vip* (vip), as an acronym. Now *rare.*

1945 *Fortune* Aug. 161 Very important persons, or 'Vips', usually travel in plush C-54's. **1968** *Listener* 22 Aug. 243/1 'Provided you are a Vip,' he added, joining the initials so that they formed a word. I was rather intrigued by this and asked him to explain what he meant by Vip, the meaning of which I feigned ignorance of. 'A Vip,' he said, 'is what in the days of you British used to be called a *bara sahib*, a senior official, but now we have been ordered to use this new Hindi word.'

2. *attrib.*, esp. as *V.I.P. lounge, treatment.*

1945 *Yank* 24 Aug. 6 The private was told by a general who had just left the VIP mess hall that 'I had a wonderful dinner'. **1958** *New Statesman* 22 Feb. 242/3 Mr Nutting, for example, was given the alpha-plus VIP treatment. **1967** MRS. L. B. JOHNSON *White House Diary* 3 Aug. (1970) 552 We drove up to an entrance and went quickly into a small VIP lounge where they shut the door. **1980** G. MCDONALD *Snatched* i. 8, I explained the situation to the head stewardess in the V.I.P. lounge.

viper. Add: **3*.** One who smokes marijuana or opium, esp. habitually. Also, a heroin addict. Now *rare.*

1938 M. BERGER in *New Yorker* 12 Mar. 36/1 They play special recordings of viper, or weed, songs with weird ritualistic themes. *Ibid.*, I was not a viper, which is the Harlem word for a marijuana smoker. **1943** I. LANG *Background of Blues* 21 The addict is a 'viper' who 'likes to smoke' or 'climbs the bush'. **1956** D. WEBB *Line-Up for Crime* iv. 69 Three good shots of heroin and you're a viper for life. A viper is an addict. **1959** MURTAGH & HARRIS *Who live in Shadow* (1960) I. iv. 54 They said I wasn't just a viper but also scumpteen of a pusher. **1977** *Canadian* 8 Jan. 15/1 He wrote that song in the late Thirties, back when people who smoked marijuana used to be called vipers.

4. a. *viper-green.*

1958 L. DURRELL *Mountolive* xvi. 300 Among the thickets of reed and sedge, in places polished to black or viper-green by the occasional clinging frosts, you could hear the chuckling..of..duck. **1976** *Star* (Sheffield) 3 Dec. 25/9 (Advt.), 1975 (N) VW *Passat* 1300... Attractively finished in viper green.

As *v. intr.*, to have an effect like that of a viper's venom. *nonce-use.*

1953 DYLAN THOMAS *Under Milk Wood* (1954) 63 Mr Pugh..mixes especially for Mrs Pugh a venomous porridge unknown to toxicologists which will scald and viper through her.

viperid (vəi·pĕrid), *sb.* and *a. Zool.* [ad. mod.L. *Viperid-æ*, f. L. *vīpera* VIPER: see -ID[3].] **A.** *sb.* A snake of the family Viperidæ, which comprises the true vipers and in most modern classifications the pit vipers, all venomous snakes having hinged maxillary bones, that are toothless except for a fang that is folded back in the mouth when not in use. **B.** *adj.* Of or pertaining to this family.

1909 WEBSTER, Viperid *a.* & *n.* **1956** L. M. KLAUBER *Rattlesnakes* II. xi. 716 The viperids were evolved directly from primitive aglyphous ancestors, rather than from either opisthoglyphs or proteroglyphs. **1965** R. & D. MORRIS *Men & Snakes* iv. 97 Generally speaking, the viperids are not as dangerous to man as the cobras and mambas, yet in some ways the symptoms of viperine poisoning are even more alarming. **1969** A. BELLAIRS *Life of Reptiles* I. v. 193 It has been suggested that the viperid or solenoglyph type of jaw was derived from that of opisthoglyphs. **1977** A. HALLAM *Planet Earth* 272 The elapids..and the viperids..are both first known from the Miocene.

vipoma (vəipōᵘ·mă). *Path.* [f. VIP s.v. *V 5 b + *-OMA.] A tumour which secretes vasoactive intestinal polypeptide (VIP).

1973 S. R. BLOOM et al. in *Lancet* 7 July 15/2 We suggest that tumours containing V.I.P., and reacting with no other hormone antisera, should be called vipomas. **1980** *Brit. Med. Jrnl.* 15 Nov. 1323/2 This patient's symptoms were unequivocally the result of a functioning vipoma of the left kidney.

viræmia (vəirī·miă). *Med.* Also (*U.S.*) **viremia.** [f. VIR(US + *-æmia*, after *anæmia, leukæmia*, etc.] The condition in which viruses are present in the bloodstream. Hence **viræ·mic** *a.*

1947 DORLAND & MILLER *Med. Dict.* (ed. 21) 1619/1 Viremia. **1954** *Jrnl. Pediatrics* XLIV. 20/1 Little is known about the presence of viremia during the course of the disease [*sc.* poliomyelitis] in man. *Ibid.* 25/2 The infectious process is now almost generally regarded as one which begins with a viremic stage. **1964** M. HYNES *Med. Bacteriol.* (ed. 8) xxv. 383 Infection with poliovirus leads first to proliferation in the intestinal mucosa. A viraemia follows and it is probably thus that the virus usually reaches the central nervous system. **1977** *Lancet* 23 Apr. 884/1 The possibility that this illness is a consequence of early viræmia should not be overlooked. **1979** *Nature*

17 May 200/2 Chickens, mice or cats neonatally infected with oncornaviruses become viraemic, develop low or no anti-tumour immunity and usually succumb to their tumours.

virago. Now usu. with pronunc. (virā·go).

viral (vəiᵊ·răl), *a.* [f. VIR(US + -AL.] Of the nature of, caused by, or pertaining to a virus or viruses.

1948 *Diagnostic Procedures for Virus & Rickettsial Diseases* (Amer. Public Health Assoc.) 15 Viral agents belonging to the psittacosis group. **1955** [see *parrot fever* s.v. *PARROT *sb.* 4]. *a* **1974** R. CROSSMAN *Diaries* (1977) III. 371 She said the viral pneumonia seemed to have cleared up, and the only area of danger was his bronchial tubes. **1976** EDINGTON & GILLES *Path. in Tropics* (ed. 2) xi. 577 Although many viruses may cause hepatitis there are two main types—infectious hepatitis and homologous serum jaundice. It is now recommended that these conditions be redesignated viral hepatitis type A and viral hepatitis type B respectively (WHO, 1973). **1983** *New Scientist* 10 Mar. 642/1 If chemicals can be found that inhibit the activity of these viral enzymes, while leaving cellular enzymes unaffected, then the path to anti-viral drugs will have been cleared.

Hence **vi·rally** *adv.*, by a virus or viruses.

1968 *Biochem. & Biophys. Res. Communications* XXXIII. 563 The normal and the virally transformed cells differ in regard to the quantity of glycolipids. **1977** *Proc. R. Soc. Med.* LXX. 559/1 Gradually interest in the viral theory was restored as examples of virally-induced tumours were discovered in mammals. **1982** *Proc. Nat. Acad. Sci.* LXXIX. 6822/1 Virally transformed rat embryo cells.

Virchow-Robin space (f-, vɜ̄·ɹko ro·bæn̄). *Anat.* [Named after R. L. K. *Virchow* (1821–1902), German pathologist, and C. P. *Robin* (1821–85), French histologist.] An extension of the subarachnoid space surrounding a blood vessel for a short distance as it enters the brain or the spinal cord.

1890 A. HILL tr. *Obersteiner's Anat. Central Nervous Organs* III. 137 Between the adventitia and the muscularis a considerable space is seen in all isolated arteries, the adventitial lymph-space (Virchow-Robin space). **1976** *Path. Ann.* XI. 298 (*caption*) Cryptococcosis involving a Virchow-Robin space in the cerebral cortex.

virement (vīᵊ·ɹman̄, vəiᵊ·ɹmĕnt). [a. F. *virement*, f. *virer* to turn (cf. VEER *v.*²).] A strictly regulated process of transferring items, esp. public funds, from one financial account to another.

[**1873** *Ann. Reg. 1872* I. 272 A dubious financial transaction, of the nature of what the French call a *virement*, had been the cause.] **1902** *Rep. Select Committee on National Expenditure* in *Parl. Papers* (H.C. 387) VII. 15 This temporary power of *virement* is vested in the Treasury by the Appropriation Act, and its exercise is conditioned by Mr Monk's Resolution of 4th and 5th March 1879. **1917** A. J. V. DURELL *Princ. & Pract. System of Control over Parliamentary Grants* I. ii. 39 In the case of the army and navy the powers of virement enable surplus appropriations in aid under one army or navy vote to be applied in making good a deficiency under another army or navy vote. **1921** W. S. CHURCHILL in M. Gilbert *Winston S. Churchill* (1977) IV. Compan. III. 1625 A supplementary estimate will not be necessary if the powers of *virement* are used to the full. **1936** W. I. JENNINGS *Cabinet Government* vii. 133 Virement is thus of two kinds, according as it is between sub-heads or between votes. **1946** *Erskine May's Law of Parl.* (ed. 14) xxv. 677 There is no definite statutory authority for this long standing facility, but it is implied by the still larger power of *virement*. **1958** *Times* 30 May 15/6 Criticism of the practice of virement whereby the Treasury allow Service Departments to use surpluses on Votes to meet deficits on other Votes is made by the Committee of Public Accounts in their second report. **1960** A. H. MARSHALL *Financial Administration in Local Govt.* xxi. 305 Most local authorities allow *virement* either formally or informally. **1975** *Language for Life* (Dept. Educ. & Sci.) xxi. 309 At one extreme, expenditure is rigidly controlled under specific 'heads', with no virement of any kind.

viremia, -ic, varr. *VIRÆMIA, -IC.

virga (vɜ̄·ɹgă). Pl. **-ae.** [a. L. *virga* rod.] ‖ **1.** *Mus.* A symbol used in plainsong notation; the note designated by this (see quots.).

1908 R. DUNSTAN *Cycl. Dict. Mus.* 439/2 *Virga*, one of the signs in Neum notation. **1925** *Ibid.* (ed. 4) 555/2 *Virga* (*L.*) 'A twig'. A square note with a stem or tail... The plainsong Virga is interpreted as a quaver. **1948** M. PIEREK *Song of Church* vii. 213 Among the Latin neums ten have Greek names.., while eight have Latin names, *clivis, pes, punctum, virga, torculus*, [etc.]. **1954** A. HUGHES *Early Medieval Music* xi. 380 The essential difference between the pre-Franconian mensural notation.. and the modal notation which preceded it lies in the fact that there is a definite sign (..the *virga* of plainsong) for a long note. **1978** *Gramophone* Aug. 365/2 But worst of all, these singers had introduced a new notion of their own, gleaned from goodness knows where, the idea that every *virga* is a long note, worth two beats.

2. *Meteorol.* Streaks of precipitation that appear to be attached to the undersurface of a cloud and usually evaporate before reaching the ground. Also *pl.* in same sense.

1947 M. A. GARBELL *Trop. & Equatorial Meteorol.* iii. 48/1 Streaks of falling cloud mass, or virgae.., are then observed under that part of the cloud base where showers are occurring. **1959** R. E. HUSCHKE *Gloss. Meteorol.* 611 Virga is frequently seen trailing from altocumulus and altostratus clouds. **1968** *New Scientist* 4 Jan. 22/1 (*caption*) An untreated cap cloud which characteristically has little if any virga or snow plumes. **1979** L. J. BATTAN *Fund. Meteorol.* viii. 151 When the water or ice particles evaporate before reaching the ground, the precipitation is called virga.

virger. For *Obs.* read '*Obs.* exc. at certain cathedrals, such as St. Paul's and Winchester' and add later examples.

1975 M. SULLIVAN *Watch How You Go* x. 174 The Canons' Virger on duty always virges the Canons in procession. **1978** *Church Times* 1 Sept. 8/2 If the Dean were still preceded by a wanded virger on his way to the divine office. **1983** *Ibid.* 11 Mar. 17/5 The Dean and Chapter of Winchester invite applications for a virger.

Hence [as back-formation] **virge** *v. trans.*, to conduct (cathedral dignitaries, etc.) in the manner of a virger.

1975 [see *VIRGER]. **1977** *Church Times* 25 Nov. 8/5 The Deacon is virged from his place to the Altar for the Gospel during the Fanfare.

virgie (vɜ̄·ɹdʒi), *a.* and *sb.* Colloq. abbrev. of VIRGIN *sb.* and *a.* Cf. -IE.

1930 [see *MUCKED *ppl. a.*]. **1965** H. GOLD *Man who was not with It* xxvii. 251 How do you know? A virgie like you were.

virgin, *sb.* and *a.* Add: **I. 2. f.** *transf.* A naïve, innocent, or inexperienced person. Freq. with adj. indicating sphere of activity. *colloq.*

1953 A. MOOREHEAD *Rum Jungle* iv. 53 A new player [at two-up]..is known as a 'virgin'. **1964** L. DEIGHTON *Funeral in Berlin* xxxii. 173 He had no strong political ideas... He described himself as a 'political virgin'. **1970** *Daily Tel.* (Colour Suppl.) 15 May 10/3 There was a competition..called 'Be a Millionaire'... I was an industrial virgin in those days but friends told me to have a go. I entered and won. **1976** E. STEWART *Launch!* 89 'That's a violation of security.' 'Stop being a virgin. People in this town bat secrets around like ping-pong balls.'

4. c. *Virgin Mary* [after *bloody Mary* s.v. *BLOODY *a.* and *adv.* C. 2], a glass of tomato juice (see quots.). Chiefly *U.S.*

1976 W. GOLDMAN *Magic* II. 90 Some girl wanted a Virgin Mary. The waiter nodded. **1977** J. PHILIPS *Five Roads to Death* I. II A waitress approached the table. 'A Virgin Mary... A Bloody Mary without the vodka.' **1981** T. HEALD *Murder at Moose Jaw* ix. 103 Crombie ordered himself a straight tomato juice with..Worcester. The Colonel did not, Bognor noted with approval, refer to the drink as 'a Virgin Mary'.

9*. A cigarette made of Virginia tobacco. *slang.* Now *Obs.* or *rare.*

1923 J. MANCHON *Le Slang* 329. **1935** C. BROOKS *Frame-Up* iv. 34 You gave me a virgin; I hadn't smoked one for nearly a fortnight. **1940** GRAVES & HODGE *Long Week-End* iii. 43 In the early Twenties..in offering a cigarette-case one would say, 'I hope you don't mind: it's only a Virgin.'

II. 17. a. *virgin bush*, bush land not brought under cultivation; *virgin country*, country that has not yet been opened up to the outside world for trade, etc.; *virgin land*, previously uncultivated land, *spec.* [tr. Russ. *tselina*] in Western Siberia and Kazakhstan, land made the subject of an intensive agricultural programme by the Soviet government since 1954; **virgin soil** (earlier *lit.* and *fig.* examples).

1905 W. B. *Where White Man Treads* 297 A heroic dare-all to share her children's father's toil to build up a home in the virgin bush. **1982** *Times* 15 Feb. 6/2 The Pope..celebrated Mass at a huge open space..which had been bulldozed out of the virgin bush a few days earlier. **1929** *Daily Express* 7 Nov. 8/4 Great tractors that will take heavy loads over virgin country where there are no roads. **1955** *Britannica Bk. of Year* 460/2 New state farms were to be set up at once mainly in Kazakhstan and western Siberia, where there were said to be many millions of acres of virgin or neglected, but fertile, land. **1959** *Listener* 10 Sept. 378/2 Mr. Khrushchev's virgin-lands scheme in Siberia and Kazakhstan. **1967** C. COCKBURN *I, Claud* xxxv. 438 Hardly anyone can be packed off to some social equivalent of the Russian 'virgin lands' for lousing things up. **1981** O. BERNIER *Pleasure & Privilege* xiii. 222 Every day men were claiming and enclosing new, virgin land. Homesteaders were at work all over the Eastern states. **1828** WEBSTER *Virgin*,..fresh; new; unused; as *virgin* soil. **1847** DICKENS *Dombey* (1848) xi. 104 We shall impart a great variety of information to our little friend... Quite a virgin soil, I believe you said.

b. *virgin wool* (see quot. 1952).

1921 *Daily Colonist* (Victoria, B.C.) 5 Oct. 7/6 (Advt.), Pure virgin wool socks at 45 c a pair. **1952** *Amer. Speech* XXVII. 262 Woolens and worsteds may be manufactured from *virgin wool*—any wool that has never before been spun, woven, knitted, felted, or otherwise made into a manufactured product. **1977** *New Yorker* 12 Sept. 106/3, 100% virgin shetland wool from the Shetland-Isles. Hand-loomed and fully-fashioned in the U.S.A.

virginalist (vɜ̄·ɹdʒinălist). [f. VIRGINAL *sb.* + -IST.] A player on the virginals; a composer for the virginals.

1913 J. E. MATTHEW tr. *C. van den Borren's Sources of Keyboard Mus. in Eng.* iv. 66 After Tallis, John Bull is the only virginalist who still used faux-bourdon as a means of figuration. **1924** M. H. GLYN *About Eliz. Virginal Mus. & its Composers* ii. 22 Had Orlando Gibbons lived out his span instead of dying in his early prime..the English Keyboard school must have attained publication... This music contains seeds which will yet fructify, unknown even to the later seventeenth century musicians, who were not true descendants of the virginalists. **1942** E. BLOM *Mus. in Eng.* xi. 183 The Elizabethan virginalists, for example, liked to base variations on them. **1960** *Times* 4 Mar. 4/6 The Elizabethan virginalists discovered that possibility and exploited it. **1979** *Early Music* Jan. 3 Clearly, there is no reason why the virginalist absolutely *must* have music, but there is a reason in this case why she should not.

virginality. Delete † *Obs.* and add later example.

1965 F. SARGESON *Memoirs of Peon* iv. 67, I was at first a little awed..by the room's too severe and uncompromising air of virginality.

Virginia. Add: **1. b. Virginia bluebell, cowslip,** a perennial herb, *Mertensia virginica*, of the family Boraginaceæ, native to eastern North America and bearing clusters of blue flowers; cf. *Virginian cowslip* s.v. COWSLIP 2 e.

1934 WEBSTER, Virginia bluebell. **1939** *Nat. Geogr. Mag.* Aug. 236/2 The pale-blue flowers and rosy-pink buds of the Virginia bluebells..are clustered on slender branches. **1978** *Detroit Free Press* 16 Apr. (Gardening Guide) 12/2 Virginia bluebells..can be purchased from special wild-flower nurseries. [**1826** W. DARLINGTON *Florula Cestrica* 23 Pulmonaria..virginica..Virginian Cowslip.] **1901** N. L. BRITTON *Man. Flora Northern States & Canada* 771 Virginia cowslip... In low meadows and along streams. **1944** G. L. NUTE *Lake Superior* 293 By July 1 the Virginia cowslips are coming into bloom. **1968** PETERSON & MCKENNY *Field Guide to Wildflowers* 322 Virginia cowslip... The nodding, trumpetlike flowers are pink in bud.

c. *Virginia rail* (cf. RAIL *sb.*³).

1828 C. L. BONAPARTE *Genera N. Amer. Birds* 334 The Virginia Rail..inhabits throughout North America. **1914** *Chambers's Jrnl.* July 439/1 The Virginia rail..is rare. **1945** *Bull. Mass. Audubon Soc.* Mar. 63 At the Sanctuary on this date we might get the Virginia Rail.

d. *Virginia cigarette, ham, tobacco* (later example).

1919 *Honey Pot* I. 1. Advt. facing p. 1, The best Virginia cigarette I have ever smoked. **1833** Virginny ham [see *MUDLARK *sb.* 1]. **1908** [see *chicken gumbo* s.v. *CHICKEN *sb.*¹ 8]. **1976** *Times* 3 Jan. 11/6 Smells of herbs and Virginia tobacco fill the air..the menu offered..Virginia ham steak from Surrey County.

2. Also, a cigarette made of Virginia tobacco. Cf. *VIRGIN *sb.* 9*.

1964 D. E. MIDDLETON in C. K. Stead *N.Z. Short Stories* (1966) 205 Now we can enjoy another of Blackie's virginias. **1971** R. DENTRY *Encounter at Kharmel* ix. 171 Do you mind if I smoke my Virginias?

Virginian. A. *sb.* **b.** (Earlier examples.)

1654 in *Colonial Rec. N. Carolina* (1886) I. 18 Sir, if you think good to acquaint the States with what is done by two Virginians born, you will honor our country. **1755** W. SMITH *Brief State Province of Pennsylvania* 15 'Tis true our Neighbours, the Virginians, have taken the Alarm, and called on our Assistance.

Vi·rgin I·slander [f. *Virgin Island*(*s* + -ER¹.] A native or inhabitant of (one of) the Virgin Islands, the westernmost islands of the Lesser Antilles, which are divided between Great Britain and the United States.

1931 *Ann. Rep. Governor Virgin Islands* 1 In replacing Navy personnel of the former administration, more than 40 per cent Virgin Islanders have been appointed to office. **1955** A. A. ALEXANDER in *Ibid.* 4 There are no colleges or schools of business administration here, and many Virgin Islanders who go to the continental United States for such training do not return. **1975** M. ORR *Rich Girl, Poor Girl* xix. 259 The lilting tones of the native Virgin Islander.

virginity. Add: **3. b.** *transf.* (The appearance of) virtue or integrity; innocence, inexperience. Also with adj. indicating a sphere of activity. Cf. *VIRGIN *sb.* 2 f.

1975 *Listener* 10 Apr. 468/1 She turned down £20,000 for half-a-day's advertising work. 'I'm selling my virginity,' she said. 'At least, that's what they're bidding for.' **1978** T. L. SMITH *Money War* I. 21 The President does not want to know... They all want it handled discreetly. And they all wish to maintain their virginity. **1982** *Times* 15 Feb. 4/2 He could claim no political virginity since he..had been an elected delegate at both Conservative and Labour conferences.

virginium (vəɹdʒi·niɒ̆m). *Obs.* exc. *Hist.* [f. VIRGINIA, name of a state of the U.S. + -IUM.] = *FRANCIUM.

1932 F. ALLISON et al. in *Jrnl. Amer. Chem. Soc.* LIV. 615 We suggest the name virginium and the symbol Va for element 87. **1936** [see *ALABAMINE]. **1938** *Encycl. Brit. Bk. of Year* 145/1 The discovery of element No. 87 has again been announced, this time with the name of Mavadium instead of Virginium. **1975** *Jrnl. Chem. Educ.* LII. 585/2 These two new elements he called virginium, after his native state, and alabamine, after the institute and state in which he worked.

Virgo. Delete ‖, for *Astr.* read *Astr.* and *Astrol.* and add: **2. a.** *attrib.* or as *adj.*, born under or ruled by the sign of Virgo (23 Aug.–22 Sept.).

1894 E. KIRK *Influence of Zodiac* xiv. 121 With proper training these Virgo people may grow into the most powerful spiritual healers. **1928** E. ADAMS *Astrol.* 74 The mercurial type of Virgo native is a very different object. **1964** L. MACNEICE *Astrol.* i. 16 'Are you Virgo?' 'Oh, no, I'm Leo.' **1970** 'D. HALLIDAY' *Dolly & Cookie Bird* ii. 15, I..said to Austin, 'When is your birthday?'..We got it worked out that he was Virgo.

b. A person born under the sign of Virgo.

1917 H. T. WAITE *Compend. Natal Astrol.* 45 The good type of Virgo is the most conscientious, methodical.. man. **1924** C. E. O. CARTER *Conc. Encycl. Psychol. Astrol.* 114 Virgo, however, is frequently extremely given over to foibles and personal idiosyncrasies which warp the mental outlook. **1938** D. ANRIAS *Man & Zodiac* vii. 82 Virgos are often witty but seldom positive. **1968** T. WOLFE *Electric Kool-Aid Acid Test* xxi. 294 'When were you born?'.. 'I'm a Virgo.' **1976** *Reader's Digest* June 75, I don't believe in this astrology business. We Virgos aren't easily taken in.

Hence **Vi·rgoan** = *VIRGO 2 b.

1946 'STELLA COELI' *Your Fate* xi. 70 The high type of Virgoan makes a good statistician, efficiency expert, [etc.]. **1960** E. CHATELHERAULT *You & Your Stars* ii. 16 Virgoans are among the most fascinating of the Zodiac tribes. **1978** *TV Times* 28 Jan.–3 Feb. 69/3 There may be a special link with a Virgoan.

‖ **virgo intacta** (vɜ̄·ɪgo intæ·ktă). [L.] A woman of inviolate chastity (in quot. 1922, *transf.* of a man); one who has never had sexual intercourse, a virgin. Freq. in legal contexts.

1726 J. AYLIFFE *Parergon Juris Canonici Anglicani* 228 The wife of one Bury was divorc'd from him upon the Score of Frigidity, it appearing that for three years after the Marriage she remain'd *Virgo Intacta* on the Account of the Husband's Impotency. **1829** J. HAGGARD *Rep. Cases Eccl. Courts* I. 728 If the parties lay together in one bed for so many years, of such ages, and the woman is certified to remain *virgo intacta*, there cannot be a stronger presumption that impotency existed, and that it was incurable. **1898** W. S. CHURCHILL *Let.* 31 Mar. in R. S. Churchill *Winston S. Churchill* (1967) I. Compan. II. 908 She too is to be pitied..as she was not originally *virgo intacta.* **1922** JOYCE *Ulysses* 483, I declare him to be *virgo intacta.* **1932** G. B. SHAW *Let.* 16 Apr. in *B. Shaw & Mrs. Campbell* (1952) 300 Ellen, though she came through with me *virgo intacta*, gave herself away heart and soul without a thought of reserve. **1968** 'A. GILBERT' *Night Encounter* iv. 48 It was later shown that she was *virgo intacta.* **1980** J. B. HILTON *Anathema Stone* x. 107 She may have teased his patience... Hence my uncertainty as to whether she was *virgo intacta.*

virgula. 3. a. For † *Obs. rare* read *rare* and add later example.

1934 PRIEBSCH & COLLINSON *German Lang.* II. x. 380 The full stop or, instead, a virgula, i.e. a short slanting strike (/) is used..to mark the end of a sentence or of a portion of a sentence followed by a pause.

virgule. Add: **1.** Now also in more general use with various functions (see quots.). Cf. *SLASH *sb.*[1] 5.

1946 G. STIMPSON *Bk. about Thousand Things* 487 The technical name of the short slanting stroke between *and* and *or* in the device is *virgule.* **1962** *Gen. Systems* VII. 299/2 Its mate is suffixed with a slant (virgule), thus: 4006 How to Silence. 4006/ How to Sound. **1980** O. M. RICCIO *Intimate Art Writing Poetry* v. 138 The vertical lines (virgules) separate the feet that make up the line.

virguncule (vəɪgʌ·ŋkiul). *nonce-wd.* [ad. L. *virguncula*, dim. of *virgo* VIRGIN *sb.*] = VIRGIN *sb.* 3 a; a young virgin.

1911 BEERBOHM *Zuleika D.* vii. 94 There are the virguncules of Somerville and Lady Margaret's Hall; but beauty and the lust for learning have yet to be allied.

virial. Add: **a.** (Further examples.) *virial theorem*, the theorem that for a steady-state system of particles obeying an inverse square law of force, the time-average of the kinetic energy equals the time-average of the virial; or equivalently, that the potential energy is twice the total energy and the kinetic energy is the negative of the total energy.

1904 J. H. JEANS *Dynamical Theory of Gases* vi. 144 The virial depends solely on the forces acting upon the molecules, and not upon the motion of the molecules. **1925** *Phil. Mag.* L. 414 By the extended theorem of the virial, the effect of the pressure of radiation can be ignored, and thus all consequences of the virial theorem which hold in the absence of radiation hold also when radiation is taken into account. **1965** PHILLIPS & WILLIAMS *Inorg. Chem.* I. i. 11 A useful theorem known as the Virial Theorem, which holds for all coulombic potential energy systems.., states that the equilibrium binding energy is equal to $\frac{1}{2}\bar{V}$ or $-\bar{T}$, where $\bar{V}$ and $\bar{T}$ are time-average potential and kinetic energies. **1974** *Encycl. Brit. Macropædia* VI. 852/2 Under such conditions the total potential energy of the cluster is exactly twice as great as the combined kinetic energy of all the cluster stars. This relation is known as the virial theorem. **1980** *Nature* 29 May 305/1 The virial theorem is often used to calculate a [galaxy] system's mass from its size and velocity dispersion.

b. *virial coefficient* [tr. G. *virialcoefficient* (H. K. Onnes 1901, in *Arch. neérlandaises des Sci. exactes & nat.* VI. 874)], each of the (temperature-dependent) coefficients of inverse powers of *V* in a polynomial series used to approximate the quantity pV/RT in the equation of state of an ideal gas or similar collection of particles; so *virial equation, expansion.*

1902 *Sci. Abstr.* V. 364 The series development $pv = A + B/v + C/v^2 + D/v^4 + E/v^6 + F/v^8$ is applied... The coefficients A, B, &c., are termed virial coefficients, and are functions of the temperature. **1955** H. B. G. CASIMIR in W. Pauli *Niels Bohr* 121 In the theory of an ideal gas interaction between atoms is neglected, but it is possible to calculate successive approximations, the so called virial coefficients. **1967** CONDON & ODISHAW *Handbk. Physics* (ed. 2) v. iv. 49/2 The virial expansion is one of the cleanest-cut developments in the subject of statistical mechanics. **1967** MARGERISON & EAST *Introd. Polymer Chem.* ii. 63 Some idea of the deviations from ideality in these dilute solutions can be obtained by evaluation of the second virial coefficients. **1978** P. W. ATKINS *Physical Chem.* i. 39 Conclusions can be drawn from the virial equation of state only by inserting specific values of the coefficients and taking note of their temperature dependence.

viricidal (vəirisəi·dăl), *a.* [f. VIR(US + -I- + -CIDE + -AL.] Fatal to viruses. So **vi·ricide**[2], a viricidal agent.

1924 *Brit. Jrnl. Exper. Path.* V. 341 Spots in which no naked-eye change whatever has taken place owing to complete neutralization by viricidal serum have been removed for study. **1946** J. R. PORTER *Bacterial Chem. & Physiol.* iv. 225 The ideal disinfectant or viricide has not been discovered. **1970** M. SKINNER *Old Rectory* 2 Who'd bred a virus which no viricide Could cope with. **1981** *Appl. & Environmental Microbiol.* XLII. 469 The results indicate that CAT may be an effective viricide against poliovirus type 2 in an acid medium. *Ibid.*, The viricidal properties of CAT [*sc.* chloramine-T] and chlorine are compared.

viridescence. Delete *rare* and add later example.

1961 G. DURRELL *Whispering Land* v. 123 Here were the vivid greens of the tropics, so many shades and some of such viridescence that they make the green of the English landscape look grey in comparison.

viridescent, *a.* Delete *rare* and add later examples.

1938 S. BECKETT *Murphy* viii. 152 The..kites rode steadily..flown by the child. She could just discern them... For a moment they stood out motionless and black, in a glade of limpid viridescent sky. **1980** P. HILL *Savages* iv. 57 The mainly deciduous trees joined branches overhead so that Leo was walking in a viridescent gloom.

viridin (vi·ridin). *Pharm.* [f. L. *virid-us* VIRID *a.*, specific epithet + -IN[1].] A crystalline antibiotic with antifungal properties, $C_{20}H_{16}O_6$, derived from the mould *Trichoderma viride.*

1945 BRIAN & MCGOWAN in *Nature* 4 Aug. 144/2 We have recently found a number of strains which produce another substance, which we propose to name 'viridin', characterized by remarkably high fungistatic activity. **1970** *Nature* 18 July 300/2 *T. viride* may retard the development of other fungi by producing the antibiotics gliotoxin or viridin, although attempts to demonstrate this with plate cultures have been unsuccessful. **1978** T. KORZYBSKI et al. *Antibiotics* III. II. 1970 Viridin is inactive against staphylococci, colon bacilli, and typhoid bacilli in concentrations up to 100μg/ml.

virile, *a.* Add: **3.** Also *virile part.*

1967 W. STYRON *Confessions Nat Turner* III. 372, I felt my virile part stiffen again beneath my trousers.

virilia (viri·liă). *rare.* [L. *virīlia* penis.] The male genitals; the penis.

1962 V. NABOKOV *Pale Fire* 123 When stripped and shiny in the mist of the bath house, his bold virilia contrasted harshly with his girlish grace.

virilism. Add: **2.** The state, of a female, of having some male sexual characteristics; also, = *VIRILIZATION.

1922 MASON & AYRES tr. *Lereboullet's Endocrine Glands* 164 Virilism may appear either in young girls after puberty, or in women after the menopause. **1945** [see *FEMINISM 3]. **1983** *Oxford Textbk. Med.* I. x. 87/1 Congenital adrenal hyperplasia can present in adult life with hirsutism, virilism, and often disturbed menstrual cycles.

virilist (vi·rilist), *sb.* (and *a.*). *nonce-wd.* [f. VIRILE *a.* + -IST.] A hearty, excessively 'manly' person; one who makes a cult of conventional masculine virtues. Also *attrib.* or as *adj.*

1910 C. E. MONTAGUE *Hind let Loose* viii. 145 To give.. to the pedant and virilist their several rights of stark rigidity and of jolly brutishness. **1922** —— *Disenchantment* v. 69 Your virilist chaplain was apt to overdo..his jolly implied disclaimers.

virilization (virilizē[i]·ʃən). [f. VIRIL(E *a.* + -IZATION.] The pathological development of male sexual characteristics, esp. in a female. Also **vi·rilized** *ppl. a.*, exhibiting virilization; **vi·rilizing** *ppl. a.*, causing virilization.

1951 L. J. SOFFER *Dis. Endocrine Glands* xxi. 689 The virilizing syndrome is an affliction essentially of females and preadolescent males. *Ibid.* 699 The Leydig cell tumours produce pseudosexual precocity in the male and virilization in the female. **1964** *Steroids* IV. 140 A virilized woman..with Cushing's syndrome due to an adrenal adenoma, had 390μg/day of testosterone in her urine. **1974** PASSMORE & ROBSON *Compan. Med. Stud.* III. xxviii. 50/1 This virilizing ovarian tumour..occurs in young adults. **1976** *Lancet* 13 Nov. 1081/1 This hormone stopped her menses and produced all the features of virilisation. **1983** *Oxf. Textbk. Med.* I. x. 85/2 Excessive hair growth is among the commoner endocrine afflictions of women. The complaint may exist in isolation or it may be one of a constellation of abnormalities found in the virilized state.

virilocal (vi:rilō[u]·kăl), *a. Anthrop.* [f. L. *virī-lis* VIRILE *a.* + LOCAL *a.* 2.] Pertaining to or designating a woman's residence after marriage in the domicile of her husband. Cf. *PATRILOCAL, *UXORILOCAL *adjs.*

1948 [see *UXORILOCAL *a.*]. **1957** V. W. TURNER *Schism & Continuity Afr. Soc.* p. xviii, It is possible that hunting, a purely masculine pursuit, and virilocal marriage, which brings together male kin in local descent groups, are parallel expressions of structural opposition between men and women in this matrilineal society. **1969** in Halpert & Story *Christmas Mumming in Newfoundland* 137 A consequence of the rigidly virilocal type of marriage and settlement pattern.

Hence **viriloca·lity; virilo·cally** *adv.*

1957 V. W. TURNER *Schism & Continuity Afr. Soc.* p. xviii, Within villages the dominant principles influencing residence were maternal descent and virilocality. *Ibid.* ii. 55 Women are often brought up patrilocally, marry virilocally, and after divorce reside avunculocally until remarriage. **1974** G. H. GOSSEN in N. Hammond *Mesoamerican Archaeol.* 219 Chamulas live virilocally in dispersed hamlets.

virion (vi·ri,ǫn). *Microbiology.* [a. F. *virion* (A. Lwoff et al. 1959, in *Ann. de l'Inst. Pasteur* XCVII. 286), f. *vir-us* VIRUS + *-i-* + *-on* *-ON[1].] The complete, infective form that a virus has outside a host cell, with a core and a capsid.

1959 *Ann. de l'Inst. Pasteur* XCVII. 288 The viral infective system, the virion, may be considered as a clathrate type of compound in which the genetic component is enclosed in a coat or capsid formed of subunits or capsomeres. **1967** K. M. SMITH *Insect Virol.* i. v The virion is, structurally and physiologically, different from any cellular organelle and from any microorganism. **1975** *Sci. Amer.* May 25/2 An electron micrograph of the poliovirus virion (the virus particle) reveals a sphere 17 nanometers (millionths of a millimeter) in diameter... The virion consists only of protein and the nucleic acid RNA.

viro- (vəi·ro), comb. form of VIRUS (sense *2 b), as in **vi·rogene**, a gene sequence corresponding to the genome of a tumour virus but occurring, normally repressed, in a cell; **viroge·nesis**, the formation or production of viruses; **virogene·tic, -ge·nic** *adjs.*, giving rise to viruses; **virope·xis** [after *colloidopexis*, f. Gr. πῆξις fixing], the process by which a virus particle becomes attached to a cell wall and incorporated into the cell by phagocytosis; **vi·rosome** [*-SOME[4]], (*a*) a particle of ribonucleoprotein and virus DNA found in the cytoplasm of certain virus-infected cells; (*b*) a liposome into which viral proteins have been introduced.

1969 Virogene [see *ONCOGENE]. **1971** *Nature* 27 Aug. 620/2 [This] suggests that activation of this sarcoma oncogene in the tumour cells is often accompanied by activation of the gs antigen of the virogene. **1976** *Ibid.* 13 May 101/1 African Old World monkeys..and African apes..possess virogenes that are useful in the taxonomic classification of these animals. **1961** Virogenesis [see *virogenetic* adj. below]. **1982** *Virology* CXXI. 296 (*heading*) The nuclear matrix is involved in herpes simplex virogenesis. **1961** *Jrnl. Insect Path.* III. 195 Inasmuch as the virogenetic network (strands) spreads over the entire cell, the virogenesis is neither confined to the cytoplasm nor to the nucleus. **1982** *Jrnl. Urol.* CXXVII. 646/2 The improved graft survival..may be an additional manifestation of unresponsiveness, not only to immunologic but also to virogenetic stimulation. **1956** *Nature* 25 Aug. 412/1 In the midgut cells of Hymenoptera infected with nuclear polyhedroses proteinaceous virogenic stromata form *de novo* in the nuclear sap... They are networks, and virus rods differentiate within vesicles in their cords. **1982** *Jrnl. Invertebrate Path.* XXXIX. 205/2 The hypertrophy is evident at a very early stage and before any obvious sign of a virus infection, such as the virogenic stroma. **1948** S. F. DE ST. GROTH in *Nature* 21 Aug. 295/1 This phenomenon strongly recalls the uptake by cells of colloidal dyes, and may..be termed 'viropexis'. **1981** *Jrnl. Gen. Virol.* LII. 329 Virosomes were taken up by Vero cells by viropexis with no evidence of fusion. **1970** DAHL & KATES in *Virology* XLII. 453/2 Since viral DNA complexes are quite poorly defined biochemically it seems appropriate to refer to such structures by the general term 'virosomes'.., in analogy with chromosomes, in order to avoid more restricted nomenclature (e.g., viral DNA, DNA 'factories', etc.), which may..create a misleading impression concerning their composition and function. **1975** J. D. ALMEIDA et al. in *Lancet* 8 Nov. 899/2 The surface hæmagglutinin and neuraminidase projections of influenza virus were removed from the viral envelope.. and relocated on the surface of unilamellar liposomes. The resulting structures were..found to resemble the original virus... The name virosome is proposed for these new bodies. **1981** *Jrnl. Gen. Virol.* LII. 329 Virosomes constitute a model system for studies on the organization of virus membrane proteins and lipids and interaction between virus particles and membranes.

viroid (vəiᵊ·roid). *Biol.* [f. VIR(US + -OID.] **1.** A virus-like particle. Also *attrib.* or as *adj.* Now *disused* in favour of next sense.

1946 E. ALTENBURG in *Amer. Naturalist* LXXX. 559 It is conceivable that there exist ultra-microscopic organisms which are akin to viruses but which are useful symbionts, and that these symbionts occur *universally* within the cells of larger organisms. We might call these supposed symbionts viroids. **1953** S. E. LURIA *Gen. Virol.* xviii. 361 Mutations of viroids could also give rise to nontransmissible, abnormal plasmagenes and be responsible..for the tumoral transformation of cells. **1959** *Oxf. Mag.* 26 Feb. 286/2 The relationship between viruses and other 'viroid' particles. **1963** *New Scientist* 20 June 652/1 If blind natural selection could conjure man out of a viroid in a couple of billion years, what could not man's conscious and purposeful efforts achieve?

2. An infectious entity similar to a virus but smaller and consisting of a strand of nucleic acid only, without the protein coat characteristic of a virus.

1971 T. O. DIENER in *Virology* XLV. 426/1, I propose the term 'viroid' for such entities. Altenburg (1946) introduced this term to designate hypothetical symbionts, akin to viruses... If, however, the 'viroid' is redefined operationally and in modern terms to encompass nucleic acid species with the properties discussed here, the term serves a useful function. To distinguish pathological conditions incited by viroids from those incited by viruses, the term 'viroid disease' is proposed. **1979** *Nature* 4 Jan. 60/2 Viroids are the smallest replicating pathogenic agents known. **1981** *Times* 2 Apr. 16 There is a parallel class of agents which infect plants, the viroids, which consist solely of strands of RNA.

virology (vəirǫ·lŏdʒi). [f. VIR(US + -OLOGY.] The branch of science concerned with the study of viruses.

1935 in DORLAND & MILLER *Med. Dict.* (ed. 17) 1502/2. **1937** *Ann. Reg. 1936* 59 In virology, two discoveries overshadowed all others. **1957** *New Scientist* 9 May 11/1 This will be the first chair in virology in this country, and its creation marks a stage in the development of virology from the young brother of bacteriology to a fully grown science in its own right. **1978** H. MCLEAVE *Borderline Case* x. (1979) 96 She no longer looked like a virology professor but an attractive, seductive woman.

Hence **virolo·gic** (chiefly *U.S.*), **-lo·gical** *adjs.*; **virolo·gically** *adv.*; **viro·logist**, a specialist in virology.

1946 *Nature* 14 Sept. 363/1 One of the main objects of the symposium, the finding of common grounds of interest between virologists, bacteriologists, mycologists and geneticists, was fully achieved. **1953** S. E. LURIA *Gen. Virol.* p. ix, In spite of many important additions to virological literature, no single volume suitable for classroom use has appeared. **1955** *Proc. Soc. Exper. Biol. & Med.* LXXXIX. 438/1 The Detroit-6 strain fulfills certain criteria..for a useful cell strain for virologic research. **1963** *Guardian* 10 Apr. 20/3 Virologists in the research laboratories at Mill Hill were exploring the possibility that some forms of human cancer may be caused by viruses. **1970** *Sci. Jrnl.* Apr. 3/3 The history of virological research is one of the continual discovery of new viruses or of new facts about old viruses. **1972** *Arch. Neurol.* XXVII. 103 (*heading*) Herpes simplex encephalitis. The course in five virologically proven cases. **1977** M. SOKOLINSKY tr. *Merle's Virility Factor* xii. 248 He was a virologist without great clinical experience. **1980** *Brit. Jrnl. Dermatol.* CIII. Suppl. No. 18. 24 Virological studies were performed on stools and throat swabs in all patients. **1980** *Amer. Jrnl. Epidemiol.* CXII. 487 There were two virologically confirmed cases with complications. **1983** *Amer. Jrnl. Veterinary Res.* XLIV. 64/1 The serologic and virologic responses of all cattle were monitored for 1 year.

virosis (vəiᵊrōᵘ·sis). Pl. **-oses** (-ōᵘ·sīz). [f. VIR(US + -OSIS.] A virus disease.

1927 *Phytopathology* XVII. 161 Certain aggregates of symptoms in potatoes (*Solanum tuberosum*) are considered to be due to corresponding degeneration diseases or viroses. [*Note*] A name for 'virus diseases' proposed on December 28, 1925, at Lincoln, Nebraska, by Dr. L. R. Jones. **1963** G. BENZ in E. A. Steinhaus *Insect Path.* I. x. 325 The most intimate association between the pathogen and its host is found in viroses. **1972** *Biol. Abstr.* LIII. 3729/2 The 'spindle virosis' of *M. melolontha* is characterized by the coexistence of 2 types of cytoplasmic inclusions: spindles and spherules.

virtu, vertu. Add: **4.** The distinctive qualities inherent in a thing or person.

1934 E. POUND *Eleven New Cantos* xxxvi. 27 Or say where it had birth What is its virtu and power. **1949** —— *Pisan Cantos* lxxiv. 11 In the light of light is the virtù. **1969** *Listener* 14 Aug. 214/3 Cromwell was shown in the same light—of a *de facto* sovereign come into power thanks to his *virtù*—by Clarendon. **1973** *Times Lit. Suppl.* 1 June 601/3 The pagan *virtù*, the 'civic humanism' of Machiavelli, had become the proud Christian freedom of the Huguenots.

virtual, *a.* (and *sb.*) Add: **4. d.** For 'momentum' read 'moment' and add: *virtual displacement,* any notional, infinitesimal displacement in a mechanical system that is consistent with the constraints of the system; *virtual work,* the work done by a force making a virtual displacement.

1877 G. M. MINCHIN *Treat. Statics* iv. 61 The virtual work of a force is the product of the force and the projection along its direction of the virtual displacement of its point of application. **1897** A. E. H. LOVE *Theoret. Mech.* viii. 139 Principle of Virtual Work. The sum of the virtual works of all the forces on a system in equilibrium vanishes in every infinitesimal displacement. **1942** SYNGE & GRIFFITHS *Princ. Mech.* ii. 60 Although the chief merit of the principle of virtual work lies in the fact that it does not involve the reactions of constraints, nevertheless it can be used to find these reactions should they be required. **1981** R. R. CRAIG *Structural Dynamics* ii. 28 Use the principle of virtual displacements to derive the equation of motion of the idealized system shown below.

e. *Nucl. Physics* Applied to an excited state of an atomic nucleus which has energy in excess of that needed for the emission of a particle but a lifetime sufficiently long for it to be regarded as a quasi-stationary state.

1931 *Proc. R. Soc.* A. CXXXIII. 228 According to the theory..the emission of α-particles by radio active nuclei is to be explained by the assumption that there exists in the nucleus a 'virtual' level of positive energy, which is occupied by an α-particle. **1955** I. KAPLAN *Nucl. Physics* xvi. 368 Each excited state of the compound nucleus, whether bound or virtual, has a certain mean lifetime. **1963** W. E. BURCHAM *Nucl. Physics* ix. 372 All nuclear levels, except the ground state, can in principle emit radiation, leaving the nucleus in a less highly excited state, and virtual levels can in addition emit particles.

f. *Particle Physics.* Applied to particles and processes that cannot be directly detected and occur over very short intervals of time and space with correspondingly indefinite energy and momenta, which are not necessarily conserved within the time involved.

1949 *Physical Rev.* LXXV. 1305/2 These divergent terms must now be interpreted as renormalization or modification of the electric charge of the proton due to virtual mesons. **1961** W. S. C. WILLIAMS *Introd. Elementary Particles* xiii. 341 If the incident photon is 140 Mev and the positron is emitted at 90° with an energy of 100 Mev, then the four-momentum of this virtual electron is about 140 Mev/c. **1971** *Sci. Amer.* June 71/3 Although it may seem that virtual particles violate fundamental conservation laws, the violation is closely delimited to those areas where the uncertainty principle applies. **1973** L. J. TASSIE *Physics Elementary Particles* viii. 15 The electron now consists of its 'bare' self together with all its virtual interactions with the electromagnetic field, corresponding to the electron emitting and re-absorbing virtual photons. **1973** *Sci. Amer.* Oct. 110/1 The scattering of the two electrons is described by saying that these particles exchange a virtual photon that transfers momentum from one particle to the other. **1979** D. R. HOFSTADTER *Gödel, Escher, Bach* (1980) v. 146 To understand how a real, physical electron propagates..the physicist has to be able to take a sort of average of all the infinitely many different possible drawings which involve virtual particles.

g. *Computers.* Not physically existing as such but made by software to appear to do so from the point of view of the program or the user; *spec.* applied to memory that appears to be internal although most of it is external, transfer between the two being made automatically as required.

1959 *Proc. Eastern Joint Computer Conf.* xvi. 82/2 The sole function of the virtual memory is to increase machine speed. **1966** R. ADAIR et al. *IBM Cambridge Scientific Center Rep.* No. G320-2007 (*title*) A virtual machine system for the 360/40. **1966** *IBM Systems Jrnl.* V. 79 A virtual-storage computer (vsc) can decode addresses that are longer than those of its memory. The longer address is treated..as a virtual address that must be transformed to the actual, shorter memory address... The virtual addressing of the word in external storage triggers a procedure that automatically brings the addressed word into memory. **1972** *Computer Jrnl.* XV. 199/2 Our system runs in a virtual machine, which is implemented by an interpreter. We can therefore easily add new instructions to our virtual hardware, merely by extending the interpreter. **1973** P. B. HANSEN *Operating System Princ.* i. 3 An operating system makes a virtual machine available to each user... The simultaneous presence of several users makes the virtual machines much slower than the physical machine. **1981** POHL & SHAW *Nature of Computation* vi. 198 The Algolic language defines an Algolic virtual machine that may be implemented on a variety of computers. The Algolic machine could be constructed with the following software on a particular machine. **1982** G. LEE *From Hardware to Software* xxvi. 444 In a multiprogramming system, several programs are being executed 'at once'... Thus the operating system has to make available to each user a virtual store, of which he appears to be the sole user. **1983** *80 Microcomputing* Feb. 232/2 Virtual-memory systems have been prevalent in mainframes and large minicomputers for at least a decade. **1985** *Which Computer?* Apr. 54/1 No doubt this is a side effect of using the disc as a virtual memory.

h. Other collocations: *virtual cathode* (Electronics), a part of a space charge or electron beam where the potential is a minimum, so that electrons are repelled and positive ions attracted; *virtual height,* the height of an imaginary reflecting plane surface which in free space would give rise to the same travel time for reflected radio waves as an actual ionospheric layer; *virtual temperature* (Meteorol.) [tr. F. *température virtuelle* (Guldberg & Mohn *Études sur les Mouvements de l'Atmosphère* (1876) I. i. 6)], the temperature that dry air would have to have in order to have the same density as a given body of moist air when at the same pressure.

1937 Virtual cathode [see *SUPPRESSOR 3]. **1964** *New Scientist* 1 Oct. 29/1 It was found that a virtual cathode could be obtained with a beam current of 3·5 milliamperes or more, and that its relaxation time was in fact inversely proportional to pressure. **1928** *Proc. IRE* XVI. 85 The heights as given in this paper are virtual heights. They are calculated on the assumption that ordinary reflection takes place and that the layer is parallel to the earth's surface. **1967** [see *IONOGRAM 1]. **1975** D. G. FINK *Electronics Engineers' Handbk.* XVIII. 107 The reflection process for plane ionosphere is equivalent to mirror-type reflection at a height equal to the virtual height h' of reflection of the equivalent vertical frequency. **1910** C. ABBE tr. Guldberg & Mohn in *Smithsonian Misc. Collections* LI. No. 4. 124 We call the quantity T the virtual temperature; for dry air the virtual temperature is the same as the absolute temperature. **1957** G. E. HUTCHINSON *Treat. Limnol.* I. vii. 468 C represents the virtual temperature of isothermal circulation prior to the development of stratification in the early summer. **1979** L. J. BATTAN *Fund. Meteorol.* v. 83 The effects of humidity can be taken into account by employing a quantity called the virtual temperature.

virtue, *sb.* **I. 4. a.** (Later example.)

1980 'J. MELVILLE' *Chrysanthemum Chain* 38 We'll make a virtue of necessity. I'll take charge of the case myself.

virtuefy, *v.* For *rare*⁻¹ read *rare* and add later example.

1884 H. JAMES *Let.* 8 Mar. (1980) III. 36, I am sorry that the divine Daudet is going to virtuefy his *souillon.*

virtuize (vɜ̄·ɹtiuəiz), *v. nonce-wd.* [f. VIRTU(E *sb.* + -IZE.] *intr.* To behave with conscious propriety; to act in a virtuous manner.

1920 D. H. LAWRENCE *Touch & Go* II. 52 If you want me to virtuise and smug with you, you had [better have stayed away].

virtuoso. Add: **3. b.** *transf.*

1921 H. CRANE *Let.* 1 Nov. (1965) 69 [Ben] Hecht is a virtuoso and arouses suspicions that one would never feel for Dreiser or Anderson. **1950** E. H. GOMBRICH *Story of Art* xviii. 268 For him to be an artist was no longer to be a respectable and sedate owner of a workshop: it was to be a 'virtuoso' for whose favour princes and cardinals should compete. **1952** A. HUXLEY *Let. c* 20 July (1969) 647 On the basis..of what I have seen done..by a man who is probably the greatest living virtuoso in the field of hypnosis..I would advise you very strongly to try hypnosis.

4. Now also passing into adj.

1947 A. EINSTEIN *Mus. Romantic Era* xi. 225 These compositions are intimate confessions, often difficult but never virtuoso. **1952** S. KAUFFMANN *Tightrope* v. 82 'Look,' he said, staring intently into her eyes, giving a virtuoso performance of sincerity, 'I can't say all this makes me happy.' **1978** J. UPDIKE *Coup* (1979) iv. 129 The virtuoso arabesques of her sullen profile. **1984** *Times* 7 Sept. 20/8 Another virtuoso set of interim figures from Bunzl left the share price up 2p at 305p.

virtuous, *a.* Add: **I. 2. g.** *virtuous circle* [after *vicious circle* s.v. VICIOUS *a.* 9 in Dict. and Suppl.], a recurring cycle of events, the result of each one being to increase the beneficial effect of the next.

1953 E. SIMON *Past Masters* III. 156 It will be a virtuous circle of publicity attracting helpers and, I trust, supplementary donations, and these begetting more publicity. **1958** *Brit. Jrnl. Sociol.* IX. 163 The child's..range and expression of discriminating verbal responses is fostered by the social structure... A virtuous circle is set up which is continually reinforced. **1982** *Times* 6 May 18/4 The rating reflects the company's virtuous circle—years of store building and modernization leading to productivity gains, which allow it to hold prices lower than its rivals but still make a better margin of 4·5 per cent.

III. 8. *virtuous-seeming* adj.

1959 S. SPENDER tr. *Schiller's Mary Stuart* III. iv. 63, I did not hide my sinful deeds behind The false show of a virtuous-seeming face.

‖**virtute officii** (vɜ̄ɹtiu·tĭ ǫfi·ʃiī), *adv. phr. Law.* [L.] By virtue of (one's) office.

1800 M. HALE *Hist. Pleas of Crown* II. xvii. 147 The court of King's bench may *virtute officii* bail any person brought before them, of what nature soever the crime is, even for treason or murder, as hath been before shewn. **1939** HENTY & REDFERN *Lewin's Pract. Treat. Law of Trusts* (ed. 14) iv. 298 The powers of trustees may be divided into (1) powers incident to the office of trustee *virtute officii*, including such powers as powers of maintenance and advancement formerly conferred by express proviso but now implied by statute, and (2) such general powers, including powers of appointment, as the settlor may expressly confer upon the trustees. **1982** *Law Q. Rev.* XCVIII. 403 He is a judge of the High Court *virtute officii.*

virucidal (vəirusəi·dăl), *a.* [f. VIRU(S + -CIDE + -AL.] = *VIRICIDAL *a.* So **vi·rucide** = *VIRICIDE².

1925 *Jrnl. Exper. Med.* XLII. 533 Animals inoculated with this strain do not become refractory to skin infection with Virus III and their sera do not become virucidal. **1975** *Water Res.* IX. 872/1 The results obtained in this present study did not confirm the greater efficiency of the OCl^- ion as a virucidal as compared with hypochlorous acid. **1977** *Lancet* 8 Oct. 760/1 Effective treatment will have to include good nursing and the use of steroids.., besides virucidal agents.

virulent, *a.* Add: **4.** *Microbiology.* Of a phage: causing lysis of the host cell immediately after replicating within it, without a period as a prophage; lytic, not lysogenic. [The sense is due to F. Jacob et al. 1953, in *Ann. de l'Inst. Pasteur* LXXXIV. 223, who used F. *virulent*.]

1953, etc. [see *TEMPERATE *a.* 8]. **1969** A. M. CAMPBELL *Episomes* i. 2 Phage types which are able to establish lysogenic systems and to reproduce as prophage are called temperate phages, as distinguished from virulent phages which are unable to do so. **1973** R. G. KRUEGER et al. *Introd. Microbiol.* xviii. 506/1 This type of virus is called a virulent virus, the agent functioning continuously as a lethal intracellular parasite.

viruliferous (viruli·fĕrəs), *a.* [f. L. *vīrul-entia* VIRULENCE + -IFEROUS.] Containing a virus: said esp. of an insect vector.

1933 K. M. SMITH *Introd. Study Viruses* 409 Viruliferous. **1937** *Jrnl. Bacteriol.* XXXIV. 132/2 Viruliferous leafhoppers held at..about 32°C. a few days frequently transmit mild strains instead of typical severe yellows. **1967** K. M. SMITH *Insect Virol.* xi. 208 Viruliferous aphids were colonized on a virus-immune plant such as Chinese cabbage for 7 days, hemolymph from these aphids was then injected into a series of known virus-free aphids. **1982** *Jrnl. Gen. Virol.* LXI. 187 The planthopper vector.. became viruliferous after injection with nB.

virus. Delete ‖ and add: **2. a.** (Later examples.) Now superseded by the next sense.

1910 HISS & ZINSSER *Text-bk. Bacteriol.* xlvii. 639 Virus dried for eight days was no longer regularly infectious. **1922** *Jrnl. Amer. Med. Assoc.* 11 Feb. 411/1 It was quickly found that the virus floats in a suspending fluid of specific gravity 1·14, while it sinks in a suspending fluid of specific gravity 1·11... To purify it,..it seems best to wash it and centrifugalize it in a suspending fluid just heavier than itself.

b. Pl. **viruses.** An infectious organism that is usu. submicroscopic, can multiply only inside certain living host cells (in many cases causing disease) and is now understood to be a non-cellular structure lacking any intrinsic metabolism and usually comprising a DNA or RNA core inside a protein coat (see also quot. 1977).

Formerly referred to as filterable viruses, their first distinguishing characteristic being the ability to pass through filters that retained bacteria.

[**1880** PASTEUR in *Compt. Rend.* XCI. 673 Le virus est constitué par un parasite microscopique qu'on multiplie aisément par la culture, en dehors du corps des animaux que le mal peut frapper.] **1881** *Sci. Amer. Suppl.* 4 June 4516/1 M. Pasteur writes: '..The virus is a microscopical parasite, which may be multiplied by cultivation outside of the body of an animal.' **1899** G. NEWMAN *Bacteria* vii. 260 The vaccination in small-pox is an inoculation of the virus of the disease;..the plague and cholera vaccinations are inoculations of pure cultures of living virus from outside the body. **1900** *Jrnl. Compar. Path. & Therapeutics* XIII. 16 The virus of foot-and-mouth disease passes through a Berkefeld filter when it is suspended in a watery liquid. **1906** *Philippine Jrnl. Sci.* I. 583 The length of time during which the virus may remain viable in the soil and in stables is not determined. **1908** *Jrnl. Compar. Path. & Therapeutics* XIII. 59 Filters which are efficient for the arrest of the smallest of the known visible microbes allow the viruses of these diseases to pass through their pores. **1912** *Jrnl. Med. Res.* XXVII. 20 The probable nature of filterable viruses, whether protozoan or bacterial. **1912,** etc. [see *FILTERABLE *a.*]. **1915** *Lancet* 4 Dec. 1242/2 We do not know for certain the nature of an ultra-microscopic virus. It may be a minute bacterium that will only grow on living material, or it may be a tiny amœba which..thrives on living micro-organisms... It is quite possible that an ultra-microscopic virus belongs somewhere in this vast field of life more lowly organised than the bacterium or amœba. **1929** *Jrnl. Amer. Med. Assoc.* 6 Apr. 1147/1 Throughout this paper the terms filtrable viruses and viruses will be used interchangeably. **1931** *Nature* 10 Oct. 599/2 But a few years ago I think that we should have had no difficulty in accepting three cardinal properties as characterising a virus, namely, invisibility by ordinary microscopic methods, failure to be retained by a filter fine enough to prevent the passage of all visible bacteria, and failure to propagate itself except in the presence of, and perhaps in the interior of, the cells which it infects. **1935** *Science* 28 June 644/1 A crystalline material, which has the properties of tobacco-mosaic virus, has been isolated from the juice of Turkish tobacco plants infected with this virus. *Ibid.* 8 Nov. 443/2 The defining characters of filterable viruses appear to be ultramicroscopic size and obligate parasitism. **1963** J. H. BURN *Drugs, Med. & Man* xix. 188 One view is that these cells contain a virus and the cancer begins when the virus is no longer kept under control. **1972** N. CALDER *Restless Earth* iv. 95/2 The Moon was declared free of viruses or spores that might infect the Earth. **1973** [see *MYCOPLASMA]. **1977** S. S. HUGHES *Virus* 112 The term 'virus' as used by bacteriologists of the 1880s and 1890s meant simply 'an agent of infectious disease'. This is the usage in Pasteur's dictum: 'Every virus is a microbe.' (1890). **1982** *Sci. Amer.* Apr. 22/3 Viruses..are not included; noncellular, they are mere genetic recipes and are not alive. **1983** W. A. STEVENS *Virol. Flowering Plants* i. 3 Bawden (1956) defined a virus as an obligate parasitic pathogen with dimensions less than 200nm. Although possibly adequate in its day, such a definition does not exclude naked nucleic acid pathogens—the viroids, or some mycoplasmas.

c. *colloq.* A virus infection.

1954 C. S. LEWIS *Lett. to Amer. Lady* (1969) 24 We mustn't let these modern doctors get us down by calling a cold a *virus* and a sore throat a *streptococcus*.

3. Also in weakened use, an infectious fear, anxiety, etc.

1982 *Economist* 25 Dec. 83/1 The virus quickly spread. First Canada extracted a promise of restraint from Japan. Then West Germany's mercurial economics minister.. hastened to Tokyo.

5. *attrib.* and *Comb.*, as (sense *2 b) *virus disease, infection, particle*; *virus-carried, -containing, -free, -induced, -infected, -like* adjs.; **virus pneumonia,** pneumonia caused by a virus rather than a bacterium.

1958 *Times* 12 June 11/3 The great diversity of virus-carried diseases. Influenza, poliomyelitis, cholera, Australian Q-fever, [etc.]. **1968** *Times* 3 Oct. 13/6 Antiserum ..was found to react positively with a virus-containing extract prepared from dahlias. **1860** Virus disease [in Dict., sense 2]. **1926** *Jrnl. Trop. Med. & Hygiene* XXIX. 19/2 The intricate processes involved in 'virus' diseases of plants and vertebrates. **1978** J. GARDNER *Dancing Dodo* xvii. 126 Rift Valley Fever..a virus disease... Usually transmitted to humans by cattle, sheep, other animals: and usually in Asia. **1946** *Nature* 26 Oct. 569/2 The great work of East Malling Research Station in raising and distributing virus-free clonal stocks. *Ibid.* 17 Aug. 217/2 M. B. Shimkin is also critical of the wide extrapolation of observations made on the relatively few virus-induced tumours to the whole range of cancer. *Ibid.* 23 Nov. 735/2 We have grown many thousands of seedlings from seeds which were obtained from virus-infected plants.. and in not a single instance have we found the seedlings diseased. **1924** *Jrnl. Exper. Med.* XL. 773 (*heading*) A filterable virus infection of rabbits. **1965** A. ROUDYBUSH *Season for Death* (1966) xxviii. 165 Mrs. Tor was suffering from a virus infection. **1982** R. RENDELL *Master of Moor* xv. 165 He was ill, he had a virus infection. **1946** *Nature* 17 Aug. 218/1 They found no evidence of the presence of a rapidly acting virus-like principle associated with the Jensen rat sarcoma. **1972** *Science* 16 June 1225/2 Electron microscopy initially revealed that HBAg consists of virus-like particles approximately 20 nanometers in diameter. **1968** *Brit. Med. Bull.* XXIV. 244/2 They [*sc.* the results] are consistent with the inactivation of a virus particle by a single interaction with radiation. **1929** *Public Health Rep.* (U.S.) XLIV. 2635 (*heading*) Vaccine virus pneumonia in rabbits. **1977** 'J. BELL' *Such Nice Client* xix. 189 She died of a virus pneumonia caught in an epidemic at the hospital. **1971** *New Scientist* 8 Apr. 82/2 The surface antigens also appear to be virus-specific. **1936** *Discovery* Oct. 329/1 Investigation of ten virus strains.

vis, *sb.*[2] Add: **2. f.** *vis comica*, humorous energy; comic force or effect.

1757 S. FOOTE *Author* I. i. 6 My disposition has, at present, very little of the Vis Comica. **1798** T. HOLCROFT *Jrnl.* 12 Oct. in *Mem.* (1925) II. v. ii. 184 This character has..not enough of the *vis comica*. **1887** G. M. HOPKINS *Lett. to R. Bridges* (1955) 261 In *vis comica*, in fun,..it is not strong: still there is enough to make me laugh aloud sometimes. **1911** BRERETON & ROTHWELL tr. *Bergson's Laughter* ii. 71 In the scene..between Sganarelle and Pancrace, the entire *vis comica* lies in the conflict set up between the idea of Sganarelle..and the obstinacy of the philosopher. **1979** F. FELSENSTEIN in Smollett *Trav.* p. xxv, Smollett's *vis comica* is..sufficiently broad to allow him to laugh at himself.

g. *vis medicatrix* (*naturæ*), the healing power of nature.

1804 *Edin. Rev.* Apr. 186 In this position arose the *vis medicatrix naturæ*, like a fairy queen, to put the wheel in motion. **1904** W. H. HUDSON *Green Mansions* xxii. 295 The *vis medicatrix* with which nature helps our weaknesses. **1949** A. HUXLEY *Let.* 30 July (1969) 601 The news of your mishap was forwarded to us... I do hope that by this time the enforced rest will have given the *vis medicatrix naturae* a chance to get busy.

visa, *sb.* Delete ‖. This form has now replaced VISÉ *sb.* as the normal term for an entry or note on a passport.

‖ **visagiste** (vīzaʒī·st). Also anglicized as **visagist** (vi·zădʒist). [Fr.] A cosmetic artist.

1958 *Observer* 14 Sept. 11/3 Elizabeth Arden..has brought over to Bond-street from Paris her *visagist*. **1965** *Harper's Bazaar* Aug. 48/2 Guy Nicolet, visagiste supreme from Revlon, designed for her the Leprechaun Look. **1979** *Courier-Mail* (Brisbane) 16 Apr. 16 (Advt.), Our visiting visagists are: [etc.]. **1981** *Times* 10 Nov. 9/1 In our pictures, visagiste Christina Saunders used Estee Lauder's shimmering bronze face powder. **1984** *Listener* 12 Jan. 26/2 The latest..has for heroine a just-post-punk visagiste.

Visakha, var. *VESAK.

‖ **visarga** (visā·ɪgă). Also 9 **viserga.** [Skr., lit. 'emission'.] A sign in the Sanskrit alphabet representing a hard (voiceless) aspiration; also, the sound itself.

1819 H. H. WILSON et al. *Dict. Sanscrit & Eng.* p. xlii, A final *Viserga* or its omission, and a final nasal mark or its omission, are always optional. **1886** *Encycl. Brit.* XXI. 270/1 The Sanskrit alphabet consists of the following sounds... visarga (ḥ) a hard aspirate, standing mostly for original *s* or *r*. **1939** *Year's Work Eng. Stud. 1937* 29 It is a pity that Flasdieck consistently uses the *visarga* (transliterated as *ḥ*) for the final letter of Sanskrit words originally ending in *s*; for only the reader familiar with Sanskrit and its rules of *sandhi* will at once realize that the first person plural of the substantive verb given as Sanskrit *smaḥ*..is to be taken for etymological purposes as equivalent to *smas*. **1953** W. S. ALLEN *Phonetics in Anc. India* ii. 50 Since these variants [sc. *-ḥ*, *-x*, and *-ø*] are not included in the alphabet, special names are devised for them [by the old Indian phoneticians], viz. *visarjanīya* (or later *visarga*) for *-ḥ*, etc... We shall perhaps be giving the most direct and phonetically appropriate translation if we render it by 'off-glide', as referring to the breathy transition from the vowel to silence. **1975** *Language* LI. 120 The first of these rules obligatorily assimilates a dental stop or continuant before any following coronal (dental, palatal, or retroflex) stop... The third converts *s* to visarga before word boundary.

vis-à-vis, *sb.* Add: **2. c.** A counterpart, an opposite number.

1900 J. K. JEROME *Three Men on Bummel* xii. 273 The Vosges peasant has not the unromantic air of contented prosperity that spoils his *vis-a-vis* across the Rhine. **1975** *Publishers Weekly* 21 July 67/1 Middleton's admiration.. [for the U.S. armed services] extends to their vis-à-vis, the Russian military.

visceral, *a.* **1. a.** Delete † *Obs.* and add later examples.

1949 *Scrutiny* XV. 152 A tendency to borrow the mantle of Mr. Wyndham Lewis in attacking the visceral and the formless in art and poetry. **1969** *Listener* 31 July 162/3 Hardly any of them fall into the tragic error of modern straight music, which eschews visceral appeal entirely. **1976** *Publishers Weekly* 1 Mar. 93/1 By accumulating a mass of homely details he gives his story of the death of Sgt. Mullen great visceral power and emotional impact. **1978** J. IRVING *World according to Garp* xvi. 321 Hoping that the visceral reality of Garp's language..somehow rescued the book from sheer soap opera.

3. c. *visceral hump*, the dorsal enlargement, containing the viscera, of snails and other gastropod molluscs in which the ventral part is a foot.

1883 *Encycl. Brit.* XVI. 635/2 As the ventral foot is clearly separate from the projecting head, so is this dorsal region, and it is conveniently spoken of as the visceral hump or 'dome' (cupola). **1927** E. STEP *Shell Life* (new ed.) i. 23 Within the shell [of the Snail] is..the 'visceral hump' containing most of the internal organs. **1972** M. S. GARDINER *Biol. Invertebrates* xi. 58/2 This and the coiling of the visceral hump has led, in a number of species, to the suppression of organs on one side (usually the right).

5. c. *visceral brain*, those parts of the brain which mediate bodily activity, esp. visceral activity, in response to emotion.

1949 P. D. MCLEAN in *Psychosomatic Med.* XI. 340 (*caption*) The shaded area of cortex represents what was formerly known as the limbic lobe of Broca and subsequently termed the rhinencephalon by Turner. It corresponds to what is arbitrarily referred to in this paper as the visceral brain. **1972** H. J. EYSENCK *Psychology is about People* i. 35 Emotionality-stability seems indissolubly linked with the *autonomic* nervous system, which regulates the expression of the emotions, and which in turn is organized and governed by the 'visceral brain'.

viscerally *adv.* (later examples).

1965 H. KAHN *On Escalation* vi. 119 Most individuals.. conclude, at least viscerally, that the dangers are simply too great. **1970** T. ROETHKE *Sel. Lett.* 173, I teach viscerally: I try to make up for ignorance by energy and enthusiasm. **1982** *Wall St. Jrnl.* 13 Aug. 16/2 Viscerally, your friends recognize that what is involved here is not one issue, but your capacity to govern.

visceralization (vi:sĕrăləizē·ʃən). *Path.* [f. VISCERAL *a.* + -IZATION.] The spreading of an infection to the viscera; the movement of a pathogen towards the viscera.

1963 *Ann. N.Y. Acad. Sci.* CXIII. 410 Visceralization of the parasites occurs as a further complication. **1969** *Current Topics in Microbiol. & Immunol.* XLVIII. 30 Subinoculation of the organisms responsible for these conditions into laboratory animals is often followed, even in cutaneous types, by extensive visceralization of the infection. **1980** *Jrnl. Exper. Med.* CLII. 605 BALB/c mice have an exceptional susceptibility to *Leishmania tropica* infection such that cutaneous lesions grow without restraint in all cases leading to fatal metastasis and visceralization in normal and x-irradiated..animals.

Also **vi·sceralize** *v. intr.*, to spread to or attack the viscera.

1969 *Current Topics in Microbiol. & Immunol.* XLVIII. 32 Sudanese or some East African infections of *L. donovani* derived from wild rodents may fail to visceralise, while the purely human kala-azar of India is usually fatal. **1974** W. H. R. LUMSDEN in *Trypanosomiasis & Leishmaniasis* (Ciba Symp.) 8 Organisms tending to 'visceralize' in man (i.e. with a predilection for infecting cells in the viscera, particularly in the spleen). **1981** *Ann. Trop. Med. & Parasitol.* LXXV. 139 The primary lesions of kala-azar may be confused with oriental sore and..some strains with the capacity to visceralize may fail to do so, causing only dermal lesions.

viscero-. Add: **viscerocra·nium** = *splanchnocranium* s.v. *SPLANCHNO-; **viscerotro·pic** *a. Med.* [*-TROPIC], tending to attack or affect the viscera; hence **viscerotro·pism.**

1925 J. S. KINGSLEY *Vertebrate Skeleton* 58 Recently the terms *neurocranium* and *viscerocranium* have been introduced. **1980** *Gray's Anat.* (ed. 36) 141/2 The trabeculae cranii may largely be derived from branchial arch (neural crest) mesoderm, i.e. from the viscerocranium, having been adapted into the cartilaginous or basal part of the neurocranium, or 'brainbox'. **1935** M. HOSKINS in *Amer. Jrnl. Trop. Med.* XV. 675 The term 'viscerotropic virus' is used to designate the strain of yellow fever virus which has been carried in *M. rhesus*. **1940** *Nature* 2 Nov. 596/1 Man ordinarily suffers only the viscerotropic attack [in yellow fever]—in his liver, kidneys and heart. **1976** *Ann. Rev. Microbiol.* XXX. 443 In the 17D strain of virus both the viscerotropic and neurotropic properties of the natural virus were markedly reduced. **1940**

Viscerotropism [see *NEUROTROPISM 2]. **1973** *Acta Virologica* XVII. 241 Street strains displaying a higher viscerotropism can actively multiply in the internal organs.

viscerotome (vi·sĕrotōᵘm). *Med.* [f. VISCERO- + *-TOME.] An instrument for obtaining post-mortem samples of liver tissue through a puncture in the abdominal wall (avoiding necropsy), used esp. when yellow fever is suspected. Hence **viscero·tomy,** the use of a viscerotome.

1934 *Amer. Jrnl. Hygiene* XIX. 553 The attempt..led one of us (E. R. R[ickard]) to attempt the design of an instrument for the removal of liver tissue without autopsy. This instrument, later christened the 'viscerotome' by Dr. Mario Biāo, reached a practicable stage of development within a few weeks. *Ibid.* 555 The opposition of relatives and friends to autopsy is greatly reduced in the case of viscerotomy. **1940** VAN ROOYEN & RHODES *Virus Dis. of Man* xxxv. 472 The viscerotome is a metal instrument..resembling a trocar, about 1 cm. square, possessing a sharp, hollow, pointed extremity fitted with a mechanically operated guillotine blade. *Ibid.*, Viscerotomy has revealed the existence of yellow fever in places in which it had hitherto passed unrecognized. **1971** P. C. C. GARNHAM *Progr. Parasitol.* iii. 24 The disease was scarcely recognized until 1934, when the introduction by Penna.. of a viscerotomy service for the diagnosis of fatal cases of yellow fever revealed its presence in Brazil. *Ibid.*, The brutal instrument, the viscerotome, is plunged through the abdominal wall of the cadaver into the liver.

viscerotonic (vi:sĕrotǫ·nik), *a.* and *sb.* [f. VISCERO- + TONIC *a.*] **A.** *adj.* Designating or characteristic of a type of personality which is comfort-loving, sociable, and easy-going, classified by Sheldon as being associated with an endomorphic physique. **B.** *sb.* One having this type of personality. So **visceroto·nia** (-tōᵘ·niă), viscerotonic personality or characteristics. Cf. *CEREBROTONIC, *SOMATOTONIC *adjs.* and *sbs.*

1937 [see *CEREBROTONIC *a.* and *sb.*]. **1938,** etc. [see *SOMATOTONIC *a.* and *sb.*]. **1956** GOACHER & WHIGHAM in E. Pound tr. *Sophocles' Women of Trachis* 60 Stigmatized as a sex crank, as a maniacal visceratonic [*sic*], he [*sc.* D. H. Lawrence] in fact made an extraordinary effort to re-establish the 'whole' man. **1969** V. DE S. PINTO *City that Shone* iii. 68, I suppose that in modern psychological jargon, as a child in those distant Edwardian days, I could be described as an introvert and cerebrotonic living in a world of extroverts, somatotonics and viscerotonics. **1980** F. J. BRUNO *Behav. & Life* xi. 379 As might be expected, viscerotonia is said to be correlated with endomorphy. The extreme endomorph with a viscerotonic personality would be a self-indulgent person.

vi:sco,elasti·city. [f. VISCO(US *a.*, VISCO(SITY + ELASTICITY.] The property of a substance of exhibiting both elastic and viscous behaviour, the application of a constant stress causing an immediate deformation that disappears if the stress is quickly removed but increases for a time and becomes permanent if the stress is maintained.

1944 *Q. Jrnl. Appl. Math.* II. 119 The solution of the first and second boundary value problems of visco-elasticity is reduced to the solution of equivalent boundary value problems of elasticity, and the determination of the response of the visco-elastic material under consideration to a simple shearing stress or a simple shearing strain. **1963** *Times* 27 Mar. 1/6 Viscosity and visco-elasticity of glasses. **1972** *Science* 2 June 1041/3 The viscoelasticity of the solutions would decrease upon continued stirring. **1976** *Nature* 12 Aug. 573/1 The explanation for the observed increase in cavitation erosion rate in polymer solution may still have its origin in polymer viscoelasticity.

So **viscoela·stic** *a.*, exhibiting or pertaining to viscoelasticity.

1944 [see above]. **1949** *Proc. Internat. Congr. Rheology 1948* II. 24 Flow birefringence in aluminium soap solutions, considered here as a typical visco-elastic system. **1963** *New Scientist* 22 Aug. 382/3 Polymer solutions.. generally show some elasticity, or tendency to preserve their shape, and are therefore called 'viscoelastic'. **1970** P. SHERMAN *Industr. Rheology* iv. 236 The Instron tester has been used to study the viscoelastic properties of potatoes, peas, and apples. **1973** J. R. RICE in A. C. Palmer *Symposium Role Plasticity in Soil Mech.* 263 Viscoelastic creep of the soil. **1978** *Sci. Amer.* Nov. 145/1 Silicone putty..is such a viscoelastic fluid.

viscometer. Add: (Further examples.)

This, rather than VISCOSIMETER, is the more usual term. **1886,** etc. [see *SAYBOLT]. **1946** *Nature* 2 Nov. 614/2 Graphs showing the flow characteristics of a grease at medium rates of shear (plunger viscometer) and at high rates of shear (pendulum viscometer) were displayed. **1967** M. CHANDLER *Ceramics in Mod. World* ii. 61 The commonest instrument for testing the fluid properties of a slip is the torsion viscometer. **1970** *British Printer* June 70/2 Mr Bisset described the functions of viscometers and tack-meters.

Hence **visco·metry,** the measurement of viscosity; the use of a viscometer; **visco·me·tric** *a.*, **-me·trically** *adv.*

1886 B. REDWOOD in *Jrnl. Soc. Chem. Industry* 29 Mar. 121/2 (*heading*) On viscosimetry, or viscometry. **1931** G. BARR *Monogr. Viscometry* iii. 48 In practical viscometry it is rarely necessary for the investigator to undertake the labour involved in the evaluation of th constants of his instrument ab initio. **1938** *Chem. Abstr.* XXXII. 1091/1 The viscometric results were in excellent agreement with those obtained by using a photoelec. nephelometer. **1946** *Chem. Rev.* XXXIX. 161 The process can be followed viscometrically, polarimetrically, or by chemical determination of the aldose end group produced. **1978** *Nature* 1 June p. xi/2 Further applications are in the field of interface rheology and viscometric determination of the molecular weight of plastic material solutions. **1982** *Lebensmittel-Wissensch. und Technol.* XV. 242 (*heading*) Viscometric study of the dispersion of whole and gelatinised cassava starch. *Ibid.*, The solubilisation of cassava starch in aqueous dimethylsulphoxide has been followed viscometrically. **1982** *Jrnl. Exper. Bot.* XXXIII. 1248 The enzyme procedure and assay, using citrus pectin, described here have enabled us to assay endo-PG by viscometry during a 6 h incubation period.

viscontial (vəikǫ·ntiăl), *a. rare*⁻¹. [f. *viscont* VISCOUNT + -IAL; cf. VISCONTAL, VISCOUNTIAL *adjs.*] Reminiscent of a viscount.

a **1916** R. ASQUITH in M. Asquith *Autobiogr.* (1920) I. xiv. 276 You beat your tangled music out Lofty, aloof, viscontial.

viscose, *sb.* For pronunc. read (vi·skōᵘs, -z). Substitute for etym. and def.: [f. VISC(OUS *a.* + -OSE².] **1.** A viscid, orange or brown solution of sodium cellulose xanthate obtained by treating cellulose successively with sodium hydroxide and carbon disulphide, and used to make regenerated cellulose by extruding it into dilute acid and either spinning it into rayon or casting it as film.

1896 C. F. CROSS *Brit. Pat.* 4713 Cellulose..requires a very much smaller proportion of alkali to convert it into alkali-cellulose suitable for use in other manufactures such..as that of the substances now known as 'viscose' and 'viscoid'. **1913** CARRIER & MARTIN in G. Martin *Industr. & Manuf. Chem.: Organic* IV. i. 189 Viscose is reconverted into cellulose (1) spontaneously, on long standing; (2) by heating; (3) by treatment with oxidising agents. **1927** T. WOODHOUSE *Artificial Silk* 30 By far the greater percentage of artificial silk is made from Viscose. **1968** *Kirk-Othmer Encycl. Chem. Technol.* (ed. 2) XVII. 179 After filtration, the viscose is transferred to a ripening tank system.., where it is deaerated and ripened to the desired level of xanthation. **1981** *Chem. Abstr.* 17 Aug. 544/1 Emulsion sausages were made in the usual way. Pork and beef casings and synthetic casings (protein, viscose, and polyamide) were used.

2. Rayon made by the viscose process.

1932 A. HUXLEY *Brave New World* iii. 58 Her jacket was made of bottle-green acetate cloth with green viscose fur at the cuffs and collar. **1949** W. GARNER *Textile Lab. Man.* iii. 77 Acetate is sometimes partly saponified, especially for the printing of mixed fabrics of viscose and acetate. **1960** *Guardian* 28 Sept. 8/6 Lilian, helion, terital and viscose are blended with wool in textiles by the high fashion houses. **1972** *Vogue* June 113/3 Candy pink and white cotton and viscose shirtwaister. **1980** GOHL & VILENSKY *Textile Sci.* ii. 32 Viscose and the other two rayon fibres have similar thermal properties to cotton.

3. Special Combs.: **viscose process,** the process for making rayon with viscose as an intermediate product; **viscose rayon,** † **silk** = sense 2 above.

1913 CARRIER & MARTIN in G. Martin *Industr. & Manuf. Chem.: Organic* IV. ix. 214 (*heading*) The viscose process. **1981** *Kirk-Othmer Encycl. Chem. Technol.* (ed. 3) XVI. 108 Considerable research is underway to replace the viscose process and to improve rayon fiber properties. **1930** *Chem. Abstr.* XXIV. 5153 Viscose rayons of 120 and 150 denier were treated with Na_2S solns. of various concns. **1957** *Woman* 16 Nov. 25/3 Viscose rayon is quite easy to do [*sc.* dye] at home. **1974** *Sci. Amer.* Apr. 57/3 The largest single use for dissolving pulp is as the raw material for the viscose-rayon process. **1913** CARRIER & MARTIN in G. Martin *Industr. & Manuf. Chem.: Organic* IV. ix. 214 The viscid solution is then spun into a solution of ammonium chloride which separates out the cellulose again, and gives..'viscose silk'. **1925** *Good Housekeeping* Apr. 142/3 The remaining variety [of artificial silk], Viscose silk, is now being made in enormous quantities.

viscosimeter. Add: (Further examples.) Cf. VISCOMETER in Dict. and Suppl.

1886, 1925 [see *SAYBOLT]. **1944** *Acta Med. Scand.* CXVII. 227 The determinations with viscosimeters having varying dimensions of the capillaries gave no real differences even in sera with very high viscosity. **1974** *Nature* 13 Dec. 572/2 This unexpected phenomenon was further investigated in a modified Couette viscosimeter device.

Hence **viscosi·metry** = **viscometry*; **vi:scosime·tric** *a.*, **-me·trically** *adv.*

1886 B. REDWOOD in *Jrnl. Soc. Chem. Industry* 29 Mar. 121/2 It is my intention..to treat the subject of viscosimetry, or the determination of viscosity, as related to the valuation of oils intended for the lubrication of machinery. **1895** BENEDIKT & LEWKOWITSCH *Chem. Anal. Oils, Fats, Waxes* xii. 621 Viscosimetric constants as determined with the new apparatus. **1904** J. LEWKOWITSCH *Chem. Technol. & Anal. Oils, Fats, & Waxes* (ed. 3) II. xv. 933 If it is desired to examine the unsaponifiable portion of a blended oil viscosimetrically. **1944** *Acta Med. Scand.* CXVII. 227 With the aid of this modified instrument it seems, as if viscosimetry would be a simple and useful clinical method. **1956** *Nature* 17 Mar. 517/1 A viscosimetric investigation into the influence of pH and ionic strength on molecular shape of a structural muscle protein. **1975** *Welding Production* May 11/1 A method is proposed of examining electrode coating mixtures by means of capillary viscosimetry. **1976** *Jrnl. Polymer Sci.* (Polymer Physics Ed.) XIV. 309 (*heading*) Abnormal viscosimetric behavior of homopolymers in mixed solvents and preferential solvation.

viscosity. Add: **1. c.** In scientific use, the tendency of a liquid or gas to resist by internal friction the relative motion of its molecules and hence any change of shape; the magnitude of this, as measured by the force per unit area resisting a flow in which parallel layers unit distance apart have unit speed relative to one another; also called *absolute* or *dynamic viscosity*; *kinematic viscosity*, the dynamic viscosity divided by the density of the fluid.

1866 J. C. MAXWELL in *Phil. Trans. R. Soc.* CLVI. 249 The viscosity of a body is the resistance which it offers to a continuous change of form, depending on the rate at which that change is effected. *Ibid.* 254 Suppose that this friction is equal to a tangential force f on every square foot, then $f = \mu v/a$, where μ is the coefficient of viscosity, v the velocity of the upper plane, and a the distance between them. **1880** *Proc. London Math. Soc.* XI. 58 If ν be the kinematic viscosity. **1913,** etc. [see *POISE *sb.*⁴]. **1921** A. W. JUDGE *Automobile & Aircraft Engines* viii. 309 The kinematical viscosity of air is thirteen times that of water. **1927** SCHODER & DAWSON *Hydraulics* xvi. 275 The unit of absolute viscosity is called a poise. **1943** R. C. BINDER *Fluid Mech.* v. 50 Viscosity = shearing stress/*rate* of shearing strain. Sometimes the foregoing term is called absolute viscosity. Probably a better term would be dynamic viscosity. **1962** J. M. MCKELVEY *Polymer Processing* ii. 41 In general, liquid viscosities decrease and gas viscosities increase with increasing temperature. **1964** [see *STOKE(S *sb.*⁴]. **1979** C. A. MARCHAJ *Aero-Hydrodynamics of Sailing* ii. 169 The kinematic viscosity of water..needed for Reynolds Number computation at the 'normal' temperature of 15°C is..$1{\cdot}23 \times 10^{-5}$ ft^2/sec.

3. Special Comb.: **viscosity index,** a number expressing the degree to which the viscosity of an oil is unaffected by temperature.

1929 DEAN & DAVIS in *Chem. & Metallurgical Engin.* XXXVI. 618/1 This system of classification permits expressing the viscosity-temperature coefficient of an oil as a simple function of its Saybolt Universal viscosities at 100 and 210 deg. F. This function, hereafter referred to as the 'viscosity index', is independent of the actual viscosity of the oil. **1977** *Lubricants Business* (Shell Internat. Petroleum Co.) 3 These [additives] are chemical compounds which supplement the properties of the mineral base oil; for example, to reduce wear of moving parts..and to improve viscosity index.

viscous, *a.* Add: **2. c.** *viscous flow*, laminar flow (see *LAMINAR *a.* 2 a).

1930 [see *TURBULENT *a.* 2 c]. **1973** FOX & MCDONALD *Introd. Fluid Mech.* viii. 311 (*caption*) Details of viscous flow around an airfoil. **1979** [see *STREAM-LINE *sb.* 1b].

viscuous, *a.* For † *Obs.* read *rare* and add later examples. Also *transf.*

In quot. 1936 perhaps a misprint. **1932** S. GIBBONS *Cold Comfort Farm* iii. 32 Growing with the viscuous light that was invading the sky. **1936** *Jrnl. R. Aeronaut. Soc.* XL. 11 Heat generated in the blades in overcoming viscuous drag also plays a part in determining the distribution of ice.

visé, *sb.* Add: (Earlier example.) Now superseded by VISA *sb.*

1842 E. LAWES *Scamper through Italy & Tyrol* iii. 32 It became necessary to obtain the *visé* of the English Consul, who demands a fee of five francs and six sous.

visé, *v.* (Later *fig.* examples.)

1917 J. AGATE *Buzz, Buzz!* 59 Every member of the audience would appear to be in possession of a passport of respectability visé'd by the police. **1927** P. HAMMOND *But—is it Art* 102 Since these New York premières are so important, let us try to attend one, carefully passported and viséd by a regular New Yorker.

Viséan (vize·ăn), *a.* Also **Visean.** *Geol.* [ad. F. *viséen* (E. F. Dupont 1883, in *Bull. de l'Acad. R. des Sci.*, etc., *de Belgique* V. 223), f. *Visé*, name of a town in Belgium: see -AN.] Of, pertaining to, or designating the upper of the two divisions of the Lower Carboniferous (Dinantian) in Europe. Also *absol.*

1905 *Q. Jrnl. Geol. Soc.* LXI. 264 If I am correct in correlating the Lower Viséan of the Belgian Geological Survey with the *Syringothyris*-Zone of the Bristol area, the terms Tournaisian and Viséan, as employed by me in this paper, do not bear their original connotation. *Ibid.* 265 The Tournaisian and Viséan facies are essentially distinct. **1956** W. EDWARDS in D. L. Linton *Sheffield* 22 The imposing scarp along the north side of the outcrop at Castleton, with its reef-aprons..referred to movements of the Derbyshire 'massif' in relation to the 'basin' north of it, during Visean times. **1969** BENNISON & WRIGHT *Geol. Hist. Brit. Isles* ix. 207 Goniatites have shown that only the Lower Limestone Group belongs to the Viséan. **1983** *Rep. Inst. Geol. Sci.* No. 82/12. 1/1 The Carboniferous rocks [exposed at Benburb, County Tyrone] fall within the Viséan Series of the Dinantian.

viseite (vī·ze,əit). *Min.* Also **viséite.** [a. F. *viséite* (J. Mélon (after G. Cesàro) 1942, in *Ann. Soc. géol. Belgique* LXVI. B53), f. as prec.: see -ITE¹.] A hydrous basic calcium and aluminium silicophosphate occurring as translucent isometric crystals of a white, bluish, or yellowish colour.

1944 *Chem. Abstr.* XXXVIII. 6244 In the examn. of the minerals which occur with delvauxite at Visé, a new mineral was found to which the name viseite was given. **1975** *Nature* 27 Feb. 722/1 Among the minerals described to have any significant degree of P(V)–Si(IV) partial substitution are viseite, nagatelite and wilkeite.

visgy (vi·zgi). Also **visgie.** *Cornish* and *Devon dial.* = BISGAY.

1777 in *Eng. Dial. Dict.* (1905) VI. 348/2. **1880** COURTNEY & COUCH *Gloss. Cornwall* 62/1 *Visgie,* an agricultural implement, in shape between a mattock and a hammer, for beating down hedges. *Ibid.* 105 Visgy. **1899** 'Q.' *Ship of Stars* iv. 35 A knife lay between his wide-planted feet, and a visgy close behind him on a heap of disturbed sand. **1915** *Blackw. Mag.* Apr. 546/1 The day being Sunday, he could not dare to risk outraging public opinion by carrying shovel or visgy through the open streets. **1954** L. WALMSLEY *Golden Waterwheel* v. 91 For the roots I had a kind of double-bladed mattock, a combination of pick-axe, chopper, adze and hoe, known in Cornwall as a visgy.

‖ **visibilia** (vizībi·liă). [L., neut. pl. of *vīsibilis* VISIBLE *a.* and *sb.*] Things seen; visual images.

1936 C. S. LEWIS *Allegory of Love* ii. 45 On the one hand you can start with an immaterial fact, such as the passions which you actually experience, and can then invent *visibilia* to express them. **1982** *Times Lit. Suppl.* 29 Jan. 97/1 Some people see things that they describe as ghosts; we can dispute the name and nature of these visibilia, but not the fact that they are seen. **1982** *PN Rev.* No. 26. 40/1 A theology of the material world..which can offer us a convincingly spiritual account of the *visibilia.*

visibility. Add: **1. d.** *fig.* The degree to which something impinges upon public awareness; prominence.

1958 MARCH & SIMON *Organizations* iv. 103 The greater the prestige of the organization..the greater the visibility of the organization. **1975** *New Yorker* 26 May 28/1 These are busy times, and our report doesn't have so very much visibility. **1981** *Nordic Skiing* Jan. 10/3 The purpose of the team is to increase skiing's visibility in this country. **1984** *Observer* 5 Aug. 15/1 From a business standpoint, the visibility Carl receives during the Olympic Games can enhance his value to the companies.

visible, *a.* and *sb.* Add: **A.** *adj.* **1. d.** Also, speech rendered into a visible record by spectrography.

1947 R. K. POTTER et al. *Visible Speech* i. 4 A sound spectrographic record for the words 'Visible Speech' is shown... The pattern is a new form of visible speech, a system of natural phonetic symbols translated from speech itself. **1953** [see *SONOGRAPH 1].

3. c. *Econ.* Descriptive of or denoting actual goods exported or imported, as opposed to 'invisible' items such as services rendered or received (cf. *INVISIBLE *a.* 1 d).

1882 R. GIFFEN *Use of Import & Export Statistics* vii. 58 As to the increase of our shipping business as a means of accounting for the non-increase of our apparent exports. It is because our invisible exports have been increasing so enormously, that there is less increase of the visible. **1917** J. A. TODD *Mech. Exchange* xiv. 184 Visible and invisible exports alike go to the debit side of the account. **1957** A. C. L. DAY *Outl. Monetary Econ.* xxviii. 365 In this way we get a balance of visible trade: quite literally 'visible', because it only includes goods that can actually be seen as they are put on board ship. **1976** *Economist* 16 Oct. 22/2 In August, 1976, Britain ran a visible trade deficit at an annual rate of £3½ billion, compared with a 1970 deficit of £25m.

d. *visible index*: an index so arranged that each item is visible.

1916 E. R. HUDDERS *Indexing & Filing* (1919) ii. 26 It is not anticipated that the visible index in any of its forms will ever supersede the card index. **1955** V. GEORGE in W. Ashworth *Handbk. Special Librarianship* iii. 45 The system most usually employed..is some form of visible index.

6. *fig.* In a position of public prominence; well-known. Cf. *VISIBILITY 1 d.

1977 *Chicago Tribune* 2 Oct. II. 28/1 (Advt.), National leader in health care field has highly visible position available on its corporate headquarters consulting staff. **1978** *Guardian Weekly* 12 Feb. 14/2 The Wilmington Ten affair makes Chavis the most visible of American political prisoners today.

B. *sb.* **1. b.** *pl.* Visible exports or imports.

1962 H. O. BEECHENO *Introd. Business Stud.* xv. 143 A country which is running an adverse balance of trade may still have a favourable balance of payments because the gain on 'invisible' items exceeds the loss on 'visibles'. **1968** *Economist* 23 Mar. 64/1 The current account (that is one 'visibles' and 'invisibles' but leaving out movements of investment funds).

3. The visible part of the electromagnetic spectrum.

1962 [see *NERNST a]. **1973** WILLIAMS & FLEMING *Spectrosc. Methods Org. Chem.* (ed. 2) i. 21 The $n \rightarrow \pi^*$ transitions of α-diketones in the diketo form give rise to two bands, one in the usual region near 290 nm..and a second..which stretches into the visible in the 340–440 nm region.

visile (vi·zəil), *a.* and *sb.* [f. L. *vīs-us* sight + -ILE, after *tactile, audile.*] **A.** *adj.* Responding most readily to visual sensations; thinking predominantly in visual images. **B.** *sb.* A person of this kind; = VISUAL *sb.* 2, VISUALIST 1.

1909 [see *AUDILE *a.*]. **1927** J. ADAMS *Errors in School* 74 This does not imply that the visiles get their knowledge entirely through the eye. **1940** *Brit. Jrnl. Psychol.* XXXI. 56 The theory of the existence of a 'visile' type. *Ibid.* 60 A theory that adolescents who draw men well tend to be of high..intelligence, to be 'visiles' in their thinking. **1954** J. EVANS *John Ruskin* 411 He [*sc.* John Ruskin] had..a visile mind. **1960** MENON & PATEL *Teaching of Eng. as Foreign Lang.* (ed. 2) iv. 26 Galton classified individuals, with reference to the sense that dominated his memory, into *visiles, audiles* and *kinaesthetic.*

vision, *sb.* Add: **2. b.** Ability to conceive what might be attempted or achieved, esp. in the realm of politics; statesmanlike foresight.

[**1904** CHESTERTON *Napoleon of Notting Hill* II. iii. 107, I fight for your royal vision, for the great dream you dreamt of the League of the Free Cities.] **1926** FOWLER *Mod. Eng. Usage* 695/2 *Vision,* in the sense of statesmanlike foresight or political sagacity, is enjoying a noticeable vogue. **1960** M. SPARK *Ballad Peckham Rye* v. 86 'How do you find Weedin?' 'Totally,' Dougal said, 'lacking in vision. It is his fatal flaw. Otherwise quite sane.' **1965** A. J. P. TAYLOR *Eng. Hist. 1914–45* xvi. 593 Truman, the new president, had none of Roosevelt's vision as international leader. **1973** E. F. SCHUMACHER *Small is Beautiful* i 243 A lack of vision on the part of the socialists themselves. **1982** D. FRASER *Alanbrooke* ix. 217 Churchill had enormous vision. He could and often did impressively surpass his supporters in his imaginative span.

5*. The visual part of a television broadcast, television images collectively; the transmission or reproduction of such images; also, the signal corresponding to them.

1910 H. N. CASSON *Hist. Telephone* ix. 287 Some future Carty..may transmit vision as well as speech. **1930** MOSELEY & CHAPPLE *Television* i. 9 On 9th February, 1928, the public were startled to learn that the Atlantic had been spanned by vision. **1934** J. H. REYNER *Television* x. 109 The radio transmission of sound or vision is usually accomplished by modulating a high-frequency carrier-wave. **1939** *Jrnl. Television Soc.* III. 8/1 Vision is amplified at an intermediate frequency of 13·2 m.c. (vision carrier). **1955** 'J. CHRISTOPHER' *Year of Comet* i. 5 He had followed the usual practice of leaving sound switched on as well as vision. **1959** G. FREEMAN *Jack would be Gentleman* i. 8 The sound came on a full minute before the vision. **1973** E. G. M. ALKIN *Sound with Vision* i. 3 In any entertainment medium in which sound and vision are combined there is a tendency to consider sound as the poor relation.

6. a. *vision-literature, poem, -world; vision-seeking* adj.; **vision quest** *N. Amer.,* the attempt to achieve a vision traditionally undertaken by mature men of the Plains Indian tribes, usu. through fasting or self-torture; **vision splendid,** the dream of some glorious imagined time; **vision-telephone** = *videophone* s.v. *VIDEO-.

1929 T. S. ELIOT *Dante* 67 The *Vita Nuova,*..a sequence of beautiful poems connected by a curious vision-literature. **1961** A. CLARKE *Later Poems* 91 The *Aisling,* or Vision poem, in which Ireland was personified, reached its pitch in the eighteenth century. **1922** R. BENEDICT in *Amer. Anthropol.* XXIV. 3 Three patterns of wide distribution are sometimes taken to characterize the vision quest of the Plains. **1966** D. ABERLE *Peyote Relig. among Navaho* xx. 340 Anthropologists have been impressed by the similarities between peyotism and the Plains vision quest. **1971** E. SHORRIS *Death of Great Spirit* iv. 40 He is a Uwipi, a medicine man and practitioner of the traditional vision quest, and there is not a Sioux Indian within two hundred miles of Pine Ridge who does not regard him with a certain amount of awe. **1922** W. B. YEATS *Trembling of Veil* II. xiv. 129 Politics, for a vision-seeking man, can be but half achievement. **1807** WORDSWORTH *Poems* II. 151 The youth, who..still is Nature's priest, And by the vision splendid Is on his way attended. **1895** A. B. PATERSON *Man from Snowy River* (1896) 21 And he sees the vision splendid of the sunlit plains extended, And at night the wond'rous glory of the everlasting stars. **1959** X. HERBERT *Seven Emus* x. 110 Such was his acting that he took in his audience along with himself, made them share his optimism, his vision splendid. **1972** I. MOFFITT *U-Jack Soc.* xii. 199, I sat obediently and listened, and Sir Philip spread his vision splendid of electricity extended—with nuclear power. **1966** *Guardian* 22 Dec. 3/3 The Post Office is exploring the possibility of..a vision-telephone for calls between individuals. **1969** *New Scientist* 16 Oct. 146/3 Big industrial concerns might..find vision telephones helpful for conferences between executives. **1915** D. H. LAWRENCE *Rainbow* xi. 267 In the vision-world He spoke of Jerusalem, something that did not exist in the everyday world.

b. In sense *5*; *spec.* **vision-mixer,** a person whose job is to switch from one camera to another in television broadcasting or recording; so **vision-mixing** *vbl. sb.*

1935 *Illustr. London News* 23 Feb. 307/1 (*in figure*) Vision control [of a television receiver]. **1937** *Discovery* Nov. 330/1 The incoming vision signal ..carries the time-sequence of light-and-shade in the original image. **1938** *Times* 7 Jan. 13/6 Behind him is the key-man, the vision-mixer. **1951** I. ASIMOV *Stars like Dust* (1958) i. 7 He jabbed at the vision control and the small screen was alive with light. **1953** AMOS & BIRKINSHAW *Television Engin.* I. i. 17 The composite signal obtained by combining a picture with a synchronising signal is known as a vision [1957: video] signal. **1956** *B.B.C. Handbk. 1957* 59 This unit..has its own VHF sound and vision transmitters. **1960** *Daily Tel.* 17 June 13/4 The present [television] centre runs more than 100 vision and 400 sound circuits. **1961** G. MILLERSON *Technique Television Production* xvi. 296 The television director is his own editor. He may himself carry out the mechanical operation of the video switching console (vision mixing desk), or have..a switcher (vision mixer), follow his instructions. **1972** D. LEES *Zodiac* 30 Zodiac's director, vision mixers, audiomen and camera men were obviously tops. **1979** ZARACH & MORRIS *Television Princ. & Pract.* ii. 8 The signal from the camera, together with the synchronising pulses.., modulate the vision carrier. **1982** A. ROAD *Dr. Who* 45/2 To the director's..right [in the gallery] are the vision mixer, the producer..and..the technical manager.

visionariness. 1. (Earlier example.)

c **1806** D. WORDSWORTH *Jrnl.* (1941) I. 286 That visionariness which results from a communion with the unworldliness of nature.

visiophone (vi·ziofōun). [f. L. *vīsio* VISION *sb.* + *-PHONE.] = *videophone* s.v. *VIDEO-.

1971 *New Scientist* 15 July 140/2 It is estimated that 125 Visiophones will be in use in that area [*sc.* Paris] within four years. **1978** *Jrnl. Communication* XXVIII. 151 The audio and video (visiophone) two-way link was reserved..each day for consultations..between staff in Nairobi and Paris.

visit, *sb.* Add: **1. f.** *Dog-Breeding.* A bitch's journey to and her stay with a dog for breeding purposes. Cf. *VISIT *v.* 8 b.

1867 *Field* 5 Jan. 5/3 The following bitches have been on a visit to Patent. **1887** G. STABLER *Pract. Kennel Guide* xii. 125 Dogs..refuse food during the time of the bitch's visit. **1910** R. LEIGHTON *Dogs* l. 320 A proper mating should be considered at the outset... It is customary for the bitch to be the visitor, and it is well that her visit should extend to two or three days at the least.

3. c. *Billiards* and *Snooker.* A turn of play at the table.

1927 *Times* 22 Feb. 16/3 At his second visit to the table he made a break of 111.

visit, *v.* **8. b.** For † *Obs. rare* read: *rare* exc. in *Dog-Breeding*: To be put to mate with (a dog) or at (a kennel). (Later examples.)

1867 *Field* 5 Jan. 5/3 The following bitches have visited Good Idea at the Blundell Arms Kennels. **1877** G. STABLES *Pract. Kennel Guide* xii. 122 In your correspondence with the owner of the bitch that is going to visit your kennel, be sure to let him know that he is to send her..as soon as there are the slightest signs of her coming in season. **1922** R. LEIGHTON *Compl. Bk. Dog* iii. 34, 40 per cent. of prize-bred bitches which visit prize-bred dogs are unproductive.

e. Also const. *at.*

1753 [in Dict.]. **1836** DICKENS *Let.* 31 Mar. (1965) I. 144, I cannot..visit at a relation's house from which my father is excluded. **1976** *Stillwater* (Montana) *News* 1 July 2/1 Ruthie Braunstadter of Billings visited at the home of her grandmother. **1978** *Times* 1 Feb. 15/5 If it were only a friendly meal around a common table, I am sure that Catholics would be only too happy to visit at the tables of their friends whenever they were invited.

f. *to visit with*: = sense 8 a in Dict. Now *U.S.*

1850 E. RUSKIN *Let.* 18 Jan. in M. Lutyens *Effie in Venice* (1965) II. 117 They visit with everybody in Venice. **1872** GEO. ELIOT *Middlem.* I. I. i. 8 The small group of gentry with whom he visited. **1903** F. NORRIS *Pit* v. 150 Almost every evening nowadays the Dearborn girls came ..to visit with the Cresslers. **1927** C. A. LINDBERGH *We* iv. 57 Perryville, Missouri, where we visited with some of Klink's friends. **1949** M. LOWRY *Let.* 1 July (1967) 179 Margerie is flying..to visit—to visit *with,* I believe I should say—her family for a week. **1973** *Black Panther* 16 June 2/1 Seale visited with David Hilliard at Vacaville (Medical Facility) Prison. **1981** C. POTOK *Bk. Lights* (1982) vii. 227 He took Karen to a movie, then visited for a while with her family. **1985** *New Yorker* 11 Feb. 70/1 A young man of Ved's age and grade level is visiting with him.

g. *intr.* To talk or chat; to exchange conversation. *U.S.*

1856 M. D. COLT *Diary* 21 Oct. in *Went to Kansas* (1862) xii. 195 Have visited some, but am now in my room again to rest. **1879** A. TOURGÉE *Fool's Errand* xix. 111 He.. stopped at the Mission-House, visiting with the teachers. **1898** M. DELAND *Old Chester Tales* 75 You can eat it while I get out and visit with the minister. **1929** *N.Y. Times Mag.* 20 Oct. 1 Having disposed of a batch of correspondence he was willing to visit in informal..fashion. It was good talk. **1967** 'P. KRUGER' *Weave Wicked Web* xi. 94, I called to see her around eight... Stella and I visited until close on eleven. **1979** N. MAILER *Executioner's Song* I. xviii. 304 Nicole drove down to the Preliminary Hearing..but they let her visit with Gary for only a moment.

visitable, *a.* **2.** (Further examples of the sense 'worth visiting'.)

1953 *John o'London's Weekly* 12 June 519/1 He was also known as a charming and eminently visitable old gentleman. **1972** *Maclean's Mag.* Mar. 57/3 While it has its share of visitable old buildings Rijeka is more European than most Yugoslav cities. **1983** R. MUIR in Muir & Welfare *Nat. Trust Guide Prehistoric & Roman Britain* ii. 27/2 There are few exciting and visitable relics of [Mesolithic] human life apart from caves.

Visitandine. b. (Earlier example.)

1871 A. J. C. HARE *Walks in Rome* I. vi. 277 It has been decided that some remains which exist in the garden of the Villa Mills (now a Convent of Visitandine Nuns) are those of the House of Hortensius.

visitation. Add: **I. 5. d.** A gathering at the home of a deceased person before the funeral takes place; a wake. *U.S.*

1974 *Amer. Speech 1971* XLVI. 70 Another interesting Boston area universal was the use, even among Protestants, of *wake* for what is elsewhere in the state often called a *visitation.* **1976** N. Thornburg *Cutter & Bone* iii. 75 'The goddamn funeral,' he explained. 'Or what do they call it the day before—visitation?' **1983** *Chicago Sun-Times* 27 Sept. 18 An acquaintance in the life insurance business showed up at the visitation and proceeded to solicit business... What kind of a person would latch onto an opportunity to solicit business at a wake?

III. 10. *visitation fee, nun*: earlier examples.

1791 J. Woodforde *Diary* 6 Dec. (1927) III. 316 Recd. of Ditto, my last Visitation Fee, 0.2.6. *a* **1700** [see *Blue Nun* s.v. ***blue** *a.* 13].

visite. Add: **1.** (Earlier example.)

c **1847** J. S. Coyne *How to settle Accounts with your Laundress* 4 I'll come in my blue *visite* and my native innocence.

‖ **3.** *visite de digestion*, a formal call paid in return for hospitality received.

1908 J. Churchill *Reminisc.* (1973) iii. 44 The writing of ceremonious notes, the leaving of cards, not to speak of *visites de digestion*, which even young men were supposed to pay, took up most afternoons. **1971** L. P. Hartley *Mrs Carteret Receives* 17, I thought it only civil to ask Madame Carteret if we could pay her a farewell visit, not a *visite de digestion*, but just an acknowledgment of her kindness.

visitee. (Earlier example.)

1710 W. King *Let.* 16 Sept. in Swift *Corr.* (1963) I. 176 There are great men here as much out of humour, as you describe your great visitee to have been.

visiting, *vbl. sb.* Add: **4.** *visiting dress* (earlier example); **visiting-book,** (*b*) = *visitors' book* s.v. *visitor 6; **visiting-card:** also in (orig. *Mil.*) *slang* phr. *to leave one's visiting-card,* to leave unpleasant evidence of having been at a place; **visiting hours,** hours when visitors may call, *spec.* to see a person in a hospital or other institution; **visiting rights,** the right to pay or receive visits (to or from a child in the custody of a divorced spouse) or to receive them (while in an institution of any kind).

1848 Thackeray *Van. Fair* lv. 500 The Bishop went and wrote his name in the visiting-book at Gaunt House that very day. **1945** Partridge *Dict. R.A.F. Slang* 60 *Visiting-card*, a bomb. Mostly in *Leave one's visiting card*... As the civilian drops visiting cards into tray or salver, so the airman drops bombs on..enemy-occupied territory. **1953** 'E. Crispin' *Fen Country* (1979) 68 All he had to do was to..leave his visiting card [*sc.* an explosive device] and collect his fee. **1972** V. Canning *Rainbird Pattern* vi. 116 He should have brought Albert [*sc.* the dog] in from the car, he at least could have left a visiting card in self-defence. **1825** E. Weeton *Jrnl.* 20 June (1969) II. 397, I am..as neat in my *every day apparel*, as any of my acquaintances; they many of them exceed me in visiting dresses. **1851** *London at Table* i. 36 A cigar is not the indispensable companion of visiting hours. **1897** *Scribner's Mag.* Sept. 384/1 Formal visiting-hours were ignored in the village of Sewanee. **1947** 'G. Orwell' *Let.* 31 Dec. in *Coll. Ess.* (1968) IV. 386 I'd love it if you did come & see me... They don't seem very lavish with their visiting hours... I've only been in the hospital abt 10 days. **1979** 'D. Kyle' *Green River High* ii. 15, I scribbled a note giving hospital visiting hours. **1971** *Deb. House of Commons* (Canada) 14 Dec. 10 460/1 Has the minister or his department investigated allegations that visiting rights were denied to members of the Black United Front? **1972** H. Kemelman *Monday the Rabbi took Off* xxiv. 159, I was divorced from his mother—he was ten at the time—I had visiting rights, of course. **1982** G. Wagner *Children of Empire* viii. 138 All the homes were surrounded by high walls to keep intruders out and the children in. Visiting rights were restricted.

visiting, *ppl. a.* Add: **1. c.** *visiting fireman* (U.S. slang): a person given especially cordial treatment while visiting an organization or place; a tourist expected to spend freely.

[**1855** *Sun* (Baltimore) 25 Oct. 1/6 A company of firemen from Rochester, N.Y.,..continue to receive the attentions of their brother firemen of Baltimore... This evening the visiting firemen will be the guests of the Washington Hose Company.] **1926** S. Lewis *Mantrap* xxi. 265, I..couldn't keep my hooks off any he-male that blows into town with the visiting firemen! **1936** H. Bernstein *Choose Bright Morning* ii. 20 He never sees people who might have legitimate business with him... But he receives all the visiting firemen. **1945** H. S. Truman in M. Truman *Harry S. Truman* (1972) x. 202 Naturally got pointed out as the visiting fireman and had a kind of reception between acts and afterwards. **1962** A. Davison *In Wake of Gemini* 115 Members of the firm, whose business it was to look after visiting firemen, had the same happy knack. **1964** *Economist* 25 Jan. 313/2 The marked-up tickets are usually sold to 'visiting firemen'. **1972** K. Benton *Spy in Chancery* i. 19 Don't they know the form for visiting firemen?..As the British delegate..I shall make a courtesy visit to the Embassy.

d. *visiting fellow, lecturer, professor*: an academic who accepts an invitation to work at another institution for a fixed term; so *visiting fellowship*, etc.

1950 *Univ. London Gaz.* 28 Oct. 178 (*heading*) Appointment of Visiting Professor of Belgian Studies. *Ibid.*, The Visiting Professorship of Belgian Studies. **1960** A. Huxley *Let.* 12 Nov. (1969) 898, I am here for the moment working as a Visiting Professor at MIT. **1962** *St. Edmund Hall Mag. 1961–2* 3 Mr. Allen was Visiting Lecturer at the University of Iowa. **1963** *Cambridge Univ. Reporter* 24 Apr. 1450 The Board of Managers of the Smuts Memorial Fund invite applications for Smuts Visiting Fellowships in Commonwealth Studies. *Ibid.*, The emoluments of a Visiting Fellow will be a sum not exceeding £1,500. **1973** *Oxf. Mag.* 1 June 2/2 Professor Levitch..has accepted a Visiting Fellowship at University [College]. **1980** A. Coppel *Hastings Conspiracy* viii. 59 Langton enjoyed a visiting lectureship at the London School of Economics. **1980** M. Drabble *Middle Ground* 156 A visiting professor..on his way to an excavation. **1982** C. Monteith in A. Thwaite *Larkin at Sixty* 41 All Souls—a College where he later stayed in his own right as a Visiting Fellow.

visitor. Add: **4. c.** *Sport.* A member of a visiting team.

1900 W. J. Ford *Cricketer on Cricket* xiv. 162 Setting aside one unpleasant incident of the present trip..our visitors can hardly complain of the treatment they have received at the hands of the players, the public, or the press. **1916, 1930** [see ***home** *a.* 2 c]. **1976** G. L. Greaves *Over Summers Again* xvi. 105 September 1966 Saw Yorkshire once again..needing an outright win over Kent to give them yet another championship... Trueman and Nicholson..soon had Kent in trouble and the visitors, all out for 119, closed 91 behind.

5. A menstrual discharge; = Visit *sb.* 4. *slang.*

1980 *Quarto* June 3/2 It was shortly before my thirteenth birthday that I first had 'Visitors'. Mother..had told me about the monthly cycle... My first 'visitor' was a light one. **1983** *Maledicta 1982* VI. 26 Menstruation (females):..visitor. **1984** *New Yorker* 29 Oct. 45/3 Girls used to say they had the curse. Or they had a visitor.

6. *Comb.*, as **visitor centre** orig. *U.S.*, a building in a tourist area in which exhibitions, slide-shows, etc., are displayed as an introduction to the locality; **visitors' book,** a book in which visitors may write their names and addresses, and, sometimes, comments; **visitors' list,** a public list of those making a visit to a place, esp. to a resort; in quot. 1864, a list of official visitors (Visitor 1 b).

1964 P. Jensen *National Parks* i. 18 Park headquarters is also here. A visitor center explains the features of the area. **1979** *Farmington* (New Mexico) *Daily Times* 27 May 3c/6 Visitor centers will tell tourists the speed limits will be enforced. **1979** *United States 1980/81* (Penguin Travel Guides) 239 A 25-minute movie about the Battle of Shiloh is shown in the Visitor Center. **1983** *Leisure, Recreation & Tourism Abstr.* VIII. iv. 205/2 A new accommodation concept, and an existing visitor centre facility. **1846** *Punch* 20 June 278/2 (*heading*) Ibrahim Pacha's visitors' book. **1870** *Ibid.* 1 Oct. 138/2 The Emperor Nicholas..'expressed himself much pleased', as the visitors' books have it. **1910** Belloc *Pongo & Bull* vii. 96 The Duke..had very properly insisted upon the retention of the visitors' book. **1976** L. Deighton *Twinkle, twinkle Little Spy* xvi. 157 There was a visitors' book..a beautiful leather-bound volume..dutifully signed by the Reid-Kennedys' guests. **1984** *Times* 25 May 7/5 (*caption*) All smiles: the Queen leaving the town hall..after signing the visitors' book. **1864** Mrs. Gaskell *Wives & Daughters* (1866) I. i. 8 Though my name has been down on the visitors' list these three years, the countess has never named me in her note... Her ladyship would be as hurt as any one when she did not see Phœbe among the school visitors. **1904** A. E. W. Mason *Truants* II. vi. 105 She..bought a visitors' list at the kiosk. **1907** E. Glyn *Three Weeks* iv. 53 The simplest thing..seemed to descend into the hall and look at the Visitors' List... There were only a few people in the hotel. **1927** E. Bowen *Hotel* iii. 27 Victor..took up the local paper and began to read the visitors' list.

Visking (vi·skiŋ). Also **visking.** A proprietary term for seamless cellulose tubing used as membranes in dialysis and as edible casings for sausages.

1931 *Trade Marks Jrnl.* 29 July 1050/1 *Visking casing.* ..sausage casings made of cellulose. The Visking Corporation,..Chicago, Illinois, United States of America; manufacturers. **1941** *Official Gaz.* (U.S. Patent Office) 15 Apr. 550/1 The Visking Corporation, Chicago... *Visking* for merchandise protectors—namely seamless cellulose tubes, and artificial sausage casings made of cellulose. **1956** *Nature* 25 Feb. 381/1 These compounds were removed..by dialysis of aqueous solutions of 2–3 mgm. of the venom, in Visking tubing. **1970** *Ibid.* 26 Dec. 1336/2 The oxidized form dialysed through visking tubing. **1977** *Times Educ. Suppl.* 21 Oct. 29/1 This apparatus was designed to simplify the setting up of experiments using visking tubing.

visna (vi·znă). Also **Visna.** *Vet. Sci.* [a. ON. *visna* to wither.] A fatal disease of sheep in which there is progressive demyelination of neurones in the brain and spinal cord. Freq. *attrib.*

1957 *Jrnl. Neuropath. & Exper. Neurol.* XVI. 389 (*heading*) Visna, a demyelinating transmissible disease of sheep. *Ibid.* 393 This experiment obviously does not prove conclusively that Visna-sera will specifically neutralize Visna-virus but it is consistent with such an explanation. **1970** Jubb & Kennedy *Path. Domestic Animals* (ed. 2) I. 269/2 The virus of visna can be transmitted by intra-pulmonary injection. **1982** *Jrnl. Neuroimmunology* III. 140 Icelandic sheep are free of natural infection since visna virus has been eradicated from the whole country.

visor, vizor, *sb.* Add: **1. a.** Also *transf.*

1957 *Time* 2 Sept. 37/2 Simons quickly clamped shut the visor of his space helmet. **1962** W. Schirra in *Into Orbit* 51 Once we are up..we can open up our visor and breathe the cabin air for a bit.

c. A shade for protecting the eyes from unwanted light while not impeding the vision; *spec.* one attached to the top of the windscreen of a motor vehicle or aircraft.

1925 J.-L. Hudon *Lexique Technique* 109 Windshield visor. **1936,** etc. [see *sun visor* s.v. ***sun** *sb.* 13 a]. **1952** *Times* 9 Jan. 3/3 Canberra pilots at Binbrook are testing a new type of visor for protecting crews against the glare at high altitudes. **1957** Rawnsley & Wright *Night Fighter* 57, I peered into the visor [of a radar], trying to accustom my eyes to the dim light. **1973** 'E. McBain' *Let's hear It* iii. 41 The visor on the driver's side was down.

visored, *ppl. a.* Add: **2. b.** Of a cap: peaked.

1950 *Manch. Guardian Weekly* 5 Oct. 15/2 The General left the 'plane, dressed in field jacket and visored, brass-encrusted cap. **1961** M. Beadle *These Ruins are Inhabited* (1963) ii. 30 The salesman spread out an impressive..array of..red-bound black blazers, visored caps, red bordered black Rugby socks. **1983** P. Chevalier *Shaft* xvii. 119 He was wearing exquisite yachting whites and a Navy-style visored cap.

vista, *sb.* Add: **5.** Comb.: **vista-dome** *U.S.*, a high glass-sided railway carriage that enables passengers to look at the view from above the normal level of the train. Freq. *attrib.*

1945 *Time* 18 June 78/3 For travelers who like to watch the country go by, Chicago, Burlington & Quincy Railroad announced a new 'Vista Dome' car, to be put in operation next week. **1948** *Sun* (Baltimore) 6 Jan. 6/5 (Advt.), The Vista-Dome affords a wonderful opportunity for camera fans. **1973** [see ***Rheingold**].

Vistavision (vi·stăviʒən). Also **vista-.** [f. Vista *sb.* + Vision *sb.*] A form of wide-screen cinematography employing standard 35 mm. film in such a way as to give a larger projected image with ordinary methods of projection. Also *fig.*

A proprietary name in the U.S.

1954 *Newsweek* 15 Mar. 104/3 A new filming process in which Paramount Pictures will produce all its films beginning with 'White Christmas'..was demonstrated last week in Hollywood. Called VistaVision, it..is designed primarily to improve wide-screen clarity. **1955** *Official Gaz.* (U.S. Patent Office) 25 Jan. TM 138/2 Paramount Pictures Corporation... *Vistavision* for motion picture films and cameras and parts therefor. **1961** *Guardian* 20 Jan. 7/3 Passion and vistavision ideas are not enough. **1976** *New Musical Express* 12 Feb. 27/5 I'll direct you to a copy of Diana Ross's 'An Evening With' (Motown) a vistavision affair on which Berry Gordy's favourite movie star provides a medley of Motown oldies.

visual, *a.* and *sb.* Add: **A.** *adj.* **2. a.** *visual acuity*, sharpness of vision; *spec.* as measured or expressed in terms of a definite scale (see quot. 1974).

1889 [in Dict.]. **1938** R. L. Rea *Neuro-Ophthalmology* iv. 86 In the early stages [of papillœdema] there may be..full central visual acuity. **1974** *Encycl. Brit. Macropædia* VII. 104/1 A visual acuity of unity indicates a power of resolving detail subtending one minute of arc at the eye; a visual acuity of two indicates a resolution of one-half minute..of arc.

b. *visual purple* [tr. G. *sehpurpur* (app. first used by W. Kühne 1877, in *Verh. d. Naturhist.-med. Verein zu Heidelberg* I. 484)]: = *rhodopsin.

[**1877** *Nature* 1 Feb. 296/1 These first observations of Kühne on the vision-purple (*Sehpurpur*), as he terms it.] **1878** M. Foster *Text Bk. Physiol.* (ed. 2) iii. ii. 415 For the restoration of the visual purple, after it has been destroyed by light, the maintenance of the circulation of the blood through the tissues of the eye is not essential. **1921** *Proc. R. Soc.* B. XCII. 232 A highly dilute visual purple may suffice for the requirements of photopic vision. **1953** *Sci. News* XXX. 116 Although as many as six visual pigments have been recognized in different species, only one, visual purple, has been obtained from the human retina. **1983** *Guardian* 4 Aug. 17/2 Retinaldehyde..is present in the retina of the eye combined with the visual pigment known as visual purple.

5. *visual field, range.*

1880 W. James *Coll. Ess. & Rev.* (1920) 169 He perceives correctly the position of objects in the visual field. **1927** B. Russell *Anal. Matter* xii. 111 The sort of relation that will not do is illustrated if we take $xy = zw$ to mean that xy and zw have the same apparent dimensions in the visual field of a certain observer. **1961** G. E. M. Anscombe tr. *Wittgenstein's Notebks. 1914–16* 45 What is a uniformly coloured part of my visual field composed of? **1953** R. Chisholm *Cover of Darkness* iii. 36 Reading the faces of cathode-ray tubes was a small part of the Observer's task. By description and instruction he had to get his Pilot to visual range. **1965** *Observer* 31 Oct. 1/1 'Visual range'—the distance one can see along the runway—is measured and passed to the pilot.

6. d. *visual aid*, illustrative matter designed to supplement written or spoken information; *spec.* in *Educ.* with reference to pictures, models, films, etc., as an aid to learning. orig. *U.S.*

1911 P. Monroe *Cycl. Educ.* V. 734/2 The last century of schoolroom practice has been marked by a great increase in the use of natural objects, models, pictures, maps, charts, and other visual aids. **1938** *Rep. Physical Educ. & Film* (Brit. Film Inst.) 1 The function of the film in education has been defined as that of a visual aid. **1958** *Economist* 29 Nov. 764/1 The visual aids which the party's television programme used to good effect. **1967** MRS. L. B. JOHNSON *White House Diary* 14 Mar. (1970) 497 In one room they were using visual-aid machines for faster reading. **1980** E. BLISHEN *Nest of Teachers* I. ii. 11 That most familiar of visual aids, an extremely tatty blackboard.

e. *visual display* (Computers) = *DISPLAY *sb.* 1 c; *visual display unit*, a device for displaying on its screen data stored in a computer, and usu. incorporating a keyboard for manipulating the data; abbrev. VDU, vdu s.v. *V 5 b.

1954 *Jrnl. Assoc. Computing Machinery* I. 57/1 Cathode ray tube equipment for providing external visual displays of information stored internally in the computer. **1967** KLERER & KORN *Digital Computer User's Handbk.* I. 77 The importance of the use of machine-produced graphs and other types of visual displays can hardly be over emphasized. **1969** *Computers & Humanities* IV. 83 For those interested in on-line text manipulation, there is special temptation in newer devices like cathode ray tubes (CRTs) or visual displays, or 'scopes', as they are variously called. **1971** J. ANDERSON in B. de Ferranti *Living with Computer* vii. 59 With..the introduction..of visual display units..there has been a resurgence of interest in applying such techniques to medical recording. **1977** *R.A.F. News* 11–24 May 7/2 When can we have our visual display unit? **1983** *Brit. Med. Jrnl.* 23 July 271 Most of the comments relating to paper records apply to visual displays for data entry. **1984** *Times* 16 Nov. 12/4 The latest scare comes from reports of women who worked on visual display units (VDUs) during pregnancy and went on to deliver handicapped babies or suffer miscarriages.

7. a. (Earlier example.)

1817 COLERIDGE *Biog. Lit.* I. iv. 76 The change of one visual image for another involves in itself no absurdity.

B. *sb.* **3.** A visual image or display, a picture; *spec.* the visual element of a film or television production. Usu. *pl.*

1951 *Brit. Kinematogr.* XIX. 110/1 A good deal has been done by..'visuals'. **1959** *Times* 4 Mar. 11/7 Exposition is particularly difficult on television—it gets confused by the visuals and the speaker's loose words. **1961** *Listener* 19 Oct. 622/3 As the commentator's voice announced that allocations for shelters by the U.S. Government had been currently increased 700 per cent, we saw a visual of President Kennedy roaring with laughter. **1966** J. DERRICK *Teaching Eng. to Immigrants* vii. 229 The Language Master..is a new transistorized machine into which can be fed visuals and reading matter on long cards. **1972** *Observer* 16 Apr. 34/6 Written entries.. should be typed, visuals (a maximum of 3ft square) carefully packed. **1974** 'D. CRAIG' *Dead Liberty* xxi. 125 The Finance lads liked your economics piece... We're getting some graphs and other visuals done. **1984** *Times* 23 Jan. 7/1 There is more porn in the [cinema] subtitles than in the visuals.

visuality. Delete *rare* and 'app. used by Carlyle only' in etym. and add: **2.** (Later example.)

1912 H. BRADLEY *Let.* in *Corr. Bridges & Bradley* (1940) 96, I do not think I can even say or hear 'bread and butter', or 'dog and cat', without an accompanying underconsciousness of the way in which these words are commonly spelt. (It may be deplorable that any human soul should have got into this degraded state of subjection to black and white visualities.)

3. Vision, sight.

1923 D. H. LAWRENCE *Birds, Beasts & Flowers* 27 You are everywhere, and I am blind, Sightless among all your visuality, You staring caryatids. **1941** *Illustr. London News* CXCVIII. 37 Immediately in front of the driver is a movable periscope, shown reflecting the other tanks ahead, whereby he can obtain full visuality when the armoured cowl has to be closed when in action.

4. Visual aspect or representation; physical appearance.

1938 R. G. COLLINGWOOD *Princ. Art* vii. 144 His [*sc.* Cézanne's] landscapes have lost almost every trace of visuality. **1975** *Physics Bull.* Apr. 165/3 Regretfully, the printed word can hardly do justice to the visuality of the afternoon. **1976** *Times Lit. Suppl.* 5 Mar. 251/1 Notable among the elements of visuality which lead to the effect of amenity is that of scale.

visualizable (viːziuălai·zăb'l), *a.* [f. VISUALIZE *v.* + -ABLE.] **a.** Capable of being visualized. **b.** Capable of being rendered visible.

1956 E. H. HUTTEN *Lang. Mod. Physics* v. 202 The models may overlap, in part, and they may become more 'abstract', i.e. less visualisable. **1968** *Amer. Speech* XLIII. 5 In the world of reality for which the elements of language are symbols, there are no visualizable objects which correspond to adjective symbols. **1980** *Nature* 8 May 100/1 We think it unlikely that the large visualizable deposits in the older birds are more than epiphenomenal.

visualization. Add: **2.** The action or process of rendering visible.

1926 [see *CHOLECYSTOGRAPHY]. **1936** *Amer. Jrnl. Cancer* XXVII. 49 The hexagonal tube..offers distinct advantages with its flat sides permitting good visualization. **1960** *New Scientist* 28 July 305/3 Echo sounding.. is now being applied to the visualization of structures within the body. **1973** *Nature* 17 Aug. 410/1 Direct visualization of biological material at this level would tell us much about the structure and mode of action of macromolecules. **1982** *Listener* 23/30 Dec. 42/3 The cinematic visualisation of the script..belongs entirely to Welles and his technicians.

visualize, *v.* Add: **3.** *trans.* To render visible.

1912 *Moving Picture World* 17 Aug. 646/2 The printed volumes of ancient history have been carefully preserved and why not the film, which is more accurate and which, supplementing the printed story, would visualize the actual occurrences so that all may readily understand? **1925** D. H. LAWRENCE in *Calendar Mod. Lett.* Dec. 269 And the camera will *visualize* the sunflower far more perfectly than Van Gogh can. **1938** *Q. Jrnl. Med.* XXXI. 462 Inflating the stomach with gas by means of an effervescing drink, a procedure we have found of great help in visualizing the apex [of the heart in radiography]. **1958** *Arch. Neurol. & Psychiatry* LXXIX. 59/1 The dorsal root axons..may then be stained and visualized. **1971** *Daily Tel.* 18 Nov. 5 (Advt.), Research has led to the building of an ultra-sensitive Schlieren apparatus, in which pulsed ultrasound may be visualised both in water and in solids.

visualizer. Add: **2.** *spec.* in *Advertising*, a commercial artist employed to design layouts.

1921 R. S. DURSTINE *Making Advertisements* ii. 23 Several arrangements suggest themselves immediately if the visualizer has a natural or a trained imagination. **1948** [see *LAY-OUT 1 b]. **1968** M. BUTTERWORTH *Walk Softly* ii. 30 She worked as a visualiser in an ad agency. **1981** *West Lancs. Evening Gaz.* 5 June 24 (Advt.), Visualisers/finished artists..required by a rapidly-expanding studio.

visuo-. Add: *visuo-spatial, tactual*, adjs.; *visuo-spatially* adv.; **vi·suomotor** *a.*, pertaining to or involving motor activity as guided by or dependent on sight; **viːsuopsy·chic** *a.*, an epithet of two cortical areas adjacent to the striate cortex, orig. regarded as sites of mental elaboration of visual sense impressions; **viːsuose·nsory** *a.*, pertaining to or involving the visual perception of sensory signals; *spec.* an epithet of the striate cortex (see *STRIATE *a.* 2), as the part of the brain that receives sensory nerve impulses from the eye.

1942 *Anat. Rec.* LXXXIV. 470 (*heading*) Reestablishment of visuomotor coordination by optic nerve regeneration. **1972** *Science* 5 May 536/2 This difference could be observed in splitbrain monkeys executing a visuomotor task with one eye covered. **1900** Visuo-psychic [in Dict.]. **1954** S. DUKE-ELDER *Parsons' Dis. Eye* (ed. 12) xxix. 500 A lesion of this vessel thus causes a crossed homonymous hemianopia often with disturbances of the visuopsychic areas. **1980** *Gray's Anat.* (ed. 36) VII. 1010/2 Not only the striate cortex (area 17, visuosensory area), but also the para- and peri-striate areas around it (areas 18 and 19—the 'visuopsychic' cortex) receive projection fibres. **1900** Visuo-sensory [in Dict.]. **1907** J. H. PARSONS *Dis. Eye* v. 90 This area, which is the primary visual or visuo-sensory area.., is the cortical projection of the corresponding halves of both retinæ. **1980** Visuosensory [see *visuopsychic* adj. above]. **1962** *Jrnl. Speech & Hearing Research* Dec. 359/2 Factor 3 is a clear-cut visuospatial factor. Tests...include matching, copying, drawing, and object-assembly tests. *Ibid.* 367/1 Visuospatial behavior..involved both visual and sensory processes. **1977** *Lancet* 10 Dec. 1227/2 Intelligence tests indicated severe intellectual deterioration on subtests measuring visuospatial perception. **1939** *Mind* XLVIII. 360 We touch surfaces of things optically known to us, and when we pass from one thing to another we leave them visuo-spatially related behind us. **1932** H. H. PRICE *Perception* ix. 277 Let us call it a visuo-tactual solid. **1959** J. L. AUSTIN *Sense & Sensibilia* (1962) ii. 8 Visuo-tactual solids.

Vita[1] (vəi·tă). Also **vita.** [L., = 'life'.] A proprietary term for glass which transmits most of the ultraviolet rays of sunlight. Usu. as *Vita-glass, Vitaglass.*

1925 *Trade Marks Jrnl.* 29 July 1649 *Vita*...Glass. Francis Everard Lamplough, 47, Bunbury Road, King's Norton, Birmingham; chemist. **1925** *Spectator* 14 Nov. 869/1 A substitute for quartz... This vitaglass is what I asked for. **1939** O. LANCASTER *Homes Sweet Homes* 60 The small tight-shut windows..will be replaced by a wide expanse of hygienic vita glass. **1948** J. BETJEMAN *Coll. Poems* (1958) 227 And many a cultivated hour they pass In a fine school with walls of vita-glass. **1957** *Oxford Mag.* 17 Oct. 18/2 The well-intended propaganda of Sir Leonard Hill and others about 1930..gave it a new lease of life by preaching that the sun was the best preventative of rickets provided that 'vitaglass' windows were used. **1981** *Times* 21 Feb. 22/3 The old Marine Spa..contained.. a Vita-glass sun lounge.

vita[2] (vī·tă). **1.** ‖ *vita nuova* [It., = new life]. The title of a work by Dante describing his love for Beatrice, used to denote a fresh start or new direction in life, usu. after some powerful emotional experience.

1934 A. J. A. SYMONS *Quest for Corvo* xii. 164 There seemed no impediment to his *vita nuova.* **1939** L. MACNEICE *Autumn Jrnl.* 43 A cultured accent alone will not provide A season ticket to the Vita Nuova. **1975** P. ORGAN *House on Cheyne Walk* xviii. 163 Not a very good way to begin *la vita nuova*, with more lies.

2. [a. L. *vīta* life.] A biography, the history of a life; *spec.* = *curriculum vitæ* s.v. *CURRICULUM.

1949 WYNDHAM LEWIS *Let.* 3 Sept. (1963) 505 You ought to cut out *cleanly* and implacably the *vita* material from this typescript. **1960** *Encounter* Mar. 82/2 Clifton Fadiman..whose credentials include..a *vita* which concludes as follows:..master of ceremonies on the popular radio programme *Information Please*, and on the television show *This is Show Business.* **1974** H. L. FOSTER *Ribbin', Jivin', & Playin' Dozens* i. 18 As far as children and their schools are concerned, the reports were simply another exercise for academicians to contribute, primarily, as a source for an additional listing on a vita or a source for citations for future papers, lectures, books, and speeches. **1979** *Amer. Speech* LIV. 257 All these observations..are summarized in the vitas of the informants.

vital, *a.* Add: **I. 4. d.** (Later examples.) Also *transf.*

1949 *Brit. Birds* XLII. 147 Vital statistics from ringed Swallows. **1956** *Newsweek* 23 Jan. 60 New eyes open on a bright wonderful world—and photography makes identification positive, records vital statistics in life's first few minutes. **1958** J. TOWNSEND *Young Devils* ii. 19 A short history of the school plus its vital statistics—i.e. number of boys, teachers, classrooms, subjects and educational standards. **1971** *Brit. Med. Bull.* XXVII. 13/2 The epidemic of iatrogenic deaths in asthmatic children shows the need for continuous monitoring of vital statistics. **1974** *Nature* 22 Mar. 306/1 The vital statistics of this second edition command respect—94 of the 1,562 pages are needed to index its 64 chapters!

e. *vital statistics*, (*a*) (see sense 4 d in Dict.); (*b*) *colloq.*, the measurements of a woman's figure, *spec.* bust, waist, and hips (cf. *STATISTICS 2 a*); similarly *vital measurements.* (Occas. of a man's figure.)

1958 *Observer* 18 May 10/4 To control and vary our vital measurements with changing fashion. **1968** G. KENT *Pictorial Hist. Wrestling* v. 119/1 *Height* 6ft. 1 in. *weight* 15 st. *chest* 48 ins. *biceps* 15 ins. *thigh* 26½ ins. Donald Dinnie and his vital measurements. **1952** C. R. COOPER *Teen-Age Vice* (1959) viii. 125 Regina..wrote haphazardly to men, giving her age and vital statistics. **1957** *Times* 1 Aug. 5/5 Those feminine measurements which have become known, in the entertainment world, as vital statistics. **1966** WODEHOUSE *Plum Pie* 60 A book like yours always involves a serious risk for the publisher owing to the absence of the Sex Motif, which renders it impossible for him to put a nude female of impressive vital statistics on the jacket. **1975** C. WESTON *Susannah Screaming* (1976) xxv. 135 I have her phone number and vital statistics.

f. Of biological stains or their use: used or carried out on living tissue. Cf. *intra vitam* s.v. *INTRA *prep.* 2, *INTRAVITAL *a.*

1907 *Chem. Abstr.* I. 734 The character of the vital staining and apparent deposition of the carmine as particles in the body cells of the rabbit was found under physiological conditions to be essentially as earlier described. **1912** *Ibid.* VI. 2453 (*heading*) The resorption of vital coloring matters in the stomach and alimentary canal. **1926** H. M. CARLETON *Histol. Technique* xiii. 194 Janus Green.—This dye..may almost be regarded as a specific vital stain for mitochondria. **1946** A. FISCHER *Biol. Tissue Cells* iii. 68 A staining of the nucleus by ordinary vital dyes is..always a sure sign of the death of the cell. **1948** *New Biol.* V. 28 Some dyestuffs do not kill the cell, and if they stain specific structures, this process of vital staining can give important information on the living cell. **1956** *Nature* 25 Feb. 387/1 A large body on one side of the nucleus stains directly..with 0·1 per cent aqueous vital red. **1974** *Ibid.* 18 Oct. 572/1 By staining with vital dyes, Bonner..showed that the cells in the anterior third of the grex become stalk cells.

Vitallium (vəitæ·liŏm). Also **-alium** and with small initial. [f. *vitall-*, of unkn. origin + -IUM.] A proprietary term for an alloy of cobalt, chromium, and molybdenum that has a high resistance to abrasion, corrosion, and heat and is used in surgery, dentistry, and engineering.

1935 *Official Gaz.* (U.S. Patent Office) 18 June 520/2 *Vitallium* for cobalt, chromium alloy. Claims use since July 8, 1934. **1947** *Richmond* (Va.) *Times-Dispatch* 13 Sept. 15/1 Short pieces of tubes made of the metal vitallium have been tried [to replace the missing link in arteries]. **1948** *Jrnl. R. Aeronaut. Soc.* LII. 16/2 The ease with which large quantities of these small supercharger blades could be produced to finished size by means of the 'lost wax' casting process, turned attention to 'Vitallium', an alloy which had been used for making special small castings by this method. **1951** *Trade Marks Jrnl.* 1 Aug. 713/2 *Vitallium*... Common metal alloys in the form of nuggets. Austenal Laboratories Incorporated.., New York, United States of America; manufacturers. **1961** *Lancet* 30 Sept. 757/1 At first a vitallium tube was used for the anastomosis. **1979** *Courier-Mail* (Brisbane) 21 July 3/1 Two teeth in the three-year old German Shepherd guard dog's armour now are capped with vitalium one of the toughest of alloys... It was Taz's enthusiasm for his work which took its toll on his teeth.

vitamin (vi·t-, vəi·tămin). orig. **vitamine** (vəi·tămin, vi·t-, -īn). [f. L. *vīt-a* life + AMINE, from a mistaken belief about the chemical nature of the compounds (cf. quot. 1920).]

1. a. Any of a diverse group of organic compounds of which small quantities are needed in the diet because they have a distinct biochemical role, often as coenzymes, and cannot be adequately synthesized by the body, so that in most cases a deficiency produces characteristic symptoms or disease.

1912 C. FUNK in *Jrnl. State Med.* XX. 342 It is now known that all these diseases, with the exception of pellagra, can be prevented and cured by the addition of certain preventive substances; the deficient substances, which are of the nature of organic bases, we will call 'vitamines'; and we will speak of a beri-beri or scurvy vitamine, which means a substance preventing the special disease. **1915** *Times Lit. Suppl.* 11 Nov. 400/3 The point about vitamines is that without them the animal ceases to grow or becomes diseased on a physiologically pure diet. **1916** McCollum & Kennedy in *Jrnl. Biol. Chem.* XXIV. 493 We would..suggest the desirability of discontinuing the use of the term vitamine, and the substitution of the term fat-soluble A and water-soluble B for the two classes of unknown substances concerned in inducing growth. **1920** J. C. Drummond in *Biochem. Jrnl.* XIV. 660 The criticism usually raised against Funk's word Vitamine is that the termination '-ine' is one strictly employed in chemical nomenclature to denote substances of a basic character, whereas there is no evidence which supports his original idea that these indispensable dietary constituents are amines... The suggestion is now advanced that the final '-e' be dropped, so that the resulting word Vitamin is acceptable under the standard scheme of nomenclature..which permits a neutral substance of undefined composition to bear a name ending in '-in'. If this suggestion is adopted, it is recommended that the somewhat cumbrous nomenclature introduced by McCollum (Fat-soluble A, Water-soluble B), be dropped, and that the substances be spoken of as Vitamin A, B, C, etc. **1932** Metcalf & Flint *Princ. Insect Life* xii. 465 Green plants can..manufacture complicated proteins, carbohydrates, fats, and vitamines from the nitrates, phosphates, sulfates, and water of the soil. **1966** V. B. Wigglesworth *Life of Insects* iv. 75 Cockroaches whose symbionts have been killed out by treatment with antibiotics must have extra vitamins in their diet. **1974** *Daily Tel.* 15 Feb. 17/4 Vitamins have received so much publicity as an essential factor for healthy living that there has been a tendency to forget that in excess some of them at least can be harmful. **1982** F. Ungar in T. M. Devlin *Textbk. Biochem.* xv. 719 Since the rat has this enzyme and ascorbic acid can be synthesized in its tissues, ascorbic acid is not a vitamin for this species.

b. *fig.*

1921 *Spectator* 16 Apr. 492/2 A book..so full of the vitamines of literature. **1971** *Where* Nov. 334/1 A diet only of football annuals would be deficient of almost every known reading vitamin.

2. With following (or occas. preceding) capital letter, denoting a particular vitamin or group of vitamins.

Some designations were abandoned when the substance concerned was shown to be a mixture, was not confirmed as a new vitamin, or became known under a chemical name.

vitamin A, either or both of two closely related fat-soluble vitamins, A_1 and A_2, esp. the former; = *retinol[2]; *vitamin* A_1, an alcohol that is present (as fatty acid esters) in egg-yolk, liver, butter, and milk, is also formed in the body from carotenoids present in green vegetables and stored in the liver, and is a component of the visual pigment rhodopsin; a deficiency of vitamin A_1 leads to night blindness and anæmia and ultimately xerophthalmia and blindness, *vitamin* A_2, the analogous component of the visual pigment porphyropsin in freshwater fish; **vitamin B,** any or all of several chemically unrelated water-soluble vitamins mostly occurring together in liver, cereals, and yeast and discovered by separation from the original 'vitamin B'; so *vitamin B complex* or *group*; **vitaman** B_1 = *thiamine 3 a; **vitamin** B_2 = *riboflavin; **vitamin** B_6, any or all of the compounds pyridoxine, pyridoxal, and pyridoxamine, esp. the first (the dietary form of the vitamin), deficiency of which is accompanied by symptoms that can include irritability, nervousness, or convulsions; **vitamin** B_{12}, cobalamin or any of several derivatives of it, cobalt, containing compounds synthesized by micro-organisms and present in food of animal origin (esp. meat, eggs, and dairy products), a deficiency leading to pernicious anæmia and neuropathy; cf. *extrinsic factor* s.v. *extrinsic *a.* 3 c; **vitamin C,** ascorbic acid; a water-soluble sugar, $C_6H_8O_6$, which is present in citrus fruits, green vegetables, and tomatoes, and in man is required for the synthesis of collagen and the maintenance of connective tissue, its deficiency leading to scurvy; **vitamin D,** each or all of the fat-soluble vitamins that cure or prevent rickets in children and osteomalacia in adults, one or other being required for the correct metabolism of calcium; *spec. vitamin* D_2 [named in Ger. by A. Windaus et al. 1931, in *Ann. d. Chem.* CDLXXXIX. 269], a compound, $C_{28}H_{44}O$, made by the ultraviolet irradiation of ergosterol and added to dairy products; also called *calciferol* or *ergocalciferol*; *vitamin* D_3 [named in Ger. by A. Windaus et al. 1936, in *Zeitschr. f. physiol. Chem.* CCXLI. 102], a closely related compound, $C_{27}H_{44}O$, formed in the skin by ultraviolet light and present in egg-yolk, liver, and fish-liver oils; also called *cholecalciferol*; **vitamin E** = *tocopherol; **vitamin G** chiefly *U.S.* = *vitamin* B_2 above; now *rare*; **vitamin H** [named in Ger. by P. Györgi 1931, in *Zeitschr. f. ärztliche Fortbildung* XXVIII. 379/2, f. *haut* skin] = *biotin; **vitamin K,** either or both of two related fat-soluble derivatives of naphthoquinone, *vitamin* K_1 (= *phylloquinone) and *vitamin* K_2 (menaquinone, $C_{41}H_{56}O_2$), one or other of which is required for proper clotting of the blood, the former occurring in green vegetables and the latter being synthesized by intestinal bacteria; **vitamin P,** any or all of the flavonoids present in food plants, formerly thought to be necessary in the diet for the integrity of the capillaries.

1920 Vitamin A [see sense 1 a above]. **1937** J. R. Edisbury in *Nature* 7 Aug. 234/1 A substance apparently identical with the 693 mμ chromogen can replace the vitamin A of rhodopsin without loss of physiological function... It..seems desirable provisionally to designate as 'vitamin A_2' the 693 mμ chromogen. **1950** [see *retinene]. **1960**, etc. [see *retinol[2]]. **1968** A. White et al. *Princ. Biochem.* (ed. 4) xl. 906 Vitamin A_2 differs from A_1 by having one additional conjugated double bond in the ring. **1976** H. R. Schiffman *Sensation & Perception* xii. 184/2 When the eye is kept in the dark, vitamin A joins with opsin to reconstitute rhodopsin. **1982** S. G. Chaney in T. M. Devlin *Textbk. Biochem.* xxvi. 1202 Vitamin A is also apparently required for mobilization of iron from the liver.

1920 *Brit. Med. Jrnl.* 31 July 151/1 The water-soluble B vitamine in rice polishings is very stable. **1920** [see sense 1 a above]. **1934** *Nature* 31 Mar. 498/2 The view has already been considered..that these two classes of dissimilar skin changes are to be ascribed to a deficiency not only of vitamin B_2 but also of another component of the vitamin B complex. **1953** D. M. Dunlop et al. *Textbk. Med. Treatment* (ed. 6) 398 Three other components of the vitamin B complex have been reported to have therapeutic effects; pantothenic acid.., pyridoxin..and biotin. **1967** *Martindale's Extra Pharmacopoeia* (ed. 25) 122/1 Dried yeast is used for the prevention and treatment of vitamin B deficiency. **1969** R. F. Chapman *Insects* v. 74 The B vitamins thiamine, riboflavin, nicotinic acid, pyridoxine and pantothenic acid are essential to most insects. **1983** A. Tull *Food & Nutrition* i. 22/2 Like the other B vitamins..nicotinic acid is also an important factor in the release of energy from food..by oxidation.

1928 Chick & Roscoe in *Biochem. Jrnl.* XXII. 790 Experiments..confirmed the conclusion of Goldberger and his colleagues..that the water-soluble B vitamin.. had two components. (1) Vitamin B_1, or the antineuritic, less heat-stable vitamin... (2) Vitamin B_2, a more heat-stable vitamin..in the absence of which the animal fails to grow. **1955** *Sci. News Let.* 26 Mar. 194/1 In each group some mothers got vitamin C (ascorbic acid) pills; some got thiamine, or vitamin B-1 pills; some got pills containing thiamine, iron, and riboflavin and niacinamide which are B vitamins; and some got placebos. **1974** Passmore & Robson *Compan. Med. Stud.* III. xxiv. 26/2 Both wet and dry beriberi occur among chronic alcoholics whose diet can be deficient in vitamin B_1.

1928 Vitamin B_2 [see *vitamin* B_1 above]. **1933** *Jrnl. Amer. Chem. Soc.* LV. 2927 Several similarities suggest its close relationship [*sc.* that of pantothenic acid] to vitamin G (B_2). **1934** [see *vitamin B* above]. **1967** H. A. Guthrie *Introd. Nutrition* xii. 236/1 Riboflavin, which has also been known as vitamin B_2, vitamin G, and the yellow vitamin, was recognized in 1917 when it became clear that vitamin B retained some growth-promoting properties after its anti-beriberi properties had been destroyed by heat.

1934 P. György in *Nature* 31 Mar. 499/1 We have for the time being named this 'rat pellagra preventive factor' in its narrow sense vitamin B_6. **1955** D. M. Hegsted in F. C. Blanck *Handbk. Food & Agric.* ix. 292 The natural occurring deficiency of vitamin B_6 has probably not been seen in any species other than recent reports of its development in infants fed certain prepared formulas. **1970** [see *pyridoxine]. **1970** [see *pyridoxamine]. **1974** [see *pyridoxal]. **1983** J. Katz in Kaye & Rose *Fund. Internal Med.* cxxxvi. 904/1 Dietary and primary pyridoxine (vitamin B_6) deficiencies are rare.

1948 M. S. Shorb in *Science* 16 Apr. 397/1 A crystalline compound, vitamin B_{12}, has been isolated from liver..and has been shown to be highly active hematopoietically.. upon cases of pernicious anemia. **1950**, etc. [see *cobalamin]. **1961** *New Scientist* 23 Feb. 457/2 The cobalt..had a selective action. Experiments showed that it was taken up by the flora of the rumen of sheep and cattle in the synthesis of vitamin B_{12}. **1982** S. G. Chaney in T. M. Devlin *Textbk. Biochem.* xxvi. 1225 The liver stores up to a 6-year supply of vitamin B_{12}. Thus, deficiencies..are extremely rare.

[**1919** J. C. Drummond in *Biochem. Jrnl.* XIII. 77 The diet has been seriously, if not totally, deficient in the anti-scorbutic factor or 'water-soluble C'.] **1920** [see sense 1 a above]. **1921** *Jrnl. Industr. & Engin. Chem.* Dec. 1115/1 We know that the antiscorbutic vitamine is water-soluble; indeed, it has been called the water-soluble C vitamine. **1942** *Ann. Reg. 1941* 344 Work on prothrombin, vitamins C, K, and P,..greatly advanced knowledge of haemorrhagic diseases. **1966** E. Birney *Selected Poems* II. 61 A hotelroom all to myself with a fan and a box of Vitamin C. **1983** *Oxf. Textbk. Med.* I. viii. 24/2 There is no convincing evidence for the claims that large doses of vitamin C (4 g or more daily) prevent or decrease severity of the common cold; the evidence for protection against cancer is stronger, but not conclusive.

1921 Funk & Dubin in *Proc. Soc. Exper. Biol. & Med.* XIX. 15 It is possible in most cases to effect an almost quantitative separation of the B-vitamine..from another substance, which we provisionally have called vitamine D. **1928** [see *ergosterol]. **1932** *Chem. Abstr.* XXVI. 1015 The isolation of cryst. vitamin D_1. *Ibid.*, An added note states that vitamin D_2 has been isolated. **1936** *Ibid.* XXX. 6423 The name vitamin D_3 is proposed for this substance. **1953** Fruton & Simmonds *Gen. Biochem.* xxxviii. 903 The term vitamin D_1 has been discarded since the material to which it was first applied has been found to be a mixture of calciferol and several sterols. **1976** H. Campion et al. in B. E. C. Nordin *Calcium, Phosphate & Mineral Metabolism* xii. 445 The compounds known as vitamin D have in common a unique arrangement of three carbon-carbon double bonds, two of which connect a hydroxylated cyclohexane ring to a substituted hydrindane system. **1983** *Oxf. Textbk. Med.* I. x. 44/2 In most respects these vitamin Ds are comparable in their metabolism and their actions.

1925 H. M. Evans in *Proc. Nat. Acad. Sci.* XI. 373 The evidence..is thus conclusively in favor of the existence of a new vitamine or food accessory to which the designation of fat soluble E may be given. [*Note*] We have adopted the letter E as the next serial alphabetic designation, the antirachitic artanine now being known as D. **1948** Martin & Hynes *Clin. Endocrinol.* viii. 157 Vitamin E deficiency..produces loss of sperm-motility in rats and is followed by atrophy of spermatogenic tissue and final loss of the sex instincts. **1968**, etc. [see *tocopherol]. **1983** *Oxf. Textbk. Med.* II. xix. 75/2 Vitamin E is necessary to prevent auto-oxidation of the unsaturated fatty acids in the red cell membrane.

1929 Sherman & Sandels in *Proc. Soc. Exper. Biol. & Med.* XXVI. 536 Experiments with reference to the more heat-stable factor of the vitamin B group (factor P-P, vitamin B_2 or G). **1934** *Jrnl. Biol. Chem.* CVI. 433 The vitamin G concentrate..was prepared by extracting hog livers with boiling water, [etc.]. **1949** R. A. & W. A. Gortner *Outl. Biochem.* (ed. 3) xxxvi. 925 Riboflavin (lactoflavin or ovoflavin or vitamin G) is 6,7-dimethylisoalloxazine-9-D-riboside. **1967** Vitamin G [see *vitamin* B_2 above].

1937 L. E. Booher in *Jrnl. Biol. Chem.* CXIX. 223 The vitamin concerned..is a relatively heat-stable component of the vitamin B complex... It will be referred to here as vitamin H. **1959** Vitamin H [see *egg-white].

1935 H. Dam in *Nature* 27 Apr. 653/1, I therefore suggest the term vitamin K for the antihæmorrhagic factor. **1939** *Jrnl. Amer. Chem. Soc.* LXI. 1295/1 (*heading*) The isolation of vitamins K_1 and K_2. **1939**, etc. [see *phylloquinone]. **1947** *Radiology* XLIX. 304/1 Vitamin K and transfusions of whole blood were ineffective in reducing clotting time. **1975** J. Marks *Guide to Vitamins* 71 Domestic animals suffering from warfarin poisoning should be treated with vitamin K_1. **1983** J. Katz in Kaye & Rose *Fund. Internal Med.* cxxxvi. 905/2 A deficiency of vitamin K cannot occur solely from an inadequate diet. Intestinal bacteria synthesize the vitamin.

1936 Rusznyák & Szent-Györgyi in *Nature* 4 July 27/2 We propose to give the name 'vitamin P' to the substance responsible for the action on vascular permeability. **1949** [see *flavonoid]. **1955** [see *citrin]. **1969** *Brit. Med. Jrnl.* 25 Jan. 235/1 No condition representing lack of vitamin P has ever been satisfactorily demonstrated. **1978** F. H. Meyers et al. *Rev. Med. Pharmacol.* (ed. 6) xli. 449/1 The flavonoids or vitamin P are of interest in relation to the question of how drug efficacy is evaluated rather than because of any nutritional effect.

3. *attrib.* and *Comb.*, as *vitamin capsule, cream, deficiency, pill, shot* (*shot *sb.*[1] 7 g (a)), *tablet, therapy*; *vitamin-containing, -enriched, -free, -poor, -rich* adjs.

1958 *Listener* 2 Oct. 523/1 Perhaps all those compact references at the foot of the page..are vitamin capsules of chapter for verse to insatiable scholars. **1965** M. Spark *Mandelbaum Gate* iii. 61 Freddy..carried small red vitamin capsules about with him to swallow after meals taken outside the British Isles. **1921** *Conquest* Sept. 498/2 The only safe rule is this..eat vitamine-containing food on every possible occasion..and avoid, as far as practicable, vitamine-free foods. **1938** *Encycl. Brit. Bk. of Year* 588/1 Preparations that have but recently come to the fore include..the group of hormone and vitamin creams, etc., known collectively as 'biological' preparations. **1979** P. Ferris *Talk to me about England* III. 133 She took the vitamin cream. **1920** *Brit. Med. Jrnl.* 31 July 147/1 It is ..still a hypothesis that the particular disease depends upon vitamine deficiency. **1946** R. Lehmann *Gypsy's Baby* 149 My *brain*..just doesn't *function* any more. Don't you think it's some vitamin deficiency? **1980** *Times* 15 Dec. 1/3 One of the hunger strikers..is in danger of irreversible loss of sight because of a vitamin deficiency. **1961** *Which?* Oct. 270/1 Wholemeal biscuits with a vitamin-enriched filling. **1921** Vitamin-free [see *vitamin-containing* above]. **1956** *Nature* 11 Feb. 271/1 Aerated cultures of *B. cereus* 569H were grown at 36° on..vitamin-free casein hydrolysate. **1945** N. Mitford *Pursuit of Love* xv. 121 A packing-case full of vitamin pills. **1981** D. Uhnak *False Witness* (1982) xi. 90 The customers..gulped down vitamin pills with swallows of juice. **1973** T. Pynchon *Gravity's Rainbow* (1975) I. 170 Nasty little fangs achop and looking to ulcerate the vitamin-poor tissue they came from. **1923** *Jrnl. Biol. Chem.* LVI. 333 The fat-soluble, vitamin-rich ration. **1944** J. S. Huxley *On Living in Revolution* 31 Sweeping measures of social security and welfare—..subsidized housing and vitamin-rich food for the under-privileged,..and so on. **1971** J. Philips *Escape a Killer* (1972) I. ii. 25, I always feel as if I'd had a vitamin shot when you turn up. **1980** J. Gardner *Garden of Weapons* II. iii. 139 Mistochenkov looked in startlingly good health. 'It's the vitamin shots they're giving me,' he told Herbie. **1951** M. Kennedy *Lucy Carmichael* II. i. 76 She..ended by saying I didn't look very well and she would send me some vitamin tablets. **1982** M. McMullen *Better Off Dead* II. xiv. 171 A little saucer was placed before him with his vitamin tablets, the B-complex and the C. **1969** *Listener* 1 May 627/2 He thinks the cure of Tobit's blindness must have been either a colossal coincidence or a primeval case of vitamin therapy, by the liberal administration of fish-guts. **1972** Vitamin therapy [see *perceptual *a.*].

Hence **vitami·nic** *a.*, pertaining to or containing a vitamin or vitamins; **vi·taminless** *a.* (*rare*); **vita·minous** *a.* (*rare*), vitaminic; also *fig.*

1914 *Nature* 12 Mar. 42/1 Vitaminous foods are fresh milk.., whole grains, potatoes, [etc.]. *Ibid.*, Such vitamineless foods as sterilised milk,..starch, and sugar. **1926** *Chambers's Jrnl.* Apr. 291/2 The milk tends to become less and less valuable from the point of view of vitaminic value. **1931** C. J. HOLMES *Gram. Arts* iii. 27 Life..is the essential thing..and we must not starve ourselves of this vitaminous element. **1980** *Acta Vitaminologica et Enzymologica* II. 75 Drug induced avitaminoses are produced more easily and are more severe if the devitaminizing power of the drug and its dosage are high.. and the vitaminic status of the patient is not optimal.

vitaminize (vi·tăminəiz), *v.* [f. prec. + -IZE.] *trans.* To add a vitamin or vitamins to (food, esp. food that lacks the vitamin concerned). Also *absol.* and *fig.* Chiefly as **vi·taminized** *ppl. a.* Also **vi:taminiza·tion,** the treatment of food in this way; **vi·taminizing** *ppl. a.*

1930 *Observer* 13 Apr. 7 Adventure, we are told, is the 'vitaminizing element' in history. **1940** *Economist* 27 Apr. 762/2 A diet of vegetables..milk, butter or vitaminised margarine..brown bread and cheese. **1942** *Endeavour* Jan. 30/2 The compulsory 'vitaminization' of margarine that has taken place since the war has merely been an extension to the whole margarine output of a practice already in partial operation. **1944** *Ourselves in Wartime* 153 Margarine was 'vitaminized', so that all categories, even the cheapest varieties, were equal in vitamin value to butter. **1960** 'R. GORDON' *Doctor in Clover* xi. 92 He has taken his vitaminised milk and played *Clair de Lune* twice on the piano. **1968** M. PYKE *Food & Society* iii. 32 Government regulations enforcing the fluoridization of drinking water or the vitaminization of margarine. **1968** M. WOODHOUSE *Rock Baby* iii. 25 You've a home-grown, vitaminized, tall-walking, all-American boy. **1970** *R. Soc. Health Jrnl.* XC. 24/1 It had been decided to vitaminize to such a level that in respect of A and D the margarine would be equal to summer butter. **1975** *Islander* (Victoria, B.C.) 3 Aug. 8/2 Vitaminized canned juices.

Vitaphone (vəi·tăfōun). Chiefly *U.S.* Also **vitaphone.** [f. L. *vita* life + PHONE *sb.*^{1}]. A process of sound film recording in which the sound track is recorded on discs and played in synchronization with the projection of the film; also, sound films made by this method. Now *disused.*

1926 *Westm. Gaz.* 20 Sept. 7/2 A method of talking-motion pictures has been developed in America. The invention is called the vitaphone... It is claimed that the synchronisation of picture and voice..is perfect. **1948** M. QUIGLY *Magic Shadows* xvii. 160 Thirty years later, magic shadow history was made... The event was the premiere of 'The Jazz Singer', starring Al Jolson and presenting the Vitaphone system of talking motion pictures. **1976** *Islander* (Victoria, B.C.) 8 Aug. 13/2 To begin with two types of sound pictures were made—Movietone and Vitaphone. **1977** *Amer. Film* Oct. 27/1 Warner theaters in every major American city were wired for Vitaphone.

vitello-. Add: **vite:lloge·nesis,** the formation of the vitellus; **vite:llogene·tic, -ge·nic** *adjs.* = VITELLOGENOUS *a.*; **vite:lloge·nin** [-IN^1], a blood-borne protein from which the substance of the vitellus is made; **vite·llophag** (-fæg), **-phage** (-fēidʒ) *Ent.* [Gr. -φαγος eating], a nucleus or energid which, during cleavage and the formation of blastoderm, remains in or moves into the vitellus and assimilates it.

1956 *Nature* 11 Feb. 277/1 (*in table*) All [honey-bee ovaries] fully regressed; no commencement of vitellogenesis. **1974** *Ibid.* 4 Jan. 72/2 Some fish are not fully regressed and have ovaries in early stages of vitellogenesis. **1961** *Biol. Abstr.* XXXVI. 1333/1 (*heading*) Vitellogenetic processes of *A. depilans* observed by electron microscopy with further considerations on the Golgi apparatus. **1978** *Nature* 23 Mar. 351/2 The last female revealed no chorionated eggs and only four late vitellogenetic proximal oocytes..in the ovarioles. **1964** *Symp. R. Entomol. Soc.* II. 37 In *Drosophila*, one vitellogenic oocyte is normally found in each ovariole. **1974** *Nature* 4 Jan. 71/2 The induction of sexual behaviour in female goldfish..by injection of ovulated eggs into the ovarian lumen of individuals with vitellogenic ovaries. **1969** *Jrnl. Insect Physiol.* XV. 1279 Two immunochemically discrete protein yolk precursors or vitellogenins appear in the blood of adult *Periplaneta americana* on day 4 or 5 after emergence. **1973** *Nature* 13 July 103/2 Insect yolk proteins, or vitellogenins, are synthesized and secreted by the fat body. **1982** *Sci. Amer.* Nov. 139/3 In the liver [of the garter snake] the phospholipids are incorporated into a lipophosphoprotein known as vitellogenin. **1892** J. P. MCMURRICH in *Zool. Anzeiger* XV. 274 In the same manner the endoderm cells are excluded from the surface of the egg, but in this case there is an actual immigration, the cells sinking down into the interior of the yolk, and becoming 'vitellophags'. **1904** [in Dict.]. **1935** [see *PRESUMPTIVE *a.* 3 b]. **1978** R. J. ELZINGA *Fund. Entomol.* iv. 86 Some of these nuclei remain behind to become vitellophags, cells for metabolizing yolk for embryonic use.

vitex (vəi·teks). [L. name used by Pliny for *Vitex agnus-castus* or a similar shrub, later adopted as a generic name by Linnæus and earlier botanists.] A deciduous shrub or small tree, often aromatic, of the genus of the same name, belonging to the family Verbenaceæ. Cf. AGNUS CASTUS.

1608 TOPSELL *Serpents* 37 The leaves of *Vitex*.. being cast on the coales for a fumigation, doe with theyr vapour chase away venomous beastes. **1829** [see *CLERODENDRUM]. **1955** E. POUND *Classic Anthol.* I. 71 Vitex in swamp ground, Branched loveliness..Vitex negundo, casting thy flowers in air. **1976** *Hortus Third* (L. H. Bailey Hortorium) 1161/2 Vitexes do well in any good soil.

vitiating, *ppl. a.* (In Dict. s.v. VITIATE *v.*) (Earlier example.)

1832 J. S. MILL in *Monthly Repos.* VI. 658 After all which has been done to break down these vitiating, soul-debasing prejudices,..where are we now?

vitiligo. Delete 'a species of leprosy' and add: In mod. use, a skin disease whose only manifestation is the post-natal development of sharply defined white patches that tend to grow in size. (Further examples.)

1842 E. WILSON *Pract. & Theoret. Treat. Dis. Skin* xii. 280 Vitiligo is the designation applied to partial leucopathia, or the diminution or absence of pigmentary secretion upon one or more parts of the body. **1855** G. B. WOOD *Treat. Pract. Med.* (ed. 4) II. 460 Vitiligo.—This term..has received various applications. Celsus embraced under it different forms of what are now known as lepra and psoriasis, and another affection which is probably identical with the *lupus non exedeus* of modern writers. **1874** W. TAY tr. *Hebra & Kaposi's Dis. Skin* III. xli. 174 The want of pigment at one time represents a substantive anomaly of formation, or a morbus *sui generis* and a wholly insignificant condition (Vitiligo alba levior, Celsus), and, at another time, forms a part of the phenomena of a very intense, constitutional disease, namely, Elphantiasis Græcorum (Vitiligo alba gravior, Celsus). *Ibid.* 176 According to the latter expressions [of Celsus], we might consider vitiligo to mean Psoriasis or Eczema.., or Elephantiasis Græcorum. In fact, these words have led to the great confusion which has existed even up to the present time..as to this matter. *Ibid.* 177 Most writers..have not been able to ignore the original meaning of Vitiligo as indicating a want of pigment, and make use of the expression to designate partial Achroma. **1887** T. M. ANDERSON *Treat. Dis. Skin* 28 Some cases of true Leprosy may be mistaken for Vitiligo. **1907** *Lancet* 16 Feb. 407/2 Leucoderma or vitiligo is doubtless familiar to you all. **1976** *Ibid.* 4 Dec. 1248/1 Since 1974 she had had psoriasis, vitiligo, and recurrent herpes labialis. **1979** E. L. RHODES *Dermatology for Physician* ii. 9/1 Although pale patches on the skin may follow eczema, psoriasis, pityriasis rosea and pityriasis_versicolor, the patches of vitiligo are absolutely white.

vitrain (vi·trēin). [f. L. *vitr-eus* VITREOUS *a.* + *-ain* in *FUSAIN (sense 2).] A black, highly lustrous, and often brittle type of coal.

1919, etc. [see *CLARAIN]. **1930** [see *DURAIN]. **1975** D. G. MURCHISON et al. tr. *E. Stach's Textbk. Coal Petrol.* v. 334 The first step..is the crushing of the run-of-mine coal... When a seam contains thick layers of bright coal, the soft and mostly brittle vitrain concentrates in the smalls, below 10 mm.

vitrectomy (vitre·ktŏmi). *Surg.* [f. VITRE(OUS *a.* + -ECTOMY.] The operation of removing the vitreous fluid from the eyeball and replacing it with another fluid.

1968 D. KASNER in *Highlights Ophthalm.* XI. 304 (*heading*) Vitrectomy: a new approach to the management of vitreous. **1975** *Courier-Mail* (Brisbane) 5 Nov. 18/6 She is the first woman in Western Australia to have the operation, known as a vitrectomy, which restored her sight. **1983** *Oxf. Textbk. Med.* I. IX. 32/2 Recently, vitrectomy has developed as a treatment for blindness from unresolved vitreous haemorrhage and as a treatment of retinal detachment subsequent to vitreous haemorrhage.

Vitremanie (vītrəmani). [f. F. *vitre* window-pane + *manie* fad.] A process of decorating window panes by the application of coloured designs in imitation of stained glass, popular in the Victorian period.

1881 *Sylvia's Bk. Artistic Knicknacks* 324 The art of vitremanie—the decoration of glass windows, &c., by the application of coloured designs so as to resemble stained-glass—is a modern invention. *Ibid.* Vitremanie may be applied to exclude unpleasing views seen through staircase or other windows. **1961** J. GLOAG *Victorian Comfort* ii. 36 A form of window decoration called 'Vitremanie', which was applied to glass 'to exclude unpleasing views'.

Vitreosil (vi·trĭosil). Also **vitreosil.** [f. VITREO(US *a.* + SIL(ICA.] A proprietary name for vitreous silica.

1909 *Trade Marks Jrnl.* 15 Dec. 2050 *Vitreosil*... Fused silica articles included in Class 15 in the form of tubes, plates, basins..and other shapes for chemical, electrical, ornamental and other similar purposes. The Thermal Syndicate, Limited,..Wallsend-on-Tyne. **1921** *Chambers's Jrnl.* 26 Mar. 272/1 Vitreosil..is composed of pure silica fused in the electric furnace by a special process. **1938** *Jrnl. R. Aeronaut. Soc.* XLII. 822 Hollow tubes of vitreosil were wound internally with spiral heating coils. **1973** *Nature* 27 July 233/1 Each portion was placed on defatted lens paper on a stainless steel mesh grid in a vitreosil dish containing Trowell's T-8 medium.

vitreous, *a.* Add: **1. a.** *vitreous silica*, an amorphous, translucent or transparent form of silica obtained by rapid quenching from the molten state.

1925 J. W. MELLOR *Comprehensive Treat. Inorg. & Theoret. Chem.* VI. xl. 288 Various names are applied to the vitrified quartz—thus, quartz-glass, vitreous-silica, fused quartz,..etc. **1971** *Materials & Technol.* II. i. 22 Transparent vitreous silica is used for the production of lenses..and other optical elements which are required to transmit ultraviolet or infra-red rays.

e. *vitreous enamel*: = ENAMEL *sb.* 1 a, *porcelain enamel* s.v. *PORCELAIN 5. So *vitreous-enamelled* adj., *vitreous enamelling.*

1916 *Chem. Abstr.* X. 261 (*heading*) Vitreous enamels or glazes for pottery, etc. **1939** BURNS & SCHUH *Protective Coatings for Metals* xvi. 381 Vitreous or porcelain enamels are essentially fused silicates or glasses holding in suspension a colloidal dispersion of color oxides, opacifiers and gases. **1963** G. S. BRADY *Materials Handbk.* (ed. 9) 281 Vitreous enameled metals are used for cooking utensils, signs, chemical tanks and piping, [etc.]. **1977** R. B. ROSS *Handbk. Metal Treatments & Testing* 389 Vitreous enamelling was very popular in late nineteenth and early twentieth centuries. With the advent of new materials, for example, aluminium in cooking ware,..the use of vitreous enamel declined and was confined very largely to articles such as baths. **1984** WORTHINGTON & KNIGHT *Home Plumbing* 96/1 Modern materials are less resistant to abrasives than the traditional vitreous enamel.

vitric (vi·trik), *a. Geol.* [f. L. *vitr-um* glass + -IC.] Of tuff: composed chiefly of glassy material.

1915 L. V. PIRSSON in *Amer. Jrnl. Sci.* CXC. 193 The use of 'vitric' and 'lithic' is suggested instead of the more common 'glassy' and 'stony' in order to avoid the misapprehension that the outward appearance of the material is referred to. **1976** *Nature* 5 Aug. 461/2 The other vertebrate remains are confined to the uppermost 30 m of aeolian tuffs beneath a widespread pale yellow vitric tuff.

vitrine, *sb.* (Earlier example.)

1880 C. SCHREIBER *Jrnl.* 19 Nov. (1911) II. 328 A small ornament... I believe it to be Spanish, [but]..I only saw it as it lay in the vitrine at the Exposition.

vitrinite (vi·trinəit). [f. *VITR(AIN + *-inite* (f. -IN^1 + -ITE^1).] One of the three major kinds of maceral that go to make up humic coal, rich in oxygen and characteristic of vitrain.

1935 M. C. STOPES in *Fuel* XIV. 11 It is now proposed to give to the individual 'macerals' a distinctive set of descriptive names with the termination *-inite*... The basis of the grouping is very simple and the names logical; and the whole therefore can easily be built up from: Rock types... Vitrain..Fusain..Clarain..Durain. Macerals... Vitrinite..Fusinite..[etc.]. **1955** *Sci. Amer.* July 62/1 The broadest attack on the problem was launched in 1951 by the British Coal Utilization Research Association, which set out to analyze..a series of vitrinites—bright black coal particles—from typical coals. **1964** *Fuel* XLIII. 123 It is..suggested that the reflectance of vitrinite A occurring in the whole coal may provide the best available index of rank. **1978** *Nature* 7 Dec. 598/1 The most common methods of estimating the degree of thermal alteration [of petroleum source rocks] are based on measurements of the residual insoluble organic material in rocks. Some of the more common methods use.. electron spin resonance, kerogen coloration and vitrinite reflectance.

Vitrolite (vi·trŏləit). Also **vitro-.** [f. L. *vitr-um* glass + -O + -LITE.] A proprietary name for opal glass.

1937 *Times* 19 Oct. 11/3 A glass floor has been laid, and glass pictures have been hung, and a bathroom lined with vitrolite is being built. **1939** *Trade Marks Jrnl.* 1 Feb. 147/1 *Vitrolite*... Opal and opaline glass. Pilkington Brothers Limited,..Liverpool, 2; glass manufacturers. **1954** *Archit. Rev.* CXVI. 268/1 Such an atmosphere is not created by stove-enamelled hardboard, vitrolite and chromium-plated barrier rails, the language of the cafeteria. **1975** [see *OPALITE].

Vittel (vite·l). The proprietary name of a type of mineral water obtained from springs in the neighbourhood of the town of *Vittel* in the Vosges department of France. Also *Vittel water.*

1895 *Army & Navy Co-op. Soc. Price List* 23 Natural mineral waters..Vichy..Vittel..Wiesbaden. **1909** *Trade Marks Jrnl.* 26 May 901 *Vittel*... A natural mineral water. Société Générale des Eaux Minérales de Vittel,..Vittel, Vosges, France. **1974** N. FREELING *Dressing of Diamond* 76 Carafe of Beaujolais and a bottle of Vittel. **1975** —— *What are Bugles blowing For?* i. 4 He..drank a little Vittel water and went to bed. **1979** 'M. HEBDEN' *Death set to Music* iii. 29, I ought to have had Vittel water, not wine.

vituperous. Delete ? *Obs.* and add: **1, 2.** (Later examples.)

1914 R. M. JONES *Spiritual Reformers 16th & 17th Cent.* v. 69 Schwenckfeld was denounced in the most vituperous language of the period. **1959** *Times Lit. Suppl.* 10 July 409/3 Venetia..watches with relief Karlo's vituperous and vulgar exit.

vivace, *adv.* (and *sb.*). Add: **a.** Also with the *adv.* used quasi-adjectivally to characterize musical composition.

1922 D. H. LAWRENCE *Aaron's Rod* xiii. 187 Lady Franks started with a *vivace* Schumann piece. *Ibid.* 188 'I always prefer Schumann in his *vivace* moods,' said Aaron.

b. as *sb.* A passage intended to be performed in this manner (see also quot. 1889 in Dict.).

1683 [see *ALLEGRO B, C]. **1922** D. H. LAWRENCE *Aaron's Rod* xiii. 188 Our Colonel began to..bounce in his chair,..doing a sitting-down jig to the Schumann *vivace.* **1959** *Times* 11 Sept. 10/6 He moved into the ensuing *vivace* with unhurried moderation. **1976** *Gramophone* Sept. 410/1 The movement's main *vivace* is a good deal less mettlesome.

vivandier. Add: (Examples of form *vivandière.*)

1848 H. GREVILLE *Diary* 29 June (1883) I. 278 Women went about disguised as *vivandières*, giving poisoned brandy to the soldiers. **1896** D. BINGHAM *Recoll. Paris* I. xiii. 221 Madame de Beaulieu..joined the Mobiles of her native province in the capacity of *vivandière.* **1963** P. FLEMING *Kolchak* xiii. 149 They were often companioned by their own or other men's wives or by ladies who played, sometimes usefully, a role roughly corresponding to the *vivandière's*.

vivarium. Add: **2. b.** Now usu. = TERRARIUM. (Earlier and further examples.)

1853 GEO. ELIOT *Let.* 13 June (1954) II. 103, I was at the Zoological gardens..and saw..the marine queerities in the Vivarium. **1958** H. N. HUMPHREYS *Butterfly Vivarium* i. 2, I am about to describe a novel kind of Vivarium, by means of which another and very distinct class of animal life—that of the 'world of insects'—may be made to exhibit its wonders. **1914** W. P. WESTELL *Boys' Bk. Pets* xvi. 217 Another type of vivarium may be constructed on similar lines to the rectangular aquarium, only making it a few inches deeper. **1978** *Nature* 19 Oct. 646/2 Lizards were housed in vivaria in a constant temperature room.

vivax (vəi·væks). *Med.* [L., = 'long-lived'.] The specific name of a protozoon of the genus *Plasmodium*, used *absol.* and *attrib.* to denote the organism and *attrib.* with reference to the relapsing type of malaria it causes, in which paroxysms occur every third day and which is usually not fatal. Freq. printed in italic.

1930 [see *FALCIPARUM]. **1946** *Jrnl. Amer. Med. Assoc.* 20 July 964/1 The patients were military personnel who had acquired vivax infections in the Pacific or Mediterranean theaters of operation. **1955** *Sci. News Let.* 23 July 52/1 The Negro seems to have a general resistance to strains of vivax from all areas. **1958** N. F. LEOPOLD *Life plus 99 Years* xxi. 321 *Vivax* malaria is also known as tertian malaria because, once the trophozoites have fallen into step and got synchronized, they sporulate every forty-eight hours. **1983** *Oxf. Textbk. Med.* I. v. 394/2 The vivax resistance factor [in many black Africans] is a blood group determinant.

‖ **vive** (vīv), *int.* [Fr., lit. 'may he (she, it) live': cf. VIVA *sb.*[1] and *int.*] **1. a.** *vive le roi* (vīv lə rwa) = *long live the king* s.v. LIVE *v.*[1] 9, used as a general acclamation to or for a sovereign. Similarly *vive l'empéreur*.

?**1594** MARLOWE *Massacre at Paris* sig. B7, *Sound trumpets within, and then all crye* Viue le Roy. *a* **1700** EVELYN *Diary* an. 1651 (1955) III. 42 The King..saluting the Ladys & Acclamators who had fill'd the Windos with their beauty, & the aire with *Vive Le Roy.* **1768** STERNE *Sentimental Journey* I. 114 Here's a couple of sous for thee—*Vive le Roi!* said the old soldier. **1815** F. BURNEY *Let.* Mar. in *Jrnls. & Lett.* (1980) VIII. 76 There was no species of enthusiasm, but..moderate cries of *Vive le roi.* **1848** E. B. BROWNING *Let.* 4 July (1897) I. v. 375 How did you feel when the cry was raised, 'Vive l'Empereur'? **1861** G. MEREDITH *Let.* 19 Nov. (1970) I. 115 The Emperor allows her £1000 a year: her mother gets £2000. *Vive l'Empereur!* **1896** C. M. YONGE *Release* II. iii. 104 Ecstatic cries of '*Vive le Roi*' broke from the populace.

b. *vive la bagatelle* (vīv la bagatel), 'success to frivolity or nonsense', an exclamation denoting a carefree attitude to life.

1732 SWIFT *Let.* 10 July in *Lit. Corr.* (1741) 150 All for want of my Rule, *Vive la bagatelle!* **1760** STERNE *Tristram Shandy* I. xix. 121 The footing of mere whims, and of a *vive la Bagatelle.* **1880** *Girl's Own Paper* 27 Nov. 144/3 *Vive la bagatelle* means 'Success to trifling'. Not a good sentiment. **1915** J. WEBSTER in *Century Mag.* Sept. 492/1, I seem to have covered a lot of paper without telling you much. *Vive la bagatelle!* **1948** M. ALLINGHAM *More Work for Undertaker* xxiii. 260 (*heading*) Vive la bagatelle!

c. Used in other phrases denoting extreme approval or enthusiasm or as a cry of acclamation. Also *joc.*

1865 G. MEREDITH *Let.* 11 Aug. (1970) I. 315 My mind is free, and vive la liberté! **1889** E. DOWSON *Let.* 24 Mar. (1967) 55 Have just finished my poulet. Vive la jeunesse: it has actually lasted 3 weeks. **1906** [see *BAN *sb.*[3]]. **1914** 'BARTIMEUS' *Naval Occasions* xi. 81 Well!..*Vive le sport!* If there were no fools there'd be no fun. **1922** E. E. CUMMINGS *Enormous Room* viii. 176 *Vive la bourgeoisie*, I said to myself. **1965** V. CANNING *Whip Hand* viii. 89 We all want to know where Mrs Vadarci is going, and you have—*vive l'amour*—a special contact there. **1980** C. Ross *Case for Compensation* v. 29 *Vive La France. Vive le sport* and where's my passport. I'm going.

d. *vive la différence* (vīv la diferañs), a *joc.* expression denoting approval of the difference between the sexes. Also in extended use. Occas. as *attrib. phr.*

1963 H. SLESAR *Bridge of Lions* (1964) xi. 164 It's your stock-in-trade, isn't it, youth and beauty? *Vive la différence*, and all that jazz. **1964** *Guardian* 21 Apr. 18/4 'Vive la difference' Tories are recognizably Tories, and Socialists are demonstrably Socialists. **1969** [see *JOCKETTE]. **1970** G. GREER *Female Eunuch* 29 Frenchmen may well cry 'Vive la différence', for it is cultivated unceasingly in all aspects of life. **1978** *Country Life* 3 Aug. 341/3 The control layout extends Citroen's *vive la différence* attitude.

2. *absol.* and as *sb.*

1919 D. H. LAWRENCE in *Athenæum* 11 Apr. 167/2 There is a new régime, sound of a new *Vive! vive!* **1922** JOYCE *Ulysses* 303 The even more excitable foreign delegates cheered vociferously in a medley of cries..*hiphip, vive, Allah.*

viverrid (vive·rid), *a.* and *sb. Zool.* [ad. mod.L. *Viverrid-æ*, f. L. *viverra* ferret: see -ID[3].] **A.** *adj.* Belonging or pertaining to the family Viverridæ, which comprises civets, genets, and mongooses. **B.** *sb.* A viverrid animal.

1910 H. F. OSBORN *Age of Mammals* iii. 197 Still more striking is the presence [in the Oligocene] of the fierce viverrid carnivores (*Amphictis, Herpestes*) of the modern civet and mongoose types. *Ibid.* iv. 259 The mustelids were becoming more numerous..while the Asiatic civets or viverrids (*Viverra*) are becoming somewhat more rare [in the Miocene]. **1964** PARKER & HASWELL *Text-bk. Zool.* (ed. 7) II. 795 The aberrant *Proteles*, the Aard-wolf or Earth-wolf of Africa is insectivorous... Like the hyænas it is obviously a highly specialised viverrid offshoot. **1976** *Nature* 5 Aug. 464/1 The carnivore fauna [of the Laetolil beds in Tanzania] is characterised by a high percentage of viverrids, constituting 32% of all the carnivore specimens.

‖ **viveur** (vivǒr). [Fr., lit. 'a living person'.] One who lives a fashionable and social life; a man of pleasure. Cf. *bon viveur* s.v. *BON *a.*

1845 THACKERAY in *Fraser's Mag.* Nov. 591/2 He became a *viveur* and jolly dog about town. **1901** 'L. MALET' *Hist. Sir Richard Calmady* III. x. 261 He has the credit of being something of a *viveur.* He knew not only his Paris, but his Baden-Baden, and his Naples, and various other warm corners where great and good men..congregate. **1921** L. STRACHEY *Queen Victoria* iii. 70 The middle-aged, hard-faced *viveur* was addressed by his young hostess. **1943** *Burlington Mag.* Aug. 201/1 Boulestin was secretary to Willy, the well-known Parisian author, journalist and *viveur*, husband to Colette.

vivianite. In etym. for 'J. G. *Vivian*' read: John Henry *Vivian* (1785–1855), of Truro and Swansea.

vivid, *a.* **2. b.** (Later example.)

1981 *Observer* 15 Nov. 2/8 The famous are shown offguard—for example,.. Sue Lawley using vivid language.

vivier (vivie). Delete † *Obs.*[−1] and add recent examples. Also *attrib.*

1964 F. WHITE *West of Rhone* ii. 31 Viviers, an old town,..was once the fish-ponds, the *viviers*, of the bishop. **1973** *Alderney Jrnl.* 8 Oct. 4 Much has been said about the politics of building vivier tanks at the end of the harbour jetty. **1979** *Guardian* 10 Oct. 12/6 The Dutch lorries..that buy shellfish from Harveys, are vivier lorries. They have huge water tanks full of sea water.

vivipary. Add: Also in *Zool.* (Further examples.)

1963 DAVIS & GOLLEY *Princ. Mammalogy* v. 118 Another approach is..to infer from changes in skull and jaw morphology the presence or absence of homeothermy..and vivipary. **1981** *Entomologica Generalis* VII. 13 Nothing..is known about the time when in the evolution of Aphidina vivipary has developed.

vivotoxin (vəi·votǫksin). *Biochem.* [f. *vivo-* (cf. VIVI-) + TOXIN.] A substance produced in an infected plant and involved in the disease process (see quot. 1953).

1953 DIMOND & WAGGONER in *Phytopathology* XLIII. 229/2 To clarify this situation a new term is suggested. A vivotoxin is defined as a substance produced in the infected host by the pathogen and/or its host, which functions in the production of disease, but is not itself the initial inciting agent of disease. **1971** *Agric. & Biol. Chem.* XXXV. 618/2 Vivotoxins are considered to be usually nonspecific to plant species. **1981** R. J. GREEN in M. E. Mace et al. *Fungal Wilt Dis. Plants* i. 11 Acceptance of the concept of the vivotoxin directed investigators to attempt to demonstrate toxins in the vascular tissues of the infected plants.

Viyella (vəi,e·lă). Also **viyella.** The proprietary name of a fabric made from a twilled mixture of cotton and wool; also, a garment made of this material. Freq. *attrib.*

1894 *Trade Marks Jrnl.* 6 June 471 *Viyella*... Yarns of wool, worsted or hair. William Hollins and company (Nottingham), Limited,..Nottingham; spinners. **1912** G. FRANKAU *One of Us* v. 41 No impious fingers groped in his Viyella. **1921** 'K. MANSFIELD' *Let.* 29 Aug. (1977) 229 That's the kind of stuff I meant, too. They had both better be lines with silver grey *viyella* or cashmere. **1932** R. LEHMANN *Invitation to Waltz* I. iii. 46 Cream viyella blouses, white piqué tennis skirts. **1942** *R.A.F. Jrnl.* 16 May 33 The pilot was wearing thick vest and pants, a Viyella shirt..and Mae West. **1969** E. MCGIRR *Entry of Death* iii. 51 She wears thick Viyella pyjamas. **1977** *Lancashire Life* Feb. 23/1 William Hollins' famous collection of mice, dressed in Viyella, that fabulous mixture of wool and cotton that keeps both mice and human mites warm in winter.

Vizeeree, var. *WAZIR[2].

vizsla (vi·ʃlă). The name of a town in Hungary used *absol.* to designate a golden-brown pointer with large pendent ears belonging to a breed developed in the region.

1945 C. L. B. HUBBARD *Observer's Bk. Dogs* 153 Of the five national breeds of dogs of Hungary, the Vizsla is the sole sporting dog. **1971** F. HAMILTON *World Encycl. Dogs* 208 The Vizsla has a lively, elegant and graceful gait. **1976** *Shooting Times & Country Mag.* 9–15 Dec. 52/1 Vizsla pups, excellent pedigree. **1977** J. WAMBAUGH *Black Marble* (1978) viii. 103 Letter openers bearing the likenesses of Vizslas and Brittany spaniels.

VJ (vī dʒēᶦ). [f. the initial letters of *V*ictory over *J*apan.] Used *attrib.* and *absol.* to denote the victory of the Allied forces over those of Japan during the war of 1939–45; esp. as *VJ-day*, designating either the day upon which Japan ceased fighting (14 August 1945) or the day of Japan's formal surrender (2 September 1945).

1944 [see *VE]. **1945** *Sun* (Baltimore) 15 June 1/8 (*heading*) 'V-J by Christmas' amazes Carlson. **1945** *Yank* 7 Sept. 9 The GIs had managed to keep their VJ spirit bottled up through most of the phony rumors, but when the real thing was popped, the cork popped with a vengeance. **1956** *B.B.C. Handbk.* 1957 169 VJ-day was recalled by the Overseas Services in a series of talks. **1968** *Listener* 19 Dec. 811/3 (*caption*) Revellers on V-J night. **1974** J. WAINWRIGHT *Hard Hit* 87 My memories ended with the war... Then—less than a week after V.J.—I married James. **1977** [see *VE]. **1978** *Jrnl. R. Soc. Arts* CXXVI. 252/1 On VJ night I was Station Duty Officer. **1982** T. FITZGIBBON *With Love* xi. 176 A little under a month after the first bomb on Hiroshima being dropped, VJ-Day as it was called was officially celebrated on 2 September 1945.

vladimirite (vlædimīᵊ·rəit). *Min.* [ad. Russ. *vladimirit* (E. I. Nefedev 1953, in *Zap. Mineral. Obshch.* LXXXII. 317), f. the name *Vladimir*: see -ITE[1].] A hydrated arsenate of calcium, $Ca_5H_2(AsO_4)_4.5H_2O$, occurring as colourless acicular monoclinic crystals.

1954 *Mineral. Abstr.* XII. 352 Vladimirite... Found in the zone of oxidation of ore deposits. **1972** [see *SAINFELDITE]. **1978** *Mineral. Rec.* IX. 73 Vladimirite... Fine, acicular, brilliant, colorless crystals in quartz cavities or with talmessite crusts were found in 1963 at the Irthem mine [in Morocco].

vlakte (fla·ktə). *S. Afr.* Pl. **vlaktes,** †**-en.** [Afrikaans, a. Du.] An extent of flat open country; a plain. Freq. *pl.*

1785 G. FORSTER tr. *Sparrman's Voy. Cape Good Hope* II. xiv. 222 Animals (probably of the gazel kind) two feet in height, which used..to herd together on the *vlaktens*, or plains. **1852** C. BARTER *Dorp & Veld* 82 The plains, or *vlakten*, occupy more than two-thirds of the whole extent of the Sovereignty. **1938** E. CAMPBELL '*Die ou Pad' & Other Rhymes* 5 The vlakte is tamed and strange. **1975** *Sunday Times* (Johannesburg) 21 Sept. 20 There was everyone wondering why the men from the vlaktes, usually so docile, suddenly seemed so fractious.

vlei. Add: Also 8 **valley. 1.** (Earlier examples.)

1793 C. R. HOPSON tr. *Thunberg's Trav. Europe, Afr., & Asia* II. p. xii, A *valley* is nothing more than a rivulet, which is sometimes over-grown with rushes, and is broad in some places, and narrow in others. **1801** TRUTER & SOMERVILLE in G. M. Theal *Rec. Cape Colony* (1899) IV. 369 We afterwards passed two other vleis or ponds about two hours distant one from another.

3. vlei lourie, loerie, one of several species of coucal of the genus *Centropus*, esp. *C. superciliosus*, found in southern Africa.

1864 T. BAINES *Expl. S.-W. Afr.* xv. 391, I shot one of the loosely-feathered birds called in the colony Vlei Lories, or Reed Hawks. **1908** [see *LOERIE]. **1936** E. L. GILL *First Guide S. Afr. Birds* 108 Burchell's Coucal, Vlei Lourie (Loerie). **1973** *Weekend Post* 28 Apr. 4 Some are just fascinating in their own right, like the vlei louries..and the Diederick cuckoo. **1978** MCLACHLAN & LIVERSIDGE *Roberts' Birds S. Afr.* (ed. 4) 253 White-browed Coucal. Vleiloerie. *Centropus superciliosus.*

Vo-Ag (vōᵘ,æ·g). *U.S. colloq.* Also **Vo. Ag.** Short for *Vocational Agriculture*, agriculture considered as a subject of study for those who intend to make it their profession. Also *attrib.*

1953 *Manch. Guardian Weekly* 5 Feb. 15/2 At Milton, Georgia, the 'Vo. Ag.' instructor took me to see Gill Brown as an example of a leading F.F.A. member... In the cultivation of the 'management' attitude..Vo. Ag. achieves distinctive success. **1976** *Columbus* (Montana) *News* 17 June 1/2 The Montana Vo-Ag teachers have selected Don Owen as the Outstanding Teacher of the 1975–76 year. *Ibid.* 1 July 4/2 Lyle has accepted a position teaching Vo-Ag at a Junior College.

vocab (vōᵘ·kæb). (Examples.)

1900 FARMER *Public School Word-Bk.* 215 *Vocab*,..(Charterhouse)..a vocabulary. **1971** 'M. INNES' *Awkward Lie* v. 94 Beadon should have said 'tailed', not 'trailed'. He hasn't got the vocab right. **1980** K. FOLLETT *Key to Rebecca* xvii. 195 'Have you done your prep?' 'Yes—French vocab.'

vocabulary, *sb.* Add: **4.** *fig.* A set of artistic or stylistic forms, techniques, movements, etc.; the range of such forms, etc., available to a particular person, etc.

1917 G. B. SHAW *How to become Musical Critic* (1960) 291 As far as mere grammar and vocabulary go, there is nothing more in the statue scene from Don Juan, which threw open the whole magic realm of modern orchestration..than in the exquisite little song of Cherubino. **1949** *Ballet Ann.* III. 109/2 Repetitions, lengthy passages, obscure symbols and movements..which ever aim not only at enriching the classic vocabulary..but at uplifting the mind. **1959** *Listener* 10 Dec. 1042/2 The extraordinary vocabulary of the latest works with their untrammelled blossoming in space, their hectic and at times almost hysterical proliferations of bumps, bulges, bags. **1960** *Economist* 22 Oct. 369/2 No country is likely to be able to rely purely on its own 'vocabulary' of styling; but British manufacturers..might be glad to escape the dependence on Italian and Swiss fashion leadership in car bodies. **1967** 'LA MERI' *Spanish Dancing* (ed. 2) vii. 86 Important is the fact that with the Pavane a vocabulary of steps appeared for the first time in dance history. **1972** E. LUCIE-SMITH in Cox & Dyson *20th-Cent. Mind* II. xiv. 474 Cubism is no longer 'analytic' but 'synthetic'. That is, it aims to create, by means of a consistent vocabulary of form, a universe which parallels the real one. **1977** *New Yorker* 25 July 62/2 Together the two enlarged the vocabulary of lawn tennis and laid the foundation for the all-court game. **1977** M. GIROUARD *Sweetness & Light* vii. 176 During the 1880s the Bedford Park vocabulary was being taken up by speculative builders and put to every kind of use. **1980** *Jrnl. R. Soc. Arts* Feb. 165/1 The vernacular building, employing the simple vocabulary of wall, sloping roof, door and small window, results in a national display of tranquil richness.

vocal, *a.* and *sb.* Add: **A.** *adj.* **2. b.** *vocal line* [*LINE *sb.*[2] 7 h].

1934 C. LAMBERT *Music Ho!* III. 190 The disparity between the vocal line and its harmonic background [in *Les Noces*]. **1961** [see *LINE *sb.*[2] 7 h]. **1963** *Listener* 7 Feb. 264/3 The orchestral skill..the command of texture and expressive colour, and the judging of instrumental comment on the vocal line.

6. a. Also *vocal fold, tract.*

1936 *Summ. Doct. Diss. Northwestern Univ.* IV. 183 Many investigations have been carried on to determine how the vocal folds vibrate. **1940** *Bell System Techn. Jrnl.* XIX. 496 Message waves are produced as muscular motions in the vocal tract. **1960** *Jrnl. Speech & Hearing Res.* III. 159/1 An investigator observed the image of the subject's vocal folds in the laryngeal mirror. **1961** *Jrnl. Acoustical Soc. Amer.* XXX. 1725/2 The generally accepted theory of speech production views the speech wave as the result of acoustic excitation of the vocal tract by one or more sources... The characteristics of the glottal source are to a large extent independent of the vocal-tract configuration anterior to the glottis. **1977** D. FRY *Homo Loquens* iii. 30 The process of articulation..depends on continual changes in the shape of the vocal tract, and hence in its acoustic properties. **1981** *Word 1980* XXXI. 152 The disruptions..due to the effects of coupling between the larynx and the supraglottal tract on the rate of vibration of the vocal folds.

b. = VOCALIC *a.* 2. (Earlier examples.)

1788 *Asiatick Res.* I. 13 This is the simplest element of articulation, or first *vocal* sound, concerning which enough has been said: the word *America* begins and ends with it; and its proper symbol therefore is A. **1818** *Trans. Amer. Philos. Soc.* I. 246 The vocal sounds are those which are represented in alphabets by the letters we call vowels.

7. *vocal-auditory* adj.

1958 *Proc. 8th Internat. Congr. Linguists* 754 Despite eloquent pleas,..that writing can and should be considered as basically a visual system independent of the vocal-auditory process, is it likely that any system of writing would be seriously proposed to-day that was not based on some attempt at a systematic correlation with the spoken language? **1981** *Amer. Speech* LVI. 130 Sign language is as adequate for the deaf as any vocal-auditory language is for a hearing person.

B. *sb.* **4. a.** Vocal music; singing.

1928 S. LEWIS *Man who knew Coolidge* I. 30 She felt more kind of called to the music line, and she was taking vocal and piano. **1968** *Blues Unlimited* Sept. 26 For strange vocal try to hear Daniel Brown's version.

b. A musical composition written for, or including a part for, the voice; a vocal part.

1934 S. R. NELSON *All about Jazz* iv. 84 A succession of vocals in radio music is sometimes tiresome. **1938** D. BAKER *Young Man with Horn* IV. 171 He had them pretty heavily arranged, with a transitional passage before every vocal. **1957** R. HOGGART *Uses of Literacy* viii. 203 Almost all [the records] are 'vocals' and the styles of singing much advanced beyond what is normally heard on the Light Programme of the B.B.C. **1975** A. AYCKBOURN *Norman Conquests* 14 He does a dance to the music and sings as the vocal starts. **1983** *Sunday Tel.* 9 Oct. 24/2 The cost of a machine with a complete package of 400 songs with the vocals edited out, is £600.

vocalese (vōᵘkălī·z). *Jazz.* [f. VOCAL *a.* and *sb.* + -ESE, perh. partly after next.] A style of singing in which singers put words to jazz tunes, esp. to solos previously improvised by jazz musicians. Also = *SCAT *sb.*[6] a.

1955 L. FEATHER *Encycl. Jazz* 248 Annie Ross, Eddie Jefferson and others imitated his idea of translating ad lib jazz into 'vocalese'. **1963** *Guardian* 5 July 11/1 Her unusual talent for simulating orchestral sounds (the jazz singing style called 'vocalese'). **1978** [see *SCAT *sb.*[6] (and *a.*) b]. **1981** *Times* 15 Apr. 16/8 King Pleasure, a pioneer of the style of modern jazz singing known as 'vocalese', has died... Vocalese is the process of putting words to improvized jazz solos.

vocalise (vōᵘkălī·z, vōᵘ·kălīz). *Mus.* Also (in imitation of VOCALIZE *v.* 5 b) **vocalize.** [a. F. *vocalise*, f. *vocaliser* VOCALIZE *v.*] **a.** A singing exercise using individual syllables or vowel sounds. **b.** A vocal passage consisting of a melody without words.

1872 *Scribner's Monthly* Feb. 481/2 When the *vocalise* was ended, I expressed my gratification and my admiration of his method to the maestro. **1949** *Scrutiny* XVI. 77 The Sonata Vocalise is an experiment in the combination of a wordless coloratura part with Medtner's habitual intricate pianism. **1959** *Listener* 2 July 37/3 The second movement..is very much in the spirit of a vocalize. **1972** J. L. DILLARD *Black English* vi. 262 If the preacher slows or hesitates, one of the older women may pick up the tempo and propel the performance forward in a *vocalise* which is strikingly like the 'breaks' utilized by New Orleans jazzmen. **1980** *Early Music* Jan. 18/2 For the virtuoso repertory of the 16th and 17th centuries exercises are available. They belong on the music stand for daily vocalises, and not on a bookshelf for theoretical research.

vocalism. 2. b. (Earlier example.)

1854 T. AUFRECHT in C. Bunsen *Christianity & Mankind* III. 93 The vowels have..been well preserved... The final consonants in the flexions have remained. The vocalism and consonantism stand in good organic relation to each other.

vocalize, *v.* Add: **5. c.** To utter any vocal sound.

1960 R. D. LAING *Divided Self* i. 20 Studying verbal behaviour in terms of neural processes and the whole apparatus of vocalizing. *a* **1961** W. LA BARRE in *Webster* (1961) s.v., The gorilla is just as likely to thump upon the upper chest..as he is to vocalize. **1972** *Sci. Amer.* Aug. 29/1 The female mallard generally vocalizes at the rate of from zero to four calls per one-minute interval.

vocalize, var. *VOCALISE.

vocalized, *ppl. a.* (Earlier example.) In *Jazz*, of the tone of an instrument: made to resemble that of the human voice.

1855 tr. *Lepsius' Standard Alphabet* 35 *French j.* This letter is the soft and vocalised sound. **1961** *John o' London's* 7 Dec. 637/1 The great jazz instrumentalists have based their styles on what is known as the 'vocalised' tone. **1970** P. OLIVER *Savannah Syncopators* 18 Emphasis is placed on the quality of blues singing and the 'vocalised tone' of jazz instrumentation.

vocation. Add: Hence **voca·tionless** *a.*

1924 *Blackw. Mag.* Apr. 445/2 Apparently we were all vocationless. **1939** A. CLARKE *Sister Eucharia* iii. 27, I stood beneath the iron gate, unveiled, Vocationless.

vocational, *a.* (Further examples.)

1910 *Proc. 1st Congr. National Conservation* 164 In conclusion..the remedies:.. *Vocational training* in high schools. **1927** W. E. COLLINSON *Contemp. Eng.* 106 The enlistment of the psychologist's help for vocational guidance. **1951, 1957** [see *GUIDANCE 1 c]. **1977** *New Statesman* 2 Sept. 294/3 The IBA is attracted to the.. Open College concept—courses in numeracy and literacy, vocational training for school-leavers, and other forms of further education.

Hence also **voca·tionalism**, training for a vocation; educational emphasis on this; **voca·tionalize** *v. trans.*, to direct towards vocational training.

1912 J. H. MOORE *Ethics & Education* 33 Schools should not be industrialized merely, nor commercialized, nor professionalized, but vocationalized. **1924** *Glasgow Herald* 1 May 8/6 The primary function of education is wider than mere vocationalism. **1959** *Oxf. Mag.* 11 June 458/2 We are so vocationalised now that we have begun to believe it is our true function to train professional scholars, professional critics and even professional readers. **1971** *Black Scholar* June 65 (Advt.), Vocationalizing higher education. **1979** *Yale Alumni Mag.* Apr. 12/2 Of all the areas in colleges and universities that will feel..the growing vocationalism of the young, the humanities will be hardest hit. **1980** [see *SUBSIDIARITY].

‖ **voce** (vō·tʃe). *Mus.* [It. = voice.] Used with qualifying phrases to designate various qualities or registers of the voice, as *voce di gola* (di gō·lā), a throaty or guttural voice; *voce di petto* (di pe·to), the chest register; *voce di testa* (di te·stā), the head register; formerly, the falsetto voice.

1742 tr. *Tosi's Observations on Florid Voice* i. 22 *Voce di Petto* is a full Voice, which comes from the Breast by Strength. *Ibid.*, *Voce di Testa* comes more from the Throat, than from the Breast. **1771** Voce di petto [see *PORTAMENTO]. **1801** BUSBY *Dict. Mus.*, *Voce di Testa*,.. a falsetto, or feigned voice. **1876** STAINER & BARRETT *Dict. Mus. Terms* 450/2 *Voce di gola*, a guttural or throaty voice. **1889** G. B. SHAW *London Music in 1888–89* (1937) 229 You are singing with your chest voice, or *voce di petto*, or long reed register, whichever you please to call it. *Ibid.*, You are singing falsetto, or in *voce di gola*, or throat voice, or short reed register. *Ibid.* 230 This high voice is what used to be called *voce di testa* or head voice. **1951** P. A. DUEY *Bel Canto in its Golden Age* xi. 124 Tenducci, the Italo-Anglican voice teacher writes briefly:.. Never force the Voice, in order to extend its compass in the *Voce di petto* upwards; but rather to cultivate the *Voce di testa* in what is called *Falsetto*. **1980** *New Grove Dict. Mus.* XVIII. 690/1 Until the late 18th and even early 19th centuries most tenors in the Italian tradition emphasized the lyrical quality of their top range and, when required, carried their voices with ease into the falsetto register (treatises of the 18th century and earlier call the falsetto range the *voce di testa*). During the first half of the 19th century, however, this traditional Italian manner of singing in the top range fell into disuse, and the expression *voce di testa* came to refer to the normal, much stronger head voice, falsetto being reserved as a special effect only for the very highest notes.

vociferative, *a.* For †*Obs.*$^{-1}$ read *rare* and add later example.

1889 G. B. SHAW *London Music in 1888–89* (1937) 167 The riot in the second act would have been better if it had either been sung note for note as written, or, as usual, frankly abandoned as impossible and filled up according to the vociferative fancy of the choristers.

vocoder (vokōᵘ·dəɹ). [f. VO(ICE *sb.* + CODE *sb.*[1] + -ER[1].] Any of various devices or systems for analysing speech or other sounds to obtain information that may be transmitted in a much reduced frequency band and used to reconstruct the sounds or synthesize new ones.

1939 H. DUDLEY in *Jrnl. Acoustical Soc. Amer.* XI. 169/1 Speech has been remade..by analyzing a talker's speech for the fundamental speech information and then using this information to remake the speech with a synthesizing device... The apparatus used has been called a 'vocoder'. **1955** *Sci. Amer.* Feb. 95/1 The Vocoder reduces to about one tenth the band width necessary to send speech. **1956** *Jrnl. Acoustical Soc. Amer.* XXVIII. 160/1 In the Scan Vocoder, we scan the envelope of the short time-frequency spectrum, for example, 30 times per second. The scan voltage is then transmitted through only one narrow band frequency channel as an envelope curve. **1970** *Sci. Jrnl.* Mar. 12/4 The main advantage of vocoders is that they require only very low digit rates of the order of 1·2–2·4 kilobits/second. **1976** *New Musical Express* 12 Feb. 24/5 The song's bridge section follows as a motley collection of barks, yelps and whines are fed through the vocoder, a device which synthesises sounds into eerie echo and resonance. **1980** *Musicians Only* 26 Apr. 13/6 The keys line-up includes..a Korg vocoder.

Hence (as a back-formation) **voco·de** *v. trans.*, to transform by means of a vocoder; **voco·ded** *ppl. a.*, produced by a vocoder.

1973 *Lang. & Speech* XVI. 293 The fundamental frequency contour of a 700-msec. vocoded utterance..was systematically varied to produce 72 contours. **1976** *New Musical Express* 12 Feb. 24/5 'Pigs' is the strongest slice of straight ahead rock the Floyd have recorded and the vocoded pig gruntings are fittingly hideous. *Ibid.* 24/6 Waters' voice is again vocoded and emerges sounding unpleasantly cybernetic. **1981** R. BROWN *Megalodon* i. 15 An electronic translator that could handle the full range of dolphin whistles and vocode them out as an ersatz humanoid voice.

vocoid (vōᵘ·koid), *a.* and *sb. Linguistics.* [f. VOC(AL *a.* and *sb.* + -OID.] **A.** *adj.* Vowel-like; articulated with no obstruction of the air-stream; contrasted with *CONTOID *a.* **B.** *sb.* A speech sound of this type.

1943 K. L. PIKE *Phonetics* v. 78 Vocoid and contoid groups are strictly delineated by the articulatory and acoustic nature of sounds. *Ibid.* vii. 143 The sounds which as a group function most frequently as syllabics are vocoids... Vocoids include practically all sounds which are usually called 'vowels'.., except that 'fricative vowels' are excluded, while 'vowel glides' such as [r], [w], and [y] are included. **1957, 1958** [see *CONTOID *a.* and *sb.*]. **1965** *Language* XLI. 476 This results in a variety of unrounded vocoid transitions between labials and following vowels. **1977** *Word 1972* XXVIII. 307 Vocoid symbolism is at most an extremely vague feeling for the appropriateness of certain vocoids to a particular meaning. **1984** *Amer. Speech* LIX. 342 One violation of (most) native English phonotactics was the *r*, which was usually a tap, even word-initially, rather than a vocoid.

vo-de-o-do, var. *VO-DO-DEO-DO.

vodka. Delete ‖, for 'used in Russia' read 'used orig. esp. in Russia', and add: Also, a glass or drink of this.

1969 M. PUGH *Last Place Left* xxix. 209 Pardoe decided to pour himself a vodka. **1981** 'J. Ross' *Dark Blue & Dangerous* xvi. 89 'Another?' he asked her. 'Thank you. A vodka and mixer.'

b. *vodka glass*; **vodka Collins**: see *COLLINS[2]; **vodka gimlet** [*GIMLET *sb.* 1 c], a cocktail made of vodka and lime-juice; **vodka martini**, a martini cocktail in which vodka is substituted for gin; **vodka-tonic**, a drink consisting of vodka and tonic water.

1953 R. & A. LONDON *Cocktails & Snacks* 46 (*heading*) Vodka martini. **1958** 'J. BYROM' *Or be he Dead* viii. 117 The vodka glasses were genuine ones. **1965** 'P. QUENTIN' *Family Skeletons* i. 4, I ordered a vodka martini. **1969** 'P. KAVANAGH' *Such Men are Dangerous* i. 13 The desk men..drink.., in the summer, vodka collinses. **1974** R. B. PARKER *God save Child* ix. 61 Can I get you a drink? .. Would you take a vodka gimlet? **1976** J. HAYES *Missing* (1977) iii. 61 She poured another vodka-tonic.

vodkatini (vǫ:dkătī·ni). Contr. of *vodka martini* s.v. *VODKA b.

1955 WILLIAMS & MYERS *What, When, Where & How to Drink* 146 (*heading*) Vodkatini (Vodka Martini). **1969** 'J. MORRIS' *Fever Grass* x. 97 You go on and get a table and order a couple of drinks. Mine is a vodkatini, a double. **1979** *Listener* 18 Jan. 80/1 'You're fighting ten pints of beer in every man.'.. The remark applies in essence (be it beer, whisky or vodkatinis) from the rough-est club to the plushiest cabaret.

vo-do-deo-do (vōᵘ:dōᵘdiˌōᵘdōᵘ·). Also **vo-do-de-o, vo-de-o-do, vo-do-deo-vo,** etc. A meaningless jazz refrain, used *attrib.* to designate a style of singing or a song characterized by speed, energy, and the repetition of such a refrain or insistent rhythm. Also *fig.*

[**1927** J. Yellen *Crazy Words, Crazy Tune* (song), Sings the same words to ev'ry song. Vo-do-de-o. Vo-do-do-de-o-do.] **1934** C. Lambert *Music Ho!* iii. 209 The most irritating quality about the Vo-dodeo-vo, poop-poop-a-doop school of jazz song is its hysterical emphasis on the fact that the singer is a jazz baby going crazy about jazz rhythms. **1937** N. Coward *Present Indicative* viii. 335 Slick American 'Vo do deo do' musical farces, in which the speed was fast, the action complicated, and the sentimental value negligible. **1946** Mezzrow & Wolfe *Really Blues* viii. 120 All the hi-de-ho, vo-de-o-do, and boop-boop-a-doo howlers that later sprouted up. **1958** V. Bellerby in P. Gammond *Decca Bk. Jazz* xvii. 214 At quick tempos some of her tricks can sound a little dated and imbued with the 'vo-do-de-o-vo' style of the late 'thirties.

vodun (voᵘ·dun). Also **vodu.** [W. Afr. (Dahomey) *vodu* (see quot. 1890).] A fetish, usu. one connected with the snake-worship and other rites practised first in Dahomey, then introduced by slaves esp. to Haiti and Louisiana. Also *attrib.* and *Comb.*, esp. in **vodunhwe, -kwe,** fetish-house. Cf. Voodoo.

1874 J. A. Skertchy *Dahomey as it Is* iii. 54 The name is derived from *Danh*, a snake, and Hweh, a residence. It is sometimes called *Vodun-hweh, i.e.*, the fetiche house. *Ibid.* vii. 154 This shrine is the Vodun-no-Demen, or fetiche-house of Demen. **1890** A. B. Ellis *Ewe-Speaking Peoples* ii. 29 The term *vōdu*..is still used..in the so-called Vaudoo, or Vaudoux worship of the negroes of Hayti..where the old python *culte* of Whydah still survives. *Ibid.*, Vōdu appears to be derived from *vō* (to be afraid), or from *vō* (harmful). **1920** *Encycl. Relig. & Ethics* XI. 400/2 The Voodoo serpent-cult in Haiti and elsewhere reproduces these W. African cults, one of the names of Dañh-sio being Vodunhwe. **1953** *Caribbean Q.* III. i. 39 The compound began with one house..a chapel or vodunkwe (house of the gods), and a tent. **1956** M. Stearns *Story of Jazz* (1957) ii. 20 A photograph by Earl Leaf of a Haitian *vodun* altar. **1963** [see *obeah 2]. **1973** E. Bullins *Theme is Blackness* 9 Black..vodun ritual-ceremony. **1985** *Times Lit. Suppl.* 11 Jan. 28/3 It is fashionable at present to argue that such African legacies as Santeria, Shango, Vodun or Camboulay provide a more promising basis for a Caribbean identity than imported European religions.

voel (voil). *rare.* [W., mutation of *moel* bald.] A bare hill or mountain.

1876 [see *roped *ppl. a.* 2 a].

voertsek, var. *voetsak *int.*

voetganger (fu·tχaŋəɹ). *S. Afr.* Also **foot-ganger.** [Afrikaans, f. Du. 'pedestrian', f. *voet* foot + *ganger* one who goes]. **1.** A locust in its immature wingless stage. Cf. Hopper¹ 2 in Dict. and Suppl.

1824 *S. Afr. Jrnl.* I. 70 The flying locusts are..less dreaded in this colony, than those which have not quite reached that stage of maturity, and are..vulgarly called 'voetgangers'. **1873** F. Boyle *To Cape for Diamonds* 300 We drove through a host of foot-gangers on the trek. These are the larvæ of locust. **1913** J. J. Doke *Secret City* 119 The locusts, the voetgangers, came in their countless millions. **1936** R. Campbell *Mithraic Emblems* 79 See there, and there it gnaws, the Rust—Voet-ganger of the coming swarm. **1966** E. Palmer *Plains of Camdeboo* xv. 244 All the world turns out to devour the voetgangers, but I remember only the white storks which appeared in numbers, and the fowls. When the first voetganger column appeared, our domestic fowls went berserk.

2. A pedestrian; also, (in quot. 1902) an infantryman.

1902 C. R. De Wet *Three Years' War* 410 It was exceedingly difficult for Colonials to rise, for they knew that not only would they have to be *voetgangers*, but also that if they were captured they would be..punished. **1950** L. G. Green *In Land of Afternoon* 144 In some ways the voetganger of a century ago fared better than the modern tramp.

voetsak (fu·tsæk), *int. S. Afr.* Also **footsack, voertsek,** and other varr. [ad. Afrikaans *voertsek, voetsek*, f. Du. *voort zeg ik* be off I say.] A command to leave (addressed esp. to a dog).

1837 J. E. Alexander *Narr. Voy. Observation W. Afr.* I. 351 Dogs attacked us as we approached; but on the cry of '*voortzuk!*' from the master..they left us. **1871** *Cape Monthly Mag.* III. 332 Cries of *foot-sek* with the slashing of a whip and the yelping of a defeated cur. **1890** *Digger's Doggerel* 22 'Bonzela Baas, Inkos!' He tell me 'Hamba, footsack!' **1899** A. Werner *Capt. of Locusts* 194 Be off with you! How dare you annoy a lady like this? *Voetsak!* **1918** C. Garstin *Sunshine Settlers* 50 He learned that when he heard the word 'Mike' he was wanted, and when he heard the word 'footsack' he was not. **1949** O. Walker *Wanton City* 74 What's White civilization in South Africa?..Social inhibitions imported from Europe? Broken accents from the world's ghettos? Fooie! Voetsak. **1950** *Cape Argus* 3 May 9/5 Betsy's only response was: 'Voetsek, you skollie.' **1963** A. Delius *Day Natal took Off* 9 He heard Bloubakkies yell to Sobisa, 'Hardloop! Run! Go! Voertsek!' **1969** A. Fugard *Boesman & Lena* 42 Few dops and a guitar and its voetsek yesterday and to hell with tomorrow.

Hence **voe·tsak** *v.*, (*a*) *trans.* to chase (a dog) away; (*b*) *intr.* to leave, to go away.

1897 E. Glanville *Tales from Veld* 227, I jes' drop in t'ask you *voetsack* all the dogs outer the place, 'fore I bring him in. **1958** *Cape Times* 4 Dec. 13/8 De La Fontaine said: 'You had better give me my money back.' I told him to *voetsak*. **1971** *The 1820* Apr. 11 But be careful who you tell to 'voetsak'..or be prepared for the consequences!

‖**vœu** (vö̃). Pl. **vœux** (vö̃). [Fr., lit. 'vow, wish': see Vow *sb.*] A recommendation made by an international conference, which is not mandatory.

1917 E. Satow *Guide to Diplomatic Practice* II. xxvi. 142 A recommendation (*vœu*)..respecting the liquor trade was adopted. **1936** R. C. K. Ensor *England, 1870–1914* xii. 420 A preamble like that..enacts nothing. It is only a *vœu*. **1939** H. Nicolson *Diplomacy* 250 *Voeux.* It sometimes happens that a conference wishes to add to its treaty certain 'recommendations' for future good conduct. These are called 'wishes' or 'voeux'. Thus the Hague Peace Conference of 1899 emitted six 'voeux'. These have no binding force upon the signatories. **1961** A. Marder *From Dreadnought to Scapa Flow* I. vi. 133 Sir Edward Fry..presented a pious *voeu*,..declaring it was 'highly desirable that the Governments should resume the serious study of this question'.

vogesite (vōᵘ·dʒēzəit). *Petrogr.* [ad. G. *vogesit* (C. H. F. Rosenbusch *Mikrosk. Physiogr.* (1887) II. 315), f. *Vogesen*, G. name of the Vosges Mountains in N.E. France: see -ite¹.] A lamprophyre consisting essentially of phenocrysts of hornblende (or augite) in a groundmass containing potash feldspar.

1891 F. H. Hatch *Introd. Stud. Petrol.: Igneous Rocks* v. 97 A second type of syenitic lamprophyre, containing hornblende instead of mica, is termed vogesite by Rosenbusch. **1937** A. Johannsen *Descr. Petrogr. Igneous Rocks* III. 37 The vogesites are greenish, grayish, or black melanocratic rocks when fresh, and reddish or brownish when weathered. **1976** *Nature* 5 Aug. 462/2 The vogesite lava is composed of approximately 85–90% olivine and augite.

vogue, *sb.* Add: **7.** *attrib.* or as *adj.* Fashionable; currently in vogue; esp. in *vogue word.*

c **1669** Howard & Villiers *Country Gentleman* (1976) i. i. 66 Pox on your Bourdeaux, Burgundie..no more of these vogue names,..get me some ale. **1915** H. L. Wilson *Ruggles of Red Gap* (1917) iii. 49 Decidedly he was not vogue. His hat was remarkable, being of a black felt with high crown and a wide and flopping brim. **1926** Fowler *Mod. Eng. Usage* 697/1 *Vogue-words.* Every now & then a word emerges from obscurity, or even from nothingness or a merely potential & not actual existence, into sudden popularity. **1947** Partridge *Usage & Abusage* 351/1 *Brave new world* is perhaps as much a cliché as it is a vogue-term. **1958** *Listener* 16 Oct. 621/2 Psychosomatic is the vogue-word of today. **1960** Partridge *Charm of Words* i. 47 One of the main differences between vogue-phrase and cliché: the majority of clichés last for generations. **1972** P. D. James *Unsuitable Job for Woman* iii. 106 Typical of the worst kind of academic writing. Contempt for logic; a generous sprinkling of vogue names; spurious profundity. **1978** *Forum on Med.* Apr. 84/1 Clichés and vogue expressions are equally plentiful. **1981** W. Safire in *N.Y. Times Mag.* 22 Feb. 9/1 Vogue words are his specialty [*sc.* Alexander Haig's]. The academic joyword of the 70's was 'exacerbate'. **1982** *Sunday Times* 5 Dec. 55 It was Chinese orders that made the mining machinery companies vogue stocks in the late seventies.

‖**vogue la galère** (vog la galę̄r), *int.* [Fr., lit. 'let the galley be rowed'.] Let's get on with it! Let's give it a go!

[*c* **1525** Wyatt *Coll. Poems* (1969) 59 My fearful trust, 'en vogant la Galère'.] **1744** Lady Hervey *Let.* 20 Oct. (1821) 86 As long as Mrs. Phipps is well, and Mr. Phipps happy, *vogue la galère.* **1822** Scott *Peveril of Peak* IV. xi. 258 '*Vogue la Galere!*' he exclaimed, as the carriage went onward; 'I have sailed through worse perils than this yet.' **1850** Thackeray *Pendennis* II. vi. 63 Eh, *vogue la galère*, I say. It's good sport, Warrington—not winning merely, but playing. **1909** L. Strachey *Let.* 13 Oct. in *V. Woolf & L. Strachey: Letters* (1956) 35 My health seems still to be something of a Mahomet's coffin. However, vogue la galère! *a* **1918** D. H. Lawrence *Phoenix* (1936) v. 594 We'll embark on a new course of education, and *vogue la galère.*

voguey (vōᵘ·gi), *a.* [f. Vogue *sb.* + -y¹.] = next.

1928 *Observer* 22 July 9/2 An achievement..which steers a happy course between the 'arty' and the 'voguey'. **1980** *Listener* 21 Feb. 228/1 'Don't have' has become voguey and displaced 'haven't got'.

voguish (vōᵘ·giʃ), *a.* [f. Vogue *sb.* + -ish¹.] That is in vogue or temporarily fashionable.

1927 *Daily Express* 26 Mar. 8 (Advt.), Hundreds of the voguish Jumper Suits await your selection. **1951** G. Greene *End of Affair* i. ii. 18 A voguish choice of reading matter in the waiting-room..*Harper's Bazaar* and *Life.* **1960** *News Chron.* 11 Oct. 4/3 An obsessive interest in [James] Dean..is voguish. **1980** *Times Lit. Suppl.* 31 Oct. 1220/1 Couples steer impeccably towards 'the smart upper floor' of a voguish restaurant.

Vogul: see Wogul, vogul in Dict. and Suppl.

voice, *sb.* Add: **I. 3.** (Further examples, esp. of the names of radio stations supposedly representing national or local opinion.)

1775 W. H. Drayton in R. W. Gibbes *Doc. Hist. Amer. Revol.* (1855) I. 181 These men..have practised every art, fraud, and misrepresentation, to raise in this Province an opposition to the voice of America. **1925** *Country Gentleman* 22 Aug. 14/1 If you tune in on WSB any evening at 8 or 10:45, you hear 'The voice of the South'—the Atlanta Journal. **1932** G. B. Shaw *Platform & Pulpit* (1962) 246 Mussolini is the most responsible ruler in Europe because he gives his orders with his own voice and not through an imaginary megaphone called 'The Voice of the Italian People'. Mr MacDonald's voice is a National Voice. **1942** *N.Y. Times* 9 Oct. 19/1 With all the short-wave stations under control of two Federal agencies.., it is expected that 'the Voice of America' will tell more nearly the same story. **1956** *B.B.C. Handbk. 1957* 132 The violently anti-British station, 'The Voice of the Arabs'. **1959** *Listener* 24 Sept. 490/2 In war time the Continental European and British colleagues broadcasting from Bush House, London, to Europe, represented not only 'the voice of London' but the true voice of the nations under Hitler's occupation. **1962** E. Snow *Other Side of River* (1963) vi. 51 The main building had a hundred large rooms, each with modern bath and each with an all-wave radio set; on mine I heard the Voice of America from Manila and United States Army broadcasts from Tokyo. **1970** D. Caute *Fanon* iv. 51 In 1956 the Voice of Free Algeria came on the air and within twenty days..the entire stock of radio sets was sold out. **1982** T. Keneally *Schindler's Ark* xxxvii. 397 The radio technicians.. listened with an earphone to the 2 p.m. news, from the Voice of London.

II. 8. e. (The utterance of) an invisible guiding or directing spirit (merging with fig. uses as sense 8 c). Chiefly *pl. direct voice*: see *direct *a.* 6 i.

1911 G. B. Shaw *Doctor's Dilemma* i. 12 When my patients tell me that theyve made a greater discovery than Harvey, and that they hear voices, I lock them up. **1924** —— *St. Joan* p. xv, Joan must be judged a sane woman in spite of her voices because they never gave her any advice that might not have come to her from her mother wit. **1924** W. Holtby *Crowded Street* xxxv. 260 Things happen against our will. Always being driven and we follow—voices. **1956** 'C. Blackstock' *Dewey Death* vii. 166 Do you think, perhaps, I am mad? Will I hear voices? **1973** A. Morice *Death & Dutiful Daughter* vi. 65, I ought to check up... My voices tell me that all is not..plain sailing there... Still, I may be wrong. **1975** 'J. Lymington' *Spider in Bath* ii. 30 A voice come to me in the night... Me Mum used to 'ave voices. Told 'er all sort er things.

10. In Parliament, etc., *spec.* a vote given with the voice, esp. by like-minded voters in unison; esp. in phr. *to collect the voices*, to take a vote by noting the relative strength of the calls of *ay* and *no* (cf. *voice vote*, sense 14 below).

1844 Erskine May *Law of Parl.* viii. 179 It must be well understood by members that their opinion is to be collected from their voices in the house, and not by a division; and if their voices and their votes should be at variance, the former will be held more binding than the latter. **1898** [see Dict.]. **1924** [see *voice vote*, sense 14 below]. **1976** S. Lloyd *Mr Speaker, Sir* 179 He then 'collects the voices' by saying, 'As many as are of that opinion say aye: of the contrary noe'.

III. 13. a. *voice-producer, -production* (earlier example) sbs.; *voice-activated, -operated* adjs.

1889 G. B. Shaw in *Star* 13 Dec. 2/4 Teacher of voice production. **1931** H. Nicolson *Diary* 6 May (1966) 73 He told me that Joseph Chamberlain was the best voice-producer he had ever heard. **1937** *Bell Telephone Q.* Apr. 113 This voice operated gain adjusting device operates on the speech coming into the control office to iron out the differences between loud voices and weak ones. **1972** *Computers & Humanities* VII. 50 Another hardware development used in teaching languages with computers is..a highly sophisticated (and rather expensive) tape recorder... It features the ability to stop a tape automatically for learner control decisions, voice-activated starting and stopping of recording, and automatic replay after each exercise. **1976** K. Benton *Single Monstrous Act* i. 11, I want Clancy's room bugged. Use a voice-operated mike. **1983** *Listener* 11 Aug. 33/2 It can't be long before voice-activated equipment enters the modern home, making remote controls a thing of the past.

b. *voice-pitch, -quality, -range.*

1932 D. Jones *Outl. Eng. Phonetics* (ed. 3) vi. 23 Some sounds are more sonorous than others, that is to say they carry better or can be heard at a greater distance, when pronounced with the same length, stress, and voice-pitch. *Ibid.* xxxi. 282 When there is more than one stressed syllable, the fall of the last stressed syllable generally begins at a pitch near to that of the initial unstressed syllables, and falls to the lower limit of the voice-range. **1946** K. L. Pike *Intonation Amer. Eng.* iv. 100 These characteristics—relaxed vocal cords, open throat..—are the goals of the trainer of voices... Voice quality..is comprised of such characteristics plus some..other differences. **1964** J. C. Catford in D. Abercrombie et al. *Daniel Jones* 29 Phoneticians should be able to classify 'voice-qualities' and other phonatory activities in as systematic a way as they classify supralaryngeal articulation. **1977** *Early Mus.* Oct. 492/2 It is actually a difficult piece, requiring..voice-ranges quite different from our standard choral division into soprano, alto, tenor, bass. **1977** P. Strevens *New Orientations Teaching of Eng.* xi. 144 Range of voice pitch, voice quality, and several more dimensions.

14. voice-box, (*b*) = *speak-box* s.v. *speak *v.* 36; **voice channel** *Telecommunications*, a channel with a bandwidth sufficiently great to accommodate speech; **voice coil** = *speech coil* s.v. *SPEECH *sb.* 13; also, a similar coil with the converse function in a moving-coil microphone; **voice frequency,** a frequency within the range required for the transmission of speech (commonly taken as 200 or 300 Hz to 3000 Hz or higher); usu. *attrib.*; **voice leading** *U.S.*, = *part-writing* s.v. PART *sb.* (*adv.*) 29; **voice level,** the volume of a voice measured for recording purposes; **voice-part** (earlier example); **voice radio,** a two-way radio; = *TRANSCEIVER; **voice synthesizer,** a synthesizer for producing sounds in imitation of human speech; **voice vote** (orig. *U.S.*), a vote taken by noting the relative strength of the calls of *ay* and *no* (cf. sense 10 above).

1971 'K. ROYCE' *Concrete Boot* i. 18, I rang the bell and a voicebox crackled in my ear. I told him who I was and pushed the door. **1959** *Listener* 18 June 1057/2 Current costs of this means of trans-oceanic telephone communication is about £70 per voice channel per mile. **1971** E. F. SCHOETERS in B. de Ferranti *Living with Computer* viii. 67 To every terminal must be assigned..equipment able to transform computer signals into a form suitable for long-distance transmission over what the Post Office calls 'voice channels'. **1934** *Discovery* Oct. 301/2 Goodmans' new '12 Watt' permanent magnet moving coil speaker.. has a totally enclosed voice coil. **1961** G. A. BRIGGS *A to Z in Audio* 126 The moving coil or dynamic microphone has been widely used... With low impedance voice coil windings..a wide frequency response with good sensitivity can be achieved. **1977** *Rolling Stone* 7 Apr. 87/3 (Advt.), With voice-coils wound with hi-temp wire on aluminum heat-sinking formers to handle the power of modern amps without burnout. **1925** *Telegraph & Telephone Jrnl.* XI. 151/2 Voice frequency telegraph. 200 to 2,000. **1944** *Electronic Engin.* XVI. 360 The transmitters are keyed by means of voice-frequency tone signals. **1975** R. L. FREEMAN *Telecommunication Transmission Handbk.* viii. 389 In practice voice frequency carrier telegraph techniques handle data rates up to 1200 bps. **1934** WEBSTER, Voice leading. **1942** [see *FAUX-BOURDON]. **1980** *Dædalus* Spring 198 The upward gap of a sixth..has here been masked by voice-leading. **1984** *Listener* 30 Aug. 30/4 With the increasingly frequent appearance of tonal triads and ever more connected voice-leading, something very much akin to the use of commonplace words has been creeping into his music. **1962** A. NISBETT *Technique Sound Studio* 258 *Voice level* is the acoustic volume produced by a voice in the studio. **1981** P. NIESEWAND *Word of Gentleman* xxvi. 180 Will you read a couple of sentences so we can get a voice level. **1776** J. HAWKINS *Hist. Music* I. p. lxxix, Instrumental aids to the voice-parts. **1959** C. OGBURN *Marauders* (1960) iv. 132 Tom Senff..had..got hold of a voice radio. **1962** *Sunday Express* 25 Nov. 3/2 Back in the cockpit, Harvey called George Bell on the voice radio. **1974** G. JENKINS *Bridge of Magpies* ii. 39 I've got a special transceiver—voice radio—laid on. RCA Navy job. [**1939, 1958** Speech synthesizer: see *SYNTHESIZER 2.] **1967** *Electronics* 3 Apr. 266/1 A voice synthesizer that Fujitsu Ltd. has developed as an audible output for its computers... When 'good morning' is fed into the computer by typewriter, the printed-out response is 'ohayo gozaimasu' and at the same time the robot-sounding voice of the synthesizer says it in Japanese. **1975** *Minicomputer Forum* 333 A voice synthesizer driven by a minicomputer and coupled to a telephone answering device and an automatic calling unit is an economical way of providing online computer services to the general public. **1979** *Personal Computer World* Nov. 58/3 On show will be two new line printers, a voice synthesizer, a P2 Quick printer and the new TRS-80 Model II. **1985** *Listener* 30 May 23 (Advt.), You won't have to ask the computer for essential information updates. The voice synthesiser will offer them. **1924** E. W. HUGHES *Man. Amer. Parl. Law* x. 241 If the voices and vote on division be at variance, do not agree, the voice vote will bind. **1955** H. W. DONAHUE *How to manage your Meeting* v. 217 In the *voice vote* all those in favor of the motion say *aye* and those opposed say *no*. This is the method usually used in deliberative assemblies. **1976** H. WILSON *Governance of Britain* iii. 55 Perhaps after suggesting a formula which appears to command assent, the prime minister asks 'Cabinet agree?'—technically a voice vote, sometimes just a murmur.

b. voice-over, narration spoken by an unseen narrator on a film or television broadcast; also, the unseen person whose voice is heard; also *attrib.*

1947 H. C. GIPSON *Films in Business & Industry* 284 *Voice-over*, narration-type recording as opposed to live sound. **1964** *Listener* 16 Apr. 629/1 The BBC..trying to find a way of avoiding naturalistic dialogue by the use of images with 'voice over' narration. **1964** *Punch* 21 Oct. 594/1 How would you like to do some voice-overs? **1966** G. N. LEECH *Eng. in Advertising* iv. 37 In the scripts, the speaker of commentaries is variously designated 'commentator', 'announcer' and 'voice over'. **1968** *Listener* 19 Sept. 379/2 In slow motion she loped muzzily through sylvan glades, and it was a matter of judgment whether the voice-over announcer would come on to plug the sexual properties of petrol, hand lotion or tooth-paste. **1974** K. MILLETT *Flying* II. 225 What I'm trying to do is to supply the voiceover for the pictures I make. **1983** *Daily Tel.* 18 Aug. 13/1 The minister gives up the cloth and takes off..to earn modest fame as a voice-over for TV commercials. **1984** *Daily Mail* 17 May 3/1 His [*sc.* Prince Andrew's] recorded voiceover will be heard by a total of around 300,000 spectators and a TV audience of millions.

voice, *v.* Add: **I. 5. d.** = *NARRATE *v.* 1 b.

1961 *Listener* 14 Dec. 1044/2 Scripted by Roger Fulford ..voiced by Andrew Cruickshank in sub-Dimbleby, it recaptured little of the emotion of the Abdication crisis. **1969** *Radio Times* 6 Feb. 31/1 The films we want to see are prized out of Continental cutting rooms by our multi-lingual production team who make translations of the original commentaries. The English versions are then voiced by nationals of each appropriate country.

7. b. Also *transf.*

1933 *Metronome* Mar. 34 Voicing ensembles should be considered entirely differently from voicing separate sax or brass trios.

8. In same sense as part of a phonological change. Also *intr.*, to become voiced.

1959 A. CAMPBELL *OE. Gram.* viii. 163 A system by which a voiceless spirant was voiced if the preceding vowel did not bear the main stress. **1964** *Language* XL. 26 The sibilant affricated in close juncture with /l/ but did not voice.

voi·ceprint. [f. VOICE *sb.* + PRINT *sb.*, after *fingerprint.*] A sonogram of a person's voice. Also *attrib.*

1962 *New Scientist* 14 June 598/2 'Voiceprint' identification may eventually supplement that from fingerprints. **1968** M. GUYBON tr. *Solzhenitsyn's First Circle* xxxiii. 198 This was really something quite new—tracing a criminal by his voice-print. **1973** *Daily Tel.* 5 Apr. 15/3 A Californian appeal court has ruled after years of controversy that voiceprints are acceptable as evidence in criminal cases. **1981** I. ST. JAMES *Balfour Conspiracy* ii. 49 The voice print library is still limited.

Hence **voi·ceprinter, voice printer,** an apparatus for producing voiceprints; **voi·ce-printing** *vbl. sb.*, the production or use of voiceprints.

1962 *Nature* 29 Dec. 1253/1 Voiceprinting uses the spectrographic impressions of the utterances of ten words frequently used in telephone conversations. **1966** *Economist* 20 Aug. 734/2 A young Negro..has been brought to trial in Los Angeles..on evidence provided by an electronic device known as a 'voiceprinter'. **1978** S. BRILL *Teamsters* iv. 144 Nine days after the voice printing Faugno disappeared. **1979** J. CROSBY *Party of Year* (1980) i. 13 If you'd just state your name again, for the Voice Printer.

voicespond (voi·spǫnd), *v.* [f. VOICE *sb.* + CORRE)SPOND *v.*] *intr.* To correspond by means of recorded oral messages. So **voi·cespondence, voi·cespondent.**

1954 *Sun* (Baltimore) 1 Feb. 4/1 A new type of friend-to-friend communication—'voicespondence'—is gaining fans in Europe. To 'voicespond' you have to own..a wire or tape recorder. *Ibid.*, Some 'voicespondents' collect recordings of famous voices... These they exchange by re-recording them for others. **1960** *Guardian* 9 Nov. 11/1 The amateur tape recording enthusiast..[may] 'voicespond' and 'tapespond'..with others at home and abroad. **1973** *Britannica Bk. of Year* (U.S.) 732/3 *Voicespondence*, communication between persons by an exchange of tape-recorded messages; *voicespond*, vb.; *voicesponder*.

voicing, *vbl. sb.* Add: **4. b.** *Jazz.* The tonal quality of a group of musical instruments in an ensemble; a blend of instrumental sound; harmonization.

1946 MEZZROW & WOLFE *Really Blues* ix. 152 We wrote..figuring out the right voicing by playing clarinet duets until it sounded good to us. **1949** L. FEATHER *Inside BeBop* i. 6 He was a third horn, blending the guitar with the tenor and trumpet for three-part voicings that produced a sound new to jazz. **1958** S. RACE in P. Gammond *Decca Bk. Jazz* x. 127 A technique of voicing for one clarinet and four saxes. **1977** *Zigzag* Mar. 5/1 What I do now is get a piano player who I really like and show him how the song was written, what kind of voicings, etc.

5. In same sense as part of a phonological change.

1959 A. CAMPBELL *OE. Gram.* ix. 180 The voicing of medial spirants was followed by the unvoicing of final spirants.

void, *a.* and *sb.*[1] Add: **A.** *adj.* **10*.** *Cards.* Of a hand: having no cards in a given suit.

1934 F. D. COURTENAY *System Experts Play* (ed. 3) 17 A void suit at a trump declaration is equivalent to an A. **1958** *Listener* 6 Nov. 753/3 One never lives to enjoy the double, for either dummy or partner will be void and will remove the double. **1972** R. MARKUS *Aces & Places* 25 When West showed void he went into a huddle. **1980** [see sense B. 8 below].

B. *sb.*[1] **3. d.** *spec.* (*a*) A defect in a crystal lattice consisting of a space larger than a single vacancy. (*b*) An interatomic space in any crystal lattice.

(*a*) **1947** *Trans. Amer. Inst. Metallurgical Engineers* CLXXI. 136/2 Supposedly these voids do not equal in volume the sum of lattice-volume change plus the direct zinc transfer. **1952** *Proc. Physical Soc.* B. LXV. 522 It remains now to discuss the generation and removal from the lattice of the large number of vacancies which do not form voids. **1965** J.-I. TAKAMURA in R. W. Cahn *Physical Metallurgy* xiv. 722 In these crystals voids are formed at grain boundaries as a result of large amount of strain. **1974** *Physics Bull.* Dec. 582/3 A nice illustration..was the discovery by Evans of the void lattice in molybdenum, voids of a few tens of Å in radius being ordered on a lattice with a spacing of one or two hundred Å.

(*b*) **1964** WERT & THOMSON *Physics of Solids* ii. 32 The fcc structure has small voids (called interstices) between the atoms. **1982** J. V. SMITH *Geom. & Structural Cryst.* v. 145 (*caption*) Tetrahedral and octahedral voids in (*a*) cubic closest-packing and (*b*) hexagonal closest-packing.

8. *Cards.* The absence of any cards in a particular suit in a player's holding.

1933 C. VANDYCK *Contract Contracted* ii. 20 The Short Suits are the Doubletons, Singletons and Voids. **1944** *Times* 17 May 6/3 Provision was made for revaluation after the first round of bidding to count three points for a void. **1980** M. DUMMETT *Twelve Tarock Games* vii. 125 Singleton Kings are usually even better than voids, unless..there is a danger that one of the opponents is void in [that suit].

9. *Med.* An emptying of the bladder.

1980 *Brit. Med. Jrnl.* 29 Mar. 889/2 Residual urine was estimated..by catheterisation after a normal void.

Hence **voi·dward** *adv.* (*rare*).

1927 JOYCE *Nightpiece* in *Pomes Penyeach*, As the bleak incense surges, cloud on cloud, voidward from the adoring Waste of souls.

void, *v.* **I. 2. b.** Delete † *Obs.* and add later example.

1876 *Fur, Fin & Feather* Sept. 167 They [*sc.* squirrels] should be voided..and kept several days in cold weather.

7. b. (Examples in *Med.* of sense 'to empty the bladder'.)

1947 STAFFORD & DILLER *Textbk. Surg. for Nurses* xlix. 500 The patient's bladder must be empty; therefore ..she should void before being draped for examination. **1966** *Amer. Jrnl. Obstetrics & Gynecol.* XCIV. 796/1 Sixteen patients were investigated who were unable to void following operations. **1977** *Lancet* 21 May 1072/2 The patient voided, was catheterised, and then lay comfortably on a..couch.

voidage (voi·dėdʒ). [f. VOID *sb.*[1] + -AGE.] Voids collectively; the proportion of a volume occupied by voids.

1946 *Nature* 17 Aug. 236/1 At 1,000°C. and with an inlet total gas rate of 200 litres/hr., sufficient to expand the bed of coke particles to a voidage of 0·7 so that the whole bed was agitated, the exit gas analyses..were [etc.]. **1966** R. D. WEST in P. Hepple *Petroleum Supply & Demand* 70 Injection wells scattered across the reservoir to inject the relatively large volumes of water required, not only to replace new oil, but also to fill the voidage left by the natural depletion. **1970** *Nature* 11 Apr. 158/2 The variation in local voidage occurring near the wall of a large cylindrical container filled with a mixture of spheres. **1983** *Chem. & Engin. Sci.* XXXVIII. 350/1 There is little difference between the surface settling rate of a bubbling bed and of a uniformly expanded bed of the same voidage.

voider. Add: **6. b.** *Med.* One who passes urine.

1969 *Radiology* XCII. 1178/1 Two of the patients were troubled by fecal retention and soiling and were thus infrequent defecators as well as infrequent voiders. **1974** *Amer. Jrnl. Roentgenol.* CXX. 407/1 We can enlarge the clinical application of these observations to patients with so-called megacystis syndrome..and the 'infrequent voider' syndrome.

voiding, *vbl. sb.* **1. a.** Delete 'Now *rare*' and add: Now only of the bladder or bowel.

In quot. 1976 perh. *concr.* (cf. sense 8 a).

1926 J. S. HUXLEY *Ess. Pop. Sci.* 281 Underlying the voiding of the bladder is a reflex mechanism. **1972** *Jrnl. Urol.* CVIII. 259/2 During voidings, rectal pressure was monitored. **1976** *Lancet* 9 Oct. 773/1 Urine from each voiding was poured into a funnel and allowed to drip. **1980** *Brit. Med. Jrnl.* 29 Mar. 889/2 Radiographic screening of the outflow tract was carried out during voiding.

voidless, *a.* For *rare*[−1] read *rare* and add: **b.** *poet.* Unavoidable.

1908 HARDY *Dynasts* III. III. i. 382 All must prepare to grip with gory death In the now voidless battle.

‖ **voilà** (vwala), *imp.* as *prep.* and *int.* [Fr., f. imp. of *voir* to see + *là* there.] There is, are, etc. As *int.*: there it is! there you are! lo! *voilà tout* (tu) [= all], that is all, there is nothing more to do or say.

1739 GRAY *Let.* 12 Apr. (1971) I. lx. 102 The minute we came, voila Milors Holdernesse, Conway, and his brother. **1778** H. WALPOLE *Let.* 12 Feb. (1955) XXVIII. 356 *Voilà* a truly long letter. **1801** JANE AUSTEN *Let.* 11 Feb. (1952) 121 Mr Bramston called here the morning before,—et voila tout. **1824** B. HAYDON *Jrnl.* 20 July in *Autobiogr.* (1926) I. 352, I have..no thoughts; I am painting portraits; *voilà tout.* **1858** LYTTON *What will he do with It?* (ed. 2) II. VI. i. 236 Ah, *voilà!* there he comes, the laggard! **1910** W. J. LOCKE *Simon* vi. 78 Dale asked me if he could call. I said 'Yes.' Perhaps I was wrong. Anyhow, *voila!* **1920** D. H. LAWRENCE *Let.* in C. Mackenzie *My Life & Times* (1966) V. 169 One of F's diamond rings was stolen... One shouldn't have diamonds voila tout! **1973** *Philadelphia Inquirer* (Today Suppl.) 7 Oct. 5/1 Plain junk that becomes—voila!—a memento when a 'Historic Philly' decal is affixed. **1980** *Quilt World* Sept./Oct. 42/3 The batting and backing were then trimmed and the edges of the quilt sewn shut. Voila! a completed quilt. **1981** 'D. JORDAN' *Double Red* xxxiv. 156 Live all your life! That is all I know, *voilà tout*

voilette. 1. (Earlier example.)

1842 C. RIDLEY *Let.* 9 Oct. in *Cecilia* (1958) viii. 101 She had on..a blue silk bonnet with a long veil (not a *voilette*).

voir dire. For 'Also 7 **voire**' read 'Also **voire**' and add: Also, an investigation into the truth or admissibility of evidence, held during a trial. Also *attrib.*

1968 *Daily Colonist* (Victoria, B.C.) 13 Sept. 42/3 Police testimony was called and a voir-dire—a trial within a trial—was held to determine whether a statement from one of the accused was admissible evidence. Immediately after the voir-dire, Magistrate Fraser questioned Dr. Carpenter. **1973** *N.Y. Law Jrnl.* 19 July 12/3 The voire dire examination as to the qualifications of this witness.. revealed that he lacked the background which would qualify him as an expert. **1980** *Times* 18 Jan. 10/4 His Lordship was prepared to assume that the voire dire (trial within a trial) and the verdict taken together did constitute a final judgment on the same issues. **1981** *Daily Tel.* 26 June 6/3 The purpose of the 'trial within a trial' known to lawyers as a *voir dire*, had been to decide whether Brophy had been induced to make a number of alleged statements [etc.].

‖ **voix** (vwa). [Fr. = voice.] Used in various phrases, as *voix blanche* (blɑ̃ʃ) [lit. 'white voice'], a toneless voice; *voix céleste* (selest) [lit. 'heavenly voice'] = *vox angelica* s.v. Vox 2; also *fig.*; *voix d'or* (dɔ̄r) [lit. 'voice of gold'] a rich dramatic voice; *voix grave* (grāv), a low-pitched or deep voice; *voix moyenne* (mwayen) [lit. 'middle voice'] a voice of middle range.

1876 Stainer & Barrett *Dict. Mus.* 452/2 *Vox angelica*... Called also *Voix céleste*, unda maris, &c. **1895** G. B. Shaw *Our Theatres in Nineties* (1932) I. 137 The inevitable stale, puerile love scene is turned on to shew off that 'voix céleste' stop which Madame Berhardt, like a sentimental New England villager with an American organ, keeps always pulled out. **1897** *Ibid.* III. 210 Sarah Bernhardt's *voix d'or.* **1907** Voix celeste [see *suabe]. **1920** D. H. Lawrence *Lost Girl* x. 232 The muted *voix blanche* came through his lips. **1935** Joyce *Let.* 19 Mar. (1966) III. 351, I sent The Dupan collection. There is none for *voix grave*. So I sent the best I could: *voix moyenne.* **1962** *Listener* 8 Nov. 779/2 Her verse has always lacked intellectual content, and..the later and more ambitious manner comes to seem one-tenth genuine poem-making to nine-tenths *voix d'or* and delphic vapour.

volant, *sb.* **3.** (Earlier example.)

1851 *Harper's Mag.* Jan. 288/1 Five volants are set on full, each being trimmed at a little distance from the edge by a narrow guimpe.

‖ **volapié** (vǫlapi͵eˑ). [Sp., lit. 'flying foot', f. *volar* to fly + *pie* foot.] In *Bullfighting*, a manner of killing in which the bullfighter runs in to kill a stationary or slowly-moving bull. Also *à volapié* adv. phr., in this manner.

1838 *Q. Rev.* LXI. 418 The 'volapie'..is dangerous but beautiful; the bull is met half way. **1910** *Encycl. Brit.* IV. 790/1 The stroke..is usually given *à volapié* (half running), the *espada* delivering the thrust while stepping forward, the bull usually standing still. **1932** E. Hemingway *Death in Afternoon* xix. 244 The volapié to be properly executed demands that the bull be heavy on his feet. **1967** McCormick & Mascareñas *Compl. Aficionado* ii. 58 This time a three-quarter sword follows a good *volapié.*

volatile, *a.* Add: **4. c.** Of markets, shares, etc.: showing sharp changes in price or value (merging with uses of sense 5).

1931 *Daily Express* 31 Jan. 2/6 Some volatile issues.. recorded..advances. **1977** *Time* 19 Dec. 10/1 It stabilized the volatile lira. **1981** *Times* 25 Sept. 1/6 The pound slipped further against all leading currencies on nervous and volatile foreign exchange markets. *Ibid.* 26 Sept. 23/6 Leading shares..remained volatile until after-hours trading when prices steadied a little. **1985** *Times* 26 Jan. 23/1 It has been one of the most volatile [Stock Exchange] accounts in recent history.

5. b. *Computers.* Of a memory: retaining data only as long as there is a power supply to it.

1950 W. W. Stifler et al. *High-Speed Computing Devices* xiv. 305 In a volatile storage medium, like a delay line, retransmission of each signal once during each storage cycle period is required. **1970** O. Dopping *Computers & Data Processing* x. 136 The flip-flop register is a fast, expensive, volatile memory. **1979** R. Mutch *Gemstone* viii. 95, I need two microprocessors, read-only and volatile memories,..and a battery.

volatility. Add: **5.** *Computers.* The property of a memory of not retaining data after the power supply is cut off.

1969 *IEEE Trans. Magnetics* V. 583/1 Progress in the overall field of semiconductor memories to date is surveyed... The problems of power, reliability, and volatility are yielding to practical solutions. **1981** *Appl. Solid State Sci.* Suppl. II. A. 122 Many investigations into lessening the impact of the volatility of the semiconductor memory have been made.

volcaniclastic (vǫlkæ:niklæ·stik), *a.* and *sb. Geol.* Also **vo:lcano-.** [Blend of Volcanic *a.* (and *sb.*) and Clastic *a.*] **A.** *adj.* Both volcanic and clastic. **B.** *sb.* A volcaniclastic rock.

1961 R. V. Fisher in *Bull. Geol. Soc. Amer.* LXXII. 1409/1 Only recently..have attempts been made to group all volcanic clastic (termed *volcaniclastic* in this paper) rocks into a single system... Rocks of pyroclastic origin are only one category of volcaniclastic rocks. **1972** F. J. Pettijohn et al. *Sand & Sandstone* vii. 261 The erosional volcaniclastics are comparable—in sedimentary structures, geometry, and thickness—to other terrigenous sandstones. **1975** *Nature* 17 Apr. 581/2 The rock types include..a variety of reworked volcanic ashes, volcaniclastic and fluviatile sediments. **1980** *Ibid.* 29 May 289/2 The Savage Mountain Formation consists of up to 5,000 m of..pillow basalt and massive subaerial flows with associated volcanoclastics.

volcanist. Add: **1.** (Further example.) Cf. *vulcanist 3.

1971 H. Kondo *Moon* (1972) 14 The volcanists have three main arguments for believing that their theory is correct.

volcano, *sb.* Add: **2. b.** In phr. *to sit on a volcano* and varr.

[**1908** L. Mitchell *New York Idea* i. 32, I feel as if we were all taking tea on the slope of a volcano.] **1909** Galsworthy *Silver Box* i. iii. 16 You're sitting upon a volcano, John. **1930** G. B. Shaw *Apple Cart* i. 26 The more I see of the sort of prosperity that comes of leaving our vital industries to big business men as long as they keep your constituents quiet with high wages, the more I feel as if I were sitting on a volcano. **1954** J. Whiting *Marching Song* ii. 42 Is it a volcano I'm sitting on and not, as I'd supposed, a dung-hill? **1983** *Listener* 27 Jan. 28/3 As in Ragtime, he exposes to white, middle-class America the nature of the volcano (racism; social injustice; competition; aggression) on which it blithely sits.

3. volcano rabbit, a small, dark brown rabbit, *Romerolagus diazi*, found only in the mountains of central Mexico and very similar to the pika, having short ears and no tail.

1969 J. Fisher et al. *Red Bk.* 54/2 The volcano rabbit is covered with fur, which is a uniform dark brown on its back and dark brownish-grey beneath. **1972** G. Durrell *Catch me a Colobus* ix. 173 The Volcano rabbit lives at a very high altitude..in the pine forests.

volcano-. The sb. used as a formative element: **volcanoclastic,** var. *volcaniclastic *a.* and *sb.*; **vo:lcanoge·nic** *a.* [*-genic], of volcanic origin; **volca:notecto·nic** *a.*, involving or pertaining to both volcanic and tectonic processes.

1965 E. Lehner et al. in G. J. Williams *Econ. Geol. N.Z.* xix. 353/2 Their survey left little doubt that the marine late Eocene and Oligocene strata which overlie the basement cover..are..intercalated with volcanogenic beds. **1977** A. Hallam *Planet Earth* 59/2 Glacial or volcanogenic sediments contain coarse particles which can be very unstable. **1907** W. H. Hobbs in *Beiträge zur Geophysik* VIII. 224 The seismotectonic lines often intersect lines of volcanoes (volcanotectonic lines) at volcanic vents. **1941** *Univ. Calif. Publ. Geol. Sci.* XXV. 242 Calderas are volcanic and therefore centric forms of destruction, volcano-tectonic engulfments of the roofs of magma reservoirs, regardless of the number of vents involved. **1965** G. J. Williams *Econ. Geol. N.Z.* xv. 235/2 The relatively high permeability of the pumiceous volcanics deposited in the large volcano-tectonic basins so typical of this active tectonic and volcanic zone. **1979** *Nature* 26 July 286/2 Zukwala volcano..lies on an isolated (non-WFB) volcanotectonic line that projects NNE via a Holocene basalt lava cone.

volcanological (vǫ:lcănǫlǫ·dʒikăl), *a.* [f. Volcanolog(y + -ical.] = Vulcanological *a.* Also **vo:ocanolo·gic** *a.*

1889 *Cent. Dict.*, Volcanological. **1931** G. W. Tyrrell *Volcanoes* i. 12 With the establishment of volcanological observatories on Vesuvius and Etna..the study of volcanoes has entered upon a new phase. **1961** Webster, Volcanologic. **1974** *Encycl. Brit. Macropædia* XIX. 98/2 Numerous stations have been set up [on Vesuvius] at various heights for making volcanologic measurements. **1982** *Encycl. Brit. Bk. of Year* 307/2 Mt. St. Helens remained active,..providing an excellent volcanological laboratory.

volens (vōᵘ·lenz), *ppl. a. Law.* [L., f. *velle* to will.] Consenting to a dangerous course of action. Cf. next.

1872 *Law Jrnl.* (Court of Exchequer) XLI. ii. 101/2 Then comes the great difficulty; it is said 'volenti non fit injuria'. It is true that he was 'volens', in the sense that he entered the employment voluntarily. **1951** *Law Rep. House of Lords* (Appeal Cases) 765 He was not volens or careless. **1965** *Mod. Law Rev.* XXVIII. v. 519 A finding that a workman was *sciens* was sufficient to defeat his claim as an invitee, even if he was not *volens.*

‖ **volenti non fit injuria** (vōᵘle·nti nōᵘn fit indʒiu·riă). *Law.* [L.] No injury is done to a willing person: a defence to an action whereby it is claimed that a person who sustained an injury agreed to risk such injury.

1658 E. Wingate *Maximes of Reason* cxxii. 482 If the Tenant in an Assise of an house desire the Plaintiffe to dine with him in the house, which the Plaintiffe doth accordingly, but doth not clame the house at that time; this is no entry or possession to cause the Assise to abate; because if he had been a stranger, he had been no trespasser for *volenti non fit injuria.* **1743** C. Cibber *Egotist* 6 *Volenti*, you know, *non fit injuria.* The publick is not obliged to buy. **1872** [see prec.]. **1933** *Law Rep.* (King's Bench Division) II. 299 We are at present disposed to take the view that the respondent is precluded from recovering on the principle volenti non fit injuria. **1980** *Oxf. Compan. Law* 1280/1 *Volenti non fit injuria*.., the principle that an injured person cannot complain of harm done him if he knew of and voluntarily incurred the risk of that harm... The plea is practically excluded in employment cases but is still relevant to cases of participation in dangerous sports.

Volga (vǫ·lgă). The name of a Russian river used *attrib.* in **Volga German,** a member of an ethnic minority living near the Volga from the seventeenth century until the Second World War; also *adj.*, of or pertaining to this people.

1941 *Times* 9 Sept. 3/3 (*heading*) Volga Germans to go. *Ibid.*, The Volga German region is an autonomous republic, with its own supreme council. **1947** W. Baczkowski *Towards Understanding of Russia* v. 199 The following Autonomous Republics were liquidated: the Republic of Volga Germans, the Kalmyk Republic, [etc.]. **1973** A. Price *October Men* xii. 176 Korbel deserted to the Wehrmacht... Told 'em he was a Volga German. **1985** *Observer* 28 July 17/1 Muscovites say this is to keep out troublemakers (Volga Germans? Crimean Tartars?).

Volgian (vǫ·lgiăn), *a. Geol.* [f. as prec. + -ian.] Of, pertaining to, or designating a stage of the Upper Jurassic and Lower Cretaceous in Russia. Also *absol.*

1893 A. Geikie *Text-bk. Geol.* (ed. 3) 919 Some of the recognized [Jurassic] life-zones of western Europe can be detected in Russia... [These include] Volgian, consisting of green, brown and dark sandstones and sands. **1955** E. Neaverson *Stratigraphical Palaeont.* (ed. 2) xii. 473 The lower beds of the Russian Volgian stage..may be correlated with the Upper Kimmeridge Clay of England. **1978** *Nature* 13 July 132/2 The fault-controlled stepwise submergence of the block-faulted basin culminated in Middle Volgian times with the most important Mesozoic phase of block-faulting in the region.

volitive, *a.* **4.** (Earlier example.)

1846 Monier Williams *Elem. Gram. Sanscrit Lang.* vi. 129 Certain roots..take a desiderative form, without exactly yielding a volitive signification.

‖**Volk, volk** (fǫlk). [G., Du., Afrikaans = nation, people: see Folk.] **1.** *S. Afr.* **a.** The Afrikaner people.

1880 G. Hudson *Let.* 1 Dec. in B. Bellairs *Transvaal War* (1885) 424, I met with a very sullen reception, and Mr Paul Kruger appeared..very anxious that I should keep out of sight of the 'volk' (people) as much as possible. **1928** E. A. Walker *Hist. S. Afr.* xiii. 515 The *Afrikaner Volk* proceeded to find itself along cultural and then along political lines. The Old Colony led the way. **1948** *Press Digest* (S. Afr. Jewish Board of Deputies) No. 2. 16 What the nationally-minded Afrikaner wishes for himself and for his volk, he wishes also for other peoples, namely a national home. **1953** P. Abrahams *Return to Goli* 175 It is not only the Afrikaans-speaking Whites, not only 'Die Volk', who believe in the colour bar. **1979** J. Drummond *Patriots* iii. 24 We have to throw out white privilege... That's being said..in the..strongholds of the Afrikaner volk.

b. The Coloured employees of an Afrikaner.

1882 *Cape Q. Rev.* 317 The water to be utilised for medicinal purposes in a bathing-house adjacent, which at present serves as a habitat for the 'volk' (workmen) of the farm. **1900** B. Mitford *Aletta* 79 Come this way. My *volk* will see to your horse. **1939** J. S. Marais *Cape Coloured People* i. 5 In the western Cape a farmer calls his labourers his 'volk'—the same word that Adam Tas used for his slaves, as distinguished from his Hottentot labourers, in the early eighteenth century. **1968** K. McMagh *Dinner of Herbs* 30, I get the volk to drag away the carcasses and skin them.

2. The German people, esp. in the ideology of National Socialism.

1933 C. B. Hoover *Germany enters Third Reich* vii. 175 *Das Volk* is thought of not as a juridical organization to which one might belong by obtaining citizenship rights through naturalization, but as a community held together by the sacred ties of common blood. **1937** *N.Y. Times Mag.* 21 Nov. 2/3 Like most nations of today, what is known as the Deutsche Volk is in itself a hybrid people composed of Germanic, Celtic, Slavic and Lithuanian elements.

3. *Comb.* **a.** In sense 1 (of the Afrikaner people): **vo·lkspele** (-spiᵊlə) *pl.*, Afrikaner folk dances; hence **vo·lkspeler,** a dancer of these; **vo·lkswil** (-vil), the will of the people.

1949 *Cape Times* 24 Sept. 9/2 There would be volkspele demonstrations, recitations and singing. **1972** *Evening Post* (Port Elizabeth) 5 Feb., Dancing that night will be confined to volkspele and other typically South African dances. **1953** *Cape Times* 17 Apr. 9/8 The group of *volkspelers*..will sail on an oversea tour in to-day's mailship. **1948** *Cape Argus* 2 Dec. 1/5 The numerical question apparently no longer applies, and it is now just a question of 'volkswil' and the support of the people. **1956** *Star* (Johannesburg) 23 Feb. 12/7 South Africa..has heard much sanctimonious talk of the 'volkswil' from members of a minority government.

b. (In English some of these words are used without proper regard for the inflexional endings customary in German itself.) In the possessive in sense 2 (of the people): **Volksdeutsch** (fǫ·lks͵doitʃ) *a.*, fem., pl., **-deutsche** (-tʃə), belonging to or characteristic of the *Volksdeutsche*, ethnically German; **Volksdeutsche** *sb. pl.*, people of German origin resident outside Germany and Austria; ethnic Germans; **Volksdeutscher,** a member of the *Volksdeutsche*, an ethnic German; also *attrib.*; **Volksgeist** (fǫ·lksgəist), the spirit or genius which marks the thought or feeling of a nation or people; **Volkskammer** (fǫ·lks͵kamǝɹ), the parliament of the German Democratic Republic; **Volksoper** (fǫ·lksōpəɹ), the light opera house in Vienna; also *transf.*; **Volkspolizei** (fǫ·lks͵politsəi), a police force of the German Democratic Republic; members of this; **Volkspolizist** (fǫ·lks,poli̇tsi·st), a member of the *Volkspolizei*; **Volkssturm** (fǫ·lks,ʃturm) a territorial army established in Germany during the last years of the Third Reich; also *attrib.*; **Volkswanderung** (fǫ·lks-vandəruŋ) = *Völkerwanderung.

1952 E. F. Davies *Illyrian Venture* x. 177 The housekeeper matron, a fat, grim *Volksdeutsche* woman. **1962** *Listener* 7 June 1004/2 The old Volksdeutsch grannie who has nothing left to do except learn to die. **1981** I. Boland tr. *Ginzburg's Within Whirlwind* i. x. 83 She..expostulated in her *Volksdeutsch* dialect that people must be fed before they are turned out to work. **1937** *N.Y. Times Mag.* 21 Nov. 16/3 The Germans of foreign citizenship are called 'Volksdeutsche', or 'racial Germans'. **1944** I. Origo *Diary* 7 June in *War in Val d'Orcia* (1947) 193 The Italian patriots..are..to give shelter to *Volksdeutsche* who have deserted from the German Army. **1961** R. Kee *Refugee World* iii. 20 Ethnic Germans (*Volksdeutsche*) living in east and south-east Europe. **1961** Webster, Volksdeutscher. **1978** H. Wouk *War & Remembrance* xlvi. 463 A tall thin horribly pimpled *Volksdeutscher* burglar from Prague. **1981** I. Boland tr. *Ginzburg's Within Whirlwind* i. xiii. 108 He was a German. A Crimean *Volksdeutscher*. **1936** Wirth & Shils tr. *Mannheim's Ideology & Utopia* ii. 59 During this period the *Volksgeist*, 'folk spirit', comes to represent the historically differentiated elements of consciousness. **1977** D. Watkin *Morality & Archit.* iii. i. 79 Our fundamental concern is..with the impression left by the emphasis on national character or *Volksgeist* as a determinant of artistic style. **1949** *Times* 8 Oct. 4 The German 'People's Council' proclaimed itself in Berlin yesterday to be the provisional Volkskammer, or Lower House, of the Parliament of the new 'German Democratic Republic'. **1977** *Whitaker's Almanack 1978* 865/1 Further amendments came into force on October 7, 1974 after adoption by the *Volkskammer* on September 27, 1974. **1928** J. A. Mahan *Vienna of Yesterday & Today* ix. 210 Two opera houses, the Staatsoper..and the Volksoper..are in use every day of the season. **1968** *Vogue* 15 Apr. 23/1 Theoretically, the difference between the Wells and the Garden is that between *Volksoper* and *Staatsoper* in Vienna. **1980** *Times* 31 Dec. 3/5 The report rejects the idea that the D'Oyly Carte company should be built up..to become a British 'Volksoper', performing light music and operetta. **1964** L. Deighton *Funeral in Berlin* vi. 38 A volkspolizei troop carrier was parked at the roadside. **1967** R. V. Beste *Repeat Instructions* (1968) ix. 94 He walked past *Volkspolizei*, who eyed him suspiciously. **1980** A. Coppel *Hastings Conspiracy* vii. 52 Two uniformed officers of the Volkspolizei..had hurried him to the military airfield at Bützow. **1974** J. D. White *Leipzig Affair* vii. 63 There was a volkspolizist waiting outside my room. **1944** *Nation* (N.Y.) 25 Nov. 653 The *Volkssturm* is necessarily largely composed of men between fifty and sixty, with a sprinkling of sixteen- and seventeen-year-old boys. **1969** A. Marin *Rise with Wind* ii. 12 He could still remember the..day when a Volkssturm officer dug him out of the rubble. **1855** Geo. Eliot *Let.* 9 Jan. (1954) II. 190 The subject I now propose is 'Women in Germany'..through the periods of the Volkswanderung and the romantic..life of the Middle Ages up to our own day.

‖ **Völkerwanderung** (fö·lkərva:nduruŋ). Pl. **-ungen.** [G., f. *völker* pl. of *Volk + *wanderung* migration.] A migration of a people or peoples *en masse*, *spec.* that of Germanic and other peoples in Europe during the later Roman Empire and the early Middle Ages. Also *attrib.*

[**1885**: see *Volkswanderung* s.v. *Volk 3 b.] **1934** A. Toynbee *Study of Hist.* II. 97 The last convulsion of the post-Minoan Völkerwanderung along the west coast of Anatolia. **1946** Priebsch & Collinson *German Lang.* (ed. 2) ii. ii. 24 Subsequent encroachments..by Goths, Franks and others during the Age of Migration (Völkerwanderung) are discussed. **1961** L. F. Brosnahan *Sounds of Language* iii. 52 The Germanic expansion of the Völkerwanderung period. **1969** J. Mander *Static Society* i. 46 The Germanic *Völkerwanderungen* after the fall of the Roman Empire.

‖ **völkisch** (fö·lkiʃ), *a.* [Ger.: see *Volk, -ish[1].] Populist, nationalist, racialist.

1939 *Times Lit. Suppl.* 7 Jan. 8/3 Saratoga and Yorktown are more familiar to the British schoolboy than a more *völkisch* school of history would tolerate. **1962** *Listener* 26 Apr. 739/3 As Franco grew strong enough to disembarrass himself of any kind of *völkisch* institutions, he encouraged the Falange to fade away. **1975** *Times Lit. Suppl.* 21 Nov. 1392/2 Whether the *völkisch* ideology and antisemitic sentiment suffered a similar setback or penetrated to other parties... There was much less personal..continuity of this older generation of *völkisch* leaders.

volkonskoite (vǫlkǫ·nsko,ǝit). *Min.* Also 9 **wolch-, wolk-; volch-.** [ad. G. *wolchonskoit* (A. Kämmerer 1831, in *Jahrb. f. Mineral.*, etc. II. 420), f. the name of Prince 'Wolchonskoy' (? i.e. Volkonsky): see -ite[1].] A green or bluish-green amorphous clay mineral of the montmorillonite group in which there is some substitution by chromium, now regarded as a variety of nontronite.

1844 J. D. Dana *Syst. Min.* (ed. 2) vi. 533 Wolchonskoite. Amorphous. Dull-shining. **1852** *Amer. Jrnl. Sci.* LXIV. 62 Silicated Chrome (Wolchonskoite?). **1892** E. S. Dana *Dana's Syst. Min.* (ed. 6) 696 Wolchonskoite. .. Volchonskoite. **1953** R. E. Grim *Clay Mineral.* iv. 58 Substitutions within the octahedral sheet [of montmorillonite] may vary from few to complete... Replacement of aluminum by iron yields nontronite; by chromium, volkonskoite; by zinc, sauconite. **1973** *Norsk Geol. Tidsskr.* LIII. 329 The Cr_2O_3 content of volkonskoite may vary within wide limits, and values up to 15–20% have been reported from Russian occurrences.

Volkslied (fǫ·lks,līt). Also **volkslied.** Pl. **-lieder** (-līdəɹ). [Ger. and Du., f. *volks* gen. of *Volk + *Lied, lied.] **1.** A German folk song; a popular song in a German folk idiom.

1858 Geo. Eliot *Jrnl.* 23 May in *Life* (1885) II. viii. 41 His wife..sang us some charming Bavarian *Volkslieder.* **1882** F. A. Kemble *Rec. Later Life* ii. 8 Dr. Charles Follen, known in his own country as Carl Follenius ..wrote some fine spirited Volkslieder. **1934** C. Lambert *Music Ho!* iii. 159 The second [*sc.* Glinka's wedding song in five-four time]..freed music from the restricting and lumbering rhythms of the German Volkslied. **1977** *Early Music* Apr. 213/1 Only two songs are true 'volkslieder' with the usual upbeat opening and steady chorale-like melody.

2. *S. Afr.* **a.** *Hist.* The national anthem of the 19th-century Transvaal Republic. **b.** A simple popular folk song.

1874 *Cape Monthly Mag.* 254 We should, in the pages of the *Magazine*, from time to time collect some of the ..'Volks-liedjes' written in the Cape Dutch patois. **1898** C. Rae *Malaboch* 217 *Volkslied*, the Transvaal National Anthem. **1921** *Eastern Province Herald* 18 Jan., The singing of the Volkslied and a vote of thanks to General Hertzog closed the meeting. **1954** H. Gibbs *Background to Bitterness* ii. ix. 149 So they had ridden off, farmers, shop assistants, civil servants, lawyers, singing the *Volkslied* as they camped close to the southern frontier with Natal. **1961** *Sunday Times* (Johannesburg) 19 Mar. 10/7 The 16 girls and 14 boys in the choir will give Volksliedjie recitals and volkspele performances.

Volksraad. Add: **1.** Now, the House of Assembly of the Republic of South Africa. (Earlier example.)

1840 in J. C. Chase *Natal* (1843) II. 127 On the 14th [Feb. 1840], the Chief Commandant..caused the following Proclamation to be read..:— I, Andries Wilhelmus Jacobus Pretorius, Chief Commandant..of all the Burghers of the..Volks-Raad of the South African Society of Port Natal..&c &c &c.

2. *Netherlands East Indies.* A council advisory to the Governor-General.

1920 *Manual Netherlands India* (Admiralty) viii. 248 This council, under the name of the *Volksraad*.. is a representative body of 38 members. **1948** A. J. Barnouw *Making of Mod. Holland* xi. 210 By an act of December 16, 1916, a *Volksraad* or People's Council was set up. **1974** *Encycl. Brit. Macropædia* IX. 488/1 At the end of World War I the Dutch..created the Volksraad (People's Council). Composed of a mixture of appointed and elected representatives of the three racial divisions defined by the government—Dutch, Indonesian, and 'foreign Asiatic'—the Volksraad provided opportunities for debate and criticism but no control over the government of the Indies.

volley, *sb.* Add: **1. c.** (Examples in *Physiol.*)

1928 *Jrnl. Physiol.* LXV 276 The rhythmic discharge is due to a more or less synchronous activity in a large number of the optic nerve fibres. The different ganglion cells have given up their usual independent fire of impulses and have taken to firing volleys. **1968** *Brit. Med. Bull.* XXIV. 253/2 Small localised changes in cortical potential, such as may follow the arrival of a sensory volley from the periphery, are completely lost in the background of much larger voltages produced by the rest of the cortical surface.

6. b. (Earlier example.)

1851 J. Pycroft *Cricket Field* v. 79 At Woolwich he hit a volley to long field for *nine*.

7. volley-ball, for *U.S.* read 'orig. *U.S.*' and add: also **volleyball**; (examples); also *attrib.*; also, the ball used in this game.

1896 *Physical Education* V. 50/1 Mr. W. G. Morgan of Holyoke, Mass., has developed a game..which is called Volley Ball... The play consists in keeping a ball in motion over a high net,..thus partaking of the character of two games,—tennis and hand ball. **1936** P. Fleming *News from Tartary* vii. i. 325 In the evening we played tennis with the Russians, or football or volley-ball with the Hunza guard. **1949** *Dziennik Zwiazkowy* (Chicago) 19 Nov. 6/3 Last year two of our volleyball teams finished in a tie for second place. **1976** *Milton Keynes Express* 4 June 39/7 Stoke Mandeville has told the club that any money raised for them will be used to purchase table tennis nets and volleyballs for the National Spinal Injuries Centre.

volley, *v.* Add: **1. c.** Also, *Association Football*, to kick (the ball) before it touches the ground; to score (a goal) in this way.

1909 in Webster. **1972** G. Green *Great Moments in Sport: Soccer* viii. 85 He vollied [*sic*] in Bowen's clever lob with half an hour left. **1976** *Scotsman* 25 Nov. 25/1 In 52 minutes Somner volleyed a goal from McQuade's cross. **1976** *Norwich Mercury* 10 Dec., It was he who provided the perfect pass for Mann to volley the ball against the St. Andrews crossbar before the interval.

e. To fire a volley or volleys at.

1908 Hardy *Dynasts* III. vii. ii. 489 Kempt's brigade.. volleys murderously Donzelot's columns..and repulses them.

Volnay (vǫ·lnēⁱ). Also 7 **Volne.** [Name of a commune in the department of Côte-d'Or, France.] A red wine of Burgundy, produced near Beaune (formerly also a white wine).

1699 M. Lister *Journey to Paris* 161 Volne, a pale Champagne, but exceeding brisk upon the Palate...is said to grow upon the very borders of Burgundy, and to participate of the Excellency of both Counties. **1833** [see Pomard]. **1889** [see *Corton]. **1961** A. Wilson *Old Men at Zoo* i. 48 'They've got two good burgundies here,' he said, 'this and the Volnay '57.' **1979** R. Lewis *Violent Death* v. 140 A good lunch of roast beef with an excellent Volnay.

‖ **volost** (vǫ·lǫst). [a. Russ. *volost'*.] The smallest rural administrative subdivision in Imperial Russia and the U.S.S.R. (abolished in 1930).

1889 in G. N. Curzon *Russia in Central Asia* v. 114 There are forty *volosts*, or sub-districts, in the Merv circuit. **1920** B. Russell *Pract. & Theory Bolshevism* i. v. 75, I asked in the villages how they were represented on the Volost (the next larger area) or the Gubernia. **1948** J. Towster *Political Power in U.S.S.R.* iv. 66 The Baltic republics..are still divided into *uyezds* and *volosts* as in Imperial Russia. **1959** *Chambers's Encycl.* XIV. 102/2 The terms *okrug* (national enclave), *uyezd* (district) and *volost* (rural area) are obsolescent. **1974** *Encycl. Brit. Macropædia* XVI. 59/1 Kiselev..provided for a measure of self-government under which the mayor of the *volost* (a district grouping several villages or peasant communes) was elected by male householders.

volplane, *v.* (In Dict. s.v. Volplane *sb.*) Add: Also *transf.* (esp. with bird as subj.) and *fig.* Hence **vo·lplaning** *ppl. a.*

1922 'Klaxon' *Heather Mixture* xi. 223 Two cocks [*sc.* pheasants] came over the brow.., and with steady wings volplaned down the line from the right. **1929** E. Booth *Stealing through Life* x. 243, I..volplaned down a flight of steps and hit the..sidewalk on my hands and knees. **1936** D. McCowan *Animals Canad. Rockies* xx. 182 You may be fortunate enough to see one of these [*sc.* flying] squirrels as it volplanes gracefully from a high branch to the ground. **1937** *Discovery* Dec. 364/1 Volplaning marsupials. **1970** 'E. Lindall' *Gathering of Eagles* v. 46 They could all..die together..watched by the eagles, seeing..the huge birds volplaning in.

Volscian, *sb.* **2.** (Earlier example.)

1859 B. W. Dwight *Mod. Philol.* I. 187 The Umbro-Samnite Dialects: Umbrian; Samnite or Oscan; Volscian; Marsian.

Volstead (vǫ·lstėd). The name of Andrew J. *Volstead* (1860–1947), American legislator, originator of the legislation to enforce prohibition (sense *4) which was passed in 1919 by the U.S. Congress, used *attrib.* to designate this legislation or the period during which prohibition was in force.

1920 *Current Opinion* Apr. 451/1 The Wet leaders..will wage a campaign for the election..of Congressmen favorable to changes in the Volstead Act. **1935** A. G. Macdonell *Visit to Amer.* xiii. 229 The Volstead amendment led to some pretty confusion, but the repeal of the Volstead amendment seems to be almost worse. **1949** *Chicago Tribune* 8 Sept. 22/2 In the Volstead era, corrupt politicians talked to exactly the same effect with the leaders of the Anti-Saloon league. **1977** H. Fast *Immigrants* iii. 179 The Congress of the United States was overriding President Wilson's veto of the Volstead Act and making Prohibition the law of the land. *Ibid.* 203 This is the finest wine country in the world, and some day the world is going to discover that—if we ever rid ourselves of this lousy Volstead thing.

Hence **Vo·lsteadism,** the policy of the Volstead Act; prohibition.

1920 *Harvey's Weekly* 27 Mar. 11/2 The Republicans would have to stand for Volsteadism or incur defeat. **1947** *Chicago Daily News* 23 Jan. 14/1 Volstead didn't write the law. Nor was he an apostle of the fanaticism called 'Volsteadism'.

volt (vōᵘlt), *v.*[2] *literary.* [f. the sb.] **a.** *trans.* To charge (something) as with electricity; to energize; to shock. **b.** *intr.* To travel like an electric current. Hence **vo·lted** *ppl. a.*

1930 R. Campbell *Adamastor* 48 Dainty one, deadly one..Whose coils are volted with electric power. *Ibid.* 61 A starved mongrel... Fierce tremors volted through his bony notches. **1936** —— *Mithraic Emblems* 21 The volted ecstasy outglows A dolphin dying in the noon. **1936** *Times Lit. Suppl.* 28 Mar. 266/4 Give man the grace to find a firm abode,..Not in power's seat that volts the sitter dead. **1942** S. Spender *Ruins & Visions* ii. 38 Driven by intolerance and volted with lies. **1962** N. Coghill in Davis & Wrenn *Engl. & Medieval Stud.* 207 All that is finest and most central in this figure is 'made' by a coalescence or fusion of allegory, parable, and symbol, and that is the poetic fact that volts it with imaginative power.

voltage[2]. Add: **a.** (Later *fig.* examples.)

1949 E. Pound *Pisan Cantos* lxxx. 85 Whoi didn't he [*sc.* Padraic Colum] keep on writing poetry at that voltage. **1961** *Times* 24 Mar. 18/4 Walton's first symphony is a work of extraordinarily high voltage. **1978** F. Olbrich *Desouza pays Price* xx. 125 Beaming the full voltage of her smile at Habib.

b. Also in *fig.* use.

1959 *Listener* 8 Oct. 590/1 Synge's brief but high-voltage career. **1966** N. Freeling *King of Rainy Country* 128 Her high-voltage emotions injected into the situation would doubtless tangle things still further.

c. *Comb.*, as *voltage doubler*, *-regulation*, *regulator*; *voltage-doubling* adj.; **voltage clamp** *Physiol.*, (the application of) a constant voltage maintained across a cell membrane by artificial means; so **voltage-clamped** *a.*, **-clamping** *vbl. sb.*; **voltage-controlled** *a.*, controllable by varying the applied voltage; **voltage divider** a linear resistor or series of resistors which can be tapped at any intermediate point to obtain a voltage equal to a desired fraction of the voltage applied between its ends.

1952 *Jrnl. Physiol.* CXVII. 504 (*heading*) Mathematical description of membrane current during a voltage clamp. **1964** G. H. Haggis et al. *Introd. Molecular Biol.* vi. 159 These ionic permeability changes associated with the action potential have been studied in squid axons and frog muscle cells..with the very elegant 'voltage clamp' technique. **1979** *Acta Protozoologica* XVIII. 183 Instantaneous I/V plots of voltage-clamped deciliated cells lack the negative resistance property characteristic of ciliated cells. **1981** *Nature* 15 Oct. 517 Although the principle is simple enough—to keep the voltage across a cell membrane constant—the technology of voltage-clamping has become a sophisticated exercise in electrical engineering. **1962** Simpson & Richards *Physical Princ. Junction Transistors* xiv. 359 External methods of gain control usually employ auxiliary diodes..to act as a voltage-controlled potential divider. **1976** *Electronic Engin.* Nov. 27/1 It [*sc.* a waveform generator circuit] can be used..in many other applications where a voltage controlled waveform is required. **1930** *Sci. Abstr.* B. XXXIII. 846 (Index), Voltage dividers, capacity and resistance types. **1932** *Bureau of Standards Jrnl. Res.* (U.S.) IX. 81 (*heading*) Theory of voltage dividers and their use with cathode ray oscillographs. **1983** *IEEE Trans. Instrumentation & Measurement* XXXII. 33/2 The attenuation reference standard in this system is a high class..inductive voltage divider. **1947** R. Lee *Electronic Transformers & Circuits* iii. 51 (*heading*) Voltage doublers. *Ibid.* (*caption*) Relation of peak sine voltage to d-c voltage in voltage-doubling circuit. **1956** *Nature* 18 Feb. 298/1 Electrical characteristics are next treated, including..descriptions of..voltage-regulation methods and apparatus. **1902** *Encycl. Brit.* XXVIII. 90/2 (*heading*) Voltage regulators. **1962** Simpson & Richards *Physical Princ. Junction Transistors* 496 We consider a voltage regulator whose input voltage..and output voltage and current..are connected by the equation [etc.].

Voltaic, *a.* Add: **3. c.** *fig.*

1920 D. H. Lawrence *Lost Girl* iii. 45 A superhuman, voltaic force filled her.

Volta·ic, *sb.* and *a.*[2] [f. the name of the West African river *Volta* + -ic.] **A.** *sb.* **a.** A group of Niger-Congo languages of West Africa. **b.** A speaker of one of these languages; a citizen of the Republic of Upper Volta. **B.** *adj.* Of or pertaining to this group of languages, or to this republic or its citizens. Cf. *Upper Voltan *a.* and *sb.*

1939 L. H. Gray *Foundations of Lang.* xii. 402 The divisions of Sudano-Guinean, according to Delafosse, may now be enumerated:..Voltaic (fifty-three languages)..apparently possessing inclusive and exclusive pronouns for the first person plural. **1949** L. Homburger *Negro-African Languages* i. 22 The people who speak Voltaic languages number about 3,000,000. **1967** M. Schlauch *Language* ii. 39 Suffixes are also used to indicate nominal classes (e.g. in Voltaic). **1969** [see *Senufo]. **1970** P. Oliver *Savannah Syncopators* 66 The use of a drone or continuous humming between sung phrases is also a vocal feature shared by Voltaic peoples and some blues singers. **1976** *New Society* 11 Nov. 293/3 Doing their military service by teaching in Voltaic schools. *Ibid.* 294/3 Educated Voltaics like to discount the CIA theory with one of their own. **1979** *Observer* (Colour Suppl.) 17 June 56/3 France for example in 1976 exported 64 million dollars worth of goods to Upper Volta (43 per cent of Voltaic imports). **1984** *Chicago Sun-Times* 9 Jan. 18 The government is treated with some skepticism by older Voltaics.

Voltairean, Voltairian, *sb.* and *a.* Add: **A.** *sb.* *β.* (Earlier example.)

1842 J. S. Mill *Let.* 10 Jan. in *Wks.* (1963) XIII. 497 We are all either bigots or Voltairians.

B. *adj.* *α.* (Earlier example.)

1846 Bp. of Meath in J. O'Connor *Hist. Ireland 1798–1924* (1925) I. viii. 249 Voltairean newspapers.

β. (Earlier example.)

1833 J. S. Mill *Lett.* (1910) I. 75 The little *feuilles* which one buys as one goes into a theatre, are the representatives of the Voltairian philosophy at present.

Voltairianism. Add: (Examples of form *Voltaireanism.*)

1901 *Q. Rev.* CXCIV. 599 Sir Henry Craik pounces with perhaps unnecessary severity upon the flippant Voltaireanism, the dapper self-assurance, and the 'slovenly omniscience' of Jeffrey and his allies. **1942** *Scrutiny* X. 400 Dostoyevsky's denunciation of the deracinated nobility who despised their own language and national character and lived in a froth of Voltaireanism and French *bons mots*.

Voltairish, *a.* For *rare*⁻¹ read *rare* and add further example.

a **1846** B. R. Haydon *Autobiogr.* (1927) iii. xiii. 252 '*Ah*,' shrugged out monsieur le valet, with a sparkling Voltairish look which every Frenchman has when convicted, as if planning a repartee, '*c'est très vrai.*'

voltammetry (vǫlt-, vǭ͡ultæ·mĕtri). *Physical Chem.* [f. Volt *sb.* + Am(père + -metry.] An electroanalytical technique for establishing the identities and concentrations of various ions in solution (see quot. 1978). Hence **voltamme·tric** *a.*, by means of or employing voltammetry; **voltamme·trically** *adv.*

1940 Kolthoff & Laitinen in *Science* 16 Aug. 152/1 (*heading*) The voltammetric determination of oxygen. *Ibid.*, By the term 'voltammetry' we mean the determination and interpretation of current-voltage curves obtained in electrolysis experiments using a suitable microelectrode as an indicator electrode. *Ibid.* 153/1 Oxygen can also be determined voltammetrically by using a platinum wire microelectrode. **1976** *Nature* 8 July 146/1 An efflux of 5-hydroxyindole acetic acid..into the CSF was observed by the voltammetric monitoring. **1978** *Kirk–Othmer Encycl. Chem. Technol.* (ed. 3) II. 618 Voltammetry is the general procedure of studying the current-voltage behavior of a microelectrode in a system which also contains a large nonpolarizable reference electrode and a large excess of an electrolyte... Polarography is a special case of voltammetry in which the small, polarizable electrode is a capillary tube from which small mercury droplets emerge at regular intervals... The plot of current vs voltage..provides qualitative and quantitative information about the solution composition. **1983** *Jrnl. Chem. Soc. Dalton Trans.* 991 (*heading*) Electron-transfer processes and electrodeposition involving the iron hexacyanoferrates studied voltammetrically.

Volterra (vǫlte·ră). The name of a town in the Tuscany region of Italy, used *attrib.* to designate alabaster quarried there. Hence also **Volte·rran** *a.*

1924 D. H. Lawrence in M. Magnus *Mem. Foreign Legion* 20 So at last coming down to the Mercato Nuovo we saw little bowls of Volterra marble, a natural amber colour, for four francs. *a* **1930** —— *Etruscan Places* (1932) vi. 183 Everybody knows Volterra marble—so called—nowadays, because of the translucent bowls of it which hang under the electric lights, as shades, in half the hotels of the world. *Ibid.*, There is no love lost between a Volterran alabaster worker and the lump of pale Volterran earth he turns into pale marketable form.

volume, *sb.* Add: **I. 3. b.** (Earlier example).

1803 M. Wilmot *Let.* 3 May in *Russ. Jrnls.* (1934) I. 13 A sentimental story that speakes Volumes in favour of the Count and his Daughter.

IV. 12. Special Combs.: **volume control**, (*a*) control of the volume of sound, esp. when reproduced or transmitted; (*b*) a knob or other device for achieving this; **volume-density**, the number *of* anything per unit volume; **volume indicator** *Electronics*, a device for measuring the power of a complex electrical signal corresponding to a sound pattern, so as to indicate the volume of the sound that is represented; **volume table** *Forestry*, a set of empirically derived figures relating the volume of timber in a given type of tree or log to measurable parameters such as height and girth, thus enabling such measurements to be used in estimating timber volumes in the field; **volume unit** = VU, vu s.v. *V 5 b.

1927 *Star* 4 June 6/4 Volume Control... Noises, etc. in the loud speaker can be very easily reduced. **1931** T. H. Pear *Voice & Personality* 78 It [*sc.* a preacher's voice] should be articulate, but with an efficient and graded volume-control. **1933** *Boys' Mag.* July 108/2 One of the all-important components..is the volume control. **1956** *B.B.C. Handbk. 1957* 100 They are also responsible for the volume control and technical quality of programmes leaving studios. **1977** 'E. Crispin' *Glimpses of Moon* viii. 152 Titty..was wearing the hearing-aid, so Ling..addressed himself..to her, while she fiddled with volume control. **1956** *Nature* 4 Feb. 226/1 These photographs have been useful for determining..the area-density and volume-density of the flying locusts. **1968** R. A. Lyttelton *Mysteries Solar Syst.* v. 155 The time that an individual particle would take to cross the cylinder..would be of the order of $2s/V$, and for this time the particle would be contributing to the average volume-density within the cylinder. **1923** *Trans. Amer. Inst. Electr. Engineers* XLII. 77/2 There has been developed a device which is called a 'volume indicator'. This consists of an amplifier detector working into a direct-current meter. **1961** G. Millerson *Technique Television Production* i. 16 His [*sc.* the sound mixer's] attention is divided mostly between the flickering needle of his volume indicator and his picture monitor. **1895** W. Schlich *Man. Forestry* III. 39 (*heading*) Estimate of volume by means of volume tables. **1902** *Forestry Q.* I. 6 The Bavarian government, in 1846, instituted a very extended study..of the stems of the more important forest trees of that country. The volume tables which resulted..involved a complete analytical measurement of over forty thousand trees. **1981** *Southern Jrnl. Appl. Forestry* V. 186/2 Users of volume tables are cautious about applying them outside the region from which they were derived, because the effects of geographic location are unknown. **1940** *Chambers's Techn. Dict.* 897/1 *VU*, the number of volume-units above or below zero power-level..indicated by the standardised volume-indicator. **1960** *McGraw-Hill Encycl. Sci. & Technol.* XIV. 374/2 Meters which give readings in volume units, called VU meters, are widely used for monitoring radio broadcasts and for sound recording.

volumeless (vǫ·liumlės), *a.* [f. Volume *sb.* + -less.] Occupying no volume; *spec.* applied to an idealized polymer chain having this property.

1946 *Nature* 26 Oct. 571/1 An ideally flexible and volumeless [polymer] chain. **1967** Margerison & East *Introd. Polymer Chem.* i. 17 Certain configurations open to the 'volumeless' chain are not available to the real polymer chain. **1974** *Jrnl. Polymer Sci.: Polymer Symposia* No. 46. 97 An expression for Γ, suggested by a well known equation for a regular cubic network of freely jointed volumeless chains, is derived. **1983** [see *voluminal *a.*].

volumetric, *a.* Add: (Earlier example.) *volumetric efficiency* (Mech.), the ratio of the volume of fluid actually displaced by a piston or plunger to its swept volume.

1857 H. E. Roscoe tr. *R. Bunsen's Gasometry* 170 The saturated solution..becomes sufficiently diluted..to allow the ammonia to be determined by a volumetric analysis with sulphuric acid. **1912** *Proc. Inst. Automobile Engineers* VI. 78 In the writer's opinion, volumetric efficiency is almost entirely a function of port area. **1930** *Engineering* 11 July 31/2 The standard valve tuning of the E.35 engine is arranged for the best possible volumetric efficiency at 1,500 r.p.m. **1973** A. Parrish *Mech. Engineer's Ref. Bk.* ii. 51 Leakage tends to be greater than in a reciprocating design but as they [*sc.* rotary positive displacement pumps] are often used for viscous fluids such as oil, this effect may be reduced to give a volumetric efficiency of 95%.

volumetrically, *adv.* (Earlier example.)

1863 W. O. Markham tr. *Neubauer & Vogel's Anal. Urine* 305 The determination of the albumen volumetrically by means of ferrocyanide of potassium.

voluminal (vŏliū·minăl), *a.* [f. L. *volūmin-*, *volūmen* (see Volume *sb.*) + -al.] Of, pertaining to, or possessing volume.

1872 *Proc. R. Soc.* XX. 5 The remarkable phenomena of the voluminal conditions at and near the critical point of temperature and pressure. **1925** J. Joly *Surface-Hist. Earth* vii. 113 A small upward displacement must then be attended with voluminal expansion. **1983** *Nucl. Instruments & Methods* CCV. 211/1 Many works..have been published for volumeless sources such as point isotropic and beam sources. But only a few papers deal with voluminal sources in which self-absorption and self-scattering of gamma rays cannot be disregarded.

voluntarism. Add: **3.** orig. *U.S.* **a.** The principle of relying on voluntary action rather than compulsion; *spec.* with reference to political and trade-union activities. Cf. Voluntaryism 2 in Dict. and Suppl.

1924 S. Gompers in *Rep. Proc. 44th Ann. Convention Amer. Federation Labor* 5/2, I want to urge devotion to the fundamentals of human liberty—the principles of voluntarism. **1948** *Sun* (Baltimore) 6 Dec. 12/3 There is reason to think that voluntarism is preferable to compulsion on racial matters as on everything else. **1973** *Times* 15 Jan. 18/6 From an almost exclusive reliance on 'voluntarism', *ie.* the promotion of negotiating procedures drawing at most indirectly upon law, Great Britain has now imposed upon the conduct of unions and employers more formal..regulations. **1983** *Listener* 22 Sept. 5/1 So much for voluntarism, the golden rule of the British TUC.

b. Denoting the involvement of voluntary organizations in social welfare. Also *spec.* in U.K. use = *volunteerism 2.

1957 *Observer* 8 Sept. 15/4 This is the essence of the American economic achievement to-day: an emphasis on the importance of the individual... And an increasing knowledge of the techniques by which men can cooperate in 'free collectivism'—voluntary private organisation. Voluntarism in our social structure is tremendously important. Without it the whole system would break down. **1969** *Wall St. Jrnl.* 21 Mar. 1/1 'Voluntarism'—President Nixon's program to enlist the help of private groups in solving social problems. **1979** *Guardian* 10 Aug., Voluntarism is one of the central characteristics of a number of organisations with which the Prince of Wales has specific connections. **1981** *Times Lit. Suppl.* 7 Aug. 911/2 When their representatives attained some municipal power, they clung to a weedy sort of voluntarism and missed their chance of creating active local democracy. **1981** *Times* 7 Sept. 2/4 The Government's emphasis on the role of volunteers in providing social services could be counterproductive... Some Labour councils connected the twin themes of public spending cuts and the strong emphasis on voluntarism. **1982** *Chicago Sun-Times* 31 Aug. 30 Bernardin could be the key to the rebirth of a larger sense of community—at a time when its implicit sense of voluntarism would be in keeping with the Reagan era and with the voluntaristic spirit alive today. **1984** *Listener* 14 June 12/2 We are going back to reliance on 'voluntarism' in this vital field.

voluntaristic, *a.* Add: **2.** Pertaining to voluntary action.

1961 B. R. Wilson *Sects & Society* i. iv. 89 Where voluntaristic activities are concerned the sectarian's feud with society remains latent. **1969** A. Stewart in Ionescu & Gellner *Populism* 194 Populist movements which are basically protest movements are threatened by the anti-institutional, voluntaristic character of grass-roots populism. **1974** B. Pearce tr. *Amin's Accumulation on World Scale* I. 29 Being voluntaristic in character, development policy draws upon new techniques of economic planning in order to work out the series of choices involved. **1977** *Dædalus* Summer 72 The obligatory component in social relationship yields to the optional or voluntaristic, status gives way to contract. **1982** [see *voluntarism 3 b].

voluntary, *a.* Add: **1. b.** *Voluntary Service Overseas*, an organization promoting voluntary work by young people (in education, social welfare, etc.) in developing countries; the service so offered or the scheme itself.

1960 *Voluntary Service Overseas* 1 Voluntary Service

Overseas enables as many as possible of these young people to have this opportunity—and, in meeting the needs of others, to deepen their own experience. *Ibid.*, Governments and agencies overseas are asking for volunteers to serve as temporary auxiliaries in many fields—social welfare, schools, youth clubs... It is in response to these requests that Voluntary Service Overseas is sending selected volunteers. **1964** M. DICKSON *World Elsewhere* ii In September 1958 ten young men left Britain for Sarawak. Three flew to Nigeria and two set off for Ghana. All were eighteen years old... They were the spearhead of the scheme which was Voluntary Service Overseas. **1965** *Listener* 7 Jan. 21/2 One finds British young people doing voluntary service overseas in all sorts of out-of-the-way places.

7. d. *voluntary patient*, one who enters a mental hospital without being committed to it.

1930 *Daily Express* 6 Sept. 9/4 Instructions sent by the Board of Control to local authorities regarding the working of the Mental Treatment Act (1930) stipulate that 'mental hospital' is to be substituted for 'asylum', and 'voluntary patient' is to be used instead of 'voluntary boarder'. **1943** G. GREENE *Ministry of Fear* III. i. 167 If only someone would complain—they are all voluntary patients. **1979** J. THOMSON *Deadly Relations* xiii. 189, I had a nervous breakdown... I..was sent to a clinic..as a voluntary patient.

9. a. (Later examples.) *spec.* in *Educ.* with reference to schools, etc., maintained by voluntary bodies.

1944 *Act* 7 & 8 *Geo. VI* c. 31 § 8 Primary and secondary schools maintained by a local education authority, not being nursery schools or special schools, shall, if established by a local education authority..be known as county schools and, if established otherwise than by such an authority, be known as voluntary schools. **1969** L. TINKHAM in Cockburn & Blackburn *Student Power* 84 There are now about one hundred Local Education Authority colleges and half as many independent voluntary colleges. **1976** *Star* (Sheffield) 29 Nov. 9/1 Pupils will be transferred to the Perlethorpe Church of England Voluntary Aided Primary School.

voluntaryism. Add: **2.** (Later examples.) Now usu. with reference to voluntary labour. Cf. *VOLUNTEERISM 2.

1946 *Organisation & Finance Adult Educ.* (Min. Educ.) 36 We are unanimously of the opinion that voluntaryism as exemplified by the Workers' Educational Association is essential if the spirit of adult education is to be preserved. **1967** *Listener* 1 June 709/2 In the light of the present arguments about the prices and incomes policy, Bevin's insistence on what he called 'voluntaryism' is most significant... Bevin resisted strong pressures in parliament to conscript labour on the home front.

volunteer, *sb.* and *a.* **A.** *sb.* **4.** Delete † *Obs.*$^{-1}$ and add: A self-sown plant. (Later examples.)

1960 *Jrnl. Forestry* LVIII. 402/3 The stand was planted on a 6 × 6-foot spacing, with some interspersed volunteers. **1978** *New Yorker* 3 July 42/1 Around the buildings ..are some of the tallest volunteers in New York, top-heavy plants.

B. *attrib.* or as *adj.* **1. d.** *Volunteer State*, a nickname for Tennessee (see quot. 1950).

1853 J. C. M. RAMSEY *Ann. Tennessee* 116 Thus early did the 'Volunteer State' commence its novitiate in arms. **1950** *Newsweek* 20 Mar. 96/2 A call for 2,800 volunteers [in the Mexican War of 1847] in Tennessee brought out 30,000 men and gave Tennessee its nickname, 'The Volunteer State'. **1973** *Guardian* 14 June 13/2 There was a spectacular..murder deep in the hills of Tennessee..as could only happen in the deepest by-ways of the Volunteer State.

volunteer, *v.* Add: **5.** (Earlier examples.)

1805 JANE AUSTEN *Let.* 27 Aug. (1952) 166 She volunteers, moreover, her love to little Marianne, with the promise of bringing her a doll. **1813** —— *Let.* 14 Oct. (1952) 354, I talk to Cassy about Chawton; she remembers much but does not volunteer on the subject.

6. (Earlier *fig.* example.)

1814 JANE AUSTEN *Mansfield Park* II. ix. 200 Thursday ..opened with more kindness to Fanny than such.. unmanageable days often volunteer.

volunteered, *ppl. a.* (Earlier examples.)

1845 *Times* 1 Nov. 4/4 The members of the press retired..from the hall, into which they had been invited by the volunteered cards of admission from the benchers. **1879** GEO. ELIOT *Theophrastus Such* i. 7 The fellow-feeling which should restrain us from turning our volunteered and picked confessions into an act of accusation against others.

volunteerism. Add: **2.** *N. Amer.* The use of volunteer labour, esp. in the social services. Cf. *VOLUNTARISM 3 b, *VOLUNTARYISM 2.

1977 *New Yorker* 1 Aug. 48/2 Still another productivity proposal is that as the city work force shrinks, volunteerism should be encouraged; citizen volunteers could serve as auxiliary policemen, park attendants, case-workers, and school aides, for instance. **1979** *Globe & Mail* (Toronto) 28 May S14 A closer examination of voluntary action or 'volunteerism' as it relates to volunteer support staffs in amateur sport. **1983** *United Airlines Mag.* June 48 Minnesota's Corporate Volunteerism Council, a clearinghouse designed to help match community needs with people willing and able to give some time to others.

‖ **volupté** (volüpte). [Fr.: see VOLUPTY.] = VOLUPTUOUSNESS.

1712 M. W. MONTAGU *Let.* 12 Aug. (1965) I. 155 All things would have contributed to make your Life passe in (the true volupté) a smooth Tranquillity. **1937** L. BROMFIELD *Rains Came* III. xxxvi. 435 The lingam, symbol of creation, of *volupté* and strange desires and pleasures. **1962** W. NOWOTTNY *Lang. Poets Use* viii. 216 The elements of *volupté* and masochism in a fervent devotional tradition. **1981** *Times Lit. Suppl.* 13 Feb. 158/3 The narrative's need to shock, its dedicated oscillatings between *volupté* and vomit, are adolescent.

volupty. Delete † *Obs.* and add later example.

1929 S. LESLIE *Anglo-Catholic* xv. 216 Edward could see every brick in position with that strange microscopic vision which makes seeing a volupty of the eye.

volutin (vǫ·liūtin). *Biochem.* Also † **-ine.** [a. G. *volutin* (A. Meyer *Practicum der bot. Bakterienkunde* (1903) xiii. 80), f. L. *volūt-ans* (pres. pple. of *volūtāre* to roll), specific epithet of the bacterium *Spirillum volutans*: see -IN[1].] A basophilic compound containing polyphosphate found in metachromatic granules in the cytoplasm and vacuoles of various micro-organisms and fungi.

1908 *Q. Jrnl. Microsc. Sci.* LIII. 298 The granules ('metachromic granules', 'red granules', 'volutine granules', etc.) probably consist of some reserve material. **1947** *Nature* 11 Jan. 63/2 Volutin is a cytological entity which has long been recognised as an important constituent of the yeast cell. **1970** PASSMORE & ROBSON *Compan. Med. Stud.* II. xviii. 14/1 Volutin granules.. have a special significance in the genus *Corynebacterium* since they are produced typically by the diphtheria bacillus.

volva (vǫ·lva). [ad. ON. *völva* (also used) (Norw. *volve*) prophetess, sibyl.] In Scandinavian mythology, a prophetess, a soothsayer, a witch.

1889 P. B. DU CHAILLU *Viking Age* I. iv. 27 The Völuspa was an inspired poem of a Völva or Sibyl, and embodies the records of the creation of the present world. **1927** E. V. GORDON *Introd. Old Norse* v. 40 It is the most complete description extant of the vǫlva or sibyl of Scandinavian heathen times. **1966** S. WAVELL et al. *Trances* xvi. 133 The priestesses of Freyja known as *volva* were the shamans of their time. They wore animal skins, their boots made of calf skin, their gloves lined with the fur of arctic cats, their goddess being drawn in a cat carriage.

volve, *v.* Restrict † *Obs.* to senses 2 and 3 and add: **1.** (Later example.) *rare.*

1910 GALSWORTHY *Inn Tranq.* in *Nation* 12 Nov. 266/2 If It did not volve and revolve on Itself, It would peter out at one end or the other.

vomit, *sb.* Add: **6.** *Comb.*, as *vomit-green* adj.; **vomit bag** = *sick-bag* s.v. *SICK *a.* 12.

1975 D. LODGE *Changing Places* i. 42 The passengers swallow to relieve the pressure on their eardrums, close their eyes, finger their passports and vomit-bags. **1978** D. MURPHY *Place Apart* i. 6 The sleazy plastic Lounge Bar had a vomit-green carpet.

vomit, *v.* **4. b.** (Later examples.)

1922 JOYCE *Ulysses* 750 If there was a row on you vomit a better face. **1946** E. O'NEILL *Iceman Cometh* III. 182 You'll be saying something soon that will make you vomit your own soul like a drink of nickel rotgut that won't stay down! **1955** E. BOWEN *World of Love* x. 185 Bent in two, she vomited laughter; though also, mortified by the exhibition, she let out penitent sobs and moans.

vomiter. 1. (Later example.)

1962 'R. GORDON' *Doctor in Swim* xxiii. 160 'Also,' he added, 'one is being sick into the swimming pool.' 'All right,' I told him wearily. 'I'll do my best. Perhaps we'd better start with the little vomiter,' I suggested, putting professional things first.

vomitorial, *a.* Restrict *rare*$^{-1}$ to sense in Dict. and add: **2.** = VOMITORY *a.* (in quot. *fig.*). *rare.*

1868 SWINBURNE *Let.* 1 Jan. (1959) I. 284 What abject and vomitorial rot of Tennyson's is this in Once a Week!

vomitorium. Add: **2.** *erron.* A room in which ancient Romans are alleged to have vomited deliberately during feasts.

1923 A. HUXLEY *Antic Hay* xviii. 252 There strode in, like a Goth into the elegant marble vomitorium of Petronius Arbiter, a haggard and dishevelled person. **1965** R. EBERHART *Sel. Poems* 40 Good Boy Man! Your innards are put out, From now all space will be your vomitorium.

vo·mitous, *a. U.S.* [f. VOMIT *sb.* + -OUS.] Repugnant, loathsome, nauseating.

1952 S. KAUFFMANN *Tightrope* xiv. 241 What kind of world is this..having to trudge back from bad restaurants in sickening heat to face mountains of vomitous, meaningless, commercial tripe? **1976** *Publishers Weekly* 24 May 57/2 Those descriptions of methods of murdering human beings as dishes for the table end up being more than a little vomitous.

vomitus (vǫ·mitʊs). [L.] = VOMIT *sb.* 2 a. Also *fig.*

1904 J. M. FRENCH *Text-bk. Pract. Med.* III. 724 The presence of HCl, pepsin, and rennet is generally sufficient evidence that the vomitus has come from the stomach. **1948** *Diagnostic Procedures for Virus & Rickettsial Diseases* (Amer. Public Health Assoc.) 11 The material available for examination may be blood, sputum, vomitus, or pleural fluid obtained during illness, or tissues, etc., collected at autopsy. **1973** *Nature* 23 Mar. 265/1 Stools, urine and vomitus were collected for a total of 48 h. **1978** J. UPDIKE *Coup* (1979) v. 211 Fighting down the vomitus of superstitious terror rising in my craw.

vo·mity, *a. U.S.* [f. VOMIT *sb.* + -Y[1].] Redolent of vomit.

1951 J. D. SALINGER *Catcher in Rye* xii. 106 The cab I had was a real old one that smelled like someone'd just tossed his cookies in it. I always get those vomity kind of cabs if I go anywhere late at night. **1967** I. A. BARAKA in W. King *Black Short Story Anthol.* (1972) 125 Oh, I am drunk and vomity in my room, with only Charley Ventura to understand my grace. **1984** *Listener* 20–27 Dec. 68/3, 80 per cent of the material is American, vomity kind of lampoons of great American institutions such as Advertising and the Presidency.

von Recklinghausen's disease (fǫn re·kliŋˌhauzěn). *Path.* [Named after Friedrich *von Recklinghausen* (1833–1910), German pathologist.] **1.** A familial disease in which numerous neurofibromas develop on various parts of the body, esp. the skin, the nerve trunks, and the peripheral nerves (described by von Recklinghausen in 1882). Also **Recklinghausen's disease.**

1899, etc. [see *NEUROFIBROMATOSIS]. **1900** H. A. THOMSON *Neuroma & Neuro-Fibromatosis* iv. 55 There is not even a good general name for the group which will include all its members, unless we adopt that suggested by certain French authors, viz.—'von Recklinghausen's Disease'. **1935** [see *NEURILEMOMA, NEURILEMMOMA]. **1969** S. JABLONSKI *Illustr. Dict. Eponymic Syndromes & Dis.* 256/1 (*caption*) Recklinghausen's disease. **1976** *Path. Ann.* XI. 371 A total of 15 schwannomas were studied ultrastructurally. Of these, two were classified as neurofibromas by light microscopy and were associated with von Recklinghausen's disease.

2. A disease in which bones are weakened by diffuse resorption and fibrous replacement of the bone substance as a result of hyperparathyroidism, leading to bowing of long bones and sometimes deformities of the chest and spine (described by von Recklinghausen in 1891); osteitis fibrosa cystica.

1910 *Ann. Surg.* Aug. 163 Crile and Hill interpret..as multiple giant-cell sarcoma, but it seems to me that it belongs to the group of Von Recklinghausen's disease. **1949** *New Gould Med. Dict.* 862/1 Generalized osteitis fibrosa cystica is called von Recklinghausen's disease of the bone. **1966** WRIGHT & SYMMERS *Systemic Path.* II. xxxii. 1129/1 Some forty years elapsed before it was recognised that von Recklinghausen's disease of the bones was..directly due to an excess of circulating parathyroid hormone. **1984** TIGHE & DAVIES *Pathology* (ed. 4) xxi. 209 These changes produce the 'brown tumours' of osteitis fibrosa cystica (von Recklinghausen's disease of bone) which may be misdiagnosed as giant cell tumours of bone (osteoclastoma).

vonsenite (vǫ·nsĕnait). *Min.* [f. the name of Marcus *Vonsen* (1879–1954), U.S. amateur mineralogist who collected the original material + -ITE[1].] A borate of ferrous and ferric iron, $Fe^{II}_2Fe^{III}BO_5$, that occurs as black, lustrous, orthorhombic crystals and is the magnesium-free end-member of a series with ludwigite.

1920 A. S. EAKLE in *Amer. Mineralogist* V. 143 Its distinctive difference in composition, and its manifest difference in structural and optical characters from ludwigite, justifies the writer in proposing the new name vonsenite. **1976** *Mineral. Abstr.* XXVII. 279/2 The first Spanish occurrence of vonsenite, end-member of the magnesium and iron borate series, is reported from the 'Monchi' mine [Badajoz].

von Willebrand (von wi·ləbrænd). *Path.* The name of E. A. von *Willebrand* (1870–1949) Finnish physician, used *attrib.* and in the possessive to designate a hereditary disease described by him that is characterized by prolonged bleeding, chiefly caused by abnormalities of the capillaries and mucous membranes.

1941 *Q. Jrnl. Med.* XXXIV. 18 It [*sc.* athrombocytopenic purpura] has also been called Von Willebrand's disease, Glantzmann's disease, and 'hemogenia'. **1966** WRIGHT & SUMMERS *Systemic Path.* I. iv. 190/1 In von Willebrand's disease the platelets are morphologically and functionally normal, but the capillaries show both structural and functional changes. **1977** [see *replacement therapy* s.v. *REPLACEMENT 3].

voodoo, *sb.* Add: Also **vodoo. 3.** *voodoo adorer, king, queen.*

1868 *De Bow's Rev.* Aug. 724 But may not the agent be met, then, by some such valid objection, on the part of the *Vodoo* adorers? **1872** *New Orleans Times* 28 June, Soon there arrived a skiff containing ten persons, among which was the Voudou queen. **1974** A. MURRAY *Stomping Blues* ii. 10 Some specific..charm, or talisman, which can be counteracted only with the aid of a voodoo queen or madam (or somewhat less often, a voodoo king, doctor, witchdoctor, or snakedoctor).

voodooist (vū·duist). [f. VOODOO *sb.* + -IST.] A practitioner of voodoo. Also *fig.*

1929 W. B. SEABROOK *Magic Island* 289 The connection which Haitian Voodooists believe exists between Dangbé and Ayida-Ouèdo. **1935** *Sun* (Baltimore) 2 Jan. 10/1 Full payment of the bonus will be accomplished..by the addition of the strength of the miracle workers in finance, the monetary voodooists, to the strength of the veterans' bloc. **1958** *Times* 18 Sept. 13/2 On the one side are set a young American officer, his wife..and others of his race, and, on the other, well, the others: the dark, the alien, the voodooists. **1966** G. GREENE *Comedians* I. ii. 57 Joseph was a good Catholic as well as a good Voodooist.

voom (vūm), *int. U.S.* [Echoic.] Indicating the sound of an explosion; usu. in *fig.* contexts. Occas. redupl. as *sb.*, the roar of an engine being revved. Cf. *VROOM.

1964 in Hamblett & Deverson *Generation X* 115 Ideally, according to them, young people should be seen and not heard. The moment they do something to draw attention to themselves, voom: trouble. **1966** S. J. PERELMAN in *New Yorker* 23 Nov. 58/1 The inspiration came to me—*voom*. **1978** *New York* 3 Apr. 56/1 The screeching car brakes, honking horns, the voom-voom of motorcycles, and the thundering of First Avenue buses exhausted me. **1985** *Observer* 12 May 1/1, I thought someone had let off a smoke bomb, then voom it all went off.

‖ **voorbok** (fūᵊ·ɹbǫk). *S. Afr.* Pl. **voorbokke.** [Afrikaans.] A goat which acts as bell-wether to a flock of sheep. Also *fig.* Cf. BELL-WETHER 2.

1913 C. PETTMAN *Africanderisms* 540 *Voorbok*... A goat ..is generally used on South African sheep-farms, instead of a bell-wether as in England. **1947** *Cape Argus* 29 Mar. 6 Many English-speaking South Africans regarded him as a man wielding a moderating influence upon racial politics. Why then should he not be useful as a bell-wether ('voorbok') leading United Party sheep into the Herenigde kraal? **1951** *Cape Times* 15 Aug. 2/6 A delivery van ran into a flock of sheep.., killing 25 sheep and the voorbok. **1972** *Daily Dispatch* (East London) 6 May 10 It reminds me of days long ago when farmers trekked their sheep from the Free State to the better winter grazing of the Natal lowveld. Each flock was led by a goat, the voorbok. The sheep..would never cross a river or enter a gate unless led by the more clever voorbok. **1976** *Evening Post* (Port Elizabeth) 20 Nov., The woman..was described in court as one of the 'voorbokke' of the riots who incited children to throw stones at White people's cars.

‖ **voorhuis** (fūᵊ·ɹhœis). *S. Afr.* [Cape Du., a. Du. *voorhuis* fore-part, hall of a house.] In a Cape Dutch house, an entrance hall, or a room into which the front door opens; a front room or sitting-room.

1822 W. J. BURCHELL *Trav. Interior S.Afr.* I. vi. 118 At about half an hour after nine, all retired to rest; some to a mat on the floor in the *voorhuis* (entrance-room, or hall). **1867** E. L. LAYARD *Birds S. Afr.* 118 Perhaps one or two would have found their way into the *voorhuis*, or entrance-hall. **1923** [see *REIMPJE, REIMPIE]. **1946** *Cape Times Week-end Mag.* 16 Nov. 4 The thatched cottage..had only two rooms; a *voorhuis* and bedroom. **1981** *N. & Q.* June 193/2 The *voorhuis* was the large central space or hall, often running right through the house, off which the other rooms opened.

‖ **voorkamer** (fūᵊ·ɹkāməɹ). *S. Afr.* [Afrikaans.] = prec. Occas. partially anglicized as *fore-kamer*.

1775 S. PIGOT *Let.* Aug. in 'V. M. Fitzroy' *Dark Bright Land* (1955) i. 16 Papa and Leonora..are at Whisk in mijnheer's fore-kamer as they style it. **1827** G. THOMPSON *Trav. & Adv. S. Afr.* (ed. 2) I. I. iii. 49, I slept this night in the outer apartment (voorkamer) or sitting-room of the house. **1896** *Cape Argus* 2 Jan. 5 The flash entered at the front doorway, and the shock was felt by all the occupants of the *voorkamer*, fourteen in number. **1940** 'B. KNIGHT' *Piping on Wind* IV. xx. 298 The voorkamer had been cleared of its furniture for dancing. **1981** *N. & Q.* June 193/2 The sitting-room or *voorkamer* appears to have been most often one of the smaller rooms, and with a fireplace.

voorlooper. Add: Now usu. **voorloper.** (Earlier and later examples.) Also *fig.*

1837 J. E. ALEXANDER *Western Afr.* I. xiii. 323 Then a long wagon would pass..drawn by a span of ten or fourteen oxen under the guidance of a *voorlooper*, a brown boy, holding occasionally a small rope attached to the horns of the leading bullocks. **1899** G. H. RUSSEL *Under Sjambok* 50 But, have you not got me a driver and voorloper? **1947** *Cape Argus* 22 Feb. 4 We in the pilot train are at first sight everywhere mistaken for the royal train itself. In time..the fact that we are merely the 'voorloper' of royalty will become more generally known. **1974** *Weekend Post* 21 Dec. 2 Clandestine trips were made across the Great Fish River, and it was on these that George Wood became a 'voorloper' of the oxen.

‖ **voorskot** (fūᵊ·ɹskǫt). *S. Afr.* [Afrikaans, f. *voorskiet* to advance (money).] The advance payment for a crop, wool clip, etc., by a farmers' co-operative society or similar body to its members. Also *transf.* Cf. *AGTERSKOT.

1948 *Cape Times* 22 Nov. 14 The Land Bank had fixed the *voorskot* price for first grade lucerne at 3s. for 100 lb. **1958** *Ibid.* 6 Nov. 1/1 Importers of raw materials and machinery would..receive 33⅓ per cent. of 1958 issues as *voorskot*. **1961** *Ibid.* 15 Feb. 9/7 A figure of R50m. is being mentioned as a *voorskot* for Bantu homelands. **1974** *Eastern Province Herald* (Port Elizabeth) 9 Sept., The Voorskot for the 1974/75 wool season has been fixed at an average of R1.50 a kilogram for clean wool.

‖ **voorslag** (fūᵊ·ɹslaχ). [Afrikaans.] The lash of a whip.

1833 *Graham's Town Jrnl.* 4 Apr. 3 He then took his whip and in endeavouring to frighten them began using the 'voor slach' of the whip. **1852** C. BARTER *Dorp & Veld* v. 43 Putting a new *voorslag* (lash) to the wagon-whip, that its smack might be clear and loud. **1910** J. BUCHAN *Prester John* iii. 59 He roared with laughter at my way of tying a *voorslag*. **1939** 'D. RAME' *Wine of Good Hope* I. v. 71 The great twelve foot driving whip with its thong of eland hide..and its thin, cutting voorslag. **1973** *Farmer's Weekly* (Suppl.) 30 May 37 Voorslags 86c doz.

Vopo (fōᵘ·po). [a. Ger., f. *vo*lks*po*lizei people's police.] (A member of) the *Volkspolizei* (see *VOLK 3 b).

1954 *Ann. Reg. 1953* 216 Members of the 'people's police', or *Vopos*, threw away their weapons. **1959** *News Chron.* 9 July 4/6 The Vopo—the People's Police. **1966**, **1967** [see *GREPO]. **1978** L. HEREN *Growing up on The Times* vi. 237 The young Vopo returned with a sergeant .., who returned our passports with an apology.

voraciousness. (Later example.)

1974 R. HELMS *Tolkien's World* iv. 80 The Orcs are covered with hair, in part to represent their sexual voraciousness and animality.

vorlage (fōᵊ·ɹlagə). [a. Ger. (both senses). Cf. G. *vorlegen* to lean forward.] **1. a.** *Skiing.* (see quot. 1939.) **b.** *pl.* Skiing trousers. Also **vorlagers.**

1939 WEBSTER Add., *Vorlage*... A position in which one leans forward from the ankles without lifting the heels from the skis, keeping the body, as a rule, at least perpendicular to the slope. **1958** *Vogue* Jan. 1 (Advt.), The Winter Sports Shop..has everything for the skier:.. Luis Ebster designs and cuts the vorlages. *Ibid.* 35/1 Tattersall checks of black and caramel match caramel vorlagers. **1959** H. LANTSCHNER *Ski-ing for Beginners* 89 One must..have the necessary Vorlage to take the weight off the skis when necessary. **1961** *Times* 27 Nov. 13/2 'Tailormade' vorlagers in a large range of sizes. **1963** C. GLYN *Don't knock Corners Off* xxii. 184 Our beanies, vorlages, ankle-length tomato coloured pants.

‖ **2.** An original version of a manuscript or a book from which a copy is produced.

1965 K. MALONE in Bessinger & Creed *Medieval & Linguistic Stud.* 120, I conceive that our scribe copied as *heol* the *hleo* of his *vorlage*. **1975** *Times Lit. Suppl.* 25 Apr. 462/4 This was first published in a French translation..in 1930 and was not followed by the Amharic original till more than thirty-five years later... More than one Amharic original was in existence, and the published text was not the *Vorlage* used for the 1930 French edition.

vorlaufer (fōᵊ·ɹlaufəɹ). [ad. G. *vorläufer* precursor, forerunner, f. *vorlaufen* to run on ahead.] A skier who travels a course before a race in order to establish a standard by which the competitors are marked.

1961 *Times* 11 Jan. 16/1 As a result of the *vorlaufers's* times, the announcer..foresaw a winning time in the region of '1·55, 1·60'. **1964** *Times* 4 Feb. 4/1 Miss T. Hecher..had followed down the *vorlaufers*.

vorpal (vǭ·ɹpăl), *a.* A word invented by 'Lewis Carroll' app. with the sense 'keen, deadly'; also in subsequent allusive uses.

1871 'L. CARROLL' *Through Looking-Glass* i. 22 The vorpal blade went snicker-snack! **1941** AUDEN *New Year Let.* II. 44 Wave at the mechanized barbarian The vorpal sword of an agrarian. **1970** [see *FRABJOUS *a.*].

‖ **vorspiel** (fōᵊ·ɹʃpīl). *Mus.* Pl. **-e.** [Ger., f. *vor* before + *spiel* (see *SPIEL *sb.*²).] A prelude.

1876 STAINER & BARRETT *Dict. Mus. Terms* 452/2 *Vorspiel* (*Ger.*), prelude, introductory movement, overture. **1889** G. B. SHAW *London Music 1888–89* (1937) 66 It was not surprising to find a charm in this 'Vorspiel' that is wanting in the empty and violently splendid overture to Rienzi. **1895** G. KOBBÉ *How to understand Wagner's Ring* (ed. 6) 66 This vorspiel is a masterly representation..of a storm gathering. **1974** *Encycl. Brit. Macropædia* XIII. 680/1 By the time of Bach, the written *Choral-Vorspiel*, or chorale prelude (as opposed to the improvised prelude to the chorale within the Lutheran service), prelude and fugue..were firmly established forms for the organ. **1983** *New Oxf. Compan. Mus.* II. 1949/2 *Vorspiel* (Ger.), 'prelude'. Wagner called the introductions to his operas *Vorspiele*, and described *Das Rheingold* as a *Vorspiel* to the *Ring*.

‖ **vorstellung** (fōᵊ·ɹʃteluŋ). *Psychol.* Pl. **-en.** [Ger.] An image, idea, mental picture, or presentation.

1807–8 COLERIDGE *Notebks.* (1962) II. I. 3217 Emptiness & absence, silence, darkness as Spinoza observed whose pocket Mr Locke picked of it without after confession, are as positive Vorstellungen as Light, Sound, Image. **1865** J. GROTE *Exploratio* I. iv. 60 Knowledge as acquaintance..is the kind of knowledge which we have of a thing by the presentation of it to the senses or the representation of it in a picture or type, a 'vorstellung'. **1890** W. JAMES *Princ. Psychol.* I. ix. 236 A permanently existing 'idea' or 'Vorstellung' which makes its appearance before the footlights of consciousness at periodical intervals, is as mythological an entity as the Jack of Spades. **1959** J. L. AUSTIN *Sense & Sensibilia* (1962) vi. 61 In Berkeley's doctrine there are *only* ideas, in Kant's only *Vorstellungen* (things-in-themselves being not strictly relevant here).

vortex. Add: **1. b.** Also *spec.* (with capital initial) a group of artists practising vorticism (see next).

1913 E POUND *Let.* 19 Dec. (1950) I. 28 You may get something that you would miss in *The Vortex*. **1914** *Blast* 20 June 8 Do you think Lloyd George has the Vortex in him? **1969** *Listener* 30 Jan. 138/1 The so-called Great English Vortex, i.e. the group of painters, sculptors and writers who..formed and represented the Vorticist movement.

7. vortex shedding, the periodic detachment of vortices from an object in a fluid flow, causing a varying force to be experienced by the object; **vortex sheet**, a region of vortices that is created at the interface of two masses of fluid having different velocities along the interface; **vortex street**: see *STREET *sb.* 2 g.

1953 A. ROSHKO *Devel. Turbulent Wakes from Vortex Streets* (U.S. Nat. Advisory Comm. Aeronaut. TN 2913) 45 There is yet no adequate theory of the periodic vortex shedding and it is not clear what is the principal mechanism which determines the frequency. **1975** *Offshore Engineer* Dec. 42/1 Vortex shedding can impose periodic forces on a pipeline. **1982** *New Scientist* 27 May 566/1 Vortex shedding is quite harmless until it begins to interfere with the safety or the function of man-made structures. **1879** H. LAMB *Treat. Math. Theory Motion Fluids* vi. 154 Let us suppose we have a series of vortex-filaments arranged in a thin film over a surface... The infinitely thin film is then called a 'vortex-sheet'. **1926** [see *SEPARATION 13**]. **1983** *Jrnl. Fluids Engin.* CV. 53 Nascent vortex strength and position are determined from the Kutta condition so that the nascent vortex has the same strength as a vortex sheet of uniform strength.

vorticism (vǭ·ɹtisiz'm). Also **Vorticism.** [f. L. *vortex, vortic-* VORTEX + -ISM.] A British art-movement of the early twentieth century, characterized by abstractionism and machine-like forms. Also applied to similar tendencies in literature.

1914 E. POUND in *Fortn. Rev.* Sept. 470 The image is not an idea. It is a radiant node or cluster; it is what I can..call a *Vortex*, from which..ideas are constantly rushing... And from this necessity came the name 'vorticism'. **1915** *Drawing* July 56/1 Vorticism..is in reality our old and amusing friend Cubism, but Cubism heavily charged with electricity. **1926** F. V. P. RUTTER *Evolution in Mod. Art* v. 105 Impressionism..was succeeded by Fauvism, Cubism, Expressionism, Futurism, Vorticism, and what not. **1962** *Listener* 5 Apr. 599/1 He [*sc.* Ezra Pound] was fighting under the banner of 'vorticism'. **1977** P. L. FERMOR *Time of Gifts* iii. 69 Pale woods and plastics were juggled together with stale and pretentious vorticism. **1980** *Daily Tel.* 6 Feb. 18 Nevinson was one of the first artists to use the contemporary techniques of vorticism and futurism for depicting the war [of 1914–18].

vorticist. Add: **2. a.** An exponent of vorticism in art.

1914 *Daily News* 7 July 6 My Scot one morning preached me a fiery sermon on the poetry of lawn tennis, and..I became a Vorticist. **1914** E. POUND *Let.* 10 Nov. (1971) 47 While the vorticists are well-represented, the College does not bind itself to a school. **1915** [see *FAUVE]. **1930** J. W. MACKAIL *Largeness in Lit.* 15 Imagists, contortionists, vorticists..have had their little day. **1970** *English Studies* LI. 269 This period [*sc.* 1910–1922] also saw the birth and death of other more obviously revolutionary groups such as the Vorticists, Imagists and Futurists. **1980** *Illustr. London News* Mar. 58/1 Even the brief and feeble spark of abstraction in England, fanned by the Vorticists and almost immediately snuffed out by the First World War, became the subject of intensive investigation.

b. *attrib.* or as *adj.*

1914 *Blast* 20 June 8 We will convert the King if possible. A Vorticist King! Why not? **1914** E. POUND in *Fortn. Rev.* Sept. 461, I shall be..more lucid if I give.. the history of the vorticist art with which I am most intimately connected, that is to say, vorticist poetry. **1923** *Daily Mail* 3 Mar. 12 Mr Wadsworth has all the qualifications of a tempera painter. In his vorticist past he was inclined to transform the world and its people into rigid, machine-like shapes. **1962** *Listener* 5 Apr. 599/1 The imagist and vorticist movements of less than fifty years ago. **1966** A. L. COBURN *Autobiogr.* ix. 102 It was in 1914 that Wyndham Lewis..founded the *avant-garde* movement named by..Ezra Pound 'Vorticist', the ideas of which derived partly from Futurism and partly from Cubism. **1981** V. GLENDINNING *Edith Sitwell* v. 83 Wyndham Lewis..was five years older than Edith herself; his Vorticist period, the editorship of *Blast*..already lay behind him.

vorticity. Add: (Earlier and later examples.) In mod. use, a vector quantity equal at any given point in a fluid to twice the angular velocity of a small element of fluid about the point.

1888 A. B. BASSETT *Treat. Hydrodynamics* I. 75 Let P be any point on the axis of one of these [vortex] filaments, dm the mass of the filament which contains P, ω and dS the molecular rotation and cross section of the filament... Then the quantity $\omega dS/dm$ is called the vorticity of the fluid at the point P. **1896** *Proc. London Math. Soc.* XXVII. 14 The component velocities..u and v, are connected with a stream-function Ψ by the relations $u = d\Psi/dy$, $v = -d\Psi/dx$. The vorticity is represented by $\frac{1}{2}\nabla^2\Psi$. **1916** H. LAMB *Hydrodynamics* (ed. 4) iii. 30 The component angular velocities of the rotation being ½ξ, ½η, ½ζ. The vector whose components are ξ, η, ζ may conveniently be called the 'vorticity' of the medium at the point (*x*, *y*, *z*). **1938** L. M. MILNE-THOMSON *Theoret. Hydrodynamics* xix. 511 Either sense of rotation can be obtained according as the bath is filled with the hot or the cold tap, the fluid from one or the other acquiring opposite vorticities as it moves near the boundary. **1958** *Science* 4 Apr. 731/3 On the surface of a fluid, the vorticity may be observed by following a cork marked with a cross... If the arms of the cross do not rotate, the vorticity is zero; if they do rotate, there is vorticity. **1976** *Nature* 1 Apr. 457/1 A motor vehicle or any other projectile in air produces vortices in its wake, but no net vorticity.

vortograph (vǭ·ɹtŏgrɑf). Also **Vortograph.** [f. VORT(EX + -O + -GRAPH.] An abstract photograph taken with a camera and a vortoscope.

1917 E. POUND *Let.* 24 Jan. (1971) 104 The vortographs are perhaps as interesting as Wadsworth's woodcuts, perhaps not quite as interesting. **1963** *Times* 29 Apr. 7/2 Mr. Coburn..went on to show the parallels between his photography and the work of painters and sculptors at a later period with his astonishing series of 'vortographs'—photographic abstractions very close in feeling to the vorticist paintings of Wyndham Lewis and such early Epstein sculptures as 'The Rock Drill'. **1966** A. L. COBURN *Autobiogr.* ix. 102 Photography depends upon pattern..as well as upon quality of tone and luminosity, and in the Vortograph the design can be adjusted at will. **1982** M. WEAVER *Alvin Langdon Coburn* 26 Prismatic, triangular effects appeared in the Vortographs in which abstraction and conception superseded observation and perception.

vortoscope (vǭ·ɹtŏskōᵘp). Also **Vortoscope.** [f. VORT(EX + -O + -SCOPE.] A mirror device used for producing abstract photographs (see quot. 1966).

1917 E. POUND *Let.* 24 Jan. (1950) 104 The vortescope [*sic*] isn't a cinema. It is an attachment to enable a photographer to do sham Picassos. That sarcastic definition probably covers the ground. **1918** —— *Pavannes & Divisions* App. IV. 252 The vortoscope is useless to a man who cannot recognise a beautiful arrangement of forms on a surface. **1966** A. L. COBURN *Autobiogr.* ix. 102, I aspired to make abstract pictures with the camera. For this purpose I devised the Vortoscope late in 1916. This instrument is composed of three mirrors fastened together in the form of a triangle... The mirrors act as a prism splitting the image formed by the lens into segments. **1982** M. HARKER in M. Weaver *Alvin Langdon Coburn* 2 He made a Vortoscope in 1916. Based on the principles of the kaleidoscope the instrument was composed of three mirrors fastened together in the form of a triangle.

Vöslauer (fœslɑu·ˌəɹ). Also **Voslauer.** [a. Ger., f. *Vöslau* name of a district in Lower Austria: see -ER¹.] An Austrian red or white table wine from Vöslau in the Vienna Woods.

1920 [see *CARLOWITZ]. **1960** *Times* 11 June 11/6 A local red wine, Voslauer, which is among the best in the country.

Vosne Romanée (vōᵘn romane). The name of a commune in the department of Côte-d'Or in France, used *absol.* to designate the wines produced there. Cf. *ROMANÉE.

1930 G. KNOWLES tr. *P. de Cassagnac's French Wines* vi. 140 The Côte-de-Nuits begins at Dijon. It includes... Flagey, with Grands-Echezeaux; Vosne-Romanée and the estates of Romanée [etc.]. **1952** A. LICHINE *Wines of France* 126 Wines from Les Verroilles..are never sold under their own name..while the third *cuvées* are sold simply as Vosne-Romanée. **1963** N. FREELING *Gun before Butter* III. 164 We'll have some burgundy. I've a Vosne Romanée; just the trick. **1980** E. LEATHER *Duveen Letter* xiv. 160 Rupert..ordered a bottle of Vosne-Romanée 1961.

vote, *sb.* Add: **8. a.** *vote on account*, a resolution at the close of the financial year to assign a sum of money to a government department as an advance payment before its full annual expenditure is authorized by law.

1859 ERSKINE MAY *Law of Parl.* (ed. 4) 531 Votes on account. The entire sums proposed to be granted for particular services, are not always voted at the same time, but a certain sum is occasionally voted on account of such grants. **1910** W. S. CHURCHILL *Let.* 11 Mar. in R. S. Churchill *Winston S. Churchill* (1969) II. Compan. II. xiii. 992 The Vote on account is the most powerful and the most simple Parliamentary engine by which the House of Commons is assured of its influence upon the Executive Government. **1963** *Economist* 24 Feb. 71/3 Part of the central government's expenditure, as recorded in the 'vote-on-account', is simply of a transfer kind; it includes, for instance, not only such personal payments as family allowances but also grants to local authorities made out of the central tax pool. *a* **1974** R. CROSSMAN *Diaries* (1977) III. 332, I am worried about this year's Vote on Account.

b. *vote of confidence*, a resolution showing majority support for a government, policy, etc. Similarly *vote of no* (or *want of*) *confidence*. Also *fig.*

1846 G. BENTINCK in *Hansard Commons* 8 June 182, I should certainly have preferred an Amendment which took the shape of a direct vote of want of confidence in Her Majesty's Ministers. **1870** LD. RUSSELL *Sel. Speeches* I. 154 Institutions..whose ministers resign on a vote of want of confidence. **1955** *Times* 10 May 14/4 The Government are asking for a vote of confidence. **1962** *Listener* 13 Dec. 1002/1 Why is it that grown men and women, no less than teenagers, are registering this unmistakable vote of no confidence in a society which has in so many ways improved their physical and material conditions of life? **1963** *Ibid.* 14 Feb. 281/2 The government survived..a vote of no confidence in the Parliament. **1976** *Glasgow Herald* 26 Nov. 1/8 Derby County's Scottish manager, Dave Mackay, was dismissed last night after three years at the Baseball ground. He had asked the club's directors for a vote of confidence.

10. *vote-catcher* (examples), *-collector*, *-getter* (examples), *-getting*, *-loser*, *-rigging*, *-splitting*; *vote-orientated*, *-proof* adjs.; *vote-wise* adv.; **vote bank**, in India, a group of people who can be relied upon to vote together in support of the same party.

1963 H. TINKER *Democratic Ideal in Asia* 17 The tribe, caste, or other association represents a 'vote bank'. **1982** *Jrnl. Commonwealth & Comparative Politics* XX. 9 The kinship group became an important vote-bank. **1923** *Weekly Dispatch* 13 May 2/2 The wild men pin their faith to the Capital Levy as a vote-catcher. **1977** *Cork Examiner* 6 June 1/7 Mr Leddin felt that Ald. Lipper was being victimised because he was a 'vote catcher' for the party in Limerick. **1859** MILL *Parl. Reform* 32 Why should the vote-collector make a distinction where the tax-gatherer makes none? **1906** *Springfield* (Mass.) *Weekly Republ.* 1 Nov. 3 He is also a strong campaigner, and has proved himself a vote-getter. **1981** *Times* 13 June 16/7 Mrs Williams..is..the party's outstanding vote-getter. **1984** *Listener* 4 Oct. 5/1 Margaret Thatcher has held doubting Conservatives loyal by a mixture of unrelenting leadership and a formidable reputation as a vote-getter. **1892** *Courier-Jrnl.* (Louisville, Kentucky) 3 Oct. 3/3 Mr. Needy..was made a victim of the vote-getting machine. **1929** *Daily Tel.* 8 Jan. 10/4 Acidulated suggestions of a lack of moral principle one day, want of suppleness the next, and ignorance of the elementary arts of vote-getting the day after do not help the cause. **1963** A. HOWARD in Sissons & French *Age of Austerity* I. 16 The Conservatives ..seem to have based their whole vote-getting strategy on a fundamental misreading of the nation's mood. **1963** *Guardian* 25 Feb. 8/1 Nationalisation is a fully certified vote-loser when it comes to election campaigning. *a* **1974** R. CROSSMAN *Diaries* (1975) I. 150 Immigration can be the greatest potential vote-loser for the Labour Party. **1971** H. WILSON *Labour Government* xxxvi. 744 Vote-orientated promises to increase most individual spending programmes. **1928** G. B. SHAW *Intelligent Woman's Guide Socialism* lxiii. 291 Those who do understand it will never be unanimous in resisting it; consequently it is voteproof at the parliamentary elections. **1958** *New Statesman* 22 Feb. 230/3 He also ignored the detailed figures I gave of 10 other branches which recorded votes in excess of the number of members entitled to vote in September 1948; nor does he deal..with any other of the numerous illustrations I gave of vote-rigging. **1983** *Listener* 20 Dec. 32/2 A 1981 BBC play about the famous ETU vote-rigging scandal of the Fifties. **1931** *Economist* 17 Oct. 723/1 Vote-splitting will be avoided as far as possible. **1950** W. S. CHURCHILL *In Balance* (1951) 391 Great harm was done to national interests at the General Election by the policy of the Liberal Party in running hopeless or vote-splitting candidatures in hundreds of constituencies. **1959** *Punch* 16 Sept. 158/2 The wing-collared politicians who emancipated women vote-wise probably had minds awhirl. **1969** G. KIRKLAND in R. Blythe *Akenfield* iv. 86 We are all mainly Socialists vote-wise.

vote, *v.* Add: **3. a.** Also *fig.* Cf. sense 3 c below.

1970 *Globe & Mail* (Toronto) 26 Sept. 23/1 They said its auditorium was poorly designed—dead acoustics, too many seats too distant. But the audiences, voting at the box-office, have continued to come for almost 40 weeks of every season.

c. In *fig.* phr. *to vote with one's feet*, to indicate an opinion by presence in or absence from a country, institution, activity, etc.

1965 *Listener* 16 Dec. 983/1 Politically, emigration provided a useful safety valve, anyone who hated the regime..could just vote with his feet and get out. **1968** *Ibid.* 31 Oct. 567/2 The McCarthy supporters began to realise that if the only choice was Nixon or Humphrey, perhaps the streets were the only true political arenas... On and after 5 November there will be plenty of voting with the feet. **1970** *Guardian* 30 July 9/6 The children.. just vote with their feet and join in. **1972** M. JONES *Life on Dole* vii. 56 Welshmen, in fact, were voting with their feet against the hopelessness that surrounded them. Those who were qualified scattered themselves across England. **1982** *Christian Order* Nov. 546 Uncounted thousands have 'voted with their feet', i.e., have left the Church. **1985** *Times* 7 Jan. 15/1 With another 16,000 to 20,000 miners returning to work an effective majority would have voted with its feet to end the strike.

5. f. With the name of a political party or of a candidate as object.

1926 *Socialist Rev.* Oct. 48 There are still hundreds of thousands of voters who cannot bring themselves to vote Conservative. **1938** *Sun* (Baltimore) 6 Sept. 20 (*caption*) Vote Lewis. **1949** C. P. SNOW *Time of Hope* I. iv. 42 He voted radical and she was a vehement tory. **1977** R. BARNARD *Blood Brotherhood* i. 11 The parishioners.. voted Conservative, when they did not vote National Front.

g. *to vote stock* or *shares*, to cast votes representing stock held in a company. *U.S.*

1957 R. A. HEINLEIN in *Mag. of Fantasy & Sci. Fiction* Oct. 30/2, I had assigned the stock to her but she knew.. that I always voted it, that I had had no intention of parting with control of the company. **1978** *N.Y. Times* 29 Mar. D10/1 The state pension agencies can vote the stock but the banks must confer with others first.

9. b. (Later examples.)

c **1850** J. M. MORTON *Box & Cox* 23, I vote, Box, that we stick by her. **1880** TROLLOPE *Duke's Children* I. xviii. 222 We've got the trap and the horses..and I vote we make a start. **1927** E. BOWEN *Hotel* ii. 15, I vote we take those two on again.

10. b. To present for voting; to record the votes of (electors). *U.S.*

1859 BARTLETT *Dict. Amer.* (ed. 2) 98 They..are taken to the polls, and 'voted', as it is called, for the party. **1884** E. W. NYE *Baled Hay* 217, I believe they vote people there who have been dead for centuries. **1904** *N.Y. Even. Post* 8 Nov. 1, 25 men were in line in many places, and they were voted at a rate of nearly one a minute.

voter. Add: **1. c.** *attrib.*, as *voter registrar*, *registration*. *U.S.*

1960 *Nation* (N.Y.) 23 Jan. 72/3 HR7597, introduced by Congressman Powell..provides for the establishment of a Federal Voter Registration Commission. **1964** *Federal Suppl.* CCXXIX. 933/2 The suits filed by the United States against several county voter registrars..were matters of common knowledge throughout the State of Mississippi. **1976** *National Observer* (U.S.) 10 July 5/5 He hopes to raise all he can—$3 million— for the Carter campaign, and raise even more, maybe $8 million, for voter registration and training schools for candidates and things like that.

Votiak, var. *VOTYAK.

Votic (vōᵘ·tik). [Origin uncertain.] A language of the Finnish group of the Finno-Ugrian family of languages, used by a small number of speakers in the Ingrian region, now in the north-west part of the U.S.S.R. Also **Vo·tian.**

1908 T. G. TUCKER *Introd. Nat. Hist. Lang.* 132 Tchudic and the cognate dialects Vepsic and Votic, about Lake Onega. **1933** [see *LUDIAN]. **1939** L. H. GRAY *Foundations of Language* 369 The languages of the Uralic family are as follows:..*Finnish* group: Finnish proper.., Karelian.., Olonetzian, Ingrian, Lüdish, Vepsian, Votian, Esthonian, etc. **1954** PEI & GAYNOR *Dict. Linguistics* 229 *Votian*, a member of the Finnish group of the Finno-Ugric (or Uralic) sub-family of the Ural-Altaic family of languages. **1964** *Language* XL. 98 The Veps, Votic, and Estonian cognates..are hardly necessary. **1977** *Ibid.* LIII. 477 The last ten are Yurak Samoyed, Lapp, Judeo-Spanish, Vepsian, Kashubian, Karaim, Ingrian, Livonian, Votic, and Manx Gaelic.

voting, *vbl. sb.* Add: **2.** *voting age*, *urn.*

1937 V. BARTLETT *This is my Life* x. 165 That mass of people..saluting with religious intensity the dustbin-like voting urns. **1966** M. WOODHOUSE *Tree Frog* viii. 60 He must have reached voting age, but you couldn't tell by looking at him. **1978** *Listener* 2 Feb. 145/2 Those recently reaching voting age. **1978** K. J. DOVER *Greek Homosexuality* III. 111 The funnel of the voting-urn used in a lawcourt.

votive, *sb.* Delete *rare*⁻¹ and add later examples.

1975 Y. YADIN *Hazor* iv. 61 We found..an elevated rectangular platform that looked like an open high place, or *bamah*, where the votives..were laid. **1976** *Scotsman* 27 Dec. 7/4 Archaeologists have recently dug up 8395 such terra cotta votives, as they are called.

Votyak (vōᵘ·tiˌak). Also **Votiak.** [Russ.] **1.** A member of a Finno-Ugrian people inhabiting the Udmurt republic in the north-western region of the U.S.S.R. Also *attrib.* or as *adj.*

1841 *Penny Cycl.* XX. 247/1 The Votiakes are settled west of the Permians, on both sides of the upper course of the river Viatka, and in the country about the source of the Kama. **1845** *Encycl. Metrop.* XXV. 866/2 Near Perm..are the Votyáks, who call themselves 'Uhdmurd, *i.e.*, Hospitable men. **1938** *N. & Q.* 23 Apr. 291/2 Votyak folk-lore is influenced by the Persians. **1948** D. DIRINGER *Alphabet* II. viii. 482 The Votiaks,..living in the Vyatka region. **1968** BETHELL & BURG tr. *Solzhenitsyn's Cancer Ward* (1971) I. viii. 110 Now, as he paced up and down the ward, he remembered how the old folk used to die back home on the kama—Russians, Tartars, Votyaks or whatever they were. **1974** *Encycl. Brit. Macropædia* VII. 313/1 In the *lud* sanctuaries of the Votyaks.. worship was performed by members of the family.

2. The language of this people, belonging to the Permian branch of the Finno-Ugrian family.

1878 *Encycl. Brit.* VIII. 700/1 *Finnic* or *Ugrian* represented by..(*b*) Karelian..(*m*) Votiak. **1908**, etc. [see *PERMIAN *a.* (*sb.*) 2]. **1932** W. L. GRAFF *Language & Languages* 406 Votyak (about 400,000) is situated between the Viatka and the Kama. **1951** W. K. MATTHEWS *Languages U.S.S.R.* iii. 24 The Permian branch, which comprises two languages, Zyryan and Votyak (Udmurt) **1977** [see *VEPSIAN].

voucher, *sb.*¹ Add: **2. d.** A document which can be exchanged for goods or services as token of payment made or promised by the holder or another (see also quot. 1947).

1947 *Sun* (Baltimore) 12 May 2/5 Stefan has gone through a stack of vouchers—expense accounts—from the American Embassy. **1955**, etc. [see *LUNCHEON 3]. **1960** S. UNWIN *Truth about a Publisher* II. xix. 353 The New Zealand Company had not given me an actual ticket..but a voucher instructing their agent to issue me a ticket. **1970** *Phi Delta Kappan* LII. 49 For some time Christopher Jenks has believed that voucher plans offer an exit from the bureaucratic morass in which many major school systems are mired. **1980** *Jrnl. R. Soc. Arts* July 475/1 It could be done through some kind of voucher scheme.

voudoun (vū·dūn), var. of VOODOO *sb.* Also **voudon.**

1939 M. STEEDMAN *Unknown to World: Haiti* xvii. 159 The gods and goddesses of the Voudon pantheon are known as the 'Lois'. **1953** M. DEREN *Divine Horsemen* 60 Voudoun (which is the Fons word for god) includes the loa (the Congo word for the spirits) of many nations. *Ibid.* 15 Voudoun is the religion, primarily African in origin, of the vast majority of the Republic of Haiti in the West Indies. **1953** *Times Lit. Suppl.* 2 Aug. 510 A Voudoun, as some purists insist, with little basis, in spelling it. **1958** J. SYKES *Quakers* I. i. 34 Almost any gathering of English citizenry could run to a pitch one associates more with a Haitian voudoun possessed by 'the loa'.

‖ **voulu** (vūlu), *a.* (*sb.*) [Fr., pa. pple. of *vouloir* to wish, want.] Contrived, deliberate, studied. Also as *sb.* (esp. *collect*).

1909 E. NESBIT *Daphne in Fitzroy St.* xiii. 207 Perhaps there's something more delicate, less *voulu*, in our little dinner as it is. The poignant beauty of the incomplete. **1938** E. BOWEN *Death of Heart* III. iv. 389 There is a narrowness about fantasy: it figures only the *voulu* part of the self. **1948** F. R. LEAVIS *Great Tradition* ii. 81 There is certainly something of that quality [*sc.* insincerity] in *Daniel Deronda*..an element of the tacitly *voulu*. **1957** L. DURRELL *Justine* II. 132 The idea is not spontaneous, but *voulue*. **1959** *Encounter* Dec. 64/1 All de Sade's excesses were '*voulus*'. They were a scientific investigation into sex. **1962** *Listener* 17 May 885/3 Here and there the impression of the *voulu* and the freakish cannot be avoided. **1968** *Punch* 3 Apr. 507/1 They simply give an impression of *voulu* oddity, nearer to a harsher, more explicitly sexual A. E. Coppard than to Carson McCullers. **1974** *Times* 2 Feb. 7/6 But her knowledge of people as such? Sometimes profound, sometimes *voulu*.

Vouvray (vūvrēⁱ·). The name of a commune in the department of Indre-et-Loire in N.W. France, used chiefly *absol.* to designate the wines produced in this and neighbouring communes.

1885 H. JAMES *Little Tour in France* vii. 60 She uncorked for us a bottle of Vouvray mousseux. **1920** G. SAINTSBURY *Notes on Cellar Bk.* vi. 97, I have said nothing, in the chapter on Champagne, as to Saumur, Vouvray, and the Swiss imitations... Vouvray..seems to me feeble. **1934** E. WAUGH *Handful of Dust* v. 246 One of them..got drunk for the first time on sparkling Vouvray. **1955** 'W. MOLE' *Hammersmith Maggot* vi. 68 Lunch, properly accompanied by a glass of Vouvray. **1981** 'A. CROSS' *Death in Faculty* xii. 141 I'm going to have a bottle of Vouvray, Clos de Nouys, 1971.

vowel, *sb.* Add: **3.** *vowel-alternation, -articulation, -consonant* (later examples in sense 'vowel followed by consonant', chiefly *attrib.*), *-length, -letter, -like* (earlier example), *-loveliness, -phoneme, -rhyme, -sequence, -shade, -sign* (earlier example), *-sound* (earlier example), *-space, -symbol, -system* (earlier example), *triangle*; *vowel-initial* adj.; **vowel colour,** the precise timbre and quality of a vowel sound; so **vowel colouring; vowel diagram,** a diagram showing relative degrees of closeness or openness, front-raising or back-raising of the tongue, in the articulation of individual vowels; **vowel-glide** [cf. GLIDE *sb.* 4], the gliding movement from one vowel component to another, as in a diphthong; also, = GLIDE *sb.* 4; **vowel gradation** = ABLAUT; **vowel harmony,** a feature of the Finno-Ugric, Turkish, and other languages, whereby successive syllables of words are limited to a particular class of vowel; **vowel height,** the degree to which the tongue is raised or lowered in the pronunciation of a particular vowel; **vowel-laxing,** the enunciation of a vowel with the speech organs relaxed (cf. *LAX *a.* 5 c); **vowel-quality,** the identifying acoustic characteristic of a vowel; **vowel-quantity,** the duration of time needed for the pronunciation of a vowel; **vowel shift,** a phonetic change of vowel or vowels, *spec.* applied to a series of changes between medieval and modern English affecting the long vowels of the standard language; freq. in phr. *great vowel shift*; cf. *SHIFT *sb.* 14 d.

1951 W. K. MATTHEWS *Languages U.S.S.R.* iv. 57 The already noticed Manchu vowel-alternation to express sex-gender may be paralleled by Evenki examples. **1937** J. R. FIRTH *Tongues of Men* 42 Instead of referring to the vowel-articulations, we refer to the resulting sounds. **1948** M. JOOS *Acoustic Phonetics* ii. 59 It seems that a listener can hear a difference of vowel color [in the [ɛ] of *hotel* spoken by three American speakers] equivalent to a distance of 1 semitone on the formant chart. **1978** *Amer. Speech* LIII. 291 Different arrays of formants constitute different vowel colors. **1939** F. M. FORD *Let.* May (1965) 321 The mere sequence of the vowel coloring of that phrase will give you acute pleasure. **1979** *Archivum Linguisticum 1978* IX. 156 Pajares notes that the loss of laryngeal and the lengthening (and in some cases vowel coloring) of the preceding vowel can also be considered a monophthongization. **1960** *Amer. Speech* XXXV. 227 Vowel-consonant syllables [are] less intelligible than consonant-vowel syllables. **1977** P. STREVENS *New Orientations Teaching of Eng.* xii. 151 Permissible consonant-clusters and vowel-consonant sequences are similar. **1932** D. JONES *Outl. Eng. Phonetics* (ed. 3) viii. 36 (*caption*) Fig. 23 Diagram illustrating the Tongue-positions of the eight primary Cardinal Vowels. Fig. 24. A more accurate form of Vowel Diagram. **1976** C. BARBER *Early Mod. Eng.* vi. 299 The long and short pure vowels in StE in the middle of our period are shown on the vowel diagrams in Figure 3 and Figure 4. [**1856** Vocal glide: see GLIDE *sb.* 4.] **1878** H. SWEET *Handbk. Phonetics* 63 (*heading*) Initial and Final Vowel-Glides. **1932** D. JONES *Outl. Eng. Phonetics* (ed. 3) 25 Such vowel-glides are often called semi-vowels. **1962** A. C. GIMSON *Introd. Pronunc. Eng.* II. vii. 121 Diphthongal Vowel Glides. The sequences of vocalic elements included under the term 'diphthong' are those which form a glide within one syllable. **1973** J. D. O'CONNOR *Phonetics* vii. 220 A diphthong..is phonetically a vowel glide or a sequence of two vowel segments which functions as a single phoneme. *Ibid.* 221 Other vowel glides such as /eu, øu, iu, ɔu/ which also occur [in Danish], must be interpreted as vowel + /v/ since they do not occur freely in the same sorts of context as the remaining vowels and diphthongs. **1887** W. W. SKEAT *Princ. Eng. Etym.* x. 158 To discover the original Teutonic vowel-gradation ..we must compare with one another the oldest known forms of the verbs in the various Teutonic languages. **1938** *Amer. Speech* XIII. 209 The term 'vowel-change' is evidently a new attempt (like 'vowel gradation'..) to avoid the German word *Ablaut*. **1973** A. H. SOMMERSTEIN *Sound Pattern Anc. Greek* ii. 70 As is well known, vowel gradation, or ablaut, was an important feature of proto-Indo-European morphology. [**1893** J. CLARK *Man. Linguistics* vi. 151 The Ural-Altaic languages..which are dominated by a law of vocalic harmony that, to speak generally, requires that one class of vowels..should obtain in the various syllables of a word.] **1900** H. SWEET *Hist. Lang.* vii. 122 In Finnish, the vowels are divided, from the point of view of vowel-harmony, into the three classes hard, soft and neutral. **1972** *Language* XLVIII. 365 The nature of the rules of vowel harmony is and has been the subject of some discussion... The traditional view is as follows: the vowel harmony rule in Turkish specifies that, for any vowel, the distinctive feature in question is determined by the value of the previous vowel. **1977** *Archivum Linguisticum* VIII. 71 This is obscured by a distinctive feature system which uses a binary classification of [±high] and [±low] to define vowel height. **1949** E. A. NIDA *Morphology* (ed. 2) ii. 16 Note that *h-* occurs before the consonant-initial stem *k'ab* and *k* before the vowel-initial stem *akan*. **1978** *Language* LIV. 23 Before apparently vowel-initial nouns like *héros* and *honte*, we find no elision. **1977** *Stud. in Eng. Lit.: Eng. Number* (Tokyo) 155 Rule (24) succeeds in formally expressing a linguistically significant generalization underlying various vowel-laxing processes. **1980** *English World-Wide* I. 250 The linguistic variables analyzed in the remaining six chapters are: (i) vowel laxing in monosyllabic personal pronouns and a number of nonpronominal forms. **1932** D. JONES *Outl. Eng. Phonetics* (ed. 3) 237 Vowel-length depends to a considerable extent on the rhythm of the sentence. **1977** P. STREVENS *New Orientations Teaching of Eng.* xii. 151 The relation between stress and vowel-length is of the same general type. **1846,** etc. Vowel-letter [see *MATER LECTIONIS]. **1933** L. BLOOMFIELD *Language* 292 We use the Latin vowel-letters not only in entirely new values..but in inconsistent ways. **1855** tr. *Lepsius' Standard Alphabet* 28 The Indian grammarians, who express the nasalisation..by a vowel-like sign, namely, by placing a dot over the letter. **1910** D. H. LAWRENCE *Let.* 26 Oct. (1962) I. 67 One can get good Swinburnian consonant music by taking thought, but never Shakespearean vowel-loveliness. **1935** G. K. ZIPF *Psycho-Biol. of Lang.* (1936) 316 All the short vowel-phonemes. **1964** C. BARBER *Present-Day Eng.* iii. 38 There is no pair of English vowel-phonemes which is distinguished solely by length. **1977** D. FRY *Homo Loquens* ii. 13 In English..about twenty are the vowel phonemes, exemplified by the word group *beat, bit, bet, bat,* etc. **1920** W. PERRETT *Peetickay* 23 A notation of vowel-quality, derived from the 'organic' positions of the tongue, lips, etc., already exists in Alexander Melville Bell's *Visible Speech.* **1965** W. S. ALLEN *Vox Latina* ii. 52 The Latin vowel-quality is vouched for by Italian *borsa.* **1933** L. BLOOMFIELD *Language* 294 For the writers, the *gh* was now a mere silent graph, indicative only of vowel-quantity. **1977** *Archivum Linguisticum* VIII. 93 According to the Introduction, it has two aims: firstly to examine the various factors involved in the vowel-quantity changes that took place between Middle High German and New High German. **1873–4** G. M. HOPKINS *Jrnls. & Papers* (1959) 287 Alliteration is initial half-rhyme, 'shothending' is final half-rhyme, assonance is vowel rhyme. **1961** A. CLARKE *Later Poems* 89 In simple patterns, the tonic word at the end of the line is supported by a vowel-rhyme in the middle of the next line. **1939** F. M. FORD *Let.* May (1965) 321 The mere vowel sequences of certain passages will be sufficient to call back to you all the associations of your youth. **1965** *Language* XLI. 482 It gives a desirable economy of phonemes, which the vowel-sequence solution does not. **1955** J. R. R. TOLKIEN *Return of King* 409 The language that they [*sc.* the Ents] had made was..slow, sonorous..; formed of a multiplicity of vowel-shades and distinctions of tone and quantity. **1909** O. JESPERSEN *Mod. Eng. Gram.* I. viii. 231 The great vowel-shift consists in a general raising of all long vowels. **1933** —— *Essentials Eng. Gram.* iii. 34 The greatest revolution that has taken place in the phonetic system of English is the vowel-shift. **1936** *Essays & Studies* XXI. 10 The great vowel-shift of the late Middle Ages was followed by numerous other changes. **1964** C. BARBER *Present-Day Eng.* iii. 51 The great vowel-shift which took place between Middle English and Modern English. **1977** *Canad. Jrnl. Linguistics 1976* XXI. II. 177 After the application of the degemination rule and the vowel shift rule one obtains [eksid]. **1849** *Jrnl. Amer. Oriental Soc.* I. 523 We begin with the Vowel-signs, of which there are three in the Persian cuneiform alphabet. **1795** *Monthly Rev.* Aug. 410 All the simple sounds, vowel and consonantal. **1965** W. S. ALLEN *Vox Latina* ii. 54 There would have been more vowel-space to accommodate the new sound. **1979** *Amer. Speech 1978* LIII. 294 Suppose the available 'vowel space' for a community's language were constrained to the relatively small triangular region bounded by the calculated Neanderthal approximations to the three reference vowels. **1932** D. JONES *Outl. Eng. Phonetics* (ed. 3) 5 The naming of vowel-symbols presents some difficulty. **1957** R. W. ZANDVOORT *Handbk. Eng. Gram.* 337 Words in silent *e* drop it before endings beginning with a vowel-symbol. **1855** tr. *Lepsius' Standard Alphabet* 11 He contended successfully against the English vowel-system. **1918** D. JONES *Outl. Eng. Phonetics* vi. 16 If we examine the tongue positions of the typical sounds of these five classes [of vowels] we find that the highest points of the tongue lie roughly on the sides of a triangle... This triangle is known as the 'Vowel Triangle'.

vowel, *v.* Add: Hence (nonce-uses) **vo·welled** *ppl. a.*; **vo·welling** *vbl. sb.*

1873–4 G. M. HOPKINS *Jrnls. & Papers* (1959) 284 This is given by vowelling, which is either vowelling on (assonance) or vowelling off. *Ibid.* 287 In Norse poetry..the vowels..seen to be sided or intentionally changed, vowelled off. **1934** DYLAN THOMAS in *Listener* 24 Oct. 691/2 Some let me make you of the vowelled beeches.

vox. Add: **3.** *vox nihili*, a worthless or meaningless word, *spec.* one produced by a scribal or printer's error; used *transf.* to denote abstract concepts whose meaning is deemed to be indistinct when analysed.

1892 in *Stanford Dict. Anglicised Words & Phrases.* **1916** H. W. B. JOSEPH *Introd. Logic* (ed. 2) xix. 404 Words like *agency* or *power*, on this view, are *voces nihili*; we think we mean something more by them than habitual sequence, but we do not. **1933** *Mind* XLII. 170 That they [actions] cannot be right *merely* as causes of effects..I have already proved, if I have proved that 'rightness' in this sense is a *vox nihili* or a mere synonym for 'causality'. **1960** *Analysis* XXI. 10 'Inductive *inference*' is a *vox nihili*, unless used—as it is sometimes confusingly used—to denote the concrete factual predictions and retrodictions that the mechanic, the seedsman, the palaeontologist and the astronomer make.

vox pop (vǫks pǫp), *sb.* (*a.*) *colloq.* Also **voxpop.** [Abbrev. of *vox populi* s.v. VOX 1.] **a.** Popular opinion as represented by informal comments from members of the general public, esp. when used for broadcasting; statements or interviews of this kind.

1964 HALL & WHANNEL *Popular Arts* ix. 225 In television..we could include..the use of the brief survey of popular opinion on any topic by means of the posed question (the so-called 'vox pop'). *Ibid.* 257 The short interview and the occasional 'vox pop' of the local news and sports programmes on radio. **1968** *Listener* 8 Feb. 164/2 A BBC camera crew went round Washington collecting vox pops—close-ups of men in the street saying pithily what they think of things. **1972** D. HURD *Truth Game* 59 Follow him close with the mike and get odds and ends of vox pop. **1975** *Listener* 18 Sept. 377/2 The audience was asked for comments, and very dim the voxpops sounded after the fluency of the two main speakers. **1981** *Times Lit. Suppl.* 25 Dec. 1501/5 There are wonderfully dreadful quotations in these chapters, including paragraphs of vox pop.

b. *attrib.* or as *adj.*

1966 *New Society* 17 Mar. 5/3 A *vox pop* survey I made among 17 housewives of St Ives. **1967** *Punch* 22 Nov. 794/1 Brandish a vox pop microphone in the concrete jungles and the cry..will recur monotonously, interspersed with blank looks. **1973** G. TALBOT *Ten Seconds from Now* iii. 35 'Vox pop' interviews on what the king ought to do. **1983** *Listener* 2 June 20/2 His suitability for the box is being questioned by whipper-snappers who would not have rated a vox-pop appearance..in the Fifties. **1985** *Spectator* 5 Jan. 7/3 A recent sermon included a vox pop poll on who in the congregation, average age 70, was familiar with Michael's song 'Thriller'.

‖ **voyagé** (vwayaʒe), *a. Ballet.* [Fr., pa. pple. of *voyager* to travel.] Designating a movement in which the pose is held during progression; usu. as *arabesque(s) voyagée(s).* Also *absol.* as *sb.*

1931 G. W. BEAUMONT *Dict. Technical Dance Terms* 30 *Voyagé*,..travelled, travelling. E.g., *arabesque voyagée.* **1957** G. B. L. WILSON *Penguin Dict. Ballet* 278 *Voyagé*,.. a movement across the stage during which the dancer holds a particular pose, usually an arabesque, and progresses in a series of hops or small jumps. **1976** *New Yorker* 26 Jan. 94/3 Tharp several times reinforces the point with moments swiped from the classics: the Wilis' arabesques voyagées.

voyageur. (Earlier example.)

1793 J. MACDONELL *Diary* 6 June in C. M. Gates *Five Fur-Traders* (1933) 75 Lost the half of this day by rain.. a perfect nuisance to us voyageurs.

‖ **voyant** (vwayaṅ), *a.* Fem. **voyante** (-aṅt). [Fr.] Showy, gaudy, flashy; *spec.* of clothes, appearance, etc.

1906 *Punch* 18 Apr. 286/3 'Anno Domini'..whom one would *expect* to be smart and *voyante*, is simply the dowdiest, quietest of mice. **1927** U. M. LYON *Etiquette* x. 113 Anything *voyant* in ties, deplorable always, is doubly so at his wedding. **1937** G. FRANKAU *More of Us* xv. 162 Tactful then mentioned he, maybe the hat—The whole costume indeed—was 'rather voyant'. 'Looks the complete tart if it comes to that', Hissed Innocent.

‖ **voyant,** *sb.* [Fr., lit 'seer'.] A visionary; one gifted with an especial degree of mental perception.

[**1924** E. Rickword tr. A. Rimbaud in *Rimbaud: Boy & Poet* 203, I say that one must be a *visionary* (voyant), make oneself a *visionary*. The Poet makes himself a *visionary* by a long immense and reasoned *derangement* of *all the senses*.] **1938** *Times Lit. Suppl.* 21 May 353/2 The systematic derangement of all the senses that he [*sc.* Rimbaud] envisaged as one of the duties of the *voyant* or visionary poet has been attempted. **1958** *Spectator* 22 Aug. 257/3 The emblem of this evil society is the head of a dead pig..animated by flies and by the imagination of the *voyant*, Simon. **1972** E. Lucie-Smith in Cox & Dyson *20th-Cent. Mind* II. xiv. 483 A way of linking Dada to an older and more specifically French tradition, that of the *voyant*, which could be traced to nineteenth-century writers such as Rimbaud and Lautréamont.

voyeur (vwayǒ·ɹ). Fem. **-euse** (ǒz). [a. Fr., f. *voir* to see.] **1.** A person whose sexual desires are stimulated or satisfied by covert observation of the sex organs or sexual activities of others. Cf. *peeping Tom* s.v. *peeping *ppl. a.*²; *scopophiliac* s.v. *scopophilia.

1900 H. Blanchamp tr. *Féré's Sexual Instinct* vi. 142 The houses of ill-fame have a *clientèle* of 'voyeurs' of both sexes. **1913** E. Jones *Papers on Psycho-Anal.* xv. 341 The patient, who had frequently indulged in pædicatio, was a pronounced *voyeur*. **1937** L. Bromfield *Rains Came* i. xlv. 192 A moment after she had disappeared the Major came out, and like a *voyeur* Ransome regarded him sharply to discover..whether she had made any progress. **1952** S. Kauffmann *Philanderer* (1957) xii. 188 The same Jake Simon who later made him a *voyeur* before puberty. **1956** C. P. Snow *Homecomings* xxxi. 214 Mrs Beauchamp, day-dreaming of a voyeuse's paradise, seeping herself into invisibility. **1972** *Daily Tel.* 7 Jan. 11/4 The hopeful voyeurs were to be disappointed for after this first fine flurry of bosoms and buttocks not a stitch was shed in the rest of the 45 minutes. **1978** C. P. Snow *Realists* viii. 236 He may have been a bit of a voyeur (he took extravagant pleasure in studying a love-object in bed). **1980** *Times Lit. Suppl.* 10 Oct. 1139/2 The film seems to miss a trick.., in that these two never get it together, but most voyeurs should be satisfied with what is otherwise on offer.

2. *transf.* and *fig.*

1956 C. W. Mills *Power Elite* vii. 162 The miser.. is an impotent voyeur of the economic system. **1958** *Times* 2 Oct. 3/2 The play..draws a firm line between those immersed in living and those plaintively watching them at it; and Hauptmann's sympathy goes to the *voyeurs*. **1967** *Spectator* 6 Oct. 404/3 Those films and TV programmes which argue that these are realities only moral cowards would evade seem to me to risk turning us all into *voyeurs* of pain, connoisseurs of private misery. **1978** J. Irving *World according to Garp* iii. 56, I was brought up to be a spectator... I was raised to be a voyeur.

Hence **voyeu·r** *v. intr.*, to obtain gratification in the manner of a voyeur; usu. as *pres. pple.* or *vbl. sb.*

1959 P. Bull *I know Face* xi. 195 She found herself dressing and undressing between two rows of hanging wardrobes, which involved delightful voyeuring for the gents manipulating the lights on the gantry above. **1970** K. Giles *Murder Pluperfect* iii. 72 'My girl,' said the Inspector, shamelessly voyeuring, lusciously and rashly voyeuring. **1980** M. Gilbert *Death of Favourite Girl* xxv. 240 His conscience wasn't all that clear, if he'd been out doing a spot of voyeuring.

voyeurism (vwayǒ·riz'm). [f. prec. + -ism.] The state or condition of being a voyeur; scopophilia. Also *transf.* and *fig.*

1924 J. S. van Teslaar tr. *Stekel's Disorders of Instincts & Emotions* II. 341 *Voyeurism*, erotic gratification experienced at looking at another's sexual organs; morbid desire to peep into secrets. **1927** Bryan & Strachey tr. *K. Abraham's Sel. Papers* iii. 83 If sublimation does not take place then a perversion (*voyeurism* and exhibitionism) arises. **1953** E. Podolsky *Encycl. Abberrations* 538/1 Voyeurism takes the place of the normal sexual act. **1958** *Oxf. Mag.* 8 May 409/1 Oxford.. seems to appeal to a disagreeable mixture of envy and voyeurism. **1969** *Daily Tel.* 25 Apr. 19/5 There is a feeling that more and more actresses are being asked to take their clothes off at auditions.. as a form of voyeurism. **1976** *Listener* 25 Nov. 682/3 A beggar's expression captured by a camera costing enough to feed, clothe and house him for..maybe five years. Is this kind of photography good or bad?..Is it just an obscene form of voyeurism, a record of what one privileged class finds quaint or interesting in another? **1980** *Times Lit. Suppl.* 7 Nov. 1258/3 *Rain on the Roof* is not much more than the averagely good television play featuring voyeurism, adultery and sudden bloody death. **1985** *Times* 21 Jan. 3/3 Many senior politicians have been appalled by the fate of the women, whose sexual activities have been exposed in a bout of national voyeurism.

voyeurist (vwayǒ·rist), *sb.* and *a.* [f. as prec. + -ist.] **A.** *sb.* = *voyeur 1. **B.** *adj.* = *voyeuristic *a.*

1955 J. F. Oliven *Sexual Hygiene & Pathol.* xxi. 424 The severe 'compulsive' voyeurist..is an obsessed.. individual. **1960** *Guardian* 6 Jan. 1/7 One father..'yielding to his exhibitionist-voyeurist impulses', regularly went off and joined a nudist colony. **1970** G. Greer *Female Eunuch* 165 Such observers have a vested interest in the detection of love affairs because of the particular voyeurist pleasures they afford. **1980** *Times Lit. Suppl.* 3 Oct. 1112/3 The cool meticulous detail in which these and other depravities are related..has an obsessive and at times voyeurist tone.

voyeuristic (vwayǒri·stik), *a.* [f. as prec. + -istic.] Of or pertaining to voyeurism. Cf. *voyeurist *a.*

1929 in Calverton & Schmalhausen *Sex in Civilization* 593 One day when we were stopping at a hotel he made me gratify his voyeuristic tendency. **1960** *Arch. Gen. Psychiatry* III. 317/2 N.T. is interesting because of his unusual voyeuristic habits. **1973** *Daily Tel.* 12 June 14/2 The British censor has made his cutting mark..so that the camera does not linger with quite the same sort of voyeuristic dedication as it did when the original version was shown at the Berlin Film Festival. **1981** *Times* 14 Sept. 18/8 The dangers of 'voyeuristic' leisure centred on the television set. **1984** *Listener* 26 Apr. 38/3 A certain arrogance in their dealings with the Divis Street tenants, a voyeuristic interest in the more sensational aspects of life in Belfast.

Hence **voyeuri·stically** *adv.*

1967 *Spectator* 14 July 48/1 The sexual autobiography ..of a Victorian gentleman who early in life became voyeuristically obsessed. **1982** *New Musical Express* 30 Oct. 28/1 A slick, flashy, voyeuristically nasty horror movie. **1985** *Times* 6 Mar. 10/1 The fact that the majority of AIDS patients are homosexual dramatizes the illness almost voyeuristically for the population at large.

‖ **voyou** (vwayū̆). [Fr.] A street urchin; a lout or hooligan.

1901 *Pall Mall Mag.* Feb. 195 But indeed the Hooligan, under the name of rough,..*voyou*..has been with us long, and not in this country alone. **1913** G. du Maurier *Martian* 61 'La flotte de Passy', as we called the Passy voyous. **1933** *Times Lit. Suppl.* 4 May 308/3 His curious friendship with a *voyou*. **1980** R. Grayson *Monterant Affair* vi. 50 She had fallen in love with one of the 'voyous' of Paris, a brash scoundrel living on his wits.

‖ **vozhd** (vǫʒd). [Russ., lit. = 'chief'.] A leader, one who is in supreme authority: applied esp. to the Russian statesman Joseph Stalin (1879–1953).

1940 E. Lyons *Stalin* xxvii. 247 The 'leader of the world proletariat', the greatest representative of creative Marxism', the 'great machinist of locomotive history'... These are typical titles bestowed on the *Vozhd*, the Leader, by officials who owed their jobs and their lease on life to Stalin. **1959** D. W. Treadgold *Twentieth Cent. Russia* xviii. 289 Even the top functionaries were subject to Stalin's supreme power, and the word *Vozhd* (Leader) came to be used openly to acknowledge and proclaim that fact. **1978** *Encounter* Feb. 42/1 The *Vozhd* of Moscow made his exit in triumph.

‖ **vrai réseau** (vrę rezo). [Fr., = true net.] The fine net ground used in making Brussels lace; also, any net ground for lace made by needle or bobbins as opposed to machine. Cf. *réseau 1.

1865 F. B. Palliser *Hist. Lace* vii. 104 It is the fineness of the thread which renders the real Brussels ground (vrai réseau) so costly. **1900** E. Jackson *Hist. Hand-Made Lace* vii. 58 The ground was of the *vrai réseau*, or needle-point mesh, now seldom seen. **1953** M. Powys *Lace & Lace-Making* iv. 29 This specimen has the Fond Rond which was used just before and contemporary with the Vrai Réseau de Valenciennes which is a diamond mesh. **1973** G. Pond *Introd. Lace* iii. 28 Old Brussels lace is of fine texture and rich in design..It was often made..in separate sprays sewn on net, which in the earlier days was hand-made and known as 'Vrai réseau' to distinguish it from the machine-made net.

‖ **vraisemblable** (vręsaṅblābl'), *a.* [Fr., f. *vrai* true + *semblable* like.] Believable, likely, plausible. Also *absol.* as *sb.* (esp. *collect.*).

1830 *New Monthly Mag.* XXX. 5/1 How far all this is fact, we have no means of ascertaining, but the vraisemblable is well preserved, and if not true..is bien trouve. **1841** Geo. Eliot *Let.* 13 Nov. (1954) I. 121, I was amused with your sharp remarks on the advertisement... I immediately perceived them to be vraisemblable. **1876** J. D. Hooker *Let.* 17 Aug. in L. Huxley *Life & Lett. J. D. Hooker* (1918) II. xlv. 366 The whole of the vraisemblable of the latter falls before the Darwinian Gospel. **1898** E. Lynn Lynton *Let.* 23 Feb. in G. S. Layard *Mrs. Lynn Linton* (1901) xvii. 228, I have had your sketch... Cleverly done..not very *vraisemblable* in the man's character. **1957** D. Piper *Eng. Face* ii. 37 The portrait that Sittow painted of Henry VII..is completely *vraisemblable*. **1969** *Listener* 24 July 99/1 A nobleman.. reproved an actor for not holding a scythe as a labourer does: he got a lecture on the elements of the *vraisemblable*. Stage-scything is not like scything. **1978** *Times* 22 Aug. 13/4 Sir John Colville's delightful speculations..on what would have happened if George Washington had lost seemed to be remarkably *vraisemblable*.

vraisemblance. 1. (Earlier example.)

1802 Scott *Let.* 8 Sept. (1932) I. 156 To give to fiction itself the charms of truth or at least of *vraisemblance*.

vrbaite (vəbā·əit). *Min.* [ad. Czech *vrbait* (B. Ježek 1912, in *Rozpravy České Akad.* XXI. xxvi. 2), f. the name of K. *Vrba* (1845–1922), Bohemian mineralogist: see -ite¹.] A sulphide of thallium, mercury, arsenic, and antimony, $Tl_4Hg_3Sb_2As_8S_{20}$, found as dark grey, tabular or prismatic, orthorhombic crystals.

1913 *Mineral. Mag.* XVI. 375 Vrbaite... Found.. embedded in realgar and orpiment from Allchar, Macedonia. **1973** *Mineral. Abstr.* XXIV. 22/2 The structure was determined on vrbaite from Allchar, Macedonia, the type locality... Vrbaite is the first structure with mixed (As, Sb) chains.

‖ **vṛddhi** (vri·dhi). Also **vriddhi.** [Skr., lit. 'increase'.] In Sanskrit grammar, the strongest grade of an ablaut-series of vowels; also, the process of phonetic change whereby vowels of the middle grade are strengthened to achieve this grade. Cf. Guna.

1841 [see Guna sb.]. **1916** A. A. Macdonell *Vedic Gram. for Students* 5 Beside the Guṇa syllables appear, but much less frequently, the syllables **ai, au, ār** (**āl** does not occur), which are called Vṛddhi by the same authorities [*sc.* the Indian grammarians] and may be regarded as a lengthened variety of the Guṇa syllables. **1965** G. Y. Shevelov *Prehist. of Slavic* 116 More important features which led to the rise of length in I[ndo-]E[uropean] were the special kind of morphological analogy called *vṛddhi* (the name used by O[ld] I[ndian] grammarians to denote reflexes of long diphthongs in OI) and the loss of laryngeals. **1979** *Trans. Philol. Soc.* 150 It is time to break away from Herzfeld's notion that fortresses are 'pflanzenbewachsener boden' or 'saatland', and that the vriddhi of initial *u* was *ā*.

vriesia (vrī·ziă). [mod.L. (J. Lindley 1843, in *Bot. Reg.* XXIX. 10), f. the name of W. H. de *Vriese* (1806–62) Dutch botanist + -ia¹.] A perennial herbaceous plant of the genus *Vriesia* (family Bromeliaceæ), native to South or Central America and bearing rosettes of linear leaves and spikes of yellow, red, or white flowers.

1843 *Bot. Reg.* XXIX. 10 (*heading*) Parrot-flowered Vriesia. **1902** L. H. Bailey *Cycl. Amer. Hort.* IV. 1957/1 Vriesias are..tropical American stiff-leaved plants. **1979** *Daily Tel.* 17 Nov. 10/1 Another group [of bromeliads], the vriesias, have flowers that at one moment look like tongues of flame, and at others you think they are formed like cuttlefish.

‖ **vrille** (vrīl). *Aeronaut.* [Fr., = spin.] A tail-spin; also, a spinning manœuvre engaged in deliberately as part of an aerobatic display.

1918 B. Hall *In the Air* iv. 32 He is trained on the rapid machines and when perfected is sent to the acrobatic school where they are taught all sorts of stunts, such as looping, vrille, tail and wing slips, and all the modern stunts. **1918** W. J. Abbot *Aircraft & Submarines* 115 The modern airplane is naturally so stable that if *not* interfered with it will always attempt to right itself before the dreaded *vrille* occurs. **1919** [see *tailspin *sb.* a]. **1965** *Amer. Speech* XL. 13 /vr-/ can be attested, also in more recent *vrille* and in a proper name.

vroom (vrum). *colloq.* (orig. *U.S.*). Also **varoom.** [Echoic.] The roaring noise of a motor vehicle accelerating or travelling at speed. Also as *v. intr.*, to make such a noise; to travel or accelerate at speed; as *v. trans.*, to rev (an engine) with such a sound. Also reduplicated and as *int.*

1967 M. J. Arlen in *New Yorker* 21 Jan. 76 To go varooming all over the desert in a couple of jeeps. **1968** L. Deighton *Only when I Larf* iv. 48, I..shaved off my moustache. Vroom vroom. **1969** *Time* 2 May 33 The foursome would prefer tough scramblers, 'with big drive sprockets, knobby wheels—and more vroom'. **1970** *Atlantic Monthly* Oct. 75 The trooper lies on his back.. reading *Hot Rod* magazine, hearing the vroom-vroom of engines. **1971** 'H. Calvin' *Poison Chasers* vii. 93 The car stood at the red light with the engine making impatient vroom noises. **1971** *Time* 19 July 59/2 Just give me ten showgirls out here, and varoom, the young guys'll come out of Los Angeles in first gear. **1973** J. Di Mona *Last Man at Arlington* (1974) iv. xv. 195 A bullet varoomed over his head. **1974** *Guardian* 21 Mar. 11/2 A score of big bad BSA's vrooming through a sleepy one-pub town. **1975** D. Lodge *Changing Places* 190 Morris pulled out and varoomed down the wrong side of the road. **1976** B. Jackson *Flameout* iv. 51 A gang of youths sitting astride motorcycles vroomed their engines. **1979** J. Hansen *Skinflick* x. 77 'How about a sports car?.. Let it roll off a cliff and catch fire. Just like TV. Sensational.' 'Varoom!' Spence said. **1984** *New Yorker* 14 May 41/2 It wasn't the *varooms* and the screeching tires that spooked people.

vrouw, vrow. Add: Also **vrou.** *spec.* in S. Afr. (Further examples.)

1798 A. Barnard *Jrnl.* 21 May in A. W. C. Lindsay *Lives of Lindsays* (1849) III. 455 We were received by the vrow, the mistress of the house—O house, unworthy such a mistress! **1827** T. Phillips *Scenes & Occurrences in Albany & Caffer-Land* i. 12 Distance to them is no consideration; the boor puts his *vrouw*..into the waggon,.. and sets off to travel five hundred miles, with as much ease as we should ten in England. **1946** *Cape Times Weekend Mag.* 16 Nov. 27 Yesterday your vrou brought to my store a cupboard that she would sell. **1972** A. A. Telford *Yesterday's Dress* 79 The 'vrouw' is wearing the thick quilted cap.

V-shaped: see V 2 c in Dict. and Suppl.

V-sign. Also **V sign.** [f. *V* = Victory: see *V 5 b.] **1. a.** The letter V used as a written symbol of victory during the war of 1939–45. **b.** The Morse Code representation of this letter or the first four notes of Beethoven's Fifth Symphony, which have the same rhythm. Also *transf.*

1941 W. S. CHURCHILL *Unrelenting Struggle* (1942) 198 The V sign is the symbol of the unconquerable will of the occupied territories, and a portent of the fate awaiting the Nazi tyranny. **1959** *Listener* 24 Sept. 489/2 The start of the 'V-sign' by Victor de Lavelaye of the Belgian Section [of the B.B.C.] in July 1941. **1972** *Times* 26 Sept. 4/8 The old V-sign, first used for the Belgian service in 1941, was a low-frequency signal. **1978** L. THOMAS *Ormerod's Landing* v. 95 There came a V-sign knock on the street door.

2. a. = *victory sign* s.v. *VICTORY *sb.* 5. **b.** A similar gesture made with the back of the hand outwards as an obscene gesture of contempt (see also quots. 1948, 1973).

a. 1942 H. NICOLSON *Diary* 23 Apr. (1967) 224 Winston ..gives the V-sign to an audience which does not greet him with any tumultuous applause. **1943** A. MOOREHEAD *End in Africa* xiv. 148 They gave the V sign, they shouted and waved flags, the girls kissed the soldiers and the men ran out with bottles of wine and fruit.

b. 1948 PARTRIDGE *Dict. Forces' Slang* 202 *V-sign*, the first and middle fingers uplifted in the form of the letter *V*, for victory. When the hand making the sign was jerked upwards, it was a sign of recognition between two acquaintances passing on a road, or of complete disagreement with the statements or actions of another, adequately replacing a vulgar monosyllable of the same significance. **1959** *Spectator* 4 Sept. 297/2 Congreve's *Double Dealer* is a sex-play... To his immediate predecessors the dirty joke was still a political gesture, a deliberately ambiguous V-sign which semaphored both political and marital freedom. **1973** *Daily Tel.* 29 Nov. 3/8 Two 'louts'..taunted him outside his home by shouting obscenities and making V-signs. **1981** B. HINES *Looks & Smiles* 36 They turned round and gave him the V-sign generously with both hands..the gatekeeper hurried inside his office and slammed the door.

vuagnatite (vwā·nyătəit). *Min.* [f. the name of M. *Vuagnat* (b. 1922), Swiss petrologist + -ITE[1].] A basic silicate of calcium and aluminium, $CaAl(OH)SiO_4$, found as white, usu. anhedral, orthorhombic crystals.

1976 H. SARP et al. in *Amer. Mineralogist* LXI. 825 Vuagnatite..occurs with prehnite, hydrogrossular, vesuvianite, and chorite in rodingitic dykes from an ophiolitic zone in the Taurus Mountains, southwest Turkey. **1979** *Mineral. Abstr.* XXX. 413/2 Vuagnatite occurs as veinlets less than 5 mm wide or as small lenses less than 15 mm long in pectolite veins cutting serpentinite in the Toba district, central Japan.

‖ **vue d'ensemble** (vü daṅsaṅbl'). [Fr.] A general view; an overall view of matters.

1865 MILL *Auguste Comte* 159 A philosopher's business is with general truths and connected views (vues d'ensemble). **1886** W. JAMES *Let.* 29 Aug. in R. B. Perry *Tht. & Char. W. James* (1935) I. 601, I gained a *vue d'ensemble* of the philosopher. **1975** *Times Lit. Suppl.* 29 Aug. 972/1 The *vue d'ensemble*..shows an enviable mastery of essentials. **1976** *Ibid.* 9 July 843/1 The impetus to crystallize his professional opinions, to create a *vue d'ensemble* of his life's work.

‖ **vuelta** (vwe·lta). *Bull-fighting.* [Sp., lit. 'turn, round'.] The triumphal circuit of the ring awarded to the successful matador.

1932 [see *RECORTE]. **1954** H. CASTEEL *Running of Bulls* vii. 134 If the applause continues he [*sc.* the matador] may make another circuit (dos vueltas). **1967** MCCORMICK & MASCAREÑAS *Compl. Aficionado* ii. 62 This is another sort of beauty, and the matador has his full award, of two ears and three vueltas.

vug. Add: (Further examples.)

1927 in M. Terry *Through Land of Promise* vi. 90 In places there are small 'vugs' containing quartz crystals. **1953** *Amer. Mineralogist* XXXVIII. 7 The vugs are commonly almond-shaped and range in size from 10 cm. down to microscopic dimensions. **1976** *Nature* 29 Apr. 813/1 The eye is captivated by the beautiful scanning electron microscope photographs of iron crystals deposited in vugs.

vuggy *a.* (further examples).

1953 *Amer. Mineralogist* XXXVIII. 7 Some of the replaced rock has a very vuggy texture. **1970** [see *PYROXFERROITE]. **1971** V. A. FIRSOFF *Gemstones Brit. Isles* iv. 25 Amethyst occurs in druses and 'small vuggy veins' in the former haematite mines of Mwyndy and Garth Ward.

vugular (vʊ·giŭlăɹ), *a. Geol.* [f. VUG + -ULAR.] **a.** Containing vugs. **b.** Of the nature of a vug.

1967 *Trans. Soc. Professional Well Log Analysts* P-1 Non-homogeneous carbonates such as vugular limes or dolomites. **1975** G. ANDERSON *Coring* i. 2 The individual pore may be like a capillary tube or it may be vugular with druzy crystal infilling. **1977** *Géotechnique* XXVII. 435 It is difficult to determine the porosity of a vugular rock sample by conventional techniques because of the problems encountered in measuring the bulk volume of the specimen.

Vuitton (vwītoṅ). In full **Louis Vuitton.** A proprietary name for the products of a French firm making high-quality luggage and other personal items.

1975 *Vogue* Sept. 305/4 (Advt.), A Louis Vuitton in the hand. **1976** *Official Gaz.* (U.S. Patent Office) 18 May TM182/2 *Louis Vuitton.* For luggage and ladies' handbags. **1977** C. WOOD *James Bond, Spy who loved Me* vii. 60 His travel-weary Vuitton suitcase. **1978** H. MACINNES *Prelude to Terror* iv. 32 An amazing hodgepodge of luggage..Vuitton combined with cardboard boxes. **1980** *Trade Marks Jrnl.* 6 Feb. 280/2 *Louis Vuitton* ...1,081,942. Handbags, suitcases, trunks, umbrellas, pocket wallets, purses..key cases. **1982** C. HOUCK *Fashion Encycl.* 220 Vuitton luggage is the most status-ridden luggage in the world, and some of the cachet has seeped over into Vuitton handbags. **1983** *Time* 1 Aug. 40/2 Louis Vuitton handbags.

Vulcanian, *a.* Add: **6.** [f. *Vulcano*, name of one of the Lipari Islands (cf. quot. 1976).] Of, pertaining to, or designating (the stage of) a volcanic eruption characterized by periodic explosive events.

1912 *Amer. Jrnl. Sci.* CLXXXIV. 412 This hypothesis does not..invalidate the division of the eruption into a 'Strombolian' and a 'Vulcanian' phase—on the contrary, it supplies a cause for the great and continued dynamism of the 'Vulcanian' phase... It is interesting to note that the 'Vulcanian' phase, as far as actual, external eruption is concerned, is cooler than the 'Strombolian'. **1944** [see *PELÉAN *a.*]. **1976** P. FRANCIS *Volcanoes* v. 169 Probably the best known Vulcanian deposit is one produced by an eruption of Vulcano itself in the 1880s. **1985** E. A. K. MIDDLEMOST *Magmas & Magmatic Rocks* i. 28/2 Vulcanian eruptions usually begin with a series of phreatic explosions that eject lithic debris from the volcanic conduit.

vulcanist. 3. (Further examples.)

1969 *New Yorker* 19 Apr. 52/2 Baldwin..was the first person to suggest convincingly that meteors might have made many of the moon's craters; previously, almost all selenologists had been vulcanists. **1971** *Nature* 27 Aug. 600/3 Although there is now a vast amount of data on the physics, chemistry and shape of the Moon, the 'vulcanists' and 'impacters' at the symposium on this subject seem to be as widely divided as ever.

vulcanizable, *a.* (Earlier example.)

1860 [see *PARTIAL *a.* 3 g].

vulcanizate (vʊ·lkănəizē[i]t). [f. VULCANIZE *v.*, after *filtrate, precipitate*, etc.] A material that has been vulcanized.

1942 *Trans. Faraday Soc.* XXXVIII. 345 The vulcanizates. **1959** *Times* 27 Apr. (Rubber Industry Suppl.) p. ii, The general purpose synthetic rubber..does not readily form crystals and so as a gum vulcanizate it is very weak. **1983** *Jrnl. Materials Sci.* XVIII. 515 The abrasion of NR/BR blend vulcanizates has been studied in three different testing machines.

vulgarian, *a.* and *sb.* Add: Hence **vulga·rianism.**

1920 D. H. LAWRENCE *Lost Girl* x. 243 She saw his modern vulgarianism, and decadence. **1963** *New Society* 21 Nov. 22/1 The rising generations of eggheads is notorious for its vulgarianism, admiring Brigitte, canonizing Marilyn.

‖ **vulgarisateur** (vülgarizatœr). [Fr.] = *vulgarizer* s.v. VULGARIZE *v.*

1933 D. L. SAYERS *Murder must Advertise* xiv. 238, I obtained an introduction to her through what..that incomparable *vulgarisateur*, Charles Dickens—abominably calls a mutual friend. **1948** *Mind* LVII. 383 The introductory chapter..consists of a defence of the philosophical *vulgarisateur*. **1955** J. WAIN *Interpretations* p. xiii, The making of large generalizations could safely be left to the *vulgarisateurs*. **1971** LD. BUTLER *Art of Possible* viii. 157 The less voluble and extrovert Hall, to act as *vulgarisateur* or publicist for his ideas.

‖ **vulgarisation** (vülgarizasyoṅ). [Fr.] = VULGARIZATION 1. Cf. *HAUTE VULGARISATION.

1939 *Year's Work Eng. Stud. 1937* 25 J. R. Firth's popular little sketch, *The Tongues of Men*, is an excellent example of that *vulgarisation* by experts which is becoming so fashionable to-day. **1959** *Times Lit. Suppl.* 11 Sept. 520/1 But Porché's later work had to stand up to the essays of..Sartre and Blanchot, and the propitious moment for his *vulgarisation* had come and gone. **1968** J. A. W. BENNETT *Chaucer's Bk. of Fame* ii. 75 Witness his book on the Astrolabe, an admirable piece of *vulgarisation* which we ought not to dissociate severely from his poetry and which may reflect the study of astronomy in the Oxford of his day.

vulgarizing, *vbl. sb.* (Example.)

1946 J. S. HUXLEY *Unesco* II. 60 They [*sc.* press and radio] have already rendered many disservices—in the vulgarising of taste, in the debasement of intellectual standards.

vulnerability. Add: **c.** *spec.* in *Contract Bridge*, the quality or state of being vulnerable (sense 2 d below).

1927 M. C. WORK *Contract Bridge* ii. 10 Trick values, the number of points to a game, game and rubber bonuses..are not affected by vulnerability. **1942** E. CULBERTSON *Official Bk. Contract Bridge* 239 The consequence of vulnerability is exposure to greater penalties and entitlement to greater premiums. **1975** *Times* 15 Nov. 13/5 In May 1925, Mr Vanderbilt..joined in a rubber of the continental game of plafond. He saw possibilities in the game, added the attraction of vulnerability..and..introduced it to the Whist Club under the name of Contract Bridge.

d. *pl.* The weaknesses in a military defence system.

1972 *Science* 19 May 819/1 The purpose of this conference is to define a comprehensive but balanced assessment of the risks, vulnerabilities, capabilities, and intentions for subversive disruption. **1978** *Time* 3 July 36/3 'There is no doubt in my mind,' he said, 'that the U.S. is the most powerful country in the world.' He admitted 'concern' about 'vulnerabilities' in NATO, but said he felt the U.S. could 'outthink, outdesign and outperform the Soviets with the resources we have and the steady increases we are requesting'.

vulnerable, *a.* Add: **2. d.** *Contract Bridge.* Of or pertaining to the liability of one side to be awarded increased penalties or increased bonuses as result of having won a game.

[**1925** *Work-Whitehead Auction Bridge Bull.* Oct. 5 In circles where high play predominates, there was introduced a variation of the above count, called 'Le Vulnerable'.] **1927** [see *danger-zone* s.v. *DANGER *sb.* c]. **1965** *Listener* 23 Sept. 474/3 Playing the Two Club system, my partner, the dealer, opened a vulnerable No Trump (strong). **1977** M. KENYON *Rapist* i. 10 Five no trumps! Don't get vulnerable!

vulture, *sb.* Add: **4. d.** *vulture-wise* adj.

1892 STEVENSON & OSBOURNE *Wrecker* xiii. 206 Towards her the taut *Norah Creina*, vulture-wise, wriggled to windward: come from so far to pick her bones. **1906** W. DE LA MARE *Poems* 82 This beast in one flat hand clasped vulture-wise A glitt'ring image.

vulture, *v.* Delete *rare*[−1] and add later examples. Also *intr.* with *down*, to descend like a vulture.

1922 JOYCE *Ulysses* 47 He rooted in the sand..vulturing the dead. **1948** M. ALLINGHAM *More Work for Undertaker* xiii. 164 The tax harpies vultured down for death duties. **1955** *Newsweek* 10 Jan. 49/1 Contestants had vultured the library's reference and guidebooks for the names of the mystery towns. **1977** L. GORDON *Eliot's Early Years* 147 From 'Proteus' came the dog vulturing the dead in part I of *The Waste Land.*

Hence **vu·ltured** *ppl. a.* (*poet.*).

1946 DYLAN THOMAS *Deaths & Entrances* 47 O spiral of ascension From the vultured urn Of the morning Of man.

vulvectomy (vʊlve·ktŏmi). *Surg.* [f. VULV(A + *-ECTOMY.] Excision of (part of) the vulva.

1917 *Amer. Jrnl. Obstetr. & Dis. Women* LXXVI. 797 A vulvectomy was done on June 27th and the patient left the hospital August 13th. **1962** *Lancet* 1 Dec. 1171/1 The histological findings of atypical basal-cell hyperplasia in any section can then justify vulvectomy.

vurry (vʊ·ri), *a. colloq.* Repr. a supposed Amer. pronunciation of VERY *a.* and *adv.*

1889 KIPLING *From Sea to Sea* (1899) I. xii. 306 The tourists..call to one another: 'Sa-ay, don't you think it's vurry much the same all along?' **1913** E. POUND *Let.* (1971) 14 Have just discovered another Amur'kn [*sc.* Robert Frost]. *Vurry* Amur'k'n. **1943** C. S. CHURCHILL *Let.* 19 Dec. in M. Soames *Clementine Churchill* (1979) xxii. 344 The food, however, is 'vurry' American. **1972** K. BONFIGLIOLI *Don't Point that Thing at Me* vii. 65 [He] wished me a vurry, vurry happy visit to the US of A.

vygie (fəi·χi). *S. Afr.* [Afrikaans, f. *vy(g)*, f. Du. *vijg, vig* fig + *-ie* diminutive suffix.] Any of several small succulent plants belonging to the genus *Mesembryanthemum* or a closely related genus, or the brightly coloured flower of one of these plants. Also **vy·gebosch** [Afrikaans *vyebossie*].

1795 tr. *C. P. Thunberg's Trav. Europe, Afr., & Asia* II. 35 The field was here of the Carrow kind, and the sheep were said to feed on those succulent plants, the Mesembryanthemums (*vygebosches*). **1892** *Jrnl.* (Grahamstown) 11 July 1/2 (Advt.), The Veld consists of much-sought-after Karoo, Vygebosch,..with Mimosas in the valley. **1931** *Farming in S. Afr.* 393 The mineral and feeding-stuff analyses of a vygie give no clue to its probable palatability. **1950** *Cape Argus* 5 Aug. 7/5 Vygies or sour figs.. blossom in a wide range of colours—scarlet, blue, purple, pink or flaming yellow. **1966** E. PALMER *Plains of Camdeboo* xvii. 271 The little vygies on the flats. **1971** [see *GOUSBLOM].

Vynide (vəi·nəid). Also **vynide.** A proprietary name for a plastic used as a substitute for leather in upholstery, clothing, etc.

1943 *Trade Marks Jrnl.* 16 June 257/2 *Vynide*...Leather cloth. Imperial Chemical Industries Limited, Wexham Road, Slough, Buckinghamshire; manufacturers and merchants. **1958** *Archit. Rev.* CXXIV. 395/2 The bookcase shelves and backs, and the wall opposite the window are covered in white vynide. **1960** *Housewife* Feb. 58/2 Thankful I brought good country-looking Vynide jacket ..(looks like leather, won't leak, will sponge clean). **1976** *Lancs. Evening Post* 7 Dec. 12/8 (Advt.), Reupholstery. Your three piece suite made as new in moquette or vynide.

vysotskite (vīsǫ·tskəit). *Min.* [ad. Russ. *vȳsotskit* (Genkin & Zvyagintsev 1962, in *Zap. Vsesoyuz. Min. Obshch.* XCI. 718), f. the name of N. K. *Vysotsky* (d. 1932), Russian mineralogist: see -ITE[1].] A sulphide of palladium and often nickel, (Pd,Ni)S, found as minute silvery tetragonal crystals having a metallic lustre.

1963 *Chem. Abstr.* LVIII. 8777 For the genesis of vysotskite is characteristic the assocn. with Pt ores, pentlandite, millerite, and other sulfides, in effusive andesite-diabase in gabbro-diabase intrusions. **1978** *Amer. Mineralogist* LXIII. 832/1 Vysotskite has since been reported..from the Stillwater Complex of Montana ..and the Lac des Isles deposit, Ontario. *Ibid.* 838/1 We conclude that braggite and vysotskite are simply compositional variants of the same phase, (Pd,Pt,Ni)S... We suggest that the family of minerals be called the braggite series and that all compositions containing less than 10 mole percent PtS be called vysotskite.

W

W. Add: **3.** W, colloq. shortening of W.C.; a lavatory or water-closet; W., women('s size) (WX, extra-large women's size); W.A., Western Australia; WASP (*U.S.*), Women's Airforce Service Pilots; WAT (*Aeronaut.*), Weight and Temperature; WATS (*U.S.*), Wide Area Telephone Service; W.C. (examples of 'West Central'); W.C.C., World Council of Churches; WCT, World Championship Tennis; W.C.T.U. (*N. Amer.*), Women's Christian Temperance Union; W.D., War Department; W.D.C., Woman Detective Constable; W.D.S., Woman Detective Sergeant; W.E.A., Workers' Educational Association; w.e.f., with effect from; W.E.U., Western European Union; wff (*Logic*) = *well-formed formula* s.v. *WELL-FORMED *ppl. a.* c; WFTU, World Federation of Trade Unions; w.h.b., wash-hand basin; W.H.O., World Health Organization; W.I. (also † West India) (examples); W.I., Women's Institute; W.I.Z.O., Wizo (wī·tzo), Women's International Zionist Organization; WKB (*Physics*) [initials of G. Wentzel, H. A. Kramers, and L. Brillouin, who each published papers on the method in 1926], used *attrib.* with reference to a method for obtaining an approximate solution of the Schrödinger equation based on the expansion of the wave function in powers of Planck's constant, *h*; W.L.A., Women's Land Army; W.M.O., World Meteorological Organization; W.O., War Office; W.O., Warrant Officer; W.O.C.(S), waiting on cement (to set); W.O.S.B. (also with pronunc. (wǫ·zbi)), War Office Selection Board; W.O.W., waiting on weather; w.p., weather permitting; WP, word processing; WPA (*U.S.*), Works Progress Administration; W.P.B., w.p.b. (*slang*), waste-paper basket; W.P.C., Woman Police Constable; w.p.m., words per minute; W.R.A.N.S. (ræ̂nz) (*Austral.*), Women's Royal Australian Naval Service; hence WRAN, Wran, a member of this; W.R.N.S., Women's Royal Naval Service; cf. *WREN[2]; w.r.t., with respect to; W.R.V.S., Women's Royal Voluntary Service, formerly *W.V.S.; W.S. (earlier example); W.S.P.U., Women's Social and Political Union; W/T, W.T., wireless telegraphy; freq. *attrib.*; w/v (see quot. 1907); W.V.S., Women's Voluntary Service; WW (I. II), World War (One, Two); W.W.W., World Weather Watch. See also *W.A.A.C., *W.A.A.F., *W.A.C., *WASP, *W.R.A.C., *W.R.A.F., *WREN[2].

1953 DYLAN THOMAS *Under Milk Wood* (1954) 11 Talking to the lamp-post..Using language..Singing in the W. **1954** A. S. C. Ross in *Neuphilol. Mitteilungen* LV. 41 *W.* either 'the letter W' or 'W.C.' (a frequent non-U expression for 'lavatory'). **1978** E. MALPASS *Wind brings up Rain* x. 105 A small garden of weeds, with a cinder path leading to a W. **1926–7, 1974** W [see S.W. s.v. *S 4 a]. **1900** *Morning Post* 12 July 9/4 Town Pro. W.A. **1971** *Sunday Australian* 8 Aug. 5/2 The State shipping service in WA has been made the scapegoat for Government indecision. **1943** *Yank* 24 Sept. 17 WASP, which stands for 'Womens Air Force Service Pilots' is the new official title of women pilots of the AAF. **1957** *Times* 9 Dec. 12/7 There is an additional requirement governing the maximum take-off and landing weights for the altitude and weight prevailing (known as the 'WAT curve'). **1976** B. LECOMBER *Dead Weight* xi. 136 Those coins weigh 600 lb..if we pile in three people on top of that that we'll be totally WAT-limited... WAT—Weight and Temperature. **1962** *Fleet Owner* Aug. 73/1 With WATS you pay a monthly fee for a special line over which you can call any telephone number in prescribed States. **1977** *New Yorker* 12 Sept. 68/3 Harry has a WATS line, so Henny called Sadie again, this time for free. **1857** *Punch* 7 Feb. 51/2 Rowland Hill has just divided London's waste of brick by ten... Lawyers, and good *Coram*'s Foundlings, All are found in W.C. **1935** E. FARJEON *Nursery in Nineties* I. viii. 63 We found the little oblong envelope..with..the London W.C. postmark. **1948** *Ecumenical Rev.* Autumn 118 The work of two Conferences convened by the Study Department of the W.C.C... is reported in this book. **1971** K. GRUBB *Crypts of Power* viii. 168 Many Churches of Asia, Africa and Latin America joined the W.C.C. **1969** *N.Y. Times* 19 Feb. 54/5 Robert A. Briner of W.C.T. said: 'This is a truce.' **1982** *Tennis Today* June 12/3 Dallas had its best field for a few years, which was an effective answer to those who would suggest WCT are on the way out after the split with the Grand Prix. **1888** LINDLEY & WIDNEY *California of South* 109 The W.C.T.U. was first organized here in 1883. **1956** B. HOLIDAY *Lady sings Blues* (1973) xix. 157 Nobody who has a police record can hold a liquor licence. This was a sop to the WCTU. **1855** *Admiralty Circular* 27 Aug., In future the mark W.D. (War Department), with the Broad Arrow, shall be used for Stores provided by the Ordnance Department. **1920** *Punch* 7 Jan. 9/1 The orders are dead strict against civilians riding in W.D. vehicles. **1942** E. WAUGH *Put out More Flags* II. 149 Patches of rank land marked on the signposts W.D., marked on the maps as numbered training areas. **1976** 'J. CHARLTON' *Remington Set* xviii. 86, I need something on a three-ton chassis.. ex-WD Bedford would do nicely. **1970** G. F. NEWMAN *Sir, You Bastard* viii. 217 Find two WDC's to accompany the women. **1972** *Police Rev.* 8 Dec. 1597/1 We in Nottinghamshire have not yet decided whether we have D.P.W.s or W.D.C.s or whether they are W.D.S.s or D.P.W. Sergts. **1910** S. A. BARNETT *Let.* 10 Mar. in H. Barnett *Canon Barnett* (1918) II. l. 332 The W.E.A. has life. **1936** A. HUXLEY *Eyeless in Gaza* xxix. 393 W.E.A. lecture-rooms. **1981** D. ROWNTREE *Dict. Educ.* 350 *Workers' Educational Association* (*WEA*), a UK organisation founded in 1903 to stimulate and satisfy the demand for education among working class people... The WEA now arranges adult education classes and courses throughout the UK (no longer primarily for working class people). **1942** PARTRIDGE *Dict. Abbrev.* 101/2 *w.e.f.*, with effect from (a given date). **1954** J. MASTERS *Bhowani Junction* xxxii. 275 It terminated her duty with my battalion w.e.f. June the twelfth. **1978** T. ALLBEURY *Lantern Network* viii. 93 The official notification of his promotion to major w.e.f. 1 Jan. 44. **1954** *Times* 11 Nov. 8/7 The first [of the protocols] modifies the older treaty to allow for the adherence of Italy and the German Federal Republic..and emphasizes close cooperation with the North Atlantic Treaty Organization, on which W.E.U. will rely. *a* **1974** R. CROSSMAN *Diaries* (1976) II. 401 George [Brown] proposes to go to a meeting of the W.E.U. next Tuesday and wants to make an important declaration there on Europe. **1944** w.f.f. [see *PRENEX *a.*]. **1956** A. CHURCH *Introd. Math. Logic* (rev. ed.) I. i. 70 We shall hereafter use the abbreviations 'wf' for 'well-formed', 'wff' for 'well-formed formula', and 'wffs' for 'well-formed formulas'. **1967** *Encycl. Philos.* V. 2/2 This property will clearly be perceived if a small letter is systematically replaced by any wff. **1971** G. HUNTER *Metalogic* i. 4 What things are to be wffs. **1947** *Times* 17 Nov. 5/6 The International Transport Workers' Federation will meet.. to consider further its decision recently taken in Washington not to affiliate to the W.F.T.U. **1978** *Statesman's Year-Bk.* I. 39 The WFTU formally came into existence on 3 Oct. 1945. **1975** *Evening Herald* (Dublin) 8 May 10/3 (Advt.), Cloakroom with w.c. and w.h.b. **1946** *N.Y. Times* 28 July IV. 2/3 Dr Thomas Parran..described the constitution of the WHO as a major contribution to world peace. **1960** *New Statesman* 2 Apr. 478/3 The Americans are..working with the WHO to build hospitals and eliminate malaria. **1977** G. SCOTT *Hot Pursuit* xi. 98 If this was a WHO team..we could be passing up the one opportunity we had. **1848** *Brit. Army Despatch* 17 Nov. 292/2 Late Captain 2nd W.I. Regt. **1900** *Naval & Mil. Rev.* July 5 Name of Vessel. Pearl. Present Station. N.A. and W.I. **1973** *Advocate-News* (Barbados) 17 Jan. 2/5 (*heading*) Deep concern over W.I. **1928** *Mid-Sussex Times* 18 Dec. 8/1 A tangible result of the W.I. trading scheme. **1940** C. MILBURN *Diary* 26 Mar. (1979) 28 A W.I. Produce Meeting..to hear about sugar for jam and the arrangements about getting it for W.I. members. **1965** *New Society* 7 Jan. 5 At Stony Creek, Ontario, in 1897, the first WI meeting was held... It wasn't until the outbreak of World War I that a Canadian widow named Mrs. Watt introduced the WI to Britain... The first meeting was held in September 1915. **1981** J. SCOTT *Distant View of Death* xii. 158 Jars of home produce to transport to the WI stall set up in the square. **1925** *Zionist Rev.* IX. 50/2 The growing edifice of the W.I.Z.O. **1940** A. ULITZUR *Two Decades of Keren Hayesod* iii. 47 The Women's International Zionist Organisation (*Wizo*). **1978** *Jewish Chron.* 6 Oct. 14/3 Coventry and Leamington Wizo held a three-day nearly new sale and raised £350 for Israel. [**1932** J. L. DUNHAM in *Physical Rev.* XLI. 713 The Wentzel-Brillouin-Kramers method of handling the wave equation (hereinafter referred to as the W.B.K. method) is very well suited to the calculation of energy levels in heavy systems.] **1935** *Ibid.* XLVII. 748/2 The wave function can be represented by the WKB (Wentzel-Kramers-Brillouin) solution. **1961** POWELL & CRASEMANN *Quantum Mech.* v. 142 The WKB solutions cannot be valid near a classical turning point, where the momentum is zero. **1974** G. REECE tr. *Hund's Hist. Quantum Theory* vii. 97 This was confirmed by later proofs using the Schroedinger equation and the WKB approximation. **1939** *Times* 26 Oct. 11/5 The farmer who is loth to employ one of the W.L.A. may see his more progressive neighbour very well served. **1942** C. MILBURN *Diary* 17 Oct. (1979) 155, I did a little W.L.A. work, going down to the hostel with some magazines. **1951** *Bull. Amer. Meteorol. Soc.* XXXII. 239/1 The International Meteorological Organization wound up its affairs in Paris on March 15–17, 1951 and handed over its assets, obligations and numerous resolutions to the new World Meteorological Organisation... Sir Nelson Johnson aptly put it when he said.. 'The IMO is dying, long live the WMO.' **1977** *Whitaker's Almanack 1978* 810/1 World Meteorological Organization (WMO), Geneva... The present membership is 139 States and 8 Territories. **1860** F. NIGHTINGALE *Let.* 8 Dec. in C. Woodham-Smith *Florence Nightingale* (1950) xvi. 358, I do hope you won't have any vain ideas that you can be spared out of the W.O... You are necessary to the re-organising of the W.O. **1914** R. BROOKE *Let.* 24 Sept. (1968) 619 He may go out as an interpreter... The W.O. has his name. **1931** *N. & Q.* 5 Dec. 408/2 Who was Capt. Robert Holden, of the 130th Regt.? From Army Lists and W.O. Commission Books, it seems that he was commissioned Lieutenant in the 115th Regt., 14 Nov., 1794. **1887** O. L. PERRY *Ranks & Badges H.M. Army & Navy* ix. 102 Such W.O.'s, N.C.O.'s and men as may be specially placed under their orders. **1977** 'O. JACKS' *Autumn Heroes* iv. 65 He's an ex W.O.II in the Paras. **1949** *Amer. Speech* XXIV. 35 The verbal *wocsing*..is derived from the initials W.O.C.S., which stand for *waiting on cement to set* (the written form is often simply *woc* without capitalization or punctuation)... A field worker tells me I must have misspelled the word, as it is always pronounced ['wɑkəsɪŋ] in the field. **1974** D. K. SMITH in P. L. Moore et al. *Drilling Practices Manual* xvi. 400 Improvements in cements, understanding WOC times, and the use of admixes have reduced WOC time to a few hours under present-day practices. **1945** *Jrnl. R. Army Med. Corps* LXXXIV. 75 W.O.S.B.'s which followed the pattern of the experimental Board. **1978** *Jrnl. R. Soc. Arts* CXXVI. 268/1 The need for skilful selection of officers..led to the WOSB or War Office Selection Board. **1982** S. RAVEN *Shadows on Grass* (1983) v. 95, I was summoned to a W.O.S.B...which would finally determine whether I was fit to be trained for a Commission. **1967** R. DE SOLA *Abbrev. Dict.* (rev. ed.) 277/1 *WOW*, waiting on weather. **1975** *Oil & Gas Industry Gloss. Terms* (Bank of Scotland) 5/2 *W.O.W.*, Waiting on Weather; usually applied to mobile offshore drilling platforms but can also refer to other offshore operations. **1889** E. C. DOWSON *Let.* 2 Mar. (1967) 43, I shall be at Baker St. as you prefer—w.p. before 3.0, to-morrow. **1931** JOYCE *Let.* 17 Apr. (1966) III. 217, I..hope to arrive in London..that evg. (w.p.). **1974** *New Acronyms & Initialisms* (Gale Research Co.), *WP*, word processing. **1980** *City Recorder* 10 Jan. 7/3 In a really small company, the executive who can operate a WP machine can work almost as a one man band. **1936** *N.Y. Herald Tribune* 1 June 8/4 (*heading*) W.P.A. must increase efficiency, says Ridder. **1943** J. S. HUXLEY *TVA* ix. 69 In the reception room..the mural by a WPA artist helps the guide to explain the project. **1979** *Listener* 16 Aug. 214/1 The Roosevelt WPA project and other attempts at a social art in the Thirties. **1903** *Photogram* X. 320/1 Anonymous letters are strongly objected to, and ..go into the W.P.B. **1934** T. E. LAWRENCE *Lett.* (1938) 815 Please dump it in the W.P.B. when it begins to bore you. **1939** *War Illustr.* 16 Dec. p. ii/3 Possessing a very large wastepaper basket, I give short shrift to all anonymous correspondents. A glance at any missive signed with a nom-de-plume and into that w.p.b. it goes. **1974** P. FLOWER *Odd Job* iii. 26 He..let it fall into the w.p.b. **1984** *Times* 20 Jan. 10/1 So presumably it's someone's job to empy wpbs and clean already clean ashtrays for part of the year. **1963** F. B. FAWCETT *Cycl. Initials & Abbrev.* 158/2 *WPC*, Woman Police Constable. **1966** L. SOUTHWORTH *Felon in Disguise* i. 17 'I'll send in the W.P.C. right away.'.. The Inspector left the room. **1981** 'J. ASHFORD' *Loss of Culion* xiii. 94 Why hadn't she accepted the offer of having a WPC with her? **1936** G. DEWEY *GS Teacher* p. xxiii, Suggested dictation rate: 30 wpm. **1977** *Belfast Tel.* 17 Jan. 17/1 (Advt.), Applicants should have a typing speed of at least 40 w.p.m. and also 80 w.p.m. shorthand. **1945** BAKER *Austral. Lang.* viii. 159 *W.R.A.N.S.*, Women's Royal Australian Naval Service (called *Wrans* or *Rons*). **1970** M. KELLY *Spinifex* ii. 30 One of the WRANS hurried over, 'Telephone, sir'. 'Thanks, Betty.' **1919** *Daily Mail Year Bk.* 49/2 The Admiralty must feel justly proud of their W.R.N.S. **1977** *Navy News* Dec. 20/1 Two world wars played a decisive part in the story of the WRNS. The First saw its formation..The Second swung those doors wide to a tremendous range of opportunities. **1956** W. L. FERRAR *Differential Calculus* iii. 33 Let. $z = f(y)$, $y = \phi(x)$; let z have a finite derivative $f'(y)$ w.r.t. y. **1979** *Nature* 30 Aug. 845/2 A measure *D* of the depth of this minimum is defined as the average VAI near days −2 and +4 (w.r.t. day 0 as the boundary transit time) minus the average VAI near day 1. **1966** *Care & Distribution of WRVS Processed Clothing* (Women's Royal Voluntary Service) p. iii, The reputation built up by WRVS in the war years for skilled care..has been enhanced in post-war years. **1978** *Morecambe Guardian* 14 Mar. 13/1 She holds a long service medal from the WRVS and still retains very strong links with the village of Holme. **1852** THACKERAY *Let.* 24 May in J. Brown *Lett.* (1912) 403 Blackwood the W.S. I saw in the Park yesterday. **1907** N. A. MARTEL in B. Villiers *Case for Women's Suffrage* 145 A young girl.. came from Huddersfield..in the care of one of the leaders of the W.S.P.U. **1967** R. S. CHURCHILL *Winston S. Churchill* II. xi. 402 The WSPU now resorted to stone throwing and later to arson. **1914** W. S. CHURCHILL in M. Gilbert *Winston S. Churchill* (1972) III. Compan. I. 292 A submarine off Sylt report by W/T (or by pigeons) at night to a waiting destroyer that the weather is favourable. **1923** *Man. Seamanship* (Admiralty) II. 23 Visual and wireless messages..sent either to the flag deck or the W.T. office for transmission. **1965** 'J. LE CARRÉ' *Looking-Glass War* vii. 84 'He was a trainer in wireless transmission.'..'The WT man?' **1978** R. V. JONES *Most Secret War* xlix. 489 Then I saw its astonishing heading: 'Obscene W/T Traffic.' **1907** *Brit. Pharmaceutical Codex* p. ix, 'w/v' represents 'weight in volume', indicating that a weighed quantity of a solid substance is contained in solution in a measured quantity of liquid. **1973** *Nature* 5 Oct. 267/2 Here I report the use of four inhibitors at concentrations of 0·5% w/v which can each stabilize ethanol in blood. **1939** N. LAST *Diary* 4 Sept. in *Nella Last's War* (1983) 11 I've got lots of plans made to spare time so as to work with the W.V.S. **1976** R. BARNARD *Little Local Murder* iii. 30 The compère talked..to the head of the town's WVS. **1960** *Acronyms Dict.* (Gale

Research Co.) 210 WWI, World War I. WWII, World War II. **1976** *Greenlist* (J. R. Wrigley Catal.) No. 23. 30 Crascredo—No Joke... (The humour of W.W.I.) **1979** G. F. NEWMAN *List* iii. 25 The bank had been..incorporated in '41, shortly before America entered WWII. **1963** *Times* 29 Apr. 9/1 It was pointed out during the congress that as ancillary measures must take several years the full realization of plans for a world weather watch (W.W.W.) was as yet a distant prospect but the interval would enable scientists to ascertain weather potentialities. **1970** *Sci. Jrnl.* Apr. 48 At the time of its inception in 1967 the WWW plan relied entirely on improving and extending existing systems. **1942** A. P. JEPHCOTT *Girls growing Up* i. 33 My biggest tragedy is I am fat & wear W.X. clothes. **1971** J. THOMSON *Not One of Us* (1972) vii. 79 Cardboard boxes were piled everywhere..'Gents' Hose. Assorted Colors.' 'Ladies Knickers. W.X.' **1984** W. BEECHEY *Rich Mrs Robinson* xii. 103 Customers..[who] thought of themselves as Small Women size when really they were WX.

4. Symbolic uses. **a.** *Genetics.* *W* is used to designate the female-determining sex chromosome in species in which the female rather than the male is the heterogametic sex.

1917 T. H. MORGAN in *Amer. Naturalist* LI. 533 In moths in which the female is the heterogametic sex, the Y chromosome (or the W chromosome to use a different nomenclature) is transmitted only by the female line. **1925** *Amer. Naturalist* LIX. 133 The locus of the F genes is in the W-chromosome that descends from mother to daughter. **1964** R. A. BEATTY in Armstrong & Marshall *Intersexuality* ii. 35 There is one kind of spermatozoon (Z) in animals with the ZW:ZZ mechanism. **1971** [see *HETEROGAMETIC *a.*]. **1984** *Nature* 23 Feb. 690/3 Natural populations [of the platyfish, *Xiphophorus maculatus*] are polymorphic for three sex factors (W, X and Y)... The XY and YY genotypes usually develop as males and XX, WX and WY become females; WW genotypes do not in fact occur because male gametes can never bear W factors.

b. *Particle Physics.* [Initial letter of *weak.*] *W* is the symbol for a heavy, charged vector boson that is probably the quantum of the weak interaction.

1960 LEE & YANG in *Physical Rev. Lett.* IV. 310 Possible existence of a weakly coupled boson $W^{\pm}$. *Ibid.*, The question of a neutral W^0 will not be examined here. **1971** *New Scientist* 2 Sept. 498/3 The experimental results agree with this theory if the W particle has a mass of about 36 proton masses. **1977** *Dædalus* Fall 32 Exchange of the W produces the familiar weak interactions, like nuclear beta decay. **1982** *Nature* 23 Sept. 295/2 The heavy W and Z bosons..can be produced in $p\bar{p}$ reactions. **1983** *Sci. Amer.* Apr. 62/2 With the discovery of the *W* particle a major goal of experimental elementary-particle physics has been achieved.

Wa (wā), *sb.* (and *a.*) [Native name.] **a.** (Any of) a group of hill-dwelling peoples of eastern Burma and southwestern Yunnan; a member of one of these peoples. **b.** Their (Mon Khmer) language or dialect. Also *attrib.* or as *adj.*

1860 F. MASON *Burmah* (ed. 2) ii. 69 There is a wild tribe called Lawa on the mountains between the Irrawaddy and the Meinan... There is a small settlement of them..in..Amherst; there formerly was one in Tavoy, where the Karens called them *Wa.* **1902** *Encycl. Brit.* XXX. 519/2 It [*sc.* the Burmese state Mang Lön] is the chief state of the Vü or Wa tribes. **1911** *Ibid.* XXVIII. 223/2 They are popularly divided into Wild Was and Tame Was. The Wild Was are remarkable as the best authenticated instance of head hunters in the British Empire. **1942** [see *PALAUNG *sb.* and *a.*] **1966** D. WILSON *Quarter of Mankind* xvi. 211 They [*sc.* Communist maps] acknowledged the Burmese claim to one piece of territory depicted in Peking as Chinese, but they took an entirely new bite out of the Wa territory shared between the two. **1974** *Encycl. Brit. Micropædia* IV. 272/1 Ethnolinguistic Groups in China..Wa (Kawa).

W.A.A.C., WAAC, Waac (wæk). Also **wack.** Acronym f. the initial letters of *W*omen's *A*rmy *A*uxiliary *C*orps (1917–19); also *U.S.*, the orig. name of the Women's Army Corps (see *W.A.C.), formed in 1942, a member of this. Also *attrib.*

1917 M. MACDONAGH *Diary* 29 Mar. in *In London during Great War* (1935) III. ii. 186 The W.A.A.C.s (Women's Auxiliary Army Corps). *Ibid.*, One of the riddles of the day is: 'Which would you like: a whack on the head or a Waac on your knee?' **1917** W. OWEN *Let.* June (1967) 472 The WAAC's now wait on us. It is rather pleasant. **1918** J. M. GRIDER *Diary* 5 Mar. in *War Birds* (1927) 85 A Waac officer can't walk out with a Tommy any more than an army officer can be seen with a Waac private. **1919** *Times* 31 Dec. 11/4 Queen Mary's Army Auxiliary Corps. To-day the W.A.A.C.'s, to give them the name under which they first earned the gratitude and regard of the Army and the public, cease to have a corporate existence. **1930** A. BENNETT *Imperial Palace* lviii. 456 What do you know of the Western Front, my dear? You aren't old enough to have been a Waac. **1935** A. J. CRONIN *Stars look Down* II. xiii. 379 ''S war work,' Stokes suggested with a ribald leer ''S war work wish [*sic*] a wack.' **1942** *Time* 18 May 62/3 WAAC at last... The Women's Army Auxiliary Corps will provide women for the Army's humbler jobs. **1957** H. H. JENKINS *Diction of 'Yank'* (Univ. Florida thesis) vi. 59 Ordnance announced the addition of the WAAC-Cycle, a light-weight, streamlined bike for the ladies. **1976** 'A. CROSS' *Question of Max* x. 134 Everyone was just WAACs and Tommies together.

W.A.A.F., WAAF, Waaf (wæf). Acronym f. the initial letters of *W*omen's *A*uxiliary *A*ir *F*orce (1939–48, subsequently reorganized as part of the Women's Royal Air Force); a member of this.

1939 *Daily Tel.* 18 Dec. 12/4 (Advt.), Women between the ages of 18 and 43 are required immediately for enrolment in the W.A.A.F. **1942** J. PUDNEY *Dispersal Point* 11 Weather at base closes down for the night: And the ash-blonde Waaf is waiting tea. **1948** W. FORTESCUE *Beauty for Ashes* xxvii. 209 W.A.A.F.s and airmen climbed into a private auto-bus. **1956** R. MACAULAY *Towers of Trebizond* xv. 179 Now the women who go with armies are..called Ats and Wrens and Waafs and Wracs. **1969** G. MACBETH *War Quartet* 42, I had chosen a WAAF, Needing her flesh and heat. **1982** J. AIKEN *Whisper in Night* 25 They wouldn't allow W.A.A.F. girls to fly. **1984** *Sunday Tel.* 16 Sept. 10/3 The contribution by the WAAF to the anti-aircraft defence of this country lay in manning..many of the balloons of Balloon Command.

waal (wæl, wāl). Also **wal.** Repr. a U.S. colloq. and dial. pronunc. of WELL *adv.* 23.

1863 [see *heater-piece* s.v. *HEATER 3]. **1897** KIPLING *Captains Courageous* vi. 129 'D'you suppose we can run her blind?' he shouted. 'Wa-al', *I* can,' Disko retorted. **1978** M. Z. LEWIN *Silent Salesman* xxxvi. 195 Wal, I guess that'll be all right.

wabe (wēɪb). A factitious word introduced by 'Lewis Carroll' (see quot. 1855[2]).

1855 'L. CARROLL' *Rectory Umbrella & Mischmasch* (1932) 139 The slythy toves Did gyre and gymble in the wabe. *Ibid.* 140 *Wabe*, (derived from the verb to *swab* or *soak*). 'The side of a hill' (from its being *soaked* by the rain). **1871** —— *Through Looking-Glass* 24 The slithy toves Did gyre and gimble in the wabe.

Wabenzi (wabe·nzi). Also **Wabenze, Wa-Benzi.** [Invented to resemble the name of an African people (viz. *WATUSI, etc.), with inserted (Mercedes-)*Benz*: see def.] In Africa, 'the Mercedes-Benz tribe': used *joc.* to designate those Black politicians, businessmen, and others whose success is characterized by their ownership or use of a Mercedes-Benz car.

1967 *Economist* 8 Apr. 112/1 Africa is rapidly earning itself the reputation of the world's biggest joke..the 'Wabenze', the new but already well-known African people whose tribal mark is a ministership and a Mercedes. **1972** J. BIGGS-DAVISON *Africa—Hope Deferred* x. 92 The sweeteners of deference and the shining, pennanted cars that have given their name to such new and privileged tribes as the 'Wa-Benzi'. **1978** S. NAIPAUL *North of South* I. i. 42 'Wabenzi' is the pleasantly jocular term used to describe the nouveau-riche black middle-class... They signal their status by the acquisition..of a Mercedes Benz. Hence, the Wabenzi—the Benz tribe. **1980** *Times* 17 July 11/1 The Wa-Benzi are the new tribe of Mercedes-Benz mounted black bureaucrats and politicos.

‖ **wabi** (wā·bi). [Jap.] In Zen Buddhist philosophy, a quality of simple, serene, and solitary beauty of a slightly sombre kind (see also quot. 1962). Cf. *SABI.

1934 D. T. SUZUKI *Essays in Zen.* III. vii. 312 This spirit of 'Eternal Loneliness' is something known pre-eminently in Japan. By this spirit..I mean what is popularly known in Japan as 'Sabi' or 'Wabi'. **1962** J. PETRIE tr. *Hasumi's Zen in Japanese Art* iv. 51 The essential features of Higashiyama art, extending into all fields, can be summarized in..the idea of 'Wabi', which is supposed to express the highest beauty and can also be carried over into other fields of art. Fundamentally it means poverty, and at the same time simplicity and calm, but it also implies an inexpressible inner joy hidden in deep modesty. Out of 'Wabi' developed harmony, respect, purity, poverty... That is what the special designation of 'Wabi' amounts to: it was the favourite expression of the Haiku masters. **1965** [see *SABI]. **1979** S. COE in I. Webb *Compl. Guide to Flower & Foliage Arrangement* xvii. 227/3 Then comes *wabi*, a recognition of ordinary things but seen in a very clear, almost transparent light.

waboom, var. WAGENBOOM in Dict. and Suppl.

WAC (wæk). *U.S.* Also **W.A.C., wac.** Acronym f. the initial letters of *W*omen's *A*rmy *C*orps, formed in 1943 (cf. *W.A.A.C.); a member of this.

1943 *Yank* 30 July 18 The fellows sent the girls to the WAC barracks to get dressed while they finished the KP jobs. *Ibid.*, When the first bunch of Wacs arrived here recently a group of GIs made dates with the prettiest one night for the Camp movie. **1956** B. HOLIDAY *Lady sings Blues* (1973) xxiii. 198 There was a war on and no damn way for me to get to England except to swim or join the WACs. **1962** E. SNOW *Other Side of River* (1963) xxxix. 290 Women are not recruited for combat training except as parachutists..but a few are used in auxiliary tasks, like WACs. **1976** 'R. B. DOMINIC' *Murder out of Commission* xiv. 100, I fetched and carried for a WAC from Camp Pendleton.

wack[1] (wæk). *slang* (orig. *U.S.*). Also **whack.** [Prob. back-formation f. *WACKY *a.*] An eccentric or crazy person; a madman, a crackpot.

1938 'E. QUEEN' *Four of Hearts* (1939) i. 9 All you wacks act this way at first. Them that can take it snaps out of it. **1951** E. PAUL *Springtime in Paris* xi. 198 The show place, the rendezvous of eccentrics, Bohemians, playboys, sightseers and international whacks is the St. Germain des Prés quarter. **1959** R. GRAVES in *Lilliput* Dec. 48/2 'I don't get the joke,' Len grumbled. 'That wack gave me the creeps! One of those 'creative artists' who create chaos'. **1982** G. F. NEWMAN *Men with Guns* xi. 81 The cop shrugged. 'Some wack with a grudge.'

wack[2] (wæk). *dial.* (chiefly *Liverpool*). Also **whack.** [Cf. *WACKER.] A familiar term of address; 'pal', 'mate'.

1963 *Beatles* 18 Said Ringo: 'Do you want an anaesthetic, wack?' **1966** P. MOLONEY *Plea for Mersey* 50 I'll get you wack! You must come back! **1972** 'K. ROYCE' *Miniatures Frame* ix. 124 'How's it, whack?' He..eyed me affectionately. **1976** *New Musical Express* 12 Feb. 18/6 Gorra light 'ave yer, wack?

wacker (wæ·kəɪ), *sb.* (and *a.*) *Liverpool dial.* [Origin unknown.] A Liverpudlian; also = *WACK[2]. Also *attrib.* or as *adj.*

1768 T. BOULTON *Sailor's Farewell* III. 32, I was told for certain, that th' king o' th' blacks had as many wenches as would stond i' th' cumpus of seven acres of graund; and, if it be true, he must be a wacker, e'cod! **1966** P. MOLONEY *Plea for Mersey* 21 The typical wacker is descended from a long line his mother listened to. *Ibid.* 22 We will consider the refinements of Wacker figures of speech later. **1970** A. ROSS *Manchester Thing* 122, I can't help you, wacker... Five o'clock shut, on Friday, wack.

wacko (wæ·ko), *a.* and *sb.* *slang* (orig. and chiefly *U.S.*). Also **whacko.** [f. *WACK(Y *a.* + *-O.] **A.** *adj.* Crazy, mad; eccentric.

1977 J. WAMBAUGH *Black Marble* (1978) ix. 182 What if he doesn't always go whacko when you make him remember the bad old days? **1977** E. LEONARD *Unknown Man* v. 46 You never know, the guy's fucking wacko. **1978** C. BLACK *Asterisk Destiny* iii. 58 Without a sense of balance..and a touch of humor, you could go whacko. **1981** D. UHNAK *False Witness* iv. 39 She's gone slightly wacko politically. **1984** *Miami Herald* 30 Mar. 3E/2 'Anyone in this business relishes the pressure,' Hazzard, 41, said. 'Maybe I'm a little wacko, but I love it.'

B. *sb.* = *WACK[1].

1977 *Telegraph* (Brisbane) 24 Mar. 4/1, I am not a weirdo, a wacko or an eccentric for wanting to do good, honest work on a day to day basis. **1980** *Washington Post* 22 Aug. A1 Billy Carter, the president's brother, testified yesterday that he is not 'a buffoon, a boob or a wacko'. **1982** R. LUDLUM *Parsifal Mosaic* xiii. 197 'They catch a whack-o now and then.' 'Whack-o?' 'Someone who's crossed over the mental line, thinks he's someone he's not.'

wacko, var. *WHACKO *int.*

wacky (wæ·ki), *a. slang* (orig. *U.S.*). Also **whacky.** [f. WHACK *sb.* + -Y[1]: cf. *out of whack* s.v. *WHACK *sb.* 4. For earlier uses ('a fool; left-handed') see *Eng. Dial. Dict.*] Crazy, mad; odd, peculiar. **a.** Of persons.

1935 J. HARGAN in *Jrnl. Abnormal Psychol.* XXX. 365 *Wacky*, insane. **1938** J. DIGGES *Bowleg Bill* 28 They all want to know why he done it, and is he gone clean whacky. **1942** *Sun* (Baltimore) 25 July 8/1 Her grandmother, wackier than she is, haunts the place. **1950** 'S. RANSOME' *Deadly Miss Ashley* xv. 172 She might..leave..her kids to that wacky aunt of theirs. **1964** *Economist* 13 June 1242/2 Departed, prostrate or, in former President Eisenhower's recent phrase, 'a little bit whacky'. **1978** J. IRVING *World according to Garp* xix. 420 It did much to drive the Ellen Jamesians even wackier or simply away. **1984** *Observer* (Colour Suppl.) 18 Mar. 7/2 She plays the wacky mother of Debra Winger.

b. Of things or abstract concepts.

1937 *Sun* (Baltimore) 19 Aug. 8/1 This picture is described as 'the wackiest'. **1941** B. SCHULBERG *What makes Sammy Run?* i. 14 The whole office was afraid of him. I know that sounds wacky. Hardened newspapermen being afraid of a..little office-boy? **1959** S. H. COURTIER *Death in Dream Time* x. 141 Your cousin's death was wacky—why go to the trouble of staging an accident? **1969** L. HELLMAN *Unfinished Woman* iv. 37 The office was a wacky joint in a brownstone house on 48th Street. **1975** D. LODGE *Changing Places* v. 191 A characteristically whacky, yet somehow endearing tenderness for individual liberty. **1984** *Listener* 24 May 39/3 In his fear of death Betjeman's hand shook, and lines were created more from wacky fright than profound or energising contemplation.

Hence **wa·ckiness,** the state or quality of being 'wacky'; craziness, oddness.

1941 *Sun* (Baltimore) 1 Oct. 10/2 Maybe the majority won't think that 'the wonderful bums' [*sc.* the Brooklyn Dodgers] can win, but they will be out by the thousands..hoping that wackiness will be more than its own reward. **1980** R. L. DUNCAN *Brimstone* iv. 80 For all her wackiness, Annie knew how to live.

wad, *sb.*[1] Add: **4. b.** In fig. phr. *to shoot one's wad*, to do all that one can do. Cf. *to have shot one's bolt* s.v. SHOOT *v.* 21 b. *colloq.* (chiefly *U.S.*).

1914 *Dialect Notes* IV. 112 *Shoot one's wad*, to do or say what one can. **1970** A. CAMERON et al. *Computers & O.E. Concordances* 31 Well, I'm really not an expert on it. I've practically shot my wad. **1971** B. MALAMUD *Tenants* 8, I want to be thought of as a going concern, not a freak who had published a good first novel and shot his wad.

5. c. A bun, a cake; also, something to eat, a sandwich. *slang* (orig. *Services*).

1919 *War Terms* in *Athenæum* 1 Aug. 695/1 *Wad*, a bun. **1927** T. E. LAWRENCE *Let.* 8 Feb. (1938) 506 No wads, so I'm able to do without money. **1937** D. JONES *In Parenthensis* 4 We've got too many buns—and all those wads. **1942** G. Kersh *Nine Lives Bill Nelson* i. 3 I'm in a caff, getting a tea 'n' a wad. **1960** 'A. Burgess' *Doctor is Sick* 226 Give us a bob for a cuppa and a wad, guv. **1973** *Guardian* 2 June 13/4 He found himself..in Kashmir sharing a char and wad with Sikh pilots. **1983** *Verbatim* Autumn 8/2 Like a 'pick', a 'wad' is also eaten standing up. A 'wad', however, is a solitary piece of inferior, if not disgusting food. The diner falls upon it with little pleasure, merely to quiet the beast in his belly.

7. wadcutter chiefly *U.S.*, a bullet designed to cut a neat hole in a paper range target.

1957 *Amer. Speech* XXXII. 195 *Wadcutter*, a lead bullet designed to be used on paper targets and having no ogive but abrupt shoulders so that a full caliber hole is punched in a target. **1981** D. Boggis *Time to Betray* xi. 61 A potential opportunity to..loose the five rounds of .32 wadcutter from the Walther GSP precision automatic.

waddy. Add: **1. a.** (Earlier examples.)

[**1788** D. Southwell in *Hist. Rec. New South Wales* (1893) II. 698 *A stick or club*, wad-di or wad-dty.] **1800** J. Hunter in *Hist. Rec. Austral.* (1914) I. ii. 406 They had each a Spear and a Warmaraa and a Waddy. **1807** J. Savage *Some Acct. N.Z.* viii. 52 The men..carry a waddy..in figure somewhat resembling a large battledore..usually formed of hard black stone.

b. *transf.* Any club or stick; *spec.* a walking-stick. (Examples.)

1899 'S. Rudd' *On Our Selection* 19 We each carried a kerosine tin, slung like a kettle-drum, and belted it with a waddy. **1936** M. Franklin *All that Swagger* 88 None of that bad language or I'll take a waddy to you. **1972** *Southerly* XXXII. 200 Freeth had offered him the use of his cane—his 'waddy', as he called it—after the first week. **1974** K. Cook *Bloodhouse* 31 She had seen him..smash his ebony waddy hard down on his neck.

waddy[2] (wǫ·di). *U.S. slang.* Also **waddie.** [Origin uncertain.] A cattle rustler; a cowboy, esp. a temporary cowhand.

1897 E. Hough *Story of Cowboy* 279 A genuine rustler was called a 'waddy', a name difficult to trace to its origin. **1927** J. Lomax *Cowboy Songs* 374 He rides a fancy horse, he's a favorite man, Can get more credit than a common waddie can. **1931** W. Rogers in S. K. Gragert *Will Rogers' Weekly Articles* (1982) V. 470 You town waddies know what a Combine is?

wade, *v.* Add: **3. e.** *to wade in*: to make a vigorous or concerted attack on one's opponent; to intervene, esp. vocally; *to wade into* (*colloq.*, orig. *U.S.*): to assail or confront energetically.

1863 B. Harte in *U.S. Sanitary Commission Bull.* (1864) I. vii. 201/1 Phrases such as camps may teach... Such as 'Bully!' 'Them's the peach!' 'Wade in, Sanitary!' **1893** H. A. Shands *Some Peculiarities of Speech in Mississippi* 66 *Wade into.* One man is said to *wade into* another when he attacks him very vigorously with either fist or tongue. This phrase is used by all classes. **1904** J. London *Let.* 17 Nov. (1966) 165 The lawyers..waded into me good and hard for the cash. **1905** *N.Y. Even. Post* 2 Sept., When a herd of sheep wades in on a patch of bluebells, they stand still and eat all day. **1928** *Daily Express* 30 July 13/6 Though severely punished by Pattenden's lefts to the face he repeatedly waded in. **1935** D. L. Sayers *Gaudy Night* ii. 33, I don't stop to think... I just wade right in and ask for what I want. **1952** E. F. Davies *Illyrian Venture* vi. 104 Luckily the Germans had not known how easily they could have waded into us. **1967** N. Marsh *Death at Dolphin* v. 125 Don't let it give you a moment's pause... Just you wade in to Conducis. **1976** *Sun* 11 Mar. 11/4 Miss Georgina Burton..waded in with her shopping bag and chased the gang away. **1984** J. Barnes *Flaubert's Parrot* x. 132 The writer must wade into life as into the sea, but only up to the navel.

Wade-Giles (wē[i]d dʒəi·lz). [The names of Sir Thomas Francis *Wade* (1818–95), diplomatist and first Professor of Chinese at the University of Cambridge, and Herbert Allen *Giles* (1845–1935), Wade's successor at Cambridge.] Used *attrib.* and *absol.* to designate a system for the romanization of Chinese script devised by Wade, and subsequently modified by Giles. (Now widely superseded by *Pinyin.) Also *ellipt.* as **Wade.**

[**1871** G. C. Stent *Chinese & Eng. Vocab.* p. vi, The tones are also according to Mr. Wade's system.] **1943** Y. R. Chao in *Mathews's Chinese-Eng. Dict.* (1945) p. ix, Now that the standard has come back to the pronunciation of Peiping, we can almost use the unmodified Wade's *Syllabary* or the more widely used Wade-Giles system. *Ibid.*, In Chauncey Goodrich's *Pocket Dictionary*, the syllables *ko k'o, ho* and *o* of Wade-Giles are given as *kê, k'ê, hê*, and *ê*. **1944** Chang & Maxwell *Conc. Eng.-Chinese Dict.* 10 People have become accustomed to the Wade form of spelling. **1947** C. F. Hockett in *Jrnl. Amer. Oriental Soc.* LXVII. 256/2 The numbering /¹/ through /⁴/ is as in Wade-Giles Romanization. **1950** J. De Francis *Nationalism & Lang. Reform in China* xii. 200 Those who have learned Wade as their first transcription of Chinese case are annoyed at the French use of another system. **1961** *Amer. Speech* XXXVI. 190 The Wade-Giles system of romanization of the Peking dialect will be followed. **1966** *Guardian* 29 Nov. 8/2 The Chinese system of romanization will certainly displace Wade-Giles eventually. **1971** R. Newnham *About Chinese* 172 Wade-Giles is the oldest and most widely used of all current romanizations, and its chief merit lies in that wide use. **1979** *Time* 2 Apr. 15/2 The changeover was started by Peking (um, er, Beijing) on Jan. 1, when the government of Zhongguo (otherwise known as China) decreed that in all its foreign-language publications Pinyin would replace the traditional Wade-Giles system of romanization.

wadeite (wē[i]·dəit). *Min.* [f. the name of Arthur *Wade* (1878–1951), British geologist + -ite[1].] A hexagonal silicate of potassium and zirconium, approximately $K_2ZrSi_3O_9$.

1938 Wade & Prider in *Rep. Brit. Assoc. Adv. Sci.* 1. 419 Nineteen occurrences of post-Permian volcanic rocks have been found in the West Kimberley area... The rocks are made up..of leucite, phlogopite,..wadeite (a new K-Zr silicate), [etc.]. **1980** *Contrib. Mineral. & Petrol.* LXXII. 191/1 The restricted occurrence of wadeite to rocks of West Kimberley, Australia and Leucite Hills, Wyoming is believed to be due to their high K/Al and Zr contents relative to other high potash rocks.

wadge: entry now merged with Wodge (in Dict and Suppl.).

Wadhamite (wǫ·dæməit). [f. the name of *Wadham* College, founded by Nicholas and Dorothy Wadham in 1612 + -ite[1].] A member of Wadham College, Oxford.

1760 J. Woodforde *Diary* 20 May (1924) I. 14 Hooke, Boteler and myself went to Welch's of Wadham College, where we designed to sup and spend the evening, but our entertainment was thus, one Lobster of a Pound, a half-pennyworth of Bread, and the same of Cheese... N.B. A Wadamite. **1976** A. Powell *Infants of Spring* xi. 191 'But', added the young Wadhamite, 'I've heard he's an absolute fish out of water when he's away from the academic world he's accustomed to.'

wadi, wady. Add: Also *attrib.*

1902 D. G. Hogarth *Nearer East* 139 The palm-lined wadi beds of Jebel Akhdar. *Ibid.* 143 Aromatic scrub and an occasional thorn is all that can be expected in the wadi bottoms. **1980** *Encounter* May 90/2 Off we go, with me stumbling after him over the rough stony ground of the wadi bed.

wading, *vbl. sb.* Add: **b.** *wading pool*; *wading shoes.*

1866 J. Macgregor *Thousand Miles in Rob Roy Canoe* (ed. 2) i. 10, I took for this tour..canvas wading shoes,..a waterproof overcoat, [etc.]. **1921** Wading pool [see *sand-pile* s.v. *Sand *sb.*[2] 9 a]. **1977** *New Yorker* 15 Aug. 42/3 He inflated and filled a plastic wading pool for the children.

Wafd (wǫft). [a. Arab. *wafd* arrival, deputation, in full *al-wafd al-miṣrī* the Egyptian delegation.] The name of an Egyptian nationalist organization formed in 1918 (from 1923, a political party) whose original aims included the establishment of autonomous government in Egypt and the abolition of the monarchy. (The party was dissolved in 1953, but reconstituted as the *New Wafd* in 1978.)

1922 *Times* 24 Jan. 9/1 The Wafd el Masri, or Zaghlul Delegation..has just issued a detailed programme of non-cooperation. *Ibid.* 27 Jan. 11/2 The reconstituted *Wafd.* **1928** E. W. P. Newman *Great Britain in Egypt* x. 239 The Wafd had been constituted in order to lay the case of Egypt before the Peace Conference of Paris. **1932** *Palestine Post* 13 Dec. 7/1 The quarrel between the Wafd and its dissidents continues. **1943** Visct. Wavell *Allenby in Egypt* i. 40 Zaghlul Bey..had not, however, been the originator of the Wafd (or Delegation), as his party came to be known. It was the creation of others, notably men like Mohammed Mahmoud. **1962** *Listener* 15 Nov. 795/1 Saad Zaghloul, the founder and leader of the Wafd party. **1974** *Great Soviet Encycl.* IV. 649/2 Some of the Wafd members unsuccessfully fought the government of Nasser in actions of 1954, 1957, and 1961. **1978** *Facts on File World News Digest* 24 Feb. 131/1 The New Wafd had 24 supporters in the 360-seat People's Assembly.

Wafdist (wǫ·ftist), *a.* and *sb.* [f. prec. + -ist.] **a.** *adj.* Of or pertaining to the Wafd. **b.** *sb.* A member or supporter of the Wafd; an Egyptian Nationalist.

1926 *Glasgow Herald* 3 June 8 Doubts..were entertained of the prospect of the Wafdist leader taking such a moderate course. **1926** *Spectator* 19 June 1032/2 The Wafdists..are likely to be restrained by the knowledge that any too free indulgence of their characteristic tactics ..would quickly make Adly throw up his office in disgust. **1958** J. W. Day *Lady Houston* xv. 235 That is, indeed, a 'Capitulation', and the worst and most fatal, by Great Britain to the Wafdist mob! **1973** *Times* 29 Oct. 17/7 From being a Liberal Constitutionalist in the days of Sarwat, his protector, he became an active Wafdist under Nahhas Pasha.

wafer, *sb.* Add: **1. b.** *ellipt.*, a sandwich of ice-cream between wafers.

1936 N. Coward *Still Life* in *To-night at 8.30* III. i. 48 An old girl..asked if I'd got an ice-cream wafer... What did she think I was, a 'Stop me and buy one?' **1979** *Listener* 6 Sept. 303/2 The vanilla wafer..proved a great healer.

4. (Earlier example.)

1848 C. Brontë in C. Shorter *Charlotte Brontë & her Circle* (1896) vi. 173 She has taken no medicine, but..Locock's cough wafers, of which she has used about 3 per diem.

5*. *Electronics.* A very thin slice of a semiconductor crystal used as the substrate for solid-state circuitry.

1956 *Bell Syst. Techn. Jrnl.* XXXV. 3 After diffusion the entire surface of the silicon wafer is covered with the diffused n- and p-type layers. **1967** *Electronics* 6 Mar. 25 Litton engineers haven't decided whether to use single or two-layer metalization to interconnect the circuits within the wafers. **1975** D. G. Fink *Electronics Engineers' Handbk.* viii. 84 After the completion of the test sequence, the probe assembly is automatically lifted up and the probes are indexed over to the next chip to be tested on the wafer. **1979** *Maclean's Mag.* 2 Apr. 37/3 'Wafers' containing hundreds of memory chips (each with 64,000 transistors): dispensing liquor, guiding spaceships. **1984** *QL User* Dec. 18 Currently, chips are manufactured in batches on discs of silicon about four inches in diameter called wafers.

6. (sense 1) *wafer-thin* adj.; (sense 3) *wafer box.*

1837 Dickens *Pickw.* liv. 591 Wilkins Flasher, Esquire, was..spearing a wafer-box with a penknife. **1968** *Canad. Antiques Collector* Nov. 26/1 When envelopes were introduced, the wafer box became a stamp box. *a* **1911** D. G. Phillips *Susan Lenox* (1917) I. xxi. 371 Wafer-thin. **1958** *Times* 15 Nov. 11/6 There is dried meat of the Valais cut in wafer-thin slices. **1976** *Times* 1 June 1/1 Pitmen in north Derbyshire are understood to have voted by a wafer-thin majority against continuing wage restraint. **1984** B. Francis *AA Car Duffer's Guide* 63/2 The radiator is made up of a collection of very narrow tubes linked by wafer-thin strips of metal which are exposed to the air-flow.

‖ **Waffen SS** (va·fən es,es). [ad. G. *Waffen-SS*, in full *Waffen-Schutzstaffel* armed defence squadron: see *Schutzstaffel and S.S. s.v. *S 4 a.] In Nazi Germany during the war of 1939–45: the combat units of the S.S.

1943 *Rev. Foreign Press* (F.O. Research Dept.) 18 Oct. 125/1 By a law of the 22nd July, Laval..authorised French citizens to join those units of the Waffen S.S. fighting on the Eastern Front. **1949** 'R. West' *Meaning of Treason* 1. vii. 164 He wanted to join the Waffen S.S. and fight the Russians. **1957** *Times Lit. Suppl.* 20 Dec. 771/2 A nucleus of the 'commandoes', but also with parachutists, Waffen S.S. **1966** G. Stein *Waffen SS* p. xxx, At the beginning of World War II the term Waffen SS was unknown. Five years later, prefaced by such adjectives as elite and fanatical, it appeared regularly in Allied war communiqués. By 1940 *Waffen SS* had become the official designation for the combat units of the SS, which had grown from the handful of armed troops maintained by the Reichsführer SS, Heinrich Himmler, for security and ceremonial purposes. *Ibid.* p. xxxi, By 1943, the exigencies of war had forced the Waffen SS to give up some of its exclusiveness. Large numbers of foreigners were recruited or conscripted. **1972** F. Forsyth *Odessa File* ii. 28 He carried the twin-lightning strikes of the Waffen SS on the right collar lapel.

waffle, *sb.*[1] Add. **a.** (Earlier examples.)

1744, 1794 [see sense *b]. **1809** A. Burr *Jrnl.* 26 Aug. (1903) I. 214 Everywhere, too, you get *wafen*; our wafles, and made and eaten in the same way.

b. *waffle frolic*; **waffle-iron** (earlier example); **waffle stomper** *U.S. slang*, a boot or shoe with a heavy, ridged sole.

1744 in *Mag. Amer. Hist.* (1878) II. 442 For my own part I was not a little grieved that so luxurious a feast should come under the name of a wafel frolic. **1794** *S. Carolina State Gaz.* 30 Aug. 1/2 (Advt.), Waffle irons. **1974** *Sunday* (Charleston, S. Carolina) 7 Apr. 10-c/8 'Waffle stompers', should anybody be wondering, are hiking shoes.

c. *Textiles.* Used *attrib.* of a style of fine honeycomb weaving (see *Honeycomb *sb.* 5 b). Also applied to the fabric woven and to the effect produced.

[**1948** *Sears, Roebuck Catal.* Fall-Winter 45/2 Cotton Chenille Spread. Sturdy white cotton sheeting tufted with fluffy chenille in regular, even waffle pattern.] **1949** *Good Housek.* Apr. 261/2 Waffle piqué is characterized by a honeycomb weave; it is not a true piqué. **1951** in M. McLuhan *Mech. Bride* (1967) 74 We had it copied faithfully for you in the..white Birdseye waffle pique. **1953** *Sun* (Baltimore) 7 Mar. (B ed.) 3/4 Part of the secret lay in the 'waffle-weave', a..technique which required special machinery... It produces a cloth that looks like a waffle, or a honeycomb. **1961** *Sunday Express* 28 May 14/2 (*caption*) Tops in waffle-knit cotton. **1962** W. Schirra in *Into Orbit* 49 A series of waffle-weave patches on our long john underwear helps to keep the oxygen moving. **1975** G. Howell *In Vogue* 242/2 (*caption*) Elements of the mid-fifties—the 'sloppy Joe',..the waffle cotton shorts. **1979** *Men's Wear* 3 May 24 Texture returns with fine seersuckers and waffle cloth.

waffle, *sb.*[2] Add: Also **woffle. 2.** Now in *gen.* colloq. use, verbose but inconsequential talk or writing; empty verbiage (see also quot. 1937).

[**1866** J. E. Brogden *Provinc. Words Lincs.* 219 *Waffle-bags*, a great talker.] **1937** Partridge *Dict. Slang* 935/1 *Waffle*, nonsense; gossip(ing); incessant or copious talk. **1953** *Times Lit. Suppl.* 13 Mar. 164/1 A little technical detail and a good deal of emotional waffle. **1957** *Economist* 21 Dec. 1041/2 His ability to distinguish the essence and to cut the waffle in any discussion are exceptional. **1961** C. S. Lewis *Let.* 9 May (1966) 298 For a good..defence of our position against modern woffle... I know nothing better than G. K. Chesterton's *The Everlasting Man.* **1965** *Spectator* 22 Jan. 96/1 There is a special relationship between Britain and the United States, a special relationship more serious than the waffle we get at banquets. **1973** C. Bonington *Next Horizon* i. 20 Cut out the waffle, and let's see your application.

waffle, *v.* Restrict Now *dial.* to sense in Dict.

and add: Also **woffle, wuffle. 2. a.** To waver; to vacillate or equivocate; to 'dither'. orig. *Sc.* and *north. dial.* Now *colloq.* or non-Standard.

1803, etc. [see *WAFFLER 1]. **1868** [see *WAFFLING *ppl. a.*]. **1893–4** R. O. HESLOP *Northumberland Words* II. 762 *Waffle*, to waft about, to waver, to walk hesitatingly, to act with indecision. **1898** B. KIRKBY *Lakeland Words* 152 Thoo'l waffle aboot an' say owt. **1943** *Horizon* Apr. 234 While I was still waffling I read 'The Mint'. **1961** C. H. D. TODD *Popular Whippet* 51 Have we an ideal or are we just 'waffling around' following this, that and the other. **1976** *Telegraph-Jrnl.* (St. John, New Brunswick) 4 Sept. 17/1 She defends the board against suggestions that it waffled on the issue because of political pressure.

b. To talk (or write) in a verbose but inconsequential manner; to ramble *on*. Also *trans.* with direct speech as obj.

[**1701** J. WHITE *Countryman's Conductor* 128 *Waffling*, all speakers and no hearers.] **1900** FARMER *Public School Word-Bk.* 216 Waffle,..(Durham) to talk nonsense. **1936** R. LEHMANN *Weather in Streets* I. v. 83 Nanny would wuffle on, and make me change my stockings. **1937** G. HEYER *They found him Dead* iv. 83 He woffled a whole lot to me about people bothering his life out. **1949** J. B. PRIESTLEY *Delight* 15 The wise men woffled on about violence and crime, missing the point by miles. **1957** G. SMITH *Friends* 60 'Funny thing is, it seems to improve my game,' waffled Bill amiably. **1960** L. MEYNELL *Bandaberry* i. 8, I under-estimated his shrewdness... I thought he was waffling. **1982** P. DICKINSON *Last House-Party* ii. 22 You can make the correct noises while all the old buffers are woffling on.

waffling *ppl. a.* (later examples); also as *vbl. sb.*

1847 J. HALLIDAY *Rustic Bard* 145 'Tis you I punch at, worthless, wafflin crood. **1868** J. C. ATKINSON *Gloss. Cleveland Dial.* 554 A windy, *waffling* soort o' chap, wheea nivver kens his ain mind. **1945** J. REITH *Diary* 11 Apr. (1975) vii. 346 A typical silly, waffling letter which Cranborne had written. **1958** J. CANNAN *And be Villain* v. 118 His sharp harsh tones were a joy to hear after the wafflings of the soft voiced Highlander. **1967** *New Yorker* 8 July 67 There will be..a large majority for a waffling resolution..calling for Israel to withdraw from the conquered territories but not passing judgement on the original conquests. **1973** J. WAINWRIGHT *Touch of Malice* 231 Waffling, thoughtless stupidity. **1976** *Sunday Mail* (Brisbane) 23 May 44/6 They should not be regarded as the wafflings of people sounding off in the papers.

waffler (wǫ·flǝɹ). [f. WAFFLE *v.* + -ER^{1}.] **1.** An unreliable person; an idler or waverer. Chiefly *Sc.* and *north dial.*

1803 R. ANDERSON *Ballads in Cumberland Dial.* (1805) 59 Saint Gworge, the girt champion, o' fame and renown, Was nobbet a waffler to Matthew Macree. **1819** in Carlyle *Early Lett.* (1886) I. 215 The waffler did not get his cart home till Monday. **1927** N. DUNDAS *Castle Adamant* iv. 60 Of course there are wafflers, ye could look or no less in a town o f five thousand souls. **1977** B. LANGLEY *Death Stalk* ii. 15 He had an instinctive distrust of all wafflers and ditherers.

2. One who indulges in waffling talk or writing. Cf. *WAFFLE *sb.*^{2} 2.

1959 *Viewpoint* July 4 It was a field day for the professional analysts and wafflers. **1968** *Sunday Truth* (Brisbane) 8 Dec. 41 It amazes me that Peter Evans was ever selected to conduct 4QR's Breakfast Show. He must be the original waffler.

waffly (wǫ·fli), *a.* [f. WAFFLE *sb.*^{2} and *v.* + -Y^{1}.] **a.** Wavering, vacillating, imprecise. **b.** Characterized by or indulging in waffling speech or writing.

1890 J. SERVICE *Thir Notandums* xix. 125 Let the waffly body tak ocht I hae written and mak a kirk or a mill o't as pleases himsel'. **1928** A. E. PEASE *Dict. Dial. N. Riding* 149 *Waffly*,..wavering, undecided, shaky, not coherent. **1957** *Economist* 23 Nov. 673/2 The Labour party's attitude to the federation has always been waffly. **1964** *Ibid.* 16 May 691/2 Mr. Duncan Sandys could never be called a waffly man. **1978** *Times* 18 Nov. 11/8, I thought the first part about the World Tree and the Green Man a little thin and waffly.

wafty, *a.* Add: **3.** That wafts or moves to and fro in the wind. *nonce-use.*

1922 JOYCE *Ulysses* 289 The wafty sycamore, the Lebanonian cedar, the exalted planetree.

wag, *sb.*^{2} Add: **3.** Also, *to hop the wag*: see *HOP *v.*^{1} 6 a.

wag (wæg), *sb.*^{3} *Archæol.* [ad. Gael. *uamhag*, dim. of *uamh* cave, hollow: cf. WEEM.] In Caithness, an Iron-age galleried structure set partly below ground-level (see quot. 1963).

[**1776** A. POPE in T. Pennant *Tour in Scotl. 1769* (ed. 4) 338 Figures 2 and 3 are what are styled *forest* or *hunting houses*... They consist of a gallery, with a number of small rooms on the sides..made with the vast flags [stones] this country is famous for... Their length is from fifty to sixty feet. These buildings are only in places where the great flags are plentiful. In Glen-Loch are three, and are called by the country people *Uags*.] **1911** A. O. CURLE in *Proc. Soc. Antiquaries Scotl.* 11 Dec. 89 To the galleried structure the name 'wag' in former times was evidently applied and still remains in use, though now transferred from the structure to the place or site, *e.g.* 'Wag-more rig', 'Wag-burn' and 'the Wag'. **1921** *Ibid.* 10 Jan. 93 Interesting as the discovery of these post-holes is in the elucidation of the broch construction, the interest it evokes does not stop here. The arrangement at once recalls the plans of the wags or galleried dwellings in Caithness. **1963** *Field Archaeol.* (Ordnance Survey) (ed. 4) 63 In Caithness there is the local variant structure known as a wag... The dwelling part is represented by a strongly-built hut circle of ordinary plan, but to this is added an oval stone-built chamber about twice as big as the hut with its floor excavated somewhat below the general ground level. **1972** E. M. MACKIE in *Dark Ages in Highlands* 16 One site at Forse..could well be a pre-broch defensive structure... This is the so-called 'wag' or 'pre-historic cattlefold' excavated by Alexander Curle.

waganga, pl. of *MGANGA.

wage, *sb.* Add: **4. a.** Simple attrib., as *wage(s) bill, board, -book, claim, clerk, contract, cost, cut, demand, dispute, inflation, labourer, -level, negotiation, packet, payment, policy, push, restraint, -rigidity, -slavery* (earlier example), *-snatch, spiral, structure, system*; *wage-related, -working* adjs.; **b.** Objective, as *wage-bargainer, -bargaining, control, -fixing*; **c.** Appositive, as *wage-price* attrib., esp. in phr. *wage-price spiral*; **wages council,** any of a number of joint management and employee councils succeeding the trade boards (from 1945), and responsible for determining the conditions of employment in certain trades; **wage differential** = *DIFFERENTIAL *sb.* 3 b; **wage drift,** the tendency for wages to rise above national rates through local overtime and other agreements; the extent of this increase; **wage freeze,** a temporary fixing of wages at a certain level; cf. *pay freeze* s.v. *PAY- 4 and *FREEZE *sb.*^{1} (ii); **wage hike** *N. Amer.*, a wage increase (cf. *HIKE *sb.* 2); **wage scale,** a graduated scale of wage rates for different levels of work; **wage stop** (also *wages stop*), the limitation of supplementary benefit to the level of the normal wage; hence **wage-stop** *v. trans.*; **wage-stopped** *ppl. a.*; **wage unit** (see quot. 1936).

1968 *Economist* 23 Mar. 16/3 Any wage bargainer worth his salt should be able to dress up a claim to fit the loose criteria 'justifying' a 3½ per cent increase. **1928** *Britain's Industr. Future* (Liberal Industr. Inquiry) III. xvii. 209 In the boot and shoe trade..it has been thought desirable to keep wage-bargaining apart from the general discussions carried on by the Joint Industrial Council. **1983** *Times* 24 June 7/6 The fear that mass hunger striking will become a common tool of wage bargaining. **1919** M. BEER *Hist. Brit. Socialism* I. II. v. 169 The total wage bill of the country diminished. **1923** H. W. B. JOSEPH *Labour Theory of Value in Karl Marx* ii. 49 If all this is true..a capitalist ought not to be indifferent whether he economizes in his wages-bill or in his other expenditure. **1982** T. KENEALLY *Schindler's Ark* viii. 96 The meeting of his wage bill was the least of Oskar's worries. **1925** *Scribner's Mag.* Oct. 415/2 The regulation of wages has been put in the hands of wage boards. **1930** *Economist* 22 Mar. 651/1 The success of the Wages Boards..should be carefully considered. **1970** *Washington Post* 30 Sept. B 11/5 A 6 per cent raise to 850,000 hard-pressed blue-collar (wage board) people. **1864** TROLLOPE *Can you forgive Her?* (1865) II. vii. 54, I don't suppose I've opened the wages book half a dozen times since last July. **1960** G. E. EVANS *Horse in Furrow* ix. 115 These wages-books..contained the lists of jobs allocated to people employed on the farm, and the amount of wages due to them. **1971** H. WILSON *Labour Govt.* xxxviii. 787 One of the main groups of printing unions, SOGAT, put in a large wage-claim. **1921** *Dict. Occup. Terms* (1927) § 939 Wages clerk. **1961** *Evening Standard* 18 July 23/5 Wages clerk to head.. wages section. **1921** *Daily Colonist* (Victoria, B.C.) 20 Mar. 1/3 We deny that any wage contract with the miners has been broken. **1977** P. JOHNSON *Enemies of Society* iii. 39 The medieval manor..yielded to a cash-nexus society based on wage-contracts between freely-negotiating individuals. **1910** *Encycl. Brit.* V. 879/1 This argument, which combined statutory wage control and statutory poor relief, seems to have been firmly embedded in the English legislative mind..till after 1600. **1978** *Economist* 18 Feb. 75/1 The [Argentine] government..has relaxed wage controls on private industry. **1985** *Financial Times* 4 Mar. 6/4 The most apparent difference is in their approach to inflation and wage control. **1958** *Spectator* 4 July 33/3 Wage-cost inflation. **1975** J. DE BRES tr. *Mandel's Late Capitalism* vi. 203 Economies in costs will thus always be accompanied in the long-run by a relative decrease in the share of wage costs in the value of the commodity. **1945** *Wages Councils Act* (8 & 9 *Geo. VI c.* 17) 116 An Act to provide for the establishment of wages councils. **1971** *Observer* 7 Nov. 16/6 Many trade unionists argue that the very existence of wages councils discourages poorer workers from joining trade unions. **1984** *Listener* 1 Nov. 11/3 The Wages Councils, providing legal minimum wages and conditions for 2·7 million of Britain's lowest-paid workers..are threatened. **1925** *Daily Herald* 30 June 2/4 (*heading*) Folly of wage-cuts. **1974** J. AIKEN *Midnight is Place* iii. 102 Protests about the wage-cut had been nipped in the bud. **1970** *Guardian* 2 Mar. 1/2 The biggest disagreement is about the effect of wage demands. **1950** Wage differential [see *DIFFERENTIAL *sb.* 3 b]. **1957** *Observer* 6 Oct. 10/2 The pension scheme, by relating superannuation to wages, strengthens the value of wage differentials and hence the incentive to acquire greater skills. **1977** *China Now* Apr.–May 7/1 They were cutting down wage differentials. **1919** in M. Gilbert *Winston S. Churchill* (1977) IV. Compan. I. 498 The moment the revolt advanced over the line of a pure wage dispute, and the strikers were guilty of a serious breach of the law, then was the moment to act. **1955** W. GADDIS *Recognitions* II. i. 322 Not written to be played by men in worn dinner jackets,..involved in wage disputes. **1963** *Times* 22 Jan. 4/6 This is a comparatively rare phenomenon, 'wage drift' in reverse, and reflects increased short time and lower earnings from bonuses, overtime and so on. *a* **1974** R. CROSSMAN *Diaries* (1976) II. 703 As for the 3½ per cent ceiling, he told me it was quite unrealistic since wage drift by itself probably comes to 3½ per cent. **1928** *Britain's Industr. Future* (Liberal Industr. Inquiry) II. xvi. 181 The practical considerations which ought to govern the process of wage-fixing. **1942** Wage freeze [see *FREEZE *sb.*^{1} (ii)]. **1967** *Spectator* 1 Sept. 238/2 The wage freeze has been imposed without a murmur of national strike action. **1980** C. MOOREHEAD *Fortune's Hostages* v. 104 The President [of Uruguay]..tried to introduce economic restraint by wage freezes. **1976** *Washington Post* 19 Apr. A 23/4 By last spring, some unions were putting in for wage hikes up to 60 per cent. **1976** *Morecambe Guardian* 7 Dec. 21/7 One woman waving a placard saying 'Wage Inflation' [etc.]. **1957** V. W. TURNER *Schism & Continuity in Afr. Society* v. 135 A man can acquire wealth by working in the White economy as a wage labourer. **1928** *Britain's Industr. Future* (Liberal Industr. Inquiry) III. 139 A wise wage-policy should aim at the highest practicable wage-levels. **1965** J. MEUVRET in Glass & Eversley *Population in Hist.* xxi. 517 In normal times wage-levels and price-levels were both very low. **1928** *Britain's Industr. Future* (Liberal Industr. Inquiry) III. xvi. 188 It is not even enough that the wage-system should be just in itself; it must be visibly and demonstrably just. And this conception ought to inspire the whole system of wage-negotiation. **1974** *Guardian* 23 Jan. 3/1 Today's wage negotiations were conducted with the Frame group. **1951** R. FIRTH *Elem. Social Organiz.* iv. 140 One point of view is that the size of the wage-packet remains the most important factor still in the incentive to work. *a* **1974** R. CROSSMAN *Diaries* (1976) II. 638 The trade unionists want to see us spending much less on social services so that there'll be more for wage packets. **1923** H. W. B. JOSEPH *Labour Theory of Value in Karl Marx* vii. 154 In the absence of definite agreements or enactments, we can produce no rule of universal application, to which wage-payments ought to conform. **1928** Wage-policy [see *wage-level* above]. **1965** *New Statesman* 9 Apr. 576/3 The principles (but not the practice) of a wages policy. **1946** *Sun* (Baltimore) 1 Mar. 1/3 The situation, therefore, presents possibilities of a critical test of the administration's new wage price line. **1958** *Engineering* 11 Apr. 460/1 There appeared to be no doubt whatever in Lord Cohen's mind that this painful process of breaking the wage-price spiral had to be adopted. **1977** M. EDELMAN *Political Lang.* viii. 147 A wage-price freeze from which major industries quickly won exceptions. **1968** *Manch. Guardian Weekly* 14 Mar. 13 It has become fashionable to say that the British..manage to keep a wage-push inflation in times of crippling deflation. **1979** *Dædalus* Spring 53 Other things being equal, the greater the wage push, the tougher and more 'lesson-teaching' a policy is necessary to control inflation. **1963** *Punch* 20 Mar. 398/2 There must..be a wage-related contributory insurance system. **1958** *Listener* 4 Dec. 930/2 Don't think it's a matter of wage restraint only. **1977** M. EDELMAN *Political Lang.* viii. 153 Employers perceive wage restraint by workers as in the public interest. **1930** W. K. HANCOCK *Australia* ix. 187 It is apparent that wage-rigidity is less important in its social consequences than in its economic and psychological consequences. **1983** *Economist* 18 June 21/3 Some belief in wage-rigidity is deeply rooted in his work. **1960** F. LYNDE *Quickening* 310 His father was deep in the new wage scale submitted by the miners' union. **1979** *Gloss. Terms Work Study (B.S.I.)* 27 *Wage scale determination*, the construction of a scale of wages reflecting the relative values of jobs. **1886** D. DONOHUE *Let.* 21 Oct. in *N.Y. Times* 24 Oct. 1/5 It is therefore but natural that we should vote for a man who proposes to use his best endeavors to bring about legislation by which wage slavery and land monopoly shall be abolished. **1962** *Observer* 25 Feb. 23/3 They were working themselves at the wage-snatch business, with a bit of smash-and-grab on the side. **1964** J. CREASEY *Look Three Ways at Murder* xx. 183 There's a hold-up... Wages snatch! **1977** L. MEYNELL *Hooky gets Wooden Spoon* xii. 149 She wasn't doing anything for the police in the wages snatch. **1948** *Ann. Reg. 1947* 20 A wage spiral was only prevented by distortion which would soon become intolerable. **1940** *Economist* 28 Dec. 799/1 The attempt to carry out a wage stop similar to the price stop had to be abandoned. **1954** E. H. CARR *Interregnum* 73 This quasi-official wages-stop remained in force throughout 1923. **1963** *Guardian* 25 Feb. 11/7 If a man is wage-stopped, he will not get anything at all from the increases. **1971** *Daily Tel.* 16 June 3/3 The wage stop is the system by which men are prevented from drawing more in State benefits than they had earned while in work—even if this means they get less than the commission's official poverty level. **1963** *Times* 18 Feb. 11/6 To suggest..that all the 15,000 wage-stopped families were outsize would, on the board's own figures, be plainly absurd. **1955** *Ann. Reg. 1954* 1 The commission..undertook to make a thorough examination..of the whole wage structure. **1898** *Kansas City* (Missouri) *Star* 18 Dec. 2/1 The ultimate outcome of the labor movement..will be the destruction of the wage system. **1929** D. H. LAWRENCE *Pansies* 75 Ultimately, we are all busy buying and selling one another. It began with Judas and goes on in the wage-system. **1936** J. M. KEYNES *Gen. Theory Employment* iv. 41 The money-wage of a labour-unit we shall call the wage-unit. **1976** F. ZWEIG *New Acquisitive Society* II. iv. 106 Economic planning which is based primarily on a 'wage unit' determined by the planning authorities as the pivot of economic planning. **1898** G. B. SHAW *Perfect Wagnerite* 29 The starving wage-working class.

wagenboom. Add: Also 8 **wage-boom; waboom.** (Earlier and later examples.)

1790 E. HELME tr. *Le Vaillant's Trav. Afr.* I. 255 A few paltry woods..had some resemblance to that named *Wage-boom*. **1946** *Cape Times* 5 Feb. 6/8 He is collecting waboom and kreupelbos seeds above the Camps Bay slopes so that the bare areas..can be covered with these handsome proteas. **1972** PALMER & PITMAN *Trees S.*

Afr. I. 525 The waboom is one of the tallest of the genus *Protea* and is conspicuous in dry rocky areas of the Cape.

Wagener (vā·gənəɹ). Also *erron.* **Wagner.** The name of Abram *Wagener* (fl. 1796) American farmer, used *absol.* or *attrib.* to designate an apple tree or its fruit belonging to a variety developed on his farm in Penn Yan, New York State (see quot. 1956).

1848 *Trans. N.Y. State Agric. Soc. 1847* VII. 315 The apple for which it is proposed to award the second premium of the society, is called the 'Wagener apple'. **1886** L. H. Bailey *Field Notes on Apple Culture* iv. 21 For winter:..Jonathan,..Northern Spy, Wagener. **1915** A. E. Wilkinson *Apple* ii. 24 The Wagener thus fits in well with the Northern Spy in soil requirements. **1925** E. Hemingway *In our Time* (1930) iv. 45 Nick stopped and picked up a Wagner apple. **1956** *Dict. Gardening* (R. Hort. Soc.) Suppl. 95/2 Wagener..Medium size, round, flattish, irregular, shining yellowish-green, striped and flushed with bright scarlet. **1969** *Oxf. Bk. Food Plants* 48/2 'Wagener'..is an example of many good apples raised in the U.S.A. from European stock.

wagery (wēⁱ·dʒəri). [f. Wage *sb.* + -ery, after *slavery.*] The wage system, wage slavery (esp. as opposed by the guild socialists); wage-earners *collect.*

1917 A. S. Neill *Dominie's Log* xv. 162, I wonder when people will begin to realise what wagery means. When they do begin to realise they will commence the revolution by driving women out of industry. **1917** S. G. Hobson *Guild Principles in War & Peace* ii. 33 Two generations of wagery were to live their squalid life.. before we find singers..grasping the true meaning of industrial oppression. **1972** A. M. Quinton in Cox & Dyson *20th-Cent. Mind* I. iv. 128 Personal fulfilment through work and the production of honest and emotionally satisfying goods could be secured only by the abolition of 'wagery', the wage system in which men sold their labour power unconditionally.

Wagga (wǫ·gă). *Austral. slang.* Also **wagga.** [f. *Wagga Wagga,* the name of a town in New South Wales.] In full, *Wagga blanket, rug.* A blanket or covering made by opening out two sacks, chaff bags, etc., and stitching them together along one edge.

1900 H. Lawson *Darling River* in *Stories* (1964) 1st Ser. 388 The live cinders from the firebox..fell in showers on deck. Every now and again a spark would burn through the Wagga rug of a sleeping shearer. **1938** X. Herbert *Capricornia* (1939) xxviii. 417 The nap..consisted of two greasy bran-sacks, or, as bushmen call them, Wagga Rugs. **1941** Baker *Dict. Austral. Slang* 80 *Wagga blanket,* a rough covering used by tramps. **1944** J. Devanny *By Tropic Sea & Jungle* 156 When you crawl under your wagga you get in one position and aren't game to move. **1969** L. Hadow *Full Cycle* 248 She went to his camp bed. 'Take your wagga, then.' 'No, it's too heavy.' **1978** *Weekend* (Austral.) 25–26 Nov. 11/4 I'm due to slip under my Wagga blankets.

wagger (wæ·gəɹ), *sb.*² *slang* (orig. *Oxford University*). More fully, **wagger-pagger (-bagger).** [One of a collection of words jocularly formed by adding *-agger* (see *-er⁶) to the initial consonants of a word or expression, in this case *waste-paper basket.*] A waste-paper basket.

1903 [see *-er⁶]. **1925** O. Jespersen *Mankind, Nation & Individual* viii. 162 There is an interesting class of words with an inserted *g*:..*wagger pagger bagger* for *waste paper basket.* **1927** W. E. Collinson *Contemp. Eng.* 125 Such playful formations as the Pragger Wagger (the Prince of Wales..) and wagger pagger bagger *waste-paper basket.* **1934** *Neuphilologische Mitteilungen* XXXV. 130 Public-school slang..*wagger* 'waste-paper-basket'. **1961** Partridge *Dict. Slang* Suppl. 1086/2 *Wagger-pagger,* a waste-paper basket. Short for *wagger-pagger-bagger.*

wagging, *vbl. sb.* Add: **2.** Special Comb. **wagging dance** = *waggle dance* s.v. *waggle *sb.* 2. Cf. *wag-tail dance* s.v. *wagtail *sb.* 5.

1950 [see *round *a.* 5 a]. **1967** *Science* 24 Nov. 1072/3 Successful forager bees..inform their hive mates of the location of the feeding place by wagging dances.

waggle, *sb.* Add: **2. waggle dance** [tr. G. *schwänzeltanz* (K. von Frisch 1923, in *Zool. Jahrb., Abt. f. Allgemeine Zool.* XL. 72)], a movement performed by honey-bees at their hive or nest, believed to indicate to other bees the site of a source of food. Cf. *wagging dance* s.v. *wagging *vbl. sb.* 2.

1952 [see *round *a.* 5 a]. **1961** *Guardian* 15 Sept. 6/6 The waggle dance of the hive bee can convey precise indications as to distance and direction of a food source. **1978** *Sci. Amer.* July 80/3 By means of the 'waggle dance' elucidated by von Frisch the bees inform their hive mates of this source of food.

waggle, *v.* Add: **1. e.** *Aeronaut.* To rock (the wings of an aircraft in flight) rapidly from side to side, usu. to convey a signal.

1918 J. M. Grider *Diary* 18 June in *War Birds* (1927) 200 Springs waggled his wings and pointed and we waggled back. **1950** *Sun* (Baltimore) 25 Nov. 2/1 The plane waggled its wings in salute to the troops. **1972** *Daily Express* 29 June 1/1 The Nimrod [aircraft] then waggled its wings and started back.

Wagner (vā·gnəɹ). The name of the German operatic composer Richard *Wagner* (see Wagnerian *a.* and *sb.*) used *attrib.* in **Wagner tuba,** a valved brass instrument resembling a wide-bore horn devised for Wagner (see quots.).

1938 *Oxf. Compan. Mus.* 963/2 What are sometimes heard to-day under the name of 'Wagner Tubas' represent a considerable modification of the [tenor, bass, and double-bass tubas].., so far as the tenor tuba and bass tuba are concerned, departing more from the French horn model as to bore, and approaching more to that of the saxhorn; they retain..the funnel-shaped mouthpiece of the horns. **1948** *Penguin Music Mag.* June 132 No one explained that the 'Wagner tubas'..were assorted saxhorns, with cup-shaped and not funnel-shaped mouthpieces. **1961** A. Baines *Mus. Instruments* 315 *Wagner tubas,* 'tuba' here is really a misnomer, the proper name for these instruments being *Wagner-Tuben*... These *Tuben,* conceived by Wagner to bridge certain gaps in the brass tone, are made in two sizes, in B♭ and F, at the same pitches respectively as the B♭ and F horns and using the same part of the harmonic series. In bore they are midway between the horn and the saxhorn... They are fitted with four valves, the purpose of the fourth being to improve the intonation of the lower octave. **1965** *Listener* 3 June 837/3 A platoon of Wagner tubas. **1980** *New Grove Dict. Mus.* XX. 152/1 *Wagner tuba,* a special kind of tuba devised by Wagner for the *Ring* with the object of bridging the gap between the horns and trombones... The main body of the instrument is elliptical, like most German tenor horns, with the bell emerging from the top at a slightly oblique angle, while the lower end almost rests on the player's lap.

Wagnerian, *a.* and *sb.* Add: **Wagne·rianly** *adv.,* in a Wagnerian manner; **Wagnerism** (earlier example); **Wagnerite** (earlier example); **Wagneri·tis** *joc.* [*-itis], excessive admiration for Wagner, viewed as a morbid condition; **Wagnerize** (*b*) *intr.* (earlier example, perh. in sense 'to play (in the style of) Wagner).

1852 *Punch* 19 June 252/2 The infection called Wagnerism is spreading most rapidly throughout the musical profession. **1855** Geo. Eliot in *Fraser's Mag.* July 50/2 *Tannhäuser*..is still the music of men and women, as well as of Wagnerites. **1866** Swinburne *Let.* 26 Dec. (1959) I. 215 My art is at a discount here, but yours is idolized; you could Schumannize and Wagnerize among us to some purpose. **1889** G. B. Shaw in *Eng. Illustr. Mag.* Oct. 55 Wagneritis (a disease not uncommon among persons who have discovered the merits of Wagner's music by reading about it, and among those disciples who know no other music than his). **1897** —— in *Sat. Rev.* 13 Nov. 514/1 In 'Hamlet' he is quite enthusiastic about naturalness in the business of the stage, and makes Hamlet hold forth about it quite Wagnerianly. **1977** *N.Y. Rev. Bks.* 26 May 15/3 He recovered from his Wagneritis sooner than most worshippers.

wagon, waggon, *sb.* Add: **9. b.** Short for *patrol-wagon* s.v. Patrol *sb.* 4 in Dict. and Suppl. *slang* (orig. and chiefly *U.S.*).

1890 J. P. Quinn *Fools of Fortune* xii. 404 When a raid is made..enough 'pluggers' are captured to fill one or two wagons and are driven to the nearest police station with much clatter and display. **1926** J. Black *You can't Win* iv. 31 I'll phone for the wagon. We'll have to take them all to the station. **1953** [see *ice *sb.* 2 c].

c. Short for *station-wagon 2. Also more *gen.,* a motor car (*colloq.*).

1955 M. Allingham *Beckoning Lady* vi. 90 'Is this the wagon?' Amanda rose to meet the car. **1968** K. Weatherley *Roo Shooter* 59 When he was ready to go, the wagon wouldn't start. **1975** 'E. Lathen' *By Hook or by Crook* xviii. 173 'Do you want to take my car, Paul?'.. 'The wagon or the sports car?'

10*. Figurative phrases. **a.** *to hitch one's wagon to a star,* to set oneself high aspirations; to aspire to another's admirable example.

1870 Emerson *Society & Solitude* 27 Hitch your wagon to a star. Let us not fag in paltry works... Work..for ..justice, love, freedom, knowledge, utility. **1929** D. H. Lawrence *Paintings of D. H. Lawrence* 22 What you mentally or 'consciously' desire is nine times out of ten impossible: hitch your wagon to a star, and you'll just stay where you are. **1939** R. Boothby *Let.* 27 May in M. Gilbert *Winston S. Churchill* (1976) V. li. 1072 One of the few things in my life of which I am proud is that in all matters of major policy during the past 5 years I have hitched my waggon to your star. **1953** E. Waugh *Love among Ruins* i. 10 'The Minister of Welfare and the Minister of Rest and Culture,' continued the Chief Guide. 'The stars to which we have hitched our waggon.' **1978** J. Hyams *Pool* iv. 44 Overweight and sedentary, he was content to hitch his wagon to David's star.

b. *on the wagon,* abstaining from alcoholic drink, teetotal. See *water-wagon* (*a*) s.v. Water *sb.* 29. orig. *U.S.*

1906 B. J. Taylor *Extra Dry* 14 It is better to have been on and off the Wagon than never to have been on at all. **1917** J. M. Grider *War Birds* (1927) 23 Springs put him on the wagon for a week. **1934** J. T. Farrell *Young Manhood* xiv. 218 'Was he oiled when the accident happened?' 'No, he was on the wagon again.' **1951** L. Hellman *Autumn Garden* iii. 138 A few years ago I'd go on the wagon twice a year. Now..I don't care. **1976** L. Deighton *Twinkle, twinkle, Little Spy* viii. 83 They dug him out of a bar.., stoned out of his mind... He stayed on the wagon for years.

c. *to fix* (someone's) *wagon,* to bring about (a person's) downfall, to spoil (his) chances of success. Cf. Fix *v.* 14 c in Dict. and Suppl. *U.S. slang.*

1951 T. Capote *Grass Harp* i. 13 She said her brother would fix my wagon, which he did; right here at the corner of my mouth I've still got a scar where he hit me. **1959** J. D. Salinger in *New Yorker* 6 June 119/1 What ever became of that stalwart bore Fortinbras? Who eventually fixed *his* wagon? **1978** M. Puzo *Fools Die* xxvii. 322 At least he could fix Merlyn's wagon, Ford was beyond his reach. He tried getting her fixed by organizing a campaign of hate mail from fans.

11. a. *wagon-spoke* (later example), *-tongue* (earlier example).

1940 W. Faulkner *Hamlet* ii. ii. 129 Her companion used the reversed pistol-butt against the wagon-spoke and the brass knuckles of the other two. **1845** J. Palmer *Jrnl. Trav. Rocky Mts.* (1847) 18 Our pilot notified us that this would be our last opportunity to procure timber for axle trees, wagon tongues, etc.

12. wagon-bed (earlier example); **wagon boss** *N. Amer.,* the man in charge of a wagon-train; a wagon-master; **wagon box,** (*a*) *U.S.,* the body of a wagon; a wagon-bed; (*b*) a large storage chest, usu. kept under the front seat of a wagon (also used as an article of domestic furniture); **wagon chest** = *wagon box* (*b*); **wagon-master** (later U.S. examples); **wagon-tent** *S. Afr.,* the tent-like canopy of a covered wagon.

1853 A. S. Knight in *Trans. Oregon Pioneer Assoc.* (1933) 40 There is no ferry here and the men will have to make one out of the tightest wagon-bed. **1873** J. H. Beadle *Undeveloped West* 98 Our 'wagon-boss', absolute monarch of a train while on the road, rejoiced in the name of John Monkins. **1973** R. Symons *Where Wagon Led* i. vi. 92 The wagon boss is an important man. You don't talk to him, but when he talks *to you,* you keep your ears clean. **1810** in *Austin Papers* (1924) I. 168, 13 Wagon Boxes. **1852** M. B. Hudson *S. Afr. Frontier Life* I. 206 We come to a door's been off a long while, Near to which stands a wagon-box sacred to books. **1853** V. Williams in *Trans. Oregon Pioneer Assoc.* (1922) 196 A number of other wagon boxes have been ripped for skiffs and ply singly. **1946** G. Foreman *Last Trek* 250 The camp was devastated by a tornado that carried wagon boxes, camp equipage, and some of the people through the air. **1969** N. W. Parsons *Upon Sagebrush Harp* i. 2 The double wagon box on the stoneboat was our own, and it was full of our household goods. **1827** G. Thompson *Trav. S. Afr.* II. 134 A couple of waggon-chests. **1968** S. Stander *Horse* 75 He sat on the wagon-chest. **1861** Wagon-master [see *forage-master* s.v. *forage *sb.* 4]. **1976** *Billings* (Montana) *Gaz.* 17 June 1-c/5 Actor John MacIntire, known as wagonmaster on the television program, 'Wagon Train'. **1845** *Cape of Good Hope Almanac* (Advt.), Country people can be supplied with..3-inch Canvas for wagontents. **1926** P. Smith *Beadle* 59 The women wore stiffly starched plain white sun-bonnets, like miniature wagon-tents. **1955** W. Robertson *Blue Wagon* viii. 72, I was in the wagon-tent when those kaffirs came.

wagon, waggon, *v.* **1.** (Earlier U.S. example.)

1794 E. Denny *Jrnl.* 18 Oct. (1860) 403 The French had opened the Indian path..and wagoned considerably upon it.

wagoning, waggoning, *vbl. sb.* (Earlier examples.)

1782 in L. P. Summers *Ann. Southwest Virginia* (1929) 770 He ought to be paid..for one day waggoning. **1837** *Southern Lit. Messenger* III. 87 There never was such a time for wagoning before.

‖ **wagon-restaurant** (vagoṅ, rẹstoraṅ). [Fr.: cf. Wagon-lit and Restaurant.] A dining-car on a Continental train.

1910 *Bradshaw's Railway Guide* Jan. 958 Special Wagon Restaurant Corridor Train leaves Paris for Cherbourg on morning of sailing. **1938** H. Nicolson *Let.* 26 Apr. (1966) 337 This man would be delightful if one met him in a *wagon-restaurant* and got into conversation. **1983** W. Blunt *Married to Single Life* vii. 199 Seated in the overheated *wagon-restaurant* of the Continental express.

wag-on-the-wall. *Horology.* Also **wag-at-the-wa',** etc. [Wag *v.*: see *Sc. Nat. Dict.* for other uses of the expression.] A variety of wall-clock with unenclosed pendulum and weights. Also *attrib.*

1825 Jamieson Suppl. II. 637/2 *Wag-at-the-Wa',*..a name given to a clock, which has no case, frequently used in the country. **1858** G. Roy *Generalship* 55 To take a fancy to a waggitonawa clock. **1904** J. Smith *Handbk. Old Scottish Clockmakers* 45 The poorer members of the community could not afford the price demanded for the long case clocks and would be content with a 'Wag at the Wa'. **1911** N. H. Moore *Old Clock Bk.* 59 Many Dutch works were sent to England without their cases... Such clocks went till the dirt and dust clogged their wheels... Such clocks as these are often called in rustic communities by the quaint name of 'wag-on-the-wall'. **1966** P. Boyle *At Night All Cats are Grey* 221 What was this nagging memory of a wag-o'-the-wall?.. With a bottle of water used as a driving weight.

wagtail, *sb.* Add: **4*.** *Joinery.* A parting-strip (see Parting *vbl. sb.* 7 b) used in the construction of a sash window.

1940 in *Chambers's Techn. Dict.* **1950** M. T. Telling *Carpentry & Joinery* 43 To prevent this happening a long thin sliver of wood called a parting slip or wagtail is placed between them *sc.* the weights] inside the box.

5. wag-tail dance = *waggle dance* s.v. *WAGGLE *sb.* 2; **wagtail kite** *nonce-use*, a toy kite with a wagging or swinging tail.

1949 C. G. BUTLER *Honeybee* viii. 120 Von Frisch described two dances, a round-dance and a wag-tail dance. **1973** Wag-tail dance [see *ROUND *a.* 5 a]. **1922** JOYCE *Ulysses* 495 Ragged barefoot newsboys jogging a wagtail kite.

wahine (wahī·ni). Also 8 **whinie**, 9 **whyenee, wiena, wyeena; wahini.** [Maori, Hawaiian, and other Polynesian languages: cf. *VAHINE.]

1. *N.Z.* A Maori woman or wife.

1773 W. BAYLY *Jrnl.* in R. McNab *Hist. Rec. N.Z.* (1914) II. 204 Their Whinies (or women) are not regular featured in general as the men. **1807** J. SAVAGE *Some Acct. N.Z.* xi. 74 *Wyeena*, a woman. **1841** *N.Z. Jrnl.* II. No. 32. 92/2 The chiefs and 'Wienas', or wives, partook. **1845** E. J. WAKEFIELD *Adventure N.Z.* I. ii. 29 Having enquired how many [wives] the Kings of England had, he laughed heartily at finding they were not so well provided, and repeatedly counted 'four *wahine*' (women) on his fingers. **1863** V. LUSH *Jrnl.* 28 Sept. (1971) 253 By noon the following day all the wahines had gone back to the Pah, cockles and all. **1911** W. H. KOEBEL *In Maoriland Bush* viii. 128 Two or three Wahines ply the men lustily with..somewhat broad banter. **1944** *Coast to Coast 1943* 105 You meet te nice girl at te dance. Plenty wahine! **1963** *Times* 7 Feb. 12/3 The warriors and their *wahine* turned away 'towards God', as I was told by an old Maori who sat with me on the grass.

2. In Polynesia: = *VAHINE.

1847 H. BINGHAM *Residence 21 Yrs. Sandwich Islands* 188 Give our *aloha* to all the new teachers and their *wahines*. **1865** H. W. BAXLEY *What I saw on West Coast of S. & N. Amer.* 515 The wahine disputes with them the palm of superiority.

3. *Surfing slang.* A girl surfer.

1963 *Surfing Yearbk.* 43/2 *Wahini*, a girl surfer. **1966** *Surfer* VII. 39 There are other things he did on the board, too, especially the full-moon tandem rides with wahines. **1971** *Studies in English* (Univ. Cape Town) II. 26 *Wahine* meaning woman in Hawaiian, a term popular among writers, has never been used in Cape Town.

wahoo. Add: **2.** *U.S.* The winged elm, *Ulmus alata*, or a closely related tree. Also *attrib.*

1770 E. MEASE *Jrnl.* 28 Nov. in *Publ. Mississippi Hist. Soc. Centenary Ser.* (1925) V. 62 The Trees which I remark'd to be the largest were Oaks of different kinds, Wahoos, Button Wood, [etc.]. **1832** D. J. BROWNE *Sylva Amer.* 308 The Wahoo is a stranger to the Middle and Northern States. **1873** *Newton Kansan* 27 Mar. 1/7 One ounce of wahoo (winged-elm) bark, added to a quart of pure whiskey..is very excellent in dyspepsia. **1969** T. H. EVERETT *Living Trees of World* xiv. 130/2 The wahoo elm..is usually characterized by branchlets having two broad corky wings.

wahoo² (wahū·) [Origin unknown.] A large marine fish, *Acanthocybium solandri*, belonging to the family Scombridæ and found in tropical seas.

[**1905** D. S. JORDAN *Guide to Study of Fishes* II. xvi. 266 Still larger is the great guaho, or peto, an immense sharp-nosed, swift-swimming mackerel found in the East and West Indies.] **1909** *Cent. Dict.* Suppl. 1429/2 Wahoo.. A common name of *Acanthocybium solandri*, a scombroid fish of tropical seas. **1920** *Outing* July 248/3 He had fished for—and caught—many a most unheard of species, as well as sharks, sword-fish, wahoo, etc. **1940** *Geogr. Jrnl.* XCV. 130 These fish [*sc.* kingfish] which the Americans call wahoo, are beautifully shaped surface feeders. **1979** *United States 1980/81* (Penguin Travel Guides) 517 The white marlin capital of the world sends fishermen out to the Jackspot..for dolphin, bonita, tuna, and wahoo.

wah-wah¹, var. Wow-wow¹.

1883 [see Wow-wow ¹]. **1891** E. ARNOLD *Seas & Lands* xl. 520 A 'wah-wah' monkey..was a delightful little creature, with very long silky arms. **1939** A. KEITH *Land below Wind* xvii. 291 *Wah wah* was the native name for gibbon ape. **1959** 'M. DERBY' *Tigress* iii. 145 The birds and the *wah-wahs*..woke. **1964** J. POPE-HENNESSY *Verandah* II. ii. 78 He [*sc.* Hugh Low] once wrote to his daughter Kitty that he loved only two creatures in the world—his wah-wah monkey, Eblis, and herself. **1975** *Blackw. Mag.* June 542/1 The only members of the ape family found in Malaya are the gibbons, the commonest of which is locally known as the *wah-wah*.

wah-wah² (wā·wā). Also **wa-wa, wha-wha, wow-wow.** [Echoic.] **1.** *Jazz.* A musical effect achieved on brass instruments by manipulation of a mute and on an electric guitar by means of a pedal controlling output from the amplifier.

1926 H. O. OSGOOD *So this is Jazz* 98 Then there is the clown of mutes. Leading philologists of the jazz world are at odds over the correct spelling of the name; some favour wow wow, others prefer wha wha, but there is authority for the simplification wa-wa. **1936** *Amer. Mercury* XXXVIII. p. x/2 *Wah-wah*, a brass effect gotten by favoring a bell of a horn with a mute. **1949** R. BLESH *Shining Trumpets* viii. 183 The 'wa-wa', produced by the cupped hand moved in front of the cornet or trumpet bell. **1950** A. LOMAX *Mr. Jelly Roll* (1952) 64 There were many other imitations of animal sounds we used—such as the wah-wahs on trumpets and trombones. **1976** *New Musical Express* 12 Feb. 25/2 You can thrill again to..Clapton playing his insidious wah-wah on 'Get Back Home'. **1977** 'E. CRISPIN' *Glimpses of Moon* iii. 38 One spends his working life in a perpetual seascape, another writing wah-wahs on trumpet parts for people surfacing in mud-baths into which they have comically fallen..and so on.

2. The sound of a baby's crying, or a noise resembling this.

1938 D. RUNYON *Furthermore* viii. 156 Something goes wa-wa, like a sheep..because..Isadore is sitting on John Ignatius Junior's doll, which says 'Mamma' when you squeeze it. **1958** HAYWARD & HARARI tr. *Pasternak's Dr. Zhivago* I. vi. 158 'Wa, wa,' yelled the babies all on one note... Only one voice stood out from the others. It was also yelling 'wa, wa',..but it was deeper.

3. *attrib.*, esp. as (sense 1) *wah-wah effect, mute, pedal.*

1925 G. GERSHWIN *Rhapsody in Blue* (music score) (1939) 1 (*direction*) Wha Wha effect. **1926** *Melody Maker* Feb. 23/2 (Advt.), The wow-wow mute is made of spun aluminium. **1926** WHITEMAN & MCBRIDE *Jazz* ix. 200 The first time I ever heard what I call the wawa mutes, used with the cornet... The players got that effect by inverting glass tumblers over the bells of the instruments. **1930** R. PAGET *Human Speech* 240 The so-called 'wow-wow' mutes for cornets and the like. **1935** *Vanity Fair* (N.Y.) Nov. 71/3 The wah-wah notes of intermittently muted brass. **1943** R. BLESH *This is Jazz* 24 This bad tone..like dirty tone, growl or wah-wah trumpet work, is expressive and therefore good from the Jazz point of view. **1954** *Grove's Dict. Mus.* (ed. 5) IV. 601/1 The trumpets and trombones very frequently use peculiar mutes, such as the 'wa wa mute', which can make the instrument weep or laugh rather like a human voice. **1969** *It* 13–28 June 13/2 Frank proved quite conclusively that he's a brilliant guitarist, especially with a 'wah-wah' pedal. **1979** R. L. SIMON *Peking Duck* xxiii. 175 It's an old song... Now they use a wah-wah pedal and a Moog Synthesizer.

waiata (wai·ata). *N.Z.* Also 9 **wyata.** [Maori.] A Maori song.

1807 J. SAVAGE *Some Acct. N.Z.* xi. 75 *Wyata*, singing. **1843** E. DIEFFENBACH *Trav. N.Z.* II. I. iv. 57 E' Waiata is a song of a joyful nature. **1905** W. BAUCKE *Where White Man Treads* 88 Then Puke..sang a waiata. **1978** P. GRACE *Mutuwhenua* xiv. 104 Singing or chanting the waiata at the conclusion of each speech. **1984** *Metro* (Auckland) Jan. 72/3 Indeed the Maori name for the racecourse is Waiatarua (Two Songs) and tradition suggests it was so named because the sound of the flood waters escaping through the underground caverns closely resembled the singing of waiatas.

waif, *sb.*¹ (and *a.*) Add: **A.** *sb.* **3.** *waif-like* adj.

1924 R. CAMPBELL *Flaming Terrapin* ii. 35 Their waif-like corpses on a stormy bed Toss in their deep deliriums. **1962** I. MURDOCH *Unofficial Rose* xv. 149 How young she looked, how waif-like.

Hence **wai·fish** *a.*, **wai·fishly** *adv.*

1936 S. SMITH *Novel on Yellow Paper* 220 Such.. wispish, waifish progeny. **1977** *Time* 31 Jan. 21/3 The waifish face beneath the jaunty white cap never loses its ethereal Pre-Raphaelite look. **1980** *Times Lit. Suppl.* 20 June 703/1 *Hurricane's* Samoan scenery is enticingly picturesque: doesn't art student Charlotte—waifishly played by Mia Farrow—arrive on her vacation exclaiming 'I can't wait to get out my paintbox'?

waif, *sb.*² Add: **2.** (Earlier *Naut.* examples, *spec.* in whaling.) Also *attrib.*, as *waif-pole.*

1839 *Knickerbocker* XIII. 382 Line-tubs, water-kegs, and wafe-poles, were thrown hurriedly into the boats. **1846** T. B. THORPE *Mysteries of Backwoods* 85 As the waiffe of the whaleman [marks] his victim on the sea. **1851** H. MELVILLE *Moby Dick* III. iii. 27 The allusion to the waifs and waif-poles..necessitates some account of the laws and regulations of the whale fishery.

wail, *v.* Add: **2. c.** Of a jazz musician: to play very well, with great feeling, etc. (*U.S. slang*). Also *U.S. colloq.*, to perform well.

1955 SHAPIRO & HENTOFF *Hear me talkin' to Ya* 231, I revered the amazing Fats Waller, who had lately made a splash wailing on organ at the Lincoln. **1959** *Encounter* June 43/2 The Beat 'cat' approaches the Beat 'chick' with the ritualistic 'Pad me'..the 'chick's', approach to the male is..'I'm frigid,' to which he can either reply 'I'll make you wail' (function) or, otherwise, 'Don't bug.' **1962** [see *BLOW *v.*¹ 14 e]. **1977** C. MCFADDEN *Serial* (1978) xxxix. 85/2 Despite his back, he was really wailin' when he hung a sharp right into his driveway, pretending Sutton Manor was a picturesque village along the route of the Tour de France.

wailing, *vbl. sb.* **c.** For '**wailing place**.. (also occas. *wailing wall*)' read **Wailing Wall,** the remaining part of the wall of the Second Temple of Jerusalem, destroyed in 70 B.C., revered by Jews as a place of prayer (also † *wailing place*) (earlier and later examples); also *transf.* and *fig.*

1878 J. FERGUSSON *Temples of Jews* II. xii. 183 The most interesting particular mentioned by the Pilgrim is the 'Lapis Pertusus', which was then the Wailing Place of the Jews. **1922** JOYCE *Ulysses* 532 Darkshawled figures of the circumcised, in sackcloth and ashes, stand by the wailing wall. **1934** C. LAMBERT *Music Ho!* III. 212 Tin Pan Alley has become a commercialized Wailing Wall. **1955** W. GADDIS *Recognitions* III. v. 945 I've just visited the Wailing Wall, and had a good cry. **1963** *Daily Tel.* 23 Dec. 12/2 The dividing wall [in Berlin] becomes a wailing wall at midnight each night. **1980** K. FOLLETT *Key to Rebecca* xxix. 308 Today I went to the Western Wall, which is also called the Wailing Wall.

wainage. 2. (Earlier example.)

1810 G. CHALMERS *Caledonia* II. ii. 134 The waynage' or cultivable lands, and meadows of each district or manor, were possessed, and laboured, in separate portions, by the individuals of the manor.

wainscot, *sb.* Add: **6. wainscot chair,** a panel-back chair (see *PANEL *sb.*¹ 20).

1663 in *Farm & Cottage Inventories of Mid-Essex 1633–1749* (Essex Record Office) (1950) 95 One Wainsscott Chair. **1891** I. W. LYON *Colonial Furnit. New Eng.* v. 145 The wainscot chairs which figure in the early records were doubtless those made up—back, seats, and all—of wood, the wood being most invariably oak. *Ibid.* 146 Wainscot chairs were quite common in England and Scotland in the seventeenth century. **1925** [see *panel-back* adj. s.v. *PANEL *sb.*¹ 20]. **1978** P. VAN GREENAWAY *Man called Scavener* i. 11 A long passage lined with Pembrokes, a Wainscot chair, a rare Caquetoire.

‖ **waipiro** (waipiro). *N.Z.* Also **waipera, waipero, waipirau.** [Maori, f. *wai* water + *piro* putrid.] Alcoholic liquor, spirits.

1845 W. BROWN *N.Z.* I. iii. 132 Another native.. keeps a grog-shop, and sells his *Waipero*..to *Hourangi* (drunken) pakehas. **1847** S. C. BREES *Pictorial Illustr. N.Z.* 13 The natives..say, it is '*all the same as te waipe-ra*', or spirits. **1863** F. E. MANING *Old N.Z.* xi. 152 He *would* go on shore..to get some water to mix with his *waipiro*, and was not his canoe found next day floating about with his paddle and two empty case-bottles in it? **1881** J. L. CAMPBELL *Poenamo* xi. 341 We had the inevitable percentage of indulgers in 'waipirau'. **1933** *Bulletin* (Sydney) 20 Dec. 20/3 Under the influence of waipiro a Rotorua Maori pinched a sedan car. **1972** P. NEWTON *Sheep Thief* xx. 169 She had no time for the waipera... 'Charles,' she said... 'You can decide right now. Me or the drink.'

wairakite (wəi·răkəit). *Min.* [f. *Wairakei*, name of a place in New Zealand + -ITE¹.] A hydrous silicate of calcium and aluminium, $CaAl_2Si_4O_{12}.2H_2O$, the calcium analogue of analcime, that occurs as colourless to white monoclinic crystals and is common in low-grade metamorphic rocks.

1955 A. STEINER in *Mineral. Mag.* XXX. 691 During the study of hydrothermal alteration of cores recovered from holes drilled at Wairakei..an unusual zeolite mineral was found... The name wairakite is given to the new mineral. **1979** *Amer. Mineralogist* LXIV. 993/1 A marked feature of wairakite crystals is the presence of complex, fine lamellar twinnings.

waist. Add: **3. c.** The middle section of the fuselage of an aeroplane, esp. a bomber. *U.S.*

1942 [see *waist gunner* in sense 7 below]. **1956** *U.S.A.F. Dict.* 560/2 *Waist*, the middle section of an airplane's fuselage. Applied esp. to the middle section of a bomber.

6. Simple attrib., as *waist height, size*; *waist-length* adj.; 'worn from the waist', as *waist petticoat, slip.*

1953 E. SIMON *Past Masters* I. i. 21 The tops of the bookshelves which at waist-height ran along the walls. **1944** R. LEHMANN *Ballad & Source* I. ii. 14 She wore a waist-length cape called a dolman. **1977** 'L. EGAN' *Blind Search* i. 1 Her waist-length brown hair [was] untidily braided. **1939–40** *Army & Navy Stores Catal.* 642/2 *Waist petticoats*..Moiré poplin. **1918** *T. Eaton & Co. Catal.* Spring & Summer 188/1 Women's overalls, made of fine khaki drill... Waist sizes 24 to 38. **1974** *Country Life* 12 Dec. 1903/1 Tartan skirts..in waist sizes 24–30 in. **1955** M. HALL *Let's make some Undies* (Let's Make It Ser.) 44 (*heading*) Straight placket for waist slips and knickers. **1976** T. STOPPARD *Dirty Linen* 9 Maddie is.. wearing..a waist-slip which is also pretty, silk and lace, with a slit.

7. waist-gun, a gun set in the waist of an aircraft; also **waist-gunner; waistline,** (*a*) (in Dict., sense 6) (earlier example); (*b*) a person's waist, esp. with reference to its size; (*c*) = sense 1 c in Dict.; (*d*) a notional line running round the body of a motor vehicle at the level of the bottom of the window frames.

1942 *Yank* 7 Oct. 3 The waist gunner sits patiently in the waist of the fuselage. *Ibid.* 23 Dec. 4 From his waist-gun position he interphoned the appearance of two Jap nightfighters off to the right. **1978** J. IRVING *World according to Garp* i. 15 Sergeant Garp had experience as.. a waist gunner in the B-17E. *Ibid.* 16 Technical Sergeant Garp, at his waist gun position. **1896** *Woman's Life* 15 Feb. 448/1 Your velvet vest should end in a narrow V at the waist line. **1928** *Daily Mail* 25 July 8/5 Even if you are one of the fortunate few who need not keep a watchful eye on their waistline, you'll eat Vita-Weat for pleasure and health. **1930** R. CAMPBELL *Adamastor* 25 Our Drakensberg's most lofty scalps Would scarcely reach the waist-line of the Alps. **1941** *Ann. Reg. 1940* 254 The Russians..attacked the 'waist-line' [of Finland] from further north. **1959** *Times* 2 Oct. 9/1 These cars..have an entirely new top from the waistline upwards. **1970** J. PHILIPS *Nightmare at Dawn* (1971) I. 41, I don't have to worry about my waistline. **1974** *Country Life* 28 Feb. 446/1 This latest Capri..has a much bigger window area with a lower waistline.

waistcoat. Add: **5.** *waistcoat-piece* (earlier example).

1789 J. WOODFORDE *Diary* 19 Sept. (1927) III. 193 Gave my Servant Man Ben a Waistcoat Piece.

waistcoateer. 1. (Later *Hist.* examples.)

1916 JOYCE *Portrait of Artist* (1969) v. 176 The grave and mocking music of the lutenists or the frank laughter of waistcoateers. **1922** [see *FLAT-CAP 2].

wait, *v.*[1] Add: **I. 5. d.** Phr. *wait for it*, said (often parenthetically) to create an interval of suspense before imparting something remarkable or amusing, in order to heighten its effect. Also *ironically*. *colloq.*

1930 M. Allingham *Mystery Mile* xviii. 170 'Wait a minute,' said Mr. Knapp. '*Wait* for it... That is just exactly wot I do know.' **1958** S. Hyland *Who goes Hang?* xvi. 74 'You're hiding something...' 'Wait for it my dear.' **1966** 'H. Calvin' *Italian Gadget* ii. 21 We can have a shower and..wait for it, dinner at the Palazzo Capucci. **1979** R. Laidlaw *Lion is Rampant* xviii. 139 The real attack will come from, wait for it, wait for it—anither direction a'thegither.

6. c. *to wait out*: (*a*) *U.S. Baseball*, (of a batter) to force (a pitcher) to throw a maximum number of pitches by refraining from striking at pitches in the hope of getting a base 'on balls', i.e. because they were not pitched over the home-plate; hence (chiefly *U.S. colloq.*), to wait during (a period of time, an event, etc.); to wait for the end of; also, *to wait it out*, to endure a period of waiting; (*b*) = *to wait for* (sense 7).

1909 *Amer. Mag.* Aug. 401 Still Chance commanded: 'Wait—wait him out.' Every batter went to the plate intent on making Donovan pitch as many balls to them as possible. **1936** *Philadelphia Rec.* 31 July 15/1 Alf M. Landon is up there under instructions from the bench to wait 'em out. **1956** H. Kurnitz *Invasion of Privacy* xv. 95 He monopolized the phone in the bedroom, where Shelly and Zorn were waiting it out. **1959** *N.Y. Times Mag.* 11 Oct. 18/1 He is sealed into the container and.. lies there in his 'contour couch' and waits out the long countdown. **1966** D. Francis *Flying Finish* x. 131, I retired to the snack bar..to wait out the twenty minutes. **1977** R. Perry *Dead End* i. 9 Unfortunately, I couldn't afford to wait him out. Daley was already overdue.

7. d. *to wait on*: (*d*) *dial.* (esp. *Austral.* and *N.Z.*), to wait for a while, to 'hold on'. Freq. *imp.*

1943 N. Marsh *Colour Scheme* xiii. 228 'Wait on, wait on,' Dikon heard Webley mumble, 'You'll get it back all right.' **1946** K. Tennant *Lost Haven* (1947) x. 138 Wait on, Patsy... Wait on, Patsy. You talk of letting the water out, but what about the fish?—bloody fish'll go too. **1967** 'G. Douglas' *Death went Hunting* xviii. 161 For some reason I can't define, he seems quite willing to accept his present position... As we say in Yorkshire, he appears to be waiting on. **1968** S. L. Elliott *Rusty Bugles* in E. Hanger *Three Austral. Plays* 92 *Andy*: Open the one from Darky. *Gig*: I am blast you... Wait on, can't you?

g. *to wait and see*. (Example with reference to Asquith's use, and earlier and later *attrib.* examples.) Also *wait and see* sb. phr.

1910 *Blackw. Mag.* May 747/1 Mr. Asquith has deemed it not incompatible with the gravity of his office to elude the curiosity of his opponents with the absurd formula, 'Wait and see'. **1969** S. Hyland *Top Bloody Secret* ii. 121 The philosophy of wait and see..was getting him nowhere. **1976** *Scottish Daily Express* 23 Dec. 11/2 The rest of the back row is in a similar state of 'wait and see'. *attrib.* **1870** L. M. Alcott *Old-Fashioned Girl* xiv. 231 She..thought she would 'wait and see.'.. The 'wait-and-see' decision was making her friend unhappy. **1930** [see *flop *adv.* and *int.*]. **1977** A. J. Russell *Pour Hemlock* xii. 147 His was a wait-and-see posture. **1984** *Times* 8 June 20/1 An understandable wait-and-see management caution.

i. (Earlier examples.)

1788 J. Woodforde *Diary* 29 Feb. (1927) III. 8 Mr. Taswell..desired us to send to Mr. Custance that they might not wait dinner for him. **1836** Dickens *Let.* 17 Sept. (1965) I. 174, I hope and trust you did not wait dinner for me.

j. *to be unable* (etc.) *to wait* (*for* or *to do* something), to be very eager or anxious for or to do it. *colloq.*

1938 D. Du Maurier *Rebecca* xvi. 232 'Oh, Madam, how exciting,' breathed Clarice. 'I don't know how I am going to wait for the day.' **1958** I. Murdoch *Bell* xix. 234 We're all so excited, we can hardly wait for tomorrow morning. **1971** J. Osborne *West of Suez* ii. i. 63 Can't wait! Let's go home *now*. **1972** *National Observer* (U.S.) 27 May 10/3 Now the young musicians can't wait to get at their instruments.

k. (you) *wait till* (or *until*).., used to imply a threat, warning, etc., or promise of something interesting or exciting, when the specified event has occurred. Also *ellipt.* as *you wait!*

1938 G. Greene *Brighton Rock* iii. i. 99 'I dunno who Brewer is,' Ida said, 'but things seem lively.' 'You wait till the races start,' the man said. 'They'll be lively all right then.' **1953** E. Simon *Past Masters* iii. iii. 154 Parents brazened out their children's tantrums with the key-phase of, 'You wait!'. **1960** S. Barstow *Kind of Loving* ii. ii. 162 Seventy-four guineas, Henry. Seventy-four bloody lovely guineas. Just wait till we tell Mr. Van Huyten about this. **1975** J. Gores *Hammett* xix. 130 She was going over to..tea with the George F. Biltmores! Wait until she wrote her mother about *that*! **1984** *Guardian* 5 Oct. 14/3 Mr Scargill..will soon, very soon—just you wait—emerge triumphant.

9. d. (Earlier example.)

1827 Carlyle tr. L. Tieck in *German Romance* II. 135 Andres waited supper.

II. 14. wait on or **upon** —. **h.** (Later examples.) Cf. Waiter 4 b.

1840 Geo. Eliot *Let.* 20 July (1954) I. 58 That constant waiting on God for instruction and comfort which [the Quietists]..make the sum total of religion. **1931** J. Buchan *Blanket of Dark* xvi. 307 Be still and wait on God. **1979** R. Blythe *View in Winter* ix. 300 One of the best things which all these new changes have brought about is this notion of waiting upon God.

i. Delete † *Obs.* and add later, chiefly *U.S.*, examples. Also, more generally, to wait for.

1817 W. Sewall *Diary* 2 May (1930) 14/1, I proceeded to the Academy and agreed to enter there upon condition that the Professor would wait on me until the next winter. **1865** O. L. Jackson *Colonel's Diary* (1922) 227 We have been waiting on the pay department. **1915** J. Buchan *39 Steps* vi. 135 He..raised his placid eyebrows and waited on me to speak. **1931** *Amer. Speech* VII. 20 *Wait on*, wait for, the Biblical sense. 'When I got there, John was waiting on me.' (Widespread.) **1955** F. O'Connor *Wise Blood* v. 85 He..darted after Hazel Motes. 'Wait on me!' he shouted. **1960** *Observer* 7 Feb. 13/4 The nation waits on the railwaymen, to see if there will be a strike or not. **1984** P. Turnbull *Big Money* ix. 153, 'I was just waiting on you two coming back.' He stood and reached for his coat.

wait-a-while. 1. (In Dict. s.v. Wait-a-bit a.)

2. In Australia, any of several plants with prickles or spiny leaves, esp. *Acacia colletioides*.

1889 J. H. Maiden *Useful Native Plants Austral.* 306 *Acacia colletioides*..'Wait-a-while' (a delicate allusion to the predicament of a traveller desirous of penetrating a belt of it). **1940** F. D. Davison *Woman at Mill* 86 Clumps of prickly wait-a-while gave back the light from millions of small shiny leaves. **1967** [see *Bathurst burr].

waiter. Add: **III. 6. b.** Restrict † *Obs.* to sense in Dict. and add: More recently, (*U.S.*) an attendant upon the bride or groom at a wedding. *Obs.* exc. *dial.* or *Hist.*

1830 in N. E. Eliason *Tarheel Talk* (1956) 303 [She] says she hears you are to be married. She wishes to know..when..as you promised she would be one of the waiters. **1927** *Dialect Notes* V. 470 *Waiter*,..an attendant of the bride or groom at a wedding. **1959** *Daily Progress* (Charlottesville, Va.) 19 Mar. 14/1 Four young men and four young women were appointed to be 'waiters' on the bride and groom.

†**7. d.** *Mil.* A soldier, etc., employed as a domestic servant to an officer. *U.S. Obs.*

1828 A. Sherburne *Mem.* i. 20, I was waiter to Mr. Charles Roberts the boatswain. *Ibid.* ii. 26 Part of our officers with five or six waiters..occupied an elegant house. **1861** *Army Regulations* 559 Non-commissioned officers not employed as waiters.

8*. A uniformed attendant on the floor of the Stock Exchange, Lloyd's of London, or other City of London institution.

1887 [see Hammer *v.* 2 d]. **1904** C. Duguid *Stock Exchange* ii. 12 We have also noticed the Waiters' Stands, about twenty in number, placed in various parts of the House, pulpit-like..so that the important announcements which emanate from these stands may be well heard in the House. **1934** F. E. Armstrong *Bk. Stock Exchange* xvii. 356 It is known that dealers used to foregather in the coffee houses of Change Alley, Cornhill. .. Here, probably, it was that 'waiters', plying their trade, and seeking out from the interior fastnesses of these refreshment rooms some particular Stock-jobber wanted by his client, gave the name to the uniformed 'waiter' who calls the Members within the walls of the present Stock Exchange. **1962** A. Sampson *Anat. of Britain* xxiii. 380 Merchant bankers work in a formal atmosphere... Mahogany, black-coated waiters and grandfather clocks set the tone of privacy. *Ibid.* xxv. 400 The Room [at Lloyd's]... When a broker is wanted, one of the 'waiters' (who stand round the room in scarlet uniform) writes his name on a special instrument. **1976** *Times* 22 Apr. (Baltic Exchange Suppl.) p. i/9 As in other City institutions, attendants wear livery and are called waiters.

IV. 12. *Chess.* = *waiting problem* s.v. *Waiting *vbl. sb.*[1] 2 c.

1906 A. C. White *Tours de Force* p. xxxii, If a problem has no threat, it is called a 'waiter', and all the different continuations are variations. **1935** *Encycl. Sports* 150/1 There is no simple waiting move for white. The key is, indeed, a 'waiter', but four of the resulting mates are different from those in the set position. **1963** M. Lipton et al. *Chess Problems* iv. 72 White can neither retain all the set mates as in a Waiter, nor change some of them while still maintaining zugzwang as in a mutate.

waiting, *vbl. sb.*[1] Add: **2. c. waiting list**, a list of people waiting for appointments, selection for any purpose, or the next chance of obtaining something; **waiting (move) problem** *Chess* (see quots.); **waiting race** (earlier example); **waiting time**, time spent waiting, *spec.* in *Computing* (see quot. 1962) or *Work Study* (see quot. 1979).

1897 *Outing* XXX. 347/2 The Michaux Club is composed of two hundred members, with a large 'waiting list'. **1916** A. Huxley *Let.* 5 Feb. (1969) 90 There is a huge waiting list for the better jobs on all the Govt. Depts. **1921** *Tax Clerks' Jrnl.* IV. 387 The right to a place on the 'waiting list' for a permanent post. **1976** *Times* 23 Feb. 13/1 Local councils were able to do little to reduce overlong waiting lists. **1891** J. Rayner *Chess Problems* 9 Waiting-move problems—*i.e.*, those in which the first move would not lead to a mate if it were not that Black is forced to reply and thereby weaken his position. **1896** *Chess Monthly* May 280 There is another class of waiting problem which is usually found very interesting... A primary position which has every indication that White has but to linger without discouraging the mates as 'set', but..one of the mates has to be given up in exchange for another to be created. **1907** S. S. Blackburne *Chess Problems* 25 *Block problem*—Otherwise called a 'Waiting Problem' is one in which White's first move leads to mate after every reply of Black, in consequence of such reply. **1962** K. S. Howard *One Hundred Years Amer. Two-Move Chess Problem* 5 Another type [of problem]..was the complete block, or waiting-move problem, especially where some of the mating moves apparently set in the initial position were changed by the key, for which Brian Harley..coined the apt name *mutate*. **1868** H. Woodruff *Trotting Horse* xxxvi. 297 Tallman made a waiting-race of it, and pulled Flora back three lengths. **1962** *Gloss Terms Automatic Data Processing* (*B.S.I.*) 85 *Waiting time*, of a store. The time interval between the instant the control unit calls for a transfer of data to or from the store and the instant the transfer commences. **1976** P. R. White *Planning for Public Transport* v. 115 Waiting time is a function of service frequency and thus is not affected directly by spacing. **1979** *Gloss. Terms Work Study* (*B.S.I.*) 16 *Waiting time*, the period of time for which an operator is available for production but is prevented from working.

waiting-man. For † *Obs.* read *Obs.* exc. *U.S.* and add later U.S. examples.

1839 *Southern Lit. Messenger* V. 752/1 The door of the bachelor's hall was assaulted by a repetition of raps, which quickened the steps of Mr. Singlesides' sedate waiting-man. **1884** G. W. Cable *Dr. Sevier* I. x. 73 The speaker ceased as the mulatto waiting-man appeared.

wait-list. orig. and chiefly *U.S.* [Wait *v.*[1]] = *waiting list* s.v. *Waiting *vbl. sb.*[1] 2 c.

1960 *Amer. Speech* XXXV. 312 There's a wait list on that one too,' one is told somberly by steamship agents. **1977** in H. J. Eysenck *You & Neurosis* vi. 185 On a rating scale of overall improvement, 93 per cent of the behaviour therapy patients contrasted to 77 per cent of the psychotherapy and wait-list patients were considered either improved or recovered. **1979** *United States 1980/81* (Penguin Travel Guides) 16 *How to Use an Airline*; it's full of information on how to make reservations, the difference between waitlist and stand-by, [etc.].

Hence as *v. trans.*, to put (a person) on a waiting list; to draw up a waiting list for places on (an aircraft, ship, etc.); **wait-listing** *vbl. sb.*

1960 *Amer. Speech* XXXV. 312 A boat is said to be *wait listed*... What gloomy fate, then, awaits the prospective passenger who is *wait listed*? **1971** *Financial Mail* (Johannesburg) 26 Feb. 656/2 What about his wait-listing for an earlier flight? **1973** *Daily Tel.* 5 Sept. 6/7 On less frequent services..overbooking is not employed. Instead, 'wait-listing' is effected, and passengers who learn that their flight is full wait at the airport on the chance of a seat becoming available.

waitress. Add: **2. b.** Chiefly *U.S.* A female servant in a private house whose duty is to wait upon those at table (cf. Waiter 7 c); in extended use, a housemaid.

1875 Mrs. Stowe *We & our Neighbors* 323 Maggie was parlor-girl and waitress, and a good one too. **1906** *N.Y. Herald* 5 Mar. 14 A competent girl as waitress and to take charge of parlor floor; private family. **1937** C. Day *Life with Mother* 215 Each brother had his own sacred place where his own toys were kept, except when the waitress cleaned the room and mixed everything up. **1953** A. Christie *Pocket Full of Rye* iv. 32 Gladys Martin is the parlourmaid or waitress, as they like to call themselves nowadays.

3. Comb.: **waitress service**, service by waitresses in a restaurant, opp. *self-service*.

1960 C. Dale *Spring of Love* i. 3 The floor with waitress service was always crowded. **1970** E. McGirr *Death pays Wages* vii. 150 The main room had tables with white cloths and a waitress service.

Hence **wai·tressing**, service as a waitress; hence (as a back-formation) **wai·tress** *v. intr.*, to work as a waitress.

1936 J. B. Priestley *They walk in City* xi. 335 Well, you're a nice-looking girl and you have done some waitressing—so it oughtn't to be hard for you to get a place. **1950** *Landfall* Dec. 308 There were pretty good ones [*sc.* jobs] going now—cooking and waitressing in town. **1974** K. Millett *Flying* (1975) iii. 311, I was a kid from St. Paul waitressing in Glacier Park. **1984** *Times* 15 Oct. 10/4 The waitress..can..make waitressing into a performing art. **1984** *New Yorker* 29 Oct. 43/1 Jenny was waitressing in Denver.

waive, *v.*[1] Add: **9. b.** *N. Amer.* Of a sports club: to waive its right to buy (a player from another club in the same league). Also *intr.* Cf. *Waiver 1 d.

1908 *Evening Star* (Washington, D.C.) 26 Feb. 13/2 The Giants have given Mike Lynch his unconditional release, as all clubs have waived. **1970** *Globe & Mail* (Toronto) 26 Sept. 36/2 John Schneider..finally was cut and.. waived through the Canadian Football League. **1979** *Tucson* (Arizona) *Citizen* 20 Sept. 2D/4 Atlanta Hawks—Waived Tim Claxton, guard, and Rickey Brown, forward.

waiver. Add: **1. d.** *spec.* The formal relinquishment by a club in a professional sports (esp. baseball) league of its right to buy the contract of a player from another club in the same league, before he is offered to a club in another league. Freq. *on waivers*. *N. Amer.*

1907 HERRMANN & PULLIAM in *4th Ann. Rep. Nat. Commission* (1908) 99 The Club never had any intention to let the player go;..they only asked for waivers as a bluff. **1946** *Encycl. Brit.* III. 167/1 There is a fixed price in each league that must be paid by the club obtaining a player by this waiver method. The player is said to be sent by club A to club B on waivers. **1951** *Britannica Bk. of Year* 88/2 The Giants claimed pitcher Jim Hearn from the Cardinals on waivers in mid-season. **1972** J. MOSEDALE *Football* v. 75 He was put on waivers at the end of the season. **1978** *N.Y. Times* 29 Mar. B4/4 Oakland.. put Dick Allen, first baseman, on waivers for purpose of giving him unconditional release.

‖ **waka**[1] (wa·ka). *N.Z.* Also 9 **walker, wauka.** [Maori.] A Maori canoe (see quots.).

1807 J. SAVAGE *Some Acct. N.Z.* xi. 77 *Wauka*, a canoe. **1834** E. MARKHAM *N.Z. or Recoll. of It* (MS.) 3 Canoes, or in the Native Mourie Tongue, Walker Mouries, or Native boats. **1841** J. C. BIDWILL *Rambles in N.Z.* (1952) 61 Those [Canoes] with topsides..are called Wa-kaw, or in common pronunciation 'Walkers'. **1845** R. TAYLOR *Jrnl.* 19 June (MS.) III. 222 We had a large waka which just held our large party. **1874** W. M. BAINES *Narr. E. Crewe* 81 'Whaka' is the native name, or rather the native generic term, for all canoes, of which there are many different kinds, as tete, pekatu, kapapa and others. **1921** H. GUTHRIE-SMITH *Tutira* x. 73 A miniature *waka* or canoe..was moved..from place to place. **1936** *Discovery* Jan. 13/2 A Moriori Waka or fishing boat. **1949** P. BUCK *Coming of Maori* (1950) II. vii. 203 River canoes (*waka tiwai*), also used on inland lakes, consisted merely of the dug-out hull. Seagoing canoes (*waka tete*)..were larger.

‖ **waka**[2] (wa·ka). [Jap.] **1.** A form of classic Japanese poetry, lyrical in nature and developed from the ancient traditional ballads.

[**1880** B. H. CHAMBERLAIN *Classical Poetry of Japanese* p. vi, *Kokiñ Wa-Ka Shifu Uchi-Giki* ('Memoranda Concerning the Collection of Japanese Odes Ancient and Modern'), by Kamo-no-Mabuchi.] **1932** B. L. SUZUKI *Nōgaku* 24 The forms sung in the Nō are the *shidai*,.. *rongi*, *waka*, and *kiri*. **1948** *Introd. Class Jap. Lit.* p. iv, In the sphere of *waka* poetry also, the *Kokinshū* anthology ..shows the transition from 'sincerity' to 'sentimentality'. **1968** *Encycl. Brit.* XII. 953/2 The poetic form used—the *waka*, deriving from the earlier folk songs—consists of an alternation of five- and seven-syllable lines, without rhyme, stress, metrical pattern or other technical device.

2. A Japanese poem of thirty-one syllables, a *tanka*.

1938 D. T. SUZUKI *Zen Buddhism* I. iv. 95 The secret documents also contain a number of *waka*, versified epigrams, in regard to the mastery of swordsmanship. **1956** D. KEENE *Anthol. Jap. Lit.* 25 His *waka*—thirty-one syllabled poems—are among the most beautiful and melancholy in the language. **1977** *Times Lit. Suppl.* 15 Apr. 448/4 The most striking qualities of the haiku and the waka.

Wakamba (wakæ·mbă). [Bantu.] = *KAMBA.

1888 *Encycl. Brit.* XXIV. 828/1 [Bantu tongues of eastern group] Wa-Kamba, Wa-Nika, Wa-Pokomo. **1935** [see *SIMBA]. **1937** K. BLIXEN *Out of Afr.* II. 138 The immigrant Somalis..have a moral code... But the unprejudiced Kikuyu, Wakambas, or Kavirondos..judge you not. **1955** *Times* 13 July 6/5 Many Nyanza and Wakamba tribesmen in the Nairobi area had taken Mau Mau oaths in the last 18 months. **1977** H. INNES *Big Footprints* I. i. 24 'A Masai?' I asked... 'No, no. He's of the Kamba people—the Wakamba.'

wake, *v.* Add: **I. 6. b.** (Further examples, chiefly *Anglo-Irish*.)

1829 M. EDGEWORTH *Garry Owen* (1832) vii. 46 You were right, dear, from first to last concerning the poor cratur's dead child; she did not want to have it *waked* at all, for she is not that way—not an Irishwoman at all. **1898** F. P. DUNNE *Mr. Dooley in Peace & War* 188 They waked th' oldest son in small beer, an' was little thought of. **1959** T. H. WHITE *Godstone & Blackymor* 168 Everybody was trying to amuse Charlie Plunkett. Otherwise, why 'wake' him? **1974** D. SEARS *Lark in Clear Air* ix. 117 They waked Holly Dallan in the parlour of the log house where she had been born and reared.

III. 8. c. *to wake snakes*: see also SNAKE *sb.* 2 d in Dict. and Suppl.

wakeaday, wake-a-day (wē[i]·kădē[i]). ?*nonce-wd.* [f. WAKE *v.* + DAY *sb.*, after WORKADAY.] Of life, etc.: such as one wakes up to each day; that is experienced by ordinary people; regular.

1893 G. B. SHAW *Let.* 21 Aug. (1965) I. 401 All these terrible combats..on behalf of Wilde, Pinero, [Frank] Harris &c. &c. &c. belong to Piona and not to the wake-a-day world. **1951** M. MCLUHAN *Mech. Bride* (1967) 97/2 Synthetic gods and goddesses (stars) appear to assume the roles of our wakeaday existence. **1962** —— *Gutenberg Galaxy* 269 The electric puts the mythic or collective dimension of human experience fully into the conscious wake-a-day world.

wakee-wakee, var. of *WAKEY-WAKEY.

waker, *sb.*[1] Add: **2.** Also *waker-upper* (with qualifying adj.). *colloq.*

1971 'E. FENWICK' *Impeccable People* vi. 35 Louise.. stood quiet, blinking... 'Sorry,..I'm a slow waker-upper. Let's go and have the coffee.'

4. Also *waker-upper*. Cf. sense 8 a of the vb. *colloq.*

1935 *Morgantown* (W.Va.) *Post* 7 Jan. 5/1 Henderson.. serves as..waker-upper, and general handy man. **1966** 'D. SHANNON' *With a Vengeance* x. 132 He slept so heavily as to need an 'arrangement' with a waker-upper.

5. (Later example.)

1974 D. SEARS *Lark in Clear Air* xi. 139 But to hear the wakers at their trade you would think the deceased was Giant MacCaskill.

wa·ke-up, *a.* and *sb.* [f. vbl. phr. *to wake up*: see WAKE *v.* 8 a.] **A.** *adj.* † **1.** *wake-up kittle*: prob. the Pacific kittiwake. *Obs.*

1832 B. MORRELL *Narr. Four Voyages Chinese Seas* iii. 216 Whale-birds, wake-up-kittles, man-of-war birds, gulls, and tropic-birds.

2. Special collocations: *wake-up call*, a telephone alarm call for awaking a sleeper, usu. in the morning; *wake-up pill* (slang), a pep-pill; *wake-up service*, a telephone service specializing in wake-up calls.

1976 P. HENISSART *Winter Quarry* xxii. 219 He obtained his key from the night desk clerk and..left a wake-up call for eight a.m. **1979** *Listener* 30 Aug. 274/1 Her addiction to the sleeping pills and the wake-up pills had, on more than one occasion, led to an overdose. **1946** *Birmingham* (Ala.) *News-Age-Herald* 3 Feb. 9A/3 Because his wakeup service requires that he arise early in the morning, Harvey has acquired the habit of remaining up all night. **1969** *New Yorker* 14 June 31/1 A number of young bachelors use us simply as a wake-up service—we're cheaper than Western Union.

B. *sb.* **1.** = *pigeon-woodpecker* s.v. *PIGEON *sb.* 6.

1844 [see *pigeon-woodpecker* s.v. *PIGEON *sb.* 6]. **1897** *Scribner's Mag.* June 773/2 The flicker has a long array of names,..like flicker, clape, wake-up,..derived from his notes.

2. [perh. orig. belonging to AWAKE *a.*] *to be a* (*full*) *wake-up* (also, of several persons, *to be wake-ups*): to be alert or wide awake (*lit.* and *fig.*). Often const. *to*. *Austral.* and *N.Z. slang.*

1930 *Bulletin* (Sydney) 16 Apr. 58/2 'Cripes, you're a full wake-up to that at last, are you?' Snow exclaimed. [**1934** W. S. HOWARD *You're telling Me!* i. 12 Well, I'm awake-up; they don't get nothing out of *me!*] **1943** F. SARGESON in *Penguin New Writing* XVIII. 68 Now I was a wake-up to what was in Maggie's mind. *Ibid.* 69 The pair of us were wake-ups when we heard somebody coming up the stairs. **1946** M. TRIST in Hadgraft & Wilson *Century of Austral. Short Stories* (1963) 214 'Don't you think we ought to have a cow?'..'No, I'm a wake-up to cows', said Dan. 'Saw enough of them when I was a kid.' **1955** D. NILAND *Shiralee* 19 A man should have hauled the cap off his head and chucked ninepence into it just to show him who was a wake-up to who. **1960** N. HILLIARD *Maori Girl* III. x. 248, I never knew till now! Well, I'm a wake-up! **1977** C. MCCULLOUGH *Thorn Birds* ii. 46 When he saw the army lads were a wakeup he was off like a shot.

3. *ellipt.* for *wake-up pill* above. *slang.*

1969 in Howe & Loraine *Environmental Med.* (1973) xvii. 227 Wake-ups and stay-awakes. **1972** *Sunday Sun* (Brisbane) 2 July 14/3 He calls the pep-pills he swallows wake-ups, truck drivers, [etc.].

4. The act of waking a person from sleep, or of being woken from sleep.

1975 *Globe & Mail* (Toronto) 2 June 27/5 Out of that $609 she could easily hire someone to do all the dirty work, such as housekeeping, and leave the easy work such as cooking and wakeups to herself. **1977** M. HERR *Dispatches* (1978) 80 All of my stuff was..ready for the five-o'clock wake-up.

wa·key-wa·key, *sb.*, (*a.*,) and *vbl. phr. colloq.* and *slang* (orig. *Services'*). Also **wakee-wakee, waky-waky.** [Reduplicated arbitrary or childish extension of WAKE *v.* 7 a, b.] **A.** *sb.* = REVEILLE.

1941 C. GRAVES *Thin Blue Line* iii. 46 At the moment all I want to do is to sleep, sleep, sleep. The thought of 'Wakey, wakey' in the morning terrifies me. *a* **1963** J. LUSBY in B. James *Austral. Short Stories* (1963) 221 Three to a tent, chums, wakey-wakey 0430 hours.

2. as *adj.* That awakens or induces wakefulness, esp. as *wakey-wakey pill*.

1946 V. TEMPEST *Near Sun* iii. 29 When the 'wakey-wakey', as the caffeine tablets are called..have been doled out, the crews climb into the W.A.A.F.-driven aircrew buses. **1952** M. TRIPP *Faith is Windsock* xi. 172 Bergen swallowed a couple of wakey-wakey tablets, and Flute did likewise. **1977** *Milestones* Spring 15/2 Rally drivers thought they had found the ideal wakey-wakey pill in amphetamines to help them combat fatigue during marathons. **1979** *Guardian* 4 Aug. 22/9 The last ever Butlin's 'wakey-wakey' call goes out to the snoring chalets.

B. *vbl. phr.* used *imp.* Also **wakey, wakey.** 'Wake up', formerly esp. as a command to soldiers at reveille. Often comb. with phr. *rise and shine* (see *RISE *v.* 3 c). Now freq. *joc.*

1945 *Gen* 30 June 51/2 The sarnt came round yelling wakey-wakey. **1948** PARTRIDGE *Dict. Forces' Slang* 203 *Wakee, wakee!*, orderly Corporal's cry at reveille. 'Wakee, wakee! Rise and shine!' **1953** E. SIMON *Past Masters* I. iii. 32 With a start I woke up... 'Waky-waky,' said Gabrielle. **1968** M. WOODHOUSE *Rock Baby* xxi. 199 'Wakey-wakey,' he said. 'Stand by your beds.' **1973** T. HEALD *Unbecoming Habits* v. 149 'Wakey Wakey, rise and shine,' said Brother Barnabas in an unconvincing demonstration of joviality.

‖ **wakf, waqf** (wǫkf). [Arab. *waqf.*] In Islamic countries, the custom of giving a piece of land, etc., to a religious institution, so that the revenue can be used for pious or charitable purposes; also, the property given in this way.

1836 E. W. LANE *Acct. Manners & Customs of Mod. Egyptians* I. 159 He first imposed a tax (of nearly half the amount of the regular land-tax) upon all land which had become a *wuckf* (or legacy unalienable by law) to any mosque, fountain, public school, &c. **1877** *Encycl. Brit.* VII. 113/2 The regular dervishes live in..khanakahs, or convents, which are endowed with lands or wakf. **1911** *Ibid.* XVII. 413/1 The law and usage of religious foundations in perpetuity (*waqf*, mortmain) became as important in Islam as monastic endowments in mediaeval Europe... It was the only safe way of providing for posterity. **1917** *Chambers's Jrnl.* July 477/1 The partisans are, on the one side, the clergy, who control the *wakfs* (religious endowments). **1976** M. S. HOQUE *Hunger* I. iv. 27 Yes, the Karaitali plot I shall give to Judge by wakf. **1976** S. R. SIMPSON *Land Law & Registration* i. 11 The inalienability of *waqf* land in Islamic countries similarly holds up development.

waking, *vbl. sb.* Add: **5.** Also **waking-time,** the time when one is awake; the moment at which one wakes up.

1959 T. S. ELIOT *Elder Statesman* 5 To my wife, To whom I owe the leaping delight That quickens my senses in our wakingtime. **1971** H. WILSON *Labour Govt.* xv. 263, I asked for a sleeping pill, in case I came to at English waking-time, 4.00 a.m. in Washington.

waky-waky, var. *WAKEY-WAKEY *sb.*, (*a.*,) and *vbl. phr.*

Walach, Wallach. 2. For *rare*$^{-0}$ read *rare*$^{-1}$ and add example.

1794 J. B. S. MORRITT *Let.* 24 June (1914) iii. 51 The languages spoken here are Hungarian, Wallach, Sclavonian and a little German.

Walachian, Wallachian, *sb.* **2.** (Earlier examples.)

1718 M. W. MONTAGU *Let.* 16 Mar. (1965) I. 390 In Pera they speak Turkish, Greek,..Sclavonian, Walachian, German. **1846** BORROW *Zincali* (ed. 4) III 257 The Hungarian Gypsy tongue..contains many words borrowed from the Wallachian.

Walden inversion: see *INVERSION 5 b.

Waldensian, *sb.* (Earlier examples.)

1604, 1832 [see **Albigensian* adj. and sb.]. **1847** J. T. MULLOCK tr. *St. Alphonsus's Hist. Heresies* I. x. 260 Rainer..for seventeen years was a Waldensian.

Waldenström (vā·ldenström). *Path.* The name of Jan *Waldenström* (b. 1906), Swedish biochemist, used in the possessive to designate a disease described by him in 1944 (see *MACROGLOBULINÆMIA).

1961, 1971 [see **macroglobulinæmia*]. **1980** *Daily Tel.* 3 Jan. 1/3 The deposed Shah of Iran is suffering from Waldenstrom's Disease, a rare blood disease which killed President Boumedienne of Algeria a year ago.

waldo, Waldo (wǫ·ldo). Pl. **waldos, waldoes.** [f. the name of *Waldo* F. Jones, the inventor of such gadgets in a science-fiction story by Robert Heinlein (see quot. 1942).] A device for handling or manipulating objects by remote control.

1942 'A. MACDONALD' (R. A. Heinlein) in *Astounding Sci. Fiction* 9 Aug. 16 Even the..humanoid gadgets known universally as 'waldoes'..passed through several generations of development..in Waldo's machine shop before he redesigned them for mass production. The first of them..had been designed to enable Waldo to operate a metal lathe. **1966** I. ASIMOV *Fantastic Voyage* vii. 75 A handling device (a gigantic 'waldo'—so named by the earlier nuclear technicians from a character in a science fiction story of the 1940s). **1978** D. A. STANWOOD *Memory of Eva Ryker* iii. 30 The bathyscaphs are both equipped with remote manipulators—the experts call them 'Waldos'—for working under the extreme pressure.

Waldorf salad (wǫ·ldɔɹf). [Named after the *Waldorf*-Astoria Hotel in New York, where it was first served.] A salad made from apples, walnuts, lettuce and/or celery, dressed with mayonnaise.

1911 LEITER & VAN BERGH *Flower City Cook Bk.* 103 Waldorf salad [recipe follows]. **1930** E. FERBER *Cimarron* 300 She was the first to electrify the ladies of the Twentieth Century Culture Club by serving them Waldorf salad —that abominable mixture of apple cubes, chopped nuts, whipped cream, and mayonnaise. **1979** A. HAILEY *Overload* III. iii. 206 A Waldorf salad, followed by a chicken casserole.

waldrapp (wǫ·ldˌræp). [a. Ger., f. *wald* wood, forest + *rapp* (var. *rappe*, *rabe*) crow: cf. RAVEN *sb.*[1]] The hermit ibis, *Geronticus eremita*, found in parts of North Africa and the Middle East.

1924 W. L. SCLATER *Systema Avium Ethiopicarum* 35 Waldrapp..Morocco, Tunis, and Asia Minor; formerly in Switzerland and other parts of southern Europe. **1964** A. L. THOMSON *New Dict. Birds* 390/1 The Hermit Ibis (or Waldrapp)..is a bird of dry country, feeding largely on beetles and nesting in colonies on cliffs. **1970** *New Scientist* 3 Sept. 457/1 The waldrapp..has a strong, unpleasant odour. **1976** G. DURRELL *Stationary Ark* iv. 81 The Waldrapp..is a medium-sized ibis, with a long curved beak, sombre black plumage.., a bare reddish-coloured face and a strange crest of long feathers on the back of its head.

wale, *sb.*[1] Add: **5.** Also, = *WALING 1.

1886 H. C. SEDDON *Builder's Work* i. 7 When the ground is firm enough to admit of it, deep and narrow trenches..may be secured by horizontal planks or wales, placed opposite each other..and kept apart by struts. **1926** A. E. WYNN *Design & Construction of Formwork* viii. 84 Above 6 ft. high there is always danger of the form twisting..from the impact of the concrete if wales are not used. **1964** R. L. PEURIFOY *Formwork for Concrete Structures* ix. 158 The bottom wale should be placed not more than 8 in. above the bottom of the form.

Waler[2]. Restrict *Anglo-Indian* to sense in Dict. and add: Also **waler. 1.** Also, a type of light Australian horse.

1897 'R. BOLDREWOOD' *My Run Home* xxxiv. 330, 'I can't imagine any thing but the English thoroughbred worthy to be named in the same day with a high-caste Arab.'.. 'I'll show you a Waler to-morrow that may convert you.' **1900** H. LAWSON *Ballad of Cornstalk* in *Coll. Verse* (1967) I. 380 He mounted his waler and rode to the sea (He was sick of the Bush and he longed for a spree). **1945** BAKER *Austral. Lang.* iii. 71 *Waler*, originally a horse exported from New South Wales to India (in modern times, a light type of army horse used in Australia). **1963** *Weekly News* (Auckland, N.Z.) 8 May 38/4 The farm hack is a multi-breed horse—a dash of cob, a little thoroughbred, maybe a touch of the Australian 'waler' whose ancestry lies with Dutch and Spanish strains. **1968** J. KIDDELL *Euloowirree Walkabout* (1970) xiii. 123 Lord, he exulted, but he's a fast horse. A Waler. One of the descendants of the bush-bred stock, the thoroughbreds of the Outback.

2. (With capital initial.) A native of New South Wales (or of Australia generally). *slang.*

1880 J. INGLIS *Our Austral. Cousins* xiii. 159 In the matter of awnings and verandahs the 'Walers' had a grand chance for a bright, cheerful..display. **1924** G. H. A. WILLIS *Royal Navy as I saw It* 270 We left the *Oceana*, which continued her voyage to Australia with the 'Walers' (as the Australian passengers were called). **1949** *Geogr. Mag.* Feb. 373 *Sydneysider* or *Waler*, a resident of New South Wales.

walia (wā·liă). [a. Amharic.] The Ethiopian ibex, *Capra walie*. Also *walia ibex*.

1932 *Nat. Hist.* XXXII. 69/2 The walia lives in a much worse place. **1965** L. BROWN *Ethiopian Episode* II. 45 The Walia Ibex were..the principal object of my expedition to Semien. **1971** *Observer* (Colour Suppl.) 31 Oct. 19/2 In the rugged Simien Mountains, where the few remaining walia dwell, farmers continue to destroy the animal's habitat. *Ibid.* 20/1 (*caption*) Fewer than 150 walia ibexes remain on earth.

Walian (wē·liăn), *sb.* and *a.* [f. *Wale-s* + -IAN.] *South* (or *North*) *Walian*. **A.** *sb.* A native or inhabitant of South (or North) Wales. **B.** *adj.* (Characteristic) of or pertaining to this region.

1894 *Wales* Aug. 170/1 He was a Methodist preacher, though he was a South Walian. **1924** J. O. FRANCIS *Legend of Welsh* 63 The best story I have heard of Welsh-speaking Englishmen was told me..by a South Walian. **1936** *Antiquity* X. 461 Richards was a South Walian. **1968** D. E. ALLEN *British Tastes* iv. 100 The stern Protestant ethos, originally adopted by..a people that then resembled the stern North Walian. **1977** D. JONES *My Friend Dylan Thomas* viii. 98, I thought this was a particularly South Walian expression until I read..*The Lore and Language of Schoolchildren*.

waling. Add: **1.** Also, a long horizontal member used to brace the lining of an excavation or the walls of a form.

1891 T. POTTER *Concrete* (ed. 2) I. v. 157 If the sides are loose it is better to stand some boards against them, lifting or removing the latter..as the concrete is being filled in. This is assuming they are not planked or waled, and stretchers are employed to keep the waling planks in position. **1893** J. P. ALLEN *Practical Building Construction* xxii. 349 Where the ground is looser the poling boards must be placed closer together, perpendicularly, with walings, which are placed horizontally inside them. **1932** [see *SOLDIER *sb.* 6*c]. **1966** C. K. AUSTIN *Formwork to Concrete* (ed. 2) 282 The principle on which this system works, is that of a single form consisting of standard steel panels supported by steel channel walings sliding between soldiers against the concrete face. **1972** V. C. LAUNDER *Foundations* x. 132 Vertical planks or baulks are driven into the ground at the sides of the excavation as it proceeds and held vertical by horizontal timbers called walings, strutted across the trench width.

3. *Basket-making.* (The process of weaving) a band of rods which forms a wale (see WALE *sb.*[1] 6); the wales of a basket.

1912 T. OKEY *Art of Basket-Making* vii. 80 The butts of the waling being pieced in at the front. *Ibid.* xi. 135 The waling of the upsett will be begun at each side. **1949** K. S. WOODS *Rural Crafts of England* III. x. 164 The uprights must now be set very firmly in position by several strong rows of waling. **1964** H. HODGES *Artifacts* x. 146 Where three rods were used simultaneously with a crossing..the weave is referred to as waling. **1983** *Daily Tel.* 20 Sept. 15/5 There is a border of 'waling' at the base of the basket.

walk, *sb.*[1] Add: **I. 1.** *to take a walk*: also, to 'receive one's marching orders', to be dismissed; freq. *imp.* in formulas of impatient dismissal, sometimes in extended form. Also *transf.* Also, to 'walk out' in a labour dispute (*WALK *v.*[1] 12*b). *U.S. slang.*

1871 'MARK TWAIN' *Sketches New & Old* (1875) 248 The first time he opened his mouth and was just going to spread himself, his breath took a walk. **1881** —— in *Century Mag.* Nov. 37 They ring out, 'Oh, dry up!' 'Give us a rest!'..'Oh, take a walk!' **1888** in Farmer *Americanisms* (1889) 550/2 The cash returns were so out of proportion to the sales, that Mr. Berry concluded to make a change and Tascott took a walk. **1937** *Amer. Speech* XII. 4 The so-called Jeffersonian Democrats took a walk from their party allegiance. **1946** *Sun* (Baltimore) 19 Nov. 2 (*caption*) Miners 'take a walk'—Black Diamond mine workers at Monongahela, Pa., are shown waiting for a car after quitting their jobs. **1961** *Lebende Sprachen* VI. 99/2 Go take a long walk off a short pier... Go jump in the lake.

e. *Baseball.* = *base on balls* s.v. *BASE *sb.*[1] 15 c. Cf. *WALK *v.*[1] 5 q.

1905 *Sporting Life* (Philadelphia) 16 Sept. 2/1 Taking the totals, or hits and walks, and such a famine in tallies would seem impossible, but there are the figures. **1948** *Daily Ardmoreite* (Ardmore, Okla.) 21 Mar. 4/6 Rice, on second from a walk and a sacrifice, crossed the home plate on a fly which Charley Gilbert misjudged. **1967** *Boston Sunday Herald* 7 May (TV Mag.) 14/2 Even the worst of ballplayers can still reach first base on a walk and even get to second should the pitcher throw wild. **1979** *Arizona Daily Star* 5 Aug. c 2/3 Dwight Evans, who had been behind 0–2 in the count, drew a two-out walk.

f. = *sponsored walk* s.v. *SPONSORED *ppl. a.* 2.

1971 M. LEE *Dying for Fun* xliv. 213 You ought to get one of the newspapers to sponsor it. Walks and demonstrations and things. **1971** *Guardian* 24 May 11/6 From 1965–69, Oxfam depended on walks for up to £175,000 of its year's £2½ millions budget.

4. e. *to win in a walk*: to win easily and without effort. *U.S. colloq.*

1896 ADE *Artie* xii. 106 'Does he stand a good chance of being elected?' 'That's what keeps me guessin'. Two years ago he win in a walk [etc.].' **1903** A. H. LEWIS *Boss* 138 He won in a walk. **1936** E. S. GARDNER *Case of Sleepwalker's Niece* xiv. 130 The whole thing..gets back to Duncan. If I can break down Duncan's identification I can win the case in a walk.

f. Any dance modelled on or resembling a walk; chiefly as second element of a Comb., as *CAKE-WALK *sb.* 1, *camel-walk* s.v. *CAMEL *sb.* 5, *Lambeth walk* s.v. *LAMBETH 3.

1937 [see *Big Apple* s.v. *BIG *a.* B.2]. **1975** G. HOWELL *In Vogue* 9/2 In return we get syncopated music, and what to do to it—the Baleta..the Twinkle..the Missouri Walk. **1975** *N.Y. Post* 27 Dec. 23 The new Walk..is an anathema to all this talk of returning romanticism, because you do it alone, without touching.

II. 14. Delete ? *Obs.* and add: Now usu., a postman's round.

1908 *Chambers's Jrnl.* Jan. 102/2 On arriving at the office of delivery letters are at once stamped and sorted to the 'walks' of the postmen. **1977** *Times* 12 July 8/4 A complaint by a postwoman..that she had been prevented from..obtaining a particular postal 'walk'.

IV. 20. (sense 1) *walk shorts.*

1965 *Punch* 17 Nov. 745 Then we equipped ourselves for our new surroundings [*sc.* Australia]. My wife..insisted on polished cotton walk shorts for a reluctant me. **1976** *National Observer* (U.S.) 6 Mar. 11/6 (Advt.), Authentic lederhosen style classic walk shorts for men and women. **1984** *Gainesville* (Florida) *Sun* 30 Mar. 8A (Advt.), Choose from white tennis shorts or solid and patterned walk shorts in polyester and cotton blends.

walk, *v.*[1] Add: **II. 5. a.** *to walk about*: also *spec.* of an Aboriginal: cf. *WALKABOUT 1.

1908 E. J. BANFIELD *Confessions of Beachcomber* II. i. 265 This for Johnny Tritton, before alonga Cooktown; now walk about somewhere down here. Might be catch 'em alonga mainland.

g. *to walk in*: also const. *on* (cf. sense 12* c below); also *spec.* to arrive unexpectedly; to enter premises, etc., with unwonted ease; to succeed against all expectations.

1930 N. COWARD *Private Lives* II. 53 What shall we do if they suddenly walk in on us? **1975** COWIE & MACKIN *Oxf. Dict. Current Idiomatic Eng.* I. 356/2 The security is so bad here that anyone could simply walk in and take what he wanted. **1977** P. HILL *Fanatics* 125 If the Christian Democrats put enough candidates up at the next election they'll walk in. **1978** M. DUKE *Death of Dandy Dinmont* iv. 39, I couldn't think of anything else to do. I was almost relieved when Hamilton walked in on me.

h. *to walk out*: of a soldier off duty, to go into town on pass.

1911 [implied in *walking-out order* s.v. *WALKING *vbl. sb.* 1b]. **1955** *Times* 27 July 5/1 In Western Command ..young soldiers are now forbidden to 'walk out' when off duty in plain clothes of unorthodox pattern.

j. (Earlier examples.)

1827 A. MOORE *Let.* in N. E. Eliason *Tarheel Talk* (1956) 303 [He] has requested to let him have the supreme pleasure of walking out with her. I fear the poor little fellow is pretty far gone, if I may judge from the frequency of his visits. **1849** DICKENS *Dav. Copp.* (1850) v. 47 No sweethearts, I b'lieve?..No person walks with her.

n. *to walk off* (an ailment: earlier example); *to walk* (a message or the like) *through*, to take it in person.

1741 RICHARDSON *Pamela* III. xxxvii. 372 'I fear you have sprain'd your Foot—Shall I help you to a Chair?' 'No, no, Sir, I shall walk it off, if I hold by you.' **1981** C. POTOK *Bk. of Lights* (1982) v. 144 'How did the major get that memo so quickly, Roger?' 'I walked it through to his desk.'

o. Also, to haul (a balloon) by walking.

1933 *Sun* (Baltimore) 27 Oct. 7/2 The..passengers disembarked..before the huge dirigible was 'walked' into the hangar. **1938** *Times* 7 Sept. 9/1 He watched a crew 'walk' a balloon out of a shed and connect it to a winch for hoisting.

p. *to walk* (*all*) *over*—(fig.): to treat (a person) with contempt; also, to defeat (an opponent) decisively. *slang.*

1851 MRS. STOWE in *National Era* 25 Sept. 1/5 St. Clare wouldn't raise his hand if every one of them walked over him. **1884** 'MARK TWAIN' *Huck. Finn* xxii. 219 In the North he lets anybody walk over him that wants to, and goes home and prays for a humble spirit to bear it. **1909** R. E. KNOWLES *Attic Guest* viii. 105 They won't let a pack of negroes walk all over 'em. **1951** N. MITFORD *Blessing* I. vi. 65 A woman who lets her husband do exactly as he likes..lets him walk over her, in fact, would never lose him. **1976** E. DUNPHY *Only a Game?* i. 34 We played QPR in a public practice game at our place today. And won easily. We walked all over them.

q. *Baseball.* Of a batter: to secure a base on balls. Cf. *WALK *sb.*[1] 1 e.

1867 *Ball Players' Chron.* 14 Nov. 2/4 Goodrich walked to the first on called balls. **1895** *N.Y. Press* 5 July 6/1 The champions harvested a pair of tallies in the second inning. Clarke did not get them over for Kelly, and Joe 'walked'. **1948** *Chicago Tribune* 7 Mar. II. 1/4 Baker walked, filling the bases. **1979** *Arizona Daily Star* 5 Aug. c-2/5 Alfredo Griffin singled and Bob Bailor walked to start the eighth-inning burst against Rich Wortham, II-II.

r. *to walk on*: (of a theatrical performer) to go on stage with few if any lines to say.

1893 H. G. MCCLELLAND *Jack & Beanstalk* 35 She used to walk on in the comic scenes. **1913** *Confessions of Dancing Girl* vii. 127, I obtained an engagement to 'walk on' in a musical comedy... I had no lines and no part. **1920** [see *SUPER *v.* 1]. **1959** P. BULL *I know Face* i. 17 He had engaged a lot of art school students to what's known as 'walk-on' in the production.

s. *walk good* (imp.): farewell, good luck. *Caribbean.*

1929 M. W. BECKWITH *Black Roadways* xiii. 199 'Walk good, me love,' says one to another setting out on a journey. **1953** R. MAIS *Hills were Joyful Together* II. i. 147 You going further, walk good then; walk good, hear? **1979** J. BERRY *Fractured Circles* 58 Walk good, Leela, chile.

t. *to walk away from* ——: to leave the scene of (an accident or the like) on one's feet, instead of being carried on a stretcher. Cf. *walking wounded* s.v. *WALKING *ppl. a.* 3 d. Also *transf.*

1956 W. A. HEFLIN *U.S. Air Force Dict.* 561/1 *To walk away from an airplane crash or accident*, to survive an accident unhurt or without serious injury. **1966** M. WOODHOUSE *Tree Frog* vi. 50, I had a..cut..but that was all. Walking away from it, they call it. **1980** J. WAINWRIGHT *Eye of Beholder* 130 'Anybody walk away from it?'..'No. One dead, one smashed up.' **1984** *Times* 19 Apr. 19/6 The provisions for bad and doubtful debts is increased..and Mr Pattullo stated confidently 'there is no international or domestic loan that we could not walk away from. It might cause us a red face but it would not harm the bank.'

6. c. (Later example.)

1841 S. S. ARNOLD *Diary* 5 Jan. in *Proc. Vermont Hist. Soc.* (1940) VIII. 149 It was a friendly interview; but she said that she could not walk with the Ch[urc]h, and wished to be out.

7. a. *to walk through one's part* (later example); also simply *to walk through*, and *fig.*

1857 C. M. YONGE *Dynevor Terrace* I. xii. 195 Her grave, pensive character only attained to walking through her part [in society]. **1899** C. SCOTT *Drama of Yesterday & To-Day* II. xiv. 442 Often when she is tired to death,.. her strength fails her. She walks through the part, as it is called. **1922** MRS. P. CAMPBELL *Let.* 11 June in *B. Shaw & Mrs. Campbell* (1952) 256, I would like you to come and see *Hedda Gabler*—it would be nice to hear all the abominable things you might say. Some say I 'walk through'.

c. *to walk over* (further example of absol. use); also *to walk over* (an opponent), to be declared the winner of a contest because of the opponent's failure to compete; *to walk away with*, to win (a prize), steal (a show), with ease; *to walk home*, to win a contest with ease.

1903 WODEHOUSE *Prefect's Uncle* ix. 136 If you'd been there to bowl we should have walked over. **1932** *Sun* (Baltimore) 21 Dec. 12/1 Jack Biener 'Walks' Home... Jack Biener, favorite at $5 for $2, simply spreadeagled the field and won in a common canter by eight lengths. **1951** N. COWARD *Star Quality* 139 It had been the.. play's provincial try-out..and..Leonora had unquestionably walked away with the show. **1958** *Times* 11 Aug. 2/7 Treorchy—a magnificent choir—walked away with the prize for big choirs. **1973** *Times* 31 July 9/8 Major J. D. E. Edwards beat Driver D. A. Beck, 6–1, 7–5; Major P. K. Sharp walked over Captain J. B. Merritt.

f. Proverbial phrase: *to walk before one can run* (and varr.), to understand elementary points before proceeding to anything more difficult; cf. CREEP *v.* 1 b. Also *to run before one can walk*.

1762 [in Dict., sense 7 a]. **1794** G. Washington *Let.* 20 July in *Writings* (1940) XXXIII. 438 We must walk as other countries have done before we can run. **1876** J. Platt *Business* 124 We must learn and be strong enough to walk before we can run. **1927** *Melody Maker* Sept. 923/1 Beginners..commence on their instruments to dabble in so-called 'hot' choruses... They run before they can walk, for, jumping on to what they believe to be 'hot' style, they attempt to cut out all the essential months of study. **1973** *Times* 17 Apr. (Liberia Suppl.) p. ii/5 He does not want Liberia to run before she can walk. **1980** K. Amis *Russian Hide & Seek* iv. 49 At the moment we can't leave it to the English to do anything. We must learn to walk before we can run. **1984** *New Yorker* 11 June 31/1 'We can't turn you into an actor, but don't turn your back on what we have to offer.' What they meant, of course, was that you've got to learn to walk before you try to run.

g. *Jazz.* Of a bass player: to play a walking bass (see *walking *ppl. a.* 9). Also said of the beat.

1951 L. Hughes *Montage of Dream Deferred* 12 Down in the bass That steady beat Walking walking walking Like marching feet. **1952** *Mademoiselle* Dec. 118 And that's the basic jazz beat, that walking beat. Up here in the north all the jazzmen are playing too fast or too slow —nobody walks. **1956** [see *string bass* s.v. *string *sb.* 32]. **1970** *New Yorker* 23 May 88/2 Then Hall soloed, while Gomez 'walked' behind him.

8. a. Also, of a batsman in *Cricket*, to walk towards the pavilion without waiting for the umpire to give him out; also with *out*.

1960 J. Fingleton *Four Chukkas to Australia* v. 48 Three runs later..Graveney should have walked but O'Neill dropped him at third slip. **1964** D. Sheppard *Parson's Pitch* vi. 107, I never saw him not walk out immediately he was caught at the wicket. He never waited for the umpire's decision. **1973** *Advocate-News* (Barbados) 11 Dec. 14/2 Brian Close, captain of the Robins XI, said: 'A batsman who knows he is out should walk. That is the way we play the game.'

b. Restrict † *Obs.* to senses in Dict. In mod. *colloq.* use said of objects presumed borrowed or stolen.

1898 J. D. Brayshaw *Slum Silhouettes* 125 A sack o' taters, or a sieve o' cherries sometimes goes awalkin' if yer don't keep yer eyes skinned. **1978** A. Melville-Ross *Blindfold* xiv. 87 'Got much theft?' 'Lord yes, but only the sort of stuff you'd expect to "walk" anyway.'

c. *to walk off with* (earlier example).

1727 M. W. Montagu *Let.* 23 June (1966) II. 78 All the little money they had..they put into the hands of a rogueish Broker who has fairly walk'd off with it.

d. *to walk away from*: to fail to deal with (something); to refuse to become involved with; also *to walk away* simply.

1963 *Life* 8 Feb. 4/1 The Kennedy proposals walk away from most of the tax reform problems. **1973** P. O'Donnell *Silver Mistress* iii. 48 'Why look for trouble?' ..Something comes along, and you just can't turn round and walk away from it.' **1978** S. Sheldon *Bloodline* xx. 237 Roffe and Sons needs an experienced president, Elizabeth... For your own sake, as well as everyone else's, I would like to see you walk away from this. **1981** *Times* 7 Dec. 13/3 Libya and Nigeria started the year trying to maintain prices at a wide premium over the marker, but instead saw buyers walk away. **1983** *Times* 6 May 15/4 No parent which itself took deposits..could expect to walk away from a subsidiary in trouble without risking a loss of confidence on the part of its own depositors.

e. = sense 12* b below.

1976 *National Observer* (U.S.) 14 Aug. 16/3 Our baby sitter founded the Sitters' Union. They get TV, cookies, and root beer, or they walk. *Ibid.* 28 Aug. 16/1 The sentry in the lobby was a representative of Universal Pictures. His mission: to keep an anxious eye out for 'walkers' and try, if he could, to find out why they walked, since there was still time to do some patching on the film. **1978** S. Brill *Teamsters* v. 180 Carey called a strike, and all four thousand of his UPS members walked. **1983** W. F. Nolan *Hammett, Life at Edge* i. 6 He would not lie to keep a job. And he walked.

11. a. Also *to walk guard*.

1930 F. A. Pottle *Stretchers* 51 In France we always wore large automatics when we walked guard.

12. f. To get *into* an awkward situation as a result of one's own unwariness.

1911 G. B. Shaw *Doctor's Dilemma* III. 60 *Ridgeon*: I don't so much mind your borrowing £10 from one of my guests and £20 from the other—*Walpole*: I walked into it, you know. I offered it. **1942** J. Sweeney in Murdoch & Drake-Brockman *Austral. Short Stories* (1951) 384 No sooner does the gong go for the third than Irish walks into a haymaker. **1978** M. Birmingham *Sleep in Ditch* 188, I had walked into this with my eyes wide open. No one could taunt me with being always right.

12*. walk out. a. To leave a gathering or place without warning, esp. in protest or disapproval; also *fig.* Const. *on.* orig. *Theat.*

1840 W. C. Macready *Diary* 19 Feb. (1912) II. 45 Very much disgusted and irritated by Mr Elton walking out in the last scene. **1897** *Daily Tel.* 24 Feb. 10/3 New York did not take kindly to his new play... I am delighted to find, on the assurance of the author, that though New York 'walked out', Washington 'walked in' and received it warmly. **1936** H. G. Wells *Anat. of Frustration* vi. 55 Suicide..may be represented very attractively as a proud and passionate refusal to drink the cup to the dregs. You 'walk out' as they say in the film world. **1937** M. Levin in A. Cooke *Garbo & Night Watchmen* 124, I rarely walk out on a picture, and never want to walk out on a simple programme picture. **1948** W. Charvat in R. Spiller et al. *Lit. Hist. U.S.* I. xxxi. 525 When a 'stout Illinoian' walked out on his lectures, he reflected that 'the people are always right'. **1969** H. Perkin *Key Profession* iii. 103 The A.U.T. delegates to the International Conference walked out the day before Hitler arrived.

b. *spec.* Of an employee: to leave his place of work at short notice, as a form of industrial action. orig. *U.S.*

1894 W. H. Carwardine *Pullman Strike* iv. 37 The men passed the word from one to another to 'walk out', which they did orderly and deliberately. **1937** *Irish Press* 11 Feb. 1/2 (*caption*) Photo shows the nursing and boiler house staffs 'walking out'. **1951** E. Paul *Springtime in Paris* v. 95 Gas workers were about to walk out, and hamstring home cooking to a certain extent. **1979** *Daily Tel.* 27 Nov. 2/2 Last night one of the two lighting and sound engineering crews on BBC-1's 'Nationwide' walked out shortly before the programme was due to go on the air.

c. To desert a partner, esp. a spouse; to withdraw from an agreed arrangement. Const. *on* (cf. sense 5 g above). orig. *U.S.*

1896 *Typographical Jrnl.* (Indianapolis) IX. 232 The Review, Republican daily, 'walked out' on the St. Louis platform. **1921** Wodehouse *Indiscretions of Archie* xii. 127 'Has she walked out on you?' 'Left us flat!' **1937** *Sunday Times* 2 May 7/4 Father Donelly..is a fairy godfather to her after she has walked out on her guardians. **1953** *Sun* (Baltimore) (B ed.) 31 Aug. 14/3 The Southern Conference digs in Tuesday for its first football practice since seven of its greatest powers walked out to form a league of their own. **1962** *New Statesman* 7 Dec. 829/1 What surprises is the famous malleability of the two women: did neither one dream of walking out? **1973** 'E. Peters' *City of Gold & Shadows* i. 6 My father walked out on my mother when I was seven.

III. 20*. To win easily. Cf. sense 7 c in Dict. and Suppl. *slang.*

1937 Partridge *Dict. Slang* 935/2 *Walk*, to win easily: Public Schools' coll.: from ca. 1895. [*Refers to quot.* 1903 *in sense* 7 c *above.*] **1976** *Times* 12 Feb. 10/2, I went to the British [championship] thinking I'd walk it... This was a mistake... It was a close shave.

IV. 21. Also *to walk hots* (see quots.).

1958 *Washington Post* 25 Sept. D-4/1 Each got his start walking hots (leading horses to cool them out following a race or a workout). **1976** *New Yorker* 29 Mar. 109/2 He got an after-school job at a ranch, mucking out stalls and 'walking hots', as the chore of cooling out horses who have just worked or raced is called.

22. c. *Baseball.* Of a pitcher: to give (a batter) a base on balls.

1913 *Chicago Record-Herald* 20 Mar. 10/5 Lange walked Kores in the hostile part, then disposed of the next pair on easy infield flies. **1938** *Chicago Tribune* 5 Apr. 19/2 Dobernic walked three batsmen in a row. **1952** B. Malamud *Natural* 78 With two out Schultz weakened, walking one man and handing the next a good enough throw to hit for a sharp single. **1976** *National Observer* (U.S.) 16 Oct., Our pitcher had walked three men in a row and I was invited to take the mound.

24. d. To swing (a gun) so as to describe a straight line on the target with successive hits.

1944 *Sun* (Baltimore) 15 June 2/5, I..aimed for his groin and walked my tommy gun right up his middle and blew him 90 feet away. **1969** I. Kemp *Brit. G.I. in Vietnam* xi. 187 'Charlie' really seemed to be walking that mortar up behind me; he was right on target with his shots.

V. 25. walk-away: also *transf.* and as *adj.*; **walk-back** *U.S. slang*, a rear apartment; **walk-march** *v.*, to march at a walking pace; of cavalry, to proceed at the walk; also as *sb.*

1926 *Amer. Mercury* Dec. 465/2 It [*sc. Variety*] has developed..the following new terms for a [Broadway] success: 'zowied 'em',..'walk-away hit' and 'clicked heavy'. **1958** *Time* (Atlantic ed.) 6 Oct. 16 Turning from a Democratic walkaway into a neck-and-neck sprint. **1978** *Detroit Free Press* 5 Mar. C 4/1 For UCLA, the walkaway winner of the Pac-8 title, the game against U-M will be a final tuneup before going into the NCAA tournament. **1945** L. Shelly *Jive Talk Dict.* 35 *Walk back*, rear apartment. **1973** 'H. Howard' *Highway to Murder* vii. 80 One-o-four Platt Street was a rooming house... The Royales lived in a walk-back at the rear of the lobby. [**1851** *Regulations for Cavalry* 190 Commanding Officer, repeated by Squadron Leaders, '*Walk, Trot*, or *Gallop March*.'] **1904** *Mounted Infantry Training* (Provisional, H.M. Army) iv. 36 The word 'Walk' or 'Trot' will in every case precede the word 'March' when the men are mounted... The word on which they move should be drawn out and rolled thus:—'Walk—M-a-r-r-c-h', and when the pace is to be increased to a trot—'T-r-r-o-t'. **1909** *Mounted Infantry Training* (War Office) iii. 36 On the command, '*Walk—March*'..the whole company moves off..general alignment and cohesion..being secured by the section leaders riding on the same alignment, and at the proper intervals. **1926** T. E. Lawrence *Seven Pillars* (1935) ix. ci. 553 Buxton a moment later called 'Walk-March!' to his men, and the four-hundred camels..started off for Jefer. **1942** C. Barrett *On Wallaby* iv. 88 We flushed many birds as we walk-marched among rocks and stones. *a* **1977** D. Wheatley *Officer & Temp. Gentleman* (1978) xiii. 157 We had to move at a sedate walk-march.

walkable, *a.* **c.** For (*nonce-use*) read *rare* and add later example.

1943 G. G. Coulton *Fourscore Years* ii. 10 For about two years..I was the youngest walkable child.

walkabout (wǭ·kăbaut). [Pidgin Eng., f. Walk *v.*[1] + About *adv.*] **1.** *Austral.* A periodic migration by a westernized Aboriginal into the bush. Often quasi-*advb.* in phr. *to go walkabout.* Also *transf.*

[**1828** *Sydney Gaz.* 2 Jan. 3 When the executioner had adjusted the rope, and was about to pull the cap over his eyes..he said, in a tone of deep feeling,..'Bail more walk about,' meaning that his wanderings were all over.] **1908** Mrs. A. Gunn *We of Never-Never* 218 The day after that was filled in with preparations for a walk-about, and the next again found us camped at Bitter Springs. **1918** C. S. Stow (*title*) The walkabouts of Wur-run-Nah. **1927** M. M. Bennett *Christison* xxv. 227 The manager would give them [*sc.* blackfellows] rations and let them..go off for a month's 'walkabout', picnicking, and fishing at favourite waterholes. **1933** *Bulletin* (Sydney) 9 Aug. 35/3 An old bush abo., then on the 'walk-about'. **1938** X. Herbert *Capricornia* (1939) xxii. 330 Wha' name—you go walkabout? **1940** F. D. Davison in 'B. James' *Austral. Short Stories* (1963) 63 [Heifers] standing motionless..at the end of one of those walk-abouts that cattle running in wild country periodically make. **1950** 'N. Shute' *Town like Alice* iii. 82 These bloody boongs, they're always going walkabout. **1958** L. van der Post *Lost World Kalahari* ix. 203 Even the Bushman born on these few remote European farms.. rediscovers the need for a long 'walk-about' in the vast desert around him. **1973** P. O'Donnell *Silver Mistress* i. 15, I like to revert to my childhood ways now and again. Like an aborigine going walk-about. **1984** *Times* 8 Oct. 10/6 First of all the players go walkabout. Then they all return to the stage and sit down. **1985** *Truck & Driver* June 38/2 (*caption*) The crowds get up close to the racing trucks during the Supergrid walkabout.

2. a. A protracted walk or journey, or one that takes in a number of places.

1946 'M. Innes' *From London Far* I. vii. 58, I proposed a walkabout. We were to stroll through Auld Reekie's dusk together. **1956** *Richmond* (Va.) *Times-Dispatch* 17 May 22 (*heading*) End of a six month walk-about [*sc.* a global tour]. **1974** 'G. Black' *Golden Cockatrice* i. 9, I've been doing a year's exchange teaching in Hong Kong... These academic walkabouts fascinate me.

b. *spec.* An informal stroll through the crowd by a member of the Royal Family or other public figure.

1970 *Daily Tel.* 31 Mar. 15/3 The Queen realised she was on to a winner with her New Zealand 'walkabouts'. **1974** *Listener* 28 Feb. 263/1 Mr Heath's..electioneering by set speech and walkabout tour. **1980** *Church Times* 25 Apr. 2/5 On Saturday the Bishop met local people during a walkabout in the market. **1984** *Listener* 15 Mar. 20/1, I was engaged in a walkabout during last year's Darlington by-election.

walkathon (wǭ·kăþǫn). *colloq.* (orig. and chiefly *U.S.*). [f. Walk(ing *vbl. sb.*[1] + *-athon.] A long-distance or protracted walk; orig. a competitive one, now esp. one undertaken to raise money for charity.

1932 *Kansas City* (Missouri) *Times* 20 Feb. 26 Sure a hick town is a place where they have enough superhicks to put on a walkathon. **1933** *Sun* (Baltimore) 4 Nov. 6/6 Next Thursday a number of Hagerstowners will enter upon an endurance contest different from any ever tried here before—a walking marathon, or a 'walkathon', as the promoters insist on calling it. The contestants walk forty-five minutes and rest fifteen for as long as they hold out. **1951** M. Kennedy *Lucy Carmichael* v. i. 239 If I had that hall I'd put on a Walkathon... In California..after two or three weeks, when there's only a few couples left in, they chain them, see? So if the girl faints, the feller can't push her under the ropes. **1957** *Daily Mail* 27 Dec. 4/3 If Barber gets to the bottom of the world by plane, why on earth are the other boys—the Hillary-Fuchs expeditions—walking?.. I gather that the walkathon idea is the British contribution to the Geophysical Year. **1963** *Weekly News* (Auckland) 31 July 3/4 (*caption*) Representatives of harriers, scouts, bible classes and old soldiers taking part in the recent 50-mile 'walkathon' in aid of the Murray Halberg Trust for Crippled Children. **1976** *Indian Express* 8 June, Walkathon. Indian athlete Harbans Singh, 28, walked non-stop for 144 hours in the town of Jalalabad. **1979** *Honolulu Advertiser* 8 Jan. B-2/2 Manned booths for various charitable walk-a-thons or walked themselves.

walker, *sb.*[1] Add: **1. c.** *walker-on*: = *walk-on *sb.* 1 b.

1897 G. B. Shaw *Our Theatres in Nineties* (1932) III. 217 A good deal of the technique acquired by American actors no doubt makes one almost long for the fatuous complacency of the British 'walker-on'. **1936** N. Streatfeild *Ballet Shoes* xiv. 212 Pauline and Petrova were, of course, principals, and as such separated from the ballet and walkers-on. **1948** [see *stand-in 2 a].

d. A person who takes dogs for walks as an occupation; also, one who rears puppies at home for a time before they are returned to kennels.

1930 C. Frederick et al. *Foxhunting* v. 61 The training of..'morale' begins from the day when the puppy returns to kennels from its walker. **1967** C. G. E. Wimhurst *Bk. Working Dogs* vii. 45 The day will come when the walker will have to return his charge to the Kennel. **1977** Hooker & Butterworth *M*A*S*H goes to Moscow* (1979) vii. 80 A dog walker..is a person..who earns his living by collecting a dozen or so dogs and taking them all for a walk at once. **1984** *Leicester Mercury* 28 June 25/2 Until they are 12 months old, the hound puppies are in the charge of the walkers who keep them at their homes.

10. a. Short for *baby-walker* s.v. *baby *sb.* B. 2.

1934 in Webster. **1971** *E. Afr. Standard* (Nairobi) 13 Apr. 14/1 (Advt.), Children's bicycles, walkers, car-seats and play-pens at Cycle Mart and Exchange Ltd.

b. = *walking frame* s.v. *WALKING *vbl. sb.* 4 b.

1941 F. H. KRUSEN *Physical Medicine* xvi. 648 Various types of walkers..will give the patient firm support through the arms and axillae when he is taking his first hesitant steps. **1971** *Catholic Worker* May 2/3 She is living at Loretto Home for the Aged..and must use a walker since she broke her hip some time ago. **1980** U. CURTISS *Poisoned Orchard* ii. 12 She's in her seventies *and* in a walker.

Walker^{2} (wǭ·kəɹ). The name of John W. *Walker* (b. 1802) used *absol.* and *attrib.* to designate an American fox-hound, usually black, white, and tan, belonging to a strain originally developed by the Walker family.

1904 J. A. GRAHAM *Sporting Dogs* ix. 134 The Walkers are chiefly bred by men in Kentucky of that name and have been shipped to nearly every part of America where foxes are found. *Ibid.* 135 The Walker hounds are fast. **1940** W. FAULKNER *Hamlet* 58 A man named Houston, heeled by a magnificent grave blue-ticked Walker hound, led a horse up to the blacksmith shop. **1964** J. GRIFFEN *Hunting Dogs Amer.* v. 195 The Walker Hound is the most popular strain of Foxhound in America today. **1980** *Hunting Ann. 1981* 17/1 Caswell has his two best strike hounds in place: Dan is a registered Walker and a fighter; his white-brown-and-black coat is creased here and there with old scars left by the claws and teeth of a bear.

walkie-lookie (wǭ:kiˌlu·ki). *colloq.* [f. LOOK *v.*, after *walkie-talkie*.] = *PEEPIE-CREEPIE.

1946 *Sci. News Let.* 30 Mar. 195 'Walkie-lookie', the picture equivalent of the small remote voice instrument known as 'walkie-talkie', will come from the 'block' system's light-weight, easily portable television camera. **1952**, etc. [see *PEEPIE-CREEPIE].

walkies (wǭ·kiz), *sb. pl. colloq.* [f. WALK *sb.*^{1} + -IE.] A childish or jocular form of *walk* used chiefly with reference to dogs. Also as quasi-*advb.* in phr. *to go walkies.*

[**1932** *Amer. Speech* VII. 242 [Jazz jargon.] Thus, we have the line 'I Prefer the Walkies', with its last word coined to rhyme with 'talkies'. **1938** A. WOOLLCOTT *Let.* 28 Jan. (1946) 163 There are now—God help me!—four black dogs to go walkee with you.] **1939** A. THIRKELL *Before Lunch* iv. 93 'Master's stick for walkies,' said Mr. Middleton. 'Fetch stick for walkies.' **1960** J. STROUD *Shorn Lamb* x. 119, I bring Gorm along here sometimes, for his walkies. **1979** T. BARLING *Olympic Sleeper* x. 118 That's one stray piece of information... It's gone walkies some-damned-where. **1981** *Sunday Express* (Colour Suppl.) 26 Apr. 13/1 Before long the subject of walkies comes up. People are obsessed, Mrs Woodhouse says, with taking dogs out for walks.

walkie-talkie (wǭ:kiˌtǭ·ki). Also **walky-talky.** [f. WALK *v.*^{1} + TALK *v.* + -IE.] **1.** A small radio transmitter and receiver that can be carried on the person to provide two-way communication as one walks.

1939 *Sun* (Balimore) 4 Oct. 24/3 'Walkie-talkie' is the Army Signal Corps' way of speaking of unit S.C.R. 195—a recently developed radio sending and receiving set so small it is carried on the back and one talks while one walks. **1944** *Life* 3 July 12/1 Above the noise of hundreds of bombs..his voice barked through the walkie-talkie. **1945** *China at War* May 38/2 Walkie-talkie sets also are used. **1955** G. BAND *Road to Rakaposhi* xvi. 178 If we had taken portable 'walky-talky' sets there would have been no problem. **1970** *Timber Traders Jrnl.* 21 Mar. 53/3 Senior members of the yard staff have walkie-talkie radio sets with which they maintain communication with the sideloader operators. **1973** C. BONINGTON *Next Horizon* xii. 175 We talked over the problem, on the walky-talky. **1979** *Arizona Daily Star* 5 Aug. A 12/1 Secret Service agents with walkie-talkies paced the auditorium's mezzanine and surrounding grounds.

2. A doll that can be made to walk and talk. Freq. *attrib.* or as *adj.*

1952 *Landfall* VI. 82 Everything he does simply runs true to type like the tricks of a walkie-talkie doll. **1957** J. FRAME *Owls do Cry* II. xxviii. 137, I shall buy her..a sleeping doll, a walkie-talkie that cries and walks. **1958** N. MARSH *Singing in Shrouds* (1959) vi. 107 Las Palmas is known to tourists for its walkie-talkie dolls. **1961** J. WAYNE *Day Ceiling fell Down* vii. 72, I thought it was a proper big doll you'd lost... Like one of them walkie-talkies.

walk-in (wǭ·kˌin), *a.* and *sb.* [f. WALK *v.*^{1} + IN *adv.*] **A.** *adj.* **1.** Pertaining to or designating a person who walks into premises casually or without an appointment; *spec.* applied to (*a*) a thief who walks in rather than breaks in; (*b*) a person who offers his services to a foreign power unsolicited, as by walking into its embassy or consulate.

1928 *Daily Express* 6 Oct. 11/2 A criminal of the type described by the police as the 'walk-in-thief', who, if he encounters anyone, slides gently from the house, with a plausible excuse. **1962** *John o' London's* 25 Jan. 82/3 A housebreaker by day is a walk-in man. **1976** *Billings* (Montana) *Gaz.* 1 July, They will be on duty for walk-in and other services from 10.00 a.m. to midnight daily.. said the executive director of the hospital. **1978** D. BLOODWORTH *Crosstalk* x. 84 In March we got ourselves a walk-in defector from China. **1979** *United States 1980/81* (Penguin Travel Guides) 45 In larger cities, many hospitals have walk-in clinics designed to serve people who do not really need an emergency service, but who have no place to go for immediate medical attention.

2. a. Of a storage area: large enough to walk into.

1943 *Pioneering in Food Preservation* (New Dominion Ser. No. 37), A small walk-in refrigeration plant for curing meat. **1960** *Farmer & Stockbreeder* 19 Jan. 118/1 (Advt.), Makers of walk-in incubators. **1966** T. PYNCHON *Crying of Lot 49* ii. 36 Oedipa skipped into the bathroom, which happened also to have a walk-in closet. **1976** *Evening Post* (Nottingham) 15 Dec. 17/1 (Advt.), Large fitted kitchen, walk-in larder. **1982** A. MATHER *Impetuous Masquerade* vii. 105 A matching chest and fitted walk-in closets.

b. Of a cinema, etc.: entered on foot, in contrast to a drive-in. *N. Amer.*

1968 *Amer. Speech* XLIII. 157 He recognized..a desire for something more than the ubiquitous..drive-in and directed me to a walk-in restaurant a few blocks away. **1973** *Daily Colonist* (Victoria, B.C.) 3 Nov. 2/1 We can't even go to a walk-in movie because he falls asleep and snores so loud it is embarrassing. So we usually go to drive-ins where he can sleep peacefully.

c. Of a room: entered directly from a specified area rather than through an intervening passage.

1967 *Coast to Coast 1965–6* 160 Back left of the bar was a row of walk-in walk-out bedrooms surrounded by a veranda. **1971** D. E. WESTLAKE *I gave at Office* (1972) 75 A narrow walk-in kitchen was off the living room through a doorway in the short wall opposite the window.

B. *sb.* **1.** A walk-in closet or cold-storage room (see sense A. 2 a above).

1946 *Daily Progress* (Charlottesville, Va.) 21 Mar. 15/2 Deep Freeze and Frozen Food Storage Walk-In Refrigerators... Down payment required as all walk-ins are custom built to customers' own specifications. **1970** 'E. QUEEN' *Last Woman* III. 160 His wardrobe closet was a roomy walk-in.

2. A walk-in defector (see sense A. 1 above).

1975 P. AGEE *Inside Company* I. 59 The first type is known as the 'walk-in'. The walk-in is a member of the party who..decides to offer his services to the U.S. government. He makes his initial contact..by walking into the U.S. Embassy or Consulate. **1980** E. BEHR *Getting Even* ii. 23 The only really satisfactory defectors were walk-ins, as they were known in the trade.

walking, *vbl. sb.*^{1} Add: **1.** *walking on* (or *with*) *two legs*: in modern China, the use of small-scale, local methods in production and education, as well as large-scale or capital-intensive ones; also *attrib.*

1962 E. SNOW *Other Side of River* (1963) xxviii. 209 'Walking on two legs' in 1958 meant starting tens of thousands of small brick blast furnaces or 'back-yard' hearths. **1964** KANG CHAO in D. J. Dwyer *China Now* (1974) xiii. 252 Another salient feature of the Great Leap movement was a greater emphasis on indigenous methods of production and labour-intensive investment projects. This policy, officially called 'walking with two legs', represented a sharp departure from previous development strategy which had stressed only modern production techniques and large-scale investment projects. **1971** G. P. JAN in S. E. Fraser *Educ. & Communism in China* I. 141 Technical training for adults in the commune schools, a mixture of modern and native methods, was referred to as the policy of 'walking on two legs'. **1977** *China Now* June 4/1 Agricultural machinery for production (walking-on-two-legs tractors, tractors, bulldozers, pumps, harvesters, etc.).

b. *walking in, -on* (in quots. *attrib.*), *-out* (later *attrib.* example), *together.*

1857 C. M. YONGE *Dynevor Terrace* I. xix. 309 Their 'walking together' was recognised. **1911** *Encycl. Brit.* XXVII. 586/2 Undress Uniforms.—In 'walking-out' order most troops wear the tunic. **1931** E. O'NEILL *Homecoming* I, in *Mourning becomes Electra* (1932) 40 Hope you don't mind my walking in on you without ceremony. **1948** *Sporting Mirror* 21 May 5/2 At one time he wanted to be an actor and was offered a walking-on part for 'Cavalcade'. **1948** *Jrnl. R. United Service Inst.* XCIII. 470 To encourage recruiting and to make Army service more popular it would certainly seem very necessary to have a smart Walking-out dress. **1982** P. D. JAMES *Skull beneath Skin* vii. 67 She would have had at least a walking-on part in all the plays.

g. Delete †*Obs.* and add later (? *dial.*) examples.

1892 C. M. YONGE *Old Woman's Outlook* 100 The attraction of 'walking' and the gala day were lacking. **1939** F. THOMPSON *Lark Rise* xv. 269 At the club walkings there were brass bands and processions of all the club members.

4. a. *walking boot* (earlier example), *dress* (earlier and later examples), *shorts, suit, tour* (earlier example); also used to designate farm implements which are operated by someone walking behind or alongside, as *walking cultivator, plough.*

1854 M. S. CUMMINS *Lamplighter* xxx. 217 To change her slippers for thick walking-boots occupied a few minutes only. **1869** *Rep. Comm. Agric. 1868* (U.S. Dept. Agric.) 417 Field No. 3..[was] cultivated but once, when about a foot high, with a five-toothed walking cultivator. **1753** G. WASHINGTON *Diary* 23 Dec. (1925) I. 63, I put myself in an Indian walking dress. *c* **1792** JANE AUSTEN *Catharine* in *Minor Wks.* (1954) 211 She sends me a long account of the new Regency walking dress Lady Susan has given her. **1909** H. G. WELLS *Ann Veronica* iii. 72 She was in one of her old walking-dresses. **1868** *Rep. Iowa State Agric. Soc. 1867* 161 [The] ground [is] plowed and harrowed,..and cultivated with riding and walking-plows. **1965** E. L. MYLES *Emperor of Peace River* I. xi. 114 Hitched to a small walking-plow, the team plodded back and forth. **1963** Walking shorts [see *easy-care* s.v. *EASY *a.* and *adv.* C.d.]. **1880** 'MARK TWAIN' *Tramp Abr.* xi. 102 The knapsacks, the rough walking suits, and the stout walking shoes which we had ordered. **1854** C. M. YONGE *Heartsease* II. II. xviii. 48 He was going to take a walking tour in Ireland.

b. walking-beam (earlier and later examples); **walking frame,** a free-standing metal frame for use as a walking aid by a person who holds or leans on the top; = *WALKER *sb.*^{1} 10 a, b; **walking-leg,** in certain arthropods, esp. crustaceans, a limb used for walking; **walking-machine,** a mechanical or robotic device attached to a person to enable him to perform duties beyond his normal capacity or strength; **walking-papers:** for *U.S. slang* read *colloq.*; (earlier and later examples); **walking-ticket** (earlier and later examples).

1845 *Knickerbocker* XXV. 63 Some rushed to the upper deck, and climbed up the chain and up the machinery to the walking beam. **1932** *Amer. Speech* VII. 263 The walking-beam, a bar, pivoted in the center, which rocks up and down, actuating the tools in cable-tool drilling or the pumping rods in a well being pumped. **1960** [see *SAMSON'S POST 2 b]. **1973** [see *STEM *sb.*^{1} 4 j]. **1974** *Petroleum Rev.* XXVIII. 558/1 Each pile handling unit has its own walking beam system for moving from one pile driving position to the next. **1976** M. MACHLIN *Pipeline* xlii. 461 Lester, he'd been sitting out on the walking beam trying to stab the control head with a joint of pipe screwed in on the casing. **1961** J. O. WALE *Tidy's Massage & Remedial Exercises* (ed. 10) x. 202 The patient may begin with walking frames or rails. **1966** *Physiotherapy* LII. 146/2 Problems to be overcome are: (1) uneven ground; (ii) steep ground; (iii) stairs. Most walking frames can cope with (i) and (ii). **1979** D. COOK *Winter Doves* II. ii. 49 Her child..was bouncing up and down in a walking frame. **1983** S. RADLEY *Blood on Happy Highway* v. 39 Osteo-arthritis in her hips made it difficult for May to get about now, even with a walking frame. **1909** W. T. CALMAN in E. R. Lankester *Treat. Zool.* VII. xv. 271 The first pair of legs..are commonly referred to as the chelipeds, and the following four pairs are distinguished as walking-legs. **1932** J. S. HUXLEY *Probl. Relative Growth* iv. 123 The pereiopod which was enlarged as the male chela being the first of the walking-leg series. **1977** G. F. WARNER *Biol. Crabs* v. 75 They burrow by tilting backwards and digging down into the sand with their walking legs. **1971** *Sci. News* 21 Aug. 118/2 Manipulators, walking machines, artificial limbs and man amplifiers—cybernetic machines that perform as appendages of man. **1973** *Britannica Yearbk. Sci. & Future 1972* 102 A four-legged 'walking machine' mimics and amplifies the movements of its human operator. The right front leg of the machine is controlled by the operator's right arm, the left front by his left arm, [etc.]. **1978** D. MURPHY *Place Apart* vi. 110 Now he is 'out of work' and has to use a complicated walking-machine provided by the NHS. **1825** S. WOODWORTH *Forest Rose* I. iv. 18 As for the bumpkin, her lover, he must take his walking papers. **1916** JOYCE *Portrait of Artist* 23 You'll get your walking papers [*sc.* discharge from a school infirmary] in the morning when the doctor comes. **1978** L. PRYOR *Viper* viii. 141 Hassan gave me my walking papers last night. **1829** in N. E. Eliason *Tarheel Talk* (1956) 124, I heard..she had given Henry a walking ticket. **1888** 'R. BOLDREWOOD' *Robbery under Arms* I. x. 124 Every soul about the place..seemed to have got a cheque and a walking-ticket at the same time. **1970** *Islander* (Victoria, B.C.) 24 May 7/2 If a man spat on the floor, he'd get warned. If he did it again he'd get his walking ticket.

walking, *ppl. a.* Add: **1. c.** *walking delegate* (earlier example).

1889 *Lippincott's Monthly Mag.* Feb. 227, I had no experience of strikes, and 'the walking delegate' was not yet stepping westward.

3. *walking doll,* a mechanically operated doll that can be made to move its legs; *walking funeral,* one in which the coffin is wheeled by hand.

1841 DICKENS *Barnaby Rudge* ix, in *Master Humphrey's Clock* II. 285, I wish I may only have a walking funeral, and never be buried decent with a mourning-coach and feathers. **1848** Walking funeral [in Dict.]. *a* **1870** in *Country Life* (1973) 29 Nov. 1833/2 The patent Autoperipatetikos or walking-doll. **1886** C. M. YONGE *Chantry House* II. xvi. 158 A Chinese walking doll was sent..for the amusement of Miss Winslow's school children. **1968** *Canad. Antiques Collector* Dec. 14/2 In the 1820's the first walking dolls were introduced. These opened and shut their eyes and said 'mama' and 'papa'. **1983** L. TAYLOR *Mourning Dress* i. 40 Even amongst the poor there were grades of funerals. The grandest involved the use of a horse-drawn hearse, but much more common was a 'walking funeral' where the coffin was wheeled on its hearse.

d. Of a casualty: able to walk despite his injuries, not in need of a stretcher; chiefly in phr. *walking wounded,* such casualties collectively; also *fig.*

1917 P. GIBBS *Battles of Somme* 265 The long trails of the walking wounded, marvellously brave, wonderfully full of spirits. **1948** G. GREENE *Heart of Matter* II. I. i. 117 We were told to prepare for nine stretcher cases and four walking ones. **1965** *Economist* 4 Dec. 1072/2 Governor Rockefeller..has been one of the political walking-wounded since his unpopular remarriage in 1963. **1972** *Guardian* 23 Dec. 8/1 There are many less conspicuous casualties, the walking wounded of the affluent society.

4. *walking gentleman, lady* (earlier examples).

1794 C. MATHEWS *Let.* 14 June in A. Mathews *Mem. Charles Mathews* (1838) I. v. 86 And asked me if I would like to play walking gentleman. **1860** G. VANDENHOFF

Leaves from Actor's Note-bk. xii. 196 Susan..was the best walking-lady on the American Stage.

5. *walking encyclopaedia* (examples); also *walking dead.*

1868 L. M. ALCOTT *Little Women* I. xii. 181 Meg.. considered him a walking encyclopaedia of useful knowledge. **1912** T. DREISER *Financier* vi. 60 There were many, many wildcat banks, and they were sufficient in number to make the average exchange-counter broker a walking encyclopedia of solvent and insolvent institutions. **1978** *Rugby World* Apr. 28/3 He could..enlist the aid of some other members of the Irish [rugby] squad like Mike Gibson, or Johnny Robbie, or Mick Quinn, who are walking encyclopaedias on English soccer in particular. **1980** J. GARDNER *Garden of Weapons* III. iii. 247 You look terrible. Like the walking dead.

7. b. *walking catfish*: a freshwater catfish, *Clarias batrachus*, native to south-east Asia and Africa, and able to use its fins to crawl over land.

1968 *Orlando* (Florida) *Sentinel* 20 Nov. 8-C/1 The state of Florida surrendered Tuesday in its war with the weird 'walking catfish' and said the ambulating invader..is here to stay. **1984** *USA Today* 6 Apr. 3B/1 Walking catfish were imported from Thailand to Florida in 1960 by a fish farmer who sold them to aquarium owners to keep their tanks clean. They since have multiplied rapidly in the wild. Some people are working on recipes to make walking catfish a more palatable dish.

9. Jazz. *walking bass*: a bass part, often consisting of broken octaves, that goes up and down the scale in 4/4 time in steps or small intervals; so *walking beat.*

1939 L. HOBSON *Amer. Jazz Music* 51 *String bass*, more often plucked or slapped than bowed, usually playing two or four notes per bar or a 'walking' (melodic) bass. **1947** W. RUSSELL in R. de Toledano *Frontiers of Jazz* iv. 61 A rhythmic and a melodic germ motive are developed over a 'walking bass' figure. **1950** [see *STRIDE *sb.* 7 b]. **1952** Walking beat [see *WALK *v.*^{1} 7 g]. **1952** B. ULANOV *Hist. Jazz in Amer.* (1958) iv. 29 If you listen carefully to the Ellington recording of 'C Jam Blues', you will hear a definitive example of the walking bass—1234/1234/1234, over and over again. *Ibid.* vi. 67 He was reliable, he put down a good walking beat, he had learned to read music. **1967** *Crescendo* May 18/2 The way he [*sc.* James Moody] wrote led to the invention of what's called the 'walking' bass, which the Americans took up later. **1980** *New Grove Dict. Mus.* III. 39/1 George Thomas, whose *New Orleans Hop Scop Blues* (1911; published 1916) included a walking bass, used the same device.

10. Mining. *walking dragline*, a large dragline supported on movable feet.

1959 *Times Rev. Industry* June 75/1 A..walking dragline..will carry a 10 cu. yd bucket at 184 ft. radius and will strip 15 tons at each bite. **1977** *Bulletin* (Sydney) 22 Jan. 39/1 (Advt.), Queensland is rich in coal, but it has to be wrested from the ground, and it's here where the huge Marion walking dragline is in its element.

walklet (wǭ·klĕt). *nonce-wd.* [f. WALK *sb.*^{1} + -LET.] A short walk.

1832 J. ROMILLY *Diary* 21 Feb. (1967) 4 Peter Ouvry & I had a walklet. **1896** A. BEARDSLEY *Let.* c 12 Dec. (1970) 225 Yesterday I ventured out for a walklet in Winter Gardens.

Walkman (wǭ·kmăn). A proprietary name for small battery-operated cassette players and headphones capable of being worn by a person on foot.

1981 *Trade Marks Jrnl.* 25 Mar. 623/2 *Walkman*... Electrical and electronic apparatus and instruments..for transmitting, receiving, tuning, recording and reproducing audio and visual signals..batteries; aerials; loudspeakers; headphones; earphones..cassettes..Sony Kabushiki Kaisha (Sony Corporation)..Tokyo 141, Japan; manufacturers and merchants. **1981** *Japan Times* 31 Dec. 10/1 Sony Walkmans, easy-driving Honda scooters and aluminum household Buddhist altars sold like hotcakes during 1981. **1983** *Chicago Sun-Times* 22 May 9 I'll wear a Walkman in line [for the film] so I won't hear any smart alecks spill the story. **1983** *Sci. Amer.* June 130/1 The smaller zippers would be for products that reflect the current trend toward miniaturization, such as for carrying cases to fit the Walkman type of portable radio. **1983** *Official Gaz.* (U.S. Patent Office) 20 Dec. TM 288/1 Sony Corporation... *Walkman*... For audio tape player, audio tape recorders, radios and headphones. **1984** S. TOWNSEND *Growing Pains A. Mole* 54 They wear red satin side vent running shorts, sleeveless satin vests, white knee socks, Sony Walkman earphones and one gold earring.

wa·lk-off. [f. vbl. phr. *to walk off*: WALK *v.*^{1} 8 c.] An act of walking off: **a.** From a stage.

1936 N. COWARD *Red Peppers* in *To-night at 8.30* I. 85 Their exit consists of a neat walk off together, one behind the other, with their telescopes under their arms. **1970** *Time* 5 Jan. 51 The walk-off is the bittersweet image by which..Chaplin wishes to be remembered.

b. From a ship, sports field, etc. Cf. *WALK-OUT *sb.* 1.

1951 *Daily Progress* (Charlottesville, Va.) 13 June 5/1 (*heading*) Walkoff grows at new atomic plant. **1960** *Daily Tel.* 28 July 1/8, 2 liner crews return after walk-off. **1971** *Guardian Weekly* 10 Apr. 6 The 22 Springbok cricketers who held a walk-off at Newlands Ground here yesterday in protest against apartheid in cricket.

wa·lk-on, *sb.* and *a.* [f. vbl. phr. *to walk on*: see WALK *v.*^{1} 5 in Dict. and Suppl.] **A.** *sb.* **1.** *Theat.* **a.** A walk-on part.

1902, 1907 [in Dict. s.v. WALK *v.*^{1} 25]. **1936** R. LEHMANN *Weather in Streets* IV. i. 361 Or I might get a walk-on in a film. **1950** *Sun* (Baltimore) 19 May 16/2 It has the all-starriest cast of all time, with all the great ones doing walk-ons and bits. **1971** R. A. CARTER *Manhattan Primitive* (1972) xv. 142 She never got another speaking part: a few walk-ons, then she was an extra again.

b. An actor, etc., who has a walk-on part; = *walker-on* s.v. *WALKER *sb.*^{1} 1 c.

1946 *Sun* (Baltimore) 20 May 6/1 It can dispense with the star system..by concentrating on teamwork in which lead actors one night become walk-ons the next. **1964** M. DRABBLE *Garrick Year* xii. 193 A square, worried-looking girl, who was married to one of the walk-ons. **1980** *Times Lit. Suppl.* 31 Oct. 1228/5 There are several blandly handsome walk-ons, most of them recently out of drama school.

2. *Sport.* A team member without any regular status. *U.S.*

1974 *Plain Dealer* (Cleveland, Ohio) 19 Oct. 2-D/1 East Tech's Mike Lucas, a 6-4 junior college transfer from Arizona, is one of three 'walk-ons' on Ohio State's basketball team. **1980** *New Yorker* 3 Mar. 80 This year..the Highlands team looks a bit too much like the rest of the students for Martínez's taste... One player..did not even come to Highlands on a basketball scholarship—a category of athlete known in the trade as 'walk-ons'. **1981** *Washington Post* 4 Sept. D-1 He was beaten by Marty Davis, 22, who made the University of California tennis team as a walk-on.

B. *adj.* **1.** Pertaining to or designating an airline service for which prior booking is not required. orig. *U.S.*

1961 *Flight* LXXX. 488/2 The airline..earlier this year introduced 'walk-on' services to Chittagong. **1967** J. GARDNER *Madrigal* viii. 220 He..asked if there were any direct flights from Manchester to Zurich... At this time of year there should be no difficulty in getting a walk-on booking. **1977** *Times* 29 July 4/3 British Airways intends to compete with Laker Airways' walk on Skytrain air service between London and New York. **1983** *Flight Internat.* 10 Sept. 680/2 Shuttle's walk-on option with guaranteed backup aircraft.

2. Theat. *walk-on part*, etc. = sense A. 1 a above. Also *transf.* and *fig.*

1963 *Times* 25 Feb. 4/1 Before luncheon the New Zealanders were so vigorous, accurate and hostile that Illingworth, Sheppard, and even Dexter could play only walk-on parts. **1973** J. LEASOR *Host of Extras* viii. 141 If he heard of any jobs going—walk-on parts, crowd scenes, the odd TV commercial—he passed them on to me. **1976** *Private Eye* 24 Dec. 17/3 The Bank of England is determined it shall be in a supporting, if not walk-on, capacity rather than a starring role. **1977** *Time* 8 Aug. 21/1 Her striking good looks eventually won her some small walk-on parts in German films. **1983** J. JUXON *Lewis & Lewis* xxi. 223 Few..of Parnell's biographers have given Lewis more than a walk-on part in the drama. **1985** *Listener* 24 Jan. 11/3 Salman Rushdie complained that Indians were for the most part given walk-on roles.

wa·lk-out, *sb.* and *a.* [f. vbl. phr. *to walk out*: see WALK *v.*^{1} 5 j, *12*.] **A.** *sb.* **1. a.** A strike, esp. one called at short notice. Also *transf.*

1888 in Farmer *Americanisms* (1889) 550/2 The walk out of brewery employés, decided upon at last night's meeting of the union, was considerable of a fizzle. Less than thirty men left their work. **1894** *Evening Sun* (N.Y.) 10 July 1/6 Some of the big firms have already closed their works in anticipation of a walkout. **1919** [in Dict. s.v. WALK *v.*^{1} 25]. **1957** *Economist* 12 Oct. 129/1 An attempt to organise a walkout by the white pupils failed when less than one in thirty left the school. **1982** *Daily Tel.* 22 July 5/1 Porters, cooks, cleaners and other ancillary staff staged an almost complete walk-out. **1985** *Times* 7 Mar. 11/3 The planners speak of lightning strikes and walkouts.

b. An act of leaving a meeting, etc., as a gesture of protest or disapproval.

1927 *Observer* 1 May 13/4 He has fulfilled the assurance he gave on taking the Chair that he would observe strict impartiality in the conduct of business... It may be that on one or two occasions Mr. Patel's judgement has been at fault, as, for instance, in the dramatic episode of the Swarajist walk-out. **1946** *Richmond* (Va.) *Times-Dispatch* 2 Apr. 1/1 Ala presented Iran's side to the council last week after Russia's dramatic walkout. **1958** *Times* 2 Sept. 7/4 The opening film [*sc.* at a festival]..saw a rather considerable number of walk-outs. **1973** H. TREVELYAN *Diplomatic Channels* viii. 125 The pointed absence or walk out on official occasions can be overdone, but is necessary if a speech by the host is directly insulting to the ambassador's country.

2. A love affair.

1934 E. WAUGH *Handful of Dust* ii. 46 He's having a terrific walk out with a girl called Sheila Shrub. **1983** P. DEVLIN *All of us There* v. 57 Ellen has been having a walk-out with his brother Joe for years.

B. *adj.* Of a room or basement: with its own exit door, i.e. not dependent on stairs to another floor. *N. Amer.*

1958 *Washington Post* 16 Aug. B6/5 This home..has.. full walkout basement and a Hotpoint kitchen. **1968** *Globe & Mail* (Toronto) 13 Jan. 42/1 (Advt.), Lower level features striking walk-out family room and sauna. **1978** *Detroit Free Press* 16 Apr. F-10/8 (Advt.), Full finished walkout basement with fireplace.

walk-over. Add: **b.** *transf.* Anything accomplished with great ease.

1902 G. H. LORIMER *Lett. Self-Made Merchant* xv. 216 It wasn't any walk-over to hold the belt in those days. **1931** *Daily Tel.* 21 Jan. 8/4 This makes its acquisition by an American crook a walk-over. **1975** P. FUSSELL *Gt. War & Mod. Memory* (1977) i. 27 His little sporting contest did have the effect of persuading his men that the attack was going to be..a walkover.

c. *attrib.* or as *adj.*

1936 *Sunday Times* 14 June 4/2 When the law gets them in its clutches, a shady lawyer is allowed to get a walkover verdict of 'Not Guilty'. **1974** *Times* 5 Oct. 14/7 Lauda seemed set for almost a walkover trip to the title (he proved himself the fastest driver..nine times this year).

wa·lk-round, *sb.* and *a.* [f. vbl. phr. *to walk round*: WALK *v.*^{1} 5 a.] **A.** *sb.* = *walk-around* (*b*) s.v. WALK *v.*^{1} 25. *U.S.*

1861 *Temple Bar* May 199 The 'Jim Crow dance'.. soon gave place to better tunes..and 'walk rounds'. **1895** *Century Mag.* Oct. 958/1 His work with the caravan was to sing songs, chiefly darky songs, accompanied by 'hoe-downs' and 'walk rounds'. **1943** *Life* 5 July 80 After the 'walk-round', which served as an entrance for the black-faced showmen, they stood before a semicircle of chairs and waited for the interlocutor's: 'Gentlemen, be seated.'

B. *adj.* Round which one can walk: applied to a self-service shop with goods so arranged.

1974 P. WRIGHT *Lang. Brit. Industry* xiii. 120 Walk-round store (where the goods are so accessible that you may be tempted to buy far more than you need). **1979** *This England* Winter 19/3 Miss Corrie's dim, prim little shop in the market place had survived the competition of walk-round stores and boutiques.

wa·lk-through, *sb.* and *a.* [f. vbl. phr. *to walk through*: WALK *v.*^{1}.] **A.** *sb.* **1.** *Theat.* **a.** A part not requiring the performer to exert himself, one that he may 'walk through' (WALK *v.*^{1} 7 a); *transf.*, an undemanding task.

1944 *Sun* (Baltimore) 15 July 6/1 The principal roles offer no difficulties, permitting Miss Powell to be herself, as always, and giving her leading man a walk-through. **1950** *Ibid.* 13 Oct. 12/2 For Mr. Milland, an actor with 58 photo-plays to his credit, this is a walk-through. **1980** J. BALL *Then came Violence* (1981) iv. 36 We've just had a homicide and this one isn't a domestic walk-through. **1984** *New Yorker* 30 Jan. 82/2 Most skilled politicians take the measure of a crowd and find ways to relate to it specifically. It is as if Glenn were doing a walk-through.

b. A perfunctory or lacklustre performance.

1970 *Globe & Mail* (Toronto) 26 Sept. 23/1 Richard Burton in Hamlet..giving us only an insulting, offhand walk-through.

2. (See quots.)

1959 W. S. SHARPS *Dict. Cinematogr.* 91/2 *Dry run*, otherwise walk-through, a full rehearsal for a production, but without cameras. **1974** *Some Technical Terms & Slang* (Granada Television), *Walkthrough*, one stage after the tech run of a drama, but before moving into the studio proper. The cast and certain technicians will meet for a rough rehearsal in the studio set without cameras. **1977** K. T. ORR *Structured Syst. Devel.* i. 5 Today we see discussions of structured walkthroughs, structured design, and structured analysis. **1983** *Dict. Computing* 388/1 *Walk through*, a product review performed by a formal team... There is a clear statement of the contribution that each member of the review team is required to make, and a step-by-step procedure for carrying out the review... The product is..openly debated with a view to uncovering problems or identifying desirable improvements.

B. *adj.* Of a building, etc.: permitting access from either end.

In quot. 1950, for the cows to enter and leave.

1950 *N.Z. Jrnl. Agric.* May 477/3 The walk-through [milking] shed with doors at the rear of the shed in the conventional manner. **1967** *Economist* 8 July p. viii, He [*sc.* the driver] will want to reach back to his load without dismounting and walking round to open the back doors—hence the spate of 'walk-through' vans in Britain. **1981** M. C. SMITH *Gorky Park* III. i. 295 A remarkable walk-through tube that attached the plane directly to the terminal. **1984** *Buses* Nov. 488/3 A sliding door in the fixed section giving a walkthru' layout for the van.

wa·lk-up, *a.* and *sb.* [f. vbl. phr. *to walk up*: WALK *v.*^{1}] **A.** *adj.* **1.** Of an apartment, etc.: that has to be reached by stairs rather than by a lift. Also applied to a building consisting of such apartments. *U.S.*

1919 MENCKEN *Amer. Lang.* iv. 110 The term *flat* 'is usually in the United States restricted to apartments in houses having no elevator or hall service'. In New York such apartments are commonly called *walk-up apartments*. **1927** E. GLYN *It* iv. 40 Mary had a tiny two-room apartment in a walk-up building in Brooklyn. **1942** *N.Y. Times* 13 Feb. (late City ed.) 13/4 Six five-story walk-up apartment houses. **1946** MEZZROW & WOLFE *Really Blues* (1957) xiii. 235 Some crummy walk-up tenement flat. **1979** H. KISSINGER *White House Years* xxi. 906 Huang Hua and I met around six o'clock in the CIA's walk-up apartment in the East Seventies. **1984** *Business Rev. Weekly* (Austral.) 4–10 Feb. 42/3 The Myer development is a three-storey walk-up affair that has appealed to a lower age group than usual for Gold Coast units.

2. That may be approached on the street, without having to go into a building.

1963 C. J. MCCALL in A. Dundes *Mother Wit* (1973) 421 The colorful window-signs of innumerable 'readers'..cry out from their store-front or walk-up locations. **1972** *Sunday Sun* (Brisbane) 8 Oct. 16/1 The same bandit had approached Miss Avery at her outside walkup window post on Tuesday and demanded $3000.

B. *sb.* **1.** A walk-up apartment or apartment block. *U.S.*

1925 *Scribner's Mag.* Oct. 6/2 Vacation heaves into sight over the horizon..the swirling dust turned into clean sand; the only walk-up a dune; and the total night life two movie theatres. 1942 R. Chandler *High Window* xxv. 149 The kind of dentists who have shabby offices on second-floor walk-ups over stores. 1954 F. P. Keyes *Royal Box* xiii. 165 The friends he had all lived in the identical kind of six-flat walk-up. 1966 R. Stout *Death of Doxy* (1967) i. 6 The person to ask lived on the second floor of a walkup on 52nd Street. 1976 *National Observer* (U.S.) 4 Sept. 1/2 The blue-jeaned couples climbing the stairs to their walk-ups together are most usually the children of affluence. 1980 J. Krantz *Princess Daisy* xxv. 438 Daisy herself lived in a low-rent SoHo walk-up and held down a full-time job.

2. *U.S. Horse-Racing.* The walk of race-horses to a starting line or tape (as opposed to starting gates). Freq. *attrib.*

1938 *Sun* (Baltimore) 1 Nov. 12/1 The only change in the usual order will be a walkup start instead of a start from a gate. 1946 *Richmond* (Va.) *Times-Dispatch* 8 Mar. 23/3 The field might have to be started from a walkup to an old-fashioned web barrier. 1959 *Washington Post* 15 Nov. c 1 The starter who had trouble..at Laurel in the ragged walk-up, says the foreign entries could be taught in five days to break from the stall gates. 1974 *Encycl. Brit. Macropædia* VIII. 1100/2 Some starts are still effected from a barrier that springs upward when actuated by the starter, or in the 'walk-up' fashion, whereby the starter gives a verbal order when the horses are reasonably well aligned.

3. *Shooting.* The act of walking up game-birds (Walk *v.*[1] 20); also *transf.* of clay pigeons; a piece of land kept for this purpose.

1972 *Shooting Times & Country Mag.* 27 May 10/3 There are numerous Bowman traps, designed to simulate varying driven game birds and there is a walk-up with 15 traps. 1975 *Times* 1 Sept. 14/6 An increasing number of landowners..let walked-up shoots... On the Speyside walk-up the other day was a Marseille dentist.

wa·lkway. orig. *U.S.* Also **walk-way.** [f. Walk *sb.*[1] or *v.*[1] + Way *sb.*[1]] **1.** = Walk *sb.*[1] 9 c.

1792 in *Essex Inst. Hist. Coll.* (1865) VII. 37/2 John Sanders..agrees to pave the walk way in front of his Father's Estate. 1816 W. Bentley *Diary* (1914) IV. 405 A walkway for the first time has been raised in the principal streets in the eastern part of the Town. 1904 *N.Y. Evening Post* 14 May 5 A space..sufficient to provide each house with a walkway to the rear. 1976 *Outdoor Living* (N.Z.) I. ii. 42 *(caption)* Quarry tiled walkway and meandering plants leading through a painted brick archway give a pleasant first impression to this home. 1980 *Daily Tel.* 16 June 2/1 Paths affected by housing development should be retained as 'walkways' through the new estate.

2. A pedestrian passageway linking different parts of a building or structure or complex of buildings, esp. one raised above ground-level and separating the users from machinery, traffic, etc. Also, a specially built path taking sightseers through an area of natural beauty or the like.

1928 R. H. Lansburgh *Industr. Management* (ed. 2) xv. 175 Accident prevention by making floors and walk-ways safe is a big factor in the industrial accident toll. 1933 *Meccano Mag.* Feb. 109/1 There is perfect communication between all members of the crew, a walk-way from end to end of the aeroplane being provided to enable members to change places quickly. 1953 *Archit. Rev.* CXIII. 83 *(caption)* The walkway..passes under the three classroom blocks and links the two main courts. 1959 *Daily Tel.* 13 Mar. 18/4 The lay-out [of London Zoo] will include all-weather covered elevated walkways from the main gate. 1960 *Guardian* 20 May 7/2 First-floor shops, walkways and bridges for pedestrians. 1960 'N. Shute' *Trustee from Toolroom* i. 13 The long wooden walkways above the tidal mud, the yachts moored bows-on in tiers. 1968 *New Scientist* 26 Sept. 640/2 There will be..a moving walkway along the pier to the two terminals [at Heathrow Airport]. 1973 *Times* 18 Oct. (Brazil Suppl.) p. vii/4 Tourists..will have 'walkways' through special jungle reserves which will remain undisturbed. 1979 *United States 1980/81* (Penguin Travel Guide) 250 The newly restored North Beach with landscaped dunes and oceanfront walkway. 1981 *Sci. Amer.* Nov. 32/1 This environment, the home of the most diverse swarm of species,..is currently studied from walkways hung high among the treetops, steel towers rising into the leafy canopy. 1984 *Daily Tel.* 3 July 1/7 Outside there will be Tivoli-style gardens with a walkway along the Thames.

wall, *sb.*[1] Add: I. **4. g.** *The Wall*: *ellipt.* for *Wailing Wall* s.v. *wailing *vbl. sb.* c.

1895 J. Smith *Pilgrimage to Palestine* xvi. 219 The 'Wailing Place of the Jews'..is situated a little to the north... High overhead towered the..stones of the Temple Wall..with the Wall itself..rising to a height of 60 feet... There, with their faces to the wall—kissing the stones,..or joining in a loud chorus of lamentation..stood a long row of Jews. 1928 *Western or Wailing Wall in Jerusalem* 6 in *Parl. Papers 1928–9* (Cmd. 3229) XV. 105 His Majesty's Government regard it as their duty..to maintain the established Jewish right of access to the pavement in front of the Wall for the purposes of their devotions. 1967 C. Potok *Chosen* xii. 198 He died while praying at the Wall for the Messiah to come and redeem his people. 1973 *Guardian* 21 June 2/7 The present intention is to link the Wall with the historic 'upper city' (now the Jewish Quarter).

h. *The Wall*: *ellipt.* for *Berlin Wall*, the wall surrounding West Berlin and separating it from communist East Berlin and the rest of East Germany (erected in 1961).

1961 *Daily Progress* (Charlottesville, Va.) 20 Oct. 1/1 Here in Berlin communism has created one of the ugliest and most depressing sights on the face of the globe. It is The Wall—the wall of death, the new concrete curtain of communism. 1964 *Ann. Reg. 1963* 225 It was stated that 1,283,918 had crossed the Wall by the time it closed on 5 January 1964. 1977 G. Markstein *Chance Awakening* lxxviii. 243 My father had his legs blown off..when he tried to flee over the Wall.

II. 8. c. In the game of Mah Jong, the arrangement of tiles from which hands are drawn. Cf. *tile *sb.*[1] 4 b.

1922 *Lit. Digest* 30 Dec. 38 One studies the unfolding of Ma Jung, one detects Eastern cunning to whet the skill, first the building of the 'wall', undoubtedly meaning the great wall of China, one of the seven wonders of the world. 1950 E. Culbertson *Culbertson's Hoyle* 415 *Wall game*, void game by exhaustion of the wall without any declaration of a complete hand. 1974 *Encycl. Brit. Micropædia* VI. 503/3 Thereafter, the other players, in counterclockwise rotation, each draw one tile, which may be the last discarded tile or a loose tile from the 'wall'.

d. *Baseball.* The barrier marking the outer perimeter of the outfield.

1928 G. H. Ruth *Babe Ruth's Own Bk. Baseball* 25 The boys began smacking the fences with long drives, outfielders began playing with their backs to the wall and infielders had to move back on the grass or have their legs torn off with hot drives. *Ibid.* 117 The ball was hit far over his head to the center field wall. 1973 *Internat. Herald Tribune* 15 June 15/3 The closest the Reds had come to a hit was Pete Rose's long drive to left-center in the third that Jim Dwyer caught at the wall.

e. *Football.* A line of defence players who defend their team's goal during a free kick.

1948 Hankinson & Chadder *Soccer for Schools* Plate 29 *(caption)* The usual procedure for the defence to adopt is for a 'wall' of players to block the line of a direct shot for goal. 1965 D. Bacuzzi *How to play Association Football* xv. 56 *(caption)* Notice how the 'wall' of defenders allows the goalkeeper space to see. 1976 E. Dunphy *Only a Game?* v. 149, I scored direct from a free kick. Curled it round the wall into the top corner from just outside the box.

f. *Surfing.* The steep face of a wave before it breaks.

1962 T. Masters *Surfing made Easy* 66 *Wall*, the steep portion of a wave almost ready to break. 1965 J. Pollard *Surfrider* ii. 20 The steep face of that wave is called its 'wall'. 1968 *Surfer Mag.* Jan. 17/1 'Just Ken' probably doesn't know what it is like to ride a well-shaped wall while hanging ten except when he is smoking grass.

9. b. The pastry forming the sides of a pie.

1747 H. Glasse *Art of Cookery* viii. 73 Make a good Standing Crust, let the Wall and Bottom be very thick. 1894 L. Heritage *Cassell's New Universal Cookery Bk.* 785/1 Form the walls of the pie with the left hand. The sides should be smooth and of equal thickness. 1959 *Listener* 22 Jan. 191/2 Lid the flan with pastry, having egged the top of the 'wall'.

III. 14. *to send to the wall* (earlier example).

1881 E. W. Hamilton *Diary* 13 Mar. (1972) I. 115 Lord Bath..is much exercised in his mind as to the Greek question sending to the wall the interests of Servia.

16. *to give a person the wall* (later example).

1869 A. J. Munby *Diary* 24 Dec. in D. Hudson *Munby* (1972) vii. 278 'If a nigger didn't give me the wall, I'd knock him down as soon as look at him!' Here we have the British Philistine.

19*. *to go over the wall* and varr.: (*a*) to go to prison; (*b*) to escape from prison; (*c*) to leave a religious order; (*d*) to defect (to another country). Hence (*e*) *over the wall* adv. phr., escaped from prison; in prison. *slang.*

a. 1917 W. Muir *Observations of Orderly* xiv. 228 He would be observed 'going over the wall' or 'going to stir' (going to detention prison).

b. 1933 *Amer. Speech* VIII. iii. 27/1 *Go over the wall*, escape. 1936 L. Duncan *(title)* Over the wall. *Ibid.* vi. 95 Us guys..pull wires to get jobs as guards, and you convicts go over the wall whenever you can. 1963 *Times* 5 June 16/1 He knew it was an unwritten law that an escape extinguished such a debt, and so he decided to 'go over the wall'. He gave himself up at Clacton-on-Sea. 1974 P. B. Yuill *Hazell plays Solomon* vi. 66 You really think Mancini would've tried to go over the wall?

c. 1949 M. Baldwin *(title)* I leap over the wall. A return to the world after twenty-eight years in a convent. 1970 *Harper's Mag.* Apr. 110 Mr. Vizzard was a Jesuit seminarian who yearned for the world, leapt over the wall, and found what he was looking for in Hollywood. 1979 'E. Anthony' *Grave of Truth* vii. 190 A bride of Christ, eh? What happens if she jumps over the wall..decides she's had enough of convent life..?

d. 1976 M. Butterworth *Remains to be Seen* v. 84 The bloody place [*sc.* the Foreign Office]..has never been the same since Kim [Philby] went over the wall.

e. 1935 A. J. Pollock *Underworld Speaks* 85/2 *Over the wall*, escaped from prison. 1973 G. Beare *Snake on Grave* xxiii. 141 He's out. Over the wall.

19.** *up the wall*: angry, furious; distraught, mad, crazy; esp. in phrs. *to climb, run up the wall*: to become very angry or distraught; *to drive, send* (someone) *up the wall*: to infuriate or put into a frenzy. *colloq.*

1951 S. Kaye-Smith *Mrs. Gailey* 160 Your mother's running up the wall because he came to dinner. 1953 H. Clevely *Public Enemy* xvii. 101 Old Marks 'll climb up the wall if he hears I closed early. 1956 A. Wilson *Anglo-Saxon Att.* ii. ii. 307 You drive me up the wall. What sort of a mess have you got poor Dad into? 1959 *Observer* 21 June 8/8 When they found out he was a Catholic, they were up the wall. 1961 *New Left Rev.* Mar./Apr. 30/1 She was right up the wall, and poor Aunt Ada isn't in any state to help. 1966 'L. Lane' *ABZ of Scouse* 40 Sends me up ther bloody wall. 1970 *New Yorker* 3 Oct. 105/1 Success or failure hardly entered into the picture. It was this kind of argument that drove some..executives up the wall. 1975 'E. Lathen' *By Hook or by Crook* xiv. 138 The American wife, the sweetie-pie who sends Everett up the wall. 1977 *Chicago Tribune* 2 Oct. vi. 15/2 The prejudice is so acute; that country is up the wall.

19*.** *off the wall* (also with hyphens used *attrib.*): unorthodox, unconventional; instinctive, intuitive, off the cuff. (See also quot. 1966.) Also used advb. *U.S. slang.*

1966 *Current Slang* (Univ. S. Dakota) Summer 3 *Off the wall*, unimpressive... I have a lit. professor who's *off the wall.* 1968–70 *Ibid.* III–IV. 88 *Off the wall*, adj. Unusual; unorthodox; 'crazy'. 1974 *National Rev.* (U.S.) 4 Jan. 47/2 Brian knows how to startle the over-interviewed with off-the-wall questions that get surprising answers: Ever see a ghost? 1975 *San Francisco Chron.* 11 Jan. 12/3 He became suspicious when Dickenson answered extremely complex questions 'off the wall'. 1976 *Time* 5 Apr. 74, 'I just thought it was off-the-wall funny', says Lear. 1977 C. McFadden *Serial* (1978) iv. 14/1 She had decided to play the whole scene off the wall, to just go with the flow... The really authentic thing to do was to act on your impulses. 1977 *Listener* 20 Oct. 498/2 Among the many new sources of cash—it's called 'off the wall' fundraising—I have heard about a tribe of Apaches which ..invested $2 million in the making of..a western. 1982 *Penthouse* Dec. 84 He started talking off the wall about how he should go to El Salvador.

21. a. simple attrib., *wall-decoration, -front*; 'set or fixed against a wall', *wall-cupboard, light, mirror, -panel, -panelling, phone, picture, safe, sconce* (examples), *socket, switch, telephone.*

1961 *Times* 16 Jan. 13/4 It is furnished throughout with tables, chairs, wall-cupboards. 1976 'W. Trevor' *Children of Dynmouth* ii. 51 The commodious wall-cupboards, the scrubbed wooden table. 1867 D. G. Rossetti *Let.* ? 12 Nov. (1965) II. 643 There are sufficient slight representatives of it [*sc.* the severed head] on vases and in wall-decoration of classic times. 1935 *Burlington Mag.* June 272/2 The question of the connexion between the carpet patterns and the wall-decoration remains difficult enough. 1964 *Listener* 3 Dec. 883/1 This is a rare opportunity to see an important High Renaissance wall-decoration. 1923 D. H. Lawrence *Birds, Beasts & Flowers* 115 The black hole, the earth-lipped fissure in the wall-front. 1869 *Bradshaw's Railway Man.* XXI. p. xvi (Advt.), Wall Lights and Mantle Piece Lustres. 1905 E. Wharton *House of Mirth* i. iii. 42 She turned out the wall-lights. 1972 Wall light [see *penlight, pen-light]. 1934 Webster, Wall mirror. 1940 M. Sadleir *Fanny by Gaslight* i. ix. 241 She studied herself in a long wall mirror. 1981 'J. Melville' *Murder has Pretty Face* i. 20 She could see her reflection in a wall mirror. 1880 L. Higgin *Handbk. Embroidery* 62 Design for wall-panel. By Mr. E. Burne-Jones. 1933 *Burlington Mag.* July 22/1 The absence of graining on the wall panels. 1962 A. Nisbett *Technique Sound Studio* 245 Marked acoustic colouration in a studio may be due to the coincidence of dimensional resonances, to wall-panel resonances, or to frequency-selective excessive absorption of sound. 1880 L. Higgin *Handbk. Embroidery* 62 Design for wall-panelling or curtains. 1962 L. Deighton *Ipcress File* xxx. 194 The wall phone rang. 1975 'R. Butler' *Where all Girls are Sweeter* vi. 70, I.. went over to the wall-phone and dialled. 1895 Wall-picture [see *Japanese lantern* s.v. *Japanese *a.* and *sb.* b]. 1966 J. Derrick *Teaching Eng. to Immigrants* v. 195 Wall pictures to match those in the book, with suitable captions printed by the teacher..can be put up in the classroom. 1931 W. Faulkner *Sanctuary* xxiii. 254 The room contained..three over-stuffed chairs, a wall safe. 1978 A. Neave *Nuremburg* iii. 36 Two wall-safes had been found, one in Bertha's bedroom and one in Gustav's dressing-room. 1954 Wall sconce [see *Oscar[2] b]. 1974 J. Aiken *Midnight is Place* i. 11 A few candles..burned flickeringly in the wall sconces. 1890 Slingo & Brooker *Electr. Engin.* xvii. 608 A wall socket..is useful in cases where it is required to place a movable lamp in circuit at one or other of a number of positions. 1977 Wall socket [see *start button* s.v. *start *sb.*[2] 12]. 1935 D. L. Sayers *Gaudy Night* vi. 114 She found the wall-switch and went down the central corridor of the Annexe. 1981 C. Dexter *Dead of Jericho* xxv. 142 He..turned on the wall switch... But clearly the electricity had been disconnected. 1914 Wall telephone [see *extension 9 h]. 1977 *Rolling Stone* 30 June 73/2 Her kitchen is very white—walls, doors, floors, white appliances... And a white wall telephone.

b. *wall-builder* (earlier example); *wall-girdled, -hung, -mounted* adjs.

1812 E. Weeton *Let.* 15 June in *Jrnl. of Governess* (1969) II. 22, 7d a yard is the price now usually paid to wall-builders. *a* 1930 D. H. Lawrence *Etruscan Places* (1932) 50 Nowhere is far off, in these small wall-girdled cities. 1876 W. Morris *Sigurd* 2 The least of its wall-hung shields. 1970 Wall-hung [see *modular *a.* 1 b]. 1964 R. F. Ficchi *Electr. Interference* v. 67 The installation, however, is quite important:..it must be located within the shielding or 'wall-mounted' through the shield. 1980 *Sunday Times* (Colour Suppl.) 21 Sept. 50 (Advt.), Toilets and bidets can be floor standing or wall mounted.

22. wall bar, one of a set of parallel bars, attached to the wall of a gymnasium, usu. running from floor to ceiling, on which various exercises are performed; **wall bed,** a bed which can be folded up against a wall when not in use; **wallboard,** (a piece of) board, made from wood pulp, fibre, and other materials, used for surfacing walls and ceilings, etc.; **wall bracket,** a bracket (Bracket *sb.* 1 a) which is attached to a wall as a stand or support for a lamp, ornaments, shelves, etc.; **wall-chalker** (later example); hence **wall-chalking; wall chart,** a chart or poster giving information, often in pictures or diagrams, and designed for display on a wall, esp. in a classroom; **wallcovering,** material used to cover and decorate the inside walls of a building (cf. WALLPAPER 1 in Dict. and Suppl.); **wall fish** *dial.*, the edible snail, *Helix pomatia*; **wall garden,** a garden surrounded by a wall, or a border planted beside a sheltering wall; **wall-hangings,** also, embroidered, woven or other decorative drapery for display on walls; occas. *sing.*; **wall newspaper,** (*a*) a newspaper produced by an educational institution or place of work, typed or hand-written, and displayed on the wall; (*b*) (esp. in Communist countries) an official newspaper displayed on the wall in public places, esp. in the street; **Wall of Death,** a fairground sideshow in which a motor-cyclist uses gravitational force to ride his motor-cycle around the inside walls of a vertical cylinder; **wall-painting,** a mural, a fresco; **wall pass** *Football* = *one-two* (*c*) s.v. *ONE 33; **wall plug**: see *PLUG *sb.* 1 c (cf. *wall socket*, sense 21 above); **wall-pocket,** (*a*) a receptacle for small household items, designed to hang on a wall; (*b*) = *wall vase* below; **wall-poster,** a poster affixed to a public wall; *spec.* = *TA TZU-PAO; **wall-side,** (*a*) the side of a wall; (*b*) the side of a pavement, etc., where there is a wall (also *attrib.*); **wall space,** an expanse of unbroken wall surface, esp. one regarded as an area for displaying pictures, etc.; **wall system** *U.S.*, 'a set of shelves often with cabinets or bureaus that can be variously arranged along a wall' (*Webster's 9,000 Words*); **wall unit,** a piece of furniture consisting of various sections and compartments such as shelves and cupboards, and designed to stand against a wall; **wall vase,** a vase with one flat side allowing it to be hung on a wall; **wallwasher,** a type of lighting fixture designed to 'wash' a wall with light (see quot. 1983).

1903 *Handbk. Physical Training* (Admiralty) I. 53 The men are placed with one side towards, and at one pace from the Wall Bars. **1973** M. RUSSELL *Double Hit* ii. 18 I'll be getting back to the wallbars. **1913** *Maclean's Mag.* Oct. 78/1 The Pacific Wall Bed is sanitary in every respect. **1974** Wall bed [see *MURPHY[3]]. **1925** (*title*) U.S. Government master specification for gypsum wall board. (U.S. Bureau of Standards.) **1933** *Archit. Rev.* LXXIII. p. lviii, The group of materials commonly known as wallboards, but more correctly termed building-boards, may..be classified in five categories:—(1) fibre boards..(2) laminated boards..(3) wood pulp boards..(4) plaster boards..(5) composite boards. **1942** [see *storyboard* s.v. *STORY *sb.*[1] 9]. **1962** A. LURIE *Love & Friendship* iv. 59 Burned, sodden chunks of wallboard lay about. **1978** *Cornish Guardian* 27 Apr. 34/6 (Advt.), Carpet Tiles. Tools. Wallboards. **1909** WEBSTER, Wall bracket. **1926** L. ELMHIRST *Notebk.* in M. Young *Elmhirsts of Dartington* (1982) xii. 295 We eliminated the wall brackets and agreed upon..ceiling lights. **1939** [see *STANDARD *sb.* 16 c]. **1951** W. FAULKNER *Requiem for Nun* I. ii. 53 Floor-lamp, wall-bracket lamps, a door left enters from the hall. **1976** *Gramophone* Sept. 516/2 The small size can be easily accommodated particularly if the speakers are mounted on wall brackets. ? **1932** DYLAN THOMAS *Sel. Lett.* (1966) 5 We're over-ripe, we night-walkers, cunt-stalkers, wall-chalkers. **1853** DICKENS *Bleak Ho.* xli. 409 Lady Dedlock, the wall-chalking and the street-crying would come on directly. **1958** S. HYLAND *Who goes Hang?* xl. 189 He was..examining a wall-chart which depicted..the working..of a bicycle. **1980** Wall chart [see *SNAKE *sb.* 4 f]. **1970** *Times* 11 Dec. 16/4 The wallcovering on three walls is glossy yellow p.v.c. **1979** *Tucson Mag.* Apr. 73/2 (Advt.), We offer a multitude of wall coverings and coordinating fabrics. **1950** O. BLAKESTON *Pink Ribbon* v. 59 They ate snails..in Gloucester, and they called them 'wall fish'. **1980** *Times* 2 Oct. 13/3 The taste of an open mushroom grilled with garlic, parsley and butter is so splendid, and superior to snails given the same treatment, that I would never now dream of bothering to cook that delicacy known in the Mendips as *wallfish*. **1780** J. WOODFORDE Diary 26 Apr. (1924) I. 280 Busy in painting some boarding in my Wall Garden. **1936** *Discovery* Mar. 86/2 Wall Garden, 385 feet long, first planted in 1935 [at the Brooklyn Botanic Garden]. **1967** E. SHORT *Embroidery & Fabric Collage* i. 9 If the finished piece of embroidery is to be seen from a distance, as for instance a wall hanging. **1979** *Arizona Daily Star* 5 Aug. J 5/7 (Advt.), They've just had a new shipment of Oaxacan Rugs and Wallhangings. **1983** *Listener* 30 June 17/1 By 1972 I needed a small pantechnicon to convey all my books on macrobiotic cookery, my plants, wall-hangings and floor cushions. **1935** N. MITCHISON *We have been Warned* III. 295 She had been shown the wall newspapers of factories and schools. **1937** E. SNOW *Red Star over China* VIII. v. 293 There was also a wall newspaper in every club, and a committee of soldiers was responsible for keeping it up to date. **1966** J. DERRICK *Teaching Eng. to Immigrants* vi. 213 Project work involving the use of aids and apparatus..such as preparing a broadcast or TV programme or involving the class or group in the production of a wall newspaper should be considered. **1978** *China Now* Mar./Apr. 19/3 They keenly contested for the miserable prizes offered in competitions between groups and individuals in sport, literacy, public health, wall newspapers, and 'factory efficiency'. **1979** *N.Y. Rev. Bks.* 25 Oct. 40/3 The hero stands in Yuryatin reading the wall-newspapers. **1946** G. TYRWHITT-DRAKE *Eng. Circus & Fair Ground* xviii. 210 Undoubtedly the most thrilling side-show was the 'Wall of Death', first seen here..in 1928. **1959** *Listener* 26 Feb. 371/2 It might..spin quickly round the steep hollow like a rider on the Wall of Death. **1976** 'W. TREVOR' *Children of Dynmouth* i. 13 The Hall of a Million Mirrors and the Tunnel of Love and Alfonso's and Annabella's Wall of Death were in the process of erection. **1688** Wall painting [see FRESCO *sb.* 2]. **1849** *Jrnl. Brit. Archaeol. Assoc.* IV. 92 Church decoration of this kind is..not unfrequently brought to light; but specimens of domestic internal wall-painting are of much greater rarity. **1898** A. BEARDSLEY *Let.* 14 Jan. (1970) 424 I'm afraid good books on the wall paintings of Pompeii are costly and beyond my balance. **1933** *Burlington Mag.* Oct. 146/2 These..portraits..brought Holbein immediate fame and the order to decorate the King's Privy Chamber in Whitehall Palace with wall-paintings. **1964** W. L. GOODMAN *Hist. Woodworking Tools* 132 A wall-painting from Pompeii. **1958** *Mod. Soccer* (Football Assoc.) v. 41 In Fig. 38 the LB [Left Back], sensing the possibility of a 'wall-pass', quickly backs away. **1973** *Times* 6 Jan. 7/5 The 'wall pass', 'one-two', touch play, 'push and run', call it what you will, we developed it at Tottenham. **1888** Wall plug [see *PLUG *sb.* 1 c]. **1914** [in Dict., sense 21 a]. **1962** L. DEIGHTON *Ipcress File* xxv. 166 There was a big two kilowatt electric fire plugged into a wall point... It was the work of a minute to switch on the wall plug. **1880** *Scribner's Monthly* Apr. 921/1 The family comb..occupied a convenient wall-pocket at one side of the small kitchen mirror. **1947** E. BISHOP in *Nation* (N.Y.) 22 Feb. 215/1 The eighty watt bulb..Lighting as well on heads Of tacks in the wall paper, On a paper wall-pocket, Violet-embossed, glistening With mica flakes. **1957** MANKOWITZ & HAGGAR *Conc. Encycl. Eng. Pott. & Porc.* 125/1 Articles for domestic use..included..punch-bowls, wall-pockets and plaques. **1971** L. A. BOGER *Dict. World Pott. & Porc.* 365/1 *Wall Pocket*, in ceramics; a decorative object made of faïence, porcelain or pottery, having the shape of a vase, with one side being flat so that it can be hung on a wall. It is also called a wall vase. **1962** E. CLEAVER in A. Dundes *Mother Wit* (1973) 14/2 The mass media..television,..illustrated wall posters [etc.]. **1966** *China Q.* Oct.–Dec. 3 Within a week or two..20,000 'sightseers' were visiting Peking University each day, partly to read the wall-posters, partly to watch and abuse the 'criminals'. **1977** 'S. LEYS' *Chinese Shadows* (1978) ii. 70 Huge wall posters placed at random throughout the city. ('Increase our Vigilance and Protect our Fatherland!') **1979** 'J. LE CARRÉ' *Smiley's People* xxvii. 322 Wall posters offering cheap ski holidays. *c* **1400, 1887** Wall side [in Dict., sense 21 a]. **1933** AUDEN *Poems* (ed. 2) 80 Climbing over to wall-side of bed. **1959** I. & P. OPIE *Lore & Lang. Schoolch.* xii. 266 The old custom of making grottoes at the wall-side edge of the pavement. **1889** in *Cent. Dict.*, Wall space. **1898** G. B. SHAW *Arms & Man* III. 47 The rest of the wall space being occupied by trophies of war and the chase. **1978** *Lancashire Life* Sept. 101/1 True, a new library is being built in Stanley Road, where wall-space for pictures will be made available, but there will be no gallery proper, and no museum whatsoever. **1978** *Detroit Free Press* 2 Apr. 7B/1 (Advt.), Westwood wall system from Southern is a handsome backdrop for any room and provides invaluable storage. **1980** *Christian Sci. Monitor* (Midwestern ed.) 4 Dec. 17/3 Wall systems are the fastest-growing category of furnishings. **1962** *Listener* 11 Jan. 65/1 Making the best use of up-to-date methods, such as the prefabrication of large wall units, which are being successfully used already in half the European countries. **1979** A. B. EMARY *Woodworking* xxiv. 104 Many of the units purchased from stores are made from melamine-covered chipboard and since it is easy to obtain the home woodworker will find this material useful when making objects such as wall units and shelving. **1889** in *Cent. Dict.*, Wall vase. **1937** *Burlington Mag.* Dec. p. xx/1, The book contains many valuable hints..such as..the advantages of wall-vases. **1979** I. WEBB *Compl. Guide Flower & Foliage Arrangement* vii. 96/2 (*caption*) Two wall vases hold flowers which suit their differing qualities and appearance. **1966** D. PHILLIPS *Lighting* 36 The principal lighting method is by wall washer fittings recessed into the suspended ceiling. **1983** *Homes & Gardens* Nov. 138 Wall-washers have half the aperture closed off and their function is to give an even illumination of one wall surface from skirting to ceiling without lighting the floor.

wallaby. 1. a. Add to the list of genera: also *Wallabia* or *Thylogale*. (Earlier example.)

1826 J. ATKINSON *Agric. & Grazing N.S.W.* ii. 24 The wallabee and padgy mellon..inhabit brushes, and afford good sport in the chase.

b. *pl.* (With capital initial.) The name of the Australian international rugby football team.

1908 *Daily Chron.* 28 Sept. 4/6 The 'Wallabies', as the Australian football players..have christened themselves. **1945** BAKER *Austral. Lang.* ix. 178 Just as New Zealand football representatives acquired the names *All Blacks, Fernleaves*, and *Kiwis*, so did Australian representatives become known as *Kangaroos, Wallabies* and *Waratahs*. **1975** *Country Life* 4 Dec. 1528/1 The Wallabies are about to play the first international of their tour against Scotland.

2. (Earlier example.)

1865 E. J. OVERBURY *Wallaby Track* in Stewart & Keesing *Old Bush Songs* (1957) 233 There are others who stick during sheaving, Then shoulder their swags on their back; For the rest of the year they'll be steering On their well-beloved Wallaby Track.

Wallace (wǫ·lăs). The name of Alfred Russel *Wallace* (1823–1913), British naturalist, used *attrib.* or in the possessive to designate concepts originated by him or related to his work, as *Wallace effect*, the evolution of reproductive isolation between sympatric species; *Wallace('s) line*, a hypothetical boundary proposed by Wallace in 1858 as separating the Oriental and the Australasian biogeographical regions.

1966 V. GRANT in *Amer. Naturalist* C. 99 It seems fitting and desirable to designate the process of selection for reproductive isolation as the Wallace effect. **1981** *Amer. Jrnl. Bot.* LXVIII. 1247/2 The sympatric origin of isolating mechanisms, the Wallace effect, postulates that those individuals in sympatric populations of the incipient species when crossed with members of the other species waste gametes in so doing, due to sterility or inviability of their progeny. **1868** T. H. HUXLEY in *Proc. Zool. Soc.* 313 Passing south of India and Indo-Malaisia [*sic*], but north of the Nicobar islands, the boundary in question would coincide with what may be called 'Wallace's line', between the Indian and the Papuan divisions of the Malay archipelago. **1911** *Rep. Brit. Assoc. Adv. Sci.* 435 For fresh-water fishes Wallace's Line is..of fundamental importance. **1957** P. J. DARLINGTON *Zoogeography* vii. 469 A small fraction of the Oriental mammal fauna extends for a considerable distance across Wallace's Line. **1958** A. J. TOYNBEE *East to West* xv. 44 Nor am I talking here of 'the Wallace line' between the gum trees and marsupial mammals of Australasia and the standard flora and fauna of the rest of the world. **1982** *New Scientist* 3 June 653/1 Examination of the fauna..on Bali and adjacent islands led him to define the 'Wallace Line'—the division between the Oriental fauna to the west and the Australasian forms to the east and north.

wallah. Add: **1. b.** (Later examples not in Anglo-Indian contexts.)

1940 E. POUND *Cantos* lx. 90 The European church wallahs wonder if this can be reconciled. **1955** *Times* 15 June 3/5 Thousands of the lorries were being worked for 12, 14, 16, and 18 hours a night, with tragic results. The term used on the roads to describe these drivers was 'night-and-day wallahs'. **1977** J. I. M. STEWART *Madonna of Astrolabe* xvii. 248 It's marvellous what these ambulance wallas can do at a pinch. **1982** B. TRAPIDO *Brother of more Famous Jack* xxxvi. 124, I thought briefly of Roger who, being a music wallah, had always made a thing of St. Cecilia's Day.

d. One carrying out a routine administrative job; a civil servant, a bureaucrat. *colloq.*

1965 A. NICOL *Truly Married Woman* 32 There's no end to what you wallahs in the administration would do to show your damned official broadmindedness. **1974** *Courier-Mail* (Brisbane) 7 June 7/3 Some wallahs in Canberra are sitting in air-conditioned offices telling us what has been flooded and what hasn't.

wallah-wallah, walla-walla (wǫ·lă wǫ·lă). [Origin unknown.] In Hong Kong, a small boat used as a ferry for casual traffic.

1957 R. MASON *World of Suzie Wong* I. iii. 33 Ships of every shape and size..tramps, junks, sampans, walla-wallas. **1967** E. HUNT *Danger Game* viii. 152 They rode in a rickshaw, a sampan and a walla walla boat. **1969** J. BENNETT *Dragon* i. 5 Back and forth, ply ferry-boats..and hydrofoils..off to Macao; walla-wallas; scavenger-boats. **1970** D. DODGE *Hatchetman* 8 Sampans, junks, and *wallah-wallahs* caught in the open water were doomed when Tai Fung blew. **1976** W. MARSHALL *Hatchet Man* i. 2 A wallah-wallah boat transporting a sailor late back from leave worked its way to alongside..a moored destroyer.

wallaroo. (Earlier example.)

1826 J. ATKINSON *Agric. & Grazing N.S.W.* ii. 24 There is also found far in the interior another variety [of kangaroo], called wallaroos; they are much larger than any of the others.

wallbanger (wǭ·lbæŋəɹ). *U.S.* Also **W-.** [App. f. WALL *sb.*[1] + BANGER[1].] In full *Harvey Wallbanger*. A cocktail made from vodka or gin and orange juice.

1970 *Gourmet* Nov. 9 (Advt.), Harvey Wallbanger. Fill tall glass with ice cubes. Fill ¾ full with orange juice. Add 1 oz. Vodka. **1972** *New Yorker* 30 Sept. 41/2 A wallbanger is a vodka or a gin or whatever you please with orange juice. **1981** T. HEALD *Murder at Moose Jaw* xi. 130 The Mounties..ordered a brace of Harvey Wallbangers. *Ibid.* 131 Smith took a draught of Wallbanger.

walled, *ppl. a.* Add: **2. a.** *walled-in*, enclosed by walls (earlier example).

1777 P. THICKNESSE *Year's Journey* II. xlix. 132 *Bonne* is a good town, well walled-in, pleasantly situated.

wallet. Add: **4.** *wallet-carrying* adj.

1929 D. H. LAWRENCE *Pansies* 76 Men in bowler hats, hurrying And a mingling of wallet-carrying women.

walletful (wǫ·lėtful). Also **wallet-full. [**f. WALLET + -FUL.] As much as a wallet (sense 3 a) will hold.

1909 in WEBSTER. **1966** *Guardian* 9 Dec. 8/6 He has a walletful of notes. **1968** L. DURRELL *Tunc* ii. 48 'I began to carry around a wallet-full of children... Look.' He tipped out of a wallet a series of grotesque pictures of nude children.

walley, var. *WALLY *sb.*[2] (and *a.*[3]).

wall-eye. Add: Also **walleye. 3.** For 'the U.S.' substitute 'N. Amer.' and add after 'fishes': esp. the wall-eyed pike, *Stizostedion vitreum*. (Earlier and later examples.)

1876 *Fur, Fin & Feather* Sept. 163/1 All along the Minnesota Division are numerous clear lakes and ponds, teeming with..'wall-eyes' or pike-perch. **1968** [see

*MUSKY *sb.*[2]]. **1982** *Nature* 16 Sept. 202/2 Walleye fish, *Stizostedion*, eat each other 'tail first', and chains of up to four fish engaged in simultaneous cannibalism have been seen.

wallflower. Add: **1. d.** A perfume derived from the flowers of this plant.

1907 *Yesterday's Shopping* (1969) 521/1 Perfumes... Verbena. Wallflower. White Carnation. *c* **1938** *Fortnum & Mason Price List* 55/2 Wallflower.. Wild Rose.. Assorted Bath Ovals. **1972** [see *MIGNONETTE 1 d].

wallful (wǫ·lful). [f. WALL *sb.*[1] + -FUL.] As much as the surface of a wall will hold; the area of an entire side of a wall.

1959 *Times* 3 Jan. 2/6 This very personal little miscellany, with its notable Bacon and wallfuls of Keith Vaughan and Burra. **1973** *Art Internat.* Mar. 52/2 The traces in question consisted of a few wallfuls of photo collages and a couple of films. **1975** 'D. RUTHERFORD' *Mystery Tour* vii. 173 A wallful of luggage lockers.

walling, *vbl. sb.*[2] Add: **3. walling hammer,** a hammer used for dressing stones in a dry wall.

1841 S. BAMFORD *Life of Radical* (ed. 2) I. 84 This person had.. threatened to beat in their brains with a walling hammer which he had in his hand. **1881** W. WESTALL *Old Factory* I. x. 136 Them as has walling hammers comes next and next again them wi' stone-breakers' hammers and hand-hammers. **1964** H. HODGES *Artifacts* vii. 109 In dressing, the usual process was to hack away first the worst of the protruding lumps with a walling hammer. **1971** *Country Life* 9 Sept. 618/1 Prizes include.. a walling hammer for the competitor who has travelled the longest distance in order to take part.

wallop, *sb.* **4. a.** Delete 'and *humorous*'. Also *fig.*

1925 T. DREISER *Amer. Trag.* I. II. iii. 171 What a wallop, eh? An' us leavin' him and that girl in the car. **1936** 'J. CURTIS' *Gilt Kid* v. 57 The brandy went down good and packed a real wallop. **1943** E. B. WHITE *Let.* 4 June (1976) 242 K and I got a big wallop out of hearing from you. **1976** *National Observer* (U.S.) 23 Oct. 22/1 Now it assumes a vertical position on the upper half of the page. Better visibility, more wallop. So we think. **1978** S. BRILL *Teamsters* x. 390 Life for Harold Gibbons didn't pack much of a wallop anymore.

c. *colloq.* Alcohol, esp. beer; alcoholic drink.

1933 *Bulletin* (Sydney) 11 Jan. 20/2 This time the wallop was met 40 miles away. **1945** J. B. PRIESTLEY *Three Men in New Suits* viii. 133 It's drink... Booze or wollop... Nine times out of ten.. you wake up in the morning.. with the usual hangover. **1949** 'G. ORWELL' *Nineteen Eighty-Four* I. viii. 90 When I was a young man, mild beer—wallop we used to call it—was fourpence a pint. **1962** N. MARSH *Hand in Glove* ii. 40 'May Leonard fix mine?.. He knows my kind of wallop.'.. Leonard adroitly mixed two treble Martinis. **1972** L. LAMB *Picture Frame* vi. 56 Mrs Tyler could do nothing to improve the wallop she served at the Hurdlemakers [Inn].

walloper. Add: **4.** *Austral. slang.* A policeman.

1945 BAKER *Austral. Lang.* vii. 137 We also call a policeman a.. walloper. **1954** *Coast to Coast 1953–4* 175 A showman he was. Knock-around man. Always two jumps ahead of the wallopers. **1968** D. O'GRADY *Bottle of Sandwiches* 54 Roebourne boasted one pub, one police station with two wallopers in it,.. and a hospital. **1981** *Bulletin* (Sydney) 13 Jan. 391, I could quite happily call them my friends. I could never think of them as wallopers.

walloping, *ppl. a.* **2.** (Examples.)

1959 F. ASTAIRE *Steps in Time* (1960) xxviii. 317 *Funny Face* proved a walloping success in the main big-city first runs and particularly at the Music Hall, where it broke several records. **1980** M. RICHLER *Joshua Then & Now* I. ii. 55 Joshua slid behind the bar, which was unattended, and poured himself a walloping cognac.

wallow, *sb.* Add: **1. a.** (Later *fig.* examples.)

1969 J. GROSS *Rise & Fall Man of Lett.* iii. 89 Nor was he at all averse himself, as a reader, to a nice old-fashioned romantic wallow, with wedding-bells ringing out in Chapter the Last. **1975** *Listener* 4 Dec. 746/2 While we are having a wallow, let me suggest that reviewers discussing 'X' films.. should be more explicit.

b. Also *transf.*

1963 A. SMITH *Throw out Two Hands* xi. 114 Every so often came a glutinous wallow where some lorry had spent time not only in extricating itself but in deforming the track still further.

c. *fig.* A state of depression or stagnation.

1934 in WEBSTER. **1938** *Times* 19 Jan. 13/5 Cannot some effort be made to rescue from the wallow into which in the provinces it is falling that fine old British institution the Christmas pantomime? **1969** J. GASKELL *Sweet Sweet Summer* 77 And you know how inter-holed and jig-saw-slotted intricate incestuous old showbis is—*one* despairs, they're all down in the black wallow. **1975** *Bookseller* 3 May 2380/2 Lifting the *Sunday Times* novel reviews out of the terrible wallows they have been in for the last few years.

wallow, *v.*[1] **6. d.** (Earlier examples.)

1876 'MARK TWAIN' *Tom Sawyer* x. 97 But if ever I get off this time, I lay I'll just *waller* in Sunday-schools! **1881** —— *Lett. to Publishers* (1967) 136 The Earl's literary excrement charmed me like Fanny Hill. I just wallowed in it.

wall-paper. Add: Also **wallpaper. 1.** (Earlier examples.) Now also made of other materials, such as vinyl. Cf. *wallcovering* s.v. *WALL *sb.*[1] 22.

1827 DRAKE & MANSFIELD *Cincinnati in 1826* viii. 65 Two Wall Paper Factories, 9 hands. **1847** F. A. KEMBLE *Let.* 12 Dec. in *Rec. Later Life* (1882) III. 300 You know how subject I am even to such an influence as that of a ridiculous wall-paper.

2. *fig.* An unobtrusive background; esp. with reference (chiefly *derog.*) to sound, music, etc. Freq. with preceding *adj.* or in *attrib.* use.

1919 'C. DANE' *Legend* 28 They wearied me... They faded into a mere wall-paper of sound, and I forgot that they were there. **1934** C. LAMBERT *Music Ho!* III. 228 It is a matter of indifference whether jazz is a stimulant.. or a piece of mental wallpaper. **1959** A. BAILEY *Making Progress* 157 Cool jazz formed a background, like aural wallpaper. **1966** *Guardian* 4 June 6/4 Of course, we have to have wallpaper talk, in a week's broadcasting, just as some people have to have wallpaper music all the week. **1969** *Listener* 24 Apr. 588/1 The cultural wallpaper of his own childhood was the Australian commercial radio stations. **1977** *Zigzag* June 40/1 The best track, for me, is.. 'Living in The Band', but most of this is just so much wallpaper. **1980** *Jrnl. R. Soc. Arts* Mar. 223/2 Possibly television is becoming visual wallpaper in much the same way as radio has become audible wallpaper.

Hence **wa·llpaper** *v. trans.* and *intr.*, to cover a wall with wallpaper; also *transf.* and *fig.*; **wa·llpapered** *ppl. a.*

1934 WEBSTER, Wallpaper *v.t.* & *i.* **1956** *Family Handyman Magazine's Painting & Redecorating Bk.* 34/1 If you want to paint formerly wallpapered walls: 1. Use check system just described. **1962** A. NISBETT *Technique Sound Studio* xi. 198 If this technique.. does not quite come off it may be possible to wallpaper over the cracks by adding a new overall backing. **1973** *Listener* 29 Nov. 733/1 You could wallpaper St. Paul's with the free brochures. **1975** P. DICKINSON *Lively Dead* xxi. 122 She had planned to wallpaper the back room. **1977** M. FRENCH *Women's Room* (1978) ii. 108 She painted and wallpapered, refinished furniture. **1977** *Listener* 28 Apr. 537/1 Into the Cambridge Union, through the amazingly wallpapered lobby. **1978** R. MILLS *Comprehensive Educ.* 80 We did the paintwork and wallpapered the ceiling. **1979** 'P. O'CONNOR' *Into Strong City* xii. 39 The room is wallpapered with.. a section of Soho dressed as artists as distinct from the criminal section who dress in another fashion.

Wallsend. (Earlier example.)

1821 *Times* 23 Jan. 1/4 Coals 46s.. warranted Wallsend, 50s. superior.

Wall Street (wǭl strīt). orig. *U.S.* The name of a street in New York City where some of the most important American financial institutions are centred, used: **1.** *absol.* Denoting the American financial world or money-market. Also *transf.*

[**1806** *Balance* (Hudson, N.Y.) V. 228/1 Walking thro' Wall street yesterday morning, I saw a large crowd.] **1841** *Week in Wall St.* p. ix, In the expressive language of Wall-street, he has himself been 'flunked'. **1871** L. M. ALCOTT *Little Men* xiv. 244 The firm [was] broken up... The barn, which was the boys' Wall Street, knew him no more. **1872** B. JERROLD *London* xii. 104 The New York gossip of yesterday, is ours upon our breakfast table. We can almost hear the hum of Wall Street. **1905** G. B. SHAW *Let.* 3 Jan. (1972) II. 497 Finding Capel Court (our Wall St) against his conscience, he became a carpenter. **1949** *Chicago Daily News* 31 May 1/6 Wall Street traced liquidation to the many new uncertainties created by declining production. **1975** *Times* 25 Sept. 8/7 The banking and business quarter—known as Beirut's 'Wall Street'.

2. a. *attrib.*, as *Wall Street broker, method, price*, etc.

1836 *Jamestown* (N.Y.) *Jrnl.* 16 Mar. 1/2 A company—Wall street brokers and speculators—are the applicants for the loan to the New York and Erie Railroad. **1861** in L. C. Baker *Hist. U.S. Secret Service* (1867) v. 100 Such.. is the windy stuff which — uses to draw money out of the Wall Street kings. **1892** A. C. GUNTER *Miss Dividends* 188 All the rest.. [had] fallen victims to his imported Wall Street methods. **1935** G. GREENE *England made Me* II. 47 'Put through any long-distance calls.' 'The Wall Street prices?' **1940** W. FAULKNER *Hamlet* III. ii. 240 He figured if we named him Wallstreet Panic it might make him get rich like the folks that run that Wallstreet panic. **1972** R. PERRY *Fall Guy* iv. 78 His immaculate suit would have put many a Wall Street executive to shame. **1981** A. LURIE *Lang. of Costume* iv. 114 In the urban centers of the West.. bankers.. sometimes adopt an Eastern manner of speech and a Wall Street appearance.

b. Special Comb. **Wall Street crash, crisis,** the collapse of the American stock-market which took place in October 1929.

1929 *N.Y. Times* 26 Oct. 2/8 Commenting on the Wall Street crash of yesterday, the German press unanimously agrees that Germany has no reason to mourn. **1933** R. G. HAWTREY *Trade Depression* iii. 31 The Federal Reserve Banks can hardly be blamed for their policy of credit restriction up to the moment of the Wall Street crisis. **1981** E. LONGFORD *Queen Mother* ii. 38 The slump or depression of the 1930s began with the Wall Street crash of 1929 in America.

Wall Streeter (wǭ·l,strī:tər). orig. *U.S.* [f. prec. + -ER[1].] A Wall Street financier, esp. of the New York stock-market.

1885 *Weekly New Mexican Rev.* 15 Jan. 2/2 The Wall streeters and money changers want less money that they may have a better chance to grind the borrowers. **1937** [see *STEM *v.*[4] 5 b]. **1943** *Sun* (Baltimore) 2 July 17/1 Many Wall Streeters trimmed accounts to be on the safe side. **1967** *Economist* 2 Sept. 788/3 Mr Haack may also have to do something to dampen a speculative attitude which is reminding some Wall Streeters of 1929. **1979** *Listener* 1 Nov. 579/1 Wall Streeters will tell you that, since its [*sc.* the market's] high of 1968, there has been a crash of sorts.

wall-to-wall (stress variable), *a.* (*sb.*, *adv.*) [WALL *sb.*[1]] **1.** Of carpeting: covering the whole floor of a room; fitted. Also *absol.* as *sb.*

1953 A. UPFIELD *Murder must Wait* ii. 12, I detest wall-to-wall carpets. **1962** A. LURIE *Love & Friendship* vi. 97 Genuine hooked rugs scattered over the wall-to-wall carpet. **1965** G. MCINNES *Road to Gundagai* iii. 39 The room fascinated me because it had two carpets on the floor, a 'wall-to-wall' covered by an Axminster. **1977** C. MCFADDEN *Serial* (1978) xxxvi. 78/2 Harvey hated crawling around on the wall-to-wall looking for contact lenses. **1977** *New Yorker* 15 Aug. 33/1 What impressed me most about that house was the carpeting, which was mercilessly wall-to-wall. **1978** *Meridian Poetry Mag.* Autumn 10 He bestrides the wall-to-wall carpeting Like a colossus.

2. a. Of objects, etc., other than carpeting: extending from one wall to another; providing coverage of an entire space. Also as quasi-*adv.*

1959 *Observer* 12 Apr. 14/5 Underpinned with warmth—a wall-to-wall convection heater. **1977** *Washington Post* 27 Nov. M3/1 Wall-to-wall art—framed prints, posters or one enormous canvas—can cover a whole wall. *Ibid.* 3/2 I designed everything wall-to-wall... The bed,.. being 75 inches long, the distance between two of the walls, is an instant wall-to-wall component.

b. *fig.* Extending from one end or extreme to the other; allowing no unfilled space; ubiquitous.

1967 *New Yorker* 25 Nov. 222 He made a highly successful series of wall-to-wall mood-music recordings. **1973** *Listener* 19 Apr. 522/2 A respite from wall-to-wall Mozart on Radios 3 and 4. **1976** *Patriot-Ledger* (Quincy, Mass.) 10 July 3/1 The state police said it was just wall-to-wall people and wall-to-wall cars. **1977** *Time* 19 Sept. 9/3 When we kick down doors looking for these people at home, we find almost always tons of literature—wall-to-wall Marx and Marcuse. **1982** S. PARETSKY *Indemnity Only* vi. 74 Why would he agree to see me? He'd never heard of me, he has wall-to-wall appointments. **1984** *Listener* 15 Mar. 19/1 Is there any good reason why we should have news bulletins, local and national, every hour on the hour, chat shows.. and wall-to-wall discussion programmes? **1984** *New Statesman* 16 Nov. 16/2 Their sponsors include the IBA.. and the BBC (in whose Reithian corridors the epithet 'wall-to-wall *Dallas*' was reputedly coined).

wallum (wǫ·ləm). *Austral.* [Aboriginal.] **a.** A tall evergreen shrub, *Banksia æmula*, common in parts of Australia. **b.** The heathland along the Queensland coast where this is common.

1889 J. H. MAIDEN *Useful Native Plants Austral.* 383 *Banksia marginata, Cav.*,... 'Honeysuckle'. The 'Wallum' of the aboriginals of Wide Bay (Queensland). **1890** F. M. BAILEY *Catal. Indigenous & Naturalised Plants Queensland* 103/2 Wallum, Banksia æmula. **1965** *Austral. Encycl.* IX. 310/1 In Queensland, the Wallum coastal formation stretching north of Brisbane has a varied heathland type of flora. **1970** W. W. BRYAN in R. M. Moore *Austral. Grasslands* vii. 107 North of Maryborough rainfall in the Wallum is only 40–45 in. **1979** *Sunday Sun* (Brisbane) 24 June 9/6 CSIRO projects on similar tracts of coastal wallum have shown it can be transformed relatively inexpensively by the aerial application of trace elements. **1979** *Sunday Mail Mag.* (Brisbane) 29 July 18/3 The wallum banksia dominates the dune scrub with its magnificent large flowers atop the serrated leaves.

wally (wǫ·li), *sb.*[2] (and *a.*[3]) *slang.* Also **Wally.** [Origin uncertain: perh. the same word as *WOLLY. Said by some to be the dim. of the personal name *Walter*: cf. *CHARLEY, CHARLIE 6. Cf. also WALLYDRAG, WALLYDRAIGLE.] An unfashionable person; one who is foolish, inept, or ineffectual. Also as a mild term of abuse. Also *attrib.* or as *adj.*

1969 *Daily Mirror* 10 Oct. 19/1 *Wally*, out of fashion. **1974** *Times* 8 Aug. 2/4 The successors to the flat-earthers.. are at present encamped on the perimeter of the great concentric stone circles... They choose to be known as the Wallies of Wessex, Wally being a conveniently anonymous umbrella for vulnerable individuals. **1976** *Telegraph* (Brisbane) 8 Oct. 10/4 The Arnolds call anybody who wears conventional clothes, such as jeans or skirts, a Wally. **1979** *Listener* 20 & 27 Dec. 861/1 Cuban heel boots.. are.. like a Wally uniform... John Travolta, the Bee-Gees and Boney M are considered Wally acts. **1983** *Evening Star* (Ipswich) 20 June 7/1 He shrugged off Ms. Ford's throw as temperamental but I bet he felt a right wally. **1983** P. INCHBALD *Short Break in Venice* xviii. 177 Keith cracked a joke over the radio and got called a bleeding wally. **1984** *Daily Tel.* 14 June 1/4 'They looked a right load of wallies,' said an eye-witness. **1985** M. STOTT *Before I Go* iv. 77, I shall seem more of a 'wally' to them than ever because I don't know half the leading telly presenters.

walm, *v.* Add: **1. c.** (Later *poet.* example.)

1908 HARDY *Dynasts* III. III. iii. 387 Throats shout 'advance' And forms walm, wallow, and slack suddenly.

walnut.[1] Add: **2. b. black walnut** (earlier examples); **English walnut** (earlier examples); **white walnut** (examples).

1612 R. JOHNSON *New Life Virginea* sig. B3, They cut downe wood for wanscot, blacke walnut tree, Spruce, Cedar & Deale. **1714** J. LAWSON *Hist. Carolina* 99 The Walnut Tree of America is call'd Black Walnut. **1743** J. CLAYTON *Flora Virginica* 190 *Juglans alba*..White Walnuts. **1772** C. CARROLL *Let.* 9 June in *Maryland Hist. Mag.* (1919) XIV. 149 It froze Here last Thursday night .., it bit the Leaves of the English Walnut tree. **1822** White walnut [see *creek-bottom* s.v. *CREEK *sb.*[1] 8]. **1876** 'MARK TWAIN' *Tom Sawyer* xvi. 134 Perfectly round white things a trifle smaller than an English walnut. **1912** White walnut [see *OIL-NUT b, c].

4. a. (sense 1) *walnut cake, -oil* (earlier and later examples); (sense 3) *walnut-panelled* adj.

1889 H. A. DE SALIS *Cakes & Confections* 28 Walnut Cake. Rub four ounces of peeled walnuts..with the whites of three eggs, [etc.]. **1936** *New Yorker* 29 Feb. 21/1 His favourite *Linzertorte*, a walnut cake. **1977** F. PARRISH *Fire in Barley* iv. 39 Some ginger biscuits and a slice of walnut cake. **1612** W. STRACHEY *Trav. Virginia* (1953) I. v. 73 A lock of an ell long, which they annoynt often with walnut oyle. **1963** *Times* 9 Feb. 11/3 The vegetables are luscious and the salads delicately dressed with walnut oil. **1984** M. BABSON *Death Swap* xii. 90 A large tin of truffles ..and the inevitable walnut oil. **1934** WEBSTER, Walnut-paneled. **1961** M. BEADLE *These Ruins are Inhabited* (1963) ii. 24 We ducked through a narrow passageway and into the chapel, a walnut-panelled room. **1981** P. NIESEWAND *Word of Gentleman* xxv. 162 Macgregor's office was walnut-panelled.

Walpolian (wǭlpōu·liăn), *a.* and *sb.* Also **-ean.** [f. the name of Robert *Walpole* (1676–1745), politician, and of his son Horace *Walpole* (1717–97), writer and politician + -IAN.] **A.** *adj.* **1.** Of, pertaining to, or characteristic of Horace Walpole or his writings. Also applied to neo-Gothic architecture of a type popularized by Horace Walpole.

1867 H. E. H. JERNINGHAM *Life in French Château* vi. 165 She had seen through the empty-heartedness and true Walpolian sense of gratitude of those she had befriended. **1876** HARDY *Hand of Ethelberta* II. xl. 146 A tendency to talk Walpolean scandal about foreign courts was particularly manifest. **1944** J. LEES-MILNE *Jrnl.* 2 June in *Prophesying Peace* (1977) 71, I was fascinated by the Walpolian Gothic chapel. **1973** *Country Life* 14 June 1726/1 The greatest Walpolian scholar, W. S. Lewis, remarked in 1934 that Strawberry Hill was 'assembled rather than built'.

2. Of, pertaining to, or characteristic of Robert Walpole or his political career.

1909 J. M. RIGG in *Cambr. Mod. Hist.* VI. xiii. 424 He adhered to the Walpolean tradition of an *entente cordiale* with France. **1979** *N. & Q.* Feb. 76/1 His appeal..to 'custom and reason', 'the practice of former times', and 'the original principles of government' could be used equally against American radicals and Walpolian oligarchs. **1983** *Ibid.* Feb. 23/1 More substance still is given to his role as a Walpolean hack.

B. *sb.* An admirer of Horace Walpole.

1927 *Observer* 24 Apr. 6/2 No Walpolian can be satisfied with anything less than the complete Toynbee edition of the Letters.

So **Walpolia·na, -ea·na** (see ANA *suff.*).

1799 (*title*) Walpoliana. **1875** *Encycl. Brit.* I. 785/2 Of the examples England has produced of this species of composition, perhaps the most interesting is the *Walpoliana*, a transcript of the literary conversation of Horace Walpole, Earl of Orford. **1938** *Times Lit. Suppl.* 26 Feb. 136/4 If General Conway's house, grounds, and..views.. are over-praised, they are only the more authentic as Walpoliana. **1959** *Times* 16 May 8/5 There will be many on this side of the Atlantic who will be deeply grieved by the news of the death of Annie Burr, wife of Wilmarth Sheldon ('Lefty') Lewis, the eminent collector and editor of Walpoliana. **1980** *Jrnl. R. Soc. Arts* Feb. 161/2 Dr. Lewis's collector's flair and comfortable means enabled him to build up an unrivalled assemblage of Walpoleana —original Walpole letters and manuscripts, and books from Walpole's own library.

Walpurgis (vælpʊ̆·ɹgis). The name (St. Walpurga or Walburga) of an 8th-c. Anglo-Saxon saint and missionary in Heidenheim, Germany, used: **a.** in **Walpurgis night** [tr. G. *Walpurgisnacht*], in German folklore and esp. Goethe's *Faust* a feast of the powers of darkness or witches' sabbath (cf. SABBATH 3) celebrated on the Brocken, a peak in the Harz mountains, on 30 April. Also *transf.*, an orgiastic celebration or party.

1823 F. L. GOWER tr. *Goethe's Faust* 233 Walpurgis Night. The Hartz Mountain. Wild and desolate country. **1900** J. FRAZER *Golden Bough* (ed. 2) I. i. 36 The special season for thus promoting the growth of flax..in some places is Candlemas or Walpurgis Night (the eve of May Day). **1933** J. CARY *Amer. Visitor* xvi. 213 A fire which illuminated a kind of Walpurgis night of ragamuffins, soldiers, doxies from the town. **1964** L. DEIGHTON *Funeral in Berlin* xlv. 286, I sank into a vortex of imaginings in which Walpurgis Night and..the smell of petrol.. were indissolubly linked. **1980** *Amer. Scholar* Autumn 456 Walpurgis Night on the eve of Mayday is an excuse for bacchanalia.

b. In other *attrib.* uses with reference to this festival.

1857 C. KINGSLEY *Two Years Ago* III. i. 33 That Walpurgis-dance of the witches and the fiends, which will ..whirl unbidden through a mortal brain. **1899** R. WHITEING *No. 5 John St.* xxix. 300 The Bosses..have come to keep Walpurgis revel. **1979** J. TATE tr. *K. A. Blom's Limits of Pain* xx. 164 The last day of April.. he could mix in the crowds,..warming himself by the Walpurgis bonfires.

‖ **Walpurgisnacht** (valpu·ɹgisnaχt). [Ger.] = prec. a. Also *transf.*

1822 SHELLEY *Let.* 10 Apr. (1964) II. 407, I have only attempted the scenes omitted in this translation, & would send you that of the *Walpurgisnacht*. **1898** W. JAMES *Let.* 9 July (1920) II. 76 The influences of Nature, [etc.]..all fermented within me till it became a regular Walpurgis Nacht. **1909** —— *Pluralistic Universe* i. 21 Nature can have little unity for savages. It is a Walpurgis-nacht procession, a checkered play of light and shadow, a medley of impish and elfish friendly and inimical powers. **1947** *Partisan Rev.* XIV. 102/2 The *Walpurgisnacht* which is Hollywood. **1965** *Guardian* 10 Dec. 6/5, I might still avoid the woods on Walpurgisnacht. **1977** *Time* 3 Jan. 65/2 *Who's Afraid of Virginia Woolf?* An admirable revival..verifies that after 14 years this marital Walpurgisnacht has become part of the permanent canon of U.S. drama.

walpurgite (væ·lpʊ̆ɹgəit). *Min.* [ad. G. *walpurgin* (A. Weisbach 1871, in *Neues Jahrb. f. Mineral.*, etc. 870), f. *Walpurgis*, name of the vein in a mine near Schneeberg in Germany where the first specimen was found: see -ITE[1].] A hydrous arsenate of bismuth and uranium found as yellow, translucent or transparent triclinic crystals.

1872 G. J. BRUSH in J. D. Dana *Syst. Min.* (ed. 5) App. I. 16 Walpurgite. **1958** *Bull. U.S. Geol. Survey* No. 1064. 242 Walpurgite is a secondary mineral, found in the oxidized zone of a vein carrying uraninite, cobalt and nickel arsenides, and native bismuth from which the U, Bi, and As content of the mineral has been derived.

Walras (va·lra). The name of Marie Esprit Léon *Walras* (1834–1910), French economist, used in the possessive in *Walras' law* to denote the mathematical theory of general economic equilibrium devised by him. So **Walrasian** (valrēi·siăn) *a.*, of or pertaining to this theory.

1942 O. LANGE in O. Lange et al. *Stud. Math. Econ.* 50, I propose to call this identity *Walras' law* because Walras was the first to recognize its fundamental importance in the formulation of the mathematical theory of prices. **1942** W. JAFFÉ in *Ibid.* 37 The affinities..between these older Walrasian theories and their independently discovered Keynesian counterparts. **1963** *Canad. Jrnl. Economics & Pol. Sci.* XXIX. 535 (*heading*) A note on Marshallian *versus* Walrasian stability conditions. **1964** *Q. Jrnl. Econ.* LXXVIII. 485 Walras' Law..states that the value of all goods demanded, including money, is equal to the value of all goods supplied. **1972** T. SOWELL *Say's Law* i. 34 *Walras' Law* states that the sum of the respective values (quantities times money prices) of goods supplied plus money supplied equals the sum of the respective values (quantities times money prices) of goods demanded plus money demanded. **1972** *Times* 26 Oct. 8/6 Sir John [Hicks]..moved away from the partial equilibrium approach of Alfred Marshall back towards the older Continental Walrasian 'general equilibrium' approach. **1983** *Economics Lett.* XIII. 49 The possibility of transfer paradoxes in Walrasian stable markets.

walrus. Add: **3. walrus moustache,** a large moustache which overhangs the lips (thus resembling the whiskers of a walrus); similarly **walrus whiskers.**

1918 W. OWEN 31 Oct. (1967) 591 An old soldier with a walrus moustache. **1982** T. FITZGIBBON *With Love* I. xii. 88, I remember Conan Doyle as a large man with sad thoughtful eyes and a walrus moustache. **1930** J. DOS PASSOS *42nd Parallel* I. 100 A big man with walrus whiskers.

Walschaerts (væ·l-, wæ·lʃəɹts, -ʃaɹts). *Mech.* Also **Walschaert.** The name of Egide *Walschaerts* (1820–1901), Belgian mechanic, used *attrib.* and in the possessive to designate a kind of valve-gear he invented that was used on some steam locomotives (see quot. 1911).

1880 *Proc. Inst. Mech. Engineers* 435 His arrangement ..was simply a modification of the Walschaert gear. **1911** *Encycl. Brit.* XXV. 834/1 A form of radial gear very largely used in locomotives, especially on the continent of Europe, is the Walschaert or Heusinger-Waldegg gear, in which the valve receives its motion in part from the piston cross-head.., and in part from a single eccentric set at right angles to the crank. **1975** B. REED *150 Yrs. Brit. Steam Locomotives* vi. 47/1 Other Group three-cylinder classes..had three separate sets of Walschaerts motion with eccentric drive for the inside set.

Walsingham (wǭ·lsiŋăm). The name of a town in Norfolk, used *attrib.* in *Walsingham Way*, a designation of the Milky Way supposed formerly to have been used as a guide by pilgrims travelling to the shrine of Our Lady of Walsingham.

c **1878** G. M. HOPKINS *Loss of Eurydice* in *Poems* (1967) 75 A starlight-wender of ours would say The marvellous Milk was Walsingham Way. **1922** JOYCE *Ulysses* 685 The waggoner's star: Walsingham way: the chariot of David: the annular cinctures of Saturn. **1973** M. J. PETRY *Herne the Hunter* vi. 71 In certain parts of England, and especially in East Anglia, the Milky Way was also known as the *Walsingham Way*, on account of the hosts of *pilgrims* who passed along the roads..to the shrine of Our Lady at Walsingham in Norfolk.

Walt Disney (wǭlt di·zni). The name of *Walt*er Elias *Disney* (1901–66), American pioneer of cartoon films, used *attrib.* to denote the style of his films or their characters. Cf. *DISNEYESQUE *a.*

1946 R. LEHMANN *Gipsy's Baby* 12 He was a total failure with rabbits, and if he blundered on one in the course of one of his Walt Disney gallops over the fields, he winced. **1962** A. LURIE *Love & Friendship* vi. 107 Bright, cheap, sentimental in a Walt Disney style, it [*sc.* a Christmas card] depicted a group of cherubs carrying packages. **1966** 'K. A. SADDLER' *Gilt Edge* x. 144 The ancient home of the Meldmays..glistened in the moonlight like a Walt Disney castle. **1974** C. HAMPTON *Savages* (1976) ii. 26 Three young men enter. They are all wearing rubber Walt Disney masks.

Walter Mitty: see *MITTY[2].

Walther (wǫ·ltəɹ, ‖va·-). The name of a German firm of firearm manufacturers, used *attrib.* and *absol.* to designate pistols and rifles made by them.

1920 H. B. C. POLLARD *Automatic Pistols* v. 49 The *Walther Selbstlade* pistol is a pocket automatic of 6·355 mm., six shots, German manufacture. **1934** G. BURRARD *Identification of Firearms & Forensic Ballistics* ix. 203, I was informed that the defendant was using a Walther rifle at the time of the accident. **1965** I. FLEMING *Man with Golden Gun* v. 76 The Walther PPK inside the waistband of his trousers. **1968** A. DIMENT *Great Spy Race* vii. 100 He..took a gun, a baby Walther, from its hiding place. **1971** *Guardian* 28 Sept. 24/1 As a point of historical interest, this is the first time that the Walther pistol, a shoulder-holstered gun introduced into the Royal Ulster Constabulary last year..has been fired in action. **1975** [see *LUGER]. **1981** J. B. HILTON *Playground of Death* i. 7 Bielby had been discovered..with a warm-barrelled pistol in his hand..a Walther 7.65 wartime German police model.

Waltonian, *a.* (Earlier example.)

a **1828** T. BEWICK *My Life* (1981) xvii. 165 Some regulations should be laid own as a guide to the fair anglers... I think Waltonian societies would be all-sufficient to do this.

waltz, *sb.* Add: **4.** Something accomplished with ease. *slang.*

1968 *Time* 5 July 38 Though Dancer eased him up at the end, Nevele Pride won in a waltz. **1970** G. F. NEWMAN *Sir, You Bastard* vi. 179 The qualifying examinations conducted through the Civil Service Commission were a waltz.

5. *attrib.* and *Comb.*, as **waltz king** [G. *Walzerkönig*], an epithet applied to the Viennese composer Johann Strauss (1825–99), famous for his waltzes; **waltz-length** *a.*, (of a garment) calf-length.

1908 *Busy Man's Mag.* Feb. 51/2 Johann Strauss, 'the waltz king'. **1938** *Oxf. Compan. Mus.* 1013/1 It seems as likely that such a waltz as the *Blue Danube*, by Johann Strauss the younger, the 'Waltz King', will last for ever as that Beethoven's Fifth Symphony will do so. **1958** *Vogue* Nov. 40 Nightgowns with lace, or ribbons and bows, in waltz length or swirling to the ankles. **1975** *New Yorker* 17 Nov. 134/2 A waltz-length, front-fastened Edwardian robe of snowy cotton, with textured scrolls of guipure on its yokes, is $75.

waltz, *v.* **b.** For 'Chiefly *slang*' read '*colloq.*' and add: Also, to move unconcernedly or boldly, as to waltz *into, off, up* (*to*), etc. (Further examples.)

1887 in *Amer. Speech* (1950) XXV. 39/2 Out on the Mississippi Valley road when his girl waltzed up. **1935** G. HEYER *Death in Stocks* v. 63 Tony seemed to have waltzed off for the night, so I wandered out on my own. **1951** J. FLEMING *Man who looked Back* i. 10 Here she was waltzing off with this nurse and leaving Ray..alone. **1974** F. NOLAN *Oshawa Project* ii. 12 He'll walk any nomination..and waltz into the White House without even having to put up a fight. **1978** N. MARSH *Grave Mistake* viii. 240 P'raps..he'll come waltzing back with a silly grin on his face having been to stay with his auntie. **1979** C. MACLEOD *Luck runs Out* v. 50 If any student or students had..got mixed up in a mess like this, they'd hardly come waltzing up to the President in open assembly and say so. **1980** 'R. B. DOMINIC' *Attending Physician* xxiv. 218 He waltzed off to be the first one in the lounge. **1984** B. FRANCIS *AA Car Duffer's Guide* 6/1 That same afternoon..the vicar's lady waltzes in.

d. *trans.* To transport or convey (something). *U.S. joc.*

1884 'MARK TWAIN' *Huck. Finn* iii. 22 They've got to waltz that palace around over the country wherever you want it. **1901** MERWIN & WEBSTER *Calumet 'K'* xi. 197 He'd call the men off just the same, and leave us to waltz the timbers around all by ourselves.

e. *to waltz Matilda*: see *MATILDA.

waltzer. Add: **c.** A fairground ride (see quots. 1961[1], 1968).

1961 F. C. ROOPE *Come to Fair* iii. 71 *The Waltzer*, an appropriate name for an ingenious machine. The motion of the cars..is both round and round the undulating track, and also a spinning one on their own axis. *Ibid.*, The Waltzer is completely safe for everyone except the most foolhardy riders. **1965** [see *NOAH'S ARK 7]. **1968** D. BRAITHWAITE *Fairground Archit.* 176 *Waltzer*, a member of the switchback family having freely-pivoted tub-shaped cars mounted on the undulating platform. **1975** *Sunday People* 6 July 11/5 As he lurches about on the waltzer or is shoved away in a dodgem car, it's easy to give him a folded bottom note in place of two. **1980** R. Hill *Killing Kindness* vi. 50 He could be on the dodgems, or the waltzer. He helps around when they're busy.

Wampanoag (wāmpănō^u·ăg), *sb.* and *a.* Also † **Wampanong, -noug.** [Narragansett lit. 'easterners'.] **A.** *sb.* (A member of) an Indian people of south-eastern Massachusetts and the eastern shore of Narraganset Bay. **B.** *adj.* Of, pertaining to, or designating this people.

1676 R. Williams *Let.* 1 Apr. in B. F. Swan *Copy of Let. of R. Williams* (1971) 11 God has prospered us so that wee had had driven the Wampanoogs with Phillip out of his Countrie. **1782** 'J. H. St. John de Crèvecœur' *Lett. from Amer. Farmer* iv. 144 Those powerful tribes..the.. Massachusets, Wamponougs, Nipnets, Tarranteens, &c. **1820** Eastburn & Sands *Yamoyden* (1834) i. 16 The Wampanoag from the height Of Haup, who strained his anxious sight [etc.]. **1871** C. M. Yonge *Pioneers & Founders* i. 25 The Sachem nearest to Plymouth had been at the first arrival of the Pilgrim Fathers, Massasoiet, chief of the Wampanongs. **1910** F. W. Hodge *Handbk. Amer. Indians* II. 903/2 Wampanoag... One of the principal tribes of New England. Their proper territory appears to have been the peninsula on the E. shore of Narragansett bay now included in Bristol co., R.I., and the adjacent parts in Bristol co., Mass. **1948** *Sat. Even. Post* 26 June 23/3 The township of Dartmouth had been purchased from Chief Massasoit, of the Wampanoag tribe. **1979** *United States 1980/81* (Penguin Travel Guides) 642 There's also the Wampanoag Indian Museum. **1980** *Smithsonian* Aug. 22 Red Wing's museum has some nice relics from early days when the Wampanoags & Narragansets..& Mohegans & Nipmucs ranged around southern New England. **1983** *Times* 3 Oct. 3/4 (*caption*) Slow Turtle, of the Wampanoag Nation, Massachusetts, at a ceremony on Hounslow Heath yesterday.

wan, *a.* Add: **6.** *wanwood*, faded or decaying woodland (*nonce-wd.*).

c **1880** [see *leafmeal* s.v. *Leaf *sb.*[1] 17].

wan, *v.* Add: **3.** *trans.* To make pale.

1889 in *Cent. Dict.* **1903** Hardy *Dynasts* I. i. iii. 16 The grey glooms of a ghost-eyed despondency Wanned as with winter the national mind. **1938** W. de la Mare *Memory* 96 Miracle..That starry flake Can of its myriads Such wide pastures make, For sun to colour, And for moon to wan.

wan (wǫn, wan), *numeral a.*, *pron.*, etc. [See One *numeral a.*, *pron.*, etc.] Repr. dial. pronunc. of *one.*

1651 [see One *numeral a.*, *pron.*, etc. A. γ]. **1802** in G. Fraser *Lowland Lore* (1880) 70, I ame to Give to him .. wan half of Corn. **1880** L. Parr *Adam & Eve* II. ix. 191 'Twas past wan. **1907** G. B. Shaw *John Bull's Other Island* iv. 81 Larry cleared six yards backwards at wan jump. **1920** F. P. Dunne *Mr. Dooley on making a Will* 4 'Twud grieve me if some wan broke into song at th' news. *a* **1966** 'M. na Gopaleen' *Best of Myles* (1968) 47 If wan is up, all has to be up. **1973** *Black World* Sept. 64 Di ripes juices fruit is di wan Dat stan longer in di sun. **1973** 'J. Patrick' *Glasgow Gang Observed* vii. 70 He's the wan they're really efter. **1979** *Bull. Yorks. Dial. Soc.* Summer 14 Wan mornin t schoolmaister wor ill.

‖ **wananchi** (wanæ·ntʃi), *sb. pl.* [Swahili, pl. of *mwananchi* inhabitant, citizen.] The indigenous workers in Kenya and Tanzania; the labouring masses.

1969 *Busara* (Nairobi) II. ii. 55 The problem was how to unite and propel a nation *into a prosperous future and not into the African past.* The distinction between these two threads of thought has yet to be clarified to millions of expectant *Wananchi.* **1970** *E. Afr. Standard* 2 Jan. 6/7 Musical concerts..for the entertainment of the *wananchi.* **1974** *Sunday Tel.* 8 Dec. 5/6 For it was only a few weeks ago..that President Nyerere was going about giving the *wananchi* (labouring masses) the good word about how Socialist Tanzania was doing very nicely, than you. **1980** *Standard* (Nairobi) 2 June 7/2 The Machakos District Commissioner..called on *wananchi* and leaders in the district to maintain peace.

‖ **wanax** (wæ·næks). Also **Wanax.** [ad. Gr. ϝάναξ, early and dial. form of ἄναξ lord.] A Mycenæan or Minoan king or ruler.

ϝάναξ is the word for 'king' or 'ruler' in the Linear B tablets; in the Homeric poems ἄναξ and βασιλεύς are both found.

[**1955** L. R. Palmer in *Trans. Philol. Soc. 1954* 37 ϝάναξ is used in Greek of the human lord..and of the divine protectors... The Tacitean passage inclines me to the view that the *wa na ka* is a priest-king (*rex*), who stands at the apex of the social hierarchy above the military leader (*dux*).] **1956** Ventris & Chadwick *Documents in Mycenaean Greek* v. 120 A monarchical system of government is proved for both Knossos and Pylos by references to the king (*wanax*); the absence of any further qualification shows that the state knew one king only. **1958** *Listener* 11 Dec. 1004/1 The..more varied documents..have perhaps tempted Professor Webster to assume too easily that the Mycenean *Wanax* was likewise a divine King. **1960** S. Dow *Greeks in Bronze Age* 25 When the destruction of the Twelfth Century took place, the chief of state, the *Wanax,* was evidently completely abolished. **1961** C. G. Starr *Origins Greek Civilization* (1962) ii. 48 The class struggle rose through serfs or slaves..to the retainers and agents of the great king, the *wanax.* **1978** *Antiquaries Jrnl.* LVIII. 22 At the summit [of an Achaean state] was the wanax, the head of the state, chief administrator, high judge, leader of the armed forces, and absolute controller of all economic activity.

wance(t): see *once *adv.* A. δ.

wand, *sb.* Add: **12*.** The straight rigid pipe linking the cleaning head to the hose of a vacuum cleaner.

1940 E. Hemingway *For whom Bell Tolls* xi. 149 The round opening at the end of the wand of a vacuum cleaner. **1967** *Boston Sunday Herald* 9 Apr. (Advt.), Attachments include braided hose, two wands and rug-bare floor tool. **1978** *Choice* (Austral. Consumers' Assoc.) Nov. 378 Most vacuum cleaners these days have moulded plastic bodies. Hoses are plastic or cloth covered, and some are of the 'stretch' variety. Wands and cleaning heads tend to be either plastic, steel or aluminium or a combination of these.

12.** A hand-held electronic device which can be passed over a bar code to read the data it represents and convert them into a computer-compatible form.

1978 *Bookseller* 17 June 3196/1 The light pen, or 'wand', that could read machine-readable codes on books. **1980** *Sci. Amer.* Apr. 111/1 (Advt.), As part of a portable data entry system, the wand can be used to read shelf tags for inventory control and order entry. **1982** *What's New in Computing* Nov. 62/1 Intermec designs and manufactures ..scanning wands for the printing and computer reading of tickets, tags and labels.

wand, *v.* Restrict *Sc.* and *dial.* to senses in Dict. and add: **3.** *trans.* To scan the bar code on (an article) using a wand (*wand *sb.* 12**).

1979 *Bookseller* 22 & 29 Dec. 2693/2 Books could be 'wanded' at the point of sale and the information stored on cassettes. **1982** *Fortune* 27 Dec. 100/1 Go to Section X, Jack, and wand all the woofers.

Wandale[2]**.** Add: Also **Wandal.** (Later example.)

1908 W. G. Collingwood *Scandinavian Brit.* ii. 16 The tribal confederacies of the Baltic shores—Danes, Swedes, Wandals, Burgunds, Bards, Goths.

wander, *sb.* Add: **2.** A gradual change in the orientation of a gyroscope or other spinning body, esp. the earth.

1930 [see *wander *v.* 2 g]. **1963** C. A. Williams *Aircraft Instrument Control Syst.* ii. 23 In moving a gyroscope from the North Pole to the South Pole the apparent wander would change from clockwise to anti-clockwise. **1971** *Q. Jrnl. R. Astron. Soc.* XII. 61 (*heading*) Polar wander and/or plate tectonics in the Palaeozoic. **1980** *Nature* 28 Feb. 845/1 The ~1,100 Myr Grenville mobile belt of the Laurentian (North American) Shield yields a record of uplift magnetisations defining a closed apparent polar wander (APW) loop.

wander, *v.* Add: **I. 2. g.** Of a gyroscope or other spinning body: to undergo a gradual change in orientation.

1930 *Engineering* 7 Mar. 323/2 The static gyro-compass did not wander during a week's trials more than about 1 deg..per day. The wandering was always in the same direction,..but the rate of wander varied slightly with alterations of the course. **1958** *Listener* 13 Nov. 779/2 The gyroscope will wander at the slightest hint of imperfection in its manufacture or assembly.

II. 5. Delete 'Now only *poet.*' (Later examples.)

1970 *Globe & Mail* (Toronto) 26 Sept. 29/5 (Advt.), When you are wandering the attractive shops..you can pause for luncheon. **1976** *Times Higher Educ. Suppl.* 12 Nov. 9/2 Born into a London Jewish family in October, 1936, he remembers the excitement of wandering the bomb sites of postwar London. **1981** E. Ward *Baltic Emerald* x. 71 First you wander this place for me, find Suite A.

7. *Comb.*, as **wander-bird** = *Wandervogel; **wander-plug,** a plug which can be fitted into any of a number of sockets in a dry battery; **wander-spirit** = *wanderlust; **wander-witted** = *wandery (cf. *wandrynge-wytted* s.v. Wandering *ppl. a.* 2 b).

1924 A. Huxley *Little Mexican* 184 Parties of rucksacked Wander-Birds. **1926** —— *Essays New & Old* 157 Of northern Germany it is enough to say that it is the home of the wander-birds. **1923** *Daily Mail* 5 June 13/5 A few high-tension batteries (50 volts with wander-plugs). **1968** Wander plug [see *spade terminal* s.v. *spade *sb.*[1] 5]. **1927** *Observer* 19 June 22/4 There is a drive..which it is the first duty of every motor owner with the wander-spirit properly developed to explore. **1959** *Listener* 29 Jan. 225/2 A wander-witted granddad, a sad bore to his family. **1959** P. Fleming *Siege at Peking* xiv. 220 The sights he had seen had turned his hair and beard prematurely white and made him wander-witted.

‖ **Wanderjahr** (va·ndəɹyāɹ). Pl. **-jahre.** [Ger.: see Wander-year.] = Wander-year.

1893 Yonge & Coleridge *Strolling Players* xiv. 117, I had my 'Wanderjahr' once; but I think I want one about every seven years—a metaphorical spree, anyhow. *a* **1910** 'Saki' *Coll. Short Stories* (1930) 105 The mouse..seemed to be trying to crowd a Wanderjahr into a few strenuous minutes. **1911** J. Ward *Realm of Ends* xviii. 402 Memories that are revived after death or when all the soul's *Wanderjahre* are over. **1922** 'K. Mansfield' *Let.* Nov. (1977) 282, I should like very much to know what he intends to do—how he intends to live now his *Wanderjahre* are over. **1952** G. Sarton *Hist. Sci.* I. xvi. 397 When Plato completed his *Wanderjahre,* he felt in him the vocation of teaching. **1982** *Listener* 7 Jan. 9/3 Wilde..in his American *Wanderjahr.*

wanderlust (wǫ·ndəɹlʌst, ‖ va·ndəɹlust). Also **Wanderlust.** [Ger.] An eager desire or fondness for wandering or travelling.

1902 *Athenæum* 4 Jan. 15 If the present reviewer knows anything of the wanderlust and the wallaby [etc.]. **1902** D. G. Brinton *Basis Social Relations* iv. 113 The goading restlessness which has driven single tribes or groups of tribes into aimless roving. This *Wanderlust* arises as an emotional epidemic. **1928** *Daily Mail* 7 Aug. 12/5 For people who have the wanderlust there are some nice tours around these parts. **1948** *Rep. Native Laws Commission 1946–48* (Dept. Native Affairs, S.Afr.) 43/1 If.. conditions are such that, when their little interval of *wanderlust* is over, they can pass into settled family life, [etc.]. **1969** G. Greene *Trav. with my Aunt* i. vii. 71 He would get a little restless with the wanderlust. **1981** J. B. Hilton *Surrender Value* xv. 113 The literally thousands of children to whom he had offered their first experience of wanderlust.

Hence **wa·nderluster; wa·nderlusting** *a.*

1927 *Sunday Express* 24 Apr. 3/4 The young wanderluster next turned up in Samoa, and went to Bombay to live in a harem. **1936** Mencken *Amer. Lang.* (ed. 4) 219 *Wanderlust*..is used much more frequently in the United States along with its derivatives, wanderluster (Eng. *rambler*), *wanderlusting* and *wanderlust-club.* **1952** S. Spender *Learning Laughter* 31 The wander-lusting young Israelis. **1985** A. McCandless *Burke Foundation* ix. 66 Senior NCOs felt a compulsive urge to track down wanderlusting junior officers.

Wanderobo (wǫndərō^u·bo). Also **Wandorobo, Wandrobo,** etc. [Native name.] The name of a nomadic hunting tribe of Kenya. Also *attrib.* or as *adj.*

1902 *Encycl. Brit.* XXVII. 611/2 Primitive hunting tribes are the Wandorobo in Masailand and scattered tribes of small stature in various parts. **1935** E. Hemingway *Green Hills Afr.* i. i. 2 We were sitting in the blind that Wanderobo hunters had built. **1937** [see *Nandi *a.* b]. **1967** M. J. Coe *Ecol. Alpine Zone Mt. Kenya* 3 The expedition met men of the wandering nomadic Wanderobo tribe at an altitude of 12,000 ft. **1977** H. Innes *Big Footprints* ii. ii. 158 He was attacked by the men of the rain forest, the Wandrobo.

‖ **Wandervogel** (va·ndəɹfog'l). Pl. **-vögel** (¶ **-vogel -vogeln**). [G., lit. 'bird of passage'.] A member of the German youth organization founded by H. Hoffmann at the end of the 19th century for the promotion of out-of-door activities, esp. hiking, and folk culture, as a reaction against the materialistic values of middle-class city life. Also *transf.*, a rambler or hiker. Occas. as *v. intr.* So **wa:nder-vo·geling** *vbl. sb.*

1924 D. H. Lawrence *Let.* 9 Aug. (1932) 606 If it's going to be Youth, then let it be Youth on the warpath, not wandervogeling and piping imitation nature tunes to the taste of milk and chocolate. **1928** —— *Lady Chatterley* i. 3 They sang the wandervogel songs. **1935** J. Buchan *House of Four Winds* ii. 49 They were remarkable young men..not in the least like the Wandervögel whom he had met on many German roads, comfortable sunburnt folk out for a holiday. **1944** M. Samuel *Harvest in Desert* xviii. 185 In Germany the *Wandervogel,* youthful rebels against the stodginess of middle-class life. **1958** *Listener* 31 July 149/2 The *wandervogel* student of 1912 with his guitar. **1962** P. Purser *Peregrinnation 22* xlviii. 223 A couple of the young mid-century *wandervogeln* you find in any youth hostel in Europe. **1967** *Listener* 30 Nov. 705/3 Around 1930, alienated and disaffected youth was being manufactured mainly in Germany, where the First War had produced the biggest earthquake. Some of them called themselves the *Wandervögel,* and wandered around Europe with their guitars and their interchangeable girlfriends, living on what they could get wherever sympathisers would accept them. **1978** J. I. M. Stewart *Full Term* xxi. 241 A bunch of juvenile *Wandervögel.*

wandery (wǫ·ndəri), *a.* [f. Wander *v.* + -y[1].] Wandering in thought or speech; vague, distant, 'scatty'.

1912 R. Brooke *Let.* Feb. (1968) 357, I was being frightfully dim and wandery and solilocutory. **1953** W. de la Mare *Private View* p. xi, This vanished creature..was not only more assured, less wandery, more securely based, and more confident. **1976** P. Dickinson *King & Joker* x. 134 She seemed so tired and wandery.

wander-year. (Earlier example.)

1880 T. W. Allies *Life's Decision* i. 6 At Oxford and in my wander-years it was the one subject for which..I not only had no taste, but the most marked repugnance.

wang, var. *whang.

wanga (wæ·ŋgă). [ad. Haitian Creole *ouanga* witchcraft, perh. ad. Kimbundu *wanga* witchcraft, or Tshiluba *bwanga* charm, fetish.] Witchcraft, sorcery; a charm or spell; a magical object. Freq. *attrib.*

1851 *Picayune* (New Orleans) 20 July 2/6 The Voudous also threw 'Wanga' or spells into the complainant's yard. **1882** J. W. Buel *Metropolitan Life Unveiled* 532, I will make a wanga-charm to charm him with; I will make him a phantom, a ghost. **1934** B. A. Botkin in W. T. Couch *Culture in South* 585 Fragments of hoodoo and conjuration, whose spells,..grigris, wangas, luck balls, conjure bottles, and conjure, tricken, or goofer bags are the special province of the Negro 'root doctor' or 'hoodoo man'. **1946** R. Tallant *Voodoo in New Orleans* (1947) 91 Another sort held gunpowder and red pepper; these were *wangas* to be thrown into somebody's path to cause them to get into fights. **1964** 'R. SEVERN' *Blood & Gold* x. 102 It's a *Wanga* dance... Black magic... She must be a *Mambo*.. a *Voodoo* priestess. **1978** W. HJORTSBERG *Falling Angel* (1979) xxxiii. 158 Sounds like some boko's put a powerful wanga on you... A boko is a hungan [*sc.* Obeah priest] who is evil... Wanga's what you'd call an evil curse... a hex, a spell.

wangle, *v.*² Add: **1.** Also *refl.* and const. advb. phr.

1922 *Sat. Rev.* 22 Dec. 953 President Wilson had to 'wangle' through Congress an act to restore the British treaty rights. **1942** 'WYNDHAM LEWIS' *Let.* ?26 June (1963) 324 In the last war like yourself I joined the army, instead of wangling myself into some safe job in London. **1961** C. V. WEDGWOOD *Thomas Wentworth, 1st Earl of Strafford* 186 In fact, he would bribe and wangle himself back into the possession of his illicit gains.

2. *intr.* To obtain something or get somewhere by irregular means, scheming, etc.; to use irregular means to accomplish a purpose. *rare.*

1918 *Sat. Even. Post* 19 Oct. 93/1 And wet—always, always wet, unless the weather is clear and the sea is calm—but good sea boats. They [*sc.* submarine chasers] wangle through somehow. They weather it out. **1919** W. DEEPING *Second Youth* xxii. 190 He agitated for a transfer..and to his joy he wangled back to the Cockneys. *Ibid.* xxvi.222 He also knew that a man who has 'wangled'..may find himself..thrust rudely into the trenches. **1921** *Glasgow Herald* 16 June 9 We wangled in, an' we'll wangle oot.

3. *trans.* To influence or induce (a person) to do something. *rare.*

1926 G. D. H. & M. COLE *Blatchington Tangle* xxi. 147 He was always on at me just lately to get Lady Blatchington to sell him the rubies. He said I could wangle her. **1928** *Daily Express* 27 Dec. 5/4 Aren't you glad..you wangled the old lady to relinquish the key.

wangler (earlier examples).

1912 E. WALLACE *Private Selby* xxxi. 281 You're a bloomin' wangler, Short. **1915** *John Bull* 27 Mar. 16/2 We regret to see them reduced to the level of vulgar weight wanglers, and so far as the bread business is concerned, we are quite prepared to believe that it was all the fault of a..machine.

wangle (wæ·ŋg'l), *sb. colloq.* [f. WANGLE *v.*²] An act of wangling; an irregular or indirect method of working; something dishonestly contrived or manipulated.

1915 *N. & Q.* 23 Jan. 66 The explanation given was: 'It's a wangle between this Office and the Inland Revenue.' **1923** *Westm. Gaz.* 21 Feb. 11/1 Mr. Justice Sargant: You can't expect the Royal Commission to be bound to what might be called a 'wangle' of this sort. **1927** *Observer* 27 Mar. 16/5 Men who sought to achieve nothing by wangle or intrigue. **1943** H. A. SMITH *Life in Putty Knife Factory* xii. 183 They [*sc.* people of New York City] have made a precise science out of the wangle. **1959** E. POUND *Thrones* xcvii. 29 But by that time they found some other wangle. **1977** P. DICKINSON *Walking Dead* II. ii. 114, I worked a wangle. I got a line on the Minister of Tourism.

wanigan (wæ·nĭgăn). *N. Amer.* Also **wannegan, wannigan. 1.** (See WANGUN a, c.)

1902 S. E. WHITE *Blazed Trail* 323 Outside the cook and cookee were stowing articles in the already loaded wanigan. **1908** [see WANGUN c]. **1911** [see WANGUN a]. **1945** F. J. FUGINA *Lore & Lure of Upper Mississippi* 221 Wanigans were small flatboats, built of natural crook knees and planked lengthwise. **1957** *Bush News* (Port Arthur, Ontario) 1 June 1/1 Three wanegans, a floating mess hall and cook shack, and six drive camps are maintained to keep the wood moving.

2. A cabin, usu. wooden, mounted on runners; = *CABOOSE 3 b.

1949 in *Dict. Canadianisms* (1967) 834/1 The Wannegan has a sled mounted house type body made of light gauge metal, and heavily insulated for use in sub zero temperatures. **1949** *Survey* June 303/2 The industry is based no longer in isolated logging camps, with lonely men living in 'wannigans' dragged through the forests on sled-like runners. **1958** L. CRISLER *Arctic Wild* 133 At Barrow, Cris chained the wolves in front of our wanigan, one of a row of four or five empty wanigans beside the airstrip. They had made up a cat train. A wanigan is a narrow shack on runners: it can be drawn by tractor across snow or tundra. **1966** *Islander* (Victoria, B.C.) 20 Feb. 7/3 While sleeping in a wanigan, a hut on sleds, I was awakened..by native children shouting. **1979** C. KILIAN *Icequake* xii. 211 We'll have to build some wanigans that'll fit on the sledges. Otherwise we'll never be able to shelter everybody.

wank (wæŋk), *sb.* (*a.*) *slang.* Also † **whank.** [Origin unknown.] **1.** Of a male: (an act of) masturbation.

This word and its derivatives are not in polite use.

1948 PARTRIDGE *Dict. Forces' Slang* 203 *Wank-pit*,.. a bed. (Air Force.) **1951** —— *Dict. Slang* (ed. 4) 1220/1 *Whank*, (male) self-abuse: low: from ca. 1870. Perhaps echoic. **1966** P. WILLMOTT *Adolescent Boys* iii. 49 When I was 13, my friends at school asked me if I'd ever had a wank. **1970** T. LEWIS *Jack's Return Home* 18 Valerie Marshbanks showed everybody her knickers and charged a penny a wank, in the bushes, one at a time. **1971** B. W. ALDISS *Soldier Erect* 83 Oh, Christ! And there wasn't even anywhere in this wilderness where you could enjoy a decent sensuous wank—certainly not in the tent or the latrine. Nowhere. **1977** *Sniffin' Glue* July 15 Behind that bog door are you thinkin' readin' or just havin' a wank?

2. An objectionable or contemptible person or thing. Cf. *WANKER 2.

1970 P. LAURIE *Scotland Yard* vi. 158 Fred's counsel is a fat wank. **1973** *Nation Rev.* (Melbourne) 31 Aug. 1434/5 Kenneth S. Jaffrey, that naturopathic scientific wank. **1977** *Time Out* 17–23 June 14/1 Why did Aldrich direct this lengthy wank for Sinatra and Martin just after he'd made a film as interesting as 'Baby Jane'? **1977** *Maledicta* I. 11 He may be called a *jerk*, a *jerkoff* or a *jackoff*; a *wank* (Brit.), or a *whack*.

3. *attrib.* or as *adj.* Likely to induce masturbation.

1976 J. I. M. STEWART *Memorial Service* viii. 122 'He has an enormous great wank picture in his room. Makes the place like a porn shop.' 'I know that picture too... It's wanky all right.' **1981** P. PORTER *Coll. Poems* (1983) 277 But you are talking about love, you'll say. Yes, and I know the difference, Taking down a wank magazine.

wank (wæŋk), *v. slang.* Also † **whank.** [Origin unknown: see prec.] **1.** *intr.* Of a male: to masturbate. Freq. with *off.*

1950 P. TEMPEST *Lag's Lexicon* 229 *Whank, to*, to masturbate. **1951** PARTRIDGE *Dict. Slang* (ed. 4) 1220/1 *Whank*, loosely *wank*, v.i., to masturbate: low: late C. 19–20. Also *whank off*. **1966** P. WILLMOTT *Adolescent Boys* iii. 49 Some boys..think, 'I'm not going to tell anyone in case they think I'm dirty, wanking myself off.' But me and my mates, we tell everybody we wank off. **1969** F. NORMAN *Banana Boy* 108, I am certain that he could have wanked for Britain in the Olympics and won a gold medal with ease. **1977** W. MCILVANNEY *Laidlaw* xli. 192 You've been wankin'... That's no' nice in public places.

2. *trans.* To masturbate (a man). Freq. with *off.*

1966 [see sense 1 above]. **1975** O. SELA *Bengali Inheritance* xi. 94 'You like for me to wank you?'.. 'No... My wife would not like it.' **1980** 'D. KAVANAGH' *Duffy* v. 93 Lots of punters wanted you to wank them off... You'd think that was the one thing they could do for themselves. **1984** J. BARNES *Flaubert's Parrot* iv. 56, I saw a monkey in the street jump on a donkey and try to wank him off.

Hence **wanked-out** *a.*, exhausted (by masturbation).

1973 W. H. CANAWAY *Harry doing Good* ii. 23 A wanked-out shivering wreck. **1976** M. HARTMANN *Leap for Sun* i. 14 I worked on a wanked-out farming magazine.

Wankel (wæ·-, væ·ŋkĕl, va·ŋ-). The name of Felix *Wankel* (b. 1902), German engineer, used *attrib.* and *absol.* to designate a kind of rotary internal-combustion engine that he invented in which an approximately triangular, eccentrically pivoted shaft rotates continuously in a chamber with its corners touching the walls, so forming three combustion spaces that vary in volume as it turns. Also *Comb.*

1961 *Engineering* 19 May 682/1 Many other people have felt that something to replace the conventional engine is needed and a promising design to rear its head has been the Wankel engine. **1966** E. RUDINGER *Consumer's Car Gloss.* 120 The Wankel engine is much smaller than a conventional engine with a similar power output, and runs more smoothly. **1967** *Economist* 2 Sept. 811/1 The motor industry has waited a long time for the first car in production to use the wankel rotary engine. Now the small German manufacturer, NSU, has got there with the Ro 80. *Ibid.* 811/2 Will the wankel be enough to sustain NSU as an independent motor company, or will NSU one day have to close ranks further with Citroen? **1970** *Guardian* 10 Nov. 11/5 Citroën..has built and sold 500 Wankel engined cars. **1972** *Sci. Amer.* Aug. 17/3 Since the Wankel has no valves, it does not need a camshaft, valve lifters and so on, and it requires no more than two spark plugs per rotor. **1979** *Motorcycling Manual* (Motorcycling Monthly) 6/1 Apart from the few Wankel-engined bikes..all current machines have either two-stroke or four-stroke piston engines.

wanker (wæ·ŋkəɹ). *slang.* Also † **whanker.** [f. *WANK *v.* + -ER¹.] **1.** One who masturbates; *wanker's doom*, disability caused by excessive masturbation.

1950 P. TEMPEST *Lag's Lexicon* 229 A man suspected of excessive masturbation is said to be suffering from 'whanker's doom'. **1961** H. S. TURNER *Something Extraordinary* ix. 158 Because Willy always has big black circles round his eyes he is classified as 'pocket billiard player' or 'wanker'. **1971** B. W. ALDISS *Soldier Erect* 86 Failed fucker, failed wanker was an inglorious double billing. **1972** K. BONFIGLIOLI *Don't point that Thing at Me* xiii. 111 Mortdecai Minor, the likeliest candidate for wanker's doom. **1977** *Maledicta* I. 11 He is *whacky*, or *whacked to the gills*; he is *wonked goggle-eyed*, or is suffering from *Wanker's Doom.* The last refer to the old idea or threat that masturbation will make a person go blind or deaf or crazy.

2. An objectionable or contemptible person. Cf. *WANK *sb.* 2.

1972 A. DRAPER *Death Penalty* v. 36 'Get out, you fucker,' screamed a youth... Another said, 'You wanker,' and indulged in a masturbatory gesture. **1976** U. HOLDEN *String Horses* vi. 69 Her kiddies..rarely spoke except to mutter 'Wanker' or something crude. **1978** K. AMIS *Jake's Thing* xii. 123 'Damon, what's a wanker?'..'These days a waster, a shirker, someone who's fixed himself a soft job or an exalted position by means of an undeserved reputation on which he now coasts.' 'Oh. Nothing to do with tossing off then?' 'Well, connected with it, yes, but more metaphorical than literal.' **1981** P. NIESEWAND *Word of Gentleman* xxxii. 222 They're such a bunch of wankers... You can't trust them to do anything properly.

wanking (wæ·ŋkiŋ), *vbl. sb. slang.* Also † **whanking.** [f. *WANK *v.* + -ING¹.] Masturbation. Also with *off.* So *wanking couch, -pit*, a bed.

1951 PARTRIDGE *Dict. Slang* (ed. 4) 1220/1 *Whanking(-) pit*, the Army's form of *whank-pit*: since early 1920's. But used also by R.A.F. **1966** D. HOLBROOK *Flesh Wounds* 39 Wakey, wakey old mate. You want to get smartly outa that wanking pit! **1969** M. PUGH *Last Place Left* xxvi. 192 You rooting goat. Why can't you take them to your own wanking couch? **1971** P. L. CAVE *Chopper* xi. 106 He'd have so many women he could say goodbye to wanking for life. **1977** *Sounds* 9 July 23/3, I don't think the cutting was any more extreme than hanging from the rafters or wanking off on stage or vomiting.

wanky (wæ·ŋki), *a. slang.* [f. *WANK *sb.* or *v.* + -Y¹.] Objectionable, contemptible; masturbatory.

1972 K. BONFIGLIOLI *Don't point that Thing at Me* xix. 173, I was now quite calm, the wanky old avenger preparing to kill his man. **1973** M. AMIS *Rachel Papers* 78 No, man, don't get too wanky with her. And cut out all this intellectual shit. **1976** [see *WANK *sb.* (*a.*) 3]. **1977** *Zigzag* Aug. 15/3 We loved that, 'cos it's such a wanky plastic paper and they thought by slagging us early they'd be in first. **1983** W. MCILVANNEY *Papers of Tony Veitch* xxx. 188 I'm not interested in his wanky theories about why he did it—just that he did it, the bastard.

Wan-Li (wæn,li). Also **Wan Li.** The royal name of Shen Zong, emperor of China 1573–1620, used *attrib.* and *absol.* with reference to pottery and porcelain made during his reign.

1876 HOOPER & PHILLIPS *Man. Marks on Pott. & Porc.* 186 The dark rich blue of the *Kea-tching* and the white granulated surface of the *Wan-leih*, are very choice. **1885** *Jrnl. Peking Oriental Soc.* I. 98 Plain white cups of *Wan li* porcelain were several taels of silver each. **1902** C. MONKHOUSE *Chinese Porc.* I. 36 Some of the blue is fine in colour, as in some pieces which were lent by Mr. William Agnew to the Burlington Fine Arts Club in 1895. One of them has the Wan-li mark. **1915** R. L. HOBSON *Chinese Pott. & Porc.* II. v. 66 Another group of marked Wan Li ware, comprising bowls and dishes with trim neat finish.. has a soft-looking glaze. **1960** H. HAYWARD *Antique Coll.* 313/2 *Wu ts'ai* (*five-colour*) *wares.* This generally implies the characteristic Wan Li period Chinese porcelain wares, painted in underglaze blue and enamel colours (red, green, yellow and purple). **1978** K. BONFIGLIOLI *All Tea in China* i. 12 In London today they are crazy for blue-and-white wares and cannot tell Wan-Li from *De Metalen Pot.*

wanna (wǫ·nă), repr. colloq. pronunc. of *want to* or *want a.* Cf. WANT *v.* 4, 5 and *WANTA.

1896 S. CRANE *Maggie* v. 42, I see he had a still on, an' I didn' wanna give 'im no stuff. **1926–7** *T. Eaton & Co. Catal.* Fall & Winter 305/1 (*song-title*), I 'wanna' go where you go. **1941** B. SCHULBERG *What makes Sammy Run?* vi. 121 Look, do you wanna be smart? **1962** J. D. MACDONALD *Girl* (1974) x. 140, I don't wanna be no nuisance woman. **1971** *Frendz* 21 May 2/1 Right on, Paul! Wanna job? **1980** G. V. HIGGINS *Kennedy for Defence* x. 104 'That's fine by me,' I said, 'if you wanna leave.'

wannegan, wannigan, varr. *WANIGAN.

wanst (wǫnst, wanst), dial. (chiefly *Anglo-Ir.*) var. of ONCE *adv.* (*conj.*). Cf. *ONCE *adv.* A. 8.

1838 W. CARLETON *Fardorougha* (1839) iv. 81 Repeat the words at wanst. **1889** T. E. BROWN *Manx Witch* 80 Jack..bore it wanst, and bore it twicet. **1890** [see *ONCE *adv.* A. 8]. **1936** M. FRANKLIN *All that Swagger* xvi. 153 The young Delacys were all for the police at the end, but Danny said no. 'Wanst you begin law, it never ends.'

want, *sb.*² Add: **5. b.** (Further examples.) Also, something that one wishes to have (as opposed to what one needs or requires).

1946 G. M. TREVELYAN *English Social History* (ed. 2) xii. 388 Tea, porcelain and woven cotton goods were now being imported..in such quantities that they came within reach of the mass of the population. They created new wants and..demand was so great that home-manufacturers took to making cotton goods and china ware. **1950** *Sport* 24–30 Mar. 19/4 (Advt.), Clubs..can use our national net-work of experts to provide grounds, fixtures, insurance, fund-raisers and all club wants. **1955** W. J. BATE *Achievement of Samuel Johnson* (1978) ii. 70 General wishes have to localize themselves into definite wants. **1977** *Chicago Tribune* 2 Oct. XII. 1/4 The first-floor laundry room is definitely more a 'need' than a 'want' item nowadays. **1983** J. BARZUN *Stroll with W. James* 280 He did not fall into the trap of supposing that a child's needs are the same as his wants.

9. *want column* (earlier U.S. example); similarly *want ad(vertisement).*

1897 *Chicago Record* 1 Mar. 10/4 Record 'want ads' bring results. **1919** MENCKEN *Amer. Lang.* 160 *Ad-writer, want-ad*,..and *ad-man*, are already accepted in technical terminology. **1940** R. CHANDLER *Farewell, my Lovely* vii. 43 The Montgomery killing hadn't even made the want-ad section. **1977** C. MCFADDEN *Serial* (1978) xlv. 96/1 The want ads..no longer solicited secondhand Hide A Beds. **1887** *Courier-Jrnl.* (Louisville, Kentucky) 12 Jan. 5/3 The *World* is treating Mr. Conkling as it treats its circulation and its 'want' advertisements upon occasion. **1919** F. HURST *Humoresque* 116 She took to..scanning want-advertisements as she stood at the news-stand. **1884** E. W. NYE *Baled Hay* 239 The want column of the Chicago *News*..has the following: 'Twelve "frightful examples" wanted.'

want, *v.* Add: **2.** Also, in *Palæography* and *Bibliography*, to lack (a leaf or a page).

1895 M. R. JAMES *Catal. MSS. Sidney Sussex Coll.* 114 Vellum... Cent. xiv, xv... *Collation:* a⁸ (wants 1, 2) b⁸–ff⁸. **1976** *Anglo-Saxon England* V. 150, i⁸ wants 1.

5. e. (U.S. examples const. *of*.)

1855 *Knickerbocker* XLV. 136 Salt, Miss? What do you want of salt? **1884** 'MARK TWAIN' *Huck. Finn* xxxv. 357 What do we want of a saw? **1914** G. ATHERTON *Perch of Devil* II. 246 But what does he want of two cottages?

f. The phr. *want out* is now in general *colloq.* use. (Earlier and later examples.)

1836 J. D. DAVIDSON *Diary* 29 Oct. in *Jrnl. Southern Hist.* (1935) I. 354 He still called out in a plaintive, infant tone, '*I want in*'—'*I want in*'. **1925** *Amer. Speech* I. 149/2, I want out at the bank because this sack of silver is too heavy to pack around with me. **1959** E. AMBLER *Passage of Arms* viii. 219 They can keep everything... We just want out. **1973** *Time Out* 2–8 Mar. 14/1 One of the kids who had paid his money..wanted out. **1973** *Nature* 28 Sept. 173/2 Britain may just be weary of industrial growth and may be saying in quite a sophisticated way that it wants out regardless of the cost. **1977** *Zigzag* Mar. 24/1, I had no regrets about leaving... I just wanted out. **1979** A. HAILEY *Overload* III. i. 194 Well, I'm not afraid, or proud, or anything any more. I just want out. **1984** *Guardian* 5 Nov. 17/4 In recent weeks the Federal Reserve chairman Mr Paul Volcker has reportedly told friends that he wants out and would be interested in the presidency of the World Bank. **1985** *Times Lit. Suppl.* 25 Jan. 102/2 If you want out, it is just about possible to live, if only internally, a better life.

wa'n't. (Later U.S. examples.)

1893 H. A. SHANDS *Some Peculiarities of Speech in Mississippi* 67 *Want*, Negro and illiterate white for *was not* or *were not*. **1929** H. W. ODUM in A. Dundes *Mother Wit* (1973) 194/1 Wan't no hero, wan't no coward. **1942** W. FAULKNER *Go down, Moses* 144 Ah went to yo house last night, but you want dar.

wanta (wǫ·ntă), repr. U.S. colloq. pronunc. of *want to*. See *WANNA.

1894 S. CRANE in *Arena* Oct. 666 Let up, will yeh? Do yeh wanta kill somebody? **1925** T. DREISER *Amer. Trag.* (1926) I. I. i. 7 That oldest boy don't wanta be here. **1946** E. O'NEILL *Iceman Cometh* II. 98 Don't let Hickey put no ideas in your nuts if you wanta stay healthy! **1977** *New Yorker* 12 Sept. 54/3 Do fast lines and play lousy—one phrase of 'Smoke Gets in Your Eyes' and then: 'Folks, you wanta drive somebody crazy?'

wa·ntable, *a.* [f. WANT *v.* + -ABLE.] Desirable, of a kind likely to become sought after.

1970 *Times* 21 July 7 This collection [of clothes]..is extremely pretty, wantable and smart in a personal private way. **1979** *Daily Tel.* 22 Jan. 11/2 Most wantable garment in the Paris collections, a Fifties' style soft leather dress cinched with an ultra-wide cummerbund in the Claude Montana collection.

wan tan, var. *WON TON.

wanted, *ppl. a.* Add: **3.** Special collocations: *wanted list*, a list of persons sought by the police or by a similar agency; also *wanted file*; *wanted poster*, a poster displaying details of a wanted person or persons, usu. under the headline 'Wanted'.

1967 'E. PETERS' *Black is Colour* i. 20 Just take a look at 'em!..Every one of 'em straight out of the wanted file. **1964** I. FLEMING *You only live Twice* xix. 228 The C.I.A. on whose WANTED list I certainly feature. **1968** P. DURST *Badge of Infamy* v. 50, I checked with the International War Crimes commission to see if Von Friede was on the wanted list. **1970** T. LILLEY *Projects Section* xiv. 177 There would always be those in the crowd who would recognise the corpse—either from 'Wanted' posters or from personal acquaintance. **1982** A. PRICE *Old Vengeful* 12 Oh dear! A good likeness... It looks like a prison picture..or maybe a 'Wanted' poster.

wanting, *pres. pple.* Add: **6.** Also *colloq.* (Earlier and later examples.)

1839 DICKENS *Nickleby* xxxiv. 331 'He was a little wanting here,' touching his forehead. **1924** J. BUCHAN *Three Hostages* vi. 85 Had something given in my brain last night..so that now I was what people call 'wanting'? **1976** 'J. BELL' *Trouble in Hunter Ward* xvii. 180 Maisie, poor mite, wanting from birth, she was.

wanton, *a.* Add: **9.** *wanton-headed* adj.

1918 D. H. LAWRENCE *New Poems* 22 By-paths where the wanton-headed flowers doff their hood.

wantum (wǫ·ntǝm). *nonce-wd.* [Blend of WANT *sb.*² + QUANTUM.] Deficiency or desire, considered as something quantifiable.

The quot. alludes to Prov. xxx. 15 The horse-leach hath two daughters, crying, Giue, giue. There are three things that are neuer satisfied, *yea* foure things say not.

1938 S. BECKETT *Murphy* 57 The horse leech's daughter is a closed system. Her quantum of wantum cannot vary.

Wanyamwezi (wanyamwē·i·zi). Also **Wanyamwesi.** [Native name, lit. 'people of the moon', hence (prob.) 'people of the West'.] The name of a Bantu people of Tanzania.

1860 R. F. BURTON *Lake Regions Central Afr.* II. xii. 4 The correct designation of the inhabitants of Unyamwezi is, therefore, Mnyamwezi in the singular, and Wanyamwezi in the plural: Kinyamwezi is the adjectival form. *Ibid.*, According to the people..in the days of the grandfathers of their grandfathers the last of the Wanyamwezi emperors died. **1911** J. FRAZER *Golden Bough: Magic Art* (ed. 3) I. v. 268 The Wanyamwesi, a large tribe of Central Africa, to the south of the Victoria Nyanza. **1947** *E. Afr. Ann. 1946–7* 93/1 The Wanyamwezi have been one of the better known tribes of Tanganyika from the time when Arab slave raiders first set up their centre at Tabora. **1955** HILL & MOFFETT *Tanganyika* 515 The Wanyamwezi are one of the more virile and hard-working tribes of the Territory, and also one of the largest.

wap, *v.*¹ Add: **1. c.** intr. *slang.* To copulate. *Obs.*

[**1567** T. HARMAN *Caveat* sig. G4ᵛ, He tooke his Iockam in his famble, and a wapping he went.] **1611** MIDDLETON & DEKKER *Roaring Girl* sig. K4ᵛ, Wee'l couch a hogshead vnder the Ruffemans, and there you [*sc.* Moll Cutpurse] shall wap with me, & Ile niggle with you. **1699** B. E. *New Dict. Canting Crew, Wap*, c. to Lie with a Man. *If she won't wap for a Winne, let her trine for a Make*, c. If she won't Lie with a Man for a Penny, let her Hang for a Half-penny. *Mort wap-apace*, c. a Woman of Experience, or very expert at the Sport. **1725** in Farmer & Henley *Slang* (1903) VII. 293/1 This doxy dell can cut been whids, And wap well for a win.

wapping *vbl. sb.* (examples in sense *1 c); also as *ppl. a.*

1610 S. RID *Martin Mark-All* sig. E3, *Nigling*, company keeping with a woman: this word is not vsed now, but *wapping*, and thereof comes the name *wapping morts* Whoores. **1612** DEKKER *O Per Se O* sig. O1ᵛ, And wapping Dell, that niggles well, And takes loure for her hire. **1707** J. SHIRLEY *Triumph of Wit* (ed. 5) III. 198 Wapping thou I know do's love.

Wapishana (wapiʃā·na), *sb.* and *a.* Also **Wapishiana, Wapisiana**; 9 **Wapiana, Wapisiano. A.** *sb.* **a.** A member of an Arawakan people of Guyana and Brazil; also this people collectively. **b.** Their language. **B.** *adj.* Of, pertaining to, or designating this people or their language.

1855 H. G. DALTON *Hist. Brit. Guiana* I. ii. 77 The Acosi, Awake, Wapishiana..are also the names of several other tribes which have been met with by late travellers. *Ibid.* (*caption facing* p. 80) The 'Belle' of the Wapisianas. **1868** W. H. BRETT *Indian Tribes of Guiana* II. v. 280 Southward of Roraima the great range of the Pacaraima Mountains extends... Beyond it are the savannahs of the Rupununi, inhabited by the *Wabean* or *Wapisiana* nation. **1883** E. F. IM THURN *Among Indians of Guiana* vi. 165 The languages of the four branches, Warrau, Arawak, Wapiana, and Carib, will be found to be quite distinct from each other. **1924** [see *LAP *sb.*¹ 4 c]. **1949** *Caribbean Q.* I. III. 41 Of the two tribes likely to be displaced, one, the Wapisiana, is not likely to be demoralised. **1959** P. CAPON *Amongst those Missing* 167 'An Indian, isn't he?' asked Judith. 'I think so. He has the look of a Wapishana.' **1972** S. E. BROCK *Jungle Cowboy* xii. 135 *Wai-Wai* is the Wapishana for tapioca.

wappie (wǫ·pi). *West Indies.* Also **wap(p)ee, wappy.** [perh. f. WAP *sb.*¹ + -IE.] A gambling game played with cards.

1943 in Cassidy & Le Page *Dict. Jamaican Eng.* (1967) 462/2 *Wappie*, a game of cards. **1952** S. SELVON *Brighter Sun* ii. 26 The older boys and men play wapee, a gambling game with cards. *Ibid.* vii. 123 Ah play cards—Ah was a rummy test in me days, and don't talk 'bout wappee! Yuh cud play cards? **1952** *Evening News* (Port of Spain) 22 Jan. 12/3 Tom..happens to back the right cards at wappie. **1959** V. S. NAIPAUL *Miguel St.* i. 12 They played *wappee* and drank rum. **1968** K. S. LA FORTUNE *Legend of T-Marie* xii. 51 Cab-men sat on benches or on boxes talking politics or playing wappie.

waqf, var. *WAKF.

war, *sb.*¹ Add: **I. 3. a.** Freq. used with def. art. to designate a particular war, esp. one in progress or recently ended. Hence *between the wars*, between the war of 1914–18 and that of 1939–45 (cf. *INTER-WAR *a.*). *Sacred War* (earlier and later examples); *War Between the States* (esp. in the use of Southerners), the American Civil War.

1774 Sacred war [see *PHOCIAN *sb.*]. **1814** *Columbian Centinel* 18 June 2/3 The southern war-hirelings say the Administration will continue the War. **1861** *Chicago Tribune* 26 May 1/9, I, Samuel M. Fassett, photographist, ..will continue to take those fine plain photographs for the low sum of one dollar, during the war. **1867** A. H. STEPHENS (*title*) A constitutional view of the late War between the States. **1911**, etc. Sacred war [see *PHOCIAN *a.*]. **1934** *Sun* (Baltimore) 5 June 14/7 There was a time when it was almost worth one's life in the city of Richmond to refer to the Civil War as the Civil War. The Richmonder who held the memories of the sixties close to his heart always called it the War Between the States. **1936** *Punch* 2 Dec. 640/1 Our telephone system is partly British and partly German and Turkish, and all of it served through the War with varying degrees of distinction. **1942** C. S. LEWIS *Screwtape Lett.* xv. 76, I had noticed, of course, that the humans were having a lull in their European war—what they naïvely call '*The War*'! **1958** 'N. SHUTE' *Rainbow & Rose* i. 3 He lived and worked in England and the Far East all the time between the wars. **1973** R. THOMAS *If You can't be Good* vi. 46 The Maurys..had supplied the South with two generals during the War Between the States.

b. Also *war of nerves*: see *NERVE *sb.* 8 f; *war of words* (Journalese), a sustained conflict conducted by means of the spoken or printed word; a propaganda war.

[**1725** War of words: see sense 1 b in Dict.] **1981** *Times* 10 Oct. 1/7 As the war of words continued in the Tory party Mrs Thatcher arrived back from the Commonwealth Conference. **1984** *Guardian* 8 Mar. 9/1 (*heading*) Vietnamese intensify war of words on Peking.

c. *to carry the war into the enemy's camp* (*into Africa*, etc.): see *CARRY *v.* 19 b.

d. *war to end war(s)*: a war which is intended to make subsequent wars impossible; usu. *spec.* the war of 1914–18.

[**1914** H. G. WELLS (*title*) The war that will end war.] **1921** G. B. SHAW *Back to Methuselah* IV. 187 There was a war called the War to End War. In the war which followed it about ten years later, none of the soldiers were killed; but seven of the capital cities of Europe were wiped out of existence. **1932** P. QUENNELL *Let. to Mrs. V. Woolf* (1933) 17 He can recall barely five or six summers; then the War to End Wars and so good-bye. **1949** E. BENN *Happier Days* vi. 71 If..war debts between nations had been wiped off the slate, and reparations in money never attempted, the 'war to end war' might have achieved its high purpose. **1953** EARL WINTERTON *Orders of Day* xxiv. 345 The Government of that day and the then leaders of opinion in general had assured us and the nation at large that it was 'a war to end war'. **1967** W. LIPPMAN in W. Safire *New Lang. Politics* (1968) 480/2 Each of the wars to end wars has set the stage for the next war. **1978** E. MALPASS *Wind brings up Rain* ix. 99 Now..the War To End War was over.

e. *to have a good war*: to achieve success, satisfaction, or enjoyment during a war. Also with other adjs. Often ironic.

1969 P. DICKINSON *Pride of Heroes* I. 49 Harvey Singleton..had a good war. A very good war indeed. After the Raid he was parachuted into France three times. **1970** —— *Seals* ii. 35 He had a very bad war. **1972** P. D. JAMES *Unsuitable Job for Woman* iv 124 He had what the men call a good war; we'd call it a bad war I dare say, a lot of killing and fighting. **1974** 'J. LE CARRÉ' *Tinker, Tailor, Soldier, Spy* xviii. 153 He had a dazzling war... The comparison with Lawrence was inevitable.

5. b. For † *Obs.* read *Obs* exc. as *minister of* (or *for*) *war*, *secretary at war*, *secretary of* (*state for*) *war*.

1693, etc. [see SECRETARY *sb.*¹ 3 a]. **1802** C. WILMOT *Let.* 15 Nov. in *Irish Peer* (1920) 115 The six Ministers of the Interior, of the Police, of Justice, of Finance, of War, and of foreign affairs. **1867** CROWN PRINCESS OF PRUSSIA *Let.* 27 Apr. in R. Fulford *Your Dear Letter* (1971) 133 The King wishes for peace..so does the Minister for War. **1877** J. BLACKWOOD *Let.* 21 Dec. in *Geo. Eliot Lett.* (1956) VI. 434, I am happy to say that our Minister of War is I think a man who may be trusted at the helm. **1903** *Ceremonies at Laying Corner Stone of Army War College Building* (U.S. Army Corps of Engineers) 9 The master of ceremonies then introduced the honorable Secretary of War. **1964** *Act Eliz. II* c. 58 § 1 There shall be transferred to a Secretary of State the functions conferred by any enactment on the Minister of Defence, or on the Secretary of State for War or for Air (however styled). **1980** A. MARWICK *Illustr. Dict. Brit. Hist.* 64/2 He [*sc.* Churchill] served the coalition subsequently as secretary of state for war and air (1918–21).

II. 8. a. (In this and the senses that follow the use of the hyphen follows no regular pattern.) *war aim, base, camp, casualty, War Department* (later U.S. examples), *war footing* (earlier examples), *hospital, measure, neurosis* (hence *-neurotic*), *news, period, production, profiteer, propaganda, -psychosis, ration, record, restriction, scare, -service* (modern examples), *situation, strain, surplus* (chiefly attrib.), *victim, -weariness, widow, -word, wound, years, zone* (earlier and later examples).

1918 A. BENNETT *Pretty Lady* xxviii. 193 The Germans were discussing their war aims. **1972** *New Yorker* 22 July 66/3 In the My Lai massacre the soldiers abandoned the unrealistic war aims of Dean Rusk and drew their illogical but understandable conclusion..all Vietnamese have to be killed. **1947** *Daily Tel.* 19 Apr. 4/2 Its virtual disappearance yesterday..is probably the only answer to the fear of its use as a war-base once more. **1977** *South China Morning Post* (Hong Kong) 14 Apr. 5/3 Militarist forces clutch at the blocs and war bases they established in Asia. **1832** A. EARLE *Narr. Residence N.Z.* (1966) 176 Mr. Hobbs, the Wesleyan missionary,..had visited the war-camp of the assembled chiefs. **1969** G. MACBETH *War Quartet* 25 In our minds A dream of war-camps festered. **1921** G. B. SHAW *Back to Methuselah* II. 88 It was the war casualty lists and the starvation afterwards that finished me up with politics and the Church and everything else except you. **1974** A. PRICE *Other Paths to Glory* II. ix. 225 The late Turco... Another war casualty? **1866** G. B. MCLELLAN *Let.* 26 Dec. in *McLellan's Own Story* (1887) xii. 221 The entire establishment..was removed to the War Department building, without my knowledge. **1944** *Time* 2 Oct. 19/1 This was strictly a military document drafted by the War Department. **1847** THACKERAY *Van. Fair* (1848) xxviii. 242 The armies of the allied powers were all providentially on a war-footing, and ready. **1872** 'MARK TWAIN' *Roughing It* ii. 22 We were reduced to a war-footing. **1860** F. NIGHTINGALE *Notes on Nursing* iii. 23, I by no means refer only to..war hospitals, but..to..military hospitals at home, in time of peace. **1982** P. QUENNELL *Customs & Characters* ii. 33 The French Ambassadress..had promised she would visit a nearby war-hospital. **1808** W. EATON in R. C. Prentiss *Life W. Eaton* (1813) 414 The Embargo was contemplated as a war measure. **1948** *Rep. Native Laws Comm. 1946–48* (Dept. Native Affairs, S. Afr.) 32/1 A War Measure has been promulgated as a temporary attempt to relieve the situation. **1975** *Toronto Star* 1 Nov. B4/4 Pierre Trudeau invoked the War Measures Act and plunged Canada into a time of arrest without warrant and detention without charge. **1920** *Internat. Jrnl. Psycho-Anal.* I. 283 Freud's introduction gives some of the chief points of view for the psycho-analytical consideration of the war neuroses. **1944** *Yank* 31 Mar. 8 For this reason there is actually no such thing as 'war neurosis', any more than there is 'war malaria' or 'war pneumonia'. **1955** J.

Strachey tr. *Freud's Psycho-Anal. & War Neuroses* in *Compl. Wks.* XVII. 215 With the end of the war the war neurotics, too, disappeared—a final but impressive proof of the psychical causation of their illness. **1857** C. Kingsley *Two Years Ago* II. v. 200, I cannot sit here quietly, listening to the war-news. It makes me mad to be up and doing. **1915** F. H. Burnett *Lost Prince* xiii. 96 [They] sat down to read the morning paper. The war news was bad to read. **1967** C. Potok *Chosen* iii. 59 There was war news all the time, but no one got this excited unless something very special was happening. **1918** H. Crane *Let.* 12 Aug. (1965) 11 All minors,..if drafted at all, will be apprenticed in machine shops, etc., during the war period. **1939** *Ann. Reg. 1938* 260 The declared policy of Senor Negrin to look beyond the war-period to a Spain in which one day the Spaniards on both sides would have to live together. **1965** A. J. P. Taylor *Eng. Hist. 1914–45* xiv. 517 Bomber command claimed the largest share of Great Britain's war-production. **1918, 1975** War-profiteer [see *profiteer *sb.*]. **1918** W. Owen *Let.* 25 Oct. (1967) 588 He had no qualifications for War Propaganda. **1974** *Guardian* 31 Jan. 1/5 War propaganda on both sides was, of course, bad and distorted. **1927** W. E. Collinson *Contemp. Eng.* 103 Symptoms of that war-psychosis, which afflicted us in common with the other belligerent nations. **1953** H. S. Whitman tr. *Janetschek's Emperor Franz Joseph* 302 Don't worry so much, and you will soon be free of your war-psychosis. **1924** D. H. Lawrence in M. Magnus *Mem. Foreign Legion* 16 He yelled for more bread—bread being war-rations and very limited in supply. **1890** E. Custer *Following Guidon* 2 They longed individually and as a regiment for a war 'record'. **1978** F. Maclean *Take Nine Spies* iv. 126 The men were impressed by his war record. **1922** W. J. Locke *Tale of Triona* xxvi. 292 England..awoke to find war restrictions removed,..and petrol to be had. **1938** J. Charlesworth *Law of Negligence* vii. 133 Where a refuge was erected in the middle of the street, and inadequately lighted, so that a taxi-cab collided with it in the dark because..owing to war restrictions, no lights were maintained,..the local authority were held liable. **1894** W. Le Queux *Gt. War in Eng. in 1897* i. 15 War-scares had been plentiful. **1977** *Listener* 10 Feb. 177/2 The war scare in 1938. **1916** J. Bailey *Let.* 8 Oct. (1935) 168 It was a great joy to see you both and King's Weston again, and to admire your wonderful 'war service' and feel that all the beauties of the house and place are being put to such splendid use [as a War Hospital]. **1979** A. Price *Tomorrow's Ghost* iv. 47 They both looked old enough to have seen war service. **1936** C. Day Lewis *We're not going to do Nothing* 29 In an actual war-situation the trade unions are in the key-position. **1914** T. A. Baggs *Back from Front* xx. 94 It is there that human nature, exuberant or impassive under the war-strain, reveals its own true colours once again. **1952** H. Innes *Campbell's Kingdom* I. v. 110 They wore war surplus clothing relieved by bright scarves. **1968** P. Geddes *High Game* viii. 97 When the big round of war surplus prosecutions started, none of the dirt ever stuck to him. **1982** D. Williams *Copper, Gold & Treasure* 16 I'll let you know if he asks me to buy him any war surplus. **1969** *Guardian* 28 Aug. 11/5 The starving war victims. **1917** 'Contact' *Airman's Outings* p. xviii, What, then, would be the effect on German war-weariness if giant raids on fortified towns by a hundred or so allied machines were of weekly occurrence? **1976** *Classical Q.* XXVI. 294 Sinon begins the first section of his lying speech with a reference to the death of Palamedes.., the second by describing the war-weariness of the Greeks. **1866** *Ann. Rep. Commissioner Indian Affairs* (U.S.) 164 These last came from Laramie during the winter, and claim to be war-widows. **1922** F. H. Burnett *Robin* v. 44 Slim young war-widows were to be seen in black dresses and veiled small hats with bits of white crape inside their brims. **1978** R. Barnard *Unruly Son* xvii. 186 We moved to London, where she passed as a war widow. **1932** E. Weekley *Words & Names* 21 We have the war-word Minnie for the German *minenwerfer*. **1938** E. Ambler *Cause for Alarm* iii. 47 The limp? Probably a war wound. **1981** C. Miller *Childhood in Scotland* 68 He was in continual pain from his war-wound. **1920** W. J. Locke *House of Baltazar* i. 9 The strain of the war years began to tell. **1977** D. Bennett *Jigsaw Man* xiii. 231 They had hidden the microfilm in the same cache they had used during the war years for passing messages. **1914** *Wells Fargo Messenger* Oct. 27/1 A late report from the war zone states that Mr. Gaston has returned to London. **1939** *Daily Tel.* 18 Dec. 6/5 The danger of 'rupture' has been vastly reduced by Congress's prohibition of American ships from entering the war zone. **1971** D. E. Westlake *I gave at Office* 142 The bar..had temporary plywood over its glassless windows, making it look like a correspondents' hangout in a war zone.

b. *war-belt* (earlier and later N. Amer. examples), *-bow*, *-club* (later examples), *-dress* (earlier example), *material*, *souvenir*; *war-balloon* (earlier example), *-beacon*, *-chariot*, *-pony*; *war-canoe* (earlier example).

1843 *Practical Mechanic* 16 Dec. 114/1 (*heading*) War balloon. **1954** J. R. R. Tolkien *Fellowship of Ring* II. ii. 277 Such light and flame cannot have been seen on Weathertop since the war-beacons of old. **1754** P. Wraxall *Abridgement Indian Affairs* (1915) 242 He calls upon them now to..join us in our Defence & Revenge & presents the Large War Belt to them. **1847** C. Lanman *Summer in Wilderness* 17 Captain James Clarke,..when about to be murdered by a council of Indians.., threw the war-belt in the midst of the savages, with a defying shout. **1965** *Canad. Historical Rev.* June 109 In December [1775] the Iroquois delegation told Philip Schuyler that Johnson after offering them a war belt and hatchet had invited them to 'feast on a Bostonian and drink his blood'. **1934** Webster, War bow. **1958** 'W. Henry' *Seven Men at Mimbres Springs* iv. 48 Nothing so guaranteed a safe passage through Apacheland as a coach that would not tip or leave the road when the warbows were bending and the Springfields blasting back at them. **1789** *Loiterer* 18 July 5 A large War Canoe and some small fishing Proas had been forced out to Sea. **1911** Fletcher & Kipling *School Hist. England* i. 15 They [*sc.* the Celts] rode on war-ponies, and, like the Assyrians in the Bible, they drove war-chariots. **1907** J. W. Schultz *My Life as Indian* xvii. 198 The fleeing men..were overtaken and shot, or brained with war clubs. **1943** R. Peattie *Great Smokies & Blue Ridge* 24 The Cherokee weapons were the ball-headed war club, spears and bows and arrows. **1984** *Listener* 4 Oct. 13/3 They were attacked by Kukukuku..with stone war-clubs. **1724** H. Jones *Present State Virginia* 5 The Seneca Indians in their War Dress may appear as terrible as any of the Sons of Anak. **1881** W. D. Hay *300 Years Hence* iv. 67 The progress of The Final Wars was marked by a whole series of inventions in war material. **1939** *Ann. Reg. 1938* 265 Meanwhile war material from Germany and Italy continued to pour in. **1865** J. Pike *Scout & Ranger* xi. 123 Many had friends..who came after them with wagons; refusing to let them ride their war ponies. **1929** D. H. Lawrence *Pansies* 128 Prancing their knees under their tiny skirts Like war-horses; or war-ponies at least! **1963** L. Deighton *Horse under Water* xliv. 180 An old war-souvenir pistol.

c. *war-tribe*.

1825 P. S. Ogden *Jrnl.* 18 Feb. (1950) 23 The War tribes appear determined that we Shall not want for their Company this year it cannot be otherwise as we are following the main War track. **1909** 'Mark Twain' *Is Shakes. Dead?* v. 53 It *could have* gone soldiering with a war-tribe..and learned soldier-wiles and soldier-ways.

d. (used in war) *war-cheer*.

1970 R. Lowell *Notebk.* 191 Frederick the Great of Prussia's war-cheer, 'Move, you bastards, do you want to live forever?'

e. *war bond*, *debt*, *expenditure*, *gratuity*, *-insurance* (example), *-loan* (examples), *-price* (earlier example), *relief*, *savings*, *-tax* (earlier example).

1918 *Daily Mirror* 12 Nov. 6/4 It bore a poem, titled 'A Message from Mars', eulogising the airmen and urging them to buy War Bonds. **1981** B. Langley *Autumn Tiger* v. 67 A gigantic billboard..urged him to 'Buy War Bonds'. **1865** *Nation* (N.Y.) I. 386 The Reconstructing State Convention of Alabama has pronounced against the repudiation of the war debt of the state. **1924** *Lit. Digest* 9 Feb. 20/2 The whole subject of war debts should undergo a new process of accountancy. **1931** *Keesing's Archives* 76/2 The oppressive problem of war-debts and reparations. **1983** T. Pocock *1945* vii. 241 The British owed their dominions, colonies, and the rest, a war debt of £4,000,000,000. **1931** War expenditure [see *inconsequentialness]. **1945** *Ann. Reg. 1944* 80 All those returning to civil life would receive war gratuities as a reward for their service. **1978** D. Dunlop in D. Abse *My Medical School* 31 Besides ordinary freshmen like myself straight from school, many came up on their war gratuities. **1898** *Amer. Rev. of Reviews* Sept. 322/2 Newspapers were required to bear the..expense of fire, marine, accident, and war insurance. **1848** Mill *Pol. Econ.* II. III. xxiii. 185 The only instance of the kind in recent history on a scale comparable to that of the war loans, is the absorption of capital in the construction of railways. **1974** *Daily Tel.* 24 June 17/1 'War Loan is a buy when the price equals the yield' was the joke on everyone's lips in Throgmorton Street a couple of years ago. Today it is no longer a joke—almost a reality. On Friday 3½ p.c. War Loan dropped to an all time low of £23½. **1824** *Cobbett's Weekly Reg.* 7 Feb. 354/2 Corn has not reached half the war-price yet. **1940** G. Marx *Let.* 5 Sept. (1967) 25 The proceeds are given to British War Relief and the actors all donate their services. **1919** *Maclean's Mag.* Jan. 55/3 Every man, woman and child in Canada should invest in War-Savings Stamps all the money that he or she can save. **1799** *Times* 1 June 2/3 The Directory have converted his accusation into a War Tax of three per cent. upon all capital.

f. With words that denote works of art, etc., of which the subject is war, as *war-ballad*, *book*, *history*, *-impression*, *novel*, *play*, *poem* (also *poetry*), *propaganda* (see sense 8 a above), *sonnet*, *story*, *verse*; *war film*, *movie*, *photograph* (also *photography*); also their authors, as *war novelist*, *photographer*, *poet*. Cf. also *war artist*, *picture* in sense 11 below.

1854 'C. Bede' *Further Adventures Verdant Green* ii. 9 What internal evidence does the Odyssey afford, that Homer sold his Trojan war-ballad at three yards an obolus? **1916** W. Owen *Let.* 23 Nov. (1967) 416, I have suddenly seen what I wanted to do with that War Ballad. **1809** M. L. Weems *Life Gen. Francis Marion* (1814) 3, I never dreampt of such a thing as writing a book; and least of all a *war book*. **1904** J. London *Let.* 4 June (1966) 159 There won't be any war-book so far as I am concerned. **1978** A. Waugh *Best Wine Last* xviii. 235 Starting with *Journey's End*..there had been a spate of war books. **1897** C. M. Hepworth *Animated Photogr.* p. vii (Advt.), War films. **1930** P. Rotha *Film till Now* I. v. 124 Like all war films manufactured in Hollywood, *The Big Parade* carried little of the real spirit of war. **1972** J. Mann *Mrs Knox's Profession* ii. 14 She looked like an amateur vamp in a war film. **1929** E. Linklater *Poet's Pub* ii. 31 He had been offered a knighthood for his official War History of the submarines. **1966** 'G. Black' *You want to die, Johnny?* xi. 198 Split-second timing..isn't achieved as often as the writers of popular war histories tend to suggest. **1917** W. Owen *Let.* 11 Mar. (1967) 442 Do you think, now, that I am going to read the *war-impressions* of home-editors? **1914** *N.Y. Times* 14 Jan. 9/6 Real war 'movies' shown... Moving pictures of real warfare were exhibited in the Seventy-first Regiment Armory last night. **1981** J. van de Wetering *Mind-Murders* I. iv. 43 An old war movie that ended well when the bad enemies surrendered. **1923** W. J. Locke *Moordius & Co.* viii. 99 He had not read the marvellous war novel to which he alluded. **1975** D. Lodge *Changing Places* v. 178 Stephen Crane wrote his great war-novel first and experienced war afterwards. **1966** J. Frederics *Ready to Die* (1968) iv. 20 He made war novelist sound like something not discussed in polite company. **1977** M. Herr *Dispatches* (1978) ii. 18, I can remember..when I was a kid looking at war photographs in *Life*. **1978** R. Gibson *Catal. 20th. Cent. Portraits* (Nat. Portrait Gallery) 36/1 Lee Miller (1907–77), well known as a war photographer. **1980** J. Danziger *Beaton* 46/2 The naïve approach of his war photography. **1896** *Godey's Mag.* Feb. 182/1 The instrument..imitates horses' hoofs with..untiring fidelity in all war-plays. **1915** *Sphere* 26 June 322/2 The production of a war play is a perilous business at the present time. **1972** P. Black *Biggest Aspidistra* I. iv. 41 *Brigade Exchange*, a war play..created by the pre-Nazi German radio. **1857** J. A. Symonds *Let.* May (1967) I. 105 He chiefly talked about ..[Tennyson's] Maud which he considers a true war poem & praises highly. **1917** W. Owen *Let.* 25 Sept. (1967) 496, I send you my two best war Poems. **1978** *Listener* 23 Mar. 378/3 There was a fine slim anthology of war poems read [aloud]. **1857** C. Kingsley *Two Years Ago* III. vi. 177 The true war poets..have been warriors themselves. Körner and Alcæus fought as well as sang. **1931** E. Blunden in W. Owen *Poems* 39 He [*sc.* Owen] was, apart from Mr. Sassoon, the greatest of the English war poets. But the term 'war poets' is rather convenient than accurate. **1962** *Listener* 8 Feb. 259/3 By 'war poet' we now automatically assume anti-war poet. This was no tacit assumption in 1916. **1865** *Atlantic Monthly* May 589/1 We have no such war-poetry. **1917** W. Owen *Let.* 27 Nov. (1967) 513, I knew he valued War Poetry before he told me so! **1973** D. Aaron *Unwritten War* IV. x. 152 Their best war poetry tended to be philosophical and personal. **1915** W. S. Churchill in *Times* 26 Apr. 5/5 The very few incomparable war sonnets which he [*sc.* Rupert Brooke] has left behind. **1864** M. B. Chesnut *Diary* 1 Jan. in C. V. Woodward *M. Chesnut's Civil War* (1981) 524, I mapped out a story of the war. Johnny is the hero... It is to be a war story. **1982** G. Lyall *Conduct of Major Maxim* xv. 145 They weren't interested in her war story, they'd heard a million war stories. **1918** G. Frankau *Judgement of Valhalla* 41 The other Side Being a letter from Major Average..acknowledging a presentation copy of a book of war-verse. **1952** E. Wilson *Shores of Light* 780, I refrained from mentioning her war-verse.

9. *war-winner*; *war-making* (later examples), *preparation*, *-winning* (also ppl. adj.); *war-bearing* ppl. adj.; *war-hungry* adj.

1936 Dylan Thomas *Twenty-Five Poems* 10 Dumbly and divinely stumbling Over the warbearing line. **1962** E. Snow *Other Side of River* (1963) lx. 456 The Western caricature of the mad-dog war-hungry Chinese. **1833** *Niles' Reg.* XLIV. 148/1 Very few persons questioned the right of congress to lay an embargo, under the war-making power. **1982** Warner & Sandilands *Women beyond Wire* v. 69 The Japanese..could be lethal..their business in the islands was that of professional war-making. **1931** W. S. Churchill *World Crisis* VI. vi. 97 Neglect in the war-preparations. **1947** Crowther & Whiddington *Science at War* I. 49 Manufacturers found it very difficult to give up mass production, in order to make the 200 or so sets 'off', which were often the war-winners. **1978** Ld. Drogheda *Double Harness* xix. 230 He was indeed one of the real war-winners, having done more than anyone to lighten Churchill's load. **1934** V. M. Yeates *Winged Victory* I. xx. 159 Tom was afraid Miller might be feeling his responsibility and want to do an undue amount of war-winning. **1956** *Nature* 11 Feb. 251/1 This was largely due to the efforts of..Sir Henry Tizard, whose foresight resulted in such war-winning devices as radar. **1974** P. Gore-Booth *With Great Truth & Respect* 123 Their object was to go hell-bent for victory with all the stupendous war-winning momentum which the United States developed.

10. *war-battered*, *-bitten*, *-bleached*, *-blinded*, *-bright*, *-brutalized*, *-devastated*, *-mazed*, *-orphaned*, *-ravaged*, *-scarred*, *-shattered*, *-torn*, *-wounded* (freq. *absol.*), *-wracked* adjs.; *war-laden* adj.

1938 W. B. Yeats *Herne's Egg* ii. 12 A weather-stained, war-battered Old campaigner such as I. **1942** W. S. Churchill *End of Beginning* (1943) 220 We recreated and revivified our war-battered Army. **1931** —— *World Crisis* VI. xxi. 323 A hundred and twenty-five thousand ragged, war-bitten men. **1941** L. B. Lyon *Tomorrow is a Revealing* 28 Eyes, and the ploughshare, baulk at the recovery Of skeletons war-bleached a grave ago. **1960** *Farmer & Stockbreeder* 15 Mar. 99 It is made by Garden Machinery, Ltd., of Slough. Director of the firm,..extreme right, is a war-blinded South African. **1970** R. Lowell *Notebk.* 108 Regret those jousting aristocracies, War-bright. **1939** C. Day Lewis *Child of Misfortune* 144 For one of our war-brutalized soldiery, you have considerable perception. **1938** *Times* 24 Aug. 12/1 The removal of import duties on mining, agricultural, and other machinery, ostensibly designed to facilitate the rehabilitation of war-devastated areas. **1900** W. B. Yeats *Shadowy Waters* 33 War-laden galleys, and armies on white roads. **1940** C. Day Lewis *Poems in Wartime* 10 Along this war-mazed valley. **1954** W. Faulkner *Fable* 46 A wealthy American expatriate ..who was supporting near Paris an asylum for war-orphaned children. **1978** *Poland* May 48/3, In the Fifties, twice as many children were born in Poland than was thought appropriate to the poverty of the war-ravaged country. **1857** J. G. Whittier in *National Era* 11 June 94/5 When each war-scarred Continental,..Waved his rusted sword in welcome. **1980** J. Lees-Milne *Harold Nicolson* vii. 114 Harold Nicolson..considered the choice of war-scarred Paris for the site of a peace-seeking meeting a psychological mistake. **1937** *Daily Tel.* 19 Oct. 15/3 (*heading*) War-shattered shrine restored. **1939** L. Jacobs *Rise of Amer. Film* v. xix. 386 Griffith revealed his superficial understanding of the war by remarking his sets for *Intolerance* had been more impressive than anything he saw in war-torn France and Belgium. **1975** 'E. Lathen' *By Hook or by Crook* xxiii. 209 It was imperative to get the children out of their war-torn background. **1950** War-wounded [see *team *v.* 1 b]. **1968** *Guardian* 23 Feb. 10/6 Few, other than surgical cases (including occasional war-wounded) were brought to the hospital. **1909** M. B. Saunders *Litany Lane* iv. 43 Women of prayer who had raised just as many waxen palms to altars, in nunnery and in palace, for many a war-wracked generation. **1976** *Billings* (Montana) *Gaz.* 17 June 1-A/3 The driver took 'the route normally taken' by anyone wishing to cross from the Christian to the Moslem sides of war-wracked Beirut.

11. War Ag., colloq. abbrev. of 'War

Agricultural Committee'; **war artist,** an artist employed to provide paintings of a war; **war baby,** (*a*) one born during a war, esp. an (illegitimate) child of a man on active service; (*b*) *slang*, a young or inexperienced officer; (*c*) *U.S. slang*, a bond or the like which is sold during a war, or which increases in value because of a war; **war bag** *U.S.*, † (*a*) = **war budget* (*a*); (*b*) a bag containing money, clothing, or other supplies; **war-bird,** (*b*) *fig.*, a fighting aircraft or airman; **war bonnet,** a head-dress decorated with eagle feathers, worn by American Indians; **War Box** *slang*, the War Office; **war bride,** a woman who marries a man who is on active service or a man (esp. a foreigner) whom she met while he was on active service; **war bridle** *Canad.*, a harsh bridle made by placing a loop of rope round the lower jaw of a horse; **war budget,** (*a*) *U.S.*, a packet carried by American Indians, containing amulets and military trophies; (*b*) (in Dict., sense 8 e); **War Cabinet,** a Cabinet with responsibility for the political decisions of a country during a war; **war cemetery,** a cemetery composed of war graves; **war chest,** (a chest or strong box for) funds used in waging war; freq. used *fig.*, esp. of funds used by a political party to finance an election campaign; **war college** chiefly *U.S.*, a college providing advanced instruction for senior officers of the armed services; **war communism,** an economic policy, based on strict centralized control of the economy, adopted by the Bolsheviks during the Russian Civil War (1917–21); **war-correspondent** (earlier examples); **war crime,** an offence against the rules of war, formerly excluding, but since the 1939–45 war including, any such act performed on the orders of a higher authority; **war criminal,** one who has committed a war crime; **war damage,** damage caused by action taken by or against an enemy during a war; hence **war-damaged** *a.*; **war dead** *pl.*, servicemen who have died on active service; **war diary,** (*a*) a diary recording the experiences of an individual during a war; (*b*) (see quot. 1918); **war dream,** a dream about war; **war economy,** (*a*) a measure taken in order to save money or other resources because of a war; (*b*) an economy, characteristic of wartime, in which a large part of the labour force is engaged in arms production, etc., rather than in the production of goods for export or for civilian use; **war effort,** the effort of a nation to win a war, or of an individual group to contribute to that end; **war fever,** an enthusiasm for war; **war-fighting,** the fighting of wars; also *attrib.*; **warfront,** the foremost part of the field of operations of opposing armies; **war-game** (later examples); also used of any game simulating war, esp. an elaborate game played with model soldiers, or of any exercise by which a military strategy is examined or tested; **war-game** *v. trans.*, to examine or test (a strategy or the like); **war-gamer,** one who plays a war-game; **war-gaming,** the playing of war-games; the use of such games to examine or test strategies; **war gas,** a gas or other chemical agent used in war to produce irritant or poisonous effects; **war generation** a generation which has experienced a war; **war grave,** the grave of a serviceman who died from wounds inflicted, accident occurring, or disease contracted on active service; **war-guilt,** the responsibility for having caused a war; freq. with reference to the claim that Germany had caused the war of 1914–18, which was embodied in an article of the Treaty of Versailles (1919); **war-hatchet** (earlier examples); **war-head** (later examples); also, that of any missile, esp. one deriving its destructive power from the release of nuclear energy; **war hero,** a man who has acted heroically in a war; also **war heroine; War House** *slang*, the War Office; **war hysteria,** unhealthy emotion or excitement caused by war; an enthusiasm for war; **war machine,** (*a*) an instrument or weapon of war; (*b*) *transf.*, the military resources of a country organized for waging war; **war marriage,** a marriage taking place in wartime, esp. one in which the bridegroom is on active service; **war medicine** *N. Amer.*, (a form of) magic formerly used by North American Indians to ensure success in war; also *fig.*; **war memorial,** a monument, etc., commemorating those (esp. from a particular locality) killed in a war, and freq. inscribed with their names; **war-mind,** a mind attuned to or desirous of war; hence **war-minded** *a.*, having such a mind; **war-mindedness; war museum,** a museum of the history of warfare in general, or of warfare during a particular period; **war orphan,** a child orphaned by war; **war pension,** a pension paid to someone disabled or widowed by war; **war picture,** (*a*) a painting of which the theme is war; (*b*) a photograph of a scene from the theatre of war; also, a documentary film of action from a war, and *transf.* a written account of this; (*c*) a cinematographic film with war as its subject or background (the usual sense); cf. *war film, movie* (sense 8 f above); **warplane,** an aeroplane equipped for fighting, bombing, etc., in war-time; **war refugee,** one who seeks refuge in another country, etc., from the effects of war; a displaced person; **war reporter** = *war-correspondent*; hence **war-reporting; war resistance,** opposition to war, pacifism; hence **war resister,** an opponent of war or of a particular war; **war risk** *Insurance* (chiefly *Marine*), a risk of loss, etc., during war-time; freq. in *pl.* and *attrib.*; **war road** *N. Amer.* = WAR-PATH a (*concr.*); **war room,** a room from which a war or part of a war is directed; **war-substantive** *a.* [SUBSTANTIVE *a.* 1 e], confirmed (in a rank) for the duration of a war; **war-talk,** (*b*) talk about war in general; **war toy,** a toy with which a child can play war-games; **war trial,** the trial of a person for a war crime or crimes; cf. *Nuremberg trial(s)* s.v. *NUREMBERG 2; **war veteran** orig. *U.S.* = *VETERAN *sb.* 1 b; **war-weary** *a.*, (*a*) (see sense 10 in Dict.) (earlier example); (*b*) *U.S.*, *spec.* applied to aircraft badly damaged in war-time, and which are withdrawn from service for repair, conversion, or scrapping; also *ellipt.* as *sb.*; **war wedding** = **war marriage*; **war work,** special work occasioned by war, and which is intended to advance the war effort; **war-worker,** a person undertaking war work; also *transf.*; **war-worthy** *a.*, suitable for or befitting war; so **war-worthiness.**

1949 E. COXHEAD *Wind in West* vi. 152 The farmer I stay with there is a member of the War Ag. **1970** G. E. EVANS *Where Beards wag All* ix. 106 When the *War Ag.* (Agricultural Committee) took over I asked 'em would they send the gyro-tiller. **1890** KIPLING *Light that Failed* (1891) xii. 237 Some man unknown who would be employed as war artist by the Central Southern Syndicate. **1981** S. CHITTY *Gwen John* ix. 148 Augustus..was in France as a war artist. **1901** E. W. B. MORRISON *With Guns in S.A.* xxxiv. 239 (*caption*) Mrs. Jourdain's 'war baby'. **1917** 'CONTACT' *Airman's Outings* 35 Even these war babies (three of them died very gallantly before we re-assembled for breakfast next day) had bottled most of their exuberance. **1917** R. W. LARDNER *Gullible's Travels* 83 'You forgot somethin',' she says, 'You forgot them war babies.' Did I tell you about that? Last fall I done a little dabblin' in Crucial Steel. **1935** I. MILLER *School Tie* xv. 286 It was possible to join a Junior Training Battalion—commonly known as the War Babies' Brigade—at the age of seventeen and a half. **1948** *Green Bay* (Wisconsin) *Press-Gaz.* 13 July 4/2 The idle rich of Europe..clamored for war while they invested great amounts in American war babies and reaped superlative profits. **1974** G. BUTLER *Coffin for Canary* ix. 105 Born Belfast, 1944, so she was just a war baby. **1820** *Western Rev.* II. 48 After the action is over, each person returns his war bag to the commander of the party. **1897** A. H. LEWIS *Wolfville* 33 S'pose you-alls gropes about in your war-bags an' sees. I'm needin' of a drink mighty bad. **1933** J. V. ALLEN *Cowboy Lore* i. 6 What's known as the 'war bag' is carried by many of the boys in their beds to protect their wardrobe, tobacco, etc., and may be anything from a flour sack to a rather pretentious container. **1972** F. VAN W. MASON *Roads to Liberty* 241 Higsby fumbled in his war bag. **1917** G. FRANKAU *City of Fear* 3 Above, The warbirds beat And whistle. **1936** 'R. HYDE' *Passport to Hell* 206 German and British warbirds were mixing it in an aerial free-for-all. **1981** *Pilot* Jan. 23/2 Some of the warbirds flying today are quite bent, cracked, patched up. **1845** J. C. FRÉMONT *Rep. Exploring Exped.* 134 Indians ..with the long red streamers of their war bonnets reaching nearly to the ground. **1928** 'BRENT OF BIN BIN' *Up Country* xxii. 356 Adjusting her widow's cap like a warbonnet, she arose to her full height of five-feet-one-and-a-half. **1973** A. H. WHITEFORD *N. Amer. Indian Arts* 151 The flowing war bonnet of the Plains has become the symbol of the American Indian. **1952** M. ALLINGHAM *Tiger in Smoke* i. 12 The War Box cited him 'Missing believed killed'. **1969** M. PUGH *Last Place Left* xxix. 213, I flit between Downing Street and the War Box and the Ministry of Defence. **1918** A. BENNETT *Pretty Lady* xi. 61 She was becoming hysterical: the special liability of the war-bride. **1939** *Daily Tel.* 18 Dec. 9/5 Silver tea and coffee sets are being bought..as gifts to the many war brides unable to set up homes. **1978** J. KRANTZ *Scruples* i. 10 She was as alert as a vixen, as humorous as the song by Maurice Chevalier after which her homesick war-bride mother had named her. **1962** J. ONSLOW *Bowler-hatted Cowboy* xviii. 175 One summer day, they [*sc.* two horses] came home, gaunt, their heads bloody and scarred from 'war bridles' with which someone had tried to halter-break them. **1813** R. STUART *Jrnl.* 14 Apr. in *Discovery Oregon Trail* (1935) x. 236 A Pole surpassing in height any put in the roof, is put out at the chimney where are suspended their Medicine Bags and War Budgets carefully concealed in innumerable wrappers. **1916** *Times* 9 Dec. 9/2 It is an immense gain to have the Prime Minister definitely and irrevocably committed to the creation of a small War Cabinet, constantly..devoted to the prosecution of the war. **1940** J. REITH *Diary* 5 Jan. (1975) v. 237, I asked if the job carried War Cabinet rank and he said no. **1980** P. FITZGERALD *Human Voices* ii. 38, I don't know who authorised him to speak. I understand it was the War Cabinet. **1922** *Encycl. Brit.* XXXII. 953/1 It is possible that the conspicuous success with which Arlington Cemetery has been designed had a share in influencing the Imperial War Graves Commission in the construction of the British war cemeteries on somewhat similar lines. **1982** 'J. GASH' *Firefly Gadroon* xv. 145 There's a turning through the woods where the American War Cemetery stands. **1901** War chest [in Dict., sense 8 e]. **1912** W. DEEPING *Sincerity* xvi. 124 He had about forty pounds left, no great sum to start a war-chest with. **1932** *Sun* (Baltimore) 30 Aug. 1/6 (*heading*) War chests practically empty, parties curtail on campaign. **1973** R. L. SIMON *Big Fix* iv. 34 All the guilt-stricken celebrities contributing to their war chest. **1894** *Abstract of Courses* (Naval War. Coll.) 3 The summer course at the Naval War College began on the 13th of June. **1913** R. MEINERTZHAGEN *Diary* 1 Nov. (1960) 56 A joint war college for all branches of Government Services [in India] would be a God-send. **1978** H. WOUK *War & Remembrance* i. 11 Talking in a calm War College vein. **1928** M. DOBB *Russian Econ. Devel. since Revolution* iii. 64 'War communism', accordingly, sprang into life in the 'forcing-house' of a mortal struggle of the new régime—a struggle in which all things were subordinated to military necessity, and the problems of industry were simply regarded as..the problem of military supplies. **1965** B. PEARCE tr. *Preobrazhensky's New Economics* 32 The economics of War Communism were those of a state economy of the war-consumption type, when we were not accumulating but were forced to *spend* our resources. **1844** War-correspondent [see CORRESPONDENT *sb.* 4 b]. **1870** A. MAVERICK *Henry J. Raymond & N.Y. Press* 256 The 'war correspondents' who had been sent out to the battle-fields to represent the newspapers of New York throve and grew famous. **1906** L. OPPENHEIM *Internat. Law* 264 Violations of rules regarding warfare are war crimes only when committed without an order of the belligerent government concerned. If members of the armed forces commit violations by *order* of their government, they are not war criminals and may not be punished by the enemy; the latter can, however, resort to reprisals. **1945** *Daily Express* 16 May 1/1 The United Nations War Crimes Commission announced last night: Hermann Goering's name was placed..on the first list of persons charged with war crimes. **1980** *Oxf. Compan. Law* 1288/2 After World War II, three classes of offences against international law came to be regarded as war crimes, crimes against peace, as by planning or waging a war of aggression, conventional war crimes, or violations of the accepted laws or customs of warfare and crimes against humanity, including extermination, enslavement, deportation and other inhumane acts. **1906** War criminal [see **war crime*]. **1929** W. S. CHURCHILL *World Crisis* V. viii. 158 An article of the Peace Treaty obliged the Germans to stigmatize all their greatest men and potentates as War Criminals. **1943** *Ann. Reg. 1942* 190 The question of the trial of war criminals ruffled..the ever-growing friendliness between Britain and America. **1981** J. WAINWRIGHT *Urge for Justice* 121 An organisation devoted to tracking down war criminals. **1939** *Act* 2 & 3 *Geo. VI* c. 72 § 4 Where the land comprised in a lease is unfit by reason of war damage, the following provisions ..shall have effect. *Ibid.* § 24 'War damage' means damage caused by, or in repelling, enemy action, or by measures taken to avoid the spreading of the consequences of damage caused by, or in repelling, enemy action. **1950** E. HYAMS *From Waste Land* 10 Sharp and hopeful landlords claimed war-damage compensation. **1975** J. CLEARY *Safe House* iv. 177 The walls were spattered with bullet and shrapnel marks..all war damage. **1946** *Mind* LV. 380 The Secretary reported appeals from war-damaged libraries in Europe. **1978** *Times* 8 May 9/8 Volunteers.. shivering in war-damaged, makeshift offices. **1969** J. BURMEISTER *Hot & Copper Sky* i. 17 They're French war dead. From the Indo-China campaign. **1917** W. J. LOCKE *Red Planet* i. 4 To fill in my time, I first started.. a sort of War Diary. **1918** E. S. FARROW *Dict. Mil. Terms* 657 *War diary*, a record of events kept in campaign by each battalion and higher organization, each ammunition, supply, engineer, and sanitary train. **1937** KIPLING *Something of Myself* iii. 49 An accursed Muscovite paper..published the war diaries of Alikhanoff, a Russian General. **1955** E. WAUGH *Officers & Gentlemen* 142 Guy chalked the nightly wanderings of the Commandos on.. his map and recorded them next day in the War Diary. **1981** J. BARNETT *Firing Squad* II. 105 The War Diary of Sergeant Michael Lugard. **1918** W. OWEN *Let.* 18 Feb. (1967) 534, I confess I *bring on* what few war dreams I now have, entirely by *willingly* considering war of an evening. **1919** W. B. YEATS *Cutting of Agate* 16 The Print Room of the British Museum is now closed as a war-economy. **1940** *Economist* 3 Feb. 189/1 The problem of war economy is to man and equip the Forces, to raise output for war and export needs to the utmost and to cut down civilian consumption. **1948** [see *peace economy* s.v. *PEACE *sb.* 15 d]. **1972** M. J. BOSSE *Incident at Naha* 56 Like any girl caught up in a war economy. She had a pimp. **1919** *Maclean's Mag.* Jan. 49 (*heading*) Britain's wonderful war effort. **1934** W. S. CHURCHILL *Marlborough* II. v. 101 Whigs and Tories alike wished the fleet to be used as a part of the main war-effort. **1954** N. COWARD *Future Indefinite* IV. vii. 194 A job which..would be of real value to the war effort. **1977** A. WILSON *Strange Ride Rudyard Kipling* vii. 299 He would never have repeated the story lest it weakened our war effort. **1812** J. STEELE *Papers* (1924) II. 668 The late report of the Secty. of the

Treasy. will cool the war fever in some. 1908 H. G. Wells *War in Air* vi. 180 To the normal high-strung energy of New York streets was added a touch of war-fever. 1978 N. Gosling *Paris 1900–1914* 187 In 1912 the slowly developing war fever..began to show itself in sinister local symptoms. 1965 H. Kahn *On Escalation* 284 Deterrence-only is the opposite of 'war-fighting'. 1983 *Listener* 10 Feb. 7/1 They are war-fighting weapons with a first-strike capability. 1950 *Sun* (Baltimore) 29 June 1 General MacArthur left for the South Korean warfront today. 1976 *Billings* (Montana) *Gaz.* 11 July 1-A/2 Lebanon's three major warfronts resounded to artillery, rocket and mortar fire. 1910 H. G. Wells *New Machiavelli* (1911) I. iii. 84 The spectacle of volunteer officers fighting the war game in Caxton Hall. 1951 D. Knight *In Deep* (1964) 92 The cadets..carrying out one of the prescribed games under the direction of student squad leaders. 1966 *Punch* 6 July 26/2 Entertaining incidental scenes (the children's war games, the husband's home movies, haggling over the junk) keep interest always alive. 1967 *Guardian* 16 Oct. 8/5 The National Wargame Championships organised by the British Model Soldier Society. 1970 *Time* 5 Oct. 13 At one point Nixon told Kissinger: 'Let's you and me war-game this,' and they worked the plans over to see, as Nixon put it, 'where the weak points might be.' 1975 *Times* 2 June 13/1 Politicians of all parties cooped up in..Westminster have become so absorbed in their own war-games that they have lost touch with the wider world. 1981 *Washington Post* 8 Nov. L1/6 'Well,' Wakko said, 'I've got to go back to work. We're war-gaming an LNW in Monaco.' 1967 *Guardian* 16 Oct. 8/5 One thing only is causing the wargamers concern. There are so many different societies in the field. 1982 M. Leapman *Yankee Doodles* IV. 208 War-gamers are not the only people undertaking such simulations. 1954 McCloskey & Trefethen *Operations Research for Management* I. 15 They used the technique of war-gaming to develop models of possible operations, then 'tested' various tactics and weapons. 1970 *Daily Tel.* (Colour Suppl.) 30 Oct. 43/2 Today war-gaming has reached a point of sophistication where one almost needs a computer to play. 1980 J. McNeil *Spy Game* ix. 96 War gaming is like that, dashed unpredictable. 1934 Webster, War gas. 1939 L. W. Marrison tr. *M. Sartori's War Gases* p. viii, The most efficient war gases are organic compounds, the inorganic compounds which have great toxicity being unsuitable for use owing to their physical and chemical properties. 1974 M. C. Gerald *Pharmacol.* vii. 134 In 1968, 6000 sheep were accidentally killed in Utah, allegedly as a result of exposure to the war gas VX that was being tested by the Army about 17 miles away. 1930 W. S. Maugham *Bread-Winner* I. 18 They were a dreary lot that war generation. 1978 Cadogan & Craig *Women & Children First* ii. 47 The sense of isolation that characterized the war generation. 1917 *Imperial War. Conf.* 5 in *Parl. Papers* (Cd. 8566) XXIII. 323 The Conference..humbly prays His Majesty to constitute by Royal Charter an Imperial War Graves Commission. 1945 J. Reith *Let.* 11 June in *Diaries* (1975) vii. 350, I should have thought..you would have welcomed the establishment of an imperial corporation—the first to be achieved (except War Graves). 1981 J. Barnett *Firing Squad* xii. 175 Search all names against...war casualty lists, ditto War Graves Commission. 1922 *Nation* 9 Sept. 758/1 (*heading*) The myth of war-guilt. 1940 W. Temple *Thoughts in Wartime* II. i. 60 The war-guilt clause, against which many of us have protested. 1971 *Guardian* 5 Aug. 12/3 Concepts of war 'guilt' derived from the Second World War have encouraged some elements of the Left to identify the war in Vietnam with an emerging American fascism. 1981 J. B. Hilton *Surrender Value* xi. 88 And she had been intense: about war-guilt, about Borchert and Kafka. 1760 G. Groghan *Jrnl.* 4 Dec. in R. G. Thwaites *Early Western Trav.* (1904) I. 116 That you [*sc.* chiefs and warriors].. may..bury the War Hatchet in the Bottomless Pitt. *a* 1818 B. Hawkins *Sk. Creek Country* (1848) 72 He lifts the war hatchet against the nation which has injured them. 1944 *Sun* (Baltimore) 20 June 3/3 Explosive carried in a warhead [of a German robot plane] is equal to a 2,200 pound German bomb. 1955 *Bull. Atomic Sci.* Apr. 168/3 In the not too distant future we can foresee the dominance of intercontinental guided missiles with hydrogen war heads. 1978 R. V. Jones *Most Secret War* xlv. 447, I was now prepared to call everyone else's bluff, and declare for a rocket of 12 tons all-up weight with a 1 ton warhead. 1898 *Kansas City Star* 19 Dec. 1/5 Following are the names of the members of the entertainment committee who received the war heroes. 1953 L. P. Hartley *Go-Between* iv. 59, I already felt violently jealous of Trimingham, and the fact that he was a war-hero did not recommend him to me. 1982 T. Allbeury *Shadow of Shadows* v. 44 Your father was a war hero. He was awarded..the Legion of Honour. 1932 *New Yorker* 9 Jan. 34/1 On the sidewalks are..a few war heroines with nothing to sell. 1979 'D. Kyle' *Green River High* viii. 106 We..read: *War heroine returns to Sarawak.* 1925 Fraser & Gibbons *Soldier & Sailor Words* 300 *War House, the,* General Staff slang for the War Office. 1926 'Sapper' *Final Count* xii. 302 They thought I was mad at the War House. 1978 D. Wheatley *Officer & Temporary Gentleman* iii. 29 A man in control at the War House who had an enormous hold upon the popular imagination. 1940 'G. Orwell' *Inside Whale* 172 The very people who..had sniggered over their own superiority to war hysteria were the ones who rushed..into the mental slum of 1915. 1968 O. Wynd *Sumatra Seven Zero* ii. 20 Birgid is the child of my war hysteria. Her father was a blond Norwegian. 1881 W. D. Hay *300 Years Hence* iv. 70 The last inventions in war-machines. 1914 W. J. Bryan *Mem.* (1925) 390 The allies see peace only in a success so signal as to crush the German war machine. 1979 *Sci. Amer.* Mar. 123/1 With the introduction of catapults, together with other war machines just coming into use in the West, sieges became more effective. 1981 B. Langley *Autumn Tiger* xv. 244 Stalin..was wary of the German war machine. 1921 'C. Dane' *Bill of Divorcement* II. 54 If it hadn't been for the war—and the war marriages. 1805 W. Clark *Jrnl.* 11 Jan. in *Lewis & Clark Exped.* (1904) I. vi. 247 Some of our Men go to See a War Medeson made at the Village on the opposite Side of the river. 1893 *Chicago Tribune* 28 Apr. 4/1 Gov. Altgeld..proceeded to administer a dose of war medicine he had been making for some time. 1962 E. E. Evans-Pritchard in *Ess. Social Anthropol.* v. 95 He used some of these forms of magic himself, getting old commoners to bring the medicines and perform the rites, except in the case of the war-medicines, which he administered himself, from the large bongo horn in which they were kept. 1912 War memorial [see *late *a.*[1] 3]. 1930 Kipling *Limits & Renewals* (1932) 324 The little cast-iron *poilu,* which seemed to be standard pattern for War memorials in that region. 1980 P. Lively *Judgement Day* v. 55 The starling flew across the nave, crashed into the War Memorial window..and thumped to the ground. 1928 Blunden *Undertones of War* iii. 27 The joyful path away from the line..was full of pictures for my infant war-mind. 1932 H. Crane *Let.* 13 Apr. (1965) 409 Dos Passos has written a very important record of the war and the 'war mind' in 1919. 1936 *Mind* XLV. 289 A society which prefers war to peace and organises itself for success in war, may be rational in the above sense, if (a) the majority of its members are genuinely war-minded, and (b) the small minority of pacifists in its ranks is allowed to express.. its dissenting opinion. 1948 W. Fortescue *Beauty for Ashes* xxii. 172 At intervals it stopped..to allow war-minded little boys to finger the ugly noses of guns. 1936 H. Read *Surrealism* 36 Motives no less irrational than those which promote war-mindedness. 1917 *Times* 20 Feb. 11/3 At No. 6, Avenue de Malakoff..in two spacious first-floor *appartements*..is housed the War Museum which, when complete, will be presented to the French nation. 1967 O. Wynd *Walk Softly, Men Praying* x. 165 An inspirational experience in a war museum. 1979 E. Bercovici *Wolf Trap* 161 The War Museum on the upper fortress fascinated him. 1915 W. Owen *Let.* 29 June (1967) 342 All France is collecting for its War Orphans. 1971 H. McCloy *Question of Time* i. 14 The nuns kept on trying to trace the families of war orphans left in their care. 1930 E. H. Young *Miss Mole* xxv. 224 The little poultry farm which was to supplement..the hero's war pension. 1980 *Daily Tel.* 24 Apr. 14/5 His mother brought him up alone on a war pension plus what she could make by smocking children's clothes. 1883 B. Potter *Jrnl.* 28 Apr. (1966) 39 First we went to the Fine Arts Gallery..to see..the Egyptian war pictures. 1900 (*title*) War pictures. 1914 R. Grau *Theatre of Science* ii. 40 The war pictures released by this company reflected the high aims of a man. 1915 V. Woolf *Diary* 25 Jan. (1977) I. 28 The Picture Palace was a little disappointing—as we never got to the War pictures, after waiting 1 hour & a half. 1946 J. B. Priestley *Bright Day* viii. 246 Honest war pictures, made on the spot here by people who know what it's like. 1978 *Listener* 30 Mar. 410/1 *In Which We Serve* I remember as the best war picture that I have ever seen. 1911 *Flight* 16 Dec. 1078/2 No one has any very definite ideas of what the future type of war-plane will be like. 1938 C. Day Lewis *Overtures to Death* 17 Oh, look at the warplanes! Screaming hysteric treble In the long power-dive, like gannets they fall steep. 1967 A. MacLean *Where Eagles Dare* xi. 230 The Mosquito bomber, all engines and plywood, was, he was well aware, the fastest warplane in the world. 1978 *Guardian Weekly* 4 June 16/1 Categories so politically volatile as warplanes. 1942 D. Powell *Time to be Born* vii. 163 Amanda was nobly..adopting a war refugee. 1973 'B. Mather' *Snowline* iii. 33 There are three million war refugees from Bangladesh in West Bengal. 1950 E. H. Gombrich *Story of Art* 118 The final result is possibly more impressive than the accounts of our own war reporters and newsreel men. 1976 S. Hynes *Auden Generation* x. 342 Compared to war-reporting of the Spanish war..*Journey to a War* is superficial and uninformative. 1932 *Week-End Rev.* 19 Nov. 611/2 We appeal to those who wish to take part in a truly practical and effective effort at war resistance to send us a donation. 1935 J. Bell in *We did not Fight* p. xviii, The most active and ardent war resisters..are more likely to take the line of revolutionary action than conscientious objection. 1976 *Pacifist* Jan. 10/1 We remain an organisation of war-resisters. 1920 *Lloyd's List Law Rep.* 22 July 288/2, I am perfectly clear this is a case that is not brought within the War Risks Policy. 1934 Webster, *War risk insurance,* term insurance written by the United States Government for members of the military and naval forces. 1939 *Country Life* 11 Feb. 133/2 An insurance against war risks should be attached to Schedule 'A'. 1974 E. R. H. Ivamy *Marine Insurance* (ed. 2) xv. 219 The term 'war risk' in a marine policy has been held to include a civil war. 1782 in V. W. Howard *Bryan Station Heroes & Heroines* (1932) xii. 144 On the Southward side below where the War road crosses the said fork. 1968 E. Russenholt *Heart of Continent* II. iii. 41 Canadians and Indians follow the old Indian war road. 1914 A. Wilson *Let.* 29 Oct. in M. Gilbert *Winston S. Churchill* (1972) III. Compan. I. 233, I should like to have a room set apart for me near the War room. 1976 J. Lee *Ninth Man* I. 82 The War Room occupied the southwest corner of the main floor in the White House. *a* 1944 K. Douglas *Alamein to Zem Zem* (1946) ii. 13 He had..returned to his war-substantive rank of captain. 1965 *New Statesman* 10 Dec. 919/1 How could a poor war-substantive captain hope to hold his own against someone like Colonel Passy. 1861 M. B. Chesnut *Diary* 23 Apr. in C. V. Woodward *M. Chesnut's Civil War* (1981) 53, Maria—are you crying because all this war talk scares you? 1939 C. Day Lewis *Child of Misfortune* III. i. 264 You're not letting this war-talk throw a scare into you? 1973 M. Kaye *Toy is Born* xv. 144 It is interesting to note that the hue and cry against war toys a few years ago had little effect on Avalon Hill. 1949 R. Chandler *Let.* 25 Feb. (1981) 149 There is an element of hypocrisy in these war trials. 1971 P. D. James *Shroud for Nightingale* vii. 242 He'd seen her before... In Germany. She was in the dock. It was a war trial. 1906 *N.Y. Even. Post* 29 Jan. 1 A guard of honor selected from the ranks of the Spanish war veterans here. 1980 J. McClure *Blood of Englishman* x. 92 War veterans... It'd all gone a bit to their heads. 1895 W. B. Yeats *Poems* 7, I have not yet, war-weary king, Been spoken of with any man. 1945 *Sat. Even. Post* 17 Mar. 20 Thousands of once precious B-17's are now 'war-wearies'. Not worth salvaging, they clutter up foreign and domestic airfields. 1945 *Fortune* Aug. 208 Five war-weary Liberators, described with horrors by their pilots as 'clunkers'. 1915 *Truth* 4 Aug. 181/2 What do we hear from London about war-weddings? 1890 Kipling *Light that Failed* (1891) ii. 24 Do you want me to do war-work? *Ibid.* iv. 64 He has thrown up war work. 1916 A. Huxley *Let.* 2 Mar. (1969) 92 A friend of mine at Magdalen, a Quaker..objected to war-work of any kind, combatant or non-. 1954 W. K. Hancock *Country & Calling* vii. 189 The answer to that difficulty was for my wife to take up paid war work in place of the voluntary work she had been doing in Birmingham. 1977 *Belfast Tel.* 14 Feb. 9/6 Rene, who was in Mackie's on war work, lived with her widowed father and looked after her young brothers. 1915 *Political Q.* May 108 It is not clear whether or no the special.. war-workers..will be permanently shut out of the trades. 1930 Blunden *De Bello Germanico* iv. 41 War-workers varying from whizzbangs to woolly bears. 1978 Cadogan & Craig *Women & Children First* ii. 48 The experiences of the war workers had been thoroughly documented. 1909 *Q. Rev.* Oct. 578 The aim must now be..to seize every opportunity to improve its war-worthiness. 1908 Hardy *Dynasts* III. vii. viii. 510 Ney holds indignantly that such a feint Is not war-worthy.

waragi (wa·răgi). [ad. Swahili *wargi.*] In Uganda, a potent alcoholic drink made from bananas or cassava.

1916 in C. Griffin *Laws Uganda Protectorate* (1924) II. 1031 'Native liquor' means any liquor prepared or manufactured in accordance with native custom and includes ..Waragi. 1935 Thomas & Scott *Uganda* xix. 295 It is forbidden by the Liquor Ordinance, 1916, that any person shall supply natives with any liquor other than..beer.. and the Rules promulgated under the Ordinance make it an offence..to distil or even to possess the raw cassava spirit known locally as *waragi.* 1973 *Guardian* 13 Jan. 13/3 The ferocious Ugandan spirit Waragi. 1976 *Listener* 19 Aug. 195/3 He had had three tots of Waragi (a highly potent Ugandan gin made from bananas). 1977 *Time* 7 Mar. 18/3 They [*sc.* Ugandans] would rather have scarce butter or a slab of meat or a bottle of *waragi,* a potent, banana-based liquor.

Warao, var. *Warrau.

warb (wǭɹb). *Austral. slang.* [Perh. f. Warb(le *sb.*[2]] A lazy, unkempt, or contemptible person (see also quot. 1959).

1933 L. Robinson in Murdoch & Drake-Brockman *Austral. Short Stories* (1951) 215 We were both of us what, in the back country, are called 'warbs', meaning confirmed and irredeemable loafers. 1959 Baker *Drum* (1960) II. 155 *Warb,* a low-paid manual worker. 2. A dirty or untidy person. 3. A simpleton or fool. 1967 K. Tennant *Tell Morning This* 201 But it's a no-hoper's jail—a lot of old warbs and kids mixed up with coves like Amos the Cannibal and chaps that razors bounce off.

warble, *sb.*[1] Add: **2.** Special combination. **warble tone** *Physics,* a constant amplitude tone whose frequency is cyclically varied between certain limits, used in acoustic measurement to avoid irregularities associated with the use of single frequencies.

1933 *Proc. IRE* XXI. 1183 The introduction of a 'warble tone' into the technique of acoustical measurements..has also supplied a growing interest in this kind of oscillation. 1958 H. J. Gray *Dict. Physics* 527/1 A warble tone can be produced from an oscillator by rotating a small variable condenser in the tuned circuit at a constant speed. 1971 B. J. Smith *Acoustics* v. 96 To attempt to eliminate the variations due to room modes for each frequency a band of noise is used, either in the form of white noise or in warble tones.

warble, *v.*[1] Add: **4. c.** Of telephones (*spec.* Trimphones): to make a distinctive trilling sound.

1965, 1969 [see *Trimphone]. 1973 G. Moffat *Deviant Death* v. 68 The telephone was warbling softly. 1981 T. Barling *Bikini Red North* x. 206 The telephone warbled. ..'You must answer it.'

warbler. Add: **1. c.** *slang.* A female singer.

1946 B. Treadwell *Big Bk. Swing* 125/2 *Warbler,* girl singer. 1961 *Times* 21 Nov. 13/2 Barbara Holt, making her stage debut, displayed the promise of an uncommon warbler. 1981 *TV Picture Life* Mar. 16/1 (*caption*) Regardless of where her love life leads, the warbler is very much in demand for films these days.

d. *colloq.* A telephone which warbles. Cf. *warble *v.*[1] 4 c.

1973 G. Moffat *Deviant Death* vii. 106 'I didn't hear a telephone, did you?' 'It's one of the new warblers.'

Warburg (wǭ·ɹbʊ̈ɹg). *Biochem.* The name of Otto *Warburg* (1883–1970), German biochemist, used *attrib.* and in the possessive to denote apparatus for the study of the metabolism of small pieces of tissue by the manometric measurement of the rate of oxygen consumption and carbon dioxide production, a technique he pioneered.

1930 *Biol. Abstr.* IV. 2745/1 By use of suitable suspensions of *B. coli* in Warburg's apparatus a biological, direct (manometric) method of measuring the hexoses is described. 1946 *Nature* 3 Aug. 155/2 The kinetics of these reductions may be followed manometrically in the Warburg apparatus by carrying out the reactions in an atmosphere of carbon dioxide. 1975 K. Wilson in Williams & Wilson *Biologist's Guide to Princ. & Techniques Pract. Biochem.* viii. 233 (*caption*) Diagrammatic representation of a Warburg manometer.

Warburgian (wǭːɪbʊ̄·ɪgiăn), *a.* [f. the name of Aby *Warburg* (1866–1929), German-Jewish cultural historian + -IAN.] Of, pertaining to, or characteristic of Warburg or his work, or the Warburg Institute, founded (1904) by him in Hamburg as Kulturwissenschaftliche Bibliothek Warburg but subsequently (1933) transferred to London. Hence **Warbu·rgianism.**

1956 A. WILSON *Anglo-Saxon Attitudes* II. ii. 273, I have neither an aesthetic inclination towards it [*sc.* Renaissance paganism] nor a Warburgian interest in the development of myth. **1958** *Times Lit. Suppl.* 23 May 277/1 It is true that when people ask the staff of the Institute what the 'Warburgian Method' really is they sometimes receive the answer that the whole point of 'The Warburg' is that it has no method. **1974** K. CLARK *Another Part of Wood* v. 190 The parts of my writing that have given me most satisfaction, for example, the chapter in *The Nude* called 'Pathos', are entirely Warburgian. **1977** *N.Y. Rev. Bks.* 24 Nov. 36/3 In nearly all his studies Gombrich follows the Warburgian practice of studying subject rather than form; but it is a humanized Warburgianism.

warby (wǭ·ɪbi), *a. Austral. slang.* [f. *WARB + -Y[1].] Unprepossessing in appearance or disposition; unkempt; disreputable, contemptible, decrepit.

1941 K. TENNANT *Battlers* xviii. 207 'Of all the warby ideas,' he said.., 'the warbiest is you going on your own.' **1949** R. PARK *Poor Man's Orange* 181 Yeah, there she was, in a warby kind of blue dress, and low-heeled shoes. **1959** D. NILAND *Big Smoke* 183 A warby unshaven young man in working clothes walked through and right up to him at the back. **1965** E. LAMBERT *Long White Night* 135 That was one of the funniest sights the main street ever saw—my old man's warby old Model A towing Foran's dirty big gleaming new Packard! **1973** J. McNEIL *Old Familiar Juice* 74 He's down there whackin' up bumpers with a couple of 'is warby mates.

warcraft. Add: **2.** (Later examples.) Also, a warship.

1918 *Chambers's Jrnl.* May 318/1 With a whisk of her stern, the warcraft stood off. **1927** *Daily Tel.* 1 Mar. 11/3 It is believed here that the British and Japanese acceptances will pave the way for a conference of these Powers with the United States to consider the limitation of warcraft other than capital ships in line with the principles of the Washington Conference. **1930** *Tablet* 16 Aug. 202/2 These scribblers..would have us..cease building war craft.

war-cry. b. (Earlier examples.)

1836 S. HOUSTON *Let.* 25 Apr. in W. B. Dewees *Lett. from Early Settler Texas* (1852) xix. 198 Col. Sherman, with his regiment,..rung the war cry, '*Remember the Alamo*'. **1837** DICKENS *Let.* 24 Sept. (1965) I. 312 Of course we refused it—a new agreement and copyright, being the War Cry.

ward, *sb.*[2] Add: **II. 6. a.** *Ward in Chancery* (earlier example); *ward of Court* (examples).

1790 *Stevens v. Savage* in *Eng. Rep.* (1903) XXX. 277 Stevens having been committed for a contempt, by having married Miss Jeffry, a ward of the Court. **1815** H. MADDOCK *Treat. Princ. & Pract. High Court of Chancery* I. ii. 264 If a Child, a Ward of Court, would not be safe, the Chancellor would not permit it to go to *Scotland*. **1837** C. SELBY (*title*) The Irish Dragoon; or, Wards in Chancery. **1875** A. H. SIMPSON *Treat. Law & Pract. Infants* viii. 145 The general rule of the Court is that a ward of Court may not be removed out of the jurisdiction. **1928** A. BICKNELL *Law & Pract. Infants* iv. 89 To remove a ward of Court from the jurisdiction without proper leave is contempt of Court. **1977** *Jersey Even. Post* 26 July 13/4 If the children were allowed to leave, they could be made wards of Court and could find themselves in a position similar to that of the recent 'tug of love' children.

V. 18. (Later examples.)

1961 R. SHAW *Sun Doctor* I. i. 47 She looked at the two main wards of the hospital—long low rooms divided into cubicles like an old dormitory in an English public school. **1975** I. ILLICH *Medical Nemesis* vi. 111 Ailments had to be turned into objective diseases. Species had to be clinically defined..so that officials could fit them into wards. **1982** B. TRAPIDO *Brother of More Famous Jack* xlvii. 193, I was required, during the first three months, to spend occasional week-long spells in hospital in a special ward for the observation of problem pregnancies.

19. b. An administrative division of the Mormon Church (the Church of Jesus Christ of Latter-Day Saints).

1859 *Mountaineer* (Salt Lake City) 27 Aug. 2/4 If the water-masters of our district or ward will see that we have a double portion of water during the ensuing week for our garden, we will now agree not to mention them again. **1925** M. R. WERNER *Brigham Young* xii. 422 The bishop was in charge of all the families of his ward. **1979** M. P. LEONE *Roots Mod. Mormonism* ii. 36 Wards average about seven hundred people.

VII. 25. a. (sense 18) *ward clerk, sister*; (sense 19 a) *ward boss* (earlier example), *committee, committeeman, politician, politics* (examples), *school*; (sense 19 b) *ward teacher*.

1890 T. ROOSEVELT *Wks.* (1926) XIV. 110 Many forces..combine to produce the ward boss, the district heeler, the boodle alderman. **1964** G. L. COHEN *What's Wrong with Hospitals?* iii. 52 Ward clerks will relieve Sisters of paper work. **1807** *Salmagundi* 2 June 212 The secretaries of the ward committees strut about looking like wooden oracles. **1922** C. E. MERRIAM *Amer. Party System* 71 Each of the forty-eight Ward Committees [in Philadelphia]..chooses two members of the City Committee. *Ibid.* 70 Each of the thirty-five wards [in Chicago] elects by direct vote of the party in a primary a ward committeeman for a term of four years. **1976** *Honolulu Star-Bull.* 21 Dec. A-11/3 He knew the workings of the ward committeemen, who directed the precinct captains and stood ready to see that the garbage of the faithful voters was picked up and the potholes in their streets were filled. [**1807** *Salmagundi* 24 Feb. 68 He however maintained as mysterious a countenance as a seventh ward politician.] **1860** *Harper's Mag.* June 94/2 'A house-breaker or a ward politician,' thought I. **1976** *National Observer* (U.S.) 1 May B5/1 In the emerging big cities, ward politicians held control of school systems for a time in the late Nineteenth Century. **1883** *Century Mag.* Aug. 581/2 He had been a little alarmed at the sudden irruption of such men as Farnham and his associates into the field of ward politics. **1957** Ward politics [see *poker-game* s.v. *POKER *sb.*[4] b]. **1818** *Niles' Reg.* XIV. 174/1 Neither the people, nor their representatives, would agree to the plan of assessment on the wards for the expenses of the ward schools. **1904** G. STRATTON-PORTER *Freckles* 15 They sent me out to the nearest ward school as long as the law would let them. **1918** H. MATTHEWS in Murdoch & Drake-Brockman *Austral. Short Stories* (1951) 244 'She be a pretty one—the ward sister,' a Tommy patient said to him one evening. **1980** J. O'FAOLAIN *No Country for Young Men* iv. 94 'Good night now, Aunt Judith.' Grainne summoned a ward sister's authoritative manner. **1878** J. H. BEADLE *Western Wilds* xxi. 332 The ward teachers had reported every case of real or supposed heresy.

b. ward aide, a person employed to do non-medical work in a hospital ward; **ward-book,** delete † and ? and add later examples; **ward-heeling** *a. U.S.*, pertaining to, engaged in, or designating, the activities of a ward-heeler; **ward orderly,** a person employed to assist nurses in a hospital ward; **ward round,** a visit paid by a doctor, or by a group of doctors and medical students, to each of the in-patients in a ward or wards, or under the care of a particular doctor; cf. *ROUND *sb.*[1] 15.

1965 *Nursing Times* 5 Feb. 172/2 Ten hospitals in the Manchester region have been authorized by the RHB to employ ward aides. **1976** *Billings* (Montana) *Gaz.* 20 June 2-c/1 She is employed as a ward aide at Billings Deaconess Hospital. **1836** J. PAGET *Let.* 10 Jan. in *Mem. & Lett. Sir James Paget* (1901) I. iv. 66 The active new apothecary..cures the patients. The ward-books hardly know themselves, the *Mistura Cascarillæ* bottle stopper sticks from disuse, and *Emplastrum Lyttæ* is never mentioned. **1977** *Lancet* 7 May 975/2 The allocation of the patients was done automatically by the ward nurse (by reference to the ward book). **1972** R. THOMAS *Porkchoppers* (1974) xxiv. 208 Practical politics, the ward-heeling kind. **1976** *Billings* (Montana) *Gaz.* 1 July, But neither ward-heeling councilmen nor grandstanding mayors can provide the kind of leadership that gets things done. **1980** N. FREELING *Castang's City* xv. 100 Why the hell would there be any integrity in these ward-heeling affairs? **1946** *Nature* 13 July 54/1 The Government and the hospital authorities have agreed upon..the training of more male nurses and the formation of a grade of 'ward orderlies' to assist the nurses. **1971** P. D. JAMES *Shroud for Nightingale* viii. 275 She went..as ward orderly. **1938** *Amer. Speech* XIII. 228/2 Doctors regularly visit the patients under their care and for some reason their visits are called *ward rounds* or *ward walks*. **1963** *Oxford Med. School Gaz.* XV. 81 At some stage during the ward-round he would lead his flock down to the P.M. room. **1977** *Lancet* 5 Feb. 317/1 His ward-rounds were very popular and were attended by a large number of undergraduates and postgraduates.

war-dance. Delete 'by savage tribes' and add earlier examples in sense 'mimetic dance' and *transf.*

1775 J. TRUMBULL *M'Fingal* I. 1 The true war-dance of Yanky-reels. **1814** SCOTT *Diary* 7 Aug. in J. G. Lockhart *Life Scott* (1837) III. 163 In a stall pamphlet, called the history of Buckshaven [Fifeshire], it is said those fishers sprung from Danes, and brought with them their *war-dance* or *sword-dance*, and a rude wooden cut of it is given. **1851** *San Francisco Picayune* 24 Oct. 2/2 Having thus satisfied his taste for hat smashing, the tiles were kicked into a heap, and the six joining hands around them went through an extemporary war dance.

wardee (wǭɪdī·). *nonce-wd.* [f. WARD *sb.*[2] + -EE[1].] An inmate of a hospital ward.

1938 S. BECKETT *Murphy* xi. 240 No sound reached him from the adjacent female wards but the infinite variety of those made by the female wardees.

warden, *sb.*[1] Add: **7. c.** An air-raid warden.

1936 [see *AIR-RAID]. **1937** *Lancet* 13 Mar. 669/2 The wardens would probably also be used in connexion with the distribution of civilian respirators. **1951** N. MARSH *Opening Night* vi. 139 'Anyone here done respiration for gassed cases?'..'I can,' said the A.S.M. 'I was a warden.' **1978** E. MALPASS *Wind Brings up Rain* xxvi. 232 A tin-hatted Air Raid Warden was hurrying along the street. ..The Warden hurried on.

17. (Earlier examples.)

1855 R. CARBONI *Eureka Stockade* 120 A Public Meeting was held... The Resident Warden in the Chair. **1860** S. DAVISON *Discovery & Geognosy Gold Deposits Austral.* xi. 332 A number of new offices had been created for the gold fields, under the name of 'wardens'.

warden, *v.* Delete *rare*[−1] and add: *spec.* to watch over or patrol (a nature reserve, etc.) by or as a warden; also *intr.*, to act as a wildlife warden.

1971 *Times* 7 May 17/7 Having wardened at the Royal Society for the Protection of Birds reserve at Loch Garten, may I enlarge upon the letter from M. S. M. Burns? **1974** *Oxford Times* 4 Jan. 7/6 It would be wardened and visited regularly to prevent vandalism and litter. **1977** *Birds* Spring 40 Philip Coxon has wardened the RSPB Balranald reserve for the last four summers. **1982** *Lakeland Echo* 18 Mar. 5 The eyres are well wardened against egg collectors. **1984** *Natural World* Summer 14/1 Several orchids on a number of sites were wardened, efforts being concentrated on lizard, early spider, military and monkey orchids.

Hence **wa·rdened** *ppl. a.*, **wa·rdening** *vbl. sb.*

1962 *Listener* 1 Mar. 375/2 There is as yet no system of wardening for the valleys... Wardening is limited by statute to places where the Board has access-agreements or owns property. **1971** *Guardian Weekly* 3 July 15 The wardening of Exmoor, for example, with its wide acres of moorland under rising pressure of visitors, is described as rudimentary. **1980** *Birds* Autumn p. v/1 Although the most obviously efficient form of protection is to establish adequately wardened reserves, this is not possible in many cases. **1980** R. MABEY *Common Ground* I. 32 A wardening system was established for the more vulnerable eyries.

wardering (wǭ·ɪdəɪiŋ), *vbl. sb.* [f. WARDER *sb.*[1] + -ING[1].] The business of a warder.

1928 *Daily Express* 23 Nov. 10/3 He has also been a prison warder, and told me that wardering is by no means to be despised.

wardite (wǭ·ɪdəit). *Min.* [f. the name of Henry A. *Ward* (1834–1906), U.S. naturalist and dealer + -ITE[1].] A hydrated basic phosphate of sodium and aluminium, $NaAl_3(PO_4)_2(OH)_4.2H_2O$, found as transparent tetragonal crystals.

1896 J. M. DAVISON in *Amer. Jrnl. Sci.* CLII. 154 A considerable quantity of this mineral has been received by Ward's Natural Science Establishment, of Rochester, N.Y. It is in the form of nodules and shows the mineral in several shades of green, and one specimen of pure milk-white... I would give [it] the name of Wardite, in honor of Prof. Henry A. Ward, of Rochester. **1942** [see *MILLISITE]. **1952** *Amer. Mineralogist* XXXVII. 849 Wardite in well-formed, white to colorless crystals has been found in a pegmatite at Beryl Mountain near West Andover, New Hampshire.

Ward-Leonard (wǭɪdˌle·năɪd). *Electr. Engin.* Also **Ward Leonard.** The name of Harry *Ward Leonard* (1861–1915), U.S. electrical engineer and inventor, used *attrib.* to designate a method of controlling a direct-current motor in which its armature current is supplied by an auxiliary d.c. generator (driven by an a.c. motor), the field current of which is varied to vary the speed of the motor.

1902 H. A. FOSTER *Electr. Engineer's Pocket-bk.* 737 The motors are controlled by the Ward-Leonard system. **1969** *Jane's Freight Containers 1968–69* 541/1 All three designs have the following features: rack operated traversing gear driven by a motor through Ward Leonard control [etc.]. **1981** CARLSON & GISSER *Electr. Engin.* xix. 745 This arrangement, known as the Ward-Leonard system, also provides regenerative braking.

wardless (wǭ·ɪdlės), *a.*[2] *rare.* [f. WARD *sb.*[2] 24 a + -LESS.] Of a key: having no wards.

1927 R. A. FREEMAN *A Certain Dr. Thorndyke* xv. 220 These wardless pin-keys are more subtle than they look.

Wardour-street. Add: **1.** Also in other attrib. phrases.

1896 *Sat. Rev.* 8 Feb. 154/2 Our Wardour Street romancers and whimpering Scotch humourists. **1958** L. FORSTER in *Aspects of Translation* 20 The peculiar Wardour Street language which some classical scholars used for English a generation or so ago. **1976** *New Yorker* 19 Apr. 118/3 To the difficulty of following Borgese's Wardour Street diction ('Bread and wine needs a man to fight and die'; 'Us enchants he, but eke frightens') Sessions adds that of hearing the words.

2. Used *attrib.* and *absol.* with reference to Wardour Street as a centre of the British film industry.

1920 *Stage Year Bk.* 51 A still more ambitious 'ten million pound' company died even before it became more than a Wardour Street fairy tale. **1927** *Melody Maker* Aug. 818/3 A 'phone message, or note perhaps, from Wardour-street. **1948** *Daily Mail* 7 Feb. 2/5 This has caused a few long faces in Wardour-street. **1958** *Punch* 17 Sept. 360/1 Any Wardour Street film-distributor knows that the public wants a boy-girl story, a happy ending..and sensational spectacle. **1975** *Times* 20 Dec. 9/7 It amazes me how few films we manage to make in a year here: Wardour Street seems to have accepted defeat.

wardrobe. Add: **7.** *wardrobe-maid* (earlier example); **wardrobe trunk,** a travelling trunk which can be used as a wardrobe.

1865 QUEEN VICTORIA *Jrnl.* 9 Oct. (1980) 121 The Duchess took me to my room..next to which was one for my wardrobe maid, Mary Andrews. **1890** B. HALL *Turnover Club* 221 In Matt's wardrobe trunks there are very many suits. **1928** S. LEWIS *Man who knew Coolidge* I. 39 She pointed out I'd have to get my dress-suit in New York and it wouldn't get wrinkled in a wardrobe trunk. **1979** *Country Life* 16 Aug. 490/3 The murderee.. had in his Louis Vuitton wardrobe trunk, full white-tie evening dress.

ward-room. Add: **1.** (Earlier example.) Since 1948 ward-rooms have been used by warrant officers as well as commissioned officers.

1758 in *Ann. Reg. 1758* (1791) 306/1 On Thursday the 13th inst. at half an hour past one in the afternoon, word was passed into the ward room, by the centry, that the fore part of our ship, the Prince George, was on fire. The lieutenants ran immediately forward. **1948** *Admiralty Order* in *London Gaz.* 25 June 3719/1 We are of the opinion that all officers of the Warrant Officer classes should be regarded as Wardroom Officers for messing purposes and the Warrant Officers Mess as such be abolished.

-wards, *suffix.* Add: **5.** Also f. pers. pron.

1842 BROWNING *Let.* 13 July in F. G. Kenyon *Robert Browning & Alfred Domett* (1906) 39 Here is a slip just off you-wards and I write at night. **1866** H. H. FURNESS *Let.* 14 Nov. (1922) I. iii. 156 If you were anyone else than the dear.., kindly fellow that I knew & loved.., I should never dare to write this letter, my manifold sins of omission you-wards would palsy my hand and freeze my ink.

ware, *sb.*³ Add: **3. a.** (Earlier example.)

1741 W. STEPHENS *Jrnl.* 23 July in *Colonial Rec. Georgia* (1908) IV. Suppl. 199 He had lately drawn his Kiln of Ware, which was baking a second Time.

c. For *Obs.* exc. *dial.* read Now *dial.* and *Trade.* Also in attrib. phr. *ware potato.*

1961 *Ann. Reg. 1960* 509 Heavy imports of new potatoes early in the year depressed the market for old ware potatoes. **1963** *Times* 10 June 7/1 The trade for old ware potatoes in England and Wales is now largely confined to caterers.

wareful, *a.* (Later *poet.* example.)

1937 G. FRANKAU *More of Us* xv. 160 Slow went his feet, and wareful As federal agent's in some gangster joint.

warehou (wa·rehu). *N.Z.* Also 9 **wareho.** [Maori.] A large marine food-fish, *Seriolella brama,* found near the South Island of New Zealand.

1848 E. J. WAKEFIELD *Handbk. N.Z.* v. 161 The *Wareho* is a fish somewhat resembling the kawai, but of much better flavour. **1886** R. A. SHERRIN *Fishes N.Z.* 99 The fish known as trevalli in the Dunedin market is a different fish, allied to the warehou. **1949** P. H. BUCK *Coming of Maori* II. viii. 215 *Warehou*..were caught with a rod. **1966** *Encycl. N.Z.* III. 552/1 Warehou..resemble trevally in general shape and colouring (blue-green above, silver below, with a dark blotch just behind the head).

warehouse, *sb.* Add: **1. g.** Phr. *warehouse to warehouse,* used *attrib.* to designate a clause in a cargo insurance policy which provides that the insurance policy applies throughout all of the normal course of transit. Also applied to the policy itself, etc.

1922 *Lloyd's List Law Rep.* 30 Nov. 270/1, I am not sure that in a warehouse to warehouse policy the word 'theft' ought to be limited to theft by violence in the same way as it is in a purely marine policy. **1924** *Ibid.* 24 Apr. 450/2 The policy..incorporates the 'warehouse to warehouse' Clause No. 6 of the Institute Cargo Clauses. **1932** *Law Times Rep.* 27 Aug. 168/2 In my view, the practice has always been that the rule as to ship's papers applies though there is a warehouse to warehouse clause in the policy. **1974** E. R. H. IVAMY *Marine Insurance* (ed. 2) xiii. 121 The general rule is that the risk attaches when the goods are loaded, but may attach beforehand if the policy contains a 'craft' clause or the 'transit' ('warehouse to warehouse') clause. **1982** J. PHILLIPS *Dict. Trading Terms* 65/2 *Transit clause,*..one of the clauses in a marine insurance policy defining the normal course of transit, and including the warehouse to warehouse cover that many traders require.

h. *U.S. colloq.* A large and impersonal institution providing accommodation for mental patients, old people, or poor people.

1970 *Sat. Rev.* (U.S.) 3 Oct. 25/1 We have too many such 'human warehouses', staffed by underpaid and poorly trained personnel. **1972** *Time* 14 Feb. 67 But for most of Willowbrook's residents, the institution is a warehouse, a place capable of providing only shelter and the barest essentials, for those whose families are either unwilling or unable to care for them. **1974** J. FLETCHER *Ethics of Genetic Control* 157 We ought to protect our families from the emotional and material burden of such diseased individuals, and from the misery of their simply 'existing' (not *living*) in a nearby 'warehouse' or public institution. **1976** *N.Y. Times* 25 Apr. IV. 1 Subsidized public housing has been anathema to the emigres who now live in the suburbs, where the very mention conjures specters of high-rise 'human warehouses' like those that have been erected in ghetto areas.

warehouse, *v.* Add: **d.** *U.S. colloq.* To place (a person, esp. a mental patient) in a large and impersonal institution.

1972 *Tuscaloosa* (Alabama) *News* 22 Feb. 1 The current federal lawsuit against Partlow State School and Hospital may become a landmark decision in America as the country continues its 'trend away from large custodial institutions where people are warehoused and where they are denied the opportunity to develop their full potential,' Dr. Philip Roos said here Monday. **1979** *Time* 2 Apr. 42/2 Freud's dazzling and complex theory of the mind..came along when American psychiatry was doing little more than warehousing the insane and performing the occasional crude Cuckoo's Nest lobotomy.

e. *Stock Exchange slang.* To buy (shares) as a nominee of another trader, with a view to a take-over. Cf. sense *1 b of the vbl. sb.

1977 *Private Eye* 13 May 17/2 The suggested reward to the Swiss holders for 'warehousing' the ex-Bates shares would be perhaps 10p or more per share profit.

warehousing, *vbl. sb.* For **a, b** read **1, 2** and add: **1. b.** *Stock Exchange slang.* (See quot. 1974.) Cf. *WAREHOUSE *v.* e.

1971 *Daily Tel.* 23 Jan. 14/6 'Warehousing' is an old City practice. **1973** *Times* 8 June 1/3 The memorandum has proposals designed to stop the practice of 'warehousing'. **1974** *Daily Tel.* (Colour Suppl.) 22 Feb. 22/2 'Warehousing'—the technique of building up in collusion a major shareholding in a company behind the cloak of nominee names with a view to a take-over. **1983** *Observer* 27 Mar. 18/9 Not a little 'warehousing' may have proved the prelude to recent attacks from South of the border.

c. *U.S. colloq.* The placing of mental patients or other disadvantaged people in large and impersonal institutions. Cf. *WAREHOUSE *sb.* 1 h.

1973 *National Rev.* (U.S.) 7 Dec. 1259 California's shift from the 'warehousing of the mentally ill' in large state mental institutions has become a model for the nation. **1976** *National Observer* (U.S.) 10 Jan. 2/1 Mental patients have the right to receive community care as an alternative to institutional 'warehousing' or release without care, according to a ruling by a Federal court in Washington, D.C. **1983** *Chicago Sun-Times* 2 Aug. 7 Warehousing became the new 'thing'. Forget about making men better, the theory ran.

wareness. (Later *poet.* example.)

1930 AUDEN *Poems* 57 In his day-thinking and in his night-thinking Is wareness and is fear of other.

wareshi (ware·ʃi). Also **warishi.** [Origin obscure; variously asserted to be Carib and Arawak.] In Guyana, a type of basket worn on the back and held by a headband round the forehead.

1924 *38th Ann. Rep. U.S. Bureau Amer. Ethnol. 1916–17* xviii. 375 The way soldiers carry their knapsacks ..is the general mode which the Indians adopt..for carrying burdens... The names of these articles: waiyari (Arawak),..and walishi or warishi (Carib.). **1958** J. CAREW *Black Midas* vi. 102 Naked Amerindian families in single file, the men in front with wareshis harnessed to their foreheads and shoulders. **1964** C. HENFREY *Gentle People* v. 103 He was reluctant to use a wareshi, an Indian carrier made from vines. **1975** C. F. GRITZNER *Guyana in Pictures* v. 59 (*caption*) A prospector ready for the trail carries his gear in a 'warishi' (Amerindian basket) capable of carrying weights of up to 200 pounds.

warfarin (wǭ·ɹfărin). *Pharm.* Also **Warfarin.** [f. *W*isconsin *A*lumni *R*esearch *F*oundation + *-arin,* after COUMARIN: see -IN¹.] A water-soluble crystalline anticoagulant used as a selective rodenticide, and as a prophylactic against embolism in the treatment of thrombosis; 3-(3-oxo-1-phenylbutyl)-4-hydroxycoumarin, $C_{19}H_{16}O_4$; (also *warfarin sodium*) the sodium salt of this.

1950 *Chem. Abstr.* XLIV. 7019 *Warfarin,* a coined name for the anticoagulant rodenticidal chemical 3-(α-acetonylbenzyl)-4-hydroxycoumarin. S. A. Rohwer... U.S. Dept. Agr. Interdepartmental Comm. on Pest Control, June 29, 1950, 2 pp. (mimeographed). **1968** *Times* 16 Dec. 7/4 Rats which are immune to warfarin, the most widely used rat poison in the world, are spreading. **1973** *Country Life* 1 Mar. 510/1 The grey squirrel cannot be tolerated... Shortly it will be permissible to use Warfarin in hoppers. **1976** *Lancet* 25 Dec. 1414/2 Anticoagulant therapy with warfarin sodium was started.

warg (wāɹg). [ad. ON. *vargr* wolf; cf. OE. *wearg* and WARY *sb.* in Dict.] In the tales of J. R. R. Tolkien: a wolf of a particularly evil kind.

1937 J. R. R. TOLKIEN *Hobbit* vi. 107 Even the wild Wargs (for so the evil wolves over the Edge of the Wild were named) cannot climb trees. **1954** —— *Fellowship of Ring* II. i. 234 There are wargs and werewolves. **1968** *Radio Times* 26 Sept. 48 It [*sc. The Hobbit's* Middle-Earth] is..peopled by dwarves, elves, goblins, giant spiders, trolls, wargs.

war-horse. Add: **b.** (Earlier and later examples.) Also used of veterans of other activities, esp. acting.

1837 R. M. BIRD *Nick of Woods* I. 68 Ar'nt thee the Pennsylvanny war-horse, the screamer of the meeting-house? **1867** A. D. RICHARDSON *Beyond Mississippi* 151 That old war horse..threw off the black shaggy bearskin overcoat which he invariably wore. **1910** *National Police Gaz.* (U.S.) 16 July 3/1 She mixed with a lot of old war-horses and really thought she was an actress. **1933** S. LEWIS *Ann Vickers* xi. 128 If she had been nervous behind the scenes, this old war-horse, this professional who had played her Lady Macbeth to much worse houses, did not seem nervous now. **1958** *Spectator* 13 June 778/1 Dr. Inge, as an old *Evening Standard* war-horse, has even posthumously some truculent things to say.

c. A tough or determined woman.

1921 R. FRY *Let.* 13 Oct. (1972) II. 514 An old campaigning English lady artist..this excessively repulsive and brick-red old war horse. **1959** A. CHRISTIE *Cat among Pigeons* v. 67 A sharp old war-horse, called Miss Chadwick, keeps a wary eye on me.

d. *fig.* Something which is frequently used or very familiar; *spec.* a work of art, esp. music, which is frequently performed.

1947 A. EINSTEIN *Music in Romantic Era* xv. 209 There is a whole series of operatic transcriptions..all pieces that are great technical war-horses. **1952** *Mind* LXI. 495 These verbs..are important because they include such philosophical war-horses as *know, believe* and *deduce.* **1958** J. FLANNER in *New Yorker* 27 Sept. 96/2 'Ben Hur'—the old theatrical war horse that has had Ben running..since..1899. **1969** *Listener* 1 May 594/1 Deliberately constructed secondary films fall into various types. There are the old-style 'visual aids', such as the famous war-horse on medieval castles which has for long been cantering round the primary and secondary schools. **1977** *New Yorker* 10 Oct. 37/2, I turned on the radio, and there was Artur Rubinstein, playing my old war-horse, the Saint-Saëns G-Minor Concerto, live from Festival Hall.

wari (wǫrī·, wǫ·ri). Also **awari, warri.** [prob. Ashanti.] A board game, originally West African but now played also in the West Indies and Guyana, a variation of mancala.

1927 G. T. BENNETT in R. S. Rattray *Religion & Art in Ashanti* xxxii. 382 Wari..is a game for two players using ..48 pebbles and a board hollowed out into two parallel rows of six cups. **1959** *Chambers's Encycl.* VI. 162/2 *Mancala,* a sedentary game with some likeness to chess or draughts... It was carried by slaves to the West Indies (with its Ashanti name of *wari*) and into Dutch Guinea. **1960** R. C. BELL *Board & Table Games* 120 Awari is a masculine pastime though women occasionally play... Making Awari boards involves spiritual danger, and only old men who have lost a wife are allowed to make them. **1975** *Observer* (Colour Suppl.) 30 Nov. 40/2 Groups of men [in Bridgetown] play 'warri', an old game brought to Barbados from Africa.

Waring¹ (wēᵊ·riŋ). *Math.* The name of Edward *Waring* (1734–98), English mathematician, used in the possessive to designate a conjecture that he published in 1770 and which was proved by Hilbert in 1909, that every integer is equal to the sum of not more than *g s*th powers, *g* depending on *s* but not on the integer.

1920 G. H. HARDY *Some Famous Probl. Theory of Numbers* 14, I pass on..to the principal object of my lecture, the very famous problem known..as Waring's Problem. **1920** L. E. DICKSON *Hist. Theory of Numbers* II. xxv. 721 E. Maillet proved Waring's theorem for eighth powers. **1940** E. T. BELL *Devel. Math.* xiv. 294 Equally prolific of new analysis and far-reaching theorems in arithmetic was the advance beginning in 1909 with Hilbert's solution of Waring's problem. **1962** C. S. OGILVY *Tomorrow's Math* v. 92 Nineteen fourth powers are required to make up 79, and it is conjectured that 19 is the answer to Waring's problem for fourth powers.

Waring² (wēᵊ·riŋ). *U.S.* In full: **Waring blender** (also **blendor**). A trade name for a make of food processor, manufactured by Waring Products Corporation, of N.Y. (The device is also used as an agitator in scientific experiments, etc.)

1948 *Amer. Home* June 117/1 Waring blendor. **1950** *House Beautiful* May 188/2 In a Waring Blendor, you mix them in less time... Flips, frappés, fizzes..are easy hot-weather drinks. **1959** [see *HOMOGENIZE *v.* d]. **1960** *Times Lit. Suppl.* 1 July 414/2 'Never nothing like it.' The shops were filled with goods and buyers... In the houses washers, dryers, freezers and refrigerators, air conditioners, vacuum cleaners, Mixmasters, Waring-blenders, television and stereophonic high-fi sets, [etc.]. **1967** M. E. HALE *Biol. Lichens* v. 74 The fragmented mycobiont culture was mixed with the algae in a Waring blender so as to form a suspension. **1977** C. MCFADDEN *Serial* (1978) xxv. 57/1 Last year he gave me this Waring blender.

wa·rlessness. [f. WARLESS *a.* + -NESS.] Absence of war.

1928 BLUNDEN *Undertones of War* xiv. 158 The sluggish weather and the general silence and warlessness encouraged us to take life easy. *a* **1930** D. H. LAWRENCE *Last Poems* (1932) 114 Look at the young men under thirty... A certain warlessness even moneylessness, A waiting for the proper touch, not for any word or deed.

war-lord. Add: **b.** [tr. Chinese *jūnfà.*] In China, a military commander who has a regional power base and rules independently of the central government, esp. in the period 1916–28.

1922 *N.Y. Times* 31 Dec. VIII. 12/3 Each provincial Tuchun, or Military Governor, is a little or a big war lord with his own army and his own laws; and his regard for the Peking Government is proportioned inversely to the size of his army and his distance from the capital. **1926** P. WEALE *Why China sees Red* ii. 43 The whole war-lord system, which is based on the interception of national revenue at the points where it is levied and on nothing else, was about to be rudely tested. *Ibid.* 44 The Manchurian war-lord was just as sly. **1937** V. BARTLETT *This is my Life* xi. 174 Many gentlemen..at the Shanghai Club became indignant over my pronunciation of the names of Chinese war-lords. **1959** *Listener* 5 Feb. 238/2 Many millions more have died since, because of floods, drought, war lords, and civil war. **1962** E. SNOW *Other Side of River* (1963) xxxv. 264 The local warlord governor, Yang Hu-ch'eng, was also more interested in keeping the Generalissimo's troops out of Shensi than continuing the civil war. **1978** D. BLOODWORTH *Crosstalk* vii. 56 Any Chinese general who decided to play the rebel warlord in those regions..would..prove a dangerous and difficult man to suppress.

Hence **wa·rlordism**, the policies or practices of a war-lord; government by war-lords.

1962 E. Snow *Other Side of River* (1963) xxxix. 285 Throughout his struggles with provincial warlordism, 'communist-bandits', and finally with the Japanese, Chiang remained essentially an old-fashioned militarist. **1966** *New Statesman* 18 Mar. 366/3 Is Indonesia now in for a spell of regional warlordism? **1971** W. F. Dorrill in T. W. Robinson *Cultural Revolution in China* ii. 42 Individual numbers of this journal..charge that P'eng Teh-huai..instituted 'warlordism' (maltreating troops and straining relations between officers and men). **1979** *Guardian* 1 Aug. 5/6 Petty warlordism, protection rackets, the levying of 'taxes'..have alienated the natural allies of the Palestinians.

warm, *a.* (and *sb.*[2]) Add: **A.** *adj.* **17. a.** *warm-bosomed, -gloved, -seated, -veined*; **b.** **warm boot** *Computers*, a reloading or restart of an operating system, etc., without switching off the computer, esp. when changing programs; also as *v. trans.*, to reload in this way; **warm front** *Meteorol.*, the forward boundary of a mass of advancing warm air.

1980 R. Zaks *CP/M Handbk. with MP/M* i. 22 This combination..produces a 'warm start' (or 'warm boot', or 'system reboot'). A warm start essentially interrupts whatever the computer is doing and starts the operation system over again. *Ibid.* 32 If you are only *reading* from a new diskette..a warm boot is not necessary to introduce the new diskette. **1981** *Your Computer* (Austral.) May–June 100/3 *Warm boot*, to reload the operating system a second or subsequent time. **1983** *Ibid.* May 21/1 After a program has run [on the Commodore 64], CP/M warm-boots—a process that takes about 30 seconds. Once a CP/M program is loaded, it runs just fine. **1983** *Byte* May 28/2 The Model 100..did not need extra time to load the text editor and the document file from the disk and later store the document on disk and reload CP/M (do a warm boot). **1925** Blunden *Eng. Poems* 54 Warm-bosomed hawthorn stands in fruitful rest. **1921** Bjerknes & Solberg in *Geofysiske Publikationer* II. iii. 12 In the first case, the boundary line at the ground will be the front of advancing cold air, or, to introduce a shorter expression, a 'cold front'. In the latter case, the boundary line will be the front of advancing warm air, or simply a 'warm front'. **1969** A. G. Forsdyke *Weather Guide* 49 The rain belt ahead of a warm front is often 200 to 300 miles wide. **1922** Joyce *Ulysses* 536 Hobbledehoy, warm-gloved,..stunned with spent snowballs, struggles to rise. *Ibid.* 265 Sprawled, warmseated, Boylan impatience, ardentbold. **1943** Dylan Thomas *New Poems* 12 A man outside with a billhook,..The warm-veined double of Time.

B. *absol.* and *sb.*[2] **1. c.** *in(to) the warm*: indoors, out of the cold.

1969 F. Hurt *Death in Mist* vii. 74 I'll just put the spade away and then we can go into the warm. **1974** J. Aiken *Midnight is Place* viii. 231, I don't think Mr Oakapple is ready for more news until we have him sitting in the warm.

2. Also without *British* (*Service*), and (*rarely*) *attrib.*, as *warm-coat*.

1928 Blunden *Undertones of War* iii. 26 My warm-coat was not adequate. **1954** W. Faulkner *Fable* 114 His braces knotted about his waist under his open warm. **1958** *Spectator* 11 July 53/2 A florid gentleman in a military warm.

warm, *v.* **I. 2. b.** For 'Now *rare*' read 'Now usu. with *up*' and add later examples, esp. with sense 'to put (an audience) into a receptive mood'.

1892 'Mark Twain' *Amer. Claimant* xxiv. 236 I'll just go over there and warm up that House of Lords. **1923** *N.Y. Times* 14 Oct. viii. 4 Warming 'em up—Going on early as a sacrifice for the later acts. **1966** *Guardian* 28 Mar. 3/7 Mrs Bessie Braddock warmed up the meeting for him. **1974** *Times* 21 Jan. 12/8 In the studio..Llew Gardner, the chairman, warmed us up music-hall style and the three panellists appeared. **1982** N. Painting *Reluctant Archer* vii. 113 We might have warmed up his audience for him.

7. Restrict † *Obs.* to senses in Dict. and add: **c.** *to warm the bell* (see quots.). *Naut. slang.*

1924 G. H. A. Willis *Royal Navy as I saw It* 116 'To warm the bell', meaning literally to strike the bell a minute or two before the exact time, was applied to circumstances in which to be in good time was meant. **1925** Fraser & Gibbons *Soldier & Sailor Words* 300 *Warming the bell*, putting on the clock. Advancing the time illegitimately for some particular reason. **1956** H. W. Edwards *Their Lawful Occasions* xxiv. 130 'Ah! I see. All ready dressed for the shore,' I said. 'Warming the bell, eh?' **1976** *Oxf. Compan. Ships & Sea* 924/2 *To warm the bell*... On board warships in the days of sail, time was measured by a half-hour sand-glass. Each time the sand ran through the glass was turned..and the appropriate number of bells struck. It was supposed..that if the glass was warmed the expansion of the neck would allow the sand to run through a little more quickly. Hence..eight bells and the return to one's hammock, would come gratifyingly earlier than it should.

II. 9. c. With *up*. Of a sportsman, etc.: to prepare oneself by light exercise or practice immediately before the start of a contest or other physical exertion.

1883 [see *warming *vbl. sb.* 1 d]. **1926** *Amer. Speech* I. 369/2 Pitchers 'warm up' on a plot of grass called 'the bull pen'. **1955** R. Bannister *First Four Minutes* 16, I was warming up on the uneven grass near the track. **1972** J. Mosedale *Football* viii. 118 Ed Neale..used to warm up for the game by breaking beer bottles across his forearm. **1976** J. Snow *Cricket Rebel* 35 Graeme Pollock again. Warming up with his first half century in 70 minutes and dashing to his century [in]..only 35 minutes.

d. With *up*. Of an engine, electrical appliance, etc.: to reach a temperature high enough for efficient working.

1947 A. Ransome *Great Northern?* i. 24 There was a whirr from below as the engine started and a steady throbbing as it was warming up. **1955** A. Budrys in D. Knight *100 Yrs. Sci. Fiction* (1969) 255 Halsey's familiar figure appeared on the screen as the set warmed up. **1958** 'N. Shute' *Rainbow & Rose* i. 18 He went to the transceiver and turned it on to warm up. **1972** *Daily Tel.* 12 Apr. 13/5 The engine warms up rapidly and performs eagerly.

warmable, *a.* For *nonce-wd.* read *rare* and add earlier example.

1839 A. Langton *Jrnl.* in *Gentlewoman Upper Canada* (1950) 98, I must tell you then that the drawing-room is as warmable as ever.

warm-blooded, *a.* Add: **warm-bloo·dedness**, the character or condition of being warm-blooded.

1923 J. S. Huxley in *Cornh. Mag.* Apr. 427 In the birds as in the mammals,..we see the evolution..of physiological characters like warm-bloodedness or efficiency of circulation. **1946** F. E. Zeuner *Dating Past* xii. 84 Warm-bloodedness and many other characters of the mammals are probably the consequence of a single important aromorph. **1982** *N.Y. Times Mag.* 7 Feb. 34/4 High metabolisms, a characteristic of the warm-bloodedness of mammals and birds.

warmed, *ppl. a.* Add: Also with *over*, *up*.

a. (Examples.)

1897 *Private Life of Queen* xvii. 141 The Queen..made a delightful luncheon off warmed-up broth and potatoes she had helped to boil herself. **1916** B. M. Bower *Phantom Herd* 246 A midnight supper of warmed-over coffee and cold bean sandwiches. **1977** H. Greene *FSO-1* vi. 57 Warmed-over moussaka uneaten before him.

b. (Examples.) *like death warmed up*: see *death *sb.* 17 c.

1887 *Nation* (N.Y.) 2 June 465/3 They will be spared the future bitterness of finding..themselves treated to insult and warmed-over excuses. **1950** *New Yorker* 8 Apr. 96/2 *Oggi*..came out with..a warmed-over photograph taken in the Farfa displaced-persons camp. **1965** *Listener* 9 Sept. 391/1 The comfort given by warmed-up studio audiences. **1978** W. Mankowitz *Extraordinary Mr Poe* vi. 186 Verses dedicated *To F*, actually warmed-over lines written for another.

warmer. Add: **3.** *warmer-up*, something that warms oneself or another up; *spec.* (*a*) a preliminary item designed to put an audience in a receptive mood; also, one who presents this; (*b*) a simulating drink. Also *warmer-upper*, esp. in sense (*b*) above.

1960 *House & Garden* Aug. 70/1 A tipple that has been a warmer-upper for British sailors since before Nelson's day. **1962** *Guardian* 22 Dec. 5/2 As so often it is the warmers-up (in this case Gordon and Bunny Jay) who do the hard work. **1972** *Jazz & Blues* Nov. 28/1 *Shaw nuff* is a very fast warmer-up. **1976** *Ulverston* (Cumbria) *News* 3 Dec. 19/2 As a 'warmer-up' the concert began with a rather pedestrian rendering of the Hebrides overture. **1980** *Times* 9 Dec. 2/1 Stone's Ginger Wine. The original warmer-upper. On its own or as a Stone's Whisky Mac.

warming, *vbl. sb.* Add: **1. d.** With *up*: the action or condition of 'warming up' (see senses 3, 9, and 11 in Dict. and Suppl.). Freq. *attrib.*

1874 J. G. McCoy *Hist. Sk. Cattle Trade* 244 This style, ..of wintering cattle, is called 'Roughing', and the feeding of corn in the spring is termed 'Warming up'. **1883** *Chicago Inter-Ocean* 27 June 5 The players..began their practice play. This is called 'warming up'. **1952** *Times* 22 Feb. 6/4 Jet-engined aircraft have two further advantages—no preliminary 'warming up' is necessary, so they can take off in shorter time. **1960** *Practical Wireless* XXXVI. 429/1 The warming up time for the unit is about 30 seconds.

3. *warming drawer, oven.*

1972 J. Burmeister *Running Scared* vii. 95 Your breakfast will be in the warming drawer if I'm not there. **1950** in M. Cecil *Heroines in Love* (1974) 199 Jocelyn turned out the warming oven. **1973** J. Burrows *Like an Evening Gone* iii. 38 There was a square warming oven..'For keeping tins and dinner plates hot.'

warmonger. Add (Further examples.) **warmongering** *vbl. sb.* (examples).

1934 *Sun* (Baltimore) 5 Mar. 6/3 Dr. Toynbee differs from Mr. McFadden's war mongers in that he makes a suggestion for avoiding such a catastrophe. **1940** N. Coward *Australia Visited* ii. 9 Many of those in high places..dismissed his [*sc.* Winston Churchill's] eloquent prophetic words as alarmist warmongering. **1940** 'G. Orwell' *Inside Whale* 170 The war-mongering to which the English intelligentsia gave themselves up in the period 1935–9. **1944** Mrs. Belloc Lowndes *Let.* 4 June (1971) 249 Algernon Cecil..regards Churchill as 'a warmonger'. **1955** *Times* 2 Aug. 7/7 They have their war-mongers..of course, but their fervency on Palestine derives as much from a sense of injustice as from wounded pride. **1981** R. Reagan in *N.Y. Rev. Bks.* 25 June 25 It is not war-mongering to say that some things are worth dying for.

warm-up. [f. the vbl. phr. *to warm up*: see Warm *v.* 3, 9, and 11 in Dict. and Suppl.] **1.** = Warm *sb.*[1]

1878 Mrs. Stowe *Poganuc People* 156 A knot of the talkers were gathered round the stove, having a final talk and warm-up. **1960** H. Pinter *Room* in *Birthday Party* 112 Thank you for the warm-up, Mrs. Hudd. I feel better now. **1974** J. Aiken *Midnight is Place* ix. 257 'Tis a poor lad half drownded—can tha..give him a bit of a roob-down an' a warm-oop?

2. Warmth, the quality of exciting or stimulating. *rare.*

1883 'Mark Twain' *Life on Mississippi* iii. 52 The song didn't seem to have much warm-up to it, somehow.

3. a. The act or process of 'warming up' for a contest, etc., by light exercise or practice. See sense *9 c of the vb.

1915 *Baseball Mag.* Dec. 116/2 Alex, after a short warm-up, vanished from the foreground. **1949** Shurr & Yocom *Mod. Dance* iii. 31 The transition is used only when use of next warm-up is desired. **1951** *Publ. Amer. Dial. Soc.* xvi. 68 Some horses run better after a stiff warm up, others just tire. **1975** *New Yorker* 28 Apr. 32/1 Her second serve was good, was well returned by Jill, and then was driven by Sylvia to Jill's backhand in a way that left her frozen, as it had in the warmup. **1984** *Times* 22 Sept. 3/3 Warm-ups should be taken slowly, as sweating does not mean that muscles are sufficiently stretched for exercises.

b. *transf.* and *fig.*

1943 *Daily Progress* (Charlottesville, Va.) 18 Aug. 1/8 Allied guns boomed in a duel with heavy Axis batteries across the Messina Strait today in a warm-up against the European fortress. **1945** *Sun* (Baltimore) 11 July 9-0/6 Polynesian was running in the Shevlin as a 'warm-up' for Saturday's $50,000 Dwyer. **1958** *Times* 17 Oct. 20/1 It was a slow warm-up that Keenan could scarcely afford. **1976** D. Heffron *Crusty Crossed* xiv. 101 A party in the afternoon, a kind of warm-up to the night's dark devilry.

c. *attrib.*

1943 *Sun* (Baltimore) 22 May 1/7 The bombing of Nauru, Tarawa and other islands in the central Pacific, were warmup attacks. **1945** *Ibid.* 12 Mar. 7-0/2 One of Mexico's leading matadors..sharpens his skill with a 'warm-up' workout..an hour before a..performance. **1958** [see *house *sb.*[1] 4 h]. **1968** C. Drummond *Death & Leaping Ladies* v. 120 They arrived at Mexico City to play a warm-up match. **1978** L. Pryor *Viper* (1979) viii. 152 The field of cars was allowed one warm-up lap.

4. The act or process of raising the temperature of an engine, electrical appliance, etc., to a level high enough for efficient working. Also *attrib.* See sense *9 d of the vb.

1945 *Sun* (Baltimore) 18 May 1/6 Massed after on the flight deck, engines roaring for the warmup,..were more planes. **1956** H. Kurnitz *Invasion of Privacy* ii. 17 There was an even, monotonous thud emanating from the machine now—the warm-up period. **1958** *Spectator* 1 Aug. 167/2 That infuriating warm-up time necessary for many TV sets. **1966** P. O'Donnell *Sabre-Tooth* xx. 270 The Dove began to taxi forward... He wished there had been a few minutes grace for a warm-up before taking off. **1975** *Physics Bull.* Dec. 550/1 The detector has a warm-up time of 10 s. **1978** *Dumfries Courier* 13 Oct. 11/2 Another refinement the picture tube designers have incorporated is a really quick warm-up which..eliminates that infuriating delay when switching on late for an important programme. **1984** B. Francis *AA Car Duffer's Guide* 63/1 Modern water-cooled systems incorporate a thermostat to give a quick warm-up.

5. a. The 'warming up' of an audience into a receptive mood, esp. before a broadcast programme is recorded or transmitted. See sense *2 b of the vb.

1958 *New Statesman* 15 Mar. 333/1 So that spontaneity shall not degenerate into chaos, the programme is preceded by a half-hour closed-circuit 'warm-up', in which those taking part get to know each others' names and voices. **1970** *Guardian* 14 Feb. 8/4 For this particular show there is an audience..and they arrive at 7.30 p.m. and are given a 'warm up' to get them in the mood for the show. **1983** *Oxford Diocesan Mag.* Aug. 10/2 For pre-service warm-ups, say—a [tape or record of a] full orchestra playing Beethoven's Fifth for Harvest Festival, [etc.].

b. *attrib.*, esp. as *warm-up man.*

1959 R. G. Stern in N. Mailer *Advts. for Myself* (1961) 319 There was no warm-up session except thirty seconds of irrelevant talk which we used for volume control. **1966** *Observer* 30 Oct. 23/4 The warm-up man (an assistant producer) jumps on to the platform. **1974** P. de Vries *Glory of Hummingbird* xii. 159 Falconer regaling..spectators..with some intendedly relaxing 'warmup' chatter. **1979** S. Brett *Comedian Dies* xvi. 149 The audience..were greeted by..a little-known comedian who had been booked for the occasion as a warm-up man.

6. *U.S.* **a.** A garment designed to keep the wearer warm. **b.** One worn during light exercise or practice; a track suit or track-suit top.

1949 *Sun* (Baltimore) 22 Sept. 7/1 (Advt.), Make a friend of Jack Frost in smart warm-ups! **1969** *Sears Catal.* Spring/Summer 35/1 Sweatshirt warm-ups fit sizes 2 to 6x. **1983** W. Safire in *N.Y. Times Mag.* 12 June 22/2 *Exercise classes* of the 1950's, where one wore *sweat suits*; these are now *workouts* with *warm-ups*.

c. *attrib.* and *Comb.* **warm-up suit**, a track suit. (Cf. also sense 3 c above.)

1945 *Richmond* (Va.) *Times-Dispatch* 9 Jan. 16 When winter comes..it's time for warm-up clothes. **1972** *N.Y. Times* 3 Nov. 44/5 (Advt.), Stretch pants, warm-up pants, skisuits. **1975** *New Yorker* 28 Apr. 31/1 She was wearing a pastel-blue warmup suit over her tennis dress. **1984** *New Yorker* 1 Oct. 30/1 Mr. Sims..wore a Nike cap, a crisp tan warmup suit.

warn, *v.*[1] **6. f.** (Earlier example.)
The expression was finally deleted from the Jockey Club's Rules of Racing in 1969 when the Jockey Club and National Hunt Committee amalgamated, and the course and training grounds at Newmarket were transferred to the Newmarket Estates and Property Co. Ltd.
1845 *Racing Calendar 1844* p. lii, Samuel Rogers and John Braham were warned off the Course and exercising ground at Newmarket.

warning, *vbl. sb.*[1] Add: **4. d.** *the usual warning*: the caution that a police officer making an arrest is bound to give, viz. that anything the suspect says may be taken down and used in evidence against him or her.
[**1919** GREGG & MCGRATH *Police Constable's Guide* (ed. 3) p. xlix, Persons in custody should not be questioned without the usual caution being first administered.] **1931** 'G. TREVOR' *Murder at School* xiii. 255, I gave her the usual warning, of course, but she began to talk, all the same. **1975** 'R. PLAYER' *Let's talk of Graves* v. 181 Holding my warrant in my right hand, I then gave her the usual warning and arrested her.
e. The action or an instance of warning (someone) *off*: see sense 6 of the vb.
1977 K. BENTON *Red Hen Conspiracy* ix. 56 He gets an ambiguous warning-off from the Embassy, but that doesn't stop him. **1980** D. FRANCIS *Reflex* xv. 181 They could have half-killed me... All they were truly delivering was a warning off. **1981** *Times Lit. Suppl.* 30 Jan. 108/5 The warning off of the racing correspondent of the *Morning Post*.
5. d. A signal given by means of a siren, etc., to indicate that an air attack is imminent, an air-raid warning. Cf. *ALERT *sb.*[1] 1 b.
1917, 1938 [see *AIR-RAID]. **1940** H. NICOLSON *Diary* 7 Sept. (1967) 111 The all-clear sounds at 6, but there is another warning at 8 which actually lasts till 5.30 a.m. **1953** R. LEHMANN *Echoing Grove* 284 There are several regulars who bustle along the moment the Warning goes and don't stick their noses out again till the All-clear. **1982** T. FITZGIBBON *With Love* I. viii. 57 The air-raid siren had sounded..but a warning about a week previously had amounted to very little.
12. *warning light*; **warning bell,** (*c*) a bell alerting people to prepare for a meal, etc.; (*d*) *fig.*, an alarm-bell sounded 'in the head', giving a presentiment of danger; **warning gong** *rare* = *dressing-gong* s.v. DRESSING *vbl. sb.* 5 a; **warning triangle,** a triangular red frame carried by motorists, and set up on the road as a danger signal to warn approaching drivers of the proximity of a broken-down vehicle or other hazard.
1849 DICKENS *Dav. Copp.* (1850) xxi. 212 The warning-bell will ring at nine; the family take breakfast at halfpast nine. **1951** E. COXHEAD *One Green Bottle* vii. 202 Somewhere, right at the back of her head, there rang a little warning bell. **1951** *Publ. Amer. Dial. Soc.* xvi. 68 *Warning bell*, a signal made to warn that it is time to saddle the horses entered in the next race. **1981** S. BRETT *Situation Tragedy* ii. 26 'I'll join you.' Something rang warning bells for Charles. 'Well, no.' **1984** *Times* 5 June 23 (*heading*) Another warning bell for the secretaries. **1938** D. SMITH *Dear Octopus* III. i. 116 Ring the warning gong, will you, dear? **1937** *Motor Catal.* (East London Rubber Co. Ltd.) 131 Ignition replacements..warning lights. **1962** *Which? Car Suppl.* Oct. 130/2 The Fiat 1500 had a particularly comprehensive array of warning lights, including lights to show when choke, side lights and hand brake were in use. **1972** J. AIKEN *Butterfly Picnic* i. 6 The encircling mountains outlined by small red warning lights. **1974** 'W. HAGGARD' *Kinsmen* xiii. 126 The warning lights were out and flashing. Her mother had some absurd new plan. **1971** *Good Motoring* Sept. 23/3 It is essential for motorists to carry warning triangles for use in case of accident or breakdown.

wa·rningfully, *adv. rare.* [f. WARNING *vbl. sb.*[1] + -FUL + -LY[2].] = WARNINGLY *adv.*
1922 JOYCE *Ulysses* 197 Quickly, warningfully Buck Mulligan bent down:—The tramper Synge is looking for you, he said, to murder you. **1945** J. STEINBECK *Cannery Row* ix. 53 'I guess everything that comes out of the human mouth is poison,' said Doc warningfully.

warp, *sb.*[1] Add: **V. 8. b.** *Science Fiction.* = *space warp* s.v. *SPACE *sb.*[1] 19.
1936 *Astounding Stories* June 30 AKKA is the symbol for humanity's secret weapon. Its user, with simple instruments, can destroy any object in the universe—by so altering the warp of space that neither matter nor energy can exist. **1954** *Galaxy* Aug. 80/2 Halfway between Earth and Venus there was a sudden shimmer as the Vegan ship slipped out of warp into normal space.
VI. 10. warp print = *shadow print* s.v. *SHADOW *sb.* 16; hence **warp-printed** *a.*
1916 *Daily Colonist* (Victoria, B.C.) 23 July 8/7 This offering comprises Fancy Ribbons in warp-print, Dresden, Pompadour and novelty stripe and plain effects. **1968** J. IRONSIDE *Fashion Alphabet* 246 *Shadow* or *Warp print.* The warp yarns are printed with the design before weaving, giving a shadowy print effect. **1957** *Times* 16 Sept. 11/1 The short dress..is in white satin with a small warp-printed design in black.

warp, *v.* Add: **II. 18. c.** *Science Fiction.* To travel through space by way of a space warp.
1946 F. BROWN in *Astounding Sci. Fiction* May 129/1 The *Ark*..would warp through space to a point a safe distance outside the Argyle I–II system and come in on rocket power. **1957** T. STURGEON *Thunder & Roses* 117 Earth was ready for him when he warped in.

warpage. Add: **2.** The extent or result of warping (sense 6).
1950 J. OSBORNE *Dental Mechanics* (ed. 3) xi. 195 The celluloid bases of 1870..suffered from warpage in the mouth. **1952** *Shell Aviation News* No. 163. 14 (*caption*) Straight-edge laid along surface of wing leading-edge shows that the earlier warpage has been entirely eliminated. **1969** [see *POSTCURE *v.*]. **1970** R. LOWELL *Notebk.* 221 We're warpage in the drift to *fin de siècle*.

war-paint. Add: **2. b.** *colloq.* Cosmetics, make-up.
1869 B. HARTE *Luck of Roaring Camp* 84 The stranger ..[brightened] through the color which Red Gulch knew facetiously as her 'war paint'. **1945** L. SHELLY *Jive Talk Dict.* 35 *War paint*, cosmetics. **1957** *Landfall* XI. I. 41 'In a moment,' Sylvia said, clicking open her purse. 'Just a daub of warpaint.' **1970** R. LOWELL *Notebk.* 57 If I look for the unbelievably beautiful In a city, it's mostly women in their war-paint. **1977** J. GARDNER *Werewolf Trace* x. 91 She had a fresh coat of warpaint and was all breathless.

war-party. Add: **2. a.** (Earlier examples.)
1755 in J. W. Lydekker *Faithful Mohawks* (1938) 84 He had ye care of providing for all ye War-parties of Indians that went thro' that place. *c* **1800** B. HAWKINS *Sk. Creek Country* (1848) 70 The war parties all march in Indian file, with the leader in front.
b. *transf.* and *fig.*
1921 C. A. W. MONCKTON *Some Experiences New Guinea Resident Magistrate* xxiv. 293 They had dispatched..a war party..and remorselessly slaughtered the Oobudura. **1946** *Sat. Even. Post* 3 Aug. 81/2 Pass the word back to Mr. Topliff at the gallop! Here's his war party! **1957** V. W. TURNER *Schism & Continuity in Afr. Society* i. 7 He inflicted several defeats on a large war-party of Chokwe. **1969** M. PUGH *Last Place Left* xiv. 99, A solitary raven scout..was summoning the raven war party to the scene. **1976** *Classical Q.* XXVI. 257 The motives of the Spartan war-party are clearly stated.

war-path. b. (Earlier example.)
1880 'MARK TWAIN' *Tramp Abr.* xxxii. 345 She was on the war path all the evening.

warper. 3. (Earlier example.)
1847 [see *SPEEDER 3].

warping, *vbl. sb.*[1] Add: **10. b.** *warping board.*
1910 L. HOOPER *Hand-Loom Weaving* iv. 42 Although the warping board..is very useful for small warps of moderate length,..it would not be convenient for very long warps, or accurate enough for warping several thousands of fine silk threads. **1960** G. LEWIS *Handbk. Crafts* 99 The warping board and the mill have the same process in common, the main difference being that when using the board you have to walk backwards and forwards to get your length, whereas when using the mill you revolve it the required number of times.

warrant, *sb.*[1] Add: **II. 15. b.** *warrant of fitness*, a certificate of roadworthiness valid for six months, which must be carried by most classes of motor vehicle in New Zealand. (The equivalent of an M.O.T. test certificate: see *M 5.)
1936 *N.Z. Statutory Regulations 1936–37* (1938) 331 Save as provided in clause (3) hereof, the driver of every motor-vehicle used on a road after the 31st day of March, 1937, shall carry in the vehicle a warrant of fitness... The warrant of fitness shall be issued only by a city authority or a person or firm appointed or approved for the purpose by the Minister. **1948** *N.Z. Law Rep.* 1229, I am convinced that a warrant of fitness does not extend to the drag link or steering assembly of a car. **1953** *Road Code* (N.Z.) 1 Jan. 39 There must be carried on a motor vehicle a Warrant of Fitness issued within the past six months. **1961** B. CRUMP *Hang on a Minute* 23 Are you aware of the law regarding warrants of fitness for motor vehicles? **1983** *N.Z. Official Yearbk.* XIII. 371 Most lightweight vehicles are required to have a warrant of fitness which can be issued at approved garages, or at testing stations operated by local authorities or the Ministry of Transport.
IV. 18. warrant card, a document of authorization and identification carried by a police officer; **warrant chief**: in Nigeria, an African local official, esp. (formerly) one appointed by the colonial power.
1920 H. L. ADAM *Police Encycl.* III. iv. 77 All officers in plain clothes are furnished with a 'warrant card', by means of which they can, should they be challenged, at once prove their *bona fides*. **1933** D. L. SAYERS *Murder must Advertise* xvii. 296 Beware of..the plain-clothes cop without a warrant-card. **1983** R. ALLASON *Branch* xii. 169 He stresses to newcomers to the Branch that they hold the same warrant cards as the rest of the Metropolitan Police. **1922** S. M. GRIER *Rep. Eastern Provinces by Secretary for Native Affairs* 5 The Native Court Clerk.. conveys to the warrant chiefs instructions sent from the Divisional Officer. **1957** LD. HAILEY *African Survey 1956* viii. 465 The members of these Councils, who came to be known as Warrant Chiefs, were selected from villages within the Council or Court area. **1976** *Daily Times* (Lagos) 12 Oct. 5/2 The role of some warrant chiefs in the selection of the new Owa of Indanre was consistent with the chieftaincy regulations.

warrantee. Add: **2.** Also (*U.S.*), misused for WARRANTY 1.
1874 J. WANAMAKER in *Philadelphia Inquirer* 26 Sept. 8/2 (Advt.), A printed guarantee, bearing the signature of the firm, will accompany each garment as a warrantee. This binds us in every sense, and will be honored as quickly as a good draft of the Government of the United States. **1980** *Verbatim* Autumn 17/1 We have three perfectly good words in English, *guarantee, warranty*, and *guaranty*, all of the same origin and having the same meaning. Now some people are trying to add a fourth, *warrantee.* A TV salesman says, 'We have a great warrantee on this product.'

warrantless, *a.* Restrict *rare* to sense in Dict. and add: **2.** *U.S.* Without judicial authorization; without a search warrant.
1950 F. FRANKFURTER in *U.S. Reports* CCCXXXIX. 80 To tear 'unreasonable' from the context and history and purpose of the Fourth Amendment..is to make the arrest an incident to an unwarranted search instead of a warrantless search an incident to an arrest. **1968** *U.S. Rep. Cases Supreme Court* 367 The Amendment deserves.. a liberal construction in order to protect against warrantless searches of buildings. **1978** *Detroit Free Press* 14 Apr. 1A/4 The activities that are alleged in connection with the Weatherman investigation, I would categorize as warrantless activities.

warrant officer. 1. The rank was abolished in the Royal Navy in 1949.
1949 *Order in Council* (Admiralty) No. 30/C-W. 1 Whereas we are of the opinion that the title 'Warrant Officer' and the term 'Warrant List' in use in the Royal Navy and Royal Marines should no longer be used but be replaced by 'Branch Officer' and 'Branch List' respectively.

Warrau (wă·rau). Also 9 **Warow, Worrow; Warraw.** [Native name.] (A member of) an American Indian people inhabiting Guyana, Surinam, and Venezuela; also, the language of this people. Also *attrib.*
The spelling *Warao* has recently emerged as the usual spelling for the language and the people.
1807 H. BOLINGBROKE *Voy. to Demerary* vii. 151 The Worrows principally inhabit the sea coast lying between the Demerary and Surinam. **1834** W. HILHOUSE in *Jrnl. R. Geogr. Soc.* IV. 321 (*heading*) Memoir on the Warow Land of British Guiana. *Ibid.* 324 On these reefs are situated many Indian villages—Warows, Arawacks, [etc.]. **1883** E. F. IM THURN *Among Indians of Guiana* vi. 167 The Warraus are the shortest. **1891** D. G. BRINTON *Amer. Race* 354 The Guaraouna or Warrau was, and continues to be, spoken by the tribes of the [Orinoco] delta. **1910** *Encycl. Brit.* XII. 676/2 [British Guiana] The aborigines—Arawaks, Caribs, Wapisianas, Warraws, &c.—..are now estimated at about 6500. **1948** P. KIRCHHOFF in J. H. Steward *Handbk. S. Amer. Indians* III. 870 The Warrau language constitutes an independent family. *Ibid.* 869 The Warrau live in the intricate Delta of the Orinoco. **1950** J. A. MASON in *Ibid.* VI. 252 The independence of the Warrau linguistic family has been admitted by all authorities. **1965** *Internat. Jrnl. Amer. Linguistics* XXXI. 106 Warao appears to have a large number of compounds. *Ibid.*, The Warao text is divided into numbered sentences without any other punctuation. **1973** *Advocate-News* (Barbados) 18 Dec. 9/5 Several cuckoos have befouled the nests of the Arawaks, Caribs, Wapisianas, Warraws and what-nots. **1978** *Amer. Poetry Rev.* Sept./Oct. 13/3 Roth..gave the title 'The Adventures of Kororomanna' to a long Warao story. **1979** J. HALIFAX *Shamanic Voices* (1980) i. 28 The Warao shaman also believes the rattle to be the world axis.

warren, *sb.* Add: **4.** (Later examples.) Also, any area of living or office space characterized as a mass of passages and (small) rooms. Cf. *rabbit-warren* s.v. *RABBIT *sb.*[1] 3 a.
1922 JOYCE *Ulysses* 423 Figures wander, lurk, peer from warrens. **1954** J. R. R. TOLKIEN *Fellowship of Ring* i. 31 Mr. Frodo left an orphan..brought up anyhow in Brandy Hall. A regular warren, by all accounts. **1977** W. J. WEATHERBY *Home in Dark* xxi. 113 It was a house to hide in: you hardly existed in this anonymous warren. **1980** R. RENDELL *Lake of Darkness* iv. 41 A room smaller than this one divided into *three*... It's a real warren.

Warren[2] (wǫ·rĕn). *Engin.* The name of James *Warren* (fl. 1848), of Middlesex, used *attrib.* and † in the possessive to designate a truss he designed composed of alternately inclined diagonal members joining two horizontal ones, so as to form a series of non-overlapping triangles pointing alternately up and down. [Patented by Warren and Monzani in *Brit. Patent 12,242* (1848).]
[**1852** *Minutes Proc. Inst. Civil Engineers* XI. 12 He had only used the simple triangulation for spans not exceeding 60 feet and generally for shallow girders, but he believed that some girders had been made on Captain Warren's plan for much greater spans.] *Ibid.* 14 Mr. Brunel..said..it was necessary to draw a distinct line of demarcation between the lattice bridge and that kind of construction called Warren's girder. *Ibid.*, The Warren girder was decidedly superior to the lattice bridge. **1866** B. B. STONEY *Theory of Strains in Girders* I. vi. 79 This class of bracing includes girders whose web consists of a simple system of triangles, such as 'Warren's' Girder. **1911** A. SMITH *Stresses in Simple Framed Structures* xiv. 83 The Warren truss has a complete system of web members composed..of diagonals. **1952** *Archit. Rev.* CXI. 159/2 Where the roof over the drug room joins that over the mill room there is a reinforced concrete Warren girder spanning 64 ft. and 13 ft. deep. **1967** *Jane's Surface Skimmer Systems 1967–68* 18/2 The lift fan bay forms part of the plenum chamber, the top skin of which is of Warren girder construction.

warrener. Add: **2.** Also *transf.*
1929 R. Bridges *Testament of Beauty* iv. 114 Poor nomads..warreners of the waste.

warrigal, *sb.* (and *a.*) Add: Also 9 **warragle.** **A.** *sb.* **1.** (Earlier examples.)
1838 J. Hawdon *Jrnl. Journey N.S.W. to Adelaide* (1952) 25 We could find no traces of the sheep except in two places, where we could perceive they had been pursued by the Warrigals. **1848** H. W. Haygarth *Recoll. Bush Life Austral.* v. 44 His 'coolie' dogs will awaken him on the approach of a 'warragle', or native dog.
B. *adj.* (Earlier example.)
1855 in Stewart & Keesing *Old Bush Songs* (1957) 164 I'm a warragle fellow that long hath dwelt In the wild interior, nor hath felt, Nor heard, nor seen the pleasures of town.

warring, *ppl. a.* Add: **1. b.** *Warring States,* used to designate the last period (475 B.C. onward) of Chinese history prior to the unification of the country in 221 B.C.
1929 J. Joshua tr. *R. Wilhelm's Short Hist. Chinese Civilization* iii. 133 The period of 'the Warring States'..is usually regarded as lasting from 403 to 221 B.C. **1935** C. P. Fitzgerald *China* iii. 65 If the story of the period of the Warring States was merely a record of anarchy and violence it would not be worthy of detailed attention in a cultural history. **1937** R. W. Swallow *Anc. Chinese Bronze Mirrors* Pl. 3 *(caption)* Warring States type of mirror. **1963** Kwang-chih Chang *Archaeol. Anc. China* vii. 177 For our purposes, round figures are sufficient: 1100 for the conquest..450 for the beginning of the Warring-States period. **1978** *Nagel's Encycl.-Guide: China* 327 The names of the states of the Warring States period almost all survive as surnames now.

Warrington (wǫ·riŋtǒn). The name of a town in Cheshire, used chiefly *attrib.* to designate a variety of cross-peen joiner's hammer.
1935 N. R. Rogers *Technol. Woodwork & Metalwork* ix. 96 There are two patterns of cross-pane hammers, Warrington and London Riveting, or Exeter. The former..is made in twelve sizes specified by Nos. 00 to 10 consecutively. **1956** A. P. Morgan *Woodworking Tools* i. 8 The Warrington hammer, and similar types with a tapering 'pene' instead of claws, is more suitable for..joinery and finer work. **1966** A. W. Lewis *Gloss. Woodworking Terms* 42 The common woodworker's hammer with its cross pane is known as the 'Warrington pattern'...A pin hammer is merely a very small Warrington. **1979** A. B. Emary *Woodworking* ii. 14 Although joiners use the Warrington-type hammer, the claw hammer is considered the best for someone who will be doing a wide variety of jobs.

warrior. Add: **6. b.** *warrior-poet.*
1878 O. Wilde *Ravenna* 9 Her warrior-poet, first in song and fight. **1958** O. Caroe *Pathans* xv. 241 The warrior-poet whose words still kindle fire in the hearts of his compatriots.

warry (wǭ·ri), *a.*[2] *poet.*[−1]. [f. War *sb.*[1] + -y[1].] Belligerent, warlike.
1901 W. B. Yeats in Lady Gregory *Ideals in Ireland* 96 She looked 'very strong and warry and fierce, but not wicked'.

Warsaw[2] (wǭ·ɹsǭ). The name of the capital of Poland, used *attrib.* in *Warsaw Pact,* to designate a military alliance of the Soviet Union with certain other European nations (see quot. 1978), formed by the Treaty of Warsaw, signed on 14 May 1955. (Principally established as a Communist counterpart to N.A.T.O.)
1955 *N.Y. Times* 14 May 18/1 It would be a mistake to discount the Warsaw pact. **1962** *Listener* 22 Mar. 500/2 The Warsaw Pact countries. **1976** Ld. Home *Way Wind Blows* xii. 167 There was, however, a running argument among the professionals as to whether the line between the Warsaw Pact and the NATO forces should be thinly held (by a trip-wire) or more strongly manned. **1978** *Internat. Relations Dict.* (U.S. Dept. State Library) 46/2 *The Warsaw Pact,* a multilateral military alliance formed by the Treaty of Warsaw, signed May 14, 1955 by the Soviet Union, Bulgaria, Czechoslovakia, East Germany, Hungary, Poland, Romania, and Albania. Like NATO, the Warsaw Pact has military and civilian institutions.

wart, *sb.* Add: **4. a.** (Later examples, sometimes with implied reference to next sense.)
1934 J. B. Priestley *Eng. Journey* vi. 187 You can meet them, a trifle subdued perhaps but there to the last wart, in the solid downright fiction of my friend, Phyllis Bentley. **1961** *Listener* 2 Nov. 738/2 The Catholic revivalists..the author presents as no doubt they would like to be presented... No warts here, perhaps regrettably. **1982** *Times* 1 Dec. 2/5 It was [the television companies']..job to hold up mirrors, some of which showed the warts in society.
b. *warts and all*: without concealment of blemishes or unattractive parts (esp. applied to a description or likeness.) Also hyphened as *attrib. phr. colloq.*
[**1763** H. Walpole *Anecd. Painting* III. i. 15 Oliver [Cromwell]..said to him, 'Mr Lely, I desire you would use all your skill to paint my picture truly like me, and not flatter me at all; but remark all these roughnesses, pimples, warts and everything as you see me, otherwise I will never pay a farthing for it.'] **1930** W. S. Maugham *Cakes & Ale* xi. 138 Don't you think it would be more interesting if you went the whole hog and drew him warts and all? **1961** *Listener* 21 Sept. 437/1 A convincing warts-and-all likeness of Wingate. **1962** *Sunday Times* 1 Apr. 13/1 The Duke of Edinburgh presents himself warts and all, without blunting the rough edges of efficiency and enthusiasm. **1966** K. Giles *Provenance of Death* iii. 96 In fact you want a run down on Stanisgate, warts and all. Huh? **1974** *Publishers Weekly* 18 Feb. 24 An intimate, in-depth, 'warts-and-all' portrait of our new Vice President. **1976** H. A. Williams *Tensions* vii. 111 God..accepts us, accepts all men, unconditionally, warts and all. **1980** *Times Lit. Suppl.* 12 Sept. 986/3 This book..may disconcert the pious more than it jolts the sceptic, but it has the story, warts, statistics and all.
5. b. An obnoxious or objectionable person. *colloq.*
1896 Ade *Artie* i. 5 There they was, holdin' to this wart. **1925** Wodehouse *Carry on, Jeeves* vii. 167 Sippy had described them as England's premier warts, and it looked to me as if he might be about right. **1948** C. Day Lewis *Otterbury Incident* i. 6 Everyone called him the Wart because he had a huge wart on his left cheek.. And because he was a wart. **1977** C. McCullough *Thorn Birds* xvii. 431 Watch your language, you dumb wart! **1984** *N.Y. Times Bk. Rev.* 1 Apr. 33/1 What!..is the old wart going to go on some more about reading?
c. *Naval slang.* A junior midshipman or naval cadet.
1916 [see *crab *sb.*[1] 10**]. **1921** *Blackw. Mag.* July 50/2 They all ignored the six 'warts'. **1962** Granville *Dict. Sailors' Slang* 129/1 *Wart,* naval cadet or junior midshipman, the 'lowest form of Naval life'; an unseemly excrescence.
6. wart disease, a disease of potatoes caused by the fungus *Synchytrium endobioticum* and producing dark pustules on the tubers.
[**1903** *Jrnl. R. Hort. Soc.* XXVIII. p. clxxviii, Warty Disease of Potatoes..was introduced from the Continent, and first appeared in Cheshire.] **1915** [see *black scab* s.v. *black *a.* 19]. **1948** W. G. Burton *Potato* v. 103 Potato varieties vary greatly in their susceptibility to attack by wart disease. **1970** H. W. Howard *Genetics of Potato* vii. 46 Breeding for resistance..to wart disease..has been very successful.

war time. Add: **1.** (Later *attrib.* examples.)
1922 C. E. Montague *Disenchantment* viii. 121 Men's friends at home would have the agonies of false alarms added to their normal wartime miseries. **1935** D. L. Sayers *Gaudy Night* ii. 30 The present lot are the real War-time generation. **1945** *ABC of Cookery* (Ministry of Food) 1 It is intended to be used with the Ministry of Food Recipe Leaflets although it is not restricted to war-time cookery. **1965** *New Statesman* 7 May 709/3 Without the exigencies of war, he would need to have war-time powers. But he would lack..the simple war-time criterion of the need 'to maintain production'. **1978** Cadogan & Craig *Women & Children First* viii. 179 Tilli is..suffering wartime shortages bitterly.
2. *U.S. Hist.* Daylight-saving time introduced during World War II (see quots.).
1942 *Time* 9 Feb. 12/3 Franklin Roosevelt decided what he will call wartime daylight saving when it starts next week. Official name: War Time. **1979** *Sci. Amer.* May 39/3 Year-round daylight-saving time, or 'war time', as it was named by President Roosevelt, began on February 9, 1942.

war-whoop. a. (Earlier example.)
1739 W. Stephens *Jrnl.* 21 Dec. in *Colonial Rec. Georgia* (1906) IV. 474 In marching, our Indians set up the war whoop.

wasabi (wa·săbi). [Jap.] A Japanese herb, *Eutrema wasabi,* whose thick root is used in Japanese cooking.
1903 *Bull. Bureau of Plant Industry* (U.S. Dept. Agric.) No. 42. 20 There is a fresh sharpness about Japanese wasabi that not even the finest Austrian sorts of horse-radish possess. *Ibid.* 21 For two years the young wasabi plants are cared for in the field. **1972** Y. Lovelock *Vegetable Bk.* 333 The roots of the related toothworts..serve as a horseradish substitute in North America... Wasabi..is a Japanese relation cultivated for the sake of its roots, which are used as a condiment. **1981** J. Melville *Sort of Samurai* xviii. 145 Otani..watched the *sushi* master deftly season the rice-cakes with a dab of tear-jerking *wasabi* paste.

wash, *sb.* Add: **I. 1. b.** *wash and brush-up,* a quick wash together with a tidying of one's hair; also *transf.,* and as *v. trans.* and *intr.*
1899 E. W. Hornung *Amateur Cracksman* 31 We must have a wash-and-brush-up before we go,—for I'm as black as your boot. **1938** G. Greene *Brighton Rock* iii. i. 107, I had to have a wash and brush up. **1941** *Vogue* June 58/2 Wash-and-brush-up your face... Creams are rationed and soap is not. **1956** G. Durrell *Drunken Forest* v. 98 The cockroach ambled about for a bit and then stopped for a quick wash and brush-up. **1959** G. Mitchell *Man who grew Tomatoes* i. 10 I'll wash and brush up, as they say, and be down in ten minutes. **1978** R. H. Lewis *Antiquarian Bks.* viii. 167 Most old books in for rebinding have an automatic 'wash and brush-up'..before getting decked out in their new finery.
2. d. fig. phr. *to come out in the wash*: (of the truth) to be revealed, become clear; (of a situation, events, etc.) to be resolved or put right eventually. Cf. *washing *vbl. sb.* 8 a.
1903 Kipling *Five Nations* 196 An' it all went into the laundry, But it never came out in the wash. **1917** Wodehouse *Man with Two Left Feet* ii. 29 A sort of fate, what? .. Heredity, and so forth. What's bred in the bone will come out in the wash. **1930** 'Brent of Bin Bin' *Ten Creeks Run* xxii. 266 That scandal has been such a long time comin' out in the wash that you must have been mistaken. **1943** N. Coward *This Happy Breed* ii. i. 53 Ethel:..I thought everything was going to be all right... Frank: Don't worry, old girl, it'll all come out in the wash. **1947** 'N. Blake' *Minute for Murder* vii. 145 'How on earth could Bill know?'..'Oh, well, it'll all come out in the wash, no doubt.' **1971** J. R. L. Anderson *Reckoning in Ice* vii. 147 When it all comes out in the wash—if it does—I suppose the company will meet our fees. **1978** J. Dunn in Hookway & Pettit *Action & Interpretation* 161 All human scientists..practise in the fond hope that the deficiencies of description or the errors and gaps in the intelligibility of record will all come out in the wash.
3. d. A liquid preparation used to protect plants against pests or disease.
1921 *Discovery* May 130/1 The providing of suitable sprays and washes, and other material connected with the checking of plant pests. **1951** *Dict. Gardening* (R. Hort. Soc.) IV. 2081/1 Other washes have had to be derived for use against it [*sc.* the red spider mite]. **1984** *Which?* Apr. 166/3 Dirt or discoloration by lichen and algae on a wall..often isn't harmful... Brush on a sterilising wash.
e. = Sheep-wash *sb.* 1, 2.
1933 *Press* (Christchurch, N.Z.) 25 Nov. 15/7 *Wash,* place and plant for washing sheep. **1965** [see *draining-pen* s.v. *draining *vbl. sb.* 4].
II. 6. b. (*b*) The air current caused by the passage of an aircraft.
1910 R. Ferris *How it Flies* xx. 474 *Wash,* the air-currents flowing out diagonally from the sides of a moving aeroplane. **1931** *Flight* 9 Oct. 1012/1 Certain modifications have been suggested which are intended to reduce the wash from the tailplane on the rudder during a flat spin. **1972** *Daily Tel.* 9 Aug. 4/8 It was not that the hundreds of [helicopter] pilots just overflew the nudist colony, but some flew so low they knocked over tents with the wash from their rotor blades.
d. Also, the removal or displacement of soil by rain and running water (in quot. 1835, a place where this occurs); freq. in *Comb.* with preceding sb., as in *rain-wash* s.v. Rain *sb.*[1] 6 in Dict. and Suppl., *sheet-wash* s.v. *sheet *sb.*[1] 12 b, *soil wash* s.v. *soil *sb.*[1] 10.
1835 J. H. Ingraham *South-West* II. 88 Bermuda grass is used with great success to check the progress of a wash. **1859** *Trans. Illinois Agric. Soc.* III. 412 Land lying in such a position as to protect it from wash..may be kept in constant cultivation. **1913** [see *soil-binding* adj. s.v. *soil *sb.*[1] 9]. **1959** G. H. Dury *Face of Earth* iii. 17 Rivers, surface-wash, and the downhill movement of solid rock combine to remove the substance of the land. **1972** R. J. Small *Study of Landforms* vi. 209 On the upper part of the slope the increased 'erosional' effect of wash away from the crest may tend to produce convexity of profile, and this may be exaggerated..by soil creep.
IV. 12. b. (Earlier example.)
1882 [see *drifting *vbl. sb.* 2].
VI. 15. b. Nonsense, rubbish, 'twaddle'. Cf. senses 11 a *fig.* and 15 a *fig.*, and Hogwash b in Dict. and Suppl.
1913 A. Lunn *Harrovians* xvii. 287 The Housemasters call their Sixth together at intervals and gass 'em... You know the kind of wash. **1933** G. Heyer *Why shoot Butler?* vi. 86 Not strictly the clean potato, is it?..Guest in the man's house, you know. The Public School Spirit, and Playing for the Side, and all that wash.
IX. 21. wash-bag, a small waterproof bag for holding toilet articles; a sponge-bag; **wash coat,** an undercoat, esp. one for improving or preparing the surface rather than giving a colour; **wash-day** (earlier example); **wash-fast** *a.*, that can be washed without losing colour or dye; so **wash-fastness; wash primer,** a wash coat for use on metal; **wash-sale** (earlier example); cf. Washed *ppl. a.* 1 f. See also *wash *v.* 20 b.
1972 E. Thorpe *Night I caught Santa Fé Chief* i. 11, I took the wash-bag out of the grip; the face-cloth was slightly damp. **1980** G. Lord *Fortress* i. 10 She..picked up her wash-bag. She went..to the bathroom. **1951** M. Hess *Paint Film Defects* 385 On wood which has been treated with water-stains the application of wash coats of a 5 to 8 per cent. shellac solution seem [*sic*] to be popular. **1960** *McGraw-Hill Encycl. Sci. & Technol.* X. 593/1 Primers are always pigmented. In clear finishes, the coat which performs this function is described as a sealer, an undercoater, or a wash coat. **1961** J. G. E. Holloway *Mod. Painter & Decorator* (ed. 5) I. 152 Often the application of a full coat of plastic paint will be preceded by a wash coat..to produce a ground of uniform colour. **1846** *Southern Lit. Messenger* XII. 598/1 Thursday is wash-day. **1963** A. J. Hall *Textile Sci.* iv. 184 This method of dyeing can be used to produce wash-fast shades. **1977** *Private Eye* 4 Mar. 21/1 (Advt.), T-shirts and sweater shirts printed to your design in wash-fast dyes, permanent whites, gold, silver or velvet flock finishes. **1962** J. T. Marsh *Self-Smoothing Fabrics* xx. 334 The thermosetting resin..gave moderate recovery but some discolouration and great embrittlement, together with a lack of wash-fastness. **1961** Webster, Wash primer. **1963** *Times* 22 Apr. 6/5 Zinc tetroxychromate is the most commonly used pigment in the so-called 'wash primers' for metals, which concurrently etch and coat the metal surface before the application of other paint coats to ensure good adhesion. **1973** Wash-primer [see *polyvinyl acetal* s.v. *polyvinyl a]. **1848** W. Armstrong *Stocks* 19 These wash sales are of course void between parties. They are of very frequent occurrence and very mischievous.

wash, *v.* Add: **I. 1. f.** (Earlier example of *absol.* use.)

1820 J. Severn *Let.* 17 Dec. in Keats *Lett.* (1958) II. 363, I am obliged to wash up—cook—& read to Keats all day.

(ii) *fig.* To bring to a conclusion; to end or finish (something). *U.S. slang.*

1925 *World* (N.Y.) 25 Oct. II. 3/1 'That guy might be all right if he washed up [*sc.* washed, cleaned himself],' commented Buck... Just then the stage manager called out: 'What will I do with this act, Mr. Ziegfeld?' 'Wash up him and the bird,' said Flo [Ziegfeld] and that was the last of the Italian and his trained canary... Hype Igoe, the World's sporting writer, heard of the incident..and in commenting..upon Frank Moran, heavy weight pugilist, advised that matchmakers 'wash him up'. The phrase caught the sporting fancy..and has become a colloquial fixture..as a meaty synonym for finals and farewell. **1929** *Sat. Even. Post* 2 Nov. 24/3 'I had an idea,' he explained... 'Just came to me, riding back. I think I know how I can wash it up.'.. He would write it now—tonight! **1940** J. O'Hara *Pal Joey* (1952) 65 They said act of God and fire etc. wash up a contract automatically. **1972** D. Delman *Sudden Death* iv. 98 That man washed himself up with me because he couldn't keep his big, fat, fairy's mouth shut.

h. *fig.* In the game of mah-jong, to shuffle (the tiles).

1926 A. Christie *Murder of Roger Ackroyd* xvi. 196 Caroline got out the Mah Jong box and poured out the tiles upon the table. 'Washing the tiles,' said the colonel. **1929** *Encycl. Brit.* XIV. 677/1 All the tiles are..put face downward on the table and thoroughly shuffled or 'washed'. **1977** 'J. le Carré' *Hon. Schoolboy* xiv. 319 Jerry heard a ritual clicking as the habitual mah-jong party washed the pieces before distributing them.

i. *absol.* To wash table utensils as opposed to drying them. Cf. *dry *v.* 1 c, *wipe *v.* 1 c.

1943 L. I. Wilder *Those Happy Golden Years* xxi. 192 Neither of you need worry about the dishes... I'll wash and Grace will wipe. **1958** J. Cannan *And be a Villain* vii. 150 Evadne..insisted on washing while Laura dried. **1962** M. Duffy *That's how it Was* xiii. 115 Billy washes, Arthur wipes, you put away. **1978** *Listener* 13 Apr. 483/1 Let's pack away the tea. I'll wash, you dry.

2. a. *to wash through*, to wash (a garment) by hand, often individually and hastily.

1936 N. Streatfeild *Ballet Shoes* ix. 136 I'll just wash your jersey through. **1968** M. Woodhouse *Rock Baby* xvii. 168 'Isn't that one of my spare shirts?'.. 'Sorry. Yes it is. But I washed it through for you.'

f. (Earlier example.)

1786 J. Woodforde *Diary* 31 May (1926) II. 247, I paid her up to this Day and told her I would get another to wash him.

3. o. *to wash up*: = sense 3 j. *U.S.*

1934 in Webster. **1935** Marsh & Jellett *Nursing-Home Murder* iii. 42 Thoms came into the [operating] theatre. 'We ought to get washed up, sir,' he said. **1947** J. Steinbeck *Wayward Bus* 214 A neatness of a mechanic who has just washed up. **1967** L. Block *Deadly Honeymoon* ii. 26 Wash up and change your clothes. **1979** R. Jaffe *Class Reunion* (1980) i. xi. 145 She was glad when he came out of the bathroom and she could go in and wash up.

p. *to wash one's hands*: euphemistic expression for 'to go to the lavatory'.

1938 I. Goldberg *Wonder of Words* vi. 108 We are invited to wash our hands, or, if we wear dresses, to powder our noses. **1953** R. Warner *Escapade* 119 She pointed to a large oak tree... 'Stupid woman,' said Lady Average. 'If she wants to wash her hands, why doesn't she go to the house?' **1966** G. Greene *Comedians* i. iii. 84 He was out 'washing his hands', as he put it in polite English. **1974** J. Gardner *Return of Moriarty* 291, I wonder if Rosie could, perhaps, take Miss Malloney to, er, to wash her hands.

II. 11. c. *to wash up*: to retrieve (gold) from the riffles, sluices, etc., in which it has collected during washing. Also *absol.*

1869 J. Anderson *Sawney's Lett.* (ed. 2) 27 Now say, what have you 'wash'd up'? Small wages. **1874** A. Bathgate *Colonial Experiences* xi. 142 After some months' hard work, we would wash up, and my mate would go off to sell the gold. **1900** B. Harte *From Sand Hill to Pine* 103 To dig for three or four hours in the morning, smoke their pipes..for an hour at noon, take up their labors again until sunset, when they 'washed up' and gathered sufficient gold to pay for their daily wants, was..the realization of a charming socialist ideal.

IV. 13. d. (Later example.)

1972 J. Wilson *Hide & Seek* vii. 122, I am making a purse..but I pricked my finger and got a bit of blood on it, but..it will wash out.

e. *to wash out* (trans.): to obliterate, cancel, remove.

1580, etc. [in Dict., sense 13 c]. **1932** R. Niebuhr *Moral Man & Immoral Society* (1933) iii. 81 It will prevent the idea of justice, which is a politico-ethical ideal, from becoming a purely political one, with the ethical element washed out. **1983** *Sci. Amer.* Feb. 86/3 Coronal structure hinted at in ordinary photographs is largely washed out by overexposure of the bright inner corona.

(ii) *colloq.* To call off (an event), esp. because of bad weather; to eliminate (a possible course of action). Usu. *pass.*

1917 A. G. Lee *Let.* 25 May in *No Parachute* (1968) 24 Today I have two patrols, one this morning..but after an hour it was washed out through bad weather. **1933** P. MacDonald *Mystery of Dead Police* vii. 49 I'll get that murder charge washed out altogether. **1953** 'N. Shute' *In Wet* v. 149 If there's an awful lot of work before we go, I might have to wash it out. **1964** Mrs. L. B. Johnson *White House Diary* 8 Apr. (1970) 104 When the commentator inquired about the possibility of McNamara [being Vice-President] and pointed out that he had been a registered Republican at one time, Lippman rather washed that one out. **1977** *Belfast Tel.* 14 Feb. 22/4 Bangor's first ever mid-week racing fixture..was washed out today when stewards inspected the course and found it waterlogged.

(iii) *Air Force slang.* To kill (an airman) in a crash; to crash (an aircraft); also (const. *of* or *from*), to withdraw (a person) from a course. Usu. *pass.*

1918 J. M. Grider *War Birds* (1926) 87 Wholesale funerals... Six American Naval pilots..thought that Camels were as easy to fly as the Hanriots they had been flying in France and they wouldn't listen to any advice from the instructors here. Three of them were washed out one week. **1927** C. A. Lindbergh *We* v. 73 Coupled with this was the anxiety of waiting for the returns from our examination papers, the failure of any two of which would be sufficient cause for their owner to be washed out from the courses. **1928** *Pop. Sci. Monthly* May 72 That Kiwi washed out the only peppy crate in the outfit. **1942** F. H. Joseph *Lett. home from Brit. at War* 16 Three planes were washed out completely, others damaged. **1943** *Yank* 30 July 18 The air cadet needed only 20 flying hours for his commission when he was suddenly washed out of advanced training and shipped. **1979** M. Hastings *Bomber Command* vi. 145 Owen was washed out of pilot training within a fortnight, and posted to learn to be a navigator.

15. a. Also *fig.*

1929 *Times* 30 Oct. 14/1 Trans-America, which closed last night at 6¼, opened today at 20¼..—$840,000,000 ..nominally washed away over-night.

16. (*fig.* example of *to wash up.*)

1947 G. Greene *Nineteen Stories* 74 And so he'd washed up here, under my eyes, sitting all day under the band-stand.

17*. *slang.* To murder. Also with *away.*

1941 in B. A. Botkin *Treas. Amer. Folklore* (1944) i. 124 So Stack, with his gun handle filled with notches, knowed there was a reward out for him for men he had washed away. **1960** 'E. McBain' *See them Die* (1963) v. 48 'This Alfredo kid, he not sush a bad guy.' 'He's getting washed and that's it.' **1979** P. Hill *Washermen* xxiv. 54 They had broken the code... The Washermen must be washed.

VI. 19. c. = *launder *v.* 1 b.

1973 *Black Panther* 30 June 2/2 The money had been 'washed' through the Mexican bank passing off as a legal fee to the Mexican lawyer in order to conceal the source of the donation. **1977** B. Freemantle *Charlie Muffin* xii. 127 We *must* wash the money... If that money isn't broken down, Kalenin..just won't cross. **1981** R. Thomas *Mordida Man* xxvii. 237 What was their payoff for washing the money?

20. b. (Not all clearly distinguishable from the Combs. listed in sense 21 of the *sb.* above.) *wash-jug, -place* (earlier example), *-rag* (later examples; now *U.S.*); **wash-and-wear** orig. *U.S.*, the property of a garment or fabric of being easily washed, drying readily, and needing no ironing; usu. *attrib.*; **wash-bench** *U.S.*, a bench on which washing is done; **wash-cloth** *U.S.*, a facecloth; **wash-deck** *attrib. Naut.*, used in, or pertaining to, the washing of the deck of a ship; *wash-deck tub* (slang), a small boat, with decks easily washed by the sea; **wash-kettle** *U.S.*, a kettle in which water is heated for washing; **wash-kitchen** (earlier and later examples); **wash-line** chiefly *U.S.* = *washing-line* s.v. *washing *vbl. sb.* 9 a; **wash-pan** *U.S.*, a metal wash bowl; a pan for washing ore; **wash-pen**: also *N.Z.*; **wash sink** *U.S.*, a sink for washing oneself.

1959 *Sears, Roebuck Catal.* Spring/Summer 493/1 Wash and wear suits... Launder by hand or washing machine... Machine-dry or drip-dry. **1966** *Wall St. Jrnl.* 11 Feb. 1/1 Permanent press differs from wash-and-wear... Wash-and-wear doesn't involve baking, but rather depends on the blending of synthetic and natural fibers for wrinkle resistance. Also, wash-and-wear has no permanent crease. **1981** Clark & Swaine *Home Managem.* x. 251 The more sophisticated American machines may have a choice of programmes, e.g...synthetics with pre-wash, wash and wear and cold wash. **1981** M. C. Smith *Gorky Park* i. xii. 164 Parties the Film-Makers Union gave for foreign guests, where the civilized appreciation of a bottle of French perfume or a wash-and-wear skirt was routine. **1843** Wash-bench [see *ironing board* s.v. *ironing *vbl. sb.* 1]. **1884** G. W. Cable *Dr. Sevier* i. xxi. 157 She had reached down and taken from the wash-bench the lump of yellow soap. **1969** N. W. Parsons *Upon Sagebrush Harp* xxiv. 132 The man was wiping his neck on the roller towel hung above the outdoor washbench. **1915** Washcloth [in Dict.]. **1949** M. Mead *Male & Female* xii. 262 A baby's face gently washed with a supersoft wash-cloth. **1978** *Detroit Free Press* 5 Mar. (Parade Suppl.) 14E/1 (Advt.), Bath towel, hand towel & washcloth—all cuddly cotton terry. **1878** E. Wakeman *Log of Ancient Mariner* ii. 41 Him I had lowered from the bow one dark night, into the wash-deck tub, in which he paddled to a little schooner close to. **1884** *Naval Encycl.* 835/1 *Wash-deck Gear*, the brooms, squilgees, holy-stones, buckets, etc., used in washing decks. **1901** F. T. Bullen *Sack of Shakings* 98 One morning, at wash-deck time, when I was prowling around forrard [etc.]. *Ibid.* 115 The wash-deck tub was hauled forrard. **1938** C. S. Forester *Ship of Line* i. 22 His captain's admission that he, too, had baths under the washdeck pump. **1927** W. de la Mare *Stuff & Nonsense* 54 It golloped up bolsters and wash-jugs and chairs. **1946** S. Spender *European Witness* ii. 18 A large enamel wash-jug. **1787** *Kentucky Gaz.* 24 Nov. 2/3 Samuel Blair, Has for sale..a Quantity of excellent.. copper and brass wash kettles. **1882–3** W. Whitman *Specimen Days* 23 They put wash-kettles on the fire, for soup, for coffee. **1973** A. Dundes *Mother Wit* p. xiii, The custom of placing an inverted wash kettle in the center of the floor during a prayer meeting so that the sounds of the singing might go into the pot and thereby not disturb the white folks. **1838** C. Gilman *Recoll. Southern Matron* xxix. 206 Preparations were made for the wedding which she chose to have performed in the wash-kitchen instead of our parlour. **1922** Joyce *Ulysses* 601 It was the daughter of the mother in the washkitchen that was fostersister to the heir of the house. **1890** K. D. Wiggin *Timothy's Quest* 48 There's lots of baby-clothes hanging on the wash-lines. **1952** J. Steinbeck *East of Eden* vii. 56 They stole ..garments from a wash line. **1969** E. H. Pinto *Treen* 157 Wash line winders are usually strictly utilitarian objects, without any collector interest. **1851** Washpan [see *stuff *sb.*[1] 4 d]. **1857** J. D. Borthwick *Three Yrs. in Calif.* 124 A 'prospecter' goes with a pick and shovel, and a wash-pan. **1884** 'Mark Twain' *Huck. Finn* xxxvii. 375 We..scratched around and found an old tin washpan. **1946** G. Wilson *Fidelity Folks* 175 The tin washpan on the creek was good enough for that. **1855** H. Phillips *Rockwood Jrnl.* (typescript) 20 John went with him to Wash-pen in afternoon. **1774** J. Woodforde *Diary* 15 Oct. (1924) I. 141, I caught a remarkable large Spider in my Wash Place. **1925** F. Scott Fitzgerald *Great Gatsby* ii. 27 'It's more of an Airedale.' He passed his hand over the brown washrag of a back. **1964** S. Bellow *Herzog* 257 He got into her ears with the washrag as she screamed, cleaned off her face, the nostrils, wiped her mouth. **1978** J. Updike *Coup* (1979) v. 192 Her momma's a washrag and her daddy's a redneck. **1857** *Lawrence* (Kansas) *Republ.* 2 July 4 'Here are all the conveniences for washing,' said the landlord, stepping to a mahogany wash sink and raising the lid. **1873** 'Mark Twain' & Warner *Gilded Age* xxix. 270 It was a small room..with a wash-sink in one corner.

c. *wash-gravel* (example).

1860 in *Occas. Papers Univ. Sydney Austral. Lang. Res. Centre* (1966) No. 9. 27 The runs of gold and lower deposits are not traceable to reefs but to made hills, composed principally of water-worn quartz nodules and debris, often cemented together with ferruginous matter, the wash-gravel resting on whitish or yellow felspathic schist.

d. *wash pants.*

1941 *Daily Progress* (Charlottesville, Va.) 3 July 10/7 (Advt.), Mens & boys swim trunks, wash pants. slack suits, sport shirts, etc. **1972** J. Maryland in T. Kochman *Rappin' & Stylin' Out* 210 Red and grown out of wash pants and levis to Oleg Cassini imported mohair suits.

washability. Delete *nonce-wd.* and add later examples.

1958 *Times* 20 Oct. 13/2 This tweed has been woven for the school..and tested for washability. **1970** *Cabinet Maker & Retail Furnisher* 23 Oct. 173/1 Acrylic fibre is nearest to wool in its characteristics with the additional benefit of washability and recovery. **1985** *New Yorker* 20 May 7 (Advt.), The polyester-and-cotton poplin has the convenience of washability.

washable, *a.* (*sb.*) Add: **2. b.** *washable distemper.*

1894 *Country Gentlemen's Catal.* p. v (Advt.), Taylor's Washable Distemper, in all tints. **1926** F. M. Ford *Man could stand Up* i. ii. 27 Washable distemper was not like the poor—always with you. **1939** *Archit. Rev.* LXXXV. 158 (*caption*) Washable distempers.

b. *sb. pl.* Articles of clothing that may be washed without being damaged.

1951 in M. McLuhan *Mech. Bride* (1967) 95 Colors perk up—brighten up—when you suds your washables in Ivory Flakes. **1973** *Philadelphia Inquirer* 7 Oct. 6 (Advt.), Our lovable washables in Arnel triacetate/nylon pretty with satin piping and bow.

washateria, var. *washeteria.

wash-ball. For *rare* read: chiefly *Hist.* (Further examples.)

1936 *Burlington Mag.* Mar. 123/2 A plain globular soap-box (called a washball box in England some fifty years earlier). **1966** T. H. Raddall *Hangman's Beach* ii. x. 150 And now came the grey attendant with wash-ball and towel, and a small wooden tub of steaming water. **1970** *Canad. Antiques Collector* Nov. 16/1 Out of the..cupboard came a silver plated shaving bowl and ewer, while from one small drawer appeared a pair of silver soap or wash ball boxes. **1980** E. Jong *Fanny* ii. xii. 280 The true Royal Chymical Wash-Ball for the beautifying of the Hands and Face.

wash-basin. Delete 'Now chiefly *U.S.*' and add later examples.

1928 Galsworthy *Swan Song* i. v. 35 We must get some more wash-basins in. **1980** *Sunday Times* (Colour Suppl.) 21 Sept. 50 (Advt.), This soft, subtle shade.. reveals the potential..of the range of wash basins. **1984** Worthington & Knight *Home Plumbing* 103/2 The normal height for a wash-basin is 800 mm..from the rim to the floor.

washboard. Add: **I. 3. b.** (Earlier example.)

1845 J. W. Norris *Business Adviser & Gen. Directory Chicago* 95 Manufacturer of the improved zinc wash-boards.

d. A washboard (sense 3 b) used as a percussion instrument; hence, the kind of music produced by bands using this instrument. Freq. *attrib.*

1925 J. Taylor (*title of musical composition*) Wash-board blues. **1933** *Gramophone* June 26/1 Washboard bands are the red-nosed comedians of dance music... They usually play about with delightfully inconsequent tunes. *Ibid.*, There is a good deal to be said for Yes Suh.. by the Washboard Rhythm Kings... The gent on the washboard is a dexterous performer. **1946**, etc. [see *JUG *sb.*[2] 1 c]. **1947** R. DE TOLEDANO *Frontiers of Jazz* 107 The first washboard was recorded by me. **1961** W. SANSOM *Last Hours Sandra Lee* vii. 173 There came a machine slamming of washboard music and wailing voices that sounded as if they were lost in a large, echoing cave. **1973** J. MARKS *Mick Jagger* (1974) 56 Washboard was also fair enough, if you wanted that sort of sound... You know.. more or less a primitive sort of Chicago sound. **1973** J. WAINWRIGHT *Pride of Pigs* 174 Instead of a drummer there was a young kid with a washboard and thimbles.

4. *fig.* A corrugated surface, esp. of a road.

1934 in WEBSTER. **1950** J. DEMPSEY *Championship Fighting* 186 Bending exercises are best to develop the stomach muscles into a protective 'washboard' against body blows. **1968** G. JONES *Hist. Vikings* III. i. 156 Not only a 'washboard' of wide furrows is visible, but even the wheel-tracks of the viking farmer's last carting. **1976** [see *REG[2]]. **1979** *Tucson Mag.* Apr. 51/1 The long gravel drive to its shore..tends to turn into a washboard in the drier summer months.

II. 5. *attrib.* as *adj.* Corrugated, furrowed, esp. as a result of weather and usage.

1913 *Bull. Geol. Soc. Amer.* XXIV. 145 The till sheet over large areas has been rubbed into a fluted or washboard form on a large scale, but with low relief. **1936** *Trans. R. Soc. Canada* XXX. IV. 10 In the general area where these wash-board moraines were noted there are extensive sand plains. **1949** *Consumer Rep.* Jan. 8/1 Pick out a hubbly surface or a 'washboard' gravel road. **1953** W. MOORE *Bring Jubilee* (1955) i. 6 The morasses or washboard roads which were the only highways. **1968** R. W. FAIRBRIDGE *Encycl. Geomorphol.* 989/2 Steep valley slopes [in a rain forest] typically have a washboard topography, a simple parallel consequent drainage system. **1976** *New Motorcycling Monthly* Oct. 6/3 Washboard surfaces would set the rear wheel pattering.

wash-bowl. Add: **2. a.** (Earlier example.)

1816 U. BROWN *Jrnl.* in *Maryland Hist. Mag.* (1915) X. 369 His wash-bowl [is] the knot of a tree.

b. *spec.* A vessel in which gold is washed.

1848 in *Essex Inst. Hist. Coll.* (1874) XII. 106, I came from Salem City, With my wash bowl on my knee. **1850** E. CHRISTMAN *Jrnl.* 3 Apr. in *One Man's Gold* (1930) 131, I am standing in a hole to the depth of my knees, with my pick raised high in the air; my spade and washbowl are lying upon the ground by my side. **1925** E. O'NEILL *Desire under Elms* I. iv. 66 Their voices..take up the song of the gold-seekers to the old tune of 'Oh Susannah'... 'I'm off to Californi-a! With my wash bowl on my knee.'

wash-dirt. (Earlier N.Z. example.)

1862 *Otago: Goldfields & Resources* 20 All the wash-dirt is auriferous.

wash-dish. 2. Delete '?' and add earlier and later examples.

1805 *Austin Papers* (1924) I. 140, 1 Wash dish. **1857** *Quinland* I. II. i. 275 An iron kettle, which I and all the family used as a common wash-dish before breakfast. **1876** *Rep. Vermont Board Agric.* III. 628 The farmer.. was able to furnish a large maple block to set the wash-dish on. **1891** M. E. FREEMAN *New England Nun & Other Stories* 271 I've got my tin wash-dish there on the bench.

wa·shdown. [f. vbl. phr. *to wash down*: see WASH *v.* 1 g.] **1.** The, or an, act of washing down; *spec.* an act of washing oneself from top to bottom at a wash-basin as distinct from in a bath or under a shower.

1949 *Amer. Speech* XXIV. 35 Another characteristic of oil-field language is the predominance of compound words... The conversion of some verb-adverb combinations into nouns and adjectives are *back-up*, *clean-out*..and *washdown*. **1972** *Bottlers' Year Bk. 1972–73* 40 Taking washdown first—obvious waste can be reduced from running hoses left unattended. **1972** J. WILSON *Hide & Seek* vii. 132, I have a washdown every day and a bath on Sundays. **1979** *Nature* 29 Mar. p. xxx/1 The instrument eliminates bumping and smearing of the sides of the tubes thus eliminating the necessity for washdowns.

2. *attrib.* Of a lavatory: (see quot. 1967). Also *absol.*

1967 *Gloss. Sanitation Terms* (*B.S.I.*) 64 *Washdown W.C. pan*, a W.C. pan in which the excrement falls into the water in the trap and is subsequently removed by the momentum of the flushing water. **1976** *Evening Advertiser* (Swindon) 31 Dec. 4/2 (Advt.), Bathroom suite: consisting of..low level washdown toilet. **1984** WORTHINGTON & KNIGHT *Home Plumbing* 96/2 There is a choice of pan styles... The most common is the washdown.

washed, *ppl. a.* Add: **1. f.** (Earlier example.)

1886 *Harper's Mag.* July 205/1 Washed or fictitious sales, or false reports of sales, are also penal offences.

i. Of a carpet: faded, bleached; specially treated so as to soften the colours and impart a sheen.

1911 G. G. LEWIS *Pract. Bk. Oriental Rugs* iii. 40 What the trade speaks of as a 'washed' rug is not necessarily a 'doctored' one. There is a legitimate form of washing which is really a finishing process... It merely washes out the surplus color and sets the rest. **1962** C. W. JACOBSEN *Oriental Rugs* 121 The danger of your buying both chemically washed and painted rugs today is practically nil. **1969** [see *Peking carpet* s.v. *PEKIN 3]. **1970** 'D. HALLIDAY' *Dolly & Cookie Bird* ii. 20 My room had..wall-to-wall washed Chinese carpeting in quiet shades of money. **1982** G. F. NEWMAN *Men with Guns* x. 74 Wallechinsky moved agitatedly across the living room.. his expensive, imported shoes making a faint squeak on the washed silk Chinese rug.

2. a. (Earlier example.)

1796 JANE AUSTEN *Let.* 1 Sept. (1952) 9 My new coloured gown is very much washed out, though I charged everybody to take great care of it.

3. (*all*) *washed up*: finished; without prospect of further success or competence; no longer on intimate terms; exhausted, 'washed out'. *slang* (orig. and chiefly *U.S.*).

1923 *N.Y. Times* 9 Sept. VII. 2/1 [Stage slang.] *Washed up*, all through for the night. **1925** *Amer. Speech* I. 36/1 [Stage slang.] How cheery it would be, when family ties begin to irk, to use their honest, 'I'm washed up with you,' to indicate that you hope the breach is permanent. **1933** S. KINGSLEY *Men in White* (1934) III. i. 109 I'm washed up with the whole business. **1934** W. SAROYAN *Daring Young Man* 38 We're washed up as a race, we're through, it's all over. **1935** J. T. FARRELL *Judgment Day* (1945) I. xvi. 312 His lips twisted into a sneer at himself, and he thought that he was just a goddam washed-up has-been. **1942** J. B. PRIESTLEY *Black-Out in Gretley* viii. 182 You're too careless, Joe..and now you're all washed up. **1958** C. WILLIAMS *Man in Motion* (1959) ii. 23 I'm washed up as a writer. **1980** *Newsweek* 17 Nov. 7/1 Once he was the most underestimated man in American politics—a washed-up movie star, it was said, who was too old, too simple and too far right to be President.

4. *to get washed up*: to get the washing up done.

1950 J. CANNAN *Murder Included* i. 12 Have to dine early now...We've only got Mrs Witts in the kitchen, and she likes to get washed up and finished.

washer, *sb.*[1] Add: **5. f.** A machine for washing dishes; a dish-washer.

1958 I. ASIMOV *Whiff of Death* xvii. 170 Just let me put the dishes in the washer and then we'll go to bed. **1976** H. MACINNES *Agent in Place* xx. 215 She stacked dishes into the washer.

8*. A face-flannel. *Austral.*

1951 D. CUSACK *Say No to Death* xxxi. 194 Doreen had given her a washer and a drop of warm water to wash the sleep out of her eyes. **1970** P. WHITE *Vivisector* iv. 236 He was reminded of an old face-washer, often grubby, one of the maids had crocheted for him, in wide mesh.

9. washer-drier, a machine that both washes clothes and dries them.

1968 *Listener* 1 Aug. 130/1 The unappealing image of America as a country..whose highest aspirations were another car in the garage or a bigger washer-dryer. **1971** *Which?* Mar. 72/2 Contracts for automatics cost about £9, for a washer-drier (like a Bendix) about £12. **1983** *The Mag.* Dec. 59/4 Built-in kitchen equipment, including dishwashers and washer-dryers.

washerette (wǫʃəre·t). [f. WASHER *sb.*[1] + -ETTE.] = *LAUNDERETTE.

1968 *Punch* 10 Apr. 521/3 The Mariner he beats his brow; But the Guest is well away. 'She runs a mobile washerette Down here, or so they say.' **1974** *State* (Columbia, S. Carolina) 1 Apr. B-9/6 (Advt.), Philco-Bendix Quality. For the best in washerette profits. **1976** *Honolulu Star-Bull.* 21 Dec. F-3/8 (Advt.), Washerette in prime location. 10 washers & 5 dryers. Good lease.

washer-up (wǫʃərʌ·p). Pl. **washers-up.** [f. vbl. phr. *to wash up* (WASH *v.* 1 f) + -ER[1].] One who washes up dishes.

1907 *Daily Chron.* 19 Apr. 12 (Advt.), Woman (young) wanted as washer-up. **1933** D. C. PEEL *Life's Enchanted Cup* xiv. 173 An experienced washer-up in canteens. **1960** *House & Garden* Oct. 165/3 Washers-up who seem to spend one third of their life at the kitchen sink. **1978** L. DAVIDSON *Chelsea Murders* viii. 42 They always had the meal together: the patron..the chef, the under-chef, the washer-up.

So **washer-u·pper** *colloq.*

1961 *John o' London's* 21 Sept. 318/3 But Dunham was more than a washer-upper. **1968** C. DRUMMOND *Death & Leaping Ladies* v. 127 The usual two washer-uppers.. who also prepare vegetables. **1977** *New Society* 25 Aug. 381/1 Rubbish-collector, tea boy, washer-upper and so on.

washerwoman. Add: **3. b.** *washerwoman's skin*, skin that is much wrinkled as a result of immersion in water.

1981 C. A. MCLAREN *Twister over Thames* iv. 65 In the light of my discoveries, notably from the wrinkled nature of the skin—washerwoman's skin, it is called..Master Thacker had been immersed for about twelve hours before ..discovery. **1985** 'E. MCBAIN' *Snow White & Rose Red* v. 73 When a body hadn't been submerged too long..the so-called washerwoman's skin wasn't too bad.

washery. Add: Also, a laundry or wash-house. (Earlier example.)

1875 TROLLOPE *Prime Minister* (1876) I. xix. 305 We've got the steam-washery put up.

washeteria (wǫʃətiᵊ·riă). orig. and chiefly *U.S.* Also **washateria.** [f. WASH *v.* + *-ETERIA.] **a.** = *LAUNDERETTE.

1959 [see *-TERIA *suffix*]. **1966** *Sunday Times* 17 July 30 Now that we have grown accustomed to the blandishments of..something called Washeterias, the next step may be drive-in laundries. **1971** L. GRIBBLE *Alias the Victim* i. 17 She wore a skirt and jumper that had the nondescript shapeless look that derives from too many visits to a washeteria. **1976** *San Antonio* (Texas) *Express-News* 27 Nov. 1B/1 T's Washhouse—the only washeteria for 75 miles in any direction. **1982** P. D. JAMES *Skull beneath Skin* xlii. 339 She'll be at the Washateria... She always does her washing on Monday afternoons.

b. *car washeteria*: a self-service car-washing establishment.

1965 *Daily Tel.* 14 May 20/2 (Advt.), The demand from motorists for simple-to-operate inexpensive car washing facilities will go on growing. Here's how the Car Washeteria answers these requirements. **1970** *Times* 24 Dec. 9, I have long grown accustomed to a cafeteria but I now clean my car at a car washeteria.

wash-hand, *a.* **b.** (Earlier examples.)

1789 J. WOODFORDE *Diary* 17 Nov. (1927) III. 153 Ben returned home about 5 o'clock with..a wash-hand Stand. **1820** G. COLMAN *X Y Z* I. 10 Overset my wash-hand stand; —grop'd to bed in the dark.

wash-house. Add: **2. c.** (Earlier example.)

1856 *Democratic State Jrnl.* (Sacramento, Calif.) 4 Aug. 3/2 There is a washhouse on Font street which seems to imbue its occupants with a desire to quarrel.

d. (Earlier example.)

c **1806** D. WORDSWORTH *Jrnl.* (1941) I. IV. 236 In the middle of the field is a wash-house, whither the inhabitants of this large town [*sc.* Glasgow], rich and poor, send or carry their linen to be washed.

wa·sh-in. *Aeronaut.* Also **washin.** [After *WASH-OUT 5.] An increase in the angle of incidence of an aeroplane wing towards the tip.

1916 H. BARBER *Aeroplane Speaks* 82 The advantages of the wash-in must, of course, be paid for. **1943** *Jrnl. R. Aeronaut. Soc.* XLVII. (Abstr. Section) 70 As the wing tips approach the tunnel wall, both the induced drag corrections and the angles of apparent washin or of apparent twist increase rapidly. **1979** BERTIN & SMITH *Aerodynamics for Engineers* iii. 83 If the angle of incidence increases toward the tip, the wing has 'washin'.

washiness. 1. (Earlier *fig.* example.)

1763 in *Owen's Weekly Chron.* (1767) 7 May 55 Humanity ..is nothing more than a childish washiness of nature.

washing, *vbl. sb.* Add: **1. h.** (Earlier example of *washing up*.)

1858 GEO. ELIOT *Scenes Clerical Life* II. viii. 157 The necessary sum of meals and the consequent 'washing up'.

5. b. *Stockbroking.* (In sense 19 b of the vb.)

1849 *Hunt's Merchant's Mag.* XXI. 118 'Washing' will hardly go down at the board. **1870** J. K. MEDBERY *Men & Mysteries Wall St.* 138 Washing is where one broker arranges with another to buy a certain stock when he offers it for sale. The bargain is fictitious. **1894** S. LEAVITT *Our Money Wars* 287 In 1887..by the process known as 'Washing',—that is, by hiring one set of brokers to buy and another set of brokers to sell,—the price of shares was forced to fifteen times their value.

8. a. Phr. *to come out in the washing*: = *to come out in the wash* s.v. *WASH *sb.* 2 d; *to take in one another's washing*: to help one another by buying one another's goods or services, esp. where no new wealth accrues overall; to render mutual services, to be mutually dependent.

1876 TROLLOPE *Prime Minister* IV. xii. 183 The effects which causes will produce,..the manner in which this or that proposition will come out in the washing, do not strike even Cabinet Ministers at a glance. **1889** G. B. SHAW *How to become Mus. Critic* (1960) 147 The inhabitants either live in villas on independent incomes or else by taking in one another's washing and selling confectionery, scrap books, and photographs. **1913** R. BROOKE *Let.* 1 Sept. (1968) 501 Most of happiness is because one's friends are happy: so that spiritually—whatever the damned Economists may say—we *do* live by taking in each other's washing. **1937** M. BORDEN *Black Virgin* iii. 63 Quite half the women she knew were [working] in shops of one sort or another. The only drawback to that being..that they took in each other's washing... Mona and Peg bought Cimmie's clothes. Cimmie bought her hats from Mona, her nighties from Peg. **1959** J. L. AUSTIN *Sense & Sensibilia* (1962) i. 4 These two terms, 'sense-data' and 'material things', live by taking in each other's washing. **1967** G. SIMS *Last Best Friend* xviii. 169, I expect you know what dealers are like for selling among themselves, it's rather like taking in each other's washing.

b. *washing-up*, table utensils awaiting washing up.

1972 J. MCCLURE *Caterpillar Cop* xiii. 211 Lisbet had eaten and stacked the washing up ready for the girl. **1977** P. HILL *Fanatics* 6 He made his bed but left the washing-up in the sink.

9. a. *washing-room* (earlier example), *soap*; **washing basket**, a basket for holding articles newly washed or waiting to be washed; **washing bat** *Hist.* (see quot. 1898); **washing-book** (earlier example); **washing-line** = *clothes-line* s.v. CLOTHES *sb. pl.* 4; **washing-machine** (earlier and later examples); **washing powder,** a cleansing agent in powder form for adding to the water used for washing household linen; **washing-stand** (earlier examples); **washing-stool,** a stool used when washing.

1947 M. MORRIS in 'B. James' *Austral. Short Stories* (1963) 362 She went down to the lines, walking heavily with her washing-basket full. **1967** *Listener* 17 Aug. 204/3, I..used to fill a big washing-basket with books and bring it downstairs as often as I wanted to. **1898** *Eng. Dial. Dict.* s.v. *Bat*, The washing bat was used to beat the dirty clothes after they had been 'put to soak'. **1969** E. H. PINTO *Treen* 149/2 A woman hitting a man with a washing bat is carved on an oak misericord of 1401, in Carlisle Cathedral... It shows that early washing bats were more shovel-shaped, with wider, shorter blades.

1983 *Daily Tel.* 16 Nov. 15/3 These finely decorated washing bats..were once used to beat the washing. **1868** W. Collins *Moonstone* I. xiii. 216 Before we begin, I should like..to have the washing-book... I want to be able to account next for all the linen in the house, and for all the linen sent to the wash. **1939** L. MacNeice *Autumn Jrnl.* viii. 33 But Life was comfortable, life was fine With two in a bed and patchwork cushions And checks and tassels on the washing-line. **1961** J. Stroud *Touch & Go* iv. 45 Any idea where I can get a washing-line post? **1978** J. Thomson *Question of Identity* xii. 115 Betty Lovell was pegging out sheets on a washing-line. *c* **1754** in *Hermathena* (1965) ci. 40 Things to be done... Morning Caps made..Curtains Chairs Carpets for Dublin ..Washing Machine. *a* **1780** *Rake's Progress* (1977) 9 Enter Porter with a Washing Machine, puts it down—Enter Beat'em, pursued by Washerwomen, who beat him & break his washing machine. **1780** *Brit. Patent 1269* 1 Washing machine. Rogerson's specification... My invention of an entire new machine called a laundry, for the purpose of washing and pressing all sorts of household linen. **1897** *Sears, Roebuck Catal.* 139/2 Washing Machines... The Electric Washers are warranted to be well made. **1944** A. Huxley *Let.* 10 Apr. (1969) 503 Fully furnished and equipped down to an electric washing machine. **1975** *Sunday Times* 16 Nov. 44/3, I also kept rushing to the other side of the room trying to empty rubbish into the washing machine. **1869** J. G. Fuller *Uncle John's Flower-Gatherers* 182 The old Prof..calls salt 'chloride of Sodium' and sets me thinking of washing powders. **1895** [see *blueing, bluing *vbl. sb.* 2]. **1969** I. & P. Opie *Children's Games* ii. 104 The mother..asks the shopkeeper for household goods, such as..some washing-powder. **1977** A. Wilson *Strange Ride of R. Kipling* v. 244 Those who find to their surprise that washing powders wash whiter. **1838** F. A. Kemble *Let.* in *Rec. Later Life* (1882) I. 175 One towel was considered all that was requisite not even for each individual, but for each washing-room. **1720** J. Steuart *Letter-Bk.* (1915) 121 Six barells washing soap. **1947** *Daily Gleaner* (Kingston, Jamaica) 5 Nov. 3/3 (*heading*) No washing soap this weekend. **1789** J. Woodforde *Diary* 13 Nov. (1927) III. 151 Bought this day..one new Mohogany Washing-Stand. **1799** *Times* 1 June 4/1 Dressing and washing stands. **1868** Dickens in *All Year Round* 19 Dec. 62/2, I found a man, his wife, and four children, sitting at a washing stool by way of table, at their dinner.

b. The phr. *washing up* (see sense 1 h in Dict. and Suppl.) in *Comb.*, as *washing-up bowl, machine, water*; **washing-up cloth,** a square of loose-weave fabric for washing dishes, etc.; **washing-up liquid,** liquid detergent for adding to washing-up water.

1938 N. Streatfeild *Circus is Coming* vii. 98 They hurried back to the washing-up bowl. Santa..put a cup in the water. **1983** D. Clark *Vicious Circle* i. 19 Marian had emptied the washing up bowl and mopped down the draining board. **1973** L. Cooper *Tea on Sunday* xvi. 136, I wouldn't myself trust poor Charlot to sell a row of washing-up cloths. **1975** G. Seymour *Harry's Game* iii. 49 The publican pushed the washing-up cloth..across the wooden bar. **1971** C. Bonington *Annapurna South Face* 254 Washing-up liquid. **1980** P. Hill *Savages* vii. 135 Found your true occupation then?..Washin' up... What made you go mad with the washin' up liquid? **1930** *Daily Tel.* 1 Dec. 23/7 (Advt.), Electric washing-up machines..will be sold by auction. **1972** C. Drummond *Death at Bar* i. 7 He has three helpers in the kitchen, one working the washing-up machine. **1932** S. Gibbons *Cold Comfort Farm* x. 137 Niver put my liddle pretty [mop] in that gurt old greasy washin'-up water. **1981** J. Wainwright *All on Summer's Day* 161 It hasn't a head on it [*sc.* beer]... An' it tastes like washing-up water.

Washington (wǫ·ʃiŋtən). *U.S.* [Name of George *Washington* (1732–99), first president of the United States of America.] **1.** *Washington lily*: a tall lily, *Lilium washingtonianum*, that grows in the mountains of the Pacific Coast of N. America and bears white flowers.

[**1859** A. Kellogg in *Hesperian* (San Francisco) III. 340 (*caption*) Lady Washington lily. **1863** *Proc. Calif. Acad. Nat. Sci.* II. 13 Dr. Kellogg also exhibited a drawing and growing specimens of a new species of lily from the Sierra Nevada... *L. washingtonianum* (Kellogg) Lady Washington Lily... Stem erect, glabrous, three to four feet high, two or more flowers on peduncles four to five inches long.] **1869** J. Muir *My First Summer in Sierra* (1911) 43 Here and there a Washington lily may be seen nodding above its even surface. **1937** [see *Shasta lily* s.v. *Shasta *a.* 2].

2. *Washington pie*: † (*a*) some kind of pie; (*b*) a light cake made of sponge layers with a jam or jelly († or cream) filling.

1878 N. A. Donnelley *Lakeside Cook Bk.* 33/1 Washington pie. **1904** F. M. Farmer *Boston Cooking-School Cook Bk.* xxxi. 421 Mix and bake Cream Pie. Put raspberry jam or jelly between layers. **1905** J. C. Lincoln *Partners of Tide* i. 10 Won't you have somethin' to eat? One of them turnovers or some Washington pie, or somethin', hey? **1968** E. R. Buckler *Ox Bells & Fireflies* xv. 231 The taste of the Christmas ribbon candy, and the fleeting taste of the good-luck thimble and the birthday wedge of Washington pie.

Washingtonia (wǫʃiŋtōᵘ·niă). [mod. L., f. prec. + -ia[1].] Either of two species of fan palm of the genus of this name, *Washingtonia filifera* and *W. robusta*, found in California and Mexico and elsewhere.

1945 J. L. Marshall *Santa Fe* 188 There were date palms and New Washingtonia palms from the Colorado desert.., but they were tricks of irrigation. **1949** *Los Angeles Times Home Mag.* 14 Aug. 32/4 There is today an impressive row of Washingtonias..standing like sentinels to direct the way to the ocean's cove park. **1976** *Hortus Third* (L. H. Bailey Hortorium) 1168/1 Washingtonias are extensively grown in Calif., often for street planting, and are common along the Gulf Coast, and in Fla., as well as in other parts of the world, particularly those with Mediterranean type of climate.

Washingtonian (wǫʃiŋtōᵘ·niăn), *sb.* and *a.* [f. as prec. + -ian.] **A.** *sb.* † **1.** A supporter or admirer of George Washington and his political standpoint. *Obs.*

1789 *Mass. Centinel* (Boston) 11 Feb. 172/3 The following gentlemen are chosen Electors... All firm federalists —and Washingtonians. **1816** M. B. Smith *Forty Yrs. Washington Society* (1906) 134 If I was a Washingtonian you might say I worshipped the sun.

2. *Hist.* A member of an American temperance society founded in 1840.

1842 *Joliet* (Illinois) *Courier* 2 Feb. 1/4 A meeting of Washingtonians was held at the methodist church on tuesday evening the 18th inst. **1891** *Cycl. Temperance & Prohibition* 203/1 The 'Washingtonians' originated in the conversion into a temperance society in April, 1840, of a Baltimore drinking club..of six men. **1947** F. D. Downey *Lusty Forefathers* 299 The fervor of the Washingtonians, founded by self-redeemed drunkards, felled thousands of apple trees, the fruits of which might otherwise..have become hard cider.

3. An inhabitant of Washington, D.C., or of the state of Washington.

1852 M. Eastman *Aunt Phillis's Cabin* 234 The beautiful prospect, to which Washingtonians are so much accustomed that they are too apt not to notice it. **1892** *Irrigation Age* 1 May 31/3 Washingtonians know a blessing when they see it. **1945** *Maryland Conservationist* Summer–Fall 7/2 The Potomac River..is very heavily fished by Washingtonians. **1972** *Times* 22 Dec. 5/6 Other Washingtonians, who do not have Air Force One to call on to fly them off to a viewing area, have booked motel rooms in York. **1978** G. Vidal *Kalki* x. 227 'It's my fault,' she apologized. 'I'm the Washingtonian. I should have told you.' **1980** *Blair & Ketchum's Country Jrnl.* Oct. 19/3 Recently a Washingtonian informed us there's real danger that the federal government will collapse.

B. *adj.* **1.** Of, pertaining to, or characteristic of George Washington or his politics.

1812 *Salem Gaz.* 22 May 3/1 The political character of Vermont is really Washingtonian. **1858** A. Lincoln *Coll. Wks.* (1953) III. 19 Fighting it in the Jeffersonian, Washingtonian, and Madisonian fashion. **1902** 'Mark Twain' in *N. Amer. Rev.* May 614 The Washingtonian character would not have been built. **1919** G. B. Shaw *Peace Conference Hints* ii. 21 The United States were still in the Washingtonian phase of non-intervention.

2. Of or pertaining to the Washingtonian Temperance Society or the practice of temperance that it advocated.

1842 *Knickerbocker* XX. 298 The festival was conducted on the Washingtonian principle. **1880** *Harper's Mag.* Jan. 191/2 Its influence is still visible in the Washingtonian homes which usefully supplement the charities of our large cities. **1911** *Encycl. Brit.* XXVI. 579/2 In the United States a flash of enthusiasm of a similar character, but on a smaller scale, known as the Washingtonian movement, had appeared.

3. Of, pertaining to, or characteristic of an inhabitant of Washington, D.C., or the state of Washington.

1961 in Webster. **1977** L. Meyer *Capitol Crime* iv. 26 There was nothing particularly Washingtonian about Reilly... Washington is full of people..who once had.. ideas about changing things.

Washita (wǫ·ʃitǭ). The name *Washita* (see below) used *attrib.* and *absol.* to designate: **a.** [Fort *Washita*, Oklahoma.] (The rocks of) a subdivision of the Cretaceous in the central-southern U.S.A. **b.** [Ouachita or *Washita* Mountains, Arkansas.] A porous variety of novaculite used for sharpening cutting tools.

1860 *Trans. Acad. Sci. St. Louis* I. 586 Washita limestone.—This important member of our Cretaceous System is made up of a nearly white, yellow, gray and blue limestone. **1885** [see *Arkansas[1]]. **1963** A. Geikie *Text-bk. Geol.* (ed. 4) II. vi. iii. 1212 The Texas Lower Cretaceous deposits..have been divided into three formations... The highest formation, termed the Washita, consists of four groups. **1938** A. Durst *Wood Carving* 18 The largest stone shown is the Washita oilstone; the others are various slips for the smaller tools. **1958** J. R. Biggs *Woodcuts* 32 The knife should be kept sharp on the India or Washita stone. **1974** *Encycl. Brit. Micropædia* X. 562/2 The Washita Group is the uppermost member of the Comanche Series.

Washoe (wǫ·ʃo, -ʃū). Also **Washo.** [Washoe *wá·šiw* Washoe Indian, Washoe Indians.] **1.** (A member of) a North American Indian people inhabiting the area around Lake Tahoe on the border of California and Nevada. Also *attrib.*

1846 J. Clyman *Jrnl.* 4 May in C. L. Camp *J. Clyman, Frontiersman* (1960) 206 The tribe we are now passing through call themselves as well as understood Washee. *Ibid.* 8 May 207 But as the tribe of natives inhabiting this stream and the adjacent country call themselves the Washew tribe and nation I think it would [be] correct to call the stream by the same name viz Waushee River. **1860** H. De Groot *Sk. Washoe Silver Mines* 15/2 To this place, on the approach of cold weather, not only the Washoes, whose territory lies adjacent, but also bands of the Pah-Utahs, from a greater distance repair. **1879** H. R. Mighels *Sage Brush Leaves* 225 We saw..a..young Washoe brave escorting his wife and mother-in-law up towards the campoody. **1903** *Out West* Apr. 439 The colors in Washoe baskets are all natural. **1947** *Desert Mag.* Dec. 32/3 The Washoes, of whom less than 1,000 remain, live in valleys along the Sierra Nevada. **1976** *Amer. Speech 1974* XLIX. 287 The Indian nomenclature belongs principally to three major Numic-speaking groups (Shoshone, Northern Paiute, and Southern Paiute) and to two non-Numic tribes, the Washo and the Mohave.

2. The region inhabited by the Washoe Indians; hence, a nickname for Nevada. Also *attrib.*

1856 *San Francisco Bull.* 26 May 3/2 The rumored trouble from the Indians of Carson, Wash-hoe and Walker's valley, is entirely without foundation. **1872** 'Mark Twain' *Roughing It* xxi. 160 Washoe is a pet nickname for Nevada. **1896** C. H. Shinn *Story of Mine* 110 Not merchants these..but a brave, honest outdoor race whose huge Washoe wagons were the forerunners of the railroads. **1947** *Amer. Weekly* 2 Nov. 21/3 Back in Washoe, later to become the state of Nevada, the Comstock Lode waited—waited to be discovered.

3. The language of the Washoe Indians, one of the Hokan group of languages.

1882 *Mag. Amer. Hist.* Apr. 255 The area of the Washo languages borders to the west on the Maídu. **1921** E. Sapir *Language* iv. 81 Washo..an Indian language of Nevada. **1968** *Language* XLIV. 822, I am thinking of the contrast with the vowel harmony patterns in Washo.

4. Special Combs.: **Washoe canary** *U.S. colloq.*, a burro; **Washoe zephyr,** a strong west wind that blows in Nevada.

1867 *Daily Territorial Enterprise* (Virginia City, Nevada) 8 Mar. 3/1 The discouraged 'Washoe canary' refuses to cheer us with its tuneful warblings. **1877** W. Wright *Hist. Big Bonanza* 114 A queer genius thus described the donkey, called by everybody in that region, 'The Washoe Canary'. **1947** *Sat. Rev.* (U.S.) 10 May 32/2 He is..discoursing on the Washoe zephyr and the Washoe canary. **1865** *Washoe* (Nevada) *Times* 4 Mar. 3/2 We have heard of hail and chain-lightning, etc., but ye gentle Washoe zephyr can discount all and everything in that line. **1872** 'Mark Twain' *Roughing It* xxi. 159 According to custom the daily 'Washoe Zephyr' set in; a soaring dust-drift..came with it, and the capital of the Nevada Territory disappeared from view. **1947** Washoe zephyr [see *Washoe canary* above].

wa·sh-off. [f. vbl. phr. *to wash off* (Wash *v.* 15 a).] **a.** Material that is washed off. **b.** The process or fact of being washed off.

1979 *Nature* 17 May 180/2 The pollutants are the wash-off of fertilisers and pesticides from the surrounding banks, the paddy and orchard fields, and the famous Mughal gardens. **1984** *Gardening from 'Which?'* June 181/1 Surface wash-off..can occur with other chemicals.

washomat (wǫ·ʃomæt). *colloq.* Also **wash-o-mat.** [f. Wash *v.* + -o + *-mat; cf. *Laundromat.] = *launderette.

1959 *Times* 30 Dec. 8/7 Twenty-storey skyscrapers were shooting up..among the Chinese laundries, the wash-o-mats. **1983** W. Garner *Think Big, think Dirty* ix. 135 Suttin used a local washomat, launderette, what you will. **1984** T. Hillerman *Ghostway* (1985) vii. 31 Laundries are magnets... The people at the Shiprock Economy Wash-O-Mat would know their customers.

wash-out. Add: **1. b.** *Biol.* and *Med.* The removal of material, esp. from a physiological system, by means of a fluid; the fluid used for, or matter removed by, this.

1955 in *Shorter Oxf. Eng. Dict.* (ed. 3) Add. **1966** *Jrnl. Lab. & Clinical Med.* LXVI. 856 The rapidity of indicator washout..should yield information regarding fluid flow patterns within the cardiovascular system. **1971** *Nature* 23 July 266/2 With a closed system technique in which a nitrogen-free atmosphere was made with helium-oxygen washout, a substantial increase in the concentration of nitrogen was measured. **1977** *Lancet* 8 Oct. 745/1 In a check of the wash-out from swabs and surgical drapes with measured volumes of blood the maximum error recorded was +2.8% by volume. **1980** *Nature* 17 Jan. 265/1 Spontaneous synaptic activity was detected in most myotubes within 1–2 min of curare washout.

c. *Meteorol.* The removal of particles from the air by falling water droplets. Cf. *rain-out 2.

1955 A. C. Chamberlain *Aspects of Trav. & Deposition of Aerosol & Vapour Clouds* (A.E.R.E. Doc. HP/R 1261) 2 Consideration is given to the four mechanisms by which aerosol particles and vapours are removed from the atmosphere, namely: (a) Sedimentation, (b) Impaction, (c) Diffusion.., (d) Wash out by rain. **1974** [see *rain-out 2]. **1980** Iribarne & Cho *Atmospheric Physics* ii. 26 The water cycle is important in the cleansing of the atmosphere by two mechanisms: Rainout... Washout—This is the name given to the elimination of gases by dissolution and of aerosol particles through capture by falling water drops.

3. (Earlier example.)

1873 *Newton Kansan* 29 May 3/2 Owing to a wash out on the Cottonwood last Sunday night, we had no train from the east until Tuesday afternoon.

4. b. *slang.* A useless or unsuccessful person; *spec.* in *Air Force slang*, a person who is eliminated from a course of training.

1918 J. M. Grider *War Birds* (1926) 65 Yesterday was washout day so we all went into town and threw a party at the Court. **1925** [see *napoo *int., a.*, and *v.*]. **1927** C. A. Lindbergh *We* 115 We waited for the almost weekly list of washouts to be published. **1929** D. H. Lawrence *Pansies* 126 Now it's a country of..young wash-outs pretending to be in love with death. **1936** J. B. Priestley

They walk in City v. 115 Gregory Porson was no good, a blighter,..a worm, a wash-out. **1950** *Chicago Tribune* 27 Apr. IV. 1/5 But there's a redeeming feature about the washouts, etc. The Wrigley field tenants still have their perfect percentage based on three straight victories. **1973** *Times* 23 Apr. 4/7, I think I'm a washout.

c. *Air Force slang.* A wrecked aeroplane.

1928 *Pop. Sci. Monthly* May 72/1 Damage to a plane is spoken of as a..'crash' and if beyond repair as a 'washout'. **1972** in *Amer. Speech 1972* (1975) XLVII. 114 Wash out—complete wreckage.

5. *Aeronaut.* A decrease in the angle of incidence of an aeroplane wing towards the tip. [Perh. f. *WASH *sb.* 6 b (*b*), but cf. WASH *v.* 2 k, *13 e and quot. 1916[1].]

1913 *Flight* 25 Jan. 87/2 The fact of them [an aeroplane's wing tips] appearing to be negative does not necessarily imply more than a 'wash-out'. **1916** H. BARBER *Aeroplane Speaks* 25 [The Angle of Incidence.. is sometimes decreased or washed-out towards the Wing-tips.] *Ibid.* 81 The wash-out also renders the ailerons..more effective. **1939** *Jrnl. R. Aeronaut. Soc.* XLIII. 792 The designer has available in this connection not only the use of tip slots, but the use of wash-out and of varying aerofoil section along the span. **1979** BERTIN & SMITH *Aerodynamics for Engineers* iii. 83 The wings of numerous subsonic aircraft have wash out to control the spanwise lift distribution.

wash-pot. Add: **5.** A vessel in which to wash clothes over a fire; a wash-boiler. *U.S.*

1926 B. ISBELL in J. F. Dobie *Rainbow in Morning* (1965) 105 At a later dance a large wash-pot of coffee, surrounded with ample tin cups, was kept boiling under a live oak tree in the yard. **1940** W. FAULKNER *Hamlet* I. 12 The women surrounded by laden clotheslines and tubs and blackened wash pots. **1944** T. D. CLARK *Pills, Petticoats & Plows* xviii. 330 The devil had him imprisoned under an upturned washpot. **1952** F. O'CONNOR *Wise Blood* iii. 62 His mother was standing by the washpot in the yard.

washroom (wǫ·ʃrūm). orig. and chiefly *N. Amer.* [f. WASH *v.* + ROOM *sb.*[1]] **a.** A room equipped for washing oneself. **b.** A lavatory or W.C.

1806 in *Mass. Hist. Soc. Coll.* (1809) X. 77 They have usually two good rooms in front, bed-rooms, kitchen, wash-room, and other convenient apartments in the rear. **1855** 'P. PAXTON' *Capt. Priest* 160 Finally a long washroom completed the odd assemblage. **1878** R. T. COOKE *Happy Dodd* 293 He..fairly went down on his knees to her in the wash-room. **1892, 1908** [in Dict. s.v. WASH *v.* 20 b]. **1941** AUDEN *New Year Let.* III. 54 In Pullman washrooms. **1952** S. SPENDER *Learning Laughter* 140 The indoor separate lavatory and washroom with shower. **1962** A. LURIE *Love & Friendship* iv. 76 The jokes one makes in washrooms. **1978** *Detroit Free Press* 5 Mar. (Parade Suppl.) 12/3 A queasy stomach sends him dashing for the washroom on bumpy plane flights. **1980** *Ottawa Citizen* 16 June 35/2 Washroom sex can mean a hand reaching for a groin underneath toilet cubicles or it can involve two men in the cubicle.

washstand. 1. (Earlier examples.)

1789 J. WOODFORDE *Diary* 13 Nov. (1927) III. 151 For the..Mohogany Wash-stand 0.10.6. **1808** E. WEETON *Let.* 14 Nov. in *Jrnl. of Governess* (1969) I. 126 A box 7 feet by 9, with a bed, a chest of drawers, two chairs, and a washstand in it.

wash-tub. Add: **2.** *Comb.* **wash-tub (bass)**, a wash-tub converted into a musical instrument like a double-bass by stretching a string across it.

1968 *Blues Unlimited* Nov. 8 We recorded Dewey Corley, who..plays kazoo and washtub bass. **1970** *Western Folklore* XXIX. 229 Two kinds of plucked one-stringed instruments are known to Negroes in America today. One is the familiar one-stringed bass, sometimes called a 'washtub bass' or 'gutbucket' from the materials of its construction. **1972** *Time* 17 Apr. 39/3 He played a washtub in a group named the Five Hip Cats.

wash-up. Add: **1. c.** A wash; an act of washing oneself. *N. Amer.*

1887 B. HARTE *Millionaire & Devil's Ford* i. 176 You boys can go there for a general wash-up. **1917** C. MATHEWSON *Second Base Sloan* 64 They..dropped from the car and went back to the station for a wash-up. **1968** *Globe & Mail* (Toronto) 13 Feb. B-12/7 The shutdown of the assembly line for 30 minutes each shift—for rest and wash-up.

wash-work. Add: **2.** (Earlier example.)

1893 A. BEARDSLEY *Let.* c15 Feb. (1970) 44 Nobody gave me credit for caricature and wash-work, but I have blossomed out into both styles.

washy, *a.* Add: **6.** Also, exhausted, washed-out.

1922 JOYCE *Ulysses* 734, I looked a bit washy.

wasp, *sb.*[1] Add: **1.** (Examples of the dial. and joc. var. *wops.*)

1893 A. LANG *Prince Ricardo of Pantouflia* vii. 128 'Hang that wops!' said Prince Ricardo..when it buzzed in his ear. **1908** O. SEAMAN *Wearing of Whisker* in *Salvage* 82 Trained like the ampelopsis, That happy haunt of woolly bears and wopses. **1932** E. STEP *Bees, Wasps, Ants* 81 Wopses, what eat up all our fruit. **1937** D. L. SAYERS *Busman's Honeymoon* xv. 308 Out comes me lord, and they wos all on to 'im like wopses round a jam-pot.

4*. (With capital initial.) A kind of flame-thrower developed by the British army during the war of 1939–45.

1944 *Hutchinson's Pict. Hist. War* 12 Apr.–26 Sept. 467 Like that of the Crocodile, the range of the Wasp is upwards of 150 yards. Fitted to the standard bullet-proof carrier, it is a terrorising weapon. **1965** *Listener* 11 Nov. 763/3 There was this Bren gun carrier with the flame thrower, sir, a Wasp I believe they're called, and I thought it was my duty to see how it worked. **1975** *Incendiary Weapons* (Stockholm Internat. Peace Research Inst.) v. 38 British and Canadian engineers developed a lighter mechanized flamethrower, called the Ronson... This was the forerunner of the Wasp (Mark 1) flame gun of which 1000 were ordered and went into production in March 1943.

5. a. *wasp-grub* (earlier and later examples); *wasp-striped* adj.

1678 Wasp-grub [see *wasp-maggot* in Dict.]. **1919** J. MASEFIELD *Reynard* 61 Brocks eat wasp-grubs. **1952** P. ATKEY *Juniper Rock* x. 87 Wasp-striped..the helicopter reappeared. **1974** E. AMBLER *Dr. Frigo* I. 49 A black butler in a wasp-striped waistcoat.

Wasp (wǫsp), *sb.*[2] orig. and chiefly *U.S.* Also **WASP.** [Acronym f. the initial letters of *W*hite *A*nglo-*S*axon *P*rotestant.] A member of the American white Protestant middle or upper class descended from early European settlers in the U.S. Freq. *derog.* Also *attrib.* or as *adj.*

1962 E. B. PALMORE in *Amer. Jrnl. Sociol.* LXVII. 442/2 For the sake of brevity we will use the nickname 'Wasp' for this group, from the initial letters of 'White Anglo-Saxon Protestants'. **1963** *Times* 2 May 15/5 There is such a thing as a 'Human Engineering Laboratory'; whether a man is a Wasp (white Anglo-Saxon Protestant) can decide his career. **1963** *New Statesman* 10 May 716/2 This year's executive model will be over six feet tall, clean-shaven, lean, and with large fleshy ears... He should try to be or pretend to be a WASP (White Anglo-Saxon Protestant) and ought to have gone to an Ivy League college, preferably Princeton. **1964** E. D. BALTZELL *Protestant Establishment* (1965) i. 9, I should first like to show how the aristocratic process still worked quite well in the case of the family of Abraham Lincoln, and especially how the WASP establishment authoritatively retained the leadership of American society in the generation of Robert Todd Lincoln. **1968** *Times Lit. Suppl.* 4 Apr. 329/1 The Jew can choose to leave his ghetto by 'passing' or by breaking the more and more flimsy barriers put up by Wasp (and non-Wasp) anti-Semitism, but the Negro cannot. **1971** M. MCCARTHY *Birds of Amer.* 71 He was the only older WASP Peter knew. **1977** *Time* 19 Dec. 66/2 United States Secretary of State Felix John Vandenberg—slim, silver-haired, tallish, Wasp—speaks with 'the lingering trace of a British accent, which had been acquired at Eton and Oxford'. **1978** *Jrnl. R. Soc. Arts* CXXVI. 276/1 Can what one calls a WASP properly and without any discrimination select an Asian? **1979** R. JAFFE *Class Reunion* (1980) I. i. 37 Daphne's father was the senior partner of the leading prestigious Wasp law firm in New York.

wasp, *v.* Restrict *nonce-wd.* to sense in Dict. and add: **2.** *intr.* Const. *around, about.* To dart about in the manner of a wasp, in an irritating, noisy, or tenacious fashion.

1967 G. F. FIENNES *I tried to run a Railway* iii. 22 Most nights brought an intruder bumbling overhead with one of our fighters wasping around looking for him. **1981** B. HEALEY *Week of Scorpion* ii. 43 'It must be very unpleasant for her.'..'No doubt... But have you conseeded how you'll make it any less so by having the police wasping about your own ears?' **1981** B. FREEMANTLE *Madrigal for Charlie Muffin* (1982) xx. 152 Traffic wasped around the piazza.

Wa·spdom. [f. *WASP *sb.*[2] + -DOM.] The characteristics, beliefs, etc., of American white Protestant 'Wasps'.

1969 *Time* 17 Jan. 21 Thus Roman Catholics like William Buckley, Sargent Shriver and Ted Kennedy are pushed toward Waspdom by their associations, professions and life styles. **1976** *Time* 27 Sept. 39/1 *Noblesse oblige* has yielded to *bourgeoisie oblige*—even at the country club, traditionally the most closely guarded bastion of upper-class Southern Waspdom.

waspie (wǫ·spi). [f. WASP *sb.*[1] + -IE.] A ladies' corset designed to make the waist appear very small; a belt of similar design. Cf. *wasp-waist* s.v. WASP *sb.*[1] 5 b.

1957 *Housewife* Sept. 89/2 A 'waspie' to whittle your waist. **1962** P. BRACKEN *I hate to housekeep Bk.* (1963) xi. 124 If it's a snug-fitting dress, and you know you'll be wearing your waspie with it, but don't want to be stuck with it or in it while you shop, put it in your big handbag too, and change in the fitting room. **1970** *Daily Tel.* 20 Apr. 15 The belt of the season is undoubtedly the laced-up waspie in suède or leather. **1976** *Times* 27 May 6/4 There were plenty [of women] still to heave a sigh of relief (if their waspies would let them).

waspily (wǫ·spili), *adv.* [f. WASPY *a.* + -LY[2].] = WASPISHLY *adv.*

1854 B. P. SHILLABER *Life & Sayings Mrs. Partington* 231 'Because she is a low, vile creature of the town,' said she, waspily. **1928** *Sunday Dispatch* 29 July 2/3 'That's what I'm doing. Turning over a new leaf—and I'm going to do well.' 'Yeah? And what comes after that?' snapped the P.C.M. waspily.

Waspish (wǫ·spiʃ), *a.*[2] orig. and chiefly *U.S.* Also **Wasp-ish, WASPish.** [f. *WASP *sb.*[2] + -ISH[1].] Of, pertaining to, or characteristic of American white Protestant 'Wasps'. Cf. *WASPY *a.*[2]

1968 *Listener* 27 June 843/3 Charles Newman, making a most impressive debut, gives in *New Axis* a picture of a community that is diametrically the opposite of Mr Baldwin's Harlem: that of an upper-middle-class WASP-ish suburb in an Illinois dormitory town. **1974** *Times Lit. Suppl.* 31 May 591/2 Postwar antisemitism in America... Echoes of haughty Waspish outrage..are to be heard in [this] silly novel about the marriage in 1946 of a sexy, clever Jewish girl from the wrong bit of New York to a handsome booby from an aristocratic Long Island family. **1978** E. TIDYMAN *Table Stakes* II. v. 261 His WASPish good looks. **1983** *Times* 8 July 7/5 He is Scorsese's contemporary, but from a different, Wasp-ish social class.

Waspy (wǫ·spi), *a.*[2] orig. and chiefly *U.S.* Also **WASPy.** [f. *WASP *sb.*[2] + -Y[1].] = *WASPISH *a.*[2]

1968 *N.Y. Times* 23 July 41/1 Black-power stalwarts suspiciously eying the Waspy surroundings. **1975** *Publishers Weekly* 9 June 61/3 Max Herschel, a high-powered industrialist in his 60s, coarse but with all the trappings of class, has lost his..mistress Bones to Steven Routledge, who is the antithesis of Max, WASPy, idealistic, a failed novelist. **1978** M. PUZO *Fools Die* xxxiii. 383 A slim, Waspy, forty-year-old ex-debutante.

wassa (matter): see *WHASSA.

wassat, repr. *colloq.* pronunc. of *what's that.* Cf. WHAT *pron.* I.

1967 J. WAINWRIGHT *Talent for Murder* 83 'Is that usual? Or, is it unusual?' 'Wassat?' **1976** T. WILDEN *To die Elsewhere* i. 5 'I'll have to be off now,' I said... 'Wassat?' said Heyward. **1981** 'J. ROSS' *Dark Blue & Dangerous* xxi. 117 'Wassat, sir?' There was deep incomprehension in his expression.

wasser (wǫ·zəɹ). Also **was-ser.** [f. WAS, 1st and 3rd pers. sing. pa. t. of BE *v.* + *-s* + -ER[1].] = HAS-BEEN *sb.*

1924 KIPLING *Debits & Credits* 313 Bert was for it, with a few remarks from the patriotic old was-sers on the bench. **1936** F. M. FORD *Let.* 6 Sept. (1965) 259 But I don't want to be harmed by people calling me a lousy old wasser.

Wassermann (‖ va·səɹman, wǫ·səɹmăn). *Med.* Also (*erron.*) **-man.** The name of August Paul *Wassermann* (1866–1925), German bacteriologist, used *attrib.* with reference to a test for syphilis devised by him in 1906, in which antibodies to the causative organism are detected by a complement-fixation test. Also *absol.*, the Wassermann test.

1909 *Jrnl. Exper. Med.* XI. 392 Unless a great simplification of the Wassermann test can be devised, it will never attain the usefulness which it really deserves. *Ibid.* 401 Cases which were negative to the Wassermann and weakly or quite often strongly positive to the present method were met with. **1952** 'N. SHUTE' *Far Country* 214 A Wasserman test would be interesting, and probably positive. **1970** PASSMORE & ROBSON *Compan. Med. Stud.* II. xxii. 16/2 The test system consists of Wassermann antigen mixed with dilutions of the patient's serum in the presence of guinea-pig complement. **1976** H. KEMELMAN *Wednesday Rabbi got Wet* xxiii. 71 When she had last had a checkup, she had asked him to do a Wassermann, too, because 'Joe was out of town on business and you know how it is when men go out of town.'

wastage. 1. c. (Example.)

1954 M. BERESFORD *Lost Villages* v. 165 Rokeby and Mortham on the Tees had not recovered from their wastage by the Scots in the fourteenth century.

d. (*a*) The loss of students through failure to complete a course of study or training; (*b*) the loss of employees by any means other than dismissal, esp. by retirement or resignation. Freq. as *natural wastage.*

1919 M. GREENWOOD in *Jrnl. R. Stat. Soc.* LXXXII. 187 Our industrial 'death' rate would then merely be the rate at which entrants to a trade pass out of it, or,..with a..narrower circle, the rates of departure from particular factories. In this sense, 'death' or wastage rates for different factories will be *prima facie* measures of the efficiencies of the respective factories. **1944** *Min. of Fuel & Power Statistics Digest from 1938* 6 in *Parl. Papers 1943–44* (Cmd. 6538) VIII. 151 Net natural wastage... [Note] This is the gross natural wastage *less* the normal juvenile recruitment. **1948** *Ann. Rep. Nat. Coal Board 1947* iv. 45 in *Parl. Papers 1947–8* X. 387 The manpower target set for the Board..was..730,000 men... This meant a net increase..of 40,000..and, since wastage was estimated at 60/65,000 men over the year, a recruitment of 100,000 was needed. **1952** [see *FAVOURABLY *adv.* 3]. **1956** *School Sci. Rev.* June 375 The Rector of Imperial College, Dr. R. P. Linstead, in a lecture last October, said (speaking of what he called 'academic wastage'), 'This academic wastage makes itself shown in different universities, but in this College much of the wastage occurs during the first year.' **1958** *Technology* May 66/2 The question of wastage in apprenticeship. **1963** *Higher Educ.: Rep. Comm. under Ld. Robbins 1961–3* 20 in *Parl. Papers 1962–3* (Cmnd. 2154) XI. 639 We discount all those who begin courses but do not successfully complete them. This is commonly described as 'wastage'—a term that we adopt for reasons of conformity but that we regard as carrying misleading implications. Wastage rates in higher education have not varied much in recent years. **1975** *Times* 25 Nov. 1/3 Nursing staff..were liable to 'natural wastage'. **1979** 'J. LE CARRÉ' *Smiley's People* (1980) v. 65 He resigned of his own accord.., part of the wastage rate that gets everyone so worried. **1983** *Financial Times* 23 Apr. I. 34 The savings which the bank is seeking will involve natural wastage, retraining, redeployment and some measure of redundancy.

waste, *sb.* Add: **III. 11. c.** (Earlier example.)

1864 *Chambers's Jrnl.* 16 July 460/2 Smith the driver.. standing upon the foot-plate of No. 69, leisurely attempting to remove the surplus oil from his black hands with a very suspicious piece of 'waste'.

12. c. Waste water, effluent; *spec.* that which is free of excrement. Cf. *SOIL *sb.*^{3} 7.

The distinction between waste and soil is commoner in the combs. with *pipe*.

1886 *Encycl. Brit.* XXI. 715/2 To connect a water-closet soil-pipe with sinks and basins..is to multiply possibilities for the spread of disease within the house, and it is strongly advisable to convey the waste from them by a separate pipe. **1913** E. H. BLAKE *Drainage & Sanitation* vii. 239 We may next consider the kinds of waste pipe... They comprise rain-water pipes.., soil pipes taking the wastes from closets and housemaids' sinks, and pipes taking the wastes from baths, lavatories, and sinks. **1959** GOODIN & DOWNING *Domestic Sanitation* v. 127 Sanitary fitments, may be divided broadly into those intended to receive the wastes of the human body, and those designed for dirty, soapy or greasy water. **1973** [see *SOIL *sb.*^{3} 7]. **1976** *National Observer* (U.S.) 28 Aug. 12/3 One theory not in the report was that frozen plumbing may have caused a backup of wastes and a contamination of the water system. **1978** T. PETTIT *Home Plumbing* x. 51/2 Waste from WCs is discharged into the soil and vent system of pipework.

IV. 13. (sense 11) *waste disposal.*

1968 E. A. POWDRILL *Vocab. Land Planning* iv. 64 Industrial land does not include..land for..waste disposal (where this occupies a significant area detached from the industrial process). **1977** P. JOHNSON *Enemies of Society* vii. 91 We now have a good idea of the extensive damage done in the areas of Lake Baikal, the Volga, the Caspian and the Aral seas, and other Soviet areas of industrial waste-disposal.

14. waste-basket *v.* (earlier example); **waste disposal unit** (see quot. 1967); **waste-disposer** = *waste disposal unit* above; **waste-gate,** (*b*) *Engin.*, a device in a turbocharger which regulates the pressure at which exhaust gases pass to the turbine by opening or closing a vent to the external atmosphere; **waste-heap,** (*a*) a pile of refuse matter; (*b*) *transf.* in *Cards*, a pile of cards formed from the accumulation during the course of a game of those which cannot be played (cf. *rubbish heap* s.v. RUBBISH *sb.* (and *a.*) 3 b); **waste heat,** heat produced as the by-product of some process; *waste-heat boiler*, a boiler employing this; **waste maker** [f. title of book: see quot. 1961], a manufacturer of consumer goods that are intended not to be durable or to be partially wasted so that the demand for new goods is kept high; **waste mould,** in *Sculpture*, a simple negative mould which has to be broken to release the cast inside it; so **waste moulding**; cf. *piece mould* s.v. PIECE *sb.* 23; **waste-pipe** (further examples); also *spec.* a pipe for the drainage of effluent from sinks, baths, etc., in contrast to a soil-pipe; **waste plug** = *PLUG *sb.* 1 b, † 2 k; **waste silk,** the inferior silk from the outside of cocoons and from cocoons out of which the moths have been allowed to escape.

1889 'MARK TWAIN' *Lett.* (1917) II. xxix. 514 Send me the pages with your corrections on them, and waste-basket the rest. **1967** *Gloss. Sanitation Terms* (*B.S.I.*) 63 *Waste disposal unit*, an electrically operated mechanical device for reducing kitchen garbage into fragments small enough to be flushed into the *drainage system*. **1968** R. V. BESTE *Repeat Instructions* vi. 64 His first conscious memory was of being in the kitchen stuffing the torn pieces into the waste disposal unit. **1977** *Evening Post* (Nottingham) 27 Jan. 14/4 (Advt.), Lounge, hall, fitted cupboards, fully fitted kitchen with waste disposal unit. **1962** *Which?* Mar. 82/1 There are obvious advantages..in being able to get rid of kitchen scraps straight down the drain, with a waste disposer. **1980** A. N. WILSON *Healing Art* vi. 62 A new sun lounge..a waste-disposer in the sink. **1948** *Shell Aviation News* No. 115. 19/1 The closed wastegate limitation is the condition where all of the available exhaust gas energy is required to drive the compressor, and all of the exhaust gas is directed through the turbine. **1981** *Pop. Hot Rodding* Feb. 22/1 It will be a relatively simple matter of welding in sections of bent tubing to make the necessary connections (including a waste-gate, should one be required). **1983** *Which?* Dec. 559/1 So a valve is needed—the wastegate—which opens when the pressure is at its maximum safe level to divert some of the exhaust gases away from the turbine. **1873**, etc. Waste heap [in Dict., sense 13]. **1892** 'L. HOFFMANN' *Illustr. Bk. Patience Games* 4 If its [*sc.* the card's] nature does not allow of its being so played, it is laid face upwards in front of the player, the cards so deposited being known as the 'waste-' or 'rubbish-heap'. **1913** —— *Sel. Patience Games* 5 The cards so dealt with being known as the 'waste-heap' or 'rubbish-heap'. **1975** *Way to Play* 145/3 *Waste pile or heap*, cards from the stock that cannot immediately be played onto the layout are sometimes placed face up in one or more waste piles, to be brought back into the game as appropriate. **1908** A. G. KING *Pract. Steam & Hot Water Heating* xxvii. 343 When no waste heat is available, an ordinary type of pipe heater may be used. **1930** *Engineering* 8 Aug. 188/3 The utilization of exhaust gases in waste-heat boilers had improved the efficiency of the large gas engine. **1972** R. G. KAZMANN *Mod. Hydrol.* (ed. 2) iv. 130 The remainder of this energy, 'waste heat', must be disposed of into the immediate environment of the power plant. **1982** W. F. OWEN *Energy in Wastewater Treatment* xii. 281 Three basic types of heat recovery equipment are typically used in wastewater heat recovery systems: shell-and-tube exchangers, waste heat boilers, and heat wheels. **1961** V. PACKARD *Waste Makers* v. 48 In some cases the consumers have no choice but to be waste makers because of the way products are sold to them. Many paste pots come with brushes built into the cover, and the brushes fail..to reach the bottom... Thus millions of 'empty' paste jars are thrown away with a few spoonfuls of paste still in them. **1970** G. JACKSON *Let.* 17 June in *Soledad Brother* (1971) 282 You dig, no waste makers, nor harnesses on production. **1929** F. J. GLASS *Modelling & Sculpture* viii. 73 You now proceed to chip away the white portion of the waste mould. **1971** *Daily Tel.* (Colour Suppl.) 5 Mar. 8/2 From this brittle clay an impression—a 'waste-mould'—is taken, from which a plaster cast is made. **1911** A. TOFT *Modelling & Sculpture* vi. 90 The term 'waste moulding' implies that the mould is only made to serve the purpose of taking one cast. **1918** H. H. STANSFIELD *Sculpture* ii. 9 In waste moulding the plaster is chipped away so that the mould is destroyed. **1876**, etc. Waste-pipe [see *soil-pipe* s.v. *SOIL *sb.*^{3} 9]. **1946** E. MOLLOY *Plumbing & Gas-Fitting* x. 221/2 For a waste pipe from a bath, sink, bidet, or lavatory basin discharging into a soil pipe from a water-closet, or a waste pipe from a slop sink, the Model By-laws specify 'a suitable trap adequately secured against destruction of the water seal'. **1877** G. E. WARING *Sanitary Condition City & Country Houses* 79 If the waste plug is operated by a handle rising the slab, there is a considerable length of pipe between it and the bottom of the basin. **1882** S. S. HELLYER *Lect. Sci. & Art Sanitary Plumbing* v. 193 These water-closets were made of marble—A the pan; B the waste-plug; C the service-pipe; D the overflow. **1965** Waste plug [see *PLUG *sb.* 1 b]. **1797** *Encycl. Brit.* XVII. 486/1 Before you begin to wind, you must prepare your cocoons.. stripping them of that waste silk that surrounds them, and which served to fasten them to the twigs. **1875** [see SPUN *ppl. a.* 1 a]. **1921** Waste silk [see *SCHAPPE].

waste, *a.* Add: **9. c.** *waste water* (further examples); also *spec.*, water that has been used in some industrial process; also, sewage. (Freq. written as one word.)

1976 *Billings* (Montana) *Gaz.* 27 June 6-C/3 The liquifaction process could give off up to 4.8 million gallons of wastewater per day and..there could be another 100 tons of solid waste generated each day by the coal scrubbing process. **1977** *N.Z. Herald* 8 Jan. 2-12/7 (Advt.), C/1073: M. K. Morrison—to discharge wastewater from State Highway No 1 into Alexandra Creek headwaters..in connection with quarrying operations at Cuthill, Albany. **1979** *Arizona Daily Star* 1 Apr. D 3/1 Stephen J. Tencza, former project engineer with the Pima County Department of Wastewater Management, has joined John S. Collins & Associates as a project engineer for the firm's sanitary engineering department.

waste, *v.* Add: **4. c.** To beat up, kill, murder (someone); to devastate a place, to kill its inhabitants. *slang* (orig. and chiefly *U.S.*).

1964 P. MARSHALL in J. H. Clarke *Harlem* 317 Stomping and wasting our Little People. *Ibid.* 319 You.. president..since Duke got wasted? **1966** J. M. BREWER in A. Dundes *Mother Wit* (1973) 240/2, I wasted (punched) one of the studs. **1971** *Guardian* 2 Apr. 12/2 The intention to 'waste' My Lai. **1975** C. WESTON *Susannah Screaming* xxix. 147 They wasted Barrett because he blew their deal. **1977** *Courier-Mail* (Brisbane) 21 Sept. 2/4, I think Simone has been wasted (killed) by the southern heavies. **1981** M. C. SMITH *Gorky Park* I. xii. 177 You want to go chasing after the guy who wasted your detective.

14. Delete ? *Obs.* (Later examples.) Also const. *away*.

1881 'MARK TWAIN' *Prince & Pauper* xvii. 187 The afternoon wasted away. **1961** W. VAUGHAN-THOMAS *Anzio* i. 8 The year wasted to an end. **1978** J. A. MICHENER *Chesapeake* 282 The boys were only eight and seven, but already the years were wasting.

wasted, *ppl. a.* Add: **5.** Intoxicated (from drink or drugs). Chiefly used outside the U.K.

1968–70 *Current Slang* (Univ. S. Dakota) III–IV. 135 *Wasted, a.* Drunk; unable to function. **1972** J. S. GUNN in G. W. Turner *Good Austral. Eng.* iii. 56 Being under the influence is..*turned on, wasted.*

wasteland. Add to etym.: This compound is now indistinguishable from collocations of the adjective (sense 1), and all further examples are added here. Add to def.: **1. b.** Land (esp. that which is surrounded by developed land) not used or unfit for cultivation or building and allowed to run wild.

1922 W. J. LOCKE *Tale of Triona* x. 116 They walked.. through the maze of new and distressingly decorous avenues, some finished, others petering out..into placarded building lots or waste land. **1933** *Archit. Rev.* LXXIV. 166/1 Farm and meadow, hedge and coppice are all part of a system which the urban dweller takes for granted but which agricultural decay can only transform..into wasteland, flood and marsh. **1969** *Daily Tel.* 5 Sept. 18 Within a stone's throw of the Guildhall are wasteland areas created by the bombing of 25 years ago. **1974** A. J. HUXLEY *Plant & Planet* xxix. 359 Land sterilization by building and industrial use, and the subsequent creation of wastelands. **1980** *Daily Tel.* 23 July 2/2 A conference on wasteland, organised in London by Thames Television.

c. *spec.* a waterless or treeless region, a desert. (Not distinguishable from some examples in Dict., sense 1 a.)

1966 F. HERBERT *Dune* 399 The stranger might think nothing could live or grow in the open here, that this was the true wasteland that had never been fertile and never would be. **1969** *Daily Tel.* (Colour Suppl.) 3 Oct. 20/4 Horses cannot last long in that pitiless wasteland where no rain has fallen for the last five years. **1979** P. THEROUX *Old Patagonian Express* (1980) vii. 131 We were in a waterless desert: no sign of the river in this parched wasteland.

d. *transf.* and *fig.*, sometimes with allusion to T. S. Eliot's poem *The Waste Land* (1922).

1868 TROLLOPE *Phineas Finn* (1869) I. xxxvi. 310 Young members..who are green from the waste lands and road-sides of private life. **1932** H. NICOLSON *Let.* 15 Apr. (1966) 114 He [*sc.* Sir Oswald Mosley] will be edged gradually into becoming a revolutionary—and to that waste land I cannot follow him. **1934** C. LAMBERT *Music Ho!* v. 281 The composer finds himself in a spiritual waste land. **1964** S. BELLOW *Herzog* 75 The commonplaces of the Wasteland outlook. **1972** *Sat. Rev.* (U.S.) 27 May 7/1 Television's sad wasteland. **1976** *Brit. Jrnl. Sociol.* XXVII. 35 Above all, there is one fundamental chasm which divides this terminological wasteland. **1981** *N.Y. Rev. Bks.* 5 Nov. 34 The once proud and efficient public school system of the United States...has turned into a wasteland.

2. *N.Z.* (See quot. 1875.)

1844 F. MATHEW *Reports* (typescript) II. 18 Any attempt on his part to assert the right of the Crown, without purchase, to what are known as Waste Lands would have immediately been attended with serious results. **1875** J. VOGEL *Official Handbk. N.Z.* 103 Public—or as they are called, 'waste'—lands are sold on several principles. **1930** L. G. D. ACLAND *Early Canterbury Runs* 1st Ser. viii. 205 Godley..was very much against letting the 'waste lands' in large areas.

wa·stemaster. Also Wastemaster. [f. WASTE *sb.* 11 + MASTER *sb.*^{1}] The name of a type of waste disposal unit. (In quot. 1963 a similar imaginary or futuristic device.)

A proprietary name in the U.S.

1946 *Official Gaz.* (U.S. Patent Office) 5 Nov. 15/1 Wastemaster; Lockley Machine Co. For electrically driven garbage grinders... Claims use since June 14, 1945. **1949** *House Beautiful* Feb. 85 Choose from these disposers... Wastemaster—Lockley Machine Co. **1963** *Punch* 16 Oct. 569/1 The wastemasters were able to come into their own and people began buying—..for scrap. **1966** *New Statesman* 13 May 710/4 (Advt.), Mais...2 beds, k. & b., waste-master. **1973** A. HOLDEN *Girl on Beach* 12, I suppose you've got a washing-machine and a clothes-drier and a wastemaster and a pop-up toaster. **1981** I. A. GORDON in *N.Z. Listener* 27 June 86 You know all about dishmasters and maybe even wastemasters.

waste-paper. Add: **1. a.** (Earlier *fig.* example.)

1869 *Bradshaw's Railway Man.* XXI. 361 The conventions of 1858 and 1862..would thus have been almost rendered mere waste paper.

b. waste-paper basket: also *fig.*

1923 J. S. HUXLEY *Ess. Biologist* vi. 217 The waste-paper basket of outworn imaginations. *a* **1930** D. H. LAWRENCE *Last Poems* (1932) 120 All that we know is nothing, we are merely crammed waste-paper baskets Unless we are in touch with that which laughs at all our knowing. **1979** *London Rev. Bks.* 25 Oct. 23/2 Marriage, the Webbs agreed, was the waste-paper basket of the emotions.

waster, *sb.*^{1} Add: **II. 6. a.** (Further examples applied to pottery.)

1878 L. JEWITT *Ceramic Art Gt. Brit.* I. iv. 76 A kiln.. in and around the remains of which were many vessels—'wasters' as they would be technically called—of various kinds. **1928** W. B. HONEY *Old Eng. Porcelain* i. 15 Nothing short of an undoubted 'waster' can prove conclusively that a particular type was made on the factory site in question. **1950** D. T.-D. CLARKE *Roman Pottery Kiln* 4 Pots of similar grey ware have been found at Market Overton..which are undoubtedly wasters. **1961** M. KELLY *Spoilt Kill* II. 81 Pots that were twisted, shrunken and collapsed... Wasters, they called them. **1974** *Canad. Antiques Collector* Sept.–Oct. 27/2 There are remains of many little potteries scattered all over southern Ontario, and mounds of 'wasters' or broken or discarded ware.

wasting, *ppl. a.* Add: **2. a.** *wasting asset* (see quot. 1974).

1930 *Economist* 26 Apr. 951/2 Dividends to shareholders —representing return of capital, since gold mines are a wasting asset—have shown much less than a corresponding rate of increase. **1953** *Times* 31 Oct. 2/7 The cost will be almost competitive with coal-based electrical power, and it would be contrary to all experience if the cost comparison did not turn steadily in nuclear energy's favour, particularly when coal is a wasting asset and steadily more costly in real terms to extract. **1970** *Guardian* 3 Nov., Dr. Beeching breathed his kiss of death on the Inverness to Kyle [railway line] in 1963; since then it has been regarded as a wasting asset. **1974** *Terminol. Managem. & Financial Accountancy* (Inst. Cost & Managem. Accountants) 65 *Wasting assets*, assets of a fixed nature which are gradually consumed or exhausted in the process of earning income (e.g. mines or quarries).

wastrel, *sb.* and *a.* Add: Hence **wa·streldom, wa·strelism,** extravagance, esp. with reference to government spending.

1906 *Westmorland Gaz.* 14 Mar. 3/2 He was, indeed, heard to say that under our present Fiscal system the wine of our manhood was oozing out while the water of wastrelism was oozing in. Sir Wilfrid Lawson was..somewhat annoyed to think that the best of all drinks should be confounded with wastrelism. **1906** *Daily Mail* 3 Nov. 4/2 All the old strongholds of Wastreldom have been carried. St. Pancras has thrown out its Wastrels; Islington will have none of them. **1919** *Ibid.* 15 Oct. 6/2 Such arguments in the interest of wastrelism have been abundantly refuted. **1931** J. BUCHAN *Blanket of Dark* 102 It was hard to believe that this was a gathering of the kings of wastreldom.

wat[4]. (Earlier example.)

1844 *Chinese Repository* XIII. 204 The Siamese are in the habit of burning their dead, and the place selected for this purpose is near the wats.

watch, *sb.* **I. 2.** For '† *Obs.* except in *watch-night*' read 'Now *rare arch.* exc. in *watch-night*' and add later example.

1877 *Life St. Willibrord* i. 7 There for some years he served God in fast, watch, and prayer, in a little cell.

IV. 21. e. *silly* (or *crazy*) *as a two-bob watch*: extremely stupid, mad. *Austral. slang.*

1954 P. GLADWIN *Long Beat Home* 72 There now, I clean forgot. I'm getting silly as a two-bob watch. **1963** L. GLASSOP *Rats in New Guinea* 192 Crazy as a two-bob watch. Should have reported it, corporal. **1972** J. DE HOOG *Skid Row Dossier* 75 'Don't buy him a beer, Johnny, he's silly as a two bob watch', someone advised as he tapped me on the shoulder.

VII. 26. (sense 6) *watch temple*; (sense 21) *watchband, -strap.*

1924 *Sears, Roebuck Catal.* 410/1 Watch-band, woven wire. For watches. **1970** N. ARMSTRONG et al. *First on Moon* iii. 64, I found the little card..and stuck it under his watchband. **1925** *Watchmaker, Jeweler, Silversmith & Optician* LI. 138 (Advt.), The finest range of watch straps. **1977** P. THEROUX *Consul's File* 126 The woman [was] covered with welts the shape of watch-straps. **1921** D. H. LAWRENCE *Sea & Sardinia* ii. 66 Venus of the aborigines, from her watch-temple looking at Africa.

27. watch cap (later examples); **watch-care** (earlier example); **watch-chain:** hence **watch-chained** *a.*; **watch-charm** *U.S.*, a small ornament that may hang from a watch-chain; **watch-keeper:** also in gen. use, one who keeps watch or acts as a look-out; hence **watch-keeping** *sb.* and *a.*; **watch-list,** a list of items or names which require close surveillance, esp. for legal or political reasons; **watch-night,** (*b*) *W. Afr.*, a night-watchman; **watch-pocket** (earlier example); **watch-riband** (earlier example); **watch-ribbon** = *watch-riband*; **watch room,** a room from or within which a watch is kept.

1966 T. PYNCHON *Crying of Lot 49* v. 114 He opened his door and found an aged bum with a knitted watch cap on his head. **1977** J. F. FIXX *Compl. Bk. Running* xii. 139 What I've found best is a simple wool hat, the kind sailors call a watch cap. **1984** *New Yorker* 31 Dec. 64/3 Bearded young fishermen, with ponytails coming out from beneath their knitted watch caps. **1845** *Indiana Mag. Hist.* (1927) XXIII. 152 Very much..depends on the..preachers and leaders, who have the after watch-care of the persons that are brought into the church. **1944** BLUNDEN *Cricket Country* i. 12 One or two watch-chained elders. **1976** 'R. GORDON' *Doctor on Job* xi. 93 Frock-coated and gold watch-chained. **1898** H. S. CANFIELD *Maid of Frontier* 15 [How's] the little baby I gave the watch-charm to? **1929** W. FAULKNER *Sound & Fury* 99 Father brought back a watch-charm from the Saint Louis Fair. **1979** *Arizona Daily Star* 1 Apr. c4/2 His uniform number and watch-charm size aren't the only distinctive things. **1981** J. R. L. ANDERSON *Death in High Latitude* ix. 141 We must have someone on watch... And the watchkeeper must have a rifle. **1946** C. S. FORESTER *Lord Hornblower* iv. 32 Nine years as a captain had not eradicated the habits acquired during a dozen years as a watchkeeping officer. **1977** *Proc. R. Soc. Med.* LXX. 485/2 A sailor reported recurrent unilateral swelling after watchkeeping. **1974** P. GORE-BOOTH *With Great Truth & Respect* 238 There had been three categories of control, namely embargo, quantitative restriction and a 'watch-list'. **1982** 'J. PENN' *Notice of Death* xix. 178 The Watch List..a list the officials have at ports of entry, of people who are wanted for one thing or another. **1953** G. M. DURRELL *Overloaded Ark* vi. 113, I engaged what in the Cameroons is known as Watchnight... There were two reasons for engaging a night watchman: the first.. to wake me up. The second..was that he patrolled the edge of the compound..for driver ant columns. **1975** J. WYLLIE *Butterfly Flood* (1977) xxxi. 148 The watch night. Where is the watch night?.. The nightwatchman was lying in his reclining chair. **1831** M. WHALLEY *Let.* 15 Feb. in J. Constable *Corr.* (1962) I. 260 Thanks for ..a pair of tastefully & beautifully made watch pockets. **1832** *Chambers's Edin. Jrnl.* I. 82/2 Having changed the wear..of a silk watch-riband for a chain. **1804** BYRON *Let.* 29 Aug. (1973) I. 51 Do not overlook my watch ribbon, and purse as I wish to Carry them with me. **1827** DISRAELI *Vivian Grey* III. v. vii. 131 Here are Eau de Cologne, violet soap, and watch-ribbons. **1850** *Ann. Sci. Discovery* 73 On the top of the structure [*sc.* a lighthouse] is the watch-room, and lantern, or light-room. **1883** 'MARK TWAIN' *Life on Mississippi* 338 One of the two establishments where the Government keeps and watches corpses until the doctors decide that they are permanently dead... A wire led to a bell in a watch-room yonder.. where a watchman sits always alert. **1943** *Gloss. Terms Telecomm.* (*B.S.I.*) 85 *Watch room*, the room, at the fire station, which is continuously staffed and contains the alarm-recording apparatus, call-bell keys and telephonic intercommunicating equipment. **1977** *Stornoway Gaz.* 27 Aug. 1/4 The Commission also want to renovate the existing harbour watchroom to provide welfare facilities for dock workers, a new watchroom, and public toilets. **1979** N. WALLINGTON *Fireman!* iii. 37, I saw..the watchroom into which came all the emergency calls.

watch, *v.* Add: **I. 4. g.** For (U.S. *colloq.*) read (*colloq.*, orig. *U.S.*). (Earlier and further examples.)

1845 J. J. HOOPER *Some Adventures Simon Suggs* ix. 115 He determined therefore to 'watch out' and keep himself 'whole' in a pecuniary point of view if possible. **1909** J. MASEFIELD *Tragedy of Nan* I. 21 You better watch out she don't tread a thy corns. **1957** R. LAWLER *Summer of 17th Doll* I. i. 19 If you don't watch out, you're gunna start hating the poor bloke before he even gets here.

† **h.** *to watch in*: to watch a television programme. *Obs.*

1928 *Daily News* 17 Dec. 6/4 (*heading*) Pictures by Wireless. Where to 'watch-in' this week.

II. 12. d. To exercise care, caution, or restraint about (something). *to watch one's step*: see *STEP *sb.* 10 b.

1837 H. MARTINEAU *Society in Amer.* I. II. 187 The valetudinarians of the place..watch their own and each others' weight. **1958** 'CASTLE' & HAILEY *Flight into Danger* i. 23 You'd better watch that waistline, Pete. **1963** 'W. HAGGARD' *High Wire* iv. 40 Rex said deliberately: 'I have to watch champagne.' 'Really? But this one won't damage you.' **1969** G. CROUDACE *Blackadder* iv. 32 Pauline ate nothing but a small, lightly-grilled steak and a lettuce leaf; it was obvious that she had to watch her weight. **1976** M. MACHLIN *Pipeline* lvii. 573 Just watch your mouth... A man died here tonight. **1981** G. MARKSTEIN *Ultimate Issue* 26 It was a comparatively shabby office... Euram Marketing gave a distinct impression of watching the pennies.

e. *to watch it*: to be careful. Freq. as imp. (as a threat or warning). *colloq.*

1916 'TAFFRAIL' *Pincher Martin* vi. 100 'Don't yer go lendin' money to any other blokes wot ain't fit to be trusted.' 'I'll watch it.' **1943** K. TENNANT *Ride on Stranger* xviii. 203 You're not getting any younger yourself, kid. You want to watch it. **1954** W. FAULKNER *Fable* 334 'All right,' the corporal said. 'Watch it now.' **1966** 'W. COOPER' *Mem. New Man* II. iv. 144, I replied in the proletarian vernacular of the times. 'Watch it!' **1978** D. BLOODWORTH *Crosstalk* xxii. 170 We really do have to watch it a bit. Thank God we're officially engaged.

watcha (wǫ·tʃă), repr. a colloq. or vulgar pronunciation of *what do* (or *are* or *have*) *you*? Similarly **watcher.** See *WHATCHA.

1926 D. L. SAYERS *Clouds of Witness* vi. 134 Hullo! Watcher mean, nap? I had got hold of a most important train of thought. **1966** R. PETRIE *Dead Loss* xiv. 108 Watcha gonna do, Jeff? You can't leave her here. **1967** E. & M. A. RADFORD *No Reason for Murder* xxiii. 167 Watcher want with Waddy? **1969** in Halpert & Story *Christmas Mumming in Newfoundland* 95 Watcha got there, Uncle?

watcha, *int.*: var. *WOTCHER *int.*

1977 'J. GASH' *Judas Pair* iii. 38 'Watcha, Lovejoy.' 'Come in, Tinker.'

watchable, *a.* Add: *spec.*, that may be watched with pleasure or profit at the theatre or cinema, or on television. (Examples.)

1933 *Punch* 11 Jan. 51/2 There were two other dancing items: Messrs. Lee, Lee, Lee and Lee, who were very watchable and possessed in their pianist an accomplished clown; and Mr. Jerry Cole. **1970** *Daily Tel.* 12 Oct. 11 That rather unfortunate category among television documentaries—worthy but not terribly watchable. **1972** *Ibid.* 22 Nov. 15/2 He was also needed..to have the stage dressed in something more watchable than brown paper and dustsheets. **1978** *Chicago* June 130/1 Schlafly..was named one of the most influential and watchable women in America in two national polls taken in 1977. **1983** *Times* 26 Oct. 18/1 A very watchable programme.

Hence **wa:tchabi·lity.**

1966 *Guardian* 29 Mar. 10/3 For sheer watchability, the Liberals have just about won. **1975** *Daily Tel.* 10 Apr. 16/5 If watchability is part of the business of TV documentary,..then 'The Fight Against Slavery'..is surely a winner.

watch-dog. Add: **c.** Also *fig.*, esp. applied to a commission or other group appointed as a safeguard against abuses by the authorities (in government, foreign policy, etc.), business interests, etc.

1873 [see *scrub-woman* s.v. *SCRUB *v.*[1] 5]. **1947** *Toronto Daily Tribune* 21 Dec. 12/1 [Vishinsky] spoke.., raking the United States for..proposing that the assembly send a semi-permanent UN 'watchdog' commission. **1960** *Daily Tel.* 22 Aug. 1/1 He demanded the dispatch to his country of a United Nations watch-dog force. **1969** *Listener* 3 July 5/1 The watchdog function of the press depends..on the effects of publicity on a politician's own colleagues and opponents. **1977** *Time* 30 May 51/2 Last March the International Trade Commission, a six-member watchdog group appointed by the President, recommended an increase in the tariffs on Japanese sets from 5% to 25%. **1984** *Daily Tel.* 9 Oct. 8/2 The Post Office was accused yesterday by its consumer watchdog body of putting profit before service to customers. **1985** *Which?* Feb. 58/1 Our regular checks over the years (and those of other 'watchdogs' such as Trading Standards Officers) have consistently revealed a depressingly low standard of workmanship in garages. **1985** *Times* 31 May 13/7 Although climbing may be the most non-bureaucratic of sports it does need a watchdog guarding its interests.

wa·tchdog, *v.* [f. the sb.] *trans.* To attend, follow, or guard (a person); to maintain surveillance over (an activity, situation, etc.). Hence **wa·tchdogging** *vbl. sb.*

1902 C. J. C. HYNE *Mr. Horrocks, Purser* 70 There seems to be a whole regiment of ragamuffins on board here watchdogging her. **1962** *Punch* 20 June 933/1 The rigours of public watchdogging. **1964** R. F. FICCHI *Electrical Interference* ii. 9 The only way the system problem can be resolved is to have a completely formalized program to 'watch dog' the problem through to its solution. **1968** *Economist* 13 July 17/1 The job of watchdogging the constitution is second nature to Tories. **1977** M. HERR *Dispatches* 191 We [*sc.* war correspondents] were..there to watchdog the day. **1980** A. SKINNER *Mind's Eye* xiv. 196 Three more..went down with the strange attacks, and he and Holbrook watchdogged them through.

watcher. Add: **h.** With preceding *sb.* in objective relation, freq. hyphenated: an expert student or one who follows the affairs of (a particular person, country, or institution). *colloq.* (orig. *U.S.*).

1966 *N.Y. Times* 27 Dec. 10/3 That was the major question of the 'China watchers' as Mao observed his birthday without public fanfare yesterday. **1971** *N.Y. Post* 20 Dec. 40 The Nixon-watchers..would construe Kissinger's return to Cambridge as a potential calamity. **1972** *Jrnl. Linguistics* VIII. I. 125 MIT-watchers have lately been puzzled by a division within the movement. **1974** *Guardian* 26 Mar. 16/1 As one experienced Brussels-watcher put it yesterday, Mr Peart has discovered how flexible the Treaty of Accession can be. **1974** Kremlin-watcher [see *KREMLIN]. **1975** *Times* 19 June 14/8 The meeting..achieved a level of futility which left even hardened EEC watchers groggy. **1976** *New Yorker* 8 Mar. 27/3 When Confucius first came under attack, professional China-watchers speculated that the criticism had allegorical overtones. **1978** *Guardian Weekly* 23 Apr. 17/3 A veteran Shah-watcher said, 'He realises the extent of present and future problems.'

† **i.** *watcher-in.* A television viewer. Cf. *WATCH *v.* 4 h. *Obs.*

1928 *Daily News* 17 Dec. 6/4 Watchers-in will be able to judge for themselves the value of picture transmissions during this week.

watcher *int.*: see *WATCHA.

water, *sb.* Add: **I. 1. f.** *water over the dam* or *under the bridge* (*dyke, mill* and varr.): past events which it is unprofitable to revive or discuss; a way of saying 'a long time has passed'.

1913 *Wireless World* I. 34/1 Much water has flowed under London Bridge since those days. **1914** KIPLING *Let.* 15 Sept. in Ld. Birkenhead *Rudyard Kipling* (1978) xviii. 279 Your articles..are a little too remote..but of course—much water, or shall we say much blood, has flowed under the bridges since they were written. **1920** GALSWORTHY *In Chancery* I. i. 5 It was a startling remark—showing in a flash what a lot of water had run under bridges since the death of Aunt Ann in '88. **1940** *Nation* (N.Y.) 16 Mar. 364 Last year's results are water under the mill. **1940** *Amer. Guardian* 11 Oct. 1 All that is water over the dam. **1955** C. S. FORESTER *Good Shepherd* 91 He should not have brought the men to battle stations at all... But that was water over the dam; no time for regrets at present. **1964** E. F. BECKENBACH *Appl. Combinatorial Math.* x. 292 But these fees are water under the bridge, for we have paid them and they will never be returned to us. **1969** 'W. HAGGARD' *Doubtful Disciple* xi. 116 'Where did he get it?' 'From Seyer, I think—we can't escape that. But that's water over the dam by now.' **1976** *Glasgow Herald* 26 Nov. 5/4 Does he look back in anger as a result of his wartime experiences? 'Not now—perhaps a little to start with. But a lot of water has gone under the dyke since then.' **1977** J. THOMSON *Case Closed* iii. 43 It's been quite a time since we last met. Water under the bridge, as they say. **1981** *Encounter* Oct. 7 You don't want to let any of that business bother you... Water under the bridge. Just accept the fact, file it away.

3. b. (Earlier nonce-combination.)

1812 H. C. ROBINSON *Jrnl.* 13 May in E. J. Morley *Blake, Coleridge, Wordsworth, Lamb, Etc.* (1922) 50 Bar. Field called Wilson '*Wordsworth & Water*'.

6. c. *deep waters*: now usu. in phr. *in deep water*(*s*).

1861 T. HUGHES *Tom Brown at Oxford* I. v. 83 Tom felt greatly relieved, as he was beginning to find himself in rather deep water. **1867** TROLLOPE *Last Chron. Barset* I. xxxiv. 294 Once he had been very nearly in deep water because Mrs. Proudie had taken it in dudgeon that a certain young rector, who had been left a widower, had a very pretty governess for his children. **1933** N. COWARD *Design for Living* II. ii. 62 Our lives are diametrically opposed to ordinary social conventions; and it's no use grabbing at those conventions to hold us up when we find we're in deep water. **1950** D. LESSING *Grass is Singing* viii. 157 He stubbornly went his own way, feeling as if she had encouraged him to swim in deep waters beyond his strength, and then left him to his own devices.

III. 17. b. *water on the knee*: an excessive accumulation of fluid in the knee joint.

1890 A. JAMES *Diary* 7 Nov. (1965) 151 They [*sc.* the English] call water on the knee, fluid on the joint. **1902** W. S. CHURCHILL *Let.* 9 Oct. in R. S. Churchill *Winston S. Churchill* (1969) II. Compan. I. 167 He is laid up with Water on the Knee. **1976** *Liverpool Echo* 6 Dec. 1/8 A lone

Canadian sailor spent 17 days at sea clinging to his capsized trimaran before he was rescued suffering only from water on the knee.

IV. 20. b. (Earlier var. example.)

1775 *London Mag.* Nov. 556/2 She has an eye of that quick and brilliant water, that it penetrates and darts through the person it looks on.

VII. 24. a. *water-bowl, -flask, -jug* (earlier examples), *-jugjar, -sack, -skin* (earlier example), *-tin, -trough* (later examples).

1779 in *Dict. Amer. Eng.* (1944) IV. 2452/2,2 water jugs. **1807** R. Southey *Lett. from England* I. xiv. 161 A compact kind of chest holds the bason, the soap, the tooth brush, and water glass... The water-jug and water-bottle stand below. **1821** Water-skin [see *girba]. **1855** *Poultry Chron.* II. 432 The price charged for these pens ..will be 6s. 6d. each, complete, with wooden bottom, water tin, and separate cloth. **1864** J. A. Grant *Walk across Afr.* 430 Here there is a bend in the Nile, and we were able to fill all our water-sacks afresh. **1920** Water-tin [see *souvenir v. 3]. **1922** Joyce *Ulysses* 491 A man.. passes..hugging a full waterjugjar. **1926** D. H. Lawrence *David* xiv. 106 Here is the pouch and the water-flask. **1935** C. Winchester *Railway Wonders of World* II. 933 There are eleven sets of water-troughs on the West Coast main line between Euston and Glasgow. **1960** J. R. Ackerley *We think the World of You* 89 On the floor was Evie's water-bowl and the vegetable remains of her dinner of yesterday. **1970** J. H. B. Peel *Country Talk* vi. 111 Water-troughs in far fields were tepid. **1979** M. McMullen *But Nellie was so Nice* (1981) I. i. 12 She.. filled Titania's water bowl, gave jealous George an extra stroking.

b. *water-supply* (earlier example), *-well.*

1849 J. Simon *City Medical Rep.* No. 1, in E. R. Pike *Human Documents of Victorian Golden Age* (1967) 280 It may be doubted, too, whether..the tenants' water supply can be pronounced good. **1921** *Review of Reviews* Aug. 157/2 Hardships of desert travelling, when great gulfs of distance lie between one water well and another. **1976** *Billings* (Montana) *Gaz.* 30 June 5-D/1 (Advt.), Water well drilling.

c. *water tank, tender, truck.*

1834 Water tank [in Dict., sense 24 a]. **1894** *Outing* June 172 Four or five rough-looking men..were clustered about the water-tank. **1957** G. V. Blackstone *Hist. Brit. Fire Service* xxv. 443 The evolution of the water tender from the mobile dam unit produced to deal with the water shortages at air-raid fires. **1958** P. Scott *Mark of Warrior* II. 122 The water truck rendezvoused. Most of the chaps' bottles were empty. **1967** O. Ruhen in *Coast to Coast 1965–6* 193, I threw down my swag near the water-tank. **1974** D. Sears *Lark in Clear Air* i. 20 We stopped at every gopher-hole and water-tank and badger-hill. **1976** *Billings* (Montana) *Gaz.* 6 July 8-A/2 The county water truck was dispatched at 4.09 p.m. ..The truck was refilled with water, before the fire was controlled. **1978** *Dumfries Courier* 13 Oct. 17/4 Two water tenders from Dumfries brought the blaze under control.

d. *water-cutting.*

1862 E. Hodder *Memories N.Z. Life* 117 We were glad to..lie down closely together in one of the dry water-cuttings.

e. *water-feed.*

1914 *Chambers's Jrnl.* May 334/2 The..lamp..works automatically, the water-feed to the carbide being drop by drop.

g. *water-seal* (earlier examples).

1877 G. E. Waring *Sanitary Conditions City & Country Houses* 31 These gases..have..the power of passing almost unretarded and unchanged through the water-seal traps. *Ibid.* 36 The water-seal is a trap in more senses than one.

i. *water-porridge, -toast.*

1838 A. Langton *Jrnl.* in *Gentlewoman Upper Canada* (1950) 80 This morning the same party assembled to tea, coffee, and water porridge—a great favourite with most of the backwoodsmen. **1843** *Ainsworth's Mag.* V. 60 My dinner was pudding or pastry, and if these failed, there was a substitute known by the name of *water-toast*... A slice of bread was toasted, and dipped..in boiling water, and then buttered and sugared. **1848** Geo. Eliot *Let.* 8 Mar. (1954) I. 255 The sympathy in Ireland seems at present only of the water toast kind. **1947** W. de la Mare *Coll. Stories for Children* 61 A bowl of water-porridge, using up for it the last pinch of meal.

j. *water-time.*

1925 R. Graves *Welchman's Hose* 9 Our feeding and our water-time, Our breeding and our slaughter-time.

k. *water-land, -point.*

1811 W. H. Marshall *Rev. Rep. to Board Agric. from Eastern Dept. Eng.* 10 The term *Water-Lands* may be deemed a solecism. But when it represents lands that have not only been formed by water, but are liable to be annihilated, and their place reoccupied, by the same element—it is surely allowable as a *Technical Term*, to convey a joint idea of 'Fens' and 'Marshes'. **1954** J. R. R. Tolkien *Two Towers* iv. 79 The Entwives..saw the.. green herbs in the waterlands in summer. **1946** U. Krige *Way Out* xv. 194 They were taken by the Germans at the water-point. **1964** J. Hillaby *Journey to Jade Sea* 167 The Balessa Kulal, a famous water-point farther down the *lugga*.

l. *water-blowball, -brook* (later examples), *-cloud, -drip, -fount* (example), *-gush, -leak, -mist, -ripple, -song, -sphere, -spray, -surface, -swirl, -talk, -world* (later example).

c **1865** G. M. Hopkins *Poems* (1967) 122 When lily-yellow is the west. Say, o'er it hangs a water-cloud And ravell'd into strings of rain. **1869** *Bradshaw's Railway Man.* XXI. 242 The dock..measures 600 feet in length and 300 in width, giving an area of water surface of upwards of four acres. **1876** 'Mark Twain' *Tom Sawyer* xxxiii. 260 It was the treasure-box..occupying a snug little cavern, along with..some..rubbish well-soaked with the water-drip. **1888** G. M. Hopkins *Poems* (1967) 198 All in froth and water-blowballs. **1904** W. de la Mare *Henry Brocken* vi. 59 Ears that have heard only..dismal water-songs, and the yelp and quarrel and night-voice of unseen hosts in the forests. **1916** Blunden *Pastorals* 30 Mocked by the white wings of the water-swirl. **1920** J. Masefield *Enslaved* 34 The melancholy water-drip alone Broke silence near me. **1921** W. de la Mare *Veil* 32 Ice on the waterbrooks their clear chimes dumbing. **1922** Joyce *Ulysses* 698 A rockery with waterspray. **1928** Blunden *Undertones of War* ix. 98 Ahead, the German front line could not be clearly seen, the water-mist and the smoke veiling it. **1928** E. Sitwell *Five Poems* 4 The water-ripples like mosaics gold. **1935** W. Stevens in *Southern Rev.* I. 80 The statue stood in stars like water-spheres. *a* **1944** K. Douglas *Alamein to Zem Zem* (1946) 52 Few Crusader tanks would run for more than two days in action without developing either an oil-leak or a water-leak. **1952** L. MacNeice *Ten Burnt Offerings* x. 60 The water-talk ends; the scrawl on the sky Smudges and fades. **1954** J. Betjeman *Few Late Chrysanthemums* 66 Back into what a water-world Of waving weed and waiting claws? **1955** E. Pound *Classic Anthol.* II. 113 Naught stands higher than mount, Nor is hollow deeper than water-fount. *a* **1957** R. Campbell *Coll. Poems* (1960) III. 19 Amidst dead calms collapsing water-gushes, And distances cascading to the deeps. **1961** K. Reisz *Technique Film Editing* (ed. 9) ii. 137 Tiny bugs skim over the water-surface. **1967** *Jane's Surface Skimmer Systems 1967–68* 14/1 The vehicle has been used primarily for testing over land, water and ice, to investigate.. seaworthiness, water spray problems, [etc.]. **1977** *Daily Tel.* 9 July 12 Lands where hearts desire the waterbrooks and wells are of crucial importance. **1984** A. C. & A. Duxbury *Introd. World's Oceans* iv. 120 Water molecules arrange themselves at any water surface to form a weak elastic membrane.

m. *water-stair.*

1920 T. S. Eliot *Ara Vos Prec* 15 Princess Volupine extends A meagre, blue-nailed, phthisic hand to climb the waterstair.

n. *water-ballet, -music* (later examples), *-pageant* (later examples), *-song, -sonnet, -sports.*

1888 Water-music [see *paddling vbl. sb.[2]]. **1888** L. A. Smith *Music of Waters* 83 The verses and tune of this water-song..follow. **1892** Water-pageant [see *bargemaster]. **1920** L. & N. Sheffield *Swimming Simplified* viii. 150 Water sports afford a varied source of amusements. **1940** L. MacNeice *Last Ditch* 9 And as the twilight filtered on the heather Water-music filled the air. **1944** Blunden *Shells by Stream* 7 Trilling still with finch or lark Or water-sonnet. **1948** T. Wilder *Ides of March* II. 143 When the water-ballet was ended, Caesar's party rose to go in search of the Queen. **1968** Water ballet [see *synchronized ppl. a.]. **1976** *National Observer* (U.S.) 30 Oct. 3/3 We enjoy water sports. **1976** *Evening Post* (Nottingham) 15 Dec. 1 Mr Michael Hammond said he had not received a reply from the County Council to an offer of assistance in organising a water pageant on the day of the Queen's visit. **1979** *Tucson Mag.* Apr. 57/1 There are..dance exercises, water ballet classes, separate massage facilities and other services. **1980** *Early Music* Jan. 50/1 It seems likely that Weiss, Buffardin, and Hebenstreit provided 'water music' for the royal couple on the barge.

p. *water-brother, -wayfarer.*

1965 Auden *About House* (1966) 16, I should like To be to my water-brethren as a spell Of fine weather. **1923** D. H. Lawrence *Birds, Beasts & Flowers* 99 Fishes.. Outsiders. Water-wayfarers.

q. *water-fay, -ghost, -king, -shape.*

1878 O. Wilde *Ravenna* 5 And down the river, like a flame of blue, Keen as an arrow flies the water-king. **1916** Blunden *Pastorals* 32 That you shall come upon the water-fays. **1925**—— *English Poems* 90 The water-shapes steal towards his gonging drone. **1928** *Oxford Poetry* 10 Many strong men had passed the ford, nor known the presence of that jeering water-ghost Denying their true conquest of the stream.

25. a. *water-divining, -dowsing, -holding, -retaining*; also with *sbs.* and *adjs.*, as *water-retention, -retentive.*

1898 K. L. Parker in Murdoch & Drake-Brockman *Austral. Short Stories* (1951) 2 We thought you..would.. know of a goolahgool, or water-holding tree. **1909** O. Lodge *Survival of Man* ix. 128 Just as people occasionally seem able to become cognisant of facts or events by means ordinarily closed to them,—a phenomenon which appears akin to the water-dowsing faculty and to the 'homing' instincts of animals,—so sometimes they can write poetry or solve problems beyond their normal capacity. **1913** W. Owen *Let.* 13 Nov. (1967) 211 What it costs to make a Scout. For instance:.. Belt..Staff (Water-divining, extra). **1930** T. S. Eliot tr. *St-J. Perse's Anabasis* 63 Consecration of stones perfectly round, water-dowsing in dead places. **1936** *Discovery* Jan. 24/1 They [*sc.* the soils] are all highly permeable and with a small water-retaining capacity. **1946** *Nature* 13 July 58/1 The lower part of the profile consists..either of re-cemented chalk or compact sand, both of which are very water-retentive. **1952** L. MacNeice *Ten Burnt Offerings* IV. i. 38 A sage whose water-divining mind Will twitch to the smallest drop. **1958** *Yearbk. Agric. 1957* (U.S. Dept. Agric.) 770/2 *Water retention*, the physical property of soil that is based on surface force action and that makes it necessary to do work in order to remove water from soil pores and from soil surface. **1969** G. Becker in Krishna & Weesner *Biol. Termites* I. xi. 367 The water content of the soil should be slightly below its water-holding capacity. **1973** D. Robertson *Survive Savage Sea* II. 73 The unpalatable, brackish water could be administered rectally in the form of water retention enemas. **1979** *Arizona Daily Star* 5 Aug. (Advt. Section) 4/1 Applicant should have at least 3 years experience in the design of hydraulic, water-retaining structures.

b. *water-fearer, -lover, -tender.*

1842 T. W. Harris *Insects Injurious to Vegetation* 11 The water-lovers (Hydrophilidæ)..act the useful part of scavengers. **1884** *U.S. Navy Exec. Ord.* 31 Dec., New ratings are hereby established as follows: boiler maker, water tenders, oilers. *a* **1885** G. M. Hopkins *Poems* (1967) 192 Fallers in dreadful frothpits, waterfearers wild. **1922** Joyce *Ulysses* 655 Bloom, waterlover, drawer of water. **1948** H. C. Nichols *Voice at Sea* x. 145 This water-tender, or boss stoker as he was sometimes called, was the devil himself.

26. a. *water-cut, -hidden, -marrowed, -pillared, -saturated, -sealed, -shafted, -smoothed, -sorted, sprinkled, -wattled, -wound*; also with *adjs.*, as *water-dispersible, -poor, -rich.*

1876 G. M. Hopkins *Poems* (1967) 65 And mazy sands all water-wattled. **1922** J. A. Dunn *Man Trap* iv. 49 Most of the young men nowadays are water-marrowed pups. **1924** G. A. Burls *Cost of Power Production by Internal-Combustion Engines* iv. 23 A gas-holder of the familiar inverted water-sealed type. **1925** E. Sitwell *Troy Park* 19 A water-hidden sound. **1927** V. Woolf in *Forum* May 704 Her cowardice; her mean, water-sprinkled blood. **1928** 'Brent of Bin Bin' *Up Country* xix. 325 The water running on to the water-smoothed stones. **1935** L. MacNeice *Poems* 21 Set these against your water-shafted air of amethyst and moonstone, the horses' feet like bells of hair. **1939** J. Steinbeck *Grapes of Wrath* i. 1 In the water-cut gullies the earth dusted down in dry little streams. **1939** Dylan Thomas *Map of Love* 6 Down the stacked sea and water-pillared shade. **1946** *Nature* 6 July 14/1 For an ordered system, the expansion on wetting is lateral for a water-rich system, and perpendicular for a water-poor system. *Ibid.* 9 Nov. 675/1 The extent of development obtained is related to the type and throughput of solvent, which is normally 10 ml. of water-saturated ether per strip. **1946** Dylan Thomas *Deaths & Entrances* 63 Turns the moon-chained and water-wound Metropolis of fishes. **1959** *Times* 30 Nov. 18/7 Water-dispersible powders. **1959** A. H. McLintock *Descr. Atlas N.Z.* 36 Soils derived from fine volcanic ash and watersorted derivatives. **1978** J. M. Brown in *Further Perspectives Organic Chem.* (CIBA) 149 The selective terminal addition to squalene in water-rich solvents. **1979** *Amer. Jrnl. Trop. Med. & Hygiene* XXVIII. 1014/2 The Department of Health of the Philippine government..has campaigned since 1950 for the installation of cheap water-sealed toilets.

b. *water-rippling* ppl. adj.; *water-dripping* vbl. sb.

1922 T. S. Eliot *Waste Land* (1923) 33 The hermit-thrush..Its 'water-dripping song' is justly celebrated. **1924** E. Sitwell *Sleeping Beauty* xx. 77 A lady sang through water-rippling leaves. **1927** —— *Rustic Elegies* 76 And the trees' vast waterfalls Echoed this water-dripping song like flashing bright bird-calls.

27. *water-dwelling, -haunting, -living, -standing* ppl. adjs. Also *water-gifted* adj.

a **1882** Emerson *Poet* in *Compl. Wks.* (1883) IX. III. 309 Methought like water-haunting birds Divers or dippers were his words. **1919** H. G. Wells *Outl. Hist.* 12/1 Water-living creatures which are always under water, wave the freely exposed gills by which they breathe in the water. **1934** Webster, Water-dwelling. **1936** *Discovery* Jan. 7/2 South American water-dwelling frogs. **1937** *Ibid.* Aug. 252/1 The larger water-haunting birds. **1942** W. Faulkner *Go down, Moses* 340 The planters.. had wrested from the impenetrable water-standing cane and cypress..cotton patches which..became fields and then plantations. **1960** T. Hughes *Lupercal* 46 Four-legged yet water-gifted.

28. *water-chilly, -clear, -cold, -dark, -eager, -flowing, -green* (earlier example), *-precious* adjs.

1884 *Girl's Own Paper* 30 Aug. 762/3 A large range of colour..primrose, water-green, beige. **1910** W. de la Mare *Three Mulla-Mulgars* xxi. 275 An odd little water-clear song. **1923** D. H. Lawrence *Birds, Beasts & Flowers* 94 Water-eager eyes. **1923** Water-precious [see *red-gold* s.v. *red a. 13]. **1924** E. Sitwell *Sleeping Beauty* 27 'Midst brightly perfumed water-flowing Eighteenth-century silks. **1925** —— *Troy Park* 59 A flaxen lily Water-chilly. **1928** —— *Five Poems* 3 That cloud of gold, Its kernel, crackling amber water-cold. **1945** —— *Song of Cold* 11 One of the Dead who lay Beneath the earth, like the water-dark, the water-thin Effigy of Osiris. **1961** R. D. Baker *Essent. Path.* xix. 527 The adenoma has a yellowish or gray, soft cut surface... Microscopically it is composed of chief cells, although occasionally of the so-called 'water-clear' cells.

29. water-base *a.*, having water as the main ingredient; **water-based** *a.*, (*a*) operating from ships; (*b*) = prec.; **water body,** a body of water forming a physiographical feature, as a sea, reservoir, etc.; **water-bomber** *Canad.*, an aircraft used for extinguishing forest fires by dropping water on them; hence **water-bomb** *v. trans.*; so **water-bombing** *vbl. sb.*; **water-boy,** (*d*) chiefly *U.S.*, a boy or man who carries or takes round drinking water; **water-bus,** a motor-boat or steamer carrying paying passengers as part of a scheduled service; **water cannon,** a device for shooting a jet of water at high pressure, esp. to disperse crowds, etc.; **water clerk,** an employee of a ship's chandler; **water content,** (amount of) water contained in some material; **water-cool** *v. trans.*, to cool (an engine, etc.) by circulating water; hence **water-cooling** *vbl. sb.* and *ppl. a.*; so **water-cooled** *ppl. a.*; **water-cooler,** a vessel or container in which water is kept cool; *spec. U.S.*, a tank of cooled drinking water in a place of work; **water cushion,** a depth of water that acts to lessen the impact or force of something; **water drive** *Oil Industry*, the use of water to force oil out of a reservoir rock; **water drum,** a drum containing water, or placed in water, and played as a musical instrument; **water fountain,** a drinking fountain; **water-garden,** (*b*) (earlier example); hence **water-gardening; water-gilt** *a.* (earlier example); **water injection,** (*a*) *Oil Industry*, the forcing of water into a reservoir formation, esp. as a technique of secondary recovery (cf. *WATER-FLOODING *vbl. sb.*); (*b*) *Aeronaut.*, the injection of water into the cylinders of a piston engine with the fuel, to cool the charge, or into the air intake of a jet engine, to cool the air, so as to increase engine efficiency in either case; **water-insoluble** *a.*, insoluble in water; **water intoxication** *Med.*, a condition resulting from the intake of too much water, leading progressively to drowsiness and unsteadiness, confusion, convulsions, coma, and death; so **water-intoxicated** *a.*; **water-keeper** one who guards a tract of water against poachers; cf. GAMEKEEPER; **water-lain** *a. Geol.* = *water-laid* adj. (*b*) in Dict.; **water mass** *Oceanogr.*, a large body of sea water that remains distinguished by its temperature and salinity from surrounding water; **water park,** a recreational area comprising stretches of fresh water that may be used for boating, etc.; **water-polo,** a game played by teams of swimmers, usu. in a rectangular pool with goal-posts, using a ball similar to a football; **water-power** (earlier example); **water-privilege** (earlier example); **water-repellent** *a.*, not easily penetrated by water though porous; *sb.*, an agent conferring this property; so **water-repellency; water-resistant** *a.*, waterproof or water-repellent; so **water-resistance; water resources,** natural sources of water available for man's use; freq. *attrib.* (in *sing.* or *pl.*); **water-rights** (also in *sing.*), the right to the use of water in a tract of land (cf. *water-privilege* (*a*) in Dict.); **water-sail,** (*b*) a sail lowered into the water to act as a sea anchor; **water-shear, -shier** (earlier example); **water silk,** watered silk (see WATERED *ppl. a.* 5); a garment of this material; also *fig.*; **water-softener,** an apparatus for making hard water soft by chemical means; also, a chemical used for this purpose; hence **water-softening** *vbl. sb.* and *ppl. a.*; **water-soluble** *a.*, soluble in water; so **water-solubility; water-splash** (earlier example); **water-spot** *v. intr.*, of fabric: to be liable to show permanently any mark made on it by a drop of water; hence **water-spotting** *vbl. sb.*, the condition of showing such a mark; **water sprout** = WATER-SHOOT 1 in Dict. and Suppl.; **water-stain,** (*a*) a stain made on a surface by contact with water; (*b*) (see quot. 1940); **water-stop:** restrict † to sense in Dict. and add: (*b*) a place where a traveller or a train may stop for water; (*c*) a sealant to prevent water from leaking through joints (see quot. 1951); **water taxi,** a small boat used for casual passenger traffic on rivers, canals, etc.; **water toothpick** = *water-pick* (see *WATER PIK); **water-torture,** a form of torture in which the victim is made to endure an incessant drip of water on the head (see also quot. 1928); also *fig.*; **water treatment,** (*a*) = WATER-CURE; (*b*) = *water torture* above; **water-tube,** (*b*) each of the tubes carrying water through a water-tube boiler; **water-tube boiler,** delete 'marine'; (further example); **water tunnel** (see quot. 1969); **water-wagon,** (*a*): for *U.S.* read orig. *U.S.* and add later examples of *slang* use (cf. *WAGON, WAGGON *sb.* 10* b).

1949 *Sci. Digest* Dec. 93 Water-base paints have been in use for years, but in the past they could not be washed without coming off. **1975** *McGraw-Hill Yearbk. Sci. & Technol.* 300/2 Because of the cost of oil-base drilling fluids.., research is continuing so that water-base drilling fluids that can provide the properties needed..can be developed. **1955** *Sci. News Let.* 15 Jan. 37/2 The new big swept-wing plane..was described as a 'truly water-based aircraft' capable of operating in high waves and marginal sea conditions. **1981** *Sci. Amer.* Aug. 85/1 Oil-based graphites tend to give off fumes, and so the latest trend in the forging industry is toward the use of water-based graphites. **1897** Water body [see *sheet-flood* s.v. *SHEET *sb.*[1] 12 b]. **1974** R. H. BRITTON in R. Goodier *Natural Environment of Shetland* 123 The most abundant type of standing waterbody on Shetland, (accounting for 27·4% of the total), is a dystrophic loch of area less than 1 hectare. **1975** *Sci. Amer.* June 88/1 (Advt.), There are many excellent shots of the planes in action, 2 of which are shown here water-bombing the blaze. **1961** *Canada Month* 6 Oct. 42/3 The Grove and Tsus fires..could have been kept small if water bombers and helicopters had been available from the beginning. **1975** *Globe & Mail* (Toronto) 20 Aug. 8/6 He said 40 ministry firefighters, another force of 48 junior rangers,..a ministry water bomber and commercial aircraft..are all being used. **1959** *Time* (Canada ed.) 17 Aug. 13/3 Ontario has a new gadget that makes water-bombing more efficient than ever: snorkel-like water intakes on tanks attached to the aircraft floats that enable the planes to load up as they taxi along lake surfaces. **1859** *Harper's Mag.* Apr. 712/1 The 'water-boy' in his first round found me standing by the stove. **1903** *Congress. Directory* 116 He assisted himself in securing an education by working as a 'water boy' on the railroad. **1965** J. A. MICHENER *Source* (1966) 408 Trumpeters, drummers, waterboys and cooks followed in a compact nest, protected by many soldiers, and not until this stupendous preamble had passed did the actual fighting men appear. **1972** J. MOSEDALE *Football* viii. 106 Hubbard was convinced that Dobie was illegally sending in plays by arranging cups on the water tray. He kicked over the tray every time the water boy came on the field. **1979** P. THEROUX *Old Patagonian Express* xii. 185 Praising the quarterback, mocking the water-boy. **1929** A. P. HERBERT in *Times* 16 Nov. 8/1 Let no one tell us that the Londoner 'does not want' the water-bus. There was not much evidence that he wanted the Tubes..before he got them. **1940** *Economist* 21 Sept. 368/2 The waterbus service, which London Transport has been running..between Westminster and Woolwich and Greenwich, has won a popularity... It is an emergency experiment that may survive both air-raids and the war itself. **1981** T. HOLME *Funeral of Gondolas* i. 9 The Rialto Bridge humped regally over the Grand Canal... A water-bus ..churned water in mid-stream. **1964** L. DEIGHTON *Funeral in Berlin* xlii. 251 An American M.P. shouted, 'You want a goddam water-cannon to wash you across the sidewalk, fella?' **1982** *Listener* 23 & 30 Dec. 5/3 People had begun to take to the streets, defying martial law, tear-gas, water-cannon and bullets. **1898** *Barbados Freight Rep.* in F. Holm-Petersen *Fra Seil til Diesel* (1951) I. 335 Our Water Clerk will meet the Vessels on their entering the bay. **1973** P. THEROUX *Saint Jack* xiii. 156, I knew my job as a water-clerk..and pored over the shipping pages of the *Straits Times*. **1946** *Nature* 21 Dec. 899/2 Vitamin-like substances..in cells with assumed water-contents of 80 per cent. **1957** G. E. HUTCHINSON *Treat. Limnol.* I. iv. 222 The water content of the major part of the lithosphere..is unknown. **1969** Water content [see *water-holding*, sense 25 a above]. **1909** WEBSTER, Water-cool v.t. **1915** W. E. DOMMETT *Submarine Vessels* v. 50 Due to the high temperatures, it is necessary to not only water-cool the cylinder, but also to cool the piston. **1971** *Physics Bull.* July 401/2 The essential difference.. is well illustrated in this example by the need to water-cool the measuring head because of high levels of radiant heat. **1905** Water-cooled [in Dict., sense 26 a]. **1984** B. FRANCIS *AA Car Duffer's Guide* 63/1 Modern water-cooled systems incorporate a thermostat. **1984** *Mining Jrnl.* 4 May 297 China has also expressed interest in Japan's PNC heavy water moderated, light water-cooled advanced thermal reactor. **1846** *Catholic Herald* (Philadelphia) 30 Aug. 272/4 Refrigerators, water coolers, and filterers. **1899** [in Dict., sense 25 c]. **1955** R. P. JHABVALA *To whom she Will* xxiii. 168 An earthenware water-cooler. **1969** *Canad. Antiques Collector* Aug. 6/1 (Advt.), Salt glazed water cooler with incised blue decoration... Each side has riderless horse. **1978** *Amer. Speech* LIII. 5 Slang..is inexact and meaningless, but these are characteristics it shares with much of standard English, as fifteen minutes at a water cooler or a political rally will show. **1910** R. FERRIS *How it Flies* x. 198 To keep the cylinder cool enough to be serviceable, two methods are in use: the air-cooling system and the water-cooling system. **1934** *Physical Rev.* XLV. 608/1 At 3,000,000 volts, ion currents of $\frac{1}{2}$ microampere are readily obtainable and it is probable that water-cooling of the accelerators and the bombarded targets will result in considerably larger utilizable currents. **1985** *Dirt Bike* Mar. 39/2 They wanted watercooling for reasons of reliability. **1907** H. BROWN *Irrigation* vi. 120 A pressure due to $6\frac{3}{4}$ feet head of water, of which 3 feet is balanced by the water cushion on the floor. **1955** S. LELIAVSKY *Irrigation & Hydraulic Design* I. ii. 270 Finally, we must mention the method of scour prevention which in earlier times was known as the 'stilling pool' or the 'water cushion', and which is now described..as the 'cistern'. **1972** L. M. HARRIS *Introd. Deepwater Floating Drilling Operations* xvi. 169 The larger the water cushion [in a well], the larger the surface pressures required to unload it. **1938** H. S. GIBSON in A. E. Dunstan et al. *Sci. of Petroleum* I. xi. 538/1 The employment of the water drive as a process has received considerable attention. **1973** C. J. MAY in Hobson & Pohl *Mod. Petroleum Technol.* (ed. 4) v. 165 When recovery was mostly by water drive, the percentage extraction varied from 24 to 78, and the recovery per acre-foot of sand from 242 to 1165 brl. **1923** C. M. BARBEAU *Indian Days in Canad. Rockies* 120 A deep sound from the seer's lodge startled the people, a sound like that of a large water drum. **1955** M. BARBEAU *Tree of Dreams* 95 The thumping of water drums at times startled the bleak places, now covered with a mantle of snow. **1970** P. OLIVER *Savannah Syncopators* 106 Outstanding xylophone orchestras, *kora*, water-drum, harp and harp-lute. **1973** A. H. WHITEFORD *North Amer. Indian Arts* 103 The Iroquois also made water drums with plugs to change the level of the water and the tone of the drum. **1946** M. C. SELF *Horseman's Encycl.* 429 Automatic water fountains are most useful for the stable. **1975** 'E. LATHEN' *By Hook or by Crook* xxi. 194 A salt-tablet dispenser beside every water fountain. **1899** S. R. HOLE *Our Gardens* x. 214 Where there are pools of water..you may have the beautiful Water Garden. **1938** F. PERRY *Water Gardening* p. ix, When I first took an interest in water gardening the dearth of literature upon the subject was the cause of much disappointment. **1982** B. CHATTO *Damp Garden* vi. 98 Water gardening on the landscaping scale is quite a different affair from the marginal plantings. *a* **1776** DUCHESS OF NORTHUMBERLAND *Diary* in *Country Life* (1974) 7 Feb. 251/3 The Water Gilt Locks..were made at Birmingham. **1940** *Jrnl. R. Aeronaut. Soc.* XLIV. 590 Will water injection become practical? **1943** *Oil & Gas Jrnl.* 11 Nov. 230/2 Because an adequate low-cost water supply was available at Midway, the economic possibilities of experimental water injection were clear. **1947** *Shell Aviation News* No. 106. 21/1 If required water injection apparatus can be included to give additional power for take-off. **1970** M. SMITH *Aviation Fuels* ix. 62 By means of water injection, heat is taken away from the cylinders, pistons and exhaust valves, and removed out of harm's way by the steam so formed, which discharges from the exhaust system. **1982** Water injection [see *WATER-FLOODING *vbl. sb.*]. **1946** *Nature* 16 Nov. 709/2 The black, water-insoluble pigment. **1937** *Amer. Jrnl. Physiol.* CXIX. 557 The serum sodium and chloride levels are low in the water intoxicated animal. **1922** *Physiol. Rev.* II. 158 (*heading*) The effects of excessive ingestion: water intoxication. **1974** PASSMORE & ROBSON *Compan. Med. Stud.* III. xlix. 8/2 Water intoxication should be considered in any patient with unexplained cerebral dysfunction, particularly if the individual has recently undergone an operation. **1898** J. MACMANUS *Bend of Road* 118 The wather-keeper..was shot be the poochers on the Dhrowes river. **1920** D. H. LAWRENCE *Women in Love* xiv. 202 He called at the water-keeper's cottage and took the key of the sluice. **1959** *New Biol.* XXIX. 14 Any given bed of water-lain rock is usually formed of relatively uniform particles; wind-deposited sands show a similar sorting. **1977** A. HALLAM *Planet Earth* 55/1 The word 'dune' is often thought to refer only to those forms built by wind, but it is now used equally for water-lain structures. **1912** MURRAY & HJORT *Depths of Ocean* v. 261 From a study of the distribution of salinity and temperature the average direction of the drift of the water-masses may be deduced. **1976** *Nature* 19 Feb. 606/2 No influx of the Atlantic watermass into northeast Icelandic waters was observed in June 1975. **1928** *Observer* 15 July 12 In the north-eastern workmen's district of Floridsdorf,..a new 'water-park' has just been opened. It..includes two ponds, connected by canals, so that some kind of 'little Venice' has been created. **1972** *Daily Tel.* 4 Sept. 8 A national water park that would include the Norfolk Broads and the Fens is being planned. **1884** Water polo [see POLO 2]. **1888** [in Dict. s.v. WATER *sb.* 24 n]. **1919** W. T. GRENFELL *Labrador Doctor* iii. 61 Our water polo games were also a great feature here, the water being warm. **1923** T. SACHS *Compl. Swimmer* (ed. 2) 151 Water polo differs from other games, not only in the irrelevancy of its name, but also in being a game that was made to order. **1980** *Guinness Bk. Records* 334/2 Water Polo was developed in England as 'Water Soccer' in 1869. **1817** M. BIRKBECK *Notes Journey Amer.* 119 Water-mills, or, in defect of water-power, steam-mills rise on the nearest navigable stream. **1804** *New Hampshire Probate Rec.* (1916) III. 755 We set off to Deborah Shackford,..the Water Privilege belonging to said Estate. **1942** *Chem. Abstr.* XXXVI. 8428/1 (Index), Water repellency. (*See also* Waterproofness.) **1955** *Industr. & Engin. Chem.* Sept. 1980/1 Some [finishes] add functional qualities, such as water repellency and shrink resistance. **1972** *McGraw-Hill Yearbk. Sci. & Technol.* 217/2 Water birds..were generally regarded as having attained perfection in water repellency. **1922** *Encycl. Brit.* XXX. 59/1 The surface of the dope should be water-repellent. **1952** R. A. PINGREE in H. C. Speel *Textile Chemicals & Auxiliaries* xx. 408 An acetate rayon fabric may tolerate a water repellent which is unacceptable to either viscose rayon or cotton. **1974** P. DE VRIES *Glory of Hummingbird* (1975) xv. 231 Testing a line of water-repellent trenchcoats. **1980** GOHL & VILENSKY *Textile Sci.* vii. 132 Water repellent finishes can be divided into two categories: 1. water-proof finishes... 2. water resistant finishes which delay the absorption and penetration of water and..allow a degree of permeability to air. **1935** C. ELLIS *Chem. Synthetic Resins* I. xxxi. 656 A variation of this method, designed to improve the water-resistance of the resins. **1966** *McGraw-Hill Encycl. Sci. & Technol.* XIII. 541/1 Linseed oil..was used to impart water- and weather-resistance. **1934** WEBSTER, Water-resistant. **1946** *Nature* 19 Oct. 562/2 The water-proofing of soft fibre boards, surface treatment with a paraffin wax emulsion giving a water-resistant surface. **1971** C. BONINGTON *Annapurna South Face* 243 For high-altitude work it is not essential that it [*sc.* a garment] should be waterproof, but it needs to be water-resistant. **1980** Water-resistant [see *water-repellent* adj. and sb. above]. **1913** W. MCCULLOH *Conservation of Water* v. 99 The work done by the State of New York toward the..conservation of her water resources is an exemplification of what may be done by..other states. **1971** P. GRESSWELL *Environment* 218 Twenty-nine River Authorities..are responsible for husbanding the water resources of entire river basins, from springs and streams to final exit into the sea. **1976** *National Observer* (U.S.) 10 Apr. 1/3 A water-resources engineer with the World Bank. **1980** *Jrnl. R. Soc. Arts* Feb. 129/2 Workshops dealt with subjects ranging from water resource management to human resource management. **1793** *Columbian Museum* (Philadelphia) Jan. 16 The purchase of the land, including the farm buildings..and water rights, *&c.* would probably be at fifteen dollars per acre. **1891** R. WALLACE *Rural Econ. Austral. & N.Z.* xiii. 213 The question of water-right is also one urgently demanding legislation in Victoria. **1920** W. H. MALLOCK *Mem. Life & Lit.* xii. 175 He would..have had to buy from the neighbouring peasants certain way-leaves and water-rights. **1950** *N.Y. Times* 20 Apr. 1/3 He also said that bill threatened their water rights. **1925** A. B. ARMITAGE *Cadet to Commodore* 15 We dropped down on the tide, aided by a large watersail over the stern, to Garden Reach. **1933** P. MITCHELL *Deep Water* 201 [At Calcutta] the mud pilot..brought with him a water sail, like a small royal with the foot weighted and a rope fastened to each corner; this was lowered over the stern into the water. **1769** A. MENZIES *Rep. to Commissioners for Annexed Estates* (1973) 83 There is not only soil but climate to fight against, as it lies within half a mile of the water shire of Scotland. **1852** QUEEN VICTORIA *Jrnl.* 10 Sept. (1980) 74, I wore a white bonnet, a grey water silk, and..my plaid scarf over my shoulder. **1926** *Glasgow Herald* 1 Apr. 8/4 The copies are bound in magnificent leather volumes with sheets of water-silks

1953 C. DAY LEWIS *Italian Visit* iv. 47 Rosetted oxen move..The loose-kneed watersilk gait of Priestesses vowed to Love. **1906** *Engineering* 21 Dec. 834/2 In this combined grease-eliminator and make-up-water-softener there is, we understand, very little matter precipitated. **1930** L. MUNDAY *Mounty's Wife* xvii. 207 This has since been all changed owing to the installation of water softeners. **1974** *Encycl. Brit. Micropædia* X. 575/2 Water softeners usually consist of zeolite or an ion-exchange resin in a tank connected directly into the water system. **1974** *Trade Names Dict.* I. 85/1 Calgonite—Water softener. **1909** *Cent. Dict.* Suppl. 1435/3 Other types of water-softening machines employ the same general principles. **1929** A. R. MARTIN *Water Softening: Base-Exchange or Zeolite Process* 6 The base-exchange process for water softening should be considered in relation to the quality of the water to be softened. **1964** N. G. CLARK *Mod. Org. Chem.* xii. 249 It [*sc.* ethylene diamine] is used as a solvent, and as an intermediate for agricultural chemicals and 'water-softening' agents. **1979** *Jrnl. R. Soc. Arts* Dec. 59/1 Presumably water-solubility is the property which militates against the accumulation of sizeable deposits of potash (and soda) at, or near, the Earth's surface. **1922** Water-soluble [see *fat-soluble* adj. s.v. *FAT *sb.*² 6 c]. **1978** *N.Y. Times* 30 Mar. c7/4 Keep feeding lettuce with a weak application of water-soluble plant food. **1835** DICKENS *Let.* 18 Dec. (1965) I. 109 Our driver..ingeniously drove the party into a 'water-splash'. **1950** *N.Z. Jrnl. Agric.* Feb. 193/2 Delustred acetate rayons also water spot very readily; therefore,.. they should never be sprinkled with water and ironed directly, or glazed patches which are difficult to remove will be formed. **1964** *McCall's Sewing* viii. 118/1 Test a scrap of your fabric first to be sure that it does not water-spot. *Ibid.* 118/2 Press [silk] with..a piece of tissue paper next to the fabric to prevent water-spotting. **1944** U. P. HEDRICK *Fruits for Home Garden* vi. 51 Such shoots are called suckers, or water-sprouts, and numbers of them are deleterious. **1976** *Yankee* Apr. 137/2 Thinning out old watersprouts and suckers will promote better fruiting. **1913** E. F. BENSON *Thorley Weir* i. 26 There was something so completely satisfying and suitable in this rough river-dress that he would not have added any embellishment to it, nor have expunged a single water-stain or sun-bleach. **1940** *Chambers's Techn. Dict.* 901/2 *Water stain*.., a stain for wood, consisting of colouring matter dissolved in water. **1966** A. W. LEWIS *Gloss. Woodworking Terms* 114 *Water stain*, colouring matter or dyes dissolved in water and used to stain wood to the required shade. **1972** *Gloss. Terms Timber* (*B.S.I.*) 16 *Water stain*, discoloration caused by water coming into contact with the surface of the converted timber. **1912** *Chambers's Jrnl.* Apr. 220/2 The towns that cluster about these desert 'water-stops'. **1945** F. H. HUBBARD *Railroad Avenue* ii. 9 Consolidation engines have enormous tenders, but the water stops on Casey's division were far apart, and the water in his tank often would drop rather low if the engine were hauling a heavy train. **1951** *Archit. Rev.* CX. 345 (Advt.), The problem of making watertight expansion joints in flat concrete roofs can be solved by the use of Expandite rubber waterstops. These waterstops were developed in the first place for sealing joints in hydraulic structures and are widely used by hydraulic engineers. **1968** *Punch* 18 Dec. 873/1 My wife keeps urging me to diversify into coolants, sealants, waterstops, mastics and corrosion inhibitors. **1928** *Observer* 8 Apr. 6 A Budapest company has just been granted permission.. to place water-taxis for hire on the Danube. **1974** LD. MANCROFT *Chinaman in Bath* xxxix. 182 The water-taxis which could do so much to ease London's traffic problems. **1978** *New York* 3 Apr. 12/1 (Advt.), Water taxis across our incredibly blue waters to other islands. **1976** *National Observer* (U.S.) 3 July 13/6 (Advt.), Portable water toothpick for travel and the office. **1928** G. B. SHAW *Intelligent Woman's Guide Socialism* lxxxi. 415 The water torture of the Inquisition, in which the fluid was poured down the victims' throats until they were bloated to death. **1946** 'R. WEST' *Train of Powder* (1955) 8 Nuremberg..was also the water-torture, boredom falling drop by drop on the same spot on the soul. **1974** L. DEIGHTON *Spy Story* x. 105 What am I supposed to do, give them the water torture? **1976** *Times* 30 Aug. 8/5 Any individual.. is worn down by the Chinese water torture of daily stress. **1983** *Daily Tel.* 12 May 4/8 A former county sheriff..and three former deputies were charged in Houston with using water torture to extract confessions from prisoners. **1862** M. D. COLT *Went to Kansas* 197 The homeopathic physician was called to see her yesterday, so she is under his treatment, while I have the privilege of giving her all the water treatment I choose. **1966** 'G. BLACK' *You want to die, Johnny?* x. 180 That character who had apologised to himself for using the water treatment on Lee Wat. *a* **1877** KNIGHT *Dict. Mech.* III. 2646/2 When the fire passes *through* the tubes, they are properly flues. The term is, however, applied to pipes, whether water-tubes or fire-tubes, below a certain diameter. **1963** *Times* 24 May (Suppl.) p. iv/7 It had 64 Babcock and Wilcox watertube boilers and eight sets of turbines coupled to three-phase 33⅓-cycle alternators generating at 11,000 volts. **1971** B. SCHARF *Engin. & its Lang.* xiv. 204 In forced circulation boilers there is no need for the boiler drum to be above the water tubes. **1940** H. E. BAUGHMAN *Aviation Dict.* 187/2 *Water Tunnel*, a device similar to a wind tunnel, but using water as the fluid in which models are tested. **1965** *New Scientist* 5 Aug. 333/2 The commissioning..of the..outdoor test tank, and the impending completion of a flume (water tunnel), equips Hovercraft Development Limited with an entire range of skirt-testing apparatus. **1969** *Gloss. Aeronaut. & Astronaut. Terms* (*B.S.I.*) iv. 18 *Water tunnel*, an apparatus for producing a controlled stream of water or other liquid for fluid dynamic experiments. **1927** *Daily Express* 3 Feb. 5/2 'Have a drink,' said Roger.., but Red stayed his hand at the decanter. 'Water-wagon?' asked Roger, surprised. **1928** G. B. SHAW *Intelligent Woman's Guide Socialism* lxxix. 397 The vast majority of modern drinkers..do not miss the extra efficiency they would enjoy on the water wagon. **1934** *Bulletin* (Sydney) 23 May 41/2 Excuse Harrie drinking soft stuff... He's on the water-waggon at present. **1971** R. DENTRY *Encounter at Kharmel* xii. 216 What, no grog? Are you supposed to be on the water waggon, skip?

30. water-moccasin, for '(see MOCCASIN 3)' read: a venomous aquatic pit viper, *Agkistrodon piscivorus*, found in the southern United States; also, one of several harmless water snakes resembling *A. piscivorus*; = *cottonmouth* s.v. COTTON *sb.*¹ 10 and MOCCASIN 3; **water mongoose,** a dark brown mongoose, *Atilax paludinosus*, found in marshes and near rivers in central and southern Africa; **water monitor** = *Nile monitor* s.v. *NILE; **water-skater** = *water-strider* below; **water-strider** = *pond-skater* s.v. *POND *sb.* 4; **water tortoise,** an aquatic tortoise of the family Pelomedusidæ, native to Africa or South America, esp. *Pelomedusa subrufa*.

1821 T. NUTTALL *Jrnl. Trav. Arkansa* ix. 216 The other frequents water, and is called the water-mockasin. **1842, 1853** [see MOCCASIN 3]. **1884** 'MARK TWAIN' *Huck. Finn* xviii. 169 If you'll come down into de swamp I'll show you a whole stack of water-moccasins. **1931** [see *COPPERHEAD 1b]. **1976** *National Observer* (U.S.) 7 Aug. 8/5 Most of his patients have been bitten by one of the three pit vipers—rattlesnakes, copperhead moccasins, or water moccasins. **1919** F. W. FITZSIMONS *Nat. Hist. S. Afr.: Mammals* II. 26 The Water Mungoose is common throughout South Africa, and extends north as far as the Equator. **1971** *Stand. Encycl. S. Afr.* III. 246/2 The marsh or water mongoose..inhabits thick vegetation along river-banks and marshes over the greater part of Africa south of the Sahara. **1947** J. STEVENSON-HAMILTON *Wild Life S. Afr.* xxxv. 316 *Varanus niloticus*, or the water monitor, is found in reeds and rocks, close to the water's edge. **1974** M. HASTINGS *Dragon Island* v. 47 The water monitor can grow to more than seven feet. **1941** STEINBECK & RICKETTS *Sea of Cortez* xvi. 164 We had sat beside the little pool and watched..the water-skaters. **1977** *Country Life* 26 May 1394/3 All you had to do was brush aside the green weed and the spider-like 'water skaters' and bow down to slake your thirst. **1952** J. CLEGG *Freshwater Life Brit. Isles* 197 The Pond Skaters or Water Striders..are larger creatures. **1973** Water-strider [see **pond-skater*]. **1835** A. SMITH *Diary* 11 Mar. (1939) I. 309 Water has been getting more scarce every year. They eat the water tortoise. **1935** *Discovery* Nov. 330/2 Water tortoises..lay basking on the lily pads. **1974** *Stand. Encycl. S. Afr.* X. 527/1 In Southern Africa there are both land and water tortoises.

31. *water-fruit*; **water-ash,** substitute for def.: any of several North American ash trees, esp. *Fraxinus caroliniana*; also = *box elder* s.v. BOX *sb.*¹ 3 b; (earlier and later examples); **water-blossom** = *WATER-BLOOM 2; **water-elm,** substitute for def.: = *PLANER-TREE; (examples); **water hyacinth,** an aquatic herb, *Eichhornia crassipes*, of the family Pontederiaceæ, native to tropical America and bearing large blue flowers; **water maple:** see also *red maple* s.v. RED *a.* 17 d; (earlier and later examples).

1709 J. LAWSON *New Voy. Carolina* 93 The Water-Ash is brittle. **1819** E. DANA *Geogr. Sk.* 171 The soil is.. thickly covered with timber; such as various species of oak and water ash. **1958** G. A. PETRIDES *Field Guide to Trees & Shrubs* 35 Water Ash... A small tree of southern swamps. **1884** W. PHILLIPS in *Trans. Shropshire Archæol. Soc.* VII. 285 Though the appearance of the 'water-blossom' has often been observed and examined, very little is known of the causes from which it originates. **1906** *Rep. Brit. Assoc. Adv. Sci.* 759 *Microcystis roseo-persicinus*..formed a striking pink 'water blossom'. **1820** J. C. GILLELAND *Ohio & Mississippi Pilot* 257 Water elm in marshes, generally in the rear of rich bottoms. **1903** 'O. HENRY' in *McClure's Mag.* Dec. 144/1 [I] noticed a rabbit-hawk sitting on a dead limb in a water-elm. **1930, 1976** Water-elm [see *PLANER-TREE]. **1930** T. S. ELIOT tr. *St.-J. Perse's Anabasis* 65 Eaters of insects, of water fruits. **1897** H. J. WEBBER in *Bull. U.S. Dept. Agric.: Bot.* XVIII. 13 The water hyacinth is becoming a serious menace to navigation. **1927** E. THOMPSON *Indian Day* xiv. 111 A colony of water hyacinth had rooted itself..where deep water still remained. **1979** *London Rev. Bks.* 25 Oct. 5/3 In this closing scene, the water hyacinths proceed towards the sea. **1803** A. ELLICOTT *Jrnl.* x. 284 Water maple..is met with as high as the Wabash. **1912** I. S. COBB *Back Home* 137 [The] walk..[was] shaded well all the way by water maples.

water, *v.* Add: **I. 3. a.** Also const. *in*.

1885 G. NICHOLSON *Illustr. Dict. Gardening* I. 217/2 The plants [*sc.* Brussels sprouts]..should be watered-in when planted. **1958** *Listener* 21 Aug. 275/2 By taking off well-ripened shoots..and placing three shoots in three-inch pots..watering them in..and keeping them perfectly airtight and shaded, I have got a good percentage to root. **1982** *Times* 22 May 9/4, I always like to water-in my lawn fertilizers.

II. 16. Delete † *Obs.* and add later example.

1966 M. CATTO *Bird on Wing* i. 15 He went into the lav. The Major could hear him watering.

water-bag. Add: **1. b.** *Austral.* A bag, freq. of canvas, used for carrying water, esp. on journeys in dry areas.

1892 [see *SHIRALEE]. **1903** 'T. COLLINS' *Such is Life* (1937) i. 47 Helping myself to a drink from the water-bag under the rear of Thompson's wagon. **1944** *Living off Land* iii. 57 Don't carry a reserve supply of water in a waterbag; evaporation alone can dry it all up in a few hours in hot weather. **1969** P. A. SMITH *Folklore Austral. Railwaymen* 19 The water was no good. We'd bring it out in boiling buckets and then fill the gang's water bags.

water-balance. Add: **4.** (Written *water balance*.) Equilibrium between water intake and water loss.

1922 *Physiol. Rev.* II. 158 In diabetes insipidus, the water balance is set at a level higher than normal. **1957** G. E. HUTCHINSON *Treat. Limnol.* I. iv. 228 (*heading*) Water balance of the hydrosphere and of continental surfaces. **1974** PASSMORE & ROBSON *Compan. Med. Stud.* III. xlix. 9/2 The driving force of thirst normally ensures the minimum daily intake of water needed to maintain water balance.

water-bed. Add: **3. a.** (Earlier examples.)

1844 A. N. BROWN *Let.* 28 Nov. in *Church Missionary Soc. Archives: New Zealand Mission* (MS.), Our kind Bishop had him removed to his House the day he was taken ill and planned a water bed to place him on. *c* **1848** J. R. PLANCHÉ *Extravaganzas* (1879) III. 294 And something like the sort o' bed That Dr Arnolt designates a water bed.

b. A plastic mattress filled with water, designed as an alternative to a conventional bed. Also *fig.*

1970 *Time* 7 Sept. 42 His efforts to improve it led him [*sc.* C. P. Hall] to a much splashier creation... It is the water bed. **1971** *Guardian* 5 Oct. 10/1 The water-bed is simply an ultra-sonically welded vinyl bag filled..with around 150 gallons of water, and contained in a wooden frame which rests on the floor or can be raised to conventional bed height. **1977** *Time Out* 21 Jan. 43 (*caption*) 'The Odyssey', a soft, billowing water-bed of a piece that's performed at the Albert Hall on Tuesday by no less than ten keyboard players plus tympani and vocals. **1978** J. IRVING *World according to Garp* xi. 205 Garp slumps back on the water bed,..the bed rolls like a small sea. **1984** *Listener* 19 July 17/4 (Advt.), For couples who want to get away together..4 poster beds, water beds—with whirlpool bath en suite.

water-bloom (wǭ·təɹblūm). [f. WATER *sb.* + BLOOM *sb.*¹] **1.** A flower living in water. *poet. rare.*

1820 [in Dict. s.v. WATER *sb.* 31].

2. [tr. G. *wasserblüte*.] (See quot. 1957.) Cf. *RED-WATER 4.

1927, 1948 [see *BREAKING *vbl. sb.* 2 c]. **1957** *New Biol.* XXIII. 86 'Water-bloom'..describes the discoloration of the waters of ponds and lakes, sometimes slow-flowing rivers and occasionally vast areas of the sea by a super-abundance of free-floating, microscopic, plant and, in rare cases, animal life. **1963** [see *PERIDINIAN].

waterbok. (Earlier example.)

1835 A. SMITH *Diary* 20 Sept. (1940) II. 240 The flesh coarse-grained and exactly like the flesh of the waterbok.

water bottle. Add: **4.** = *hot-water bottle* s.v. *HOT WATER 1 b.

1840 J. ROMILLY *Diary* 31 Dec. (1967) 207 Lodge burnt his leg with a water bottle & laid up. **1905** S. WEYMAN *Starvecrow Farm* xxv. 230 That was not the day of bedroom fires, or rubber water-bottles. **1929** W. FAULKNER *Sound & Fury* 334 Dilsey reached the top of the stairs and took the water bottle. 'I'll fix hit in a minute... I gwine build de fire myself.'

water-buck. (Earlier example.)

1839 W. C. HARRIS *Wild Sports S. Afr.* 186 A water buck..is about the size of an ass and of somewhat browner colour.

Waterbury (wǭ·təɹbŭri). The name of a town in Connecticut, U.S.A., used *attrib.* or *absol.* to designate a low-priced watch or clock of a type manufactured there.

1884 *Official Gaz.* (U.S. Patent Office) 6 May 526/1 *The Waterbury Watch Company*, Waterbury, Conn. Application filed July 21, 1883. 'The words "*The Waterbury*".' **1887** KIPLING *Plain Tales from Hills* (1888) 73 Platte,.. being poor, had a Waterbury watch and a plain leather guard. **1890** B. HALL *Turnover Club* 16 The Reporter drew from its resting place the Waterbury chronometer. **1893** SOMERVILLE & 'ROSS' *Vine Country* vi. 105 My cousin with some trouble disinterred the Waterbury. **1908** *Sears, Roebuck Catal.* 348/1 Our new eight-day Waterbury Clock. *c* **1909** D. H. LAWRENCE *Collier's Friday Night* (1934) iii. 76 He..takes a Waterbury watch with a brass chain from the wall beside the book-case. **1920** F. E. GREEN *Hist. Eng. Agricultural Labourer 1870–1920* IV. 93 He turned up..on Sunday with a fashionable billycock, a walking stick and a Waterbury. **1939** JOYCE *Finnegans Wake* 290 O Shee who then (4.32 M.P.,..according to all three doctors waterburies) [etc.]. **1963** C. MACKENZIE *My Life & Times* II. 42, I kept surreptitiously looking at my ten-and-sixpenny Waterbury watch.

wa·ter-cart, *v.* [f. the sb.] **a.** *trans.* To provide with water-carts. **b.** *intr.* To weep. *slang.*

1851 DICKENS in *Househ. Words* 2 Aug. 433/1 The great metropolis is..so much more water-carted..than it usually is. **1920** W. DE MORGAN *Old Man's Youth* (1921) xxix. 282 She makes believe she knew Gromp, and I know she didn't. She'd watercart.

water-colour. Add: **5.** *water-colour drawing* (earlier example), *exhibition* (earlier example).

1811 JANE AUSTEN *Let.* 25 Apr. (1952) 275 Henry has been to the Watercolour Exhibition, which open'd on Monday. **1824** J. ARROWSMITH *Let.* 19 June in J. Constable *Corr.* (1966) IV. 184, I by this post write to give directions to be sent to me with my watercolour drawings.

Hence **wa·ter-colour** *v. intr.*, to paint with water-colours; **water-colouring** *ppl. a.*

1855 D. G. Rossetti *Let.* 23 Jan. (1965) I. 239, I have been water-colouring again, somewhat against the grain. **1928** R. Fry *Let.* 4 Apr. (1972) II. 621 It was a dismal audience of retired colonel water-colourists and their water-colouring daughters. **1935** A. Huxley *Lett.* (1969) 393 Are you oiling or water-colouring or gouaching?

water-coloured, *a.* **2.** (Later example.)

a **1941** V. Woolf *Haunted House* (1943) 91 Water-coloured rings set in pearls.

water-cracker. Add: **3.** (Examples.) Now *Obs.*

1825 *Missouri Intelligencer* 4 June 3/4 Ward and Parker have just received for sale at their grocery and liquor store molasses, water crackers, [etc.]. **1899** S. T. Rorer *Bread & Bread Making* 57 It [*sc.* the dough] may be rolled out into very thin sheets, cut into square crackers, pricked with a fork, baked in a moderate oven, producing what are called Virginia biscuits or water crackers.

water-cress. Add: **3.** *water-cress sandwich, soup.*

1911 W. J. Locke *Glory of Clementina Wing* xxi. 310 He picked up from a plate a little three-cornered water-cress sandwich. **1978** P. Moyes *Who is Simon Warwick?* xii. 143 Tea had been laid out..silver teapot and milk jug, wafer-thin watercress sandwiches. **1923** W. G. R. Francillon *Good Cookery* (ed. 2) 102 (*heading*) Watercress soup. **1980** *Redbook* Oct. 234/1, I am intent on the food—water cress soup and a salad of butter lettuce.

water-cure. Add: **2.** In the Philippines, torture by forcing a person to drink large quantities of water in a short time.

1902 'Mark Twain' in *N. Amer. Rev.* May 623 The torturing of Filipinos by the awful 'water-cure'..to make them confess. **1976** *New Yorker* 3 May 96/2 The Civil Liberties Union of the Philippines..accused the police and the military of employing 'water cures' and electric shocks as well as beatings with clubs.

water-dog. **3. a.** For '† *Obs.* (? exc. dial.)' read '*Obs.* exc. *W. Afr.*' (Later example.)

1960 M. Macdonald in G. Maxwell *Ring of Bright Water* xii. 164 A Senior African joined the group. 'This be the piccin of water-dog,' he intoned.

watered, *ppl. a.* Add: **4. a.** Also, *watered-down* (now the usual form). Cf. sense 4 b in Dict.

1976 P. Cave *High Flying Birds* iv. 51 He matched Lorna glass for glass, chucking the stuff down as though it was watered-down Coke. **1978** A. Gilchrist *Cod Wars* ii. 7 A watered-down beer, unworthy of the name, is legally sold.

b. (Earlier example.)

1889 'Mark Twain' *Connecticut Yankee* iv. 55 Everybody took in all this bosh..and never smiled or seemed to notice that there was any discrepancy between these watered statistics and me.

water-engine. **1.** (Later example.)

1864 Trollope *Small Ho. at Allington* II. xi. 113 Calling for the police when there is a row in the house is like summoning the water-engines when the soot is on fire in the kitchen chimney.

water-engineer. Restrict † to sense in Dict. and add: **b.** An official charged with the management of the water-supply of a district.

1937 *Discovery* Feb. 60/2 Mr Walters, a leading water engineer.

waterer. **6.** Read: A container used for supplying water to animals or plants.

1891 [in Dict.]. **1958** *Times Lit. Suppl.* 21 Nov. p. xii/5 Would you make a plant waterer or a..pea-shooter? **1960** *Farmer & Stockbreeder* 19 Jan. (Suppl.) 31/3 With deep litter, the use of a droppings pit and waterers over it [*sc.* in a poultry house] are a further help. **1970** *Jrnl. Gen. Psychol.* Oct. 240 The food cups and waterers [for the rats] were replaced with clean containers. **1981** *Farmstead Mag.* Winter 85 (Advt.), Includes choosing proper breeds [of rabbits], housing, feeders, waterers, feeding and diets, rabbit management, disease prevention, marketing.

waterfall. Add: **5.** (Earlier and later examples.)

1848 J. H. Newman *Let.* 3 Sept. (1962) XII. 268 He..looks a striking man in his Jesuit dress, though what his cut may be with a French coat and satin waterfall I can't tell. **1914** *Lit. Digest* 22 Aug. 328/2 A waterfall..is, in addition, a scarf or necktie with long drooping ends, or a chignon with pendent curls.

6. (Earlier U.S. example.)

1859 C. C. Richards *Village Life in Amer.* (1912) 119, I wore my new waterfall for the first time.

7. In a woman's garment, a fall of material or attached decoration (orig. with reference to bustles).

1886 *Girl's Own Paper* 27 Feb. 339/3 Patterns already issued:—polonaise with waterfall back. **1925** *Dialect Notes* V. 346 *Waterfall, n.*, a form of bustle for hanging the dress round the body. **1950** *New Yorker* 25 Mar. 84/2 What she calls 'waterfalls'—cascades of bustle drapery—add interest to the backs of all types of clothes. **1970** *Trafford Spring & Summer Catal.* 4 The dress is fully lined, and a waterfall frill, edged with dainty braid, tops a gently flared skirt. **1981** *Times* 30 July 2/8 The Queen's coat and dress, with its waterfall of pleated crêpe de chine.

8. *Ceramics.* A stream of glaze material used for application to the upper surfaces of tiles (see quot. 1964). Freq. *attrib.*

1961 *Brit. Ceramics Abstracts* 197 Methods of glazing wall-tiles... The second part [deals] with the 'waterfall' process of glazing. **1964** A. E. Dodd *Dict. Ceramics* 308 *Waterfall process*, a method for the application of glaze materials to a ceramic body by mechanically conveying the ware through a continuously flowing (recirculated) vertical stream of the glaze suspension. The process is used in the glazing of wall tiles. **1967** M. Chandler *Ceramics in Mod. World* iii. 99 (*caption*) 'Waterfalling' of wall tiles. Tiles to be glazed on one side only are conveyed mechanically..through a waterfall of glaze slip that covers only their upper surfaces and edges. **1973** C. W. Parmelee *Ceramic Glazes* (ed. 3) v. 149 Each color is dried between applications and the final station applies the glaze by waterfall. *Ibid.*, Tiles are placed on a conveyor..and passed under the waterfall machine.

Hence as *v. intr.*, to tumble or cascade in the manner of a waterfall; as *v. trans.*, to cover with a stream of running liquid; so **wa·terfalled** *a.*, having a waterfall (also *fig.*); **wa·terfalling** *ppl. a.* and *vbl. sb.*

1944 G. Barker *Eros in Dogma* 34 Who has not seen, over The waterfalling hair at the shoulder of Life, Death from his own face staring out of a glass? **1957** J. Frame *Owls do Cry* (1958) xxxviii. 171 Gaping idiot mouth waterfalled with slobber. **1967** [see *waterfall 8]. **1967** M. Chandler *Ceramics in Mod. World* iii. 99 Spray that misses the articles goes onto a wall at the back of the booth that is continuously 'waterfalled'. **1968** B. Hines *Kestrel for Knave* 128 One boy posed Eros-like, and allowed a jet of water to play into his palm and waterfall out on to the tiles of the drying area. **1976** *Shooting Times & Country Mag.* 16–22 Dec. 26/2 The exotic venue was..the 1,036 acre Wild Life Park at Cricket St Thomas with the waterfalled Bedpool Lakes reposing in the partly wooded valley below. **1980** J. Gardner *Garden of Weapons* II. iv. 154 The rope ladder..dislodged, waterfalling on to the balcony.

water-flood. Add: **4.** *Oil Industry.* Water-flooding; an instance of this. Freq. *attrib.*

1928 *Trans. AIME Petroleum Div.* LXXVII. 334, I was interested..to see what the pumping problem would be if it was later decided to mine a water-flood property. **1946** *Producers Monthly* Dec. 20/1 Throughout the water flood, measurements were taken of the pressure distribution. **1977** *Offshore Engineer* Apr. 20/1 (Advt.), In waterflood and other really tough uses, the McEvoy Super Mudwonder proves better than valves B or C, or any other competitor.

wa·ter-flooding, *vbl. sb.* *Oil Industry.* [f. Water *sb.* + Flooding *vbl. sb.*] The injection of water into a reservoir rock through wells drilled for the purpose, in order to force oil into neighbouring production wells.

1928 *Trans. AIME Petroleum Div.* LXXVII. 391 Of some value in water-flooding are water analyses and..data of sand conditions. **1938** H. S. Gibson in A. E. Dunstan et al. *Sci. of Petroleum* I. xi. 535/1 In the Bradford field of Pennsylvania..water flooding as a production practice was legalized in 1921. **1940** [see *secondary *a.* 5 k]. **1961** *Economist* 2 Dec. 956/1 The..water..will be injected around the flanks of the [oil] field, and not in the centre as in most 'waterflooding' projects. **1982** D. R. Skinner *Introd. Petroleum Production* II. i. 2 The first methods of secondary recovery utilized gas injection and a primitive form of water injection—saltwater disposal. Later, water injection or secondary waterflooding became the dominant form of secondary recovery.

Waterford (wǭ·təɹfǒɹd). The name of a city in the south-east of Ireland, used *attrib.* and *absol.* to designate glassware first manufactured there in the eighteenth and nineteenth centuries, esp. drinking glasses and chandeliers.

1783 *Dublin Evening Post* 4 Oct. in M. S. D. Westropp *Irish Glass* (1920) iii. 69 Waterford Glass House. George and William Penrose having established an extensive glass manufacture in this city, their friends and the public may be supplied with all kinds of plain and cut flint glass. **1852** J. F. Maguire *Industrial Movement in Ireland* 102 The Waterford glass-house was in active work up to the year 1845, and had earned the highest reputation for its glass throughout the country. **1898** *Sale Catal.* in *Country Life* (1974) 26 Sept. 854/2 Waterford and Cork cut glass. **1917** W. J. Locke *Red Planet* xxi. 269 A precious old Waterford claret jug. **1936** M. Kennedy *Together & Apart* III. 211 Come and look at this glass... It's Waterford. **1940** J. Cary *Charley is my Darling* lx. 324 A magnificent seven-branch candlestick of Waterford glass. **1964** Mrs. L. B. Johnson *White House Diary* 25 Apr. (1970) 125, I described the Savonnerie rug, the Waterford chandelier. **1977** *Daily Colonist* (Victoria, B.C.) 26 Oct. 7/3 (Advt.), Waterford crystal, a treasure hunter's delight, now on..sale. **1978** J. Carroll *Mortal Friends* I. ii. 22 The few pieces of Waterford in the village had been loaned and were out, filled with jams and preserves.

waterfowl. Add: Also **waterfowler** *U.S.*, a hunter of wildfowl; **waterfowling** *U.S.*, the hunting of wildfowl.

1976 *National Observer* (U.S.) 27 Nov. 14/4 The appeal of hunting for even old men was best described by a 68-year-old friend and lifelong waterfowler who shared a blind with me at Izembek several years ago. **1980** *Outdoor Life* (U.S.) (Northeast ed.) Oct. 80/3 Top-quality decoys are more important in puddler hunting than any other kind of waterfowling.

Wa·tergate[3]. The name of a building in Washington D.C., containing the national headquarters of the Democratic Party, which was burgled on 17 June 1972 by persons connected with the Republican administration; used *attrib.* and *absol.* with reference to this event and the circumstances leading to the resignation of President R. M. Nixon in 1974. Also *transf.*, denoting a political or commercial scandal on a large scale.

The element *-gate* has been used in recent times, preceded by the name of a relevant person, etc., to denote an actual or alleged scandal usually of a political or commercial kind. Examples are to be found in *The Second Barnhart Dict. of New English* (1980): *Koreagate* (1976), *Lancegate* (1977), *Muldergate* (1979), etc. The formative element is also discussed in *American Speech* (1978) LIII. 215–17.

1972 *New Republic* 19 Aug. 4 The very name, 'the Watergate caper', tells how funny it is. **1972** *Time* 28 Aug. 20 By coming down hard on Mitchell, the Democrats hope they can make Watergate a devasting—and durable—campaign issue. **1973** *Freedom* 2 June 1/2 Anything the Americans do we can do better. We have produced our own miniature Watergate plus two new magic ingredients—sex and drugs. **1973** 'H. Pentecost' *Beautiful Dead* (1975) III. i. 141 That's the way it goes in any kind of criminal conspiracy to hide the truth. It's like a Watergate. More and more people become involved, more and more crimes are committed to hide an initial truth. **1974** E. Ambler *Dr. Frigo* II. 101 A Central American Watergate you want now? **1974** *Times* 27 July 15/7 Your reviewer..sums up the current Chichester production of *Oedipus Tyrannus* as a 'Theban Watergate drama'... Watergate conspiracies were..frequent in the history of classical Greece. **1976** *Washington Post* 26 Jan. A 2/6 'The news has been inundated by a financial Watergate of leaked disclosures of troubled banks and bank holding companies,' said Reuss. **1977** M. Edelman *Political Lang.* viii. 150 Watergate, the Pentagon Papers, and revelations of the deception of Congress by officials of the executive branch and by intelligence agencies have made us sensitive to lying in high places. **1980** J. Melville *Chrysanthemum Chain* 175 What about a Watergate style investigation? **1982** M. Russell *Rainblast* xiii. 125 The damage is done. Fleet Street gets the signal and..everyone's sniffing the stench of another Watergate.

Hence as *v. intr.* (and *trans.*), to take part in political conspiracy or in activities directly or indirectly associated with Watergate, as the use of hidden listening devices, concealment of corrupt activities, suppression of evidence, etc. Hence **Wa·tergater**; **Wa·tergating** *vbl. sb.*

1973 *Birmingham* (Alabama) *Post-Herald* 28 Apr. A-4/3 In the political machinery of the future we may hear of a political party 'Watergating' another party. *Ibid.* A-4/4 They will be asking the voters to remember 'Watergate', for the GOP's might be Watergating again. **1973** *Black Panther* 12 May 2/3 The issue is not how high *up* Watergate goes. The issue is how far *down* watergating goes. The bug on our telephones, and yours, is the issue. *Ibid.* 21 July 2/3 (*heading*) David Hilliard, victim of Watergaters. **1974** N. Freeling *Dressing of Diamond* 20 'And if you try to keep something from the press they're apt to be vengeful.' 'You mean Watergating.' 'Right... It's easily concluded that an effort is being made to cover something, for personal or political considerations.' **1975** G. Seymour *Harry's Game* vi. 91 Not much eavesdropping in here. Need to Watergate the place. **1976** *Publishers Weekly* 1 Mar. 9/1 'When I [*sc.* Archibald Cox] was Watergating, for instance' (this appears to be a coinage of his own, but he rolls it off the tongue as if it were common usage). **1976** *Times Lit. Suppl.* 2 July 815/2 His followers perform experiments that are sadistic, pointless, and repetitive, and are given to watergating the evidence ('Not that there was anything *wrong* on those tapes'). **1979** *N.Y. Rev. Bks.* 8 Feb. 10/4 Perhaps what Jerry Ford should have done on the day he pardoned Nixon was to pardon all the Watergaters and all the Vietnam resisters in one controversially magnanimous act.

water-hole. Add: **3.** *Astr.* The part of the radio spectrum between 1420 MHz (at which hydrogen atoms radiate) and about 1660 MHz (at which hydroxyl radicals radiate). [So called because hydrogen and hydroxyl are the constituents of water.]

1976 *Sci. News* 28 Feb. 132 Between the hydrogen and hydroxyl (OH) bands..lies the 'water hole',..which..offers a frequency less drowned in deep-space static. **1979** *Daily Tel.* 10 Nov. 11/1 Scientists have argued that..the radio water-hole will be the most logical communications medium for intelligences across the universe.

water-horse. Add: **3.** *Newfoundland.* (Earlier and later examples.)

1777 G. Cartwright *Jrnl.* 5 Aug. (1792) II. 242 Fourteen quintals of fish were washed, the water-horse was carried out, and the green fish were spread. **1966** A. R. Scammell *My Newfoundland* 49 The Blanchard women were spreading out green, waterhorse fish.

Waterhouse–Friderichsen (wǭ·təɹhaus,-frī·děriksěn). *Path.* The names of Rupert *Waterhouse* (1873–1958), English physician, and Carl *Friderichsen* (b. 1886), Danish physician, used *attrib.* to designate a fulminating meningococcal septicæmia with hæmorrhagic destruction of the adrenal cortex that occurs chiefly in children and is fatal within hours if not promptly treated.

1936 *Jrnl. Amer. Med. Assoc.* 16 May 1715/2 The disease now known as the Waterhouse-Friderichsen syndrome was recognised as an entity by Little in 1901. **1974** J. D. MAYNARD in R. M. Kirk et al. *Surgery* xii. 256 Precipitating factors [of adrenal insufficiency] are septicaemia, meningococcal meningitis (Waterhouse Friderichsen syndrome..), severe abdominal trauma, [etc.].

watering, *vbl. sb.* Add: **III. 22. watering hole,** (*a*) = WATER-HOLE 1 a; (*b*) *slang*, a place where refreshment (esp. alcohol) is available, as a bar, hotel, etc. (see also quot. 1972).

1882 Watering hole [in Dict., sense 21]. **1972** B. RODGERS *Queens' Vernacular* 209 *Watering hole* [*spot*] (Brit gay sl), neighborhood cruising locale, usually a park grounds or a bar. **1975** *Telegraph* (Brisbane) 30 Oct. 35/5 The Jindalee Hotel..is a great watering hole. **1981** J. BARNETT *Firing Squad* viii. 77 'I always visit a watering hole on the way home... Cheers.' Palmer took a slow drink. **1984** *Gainesville* (Florida) *Sun* 30 Mar. 1D/5 In a simpler time, players and fans mingled at local watering holes, drinking beers together and becoming friends.

wateringly, *adv.* (Later example.)

1967 P. WHITE in *Coast to Coast 1965–6* 227 She.. gasped, looking wateringly at the bundle.

watering-place. 3. b. (Earlier example.)

1817 JANE AUSTEN *Sanditon* vi, in *Minor Works* (1954) 389 The very quietest part of a Watering-place Day.

waterish, *a.* **10.** Delete † *Obs.* and add later U.S. example.

1832 J. P. KENNEDY *Swallow Barn* I. xxvii. 283 His constitution resembles that waterish gravelly soil you see sometimes around a spring.

waterless, *a.* Add: **c.** Of processes, apparatus, etc.: employing or needing no water.

1930 *Engineering* 6 June 742/3 One advantage of the waterless gasholder was found to be the absence of a succession of sudden increases and decreases in pressure. **1951** *Good Housek. Home Encycl.* 313/2 The waterless cooker consists of a fairly deep aluminium pan, which is divided into compartments. **1971** *British Printer* Aug. 80/2 The need to maintain a critical ink-water balance.. may be overcome by the development of waterless offset-litho.

waterlog, *v.* Add: **1.** Also *intr.* for *pass.*

1780 in Laughton & Heddon *Great Storms* (1927) v. 109 The ship began to waterlog.

2. Also *intr.* for *pass.*

1950 *N.Z. Jrnl. Agric.* Mar. 224/1 Heavy soils which waterlog in wet spells should be avoided, as the plants will not tolerate 'wet feet' for long.

Waterloo. Add: *to meet one's Waterloo* (examples).

1859 W. PHILLIPS *Lesson of Hour* 11 Every man meets his Waterloo at last. **1905** A. CONAN DOYLE *Return of Sherlock Holmes* 356 We have not yet met our Waterloo, Watson, but this is our Marengo. **1961** C. MCCULLERS *Clock without Hands* iii. 67, I felt right then and there I had met my Waterloo. **1982** *Times* 20 Oct. 19/6 The main fount of the economic nightmare now engulfing the world has met with its Waterloo.

c. Waterloo ball, a frivolous entertainment preceding a serious occurrence (with reference to a ball given in Brussels by the Duchess of Richmond on the eve of the Battle of Waterloo); **Waterloo church** (see quots. 1938, 1961); **Waterloo cracker** (earlier example); **Waterloo Cup,** in Coursing, a race held annually at Altcar, near Liverpool.

1954 P. TOYNBEE *Friends Apart* xi. 132, I now see these dances as a succession of Waterloo Balls, a rapturously gay company, rapturously doomed. **1968** *Listener* 11 July 44/3 Is it a Waterloo Ball we are invited to watch, a permanent party on the eve of great events? **1938** B. F. L. CLARKE *Church Builders of 19th C.* ii. 24 In 1828 the Church Building Society was incorporated by Parliament. The same Act abolished Church Briefs... The churches built as the result of the Act were officially known as the Commissioners' Churches; the general public called them Waterloo Churches. **1961** M. H. PORT *Six Hundred New Churches* ii. 28 The popular misnomer, 'Waterloo Churches', became applied to those built with the aid of the first parliamentary grant. [*Note*] The term is sometimes applied only to the four churches built in the old parish of Lambeth (St John, Waterloo Bridge Road; St Luke, Norwood; St Mark, Kennington; St Matthew, Brixton). This may originate from St John's having been commonly termed..'Waterloo Church', which refers, of course, to its site. **1972** N. PEVSNER *Some Archit. Writers 19th c.* v. 29 This was the heyday of the Greek Revival and the so-called Waterloo churches. **1833** CARLYLE *Sart. Res.* in *Fraser's Mag.* Nov. 583/2 What vehicle of that sort have we, except *Fraser's Magazine?* A vehicle all strewed (figuratively speaking) with the maddest Waterloo-Crackers. **1836** *Bell's Life* 20 Mar. 3/5 *Waterloo Cup*, eight dogs...Deciding course.—Melanie beat Unicus, and won the Cup. **1898** [see STAKE *sb.*[2] 3]. **1939** R. GODDEN *Black Narcissus* xx. 182 Call in your mad dog, Clo. Is it the Waterloo Cup you've entered it for? **1983** *Times* 3 Mar. 3/2 More than 300 demonstrators yesterday disrupted the second day of the Waterloo Cup hare coursing meeting in Lydiate Field, Lancashire.

wa·terly, *adv. rare.* [f. WATER *sb.* + -LY[2].] After the manner of water.

1918 D. H. LAWRENCE *New Poems* 62 You undine-clear and pearly, soullessly cool And waterly The pool for my limbs to fathom.

water-mark, watermark, *sb.* Add: **6.** *watermark disease*, a disease of the cricket-bat willow, *Salix alba* var. *cœrulea*, caused by the bacterium *Erwinia salicis* and producing dying-back in the crown of the tree and stains in the wood.

1924 W. R. DAY in *Oxf. Forestry Mem.* III (*title*) The watermark disease of the cricket-bat willow. **1950** *Q. Jrnl. Forestry* XLIV. 106 Watermark disease of the cricket bat willow..spreads rapidly both upwards and downwards in the wood vessels. **1976** *Eastern Even. News* (Norwich) 9 Dec. 15/4 This was to cut the cost of services for an inspector on 'watermark disease' of willow trees.

water-miller. Delete ? *Obs.* and add later examples.

1909 E. DANIELS in *Cambr. Mod. Hist.* VI. xx. 714 Arnold, a water-miller in the neighbourhood of Züllichau in the Neumark. **1977** *New Scientist* 14 Apr. 84/1 Water millers in the 1970s can reasonably claim to be the oppressed and persecuted class among a wide range of water users.

Water Pik (wǭ·təɹ pik). Also **Water-Pik, water-pick.** A device for cleaning the teeth by directing a jet of water at them.

Water Pik is a proprietary name in the U.S.

1963 *Official Gaz.* (U.S. Patent Office) 15 Oct. TM 109 Aqua-Tec Corporation, Fort Collins, Colo. Filed Dec. 14, 1962. *Water Pik.* For readily portable oral hygiene appliance utilizing a pulsed jet of water for massaging the gums and cleaning spaces adjacent to the teeth. First use Oct. 14, 1961. **1971** *Consumer Rep.* June 387/2 Many people incorrectly use the term *Water Pik* as a generic name for dental irrigators, but there are a number of other brands on the market. Our project included 11 electric irrigators (of which three were *Water Pik*). **1971** *Better Homes & Gardens* Nov. 136/2 To use the oral irrigating device, place water in the reservoir, hold the water pick in the mouth and turn the pick on. **1978** G. GREENE *Human Factor* I. iii. 44 He turned on his electric water-pick... 'Amusing little gadget, that of yours... I suppose it really is better than an ordinary toothbrush?' **1978** J. UPDIKE *Coup* (1979) ii. 78 Her new possessions—..mechanical beauty aids, a hair-blower and a Water-Pik—were overwhelming the little pisé-walled room.

Hence **wa·ter-pick** *v. trans.*

1976 P. DICKSON *Electronic Battlefield* i. 10 Frank was brushing and water-picking his teeth.

water-pit. Add: **c.** = WATER-HOLE 1 b. *poet.*

1920 BLUNDEN *Waggoner* 19 The great pike lies.. Watching the waterpit sheer-shelving dark.

water-plane. Add: **3.** (Earlier example.) Now *Obs.* Cf. *SEAPLANE.

1912 *Q. Rev.* July 248 With this [float] Curtiss' water-plane was the first to quit the sea under its own power.

waterproofer. Add: **2.** = WATERPROOFING *vbl. sb.* 2 b.

1909 WEBSTER, *Water-proofer*... Also, a waterproofing material, as for roofs. **1923** E. G. BLAKE *Damp Walls* xii. 173 Many of these compounds completely substantiate the claims which are made for them as integral waterproofers by the manufacturers. **1951** *Archit. Rev.* CX. 402/3 To provide a waterproof backing for external tiling Tretol liquid cement waterproofer has been used. **1974** I. H. SEELEY *Building Technol.* iv. 60/1 Colourless waterproofers can make a wall surface water-repellent and less porous, without much change in the appearance.

wa·terproofness. [f. WATERPROOF *a.* + -NESS.] The state or condition of being waterproof.

1934 in WEBSTER. **1943** P. I. SMITH *Synthetic Adhesives* iv. 48 Straight ethyl cellulose cements and ethyl modified adhesives are now being employed... They offer advantages over certain other cellulose thermo-plastic adhesives by reason of their great toughness, waterproofness and heat sealing properties. **1952** *Times* 14 Mar. 6/1 It would then become an offence to describe wrongly such qualities as 'waterproofness' or resistance to fading. **1968** G. MAXWELL *Raven seek thy Brother* xiii.163 The contact of human hand can remove the 'water-proofness' of a seabird's plumage. **1978** *Detroit Free Press* 16 Apr. E 8/3 The old style boot greases were developed during World War II for government use. Waterproofness of combat boots was the main objective.

water-rat. Add: **3.** *Grand Order of Water Rats*, a philanthropic show-business society (see quot. 1951). Also *ellipt.*, as *Water Rats.*

1910 *Era Annual* 47 July..Memorabilia of Theatrical Events... Water Rats Motor Run to Brighton, 1909. **1935** A. HADDON *Story of Music Hall* xix. 90 Elvin.. founded the Grand Order of Water Rats, which led to the institution of nearly every existing artistes' organisation. **1951** *Oxf. Compan. Theatre* 835/1 *Water Rats, the Grand Order of*, a British association of members of the music-hall profession which originated in 1889 from an up-river (Thames) party to celebrate the successes of the Water Rat, a racing pony. **1956** *Golden Jubilee Bk. Show Business* (Variety Artistes Fed.) 17/3 There is the Grand Order of Water Rats..also the 'sister' section of the Water Rats—the Lady Ratlings. **1977** T. HEALD *Just Desserts* iii. 56 He..found a large lavatory decked out in Victorian tiles, original newspaper cartoons ..and a document certifying that Escoffier Savarin Smith was a member of the Grand Order of Water Rats.

wa·ter-rot, *v. U.S.* [See ROT *v.* 4 c; cf. WATER-RET *v.*] = WATER-RET *v.* So **wa·ter-rotted** *ppl. a.*, **wa·ter-rotting** *vbl. sb.*; hence **wa·ter-rot** *sb.*

1705 *Boston News-Let.* 30 July 2/2 For Hemp Water rotted,..per Ton,..Six Pounds. **1759** *Newport* (Rhode Island) *Mercury* 8 May 1/2 Some prefer Water-rotting [for flax]. **1838** H. COLMAN *1st Rep. Agric. Mass.* (Mass. Agric. Survey) 72 The superintendent states that the water-rotted flax of Scotland is much superior to ours, which is dew-rotted. **1843** *Amer. Pioneer* II. 450 The manner of making ropes of linn bark, was to cut the bark in strips..and water-rot it in the same manner as rotting flax or hemp. **1848** *Rep. U.S. Comm. Patents 1847* 246 It is of great importance in raising flax..that the water rot and dew rot must be used together to produce a fine white fibre. **1883** R. L. ALLEN *New Amer. Farm Bk.* (rev. ed.) 252 The best plan for water rotting of hemp is in vats under cover, the water in which is kept at an equable temperature.

water sapphire. [Cf. *SAPHIR D'EAU.] **a.** A colourless variety of native sapphire (sense 1 b). **b.** A type of clear blue quartz (quot. 1829). **c.** = *SAPHIR D'EAU.

1698, etc. [in Dict. s.v. SAPPHIRE 1 b]. **1829, 1850** [in Dict. s.v. WATER *sb.* 29]. **1925, 1936** [see *SAPHIR D'EAU]. **1979** HURLBUT & SWITZER *Gemology* xiii. 182/2 Iolite is the sapphire-blue gem variety of the mineral known by mineralogists as cordierite... 'Water sapphire', or 'saphir d'eau' are misleading names early applied to the gem.

water-scape[2]**.** Delete *rare* and add further examples. Also, a picture of such scenery.

1886 G. M. HOPKINS *Lett. to R. Bridges* (1935) 240, I may be able some day to let you have a better waterscape from the Dargle or somewhere near Dublin. **1908** CHESTERTON *All Things Considered* 31 The landscape (or waterscape) of my own romantic town. **1955** R. CHURCH *Over Bridge* i. 4 His aim was to establish a *real* aquarium, with fresh water-scape scenery of..mosses, rondures, recesses, mournful weeds. **1979** *Sci. Amer.* Nov. 39/1 Good maps show the virgin waterscape, the snow depth, the detail of the complex arteries that bring the water to San Francisco and to Los Angeles.

watershed[1]**.** Add: **1.** (Earlier *fig.* example.) Also *attrib.* in *fig.* use.

1878 LONGFELLOW *Kéramos* i. 87 Midnight! the outpost of advancing day!.. The watershed of Time, from which the streams of Yesterday and To-morrow take their way. **1962** *B.B.C. Handbk.* 32 The BBC's Code of Practice on Violence, its new 9.30 p.m. watershed policy, its intention to distinguish those programmes which it thinks unsuitable, and perhaps more important, suitable for children.. show that both sides are aware of the problem. **1973** T. TOBIN *Lett. G. Ade* 2 While a journalist in Chicago, Ade became one of the more astute chroniclers of the daily preoccupations of ordinary people who were living through the 'watershed period'. **1980** *Listener* 29 May 68/3 *On the Town*, which [Gene] Kelly himself describes as a watershed picture, and which opened up the musical to location shooting.

water-shoot. 1. Delete † *Obs.* and add after root:, trunk, or main branch. (Later examples.)

1953 D. M. WRIGHT *Dwarf Fruit Trees* vi. 53 All that is necessary is the annual cutting out of..strongly growing 'water shoots'. **1965** *Sunday Mail Mag.* (Brisbane) 26 Sept. 15 Water shoots are strongly growing stems, usually sappy and developing rapidly.

wa·tersider. *Austral.* and *N.Z.* [f. WATERSIDE + -ER[1].] A dockside worker.

1914 *Evening Post* (Wellington, N.Z.) 4 Feb. 10 For some time certain sections of watersiders who term themselves loyal men have been making periodic attacks on certain officials of the harbour board. **1925** *Glasgow Herald* 28 Oct. 12 The Entor is berthed at Fremantle under a police guard, with watersiders discharging her. **1949** F. SARGESON *I saw it in my Dream* xiv. 160, I see they're having trouble with those watersiders again. **1969** *Age* (Melbourne) 24 May 3/3 The watersiders' vigilance officer ..went aboard and warned the mate that if the ship sailed she would be declared 'black' in all Australian ports. **1969** *Northern Territory News* 11 July 8/2 Darwin watersiders now officially have a guaranteed minimum wage of $200 a month, but will continue to press for permanent employment with a minimum weekly wage. **1984** *N.Z. Listener* 10–16 Mar. 22/2 There, tattooed watersiders drink away the profits of a crown and anchor session down at the wharves.

wa·ter-ski, *sb.* Also **water ski.** [SKI *sb.*] **1.** One of a pair of skis enabling the wearer to skim the surface of water when towed by a motor-boat. Cf. *SKI *sb.* 1 c.

1931 *N.Y. Times* 3 May xx. 15/4 In 1928 a young Viennese student and amateur skier named Joseph Krupka, observing a long-legged waterfly racing over the surface of a rain-barrel, conceived the idea of skiing over water as he had done over snow. That night be worked out on paper the construction of a water ski. **1931** *Times Educ. Suppl.* 5 Sept. p. i/3 A schoolmaster.. crossed the Channel..on a pair of water skis. **1952** D.

Dodge *To catch Thief* v. 149 A speedboat roared by... A man and a girl on water skis rode the wake. **1973** L. Meynell *Thirteen Trumpeters* iv. 54 I'll lay odds *damage to one pair of water skis* turns up on my bill.

2. *attrib.* (repr. *water-skiing* vbl. sb.).

1931 *N.Y. Times* 3 May xx. 15/4 The 1929 water ski champion, Herr Pribitzer of the water-ski rescue section ..has attained speeds of more than twelve miles an hour. **1955** *Sports Illustr.* 1 Aug. 27 California water-ski clothes show a penchant for dressing to match from trunks to skis. **1960** *Housewife* May 54/1, I left England..with four pairs of water-skis..to start a water-ski school. **1981** *Beautiful Brit. Columbia* Spring 44/2 Here you can rent autos, water-ski boats, [etc].

wa·ter-ski, *v.* Also **water ski.** [f. the sb.] *intr.* To skim over the surface of water on water-skis. Cf. *SKI *v.* 1 b.

1953 *Time* 19 Jan. 85/3 Aristotle Socrates Onassis is a Greek-born Argentine who water-skis in the best international circles. **1960** *Sunday Express* 3 July 19/2 What does it cost to water ski? **1971** P. Gresswell *Environment* 217 It is not possible to fish and water-ski in the same place. **1979** R. Jaffe *Class Reunion* (1980) II. x. 285 They both liked to water-ski.

wa·ter-skier. Also **water skier.** [f. prec. + -ER[1].] One who water-skis. Cf. *SKIER (*b*).

1931 *N.Y. Times* 3 May xx. 15/4 The water skier can carry about sixty pounds additional weight. **1935** *Lit. Digest* 13 Apr. 46/3 Water-skiers who are of championship caliber can hold one ski above the head and swing the free leg back and forth. **1958** X. Fielding *Corsair Country* vii. 139 He..would certainly resent its [*sc.* the mole's] present use as a landing-jetty not for galleys but for water-skiers. **1978** P. Porter *Cost of Seriousness* 34 Up river the water skiers puff and plane.

wa·ter-skiing, *vbl. sb.* Also **water skiing, ski-ing.** [f. as prec. + -ING[1].] The action of the verb, esp. as a sport. Cf. *SKI-ING *vbl. sb.* 2.

1931 *N.Y. Times* 3 May xx. 15/4 Water skiing is beginning to eclipse canoeing. **1935** *Lit. Digest* 13 April 46/3 Georges Ducros, European water-skiing champion,.. hopes to popularize his speciality here this summer. **1948** M. Murray *King & Corpse* (1949) xix. 214 Water ski-ing at night is a lot more exciting than in the daytime. **1960** *Times* 15 Aug. 12/5 (*heading*) British girl fifth in water-skiing. **1973** 'G. Black' *Bitter Tea* ii. 27 Water ski-ing equipment. .including a couple of scuba masks.

watertight, *a.* Add: **2.** (Earlier example in *sing.*)

1867 J. T. Thomson *Rambles with Philosopher* iii. 14 A shoemaker..beating time with his mallet on the hob-nails of an old *water-tight* that he was repairing.

water-washed, *pa. pple.* and *ppl. a.* (Earlier example.)

1826 J. G. Whittier *Exile's Departure* in *Poet. Wks.* (1898) 521/1 The forest-crown'd hill and the water-wash'd strand.

water-wave, *sb.* Add: **3.** (Examples.) orig. *U.S.*

1882 *Harper's Mag.* Nov. 877/2 She is pasting down her wetted hair into a semblance of the 'water-waves' of fashionable society. **1923** E. F. Wyatt *Invis. Gods* I. i. 7 His grandmother..bending over him her water waves and pearl powder. **1958** J. Cannan *And be a Villain* i. 5 Passing a clean white hand over the water-waves of his naturally fuzzy hair. **1972** *Vogue* June Special 68/2 Hair in sleek water waves, by Jean Louis David, Paris.

water-waved *ppl. a.*: also of hair: set, with water, into waves; **wa·ter-wave** *v. trans.*, to set (hair), with water, in waves.

1928 A. Huxley *Point Counter Point* xxviii. 453 She readjusted a water-waved lock of hair. **1962** E. Snow *Other Side of River* (1963) lxvii. 513 A little girl with large saucy black eyes and beribboned hair her mother must have water-waved. **1975** J. Gores *Hammet* (1976) xix. 130 Goodie had spent a dollar..to have her blond ringlets water-waved by Georgia.

wa·ter-waving, *vbl. sb.* [f. Water-wave *sb.* + -ING[1].] **1.** The wavy or 'watered' appearance imparted to silk and other fabrics by pressing two pieces together.

1894 J. E. Davis *Elem. Mod. Dressmaking* v. 94 Beetled plain linings generally show a marking like a slight water-waving on the surface.

2. A method of waving hair with water.

1925 *Daily Tel.* 13 May 20/5 (Advt.), Wanted, smart man... Must be thoroughly competent in perm. waving, Marcel and water waving. **1927** *Daily Express* 30 Nov. 13/3 She can give lessons in water waving, face massage, and chiropody. **1932** [see *finger-waving* vbl. sb. s.v. *FINGER *sb.* 15].

water-way. 4. (Earlier examples.)

1797 G. Imlay *Topogr. Descr. W. Territory N. Amer.* (ed. 3) 34 Major Willis..found 1300 yards clear water-way between the lower beaches or counter-shores of the banks on both sides of the river. **1832** J. S. Mill *Let.* 24 May in *Wks.* (1963) XII. 99 Yet if such glimpses are numerous, some general tendency shall predominate even in the few furlongs of water-way which they may chance to disclose.

wa·ter-wings, *sb. pl.* Add: **4.** Inflatable floats which may be fixed to the upper arms of persons learning to swim, in order to give increased buoyancy.

1907 *Yesterday's Shopping* (1969) 323/3 All Water Wings..support a man as easily as a boy..on just the level at which a person can swim or float comfortably. **1922** Wodehouse *Girl on Boat* v. 102 A little undersized shrimp of a fellow with a green face and ears like water-wings. **1948** 'P. Woodruff' *Whatever Dies* 151 You could take it, if you would be bold and throw away your water-wings. **1976** 'G. Black' *Moon for Killers* iii. 37 Gloria's daughter was..dressed for the water..with..a pair of water wings.

wa·ter-witching, *vbl. sb. U.S.* [f. Water-witch + -ING[1].] = Water-finding *vbl. sb.* Hence **wa·ter-witch** *v. intr. rare* (in quot. *transf.*).

1877 H. Ruede *Sod-House Days* (1937) 196 Talking with Hoot about digging wells, etc., he told me about one new neighbor, Diegel, who has a firm faith in water witching. **1947** R. Bedichek *Adv. with Texas Naturalist* x. 119, I followed for a short distance an immense sow..her nose barely skimming the sand, apparently searching for something. It turned out that she was water-witching.. for presently she began rooting. Soon her..snout unearthed a spring of crystal-clear water. **1968** S. E. Roberts *Of Us & Oxen* ii. 18 Several homesteaders..had had to dig a number of wells before striking water, even though these wells had been located by 'water-witching'. **1976** *National Observer* (U.S.) 14 Aug. 11/1 One of our neighbors practiced the art of water witching.

waterwork. Add: **3. a.** (Later examples.)

1803 M. Wilmot *Let.* 6 Aug. in *Russ. Jrnls.* (1934) I. 34 The Gardens..so extensive and so beautiful and the Water works are beyond description. **1842** W. F. Tolmie *Jrnl.* 7 May (1963) 359 As the great display of waterworks was to take place at 5, I finally decided on remaining.

b. For *nonce-use* read *rare* and add later example with reference to rain.

1931 D. L. Sayers *Five Red Herrings* xvii. 179 'It's not raining... Better than yesterday.'.. 'Tons better. Really,..you'd think they'd turned on the water-works yesterday on purpose to spoil my sketching-party.'

c. *pl.* The urinary system. *euphem.*

1902 F. W. Maitland *Let.* 6 July (1965) 249, I gather from Albutt that the immediate cause of death was, as A. put it, 'in the water works'. **1922** Joyce *Ulysses* 355 Cissy..came back with her tongue out and said uncle said his waterworks were out of order. **1959** E. Ambler *Passage of Arms* v. 124 Little scotch, lot of soda. Got to keep the old waterworks going in this climate. **1977** W. Hildick *Loop* xxix. 205 I'd been plagued for a long time..by—well—let's call it waterworks trouble.

Watford (wǫ·tfə̆ɹd). The name of a town on the N.W. edge of the London conurbation, used with allusion to the view attributed to Londoners that north of the metropolis there is nothing of any significance to English national or cultural life.

1973 G. Talbot *Ten Seconds from Now* (1974) iii. 37 A man who, until he made the journey from London, thought that woad began at Watford. **1977** *Times* 17 Jan. 13/6 As an Englishman from north of Watford I sometimes suspect that the harmony [in Turkey] is.. greater than..between different regional and social sectors in this country. **1980** D. Williams *Murder for Treasure* ii. 17 'Provincial visitors'..broadly covered anyone normally domiciled north of Watford. **1983** *Oxford Diocesan Mag.* July 13/2 The urgent need is to unite the country... This does not mean watery consensus politics. It does mean recognising that.. Britain does not end at Watford. **1984** *Sunday Tel.* 21 Oct. 9/6 Yorkshire is becoming the most militant county in England... There's the rub. The line between North and South is not just drawn at Watford. Scargill is of the South.

Watson[1] (wǫ·tsən). The name of the doctor who was the stolid, faithful assistant and foil to the detective Sherlock Holmes in the stories of A. Conan Doyle, used allusively of one who acts similarly as a stooge or audience, esp. for a detective.

1927 R. A. Knox *Three Taps* vi. 52 Watson-work meant that Angela tried to suggest new ideas to her husband under a mask of carefully assumed stupidity. **1946** D. L. Sayers *Unpopular Opinions* 188 The story is told by the detective's *fidus Achates* or (to use the modern term) his Watson. **1953** Wodehouse *Performing Flea* 18, I wonder what an oesteopath does if a patient suddenly comes apart in his hands. ('Quick, Watson, the seccotine!'). **1958** B. Hamilton *Too Much of Water* x. 228 I've been..a sort of yes-man or Watson to him. *a* **1976** A. Christie *Autobiogr.* (1977) v. v. 282, I was..tied to two people: Hercule Poirot and his Watson, Captain Hastings. **1981** Craig & Cadogan *Lady Investigates* ii. 48 Mrs Lucilla Wiggins, the 'Watson' figure in the cases of Mrs Herlock Shomes.

Watson[2] (wǫ·tsən). *Austral.* [Allegedly the name of two Australian brothers who were noted betters about the turn of the century: cf. S. J. Baker *Austral. Lang.* (ed. 2, 1966) xii. 273–4.] In catch-phr. *to bet like the Watsons*: to wager large sums.

1949 L. Glassop *Lucky Palmer* 163 Bet well ? You bet like the Watsons. **1954** T. Ronan *Vision Splendid* 76 The survey-party is chequed-up to the skies and while they've got it they'll bet like the Watsons. **1967** F. Hardy *Billy Borker yarns Again* 140 I'd bet like the Watsons meself if I had a million quid in the bank.

Watson–Crick (wǫ:tsən,kri·k). *Biochem.* The names of James D. *Watson* (b. 1928), U.S. biochemist, and Francis H. C. *Crick* (b. 1916), English biochemist, used *attrib.* with reference to the pairing of adenine with thymine (or uracil) and of guanine with cytosine in the two strands of a double helix, described by them in 1953.

1964 G. H. Haggis et al. *Introd. Molecular Biol.* ix. 229 The Watson-Crick pairs are purine-pyrimidine pairs. **1966** T. H. Jukes *Molecules & Evolution* i. 5 When cells divide and multiply, this sequence [of bases in DNA] replicates itself enzymatically through the Watson-Crick complementary pairing mechanism. **1976** *Nature* 23 Sept. 289/1 Much of the pairing at the third codon position also involves the normal Watson–Crick base pairs, A–U, and G–C, but for several codon–tRNA interactions, non-Watson–Crick pairs are clearly required.

watsonia (wǫtsōu·niă). *Bot.* Also **Watsonia.** [mod.L. (P. Miller *Gardener's Dict.* (ed. 7, 1759) s.v.), f. the name of Sir William *Watson* (1715–87), Scottish naturalist + -IA[1].] A bulbous plant of the genus of this name (family Iridaceæ), native to South Africa and bearing spikes of white, pink, or red flowers similar to gladioli.

1801 *Curtis's Bot. Mag.* XV. 533 (*heading*) Aletris-like Watsonia. **1843** M. Edgeworth *Lett. from Eng.* (1971) 595 The most beautiful flowers..Gladiolis and red and white Watsonia. **1902** L. H. Bailey *Cycl. Amer. Hort.* IV. 1971/1 Great interest has been aroused in Watsonias recently. **1948** A. Paton *Cry, Beloved Country* I. iii. 20 Here..grow the blue agapanthus, the wild watsonia, and the red-hot poker. **1971** P. M. Synge *Collins Guide to Bulbs* (ed. 2) 308 All watsonias are easily raised from seed.

Watsonian (wǫtsōu·niăn), *a.* [f. the surname *Watson* + -IAN.] Of, pertaining to, or characteristic of someone called Watson; *spec.* **a.** J. B. Watson (1878–1958), U.S. behavioural psychologist; **b.** Dr. Watson of the Sherlock Holmes stories (see *Watson[1]).

a. **1923** K. Dunlap *Old & New Viewpoints in Psychol.* (1925) ii. 54 'Behaviorism' now means the Watsonian view exclusively. **1927** B. Russell *Outl. Philos.* iii. 41 His [*sc.* the ape's] behaviour when he had once realised that one stick could be made by joining the two was scarcely Watsonian. **1928** R. Frost *Let.* 22 June (1964) 188 The logic of religion by nice gradations outside of Catholicism in Protestantism, outside of Protestantism in agnosticism, and finally outside of agnosticism in Watsonian behaviorism. **1960** [see *reinforcement 3 c]. **1968** P. McKellar *Experience & Behav.* viii. 218 The stultifying limitation which Watsonian behaviourism imposed upon psychology. **1983** *Brit. Jrnl. Psychol.* LXXIV. 301 Certain influential modern psychologists have singled out attention as an aspect of cognition that fell early to the Watsonian onslaught.

b. **1940** E. Bentley *Those Days* ix. 250 Its [*sc.* the Sherlock Holmes Society's] annual dinners..were followed by discussions on points of Watsonian chronology. **1960** *Encounter* Mar. 66/2 Just one more case of Watsonian blackmail. **1968** *Listener* 4 July 22/1 What the elements of magic in the Holmes stories were, and are, I have never seen analysed. The stilted Watsonian style of sentence structure must be one major element. **1981** Craig & Cadogan *Lady Investigates* i. 32 There is no Watsonian colleague to..assist with her cases.

watt. Add: **b. watt-second,** a unit of energy equal to one joule, being the energy consumed at a rate of one watt during one second; hence (abbreviated as) **wattsec.**

1962 *New Scientist* 18 Jan. 157/1 The term 'wattsec' is..a common one among radio engineers while 'joule' appears to be seldom used in practice. **1893** G. Kapp *Dynamos, Alternators, Transformers* ii. 42 This unit [*sc.* the erg] is also inconveniently small, and for practical purposes it is customary to employ a unit 10,000,000 times as great—namely, the 'watt-second' or 'joule'. **1981** *Sci. Amer.* Dec. 37/1 A photon with a frequency in the visible region of the electromagnetic spectrum has little energy: less than 10^{-19} joule, or watt-second.

wattage (wǫ·tĕdʒ). [f. Watt + -AGE.] **a.** An amount of electrical power, esp. the operating power of a lamp, appliance, etc., expressed in watts; *colloq.*, electricity, electrical illumination.

1903 *Electr. World & Engineer* 27 June 1095 Dividing the kilowatt-hours mentioned by said number of lamps shows an average per lamp at station of 463·8 watts, deducting from which 9 per cent. for line loss, shows a net wattage per lamp at lamp terminal of 422. **1933** *Times* 5 Dec. (Electricity Supply Suppl.) p. xxiii/1 Employing lamps of comparatively low wattage. **1953** J. Cary *Except the Lord* xviii. 81 The quivering lanterns, the jumping flames..gave an elation to our saturnalia that would not have been kindled by frigid festoons of wattage. **1962** L. Deighton *Ipcress File* xxv. 165 A light of low wattage glowed in the main hall. **1976** A. Hope *Hi-Fi Handbk.* 29 That's a fairly reasonable minimum wattage rating per channel for a stereo amplifier. **1977** *Time* 21 Nov. 49/1 This Christmas may well burn record wattage. **1984** *Verbatim* Summer 4/2 From the ceiling hang bare light bulbs of such low wattage that the interior is scarcely discernible.

b. *fig.*

1964 *Listener* 10 Dec. 952/1 Peter Cushing's stolid Churchill was thrown in the shade by the high wattage of this acting. **1980** D. Francis *Reflex* xvii. 199 She had a powerful attraction..with the full wattage switched my way.

Watteau. Add: **Watteau pleat** (earlier example).

1873 *Young Englishwoman* Oct. 490/2, I have made a Princesse dress with a Watteau pleat and flounce of eleven yards of print.

Watteauesque (wɒto͵e·sk), *a.* [f. WATTEAU + -ESQUE.] Suggestive of or in the style of Watteau.

1925 *Glasgow Herald* 25 Apr. 8/3 Opposite might hang a Watteauesque diversion representing an impossibly light and brilliantly fanciful landscape. **1966** N. MARSH *Black Beech & Honeydew* xi. 256 *Twelfth Night* seemed to work its own miracle... Feste, all frill and Watteauesque stripes, was enchantingly realised. **1974** *Country Life* 7 Feb. 257/1 Throughout the decade 1720-30 Mercier both painted and engraved Watteauesque subjects.

wattle, *sb.*[1] Add: **II. 4. d.** *wattle extract.*

1955 *Times* 30 June 18/2 The price of South African wattle extract remained the same during 1954 as it was during 1953 and 1952. **1969** T. C. THORSTENSEN *Pract. Leather Technol.* ix. 141 The main source of wattle extract is the *Acacia mollissima*, or Black Wattle.

Watusi (watū·si). Also **Watussi, Watutsi.** [Native name.] **1.** The name of a minority racial group in Rwanda and Burundi, probably of Ethiopic or Nilotic origin, which formerly dominated the majority Hutu people; a member of this group. Also *attrib.* or as *adj.* Also called *TUTSI.

1899 H. A. NESBITT tr. *P. Kollmann's Victoria Nyanza* ii. 13 None of the large cattle adorned with magnificent horns which we find everywhere else among the Wahuma and Watussi are to be noticed in Uganda. **1937** *John o'London's* 5 Feb. 765/1 The Watussi still preserve certain rites and customs analogous to those which are known to have been operative in Ancient Egypt. **1959** A. MOOREHEAD *No Room in Ark* ii. 66 The Watusi are celebrated hunters, very tall and lithe. **1960** *Guardian* 7 June 4/1 Watutsi pastoralists..are encircling the Birunga. **1976** D. TOPOLSKI *Muzungu* xv. 227 Noel was a Watutsi and had been adopted at an early age by a farmer from New Zealand.

2. (Also with small initial.) A popular dance of the 1960s. Also as *v. intr.*

1964 *Time* 20 Mar. 62/3 (*caption*) Watutsiing at Whisky à Gogo. *Ibid.*, A pretty eyeful slaps on new records and dances it all by herself. That way, it's called the Watutsi. **1965** [see *hip-swinging* adj. s.v. *HIP *sb.*[1] 4 b]. **1966** *Punch* 20 July 116/1 They..fed on lotus and daiquiri, they frugged and watutsied. **1966** T. PYNCHON *Crying of Lot 49* v. 105 Nefastis had been watching on his TV set a bunch of kids dancing some kind of a Watusi. **1966** H. NIELSON *After Midnight* (1967) xvi. 213 She could teach you to watusi and swim. **1974** *Encycl. Brit. Micropædia* X. 213/3 Dances evolved from the twist, such as the frug, the jerk, and the watusi, were invariably performed by shaking the pelvis. **1979** R. JAFFE *Class Reunion* (1980) II. vi. 244 They danced the frug, the swim, and the watusi.

Waughian (wǭ·iăn), *a.* [f. the name *Waugh* + -IAN.] Of, pertaining to, or characteristic of the English novelist Evelyn Waugh (1903–66) or his writing.

1960 *Times Lit. Suppl.* 2 Dec. 783/3 Smyth strays into 1960 from some distant Waughian era. **1976** *Ibid.* 1 Oct. 1229/4 Sniping on Firbankian and Waughian lines. **1977** *Time* 19 Dec. 11/1 A country without government? The description immediately calls to mind a Waughian Third World kingdom.

Also **Waughism** (wǭ·iz'm), (*a*) the ideas or style characteristic of Waugh, or those portrayed in his novels; (*b*) a word or expression characteristic of Waugh.

1934 [see *RUSSELLISM]. **1976** A. POWELL *Infants of Spring* x. 167 The sessions he devoted to ragging ('mocking', to use a Waughism..) were likely to take certain routine forms.

wave, *sb.* Add: **I. 2. c.** Also, one of military vehicles or aircraft.

1943 R. V. JONES *Most Secret War* (1978) xli. 382 Longer raids will always be liable to attacks on their last waves whenever fighters can fly. **1951** O. BERTHOUD tr. *Clostermann's Big Show* I. 38 The airfield at Triqueville ..was going to be bombed in force by two waves of 72 Marauders. **1982** *Daily Tel.* 12 Oct. 17/8 The fly past will take place in two waves—a slow one consisting of five formations of helicopters.., then the fixed-wing aircraft, again in five formations.

3. b. Also, a sharp increase in the extent or degree *of* some phenomenon; cf. *crime wave* s.v. *CRIME *sb.* 4.

1910 *Sat. Even. Post* 29 Oct. 46/2 A good many 'waves of crime' occur in the imagination of newspapers. **1920** *Times* 21 Jan. 12/1 The probability of a 'wave' of crime after the war has been foreseen and foretold by students of social problems. **1927** *New Republic* 21 Sept. 109/2 The Metropolitan Life Insurance Company, commenting on the alleged suicide wave among young people, reports ..that the suicide rate for the population as a whole is decreasing. **1958** W. S. CHURCHILL *Hist. Eng.-Speaking Peoples* IV. x. i. 10 Throughout the country a fresh wave of demonstrations followed. **1971** *Daily Tel.* 13 Apr. 6 The pace of dismissals is accelerating as companies strive to restore profits after the massive wave of inflation in costs and wages.

c. *the wave of the future*: the inevitable future fashion or trend; the coming thing.

1940 A. M. LINDBERGH (*title*) The wave of the future, a confession of faith. **1959** *Daily Tel.* 8 July 10/3 Mr. Khruschev, in the eyes of these critics, feels that he is riding the 'wave of the future'. **1969** M. PUZO *Godfather* I. xi. 150 The business I am in is the coming thing, the wave of the future. **1971** *Sci. Amer.* Sept. 5/2 (Advt.), Fan jets are the wave of the future. You'll find them on all the 747's. **1976** L. BERNSTEIN *Unanswered Question* v. 266 They were all, including Mahler, swept along by the mighty 'wave of the future' that Wagner, in his hyper-romantic egomania, had predicted and initiated.

d. Phr. *to make waves*: to stir up trouble, make things worse, make a fuss. orig. and chiefly *U.S.*

In quot. 1925 used in the literal sense.

[**1925** 'KIMBO' *Tropical Tales* 10 Back at the foul stinking bog Potts heard himself hailed by the well-known voice of his late father. 'Hello, sonny,..slip in gently...for the Lord's sake don't make any waves.'] **1962** A. LURIE *Love & Friendship* xiv. 277, I think it will be best if she tells him herself... After I've left. We don't want to make waves. **1972** *Publishers' Weekly* 10 Apr. 58/2 Dr. Wilkins..had just been fired from Willowbrook for allegedly making waves about conditions. **1983** *Times* 19 Feb. 11/5 He is..a solid dependable Scotsman who runs a company at a profit in an orderly fashion and doesn't make waves.

4. a. *spec.* One in the hair; also, a set that leaves the hair in waves.

1864 DICKENS *Mut. Fr.* (1865) I. I. iv. 31 Bella..employed both her hands in giving her hair an additional wave. **1866, 1895** [in Dict.]. **1895**, etc. [see *MARCEL *sb.*]. **1922** JOYCE *Ulysses* 343 Gerty's crowning glory was her wealth of wonderful hair. It was dark brown with a natural wave in it. **1925** F. SCOTT FITZGERALD *Great Gatsby* ii. 44 All the things I've got to get. A massage and a wave, and a collar for the dog. **1938** E. AMBLER *Cause for Alarm* v. 79 Prolonged steaming operations take the wave out of my hair. **1959** *Chambers's Encycl.* VI. 691/2 There are three main denominations of heat waving: the 'machine wave'..the 'machineless' wave..and the 'wireless' wave. **1973** [see *KIRBY-GRIP].

5. c. (Earlier examples.)

1760 *Phil. Trans. R. Soc.* LI. 601 A large quantity of vapour may be conceived to raise the earth in a wave, as it passes along between the strata. **1848** *Trans. R. Irish Acad.* XXI. 58 The only motion that will fulfil these conditions, is the transit of a wave of elastic compression, or of a succession of these,..through the solid substance and surface of the disturbed country.

e. *Physics.* A de Broglie wave (see *DE BROGLIE).

1924 L. DE BROGLIE in *Phil. Mag.* XLVII. 450 We are then inclined to admit that any moving body may be accompanied by a wave and that it is impossible to disjoin motion of body and propagation of wave. **1930**, etc. [see *matter wave* s.v. *MATTER *sb.*[1] 26]. **1942, 1956** [see *probability wave* s.v. *PROBABILITY 4]. **1978** D. A. DAVIES *Waves, Atoms & Solids* i. 21 In order to represent the electron by a wave, or group of waves, we require to be able to state whether the wave will show dispersion.

III. 9. a. *wave-beat, energy, -noise, -wail*; (sense 7) *wave gesture.*

1979 *East Anglian Mag.* Aug. 532/2 Four wild swans came high overhead, the chanting wave-beats of their wings making a windy threnody in the great silence of the Fen sky. **1976** *Jrnl. R. Soc. Arts* CXXIV. 729/1 The seasonal distribution of wave energy fits nicely into the pattern of energy demand, that is, more in the winter than in the summer. **1922** JOYCE *Ulysses* 512 He invokes grace from on high with large wave gestures. *Ibid.* 47 At the lacefringe of the tide he halted... His snout lifted barked at the wavenoise. **1906** HARDY *Dynasts* II. IV. viii. 185 Weary wave-wails from the clammy shore.

b. (sense *4 a) *wave-curler, -setter*; *wave-compelling, -setting* adjs.; *wave-making* sb. and adj.

1890 G. NEILSON *Trial by Combat* ix. 27 The remark presents the great Dane in a light somewhat different from that suggested by his wave-compelling attitude on the wild sea shore. **1915** R. LANKESTER *Diversions of Naturalist* 61 Specially powerful wave-compelling winds. **1931** *Lady* 26 Feb. 300/1 Fix your wave-setting combs in place. **1932** *Mod. Woman* Feb. 72/1 A perfectly easy method of keeping your hair permanently waved, set and curled at home... Wave curlers 1/- pair. **1932** *Even. Standard* 1 July 9 (Advt.), A..wavesetter in your bag is almost as good as taking your hairdresser on holiday with you. **1942** Wave-making [see *SONIC *a.* 1 b]. **1961** *Guardian* 29 Apr. 1/5 Mr. Hardy sprayed on a sweet-smelling wave-setting lotion. **1979** *United States 1980/81* (Penguin Travel Guides) 235 A resort-style motel with a lake and wave-making swimming pool.

c. *wave-white.*

1922 JOYCE *Ulysses* 11 Wavewhite wedded words shimmering on the dim tide.

e. *wave-beat, -circled, -cut, -eroded, -kissed, -rusted, -shattered, -walled, -whitened, -worn* (later examples); *wave-free, -weary*; *wave erosion.*

1843 J. R. LOWELL in *Pioneer* Jan. 40 Stands a maiden..Musing by the wave-beat strand. **1854** F. W. FABER *Oratory Hymns* 67 Angelic songs are swelling O'er earth's green fields, and ocean's wave-beat shore. **1861** M. ARNOLD in A. A. Procter *Victoria Regina* 181 The wave-kiss'd marble stair. **1878** O. WILDE *Ravenna* 14, I have wandered far From the wave-circled islands of my home. **1881** —— *Poems* 131 Be not afraid To leave this wan and wave-kissed shore. *Ibid.* 161 Some wave-shattered steep. **1885** G. K. GILBERT in *5th Ann. Rep. U.S. Geol. Survey* 84 The submerged plateau whose area records the landward progress of littoral erosion, becomes a terrace after the formative has disappeared, and, as such, requires a distinctive name. It will be called the wave-cut terrace. **1889** W. B. YEATS *Wanderings of Oisin* II. 73 And she with a wave-rusted chain was tied To two old eagles. **1892** —— *Countess Kathleen* 126 When her own people ruled in wave-worn Eri. **1901**, etc. Wave-cut [see *PLATFORM *sb.* 6 c (i)]. **1906** HARDY *Dynasts* II. I. vi. 38 The Universal-empire plot Demands the rule of that wave-walled spot. **1919** D. W. JOHNSON *Shore Processes & Shoreline Devel.* iv. 161 The wave-erosion features associated with the coast, shore, shoreface, and offshore, are three in number. **1924** E. SITWELL *Sleeping Beauty* xiv. 47 Pan, with his satyrs on the rocks Feeding their wave-weary flocks. **1929** W. B. YEATS in *New Republic* 2 Oct. 173/2 A bone wave-whitened and dried in the wind. **1939** W. H. TWENHOFEL *Princ. Sedimentation* ii. 30 As sea level before the rise is assumed to have been stationary, a wave-eroded surface may be expected to have developed in places. **1952** C. DAY LEWIS tr. *Virgil's Aeneid* III. 72 Over against wave-worn Plemyrium there's an island Athwart the gulf of Syracuse. **1968** R. W. FAIRBRIDGE *Encycl. Geomorphol.* 133/1 Coasts made irregular by wave erosion are less common. **1974** C. TAYLOR *Fieldwork in Medieval Archaeol.* iv. 60 On the valley sides above the dam is ridge and furrow which ends just above the slight wave-cut platform which still marks the former edge of the water in the lake. **1979** *United States 1980/81* (Penguin Travel Guides) 611 Cruising on these wave-free waterways is relaxing.

10. wave analyser, any instrument for analysing a wave motion into its Fourier components; **waveband,** a range of (esp. radio) wavelengths or frequencies between specified limits; **wave base** *Physical Geogr.*, the greatest depth at which sediment can be disturbed by surface waves; **wave change** *Radio*, used *attrib.* to designate a switch for changing the wavelength to which a transmitter or receiver is tuned; also **wave changer; wave cloud** *Meteorol.*, an elongated cloud that is one of a parallel series formed at the crests of atmospheric waves in the lee of high ground and remaining stationary in relation to the ground; **wave drag** *Aerodynamics*, the drag experienced by a body at supersonic speeds as a result of the formation of a shock wave; **wave equation** *Physics*, an equation that represents wave motion, esp. (*a*) the differential equation $\partial^2 U/\partial t^2 = c^2\nabla^2 U$; (*b*) Schrödinger's equation (see *SCHRÖDINGER); **wave filter** *Electr. Engin.* = *FILTER *sb.* 3 e; **wave function** *Physics*, a function that satisfies a wave equation; *esp.* a Schrödinger wave function (see *SCHRÖDINGER); **wave group,** a short group of waves, not necessarily of uniform wavelength or amplitude; **wave-hop** *v. intr. colloq.* [after *hedge-hop* vb. s.v. *HEDGE *sb.* 9], to fly low over the sea; hence **wave-hopper; wave machine,** an apparatus for producing waves in water; **wave-meter,** substitute for def.: a device for measuring the wavelength or frequency of radiofrequency waves; (earlier and later examples); **wave number** *Physics* and *Chem.*, the number of waves per unit length, used esp. as a spectroscopic unit to represent the frequency of electromagnetic radiation and usu. expressed in reciprocal centimetres, cm.$^{-1}$ (see *KAYSER); the reciprocal of wavelength, or this multiplied by 2π; symbol k; **wave packet** *Physics*, a group of superposed waves which together form a travelling localized disturbance; *esp.* one described by the Schrödinger equation and regarded as representing a particle; cf. *PACKET *sb.* 1 h; **wave-particle** *Physics*, used *attrib.* to designate the two-fold description of matter and energy in terms of two seemingly incompatible concepts, waves and particles; **wave pattern** = *Vitruvian scroll* s.v. VITRUVIAN *a.* b; **wave period** *Physics*, the period between the arrival at a given point of successive maxima of a travelling wave; **wave picture** *Physics*, the conception of sub-atomic particles as waves, in accordance with wave theory; **wave-power,** power derived from the action of water waves; **waverider** *Aeronaut.*, a wing that derives lift from a shock wave close to its under-surface; an aeroplane having such wings; **waveshape** = *WAVEFORM; **wave theory,** add: more widely in *Physics*, any theory treating of something as waves, esp. such a theory of sub-atomic particles; (further examples); (*b*) *Philol.* = *WELLENTHEORIE; **wave trap,** (*b*) *Radio* = *TRAP *sb.* 8 d; **wave vector** *Physics*, a vector whose direction is the direction of propagation of a wave and whose magnitude is its wave number; **wave velocity** *Physics* = *phase velocity* s.v. *PHASE *sb.* 5; **wave winding,** substitute for def.: a kind of armature winding in which the coils are wound between commutator bars just over 180° apart so that there are two routes in parallel

between the positive and the negative brush; (examples).
1931 H. A. Brown *Radio-Frequency Electr. Measurements* ix. 314 (*caption*) Balanced modulator used in wave analyzer. **1946** *Nature* 7 Sept. 329/2 A wave-analyser was developed..in 1944 in order to analyse ocean waves and swell and ship movement. **1975** G. J. King *Audio Handbk.* v. 112 Harmonic distortion. For this test an audio wave analyser is required. **1923** *Daily Mail* 28 Apr. 5 A receiver which will function efficiently over a waveband stretching from 300 metres to 20,000 metres. **1935** *Discovery* Sept. 278/1 Recent developments..have made possible..room within this waveband (30 to 75 million cycles) to accommodate several independent high-definition sound and picture channels. **1958** *Observer* 17 Aug. 8/3 By international agreement, four wavebands are available for television. **1971** I. G. Gass et al. *Understanding Earth* x. 144/2 Ultraviolet light (primarily in the wave-band 1 500 to 2 100 angstroms). **1899** F. P. Gulliver in *Proc. Amer. Acad. Arts & Sci.* XXXIV. 177 The term wave-base is here introduced as a comparable term to river baselevel or hard stratum baselevel. It is another local baselevel, which ought to be distinguished from the grand baselevel of the sea. **1968** R. W. Fairbridge *Encycl. Geomorphol.* 1226/1 Historically, there has been much confusion about the lower limit of wave base and marine abrasion. **1930** *Telegraph & Telephone Jrnl.* XVI. 86/1 It is necessary to have a split battery at the distant end to provide the momentary impulse for the wave change relay. **1957** *Practical Wireless* XXXIII. 520/1 The front panel carries the wave-change switch. **1924** S. R. Roget *Dict. Electr. Terms* 289/1 *Wave changer*, a switching arrangement enabling connections to be altered rapidly in a wireless transmitting apparatus to cause waves of a different wave length to be transmitted. **1929** Duncan & Drew *Radio Telegr. & Telephony* xxi. 673 A five position wave-changer switch changes the wavelength of the closed oscillatory circuit..simultaneously with the open radiative circuit. **1959** R. E. Huschke *Gloss. Meteorol.* 620 Wave cloud. **1977** *Sci. Amer.* July 40/2 (*caption*) Wave clouds in the lee of a Martian crater were photographed by *Mariner 9*. **1948** *Sci. News* VII. 30 To attain very high velocities in a practicable aircraft it is obvious that wave drag must be reduced to a minimum. **1951** [see *form drag* s.v. *form *sb.* 22]. **1981** C. E. Dole *Flight Theory & Aerodynamics* vii. 217 The heat rise behind the shock wave is either radiated to the atmosphere or absorbed by the wing surface,..and this lost energy must be continuously supplied by the engines. This energy loss represents a type of drag known as wave drag. **1926** E. Schrödinger in *Physical Rev.* XXVIII. 1049 (*heading*) The wave equation and its application to the hydrogen atom. **1927**, etc. [see *Schrödinger]. **1936** P. M. Morse *Vibration & Sound* vi. 188 Plane waves of sound, longitudinal waves, obey the same wave equation as do the transverse waves on a string. **1982** W. H. Hayward *Introd. Radio Frequency Design* iv. 114 A complete solution of the voltage wave equation..is the sum of positive and negative moving voltage waves. **1908** *Phil. Mag.* XVI. 481 This machine has been used with a wave filter, consisting of series inductances of low effective resistance and parallel capacities. **1947** R. Lee *Electronic Transformers & Circuits* vi. 150 Many wave filters are composed of several sections which simulate transmission lines. **1973** S. K. Mitra et al. in Temes & Mitra *Mod. Filter Theory & Design* i. 1 The theory of filters owes its origin to Wagner and Campbell, who in 1915 advanced the concept of passive electric wave filters. **1925** *Proc. R. Soc.* A. CVII. 43 (*heading*) Spheroidal wave-functions. **1926** E. Schrödinger in *Physical Rev.* XXVIII. 1049 The wave-function physically means and determines a continuous distribution of electricity in space, the fluctuations of which determine the radiation by the laws of..electrodynamics. **1935**, etc. [see *proper *a.* 3* b]. **1961** Powell & Crasemann *Quantum Mech.* ii. 59 Until suitable boundary conditions and requirements concerning the continuity of solutions are imposed, the properties of the wave function are not completely described by the Schrödinger equation. **1979** *Sci. Amer.* Nov. 128/1 In quantum mechanics an elementary particle such as an electron is represented by the mathematical expression called a wave function, which often describes the electron as if it were smeared out over a large region of space. [**1877** *Nature* 23 Aug. 343/1 (*heading*) On the rate of progression of groups of waves.] **1923** H. Moore *Textbk. Intermediate Physics* xxxii. 317 A noise consists of a single wave or of a very short wave-group, while a musical note consists of a regular succession of similar waves constituting a regular wave-train. **1952** R. W. Ditchburn *Light* iv. 95 In a dispersive medium, the components of a wave group move with different speeds, and the phase relations between the components are altered. **1978** I. G. Main *Vibrations & Waves in Physics* xii. 210 Any isolated wave group may be viewed as a superposition of many sinusoidal waves. **1943** *Times* 21 Dec. 2/3 Sneak-raiding FW 190s which wave-hopped across the Channel and North Sea to surprise seaside towns were a daytime menace. **1952** C. Day Lewis tr. *Virgil's Aeneid* iv. 80 Like a bird which along the shore and around the promontories Goes fishing, flying low, wave-hopping over the water. **1984** J. Savarin *Wolfrun* xiii. 175 'What I can do with a chopper will surprise you.' They'd be wave-hopping all the way across [the Channel]. **1957** R. Watson-Watt *Three Steps* xxxviii. 218 Our fears about the wave-hopper. **1968** *Surfer Mag.* Jan. 46/1 They constructed a wave machine that could be a forerunner of a fantastic era of artificial surfing. **1979** *Listener* 1 Mar. 315/3 A swimming-pool..a place to bring the family..and enjoy the wave-machine. **1904** *Electrician* 1 Jan. 408/2 (*caption*) General view of wave meter. **1945** *Electronic Engin.* XVII. 720/1 The absorption wavemeter can be greatly improved by the addition of a valve which will provide the necessary energy to maintain the tuned circuit in continuous oscillation. **1979** P. Hawker *Guide to Amat. Radio* iv. 63/2 A convenient method of calibrating the wavemeter is to use a communication receiver. **1873** *Rep. Brit. Assoc. Adv. Sci. 1872* 53 The term *wave-numbers* appears preferable to the equivalent term 'inverse wavelengths' which has been hitherto used. **1936** *Physical Rev.* L. 59/2 The vector **k** is called 'the reduced wave number vector'. **1973** *Physics Bull.* July 419/2 These devices are characterized by a relatively small tuning range (a few wave-numbers). **1979** *Nature* 20–27 Dec. 887/2 It is confusing to find both the chemists' wavenumber ($1/\lambda$) and physicists' wavenumber ($2\pi/\lambda$) used in different parts of the text. **1928** *Proc. R. Soc.* A. CXVII. 276 Schrödinger has shown that for a harmonic oscillator a wave packet can be constructed which, though it spreads in the intermediate states, always returns to its original form at each end of the swing. **1955** Friedman & Weisskopf in W. Pauli *Niels Bohr* 153 More insight into this equation is provided by examining the time behaviour of a neutron wave packet. **1968** G. Ludwig *Wave Mech.* i. iv. 47 A wave packet is not to be regarded as an approximation to a corpuscle, so that the corpuscles are *in fact* more or less extended *waves*, but the ψ-wave determines only the probability..of the position of the corpuscles. **1979** *Nature* 22 Mar. 312/1 Observations in Massachusetts Bay of high-frequency internal wave packets indicate that they are caused by lee waves generated outside a submarine bank at the Bay's seaward margin during ebb tide. **1938** R. C. Tolman *Princ. Statistical Mech.* vii. 231 The foregoing considerations are sufficient to give an idea of the quantum mechanical treatment of wave-particle duality in the cases of entities which were customarily regarded solely from the particle point of view. **1968** M. S. Livingston *Particle Physics* iii. 47 The growing understanding of the wave-particle dualism in the properties of light led Louis de Broglie in 1925 to propound the hypothesis that a material particle should also have a wave property associated with it. **1905** G. W. Rhead *Princ. Design* 116 Another motive in Egyptian borders..is a kind of spiral or wave pattern, starting from a series of small circles. **1956** G. Taylor *Silver* ix. 192 All kinds of classical motifs, such as anthemion, key..and wave patterns. **1909** *Proc. R. Soc. Edin.* XXIX. 446 The energy propagated in one wave-period across a plane at right angles to the direction of the wave-motion is equal to the energy contained in one wave-length of the group multiplied by the ratio of group-velocity to wave-velocity. **1946** *Nature* 7 Sept. 330/2 These peaks are equivalent to wave-periods of submultiples of 3 × 20 or 60 sec. **1975** *BP Shield Internat.* May 13/3 Wave heights and wave periods..are the crucial statistics that spell work or no work on the crane barges. **1955** W. Heisenberg in W. Pauli *Neils Bohr* 15 The complete equivalence of the particle and wave pictures in the quantum theory was thus demonstrated for the first time. **1974** G. Reece tr. *Hund's Hist. Quantum Theory* xi. 142 Quantum and wave pictures combine to give $\Delta\ p = uh/l$. **1973** *Bull. Amer. Assoc. Petroleum Geologists* LVII. 1835/1 Wave-power gradient studies along the mainland [of the Florida coast]..indicate that the dominant wave approach direction, responsible for littoral drift towards the south-southeast, is from the west. **1974** *Times* 7 Oct. 1/3 A significant part of Britain's future energy requirements could come from cheap, pollution-free wave power. **1980** D. Bloodworth *Trapdoor* xiii. 75 There are studies for deriving solar energy from seaweed, windpower from the trades, wave-power from the surf. **1984** *Times* 8 Nov. 16/1 The pilot wave-power plant at Toftestallen, about 50 miles west of Bergen, is expected to be operational next year. **1964** *Times* 29 May 12/3 The R.A.E. had designed a new type of delta wing known as a 'waverider' which has a convex upper surface and is supported by the pressure generated by the shock wave trapped under the concave lower surface. **1978** D. Küchemann *Aerodynamic Design of Aircraft* iii. 77 In general terms, waveriders are a type of aircraft where the means for providing volume, lift, and propulsion are so closely integrated that their effects cannot readily be separated from one another. **1940** *Chambers's Techn. Dict.* 902/2 Wave-form, wave-shape. **1947** R. Lee *Electronic Transformers & Circuits* ix. 234 It is sometimes convenient to know whether a transformer, whose frequency response is known, can deliver a given wave shape. **1965** *Wireless World* July 364/1 The use of cameras to make a permanent photographic record of a waveshape on an oscilloscope screen is now commonplace. **1984** *Sounds* 1 Dec. 59/5 Vibrato is offered with four waveshapes to choose from, and may be programmed. **1926** Wave theory [see *emission theory* s.v. *emission 4 c]. **1932** *Discovery* Apr. 109/1 This new physics was soon to be revolutionized further by De Broglie and Schrödinger, with their enthusiasm for the new wave theory of matter. **1933** L. Bloomfield *Language* xviii. 318 The presentation of these factors became known as the wave-theory, in contradistinction to the older family-tree theory of linguistic relationship. **1966** C. R. Tottle *Sci. Engin. Materials* i. 8 The adaptation of classical mechanics to wave theory dates back only some forty years, so that modern concepts of the structure of atoms are very new. **1971** [see *Stammbaum]. **1974** G. Reece tr. *Hund's Hist. Quantum Theory* xi. 150 Schroedinger regarded this equation as the basis of the wave theory of particles. **1923** *Mod. Wireless* I. 247/2 The second frame aerial..is stated..to act as a 'wave-trap'. **1968** *Radio Communication Handbk.* (ed. 4) xvi. 3/1 If the generator whine remains pronounced, a fully screened tuned wave trap may be inserted in series with the output from the generator. **1955** L. Rosenfeld in W. Pauli *Niels Bohr* 88 The Fourier components of wave vector *k*. **1978** H. M. Rosenberg *Solid State* (ed. 2) ii. 21 However, in the mathematical treatment of waves it is much more convenient to use the wave vector **k** instead of the wavelength λ. **1887**, etc. Wave velocity [see *group velocity* s.v. *group *sb.* 6]. **1909** [see *wave period* above]. **1910** [in Dict., sense 9 a]. **1969** R. H. Webb *Elementary Wave Optics* v. 61 It is the wave velocity rather than the group velocity which is measured by refraction. **1892**, etc. Wave-winding [see *lap winding* s.v. *lap *sb.*³ 6]. **1980** Slemon & Straughen *Electric Machines* iv. 272 If the paths of the current through the wave winding from a positive to a negative brush are traced, only two parallel paths from the positive to the negative armature terminal will be found.

wave, *v.* Add: **I. 10. b.** Also *to wave down* [cf. *flag down* s.v. *flag *v.*⁴ 2 a], to wave at (a driver of a vehicle) as a signal to stop. Also with the vehicle as object.
1955 J. P. Donleavy *Ginger Man* xxx. 343 A taxi roaring by. Wave it down. To the Red Lion Square. Fast. **1967** J. Weatherhead *Sacred Shaft* ii. 15 There was a man..waving her down on the fast stretch near Oxted. **1972** T. Lilley *'K' Section* xl. 176 A man on a motor-bike..stopped when Carter waved him down. **1981** M. C. Smith *Gorky Park* i. xvii. 253 It took him twenty minutes to wave down a taxi.

III. 14. wave-off *Aeronaut.*, a signal or instruction to an approaching aircraft that it is not to land.
1951 *Jrnl. R. Aeronaut. Soc.* LV. 526/2 To avoid embarrassment to the pilot, the sudden increase of power on the wave-off signal should not be accompanied by violent changes of trim. **1973** *Black Panther* 20 Oct. 10/2 When a tower calls 'missed approach' to an aircraft, they are obliged to obey and accept the tower's 'wave-off'.

wa·veform. Also **wave form, wave-form.** [f. Wave *sb.* + Form *sb.*] The shape of a wave at any moment, or that of the graphical representation of a (usu. periodically) varying physical quantity; a wave regarded as characterized by a particular shape or manner of variation, esp. a varying voltage.
1845 *Rep. Brit. Assoc. Adv. Sci. 1844* i. 340 The wave of the first order has a definite form and magnitude... This wave-form has its surface wholly raised above the level of repose of the fluid. **1846, 1889** [in Dict. s.v. Wave *sb.* 10]. **1903** *Whittaker's Electr. Engineer's Pocket-Bk.* 104 The effects produced by the various wave forms may be calculated by summing the effects produced by each component having this peculiar form. *Ibid.* 108 The wave form of an alternating E.M.F. **1923** *Proc. R. Soc.* A. CIII. 84 The term 'wave-form' is used throughout as a convenient abbreviation for the 'temporal variation of the electric field'. **1947** Crowther & Whiddington *Science at War* 15 A cathode ray tube would be suitable for finding the wave-form of the atmospheric. **1958** *Engineering* 31 Jan. 160/1 Electrical waveforms can be generated electronically and fed to the speaker which transforms them into 'artificial' sounds. **1968** *Brit. Med. Bull.* XXIV. 251/2 They established that the breathing waveforms contain at least four significant components, having approximate frequencies of 0.27, 0.12, 0.07, and 0.03 cycles per breath. **1977** *Rolling Stone* 24 Mar. (Advt.), These new speakers come with a test record that lets you pinpoint the output level where your particular amplifier begins to clip the peaks of the musical waveform.

wave guide. Also **wave-guide, waveguide.** [f. Wave *sb.* + Guide *sb.*] A device which constrains or guides electromagnetic waves along a path defined by its physical structure and conducts them with minimum energy loss; *spec.* a metal tube, usu. of rectangular cross-section, doing this in the hollow space along its length. Also *transf.* Cf. *transmission line* s.v. *transmission e.
1936 *Bell Syst. Techn. Jrnl.* XV. 284 A novel form of electrical propagation by means of which extremely high-frequency waves may be transmitted from one point to another, through specially constructed wave guides. The guide..may be a hollow copper pipe. **1960** M. Redwood *Mech. Waveguides* 1 In much of the research work in which mechanical waveguides are found the waveguide itself is of only subsidiary interest. **1969** *Guardian* 7 Nov. 13/4 Experimental lengths of a kind of special pipe called a 'wave-guide'..are expected to be the very high capacity trunk telecommunications cables of the future. **1976** *Jrnl. R. Soc. Arts* CXXIV. 591/2 The electron beam is fired into a 'wave guide' carrying a very intense flow of radar waves. **1979** *Sci. Amer.* Oct. 71/3 Some whistlers have proved to be signals generated by a lightning stroke in one hemisphere of the earth and conducted to the opposite hemisphere through a natural waveguide formed by the lines of force of the earth's magnetic field. **1984** *Which?* Dec. 542/1 Microwaves..are directed into the oven by a wave guide.

wa·velength. Also **wave length, wave-length.** [f. Wave *sb.* + Length *sb.*] **1. a.** The distance between successive peaks or maxima of a wave; *esp.* this as a distinctive feature of the radio waves used to carry a particular programme service.
1850 *Rep. Brit. Assoc. Adv. Sci. 1849* ii. 11 It was well known..that Fraunhofer had most accurately measured the wave lengths of seven of the principal fixed lines in the solar spectrum. **1871**, etc. [in Dict. s.v. Wave *sb.* 10]. **1925** *Scribner's Mag.* July 47/2 He swung the dials round to where he could receive the commercial wave lengths. **1950** *Engineering* 24 Mar. 337/3 The reasons for changes in the wavelengths of European broadcasting stations..are explained. **1971** *Daily Tel.* 18 Jan. 7/4 His experts have also juggled wavelengths to make air space for both Radio 1 and the commercial network. **1977** P. B. & J. S. Medawar *Life Sci.* i. 20 Ordinary light microscopy has the disadvantage that nothing can be seen that is smaller than the wavelength of visible light.

b. Electromagnetic waves of the wavelength described.
1915 R. A. Houston *Treat. Light* xxv. 449 He assumes the existence of an enclosure containing a great number of Hertzian oscillators all radiating and absorbing the same wave-length. **1937** Jenkins & White *Fund. Physical Optics* xii. 277 Substances are said to show selective reflection when certain wave-lengths are reflected much more strongly than others. **1982** *Sci. Amer.* Aug. 52/1 Most ultraviolet wavelengths..cannot penetrate the earth's atmosphere.

c. The distance between adjacent heights or hollows in a body with a wave-like surface.
1958 *Spectator* 31 Jan. 133/3 The wavelength of the corrugations [on Persian roads] is considerably larger

than the pace of a sheep or goat. **1977** *Sci. Amer.* Apr. 30/1 Nearly constant winds blow across the basin with such force that they pile up sand dunes as much as 150 kilometres long with wavelengths of three to five kilometres, clearly visible in satellite pictures.

2. *fig.* with allusion to radio reception, implying (esp. mutual) understanding; esp. in phr. *to be on the same wavelength* (as someone else), to understand each other.

1927 *Amer. Speech* II. 276/2 *Have one's wave length,* know one's sentiments. **1929** A. E. HOUSMAN *Let.* 16 Feb. (1971) I. 276 Only the archangel Raphael could recite my poetry properly, but..you would do it quite nicely, and I shall try not to set up interfering wavelengths. *a* **1936** KIPLING *Let.* in C. Carrington *Rudyard Kipling* (1955) xx. 509 Every man has to work out his creed according to his own wave-length, and the hope is that the Great Receiving Station is tuned to take *all* wave-lengths. **1938** *Times Lit. Suppl.* 24 Sept. 617/3 She finally comes to believe that she is the only person in Riverville who was 'born civilized' and that nobody else there is of her own 'wavelength'. **1947** T. S. ELIOT *Milton* 12 It is only in the period that the wave-length of Milton's verse is to be found. **1959** *Economist* 6 June 919/2 Editors and publishers..have to..find the wave-length of their..readers. **1964** H. WALDOCK in *Barcelona Traction, Light & Power Co. Case* (Internat. Court of Justice) II. 112, I do not think that it would assist the Court if I were to deal with every contention advanced by our opponents in their Observations and Conclusions; for on some points we are really not on the same wave-length. **1976** LD. HOME *Way Wind Blows* ii. 27 In September A. W. Whitworth took over, and I like to think we were soon on each other's wave-length. **1983** D. DUNNETT *Dolly & Bird of Paradise* xiii. 168 We weren't on the same wavelength really... He was clever. And my thoughts are easy to read.

3. Special Comb.: **wavelength constant** = *propagation constant* s.v. *PROPAGATION 8.

1940 *Chambers's Techn. Dict.* 902/2 Wavelength constant. **1963** [see *propagation constant* s.v. *PROPAGATION 8].

wave mecha·nics. *Physics.* Also **wave-mechanics** (with hyphen). [f. WAVE *sb.* + MECHANICS.] A form of non-relativistic quantum mechanics introduced by E. Schrödinger in which particles are regarded as having some of the properties of waves, the waves being described by the wave functions produced as solutions of the Schrödinger wave equation.

1926 *Physical Rev.* XXVIII. 726 Schroedinger's presentation is based on his wave-mechanics, while this is based on the matrix-mechanics. **1942** J. D. STRANATHAN *'Particles' Mod. Physics* vi. 228 On wave mechanics the electron is not regarded as a localized particle. **1953** *Sci. News* XXX. 13 When wave mechanics is applied to any problem, the first step is to write down an expression for the energy of the system. **1974** *Encycl. Brit. Macropædia* XI. 796/1 The revolutionary development of quantum mechanics (of which wave mechanics and matrix mechanics are specialized partial formulations) occurred with breath-taking rapidity in the years 1925–30.

Hence **wave-mecha·nical** *a.*, **-mecha·nically** *adv.*

1928 E. SCHRÖDINGER *Four Lect. Wave Mech.* 6 In replacing the ordinary mechanical description by a wave-mechanical description our object is to obtain a theory. **1951** C. N. HINSHELWOOD *Struct. Physical Chem.* vi. 129 The number of solutions of the ψ equation, which correspond to a given value of the permitted energy value *E*, is the expression for the statistical weight in the wave-mechanical formulation. **1971** *Physics Bull.* Jan. 16/2 A molecule is harder to deal with wave-mechanically than either an atom or an atomic crystal.

waver, *v.* **1. a.** Delete † *Obs.* and add later examples.

1924 GALSWORTHY *White Monkey* I. viii. 63 Michael watched him down the corridor, saw him waver into the dusky street. **1977** D. FRANCIS *Risk* ii. 20 One of them [*sc.* the two horses in front] wavered up the straight at a widening angle. The other seemed to be stopping second by second... Tapestry scorched past both of them..and won the Gold Cup.

Waves (wē^i^vz), *sb. pl. U.S.* [See quot. 1972.] The women's section of the United States Naval Reserve, established in 1942. In *sing.*, a member of this Reserve, or, since 1948, a woman serving in the U.S. Navy. Cf. *WREN^2.

1942 *Chicago Tribune* 9 Aug. I. 6/1 The navy's new women's reserve corps — the Waves — will learn to drill, salute, wear the regular insignia of the service.. and they will receive..detailed instructions in navy customs. **1943** N. W. ROSS *Waves* 1 The initials of the WAVES stand for the words 'Women Accepted for Voluntary Emergency Service'. *Ibid.* 150 Orders tell the WAVE where she is to go next. **1972** J. B. HANCOCK *Lady in Navy* 61 In 1942, when the planning for the Women's Reserve began, the question of a short and catchy name was posed... Miss [Elizabeth] Reynard addressed herself to the problem... 'I realized that there were two letters which had to be in it: W for women and V for volunteer.... So I played with those two letters and the idea of the sea and finally came up with "Women Appointed for Volunteer Emergency Service"—WAVES.' (Later, when it was realized that *Appointed* applied only to officers, *Accepted* was the word substituted.) **1977** *Time* 10 Jan. 43/3 Mainbocher's creations graced Wallis Warfield Simpson at her marriage to the Duke of Windsor, as well as millions of WAVES and Girl Scouts, whose uniforms he fashioned.

wavicle (wē^i^·vik'l). *Physics.* [Blend of WAVE *sb.* and PARTICLE *sb.*] An entity having characteristic properties of both waves and particles.

1928 A. S. EDDINGTON *Nature Physical World* x. 201 We can scarcely describe such an entity as a wave or as a particle; perhaps as a compromise we had better call it a 'wavicle.' **1934** *Times Lit. Suppl.* 11 Jan. 20/3 It [*sc.* X-ray diffraction] has revolutionized conceptions of the electron, which has had to be looked upon as something intermediate between a corpuscle and a packet of waves — a 'wavicle' in fact. **1962** J. NEEDHAM *Sci. & Civilisation in China* IV. I. 135 Old Chinese philosophers.. thought of *chhi* as something between what we should call matter in a rarefied gaseous state on one hand, and radiant energy on the other. Though all our assured knowledge gained by experiment makes us infinitely richer than they, is the concept of 'wavicles' in modern physical theory so much more penetrating? **1976** *New Scientist* 26 Aug. 461/4 To think that a particle or wavicle or whatever, is small for us, therefore it is small for the Universe, is to be biased or homo-centred.

waving, *vbl. sb.* Add: **6. waving-base,** an observation terrace at an airport from which members of the public may watch the aircraft and wave to the travellers.

1954 *Archit. Rev.* CXV. 24 Opening off this is a roof-garden 'waving-base' from which passengers' friends can watch the departure of aircraft. **1958** [see *jet age* s.v. *JET *sb.*^{3} II]. **1965** *New Statesman* 20 Aug. 261/2 Even at dreary old Heathrow you can get out on to one of the waving-bases..for free.

wavy, *a.* Add: **7. wavy-handled; Wavy Navy** *colloq.*, the Royal Naval Volunteer Reserve, so nicknamed from the wavy braid worn by officers on their sleeves prior to 1956.

1927 PEAKE & FLEURE *Peasants & Potters* 72 The wavy-handled pots. **1928** V. G. CHILDE *Most Anc. East* iv. 94 The wavy-handled jars..have been connected by Petrie, Frankfort, and Scharff with Palestine and Syria. **1918** W. OWEN *Let.* 21 Mar. (1967) 541 Her son, a Lieut. in the 'Wavy Navy' was at home. **1944** A. JACOB *Traveller's War* iii. 40 The ship's doctor and the paymaster-lieutenant, both 'Wavy Navy' men..have been in the service only a few months and know next to nothing of the sea. **1960** D. FEARON *Murder-on-Thames* xiv. 115, I remember him when he was a Sub. He was Wavy Navy then.

waw, *sb.*^{4} Add: **waw consecutive** *Heb. Gram.* = *Vau conversive* s.v. CONVERSIVE *a.*^{1} 2 b.

1880 E. C. MITCHELL tr. *Gesenius' Heb. Gram.* II. ii. 125 (*heading*) The perfect and the imperfect with Wāw consecutive. **1880** *Encycl. Brit.* XI. 596/2 Among the points in which Hebrew differs both from Arabic and Aramaic may be mentioned..the use of Waw consecutive. **1889** J. KENNEDY *Introd. Biblical Heb.* 117 Ewald and other modern Grammarians prefer to call it *Waw Consecutive.* **1914** J. E. MCFADYEN *Davidson's Introd. Heb. Gram.* (ed. 19) xxiii. 84 Waw consecutive with the imperf. is pointed exactly like the Article. **1957** *Encycl. Brit.* XI. 362/1 Further relief was provided by '*wāw*-consecutive', a construction almost confined to Biblical Hebrew.

wa-wa, var. *WAH-WAH^2.

wax, *sb.*^{1} Add: **6. e.** (See quots.) Cf. *paraffin wax* s.v. PARAFFIN *sb.* 4.

1924 *Ski Terms* in *Tourist* (Winter Sports No.) 12/2 *Wax*, a paraffin preparation to prevent the snow balling under the ski. **1962** *Austral. Women's Weekly* 24 Oct. (Suppl.) 3/4 *Wax*, paraffin wax, rubbed on a [surf]board to prevent slipping.

f. *lost wax*: see *LOST *ppl. a.* 6.

10*. *U.S. slang.* A gramophone record; *to put on wax*, to make a gramophone record of, to record. [From the 'wax' discs in which the recording stylus cuts its groove.]

1932 *New Yorker* 11 June 56/2 An extraordinarily competent bit of manufacture is the latest wax by Miss Jeanette MacDonald (Victor 24103). **1940** J. O'HARA *Pal Joey* (1952) 107, I am going to play the tune and cut a wax of it. **1941** *Jazz Information* Nov. 28/1 Some of the most beautiful piano playing Jelly Roll ever put on wax. **1941** W. C. HANDY *Father of Blues* xvi. 219 Recording companies..made them available on wax. **1968** P. OLIVER *Screening Blues* 4 The more sophisticated types of vaudeville entertainment were to be heard on wax before the Southern rural blues. **1979** *Early Music* Oct. 469/1 Scarlatti, Rameau, Couperin, Handel and, of course, Bach were committed to wax during the 1930s, as well.

11. a. *wax dummy.*

1840 DICKENS *Master Humphrey's Clock* I. 101 A young hairdresser..opened a wery smart little shop with four wax dummies in the winder. **1969** Y. CARTER *Mr Campion's Farthing* xix. 188 A wax dummy displaying a garment for sale. **1978** J. ANDERSON *Angel of Death* xii. 139 Her body as motionless, her face as impassive as a wax dummy.

c. *wax-bleacher, -refiner.*

1881 *Instructions to Census Clerks* (1885) 77 Wax, beeswax—bleacher, refiner [etc.]. **1908** *Westm. Gaz.* 29 Apr. 1/3 He..became a wax-bleacher at Hoxton.

d. *wax-daubed.*

1942 W. FALKNER *Go down, Moses* 305 The tawny wax-daubed shapeless lump.

e. *wax-blond, -pale, -white* (earlier example).

1925 E. SITWELL *Troy Park* 92 Oh, wax-blond orange-blossoms' calice Of their hair. **1942** —— *Street Songs* 31 Dark-leaved arbutus blooms with wax-pale bells. **1883** 'MARK TWAIN' *Life on Miss.* xxxi. 338 All of them with wax-white, rigid faces.

12. wax bath, an application of warm liquid wax which is allowed to solidify to a part of the body, for cosmetic or medical purposes; also, an immersion in liquid wax; **wax bean** *U.S.* = *wax-pod bean* below; **wax-eye** *Austral.* and *N.Z.* = *silver-eye* s.v. *SILVER *sb.* and *a.* 21 c; cf. ZOSTEROPS; **wax jack,** a contrivance designed for holding a coiled taper with its end ready for lighting, to provide a flame for melting sealing wax; **wax museum,** a wax-works; also *fig.*; **wax-oil** (earlier example); **wax-pod bean,** a dwarf French bean belonging to any of several varieties having yellow, stringless pods; a butter-bean; **wax print,** cloth patterned by a batik process.

1916 *Chambers's Jrnl.* Oct. 701/1 The wax-bath has not been found beneficial in chronic rheumatoid arthritis. **1975** *Harpers & Queen* June 168/1 Sauna, steam cabinet baths, wax baths. [**1900** L. H. BAILEY *Cycl. Amer. Hort.* I. 136/2 The Wax or Yellow-podded sorts need a richer soil.] **1905** *Outing* July 502/2 White bush wax-beans are best for very early, but the pole varieties are better for late. **1967** R. M. CARLETON *Vegetables for To-day's Gardens* ii. 14 No one has produced a wax bean with better flavour than Pencil Rod Black Wax. **1874** A. BATHGATE *Colonial Experiences* xvii. 239 While some species are seemingly dying out, others, such as the moko-moko and the wax-eye..appear to be increasing. **1957** J. FRAME *Owls do Cry* ix. 39 The wax-eyes hungry for honey, will make their green and yellow cloud to follow her. **1937** *Times Lit. Suppl.* 13 Mar. 189/2 Such diversities as a coach model, a silver wax-jack and devices of human hair. **1956** G. TAYLOR *Silver* v. 114 The wax jack..is a simple framework supporting a horizontal reel which revolves to feed a length of taper up through a central nozzle. **1980** *Halcyon Days Catal.* 16/1 A bougie box or wax jack (designed to encase a flexible wax taper). South Staffordshire, c. 1770..£520. **1963** V. NABOKOV *Gift* i. 35 A Russian foodshop, which was a kind of wax museum of the old country's cuisine. **1981** J. VALIN *Dead Letter* viii. 68 There was something a little scarey about this artificial paradise... The place had the shallow charm of a wax museum. **1852** J. M. HONIGBERGER *Thirty-five Yrs. in East* I. 69, I kept the wound open for several days, and ordered the swollen parts to be embrocated with wax-oil. [**1913** L. C. CORBETT *Garden Farming* ix. 136 A different variety..may have either green or wax pods.] **1921** *Culture of Vegetables & Flowers* (Sutton & Sons) (ed. 16) 24 Many visitors to the Continent have learned to appreciate the fine qualities of the Waxpod Beans. **1951** [see *BUTTER-BEAN]. **1962** *Amateur Gardening* 5 May 19 The golden waxpod beans have always attracted a good deal of attention. **1969** *Times* 24 Nov. (Congo Suppl.) p. iv/3 English Calico is planning a factory to manufacture 20m. yards of 'wax prints' a year. **1979** *Guardian* 8 June 17/3 Accra's famous market mammies have their stalls..broken into..and their contents—waxprint cloth, provisions,..taken away.

wax, *v.*^{2} Add: **1. c.** To remove unwanted hair from (legs, etc.) by applying hot wax and then peeling off wax and hairs together.

1953 W. P. MCGIVERN *Big Heat* x. 134 When the boys talk business I go out and get my legs waxed. **1971** *Sunday Express* (Johannesburg) 28 Mar. (Home Jrnl.) 12/2, I would also like my legs waxed. **1977** J. DIDION *Bk. Common Prayer* v. ix. 232 Carmen Arrellano had been having her legs waxed in the Caribe beauty shop.

5. To make a gramophone record of (music, etc.); to record. Cf. *WAX *sb.*^{1} 10*. *slang* (chiefly *U.S.*).

1935 *Melody Maker* 12 Oct. 11/4 Mario..took his harp to the Columbia Studios, and there he well and truly waxed a couple of the classics of jazz. **1946** [see *DIXIE^2 1 c]. **1954** *Cleveland Press* 7 Aug. (Home Mag.) 31 Gertrude Berg has waxed a comedy duet with Red Buttons for Columbia records. **1976** *Daily Times* (Lagos) 13 Aug. 18/2 (Advt.), Another new LP Record waxed by the Celestial Church of Christ Choir.

wax-berry. Add: **a.** Also, *Myrica cordifolia*, native to South Africa. (Further examples.)

1855 W. A. NEWMAN *Biogr. Mem. J. Montagu* vii. 169 Parts of the reclaimed soil..were not found suitable for the waxberry-bush. **1953** [see *KANKERBOS, KANKERBOSSIE].

wax doll. 1. (Earlier examples.)

1786 J. WOODFORDE *Diary* 16 Mar. (1926) II. 231 It was a wax Doll, a female Figure, dressed with a Trumpet in her Mouth. **1816** JANE AUSTEN *Let.* 21 Apr. (1952) 455 It might do for a quilt for your little wax doll.

attrib. **1847** THACKERAY *Van. Fair* (1848) xii. 97 That silly insignificant simpering Miss Thompson, who has nothing but her wax-doll face to recommend her.

waxer. Add: **c.** *gen.*

1890 O. WILDE in *19th Cent.* July 127 The waxers and gilders of images. **1930** in C. S. Johnson *Negro in Amer. Civilization* I. vii. 100 Gas pipe layer, car washers, floor waxer. **1978** *Detroit Free Press* 16 Apr. F5/3 (Advt.), Dental technician. Experienced waxer for crown and bridge lab.

waxing, *vbl. sb.*^{2} Add: **1. d.** Depilation by means of wax (see *WAX *v.*^{2} 1 c).

1974 *Times* 27 Aug. 9/2 Services..include waxing, manicure, pedicure. **1977** *Evening Post* (Nottingham) 27 Jan. 6/1 (Advt.), Get rid of unfeminine hair with the entirely new and painless method. No needle, no scarring, no waxing. **1982** *Oxford Times* 5 Nov. 13/5 (Advt.), Beauty Therapy, facials, manicure, pedicure, waxing.

2. b. *U.S. slang.* A gramophone record or phonograph cylinder.

1936 *Metronome* Feb. 21/4 *Waxing*, phonograph record. **1941** *Jazz Information* Nov. 26/1 I'll stick to the Victor-Bluebird waxings, for they are the best. **1965** [see *FRUG]. **1981** *Listener* 1 Jan. 30/1 Buddy Bolden..is said to have recorded a phonograph cylinder, somewhere around 1902... The rumoured waxing has never been discovered.

wax-light. (Earlier example.)

1600 M. HOBY *Diary* 18 Sept. (1930) 145, I reed, praied, was busie about waxe lightes, and then I dined.

waxwork. Add: **3.** (Earlier examples.)

1763 BOSWELL *Jrnl.* 4 July in *London Jrnl.* (1950) 289, I went and saw Mrs. Salmon's famous wax-work in Fleet Street. **1773** DUCHESS OF NORTHUMBERLAND *Diary* (1926) 207 The Tower, the Venetian Lady, Westminster Abbey, Salmon's Waxworks.

4. (Earlier example.)

1818 W. P. C. BARTON *Compendium Floræ Philadelphicæ* I. 128 Wax Work. A climbing plant frequently reaching the tops of trees.

waxy, *a.*[1] Add: **5.** *Comb.*, as *waxy-faced, -looking, -skinned, -white.*

1846 Waxy-faced [in Dict., sense 3 a]. **1927** *Scots Observer* 1 Jan. 3/1 Barefoot women..some with waxy-faced infants in their arms. **1859** D. BUNCE *Trav. with Dr. Leichhardt* vi. 44 A race of plants having waxy-looking berries. **1871** [in Dict., sense 3 a]. **1964** S. DUKE-ELDER *Parsons' Dis. Eye* (ed. 14) xxii. 328 Oedema is usually not marked, but all over the posterior pole there tend to gather hard, white or yellow, waxy-looking patches of exudates. **1930** J. DOS PASSOS *42nd Parallel* I. 34 He was a sharpnosed waxyskinned young man. **1929** W. FAULKNER *Sanctuary* xxiii. 261 His nostrils were waxy white with rage. **1954** A. G. L. HELLYER *Encycl. Garden Work* 452 *Kindingeri*, waxy-white, reddish at base.

way, *sb.*[1] Add: **I. 1. f.** *Way Out sign.*

1972 L. MEYNELL *Death by Arrangement* xiii. 178 Hooky was forced to follow him along an uncomfortably empty platform towards the 'Way Out' sign. **1982** J. O'FAOLAIN *Obedient Wife* iii. 59 Just follow the Way Out signs.

II. 4. c. *everything coming* (or *going*) *one's way*: everything happening in one's favour; *to know one's way around* (or *about*): (later example); also, to have shrewdness born of experience; *to go separate ways*: to cease to work or operate together and follow different paths.

1903 G. B. SHAW *Maxims for Revolutionists* in *Man & Superman* 242 In moments of progress the noble succeed, because things are going their way. **1903** *Red Bk.* June 167/2 Everything was coming his way. **1921** GALSWORTHY *To Let* I. v. 52 'That's a young woman who knows her way about,' he said. **1932** KIPLING *Limits & Renewals* 385 They must be enjoying themselves now at a theatre. Everything's coming their way. [**1935** N. L. MCCLUNG *Clearing in West* xix. 152 Jack knew his way around, having been here many times the winter before... He drove straight down to Pacific Street to the Farmer's Home.] **1938** *Times* 1 Jan. 10/4 Much was certainly lost when the original directorate decided to go separate ways, as from the separation both parties seem to have suffered. **1943** O. HAMMERSTEIN *Oklahoma!* (1947) 18, I got a beautiful feelin' Ev'rythin's goin' my way. **1957** 'R. WEST' *Fountain Overflows* xi. 241 And whatever you could say about my Ma, you couldn't say she didn't know her way about. **1968** H. R. F. KEATING *Inspector Ghote hunts Peacock* vii. 95 That girl was a pretty slick chick.. She knew her way around. **1973** G. JENKINS *Cleft of Stars* v. 60, I cursed that old rifle for letting me down at the moment when everything was going my way.

7. j. Colloq. phr. *on the* (or *one's*) *way out* (or *down*): going down in status, position, estimation, or favour; similarly with *in* or *up*, expressing the opposite sense.

1937 *Time* 25 Jan. 12/3 Every time one of them has called on the President and emerged smiling, rumor has whispered throughout Washington that the other was 'on his way out'. **1938** *Sat. Rev.* (U.S.) 17 Sept. 17/1 The thrill of being on the way up, of being prominent, being envied. **1938** H. L. ICKES *Diary* 5 Nov. (1955) II. 497 France is but little better than a third-rate power and is on the way down. **1955** A. L. ROWSE *Expansion Eliz. Eng.* i. 27 The Scottish king could well afford to make the concession: she was on her way out, he was on his way in. **1960** *Guardian* 9 Dec. 8/5 Sunrise yellows and pinks are definitely on the way in. **1962** in R. Jarrell *Sad Heart at Supermarket* 92 Poetry is on the way out! **1975** D. BAGLEY *Snow Tiger* xx. 163 This is the last job I'll hold as chief engineer. If I lose it I'll be on the way down—I'll be assistant to some smart young guy who is on his way up. **1980** A. SCHOLEFIELD *Berlin Blind* I. 5 Calland was a good-looking young man on the way up.

8. a. *a little goes a long way* and varr.: see GO *v.* 43 c, *LITTLE *sb.* 4.

c. *by a long way* (earlier example); *to go a long* or *great way*: also, to be in agreement *with* someone; *all the way*: completely; cf. senses 8 e, f below.

1850 LADY LYTTLETON *Let.* 12 June (1912) 401, I cannot *quite* enter into his politics... But a very great way I go along with him. **1859** DARWIN *Let.* Nov. (1887) II. vi. 224 Also from Quatrefages, who is inclined to go a long way with us. **1859** T. HUGHES *Tom Brown at Oxf.* iv, in *Macmillan's Mag.* Dec. 102/1 He is more of a gentleman by a long way than most. **1973** 'N. CARTER' *Spanish Connection* x. 112 I'm saying I can't buy your story all the way, Corelli.

d. *all the way from — to —*: (*a*) throughout the specified interval, at every point in it; (*b*) *U.S.*, (estimated, etc.) at any amount between the specified quantities.

(*a*) **1791** [in Dict., sense 8 a]. **1966** *Listener* 5 May 643/2 The peak age [for crime] is during the last year at school... The rate is fairly high all the way from twelve to twenty.

(*b*) **1878** J. H. BEADLE *Western Wilds* xxxi. 493 The value of the booty taken has been estimated all the way from $150,000 to $300,000. **1931** G. T. CLARK *Leland Stanford* xi. 365 The amount said to have been wagered ..has been variously stated all the way from $5,000 to $50,000.

e. *to go all the way, the whole way*: (*a*) to continue a course of action to its conclusion; *spec.* (*slang*), to engage in sexual intercourse (*with* someone), as opposed just to fondling; (*b*) to agree completely *with* someone.

1915 J. C. POWYS *Visions & Revisions* 12 If you lack the courage, or the variability, to *go all the way* with very different masters, and to let your constructive consistency take care of itself, you may become, perhaps, an admirable moralist; you will never be a clairvoyant critic. **1922** H. J. LASKI in *Holmes-Laski Lett.* (1953) I. 412, I can't go all the way with it, for if it was as a business man that the tyrant found the path to power I should have thought there would have been mention of it in Aristotle. **1924** P. MARKS *Plastic Age* xiv. 151 'Wonder if Janet would have gone the whole way,' flitted across his mind. **1927** H. T. LOWE-PORTER tr. *Mann's Magic Mountain* I. iii. 78 'Am I right?' 'You certainly are, I can go all the way with you there.' **1961** L. P. HARTLEY *Two for River* 49 I'd sooner go the whole way with somebody than natter with them at a tea-table. **1970** W. J. BURLEY *To kill Cat* x. 186 The things we found in her room! I mean it was obvious she was going all the way and her not fifteen! **1975** *Listener* 30 Oct. 574/4, I am not sure that I go all the way with Mr Miller in some of his analysis. **1979** R. JAFFE *Class Reunion* (1980) I. i. 24 She would go to medical school... She didn't know if she would have the guts to go all the way: intern, resident, actually practice medicine. *Ibid.* vi. 86 They would do as much as they could without either removing the rest of her clothes or going all the way.

f. *to come* or *go a long way* (with personal subj.: for impersonal subj. see GO *v.* 43 c, d): to achieve much, to make much progress; *to have a long way to go*, etc., to be far short of some accomplishment; so *a long way from*, far short of, much inferior to.

1917 H. J. LASKI in *Holmes-Laski Lett.* (1953) I. 121 Your bretheren [*sic*].. have still a long way to go before they understand the meaning of a certain dissent in *Adair v. U.S.* **1922** W. S. MAUGHAM in *Pearson's Mag.* Oct. 320/2 He had come a long way since then. **1925** *New Yorker* 5 Sept. 11/3 Which is another way of saying that he will go a very long way. **1933** F. BALDWIN *Innocent Bystander* viii. 150 Sherry had a long way to travel before she would be a Fontanne or a Cornell. **1935** H. L. MENCKEN *Let.* 4 Jan. (1961) 386 You must yet go a long way, of course, before you are eligible to it. **1940** *Chatelaine* July 37/2 Pat and Rosemary have come a long way; they started their careers with Fred Waring's Pennsylvanians and ended up stars in one of the largest motion picture studios in the world. **1957** *Practical Wireless* XXXIII. 684/2 The system is a very long way from Hi-Fi, but is sufficient for the transmission of speech. **1966** *Seventeen* July 140/3 Society seems to have come a long way since the days of the Puritans, and now we're up to topless bathing suits. **1977** P. BAELZ *Ethics & Belief* vii. 79 Man has still a long way to go before he exercises his freedom responsibly and responsively.

9. b. *that way*: spec. (*a*) homosexual; (*b*) (const. *about*) in love or infatuated; also (in general sense) *that way inclined, to get that way.*

1603 [see INCLINED *ppl. a* 3 a]. **1859** T. HUGHES *Tom Brown at Oxf.* (1861) I. x. 163 Both 'smalls' and 'greats' are sufficiently distant to be altogether ignored, if we are that way inclined. **1916** A. BENNETT *These Twain* xx. 518 'He simply hates doing a thing straight off.' 'Yes, he is rather that way inclined.' **1922** C. SANDBURG *Slabs of Sunburnt West* 6 How do you get that way? *a* **1960** E. M. FORSTER *Maurice* (1971) vii. 42 The Greeks, or most of them, were that way inclined, and to omit it is to omit the mainstay of Athenian society. *Ibid.* xii. 62 In his second year he met Risley, himself 'that way'. **1960** WENTWORTH & FLEXNER *Dict. Amer. Slang* 540/2 *That way*, in love. Usu. in 'They are that way about each other.' c. 1940. **1961** V. SACKVILLE-WEST *No Signposts in Sea* 82 If I were that way inclined, which I am *not*, I can imagine falling in love with him myself. **1965** J. P. CARSTAIRS *Concrete Kimono* xxiii. 207 Sharon. Be reasonable. I thought you were 'that way' about Roderick. **1966** 'J. HACKSTON' *Father clears Out* 91 It got that way in the end that I used to look forward to seeing Nolan and his team come lumbering down from the north. *a* **1967** J. R. ACKERLEY *My Father & Myself* (1968) xvi. 185, I divined that he was homosexual, or as we put it, 'one of us,' 'that way', 'so', or 'queer'.

d. *the other way about* (earlier examples); also *the other way, the other way around.*

1834 *Edin. Rev.* Oct. 83 The fault, in the present instance, is the other way. **1879** R. L. STEVENSON in *Cornh. Mag.* Oct. 412 He [*sc.* Burns] was 'constantly the victim of some fair enslaver'—at least, when it was not the other way about. **1925** *New Yorker* 28 Mar. 25/2 It is just as good the other way around. **1963** *Christian Century* 9 Jan. 49/1 But the Augustinian, and biblical, position addresses man the other way around: Find God and you will find yourself.

f. *to have it both ways* and varr.: to have advantages from two opposed or contradictory standpoints; to make use of alternatives or contradictions as it suits one.

1914 G. B. SHAW *Fanny's First Play* II. 191 Then I suppose what I did was not evil; or else I was set free for evil as well as good. As father says, you cant have anything both ways at once. **1926** F. M. FORD *Man could stand Up* I. ii. 33 An oafish thing to do! To take a school-girl..just past the age of consent, out all night in a dog-cart... You'd think any man who *was* a man would have avoided that! Most men knew enough to know that the Woman Pays.., the school-girl too! But they get it both ways. **1964** C. HODDER-WILLIAMS *Main Experiment* vii. 73 'It was only folklore.'.. 'Yes, but you can't have it both ways. If it frightens you it must mean something.' **1967** *Listener* 13 Apr. 489/2 So our dual terminology helps us to have it both ways.

III. 12. c. *to have one's way*: *spec.* to have sexual intercourse *with* (used chiefly of a man).

1915 CONRAD *Victory* IV. xii. 399 If I had taken you by the throat this morning and had my way with you, I should never have known what you are. **1939** *Ottawa Jrnl.* 23 Aug. 15/2 He might destroy Phil..to have his way with Joan. **1961** W. BROWN *Bedeviled* 113 Although she struggled, she was no match for him and he had 'had his way with her'. **1980** E. JONG *Fanny* III. xiii. 440 Thus could Anne Bonny defend herself when she did not fancy a Man, but when she fancied one, she also had her Way with him.

14. a. (Further examples.)

1860 GEO. ELIOT *Mill on Floss* II. III. vii. 107 I'm not a-defending him, in no way, for being so hot about th' erigation. **1952** M. R. RINEHART *Pool* (1953) xx. 170 It's no way to talk about a sister, but I've had about all I can take.

d. For *no way* see NOWAY *adv.* in Dict. and Suppl.

h. (Earlier example.) Now also in weakened use: a principle or activity that governs all one's actions; a dominating interest or occupation.

1605 SHAKS. *Macbeth* v. iii. 24 My way of life Is falne into the Seare, the yellow Leafe. **1917** H. J. LASKI in *Holmes-Laski Lett.* (1953) I. 104 Education is a way of life and not the collection of information. **1938** *Amer. Jrnl. Sociol.* XLIV. 1 (*heading*) Urbanism as a way of life. **1957** *Times Lit. Suppl.* 1 Nov. 650/5 Democracy has not yet been accepted as a way of life in Germany. **1970** *Daily Tel.* 4 Sept. 5/2 The investigation..is expected to ask searching questions into the safety of supertankers, which have now become a 'way of life'. **1974** *Times* 8 Mar. 23/5 (*heading*) Hong-kong... Where a quick profit is a way of life. **1981** Q. CRISP *How to become a Virgin* 188 Giving talks to American universities could easily be converted into a way of life.

j. *there is no way* (with dependent clause) (colloq.): there is no possibility that; cf. NOWAY *adv.* in Dict. and Suppl.

1975 *New Yorker* 1 Dec. 55/2 There is no way a losing candidate can pick himself up and pretend nothing has happened to him. **1977** *Daily Tel.* 10 Oct. 12/8 We are operating an emergency service and there is no way we would strike and let the old folk down. **1978** S. BRILL *Teamsters* x. 380 There was no way he would support the President's reelection. **1978** G. A. SHEEHAN *Running & Being* xiii. 188 He had recognized the bald head and there was no way I was going to beat him.

l. (*in*) *one way or* (or *and*) *another*: by any of various methods, for any of various reasons, in any of various respects. Cf. sense 9 e in Dict.

1861 T. HUGHES *Tom Brown at Oxf.* I. iii. 40 Being a good whist and billiard player, and not a bad jockey, he managed in one way or another to make his young friends pay well for the honour of his acquaintance. **1923** R. MACAULAY *Told by Idiot* I. v. 23 One way and another, what with papa's friends and mamma's and the children's, a good deal of life flowed into the..house. **1955** L. P. HARTLEY *Perfect Woman* viii. 79 What, after all, had he to tell Alec that mattered so much, one way or another? **1965** M. ALLINGHAM *Mind Readers* xix. 211 We're in for a very busy time, my lad, one way and another. **1973** *Listener* 15 Nov. 661/3, I was quite well educated, one way and another. **1979** A. PRICE *Tomorrow's Ghost* xii. 216 Captain Fitzgibbon wouldn't come back from that last Ulster tour, one way or another.

m. *way of looking at it* or *things*: the (personal) perspective from which one views a situation or event, esp. as regards attitudes brought to it or implications seen in it; a point of view.

[**1845**: see LOOK *v.* 3 a. **1861** T. HUGHES *Tom Brown at Oxf.* III. v. 95 Mary's habits, and thoughts, and ways of looking at and judging of people and things, were much changed.] **1881** H. JAMES *Portrait of Lady* I. xvii. 218, I can't make out that what he tells me about the royal family is much to their credit; but he says that's only my peculiar way of looking at it. **1893** 'L. CARROLL' *Sylvie & Bruno Concluded* ii. 27 It's a new way of looking at it—to me..but it seems a *true* way, also. **1905** E. G. WHITE *Ministry of Healing* 483 We differ so widely in disposition, habits, education, that our ways of looking at things vary. **1911** D. H. LAWRENCE *White Peacock* II. i. 202 It's one way of looking at things. **1963** D. LESSING *Man & Two Women* 141, I mean to say, you've got to take the rough with the smooth, and there's no other way of looking at it.

n. *the way*: so that, with the result that. *Ir.*

1899 SOMERVILLE & 'ROSS' *Some Experiences Irish R.M.* v. 118 A couple o' dhraws o' th' ash plant across the butt o' the tail, the way I wouldn't blind her. **1912** J. STEPHENS *Crock of Gold* xiv. 225 Be sure and hold him tight..the way we can have a good look at him. **1924** R. MACAULAY *Orphan Island* i. 16 We must see about fermenting some of this fruit-juice, the way we'll get something fit to drink.

o. *it's this way*: a colloq. formula introducing an oral explanation.

1905 'O. Henry' *Strictly Business* (1910) But it's this way: Suppose you're a Fifth Avenue millionaire, soaring high. **1938** T. Caldwell *Dynasty of Death* (1939) I. 385 Well, it's this way, Paul: you see, a number of us must stay at home to make the guns..for our soldiers to use. **1961** *East Anglian Mag.* July 505 'It's this way,' he expounded to his cronies in the know. **1970** [see *lose *v.*[1] 9 b].

15. (*in*) *more ways than one.*

a **1600** Hooker *Wks.* (1836) III. 796 That justice exacteth punishment for offending, even after their offences be forgiven them, there is, as it seemeth, proof sufficient more ways than one. **1816** *Edin. Rev.* Dec. 464 The foreign Commissioners had not yet reached St Helena, whose presence in the island may justly have alarmed Sir Hudson, in more ways than one, for the safety of his prisoner. **1895** Hardy *Jude* v. viii. 398 Her loss was a loss to me in more ways than one! **1952** M. R. Rinehart *Swimming Pool* xiv. 129 It's a dead end, in more ways than one.

16. a. (*to put*) *in the* (or *a, that*) *way*: (to make) pregnant; cf. *in the family way* s.v. Family 10 b.

1817 Jane Austen *Let.* 23 Mar. (1952) 488 Mrs Clement too is in that way again. I am quite tired of so many Children. **1831** Mrs. Arbuthnot *Let.* 18 Feb. in C. Arbuthnot *Corr.* (1941) 140 Young Ly. C. is *not in a way*; the old housekeeper wrote to her something about it, & she wrote back word, 'God's will be done.' **1867** Queen Victoria *Let.* 25 Oct. in R. Fulford *Your Dear Letter* (1971) 155 Dearest child, why did you not tell me, your own mother, when you first began being in that way? **1960** *Pick of Today's Short Stories* XI. 215 They'd both eloped... 'I'll bet he put her in the way'. **1980** J. Rose *Elizabeth Fry* iii. 44 She suspected herself of being pregnant, 'in the way' as she called it.

19. a. *in a small way* (earlier example).

1833 Carlyle in *Fraser's Mag.* July 27/1 Next, however, as another more lasting resource, he forges; at first in a small way.

b. *in a big way*: on a large scale, intensively; (*colloq.*) with great enthusiasm or display; very much, very well. orig. *U.S.*

[**1903** *Dialect Notes* II. 306 *Big way* (to get in a), *v. phr.*, to become excited. 'The preacher got in a *big way* and you could hear him a mile.'] **1927** F. Harris *My Life & Loves* III. v. 69, I meant to take up the whole problem of journalism in a big way when I came back. **1932** *N.Y. Times Bk. Rev.* 10 Jan. 17/3 A gangster who calls himself Napoleon and who goes in for crime in a big way. **1936** H. L. Ickes *Diary* 30 June (1955) I. 626 The speech went over in a big way. **1943** J. S. Huxley *TVA* vii. 51 Over half a million acres..of fishable water..are already being taken advantage of in a big way. **1950** C. MacInnes *To Victors* II. 211, I could go for her in a big way. **1955** A. Huxley *Let.* 18 Mar. (1969) 738 Amanita muscaria..he thinks will open the doors of ESP in a big way. **1958** *Times Rev. Industry* Dec. 57/2 Users of traditional materials are looking to the..use of..plastics in a big way. **1980** A. Mars-Jones *Lantern Lect. & Other Stories* (1981) 10 The Trust people played hard-to-get until he started bequeathing the property..to the Welsh nationalists. *Then* they sat up and took notice In A Big Way.

IV. 23. c. For *dial.* read *dial.* and *U.S.* Also *a ways* (unqualified).

1927 W. Faulkner *Mosquitoes* 202 I'll carry you a ways, until we get somewhere. **1933** Bloomfield *Language* ii. 40 A speaker can be heard only a short ways and only for an instant or two. **1938** T. Wilder *Our Town* I. 52 Can I walk along a ways with you? **1976** *New Yorker* 15 Mar. 67/1 As it passed over the ridge to land on the other side it hit a tree quite a ways up. **1979** N. Mailer *Executioner's Song* (1980) I. xxix. 445 Though I suppose at some point in the future..he may be eligible for parole, that's a long long ways away.

V. 27. pay one's way. b. (Earlier example.)

1803 G. Colman *John Bull* II. iii. 22, I earned my fair profits; I paid my fair way.

34. in the way. (See also sense 16 a above.)

35. j. *in way of* (Naut.): = *in wake of* s.v. Wake *sb.*[2] 4 b (*a*).

1950 L. Baker *Design Marine Water-Tube Boilers* ix. 144 *Arboring*, a term applied to the removal of tube plate material in way of tube ends to reduce the unsupported length of tube inside the drum. **1957** *Shipping World* 21 Aug. 153/2 Longitudinal centre-line bulkheads are provided in all the main and tweendeck holds,.. and in way of the hatch openings there are steel supports for removable wooden longitudinal bulkheads. **1960** *Fishing Gaz.* (N.Y.) 15 Mar. 18/1 The propeller shaft has 5/8″ thick centrifugally cast liners or wearing sleeves shrunk on in way of the stern bearing and stuffing box.

36. on the way (this form only): *spec.* (*colloq.*) (*a*) pregnant; (*b*) (of a child) conceived but not yet born.

(*a*) **1588** [in Dict., sense 36 a]. **1865** A. Macdonald *Let.* Apr. in A. W. Baldwin *Macdonald Sisters* (1960) vi. 100 Poor Mrs Hughes..is 'on the way again, blest if she ain't'. **1941** E. Welty *Curtain of Green* (1943) 39, I bet you another Jax that lady's three months on the way. (*b*) [**1858**: cf. sense 38 b in Dict.] **1896** Kipling *Day's Work* (1898) 271 I'm a married man, an' my fourth's on the ways [*sic*] now, she says. **1919** V. Woolf *Night & Day* ix. 121 He has two children, and another on the way. **1961** G. Greene *Burnt-Out Case* vi. i. 183, I think I have a baby on the way... He doesn't want one. **1983** R. Rendell *Speaker of Mandarin* v. 69 We've..four simply adorable grandchildren with another on the way.

b. imp. (*be*) *on your way*: go away, get going; also (*U.S.*), 'get away' (Get *v.* 54 b in Dict. and Suppl.). *colloq.* (orig. *U.S.*).

1903 'O. Henry' *Trimmed Lamp* (1907) 236 Be on your way, Freddie. **1929** Wodehouse *Gentleman of Leisure* xi. 86 'We're going down with him to the country today, Spike, so be ready.' 'On your way, boss. What's dat?' **1974** 'P. B. Yuill' *Bornless Keeper* xii. 113 Toddle off back to Victoria... On your way, amigo.

c. (*I am*) *on my way*: a formula used to express the speaker's intention of hurrying or of making an immediate departure.

1919 in N. I. White *Amer. Negro Folk-Songs* ii. 124 Lord I'm on my way... Lord I'm on my way. **1948** G. Vidal *City & Pillar* ii. 35 'I'm on my way,' said Jim. **1971** 'L. Egan' *Malicious Mischief* (1972) ix. 158 'Call just in..—they had a prowler over on Jackson... He was armed.'.. 'I'm on my way!' snapped Varallo. **1972** J. Philips *Vanishing Senator* I. iv. 37 'Step on it, will you?' 'On my way,' Peter said. **1978** A. Price *'44 Vintage* xii. 152 If it's all the same to you, m'sieur, we'll be on our way.

38. under way. Now freq. as one word: see *underway *adv.*

VI. 39. a. *way-end* (earlier example); **c.** *way-weary* adj.

1869 W. Barnes *Early England & Saxon-English* 106 When the railway was taken into the hands of more learned men, we had... the *terminus* instead of the rail-end, or way-end, or outending. **1916** Blunden *Harbingers* 60 Wayweary traveller, with your broad bright eyes. **1926** T. E. Lawrence *Seven Pillars* (1935) 5 Love, the way-weary, groped to your body.

40 a. way-freight *N. Amer.*, goods that are picked up or set down at intermediate stopping places on a railway or shipping route; also, a train carrying such freight; **way letter** (earlier examples); **way-place** *U.S.*, a stopping place on a road or railway; a wayside hostelry or an intermediate station; **way-point,** substitute for *U.S.* and def.: orig. *U.S.*, a stopping-place on a journey; (earlier and later examples); also, (on an air journey) the computer-checked coordinates of each stage of a long flight; **way-port,** a port which normally serves as a port of call rather than as an ultimate destination; **way-stop,** chiefly *U.S.*, an intermediate stopping place on a journey; also *fig.*; **way train** *U.S.*, a train which stops at intermediate stations on a railway; a stopping train.

1833 *Niles' Reg.* XLIV. 260/2 The hatch..was open to get out a lot of way-freight. **1875** 'Mark Twain' in *Atlantic Monthly* Aug. 191 No way-freights and no way-passengers were allowed, for the racers would stop only at the largest towns. **1898** H. E. Hamblen *Gen. Manager's Story* 37 The way freight..had crossed over to load some freight. **1977** *Islander* (Victoria, B.C.) 8 May 2/3 The discharging of cargo and the loading of way-freight. **1773** H. Finlay *Jrnl.* 11 Nov. (1867) 38 Way letters he makes his own perquisite. **1851** E. Bowen *U.S. Post-Office Guide* 47 On the letters brought by a mail carrier to be mailed, called way-letters, one cent. is to be charged in addition to the usual postage. **1849** H. Melville *Jrnl. Visit to London* (1948) 67 In a fit of the nightmare was going to stop at a way-place, taking it for the place of my destination. **1883** 'Mark Twain' *Life on Mississippi* lii. 512 She got out of the cars at a way-place. **1880** *Harper's Mag.* Dec. 53 The Ohio is plied by a line of Cincinnati and Pittsburgh packets, and by smaller craft earning a precarious existence between 'way' points. **1899** J. London *Let.* 12 Sept. (1966) 54 And to-morrow I start out on that postponed trip of mine to Stanford University and Mt. Hamilton, to say nothing of way points. **1971** *Flying* Apr. 29/1 (Advt.), Computer and waypoint selector lets you fly direct to a destination hundreds of miles away.. forget about airways dog-legs. **1983** *Times* 6 Sept. 26/2 They plot course by typing..a series of 'way-points' into the computer. Such way-points occur every four hundred miles, so even if one were wrong, the next should put aircraft back on course. **1984** *Sunday Times* 20 May 34/2 The co-ordinates of the different 'waypoints', or intermediate stages along the flight..were checked and found correct. **1897** 'Mark Twain' *Following Equator* xxxii. 303 A good many of us got ashore at the first way-port to seek another ship. **1901** *Daily Colonist* (Victoria, B.C.) 11 Oct. 3/2 The steamer Princess Louise..has been tied up for repairs, and there will be no steamer leaving for the canneries and way ports of the north until Monday at least. **1927** *Blackw. Mag.* Mar. 330/2 'A way-port!' he sighed, after ordering coffee. 'It's turned out to be a terminus for a good many fellows like me.' **1961** Webster, Way-stop. **1969** *Islander* (Victoria, B.C.) 17 Aug. 12/3 She [*sc.* a steamboat] makes various way-stops on each trip and as Skipper McMinn says—'We stop for anyone who jumps up and down on the shore and gives us a holler.' **1981** *Southern Horticulture* (N.Z.) Spring 13 A town that's now making it. Martinborough was once just a way stop on the road to Pirinoa. **1983** C. G. Hart *Rich die Young* iv. 45 Pat was using the Academy as a way-stop while he tried to break into the movies. **1873** 'Mark Twain' & Warner *Gilded Age* xxix. 269 Next morning..he descended, sleepy and sore, from a way-train. **1920** S. Lewis *Main Street* 22 The hordes of the way-trains were not altogether new to Carol.

way, *adv.* Restrict *Obs.* exc. *Sc.*, *north.*, and *U.S.* to senses 1, 2 b, and 3, and add: **2. a.** (Later examples.)

1927 Baroness Orczy *Sir Percy hits Back* v. 35 The three men had become mere specks, 'way down the road. **1959** *Times Lit. Suppl.* 16 Oct. 589/3 You are feet deep in snow and the temperature is way below zero. **1972** *Guardian* 17 Nov. 1/6 The census figures confirm..that unemployment is way above the official figure. **1979** R. Perry *Bishop's Pawn* v. 76 You're way off course... It's back on Unter den Linden.

b. With *down, over.* For *way back, in, off, out, up* see main entries below.

1851 E. S. Wortley *Trav. in U.S.* xxiii. 138 The trading and wealthy cities of far off Alabama and Louisiana, 'way down south'. **1854** Way down [in Dict., wrongly placed in sense 2 a]. **1866** *Atlantic Monthly* May 640 Nor these ain't metters thet with pol'tics swings, But goes 'way down amongst the roots o' things. **1850** L. H. Garrard *Wah-to-Yah* xvii. 222 Calyforny! way over yonder!

c. *fig.* Much, far. *U.S.*

1941 L. I. Wilder *Little Town on Prairie* v. 34 'I wonder how much it costs,' said Ma. ''Way too much for ordinary folks,' said Pa. **1957** *New Yorker* 2 Nov. 105/2 Go by plane, train or ship. Arrive way sooner—relaxed! **1977** *Rolling Stone* 24 Mar., He was a country & western singer and he drank way too much.

wayang (wa·yaŋ). [Javanese *wajang, wayang.*] **1.** In Indonesia and Malaysia, a theatrical performance employing puppets or human dancers; *spec.* a type of Javanese shadow puppet play.

1808 *Asiatick Res.* X. iii. 181 Scenic exhibitions termed 'Wayang-wayang', were till lately, very common in the peninsula of Malayu [*sic*]. **1853** *Jrnl. Indian Archipelago* VII. 271 A very large collection of Wayang figures, cut out of hide. **1881** *Encycl. Brit.* XIII. 604/2 The wayangs or puppet plays, in which grotesque figures of gilded leather are moved by the performer, who recites the appropriate speeches, and as occasion demands plays the part of chorus. **1910** [see *shadow-play* s.v. Shadow *sb.* 16]. **1934** H. W. Ponder *Java Pageant* iv. 49 The stories have been immortalized..by the 'Wayang', or native theatre, which for countless generations has been so much a part of Javanese life. **1965** L. Palmier *Indonesia* xi. 171 The wayang performance has always had a magic and religious significance. **1973** D. May *Laughter in Djakarta* iv. 71 Tonight he was going..to see a *wayang*, an old Hindu-Javanese story acted and danced by a famous company from central Java. **1978** N. Freeling *Night Lords* xvi. 72 The wayang dollies depended..upon the skill and suppleness of the manipulator's fingers.

2. With qualifying term (see quot. 1969), as **wayang kulit** [Javanese *kulit* skin, leather], the Javanese shadow puppet play.

1893 W. B. Worsfold *Visit to Java* x. 178, I had an opportunity of witnessing..the wayang *klitik*, in which the puppets are exhibited themselves to the audience instead of being made to project shadows. **1894** J. D. Vaughan in N. B. Dennys *Descr. Dict. Brit. Malaya* 324 In a puppet show the figures are seen and in this their shadows are. The show is called *wayang kulit*, or leather puppets. **1936** G. B. Gardner *Keris* i. 21 The figures are usually grotesque, of the *wayang kulit* type. **1965** *Economist* 13 Mar. 1149/3 The traditional Indonesian *wayang purwa* puppet theatre show, usually performed at night, in which the vague shadows of leather puppets are fuzzily silhouetted on a screen. **1966** D. Forbes *Heart of Malaya* viii. 100 Figures that moved across the frame of the doorway looked like silhouettes in the *wayang kulit*, the shadow play. **1969** A. R. Philpott *Dict. Puppetry* 277 The precise nature of the performance is distinguished by a qualifying term—e.g. wayang purwa, wayang gedog,.. wayang wong—the last being a performance by human actors... The qualifying term may indicate type of puppet or the type of plays. **1976** *Times* 31 Aug. (Malaysia Suppl.) p. iv/4, Both farmers and fishermen are largely confined to their houses during the monsoon season, when some of them cut silhouette puppets from cowhide for the traditional Wayang Kulit shadow play—a long procession of characters, based on the Indian epic *The Ramayana.*

way-back, *adv.*, *a.*, and *sb. colloq.* (chiefly *U.S.*, *Austral.*, and *N.Z.*). Forms: see below. [f. Way *adv.* + Back *adv.*] **A.** *adv.* Usu. written **way back. 1.** Far away; in or *from* a remote rural area.

1855 *Merry's Museum* XXIX. 58, I did not know that there was such a fine Magazine,..for I live 'way back in the woods'. **1884** *Boston Globe* Oct., His unkempt hair, gawky appearance, and homespun suit..all bespoke the citizen from wayback. **1889** Kipling *From Sea to Sea* (1899) II. xxvi. 28 'You'll see the salmon-wheels 'fore long,' said a man who lived 'way back on the Washoogle'. **1916** G. Thornton *Wowser* 85 The condition of those living 'wayback'. **1930** M. R. E. Blair *By Pacific Waters* ii. 12 I'm sure they are getting a storm way-back. **1936** 'F. Gerald' *Millionaire in Memories* iii. 106 Blackall was much the same as any other township 'way back'. **1976** *National Observer* (U.S. 6 Nov., 'We needed something to let people know that there was a church there,' says Rector Mart Gayland Pool. 'We sat way back on a slope near a golf course, and our facility looked more like a bowling alley or a Kinney shoe store.'

2. A long time ago; *from way back*, since a long time ago; hence, through and through.

1887 *Lantern* (New Orleans) 30 July 3/3 Nick is a walker from way back. **1889** [see Way *adv.* 2 b]. **1889** Kipling *From Sea to Sea* (1899) I. xxii. 432, I am an American by birth—an American from way back. **1892** 'Mark Twain' *Amer. Claimant* 167, I tell you, he's an artist from way back! **1907** [see Way *adv.* 2 b]. **1923** J. H. Cook *50 Yrs. Old Frontier* III. 227 This occurred 'way back', when the Indians had no horses. **1939** *Country Life* 11 Feb. p. xxxvi/1 The 'Rule for Anchoresses', written way back in the thirteenth century. **1948** *Sporting Mirror* 19 Nov. 6/2 Way back in September I said that Norwich City have got what it takes and would be a power this season. **1969** J. D. A. Widdowson in Halpert & Story *Christmas Mumming in Newfoundland* 218 The real mummers we used to have way back. **1970** J. Lennon in J. Wenner *Lennon Remembered* (1972) 144 He not only knew my work, and the lyrics that I had written but he also understood them, and from *way* back. **1978** R. HILL *Pinch of Snuff* ix. 87 'You know Burkill, sir?' he asked. 'From way back.'

B. *adj.* Usu. written **way-back, wayback. 1.** Of long ago.

1885 *Santa Fé Weekly New Mexican* 10 Sept. 1/2 A writer in giving a description of the plains of Kansas in the 'way back' time, speaks of it as a 'wilderness of grasses'. **1962** *Observer* 17 June 3/6 [U.S. writer] He had an ancestor cult. There was a painting of a way-back ancestor wearing a woollen waistcoat.

2. Hailing from, or located in, a remote rural area.

1887, 1918 [see WAY *adv.* 2 b]. **1933** *Bulletin* (Sydney) 24 May 21/2 Mrs. Smallbeer sold her very wayback pub. **1950** K. S. PRICHARD *Winged Seeds* xv. 165 Sally understood that this visit to a way-back station was an experience for them. **1951** *Landfall* V. 278 Miss Dane.. imagined herself a pioneer of progress in a wayback community. **1973** M. CARNEGIE *Friday Mount* 218 No wonder some of the way-back towns had that look.

C. *sb.* Form as for the adj. **1.** A person inhabiting or coming from a remote district.

1890 E. CUSTER *Following Guidon* xvii. 261 We were, in Western terms, 'waybacks from wayback'. **1912** R. S. TAIT *Scotty Mac, Shearer* 125 At a group in front of him a thimble-rigger was expending much eloquence to induce a party of waybacks to relieve him of his surplus cash. **1924** *Contemp. Rev.* Aug. 236 The well-known resourcefulness and sense of location of the present-day way-backs of Australia..are due..to lessons taught the pioneers by the natives.

2. Remote rural areas; *spec.* the Australian outback.

1890 [see prec. sense]. **1901** F. J. GILLEN *Diary* 5 Oct. (1968) 277 The station is built on a stony rise on the western bank of the Newcastle and like most stock stations in the 'wayback' there has been no attempt made to improve the appearance of the surroundings. **1925** H. H. COOK *Far Flung* v. 39 Some 50 miles in the 'way-back'. **1933** *Bulletin* (Sydney) 27 Sept. 20/4 Waltzing Matilda in the waybacks of S.A. I came upon a well-found homestead.

way-bill. 2. (Earlier example.)

1851 W. KELLY *Excursion to California* I. x. 172 According to our way-bill, and comparing it with our computed travel, we could not be far off the next crossing of the Platte.

way-·in, *a. slang.* [f. WAY *adv.* + IN *adv.*, after *WAY OUT *a.*] Conventional; fashionable, sophisticated.

1960 *N.Y. Times Mag.* 12 June 19/1 A famous lady columnist with a way-out taste in millinery but a way-in taste in film fare. *Ibid.* 78/4 Many artists..have sought refuge in..way-in or way-out religious conversions. **1967** *Punch* 29 Nov. 817/2 There's a real way-in guy looking like how a guy on *The Times Saturday Review* ought to look like.

waying (wē^{i}·iŋ), *vbl. sb. poet. nonce-wd.* [f. WAY *v.* + -ING[1].] A going away; departure.

1922 HARDY *Late Lyrics & Earlier* 120 So, with this saying, 'Good-bye, good-bye,' We speed their waying.

way-leave, wayleave. Add: More widely, a right of way granted by the owner of land to a particular body and for a particular purpose, often in return for payment; also, a document conferring the right. (Further examples.)

1928 H. G. WELLS *Way World is Going* xi. 127 The exploitation of the air, as a means of..available travel, is hopeless without..secure wayleaves over Europe. **1930** *Times* 22 Mar. 19/2 We have also practically completed the Scottish overhead 'Grid' system for the Central Electricity Board... Owing to the difficulty of securing permission for wayleaves our work was necessarily interfered with. **1960** *Farmer & Stockbreeder* 1 Mar. 91/1 The Central Electricity Generating Board has no legal right of entry on your land without your permission or until such time as you have signed a wayleave. **1963** *Times* 24 May 16/6 A wayleave for a future subway linking the triangle with the Radcliffe Infirmary and passing under the Banbury and the Woodstock roads.

attrib.

1960 *Times Rev. Industry* Feb. 75/1 There is no way-leave payment. **1971** P. GRESSWELL *Environment* 215 Landowners are in a strong position to influence power line proposals through granting or refusing wayleave consent.

way·mark, *v.* [f. the sb.] *trans.* To provide or identify (a path) with waymarks. Hence **way·marked** *ppl. a.*, **way·marking** *vbl. sb.*

1960 *Guardian* 5 Nov. 6/3 The Ramblers' Association.. is cleft..over the question of 'waymarking' paths and routes by means of blobs of coloured paint. *Ibid.* 9 Nov. 8/3 The plan to provide 'waymarking' on some popular British fells. **1973** *Village* Autumn 51 Walkers on the Continent or in America find themselves well supplied with long-distance trails and with waymarked paths in tourist areas. **1982** *Walker's Britain* 328/2 There are still several stretches where the waymarking is incomplete because public rights of way have not been obtained. **1983** *Out of Town* July 72/2 Much effort and imagination has gone into waymarking the walks.

way off, *adv.* and *a.* orig. *U.S.* [f. WAY *adv.* + OFF *adv.*] **A.** *adv.* Far away.

1853 G. C. HILL *Dovecote* 29, I found her 'way off in them woods yonder! **1897** [in Dict. s.v. WAY *adv.* 2 b]. **1897** KIPLING *Captains Courageous* iii. 60 'Way off yander's the *Day's Eye.* **1929** D. H. LAWRENCE *Pansies* 72 Out of the soul's middle to the middle-most sun, way-off, or in every atom. **1952** *Manch. Guardian Weekly* 22 May 7/2 Way off to the right was a beery Irishman.

2. Far from the intended target; greatly mistaken, quite wrong.

1892 *Harper's Mag.* Feb. 438/2 The papers are generally 'way off in some things. **1906** A. H. LEWIS *Confessions of Detective* I. i. 10 'You're dead wrong, Doc!' broke in Mugsey... 'You're 'way off.' **1962** J. GLENN in *Into Orbit* 209 My attitude indications on the instrument panel are way off. **1973** 'H. HOWARD' *Highway to Murder* x. 118 Seemed first impressions could be 'way off. **1977** H. KAPLAN *Damascus Cover* (1978) iv. 33 On the pistol range Ari discovered..that his aim was way off.

B. *adj.* **1.** Usu. **way-·off.** Distant.

1870 A. D. WHITNEY *We Girls* (1871) xi. 229 General and Mrs. Ingleside..had come from their way-off, beautiful Wisconsin home. **1928** D. H. LAWRENCE *Woman rode Away* 93 The way-off things like the sun.

way out, *adv., a.,* and *sb.* orig. *U.S.* [f. WAY *adv.* + OUT *adv.*] **A.** *adv.* Far out, far away. *colloq.*

1868 G. A. CUSTER *Let.* 20 Feb. in E. Custer *Following Guidon* (1890) 53 They had braved the perils..in order to bring us, 'way out here, news from our loved ones. **1882** *Congress. Rec.* 9 Mar. 1758/1 Instead of that they go way out to Peoria, Illinois. **1933** L. I. WILDER *Farmer Boy* xvi. 119 This country..goes 'way out beyond Kansas.. down to the Pacific Ocean. **1944** M. LASKI *Love on Supertax* xi. 102 After a..journey by 'bus, Clarissa alighted way out on the North Circular Road. **1977** *Chicago Tribune* 2 Oct. v. 2/2 There is more clout in the Senate, you see, than way out west away from the mainstream.

B. *adj.* Also **way-ou·t. 1.** Far removed from reality or from convention; extreme; progressive, avant-garde, advanced. *slang.*

1958 G. LEA *Somewhere there's Music* xix. 164, I turn on [*sc.* smoke marijuana] a little and I get way out. **1959** *Encounter* June 42/2 The ego-ideal of the Beatnik is the 'cool hipster'—..the man who is 'way out'. **1959** N. MAILER *Advts. for Myself* (1961) 296 Mine [*sc.* my hypothesis] is interesting, mine is way out (on the avenue of the mystery along the road to 'It') but still I am just one cat in a world of cool cats. **1961** *Life* (Internat. ed.) 8 May 44 The way-out world of micro-electronics. **1964** J. DUNBAR in Hamblett & Deverson *Generation X* 179 One thing I like about Cambridge, people don't try to be too way out. At places like Oxford, or Reading, I've seen blokes going around barefoot and wearing ear-rings. **1967** *Times* 13 Apr. 23 The 'way out' field of nuclear fusion. **1972** J. PHILIPS *Vanishing Senator* III. iii. 162 Vardon thought up a way-out scheme to commit a murder. **1979** *Dædalus* Spring 141 These [*sc.* Radio Città in Bologna and Radio Alice] were 'way-out' examples of local radio. **1982** BARR & YORK *Official Sloane Ranger Handbk.* 38/1 She would not wear Art Nouveau jewels (too way out).

2. Greatly mistaken. *slang.*

1959 M. SUMMERTON *Small Wilderness* viii. 112 You're way out, Puss. If anybody has got a perfect alibi..it's Cliff. **1965** *New Statesman* 7 May 721/3, I would not presume to argue with Edward Hyams on matters botanical, but he is way out on snakes.

C. *sb.* A person who holds extreme or unconventional views.

1968 *Manch. Guardian Weekly* 17 Oct. 19 The drop-outs have copped out, the redskins have bitten the dust, the way-outs have faced the nitty-gritty (truth). **1970** *Encycl. Sci. Suppl.* (Grolier) 158 Two years ago we were considered way-outs. Nobody knew what conservation meant.

Hence **way-ou·tness** *slang*, unconventionality.

1965 *Tablet* 27 Nov. 1327/1 Some way-outness prevents him from acquiescing in the wisdom of acceptance. **1968** R. V. BESTE *Repeat Instructions* i. 10 That's the kind of way-outness that should have made Security suspicious. **1979** S. SMITH *Survivor* xvii. 185 Young people of all degrees of 'way-outness'.

ways and means. Add: **2. a.** Also *attrib.*

1867 *Oregon State Jrnl.* 5 Jan. 2/2 The Ways and Means Committee decided to postpone an action on Mr. Boutwell's bill. **1919** *Lit. Digest* 22 Mar. 21/2 Mr. Fordney, of Michigan,..will probably be..Chairman of the Ways and Means Committee. **1973** B. J. SIMS *Suppl. to Sergeant on Stamp Duties* (ed. 6) A55 This section and the associated Ways and Means Resolution provides powers whereby changes in stamp duty may be given effect to by means of a Budget Resolution. **1977** *Time* 12 Dec. 34/2 Al Ullman, the House Ways and Means chairman, has been pleading with Carter for a 'minimalist' rather than a 'maximalist' tax bill.

wayside. Add: **a.** Phr. *to fall by the wayside* [after Luke viii. 5: see quot. 1526 in Dict.], to fail to stay the course, to drop out.

1965 *New Statesman* 7 May 719/1 Responding to persuasion, young wives go back into teaching... Some toughen and survive, others fall by the wayside. **1973** *Times* 24 May 10/1 She went to San Diego for a world junior tournament last year and fell by the wayside only because of a marker's error. **1977** L. T. MILIC in Bond & McLeod *Newslett. to Newspapers* I. 41 As society changes, so must the tone of a publication or it falls by the wayside.

b. *wayside pulpit*, a board, usu. placed outside a place of worship, displaying a religious text or maxim.

1925 *Advertising World* Dec. 302/2 (*heading*) How the 'wayside pulpit' scheme was organized. **1932** Q. D. LEAVIS *Fiction & Reading Public* II. iv. 193 An inspection of the slogans displayed on Wayside Pulpits..reveals that they are largely devoted to denunciation of an attitude described as pessimistic. **1976** *Church Times* 20 Feb. 11/1 'My greed is another's need' and 'Live simply that others may simply live' have become familiar slogans on wayside pulpits and in parish magazines. **1981** F. INGLIS *Promise of Happiness* iii. 93 We most of us *know* when we are lying. My wayside pulpit-point is that we no longer care very much.

way station. *U.S.* Also **way-station. 1. a.** (In Dict. s.v. WAY *sb.*[1] 40.) Also *transf.*

1850 *Ann. Rep. Railroad Corp. Massachusetts 1849* 21 Way stations for express trains. **1854** *Harper's Mag.* VIII. 566/2 The boats touched at most of the prominent towns on the river, to land such passengers as might desire to disembark at 'way-stations'. **1855** [see *LOCK *v.*[1] 7 d]. **1856,** etc. [in Dict.]. **1912** F. J. HASKIN *Amer. Govt.* 210 Cities which are to-day mere way stations on the international routes of trade will grow into rich world centers. **1914** *Sat. Even. Post* 4 Apr. 52/2 At ten o'clock that night at a way-station the kid was ditched. **1934** A. WOOLLCOTT *While Rome Burns* 258 To fly by way of Ottawa, Point Barrow, and other way-stations. **1944** *Daily Progress* (Charlottesville, Va.) 21 July 1/8 The island [*sc.* Guam].. formerly served as a way-station on the trans-Pacific airroute to the East. **1976** N. THORNBURG *Cutter & Bone* vi. 134 It was..a way station carefully restored and preserved to offer at least a semblance of its original state. **1984** *New Yorker* 9 July 43/2 The United States may..use Moroccan facilities..as way stations for combat troops destined for service in, say, the Middle East.

b. *fig.*, or in fig. context.

1892 *Congress. Rec.* 23 Mar. 2462/2 'Will the gentleman allow me to ask him a question?'..'The gentleman will excuse me. On a fast schedule I can not stop at way stations.' **1926** [see *TECTAL *a.*]. **1948** MENJOU & MUSSELMAN *It took Nine Tailors* 10 She thought a theater was just a way station on the road to perdition. **1960** BRUNER & KLEIN in Kaplan & Wapner *Perspectives in Psychol. Theory* 65 There are corticofugal impulses that go down through the reticular formation to program selectivity of intake by way stations in the sensory system. **1973** *Sci. Amer.* July 52/1 Lymphocytes are found in high concentrations in the lymph nodes, way stations along the lymphatic vessels. **1978** W. GARNER *Möbius Trip* (1979) i. 12 The Belgravia apartment was not a home... It was a way station. **1982** H. KISSINGER *Yrs. of Upheaval* viii. 302 The cease-fire was merely a tactic, a way station toward their objective of taking over the whole of Indochina by force.

way up, *adv.* and *a.* orig. *U.S.* [f. WAY *adv.* + UP *adv.*] **A.** *adv.* Far up.

1851 'E. WETHERELL' *Wide, Wide World* I. xii. 150 Do you live 'way up there? **1862** O. W. NORTON *Army Lett.* 100 A minister of the gospel who was so wonderfully.. war-like way up in Erie. **1901** [in Dict. s.v. WAY *adv.* 2 a]. **1946** K. TENNANT *Lost Haven* (1947) vii. 95 If you owned a bath, it put you 'way, 'way up in the world. **1956** H. KURNITZ *Invasion of Privacy* xiv. 92 She came down the stairs and I thought that was funny because they live way up top. **1972** *National Observer* (N.Y.) 27 May 14/1 Way up in the high-level social circles are those who are so rich they never, ever talk about money.

B. *adj.* Usu. **way-·up.** Excellent, first-class; of high social standing. *slang* (chiefly *U.S.*).

1887 F. FRANCIS *Saddle & Mocassin* 81 A real way-up cook, who could make chile-con-carne, tamales, and all the best Mexican dishes. **1902** KIPLING *Traffics & Discoveries* (1904) 17 He's a way-up barrister when he's at home. **1909** 'O. HENRY' *Roads of Destiny* xviii. 299, I want to be manager of something way up—like a railroad or a diamond trust or an automobile factory.

way-up (wē^{i},ʊ·p), *sb. Geol.* [f. phr. (*which, this, the right,* etc.) *way up* (WAY *sb.*[1] 9 a, UP *adv.*[2] 9 a).] Orientation as regards which part is uppermost or was deposited last.

1958 *Q. Jrnl. Geol. Soc.* CXIII. 364 Way-up has been determined from graded bedding. **1969** BENNISON & WRIGHT *Geol. Hist. Brit. Isles* ii. 34 Certain characters, such as..the way-up of shells, provide evidence of bottom conditions and the strength of currents. **1982** COLLINSON & THOMPSON *Sedimentary Structures* vi. 97/1 Aeolian structures could help to establish way-up in highly dipping sequences.

Wazir[2] (wăzi^{ə}·ɹ). Also **Waziri**; 9 **Vazírí, Vizeeree, Wuzeerá,** etc. A member of a Pathan people of north-west Pakistan; also, this people collectively. Also *attrib.* or as *adj.*

1815 M. ELPHINSTONE *Caubul* III. iii. 385 The Vizeerees are said to be tall and muscular. **1838** in *Parl. Papers 1839* XL. 29 The Vezeree territory. **1842** C. MASSON *Journeys* I. vii. 100 A few Vazírí huts. **1847** H. B. EDWARDES *Diary* 3 Dec. (1911) 156 A very extensive triangular *Thull*, or sand, occupied by the Vizeeree tribes. **1851** R. G. LATHAM *Ethnol. Brit. Colonies* iv. 182 The mountaineers around them—the *Vizeri*—are a pure branch. **1873,** etc. [see *MAHSUD]. **1924** LD. RONALDSHAY *India* vii. 76 Our dealings with the Mahsud Waziris. **1957** B. J. GOULD *Jewel in Lotus* x. 134 The 'girls' were Wazir tribesmen and the welcome they received was a salvo of rapid fire. **1977** J. CLEARY *High Road to China* v. 163 The Mahsuds and Wazirs have..shot down several of our machines. *Ibid.* 175 The four Waziri..remained behind.

wch, wch., abbrev. of WHICH *pron.*

1739 T. CORAM *Let.* 15 Sept. in R. McClure *Coram's Children* (1981) iii. 31 The Attorny & Solicitor Generals Fees..wch they had for Examining the Proposals. **1793** C. BURNEY *Let.* 10 July in F. Burney *Jrnls. & Lett.* (1972) II. 171, I dread the evils into wch their sudden union w^{d} involve them. **1811** SHELLEY *Let.* 6 Jan. (1964) I. 37 Ignorant of the refinements in Love, wch. can only be attained by solitary reflexion.

wd, wd., abbrev. of *would* s.v. Will *v.*[1]

1793 [see *wch, wch.]. **1800** [see *wholesale *v.*]. **1811** Shelley *Let.* 12 Jan. (1964) I. 44 Wd. that I cd. believe them to be as [they] are represented. **1888** H. O.D. Davidson *Let.* 12 July in R. S. Churchill *Winston S. Churchill* (1967) I. Compan. I. v. 169, I thought it wd do him good to spend a day with you. **1910** [see *week-endize* vb. s.v. *week-end]. **1930** E. Pound *XXX Cantos* vi. 24 They wd. have given him poison But for the shape of his sword-hilt. **1981** J. Stubbs *Ironmaster* xiv. 188 There w[d] be an Outcry if the wedding was to fall in the month of May.

we, *pron.* Add: **1. h.** Used in conjunction with *they* to allude to the tension between two mutually exclusive groups or categories of people, or their opposing interests. Cf. *them and us* s.v. *them *pers. pron.* 1 e.

[**1884** F. Maurice *F. D. Maurice* II. xvii. 531 That division of all men into the two classes of 'we' and 'the rest',..which we most of us adopt.] **1926** Kipling *Debits & Credits* 327 Would you believe it?—They look upon We As only a sort of They! **1942** H. Haycraft *Murder for Pleasure* xv. 316 The..fundamental contradiction between the We and They in government. **1948** R. H. Tawney in F. A. Iremonger *William Temple* v. 88 The 'We and They' complex..could not survive continuous co-operation with colleagues..whose experience of life was quite different from his own. **1965** *Observer* (Colour Suppl.) 25 Apr. 13/1 The children have a chance of learning to deal with adults, without the we–they feeling. **1973** *Guardian* 30 Mar. 14/2 Anything which emphasises the 'we' and 'they' of the situation will drive men..towards the extremes of politics.

weak, *a.* Add: **2. b.** *weak sister*, an ineffectual or unreliable person (or either sex); a person of weak character; also *transf. colloq.* (orig. *U.S.*).

1857 *Call* (San Francisco) 3 May 1/1 G. W. Swerzy..is a 'weak sister' and a rather 'bad egg'. **1866** Geo. Eliot *Felix Holt* I. iv. 95 'I lack grace to deal with these weak sisters,' said the minister. **1949** R. B. West *Rocky Mt. Cities* 311 The morning *Rocky Mountain News*..dawdled along as one of the weakest sisters in the Scripps–Howard string [of newspapers]. **1955** E. Berckman *Beckoning Dream* (1956) xix. 135 Luanna was a softie.., a weak sister. She's the one you'd expect to go all to pieces, and she did. **1976** 'J. Ross' *I know what it's like to Die* xvii. 116 Birdsell was a weak sister... He was..known to be greedy and a physical coward.

12. f. (*b*) *Math.* Of a mathematical entity or concept: implying less than others of its kind; defined by fewer conditions.

1950 W. Feller *Introd. Probability Theory* I. viii. 157 The strong law of large numbers was first formulated by Cantelli (1917)... Like the weak law, it is only a very special case of a general theorem on random variables. **1964** A. P. & W. Robertson *Topological Vector Spaces* p. vii, It often clarifies results in the theory of normed spaces, especially those concerned with the weak topology, to regard them as particular cases of more general results about topological vector spaces. **1971** G. Higman in Powell & Higman *Finite Simple Groups* vi. 211 We then define E_n to be the weakest equivalence relation on Ω_n satisfying the following three conditions. **1979** *Proc. London Math. Soc.* XXXVIII. 439 Let **L** be the collection of minimal edge-sets of paths which join *s* to *s′* or *t* to *t′*. Then **L** has the weak MFMC property (but..in general, not the strong).

k. *Physics.* Applied to one of the four known kinds of force between particles, which is effective only at distances less than about 10^{-15} cm., is very much weaker than the electromagnetic and the strong interactions, and conserves neither strangeness, parity, nor isospin.

[**1953** M. Gell-Mann in *Physical Rev.* XCII. 833/2 Let us suppose that both 'ordinary particles' (nucleons and pions) and 'new unstable particles'..have interactions of three kinds:.. (iii) Other charge-dependent interactions, which we take to be very weak.] **1954** [see *strong *a.* 10 e]. **1968** M. S. Livingston *Particle Physics* vii. 139 Parity conservation is violated in this weak interaction. **1972** G. L. Wick *Elementary Particles* iii. 43 Typical weak interactions are nuclear beta decay and the slow decays of elementary particles. **1976** *Sci. Amer.* Jan. 45/1 The weak force affects every particle but one, the exception being the photon. **1982** *Ann. Reg. 1981* 385 Theorists had already inferred that electromagnetism and the weak force were two extremes of the same thing.

15. d. Of flour: made from soft wheat, so that it contains relatively less gluten and more starch, rises less with yeast, and is less cohesive. Of wheat: soft.

1889 J. Blandy *Bakers' Guide* (ed. 2) 65 It is very important that young bakers should know how to buy, and blend flour for bread-making; and we..direct them to use a hard dry flour in the sponge, with an eighth part of soft weak flour..to feed the yeast. **1914** *Times* 8 June 16/5 Some flours, among which that from English wheat may be taken as a familiar example, produce small flat close-textured and 'runny' loaves. These are called weak flours. **1924** J. Stewart *Bread & Bread Baking* ii. 15 Weak flours are..important in pastry baking and confectionery. **1951** *Good Housek. Home Encycl.* 466/2 'Soft' or 'weak' wheats contain less gluten and more starch. **1962** *Listener* 22 Mar. 510/1 As a general rule, 'strong' flour contains more nitrogen than 'weak' flour.

e. Of the mixture in an internal-combustion engine: = *lean *a.* 4 f.

1918 V. W. Pagé *Aviation Engines* iii. 114 A rich mixture ignites much quicker than a weak mixture. **1948** 'N. Shute' *No Highway* ix. 217 Mr. Honey's estimate of the time to tailplane failure, under normal weak mixture cruising conditions, was 1,440 hours. **1981** R. Bacon *Two-Strike Tuning* ix. 63 All two-stroke engines are sensitive to mixture strength. Too rich and the power and acceleration suffer, while if too weak the result can be a seized or holed piston.

16. b. *weak link*: the weakest or least dependable of a number of interdependent items; also in *Proverb.* Cf. *weak point* (*a*), sense 16 e in Dict.

1868 *Cornh. Mag.* XVII. 295 A chain is no stronger than its weakest link. **1885** [see sense 16 a in Dict.]. **1926** H. Crane *Let.* 12 Aug. (1965) 272 Mrs. Simpson was enormously pleased at your postcard; and I with your praise of the Dedication. You generally do pick the weakest link; that verse has bothered me. **1942** I. S. Shriber *Body for Bill* (1947) xiv. 183 'Stansfield was a pretty weak individual... He was threatening to give the whole thing away.'.. 'A chain is no stronger than its weakest link, remember?' **1965** M. Frayn *Tin Men* xv. 88 An unreliable man, Haugh, a weak link in the team. **1975** R. Lewis *Double Take* iv. 138 All right, he lifted the heart drug, but we..picked out the weak link in Ward too. **1984** *Bookseller* 8 Sept. 1049/2, I sometimes seek comfort in the old adage that a chain is only as strong as its weakest link.

e. (*a*) (Earlier example.)

1865 Mill *Auguste Comte* 126 M. Littré..is a disciple only of the Cours de Philosophie Positive, and can see the weak points even in that.

20. Of a variant pronunciation: usual in contexts where the word is unstressed.

1890 H. Sweet *Primer Spoken Eng.* 13 Words that occur very frequently with weak stress often develope a weak form by the side of the original strong one. **1917** D. Jones *Eng. Pronouncing Dict.* p. xix, Circumstances exist in which strong forms occur unstressed, but in no case does a weak form occur stressed. **1982** J. C. Wells *Accents of Eng.* I. iii. 227 In many accents the pronoun *you* has a weak form /jə/ (conventionally spellable *ya* in the United States, but *yer* in non-rhotic-oriented England).

21. b. (Earlier example.)

1833 *Philol. Museum* II. 385 No weak verb ever in process of time became strong, while strong verbs do become weak.

21*. Similative phrases in which *weak* may have any of various meanings. (See also sense 5 a in Dict.)

1535 Bible (Coverdale) *Ezek.* vii. 17 All knees shalbe weake as the water [**1611** (A.V.) weake as water]. **1874** Trollope *Phineas Redux* II. xxx. 244 She would not sin... Having so resolved, she became weak as water. **1926** J. Buchan *Dancing Floor* i. ii. 54 We were as weak as kittens, but..extraordinarily happy. **1980** A. Price *Hour of Donkey* ix. 123 He must have been as weak as a kitten, with all the blood he'd lost. **1983** J. Wainwright *Their Evil Ways* v. 154, I think you're mad... Mad and as weak as water.

22. a. *weak-fleshed, -limned, -principled, -skinned, -stressed* adjs.

1967 Weak-fleshed [see *raw-jawed* adj. s.v. *raw *a.* 9]. *a* **1918** W. Owen *Poems* (1963) 90 The weak-limned hour when sick men's sighs are drained. **1913** D. H. Lawrence *Sons & Lovers* ix. 246 It was the nose and eyes of her own mother's people—good-looking, weak-principled folk. **1933** Dylan Thomas *Lett.* (1966) 72 And unless you want to regard the man [*sc.* D. H. Lawrence] as a vain, weak-skinned, egocentric, domineering little charlatan, *don't* borrow the book. **1898** H. Sweet *New Eng. Gram.* II. 32 If three strong-stressed words come together—especially in immediate succession, but also with intervening weak-stressed words — the stress of the middle word is often reduced. **1966** *English Studies* XLVII. 83 In languages that use interrogatives as indefinites, such as Dutch, the latter are always weak-stressed.

weakfish. (Earlier example.)

1791 J. Baxter *Jrnl.* 21 June in *Amer. Speech* (1965) XL. 200 Went a fishing..had 350 weekfish.

weak-kneed, *a.* (Earlier example.)

1863 *Rio Abajo Press* (Albuquerque, N.M.) 24 Feb. 2 But we must forego these comforts and conveniences, because our legislators are too weak-kneed to enact a tax law.

weakly, *adv.* Add: **8.** *Math.* In a way that implies less or that satisfies fewer conditions (cf. *weak *a.* 12 f (*b*)).

1955 M. Loève *Probability Theory* ix. 443 If all sequences $\tilde{T}^n X$ are weakly compact, then it is easily proved that sup $\|\tilde{T}^n\| < \infty$. **1972** R. J. Wilson *Introd. Graph Theory* vii. 102 A digraph *D* is said to be connected (or weakly-connected) if it cannot be expressed as the union of two disjoint digraphs.

weak-minded, *a.* **1.** (Earlier example.)

1716 T. Cave *Let.* 5 Aug. in M. M. Verney *Verney Lett.* (1930) II. xxii. 43 We all continue in perfect sanity of body but very weak-minded this hott weather, as you'l judg by this Scrawll.

weald. Add: **3. wealdsman**, an inhabitant of the Weald.

1928 *Daily Tel.* 29 May 8/5 The flares signalled her triumph to the wealdsmen of Sussex.

Wealden, *a.* Add: **2. b.** Applied to a style of timber house built in the Weald in the late medieval and Tudor periods (see quots. 1961, 1963).

1956 *Archaeol. Jrnl.* CXII. 93 In Kent the aisled hall was replaced by the type of building often called the 'Wealden' house, though it has a wider distribution than that. **1961** M. W. Barley *Eng. Farmhouse & Cottage* I. ii. 27 The Wealden house has a central hall open to the roof with a storeyed wing at one end or both. The whole is under a continuous roof, but the storeyed wing is jettied out, to overhang the ground floor by a foot or more. **1963** S. E. Rigold in Foster & Alcock *Culture & Environment* xiii. 351 The characteristic hall-house of Kent and Sussex has a unitary hipped roof..covering both the hall and the two-storeyed ends... When the upper stories are jettied laterally, the façade of the hall between them is relatively recessed, and the lateral wall-plate of the jettied ends is carried right across..in front of the wall-plate of the hall... This is the so-called 'Wealden house'. **1974** *Country Life* 14 Feb. 312/4 A yeoman farmer's house of the Wealden type that existed in the mid 15th century.

we-all (wī-ǭl), *pron. U.S. dial.* [f. We *pron.* + All *a.*] Used in place of We *pron.*

1875 'Mark Twain' *Let.* 23 Nov. (1917) I. xv. 268 We-all send love to you-all. **1905** A. V. Culbertson *Banjo Talks* 25 Ter do lak we-all in de pas'. **1926** E. M. Roberts *Time of Man* vii. 266 His wife was young..and we-all made a jolly set. **1949** *Chicago Tribune* 27 Feb. vii. 6/6 Did we-all see Smokey hold? **1964** *N.Y. Times Mag.* 23 Aug. 62/2 *Soul brother*, Negro; also referred to as..*we-all,..the people.*

So **we-all's**, our; ours.

1887 *Scribner's Mag.* Oct. 475/1 O Lawd, 'lighten we-all's unnerstandin's. **1893** H. A. Shands *Some Peculiarities of Speech in Mississippi* 67 'That house is we all's' means that the house belongs to all of us. **1905** A. V. Culbertson *Banjo Talks* 160 Bin settin' yer..lak dis, So I be sut'n dat I doan' miss De train dat teck me back ter we-all's place.

wealth. Add: **6.** *wealth-creating, -holder, -making*; *wealth-fantasy*; **wealth tax**, a tax levied on the basis of a person's capital or financial assets.

1964 M. McLuhan *Understanding Media* (1967) x. 110 In the Roman world the army was the work force of a mechanized wealth-creating process. **1940** 'G. Orwell' in *Horizon* Mar. 181 This kind of thing is a perfectly deliberate incitement to wealth-fantasy. **1957** A. C. L. Day *Outl. Monetary Econ.* ii. 19 Similar considerations will influence many other wealth-holders. **1980** *TWA Ambassador* Oct. 14/1 Much of the growth in the number of wealthholders in the United States has been among the affluent, but clearly non-wealthy middle-class and upper-middle-class households. **1964** M. McLuhan *Understanding Media* (1967) x. 111 The Roman Army as a mobile, industrial wealth-making force. **1963** *Daily Tel.* 22 Feb. 26/6 (*heading*) Wealth tax statement next week. **1974** *Guardian* 23 Mar. 12/1 The Labour Party..suggested an annual wealth tax starting at 1 per cent on £50,000, and running up to 5 per cent on £400,000 and more. **1976** *Jrnl. R. Soc. Arts* Mar. 200/1 Until the final form of wealth tax has been decided it is not possible to decide whether it will be fiscally neutral as regards private woodlands.

wealthily, *adv.* (Later example.)

c **1885** E. Dickinson *Poems* (1955) III. 1123 Ill it becometh me to dwell so wealthily When at my very Door are those possessing more, In abject poverty.

wealthy, *a.* Add: **6.** (With capital initial.) Name of a N. American variety of late-ripening, red-skinned cooking or dessert apple.

1869 C. Downing *Fruits & Fruit Trees Amer.* (ed. 2) ix. 398 Wealthy. A new variety originated by Peter M. Gideon, near St. Paul, Minn., from seed gathered in Maine about 1860... Fruit medium, oblate or roundish oblate, whitish yellow ground, shaded with deep rich crimson. **1921** *Daily Colonist* (Victoria, B.C.) 7 Oct. 7/4 Seal of Quality Groceries. No. 1 Wealthy Apples, excellent, sound stock, in boxes containing about 40 lbs. **1944** *Chicago Daily News* 25 Sept. 13/3 Right now Wealthies or Maiden's Blush are the choice varieties for cooking or pie. **1975** *New Yorker* 11 Aug. 39/1 The five apples so suddenly swept from the general market were the Baldwin, the Wealthy, the Golden Grimes, the Ben Davis, and the Black Twig.

weaner. **2.** For (? *Australian*) read 'orig. *Austral.* and *N.Z.*' and add: Also, a pig or any other animal weaned during the current year. Also *attrib.* (Earlier and further examples.)

1865 R. Henning *Let.* 19 Aug. (1966) 208 He takes the heaviest flock of all, 2,200 weaners. **1928** *Daily Express* 3 Feb. 5/2 Instruction is given in..the rearing of calves for stock, for market as 'weaners', and for sale as veal. **1950** *N.Z. Jrnl. Agric.* Jan. 63/1 Pigs sold as weaners through saleyards. **1958** *Times* 29 Sept. 2/7 Though weaner prices fell..during 1957/58, high prices for fat pigs are still reflected in the store market. **1969** T. West in R. Blythe *Akenfield* xi. 179, I want to produce weaner-pigs... Are you interested? **1981–2** *Deer Farmer* (N.Z.) Summer 10/3 The trial of disbudding of 80 to 100 weaner bucks will start in March next year. *Ibid.* 16/2 A herd of 300 New Zealand wapiti and wapiti-red hybrid females, is run at Criffel, along with 200 bulls, and 30 male and 30 female New Zealand wapiti weaners. **1984** *N.Z. Farmer* 12 Apr. 12/1 The cattle policy is to winter all weaners.

weapon, *sb.* Add: **2. c.** Also *with his own weapon*(*s*).

1781 Johnson *Lives of Poets: Congreve* 17 He is very angry, and, hoping to conquer Collier with his own weapons, allows himself in the use of every term of contumely and contempt. **1850** C. Kingsley *Alton Locke* II. xvi. 259 Try no more to meet Mammon with his own weapons, but commit your cause to Him who judges righteously. **1897** B. STOKER *Dracula* xxii. 306 He has chosen this earth because it has been holy. Thus we defeat him with his own weapon, for we make it more holy still.

3. Delete † *Obs.* and add later examples. *coarse slang.*

1762 T. BRIDGES *Homer Travestie* IV. 189 She guides his weapon where she lists: Nay more, a touch of her soft hand, If fallen down, will make him stand. **1922** JOYCE *Ulysses* 529 Well for you, you muff, if you had that weapon with knobs and lumps and warts all over it. **1972** H. & R. GREENWALD *Sex-Life Lett.* (1974) 279 This sexual thrill still comes over me whenever I see a horse flashing his weapon, and although I feel guilty and try to look away, I usually look as long as decently possible.

4. simple attrib., as *weapon-hoard, -pit, -power*; *weapon-like* adj.; objective, as *weapon-delivery* (also *attrib.*); *weapon-making* vbl. sb.; **weapon(s)-carrier,** a vehicle or aircraft specially designed for carrying weapons; **weapons-grade** *a.*, applied to fissile material of suitable quality for making nuclear weapons; **weapon(s) system** orig. *U.S.*, a military weapon together with all the equipment required to make use of it, such as detection and control apparatus, a launcher, and a delivery vehicle; **weapon-training** *vbl. sb.*, training in the use of weapons.

1938 *19th Cent.* Feb. 195 The possibilities of the new weapon-carrier in the air. **1947** *Horizon* Sept. 207 A weapons-carrier flew by loaded with G.I.s. **1963** *Daily Tel.* 10 Oct. 15/8 TSR 2, the RAF's tactical and strategical bomber,..has the most secret and sophisticated all-weather weapons delivery system in the world. **1977** *R.A.F. News* 22 June–5 July 2/5 Live ammunition, bombs and missiles were, in general, carried only by aircraft flying sorties which would culminate in weapon delivery at one of the recognised ranges. **1961** *Ann. Reg. 1960* 152 Both countries..should each set aside 30,000 kilograms of weapons-grade uranium 235, as a first step in their transfer to peaceful uses. **1977** N. FREELING *Gadget* I. 11 It won't make a bomb... It's nowhere near weapons grade. **1955** J. R. R. TOLKIEN *Return of King* 50 There are no great weapon-hoards here, lord. **1922** D. H. LAWRENCE *England, my England* (1924) 36 Not what we would call love, but a weapon-like kinship. **1936** AUDEN *Look, Stranger!* 67 Built by the conscious-stricken, the weapon-making, By us. *a* **1944** K. DOUGLAS *Alamein to Zem Zem* (1946) 29 Looking down..at a weapon-pit beside us, I saw a Libyan soldier reclining there. **1958** M. K. JOSEPH *I'll soldier no More* ix. 161 The neat row of weapon-pits so convenient for sleeping. **1937** L. HART *Europe in Arms* xvii. 238 At night..an increase of man-power in proportion to weapon-power is desirable. **1956** W. A. HEFLIN *U.S. Air Force Dict.* 564/2 Weapon system. *Also* weapons system. **1958** *Engineering* 11 Apr. 450/1 The 'weapon system concept'—that is, a unified integration of airframe, weapon-firing control, and enemy identification. **1977** M. EDELMAN *Polit. Lang.* viii. 147 Americans and Russians are constantly told that the other is ahead in this or that weapons system **1980** R. L. DUNCAN *Brimstone* x. 244 There were always 10,000 diverse elements which were required to come together at precisely the right instant, the total testing of a weapons system and a defense against that system. **1945** E. WAUGH *Brideshead Revisited* 9 Had I put in the names of two corporals for the weapon-training course? **1979** R. PERRY *Bishop's Pawn* vi. 106 Their weapon training had been sadly neglected... In killing Moss, they'd used sufficient ammunition to decimate a small army.

weaponeer (wepənɪ͡ə·ɹ). *U.S.* [f. prec. + -EER.] **a.** One who has charge of a weapon of war prior to its deployment.

Orig. used *spec.* of nuclear weapons.

1945 in *Amer. Speech* (1947) XXII. 149/2 Here are the names of the Superfortress crew which carried the atomic bomb to Japan... Naval observer and 'weaponeer', Capt. William S. Parsons. **1952** *Word Study* Feb. 4/1 United States atomic weaponeers probably will set off the world's greatest explosion within the next few days.

b. An expert or specialist in the development of weapons of war.

1979 *New Yorker* 13 Aug. 67/1 Robert Wilson..head of experimental physics at Los Alamos; Philip Morrison, who had gone..to take care of the bombs..; Richard Feynman, who had been in charge of one of the computing sections... I fitted in with this bunch of weaponeers. **1982** *Christian Sci. Monitor* 22 June 22/1 Probably the most interesting to the weaponeers of the great powers was the testing of US vs. Soviet fighter planes.

So **weaponee·ring** *vbl. sb.*, the development and production of weapons of war.

1955 *Bull. Atomic Sci.* Sept. 239/3 Nearly half of our expenditure for research and development each year goes to weaponeering. **1960** *N.Y. Times Mag.* 29 May 20 You must..make those essential advances in the state of the weaponeering art which will most intercept any possible aggression by any potential enemy. **1976** *Aviation Week* 19 Jan. 54/1 It's easier to conceptualize bombs, weaponeering and 'hard kill' missiles than the wizardry of electronic detection and countermeasures equipment.

weaponization (wepənaizē͡ɪ·ʃən). *U.S.* [f. as prec. + -IZATION.] The process of equipping with weapons of war, or adapting something for use as a weapon. So **wea·ponized** *ppl. a.*

1969 *U.S. Dept. Defense Appropriation Bill 1970* (91st Congress 1 Sess., House Rep. 698) 72 Aircraft Weaponization (advanced and exploratory development) was reduced. **1973** *Black Panther* 7 Apr. 10/2 Observers worry that the fledgling crime protection industry may follow a similar line, with huge profits made in this industry supporting a new domestic lobby for more weaponized solutions to the anger of the ghetto, the barrio and the poor white hollow. **1976** *Aviation Week* 1 Nov. 19/2 He said the Navy plans to build a 3,000-ton 'weaponized' surface-effect ship. **1982** *N.Y. Times* 23 Mar. A-14/2 Chemical warfare agents were..weaponized with Soviet assistance in Laos, Vietnam and Kampuchea. **1983** *Aviation Week* 17 Jan. 27/2 He cited an alarming trend toward the weaponization of space as the reason for his new emphasis on the civilian uses of space.

weaponry. Delete *rare* and add: Now esp. weapons of war. (Further examples.)

1956 C. W. MILLS *Power Elite* viii. 184 The new weaponry has been developed as a 'first line of defense'. **1959** *Times Lit. Suppl.* 16 Jan. 27/2 War has become inevitable because of the weaponry which both sides are amassing. **1961** *New Left Rev.* Jan.–Feb. 49/1 Modern weaponry advances faster than any other branch of technology. **1972** *Daily Tel.* 27 May 1/1 The Russians have deployed 64 defensive Galesh missiles around Moscow since 1969, but the Americans are more advanced in this weaponry. **1977** *Irish Times* 8 June 5/2 The US should put aside hopes of outstripping the Soviet Union in doomsday weaponry.

fig. **1966** *New Statesman* 23 Dec. 942/1 Its weaponry of surprises..allows Miss Smith free movement in areas where the clichés lie thick.

wear, *sb.* Add: **1. b.** *the worse for wear* (further examples). Also, drunk. See also WORSE *a.* 4 c.

1857 C. M. YONGE *Dynevor Terrace* II. xvii. 270 His boots were less polished..and he looked somewhat the worse for wear. **1936** J. BUCHAN *Island of Sheep* iii. 44 When I came across him in Persia..he was rather the worse for wear. **1966** D. FRANCIS *Flying Finish* x. 127 You'll be kicking your heels about the airport for a few hours. Don't let any of them get...er...the worse for wear. **1977** M. ALLEN *Spence in Petal Park* xix. 87 The blonde girl left about ten, looking distinctly the worse for wear. **1982** T. BERGER *Reinhart's Women* iii. 46 The vehicles in view were routine automobiles, two of them the worse for wear, with dents and rust and jagged antenna-stems.

6. c. *wear-and-tear pigment* (Biochem.) [tr. G. *abnutzungspigment*]: a pigment that accumulates in cells as they age.

1928 *Amer. Jrnl. Path.* IV. 236 This pigment (lipofuscin) was recognized by Lubarsch who classified it along with melanin as 'wear-and-tear' pigment (*Abnutzungspigmente*). **1943** *Jrnl. Compar. Neurol.* LXXVIII. 45 It would be better to abandon the attempt to group all these substances [from different tissues] under the common term 'wear-and-tear' pigment. **1968** [see *lipofuscin* s.v. *LIPO-].

IV. 9. a. *attrib.* and *Comb.*, as *wear-resistance, -resisting*; *wear-proof, -resistant, -resisting* adjs.; **wear-dated** *a.* (see quot. 1968).

1897 *Sears, Roebuck Catal.* 183/2 This suit..is regular wear-resisting goods. **1921** *Daily Colonist* (Victoria, B.C.) 9 Apr. 7/1 Wearproof Suits for Boys. Specially selected materials and extra care in the making of these suits enable them to give every wearing satisfaction. **1943** *U.S. Patents Q.* LVI. 494/2 Wear-resisting, anti-fatigue, and shock-absorbing properties are relative and not absolute terms. **1946** *Nature* 5 Oct. 476/2 The advantage of these new processes is that the weight and wear-resistance of the fabrics are increased. **1960** *Farmer & Stockbreeder* 29 Mar. (Suppl.) 4/1 A wear-resistant outer lining. **1968** J. IRONSIDE *Fashion Alphabet* 102 *Wear-dated*, officially recognised guaranteeing the length of normal wear of garments. **1978** *Detroit Free Press* 16 Apr. (Detroit Suppl.) 14 (Advt.), Choice of covers includes lush acrylic velvet by Monsanto with two-year wear-dated guarantee.

wear, *v.*[1] Add: **I. 4. e.** *to wear the trousers*: see *TROUSERS *sb. pl.* 2 c.

8. c. To tolerate, accept, or agree to (a proposal, etc.). Usu. in negative with *it* as obj.

1925 FRASER & GIBBONS *Soldier & Sailor Words* 301 *To wear*, to put up with, *e.g.*, 'I won't wear it', I won't stand it. **1945** C. H. WARD-JACKSON *It's a Piece of Cake!* (ed. 2) 61 *Wear it. Agree to it, accept it.* Thus, 'I've asked the old man for permission to keep the bar open an hour later, but he won't wear it.' **1950** C. MACINNES *To Victors the Spoils* I. 70 'The new Captain would never wear it.' 'Then it's up to you to put it to him the right way.' **1961** E. WAUGH *Unconditional Surrender* III. i. 203 Presently the Lieutenant came across to them bearing a cigar-case. 'I can't wear them myself,' he said. **1970** P. H. JOHNSON *Honours Board* 61 The mother said this was very kind but that Peter would never—she was given to girlish slang—'wear it'. **1981** S. JACKMAN *Game of Soldiers* I. 53 No.. Watson wouldn't wear it... Nor will I.

10. c. With *on* or *upon*. Of a circumstance: to affect (a person) adversely; to fatigue or debilitate. Cf. WEIGH *v.*[1] 22 a.

1864 O. W. NORTON *Army Lett.* (1903) 245, I did not suppose these things were serious enough to wear upon your health. **1901** 'L. MALET' *Hist. Sir R. Calmady* v. ii. 389, I have had a detestable winter... It wore upon me. It demoralised me. **1915** D. H. LAWRENCE *Let.* ?29 Apr. (1962) 335 You can't imagine how it wears on one, having at every moment to resist this established world.

III. 14. c. *to wear thin* (*fig.* examples).

1931 J. VAN DRUTEN *London Wall* II. i. 69 You must have known yourself it's [*sc.* a love affair] been wearing him. **1942** J. S. HUXLEY in *Polit. Q.* XIII. 384 The inter-war disputation between the 'have' and the 'have-not' powers is wearing a bit thin. **1982** G. M. FRASER *Flashman & Redskins* 52, I knew Susie's first good opinion of Spring had worn thin.

V. 19. a. *to wear late* (earlier example.)

1826 SCOTT *Woodstock* I. iii. 98 It wears late, and gets dark.

wearabi·lity. [f. WEARABLE *a.* + -ITY.] The capability of being worn or of enduring wear; suitability for wear; durability.

1927 *Daily Express* 5 Sept. 5/2 A series of distinctive models to demonstrate individuality with wearability. **1958** *Vogue* Dec. 108 This is the sweater you must have this autumn for its soft lines, its beautiful wearability. **1966** *Chem. & Engin. News* 19 Dec. 13/2 Corfam sells in the U.K. for about the same as top-quality shoe leather, with which Du Pont compares its product for wearability under flexing and for 'breathability'. **1981** *Observer* (Colour Suppl.) 12 Apr. 75 (Advt.), A 100% cotton shirt with all the comfort and wearability men associate with cotton.

wearing, *ppl. a.* Add: **3.** *wearing course* (Highway Engin.) (see quot. 1954).

1940 *Gloss. Highway Engin. Terms* (*B.S.I.*) 28 *Wearing course*, the layer of material applied to form the carriageway. **1977** *Bitumen* (Shell Internat. Petroleum Co.) 2/4 The traffic load is carried mainly by the base layer, while the wearing course provides a waterproof non-skid cover which resists traffic wear.

wearisomeness. 1. (Later example.)

1882 E. W. HAMILTON *Diary* 25 Nov. (1972) I. 364 R.G. evidently wants to get out of harness also, partly from a feeling of wearisomeness and partly from bad health.

wea·r-out. *rare.* Also **wearout.** [f. vbl. phr. *to wear out*: see WEAR *v.*[1] 9, 14.] Wearing out; destruction or damage from use.

1897 C. T. DAVIS *Manuf. Leather* (ed. 2) 270 There is absolutely no wear-out to any of the working parts of the bed. **1979** *Arizona Daily Star* 5 Aug. C 4/1 (Advt.), They are..protected against premature wearout during the warranty period.

weary, *a.* Add: **1. f.** *Weary Willie*: see *Tired Tim* s.v. *TIRED *ppl. a.*[1] 1 c.

1896 *Illustr. Chips* 16 May 1/3 *Lazy Larry:* 'Watcher doin', Willie?' *Weary Willie:* 'Oh, jest wipin out a little debt I owe.' **1901** *Munsey's Mag.* Sept. 884/2 Dan had not been gone a day when the first Weary Willy appeared and demanded pie, with a horrid leer. **1906** E. DYSON *Fact'ry 'Ands* vii. 76 'Garn,' he said, 'no airs. Yer Weary Willie's brother Sam, *halias* Ther Frequent Sleeper, [etc.].' **1909** *Punch* 20 Jan. 46 (*caption to picture of two tramps*) *Weary Willie:* I'd sooner walk up 'ill than I would down, any day—it do throw yer into yer boots so. **1927**, etc. [see *TIRED *ppl. a.*[1] 1 c]. **1929** *Amer. Speech* IV. 345 *Weary Willie*, a tramp who usually hikes it and is too tired to work. **1972** [see *TIRED *ppl. a.*[1] 1 c].

III. 9. *weary-brained, -eyed* adjs.

1898 G. B. SHAW *Let.* 1 May (1972) II. 38, I finish the book at a sitting, as I don't want to be weary-brained when Charlotte comes. **1930** J. MASEFIELD *Wanderer of Liverpool* 24 Weary-eyed men came on deck.

weasel, *sb.* Add: **5.** (Earlier example.)

1845 in C. Cist *Cincinnati Misc.* I. 240 The inhabitants of..S. Carolina [are called] Weasels.

5*. A tracked vehicle capable of travelling over difficult terrain; *spec.* (*a*) a light cargo and personnel carrier (*U.S. Mil.*); (*b*) a snow tractor (see quot. 1958).

1944 *Yank* 4 Aug. 17/2 Cargo carrier M29, nicknamed the Weasel, is now in full production. **1949** [see *snow-buggy* s.v. *SNOW *sb.*[1] 7 b]. **1958** *Times* 11 Nov. 6/7 The Weasel—one of the snow vehicles used by Sir Vivian Fuchs on his trans-Antarctic journey—was invented by a civilian, the late Mr. Geoffrey Pyke. **1964** 'J. H. ROBERTS' *Q Document* (1965) ix. 206 The hotels operated what the student referred to as 'wesaru'—which..was the Japanese way of pronouncing 'weasel', a cross between a jeep and an army tank—to carry the guests. **1980** *Globe & Laurel* July/Aug. 227/2 We in fact lost two vehicles doing this, one being my own command vehicle which was a cargo LVT with a weasel in the back.

5.** An equivocal statement or claim, esp. one used in an intentionally misleading advertisement. See *weasel word*, sense 6 b below.

1959 T. GRIFFITH *Waist-High Culture* (1960) 83 The answer may have to be a 'weasel', the phrasing that avoids or begs the question. **1963** D. OGILVY *Confessions Advert. Man* xi. 155, I plead guilty to one act of *suggestio falsi*—what Madison Avenue calls a 'weasel' **1975** *Idle Moments* (Austral.) Dec. 26/2 The' weasels' are so cleverly written, so subtle, you hardly notice them at all.

6. a. *weasel-mind*; *weasel-eyed* adj.

1922 Weasel-eyed [see *peanut-brained* adj. s.v. *PEANUT b]. **1985** C. FITZGIBBON *Love lies a Loss* v. 59 The weasel-eyed creditors lined the dock. **1923** *Chambers's Jrnl.* Feb. 88/1 Simon would have dallied by the way, his weasel-mind alert to draw news of the hindering from this Heseltine.

b. weasel word orig. *U.S.*, an equivocating or ambiguous word which takes away the force or meaning of the concept being expressed; hence **weasel-worded** *a.*

1900 S. CHAPLIN in *Century Mag.* June 306/2 'The public should be protected—' 'Duly protected,' said Gamage, 'That's always a good weasel word.' **1916** *N.Y. Times* 1 June 1/2 Colonel Roosevelt began the day's speechmaking by opening his guns upon President Wilson... He accused Mr. Wilson of using 'weaselwords' in advocating universal military training, but 'only the compulsion of the spirit of America'. A weasel, the Colonel explained, would suck all the meat out of an egg and leave it an empty shell. **1939** *Florida* (Federal Writers' Project) I. 125 There were no 'weasel word' qualifications, such as 'it is alleged'. **1952** G. Sarton *Hist. Sci.* I. xvi. 404 It is perhaps a little ambiguous to call them idealists. [*Note*] The weasel word idealist is sometimes understood as the opposite of realist. **1977** P. Johnson *Enemies of Society* viii. 108 Whereas in the spheres of advertising, education and economics the use of weasel words tends to be towards gross overstatement, in the field of killing and mass destruction, the tendency is to understate and minimize. **1923** Ld. Charnwood *Theodore Roosevelt* x. 215 It is even comically reminiscent of the writer's own criticisms later of Mr. Wilson's 'weasel-worded' phrases. **1981** *N.Y. Times* 29 Mar. 4/1 The facts it contained did not support what one official termed the agency's 'weasel-worded' conclusion.

c. *attrib.* or as *adj.*, after *weasel word*, above. Of a statement, etc.: equivocating, ambiguous, quibbling.

1912 T. Roosevelt in *Outlook* 27 July 662/2 The weasel sentence about States' rights could well have been suggested by the astuteness of Mr. Bryan's fellow-Democrat Mr. Ryan. **1965** M. Naylor *Your Money* x. 59 If..other things remain equal..,the price will rise... It is now time to deal with that weasel qualification, 'other things being equal'. **1974** R. M. Pirsig *Zen & Art of Motorcycle Maintenance* (1976) IV. xxviii. 337 The whole business seemed to many of them merely a new and pretentious jargon of weasel concepts. **1979** *Financial Rev.* (Melbourne) 27 Apr. 2 The probability is that the commission will deliver another of its weasel judgements, recognising merit on all sides.

wea·sel, *v.* *colloq.* (orig. *U.S.*). [f. the sb.] **1. a.** *trans.* To render (a word, phrase, etc.) ambiguous or equivocal; to remove or detract from (its meaning) intentionally.

1900 *Century Mag.* June 305/2 I've seen him take his pen, and go through a proposed plank or resolution, and weasel every flat-footed word in it. **1919** T. Roosevelt in *Maine, my State* (Maine Writers Research Club) 20 'His words weasel the meaning of the words in front of them,' said David, 'just like a weasel when he sucks the meat out of an egg and leaves nothing but the shell'.

b. *intr.* To equivocate or prevaricate, to use weasel words.

1956 [see *dirt *sb.* 6 e]. **1963** D. Ogilvy *Confessions Advert. Man* v. 99 If you tell lies, weasel, you do your client a disservice. **1972** C. Weston *Poor, Poor Ophelia* xxv. 151 He listened to the younger detective weaseling at the other end.

2. a. To extricate oneself from or get *out of* a place in the manner of a weasel. Also with *in* (with movement in the opposite direction).

1925 J. Bone *London Perambulator* 162 How to weasel out of London, north, south, east and west, with the fewest possible obstructions. **1963** T. Pynchon *V.* vii. 171, I was always weaseling in, you know, on some show where you wouldn't expect to find naval personnel. **1968** P. Dickinson *Skin Deep* ix. 176 Pibble weaseled out of the car and ran across the road.

b. To escape from or extricate oneself *out* (*of* a situation, obligation, etc.), esp. dishonourably; to welsh *on*. Also with *one's way*.

1956 *Washington Post* 7 Aug., For this country to weasel on its obligation would be both to fracture the Atlantic alliance and to engage in the most offensive and immoral sort of appeasement. **1962** N. Maxwell *Witch-Doctor's Apprentice* ii. 10, I wanted to commit myself publicly to it so that it would be hard to weasel out after only a day or two. **1973** *New Yorker* 3 Mar. 85/1 Canterbury is one of the 'decadent' communities that gradually weaseled out of the Shaker strictures against ornament and luxury. **1978** M. Puzo *Fools Die* xxi. 239 A real fucking claim agent weaseling out of his obligations. **1980** *Logophile* IV. I. 46/1 It required weaseling his way into the confidence of his bank-manager. **1981** *Spectator* 6 June 16/2 Jilly Cooper was too kind-hearted to name those who weaseled out of the exercise.

3. *trans.* To obtain or extract (something) *out of* another, esp. by cunning.

1975 L. Deighton *Yesterday's Spy* xii. 99 He..'weaseled' luggage for the boat-train passengers and was not above stealing the occasional camera. **1975** *Observer* 30 Nov. 22/4 My sole achievement was weaselling a medical certificate out of my G.P.

Hence **wea·selling** *ppl.a.* and *vbl. sb.*

1956 H. Kurnitz *Invasion of Privacy* xii. 81 Never could get along with lawyers... Bunch of weaseling doubletalkers. **1969** *Listener* 31 July 132/2 'Legitimate puffery' is often plain lying. At best, it encourages 'weaselling'—the use of meaningless and unverifiable formulae like 'Bloggo is better'; at worst, it is demonstrably fraudulent. **1978** *N.Y. Times* 30 Mar. D 18/1 Arum says there has been heavy pressure for a return bout from all over the world. He offers this as justification for his weaseling out of a commitment to match Spinks with Ken Norton.

weaselish (wī·z'liʃ), *a. rare.* [f. Weasel *sb.* + -ish[1].] = Weaselly *a.*

1923 D. H. Lawrence *Captain's Doll* xiv, in *Ladybird* 225 The driver, who was thin and weaselish.

weaselly, *a.* Add: Also **weas(e)ly.**

1973 M. Amis *Rachel Papers* 128 He was wearing a fashionable black polo-neck jersey (fashionable, that is, among the weasly middle-aged) whose sleeves he was rolling down. **1982** Barr & York *Official Sloane Ranger Handbk.* 17/2 What a funny little weasely face he has!

weather, *sb.* Add: **I. 1. c.** (Further examples.) Also *spec.* (*Lit.*), applied to an intellectual climate, state of mind, etc.

1909 H. James *Roderick Hudson* (rev. ed.) vii. 147 He supposed that these changes of intellectual weather.. were the lot of every poet. **1922** G. Santayana *Soliloquies in England* 30 What governs the Englishman is his inner atmosphere, the weather in his soul. **1927** T. Wilder *Bridge of San Luis Rey* 17 Such authors live always in the noble weather of their own minds. **1962** K. Allott *Penguin Bk. Contemp. Verse* 18 A short introduction giving explicit attention to the poetic 'weather' of each of the last four decades.

2. f. (Earlier example.)

1827 *Austin Papers* (1924) I. 1622 The fredonians is all here rather under the wether.

h. (Earlier example.)

1829 P. Egan *Boxiana* 2nd Ser. II. 302 Asking of no favours from the clerk of the weather to keep off 'the pitiless pelting storm', as their greasy jackets were proof against all watery attacks.

j. *above* (or *over*) *the weather* (Aeronaut.), above the range of weather conditions acting at ground-level; above the clouds.

1944 *Aviation* Feb. 497/1 The plane climbs..to fly 'over the weather'. **1958** *Listener* 16 Oct. 593/1 It was said that they [*sc.* accidents] had destroyed all prospect of carrying passengers at speeds not far short of the speed of sound, far above the weather, at heights of 35,000 feet.

II. 6. a. *weather bulletin, -cast* (later example), *-journal, -lorist, -map* (earlier example), *prediction, report* (examples), *-saw, -screen.*

1926 R. Macaulay *Crewe Train* II. viii. 157 She asked Arnold..to tell her when the weather bulletin came on; that was normally the only part of the programme to which she cared to listen. **1980** P. Moyes *Angel Death* xv. 198 The weather bulletin..advised guests that Hurricane Beatrice was..moving at a brisk fourteen knots. **1980** *Time* 17 Mar. 37/1 A native American art form, the television weathercast. **1868** G. M. Hopkins *Jrnls. & Papers* (1959) 189 Henceforth I keep no regular weather-journal but only notes. **1905** *Westm. Gaz.* 21 Aug. 10/1 A remarkable dearth of acorns..which, according to the weather lorists, is a favourable augury for the coming weather. **1877** Weather map [see *facsimile 2 a]. **1909** Weather prediction [see *gaffe]. **1951** M. McLuhan *Mech. Bride* (1967) 75/1 The comment is given in the style of stock-market operations or weather predictions. **1863** R. Fitzroy *Weather Bk.* 349 Local changes should be indicated to observers..by due attention to the published Weather Reports. **1939** T. S. Eliot *Family Reunion* II. i. 97 And now it is nearly time for the news We must listen to the weather report. **1980** A. E. Fisher *Midnight Men* vii. 78 He could do without unfavourable weather reports. **1871** G. M. Hopkins 6 Aug. *Jrnls. & Papers* (1959) 213 The common weather-saw about the rainbow. **1914** 'Bartimeus' *Naval Occasions* xx. 181 The men on the bridge ducked their heads as..a shower of spray drifted over the weather-screens. **1977** P. Smalley *Trove* ii. 84 The triple-panel weather screen was fitted with heavy duty wipers.

b. *weather-caster* (so *-casting*), *-forecaster.*

c **1904** *Encycl. Dict.* Suppl., Weather-caster. **1965** *Punch* 5 May 660/2 His great ambition in life is to be a TV weathercaster. **1980** *Time* 17 Mar. 37 TV weathercasters have been much mocked for their polyester jocularity. *Ibid.* (*heading*) The wonderful art of weather-casting. **1900** *Nature* 29 Nov. 110/2 Disappointing..from the viewpoint of the weather forecaster. **1981** *Times* 9 Dec. 1 The weather forecasters were critized..for not giving enough warning..of the snowfall.

c. *weather-roughened.*

1897 W. B. Yeats *Secret Rose* 187 Her dark, weather-roughened skin.

d. *weather-resistant, -resisting.* Also *weather-resistance.*

1894 [see *roofing (*vbl.*) *sb.* 1 b]. **1934** *Archit. Rev.* LXXVI. 16/1 Many years of use have proved the method satisfactory, both as a weather-resistant and as insulation. **1942** *E. African Ann.* *1941–2* 98 (Advt.), Anti-rust paint..durable, elastic, weather-resisting. **1967** M. Chandler *Ceramics in Mod. World* iv. 117 Another property that makes both porcelain and glass insulators particularly suitable for high-voltage insulators is their weather-resistance. **1970** *New Yorker* 3 Oct. 27/2 You can bolt on anything from redwood to weather-resistant aluminum.

7. weather balloon, a balloon sent up to provide meteorological information, either by the course it takes or by means of instruments it carries; **weather bureau** *U.S.*, an agency (*spec.* one established by the Government) which observes and reports on weather conditions; **weather centre,** an office which provides weather information and analysis; *spec.* in U.K., part of the Meteorological Office; **weather clerk** = *clerk of the weather* s.v. Clerk *sb.* 6 c; **weathercoat,** a weather-proof coat, a raincoat; **weather cycle,** a recurring pattern of weather or of some tendency in the weather; **weather-fast** *a.*, secure against the weather; **weather-man,** delete † and add: (*a*) (later examples); now also *spec.* one who presents a weather forecast on radio, television, etc.; (*b*) (freq. with capital initial and in *pl.*) (a member of) a violent revolutionary group in the U.S. (see quot. 1970); cf. *Weather Underground* below; **weather modification,** the deliberate alteration of the weather in an area; **weather-monger** (later example); **weather plane,** an aeroplane designed to collect data on weather conditions at high altitudes; † **weather-prophecy** *Obs.*, the foretelling of the weather; **weather radar,** radar used for meteorological investigations (e.g. of rain); **weather satellite,** a satellite especially equipped to observe weather conditions and to provide meteorological information; **weather ship,** a ship serving as a weather station; **weather station,** a meteorological observation post; **weather-strip** orig. *U.S.* (examples); **weather-stripped** *ppl. a.*; **weather-stripping** *vbl. sb.*, material used to weather-strip a door, window, etc.; the process of applying this; **Weather Underground,** the revolutionary organization formed by the Weathermen (see above); **weather window** *Oil Industry*, a brief interval in the year when the weather is calm enough to allow construction, loading, etc., operations to be carried out at sea; **weather woman,** (*a*) (with capital initial) a female member of the revolutionary Weatherman organization; (*b*) a woman who presents a weather forecast on radio or television.

1940 *War Illustr.* 19 Jan. 614/3 (*caption*) Finnish soldiers are investigating weather conditions by sending up a weather balloon. **1979** J. Gribbin *Weather Force* vii. 160 (*caption*) Russian scientists..prepare to launch a flock of weather balloons, which will radio back information about conditions in the atmosphere's lower levels. **1871** *Harper's Mag.* Aug. 401/1 In the year 1857 Lieutenant M. F. Maury..appealed to the public and Congress, through the press, urging the establishment of a storm and weather bureau. **1890** *U.S. Statutes* XXVI. 653 The civilian duties now performed by the Signal Corps of the Army shall hereafter devolve upon a bureau to be known as the Weather Bureau. **1950** *Los Angeles Times* 12 Feb. 1/4 Weather Bureau figures show that ·34 inch fell during the rainstorm. **1978** S. Sheldon *Bloodline* iv. 71 July turned out to be the rainiest month in the history of the French weather bureau. [**1959** *Times* 19 Aug. 8/7 The Air Ministry Meteorological Office is to open a 'weather shop' where the public may call in person at the new home of the London forecasting office at Princes House, Kingsway.]. **1961** *A.A. Handbk.* 17 'Weather Centres' staffed by the Meteorological Office are open in London, in Glasgow, and in Manchester. **1973** C. Bonington *Next Horizon* xiii. 185, I..went through the daily ritual of getting the weather forecast. This entailed 'phoning..the weather centre in London. **1877** 'Mark Twain' *New England Weather* in *Index* (Boston) 11 Jan. 16/2 It must be raw apprentices in the weather-clerk's factory who experiment and learn how in New England.., and then are promoted to make weather for countries that require a good article. **1898** H. S. Canfield *Maid of Frontier* 111, I wouldn't have a weather clerk inside of me for any thing. **1897** J. L. Allen *Choir Invisible* x. 132 He got up at last and wrapped his weather-coat about him. **1930** *Daily Express* 6 Oct. 13/5 (*caption*) Real Harris tweed weathercoat. **1978** *Sunday Times* 21 May 1/6 (Advt.), A pure silk wrap-around weathercoat..to protect you from summer showers..£165. **1930** *Engineering* 31 Jan. 148/2 Based upon a weather cycle or period of almost fourteen years. **1910** J. Farnol *Broad Highway* I. xxiv, It was somewhat roughly put together, but still very strong, and seemed, save for the roof, weather-fast. **1901** Weather man [see *hot wave* s.v. *hot *a.* 12]. **1944** *Sun* (Baltimore) 15 Nov. 11/2 Nobody ever gets anywhere telling the weatherman how to behave. **1952** W. Stevens *Let.* 26 June (1967) 757 It did not go below 85° in N.Y. last night according to the weather man. **1970** *Guardian* 28 Oct. 13/3 The Weathermen have been in existence for just over a year, since the SDS [*sc.* Students for a Democratic Society] split of June, 1969... The Weathermen got their name from a line in a Bob Dylan song: 'You don't need a weatherman to know which way the wind blows.' **1971** *Times* 15 Jan. 12/6 Could this country have acquired an Anglicized offshoot of the American Weatherman—or Weathermen as these violent urban guerillas are less accurately but probably more widely known? **1979** R. Perry *Bishop's Pawn* i. 23 The West was agreed that the IRA, the Weathermen, the Red Army Faction..were composed of criminals, terrorists and murderers. **1983** *Listener* 14 July 17/3 We asked the weatherman, Jack Scott, to demonstrate some of those extraordinary regional variations for us. **1951** *U.S. Congr. Senate Committee Interior Hearings* Apr. 152 Weather modification on a small scale, such as protection against frost..is known to be possible. **1968** *Times* 1 Nov. 6/6 Russian research on methods of reducing damage to crops by hailstorms is being examined seriously in the United States, according to a National Science Foundation report on last year's activities in weather modification. **1977** *Time* 7 Mar. 55/1 The Governors also agreed to create a task force that could channel such requests for aid and coordinate weather-modification (cloud seeding) programs. **1911** J. G. Frazer *Golden Bough: Magic Art* (ed. 3) I. iv. 227 Wizards, doctors, weather-mongers, prophets. **1962** *Listener* 18 Oct. 632/2 The 'Coliseum of cloud' that a weatherplane captured for us. **1976** *Evening Post* (Nottingham) 13 Dec. 7/2 Experts..identified it as a crashed weather plane which sends wind and temperature conditions from a height of 90,000 feet. **1843** Mill *Logic* I. III. iv. 389 The reliance on astrology, or on the weather-prophecies in almanacs. **1946** *1st Technical Rep. Weather Radar Research* (Mass. Inst. Technol. Dept. Meteorol.) (AD 54113) 3 (*heading*) Weather-radar observations at M.I.T.'s Radiation Laboratory. **1979** *Atmosphere-Ocean* XVII. 78 The radar data were obtained from the McGill Weather Radar located just outside Montreal. **1960** *Aeroplane* XCIX. 90/2 After taking 22,952 photographs of the Earth's cloud cover, Tiros I, the World's first weather satellite, has ended its useful life..after the satellite's electronics had suffered a failure. **1976** L. Deighton *Twinkle, twinkle, Little Spy* xi. 115 His factories make complicated junk for communications satellites... And there are weather satellites too. **1946**

Shell Aviation News No. 100. 6/3 A proposal by the Search and Rescue Committee that weather ships should be maintained in the North Atlantic for meteorological observations. **1978** *Nature* 1 June 407/1 Following the withdrawal of US weatherships in 1973, it is the only regularly reporting deep ocean (3,000 m) station in the North Atlantic north of the tropics and south of 50° N. **1895** *Funk's Stand. Dict.*, Weather station. **1953** *Encounter* Nov. 7/1 Japan gets its weather from China, but no weather reports—at least not until the Japanese experts again manage to break the code of the Chinese weather-stations. **1981** 'E. LATHEN' *Going for Gold* vii. 87, I was on to the weather station... The forecasters are talking about the blizzard of the century. **1847** *Rep. Comm. Patents 1846* (U.S.) 94 One patent has been granted for improvement in fences, and another for a weather strip for doors. **1921** *Daily Colonist* (Victoria, B.C.) 25 Oct. 6/6 (Advt.), Weather Strip—'Stormproof', 24 feet in box. **1970** K. BALL *Fiat 600, 600D Autobook* xii. 143/2 The front windscreen and rear window are secured in place by a special weatherstrip. **1985** *Times* 19 July 13/4 In windy winter conditions the windloading presses the door up against the weatherstrip. **1908** I. N. STEVENS *Liberators* 8 The wind that shook the windows, weather-stripped as they were, crept into the room. **1945** NELSON & WRIGHT *Tomorrow's House* xiii. 147/2 A heavy flush door, weather-stripped,..would..reduce the direct transmission of sound. **1942** *Archit. Rev.* XCI. 99/3 The windows are pine with aluminium weatherstripping. **1959** 'S. RANSOME' *I'll die for You* xii. 144 A part of the weather stripping was loose, and in a heavy rain it leaked. **1975** *Globe & Mail* (Toronto) 14 Nov. 2/5 As for weather-stripping, Mrs. Macdonald said their house doesn't need it because of extra insulation and double windows. **1972** *National Observer* (U.S.) 27 May 10/2 The..'Weather Underground', which boasts that it is responsible for so many of these bombings, is down to only 15 or 20 members now, according to sources in the House Internal Security Committee. **1982** H. KISSINGER *Years of Upheaval* iv. 89 The terrorism of the Weather Underground. **1974** *Petroleum Rev.* XXVIII. 787/1 The weather-window is normally reckoned to last into September. **1983** *Sunday Times* 6 Mar. 69/4 It's been said that Esso's development of artificial islands has not merely opened the weather window further but ripped it off its hinges. **1971** *Times* 15 Jan. 12/7 Only one unconnected Weatherwoman has since been traced. **1973** *Daily Tel.* 14 Dec. 3/3 BBC Television is to have its first weather woman. She is Miss Barbara Edwards,..who at present reads weather forecasts on radio. **1982** *Times* 28 May 9/3 Diana Arp..was from a very wealthy family and became a Weather woman, making bombs.

8. weather deck, a deck exposed to the weather; the uppermost unprotected deck, other than the forecastle, bridge, and poop; **weather-dodger** *slang*, a screen on the bridge of a ship, affording protection from the weather; **weather-mark** *Sailing*, a mark on a racing course towards which boats sail into the wind.

1909 *Man. Seamanship* (Admiralty) II. xx. 409 Wood planking is now fitted only to the weather decks. **1973** H. GRUPPE *Truxton Cipher* (1974) xiii. 135 Tolley..disappeared down the weather-deck ladder. **1924** R. CLEMENTS *Gipsy of Horn* v. 84 One was..in comparative comfort under the lee of the weather-dodger. **1894** *Outing* XXIV. 36/2 The 'Una' turned the weather-mark with a lead of nearly half an hour. **1963** *Times* 8 June 5/1 By the weather mark Andromeda was in front.

wea·therable, *a.* [f. WEATHER *v.* + -ABLE.] Capable of withstanding the effects of the weather. Also **wea:therabi·lity.**

1961 WEBSTER, Weatherability. **1963** H. R. CLAUSER *Encycl. Engin. Materials & Processes* 662/1 The poor weatherability of some of the man-made fibers can be overcome by the use of special finishing and/or coating treatments. **1972** J. G. CRUICKSHANK *Soil Geogr.* ii. 52 Even where the parent material is rock in place, the weatherable minerals—or what has survived complete chemical weathering—are of continuing importance for soil profile development. **1979** *New Scientist* 17 May 547 Silicones in paint prevent colour fading, and give better long-term weatherability and heat resistance.

weatherboard. Add: **1. c.** A weatherboarded dwelling or other building. *Austral.*

1925 'H. H. RICHARDSON' *Way Home* II. i. 123 Jerry and his bride had made ready their tiny weatherboard. **1935** L. MANN *Human Drift* xxxvi. 238 Magnificently the two stories of Geelong weatherboards, new that year, overlooked on the ridge. **1975** D. MALOUF *Johnno* ii. 28 But our one-storeyed weatherboard wasn't the only one to be fortified. The whole city had taken on the aspect of an armed camp.

weathercock, *sb.* Add: **3. c.** *Aeronaut.* Used *attrib.* and as *adj.* with reference to the tendency of an aircraft to turn away from the set compass direction into the relative wind.

1898 *Aeronaut. Jrnl.* Jan. 6/2 The little vertical rudder has a little bit of a weather-cock action. If the wind suddenly shifts, it swings the machine round to head the wind. **1916** G. C. LOENING *Military Aeroplanes* xii. 166 Some tendency to head into the relative wind is necessary. This is obtained by having enough rudder or fin surface aft to bring the directional center back of the c.g. and is called 'weathercock' stability. **1928** N. MACMILLAN *Art of Flying* vii. 74 A seaplane is usually directionally stable to the wind on the water with engine stopped, a quality which is described as being 'weathercock'... If the seaplane is weathercock, she will ride head to wind and drift backward. **1935** C. G. BURGE *Compl. Bk. Aviation* 616 Weathercock instability. **1945** *Jrnl. R. Aeronaut. Soc.* XL. 461/2 Weathercock stability should be reasonably high, to cut down the magnitude of the inadvertent skid. **1970** T. HACKER *Flight Stability & Control* vii. 160 The variation of the vertical tail area will influence the weathercock stability.

weathercock, *v.* Add: **1.** (Later example.)

1824 *Blackw. Edin. Mag.* June 703/2 No change of times can ever change that feeling in me. Let others weather-cock it to and fro as they please.

4. *intr.* **a.** *Naut.* Of a ship: to (tend to) head into the wind.

1952 SMITH & VIOLET *Wind calls Tune* i. 19 She would weathercock head to seas and, under mizzen and foresail, she would sail well without anybody at the tiller. **1974** *Tel.* (Brisbane) 4 June 8/5 In these conditions the boats had a strong tendency to weathercock, making it exceptionally difficult to pick up buoys.

b. *intr.* (See quot. 1956.) Also *trans.*, to cause to weathercock.

1956 W. A. HEFLIN *U.S. Air Force Dict.* 565/2 *Weathercock.* Of an airplane, rocket, or similar body: to align, or attempt to align, its longitudinal axis with the direction of the wind. **1976** 'M. ALBRAND' *Taste of Terror* v. 38 That terrible cross-wind caught the plane's high vertical stabilizer and began to weathercock it into the wind.

Hence **wea·thercocking** *vbl. sb.*

1952 SMITH & VIOLET *Wind calls Tune* vi. 59 We had to get the mizzen as flat as possible to make it more efficient as a 'weather cocking' influence. **1985** *Flight* 4 May 23/3 The butterfly tail..actually eliminates weathercocking in crosswinds.

weather-eye. Add: *to keep one's weather-eye open*, etc. (earlier and further examples).

1829 P. EGAN *Boxiana* 2nd Ser. II. 505 Lads of the Fancy, who always keep their 'weather eye' up towards business, *i.e.* looking after the blunt. **1846** DICKENS *Dombey* x. 89 Joe is awake, Ma'am... Josh has his weather-eye open, Sir. **1851** H. MELVILLE *Moby Dick* I. xxxiv. 253 All whale-ships' standing orders, 'Keep your weather eye open, and sing out every time'. **1916** 'TAFFRAIL' *Pincher Martin* iv. 53 Even the captain and the navigator..did not seem to be taking things very seriously, though in reality they both had their weather-eyes very much lifting. **1959** B. WOOTTON *Soc. Sci.* 10, I have tried to keep a weather eye open to what is going on elsewhere: references to work in other areas..will be found scattered through these pages. **1981** *Times* 7 Apr. 6/7 The Russians..are keeping a weathereye on other navies.

weathering, *vbl. sb.* Add: **2.** (Later examples.) Also *weathering ground.*

1855 SALVIN & BRODERICK *Falconry in Brit. Isles* iii. 44 In the morning..they may be..placed upon blocks in the open air, without their hoods; this is called 'weathering'. **1960** M. WOODFORD *Man. Falconry* ii. 9 The weathering ground should be a level, well-drained area of short grass protected from the prevailing winds. **1978** *Country Life* 27 July 215/3 Hawking enthusiasts will be delighted to find a well-stocked weathering ground at Kinmount.

wea·therize, *v. U.S.* [f. WEATHER *sb.* + -IZE.] *trans.* To make weatherproof; *spec.* to render (a building) impervious to the effects of weather, by insulation, double-glazing, etc. Also **wea·therized** *ppl. a.*; **wea·therizing** *vbl. sb.*; **wea:theriza·tion.**

1946 *Woman's Home Compan.* Mar. 117/3 (Advt.), Weather-Bird Shoes for boys and girls are weatherized. **1946** *Collier's* 9 Nov. 92 (Advt.), A brand-new portable [radio] with new weatherized case. **1976** *Laurel* (Montana) *Outlook* 9 June 3/2 A project which could provide insulation and other weatherization materials... A coordinator for the Weatherizing program. **1977** *Time* 4 Apr. 52/2 Plants and office buildings will have to be weatherized to prevent energy loss. **1980** *New Age* (U.S.) Oct. 38/1 In Fitchburg, Massachusetts, people were so scared of freezing last winter that they dreamed up a program of door-to-door citizen action which was supposed to weatherize half their houses in five weeks. **1983** *Hyde Park* (Chicago) *Herald* 6 July 21 The city's weatherization program makes it worthwhile.

Weather-ometer (weðərǫ·mitəɹ). Also **Weatherometer, weatherometer.** [f. WEATHER *sb.* + -OMETER.] A proprietary name for a device which subjects substances to simulated weather conditions in order to determine their weather-resistance.

1929 *Official Gaz.* (U.S. Patent Office) 11 June 308/2 Atlas Electric Devices Company, Chicago, Ill... Weather-ometer. For Apparatus for Testing the Effect of Weather Upon the Surfaces of Objects. Claims use since Dec. 3, 1926. **1937** *Nature* 28 Aug. 353/1 For accelerated weathering tests on various paints the weatherometer..has been used. **1951** [see *FADE-OMETER]. **1965** *New Scientist* 1 July 25/3 A cyclic weatherometer developed as a screening test for new types of timber preservatives and water repellants.

weatherproof, *a.* (*sb.*). Add: **b.** *sb.* Also, a weatherproof coat; a raincoat.

1925 *Studio* (Art & Publicity Special Autumn No.) (Advt. suppl.) p. ix, Aquascutum pure wool weatherproofs come in one quality only—the best. **1935** *Times* 21 Feb. 14/2 [The Queen] saw the colour first in a crêpe de Chine weatherproof made with a cape. **1962** *N.Y. Times* 16 Nov. 3 A & F presents a selection of Burberry topcoats, overcoats and weatherproofs.

Hence as *v. trans.*, to make weatherproof or impervious to weather; **wea·therproofed** *ppl. a.*; **wea·therproofness.**

1926 T. E. LAWRENCE *Seven Pillars* (1935) VI. lxxix. 435 The Indians weather-proofed their own north-west rooms. **1929** *Punch* 17 Apr. p. xxii/2 Weatherproofed by Burberrys, their value as overcoats is enhanced in every way. **1933** *Times Lit. Suppl.* 7 Dec. 874/3 There is something animal—..in their strength, endurance, weatherproofness and capacity to live rough. **1963** *N.Y. Times* 1 Dec. 12 The 'Stormster'..all-climate coat... Weatherproofed cotton-poplin..lined. **1969** *Jane's Freight Containers 1968–69* 9/2 It is recommended that the test for weatherproofness (Test No. 9) be made last. **1976** *West Lancs. Evening Gaz.* 8 Dec. 11/9 The revolutionary roof coating system designed to protect, insulate and weatherproof your home.

weather-stained, *ppl. a.* (Earlier example.)

1849 THOREAU *Week Concord Riv.* 57 Town records, old, tattered, time-worn, weather-stained chronicles.

weather-wise, *a.* Add: **a.** Also *absol.* as *sb.*

1922 JOYCE *Ulysses* 390 Biggish swollen clouds to be seen as the night increased and the weatherwise poring up at them.

wea·therwise, *adv.* orig. *U.S.* [f. WEATHER *sb.* + WISE *sb.*[1] II.] As regards the weather.

1963 [see *personnel-wise* advb. s.v. *PERSONNEL 3]. **1971** *Country Life* 21 Oct. 1084/1 October is usually a very good month weatherwise. **1975** *Budget* (Sugarcreek, Ohio) 20 Mar. 15/6 Weatherwise the last week has been real nice.

Weatings (wī·tiŋz), *sb. pl.* Also **w(h)eatings.** [f. respelling of WHEAT *sb.* + *-ings*, as in *middlings* s.v. MIDDLING *sb.* 3 c.] A proprietary name for the residue of the milling of wheat (the sharps: see SHARP *sb.* 9), used as food for farm animals.

1931 *Trade Marks Jrnl.* 30 Sept. 1329/1 Weatings... Fine wheat offals (for food). The M.M.A., Limited,.. London E.C. 3. **1937** C. FORMAN *Pig Breeding & Feeding* vii. 79 These wheatings are advertised as not more than 5 per cent fibre. **1937** E. M. RICKARD-BELL *Handbk. Mod. Pig Farming* vii. 81 For the weatings we can substitute up to 10 per cent. with coconut cake. **1960** *Farmer & Stockbreeder* 8 Mar. 5/1 Weatings and bran both quoted at £25 per ton ex mill. **1976** G. JOHNSON *Profitable Pig Farming* (ed. 5) viii. 124 Sharps, weatings or middlings have not been included in any of the above selection of suitable rations.

weave, *v.*[2] Add: **1. b.** Also of a wild animal in captivity.

1934 [implied in *WEAVING *vbl. sb.*[2] 2]. **1973** G. DURRELL *Beasts in my Belfry* vii. 140, I could only presume that he [*sc.* a buffalo doing a sort of waltz] put on this performance for the same reason that a lion paces up and down its cage or a polar bear or an elephant will weave from side to side—a soothing and interesting habit to pass the time till the next meal.

c. *R.A.F.* Of an aircraft or its pilot: to fly a weaving course, usu. in attempting to avoid enemy planes or anti-aircraft fire. Also *transf.* (in this use *slang*).

1941 *Battle of Britain August–October 1940* (Min. of Information) 13 Enemy bomber formations were..protected by a box of fighters, some of which flew slightly above to a flank or in rear,..and..others weaving in and out between the sub-formations of the bombers. **1942** *R.A.F. Jrnl.* 3 Oct. 22, I took my Edgar Wallace from the billet and weaved out to the Nissen hut. **1943** P. BRENNAN et al. *Spitfires over Malta* 26 The remaining four 110's at once broke, and began weaving, each steering a different course home. **1952** [see *PREDICT *v.* 4]. **1973** N. MONSARRAT *Kappillan of Malta* 38 The sky above him seemed full of planes, weaving and circling like the flies in the wine-shop.

d. *to get weaving*, to apply oneself briskly to something; to 'get a move on'. Cf. *to get cracking* s.v. *CRACK *v.* 22 b. *colloq.* (orig. *R.A.F.*).

1942 *R.A.F. Jrnl.* 30 May 19 We'll knock that..place off the map. Get weaving. **1942** T. RATTIGAN *Flare Path* III. 83 We'd better get weaving, or we'll find this chemist feller has gone to lunch. **1948** A. BARON *From City, from Plough* v. 36 There won' 'alf be a queue at the NAAFI... Let's get weaving. **1959** M. PUGH *Chancer* 49 When he gets weaving, the dashboard ashtray does three thousand revs. **1964** R. BRADDON *Year of Angry Rabbit* i. 8 And this call's costing me a ruddy fortune so how's about you hang up and get weaving, eh? **1971** B. W. ALDISS *Soldier Erect* 185 Pack your night things in a small pack and get weaving, while I lay on transport.

weaver[1]. Add: **2. b.** *Boxing.* A boxer who weaves from side to side as a tactical move. Cf. WEAVE *v.*[2] 4.

1829 P. EGAN *Boxiana* 2nd Ser. II. 165 They again became weavers, till they measured their lengths upon the ground, Warren again undermost. **1950** J. DEMPSEY *Championship Fighting* xi. 54 'Bobbers and weavers'—chaps who come in bobbing low and weaving from side to side.

c. *R.A.F. slang.* A pilot (or aircraft) pursuing a weaving course. Cf. *WEAVE *v.*[2] 1 c.

1942 in Forbes & Allen *Ten Fighter Boys* 47, I called up the C.O. and said I would like to take up position as a 'weaver'. **1956** J. E. JOHNSON *Wing Leader* iv. 53 Some of our squadrons provided two weavers in an attempt to guard themselves from the bounce. The weavers flew above the squadron and continually weaved and criss-crossed.

d. A driver of a motor vehicle who moves continuously from lane to lane, esp. in order to pass other vehicles. *colloq.*

1960 *Amer. Speech* XXXV. 312 For a long time we have

heard of the *weaver*, the driver who shifts from lane to lane in driving. **1973** *Telegraph* (Brisbane) 13 Sept. 30/1 Then we have the weaver, who careers from lane to lane, passing other cars right and left.

5*. *Basket-making.* Any cane which is woven between the stakes of a basket.

1897 A. FIRTH *Cane Basket Work* ii. 17 *Weavers*, the canes which are placed alternately behind and before the spokes. **1960** E. LEGG *Country Baskets* 27 If you will just bear in mind the names of the parts—sticks or stakes, and weavers—..you will never forget the different grades required... The stakes must be stouter or stronger than the weavers.

6. a. weaver ant, a tropical ant, esp. one of the genus *Oecophylla*, which builds nests of leaves fastened together by the silk of its own larvæ.

1913 *Ann. Rep. Smithsonian Inst. 1912* 456 The highly interesting weaver ants..use their larvæ as weaver's shuttles. **1977** *Sci. Amer.* Dec. 146/1 Weaver ants are extremely abundant, aggressive and territorial.

weaving, *vbl. sb.*[2] Add: **2.** The side-to-side movement by an animal of its head and neck.

1934 MILLER & ROBERTSON *Pract. Animal Husbandry* 59 Weaving is a nervous habit acquired by many wild animals in captivity (especially bears), and occasionally by horses. **1973** G. DURRELL *Beasts in my Belfry* iv. 70 Sam had a habit—not uncommon in bears—which is called weaving.

weaving, *ppl. a.* Add: Hence **wea·vingly** *adv.*

1945 L. MACNEICE in *Horizon* Nov. 295 Loom of wind Weavingly laughingly leavingly weepingly. **1959** C. OGBURN *Marauders* (1960) vi. 183 Overby ran erect, like a halfback,..carrying his rifle weavingly before him as if it were a football.

web, *sb.* Add: **I. 5. b.** Also, a continuously moving plastic sheet or film.

1958 E. G. FISHER *Extrusion of Plastics* vii. 96 The sheet passes through one or two pairs of nip rolls which draw the web through the take-off. **1974** J. H. BRISTON *Plastics Films* xv. 191 The web of material is controlled at all stages of the wrapping operation and cut-off only takes place when the product has been fully enclosed.

III. 14. a. Also, a longitudinal vertical member joining the upper and lower components of a wooden rib, spar, or beam in an aircraft.

1909 *Flight* 11 Sept. 553/2 The rib for a double-surfaced deck [*sc.* wing] is more elaborate in construction, and is itself stiffened with 'webs'. **1918** *Ibid.* 25 July 830/2 Each of the spars is built up of spruce flanges, connected on front and rear faces by three-ply webs, the whole forming a box. **1919** PIPPARD & PRITCHARD *Aeroplane Struct.* xvii. 199 The load is transmitted by shear across the web portion of the rib, and so this portion must be very strongly attached to the web of the spar. **1962** *Flight Handbk.* (ed. 6) iii. 45 Platz's wing employed box spars with plywood sides (webs) and heavier wooden tops and bottoms (booms).

h. *pl.* Snow-shoes. *N. Amer.*

1923 *Beaver* Jan. 145 It is said they still enjoy an occasional zestful tramp on the 'webs' over leagues of new Manitoba snow. **1939** K. PINKERTON *Wilderness Wife* ix. 103 After breakfast we went out to slip on our webs. **1966** M. E. & O. MURIE *Wapiti Wilderness* xviii. 223 Snowshoes, or 'webs' as the Jackson Hole people call them, were the tried and true aids.

IV. 18. Objective, as *web-spinning* adj.; similative, as *websoft* adj.; **web-fed** *a. Printing* = *reel-fed* adj. s.v. *REEL *sb.*[1] 6; **web-nest**, a filmy tissue enclosing a group of certain caterpillars or web-spinners (sense *b); cf. *web-worm*; **web offset**, offset lithographic printing on a continuous reel of paper (cf. sense *5 b); freq. *attrib.*; **web-spinner**, (*a*) a web-spinning spider; (*b*) a brownish gregarious insect of the order Embioptera, the females of which are wingless.

1949 MELCHER & LARRICK *Printing & Promotion Handbk.* 358/1 Newspapers are printed on web-fed rotary presses. **1965** ZIGROSSER & GAEHDE *Guide Coll. Orig. Prints* iv. 73 In the rotogravure process the plate is in the form of a copperplated cylinder, functioning in a web-fed rotary press for long and speedy runs of printing. **1895** W. SCHLICH *Man. Forestry* IV. 279 The caterpillars, enclosed in the common web-nest, first gnaw the upper side of the leaves. **1903** *Biol. Bull.* IV. 100 They [*sc.* Embiidæ] still spin their web-nests. **1959** *Times Lit. Suppl.* 15 May 296/3 America, the land of newspapers on the giant scale,..is making great strides..with web-offset colour on newsprint. **1967** E. CHAMBERS *Photolitho-Offset* xv. 238 Web offset can be defined as a method of lithographic printing in..one or more colours on one or both sides of a web of paper in a single operation. **1981** *Printing World* 28 Jan. 13/1 It was printed on a new Timson T32 web offset press. *a* **1915** JOYCE *Giacomo Joyce* (1968) 7, I hold the websoft edges of her gown. **1923** *Jrnl. & Proc. R. Soc. Western Australia* IX. 1. 61 The Order Embioptera, or Web-spinners, is a small but very distinct and isolated group of insects. **1941** J. S. HUXLEY *Uniqueness of Man* ix. 193 In the spiders, we find a very interesting difference between the hunters and the web-spinners. **1944** *Proc. U.S. Nat. Mus.* XCIV. 401 (*title*) A revision of the Embioptera, or web-spinners, of the New World. **1972** SWAN & PAPP *Common Insects N. Amer.* vi. 85 Embiids or Webspinners..occur mostly in the tropics and subtropics. **1904** W. H. HUDSON *Green Mansions* v. 57 This was no web-spinning, sedentary spider. **1946** *Nature* 2 Nov. 630/2 The web-spinning Tineid caterpillar..is usually an inhabitant of hawthorn bushes.

weber. Add: **a.** (Earlier examples of the sense 'coulomb'.) Also † **veber.**

1872 *Telegr. Jrnl.* I. 11/1 The current through *a b* will then be equal to one British Association unit of current, or one veber per second. **1874** [see *FARAD 2].

† **b.** A unit of magnetic pole strength, equal to the pole strength that produces a field of 1 oersted ('gauss') at 1 centimetre. *Obs.*

1882 R. CLAUSIUS in *Phil. Mag.* XIII. 394, I would take leave to propose that for it [*sc.* the unit of magnetism] the name 'weber' be introduced. **1892** G. F. BARKER *Physics* iv. iii. 645 The unit pole just now defined..is called a weber and the unit field which it produces at unit distance is called a gauss.

c. The M.K.S. unit of magnetic flux (now incorporated in the International System of Units), equal to 100 million maxwells; one volt-second. Symbol Wb.

1891 *Trans. Amer. Inst. Electr. Engineers* VIII. 542 We can start by defining 10^8 lines of force as the unit of induction and call it, say, a weber. **1895** *Rep. Brit. Assoc. Adv. Sci.* 196 The Committee..recommend for tentative adoption the following terminology: —— 1. That as a unit for magnetic field, a hundred million 'c.g.s. lines' be called a weber. **1935** *Proc. Nat. Acad. Sci.* XXI. 579 Various International Electrical Congresses..and since then, the I.E.C., have adopted, by successive steps, the well-known series of nine practical electromagnetic units (ohm, volt, ampere, farad, coulomb, joule, watt, henry and weber). **1963** G. TROUP *Masers & Lasers* (ed. 2) v. 67 For magnetic dipole transitions, $|p_{mn}|$ is of the order of a Bohr magneton ($1{\cdot}2 \times 10^{-29}$ weber metre). **1971** I. G. GASS et al. *Understanding Earth* iv. 71/2 The [magnetic] field varies over the Earth from 7×10^{-5} to $2{\cdot}5 \times 10^{-5}$ weber metre^{-2} (Wb m^{-2}).

Weber[2] (vēi·bəɹ). *Physiol.* [The name of Ernst H. *Weber* (1795–1878), German physiologist and anatomist.] **1.** *Weber's law*: the observation made by Weber that the increase in a stimulus that is just noticeable is a constant proportion (the *Weber fraction* or *ratio*) of the initial stimulus, for any one sense.

1872 [see *PSYCHO-PHYSICAL *a.*]. **1890** W. JAMES *Princ. Psychol.* I. xiii. 537 So much for a general account of what Fechner calls Weber's law. **1935** *Brit. Jrnl. Psychol.* XXVI. 226 The obvious fact that Weber's Law is disobeyed both for very high and for very low light intensities leads to the clearly apparent result that..the various greys at either end of Dr. Ostwald's scale are never even approximately equidistant. **1938** STEVENS & DAVIS *Hearing* iv. 149 We are not here concerned with the constancy of the Weber fraction $\Delta I/I$, which was *another* of Fechner's assumptions, but only with..the ability of an added just-noticeable difference to contribute always the same increment to the total subjective effect. **1952** I. J. HIRSH *Measurement of Hearing* vii. 194 We conclude that Weber's Law holds (for white noise) from about 20 to 100 db Sensation Level. **1970** *Jrnl. Gen. Psychol.* LXXXII. 38 The results of the present experiment suggest that the use of contrasting St[andard] and Co[mparison] vibrotactile stimuli will result in relatively small Weber ratios.

2. *Weber-Fechner law* [*FECHNER] = *Weber's law* above; also, the related statement that the strength of a sensation is proportional to the logarithm of the stimulus causing it.

1891 A. D. WALLER *Introd. Human Physiol.* xv. 536 (*heading*) The Weber-Fechner law. **1968** PASSMORE & ROBSON *Compan. Med. Stud.* I. xxiv. 30/2 To increase the loudness by steps that seem equal to the listener the intensity of sound must be multiplied by approximately the same factor for each step (Weber–Fechner relation).

Weberian (vēi·bīə·riăn), *a.*[2] [f. the name of Carl Maria von *Weber* (1786–1826), German composer + -IAN.] Of, pertaining to, or characteristic of Weber or his music.

1958 *Listener* 28 Aug. 321/3 Many of the typically Weberian passages in dotted notes. **1978** *Gramophone* June 56/2, I hope I have not led you to undertstimate the quality of so much of the music—the Weberian horns at the start of No. 1.

Weberian (vēi·bīə·riăn), *a.*[3] [f. the name of Max *Weber* (1864–1920), German sociologist and political economist + -IAN.] Of, pertaining to, or characteristic of Weber, his philosophy, or his writings.

1959 G. D. MITCHELL *Sociol.* 114 The importance of this Weberian analysis is that a system of stratification is seen to depend upon the economic character of society, the way prestige is distributed, and the kind of legal and political institutions it possesses. **1969** P. A. ROBINSON *Freudian Left* 6, I consider the Weberian ideal of a *wertfreien* science misguided. **1975** *Times Lit. Suppl.* 1 Aug. 880/5 This account of the transformation of Wolof war-leaders into bureaucrats, bringing Weberian theory to bear, is a new departure. **1979** L. LERNER *Love & Marriage* vi. 231, I shall use 'sublimation' essentially in its Weberian meaning.

Webernesque (vēi·bəɹne·sk), *a.* [f. the name of Anton von *Webern* (1883–1945), Austrian composer + -ESQUE.] Characteristic of the music of Webern. So **We·bernish** *a.*, somewhat resembling the music of Webern.

1959 *Listener* 28 May 960/3 The ejaculatory, disjointed, Webernish texture. **1961** *Times* 13 Oct. 18/5 The instrumentation is carried out in characteristically Webernesque fashion. **1976** *Gramophone* Sept. 437/3 The surface is..rather Webernesque.

Weber number (vei·bəɹ, we·bəɹ). *Physics.* Also **Weber's number.** [tr. G. *webersche zahl* (F. Eisner 1932, in Wien & Harms *Handb. d. Experimentalphysik* IV. IV. 225), f. the name of Moritz *Weber* (1871–1951), German naval engineer, who first formulated it in 1919.] A dimensionless quantity used in the study of surface tension, bubbles, and waves, usu. expressed as $\rho l v^2/\gamma$ or the reciprocal of this, where γ is the surface tension of the fluid, ρ its density, l the characteristic length, and v the velocity of the fluid or of waves in the fluid; also, the square root of either quantity.

1937 O'BRIEN & HICKOX *Appl. Fluid Mech.* v. 149 Generalized Representation of Weir Coefficients... The first three terms [in the coefficient of discharge] merely represent the geometrical similarity including the roughness. The other two are Weber's number and Reynolds' number. **1946** H. ROUSE *Elem. Mech. of Fluids* x. 322 The radical form of this ratio $W = V/\sqrt{(\sigma/\rho L)}$ is known as the Weber number. **1977** R. A. DUCKWORTH *Mech. of Fluids* vii. 149 In ship testing, the influence of surface tension forces, for which the Weber number, $(\sigma/\rho V^2 l)$, provides the criterion for dynamic stability, may be ignored because..such forces are negligible compared with the viscous and gravitational forces. **1979** A. L. LYDERSEN *Fluid Flow & Heat Transfer* ii. 39 Examples of force ratios are..inertia forces/surface forces = .. $\rho L V^2/\gamma$ = We = Weber number. **1979** *Sci. Amer.* Aug. 170/3 When the beaker is made to create water sheets in the middle range of Weber numbers, the ridge sends out curved waves.

web-foot. Add: **3. b.** (Earlier example.)

1845 W. WHITMAN in *Amer. Speech* (1961) XXXVI. 297 Oregonese [are called] *Webfoots*.

c. An infantryman. *U.S. slang.*

1867 B. W. DUKE *Hist. Morgan's Cavalry* xiv. 400 When the 'webfeet' called us 'buttermilk rangers', we did not get angry with them. **1917** J. MORGAN *Recoll. Rebel Reefer* 210, I was only a poor 'webfoot'.

web-footed, *a.* Add: Also *fig.* (in quots., *Mil.*).

1945 *Tee Emm* (Air Ministry) V. 49 We feel that the web-footed boys [i.e. Coastal Command] are not the only ones who may fall into the water out East. **1980** *Globe & Laurel* July/Aug. 226/1 The Small Raids Wing of the newly established Amphibious School based at Fort Cumberland and RMB Eastney, which also absorbed former web-footed units like RM Det 385.

Webley (we·bli). The proprietary name of various types of revolver and other small arms, etc., originally made by the firm of P. Webley and Son. Also *absol.*

1889 *Field* 4 May 618/1 After an exhaustive trial..the new Webley revolver..has been adopted by the English Government. **1897** *Sears, Roebuck Catal.* 586/2, 44 caliber, center fire, Webley cartridge. **1911** *Encycl. Brit.* XXI. 656/1 In the Webley the bolt is upon the standing breech and grips the extremity of the hinged barrel. **1920** *Trade Marks Jrnl.* 24 Mar. 567 Webley... Small-arms. Webley & Scott, Limited,..Birmingham; small arms manufacturers. **1923** *Official Gaz.* (U.S. Patent Office) 16 Jan. 502/2 Revolvers, automatic pistols, and other small arms. Webley & Scott Limited, Birmingham, England. **1937** S. SMITH *Good Time was had by All* 53 A Webley, service pattern, is a useful weapon. **1979** P. COSGRAVE *Three Colonels* vi. 137 Haddad was wearing a heavy Webley ostentatiously on his hip.

Webster[2] (we·bstəɹ). The name of Noah *Webster* (1758–1843), the American lexicographer, used *absol.* to designate his Dictionary (first published in 1828), and any of its later revisions and abridgements (now published by G. and C. Merriam Co., Springfield, Mass.).

1843 *Quincy* (Illinois) *Herald* 17 Mar. 4/1 (*heading*) Definitions not found in Webster. **1928** *Amer. Speech* IV. 90 We use *Webster* (in America) colloquially as synonymous with *dictionary*. **1950** [see *OXFORD 2]. **1978** *Amer. Speech* LIII. 70 Many 'Websters' later, came the controversial dictionary edited by Philip B. Gove and published in 1961 by the G. and C. Merriam Company of Springfield, Massachusetts, to whom Webster's heirs had sold the rights to the dictionary in 1843.

Websterian (websti·ə·riăn), *a.*[1] [f. the name of Noah *Webster* (see prec.) + -IAN.] Of, pertaining to, or characteristic of Webster's Dictionary (see prec.) or any of its later versions or abridgements.

1874 B. F. TAYLOR *World on Wheels* 28 Websterian 'probabilities' says that is not the derivation of 'scale' at all. **1897** *Bookman* Nov. 201 We are quite sure that if the English were to adopt the Websterian spelling, Professor Matthews would very, very soon experience a conservative reaction. **1935** A. C. BAUGH *Hist. Eng. Lang.* xi. 442 James Fenimore Cooper..was pronouncing..*beard* as *berd* or *baird* (another Websterian pronunciation). **1962** *New Yorker* 10 Mar. 156/2 Nearly all the books that come off the press..are edited and printed in accordance with Websterian usage. **1979** *Amer. Speech* LIV. 13 Thus was the battle joined between the traditional grammarians and those who might well be called the Websterian grammarians.

Webste·rian, *a.*[2] [f. the name of the English dramatist John *Webster* (1580–1625) + -IAN.]

Of, pertaining to, or characteristic of Webster or his plays.

1928 *Observer* 12 Feb. 4 With the great Websterian passages there is mingled a great deal of melodramatic fustian. **1940** M. Lowry *Let.* 27 July (1967) 32 It is 'original' if you fear for past Websterian, not to say Miltonian, minor lacks of ethics on my part. **1950** *Scrutiny* XVII. 152 The other (*The Insatiate Countess*) a rather Websterian account of a promiscuous noble-woman's destruction. **1971** *Guardian* 19 Jan. 8/5 The true Websterian frisson is achieved on an empty stage.

websterite[2] (we·bstərait). *Petrogr.* [f. *Webster*, name of a village in N. Carolina + -ITE[1].] An ultramafic intrusive igneous rock composed essentially of orthorhombic and monoclinic pyroxenes.

1890 G. H. Williams in *Amer. Geologist* VI. 44 The specimens obtained by Mr. Merrill from Webster are such admirable representatives of the bronzite-diopside rocks that the name Websterite is suggested..for them; and there seems to be no impropriety in extending this term over all the massive intrusives which are composed entirely of monoclinic and orthorhombic pyroxene. **1978** S. R. Nockolds in S. R. Nockolds et al. *Petrol. for Students* xiii. 148 Pyroxenite with both ortho- and clino-pyroxene ('websterite') is the commonest variety, found both in connection with some great layered igneous bodies..and in small intrusions.

Wechsler (we·kslər). *Psychol.* The name of David *Wechsler* (b. 1896), American psychologist, used *attrib.* or as *adj.* in connection with various intelligence tests devised by him (and in use since 1939), esp. the *Wechsler-Bellevue Intelligence Scale*, the *Wechsler Intelligence Scale for Children* (WISC), and the *Wechsler Adult Intelligence Scale* (WAIS). Also *absol.*

1942 *Amer. Jrnl. Psychol.* LV. 608 The Wechsler-Bellevue Intelligence Scale, an individual scale adapted to ages 10–60 and consisting of 5 verbal and 5 performance-tests, with vocabulary-test as alternate. **1954** A. Anastasi *Psychol. Testing* xii. 306 Two scales for measuring 'general intelligence', namely, the Wechsler-Bellevue Intelligence Scale and the Wechsler Intelligence Scale for Children. *Ibid.*, One of the primary objectives of the Wechsler-Bellevue is to provide an intelligence test suitable for adults. **1961** *New Scientist* 16 Mar. 665/3 Special psychological tests, including the well-known Wechsler Memory Scale,were employed to assess memory. **1970** *Jrnl. Gen. Psychol.* July 69 The tasks of the Wechsler..are not composed of stimuli all of the same degree of structuredness either. **1981** D. Statt *Dict. Human Behav.* 129 *Wechsler Adult Intelligence Scale*, one of the most widely used intelligence tests for adults, combining performance and verbal ability testing.

Weddell (we·dĕl). The name of James *Weddell* (1787–1834), Scottish navigator, used *attrib.* or in the possessive as **Weddell('s) seal,** to designate a large brown Antarctic seal, *Leptonychotes weddellii*, first recorded by him and named in his honour in 1826. Cf. *sea-leopard* s.v. Sea *sb.* 23 b. Also *absol.*

1902 G. E. H. Barrett-Hamilton in *Rep. Coll. Nat. Hist. Voy. 'Southern Cross'* i. 19 Weddell's seal is probably of wide distribution. **1923** F. Wild *Shackleton's Last Voy.* vi. 118 Near by a fat Weddell seal lay asleep. **1938** [see *crab-eater 3]. **1971** R. Sale *Man who raised Hell* i. i. 14 He was trying to tag a Weddell mother seal... Weddells are big animals, going to twelve feet. **1979** *Nature* 11 Jan. 87/3 The Weddell seal has adapted to fill a specialised niche—the inshore fast ice zone—where it winters under the ice, keeping breathing holes open with its teeth.

weddellite (we·dĕlait). *Min.* [f. the name of the *Weddell* Sea, Antarctica, where it was first found + -ITE[1].] A hydrated calcium oxalate, $CaC_2O_4.2H_2O$, which occurs as colourless tetragonal crystals and is common in calculi.

1942 Frondel & Prien in *Science* 24 Apr. 431/1 Stones [formed in the body] composed wholly of carbonate-apatite are relatively rare. Whewellite ($CaC_2O_4{\cdot}H_2O$), weddellite ($CaC_2O_4{\cdot}2H_2O$) and especially struvite..are ordinarily present. **1961** *Lancet* 26 Aug. 452/1 (*caption*) The large crystals in the centre of the field were of calcium oxalate dihydrate (weddellite). **1976** *Chem. Abstr.* 20 Sept. 190/1 (*heading*) Whewellite ($CaC_2O_4{\cdot}H_2O$) and weddellite ($CaC_2O_4{\cdot}2H_2O$) from the Upper Cretaceous limestone near Zminj in Istria (Croatia, Yugoslavia).

wedding, *vbl. sb.* Add: **2. b.** *Golden Wedding* (earlier example).

1850 J. von Tautphœus *Initials* I. v. 121 'Perhaps you have no golden or silver wedding in England?' 'I confess I never heard of any thing of the kind,' said Hamilton... 'To be fifty years married and to have a golden wedding, is a sort of event in a family.'

4. a. *wedding-anniversary* (later example), *-coat* (earlier example), *-dress* (earlier example), *-journey* (earlier example), *photo, photograph, -present* (earlier example), *-suit* (later examples), *-supper* (later example), *tour, trip, visit.*

1971 'D. Halliday' *Dolly & Doctor Bird* iii. 33 It's our wedding anniversary. **1838** M. R. Walker *Let.* 27 July in C. M. Drury *Elkanah & Mary Walker* (1940) iii. 92, I was glad indeed to see him safe & sound with his cloths sadly rent having lost his coat his *wedding coat.* **1801** M. Edgeworth *Belinda* II. xxxi. 357 Something must be left to the imagination. Positively I will not describe wedding dresses. **1841** Thackeray *Gt. Hoggarty Diamond* in *Fraser's Mag.* Nov. 598/1 She lent us her chariot for the wedding journey. **1966** P. Willmott *Adolescent Boys* iii. 46 They showed us different wedding photos. **1956** *Focal Encycl. Photogr.* 1273/2 A good set of wedding photographs calls for a surprising amount of planning and organization. **1972** C. Fremlin *Appointment with Yesterday* x. 76 Cora should have received the wedding photograph. **1854** C. Schreiber *Jrnl.* 27 May (1952) 35 My wedding present to Felicia, a white and gold bookcase. **1807** Wedding suit [see *family tree* s.v. *family *sb.* 11]. **1959** W. Faulkner *Mansion* xiii. 296 Maybe he picked it up along with that-ere white wedding suit. **1961** *New Eng. Bible Rev.* xix. 9 Happy are those who are invited to the wedding-supper of the Lamb! **1847** C. M. Yonge *Scenes & Characters* xxxi. 340 The wedding had been hurried on, and the wedding-tour was shortened. **1955** C. Carrington *Rudyard Kipling* ix. 201 It will not be necessary to retrace Rudyard's steps throughout his wedding tour. **1855** Dickens *Dorrit* (1857) i. ii. 17 A clerical English husband..on a wedding trip with his young wife. **1925** F. Scott Fitzgerald *Great Gatsby* viii. 183 Tom and Daisy were still on their wedding trip. **1974** *News & Reporter* (Chester, S. Carolina) 22 Apr. 4-a/8 After a wedding trip to Charlottesville, Virginia the couple will reside on Morreene Road, Durham. **1794** J. Woodforde *Diary* 7 Apr. (1929) IV. 103 Mr. & Mrs. Carbould are gone out for a few days to make a wedding visit to Mrs. Carbould's Brother at Castor near Yarmouth. **1872** Geo. Eliot *Middlem.* II. iii. xxviii. 89 Through the next weeks there would be wedding visits received and given.

b. wedding band *U.S.* = *wedding-ring*; **wedding-breakfast,** delete 'formerly' and add earlier and later examples; cf. *breakfast *sb.* 2 b; **wedding-bush,** a shrub of the genus *Ricinocarpos*, of the family Euphorbiaceæ, esp. *R. pinifolius*, which is native to eastern Australia and bears clusters of fragrant white flowers; **wedding-cake:** also *fig.*, esp. applied *attrib.* (often somewhat dismissively) to a sumptuously ornate style of architecture, and (also *absol.*) to buildings in this style; (later examples); **wedding canopy** *Judaism* = *chuppah; **wedding-cards** (earlier example); also in *sing.*; **wedding group,** (a photograph of) a wedding party; **wedding list,** a list of acceptable wedding gifts for guests to consult and act upon; **wedding party,** the assemblage of persons at a wedding; **wedding reception,** a party at which the wedding guests are formally greeted and entertained after the marriage ceremony; cf. *reception 2 d; **wedding-ring:** also, a ring similarly presented by the bride to the bridegroom, and worn afterwards by him; later *fig.* examples, both *attrib.*

1946 R. Lyle *Mademoiselle's Handbk. Bridal Consultants* vi. 79 Wedding bands have in centuries past been made of iron as well as gold. **1977** 'E. McBain' *Long Time no See* i. 16 On the third finger of his left hand, there was a wedding band. **1850** Thackeray *Pendennis* II. xv. 144 There is a wedding breakfast. **1962** *Sunday Times* 11 Nov. 25/4 They married in church, and had a wedding breakfast but no honeymoon. **1923** *Census of Plants of Victoria* (Field Naturalists' Club of Victoria) 41 Wedding Bush. **1961** Wedding-bush [see *manna[1] 9]. **1925** F. Scott Fitzgerald *Great Gatsby* i. 8 A breeze..blew curtains,.. twisting them up toward the frosted wedding-cake of the ceiling. **1949** H. G. Alsberg *Amer. Guide* 105 *Kennebunk* ..Among numerous old mansions are..Wedding Cake H. (c. 1825), with most unusual Vict. trimmings. **1968** *N.Y. City* (Michelin Tire Corp.) 16 Others [*sc.* skyscrapers], sometimes known as *wedding cakes*, were covered with ornate sculpture in the 1900 '*Gigi style*'. **1971** J. Willett in A. Bullock *20th Cent.* 242/1 A massive piece of wedding-cake architecture (..fortunately never built) for the projected Palace of Soviets in Moscow. **1892** I. Zangwill *Childr. Ghetto* I. 37 The hope was expressed that Mr. and Mrs. Belcovitch would like..to see their daughters' daughters under the *Chuppah*, or wedding canopy. **1978** I. B. Singer *Shosha* iv. 74 You should lead your daughter to a black wedding canopy! **1847** C. M. Yonge *Scenes & Characters* ii. 9 She was putting her sister's wedding cards into their shining envelopes. **1953** Dylan Thomas *Let.* 31 Mar. (1966) 401 Had your wedding card. Congratulations. **1861** Geo. Eliot *Silas Marner* 361 The wedding group had passed on..to the humbler part of the village. **1930** R. Lehmann *Note in Music* v. 190 The texts, the wedding group, and the photograph of a grave on the wall. **1979** J. Adam Smith *John Buchan* 51 People in Scotland, she said, might like to have wedding groups, but she doubted if it was ever done in London. **1981** *Times* 7 Mar. (Bride & Home Suppl.) p. vi/1 Today's brides..confine romance to their wedding dress and..Roneo their less personal requirements... The stores still keeping wedding lists do provide a valuable service. **1873** C. M. Yonge *Pillars of House* IV. xlvii. 340 The blow was known to all that sad wedding party. **1877** W. S. Gilbert *Engaged* (?1883) ii. 31, I have ordered four flys for the wedding party. **1979** J. Gardner *Nostradamus Traitor* xxxv. 165 Another alert. This time the wedding party had to take shelter. **1871** A. J. Munby *Diary* 4 Nov. in D. Hudson *Munby* (1972) 299 We, Council and Students..offered this evening a wedding reception to Litchfield and his bride. **1965** [see *stung *ppl. a.* 2]. **1978** S. Sheldon *Bloodline* xlv. 374 After the ceremony there was a wedding reception at the Baur-au-Lac. **1953** Dylan Thomas *Under Milk Wood* (1954) 74 His mother..with her wedding-ring waist and bust like a black-clothed dining-table suffers in her stays. **1980** *Quilt World* Sept./Oct. 23/1 Sheri's mother feels that it is a single wedding ring quilt because when four blocks are pieced together a ring is formed.

‖**wedeln** (vē·dəln), *sb. Skiing.* Also **wedel.** [a. G. *wedeln* (in same sense).] A skiing technique using a swaying movement of the hips to make short parallel turns (see *parallel *a.* 1 b). Also *attrib.*

1957 J. Ceely tr. *Joubet & Vuarnet's Ski ABC* ii. 106 The skier effects a real wedeln when he is able to minimize the second step of the above progression. *Ibid.* iii. 130 In linked turns or wedeln, planting the pole adds favorable *rhythm* to the movements. **1958** *Times* 1 Mar. 7/6 The reverse shoulder technique of *wedeln*..or *godille* as the French call it, has become so universal among first-class racers of all nations that no one using the classical rotation can hope to be placed in a serious race. **1963** *New Yorker* 2 Feb. 37 Down he goes, anyway, his wedeln so crisp he never seems to care at all for the configuration of the snow. **1963** *Amer. Speech* XXXVIII. 208 Other attributive uses are *wedel track* and *wedel turn.* **1973** R. Hayes *Hungarian Game* xxxii. 195 We had skied nearly to the base of the mountain and Mary Louise shot over a drop... I did a quick wedeln series and looked for her. **1974** H. Evans et al. *We learned to Ski* 44 Those who can do the long radius parallel turn learn to make shorter linked parallel turns—the wedel. **1975** *Oxf. Compan. Sports & Games* 965/2 Between 1956 and 1958, the Austrian, *Sailer*, won seven out of eight world titles,.. and he introduced the *wedeln* style to a wide public.

‖**wedeln** (vē·dəln), *v. Skiing.* Also (app. more commonly) **wedel.** [a. G. *wedeln* (in same sense), lit. to wag (the tail).] *intr.* To use the wedeln technique in skiing. Also *transf.* in *Skateboarding.*

1961 *Times* 7 Jan. 7/7 Sign-posted high roads which shepherd each carload of uninspired humanity down from the heights..wedelning as best they can. **1963** *Amer. Speech* XXXVIII. 208 *Wedel*; *wedeln, v.* to execute a special kind of short parallel turns close to the fall line in quick succession. **1968** *Time* 15 Nov. 49 They wedeled down the 1,200-ft. slope or slammed through the slalom course. **1973** P. A. Whitney *Snowfire* iii. 36, I don't care..whether my skis are expertly parallel. I've never been able to wedel. **1977** *Skateboard Special* Sept. 3/1 Special slalom decks have a raised centre to make it easier to 'pump' or 'wedel'.

Hence **we·del(l)ing** *vbl. sb.*

1977 *Skateboard Special* Sept. 2/2 *Wedeling*, a sophisticated method of reducing speed while zig-zagging down steep hills. *Ibid.* 5/1 Slalom decks..are often slightly raised in the middle to make pumping and wedeling easier. **1979** N. Slater *Falcon* ix. 161 His *wedelling* turns between each traverse were smothered in a flurry of snow.

wedge, *sb.* Add: **2. b.** *the thin end of the wedge* (earlier examples).

1856 C. Fox *Jrnl.* 8 Nov. in *Memories Old Friends* (1882) xxii. 308 Beware, Englishmen, of the tendencies to hierarchy in your country when the thin end of the wedge is introduced: it will work its way on to all this. **1867** *Hansard Commons* 27 June 615 The thin end of the wedge.

5. i. A v-shaped sign used in various musical and other notations (see quots.).

1893 E. M. Thompson *Handbk. Greek & Latin Palæogr.* v. 68 The paragraph-mark was not..uniformly the horizontal stroke; the wedge > ..and similar forms were employed. **1970** *Language* XLVI. 78 Wedges printed after vowel symbols, e.g. [a^ a> a˅ a<], indicate raising, backing, lowering, and fronting. **1980** *Early Music* July 401/1 The most fascinating [signs] are the wedges indicating *crescendo, diminuendo* and *messa da voce* on single long notes: ◀, ▶, ◆, and a passage with second-position fingerings.

j. *Golf.* A golf club with a wedge-shaped head, used for lofting the ball at approach shots, or (= *sand wedge* s.v. *sand *sb.*[2] 10 a) out of a bunker, etc. Also, a shot made with a wedge.

[**1924** J. White *Easier Golf* iv. 100 What I attempt to do is to use this heel [of a club]..as a wedge, and by driving this into the sand behind the ball I create sufficient disturbance to force the ball out of any lie.] **1937** [see *sand wedge* s.v. *sand *sb.*[2] 10 a]. **1952** *Chambers's Jrnl.* May 300/1 Basil walked moodily off the tee, and after five minutes' search found his ball embedded in a patch of the foulest rough on the course, hacked it out with his wedge, and, playing two odd to the green, lost the hole. **1961** *Times* 1 July 4/1 He..played an overcautious wedge at the Royal. **1975** *Daily Tel.* (Colour Suppl.) 12 Sept. 9/4 Putting is out; most golfers carry just a driver, a four-wood, mid-iron and wedge.

k. A wedge heel; a wedge-soled shoe. See sense 9 b below. *colloq.*

1959 *Chambers's 20th Cent. Dict.* Add. **1965** R. Hardwick *Plotters* (1966) xi. 102 Stretch pants, wedges, and a leghorn hat. **1968** J. Ironside *Fashion Alphabet* 137 *Wedge*, a solid heel joined to the sole in one solid piece. **1976** *Washington Post* 19 Apr. A12/3 (Advt.), Casual style wedges in Oxford and slip-on styles. **1983** *Times* 14 July 11/3 Gladiator straps on stacked wooden wedge..£44.50.

l. A hair style in which the ends of the hair are slightly graduated so that they form a series of wedges. orig. *U.S.*

1976 *Time* 19 Apr. 69 There are many variations on the new wedge. Stylists at the Paul McGregor shops in New York and Los Angeles have shaped the back of the cut into three inverted pyramids. **1977** *Daily News* (Perth, Austral.) 19 Jan. 6/4 After she became a headliner, Dorothy's hairdo, called the wedge, sent girls rushing off to hairdressers to duplicate the look. **1985** *Hair* Summer 78 (*caption*), Short, sculptured sweeping version of the wedge has classy clout in the form of a pink flash.

9. a. *wedge-blade*; *wedge-balancing* adj.

1921 D. H. LAWRENCE *Tortoises* 19 Four rowing limbs, and one wedge-balancing head. **1917** —— *Look! We have come Through!* 113 The fine, fine wind... Like a fine, an exquisite chisel, a wedge-blade inserted.

b. *attrib.* and *Comb.* Designating a wedge-shaped heel extended under the instep of a woman's shoe (also, the sole which includes this), or a shoe having such a heel. Freq. as *wedge-heel, shoe, sole*; *wedge-heeled, -soled* adjs. Cf. sense 5 k above.

1939 M. B. PICKEN *Lang. Fashion* 164/3 *Wedge-soled*, having a wedge-shaped piece making a solid sole, flat on the ground from heel to toe. **1940** GRAVES & HODGE *Long Week-End* xxi. 375 A high-heeled fancy shoe..and a wedge-heeled streamlined type. **1940** *Manch. Guardian Weekly* 11 Oct. 259 Today's displays of courts..and wedge-heel, and all other of the creations of the fashion-designer, give no indication..of what was really a welcome weeding out. **1940** O. NASH in *New Yorker* 23 Nov. 18/2 Let us give thanks that women's wedge shoes weren't invented until they were. **1942** in C. W. Cunnington *Eng. Women's Clothing in Present Cent.* (1952) viii. 271 Practical [shoes], with flatter heels, square toed and wedge-soled. **1951** [see *CREEPER 1 d]. **1957** R. HOGGART *Uses of Literacy* iv. 102 Mail-order firms advertise fancy wedge-shoes. **1975** D. BEATY *Electric Train* 153 Painted faces clumping up..on six-inch wedge shoes. **1983** P. DEVLIN *All of us Here* x. 112 Her daughter, in a new permanently pleated skirt, wedge-heeled shoes.

10. wedge-tail *Austral.*, the wedge-tailed eagle (see *wedge-tailed* adj.); = *EAGLE-HAWK 2; **wedge tent** = A TENT.

1935 A. C. CHISHOLM *Bird Wonders Austral.* x. 102 The Wedge-tail is a formidable foe for any native mammal. **1965** [see *EAGLE-HAWK 2]. **1974** D. STUART *Prince of my Country* ii. 9 Watching the long effortless circling of the wedgetail high in the air. **1977** *Times Lit. Suppl.* 21 Jan. 76/2 Australia is the only place in the whole world where the wedgetail eagle is known. **1862** O. W. NORTON *Army Lett.* (1903) 49 We used to sleep on the ground or on pine boughs when we had the small wedge tents. **1940** G. W. MARTIN *Mod. Camping Guide* v. 86 The wedge tent, known also as the A tent, is a popular model with explorers and other outdoorsmen who want something a little larger than a tiny crawl-in tent. **1980** D. T. ROSCOE *Your Bk. Camping* ('Your Bk.' Ser.) ii. 22 Wedge tents.. are designed to save weight and bulk and to withstand wind better when the smaller end is pitched directly into it.

wedge, *v.*^{1} Add: **6.** *to wedge out* (Geol.): = *thin out* s.v. THIN *v.*^{1} 2 a; = *lens out* s.v. *LENS *v.*

1819 [implied in *wedging out* s.v. *WEDGING *vbl. sb.* 3*]. **1839** R. I. MURCHISON *Silurian Syst.* 140 Limestone..can be traced tapering away from a central mass to thin extremities, which really wedge out between the coal grits and the older deposits. **1945** *Bull. Amer. Assoc. Petroleum Geologists* XXIX. 1563 The distinction from the Permeability Trap Reservoirs is made by restricting the Pinch-Out Trap Reservoirs to types located in such stratigraphic intervals or zones which actually wedge out. **1966** *Earth-Sci. Rev.* I. 163 Ignimbrites tend to wedge out against or thin over topographic highs. **1979** *Nature* 27 Sept. 267/1 These nappes wedge out and converge to the west and seem to represent a telescoping of Lower Palæozoic Facies.

wedged (wedʒd), *ppl. a.*^{2} [f. WEDGE *v.*^{2} + -ED^1.] Of wet clay: that has been wedged to expel air-bubbles before it is worked.

1903 in J. Burnett *Useful Toil* (1974) III. 298 From balls of wedged or refined clay he made the pancake-like shapes of clay which he had to use in making the next set of plates. **1967** M. CHANDLER *Ceramics in Mod. World* ii. 63 However well pugged or well *wedged* (hand worked to eliminate air) his clay may be, the ceramic sculptor cannot be certain that it contains no *blebs*.

wedger (weˑdʒəɹ). [f. WEDGE *v.*^{2} + -ER^1.] A workman who wedges clay to expel air-bubbles from it.

1881 *Harper's Mag.* Feb. 361/2 The 'wedger' takes a lump of..twenty pounds, lays it on the kneading block before him, [etc.]. **1921** *Dict. Occup. Terms* (1927) §104 *Wedger, clay wedger*, cuts lump of clay into pieces or wedges with wire cutter, and beats one piece of clay vigorously against another to make it homogeneous and free of air bubbles, for use in manufacture of highest class ware.

wedgie (weˑdʒi). *colloq.* Also **wedgy.** [f. WEDGE *sb.* + -Y^6.] A wedge-heeled shoe (see *WEDGE *sb.* 9 b); more recently, also *spec.* one with a built-up or 'stacked' sole. Usu. in *pl.*

1940 *Women's Wear Daily* 15 Mar. 18/1 New streamlined wedgies that make the foot look smaller. **1943** *Consumers' Res. Bull.* (U.S.) Dec. 20/2 Brown leather 'wedgie' with bottom-sole of thin leather. **1950** [see *sling-back* s.v. *SLING *sb.*^{2} 7]. **1962** A. HUXLEY *Island* ix. 133 Soft Platform Wedgies in Wide Widths. **1974** E. BRAWLEY *Rap* (1975) I. v. 83 She always wore those white wedgies, old Marie-Claude, claimed they eased her feet on the job.

wedging, *vbl. sb.* Add: **2.** Delete 'jutting *out* or' and transfer quot. 1819 to sense 3* below.

3*. *Geol.* With *out*: the narrowing of a stratum or the like to the point of extinction. Cf. *WEDGE *v.*^{1} 6.

1819 [in Dict., sense 2]. **1883** W. S. GRESLEY *Gloss. Coal-Mining* 283 *Wedging out*, cropping or thinning out.

Wedgwood. Add: **1. a.** Now a proprietary name both in the U.K. (since 1876) and the U.S. (since 1906).

1876 *Trade Marks Jrnl.* 2 Aug. 325 Wedgwood. Godfrey Wedgwood..trading under the Firm of Josiah Wedgwood and Sons..Pottery Manufacturers... Pots. 2823. 28th Feb. 1876. **1906** *Official Gaz.* (U.S. Patent Office) 4 Dec. 1671/1 Wedgwood. Particular description of goods.—Porcelain, stoneware, and earthenware, including Jasper.

b. (Later *absol.* examples, = Wedgwood blue.)

1923 *Daily Mail* 19 Feb. 1 (Advt.), Coloured Jap silks (36 inches wide)... In pink, coral, wedgwood, helio, [etc.]. **1974** P. DICKINSON *Poison Oracle* ii. 41 Her angry Wedgwood eyes held his.

wee, *a.* Add: **e.** *Wee Frees*: also *transf.*

1953 EARL WINTERTON *Orders of Day* viii. 92 In 1919.. both the Labour and Liberal Oppositions were small and ineffective. The latter, facetiously known as the 'Wee Frees'..split into two halves led by Sir Donald Maclean and Mr. George Lambert respectively. **1966** *Punch* 20 July 123/3 His account of the way in which the Wahabis—the Calvinistic 'wee frees' of Islam—are surrendering to the worst of Western culture is a lively moral tale in itself. **1979** H. WILSON *Final Term* i. 10 The smell of power..was in their nostrils, for the first time since the 'Wee Frees', the Samuelite Liberals, had left the 1931 Coalition Government.

f. *the wee (small) hours* = *small hours* s.v. HOUR 3 b. *colloq.*

[**1787** BURNS *Death & Dr. Hornbook* in *Poems & Songs* (1968) I. 84 The auld kirk-hammer strak the bell Some wee, short hour ayont the *twal*.] **1849** C. BRONTË *Shirley* II. ii. 73 She followed the steps of the night, on its pathway of stars, far into the 'wee sma' hours ayont the twal.' **1859** [see HOUR 3 b]. *a* **1891** H. MELVILLE *To Major John Gention* in *Compl. Wks.* (1924) XIII. 366 In the wee hours..how affluent hast thou been on that theme. **1932** 'L. G. GIBBON' *Sunset Song* 232 They'd another long dram, and they argued far into the wee, small hours. **1949** P. MICHAELS *This Perverse Generation* v. 44 No one has a persistent inner compulsion to..talk about silly things in crowded, stuffy, little night-club rooms at wee hours of the morning. **1966** 'H. MACDIARMID' *Company I've Kept* viii. 193 We walked back..in the 'wee sma' 'oors' of the following morning. **1979** *United States 1980/81* (Penguin Travel Guides) 278 Several acts keep the place hopping from dinner time until the wee hours.

wee (wī), *sb.*^{2} *colloq.* [See next.] = *WEE-WEE *sb.* 1.

1968 R. CLAPPERTON *No News on Monday* vi. 61 Wanda is downstairs having a wee. **1971** P. PURSER *Holy Father's Navy* ii. 12 Hurry up, I want to do a wee. **1973** *Punch* 1 Aug. 139/1 Thought I saw someone comin' in de gate, but it only a dog havin' a wee on de magnolia.

wee (wī), *v. colloq.* [Echoic: see *WEE-WEE *v.*] *intr.* To urinate. Also *refl.* = *WET *v.* 5 d.

1934 DYLAN THOMAS *Let.* 11 May (1966) 128 Wee on the sun that he bloody well shines not. **1970** *Guardian* 13 July 9/2 Ladies always have to walk a mile and they'll wee themselves if they don't find something soon. **1976** *West Lancs. Evening Gaz.* 15 Dec., She hit her daughter because she kept on 'weeing' all the time. **1983** *Daily Mail* 30 May 17/5 Our headmaster told us that any boy caught short should if absolutely necessary wee into an empty milk bottle.

weed, *sb.*^{1} Add: **3. c.** Marijuana; a marijuana cigarette. *slang* (orig. *U.S.*).

1929 *Amer. Speech* IV. 345 *Weed*, marijuana cigarette. (A Mexican drug.) **1932, 1933** [see *REEFER^1 3]. **1939** C. R. COOPER *Designs in Scarlet* viii. 145 There are certain centers in which marihuana offers more of a menace... The peddling of the weed is dependent upon persons.. content with small profits. **1949** R. CHANDLER *Little Sister* xxiv. 173 They were looking for..a suitcase full of weed. **1955** J. KEROUAC in *Paris Rev.* Winter 14 You could smell tea, weed, I mean marijuana, floating in the air. **1965** W. SOYINKA *Road* 24 Say Tokyo reaches out a stick of weed to him which he accepts behind his back. **1978** R. HILL *Pinch of Snuff* iii. 28 She *might* be on the game. Or she might have a bit of weed about the place. Or anything.

5. b. Hence, a small, feeble, or contemptible person; a 'weedy' type (see *WEEDY *a.*^{1} 4 b). *slang.*

1953 WILLANS & SEARLE *Down with Skool!* (1954) 12 There are a grate number of other weeds and wets about the place. **1959** I. & P. OPIE *Lore & Lang. Schoolch.* ix. 170 *Little 'uns*..Tiny Tim, Tom Thumb, tot, and, very common, weed. **1960** M. SPARK *Bachelors* x. 179 She's mad in love with that little weed Patrick Seton. **1970** *Times* 4 Mar. 13/5 A girl torn between a brainy weed and a moronic body-builder. **1982** BARR & YORK *Official Sloane Ranger Handbk.* 71/1 Don't try too hard: swots are weeds.

7. a. *weed control, -drift, -growth, -life.*

1923 KIPLING *Irish Guards in Great War* I. 222 They broke and disappeared in the rank weed-growth. **1934** A. HUXLEY *Beyond Mexique Bay* 249 Lawrence wrote eloquently of Oaxaca and Lake Chapala,..of the merits of that rank weed-life of the natural man. **1948** S. B. WHITEHEAD *Reclaiming your Garden* ii. 17 Chemicals.. have a selective action in weed control. **1951** *Sport* 7–13 Jan. 8/1 It had the drawback of increasing weed-growth. ?**1953** DYLAN THOMAS *Sel. Lett.* (1966) 416 In the slimy squid-rows of the sea there's such a weed-drift and clamour of old plankton drinkers. **1966** *Listener* 1 Sept. 304/1 The improvement of cultivation techniques to make weed control possible.

b. *weed-clogged, -covered, -laden, -mantled, -ridden, -sodden, -woven* adjs.

1898 O. WILDE *Ballad Reading Gaol* 12 Every day Crawled like a weed-clogged wave. **1910** W. DE LA MARE *Three Mulla-Mulgars* xxiii. 305 Nod's raft swam last across this weed-mantled lagoon. **1922** JOYCE *Ulysses* 699 In loose allwool garments..trundling a weedladen wheelbarrow without excessive fatigue at sunset amid the scent of newmown hay. **1938** W. DE LA MARE *Memory* 29 Roofless and eyeless, weed-sodden, dank, old, cold. **1944** BLUNDEN *Shells by Stream* 15 Weed-woven the shallowing pool. **1953** L. KUPER *Living in Towns* 300 Waste land and weed-covered pit banks. **1968** E. A. MCCOURT *Saskatchewan* xvii. 195 The inscriptions on the wooden crosses in the weed-ridden settlement graveyard. **1972** R. ADAMS *Watership Down* xxxii. 245 The rough, weed-covered ground of the combe sloped away below them.

c. *weed-cutter* (earlier example); *weed-waving, -winding* adjs.; also *weed-free* adj.

1850 *Rep. Comm. Patents 1849* (U.S.) I. 297, I likewise claim the combination of the adjustive weed cutter and leveler F. **1879** G. M. HOPKINS *Poems* (1967) 78 On meadow and river and wind-wandering weed-winding bank. **1940** J. BETJEMAN *Old Lights for New Chancels* 33 The light skiff is push'd from the weed-waving shore. **1960** *Farmer & Stockbreeder* 22 Mar. 56/3 It is the modern alternative..to secure weed-free cropping. **1981** M. SELLERS *From Eternity to Here* i. 7 A well-planned and weed-free vegetable garden.

d. weedhead *slang* (chiefly *U.S.*), one who is addicted to marijuana; a marijuana smoker (see *HEAD *sb.* 7 e); **weed inspector,** an official in charge of controlling the growth of noxious weeds; **weed-killer,** for def. read: something that kills weeds, *spec.* any of various chemical preparations used for killing weeds; liquid, powder, etc., of this kind; (earlier and later examples); also *fig.*

1952 *Amer. Speech* XXVII. 30 *Weedhead*,..marijuana smoker. **1966** C. HIMES *Heat is On* xx. 157 Weedheads jabbered and gesticulated. **1973** R. PARKES *Guardians* x. 178 The students that spat and jeered at authority, the weed-heads that threw acid in a vicar's eyes. **1909** *Chambers's Jrnl.* Nov. 702/2 The writer, in his capacity as weed-inspector, has had..to direct the settlers to plough under entire fields of growing grain in order to eradicate such weeds. **1974** D. SEARS *Lark in Clear Air* iv. 48 The one in overalls was Brad-Awl Callum, weed inspector, pound-keeper, truant officer and County Constable all rolled into one. **1745** W. ELLIS *Agric. Improv'd* in *Mod. Husbandman* July xi. 88 Such Wheat commonly runs up into such rank Stalks, as to become great Weed-killers. **1901** M. FRANKLIN *My Brilliant Career* xxi. 179 Every one would be wanting to engage me as the great noxious weed-killer and poisonous insect exterminator if I made away with you. **1929** WODEHOUSE *Mr. Mulliner Speaking* i. 23 What this woman needed was a fluid ounce of weed-killer. **1967** B. PATTEN *Little Johnny's Confession* 46 Who poured weedkiller over your innocence? *a* **1974** R. CROSSMAN *Diaries* (1976) II. 291 She only talked to Anne and myself about a new weedkiller called Paraquat, pointing out of the window to a field where it was being used.

weed, *v.* Add: **4. e.** *trans.* To perform a process of selecting from (a collection of documents, a file, etc.), rejecting those items which are unimportant or not worth retaining; to select (papers, etc.) in this manner. Also, to select (papers, etc.) in order to withhold them from general inspection. Also with *out.*

1874 H. TAYLOR *Let.* 30 Sept. in J. Brown *Lett.* (1912) 412, I am not sure that when I admired his poetry most, I did not admire his letters more, but like almost every collection of letters they should be weeded. **1946** A. E. PORTER *Let.* 26 Aug. in P. Moon *Transfer of Power* (1979) VIII. 309 Dick Tottenham, who compiled most of the files and is now on leave preparatory to retirement, would be singularly well qualified to weed them out and present you with those which are in fact worth keeping. **1977** *Times* 31 Aug. 4/1 The Ministry of Defence has begun a review of the way classified papers are written, filed, preserved (or 'weeded').

f. *to weed down*, to reduce (a list of candidates, etc.) to a short-list.

1942 *R.A.F. Jrnl.* 18 Apr. 6 Those who pass are further weeded down by a ballot. **1962** J. GLENN in *Into Orbit* 17 NASA asked us to take a series of tests which would help weed us down further.

6. *Angling.* Of a trout: to bury itself in weeds when hooked (*refl.* and *intr.*). Also, to entangle (the fish) in weeds (const. in *pass.*).

1889 F. M. HALFORD *Dry-Fly Fishing* ix. 211 Do not be afraid of weedy places. Trout..seldom weed at night, probably because they do not see the angler. *Ibid.* 224 When a fish is once weeded, the following tactics are what I suggest. **1960** *Times* 2 July 11/2 The risk of allowing a fish to weed itself is much reduced..if the weedbed lies upstream. *Ibid.*, More good trout have been lost in attempts to prevent them reaching weedbeds than have been lost in efforts to get them out once they have become weeded.

weeded (wīˑdėd), *a.*^{2} *arch.* [f. WEED *sb.*^{2} + -ED^2.] Dressed in widow's weeds.

1895 HARDY *Jude* v. vii. 369 Having ascertained thus much the immensely weeded widow retraced her steps. **1971** 'A. BURGESS' *MF* i. 18 An untrustworthy young man in black spoke to the frail weeded widow.

weeder. Add: **3. b.** *spec.* A person employed

by a government department to weed documents, letters, etc.

In quots. 1976 and 1984 the process is one of selecting papers in order to withhold or suppress them rather than to discard them.

1976 SUMMERS & MANGOLD *File on Tsar* v. xx. 254 Before papers get anywhere near the Public Record Office the weeders, for that is what they are called in government circles, have first bite; beavering away in Whitehall basements, they plough through the documents accumulated by all government ministries, deciding what should be suppressed. **1983** W. GARNER *Think Big, Think Dirty* vii. 101 The weeders worked in Central Registry, thinning down documentation as it grew bulky, repetitive or outdated. **1984** *Times* 23 May 10/3 Highly secret work, so secret that the weeders will see that it is not disclosed, even after 30 years.

weedery (wī·dəri), *sb.*[2] *poet. nonce-wd.* [f. WEED *sb.*[2] + -ERY.] Mourning garments.

1908 HARDY *Dynasts* III. vi. ii. 459 Even as he For whom thou wear'st that filial weedery Was waylaid by my tipstaff nine years since.

weedicide (wī·disəid). [f. WEED *sb.*[1] + -I- + -CIDE.] A chemical preparation designed as a weed-killer; weed-killer.

1934 *Jrnl. Dept. Agric. W. Austral.* XI. 521 Sodium arsenite has been employed extensively..as a weedicide, and..proved the most successful weed killer. **1951** *Chambers's Jrnl.* Aug. 457/1 Agricultural scientists..have set themselves the task of finding efficient straight weedicides. **1975** *N.Z. Jrnl. Agric.* Sept. 21/1 Maize farmers..spend a great deal of time and money on ground preparation, seed, fertilisers and weedicide. **1979** *Indian Express* 10 Apr. 10/4 As preparatory cultivations are carried out to control weeds only, efforts should be made to use weedicides for it whenever necessary.

weeding, *vbl. sb.* Add: **2. b.** (Later examples.) Also with *out*.

1916 *Kinematograph Year Bk.* 36 (*heading*) The weeding-out process. **1932** *New Yorker* 14 May 56/2, I should like to hear some of the manuscripts that the weeding-out committee considered inferior to the final five. **1953** J. S. HUXLEY *Evolution in Action* ii. 42 This weeding-out process. **1968** *North Amer. Rev.* CVII. 589 In one case, and in one case only, could this weeding [of a library's collection] be properly made. **1977** *Times* 31 Aug. 4/1 Valuable material may have been destroyed during 'weeding'. **1981** D. FRANCIS *Twice Shy* xii. 139 He disagreed strongly with my weeding-out policy, even though I'd..discussed every dud [horse] to be discarded.

weedy, *a.*[1] Add: **3.** (Earlier example.)

1867 *Trans. Illinois Agric. Soc.* VI. 638 *Weedy*, flour made from wheat that has come in contact with a noxious weed imparting an unpleasant smell.

4. b. (Later examples.) Also without reference to physical qualities: feeble, half-hearted, weak; lacking firmness or strength.

1922 E. M. FORSTER *Life to Come* (1975) 73 The chief had developed into an affable and rather weedy Christian with a good knowledge of English. **1971** *Petticoat* 24 July 4/3 I'm just too weedy, I don't threaten to expose them. **1982** BARR & YORK *Official Sloane Ranger Handbk.* 122/1 At whatever grade, they are fearless ('Be weedy in front of the wops?').

c. Of things.

1950 *Chambers's Jrnl.* Mar. 131/1 He must have conveyed this to her in one way or another, because soon afterwards she sent back his presents, and the weedy friendship which might have blossomed into a beautiful love was nipped in the bud.

5. *weedy-brown* adj.; *weedy-slow* adv.

1958 J. BETJEMAN *Coll. Poems* 263 A mounting arch of water weedy-brown. **1923** E. SITWELL *Bucolic Comedies* 38 In the Castles drownèd long ago Where the empty years pass weedy-slow.

Hence **wee·diness**, the quality or state of being 'weedy'; lack of physical presence; feebleness.

1924 WODEHOUSE *Bill the Conqueror* v. 103 He had a certain weediness, a lack of thews and sinews. **1925** W. DEEPING *Sorrell & Son* viii. 80 He realized that in spite of the other man's weediness he was a competitor who was to be respected.

week, *sb.* Add: **1. b.** (Later examples.) Also, a week during which some event takes place, either annually or on one occasion only; a week during which attention is focused on a particular topic for promotional, charitable, etc., purposes.

1761 G. COLMAN *Jealous Wife* II. 21 How unlucky it is, that this damn'd Accident shou'd happen in the Newmarket Week! *c* **1810** W. HICKEY *Mem.* (1960) xx. 326 We had previously enjoyed private lodgings at Epsom..for the race week. **1890** W. BOOTH *In Darkest Eng.* II. vi. 231 Self-denial..[which] the Soldiers of the Salvation Army practice every year in Self Denial Week. **1917** *Wells Fargo Messenger* V. 133/2 (*caption*) Native sons of the Golden West begin 'Prune Week' ceremonies. **1965** 'E. McBAIN' *He who Hesitates* iii. 34 'How come everybody's so eager to join me this morning?' Roger asked. 'Who knows?... Maybe it's national brotherhood week.' **1977** *Lancashire Life* Mar. 99/1 He won a prize for the best money-raising poster during Warships Week.

3. Now also meaning five working days, from Monday to Friday inclusive, as opposed to the weekend; *three-day week*: see *THREE III. 2.

5. d. *week in, week out*: see IN *adv.* 2.

e. *week-to-week* (attrib. phr.), continuing or recurring in successive weeks; continual. Cf. To *prep.* 6 c.

1959 *New Statesman* 24 Jan. 92/2 The lightning flashed above Sinai, and in its glare, the starry-eyed observer, remote from the week-to-week grind of party work, saw a great machine, whirring smoothly to life. **1981** J. SUTHERLAND *Bestsellers* i. 15 The bestseller lists... Their week-to-week attention singles out sensational books of the moment.

6. c. Also † *a week of Saturdays*, an indefinite period, a long period. Cf. *Month of Sundays* s.v. MONTH[1] 3 f.

1831 *Constellation* 8 Jan. 57/3 No, you couldn't gess a week of Saturdays and so I'll tell you—cause it is *unginteel*.

weekday. Add: **3. a.** Now also used to mean a day of the week other than Saturday or Sunday.

1976 P. R. WHITE *Planning for Public Transport* ii. 32 On weekdays (Mondays to Fridays), to which many urban surveys are confined, many trips are made within a confined time budget.

week-end. Add: **1. a.** (Earlier examples). Also, the end of a week. *long week-end*: see *LONG *a.*[1] 18.

1638 in *Victoria County Hist. Yorkshire* (1912) II. 415/2 The greatest weight of the said exaction will fall upon very poor people..who making every week a coarse kersey and being compelled to sell the same at the week end..are nevertheless constrained to yield one half penny apiece. **1793** W. B. STEVENS *Jrnl.* 27 Feb. (1965) I. 70 Wrote to Dewe that I would put on my seven league boots next weekend and stretch my course to Appleby. **1870** *Food Jrnl.* 1 Mar. 97 'Week-end', that is from Saturday until Monday,—it may be a later day in the week if the money and credit hold out,—is the season of dissipation.

2. *attrib.* **a.** For use at week-ends, as *week-end bag, case, cottage*, etc.; occurring at or for the duration of a week-end, as *week-end course, leave, school, war*, etc.

1887, 1896 [sense a in Dict.]. **1911** 'SAKI' in *Bystander* 12 Apr. 70/2 I've seen a week-end cottage near Dorking that I should rather like to buy. **1924** KIPLING *Debits & Credits* (1926) 316 You live like a home defence Brigadier, besides week-end leaf [sic]. **1934** WEBSTER, Weekend case. **1944** J. S. HUXLEY *On Living in Revolution* 117 Short weekend courses and longer 'study workshops' for teachers. **1946** C. MCCULLERS *Member of Wedding* I. 10 At dark John Henry came to the back door with a little week-end bag. **1952** 'M. COST' *Hour Awaits* 136 She carried a small, smart week-end case of crocodile. **1958** O. CAROE *Pathans* xxv. 418 Roos-Keppel did indeed start his tour of office with two small operations the scale of which is sufficiently shown by the fact that one of them was called the week-end war. **1962** J. BRAINE *Life at Top* x. 136, I came to each and every week-end school here. **1967** R. V. BESTE *Repeat Instructions* (1968) xiv. 148, I haven't a week-end cottage. **1973** *Guardian* 22 Jan. 1/1 Lieutenant Mark Phillips, on weekend leave from Germany, went hunting on Saturday with Princess Anne. **1982** J. O'FAOLAIN *Obedient Wife* ii. 42 A weekend bag packed with scent, toothbrush and so forth.

b. Carrying out a specified activity or fulfilling a specified role only at week-ends or for pleasure (sometimes with the implication 'casual, amateur'); e.g. *week-end Air Force, athlete, father, gardener, motorist, sailor, soldier, writer*. Cf. *SUNDAY *sb.* 3.

1935 *Discovery* Oct. 314/1 The publisher suggests that *English Earth* will interest equally the farmer and the week-end motorist. **1941** *Time* 30 June 31/1 Week-end athletes should be careful. **1943** C. H. WARD-JACKSON *Piece of Cake* 62 *Week-end Air Force, The*, the Auxiliary Air Force. It was formed in 1925, its officers and men being citizens who gave week-ends and other part-time to their duties. **1959** *Listener* 12 Mar. 461/1 None of your present week-end, or decade-end writers realize that the present agitators are the sons of a former day, of which these writers presumably know nothing. **1962** *Jrnl. Family Law* Fall 104 The law is, in fact, uncertain as to the rights of the ex-spouse. Consequently, it seems even more uncertain about the privileges which the law should extend to the children with 'week-end fathers'. **1970** *New Yorker* 3 Oct. 40/3 Will you look at them weekend soldiers. **1974** *Harper's & Queen* Sept. 117 Humphrey Brooke was only a weekend gardener until..he decided to retire. **1976** 'D. HALLIDAY' *Dolly & Nanny Bird* ix. 120 The boat was..full of tanned, husky weekend sailors.

week-ending: also as *ppl. a.*, (in the habit of) spending the week-end away from home; **week-endize** *v. intr.*, to spend a week-end away from home (*nonce-wd.*); **week-endy** *a.*, suggestive of the week-end.

1910 R. BRIDGES *Let.* 21 June in Bridges & Bradley *Corr.* (1940) 77, I was glad to get your note saying that you wd week-endize. **1930** J. B. PRIESTLEY *Angel Pavement* xi. 567 She spent the next few minutes getting from the bus to the station, which was very crowded and week-endy. **1934** WEBSTER, Weekending *adj.* **1947** J. HAYWARD *Prose Lit. since 1939* 36 *The Long Week-end*—an ironical title which only the 'week-ending' Englishman will appreciate. **1973** A. GREY *Some put their Trust in Chariots* xiii. 72 Weekending French families setting out in their saloons for the countryside. **1976** G. EWART *No Fool* II. 61 Contrariwise, would you admire what's trendy (you were a fashion once yourself) or see virtue in what's sutburban or weekendy?

weekender. Add: **2. a.** A week-end cottage (see *WEEK-END 2 a). *colloq.*

1941 BAKER *Dict. Austral. Slang* 81 *Weekender*, a week-end holiday cottage or shack. **1967** E. HUNT *Danger Game* iii. 59 He had a week-ender at Palm Beach and a lovely car. **1976** *Billings* (Montana) *Gaz.* 16 June 10-c/5 (Advt.), Small, clean..home in Red Lodge. Perfect week-ender any season. **1983** *Austral. Women's Weekly* Aug. 21/2 There is, says Pauline, constant confusion over..shacks and holiday homes. 'A shack in NSW is a tumble-down wreck. In NSW you have a weekender.'

b. A bag large enough to carry everything needed for a week-end away from home; a week-end bag. *U.S. colloq.*

1961 *Harper's Bazaar* June 24/2 A capacious week-ender in pale coffee-bean hide. **1980** *TWA Ambassador* Oct. 99/1 You'll use the Kluge Bag like a week-ender too, because it's just as easy to carry on and a whole lot better.

weekly, *a.* and *sb.* Add: **A.** *adj.* **2. a.** *weekly boat*: a coaster on which the crew is paid by the week. Cf. *monthly boat* s.v. *MONTHLY *a.* 4.

1927 F. H. SHAW *Knocking Around* 4 She was a weekly boat, where the crew provided their own food. **1946** J. BATTEN *Dirty Little Collier* 12 These weekly boat men are quite used to slipping home for a few hours.

b. *weekly boarder*: a school pupil who boards at the school during the week and returns home at week-ends.

1841 DICKENS *Let.* 6 Mar. (1969) II. 225, I will send [him] as a weekly boarder to the best school I can find in the place... I say weekly boarder, because I should wish the boy..to be at home from Saturday night to Monday Morning. **1973** J. MANN *Only Security* i. 9 It had a school where Clovis might be a weekly boarder.

B. *sb.* (Earlier examples.)

1833 [see *MONTHLY *sb.* 2]. **1845** DICKENS *Let.* 26 July (1977) IV. 337 A notion..has occurred to me in connexion with our abandoned little weekly.

weeksite (wī·ksəit). *Min.* [f. the name of Alice M. D. *Weeks* (b. 1909), U.S. geologist + -ITE[1].] A hydrated silicate and oxide of uranium and potassium, $K_2(UO_2)_2(Si_2O_5)_3 \cdot 4H_2O$, found as soft, yellow orthorhombic crystals.

1960 W. F. OUTERBRIDGE et al. in *Amer. Mineralogist* XLV. 43 Weeksite at the Autunite No. 8 claim occurs as small spherulites of yellow radiating crystals. **1978** *Mineral. Abstr.* XXIX. 232/1 Weeksite..is described for the first time from France in the uranium deposit of Les Bois Noirs.

weeny, *a.* Add: **2.** Special collocation: **weeny-bopper** *colloq.* [after *teeny-bopper*], a very young (esp. female) pop fan (sometimes notionally of a younger age group than a teeny-bopper, but the two terms are freq. interchangeable).

1972 *Daily Express* 2 Nov. 16 Britain's 'weeny-boppers' are in danger of dancing their way to incurable deafness. **1975** *Evening News* 5 July 16/5 Being a weeny-bopper can be a problem when it comes to clothes... Our model, Karen, nearly 13, got her mum to take her round the stores. **1976** M. BUTTERWORTH *Festival!* viii. 133 A couple of weenie-boppers at a pop concert.

weeny (wī·ni) *sb.*[1] Also **weenie.** [f. the adj.]

1. *colloq.* A very young child.

1844 C. RIDLEY *Let.* Oct. (1958) xv. 180, I must tell you now about the chicks [i.e. children]. Little weeny is growing visibly. **1973** 'D. HALLIDAY' *Dolly & Starry Bird* vi. 82 Not Mr. Paladrini who was so nice to the weenies? **1977** *Ottawa Citizen* 29 June 7/1 Our five-year-old granddaughter keeps asking when the trip is going to begin. Travelling with weenies is something that Mama and I have done for most of our lives.

2. *U.S. slang.* **a.** A girl; an effeminate man. **b.** An objectionable person.

1929 [see *PHOOEY *int.* (*sb.*)]. **1963** *Amer. Speech* XXXVIII. 171 Some of the less frequent..phrases [for an effeminate young man] are: *dink*..and *weenie*. **1964** *Ibid.* XXXIX. 118 Free variation..is also established in the interchangeability of the names of smaller animals for socially unacceptable persons: *toad, squirrel*, and *shrimp* all serve for the zoologically unsound but all-inclusive *weenie*.

weeny (wī·ni), *sb.*[2] *U.S. slang.* Also **weeney, weenie.** Var. *WIENIE. Cf. *WINNY.

1906 *Dialect Notes* III. 163 *Weenie*..Wiener Wurst, sausage. 'Hot *Weenies*.' **1935** *Amer. Speech* X. 159 'Weinies', 'Wienies', and 'Weenies' are also for sale. **1960** C. HAMBLETT in *Pick of Today's Short Stories* 136 The simplest basics... Marilyn Monroe, hot dogs, weenies. **1981** P. THEROUX *Mosquito Coast* viii. 72 Father said, '..I've got other weenies to roast.' And he went back to his maps.

weep, *sb.* Add: **1. b.** Also *the weeps*: a fit of weeping or melancholy. Also *transf.*

1922 JOYCE *Ulysses* 297 And Bob Doran starts doing the weeps about Paddy Dignam. **1937** 'G. ORWELL' *Let.* 31 July in *Coll. Ess.* (1968) I. 280, I heard from Murry who seemed in the weeps about something. **1982** *Medico-Legal Jrnl.* L. 10 Leaving his Counsel to do what we call 'The weeps', i.e. to plead in mitigation of sentence.

weep, *v.* Add: **I. 4. a.** (Further examples.)

1972 *Guardian* 9 Feb. 6/8 The freighter Autolycus..was ordered to leave the harbour..after her cargo of nitro-glycerine was found to be 'weeping'. **1978** C. EGLETON *Mills Bomb* ix. 91 Gelignite... Dangerous? Only if they were handling jelly that was beginning to weep. **1982** *Times* 6 Jan. 7/7 Stirring the loyalists up was like..playing with jelly that had been weeping for two years.

weeper. Add: **6.** = *WEEPIE. *colloq.*
1934 'N. BELL' *Winding Road* xvii. 445 A few hot-eared scribes have written weepers about such things and kidded themselves they'd done the trick. **1949** M. LASKI in *Sketch* 21 Dec. 551/2 Every magazine..reckons to print at least one weeper every Christmas. **1977** *New Yorker* 8 Aug. 10/1 Irene Dunn does the suffering in this version of the Fannie Hurst classic weeper about a woman who loves a selfish married man. **1984** *Miami Herald* 30 Mar. 7D/4 We have been hearing that romance is making a comeback in the movies, and here it is: the old-fashioned, meet-ya-when-this-war-is-over weeper.

weepie (wī·pi). *colloq.* Also **weepy.** [f. WEEP *v.* + -IE; cf. *TALKIE, etc.] A sentimental film, story, play, etc.; a 'tear-jerker'.
1928 *Sunday Dispatch* 23 Dec. 12/2 There are undoubtedly times when a film calculated to raise buckets of tears has its appeal. Someone recently christened this type of picture..a 'weepie'. **1948** *Sunday Pictorial* 18 July 11/4 'If Winter Comes' (Empire) is a re-make of the famous weepie novel. **1958** *Spectator* 18 July 85/3 *Chicken Soup with Barley*..is an East End Jewish weepie. **1962** *Times* 14 May 14/1 An all-out weepy is the only possible description for *Girl in a Birdcage.* **1977** D. FRANCIS *Risk* xvi. 207 How much easier if the miscreant would confess..a sentimental solution..which happened only in weepie films. **1984** *Listener* 5 July 35/1 'Weepies' come in all shapes and sizes. Ostensibly they are women's pictures, because only women cry at them, right?

weeping, *ppl. a.* Add: **6.** *weeping cherry, myall* (earlier examples), *rose.*
1824 'A. SINGLETON' *Lett. from South & West* 62 The weeping-cherry..bears blossoms when a part of the fruit is ripe. **1859** D. BUNCE *Trav. Dr. Leichhardt* 91 Many species of *Acacia* made their appearance, including the celebrated Weeping Myall. **1869** S. R. HOLE *Bk. about Roses* viii. 124 They may soon be trained into Weeping Roses. **1889** Weeping myall [see *BOREE[3]]. **1951** *Dict. Gardening* (R. Hort. Soc.) IV. 1825/2 Newly planted bush and standard (not weeping) roses should be pruned back. **1969** *Better Homes & Gardens* (U.S.) Apr. 83 *Weeping cherry*, bright pink blossoms are artistically spaced along the gracefully hanging branches.

weeping willow. Add: **2.** Rhyming slang for 'pillow'. Now *rare* or *Obs.*
1880 D. W. BARRETT *Life & Work among Navvies* (ed. 2) II. ii. 43, I have been told..that often when a man is ready to retire to rest, he will inform his mates, 'That he's done his lot for the day, and is goin' to lay his pen'oth o' bread (head) on the weeping-willow (pillow).' **1944** N. STREATFEILD *Curtain Up* x. 123 Time young Holly was in bed... Hannah wants your head on your weeping willow, pillow to you.

weeshy, *a.* (Earlier example.)
1825 [see *DEESHY *a.*].

Weetabix (wī·tăbiks). The proprietary name of a breakfast cereal in the form of thick crumbly biscuits made from wheat.
1936 *Official Gaz.* (U.S. Patent Office) 3 Mar. 31/1 Olive Cross, Washington, D.C. Filed Jan. 11, 1936. *Weetabix* for crushed wheat breakfast food biscuits. **1938** *Trade Marks Jrnl.* 17 Aug. 1009/2 *Weetabix*... Wholemeal biscuits. Weetabix Limited,..Kettering, Northamptonshire; manufacturers. **1974** R. RENDELL *Face of Trespass* i. 14 He..poured milk over a couple of Weetabix and sat down to eat his breakfast. **1981** F. INGLIS *Promise of Happiness* ii. 47, I changed loyalties..from cornflakes to Weetabix.

wee-wee, var. WI-WI[2].

wee-wee (wī·wī), *v. colloq.* [Echoic: freq. as a child's word.] *intr.* To urinate.
1930 C. BEATON *Diary* Dec. in *Wandering Years* (1961) IX. 192 Young men..hurried into the garden to wee-wee. **1944** D. WELCH *In Youth is Pleasure* vi. 113 Orvil hated Guy... He was glad that the dog had wee-wee'd on Guy's expensive jacket. **1954** D. ABSE *Ash on Young Man's Sleeve* 167, I suddenly rushed into the sea..and wee-weed in the water for a joke. **1960** L. PINCUS *Marriage* ii. 110 Mrs. Robinson felt disgusted at the thought of 'the tail' touching her, 'because it wee-wee'd'. **1975** 'J. LYMINGTON' *Spider in Bath* ii. 40 Show us the way to the bar and the lady would probably like to wee-wee.

wee-wee (wī·wī), *sb. colloq.* [f. as prec.: cf. *PEE-PEE[2].] **1.** Urine; an act of urination; *to do (have,* etc.) *a wee-wee, to go (make) wee-wee,* to urinate. Cf. WATER *sb.* 18 a.
1937 PARTRIDGE *Dict. Slang* 943/1 *Wee-wee,* a urination; esp. *do a wee-wee*..late C. 19–20. **1938** *Life & Health* Sept. 19/2 If he wants to urinate, it's, 'Mommie, wee, wee, duty.' **1948** A. N. KEITH *Three came Home* x. 184 Our barrack..smelled of kids, pots, and wee-wee. **1955** J. P. DONLEAVY *Ginger Man* xvi. 175 If you'll excuse me a moment, I must make wee wee. **1961** J. STROUD *Touch & Go* xiii. 138 He made his voice deliberately offensive: 'He's gone to do a wee-wee.' **1969** M. BRAITHWAITE *Never sleep Three in Bed* xvii. 76 Hub and I had to go wee wee, and when advised by Mother that we were to go upstairs instead of in the back yard we took the stairs two at a time to see if such a thing could be true. **1982** J. SCOTT *Uprush of Mayhem* vi. 67 When he needed a wee-wee he did it in a corner of the hut.

2. A penis.
1964 W. & J. BREEDLOVE *Swap Clubs* xv. 233 Our grandmothers, wielding butcher knives, threatened to cut off our fathers' wee-wees if they didn't stop playing with them. **1972** *Screw* 12 June 16/3 [The] self-righteous defender of what he thought to be his threatened wee wee, could not contain his machismo.

Wegener[1] (vē̆i·gənəɹ). *Geol.* The name of Alfred *Wegener* (1880–1930), German geophysicist, used in the possessive with reference to the theory of continental drift which he first published in 1912.
1922 *Living Age* 10 June 657 Professor F. E. Weiss.. writes in the Manchester Guardian that Professor Wegener's theory 'constitutes a good working hypothesis, and the striking simplicity with which it allows many phenomena to be explained will greatly stimulate further enquiry'. **1926** [see *continental drift* s.v. *CONTINENTAL *a.* 1 d]. **1963** *Sci. Amer.* Apr. 90/1 Between 1920 and 1922 Wegener's hypothesis excited great controversy. **1982** *Nature* 23/30 Dec. 681/2 Jeffreys refers with regret to the defection of Sir Arthur Holmes to 'Wegener's theory'.
Hence **Wegene·rian** *a.*
1960 *Bull. Amer. Assoc. Petroleum Geologists* XLIV. 245 (*caption*) Early tertiary paleography and trans-Atlantic migration route for shelf benthos according to Wegenerian hypothesis of continental drift. **1967** *Oceanogr. & Marine Biol.* V. 340 Some zoologists are inclined to accept the Wegenerian idea that the Atlantic Ocean is indeed young, and of no greater antiquity than the Cretaceous. **1980** *Guardian* 20 Nov. 13/8 Pangea..probably existed for a few hundred million years before it..began to break up to generate Wegenerian drift.

Wegener[2] (vē̆i·gənəɹ). *Path.* [The name of F. *Wegener*, 20th-c. German physician.] *Wegener's granulomatosis*: an often fatal disease characterized by granulomatosis of the respiratory tract and necrotizing blood-vessels.
1948 *Acta Path. & Microbiol. Scandinav.* XXV. 582 Clinically, this case agreed well with the previously described cases of Wegener's granulomatosis. **1957** *Thorax* XII. 57/1 The syndrome has been known as Wegener's granulomatosis since his detailed description of three cases in 1936 and 1939. **1977** *Daily Colonist* (Victoria, B.C.) 4 Dec. 27/6 An autopsy showed that my grandmother died of a very rare disease called Wegener's granulomatosis.

weggebobble (we·dʒĭbǫb'l). *nonce-wd.* Humorous alteration of VEGETABLE *sb.*
1922 JOYCE *Ulysses* 163 Coming from the vegetarian. Only weggebobbles and fruit.

‖ **Wehmut** (vē·mūt). [Ger.] Sadness, melancholy, wistfulness, nostalgia.
1907 M. A. VON ARNIM *Fräulein Schmidt & Mr. Anstruther* xlii. 130 What I feel when I listen to music is chiefly *Wehmut*, and I don't think much of *Wehmut*... It is a forlorn thing, made up mostly of vague ingredients—vague yearnings, vague regrets, vague dissatisfactions. **1920** D. H. LAWRENCE *Let.* in C. Mackenzie *My Life & Times* (1966) V. 170, I get a sort of Wehmut. Quoi faire! **1933** J. HILTON *Lost Horizon* 20 A sort of universal sadness,..something remote or impersonal, a *Wehmut* or *Weltschmerz*, or whatever the Germans call it.

wehrlite (vēᵊ·ɹləit, wə·ɹləit). [f. the name of Adolf *Wehrle* (1795–1835), Austrian Councillor of Mines: see -ITE[1].] **1.** *Petrogr.* [ad. G. *wehrlit* (F. von Kobell *Grundzüge d. Mineral.* (1838) iii. 313).] A peridotite mainly consisting of olivine and monoclinic pyroxene with common accessory opaque oxides.
1861 H. W. BRISTOW *Gloss. Mineral.* 404/1 *Wehrlite*, the name given by von Kobell to a massive granular mineral, which is probably a variety of Lievrite. **1913** J. P. IDDINGS *Igneous Rocks* II. I. vi. 316 Wehrlite is closely associated with olivine-gabbro, into which it grades with increasing feldspar. **1979** *Nature* 7 June 489/2 The cumulate peridotites are recognised in thin sections which show serpentinised wehrlite with 50% clinopyroxene.
2. *Min.* [a. F. *wehrlite* (J. J. N. Huot *Nouveau Man. complet de Minéral.* (1841) I. 188).] A native rhombohedral alloy of bismuth and tellurium occurring as tin-white to steel-grey foliated masses.
1874 *Amer. Jrnl. Sci.* CVIII. 259 The following minerals are positive (+), or negative (−), in contact with copper:..Wehrlite $Bi_2(TeS)_4$ +. **1931** *Chem. Abstr.* XXV. 1762 Eleven Te minerals are found in Hungary... Tetradymite,..wehrlite..and stützite are described. **1972** *Doklady Earth Sci.* CC. 167/1 Wehrlite is a sulfur-free bismuth telluride whose composition and position in the classification of minerals are interpreted differently by various authors. Wehrlite was first described at the Deutsch Pilsen deposit, Hungary.

‖ **Wehrmacht** (vē·ɹmaχt). Now *Hist.* [Ger., lit. 'defence force'.] The name used for the German armed forces between 1921 and 1945. Also *attrib.*
1935 in *Documents on German Foreign Policy* (1959) III. 1008 Ranks and badges of rank of the members of the Reich Air Ministry..will assume a military character and resemble those of the Wehrmacht. **1945** *Daily Mirror* 8 May 3/2 The Wehrmacht commander announced that he did not recognise what he described as the 'armistice'. **1945** 'G. ORWELL' in *Tribune* 9 Nov. 10/3 He..attempted to pass himself off as an ordinary soldier of the Wehrmacht. **1959** M. CROSLAND tr. *J. Rovan's Germany* 176 Young Germans..begin travelling around the country armed with a stewpan and an old Wehrmacht kitbag. **1965** *English Studies* XLVI. 226 The Wehrmacht mentality is plain, the terrible joyous uplift in the fact of killing, the terrible satisfaction to be extracted from a sense of the irresistible. **1978** L. HEREN *Growing up on The Times* vii. 257 Of all the armies which fought in the second world war, the *Wehrmacht* was undoubtedly the best, perhaps the best in history.

Wei (wē̆i). The name of a Chinese dynasty, esp. one of the partial dynasties ruling (in the north of China) from the mid-4th to the mid-6th cent. A.D. Also used *attrib.* and *absol.* to designate works of art, esp. sculpture and pottery, produced in the period.
1894 G. N. CURZON *Probl. Far East* viii. 276 The Inner Wall is attributed to the Wei dynasty in A.D. 542. **1913** R. FRY *Let.* 31 May (1972) II. 368 I've just seen a show in Paris full of the most amazing things; among them the finest Wei Dynasty statues from somewhere away in the west of China. **1952** WATSON-GANDY & GORDON tr. *Grousset's Rise & Splendour Chinese Empire* xv. 111 Their dynasty was called Wei (often referred to as T'o-pa Wei to distinguish it from the Three Kingdoms Wei). *Ibid.* 114 Wei sculpture has been called the Far Eastern equivalent of the Romanesque and Gothic sculptures which developed six and eight centuries later in Europe. **1960** C. WINICK *Dict. Anthropol.* 556/1 *Wei*,..unglazed pottery often decorated with pigment and tomb figures of the Wei dynasty in China, A.D. 368–557. **1982** M. YOUNG *Elmhirsts of Dartington* viii. 196 Ancient Chinese pots of the Han, Wei, Tang and Sung dynasties.

weibullite (vəi·buləit). *Min.* [ad. Sw. *weibullit* (G. Flink 1910, in *Ark. f. Kemi, Mineral. och Geol.* III. xxxv. 4), f. the name of K. O. M. *Weibull* (1856–1923), Swedish mineralogist: see -ITE[1].] A mineral containing lead, bismuth, selenium, and sulphur and occurring as grey crystals at Falun, Sweden; now regarded as an orthorhombic species but for long of uncertain status.
1913 *Mineral. Mag.* XVI. 375 Weibullite... This mineral, from Falun, Sweden, was described by M. Weibull in 1885 as a seleniferous variety of galenobismutite. **1980** *Amer. Mineralogist* LXV. 789 Studies of specimens from Falun, Sweden, reported to contain the two minerals weibullite and wittite have established at least *three* selenium-rich bismuth–lead sulphosalts of similar chemistry. A nomenclature is proposed in which two of the minerals retain the old names weibullite and wittite, while the third is given the new name nordströmite.

‖ **wei ch'i** (wē̆i tʃi). Also **wei chi.** [Chinese *wéiqí*, f. *wei* to surround + *qi* chess.] A traditional Chinese board game of territorial possession, equivalent to *GO *sb.*[2]
1871 *Jrnl. North-China Branch R. Asiatic Soc.* VI. 107 The chessman of the *wei ch'i*..are generally *not* made of ivory, but of stone or a glassy substance. **1892** *Ibid.* XXVI. 80 *Wei-ch'i* is considered *par excellence* the game of the literary class, while Chess is the favourite diversion of military men. **1911** H. F. CHESHIRE *Handbk. Goh or Wei Chi* 148 To the cultured classes..'Wei Chi',..was, and is an almost essential part of their life. **1917** *Encycl. Sinica* 594/1 *Wei ch'i, surrounding chess*, often called chess by foreigners... The square board on which it is played is divided by eighteen lines each way, making 324 squares. The play..is at the points where the lines cut or meet. **1969** R. C. BELL *Board & Table Games* II. iii. 59 The eighteenth-century Chinese painting on glass reproduced as the frontispiece, shows two ladies playing Wei-ch'i on an antique form of board of 13 × 11 squares. **1976** *New Yorker* 26 Jan. 23/2 The pattern recalls the Chinese game of wei-ch'i (known here by its Japanese name, *go*), in which a player captures his opponent's counters by surrounding them with his own.

Weichsel (vəi·ksĕl). *Geol.* The German form of the name of the river Vistula in Poland, used *attrib.* and *absol.* to designate the fourth and final Pleistocene glaciation in northern Europe, corresponding to the Würm glaciation of the Alps. Hence **Weichse·lian** *a.* (also *absol.*).
1934 R. A. DALY *Changing World of Ice Age* i. 29 Recently four Glacial stages have been traced in Germany. Figure 19 shows the nested moraines of three, named in order of decreasing age, Elster, Saale, and Weichsel. **1968** EMBLETON & KING *Glacial & Periglacial Geomorphol.* 10 The links with North America, apart from the correlation of the Wisconsinan with the Würm/Weichselian, are more tenuous. **1969** BENNISON & WRIGHT *Geol. Hist. Brit. Isles* xvi. 361 After the early Weichselian glaciation the climate varied considerably. **1974** *Encycl. Brit. Micropædia* X. 598/3 The Weichsel Glacial Stage has been divided into at least two main cold phases,..separated from each other by a period of more moderate climatic conditions, an interstadial. **1979** *Jrnl. Arid Environments* II. 293 Five successive units of time, respectively the Palaeozoic, the Mesozoic, the Tertiary, the Quaternary, and the late Weichselian and Flandrian.

weigh, *sb.*[2] (Earlier example.)
1777 E. DRAPER *Let.* 25 Aug. in *N. & Q.* (1944) 15 July 28/1, I can assure you on the authority of Mr. Sullivan, that he saw him underweigh in the Bessborough and for the East Indies several Weeks ago.

weigh, *v.*^{1} Add: **II. 7. b*.** *to weigh* (someone) *against gold* (or *silver*): to perform the Indian ceremony in which (a rajah, etc.) is weighed and his weight in gold (or silver) distributed as largesse.

1969 J. OVINGTON *Voy. Suratt.* 179 The Moguls are sometimes weighed against Silver. **1934** *Times* 25 Aug. 13/2 The Maharajah..will be weighed against gold... The gold-weigh ceremony is usually performed with gold supplied by the person being weighed... This amount will be distributed in charity. **1936** *Times* 14 Jan. 13/6 At this Durbar the Aga Khan will be weighed against gold, and it is expected that 20,000 guests will attend the function.

d. *to weigh off*: to punish; to convict or sentence. *slang* (orig. *Mil.*). Now chiefly *Criminals'*.

1925 FRASER & GIBBONS *Soldier & Sailor Words* 301 *Weighed off, to be*, to be brought up before an officer and punished. **1945** *Tee Emm* (Air Ministry) V. 54 P.O. Prune will have to investigate and deal with a charge..and possibly weigh off the first delinquent of his service career. **1958** F. NORMAN *Bang to Rights* I. 22 You just got weighed off yesterday? **1963** T. & P. MORRIS *Pentonville* ii. 20 One young man..commented that he had been 'weighed off at X Assizes by some old geezer togged up like Father Christmas'. **1978** B. NORMAN *To nick Good Body* x. 81 Another was in custody..waiting to be weighed off.

e. *to weigh in*: to weigh (an air passenger's luggage) before departure; to subject (a passenger) to this procedure. See *excess luggage* s.v. EXCESS 6 b.

1934 RHYS-WILLIAMS *Diary* 1 Aug. (MS.), Left Eaton Place at 4.30 p.m. for Victoria, where we were 'weighed-in', and had our luggage weighed and labelled. **1961** L. DEIGHTON *Ipcress File* v. 30 She weighed in my wardrobe case. **1970** *New Yorker* 16 May 41/2 The porter..takes her bag and follows her to the desk to have it weighed in.

f. Angling. *to weigh in*: of an angler, to have (one's catch) officially weighed at the end of a competition. Also *absol.*

[**1928**: see *WEIGHER 3 a]. **1949** *Club Anglers' Jrnl.* Nov. 14/1 The river fished well and the winner weighed-in 6 lb. 4 oz. 12 drm. **1972** *Match Rules* (Nat. Fed. Anglers) in E. Marshall-Hardy *Angling Ways* (1973) xxxix. 306 No competitor may have his catch weighed in who has litter lying on the banks of his swim. **1976** *Wymondham & Attleborough Express* 17 Dec. 22/5 Only 10..competitors weighed in,..but..Frank Kilbourn..float fished to take 9–2 of good roach.

9. a. *to weigh in*: also, of a boxer (turning the scales *at* a particular weight) before a fight. Hence in general colloq. use.

1909 'O. HENRY' *Roads of Destiny* xviii. 307 He was six feet four and weighed in at 135. **1931** *Daily Express* 13 Oct. 1/7 Both boxers weighed in this afternoon. **1958** S. WILCOX *3 Days Running* vii. 79 When at last I was able..to 'weigh-in'..I weighed five pounds more than at the beginning of the day. **1966** *Aviation Week & Space Technol.* 5 Dec. 6/1 The complete inertial package weighs in at only 14 pounds. **1979** *SLR Camera* Mar. 35/1 The compact 'Zuiko' 1000mm measures just 26 inches and weighs in at around eight and a half pounds.

c. fig. *to weigh in*: to bring one's weight or influence to bear; to enter a forceful contribution to a discussion, etc. *colloq.*

1909 G. B. SHAW *Let.* 31 July (1972) II. 854, I want you to ask the Chief Rabbi to weigh in. **1919** BEERBOHM *Seven Men* 147 A few weeks later the Anglo-Indians weigh in. In due course we have the help of our Australian cousins. **1938** E. BOWEN *Death of Heart* III. iii. 378 The telephone crisis..had been the moment for Lilian to weigh in. **1956** A. L. ROWSE *Early Churchills* 221 The Princess Anne, in her constant rôle of fairy godmother to the Marlboroughs, weighed in; nor could it have been done with more tact and good feeling. **1976** *Milton Keynes Express* 4 June 38/4 Sim weighed in with 4–27 off eight overs.

d. To launch *into* and attack (a person, etc.). Also *fig. colloq.*

1941 BAKER *Dict. Austral. Slang* 81 *Weigh into someone*, to attack, wade into a person in a fight. **1976** F. WARNER *Killing Time* I. i. 8, I survived the war,..and then, if I was a minute after 9.30 in the evening, my Mother would weigh into me.

weighed, *ppl. a.* **3.** (Later example.)

1935 S. SPENDER in *London Mercury* May 8 The tall girl with her weighed-down head.

weigher. Add: **3. a.** Also *weigher-in*.

1906 A. H. LEWIS *Confessions of Detective* I. i. 7 I've been weigher-in at the boxing tournaments for over ten years. **1928** *Daily Tel.* 25 Sept. 12/5 It is a rule that every fish caught must be kept alive, and after being weighed must be put back into the water by the official weigher-in. **1982** J. A. SHARWOOD in *Occasional Papers Univ. Sydney Austral. Lang. Res. Centre No. 20.* 20 He may be inclined to complain to the *boundary rider*..about *the bloke with the short arm* being employed as the *weigher-in* there.

wei·gh-in. [f. the vbl. phr. *to weigh in*: see *WEIGH *v.*^{1} 7, 9.] **1.** *Boxing.* The weighing-in of a boxer before a fight. See sense *9 a of the vb.

1939 *Sun* (Baltimore) 28 June 15/1 The general might bring the subject up at the weigh-in and instruction period for the two fighters at noon to-morrow. **1946** *Daily Progress* (Charlottesville, Va.) 18 June 7/4 Louis expected to remain at Pompton Lakes until just before the weigh-in. **1952** L. A. G. STRONG *Darling Tom* 138 At the weigh-in, each man had received instructions to scow at the other. **1974** H. L. FOSTER *Ribbin', Jivin', & Playin' Dozens* vi. 251 Boxers at weigh-ins usually attempt to psych one another.

2. *Angling.* The weighing of the anglers' catch at the end of a competition. See sense *7 f of the vb.

1949 *Club Anglers' Jrnl.* Oct. 14/2 A good weigh-in, topped by a splendid bag of roach. **1971** *Rocquaine Regatta: Programme* (Guernsey) 7 Event 1–8.00 a.m. Sea Angling. Start at Imperial Hotel 8.00 a.m.—weigh-in 10.30 a.m. **1972** *Shooting Times & Country Mag.* 1 July 16/1 The weigh-in caused great excitement as individual catches were very close.

weight, *sb.*^{1} Add: **II. 8. a.** *weight for weight*: also (with hyphens) used *attrib.*

1964 W. G. SMITH *Allergy & Tissue Metabolism* vi. 71 In the perfused cat hind limb it is as active as acetylcholine on a weight-for-weight basis. **1968** *Times* 3 Dec. 10/8 Female rats were given daily doses reckoned to be about eight times as powerful on a weight-for-weight basis as those taken by the tribeswomen. **1974** *Brit. Med. Jrnl.* 19 Jan. 107/2 Special care needs to be taken over the use of Lanoxin brand [of digitalis], which is now twice as potent on a weight-for-weight basis as formerly.

c. *to lose weight*: to become thinner or less corpulent; *to put on weight*: see PUT *v.*^{1} 46 f.

1961 M. SPARK *Prime of Miss Jean Brodie* iv. 114 She had lost weight through her sad passion for Mr. Lloyd. **1970** M. PATTEN *Bedsitter Cookery* 89/1 Most sensible people today are anxious to keep a slim figure and a well-planned diet is an essential towards either losing weight or maintaining a good weight. **1982** J. MANN et al. *Diabetics' Diet Bk.* I. 20 To lose weight you should aim to have only 1,300 calories a day.

10. c. *to pull* (*one's*) *weight*: see *PULL *v.* 15 b; *to throw* (*chuck*, etc.) *one's weight about* or *around*: to assert oneself or one's authority, esp. in an objectionable way; to act officiously. *colloq.*

1917 A. G. EMPEY *From Fire Step* 31 Don't chuck your weight about until you've been up the line and learnt something. **1922** C. E. MONTAGUE *Disenchantment* viii. 104 Some typically stupid English General..was clearly throwing his weight about, as they say, without any real understanding of anything. **1926** S. JAMESON *Three Kingdoms* xii. 348 'Come to that,' he said, 'Isabel has more right than any of you to fling her weight about.' **1941** J. P. MARQUAND *H. M. Pulham, Esq.* i. 10 Bill King..always used to say that Bo-jo was a bastard, a big bastard. Perhaps he meant that Bo-jo sometimes threw his weight around. **1955** E. HILLARY *High Adventure* 163 A big, strong, swanking chap who had thrown his weight about a good deal lower down. **1966** N. MARSH *Death at Dolphin* (1967) vi. 145 Why hadn't he put his foot down?.. He should have thrown his weight about. **1982** 'M. HEBDEN' *Pel & Staghound* xv. 176 Madame Rensselaer seemed to enjoy throwing her weight about.

d. *atomic weight* (earlier and later examples); = *atomic mass* s.v. *ATOMIC *a.* 1; similarly *molecular weight*, the relative molecular mass of a molecule, equal to the sum of the atomic weights of the constituent atoms.

1820, etc. Atomic weight [in Suppl. s.v. *ATOMIC *a.* 1]. **1872** *Jrnl. Chem. Soc.* XXV. 949 The relative molecular weights of ether, alcohol and water. **1950** *Sci. News* XV. 88 Blue hæmocyanin... This molecule is the largest of any known substance, having a molecular weight of several millions. **1978** P. W. ATKINS *Physical Chem.* ii We can determine how many elementary units we have by measuring the mass of the sample..and knowing the relative molecular mass (R.M.M., the 'molecular weight').

11. b. Phr. *to take the weight off* (*one's feet*): to sit down and rest. Cf. *to take a load off* (*one's feet*) s.v. *LOAD *sb.* 3 h. *colloq.*

1936 'J. TEY' *Shilling for Candles* ix. 100 Waiters like to take the weight off their feet for a little. **1960** L. DAVIDSON *Night of Wenceslas* i. 19 We were at the seat now. 'Like to take the weight off?' I said. **1965** A. ROUDYBUSH *Season for Death* (1966) xxxii. 190, I stepped into the library..to take the weight off my feet for a minute. **1973** H. MILLER *Open City* xv. 168 Sit down, take the weight off.

III. 15. b. (Earlier and later examples.) More widely, a multiplying factor associated with each of a series of numerical quantities, esp. ones that are added together.

1825 *Phil. Mag.* LXV. 167 The arithmetical mean of a set of observations..is the particular case when the weights a, a′, a″ etc. are all equal, and the sum of the errors is equal to zero. **1868** J. C. WATSON *Theoret. Astron.* vii. 372 The relative accuracy of two or more observed values of a quantity may be expressed by means of what are called their weights. **1935** PAULING & WILSON *Introd. Quantum Mech.* iv. 100 The degree of degeneracy (the number of independent wave functions associated with a given energy level) is often called the quantum weight of the level. **1940** G. CROWTHER *Outl. Money* iii. 93 For some sorts of index numbers, weighting is essential... Weights that are correct at one time may be incorrect at other times. **1949** *Economist* 8 Oct. 775/1 If the estimate of the change in productivity had been based on calculations using post-war weights they would have indicated a larger increase in productivity in the United States. **1970** O. DOPPING *Computers & Data Processing* ii. 32 The number 491 means 4 × 100 + 9 × 10 + 1. The weights are 100, 10, and 1, respectively. **1983** *Personal Computer World* Dec. 142/2 When each digit is multiplied by its weight the sum of the products, including the check digit, whose weight is 1, is exactly divisible by 11 in a valid [Standard Book] number.

19. (Later examples.)

1938 'G. ORWELL' *Homage to Catalonia* v. 65 The Communist Party, with Soviet Russia behind it, had thrown its whole weight against revolution. **1951** C. P. SNOW *Masters* xxxiii. 268, I can't do as much as I should like, but I shall throw in my weight wherever I can. **1976** *Southern Even. Echo* (Southampton) 11 Nov. 1/1 The floodgates opened on the fluoridation of water supplies.. when the..Regional Health Authority put their weight behind the scheme.

IV. 21. d. A measure of an illegal drug; hence, the drug. Also without article. *slang.*

1971 *Frendz* 21 May 11/2 Avoid carrying weight late at night. **1972** *Listener* 23 Mar. 359/3 Your hash dealer is usually a friendly happy freak who's managed..to buy himself a weight and he deals it out to his friends. **1978** S. WILSON *Dealer's Move* i. 13 Neil was taking colossal risks, there'd be up to thirty weights sitting in the flat at one time.

VI. 25. a. *weight-gain, limit*; *weight-conscious* adj.; **weight belt**, a belt to which weights are attached, designed to help divers and underwater swimmers stay submerged; **weight cloth** (earlier example); also *fig.*; **weight function** *Physics*, a function that specifies the weight (sense *15 b) of some quantity; **weight training**, a method of physical training involving the use of weights.

[**1943** *Diving Man.* (U.S. Navy Dept.) x. 150 Next, the weighted belt is fastened on.] **1955** R. & B. CARRIER *Dive* iv. 111 Weight belts should also provide for interchangeable weights to regulate buoyancy as needed. **1966** 'L. HOLTON' *Out of Depths* (1967) xii. 115 'Here. I'll show you a diver's gear.'.. He held up a weight belt. **1978** A. P. BALDER *Sport Diving* ii. 14 The purpose of the weight belt is to help the diver achieve the weightless state. **1887** KIPLING *Plain Tales* (1888) 144 You can arrange the race with regard to 'Shackles' only. So long as you don't bury him under weight-cloths, I don't mind. *Ibid.* 181 Maybe, Fate's weight-cloths are breaking his heart. **1974** *Radio Times* 28 Feb. 280/2 A nervously weight-conscious society. **1930** Weight function [see *ORTHOGONALIZE *v.*]. **1974** G. REECE tr. *Hund's Hist. Quantum Theory* ii. 33 He made use of a weight function $G(E/\nu)$ for the enumeration of states. **1956** *Nature* 3 Mar. 423/2 (*caption*) Average weight-gains of animals fed on lime-treated maize. **1981–2** *Deer Farmer* (N.Z.) Summer 3/1 (Wapiti) Crosses with reds; the hybrids also produce good velvet and weight-gains. **1961** *Engineering* 21 July 72/1 The new 1½ litre 'weight limit' formula came into effect..in May. **1955** O. STATE *Weight Training for Athletics* i. 17 *Weight training*..implies training with light weights..for the purpose of improving one's performance in a particular sport. **1957** DUNCAN & BONE *Oxf. Pocket Bk. Athletic Training* (ed. 2) iii. 24 Weight training may now be regarded as an *essential* part of athletic training. **1976** E. DUNPHY *Only a Game?* v. 147 We have to do weights. I don't believe in weight-training.

b. *weight-bearing* (sb. and adj.), *-lifter, -puller, -putting, -reducing* (sb. and adj.), *-throwing*.

1954 MARTIN & HYNES *Clin. Endocrinol.* (ed. 2) ii. 50 Osteoarthritis of the hips, knees and spine develops from undue strains of excessive weight-bearing as life advances. **1959** *Manch. Guardian* 9 July 5/7 We cannot even tell whether the heavy walls of the new buildings are the weight-bearing structures they look to be. **1977** P. A. RING in *Bone & Joint Dis.* (Brit. Med. Assoc.) 83 It may be better to strive for union in the relatively young patient, even at the risk of a period of protected weight-bearing. [**1884** *Nat. Police Gaz.* (U.S.) 12 Jan. 13/2 Alonzo Hiwanda, the..champion heavy-weight lifter.] **1897** *Ibid.* 26 May 3/4 Bothwell, of Glasgow, is well known as a powerful man, besides a weight lifter. **1955** R. BANNISTER *First Four Minutes* 112 The waddling gait and breathlessness of a muscle-bound weight-lifter. **1980** *Sunday Times* (Colour Suppl.) 14 Sept. 99/2 A weightlifter complained that he did not like showing his tattoos in public. **1868** H. WOODRUFF *Trotting Horse* xxiii. 200 The weight-pullers..are of medium weight. **1900** A. E. T. WATSON *Young Sportsman* 84 *Weight putting*—The weight should weigh 16 lbs., and in England must be of iron. **1948** *Sporting Mirror* 21 May 14/3 Giles had never done any weight putting when he went to Germany with the army. **1922** *Times* 7 Oct. 13/5 Grilling is the great essential of the weight-reducing diet. **1958** F. C. AVIS *Boxing Ref. Dict.*, *Weight reducing*, taking off superfluous weight, often by means of vapour baths, sweating exercises, etc. **1978** N. MARSH *Grave Mistake* ii. 42 She tried..to get Verity to fix a day when she would come to a weight-reducing luncheon. **1901** J. P. PARET *Woman's Bk. Sports* 163 Weight-throwing has four or five variations. **1960** *Times* 29 Apr. 16/6 The investigation covered swimming, track running, weight-throwing.

weight, *v.* Add: **2. d.** Also, to treat (the components of any numerical quantity) similarly.

1927 C. SPEARMAN *Abilities of Man* App. p. xviii, We urgently require to know how the single tests should be relatively 'weighted' in their combination. **1971** I. G. Gass et al. *Understanding Earth* v. 82 The individual data were weighted according to quality, so that a poorly determined result makes a smaller contribution to the mean than a precisely determined value. **1976** *Daily Record* (Glasgow) 30 Nov., Replies were weighted by age and General Election voting to make sure they were representative of all Record readers. **1977** *Whitaker's Almanack 1978* 1219 In working out the [cost-of-living] index figure, the price changes are 'weighted'—that is, given different degrees of importance—in accordance with the pattern of consumption of the average family.

4. a. (Earlier example.)

1734 J. STEUART *Letter-Bk.* (1915) 378 Your meall to be weighted with the common standard weights of Mariebrugh.

weightage (wē^i·tėdʒ). Chiefly *Pol.* or in *Pol.* contexts. [f. WEIGHT *v.* + -AGE.] The assignment of a weighting factor to compensate for some (numerical) disadvantage, esp. in favour of a sparsely populated area, or to a minority party, interest, etc.; the amount so added. See *WEIGHTING *vbl. sb.* 3.

1906 in A. Husain *Fazl-i-Husain* (1946) vi. 96 Weightage, not by numerical strength but by political importance and value of the contribution made to the defence of the Empire. **1937** *Times* 24 Dec. 13/3 The Liberals [in Romania] only managed to secure 38 per cent. of the votes... They do not, therefore, qualify for the 'weightage' provided by the law of 1926. **1949** I. JENNINGS *Constitution of Ceylon* ii. 189 In agricultural countries like South Africa and Australia..the rural population, on whom the wealth of the country largely depends, must be given some weightage against the more concentrated and more highly organized urban population. **1957** L. F. R. WILLIAMS *State of Israel* 159 Does the present plan give these fractional groups a weightage in public affairs.. which their relative unimportance cannot justify? **1971** *Queen's College* (Oxford) *Record* Dec. 22 The geographical distribution of men who have gone down does not reflect quite the same northern weightage as do schools of origin. **1980** *Sunday Mail* (Brisbane) 9 Nov. 25/1 The National Party yesterday reaffirmed its policy of electoral distribution based on the electoral 'weightage' principle.

weighted, *ppl. a.* Add: **2. c.** *weighted* is similarly used of numerical quantities other than averages. (Earlier and later examples.)

1845 *Encycl. Metrop.* II. 443 We may..call the constant *c* the specific weight of the observations to which it applies, and $\Sigma c\mathrm{A} \div \Sigma c$ the weighted mean. **1962** A. NISBETT *Technique Sound Studio* 277 Quoted noise levels are sometimes 'weighted' against bass according to standard loudness contours. Weighted and unweighted measurements may differ by 20 dB or more at low frequencies. **1970** G. K. WOODGATE *Elem. Atomic Struct.* vii. 137 The identity..simply states that the weighted mean of the energies of the levels belonging to a term coincides with the energy of the unperturbed term. **1972** *Times* 27 Sept. 2/2 (*heading*) 'Weighted' vote at Labour conference suggested.

weighting, *vbl. sb.* Add: **3.** The assignment of weights (WEIGHT *sb.* 15 b in Dict. and Suppl.); the weights so used.

1905 [in Dict., sense 1 a]. **1940** [see *WEIGHT *sb.* 15 b]. **1965** PHILLIPS & WILLIAMS *Inorg. Chem.* I. iii. 75 One general technique for improving on the first approximation by the V.B. method is to include additional structures..in the complete wave function, with appropriate weighting factors. **1972** *Guardian* 18 Feb. 13/5 Rents and eating out..accounts for 22 per cent of the 'weighting' of the [retail price] index. **1983** *Personal Computer World* Dec. 142/2 Each of the eight digits of the base number is given a weighting.

4. An amount added to a salary for a special reason; esp. *London weighting*, that paid to compensate for the higher cost of living in the London area.

1946 *Scheme of Conditions of Service* (National Joint Council for Local Authorities' Admin., Profess., Techn. & Clerical Services) 19 The salary scales shall be weighted, as follows, in favour of officers employed in the London area:..£20 weighting with proportionate weighting of female scales. **1952** *Times* 25 Jan. 2/7 The wording of the statement relating to the award did not make clear whether the recommended increase was meant to be over and above the weekly 10s. 'weighting allowance' granted to London [fire]men. **1958** *Times* 5 Dec. 3/2 Salary (including London Weighting) according to age and experience. **1976** *Broadcast* Dec. 17/1 Brief consideration was given to a number of items including: weighting for major towns and cities other than London, London weighting, interest on monies owed to staff, [etc.]. **1982** *Daily Tel.* 20 Oct. 1/1 The government is to end the annual publication of the London weighting index which is widely used as the basis for calculating extra payments for employees in London.

weightless, *a.* Add: **a.** Also (of a body having mass), not apparently acted on by gravity, either because the gravitational field is locally weak, or because both the body and its surroundings are freely and equally accelerating under the field (as in an orbiting satellite).

1929 *Science Wonder Q.* Fall 55/2 Do you mean that.. we will be weightless as soon as you..set the lever at zero? **1950** *Jrnl. Aviation Med.* XXI. 396/2 A body is weightless as soon as it is allowed to move freely under the influence of gravity and of its own inertia. **1953** A. C. CLARKE *Prelude to Space* v. 28 The perfect [spaceship] pilot..must be capable of operating efficiently..when he was 'weightless'. **1978** *Nature* 20 July 236/1 We report here the results of an experiment in the weightless environment of space. **1983** A. MASON *Illusionist* i. 15 A man who could command his body to float weightless through the air could not command the necessities of life.

weightlessness (further examples).

1929 *Science Wonder Q.* Fall 58/2 If they had not already been accustomed to weightlessness, the first heedless step would have carried them far from the ship. **1932** D. LASSER *Conquest of Space* xiii. 192 The terrors of weightlessness. **1959** *Observer* 31 May 1/4 The two monkeys spent a number of minutes in a condition of weightlessness or zero G. **1974** R. ADAMS *Shardik* x. 74 Her stance gave a curious impression of weightlessness, as though she might actually be about to float down into the hollow. **1983** *Brit. Med. Jrnl.* 13 Aug. 479/2 The most important vestibular disturbance encountered in weightlessness is motion sickness.

Weight Watcher. orig. *U.S.* Also **weight-watcher.** [WEIGHT *sb.*¹: see *WATCH *v.* 12 d.] **1.** *pl.* A proprietary name used esp. for (members of) an organization, Weight Watchers International Inc., formed to promote dietary control as a means of slimming, or any of its associated clubs. Occas. in *sing.*

1961 *Official Gaz.* (U.S. Patent Office) 28 Feb. TM 130/2 The Low Calorie Candy Co., Inc... Filed Mar. 14, 1960. *Weight Watcher.* For dessert and pie mixes sold in combination packages... First use Feb. 1, 1960. **1964** *N.Y. Herald Tribune* 1 Nov. 11 4/3 Weight Watchers is an Alcoholics Anonymous for compulsive eaters. *Ibid.* (*caption*) Novice Weight Watchers line up for the first session of a new group. **1966** J. NIDETCH (*title*) The Weight Watchers Cookbook. **1966** *Sunday Tel.* 28 Aug. 2/4 A Long Island housewife has successfully tackled the American problem of compulsive eating with her movement Weight Watchers Incorporated, which now has hundreds of thousands of members in 15 States. **1967** *Business Week* 4 Mar. 106/3 They..transplant the Weight Watcher idea..under a system of franchises. **1967** *Trade Marks Jrnl.* 25 Oct. 1628/2 *Weight Watchers*... Books, printed publications, stationery, diaries, printed matter and pocket portfolios..all containing data pertaining to dieting and weight control. Weight Watchers International Inc. **1967** *Official Gaz.* (U.S. Patent Office) 5 Sept. TM 21/2 I. B. Kleinert Rubber Company, New York... *Weight Watcher.* For girdles. **1968** *Ibid.* 16 Jan. TM 133/1 Weight Watchers International, Inc... Filed Sept. 26, 1967. *Weight Watchers*... For indicating membership in the applicant association. **1968** *Ibid.* 18 June TM 146/1 *Weight Watchers.* For planning, executing and supervising diet programs by means of group meetings, courses [etc.]... First use May 15, 1963. **1972** J. ANDERSON in *Clin. Endocrinol.* (1973) 80 Group therapy should not be derided and is probably one of the main reasons for the apparent success of 'Weight-Watchers' clubs. **1977** P. HILL *Liars* xi. 144 You should join Weightwatchers... They'd slim you down in no time. **1978** *Cornish Guardian* 27 Apr. 12/5 Mr. Arthur spoke of the health campaign in arranging a 'fun and jog' for all ages, involving the local Weight Watchers, Keep Fit Classes. **1984** S. MOODY *Penny Dreadful* xi. 144 Half the world starved while the other half joined Weight Watchers.

2. (With small initials.) A person who tries to lose weight, esp. by dieting; one who is weight-conscious.

1966 *Family Circle* Jan. (recto front cover), Meal plans for weight-watchers. **1968** *Sunday Times* 10 Nov. 35 Italians are not exactly the keenest weight-watchers in the world and hardly let a day go by without forking into the pasta. **1970** *Guardian* 6 June 12/5 What the intelligent weight watcher needs is a diet which keeps her fit. **1971** *New Scientist* 4 Feb. 231/3 The hint to weight-watchers is obvious: keep food out of sight, and it should stay out of mind. **1983** *Daily Tel.* 9 Feb. 17/4 The old message that it was good for weight watchers to eat a slice of cheese on a cream cracker has gone out of the window.

Hence **wei·ght-watching** *ppl. a.* and *vbl. sb.*

1970 *Globe & Mail* (Toronto) 26 Sept. 29/2 (Advt.), Luncheon here is to be recommended..and for the weight watching girls..there are tempting light suggestions. **1978** *Dumfries Courier* 20 Oct. 28/3 Martin..decided that dieting or weight-watching were not for him. **1982** W. J. BURLEY *Wycliffe's Wild-Goose Chase* iv. 66 'Beef casserole with boiled potatoes and carrots.' Good! But not for weight watching.

Weil (vəil). *Path.* [The name of H. A. *Weil* (1848–1916), German physician, who described the disease in 1886 (*Deutsch. Archiv f. Klin. Med.* XXXIX. 210).] *Weil's disease*, a severe, sometimes fatal, form of leptospirosis that is characterized by fever, jaundice, and muscle pains and is acquired by infection from the urine of rats.

1889 *Brit. Med. Jrnl.* 6 July 11/1 (*heading*) Notes on a case of Weil's disease. **1934** [see *LEPTOSPIROSIS]. **1961** R. D. BAKER *Essent. Path.* ix. 200 The mortality of Weil's disease (spirochetal jaundice), the common leptospirosis of man, is about 10 per cent. **1977** C. MCCULLOUGH *Thorn Birds* xii. 276 He looked thin, wrinkled and yellow... 'What is Weil's disease, Luke?'.. 'Oh, it's just some sort of jaundice most cutters get sooner or later. The cane rats carry it.'

Weil–Felix (vəil,fī·liks). *Med.* [The names of Edmund *Weil* (1880–1922), Austrian physician, and Arthur *Felix* (1887–1956), Polish bacteriologist, who described the reaction in 1916 (*Wien. klin. Wochenschr.* XXIX. 33).] *Weil–Felix reaction*: an agglutination reaction which takes place when serum from a patient infected with typhus is added to certain strains of bacteria of the genus *Proteus*, used as a diagnostic test for the disease.

1919 *Public Health Rep.* (U.S.) XXXI. 2446 The Weil–Felix reaction..has recently come into use as a means of diagnosing typhus fever. **1956** *Nature* 11 Feb. 257/2 The Weil–Felix reaction..proved of immense value in the differential diagnosis of typhus from typhoid and other fevers of unknown origin, and stimulated a great deal of research to explain why it was possible to obtain a specific agglutination reaction with an organism playing apparently no part in the causation of the disease. **1978** *Jrnl. R. Soc. Med.* LXXI. 509 The Weil–Felix reaction, which is the only generally available diagnostic test, failed to detect over 50% of proven cases in several series.

Weimar (vəi·māɹ). The name of a city in Thuringia, Germany, where the democratic constitution under which Germany was governed from 1919 until the start of the Third Reich in 1933 was drawn up. Used *attrib.* and *absol.* with reference to the political, social, and cultural aspects of Germany during this period, esp. in phr. *Weimar Republic.*

1932 *Internat. Affairs* XI. 770 The return pure and simple to the Weimar system. **1934** H. P. GREENWOOD *German Revolution* iii. 39 The National Assembly at Weimar epitomised..the whole Weimar Republic. **1958** *Listener* 20 Nov. 828/2 The liberal fancies of the Weimar Republic. **1963** W. H. CHAMBERLIN *German Phoenix* xiii. 244 In distinct contrast to the Weimar period, a political system based on free elections.. has had time to strike deep roots. **1968** P. GAY *Weimar Culture* (1969) p. xiv, The dazzling array of these exiles..tempts us to idealize Weimar as unique, a culture without strains.., a true golden age... But to construct this flawless ideal is to trivialize the achievements of the Weimar Renaissance. **1974** W. LAQUEUR *Weimar* vii. 224 There was..a light side to Weimar culture: Fritzi Massary and Richard Tauber, Marlene Dietrich and the *White Horse Inn.* *Ibid.* ix. 273 The Weimar revival reached its apogee in the late 1960s with the rise of the New Left. **1982** S. G. DUFF *Parting of Ways* vii. 74 The Weimar Government tried to meet..obligations by printing money.

Weimaraner (vəimărā·nəɹ, wəi-). [Ger., f. *Weimar* (see prec.) + *-aner* (something) of this place, region, etc.] A (breed of) grey, short-coated, drop-eared pointer, which was originally bred as a hunting dog in the Weimar region.

1943 *Amer. Kennel Gaz.* Jan. 77/1 The admission to registration of the Weimaraner..brings to 109 the breeds now recognized as pure-bred. **1952** L. ROSS *Picture* 35 He had..a pen for eight Weimaraner puppies. **1954** *Time* 1 Mar. 19/1 Republican speechwriters came to a point like so many Weimaraners last November. **1968** *Globe & Mail* (Toronto) 17 Feb. 49/5 (Advt.), Weimaraners are medium size sporting dogs. **1979** *Daily Mail* 26 Oct. 25/2 The upper middles have recently taken to foreign breeds—weimaraners and rotweilers.

weiner (wī·nəɹ), var. of *WIENER *sb.* a. Cf. *WEENY *sb.*² *N. Amer.*

1961 in WEBSTER. **1965** P. TAMONY *Americanisms* (typescript) No. 10. 8 In Frankfurt small sausages were termed *Wein*; this turns up in American colloquialism as *weiner* and *weenie.* **1973** H. NIELSEN *Severed Key* iv. 45 We got a little cold beer and some weiners, and we thought we'd have us a picnic. **1980** J. M. BICKHAM *Regensburg Legacy* iv. 56 The hotel supper..sauerkraut, weiners, green beans.

‖ **Weinstube** (vəi·nʃtūbə). [Ger., f. *wein* WINE + *stube* *STUBE, room.] A small German wine-bar or tavern. Cf. *BIERSTUBE.

1899 F. NORRIS *McTeague* 126 Its place was taken by a German saloon, called a 'Wein Stube'. **1936** C. BEATON *Diary* Sept. in *Wandering Years* (1961) xvi. 297 We sit in the Weinstube drinking white wine. **1946** S. SPENDER *European Witness* 138 The Weinstube was one of those German drinking cellars which resemble a chapel. **1969** K. BENTON *Twenty-Fourth Level* vi. 101 He dined in a noisy, cheerful German *Weinstube.* **1981** L. DEIGHTON *XPD* vi. 36 The wreckage of a German Weinstube.

‖ **Wein, Weib, und Gesang** (vəin vəip unt gəza·ŋ), *phr.* [Ger.] Wine, women, and song, proverbially considered the essential ingredients for carefree entertainment and pleasure by men.

First popularized as the title of a Strauss waltz (1869). Strauss prob. took it from the anon. couplet found in the Luther room at Wartburg: Wer nicht liebt Wein, Weib und Gesang /Der bleibt ein Narr sein Leben lang (see WINE *sb.*¹ 1 f (b), quot. 1862).

1885 G. B. SHAW in *Dramatic Rev.* 27 June 341/1 The '*Wein, Weib, und Gesang*' waltzes which the Inventions Council offer us as the flower of modern European music. **1924** G. B. STERN *Tents of Israel* vi. 87 Franz..was a typically Viennese Rakonitz, in the famous Wein-Weib-und-Gesang style. **1935** C. ISHERWOOD *Mr. Norris changes Trains* iii. 38, I shall..prepare myself to enjoy an evening of *Wein, Weib, und Gesang.* More particularly *Wein.* **1959** M. CROSLAND tr. *J. Rovan's Germany* 21 The famous trilogy '*Wein, Weib und Gesang*' (wine, woman and song) which form the subject of numerous drinking songs on both sides of the Rhine.

weir, *sb.* Add: **6.** *weir-stream* (earlier example).

1889 J. K. JEROME *Three Men in Boat* ix. 143 We might have somehow got into the weir stream, and be making for the falls.

weird, *a.* Add: **4. b.** Colloq. phr. *weird and wonderful*, marvellous in a strange or eccentric way; both remarkable and peculiar or unfathomable; exotic, outlandish. Freq. *iron.* or *derog.*

1859 J. H. STIRLING in *Meliora* Oct. 231 These [poems] are doubtless meant to be very weird and wonderful, but they are mere breath, and..barren as the wind. **1886** O. WILDE in *Pall Mall Gaz.* 1 Feb. 5/1 There is psychology of a weird and wonderful kind. **1908** T. E. LAWRENCE *Let.* 9 Aug. (1954) 70 Their food is weird and wonderful. **1946** VISCT. KNEBWORTH *Boxing* xiv. 176 The beginner so often ets the idea that he is going to do the most weird and ronderful movements. **1962** *Friend* 3 Aug. 947/1 Nearly ll the weird and wonderful decorations were provided by decorator member of the club. **1978** S. NAIPAUL *North f South* II. vi. 227 A weird and wonderful place is Jo'burg.

veirdie (wīᵊ·ɹdi). *slang.* Also **weirdy.** [f. VEIRD *a.* + -IE.] **1.** An odd or unconventional person; one who is considered 'weird'; *spec.* applied to any young man with long air and a beard. Freq. in *pl.*

1894 A. S. ROBERTSON *Provost o' Glendookie* 101 'He's wa without his curran' loaf.' 'He's a weerdie.' **1949** V. R. BURNETT *Asphalt Jungle* (1950) ii. 19 Cobby.. hought to himself: 'He's a weirdy, all right.' **1954** 'P. QUENTIN' *Wife of Ronald Sheldon* vii. 57 God, is that one a weirdie!.. There was a cobweb in her hair. **1959** *Listener* 3 Dec. 975/1 The weirdies that Kerouac seems always to meet wandering and muttering in the mall hours. **1960, 1961** [see *BEARDIE 2]. **1962** *Punch* 4 Feb. 268/2 One [bedsitter]..advertiser..added 'No Weirdies either'. **1966** *Daily Tel.* 17 Nov. 18/8 There was not an unwashed bearded weirdie in sight! **1974** K. MILLETT *Flying* (1975) I. 94 I'm not a friend, just the visiting weirdie.

2. Something that is 'weird', fantastic, bizarre, or grotesque. Freq. applied to a film, book, etc.

1948 *Astounding Sci. Fiction* Jan. 15 The *Cosmos* had one of its feature writers compose a weirdie about a world consisting of beings of pure mind. **1962** *Listener* 14 June 1043/3 *The Lake Lovers* is a weirdie. **1968** *Blues Unlimited* Nov. 25 Country Jim is a weirdie. **1969** R. PETRIE *Despatch of Dove* i. 26 No mistake, it was a weirdy of a day.

weirdo (wīᵊ·ɹdōᵘ), *sb.* and *a. slang.* [f. WEIRD *a.* + *-O².] **A.** *sb.* = *WEIRDIE 1.

1955 L. FEATHER *Encycl. Jazz* 347 *Weird-o*, a weird person. **1958** *Observer* 13 Apr. 15/3 He is worried by Press reports which represent him as 'a weirdo—there is another word for it'. **1967** *Courier-Mail* (Brisbane) 13 Apr. 22/3 Another set of weirdos using a slick philosophy of revolt against the established order as camouflage for a lazy or corrupt existence. **1972** J. McCLURE *Caterpillar Cop* iv. 45 A shock-haired, bearded weirdo in a tartan dressing-gown and wellington boots. **1976** M. MACHLIN *Pipeline* xli. 448 We are near the village and I go back a lot, but like I said, they all treat me like I was some weirdo. **1981** *London Rev. Bks.* 3–16 Sept. 3 Santa Fe is acknowledged as a milieu of aesthetes and weirdos. **1984** *Melody Maker* 6 Oct. 34/4 This record is for the real weirdos.

B. *adj.* Bizarre, eccentric, odd.

1962 *Sunday Times* 5 Aug. 20/6 Frankly, I'm sick of your whole weirdo line. Leave me alone. **1969** C. BURKE *God is Beautiful, Man* (1970) 46 About halfway through the party a real weirdo thing happened. **1974** M. MOORE *Silver Birch Country* 43 The lady I'm looking after is a dear old duck, completely weirdo, but she's got a terrible sense of humour, and I like her. **1979** *Tucson* (Arizona) *Citizen* 20 Sept. 2A/6 It..makes us sound like some sort of weirdo fanatics opposed to all medicine.

weisenheimer, var. *WISENHEIMER.

Weissenberg (vəi·sənbɜːg). [The name of Karl *Weissenberg* (b. 1893), Austrian-born physicist.] **a.** *Cryst.* Used *attrib.* with reference to a technique of single-crystal X-ray diffraction introduced by him, in which a metal shield allows the diffracted X-rays to produce only one set of parallel lines of spots which are recorded over the whole of the photographic film by rotating it synchronously with the crystal, enabling the Miller indices and other crystal parameters to be easily obtained.

1934 W. P. DAVEY *Study of Crystal Struct. & its Applic.* vii. 205 The Weissenberg camera may be used..in the indexing of diffraction spots which are so thickly clustered on layer lines as to require otherwise a large number of oscillation photographs. **1962** Weissenberg photograph [see *SALESITE]. **1976** D. SHERWOOD *Crystals, X-rays & Proteins* xiv. 507 To obtain full three-dimensional information, we may take a series of photographs corresponding to each layer line in which we are interested. This was realised by K. Weissenberg, and in 1924, he published an experimental method which enables this to be done. This is now known as the Weissenberg method.

b. Physics. *Weissenberg effect*: an effect observed when a visco-elastic liquid is stirred, when the liquid rises in the centre and climbs the stirring rod rather than forming a concave surface like normal fluids.

1949 M. REINER et al. in *Jrnl. Soc. Chem. Industry* LXVIII. 327/2 When a vertical rod is rotated in certain viscous elastic liquids, the liquid climbs up the rod and when a disc is rotated in such a liquid near the bottom of a beaker containing it, the liquid is drawn radially towards the centre... Freeman and Weissenberg claim that the first experimental observations were made by Weissenberg and Russell... In view of this it would seem justifiable to describe such phenomena as 'the Weissenberg Effect'. **1978** *Sci. Amer.* Nov. 148/2 If you would like to produce the Weissenberg effect, you might use a mixing bowl mounted on a turntable.

weissite² (vəi·səit). *Min.* [See quot. 1927 and -ITE¹.] A copper telluride, Cu_5Te_3, occurring (often in association with rickardite) as bluish black or bluish grey pseudocubic crystals with a metallic lustre that darken on exposure to air.

1927 W. P. CRAWFORD in *Amer. Jrnl. Sci.* CCXIII. 346 The mineral is named Weissite after the late Loui Weiss, owner of the Good Hope mine [at Vulcan, Colorado]. **1980** *Mineral. Abstr.* XXXI. 354/1 Rickardite and weissite occur with pyrite, tetrahedrite, chalcopyrite, and altaite in this orebody in andesites and dacite porphyrites.

‖ **Weisswurst** (vəi·svuɹst). [Ger., f. *weiss* white + *wurst* sausage.] (A) whitish German sausage made chiefly of veal.

1963 I. FLEMING *On H.M. Secret Service* xxvi. 289 At the Franziskaner Keller..they ate mounds of Weisswurst and drank four steins of beer each. **1970** *Sat. Rev.* (U.S.) 12 Sept. 107/3 Germany's never-stale variety of sausages, particularly..the delicate Weisswurst. **1983** *N.Y. Times* 7 Sept. c7 Weisswurst, the great specialty of Munich, is generally made with veal, pork, bread crumbs, nutmeg, salt, pepper and, sometimes, lemon peel or parsley. It is also stuffed into casings before cooking.

welcome, *sb.*¹, *int.* and *a.* Add: **B. 4. d.** *you are* (or *you're*) *welcome*: a polite formula used in response to an expression of thanks.

[**1907** W. W. JACOBS *Short Cruises* ii. 34 'Thank you,' said the girl, with a pleasant smile. 'You're quite welcome,' said the skipper.] **1960** *Times* 14 Sept. 12/7 The coloured lift attendant in South Carolina who had that attractive way of saying, almost singing, 'You're welcome' whenever we thanked her. **1977** P. DICKINSON *Walking Dead* I. iv. 55 'Thanks,' said Foxe..'You're welcome,' said Dreiser. **1980** A. E. FISHER *Midnight Men* viii. 93 He dialled Directory Enquiries and asked the girl if she had a number. She gave him one and told him he was welcome.

e. *you are welcome* (*to* something): said ironically of something one is glad to be without.

1937 A. THIRKELL *Summer Half* i. 10 'Fine Old English Gentleman,' said the applicant enthusiastically. 'You are welcome to him.' **1969** J. N. SMITH *Is he Dead, Miss finch?* xviii. 118 My Uncle Len and Aunty Marge live there in a caravan. (They're welcome.)

C. 5. d. *welcome aboard*, said (in allusion to nautical usage) as a joc. greeting to someone joining a particular group, enterprise, etc.

1962 J. D. MACDONALD *Key to Suite* ii. 28 He put Hubbard's material in the envelope, hesitated, then scrawled across the front of it, 'Welcome aboard!' **1970** J. SANGSTER *Touchfeather, Too* iii. 79 We headed across the cool green lawn to the clubhouse... I was introduced to the manager..[who] had once served..in the navy. 'Welcome aboard, Miss Touchfeather,' he said. **1977** 'J. LE CARRÉ' *Hon. Schoolboy* v. 111 'Welcome aboard,' said Guillam... They had reached the fifth floor.

welcome, *sb.*² Add: **2. a.** Also freq. *attrib.*

1955 B. PYM *Less than Angels* vi. 71 We aren't getting on very fast with your welcome-home party. **1966** B. KIMENYE *Kalasanda Revisited* 32 He would take the creature up to the Musaka's and ask Miriamu to prepare it as a special 'welcome home' supper for Yosefu. **1974** M. BIRMINGHAM *You can help Me* viii. 178 It gives me the chance to be part of your welcome-home committee.

c. *dial.* A bell tolled on the occasion of a person's death. Also *transf.*

1878 F. KILVERT *Jrnl.* 25 Dec. (1977) 328 The Welcome Home, as it chimed softly and slowly to greet the little pilgrim coming to his rest, sounded bleared and muffled through the thick snowy air. **1948** F. THOMPSON *Still glides Stream* xii. 226 It was a small, homely procession which..accompanied Reuben on the last of his many journeys. The silvery sweet strain of a robin threaded the silence. 'The welcome home!' said Mrs. Finch.

6. *attrib.* and *Comb.*, as **welcome mat** *U.S. colloq.*, a mat put out to greet welcome visitors; chiefly used in *fig.* phrs. to indicate a friendly welcome (cf. *red carpet* s.v. *RED *a.* 19 a); **welcome song**: *spec.* the first ode composed by Purcell (see quots.); **welcome wagon** *N. Amer.*, a car bringing gifts and samples from local merchants to newcomers in a community; also *fig.*

1951 I. ASIMOV *Foundation* (1953) II. v. 73, I certainly don't intend to lay down the welcome mat. **1963** M. MCCARTHY *Group* iii. 50, I can only ask you to come here whenever you're in town. The welcome mat will be out. **1978** R. NIXON *Mem.* 622 The door will not only be open—I've been weaving a welcome mat. **1681** H. PURCELL (*song-title*) A Welcome Song in the year 1681 for the King. **1883** GROVE *Dict. Mus.* III. 47/1 In 1680.. [Purcell] produced the first of his numerous odes, viz. 'An Ode or Welcome Song for his Royal Highness [the Duke of York] on his return from Scotland'. **1942** Welcome song [see *birthday ode* s.v. *BIRTHDAY 3]. **1961** WEBSTER, Welcome wagon. **1970** A. TOFFLER *Future Shock* (1971) vi. 104 We have in many American suburbs a commercial 'Welcome Wagon' service that accelerates the process by introducing newcomers to the chief stores and agencies in the community. **1971** H. T. WALDEN *Anchorage Northeast* 13 The welcome-wagon type of hospitality is not here. **1976** *Times Lit. Suppl.* 2 Jan. 4/3 He was never serious about moving to America, fearing perhaps that the American welcome wagon, by killing his habit of resentment with kindness and pelf, might stultify his..literary gifts.

welcomeness. (Later example.)

1977 [see *picnic party* s.v. *PICNIC *sb.* 3].

weld, *sb.*² Add: **3. weld decay,** (increased susceptibility to) corrosion in chromium-nickel stainless steel that has been kept at 600° to 900°C for a time (as in welding), owing to the precipitation of chromium carbide and the consequent lowering of the chromium content; **weld pool,** the pool of molten metal formed about a joint in welding.

1932 E. GREGORY *Metallurgy* vii. 275 The heating of alloy steels of the 18 per cent chromium, 8 per cent nickel type in the range 650°–900° C. greatly decreases their corrosion resistance... This phenomenon is known as weld-decay. **1973** A. PARRISH *Mech. Engineer's Ref. Bk.* v. 74 This local depletion of chromium causes lack of passivity in acid corrodants with consequent attack along grain boundaries (weld decay). **1964** W. STEEDS *Engin. Materials, Machine Tools & Processes* (ed. 4) vii. 169 With coated electrodes too high a current..makes control of the weld pool difficult. **1975** BRAM & DOWNS *Manuf. Technol.* ii. 55 The arc and the weld pool are protected from atmospheric contamination.

weld, *v.* Add: **2. b.** (*b*) (Earlier example.)

1802 J. PLAYFAIR *Illustr. Huttonian Theory* 283 The *line* of separation..has, on the whole, been marked out with great precision; and, though the stones have been firmly united, or, as one may say, welded one upon another, yet, when a fresh fracture was obtained, the stratified and unstratified parts have rarely failed to be distinguished.

weldability. (Earlier example.)

1869 H. S. OSBORN *Metallurgy Iron & Steel* iii. 85 There is a degree of weldability in platinum which causes that metal to be classified with iron as a weldable metal.

weldable, *a.* (Earlier example.)

1855 D. LARDNER *Hand-bk. Nat. Philos.: Hydrostatics* III. v. 304 Weldable metals.—The metals capable of being welded soften before they are fused.

welded, *ppl. a.* Add: **3.** *Geol.* **a.** Applied to pyroclastic rock formed by the union of small, heat-softened particles.

[**1802**: see *WELD *v.* 2 b (*b*). **1899** J. P. IDDINGS in A. Hague et al. *Geol. Yellowstone Nat. Park* II. x. 406 The mass is compact of glass, but it consists of irregularly shaped streaks and patches of different color. These twist and curve about one another and appear like a perfectly welded mass of strips or ribbons and irregular fragments of variously colored glass.] **1909** —— *Igneous Rocks* I. I. viii. 333 These examples of welded pumice are from rhyolitic lavas in the Yellowstone National Park. **1935** *Trans. Amer. Geophysical Union* 309 Although commonly and perhaps generally associated with deposits of light-colored volcanic ash of rhyolitic composition, the welded tuff is not confined to this association but occurs also on older rocks. **1962, 1970** [see *IGNIMBRITE]. **1977** A. HALLAM *Planet Earth* 74/1 There may also be intercalations of submarine pillow lavas or welded tuffs indicative of volcanic islands.

b. Applied to an intimate, close-fitting contact between two bodies of rock that have not been heat-softened or tectonically disrupted.

1939 *Q. Jrnl. Geol. Soc.* XCV. 354 The contact is, as usual, welded, and the base of the overlying sediments consists of current-bedded, brown-weathering, fine sandstone. **1948** R. R. SHROCK *Sequence in Layered Rocks* ii. 55 There are examples..where an entire geological system is represented by the hiatus along the welded contact. **1976** *Jrnl. Geol. Soc.* CXXXII. 125 The contact of the slump sheets with the overlying mega-beds is welded, i.e. depositional fit is present.

welding, *vbl. sb.*¹ Add: **3. welding torch,** a blow-pipe used in welding.

1921 *Engineering Index 1920* 417/2 A new carriage for welding torches. **1975** BRAM & DOWNS *Manuf. Technol.* ii. 42 The welding torch used with these systems must be designed to aspirate the acetylene.

weldment (we·ldmĕnt). [f. WELD *v.* + -MENT.] A unit consisting of pieces welded together.

1945 in WEBSTER Add. **1950** *Engineering* 10 Feb. 149/1 In fabricated 'weldments'..it might not be necessary to stress-relieve. **1962** *B.S.I. News* Nov. 21/1 Fabricators may be taking a grave risk when they accept orders for weldments..furnished to inadequate specifications. **1979** *Railway Age* 31 Dec. 50/2 New features include..use of alloy steel castings in place of weldments.

Weldmesh (we·ldmeʃ). Also **weldmesh.** [f. WELD *sb.*² or *v.* + MESH *sb.*] The proprietary name of wire mesh formed by welding together two series of parallel wires crossing at right angles. Freq. *attrib.*

1935 *Trade Marks Jrnl.* 24 Apr. 516/1 *Weldmesh*... screens, partitions, guards, frames, sieves and seatings, all made of welded steel wire. The British Reinforced Concrete Engineering Co. Limited,..Stafford; manufacturers and merchants. **1957** *Archit. Rev.* CXXI. 116 The balcony rail is of weld-mesh panels, with teak handrail. **1971** *Country Life* 11 Nov. 1255/1 It [*sc.* a cage] is made of weldmesh, used for tiger cages. **1978** *Cornish Guardian* 27 Apr. 10/3 (Advt.), 8 ft weldmesh pig lamps. **1984** *Times* 28 July 2/3 The committee recommended that the chain-link fence should be supplemented by weldmesh fencing which is more difficult to breach.

welfare, *sb.* Add: **3*. a.** The maintenance of members of a group or community in a state of (esp. physical and economic) well-being, esp. as provided for and organized by legislation or social effort. See also sense 4 in Dict. and Suppl.

1918 [see *rest room* s.v. *REST *sb.*[1] 14 a]. **1965** A. J. P. TAYLOR *Eng. Hist. 1914–45* IV. 121 Free treatment of venereal disease was the sole innovation in 'welfare' directly attributable to the first World War. **1968** M. PYKE *Food & Society* v. 66 And a Western community converted to the principles of welfare will supply vitamins and much else without requiring profit. **1977** M. FRENCH *Women's Room* (1978) ii. 139 Welfare..was starting to be a big thing. A lot of Puerto Ricans coming up to New York to get a free handout.

b. *ellipt.* (Usu. with capital initial.) A welfare centre or office; (the officials of) a welfare department.

1928 [see *PALLY]. **1960** D. LESSING *In Pursuit of English* IV. 135 Once she asked Welfare if Aurora could go to a council nursery. **1972** J. MANN *Mrs. Knox's Profession* vii. 57 That poor mite... The mother didn't ought to leave it like that... They ought to get the welfare to that woman. **1984** *Observer* (Colour Suppl.) 18 Mar. 6/2 First I rang the Welfare to make sure they would get me a flat.

c. = *welfare benefit*, sense 4 below. Esp. in phr. *on* (*the*) *welfare*. orig. *U.S.*

1946 [see *SNAG *v.*[2] 4]. **1964** S. M. MILLER in I. L. Horowitz *New Sociol.* 295 Women on welfare strongly demonstrated against the cessation of allowances. **1970** *Toronto Daily Star* 24 Sept. 1/1 People receiving welfare in Metro broke all previous records. **1974** K. MILLETT *Flying* (1975) II. 141 Half the people I know feed on welfare. **1976** F. ZWEIG *New Acquisitive Society* II. v. 111 If a man with four children on supplementary benefits would only be better off working if he could earn about £75 a week, it would..need a very conscientious man, keen on his work, to resist the temptation to stay on welfare.

4. *welfare centre, clinic, committee* (example), *department, office, officer, service, work* (earlier example); also, provided by the State for those in need, as *welfare benefit, cheque, food, milk*; subsisting on benefits provided by the State, as *welfare family, mother*; **welfare capitalism**, a capitalist system seeking to combine a desire for profits with concern for the welfare of its employees; **welfare fund**, a fund or funds from which payments are made in time of sickness, etc.; **welfare hotel** *U.S.*, a hotel in which people on welfare are housed until more permanent quarters can be found for them; **welfare roll** *N. Amer.*, a list of those entitled to welfare benefits from the State.

1977 M. EDELMAN *Political Lang.* vii. 125 Through disorder the poor have increased welfare benefits in the United States. **1960** *New Left Rev.* Sept.–Oct. 10/2 The very real achievements of 'welfare capitalism'. **1978** P. BAILEY *Leisure & Class in Victorian Eng.* ii. 43 Robert Owen's New Lanark mills had included an annexe comprising a school, museum, music hall and ballroom..and there were several other examples of this kind of welfare capitalism. **1917** *New Witness* 28 June 202/1 It is continually stated that Maternity Clinics and Infant Welfare Centres have met with the greatest success in France. **1941** J. S. HUXLEY *On Living in Revolution* (1944) 21 Communal feeding centres, crèches or welfare centres. **1947** *Sun* (Baltimore) 6 May 22/8 The cashing of four welfare checks sent to one of her male inmates after his death. **1976** *Billings* (Montana) *Gaz.* 17 June 1–D/2 When he got his Social Security and welfare checks. **1937** 'G. ORWELL' *Road to Wigan Pier* v. 93 The baby was getting its weekly packets of milk from the Welfare Clinic. **1952** *Oxf. Jun. Encycl.* X. 282/1 The welfare committees also provide welfare services for the blind, deaf, dumb and crippled. **1922** S. LEWIS *Babbitt* ii. 17, I wonder if I could get one of the department-stores to let me put in a welfare-department. **1977** M. EDELMAN *Political Lang.* v. 79 A welfare department or education department bears a name that is even less adequate in defining the priorities to which it must respond. **1977** *New Yorker* 27 June 88/3 The Spencers were far from being a welfare family; the house cost forty thousand dollars, which they could afford. **1948** *Ann. Reg. 1947* 487 There were..subsidies on animal feedingstuffs, welfare foods, milk in schools. **1958** Welfare food [see *family allowance* s.v. *FAMILY *sb.* 11]. **1947** *Ann. Reg. 1946* 205 Mr Lewis [*sc.* a trade-union leader]..refused even to discuss his demands until he had been granted a 'welfare fund' financed by a royalty on coal. **1978** S. SHELDON *Bloodline* xxxix. 348 They were listed if they had paid taxes or drawn unemployment insurance or welfare funds. **1971** *Times* 8 Jan. 5/1 The scandal of the 'welfare hotels' [in New York] where the city places homeless families has been simmering for many weeks. **1977** *N.Y. Rev. Bks.* 15 Sept. 3/1 One welfare hotel in New York, the scene of repeated mayhem, is next to the local police station. **1958** Welfare milk [see *family allowance* s.v. *FAMILY *sb.* 11]. *a* **1974** R. CROSSMAN *Diaries* (1976) II. 560 Increased family allowances with supplementary allowances and children's tax allowances, the price of school meals, the price of welfare milk, [etc.]. **1971** *N.Y. Times* 9 June 43 The needs of..the pressured pensioner, the welfare mother and the harried commuter in our cities involve the whole range of vital urban services. **1978** *Guardian Weekly* 8 Jan. 16/4 Welfare mothers should get off the dole and go to work. **1976** *National Observer* (U.S.) 12 June 4/3 I'd rather see people employed than at the welfare office. **1944** Welfare officer [see *SAY *v.*[1] 1 c]. **1963** T. PARKER *Unknown Citizen* ii. 58, I have been to see the C.A.C.A. welfare officer responsible for Smith's after-care. **1970** *Toronto Daily Star* 24 Sept. 1/1 The number of family units on the welfare rolls has more than doubled in the past year. **1979** *United States 1980/81* (Penguin Travel Guides) 300 A city where the list of places that offer poor boy sandwiches is probably longer than the welfare rolls. **1952** Welfare service see *welfare committee* above]. **1903** *Review of Reviews* July 79/1 The term 'industrial betterment', or 'welfare work', is used in a wider sense to include all of those services which an employer may render to his work people over and above the payment of wages. It has even been used to include the provision of homes for employees, kindergartens, schoolhouses [etc.].

we·lfare state. Also **Welfare State.** [STATE *sb.* 30.] A country in which the welfare of members of the community is underwritten by means of State-run social services.

The term is sometimes said to have been coined by Sir Alfred Zimmern in the 1930s, but it has not been traced in his published writings.

1941 W. TEMPLE *Citizen & Churchman* ii. 35 We have.. seen that in place of the conception of the Power-State we are led to that of the Welfare-State. **1948** *Economist* 24 Jan. 135/2 The welfare state got its start in the deepest depression this country [*sc.* the U.S.] has ever known. **1950** *Times* 19 May 5/3 This is one of the achievements for which the 'welfare State', with its vast apparatus of taxation, subsidies, family allowances, school meals, and other services, can claim credit. **1959** B. WOOTTON *Social Sci. & Social Path.* 16 The myth of the 'welfare state' has turned the minds of investigators away from the study of material want. **1967** M. DRABBLE *Jerusalem the Golden* ix. 214 She wondered whether she should fall on her knees and thank..the Welfare State. **1976** *New Yorker* 22 Mar. 48/3 They came because Sweden, more than any other country in the industrial West, is a workers' state—not a Socialist state..but a stunning experiment in welfare-state capitalism. **1977** M. WALKER *National Front* 8 A scholarship kid who went to grammar schools and won a scholarship to Oxford because of the 1944 Education Act and the Welfare State. **1984** *Listener* 22 Mar. 9/3 Repeated assertions that the welfare state is to be dismantled and the counter-assertion that Mrs Thatcher's administration is committed to maintaining welfare expenditure. **1985** *New Statesman* 9 Aug. 3/1 The welfare state will have to retain the power to take away children from danger.

Hence **we:lfare-sta·tism** orig. *U.S.*, the social conditions or organization associated with a welfare state; **we:lfare-sta·tist**, one who advocates such organization. Cf. *WELFARISM, *WELFARIST 1.

1949 in *Amer. Speech* (1957) XXXII. 296 Welfare statism advanced slowly and gradually. **1958** *Spectator* 31 Jan. 143/1 The combined effects of high taxation, continuous inflation, welfare statism and the tempting array of consumer goods. *Ibid.* 13 June 761/1 The demands of the welfare-statists in Congress for increased Government spending and tax cuts are now only occasionally heard. **1971** P. WORSTHORNE *Socialist Myth* v. 76 Labour Governments have to make too many economic concessions to the rich.., which places very strict limits on the scope and scale of welfare-statism. **1980** *London Rev. Bks.* 3–16 July 15/3 'Welfare statism' came into being in the 1940s... It consisted in..the extension to the whole population of adequate health, education and social insurance.

welfarism (we·lfe^əriz'm). orig. *U.S.* [f. WELFARE *sb.* + -ISM.] The principles or policies associated with a welfare state; also = *WELFARE-STATISM.

1949 *Life* 25 July 17/2 There must be safeguards so that welfarism does not end in economic or political tyranny. **1961** *Engineering* 17 Feb. 249/1 All Germans.. also agree that the term 'welfarism' is likely to have widely different meanings in the U.K. and in Germany. **1962** *Times* 23 Jan. 9/7 Text-books..are slanted towards welfarism, socialism, and world government. **1968** P. B. AUSTIN *On being Swedish* ix. 72 'The Swede,' said old Sundbärg, before welfarism or modern Swedish prosperity were born or thought of, 'would not mind Sweden being prosperous, providing that no one in it were better off than himself.' **1976** R. DELMAR in Mitchell & Oakley *Rights & Wrongs of Women* ix. 283 State regulation of the family through welfarism (family allowances etc.).. means that the working class..has the law available to them. **1984** *Times* 21 Apr. 9/2 The proposition that the ills of Britain..are more or less the fault of capitalism is no more self-evident than the proposition that they are more or less the fault of welfarism.

welfarist (we·lfe^ərist), *sb.* (*a.*) [f. as prec. + -IST.] **1.** One who is concerned with welfare, esp. that of animals. Also *attrib.* or as *adj.*

1941 I. BROWN in *Manch. Guardian Weekly* 14 Mar. 214/3 There is in this country an enormous and semi-official bureaucracy which deals in social welfare and all manner of educational and uplifting matters. It is rapidly developing a jargon of its own... The Uplifters and Welfarists are assaulting us with the Scorpions of their Jargantuan. **1979** *Country Life* 15 Feb. 428/1 How does one define 'Animal Welfare'?.. To some the term 'welfarist' is almost one of contempt. **1980** *Times* 13 Feb. 3 The union has failed on our behalf to respond to the lies and unfair allegations of the welfarists. **1980** *Observer* (Colour Suppl.) 16 Mar. 41/3 The animal welfare movement—or the 'welfarist' movement as it is now widely called. **1983** *Sci. Amer.* Aug. 5/2 The pork producer of today generally is an animal protectionist and an animal welfarist in the best practical sense.

2. orig. *U.S.* One who supports the principles or policies associated with a welfare state. Also *attrib.* or as *adj.* Cf. *WELFARE-STATIST.

1968 *New Yorker* 12 Oct. 201 The welfare state..is not incompatible with the police state. George Wallace is a welfarist, and so is Mayor Daley. **1977** *Daily Tel.* 30 June 16 Questions arise which, in recent years, have been rendered almost taboo by the near-universal acceptance of facile welfarist orthodoxy. **1985** *Daily Tel.* 6 May 14/ It has often been said..that he is the prisoner of . Californian perspective which scorns the moribun welfarist states of Western Europe for the growth an dynamism of the Pacific basin area.

well, *sb.*[1] Add: **8. a.** (Earlier example i sense 'the open space in which a lift operates'.

1890 B. HALL *Turnover Club* viii. 87 But Gean hustle the man out to the elevator shaft and dropped him int the well beneath.

d. = *orchestra pit* s.v. *ORCHESTRA 4.

1933 P. GODFREY *Back-Stage* i. 15 The orchestra are i position in the 'well'. **1951** *Oxf. Compan. Theatre* 836/ The Orchestra Well for the accommodation of the theatr musicians is in front of and below the stage itself.

11. c. Also *spec.* in *Ceramics*, the depresse central portion of a plate, saucer, or dish.

1937 *Crockery & Glass Jrnl.* Nov. 28 The Fleurett shape..with flower grouping in the well and repeated o the shoulder. **1971** *Country Life* 21 Oct. 1055/1 Th saucer is decorated with a circular medallion of The Bul and the Mouse, its well with four sprigs of flowers, th bowl with the Bull and the Frogs.

11*. *Physics.* = *potential well* s.v. *POTENTIA *sb.* 4 c.

1942 *Rep. Progress Physics* VIII. 302 The..way t estimate the depth of the well is to postulate that th binding energy of the least strongly bound particle shal be equal to the experimental value for this quantity **1972** *Sci. Amer.* Apr. 27/1 The original aim was to creat a well so deep (from 10 to 20 million volts deep) that th ion-ion collisions could be energetic enough for nuclea transmutations to occur.

12. *well-conductor, -pulley, -site; well-like* adj (earlier example).

1974 *BP Shield Internat.* Oct. 2/1 The jacket..wrap round the well-conductors which go down into th ground. **1854** THOREAU *Walden* 195 We have one othe pond just like this, White Pond..but I do not know a third of this pure and well-like character. **1940** W FAULKNER *Hamlet* I. i. 18 He had already begun to hea the mournful..plaint of a rusted well-pulley. **1972** L. M HARRIS *Introd. Deepwater Floating Drilling Operation* iii. 22 The wellsite geologist should..provide technica assistance to the drilling supervisor. **1979** *Jrnl. R. Soc Arts* CXXVII. 406/2 This led in due time to the adoptio of a system of deep ditches around the various well sites

13. well-fire = *well-grate* below; **well-grate** (see quot. 1910); **well-kick**, the exerting by an oil-well of pressure in excess of that of the drilling fluid pumped into it, leading to loss o circulation; **well-sweep** (earlier example).

1906 *Studio* XXXVIII. 127/1 Well-fires are used in al the rooms. **1910** *Encycl. Brit.* XII. 378/2 In the closing years of the 19th century a 'well-grate' was invented, in which the fire burns upon the hearth, combustion being aided by an air-chamber below. **1927** W. E. COLLINSON *Contemp. Eng.* 90 Fires..are more often well-grates (i.e low) than basket-grates (with hobs for the kettle). **1972** L. M. HARRIS *Introd. Deepwater Floating Drilling Operations* x. 97 Closing in around the drill pipe and circulating a conventional well kick. **1974** P. L. MOORE et al. *Drilling Practices Manual* xi. 277 Failure to recognize a well kick could be disastrous. **1836** C. A. GOODRICH *Universal Traveller* (ed. 2) I. i. 27 Here and there, by the side of the older houses, may be seen a well-sweep, a primitive contrivance to draw up water by a pole, which is attached to a beam, moving up and down on an axle.

well, *a.* **5. c.** For 'Now only *U.S.*' read 'Now chiefly *U.S.*' and add: Also *well-baby*, used *attrib.* to designate clinics or health care arrangements for routine checking of healthy children, as a form of preventive medicine; **well woman** (usu., with hyphen, *attrib.*), a woman who has undergone satisfactory gynæcological tests.

1921 *Daily Colonist* (Victoria, B.C.) 5 Oct. 6/4 A well-baby clinic will be held at the Saanich Health Centre.. An invitation is extended to all mothers to bring their infants. **1963** *Jrnl. Amer. Med. Assoc.* 2 Nov. 459/1 She had been advised to bring the child to the well-baby clinic. **1976** G. E. GODBER *Brit. National Health Service* i. 5 Many of the elected councils of cities and counties had not used their powers to provide antenatal and well-baby care. **1981** 'G. GAUNT' *Incomer* xxvi. 173 That Thursday's well-baby clinic functioned with the slick accuracy of a Jesuit mass. **1977** *PEN Broadsheet* No. 3. 3/3 A range of leaflets on contraceptive methods, well-women care, sex-related diseases. **1980** *Brit. Med. Jrnl.* 29 Mar. 958/2 The new hospital will have a 40-bed gynaecological unit with a wide range of outpatient services and a specially designed 'well woman clinic' to provide urgently needed health screening. **1984** S. TOWNSEND *Growing Pains A. Mole* 13 She says she needs the money for her 'Well Woman' test. She is having primary and secondary sexual organs checked. **1985** *Observer* (Colour Suppl.) 14 Apr. 23/3 She looked every inch the part of the world's most glamorous well-woman.

well, *adv.* Add: **II. 5. a.** *well taken*: of a point in an argument, aptly or judiciously raised. orig. *U.S.*

To be distinguished from the phr. *to take* (someone's) *point*, where *take* = to understand the significance of.

1863 A. LINCOLN *Coll. Works* (1953) VI. 245 The point made in your paper is well taken. **1907** *Nation* (N.Y.) 14 Feb. 146 One of Mr. Hearst's points seems to us well taken. **1936** E. B. WHITE in *New Yorker* 14 Mar. 16/2 The question is well taken. **1943** [see *POINT *sb.*[1] 28 c].

IV. 18. e. *to be* (or *get*) *well away*: to have (or obtain) a good start over one's pursuers; usu.

g., to make good progress in an activity esp. drinking). *colloq.*

1910 *Glasgow Herald* 7 Feb. 13/2 From the drop out Andrew got well away but Henry pulled him up. **1927** W. E. COLLINSON *Contemp. Eng.* 101 Expressions..like.. he's well away' (he has got into his stride or into swing whether in tackling a meal or a flirtation or in drink). **1947** 'N. SHUTE' *Chequer Board* iii. 51 Bristow had a bottle of whisky and I had one of gin so we were well away. **1950** J. CANNAN *Murder Included* vii. 141 'What's happened?'.. 'If we knew that, we should be well away.' **1956** C. BLACKSTOCK *Dewey Death* vi. 128 He paused again, but Sergeant Robins saw no point in making any comment; the young gentleman was plainly well away. **1973** J. PORTER *It's Murder with Dover* viii. 72 Many great men..[can] drop off to sleep at any time..and Chief Inspector was no exception. He was well away by the time MacGregor climbed back into the car. **1984** A. CARTER *Nights at Circus* III. v. 233 The Colonel..overcomes his resistance to vodka to such an extent he is soon well away and sings songs of Old Kentucky.

V. 22. c. With intensive (usu. *slang*) adv. or adj. prefixed, as *bloody well, damn well*, etc.

1884 [see *BLEEDING *ppl. a.* 6]. **1898** [see JOLLY *adv.* 2]. **1903** [in Dict., sense 22 (*a*)]. **1921** E. O'NEILL *Emperor Jones* i. 160 Ring the bell now an' you'll bloody well see what I means. **1928** E. WAUGH *Decline & Fall* III. iii. 240, I should bleeding well say there was. **1933** [see RUDDY *adv.*]. **1941** [see *DAMN *a.* and *adv.*]. **1943** D. WELCH *Maiden Voyage* iii. 14 Someone in the next cell was shouting, 'Bloody well let me out, you bastards.' **1962** L. R. BANKS *End to Running* I. vi. 96 Because actually, as a matter of fact, don't y'know, I'm not kidding well coming.

VII. 28. *well-vascularized.*

1959 W. ANDREW *Textbk. Compar. Histol.* iv. 113 (*caption*) The 'hairs', covered with well-vascularized epidermis, may be as much as 20 mm. long.

well-adjusted, *ppl. a.* Add: **b.** With reference to emotional adaptation. Cf. *ADJUSTED *ppl. a.* 4.

1939 L. MACNEICE *Autumn Jrnl.* xii. 49 A civilised, articulate and well-adjusted Community where the mind is given its due But the body is not distrusted. **1940** [see ADJUSTED *ppl. a.*]. **1952** C. P. BLACKER *Eugenics: Galton & After* 307 Able and well-adjusted children. **1977** E. AMBLER *Send no More Roses* i. 11 The Able Criminal.. may be presumed..to be emotionally stable and 'well-adjusted'.

well-aged, *a.* For '† *Obs.*' read 'Now *rare*' and add later example.

1979 [see *road-bed* s.v. *ROAD *sb.* 9 b].

well-aired, *ppl. a.* **2.** (Earlier example.)

1789 H. NEWDIGATE *Let.* 1 July in A. E. Newdigate-Newdegate *Cheverels of Cheverel Manor* (1898) vi. 89, I came home to a well-air'd Comfortable Bed.

well-argued, *ppl. a.* (Later examples.)

1964 K. G. GRUBB *Layman looks at Church* iv. 100 Laymen make contributions in Assembly debates..which are often serious and well-argued. **1975** *Amer. Speech 1971* XLVI. 261 Vennemann's paper is a well-argued proposal for modifying marking theory in TG grammar.

well-arti·culated, *ppl. a.*

1951 W. K. MATTHEWS *Languages U.S.S.R.* iii. 33 Mordvin..shares with Cheremiss a well-articulated system of word-formation. **1977** *Jrnl. Commonw. & Compar. Politics* XV. 5 Pre-unionists parties in some colonies and republics of South Africa were functionable, rather well-articulated units.

well-atte·nded, *ppl. a.* Of a meeting: attended by a large number of people.

1946 *Nature* 21 Dec. 918/1 Dr. W. H. Taylor presided over a well-attended meeting. **1979** G. POTTINGER *Secretaries of State for Scotland 1926–76* xix. 193 The Scottish Covenant Movement..held two well-attended assemblies in 1947 and 1948.

well-behaved, *ppl. a.* Add: **2.** *Math.* Applied to different entities with varying implications as to their susceptibility to manipulation, as continuity or differentiability (of a function), convergence (of a series).

1939 C. B. BOYER *Concepts of Calculus* vi. 246 Inasmuch as Euler restricted himself to well-behaved functions, he did not become involved in those subtle difficulties connected with the notions of infinity. **1965** PATTERSON & RUTHERFORD *Elem. Abstr. Algebra* iii. 60 Of the two operations in a ring *R*, addition is 'well-behaved' in that it satisfies the commutative and associative laws and there exist an identity element and inverses... Multiplication is not so well-behaved. **1968** FOX & MAYERS *Computing Methods for Scientists & Engineers* i. 13 Since $x = 0$, and $J_0(x)$ is perfectly 'well-behaved', then also $y'(0) = 0$.

3. Of a computer program: communicating with hardware via standard operating system calls rather than directly, and therefore able to be used on different machines.

1984 *Austral. Microcomputer Mag.* Jan. 42/1 The disk drives can read and write IBM-PC format disks, and of several programs tried on the system, those that were 'well behaved' worked and those, such as word processors, that tend to directly address the machine's hardware would not always work. **1984** *Austral. Personal Computer* May 65/3 PC mode handles all well-behaved programs... In the case of direct hardware calls, problems usually arise if a 'not quite IBM-compatible' machine is used.

well-braced, *ppl. a.* (Earlier lit. example.)

1785 T. DWIGHT *Conquest of Canäan* VI. 141 The well-brac'd buckler glittered o'er his breast.

well-bred, *ppl. a.* **2.** (Earlier example.)

1805 *Times* 7 Nov. 1/1 To be sold..four capital well-bred hunters.

well-bree·ched, *ppl. a.* Prosperous, well-to-do. Cf. BREECHED *ppl. a.* 4.

1821 P. EGAN *Life in London* II. ii. 178 Jerry is in Tip Street upon this occasion, and the Mollishers are all nutty upon him, putting it about, one to another, that he is a well breeched Swell. **1860** HOTTEN *Dict. Slang* (ed. 2) 104 *Breeched*, or *to have the bags off*, to have plenty of money; 'to be well breeched', to be in good circumstances. **1968** P. SCOTT *Day of Scorpion* I. ii. 64 Her first husband..died well-breeched. **1980** *Jrnl. R. Soc. Arts* Apr. 266/1 That they had been able to become rich or well-breeched in a worldly sense is incidental. **1985** *Times* 22 Mar. 23/8 Britoil presents the spectacle of a fairly well-breeched oil group.

well-ca·red-for, *ppl. a.* [See CARE *v.* 3.]

1942 W. FAULKNER *Go down, Moses* 129 He..watched Lucas cross the Square,..erect beneath the old, fine, well-cared-for hat. **1959** J. CARY *Captive & Free* 116 An envied minority of cherished, well-bred, well-educated, well-cared-for families. **1979** V. L. PANDIT *Scope of Happiness* xx. 136 A lovely well-cared-for garden.

well-caulked, *ppl. a.* (Later example.)

1969 *Jane's Freight Containers 1968–69* 464/2 Liberal use of adhesives and sealants to provide a well-caulked box.

well-chosen, *ppl. a.* Add: **b.** Freq. in phr. *a few well-chosen words*, a short and telling speech or piece of writing. Also *ironically*.

1854 *Harper's Mag.* Feb. 423/2 Thomas Carlyle..has excelled all his contemporaries in the graphic pictures which he has painted in a few well-chosen and expressive words. **1912** BEERBOHM *Christmas Garland* 46 You figure him at the gate, shaking hands all round, and speaking perhaps a few well-chosen words about the future. **1957** D. ROBINS *Noble One* xix. 177, I can and shall go down and settle *her* with a few well-chosen words.

well-concea·led, *ppl. a.*

1925 F. SCOTT FITZGERALD *Great Gatsby* vii. 139 He put out his..hand with well-concealed dislike. 'I'm glad to see you, sir.' **1982** *N.Y. Times* 3 Feb. A 8/1 This correspondent visited the wellconcealed underground location of Venceremos radio in the mountains.

well-concei·ved, *ppl. a.*

1836 J. S. MILL in *London Rev.* II. 368 A well-conceived and well-executed work of fiction. **1862** —— *Pol. Econ.* (ed. 5) II. v. ii. 395 Mr. Hubbard..whose well-conceived plan wants little of being..an approximation to a just settlement. **1919** W. S. CHURCHILL *Let.* 20 Jan. in M. Gilbert *Winston S. Churchill* (1977) IV. Compan. I. 472 Executive Heads of well-conceived Branches. **1979** *Jrnl. R. Soc. Arts* Apr. 259/2 The latter Council has gradually built up a series of well-sited, well-conceived and well-run centres.

well-conditioned, *a.* Add: **2. c.** *Surveying* and *Math.* Such that a small error in measurement or change in data gives rise to only a small change in the calculated result.

1882 J. L. ROBINSON *Treat. Marine Surveying* viii. 141 If the equilateral triangles are not obtainable, then they must be as 'well-conditioned' as possible, i.e. the angles must lie between 30° and 75°. **1952** D. R. HARTREE *Numerical Analysis* viii. 155 The normal equations are less well-conditioned than the original equations. **1973** C. W. GEAR *Introd. Computer Sci.* vi. 261 Is the problem of computing the hypotenuse of a right-angled triangle, given the other two sides, well-conditioned?

well-constructed, *ppl. a.* Add: (Later examples.) Hence **well-constru·ctedness.**

1893 W. S. GILBERT *Utopia (Limited)* I. 25 Oh admirable art! Oh neatly-planned intention! Oh happy intervention—Oh well-constructed plot! **1915** A. J. BALFOUR in M. Gilbert *Winston S. Churchill* (1972) III. Compan. II. 1281 Well-constructed trenches. **1975** *Studies in Eng. Lit.: Eng. Number* (Tokyo) 138 The defect of Mr. Halliburton's well-constructed volume, it seems to me, lies in its well-constructedness.

well-co-o·rdinated, *ppl. a.*

1940 W. FAULKNER *Hamlet* II. ii. 127 Precocious, well-co-ordinated and quick to learn..he acquired enough credits in three years to enter college. **1983** *N.Y. Times* 7 May I. 14/5 A buoyant and wellcoordinated performance of the Vivaldi.

well-covered, *ppl. a.* Add: In quot. 1884 in Dict., used in sense 'thickly covered with flesh'. Hence in *colloq.* use of a person: plump, corpulent. (Later examples.) Cf. *WELL-UPHOLSTERED *ppl. a.*

1943 D. WELCH *Maiden Voyage* xvii. 136 A mild, well-covered person, with crinkly hair and rather piggy eyes. **1972** 'E. FERRARS' *Breath of Suspicion* I. 7 He was rosy, bland and very well-covered.

well-cra·fted, *ppl. a.* [*CRAFT *v.* 2.]

1976 *Nature* 15 July 169/3 A well-crafted murder mystery. **1983** *Listener* 16 June 29/3 It is gripping, slick, well-crafted and beautifully shot.

well-crea·med, *ppl. a.*

1922 JOYCE *Ulysses* 527 Your wellcreamed braceletted hands.

well-designed, *ppl. a.* (Later examples.)

1934 *Archit. Rev.* LXXV. 39/1 Well-designed manufactures are, after all, not so rare in England. **1975** *Language for Life* (Dept. Educ. & Sci.) xxvi. 540 There is evidence in some schools that well-designed measures can be successful.

well-dete·rmined, *ppl. a.*

1905 W. JAMES *Ess. Radical Empiricism* (1912) iv. 128 Its successors differ from it in another well-determined way. **1968** FOX & MAYERS *Computing Methods for Scientists & Engineers* iii. 50 If the problem is well-conditioned the constants of this combination are well-determined.

well-do·cumented, *ppl. a.* Supported or attested by much documentary evidence.

1937 *Burlington Mag.* Apr. 156/1, 1465, in which year he [*sc.* Bellini] produced his first well-documented painting. **1946** *Nature* 30 Nov. 770/1 Well-documented studies of the Tehuelche and Puelche of Patagonia. **1978** *Jrnl. R. Soc. Med.* LXXI. 697/1 The well-documented increases in prescribing represent therapeutic irresponsibility.

well-doer. (Later example.)

1961 NEW ENG. BIBLE *John* iii. 11 The well-doer is a child of God; the evil-doer has never seen God.

well(-)done, *ppl. a.* **3.** (Earlier example.)

1747 H. GLASSE *Art of Cookery* i. 4 Pork must be well done, or it is apt to Surfeit.

well-drai·ned, *ppl. a.*

1871 W. ROBINSON *Subtropical Garden* II. 198 A well-drained, sandy soil..is the best for this plant. **1912** J. W. WHITE *Flora of Bristol* 251 The well-drained banks of railway lines. **1960** *Farmer & Stockbreeder* 15 Mar. (Suppl.) 10/3 Most herbs will grow in any ordinary well-drained ground.

well-endowed, *ppl. a.* Add: Also *spec.*, with reference to sexual potency or size of sexual organs. *colloq.*

1951 N. MONTSARRAT *Cruel Sea* v. 302 'I'm not rich.'.. 'You are doubtless well-endowed... It's better, really... A lot of women think so.' **1968** in H. & R. Greenwald *Sex Life Lett.* (1974) 79 By the age of ten, my member was already larger than that of a well-endowed adult. **1983** *Maledicta 1982* VI. 157 He says he has been well endowed and you must know this means 'heavily equipped sexually'.

‖ **Wellentheorie** (ve·lĕnteˌori). *Philol.* [G., f. *welle* wave + *theorie* THEORY¹.] The theory that linguistic changes spread like waves over a speech-area and the dialects of adjacent districts resemble each other most; = *wave theory* (*b*) s.v. *WAVE *sb.* 10.

1939 L. H. GRAY *Foundations of Lang.* ii. 42 To account for the spread and relationship of languages, two main hypotheses have been advanced, both, it is true, primarily for the Indo-European group, but, in principle, equally applicable to all others. These are the *pedigree-theory* (*Stammbaumtheorie*) advanced by August Schleicher in 1866 and the *wave-theory* (*Wellentheorie*) proposed by Johannes Schmidt in 1872. **1964** R. H. ROBINS *Gen. Linguistics* viii. 349 The theory of common characteristics resulting from the spreading of linguistic features 'in waves' over adjacent dialects within a family is called the 'Wellentheorie'. **1965** [see *STAMMBAUM]. **1975** *Amer. Speech 1971* XLVI. 254 Real change..may in some sense be systematic (as in the analysis of style and social variables and the Wellentheorie of linguistic geographers).

well-entre·nched, *ppl. a.*

1929 W. S. CHURCHILL *World Crisis* V. xix. 432 We had a rather restricted but well-entrenched and well-wired position. **1979** P. BUCKLAND *Factory of Grievances* v. 108 A handful of well-entrenched free-traders.

well-equipped, *ppl. a.* (Earlier example.)

a **1854** MILL *Early Draft Autobiogr.* (1961) 120 A well-equipped ship.

Wellerian, *a.* (Earlier example.)

1839 DICKENS *Let.* 25 Jan. (1965) I. 359 Your agreement is—in Wellerian phraseology—gammon.

Wellerism. Add: Usu. *spec.*, a form of comparison in which a familiar saying or proverb is identified, often punningly, with what was said by someone in a specified but humorously inapposite situation. (Earlier and later examples.)

1839 *Boston Morning Post* 9 Jan. 2/2 *Wellerisms.*—'It does one's heart good to look at you,' as the fox said to the chickens, when he found he couldn't get over the barn-yard wall, to eat them. **1854** *Yankee Notions* III. 142 (*heading*) Phrenological Wellerisms. **1931** A. TAYLOR *Proverb* IV. 219 Wellerisms involving a temporal clause, e.g. '*Much noise and little wool,' said the Devil when he sheared a pig*, are largely used of women. **1959** [see *knock-knock* sb., v., and int. s.v. *KNOCK-.] **1975** *New Society* 25 Dec. 685/1 Sam Weller has joined Dr Spooner and fathered the wellerism: 'Meet you at the corner as one wall said to another,' but the wellerism can also be transformed into a riddle.

well-e·xecuted, *ppl. a.*
1836 [see *WELL-CONCEIVED *ppl. a.*]. **1978** R. LUDLUM *Holcroft Covenant* xxxvii. 425 It was a well-executed trap.

well-expre·ssed, *ppl. a.*
1845 MILL in *Westm. Rev.* XLIII. 331 It is a well-thought and well-expressed explanation. **1943** *Mind* LII. 354 What he [*sc.* Roger Bacon] has to say on *privatio* is sound and well-expressed.

well-farmed, *ppl. a.*
1848 MILL *Pol. Econ.* I. I. xii. 214 The careful cultivation of a well farmed district. **1955** P. C. WINTERTON *Fifty Tumultuous Years* 216 Well-farmed land.

well-fixed, *ppl. a.* Add: **2.** Reasonably affluent, comfortably off. *U.S. colloq.*
1822 A. D. MURPHEY *Let.* 22 Aug. in *Papers* (1914) I. 263 His Brother is well fixed, has one of the best tracts of land in Tennessee, and is growing rich *fast.* **1912** N. M. WOODROW *Sally Salt* 228 I'm well to do, Hilda, well fixed in the world. **1952** J. STEINBECK *East of Eden* ix. 78 He was better than well fixed—he was rich. **1970** J. BLACKBURN *Land of Promise* i. 11 He..had become 'well fixed', as the family colloquialism expressed moderate wealth.

well-formed, *ppl. a.* Add: **b.** Also *spec.*, formed according to stated grammatical rules.
1961 A. G. OETTINGER in *Proc. Symposia Appl. Math.* XII. 104 One important common problem is that of obtaining an algorithm for distinguishing sentences from nonsentences or..well-formed strings from not well-formed strings. **1969** R. A. HALL in *Neuphilologische Mitteilungen* LXX. 204 The oft-repeated claim that all 'well-formed' sentences of a language are derivable from a single syntactic kernel is clearly unfounded. **1980** *Amer. Speech* LV. 90 'Le crabmeat cocktail' is well-formed in that *cocktail* has been borrowed into French as a masculine noun.

c. *Logic.* Applied to any sequence of symbols conforming to the formation rules of a logical system. Esp. as *well-formed formula.*
1936 A. CHURCH in *Amer. Jrnl. Math.* LVIII. 346 We select a particular list of symbols... And we define the word *formula* to mean any finite sequence of symbols out of this list. The terms *well-formed formula*, [etc.],..are then defined by induction. **1954** I. M. COPI *Symbolic Logic* vi. 184 In a logistic system..any formulas which on the intended interpretation do *not* become significant statements are *not* well formed formulas. **1967** *Encycl. Philos.* V. 22/2 A formal language *L* is given by specifying (*a*) a list of *symbols* of *L* and (*b*) a set of *formation rules* for combining these symbols into acceptable, or well-formed, expressions (terms, formulas, sentences) of *L.* **1978** A. G. HAMILTON *Logic for Mathematicians* iii. 53 The use of parentheses in well-formed formulas is precisely given in the definition.

Hence **well-fo·rmedness** (chiefly in *Linguistics*).
1957 *Encycl. Brit.* XIV. 306/1 The condition of well-formedness [in logical formulas]. **1961** N. CHOMSKY in *Word* XVII. 221 Information as to whether the sequence of phones is a properly formed or *grammatical* sentence and if not, in what respect it deviates from well-formedness. **1970** J. P. THORNE in J. Lyons *New Horizons in Linguistics* ix. 186 Between..extremes of well-formedness occur sentences of varying degrees of grammaticalness. **1979** F. KERMODE *Genesis of Secrecy* iii. 64 We depend upon well-formedness..in written language.

well-fo·rmulated, *ppl. a.*
1968 C. G. KUPER *Introd. Theory Superconductivity* i. 2 A well-formulated problem. **1977** P. STREVENS *New Orientations Teaching of Eng.* ii. 23 Well-formulated propositions.

well(-)founded, *ppl. a.* Add: Hence **well-fou·ndedness.**
1920 *Glasgow Herald* 25 Feb. 9/3 There can be no discussion..with regard to..the well-foundedness of the charges. **1970** B. BREWSTER tr. *Althusser & Balibar's Reading Capital* (1975) III. i. 212 Interpretations..whose well-foundedness will, I hope, emerge later in the paper.

well-gowned, *ppl. a.*
1920 E. POUND *Hugh Selwyn Mauberley* 20 Doubtful, somewhat, of the value Of well-gowned approbation Of literary effort. **1975** S. MILLIGAN in C. Allen *Plain Tales from Raj* xv. 158 Always very pale and very beautiful and well-gowned and never moving very fast if they were on horses.

well-head. Add: **3. b.** The structure surmounting an oil- or gas-well. Freq. *attrib.*
1951 *U.S. Rep. 1950* CCCXL. 180 The issue in this case is the power of a state to fix prices at the wellhead on natural gas. **1969** *Times* 16 Dec. (Bahrain Suppl.) p. iv/3 (Advt.), Well-head structures for undersea drilling. **1972** L. M. HARRIS *Introd. Deepwater Floating Drilling Operations* ix. 93 The wellhead is installed on top of, and run with, the conductor pipe. **1983** *Fortune* 13 June 60/2 For each $1 drop in the wellhead price, producers' net income falls only 25 cents.

well-heeled, *ppl. a.*: see *HEELED *ppl. a.* 2 b.

well-hung, *ppl. a.* Add: **1. a.** Chiefly (now always) in *spec.* sense, having large genitals. (Later examples.)
1868 *Index Expurgatorius of Martial* 3 In Rome well-hung youths made a good profit by their amours. **1958** L. DURRELL *Balthazar* v. 103 They love a well-hung diplomat. **1977** D. WILES *Death Flight* xviii. 177 Hey, man... You sure is well hung for a priest!

wellie: see *WELLY.

well-in, *adj. phr.* Add: (Earlier example.)
1845 T. MCCOMBIE *Arabin* 241 They had a pretty little farm, and were well in.

Wellington. Add: Also **wellington. 1. a.** *Wellington boot*: in recent use = sense 2 b below.
1971 [see *DELPHINIUM b]. **1980** L. LEWIS *Private Life of Country House* vi. 79 Snowboots..were virtually superseded by rubber wellington boots, which I first saw when I was about eleven [i.e. *c.* 1920].

b. *Wellington hat* (earlier example, applied to a type of lady's hat).
1815 [see *half-dress* s.v. *HALF- II. n].

c. *Wellington chest* (*of drawers*): a tall narrow chest of drawers used for keeping specimens. Occas. ellipt. as *Wellington.*
1953 'N. BLAKE' *Dreadful Hollow* iv. 50 There was the wellington to which Stanford Blick had directed him. Nigel opened one of its drawers. **1960** H. HAYWARD *Antique Coll.* 304/2 *Wellington chest*, a tall narrow chest containing about a dozen drawers which can be locked by a single hinged flap securing all the drawers. **1971** *Country Life* 7 Oct. (Suppl.) 23 (Advt.), A small antique mahogany Wellington chest of drawers measuring only 19½ inches wide, 14 inches deep and 41 inches high. **1982** 'J. GASH' *Firefly Gadroon* v. 53 There's a space where I used to have my Wellington chest before I flogged it for bread.

2. b. A waterproof boot usu. reaching the knee, worn in wet or muddy conditions. Usu. *pl.*
1907 *Yesterday's Shopping* (1969) 326/1 Black glazed rubber boots. Ladies' Wellingtons. **1944** D. WELCH *Jrnl.* 25 Jan. (1973) 107 He wore an old thick jersey, and grey flannels tucked into Wellingtons. **1984** *Brian Mills Catal.* Spring & Summer 337/4 Waterproof wellington in PVC.

well-i·ntegrated, *ppl. a.*
1943 *Mind* LII. 127 A well-integrated body of..laws. **1976** B. GIBSON *Birmingham Bombs* ix. 74 They got on with their neighbours and most of them were regarded as well-integrated members of the community.

wellish, *adv.* For *dial.* read *dial.* and *colloq.* and add further examples.
1830 H. COCKBURN *Let.* 30 Dec. (1932) 30 How are you? All wellish here. **1856** D. G. ROSSETTI *Let.* 6 Mar. (1965) I. 293, I fancy it will pay wellish, too. **1934** E. BOWEN *Cat Jumps* 230 '[Do you] know him fearfully well?' 'Wellish,' said Rachel.

well-kempt, *ppl. a.* Delete † *Obs.* and add later examples. Also tidy, well cared for.
1922 JOYCE *Ulysses* 212 A wellkempt head, new-barbered. **1934** P. FLEMING *One's Company* II. xviii. 306 The numerous temples were so well-kempt. **1973** *Observer* (Colour Suppl.) 23 Sept. 43/1 Tall, improbably athletic, handsome, bearded, he looked like a well-kempt prophet.

well-known, *ppl. a.* Add: Hence **well-kno·wnness.**
1961 D. J. BOORSTIN *Image* viii. 162 The star system.. puts a premium on well-knownness for its own sake. **1978** J. PEARSON *Façades* xxiii. 401 A celebrity has been defined by Daniel Boorstin as a person who is known for his well-knownness. **1984** *Listener* 15 Mar. 31/2 Telly persons are, as it were, well known for their well-known-ness.

well-languaged, *a.* For '† *Obs.*' read 'Now *arch.*' and add later examples.
1938 *Times Lit. Suppl.* 20 Aug. 548/2 Sir Robert Cordell, whose well-languaged seventeenth-century will.. makes interesting reading. **1954** L. HOTSON *First Night of 'Twelfth Night'* i 29 The well-languaged Elizabeth kept helping Lord Grey interpret the gist of it.

well-lit, *ppl. a.*
1866 GEO. ELIOT *Felix Holt* III. xlix. 249 Esther had to seat herself in the..drawing-room, in a well-lit solitude. **1931** W. S. CHURCHILL *World Crisis* VI. xii. 179 Hindenburg, who was waiting in the 'well-lit station hall' at Hanover. **1965** *Motor* 17 July 5/1 Dipped headlights are probably of benefit on less well-lit roads.

well-made, *ppl. a.* Add: **2.** Also *well-made play* [tr. F. *pièce bien faite*], a type of play written according to a prescribed formula and aiming at neatness of plot and dramatic incident rather than profundity of characterization, truth to nature, etc.
[**1895** G. B. SHAW in *Sat. Rev.* 2 Nov. 576/1 Then 'The New Magdalen' was a fashionable and well-made piece.] **1910** —— *Brieux* 13 Commercially, the classic play was supplanted by a nuisance which was not a failure: to wit, the 'well made play' of Scribe and his school. The manufacture of well made plays is not an art: it is an industry. **1962** *Listener* 11 Oct. 574/1 The merits and the demerits of a Galsworthian 'well-made' play.

well-meant, *ppl. a.* Add: **c.** Of persons: well-meaning. *rare.*
1849 C. BRONTË *Shirley* I. vii. 153 A well-looked, well-meant, and on the whole, well-dispositioned girl.

well-me·rited, *ppl. a.*
1827 J. S. MILL in *Arch. für Sozialwissensch.* LXII. 456 Reformed patriots whose exertions in the cause of liberty have at length earned the well-merited award of a place. **1899** BELLOC *Moral Alphabet* 48 So he wrote, without stopping, for several days In terms of extreme but well merited praise. **1946** *Nature* 26 Oct. 576/2 Under his wise guidance a well-merited reputation both in teaching and in research was rapidly built up.

well-mo·dulated, *ppl. a.*
1845 POE in *Broadway Jrnl.* II. 354/2 The rhythm is.. well-modulated. **1934** C. LAMBERT *Music Ho!* IV. 235 Mr Christopher Stone whose well-modulated voice has doubtless given pleasure to millions.

well-mo·tivated, *ppl. a.*
1965 N. CHOMSKY *Aspects of Theory of Syntax* 210 A stronger but rather well-motivated condition is proposed by Postal. **1977** P. STREVENS *New Orientations Teaching of Eng.* v. 59 A theory of language teaching, on the other hand, with well-motivated links to specific areas of linguistics and psychology—*that* might be attractive.

well-natured, *a.* For *Obs.* read *rare* and add **1. a.** (Later example.)
1921 GALSWORTHY *To Let* II. i. 119 He went as a well-natured dog goes for a walk with its mistress, leaving a choice mutton-bone on the lawn.

well-oiled, *ppl. a.*: see *OILED *ppl. a.* 3.

well-o·rchestrated, *ppl. a.*
1947 A. EINSTEIN *Mus. Romantic Era* xvii. 315 The opinion that has become current with critics and with the public that the *Capriccio* is an unusually well-orchestrated piece is wrong: the Capriccio is a splendid composition for orchestra. **1979** *Wall St. Jrnl.* 20 Dec 6/3 Why has such a well-orchestrated masking of political repressions been necessary?

well-ordered, *ppl. a.* Add: **2.** *Math.* [tr. G. *wohlgeordnet* (G. Cantor in *Math. Ann.* (1883) XXI. 548, (1898) XLIX. 207).] Of an ordered set: having the property that every non-empty subset of it has a first or least element.
1902 *Amer. Jrnl. Math.* II. 384 The usual notation $\alpha+\beta+\gamma+$ ..is only suitable for a finite, or at least for a well-ordered set of numbers. **1931** P. DIENES *Taylor Series* iii. 95 All these definitions..extend to every type of transfinite sequence (well-ordered set) of numbers. **1975** R. A. SILVERMAN tr. *Kolmogorov & Fomin's Introd. Real Analysis* i. 23 The set *M* of rational numbers in the interval [0, 1] is ordered but not well-ordered.

well-ordering, *vbl. sb.* Add: In *Math.*, the property of being well-ordered; also, a well-ordered set. Freq. *attrib.*
1941 BIRKHOFF & MACLANE *Survey Mod. Algebra* i. 9 The integers have one further important property, not characteristically algebraic and not shared by other number systems. This is the well-ordering principle. **1963** W. V. QUINE *Set Theory* 145 Well-orderings are notable for their exemplary behavior. **1966** *Math. Rev.* XXXI. 6/1 Only denumerable well-orderings are considered. **1970** A. G. HOWSON *Handbk. Terms Algebra & Analysis* xvi. 80 Zermelo's Well-Ordering Theorem states that if *X* is any set whatsoever, then there exists a well-ordering of *X.*

So **well-o·rder** *v. trans.*, to arrange the elements of (a set) in such an order as to produce a well-ordered set.
1944 *Ann. Math. Stud.* XIII. 117 For a finite set can be well-ordered in obvious fashion and hence must obey the axiom of choice. **1966** *McGraw-Hill Encycl. Sci. & Technol.* XII. 206/1 One considers the collection *Z* of all subsets of *X*, selects a point $x_\alpha = f(z_\alpha)$ from each element z_α of *Z*, and well orders *X* so that [etc.].

well-pa·dded, *ppl. a.* Provided with sufficient padding. Also *transf.* and *fig.*
1933 J. BUCHAN *Prince of Captivity* II. ii. 190 What has become of the nice, easy-going, well-padded people with soft voices and wide smiles. **1945** WYNDHAM LEWIS *Let.* 29 June (1963) 384 However well-padded with dollar-bills you might be. **1976** 'R. GORDON' *Doctor on Job* vii. 62 Mr Clapper rocked back in his well-padded chair.

well-plucked, *a.* *colloq.* [PLUCKED *a.*] Plucky, fearless.
1873 M. A. BARKER *Station Amusements in N.Z.* 148 He was a well-plucked one... He told me it took five mortal hours to come the last mile. **1936** M. DE LA ROCHE *Whiteoak Harvest* xviii. 230 'That gray one is a 'andful for you'... 'I'm not afraid.' 'You're wot I call a well-plucked 'un.'

we·ll-point. *Civil Engin.* [WELL *sb.*[1]] One of a system of pipes sunk into the ground around an excavated area in order to lower the water-table. Hence as *v. trans.*, to supply with well-points.
1951 *Engineering* 4 May 536/3 The consulting engineers considered..that lowering of the ground-water level by means of well-points would be the most efficient method of keeping the excavation dry. **1958** J. S. SCOTT *Dict. Civil Engin.* 409 An excavation in sand cannot become quick if effectively wellpointed. **1971** O. H. BULLITT *Search for Sybaris* xvii. 169 The most effective way of dewatering an area..would be by means of a well-point system.

well-pu·blicized, *ppl. a.*
1973 G. TALBOT *Ten Seconds from Now* xii. 165 The Queen's well-publicised love of horses. **1979** *Jrnl. R. Soc. Arts* CXXVII. 645/2 The discussion should be open and well-publicized.

well-reasoned, *ppl. a.* (Earlier example.)
1834 J. S. Mill in *Monthly Repos.* VIII. 593 Lord Brougham..delivered a firm, steady, and well-reasoned opinion.

well-resea·rched, *ppl. a.*
1958 *Times Lit. Suppl.* 15 Aug. 13 (Advt.), This well-researched book has been highly acclaimed. **1966** [see *researched *ppl. a.* 2]. **1978** *Jrnl. R. Soc. Med.* LXXI. 597/1 There is a respectable weight of well-researched evidence.

well-re·sted, *ppl. a.*
1890 W. James *Princ. Psychol.* II. xvii. 15 Successive contrast..can be avoided only by carefully fixating with the well-rested eye a point of one's field. **1965** J. A. Michener *Source* (1966) 798 At dusk on the afternoon of Tuesday, April 13, the Palmach men roused Ilana and her two well-rested companions.

well-scrubbed, *ppl. a.*
1916 Joyce *Portrait of Artist* (1969) ii. 64 A well-scrubbed kitchen. **1949** C. Fry *Lady's not for Burning* II. 49 Always fornicate Between clean sheets and spit on a well-scrubbed floor. **1976** 'R. Gordon' *Doctor on Job* iii. 18 A small, round, well-scrubbed looking man.

well-shaved, *ppl. a.* = well-shaven *ppl. a.*
1940 W. Faulkner *Hamlet* i. i. 15 He just sat there.. well-shaved and clean in his perfectly clean faded shirt.

well-shod, *ppl. a.* (Later example.)
1916 Joyce *Portrait of Artist* (1969) v. 227 He..passed out, his wellshod feet sounding flatly on the floor.

Wellsian (we·lziăn), *a.* (and *sb.*) Also **Wellsean.** [f. the name of H. G. *Wells* (1866–1946) + -ian.] Of, pertaining to, or resembling the ideas and writings of H. G. Wells, esp. in his science fiction, social comment, etc. Occas. as *sb.*, a devotee or follower of H. G. Wells.
1912 *Westm. Gaz.* 9 Nov. 4/2 The delightful comments on the Wellsian philosophy. **1916** J. Freeman *Moderns* 93 The extension of such a rigid word as morality, until it includes its own contradictions, is typically Wellsean. **1916** G. B. Shaw *Pygmalion* 200 The new-born Wellsian had to find her bearings almost as ridiculously as a baby. **1923** A. Huxley *Antic Hay* iv. 55 'Let me put you down for a couple of pairs [of pneumatic trousers].' Mr. Mercaptan shook his head. 'Too Wellsian,' he said. 'Too horribly Utopian.' **1946** R. G. Collingwood *Idea of Hist.* 252 Some Wellsian machine for looking backwards through time. **1962** E. Snow *Other Side of River* (1963) lxvi. 503 One Wellsian exhibit showed the long-range plan of a canal and river system which would virtually encircle China. **1977** M. Drabble *Ice Age* i. 69 He thought of a Wellsian paradise, a Welwyn Garden City, with neat boxes.

well-si·ted, *ppl. a.*
1925 J. G. Macleod in *Oxf. Poetry* 27 Or that old solemn cormorant Who sits like a well-sited statue carved in black. **1979** [see *well-conceived *ppl. a.*].

well-spa·ced, *ppl. a.* Of items that are neither too close nor too far apart from each other.
1939 M. Spring Rice *Working-Class Wives* iv. 70 She..has four children, well-spaced. **1962** E. Snow *Other Side of River* (1963) lxxv. 576 Large blocks of well-spaced three-story apartments. **1977** N. Sahgal *Situation in New Delhi* xiii. 128 Sometimes during a Cabinet meeting he said not more than five well-spaced words of one syllable each.

well(-)spoken, *ppl. a.* **3.** (Later example.)
1963 Wodehouse *Stiff Upper Lip, Jeeves* ii. 18 Knowing where I could get a couple of tickets for a well-spoken-of musical.

well-stru·ctured, *ppl. a.*
1974 tr. *Wertheim's Evolution & Revolution* 97 To provide a model of an integrated, well-structured whole in which any conflict could be smoothed down. **1978** *Language* LIV. 205 There is a well-structured account for Korean by Martin 1962.

well(-)sui·ted, *ppl. a.* **1.** [Suit *v.* 10 b.]
The examples in quots. 1771 and 1837 can equally be analysed as *well* adv. + *suited* rather than as a ppl. adj.
1771, 1837 [see Suit *v.*[1] 10 b]. **1950** T. S. Eliot *Cocktail Party* ii. 109, I consider That you are exceptionally well-suited to each other.
2. [Suited *ppl. a.* 2.]
1855 W. Whitman *Leaves of Grass* 69 Do you think I could walk pleasantly and well-suited toward annihilation? **1980** D. K. Cameron *Willie Gavin* xiii. 127 His likeness..shows him as well-suited as any eminent Edwardian, the wide skirt of the jacket falling away from a high button.

well-tanned, *ppl. a.* Add: Now chiefly with sense 'tanned by the sun, sunburnt'.
1867 W. Whitman *Leaves of Grass* (ed. 4) xlvii. 89 Preferring..those well-tann'd to those that keep out of the sun. **1892** 'Mark Twain' *Amer. Claimant* xvi. 164 He had a well-tanned complexion. **1916** Joyce *Portrait of Artist* (1969) ii. 60 Uncle Charles was a hale old man with a welltanned skin.

well-tempered, *ppl. a.* **4.** (Earlier example.)
1820 tr. *J. N. Forkel's Life John Sebastian Bach* 93 The well-tempered clavichord; or preludes and fugues in all the keys.

well-turned, *ppl. a.* Add: **5.** *well turned-out*: smartly dressed, well-groomed.
1903 [see *classy *a.*]. **1919** E. P. Oppenheim *Strange Case Mr. Jocelyn Thew* i. ii. 17 A very distinguished-looking and exceedingly well-turned-out caller. **1976** G. Ewart *No Fool* i. 20 Well-turned-out were the waisted women.

well-upho·lstered, *ppl. a.* Having soft and thick upholstery; usu. *transf.* in *colloq.* use, plump, 'well-covered'.
1932 H. R. Wakefield *Ghost Stories* 44 Mrs. C., a handsome well-upholstered matron, had a shrewd Scottish flair for entertainment. **1939** H. Hodge *Cab, Sir?* v. 48 She looks a bit second-hand, though she's well-upholstered. **1964** in Hamblett & Deverson *Generation X* 171, I have a preference for dark girls with warm brown eyes and I like them well-upholstered. **1971** E. Lemarchand *Death on Doomsday* ii. 26 Well-upholstered elderly women.

well-weaponed, *ppl. a.* (Later example.)
1917 Kipling *Diversity of Creatures* 405 To the sound of trumpets shall their seed restore my Cities, Wealthy and well-weaponed.

well-willing, *a.* **a.** (Later example.)
1931 *Times Lit. Suppl.* 20 Aug. 631/1 Not even the most well-willing of critics can escape from its two main flaws.

well-written, *ppl. a.* (Later example.)
1911 G. B. Shaw *Blanco Posnet* Pref. 360 An able and well-written statement of the case.

welly (we·li). Also **wellie.** Abbrev. of *Wellington 2 b. **a.** *colloq.* A wellington boot. Also *Comb.*, as *welly-boot.*
1961 *Guardian* 2 June 9/5 The ground floor we converted back into a hall, for coats and wellies, etc. **1971** J. Osborne *West of Suez* i. 42 Huge surgeons who tower over you in green and rubber wellies. **1972** D. Haston *In High Places* i. 15 We only have welly boots and gym-shoes. **1976** *Printing World* 30 Apr. 8/2 Wellington, who, as we all know, has a boot named after him... The influence of the child is apparent today as I gather it is now widely known as a 'wellie'. **1982** S. Radley *Talent for Destruction* iii. 20 Perhaps it wasn't done for a parson to wear welly boots under his cassock.
b. *slang.* A kick, acceleration. Also *fig.*
1977 *Daily Mirror* 10 May 23/1 The girl they call 'Daredevil Divi' gave the car a bit more wellie. In racing language, this meant she was stepping on the accelerator. **1979** *Guardian* 12 Feb. 20/3 The tactic most likely to succeed in the conditions was the long welly upfield. **1983** D. Gethin *Wyatt & Moresby Legacy* xxv. 174 'When I say go, give it some welly... Go.'.. Explosions sounded.
Hence **welly** *v. trans.*, to kick or trip up with one's foot. *slang.*
1966 F. Shaw et al. *Lern Yerself Scouse* 48 *Eee wuz wellied*, he was kicked. **1980** D. Morris *Tribal Words* (typescript), *Wellied*, heavily tackled and brought down. To *welly* is to make a savage tackle, boot-first... 'He must expect to be wellied a few times' is a typical expression.

wels (wels, vels). [a. Ger. *wels.*] = *sheatfish.
1880 A. C. L. G. Günther *Introd. Study of Fishes* 565 The species which has given the name to the whole family is the 'Wels' of the Germans, *Silurus glanis.* **1905** D. S. Jordan *Guide to Study of Fishes* II. ix. 182 The huge sheatfish, or wels,..next to the sturgeon, is the largest river fish in Europe. **1931** J. R. Norman *Hist. Fishes* vii. 138 The Wels or Glanis..of Europe normally feeds on fishes, frogs, and crustaceans. **1969** A. Wheeler *Fishes Brit. Isles & N.W. Europe* 221/2 Wels have been introduced in a number of private lakes in southern England.

Welsbach (ve·lzbaχ). The name of Carl Auer Freiherr von *Welsbach* (1858–1929), Austrian chemist and engineer, used *attrib.* to designate the gas mantle (Mantle *sb.* 5 g), invented by him, and the lamps employing it.
A proprietary name in the U.S.
1887 *Pall Mall Gaz.* 18 Mar. 12/1 The Welsbach burner would produce a purer light..with two cubic feet of gas per hour. **1901** *Daily Colonist* (Victoria, B.C.) 1 Oct. 5/4 The Victoria Gas Co., Ltd., are now installing complete Welsbach Lamps free of cost, charging the nominal sum of 5 cents per lamp per month for mantle renewal. **1912** A. Bennett *Matador* 308 The Welsbach incandescent mantles on the chandelier saved thirty per cent in gas-bills while increasing the light by fifty per cent. **1964** *Official Gaz.* (U.S. Patent Office) 21 July tm 119/2 The Welsbach Corporation, Philadelphia, Pa... *Welsbach.* For gas lamps..and gas mantles. **1980** *Sci. Amer.* May 123/2 The Welsbach mantle, a type of gas burner widely used for home lighting around the turn of the century, proved to be a rich source of N rays.

Welsh, *a.* and *sb.* Add: *adj.* **2. b. Welsh flannel** (earlier example); **Welsh mutton** (earlier example).
1771 Smollett *Hump. Cl.* I. 126 These sums she has more than doubled, by..dealing in cheese and Welsh flannel, the produce of his flocks and dairy. *Ibid.* II. 228, I dined upon a delicate leg of Velsh mutton and cully-flower.
c. Welsh Black, a black-coated ox or cow of a breed originally developed in north Wales, now usually kept for both meat and milk production; **Welsh cattle** (earlier example); **Welsh hound,** a dog similar to an English foxhound but wire-haired; **Welsh mountain (sheep),** a small, hardy sheep of a breed developed in high regions of Wales; **Welsh terrier,** a stocky, rough-coated, usually black and tan terrier with a square muzzle and drop ears, belonging to a breed originally developed in Wales to hunt vermin.
1919 K. J. J. Mackenzie *Cattle* xi. 149 Welsh Black Cattle. Some 20 years ago there were two distinct types of black cattle in Wales. **1953** A. Fraser *Beef Cattle Husbandry* ix. 134 The modern Welsh Black is the outcome of two types or breeds. **1977** *S. Wales Guardian* 27 Oct. 2/3 (Advt.), Welsh Black cow, 5th calver, with Cross-Friesian Steer calf at heel. **1747** H. Glasse *Art of Cookery* xiii. 129 Take the leg of a fat but small Beef, the Fat Scotch or Welch Cattle is best. **1893** R. B. Lee *Mod. Dogs* (*Sporting Division*) iv. 86 The harrier is oftener coarser in his coat than the foxhound, which may be ascribed to crossing with a rough Welsh hound that I believe is still to be found in some parts of the principality. **1930** J. D. D. Evans in C. Frederick et al. *Foxhunting* xxxi. 306 The Welsh hound is probably in some degree of later origin. **1973** *Country Life* 27 Dec. 2173/2 The three Welsh hounds he is shown holding have long, hairy coats, whitish-grey in colour. **1899** W. J. Malden *Sheep Raising & Shepherding* ii. 5 Such breeds as the Welsh Mountain..have soft short wool. **1960** [see *Exmoor]. **1979** *Country Life* 7 June 1769/3 A black version of the Welsh Mountain sheep. **1885** *Kennel Chron. & Pedigree Register* VI. 161/1 Welsh terriers.—*Dog:* 2nd, W. C. Whiskin (Welsh Dick). **1894** R. B. Lee *Mod. Dogs* (*Terriers*) x. 231 The dog of which I write as a Welsh terrier was unknown until some eight years..ago. Then he appeared in some of our shows; he was given a place in the Stud Book; a club was formed in 1886 to look after his welfare. **1950** A. C. Smith *Dogs since 1900* xi. 193 In 1942 Welsh Terriers came into prominence in the United States. **1980** E. Leather *Duveen Letter* i. 13 The Welsh terrier removed himself from the tapestry-covered Gainsborough chair.
d. Welsh cake, a kind of individual spicy cake made in Wales with currants and ginger; **welshcomb** *v. trans.*, to comb one's hair by using one's thumb and fingers instead of a comb; **Welsh dragon,** a heraldic dragon as the emblem of Wales; also *fig.*; **Welsh Nationalist,** someone wanting home rule for Wales; *spec.* a member of the Welsh Nationalist Party; **Welsh Office,** an administrative department of the British Government with responsibility for Welsh affairs; the building where this is housed; **Welsh Wales** *colloq.*, the parts of Wales where Welsh culture is especially strong or which are most distinctively Welsh; **Welsh wizard** or **Wizard,** a nickname for David Lloyd George (1863–1945), Welsh politician and British prime minister.
1932 Dylan Thomas *Sel. Lett.* (1966) 6 Mother has made Welshcakes. **1975** B. Meyrick *Behind Light* xiv. 184 Sandwiches, spice buns, Welsh cakes and bread and margarine. **1980** B. Freeman *First catch your Peacock* viii. 163 *Welsh Cakes* (*Pice ar y maen*). There are two ways of making these traditional little spicy cakes. The most usual is on the bakestone or griddle, which produces them in a rather dry, biscuity form... The other method is to make them..in a Dutch oven, and this produces cakes which are firm on the outside, soft and melting within. **1922** Joyce *Ulysses* 125 He took off his silk hat and..welshcombed his hair with raking fingers. **1971** 'A. Burgess' *MF* x. 111 Dressed and welshcombed, I pocketed my luggage and went downstairs. **1857** C. M. Yonge *Dynevor Terrace* I. xxi. 349 If she had let the Welsh dragon show his teeth in style, he would only have had to make unpleasant apologies. **1909** A. C. Fox-Davies *Compl. Guide Heraldry* xiii. 225 His Majesty the King has recently added the Welsh dragon differenced by a label of three points argent as an additional badge to the achievement of His Royal Highness the Prince of Wales. **1980** *Times* 16 Dec. 3/6 They..see the Welsh dragon flying over public buildings in the principality. **1891** *Dod's Parl. Compan. 1890–91* 246 George, David Lloyd... 'A Welsh Nationalist', supporting 'Home Rule', 'Temperance', 'Disestablishment', and other items in the programme of the Advanced Liberal Party. **1925** *North Wales Observer* 13 Aug. 5/3 The proposals of the new Welsh Nationalist Party were calmly received..at the Baptist Church, Pwllheli, on Thursday. **1937** W. H. Jones *What is happening in Wales?* iii. 9 What makes the Welsh Nationalist movement essentially a literary movement? **1966** M. Woodhouse *Tree Frog* xviii. 131 'Patriotism dictates,' he said. 'Don't give me that,' I said. 'I'm a Welsh Nationalist.' **1972** *Guardian* 19 June 24/8 Welsh Nationalists intend to set up a mobile pirate radio station. [**1964** *Times* 20 Nov. 6/7 Mr. Harold Wilson, Prime Minister.., in a statement defining the responsibilities of the Secretary of State for Wales, said:— . The interests of Wales are now represented in the Cabinet by the Secretary of State. .. He will have a Welsh office in Cardiff..and a small ministerial office in London.] *Ibid.* 22 Dec. 10/4 Mr. Griffiths, Secretary of State for Wales, yesterday opened the first permanent home of the Welsh Office in London. **1976** *S. Wales Echo* 26 Nov., Demonstrations by angry parents outside the Welsh Office now seem certain after South Glamorgan County Council's controversial decision to turn a Cardiff high school into a Welsh-speaking secondary. **1976** *Flintshire Leader* 10 Dec. 1/2 The call for a crossing did not meet Welsh Office conditions because there were not enough houses or people living in the village. **1977** *Western Mail* (Cardiff)

5 Mar. 3/2 The council has had to go to the Welsh Office for money for industrial development. **1954** G. Daniel *Welcome Death* x. 125 'The Vale of Glamorgan is legally Wales, isn't it, although no one speaks any Welsh here?' 'Quite right... This is Wales, if not Welsh Wales'. **1971** D. Ayerst *Guardian* xxi. 290 In the hills behind the coastal resorts, Welsh Wales with its roots in the chapels had an intense cultural life of its own. **1983** A. Beevor *Faustian Pact.* i. 8 The sight of the sheep-cropped hills... There was Welsh Wales. **1917** M. MacDonagh *Diary* 9 July in *London during Gt. War.* (1935) iii. iv. 203 Is not 'L.G.' known as the 'Welsh Wizard'. **1922** *National Rev.* July 652 We are told..that several of His Majesty's Ministers are acutely uncomfortable in the impasse into which they have allowed themselves to be manœuvred by the Welsh Wizard. **1976** W. J. Burley *Wycliffe & Schoolgirls* vii. 126 There had never been a real statesman since the little Welsh wizard.

welsh, *v.* Restrict *Racing* to sense in Dict., for †**welch** read **welch** and add: **2.** *intr.* Const. *on.* To fail to carry out one's promise to (a person); to fail to keep (an obligation).

1932 H. Crane *Let.* ?Jan. (1965) 395, I really can't welsh on Eyler Simpson (who is equally responsible, since he signed the lease with me). **1971** H. Wouk *Winds of War* i. 4 The real shadow on this couple was that Commander Henry thought Rhoda had welshed on their courtship understanding. **1974** *Socialist Worker* 2 Nov. 5/1 When the brothers were captured on a bank raid, the British government welched on them, dropped them like a hot penny. **1978** *Lancashire Life* Apr. 73/4 Very few people welsh on paying their taxi fare. **1982** T. Keneally *Schindler's Ark* v. 72 Across his desk..had crossed copies of angry SS memoranda addressed to army officials and complaining that the army was welching on its arrangement.

Welshie, var. *Welshy *sb.*

Welshwoman. (Later example.)

1964 C. Mackenzie *My Life & Times* iii. 282 Nurse Williams..was a plump little Welshwoman from Rhyl.

Welshy (we·lʃi), *sb. slang.* Also **Welshie.** [f. Welsh *a.* and *sb.* + -y[6].] A Welshman or Welshwoman.

1951 E. Coxhead *One Green Bottle* ii. 46 You'd think I was a Welshy by my name, Gwen Evans, but I'm a proper Cockney. **1978** E. Malpass *Wind brings up Rain* ii. 23 Alice was still staring at her unblinking. 'You deep little Welshie', she said.

welt, *sb.*[1] Add: **7. welt pocket,** a slot pocket having a welt on the lower edge that extends upward to cover the slit.

1932 D. C. Minter *Mod. Needlecraft* 134/1 Welt pocket... Mark opening with tack 4½ inches long. Cut welt 5 inches long and width required. **1978** *Detroit Free Press* 5 Mar. a 16/2 (Advt.), Single-breasted styling with self-belt, epaulets, welt pockets.

welt (welt), *sb.*[3] *dial.* [Origin unknown.] The practice by which some members of a gang of dockers take an unauthorized break while the rest work, and so turn and turn about. Hence as *v. intr.*, to take a break thus; **we·lting** *vbl. sb.*[3]

1964 *Guardian* 7 Dec. 4/1 It is 1 30 p.m...and the afternoon 'welt' is settling in. *Ibid.*, 'Welting'—the practice whereby part of a gang takes an unofficial break while the rest continues working—is firmly entrenched in Liverpool. **1965** *Wall St. Jrnl.* 13 Jan. 11 A visitor dropping into almost any waterfront cafe beside the forest of ship masts rising along the River Mersey in Liverpool will quickly discover one reason. He'll find stevedores 'welting' or enjoying their stout and porter at the bar on company time. Work crews allow members to 'welt' on a share-and-share alike basis. **1967** *Economist* 4 Nov. 490/1 Ending the welt would make possible higher basic rates of pay. **1977** *Guardian* 4 Sept. 2/2 In some docks..there is still tension because of managers' attempts..to crack down on the 'welt'.

‖ **Weltanschauung** (veltanʃau·uŋ). Also with small initial. Pl. **-ungen.** [Ger., f. *welt* World *sb.* + *anschauung* perception.] A particular philosophy or view of life; a concept of the world held by an individual or a group; = *world-view* s.v. World *sb.* 25.

1868 W. James *Let.* in R. B. Perry *Tht. & Char. W. James* (1935) I. viii. 160, I remember your saying.. that the characteristic of the Greek '*Weltanschauung*' was its optimism. **1906** *Nature* 10 May 26/2 In 1863 Haeckel entered the lists as the champion of the evolutionist 'Weltanschauung'. **1917** A. S. Pringle-Pattison *Idea of God* iv. 69 The intimate appreciation of living experience forms the basis of the whole *Weltanschauung* which he [*sc.* Bergson] offers us. **1934** M. Bodkin *Archetypal Patterns in Poetry* 326 A man's philosophy..is his *Weltanschauung*—the individual vision, or perspective of reality. **1938** E. Quinn *Mission of Austria* iii. 30 Both Catholicism and National Socialism are *Weltanschauungen.* **1952** G. Sarton *Hist. Sci.* I. iv. 121 The creation of that astrological *Weltanschauung* which dominated late ancient and medieval thought and is not yet extinct today proves the survival through the Dark Interlude of some astronomical ideas of immemorial antiquity. **1958** J. Jocz *Theol. of Election* i. 11 The impact of the Christian *Weltanschauung* upon the Jewish mind. **1972** *Science* 2 June 988/1 The main reason why evolutionism..made such slow progress is that it was the replacement of one entire *weltanschauung* by a different one. **1978** N. Jardine in Hookway & Pettit *Action & Interpretation* 124 Speakers of different cultures, having different *Weltanschauungen*, ideologies, interests, paradigms, etc.

‖ **Weltansicht** (ve·ltanziχʸt). *rare.* [Ger., f. as prec. + *ansicht* view.] A world view.

1892 W. James *Let.* 19 Sept. (1920) I. 324, I realized how exactly a philosophic *Weltansicht* resembles that from the top of a mountain. **1977** *Archivum Linguisticum* VIII. 49 The following statement that every language represents a 'Weltansicht' (world view) of its own also proves the significance of the non-uniformity of languages for von Humboldt.

‖ **Weltbild** (ve·ltbilt). [Ger., f. as prec. + *bild* picture.] A view of life.

1934 L. Mumford in W. Frank et al. *Amer. & Alfred Stieglitz* ii. 47 Stieglitz..helped restore those values that had been left out of the narrow *Weltbild* of his contemporaries. **1963** J. Lyons *Structural Semantics* iii. 40 The suggestion that we are influenced in our 'Weltbild' by the language we have been brought up to speak is open to different interpretations. **1973** I. Robinson *Survival of Eng.* iii. 82 The automatic wage-increase is so much taken for granted as a necessary part of the world that it is perhaps more *Weltbild* than what is usually thought of as language. **1983** *Bull. Amer. Acad. Arts & Sci.* Oct. 35 Mahler's *Weltbild* bore the marks not only of intellectual populism but of his class and ethnic origins.

welter, *sb.*[3] **1. b.** *Welter Stake* (earlier example).

1820 *Sporting Mag.* VI. 2/1 A capital gentleman jockey for a *Welter* stake.

welter weight. 1. b. (Earlier example.)

1832 *Q. Rev.* XLVII. 240 'Out upon this great carcass of mine,' says one of the best of the welter-weights.

‖ **Weltliteratur** (ve·lt,litĕrătūᵊːɹ). Also **-litteratur.** [Ger., f. *welt* World *sb.* + *literatur* Literature.] A literature of all nations and peoples; a universal literature.

[**1827** Goethe *Gespräche mit Eckermann* (1836) I. 325 National-Literatur will jetzt nicht viel sagen, die Epoche der Welt-Literatur ist an der Zeit.] **1913** E. Pound *Let.* 7 Nov. (1971) 24 Until 'we' accept what I've been insisting on for a decade, i.e., a universal standard which pays no attention to time or country—a Weltlitteratur standard—there is no hope. **1962** *Listener* 6 Sept. 358/2 It gives a new meaning to Goethe's dream of *Weltliteratur.* **1974** *Times Lit. Suppl.* 17 May 526/2 A truism, that Pound and Eliot were rebels against American provincialism and proponents of a *Weltliteratur.*

‖ **Weltpolitik** (ve·ltpǫliti:k). [Ger., f. as prec. + *politik* politics.] International politics; world affairs from a political standpoint; a particular country's policy towards the world at large.

1903 J. Bailey *Diary* 19 Feb. (1935) 90 Lord George Hamilton said..that the one thing needed to make the U.S.A. friends with us was their going into *Welt Politik.* **1905** D. M. Wallace *Russia* II. xxxviii. 428 Never, perhaps, has the construction of a single line [*sc.* the Trans-Siberian Railway] produced such deep and lasting changes in the sphere of *Weltpolitik.* **1941** *N. & Q.* 26 July 43/2 The ineffectiveness of the Kruger telegram opened German eyes to the need of a fleet if Germany was to play a successful, or even a real, part in *Weltpolitik.* **1979** G. St. Aubyn *Edward VII* vii. 363 The Triple Entente was a direct reaction to Germany's *Weltpolitik.*

‖ **Weltschmerz** (ve·ltʃmēᵊɹts). Also **weltschmerz.** [Ger., f. as prec. + *schmerz* pain.] A weary or pessimistic feeling about life; an apathetic or vaguely yearning attitude.

1875 J. A. Symonds *Renaissance in Italy* I. iv 232 The Weltschmerz did not exist for the men of the Renaissance. **1896** W. Caldwell *Schopenhauer's System* 523 His philosophy is a study of the *Weltschmerz* that we all feel at times. **1923** A. Huxley *Let.* 2 Sept. (1969) 218, I have also been having a..jaundice lying on my liver, which reduced me to a fearful state of weltschmerz and incapacity to do anything. **1935** C. Isherwood *Mr. Norris changes Trains* ix. 150 'What's the matter?' I asked. 'Things in general... The state of this wicked world. A touch of *Weltschmerz*, that's all.' **1947** [see *accidia]. **1960** C. Geertz *Religion of Java* vi. 75 He said..the young good ones..die early, as a kind of reward, for it is a good thing to be dead. He spoke happily, not in any *Weltschmerz* mood. **1965** W. Golding *Hot Gates* 136 The sadness, the *weltschmerz* resulting from the constant movement of the ship. **1981** J. D. MacDonald *Free Fall in Crimson* i. 6 'It is like *weltschmerz*.' 'Which, as you have so often told me, is homesickness for a place you have never seen.'

wen[1]**.** Add: **3.** Comb.: **wen-man** *nonce-wd.*, a city-dweller.

1937 Auden *Lett. from Iceland* viii. 102 The mountain-snob is a Wordsworthian fruit... He calls all those who live in cities wen-men.

wen, repr. a pronunc. of When *adv.* (*conj.*, *sb.*) in dialect or in uneducated speech.

1893 H. A. Shands *Some Peculiarities of Speech in Mississippi* 67 *Wen*, sometimes used by illiterate whites and negroes for *when.* **1901** M. Franklin *My Brilliant Career* iii. 16 It puts me in mind ev the time wen the black fellers made the gins do all the work. **1952** [see *queen *sb.* 5 e]. **1979** *Amer. Speech* LIV. 67 W'en you see the fire come from the brimstone..this earth ain' gon' be burnin'.

wend, *v.*[1] **15.** (Later example without poss. pron.)

1883 [see Fairway].

Wendic, *a.* and *sb.* (Earlier examples.)

1848 *Rep. Brit. Assoc. Adv. Sci. 1847* 267 The Old Slavonic of the Bible and of Nestor, the Russian, Servian, Croatic, and Wendic. **1856** Max Müller in *Oxford Ess.* i. 14 We know nothing of the Arian race, before it was broken up into different nationalities, such as Indian, German, Greek, Roman, Windic, Teutonic, and Celtic.

wendigo, var. *windigo.

Wendy house. Also with small initial or hyphen. [Named after the small house built around Wendy in J. M. Barrie's play *Peter Pan* (1904).] A small house-like structure for children to play in.

1949 M. Atkinson *Junior School Community* 11 Wendy house—made by a joiner: two large pieces of plywood hinged together. **1957** *Listener* 9 May 743 There is a Wendy-house in the corner [of the class room]. **1971** *Where* Dec. 356/1 They have performed wonders in getting the bus and re-equipping it with ladders, a wendy house and even a telephone. **1977** J. McClure *Sunday Hangman* viii. 80 The rocking horse was legless.., the pedal car was a write-off, and the Wendy house had been trampled flat.

wenge (we·ŋge). [Local name in Zaïre.] The dark brown timber of *Millettia laurentii*, a tree of the family Leguminosæ found in Central Africa.

1963 *House & Garden* Feb. 60 (*caption*) Seating unit series..teak and wenge frame, latex foam cushions. **1972** *Handbk. Hardwoods* (Building Res. Establishment) (ed. 2) 164 The timber wengé..from Zaire is generally similar in appearance and properties to panga panga.

‖ **wên jên** (wɔ̄n ʒɔ̄n, wɔ̄n rɔ̄n). Also with hyphen. [Chinese *wénrén* man of letters, f. *wén* writing + *rén* (*jên* in Wade-Giles) man.] Chinese men of letters.

1958 W. Willetts *Chinese Art* II. vii. 509 From early Ming times until quite recently, the history of Chinese painting has been written by that highly articulate but alarmingly unanimous body of people, the *wên jên* or *literati.* **1970** *Oxf. Compan. Art* 232/2 Though *wên-jên*, many of them were also professional painters.

‖ **wen li** (wɔn lī). Also **wenli** and with capital initial. [Chinese *wén lǐ* grammar, literary style, f. *wén* writing + *lǐ* texture, reason.] = *wen-yen.

The synonymy is based on a misconception of the Chinese meaning, and does not exist in that language.

1887 *Chinese Times* 11 June 502/1 The bishop's style, call it *Wen li* or *Mandarin*, is admirably clear and idiomatic. **1917** S. Couling *Encycl. Sinica* 597/2 The term *Wên li* is now in constant use especially among foreigners, to denote the Chinese literary style, which differs in degrees of conciseness or obscurity, and hence is sometimes divided into 'high' and 'low' *Wên li.* **1972** E. A. Nida *Bk. of Thousand Tongues* 70/1 Wenli was a written language which could be used throughout the whole of China. **1977** C. F. & F. M. Voegelin *Classification & Index World's Lang.* 114 The descendant of an earlier form of Chinese known as Wen Yen or Wen Li continues to be used by all educated Chinese..for special purposes.

Wenlock. Add: In mod. use, the name of the middle of three divisions of the Silurian, lying below the Ludlovian and above the Valentian (Llandoverian); used *attrib.* and *absol.* (Further examples.)

1946 [see *Ludlovian *a.*]. **1969** Bennison & Wright *Geol. Hist. Brit. Isles* vi. 116 A great deal of relatively recent work has been done on the limestone and shale shelf-sea facies of Wenlock and Ludlow age in the Welsh Borders. **1979** R. Anderton et al. *Dynamic Stratigr. Brit. Isles* vii. 96/1 Turbidity currents deposited sands in a separate turbidite zone during the Wenlock and lower Ludlow.

Wenlockian, *a.* Add: Also, of or belonging to the Wenlock series. Freq. *absol.*

1946 [see *Ludlovian *a.*]. **1969** Bennison & Wright *Geol. Hist. Brit. Isles* vi. 124 The thickness of the Wenlockian strata may amount to about 25,000 feet. **1974** *Encycl. Brit. Macropædia* XVI. 774/2 The Llandoverian.. saw the beginning of a sharp distinction between basin graptolitic shale facies and calcareous and..sandy shelf facies. This distinction was well marked in the Wenlockian.

Wensleydale. Add: **b.** Also, a white cheese (see quot. 1963).

1963 A. L. Simon *Guide Good Food & Wines* 648/2 The best-known variety of Wensleydale cheese, cylindrical in shape, like Stilton, but of smaller dimensions, which grows 'blue' when ripe, like Stilton... The other sort of Wensleydale cheese is a flat-shaped, white cheese which is eaten fresh and does not generally go blue. **1985** D. Clark *Performance* iv. 105 Brawn and Wensleydale cheese sandwiches.

‖ **wen-yen** (wɔn yen). Also **wenyan, wenyen,** and with capital initial. [Chinese *wényán*, f. *wén* writing + *yán* speech, words.] The traditional literary language or style of China, superseded in the twentieth century by *PAI-HUA.

1936 N. WALES in E. Snow *Living China* 336 Until 1917 there existed in..stalemate three fairly distinct strata of literature: (1) the ancient cult of the *literati* in the dead *wen-yen* classical written language, ..(2) the healthy parvenu *pai-hua*, 'plain speech', literature of the people in the spoken language, and..(3) the story-tellers' literature in the provincial dialects. **1964** *Anthropol. Linguistics* Mar. 31 Many words which require two characters in Han Chinese can be written with one character in Wenyen. **1968** [see *PAI-HUA]. **1969** *Language* XLV. 690 One is the Classical Chinese, *wényán*, which has been used from antiquity up to recent years. **1980** *Times Lit. Suppl.* 27 June 725/1 He has been engaged..in an immense study of the ancient Chinese classics written in the elegant but archaic *wenyen* Chinese favoured by old-fashioned scholars—a language almost as remote from present-day speech as Latin from the modern European vernaculars.

Werdnig–Hoffmann (və̄·ɹdnig). *Path.* The names of Guido *Werdnig*, 19th-century Austrian neurologist, and Johann *Hoffmann* (*HOFFMANN 3), who described the disease in 1890 and 1893 respectively, used in the possessive and *attrib.* to designate a fatal familial disease that is present at birth or develops soon afterwards and is characterized by muscular atrophy, paralysis, and loss of sucking ability.

1903 *Trans. Clin. Soc.* XXXVI. 226 (*heading*) Three cases of family progressive spinal muscular atrophy (Werdnig–Hoffman [*sic*] type). **1920** *Brain* XLIII. 170 The case was scarcely one of amyotonia congenita, but rather was related to Werdnig–Hoffmann's progressive muscular atrophy, in spite of there being no obvious element of heredity. **1978** *Arch. Dis. Childhood* LIII. 921/1 Werdnig–Hoffmann disease—the acute severe infantile form of spinal muscular atrophy—often presents in the neonatal period with profound weakness.

were-. Add: **we·re-jaguar,** in Olmec mythology, a creature partly human and partly feline.

1967 L. DEUEL *Conquistadors without Swords* xviii. 235 Today,..more than 400 years after the Spanish Conquest and 2,000..years since its origin, the were-jaguar, the *nawal*, is still invoked to frighten children who will not go to sleep. **1967** E. P. BENSON *Maya World* ii. 24 Olmec art is full of creatures who are part human and part feline... Often they are a combination of human infant and jaguar. They are called 'were-jaguars'. **1979** E. ABRAMS tr. *H. Stierlin's Precolombian Civilizations* 68 This werejaguar figure tenoned into the wall of the pyramid at Chavín.

werewolf. Add: **2*.** A member of a right-wing paramilitary German underground resistance movement.

1945 in *Amer. Speech* (1949) XXIV. 289/2 It boasted that..underground killers—'Werewolves'—had carried out the sentence. **1946** E. LINKLATER *Private Angelo* xxi. 266 A company of Free Austrians who..handed him over to a ridiculous little party of people who called themselves Werewolves. **1950** C. MACINNES *To Victors the Spoils* I. 111 Isn't it going to be dangerous..? What about the Gestapo and the werewolves? **1982** C. THOMAS *Jade Tiger* 48 The subject matter of the interrogation—local conditions, Werewolf units, SS and Gestapo individuals' whereabouts.

Werner (wə̄·ɹnəɹ, ‖ vę̄·rnər). *Path.* [The name of Carl W. O. *Werner* (b. 1879), German physician, who described the syndrome in 1904.] *Werner's syndrome*: a rare hereditary syndrome whose symptoms include short stature, endocrine and vascular disorders, and premature ageing and death.

1934 OPPENHEIMER & KUGEL in *Trans. Assoc. Amer. Physicians* XLIX. 359 After careful consideration we have selected the patronymic name, Werner's syndrome, rather than Rothmund's syndrome, for on reading Rothmund's original paper (1868)..we are convinced that he described a quite different condition. **1962** A. SORSBY in A. Pirie *Lens Metabolism Rel. Cataract* 298 The association of cataract with such affections as.. Werner's syndrome has been known for many years. **1980** *Practitioner* Nov. 1170/2 Rapid whitening of scalp hair associated with rapid ageing of the face..are features reported in Werner's syndrome, a heredo-familial disease in young adults who age rapidly.

Wernicke (v-, wə̄·ɹnikə). *Path.* The name of Karl *Wernicke* (1848–1905), German neurologist, used in the possessive to designate: **a.** A neurological disorder in which there is an inability to understand speech and, usually, to speak sensibly, caused by a lesion of *Wernicke's area*, an area of the cerebral cortex comprising parts of the temporal and parietal lobes.

1887 VICKERY & KNAPP tr. *Strümpell's Text-bk. Med.* 679 The word, when it is heard, may fail to call up the appropriate mental image. Kussmaul has given this condition the name of word deafness (Wernicke's sensory aphasia). The patient is not really deaf, for he hears everything, but he no longer understands what he hears, and has forgotten what the words signify. **1907** *Practitioner* Oct. 545 In the Aphasia of Broca..the cases.. closely resemble those of Wernicke's aphasia, with the difference that, in Broca's aphasia, the patient cannot speak. **1908** A. GORDON *Dis. Nervous Syst.* vii. 118 Pierre Marie..holds that aphasia..is caused by a lesion in the lenticular nucleus and in Wernicke's zone; the latter comprises the following portions: supra-marginal gyrus, angular gyrus, the posterior portions of the first two temporal convolutions. **1965** [see *LOGORRHŒA, LOGORRHEA]. **1976** *New Yorker* 15 Nov. 152/2 There are two areas of the cortex that have been shown to be directly involved in speaking. Those areas—known since the late nineteenth century as Broca's area and Wernicke's area—are on the side of the brain (usually the left) that is dominant for speech. **1979** *Sci. Amer.* Sept. 161/1 In Wernicke's aphasia speech is phonetically and even grammatically normal, but it is semantically deviant.

b. An encephalopathy caused by vitamin B_1 deficiency and characterized by mental confusion and uncontrolled movements, esp. of the eyes. So *Wernicke–Korsakoff* [see *KORSAKOFF], applied to Wernicke's syndrome and Korsakoff's syndrome when both are present in an individual.

1910 E. E. SOUTHARD in Osler & McCrae *Syst. Med.* VII. xiii. 631 (*heading*) Hemorrhagic superior polioencephalitis (Wernicke's disease). *Ibid.*, The non-alcoholic and the alcoholic forms of Wernicke's disease are considered. **1939** *Jrnl. Path. & Bacteriol.* XLVIII. 259 We suggest therefore that, as in chronic alcoholism so in pregnancy, B_1 deficiency may play a part in producing Wernicke's encephalopathy as well as polyneuritis. **1966** *Trans. Amer. Neurol. Assoc.* XCI. 31 The Wernicke–Korsakoff syndrome is..both a clinical and a pathological entity. **1978** *Sci. Amer.* Oct. 76/3 The Wernicke-Korsakoff syndrome is a neurological disorder that begins with an acute phase characterized by palsy and poor muscular coordination; with treatment the acute phase gives way to a chronic phase, Korsakoff's psychosis, characterized by severe amnesia.

werrit, *v.* Add: Also **we·rriting** *ppl. a.*

1808 E. WEETON *Let.* 5 Oct. in *Jrnl. of Governess* (1969) I. 111, I was laughed at, or found I had displeased. I had a most werreting life of it. **1865** [in Dict.].

‖ **wertfrei** (vēᵊ·ɹtfrəi), *a.* [Ger., f. *wert* value, WORTH *sb.*[1] + *frei* FREE *a.*] Free of value-judgements; morally neutral. Hence **we·rtfreiheit** (also with capital initial) [-HOOD], the quality of being *wertfrei*.

1909 W. M. URBAN *Valuation* xiv. 422 The more neutral or '*wertfrei*' judgments of science. **1944** H. A. HODGES *Wilhelm Dilthey* v. 80 It is generally recognized that the natural sciences have no interest in judgments of value. Their *Wertfreiheit* is one of their most treasured attributes. **1964** ROUSSEAS & FARGANIS in I. L. Horowitz *New Sociol.* 289 Max Weber distinguishes between science as being *wertfrei* and *wertlos*. *Wertfrei* is defined as being free from prevailing passion and prejudice. **1975** *Times Lit. Suppl.* 25 July 848/1 What specially distinguishes Ontology, American Style, however, is that it is far more *wertfrei*, uncommitted, cool, detached and technical. *c* **1978** C. R. TAME *Against New Mercantilism* 8 No one would abandon the heritage of *wertfreiheit* in economics and the social sciences.

Wesak, var. *VESAK.

‖ **Wesen** (vē·zən). *rare.* [Ger.] **a.** A person's nature (as shown in characteristic behaviour).

1854–5 GEO. ELIOT in J. W. Cross *George Eliot's Life* (1885) I. vi. 353 Fräulein Solmar is..probably between fifty and sixty, but of that agreeable *Wesen* which is so free from anything startling in person or manner. **1884** MRS. H. WARD *Miss Bretherton* i. 10 And then her *Wesen* is so attractive; she is such a frank, unspoilt, good-hearted creature.

b. The distinctive nature or essence of anything.

1959 *Listener* 22 Oct. 689/2, I believe myself that it is only in the totality of its historic manifestations that Christianity can be understood, and that so long as it does survive, its *Wesen*, its nature, will continue to reveal new potentialities.

Wessex (we·seks). [OE. *West Seaxe* West Saxons.] **1.** The name of a kingdom in south-west England in Anglo-Saxon times, used by Thomas Hardy as the name of the county in which his stories are set (corresponding approximately to Dorset, Somerset, Hampshire, and Wiltshire) and since used as a name for south-west England or this part of it.

1868 W. BARNES *Poems of Rural Life in Common Eng.* Pref., As I think that some people, beyond the bounds of Wessex, would allow me the pleasure of believing that they have deemed..my homely poems in our Dorset mother-speech to be worthy of their reading, I have written a few of a like kind, in common English. **1874** HARDY in *Cornh. Mag.* Nov. 624 Greenhill was the Nijnii Novgorod of Wessex; and the busiest..day of the whole statute number was the day of the sheep-fair. **1876** *Examiner* 15 July 794/1 The Wessex man knows that these passages have in them the real ring, all equally true to life and scenery. **1938** *Proc. Prehistoric Soc.* IV. 52 The work..was..undertaken with a view to examining the cultures of the geographical area usually comprised in the term 'Wessex' in the period immediately following the Beaker phase. **1979** *N. & Q.* June 193/2 All [volumes] share a chronology of the life and works, Hardy's General Preface to the Wessex Edition, and notes on Wessex and Wessex names.

2. *attrib.* = *SADDLEBACK *sb.* 4 h.

1919, etc. [see *SADDLEBACK *sb.* 4 h]. **1919** [see *KILLER 4 b]. **1978** A. WILLIAMS *Backyard Pig Farming* iv. 27 There used to be a Wessex Saddleback originating in Dorset; it had black back legs.

3. *Archæol.* Of, pertaining to, or designating an Early Bronze Age culture in southern England, *c* 2000–1500 B.C., represented by grave-goods of native and European provenance.

1938 S. PIGGOTT in *Proc. Prehistoric Soc.* IV. 52 Many elements..here described as typical of the Wessex Culture of the Bronze Age are..found in associations which are late and outside the main culture-area. **1954** *Antiquity* Mar. 28 The axes..of this broad-butted type,.. characteristic..of Piggott's Wessex Culture. **1963** E. S. WOOD *Collins Field Guide to Archaeol.* I. iv. 64 The Wessex nobility seem to have come from Germany. **1975** *Times Lit. Suppl.* 14 Mar. 282/1 The unlikelihood of Mycenaean influence on Stonehenge and the 'Wessex culture' of southern England. **1983** P. A. CROWL *Prehist. Britain* i. 33 The Wessex urns..lacking the refinement one would have expected of this..culture.

west, *adv.*, *sb.*[1], and *a.* Add: **B. 3.** *Bridge.* (With capital initial.) The player sitting opposite and partnering East, and having South to his right.

1926 [see *EAST *sb.* 4]. **1958** *Listener* 2 Oct. 541/1 West was a good enough player to have a chance of succeeding. **1974** *Country Life* 3 Oct. 975/1 Warned off Hearts and Clubs, West had to lead a Spade or a Diamond.

C. *sb.* **3. b.** (Earlier example.) See also *WILD WEST.

1796 G. WASHINGTON in *Claypoole's Amer. Daily Advertiser* 19 Sept. 2/2 The West derives from the East supplies requisite to its growth and comfort.

e. (With capital initial.) The non-Communist states of Europe and America.

1946 H. NICOLSON *Diary* 22 Aug. (1967) 75 He is convinced that the Russians wish to dominate the world... The only way in which the West can counter this is to pool their philosophy of liberalism, put up a united front. **1951**, etc. [see *EAST *sb.* 2 b]. **1957** *Ann. Reg. 1956* 228 Some 5,000 citizens a week continued to flee to the West. **1964** M. MCLUHAN *Understanding Media* (1967) ii. 40 Competitive sports between Russia and the West. **1979** T. BENN *Arguments for Socialism* i. 38 It is not only in the West that Marxism is seen as one of the main sources of democratic socialist philosophy.

D. *adj.* **1. c.** *the West Bank*, a region west of the River Jordan and north-west of the Dead Sea which became part of Jordan in 1948 and was occupied by Israel in the Arab–Israeli War of 1967; hence *West Banker*, an inhabitant of the West Bank.

1967 *Times* 3 Aug. 16/7 Making the Israeli pound legal tender side by side with the Jordanian dinar on the Israeli-occupied West bank should go a long way towards increasing imports of goods from Britain. *Ibid.* 10 Aug. 7/1 Even those Israelis who would gladly abandon Sinai, Gaza and the West Bank would prefer to keep the Syrian heights overlooking the Sea of Galilee. **1968** *N.Y. Times* 22 Dec. IV. 4/6 The many interviews given by King Hussein who often refers to granting more self-government to the West Bankers. **1972** *Guardian* 10 Apr. 11/3 Hussein..is seeking to prevent disaffected West Bankers..from reversing their links with the Hashemite throne. **1978** *Internat. Relations Dict.* (U.S. Dept. State Library) 35/2 These groups rejected..the establishment of a Palestinian state on the West Bank. **1983** 'J. LE CARRÉ' *Little Drummer Girl* ii. 32 Miss Bach had been talking wistfully of taking up the wagon-trail life of a West Bank settler.

2. b. *West Briton*: † (*a*) a native of Wales; (*b*) a native of Ireland; in mod. use, (chiefly derogatory) one who favours a close political connection with Great Britain; hence *West Britonism*.

1712 P. LEIGH *Life S. Wenefride* 46 Whatever this incredulous Age may think of..our Saint's Return to Life; it appear'd so evident to the West Britains..that many Pagan People..came..to receive Baptism. **1816** J. GIFFARD *Let. to Sir Robert Peel* 19 Mar. (Brit. Library Add. MSS. 40,253, f. 258), The periphrastic Title of the United Kingdom of Great Britain and Ireland..goes out of its way—to remind people that they were once disunited and to keep them so—had the whole been called by one common name *Britain*—we should have had the Inhabitants proud of the glorious Title *Britons* and we West *Britons* would have been as much conciliated and attached as the North Britons are. **1836** D. O'CONNELL in J. O'Connor *Hist. Ireland 1798–1924* (1925) I. vii. 226 The people of Ireland are ready to become portion of the Empire, provided they be made so in reality and not in name alone; they are ready to become a kind of West Britons, if made so in benefits and justice; but if not, we are Irishmen again. **18..**, **1909** [in Dict.]. **1910** D. HYDE in R. M. Dorson *Peasant Customs* (1968) II. 718 The men who..while protesting..against West Britonism, have helped..to assimilate us to England and the English. **1918** West Britonism [see *SHONEEN]. **1925** in J. O'CONNOR *Hist. Ireland 1798–1924* II. xxiv. 368 The American friends of Irish liberty are both grieved and resentful at some of the recent exhibitions given there of the revival of West Britonism. **1944** JOYCE *Stephen Hero* xvii. 54 No West-Briton could speak worse of his Countrymen. **1960** C. C. O'BRIEN *Shaping of Mod. reland* 19 When Moran and his friends talked of Weste lBritons they had in mind, I imagine, some archetyp of a dentist's wife who collected crests, ate kedgeree for breakfast and displayed on her mantelpiece a portrait oj the Dear Queen. **1962** B. INGLIS *West Briton* viii. 143, I never heard of West Briton being used except pejoratively. **1972** C. C. O'BRIEN *States of Ireland* iv. 77

Protestant loyalists—that is to say, most Protestants—also came inevitably under attack, usually as West Britons.

c. (Further examples.)

1824 COLLIER & MACCARTHY (*title*) West-African sketches. **1863** *Irish People* 5 Dec. 24/3 The West-British press chimed in. **1865** R. F. BURTON *Wit & Wisdom from W. Afr.* iii. 121 The practical selfishness and feelinglessness of the wild West African, who, when, tamed by slavery, becomes one of the most tender of men. **1925** J. O'CONNOR *Hist. Ireland 1798–1924* II. xxiv. 373 People dance the same dances as were the fashion in the old West-British days. **1950** *New Yorker* 16 Sept. 83/1 They [*sc.* the Germans] think that German rearmament is inevitable, and suggest that a sort of Foreign Legion.. be activated immediately, in which all West European men willing to go to war against Communism could volunteer. **1958** *Listener* 11 Dec. 977/2 He [*sc.* Herr Brandt] is coming gradually to symbolize for many West Berliners their determination to remain free. **1969** A. MARIN *Rise with Wind* (1970) vi. 75 Clay sank into a chair, his eyes fixed coldly on the West German. **1973** *Times* 27 Nov. 9/1 (*heading*) Fewer West Berliners visit the East. **1976** W. LAQUEUR in D. Villiers *Next Year in Jerusalem* 86 The non-Jewish Jew is a specifically West European phenomenon. **1976** M. BIRMINGHAM *Heat of Sun* iii. 34 To build a house in his home town, to which all West Africans dream of retiring. **1981** J. JOHNSTON *Christmas Tree* 114 It wasn't that I objected to De Valera's neutrality... I had no political feelings of being West British..no Crown fever. **1983** *Spectator* 14 May 8/1 It is unsettling to find a pillar of West German industry collecting Nazi memorabilia.

d. With abstract sbs. derived from the sbs. and adjs. of prec. sense.

1895 *Dundalk Examiner* 24 Aug. 2/6 A slogan cry which would..sound the death-knell of ascendancy and West Britishism in this country? **1971** J. SPENCER *Eng. Lang. W. Afr.* 28 There is certainly a sufficiency of terms and expressions peculiar to the use of English in this region to justify the term West Africanism. **1980** *English World-Wide* I. i. 76 AVE [*sc.* African Vernacular English] is ..characterized by a vocabulary adapted to its environment, which shows itself in oft-quoted West Africanisms.

west coast. 1. The western coast of a country or region; in some cases with capital initials as a proper name. Also *attrib.*

1377, 1689, 1801 [in Dict. s.v. WEST *a.* 1 a]. **1845** *N.Z. Jrnl.* 13 Sept. 234/2 Of the west coast of the Middle Island, commonly called by the whalers the 'West Side', we heard a good deal. **1850** *Calif. Courier* (San Francisco) 2 Dec. 2/1 Our position here on the West Coast has been and still is a peculiar one. **1862** *Jrnl. R. Geogr. Soc.* XXXII. 294 Arrangements entered into with the Provincial Government of Nelson for the survey of the West Coast district of that province. **1897** M. KINGSLEY *Trav. W. Afr.* 8 Sound knowledge..collected during an acquaintance with the West Coast of over thirty years. **1926** A. HUXLEY *Jesting Pilate* IV. 287 The stranger coming to the West Coast will be astonished by the amount of casual embracement. **1959** A. MCLINTOCK *Descr. Atlas N.Z.* p. xvi, The road..here swings in a northerly direction..towards Arthur's Pass, 3,020ft, and thence to the West Coast. **1971** *Country Life* 9 Dec. 1642/2 Last year..the west-coast herrings proved to be the only plentiful supply in northern Europe. **1977** H. FAST *Immigrants* II. 88 We're the lifeline, the West Coast, San Francisco.

2. (Usu. with capital initials.) Used *attrib.* with reference to a style of modern jazz playing that was centred on Los Angeles in the 1950s, typified by small ensembles, technical sophistication, and elaborate writing. orig. *U.S.*

Cf. *West Coaster* below, quot. 1954.

1954 *Downbeat* 7 Apr. 6/1 The latest example of this thinking-by-pigeonholes is the attempt to convince the populace that there is a growing west coast school of jazz. *Ibid.* 19 May 16/3 Nat Hentoff's comments on 'west coast jazz' aroused considerable comment. **1959** *News Chron.* 12 Aug. 6/5 He is not only benevolent about West Coast jazz but aware of its technical ins and outs. **1961** *Times* 4 Feb. 11/5 Music of considerable variety, ranging from some vigorous Dixieland..to West Coast Jazz (with Palm Court cello). **1962** *Melody Maker* 21 July 7/1 Some of the 1954 tracks have a nostalgic, almost dated, appeal, in the writing, it is so typical of West Coast jazz of the time—neat, smooth and often very clever. **1980** *New Grove Dict. Mus.* XX. 371/2 Miles Davis's 1949–50 recordings were an initial influence as is shown by such archetypal West Coast performances as Rogers's *Didi* (1951).

3. Used *attrib.* to designate a kind of large rear-view mirror (see quot. 1963). orig. *U.S.*

1963 *Amer. Speech* XXXVIII. 46 *West coast mirror*,.. a large, square, rear-view mirror attached to the side of a cab. **1968** *Globe & Mail* (Toronto) 17 Feb. 41 (Advt.), Mercury ¾ ton pickup... 4 speed transmission, west coast mirrors. **1980** *Truck & Bus Transportation* (Austral.) Mar. 96/1 All-round vision is generally good, but Cronulla Carrying have gone one step further by replacing the meagre standard mirrors with the efficient west-coast type.

Hence **West Coaster**, (*a*) one who lives on the West Coast; *spec.* (*N.Z.*) = *COASTER 3 c; (*b*) a player or devotee of West Coast jazz.

1896 *N.Z. Alpine Jrnl.* II. 157 He was..not a native born West Coaster. **1936** 'R. HYDE' *Passport to Hell* ii. 54 He washed shirts for the brawny West Coasters. **1941** O. DUFF *N.Z. Now* v. 71 The people are never 'Southlanders'..as the people of the West Coast are 'West Coasters'. **1949** M. STEEN *Twilight on Floods* II. ii. 198 Eighty-five per cent West Coasters die of fever, or return home total wrecks! **1954** *Time* 1 Feb. 38/2 Today, the liveliest center of developing jazz is California... The West Coasters include such names as..Shelly Manne.., Shorty Rogers.., Gerry Mulligan and Stan Getz.., Dave Brubeck. **1958** K. GOODWIN in P. Gammond *Decca Bk. Jazz* xiii. 148 Groups from four to nine pieces have been most popular among the West Coasters. **1974** M. BRAITHWAITE *Ontario* ii. 7 It is nonsense to maintain that there are no special characteristics of Canadians from different regions of the country. West Coasters *are* different from those who live on the East Coast. **1977** *Times* 16 May 8/7 Their effect on humourless West Coasters [*sc.* in California] was..devastating.

west end. Add: **2.** (Earlier example.)

1776 *Gazetteer & New Daily Advertiser* 11 Sept. in Bond & McLeod *Newslett. to Newspapers* (1977) III. 186 A gentleman in a certain coffeehouse at the Westend of town.

b. The theatres of the West End, or their personnel.

1894 *Theatre* Oct. 155 The influence of the west end is felt both in the cheaper London houses and throughout the provinces. **1979** *Listener* 16 Aug. 206/3 No one wanted a National Theatre. The West End didn't want it because they feared a new rival.

4. (Examples relating to West End theatres.) Also passing into *adj.*

1890 G. B. SHAW *London Music 1888–89* (1937) 322 The more commercial atmosphere of the West-end theatre. **1890** O. WILDE *Pict. Dorian Gray* iii, in *Lippincott's Monthly Mag.* July 29, I will take a West-End theatre and bring her out properly. **1928** A. HUXLEY *Point Counter Point* x. 159 So well travelled, so brilliantly cosmopolitan and West-End. **1936** N. COWARD *To-Night at 8.30* I. 103 If you're so bloody West End why the hell did you leave it? **1954** 'M. COST' *Invitation from Minerva* 171, I got my first West-End engagement. Since then, I've never looked back. **1983** S. VIZINCZEY *Innocent Millionaire* iii. 14 Occasionally his London agent got him a part in the West End production of an American play.

west-ender (earlier example); **west-endian, -endy** *adjs.*, characteristic or suggestive of a west end, *spec.* that of London.

1833 *Chambers's Jrnl.* 30 Mar. 66/2 There have been instances of 'west-enders' going on a tour of discovery.. within the precincts of Wapping. **1856** J. M. LUDLOW *Let.* Nov. in C. L. Graves *Life & Lett. A. Macmillan* (1910) ii. 91 [A London shop] more West-endian than Bell's or Nutt's. **1911** J. BONE *Edin. Revisited* i. 12 A minister of the Gospel from the West Coast identified Edinburgh as an 'east-windy, west-endy city'. **1959** *New Chron.* 25 July 4/5 Most of it proved too precious and West Endy for television.

westerliness. (Example.)

1927 [see *EASTERLINESS]

western, *a.* and *sb.*[1] Add: **A.** *adj.* **3. a.** *Western Approaches*, the area of sea immediately to the west of Britain; *Western Islands* = *Western Isle* (*a*), (*b*); *Western Isle*, (*a*) *pl.*, the Hebrides; cf. *west isles* s.v. WEST *a.* 1 c; (*b*) *pl.*, the Azores; † (*c*) Ireland (*rare*$^{-1}$); *Western Ocean*, the Atlantic.

1697 W. DAMPIER *New Voyage round World* v. 107 The most remarkable places that I did ever hear of for their breeding, is at an Island in the West Indies called Caimanes, and the Isle Ascention in the Western Ocean. **1758** J. ARMSTRONG *Let.* 21 Oct. in *N. & Q.* (1979) Feb. 44/2, I hope you have had an agreeable View of the Western Isles. **1760** F. FAUQUIER *Let.* 28 Oct. in G. Reese *Official Papers* (1980) 422 The Vessel is cleared out for Gibraltar, and then under pretence of being drove by stress of Weather into Madeira or some of the western Isles. **1775** JOHNSON (*title*) Journey to the Western Islands of Scotland. **1776** GIBBON *Decl. & Fall* I. i. 5 The western isle might be improved into a valuable possession. **1805** in *Naval Documents U.S. Wars with Barbary Powers* (U.S. Office Naval Rec.) (1944) V. 366 It is my opinion, she is competent to be sent across the Western Ocean, and should it be deemed necessary to send her to the Mediterranean, she could be speedily equipped. **1810** J. E. CALDWELL *Tour through Part of Virginia* (ed. 2) (1951) 47 The Azores, or Western Islands, are nine in number. **1870** Western Islands [in Dict.]. **1920** *Times* 1 Mar. 9/3 The title of Admiral Sir Reginald Tupper..has now been changed to Commander-in-Chief of the Western Approaches. There are three captains, R.N., in charge of Naval Areas under his orders. Captain Denis B. Crampton..commands the Irish Sea Area; Captain William D. Church..the Kingstown Area; and Captain E. G. Lowther-Crofton..the Buncrana Area. **1935** J. MASEFIELD *Victorious Troy* 8 Did you ever see a storm, a real storm, a Western Ocean Hurricane? **1946** W. S. CHURCHILL *Secret Session Speeches* 38 The powerful reinforcement of large-range aircraft..which were sent.. to the Western Approaches are now active. **1961** G. FOULSER *Seaman's Voice* ii. 33 Western Ocean gales are notorious for their ferocity. **1976** *Mariner's Mirror* LXII. 177 Sometimes homeward-bound convoys would be routed away from the Western Approaches, the Bay of Biscay, and the English Channel. **1976** *Scotsman* 15 Dec., The rents of the 2000 local authority houses in the Western Isles are to be increased by £39 a year from April. **1979** *N. & Q.* Feb. 44/2 We can now be fairly certain that John Wilkes..also made a journey to the Western Islands of Scotland.

f. *Western Front*, the front in Belgium and northern France in the wars of 1914–18 and 1939–45.

[**1914** *Parl. Deb. Written Answers* (*Commons*) 12 Nov. 167 The British casualties in the Western area of the war up to 31st October are, approximately, 57,000. **1914** M. HANKEY *Memo.* 28 Dec. in M. Gilbert *Winston S. Churchill* (1972) III. Compan. I. 337 The remarkable deadlock which has occurred in the western theatre of war.] **1914** LLOYD GEORGE *Memo.* 31 Dec. in *Ibid.* 352 These objects cannot be accomplished by attacks on the Western Front. **1915** *Times* 7 Jan. 9/6 Lord Kitchener..explained that the operations on the Western front have for some time resolved themselves into a state of siege warfare. **1915** A. BENNETT (*title*) Over there: war scenes on the Western Front. **1917** *Weekly Dispatch* 3 June 1/3 (*heading*) Mystery of the Western Front. **1939** *War Weekly* 3 Nov. 35/1 The incalculable factor on the Western Front is the mind of Hitler. **1983** P. A. CROWL *Intelligent Traveller's Guide Historic Britain* x. 502 What was lost were thirty-six Czech divisions delivered to Hitler free of charge at Munich plus a greatly improved German position on her western front.

g. *Western American*: = *general American* s.v. *GENERAL *a.* 2 a.

1919 G. P. KRAPP *Pronunc. of Standard Eng. in Amer.* 147 If your own speech is of the Eastern American type, transcribe a passage illustrating it into Western American speech. **1925** —— *Eng. Lang. in Amer.* II. i. 30 The consonant *r* is more distinctly sounded in northern British and Western American. **1936** MENCKEN *Amer. Lang.* (ed. 4) vii. 358 The chief characters of Western, or General American and of New England and Southern American have been indicated. **1959** L. M. MYERS *Guide to Amer. Eng.* (ed. 2) ii. 30 Three major dialect areas have long been recognised in American English—New England, Western or General American, and Southern. Linguistic geographers now prefer the terms Northern, Midland, and Southern.

h. *Western European Union*, an association formed in 1955 from the former Western Union, with the addition of Italy and (West) Germany, in order to coordinate defence and promote cooperation in economic matters and (until 1960) in social and cultural ones; abbrev. W.E.U. s.v. *W 3; *Western Union*, an association of West European nations (Belgium, France, Luxembourg, the Netherlands, and the United Kingdom) which was formed in 1948 for purposes of military and economic cooperation and became the Western European Union in 1955.

1948 E. BEVIN in *Hansard Commons* 22 Jan. 390 The European Recovery Programme brought all this to a head, and made us all face up to the problem of the future organisation. We did not press the Western Union..in the hope that when we got the German and Austrian peace settlements, agreement between the Four Powers would close the breach between East and West. **1950** *Times* 22 Aug. 4/6 About 50 squadrons of fighters and bombers will take part in the first Western Union air defence exercise. **1954** *Times* 11 Nov. 8/7 Some of the preparations for bringing the Western European Union into existence have been made by a committee in London. **1973** B. COCKS *European Parliament* viii. 67 The Assembly of the international organisation known as Western European Union has a close relationship with the Council of Europe since its entire membership is composed of the Representatives from the seven WEU countries to the Consultative Assembly. **1974** P. GORE-BOOTH *With Great Truth & Respect* 351 Mr Brown has recounted the strategem he employed at a Ministerial Western Union meeting to ensure that the application was formally presented in a way that could not run into procedural objections. **1976** J. WHEELER-BENNETT *Friends, Enemies & Sovereigns* iv. 125 He..expressed considerable concern as to what the effect would be of Germany's rearmament in accordance with her membership of the European Defence Community (or, as it turned out to be, the Western European Union).

4. a. In mod. use also *spec.* (*a*) applied to the countries of western Europe that opposed Germany in the wars of 1914–18 and 1939–45; (*b*) of, pertaining to, or designating the non-Communist states of Europe and America.

(*a*) **1914** *Times* 23 Nov. 9/2 The appearance of Turkey as the ally of Germany and Austria against the Western Powers and Russia necessarily put an end to negotiations between Sofia and Constantinople. **1917** I. F. MARCOSSON *Rebirth of Russia* viii. 141 German imperialism, after having defeated our Western Allies, will turn against us the whole power of its arms. **1938** E. AMBLER *Cause for Alarm* viii. 132 The Nazis and the Fascisti..agreed to present a united front to the Western powers. **1940** *Economist* 13 Jan. 51/2 The outbreak of open hostilities between the U.S.S.R. and the Western Powers. **1974** *Encycl. Brit. Macropædia* XIX. 958/1 The Russian Revolution of March..1917 dismayed the western Allies and delighted the Central Powers. *Ibid.* 1006/1 The western Allies' 'Operation Overlord'..took place on June 6, 1944.

(*b*) **1918** *Times* 4 June 5/2 The greatest question in the world to-day is whether Russia is to be abandoned, or whether she is to be saved; whether Western ideals are to prevail in the country whose potential power will be the balance in history. **1947** *Ann. Reg. 1946* 218 A pointed appeal to the Russian people to regard their two Western Allies [*sc.* Great Britain and the United States] as the only blot on the Soviet horizon. *Ibid.* 219 The need [of Russia] for an American loan and the consequent recognition of the desirability of making some concessions to the Western Powers. **1956** *B.B.C. Handbk. 1957* 60 The jamming..of certain language transmissions of the BBC and other Western Bloc broadcasters. **1959** *Daily Tel.* 18 Dec. 1 Expectations of some progress in Western politics rose in Paris to-night on the eve of the 'Western Summit' meetings which will take place here this weekend. **1982** *Ann. Reg. 1981* 67 The fourth [proposal] called on the Soviet Union to accept Western plans for reducing the risks of surprise attack.

e. *western man* (also with either one or two initial capitals): man as shaped by the culture and civilization of Western Europe and North America.

1909 CHESTERTON *Orthodoxy* i. 14 An active and

imaginative life, ..a life such as western man at any rate always seems to have desired. **1927** WYNDHAM LEWIS (*title*) Time and western man. **1962** E. CLEAVER in A. Dundes *Mother Wit* (1973) 10/2 The traditional judgments which Western Man has made..are now..the cause of very serious maladjustments in our society and..the world at large. **1970** C. C. O'BRIEN *Camus* i. 27 The role often claimed for Camus, as an expression of the conscience of Western man. **1981** *Times Lit. Suppl.* 20 Mar. 321/2 Edward Bond's cloudy gropings towards a view of Western man.

5. a. (Earlier example.)

1794 T. COOPER *Some Information respecting Amer.* 8 These parts..furnish yearly a very considerable number of emigrants to the middle and western states.

b. (Earlier examples.) *western equine encephalitis* or *encephalomyelitis*, a mosquito-borne viral encephalitis in the U.S., South America, and eastern Europe that affects chiefly horses but also people and is sometimes fatal, esp. to children; *western roll* (Athletics), a method of high-jumping in which the athlete jumps from the inside foot, swings up the other leg, and rolls across the bar on his side; *Western saddle* (see quot. 1946); *western sandwich* (N. Amer.), a sandwich in which the filling is an omelette containing onion and ham.

1703 in *Mass. Hist. Soc. Coll.* (1838) 3rd Ser. VII. 61 Letters from Piscataqua come in the Western mail. **1784** G. WASHINGTON *Diary* 4 Oct. (1925) II. 326 The Western Settlers—from my own observation—stand as it were on a pivot. **1929** G. M. BUTLER *Mod. Athletics* viii. 108 (*caption*) The 'western roll'. **1933** *Proc. Soc. Exper. Biol. & Med.* XXXI. 217 (*heading*) A serological difference between Eastern and Western Equine Encephalomyelitis virus. **1946** M. C. SELF *Horseman's Encycl.* 346 The Western or cowboy saddle which is similar to that used..in all countries where men spend long hours in the saddle..is characterized by its deep seat, high cantle and pommel... The stirrups are set about midway and the cowboy rides with an almost straight leg. **1959** M. CALLAGHAN in R. Weaver *Canad. Short Stories* (1968) 2nd Ser. 8 He thought of having a western sandwich in the café across the road from the hotel. **1959** *Jrnl. Infectious Dis.* CV. 295 A similar situation may exist with respect to western equine encephalitis infection in swine. **1961** *Canad. Jrnl. Microbiol.* VII. 295 Western equine encephalitis has been a disease of public health importance in Saskatchewan since it was first recognized in 1935. **1964** Western roll [see *SCISSORS *sb. pl.* 2 b]. **1964** M. MCLUHAN *Understanding Media* (1967) xxxi. 341 The varied and rough textures of Western saddles, clothes, hides. **1973** D. HUGHES *Along Side Road* xx. 155 He stopped to have a western sandwich and a cup of tea. **1976** *Western Mail* (Cardiff) 27 Nov. (Advt.), Just arrived from America: New selection of Western saddles. **1978** G. WRIGHT *Illustr. Handbk. Sporting Terms* 23/3 The western roll is rarely practised today, the favoured methods being the straddle and the flop. **1983** *Amer. Rev. Respiratory Dis.* CXXVII. 132/3 We report here a patient with western equine encephalitis who developed hypoventilation. **1983** *Amer. Jrnl. Trop. Med. & Hygiene* XXXII. 1130 *Culex tarsalis* was a less competent vector of western equine encephalomyelitis (WEE) virus after 2–3 weeks' extrinsic incubation at 32°C than after incubation at 18° or 25°C.

c. *western hemlock*, a conifer, *Tsuga heterophylla*, native to the western coast of North America; also, its light brown timber; *western red cedar*, a large columnar conifer, *Thuja plicata*, native to western North America; also its reddish-brown timber; *western white pine*, a pine with grey-green needles, *Pinus monticola*, native to high ground in western North America; *western yellow pine* = *PONDEROSA.

1869 *Amer. Naturalist* III. 410 Western White Pine... I found scattered trees of this beautiful species on the highest parts of the Rocky Mountains. **1886** J. MACOUN *Catal. Canad. Plants* I. 461 *J[uniperus] occidentalis*, Hook. Western Red Cedar... I place all our western 'red cedar' under this species. *Ibid.* 471 *T[suga] Mertensiana*, Carr. Western Hemlock... In the Selkirk Mountains it is a tall, beautiful tree, over 150 feet high. **1901** *World's Work* July 888/2 The wood of the western yellow pine..is used by them for mine timbers. **1905** *Bull. Bureau of Forestry* (U.S. Dept. Agric.) LXVI. 33 The rock pine, western red cedar,..have, without doubt, come down from the Rocky Mountains. **1908** N. L. BRITTON *N. Amer. Trees* 67 Western Hemlock..grows in rich, moist soil. **1923** Western yellow pine [see *heavy-wooded pine* s.v. *HEAVY *a.*[1] 30]. **1957** *Handbk. of Softwoods* (Forest Products Res. Lab.) 22 Consignments of western hemlock frequently contain a percentage of fir. **1963** Western hemlock [see *KAPUR]. **1969** Western red cedar [see *RED CEDAR a]. **1977** *Weekly Times* (Melbourne) 19 Jan. 4/1 (Advt.), The following is included in your kit: Council plans and specifications, flooring,..glazed Western Red Cedar windows, [etc.]. **1978** W. H. HARLOW et al. *Textbk. Dendrology* (ed. 6) 66 Western white pine was first observed along the banks of the Columbia and Spokane Rivers in 1831.

d. (Also with capital initial.) Applied to the films and novels called 'westerns' (see sense B. 4 below). orig. *U.S.*

[**1909** *Moving Picture World* 6 Nov. 638 The success of their Western series of last year was abundantly satisfying and added greatly to the reputation of the firm. *Ibid.*, Western subjects, in which the wild and woolly plays the leading part, have won immense popularity.] **1910** *Ibid.* 21 May 834/1 It is almost impossible to criticize these Wild Western films, because cowboys are likely to do almost anything. **1913** *Moving Picture Ann. 1912* 29 Many film makers still turn out great quantitites of so-called Western and Indian pictures. **1931** *Ann. Reg. 1930* 49 Garry [*sic*] Cooper has revived the popularity of Western pictures. **1959** *News Chron.* 5 Aug. 6/4 Many Western novels are abominably written. **1967** M. ARGYLE *Psychol. Interpersonal Behaviour* i. 28 An indirect form of aggression will occur, which may consist of..mere aggression in fantasy, such as watching western films or wrestling matches. **1974** *Encycl. Brit. Micropædia* X. 624/2 The western film can be dated from *The Great Train Robbery* (1905).

9. *Comb.* (chiefly in sense 4 a), as *western-educated, -European, -style, -trained, -type* adjs.

1933 N. WALN *House of Exile* I. vi. 96 A Western educated woman doctor. **1974** M. FIDO *R. Kipling* 50/2 Kipling['s]..generation made 'Bengali' almost a synonym for 'western-educated Indian', and always used the word with a touch of contempt. **1949** M. MEAD *Male & Female* vi. 132 Almost any Balinese male placed in a series of western-European males would look 'feminine'. **1969** 'E. LATHEN' *When in Greece* ii. 17 Greece..was an associate in the Common Market, which would bring every Western European banker into the picture. **1895** *Montgomery Ward Catal.* Spring & Summer 330/1 Three-Horn Western Style Side Saddle. **1953** *Archit. Rev.* CXIV. 255/2 Peking of course offers a complete contrast to such cities as Shanghai where large areas have been covered with western-style multi-storey buildings. **1977** P. JOHNSON *Enemies of Society* xi. 160 The abolition of western-style academic research, and the substitution of acupuncture for standard medical practice. **1962** E. SNOW *Other Side of River* (1963) xlii. 309 Since 1958 all Western-trained doctors have been required to devote at least six months to the study of Chinese medicine. **1958** *Times* 13 Aug. 12/4 In West Africa they hold to the traditional styles, though the more sophisticated often keep western-type frocks in their wardrobe.

B. *sb.* **4.** (Also with capital initial.) A film or novel belonging to a distinct genre in which life in the American West in the nineteenth century is portrayed, usu. through idealized stock situations and characters, esp. cattle-men (cowboys) and gun-fights. Cf. sense A. 5 d above. orig. *U.S.*

1912 *Moving Picture World* 27 July 306 (Advt.), 'The Fight at The Mill'... A powerful Western, distinctly unusual among typical 'Westerns' containing a beautiful story and a dashing Indian battle that will interest and instruct. **1915** [see *SUPE]. **1918** *Wells Fargo Messenger* VI. 178/1 What would the good old 'Western' be without the historic Wells Fargo stage coach and its treasure box? **1923** *Time* 11 June 15/1 Love stories are their first choice, comedies second, society life as known to the De Mille brothers third, and then come the Westerns. **1927** *Sat. Rev. Lit.* 15 Oct. 232 (Advt.), The Gun-Slinger by George M. Johnson. A Western with the kick of a .45. **1930** *Publishers' Weekly* 8 Feb. 689 (Advt.), Five sure-shot Westerns... Salesmen and booksellers everywhere report to us a keen and growing demand for this type of story. **1954** E. E. CUMMINGS *Let.* 9 Mar. (1969) 227 'William S. Hart' was a vastly popular..hero of our early Westerns: i.e. melodramatic movies featuring terrific battles between noble & wicked hardriding sharpshooting super cowboys. **1958** *Listener* 9 Jan. 60/1 Twenty-five per cent of the best television time is still given over to 'Westerns'. **1962** L. DEIGHTON *Ipcress File* xviii. 110 On the army table were a few books; German grammar..two paperback westerns. **1977** B. PYM *Quartet in Autumn* xviii. 171 Watching a Western on the other channel.

C. *adv. Equestrianism.* In the manner of a cowboy; in a relaxed style with a deep-seated saddle and almost straight legs.

1972 *Country Life* 5 Oct. 817/1 In a year Lady Sarah was so used to riding Western that she found it almost strange to revert to English for hunting. **1980** *Times* 28 June 13/7 Riding western is not like riding Badminton style.

westerner. Add: **2.** (Earlier example.)

1880 W. JAMES in *Atlantic Monthly* Oct. 449/2 *Not* to fall back on the gods, where a proximate principle may be found, has with us Westerners long since become the sign of an efficient..intellect.

4. *Hist.* An advocate of or believer in the concentration of forces on the Western Front during the war of 1914–18.

1928 F. B. MAURICE *Rawlinson of Trent* p. xi, Upon the problems of the Great War, Rawlinson has naturally much light to throw. Who was right, the Easterner or the Westerner? **1931** W. S. CHURCHILL *World Crisis* VI. xix. 282 Falkenhayn was a convinced and inveterate 'Westerner'. **1960** *Times Lit. Suppl.* 20 May 318/3 Captain Falls is a firm 'Westerner' although he believes that the Dardanelles enterprise was 'a well-inspired venture'. **1977** G. H. CASSAR *Kitchener* xiv. 295 Kitchener's difficulties were exacerbated by the two prevailing schools of strategical thought, the Easterners and the Westerners.

5. a. *Hist.* A 19th-century Russian who adopted or advocated Western attitudes and behaviour.

1949 I. DEUTSCHER *Stalin* vi. 207 But Lenin remained a 'Westerner' in several senses. **1950** E. H. CARR *Bolshevik Revolution* I. i. 8 The westerners held that it was the destiny of Russia, as a backward country, to learn from the west.

b. One belonging to the non-Communist West.

1964 M. MCLUHAN *Understanding Media* (1967) xxi. 222 Are we to suppose that this kind of media illiteracy is characteristic only of Westerners, and that Russians know how to correct the bias of the medium? **1975** P. THEROUX *Great Railway Bazaar* xxx. 330, I was now the only Westener on the train.

westernism. 1. (Earlier example.)

1838 *Knickerbocker* XI. 447, I now recollect but few specimens of Jack's *westernisms*, and these I think were not his best.

westernize, *v.* Add: **b.** *intr.* To become western in character. *rare.*

1903 L. F. WARD *Pure Sociol.* 33 Some of the nations of the East, notably Japan, are rapidly westernizing.

Hence **we·sternizer,** one who makes a country or culture more Western.

1935 *Times Lit. Suppl.* 2 May 287/2 French and English incursions..entered [Afghanistan] from the East, and..carried Dravidian ideas with them against that tide of Westernizers of whom Alexander was one of the earliest. **1958** *Listener* 27 Nov. 864/2 Arab Westernizers. **1964** *Economist* 13 June 1251/2 Ch'en Tu-hsiu was a westerniser. **1976** *Times Lit. Suppl.* 23 Apr. 490/3 The dispute between Slavophiles and Westernizers, originally a literary controversy, spawned a vast secondary literature, first in Russia and then in the wider world.

westernly, *adv.* Restrict † *Obs.* to sense in Dict. and add: **2.** In a Western manner.

1588 [see KENTISHLY *adv.*]. **1976** M. H. KINGSTON *Woman Warrior* (1977) 59 The one [Chinese] faculty member in the western suit smiles westernly. **1982** C. THOMAS *Jade Tiger* iii. 59 A stylised, dignified, almost Westernly-handsome Chinese. **1983** *Christian Science Monitor* 15 Feb. 12/1 Dressing more stylishly—and often, more Westernly—is a preoccupation... Young Russians pass quick and critical judgement on the clothes of their peers.

westernness (we·stəɹnˌnés). Also with capital initial. [f. WESTERN *a.* + -NESS.] The quality of belonging to a Western country or culture, or having Western attitudes and ideas.

1953 *Essays in Crit.* III. 132 We become aware..in the work of Conrad of the co-existence of two 'moralities': that derived from a simple tradition of 'Westernness'..and that derived from an awareness of the force..of '*égoïsme*' in a decaying order. **1977** P. LASLETT *Family Life & Illicit Love in Earlier Generations* i. 13 Westernness or any other cultural attribute.

westerveldite (we·stəɹveldəit). *Min.* [f. the name of Jan *Westerveld* (1905–62), Dutch geologist + -ITE[1].] An orthorhombic arsenide of iron or iron and nickel (see quot. 1972).

1972 I. S. OEN et al. in *Amer. Mineralogist* LVII. 354 A Co-bearing nickel-rich iron monoarsenide corresponding in composition and structure to a Ni-rich member of the orthorhombic FeAs-(Fe,Ni)As solid solution series of synthetic alloys occurs in chromite-niccolite ores from La Gallega, Spain. The name westerveldite is proposed for minerals in this solid solution series. **1977** *Neues Jahrb. f. Mineral. Abhandlungen* CXXX. 209 Recently westerveldite with the ideal composition FeAs was found at four localities within the Ilímaussaq alkaline intrusion in South Greenland.

West Highland. Used *attrib.* and *absol.* to designate animals associated with the West Highlands of Scotland, as (*a*) a breed of cattle also called kyloes (see KYLOE); (*b*) a kind of terrier (see *POLTALLOCH).

1875 *Encycl. Brit.* I. 389/1 The Kyloes or West Highland cattle are the most prominent of this group [*sc.* mountain breeds]. **1906** *Our Dogs* 15 Sept. 548/1 White West Highland Terriers.—Here truly may be written there is ample room for improvement. **1910** 'SAKI' *Reginald in Russia* 28 A lady..was expressing to me..her interest in West Highland terriers. **1950** [see *POLTALLOCH]. **1953** A. FRASER *Beef Cattle Husbandry* ix. 122 This breed, sometimes called the 'West Highland' or 'Kyloe', is descended from the native breed of the Scottish highlands. **1968** P. DICKINSON *Skin Deep* ix. 174 She's a nice lass, Roedean, breeds West Highlands down at Sonning. **1976** *Daily Record* (Glasgow) 4 Dec. 25/3 (Advt.), West Highland pups..suitable for Christmas. **1978** *Country Life* 24 Aug. 489/3 The White West Highland was let out of the front door.

So **West Highlander,** a kyloe.

1832 *Chambers's Edin. Jrnl.* I. 70/2 On many farms I observed a variety..resembling the heavy class of our West Highlanders. **1882** [see KYLOE]. **1979** *Country Life* 22 Nov. 1950/1 No breed of cattle more perfectly graces its native habitat than the West Highlander.

westie (we·sti). Also **westy.** [f. WEST *a.* + -IE, -Y[6].] A West Highland white terrier.

1959 *Observer* 1 Feb. 12 The 'Westie' is one of the few terriers to maintain its position. **1978** *Country Life* 24 Aug. 489/3 The Westy returned and sat down. **1979** *Daily Mail* 26 Oct. 25/4 Mr Definitely-Disgusting..[is] particularly partial to 'Westies' as he calls West Highlands.

West Indian, *sb.* and *a.* Add: Also (as one word) **Westindian. 1.** *sb.* **c.** A person of West Indian ancestry.

1928 *Times* 25 June 5/1 The out-cricket of the West Indians on Saturday indicates that the compliment, which has been paid to them, has not been prematurely offered. **1957** *Times* 18 Feb. 4/7 Statistics show that more than 26,000 West Indians migrated to Britain during 1956. **1961** *Ann. Reg. 1960* 122 In his message to West Indians on Christmas Day the Prime Minister of the Federation, Sir Grantly Adams, spoke of West Indian unity. **1971** *Observer* 21 Feb. 5/1 The Scots West Indian... Born in Edinburgh, he has Jamaican blood from his father's side. **1973** *Montserrat Mirror* 23 Mar. 5/2 Trinidad is the home of calypso but this form of music belongs to all

Westindians. **1981** *Westindian World* 31 July 2/3 My findings demolished a myth about Westindians.

Hence **West Indianness**, West Indian quality or character.

1953 *Caribbean Q.* III. III. 181 We are..still trying to discover what..makes us characteristically West Indian, or if you like, what is the essence of our West Indianness. **1972** Ramchand & Gray *West Indian Poetry* 89 The West Indian poet's confidence about his West Indian-ness.

Westinghouse (we·stiŋhaus). The name of George *Westinghouse* (1846–1914), U.S. inventor and manufacturer, used *attrib.* and *absol.* to designate a kind of air brake he invented in 1868 for use on railway trains, operated by compressed air on a fail-safe principle.

a **1877** Knight *Dict. Mech.* I. 356/1 The Westinghouse Atmospheric Brake..was patented in 1869, and has been adopted on many railway lines in the United States and Europe. **1886** *Encycl. Brit.* XX. 248/2 The Westinghouse brake was greatly in advance of previously existing systems. **1933** *Times Lit. Suppl.* 2 Nov. 738/3 Many will regret the gradual abandonment of the Westinghouse brake on steam-hauled trains. **1949** D. M. Davin *Roads from Home* I. v. 75, I jammed on the Westinghouse, saying to myself I'd look a fine bloody fool if I'd stopped the train for nothing. **1967** G. F. Fiennes *I tried to run a Railway* iv. 40 Only the Stratford District had kept the Westinghouse brake.

Hence **Westinghou·sian** *a.* (*fig. nonce-use*).

1948 V. Nabokov in *New Yorker* 31 July 20/1 The train stopped with a long-drawn Westinghousian sigh.

Westmark (we·st-, ‖ ve·stmāɹk). Also **westmark, west mark.** [Ger., f. *west* West *sb.*[1] + *mark* Mark *sb.*[2] 2 c.] The currency unit of West (formerly western) Germany, as distinguished from the *Ostmark of East Germany.

1948 *Times* 2 Sept. 4/6 In view of the report that the east-mark is going to be recognized Berliners have been getting rid of the west-mark. **1959** [see *Ostmark]. **1964** L. Deighton *Funeral in Berlin* v. 31 'How much money are you carrying?' I spread the few Westmarks and English pounds on the desk. **1980** A. Scholefield *Berlin Blind* iii. 129, I have postcards in the bus which you may buy with Westmarks. **1980** *Times Lit. Suppl.* 31 Oct. 1230/3 In Germany..the Bundesrepublik offers 10,000 west-marks as the Thomas Mann prize, and the DDR 18,000 east-marks for the Heinrich Mann.

Westminster. Add: **2.** The Palace of Westminster; hence, Parliament, of which the Palace is the seat. Freq. *attrib.*

The present Palace of Westminster (built 1840–67) is more commonly known as the Houses of Parliament.

1807 *Morning Chron.* 13 Apr. 3/2 The Westminster Company of Independent Performers being lately dissolved. **1869** Trollope *Phineas Finn* II. lxxiv. 306 The girl whom he loved..better even than Westminster and Downing Street. **1918** G. Frankau *One of Them* xvii. 127 What art thou, Westminister? A caucused lobby? An oratorial-acrobatic stadium..? Or art indeed the Common Weal's palladium? **1961** S. A. de Smith in *Jrnl. Commonwealth Political Stud.* I. 3 In its narrow sense the Westminster Model can be said to mean a constitutional system in which the head of state is not the effective head of government; [etc.]. **1972** *Guardian* 11 July 13/8 It is sometimes suggested that what de Gaulle did for France in Algeria, Westminster should do for Britain in Ulster. **1977** *Time* 27 June 20/1 One of the most frequently heard catch phrases has to do with moving away from the 'Westminster system' of parliamentary representation toward some form of presidential or federal system.

b. *Westminster chimes* or *quarters*: the pattern of chimes struck at successive quarters by Big Ben in the Palace of Westminster, and used for other clocks and (more recently) door chimes; it uses four bells struck in five different four-note sequences, each of which occurs twice in the course of an hour.

1860 E. B. Denison *Rudimentary Treat. Clocks* (ed. 4) p. vii, Cambridge and Westminster chimes. *Ibid.* 191 A very grand G hour bell to the BAGD bells of the peel, on which the Cambridge and Westminster quarters might then be struck. **1923** W. I. Milham *Time & Timekeepers* xvii. 298 To make and place a clock.. striking the hours and Westminster quarters on five bells. **1924** *Eng. Clocks & Watches* (Horol. Jrnl.) 42 The clock can be fitted with Whittington and Westminster Chimes. **1962** V. Nabokov *Pale Fire* 43 Four hundred thousand times The tall clock with the hoarse Westminster chimes Has marked our common hour. **1967** 'R. Simons' *Taxed to Death* iv. 63 When Wace pressed the bell-button they heard Westminster chimes ringing in the hall. **1980** *New Grove Dict. Mus.* IV. 244/2 The best known of all clock chimes, the Westminster Quarters.., was derived from a quatrain in Handel's *Messiah*. In 1794 William Crotch wrote four variations on the fifth and sixth bars of 'I know that my Redeemer liveth'..for the new Cambridge University clock in Great St Mary's Church. They were accepted, and in 1845 were copied on the Royal Exchange clock, London. **1981** *Country Life* 12 Feb. 362 (Advt.), A superb clock..the three chimes, Westminster, Whittington and Winchester, obtainable at will.

West Nile. *Med.* [f. West *a.* + name of the river *Nile*.] Used *attrib.* to designate a mosquito-borne virus and the disease it causes, usu. a mild fever but sometimes a fatal encephalitis.

1940 K. C. Smithburn et al. in *Amer. Jrnl. Tropical Med.* XX. 471 The purpose of this paper is to report the isolation of one such [infective] agent, which we call the West Nile virus, and to describe some of its properties. **1955** *Sci. Amer.* Mar. 64/3 He concluded that West Nile fever was predominantly a disease of childhood. **1961** M. Hynes *Med. Bacteriol.* (ed. 7) xxv. 392 Antigenically related viruses have a similar ecology..in central Africa (West Nile encephalitis). **1983** *Oxf. Textbk. Med.* I. v. 104/2 Recognizable disease due to West Nile virus infection has been observed in Israel... No vaccine is yet available.

West of England. Also with hyphens. The name of a region of England, used *attrib.* and *absol.* to designate high-quality woollen broadcloth for which it has long been noted.

1843 *Penny Cycl.* XXVII. 555/2 In the West of England..each workman confines himself exclusively to a particular branch of the manufacture; and this has been supposed to have led to the excellence of the West of England cloth. **1882** *Queen* 23 Dec. (Advt.), Homespuns, Tweeds,..West of England cloths. **1936** 'N. Blake' *Thou Shell of Death* i. 8 His waistcoat..[of] West-of-England cloth. **1972** E. Kerridge in J. G. Jenkins *Wool Textile Industry in Gt. Brit.* 33/1 The same [*sc.* a more intensive use of capital and skilled labour] was true to a lesser extent..of the new superfine West of Englands. **1976** F. Greenland *Misericordia Drop* I. vii. 49 He wore ..grey West-of-England flannels.

Weston (we·stən). The name of Edward *Weston* (1850–1936) English-born electrical engineer, used *attrib.* **a.** In *Electr.*, designating a primary cell with electrodes of mercury and of cadmium amalgam and electrolyte of cadmium sulphate, used as a standard voltage source for calibrating electrical instruments.

1901 [see *metastability]. **1963** G. L. Pickard *Descriptive Physical Oceanogr.* vi. 94 The Weston cell has a limited sensitivity. **1972** *Physics Bull.* Jan. 40/2 The Bureau is..interested in the Josephson effect for possible use in electrical standards, although for the moment the standard Weston cell is preferred for convenience.

b. In *Photogr.*, designating an obsolescent system of film speeds based on exposure meters made by the Weston Electrical Instrument Company or its successors.

1940 *Chambers's Techn. Dict.* 905/2 Weston film-speed. **1950** W. F. Berg *Exposure* 167 The introduction of Weston speed figures was of considerable importance. **1963** Jerrard & McNeill *Dict. Sci. Units* 105 The Weston number, the British Standards Institute speed number and the American Standards Association system also indicate the speed of the emulsion at its maximum sensitivity.

Westphalian, *a.* and *sb.* For **a, b** read **A, B** and add: **A.** *adj.* **2.** *Geol.* [ad. F. *westphalien* (A. de Lapparent *Traité de Géologie* (ed. 3, 1893) 819).] Of or belonging to a stratigraphic division of the Upper Carboniferous in Europe, above the Namurian and below the Stephanian. Also *absol.*

1901 [see *Stephanian *a.*]. **1915** C. Schuchert *Text-bk. Geol.* II. xl. 729 The Coal Measures formation is again divided into two series, the earlier half, or Middle Carboniferous, being widely known as the Westphalian.. when coal bearing. **1969** Bennison & Wright *Geol. Hist. Brit. Isles* ix. 221 In Britain the greater part of the Coal Measures belongs to the Westphalian. **1976** *Nature* 22 July 277/1 The age of this late retrogression..is synchronous with the intrusion of younger Variscan granites, a major break in sedimentation and the main phase of Hercynian folding (Sudetic phase: Westphalian in age).

west side. Add: **c.** Also **West Side.** That district of New York City which lies on the west side of Manhattan. Also *attrib. U.S.*

1858 *Harper's Mag.* July 283/2 As our friend entered the door a well-known 'West side' operator made his bid. **1903** *Ibid.* July 213 The abysmal craving of New Yorkers —West Side or East Side—is for friends. **1958** A. Laurents (*title of play*) West Side story. **1976** Botham & Donnelly *Valentino* iii. 25 He left the West Side and moved into a stable garret adjoining the home of millionaire Cornelius Bliss. **1981** J. Valin *Dead Letter* xix. 182 That region of worn houses..that is the westside ghetto.

West Sider. *U.S.* [-er[1].] A resident of Manhattan's West Side.

1903 *N.Y. Even. Post* 14 Nov. 4 The persistence with which the West Siders have followed up this question of the Broadway trees. **1914** G. Atherton *Perch of Devil* I. 2 Ida, forced..to accept employment with a fashionable dressmaker and consumed with envy of the 'West Siders' whose measurements she took. **1980** *N.Y. Times* 21 July A-8/2 Because the West Sider usually has so much money and time tied up in his lawn, plants and trees..he finds himself in a constant struggle to keep growing things from turning brown.

west wind, west-wind. Add: **b.** (Usu. with capital initials.) One of the four 'tiles' or discs called winds in the game of mah-jong; the player who takes this tile at the beginning of the game and sits opposite East Wind, or a player who succeeds him in being so designated.

1922 R. E. Lindsell *Ma-Cheuk or Mah-Jongg*, 13 East discards a West wind. North..exposes a pair of West winds. **1952** M. Steen *Phoenix Rising* vii. 154 She slid the West Wind on to her ebony rack. **1960** [see *east wind b]. **1976** R. C. Bell *Discovering Mah-jong* 15 The third round is West Wind's round.

westy, var. *westie.

wet, *sb.*[1] Add: **6.** A 'wet' person (see *wet *a.* 15 b); *spec.* a politician with liberal or middle-of-the-road views on controversial issues (often applied to members of the Conservative Party opposed to the monetarist policies of Margaret Thatcher).

1931 F. L. Allen *Only Yesterday* x. 254 The Government putting wood alcohol and other poisons into industrial alcohol to prevent its diversion, and the wets thereupon charging the Government with murder. **1933** D. L. Murray *Eng. Family Robinson* vii. 159 He's quite right... You *are* a wet! Who does pay regularly? **1939** G. Heyer *No Wind of Blame* xvi. 299 He's a regular wet, that chap: doesn't hold with blood sports. **1948** C. Day Lewis *Otterbury Incident* ix. 111 Don't be a wet. We'll get off all right. **1961** C. Willock *Death in Covert* xi. 201 'That wet,' said fford, reverting to a school-boy expression. 'Wet he may be, but he knows about lighters.' **1974** I. Murdoch *Sacred & Profane Love Machine* 76 You've made me into a bloody wet. I'm a fighter and you've made me into a weak person. **1976** S. Barstow *Right True End* III. xii. 180 She likes to throw out these challenges that put me to the test and make me feel a weak-kneed wet. **1980** B. W. Aldiss *Life in West* ii. 42 He's a bit of a wet, but quite a sound art-historian. **1980** *Sunday Tel.* 6 Apr. 9 At least Sir Ian Gilmour and other political wets do not have their hair pulled. **1980** *Times* 7 Apr. 9/1 Mr James Prior, Secretary of State for Employment, is described in one Sunday paper as 'the champion of the Tory wets'. *Ibid.*, Who..are to be counted among the wets? The answer seems to be anybody who crosses the Prime Minister in fashioning a particular policy. **1980** W. Whitelaw in *Observer* 23 Nov. 11, I don't really know what a wet is. **1983** *Age* (Melbourne) 5 Oct. 13 [Of U.K. politics] In contrast to the expansionist, protectionist and welfare-oriented Wets, the Dries stand for small government, economic rationality and individual responsibility.

7. *U.S. slang.* = *wetback* s.v. *wet *a.* 20.

1973 *Daily Tel.* (Colour Suppl.) 16 Feb. 13/1 In the past, unscrupulous employers would employ a 'wet' for a month, then denounce him to the Immigration authorities before pay day. **1979** *Time* 8 Oct. 33/1 A group of 'wets', or 'undocumented workers', as official jargon calls them. Most of the Mexican aliens are poor, frightened and docile people whose only crime is seeking to find work and a better life in the U.S. **1979** G. Swarthout *Skeletons* 104 Why doesn't this [system] detect every wet who puts a toe across the line?

wet, *sb.*[2] Add: **2.** *slang.* Urination, the act of urinating; urine. *rare.*

1925, 1975 [see *wet *v.* 17].

wet, *a.* Add: **2. f.** (Later examples.) Freq. with def. article and also with capital initial. *colloq.* (chiefly *Austral.*).

1908 Mrs. A. Gunn *We of Never-Never* i. 5 He..wired an inane suggestion about waiting till after the Wet. **1934** *Bulletin* (Sydney) 29 Aug. 20/4 In the 'wet' it became a miniature lake at which one cocky's horses were wont to drink. **1941** I. L. Idriess *Great Boomerang* vii. 51 An early and heavy wet would set in that would spill water for a thousand miles south-west. **1968** S. L. Elliott *Rusty Bugles* in E. Hanger *Three Austral. Plays* I. ii. 41 That's what everyone tells me. Wait until you've done a Wet. **1981** P. Carey *Bliss* iii. 135 Each year when the wet ended she found herself looking forward to it again.

4. e. Applied to a removable liner for the cylinder of an internal-combustion engine that has cooling water flowing between it and the cylinder wall.

1935 *Jrnl. R. Aeronaut. Soc.* XXXIX. 470 The four cylinders 63 m/m. bore by 120 m/m. stroke were steel jacketed, wet liners, having four valves per cylinder. **1959** *Motor* 14 Oct. 304/2 Cylinder blocks with individual wet liners of cast iron. **1975** M. J. Nunney *Automotive Engine* iii. 94 Positive sealing arrangements must be made with wet cylinder liners to prevent leakage of coolant into the crankcase. **1981** H. E. Ellinger *Automotive Engines* x. 157/2 Coolant flows around the cylinder sleeve, so this type of sleeve is called a wet sleeve.

5. d. *to get wet*: to lose one's temper, become angry. *Austral. slang* (? *Obs.*).

1898 *Bulletin* (Sydney) 17 Dec. Red Page, To *get narked* is to lose your temper; also expressed by *getting dead wet*. **1916** C. J. Dennis *Songs of Sentimental Bloke* 42 Romeo gits wet as 'ell. **1945** Baker *Austral. Lang.* 121 A man in a temper is said..*to get wet*.

e. *to get* (someone) *wet*: to gain the upper hand over; to have at one's mercy. *N.Z. slang.*

c **1926** 'Mixer' *Transport Workers' Song Bk.* 29 He skites about in-fighting. Stick to him, Mick; you've got him wet. **1941** *Coast to Coast 1941* 124 'Got you wet, haven't they?' He flung the remark over his shoulder as he went over to his bed. **1945** F. Sargeson *When Wind Blows* vi. 40 Now we've got 'em wet.

f. Of those activities of intelligence organizations, esp. of the K.G.B., that involve assassination. *slang.*

1972 A. Price *Col. Butler's Wolf* vi. 58 The Russian slang for Spetsburo Thirteen was *Mokryye Dela*—'The department of wet affairs'..and to get wet was the feared, inevitable fate of traitors pursued by the special bureau. **1975** J. GRADY *Shadow of Condor* ii. 47 'The courier made other mistakes... It was a wet affair.'.. Ryzhov like to use the old KGB liquid euphemism for executions. **1980** J. GARDNER *Garden of Weapons* II. vii. 191 He had seen men killed: and killed them himself: he had directed 'wet operations', as they used to be called.

15. b. Inept, ineffectual, effete; also as quasi-*adv.* and in comb. *wet fish*, a wet individual, a 'drip'. Also *spec.* in *Politics* (see quots. 1981 and 1983). Cf. *WET *sb.*[1] 6.

1916 'TAFFRAIL' *Pincher Martin* ii. 27 I'll give yer a clip 'longside the ear'ole if you ain't careful. Don't act so wet. **1924** P. MARKS *Plastic Age* 94 They attended a performance of Shaw's 'Candida' given by the Dramatic Society and voted it a 'wet' show. *Ibid.* 192 A man is wet if he isn't a 'regular guy'; he is wet if he isn't 'smooth'; he is wet if he has intellectual interests..; and he is wet.. if he is utterly stupid. **1938** E. BOWEN *Death of Heart* II. iv. 239 Cecil is so wet! Coming early like that, then sticking round like that. **1944** A. CHRISTIE *Towards Zero* 86 Audrey marry that wet fish? She's a lot too good for that. **1963** Wet fish [see *MOOSE[1] c]. **1969** K. AMIS *Green Man* iv. 180 The Jesus of the Gospels can be a bit of a wet liberal at times. **1973** P. O'DONNELL *Silver Mistress* iv. 74 Don't talk wet, Jan. There's nothing you could do. **1980** *Times Lit. Suppl.* 28 Nov. 1355/2 The contrast between the splendid façade and the rather wet interior of the man [*sc.* Havelock Ellis], who was kind and gentle and distinguished, but also distressingly absent, indifferent and faint.

1981 *Observer* 26 July 12/3 The term 'Wet' was originally used by Mrs Thatcher, who meant it in the old sense of 'soppy', as in 'What do you mean the unions won't like it, Jim? Don't be so wet.' It meant feeble, liable to take the easy option, lacking intellectual and political hardness. Like so many insults, it was gleefully adopted by its victims, and so came by its present meaning of liberal, leftish, anti-ideological. **1982** *Listener* 23/30 Dec. 6/3 In considering the promotion of wet (or wettish) Ministers, she will tell herself that Pope was right. **1983** *Age* (Melbourne) 5 Oct. 13 Britain's Tory Prime Minister, Mrs Margaret Thatcher, began this vogue terminology by contemptuously dismissing dewy-eyed dissenters from her arid Right-wing policies as 'wet'.

c. *all wet*: mistaken, completely wrong. orig. and chiefly *U.S.*

1923 *N.Y. Times* 9 Sept. VII. 2/1 *All wet*, all wrong. **1931** *Kansas City Times* 29 Aug., Alfalfa Bill Murray may be 'all wet' in his state-line bridge and oil production controversies. **1940** G. ADE *Let.* 5 June (1973) 221 Regarding the Rotary Clubs, I..am an honorary member. I think the organization is alright and that Sinclair Lewis was all wet when he tried to poke fun at the small town booster. **1941** E. B. WHITE *Let.* Summer (1976) 216, I haven't had much time to think things over and I am probably all wet on a lot of things in here. **1951** A. BARON *Rosie Hogarth* 282 You're all wet if you think I'm giving up that easy.

d. *wet behind the ears*: see *EAR *sb.*[1] 1 c.

16. c. For *U.S.* read 'orig. and chiefly *U.S.*' (Earlier and later examples.) Hence as quasi-*adv.* in phr. *to go* or vote *wet*. Cf. *DRY *a.* 11 a.

1870, etc. [see *DRY *a.* 11 a]. **1888** *North American* (Philadelphia) 3 Apr. 1/1 Forty-nine counties have voted 'dry', and thirty-three 'wet'... Thirteen of twenty towns went 'dry', and seven 'wet'. **1954** K. AMIS *Lucky Jim* 109 The still recent tradition of a 'wet' Summer Ball. **1974** *Times* 7 Oct. 4/1 Flintshire, Radnorshire, Breconshire.. voted to go wet. *Ibid.* 4/2 That poll ended the curious situation of one inn which straddled on the wet-dry border... The public bar was dry and empty, but the lounge bar was wet and crowded.

d. (Earlier and later examples.)

1888 *Battle Creek* (Michigan) *Weekly Jrnl.* 29 Feb., This is the first great victory for the 'wets'. **1896** [see *DRY *sb.* 5]. **1968** *Daily Tel.* 8 Nov. 1/4 The 'wets' gained three counties..in the Welsh referendum on Sunday drinking.

17. b. Designating chemical tests and analysis involving the use of solvents or other liquids; = HUMID *a.* c; so *wet-chemical* adj. Cf. WAY *sb.*[1] 14 c.

1800, etc. [see sense 17 in Dict.]. **1858** *Phil. Mag.* XVI. 331 This method is particularly adapted..when the substances of this group occur in so small quantities that they are no longer recognizable in the wet way. **1932** F. SODDY *Interpretation of Atom* xv. 253 Almost all the ordinary chemical tests for the common elements, by which they are identified in the ordinary reactions of 'wet' analysis, are not tests for the elements, but for their ions. **1967** *Electronics* 6 Mar. 29 (Advt.), You can be sure of a complete refinery service... Including, under one roof..laboratory facilities for wet chemical analysis and electrolytic methods of analysis. **1973** *Nature* 8 June 365/1 Since the Second World War, physical methods of analysis..have increasingly displaced wet chemistry from the industrial routine analytical laboratory. **1977** *New Scientist* 17 Feb. 384/1 Traditional methods of detecting nitrogen oxides as air pollutants monitor the change in colour of an acid permanganate solution as the oxides are absorbed. These wet-chemical methods.. require relatively large samples of gases.

18*. Of natural gas: containing significant amounts of the vapour of higher hydrocarbons.

1926 *Daily Colonist* (Victoria, B.C.) 18 July 16/7 Wet gas flow of 3,000,000 feet a day was struck at McLeod No. 2 well in Turner Valley last night. **1948** *Petroleum Handbk.* (Shell Petroleum Co. Ltd.) (ed. 3) ix. 154 Gases produced in contact with oil can be either 'dry' or 'wet', depending on the nature of the crude oil and the method of separating the gas from the oil. **1982** *Shell Briefing Service* No. 5. 5/2 LPG is essentially a mixture of propane and butane stored at ambient temperature under moderate pressure. It can be derived from the gas associated with crude oil or from 'wet' natural gas directly at the well.

19. a. *wet-plucked.*

1960 *Farmer & Stockbreeder* 19 Jan. Suppl. 41/3 At slaughter the birds are all..wet-plucked by machine and then eviscerated. **1969** R. ADLARD in R. Blythe *Akenfield* xiv. 234 The feathers are no use because the chickens [in factory farms] are wet-plucked, so there is only a mess.

b. *wetmouthed.*

1951 DYLAN THOMAS *Sel. Lett.* (1966) 352 [Fresh recruits] see before them in the hot moonlight wet-mouthed Persian girls from the bazaar.

20. wetback orig. and chiefly *U.S.*, an illegal immigrant who crosses the Rio Grande from Mexico to the U.S.; also *attrib.* and *transf.*; **wet bar** *N. Amer.*, a bar or counter in a private house from which alcoholic drinks are served; **wet bob**: so **wet bob** *v. intr.*; **wet-bobbing** *vbl. sb.*; **wet diggings** orig. *U.S.*, gold diggings in or near a river or stream; cf. *dry diggings* s.v. *DRY *a.* C. 3; **wet dream**, an erotic dream which causes a man or boy to have an involuntary sexual orgasm during sleep; also *fig.*; **wet-eared** = *wet behind the ears* s.v. *EAR *sb.*[1] 1 c; **wet end**, that end of a paper-making or drying machine into which the wet material is passed; **wet lease** (see quot. 1979); so **wet lease** *v. trans.*, **wet-leased** *ppl. a.*; **wet leg** *slang*, a self-pitying person; **wet look** [LOOK *sb.* 2 f], an appearance of a wet or shiny surface; usu. *attrib.*, esp. of fabrics (see quot. 1968); **wet pack**, a compact waterproof bag which folds or rolls up and is designed for carrying toilet articles; **wet-point** *a.*, of villages, settlements, etc.: having an available water supply; **wet process**, a manufacturing process involving the use of water or other liquid; freq. *attrib.*; **wet rent**, a levy paid to a brewery by a publican in a tied public house in proportion to the amount of beer sold (see also quot. 1907); **wet shave**, a shave (SHAVE *sb.*[2] 2) carried out with the aid of a razor, soap, and water as opp. to a (usu. electric) razor alone; so **wet shaver**, someone who shaves by this method; **wet shaving** *vbl. sb.*; **wet smack** *slang* (chiefly *U.S.*), a spoil-sport; **wet spinning**, (*a*) spinning of natural fibres when they are wet from passage through a water bath; (*b*) spinning of man-made fibres in which the spinneret extrudes the streams of liquid into a coagulating bath; so **wet-spin** *v. trans.*, **wet-spun** *ppl. a.*; **wet strength**, the strength of paper and textiles when wet; **wet suit**, a suit, usu. of rubber, worn by divers, surfers, etc., to protect them from the cold; hence **wet-suited** *a.*; **wet time**, in the building trade, time during which work cannot be carried out owing to bad weather; **wet trade** (see quots.); **wet-weather** *a.*, (*a*) associated with or occurring in rainy weather; (*b*) designed for use in rainy weather; **wet-white**, liquid white theatrical make-up; **wet wing** *Aeronaut.* (see quot. 1969); usu. *attrib.*

1929 *Foreign Affairs* Oct. 101 The peon walks or swims across..and is welcomed by his countrymen here as a 'wet back'. **1972** *Observer* (Colour Suppl.) 28 May 28/1 Last year in California alone, border patrols turned back 27,000 wetbacks (the contemptuous name derives from their practice of swimming the Rio Grande to reach the US). **1978** *N.Y. Times Mag.* 23 July 23/2 Wetbacks (a derogation of Mexicans swimming the Rio Grande to slip into the U.S.) became illegal aliens, and are now referred to as undocumented persons. **1979** *Guardian* 8 June 5/2 Illegal migrants from South China..are getting into Hong Kong..usually swimming the last part of the trip. The total of Chinese 'wetbacks' intercepted..in the first week of June alone came to 3,722. **1982** T. BEATTIE *Diamonds* xii. 100 It might be that wetback job I did... But they can't prove anything. **1968** *Globe & Mail* (Toronto) 15 Jan. 23/6 (Advt.), Panelled family room, games room, wet bar. Real executive home! **1978** R. THOMAS *Chinaman's Chance* xx. 206 Ploughman turned to find Reginald Simms standing by a small wet bar across the room. **1884** J. MONTAGU *Let.* Mar. in Troubridge & Marshall *John Ld. Montagu of Beaulieu* (1930) 31, I have been out wet-bobbing several times and am getting coached. **1901** G. FRANKAU *Eton Echoes* 40 (*heading*) Wet Bobbing. **1926** *Spectator* 3 July 11/1 Any alternative summer game or sport..such as is provided by 'wet-bobbing' at a school like Eton. **1849** J. WYLD *Geogr. & Mineral. Notes* 21 The works are divided into two classes,—Dry Diggings and Wet Diggings. **1862** J. L. C. RICHARDSON *Sk. Otago* 48 See how the wet diggings will pay in the summer time. **1935** E. B. BUCKBEE *Saga Old Tuolumne* 11 He worked ceaselessly throughout the day lifting gold from the 'wet diggings'. **1965** G. J. WILLIAMS *Econ. Geol. N.Z.* vii. 72/1 The conglomerates accumulated on the slopes of the mountains are the proper field for the 'dry diggings', while from the gravel and sand of the beds of rivers and smaller streams the gold is obtained by 'wet diggings'. **1851** W. ACTON *Pract. Treatise Diseases of Urinary Organs* (ed. 2) I. ii. 226 Spermatorrhœa..is known..as nocturnal or diurnal emissions, pollutions, wet-dreams, [etc.]. **1921** H. CRANE *Let.* 11 Feb. (1965) 53 The wet-dream explosions of Virgil Jordan and McAlmon. Their talk is all right—but what is true of it has been said adequately before. **1946** B. MARSHALL *George Brown's Schooldays* 170 Well, what are you standing there looking like a wet dream for? **1963** A. HERON *Towards Quaker View of Sex* ii. 16 It is at this stage that nocturnal emissions or 'wet dreams' as they are often called, are frequently the first clear sign of sexual maturity in the boy. **1971** B. W. ALDISS *Soldier Erect* 10 Jesus, what a wet dream of a party that was! **1978** A. NEAVE *Nuremburg* viii. 86 He was said by the prosecution to have boasted to his chauffeur of nightly wet dreams and exhibited the semen to prove it. **1967** E. MCGIRR *Hearse with Horses* iii. 50 If a race was fixed they wouldn't need a wet-eared kid mixed up with it. **1971** F. FORSYTH *Day of Jackal* I. i. 21 Apart from a few wet-eared ninnies who refused to come, Rodin led his entire battalion into the military putsch of April 1961. **1888** CROSS & BEVAN *Text-bk. Paper-Making* x. 154 This part of the machine, which is called the 'wet-end', is placed at a slight slope. **1927** T. WOODHOUSE *Artif. Silk* iii. 25 The wet pulp is now run on to the feed end, usually termed the 'wet-end', of the drying machine. **1962** Wet end [see *dry end* s.v. *DRY *a.* C. 3]. **1962** *Aeroplane & Astronautics* CII. 88/2 Philippine Air Lines has wet-leased (i.e., aircraft plus flight crew) a Boeing 707 from Pan American. **1977** *Indian Express* 18 May 1/2 The Airbus will be either wet leased or chartered by Air-India. **1979** *Daily Tel.* 8 June 36/6 Aircraft can be leased by the hour, day, week, month, quarterly or longer on a 'dry' lease which means that crews are not provided, or on a 'wet' lease which means that the owner of the aircraft also supplies crew and, in some cases, the necessary fuel. **1978** *Observer* 29 Jan. 1/5 These too will have to be taken out of service for modifications, and their place taken by 'wet leased' foreign aircraft (that is, planes taken complete with their own crews). **1922** D. H. LAWRENCE *Let.*? 12 Oct. (1962) II. 726 Being too much of a wet-leg, as they say in England, nakedly to enter into the battle. **1929** —— *Pansies* 124 It is strange to think of the Annas, the Vronskys, the Pierres, all the Tolstoyan lot Wiped out... And the Tchekov wishy-wambly wet-legs all wiped out. **1981** *Times Lit. Suppl.* 3 July 745/1 We know how much Auden hated wet-legs, how constantly he repeated his many litanies of his own good fortune. **1968** J. IRONSIDE *Fashion Alphabet* 102 The 'Wet Look' is a chemical finish to fabrics to make them appear shiny and wet. **1969** *Times* 24 Nov. 16/2 Natural coloured python or wet-look patent are the most fashionable finishes for day. **1970** D. UHNAK *Ledger* (1971) ix. 114 Her lips, shining with a wet-look lipstick, quivered. **1971** *Daily Tel.* 2 Feb. 11 (*caption*) The chair and stool covered in white wet-look fabric. **1981** *Westindian World* 31 July 14/2 (Advt.), Hot & cold straightening, curly perm, wet look. **1928-9** *Army & Navy Stores Catal.* 419/1 Wet Pack. Fitted with comb and nail file, etc. Size closed, 5½ × 4½ in... Pigskin 12/–. **1974** *Harrods Christmas Catal.* 18/2 For travelling men... Two wet packs with waterproof linings. **1920** Wet-point [see *dry-point village* s.v. *DRY *a.* C.3]. **1969** G. C. DICKINSON *Maps & Air Photographs* xiv. 216 (*heading*) 'Wet-point' sites—i.e. places with an available water supply. **1909** WEBSTER, *Wet... Chem., etc.* Employing, or done by means of, or in the presence of, water or other liquid... The *wet* process or way. **1930** *Engineering* 3 Jan. 18/3 The Assano Portland Cement Company's works at Nishitama. This is a wet-process plant. **1945** H. D. SMYTH *Gen. Acct. Devel. Atomic Energy Mil. Purposes* vii. 75 Study of product recovery processes as a whole (wet processes, physical methods). **1969** Wet process [see *BY-PRODUCT b]. **1907** F. E. E. BELL *At Works* v. 122 Some of the yearly benefit clubs of which the head-quarters are at public-houses demand..an extra contribution, from 1d. to 3d., what is called the 'wet rent', which is quite deliberately allowed for drink each meeting-night. **1967** *Economist* 29 Apr. 480/2 The Jones board has implicitly accused the brewers of subsidising too many low volume country pubs, by charging less than the market rents but rather more for their beer, a practice known in the trade as a 'wet rent'. In actual fact, wet rents are steadily becoming proportionately less important, and the brewer's idea is to protect the publican against the ups and downs of trade by charging him, in effect, a rent that varies slightly with beer sales, thus identifying his interest more closely with that of the brewer. **1978** *Times* 3 May 19/6 The brewers ..continue phasing out 'wet' rents under which a tenant pays more or less to the brewery according to the amount of beer sold through the pub. **1976** *NBR Marketplace* (Wellington, N.Z.) III. 2/1 Something over 50 per cent of the estimated 900,000 regular shavers in New Zealand prefer a wet shave start to the day. *Ibid.* 2/3 About 94 per cent of wet shavers use the safety razor with double-edge blades or the modern single-edge blade systems. **1964** *Financial Times* 25 Feb. 11/8 The chief obstacle at present is the wet-shaving industry's promotion of the new stainless steel blades. **1980** 'D. KAVANAGH' *Duffy* iii. 44 They only took the television set and his electric razor... He went back to wet shaving. **1927** *Amer. Speech* III. 221 *Wet smack*,..something unsatisfactory; applies particularly to an individual who spoils a party; a kill-joy. **1929** WODEHOUSE *Mr. Mulliner Speaking* i. 33 The man is beyond question a flat tyre and a wet smack. **1977** *Maledicta* Summer 17 If she is actually frigid, she's a *wet smack*. **1963** A. J. HALL *Textile Sci.* ii. 75 Some of these polymers are soluble in organic solvents..and thus allow the preparation of solutions which can be *dry* spun..or wet spun—that is, extruded into a coagulating bath. **1973** *Materials & Technol.* VI. iv. 328 Polyacrylonitrile solutions have been wet-spun..into a coagulating bath. **1864** Wet spinning [see *dry spinning* s.v. *DRY *a.* C.3]. **1927** T. WOODHOUSE *Artif. Silk* 28 The coagulation by means of liquid of any kind has given rise to the term 'wet spinning', whereas the term 'dry-spinning' has been applied in all cases where the solvent is vaporized. **1969** A. J. HALL *Stand. Handbk. Textiles* (ed. 7) iii. 127 In wet spinning the roving is led through a trough of hot water..so that the fibres are softened. **1973** *Materials & Technol.* VI. iv. 295 Another method of taking up the wet spun yarn. **1960** R. W. MARKS *Dyma-*

xion World of B. Fuller 59/1 Even in 1954 Kraft paper having exceptional 'wet tensile strength' had been developed—'wet strength' meaning the ability of the paper to retain its structural quality when saturated. **1962** J. T. Marsh *Self-Smoothing Fabrics* xiv. 211 These examples of dimensional stability are of some consequence, and indeed of great consequence with fibres of regenerated cellulose whose low wet-strength is a serious defect but one which is remedied by the crease-resisting process. **1973** *Nature* 27 Apr. 588/1 Cross linking has been used for over thirty years in making 'wet strength' papers. **1955** Wet suit [see *dry suit* s.v. *dry *a.* C.3]. **1964** *Skin Diver* Oct. 19 An American skin diver aboard an Irish fishing boat..had a difficult time convincing the skipper that his 'wet' suit would save a man's life if he fell into the freezing water. **1970** *Daily Tel.* (Colour Suppl.) 18 Sept. 12 On deck three of us, clad in rubber wetsuits, prepared to slip over the side. **1972** *Islander* (Victoria, B.C.) 4 June 16/1 The wet suit, worn to keep the diver warm, is almost a necessity in these northern waters. **1984** S. Townsend *Growing Pains A. Mole* 78 She looked dead erotic in her black wetsuit and crash helmet. **1972** *Nat. Geographic* Oct. 584 Wet-suited author examines the giant wraparound grin of a right whale. **1978** D. Williams *Treasure up in Smoke* xix. 174 The alerted wet-suited figure had..waded to the beach. **1938** *Times* 5 May 10/4 For nearly 20 years the building trade operatives have..claimed that for uncontrollable irregularities of employment..there should be a scheme of compensation for loss of earnings. The phrase which they used to focus the claim was 'payment for wet time'. **1952** *Economist* 12 July 118/2 Steel erectors on American building sites do not enjoy either a guaranteed week or payment for 'wet-time'. **1962** *Listener* 26 July 154/3 The 'do-it-yourself' enthusiast who is preparing to tackle garden operations involving the use of cement, lime, and water—the so-called 'wet trades'. **1973** *Times* 24 Feb. 13/1 The shortage of skilled workers, particularly in the 'wet trades' of bricklaying and plastering. **1858** T. S. Woodward *Let.* 20 Dec. in *Reminisc.* (1939) 157 Fortunately, we found a little wet-weather spring near the top. **1901** [see Wet *a.* 2 e]. **1922** M. A. von Arnim *Enchanted April* i. 8 Big grey eyes almost disappearing under a smashed-down wet-weather hat. **1934** M. V. Hughes *London Child* iii. 28 The boys were off on some long wet-weather tramp. **1978** 'D. Rutherford' *Collision Course* 182 I'm gambling on rain... We're giving you wet-weather tyres. **1922** M. Arlen *Piracy* iii. xiv. 256 Just look how depraved they are! They are covered with verdigris, but they call it wet-white! **1976** 'D. Fletcher' *Don't whistle 'Macbeth'* 51 The first time I sang Elvira, I had to cover myself from head to toe with wet-white. [**1958** *Flying Rev.* Oct. 37/1 Scheduled to Supplement earlier Stratofortresses currently serving with the Strategic Air Command, the B-52G employs a 'wet' integral-tank wing which substantially increases the bomber's unrefuelled range.] **1961** *Flight* LXXIX. 818/2 These new 'wet wing' versions, with greatly increased weight and machined-plank wing skins, have suffered local stresses greater than any experienced with the earlier versions of lower weight and performance. **1969** *New Scientist* 25 Sept. (Microbes in Industry Suppl.) 23/2 In modern 'wet-wing' aircraft, such as Concorde, the fuel is simply pumped into the wings which are coated internally with sealants. In older aircraft..the fuel is contained in rubber bags in the wings.

wet, *v.* Add: **I. 1. b.** *Sci.* Of a liquid: to cover or penetrate (a substance or object) readily, so that a small quantity spreads uniformly over it rather than lying as droplets upon it.

A common criterion of wetting is the angle that the surface of a droplet makes, at its point of contact, with the surface on which it rests (as measured through the liquid): the liquid is said to wet or not to wet the surface according as the angle is less or greater than 90 degrees.

1855 D. Lardner *Hand-bk. Nat. Philos.: Hydrostatics* i. v. 69 If a liquid be poured into a vessel whose sides are of such a nature as to be wetted by it, the liquid.. will be curved upwards near the points where it touches the side. **1884** A. Daniell *Text Bk. Princ. Physics* xi. 246 Objects which are wetted by the liquid in which they float are thus apparently attracted by it; those which are not so are apparently repelled. **1932** *Phytopathology* XXII. 926 The presence of an appreciable quantity of sodium hydroxide..increases the ease with which the leaves can be 'wetted' in the solution. **1967** M. Chandler *Ceramics in Mod. World* vi. 171 Silicon nitride..is not wetted by molten metals. **1974** *Encycl. Brit. Macropædia* XI. 782/1 The adhesion of water to glass at an air-water-glass interface is greater than the cohesion of water, and hence water is said to wet the glass... The cohesion of mercury is greater than its adhesion to glass and it does not wet the glass. **1978** *Nature* 20 July 237/1 An example of this is a droplet of the liquid resting on a solid surface. When the contact angle is less than 90°, the liquid wets the solid. Molten beryllium does not wet BeO because the contact angle exceeds 90°.

5. c. Also *fig.*, to become excited or upset (as if about to void urine in one's clothes).

1979 'M. Underwood' *Smooth Justice* i. 35 There are quite a few people who'll wet their pants if I get sent down. **1981** A. Price *Soldier no More* 184 We did see the *Histories* season at Stratford, I grant you. But I don't remember any schoolgirls wetting their pants next to me.

d. *refl.* To urinate involuntarily. Also *fig.* (cf. sense 5 c above).

1922 Joyce *Ulysses* 730 What do I care with it dropping out of me and that black closed breeches he made me buy takes you half an hour to let them down wetting all myself. **1970** G. F. Newman *Sir, You Bastard* 258 The Sunday editors would wet themselves; they liked nothing better than a sordid purge in an institution. **1976** *Times Lit. Suppl.* 30 Jan. 100/5 She also sweats, weeps, vomits and wets herself.

7. a. Also, *to wet* (one's) *beak, beard.*

1939 T. S. Eliot *Old Possum's Bk. Pract. Cats* 16 For to the Bell at Hampton he had gone to wet his beard. **1978** J. Carroll *Mortal Friends* i. v. 53 Is there a public house here where a fellow could wet his beak?

e. (Earlier example.)

1783 J. Woodforde *Diary* 9 Oct. (1926) II. 97 With the latter I walked to the Swan and there wetted with him that is, drank a glass of Wine.

8. b. *to wet the baby's head* and varr.: to drink to celebrate the birth of a child. *colloq.*

1885 W. Westall *Old Factory* xxiv. 161 'We'll wet little Mabel's head with some of it.' 'What mean you?'.. 'Why my wife was brought to bed last night of a little lass as we are going to call Mabel, and I'd like us to drink to her health. That's what we call wetting a child's head in these parts.' **1924** Lawrence & Skinner *Boy in Bush* xiv. 210 Come along in—all welcome!—an' wet the baby's eye. **1953** E. Simon *Past Masters* iii. v. 173 At the party given to 'wet the baby's head' the McGillivrays' friends and relations produced only large and expensive gifts. **1970** *Guardian* 2 May 3/7 If he had not been wetting the baby's head, and so been slightly above proof, he might have run for it.

10. b. For *'dial.'* read *'dial.* and *colloq.'* (Earlier and later examples.) Also with tea-leaves as *obj.*

1902 *Cornh. Mag.* Dec. 776, I ha' wetted th' tea pretty nigh half-an-hour ago. **1939** Joyce *Finnegans Wake* 585 You never wet the tea! **1944** M. Laski *Love on Supertax* viii. 77 Make yourself at home, and I'll just wet the tea-leaves. **1978** I. Murdoch *Sea* 419 'I'll wet the tea,' said Hartley and disappeared into the kitchen.

II. 17. To urinate. Also *fig.*

1925 D. H. Lawrence *Novel* in *Reflections on Death of Porcupine* 122 But see old Leo Tolstoi wetting on the flame. As if even his wet were absolute! **1935** V. Woolf *Let.* 21 June (1979) V. 403 The marmoset is just about to wet on my shoulder. **1954** J. Steinbeck *Sweet Thursday* xiv. 82 House-broken dogs wet on the parlor rug. **1975** J. Cleary *Safe House* ii. 71 The children want to wet... Come on, love. Have your wet.

III. 18. The vb. stem in comb., as **wet-bed** = *bed-wetter* s.v. *bed *sb.* 19.

1934 'J. Spenser' *Limey breaks In* iv. 61, I lay awake for so long that I heard the night watchman come to call the wet-beds. **1960** J. Stroud *Shorn Lamb* xviii. 204 Does he enurete?.. I've got four chronic wet-beds already.

weta (we·tă). *N.Z.* [Maori.] Any of several wingless orthopteran insects of the genus *Deinacrida, Pachyrhamma,* or *Hemideina.*

1843 E. Dieffenbach *Trav. N.Z* II. iii. 396 Weta—an insect so called. **1857** C. Hursthouse *N.Z.* I. v. 123 The Weta, a suspicious-looking scorpion-like creature, apparently replete with 'high concocted venom', but perfectly harmless. **1863** S. Butler *First Year in Canterbury Settlement* ix. 441 One of the ugliest-looking creatures..is called 'weta', and is of tawny scorpion-like colour, with long antennae and great eyes, and nasty squashy-looking body, with (I think) six legs. **1888** *Trans. N.Z. Inst.* XXI. 41 Not a sound was heard in that lonely forest, except..the sharp noise produced by the *weta*. **1949** [see *huhu]. **1961** R. Park *Hole in Hill* (1962) xiv. 115 A giant glistening black insect..waving its antennae... 'It's only a *weta*!' **1975** E. Hillary *Nothing Venture, Nothing Win* ii. 40 When I was making up the bed I found a huge weta..in one of the blankets.

wetland (we·tlænd). [f. Wet *a.* + Land *sb.*] An area of land that is usually saturated with water, often a marsh or swamp. Also *attrib.* Also *pl.* (sometimes const. as *sing.*).

1743 M. Catesby *Nat. Hist. Carolina* II. p. iv, On this wet Land grows a variety of Evergreen Trees and Shrubs. **1847** H. Howe *Hist. Coll. Ohio* 98 'Wet land'..by judicious cultivation..rapidly improves in fertility. **1955** *Sci. News Let.* 29 Oct. 281/2 The wetland partridge is about twice the size of the valley quail. **1965** *New Scientist* 17 June 763/3 Wetlands are defined to include marshes, bogs, swamps and any still water less than six metres deep. **1969** *Nature* 19 Apr. 239/2 Wetland ecosystems in the limited sense of this work are defined as ecosystems with a watertable, above, at or very near the substrate surface, the substrate remaining saturated throughout the year. **1979** *Daily Tel.* 25 Oct. 11/4 Plans to protect the Somerset wetlands—an area of rare wildlife, whose future has been in dispute—are to be prepared. **1980** *National Trust* Spring 16/3 We intend to preserve this swamp area in its natural state as a haven not only for wetland flora but also for birds and animals. **1985** *Daily Hampshire Gaz.* (Northampton, Mass.) 9 Aug. 17/5 Under state law construction can not take place on a wetlands unless there are plans to replace the wetlands

wetly, *adv.* (Examples in sense *15 b of the adj.)

1975 *Times Lit. Suppl.* 12 Dec. 1486/3 Raffles's relations with his accomplice, Boswell, and room-mate, the wet and unendearing Bunny. Bunny..went to prison..to shield A.J., who rather let him down; but Bunny wetly forgave him. **1978** *Guardian Weekly* 12 Mar. 21/3 A peaceable fellow-officer, played slightly wetly by the American Beau Bridges.

Wetmore (we·tmōᵊɹ). The name of Alexander *Wetmore* (1886–1978), American ornithologist, used *attrib.* in *Wetmore order* to designate the system of bird classification developed by him.

1965 *Jrnl. Lancs. Dial. Soc.* Jan. 5 They are listed in Wetmore Order, i.e. the system of classification which is generally accepted in modern bird books. **1979** *Nature* 29 Mar. 490/1 Indeed Wetmore's name has become a household word among ornithologists, for his classification of the birds of the world, forming the basis for the well known 'Wetmore order', has, with modifications necessitated by new knowledge, become the generally accepted arrangement, as adopted in Peters' *Checklist of Birds of the World* and other authoritative compilations.

wetness. Add: **c.** Feebleness, ineptness. Cf. *wet *a.* 15 b.

1977 *Times* 29 Sept. 4/1 It was surely not Liberal 'wetness', as the incoming president, Mr. Gruffydd Evans, termed their traditional virtues of niceness and fair-mindedness. **1981** R. D. Edwards *Corridors of Death* vii. 33 A profession which regards loyalty as weakness and decency as wetness. **1983** *Times* 4 Nov. 7/1 The idea that an ally has a right to independent judgment is too easily dismissed as what Mrs Thatcher might describe..as wetness.

wettable, *a.* Add: (Examples corresponding to *wet *v.* 1 b.)

1903 W. R. Fisher tr. *Schimper's Plant-Geogr.* iii. i. 225 The foliage in a constantly humid climate is as a rule easily wettable. **1955** [see *captan]. **1976** *McGraw-Hill Yearbk. Sci. & Technol.* 208/2 Spraying the wettable powder or flowable formulation results in distribution patterns that are particulate in form rather than lamellar.

Hence **wettabi·lity,** the property of being wettable; the degree to which something may be wetted (*wet *v.* 1 b).

1913 *Chem. Abstr.* VII. 3441 The wetting of glass by different pairs of liquids was investigated with special reference to the effect of prolonged wetting upon the 'wetability'. **1933** *Amer. Jrnl. Sci.* XXV. 329 The 'wettability' of the particle in water. **1973** *Nature* 2 Mar. 14/1 The wettability of leaf surfaces is influenced by the fine structure and chemical composition of the wax. **1977** J. L. Harper *Population Biol. Plants* xi. 379 *Larrea* affects the water relations of the soil surrounding the plants, reducing soil wettability.

wetted, *ppl. a.* Add: **2.** *Aeronaut.* Of an aircraft surface: in contact with the moving airflow.

1916 F. W. Lanchester *Flying Machine from Engin. Standpoint* 110 If the direct resistance is properly assessed on the basis of 'wetted' surface, whether we call it a *surface* coefficient or a *skin-frictional* coefficient is merely a question of terminology. **1958** *Observer* 11 May 13/4 The plan form of the 'nicked delta' or delta with the inner middle rear part cut out, was adopted to reduce to a minimum the 'wetted' area or part over which air flows, without reducing the part that does useful work. **1983** D. Stinton *Design of Aeroplane* v. 208 When an aeroplane is very clean and highly streamlined, parasite drag may be attributed to skin friction drag... For this we need to work out wetted area.

wetting, *vbl. sb.* Add: **4*.** Urination, usu. resulting from incontinence or stress.

1943 [see *soiling *vbl. sb.*[1] 1 b]. **1960** I. Bennett *Delinquent & Neurotic Children* viii. 252 Soiling, wetting, and difficult behaviour.

wetting, *ppl. a.* Add: **a.** (Examples corresponding to *wet *v.* 1 b.)

1948 *Nature* 28 Feb. 313/2 A non-polar 'wetting' liquid such as carbon tetrachloride is floated on mercury in the reservoir beneath the U-tube. **1980** *Brit. Med. Jrnl.* 18 Oct. 1047/2 A wetting solution coats a hard lens with a chemical that permits water to spread and form a surface that is less traumatic to eye tissues.

b. *wetting agent*, a chemical that can be added to a liquid to reduce its surface tension and make it more effective at wetting.

1927 *Chem. Abstr.* XXI. 414 The Na salts of the products may be used as wetting agents. **1950** *Engineering* 5 May 517/1 The success of Teepol as a wetting agent is due to its effectiveness in reducing the surface tension of water. **1977** J. Hedgecoe *Photographer's Handbk.* 39 Rinsing the film in 'wetting agent' (weak detergent) at the end of washing helps to prevent the accumulation of drops of water.

wetware (we·twēᵊɹ). [f. Wet *a.* after *hardware, software.*] Chemical materials organized so as to perform arithmetic or logical operations; brain substance, as having this ability.

1975 *Nature* 23 Oct. 634/1 An electronic computer is made up of hardware and software; a chemical automaton needs an additional component, a chemical reaction system which might be called 'wetware'. **1977** *N.Y. Times* 8 May i. 34/6 Computer scientists have lately begun talking about 'wetware', which is the human brain. **1984** *Times Lit. Suppl.* 14 Dec. 1442/3 There is no obvious reason why biological 'wetware' should be any better at impuing internal structures with semantic significance than silicon 'hardware'. **1985** *Listener* 10 Jan. 9/3 The whole claim of strong AI is that the physical and chemical hardware or wetware of the system are quite irrelevant.

we-uns (wī·ɒnz), *pron. U.S. dial.* Also **we uns, we'uns.** [f. We *pron.* + *uns*, dial. var. *ones* (One *pron.*).] Used in place of We or Us *prons.*

1864 *Harper's Mag.* Dec. 16/2 'What for you uns', said they, in their barbaric dialect, 'come down here to fight we uns?' **1865** O. L. Jackson *Colonel's Diary* (1922) 208 If we 'uns were to go down to Goldbro or Raleigh, do you think we 'uns could get any old creetur?.. A horse or a mule? **1907** H. B. Wright *Shepherd of Hills* xi. 105 You can get out o' these hills an' be somebody like we'uns. *Ibid.* xii. 109 He sure talks so we'uns can understand. **1913** H. Kephart *Our Southern Highlanders* xiii. 286 Let's we-uns all go over to youerunses house. **1938**

C. H. MATSCHAT *Suwannee River* iii. 53 We-uns'll..light for home.

Weymouth. Add: **2.** *Horseriding.* Designating a type of curb bit (see quot. 1963) or a double bridle comprising this bit and a snaffle with two sets of reins.

1792 T. H. MORLAND *Every Man his Own Judge* 70 A Weymouth bridle, with bit, and bradoon, is in my opinion preferable to any other sort for the road. **1919** R. S. TIMMIS *Notes on Riding & Driving* iii. 39 A few good snaffles, both racing and exercising (with cross-pieces outside the cheek), and a Weymouth or a Pelham bit and bridoon are all that are necessary for practically all horses. **1938** F. C. HITCHCOCK *To Horse!* ix. 274 The only objection to a double bridle is that its use entails two separate mouthpieces in the horse's mouth. The usual pattern bit used is called the Weymouth. **1946** M. C. SELF *Horseman's Encycl.* 433 The Weymouth bridle consists of a bit and bridoon. It is the bridle most usually used for the finished saddle horse. **1963** BLOODGOOD & SANTINI *Horseman's Dict.* 21 *Weymouth or Ward Union bit,* bit consisting of straight, moderately long cheek-pieces, stationary or sliding mouthpiece, either straight or with a slight Muller or Cambridge port. Simplest of all curb bits and most generally used. **1965** C. E. G. HOPE *Riding* v. 59 The curb used with a double bridle, known as the Weymouth or Ward Union, invariably has a plain port mouth.

wh. **1.** (Also **wh-**, **wh'**) Informal written abbrev. of WHICH *a.* and *pron.*, in relative use.

c **1858** E. DICKINSON *Poems* (1955) I. 16 Sleep is the station grand Down wh', on either hand The hosts of witness stand! **1865** HARDY *Let.* 20 Oct. (1978) I. 5 You will know wh. part of the Abbey I mean if you think of Salisbury Cathedral & of the row of small arches over the large arches. **1889** W. WHITMAN *Daybks. & Notebks.* (1978) II. 528 Paid $3.15 for insurance for $300 on stock at 1213 Filbert st. wh- is continued on to Feb: 8 '90.

2. *Linguistics.* A symbol representing an interrogative or relative pronoun (most of which begin with the digraph *wh*). Freq. *Comb.*, as *wh-clause, -question, -transformation*, etc.

1957 N. CHOMSKY *Syntactic Struct.* vii. 69 In the morphophonemics of English we shall have rules: *wh + he*→/huw/, *wh + him*→/huwm/, *wh + it*→/wat/. **1960** *Internat. Jrnl. Amer. Linguistics* XXVI. III. ii. 36 Again adopting Chomsky's excellent analysis of interrogative sentences, we wish now to produce those structures introduced by words beginning, for the most part, with *wh-*, i.e. WH-questions and their affirmative counterparts, relative clauses and question-word clauses. **1962** N. CHOMSKY in *3rd Texas Conf. Probl. Linguistic Anal. in Eng.* 147 Application of the *wh*-transformation is conditional on the interrogative transformation 3. **1964** *Language* XL. 5 The interrogative specifier *Wh* can remain unattached or can have attached to it (indicated by +) various elements of the sentence. **1966** G. N. LEECH *Eng. in Advertising* vi. 61 It is the type which consists of an embedded *wh-* clause. **1975** J. GOULET *Oh's Profit* v. 31 *Trabasso:* You mean he demonstrates nonkernel sentences? *Liedlich:* Passive, interrogative, imperative, and he's beginning to get the hang of WH-subordination, too. **1980** B. NEWMAN in *Bible Translator* XXXI. 326 Lengthy sentences are found throughout NIV... Romans I. 1–4 is a single sentence consisting of 72 words, involving at least one case of ellipsis, one dash, one colon, two 'wh'-clauses, and several appositions. **1981** R. BURCHFIELD *Spoken Word* 30 *Wh*-questions: Which hotel is he staying *at*? Who are you voting *for*?

whack, *sb.* Add: **2. b.** Also more generally, a sharing-up or distribution.

1896 ADE *Artie* xii. 107 He hadn't been in on the whack-up six weeks till he was wearing one o' them bicycle lamps in his neck-tie. **1912** R. A. WASON *Friar Tuck* xi. 85 'What ya goin' to kill her with?' he asked, his eyes dancin' like an Injun's at the beef whack-up.

c. *U.S.* A bargain or agreement. Esp. in phr. *it's* (or *that's*) *a whack*.

1860 *Johnson's Orig. Comic Songs* (ed. 2) 45, I axed her for to marry me, she said it was a whack. **1876** 'MARK TWAIN' *Tom Sawyer* vi. 70 'I'll stay if you will.' 'Good—that's a whack'. **1884** J. HAY *Bread-Winners* x. 149 Say the word, and it's a whack. **1903** A. D. MCFAUL *Ike Glidden in Maine* xviii. 146 'I'll guarantee to get him to take you to Grand Menan with him.' 'It's a whack,' said Jim. **1911** *Dialect Notes* III. 540 *Whack,*..an agreement, a 'go'; e.g., 'That's a whack!'

4. *out of whack*: disordered, malfunctioning; out of order or alignment. Cf. *WACKY *a.* Chiefly *U.S.* **a.** Of a person or a part of the body.

1885 C. A. SIRINGO *Texas Cowboy* v. 33, I was too weak to walk that far on account of my back being out of whack. **1899** ADE *Doc' Horne* viii. 79 My stomach seems to be out of whack. **1903** A. M. BINSTEAD *Pitcher in Paradise* vi. 146 At last he utterly gets his thinker out of whack an' goes back to the villa. **1918** H. A. VACHELL *Some Happenings* xii. 205 His liver is out of whack and no mistake. **1969** 'V. PACKER' *Don't rely on Gemini* (1970) xviii. 150 Margaret had had symptoms of early menopause last winter: that had thrown her way out of whack, could conceivably explain such erratic and erotic behaviour.

b. Of a mechanism.

1906 *McClure's Mag.* Feb. 34 Being able to get at any part of the mechanism which may be 'out of whack' is important. **1934** D. HAMMETT *Thin Man* xi. 77 The phone in the apartment was out of whack. **1949** *Time* 30 May 53/2 With normal vibration a lot of them would have gone out of whack. **1975** *New Yorker* 28 Apr. 40/3 He sends no message on the tape recorder to the little boys, because they have already put the machine out of whack. **1985** *Mail on Sunday* (Colour Suppl.) 3 Mar. 20/2 The body's like an automobile. You have to rest and repair it, not run with the motor out of whack.

c. *fig.*

1952 C. ARMSTRONG *Black-Eyed Stranger* xiv. 117 Ambielli's got principles. They are a little off, slightly out of whack. **1973** in G. Gibson *Eleven Canad. Novelists* 123, I don't know whether it is because my own sense of sexual timing or whatever is out of 'whack' with everybody else's. **1975** M. AMIS *Dead Babies* v. 33 Everything is out of whack at Appleseed Rectory; its rooms are without bearing and without certainty. **1978** S. BRILL *Teamsters* vi. 250 In the next decade..the bad loans and poor investment management would..start to throw the cash-flow projections out of whack.

whack, *v.* Add: **3.** (Examples with *up*.)

1893 H. A. SHANDS *Some Peculiarities of Speech in Mississippi* 77 *Whack up,* an expression employed by all classes, probably as semi-slang, to mean *to divide, to share.* **1961** *Coast to Coast 1959–60* 126 I'll whack up the breakfast, then, and see how poor bloody Bill's getting on. **1981** *Amer. Speech* LVI. 27 The DARE project has turned up *whack it up, whack up* (two informants for each).

4. *intr.* With *off*: to masturbate. *U.S. slang.*

1969 P. ROTH *Portnoy's Complaint* 78 Did I mention that when I was fifteen I took it out of my pants and whacked off on the 107 bus from New York? **1969** *Listener* 17 Apr. 538/3 Fellatio with the Monkey does not present the same practical difficulties as whacking off in Momma's bathroom. **1977** *Transatlantic Rev.* LX. 36 'What-in-hell you do for sex anyway?' he asked the boy one night. 'Whack off into the tin pot where they keep the mashed potatoes?'

whack, var. *WACK.

whacked (hwækd), *ppl. a. slang.* [f. WHACK *v.* + -ED[1].] **1.** Tired out, exhausted.

1919 *Athenæum* 15 Aug. 759/1 'Whacked to the wide' means to be tired out. **1952** J. CANNON *Body in Beck* v. 82 He had been on the job since dawn, was whacked and must call it a day. **1960** L. MEYNELL *Bandaberry* vi. 100 I'm whacked. How far have we done? **1976** J. SNOW *Cricket Rebel* 118 In addition to recovering from the injury to my right hand I was whacked when I arrived back in England from the MCC tour.

2. *whacked out*: mad, crazy; *spec.* intoxicated with drugs. Cf. *WACKY *a. U.S.*

1969 *Current Slang* (Univ. S. Dakota) Summer 17 *Whacked out,* unorthodox; inclined toward foolish acts. **1969** 'V. PACKER' *Don't rely on Gemini* (1970) i. 8 You Cancers are whacked out because the moon rules you. **1975** *High Times* Dec. 68/3 Then there's the pilot who was whacked out of his skull and landed a hundred-grand rented Cessna 411 gear up in Las Vegas. **1980** W. SAFIRE in *N.Y. Times Mag.* 14 Sept. 11/2 In America, the term 'whacked-out' is current, as an intensified form of 'spaced out' or 'zonked out', meaning soft-headed after prolonged and excessive use of drugs.

whacking, *vbl. sb.* Add: **1. b.** *transf.* A beating or defeat in a contest; a 'thrashing'.

1951 *Sport* 27 Apr.–3 May 3/2 If Wednesday gets a whacking from Spurs this time..they can hardly grumble.

whacking, *ppl. a.* (Earlier examples.)

1806 J. DAVIS *Post Captain* iv. 19 She looks..like a whacking frigate. **1819** J. THOMSON *Poems* (ed. 2) 201 A whakin' fee gets tauld them down for sorry haet, I trow.

whacko (stress variable), *int.* Also **wacko.** [f. WHACK *sb.* + *-O[2].] An exclamation of delight or excitement: Splendid! Excellent! Hurrah!

1941 BAKER *Dict. Austral. Slang* 81 *Whacko,* good! Hurrah! A popular ejaculation. **1944** A. F. BRUNO *Desert Daze* 7 Chips let his [Mills bomb] go..Whacko! **1961** J. MACLAREN-ROSS *Doomsday Book* I. vii. 74 'All's well,' Marsh said elatedly... 'Whacko!' Eustace cried. **1967** *Southerly* XXVII. 75 This is the message. 'Home Friday. Wacko.' **1978** L. DAVIDSON *Chelsea Murders* xvii. 94 After all it was only two days to—whacko!—Monday.

whacko, whacky, varr. *WACKO, *WACKY.

whadd(a)ya, etc., repr. colloq. pronunc. of 'what do you'.

1927 C. HOPLEY-WOOLRICH *Children of Ritz* iv. 72 Gaffney shook hands. 'Whaddya know, eh?' he greeted him breezily. **1945** A. KOBER *Parm Me* 33 'Waddeya mean,' she says back to me. **1952** E. WILSON *Equations of Love* 34 'Well, whaddaya know!' exclaimed Mort. **1955** W. GADDIS *Recognitions* II. iv. 446 Whadda you say? **1967** J. WAINWRIGHT *Talent for Murder* 205 Wadya mean, copper? **1975** *New Yorker* 20 Oct. 38/2 'Hey, hey, whaddya say!' he shouts. **1981** J. D. MACDONALD *Free Fall in Crimson* xiii. 147 'Peter Kesner in, please?' 'Whaddaya want with him?'

‖**whakapapa** (fakăpa·pa). [Maori.] (Maori) genealogy; a genealogical table.

1960 N. HILLIARD in C. K. Stead *N.Z. Short Stories* (1966) 249 You don't even know your own *whakapapa*! **1966** *Encycl. N.Z.* II. 438/2 Most Maori traditional narrative includes some whakapapa or genealogical record of a connection between the characters in the story. The web of the tale is often so entwined as to require the explanation afforded by the whakapapa. **1974** *N.Z. Listener* 20 July 10/4, I can..make a brief and somewhat tentative reference to the links in our whakapapa, between our tribes they are a long way back **1975** D. BAGLEY *Snow Tiger* iv. 53 Turi's *whakapapa* stick, his most prized possession,..which gave his ancestry.

whale, *sb.* Add: **1. b.** (*a*) **black whale** (earlier example).

1831 in R. McNab *Old Whaling Days* (1913) i. 3 The black whales visit the bays and coasts of New Zealand for the purpose of calving.

(*b*) (Earlier example of *right-whaling*.)

1849 H. MELVILLE *Mardi* I. i. 5 This horrid and indecent Right Whaling..is as the butchery of white bears upon blank Greenland icebergs.

5. c. *a whale of*: for (U.S.) read (orig. U.S.) and add later examples.

1921 *Chambers's Jrnl.* May 308/1 He had come here to have one whale of a time. **1938** G. HEYER *Blunt Instrument* iii. 45 It doesn't look such a whale of a case to me. **1954** J. B. PRIESTLEY *Magicians* i. 15 An equally dashing, whale-of-a-fellow, R.A.F. type. **1963** N. MARSH *Dead Water* (1964) i. 22 She's having a whale of a time with Mr. Joyce. **1980** B. CASTLE *Castle Diaries* 363 They regaled us with drinks and a superb buffet and we had a whale of a time.

6. a. *whale-cry, -ground, -hole, -hunt, -steak* (examples); (as weapons, etc.) *whale-pike, -pole, -rope* (earlier example); *whale-blue, -mouthed* (later example), *-shaped* adjs. **b. whale-louse** (later examples).

1946 DYLAN THOMAS *Deaths & Entrances* 55 The coast Blackened with birds took a last look At his thrashing hair and whale-blue eye. **1851** H. MELVILLE *Moby Dick* II. xii. 78 The ancient whale-cry upon first sighting a whale from the mast-head. **1851** Whale-ground [see *oil-ship* s.v. *OIL *sb.*[1] 6 e]. **1897** KIPLING *Captains Courageous* v. 111 'Whale-hole.'..He had led them to the edge of the barren Whale-deep, the blank hole of the Grand Bank. **1851** H. MELVILLE *Moby Dick* III. xix. 134 The far different nature of the whale-hunt. **1916** R. C. ANDREWS *Whale Hunting* xxi. 248 This growth [on the snout of the right whale] is produced by whale lice. **1952** J. FISHER *Fulmar* xviii. 423 He writes of the fulmars 'searching out' whale-lice. **1972** *Nat. Geographic* Oct. 579 (*caption*) Communities of whale lice.. some of them half an inch long, cling to the growths [on the head of each right whale]. **1952** L. MACNEICE *Ten Burnt Offerings* ii. 23 The whale-mouthed arch the bones of the future. **1851** H. MELVILLE *Moby Dick* II. xii. 94 The valiant Captain danced up and down with a whale-pike. *Ibid.* xiv. 124 The flag of capture lazily hanging from the whale-pole inserted into his spout-hole. **1849** —— *Redburn* I. xx. 194 Coiled away in a tub. Like a whale-rope. **1930** *Times Educ. Suppl.* 25 Oct. p. iv/1 In the whale-shaped head is a window for the driver. **1978** M. PUZO *Fools Die* ii. 16 White-dotted red square dice were dazzling flying fish over the whale-shaped crap tables. **1851** H. MELVILLE *Moby Dick* II. xii. 166 Don't I always say that to be good, a whale-steak must be tough? **1969** *Listener* 14 Aug. 206/3 What *did* we eat? Well, we ate whale-steak for one thing.

whale, *v.*[2] **2.** (Earlier examples.)

a **1852** F. M. WHITCHER *Widow Bedott Papers* (1883) vi. 67 You remember that one that come round a spell ago a whalin' away about human rights. **1886** *Harper's Mag.* July 322/1 In tones of wrath..he whaled it at his opponent throughout the fifteen minutes alloted to him.

whaleback. Add: **3.** More widely, any land form or land mass likened to the back of a whale; *spec.* (*a*) = *ROCHE MOUTONNÉE; (*b*) an elongated sand dune.

1913 *Proc. Geologists' Assoc.* XXIV. 247 A characteristic rounded form resembling..the 'whale-back' of glaciated areas. **1918** *Geogr. Jrnl.* LI. 23 In these whalebacks and crescents the cross-section that has the longest base passes through the summit of the dune. **1928** *Chambers's Jrnl.* Jan. 1/2 Behind all, a dim whale-back that might be Stroma, or Ultima Thule. **1933** *Geogr. Jrnl.* LXXXII. 125 A whaleback is a flat-topped ridge of sand anything up to 100 miles in length, of the order of half a mile wide, and up to 100 feet high. **1952** V. CANNING *House of Seven Flies* xi. 155 A long stretch of sand..the long ridges of wave marks from the last tide shadowed across the rising whaleback. **1955** *Geogr. Jrnl.* CXXI. 476 Some British whalebacks are undoubtedly *roches moutonnées*, some others, and probably many tropical examples, are genetically related to tors. **1974** M. GILBERT *Flash Point* x. 82 Behind the whaleback of Kinder Low and Edale Head a storm was brewing up. **1977** A. HALLAM *Planet Earth* 67/2 Where folds can be traced in three dimensions, it is found that the structures die out along their fold axis and, where suitably exposed, form whalebacks.

whalebacked *a.* (earlier example).

1869 'MARK TWAIN' *Innoc. Abroad* 441 We can see th long, whale-backed ridge of Mount Hermon projecting above the eastern hills.

whalebone, *sb.* Add: **wha·leboning,** a beating with a piece of whalebone (sense 3).

1851 H. MELVILLE *Moby Dick* I. xxx. 205 Only a whaleboning that he gave me—not a base kick.

whaler. Add: **4.** Also **waler.** [ellipt. f. *Murrumbidgee w(h)aler* s.v. *MURRUMBIDGEE: (see also quot. 1945).] A tramp or 'sundowner'. *Austral. slang.*

1883 R. E. N. TWOPENY *Town Life in Australia* 244 A 'waler' is a bushman who is 'on the loaf'. He 'humps his drum', or 'swag', and 'starts on the wallaby track'. **1886** F. COWAN *Australia* 31 The Whaler: of the Murrumbidgee and the Darling; when it suits his pleasure and convenience, a dolce-far-niente outcast in the fertile valleys of the rivers named, beyond the running of a warrant or a writ. **1903** 'T. Collins' *Such is Life* 4 Willoughby, who was travelling loose with Thompson and Cooper, was a whaler. **1945** Baker *Austral. Lang.* v. 102 According to an old-timer correspondent: 'They were so apt to lie about the size of the 'whales' they caught that a generic name for this class of unemployable traveller came into being.' This explanation is open to some doubt... In our early days New South Welsh horses exported to India for army use were known as *walers*. The original *Murrumbidgee whalers* may therefore have been N.S.W. tramps... Blood brethren of the *whaler* (this spelling is retained because tradition holds mainly to the 'whale' theory)..are the *Domain dosser*, [etc.]. **1963** A. Marshall *In Mine Own Heart* (1964) xx. 164 The whaler, a term that had originated from the name given to those swagmen who in the early days spent their time moving up and down the Murrumbidgee River..now applied to those who walked from town to town in preference to jumping trains. **1965** B. Wannan *Fair Go, Spinner* ii. 53 After drinking some Wilcannia beer, a whaler I once saw got up and started to fight with himself.

4. Special Combs. **whalerman** = Whaler 1; **whaler shark,** any of several sharks of the genus *Galeolemma,* found in Australasian waters.

1891 R. L. Stevenson *In South Seas* (1896) i. xiii. 128 Captain Chase, they called him, an old whaler-man. **1963** *Times* 18 May 9/7 The first big bang was at night and the Norwegian whalermen heard it six miles away. **1974** G. Jenkins *Bridge of Magpies* ii. 33 Old whalermen's graves in New England. [**1882** J. E. Tenison-Woods *Fish New South Wales* iv. 92 The following list [of sharks] includes all that are known to occur in our seas:..the Whaler, [etc.].] **1937** Z. Grey *Amer. Angler in Austral.* vii. 70 Among the trawlers it was not unusual to see a dozen whaler sharks all in a bunch. **1972** *Islander* (Victoria, B.C.) 9 Apr. 7/1 A whaler shark darting over the reef flat with a sudden burst of speed.

whaling, *vbl. sb.*[1] Add: **1. b.** (Earlier examples.)

1722 *New-England Courant* 18 June 2/2 Huffey of Nantucket..went out from thence on the Whaling Account. **1767** M. Cutler in W. P. & J. P. Cutler *Life & Corr. M. Cutler* (1888) I. i. 19 Our whaling vessels sailed for the Western Islands. **1782** 'J. H. St John de Crèvecœur' *Lett. from Amer. Farmer* v. 158 They have greatly cheapened the fitting out of their whaling fleets.

2. Comb. **whaling station,** a land base where whales which have been caught are flenched and rendered.

1874 C. M. Scammon *Marine Mammals N.W. Coast N. Amer.* iii. v. 247 At the point where the enormous carcass was stripped of its fat, arose the 'whaling station', whose trypots were set in rude furnaces..and capacious vats were made of planks, to receive the blubber. **1930** L. G. D. Acland *Early Canterbury Runs* 1st Ser. vi. 116 The country..was accessible on foot from the old shore whaling station. **1963** L. Diack *Labrador Nurse* v. 25 One night we tied up at a whaling station. **1977** C. McCullough *Thorn Birds* ii. 20 The eleven men..came out at the whaling station of Hobart.

wham (hwæm), *sb.*[2] *colloq.* [Echoic. Cf. next.] **1.** A heavy blow; the sound of a heavy blow (or of an explosion, etc.). Also, a resounding success, a 'knock-out'; an attempt *at* something (cf. Whack *sb.* 1 b).

1923 *N.Y. Times* 9 Sept. vii. 2 *Wham,* a success, a knock-out. **1924** *Dialect Notes* V. 257 Onomatopoetic words.. bam, blam, ca-blam, slam, wham, zam..(all= sound of blow). **1949** J. R. Cole *It was so Late* 90 The occasional echoing wham of a charge of gelly. **1957** 'J. Wyndham' *Midwich Cuckoos* iv. 38 Might be a good idea to have a wham at it. **1973** C. Bonington *Next Horizon* viii. 121 Have another try... This time the peg held, another half-dozen whams of the hammer, and it was in to the hilt.

2. As *int.* or *adv.*: with a wham.

1924 E. Hemingway *In our Time* 10 The bull rammed him wham against the wall. **1934** J. M. Cain *Postman always rings Twice* xi. 126 And then, wham, I pleaded her guilty. **1948** 'J. Tey' *Franchise Affair* viii. 90 They go that short step too far and wham! out comes that business-like paw. **1958** P. Mortimer *Daddy's gone a-Hunting* xxx. 170 He..walked through the front door and wham. She did it with a clock. **1965** M. Frayn *Tin Men* xxvi. 144 When the iron was hot, wham!—he would come out like a tiger and knock it for six. **1975** A. Ayckbourn *Norman Conquests* 5 It was just wham, thump and there we both were on the rug.

wham (hwæm), *v. colloq.* [Echoic. Cf. prec.] **1.** *trans.* To strike violently; to propel with great force, by hitting, throwing, kicking, etc. Also *fig.*

1925 *Sat. Even. Post* 14 Feb. 16 The wow finish, properly, is the legitimate successor to the old apple-sauce flag-waving finish for whamming an audience. **1930** E. Ferber *Cimarron* xxi. 349 Standing Bear whams it out so straight and so far that he makes the [golf] pro look like a ping-pong player. **1933** J. Thurber *My Life & Hard Times* iv. 57 She..picked up a shoe, and whammed it through a pane of glass across the narrow space that separated the two houses. **1950** A. Buckeridge *Jennings goes to School* xii. 239 You must have put all your weight behind it, or you wouldn't have gone down flat like that, after you'd whammed it in. **1951** *Sport* 7–13 Jan. 15/2 Basically the same team, which had been languishing generally on the wrong side,..whammed in six against Derry. **1962–3** E. Birney *Sel. Poems* (1966) ii. 59 Nine shoeboys wham their boxes Slap at my newshined feet. **1971** C. Bonington *Annapurna South Face* xiii. 161 He whammed in the ice-hammer, pulled up on it, kicking with the two front points of his crampons into the ice.

2. *intr.* To pound or strike violently; to move with speed, violence, or noise. Also *fig.*

1948 W. C. Williams in *Poetry* June 147 Each time he'd swing the axe and I heard it wham into the wood, I'd let out a wild cackle of delight. **1948** D. Ballantyne *Cunninghams* 135 The nausea rushes that made his head wham. **1954** A. C. Clarke *Silence Please* in *Tales from White Hart* (1957) 3 Bert's blast whammed overhead. **1962** K. Kesey *One flew over Cuckoo's Nest* i. 51 The black boy whammed flat against the wall and stuck, then slid down to the floor. **1973** P. White *Eye of Storm* xii. 586 A partition of the door still in motion whammed against an ear and sent his hat spinning. **1980** *Daily Tel.* 27 Aug. 2 (Advt.), The incredible Casio FX39..whams through complicated equations and elementary statistical formulae.

wham-bam, -bang, *adv.* (or *int.*), *a.*, (*sb.*). [f. *Wham *sb.*[2] 2 + *Bam *int.* or Bang *v.* 8.]

A. *adv.* or *int.* With a wham and a bang: used to denote a sudden or forceful effect (*lit.* or *fig.*); *spec.* with reference to sexual intercourse conducted quickly and without tenderness, esp. in phr. *wham, bam, thank you ma'am.*

1956 B. Holiday *Lady sings Blues* (1973) ii. 22 With my regular white customers, it was a cinch. They had wives and kids to go home to. When they came to see me it was wham, bang, they gave me the money and were gone. *Ibid.* 25 'I thought I was giving you a chance,' she spouted at me. 'But you turned out to be a girl of bad character.' Wham, bang, four months she handed me. **1971** S. Firestone *Dialectic of Sex* vi. 152 Men are interested in nothing but a screw (wham, bam, thank you M'am!). **1977** *Ripped & Torn* vi. 9/1 We play a set that starts at the beginning and goes Wham Bam Bam to the end. **1977** *Playgirl* May 13/1 Not all men are 'wham bam thank you ma'am' types.

B. *adj.* Loud, violent, forceful (see also quot. 1960).

1960 Wentworth & Flexner *Dict. Amer. Slang* 573/1 *Wham-bam,* quick(ly) and rough(ly); displaying more energy than finesse. **1976** *Publishers Weekly* 4 Oct. 65/2 Harbinson on Elvis..ticks off the outrageous 'Hound Dog' of pop music in wham-bam style. **1977** *Listener* 20 Oct. 498/3 Screenwriters..know that it's mainly wham-bang shock effect that sells.

C. *sb.* A sudden, violent effect.

1975 *Listener* 17 July 68/3 Now it is the big wham-bang of sudden [price] rises.

whammer (hwæ·məɹ). *Mountaineering.* [f. *Wham *v.* + -er[1].] A kind of piton hammer.

1971 [see *piton hammer* s.v. *Piton 3]. **1974** H. MacInnes *Climb to Lost World* ix. 142 The Whillans 'Whammer'—a multi-purpose piton hammer.

whammo (hwæmōᵘ: stress variable), *int.* Also **whamo.** [f. *Wham *sb.*[2] + *-o[2].] = *Wham *sb.*[2] 2; an exclamation suggesting a sudden violent blow or surprising event, etc.

1932 *Fitchburg* (Mass.) *Sentinel* 7 May, But the heavy comes to, and Whamo! The boy goes down bam. **1945** *Record* (Philadelphia) 4 July 11/1 'Ring out the tidings, Grandpa!' and the old gent spit on his hands, and Whammo! went the Liberty Bell. **1959** N. Mailer *Advts. for Myself* (1961) 97 They meet again in New York.. and whammo do they get together. I mean drinking and making love, nothing can stop them. **1969** P. Dickinson *Pride of Heroes* i. 45 Everyone a bit nervy for about a fortnight, and then, whammo, something happens. **1981** *Daily Express* 24 July 14/4, I put the telephone down and whammo! Another 'little twinge'.

whammy (hwæ·mi). *colloq.* (orig. and chiefly *U.S.*). [f. *Wham *sb.*[2] + -y[6].] An evil influence or 'hex'. From the 1950s, often with reference to the comic strip Li'l Abner (see quot. 1951), esp. in phr. *a double whammy* and varr. Hence, an intense or powerful look, etc.; something effective, upsetting, problematic, etc.

1940 J. R. Tunis *Kid from Tomkinsville* x. 151 Interest round the field now centered in the Kid's chances for a no-hit game... On the bench everyone realized it too, but everyone kept discreetly quiet on account of the Whammy. Mustn't put the Whammy on him! **1951** *Al Capp's Li'l Abner* July, *Evil-Eye Fleegle* is th' name, an' th' '*whammy*' is my game. Mudder Nature endowed me wit' eyes which can putrefy citizens t' th' spot!.. There is th' '*single whammy*'! *That,* friend, is th' full, *pure power* o' *one* o' my evil eyes! It's *dynamite,* friend, an' I do not t'row it around lightly!.. And, lastly—th' '*double whammy*'—namely, th' *full power o' both eyes*—which I hopes I never *hafta* use. **1952** B. Malamud *Natural* 75 They were afflicted with more than the usual number of hexes and whammies and practised all sorts of magic to undo them. **1964** J. Masters *Trial at Monomoy* ii. 66 You heard that our local witch has put her whammy on you now? **1970** *Daily Tel.* (Colour Suppl.) 30 Oct. 19/2 That smile, a huge, sweet, melting smile, a whammy of an MRA smile, a West-Coast switched-on-sincere smile, which envelops just everybody. **1976** *New Yorker* 16 Feb. 107/1 In the Germany scenes, Wertmuller achieves the effect of liveliness through one whammy after another. The starving prisoners in the camp are beaten and murdered to the tune of the Ride of the Valkyries. **1979** C. James *Pillars of Hercules* iii. xi. 122 Holmes was a nonconformist in a conformist age, yet still won all the conformist rewards. It was a double whammy.

whang, *sb.*[1] Restrict *Sc.* and *dial.* to senses in Dict. and add: Also **wang. 3.** The penis. *slang* (orig. and chiefly *U.S.*).

1935 H. L. Davis *Honey in Horn* iii. 34 Leave them horses alone or I'll cut your whang off. **1949** H. Miller *Sexus* viii. 250 You say he's got a terrific wang, Bill. I don't know how he ever gets it in there. **1952** N. Mailer *Barbary Shore* x. 89 Guinevere..went on at length with one of her inexhaustible stories about a lover and his whang. **1959** M. Richler *Apprenticeship D. Kravitz* i. x. 60 He's got a whang that could choke a horse. I know, we had a leak together once. **1969** K. Vonnegut *Slaughterhouse-Five* v. 115 Montana was naked, and so was Billy, of course. He had a tremendous wang. **1981** G. Hammond *Revenge Game* ix. 102 Maybe you're not as ready with your whang as you were, or maybe you couldn't keep it up——.

whang, *v.*[1] Restrict *Sc.* and *dial.* to other senses in Dict. and add: Also **wang. 1. b.** *trans.* and *intr.* (Later examples.) *dial.* and *colloq.*

1905 in *Eng. Dial. Dict.* VI. 439/2 He wanged a stone at me. **1914** C. Mackenzie *Sinister Street* II. iii. i. 500 The governor wanged them into my lap. **1965** *Punch* 22 Sept. 420/1 Anybody wanting to wang up a skyscraper or indeed any building of size and importance will have to publish a comprehensible model or drawing. **1980** D. Bogarde *Gentle Occupation* ix. 249 Suddenly a stone spun out of nowhere and whanged harmlessly against the bonnet of the car. **1984** *New Yorker* 23 Apr. 80/3 Bad bush pilots..cross the margins of heavy weather and whang into mountains. *Ibid.* 29 Oct. 140/3 Mondale was ready for him and whanged the line back.

whang, *v.*[2] Add: Also **wang. a.** Also, as of the noise of a loudspeaker, the speed of a car, etc.

1952 *Observer* 2 Nov. 3/5 The words from the loudspeaker wang back from the quiet village houses, but the doors remain closed. **1977** *Motor* 19 Feb. 24/1 You rush from the pits just as the leading Porsches wang past.

whangdoodle, whang-doodle. *N. Amer.* Also **whangydoodle.** [Fanciful.] **a.** An imaginary creature. **b.** Something unspecified, a 'thingummy'. (See also quot. 1904.)

1858 H. T. Lewis in *Salem* (Illinois) *Advocate* 27 Jan. 1/2 They shall..flee unto the mountains of Hepsidam, where the lion roareth and the wang-doodle [*Yankee Notions* Feb. 52/1 whang doodle] mourneth for his first-born. **1870** *Punchinello* (N.Y.) 9 Apr. 30/1 In his own State the Ku-Klux raged, together with the fierce whang-doodle. **1890** *Boston Jrnl.* 24 July 2/5 The rougher element among the boys..formed the 'Whang Doodle' Club for the purpose of settling him. **1904** R. F. Foster *Practical Poker* 11 The 'whangdoodle', a round of compulsory jack-pots after a big hand has been shown. **1923** *Nation* (N.Y.) 22 Aug. 179 The downtrodden and oppressed force on the *Gazette*..has to live with this old whang-doodle and listen to his preterbacious scandulations. **1931** *Amer. Speech* VI. 259 Whangdoodle, whangydoodle, what have you, whatsis, whatsit, [etc.]. **1979** *Globe & Mail* (Toronto) 24 Jan. 6/1 In 1976... A new company sprang to the fore in Quebec... PQ Productions claimed to have invented the whangdoodle.

whangee. (Earlier example.)

1790 in W. Roughead *Bad Companions* (1930) 6 He.. sometimes wears a cocked hat,..and generally carries a Wangee cane in his hand.

whanger (hwæ·ŋəɹ), *sb.*[2] *U.S. slang.* Also **wanger.** [f. Whang *v.*[1] + -er[1].] = *Whang *sb.*[1] 3.

1939 J. Steinbeck *Grapes of Wrath* ii. 14 An' there we spied a nigger, with a trigger that was bigger than an elephant's proboscis or the whanger of a whale. **1976** M. Machlin *Pipeline* xiv. 160 She didn't get the idea so fast, so he whipped the old wanger out of his union suit and laid it on the table in front of her.

whank, whanker, occas. varr. *Wank, *Wanker.

whare. Add: Also with pronunc. (fa·re). Also 9 **wurrie. 1.** (Earlier examples.)

1807 J. Savage *Some Acct. N.Z.* xi. 77 *Wurrie,* a house, or hut. **1817** J. L. Nicholas *Voyage to N.Z.* I. xii. 352 A young woman..beckoned to me to accompany her to her *warree* or hut.

2. Hence *gen.*, a hut or shed; *spec.* on a sheep station, a building where the hands sleep or eat. Also with defining word.

1853 A. S. Atkinson *Jrnl.* 26 Oct. in *Richmond-Atkinson Papers* (1960) I. 135 James and I went to the site chosen for our new whare. **1853** J. M. Richmond *Let.* 11 Nov. in *Ibid.* 133 Their 'wharre', as it is called, is a most romantic tho' not v. commodious dwelling;..it is in fact a roof on the ground, thatched with nikau, a palm, the only one in N.Z. **1891** R. Wallace *Rural Econ. Austral. & N.Z.* xv. 225 Pioneering, or cutting a place out of the bush and building a log 'wharë', is extremely rough and lonely work. **1904** 'G. B. Lancaster' *Sons o' Men* 4 He scudded across the tussock flat to the eating-wharé; burst open the door, and cast the word loose on the boys. **1926** A. F. Webb in D. M. Davin *N.Z. Short Stories* (1953) 205 We had dinner at twelve and made a plum duff because there was time to cook it while we were all about the whare. **1939** J. Mulgan *Man Alone* viii. 95 You'll be sleeping in the *whare* down there... There's no room in the house. **1963** B. Pearson *Coal Flat* vii. 141 Eventually Miss Dane said: 'Time I got back to the *whare.*' **1972** M. Shadbolt

Strangers & Journeys i. 29 They found he had built a whare. A one-room shack of roughly-split timber.

3. Special combinations. **whare puni**, a (Maori) family sleeping-house (see also quot. 1911); **whare runanga** [*RUNANGA], a Maori council chamber.

1911 W. H. KOEBEL *In Maoriland Bush* xx. 262 It is regrettable that the interpretations of the carvings upon the beams and panels of the old *whare-punis* or meeting-houses have been lost. **1926** H. GUTHRIE-SMITH *Tutira* (ed. 2) 86 A *whare-puni* or sleeping-house. **1950** *N.Z. Jrnl. Agric.* May 502/2 The great michi, the barge boards of a whare-puni (a sleeping house). **1891** R. WALLACE *Rural Econ. Austral. & N.Z.* xiv. 218 A special house of assembly, the *whare runanga*..is set apart in which to receive and entertain strangers. **1910** J. COWAN *Maoris of N.Z.* xii. 163 Most Maori villages of any importance contain at least one *whare-whakairo*, a large house..used as the communal assembly hall, council-place (*whare-runanga*),..and guest-house (*whare-manuhiri*). **1955** W. J. PHILLIPS *Maori Carving Illustr.* 40 The Assembly House or whare runanga is often well adorned with carvings.

wharf, *sb.*¹ Add: **3.** *wharf-labourer, -master* (later examples), *-shed*; **wharf crane**, a crane fixed in position on a wharf (see quot. 1968); a wharf-side crane; **wharf-lumper** *Austral.* [LUMPER *sb.* 1 a], a wharf-labourer; **wharf-rat** (earlier examples in both senses).

1893 K. P. DAHLSTROM tr. *Weisbach & Herrmann's Mech. Hoisting Machinery* vi. 243 The ordinary wharf crane with capacity to lift 100 to 200 cwt. **1903** J. HORNER *Elem. Treat. Hoisting Machinery* xvii. 195 There is a class of fixed jib cranes which have no other name than that which designates the nature of their service, fixed wharf cranes... But by the term wharf crane, a broad type only is understood. **1968** *Gloss. Terms Materials Handling* (*B.S.I.*) IV. 14 *Dockside or wharf crane*, a jib crane designed for loading and unloading ships, consisting of a full or semi-portal, fixed or rail mounted, supporting a revolving superstructure and jib. **1890** *Evening Post* (Wellington, N.Z.) 11 July 2 A wharf-labourer who stands charged with the theft of an oil skin coat... The accused was at work discharging coal on the Mawhera. *a* **1948** L. G. D. ACLAND *Early Canterbury Runs* (1951) xi. 321 Trouble with wharf labourers.. kept them six weeks in Auckland. **1906** E. DYSON *Fact'ry 'Ands* iii. 39 Three weeks..later, Sarah was married to a wharf-lumper..and Fuzzy's dream of love was over. **1951** V. PALMER in *Landfall* V. 292 In Victoria..it was read by nearly everybody, from wharflumpers to politicians. **1836** J. M. PECK *New Guide for Emigrants to West* xii. 320 The following, from the register of a wharf master, will exhibit the commerce for 1835. **1968** M. M. SIBLEY *Port of Houston* iii. 59 Wharfmaster Daniel G. Wheeler reported that in that year [*sc.* 1844] 6.892 bales passed over the Houston wharves. **1823** J. F. COOPER *Pilot* II. i. 13 To burrow like a rabbit, or jump from hole to hole, like a wharf-rat. **1836** *Franklin Repository* (Chambersburg, Pa.) 4 Oct. 1/3 I've an idea, my man, that you are one of the wharf rats; and, if so, the less lip you give me the better. **1952** R. FINLAYSON *Schooner came to Atia* xi. 61 In the..market place by the wharfshed.

wharfie (hwǭ·ɹfi). *Austral.* and *N.Z. colloq.* [f. WHARF *sb.*¹ + -IE.] A wharf-labourer; a stevedore or docker.

1912 *Lone Hand* 1 May 40 The best testimonial to Hughes' ability is the fact that he has so often swayed the unruly 'wharfies', and controlled their organisation for so long. **1926** J. DEVANNY *Lenore Divine* vii. 47 Imagine Holly haranguing the wharfies from the soap-box. **1928** *Bulletin* (Sydney) 21 Mar. 12/1 'Twas Bill the wharfie grinned and stuck his hook into his belt. **1938** W. E. DEXTER *Rope Yarns* 234 Ships arrived [at Melbourne] with general cargo—oddments from a needle to an anchor—and were looked upon as legitimate prey by the warfies and lumpers. **1949** D. M. DAVIN *Roads from Home* 226 They..watched the wharfies unloading. **1963** B. PEARSON *Coal Flat* xx. 355 Sid Holland would put those bloody wharfies and miners in their place. **1978** B. MASON in *Islands* (N.Z.) Aug. 18 But one of his wharfie mates had given him a ticket for his birthday. **1981** *National Times* (Austral.) 25–31 Jan. 24/2 A lazy wharfie would be known as 'the Judge' because he was always sitting on a case, and another 'the London Fog' because he would never lift.

Wharncliffe (hwǭ·ɹnklif). The name of James Archibald Stuart-Wortley-Mackenzie, 1st Baron *Wharncliffe* (1776–1845), used *attrib.* and in the possessive to designate a standing order in Parliament which requires the directors of a company wishing to promote any private Bill for the extension of the company's powers to secure the consent of its members or shareholders, or a meeting at which this consent is sought.

1846 *Hansard Lords* 23 Apr. 874 Their Lordships had already required further securities, in particular cases, by the Order called Lord Wharncliffe's Order, which required in the case of established companies, if they.. demanded powers beyond their original powers—that..a meeting consisting of three-fifths of the company should have sanctioned the proposed alteration. **1851** ERSKINE MAY *Law of Parl.* (ed. 2) xxvii. 560 It is directed by an order commonly known as 'Lord Wharncliffe's order'. **1887** F. CLIFFORD *Hist. Private Bill Legislation* II. xx. 784 In order to prevent directors of companies from promoting Bills without the knowledge or sanction of shareholders, the House of Lords framed, in 1846, a series of Orders, under which 'Wharncliffe meetings', as they were afterwards termed, must be held, to consider each Bill so promoted. **1923** *Daily Mail* 24 Feb. 3/2 Your approval will be asked at a Wharncliffe Meeting which will be held in the near future. **1948** O. C. WILLIAMS *Hist. Devel. Private Bill Procedure* I. vi. 166 The Wharncliffe Order, then, was *not* first framed in 1846, as Clifford says, but in 1838; it was *not* one of a series of orders, but developed into a series by processes of division and addition; its object was *not* simply to prevent directors of companies from promoting bills without the knowledge and sanction of shareholders but to prevent the promotion of bills to obtain further powers (especially to construct branch lines—always a speculative project) without such sanction.

whassa (hwǫ·sǎ). Also **wassa**. Repr. colloq. or careless pronunc. of 'what is the (matter, etc.)'. Cf. *WHAT'SA MATTER.

1906 E. NESBIT *Railway Children* ii. 28 Roberta woke Phyllis... 'Wassermarrer?' asked Phyllis. **1942** BERREY & VAN DEN BARK *Amer. Thes. Slang* § 256/14 *What's the matter?*..wha'sa mat?, wha'sa matter?..wazzo maro? **1951** C. M. KORNBLUTH *Marching Morons* in *Best of C. M. Kornbluth* (1977) 156 'Wassamatter?' snorted her husband. **1967** 'W. WRIGHT' *Shadows don't Bleed* v. 84 Whassa matter? You don' believe me? **1973** J. DRUMMOND *Bang! Bang! You're Dead!* xxv. 86 'Wassermatter?' 'I want to join, is all.' **1978** M. KENYON *Deep Pocket* ix. 102 'Whassa time?' A quarter to three.

what, *pron., a.*¹, *adv., conj., int.* (*sb.*) Add: **A. I.** *pron.* **5. b.** Also *what say?* (*slang*, orig. *U.S.*), what did (or do) you say? shall we? (cf. *SAY *v.*¹ 2 m); *what's with..?* (*colloq.*, orig. and chiefly *U.S.*), what's the matter with..?, what has happened to? (see also quot. 1962).

1825 J. NEAL *Bro. Jonathan* I. 357 'Was he hurt, uncle Harwood?' 'What say?' **1855** W. G. SIMMS *Forayers* 52 What 'say, boys—won't a back-and-rush of the nags do it? **1934** S. LEWIS *Work of Art* 294, I think it would be fun to run up the Hudson to Ye Bunche of Grapes some noon. What say? **1966** *New Yorker* 24 Dec. 25 What say we skip a few 'fa-la-la's'? **1972** 'B. GRAEME' *Tomorrow's Yesterday* iii. 32 What say we have coffee at home for once? **1940** J. O'HARA *Pal Joey* 125 Nick what's with the free food? Explain. **1960** 'E. MCBAIN' *Killer's Choice* ix. 97 'What's with this kosher bit?' he asked. 'Get me some butter.' **1962** *Amer. Speech* XXXVII. 203 The elliptical 'What's with..?' (*Vos iz mit..?*) also has occurred, not only in the sense of 'What's new?'..but also as a substitute for 'What's the matter with..?' (a sense common in Yiddish). **1976** *National Observer* (U.S.) 24 Jan. 1/1 But it's not easy, because an interloper keeps asking depressing questions—such as: How do you feel about the state of the country? What's with the economy? **1977** H. FAST *Immigrants* III. 172 There are ways to find out what's with Jake.

c. *what about it?*: an enquiry as to the course of action to be adopted.

1927 H. A. VACHELL *Dew of Sea* 259 Your head keeper says we must have two guns apiece. Now—what about it? **1935** D. L. SAYERS *Gaudy Night* viii. 163 'I say,' said Mr. Farringdon, '..you simply *must* come.'.. 'What about it?' said Harriet, deferring to Mr. Pomfret.

8. b. (Later examples of *what all* without the negative verb.)

1901 H. SUTCLIFFE *Barbara Cunliffe* 9 Some reckon Tib helps him wi' his black magic, an' his turning stones to gold, an' what all. **1942** W. FAULKNER *Go down, Moses* 76 My mind gonter change about whatall I seed. **1947** E. MEYNELL *Sussex* ix. 225 Sheep are most unfortunate creatures in the infections to which they are liable—the foot rot..and the liver-fluke and what all. **1957** J. KEROUAC *On Road* (1958) III. iv. 202 Weariness and.. sorrow and what-all was on his mind. **1962** A. LURIE *Love & Friendship* vii. 123 That old Mr Higginson... Got his house full of bird dirt and what-all.

d. Also *that's what*; *you know what?*

1902 *Dialect Notes* II. 247 *That's what*, exclamation of affirmation or assent. **1908** L. M. MONTGOMERY *Anne of Green Gables* xv. 165 She'll..be ready enough to go back of her own accord, that's what. **1960** H. PINTER *Room* 98 You know what though? It looks a bit better. It's not so windy. **1965** 'LAUCHMONEN' *Old Thom's Harvest* ii. 29 'You don't bring anybody.'.. 'Oh—oh. That's what.' **1982** H. ENGEL *Murder on Location* xviii. 164 'You know what, Chris?' 'What?' 'You know it stinks to heaven as well as I do.'

11. a. (Further examples of *what for* introducing a clause.) (A non-standard use.)

1948 E. WAUGH *Loved One* 51 What for you want new ideas? **1984** J. PLATT et al. *New Englishes* vii. 127 *What for* you want to do that?

c. Also, *to show* (someone) *what for*: to make him take notice; to show who is in charge.

1960 N. HILLIARD *Maori Girl* 142 If a man came here I took a liking to, I'd show him what-for soon enough. **1966** *Listener* 18 Aug. 229/1 The stereotype of 'the wily oriental gentleman..the half-civilized levantine..the type of fellow who must be shown what for'.

C. I. *pron.* **3. b.** (Later examples.)

1966 I. MURDOCH *Time of Angels* iii. 32 Pattie resented too, what before she had scarcely noticed, Carel's assumption that Muriel and Elizabeth were socially her superiors. **1970** C. W. K. MUNDLE *Critique Linguistic Philos.* 16 Their claim is sometimes that so and so is..incorrect English, sometimes (what is very different) that it is absurd or meaningless. **1976** *Times* 7 June 14/6 To this he added, what could hardly be encouraging to other aspirants to riches, 'In building a large fortune it pays to be born at the right time.'

4. e. *what have you*: anything else (similar) that there may be, or that one can think of. orig. *U.S.*

1925 *New Yorker* 10 Oct. 28/2 New Yorker, Newarker, or what have you? **1930** H. CRADDOCK *Savoy Cocktail Bk.* I. 113 Fill the said tumbler with Water, Ginger Ale, or What Have You, until almost to the top. **1944** AUDEN *For Time Being* (1945) 115 Disguising himself as a swan or a bull or a shower of rain or what-have-you. **1956** A. WILSON *Anglo-Saxon Attitudes* 163 Too busy or going on leave or what-have-you. **1968** K. WEATHERLY *Roo Shooter* 110, I must have been away about two hours, buying the stores and what-have-you. **1973** C. BONINGTON *Next Horizon* iv. 66, I was eager to snatch at every opportunity to get myself established as a writer, film-maker, what-have-you, in an effort to find a clearly defined career.

5. b. (Earlier example of *not but what.*)

c **1883** E. FITZGERALD *Let.* in A. C. Benson *E. Fitzgerald* (1905) i. 19 Never having read his father's [poems] ..till drawn to them by me... Not but what he loved and admired his father in every shape but that.

6. Likewise with *as*.

1960 M. SPARK *Ballad Peckham Rye* iii. 29 'He's the same as what we are,' Dixie said. **1966** P. WILLMOTT *Adolescent Boys* ii. 26 They're all about the same age as what we are.

II. *adj.* **10.** (Later examples of *what time* used as a deliberate archaism.) Also, *what while* (poet.).

1861 D. G. ROSSETTI tr. *Dante's Vita Nuova* in *Early Italian Poets* II. 299 It is your fickleness..makes me tremble thus What while a lady greets me with her eyes. *c* **1882** G. M. HOPKINS *Poems* (1967) 93 Walked with the wind what while we slept. **1936** W. B. PEMBERTON *Carteret* ix. 253 He and his brother were quietly mobilising their forces what time a rollicking..Carteret dictated optimistic despatches. **1945** R. HARGREAVES *Enemy at Gate* 24 One side getting ready for the next time what-time the other as carefully and methodically prepared themselves to fight the last.

whata, var. *FUTTAH.

whatcha (wǫ·tʃǎ), repr. a colloq. or vulgar pronunciation of *what do* (or *are*, or *have*) *you*? See *WATCHA.

1934 J. T. FARRELL *Calico Shoes* 43 H'lo, baby! Whatcha say, kid! **1966** M. & G. GORDON *Undercover Cat prowls Again* (1967) v. 44 Whatcha getting me today, Tim? **1973** *Black World* June 65 Awwwwh, Baby what'-cha done to me-ee. **1978** 'M. CRAIG' *Were he a Stranger* xvi. 128 'Whatcha want?'..'We're looking for a man,' Ted called.

whatchamacallit (wǫ·tʃămăkǭ:lit), repr. a pronunciation of *what-you-may-call-it* (see WHAT-D'YE-CALL-'EM, etc. *γ*). Chiefly *U.S.*

[**1928** M. OSTENSO *Mad Carews* xii. 160 It's your—whatcha-may-call-it—your dowry!] **1942** BERREY & VAN DEN BARK *Amer. Thes. Slang* § 75/4 *Contrivance*.. *gadget*, whatchamacallit. **1974** R. B. PARKER *God save Child* (1975) ii. 13 A pet whatchamacallit... Guinea pig. **1979** *Globe & Mail* (Toronto) 24 Jan. 6/2 Wouldn't everyone feel silly if it turned out..that the whang-doodle was just a whatchamacallit with speed stripes?

whatever, *pron.* and *a.* Add: **3. c.** *adv.* Whatever may be the case, at all events. *dial.* (and *colloq.*).

1870 'R. PIKETAH' *Forness Folk* 15, I cuddent leave t' pleass whativver wi'out seein' her. **1900** 'A. RAINE' *Garthowen* 93 She's got a tidy pair of ankles, whatever. **1933** 'R. CONNOR' *Girl from Glengarry* 120, I am doing my utmost whatever. **1960** R. WILLIAMS *Border Country* I. ii. 58 What do it matter it's down?.. He is Will whatever. **1962** *Amer. N. & Q.* I. 15/1 Whatever, from the early 1700s to the present day..it was the musical that struck root as an indigenous form. **1980** *New Musical Express* 12 Jan. 33/1 Whatever, the myth looks momentous in its sleek new American threads.

4. c. *or whatever*: used after a noun (or nouns) to suggest that some other unspecified term might be employed instead, as being more usual, preferable for any reason, or more applicable; or something similar; or the like. *colloq.*

1905 W. JAMES *Let.* 25 Apr. (1920) II. 225 Poor Professor De Sanctis, the Vice President or Secretary or whatever. **1913** E. POUND *Let.* 7 Nov. (1971) 24 *If* Chicago (or the U.S.A. or whatever) will slough off its provincialism, if it will begin to be aware of Paris (or of any other centre save London),..there is no reason for Chicago or *Poetry* or whatever not being the standard. **1917** H. JAMES *Sense of Past* II. 83 One of those concentrated terms of pious self-dedication or whatever by which the aspirants of the ages of faith used to earn their knighthood. **1958** P. SCOTT *Mark of Warrior* II. 167 I'd get on to battalion or brigade, or whatever, and tell 'em. **1964** [see *KIWANIS]. **1975** I. MURDOCH *Word Child* 47 And even if we are all thoughts in the mind of God or whatever why should you be able to become God? **1981** 'M. INNES' *Lord Mullion's Secret* ii. 21 There isn't a handy second title around. Viscount Tom Noddy, or whatever. **1984** J. BARNES *Flaubert's Parrot* x. 129 Bourgeois monarchy, or bureaucratised totalitarianism, or anarchy, or whatever.

d. Similarly replacing other parts of speech.

1947 *Periodical* XXVII. 93 It was in one with a brown (or whatever) cover. **1976** *Church Times* 6 Aug. 9/1 Now that the Archbishop of Canterbury has 'relinquished', 'delegated' or whatever his metropolitical authority to the local Arab Anglicans.., is it not proper [etc.].

what-ho (hwǫt,hōᵘ·), *a.* [The exclamation *what ho!* s.v. WHAT B. I. 3 a used as an adj.] Superior, smart, stylish; designating the type

of person supposed to use the exclamation, esp. the heartier kind of officer and gentleman.
1937 in *Amer. Speech* (1938) XIII. 239/1 At the time of their installation the elevators at the Ritz Carlton were considered the What-ho-iest in town. **1973** *Times Lit. Suppl.* 21 Sept. 1074/3 Those who survive to be relieved by what-ho young soldiers in scarlet tunics and white bandoliers. **1977** *Time* 22 Aug. 37/1 The Legionnaires are a carefully assorted lot,..a soulful French musician, a what-ho English blueblood, a hulking Russian who once guarded the Czar's family, and so on.

what-if (hwǫ·tˌif), *a.* and *sb.* [An extended use of the phr. *what if..?*: see WHAT A. I. 5 a.] (That involves) speculation as to what might have been, had antecedent conditions been different; an instance of this.
1973 *Nation Rev.* (Melbourne) 31 Aug. 1455/1 The whatif game, a futile exercise in hindsight, poses such unanswerable questions as whatif Romulus and Remus had fallen foul of a hostile..wolf? **1974** J. IRVING *158-Pound Marriage* (1980) III. 57 Joseph Stalin..was himself a figure surrounded by a horde of *what if's*. **1977** *New Yorker* 29 Aug. 66/2 'The Eagle Has Landed', one of the current unalarming terror films about what-if, the what-if being, in this case, what if the Germans had tried to capture Churchill? **1982** *Times* 14 Jan. (Information Technology Suppl.) p. v/4 *What-If Games.* Computer software is available which allows users to change one variable in a set of data, and see how this affects all the other variables. **1984** *Computers in Teaching* No. 1. 29 All of the models are theoretically realistic and allow the undergraduate student to pose the 'What if..?' kinds of question, which are so difficult to answer without recourse to simulation.

what-is-it, var. *WHATSIT.

what-like, *interrog. a.* (*sb.*) Add: **a.** Also, of what kind or character. (Earlier and further examples.)
1719 A. RAMSAY *Poems* (1945) I. 214 To speer what like a Carlie is he. **1810** R. H. CROMEK *Remains of Nithsdale & Galloway Song* 37 What like may your lassie be? **1865** DICKENS *Mut. Fr.* II. III. ii. 16 She knows Miss Abbey of old, remind her, and she knows what-like the home, and what-like the friend, is likely to turn out. **1905** in *Eng. Dial. Dict.* VI. 443/1 What-like hat had he on? **1953** 'N. BLAKE' *Dreadful Hollow* xii. 150 Now you tell me—what like are the Blick laddies?

Whatman. Add: A proprietary term. (Later examples.)
[**1876** *Trade Marks Jrnl.* 8 Nov. 748 *J. Whatman*... W. and R. Balston, Springfield, Maidstone, Kent; Paper Manufacturers... Writing paper and drawing paper.] **1916** *Ibid.* 26 July 763 W. E. R. Balston Limited Genuine Whatman folded filter papers. **1976** *Ibid.* 28 Apr. 890/2 *Whatman*..paper and paper articles..not including printed publications. Whatman Limited, Springfield Mill, Maidstone, Kent, Paper manufacturers.

what-not, whatnot. Add: **1. a.** Also, 'whatever you like to call it'.
1876 E. W. HEAP *Diary* 11 June in *Publ. Amer. Dial. Soc.* (1969) LII. 56 [We] all started out on our grand excursion Picnic fishing party or what not.
c. Used as a euphemism for something the speaker does not wish to name.
1964 in Hamblett & Deverson *Generation X* 85 By the time I was fourteen I'd been a court witness in an indecent exposure case after an Indian doctor had been caught flashing his whatnot at me in an Adventure Playground. **1977** *Custom Car* Nov. 28/2 What ho, a twace of the fairer whatnot in the old Panther eh? **1977** M. RILEY *Ideal Friend* iv. 30 She said..tapping the Cellophane-covered éclairs, 'I don't know about you but these always put me in mind of nignogs' whatnots.'
Hence **wha·tnotism,** any or every kind of 'ism' (as a final term in an enumeration of 'isms').
1915 GALSWORTHY in *Fortn. Rev.* 1 Nov. 928 What is wanted in a work of art is an..adequate correspondence between fancy and form..so that one shall not be distracted by its naturalism, mysticism, cubism, whatnotism. **1951** KOESTLER *Age of Longing* I. v. 113 Those convicted of formalism, neo-Kantianism,..and whatnotism were given their deserved punishment.

what'sa matter (wǫ:tsăˌmæ·təɹ). Also **whatsamatter,** etc. Repr. colloq. or careless pronunciation of 'what is the matter?' Cf. *WHASSA.
1935 *New Yorker* 12 Jan. 18/3 What'sa metta with Kitty Shapiro? **1950** *Commentary* Sept. 255/2 'Whatsamatter,' he shouted at Rosa, 'you want her blood?' **1960** 'E. MCBAIN' *Heckler* (1962) xiv. 136 Whattsa matter? Something wrong? **1977** D. E. WESTLAKE *Nobody's Perfect* (1978) II. i. 102 Whatsa matter don't you wanna go home!!!

what's-her-face (wǫ·tsəɹfē̆ⁱs), occas. U.S. var. *what's-her-name* s.v. WHAT'S-HIS-NAME. Cf. *WHATSISFACE.
1980 in S. Terkel *Amer. Dreams* 5 Several times during my year as what's-her-face I had seen the movie *The Sting*.

what's-his-name. Add: Also **whatsisname; what's-your-name** (later example).
1942 W. FAULKNER *Go down, Moses* 87 Is that so? Look here, Mister What's-your-name—. **1943** K. TENNANT *Ride on Stranger* x. 114 And then Bleeby.. accusing me..of turning Whatsisname against him. **1979** S. WILSON *Glad Hand* I. i. 11 *Marilyn.* What is going on? *Brian.* Same old thing: raising the whatsis-name—the Antichrist.

whatsisface (wǫ·tsizfē̆ⁱs), U.S. var. WHAT'S-HIS-NAME.
1967 *Current Slang* (Univ. S. Dakota) Spring 5, [1964] *What's his face*, one whose name is forgotten. **1977** J. WAMBAUGH *Black Marble* (1978) vi. 79 They're having another Save Harry Whatzisface party there today. **1978** *N.Y. Times Mag.* 23 July 23/3 The derivation of some vogue phrases is a mystery:.. What visual need caused the unforgettable 'whatsisname' to become whatsisface?

whatsit (wǫ·tsit). *colloq.* Also **what-is-it, what's-it,** and (*U.S.*) **whassit.** [The phr. 'what is it?' used as a sb.: see WHAT A. I. 1.] = WHAT'S-HIS-NAME, WHAT'S-ITS-NAME, etc. (used variously of a person or thing); a 'thingummy'.
a **1882** *Philad. Times* in *Dict. Americanisms* (1951) II. 1855/1 The two negro girls, who figure as 'what-is-its', are paid $200 a week. **1898** J. D. BRAYSHAW *Slum Silhouettes* 158 'Now,' said Joe, 'who says pudden? Mister What's It—a little piece?' **1922** S. LEWIS *Babbitt* vi. 77 He's a what-is-it from Columbia. **1931** *Kansas City Times* 29 Sept., A Whassit. Excitement..Friday afternoon was caused by the appearance of an insect which [etc.]. **1954** P. FRANKAU *Wreath for Enemy* III. v. 215, I couldn't even walk along the passage to the whatsit. **1979** P. ALEXANDER *Show me Hero* xvii. 178 Suddenly you're a man. Not just because you happen to have a couple of whatsits, but because you *feel* it. **1984** B. FRANCIS *AA Car Duffer's Guide* 14 Do you think I ought to check the strength of the whatsit—electrolyte—while I'm at it?

wha:t-the-he·ll, *v. slang.* [The phr. 'what the hell?' used as an expression of irritation: see HELL *sb.* 9.] *intr.* To exclaim 'what the hell..?'; to make an angry demand for an explanation.
1924 WODEHOUSE *Leave it to Psmith* x. 211 While everybody's cutting up and what-the-helling. **1939** H. HODGE *Cab, Sir?* 181 The yawper, of course, is convinced that if he doesn't what-the-hell a little..we shall deliberately go a long way round. **1963** WODEHOUSE *Stiff Upper Lip, Jeeves* xvii. 132 This telephone call was Aunt Dahlia what-the-helling.

wha:t-the-he·ll, *adj. phr. slang.* [The phr. *what the hell!* s.v. *HELL *sb.* 9.] Casual, insouciant, devil-may-care.
1968 *Listener* 1 Aug. 130/1 Much of this is due to his casual 'What the hell?' attitude to the over-familiar pomposities of public life. **1977** *Time* 19 Dec. 47/2 The only real stumbling block is fear of failure. In cooking you've got to have a what-the-hell attitude.

whau (fau, wau). *N.Z.* Also **wou.** [Maori.] A shrub or small tree, *Entelea arborescens*, of the family Tiliaceæ, native to New Zealand and bearing serrate leaves and clusters of small white flowers; = *CORKWOOD 2. Also, the light wood of this tree.
1840 J. S. POLACK *Manners & Customs New Zealanders* 263 The *Pongo* and *Wou*..are varieties of the cork-tree. **1868** *Trans. N.Z. Inst.* I. III. 35 For floats, the light wood of the small tree Whau..was used. **1889, 1946** [see *CORKWOOD 2]. **1980** J. T. SALMON *Native Trees N.Z.* 120 Whau is an attractive New Zealand tree with an unusual, almost tropical appearance.

wheal, *sb.*³ (Later example.)
1857 C. M. YONGE *Dynevor Terrace* I. iii. 38 The last unfortunate wheal failed when the rope broke.

wheat, *sb.* Add: **2. b.** The pale gold colour of ripe wheat. Also *wheat-gold*.
1915 WODEHOUSE *Something Fresh* iii. 83 Joan Valentine was a tall girl, with wheat-gold hair. **1965** [see *French roll* s.v. *FRENCH 3 b]. **1970** *New Yorker* 8 Aug. 1 (Advt.), Great embroidered coat of cotton-polyester in wheat with pumpernickel trim. **1977** M. HERR *Dispatches* 175 He was wearing a denim workshirt and wheat jeans. **1983** *Harrods Mag.* Spring & Summer 104/2 Cotton trousers in White, Wheat, Slate Blue or Navy. **1984** H. HIRT *Heat of Winter* i. 2 His face was.. very fair—what the Indian matrimonial advertisements describe as a 'wheat' complexion.
4. a. *wheat-acre, -belt* (BELT *sb.*¹ 5 a in Dict. and Suppl.), *-bran* (later example), *-bread* (later examples), *-breeder, -breeding, -cake, cocky* Austral. (COCKY *sb.*² 2), *country, -farm, -farmer, -farming, -feed, futures* (FUTURE *sb.* 6), *-lumper, -lumping, ranch, rancher, -straw, -wine*; *wheat-bellied, -blazing* adjs.; *wheat-midge* (earlier and later examples). **b. wheat berry** (earlier example); **wheat-bird** (later examples); also, in North America, the horned lark, *Eremophila alpestris*; **wheat bulb fly,** the larva of a muscid fly, *Hylemyia coarctata*, which attacks the base of wheat stems; **wheat-duck** (examples); **wheatflakes** *sb. pl.* (orig. *U.S.*), a breakfast cereal made from flaked and flavoured wheat (cf. *cornflakes* sb. pl. s.v. *CORN *sb.*¹ 11); **wheat germ,** the embryo of the wheat grain, extracted during milling, and valued as a source of vitamins; **wheat-grass,** (*b*) a creeping perennial grass of the genus *Agropyron*; **wheat roll,** a roll made of wheatmeal bread; **Wheat State,** in the U.S., a popular nickname for Kansas or Minnesota; also used of South Australia.
1876 G. M. HOPKINS *Poems* (1967) 177 The blue wheat-acre is underneath. **1922** JOYCE *Ulysses* 196 Eve. Naked wheatbellied sin. **1863** *Harper's Mag.* Oct. 718/1 The enterprising town..is the wheat-market for a considerable section of the wheat-belt of the state. **1910** *Chambers's Jrnl.* Mar. 205/2 The laying out of ready-made farms in the wheat-belts of North-West Canada. **1980** *Jrnl. R. Soc. Arts* Mar. 175/2 In the wheat belts in the USA and Australia there were..large areas still undeveloped. **1848** *Rep. Comm. Patents 1847* (U.S.) 373 Taking the outer coating or bran from the wheat berry previous to grinding produces the following important results. **1865** Wheat bird [see *PEABODY]. **1917** T. G. PEARSON *Birds Amer.* II. 212 Horned Lark.. [also called] Prairie Bird; Road Trotter; Wheat Bird. **1937** BLUNDEN *Elegy* 60 seek the wide wheat-blazing plain. **1946** *Nature* 31 Aug. 293/1 The fungus was grown in various modifications of Czapek-Dox medium with addition of manganese sulphate, in some cases with.. autoclaved wheat-bran extract. **1862** M. D. COLT *Went to Kansas* 83, I live entirely on food made of corn.. leaving the wheat bread for grand-ma and grand-pa. **1880** [see *SOUTHERN *a.* 4 c]. **1978** *Listener* 10 Aug. 180/3 Oatcakes, potato cakes and wheat bread were cooked deliciously on a griddle. **1912** *Rep. 13th Meeting Australasian Assoc. Adv. Sci.* 536 (*heading*) The realization of the aims of William J. Farrer, wheat breeder. **1974** *Encycl. Brit. Macropædia* III. 1157/2 Wheat breeders regularly produce new varieties. **1898** W. J. FARRER *Let.* 30 Aug. in R. Archer *William James Farrer* (1949) xiv. 109, I should continue to carry on the wheat-breeding work at Lambrigg. **1965** *Austral. Encycl.* IX. 284B (*caption*) Wheat-breeding plots at the Temora Experiment Farm. **1883** E. A. ORMEROD *Rep. Observations Injurious Insects 1882* 20 Wheat-bulb fly..was observable early in March. **1921** *Jrnl. Agric. Sci.* XI. 98 Wheat-bulb fly..does not appear to do much harm in a wet, cold, or damp summer. **1975** *N.Z. Jrnl. Agric.* Sept. 67/1 The topics covered in the first few months of the scheme include cereal mildew, wheat bulb fly, yellow rust. **1772** M. PATTEN *Diary* (1903) 293 His wife baked a parcel of Wheat Cakes for me when I went up to Cockermouth. **1865** A. D. WHITNEY *Gayworthys* 218 There are wheat-cakes and maple syrup for your breakfast. **1981** J. DUNNING *Deadline* (1982) xix. 191 Trudy fixed him a breakfast of eggs and bacon and wheat cakes. **1933** *Bulletin* (Sydney) 1 Mar. 13 A good, typical S. Australian public man—a wheat cocky. **1941** K. TENNANT *Battlers* xxi. 228 Like many another broken 'wheat cocky'..Jim might be packing his kids and wife into his old truck any time now. **1776** *New-York Gaz.* 24 June 3/3 To be Sold..a very good Grist-Mill.. in a very good Wheat Country. **1890** *Stock Grower & Farmer* 29 Mar. 5/3 The panhandle country..is a fine wheat country. **1979** TANOUS & RUBINSTEIN *Wheat Killing* (1980) ix. 55 We were in the flat wheat country drained by the Missouri River. **1888** G. TRUMBULL *Names & Portraits of Birds* 21 He found this species [*sc.* the American widgeon] in enormous flocks on the wheat-fields, and..it was there called the wheat-duck. **1917** T. G. PEARSON *Birds Amer.* I. 120 Wheat Duck..is very fond of wild celery. **1980** *Hunting Ann. 1981* 40/3 A wigeon in one region would be called a baldpate in another area or wheatduck in another. **1958** *Publ. Amer. Dial. Soc.* XXX. 6 Farmers who have large wheat-farms. **1870** *Rep. Comm. Agric. 1869* (U.S. Dept. Agric.) 5 The wheat farmer..is not joyous over his market returns. **1959** *Cape Times* 18 July 2/5 Wheat farmers welcomed the good rains. **1965** *Austral. Encycl.* IX. 285/2 The most spectacular change in wheat-farming practice in recent years. **1932** *Daily Tel.* 8 Oct. 4/2 Oats quiet of sale... Millers' wheatfeed quiet. **1960** *Farmer & Stockbreeder* 29 Mar. 4/2 Demand for wheatfeed is steady. **1903** *Bull. Maine Agric. Exper. Station* No. 84, 143 Fruen's Best Wheat Flakes, 'made from the best Pacific Coast White Wheat'. **1939** G. GREENE *Lawless Roads* ii. 45 He looked up from his dry wheat flakes. **1970** M. KELLY *Spinifex* ii. 37 A grocer size wheatflakes box. **1908** 'O. HENRY' *Strictly Business* 252 After I had taken some $9,000,000 out of the soap business I made the rest in corn and wheat futures. **1979** TANOUS & RUBINSTEIN *Wheat Killing* (1980) ii. 13 The rise in the wheat price will mean a fortune to them if they own the wheat futures. **1897** *Sears, Roebuck Catal.* 15/3 Wheat Germ Meal... Cooked in 5 minutes. **1933** *Discovery* May 160/1 The richest source of vitamin E is wheat germ. **1980** *Sunday Times* (Colour Suppl.) 20 Jan. 57/3 Wheatgerm Loaf. A good hearty farmhouse loaf. **1762** W. HUDSON *Flora Anglica* 45 Common Wheat-grass, Dog's-grass, Quick-grass or Couch-grass. **1871** *Harper's Mag.* July 187/2 Among the more important of these plants the wheat-grass stands pre-eminent. **1968** F. W. GOULD *Grass Systematics* 186 Several species of *Agropyron* are important forage grasses on western rangelands, outstanding among which are.. bluebunch wheatgrass, and..western wheatgrass. **1934** *Bulletin* (Sydney) 3 Jan. 14/3 Harrison, a Wallendbeen (N.S.W.) wheat-lumper, carried 1170 bags of wheat the other day. **1957** Wheat-lumping [see *RING *v.*¹ II]. **1840** J. & M. LOUDON tr. *Kollar's Treat. Insects* II. 123 The Wheat Midge.. The perfect insect has a distant [*sic*] resemblance to the common midge, but is smaller. **1931** K. M. SMITH *Textbk. Agric. Entomol.* xi. 169 Wheat midge was especially destructive in 1926 in the eastern counties. **1874** Wheat ranch [see *sheep ranch* s.v. *SHEEP *sb.* 7 c]. **1947** *Mazama* Dec. 1/1 An overnight trip to the 500-acre wheat and stock ranch..near Wamic. **1947** *Chicago Tribune* 1 Nov. 11/4 A former life term prisoner..admitted the..slaying of a retired Canadian wheat rancher. **1977** J. GILLIS *Killers of Starfish* (1979) v. 32 Maybe he was a big wheat rancher. **1962** E. SNOW *Other Side of River* (1963) lix. 447 The dining room I saw was serving wheat rolls, turnips, cabbage and spinach which looked adequate and wholesome. **1978** H. MCLEAVE *Borderline Case* (1979)

iv. 49 Shigo brought hot coffee, wheat rolls baked on the spot, butter. **1911** D. MALLOCH *Resawed Fables* 65 He had a Friend in the Retail Lumber Business..and he sent him enough Money to get Home to the Wheat State. **1945** BAKER *Austral. Lang.* x. 187 Popular names for the various Australian states are:..South Australia: the Wheat State. **1950** R. MEYER *Festivals U.S.A.* 225 Kansas is sometimes called the Wheat State, but it is more familiarly known as the Sunflower State. *c* **1903** O. READ in *Library Southern Lit.* (1909) X. 4374 The Squatter, with his wheat-straw beard, his hay hair and his autumn leaf complexion. **1941** L. B. LYON *Tomorrow is Revealing* 44 A son with a bird's glint, and wheat-straw hair. **1954** E. POUND *Cantos* liii. 281 With gold cup of wheat-wine that he go afield to spring ploughing. **1982** C. THOMAS *Jade Tiger* 52 Wheat wine, almost pure alcohol.

wheatear[1]. Add: **2.** A pattern in embroidery, lace, weaving, etc., or an ornament in wood-carving, etc., resembling an ear of wheat.

1882 [in Dict.]. **1911** *Encycl. Brit.* XIII. 306/1 The backs of Hepplewhite chairs were often adorned with galleries and festoons of wheat-ears or pointed fern leaves. **1919** T. WRIGHT *Romance Lace Pillow* ix. 83 The ancient pattern called the *Wheat-ear and Cornflower*.. is still made. **1955** R. W. MILLAR tr. *Daniel-Rops' Jesus in His Time* ix. 366 Heavy columns of porphyry with rather ungainly capitals carved with grapes and wheat-ears. **1957** SIMPSON & WEIR *Weaver's Craft* xii. 151 The patterns most generally used for tweeds are..Twill.. Goose eye..Wheatear. **1977** *Penguin Dict. Decorative Arts* 374/2 Typical of the [Hepplewhite] style are.. wheat-ears with which the central splat of shield-back and other chairs are decorated.

wheaten, *a.* Delete 'Now *rare.*' and add: **1.** (Later examples.)

1922 JOYCE *Ulysses* 503 Wheatenmeal with honey and nutmeg. **1944** L. MUMFORD *Condition of Man* vi. 202 Wheaten bread.

4. Of a pale honey colour. *Wheaten terrier*, a soft-coated terrier belonging to a breed originally developed in Ireland and distinguished by its pale golden wavy coat. Also *absol.* as *sb.* denoting the dog (also, the colour).

1943 *Our Dogs* 5 Mar. 234/5 The soft-coated Wheaten Terrier has now been recognised by the English Kennel Club. *Ibid.* 19 Mar. 281/2 There were 30 entries of Wheatens at the Irish Kennel Club show. **1945** C. L. B. HUBBARD *Observer's Bk. Dogs* 146 Wheaten-coloured Terriers of soft coats have existed in Ireland for a considerable time. **1959** *Times* 14 Aug. 1/7 (Advt.), Soft-coated Wheaten Terrier puppies. **1971** F. HAMILTON *World Encycl. Dogs* 480 The mature Wheaten is an attractive, compact, well-built dog, strong and energetic. **1975** *Country Life* 6 Feb. 311 The Border terrier..coat of either wheaten, red, grizzle and tan, or blue and tan.

Wheaties (hwī·tiz), *sb. pl.* Also **wheaties.** [f. WHEAT *sb.* + -IE.] The name of a breakfast cereal made from wheat.

A proprietary name in the United States.

1925 *Official Gaz.* (U.S. Patent Office) 24 Mar. 738/2 Washburn Crosby Company, Minneapolis, Minn. *Wheaties* ..Cereal food products. **1935** *Good Housekeeping* (N.Y.) June (Advt., rear cover), Wheaties bring real whole wheat..in a ready-to-serve form that children adore. **1952** *Galaxy* Sept. 50/1 An institution is where they put Aunt Maggy when she started collecting Wheaties in a stamp album. **1968** *Shakes. Q.* Winter 38 For Ryot..to tempt Youthe with archery, would be as if Gluttony tried to corrupt his appetite with a bowl of wheaties. **1981** I. ST. JAMES *Balfour Conspiracy* vii. 241 Their morning wheaties came wrapped in a..Press Release.

Wheatstone. Substitute for def. of *Wheatstone('s) bridge*: a simple circuit for measuring a resistance by connecting it so as to form a quadrilateral with three known resistances and applying a voltage between a pair of opposite corners: a galvanometer connected between the other two corners registers no current when the ratios of the two pairs of adjacent resistances are equal. (Further examples.)

1901 *Phil. Trans. R. Soc.* A. CXCVI. 29 The two grids A and A′ formed two arms of a Wheatstone bridge. **1953** A. SMITH *Blind White Fish in Persia* i. 25 He had with him..a Wheatstone's bridge—a gadget of complex appearance for measuring the electrical resistance of the soil. **1979** E. N. LURCH *Electric Circuit Fundamentals* ix. 296 The Wheatstone bridge..is the elementary bridge circuit that is the prototype of all the more complex bridges used in electric circuit analysis.

b. Used in the possessive, *attrib.*, and *absol.* to denote forms of electric telegraph invented by Wheatstone.

1858 FARADAY in *Notices of Proc. R. Inst.* II. 555 (*heading*) On Wheatstone's electric telegraph in relation to science. **1881** *Ibid.* IX. 302, I found that one of our Wheatstone instruments was actually working at the rate of 180 or 190 words a minute. **1898** [in Dict.]. **1922** GLAZEBROOK *Dict. Appl. Physics* II. 788/2 Wheatstone simplex circuits are used extensively for the transmission of press telegrams to all parts of Great Britain. **1949** *Brit. Jrnl. Psychol.* XL. 37 A Wheatstone transmitter was driven at 6 and 14 words a minute by a variable speed gear.

wheaty, *a.* Restrict † *Obs.* to sense in Dict. and add: **b.** Of or pertaining to wheat.

1933 L. I. WILDER *Farmer Boy* vii. 47 The wheaty smell of new bread.

whee (hwī), *int.* [Echoic.] An exclamation of joy, exhilaration, astonishment, etc. Occas. as *sb.*, a high-pitched sound resembling this.

[**1918** E. A. MACKINTOSH *War, the Liberator* IV. 145 Whee-ee-ee-errump! The air was full of dust and smoke from a little way up the trench.] **1920** S. LEWIS in *Sat. Even. Post* 11 Dec. 10/1 'Whee!'..He sprang up, posed like the Statue of Liberty, hurled a pillow at her. **1944** E. S. GARDNER *Case of Black-Eyed Blonde* (1948) xx. 205 The little boy shrieked with delight. 'Whee-eee-ee,' he cried. **1960** M. MACDONALD in G. Maxwell *Ring of Bright Water* xii. 168 Her [*sc.* the otter's] basic conversational vocabulary was a high-pitched whistling 'Whee'. With loud and soft, short and long and other variations of 'Whees' she had quite a lot to say. **1978** N. FREELING *Night Lords* v. 24 Whee, thought Castang: he has worked fast. **1981** *Studia Mystica* IV. iv. 34 A cry of 'Whee!'

whee (hwī), *v.* [f. prec.] **a.** *trans.* With *up.* To stimulate, excite. *U.S. colloq.* **b.** *intr.* To utter a high-pitched sound.

1949 *Sat. Even. Post* 3 Dec. 3/3 And did that whee him up to do his Christmas shopping early? **1960** M. MACDONALD in G. Maxwell *Ring of Bright Water* xii. 171 She [*sc.* an otter] would lie on the floor..'wheeing' plaintively. **1966** *N.Y. Times* 17 Apr. v. 2, I was all wheed up, feeling great, I knew I would win. **1971** *Atlantic Monthly* Mar. 36, I got so patriotically wheed up that I ended by calling for three cheers for General Douglas MacArthur.

wheel, *sb.* Add: **II. 3. h.** (Later examples.)

1929 J. B. PRIESTLEY *Good Compan.* I. ii. 67 For the next hour she sat at the wheel under his tuition. **1972** T. P. MCMAHON *Issue of Bishop's Blood* (1973) xvi. 229 The long-haul truckers drove themselves right into a ditch after too many hours at the wheel.

7. a. (Earlier examples.)

1880 *Scribner's Monthly* Feb. 483/1 A few possessors of the birotate chariot, numbering some forty odd, enjoyed a 'wheel around the Hub'. **1882** *Wheelman* I. 13 'I love my wheel,' he said, 'as the yachtsman loves his boat.'

b. *to be on someone's wheel*: to be close behind someone, to be on his track; to put pressure on someone (to do something). *slang* (chiefly *Austral.*).

1941 V. DAVIS *Phenomena in Crime* vi. 78 Don't come here if there's a busy on your wheel! **1954** V. KELLY *Shadow* 89 Down there the cops'll give you a go. Here they're on your wheel all the time. **1959** A. UPFIELD *Bony & Mouse* 104 I'll be ready for it. I'm going to be right on Tony's wheel when it happens. **1969** O. WHITE *Under Iron Rainbow* 118 The inspector's been on my wheel to trace him.

c. *pl.* A car. *slang* (orig. *U.S.*).

1959 *Esquire* Nov. 70 J, *Wheels*, car. **1970** K. PLATT *Pushbutton Butterfly* (1971) v. 51 'Can I drive you to where you're agitating today?' 'Beautiful. I don't have wheels,' he said. **1971** 'H. CARMICHAEL' *Quiet Woman* iv. 33 I'd be out and about if I had wheels. Damn car won't be ready until tomorrow. **1982** G. LYALL *Conduct of Major Maxim* xxv. 222 'Did you find me some wheels?'.. 'Yep: a Renault 16TX.'

7*. *we had one but the wheel came off*, joc. phr. used to indicate that the speaker has not understood the subject of the foregoing conversation.

1937 PARTRIDGE *Dict. Slang* 366/1 *Had one and* (or *but*) *the wheel came off* (,*we*), a lower-class and military c.p. directed at an unintelligible speaker or speech. **1974** P. WRIGHT *Lang. Brit. Industry* xiv. 128 If asked for something foolish, you can say,..'I had one but the wheels came off.'

III. 8. b. *U.S. slang.* A dollar; = CART-WHEEL 2.

1807 H. TUFTS in E. Pearson *Autobiogr. of Criminal* (1930) II. iv. 293 *Wheel*, a dollar. **1825** J. NEAL *Brother Jonathan* I. 160, I shows him a double handful o' the royal goold; the ginooine yeller stuff—wheels. **1902** W. N. HARBEN *Abner Daniel* 143 How will fifteen hundred round wheels strike you? **1907** C. E. MULFORD *Bar-20* v. 47, I paid twenty wheels for that eight years ago.

c. A whole cheese, flan, or other food which is made with a circular form but may be cut into sections. Usu. with *of* and defining term.

1977 *New Yorker* 3 Oct. 53/3 A feast of varied delicacies, its principal ornament a small wheel of Camembert. **1978** C. CONRAN *British Cooking* 233/2 On May Day in the city of Gloucester a huge golden wheel of cheese, festively garlanded, used to be carried in procession round the town. **1978** *Neiman-Marcus Christmas Bk.* 93 A full three pound wheel, covered with protective black wax. **1982** M. BABSON *Death warmed Up* viii. 75 The wheels of pizza and quiche lorraine in the makeshift rack. **1985** *Sci. Amer.* May 67/1 The semisoft, blue-mold cheese is made from sheep's milk and formed into wheels weighing about 2·5 kilograms (5·5 pounds) each.

IV. 11. a. Also in phr. *the wheel has come full circle* and varr. (in allusion to SHAKES. *King Lear* v. iii. 174), the same situation has come about again, things have returned to their original position.

1944 W. S. MAUGHAM *Razor's Edge* v. 176 The wheel comes full circle... There was a time when the black sheep of the family was sent from my country to America; now apparently he's sent from your country [*sc.* America] to Europe. **1954** J. A. SHEARD *Words we Use* iv. 158 Old English had a derivative noun, *godspellere*, but this..was later replaced by a foreign loan-word,..*evangelist*... But in recent years the wheel has come full circle, and by a new process of derivation the Americans have their *hot gospellers*! **1966** W. H. LEWIS in *Lett. C. S. Lewis* 24 The wheel had come full circle: once again we were together in the little end room at home. **1977** J. CROSBY *Company of Friends* xviii. 117 The wheel was coming full circle. The public was fed to the teeth with disclosure. It yearned for the security of secrecy.

12. b. *on wheels.* (*a*) (later examples); (*c*) used as an intensive: in the extreme.

1914 [see *JOB *sb.*[2] 4 d]. **1943** S. LEWIS *Gideon Planish* 127 Looks just like a sweet little ivory statue, but is she hell on wheels! **1958** M. DICKENS *Man Overboard* iv. 59 It was his wife. She's a bitch on wheels, from what he tells me. **1970** 'D. HALLIDAY' *Dolly & Cookie Bird* iv. 42 Look at the time... If you're going to show us your balloons, you'll have to do it on wheels. **1978** S. BRILL *Teamsters* vii 275 In the 1930s and '40s and into the '50s, truck driving was sweatshop labor on wheels. **1980** N. FREELING *Castang's City* xxv. 174 Local wine-shipper in quite a high-class way... The business ran on wheels.

d. *silly as a wheel*: extremely silly. *Austral. slang.*

1952 T. A. G. HUNGERFORD *Ridge & River* 57 Oscar was sound, but silly as a wheel. **1966** J. MORRISON in *Coast to Coast 1965–66* 157, I warned Rose. She was as silly as a wheel, too, but a man's got to do what he can to protect his daughters.

13. c. *to see* (*what makes*) *the wheels go round* and varr: to see how things work; chiefly *fig.* with reference to the operation of a business, organization, etc. *colloq.*

[**1876** J. HABBERTON *Helen's Babies* 11 'I want to see the wheels go round,' said Budge.] **1923** R. D. PAINE *Comrades of Rolling Ocean* ix. 160, I want to watch a supercargo and see his wheels go round. **1922** *Broadcaster* Oct. 149/1 The natural indifference of the fair sex to any knowledge of what 'makes the wheels go round.' **1979** P. LEVI *Head in Soup* iii. 58 How amateur we were. Those who know how the wheels turn are always bored. **1980** N. FREELING *Castang's City* xv. 100 There's any amount of what makes the wheels go round... Featherbedding and barrel-rolling.

d. = *big shot* s.v. *SHOT *sb.*[1] 22 c. Cf. *big wheel* (*b*) s.v. *BIG *a.* B. 2. *slang* (orig. and chiefly *U.S.*).

1933 *Amer. Speech* VIII. II. 55/2 *Wheels*, substitute for big shots, leaders of a gang. **1956** B. HOLIDAY *Lady sings Blues* (1973) xviii. 149 After I got to be a wheel in the kitchen, I used to take care of Marietta by saving her the best of the food. **1963** J. N. HARRIS *Weird World Wes Beattie* (1966) iii. 36 Well, in business, Howie is a sort of minor wheel... He owns pieces of things. Radio stations, a commercial film company, a night club. **1975** *Globe & Mail* (Toronto) 12 Sept. 27/8 If politicians and business people and other wheels don't like it, he couldn't care less. **1980** A. FOX *Kingfisher Scream* vi. 94 Some Pentagon wheel's flying in and Don feels he has to travel up there with him.

15. c. In *Rugby Football.* (See quot. 1897.)

1897 [see *BACK *a.* 1]. **1927** H. WALPOLE *Jeremy at Crale* xvi. 284 Back they went, down again, the ball flung in. The Callendar forwards had it and manœuvred the finest wheel of the match, swinging round against all opposition.

V. 17. a. Of or pertaining to a wheel, etc., as *wheel alignment, arch, brake, trim*; furnished with a wheel, etc., as *wheel hoe, loader.*

1908 *Motor Man.* (ed. 10) vi. 165 (*heading*) To test wheel alignment. **1971** 'D. RUTHERFORD' *Clear Fast Lane* 70 I'm not going on till we've had the wheel-alignment checked. There's..a service station ten kilometres on. **1935** *Automobile & Carriage Builders' Jrnl.* Mar. 45 (*caption*) Details of the wheelarch, scuttle ventilator and rear locker. **1983** *Buses* Feb. 57/1 Longitudinal seating provided over the rear wheelarches. **1936** *Discovery* July 228/2 The average pilot regards his wheel brakes as an assistance to ground taxying rather than as a means of arresting his run. **1974** *Encycl. Brit. Macropædia* I. 378/1 Wheel brakes are generally hydraulically operated. **1858** C. FLINT *Milch Cows* 193 In weeding, a little wheel-hoe is invaluable. **1911** *Daily Colonist* (Victoria, B.C.) 22 Apr. 9/6 (Advt.), We carry a full line of Garden Drills, Double and Single Wheel Hoes. **1971** Wheel loader [see *DOZER[2]]. **1976** *Ilkeston Advertiser* 10 Dec. 3/4 (Advt.), Morris 1800 (Princess style) Saloon (1975 'P')... Fitted radio, wheel-trims etc. **1983** *Which?* Sept. 435/2 However, all of the 'MG' wheel trims fell off at some time.

b. Objective, as *wheel-changing*; instrumental, as *wheel-driven, -worn* (later example) adjs.

1974 *Harrod's Christmas Catal.* 69/2 Lotus..scale model: complete with wheel brace for wheel changing. **1972** Wheel-driven [see *SALT *a.*[1] 1 c]. **1944** BLUNDEN *Shells by Stream* 13 Its kingdom is the farm, the farmer's lane Its wheelworn churchway from the lonely road.

18. wheel arrangement, the relative positioning of driving wheels and idle wheels on a locomotive; **wheel-back** (earlier example); also a chair with such a back; **wheel balance** *Mech.*, an even distribution of mass about the axis of a wheel so that it rotates without wobbling or vibrating; so **wheel balancing,** the process of achieving this for the wheels of a motor vehicle; **wheel bay** = *wheel well* below; **wheel brace,** (*a*) a tool for screwing and unscrewing nuts on the wheel of a vehicle; (*b*) a kind of hand drill worked by the turning of a wheel; **wheel car,** a simple farm-cart (see quot. 1931); **wheel clamp,** a clamp designed to be locked to one of the wheels of an illegally parked motor vehicle to immobilize it; hence as *v. trans.*; so **wheel clamping** *vbl. sb.* and *ppl. a.*; **wheel-dog** *Canad.*, the dog harnessed nearest to the sleigh in a dog team; **wheel-dwelling, -hut** *Archæol.* = *WHEEL-HOUSE 3; **wheel landing** *Aeronaut.*, a landing (of an aircraft with a tail-wheel or tail-skid) in which the main wheels touch down first, followed by the tail; **wheel pants** *Aeronaut.* (see quot. 1956); **wheel-pit,** (*a*) (earlier example); **wheel-set,** a pair of wheels attached to an axle; **wheel slip,** the failure of the wheels of a vehicle to grip the surface on which they are travelling, so that they slip instead of rolling; also (*rare*) as *v. intr.*; **wheel spin,** the spinning of the wheels of a vehicle, caused by hard acceleration of the engine combined with the failure of the wheels to take a grip on a slippery surface; **wheel-tax** (earlier example); **wheel well,** the recess, under the wing of a vehicle, into which the wheel fits, or, on an aircraft, into which the landing gear is retracted; **wheel-window** (earlier example); **wheel wobble,** vibration of the wheels of a vehicle in motion, usu. when travelling at some speed; also *fig.*

1912 *Railway Mag.* Mar. 203/1 Of the total number of engines mentioned, 80 were of the 2–2–2–0 wheel arrangement. **1966** K. MÖLLER *Amer. & Brit. Railway English* 43, 0–8–0 is a notation for a wheel arrangement of eight driving wheels and no leading or trailing wheels. A great number of wheel arrangements have special names, originating with the railway on which they were first used. **1902** W. H. HACKETT *Decorative Furnit.* xi. 133 A set of six typical Heppelwhite [*sic*] chairs..had 'wheel' backs, on taper legs, with cross stretchers. **1927** W. E. COLLINSON *Contemp. Eng.* 90 The revival of Welsh dressers, wheel-backs and ladderbacks. **1968** J. ARNOLD *Shell Bk. Country Crafts* 133 In the hand-made 'wheel-back' there is the vestigial hub in the centre, but for economy this is absent from the factory-made splat. **1946** W. H. CROUSE *Automotive Mech.* xxiv. 533 Wheel balance can be checked in several ways. **1962** *Which? Car Suppl.* Oct. 139/2 Severe vibration developed throughout the car at speeds over 65 mph and a further check of wheel balance failed to overcome this. **1951** I. FRAZEE et al. *Automotive Suspensions* x. 276 (*heading*) Wheel balancing. **1977** Wheel balancing [see *SHIMMY *sb.*² 2]. **1976** 'A. HALL' *Kobra Manifesto* xv. 200 The problem was to keep my body arched against the curved top of the wheelbay, giving me a chance of escaping the wheels when they slammed home and locked. **1920** *Motor Man.* (ed. 23) xiv. 144 The most popular form of fitting is by means of separate bolts carried on the fixed hub, to which the pressed-steel wheel is held by a number of capped nuts which can be detached by a wheel brace. **1964** F. PRESTON *Man makes Hole* 6/2 The hand drill or wheel brace is of fairly recent origin, although it derives from the so-called bevel drill widely made in Germany. **1974** Wheel brace [see *wheel changing*, sense 17 b above]. **1975** R. A. SALAMAN *Dict. Tools* 187/2 *Drill, hand* (Wheel Brace..).. The modern form of Hand Drill was an American innovation of about 1870 which reached this country about the turn of the century. **1984** B. FRANCIS *AA Car Duffer's Guide* 38/2 Then, with the wheelbrace, slacken off all the wheel nuts about half a turn. **1931** *Antiquity* June 185 The special features of the wheel-car are..(a) the great length..of the body..; (b) the position of the axle tree *above*..the main beams of the frame; (c) the bumpers..; and (d) the embryo cart structure. **1968** J. ARNOLD *Shell Bk. Country Crafts* xi. 163 Round about Clun, they knew it [*sc.* a gambo] as a wheel-car. **1980** *Daily Tel.* 2 Jan. 3 (*heading*) Car park offenders face wheel clamps. **1981** *Times* 19 Nov. 3 Illegal parking in London has become so widespread that the Government may bow to police demands to be allowed to use wheel clamps to immobilize offending vehicles. **1983** *Daily Tel.* 14 July 19/1 Cars belonging to diplomats will no longer be wheel-clamped. **1980** *Daily Tel.* 2 Jan. 3/2 More officers will be available to tow away dangerously parked vehicles and the use of the 'Denver Shoe' a wheel clamping device, is being considered. **1983** *Sunday Tel.* 15 May 3/1 The wheel clamping team..will consist of one sergeant, eight police constables, 28 vehicle removal officers and eight traffic wardens. **1922** G. C. F. PRINGLE *Tillicums* 85, I put a smaller dog..in the lead and hitched Steal up next the sleigh as my 'wheel-dog'. **1965** A. V. WILSON *No Man stands Alone* 29, I firmly believe that the 'wheel-dog', next to the sled, can upset one any time he wishes. **1931** V. G. CHILDE *Skara Brae* vii. 174 The Jarlshof hut..illustrates..the normal construction of a wheel-dwelling. *Ibid.* 173 The relics from the wheel-huts round the broch of Jarlshof cannot be distinguished from those from the broch itself. **1928** N. MACMILLAN *Art of Flying* x. 142 With many aeroplanes..too slow speed of approach makes the elevator unable to apply the necessary load quickly enough. This results in a wheel landing with the tail up. **1942** *R.A.F. Jrnl.* 13 June 8 The second pilot..said that the impact was no worse than a bad wheel landing. **1956** *U.S. Air Force Dict.* 567/1 *Wheel pants*, a set of streamlined fairings around each wheel in certain fixed landing gears. **1971** *Flying* Apr. 40/1 The 172 did appear with clean, 175-style wheel-pants. **1850** S. JUDD *R. Edney* iii. 43 The subordinate branches were carried on below, under the 'bed' or main floor of the mill, near the wheel-pit. **1969** *Jane's Freight Containers 1968–69* 102/1 Provision has to be made for wheelsets to be available at the destination terminal. **1980** *Sci. Amer.* Aug. 33/3 A revolutionary bogie design which prevents wear on the wheel flange as the train negotiates a bend. No longer is the wheelset banging from side to side, abrading the flanges. **1945** H. J. MASSINGHAM *Wisdom of Fields* x. 193 A tractor was ploughing in the stubble... The machine was wheel-slipping. Wheel-slip means [*sc.* causes] soil-panning and winter-souring of it;..it means waste. **1960** *Times* 14 Mar. 21/2 Wheel-slip, with wheeled tractors, can be an intolerable nuisance. **1983** *Austral. Transport* Feb. 21/2 The locomotives are equipped with greatly improved wheel slip controls. **1928** *Daily Tel.* 11 Sept. 15/6 He took a grassy approach too wide, and had a wheel spin, from which he cleverly recovered. **1937** *Times* 13 Apr. p. xvi/4 On a sandy gradient of about 1 in 2, the vehicle was stopped and started, ascending and descending. No wheel spin or baulking was noticed. **1956** *Railway Mag.* Nov. 722/1 Steps already had been taken to check wheelspin. **1979** R. LEWIS *Violent Death* i. 7 The van came lurching..from under the trees... Wheel-spin threw up a mist of pine needles. **1780** A. YOUNG *Tour in Ireland* II. xvii. 75 Taxes are inconsiderable, for there is no land tax, no poor rates..only half a wheel tax. **1959** F. D. ADAMS *Aeronaut. Dict.* 181/2 *Wheel well*, a recess or hollow in a wing, fuselage, etc. for a retractable landing-gear wheel. **1961** N. D. VAN SICKLE *Mod. Airmanship* (ed. 2) iv. 103 Having the openings closed while the gear is down is advantageous because the tires will not throw foreign matter into the wheel well during ground movement. **1974** *Hot Rod Yearbk.* XIV. 219/1 Epoxy paint..was also sprayed on rear inner wheel wells. **1975** *Times* 31 Mar. 4/1 (*caption*) A Boeing 727 arrives at Saigon airport..with the body of a South Vietnamese soldier hanging from the wheelwell. **1821** M. BROWNE *Jrnl.* 2 May in *Diary of Girl in France* (1905) 25 There are [in Amiens Cathedral] two pretty painted wheel-windows. **1930** *Engineering* 7 Feb. 163/1 Concerned with problems of suspension and wheel wobble and shimmy. **1961** *Times* 17 Jan. 14/1 Apart from an alarming wheelwobble early in their second innings West Indies have had by far the best of today's play. **1978** A. WAUGH *Best Wine Last* vii. 56 It [*sc.* a car] developed a wheel wobble at between forty-eight and fifty miles an hour.

wheel, *v.* Add: **II. 8. c.** *colloq.* To bring (someone) *in*, as for an interview, meeting, performance, etc. Also, with similar meaning, const. *on, out.* Also *fig.*

1970 *New Yorker* 28 Feb. 29/3 The Administration wheels out what are at the moment issues..which everyone can agree on. **1977** M. ALLEN *Spence in Petal Park* xviii. 78 Wheel Prendergast straight in when he arrives. **1978** *Daily Mirror* 12 Jan. 2/4 The agreed quota for Japanese car imports in 1977 should be wheeled out again for 1978. **1983** *Listener* 20 Oct. 27/1 'Celebrities' were wheeled in before a studio audience. **1984** *Times* 9 Feb. 11/5 This new element is wheeled in when cousins come to stay. *Ibid.* 15 Aug. 11/1 Kenny Everett..was wheeled on with other celebrities to warm up a Conservative rally for the Leader in the course of last year's general election campaign here. *Ibid.* 8 Dec. 6/4 Although his field is limited to southern France from the fourteenth to the eighteenth century, the French media wheels him out to make pronouncements on Giscard's reign, his reservations about Mitterand's regime, or whether Nazi war criminals like Barbie should be executed.

10. b. To drive a car slowly, as when manœuvring into or out of a car park.

1962 R. UNEKIS *Chase* (1963) vii. 20 Grozzo wheeled the Olds into the big parking area. **1974** N. FREELING *Dressing of Diamond* 182 It was Castang who wheeled the Citroën out of the parking-lot. **1976** *National Observer* (U.S.) 11 Dec. 8/2, I wheeled the bright-blue test car into a parking space.

wheel and dea·l, *v. colloq.* (orig. and chiefly *U.S.*). Pa. t. **wheeled and dealed.** [f. *WHEEL *sb.* 13 d + DEAL *v.*] **1.** *intr.* To engage in scheming or shrewd bargaining, esp. of a political or commercial nature. Cf. *WHEELER-DEALER.

1961 WEBSTER, *Wheel and deal*, to take the part of a leader or wheel and to take charge of affairs or arrangements (showed the town how an absolute dictator wheels and deals—*Newsweek*). **1962** 'K. ORVIS' *Damned & Destroyed* vii. 53 You don't act like you really know where to wheel-and-deal yet. **1967** *National Observer* (U.S.) 3 July 13 Reagan could break loose votes from the Democrats if he really wanted to. You can always wheel-and-deal and get at least part of what you want. **1967** *Listener* 24 Aug. 250/1 Frost is wheeling and dealing off camera. **1974** *Publishers Weekly* 24 June 58/1 Lads who..wheeled and dealed with megacorporations. **1976** J. I. M. STEWART *Memorial Service* xiv. 234 What's in the wind is a little quiet wheeling and dealing about the black sheep of the family.'..'Why should the Provost wheel and deal about you?'

2. *trans.* To obtain by scheming; to deal or bargain in.

1971 R. DENTRY *Encounter at Kharmel* xii. 217 In other words, if we agree to shut up, you'll wheel and deal some pin money for us. **1974** *Scottish Daily Express* 16 Apr. 4/3 Dr. Henry Kissinger, due here shortly to wheel and deal hi way to stilling the guns. **1979** *Tucson Mag.* Mar. 49/1 The Inn was originally built to wheel and deal Arizona land.

Hence **wheeling and dea·ling** *vbl. sb.* Cf. *wheeler-dealing* vbl. sb. s.v. *WHEELER-DEALER.

1969 *Listener* 9 Jan. 60/3 As a proof of his mischievous intentions, he [*sc.* Henry II] invites the devious King of France to this gathering. It would need a Norman Mailer to describe accurately the wheeling and dealing that follows. **1976** [see sense 1 above]. **1981** *Beautiful Brit. Columbia* Summer 9 When silver prices rode the crest and silver-miners and promoters flocked to the Slocan.. the streets of New Denver..were alive with wheeling and dealing.

whee·lbarrowing, *vbl. sb.* [f. WHEELBARROW *sb.* + -ING¹.] **1.** Conveyance in a wheelbarrow.

1893 [in Dict. s.v. WHEELBARROW *sb.*].

2. *Aeronaut.* Landing where only the nose-wheel (of an aircraft with a tricycle under-carriage) is in contact with the ground.

1977 *Flight* 13 Aug. 480/2 We found the nose could be held up. We thought that there could be little excuse for nosewheel landings or wheelbarrowing. **1983** D. STINTON *Design of Aeroplane* x. 370 Sloppier landing habits, failure to get the tail down on landing..cause too many ballooning, wheelbarrowing and mishandling incidents.

wheel-chair. (In Dict. s.v. WHEEL *sb.* 18.) Also **wheelchair, wheel chair.** Substitute for def.: **1.** A chair on wheels used by invalids or the disabled; also = *Bath-chair* s.v. BATH *sb.*² 2. (Further examples.)

1817 JANE AUSTEN *Let.* ? May (1952) 497, I..am to..be promoted to a wheel-chair as the weather serves. **1841** THACKERAY *Second Funeral of Napoleon* iii. 77 A servant passes, pushing..a shabby wheel-chair. **1890** *Harper's Mag.* Mar. 613/1 Mrs. Aydler flitted backward and forward in her wheel chair. **1958** *Times* 15 Sept. 11/1, I was in no condition to register the details of arriving in the hospital ward in a wheelchair. **1977** *Whitaker's Almanack 1978* 584/2 Britain banned a team of 5 White and 5 Black young Rhodesians confined to wheelchairs from coming to the U.K. to participate in games for the disabled at Stoke Mandeville, Bucks. **1981** *Sunday Times* 14 June 86 A lot of people seem slightly on edge at meeting me in a wheelchair but my main aim is to dispel this straight away.

2. *attrib.* and *Comb.*, as *wheelchair patient, wounded*; *wheelchair-bound, -ridden* adjs.; also with reference to sporting events for those confined to wheelchairs, as *wheelchair athlete, games, Olympics, slalom.*

1972 Wheelchair athlete [see *wheelchair games* below]. **1981** *Daily Mail* 17 June 38/5, I am fortunate enough not to be wheelchair-bound. **1972** R. C. ADAMS et al. *Games, Sports & Exercises* (ed. 2) iii. 10/2, 1960..marked the first time the wheelchair games were held along with the Olympic Games... Wheelchair athletes from all over the globe were greeted by the Pope. **1972** *Even. Telegram* (St. John's, Newfoundland) 5 Aug. 18/1 The Wheelchair Olympics..were started after the Second World War for crippled war veterans. They have since become games for athletes with spinal cord injuries or those who have been paralysed by polio. **1970** *Stoke Mandeville Dict. Managem. Paraplegic Patients* 4 Occasionally indicated on the stiff hip or knee of wheelchair-patients. **1968** T. STOPPARD *Real Inspector Hound* 16 Magnus, the wheelchair-ridden half-brother of her ladyship's husband Lord Albert Muldoon. **1964** *Times* 12 Nov. 11/3 Carol Bryant..won a gold medal in the wheelchair slalom. **1982** *Daily Tel.* 5 Oct. 15/1 He would not change his mind about excluding 'wheelchair wounded' from the Falklands victory parade.

Hence **whee·l-chaired** *a.*, in or confined to a wheelchair.

1938 *Amer. Speech* XIII. 196 Wheel-chaired. **1973** *Times* 11 Apr. 8/6 A mini-bus is used in one of our split-site comprehensives to carry wheelchaired pupils from building to building. **1977** *New Scientist* 3 Mar. 499/1 Another council decision..caused the AAAS's wheel-chaired delegates to wheel themselves out of the room in disgust.

wheeled, *a.* Add: **1. a.** Also freq. in *wheeled chair*, = *WHEEL-CHAIR.

1847 DICKENS *Dombey & Son* (1848) xxx. 300 Withers the page, released..from the propulsion of the wheeled-chair. **1911** F. H. BURNETT *Secret Garden* xx. 213 The strongest footman in the house carried Colin down-stairs and put him in his wheeled chair. **1981** J. MANN *Funeral Sites* i. 11 I'm too fat for an operation, they say... It's endurance or a wheeled chair.

whee·l-engraving. [f. WHEEL *sb.* + ENGRAVING *vbl. sb.*] The art or craft of engraving patterns, etc., on glass by means of a rotating copper wheel and an abrasive mixture of emery and oil, sand and water, or the like.

1884 Wheel engraving [in Dict. s.v. WHEEL *sb.* 17 b]. **1929** W. BUCKLEY *Diamond Engraved Glasses of 16th Cent.* 8 Wheel engraving became common before the end of the 17th century and superseded the use of the diamond as the usual method of engraving glasses. **1957** *Encycl. Brit.* X. 413/1 By the end of the [17th] century this type of diamond point work was superseded in popularity by wheel engraving. **1975** *Oxf. Compan. Decorative Arts* 403/2 English glass..was greatly in demand in the Netherlands for the flourishing school of wheel-engraving in the German manner.

Hence (as a back-formation) **whee·l-engrave** *v. trans.*; also **whee·l-engraved** *ppl. a.*; **whee·l-engraver.**

1926 B. RACKHAM in W. Buckley *European Glass* p. x, The wonderful skill of technique shown in the finest German wheel-engraved glasses may make up..for the loss of nobility involved. **1937** *Burlington Mag.* Nov. 221/1 The lines are crudely wheel-engraved. **1961** E. M. ELVILLE *Collector's Dict. Glass* 55/2 There are quite a number of diamond point and wheel engravers today who have constant employment in such work. **1972** *Country Life* 30 Nov. 1499/1 A later tumbler in the same sale was wheel-engraved with a bust portrait of Prince Charles Edward. **1979** *Homes & Gardens* June 83/1 Often these declare their purpose at a glance, with wheel-engraved patterns of the ale brewer's hop leaves and barley.

wheeler. Add: **II. 13.** (Earlier and later examples.)

1886 H. BAUMANN *Londinismen* 232/1 *Wheeler*, velocipedist. **1929** *Newport & Market Drayton Advertiser* 28

June 3/4 Shropshire wheelers. Sunday's run to Bala. **1979** *Guardian* 8 Aug. 7/4 A posh camping shop..no shop for humble wheelers.

wheeler-dea·ler. *colloq.* (orig. and chiefly *U.S.*). [f. *WHEEL AND DEAL *v.*: cf. -ER[1].] A schemer, esp. in business or politics; one who wheels and deals (see quot. 1960).

1960 WENTWORTH & FLEXNER *Dict. Amer. Slang* 574/2 *Wheeler-dealer*..one who wheels and deals; an adroit, quick-witted, scheming person; a person with many business or social interests. **1963** *Economist* 24 Aug. 666/1 Two Dallas oil millionaires,..described as 'a pair of old-line Texas wheeler-dealers'. **1968** G. WYCKOFF *Image Candidates* iii. 20 Ted had been known as the Wheeler-Dealer because he always had important phone calls to make from his hotel room when we arrived on location. **1973** *Guardian* 23 Mar. 15/3 Old-style American corruption of the wheeler-dealer variety. **1978** L. HEREN *Growing up on The Times* ix. 301 He [*sc.* Lyndon Johnson] was a shop-soiled old politico, a wheeler dealer, and past master of consensus politics.

Hence **wheeler-dea·ling**, the activity of a wheeler-dealer; = *wheeling and dealing* vbl. sb. s.v. *WHEEL AND DEAL *v.*

1968 *N.Y. Times* 1 Feb. 42 Wondering what wheeler-dealing was going on over telephone lines among the various managements. **1976** *Listener* 5 Feb. 135/3 To ensure that..councils (or the community) got the upper hand in any wheeler-dealing between councils and developers. **1979** *Daily Tel.* 27 Apr. 36/6 Mr Prior also stressed that voting liberal could mean another 'hung' Parliament which would mean more 'wheeler dealing' at Westminster. **1984** *Listener* 22 Mar. 4/1 It is here in the intricate wheeler-dealing of the Common Market, the Atlantic alliance and international trade and finance that the 'diplomatic' reputations of the future will be made.

wheel-house. Add: Also **wheel house, wheelhouse. 1.** (Earlier and later examples.)

1835 J. H. INGRAHAM *South-West* I. xxiii. 247 The pilot (as the helms-man is here called) stands in his lonely wheel-house. **1846** A. HAWKINS *Let.* 20 Nov. in N. E. Eliason *Tarheel Talk* (1956) 304 The carpenter in coming out of the wheel house whare he had been mending the wheel dropd the candle on some loose cotton. **1906** 'MARK TWAIN' *Autobiogr.* I. 310 Rush..astern to the solitary lifeboat lashed aft the wheelhouse on the port side. **1976** *Southern Even. Echo* (Southampton) 2 Nov. 20/1 On the roof of the main building is a full-size replica of a ship's wheelhouse which is used for training.

2. b. = ROUND-HOUSE *sb.* 3 a.

1971 [see *ROUND-HOUSE *sb.* 3 a].

3. *Archæol.* A circular stone dwelling of the late Iron Age of a type widespread in northern and western Scotland, having partition walls radiating from the centre. Cf. *wheel-dwelling, -hut* s.v. *WHEEL *sb.* 18.

1935 V. G. CHILDE *Prehist. Scotland* x. 217 A wheel-house is in essence a walled area roughly circular or oval.. divided up into a number of voussoir-shaped rooms or compartments by radial walls arranged like the spokes of a wheel. **1957** T. C. LETHBRIDGE *Gogmagog* viii. 149 A considerable mass of pottery of what must be considered Iron Age culture, though of Roman date, has now been recovered from brochs and wheel-houses in the Hebrides. **1970** BRAY & TRUMP *Dict. Archaeol.* 254/2 Wheelhouses survived well into the Roman period as dwellings and farmhouses.

wheelie (hwī·li). *slang.* Also (*rare*) **wheely.** [f. WHEEL *sb.* + -IE.] **1.** orig. *U.S.* **a.** The stunt of raising the front wheel off the ground while riding a bicycle or motor-cycle.

1966 *N.Y. Times* 12 Nov. 45 A popular sport for young bicycle riders is 'doing a wheelie'. This means lifting the front wheel off the ground and balancing on the rear wheel alone. **1969** *Oz* Apr. 31/1 Odd Job tries to do a few wheelies but can't quite get the front wheel off the ground. **1975** *Courier-Mail* (Brisbane) 6 Dec. 2/4 Wheelies are no trouble to the world 125cc motocross champion... But..it's a technique he uses strictly off the road. **1982** *Daily Tel.* 25 June 6/7 Acquitting a motor-cyclist.. of careless driving by performing a 'wheelie'—driving with his front wheel off the road. **1985** *Daily Mail* 6 Apr. 25/1 That's the bike seen on TV with crash-hatted kids doing wheelies.

b. *transf.* In skateboarding, the stunt of riding on only one pair of wheels, with either the nose or tail of the board in the air. (In quot. 1978 further *transf.*)

1976 A. CASSORLA *Skateboarder's Bible* 10 Many of the tricks now popular originated that era, including nose and tail wheelies. **1978** *Evening Standard* 10 May 8/1 Wheelies centre rolls to a close. A pioneer skateboard centre is closing through lack of support. **1979** W. JONES in *Voices 20* Autumn 43 Down the subway he doth go.. Out the other end and into a wheely.

2. A sharp U-turn made by a motor vehicle, causing skidding of the wheels. orig. *Austral.*

1973 *Sunday Mail* (Brisbane) 29 July 3/1 'Hoons' felt free to do 'wheelies'—making U-turns at high speed to make their tyres scream. **1977** *Custom Car* Nov. 63/2 One of the most hair-raising wheelies I've ever seen.. necessitating an extensive chassis rebuild. **1982** J. S. BORTHWICK *Case of Hook-Billed Kites* xxxvi. 122 Tom did a wheelie into Route 77.

3. *Austral.* A person in or confined to a wheelchair.

1977 *Courier-Mail* (Brisbane) 14 Nov. 2/3 Terry Valentine braces the wheelchair as wheelie-shotputter Rene Ahrens..prepares to make his toss. **1978** *Sunday Mail* (Brisbane) 10 Sept. 34/3 So many places and things are inaccessible to the 'wheelie'. **1981** *Telegraph* (Brisbane) 14 Jan. 44/2 The wheelie symbol on selected parking spaces..is often ignored.

wheeling, *vbl. sb.* Add: **e.** (Earlier example in sense 'travelling in a wheeled vehicle'). Also, the condition of a road suitable for the passage of (wheeled) vehicles.

1850 L. SAWYER *Jrnl.* 3 July in *Way Sketches* (1926) v. 81 Our road lay over deep barren sand, which rendered the wheeling very difficult. **1864** *Ret. Agric. Soc. Maine* 52 The January thaw..gives us bare hills and wheeling. **1873** 'G. HAMILTON' *Twelve Miles* ii. 25 He told her he would give her a sleigh-ride when it came wheeling.

j. *wheeling and dealing*: see *WHEEL AND DEAL *v.* Also **wheeling-dealing** *vbl. sb* and *ppl. a.*

1973 *Guardian* 21 June 2/3 The cliché of the moment is that Mr Brezhnev is..a sort of wheeling-dealing gladhander. **1977** *Guardian Weekly* 28 Aug. 22/4 The wheeling-dealing that went on within the tribunal when it came to considering the verdicts.

wheel-lock. Add: **3. b.** = LOCK *sb.*[2] 15.

1927 *Observer* 20 Feb. 21/3 The majority of our fire-fighting appliances are not provided with adequate wheel-locks.

wheelman. Add: **1.** (Earlier examples.)

1865 *Oregon State Jrnl.* 12 Aug. 2/5 The wheelman says that large fragments of the bottom and a part of the rudder were afterwards seen alongside the wreck. **1866** 'MARK TWAIN' *Lett. from Hawaii* (1967) 195 Four other gentlemen and the wheelsman were all assembled on the little after portion of the deck.

3. A driver, *spec.* (*Criminals' slang*) the driver of a getaway vehicle. orig. *U.S.*

1935 J. HARGAN *Gloss. Prison Lang.* 8 *Wheelman*, driver of a getaway car. **1962** 'K. ORVIS' *Damned & Destroyed* xii. 80 Later on,..he began driving a cab. Also being a wheel-man for the mobs. **1967** M. PROCTER *Exercise Hoodwink* vi. 44 The thieves had locked themselves in, and when they had emptied the safe, they had phoned for their wheel man like calling for a taxi. **1975** *Publishers Weekly* 27 Jan. 283/3 (Advt.), When a young California hoodlum blew the brains out of a helpless store clerk last year Ken Pestana was the unwitting wheelman waiting outside.

wheelwork. Add: **c.** Applied to the works of a watch or other time-piece. Also *fig.*

1843 *Penny Cycl.* XXVII. 107/2 In a repeater there is an additional train of wheels between the frame-plates, called the runners, or little wheel-work. **1868** *Chambers's Encycl.* X. 82/1 The arrangement of the wheel-work in a watch. **1890** W. JAMES *Princ. Psychol.* II. xix. 112 There seem no good grounds for supposing this additional wheelwork in the mind. **1981** *Times* 2 May 15/4 Examination of the instrument reveals nothing inconsistent with it being a bench-timer, possibly contrived from an early frame and wheel work.

wheelwrighting. (Earlier example.)

1883 *Rep. Indian Affairs* (U.S.) 253 Carpentry, harness-making, wheelwrighting.

whelk[1]. Add: **d. whelk-stall** (later examples); freq. in phr. *to be unable to run a whelk stall* and varr., to be incompetent, esp. in business; **whelk-tingle,** substitute for def.: = *TINGLE *sb.*[3]; (later example).

1894 J. BURNS in *South-Western Star* 13 Jan. 3/4 From whom am I to take my marching orders? From men who fancy they are Admirable Crichtons,..but who have not got sufficient brains and ability to run a whelk stall? **1928** 'N. SHUTE' *So Disdained* iv. 159 If you try to run him as a manager as well, then your luck'll be out... He couldn't run a whelk stall to make it pay. **1960** C. STORR *Marianne & Mark* iii. 42 The beaches and the whelk stalls. **1965** O. MANNING *Friends & Heroes* xiv. 148, I said we were all disgusted at the way the School had gone down; and I said things would be no better under Callard. I said Callard couldn't run a whelk-stall. **1966** *Hansard Commons* 22 Nov. 1283 The great majority of hon. Gentlemen opposite have not the qualifications to run a whelk stall profitably. **1980** M. DRABBLE *Middle Ground* 25 Which should she pick?..vain Albert from the whelk stall? **1981** *Financial Times* 1 Apr. 15/2 None of them [*sc.* the 364 economists] has had enough practical experience to run the proverbial whelk stall. **1959** *Times* 25 Aug. 5/6 A survey of the damage done on English oyster beds by the American whelk tingle..has just been concluded.

whelp, *sb.*[2] Erron. for WELT *sb.*[1]

1912 in *Dialect Notes* III. 593 She whipped the horse till she raised great whelps on him. **1952** *Publ. Amer. Dial. Soc.* XVII. 34 Time was in the upcountry when the teacher would, with a hickory, raise whelps on the legs of a recalcitrant pupil. **1962** W. FAULKNER *Reivers* viii. 181 How the hell did Sugar Boy ever let him get this far without at least one whelp on him? **1980** *Verbatim* Autumn 17/2 A quite common mispronunciation is 'whelp' for 'welt': 'He has some big whelps on his arm.'

whelphood. (Earlier example.)

1847 E. BRONTË *Wuthering Heights* I. xiii. 325 It [*sc.* a dog] had spent its whelphood at the Grange.

whelping, *vbl. sb.* Add: *whelping ice* (see quots.).

c **1900** J. P. HOWLEY in *Regional Lang. Stud.—Newfoundland* (1978) VIII. 23 Whelping ice. The part of an ice field where they [*sc.* seals] bring forth their young. **1919** W. T. GRENFELL *Labrador Doctor* (1920) ix. 174 The smoother, whiter variety known as 'whelping ice'—that is, the Arctic shore ice..on which the seals give birth to their pups. **1969** H. HORWOOD *Newfoundland* xii. 83 The drift ice where they [*sc.* seals] give birth to their young is the whelping ice.

when, *adv.* (*conj.*, *sb.*). Add: **I. 2.** Also as a reply to the formula *say when.*

1911 *Maclean's Mag.* Oct. 297/2 'Say when?' I held the glass with a shaking hand: 'When.' **1931** A. POWELL *Afternoon Men* I. 13 'Say when, sir,' said the waiter. 'When,' said Pringle. **1948** E. WAUGH *Loved One* 3 'When,' he added aside to the young man, who helped him to whisky. 'Right up with soda, please.'

II. 4. a. Also with ellipsis of following clause: in the past, in the old days. *N. Amer. colloq.*

1962 M. RICHLER in *Kenyon Rev.* Winter 88 Six months from now..I'll be saying I knew you when. **1968** H. WAUGH *'30' Manhattan East* (1969) 163 She needn't try those airs with me. I knew her when. **1984** M. HINXMAN *Night they murdered Chelsea* viii. 65 The Hearst newspaper group are even flying in Gloria Beesley to cover the case. She knew Charlotte when.

whenabouts. Add: Also, the approximate time at which a thing happened. Also *interrog.*

1952 V. GOLLANCZ *My Dear Timothy* 74 By eighteen hundred and ninety-eight, when or whenabouts I first heard it. **1966** A. E. LINDOP *I start Counting* xx. 247 'When? Whenabouts?' '..Lemme see. Be about four o'clock in the afternoon.'

whenceness (hwe·nsnės). *rare.* [f. WHENCE *adv.*, *conj.* (*sb.*) + -NESS.] The place or source from which something comes or arises; place of origin.

1922 JOYCE *Ulysses* 388 All is hidden when we would backward see from what region of remoteness the whatness of our whoness hath fetched his whenceness. **1980** *Dædalus* Spring 248 Given the group's oblique disposition, the 'whenceness' of this saved soul seems unmistakable.

whenever, *adv.*, *conj.* Add: **I. 1.** Also as adv. with loss of relative force: at whatever time. *colloq.*

1917 H. JAMES *Ivory Tower* in *Amer. Novels* III. v. 221, I said to myself..three weeks ago, or whenever, that it wasn't for that I was going to come over. **1982** J. D. MACDONALD *Cinnamon Skin* xi. 107 Maybe we can leave it that you can come over to Lauderdale whenever.

where, *adv.* and *conj.* Add: **II. 10. c.** In U.S. use freq. equivalent to THAT *conj.* (see also quot. 1931).

1927 E. O'NEILL *Marco Millions* II. ii. 122, I can see where I'll have to be telling her what to do every second. **1931** G. O. CURME *Syntax* 245 This old use of *where* with the force of a noun + *in which* is still heard in colloquial speech: 'This morning I read in the Tribune *where* (in the literary language *an account in which*) *a boy killed his father*.' **1938** D. RUNYON *Furthermore* iii. 51, I see by the papers where three Brooklyn citizens are scragged. **1958** T. CAPOTE *Breakfast at Tiffany's* 110 [I] had read where the Trawlers were countersuing for divorce. **1965** *New Yorker* 15 May 45, I see where the St. Regis has changed hands again. **1976** *National Observer* (U.S.) 14 Aug. 2/4, I can see where people might think that Kelley doesn't know what's going on in his own organization.

d. In *colloq.* phr. *where it's* (*he's, she's*) *at*: the true or essential nature of a situation (or person); the true state of affairs; a place of central activity. Cf. *AT *prep.* 1 d. orig. *U.S.*

1903 [see *AT *prep.* 1 d]. **1965** *Daily Mail* 2 Oct. 5/2 What's the phrase you use for being in touch?.. Where it's at. **1967** *Listener* 26 Oct. 522/3 As Dylan says, 'I'll let you be in my dream, if I can be in yours.' I think I know where he's at. **1971** *Melody Maker* 9 Oct. 17/5 The musicians frequently became frustrated..not really believing their own bands were where it was at. **1974** R. M. PIRSIG *Zen & Art of Motorcycle Maintenance* x. 117 That, today, is where it is at, and will continue to be at for a long time to come. **1977** W. J. WEATHERBY *Home in Dark* xiii. 69 She was always a housewife at heart. She just took too long to find out where she was at.

e. U.S. dial. *to where*, to or at a point, position, etc., such that; to such an extent that. Occas. with omission of *to.*

1933 M. K. RAWLINGS *South Moon Under* xvi. 157 Is your loggin' to where you kin leave it for a whiles? **1938** —— *Yearling* xvi. 181 My grand-pappy got hisself stung oncet to where he was in the bed a fortnight. **1960** H. LEE *To kill Mockingbird* xi. 109 Having developed my talent to where I could throw up a stick and almost catch it coming down. **1969** B. K. GREEN *Wild Cow Tales* 247, I would pitch a rope over a steer's neck and give it a whip-like motion to where the knot would come back under his neck on the ground back on my side. **1974** N. GUIDICI in S. Terkel *Working* VI. 316, I want to have enough money where I wouldn't have to be a bum on the street.

11. c. *to the point where*, to a situation, condition, extent, etc., such that.

1938 F. SCOTT FITZGERALD *Let.* 22 Feb. (1964) 569 If t ever came to the point where you thought you ought to lay up under medical care, his is the sanitarium which I should choose. **1960** *Radio Amateur's Handbk.* (ed. 37) 190/2 Adjust the potentiometer..to the point where the oscillator cannot be heard between dots and dashes at normal keying speed. **1968** CHOMSKY & HALLE *Sound Pattern Eng.* 329 Our investigations of these features have not progressed to a point where a discussion in print would be useful. **1970** P. WHITTLE *Probability* v. 100 Models which can be simple, without being idealized to the point where they have no practical value.

12. b. (Later example.)

1929 R. A. CRAM *Catholic Church & Art* iv. 57 Where the pagan architecture had been an *exterior* art..and where Roman and Byzantine art had striven to achieve space in its simplest form, the North worked for interior space.

IV. 15. b. *whereamong* (later example), *wherewithout* (later example).

1929 R. BRIDGES *Testament of Beauty* I. 17 Whereamong hath the sceptic honourable place. **1899** BEERBOHM *More* 95 Mere masses of colour, crude intensity of conception, wherewithout posters fail, were quite unnecessary.

whereof, *adv.* Add: **II. 5. b.** Phr. *to know whereof one speaks* (or *writes*, etc.): to know what one is talking about, to speak from experience.

1922 H. VAN LOON *Story of Mankind* xliii. 256 He [*sc.* Erasmus] had travelled a great deal and knew whereof he wrote. **1967** R. STEIN *Great Cars* 165/1 Ettore Bugatti knew whereof he spoke when he advised people griping about hard starting to keep their cars in heated garages. **1975** *Publishers Weekly* 24 Mar. 42/2 Fischer has been a lifelong reporter on public affairs and was on LBJ's Commission on Rural Poverty, so he knows whereof he writes.

whereso, *adv., conj.* **4.** (Later *arch.* example.)

1889 'MARK TWAIN' *Connecticut Yankee* xi. 130 Whereso if ye be minded..it is in the east.

wheresomever. 3. (Later example.)

1837 R. BIRD *Nick of Woods* iii. 43 He haunts about our woods..and kills 'em [*sc.* Indians] wheresomever he catches 'em.

whereto, *adv.* **I. 2.** (Later *arch.* example.)

1900 A. MEYNELL *John Ruskin* vii. 119 Whereto, then, is the persuasion of this book directed?

wherever, *adv., conj.* **2. b.** For 'Now *rare* or *Obs.*' read: Now usu. preceded by *or*, whatever place. (Later examples.) Cf. *WHATEVER *pron.* and *a.* 4 c; *WHENEVER *adv., conj.* 1. *colloq.*

1917 H. JAMES *Sense of Past* IV. iii. 242 A pot of about the size..of that one..on the cabinet or wherever. **1952** A. HOCKING *Best Laid Plans* vi. 90 This committee will now adjourn to The Pig and Whistle or wherever, for liquid refreshment. **1976** *Bookseller* 24 Apr. 2088/1 A jet flies off to London, New York, Paris, or wherever. **1978** *Jrnl. R. Soc. Arts* CXXVI. 220/1 In times of trouble, whether in Cyprus, or Karachi, or wherever, you would see everybody tuning in to the BBC. **1981** W. BRONK *Life Supports* 31 The terrible world where hollow catastrophe Hangs wherever.

whet, *v.* Add: **3.** Also with *up*.

1823 T. BEWICK *Memoir* (1975) xii. 105 The extreme interest I had always felt in the hope of administering to the pleasures & amusement of youth..whetted me up & stimulated me to proceed.

absol. **1877** 'MARK TWAIN' in *Atlantic Monthly* Nov. 586/2 You see 'em begin to whet up whenever they smell argument in the air. **1893** —— in *Century Mag.* Jan. 342/2 The people were still in the drawing-room, whetting up for dinner.

whew, *sb.*[1] Add: **2. b.** *dial.* A factory hooter.

1869 J. HARTLEY *Halifax Clock Almanack* 48 Yond's th' whew, soa we mun goa an' do another bit for th' maister. **1929** J. B. PRIESTLEY *Good Compan.* iv. 118 Bruddersford has an elaborate system of factory buzzers—usually known as whews. **1934** —— *Eng. Journey* vi. 194 Time for them had been marked by the sound of its [*sc.* the mill's] hooter—locally known as a 'whew'.

whew, *sb.*[2] *dial.* [f. WHEW *v.*[2]] A hurry; *esp.* in phr. *all of a whew*, in a hurry, impatient or excited.

1905 in *Eng. Dial. Dict.* VI. 453/1 Sec a whew he's in. **1922** A. BROWN *Old Crow* xi. 119 He wants me to go down in his river pastur', choppin'. All of a whew to git at it.

whey, *sb.* Add: **3.** *wheyhued, -pale* (examples), *-sour* adjs.; **wheygoose** *nonce-wd.*, used as a term of opprobrium.

1949 C. FRY *Lady's not for Burning* I. 8 What shall I do With this nattering wheygoose, Alizon? Shall I knock him down? *a* **1915** JOYCE *Giacomo Joyce* (1968) 2 Smitten by the hot creamy light, grey wheyhued shadows under the jawbones. **1916** —— *Portrait of Artist* v. 193 He saw in a moment the student's wheypale face. **1978** H. WOUK *War & Remembrance* xiii. 129 Ascher's whey-pale face wanly lit up at the comparison. **1922** JOYCE *Ulysses* 29 With her weak blood and wheysour milk she had fed him.

which, *a.* and *pron.* **B. I. 2. b.** For 'humorous' read '*dial.* or humorous' and add later examples.

1835 A. PARKER *Trip to West & Texas* 88 Ask a question, and if they do not understand you, they reply '*which?*' **1910** P. W. JOYCE *Eng. as we speak it in Ireland* 348 When a person does not quite catch what another says, there is generally a query... Our people often express this query by the single word 'which?' **1938** W. FAULKNER *Unvanquished* 83 Yankee say, 'Sartoris, John Sartoris,' and Marse John say, 'Which? Say which?' **1950** —— *Coll. Stories* 752 'Here,' Weddel said, extending the tumbler... The Negro stopped... 'Which?' he said. He looked at the glass.

III. 7. c. (Further examples.) Now very common in spoken English.

Quot. 1950 is a mixed construction. Cf. AND *conj.* 11 a. **1902** H. JAMES *Wings of Dove* I. iv. 85 He imaged it—which was enough as some proved vanity. **1950** PATTERSON & CONRAD *Scottsboro Boy* II. v. 122 He..said, 'Haven't I told you black sons of bitches about talking after bed hours?' 'I wasn't talking,' I said. And which I wasn't. **1981** *London Rev. Bks.* 19 Feb.–4 Mar. 9/2 To be fair, Frances Partridge is concerned in this book to put the record straight on the central episode of Carrington's suicide: to emphasize Ralph Partridge's fear that this would happen, and his desperate efforts to avert it. Which is reasonable enough.

whi·ch-a-way, *pron.* *U.S. colloq.* and *dial.* [Cf. WHICH *a.* and *pron.* B. 12; *every which way* s.v. EVERY *a.* 1 f in Dict. and Suppl.] Which way, in what direction. Cf. *THAT-A-WAY *adv.*

1909 *Dialect Notes* III. 381 *Which-a-way*,..which way. **1938** M. K. RAWLINGS *Yearling* i. 13 Which-a-way will we begin huntin' him? **1968** O. SPANN in P. Oliver *Screening Blues* iii. 125 Well, you know I'm so mad this morning, don't know whichaway to go.

whichever, *a.* and *pron.* Add: (Later examples of a person.)

1880 HARDY *Trumpet-Major* I. ix. 178 Whichever of us she likes best, he shall take her home. **1919** G. B. SHAW *Inca of Perusalem* in *Heartbreak House* 205 The Inca is to come and look at me, and pick out whichever of his sons he thinks will suit.

whi·chway(s, *adv.* Chiefly *U.S.* = *every which way* s.v. EVERY *a.* 1 f in Dict. and Suppl. Often prec. by *all*.

1961 in WEBSTER, Leaving her towel and brush and comb lying whichway. **1968** 'J. WELCOME' *Hell is where you find It* xiv. 166 He told me they [*sc.* drugs] took everyone all whichways. If you'd ever had a drink or two before, you want a lot more where you were on the pills kick—sometimes. **1978** *People's Friend* 13 May 19/1 She pictured the scene and winced at the idea of Gregory seeing her without make-up, her hair all-which-way from the steam. **1975** 'MISS READ' *Battles at Thrush Green* i. 16 What chance is there of pushin' a mower up these 'ere paths with the graves all going which-way? *Ibid.* xix. 223 He was on a bike far too big for him—sawing away he was, wobbling all whichways.

whick, *a.* North. var. of QUICK *a.* Cf. *WICK *a.*[2]

c **1760** W. HUTTON *Dialogue in Vulg. Lang. Storth & Arnside* (*c* 1900) 4 Was It whick, says Ta? **1790** [see QUICK *a.* 2]. **1879**— [see *Eng. Dial. Dict.*].

whicker, *v.* Add: **2.** (Earlier examples.)

1753 J. POULTER *Discoveries* (ed. 5) 7 The Horse, as soon as the others past began to whicker, so that we were obliged to gag him.

3. To make a sound as of something hurtling through or beating the air.

1926 *Spectator* 28 Aug. 313/2 Bid Jove send down a thunderbolt to whicker through the sky. **1965** G. MAXWELL *House of Elrig* xiii. 167 My aunt's black-and-white nun pigeons whickered past my window and drank at the bird-table.

whicker *sb.*: also, the sound of something beating the air; hence also **whi·ckering** *vbl. sb.* and *ppl. a.*

1899 SOMERVILLE & 'ROSS' *Some Experiences Irish R.M.* xi. 277 A pale, yellow foal sprinted up beside us, with shrill whickerings of joy. **1920** J. MASEFIELD *Right Royal* 73 Far over his head with a whicker of wings Came a wisp of five snipe from a field full of springs. **1937** E. SITWELL *I live under Black Sun* I. iii. 48 The door of her room..opened with a dark strawy noise like the wickering voice of a bear. **1940** H. SPRING *Fame is Spur* i. 11 And so great was the silence that the whickering of banners could be heard. **1965** G. MAXWELL *House of Elrig* ii. 27 Black rock cliffs with deep mysterious caves full of the whicker of rock-pigeons' wings.

Whieldon (hwī·ldŏn). The name of Thomas *Whieldon* (1719–95), Staffordshire potter, used *attrib.* to designate the kind of coloured earthenware made in his factory (founded 1740). Also *Comb.*, as *Whieldon-type* adj., resembling this ware.

1869 C. SCHREIBER *Jrnl.* 1 Oct. (1911) I. 42 One Wheildon Ware plate. **1900** F. LITCHFIELD *Pott. & Porc.* vii. 317 Whieldon ware is peculiarly light and the articles well potted. **1929** H. READ *Staffordshire Pottery Figures* Pl. 14 (*caption*) The term 'Whieldon type' [is used] when the figure depends entirely for its decoration on coloured glazes. **1942** *Burlington Mag.* Oct. 260/1 Most dangerous are the increasingly skilful fakes of Astbury and Whieldon figures. **1968** *Canad. Antiques Collector* July 13/1 What is Whieldon Ware? This is a term referring to all types of ware of a mottled, cloudy or splashed character. **1978** *Times* 28 Jan. 12/6 (*caption*) A Whieldon-type teapot and cover, c. 1765. **1983** *Country Life* 2 Dec. (Suppl.) 72/2 A Whieldon pottery horse, decorated in underglaze colours of green, yellow and brown.

whiff, *sb.*[1] Add: **I. 1. d.** *U.S. slang.* A miss, a failure to hit (a ball).

1952 *N.Y. Herald Tribune* 15 May 21/6 On the first tee he took a careful stance and then fanned the air four times. After the fourth whiff he growled, 'This is the hardest course I ever played.'

6. (Earlier example.)

1800 M. EDGEWORTH *Parent's Assistant* (ed. 3) VI. 158 Lean on my arm, madam, and we'll have you in and at home in a whiff.

whiff, *v.*[1] Add: **6.** *U.S. slang.* **a.** *intr.* Of a batter in Baseball or a golfer: to miss the ball. Cf. *FAN *v.* 8 b.

1913 *Wells Fargo Messenger* I. 93/2 When he has to line 'er out he does, but he doesn't whiff at random. **1926** *Amer. Speech* I. 369/2 He [*sc.* a baseball player] 'whiffs' when he fails to hit. **1942** BERREY & VAN DEN BARK *Amer. Thes. Slang* § 677/34 *Miss the ball*,..whiff.

b. = *FAN *v.* 8 a.

1914 R. LARDNER in *Sat. Even. Post* 7 Mar. 7/2, I whiffed eight men in five innings in Frisco yesterday. **1951** in Wentworth & Flexner *Dict. Amer. Slang* (1960) 575/1 Vic Raschi whiffed twelve batters in gaining his 15th win of the year. **1941** *Nebraska State Jrnl.* 20 June (*heading*), Hurler whiffs 20.

whiffet. Add: **1.** (Earlier example of *whiffet dog.*)

1848 *Ladies' Repository* VIII. 315 The best protection to a house, with a family in it that can be named—that is, a little, barking, noisy, cowardly, whiffet dog.

whiffle, *sb.* Add: **3.** A soft sound as of gently moving air or water.

1972 F. FORD *Atush Inlet* i. 9 Their subdued cries could be heard faintly against the gentle whiffle of falling water. **1976** J. CROSBY *Snake* (1977) xxx. 179 She listened to..the soft whiffle of her breathing.

4. *Comb.*, as **w(h)iffle-ball** *U.S.*, a light hollow ball (orig. designed for golf practice in a confined space), used for playing a variety of Baseball; also the game itself; **whiffle-minded** *a.* (*U.K.* and *U.S. dial.*), changeable fickle.

1965 F. KNEBEL *Night of Camp David* xvii. 273 The boys of Saybrook were playing whiffle ball. **1970** *Time* 25 May 43 [David Eisenhower]..passing the afternoon playing wiffle ball on the south lawn of his father-in-law's White House. **1970** *New Yorker* 11 July 20 Kids playing with whiffleballs and baseballs. **1976** WOODWARD & BERNSTEIN *Final Days* 242 He would get a whiffle-ball game going on the White House tennis court. **1980** *N.Y. Sunday News Mag.* 2 Mar. 12/2, I would chase the whiffleball across the street. **1902** H. F. DAY *Pine Tree Ballads* 47 Hate to act so whiffle-minded, but my father used to say, 'Men would sometimes change opinions; mules would stick the same old way'. **1905** in *Eng. Dial. Dict.* VI. 456/1 'e's so w'iffle-minded—'e dunna know 'is own mind two minutes together.

whiffled (hwi·f'ld), *a.* *slang.* [Origin obscure: cf. SQUIFFY *a.*] Intoxicated, drunk.

1927 WODEHOUSE *Meet Mr. Mulliner* vi. 191 Intoxicated? The word did not express it by a mile. He was oiled, boiled, fried..whiffled, sozzled, and blotto. **1930** —— *Very Good, Jeeves!* ii. 46 'Have you forgotten that I did thirty days..for punching a policeman..on Boat-Race night?' 'But you were whiffled at the time.' **1956** J. D. CARR *Patrick Butler for Defence* xiv. 157 Helen.. was much too clear-headed..ever to let herself get whiffled.

whiffletree. (Earlier example.)

1842 W. P. HAWES *Sporting Scenes* II. 69 Our whiffletree became detached from the vehicle, and fell upon the horse's heels.

whiffling, *vbl. sb.*[1] (s.v. WHIFFLE *v.*[1] in Dict.) Add: **2.** Vacillation, evasion.

1841 J. F. COOPER *Deerslayer* I. i. 23, I would carry the gal off to the Mohawk by force, make her marry me in spite of her whiffling. **1906** *Springfield* (Mass.) *Weekly Republ.* 18 Oct. 3 This outcome of a week of doubt and whiffling will be viewed with mixed emotions. **1984** *Daily Tel.* 13 Feb. 12/5 When first I heard these whifflings, a couple of years ago, I thought they must be satiric.

whifflow (hwi·flōu). *Naut. slang.* [Fanciful formation.] (See quot. 1961.)

1961 F. H. BURGESS *Dict. Sailing* 222 *Whifflow*, an unnamed gadget; used when a proper name is forgotten. **1971** 'A. BURGESS' *MF* v. 64 The cabin was still a mess of smashed and battered whifflows.

whiffy, *a.* Add: (Earlier and later examples.) Also *fig.*

1849 H. MELVILLE *Mardi* II. xxvii. 109 A pithy, whiffy sentence or two. **1934** R. MACAULAY *Going Abroad* xi. 77 'A bit whiffy,' Hero said, as they passed among the cottages that encircled the muddy..pool. **1962** AUDEN *Dyer's Hand* (1963) 520, I have always found the atmosphere of *Twelfth Night* a bit whiffy. **1978** *Birds* Summer 45/2 The area is dusty and whiffy with lorries arriving to tip every four minutes.

Whig, *sb.*[2] and *a.* Add: **C. Whig historian,** a historian who interprets history as the continuing and inevitable victory of progress over reaction; **Whig history,** history written by or from the point of view of a Whig historian.

1924 G. B. SHAW *Saint Joan* Pref. p. x, Her [*sc.* Joan's] ideal biographer..must understand the Middle Ages ..much more intimately than our Whig historians have ever understood them. **1980** H. TREVELYAN *Public &*

Private 149 George Macaulay Trevelyan..was essentially a Whig historian, thus continuing the family tradition derived from his father and his kinsman Macaulay. **1931** H. C. BUTTERFIELD *Whig Interpretation of Hist.* i. 6 The truth is that there is a tendency for all history to veer over into whig history. **1973** *Listener* 28 June 869/1 Macaulay..wrote consciously Whig history: yet.. enunciated the principles of historical criticism which explains why Whig history is a distortion.

Whiggish, *a.*² Add: (Later example with reference to historical interpretation: see *Whig historian, history* s.v. *WHIG *sb.*² and *a.* C.)

1975 *Times Lit. Suppl.* 28 Nov. 1404/3 The danger, ever-present in women's history (as in labour history) of whiggish perspectives: of self-indulgently allowing enthusiasm for the women's cause today to obstruct sensitive understanding of women's situation yesterday.

Whiggishly *adv.* (later examples in corresponding sense).

1975 *University* (Princeton Univ.) Winter 4/1 This is not to say whiggishly that science at any juncture has been the only description of physical reality that was historically possible. **1980** *Times Lit. Suppl.* 25 July 837/1 Authors tend to win a place in the history of social and political thought by making what is usually, and whiggishly, referred to as a 'theoretical contribution'.

while, *sb.* **II. 6. b.** Restrict † *Obs.* to senses in Dict. and add: Also *U.S.*, a long time.

1836 T. C. HALIBURTON *Clockmaker* (1837) 1st Ser. xvi. 136 You'll search one while..afore you'll find a man that..is equal to one of your free and enlightened citizens. **1852** MRS. STOWE *Uncle Tom's Cabin* I. xi. 159 I'd mark him..so that he'd carry it *one* while. **1897** 'MARK TWAIN' *Following Equator* liii. 511 If India knows about nothing else American, she knows about those, and will keep them in mind one while.

while, *conj.* Add: **4. a.** (Later example.)

1918 W. DE LA MARE *Motley* 68 How do the days press on, and lay Their fallen locks at evening down, Whileas the stars in darkness play.

C. while-you-wait *adj.* or *adv. phr.* (orig. *U.S.*), designating a service that is performed immediately (as opp. to one for which the customer must leave his property and collect it later); also *fig.*; also *absol.* as *sb.*, an establishment providing such a service; freq. (in advertisements) spelt *while-u-wait.*

1929 *Amer. Speech* V. 24 Those who are selling 'service' are fond of using expressions of this sort:..Shine While U Wait, Hats Cleaned While U Wait, [etc.]. **1936** MENCKEN *Amer. Lang.* (ed. 4) 209 Q-room.., While-U-wait, and Bar-B-Q.., all of them familiar signs. **1965** H. GOLD *Man who was not with It* xxix. 271 We were at a low office block.., shoe repair and while-you-wait. **1972** *Guardian* 11 July 10/6 The..catalogue essay..is a masterpiece of myth-making, art history while-u-wait. **1972** *Times* 9 Aug. 12/7 (*caption*) A while-you-wait parts replacement service. **1977** *Evening Gaz.* (Middlesbrough) 11 Jan. 13/2 (Advt.), M.O.T. test while-u-wait.

whilie (hwəi·li). *Sc. dial.* Also **whiley, whyllie.** [f. WHILE *sb.* + -IE.] A short time.

1819 J. BURNESS *Plays* 29 Master Clinton is out a whyllie syne. **1908** *Old-Lore Misc.* I. IV. 183 After it was burned a whiley. **1920** J. L. WAUGH *Heroes* 18 When ye've been a whilie here. **1951** N. M. GUNN *Well at World's End* xxiv. 214 'Be quiet!' she said... 'I just came for a whilie to see them.' **1981** G. HAMMOND *Revenge Game* vi. 55 The inspector's house..was let to a retired couple for a whilie, but they moved away up to Inverness.

whillaloo. Add: Also 7 **fuillilaloo.** Also as *int.* and *v. intr.* Cf. *PILLALOO *sb.* (*int.*).

1663 R. HEAD *Hic et Ubique* I. vi. 18 Enter Patrick crying..Fuillilaloo! **1977** *Times Lit. Suppl.* 22 Apr. 480/4 All those uncles trailing their coats and shouting whillaloo and clear the way. **1899** [see *PILLALOO *sb.* (*int.*)].

Whillans (hwi·lănz). The name of Don *Whillans* (1933–85), mountaineer, used *attrib.* of objects devised by him for the assistance of climbers, as *Whillans box*, a kind of frame tent (see quot. 1971¹); *Whillans harness*, a harness designed for use by mountaineers climbing fixed ropes; *Whillans whammer*, a kind of peg hammer or piton.

1971 C. BONINGTON *Annapurna South Face* v. 66 At this stage, Base Camp was no more than a staging camp, with a two-man tent and two Whillans Boxes... We had been worried that ordinary tents might prove inadequate on the very steep ground... Don had come up with the solution, designing a prefabricated, box-like structure, with a framework of timber and an outer covering of proofed nylon. *Ibid.* xii. 147 This [*sc.* being on an ice cliff] was one place where Dougal found a use for the Whillans Whammer, Don's space-age climbing tool, for its squat, triangular-shaped pick proved ideal for this type of ice. **1972** D. HASTON *In High Places* xi. 118 Huddled into the back of the Whillans box—a super-strong frame tent designed by Don—we could only sit and wait. **1974** H. MACINNES *Climb to Lost World* ix. 137 It was ironic that the designer of the Whillans harness was the only member of the expedition who didn't have..one which would fit his ample girth. **1978** P. GILLMAN *Fitness on Foot* v. 73 The Willans harness is manufactured by the Lancashire company Troll.

whimp, *v.* Add: (Later example.) Hence as *sb.*

1925 *Blackw. Mag.* Aug. 169/2 'Don't whimp,' I said to Irene. 'I am not whimping, daddy.' *Ibid.* 173/1 This was something beyond a whimp.

whimper, *sb.* Add: **2.** *not with a bang but a whimper*: see *BANG *sb.*¹ 2 a.

whimsily, *adv.* (In Dict. s.v. WHIMSY, WHIMSEY *sb.* (*a.*).) (Later example.)

1980 P. MOYES *Angel Death* xviii. 237 The whimsily-drawn pamphlet which they gave to visitors.

whimsy, whimsey, *sb.* (*a.*) Add: **7. b.** A small object made by a glass-maker or potter for his own amusement.

1938 A. FLEMING *Scottish & Jacobite Glass* ix. 109 Dame Fashion..seems to settle upon glass as a favourite and satisfactory medium of decoration. Other 'wimsies' are cheap little fantastic groups of figures, fruit and flowers delicately made from a tube modelled by a tool with infallible dexterity. **1976** *Canadian Collector* (Toronto) Mar.–Apr. 23/1 We were able to locate several more examples of the whimseys produced by the last potter.

whimsy-whamsy. Add: (Earlier and later examples.) Also *attrib.*

1807 SOUTHEY *Lett. from England* III. lix. 109 An old Welsh baronet..chose some years ago to set up a heresy of his own... He himself called it Rational Whist; his friends, in a word of contemptuous fabrication, denominated it his *whimsy-whamsy.* **1931** *Time & Tide* 26 Sept. 1118 Have we not whimsy-whamsy authors of our own without importing the too, too, quaint devices of foreign playwrights? **1945** S. LEWIS *Cass Timberlane* xl. 302 Sure, the jolly little playboy, and underneath his whimsy-whamsy, he's the coldest-hearted rich-man's lawyer. **1951** MCLUHAN *Mech. Bride* (1967) 101/1 It is not a laughter or comedy to be compared with the whimsy-whamsy article of James Thurber.

whin¹. Add: **4. whin-mill,** a mill for crushing whin for horse-feed.

1793 in *Trans. Buchan Field Club* (1935) XIV. 76 Carrying wood for the whine mile. **1893** C. A. MOLLYSON *Parish of Fordoun* 188 With a plentiful supply of oilcake and other nutritious feeding stuffs there is no place now for the whin-mill. **1957** E. E. EVANS *Irish Folk Ways* viii. 110 The knocking stones..where the whins were 'melled' with a wooden maul, are sometimes to be seen in the farmyard, and there were a few water-driven 'whin-mills'.

whine, *sb.* (Examples referring to the sound of machinery.)

1928 E. WALLACE *Double* xx. 295 They heard the whine of a car draw up on the ground below. **1942** W. FAULKNER *Go down, Moses* 143 The air pulsed with..the whine and clang of the saw. **1962** *Which? Car Suppl.* Oct. 127/2 Other noises of which our drivers complained were rear axle whine in all the cars.

whine, *v.* **1. c.** (Examples referring to machinery.)

1962 *Which? Car Suppl.* Oct. 140/1 Engine always whined when started from cold. **1972** *Daily Tel.* 16 May 9 Two minutes after the jet engines whine to a standstill she walked slowly down the special lateral gangplank. **1974** S. MIDDLETON *Holiday* iv. 42 Lawn-mowers whined.

whinge, *sb.* For '*Sc.* and *dial.*' read 'orig. *Sc.* and *dial.*' (Later examples.) Now *esp.* a peevish complaint.

1938 S. BECKETT *Murphy* iii. 37 He threw his voice into an infant's whinge. 'I cudden do anything, Maaaammy.' **1947** I. L. IDRIESS *Isles of Despair* xxxviii. 254 The bull [whale] complained with a stupid little grumbling whinge and edged a few yards farther away. **1963** [see *PEANUT 2 b]. **1973** P. WHITE *Eye of Storm* i. 64 'You're so *unfair*!' A whinge developed through a moan into a downright blub. **1981** *Listener* 4 June 749/1 This is not just an envious whinge. **1982** J. THOMSON *To make a Killing* xiii. 231, I knew bloody well he'd shop me and make a fuss... He'd already had a whinge about the rubbish I'd left. **1985** *Times* 10 Jan. 10/6 In my one-but-last whinge I was going on about the burdensome duties of The Talk.

whinge, *v.* For '*Sc.* and *north. dial.*' read 'orig. *Sc.* and *north. dial.*' and add: Now also **winge.** *Esp.* to complain peevishly. (Further examples.) **whinging** (also **w(h)ingeing**) *vbl. sb.* and *ppl. a.* (further examples).

1907 J. M. SYNGE *Let.* 31 Mar. (1971) 121 Forgive this contemptible sort of whinging. I am so lonely and miserable I cant help it. **1922** JOYCE *Ulysses* 10 You crossed her last wish in death and yet you sulk with me because I don't whinge like some hired mute from Lalouette's. **1946** K. TENNANT *Lost Haven* (1947) xvii. 272 She had lifted up her brief skirt..to exhibit her sand-fly bites. ..'You don't want to whinge about them... You had a good time, didn't you?' **1955** S. BECKETT *Molloy* II. 172, I forgot that my son would be at my side,..whinging for food. **1965** *Listener* 2 Sept. 339/2 There is a stinging phrase in use, 'wingeing Poms' (translate into 'complaining English'). **1969** *Advertiser* (Adelaide) 12 May 5/4 Stop whingeing and give a bloke a go, mates. **1973** B. BAINBRIDGE *Dressmaker* 8 If that girl didn't stop her wingeing, the neighbours would be banging on the wall. **1983** *Times Lit. Suppl.* 11 Mar. 236/1 In 1849, Arnold whinged to Clough that the age was '..unpoetical'. **1983** *Sunday Times* 31 July 33/1 'What sort of people do Australians hate most?' 'The whingeing Pom... Poms that come over and do nothing but whinge.' **1984** *Times* 20 Jan. 10/7 This is not the month for whingeing criticisms. **1984** *Sunday Times* 9 Dec. 7/1 All must drill most Tuesday nights..and not whinge when the trousers of their best suits are crumpled and smutted under the uniform.

whinger, *sb.*² For '*Sc.* or *dial.*' read 'orig. *Sc.* or *dial.*' and add later examples.

1934 *Bulletin* (Sydney) 27 June 11/2 Touching the query about 'whinger'.., 'winjer' was accepted slang for 'grumbler' at Q. Uni. a few years ago, and probably still is. I have seldom heard it elsewhere, and no one who uses it seems to know the derivation. **1959** I. & P. OPIE *Lore & Lang. Schoolch.* x. 186 Other local terms for crying... In Dublin the usual word is 'whinging', hence 'whinger', a term also still used in Cumberland, and occasionally heard in Liverpool. **1983** *Listener* 14 Apr. 17/2 Certainly, no whinger like me will ever turn Simon into a dissident.

whiny, *a.* Add: *whin(e)y pin(e)y*: so *whiney-pine* vb. intr., to make whining noises.

1920 'K. MANSFIELD' *Let.* 27 Sept. (1977) 182 Two infant wasps..each caught hold of a side of a *leaf* and began to tug... They became furious. They whimpered, whiney-pined—snatched at each other—wouldn't give way.

whio (fi·o, wī·o). *N.Z.* Also 9 **wihu, wio.** [Maori.] The blue duck, *Hymenolaimus malacorhynchos*, native to New Zealand.

1847 T. BRUNNER *Jrnl.* 2 Apr. in N. M. Taylor *Early Travellers N.Z.* (1959) 272 Shot a *wihu*, or blue duck. **1855** R. TAYLOR *Te Ika a Maui* xxv. 407 *Wio*,..the blue duck, is found abundantly in the mountain streams of the south part of the North Island..; it takes its name from its cry. **1880** J. C. CRAWFORD *Trav. N.Z. & Austral.* 122 At Kai-inanga, Deighton shot a pair of *whio*, or blue-ducks. **1966** *Encycl. N.Z.* I. 499/2 The most peculiar is undoubtedly the blue duck, mountain duck, or *whio.*

whip, *sb.* Add: **I. 1. d.** *a fair crack of the whip* (colloq.): a fair chance to participate or act.

1929 K. S. PRICHARD *Coonardoo* 179 I'll see you get a fair crack of the whip now, Mr. Watt. **1944** L. GLASSOP *We were Rats* 2, I am sorry to have to tell you that the Lord's had a fair crack of the whip and He's missed the bus. **1957** *Technology* Oct. 271/1 We should give the technical high school a trial..with a fair crack of the whip when the talent is being handed round. **1971** *Radio Times* 19 Aug. 50/1 It is the first time in 4½ years that those opposing the present abortion law have been given a really fair crack of the whip on a B.B.C. panel.

2. b. = *whip aerial* s.v. *WHIP- 1 c.

1940 *Electronics* July 68/2 The whip is used to increase the capacitance and to carry some current to greater heights. **1960** *Practical Wireless* XXXVI. 342/2 The aerial is an 8 ft. 'whip' which is swung into the vertical on arrival at a stopping place, being attached to the side of the caravan permanently, on an insulator. **1976** *S9* (N.Y.) Feb. 34/1 They are factory pretuned..and will take up to 500 watts of power, radiating from a 46-inch stainless steel whip.

3. c. For *dial.* read *dial., Austral.,* and *N.Z.* (Earlier and later examples.)

1888 G. G. B. SPROAT *Rose o' Dalma Linn* 242 He'll hae whups o' tabacca. **1897** I. SCOTT *How I stole 10,000 Sheep* vii. 29, I was glad to hear Jim come cantering up with 'whips' of bread, cheese, beer and horse-feed. **1928** 'BRENT OF BIN BIN' *Up Country* xi. 183 Whips of room for us both. **1948** R. FINLAYSON *Tidal Creek* I. vi. 59 'Didn't think old Podder would ever bother about that bit of land,' says Uncle Ted. 'Got whips of land.' **1961** G. FARWELL *Vanishing Australian* 182 Then you want capital—whips of it.

4. b. *Printing.* A compositor who sets type speedily.

1890 BARRÈRE & LELAND *Dict. Slang* II. 409/1 *Whip*... (Printers), quick setter of type. *a* **1974** P. EVETT in J. Burnett *Useful Toil* (1974) III. 333, I was put into the piece 'ship' on the paper, where I can truly say I held my own, though I was no whip. **1978** *Times Lit. Suppl.* 15 Sept. 1022/4 An average compositor at that time would have set a thousand characters or ens an hour, and a 'whip', or fast setter on piece-work, would have set upwards of fifteen hundred.

6. (Earlier example.)

1850 THACKERAY *Pendennis* II. vi. 52 Captain Raff, the honourable member for Epsom,..retired after the last Goodwood races, having accepted, as Mr. Hotspur, the whip of the party, said, a mission to the Levant.

7. a. (Earlier example of *whip-up.*)

1884 E.W. HAMILTON *Diary* 2 May (1972) II. 608 It was carried..by a majority of 2 to 1, owing no doubt in great measure to the whip-up which the Prince of Wales had made.

b. Now usu. *whip-round* (not restricted to charitable collections). (Further examples.)

1874 HOTTEN *Slang Dict.* 339 Whip-round. **1887** *Echo* 23 Nov. 4/4 Neighbours, who knew that she had no money, instituted a 'whip round', and soon raised the necessary amount. **1948** M. LASKI *Tory Heaven* i. 12 The whip-round for garments and the ladies' little cries when they were told that clothes were rationed at home. **1977** *Centuryan* (Office Cleaning Services) Christmas 2/3 It appears a whip-round for the drinks was suggested. **1980** A. MORICE *Death in Round* xiv. 107 She..handed over the money that had been raised by the whip round. **1985** *Times* 14 June 5 The extra money will have to be found by a nonrepayable whip-round among member states.

d. *the whip*: the discipline that goes with

being a member of a party in Parliament; an MP's membership of a party.

1950 THEIMER & CAMPBELL *Encycl. World Politics* 458/2 To decline the whip is a method of resignation from the party. **1955** *Times* 24 May 15/1 Some effort had been made to arrive at a non-intervention arrangement, but it broke down when Mr. Walker was asked if he would accept the Conservative whip. **1966** *Listener* 25 Aug. 289/1 If he is a member of the Labour Party, he is bound by the standing orders of the Parliamentary Labour Party... To defy the standing orders may involve the withdrawal of the whip. **1980** B. CASTLE *Castle Diaries* 12 The bitterness intensified when, in October 1971, sixty-nine Labour MPs, headed by Roy Jenkins, defied the Labour whip and voted for Mr. Heath's motion.

9. b. *Cricket.* A whipping or springy action of the batsman's or bowler's wrist in playing or delivering the ball.

1903 [see *FLICK *sb.*[1] 1 d]. **1923** *Cricketer Ann. 1922–3* 78 Kilner bowls left hand slow..has a good action with a nice 'whip' in it.

III. 15*. A fairground roundabout in which a continuous revolving chain carries a number of cars or tubs round an oval track, the tubs being pivoted so as to swing freely about their point of attachment to the chain.

A proprietary name in the U.S.

1925 WODEHOUSE *Carry on, Jeeves!* vi. 152, I could hardly drag him away from the Whip, and as for the Switchback, he looked like spending the rest of his life on it. **1937** HULL & WHITLOCK *Far-Distant Oxus* xx. 277 Bridget, Anthony, and Peter went off for a ride on the 'Whip'. **1969** L. MOODY *Ruthless Ones* ix. 96 They went into the fun fair and tried the big dipper, the wheel, the whip. **1976** *Official Gaz.* (U.S. Patent Office) 8 June TM89 A. G. Mangels Co., Inc., Bay Shore, N.Y... *Whip.* For carnival type amusement ride... First use since at least as early as 1914. **1979** C. WOOD *Bond & Moonraker* v. 61 'The Whip' of his childhood days, but revolving at a speed that would have..hurled it half-way across the fairground.

whip, *v.* Add: **I. 2. d.** To pinch or steal, to make off with; †to swindle. *slang* (orig. *Criminals'*).

1859 G. W. MATSELL *Vocabulum* 95 *Whipped,* cheated out of a share, or equal part of the plunder. **1904** 'No. 1500' *Life in Sing Sing* xiii. 259 *Holding the mark till the tool whips his stone.* Engaging a person's attention till the thief succeeds in stealing his diamond. **1946** G. KERSH *Clean, Bright & Slightly Oiled* ii. 11 Hi, you, you give me back that dog-end you whipped. **1958** M. K. JOSEPH *I'll soldier no More* 19 'Where's your hat, Barnett?'.. 'Dunno, Someone musta whipped it.' **1976** A. MILLER *Inside Outside* xi. 173 One of them was rightly furious as the escaper had whipped (stolen) his overcoat. **1981** P. O'DONNELL *Xanadu Talisman* ix. 182 The Shah must've whipped this... Stashed it away in a Swiss bank.

II. 7. b. *intr.* Of cream: to be capable of being whipped.

1943 *Mod. Lang. Notes* LVIII. 13 Cream *whips* quickly. **1979** A. PARKER *County Recipe Notebk.* viii. 108 Single cream..will not whip.

12. Phr. *to whip one's weight in wildcats* and varr.: (to be able) to fight vigorously; to be fit and strong. Chiefly *U.S.* ? *Obs.*

1828 *Spirit of Seventy-Six* (Frankfort, Kentucky) 17 Jan. 3/5, I can ride upon a streak of lightning, whip my weight in wild cats. **1834** [in Dict.]. **1852** H. C. WATSON *Nights in Block-House* 20 Not as long as I can whip my weight in catamounts or bar, I'll never give in. **1870** G. H. LEWES *Let.* 17 May in *Geo. Eliot Lett.* (1956) V. 96 We hope to see you both come back ready to 'whip your weight in polecats'. You will not find us in that vigorous condition! **1878** [see *ONCE *adv.* A. γ].

14. (Earlier example.)

1742 H. FINCH *Let.* 18 Nov. in P. D. G. Thomas *House of Commons in 18th Cent.* (1971) vi. 114 The Whigs for once in their lives have whipped in better than the Tories.

16. a. (*h*) *Austral.* and *N.Z.* To complain or moan.

1892 *Bulletin* (Sydney) 7 May 10/3 Now he only 'whips the cat' at the bottom of the Carlton poll. **1909** H. THOMPSON *Ballads about Business* 12 You could make tenners den like vinkin', dough Now you are vippin' der cat. **1911** *Triad* 10 June 18 Tell him [*sc.* a misled person] he has leave to go and whip the cat. **1948** V. PALMER *Golconda* xxiii. 194 If there's anything wants doing you've only got to ask Macy Donovan... And he makes light of it, too. No whipping the cat: no setting himself up as a little tin god.

whip-. Add: **1. a.** *whip-flick, -stroke, -thong* (earlier example). **b.** *whip-cracking*: also as *adj.*; *whip-minder, -scarred, -smacking* (earlier example). **c. whip aerial, antenna,** an aerial in the form of a flexible wire or rod with a connection at one end; **whip-club** (earlier example); **whip-grass** (earlier example); **whip-scorpion,** substitute for def.: an arachnid of the order Pedipalpida, having a flattened abdomen and long flagella attached to the first pair of legs; (examples); **whip-stall** *Aeronaut.*, a stall in which an aircraft changes suddenly from a nose-up attitude to a nose-down one.

1941 *Electronics* Jan. 60/2 It was necessary to vary the height of the whip aerial which was mounted on the top of the solenoid. **1979** A. JUTE *Reverse Negative* (1980) 42 The car had a prominent whip aerial of the kind police mobile patrols use mounted on its rear fender. **1943** F. E. TERMAN *Radio Engineers' Handbk.* 1019/2 (Index), Whip antennas. **1974** R. B. PARKER *Godwulf Manuscript* xviii. 141 An aggressively nondescript car made noticeable by the big whip antenna folded forward over the roof and clipped down. **1808** *Monthly Pantheon* I. 416/1 A new new Whip-club is now about to be established. **1934** WEBSTER, Whip-cracking, *adj.* **1939** R. CAMPBELL *Flowering Rifle* I. 17 For whom I sent the gay whip-cracking words To round them up in flabbergasted herds. **1976** A. MURRAY *Stomping Blues* ix. 166 He also behaves for all the world like a whip-cracking trail driver. **1960** C. DAY LEWIS *Buried Day* vi. 126 Our instructor..was a ..man with..a word of command like a whip-flick. **1976** *Sunday Sun* (Brisbane) 23 May 115/1 *The whip flick.* Done in a tight finish. You flick your whip across the other horse's nose, up goes his head and you have the advantage in the photo. **1814** O. RICH *Synopsis Genera Amer. Plants* 106 Scleria... Whip-Grass. **1928** R. NEVILL *Romantic London* vii. 143 A quaint old-world calling..was that of 'whip-minder'; a number of people formerly making a living by looking after the whips of drivers of vehicles, while the latter were engaged on pleasure or business. **1961** *Times* 23 Mar. 17/3 When Covent Garden boasted 'whip minders'. **1849** J. R. LOWELL *King Retro* in *Nat. Anti-Slavery Standard* 10 May 199/2 From whip-scarred flesh the soul can soar To him who made and sees us. **1966** R. HAYDEN in S. Henderson *Understanding New Black Poetry* (1973) 158 Harriet Tubman, Woman of earth, whipscarred, A summoning, a shining. **1912** J. H. COMSTOCK *Spider Book* i. 16 The common name whip-scorpions was doubtless suggested by the slender caudal appendages of the Thelyphonidæ. **1981** *Sci. Amer.* Dec. 32/1 Watch out for the fungus-ridden whip scorpion and the vampire bats. **1845** POE in *Broadway Jrnl.* 2 Aug. 60/2 The 'Katherine and Petruchio' of Niblo's, is absolutely beneath contempt —a mere jumble of unmeaning rant, fuss, whip-smacking, crockery-cracking, and other Tom-Foolery. **1927** C. A. LINDBERGH *We* ii. 33 For an instant we hung motionless in the perfect position for a whipstall. **1936** *Aircraft Engin.* Apr. 111/1 The mechanics of the whip-stall or uncontrollable nose dive are simple. **1953** C. A. LINDBERGH *Spirit of St. Louis* II. vi. 326 A whipstall at 1500 feet, with nothing but needles by which to orient myself! **1889** 'MARK TWAIN' *Connecticut Yankee* xxvii. 354 A precaution which had been suggested by the whip-stroke that had fallen to my share. **1958** L. DURRELL *Mountolive* xii. 229 Nessun felt the heat of the whip-stroke on his hand though the lash had not touched him. **1827** *Hallowell* (Maine) *Gaz.* 20 June 4/5 They have also received a large supply of..Whips and Whipthongs.

2. b. whip-pan *Cinemat.* and *Television,* a panning movement fast enough to give a blurred picture; also as *v. intr.*

1960 D. DAVIS *Grammar of Television Production* 33 The 'whip pan', a device..whereby the camera sees one object, then pans very quickly and sees another, is.. legitimate because it does what the eye does and blurs the intervening detail. **1965** P. JONES *Technique of Television Cameraman* x. 136 Some television directors..instruct the cameraman to whip pan across a scene, but cut to the next static shot on another camera before the pan has ceased. **1979** *Observer* 26 Aug. 20/8 The cameras..zooming in and out, whip-panning, busying about the place looking for new angles. **1980** *Times Lit. Suppl.* 3 Oct. 1098/3 Unlike Brian De Palma in his movie version of King's earlier novel, *Carrie,* Kubrick doesn't use whip-pans, sudden zooms on neck-wrenching shocks: the horrors are revealed discreetly, almost lovingly.

whipcord, *sb.* **2. b.** (Earlier example.)

1895 *Montgomery Ward Catal.* Spring & Summer 4/2 All Wool Black Whipcord Suiting..shows fine raised satin finished cords running diagonally through the cloth.

whipcord, *v.* Delete (*nonce-wd.*), substitute quot. 1784 for quot. 1811 in Dict., and add later example.

1784 R. ROBINSON *Jrnl.* 26 May in *Belfast Monthly Mag.* (1809) June 435/1 Whip-corded the boys' plough whips. **1863** MRS. GASKELL *Cousin Phillis* i, in *Cornh. Mag.* Nov. 627 He has often to whip-cord the plough-whips.

whip-hand. Add: **1.** (Earlier example.)

1806 *Ann. Reg. 1804* 413/1 For a morning's ride this might be *complimentary;* but it was here depriving me of the *whip hand.*

2. Now usu. without *of.*

1947 *Sun* (Baltimore) 22 Dec. 2/1 Its objective will be to outstrip the Marshall plan and so to gain the political whiphand over Europe. **1951** F. YERBY *Woman called Fancy* (1952) xvi. 302 In that election year of 1894, the white vote was so hopelessly divided that the blacks.. held the whip hand. **1974** *Howard Jrnl.* XIV. 49 The white population who have for so many centuries held, both literally and metaphorically, the whip hand. **1977** M. THATCHER in *Observer* 25 Sept. 10/1 If trade unions hold the whip hand, upon whose back does the lash fall? **1985** *Times* 26 Jan. 21/2 Sir Owen, however, still has the whip hand: he has the money and can bail the banks out of the whole complex exercise.

whip-lash, *sb.* Add: Also **whiplash. 3.** An injury to the head, neck, or spine caused by the head's being dashed to and fro on the less mobile trunk when a seated person is jerked forwards or backwards, as in a car accident. Usu. *attrib.*, esp. in *whiplash injury.*

1955 *Jrnl. Amer. Med. Assoc.* 5 Nov. 983/2 Poor seat-design accounts for thousands of so-called whiplash injuries. **1962** *Times* 23 Jan. 5/5 They discount arguments that 'whiplash' injury is common among safety belt wearers. **1971** H. PACY *Road Accidents* i. 21 In damage to rear of vehicle think of whiplash. **1975** *Year Bk. Ear, Nose & Throat* 14 This article documents another useful study regarding the effects of cervical spine trauma, or 'whiplash' trauma. **1977** *Woman's Day* (Austral.) 24 Oct. 47/1 My husand had a car accident at the beginning of last year and received a whiplash injury. **1983** *Which?* Sept. 402/3 If no effective head restraint is provided, the head tends to get left behind, causing major bending and straining of the neck—'whiplash' injuries.

whiplash (hwi·plæʃ), *v.* [f. prec. sb.] **1.** *trans.* **a.** To inflict sudden or severe harm on.

1957 A. MACNAB *Bulls of Iberia* viii. 83 The bull's trajectory is accordingly also bent in an arc... The bull is not now being violently whip-lashed as in the 'benders', but is being smoothly worn down. **1975** *Business Week* 14 July 50 Whether such a complex plan can be managed effectively, or whether it will be whiplashed by the short-term interest of elected officials and mired in a new superbureaucracy is perhaps the most important unanswered question. **1980** *N.Y. Times* 28 June 9/5 Much of the playing was perfunctory. Mr. Getz had a ghastly time, whiplashed between feedback and reed trouble that led to a classic climactic squeak. **1982** *Christian Sci. Monitor* 5 Oct. B 2/2 Oil field service companies have been 'whiplashed' as profit-starved major oil companies have sharply cut back drilling programs.

b. To jerk in a contrary direction; *spec.* to cause a whiplash injury to.

1971 *Daily Colonist* (Victoria, B.C.) 27 May 55/1 Parents who shake their babies in a fit of temper are threatening their lives, a surgeon has warned. Severe shaking can 'whiplash' the baby's head, causing blood clots on the brain. **1980** *Washington Post Mag.* 30 Nov. 53/1 (*caption*) The final solution to the problem of the hook on your tape measure slipping off the edge of the credenza to which you've attached it, whiplashing the tape into your eye. **1982** J. GARDNER *For Special Services* xiii. 133 The force of impact had whiplashed the man's head, breaking his neck.

2. *intr.* To move suddenly and forcefully, like a whip that is cracked. Also *fig.*

1963 *Lebende Sprachen* VIII. 169/3 [Drivers' vocabulary.] To whiplash. 1. his head whiplashed. 2. the trailer whiplashed. **1971** *Daily Tel.* 13 Dec. 3/2 The Environment Department is investigating methods used to fix posts for motorway crash barriers. It fears that if they have not been planted deep enough, a crash might uproot them and allow a stretch of high-tension metal barrier to 'whiplash' across the carriageways. **1972** D. DELMAN *Sudden Death* (1973) iii. 77 He set us against each other. And he figures..one of us..is going to whiplash with something he can use. **1977** *Washington Post Mag.* 27 Nov. 40/3 Conservatives say they can't do or say anything because it will hurt their careers. It's like the old back-lash has whiplashed. **1983** *Washington Post* 20 Feb. G3/6 The cable that catches the planes when they come in snapped. It whiplashed around the deck and caught the Chief in the spine. **1983** D. BOGGIS *Women they sent to Fight* xxxviii. 220 Margaret released her... Zelaszny whiplashed round..terrified.

whi·pless, *a.* [-LESS.] Of a Member of Parliament: having resigned, or having been deprived of, the whip.

1962 *Guardian* 13 Dec. 2/3 Mr Emrys Hughes, the 'whipless' Labour member for South Ayrshire. **1967** R. BUTT *Power of Parliament* xii. 317 Opinions varied as to how far the 'Whipless' MPs suffered from social or other pressures from the parties they had deserted during their period in isolation. **1976** *Times* 23 Feb. 13/2 A small and whipless group of independent Labour MPs.

whipped, whipt, *ppl. a.* Add: (The spelling whipt is now *arch.*) **8.** Subject to a Parliamentary whip.

1970 P. G. RICHARDS *Parliament & Conscience* iii. 60 This was duly debated and defeated on a straight party whipped vote. **1976** *Times Lit. Suppl.* 12 Mar. 300/2 In the 1970–74 Parliament, two thirds of the Conservative members voted against their party whip on at least one occasion, and one (Enoch Powell) did so in 113 whipped divisions. **1981** MARSH & CHAMBERS *Abortion Politics* vii. 194 MPs..are subject to constituency and interest group pressure on whipped issues.

whipperginnie. Add: **3.** (Later *arch.* example.)

1923 R. GRAVES *Whipperginny* 45 The minds of these two princes Were of such subtlety and such nimbleness That Whipperginny on the fall of a card Changed to Bézique or Cribbage or Piquet.

whipper-in. 1. (Ear er *fig.* example.)

c **1771** S. FOOTE *Maid of Bath* Prol. p. vi, To change the figure—formerly I've been To straggling follies only *whipper-in.*

whi·pper-snap, *v.* [Back-formation f. WHIPPER-SNAPPER.] *intr.* To behave like a whipper-snapper; to be impertinent. Hence **whi·pper-snapping** (and varr.) *vbl. sb.* and *ppl. a.*

1908 W. DE MORGAN *Somehow Good* xi. 100 The lines they might elect to whipper-snap on were not to be those of sentimental nonsense. **1913** D. H. LAWRENCE *Sons & Lovers* xiii. 349 Think I'm goin' ter have *you* whipperty-snappin' round? **1925** —— *Refl. Death Porcupine* 231 Oh, the universe has a terrible hole in the middle of it, an oubliette for all of you, whipper-snappering mongrels. **1973** *Times* 11 Apr. 13/5 Jackie Rea, a former champion, there to match whipper-snapping with an old dog's tricks.

whippet. Add: **4. b.** Usually *attrib.* as *whippet tank.*

1918 E. W. FARROW *Dict. Mil. Terms* 664 *Whippet tank,* an English armored car equipped with caterpillar treads. **1920** J. C. F. FULLER *Tanks in Gt. War* 176

March 26 [1918] is an interesting date in the history of the Tank Corps, for, on the afternoon of this day, the Whippet Tanks made their debut. **1938** G. GREENE in *Spectator* 22 July 139/2 Whippet tanks—camouflaged as in war. **1946** *New Yorker* 9 Mar. 83/1 Solid city blocks of whippet and giant tanks.

whippiness (hwi·pinės). [f. WHIPPY *a.* + -NESS.] Pliable quality; flexibility.

1881 *Sportsman's Year-bk.* 70 Some successful anglers use the two extremes of whippiness and stiffness [in fly-rods]. **1913** W. E. DOMMETT *Motor Car Mech.* 130 This control has the objection..that the gear box has to be long with possible whippiness of the shafting. **1975** *Daily Tel.* 5 Apr. 8/1 All you have to do is to choose a branch of sufficient whippiness to be pulled down to the ground and fixed there.

whipping, *vbl. sb.* Add: **1. a.** (Further U.S. *fig.* example.)

1835 F. A. CHARDON *Jrnl.* 10 July (1932) 37 Went to the Medicine dance last—Came back late and got a whipping from my Wife for my bad behaviour.

f. The action of stirring *up* strong feelings or the like (see WHIP *v.* 13).

1952 C. DAY LEWIS *Grand Manner* 12 This whipping-up of words into a frenzy. **1955** *Times* 18 July 4/7 He had emphasized that the 'whipping up' of public opinion against South Africa..would..estrange the great majority of South Africans. **1959** *Daily Tel.* 29 Dec. 6 This prospect suggests a possible explanation for his deliberate whipping-up of patriotic frenzy.

4. a. whipping-block, a block on which offenders are laid to be whipped; **whipping cream**, a grade of cream suitable for whipping; **whipping-house** *U.S.*, a building in which at one time Blacks were whipped.

a **1877** SWINBURNE *Lesbia Brandon* (1952) 504 He.. begged..that he might not be hoist across the whipping-block by a servant. **1953** R. GRAVES *Poems* 26 And taught St. Dominic's to baulk At gown and hood and whipping-block. **1924** *Techn. Bull. N.Y. State Agric. Exper. Station* No. 113. 3 Good whipping cream gave a reduced volume of whipped cream when compared to poor whipping cream. **1978** *Chicago* June 248/2 Pure whipping cream for coffee and batters. **1852** MRS. STOWE *Uncle Tom's Cabin* II. xxix. 147 It was the universal custom to send women and young girls to whipping-houses.

d. whipping side *Austral.* (see quot. 1965).

1957 STEWART & KEESING *Old Bush Songs* IX. 259 You see our ringer already turned and he's on the whipping side. **1965** J. S. GUNN *Terminol. Shearing Industry* II. 37 *Whipping side*, the name given to the last side of the sheep to be shorn and the blow here is down from the shoulder.

Whipple (hwi·p'l). *Path.* [The name of George Hoyt *Whipple* (b. 1878), U.S. pathologist, who described the disease in 1907 (*Bull. Johns Hopkins Hosp.* XVIII. 382).] *Whipple's disease*: = *intestinal lipodystrophy* s.v. *LIPODYSTROPHY.

[**1939** *Amer. Jrnl. Path.* XV. 483 (*heading*) Malabsorption of fat (intestinal lipodystrophy of Whipple).] **1945** *Ibid.* XXI. 1079 The pathologic findings in Whipple's disease are characterized by deposits of fat and fatty acids in the small intestine and mesenteric lymph nodes. **1978** *Price's Textbk. Pract. Med.* (ed. 12) VIII. 652/2 Whipple's disease, characterized by fever, joint pains, wasting, and diarrhoea, can initially be suspected [in cases of Crohn's disease].

whip-poor-will. (Earlier and later examples.)

1709 J. LAWSON *New Voy. Carolina* 146 Whippoo-Will, so nam'd, because it makes those Words exactly. **1920** W. D. HOWELLS *Vacation of Kelwyns* 42 The whippoorwills..whirred through the cool, damp air. **1938** J. M. GORDON *Canad. Mosaic* (1939) ix. 218 Dreamily lying with prairie for pillow Clear I hear calling the lone whip-poor-will. **1960** R T. PETERSON *Field Guide Birds of Texas* 134 Whip-poor-will... Best known by its vigorous cry repeated in endless succession at night.

whipsaw, *sb.* Add: **2.** *fig.* Something that is disadvantageous in two ways. orig. and chiefly *U.S.*

1873 *Kansas Mag.* Mar. 232/1 There was fifteen hundred on the turn—seven hundred and fifty on each side of it—and the run was tray, ace; a whipsaw. **1929** L. F. CARR *Amer. Challenged* 79 The whip-saw of paying high prices for what they bought and being forced to receive low prices for what they sold. **1967** *Listener* 23 Nov. 656/3 The wage push..and the rising interest rates.. have together caught the American economy in a cruel and sharp whipsaw... The worst sort of inflation of costs and the worst sort of deflation of values. **1977** *Time* 25 July 48/3 By the spring of 1974, the whipsaw effect of recession and rising costs—particularly for oil which fuels 80% of Con Ed's generating capacity—left the company strapped.

whip-saw *v.* (earlier and later examples); hence **whip-sawing** *vbl. sb.* (lit. and *fig.*).

1842 *Amer. Pioneer* I. 83 Dwellinghouses, made of wood, whip-sawed into timbers, four inches thick, and of the requisite width and length. **1873** *Kansas Mag.* June 497/1 On the next Budd whipsawed him, and that closed that deal. **1885** *Mag. Amer. Hist.* May 496/1 *Whip-sawing*, the acceptance of fees or bribes from two opposing persons or parties. **1903** *Sun* (N.Y.) 8 Nov. 10 The speculators have subjected themselves to the process known in Wall Street as whipsawing, that is, they have bought when the market was strong and sold when the market was weak, and found each time that they bought at the top and sold at the bottom. **1930** H. A. INNIS *Fur Trade in Canada* II. v. 140 Men were engaged in cutting, squaring, whipsawing, and hauling timber for the construction and repair of the forts. **1957** *Listener* 12 Dec. 970/1 Mr [Adlai] Stevenson has been whip-sawed by conflicting advice. **1958** F. G. SLAUGHTER *Daybreak* III. xiii. 176 The tendency to whipsaw all society into robots who work, think and eat alike is hardly an end product of intelligence. **1969** D. BAGLEY *Spoilers* ii. 58 'Okay, so you've whipsawed me,' said Follet sourly. **1975** *Weekend Mag.* (Montreal) 12/1 Whip-sawing, industrial relations slang for the union practice of wringing a high settlement from a weak company and then using that settlement as a floor for bargaining with a big company, was rampant. **1976** *Billings* (Montana) *Gaz.* 27 June 8-C/3 A major problem occurs when one small union negotiates a salary increase for its workers and all other state employes in the same job classification want the same increase. The effect is to 'whipsaw' the state between their competing demands. **1979** C. E. SCHORSKE *Fin-de-Siècle Vienna* vii. 351 Schoenberg whipsaws us upward out of the crepuscular calm.

whip-snake. Add: Also, in southern Africa, a grass or sand snake of the genus *Psammophis*, esp. *P. notostictus*.

1880 J. NIXON *Among Boers* ii. 45 He had all but put his foot upon a whip snake. These snakes are small and slender, being only as thick as the little finger. **1912** F. W. FITZSIMONS *Snakes S. Afr.* (new ed.) 462 The Grass and Sand Snake, when alarmed, glide off over the stunted herbage... Colonists know these as Whip Snakes. **1952** *Cape Times* 24 Apr. 9/2 As schoolboys were walking along the road..they saw a whipsnake.

whip-stitch, *sb.* Add: **2.** (Earlier example.) Also (without *at*), each item without exception; 'every last thing'.

1824 P. HOBBY *Life of Marion* p. i, What can one do, when one's friends are..calling out at every whipstitch.. 'Well, but sir, where's Marion?' **1888** F. R. STOCKTON *Dusantes* III. 130 Every whip-stitch of his bag and baggage shall be trundled after him.

whipstock. Add: **4*.** *Oil Industry.* A long, tapered steel wedge which can be placed at the bottom of a hole to cause the drilling bit to deviate sideways, e.g. in directional drilling.

1903 *Dialect Notes* II. 345 *Whip-stock, n.*, an implement used in drilling past a set of tools when fast. **1935** *Econ. Geol.* XXX. 740 Controlled deflection of a hole toward a specific objective through the use of whipstocks, knuckle-joints and improved methods of well surveying has given added flexibility to rotary tools. **1973** J. W. JENNER in Hobson & Pohl *Mod. Petroleum Technol.* (ed. 4) iv. 128 The whipstock had to be pulled out of the hole and reset every 25 ft or so..in order to achieve sufficient angle build up.

whirl, *sb.* Add: **11.** *colloq.* (orig. *U.S.*). An attempt, esp. an initial or tentative attempt. Freq. in phr. *give it* (and varr.) *a whirl*. Cf. *BURL *sb.*[2] 2.

1884 C. B. LEWIS *Sawed-Off Sk.* 277 After licking the best man in his own camp he came down to give us a whirl. **1889** 'MARK TWAIN' *Connecticut Yankee* xix. 234 No sound and legitimate business can be established on a basis of speculation. A successful whirl in the knight-errantry line... It's just a corner in pork, that's all, and you can't make anything else out of it. **1904** 'O. HENRY' *Sixes & Sevens* (1911) 75 I'd been saving up for a year to give this New York a whirl. **1922** S. LEWIS *Babbitt* vi. 90 But—I wish I could've had a whirl at law and politics. **1923** WODEHOUSE in *Strand Mag.* Apr. 335 Jeeves, if he cared to take a whirl at it, could be Prime Minister or something to-morrow. **1949** A. MILLER *Death of Salesman* I. 66 Come on up. Tell that to Dad. Let's give him a whirl. **1965** K. ROBERTS in J. Carnell *New Writings in S-F* III. 127 I'm going up again next weekend. Give it another whirl. **1979** S. WILSON *Greenish Man* 11 You've nothing to lose. Give it a whirl, try it for a month. **1985** *Times* 28 Feb. 20/2 John Syer came to me and said he could help... So I thought I would give it a whirl.

whirligig, *sb.* **2.** (*b*) (Earlier example.)

1816 E. WEETON *Let.* 22 May in *Jrnl. of Governess* (1969) II. 145 Large caravans enter the town with.. wooden horses, whirligigs, gambling tables, barrel organs.

whirling, *vbl. sb.* Add: **4.** *attrib.* and *Comb.*, as *whirling speed*; **whirling disease**, a disease of trout caused by the parasitic sporozoan *Myxosoma cerebralis*, which affects the balance of the fish it attacks.

1961 J. I. LENGY et al. tr. A. V. Uspenskaya in G. P. Petrusheveski *Parasites & Dis. Fish* 47 One of the most dangerous of the known parasitic diseases is the so-called 'whirling disease'. **1962** *Spec. Sci. Rep. U.S. Fish & Wildlife Service* No. 427. 2/2 Whirling disease appeared in brook trout at the Benner Spring Fish Research Station..in 1956. **1982** *Times* 12 Feb. 4/5 Whirling disease..is a parasite which gets into the skull of trout fry, causing a fish to lose its balance so that it swims round and round until it eventually dies. **1894** *Phil. Trans. R. Soc.* CLXXXV. 283 The whirling speed was taken to be at the commencement of whirl, that is to say, the lowest speed at which the shaft definitely whirled.

whirlpool[2]. Add: **1. c.** A bath or pool with underwater jets of hot, usu. aerated, water, used for purposes of physiotherapy or relaxation; also, a pumping unit for producing such jets. orig. *U.S.*

1975 *Sports Illustrated* Aug. 41 Sportswriters let you know they are on such intimate terms with an athlete that they can interview him in 'the whirlpool'. *Ibid.* 42/3 Last year Underwriters' Laboratories..dropped its long-standing approval of portable whirlpools whose unit, motor and all, goes into the water. **1976** *Billings* (Montana) *Gaz.* 16 June 8-A/3 (Advt.), Relaxing, soothing whirlpool... Directional nozzle, aerator, timer, handle. **1978** *Detroit Free Press* 5 Mar. D17/2 (Advt.), Entertainment and dancing in the Wharf Lounge. Indoor pool, sauna, whirlpool, charming restaurants. **1980** D. WILLIAMS *Murder for Treasure* ix. 86 The heated indoor whirlpool..measures twelve feet across. **1985** *Brit. Med. Jrnl.* 6 Apr. 1024/1 The whirlpool or Jacuzzi is a North American invention which has flourished there since the early 1970s but has only recently been introduced into Britain. Hot water is agitated mechanically through pressurised jets in a large tub and gives the bather a pleasurable sensation. Bathing in the company of others is usual.

2. b. (In sense 1 c above.)

1950 *Life & Health* Oct. 8/2 Whirlpool baths have stimulating effects. **1972** 'E. LATHEN' *Murder without Icing* (1973) xii. 113 It's more like a country club.. saunas and whirlpool baths, cocktail bars and singles nights. **1975** *Sports Illustrated* Aug. 42/2 Doctors generally agree on the salubrious effects of whirlpool therapy. **1978** *Official Gaz.* (U.S. Patent Office) 13 June TM 88/1 Jacuzzi Bros Inc., Little Rock, Ark... *Jacuzzi*... For hydro-therapy products..therapeutic whirlpool baths and parts thereof. **1984** *Miami Herald* 6 Apr. 15D/5 (Advt.), Bayside pool, sundeck and whirlpool spa. **1984** *Listener* 19 July 17/4 (Advt.), For couples who want to get away together..4 poster beds, water beds—with whirlpool bath en suite.

whirlwind, *sb.* Add: **3.** *spec.* applied to something done in great haste.

1865 [in Dict.]. **1942** [see *ROMANCE *sb.* 5]. **1952** J. L. WATEN *Alien Son* 87 Auntie Fanny lived her own life, never commenting on her husband's whirlwind comings and goings. **1969** 'D. SHANNON' *Crime on their Hands* vii. 99 We only got engaged last week. It was a whirlwind romance. **1977** D. E. WESTLAKE *Nobody's Perfect* 65 Jet-setter Arnold Chauncey, just back from his whirlwind tour of Brasilia. **1984** *Times* 20 Feb. 10/2 His whirlwind investigation of NHS management.

whirlwind *v.* (earlier example).

1894 'MARK TWAIN' *Let.* 22 Dec. (1917) II. 617 These salvation-notions that were whirl-winding through my head.

whirly-. Add: **whirly-whirly**, (*a*) a dentist's drill (*nonce-use*); (*b*) *Austral.*, a whirling air current or dust cloud.

1928 A. P. HERBERT *Trials of Topsy* xii. 73 He *thrust* the whirly-whirly *inch* by *inch* into the very *dome* of a girl's head. **1930** V. PALMER *Men are Human* xiii. 112 A cool breeze..raised little whirly-whirlies of dust. **1959** *Listener* 15 Jan. 113/1 The dust whirls and capers into fantastic whirlie-whirlies. **1972** *Southerly* XXXII. 4 A small whirly-whirly swept down the verandah, lifting dust and lolly papers in a mini-spiral.

whirlybird (hwə̄·ɹlibəɹd). *slang.* (orig. *U.S.*). [f. WHIRLY- + BIRD *sb.*] A helicopter.

1951 *Air Facts* 1 July 30/1 The biggest untold story out of Korea is of a few score unarmed American helicopters and a handful of pilots who have flown themselves and their 'whirlybirds' into military history. **1959** *Sunday Times* 26 Apr. 31/4 The noise which piston-engined 'whirly-birds' inevitably make causes no nuisance to workers in London. **1983** *Chicago Sun-Times* 28 July 82/1 The Bellwood-based whirlybird company has asked Civil Aeronautics Board approval to operate regularly scheduled flights.

whirra (hwi·ră). [f. WHIRR, WHIR *sb.*] A whirring sound that varies in quality. (The examples are *Austral.*)

1929 K. S. PRICHARD *Coonardoo* i. 14 The pigeon flew off with a whirra of grey silken wings. **1969** H. WILLARD in P. A. Smith *Folklore Austral. Railwaymen* 174 Within two minutes whirra whirra whirra, the spears and boomerangs were coming over our heads.

whirry, *v.* **2.** (Later example.)

1920 BLUNDEN *Waggoner* 24, I whirry through the dark.

whirry (hwə̄·ri), *a.* [f. WHIRR, WHIR *sb.* + -Y[1].] Characterized by, or of the nature of, a whirr.

1936 E. DARK *Return to Coolami* xiv. 142 There are the locusts beginning... A nice noise, whirry, hot, drowsy. **1982** *Financial Times* 25 Sept. 6/6 Intal suffered from the disadvantage that it could only be taken by the patient by means of a rather complex, whirry machine called the 'Spinhaler'.

whish, *v.*[1] **2.** (Later examples.)

1929 R. GRAVES *Good-bye to all That* xiii. 153, I heard one shell whish-whishing towards me. **1939** L. MACNEICE *Autumn Jrnl.* xiv. 54 The wheels whished in the wet. **1959** R. BRADBURY *Day it rained Forever* 214 Wouldn't it be nice to take a Sunday walk the way we used to do, with your silk parasol and your long dress whishing along?

whisk, *v.* **1. b.** (Later examples.)

1916 'BOYD CABLE' *Action Front* 12, I heard..something else goin' *whisk* like a cane switched past your ear. **1919** H. WALPOLE *Secret City* II. v. 353 A beautiful fruit just within his grasp... He's going to taste it, when whisk! it's gone.

whisker, *sb.*[1] Add: **4. d.** Phr. *to have whiskers* and varr.: (of news, a subject, etc.) to be no longer novel or fresh; similarly *to grow whiskers*. Also concr., of food: to become contaminated with mould.

1935 D. L. Sayers *Gaudy Night* viii. 182 That old story... It's got whiskers on it—it's six years old. **1951** M. Kennedy *Lucy Carmichael* vii. i. 345, I am putting on Čapek's *R.U.R.* But it has got whiskers. It was quite a novelty when it was first put on. **1959** *Times* 6 May 4/6 The subject is beginning to grow whiskers. **1977** D. Francis *Risk* vii. 78 The steak in the fridge had grown whiskers. **1977** D. O'Sullivan in D. Marcus *Best Irish Short Stories* II. 90 'Did I ever tell you the one about the Scotsman and the octopus?'..'It has whiskers.'

5. b. *fig.* A very small distance or amount, a fraction: used chiefly in comparisons. *colloq.* (orig. *U.S.*).

1913 *Dialect Notes* IV. 6 *Whisker, n.*, a little; a trifle. 'Move it just a whisker.' **1953** *Wall St. Jrnl.* 11 Aug. 1/5 The London price is still a whisker below the 30 cents a pound charged by major U.S. producers. **1973** P. O'Donnell *Silver Mistress* i. 13 Sooner or later they would go on a job and not come back... Even in the past year they had come within a whisker of it twice. **1980** *Jrnl. R. Soc. Arts* Mar. 236/2 In these storms at sea, sunsets, sunrises, cloud formations and light conditions, Turner was within a whisker of pre-empting the great Monet himself. **1983** *Times* 15 July 18/3 Yesterday the shares rose 2p to 99p—a whisker from the year's high. **1984** *Listener* 14 June 15/3 Someone shoots for goal, and he either misses it by a whisker or by miles.

c. *Electr.* A wire used to form a rectifying contact with the surface of a semiconductor; cf. *cat's whisker* s.v. *cat *sb.*[1] 18 and 19.

1915, etc. [see *cat(s') whisker* s.v. *cat *sb.*[1] 18 and 19]. **1949** *Ann. Reg. 1948* 418 By the addition of a second wire whisker touching the germanium within a few thousands of an inch of the first the diode was converted into a triode. **1959** K. Henney *Radio Engin. Handbk.* (ed. 5) ix. 15 These diodes are representative of a family of germanium point-contact diodes using unplated whiskers. **1975** D. G. Fink *Electronics Engineers' Handbk.* ix. 62 Until 1965 point contact diodes were fabricated utilizing moderately low resistivity material with the rectifying contact established by contacting the semiconductor surface with a metal whisker.

6.* A single crystal that has grown in a filamentous form a few microns thick, characterized by a tensile strength much greater than the bulk material and used in quantity as reinforcing agents.

1946 *Monthly Rev. Amer. Electroplaters' Soc.* Jan. 28/1 The growth of needle-crystals on cadmium deposits has caused considerable annoyance in the radio industry. These crystals are known as 'whiskers'. They grow between condenser plates of variable condensers, and, being electrical conductors, actually short-circuit the plates. **1951** *Corrosion* VII. 329/1 An attempt was made to develop whisker growths in the laboratory. **1961** *New Scientist* 28 Dec. 776/3 Whiskers, the hair-like crystals which are far stronger than steel, are now being incorporated in bonding materials: for example, General Electric's silver reinforced with sapphire whiskers. **1973** *Sci. Amer.* July 44/2 Alumina whiskers have a tensile strength of up to three million pounds per square inch and a modulus of 62 million pounds per square inch.

7. whisker pole *Naut.* (see quot. 1976); = sense 6 a in Dict.

1954 *Motor Boating* Dec. 27/1 *Iris* was flying all her kites—main, mizzen, genoa winged out on the whisker pole, and mizzen staysails. **1960** J. J. Rowlands *Spindrift* 204 On the yacht-club float a girl..is rubbing down the last coat of varnish on a whisker pole. **1976** *Oxf. Compan. Ships & Sea* 938/1 *Whisker pole*, a short bearing-out spar used in yachts and sailing dinghies to bear out the clew of the jib on the opposite side of the mainsail when running before the wind, thus obtaining some of the advantage which would be gained in a larger vessel when she sets a spinnaker. **1980** *Yachts & Yachting* 29 Feb. 651/2 'American Express' carried two poles that extended from 11.5 ft to 18 ft plus a standard pole of 7.5 ft. The long ones were used as a spinnaker pole in the collapsed position, as whisker pole in the fully extended position, and as a bowsprit in the 14ft length.

whiskerless *a.* (earlier example).

1843 Dickens *Mart. Chuz.* (1844) ii. 10 His very throat was moral... Serene and whiskerless.

whiskered, *a.* **1. a.** (Earlier example.)

1769 T. Warton *Let.* 10 Oct. in D. Garrick *Private Corr.* (1831) I. 369, I went on board one of the Russian ships, and had the pleasure of being surrounded with a thousand whiskered sailors and soldiers from Archangel.

whiskery, *a.* (In Dict. s.v. Whisker *sb.*[1]) Add: **2.** Suggestive of or resembling whiskers or a whisker; having whiskers.

1927 H. V. Morton *In Search of England* v. 98 The dark room smelt of..that indefinite whiskery smell of old men. **1959** *Times* 4 May 4/5 They fluffed a chip out of whiskery grass. **1984** *Listener* 10 May 3/1 Streets with a few measly roadside stalls peddling second-rate oranges and whiskery root vegetables.

whisky, whiskey, *sb.*[1] Add: In addition to the distinction mentioned in Dict., *whisky* is the usual spelling in Britain and *whiskey* that in the U.S. **a.** *whisky-and-soda* (examples).

1898 G. B. Shaw *Mrs. Warren's Profession* ii. 177, I could do with a whisky and soda now very well. **1924** H. Crane *Let.* 30 Nov. (1965) 195 As whiskey and soda was served I quickly revived. **1979** G. St. Aubyn *Edward VII* vii. 316 Offering him a whisky-and-soda and a cigar.

b. *whisky bottle, decanter, glass, -shop* (earlier example); *whisky-drinking* sb. and adj. (earlier examples); *whisky-gold, -soaked, -sodden* (earlier example) adjs.; **whisky-head** *U.S. slang*, one who consumes a great deal of whisky; **whisky-house** *Obs.*, a place where whisky is sold; **whisky mac** (also **Whisky Mac**), whisky and ginger wine mixed in equal proportions; a drink of this; **whisky money** *Hist.*, the proportion of the beer and spirit duty which was allocated to technical education by the Local Taxation (Customs and Excise) Act of 1890; **whisky priest**, an habitually drunken priest; **whisky-skin** *U.S. slang*, a drink containing whisky; **whisky-soda** (not in U.K. use), whisky-and-soda; **whisky sour** orig. *U.S.*, a drink of whisky acidulated with the juice of citrus fruit; **whisky-straight** (earlier example); **whisky voice**, a hoarse or alcoholic voice; **whisky-water** = *whisky-and-water*.

1843 'R. Carlton' *New Purchase* ii. lvi. 242 He abstained..from his whiskey bottle. **1981** M. Hatfield *Spy Fever* i. vi. 53 The whisky bottle was still in play, though its contents..had not shrunk catastrophically. **1931** M. Allingham *Police at Funeral* xi. 151 He..shot a hopeless glance at the whisky decanter. **1976** E. Ward *Hanged Man* xxi. 129 Galbraith placed the whisky decanter within reach. **1883** 'Mark Twain' *Life on Mississippi* lviii. 571 Whiskey-drinking, breakdown-dancing rapscallions. **1884** —— *Huck. Finn* xxi. 212 There was considerable whisky drinking going on. **1940** R. Chandler *Farewell my Lovely* xiii. 82 She wore a hat with a crown the size of a whisky glass. **1918** E. Sitwell *Clown's Houses* 15 The sunlight pours all whisky-gold. **1944** S. Bellow *Dangling Man* 179 'Took you in it at last, didn't I!' I exclaimed. 'You damned old whisky-head.' **1968** P. Oliver *Screening Blues* 23 Blues about liquor and the 'whisky-head man', about prostitution, gambling, vagrancy and intended violence, figure in the work of singers of all generations. **1767** *Scots Mag.* Apr. 222 Grant kept a whisky-house. **1835** R. M. Bird *Hawks of Hawk-Hollow* II. 6 You would have some of the wherewithall smuggled up to this identical old woman's whiskey-house! **1960** *Spectator* 14 Oct. 579 It [*sc.* Stone's Ginger Wine] is a little cloying taken neat, but mixed with an equal quantity of whisky it becomes 'Whisky Mac'. **1961** L. Payne *Nose on my Face* iv. 63, I..said I'd have a whiskey mac. **1976** *Liverpool Echo* 22 Nov. 7/5 A thief stole a £45 cask of whisky mac from an off-licence in Pasture Road, Moreton. **1982** Barr & York *Official Sloane Ranger Handbk.* 92/2 You drink beer, whisky macs, cherry brandy, sloe gin—or neat whisky. **1911** *Encycl. Brit.* XXVI. 495/1 If the 'whisky' money..were found to be well and carefully expended, no future Chancellor would be able to divert it to any other purpose. **1937** G. A. N. Lowndes *Silent Social Revolution* ii. 39 Action taken by the Technical Education Committees of the County Councils..to encourage the formation of classes and guarantee them financial support out of the 'Whiskey Money'. **1973** L. Holcombe *Victorian Ladies at Work* ii. 30 A portion of the 'whisky money', the proceeds from the increased duties on beer and spirits, to be spent on technical education by the county and county borough councils. **1939** G. Greene *Lawless Roads* vi. 161 'He was just what we call a whisky priest.'.. He had taken one of his sons to be baptized, but the priest was drunk. **1971** H. C. Rae *Marksman* i. iii. 19 With cheap striped pyjamas buttoned close around his throat Doyle looked like a whisky priest in a penal settlement. **1977** *Times* 4 Aug. 10/5 The communist equivalent of one of those Greeneland fables wherein a whisky priest rallies..to strike a blow for the God he no longer believes in. **1804** Lewis & Clark *Orig. Jrnls. Lewis & Clark Expedition* (1904) I. 10 Such as have made hunting..a pretext to cover their design of visiting a neighbouring whiskey shop. **1856** *Yale Lit. Mag.* XXI. 146 (Th.), Nine whiskey skins, and our spirits rushed together. **1891** *Sunday Times* 22 Feb. 2/3, I heard of the contemplated establishment of a London American club, the scheme of which seemed to comprise unlimited cocktails, whiskey skins, corpse revivers, [etc.]. *a* **1910** 'Mark Twain' *Autobiogr.* (1924) I. 209 Some old whisky-soaked, profane..infidel of a tramp captain. **1978** R. Ludlum *Holcroft Covenant* xiii. 153 Ellis made arrangements for the whiskey-soaked clothes to be picked up by the cleaners and returned by mid afternoon. **1915** H. L. Wilson *Ruggles of Red Gap* 50 Here, Charley, veesky-soda! **1975** O. Sela *Bengali Inheritance* xxv. 220 Shaking heads over their whisky-sodas saying, what could you expect. **1883** 'Mark Twain' *Life on Mississippi* lvi. 548 A harmless whiskey-sodden tramp. **1889** *Cent. Dict.*, Whisky sour. **1904** R. M. Lovett *Richard Gresham* 186 Bring a couple o' whiskey sours there, barkeep. **1975** D. Lodge *Changing Places* iii. 116 The lavish whisky-sours and daiquiris being prepared by the host. **1980** L. Birnbach et al. *Official Preppy Handbk.* 102/2 Tailgate picnics, whiskey sours in the stadium, and the general complexity of the sport guarantee that nobody knows what is going on. **1864** *Congressional Globe* 21 Apr. 1876/2 From the impassioned tone of the gentleman from Illinois..one would suppose that he had been investing in whisky straight. **1964** J. C. Catford in D. Abercombie et al. *Daniel Jones* 32 Simultaneous whisper + voice + creak: one form of 'beery' or 'whisky' voice. **1978** J. Updike *Coup* (1979) vii. 294 The women in the souk, with those long red finger-nails and blue hair in bandanas and those cracked whiskey voices. **1919** 'Etienne' *Strange Tales from Fleet* 5 'Thank you,' said the Captain, 'a whisky water, please.' **1978** T. Willis *Buckingham Palace Connection* i. 7 The ice-machine had broken down and I had to put up with a tepid whisky-water.

whisky, *v.* (In Dict. s.v. Whisky, Whiskey *sb.*[1]) (Earlier *refl.* example.)

1830 G. Colman *Random Rec.* II. 139 Post-boys and waggoners water'd their horses, and *whisky'd* themselves.

whiskyish (hwi·skiˌiʃ), *a. rare.* [f. Whisky, whiskey *sb.*[1] + -ish[1].] **a.** Inclined for whisky. **b.** Tainted with whisky.

1929 W. Deeping *Roper's Row* ii. 11 Don't be in a 'urry, my lad. Wait till they're warm. If they're whisky-ish, wait till the whisky's got 'em. **1929** E. Bowen *Last September* vi. 73 Some one tried to kiss you with whisky-ish breath.

whisper, *sb.* Add: **4.** *whisper-like, -proof* adjs.; **whisper-shot** (further example).

1876 *Gentl. Mag.* Sept. 339 To ascertain whether..our boasted right of asylum was really whisper-proof. **1904** W. H. Hudson *Green Mansions* iii. 45 The mysterious melody began... It was uttered by the same being heard on former occasions..that low, whisper-like talking. **1936** N. Streatfeild *Ballet Shoes* xviii. 278 Petrova looked round to see that Posy was out of whisper-shot. **1964** J. C. Catford in D. Abercombie et al. *Daniel Jones* 37 What *feels* like *breath*..begins to *sound* more whisper-like at rates of flow above about 300 cl/sec.

whisper, *v.* **2.** (Earlier example with the words uttered as obj.)

1836 E. B. Browning *Poet's Vow* v, in *New Monthly Mag.* XLVIII. 217 They whispered oft, 'she sleepeth soft'.

whispering, *vbl. sb.* Add: **4. whispering campaign**, a systematic circulation of rumours, esp. in order to denigrate someone or something (orig. in *U.S. Politics*); **whispering Willie** *slang* (see quots.).

1920 *Nation* (N.Y.) 10 Nov. 517/1 The scandalous underhandedness of the whispering campaign of the Democrats..only prove[s] the spuriousness of all their protestations of belief in equal rights for black and white. **1949** 'R. West' *Meaning of Treason* i. vi. 118 A whispering campaign designed to weaken public confidence. **1962** D. Lessing *Golden Notebk.* i. 139 He was desperately depressed—a whispering campaign around the party and near-party circles, that he was and had been 'A capitalist spy'. **1978** D. Bloodworth *Crosstalk* viii. 69 The Chinese have been mounting a whispering campaign against the Soviet Union, quite distinct from their overt anti-Soviet propaganda. **1918** H. W. McBride *Emma Gees* 135 The..'Whispering Willies' belong to the class of large caliber, long range naval gun shells which pass over the front line so high that only a sort of whistling sound is heard. **1937** Partridge *Dict. Slang* 952/2 *Whispering Willie*, a type of big naval gun used by the Germans: East African campaign of the G.W.

whist, *sb.*[2] **2.** (Earlier example.)

c **1874** D. Boucicault *Shaughraun* (*c* 1884) i. iii. 7/2 Hould your whist now! Wipe your mouth, an' give me a kiss!

whist, *sb.*[3] Add: **a.** *short whist* (earlier example).

1829 E. M. Arnaud *Epitome Whist* 29 The game is won by the party whose score first amounts to ten points in Long Whist, or five in Short Whist.

b. *whist party* (earlier example), *-player* (earlier example); **whist-drive** (further examples); now often as a means of raising funds for charities.

1915 T. Burke *Nights in Town* 179 When I received the invitation to the whist-drive at Surbiton my first thought was, 'Not likely!' **1924** [see *institute *sb.*[1] 4]. **1959** [see **community centre* s.v. *community ii]. **1977** *Lancs. Life* Nov. 73/1 They raised the money themselves (with hot pot suppers, whist drives, amateur drama and dances). **1981** G. Markstein *Ultimate Issue* 196 In the lobby of the officers' club the wives were having a whist drive. **1744** S. Fielding *Adv. David Simple* I. ii. i. 144 One of the Ladies, who was of the Whist-Party the Night before. *Ibid.* 147 Your Curiosity seems to be fully satisfied with what you have seen of the whist-players.

whistle, *sb.* Add: **1. b.** (*d*) *to blow the whistle on* (a person or thing): to bring an activity to a sharp conclusion, as if by the blast of a whistle; now usu. by informing on (a person) or exposing (an irregularity or crime). Also without *on*.

1934 Wodehouse *Right Ho, Jeeves* xvii. 222 Now that the whistle had been blown on his speech, it seemed to me that there was no longer any need for the strategic retreat which I had been planning. **1953** R. Chandler *Long Good-Bye* vi. 38 Come on, Marlowe. I'm blowing the whistle on you. **1965** *Midnight* 12 July 20/1 More and more frequently though, a whistle is being blown on the more exuberant borrowers. **1978** S. Wilson *Dealer's Move* v. 98 So Arnie and Alfie blew the whistle on you all. What are you going to do about it? **1984** *Gainesville* (Florida) *Sun* 29 Mar. 5A/4 Jim Kirkland, the man who first blew the whistle on Gainesville's deteriorating financial condition, has resigned after less than three months on the job.

d. *whistle and flute*: rhyming slang for 'suit' (Suit *sb.* 19). Chiefly *ellipt.* as *whistle*.

1931 Brophy & Partridge *Songs & Slang of Brit. Soldier, 1914–18* (ed. 3) 375 *Whistle and flute*, a suit (of clothes). **1941** G. Kersh *They die with their Boots Clean* i. 27 He is the one permanent type of Londoner..the.. Cockney... To Barker..a suit is a Whistle, or Whistle-an'-Flute. **1960** A. Prior in *Pick of Today's Short*

Stories XI. 180 Half-Nelson lives for clothes... He never keeps a whistle more than a month. **1970** A. DRAPER *Swansong for Rare Bird* vii. 51 My best whistle was in a big heap on the floor. **1980** 'J. GASH' *Spend Game* ix. 97 'Him with the fancy whistle.' Whistle-and-flute, suit.

4. *whistle-call* (earlier example); **whistle-blower** chiefly *U.S.*, one who 'blows the whistle' on a person or activity (see sense 1 b (d) above), esp. from within an organization; also **whistle-blowing** *vbl. sb.* and *ppl. a.* (lit. and *fig.*); **whistle-language** = *whistle-speech* below; **whistle punk** *N. Amer. Logging*, a workman who sends signals by means of a whistle to those operating a donkey-engine; **whistle-speech**, a system of communication by whistling based on the spoken language, found esp. among peoples of mountainous districts and used to communicate over long distances.

1970 *N.Y. Times* 23 Mar. 40 When they reflect more fully on how well the majority leader handled a whistle-blower and protected their interests. **1983** *New Scientist* 23 June 838/1 A whistleblower who tries to alert his own organisation to a problem and fails will, if he feels strongly enough about the matter, go outside. **1971** *Ibid.* 9 Dec. 69 The Code [of Good Conduct of The British Computer Society] contains secrecy clauses that effectively prohibit Nader style whistle-blowing. **1978** *Monitor* (McAllen, Texas) 21 May 16A/6 He has introduced legislation to protect 'whistleblowing' federal employees from reprisals if they reveal wasteful, illegal or improper government activities. **1980** *Times* 1 Apr. 3/4 The growth in Britain of 'whistle-blowing' journalism (blowing the whistle on the secret parts of the state and its servants by disclosing their activities) would seem to have sealed the fate of the D-notice system. **1983** D. DUNNETT *Dolly & Bird of Paradise* vii. 80 Whistle-blowing guys in white helmets. **1746** W. ELLIS *Agric. Improv'd* May xvi. 100 In a certain Park, where Pheasants and Partridges come at the Whistle-call. **1956** J. WHATMOUGH *Language* iii. 48 In this book we are not concerned with such departures from true speech as the so-called whistle 'languages' of Mazateco..and of the Canary Islands. **1957** *Amer. Anthropologist* LIX. 487 My direct interest in the subject stems from a brief encounter with a whistle-'language' and a slit-gong xylophone..among the Northern Chins of Burma. **1978** *Maledicta* II. 254 Whistle-Languages: Who knows whether there are insults or other abuses in whistled languages of the Canary Islands, Kuskoy/Turkey, etc.? **1925** *Amer. Speech* I. 136 The 'whistle-punk', who handles the signal wire that runs from the timber to the whistle of the donkey-engine. **1945** B. MACDONALD *Egg & I* xiv. 184 Sharp and clear came the whistle punk's signals for a skidder. **1965** M. MCINTYRE *Place of Quiet Waters* ix. 172 He might get a job as a whistle punk in a logging camp. **1948** *Language* XXIV. 280 (*heading*) Mazateco whistle speech. **1972** HARTMANN & STORK *Dict. Lang. & Linguistics* 255/2 Young English children often use whistle speech as a game. **1979** L. CAMPBELL in Campbell & Mithun *Lang. Native Amer.* 958 Whistle speech is shared by Amuzgo, Mazatec,..some Nahua dialects, and Mexican Kickapoo.

whistle, *v.* Add: **II. 9. b.** *to whistle in the dark*: to put on a brave front; to make a pretence of confidence.

1939 [implied in *WHISTLING *vbl. sb.* 1 d]. **1958** *Spectator* 8 Aug. 185/3 At his press conference, Mr. Dulles was whistling bravely in the dark. **1971** 'L. EGAN' *Malicious Mischief* (1972) ii. 29 That fellow's whistling in the dark. And I think he knows it. **1983** S. HILL *Woman in Black* 92 'I am finding the whole thing rather a challenge.' 'Mr Kipps..you are whistling in the dark.'

10. (Later example.)

1917 H. A. VACHELL *Fishpingle* xii. 236 He hurried on, now doubly assured that Joyce had 'whistled'.

11. To smell unpleasantly or strongly. *slang. rare.*

1935 AUDEN & ISHERWOOD *Dog beneath Skin* II. v. 113 Wot wouldn't I give for a bath? Cor! I don't 'alf whistle!

whistleable (hwi·s'l,ăb'l), *a.* [f. WHISTLE *v.* + -ABLE.] Of a tune, etc.: capable of being whistled; suitable for whistling.

1962 *Guardian* 9 Oct. 7/1 This movement contains no fewer than four very singable and whistleable tunes. **1973** *Daily Tel.* 19 Apr. 10/4, I want to sit light to the glorious fantasy, to let it ride through my mind like a whistleable tune.

whistled, *ppl. a.* Add: **1. a.** (Earlier example.)

1816 J. HECKLEWELDER *Let.* 24 July in *Trans. Hist. & Lit. Comm. Amer. Philos. Soc.* (1819) I. 396 Where *w* in this language is placed before a vowel, it sounds the same as in English; before a consonant, it represents a whistled sound.

b. *whistled language* or *speech*: = *whistle-language, -speech* s.v. *WHISTLE *sb.* 4.

1948 *Language* XXIV. 283 Many words and phrases in Mazateco have identical tonal patterns. In the spoken language segmental phonemes usually distinguish tonally identical words and phrases. In the whistled language the absence of the segmental features gives opportunity for ambiguities. **1957** *Archivum Linguisticum* IX. 44 The Silbo Gomero is not the only whistled language in the world..but..is unique in being based not on prosodic but on purely articulatory features. **1978** *Verbatim* Sept. 13/1 Such systems of communication by whistling, based on the language of the user, are conventionally referred to as 'whistled languages' or 'whistled speech'.

3. Drunk, (mildly) intoxicated. *slang* (orig. *Mil.*).

The relationship, if any, to *whistled drunk* in Dict. is obscure.

1938 G. MARCH-PHILLIPPS *Ace High* II. iv. 216 They would be drunk as lords, tight as owls, screwed, canned, whistled. **1942** H. E. BATES *Greatest People in World* 8 He bounced in very late..and then began to eat as if he had returned from a hunting expedition. 'Pretty whistled last night, boys,' he would say. 'Rather off my feed.' **1968** 'O. MILLS' *Sundry Fell Designs* viii. 83 He'd taken a skinful aboard, somewhere. He sounded more than a bit whistled. **1979** *Private Eye* 6 July 15/1 We all sidled off to a very nice little snug at the Golden Goose, where.. all of us got faintly whistled.

whistler. 2. b. For *Arctomys pruinosus* substitute *Marmota caligata*; = *SIFFLEUR. (Earlier and later examples.)

1703 tr. *Lahontan's New Voy. N.-Amer.* I. 110 [We saw] little beasts called Siffleurs or Whistlers. **1866** J. K. LORD *Naturalist in Vancouver Island* II. 195 The Redskin is the whistler's most implacable enemy; he never tires of hunting and trapping the little animal. **1912** *Canad. Alpine Jrnl.* (Special No.) 28 The big hoary marmots are well named 'whistlers' by all mountain climbing people of the Canadian Rockies. **1973** *Islander* (Victoria, B.C.) 4 Feb. 4/3 Here we saw ptarmigan and heard the marmots, or whistlers.

3. b. An atmospheric heard as a whistle that falls in pitch, caused by radio waves generated by lightning and guided by the lines of force of the earth's magnetic field.

1928 *Nature* 17 Nov. 768/1 These observations refer to a peculiar class of atmospheric, which from their musical nature are appropriately termed 'whistlers'. **1963** G. M. B. DOBSON *Exploring Atmosphere* viii. 141 It is also possible to get some information about the ionization at very great heights above the earth from the curious phenomenon of 'whistlers' or 'whistling atmospherics'. **1974** [see *MAGNETOSPHERIC *a.*]. **1979** [see *WAVE GUIDE].

Whistlerian (hwislī^ə·riăn), *a.* [f. the name *Whistler* + -IAN.] Of, pertaining to, or characteristic of the American painter and wit James Abbott McNeill Whistler (1834–1903) or his work; after the style of Whistler.

1891 E. DOWSON *Let.* 2 Feb. (1967) 183 Oscar arrived late looking more like his Whistlerian name, in his voluminous dress clothes, than I have ever seen him. **1905** W. J. LOCKE *Morals of Marcus Ordeyne* ii. 19 A sort of Whistlerian nocturne of golden fog! **1927** CHESTERTON *Robert Louis Stevenson* iv. 92 We talk of some Whistlerian satire as a squib; but satire can only shine in the dark. **1956** D. JONES *Let.* 24 Aug. in R. Hague *Dai Greatcoat* (1980) III. 170 I'm glad to have found one surviving little oil study from this almost Whistlerian world. **1960** *Times* 15 Nov. 16/5 This is all very well in an aesthetic and Whistlerian sense. **1979** S. WEINTRAUB *London Yankees* vi. 180 His [*sc.* Sargent's] icily elegant and Whistlerian portrait..of Madame Judith Gautreau.

Also **Whistlerism** (hwi·slərizʼm), the style or æsthetic theory of Whistler; **Whi·stlerish** *a.*

1912 C. ROWLEY *50 Yrs. Work without Wages* 147 We discussed the prevailing fashions of Whistlerism, Impressionism, and..post-Impressionism. **1918** G. B. SHAW *Pen Portraits* (1932) 40 They are art for art's sake: the political variety of Whistlerism. **1979** *Times Lit. Suppl.* 23 Nov. 10/4 The subject of the Thames..her Whistlerish visual evocations.

whi·stle-stop, *sb.* orig. *U.S.* Also **whistle stop.** [WHISTLE *sb.*] **1.** A small station or town at which trains do not stop unless requested by a signal given on a whistle.

1934 M. H. WESEEN *Dict. Amer. Slang* 418 *Whistle Stop*, a small town. **1944** *Sat. Rev.* (U.S.) 2 Sept. 2/4 The frank..and..challenging story of the men of the U.S. Foreign Service who represent America in the whistle-stops of the world. **1948** *N.Y. Times* 7 Sept. 18/8 President Truman told a railroad station crowd here tonight that 'before this campaign is over I expect to visit every whistle stop in the United States'. **1949** *Time* 9 May 29/3 To protest making Electra a whistle stop for express trains, he had thousands of plastic whistles molded in the shape of locomotives. **1949** 'H. ROBBINS' *Dream Merchants* (1950) 290 He thought Rock had been acting strangely yesterday when they had been married at that whistle stop just inside the California border. **1957** B. HUTCHISON *Canada* 217 The railway traveler sees only the dismal villages of the main line, the whistle stops around a wooden grain elevator..and a garage. **1965** S. G. LAWRENCE *40 Yrs. on Yukon Telegraph* xvii. 102 The railway company only recognized the town as a whistle stop.

2. One of a series of rapid, superficial visits.

1952 *Manch. Guardian Weekly* 7 Aug. 3 Truman opens his trap at the first whistle-stop. *Ibid.* 9 Oct. 3 As for Mr Truman's contribution by whistle-stop, his speeches have been..violently abusive. **1959** *Observer* 2 Aug. 9/4 We have gone on the marathon round of the dress shows (making whistle stops at breakfast and lunchtime at the smaller houses). **1976** *Courier-Jrnl.* (Louisville, Kentucky) 17 Sept. A2/1 President Ford is making a three-day tour..that will include a series of 'whistlestops' aboard a Mississippi riverboat.

3. Used *attrib.* to designate a journey with a lot of brief halts; *spec.* one by a campaigning politician that takes in many undistinguished places in this way. Also *fig.*

1949 *Time* 6 June 22/1 Louis Johnson..raised enough money..to pay for Harry Truman's whistle-stop campaign. **1952** *Manch. Guardian Weekly* 18 Sept. 3/1 On the whistle-stop tour down California's Central Valley. **1959** *Manch. Guardian* 23 July 1/3 The Queen and the Duke of Edinburgh..continued their 'whistle stop' journey to Moose Jaw. **1972** G. DURRELL *Catch me a Colobus* v. 94 Our whistle-stop tours of the villages round about had paid dividends and when we went to visit them again we rarely came away empty handed. **1973** M. TRUMAN *Harry S. Truman* i. 1 We had left Independence, Missouri, earlier in the day, and made a whistle-stop visit to Junction City, Kansas, at 11:05 p.m. **1976** *Times Lit. Suppl.* 23 July 904/4 She goes on to a whistle-stop history of attitudes to female inversion from Ancient Greece to the present day. **1978** *Broadcast* 17 July 15/1 BBC Radio 1's Roadshow set off again this week with a seven-week whistle stop tour of Britain's holiday resorts. **1981** *N. & Q.* Dec. 556/1 The result is an unremitting whistle-stop tour through barren regions.

Hence **whi·stle-stop** *v.*, (*a*) *trans.*, to travel through (a region) on a whistle-stop tour (*rare*); (*b*) *intr.*, to make a whistle-stop tour; also **whi·stle-stopping** *vbl. sb.*

1952 *News* (Birmingham, Ala.) 26 July 1/3 In a sort of swan song to the Democratic Party as its leader, he offered to whistle-stop the country for his successor. *Ibid.* 23 Sept. 14/5 Ike Eisenhower had settled down to whistle-stopping. **1952** *Time* 13 Oct. 23/3 In Michigan last week, nearly 100,000 people turned out to see Eisenhower as he whistlestopped across the state. **1957** *Ann. Reg. 1956* 183 Most of the 'whistle-stopping' was left to the assiduous Mr. Nixon. **1959** *Observer* 12 July 4/7 The Queen and the Duke of Edinburgh have been whistle-stopping their way across British Columbia. **1964** J. RESTON in M. McLuhan *Understanding Media* xxxii. 339 Everybody's now whistle-stopping through somebody else's country, usually ours. **1972** *Observer* 23 Apr. 6/4 Italian politicians are whistle-stopping around the country this weekend in..the..election campaign. **1978** *Guardian* 14 Dec. 15/4 Howard Jarvis.. the Messiah of taxpayers..has whistle-stopped across the United States with..226 events every 10 days.

whistling, *vbl. sb.* Add: **1. d.** In *fig. phr. whistling in the dark*: see *WHISTLE *v.* 9 b.

1939 *Time* 18 Dec. 21/3 Since precious little German trade can be sailed, submarined or flown overseas, writing about 'new possibilities'..sounded like official whistling in the dark. **1968** J. M. WHITE *Nightclimber* xix. 132 He, like me, hated and feared being carried in this ship, for all his whistling in the dark. **1977** *Listener* 10 Feb. 169/3 Lenin and his wife..were not above a little whistling in the dark to keep up their spirits.

whistling, *ppl. a.* Add: **1. a.** *whistling kettle*, a kettle fitted with a device that emits a whistle as the water boils.

1928–9 *Army & Navy Stores Catal.* 173/4 *The Whistling kettle.* When the water boils the kettle whistles. **1961** J. STROUD *Touch & Go* iv. 43 The whistling kettle.. burst into an unnerving shriek. **1974** R. INGHAM *Yoris* xx. 63 She put a small whistling kettle on the gas ring.

c. *Mil.* Designating a missile which makes a whistling sound in flight, or a gun from which such missiles are fired. Freq. in the nicknames of these.

1864 J. BROBST *Let.* 28 May in M. B. Roth *Well, Mary: Civil War Lett. Wisconsin Volunteer* (1960) iv. 67 We dare not show our heads unless we want them to send one of their whistling jimmies at us. **1902** J. MILNE *Epistles of Atkins* iv. 67 At Ladysmith 'Sighing Sarah' and 'Whistling Willie' proclaim their own shots from Umbalwana. **1926** T. E. LAWRENCE *Seven Pillars* xcv. 507 The aeroplanes circled round in their cold-blooded way, to drop whistling bombs into its trenches. **1948** W. WHITE *Man called White* 256 Three heavy German guns which the Americans nicknamed 'The Anzio Express' and 'Whistling Willies'.

2. b. *whistling atmospheric*: = *WHISTLER 3 b.

1953 *Phil. Trans. R. Soc.* A. CCXLVI. 128 The main facts of observation concerning the whistling atmospherics..are summarized above. **1959** DAVIES & PALMER *Radio Stud. Universe* ix. 174 Storey at Cambridge in 1952..was investigating a phenomenon known as whistling atmospherics or simply 'whistlers' which are groups of radio waves at audio frequencies (15 kc/s). **1963** [see *WHISTLER 3 b].

4. b. whistling thorn, a small prickly tree, *Acacia drepanolobium* or *A. zanzibarica*, found in East Africa.

1949 R. O. WILLIAMS *Useful & Ornamental Plants in Zanzibar* 102 *Acacia zanzibarica*..Coast Whistling Thorn. A thorny tree..bearing balls of bright yellow flowers. **1966** C. A. W. GUGGISBERG *S.O.S. Rhino* iii. 53 The rapid spread of the whistling thorn over vast areas.. is probably a result of the reduction..of this animal! **1976** K. THACKERAY *Crownbird* i. 9 The cab was full of whistling thorn, and swarming with red ants.

Whit (hwit). [The first element of WHITSUN, WHIT SUNDAY, etc.] = WHITSUN 1, WHITSUNTIDE. **Whit walk,** a Whitsuntide event in which church congregations walk in procession through the streets.

For *Whit Monday*, etc., and *Whit-week* see s.v. WHIT SUNDAY, WHITSUNDAY.

1959 I. & P. OPIE *Lore & Lang. Schoolch.* xii. 232 Well-dressing,..and the children's great Whit walks in Manchester and elsewhere, are undoubtedly exciting occasions in the lives of local youngsters. **1963** *Times* 5 June 7/1 (*heading*) Whit road toll down by 19. **1976** NICHOLS & ARMSTRONG *Workers Divided* 108 This morning our foreman told us that we've got to work Whit Bank Holiday. **1978** P. BAILEY *Leisure & Class in Victorian Eng.* ii. 46 The popular holiday ritual of the Whit walks—street processions of witness complete with flags and decorations and marching bands. **1979** *Guardian*

30 May 10/8 In Lancashire... Whit Walks in most towns and many villages.

whitbed (hwi·tbed). Also 9 **white bed.** [f. WHITE *a.* + BED *sb.*] One of the upper beds of Portland Stone, lying next below the roach; stone from this, valued as a clean freestone for building.

1829 T. WEBSTER in *Trans. Geol. Soc.* II. 38, I obtained from the quarrymen the thickness of the several beds, and the names by which they distinguished them from each other: but..these local appellations are not used by London architects and builders, the whole together passing here under the name of Purbeck stone only. The following is a list of the strata of limestone... 13. White bed, excellent. **1860** R. DAMON *Handbk. Geol. Weymouth* 78 Whit Bed or Upper Tier.—This bed, the best stone that the island produces in point of quality, is of a whitish brown colour when first raised, but becomes paler on parting with its quarry water. **1911** *Encycl. Brit.* XXII. 122/1 The Portland limestones have been much in demand for building purposes; at Portland the 'Top Roach', the 'Whit Bed' or top freestone, and the 'Best Bed' (or Base Bed) are the best known. **1925** J. BONE *London Perambulator* ii. 32 You can see shell imprints on the freshly cut whitbed stone on the top of the new Bush Building. **1934** *Archit. Rev.* LXXV. 27 (*caption*) A 'close up' of the polished Portland stone wall sheathing—a new compact crystalline limestone, with a lovely fossil formation, discovered under the tiers of whitbed at the Portland quarries. **1936** [see *CURF]. **1980** *Univ. Coll. London Bull.* Mar. 2/2 The thickest and most sought after unit in the local sequence is the Whitbed, noted for its homogeneity stemming from its lack of fossils or flint masses which may blemish other horizons above or below in the succession.

whitchet, var. *WICHERT.

white, *sb.* Add: **9. b.** (*b*) (Later examples.)

1922 E. RAYMOND *Tell England* II. iv. 207 All honest boys, we know, fancy themselves in their whites. **1974** K. MILLETT *Flying* (1975) I. 101 Rich playing championship tennis..in his whites. **1978** G. MCDONALD *Fletch's Fortune* (1979) xiv. 96 Stop at the pro shop... We'll fix you up with a racket and balls... Have whites?

d. *pl.* White articles of washing.

1962 *Which?* Aug. 231/2 The programme you choose for the washing you want to do ('whites', for example, or 'delicate fabrics' are possible settings on both machines) automatically determines washing and spin drying times. **1979** A. PRICE *Tomorrow's Ghost* xiii. 229 It used to be right dirty rain... Woman couldn't put her whites out.. when it was raining.

10. a. (Later example of *pl.* use.) Also (*sing.*) in general sense, money (*slang*).

1903 A. M. BINSTEAD *Pitcher in Paradise* viii. 204 Again and again the needy one implored his obdurate chum to shake out at least a deuce of whites. **1960** [see *CABBAGE *sb.*[1] 1 e].

11. (Later examples.)

1961 [see *RED *sb.*[1] 5 b]. **1972** 'W. HAGGARD' *Protectors* ix. 111 He..had drunk most of a bottle of wine. He had discovered the local whites with pleasure. **1978** T. L. SMITH *Money War* III. 182 He would have the filet of sole amandine... He couldn't quite make up his mind which of the wonderful whites to choose to go with it.

13. *poor whites* (examples); also *sing.* and *fig.*

1819 W. FAUX *Jrnl.* 28 July in *Memorable Days in Amer.* (1823) 118 The poor white, or white poor, in Maryland,..scarcely ever work. **1833** in *Maryland Hist. Mag.* (1918) XIII. 338 The poor whites at the South are not as well off in their physical condition as the slaves, and hardly as respectable. **1886** J. A. FROUDE *Oceana* xviii. 326 When he dies, the Maori and the poor whites in New Zealand will have lost their truest friend. **1896** R. WALLACE *Farming Industries of Cape Colony* 406 The so-called 'poor whites' are chiefly the descendants of French protestant refugees, and, in some districts, of early Dutch settlers. **1934** A. N. J. DEN HOLLANDER in W. T. Couch *Culture in South* xx. 414 In discriminating southern speech, it was not used to include all white persons who were poor... The 'poor-whites' were those who were both poor and conspicuously lacking in the common social virtues and especially fell short of the standard in certain economic qualities. **1958** L. VAN DER POST *Lost World Kalahari* iii. 56 All who worked for my grandfather no matter whether Griqua, Hottentot,.. Cape-coloured or poor white, were ultimately held in equal affection. **1974** 'J. LE CARRÉ' *Tinker Tailor* i. 9 Jim Prideaux was a poor white of the teaching community.

14. (*b*) Also, the white ball in pool.

1981 P. QUINN *Tackle Pool* ii. 25 If the white is at point A it must be played into the black almost full ball.

15. c. A white diamond.

1878 [see OFF COLOUR, OFF-COLOUR *phr.* and *a.* 2]. **1895** [see *BYWATER]. **1928** [see *BYE *sb.* 3]. **1972** V. CANNING *Rainbird Pattern* xi. 227 The diamonds were genuine,..blue whites, fine whites and whites. **1973** *Times* 25 Aug. 17/3 The (more or less) accepted English classes run thus in descending order: (1) finest fine white or river *alias* blue-white; (2) fine white; (3) commercial white.

d. A white ostrich-feather.

1881 A. DOUGLASS *Ostrich Farming S. Afr.* xiii. 81 The cocks' quill feathers..he will..sort first... Prime whites, first whites, second whites, tipped whites. **1890** A. MARTIN *Home Life on Ostrich Farm* vi. 103 A large and magnificent bunch of *wing*-feathers, the finest and longest of 'prime whites'.

e. *slang.* Morphine. Cf. *white stuff* s.v. *WHITE *a.* 11 e.

1914 JACKSON & HELLYER *Vocab. Criminal Slang* 87 *White, noun,* current amongst morphine habitues. Morphine. Example: 'How many times a day are you shooting the white?' **1977** N. ADAM *Triplehip Cracksman* iii. 32 By 1965 they were growing poppies for half the world's white.

f. White bread; a white loaf. *colloq.*

1960 WENTWORTH & FLEXNER *Dict. Amer. Slang* 576/1 *White,* white bread. **1974** 'A. GILBERT' *Nice Little Killing* iv. 55 Last of all came the baker... Leave a small white to be on the safe side. **1977** D. E. WESTLAKE *Nobody's Perfect* 45 A luncheon-loaf sandwich on white with mayo in his left hand. **1978** R. WESTALL *Devil on Road* vi. 35, I got thick-sliced white and corned-beef.

g. An amphetamine tablet. *slang.*

1967 [see *PILL *sb.*[2] 1 d]. **1969** *Observer* 21 Dec. 1/1 The street pusher with his 'wanna score some whites (Benzedrine)? Dollar a roll.' **1972** H. C. RAE *Shooting Gallery* I. 19 He had anticipated a rash of arrests for possession of brown drugs and amphetamines—but not this, not a straight leap into the lethal whites.

17. e. Phr. *white-on-white,* used *attrib.* to designate articles made of white cloth with a white woven-in design; also *fig.*

1955 W. GADDIS *Recognitions* II. vii. 572 A bow tie of propeller proportions stood out over extra-length collar bills on a white-on-white shirt. **1958** J. BLISH *Case of Conscience* xi. 113 'Why don't you give *me* a chance?' Michelis said raggedly. Then he turned white-on-white. **1976** A. GOLDMAN in D. Villiers *Next Year in Jerusalem* 221 Perhaps it was radio..that forced American humor in the thirties to enter a phase of white-on-white neutrality. **1978** *Detroit Free Press* 5 Mar. D9/2 The Smithsonian Institution has several white-on-white quilts done in this manner.

19. a. For 'an Italian Ghibelline' read 'a member of one of the two factions into which the Guelphs split (see *BLACK *sb.* 8 a)'. Now, a member of any of various counter-revolutionary or strongly conservative parties.

1802, etc. [see *BLACK *sb.* 8]. **1942** 'A. BRIDGE' *Frontier Passage* i. 6 There were a few Whites in Madrid..and.. they had a pretty thin time of it. **1954** B. & R. NORTH tr. *M. Duverger's Pol. Parties* II. i. 216 In small French villages public opinion spontaneously distinguishes between 'Whites' and 'Reds', 'clerical' and 'anti-clerical'. **1965** M. MICHAEL tr. *Myrdal's Rep. from Chinese Village* (1967) IV. 186, I joined the Young Pioneers. There we had classes about which districts were red and liberated and which were held by the Whites or the Japanese.

b. *spec.* An opponent of the Bolsheviks during the Russian Civil War (1918–21).

1921 F. MCCULLAGH *Prisoner of Reds* iii. 26 A few miles off, on the west, was a large force of whites, which intended to advance on Krasnoyarsk that night. **1924** E. G. JELLICOE *Playing the Game* xiii. 224 Expeditionary Armies of Britain and the United States, invaded Northern Russia..in order to link up with Russian Whites against Russian Bolsheviks. **1944** M. LASKI *Love on Supertax* ix. 86 She *is* Russian... Her parents were Whites who fled to Paris just before the October Revolution. **1950** E. H. CARR *Bolshevik Revolution* I. 325 In all these regions the ultimate effect of the civil war waged by the 'whites' with foreign backing had been to consolidate the prestige..of the Russian Soviet Government. **1964** L. DEIGHTON *Funeral in Berlin* 318 Chekist operators... Originally these were an anti-sabotage, anti-revolutionary force..during the civil war..empowered to..execute Whites, or Reds who were getting a little bleached. **1976** [see *RED *sb.*[1] 6 b].

22. *in the white* (further examples).

1957 *N.Z. Timber Jrnl.* Aug. 59/2 *In the white,* applied to finished furniture ready for polishing or other treatment. **1965** *Wireless World* July 9 (Advt.), This range includes..ready-assembled cabinets in the white for finish to own requirements. **1968** J. ARNOLD *Shell Bk. Country Crafts* 130 Factory-made chairs are often dispatched for later finishing, 'in the white' they call it. **1971** *Country Life* 10 June 1416/2 James Giles..bought consignments of Worcester porcelain in the white for decorating to commission. **1981** *Sci. Amer.* Oct. 134/3 Violinmakers often say that a violin sounds better in the white than it does after it is varnished.

23. white(s)-only *a.*, reserved for white people.

1968 *Listener* 18 July 86/3 In 1958, the Court of Appeal supported the Musicians' Union in their boycott of a whites-only dance-hall in dear old Wolverhampton. **1971** *Sunday Times* (Johannesburg) 28 Mar. 1/3 It was a Whites-only compartment. **1971** *Guardian* 29 Sept. 19/2 In Salisbury [Rhodesia], there are perhaps half a dozen 'Whites Only' signs—mainly on public lavatories. **1980** *English World-Wide* I. I. 55 In the 1950's Nassau's whites-only schools, cinemas, and restaurants were desegregated.

White (hwəit), *sb.*[2] The name of Gilbert *White* (1720–93), English naturalist, used in the possessive to designate *Zoothera dauma,* a yellowish-brown and white thrush with black markings native to Asia, eastern Europe, and Australia, and orig. named *T. whitei* in his honour by T. Eyton (1836).

1836 T. EYTON *Hist. Rarer Brit. Birds* 93 The general colour of White's Thrush, on the upper surface, is ochraceous yellow. **1893** *Ibis* 371 (*heading*) On the occurrence of White's thrush in European Russia. **1954** D. A. BANNERMAN *Birds Brit. Isles* III. 165 In its plumage White's thrush is characterized by the very prominent black crescentic markings.

white, *a.* Add: **1. e.** *whiter than white*: extremely white; freq. *fig.*

In mod. use popularized as an advertising slogan for Persil soap-powder.

[**1592**: see WHITE *sb.* 17 a.] **1924** *O.E.D.* s.v. *White* sb. 23, Exceeding or surpassing white, 'whiter than white'. **1949** D. SMITH *I capture Castle* vii. 95 The strangeness of her face: that look she has of belonging to a whiter-than-white race. **1962** *Daily Tel.* 28 June 1/3 He is said to have said that the report made out the BBC to be 'whiter than white'. **1974** 'A. GARVE' *File on Lester* vii. 31 Where their leaders are concerned, the masses are puritan—they expect standards of personal behaviour whiter than white. **1979** K. BONFIGLIOLI *After you with Pistol* xxii. 180 My knuckles were now Whiter-Than-White.

f. *Sci.* and *techn.* Applied to (non-optical) radiation, esp. sound and X-rays, having approximately equal intensities at all the frequencies of its range; esp. *white noise* (also *fig.*).

This use arises by analogy with the spectral composition of white light.

1922 *Nature* 1 Apr. 414/2 Just as the spectrum of a hot body normally consists of a continuous spectrum of white light, together with certain spectrum lines the wavelengths of which are characteristic of the radiating material, so an element emitting X-rays not only gives out 'white' radiation, but superposes its characteristic lines on the general spectrum. **1943** *Jrnl. Aeronaut. Sci.* X. 129/1 Inside the plane it is different; there all frequencies added together at once are heard, producing a noise which is to sound what white light is to light... That white noise is annoying needs little argument. **1948** *Bell Syst. Technical Jrnl.* XXVII. 642 If the noise is itself white..the result reduces to the formula proved previously. **1959** *Lancet* 12 Sept. 342/2 'White-sound' generators, which blind out extraneous noises, are unsatisfactory [for use in perceptual isolation experiments]. **1976** *Jrnl. R. Soc. Arts* CXXIV. 588/2 The proportion of power converted into the more penetrating 'bremsstrahlung'—or 'white' radiation—is approximately proportional to the atomic number of the target material. **1977** P. B. & J. S. MEDAWAR *Life Science* i. 14 When the noise signals are so subdued, random and heterogeneous that their pretensions to conveying information are negligible, we may speak of 'white noise', e.g. the sound—as of innumerable mice eating Rice Crispies—that sometimes accompanies long-distance telephone calls. **1980** P. WAY *Icarus* ix. 57 Maybe they *could* listen in, even through the white noise of the running water. **1984** *Mail on Sunday* (Colour Suppl.) 2 Dec. 6/2 (Advt.), At standard or even very low listening levels, you will never be harassed by hum or white noise.

2. e. [tr. It. *voce bianca* white voice.] Of a singing voice or its sound: lacking any emotional coloration (such as may be imparted by vibrato). Also *transf.* Cf. *voix blanche* s.v. *VOIX.

1884 F. NIECKS *Dict. Mus. Terms* 257 *Voce bianca* (It.), lit. 'white voice'. The female and children's voices, and also some bright-sounding instruments, are thus called. **1904** S. JOYCE *Dublin Diary* (1962) 39, I called McCormack's voice 'a white voice'—it is a male contralto. **1921** L. TETRAZZINI *My Life of Song* xix. 316 Be careful not to simulate too broad a smile. Too wide a smile often accompanies what is called 'the white voice'. This is a voice production where a head resonance alone is employed, without sufficient of the appoggio or enough of the mouth resonance to give the tone a vital quality. This 'white voice' should be thoroughly understood, and is one of the many shades of tone a singer can use at times.. to produce certain atmospheric effects. For instance, in the mad scene in *Lucia,* the use of the 'white voice' suggests the babbling of the mad woman, as the same voice..in the last act of *La Boheme* suggests utter physical exhaustion, and the approach of death. An entire voice production on this colourless line, however, would always lack the brilliancy and the vitality which inspires enthusiasm. **1951** W. MORUM *Gabriel* I. iv. 56 That vibrato ..[is] no use for symphony work. In the big orchestras the trumpeter employs what we call a *white* tone. A pure tone. **1957** V. NABOKOV *Pnin* 182 'I want a last piece of advice from you,' said Liza in what the French call a 'white' voice. **1961** *Times* 28 Sept. 16/1 An attractive, brightly ringing voice, rather white at the top but pleasantly dark below. **1975** *Gramophone* Dec. 1075/1 The soprano, Emma Kirkby, produces a 'white tone' which is scarcely distinguishable from that of a choir boy in some items, and this makes for a commendable purity of intonation. **1976** *Times* 8 Nov. 8/6 Where another team might produce a remote, 'white' sound, without vibrato..the Amadeus [Quartet] permitted a more human, warm tone. **1981** LD. HAREWOOD *Tongs & Bones* xiii. 209 He contented himself for the first act with accurate, small-scale singing in a rather small, white voice.

f. Of a drink of coffee: with milk or cream added.

[**1900** G. BELL *Let.* 25 May (1927) I. 113 Besides the bitter black coffee, we were handed cups of what they [*sc.* Hasineh Arabs] called 'white coffee'—hot water, much sweetened and flavoured with almonds.] **1925** X. M. BOULESTIN *Conduct of Kitchen* 10 It is somewhat distressing..to have to stop at the coffee-stall on the way home for an honest sandwich and a cup of 'white' coffee. **1940** *Punch* 6 May (Summer No., unpaginated) (*caption*), Please don't hesitate to say if you prefer your coffee white. **1982** H. SHAW *Death of Don* i. 3 'Black or white, Master?' 'White, please.'..They took their coffee and brandy and sat down.

4. a. *poor white folks* (also *folk*), *trash* (examples); so *poor white, poor-white* as compound adj. (not always contemptuous, and in wider use, esp. in *S. Afr.*); also *fig.* Hence *poor-white-folksy, -trashy* adjs. Cf. TRASH *sb.*[1] 4 in Dict. and Suppl., *WHITE *sb.* 13.

1821 *Austin Papers* (1924) I. 446 My friend could probably take with him about twenty negroes and perhaps a poor white family consisting of a man and his wife. **1833** [see *TRASH *sb.*[1] 4]. **1836** J. K. PAULDING *Slavery in U.S.* 205 The slave of a gentleman universally considers himself a superior being to 'poor white folks'. **1864** *Harper's Mag.* Aug. 412/2, I wouldn't do my hair in a three strand braid on no account; it is too poor-white-folksy for me. **1911** *Chambers's Jrnl.* Jan. 6/1 An effort has also been made to enrol men of the 'poor white' class in the police force, for which they appear well adapted. **1949** *Race Relations in S. Afr.* 413 It was not until 1898 that the first organized effort at their rehabilitation was made. In that year the Dutch Reformed Church in the Cape Colony established the Kakamas Labour Settlement for 'Poor White' families. **1951** H. Giles *Harbin's Ridge* 63 He never had been much account. Always content just to make out, which we considered poor-white-trashy in our parts. **1958** *New Statesman* 1 Feb. 143/1 In *The Hamlet* Faulkner describes the infiltration out of nowhere into..that sequestered poor-white corner of Yoknapatawpha County, Mississippi, of the Snopes family. **1958** *Times Lit. Suppl.* 13 June 328/5 Mr. Chase's thesis allows us to see them [*sc.* many popular American novels] as, so to say, poor-white relations of incomparably more distinguished works, relations that all the same show, in however degenerate a way, similar fundamental responses to the nature of American experience. **1958** A. Jackson *Trader on Veld* 43 As a matter of course, every property was divided equally among the owner's sons upon his death... Few things contributed more effectively to the creation of a Poor White class than did this usage. **1979** J. Drummond *Patriots* xv. 77 He'd been poor, the son of a poor-white farmer.

c. Of or pertaining to white people.

1852, etc. [in Dict., sense 4 a]. **1868** *N.Y. Herald* 4 July 5/2 The registered white vote has been very greatly increased. **1933**, etc. [see *white jazz*, sense 11 e below]. **1937** L. & E. Dowling tr. *H. Panassié's Hot Jazz* ii. 28 White musicians were playing..a so-called 'white' hot style intended to compete with the other style. **1944** *Living off Land* iv. 64 Natives are always hunting the coast for food. Also, there will be cattle stations, or white camps along the coast. **1959** 'F. Newton' *Jazz Scene* iv. 70 The most characteristically 'white' style in the history of jazz. **1965** F. Symington *Tuktu* 59 Most missionaries tried to teach their charges how to cope with the 'white' culture and economy. **1977** *Times of Swaziland* 25 Feb. 12 (Advt.), Farming estate... Strategically situated in centre of largest white area of popular Natal Midlands. **1984** J. McClure *Artful Egg* xi. 156 A couple..who affected sophisticated white manners and even spoke English with an almost white accent.

5. b. *to bleed white*: (*b*) (examples).

1935 *Sabbath School Worker* Nov. 6/1 'There are too many appeals for money', the people are 'bled white', and 'we can't give another penny'. **1945** R. Chandler in *R. Chandler Speaking* (1966) 113 It is the writers' own weakness as craftsmen that permits the superior egos to bleed them white of initiative, imagination, and integrity. **1982** 'W. Haggard' *Mischief-Makers* i. 16 Her husband had been a wealthy man, the lady's solicitors sharp and ruthless, and her husband had been bled white to get rid of her.

6. a. *white nun*, a Cistercian nun (cf. White monk).

1877 J. Penderel-Brodhurst *Guide to Boscobel* v. 20 Whiteladies... The name is derived from the circumstance that the house was once a Priory of Cistercian or White Nuns. **1954** A. Seton *Katherine* xxxii. 536 Katherine..surveyed the two nuns... White nuns, Cistercians, shrouded in snowy wimples and habits.

b. (Further examples.) In recent use applied to the Kuomintang in China and to the Christian Democrats in Italy.

1937 E. Snow *Red Star over China* i. i. 21 To get in touch with Communists in the 'White' areas [of China] was extremely difficult. **1952** [see *Kuomintang]. **1965** C. D. Eby *Siege of Alcázar* (1966) iii. 63 In less than forty-eight hours the Alcázar had become a solitary White island in the middle of a raging Red sea. **1965** M. Michael tr. *Myrdal's Rep. from Chinese Village* (1967) iii. 131 My father was taken by the white bandits and beheaded. **1967** C. Seton-Watson *Italy from Liberalism to Fascism* xii. 514 A left wing, led by Miglioli, the pacifist and 'white' trade unionist, called for a Christian proletarian party that would make capitalism its main enemy. **1973** P. A. Allum *Politics & Society in Post-War Naples* 326 The DC and PCI are heirs to particular Italian subcultures, the Catholic and the marxist. Both.. ensure..the electoral strengths of both parties in North and Centre, and above all in those regions (e.g. the 'white' provinces of the NE and 'red' provinces of the Centre, etc.) where they organise specific populations.

7. c. Of propaganda: truthful.

1965 B. Sweet-Escott *Baker Street Irregular* i. 29 The Ministry of Information..confined itself to straight or 'white' propaganda in neutral and friendly countries. **1976** [see *propaganda 3].

11. a. In names of animals. **white † admirable, admiral** [Admiral *sb.* 6], a dark-coloured butterfly, *Limenitis camilla*, with white markings; **white-bird,** (*c*) (without hyphen) in Irish folklore, a bird of fairyland; **white egret** = *white heron* (*a*) below; **white-fly,** a small bug of the family Aleyrodidæ, usually covered with pale, powdery wax, esp. *Trialeurodes vaporariorum*, which is a pest of greenhouse plants; **white fox,** a small fox, *Alopex lagopus*, native to northern Canada, Greenland, and Iceland, which has white fur in winter; also, the fur of this animal; **white goat** = *Rocky Mountain goat* s.v. *Rocky *a.*[1] 1 b; **white heron** (usu. qualified by *great*), (*a*) the common egret, *Egretta alba*, a large white bird with a yellow bill and dark legs found in parts of Europe, Asia, North Africa, the Americas, and Australasia; (*b*) a white subspecies of the great blue heron, *Ardea herodias*, found in Florida; **white owl:** see Owl *sb.* 1 b; **white perch** *U.S.*: see Perch *sb.*[1] 2; (examples); **white pointer:** see *pointer 12; **white rhino(ceros),** a large, wide-mouthed rhinoceros, *Ceratotherium simum*, native to parts of Sudan, Uganda, and South Africa; **white steenbras,** a large marine food fish, *Lithognathus lithognathus*, found in coastal regions of South Africa; **white whale** = Beluga 2.

b. In names of plants. *white grape* (example); **white ash,** (*a*) add: *esp.* a North American ash, *Fraxinus americana*; (earlier and later examples); *white-ash breeze* (earlier example); **white-bark pine,** a pine with pale, flaky bark, *Pinus albicaulis*, native to north-western North America; **white birch:** see Birch *sb.* 1 b; (earlier and later examples); **white box,** either of two Australian trees, the evergreen *Bursaria spinosa*, which bears clusters of fragrant white flowers, or a box eucalypt, *Eucalyptus albens*, which has pale leaves; **white campion:** see Campion[2]; **white cedar,** (*a*) any of several North American conifers, esp. one of the genus *Chamæcyparis*; (*b*) *Austral.*, a name used for species of *Melia*, deciduous trees native to the East Indies and Australia; **white clover:** see Clover 1 b; (later examples); **white elm,** the American elm, *Ulmus americana*; also, the European elm, *Ulmus lævis*, which resembles it closely; **white fir,** any of several North American firs, esp. *Abies concolor*, native to the south-western United States; **white mangrove:** see Mangrove[1] 2; **white maple,** any of several maples with pale bark, esp. the silver maple, *Acer saccharinum*, or the mountain maple, *A. spicatum*; **white mulberry,** a round-topped mulberry, *Morus alba*, or its white or pink fruit; **white oak,** any of several species of North American oak, esp. *Quercus alba*, which is native to the eastern part of the continent; also, the wood of this tree; **white poplar,** (*a*) (see Poplar 1 b); (*b*) *N. Amer.*, the aspen, *Populus tremuloides*; (*c*) *N. Amer.*, the tulip-tree, *Liriodendron tulipifera*; **white-rot:** see Rot *sb.*[1] 2 c and sense 11 e below; **white spruce,** a spruce with bluish foliage, *Picea glauca*, native to North America; **white walnut** = Butter-nut 1.

c. In names of minerals, chemical products, etc. *white clay*; **white brick,** (*b*) a hard, durable variety of brick made from gault; **white cast iron** = White iron b; cf. *grey* (*cast*) *iron* s.v. *grey, gray *a.* 8 c; **white earth,** earth material (as clay) that is light-coloured; *spec.* in *Painting*, a white earth-colour; **white oil,** (*a*) crude oil that is pale in colour; (*b*) a colourless petroleum distillate; *spec.* a highly refined heavy distillate used medicinally and in the food and plastic industries; **white phosphorus,** (*a*) the white opaque incrustation that forms on phosphorus when it is kept under water (? *obs.*); (*b*) the ordinary allotrope of phosphorus, a translucent waxy whitish or yellowish solid which unlike red phosphorus is poisonous and very reactive; **white precipitate,** either of two mercuric amidochlorides obtained by treating mercuric chloride with ammonia: *fusible white precipitate*, $HgCl_2(NH_3)_2$, and *infusible white precipitate*, $HgClNH_2$ (ammoniated mercury), obtained when there is excess ammonia and used in ointments against worm infection; **white rust,** a white coating that forms on zinc in air, consisting of some or all of the oxide, hydroxide, and carbonate (see also sense 11 e below); **white sapphire,** a variety of corundum that is colourless owing to the absence of the impurities responsible for the blue colour of ordinary sapphire; **white spirit,** a volatile colourless liquid distillate of petroleum that boils between about 150°C and 200°C and is widely used as a paint thinner and solvent; **white tin,** (*a*) refined metallic tin, in contrast to black tin; (*b*) the ordinary allotrope of tin, in contrast to grey tin.

d. white cell = *white corpuscle* in Dict.; **white finger(s)** = *Raynaud's phenomenon* s.v. *Raynaud; also *attrib.*; **white scour,** a disease of calves, freq. due to infection with *E. coli*, causing severe diarrhœa, dehydration, and often death.

1798 E. Donovan *Nat. Hist. Brit. Insects* VII. 75 The White Admirable Butterfly feeds upon the common honey suckle or woodbine. **1906** R. South *Butterflies Brit. Isles* ii. 59 The White Admiral (*Limenitis sibylla*). The 'White Admirable Butterfly', as it was called by some of the older English entomologists, needs only to be seen to be at once recognized. **1717** J. Petiver *Papilionum Britanniæ Icones* 1/2 in *Opera* (1764) II. vii, White Admiral. Found about Dullidge and Wickham near Croydon, as also at Henly upon Thames. **1826** J. Curtis *Brit. Entomol.* III. 124 (*heading*) Limenitis camilla. The White Admiral. **1857** H. T. Stainton *Man. Brit. Butterflies & Moths* I. 33 White Admiral..Blackish brown, with a broad white band crossing the centre of the wings. **1922** V. Woolf *Jacob's Room* ii. 36 He had seen a white admiral circling higher and higher round an oak tree, but he had never caught it. **1968** *Oxf. Bk. Insects* 46/2 White Admiral..belongs to the same family as the Fritillaries. **1683** *Coll. New Hampshire Hist. Soc.* (1866) VIII. 146 [They] did feloniously..use about one cord of white ash. **1784** [see *red ash* s.v. *red *a.* 17 d]. **1851** H. Melville *Moby Dick* II. xxxix. 262 There she slides, now! Hurrah for the white-ash breeze! **1950** *Chicago Tribune* 27 Apr. iii. 10/1 Under each cutting spindle is placed a block of white ash. **1908** N. L. Britton *N. Amer. Trees* 12 White Bark Pine..a rather small tree of alpine habitat. **1949** *Sierra Club Bull.* Dec. 24, I knew I could not get any sleep just by crawling under the low branches of a white-bark pine. **1974** *Blackw. Mag.* Oct. 307/1 Stands of whitebark pine mingled with spruce..provide welcome shade. **1789** J. Morse *Amer. Geogr.* 197 On the high lands are..beech and white birch. **1961** H. MacLennan *Rivers of Canada* 48 Otherwise nothing but the immense low forest of spruce with the occasional splash of white birch. **1980** *Family Handyman* Sept. 63/2 Because hardwoods are more dense, there is more energy in a cord of oak, say, than a cord of white birch or white pine. **1892** W. B. Yeats *Countess Kathleen* 106 (*title*) The white birds. **1894** —— *Land of Heart's Desire* 41 The Child (*from the door*): White bird, white bird, come with me, little bird! Maire Bruin: She calls my soul! **1940** E. Pound *Cantos* lvi. 60 May the white birds remember this warrior. **1909** A. E. Mack *Bush Calendar* 67 Flowers blooming [in January]. *Bursaria spinosa.* White box or black thorn. **1923** *Census of Plants of Victoria* (Field Naturalists Club of Victoria) 46 *Eucalyptus albens* Miquel White Box. **1936** F. Clune *Roaming round Darling* xvii. 161 White box is a good burning wood, sheds a brown bark in springtime, then has a white surface. **1946** K. Tennant *Lost Haven* (1947) xvii. 289 'What are those trees down there?'..'Blueberry ash, white box, whipwood.' **1965** *Austral. Encycl.* III. 406/2 White box..having pallid glaucescent foliage. **1845** J. H. Parker *Gloss. Terms Archit.* (ed. 4) I. 72 In colour they are paler than ordinary red bricks, but are redder than the common white brick of Suffolk. **1969** R. Blythe *Akenfield* ix. 140 The school at Akenfield..is a stark, knife-edged building constructed of Suffolk white-brick, [etc.]. **1979** *Guardian* 10 July 19/7 The famous Suffolk whitebrick which Georgian architects favoured for the region's grander houses. **1795** White cast iron [see Iron *sb.*[1] 2]. **1967** A. H. Cottrell *Introd. Metall.* xxv. 518 In white cast irons, which are usually made by limiting the content of graphite-forming elements such as silicon to low levels.., all the carbon exists as cementite and the name white refers to the bright fracture produced by this brittle constituent. **1674** J. Josselyn *Acct. Two Voy. New England* 67 The white Cedar is a stately Tree. **1709** [see *pitch pine]. **1856** [see Cedar 3]. **1884** A. Nilson *Timber Trees New South Wales* 97 White Cedar.—An elegant tree. **1908** E. J. Banfield *Confessions of Beachcomber* i. i. 20 The white cedar..is a welcome and not unworthy substitute in appearance and perfume for English lilac. **1941** *Sun* (Baltimore) 12 Aug. 15/2 The hulls will be of two thicknesses, mahogany over white cedar. **1980** P. Moyes *Angel of Death* xi. 148 A fallen tree—a biggish white cedar with a trunk about a foot in diameter. **1861** *Q. Jrnl. Microsc. Sci.* I. 167 Colourless corpuscles, or white cells, exist in the blood in a comparatively small number. **1885, 1968** White cell [see *red cell 1]. **1480** White clay [see Clay *sb.* 1 a]. **1783** J. Wedgwood *Let.* 13 Oct. (1965) 272 Having seen a specimen of fine white clay.. and being told it came from the Apalachian mountains..I was so delighted with the appearance of this beautiful raw material..that..I determined upon sending an agent to the spot. **1852** in *Proc. Amer. Antiquarian Soc.* (1933) XLIII. 373 Mr Nichols..has in contemplation the purchase of a tract of land containing a mine of white or China Clay. **1790** S. Deane *New-England Farmer* 58/2 Red and white clover are the only sorts known and esteemed in this country. **1884** F. J. Lloyd *Science of Agriculture* xv. 268 White or Dutch clover..is a well-known variety of good feeding quality. **1977** J. L. Harper *Population Biol. Plants* i. 25 The useful measure is the number of leaves, for example in..white clover. **1832** W. A. Ferris *Diary* 8 May in *Life in Rocky Mts.* (1940) xxv. 143 It is sometimes found in various parts of the country, and is sometimes called 'white earth'. **1910** A. P. Laurie *Materials of Painter's Craft* iv. 42 Then among the whites we have a large number of white earths, of which chalk is of course the most important. **1969** R. Mayer *Dict. Art Terms & Techniques* 430/1 Because of its clarity and high absorbency, white earth is well suited for, and in limited use as, a base for certain lakes. **1835** J. J. Audubon *Ornith. Biogr.* III. 137 [The Louisiana Heron] is at all seasons a social bird, moving about in company with the Blue Heron or the White Egret. **1872** E. Coues *Key to N. Amer. Birds* 267 Genus *Ardea* Linnæus... Great White Egret, White Heron... *Egretta*...Little White Egret, Snowy Heron... *Candidissima.* **1939** *Florida* (Federal Writers' Project) i. 26 The handsome white egret, once nearly extinct, is now protected. **1957** D. A. Bannerman *Birds Brit. Isles* VI. 68 The great white egret, though included in the genus *Egretta*, is in habit more like the grey heron and the purple heron and less like the egrets. **1770** White elm [in Dict.]. **1860** *Trans. Illinois Agric. Soc.* IV. 451 The White Elm..is not good timber—is hard to split. **1948** *N.W. Ohio Q.* Winter 10 It was made of a strip of white elm bark about one foot wide. **1981** *Sci. Amer.* Aug. 40/3 Most European elms, including the European white elm (*U. laevis*), the English elm (*U. procera*) and the various cultivars of the species *U. carpinifolia* are also susceptible.

1939 STEDMAN *Med. Dict.* (ed. 14) 1231/2 *White fingers*, an occupational disease occurring in operators of pneumatic hammers who are exposed to cold, affecting usually the fingers of the left hand. **1947** [see *PNEUMATIC *a.* (*sb.*) 1 a]. **1971** *New Scientist* 15 Apr. 154/3 Researchers have found bone softening in chain saw operators and there is also the 'white fingers' complaint, with fingers going cold and numb. **1973** [see *RAYNAUD]. **1978** *Kingston* (Ontario) *Whig-Standard* 18 July 15/2 Regular users of chain saws, grinders, and pneumatic hammers, drills and chisels often develop a condition called 'white finger' disease. **1850** A. J. ALLEN *Ten Years in Oregon* v. 52 They found the red and white fir, spoken of by Clark and Lewis. **1897, 1913** [see *grand fir* s.v. *GRAND *a.* 12]. **1948** *Pacific Discovery* Mar. 7/2 Sequoias become established most easily..on cool north and east slopes with sugar pine and white fir. **1900** *Technical Ser. Div. Entomol., U.S. Dept. Agric.* No. 8 10 The minute 'white-flies'..may be flying around. **1925** A. D. IMMS *Gen. Textbk. Entomol.* 360 The 'white flies' are a much neglected group. **1946** *Nature* 14 Dec. 852/1 A few [gall midges] are carnivorous, preying upon..white-flies, other gall midges and the like. **1981** *Farmstead Mag.* Winter 35/3 Mites, aphids and whiteflies sometimes bother greenhouse cukes, but don't let this panic you into using a chemical spray. **1696** in H. Kelsey *Papers* (1929) 54 They [*sc.* Indians] brought nothing but 2 white fox skins. **1774** [in Dict.]. **1862** *Canad. Naturalist* May 138 White foxes have been killed on the south shore of Great Slave Lake. **1926** *Daily Colonist* (Victoria, B.C.) 22 July 19/6 The average price for white fox was $34.85. **1930** R. W. SERVICE *Coll. Verse* 269 Fur had they, white fox, marten, mink, to trade. **1969** *Beaver* (Winnipeg) Summer 10/2 The white fox is the principal source of fur income at Rankin [Inlet] as elsewhere. **1877** C. HALLOCK *Sportman's Gazetteer* 40 The White Goat is confined to the loftiest peaks of the Rocky Mountains. **1936** D. MCCOWAN *Animals Canad. Rockies* xiv. 122 A full grown male White goat has a body length of about five feet, stands approximately forty inches high at the shoulder and is from two hundred to two hundred and fifty pounds in weight. **1846–7** THOREAU *Walden* (1957) 114 The red pine and the black ash, the white grape and the yellow violet. **1624**, etc. White heron [see HERON, HERN 1 b]. **1813** A. WILSON *Amer. Ornithol.* VII. 106 The opportunities which I have ..had, of observing them with the train..from its first appearance to its full growth, satisfies me that the Great White Heron with, and that without the long plumes are one and the same species, in different periods of age. **1846**, etc. [see *KOTUKU]. **1917** *Auk* XXXIV. 86 The Great White Heron is of more social habits than the Blue Heron. **1939** *Florida* (Federal Writers' Project) I. 26 The great white heron, a Florida native, nests on the keys. **1957** D. A. BANNERMAN *Birds Brit. Isles* VI. 71 The great white heron is..very rare in North Africa in winter west of Egyptian territory. **1964** A. L. THOMSON *New Dict. Birds* 367/2 The Great White Heron *A*[*rdea*] '*occidentalis*' of Florida..may be no more than a local population of a colour phase. **1966** *Encycl. N.Z.* I. 209/1 Swamp and lake-edge birds include the rare white heron.. (*Egretta alba*). **1966** P. SHERLOCK *West Indian Folk-Tales* 57 A flock of white herons flew across the river. **1774** in *Rep. Bd. Trustees Publ. Archives Nova Scotia* (1945) 34 This town..affords a great store of fine timber.. white and black ash; white mapple; rock mapple. **1832** D. J. BROWNE *Sylva Amer.* 101 The white maple puts forth green and yellow flowers early in the spring. **1916** E. T. SETON *Woodcraft Man.* 291 Silver Maple, White or Soft Maple..usually a little smaller than the Sugar Maple. **1981** *Publ. Amer. Dial. Soc.* LXVII. 37 Sugar maple... All of the Iron Range respondents [in Minnesota] use the generic *maple*... On the Mesabi single instances of *soft maple, sugar maple,* and *white maple* are recorded. **1610** *True Decl. Estate of Virginia* 55 There are innumerable White Mulberry trees. **1737** J. WESLEY *Jrnl.* 2 Dec. (1910) I. 402 The white mulberry is not good to eat. **1850** [see MULBERRY 1]. **1957** M. HADFIELD *Brit. Trees* 248 The white mulberry..(so called from its white or pinkish, insipid fruit), is cultivated as the principal food plant of the caterpillar of the silkworm moth. **1975** E. WIGGINTON *Foxfire 3* 276 Dried white mulberries were used as a substitute for raisins or figs. **1634** White oak [see *red oak* s.v. *RED *a.* 17 d]. **1770** [in Dict.]. **1873** 'MARK TWAIN' & WARNER *Gilded Age* xvii. 163 You kin git all the rails you want outen my white-oak timber over thar. **1883** J. MACAULAY *Grey Hawk* iii. 44 The banks on both sides are covered with poplar and white oak and other trees, which grow to a considerable size. **1930** W. FAULKNER *As I lay Dying* 132 Tull take and cut them two big whiteoaks. **1941** *Sun* (Baltimore) 12 Aug. 17/2 They had in storage enough Dorchester county white oak to construct keels and frames. **1975** White oak [see *pin oak* s.v. *PIN *sb.*[1] 18]. **1913** V. B. LEWES *Oil Fuel* 38 In some parts of the world small deposits of what are called 'white oil' are..found. **1919** *Electric Jrnl.* XVI. 336/2 Lectroseal transformer oil and white oil of paraffin have marked absorption. **1925** A. B. THOMPSON *Oil-Field Explor. & Development* I. xi. 504 The so-called 'white' oils occasionally encountered in oil-fields are usually transparent and amber or sherry tinted, and are evidently filtration products of darker varieties commonly found in the neighbourhood. **1938** F. M. ARCHIBALD in A. E. Dunstan et al. *Sci. of Petroleum* IV. 2838/1 Petrolatum liquidum is the highest grade of white oil. **1977** *Lubricants Business* (Shell Internat. Petroleum Co.) 4 Technical and medicinal white oils are also important. **1775** A. BURNABY *Trav. N. Amer.* 15 These waters are stored with incredible quantities of fish, such as sheeps-heads, rock-fish, drums, white perch. **1851** T. A. BURKE *Polly Peablossom's Wedding* 129 The trout and white perch bit beautifully. **1949** *Sat. Even. Post* 12 Mar. 46/4 About the best fun was going out to the pond after white perch. **1849** H. WATTS tr. *Gmelin's Hand-bk. Chem.* II. v. 107 Phosphorus, kept under water ... gradually becomes covered with an opaque crust which..afterwards turns white... This white phosphorus retains its original appearance when dried over oil of vitriol. **1865** *Chem. News* 24 Nov. 251/1 He establishes that white phosphorus is neither a hydrate nor an allotropic state of ordinary phosphorus,..but that it is, in fact, merely ordinary phosphorus irregularly corroded on the surface by the action of air dissolved in the water. **1884** FRANKLAND & JAPP *Inorg. Chem.* xxx. 371 Amorphous phosphorus, prepared by any of the above methods, invariably contains a small quantity of white phosphorus, the presence of which renders the product dangerously inflammable. **1976** *New Yorker* 15 Mar. 80/3 Two white-phosphorus rounds were exploded over the landing zone to indicate the 'all clear'. **1774** in J. L. Peyton *Adventures my Grandfather* (1867) 127 The forest of Kentucky consists of yellow and white poplar, walnut, [etc.]. **1814** F. PURSH *Flora Americæ Septentrionalis* II. 383 *Liriodendron*..generally known by the name of Tulip-tree, or White and Yellow Poplar. **1908** C. MAIR *Through Mackenzie Basin* 81 It was well-timbered..with the finest white poplar I had yet seen. **1954** H. EVANS *Mist on River* 19 The wide and sunny freedom of his valley, with birches and white poplars between the belts of jackpine. **1825** *Phil. Mag.* LXV. 227 With common salt I obtained the same results, mercury remaining, and white precipitate being thrown down from the solutions, by liquid ammonia. **1887** [in Dict.]. **1923** J. W. MELLOR *Comprehensive Treat. Inorg. & Theoret. Chem.* IV. xxxi. 786 Conversely, infusible white precipitate is converted back to fusible white precipitate by the action of a soln. of ammonium chloride in liquid ammonia. **1956** J. S. ANDERSON tr. *Remy's Treat. Inorg. Chem.* II. ix. 474 The most important example of an ammonia addition compound is the 'fusible white precipitate', and important examples of mercury-substituted ammonia or ammonium derivatives are the 'infusible white precipitate' and 'Millon's base'. **1838** W. C. HARRIS *Narr. Exped. S. Afr.* xix. 184 A pair of white Rhinoceroses opposed our descent. **1941** J. S. HUXLEY *Uniqueness of Man* viii. 184 The numerous creatures which would have become extinct but for vigorous protection..such as the..white rhinoceros. **1972** *Islander* (Victoria, B.C.) 9 July 2/3 In South Africa the white rhino has increased from 20 to 2,000. **1981** P. TURNBULL *Deep & Crisp & Even* vii. 125 He stuck out like a white rhino at a tea party. **1932** *Iron Age* Jan. 232/1 A common corrosion found on the surface of zinc-coated products has been called by the industry 'White Rust'. **1976** A. R. L. CHIVERS in L. L. Schrier *Corrosion* (ed. 2) I. iv. 156 Zinc which has been properly aged..is safe against white-rust formation. [**1668** White sapphire: see SAPPHIRE 1 b.] **1884** E. W. STREETER *Precious Stones & Gems* (ed. 4) III. ii. 160 The varieties of Precious Corundum ascertained to exist in the Burmese dominions are the Oriental Sapphire..the Oriental Ruby..the Opalescent Ruby, the Star Ruby, the Green, the Yellow, and the White Sapphires, and the Oriental Amethyst. **1904** L. J. SPENCER tr. *Bauer's Precious Stones* III. 566 Zircon and corundum ('white sapphire'). **1942** B. W. ANDERSON *Gem Testing for Jewellers* ix. 88 Perfectly colourless corundum, usually referred to as 'White Sapphire', is not common in nature... Synthetic corundum..is, however, manufactured on a large scale. **1744** W. ELLIS *Mod. Husbandman* Jan. xii. 79 He lost several of his Flock by the Gripes and the White-scour. **1897** W. HOUSMAN *Cattle* viii. 251 Inflammation of the stomach and bowels [of calves]..is also commonly spoken of as 'white scour'. **1963** *Times* 17 May 5/7 (Advt.), Today the vet can control mortality from diseases like white scours. **1920** *Chem. Abstr.* XIV. 3786 Eight samples of light, medium and heavy types of petroleum distillate (white spirit) were examd. and compared with turpentine as to boiling range. **1977** *Reader's Digest Bk. Do-It-Yourself Skills & Techniques* 11/2 For cleaning out oil-based paints, wash the brush in white spirit. **1770** G. CARTWRIGHT *Jrnl.* 27 Aug. (1792) I. 30 About four miles above, are several small low islands, on which grow many fine white, and black spruces. **1832** [see SPRUCE *sb.* 4 b]. **1949** *Sat. Even. Post* 12 Mar. 50/3 Banks..were covered with a growth of fir and white spruce. **1968** R. KROETSCH *Alberta* IV. 164 Heavy stands of white spruce grow on the islands in Astotin Lake—the kind of spruce that covered much of the vicinity perhaps five hundred years ago. **1977** *New Yorker* 9 May 95/1 He thought that white spruce and other species could live farther north. **1801** White steenbras [see STEENBRAS]. **1905** [see *mussel-cracker* s.v. *MUSSEL *sb.* 4]. **1959** [see *foul-hooked* s.v. *FOUL *adv.* 6]. **1974** *Stand. Encycl. S. Afr.* X. 263/2 White steenbras... One of the best-known angling-fishes in Southern Africa. **1610** White tin [in Dict.]. **1706** [see TIN *sb.* 1 b]. **1902** A. FINDLAY tr. *Ostwald's Princ. Inorg. Chem.* xli. 720 Besides the ordinary white tin, a grey form is also known which has a much smaller density. **1944** C. PALACHE et al. *Dana's Syst. Min.* (ed. 7) I. 127 Solid white tin (β-tin) by contact with gray tin (α-tin), alters to a gray powder ('tin plague'). **1950, 1965** [see *grey tin* s.v. *GREY, GRAY *a.* 8 c]. **1973** J. J. LAGOWSKI *Mod. Inorg. Chem.* xi. 334 (*caption*) Each atom in white tin is surrounded by six other atoms arranged in a distorted octahedral structure. **1743** J. CLAYTON *Flora Virginia* 190 *Juglans alba*... White Walnuts. **1822** J. WOODS *Two Years' Residence Eng. Prairie* 228 White-walnut, or butter-nut, and black-walnut, are not so good as the English walnut. **1916** E. T. SETON *Woodcraft Man.* 275 White Walnut, Oil Nut, or Butternut..rarely 100 feet high. **1958** G. A. PETRIDES *Field Guide Trees & Shrubs* 86 Butternut.. also known as White Walnut, wood lighter in colour than that of its more valuable relative. **1697** H. KELSEY *Jrnl.* 6–7 July in *Papers* (1929) 88, 2 hands..brought news of a white whale drove a shore. **1834** [see WHALE *sb.* 1 b]. **1923** *Beaver* June 340/2 Indian reports were received that porpoises, or white whales, were..making excursions..up a certain creek. **1978** *Weekend Mag.* (Toronto) 22 July 16/1 White whales or belugas..become progressively lighter with age. **1985** *Times* 6 Mar. 8/4 Soviet seamen trying to save a large pod of white whales..trapped in the ice.

e. White Africa, the white inhabitants of Africa; the parts of Africa ruled by white people; **White Army,** any of the armies which opposed the Bolsheviks during the Russian Civil War (1918–21); also, a group which opposed the Red Guards in Finland in 1918; **White Australia,** used *attrib.* and *absol.* to designate a policy of restricting immigration into Australia to white people; **white backlash,** resentment felt by white people against demands made by, or concessions made to, black people; hence **white backlasher; white book:** *spec.* (with capital initials) the book first published in 1882 as *Annual Chancery Practice* and now entitled *Supreme Court Practice*; (further examples); **white cane** = *WHITE STICK 3; **white chauvinism** orig. *U.S.*, a white person's excessively high regard for his own race; so **white chauvinist; white Christmas,** a snowy Christmas; **white coal:** more commonly, flowing water as a source of energy; also, electricity; cf. *white fuel* (a) below; (earlier and later examples); **white dominion,** a dominion (sense *2 b) in which the majority of the inhabitants are white; **white dwarf** *Astr.*, a small, faint, very dense star (usu. but not necessarily white in colour) lying below the main sequence, and representing the stable phase assumed by stars having less than 1·4 solar masses when their nuclear reactions cease; (not regarded as a type of dwarf: see quot. 1978 and cf. *DWARF *sb.* 2 b); **white elephant:** see ELEPHANT 2 in Dict. and Suppl.; **white embroidery,** white-thread embroidery on a white ground; = *white work* below; **White English,** term occas. used in contrast to Black English, in the sense 'the English of white speakers'; **White Father,** (*a*) a white man regarded as protecting or controlling people of another race; (*b*) [tr. F. *Père Blanc*], a member of the Society of Missionaries of Africa, a Roman Catholic order founded in Algiers in 1868; **whitefellow** (earlier examples); **white flag,** (*c*) used *attrib.* (with capital initials) to designate a communist group active in Burma since 1946; **white flight** chiefly *U.S.*, the migration of white people from inner-city areas (esp. those with a large black population) to the suburbs; **white folk(s), white-folk(s),** applied by U.S. Blacks to white people; **white frost,** hoar-frost; **white fuel,** (*a*) flowing water as a source of power; cf. *white coal* above; (*b*) lead-free petrol; **white goods,** (*a*) domestic linens, as sheets, towels, etc. (now not necessarily white); (*b*) electrical goods that are conventionally white, such as washing machines and refrigerators; **White Guard, Guardist,** (*a*) a member of a force which fought for the Finnish government against left-wing insurgents in the civil war of 1918; (*b*) a member of a counter-revolutionary force in Russia during the civil war of 1918–21; also *transf.*; **White Highlands,** an area in western Kenya formerly (1904–59) reserved for Europeans; hence **White Highlander; white hole** *Astr.* [opp. *black hole*], a celestial object which expands outwards from a space–time singularity emitting energy, in the manner of a time-reversed black hole; **white hope,** orig., a white boxer who might beat Jack Johnson, the first Black to be world heavyweight champion (1908–15); hence, a person who, or a thing which, it is hoped will achieve much or on whom or which hopes are centred; **White Hun,** a member of a nomadic people of uncertain origin, also called Ephthalites or Hephtalites, who lived in Bactria in the fifth and sixth centuries A.D.; **white hunter,** a white man who hunts big game professionally; **white jazz,** jazz as played by white musicians; **white knight,** (*a*) (with allusion to a character in *Through the Looking-Glass*), an enthusiastic but ineffectual person; (*b*) a hero or champion; *spec.* (*Stock Exchange slang*) a company that comes to the aid of one facing an unwelcome take-over bid; **White Lady,** (*a*) a cocktail made of two parts of dry gin, one of orange liqueur, and one of lemon juice; (*b*) *Austral. slang*, a drink of methylated spirits, sometimes mixed with another ingredient; **white land** *slang*, open land that is not designated for development or change of use, or on which development is not allowed (so called from its being uncoloured on planning maps); **white level** *Television*, the signal level corresponding to the maximum brightness in transmitted pictures; **white lightning** *slang* (orig. *U.S.*), (*a*) inferior or illicitly distilled whisky; (*b*) a kind of LSD; **white list** *colloq.* [after BLACK LIST in Dict. and Suppl.], a list of people or things considered acceptable; **white market** [after

*BLACK MARKET], authorized dealing in things that are rationed or of which the supply is otherwise restricted; **white meter,** a meter that registers off-peak consumption of electricity; **white mule** *U.S. slang*, a potent colourless alcoholic drink; *spec.* illicitly distilled whisky; **white Negro,** (*a*) a Negro, or a person with Negro ancestry, who has a pale or albino complexion; (*b*) a white person who defends the rights or interests of Negroes, or identifies with them; (*c*) *nonce-use* (see quot. 1949); **white nigger** *slang* (chiefly *U.S.*), (*a*) a derogatory term for a white person who does menial labour; (*b*) a Negro who is regarded as deferring to white people or accepting a role prescribed by them; (*c*) (see quot. 1970); **white night,** (*b*) a night when it is never properly dark, as in high latitudes in summer; **white note,** (*b*) a note corresponding to a white key on a keyboard; = NATURAL *sb.* 7 a; **white paper,** (*c*) *spec.* (with capital initials) before 1940, an Order Paper of the House of Commons which was a corrected and revised version of one issued earlier the same day (a Blue Paper); (*d*) (with capital initials) a government publication presented to Parliament and having white covers rather than blue ones (usu. less bulky than those with blue covers); *esp.* one outlining proposed legislation or stating policy; also *transf.*; *White Paper candidate* Naval slang (see quot. 1962); **white plague,** tuberculosis; cf. *white death, scourge* in Dict.; **white port,** port wine made from white grapes; **whitepox** [see quot. 1972], epithet of a pox-virus isolated from monkeys that is very similar to the smallpox virus; **white-print,** a document printed in white on a dark ground; **white rabbit, White Rabbit,** used with allusion to the White Rabbit in Lewis Carroll's *Alice's Adventures in Wonderland* (1865), who was running because he was in danger of being late; also as *adj.* and *adv. phr.*; **white racism,** belief in the superiority of the white race, leading to antagonism towards people of other races; hence **white racist** *a.* and *sb.*; **White Rajah,** any of the three Rajahs belonging to the English family of Brooke who ruled Sarawak between 1841 and 1941; also *transf.*; **white ribboner,** one who wears a white ribbon as a badge of temperance; a teetotaller; **white room,** a clean and dust-free room used for the assembly, repair, or storage of spacecraft or delicate mechanisms; **white rot,** any of several fungal diseases of wood or living plants indicated by white patches of decay or mould (see also ROT *sb.*^{1} 2 c); **white rum,** a colourless variety of rum; **white rust,** a fungus disease of certain plants indicated by white blisters on leaves or stems, esp. one caused by *Albugo candida* affecting cruciferous plants or one caused by *Puccinia horiana* affecting chrysanthemums (see also sense 11 c above); **white sale,** a shop sale of white goods and household linen; **white settler,** (*a*) a white inhabitant of a non-white territory; (*b*) *transf.* (see quot. 1976); **White Sister,** a nun wearing a white habit; *spec.* a member of the Congregation of the Missionary Sisters of Our Lady of Africa, founded in 1869 to assist the White Fathers, or of the Congregation of the Daughters of the Holy Ghost, founded in 1706 in Brittany; **white slave** (earlier and later examples); *spec.* a prostitute, esp. one trapped into prostitution by others; also (with hyphen) as *v. trans.*, to sell or trap (a girl) into enforced prostitution, esp. abroad; **white-slaving** *vbl. sb.*; **white soup,** soup made with white stock; **white stock,** stock made with chicken, veal, or pork; **white stone, whitestone,** (*b*) a colourless gemstone; (*c*) a form of rendering; **whitestone** *v. trans.*, to whiten with stone (cf. HEARTHSTONE *sb.* and *v.*); **white stuff** *slang* (chiefly *U.S.*), morphine, heroin, or cocaine (cf. *WHITE *sb.* 15 e); **white supremacism,** a doctrine or the practice of white supremacy; hence **white supremacist** *sb.* and *a.*; **white supremacy,** domination by white races over non-white, esp. black, races; **white suprematist** *rare* = *white supremacist* sb. above; **White Terror** (see TERROR *sb.* 4; further examples); also *spec.* a similar period in Hungary in 1919–20 and in China in the years following 1927; **white tie,** *spec.* a man's white bow-tie worn with a black tailcoat; also *ellipt.*, a man's formal evening dress including a white tie; freq. *attrib.*; **white trash:** see TRASH *sb.*^{1} 4 in Dict. and Suppl.; **white war,** war without bloodshed; economic warfare; **white ware** (earlier example of sense 'white earthenware'); **white way** *U.S.* (usu. with capital initials), a brilliantly lit city street; *spec.* (usu. *Great White Way*), the part of Broadway either side of Times Square, the heart of New York's theatre district, or a similar street in any other town; **whitewear** = *white goods* (*a*) above; **white wedding,** a wedding at which the bride wears a formal white dress; **white whisky,** colourless whisky; *spec.* (*N. Amer.*) home-made or illicit whisky; **white work,** embroidery worked in white thread on a white ground.

1910 J. BUCHAN *Prester John* xxii. 353 The amnesty came..and white Africa drew breath again. **1974** A. WILLIAMS *Gentleman Traitor* i. 16 The armies and police forces of White Africa. **1918** White Army [in Dict., sense 6 b]. **1960** O. MANNING *Great Fortune* II. 109 It makes you look like a White Army officer. **1977** J. CLEARY *High Road* iii. 95 He had come out of Russia, a cavalry commander in one of the White Armies. **1921** White Australia [in Dict., sense 4 a]. **1930** W. K. HANCOCK *Australia* iv. 77 The policy of White Australia is the indispensable condition of every other Australian policy. **1979** *Guardian* 5 Jan. 7/2 Mr Gough Whitlam's Labour Government abolished the 'white Australia' policy five years ago. **1964** *Courier-Mail* (Brisbane) 29 July 2 Goldwater is no racist, but there's little doubt that his supporters hope to win votes from the 'white backlash', the so-far unmeasured resentment among many whites to some of the negro demonstrations and riots. **1974** *Spartanburg* (S. Carolina) *Herald* 25 Apr. c2/1 He said a serious white backlash had developed against aboriginal advancement programs. **1966** *Economist* 17 Sept. 1130/2 The result leaves 'white backlashers' little choice in November: Mr Peabody, a staunch liberal.., will oppose a Negro, Mr Edward Brooke, who has won the Republican senatorial nomination. **1968** *Listener* 7 Nov. 625/1 The spies converge on Shaefer, and the homely white-backlashers adroitly lay them flat. **1965** J. DEDHAM *Young Man's Guide to Law* xiii. 150 Great industry has to be employed in really absorbing the procedure of the courts both from the 'White Book' (the High Court practice) and the 'Green Book' (the County Court practice). **1982** I. H. JACOB *Supreme Court Pract.* I. p. vii, It may fairly be claimed that the year 1982 is the hundredth anniversary of the White Book. **1973** *Times* 8 June 7/7 (Advt.), Nowadays it takes more than a white cane to help blind people. **1980** D. MACKENZIE *Raven & Paperhangers* vi. 85 There's a special place for blind men. *And* you get a white cane. **1946** *Political Affairs* XXV. 935/2 The corrupting influence of white chauvinism has operated to maintain the most harmful division in the ranks of American labor. **1951** W. Z. FOSTER *Outl. Polit. Hist. U.S.* xxxiv. 563 White chauvinism—race hatred—has been, and still is, a question of hard cash to the big capitalists and landowners of the United States. *Ibid.*, Much of the race prejudice that does exist among the Latin American peoples..is due to the corrupting attitudes of white chauvinists (diplomats, tourists, and businessmen) from the United States. **1984** *Washington Post* 26 Feb. 10/1 White chauvinism in jazz writing has in large part replaced the tentative thrust toward 'ethnomusical' and socially aware analysis that were evident in the 6o's and 7o's. **1857** C. KINGSLEY *Two Years Ago* III. x. 305 We shall have a white Christmas, I expect. Snow's coming. **1913** *Collier's* 13 Dec. 8 (*heading*) A white Christmas. **1942** I. BERLIN (*song-title*) White Christmas. **1976** *Weekend Echo* (Liverpool) 4–5 Dec. 1/2 The weather men say the big shiver could bring our first white Christmas for years. **1885** *Neepawa* (Manitoba) *Star* 21 Aug. 2/1 Nor should those intrusted with the people's money.. embezzle..the least portion of that money, under colour of black coal or white coal, ditch contracts, or any other pretext. **1963** *Daily Tel.* 18 Sept. 14 All may not think electricity the best heating or cooking or even lighting agent. But it is the cleanest and simplest and deserves its title of 'white coal'. **1971** *Nat. Geographic* July 25/2 Many former waterfalls now slip submissively through penstocks and turbines, and this abundant 'white coal' has drastically altered the country's age-old fish-forest-and-farm economy. **1966** *Guardian* 6 Sept. 8/4 Assuming that the crumbling process would continue, Britain would be left with the 'white dominions'. **1973** C. CARRINGTON in Kipling *Compl. Barrack-Room Ballads* 23 After..1871, there were no British regular troops in the new 'White Dominions'. **1977** A. WILSON *Strange Ride R. Kipling* v. 253 Canada was the white dominion that Kipling had known longest. **1924** *Monthly Notices R. Astron. Soc.* LXXXIV. 322 The white dwarfs Sirius (*comes*) and O_2 Eridani. **1925** *Nature* 5 Dec. 834/1 Invoked to decide the truth of a suspicion of transcendently high density in the 'white dwarf' stars, it [*sc.* Einstein's theory of gravitation] has decided that in the companion of Sirius matter is compressed to the almost incredible density of a ton to the cubic inch. **1935** B. RUSSELL *Relig. & Sci.* viii. 217 If none of these things happen first, we shall in any case be all destroyed when the sun explodes and becomes a cold white dwarf. **1969** *Listener* 2 Jan. 10/3 White dwarfs are stars like the Sun which have collapsed into a sphere the size of a planet. **1978** PASACHOFF & KUTNER *University Astron.* x. 283 Do not confuse the term 'white dwarf' with the term 'dwarf'. The former refers to the dead hulks of stars.., while the latter refers to normal stars on the main sequence. **1876** GEO. ELIOT *Dan. Der.* II. IV. xxix. 223 Gwendolen..held a piece of white embroidery which on examination would have shown many false stitches. **1931** A. K. ARTHUR *Embroidery Bk.* viii. 83 Bullion knots are frequently used in white embroidery. **1971** S. LEVEY *Discovering Embroidery of Nineteenth Cent.* 9 White embroidery flourished throughout the century. **1974** *Florida FL Reporter* XIII. 3/3 *Black English* origins are almost entirely, if not entirely, rooted in *White English* dialect usage. **1974** *Newslet. Amer. Dial. Soc.* Nov. 44 Intonation patterns of Black English were studied and compared with those occurring in White English and formal Black English. **1835** C. F. HOFFMAN *Winter in West* I. 251 The unfortunate agent..was shot in the act of appealing to the Indians as their friend and 'father',—the reply being..'We have no longer any white father.' **1889** R. F. CLARKE *Cardinal Lavigerie* I. iv. 100 The White Fathers—a name given to the Algerian missioners on account of their wearing the long white robe of the Arab. **1894** *Harper's Mag.* Sept. 516/2 The White Father has sent me. **1969** *Telegraph* (Brisbane) 18 Sept. 2/2 The people we detest are the 'White Fathers'—those who control our destiny. **1977** B. LUCAS tr. *De Foucauld's Lett. from Desert* vii. 130 The Apostolic Prefect will probably tell him to spend a few days at Maison-Carrée, near Algiers, the mother-house of the White Fathers. **1832** Whitefellow [see *BUDGEREE *a.*]. **1853** C. B. HALL in T. F. Bride *Lett. Vict. Pioneers* (1898) 218 My black boy..showed me three or four bodies, partially concealed by logs. There were numerous tracks of horses round about. He explained the occurrence in his way—'I believe blackfellow bimbulalee sheep all about. Then whitefellow gilbert and put 'em along o' fire.' **1949** *New Statesman* 12 Feb. 147/1 The story begins last March. Then the Communists (White and Red Flag), who had already gone underground, began guerilla warfare on Government treasuries. **1959** *Listener* 18 June 1051/1 The so-called White Flag Communists who followed the Stalinist line. **1974** White Flag [see *RED FLAG 3 a]. **1967** *New Republic* 22 July 19/2 School quality is a far more important factor than racial feeling in this white flight from desegregated schools. **1975** *Political Sci. Q.* XC. 675 White flight from cities has been a much discussed phenomenon in the last decade. **1978** *Sci. News* 23 Sept. 216 Previous studies of this so-called 'white flight' phenomenon have been criticized for not taking into account the type of desegregation involved and for ignoring other factors that might have induced white families to leave the central city anyway. **1929** W. FAULKNER *Sound & Fury* 101 If it hadn't been for my grandfather, he'd have to work like whitefolks. **1932** E. CALDWELL *Tobacco Road* xv. 179 What's the matter with your automobile, white-folks? **1973** *Black World* May 20/1 In his essays on whitefolk, Du Bois invokes two specific historical occurrences which reflect the paradoxes, lies and hypocrisy of white civilization. **1981** A. MACKAY *Death on River* (1983) 120 She dressed conservatively. White folks' clothes, she thought wryly. **1382, 1563, 1739** White frost [see FROST *sb.* 2]. **1780** W. FLEMING *Jrnl* 14 Mar. in N. D. Mereness *Trav. Amer. Colonies* (1916) 634 Monday night there was a smart white frost. **1835** J. MARTIN *Comprehensive Descr. Virginia* 66 Our white frost is generally harmless, it being simple dew slightly congealed. **1967** White frost [see *HOAR-FROST a]. **1913** F. SODDY *Matter & Energy* v. 135 The 'white fuel' of the Norwegian hill-sides. **1928** *Daily Tel.* 27 Mar. 10/7 Italy has..greater advantages for the development of 'white fuel', for Egypt has but one single river. **1958** *New Scientist* 6 Feb. 19 When the catalyst is used with 'white' or unleaded fuel (as on motorised trucks for indoor use in factories) this difficulty does not arise. **1900** *T. Eaton & Co. Catal.* White Goods & Midwinter Sale 12 These prices for Shirt Waists and Wrappers are special for the White Goods Sale only. **1943** L. I. WILDER *These Happy Golden Years* xxxi. 276 Busily working with the white goods, Ma and Laura discussed Laura's dresses. **1960** *Economist* 8 Oct. 158/1 Refrigerators, deep freezers, washing machines, clothes dryers and other so-called 'white goods'. **1976** *Which?* Mar. 61/1 Electrical equipment..includes things like washing machines and fridges (what the trade calls white goods) as well as TVs and audio (which the trade calls brown goods). Specialist TV and audio shops don't normally sell white goods. **1981** *Times* 9 Mar. 19/6 An abiding problem for the white goods manufacturers is the high level of imports. **1922** White Guard [see *RED GUARD 1 b]. **1970** G. HUIZER in I. L. Horowitz *Masses in Lat. Amer.* xiii. 454 Tapia continued to have meetings with peasants in their houses although the soldiers or 'white guards' sent by the Cantabria hacienda tried several times to capture him. *Ibid.* 497 'White guards'..were groups of armed men hired by the landowners [in Mexico] to fight against those peasants who petitioned for land. **1971** H. TREVELYAN *Worlds Apart* xxiii. 267 The house was lucky to escape destruction during the Revolution, when it was said to have been for a time in the front line as a White Guard post opposite the Kremlin. **1974** J. WHITE tr. *Poulantzas's Fascism & Dictatorship* IV. iii. 210 The fascist phenomenon was constantly identified with the Russian White Guards, as a change to a revolutionary situation. **1951** in J. Degras *Soviet Documents on Foreign Policy* I. 131 A White Terror eclipsing the atrocities of the Finnish White Guardists. **1964** V. NABOKOV *Defence* xiii. 211 Yes, yes, I know he's a chess player... But what is he? A reactionary? A White Guardist? **1971** S. TALBOTT tr. *Khrushchev Remembers* i. 15 Our army won many important victories against our White-Guardist class enemies in the first years of the Revolution. **1976** P. DRISCOLL *Barboza Credentials* I. i. 24, I had seen Kenya..prosper in spite of the White Highlanders sneering. **1935** E. HUXLEY *White Man's Country* I. ix. 208 In East Africa the settlers' principal anxiety was that Indians would permeate the relatively small area of land suitable for colonisation—the 'white highlands'. **1957** W. M. HAILEY *Afr. Survey* (rev. ed.) xi. 719 The reservation of the White Highlands for Europeans prevented the process of expansion by which the more populous tribes would normally have found relief from congestion. **1978** S. NAIPAUL *North of South* I. iv. 114 Soil erosion had been one of the great settler obsessions. The battle against it had become part and parcel of the battle for civilisation, providing a powerful argument for the preservation of the status quo in the 'White' Highlands. **1971** *Nature Physical Sci.* 3 May 20/1 Black holes..are related in a genitive manner to 'white holes', defined to be singularities from which matter and energy emerge. **1977** *N.Y. Rev. Bks.* 29 Sept. 22/2 There is speculation..that every black hole is joined to a 'white hole'—a hole that gushes energy instead of absorbing it. **1911** *Daily Colonist* (Victoria, B.C.) 28 Apr. 11/4 A New York promoter has succeeded in arranging for a match between Albert Palzer, New York's most prominent white hope, and Carl Morris, the giant locomotive engineer. **1912** I. S. Cobb *Back Home* 233 Judge Priest was a celebrity, holding the limelight to the virtual exclusion of grand opera stars, favourite sons, white hopes, [and] debutantes. **1919** *Observer* 16 Nov. 12/6 In the south, based on the Black Sea and liberally furnished with British material, Denikin and his Cossacks were the 'white hope' of the anti-Bolshevists. **1941** Ld. Berners *Far from Madding War* iii. 50 He was a composer: the white hope (thus a critic had described him) of English music. **1948** *Time* 5 July 40/2 Idol of the Negro race, and so popular with the whites that the old cry for a 'white hope' never came up, Joe Louis..was a champion the whole U.S. was proud of. **1952** M. Allingham *Tiger in Smoke* iv. 81 Detective Coleman had been one of Luke's white hopes. He had liked the boy for his eagerness. **1969** *Daily Tel.* 6 Oct. 12 In the immediate post-war years cheap and almost limitless atomic power was the white hope of a small island sadly short of raw materials. **1979** *Nature* 23 Aug. 638/1 Interferon is the great white hope of cancer therapy. **1781** Gibbon *Decl. & F.* II. xxvi. 584 The white Huns, a name which they derived from the change of their complexions. **1866** H. Yule *Cathay & Way Thither* I. p. liv, The Yueichi..who became known in the West as Indoscythians, and at a later date as White Huns. **1965** G. Wheeler *Soviet Central Asia* i. 5 In the fifth century southern Turkestan was conquered by the Ephthalites or White Huns. **1945** N. Mitford *Pursuit of Love* xi. 90 She's happy now, isn't she, with her white hunter? **1964** D. Varaday *Gara-Yaka* xiv. 124 Two white hunters lay in wait, and each shot one of the pride. **1980** G. M. Fraser *Mr American* xxvi. 546 He's an elephant hunter to trade—what they call a white hunter. **1933** (*record-title*) White jazz. **1946** R. Blesh *Shining Trumpets* i. 23 No heterophony in white jazz except a chaotic sort in Chicago-style jazz. **1950** [see *schmaltz 2]. **1976** J. Berendt *Jazz Bk.* 11 There seem to have been white bands almost from the start. 'Papa' Jack Laine led bands in New Orleans from 1891. He is known as the 'father' of white jazz. **1895** M. Kingsley *Jrnl.* 23 May in *Trav.* (1897) vi. 110 The chief..bows with a jerk that causes the pantaloons to faint in coils, like the White Knight in 'Alice in Wonderland'. **1956** N. Marsh *Off with his Head* (1957) ii. 41 'I believe I have made a really significant discovery..' cried Dr. Otterly with the infatuated glee of a White Knight. **1970** *Times* 23 Apr. 7 The Italian Communist Party..will take its members into the regional election campaign next month as white knights dealing with the joint evils of corruption and reaction. **1976** J. Philips *Backlash* (1977) III. ii. 130 Woody would like nothing better than to play the white knight to my damsel in distress. **1979** *N.Y. Times Mag.* 30 Sept. 24/4 The Rangers' problems stemmed from the habit that.. the team's general manager..had of hiring ineffectual cronies to coach the club, and then replacing them with himself when they failed—a kind of 'white knight' compulsion. **1981** *Guardian* 30 Oct. 15/1 Thomas Tilling.. emerged yesterday as the white knight appointed by Berec to save the Ever Ready battery maker from the clutches of Hanson Trust. **1930** H. Craddock *Savoy Cocktail Bk.* I. 175 *White Lady Cocktail.* ¼ Lemon Juice, ¼ Cointreau. ½ Dry Gin. **1935** K. Tennant *Tiburon* 19 Two old men in the corner lying stupefied over a mixture of 'white lady'—boiled methylated spirit with a dash of boot polish and iodine. **1952** B. Hamilton *So Sad, so Fresh* xviii. 117 He indicated a cocktail cabinet..and proceeded to mix two 'White Ladies'. **1964** *Telegraph* (Brisbane) 24 Sept. 5/2 Aborigines..used to swill cheap wines and other concoctions like 'White Lady'—a fiendish brew of methylated spirit and powdered milk. **1975** R. Beilby *Brown Land Crying* 225 'Ya was on the White Lady at the finish, mixin' it with Coke.'.. 'But jees, meths'n Coca Cola.' **1978** White lady [see *sidecar 2]. **1960** *Guardian* 14 July 8/5 How much 'white land' the planning authorities have left between the limits of development shown on the town map and the beginning or inner edge of the green belt. **1971** P. Gresswell *Environment* 270 Open country and villages, both of which may be included in 'white land', have suffered. **1974** *Times* 19 Feb. 2/1 Mr. Rippon, Secretary of State for the Environment, should be challenged in the courts if he allows more 'white land' in the Worcestershire county structure plan to be used for development, a report by the county planning committee states. **1940** W. T. Cocking *Television Receiving Equipment* 298/2 (Index), White level. **1950** Rabinoff & Wolbrecht *Questions & Answers Television Engin.* x. 233 The maximum white level shall be 15 per cent or less of the peak carrier amplitude. **1953** Amos & Birkinshaw *Television Engin.* I. i. 17 White level may be positive or negative with respect to black level. **1982** J. Goldberg *Fund. Television Servicing* i. 5 Television standards identify a white level and a black level of picture information. **1921** *Double Dealer* July 20/1 The men lean or sit on the counter and talk politics, hard times..and more enthusiastically, the devastating and withering qualities of the current 'white lightning', 'white mule', or just plain 'corn', as the local moonshine whiskey is called. **1940** C. McCullers *Heart is Lonely Hunter* II. iv. 119 He had a pint of bootleg white lightning. **1969** *Times* 9 Dec. (Taiwan Suppl.) p. ii/3 The distillery's main product is kaoliang, a potent liquor made out of Quemoy-grown sorghum and known as White Lightning. **1972** *Village Voice* (N.Y.) 1 June 77/3 Ellen..unfolded some tinfoil which she said contained three tabs of Owsley's original 'white lightning', the Mouton-Rothschild of LSD. **1975** B. Garfield *Hopscotch* xii. 128 It was white lightning country and the backhill bootleggers were numerous. **1979** R. L. Simon *Peking Duck* vi. 50 Mao tai, the Chinese version of White Lightning. **1900** G. B. Shaw *Let.* 31 Aug. (1972) II. 182 The Labor Leader's 'white list' is the final stroke—the white flag held up to Liberalism at the moment when we are on the verge of victory over it. **1939** *Country Life* 11 Feb. p. xxi/1 (Advt.), Furs.—Avoid those tortured to death. Buy only those named on the Fur Crusade White List. **1977** *Lancet* 30 Apr. 963/1 One idea is a 'white list' of preferred drugs or a list of excluded drugs for which the N.H.S. would not expect to pay. **1943** *New Yorker* 25 Dec. 36/2 Britons buying legally and mournfully on the white market. **1968** P. Oliver *Screening Blues* vi. 181 There appears to have been no relaxing of the strict segregation of record catalogues, nor any apparent attempt to secure a white market for Negro records of this [*sc.* pornographic] character. **1973** *Times* 28 Dec. 1/4 A feature of the system would be a 'white market' in which unused coupons could be sold freely or bartered. **1972** *Times* 2 Oct. 9/3 It is connected to a separate wiring circuit and an offpeak or white meter. **1974** *Ecologist* Oct. 299/2 Measures such as low-tariff electricity ('White Meter') in off-peak periods only, have already made consumers prepared to group their demand for an intermittent supply. **1889** H. H. McConnell *Five Years a Cavalryman* 60 About this time I first became acquainted with a..drink known as 'pine-top' or 'white-mule' whiskey. **1928** *Collier's* 29 Dec. 8/1 What do you think about a bunch of boys and girls..stealin' a keg of white mule from a dealer? **1942** W. Faulkner *Go down, Moses* 156 Gets himself a whole gallon of bust-skull white-mule whisky. **1973** *Globe & Mail* (Toronto) 23 Feb. 37/8 At other times..the stuff would..lash out with its hind hooves at the little old wine-maker like the white mule once so respected in the Ozarks. **1765** *Phil. Trans. R. Soc.* LV. 45 (*heading*) An account of the White Negro shewn before the Royal Society. **1790** W. Wilberforce *Jrnl.* 5 Apr. in R. I. & S. Wilberforce *Life W. Wilberforce* (1838) I. vii. 264 Hard at work on Slave Trade evidence all day with 'white negroes', two Clarksons and Dickson. **1824** J. Doddridge *Notes Settlement & Indian Wars W. Parts Virginia & Pennsylvania* 52 Mulattoes.. are denominated white negroes. **1838** R. I. & S. Wilberforce *Life W. Wilberforce* I. vii. 255 Messrs. Clarkson, Dickson, &c. jocosely named by Mr. Pitt, his 'white negroes'. **1850** 'M. Tensas' *Odd Leaves Life Louisiana 'Swamp Doctor'* 76 He was one of that peculiar class called Albinoes, or white negroes. **1949** Koestler *Promise & Fulfilment* I. vii. 69 The Jewish Defence organization became another white negro, which changed its colour according to the political situation. **1957** N. Mailer in *Dissent* IV. 279 The hipster had absorbed the existentialist synapses of the Negro, and for practical purposes could be considered a white Negro. **1980** E. G. Wilson *John Clarkson* iv. 51 Both Clarksons were counted among the activists whom Pitt in a rare jest called the 'white Negroes'. **1837** R. M. Bird *Nick of Woods* I. 170 Hanging too good for him, white niggah t'ief, hah! **1871** E. Eggleston *Hoosier Schoolmaster* 52 'Ole Miss Meanses' white nigger', as some of them called her, in allusion to her slavish life. **1934** *Esquire* Feb. 96 Art Hickman and other purveyors of sweet rose to meteoric fame while white men who continued to play hot received the chauvinistic appellation of 'white niggers'. **1965** *Listener* 15 Apr. 545/2 The intellectual West Indian is being told to stand up and be counted. Will he commit himself to his people or remain what our radical Negroes in the Southern United States would call a 'white nigger'? **1970** R. D. Abrahams *Positively Black* vi. 135 Hippies and other recent Bohemian groups have openly proclaimed themselves 'white niggers' by which they seem to mean that, like blacks, they represent an alternative to the life style of majority-group American culture. **1975** *Times Lit. Suppl.* 7 Nov. 1320/4 Dr Marcus Foster, a black,..suggested that the children be equipped with identity passes... The unfortunate Foster was widely accused of being an Uncle Tom and a white nigger. **1960** G. Blanchet *Search in North* ii. 28 There was a brief pause while the sun was just below the horizon—the 'white night' as it is called. **1981** *Times* 6 June 14/3 If you go to Leningrad at this time of year you catch the celebrated 'white nights', when there is only a brief twilight around midnight. **1959** D. Cooke *Lang. of Music* ii. 44 The white-note scales on C (Ionian mode) and A (Aeolian mode) were already our C major and A minor scales. **1983** *Listener* 14 July 35/3 With its use of the traditional plainchant melody of the Psalm, its 'white-note' counter-melodies and harmonisations..it struck a fresh note after the highly-wrought complexity and chromaticism of most of Goehr's earlier works. **1906** *Minutes Evidence Sel. Comm. Official Publ.* 15/1 in *Parl. Papers* (Cd. 279) XI. 95 With regard to the White Paper, which is printed, and which is handed to Members with the notices of the day, that is printed from the same type, I presume, as the Blue Paper, which is sent to us in the morning? **1920** [see *White Terror* below]. **1922** C. E. Montague *Disenchantment* viii. 115 Our rulers have continued to issue to the Press, at our cost as Blue Books and White Papers, long passages of argument and suggestion. **1924** H. B. Lees-Smith *Guide to Parl. & Official Papers* ii. 19 Corrections in the Blue Paper, such as putting amendments to Bills in their right order, are made during the morning and sent to the printer in time for the White Paper. **1950** Kerr & James *Wavy Navy* 255 These ratings had been earmarked as suitable 'White Paper' candidates by their Commanding Officers and recommended to the Admiralty. **1955** *Times* 16 June 8/5 The text of the two agreements would be published in the next few days and laid before Parliament as White Papers. **1962** Granville *Dict. Sailors' Slang* 132/2 *White Paper candidate*, candidate for a temporary (wartime) commission in the RNVR. The White Paper was passed in Parliament for a scheme of promotion for suitable ratings who had served on the lower deck for at least three months in a ship at sea in time of war. **1967** *Listener* 8 June 739/2, I first hastened to read President Nyerere's 'White Paper' on education. **1971** H. Wilson *Labour Govt.* xiii. 201 Some of our major commitments.. had been worked out only to White Paper stage. **1978** *Dædalus* Fall 3 He would have been..the venerable statesman who delivered the White Paper on Defense in the postwar period. **1906** *Daily Colonist* (Victoria, B.C.) 10 Jan. 2/2 To Fight White Plague... The tuberculosis convention..has been a great success. **1926** H. V. Morton *Spell of London* 68 The peril of youth, the horrible white plague. **1961** L. Mumford *City in Hist.* xvii. 547 As early as the eighteenth century Mercier had observed this metropolitan form of the White Plague. **1723** J. Nott *Cook's & Confectioner's Dict.* sig. Pp. 7^v, Two Gallons of White-port Wine. **1892** Mew & Ashton *Drinks of World* 100 of white Ports the best are *Muscatel de Jesus*..and the *Lachryma Christi*. **1920** G. Saintsbury *Notes on Cellar-bk.* vi. 88 White Port..I think nearly deserving of the curse above pronounced on sparkling claret. **1978** M. Walker *Infiltrator* xiii. 144, I was given a glass of white port. [**1972** Gispen & Brand-Saathof in *Bull. World Health Org.* XLVI. 591/1 The parental Copenhagen virus..continually gives rise to a few white-pock forming virus particles by mutation. *Ibid.*, The occurrence of wild white poxvirus in healthy monkeys cannot be explained by the instability noted above.] **1977** *Brit. Med. Jrnl.* 26 Feb. 530/2 Viruses as yet indistinguishable from variola virus were isolated from the kidneys of six healthy monkeys and two rodents; these have been termed 'whitepox viruses'. **1979** *Nature* 24 May 295/2 Vaccinia, cowpox and camelpox viruses lack continuous transmissibility in man, but the situation with monkeypox virus and whitepox virus deserves further comment. **1919** H. Leverage *White Cipher* 84 He memorized the details like a draughtsman reading a white-print. **1967** White-print [see *Ozalid]. **1930** R. Lehmann *Note in Music* iv. 154 'I must hurry, I must hurry,' she said... Like the white rabbit, he thought. **1979** S. Brett *Comedian Dies* v. 52 Her pretty little face looked anxious... 'Oh, um. If you'll excuse me...' And she scuttled out, all White Rabbit. **1982** J. Elliott *Country of her Dreams* xii. 144 Off he went, scuttling.., White Rabbit late for a date. **1970** *Rep. 20th Ann. Round Table Meeting Linguistics & Lang. Stud.* 221 Because such quasi-militants feel that Negro dialect is inherently 'bad' (as did conservative Negroes before them), they regard it as a product of white racism. *Ibid.*, They see any attempt to describe and scientifically record Negro dialect as nothing more than a white-racist exploitation of Negroes. **1973** *Black Panther* 17 Mar. 6/3 No charges were pressed against any of the club-wielding, epithet-sputtering white racists clearly because the Navy felt that only 'they' (Blacks) had been in the wrong. **1977** M. Walker *National Front* 9, I despise nationalism, whether it be British, White Racist or Martian. **1909** Baring-Gould & Bampfylde (*title*) A history of Sarawak under its two White Rajahs, 1839–1908. **1966** *New Statesman* 1 July 21/1 Her role is somewhere between a White Rajah and a VSO. **1974** *Radio Times* 19 Mar. 37/3 The story of the last White Rajah of Sarawak. **1887** *Voice* (N.Y.) 15 Dec. 2/2 Brother Finch endeared himself to all White Ribboners. **1970** 'O. Henry' *Trimmed Lamp* 32 The 'demon rum'—as the white ribboners miscall whiskey. **1974** *Daily Tel.* 3 July 17/7 The National British Women's Total Abstinence Union, which has 6,000 members, still issues a white ribbon bow in the form of a badge to its followers, who are known as the 'white ribboners'. **1961** *Aeroplane & Astronautics* CI. 684/1 The new factory incorporates the latest production methods and in view of its development of special-purpose connectors—particularly in the micro-miniature field—a 'white room' is being fitted out so as to give the cleanest manufacturing conditions for this type of component. **1965** *Life* 5 Nov. 111/4 The capsule itself will be stored in the pristine solitude of a 'white room' near Cape Kennedy until Schirra and Stafford are ready to fly again. **1970** N. Armstrong et al. *First on Moon* iii. 66 The other five members of the close-out crew were in the 'white room' on swing arm No. 9. **1906** M. C. Cooke *Fungoid Pests of Cultivated Plants* 155 White rot of Grapes..occurs on the fruit, leaves, and rarely on twigs. **1946** Cartwright & Findlay *Decay of Timber* iv. 48 Decomposition of wood by fungi is of two main types, which have been described as brown rots and white rots respectively... In a white rot all the components of the wood, including the lignin, are decomposed. **1951** *Dict. Gardening* (R. Hort. Soc.) III. 1426/1 White Rot of onions due to the fungus *Sclerotium cepivorum* shows when..affected plants are seen to have rotten roots while the base of the bulb is covered with a very white, fluffy mycelium. **1969** G. Becker in Krishna & Weesner *Biol. Termites* I. xi. 356 A large number of mold fungi, white-rot fungi, and bacteria can produce toxic substances. **1962** S. Wynter *Hills of Hebron* xvi. 198 With the money he bought bags of rice..and even a few bottles of white rum. **1972** *Times* 19 Aug. 10/1 White rum promises to be the spirit of the 1970s. **1848** M. J. Berkeley in *Jrnl. R. Hort. Soc.* III. 266 Nothing can have been more general than the white rust..which is so common on cruciferous plants. **1937** F. D. Heald *Introd. Plant Path.* vii. 97 The greatest development of the white rusts is during the cool periods of early spring. **1981** *Daily Tel.* 16 May 19/2 Several cases of white rust.. have been found in imported plants [*sc.* chrysanthemums]. **1914** *Photo-Era* XXXIII. 168 (*caption*) A spring white-sale. **1970** *New Yorker* 10 Oct. 158/2 The season of White Sales. **1937** K. Blixen *Out of Afr.* iv. 298 Kitosch was a young Native in the service of a young white settler of Molo. **1969** J. Mander *Static Society* vi. 154 A White Settler minority, as in South Africa, can usually keep power if it is sufficiently determined and has a monopoly of arms. **1972** [see *holiday home* s.v. *holiday *sb.* 4 a]. **1974** *Daily News* (Tanzania) 13 Sept. 1/2 The three-day occupation of the main radio station here by the criminals (white settlers) protesting at the independence settlement, and the subsequent fighting and looting in the city's African suburbs, have shattered Portuguese hopes of a peaceful and amicable transfer of power in the colony. **1976** *Listener* 3 June 716/2 'White settlers' is a phrase now in common currency in the Highlands to describe refugees from that well-known rat race who buy any old wreck of a cottage, spend a lot of money on it and live there, many of them, for a month or so in the summer. **1659** White Sister [in Dict., sense 6 a]. **1890** E. H. Barker *Wayfaring in France* vi. 305 It was a White Sister kneeling and praying. **1908** *Catholic Times* 6 Mar. 11/2 We have in the Katanga many missions..and everywhere are White Fathers, religious women (White Sisters). **1957** G. D. Kittler *White Fathers* vii. 81 The answer, Lavigerie realized, would be in establishing the White Sisters. **1789** *Deb. Congress U.S.* 13 May (1834) 350 He hoped it would comprehend the white slaves as well as black, who were imported from all the jails of Europe. **1807** Southey *Lett. from England* II. xxxviii. 150 Let us leave to England..the distinction.. of being the white slaves of the rest of the world, and doing for it all its dirty work. **1913** C. Pankhurst

Great Scourge p. viii, Regulation of vice and enforced medical inspection of the White Slaves. **1917** A. Huxley *Let.* May (1969) 125, I am safe from these body-snatchers, kidnappers, baby killers and white slave traffickers, the Recruiters. **1970** 'J. Quartermain' *Diamond Hook* xvi. 99 If you stop me.., I'll white-slave Jessie to South America. **1977** D. Wheatley *Young Man Said* x. 147 Was she white-slaved—a fate which befell more than a few girls of her type and class in those days? **1960** D. Lessing *In Pursuit of English* i. 16 A father-figure.. with a [*sic*] strong white-slaving propensities. **1723** J. Nott *Cook's & Confectioner's Dict.* sig. L8v, To make White Cullis... Use this with White Soops and Ragoos. **1813** Jane Austen *Pride & Prejudice* I. xi. 123 As for the ball..as soon as Nicholls has made white soup enough I shall send round my cards. **1977** J. Aiken *Five-Minute Marriage* vi. 95 Next week Mrs. Andrews really must start making white soup; and I must write.. to Gunter's about the ices. **1853** R. Riddell *Indian Domestic Econ.* 63 Take three quarts of good white stock. **1905** *Tasty Dishes* (new ed.) 10, 3 pints of white stock. **1960** *Good Housek. Cookery Bk.* (rev. ed.) 196/1 Vegetable water or stock made from bones should be used for gravies and brown sauces; milk, or milk and white stock for white sauces. **1861** H. W. Bristow *Gloss. Mineral.* 320/2 When cut for jewelry, it [*sc.* rock crystal] is called by lapidaries, 'white stone'. **1937** *Burlington Mag.* Nov. p. xix/2 A gold ring with a telling portrait carved in whitestone. **1941** F. Thompson *Over to Candleford* vi. 98 She kept the whole of the fair-sized house cleaned and polished and whitestoned. **1963** *Times* 11 June 15/4 The whitestone and glass frontage gives the impression of verticality. **1978** R. Doliner *On the Edge* (1979) iv. 62 A whitestone Italian Renaissance mansion on Sixty-third Street. **1908** J. M. Sullivan *Criminal Slang* 27 *White stuff*, morphine. **1915** G. Bronson-Howard *God's Man* I. iv. 39 There's quite a trade in laudanum... The 'White Stuff's' on the up-and-up too. **1953** W. Burroughs *Junkie* (1972) xiii. 129, I had never been able to drink before when I was on the junk, or junk-sick. But eating hop is different from shooting the white stuff. You can mix hop and lush. **1967** N. Lucas *C.I.D.* x. 135 Luckier still not to have graduated from pep pills to..'The White Stuff'..heroin. **1958** *Listener* 12 June 967/1 The steady propulsion towards white supremacism. **1979** *Daily Tel.* 5 Sept. 6 He [*sc.* Ian Smith] is well aware that the noisy and active minority who regard him as the totem of white supremacism will call for his blood. **1959** *New Statesman* 30 May 751, I have wondered..whether there was any link between the demagogues of Notting Hill and white supremacists elsewhere. **1961** *Spectator* 20 Jan. 65 A way of life..that is white-supremacist. **1964** L. Nkosi *Rhythm of Violence* II. i. 26 The White Supremacists will not get away so easily! **1977** *Times* 30 Aug. 10/3 Mr John Tyndall, the National Front's founder and chairman..describes himself as 'an unashamed white supremacist' and regards whites as intellectually.. superior to blacks. **1981** *Times* 17 Mar. 12/3 The real contest in next month's general election will be between the ruling National Party and the white supremacist parties to the right of it. **1902** A. Tourgée *Let.* 15 May in T. L. Gross *Albion W. Tourgée* (1963) viii. 143 It is the very highest form of blasphemy to claim that the idea of 'white supremacy' and the later barbarism which demands race-subjection or extermination is pleasing to God or conformable to the religion of the Man of Nazareth. **1931** W. S. Churchill in J. C. Squire *If it had happened Otherwise* 179 Upon the rebound from this there must inevitably have been a strong reassertion of local white supremacy. **1981** *Times* 18 Mar. 8/6 The Rustenburg constituency..represents some of its most far-right votes for white supremacy. **1958** *Times Lit. Suppl.* 11 July 386/3 They imply that, had the Supreme Court said 'desegregate by the so-and-so of this year', and had President Eisenhower backed the Courts to the limit, the Southern white supremastists would not have 'fought back', or would only have done so unsuccessfully. **1971** J. Bishop *Days of Martin Luther King, Jr.* iv. 332 A few White Supremacists said that there was no doubt that the bombing was the work of..a militant black who wanted to incite his people to riot. **1920** *Glasgow Herald* 7 May 9 A report on the alleged existence of a 'White Terror' in Hungary has been issued in the form of a White Paper. **1965** J. Ch'ên *Mao & Chinese Revolution* (1967) I. v. 125 The less hesitant Wuhan declared the CCP [*sc.* Chinese Communist Party] outlawed on that fateful day of 13 July 1927. The so-called White Terror thus began and chaos ensued. **1970** G. Huizer in I. L. Horowitz *Masses in Lat. Amer.* xiii. 480 The secretary-general..noted the continuous struggle of the CNC [*sc.* National Confederation of Peasants] against the 'white terror' of landowners and caciques. **1977** *Time* 21 Mar. 26/2 In the 1930s leftists lived in constant fear of the so-called White Terror imposed by the [Chinese] Nationalist secret police. **1980** *Times Lit. Suppl.* 25 Apr. 471/2 After the collapse of [Béla] Kun's regime, the White Terror raged, but Korda somehow survived unharmed. **1853** 'C. Bede' *Adventures Verdant Green* vii. 65 You are going to wine with Smalls this evening... I suppose you would go properly dressed,—white tie, kids, and that sort of thing, eh? **1930** M. Kennedy *Fool of Family* xx. 208 'Is it a grand party?' asked Caryl nervously... 'I mean is it white tie?' explained Caryl. 'Oh yes, of course it's white tie.' 'Then it is grand.' **1936** [see *black tie* s.v. *black a. 19]. **1942** D. Powell *Time to be Born* iv. 83, I will give a white-tie dinner for eighteen. **1981** Ld. Harewood *Tongs & Bones* i. 29 The glamour of the occasion impressed me greatly—I was probably the only person in the boxes not in a white tie. **1932** H. G. Wells *Work, Wealth & Happiness* xii. 607 Tariff obstruction at this higher level is, for all practical ends, *war at the frontier*, White War, the chronic as distinguished from that acute form in which invasion, bomb, bayonet and poison gas play leading parts, which more emphatic sort of warfare we may call Red War. **1939** *New Statesman* 3 June 878/2 Armament firms will boom more conspicuously, but the promised Government limitation of earnings or special taxations of 'whitewar' profits must deprive the armament or semi-armament equities of their usual attraction. **1776** J. Wedgwood *Let.* 14 Jan. (1965) 189 But for *Usefull China*, or such a *white-ware* as you mention, I must beg a longer time. **1909** *Sat. Even. Post* 20 Feb. 8/1 Start at Fifty-ninth Street and walk down what the Manhattanese call the 'Great White Way'. **1920** S. Lewis *Main Street* 416 Then, glory of glories, the town put in a White Way. **1933** E. Caldwell *God's Little Acre* xi. 170 Out of the grey darkness of the building the girl suddenly appeared in the glow of the whiteway lights. **1939** *Florida* (Federal Writers' Project) II. 259 Central Avenue [in St. Petersburg], the city's 'White Way', extends rulerlike for 7 miles across the peninsula. **1977** *Washington Post* 30 Jan. E-1/1 When dancer-choreographer Merce Cunningham..appeared.. at New York's Minskoff Theater recently..one might have supposed..that the Great White Way had suddenly gone avant-garde. **1980** *N.Y. Times* 10 Dec. A-14/2 'Welcome to Boston's Great White Way,' the sign on a theater marquee pridefully proclaimed. **1905** H. G. Wells *Kipps* I. ii. 40 Cretonnes, chintzes, and the like; serviettes, and all the bright hard whitewear of a well-ordered house. **1949** N. Mitford *Love in Cold Climate* I. xvi. 170 She was awfully old for a white wedding, thirty or something terrible. **1962** *Daily Herald* 8 Jan. 6/8, I had a lovely white wedding... Given my time again I would cheerfully splash everything on one. **1976** *Listener* 29 July 105/1 Young black girls [in Soweto] now demand white weddings with lots of bridesmaids and floating veils. **1901** G. Parker *Right of Way* 23 Rouge Gosselin flung off his glass of white whisky, and threw after it another glass of cold water. **1957** W. Faulkner *Town* xxiv. 357 Ratliff..took a pint bottle of white whiskey from inside his shirt. **1968** 'N. Blake' *Private Wound* i. 17 Padraig, another Jamieson for Mr. Eyre. The white whiskey, mind, this time. Did y'ever try Jamieson's white? **1863** Mrs. Gaskell *Sylvia's Lovers* III. i. 2 Sitting in the dark parlour..and doing 'white work', was..wearying to her. **1936**, etc. [see *Mountmellick]. **1967, 1975** White work [see *Richelieu].

12. a. *white-fiery, -yellow.*

1876 G. M. Hopkins *Wreck of Deutschland* xiii, in *Poems* (1967) 55 Wiry and white-fiery and whirlwind-swivellèd snow. **1922** Joyce *Ulysses* 179 He..felt a slack fold of his belly. But I know it's whiteyellow.

b. *white-enamelled, -flattened, -heaped, -pointed, -quartered, -spread; white-shining, -steaming* adjs.; **white-burning** *a.*, applied to clay that gives a white product when fired; **white-dominated** *a.*, dominated by white people.

1965 G. J. Williams *Econ. Geol. N.Z.* xx. 359/2 The clays so formed are plastic, refractory and white-burning. **1967** M. Chandler *Ceramics in Mod. World* ii. 49 A small proportion of more plastic white-burning clay is sometimes included. **1960** White-dominated [see *question mark 2]. **1981** *Listener* 31 Dec. 810/1 Blacks tend to regard journalists as part of the white-dominated, Establishment-prone media. **1915** 'Bartimeus' *Tall Ship* iii. 51 Forward, the white-enamelled bulkhead was pierced by two entrances. **1918** D. H. Lawrence *New Poems* 47 Oh, masquerader, With a hard face white-enamelled. **1922** Joyce *Ulysses* 86 Nose whiteflattened against the pane. *Ibid.* 39 Belly without blemish, bulging big, a buckler of taut vellum, no, whiteheaped corn. **1948** D. Ballantyne *Cunninghams* 165 The dark blue sea, white-pointed by the wave tops. **1962** White-quartered [see *pink-scrolled* s.v. *pink *a.*[1] C. b]. **1851** J. G. Whittier *Benedicite* in *Nat. Era* 16 Oct. 166/5 God's love—unchanging, pure, and true—The Paraclete white-shining through His peace. *a* **1973** J. R. R. Tolkien *Silmarillion* (1977) 262 A city white-shining on a distant shore. **1918** D. H. Lawrence *New Poems* 26 Daisies that waken all mistaken white-spread in expectancy. **1921** R. Graves *Pier-Glass* 26 And a white-steaming mist Obscures desire.

c. *white-aproned, -barked, -bloomed, -blossomed, -bodied, -coned, -curtained, -fanged, -fronted* (later examples), *-gaitered, -glanced, -hooded, -jacketed, -maned* (later examples), *-naped, -necked, -polled, -smocked, -souled, -spatted, -stockinged, -tied, -tiled, -tilted* [Tilt *sb.*[1]], *-walled* (later examples); **white-arsed** *slang*, a term of abuse; **white-backed vulture**, an African vulture of the genus *Pseudogyps*; **white-breasted** (later examples); *white-breasted nuthatch*, a North American nuthatch, *Sitta carolinensis*; **white-crowned**, having a white crown; *white-crowned sparrow*, a North American sparrow, *Zonotrichia leucophrys*; **white-elephantine**, of the nature of a white elephant; uselessly splendid; **white-floured**, with the face whitened by flour; **white-throated sparrow** = *Peabody.

1868 J. G. Whittier in *Atlantic Monthly* 3 Jan. 1 Bare-armed..she came, White-aproned, from her dairy. **1977** J. Gillis *Killers of Starfish* x. 76 A white-aproned waiter appeared..bearing little plates of cheese squares. **1922** Joyce *Ulysses* 587 He's a whitearsed bugger. **1975** *Daily Colonist* (Victoria, B.C.) 18 May 1/1 Delegates.. sat in shocked silence when an Indian leader accused them of being 'white-arsed Liberals'. **1884** R. B. Sharpe *Layard's Birds S. Afr.* (ed. 2) 794 African White-backed Vulture... General colour deep brown. **1964** D. Varaday *Gara-Yaka* ix. 78 The sitters were white-backed vultures, the most common in this area [by the Limpopo]. They were so dark brown in parts that they looked dirty, but their lighter parts appeared immaculate in contrast. **1779** *U.S. Mag.* (Philadelphia) Feb. 85 The lowly mangrove fond of wat'ry soil; The white barked gregory rising high in air. **1948** White-barked [see *Engelmann]. **1922** Blunden *Shepherd* 43 From white-bloomed plum. **1911** J. Masefield *Everlasting Mercy* 79 That white-blossomed pond. **1904** W. B. Yeats *King's Threshold* 55 It was praise of that great race That would be haughty, mirthful, and white-bodied. **1808** A. Wilson *Amer. Ornithol.* I. 41 The White-breasted Nuthatch is common almost everywhere in the woods of North America. **1946** G. Stimpson *Bk. about Thousand Things* 491 The white-breasted cormorant is largely responsible for the production of the vast guano deposits on the islands off the coast of Peru. **1972** L. Hancock *There's a Seal in my Sleeping Bag* i. 14 Searching for the white-breasted sea eagle. **1980** *Northeast Woods & Waters* Dec. 23/2 Hairy and downy woodpeckers, white-breasted nuthatches..attack the suet on the old pear tree. **1920** Blunden *Waggoner* 40 Smoke's light blue pennants coil From white-coned oasts. **1836** R. King *Narrative of Journey* II. 196 The *fringilla leucophrys*, or white-crowned finch..perched on the topmost branch. **1839** W. B. O. Peabody *Rep. Ornithol. Mass.* 32 The White-crowned sparrow..is one of the finest of this family of birds. **1894** B. Torrey *Florida Sketch-bk.* 235, I discovered..perched at the top of the oak, tossing back his head and warbling—a white-crowned sparrow. **1975** *Nature* 18 Sept. 182/1 The Californian scrub habitat is occasionally devastated by fire, so that the white-crowned sparrow population is reduced to a few birds living in isolated patches of surviving scrub. **1977** *New Yorker* 19 Sept. 123/1 The twisted fig tree, the almond, not yet white-crowned, the slow tendrils of grape reaching into the sky are companions for a time. **1914** D. H. Lawrence *Widowing of Mrs. Holroyd* I. i. 3 At the back is a white-curtained window. **1959** *Economist* 28 Mar. 1152/1 The white elephantine palace by the lake at Geneva may be good enough for the foreign ministers. **1971** A. Sampson *New Anat. of Britain* xvii. 335 Sir John Hill..had applied quite drastic economies to its white-elephantine operations [*sc.* those of the Atomic Energy Authority]. **1952** C. Day Lewis tr. *Virgil's Aeneid* xi. 254 His head was helmeted in a wolf's mask Whose gaping mouth with its white-fanged jaws served for a visor. **1925** E. Sitwell *Troy Park* 21, I saw the white-floured zanies go. **1908** E. J. Banfield *Confessions of Beachcomber* I. iii. 98 White-fronted Heron, *Notophoyx novæ-hollandiæ*. **1909** A. E. Mack *Bush Calendar* 23 Birds breeding in September... *Ephthianura albifrons*. White-fronted chat. **1955** E. Pound *Classic Anthol.* I. 60 Chariots, rank on rank With white-fronted horses. **1971** *Country Life* 27 May 1292/3 The famous Wexford Slobs, main winter headquarters of the Greenland race of white-fronted geese. **1922** Joyce *Ulysses* 558 His nag, stumbling on whitegaitered feet, jogs along the rocky road. **1930** Blunden *Poems* 290 Those white-glanced pools. **1900** W. S. Churchill in *Morning Post* 17 Feb. 8/1 White-hooded, red-crossed ambulance waggons. **1927** A. Clarke *Son of Learning* II. 38 The Abbot said There is a barrel of white-hooded ale Here. **1910** W. J. Locke *Simon the Jester* xxiii. 323 White-jacketed waiters darting to and fro. **1980** H. R. F. Keating *Murder of Maharajah* xiii. 156 White-jacketed Goan bearers. **1883** W. Whitman *Daybks. & Notebks.* (1978) II. 319 The sea-beach and surf—its myriad ranks like furious white-maned racers, urged by demoniac emulation to the goal, the shore. **1955** E. Pound *Classic Anthol.* IV. 212 White-maned black stallions Pull with due order. **1932** *Discovery* July 232/2 The white-naped ravens and the mountain buzzards swing overhead. **1975** *New Yorker* 24 Mar. 34/2 The white-naped crane, fifteen hundred left, fifty in zoos. **1912** J. Stevenson-Hamilton *Animal Life Afr.* xvii. 299 The ravens are represented by the white-necked raven (*Corvultur albicollis*) in the south.. of the Ethiopian region. **1965** G. B. Schaller *Year of Gorilla* vii. 161 The most regular visitors to our meadow were a pair of white-necked ravens, lovely birds with iridescent black plumage and a striking white collar around the neck. **1968** *Sunday Mail Mag.* (Brisbane) 8 Sept. 6/1 Only two species of seals now live on the southern Australian coast-line, namely the white-necked hair-seal [etc.]. **1922** Joyce *Ulysses* 537 Staggering Bob, a whitepolled calf, thrusts a ruminating head.. through the foliage. *Ibid.* 102 The whitesmocked priest came after him tidying his stole with one hand. **1973** M. Amis *Rachel Papers* 186 There—round-eyed, white-smocked and spotless—was Rachel. **1874** J. G. Whittier *Sumner* in *Memorial to Charles Sumner* 100 He never brought His conscience to the public mart; But lived himself the truth he taught, White-souled, clean-handed, pure of heart. **1902** G. W. E. Russell *Londoner's Log-Book* iii. 40 Sir William Harcourt as the white-souled champion of spiritual religion. **1922** White-spatted [see *slew-foot]. **1934** Dylan Thomas *Let.* 14 Jan. (1966) 93 The white-spatted representatives of a social system that has, for too many years, used its bowler hat for the one purpose of keeping its ears apart. **1916** E. Pound *Lustra* 48 Her white-stockinged feet. **1957** J. Agee *Death in Family* III. xvii. 284 Catherine stood..looking at the skirt and at her white-stockinged feet. **1811** A. Wilson *Amer. Ornithol.* III. 51 White-Throated Sparrow.. [winters] in most of the states south of New England. **1865**, etc. White-throated sparrow [see *Peabody]. **1977** *New Yorker* 5 Sept. 23/3 Dozens of white-throated sparrows..have appeared among the cattails. **1848** A. H. Clough *Bothie of Tober-na-Vuolich* i. 5 The Tutor.. White-tied, clerical. **1972** A. Roudybush *Sybaritic Death* (1974) ii. 5 Tail-coated, white-tied and silk-hatted men. **1924** G. B. Stern *Tents of Israel* xiii. 182 I've wanted things, too... Hundreds of baths; baths in white-tiled rooms, and not skimping the hot water. **1978** T. Gifford *Glendower Legacy* (1979) 53 An ancient wino was mopping one corner of the long, narrow, white-tiled floor. **1939** F. Thompson *Lark Rise* i. 2 The baker's little old white-tilted van. **1958** *Punch* 21 May 670/3 Dunlop white-walled tyres, white pedals, and white pump. **1985** A. McCandless *Burke Foundation* i. 4 White-walled houses with red-tiled roofs.

d. (*a*) *white-duck*; (*c*) **white-shoe** *slang* (chiefly *U.S.*), effeminate, immature; **white telephone**, (of a film) telling an unrealistic story set in elegant surroundings; **white-wall**, (of a tyre) having white sidewalls.

1849 White duck [see Duck *sb.*[3] 3]. **1925** H. Crane *Let.* 19 Aug. (1965) 214 White undershirt and loose white duck pants. **1966** in *Islands* (N.Z.) (1978) Aug. 93 White-duck curtains..Hang at the windows. **1957** J. D. Salinger *Zooey* in *New Yorker* 4 May 62/2 Phooey, I say, on all white-shoe college boys who edit their campus literary magazines. Give me an honest con man any day. **1974** G. JENKINS *Bridge of Magpies* vi. 85 What sort of white-shoe captain are you? **1975** *N.Y. Times* 22 Sept. 33/1 Covert operations can be stripped from the CIA... So can such monkey business as dropping simulated poison cannisters in the New York subways—the games of white-shoe boys who never grew up. **1958** *Oxf. Mag.* 22 May 462/2 Then from Italy, which had hitherto only produced 'white telephone' films, came this simple, humble and extremely moving story. **1975** *New Yorker* 5 May 24/3 This is an icy high-minded white-telephone movie. **1953** L. Z. HOBSON *Celebrity* viii. 116 A Buick Roadmaster... Fully equipped, radio, heater, white wall tyres. **1965** *Punch* 20 Oct. 567/2 Then I shall buy this year's model, too, my beloved,..with whitewall tyres and a cigar-lighter. **1978** *Listener* 2 Feb. 158/2 When film makers go 'period', as they did for *Chinatown*, the bulky Buicks and Oldsmobiles have to be lovingly rebuilt, white-wall tyres, teeth-like radiator grills and bonnet 'ventiports', almost from scratch.

e. † **white-choker** *slang*, a clergyman (cf. CHOKER 2); so **whitechokerism; white-hat,** (*b*) *U.S. Naval slang*, an enlisted man; (*c*) *slang* (orig. *U.S.*), a good man; a hero; **white-leg** (examples); **whitewall,** a white-wall tyre (see sense 12 d above).

1903 A. H. LEWIS *Boss* xxi. 292 It's that same Reverend Bronson who gives Melting Moses th' office to dog me. I'll put Mr. Whitechoker onto my opinion of th' racket. **1912** A. BENNETT *Matador of Five Towns* 100 You belong to that Methody lot... I seed you talking to them white-chokers. **1866** J. R. LOWELL *Let.* 10 Apr. (1894) I. 361, I don't understand your English taste for what you call 'respectability' (I should call it 'whitechokerism'), thinking, as I do, that the one thing worth striving for in this world is a state founded on pure manhood. **1956** E. N. ROGERS *Queenie's Brood* 241 There's a white hat out here who has gone crazy. **1975** *Courier-Mail* (Brisbane) 28 Feb. 5/2 Laver's the last of the white hats (the good guys who wear the white hats in cowboy movies). **1975** W. SAFIRE *Before the Fall* III. vii. 191 Nixon and Haldeman clung to the original game plan..against the urging of..Garment, and other 'white hats'. **1978** *Guardian Weekly* 15 Jan. 18/2 His judgments of the men he dealt with... The white hats are Truman [etc.]. A prime villain is Britain's postwar foreign secretary. **1811** R. HOOPER *Lexicon-Medicum* (new ed.) 615/2 *Phlegmasia dolens*... By the Germans it is called Œdema lacteum, and by the English the white leg. **1899** [see *milk leg* s.v. MILK *sb.* 10 a]. **1939** M. SPRING-RICE *Working-Class Wives* v. 122 She is very anæmic, has 'whiteleg', constipation and piles. **1976** *Lancet* 27 Nov. 1197/2 Iliac-vein thrombosis or 'white leg' affects the left side more commonly than the right. **1982** P. BARKER *Union Street* 250 After our May was born she never walked properly again. She had what they called the white leg. **1958** *Autocar* 31 Oct. 675 (*caption*) Bentley Flying Spur, sans fins, sans whitewalls, sans tinsel. **1968** *Globe & Mail* (Toronto) 5 Feb. 26/5 (Advt.), Hardtop, big 6 with automatic, radio and whitewalls. **1978** *Detroit Free Press* 5 Mar. c7/2 (Advt.), A built-in Scuff Bar that helps keep whitewalls white.

f. *white-breast.*

1933 D. H. LAWRENCE *Mod. Lover* (1934) 11 The fallow flickered over with pink gleams of birds white-breasting the sunset.

white, *v.*[1] Add: **1. b.** Const. *out.* Of vision: to become impaired by exposure to a sudden bright light (see also quot. 1981). Also *trans.*, to 'blind' (an audience in a theatre) by such means.

1978 'A. STUART' *Vicious Circles* 22 At once my eyes whited out—as disoriented by the brilliant evening sun as a bat caught by a searchlight. **1981** *Times Lit. Suppl.* 30 Jan. 112/1 As the women lie down to sleep in the hot summer morning, the stage lights white out to mime the atomic fireball. **1983** *Listener* 3 Feb. 32/3 In Bristol the Little Theatre performs the stage play, using lasers and whiting-out audiences.

2. c. Delete † and add later example.

1972 E. WIGGINTON *Foxfire Bk.* 181 And it was the sulfur that whited the apples, and they had a little sulfur flavor.

f. *to white out*: to obscure or cover with something white, esp. a white fluid used by typists. Also *fig.*

1975 J. BUTCHER *Copy-Editing* iii. 25 If you want to cancel an underlining for italic, white it out, or put two or three short lines through it, not a wavy line. **1978** M. DUFFY *Housespy* vi. 141 Its long shop window was whited out. **1982** R. LEIGH *Girl with Bright Head* xi. 74 There's also a couple of places where she has had to white out mistakes and type over them. **1983** 'J. LE CARRÉ' *Little Drummer Girl* xiii. 224 She drove with her mind whited out and her thoughts deliberately foreshortened. **1984** *Times Lit. Suppl.* 13 July 771/3 The embarrassed printer explained that he'd whited the little dot out, thinking that it was a dust spot.

g. To make *up* (an actor) to look white.

1977 R. BARNARD *Death on High C's* xv. 148 He was already 'whited up' for the part of the Duke of Mantua... He must look odd, with his deadly white colouring and negroid lips.

white ant, *sb.* [f. WHITE *a.* + ANT.] **1.** (See ANT 3.)

1684 LOCKE *Jrnl.* 17 Nov. in K. Dewhurst *Locke* (1963) 265 Told me of a sort of white ants that there mightily infests them. **1699,** etc. [see WHITE *a.* 11 a]. **1729,** etc. [see ANT 3]. **1908** E. J. BANFIELD *Confessions of Beachcomber* I. vii. 227 The 'white ant' (which is not an ant).. would literally eat us out of house and home. **1928** R. CAMPBELL *Wayzgoose* i. 20 White-ants and borers, turning boards to dust. **1938** X. HERBERT *Capricornia* (1939) viii. 102 The white-ants have eaten the wheels of my buckboard. **1974** D. STUART *Prince of my Country* v. 40 The wind and the rain and the white ants will level the camps.

2. With allusion to the supposed destruction of the brain by white ants, implying loss of sanity, sense, or intelligence. *Austral. slang.*

1908 H. FLETCHER *Dads & Dan: between Smokes* 64 It wants a fool or a very sane cove indeed ter live in ther lonely bush an' keep ther white ants out o' his napper. **1926** L. G. E. GEE *Bushtracks & Goldfields* 65 And so he rambles on..and in the unsteady glance of his honest, old eyes and his disconnected speech, I read the mark of the Australian solitudes—'white ants' they call it up north. **1938** H. DRAKE-BROCKMAN *Men without Wives* 27 ' "Get the white ants?" What do you mean?' 'Go ratty. Mad.' **1948** V. PALMER *Golconda* vii. 49 They had a definite respect for Christy. He might have a few kinks ..but there was something dinkum about him, and if there were white ants behind his forehead they had a lot of work ahead of them. *a* **1951** E. HILL in Murdoch & Drake-Brockman *Austral. Short Stories* (1951) 292 My brownie days are over... I reckon I've got white ants.

white-a·nt, *v.* Chiefly *Austral.* [f. prec.] *trans.* To destroy in the manner of termites or white ants; to undermine, eat away, or sabotage.

1925 *Glasgow Herald* 14 Nov. 9/6 The extremists..have deliberately 'white-anted' the Labour movement..and squandered the funds of the wealthy unions. **1952** L. OVERACKER *Austral. Party System* vi. 182 The Communists have 'white anted' the unions, elected their members to offices in the Miners' Federation, the waterside workers' and ironworkers' unions, and developed 'shop committees' as basic units in the factories. **1962** R. WALLIS *Point of Origin* 96 After hearing..about me.. he decided he'd have to do his duty as a gentleman and tell Rockdale he was being white-anted. **1968** D. IRELAND *Chantic Bird* xi. 102 Television had white-anted their audiences, and they had to use the place for other things besides films.

Hence **white-a·nted** *ppl. a.*, **white-a·nting** *vbl. sb.*

1936 F. CLUNE *Roaming round Darling* xx. 205 The piece of the boat is five feet long and is made of soft wood, badly white-anted. **1945** BAKER *Austral. Lang.* xiv. 245 White-anting. **1950** D. CUSACK *Comets Soon Pass* in *Three Austral. Three-Act Plays* II. ii. 55 *Dr. John.* Each man must find his own pole to swing to. I have found mine. *Mrs. Ellington-Brown.* I think that's too wonderful, so mystic. *Talbot.* White-anting society! *Jack Smith.* Too mystic for my taste, Doc. I think you've got to get out and fight for things. **1973** *Sydney Morning Herald* 30 Aug. 6/4 We are promised largesse in the form of harbourside parks in the same breath as the white-anting of a remote scenic gorge is sanctioned.

white bear. Chiefly *N. Amer.* **a.** = *polar bear* s.v. *POLAR *a.* b.

1600 HAKLUYT *Princ. Navigations* III. 6 The soile is barren in some places,..but it is full of white beares. **1823** *Canad. Mag.* I. 394 The great white bear takes refuge in the most icy climates. **1860** P. H. GOSSE *Romance Nat. Hist.* 62 The white bear, seated on a solitary iceberg in the Polar Sea. **1953** W. B. MOWERY *Tales of Mounted Police* 149 [He had] several livid weals across his left cheek where a white bear had once clawed him.

b. A grizzly bear (*Ursus horribilis*) in a light-coloured phase.

1791 J. LONG *Voy. Indian Interpreter* 95 The large white bear, commonly called the grizly bear, is a very dangerous animal. **1852** J. REYNOLDS *Hist. Illinois* 172 He was destroyed there [in the Rocky Mountains] by a white bear. **1952** J. JENNINGS *Strange Brigade* (1954) 105 There were also red deer or *biche*, and white bears and white partridges.

white-bea·rded, *a.* [WHITE *a.* 12 c.] Having a white beard. **a.** Of a man.

1596 [in Dict. s.v. WHITE *a.* 12 c]. **1914** D. H. LAWRENCE *Widowing of Mrs. Holroyd* III. 81 A little stout, white-bearded man.

b. Of wheat.

1788 G. WASHINGTON *Diary* 8 Sept. (1925) III. 417 Also sowing..one bushel of the White bearded Wheat sent me by Beale Boardly. **1850** *Rep. U.S. Comm. Patents 1849: Agric.* 132 The white-bearded wheat, a valuable kind less liable to total failure than any other; not very popular with millers.

c. *fig.*

1920 E. SITWELL *Wooden Pegasus* 100 And, mourners too, white-bearded seas Walk slowly by them as they come. **1960** *Farmer & Stockbreeder* 19 Jan. (Suppl.) 1/1 Waves came solid green and white-bearded, like frost giants racing.

whiteboard (hwəi·tbōᵊɹd). [f. WHITE *a.* after *blackboard.*] A white surface for use like a blackboard but accepting felt-tipped pens and wax crayons.

1966 'W. COOPER' *Mem. New Man* II. v. 160 He.. went to the blackboard. (Actually it was an up-to-date plastic white-board, on which one wrote with a coloured wax crayon.) **1977** *Times Educ. Suppl.* 21 Oct. 28/1 (Advt.), They are whiteboards that stay white, year after year. **1978** J. MCNEIL *Consultant* ix. 106 They came to a meeting room... The walls were bare except for a white-board. **1985** *Times Educ. Suppl.* 19 July 20/5 We should also bear in mind that partially-sighted pupils often fare better if a white-board is used rather than a blackboard.

white boy, whiteboy. 1. Delete † *Obs.* and add later example.

1919 T. S. ELIOT *Let.* 9 July in *Waste Land Drafts* (1971) p. xvii, The small public which *I* could bring to it [*sc.* the *Egoist*] now reads the *Athenaeum* every week. There I am a sort of white boy; I have a longish critical review about three weeks out of four.

whi·tecap, *v. U.S.* [f. the sb., sense 4.] *trans.* To commit an outrage upon (a person) in the style of the whitecaps. Chiefly as **whi·tecapping** *vbl. sb.* Also **whi·tecapper.**

1895 T. ROOSEVELT in *Century Mag.* Nov. 72/2 The law-breaker, whether he be lyncher or whitecapper, or merely the liquor-seller who desires to drive an illegal business. **1900** M. NICHOLSON *Hoosiers* 45 The milder form of outlawry, known as 'white-capping', has also been practised in Indiana occasionally. **1904** *N.Y. Even. Post* 28 Jan. 9 The Mississippi has voted Gov. Vardaman a special appropriation to enable him to suppress the 'white cappers'. **1908** D. G. PHILLIPS *Old Wives for New* iv. 68 If he wasn't such a wonderful doctor he'd have been white-capped long ago—tarred and feathered and railed out of town. **1943** A. G. POWELL *I can go Home Again* 167 During the short time I served as county judge, a series of 'whitecappings', directed against Negroes, occurred in the lower part of the county. **1970** [see *KU-KLUX 1 a].

whi·tecapping, *a. rare*[−1]. [f. as prec. + -ING[2].] Covering with or as with a white cap.

1912 J. LONDON *Son of Sun* v. ii. 175 Their long slopes.. were broken by systems of smaller whitecapping waves.

white cliffs, *sb. pl.* [f. WHITE *a.* + CLIFF.] **1.** Chalk cliffs; *spec.* those of Dover, regarded as a symbol of Great Britain.

1879 [see CLIFF 1 b]. **1902** KIPLING *Just-So-Stories* 7 Take me to my natal-shore and the white-cliffs-of-Albion. **1940** N. BURTON (*song*) There'll be blue-birds over the white cliffs of Dover. **1940** R. S. LAMBERT *Ariel & All his Quality* iii. 84 Full of a mystic vision of Empire..inspired by the sight of the white cliffs of Dover. **1978** M. KENYON *Deep Pocket* xiv. 181 You'll be deported, you'll never see the White Cliffs again.

2. (With capital initials.) The name of a town in New South Wales, used *attrib.* to designate opals mined there.

1911 C. E. W. BEAN *'Dreadnought' of Darling* xxv. 222 The Wilcannia banks live on the White Cliffs opal. **1936** H. P. WHITLOCK *Story of Gems* x. 127 The White Cliffs opals are not unlike those from Hungary, but they show broader flashes of colour. **1975** R. WEBSTER *Gems in Jewellery* xi. 57 The White Cliffs opal is cream in colour and found in seams in sandstone.

whitecoat. Add: **3.** A doctor or hospital attendant who wears a white coat. (In this sense the form *white coat* is not *Obs.*)

1911 [see *SCHMERZ]. **1932** 'JOCK' *Dartmoor from Within* vi. 134 He makes straight for the tub, and 'White Coat' alters his course to cut him off. **1980** *Brit. Med. Jrnl.* 29 Mar. 934/2 We roar into the hospital. White coats run out.

white-collar, *sb.* and *a.* orig. *U.S.* **A.** *sb.* **a.** (As two words.) A white collar regarded as characteristic of a man engaged in non-manual work.

1919 U. SINCLAIR *Brass Check* xiii. 78 It is a fact with which every union workingman is familiar, that his most bitter despisers are the petty underlings of the business world, the poor office-clerks..who, because they are allowed to wear a white collar.., regard themselves as members of the capitalist class. **1976** M. HINXMAN *End of Good Woman* i. 9 Tom emigrated to Canada. Dick put on a white collar and became a bank clerk.

b. A person engaged in non-manual work.

1930 A. P. HERBERT *Water Gipsies* iv. 39 That family over there..come here every Thursday of their lives for a little family reunion, and white collars, too, all of them. **1938** W. SMITTER *F.O.B. Detroit* 32 It wasn't long before the white-collars up front began taking notice of what was going on on the floor. **1954** E. PANGBORN *Mirror for Observers* (1955) I. i. 19 A residential backwater for factory workers, white-collars, transients. **1962** 'K. ORVIS' *Damned & Destroyed* i. 12 A pair of white-collars from a near-by St. James Street brokerage office pounded the bar for fresh drinks. **1971** W. J. BURLEY *Guilt Edged* i. 5 [The] passenger ferry..had made only two return trips, one for the workers at seven-thirty and one for the white-collars at eight-thirty.

B. *adj.* **a.** Of a person: engaged in non-manual, esp. clerical, work.

1921 *Ladies' Home Jrnl.* May 98/4 Urban chain restaurants have accustomed white-collar boys and girls to tasty viands, albeit in limited amounts. **1924** W. MCDOUGALL *Ethics & Some Mod. World Probl.* iv. 125 The strata of brain-workers made up the white-collar class or middle classes. **1937** *Atlantic Monthly* Dec. 750/1 Proletarian literature..has been accompanied by books on the white-collar worker, the storekeeper..the scientist, and the millionaire in situations equally disastrous or degrading. **1948** *Chicago Tribune* 3 Apr. II. 1/4 The modern white collar girl wants a job which not only offers opportunities but advances as well. **1959** [see *blue-collar* s.v. *BLUE *a.* 13]. **1969** *Times* 30 Apr. 26/6 The first strike action by manual workers against the British Steel Corporation's new policy of white collar union recognition broke out yesterday. **1982** D. GORHAM *Victorian Girl* ii. 29 Teachers and nurses..were of less importance numerically than [female] 'white collar' workers.

b. Of work or an occupation: not manual or industrial; *spec.* clerical.

1926 *Amer. Speech* II. 96/2 The uneducated and uneducable found a new field opening to them, and rushed in, to take advantage of the 'white-collar' work. **1937** 'G. ORWELL' *Road to Wigan Pier* xi. 205 The typical Socialist..is either a youthful snob-Bolshevik..or, still more typically, a prim little man with a white-collar job. **1962** AUDEN *Dyer's Hand* (1963) 123 He has a dingy white-collar job. **1979** T. BENN *Arguments for Socialism* ii. 41 The definition of a worker is extended to include all wage and salary earners and paves the way for the extension of trade unionism into the realms of clerical white collar, scientific and technical and managerial work.

c. (See quot. 1937.) *U.S.*

1932 [see *dirt farmer* s.v. *DIRT *sb.* 7 d]. **1937** *Amer. Speech* XII. 105 The adjectives *suitcase* and *bonanza* and *whitecollar* are applied in recently developed wheat-farming areas to large owner-farmers who live outside the community and appear during the sowing and harvesting seasons.

d. Applied to a person who takes advantage of the special knowledge or responsibility of his position to commit non-violent, often financial, crimes; also to the crime itself.

[**1932** E. H. SUTHERLAND in *Publ. Amer. Sociol. Soc.* Aug. 60 The financial crimes of the white-collar classes.] **1934** —— *Princ. Criminol.* ii. 32 These white-collar criminaloids..are by far the most dangerous to society.. from the point of view of effects on private property and social institutions. **1964** M. ARGYLE *Psychol. & Social Probl.* v. 65 Older middle-class people are tempted to commit offences other than theft or violence, and the various kinds of 'white collar crime' are hard to detect—income-tax avoidance, bogus expense claims and complex business illegalities. **1977** *Wandsworth Borough News* 7 Oct. 5/3 Dangerous drivers and white-collar criminals are far more likely to receive lenient treatment than the petty habitual thief. **1984** *Daily Tel.* 12 Nov. 20/2 White-collar crime like fraud is..on the increase.., and the computer has opened enormous vistas of extra opportunity.

white-co·llared, *a.* [-ED².] **1.** Wearing a white collar; also *fig.*

1932 H. G. WELLS *Work, Wealth & Happiness of Mankind* vii. 237 The black-coated, white-collared clerk. **1947** J. MULGAN *Report on Experience* 18 Ten millions of the rest, bowler-hatted, white-collared, moved in monotonous rhythm. **1951** D. GLOVER *Sings Harry* 41 It's plain hard hazardous work To work with the white-collared wave.

2. = *WHITE COLLAR *a.* a.

1933 *Sun* (Baltimore) 14 Apr. 4/6 Hands blistered and backs sore from hard physical labor, so-called 'white-collared men' of West Virginia are calling for more and yet more work. **1947** *Hist. 'The Times'* III. v. 117 That public was the great and growing, vigorous 'white-collared' lower-middle class. **1959, 1967** [see *blue-collared* adj. s.v. *BLUE *a.* 13]. **1977** M. GREEN *Children of Sun* (rev. ed.) x. 460 *Lucky Jim*..described a new class on the British scene, the white-collared proletariat, trained technicians but not educated gentlemen.

whited, *ppl. a.* Add: **1.** *whited sepulchre* (earlier example).

1835 J. E. ALEXANDER *Sketches in Portugal* i. 13 What a whited sepulchre we found the city to be!

white-eared, *a.* Add: *white-eared flycatcher*, a monarch flycatcher, *Monarcha leucotis*, found in Australia; *white-eared pheasant*, an eared pheasant, *Crossoptilon crossoptilon*, found in forest regions of eastern Tibet and neighbouring China.

1869 J. GOULD *Birds Austral. Suppl.* 12 (*heading*) White-eared Flycatcher. [**1918** W. BEEBE *Monogr. Pheasants* I. 187 Once only was a glimpse permitted to us of the wonderful White Eared-pheasants.] **1976** G. DURRELL *Stationary Ark* iv. 78 Our chances of establishing the White-eared pheasant in captivity seemed..slim. **1980** G. PIZZEY *Field Guide Birds Austral.* 258 White-eared Monarch Flycatcher..has been likened to a miniature Magpie Lark.

whi·te-face, *sb.* and *a.* Also **whiteface, † white face. A.** *sb.* **† 1.** The widgeon. *Obs. rare.*

1709 [see *BALD-FACE 1].

2. One of a Hereford herd of cattle. Now chiefly *N. Amer.*

1860 [in Dict. s.v. WHITE *a.* 12 e]. **1965** E. MCCOURT *Road across Canada* 152 Herds of white-faces dot the slopes.., grazing knee-deep in the lush grass of the wide valley-bottoms. **1970** M. G. EBERHART *El Rancho Rio* (1971) viii. 85 I've been breeding white-faces—pure-bred Herefords.

3. White or light-coloured make-up, esp. as worn by a clown, or by a black actor playing a white character. orig. *U.S.*

1895 *N.Y. Dramatic News* 9 Nov. 14/4 Lew Dockstader, in his new white-face act,..will be seen at Keith's, November 18. **1947** *Partisan Rev.* Jan.–Feb. 65 The selection of Canada Lee, a negro in white-face, to play Bosola. **1948** M. WINTER in P. Magriel *Chron. Amer. Dance* 53/1 English clowns..returned to whiteface, but kept certain characteristics of blackface performers. **1981** *Times* 11 Apr. 7/1 We find him grovelling on the floor like a mock Othello in whiteface.

B. *adj.* Of an animal: having a white face.

1785 T. JEFFERSON *Notes Virginia* vi. 126 White face teal. **1961** R. P. HOBSON *Rancher takes Wife* xvii. 217 There's a herd of top whiteface cows. **1978** *Detroit Free Press* 5 Mar. C20/5 (Advt.), Whiteface Capuchin male, 2 years old. **1984** *Properties Open in 1984* (National Trust) 40 A Country Park surrounds the property and contains a flock of Whiteface Woodland sheep.

white-footed, *a.* Add: *white-footed mouse*, any of several species of North American mice of the genus *Peromyscus*, esp. *P. maniculatus* or *P. leucopus*.

1857 *Rep. Comm. Patents 1856: Agric.* (U.S.) 86 The food of [the Northern shrike]..consists almost wholly of arvicolae and a few white-footed prairie mice. **1869** *Amer. Naturalist* III. 120 When the axe-man struck the tree, a Whitefooted Mouse..rushed from the nest. **1936** D. MCCOWAN *Animals Canad. Rockies* viii. 68 The White-footed mouse is of medium size and has a silky coat that is dark brown above and light on the underparts. **1977** J. L. HARPER *Population Biol. Plants* xv. 465 The seed was collected and buried mainly by white-footed mice.

white gold. 1. † a. Platinum. *Obs.*

1764 *Gentl. Mag.* XXXIV. 128/1 (*heading*) A farther Account of a Metal, called Platina, or White Gold. **1798** [in Dict. s.v. WHITE *a.* 11 c].

b. A name applied to various silvery-coloured alloys of gold with nickel, palladium, platinum, or silver.

1893 *Funk's Stand. Dict.* s.v. *Gold*, *White gold*, an alloy of about five parts of silver to one of gold. **1921** *Daily Colonist* (Victoria, B.C.) 12 Mar. 2/1 Modern Wedding Rings... White Gold Rings, $10. **1940** *Chambers's Techn. Dict.* 382/1 *White gold* is usually an alloy with nickel, but as used in dentistry this alloy contains platinum or palladium. **1946** G. STIMPSON *Bk. about Thousand Things* 242 White gold jewelry nowadays differs from regulation gold, not in the quality or the quantity of gold used, but in the kind of alloy. **1956** J. N. ANDERSON *Appl. Dental Materials* vii. 78 Casting alloys [of gold] containing a large amount of palladium together with silver are called white golds. **1971** *Nature* 18 June 443/1 Two basically gold-silver alloys were known to the Greeks and Romans: (1) 'white gold'—a haphazard mixture derived from grains of weathered auriferous ore; and (2) 'electrum'—an alloy of controlled quality. **1974** *Country Life* 26 Dec. 2002/3 Platinum has largely been superseded by white gold as a jewellery metal. **1980** 'E. MCBAIN' *Ghosts* ii. 28 One rope choker of eighteen-karat yellow and white gold.

2. Any white substance regarded as valuable.

1966 *Times* 28 Feb. (Canada Suppl.) p. xi/1 Most of the subterranean 'white gold' [*sc.* potash] lies beneath Saskatchewan. **1974** G. JENKINS *Bridge of Magpies* ii. 27 My job was to police the Sperregebiet from the sea... There is..on this God-forsaken shore: a string of rocky little inshore islands coated in bird guano—white gold, they call it.

white-haired, *a.* Add: **2.** *white-haired boy*, a favourite. *colloq.* Cf. WHITE-HEADED *a.* 2 b.

1910 *Nat. Police Gaz.* (U.S.) 29 Jan. 3 (*heading*) The white haired boy. *Ibid.* 3/4 He, this white-haired Willie-boy, really wanted her to become his wife. **1923** H. C. BAILEY *Mr. Fortune's Practice* ii. 38 His mother's white-haired boy, he is. Not 'alf. **1936** J. DOS PASSOS *Big Money* 496 You're the whitehaired boy around here. **1977** I. SHAW *Beggarman, Thief* II. iii. 147 Rudy..was the white-haired boy of the family.

Whitehall¹ (hwəi·thǫl). **1.** The name of a street in London, used to designate the government offices situated there, or the civil service in general.

1827 *Morning Post* 24 Mar. 3/2 In consequence of that accommodation, an equal amount of Exchequer Bills before locked up at Whitehall are afterwards to be locked up in Threadneedle-street. **1850** *Daily News* 13 Mar. 5/2 The infection of..'Christian Socialism' is spreading to Whitehall. **1910** *Times Educ. Suppl.* 6 Sept. 13/2 The introductory remarks..breathe a very different spirit from that of earlier official utterances of Whitehall. **1946** C. S. FORESTER *Lord Hornblower* ix. 79 Heaven only knew what Whitehall and Downing Street would say. **1958** *Radio Times* 23 Feb. 6/1 This is a tense story of sea warfare... The mess-room talk is most authentic..and Mr. White is obviously familiar with his 'Whitehall types'. **1977** *Listener* 7 Apr. 442/1 British Leyland..is almost entirely a Whitehall creation.

2. Special Combs.: **Whitehall farce**, any of a series of bedroom farces produced at the Whitehall Theatre, London, esp. those presented between 1950 and 1967 by Brian Rix; **Whitehall Warrior** *slang*, a civil servant; an officer in the armed forces employed in administration rather than on active service.

1966 N. MARSH *Black Beech & Honeydew* x. 233 My uncle..was like a Professor in a Whitehall farce. **1966** *Guardian* 20 Aug. 4/4 Blackpool..fulfils a socal need. Like a Whitehall farce, it dictates its own terms and makes general criticism futile. **1976** M. GILBERT *Night of Twelfth* v. 42 The play [sc. *Twelfth Night*].. [is] a love story mixed up with a Whitehall farce. **1973** K. GILES *File on Death* vii. 174 I'm Quarles, a battered old Whitehall Warrior. **1976** W. WHITE *Long Silence* vii. 57, I didn't want anybody to think I was a chairbound officer, a Whitehall Warrior. **1978** P. O'DONNELL *Dragon's Claw* v. 81 Roger was a Whitehall Warrior until he retired.

Hence **Whitehalle·se**, jargon regarded as typical of the civil service; **Whiteha·llism**, attitudes or personnel regarded as typical of the civil service.

1915 LD. ESHER *Let.* 21 Oct. in M. Gilbert *Winston S. Churchill* (1972) III. Compan. II. 1232 In the Navy.. there seems to be a trifle too much of 'Whitehallism'. **1940** *Manch. Guardian Weekly* 15 Mar. 216 Shortage of paper may now prompt economy of speech, and if it sloughs away some of the pomposities of business English and Whitehallese, which is slightly more correct in its heavy Latinity but just as lacking in sense and suppleness, the war may be said to have done us a little good. **1958** *Times* 15 Nov. 8/3 At the time he said the Government were snubbing Wales and there was no prospect of 'Whitehallism' ever understanding Welsh aspirations. **1975** *Economist* 15 Feb. 115/2 In spite of long exposure to Whitehallese, she writes in English. He lapses far too often into gobbledygook. **1984** *Guardian* 1 Jan. 4 Phrases that take two words to say what one used to—'check out', 'meet with', 'consult with' (although Mrs Thatcher may shortly ban the last one from Whitehallese).

† Whiteha·ll². *U.S. Obs.* The name of a district of New York, used *attrib.* to designate a type of rowing-boat. So **† Whiteha·ller,** one who uses a Whitehall boat.

1828 J. F. COOPER *Notions of Americans* I. 40 The latter [*sc.* New York boatmen], it appears, are of a class of watermen, that are renowned in this country, under the name of Whitehallers. **1835** C. J. LATROBE *Rambler in N. Amer.* i. 25 The light skilfully managed wherry of the Whitehaller. **1849** H. MELVILLE *Redburn* II. xxix. 289 The Whitehall boats were around us. **1890** N. P. LANGFORD *Vigilante Days* II. 129 To attempt the passage..in a whitehall boat would be madness.

whitehead¹, *sb.* Add: **4.** Also **white head. a.** A disorder in which the scalp is covered with white spots or crusts. **b.** [After *BLACK-HEAD 4.] A white or white-topped pustule.

1911 *Trans. S. Afr. Med. Congr.: 12th Meeting* 165 The so-called 'white head', so often seen in Bechuanaland..is a pustular syphilide affecting the scalp. The pustules..tend to coalesce, forming thick whitish crusts. ..In some cases the head becomes covered, giving the appearance of a solid white cap. **1922** *Brit. Jrnl. Dermatol. & Syphilis* XXXIV. 267 The scalp condition we are about to discuss is known to the natives..by the name of wit kop, dikwakwadi, or white head. **1940** BECKER & OBERMAYER *Mod. Dermatol. & Syphilol.* xxix. 521 Milium or 'white head' is the name for a tiny, pearly-white globular lesion..with a shiny, translucent surface. **1978** PARSONS & SOMMERS *Gynecology* (ed. 2) xx. 308/1 Closed comedones ('whiteheads') are the precursors of the inflammatory papules and pustules that commonly occur. **1982** P. M. MARGOLIN *Last Innocent Man* I. vii. 70 The boy's right hand raised slowly and began to pick at a whitehead on his cheek.

Whitehead². Add: (Earlier example.) Also *attrib.*

1877 *Sci. Amer.* 2 June 337/2 The Whitehead torpedo can be made to go at the rate of 20 knots for 1,000 yards, and at any depth that is desired from 1 foot to 30 feet.

white-headed, *a.* Add: **2. b.** (Later examples.) Not now restricted to Ireland.

1933 A. CHRISTIE *Lord Edgware Dies* xxii. 186 You're positively convinced now that Ronald Marsh is a white-headed boy who can do no wrong. **1954** T. S. ELIOT *Confidential Clerk* II. 60 Perhaps you think it would be bad for your prospects Now that you're Claude's white-headed boy.

Whiteheadian (hwəithe·diăn), *a.* [f. the name *Whitehead* + -IAN.] Of, pertaining to, or characteristic of the English mathematician and philosopher A. N. Whitehead (1861–1947) or his ideas.

1943 *Mind* LII. 68 The Whiteheadian attempt to reconcile permanence and flux, time and eternity. **1977** *Church Times* 25 Feb. 6/5 Process theology has taken over the Whiteheadian scheme and used it as a means of expounding the Christian faith. **1978** *Christian* IV. IV. 328 The last point..follows if it is true—as the Whiteheadian conceptuality to which I happen to subscribe would say—that 'a thing *is* what a thing *does*'.

white-heart, *sb.* and *a.* For **1, 2** read **A, B** and add: **A.** *sb.* **1.** (Earlier example.)

1707 [see *black heart* s.v. *BLACK *a.* 19].

2. *Metallurgy.* Malleable cast iron made by keeping white iron at a high temperature for several days in an oxidizing environment, so as to remove the carbon from the surface layers and increase the ductility and strength. Freq. *attrib.*

1925 *Jrnl. Iron & Steel Inst.* CXII. 433 The material examined consisted of metal from the open-hearth furnace only, corresponding to that used for whiteheart castings and blackheart castings in Europe and America. **1949** [see RÉAUMUR b]. **1960** [see *GRAPHITIZE *v.* 1 b]. **1968** A. H. COTTRELL *Introd. Metallurgy* xxv. 519 Whiteheart malleable iron is made by heating the casting in an oxidizing environment.

B. *adj.* (Earlier example.)

1747 H. GLASSE *Art of Cookery* iv. 57 Take a fine White-heart Cabbage.

white horse. 5. (Examples.)

1846 J. R. BROWNE *Etchings of Whaling Cruise* 130 The white, hard blocks, containing but little oil, and which are found near the small, and at the flukes, are called 'white horse'. **1851** H. MELVILLE *Moby Dick* II. xcix. 173 White-horse,..obtained from the tapering part of the fish, and also from the thicker portions of his flukes.

white house. [HOUSE *sb.*¹] **1.** (With capital initials.) **a.** The popular name for the official residence of the President of the United States at Washington; hence, the President or his office.

1811 F. J. JACKSON *Let.* 24 Apr. in H. Adams *Documents New-Eng. Federalism* (1877) 385 [Foster] goes..to act as a sort of political conductor to attract the lightning that may issue from the clouds round the Capitol and the White House at Washington. **1812** A. BIGELOW *Let.* 18 Mar. in *Proc. Amer. Antiquarian Soc.* (1930) XL. 331 There is much trouble at the white house, as we call it, I mean the President's. **1833** [in Dict. s.v. WHITE *a.* 11 e]. **1884** *Century Mag.* Apr. 803/1 There is no building quite as satisfying to my eye as the White House. **1927** S. BENT *Ballyhoo* iii. 80 Conversationally they referred to the 'White House Spokesman', when he existed, as the Executive Larynx or the Presidential Ghost. **1950** *Daily Ardmoreite* (Ardmore, Okla.) 14 Feb. 1/7 The White House said no further action on its part is contemplated at this time. **1958** *New Statesman* 11 Jan. 30/1 He has no influence in the White House, and in recent months the requests for his advice have been little more than perfunctory. **1977** M. EDELMAN *Political Lang.* vi. 111 The White House tapes exemplify this common form of public language.

b. *transf.* Applied to other buildings serving as official residences.

1860 *Southern Enterprise* 3 Oct. 2/5 He announces himself, in the event of Lincoln's election, as candidate for *'the White House'* of the independent State of Georgia! **1878** *Trans. Illinois Dept. Agric.* XIV. 146 Tecumseh had his thousands of braves encamped above and below Vincennes, Indiana, where Gen. Harrison occupied the 'White House' of this great Northwest. **1947** F. D. DOWNEY *Our Lusty Forefathers* 101 George Washington had been elected President, inaugurated in New York, and had established his 'White House' at No. 3 Cherry Street. **1974** *Encycl. Brit. Micropædia* VIII. 844/1 It [*sc.* San Clemente] gained national prominence in 1969 when Pres. Richard M. Nixon purchased property there for use as a summer White House. **1975** *Caribbean Contact* Feb. 16/1 Speaking with Mr. Ebenezer Joshua at his 'white house' home overlooking the prison compound—as I did during my visit to St. Vincent to cover the recent election—one immediately appreciates the feelings of St. Vincent's radical and disenchanted youth.

2. *Sc.* In north-western Scotland and the Hebrides, a house built of mortared stone; *spec.* one having single-thickness walls cemented with lime mortar. Cf. *BLACK HOUSE 2. *Obs.* exc. *Hist.*

1824 J. MACCULLOCH *Highlands & Western Isles* I. 112 The true white house consists of masonry and slate..but the heteroclite, 'kind of white house', is covered with thatch, and, what is much more essential, possesses a chimney. **1870** *Proc. Soc. Antiq. Scotland* VII. 154 The distinctive terms for a house built with lime-mortar, or without it, remain the same... In the northern islands it is still a White-house, and in the Western Highlands it is Tigh-gal. **1955** A. GEDDES *Isle of Lewis & Harris* i. 27 Here and there new houses stand out, the 'white houses' (*tighean geala*)..are usually grey... These dwellings have generally been stone-built and were often slate-roofed. **1974** *Northern Stud.* IV. 22 The 1924 [Crofters] Act afforded an opportunity to improve housing and in the next decade the 'white house' began to replace the traditional 'black house' or 'taigh dubh'.

white iron. b. For 'a large proportion of carbon' read 'most or all of its carbon'.

white line, white-line, *sb.* Add: **2. a.** (Later examples.)

1863 [see *EM]. **1960** G. A. GLAISTER *Gloss. Bk* 28/2 *Blank line*, a line which is filled with quads, leads, or blank slugs; a white line in which no letters or other type characters appear.

b. *Engraving.* An engraved line which prints white; the art or technique of using such lines.

1884 H. A. DOBSON *Thos. Bewick & his Pupils* 145 The other difference, of which Bewick is said to be the inventor, consisted in the employment of what is known technically as 'whiteline'. **1906** A. HAYDEN *Chats on Old Prints* iii. 86 He [*sc.* Bewick] was not the inventor of the white line, but he used it freely and adapted his designs accordingly. **1924** H. FURST *Modern Woodcut* i. 10 The black line method keeps the woodprint..in a servile reproductive state, the onus of design falling..on the original designer... The problem of the designer in white line is an entirely different one, requiring..more forethought. **1938** F. WEITENKAMPF *Illustrated Bk.* ii. 52 For the woodcutter the white line was assuredly an easier method of producing tonal effect than elaborate cross-hatching in black. **1973** *Times* 31 July 10/6 His first two prints were from wood blocks, the wood-engraver's 'white line' being used with decision in the silhouetted *Reclining Nude* of 1931.

3*. Alcohol as a drink; also, one who drinks alcohol. *U.S. slang.*

1908 J. M. SULLIVAN *Criminal Slang* 27 *White-line*, an alcohol drinker. **1914** JACKSON & HELLYER *Vocab. Criminal Slang* 88 *White line, white lime.* Current amongst yeggs and hoboes. Alcohol. Example: 'You'll have to go to the croker and get a stiff for the white line.' **1926** J. BLACK *You can't Win* vi. 66 'A four-bit micky, a fifty-cent bottle of alcohol—Dr. Hall, white line,' he translated in disgust. **1926** *Flynn's* 16 Jan. 640/1 All we could glom was a shot of white line.

3.** A narrow white strip painted on the road surface to guide or direct motorists; *esp.* one that separates adjacent traffic lanes.

1924 *Oxford Times* 29 Aug. 9/4 The experiment of the white line, which has proved so successful in encouraging the careful driving of motors round corners in Worcestershire, might with advantage be tried in this district. **1930** *Motor* 10 June 892/2 We do think that observations might be directed at white line offences where they occur in really dangerous places. **1971** *Daily Tel.* (Colour Suppl.) 22 Oct. 25/3 White lines broken but close together can mean a corner or hillcrest is coming. **1976** *Evening Chron.* (Newcastle) 26 Nov., Mr. Cook ruled that the council was guilty of maladministration because it could have speeded up the painting of white line markings.

4. white-line dart (moth), *Euxoa tritici*; (earlier and later examples).

1840 J. & M. LOUDON tr. *Köllar's Treat. Insects* II. 102 The White-line Dart Moth... A moth injurious to buckwheat and autumn-sown grain. **1948** W. J. STOKOE *Caterpillars Brit. Moths* I. 178 The White-line Dart..is widely distributed.

white man. Add: **2. a.** (Later examples of spelling *whiteman.*) *the white man's burden*: see *BURDEN *sb.* 2 a; *the white man's grave*, equatorial West Africa considered particularly unhealthy for white people.

1836 F. H. RANKIN *White Man's Grave* I. p. viii, [Sierra Leone] bears the terrific and poetic title of the 'White Man's Grave'. **1897** M. H. KINGSLEY *Trav. W. Afr.* 2 My friends..said, 'Oh, you can't possibly go there; that's where Sierra Leone is, the white man's grave, you know.' **1924** MAURICE & ARTHUR *Life Ld. Wolseley* iv. 65 The Gold Coast had well earned the name of 'The White Man's Grave'. **1938** X. HERBERT *Capricornia* (1939) iii. 24 The whitemen left the hunting to the [Australian] natives. **1944** F. CLUNE *Red Heart* 19, I dug up his body, souvenired his false teeth and diaries, and reburied him in whiteman fashion. **1952** P. ATKEY *Juniper Rock* xiv. 127, I was a bride at eighteen... I went out to the white man's grave. **1956** A. SAMPSON *Drum* xi. 156 As whites regard Africans as natives or boys, not people or men so Africans never describe whitemen (which they spell, significantly, in one word), as *abantu*, or people. **1970** G. F. NEWMAN *Sir, You Bastard* ii. 67 The street in Hammersmith where Whitmarsh lodged was so overrun with immigrants that an English-speaking whiteman was a latterday Livingstone.

white meat, whitemeat. Restrict *Obs.* exc. *dial.* to senses a, c, and d and add: **b.** Also *sing.*

1973 *Guardian* 19 Mar. 7/5 People in Britain ate less red meat last year, but more 'white' meat such as pork and poultry. **1975** P. V. PRICE *Taste of Wine* vii. 134/1 White meat is generally taken to include pork, veal, chicken and turkey, while the 'reds' are beef, lamb, duck and goose. **1985** *Which?* Feb. 54/2 In general, nutritionists recommend that the average British diet should contain less fat and more fibre... They say a good way to achieve this change is to eat more white meat (especially poultry) and fish in place of red meat.

2. *slang* (chiefly *U.S.*). White women considered as sexual partners or conquests. Cf. *MEAT *sb.* 3 e.

[**1937** *Printers' Ink Monthly* May 45/3 *White meat*, an actress.] **1940** 'J. CRAD' *Traders in Women* v. 134 The..liner took me to Shanghai, and here once again I met the European procurer and salesman of 'white meat'. **1972** [see *HOME *sb.*[1] 13*]. **1976** M. MAGUIRE *Scratchproof* x. 152 I'm off white meat. I have a good thing going with a negro film editor. **1982** J. PHILIPS *Target for Tragedy* (1983) I. iii. 52 Some stranger who sees a piece of white meat he thinks might come his way.

whitener. 2. (Later example.)

1971 D. POTTER *Brit. Eliz. Stamps* ii. 22 Optical whitener is used in the making of the paper.

white-out (hwəɪ·taʊt). Also **whiteout.** [f. phr. *to white out* (cf. *WHITE *v.*[1]), by analogy with *BLACK-OUT.] **1. a.** *N. Amer.* A heavy snow-storm, a blizzard.

1942 *Sun* (Baltimore) 30 Mar. 8 (*caption*) Whiteout. **1980** *Sat. Rev.* (U.S.) May 66 Blizzards—white-outs they call them here [*sc.* in Labrador]—bring snow that whirls and thrashes and blinds, stinging noses, and cabins disappear in the whiteness.

b. A condition in which neither shadows nor the horizon can be seen and physical features are lost in the background, caused by an evenness of lighting such as sometimes occurs in cloud or in snow- or ice-covered regions.

1946 *Sun* (Baltimore) 20 Apr. 7/2 Hedine, of the United States Weather Bureau at Winnemucca, Nevada, described the 'Arctic whiteout' today, defining it as a condition of the snow country wherein all land features are camouflaged, 'blending earth and sky so that the horizon and all landmarks are indistinguishable'. **1955** *Sci. Amer.* Apr. 54/3 Lieutenant John P. Moore, a Navy pilot, was killed when his helicopter crashed during a 'white-out'. This condition, one of the chief hazards of Antarctic travel, occurs when sunlight diffuses through a solid overcast. **1959** V. FUCHS *Antarctic Adv.* vii. 96 A whiteout is something like a blackout in reverse... No surface irregularities in the snow are visible in the diffused, opaque light, but a dark object like a man or a vehicle may be clearly seen. **1966** F. HOYLE *October 1st* viii. 95 It was impossible to know whether you were looking ten yards..or even a hundred miles. The effect..was far more weird than the kind of white-out you sometimes get on a snowfield in the mountains. **1976** M. MACHLIN *Pipeline* i. 7 White-out had set in just after Takolik had seen The-Man-Who-Hides. **1980** *Daily Tel.* 30 July 16 Bad weather, including white-outs caused by low cloud, hampered the early stages and Bonington is reported as saying he can well understand why the peak has never been climbed before. **1984** *Times* 5 Jan. 9/4 When whiteout exists, by the interaction of sunlight, snow, cloud and reflection, it induces the belief in a pilot that he is flying over flat terrain with unlimited forward visibility.

2. A white liquid that can be brushed on to paper to obliterate marks and provide a white surface on which to type or write afresh.

1977 L. O'DONNELL *Aftershock* xiii. 180 You changed the date... Did you cover the original entries with a strip of paper, or did you use white-out? **1984** *New Yorker* 23 Jan. 44/2 A Chinese version of typists' white-out.

white pine. [WHITE *a.* 11 b.] **1.** *N. Amer.* Any of several North American pines, esp. *Pinus strobus*, which is native to eastern and central parts of the continent; also, the pale soft wood of such a tree. Cf. WEYMOUTH.

1682 *Early Rec. Providence, Rhode Island* (1899) XIV. 113 From y[e] said heape of stones to range north..to a great white pine. **1767** *Quebec Gaz.* 8 Dec. 3/1 They are hereby forbid to cut down..White Pine..on the lands above described. **1785,** etc. [see PINE *sb.*[2] 2]. **1948** *Reader's Digest* Jan. 68/2 Of all American woods none has been more significant than white pine. **1961** H. MACLENNAN *Rivers of Canada* 97 When Wright surveyed the Ottawa forests he found an abundance of white pine standing two hundred feet tall. **1973** A. H. WHITEFORD *North Amer. Indian Arts* 107 White pine bark canoes were made by the Kutenai. **1974** M. BRAITHWAITE *Ontario* ix. 134 All about him..were great stands of white pines, tall trees stretching as straight as a ruler.

2. *Austral.* A tree belonging to any of several species of *Podocarpus* or *Callitris*. Cf. KAHIKATEA, *PODOCARP.

1855, etc. [see PINE *sb.*[2] 2]. **1975** D. BAGLEY *Snow Tiger* ii. 33 Gone were the stands of tall white pine and cedar, of kahikatea and kohekohe.

3. Special Combs.: **white pine blister (rust),** a rust disease of certain pines, caused by the fungus *Cronartium ribicola*, which spends part of its life cycle on gooseberry or currant bushes; **white pine weevil,** the larva of a brown beetle, *Pissodes strobi*, which tunnels in new shoots of certain pines.

1911 *Bull. U.S. Bureau Plant Industry* No. 206. 9 The white-pine blister rust now imported into this country from Germany is caused by a heterœcious fungus. **1974** M. HOYT *Thirty Miles* vi. 66 We had currant bushes..before anybody knew they were an intermediate host to..white-pine blister. **1905** *Bull. Forestry Bureau* (U.S. Dept. Agric.) No. 63. 14 The white pine weevil..is a reddish-brown snout beetle. **1976** *Columbus* (Montana) *News* 27 May (Joliet Suppl.) 4/5 Whitepine weevil..can kill twigs and branches of some evergreens.

White Russian, *sb.* and *a.* [f. WHITE *a.* + RUSSIAN *sb.* and *a.*; cf. *BELORUSSIAN *a.* and *sb.*] **A.** *sb.* **1. a.** The Russian dialect or language spoken in Belorussia, a district in the western part of Russia which is now one of the constituent republics of the Soviet Union.

1850 'TALVI' *Hist. View Lang. & Lit. Slavic Nations* II. i. 51 The White-Russian is the dialect spoken in Lithuania and a portion of White Russia, especially Volhynia. **1932** C. A. PHILLIPS tr. *H. von Eckardt's Russia* VI. ii. 475 Up to the sixteenth century the Lithuanian Grand Princes and boyars regarded White Russian as their language. **1949** ENTWISTLE & MORISON *Russian & Slavonic Lang.* i. 30 White Russian became a chancery language, not a literary tongue. **1960** W. K. MATTHEWS *Russian Hist. Gram.* I. ii. 34 There are seven groups of Slavonic languages, viz. the East Slavonic (Russian, White Russian, and Ukrainian) [etc.].

b. A native or inhabitant of Belorussia.

1886 [see RUSSIAN *sb.* 1 a]. **1912** [in Dict. s.v. WHITE *a.* 11 e]. **1918** R. WILTON *Russia's Agony* i. 9 The White Russians, a comparatively small section of the Northern Slav people, inhabiting Smolensk and the upper reaches of the Dnieper. **1960** W. K. MATTHEWS *Russian Hist. Gram.* III. ii. 309 The grammatical treatises of the time..are mainly the work of non-Russian scholars—White Russians and Ukrainians.

2. = *WHITE *sb.* 19 b.

1927 *Daily Tel.* 29 Mar. 11/6 The White Russians in the Northern Army..were purely soldiers, while the Reds were carrying on propaganda. **1930** *Times* 17 Mar. 12/6 Yesterday afternoon 'White' Russians, most of them women, made a demonstration at the offices of Amtorg Trading Corporation, the Soviet's American commercial agency. **1943** tr. *N. Basseches's Unknown Army* iv. 59 If they were in the territory of the Soviets, they either broke through in time to join the White Russians or they were caught by the Red mobilization. **1973** 'D. HALLIDAY' *Dolly & Starry Bird* xii. 184 Innes was sitting looking at the Director like a White Russian receiving word of Biological Ajax. **1976** *New Yorker* 15 Nov. 39/1, I was surrounded by..some of those privileged White Russians who abandoned their first-adopted countries of Europe to come to the States at the onset of the Second World War.

B. *adj.* **1.** Of or pertaining to Belorussia or its people.

1886 *Encycl. Brit.* XXI. 71/1 In 1879 in European Russia,—exclusive of six Lithuanian and White Russian governments,—42,530 persons were tried before the courts. **1918** TROFIMOV & SCOTT *Handbk. Russian* I. I. 4 The White Russian dialect covers the smallest area of all the Russian dialects. **1926** L. H. GUEST *New Russia* i. 21 The following are Independent Republics: The Ukrainian Socialist Soviet Republic..The White Russian Socialist Soviet Republic. **1944** [see *BELORUSSIAN *a.* and *sb.*]. **1960** W. K. MATTHEWS *Russian Hist. Gram.* II. xii. 276 In the latter part of the seventeenth century the influence of the White Russian and Ukrainian scholars and writers began to be felt.

2. Of or pertaining to the Whites in the Russian Civil War.

1929 W. S. CHURCHILL *World Crisis* V. xii. 247 We have seen them [*sc.* the Czechs] already in October 1918.. exasperated by White Russian mismanagement. **1957** P. KEMP *Mine were of Trouble* iii. 39 The Requetés were raising two squadrons in Seville, under a White Russian colonel named Alkon. **1964** R. PERRY *World of Tiger* ii. 24 The White Russian hunter Yankovsky. **1974** *Encycl. Brit. Macropædia* XVI. 70/2 The Red Army..drove him [*sc.* Wrangel] and his army into exile. There remained only the Japanese and White Russian forces in eastern Siberia.

whitesmithery. (Earlier example.)

1812 *Niles' Weekly Reg.* 25 Jan. 390/2 Emery..is an article of the first consequence in the cotton and woolen manufacturies, and in white smithery.

whitesmithing (hwəi·tˌsmiþiŋ), *vbl. sb.* [f. WHITESMITH¹ + -ING¹.] = WHITESMITHERY.

1835 *Lexington* (Kentucky) *Observer* 10 June, Whitesmithing. Frederick Klaiber lately from Germany..has just commenced the above business. **1900** *Daily Chron.* 2 Jan. 3/1 Part of the bench at which the missionary-explorer learnt whitesmithing is exhibited.

white stick. Add: **3.** A white walking-stick carried by a blind person both as a distinguishing feature and to locate obstacles. Cf. *white cane* s.v. *WHITE *a.* 11 e.

1961 *A.A. Handbk.* 20 Responsible blind welfare organizations strongly recommend all blind persons to carry a white stick. **1967** S. BECKETT *Stories & Texts for Nothing* VIII. 110 But what is this I see, and how, a white stick and an ear-trumpet. **1974** *Times* 21 Feb. 10 His first perilous adventures with the white stick. **1978** 'H. CARMICHAEL' *Life Cycle* xiv. 150 The man who doesn't admire you shouldn't be allowed out in the street without a white stick.

white-tail. **2.** For *Cariacus* read *Odocoileus*. (Earlier and later examples.)

1872 R. G. MCCLELLAN *Golden State* 241 There are several varieties: the mule-deer, black-tail, antelope, and white-tail. **1936** D. MCCOWAN *Animals Canad. Rockies* vii. 59 The hoofs of the wapiti and whitetail deer are too small to propel these animals through the water with any great speed. **1968** R. KROETSCH *Alberta* I. 12 White-tails and mule deer and mallards and grouse tumble before the unerring aim. **1980** *Hunting Ann. 1981* 29/1 My mountain-hunting buddy..came down out of his renowned mule deer country..to join me in a search of a big Colorado whitetail.

white-tailed (hwəi·tˌtēⁱld), *a.* [WHITE *a.* 12 c.] Having a white tail; *white-tailed deer* = WHITE-TAIL 2 in Dict. and Suppl.; *white-tailed eagle*, the European sea eagle (see EAGLE *sb.* 1 a); *white-tailed gnu*, the common (as distinct from the brindled) gnu, *Connochætes gnou*; *white-tailed ptarmigan*, a ptarmigan, *Lagopus leucurus*, found in western North America.

1642 [in Dict. s.v. WHITE *a.* 12 c]. **1678** J. RAY tr. *Willughby's Ornithol.* II. 61 Of the Pygarg or white-tail'd Eagle. **1832** W. A. FERRIS *Jrnl.* 27 Aug. in *Life in Rocky Mts.* (1940) 131 In the afternoon..we killed a white-tailed fawn. **1887** White-tailed deer [in Dict. s.v. WHITE *a.* 12 c]. **1889** *Cent. Dict.*, (caption s.v. *Gnu*) Common or White-tailed Gnu. *Ibid.*, White-tailed ptarmigan. **1912** J. STEVENSON-HAMILTON *Animal Life Afr.* vii. 106 There is no more remarkable beast, either in appearance or manners,..than the white-tailed gnu. **1926** F. C. R. JOURDAIN in J. J. Walker *Nat. Hist. Oxford Distr.* 146 White-tailed Eagle.. has occurred on Wantage Downs. **1941** J. S. HUXLEY *Uniqueness of Man* viii. 184 Other species now exist only in captivity. Such are the beautiful and fantastic white-tailed gnus. **1948** A. L. RAND *Mammals Eastern Rockies* 208 When the alarmed white-tailed deer goes bounding away, its tail usually stands straight up, and it is a great snowy banner that leaves no doubt of identity. **1968** R. KROETSCH *Alberta* II. 59 Soon after, we saw two white-tailed deer, just on the timberline. **1973** *Islander* (Victoria, B.C.) 1 Apr. 2/2, I have found myself staring at a whitetailed ptarmigan in the high mountains believing that he was snow. **1981** *Birds* Autumn 55/3 (*caption*) White-tailed eagle—last bred in Britain in 1916... A scheme to reintroduce these birds to Scotland is now underway.

whitethroat. **2.** (Earlier and later examples.)

a **1862** THOREAU *Maine Woods* (1864) 198 We heard the white throats along the shore. **1916** D. C. SCOTT *Poems* (1927) 47 A rocky islet followed With one lone poplar and a single nest Of white-throat-sparrows that took no rest. **1939** [see *PEABODY]. **1978** A. LAMPMAN *Lyrics of Earth* 32 The white-throat's distant descant with slow stress Note after note upon the noonday falls.

whitewash, *sb.* Add: **2.** (Earlier *attrib.* examples.)

1814 *Austin Papers* (1924) I. 240, 1 White Wash Brush. **1848** D. G. ROSSETTI *Let.* 20 Jan. (1965) I. 34 All my traps have been moved up into an attic, to make room for ladders, whitewash-pails, and such-like gear.

4. (Further examples.) For *U.S. colloq.* read *colloq.* (orig. *U.S.*). Also, a victory in a series of games of which the opponents fail to win any.

1867 *N.Y. Clipper* 31 Aug. 164/2 The first 'whitewash' of the [baseball] game was drawn by the Mutuals. **1874** *State Jrnl.* (Lincoln, Nebraska) 26 June 4/1 The second match game of croquet took place yesterday morning, and resulted in a second whitewash for the latter named gentleman. **1961** *Times* 4 May 4/6 Miss Truman who yesterday allowed Mrs. Cawthorn but 23 points in what the players of darts would term a 'whitewash'. **1962** *Times* 26 May 3/5 England nearly scored a whitewash over France..only the victory of G. Mourgue d'Algue standing between them and a 12–0 lead on the first day. **1977** *Evening Gaz.* (Middlesbrough) 11 Jan. 14/1 Only one whitewash this week in the Friendly League. **1978** *Rugby World* Apr. 4/1 Scotland must be bitterly disappointed that they have suffered their first whitewash for ten years.

†**5.** *slang.* (See quot. 1864.) Cf. WHITEWASHER 3. *Obs.*

1864 HOTTEN *Slang Dict.* 270 *Whitewash*, a glass of sherry as a finale, after drinking port and claret. **1879** TROLLOPE *John Caldigate* III. x. 142 'Take another glass of port, old boy.' Bagwax did take another glass, finishing the bottle... 'Take a drop of whitewash to wind up, and then we'll join the ladies.'

6. *Comb.*: **whitewash gum**, either of two eucalypts with powdery white bark, *Eucalyptus apodophylla* and *E. terminalis*, found in northern and central Australia.

[**1926** J. M. BLACK *Flora S. Austral.* III. 420 *E*[*ucalyptus*] *terminalis*... Whitewashed gum; bloodwood.] **1934** *Bulletin* (Sydney) 2 May 21/2 The whitewash gum.. forms a striking feature of the landscape about Alice Springs. **1965** *Austral. Encycl.* III. 406/2 Whitebark or 'whitewash gum'..of Arnhem Land has perfectly smooth trunks covered with a white mealy 'bloom' that rubs off when touched.

whitewash, *v.* **3.** For *U.S. colloq.* read *colloq.* (orig. *U.S.*). Also *loosely*, to beat by a large margin. (Earlier and later examples.)

1867 *Chicago Republican* 6 July 2/6 The Unions were whitewashed 3 times, and the Forest Citys 5 times. **1972** *Korea Times* 19 Nov. 1/5 Husky south Korean girls white-washed Thailand 106–17..in the second game. **1981** R. LEWIS *Seek for Justice* vi. 193 He took the first game [of darts]... He all but whitewashed Freddy in the second.

whitewashed, *ppl. a.* Add: **3.** *whitewashed American, Yank*, or *Yankee*, a person who affects American manners, or who has spent a short time in America; also *transf.*

1855 in *Occas. Papers Univ. Sydney Austral. Lang. Res. Centre* (1966) No. 10. 26 'I have heard people say they would like to see us clear altogether of British rule.'.. 'Have you heard that said here?'—'Yes, by a few of those disaffected persons; very few; they are generally what are termed "white-washed Yankees".' **1898** A. J. BOYD *Shellback* 73 He was not one of the low, bullying, half-Irish, half-American sort of men who are called 'whitewashed Yankees'. **1926** W. S. DILL *Long Day* 147 This particular story concerns a 'white-washed American', *i.e.* a native of Canada who had been naturalized in the United States and then secured repatriation in his own country. **1938** F. A. WORSLEY *First Voy. in Square-Rigged Ship* 82 Whitewashed Yanks (Europeans who had served a voyage in American ships or spent a short period in the States) were numerous. **1970** J. F. LEAVITT *Wake of Coasters* 62/2 Some of the schooners in later years were 'white-washed yankees': American built vessels kept under U.S. registry but with the controlling interest actually owned across the border in New Brunswick or Nova Scotia.

whitewasher. Add: **1.** (Earlier example.)

1733 *S. Carolina Gaz.* 24 Feb., He's a Bricklayer, Plaisterer and White-washer.

2. (Earlier example.)

1820 M. WILMOT *Let.* 27 Sept. (1935) 84 On recollection his cause is too *good* to be successful in such clever hands as her [*sc.* Queen Caroline's] whitewashers.

whiteweed. (Earlier example.)

1803 in *Mass. Hist. Soc. Coll.* (1804) IX. 200 On the upland and meadows grow burdens grass, ribwort, white weed, [etc.].

Whitgiftian (hwitgi·ftiăn), *sb.* and *a.* [f. *Whitgift* + -IAN.] **A.** *sb.* A pupil or former pupil of Whitgift School, Croydon. **B.** *adj.* Of, pertaining to, or characteristic of John Whitgift (*c* 1530–1604), Archbishop of Canterbury and founder of Whitgift School.

1880 *Whitgift Mag.* Jan. 13/2 We were glad to notice among the Chorus several 'Old Whitgiftians'. **1905** (*title*) The Whitgiftian. [*Previously* The Whitgift Magazine.] **1962** *Hist. Mag. Protestant Episcopal Church U.S.* XXXI. 128 The picturesquely rhetorical phrase of F. W. Maitland has been considered the most decent dismissal of the whole Whitgiftian flavour: 'a remorseless predestinarian'. **1967** P. COLLISON *Elizabethan Puritan Movem.* v. i. 245 Of this generation of clergy, few with minds of their own would subscribe to the Whitgiftian formula without a qualm. **1977** P. CLARK *Eng. Provincial Soc. from Reformation to Revolution* v. 184 In the county [of Kent]..the Whitgiftian reaction caused a marked polarisation between moderate Puritans and conformist Presbyterians on the one hand, and less respectable radicals and separatists on the other.

whither, *adv.* Add: **2. b.** Followed by a single word or short phrase.

1982 *English Studies* LXV. 90 The recently recycled interrogative adverb *whither* (as in *Whither Democracy?*).

whiting, *sb.* Add: **1. b.** (*d*) *blue whiting*, an oceanic fish of the cod family, *Micromesistius poutassou*, found in north-western Europe and the Mediterranean; = POUTASSOU.

1959 A. C. HARDY *Open Sea* II. xi. 229 The blue whiting..lives over the deep water off the edge of the continental shelf. **1974** *Guardian* 20 Mar. 11/1 The blue whiting..cod-like in taste and texture, slender in shape, about a foot long. **1977** *Grimsby Even. Tel.* 5 May 8/4 Certainly its size makes it an easier fish to process than the more publicised blue whiting.

whitishness. (Later example.)

1929 S. LESLIE *Anglo-Catholic* xii. 158 In the lamplight he noticed her deathliness of hue, the whitishness of lead-poisoning.

whitleather. Add: **1. a.** α. (Later example.)

1960 G. E. EVANS *Horse in Furrow* xvii. 213 Sidney Austin, the harness-maker, still uses strips of whitleather to repair..the collars of farm-horses.

b. (Later example.)

1913 D. H. LAWRENCE *Love Poems & Others* 44 A widow o forty-five As has sludged like a horse all her life, Till 'er's tough as whit-leather.

Whitley (hwi·tli). The name of J. H. *Whitley* (1866–1935), chairman of a committee set up in 1916 to consider relations between employers and employees, used *attrib.* with reference to the recommendations of this committee concerning good industrial relations, etc.

1917 in *State Service* (1969) Sept. 226/3 The application of the Whitley report should be extended to occupations of a purely commercial or clerical character. **1919** *Manch. Guardian* 11 Feb. 7/3 (*heading*) The Whitley councils. **1923** *Daily Mail* 29 Jan. 7 Mistress and maid should be their own Whitley Council. **1924** *Glasgow Herald* 20 Sept. 11 During the war and after the war Whitley bodies were set up in industries which up till then had nothing of the kind. *Ibid.*, The Whitley machinery could be used to discuss reduction in wages. **1928** *Britain's Industr. Future* (Liberal Industr. Inquiry) III. v. 174 It is important to understand the causes of the limited degree of success which has attended the Whitley scheme. **1976** *Star* (Sheffield) 3 Dec. 5/2 He recommends that a national forum be set up where Ministers can discuss policies with staff representatives, along with new regional Whitley Councils, and local committees.

Hence **Whi·tleyism**, the use of Whitley Councils or similar methods for dealing with relations between employers and employees.

1919 *Manch. Guardian* 28 Feb. 14/4 Judge Parry.. criticised the bureaucracy for its failure to apply the principles of 'Whitleyism' to departments of the Government service. **1928** *Daily Tel.* 14 Aug. 10/6 There has now followed a striking development, completing the destruction of Whitleyism in the Post Office. **1969** *State Service* Sept. 226/1 (*heading*) Whitleyism in the Civil Service.

whitlockite (hwi·tlǫkəit). *Min.* [f. the name of Herbert P. *Whitlock* (1868–1948), U.S. mineralogist + -ITE¹.] A calcium hydrogen phosphate containing ferrous iron and magnesium, $Ca_9(Mg,Fe)H(PO_4)_7$, found as transparent or translucent rhombohedral crystals of various colours and often occurring in dental calculi.

1940 C. FRONDEL in *Program & Abstr. 21st Ann. Meeting Mineral. Soc. Amer.* 7 Whitlockite is anhydrous calcium triphosphate..with Ca substituted for by Mg.. and Fe... The mineral is named after Herbert P. Whitlock,..at present Curator of Minerals and Gems in the American Museum of Natural History. **1971** *Nature* 3 Dec. 264/1 The rock contains relatively small amounts of the phases that we have found in other Apollo basalts (..whitlockite, baddeleyite). **1979** WILLIAMS & ELLIOTT *Dental Biochem.* xii. 226 Whitlockite is more common in subgingival compared with supragingival calculus.

Whitmanesque (hwitmăne·sk), *a.* [f. the name *Whitman* + -ESQUE.] Characteristic or suggestive of Walt Whitman (1819–92), U.S. poet, or of his poetry.

1882 *Good Lit.* Sept. 2 Clever persons can manufacture Whitmanesque verse quite equal to the average of the original. **1901** E. CROSBY *Edward Carpenter* 6 The long series of poems in Towards Democracy is with few exceptions written in the Whitmanesque meter, or lack of meter. **1913** W. DE LA MARE in *Edin. Rev.* Jan. 193 Eloquence and facility are the danger of Whitmanesque verse of this nature. **1934** C. LAMBERT *Music Ho!* v. 281 There is very little Whitmanesque acceptance of life about the artist of today. **1957** P. WILDEBLOOD *Main Chance* 152 They have a Whitmanesque simplicity that we've quite lost. **1977** *Time* 1 Aug. 50/2 Such a collage has an effect of Whitmanesque tenderness.

So (mostly somewhat *nonce*) **Whitmane·se**, the characteristic style or diction of Whitman; **Whitma·nia**, (*a*) [-MANIA], (a punning word for) exaggerated admiration for Whitman; (*b*) [-IA¹], writings pertaining to Whitman; **Whitma·niac**, a devotee of Whitman; **Whitma·nian** *a.* = *WHITMANESQUE *a.*; **Whitma·nian** *sb.*, an admirer or imitator of Whitman; **Whi·tmanish** *a.* = *WHITMAN-

ESQUE *a.*; **Whi·tmanism,** Whitman's metrical or poetical style; a feature of this; **Whi·tmanist, Whi·tmanite,** a Whitmanian; **Whi·tmanize** *v. intr.*, to write in the manner of Whitman; **Whitma·nnic** *a.* = *WHITMAN-ESQUE *a.*

1887 Whitmania [see *BRONTËAN *a.*]. **1887** M. BERENSON *Let.* 6 Jan. in Strachey & Samuels *M. Berenson* (1983) ii. 36, I was a Whitmanite at Smith College. **1889** *Pall Mall Gaz.* 25 Jan. 3/2 Having thus to a certain degree settled upon what one might call the *technique* of Whitmanism, he began to brood upon the nature of that spirit that was to give life to the strange form. **1893** R. LE GALLIENNE *Retrosp. Rev.* (1896) I. 213 'I see twenty-two young men from Foster's watching me, and the trousers of the twenty-two young men' is irresistible Whitmanese. **1894** *Nation* 7 June 433/1 One of the worst of Whitmanisms, the interlarding of foreign words. **1902** *Academy* 16 Aug. 173/1 Mr. Moody does not Whitmanise on the one hand, or follow the outworn Tennysonian convention on the other. **1906** *Dial* (Chicago) 1 Mar. 144/2 Much of the conversation reported is trivial to all but ardent Whitmanites. **1918** *Cambr. Hist. Amer. Lit.* II. III. i. 267 Whitmanism..has already had the ironical fate of developing something not unlike a cult. **1934** *Times Lit. Suppl.* 30 Aug. 586/3 Before Rossetti established himself publicly as the principal English Whitmanist, 'Leaves of Grass' had been the subject of several reviews. *a* **1930** D. H. LAWRENCE *Phoenix* (1936) 269 Whitmanish 'adhesiveness' of the social creature. **1948** L. SPITZER *Linguistics & Lit. Hist.* 218 The first [*sc.* the old alexandrine], Claudel replaced by the Biblical and Whitmanian verset. **1953** A. ALPERS *Katherine Mansfield* 124 Thus reminded that she had a country of her own, Katherine addressed to Wyspiański another of her Whitmanish declamations. **1959** *Times Lit. Suppl.* 16 Oct. 594/4 A foreword by Mr. Charles E. Feinberg, the noted Whitmaniac of Detroit. *a* **1960** E. M. FORSTER *Maurice* (1971) 217 Edward Carpenter..was..a Whitmannic poet whose nobility exceeded his strength. **1964** *New Statesman* 13 Mar. 414/3 The presses groan with Whitmania. **1977** *Listener* 30 June 866/3 The Fabian Society..sprang from an idealistic society called the Fellowship of the New Life, much influenced by the Whitmanian, Edward Carpenter.

whitmoreite (hwi·tmǫrəit). *Min.* [f. the name of Robert W. *Whitmore* (b. 1936), U.S. mineral collector + -ITE[1].] A secondary hydrated basic phosphate of ferric and ferrous iron, $Fe^{2+}Fe^{3+}{}_2(PO_4)_2(OH)_2.4H_2O$, found as twinned monoclinic crystals of a brownish colour.

1974 P. B. MOORE et al. in *Amer. Mineralogist* LIX. 900/2 Whitmoreite occurs as thin acicular crystals five to ten times as long as they are thick, which range from 0·1 to 2 mm in length. **1979** *Mineral. Abstr.* XXX. 450/1 The occurrence and parageneses of the following newly recognized secondary phosphates in the pegmatite of Hagendorf, West Germany, are recorded: whitmoreite, schoonerite, [etc.].

Whitstable (hwi·tstăb'l). The name of a coastal town in Kent, used *attrib.* and *absol.* to designate oysters bred there.

1883 *Queen* 20 Oct. (Advt.), Any others that are advertised at a low price..*cannot possibly* be the *genuine* Medina or Whitstable Oysters. **1940** A. L. SIMON *Conc. Encycl. Gastron.* II. 69/2 Most Whitstable oysters to-day are..relaid Brittanys or Belons. The oysters known as *Royal Whitstables* are, however, genuine natives, taken from a breeding ground the boundaries of which were settled by law about 1900. **1960** *Times* 2 Nov. 13/6 They may not be Whitstables, but they are oysters of a kind. **1971** *Vogue* 15 Sept. 43/1 One of London's best fishmongers. Ask for fresh sardines, Whitstable oysters, game. **1973** 'J. STURROCK' *Wicked Way to Die* x. 142 They've got as fine a barrel of Whitstables here as ever I've seen.

whitter, *v.* Restrict *Sc.* to senses in Dict. and add: **3.** Now usu. in form **witter.** To chatter or mutter; to grumble; to speak with annoying lengthiness on trivial matters. Occas. *trans.* Freq. const. *on.* Hence **w(h)i·ttering** *ppl. a. colloq.* (orig. *Sc.* and *dial.*).

1808 A. SCOTT *Poems* 82 The winking swankies whitter, An' fondly ee some female band. **1854** A. E. BAKER *Northamptonshire Gloss.*, *Whitter*, to murmur, to grumble, to complain... 'Don't *whitter* so.' **1886** R. E. G. COLE *Gloss. Words S.W. Lincs.* 168, I witter my-sen at times, and my husband tells me I'm a regular wittering old woman. **1925** E. C. SMITH *Mang Howes* 21 A clecken o guidweives at a gairdeen-yett whuttert ti other whan they eyed iz. **1959** [see *suicide blonde* s.v. *SUICIDE *sb.*[2] d]. **1966** 'O. MILLS' *Enemies of Bride* ii. 16 You might..try making the tea, instead of wittering on about Cordon Bleu methods. **1973** *Where* Jan. 13/2 Don't whitter away at every item [on the agenda], giving up at the first unsatisfactory explanation. Make your choice of issue, then take your time. **1981** R. D. EDWARDS *Corridors of Death* i. 4 The questions which those who had spotted him as the man-in-the-know were wittering at him. *Ibid.* xxxvi. 164 It wasn't like Robert to witter on like this. **1982** *Observer* 3 Oct. 9/2 If I wasn't going to hear the Tories wittering on in Brighton this week, I'd be in Frankfurt listening to publishers wittering on at the annual Book Fair. **1983** *Listener* 20 Jan. 5/2 A really wittering, patronising speech programme is a worse insult to the intelligence than the most fatuous disc jockey.

whittle, *v.*[2] Add: **I. 1. a.** Also with *down* (cf. sense 2).

1972 D. BLOODWORTH *Any Number can Play* xii. 103 A young orang..tried poking it [*sc.* a hole in a log] with a twig that was too thick, then whittled down the twig. **1979** J. HARVEY *Plate Shop* xv. 72 Ted put his feet up on the tin waste-paper box..and started absorbedly hewing and whittling a pencil down to the stub.

II. 4. *intr.* To worry or fret. Occas. *trans. dial.*

1880 *N. & Q.* 6 Mar. 205/2 When I was a boy my mother daily used this word to express fidgetiness or uneasiness. 'What are you *whittling* about?' seems to ring in my ears at this moment. **1913** D. H. LAWRENCE *Sons & Lovers* viii. 202 'How do you think I'm going to manage?' 'Well, it won't make it any better to whittle about it.' **1984** *Daily Tel.* 23 Oct. 10/3 'I'm whittled to death about the future of the mining industry.' These, or words like these, are attributed to Mr. Michael Eaton, the new character in the long-running serial story of the mining dispute.

whittled *ppl. a.*: also *whittled-down*.

1961 A. BROWNJOHN in E. Lucie-Smith *Brit. Poetry since 1945* (1970) 266 Farmers call hillocks And ponds.. By the first words to hand; a heavy, whittled-down Simplicity meets the need. **1962** E. SNOW *Other Side of River* (1963) xxiv. 183 If any of these somewhat blind guesses are right, the whittled-down results still remain impressive. **1980** M. BOOTH *Bad Track* ii. 34 Long streets with a whittled-down green, a church..a pub.

Whitworth. Add: **b.** Used *attrib.* and † in the possessive to designate a series of screw threads proposed by Whitworth in 1841 (and later additions to it), fasteners having one of these threads, and tools for use with the fasteners.

[**1841** *Proc. Inst. Civil Engineers* I. 157 (*heading*) 'On an uniform system of screw threads.' By Joseph Whitworth.] **1877** *Calvert's Mechanics' Almanack* 4 The terms, 'Whitworth's Threads', 'Whitworth Taps'..have sprung from the lips of all concerned with the iron trade. **1916** *Proc. Inst. Automobile Engineers* XI. 176 We all imagined that the Whitworth system for the larger sizes of screws was so perfect that there would be no difficulty in making sure that Whitworth nuts would fit Whitworth bolts sufficiently well for all practical purposes. **1968** J. ARNOLD *Shell Bk. Country Crafts* 160 Until the advent of the Whitworth thread, which standardized threads all over the country, it was the practice for smiths to tap their own threads. **1970** *Kay & Co.* (Worcester) *Catal.* 1970–71 Autumn/Winter 770/2 Ring Spanners... Available in Whitworth, AF or Metric sizes. **1972** *Practical Motorist* Oct. 209/1 Whitworth fasteners are no longer in general use, although you will encounter them on older cars.

whity, *sb.* Add: Also **whitey** (the usual form), **whitie. 1.** (Also with capital initial.) Also, a white woman; white people collectively. Freq. derog. *slang* (chiefly *Blacks'*).

1942 BERREY & VAN DEN BARK *Amer. Thes. Slang* § 385/2 *White person*,..whitie. **1952** S. SELVON *Brighter Sun* iv. 61 A white-skinned girl..was called 'Whitey cockroach!' **1964** *Time* 31 July 12/3 Harlem..is where the white man is no longer the 'ofay' but 'Mr. Charlie' or 'the man', and mostly 'whitey', derived from the Black Nationalist talk of 'the blue-eyed white devil'. **1967** C. DRUMMOND *Death at Furlong Post* xi. 138 Get to hell away from me! You Whities stink! **1968** *Times Lit. Suppl.* 4 Apr. 329/2 The world of 'Whitey' into which these Negroes no longer want to be integrated. **1971** A. KING *One Love* 19 There's a Whitey in every Black man that has to come out, or die, before he's ever himself. **1972** R. K. SMITH *Ransom* I. 24 We're gonna hit Whitey and hit him again. **1976** *Listener* 15 Apr. 462/1 There is a pub in south London where black intellectuals meet, and if you happen to be a white man, the landlord—who is of West Indian origin—delights in calling you 'whitie'. As far as he is concerned, it's all in fun. **1977** *New Yorker* 26 Sept. 131/1 He's no more than a trivial whitey to be squished. **1980** *Amer. Speech* LV. 211 It encompassed a protest of whitey's 'theft' of yet another style of jazz—swing.

whizgig. (Earlier example.)

1821 M. EDGEWORTH *Let.* 22 Nov. (1971) 279 A Whizgig for Pakenham in my next.

whizz, whiz, *sb.*[1] Add: **1. b.** The practice of picking pockets (chiefly in phr. *on the whizz*); a pickpocket. *slang* (orig. and chiefly *U.S.*).

1925 E. JERVIS *25 Yrs. in Six Prisons* i. 17 Some of the boys are 'on the whiz' (pickpockets). **1931** *Amer. Speech* VII. 117 *Whiz*, n. A pick-pocket. **1936** 'J. CURTIS' *Gilt Kid* 245 They might pinch him for being on the whizz. **1963** T. TULLETT *Inside Interpol* xii. 162 The pickpocket, known in the underworld as the 'whiz'..is always a specialist.

3. An act of urination. *slang.*

1971 D. CLARK *Sick to Death* i. 21 She could have left him alone..while she went for a whizz or changed her clothes.

4. *attrib.* and *Comb.*, as **whizz-boy, -man** *slang*, a pickpocket; **whizz-mob** *slang*, a gang of pickpockets.

1931 M. ALLINGHAM *Police at Funeral* vii. 95 How many murders do we get in this class... It's navvies, whizz-boys, car thieves..who run off the rails and commit murder. **1938** F. CHESTER *Shot Full* xxv. 285, I used to frequent a number of public-houses, used by 'the boys', as criminals are known among the English. There were screwsmen,..'whizz-men',..and 'drag-men'. **1959** *Listener* 12 Mar. 485/1 The quick-fingered craft of those whom the Elizabethans called nips and we call whizz boys. **1932** 'S. WOOD' *Shades Prison House* xix. 278 There one may rub shoulders with..thieves of every type, whiz-men, burglars, car-bandits. **1929** G. DILNOT *Triumphs of Detection* iv. 47 A 'wizz mob' which operated, say, at Hammersmith Broadway, would immediately suspend business..if they saw a local detective in the vicinity. **1941** J. PHELAN *Murder by Numbers* v. 53 'Putting a smother they call it... Crowd cover up something...' 'I see. Like a whizz mob—pickpockets, I mean.' **1955** D. WEBB *Deadline for Crime* iii. 52 Provincial police forces looked to him for help when they wanted their towns cleared of the 'whiz mob', as English pickpockets are known in the underworld.

whizz, whiz (hwiz), *sb.*[2] Also **wiz** (wiz). *slang* (orig. *U.S.*). [Perh. identical with WHIZZ *sb.*[1], but in sense 1 b also regarded as f. WIZ(ARD *sb.*] **1. a.** Something very remarkable.

1908 G. H. LORIMER *Jack Spurlock* vii. 157 It is not only a whiz, but a hummah! You are in on the ground flo' of King Solomon's Mines, Limited. **1920** F. SCOTT FITZGERALD *This Side of Paradise* I. ii. 45 'Wonderful night.' 'It's a whiz.' **1959** *Times* 7 Dec. 13/3 Here are some of the gifts I have given to children in recent years: a massive iron key that could surely unlock the deepest dungeon in Nottingham Castle and makes a whizz of a paper-weight.

b. A person who is wonderfully skilful or talented in some respect.

1914 'HIGH JINKS, JR.' *Choice Slang* 20 A person is designated as a 'Whizz' when he has exceptional ability along one or more lines. **1921** H. CRANE *Let.* 1 Oct. (1965) 66, I..have a strong notion that as a copy writer I will eventually make a 'whiz'. **1924** W. M. RAINE *Troubled Waters* xiii. 142 Millie done fixed my game laig up with that ointment good as new. I want to tell you-all that girl is a wiz. **1928** S. LEWIS *Man who knew Coolidge* I. 36 He thinks he's such a wiz at cars, but..he couldn't locate that squeak. **1948** A. HUXLEY *Ape & Essence* (1949) 69 He's an absolute whizz at Malicious Animal Magnetism. **1962** E. B. WHITE *Let.* 13 July (1976) 493 You chose a real whiz..when you picked me for your grammarian. **1978** S. BRILL *Teamsters* vi. 211 Malnik was well known..as an associate of long-time mob financial wiz Meyer Lansky. **1982** *Financial Times* 22 June 9/2 He has since become a whizz at ping pong. **1984** *New Yorker* 9 July 35/3 Little Nick Silver, a math whiz from Toughkenamon..was the youngest kid at camp. **1984** *Times* 18 Oct. 14/6, I have a whizz of an accountant who will probably arrange things.

2. Comb.: **whiz(z)-kid,** an exceptionally successful or brilliant young person, esp. in politics or business; hence **whiz(z)-kiddery,** the phenomenon of whizz-kids; the style or mode of work of a whizz-kid.

1960 *Time* 21 Nov. 100/1 The 'Whiz Kids'—as the team soon was known. **1962** *Economist* 22 Dec. 1202/1 Critics..regard President Kennedy as a quiz-kid surrounded by whiz-kids. **1966** OGILVY & ANDERSON *Excursions in Number Theory* ix. 103 Zerah Colburn was an early nineteenth-century mathematical whiz-kid. **1967** *Economist* 24 June 1353/3 The whole programme has been a curious hotch-potch of whiz-kidery, preconceived theory and painstaking trial-and-error pragmatism. **1976** *Observer* 26 Sept. 8/1 Many in the institutions—banks insurance companies, investment funds, Stock Exchange and so on—who swallowed whizz-kiddery in its myriad forms. **1976** *Time* 27 Dec. 13/1 The sin of Whiz Kid Shelepin was that he tried to build a political base from which to promote his own post-Brezhnev candidacy for the top post. **1977** M. DRABBLE *Ice Age* I. 27 Anthony was watching unedited film of an interview with Len the property whizz kid. **1977** *Times* 4 July 22/3 Whizz-kiddery is out; gravitas is in. **1980** *Times Lit. Suppl.* 3 Oct. 1079/5 Editors are a humble and obscure race; lacking the glamour of the whiz-kids and wheeler-dealers.., they are rarely seen in polite society, their names unknown to the columns of *The Bookseller*. **1981** *Sunday Express* 25 Jan. 17/1 Prime Minister Margaret Thatcher will meet Britain's latest whizz-kid inventor when she hosts a unique gathering of inventors and financiers at Downing Street tomorrow. **1985** *Times* 22 June 9/5 We have often been tempted to listen to the siren voices of those who would advise..the latest radical church services, guitars and steel bands and other forms of whizkiddery.

whizz, whiz, *v.* Add: **4.** *intr.* To urinate. *slang.*

1929 D. H. LAWRENCE *Pansies* 24, I wish I was a gentleman As full of wet as a watering-can To whizz in the eye of a police-man. **1976** R. B. PARKER *Promised Land* vii. 37, I wondered if anyone had ever whizzed on Allan Pinkerton's shoe.

whizz, whiz, *int.* Add: Cf. *GEE WHIZ(Z *int.*

whizz-bang (hwi·zbæŋ), *int.*, *sb.*, and *a. slang.* Also **whiz-bang,** without hyphen, and as two words. [f. WHIZZ, WHIZ *v.* or *int.* + BANG *sb.*[1]] **A.** *int.* Expressing a whizzing sound that ends with a thud or explosion, such as may be heard as a bullet or shell strikes a target.

1836 DICKENS *Pickw.* (1837) ii. 9 Fired a musket.. rushed into wine shop..back again—whiz, bang. *c* **1838** C. MATHEWS in M. R. Booth *Eng. Plays of 19th Cent.* (1973) IV. 133 She called in a farmer..Who loaded his blunderbuss..Whizz, bang! Lord, I thought I was murdered outright. **1920** [in Dict. s.v. WHIZZ, WHIZ *int.* and *adv.* b].

B. *sb.* **1.** (In Dict. s.v. WHIZZ, WHIZ *int.* and *adv.* b.)

1915 [in Dict.]. **1918** W. OWEN *Poems* (1920) 16 What murk of air remained stank old, and sour With fumes of whizz-bangs. **1923** KIPLING *Irish Guards in Gt. War* I. 143 Three men killed in the line by a single whizz-bang.

1968 J. R. ACKERLEY *My Father & Myself* vi. 51 In 1918, just before the Armistice, he was killed by a whizz-bang. **1979** S. WILSON *Vampire* II. 56 Those guns. Those ever present guns. Eighty-eights. Whizz-bangs. None of us need to be reminded of the names.

2. A resounding success; a marvel.

1916 in *Amer. Speech* 1972 (1975) XLVII. 116 Masson is a whizbang at getting up the kind of food that makes the troops want to fight. **1944** T. H. WISDOM *Triumph over Tunisia* 182 The raid was a whizz-bang, the R.A.F. expression denoting something highly successful. **1978** M. PUZO *Fools Die* xvi. 169 These were the sharpest kids in America, the future business giants, judges, show business whizbangs. **1983** *Listener* 14 July 37/1 George Stevens..knew how to make box-office whizz-bangs but not very interesting movies.

3. A firework that jumps around making a whizzing noise and periodic bangs.

1960 J. LODWICK *Asparagus Trench* 53, I carried.. whizz-bang fireworks, harmless but disconcerting pyrotechnical trivia these, by reason of their strange gyrations. **1983** D. LAMBERT *Judas Code* iii. 55 He lit three more firecrackers—Whizz Bangs they were called.

C. *adj.* **a.** Excellent. **b.** Fast-paced, very lively; spectacular.

1959 I. & P. OPIE *Lore & Lang. Schoolch.* ix. 161 Other superlatives currently in favour are:..swell, whizzing, whiz-bang, whizzo. **1963** *Economist* 5 Jan. 28/1 Americans are often the first to admit that sometimes a whiz-bang quality about their methods tends to upset their friends. **1965** *Listener* 16 Sept. 431/1 I'm not suggesting that programmes on the arts should be as whizz-bang as *The Dick Van Dyke Show*, but I do suspect that Drama and Light Entertainment could teach them a lot. **1967** *Spectator* 8 Dec. 725/2 A sculptor whose inventions..are made for prolonged contemplation when much work is made for whizzbang impact. **1972** *National Observer* (U.S.) 27 May 20/5 Bernstein inclines to brisk tempos; it would be interesting to see a regiment actually try marching to his whiz-bang 'Stars and Stripes Forever'. **1984** *Listener* 5 Jan. 8/3 As for home-grown, whizzbang, laugh-a-line comedy—Channel 4, where are you?

Hence as *v. trans.*, to shoot whizz-bangs at; **whizz-banged** *ppl. a.*

1918 G. FRANKAU *One of Them* ix. 66 How oft, in some wild Western whizz-banged dug-out..Has my soul flown from Staff-emitted paper To the glad days, when from my purse I'd lug out That last fat stake. **1919** *King's Royal Rifle Corps Chron. 1916* 139 This line was whizz-banged heartily. **1928** BLUNDEN *Undertones of War* iv. 35 Some of us were just in time, when next the enemy gunners whizzbanged here, to jump down from the fire-step into a dugout stairway.

whizzer. Add: **2.** Something or someone extraordinary or wonderful; a 'stunner'. *slang.*

1888 E. L. DORSEY *Midshipman Bob* I. x. 93 'Fore-top-gallant studdingsail-boom-tricing-line-block strap-thimble.' Ain't that a whizzer? **1947** 'N. BLAKE' *Minute for Murder* v. 98, I must say she was a whizzer in those days. **1976** *Zigzag* Apr. 28/1 'She's long' features Bill's best guitar solo (despite many other whizzers). **1977** 'J. GASH' *Judas Pair* viii. 95 It's a whizzer... I've found a cased set.

3. A pickpocket. *slang.*

1925 N. LUCAS *Autobiogr. Crook* vii. 108 The stalls of theatres at matinees are sometimes patronized by 'whizzers'. **1941** V. DAVIS *Phenomena in Crime* xiv. 195 There are a score of girl 'whizzers' in London who can get a man's pocket wallet..with conjuring skill. **1974** R. EDWARDS *Dixon of Dock Green* 17 It was also a right place for 'whizzers'—pick-pockets.

4. *on a whizzer*: on a drinking spree. *N. Amer. slang.*

1910 B. EDWARDS *Best of Bob Edwards* (1975) v. 104 He was only off on a little bit of a whizzer. **1936** *Univ. Texas Stud. in Eng.* XVI. 51 A number of phrases with *go* refer to the act of 'getting drunk': one may *go on..a whizzer*.

whizzing, *vbl. sb.* Add: **2.** Pick-pocketing. *slang.*

1925 N. LUCAS *Autobiogr. Crook* vii. 98 My pals went in for every known form of getting other people's property. .. 'Drumming', 'parlor jumping', 'whizzing'. **1941** V. DAVIS *Phenomena in Crime* xv. 209 Nearly all classes of 'whizzing' take place on the 'shove-up' principle.

whizzing, *ppl. a.* Add: **2.** Excellent, 'smashing'. *slang.*

1953 [see *KNOCK-OUT *sb.* 4]. **1959** [see *WHIZZ-BANG *a.*].

whizzo, wizzo (hwi·zo, wi·zo), *int.* and *a. slang.* [f. WHIZZ, WHIZ *sb.*¹ + *-O².] **A.** *int.* An exclamation expressing delight.

1905 in *Engl. Dial. Dict.* **1943** *Penguin New Writing* XVI. 28 Wizzoh! No night fighters! **1954** D. AMES *Crime, Gentlemen, Please* xxi. 123 'It's really a little surprise for the kiddies.' 'Whizzo!' cried Anna, grabbing it. **1959** J. VERNEY *Friday's Tunnel* xxviii. 269 Friday.. yelled, 'Oh, whizzo!'

B. *adj.* Excellent, wonderful.

1948 *R.A.F. Rev.* Jan. 20/2 It's whizzo when you get a fried egg sunny-side-up for tea. **1948** I. BROWN *No Idle Words* 97 A father who told his son that he had..arranged for the boy to visit Norway received the following answer: 'Absolutely wizard, flash, whizz-o, grand, lovely to beetle up to Norway.' **1955** M. ALLINGHAM *Beckoning Lady* xiii. 185, I wanted to look at some wizzo lettering on..the Tomb. **1968** *Listener* 19 Dec. 810/3 The Squadron-Leader and I decided to give a party—what the Squadron-Leader called a proper whizzo party with marks on the ceiling.

whizzo (hwi·zo), *sb. slang.* [f. *WHIZZ, WHIZ *sb.*² + *-O².] = *WHIZZ, WHIZ *sb.*² 1.

1977 *Daily Express* 29 Mar. 20/3 Keyboard whizzo Keith Emerson uses his [side of an album] for a neo-classical piano concerto, accompanied by the London Philharmonic Orchestra. **1981** *Sydney Mirror* 2 July 8/4 Electronics whizzo Dick Smith..aims to become the taxman's friend in another way.

who, *pron.* (*sb.*) Add: **I. 4. a.** *Who's Who*: (earlier and later *transf.* examples); also *fig.* Also, *you and who else?*: a contemptuous expression of incredulity, conveying scepticism about a person's ability to do some past or threatened deed, esp. of violence.

1917 *Wells Fargo Messenger* V. 183/2 The Messenger is no 'Who's who'. **1917** *National Police Gaz.* (U.S.) 18 Aug. 2/4 We don't believe that Ed W. Dunn's latest effusion would win a place for him in the poet's 'Who's who!' corner. **1929** 'E. QUEEN' *Roman Hat Mystery* xviii. 260 'Forget, and I'll dip you into the East River.' 'You and who else?' breathed Djuna. **1929** *Times Lit. Suppl.* 18 Apr. 308/2 First he [*sc.* the biographer] gets out of the way the 'Who's Who' of Wallace Williamson's career in a terse opening chapter. **1951** P. BRANCH *Lion in Cellar* iii. 38 ''Oo creased 'im?' he asked... 'I did,' he said firmly... 'You an' 'oo else?' he jeered. **1962** W. NOWOTTNY *Lang. Poets Use* ii. 34 Whilst using obituary or *Who's Who* language, it [*sc.* the diction] subtly detaches itself from the social attitudes such language is normally associated with. **1971** A. MORICE *Murder in Married Life* xiii. 124 Julian: 'Then I'll throw you out.' Murderer: 'You and who else, ha ha.' **1974** *Advocate-News* (Barbados) 19 Feb. 12/1 The list of batsmen to come is straight out of the 'who's who' of attacking cricketers. **1981** *Country Life* 16 July 205/4 *Women in History*..is a sort of *Who's Who* and *Who Was Who* of women who..should be known.

b. *who does what*(?): which person will do which task; *esp.* (in a demarcation dispute) members of which trade union will do a certain job.

1922 H. S. WALPOLE *Cathedral* II. iii. 194 But who's going to decide who does what?.. We're not much in the sewing line. **1960** *Guardian* 13 Sept. 3/2 A who-does-what dispute between the Amalgamated Engineering Union and the Electrical Trades Union. **1962** *Economist* 13 Oct. 118/1 The squabble over who-does-what. **1962** *Daily Tel.* 28 Nov. 1/1 The Trades Union Congress will seek to settle future 'Who does what?' demarcation disputes with quick and decisive action. **1979** *Now!* 21–27 Sept. 60/1 The £100 million complex has stood idle, paralysed by an inter-union 'who does what' row over 42 jobs.

¶ **5.** (Later examples.)

1941 V. WOOLF *Between Acts* 101 Who was she looking for? **1958** *Observer* 6 Apr. 3 (*heading*) Who do you want to save? **1966** I. MURDOCH *Time of Angels* x. 106 Who, after all, could I possibly be in love with? **1969** *Listener* 13 Nov. 664/1 One of the policemen..went up to him and almost shouted: 'Who do you think you're talking to?' **1980** J. GERSON *Assassination Run* ii. 35 The days of Philby and Blake when no one knew who to trust.

II. ¶ **13.** For the note read simply: Still common colloquially. (Examples of the use described in Dict. as *rare* or *obs.*)

1979 *Globe & Mail* (Toronto) 27 Aug. 14/5 They come to see Bowser, who they equate not only with The Fonz, but the Cookie Monster and Mork from Ork, too. **1984** *Times* 6 Feb. 12/3 Just over half..of our sample who we assessed as working class concurred.

III. 14. c. (Later example.)

1955 *Bull. Atomic Sci.* June 228/3 The 'who' and 'why' of ethical judgments may lie in the realm of metaphysics; but the 'how' are phenomena in the natural world.

whoa, *int.* **2.** (Earlier example.)

1843 [see *HAW *int.*² and *sb.*⁵].

who-all (hū·ǭl), *pron. U.S. dial.* Also **who all.** [f. WHO *pron.* + ALL *a.*] Used for WHO *pron.* in interrogative and relative functions (with sing. as well as pl. sense).

1899 B. W. GREEN *Word-bk. Virginia Folk-Speech* 424 Who-all *interrog.* Meaning all who: as '*Who all* were there.' **1905** A. V. CULBERTSON *Banjo Talks* 15, I ain' care who-all come dis way! **1916** R. FROST *Let.* 21 Mar. (1964) 27, I wish I could remember..who-all I've baptized into my heresies. **1938** M. K. RAWLINGS *Yearling* vii. 67 Jody asked brashly, 'Who-all's your sweetheart?' **1938** J. STUART *Beyond Dark Hills* vii. 184 Will you get up and tell the student group just why you were out there..and who all were with you? **1944** in *Amer. Speech* (1946) XXI. 52 We always said, as the town [*sc.* Hawley, Minnesota] still does, 'Who-all was there?' and 'What all did you do?' Many of the Irish also use 'who-all' and 'what-all'.

whodunit (hūdʌ·nit). *colloq.* Also **whodunnit** and (*rare*) other varr. [repr. *who done* (= illiterate for *did*) *it?*] A story or other work of fiction about the solving of a mystery, esp. a murder; a detective or murder story. Occas. used for 'who did it' in other contexts.

1930 D. GORDON in *News of Bks.* (U.S.) July 10 *Half-Mast Murder*, by Milward Kennedy—A satisfactory *whodunit.* **1942** G. MITCHELL *Laurels are Poison* vi. 61 That was another case of Oo-dun-it. Or was it? **1943** *Britannia & Eve* Feb. 16/1 Clifton Fadiman..moved in with an intellectual slap-stick show, which could be appreciated equally by professors and the public for 'who-dun-it?' books. **1951** M. MCLUHAN *Mech. Bride* (1967) 104/2 Would the thriller fan be abashed to learn that the whodunit anticipated the techniques of modern science and art? **1959** 'A. GILBERT' *Death takes Wife* xiii. 173 The whodunnit writers have got us all educated. **1961** *Times* 26 July 15/5 A new 'whodunit'..is to be produced at St. Martin's theatre. **1971** WODEHOUSE *Much Obliged, Jeeves* vii. 69, I..go in mostly for who-dun-its and novels of suspense. For the who-dun-it Agatha Christie is always a safe bet. **1971** E. LEMARCHAND *Death on Doomsday* xi. 169, I think sleeping dogs will be let lie, provided we can establish whodunit. **1975** *New Yorker* 21 Apr. 2/1 (Advt.), *Equus*—A brilliant psychological whodunit by Peter Shaffer. **1980** *Times Lit. Suppl.* 30 May 615/5 In the whodunnit, we are conditioned to look for not the most obvious but the *least likely* suspect.

Hence **whodu·n(n)itry,** material or writing such as occurs in a 'whodunit'.

1961 *Daily Tel.* 18 Dec. 10/4 'The Judge and his Hangman' on BBC television last night. This is whodunitry with undertones. **1966** *Punch* 8 June 859/2 His *The Weekend Girls*..settles for whodunitry rather than sociology. **1972** *Daily Tel.* 4 Apr. 9/8 There is no sexual element whatever, and..it doesn't dabble in whodunnitry.

whole, *a.*, *sb.*, *adv.*, (*int.*). Add: **D. 1. whole caboodle:** see *CABOODLE; **wholefood,** unrefined food containing no artificial additives; an article or kind of such food; **whole hog:** also (usu. with hyphen) *attrib.* as *adj.*, thorough-going, out-and-out; *whole-hogger* (further examples); *whole-hogging* adj. = *whole-hog* adj.; *whole-hoggism* (earlier examples); **whole kit and boiling,** etc.: see *KIT *sb.*¹ 3; **whole meal:** also (*colloq.*), a wholemeal loaf; **whole milk,** milk from which no constituents have been removed; also *attrib.*; **whole nine yards** *U.S. colloq.*, everything, the whole lot; also as *adv.*, all the way; **whole tone** *Mus.* = *whole note* (*a*) in Dict.; *whole-tone scale* (see quot. 1928); freq. with reference to compositions based on this scale, particularly those of Debussy; **whole wheat,** wheat which has not been deprived of some constituents by sifting; usu. *attrib.* (with hyphen or as one word), designating flour or foodstuffs made from this.

1960 *Mother Earth* Oct. 341 We should like to hear from further growers who may have available supplies of wholefood, especially winter salads, parsnips [etc.]. **1971** *It* 2–16 June 23/3 (Advt.), The Country Bizarre is a little seasonal magazine on traditions, crafts..whole food culture, poetry, drawings. **1978** *Peace News* 25 Aug. 19/3 (Advt.), If you are interested in wholefoods, running a shop collectively and a political awareness of food please contact us. **1980** *Times* 21 Feb. 12/3 The longest lunch queues in London now are for wholefood... Vegetarian restaurants and health food shops are not new. What is changing is their style. **1829** *Virginia Herald* (Fredericksburg) 28 Mar. 2/3 Of late he has shown a disposition to become 'a whole hog man'. **1855** I. C. PRAY *Mem. J. G. Bennett* 141 James Gordon Bennett..is a thoroughgoing, 'whole-hog' Jackson man. **1935** *Planning* 23 Apr. 8 Once you start planning you cannot stop half-way, and whole-hog planning means tyranny. **1956** N. PEVSNER *Englishness of Eng. Art* iii. 61 In the architecture of about 1900 there is in England the fresh yet friendly and human style of Voysey, not the whole-hog throwing overboard of all traditions as in Frank Lloyd Wright in America. **1977** *Rolling Stone* 30 June 69/2 My guess is that few white Rhodesian soldiers out there in the bush are wholehog white supremacists anymore. **1904** *Daily Chron.* 28 July 5/6 The country is sick of the whole-hoggers, the half-hoggers,..and the whole lot of them. **1907** E. NESBIT *Enchanted Castle* xi. 333 Your ancestors were whole-hoggers. They have done the thing as it should be done—every detail attended to. **1920** D. H. LAWRENCE *Women in Love* xxix. 438 He is such a whole-hogger. **1923** R. MACAULAY *Told by Idiot* I. xvii. 60 Stanley was like that—enthusiastic, headlong, a deep plunger, a whole-hogger. **1966** *Listener* 26 May 749/1 In the matter of theatre censorship, I am a whole-hogger. **1934** C. LAMBERT *Music Ho!* v. 301 He [*sc.* Berg] cannot be described as a wholehogging atonalist. **1943** WYNDHAM LEWIS *Let.* 24 Nov. (1963) 370 He is a whole-hogging Thomist. **1960** *Guardian* 27 June 7/2 Whole-hogging festival visitors. **1838** *Carlisle Patriot* 18 Aug. 2/5 The quaint version which the *Times* gave the other day of 'whole hoggism'. **1848** *Blackw. Mag.* July 54 Purge the land of moderatism and anti-whole-hog-ism. **1967** Wholemeal [see *HOVIS]. **1983** A. T. ELLIS *Other Side of Fire* xvi. 102 Small white, small wholemeal and a couple of croissants. **1970** *Kenya Farmer* Feb. 9/2 We send 110 gallons whole milk per day to Eldoret and separate all the rest for rearing stock. **1977** *Lancet* 19 Feb. 388/1 Sensitivity to cow's whole milk was investigated in six patients. **1982** P. RANCE *Great Brit. Cheese Bk.* I. v. 97 These wholemilk cheeses, traditional in this area, vary considerably. **1970** *Word Watching* Apr. 7/2 *Whole nine yards*, the entire thing. **1981** *Washington Post* 16 Jan. (Weekend sect.) 20/3 A Japanese disaster film, *Virus*, goes the whole nine yards, showing the city as a deserted freeway underpass. **1983** *Aviation Week* 7 Mar. 46/2 The Army came out and gave us the whole nine yards on how they use space systems. **1897** J. S. SHEDLOCK tr. *Riemann's Dict. Mus.* 863/1 *Whole-tone*, the larger of the two progressions by tone within the fundamental scale. **1928** *Melody Maker* Feb. 209/3 The Whole Tone Scale.. is composed entirely of intervals of a Tone, thus having only *seven degrees* between its Tonic and its Octave. It has only come into use quite recently and is employed by the school devoting itself to..'futuristic' harmony. **1934** [see *ELEVENTH *sb.* 2]. **1935** G. ABRAHAM *Stud. Russ. Mus.* iv. 77 Dargomïzhsky's fondness for the sharpened fifth of the scale, for the augmented triad which is, so to speak, the 'common chord' of the whole-tone scale.

1952 B. Ulanov *Hist. Jazz in Amer.* (1958) 284 The augmented chords and whole-tone melodies reveal their Debussyan source more clearly. **1977** *Time* 21 Mar. 62/3 His inclusion of Russian fold music, Turkish airs, even the whole-tone scale from the Orient (more than half a century before Debussy) suggests that he was exceptionally curious and openminded. **1903** Wholewheat bread [see *peanut butter* s.v. *PEANUT b]. **1946** *Sun* (Baltimore) 14 Feb. 14/1 As everybody knows, whole-wheat bread is more nutritious than white bread. **1971** *Times* 11 Sept. 10/4 The distinction between *galettes* (made from buckwheat or wholewheat) and crêpes. **1980** *Sunday Times* (Colour Suppl.) 20 Jan. 57/1 The most basic, natural loaves of all, contain 100 per cent whole wheat flour.

2. a. *whole-body, -grain* (examples), *-house, -word.*

1947 *Radiology* XLIX. 283/1 To determine whether a daily dose of whole-body irradiation when given over a period of several hours produced the same injury as when given within minutes. **1961** *Lancet* 7 Oct. 784/2 Modification..would require interference with the normal whole-body response to injury. **1977** *Times* 10 Sept. 2/1 Patients from several London hospitals are being sent to BUPA's medical centre to be X-rayed by their EMI whole-body scanner. **1983** P. Niesewand *Scimitar* xx. 566 Lyle and Ross were..subjected to everything from lumbar punctures and sperm tests to whole body scans. **1960** *Farmer & Stockbreeder* 15 Mar. (Suppl.) 10/1 Second-class protein..is found in whole-grain cereals, nuts, lentils and soya beans. **1976** *Woman's Day* (U.S.) Nov. 158/2 Unleavened whole-grain bread should be served generously to assure that your family fills up on fat- and cholesterol-free foods. **1985** *N.Y. Times Mag.* 6 Jan. 6/4 Popular among runners of marathons who stuff themselves with whole-grain pasta before trotting off to the day's race. **1952** *Archit. Rev.* CXI. 212/2 The Radiation 'whole-house' warming system. **1976** *National Observer* (U.S.) 19 June 8 (Advt.), Your Trane Comfort Corps consultant is a full-time specialist in whole-house air conditioning. **1964** P. A. D. MacCarthy in D. Abercrombie et al. *Daniel Jones* 157 This in turn facilitates the recognition of whole-word patterns. **1975** *Language for Life* (Dept. Educ. & Sci.) xxvi. 521 Word recognition is not merely a matter of learning unique whole-word forms. **1980** *Redbook* Oct. 220/1 Most important, the teaching of beginning reading was dominated by the 'whole-word' or 'look-say' method, in which children learned to recognize entire words, rather than by the method of 'phonics' in which they learned to sound out letters and groups of letters.

d. whole-earther *colloq.*, somebody who is actively concerned about the protection and wise use of natural resources and wildlife; **whole-life** *a.*, pertaining to or designating an insurance policy for which the premiums are payable until the death of the insured person; **whole-number rule** *Physics*, the empirical law that the atomic weights of the elements are mostly close to being whole numbers; **whole rock** *a. Geol.*, designating the use of a complete rock sample in an analytical procedure, as distinct from the individual minerals composing it.

1975 *Times* 5 Aug. 12/7 The 'amenity lobby'..includes a new wave of 'whole earthers': notably the Conservation Society founded in 1966..and Friends of the Earth. **1980** *Blair & Ketchum's Country Jrnl.* Oct. 67/1 It includes..neo-Jeffersonians, back-to-the-landers, whole-earthers, communists, and neopioneers seeking to revive old country ways. **1845** *Williams's Directory of Leeds* 46 (Advt.), One-third of the 'Whole Life' Premium may remain unpaid..as a Debt upon the Policy. **1881** *Harper's Mag.* Jan. 79/1 Never take a whole-life policy to embarrass the declining and unproductive years of life. **1977** *National Observer* (U.S.) 15 Jan. 9/2 Whole life—also called cash-value, straight, permanent, ordinary and endowment life—combines insurance protection with a savings or endowment plan. [**1919** F. W. Aston in *Nature* 18 Dec. 393/2 Of more than forty different values of atomic and molecular mass so far measured all, without a single exception, fall on whole numbers.] **1923** E. N. da C. Andrade *Structure of Atom* vii. 111 The whole number rule allows us to suppose that all nuclei are built up of the same mass elements, *i.e.* protons. **1967** Oldenberg & Holladay *Introd. Atomic & Nuclear Physics* (ed. 4) xvi. 238 The great simplification was finally introduced through the whole-number rule, which indicates a few fundamental particles as building blocks of all matter. [**1955** *Bull. Geol. Soc. Amer.* LXVI. 1711 Approximate minimum ages have been determined for the Cranberry gneiss..and Henderson gneiss by measuring A^{40}/K^{40} ratios on samples of the whole rock.] **1964** *Geochem. Internat.* I. 739/2 It was decided to determine the age of the granites by the Rb-Sr method on whole rock samples. **1979** A. W. Hofmann in Jäger & Hunziker *Isotope Geol.* 215 The evidence for a Caledonian age of the pre-Hercynian gneisses rests in part on two whole-rock Rb-Sr isochrons.

wholesale, *sb., a., adv.* Add: **4. c.** As *sb.*, a wholesale dealer or organization.

1851 [see *RETAIL *sb.*[1] (and *a.*) 3]. **1884** [see Retail *sb.*[1] (and *a.*) 3]. **1928** *Daily Express* 29 May 7/4 The ability of the wholesales to adopt methods of mass production..must be lessened.

wholesale *v.* (earlier and later examples); also *absol.*; hence **who·lesaling** *vbl. sb.* and *ppl. a.*

1800 M. L. Weems *Let.* 17 Dec. in *M. L. Weems: Wks. & Ways* (1929) II. 152 But for this I wd instantly wholesale my books & quit the business forever. **1837** Dickens in *Bentley's Misc.* Oct. 413 We have been prevailed upon to allow this number of our Miscellany to be retailed to the public, or wholesaled to the trade, without any advance upon our usual price. **1881** *Oregon State Jrnl.* 1 Jan. 7 We are prepared to Wholesale and Retail Cheaper than any place in this city. **1906** S. E. Sparling *Introd. Business Organization* xi. 254 In the trade jobbing is virtually synonymous with wholesaling. **1926** N. S. B. Gras in Crump & Jacob *Legacy of Middle Ages* 440 Although many merchants might prefer the wholesale trade, they were not allowed to be exclusively wholesaling merchants. **1962** R. B. Fuller *Epic Poem on Industrialization* 134 'Science News Service' An industrial syndicate Wholesaling to publishers Reported thirty thousand technical innovations. **1972** *Vogue* Jan. 12/2 They wholesale to many shops. **1975** 'E. Lathen' *By Hook or by Crook* xiv. 137 Gregory takes care of the wholesaling in this country. Paul runs the retail stores. **1982** *Electr. Wholesaler* Sept. 40/1 He started a general electrical wholesaling firm. **1984** *Listener* 23 Feb. 9/2 There is the jobber, wholesaling shares and making money out of the margin.

wholescale (hōu·lskēil), *a.* [f. Whole *a.* + Scale *sb.*[3], influenced by Wholesale *sb., a., adv.*] = Wholesale *a.* 5. Cf. *full-scale.

1960 B. Bergonzi in F. Kermode *Living Milton* x. 168 Leavis's case..is not a mere critical reappraisal of Milton, but a whole-scale demolition. **1983** M. Edwardes *Back from Brink* v. 76 If we were going to run into this sort of problem over £22 million of investment in one factory, how could we contemplate a wholescale modernisation and new product programme across BL, running into hundreds of millions of pounds in dozens of locations? **1984** *Amer. Banker* 5 June 3/1 For middle-level executives, there will be some 'shifting, but not on a wholescale scale', he said.

wholewise, *adv.* Add: Also as quasi-*adj.*

1937 *Mind* XLVI. 252 The whole-wise working of the organism is further illustrated by the 'privileged postures' which we take up as a convenient background to various performances.

wholism (hōu·liz'm). [Alteration of *HOLISM, after Whole *sb.*] The doctrine or belief that wholes must be studied as such, and that the parts can only be understood in relation to the wholes to which they belong; the doctrine that evolutionary forces tend towards the forming of new and more complex wholes; = *HOLISM.

1939 J. E. Boodin *Social Mind.* p. vii, Two conceptions ..have recently been emphasized in philosophy and social theory, namely creative synthesis or emergence and wholism or gestaltism... Wholism means that..events can be understood only as figuring in a whole or gestalt. **1941** *Mind* L. 394 Boodin is fully justified in claiming both that he thought and wrote in the spirit of 'creative synthesis' and 'wholism', before these terms had been invented or had, at any rate, become popular. **1962** R. & H. Hauser *Fraternal Soc.* 9 The keynote of their work is 'Wholism'. **1981** *Amer. Jrnl. Clin. Biofeedback* IV. 33 The biofeedback experience also highlights the concept of wholism.

Hence **who·list** *a.* and *sb.*, **wholi·stic** *a.*, **wholi·stically** *adv.*

1941 *Mind* L. 397 As everyone knows who has studied the use of the concept of 'creative synthesis', and, in general, all 'wholistic' types of philosophy, thinkers of this school are not content to describe the Universe merely as making and unmaking wholes of various sorts. **1956** J. S. Bruner et al. in J. S. Bruner *Beyond Information Given* (1974) ix. 163 We shall refer to the ideal strategy just described as the wholist strategy. **1962** R. & H. Hauser *Fraternal Soc.* ii. ii. 121 As wholists we ask, is not all this..activity..useless. *Ibid.* iv. 181 Our approach to the problems of violence is wholistic. **1964** F. H. Blum in I. L. Horowitz *New Sociol.* 166 Being concerned with the totality of the human situation, he [sc. Mills] dealt with them [sc. key problems] wholistically. **1972** L. S. Hearnsaw in Cox & Dyson *20th-Cent. Mind* I. vii. 232 Between the wars a new brand of psychology was born, the psychology of personality, wholistic in its presuppositions. **1974** H. J. Klausmeier et al. *Conceptual Learning & Devel.* iii. 67 We rarely receive information in a nice sequence of positive instances so that we may adopt a wholist strategy. **1980** R. Herink *Psychotherapy Handbk.* 698 Wholistic therapy.

wholly, *adv.* Add: **1.** (Later example of *wholely.*)

1915 D. H. Lawrence *Rainbow* xii. 327 Then, and then only..could he act wholely, without cynicism and unreality.

3. Comb.: **wholly-owned** *a.*, applied to a company all of whose shares are owned by another company.

1964 *Financial Times* 11 Feb. 12/1 The directors..have decided to give the holders of Ordinary shares the opportunity of acquiring an interest in the wholly-owned subsidary. **1972** *Accountant* 21 Sept. 360/1 The UK company is a subsidiary—although not wholly-owned. **1976** *Scotsman* 20 Nov. 3/2 The plan is recommended by the boards of all the companies, who will become wholly-owned subsidiaries of the new Malaysian group.

whomp (hwǫmp), *sb. colloq.* (orig. and chiefly *U.S.*). [Echoic.] **a.** A heavy, low sound. **b.** A heavy blow; also *fig.*

1926 *Blackw. Mag.* May 595/2 Ever think of Piccadilly in the evening, and the 'whomp' of an orchestra starting up in some theatre? **1970** J. H. Gray *Boy from Winnipeg* 145 We got some special whomps just in case we had sneaked anything. **1977** R. L. Duncan *Temple Dogs* I. iii. 104 Corbett realized that he had heard a sound, a kind of muted whomp and the Colonel had been shot. **1979** *Washington Post* 4 Oct. A15/2 Liberal and conservative journals are good at least once a year for a whomp at the fat, spoiled, arrogant and pricey world they believe the average bureaucrat to live in. **1983** *Ibid.* 16 Oct. G4/4 He recruited bassist Tony Butler and drummer Mark Brzezicki. The massive and dramatic rhythmic whomp they provide reflects their studio work.

whomp (hwǫmp), *v. colloq.* (orig. and chiefly *U.S.*). [f. the sb.] **1.** *trans.* **a.** To defeat decisively. **b.** To strike (a person) hard, to hit, thump.

1952 *Britannica Bk. of Year* 667/1 *Whomp*, to defeat decisively. **1973** 'D. Shannon' *Spring of Violence* xi. 194 If you did something wrong at school you got whomped. **1979** D. Anthony *Long Hard Cure* ix. 79 He had a history of whomping women. **1984** *New Yorker* 1 Oct. 113/1 Tuggle keeps whomping us on the skull.

2. *trans.* With *up.* **a.** To produce quickly, with little preparation or planning.

1955 T. Taylor *Grand Inquest* ix. 241 This procedural paraphernalia was, to borrow Al Capp's apt expression, stricly 'whomped up'. **1957** *New Yorker* 23 Nov. 67/1, I remember the agreement very well. The two of you whomped it up the day after Bob got his overseas orders. **1961** J. Steinbeck *Winter of our Discontent* 190 Wives whomping up a last-ditch dinner. **1980** *Christian Sci. Monitor* 22 May B-16/3 When people ask questions about things I really don't know the answer to..the temptation is to put on my sage mantle and whomp up something.

b. To arouse or stir up (feeling, a disturbance, etc.).

1961 in Webster. **1970** *Daily Colonist* (Victoria, B.C.) 5 May 1/3 Antiwar groups held rallies at dozens of colleges and universities..to whomp up student interest in a national student strike during the closing weeks of the academic year. **1975** M. Amis *Dead Babies* xv. 74 To his hopelessness and grief, Philboyd could not act immediately; time was—when there'd have been enough tubby little rednecks like himself still living in Tara—they could have pitched right in there and whomped up a storm.

3. *intr.* To fall with a 'whomp'.

1960 *New Scientist* 14 Apr. 933/1 The Sunday edition of the *New York Times*..whomped to the floor outside my apartment door.

whoness (hū·nės). *rare.* [f. Who *pron.* (*sb.*) + -ness.] **a.** That which makes a person who he is. **b.** The state of being an isolated individual.

1922 [see *WHENCENESS]. **1931** *Times Lit. Suppl.* 28 May 422/4 A crisis of spiritual rebirth in which the personal will submit only after long struggle to an ineluctable impersonal destiny..thus escaping from the anguish of 'whoness'..into the peace of 'wholeness'.

whoof, *int.* (*sb.*). Add: **2.** Also **woof** (wŭf, wuf). (Expressing) a sound like that of a sudden expulsion of air (less sibilant than 'whoosh').

1921 [in Dict.]. **1921** 'K. Mansfield' *Scrapbk.* (1939) 182 The heavy baize door swung to with a 'woof'. **1936** Wodehouse *Laughing Gas* vii. 88 He came over to the arm-chair and sank into it with a luxurious whoof. **1945** *Penguin New Writing* XXIII. 10 Her great guns swing up... Then woof! with a sheet of flame that hides the ship she's hurled a packet of one-ton bricks at something out of sight. **1966** R. H. Rimmer *Harrad Experiment* (1967) 34 Woof! I'm pooped.

whoof, *v.* (in Dict. with Whoof *int.* (*sb.*)). Add: **2.** To make a sound as of air being expelled. Also *fig.*

1966 'L. Lane' *ABZ of Scouse* 117 *Whoof*, to pass wind. **1978** J. Updike *Coup* (1979) vi. 248 He took up a hand mike.., *whoofed* into it experimentally. **1979** *Homes & Gardens* June 126/1 'I am getting seriously worried about prices. They are going to whoof, like this.' And his arm rose at a steep angle from his desk and pointed somewhere in the direction of the stratosphere.

whoofle (hwŭ·f'l, hwu·f'l), *v.* [Echoic; cf. Whoof *int.* (*sb., v.*) and Whuffle *v.*] *intr.* To make a snorting, gurgling, or snuffling sound; (in quot. 1902 *trans.*, to take *up* with such a sound). Hence **whoo·fling** *vbl. sb.*

1902 H. F. Day *Pine Tree Ballads* 225 To have him fill his saucer and go whoofling up his tea. **1934** L. A. G. Strong *Don Juan & Wheelbarrow* 156 A whoofling and puffing behind him announced Joey. **1944** 'Brahms' & 'Simon' *No Nightingales* vi. 27 Mr. Blount sighed his content and moved the ledger to one side. He moved it over the chessboard and upset all the pieces. General Burlap whoofled.

whoom (hwum), *v.* [Echoic.] *intr.* To make a resonant booming or rushing sound. Hence as *sb.*

1936 L. Durrell *Spirit of Place* (1969) 41 Wild pigeon whoomed over. **1942** D. M. Crook *Spitfire Pilot* 90 The deep 'whoom' of a bursting bomb could be heard. **1956** C. D. Simak *Strangers in Universe* (1958) 21 He heard another jet whoom upward from the field. **1956** B. Holiday *Lady sings Blues* (1973) xi. 105 There was a whoom and this big tree crashed over with a wham and a bang.

whoompf (hwum(p)f), *int.* (*sb.*) Also **whoomph,** etc. [Echoic.] (Expressing) a sudden, violent rushing sound, as when a quantity of flammable material bursts into flame. Cf. the synonymous *WOOMPH *int.* (*sb.*, *adv.*).

1958 'W. HENRY' *Seven Men at Mimbres Springs* xv. 170 Then *whoomff!* land on it with all fours. **1962** *John o' London's* 6 Dec. 527/2 The whole place goes up in flames.., *whoomph.* **1973** D. LEES *Rape of Quiet Town* vii. 122 A rending crash of metal and a whoompf of flame. **1983** J. MANN *No Man's Island* xi. 145 Check for gas leaks. Light a match and—whoomph.

whoop, *sb.* Add: **1. c.** Slang phrases (orig. and chiefly *U.S.*): *a whoop and a holler* (and varr.): a short distance; *not to care a whoop* (and varr.): not to care one bit; to be indifferent.

[**1753** C. GIST *Jrnl.* 27 Dec. (1893) 85 We grew uneasy, and then he said two whoops might be heard to his cabin.] **1815** [see sense 1 a in Dict.]. **1904** *Baltimore American* 30 Aug. 6 The voting public as a whole doesn't care a whoop about the question. **1908** J. LONDON *Let.* 27 Oct. (1966) 268, I don't care a whoop in high water whether you get married..or not. **1920** E. H. JONES *Road to En-Dor* (ed. 2) xxvii. 313, I don't believe Enver Pasha cares two whoops whether I've had syphilis or not. **1924** WODEHOUSE *Bill the Conqueror* vii. 141 'It isn't as if she cared a hang about him.' 'Doesn't she?' 'Not a whoop.' **1936** E. B. WHITE *Let.* 24 Dec. (1976) 145, I don't give a whoop about dignity. **1951** L. CRAIG *Singing Hills* 155 They lived in a cabin which Miriam said was three whoops and two hollers away. **1957** J. AGEE *Death in Family* II. x. 157, I wouldn't give a whoop if you got blind drunk, best thing you could do. **1974** D. SEARS *Lark in Clear Air* i. 14 A string of hounds..were only a whoop and a bellow behind father.

whoop, *v.* Add: Also with pronuncs. (hwūp, wūp). **1. e.** *whoop it up*: for 'U.S. slang' read colloq. (orig. U.S.)'; also, to stir up political enthusiasm; also *whoop things up*. (Further examples.)

1888 *Century Mag.* May 156 His rival is a prominent politician, with an abundance of party workers to 'whoop it up' for him. **1891** B. HARTE *First Family Tasajara* i. 8 What did we whoop things up here last spring to elect Kennedy to the legislation [*sic*] for? **1935** WODEHOUSE *Luck of Bodkins* iii. 37 You didn't by any chance..whoop it up with those mysterious foreign adventuresses who haunt those parts? **1951** E. PAUL *Springtime in Paris* ii. 19, I supposed that elsewhere in France there might be as many young enthusiasts whooping it up for De Gaulle. **1954** B. HECHT *Child of Century* IV. 230 Sherwood [Anderson] would be able to whoop it up for me in a half-dozen periodicals which had come to consider his word as artistic law. **1956** 'J. WYNDHAM' *Seeds of Time* 136 Thousands of trippers whooping it up with pandemonium for most of the night. **1959** 'N. BLAKE' *Widow's Cruise* 93 Some premonition seemed to cast its shadow over the revellers, in spite of Mr. Bentinck-Jones's efforts to whoop things up. **1983** *Listener* 8 Sept. 24/2 The broadcasting moguls and their groupies whooped it up in Edinburgh and other select watering holes.

f. *whoop up* (trans.): to arouse enthusiasm for; to promote or praise with vigour; also, to give a boost to.

1885 *South Florida Sentinel* (Orlando) 5 Aug. 3/3 Whoop up Florida to those Yankees. **1893** [see *STAND-OFF *sb.* 3]. **1904** *Sun* (N.Y.) 8 Sept. 10 The bail was reduced to $10,000, but was whooped up to $15,000 when Larry was re-arrested. **1950** *Sun* (Baltimore) 6 Nov. 3/2 Spokesmen for each party whooped up interest in the outcome. **1970** *Globe & Mail* (Toronto) 26 Sept. 6/5 All human progress, even in morals, has been the work of men who have doubted the current moral values, not of men who have whooped them up and tried to enforce them. **1976** *Listener* 23 Sept. 375/1 If there was any temptation to whoop the original up into contemporary shape, he resisted it. **1983** *Listener* 14 July 19/2 It somehow won that year's Prix Italia,..which so immensely whooped me up that I galloped down to Venice to collect.

whoop-de-do (hū:pdidū·, hw-, w-). *U.S. colloq.* Also **whoop-de-doo**, etc. [A fanciful extension of WHOOP *v.* or *WHOOPS *int.*] A fuss, bustle, or commotion; a 'to-do'; *spec.* in *Motor-cycling*, a very bumpy stretch of road.

[**1895** S. CRANE *Red Badge of Courage* xvi. 160 'Whoop-a-dadee,' said a man, 'here we are! Everybody fightin'.'] **1929** W. FAULKNER *Sound & Fury* 321 But I cant have all this whoop-de-do and sulking at mealtimes. **1949** S. LEWIS *God Seeker* vi. 34 But what's the use of a loud-mouthed evangelical like your Reverend Chippler,..with his..general circus whoop-tee-do? **1962** J. STEINBECK *Trav. with Charlie* 186 This is not patriotic whoop-de-do; it is a carefully observed fact. **1976** B. KAYSING *Fell's Beginner's Guide to Motorcycling* 256 *Whoop-de-doo*, a road that goes up and down like a roller coaster track. **1980** *Dirt Bike* Oct. 15/1 Very soon we were all lying beside the road, for even though the road looked good at first, it was plagued with whoopdiedoos, and we came into them a little hot. **1981** *Verbatim* Spring 24/1 There was many an angry powwow and much whoop-de-do, but in the end, of course, the bigwigs won. **1985** *Dirt Bike* Mar. 27/1 Through whoopdedos it takes a full stroke without bottoming harshly and keeps giving you maximum ground contact.

whoopee (see below), *int.* and *sb.* [f. WHOOP *int.* + -EE[2].] **A.** *int.* (hw-, wupī·) An exclamation of exuberant joy. Cf. *HOOP-EE *int.*

1862 *Harper's Mag.* July 282/1 He yelled at the top of his voice, 'Whoopee! Whiskey only twenty-five cents a gallon!' **1890** KIPLING *Barrack-Room Ballads* (1892) 32 Whoopee! Tear 'im, puppy! **1895** *Outing* XXVI. 428/2 John's 'whoopee' had caused a little ebon..to set open the gates. **1932** B. C. PLOWRIGHT *For Groupers Only* iii. 23 Whoopee!! this is great news! **1974** *Listener* 19 Sept. 355/3 You take your second MB..and once you've passed this—whoopee! You're virtually guaranteed to qualify.

B. *sb.* (hw-, wu·pī; hw-, wū·pī) Exuberant or boisterous merry-making; revelry; †a lively or rowdy party; phr. *to make whoopee*, to indulge in such behaviour; (in quot. 1928, to behave amorously). Cf. *WHOOP-UP. *colloq.*

1928 G. KAHN *Makin' Whoopee* (song), Another bride, another June, Another sunny honeymoon, Another season, another reason for making whoopee! **1929** *Punch* 24 July 86/2 A London hostess, writing to a gossip page, said—'I am giving a Whoopee. Do come to it.' **1930** *Sat. Even. Post* 13 Dec. 25/1 Novelists portray him as the gin-drinking patron saint of whoopee. **1930** E. WAUGH *Vile Bodies* iv. 51 Noel and Audrey are having a little whoopee on Saturday evening. **1933** DYLAN THOMAS *Poems* (1971) 84 Even heaven has a smell Of putrefying angels who Make deadly whoopee in the blue. **1938** F. D. SHARPE *Sharpe of Flying Squad* ii. 27 Boys and girls at the end of an evening's 'whoopee', would come out of a night club and take the first car they saw for a joy-ride. **1945** M. SOAMES *Let.* 24 July in *Clementine Churchill* (1979) xxiv. 385 The evening broke up about midnight, in a general atmosphere of whoopee and goodwill. **1949** F. SWINNERTON *Doctor's Wife comes to Stay* 109 'I thought you and Mother would make whoopee here—' 'Whoopee!' muttered the Doctor. 'Disgusting word for a disgusting occupation!' 'Oh, just noisy hopelessness,' explained Rex. 'Despair set to rhythm.' **1972** D. FRANCIS *Smokescreen* ii. 26 We had left the bright lights, the adulation, and the whoopee, and gone to live in the country. **1976** *Times Lit. Suppl.* 13 Aug. 1009/5 Frustrated laughers, dancers and makers of whoopee. **1984** Q. CRISP *Manners from Heaven* vii. 74 'It often happens that when we think we're making whoopee we're only making a *whoops*! instead,' I replied.

2. Comb.: **whoopee cushion,** a cushion which when sat upon emits a sound like that of the breaking of wind.

1960 *Spectator* 3 June 804 The comically battered face of a whoopee cushion. **1975** P. THEROUX *Great Railway Bazaar* viii. 98 These people..were as hard to silence as whoopee cushions. **1977** *Sunday Times* (Colour Suppl.) 6 June 42/3 Andrew..has..a taste for practical jokes..slipping whoopee-cushions where his father or mother was likely to sit.

whooper. Add: **a.** Also **whooper-up.**

1904 *N.Y. Times* 4 July 1 The only candidate who has back of him a boom which is not characterized by 'whooper-up' methods. **1909** J. R. WARE *Passing Eng.* 266/1 *Whooperups*.., inferior, noisy singers. **1932** H. CRANE *Let.* 12 Apr. (1965) 408 They're generally preferable to all the trained and professional strummers and whoopers-up I've ever heard.

b. Also, = *whooping crane* s.v. WHOOPING *ppl. a.* in Dict. and Suppl.

1860 *Southern Cultivator* XVIII. 324 Here [in Florida] is found every grade, kind, size, and color..from the beautiful little mourning Dove..to the tall Whooper, of 5 or 6 feet high. **1838** C. H. MATSCHAT *Suwannee River* 286 It is the favorite haunt of the gray whoopers. **1979** *Time* 2 Apr. 23/3 Whatever he felt about the whooper, Carter appreciated the award, which recognized his support for environmental protection and recreation.

whooping, *ppl. a.* Add: **a. whooping crane** (earlier and later examples).

1731, 1837 Whooping crane [see HOOPING *ppl.a.*[1]]. **1879** N. H. BISHOP *Four Months in Sneak-Box* 108 Whooping-cranes..in little flocks, dotted the grassy prairies. **1938** M. K. RAWLINGS *Yearling* x. 94 He pointed. 'The whoopin' cranes is dancin'.' **1976** *Daily Colonist* (Victoria, B.C.) 7 May 10/6 A scraggly-looking whooping crane chick, hatched this week at the government wildlife centre here.

c. *fig.* Unusually large; whopping; also, very noisy, wild, uproarious. Also as quasi-*adv.*, hugely, immensely. *slang* (chiefly *U.S.*).

1866 'MARK TWAIN' *Let.* 30 July (1917) I. v. 115 The first few days we came at a whooping gait. **1906** E. DYSON *Fact'ry 'Ands* vii. 88 Odgson..was then lyin' in ther City cells, whoopin' delirious. **1939** G. ADE *Let.* 7 June (1973) 211 Let's make each one of these parties a whooping success. **1969** FABIAN & BYRNE *Groupie* (1970) xiii. 94 They unstrap me and shoot two whooping great penicillin injections into my backside.

whoops (hwūps, hwups), *int.* [Var. of *OOPS.] An exclamation of dismay or surprise, usu. upon stumbling, or realizing an obvious mistake. Also **whoo·psie(-daisy)** *int.* = *UPSIDAISY.

1925 *New Yorker* 26 Sept. 8/2 (*caption*) Whoopsie Daisy! **1937** E. POUND *Let.* Jan. (1971) 287 Whoops! And do I *envy* you. I *do.* **1957** J. KEROUAC *On Road* (1958) II. viii. 159 Whoops, I thought I was on the wrong side of the road. **1969** C. ARMSTRONG *Seven Seats to Moon* xiii. 126 The woman said, 'Whoopsie', and her strong hand came under his armpit. **1973** G. TALBOT *Ten Seconds from Now* xii. 161, I was appalled at the tape playback to hear that I had punctuated my commentary by a 'whoops!' every minute or so. **1980** G. M. FRASER *Mr American* xviii. 328 'Whoops!' said Pip... 'Claridge's, eh? That's what I like to hear!'

whoop-up (hū·pʌp, hw-, w-). Chiefly *N. Amer.* f. vbl. phr. *to whoop it up*: see WHOOP *v.* 1 e.] An instance of 'whooping it up'; a noisy celebration or party; revelry.

1913 I. COWIE *Company of Adventurers* 319 As soon as the general 'whoop-up' began, all the traders..packed up their outfits snugly and retired. **1927** *Daily Express* 5 Oct. 3/3 The Ward Room is—apart from the 'whoops up' natural to lonely men—noted for its air of sober responsibility. **1953** D. CUSHMAN *Stay away, Joe* 22 Ain't you going to have no dance, no rodeo, whoop-up? **1968** E. S. RUSSENHOLT *Heart of Continent* III. ix. 153 For 'whoop-up juice' they [*sc.* whisky traders] reclaim the rifles Indian hunters have just bought with a year's hunting. **1976** D. HEFFRON *Crusty Crossed* xiv. 101, I thought it quite..sensible of Big Point to have one great annual public whoop-up in which to give a little exercise to the witch and devil of one's soul.

whoosh, *v.* Add: Also **woosh. 1.** (Later examples.) Also, to move rapidly with a rushing sound.

1909 H. G. WELLS *Tono-Bungay* II. ii. 163 Make it all slick, and then make it woosh. **1922** D. H. LAWRENCE *Aaron's Rod* xxi. 306 You want to whoosh off in a nice little love-whoosh and lose yourself. **1966** I. JEFFERIES *House-Surgeon* viii. 156 The blood was wooshing in and Bernard nodded.

2. *trans.* To cause to move rapidly with a rushing sound. Also *fig.* Const. *up*, to enliven.

1909 H. G. WELLS *Tono-Bungay* II. ii. 162 A Real Live Thing! Wooshing it up! Making it buzz and spin! **1920** D. H. LAWRENCE *Touch & Go* 7 A system of vacuum tubes for whooshing Bradburys about from one to the other. **1956** W. SANSOM *Loving Eye* 102 Cars wooshed water-spray on the wet macadam. **1968** B. HINES *Kestrel for Knave* 27 He whooshed the curtains open and switched the light off. **1971** *Sunday Express* (Johannesburg) 28 Mar. (Home Jrnl.) 2/2 (Advt.), Removable Fibre-fill padlets whoosh you into high young curves, naturally. **1982** *Nature* 13 May 91/1 Chrétien will be the first Western astronaut to be whooshed into space by a Soviet rocket.

whoosh, *sb.* Add: Also **woosh.** (Earlier and later examples.) Also, an exclamation 'whoosh!'; a movement accompanied by a rushing sound; a gushing or 'whooshing' style.

1880 'MARK TWAIN' *Tramp Abroad* xx. 194 He fetched a prodigious '*Whoosh!*' to relieve his lungs. **1909** H. G. WELLS *Tono-Bungay* III. iv. 391 Once or twice before you've stepped in—with that sort of Woosh of yours. **1934** —— *Exper. in Autobiogr.* I. i. 37 Just because of that constitutional apathy it will be characteristically free from individual Woosh. **1962** 'R. GORDON' *Doctor in Swim* i. 9 We sat for a moment listening to the woosh of the jets. **1976** *Globe & Mail* (Toronto) 8 Nov. 16/6 When I develop a mental picture of the person I'm affecting, my objectivity goes out the window in a woosh of sympathy. **1984** *Listener* 14 June 32/3 We may be used to the idea of pressing buttons on commercial synthesisers and summoning whooshes of space-age sound.

whoosh, *int.* Also **woosh.** [f. the vb.] An exclamation evocative of or accompanying a sudden explosive rushing sound or movement.

1899 S. R. CROCKETT *Kit Kennedy* xxxvii. 261 The cravin' wad juist bank up like a water ahint a dam—and then—*whoosh*, awa' she gaed. **1909** H. G. WELLS *Tono-Bungay* II. ii. 162 That's you, steady and long and piling-up,—then, wo-oo-oo-oo-osh. **1927** *Blackw. Mag.* Apr. 488/1 John said, 'Woosh! some armful. Look out for the eggs.' **1936** 'R. HYDE' *Check to your King* 69 The Princess..shouts 'Whoosh!' **1949** DYLAN THOMAS *Let.* 13 Oct. (1966) 328 Bills and demand notes, at me like badgers, whoosh! **1965** *Family Circle* Oct. 13/1 Plain lonesome? Whoosh, it's a friend. **1977** *Sounds* 9 July 19/2 Onstage we just go like, woosh!

whoosy, whoozy, varr. WOOZY *a.* in Dict. and Suppl.

whop, *sb.* Add: Also **wop.**

1895 KIPLING in *Youth's Compan.* 19 Sept. 442/4 Then he..drew up with a doleful *wop! wop! wop!* by the side of the great forty-five-ton, six-wheel coupled,..Number Twenty-five. **1899** W. S. CHURCHILL *River War* I. xiii. 423 The *wop!* of the distant explosion came back, like the echo of the report.

whore, *sb.* Add: **1. c.** A male prostitute; any promiscuous or unprincipled person. (Esp. as a term of abuse.)

1633 [see WORM *sb.* 10 b]. **1906** J. JOYCE *Let.* 19 Aug. (1966) II. 152 He began to shout..when the lazy whores of priests began to chant. **1957** P. KEMP *Mine were of Trouble* vi. 108 Lyall would interrupt with..'But surely you can't expect the Irish to be any use in Spain? There aren't any hedges here for them to shoot from behind.'.. Lawler would storm out, shouting: 'Ye great buckin' whore!' **1968** E. GAINES in A. Chapman *New Black Voices* (1972) 103 'You hear me whore?' 'I might be a whore, but I'm not a merciless killer,' he said. **1976** *New Yorker* 12 Jan. 73/2 Gig Young can play the top whore in 'The Killer Elite' because his sad eyes suggest that he has no expectations and no illusions left about anything.

4. *whore-like* adj. (later example); **whore-hunt** *v.* (later example); **whoremistress,** a brothel-keeper; **whore's egg** *N. Amer.* (chiefly *Newfoundland*) = SEA-URCHIN 1; **whore-shop** *slang*, a brothel.

1931 R. CAMPBELL *Georgiad* i. 15 Lovelorn poets..troop whore-hunting down the country lanes. **1974** H. J. PARKER *View from Boys* 213 'A right scrubber' is a girl who's rough-looking, whorelike. **1922** JOYCE *Ulysses*

515 Bella Cohen, a massive whoremistress enters. **1969** A. MARIN *Rise with Wind* xii. 154 Consejo..works for a whoremistress we call Tía Concha. **1829** T. C. HALIBURTON *Hist. & Statist. Acct. Nova Scotia* II. ix. 405 Shell fish. Whore's egg. **1930** *Amer. Speech* V. 393 *Whore's egg,*..a small spring crustacean esteemed by the Italians as a delicacy. **1948** Z. N. HURSTON *Seraph on Suwanee* 296 That damn whore's egg! Ruin you if only one spine gets into your hand. **1972** E. STAEBLER *Cape Breton Harbour* ix. 85 You be careful when you's swimming that you don't step on a whore's egg, they sea urchins is full o' prickles will give you a fester. **1938** V. S. PRITCHETT *You make your own Life* 79 What a town like this wants is a couple of good whore shops and a factory. **1972** A. MACVICAR *Golden Venus Affair* vi. 67, I hate The Golden Venus... It's just a whoreshop.

whore, *v.* Add: **1. c.** *intr.* fig. To pursue or seek *after* (something false or unworthy). In allusion to Exod. xxxiv. 15. Cf. WHORING *vbl. sb.* (quot. 1535).

1913 E. POUND *Let.* 13 Aug. (1971) 21 The unspeakable vulgo will I suppose hear of him [*sc.* F. M. Hueffer] after our deaths. In the meantime they whore after their Bennetts and their Galsworthys and their unspeakable canaille. **1937** J. M. MURRY *Necessity of Pacificism* 24 The intellience of Socialism went a-whoring after the strange gods of Russia. **1970** R. LONG in A. Chapman *New Black Voices* (1972) 421 The University was whoring after strange gods, they all seemed to say: technology, athletics, materialism. **1972** *Language* XLVIII. 425, I do not accept Chomsky's conception of social scientists as universally whoring after the surface features of other sciences, neglecting all fundamental problems, and taking refuge in spurious precision and trivialities.

2. For ? *Obs.* read Now *rare* and add later example.

1969 A. HUNTER *Gently Coloured* iii. 33 Some friend squeezing you dry, whoring your sister.

whore-house. 1. For † *Obs.* read: Revived in recent (chiefly *U.S.*) use. (Later examples.)

1909 in J. A. & A. Lomax *Amer. Ballads & Folk Songs* (1960) 104 Frankie went down to de whore-house, Rang de whore-house bell, Says 'Tell me, is my lovin' Albert here? Caze Frankie's gwine to raise some hell—Oh, he's my man, but he's a-doin' me wrong.' **1935** J. STEINBECK *Tortilla Flat* i. 25 'Pilon!..I am an heir! I own two houses.' 'Whore houses?' Pilon asked hopefully. **1951** J. MASTERS *Nightrunners Bengal* I. vi. 82 Every one knew her as the madam of a high-grade whore-house. **1978** G. GREENE *Human Factor* III. iii. 123 'If you want to fuck a black whore,' Captain Van Donck interrupted with impatience, 'why don't you go to a whore-house in Lesotho or Swaziland?' **1982** *Times* 22 May 8/1 Prospectors came by the thousand, saloons and whore-houses were erected.

2. *attrib.* and *Comb.* **a.** Simple attrib., as *whore-house bell, owner, perfume, scum.* **b.** Designating or pertaining to a style of music, esp. jazz, played in brothels, as *whore-house music, piano.* **c.** *Comb.*, as *whore-house madam* = *MADAM 3 c (*d*).

1909 Whore-house bell [see sense 1 above]. **1938** D. BAKER *Young Man with Horn* III. i. 141 You certainly play whorehouse piano, fella, and nigger whorehouse at that. **1946** R. BLESH *Shining Trumpets* xiii. 295 This rich and earthy piano playing, called by extreme jazz purists with an ear for the picturesquely accurate, 'whore-house piano'. **1949** R. CHANDLER *Little Sister* xvii. 110 A very cheap grade of whore-house perfume. **1954** W. FAULKNER *Fable* 379 Shoot now, you whorehouse scum. **1956** B. HOLIDAY *Lady sings Blues* (1973) i. 8, I guess I'm not the only one who heard their first good jazz in a whore-house... A lot of white people first heard jazz in places like Alice Dean's, and they helped label jazz 'whorehouse music'. **1975** G. V. HIGGINS *City on Hill* vi. 150 When you try to talk about something else, it's like trying to discuss cryogenics with a whorehouse madam.

whoremaster. Delete bracketed etymological note and *Obs.* or *arch.*, and add: **2.** *spec.* A procurer or pimp.

1864 in WEBSTER. **1922** E. E. CUMMINGS *Enormous Room* vii. 163 Now I must tell you what happened to the poor Spanish Whoremaster. **1964** in Hamblett & Deverson *Generation X* 94 Johnny knew just when to corrupt and when to give the old ego a boost. He's one of the great whoremasters of all time, working on the principle of the carrot and the stick. **1977** M. T. BLOOM *13th Man* (1978) vii. 133 The newcomers had little money and.. they got tempted by the whoremasters.

whoreson. For *Obs.* or *arch.* read Now *arch.* and add: **a.** (Later examples.)

1926 [see *INGLE *sb.*[2]]. **1975** *Weekend Mag.* (Montreal) 1 Nov. 21/1 If the whoreson who dropped his socks into the chamber pot and sold the results to a lantern jaws like you is not at a rope's end since this fortnight, there is no justice left on earth!

b. (Later example.)

1909 E. POUND *Exultations* 14 You whoreson dog, Papiols, come!

Whorfian (hwǭ·ɹfiăn), *a.* [f. the name of the American linguist Benjamin Lee *Whorf* (1897–1941) + -IAN.] Designating the views and theories of B. L. Whorf, esp. in *Whorfian hypothesis*, the theory that one's perception of the world is influenced or determined by the structure of one's native language (also *Whorf hypothesis*). Cf. *SAPIR-WHORF HYPOTHESIS.

1957 R. K. MERTON *Social Theory* (rev. ed.) ii. 92 It is the extreme Whorfian position which Joshua Whatmough attacks. **1963** J. LYONS *Structural Semantics* iii. 40 The view expressed in this quotation from Sapir has been championed more recently by Whorf, and has come to be known within linguistics as the 'Whorfian hypothesis'. **1964** R. H. ROBINS *Gen. Linguistics* ii. 80 This is part of what has come to be known as the 'Whorf hypothesis'. **1968** M. BLACK *Labyrinth of Lang.* iv. 75 Some interesting attempts have been made to determine the validity of Whorfian ideas. **1978** *Language* LIV. 167 His chapter on personal context contains discussions of the Whorfian hypothesis.

Hence **Who·rfianism**, a Whorfian conception; Whorf's theories regarded *collect.*

1963 J. LYONS *Structural Semantics* iii. 40 For a strong and convincing attack on the more extreme aspects of 'Whorfianism', cf. M. Black, 'Linguistic relativity'. **1978** *Language* LIV. 267 Parry's notion that formulaic language imposes formulaic thought is a kind of Whorfianism run wild.

whorish, *a.* For *rare* or *Obs.* read *arch.* and add: **1. a.** (Later examples.)

1948 D. WELCH *Brave & Cruel* 245 Mary..had nothing to take her mind from the hideous picture of a breast pump, a whorish wife and an idiot baby. **1981** V. CANNING *Boy on Platform One* iv. 60 Whorish..the word swam gently into his mind. Whore, too, she was.

b. (Later examples.)

1942 D. WELCH *Jrnl.* 30 Aug. (1952) 7 When we had.. pushed back the whorish, dirty red satin curtain. **1967** A. LASKI *Seven Other Years* iv. 56 It was a charming dress..virginal in colour, whorish in cut. **1980** A. E. FISHER *Midnight Men* iv. 45 Bathrooms should reflect.. the woman of the house... I'd like a sort of whorish pink.

whorishly *adv.* (later example).

1977 *Listener* 25 Aug. 246/3 The gratuitous violence, slotted whoreishly into the sequences.

whorl, *sb.* Add: **3. b.** A configuration in finger-prints.

1880, etc. [see *LOOP *sb.*[1] 4 h]. **1954** F. CHERRILL *Cherrill of Yard* vi. 62, I noticed particularly the patterns on the ends of the fingers, for they were of the whorl type. **1977** *Sci. Amer.* Dec. 141/1 The resulting patterns are known to the dermatologist respectively as loops, triradii and whorls.

whory, *a.* For *rare* read Formerly *rare* and add later examples.

1955 J. KEROUAC in *Paris Rev.* Winter 11 The whorey smell of a big city. **1967** K. GILES *Death & Mr. Prettyman* i. 18 London was as whorey then as now. **1976** *New Yorker* 15 Nov. 180/3 At twenty she was taking care not only of herself and her child but also of a tubercular half sister, also cast off by their whorey mother. **1980** N. FREELING *Castang's City* xxii. 148 It's not a whory setup; three of these dames live there and they're secretarial types.

whose, *pron.* **3.** (Later examples.)

1906 CONRAD *Mirror of Sea* vii. 33 A newspaper of sound principles, but whose staff *will* persist in 'casting' anchors. **1927** E. BOWEN *Hotel* vi. 57 She looked down.. and saw a little house, with a blue door whose colour delighted her. **1958** I. MURDOCH *Bell* iv. 47 Toby.. marvelled at this light which is no light..and whose strength is seen only in the sharpness of cast shadows. **1968** J. LYONS *Introd. Theoretical Linguistics* 55 Whether there are, or could be, two languages whose vocabularies are to no degree whatsoever isomorphic with one another is a question with which we need not be concerned. **1981** I. MCEWAN *Comfort of Strangers* ix. 122 There were pictures whose context she understood immediately.

whosis (hū·zis). Also **whoosis.** [Colloq. contraction of 'who is this?' (WHO *pron.*); in quot. 1923, perh. repr. 'whose is this?'] 'What's-his-name', 'so-and-so'. Often following a title, as *Mr. Whosis.*

1923 J. E. BAXTER *Locker Room Ballads* 8 That number one's a Big League Green As slick as Whoosis Vaseline. **1939** R. STOUT *Some buried Caesar* vi. 72 He.. introduced himself as Mr. Whosis, Assistant District Attorney. **1953** G. W. BRACE *Spire* xxiii. 229, I suppose.. you mean he should go and see your precious Dr. Whoosis? **1962** J. D. SALINGER *Franny & Zooey* 130 How was the script? Did it come? You said Whosis—Mr. LeSage or whatever his name is—was going to drop it off with the doorman. **1965** I. FLEMING *Man with Golden Gun* vi. 89 Don't forget one thing, Mister Whoosis. I rile mighty easy.

whosit (hū·zit). Also **whoosit, whoozit, whozit.** [Colloq. contraction of 'who is it' (WHO *pron.*).] = prec.

1948 'P. QUENTIN' *Run to Death* xxi. 156 *Ye Old Antique Shoppe* with little leaded glass panes. *Mother Whosit's Chicken Kitchen.* **1951** *Blue Bk. Mag.* Jan. 24/3 Mr. Whoozit—please come quickly. **1951** 'J. TEY' *Daughter of Time* viii. 112 Someone, say, insists that Lady Whoosit never had a child. **1967** O. NORTON *Now lying Dead* i. 9 That's what I've got to work out... Like Angela Whoosit was telling us. **1977** J. FLEMING *Every Inch a Lady* I. i. 7 Arrival..of Mrs Whozit, the lady help.

whump (hwɒmp), *v.* Also **wump.** [f. as next.] **1.** *intr.* To make a dull thudding sound; to move with a 'whump'; to bang or thump; to strike (with a thud).

1897 E. TERRY *Let.* 5 Feb. in *Ellen Terry & Shaw* (1931) 126 Not a single speech do I know yet, and my head is thumping and wumping. **1928** *Blackw. Mag.* Jan. 5/1 The look-out sentry..whumped twice, briskly, on his hand-gong. **1939** *Life* 11 Dec. 26 Taft of Ohio sturdily whumped at the New Deal's 'insane deficit policy'. **1981** B. GRANGER *Schism* xi. 89 The windshield wipers whumped, whumped slowly across the streaky glass.

2. *trans.* To strike heavily or with a 'whump'.

1974 D. E. WESTLAKE *Help* (1975) iii. 20, I would then adjust the rubber stamp.., wump it onto the stamp pad, wump it onto the envelope. **1976** *National Observer* (U.S.) 24 Jan. 19/3 What had been lost at Waterloo and Sedan could be won back by whumping mud forts in the Sahel.

Hence **whu·mping** *vbl. sb.* and *ppl. a.*

1928 *Blackw. Mag.* Jan. 2/2 The occasional whumping and booming of war-gongs. **1977** P. DICKINSON *Walking Dead* II. viii. 206 There was a slow, wumping explosion

whump (hwɒmp), *sb.* (and *int.*) Also **wump.** [Echoic: cf. *bump, thump,* etc.] A dull thudding sound, as of a body landing heavily. Also *int.* Cf. *WHOMP.

1915 D. O. BARNETT *Let.* 6 May (1915) 130 Then there was a wump over beyond, and a young howitzer shell went zip over my trench. **1922** *Chambers's Jrnl.* 7 Oct. 707/1 The globe suddenly swung in a long arc across some hidden gully in the bottom and fetched up with a stunning 'wump' on the slope of the other side. **1926** GALSWORTHY *Escape* I. ii. 32 Still—up on the ladder and down with a whump—it hits 'em [*sc.* gentlemen] harder than it does the others. **1930** C. R. SAMSON *Fights & Flights* II. iv. 181 '*Wump*' fell a second bomb. **1967** *Boston Herald* 1 Apr. 20/2 (*caption*) Whump! **1976** *New Yorker* 8 Mar. 106/2, I heard this funny sound: a kind of *whummpp.*

whunk (hwɒnk), *sb.* (and *v.*) *rare.* Also **whonk.** [Echoic.] A dull hollow sound, as of a bullet striking something. Also as *v. intr.*, to strike with a 'whunk'.

App. only in the work of Hemingway.

1935 E. HEMINGWAY *Green Hills Afr.* II. iii. 53 We had both heard the whunk of the bullet. *Ibid.* II. iv. 76, I heard the *whonk* of the bullet. **1936** —— in *Hearst's Internat.* Sept. 168/1 He heard a *whunk* that meant that the bullet was home. *Ibid.* 170/3 Hearing the bullets whunk into him.

whup (hwɒp), Sc. var. of WHIP *v.* (q.v.). Also *U.S. colloq.* and *dial.* (Examples, esp. of senses 6, 12 of the vb.) Also **whu·pping** *vbl. sb.*

1893 H. A. SHANDS *Some Peculiarities of Speech in Mississippi* 68 *Whup,*..Negro for *whip.* **1906** *Dialect Notes* III. 164 *Whup,*..to vanquish, to punish, to tire. 'That *whups* me.' **1929** W. FAULKNER *Sanctuary* (1981) xi. 132 You done whupped him. **1939** J. STEINBECK *Grapes of Wrath* xxviii. 504 Whyn't ya whup her, Ma?.. Go on, give her a whup. **1948** A. LOMAX in A. Dundes *Mother Wit* (1973) 481/1 Give him a whuppin'. **1950** PATTERSON & CONRAD *Scottsboro Boy* III. ii. 193, I told the warden I was not guilty of the charge and didn't want to be whupped. **1968** *Punch* 25 Sept. 451/2 The Matt Dillon urge to 'whup' the Commies. **1972** J. GORES *Dead Skip* v. 31 He might have come after Bart..because he wanted to whup a nigger? **1974** W. GARNER *Big enough Wreath* vii. 94 You swore there never was a whupping could make you holler.

whuss (hwɒs). U.S. (chiefly Black English) colloq. abbrev. of 'what is..?'

1935 Z. N. HURSTON *Mules & Men* (1970) I. iii. 74 Whuss de matter, Jack? **1938** C. HIMES *Pork Chop Paradise* in *Black on Black* (1973) 174 Whuss yo' name? **1977** *Rolling Stone* 16 June 11/2 Whuss happnin'?

whut (hwɒt), U.S. dial. and Black English var. of WHAT *pron.*

1909 *Dialect Notes* III. 387 *Whut,* what. A common pronunciation. **1929** W. FAULKNER *Sanctuary* (1981) viii. 94, I couldn't tell and wouldn't even keer whut I was eatin. **1936** M. MITCHELL *Gone with Wind* v. lix. 996 Miss Melly, you know whut he done? **1961** J. JAHN in A. Dundes *Mother Wit* (1973) 101/1 Whut makes yore head so red. **1973** *Black World* July 62/2 Well, so whut.

why, *adv.* (*sb., int.*) Add: **I. 1. d.** With the negative form of the simple present tense in formulating a positive suggestion, as 'why don't I (we, etc.)..?'

1949 D. SMITH *I capture Castle* xii. 212 Why don't I drive you over to hear it now? **1974** G. MITCHELL *Winking at Brim* vi. 54 Mummy brought a couple of thermos flasks... Why don't I go and collect one? **1982** R. DOYLE *Havana Special* vii. 182 Why don't I stop by her compartment..and see how she is?

3. b. Duplicated in phr. *why, oh why..?*, as an emphatic interrogative, expressing dismay, disapproval, or complete lack of comprehension of another's actions; 'why on earth..?'

1865 M. ARNOLD *Let.* 23 July (1895) I. 294 Why, oh, why do not you and Edward come to the Black Forest and join us? *a* **1884** T. H. HUXLEY *Let.* in *Henry Bristow Ltd. Catal.* (1981) No. 269. 14 My students..cannot get copies of the second edition of the Biology book. Why oh why was it not ready by October. **1934** N. MARSH *Man lay Dead* xi. 194 Why, oh why, did the murderer sound the gong? **1961** 'E. LATHEN' *Banking on Death* (1962) viii. 70 Why, oh why, had she been so bitchy to his wife? **1975** *Times* 8 Mar. 13/7 Why, Oh why does Rolls-Royce.. name its latest product after an area of French marshland?

VI. 9. *Comb.* **why-question,** a question inquiring after the reason for something; one which is introduced by the word 'why'. Cf. *WH 2.

1973 A. DUNDES *Mother Wit* 568 'Why' questions are always difficult to answer. **1978** *Language* LIV. 71 A *that*-clause can be the basis of a *why*-question when it is assigned the semantic status of the volunteered stance of the subject of the verb whose complement it is.

Hence as *v. intr.*, to ask the question 'why?' (chiefly as *pres. ppl.*); also **why·ing** *vbl. sb.*

1926 H. PEARSON *Whispering Gallery* ii. 19, I made the mistake of doing or dying, but at the same time why-ing. **1928** D. H. LAWRENCE *Phoenix II* (1968) 520 Why indeed? But once you start whying, there's no end to it. **1932** E. M. BRENT-DYER *Chalet Girls in Camp* i. 24 'Why?'..'For goodness' sake don't start why-ing, Rix!' **1959** *Times Lit. Suppl.* 2 Jan. 7/1 (*heading*) Howing and whying.

whydunit (hwəidʊ·nit). *slang.* Also **why-dunnit.** [f. WHY *adv.* + *WHO)DUNIT.] A story, play, or film in which the main interest lies in the detection of the motive for some crime or other action.

1968 *Guardian* 1 May 7/2 Patricia Highsmith..writes why-dunnits rather than who-dunnits, psychological thrillers. **1970** *Homes & Gardens* Feb. 122/2 This novel isn't so much a whodunit as a whydunit, with a revolver doing the deed. **1984** *Listener* 17 May 35/3 It is a terrific whodunnit, constantly hinting at whydunnit, at the ethical squalor of all the participants.

whyness (hwəi·nės). [f. WHY *adv.* + -NESS.] That which causes a thing to be as it is; the essential reason for something. Cf. WHATNESS.

1896 R. FRY *Lett.* (1972) I. 116 You who..care nothing about the *whyness* of the *what.* **1932** *Times Lit. Suppl.* 20 Oct. 765/3 But it is the whatness not the whyness of things that matters. **1950** *Mind* LIX. 405 Logical empiricism indicates the 'howness' of the world, but not the 'whyness'. **1962** *Time* 11 May 70 Teacher Foote reports that *-ness* added to nouns, pronouns, verbs, and phrases—a custom thought until now to be mostly whimsical, as in *whyness*, and *everydayness*—has become popular among distinctly unjocose people.

wibbly-wobbly, *a.* Add: Also as *sb.*, in phr. *all of a wibbly-wobbly. nonce-use.*

1922 JOYCE *Ulysses* 399 Bless me,..I'm all of a wibbly-wobbly.

wichert (wi·tʃəɹt). *dial.* Also **whitchet, witchert,** etc. [Orig. uncertain; perh. repr. a local pronunc. of 'white earth'.] A variety of chalk marl subsoil found near the Chilterns in Buckinghamshire, which is mixed with chopped straw and used locally for walling.

1912 *R. Comm. Hist. Monuments: Buckinghamshire, South* 342 *Wichert* or *Whitchet* (white earth).—A local term for a kind of white marl or mud found at Haddenham, Dinton, and in the district, and used unburnt mixed with chopped straw for walling. **1916** C. F. INNOCENT *Devel. Eng. Building Construction* x. 136 In Buckinghamshire, where the walls were built of a kind of white clay called 'witchit', found about eighteen inches below the surface of the ground. **1929** H. HARMAN *Bucks. Dial.* 165 The wichert (or whitchet), which is a kind of white marl found locally, is laid in heaps beside the line of the intended wall and well soaked with water. When the stonework is in position, the wichert is turned and short straw is trodden into it; the purpose of this is merely to keep it fairly compact whilst it is wet. **1942** W. ROSE *Good Neighbours* iv. 42 He also made the curious three-pronged forks, with flat tines, with which the masoners built the wichert walls of the village. **1951** P. OYLER *Feeding Ourselves* iii. 32 Hand-made bricks and tiles, stone and thatch, cob or wichert cannot be out of place in the scenery from which they come. **1958** *Records of Buckinghamshire* XVI. III. 136 It is considered most probable that the main walls were built of the local chalk mud charged with chopped straw, known in these parts as *witchert.* **1977** *Oxford Times* (S.E. ed.) 4 Mar. 1 The cottage was built of Witchert, a sophisticated sort of mud, of which there are many examples in Haddenham. The material crumbles when demolished.

wichetty, var. WITCHETTY in Dict. and Suppl.

Wichita (wi·tʃətǭ). Also 9 **Wichataw.** [f. the name of *Wichita*, in Kansas.] **a.** (A member of) a Caddoan Indian people of southern central N. America (now Oklahoma, formerly also Kansas and Texas). **b.** Their language. Also *attrib.*

1841 H. S. FOOTE *Texas & Texans* I. xiv. 299 There are several other remnants of tribes in Texas..the *Wichataws*, who live far North, on the Brassos. **1883** W. F. CODY in B. A. Botkin *Treas. Amer. Folklore* (1944) Music. Enter a group of Wichita Indians. **1960** R. W. MARKS *Dymaxion World of B. Fuller* 37/1 When the first Wichita house finally was opened to the public, many were struck by its spaciousness and air of luxury. **1965** *Language* XLI. 84 The consonantal opposition nasal/oral occurs in all the languages of the world except Wichita. **1978** *Ibid.* LIV. 503 Of the three American Indian linguistic groupings discussed here, those of the Cadoan family, spoken in the Southern Plains, are perhaps the least described; of the surviving languages—Caddo, Wichita, and Pawnee—none is being learned by children.

wichuraiana (witʃuːrəi,ā·nă). a. specific epithet of *Rosa wichuraiana* (F. Crépin 1886, in *Bull. Soc. Bot. Belgique* XXV. 189), f. the name of Max Ernst *Wichura* (1817–66), German botanist + *-IANA.] A climbing, almost evergreen, rose belonging to the species *Rosa wichuraiana*, which is native to eastern Asia and bears white flowers, or one of many cultivars developed from it, usually distinguished by small glossy leaves and flowers in clusters. Freq. *attrib.*

1907 [see *PENZANCE]. **1913** [see *DOROTHY PERKINS]. **1923** *Daily Mail* 10 Mar. 15 The top growth of roses, excepting..wichuraianas, should be severely pruned in the first season. **1945** G. M. TAYLOR *Roses* xv. 76 Some of the Wichuraianas..will cover a wall very quickly. **1960** *News Chrons.* 6 Aug. 6/1 The wichuraiana ramblers are a case in point. **1962** R. PAGE *Education of Gardener* vi. 199 Among rambler roses I like to use the wichuraiana varieties.

wick, *sb.*[1] For sense numbers read **1. a, b, c,** and **3,** and add: **1. d.** In fig. phr. *to turn the wick up* (or *down*), to open (or close) the throttle of an engine; to accelerate (or decelerate). *colloq.*

1948 [see *THROTTLE *sb.* 4 b]. **1965** PRIESTLEY & WISDOM *Good Driving* iii. 28 The gas pedal can be likened to the wick of an oil lamp. Turn it up and you get more light... Indeed it is a simile much used by motor cyclists who talk of 'turning the wick up' as a more graphic and descriptive way of saying 'I accelerated'.

2. a. to *get on* (one's) *wick*, to irritate or annoy (a person); to exasperate; to get on one's nerves (*NERVE *sb.* 8 e). *colloq.*

It is sometimes suggested that both this and the next sense derive from (Hampton) *Wick*, rhyming slang for PRICK *sb.* 17. See Partridge and WICK *sb.*[2] 2.

1945 *Penguin New Writing* XXVI. 56 Parades and bullshit get on his wick. **1958** K. AMIS *I like it Here* 32 But I wish he wouldn't think he'd got the right to knock the English. That's what really gets on my wick. **1961** 'B. WELLS' *Day Earth caught Fire* iv. 54 'Strewth, these licensing laws get on your wick, don't they,' they grumbled. **1977** K. BENTON *Red Hen Conspiracy* iii. 22 The way you talk about Pat gets on my wick. **1984** B. FRANCIS *AA Car Duffer's Guide* 6/2 Gets on my wick, she do.

b. *to dip* (one's) *wick*: of a man, to engage in sexual intercourse. *slang.*

1958 J. CAREW *Black Midas* vi. 96 'Come on!' Santos bellowed. 'If every time you dip your wick you going to fall in love, then God help you!' Belle jumped out of bed and pulled on her dress. **1969** D. NILAND *Dead Men Running* iv. 159 When you're starved for a woman dip your wick, and the starvation's gone. **1971** B. W. ALDISS *Soldier Erect* 111 Di asked, 'You don't feel like a bit of a bunk-up this evening, Stubby, by any chance?' 'A bit of what?' 'Dipping your wick, man!' **1981** R. BARNARD *Sheer Torture* xiii. 137 None of your barmaids or local peasant wenches for Pete. He's very calculating where he dips his wick.

wick, *a.*[2] *North.* var. of QUICK *a.* Cf. *WHICK *a.*

1848 MRS. GASKELL *Mary Barton* I. viii. 127 In th' Infirmary..there be good chaps there to a man, while he's wick, whate'er they may be about cutting him up at after. **1911** F. H. BURNETT *Secret Garden* xi. 105 'It's as wick as you or me,' he said;..Martha had told her that 'wick' meant 'alive' or 'lively'. **1970** 'J. HERRIOT' *If only they could Talk* ix. 69 This 'oss is as wick as an eel. **1972** *Observer* 23 Apr. 23/4 Knott is, to use a Yorkshire expression, 'wick', but wick cricketers are rare these days. **1978** *Lancashire Life* Oct. 99/1 Granny Martha Mosscropp, approaching her century and as wick as a flea, had known in girlhood the enclosed life of Victorian Ramstwistle.

wicked, *a.*[1] (*sb., adv.*). Add: **I.** *adj.* **1. c.** Designating a stock evil character in a fairy-tale, as *Wicked Fairy, Stepmother, Uncle*, etc. Freq. *transf.*

1897 KIPLING *Stalky & Co.* (1899) 39 He owned a soft, slow smile which well suited the part of the Wicked Uncle. **1906** *Sleeping Beauty* ('Tales for Little People' ed.) 8/2 'That looks like the wicked fairy, I'm sure,' said his majesty to himself. **1946** A. HUXLEY *Let.* 26 May (1969) 544 That blessing and curse of cleverness, with which the Fairy Godmother, who is also the Wicked Fairy, endowed me. **1978** M. BABSON *Tightrope for Three* xv. 78 He could not see Lillian in the classic 'wicked stepmother' situation. **1982** 'J. MELVILLE' *Painted Castle* i. 21 If you left Tad out of consideration, uncomfortable things were apt to happen. He had a touch of the Wicked Fairy about him.

3. b. Excellent, splendid; remarkable. *slang* (orig. *U.S.*).

1920 F. SCOTT FITZGERALD *This Side of Paradise* I. iii. 119 'Tell 'em to play 'Admiration'!' shouted Sloane... 'Phoebe and I are going to shake a wicked calf.' **1977** *Western Mail* (Cardiff) 5 Mar. 8/2 He could, as I say, sidestep off either foot, but what sped him on was a wicked acceleration over 20 yards.

II. *absol.* or as *sb.* **4. a.** Also in phrs. *no peace for the wicked*: see *PEACE *sb.* 14*; *no rest for the wicked.*

1935 MARSH & JELLETT *Nursing-Home Murder* iv. 57 The throat specialist..remarked: 'No rest for the wicked, nurse.' **1958** A. SILLITOE *Sat. Night & Sunday Morning* i. 20 'No rest for the wicked,' she laughed. **1965** T. CAPOTE *In Cold Blood* iv. 321, I wish you'd send me earplugs. Only they wouldn't allow me to have them. No rest for the wicked, I guess. **1979** M. BABSON *So soon done For* vii. 54 'I wish *I* could take some time and get away. But there's no rest for the weary.' 'Or the wicked.'

wicket. Add: **3. a.** *double wicket* (earlier examples); *to keep wicket* (earlier example).

1773 J. BURNBY *Kentish Cricketers* 14 Davis, who loves a Game of Cricket, And shines whene'er he keeps the Wicket. **1778** *Coventry Mercury* 6 July 3/4 On Tuesday last..a Cricket Match, (full set at double wicket) was played between the Wappenbury and Coventry players. **1801** J. STRUTT *Sports & Pastimes Eng.* II. iii. 83 Cricket. ..This game which is played with the bat and ball, consists of single and double wicket.

d. Fig. phrs.: *to be on a good wicket*, to be in an advantageous or favourable position; *to bat* (or *be*) *on a sticky wicket*: see *STICKY *a.*[2] 1 c.

1941 *Punch* 24 Dec. 551/1, I wondered why I was so anxious to conceal my age; for the old *are on a good wicket.* **1961** *Listener* 2 Nov. 737/2 Perhaps the most satisfactory contributions are those of Lord Birkett, who is on a good wicket in describing the change in legal attitudes to obscenity, and Dr. Robert Gosling. **1977** *Verbatim* Dec. 3/2 To *be on a good wicket* is, like *being on a good pitch*, to 'be in a good spot'. To *be on a good wicket* with someone is to 'be in favor' with him.

6. (sense 3) *wicket-bag, -taker.*

1916 JOYCE *Portrait of Artist* (1969) 90 A team of cricketers passed,..one of them carrying the long green wicketbag. **1962** *Times* 20 June 4/1 In the second Test match..Coldwell wins his [cap] as the season's premier wicket-taker. **1976** J. SNOW *Cricket Rebel* 76 Barry Knight had been the main wicket-taker in the West Indies first innings with four.

wicket-keep. (Earlier example.)

1867 *J. Lillywhite's Cricketer's Compan.* 107 [He] promises very well as a wicket-keep.

wicket-keeping. Add: (Earlier examples.)

1826 F. REYNOLDS *Life & Times* II. xiv. 170 No man could..surpass..Hammond in wicket keeping. **1833** *Sporting Mag.* LXXXII. 353/2 The wicket-keeping of Wenman.

Hence (as a back-formation) **wi·cket-keep** *v. intr.*, to keep wicket; **wi·cket-keeping** *ppl. a.*

1891 W. G. GRACE *Cricket* v. 138 Lillywhite was bowling and I was wicket-keeping. **1955** I. PEEBLES *Ashes* i. 13 Two wicket-keeping batsmen. **1976** *Milton Keynes Express* 25 June 49/5 In his nine games for the club so far this season the wicket keeping batsman has claimed 19 victims.

wicking, *sb.* (Earlier example.)

1847 *Rep. Comm. Patents 1846* (U.S.) 220 This is combined with a small tube within it, through which the wicking is introduced, to cause the tallow to unite around the wicking.

wickiup, var. WICKYUP in Dict. and Suppl.

wi·ckless, *a.* [f. WICK *sb.*[1] + -LESS.] That burns without a wick; not fitted with a wick.

1899 *T. Eaton & Co. Catal.* 'Summer Needs' 13 (*heading*) Wickless blue flame oil stoves. **1924** *Chambers's Jrnl.* Sept. 638/1 In all wickless stoves and lamps particles of carbon are deposited in the vaporiser. **1950** [see *gun-flash* sv. *GUN *sb.* 14 a].

wickmanite (wi·kmănəit). *Min.* [f. the name of F.-E. *Wickman* (b. 1915), Swedish mineralogist + -ITE[1].] A cubic hydroxide of manganese and tin, $MnSn(OH)_6$, found as small yellowish or colourless octahedral crystals.

1967 MOORE & SMITH in *Arkiv för Mineral. och Geol.* IV. 398 Wickmanite..is of interest since it is the first tin mineral reported from Långban. **1977** *Canad. Mineralogist* XV. 437/1, Wickmanite, $MnSn(OH)_6$, schoenfliesite, $MgSn(OH)_6$, and manganoan schoenfliesite occur in separate low-temperature parageneses in hydrothermally mineralized skarns at Pitkäranta, Karelia.

wicky. b. (Examples.)

1804 A. F. M. WILLICH *Domestic Encycl.* I. 53/1 The plant [*sc.* Andromeda] is there [*sc.* in the southern states] called 'wickie'. **1901** C. T. MOHR *Plant Life Alabama* 654 Wicky..Louisianian area..Low sandy pine barrens.

wickyup. The standard form is now *wickiup.* (Further examples.)

1876 *Sun* (N.Y.) 10 May 2/6 Come up and see me at my wickiup in Montana. **1930** E. FERBER *Cimarron* i. 11 He was raised in a tepee; a wickiup had been his bedroom, a blanket his robe. **1959** E. TUNIS *Indians* 110/1 In winter the Diggers put their wickiups over pits for additional warmth, just as the Basketmakers did. **1973** 'P. BUCHANAN' *Requiem of Sharks* xi. 111 In the slang of the Pascagoula Indians, she was built like a brick wickiup.

wid (wid), repr. colloq. and dial. pronunc. of WITH *prep.*

[See WITH *prep.* for pre-16th cent. examples.] **1869** S. H. BRADFORD *Scenes in Life Harriet Tubman* 26 Jesus will go wid you. **1884** D. BOUCICAULT *Shaugraun* I. i. 3 Never fear, I'll be even wid your honour yet. **1895** BAINES & SMILEY in A. Dundes *Mother Wit* (1973) 256/2 You an' I was sittin' at de table wid but one dish ob soup. **1897** KIPLING *Capt. Cour.* iii. 77 We do be condescending to honour the second half wid our presence. **1935** [see *JACK *sb.*[1] 2 e]. **1953** K. TENNANT *Joyful Condemned*

xii. 106 What's up wid yuh now? **1978** J. IRVING *World according to Garp* xix. 432 She didda lot for people wid *complicated* lives.

Widal (vi-, widā·l). *Path.* The name of G. F. *Widal* (1862–1929), French physician, used *attrib.* and in the possessive to designate an agglutination test for typhoid and other *Salmonella* infections described by him in 1896.

1899 H. M. BIGGS in *Typhoid Fever* (N.Y. State Med. Assoc.) 272 A negative result from the Widal test cannot be regarded as having much significance. *Ibid.*, While the Widal reaction may be very late in its appearance,.. when present it is of the greatest possible value in the diagnosis. **1908** *Practitioner* Sept. 423 The absence of spots, Widal's reaction,..and the presence of a marked leucocytosis and of localised pain, will settle any doubt. **1974** R. M. KIRK et al. *Surgery* ii. 35/2 This is the basis of Widal's reaction..for the diagnosis of typhoid, and it can also be used to detect dysenteric infection. **1976** *Lancet* 20 Nov. 1143/2 Stool microscopy, stool culture (including viral culture), and a Widal test failed to establish a diagnosis.

widdle (wi·d'l), *sb.*² *colloq.* [Echoic: cf. *PIDDLE *sb.*, *WEE *sb.*², and next.] An act of urination.

1954 J. PUDNEY *Smallest Room* 36 The *wee-wee*, the *widdle*, the *pee-pee*, and the *piddle*. **1969** D. CLARKE *Nobody's Perfect* iii. 77, I hardly ever saw him unless I.. wanted a widdle. **1977** A. COREN *Lady from Stalingrad Mansions* 63 Love is..mekkin' sure yer betrothed 'as a pensionable position wi' luncheon vouchers an 'gets out of 'is bath when he wants a widdle.

widdle (wi·d'l), *v.*³ *colloq.* [f. as prec.: cf. PIDDLE *v.* 2.] *intr.* To make water, to urinate. Hence **wi·ddling** *ppl. a.*

[**1956** G. DURRELL *My Family & Other Animals* xi. 143 Larry's suggestion that [the puppies]..be called Widdle and the Puke was greeted with disgust by Mother.] **1968** *Listener* 13 June 785/2 *Work is a Four-Letter Word*, with its short-term expedients (including some inferior pop music and a widdling dog), is grimly unrisible. **1970** 'R. GORDON' *Doctor on Boil* ii. 15 From some of the receptacles you physicians produce, you seem to imagine a camel could widdle through the eye of a needle. **1974** 'D. MEIRING' *President Plan* xii. 95 Martinez was practically widdling with excitement. **1983** W. HARRISS *Bay Psalm Bk. Murder* ix. 82 He headed straight for me... I damn near widdled.

widdy-widdy-way (wi:di,wi:di,wēⁱ·). *dial.* Also **widdy(-way)**, etc. [A rhyme used during the game: see also in *Eng. Dial. Dict.* and quot. 1969 source below.] A children's game of tag.

1846 J. R. PLANCHÉ *Invisible Prince* I. ii. 9 And hail the scenes where I was wont to play At marbles, hopscotch, hoop, and widdy way. **1859** *Games & Sports for Young Boys* 1 *Widdy.* This is a very spirited game, and is peculiarly adapted for wintry weather. **1893–4** R. O. HESLOP *Northumb. Words* II. 788 *Widdy-widdy-way*,..a boys' game. Two boys start hand in hand from a 'bay', and endeavour to touch their opponents. Anyone touched must return with them to the bay and join hands with the first to make a fresh sally... If the chain of hands be broken, the sally has proved a failure, and each outsider endeavours to capture and ride in triumph on the back of one of his quondam pursuers. **1897** H. G. WELLS *Plattner Story* 250 Figures kept moving from one line to another, like children playing at Widdy, Widdy Way. **1969** I. & P. OPIE *Children's Games in Street & Playground* ii. 94 In Peckham Rye the game is known as 'Chain Widdy'.

wide, *sb.* Add: **3.** (Earlier example.)

1846 W. DENISON *Cricket* 5 The parties deliver beyond their natural powers; control of the ball is thus lost, and a 'wide' is the consequence.

4. *to the wide*: to the extreme; entirely, utterly. Used in various slang phrs., as *blind* (*broke, dead, out,* etc.) *to the wide*; *done to the wide*: see *DO *v.* 11 e.

1915 G. FRANKAU *Tid'apa* iii. 19 'Blind, blind to the wide.' It *was* shaky, his hand on the dipper-bar, As the water slopped over, gurgling, from its Ali-baba jar. **1920** WODEHOUSE *Jill the Reckless* xiv. 208 Here was a girl who seemed to like him although under the impression that he was broke to the wide. *a* **1936** KIPLING *Something of Myself* (1937) vi. 155, I have seen a Horse Battery 'dead to the wide' come in at midnight in raging rain. **1946** *Coast to Coast 1945* 29 Now yer broke to the wide—I'd rather yer died. **1958** F. C. AVIS *Boxing Dict.* 96 *Out to the wide*, completely unconscious. **1959** L. LEE *Cider with Rosie* 90 Wake up, lamb... He's wacked to the wide. Let's try and carry him up. **1963** M. DUGGAN in C. K. Stead *N.Z. Short Stories* (1966) 97 Honest, simple and broke to the wide.

wide, *a.* Add: **I. 1. b.** Also (Austral.) *the wide brown land*, Australia; *wide open spaces*: see *OPEN *a.* 8 a.

1914 D. MACKELLAR *Witch Maid* 29 Her beauty and her terror—The wide brown land for me. **1934** J. & G. MACKANESS (*title*) The wide brown land. **1973** *Australian* 4 May 11 Migrants are staying away in droves from the widest and brownest part of this wide, brown land.

II. 5. c. As the final element in comb. with sbs. which denote regions, organizations, etc., as WORLD-WIDE, and *country-wide, nation-wide, state-wide* (see at first element in Suppl.), in the sense 'as wide as the——' or 'extending throughout the whole——'.

III. 11. c. Quot. 1887 may be redated 1879 (*Macmillan's Mag.* Oct. 502/1). Also, shrewd, sharp-witted; (dishonestly) cunning or knowledgeable; skilled in sharp practice; engaging in shady dealings. See also *wide boy*, sense 12 c below. (Later examples.)

1928 E. WALLACE *Gunner* xxviii. 226 You can handle these swells, Danty, and you're wide enough to keep yourself out of trouble. **1938** F. D. SHARPE *Sharpe of Flying Squad* i. 13 Underworld men and women..refer to themselves as 'wide people' or 'one of us'. They're a colourful, rascally lot these 'wide 'uns'. **1956** T. HUDDLESTON *Naught for your Comfort* ii. 28 He must become a 'tsotsi', a cosh-boy, a wide-guy—because at least there's excitement that way, while it lasts. **1981** *Event* 16 Oct. 101/3 They've never struck me as a bunch of wide-persons.

IV. 12. a. *wide-armed* (earlier example), *-beaked, -bellied, -lapped, -legged, -margined, -shouldered, -sleeved* (later examples), *-waked, -windowed.* **c. wide-angle** *a.* (examples of *wide-angle lens*); also in extended use and as *sb.*; **wide-aperture** *a.*, applied to (an instrument having) an objective lens of large diameter; **wide-band** *a.*, capable of transmitting or handling signals in a wide frequency band; **wide-bodied** *a.*, of a large jet aeroplane: having a wide fuselage (cf. *JUMBO 1 b); also **wide-body** (usu. *attrib.*); **wide boy** *slang*, one who lives by his wits, often dishonestly; one who engages in petty-criminal activities, a 'spiv'; cf. sense *11 c; **wide-cut** *a. Oil Industry*, involving or produced by fractional distillation over a wide temperature range, or the fraction so obtained (see quots. 1958, 1966); **wide-eyed** *a.*: also *fig.*; **wide gauge** *Railways* = BROAD GAUGE; **wide-leafed** *a.* (earlier example, *transf.* of a table); **wide-meshed** *a.*, of a net: having wide meshes or interstices; (in quots., *fig.* of a survey); **wide receiver** *Amer. Football*, a pass receiver who stands several yards to the side of an offensive formation; cf. *FLANKER *sb.*¹ 3 d, *RECEIVER¹ 1 c (*a*); **wide-scale** *a.*, that occurs on a wide scale; extensive; cf. *large-scale* adj. s.v. *LARGE *a.* 15 c; **wide screen**, a cinema screen which presents a wide field of vision in proportion to its height (see quot. 1957); freq. *attrib.*; **wide-spectrum** *a.*, (*a*) *fig.*, effective against a wide range of organisms; = *broad-spectrum* s.v. *BROAD *a.* D. 2; (*b*) *lit.*, characterized by light of a wide range of wavelengths; **wide-wale** a., of fabrics, esp. corduroy: broad-ribbed.

1897 C. M. HEPWORTH *Animated Photogr.* xiii. 97 The use of a wide-angle lens..is..abominable in connection with the production of a living photograph. **1947** H. LEWIS *Photogr. Today* 53 On analysing my shots..I usually find that 70 per cent. have been taken with a 5 cm. lens, 2 per cent. with a long-focus lens, and the rest with a 3.5 cm. wide-angle lens. **1955** *Mademoiselle* Mar. 113 *Oklahoma!* is made in 'fabulous new Todd-AO wide-angle, large-screen process'. **1965** C. FORSYTE *Double Death* iii. 22 He kept most of his attention on the special wide-angle driving mirror that raked the traffic on his tail. **1974** J. IRVING *158-Pound Marriage* i. 11 Forget the wide-angle. (I see Edith and Severin Winter only in close-ups.) **1983** *Which?* Sept. 388/3 A zoom lens lets you move in from a wide-angle view to a closer shot. **1958** *Amateur Photographer* 31 Dec. 914/2 For colour work a wide-aperture lens is invaluable. **1966** D. G. BRANDON *Mod. Techniques Metallogr.* i. 57 With a wide-aperture telescope..there is no loss of brightness on magnification. **1869** J. R. LOWELL *Poet. Works* (1912) 415 The friend of all the winds, wide-armed he towers. **1935** *Wireless Engineer* XII. 251/1 A means of examining the behaviour of wide-band amplifiers when supplied with transient input waves. **1967** E. CHAMBERS *Photolitho-Offset* iv. 42 Although this ideal is not fully realised the fact remains that very acceptable results can be obtained using either wide-band (trichromatic) or narrow-cut filters. **1982** *Economist* 6 Mar. 25/2 The government wants Britain's cities to be cabled quickly with wideband cable. **1807** J. BARLOW *Columbiad* III. 131 The wide-beak'd hawk, that now beholds me die, soon with his cowering train my flesh shall tear. **1921** D. H. LAWRENCE *Birds, Beasts & Flowers* 30 An enormously wide-beaked mouth. **1921** W. DE LA MARE *Veil* 6 Dipped the wide-bellied boat. **1980** *Jrnl. R. Soc. Med.* LXXIII. 7 A wide-bellied, ungainly but functional ambulance. **1970** *Times* 4 Sept. (Aviation Suppl.) p. i/4 About £200m. is being requested to get the proposed BAC 3-11 wide-bodied, 250-seater subsonic airliner off the ground. **1983** *Times* 12 Feb. 20/8 Western airlines..were not allowed to fly wide-bodied jets such as the Airbus into Moscow until the Russians had developed their own Il 86. **1968** *Flight Internat.* 14 Nov. 777/1 BAC foresees a demand for standards matching the high-capacity wide-body aircraft of the long-haul routes on short/medium-haul routes. **1979** T. GIFFORD *Hollywood Gothic* (1980) xxx. 308 The wide-bodies slid down..into the bustle of Los Angeles International Airport. **1983** *Listener* 9 June 6/2 Only two companies are now producing wide-body airliners. **1937** R. WESTERBY *Wide Boys never Work* 232 Jim was turning, or had already turned, into a Smart Aleck, a Wide Boy, a despiser of the Mugs who worked. **1947** *People* 22 June 5/3 It seems the wide boys are trying to muscle in and buy these dogs to pit against one another in private fights. **1952** 'J. TEY' *Singing Sands* iv. 57 He was a wide boy. Wide boys don't want trouble. **1960** V. GIELGUD *To Bed at Noon* III. i. 159 Blackmailed—for the murder? Not even the widest of the local wide-boys could have got on to it. **1976** J. O'CONNOR *Eleventh Commandment* iii. 38 All the wide boys thought I had gone mad when they saw me in khaki. **1958** *Chambers's Techn. Dict.* 1027/2 *Wide-cut fuel*.., low octane petrol (gasoline) obtained from wide-cut distillation used in turbojets in order to conserve kerosene. **1966** *McGraw-Hill Encycl. Sci. & Technol.* X. 54/2 Petroleum is separated by distillation into fractions designated as (1) straight-run gasoline..; (2) middle distillate..; (3) wide-cut gas oil, which boils at about 345–540°C,.. and (4) residual oil. **1982** *Fuelling Aviation* (Shell Internat. Petroleum Co. Ltd.) 5/2 The military wide-cut fuel is called JP-4 and this is the major fuel for the airforces of the world. **1923** D. H. LAWRENCE *Birds, Beasts & Flowers* 109 The human soul is fated to wide-eyed responsibility In life. **1983** L. DEIGHTON *Berlin Game* ix. 95 You ask him all those wide-eyed innocent questions about making profits from cheap labour. **1841** Wide gauge [see WIDE *a.* 5 a]. **1982** S. G. DUFF *Parting of Ways* iv. 43 We all boarded the train for Moscow, changing onto the wide-gauge railway at the Soviet frontier. **1856** J. G. WHITTIER *Poet. Works* (1898) 353/1 Pacific rolls his waves a-land, From many a wide-lapped port and land-locked bay. **1928** BLUNDEN *Japanese Garland* 19 Fine fields, wide-lapped, whose loveliest-born Day's first bright cohort finds. **1779** P. FRENEAU *House of Night* in *U.S. Mag.* Aug. 356 A wide-leaf'd table stood on either side. **1938** R. GRAVES *Coll. Poems* 28 The wide-legged robin with his breast aglow. **1889** O. WILDE in *Fortn. Rev.* Jan. 43 Book-bindings, and early editions, and wide-margined proofs. **1938** *Dialect Notes* VI. 626 Professor A. H. Marckwardt..has begun a wide-meshed survey of the Great Lakes region and the Ohio River valley. **1980** *English World-Wide* I. 1. 28 Unfortunately..his survey is even more wide-meshed than Orton's. **1968** *Redskins* 17 Nov. 77/3 Depth at wide receiver is strong, too, in rookie Dennis Homan. **1981** *Washington Post* 8 Apr. D1 We will have to take the best athlete available... That could be an offensive lineman, a running back or a wide receiver. **1958** G. LIENHARDT in Middleton & Tait *Tribes without Rulers* 108 There was little wide-scale co-operation against the common enemies. **1980** *Daily Tel.* 26 May 6/7 By confining the emergency arrangements as far as possible to the Bristol line, BR has avoided widescale timetable changes. **1931** *Ann. Reg. 1930* II. 48 The Wide Screen is still only a matter for experiment, as standardisation has not yet been achieved. **1932** *Ibid. 1931* 47 The 'Wide Screen' invention, though perfected, was not offered to the public by the big producing concerns, seeing that it would involve the studios in huge expenditure. **1953** *Manch. Guardian* 13 Aug. 4/7 Hollywood..has decided to coast for the present on a compromise between 3-D and Cinemascope—namely on the less spectacular development known as Wide Screen. **1957** *Encycl. Brit.* XV. 862/1 Basically 'wide screen' means any departure from the screen proportions fixed by Edison and his contemporaries at 4 to 3 (or 1·33 to 1); *i.e.*, three units high for every four wide... If the aspect ratio were to be changed there was only one practical way—screens would have to be wider. **1967** H. HARRISON *Technicolor Time Machine* (1968) iii. 27 An accurate, full-length, wide-screen, realistic, low-budget, high-quality historical. **1976** *National Observer* (U.S.) 16 Oct., Imagine, right before your eyes on the wide screen, the stern of the Titanic..comes shooting out of the water as if the projector had been reversed. **1935** KIPLING *Two Forewords* 19 But *thou*, O Nakhoda, art young and wide-shouldered. **1973** T. PYNCHON *Gravity's Rainbow* I. 127 A few women in clinking boots and wide-shouldered swagger coats, but no children. **1926** D. H. LAWRENCE *David* viii. 63 Takes off striped coat, or wide-sleeved tunic. **1980** *Catal. Fine Chinese Ceramics* (Sotheby, Hong Kong) 214 A Jade Carving of a lady wearing a wide-sleeved robe. **1959** S. DUKE-ELDER *Parsons' Dis. Eye* (ed. 13) xv. 175 One of the wide-spectrum antibiotic drugs such as the tetracyclines. **1972** *Country Life* 25 May 1351/1 The farmer uses..a wide-spectrum weedkiller, which is a mixture of chemicals designed to control a whole range of weeds. **1977** J. L. HARPER *Population Biol. Plants* x. 321 They inserted wide-spectrum fluorescent tubes between the rows of a close canopied crop of soyabeans. **1982** *Sci. Amer.* Mar. 98 Snakes of two families can detect and localize sources of infrared radiation. Infrared and visible-light information are integrated in the brain to yield a unique wide-spectrum picture of the world. **1856** J. G. WHITTIER *Poet. Works* (1898) 52/2 With steeds of fire and steam, Wide waked Today leaves Yesterday behind him like a dream. **1957** M. B. PICKEN *Fashion Dict.* 374/2 *Wide-wale serge*, serge with broad diagonal weave. **1980** L. BIRNBACH et al. *Official Preppy Handbk.* 98 Wide wale corduroy pants. **1869** J. R. LOWELL *Poet. Works* (1917) A life wide-windowed, shining all abroad, Or curtains drawn to shield from sight profane. **1970** *Daily Tel.* 30 Apr. 17 A wide-windowed bar parlour.

wide, *adv.* Add: **3*.** Transferred senses of *wide open*. **a.** *Boxing*, etc. Fully exposed to assault; unprotected, off one's guard. Freq. *fig.*, esp. in phr. *to leave* (*lay*, etc.) (*oneself*) *wide open*.

1915 E. CORRI *30 Yrs. Boxing Referee* 150 Johnny Summers..in an unguarded moment, left himself wide open and encountered one of the most decisive knock-out punches I ever saw. **1941** B. SCHULBERG *What makes Sammy Run?* i. 14 You never find me going in for favors... It leaves you wide open. **1948** 'N. SHUTE' *No Highway* vi. 148 Honey lays himself wide open to that sort of thing. **1966** 'A. HALL' *9th Directive* iv. 42 One fine day he would catch me wide open and slam me down.

b. Of an issue, case: not circumscribed or prejudiced by conditions; unrestricted (in its implications, effects, etc.); not resolved or decided; *spec.* of a police investigation.

1963 'J. MELVILLE' *Burning is Substitute* iii. 51 Charmian suddenly had the feeling that this affair..was wide open, could reach anywhere. **1970** *Daily Tel.* 10 July 19 The fate of Penguin Publishing Company is still wide open. **1973** J. THOMSON *Death Cap* iii. 41 They're the only people who so far have entered the case... As far as I'm concerned, it's still wide open. **1982** C. AIRD *Last Respects* xiii. 137 It's [*sc.* a murder enquiry] what you might call wide open still... You'll have to look on it as a challenge.

6. *wide-ranging* (later examples), *-rolling* (earlier example), *-sweeping*; *wide-apart*; **wide-open** *a.*, (*b*) *U.S.*, of a town: not oppressed by laws or law enforcement.

1941 E. BOWEN *Look at all those Roses* 39 The wide-apart birch-trees. **1983** T. HUGHES in *Listener* 21 Apr. 27/1 They have a chirruppy, chicken-sweet expression With goo-goo starlet wide-apart eyes. **1892** *Harper's Mag.* June 103/1 It is what they call in Montana 'a wide-open town'. **1975** J. GORES *Hammett* xi. 79 He has been elected three times because the citizens *want* a wide-open town. **1958** *Times Lit. Suppl.* 7 Feb. 76/4 A representative antnology, which is so wide-ranging in its material..that its final effect is rather of confusion than of enlightenment. **1980** B. HILL in *Beautiful Brit. Columbia* Summer 39 The wide-ranging sheep that are one of the island's main farm products provide the source of wool for local weavers. **1785** T. DWIGHT *Conquest of Canāan* XI. 295 Wide-rolling dust the neighbouring concave fills. **1924** *Motor* 14 Oct. 491 (*caption*) One of the two wide-sweeping bankings on the new speedway at Montlhery, near Paris. **1979** *Jrnl. R. Soc. Arts* CXXVII. 409/2 Wessex..will therefore not be subjected to wide-sweeping environmental problems.

wide-awake, *sb.* Add: **2.** (Earlier example.)

1877 R. L. PRICE *Two Americas* iv. 57 Sea-gulls and wide-awakes hovered in hundreds over the water.

3. (Earlier example.)

1865 DICKENS *Mut. Fr.* II. II. xii. 111 You have been told that he might pull through it.., Wide-Awake; have you?

wide-mouth, *a.* Add: **B.** *sb.* One who speaks loudly, boastfully, or without restraint. Cf. *big mouth* s.v. *BIG *a.* B. 2.

1959 I. & P. OPIE *Lore & Lang. Schoolch.* x. 189 The tell tale is christened ..a tout, traitor, quisling, or wide-mouth. **1978** *Times Lit. Suppl.* 28 Apr. 462/2 You feel, frequently, like booing him for a bighead and a wide-mouth.

widger (wi·dʒəɹ). Also *erron.* **wigger.** [See quot. 1956.] A gardening tool consisting of a small strip of metal with a shallow furrow down the centre, used as a miniature trowel to move seedlings, cultivate pot plants, etc.

1956 *Dict. Gardening* (R. Hort. Soc.) Suppl. 333/1 The original widger..is the shape of a small spatula... The name 'Widger' was transferred to this horticultural tool by Mr. Clarence Elliott; it comes from one of a series of nonsense definitions used to test the memorizing ability of British Naval Cadets. **1962** *Listener* 22 Nov. 887/3 A stainless steel 'wigger' is a very useful little gadget for pricking out seedlings. **1973** *Country Life* 5 Apr. 940/1 Seedlings..I move ..with a widger—an invaluable narrow-bladed, long trowel-like hand tool.

widget (wi·dʒėt). orig. *U.S.* [Perh. alteration of *GADGET.] An indefinite name for a gadget or mechanical contrivance, esp. a small manufactured item.

1931 *Amer. Speech* VI. 259 Widget. **1937** E. LYONS *Assignment in Utopia* (1938) III. iii. 299 Every time the percentage of widgets turned out by her factory rose her features shone. **1961** *N.Y. Times Mag.* 26 Nov. 109 Widgets by wire... Suppose something goes wrong with your Westinghouse appliance. What then? Your Westinghouse dealer can get you any new part faster than anyone around. He orders it by special telegraph line. **1966** 'E. LATHEN' *Murder makes Wheels go Round* i. 5 The corporation would..go about its business of producing bigger and better widgets. **1973** S. ALSOP *Stay of Execution* (1974) II. 193, I asked Joe if the widget could be protected by patent. Joe said ..it couldn't... A few weeks ago,..IBM began to make its own widget, cheaper and better serviced than the Intercomp widget. **1982** BARR & YORK *Official Sloane Ranger Handbk.* 11/1 You never have to see the industry ('widget factories') and commerce ('selling brushes') that make the money.

widgie (wi·dʒi). *Austral.* and *N.Z.* Also **weegie.** [Origin uncertain.] An Australasian teddy-girl, the female counterpart of a *BODGIE.

1950 *Sun* (Austral.) 5 July 19 There'll be ..prizes for the most colorfully dressed 'bodgy' and 'weegie'. **1956** S. HOPE *Diggers' Paradise* 86 A popular district with bodgies and widgies is 'the Cross'. **1965** E. BROWN *Big Man* xix. 168 A mob of bodgies and widgies on a camping holiday. **1977** *Times* 13 May 14/1 Gang delinquency..has made its mark around the world..in Australia the bodgies and widgies.

Widmanstätten (vi·t-, wi·dmănʃtetən, -st-). Also **-staetten, -statten.** The name of A. J. *Widmanstätten* (1754–1849), Austrian scientist, used *attrib.* with reference to an orderly pattern of intersecting bands seen in some meteorites and steels when a polished section is etched, attributed to the crystallization or precipitation of a new solid phase along the crystal planes of a parent solid phase.

1861 *Q. Jrnl. Geol. Soc.* XVII. II. 9 The plane of the cutting shows strings of whitish colour indicative of crystalline structure ('Widmannstetten's figures'). **1881** L. FLETCHER *Guide Meteorites Brit. Museum* 16 The want of homogeneity in meteoric iron is beautifully shown by the 'Widmanstätten' figures. **1927** *Jrnl. Iron & Steel Inst.* CXVI. 584 He points out the difference between the needle-like structure of the ferrite and the Widmanstätten structure. **1971** I. G. GASS et al. *Understanding Earth* viii. 116/2 Those irons..usually show the Widmanstaetten structure.

Hence † **Widmanstä·ttian** *a.*

1842 *Amer. Jrnl. Sci.* XLIII. 359 The powder arranged itself in directions coinciding with the Widmanstättian figures. **1883** *Phil. Trans. R. Soc.* CLXXIII. 889 It is the constituent of nickel-iron which forms the fine lines constituting the Wiedmannstättian figures, and not schreibersite, as usually stated in writings on the etched figures of meteoric iron. **1886** [see *NEUMANN].

widow, *sb.*[1] Add: **1. d.** (Later allusive examples.)

1952 W. M. MILLER in *Galaxy* Nov. 153/1 It was different if the business-widow called on a couple. Then the lone male could retire. **1965** *Guardian* 30 July 10/5 One Scottish TA unit, aware of the dangers of creating 'TA widows' opens its bar on drill nights to wives and girl-friends. **1973** R. BUSBY *Pattern of Violence* ii. 32 You tell her to come and see me. We police widows have got to stick together. **1980** *Financial Rev.* (Austral.) 14 Jan. 8/2 Dick Smith's resident computer expert..said the key-boards, screens, printers and central processors are giving birth to a new social problem, 'computer widows'.

h. *The Widow* (*of* or *at Windsor*): a familiar epithet for Queen Victoria, whose husband predeceased her by forty years. orig. chiefly *Services'.*

1888 KIPLING *Private Learoyd's Story* in *Soldiers Three* 14 They tell me t' Widdy herself is fond of a good dog. **1890** —— *The Widow at Windsor* in *Barrack-Room Ballads* (1892) 39 Then 'ere's to the Widow at Windsor, An' 'ere's to the stores an' the guns, The men an' the 'orses what makes up the forces O' Missis Victorier's sons. **1900** *Captain* III. 235/1 The design..shows the Queen as a widow—the 'Widow of Windsor'. **1932** *Times* 12 Feb. 14/2 'The Widow' (as we subalterns had irreverently nicknamed the Empress of India). **1964** E. LONGFORD *Victoria R.I.* xxxvi. 562 She died just after half-past six... The famous 'hush' which had always surrounded 'The Widow at Windsor' was shattered. **1980** R. HALL *Lovers on Nile* xiv. 216 The 'Widow of Windsor' would feel herself justified in having ostracized Sam and Florence.

3. c. (Earlier example.)

1781 BOSWELL *Jrnl.* 28 Apr. (1977) 333 He [*sc.* Lord Townshend] had called Sir Joshua, 'Will you give us one cool bottle of claret?' They were taking away the former. 'No,' said Lord Townshend, 'Let us first take the widow.'

d. *Typogr.* A short line at the end of a paragraph, esp. one which is set at the top of a page or column, or which contains only (part of) one word, and is therefore considered unsightly.

[**1904** *Man. Rules Compositors S. S. McClure Co.* 25 All running heads are to be set one nonpareil from the body, unless otherwise instructed. Care must be taken to overcome 'rivers', and to this end indiscriminate division of words is allowed. Care should also be exercised to overcome 'widdies' at the top of pages.] **1925** [see *SLUG *sb.*[2] 4 f]. **1932** P. VAN D. STERN *Introd. Typogr.* ii. 15 When a single word runs over, it is often desirable to alter the copy ..so that the words can be run back. Single words standing in a line are called 'widows'. **1948** *Bull. N.Y. Public Library* Jan. 3 Early in 1936, H. M. Lydenberg.. began a quiet, and not quite humorless, investigation into the origin and identity of the typographical 'widow', that awful slattern of the printed page. **1954** M. LASKI in *Author* Winter 30/2 It is a common experience, when working for *Vogue*, to be asked to add a few words to a paragraph so as to avoid unsightly 'widows' or single-word lines. **1963** D. OGILVY *Confessions Advertising Man* vii. 124 It has been discovered that 'widows' increase readership, except at the bottom of a column. **1980** B. CRUTCHLEY *To be Printer* 55 Our best customers were those who looked to us..to..print well, which meant avoiding 'widows'.

e. *five-fingered* (also *dry-mouthed*) *widow*, in phrs. alluding to the act of masturbation. *slang* (chiefly *Services'*).

1971 B. W. ALDISS *Soldier Erect* 44 In there [*sc.* the 'shithouse'], behind the stable-like door of one compartment or another, I went to a regular evening rendezvous with my dry-mouthed widow. **1975** C. ALLEN *Plain Tales from Raj* xv. 159 Many turned, as a last resort, to the 'five-fingered widow'.

4. a. *widow mother* (later example). **c.** *widow-making* (later example). **d. widow-maker,** (*b*) *N. Amer. slang*, a dead branch caught high in a tree which may fall on someone below; (c) *slang* [tr. G. *witwemacher*], a nickname for the Lockheed F-104 Starfighter strike and reconnaissance aircraft (see quot. 1975); also (*U.S. Mil.*), a grenade launcher; **widow-man** *dial.* = WIDOWER[1] 1 a.

1945 M. H. ALLEE *Smoke Jumper* iv. 47 He remembered the Kid's caution about widow-makers, limbs falling from high overhead. **1965** M. MCINTYRE *Place of Quiet Waters* ix. 163 Now's the time to look out for widow-makers... Don't you go walking about in the woods when she's blowing like this. **1975** *Times* 26 Sept. 7/2 The loss of 178 aircraft in Germany earned it [*sc.* the Starfighter] the title of 'Witwemacher', or widow-maker. **1976** *Courier-Mail* (Brisbane) 13 Feb. 4/4 They opened up with automatic rifle fire, a Browning machine-gun, and 66 anti-tank rockets, and a 'widow-maker'—a grenade launcher. **1876** G. M. HOPKINS *Wreck of Deutschland* xiii, in *Poems* (1967) 55 The widow-making unchilding unfathering deeps. **1887** T. E. BROWN *Doctor & Other Poems* 35 Sir John, it appears, Was a widda man. **1946** C. MCCULLERS *Member of Wedding* II. 43 He was a widowman, for her mother had died the very day that she was born—and, as a widowman, set in his ways. **1937** C. DAY LEWIS *Starting Point* 36 Theo's getting as fussy as a widow-mother.

5. widow's cruse *fig.* (with allusion to I Kings xvii. 12–16) [see CRUSE], a supply which, though apparently meagre, is, or seems to be, inexhaustible; **widow's walk** chiefly *N. Amer.*, a rectangular balustraded platform (characteristic of New England architectural styles in the 18th and 19th cent.) built on top of the roof of a house, esp. for providing an unimpeded view of the sea (see quot. 1978).

1816 SCOTT *Old Mortality* in *Tales my Landlord* 1st Ser. IV. xii. 268 'Can you lodge a stranger for a night?' 'I can, sir, if he will be pleased with the widow's cake and the widow's cruize.' **1915** D. H. LAWRENCE *Phoenix II* (1968) 382 Wherein..is the immortality, in the constant occupation of the nest, the widow's cruse, or in the surpassing of the phoenix? **1977** *Jrnl. R. Soc. Arts* CXXV. 463/1 Information is infinitely reproducible without diminishing it: it is a veritable widow's cruse. **1939** S. CHAMBERLAIN *Nantucket* 25 Variously termed a 'Captain's Walk', or the 'Widow's Walk', it is just 'The Walk' in Nantucket. **1961** J. STEINBECK *Winter of our Discontent* i. 14 The fine old house,..his great-grandfather's,..with..Adam decorations and a widow's walk on the roof. **1978** J. A. MICHENER *Chesapeake* 463 The name *widow's walk* derived from romantic tales of those loyal women who continued to keep watch for a ship that had long since gone to the bottom of some coral sea.

widower[1]**.** Add: **1. c.** The counterpart of WIDOW *sb.*[1] 1 d in allusive use, as *football widower*, etc. *colloq.*

1969 *Listener* 17 Apr. 534/3 He's a football widower because I'm the one who's always trooping away to football matches. **1971** A. NIXON *Attack on Vienna* xi. 109 Mr Fletcher had had a quiet drink with another bridge widower. **1973** *Guardian* 25 May 11/2 The age of golf widowers is developing.

width. Add: **4. a.** (Earlier example.)

1872 D. G. ROSSETTI *Let.* 26 Sept. (1967) III. 1076 It would be quite enough to make four curtains..6 ft ½ wide (or under would do if more convenient with the widths of the velvet).

b. The width of a swimming-bath taken as a measure of the distance swum. Cf. *LENGTH *sb.* 4 d.

1930 *Swimming Instruction* (Amateur Swimming Assoc.) 55 From this stage the class should proceed to swim.. several widths, legs only, using supports or 'Dog Paddle'. **1971** *Daily Tel.* 17 Nov. 3/6 Mrs Annie Oakley, 86,.. has been presented with a certificate for swimming two widths at Soundwell Swimming Club. **1981** H. ENGEL *Ransom Game* (1982) xxx. 198 She went off the board again... She did two lengths to each of my widths.

Wiedemann–Franz (vī·dəman frɑnts). *Physics.* [The names of G. H. *Wiedemann* (1826–99) and R. *Franz* (1827–1902), German physicists, who published the law in 1853 (*Ann. d. Physik* LXXXIX. 497).] *Wiedemann–Franz law*: the law that at any given temperature the ratio of the thermal to the electrical conductivity has approximately the same value for all metallic elements; *Wiedemann–Franz ratio*: this ratio or the Lorenz ratio (see *LORENZ).

1924 J. R. PARTINGTON in H. S. Taylor *Treat. Physical Chem.* I. xi. 490 The Wiedemann-Franz law is only approximate. **1966** PHILLIPS & WILLIAMS *Inorg. Chem.* II. xix. 23 The transition metals are also good conductors of heat. On the free-electron theory it is predicted that there should be a direct relation between the thermal, k, and electrical, σ, conductivities, the Wiedemann–Franz ratio. **1975** D. G. FINK *Electronics Engineers' Handbk.* VI. 10 The Wiedemann-Frantz [*sic*] ratio L is defined as $L = \lambda/\sigma T$. **1975** *Jrnl. Low Temperature Physics* XX. 691 The Lorenz numbers..are very close to the theoretical value..predicted by the Wiedemann–Franz law for pure electronic heat conduction limited by impurities.

wiederkom (vī·dəɹkǫm). Also **wiederkomm** and with capital initial. [ad. F. *vidrecome* goblet (Robert, 1752), ult. ad. G. *wiederkommen* to return, come again (see quots.).] A tall, cylindrical, German drinking-vessel, made of (usu. coloured or painted) glass.

The Eng. form reflects the original Ger. derivation. F. *vidrecome* is sometimes understood as a fanciful corruption of G. *willkomm* loving-cup, but this suggestion appears to be unsubstantiated.

1878 A. NESBITT *Descr. Catal. Glass Vessels S. Kensington Museum* p. cxxiii, The cylindrical drinking vessels, generally called wiederkoms..are sometimes very large, some being as much as 20 in. in height. **1881** C. C. HARRISON *Woman's Handiwork* III. 229 For side-board decoration, the Wiederkom or 'come again' drinking-cups in emerald-hued [Bohemian] glass, have always been popular. **1897** A. HARTSHORNE *Old Eng. Glass* xv. 82 A glass called a 'Wiederkom' was one which was filled, passed round the table..and 'came again' empty. **1907** E. DILLON *Glass* xvi. 266 The term *wiederkomm* given by so many English..writers to the large broad forms [of drinking-glasses], is unknown in Germany, so that I think the expression may be definitely abandoned and replaced by the word *humpen* or *willkomm humpen*. **1926** N. H. MOORE *Old Glass* I. 81 The huge glasses known as 'Willkommen'..were originally used by a host to welcome his newly arrived guest... The term 'Wiederkom' by which these glasses are known in England is a misnomer. **1946** W. B. HONEY *Glass* vi. 75 The *Stangenglas*..became popular in a modified form as the *Willkomm*, or 'greeting-glass' (sometimes mistakenly called a *Wiederkom*), in thin metal. **1977** H. NEWMAN *Illustr. Dict. Glass* 342 *Wiederkomm* (*humpen*),..literally, come again beaker. A term used by A. Nesbit [*sic*]..in referring to *Willkomm* (*humpen*) and many other types of enamelled *Humpen*... It is a term not used by German museums.

Wien[1] (vīn). *Physics.* The name of Wilhelm *Wien* (1864–1928), German physicist, used *attrib.* and in the possessive to denote (*a*) an approximation to Planck's law that holds at short wavelengths, according to which the flux of radiant energy of wavelength λ emitted by a black body at temperature T is proportional to $1/\lambda^5 \exp(hc/\lambda kT)$; (*b*) the displacement law (sense (i) s.v. *DISPLACEMENT 2 e).

1899 *Astrophysical Jrnl.* X. 40 My observations..make it seem possible that the law derived by W. Wien represents the emission of 'the absolutely black body'. In Wien's formula, J = [etc.]. **1900** *Sci. Abstr.* III. 383 Wien's laws, according to which the wave-length of the maximum radiation is inversely proportional to the absolute temperature, and the corresponding maximum energy proportional to the fifth power of the absolute temperature, were confirmed. **1904** Wien's displacement law [see *DISPLACEMENT 2 e]. **1948** [see *RAYLEIGH-JEANS]. **1963** G. L. PICKARD *Descriptive Physical Oceanogr.* v. 52 According to Wien's Law this energy is concentrated round a wavelength of 0.5μ. **1978** PASACHOFF & KUTNER *University Astron.* ii. 24 From Wien's displacement law, we can see that the colors of stars in the sky are telling us something about their temperatures.

Wien[2] (vīn). [The name of M. C. *Wien* (1866–1938), German physicist.] **a.** Electr. *Wien bridge*: an alternating-current bridge circuit devised by Wien which is used to measure capacitance (or frequency) in terms of resistance and frequency (or capacitance); *Wien bridge oscillator*: an oscillator based on this circuit.

1922 GLAZEBROOK *Dict. Appl. Physics* II. 1029/1 *Wien bridge*, for the measurement of the capacity and power factor of a condenser. **1957** *Practical Wireless* XXXIII. 709/2 In Fig. 2 a simple bridge for capacitor testing is given. This is known as a Wien bridge. **1967** *Electronics* 6 Mar. 63/3 (Advt.), Here, the RA-240 is used in the design of a highly stable, uncompensated Wien bridge oscillator. **1979** R. HAMILTON *Electronics for Technicians* vii. 157 The other type of *R–C* oscillator to be considered is known as a Wien bridge oscillator. (The name derives from a type of bridge circuit used in measurements, the feedback network of the oscillator being part of a balanced Wien bridge.)

b. Physical Chem. *Wien effect*: the increase in the electrical conductivity of an electrolytic solution as the field strength is increased.

1934 R. P. BELL *Electrolytes* v. 90 The increase in conductivity [with frequency] is..of the same order of magnitude as the Wien effect. **1978** P. W. ATKINS *Physical Chem.* xxv. 832 The Wien effect is the observation of higher mobilities [of ions] at higher electric fields. (There are two Wien effects. The first Wien effect is the one just described: the second Wien effect is the enhancement of the degree of ionization of an ionogen, or weak electrolyte, by the applied field.)

wiener (vī·nəɹ), *a.* and *sb.* Also erron. **weiner.** [a. Ger., of Vienna.] **A.** *adj.* **1.** *wiener schnitzel*: see *SCHNITZEL.

2. *wienerwurst* [G. *wurst* sausage]: = *Vienna sausage* s.v. *VIENNA 1 a. *U.S.*

1889 *Gallup* (New Mexico) *Gleaner* 27 Mar. 3/3 We..are willing to bet our unpaid debts, against a weiner-wurst [*sic*] that the modest local of the *Democrat* blushed more than the bride when he saw her in the diaphanous costume he describes. **1899** F. NORRIS *McTeague* v. 75 The lunch baskets were emptied... There were wienerwurst and frankfurter sausages. **1949** *Los Angeles Times* 15 May II. 5/2 I've never lamped a crooked dime, not e'en a wienerwurst.

‖ **3.** *Wiener Kreis* [G. *kreis* circle]: = *Vienna Circle* s.v. *VIENNA 1 a.

[**1929** (title) *Wissenschaftliche Weltauffassung. Der Wiener Kreis* (E. Mach Verein).] **1932** *Jrnl. Philos.* XXIX. 122 The philosophy of the 'Wiener Kreis' is unique in that it was formulated for the first time in a concise joint manifesto. **1950** B. RUSSELL *Logic & Knowl.* (1956) 370 Wittgenstein's *Tractatus Logico-Philosophicus*..provided a stimulus which helped in the formation of the 'Wiener Kreis', where logical positivism first took the form of a definite school. **1964** *New Statesman* 10 Apr. 574/2 The early chapters are full of perception theory, Chicago School aesthetics, *Wienerkreis* linguistics, ..Platonic misconceptions and all stations to the Hochschule at Ulm.

B. *sb.* **a.** = *wiener wurst* above. Cf. *WEINER. *N. Amer.*

1904 H. R. MARTIN *Tillie* iii. 34 I'm havin' fried smashed potatoes and wieners. **1935** *Motion Picture* Nov. 79/1 Hot dogs are just wiener sausages! **1970** S. J. PERELMAN *Baby, it's Cold Inside* 81 Platters of smoking hot wieners flanked by creamed spinach.

b. *Comb.* **wiener roast** *N. Amer.*, a barbecue at which wieners are cooked and served.

1920 *Outing* July–Aug. 245/1 All over France they introduced the women war workers to American hikes, wiener roasts, camping in the open, and games of all sorts. **1970** J. H. GRAY *Boy from Winnipeg* 53 Snowshoeing clubs..given to walking for miles after every snow, usually stopping for a wiener roast somewhere along the way.

wienie (wī·ni). *N. Amer. slang.* Also erron. **weinie.** [f. *WIENER *a.* and *sb.*: see -IE.] = *WIENER *sb.* a. Cf. *WEENY *sb.*[2], *WINNY.

1911 *Daily Colonist* (Victoria, B.C.) 26 Apr. 7/3 Weinies, pretzels and coffee were served and German relishes. **1919** U. SINCLAIR *Jimmie Higgins* xx. 195 Mocking soldier-boys, who made merry..over sauerkraut and..'wienies', otherwise known as 'hot dogs'. **1940** R. CHANDLER *Farewell, my Lovely* xxxiv. 161, I spotted him [*sc.* the hot dog man] in a white barbecue stand tickling wienies with a long fork. **1959** E. AMBLER *Passage of Arms* iv. 103 The barman opened up a can of weinies. **1977** *Time* 4 July 37/1 One man's meat is another man's corndog (a wienie impaled on a stick and dunked in a bubbling cornbread batter).

wife, *sb.* Add: **1. c.** *Wife of Bath*, one of the pilgrims in Chaucer's *Canterbury Tales*; used allusively (usu. *attrib.*), chiefly with reference to sexual appetite and outspokenness.

1926 A. HUXLEY *Essays New & Old* 178 Her comments on the connubial state were so very Juliet's Nurse, so positively Wife-of-Bath, that we were made to feel quite early Victorian. **1946** 'J. TEY' *Miss Pym Disposes* xviii. 185 The wide flat hat planked slightly to the back of her head on top of her wimple—Wife of Bath fashion—gave her an air of innocent astonishment. **1974** K. MILLETT *Flying* (1975) II. 183 Alison sings, a great lusty Wife of Bath woman. **1978** R. RENDELL *Sleeping Life* iii. 23 Horrifyingly, she added, with a Wife of Bath look, remembering the old dance, 'Wouldn't be for sex, not so likely.'

2. b. (*d*) *wife and mother*, a conventional epithet describing a woman who shows a zealous devotion to her family (now also somewhat *joc.*).

1798 MRS. INCHBALD *Lovers' Vows* (ed. 3) II. iii. 31 Go to Amelia—explain to her the duties of a wife and of a mother. **1850** MRS. GASKELL *Let.* Apr. (1966) 108 One of my mes is a true Christian..another of my mes is a wife and mother, and highly delighted at the delight of everyone else in the house. **1911** G. B. SHAW *Getting Married* 196 She's a born wife and mother, maam. Thats why my children all ran away from home. **1930** A. CHRISTIE *Murder at Vicarage* xxxii. 252 I'm going to be a real 'wife and mother' (as they say in books). **1974** M. CECIL *Heroines in Love* v. 128 They could remain devoted wives and mothers *and* do their bit for the Cause.

(*e*) preceded by an adj. or sb. denoting the husband's occupation (freq. of a Mil. character, as *navy, service wife*), and esp. connoting a wife who fulfils official expectations of this role.

1951 'J. TEY' *Daughter of Time* II. 9 The present Valerie or Angela or Cecile..must be a naval wife. **1975** 'J. BELL' *Victim* i. 17 All the vulgar arrogance of an overseas army wife between the wars. **1981** P. MCCUTCHAN *Shard calls Tune* ii. 18 Beth had been a police wife..and a Foreign Office Security wife... She knew she mustn't ask where Simon was going.

c. (*b*) *a wife in every port*, a licence or indulgence (jocularly) said to be enjoyed by sailors.

1761 I. BICKERSTAFFE *Thomas & Sally* I. iii. 5 'Tis pretty sport, for one that gets a wife at ev'ry port. **1907** *Punch* 22 May 365/2 (*caption*) *Admiral.* And what made *you* wish to become a sailor, my boy? *Navy Candidate* (*in perfect good faith*). Because he's got a wife in every port, sir. **1933** SOMERVILLE & 'ROSS' *Smile & Tear* xi. 132 'The wife in every port', supposed to be the perquisite of sailors, is no more than the constant aspiration of every self-respecting dog.

g. The passive member of a homosexual partnership. *slang.*

1883 W. A. HAMMOND *Sexual Impotence in Male* i. 57 The one who was in this disgusting arrangement to act the part of 'husband' came to his 'wife's' bed and remained there during the night. **1957** DANFORTH & HORAN *D.A.'s Man* (1958) i. 3 He's got a new girl. His 'wife' went home last week. **1978** J. HYAMS *Pool* xiii. 199 The group's leader [a homosexual]..made his 'wife' head of production.

5. b. (*a*) *wife-basher*; (*b*) *wife-bashing, -battering, -beating* (earlier example). **d. wife-bound** *a.* (later example); **wife-swapping**, the interchange of marital partners for sexual purposes within a social group; hence **wife-swap** *sb.* (occas. as *v. intr.*); **wife-swapper.**

1909 *Practitioner* Dec. 828 Poisoning conducted on these lines..resembles the action of the wife-basher, who attacks his victim with a poker... The wife-basher, however, is aware of the obviousness of his crime. **1979** J. WAINWRIGHT *Tension* 98 She walked to the home of the 'wife-basher'..and..went into action. **1978**—*Thief of Time* 221 'Why should some wandering female run to the nearest doctor?'..'Wife-bashing. Unwanted pregnancy. A score of reasons.' **1978** *Times* 16 Feb. 4/7 Wife-battering is most likely to occur among couples with a family history of violence. **1856** GEO. ELIOT *Let.* 18 Jan. (1954) II. 225 A Petition..that married women may have a legal right to their own earnings, as a counteractive to wife-beating and other evils. **1820** KEATS *Let.* 28 Jan. (1958) II. 247 Henry is wife-bound in Cambden Town there is no getting him out. **1976** *Private Eye* 24 Dec. 8/2 M. Phillipe Dannat..told the magistrates of Nice that he had assaulted M. Georges David at a wife-swap rendezvous in the hills above St. Tropez. **1978** F. WELDON *Praxis* xx. 184 They played strip poker; they wife-swapped. **1969** C. HIMES *Blind Man with Pistol* x. 111 Wife swappers, gang fuckers, seekers of depravity. **1959** M. PUGH *Chancer* xiv. 170 He began to discuss the wife-swapping parties held locally... 'But how do they get away with it here?... The town's so small. I would have thought that after six months..they'd have to convene a mass divorce trial.' **1967** W. & J. BREEDLOVE *Swinging Set* x. 119 They brought up the subject of 'wife-swapping' with four other couples. **1976** 'W. TREVOR' *Children of Dynmouth* iii. 77 There was wife-swapping every Saturday night at parties on the new estate.

wifie. (Earlier examples.)

1786 BURNS *Poems, chiefly in Scottish Dial.* 126 His clean hearth-stone, his thrifty Wifie's smile. **1819** KEATS *Let.* 18 Sept. (1931) II. 439, I intend to write a letter to you[r] Wifie.

wifing (wəi·fiŋ). *rare.* [f. WIFE *sb.* + -ING[1].] The activity or condition of being a wife or housewife.

1905 G. B. SHAW *Let.* 3 Jan. (1972) II. 499 As to ordinary domestic mothering and wifing she [*sc.* Shaw's mother] was utterly unfitted for the sentiment of it. **1952** S. KAUFFMANN *Philanderer* (1953) ii. 28 If there was one kind of wife he didn't want..it was one who made a career of 'wifing'.

wig, *sb.*[3] Add: **1. e.** *Austral. Sheepshearing.* The wool of a sheep growing around the eyes and on top of the head, removed during shearing. Cf. *TOPKNOT 1 b.

a **1964** H. P. TRITTON in R. Ward *Penguin Bk. Austral. Ballads* (1964) 228 Two blows to chip away the wig. **1972** J. S. GUNN in G. W. Turner *Good Austral. Eng.* iii. 61 One thing I did notice about shearing was..two terms for the one idea..for example *rouseabout/shedhand..topknot/wig.*

4. (Earlier example.)

1789 J. WOODFORDE *Diary* 1 Feb. (1927) III. 81 Thomas Carr dined with our Folks in Kitchen. Gave him a tolerable good Wigg.

5. wig-picker *U.S. slang*, a psychiatrist; **wig-stand,** a support, usu. of wood or porcelain, comprising a base and rounded stem upon which a wig may rest when not in use (cf. *wig-block*).

1961 *Amer. Speech* XXXVI. 147 *Wig picker*,..a psychiatrist. **1971** M. MCCARTHY *Birds of Amer.* 153 Was I afraid of what a wig-picker might say? **1883** R. W. PROCTER *Barber's Shop* (rev. ed.) xix. 189 Here is the lost one's original epitaph (with the wig-stand and block to match)..*The Barber's Epilaph.* **1911** O. ONIONS *Widdershins* i. 18 A couple of mushroom-shaped old wooden wig-stands. **1970** *Country Life* 17–24 Dec. 1245/2 Hand-painted wig stands from Dodo Designs.

wiglet (later examples).

1964 *Sun-Herald* (Brisbane) 21 June 56/3 Wiglets, or half wigs start from 11 gns and full wigs are from 32 gns. **1979** L. KALLEN *Introducing C. B. Greenfield* xi. 131 A stand bearing wigs and wiglets.

wig, *v.*[2] Add: **3.** *intr.* With *out.* To be overcome by extreme emotion; to be stimulated to the point of imbalance; to go mad, 'freak out'. *U.S. slang.*

1955 *Amer. Speech* XXX. 305 He wigged out at the prof's gag. **1968** P. WELLES *Babyhip* xx. 139 'The Boss Pornographers,' he said, 'it's LSD Music, to wig-out by.' **1975** *Time* 27 Oct. 70/3 Some in the startled crowd recall him saying, 'The company is now in God's hands.' One executive wondered if Goshorn had 'wigged out'. **1978** J. GORES *Gone, no Forwarding* (1979) xi. 69 Kearney was going to wig out when the expense voucher for $100 worth of cocaine came in.

Hence **wigged-out** *ppl. a.*

1977 *New Yorker* 24 Oct. 152/2 The lunacies..just function as part of a normally wigged-out mode of existence. **1980** *San Francisco Bay Guardian* 16–23 Oct. 21/2 It's a barbed, wigged-out satire on hypocrisy and authoritarian therapy via the problem of alcoholism.

wigger, var. *WIDGER.

wiggle, *v.* **1.** (Later *fig.* example.)

1927 H. A. VACHELL *Dew of Sea* 260, I must wiggle out of the mess.

wiggle, *sb.* (In Dict. s.v. WIGGLE *v.*) Add: **1.** (Earlier examples.) *to get a wiggle on* (earlier example).

1816 J. K. PAULDING *Lett. from South* I. 235 They suffered their hair to grow into a mighty bunch behind, and walked with the genuine *Rutland wiggle*; that is to say, on tiptoe, and with a most portentous extension of the hinder-parts. **1869** L. M. ALCOTT *Little Women* II. xxiv. 355 Rob's footstool had a wiggle in its uneven legs. **1896** *Inlander* Jan. 147 *Get a wiggle on you*, hurry up; bestir yourself.

2. = WIGGLER in Dict. and Suppl.

1831 T. BUTTRICK *Voy., Trav., & Discoveries* 78 The

water was very bad... After straining it would still exhibit live insects, which they call wiggles.

3. A wavy line drawn by a pen, pencil, etc.

1942 *Punch* 12 Aug. 127/1 An old envelope bearing the regimental Paymaster's stamp, partly obliterated by adhesive tape, and the word 'Confidential' crossed out with a wiggle in pencil. **1967** R. D. Mattuck *Guide to Feynman Diagrams in Many-Body Problem* iv. 63 The majority of writers draw the above interaction with a dashed line... However, we shall always use the wiggle.

wiggler. (In Dict. s.v. Wiggle *v.*) Add: **1.** Applied esp. to the larva of a mosquito. (Earlier and later examples.)

1859 J. R. Bartlett *Dict. Americanisms* (ed. 2) 492 *Waggletail*, the larva of the mosquito, etc.; also called a wiggler. **1938** J. Steinbeck *Long Valley* 186 The mosquito wigglers tumbling up and down, end over end, in the water. **1969** K. M. Wells *Owl Pen Reader* iv. 365 In a month or two this bog hole will be full of wigglers.

2. *Physics.* A magnet designed to make a beam of particles in an accelerator describe a sinusoidal path in order to increase the amount of radiation they produce. Freq. *attrib.*

1974 *IEEE Trans. Nucl. Sci.* XX. 984/1 This proposal projects the installation of many additional beam runs and 'wiggler' magnets. **1981** *Science* 16 Oct. 316/2 A wiggler is a special magnet that fits into one of the straight sections of a storage ring between the bending magnets. The wiggler bends the electrons into a sine wave-shaped path whose local radius of curvature is smaller than that of the smooth circular arc of the bending magnets.

wiggletail. (In Dict. s.v. Wiggle *v.*) (Earlier example.)

1855 *Chicago Times* 9 Aug. 4/6 The mosquito proceeds from the animalcule commonly termed the wiggle-tail.

wiggle-waggle, *sb.* Add: **2.** = *cake-walk *sb.* 2. Also *wiggle-woggle.*

1910 *Penny Guide Japan-British Exhib.* 25 Fun on the Wiggle Waggle. **1923** R. Macaulay *Told by Idiot* iii. xxi. 256 The establishment of the White City at Shepherd's Bush, with the Franco-British Exhibition..and flip-flaps, switchbacks, wiggle-woggles, and scenic railways. **1938** 'G. Orwell' *Homage to Catalonia* xii. 254 A dreadful thing called the Wiggle-Woggle at the White City Exhibition.

wiggy, *a.* Add: **2.** [f. *wig *v.*[2] 3.] Mad, crazy, 'freaky'. *U.S. slang.*

1963 L. Deighton *Horse under Water* xxii. 96, I just got some new jazz records from the States, Ace. Pretty wiggy. **1972** *Last Whole Earth Catalog* (Portola Inst.) 31/1 Traditionally considerations such as his—economics, organizations, the future—turn a prophet's soul terrible and dark or at least partially wiggy. **1978** *Amer. Poetry Rev.* Nov./Dec. 26/2 'Poor devil,' she added, 'he blew the star's fuse when we went wiggy for the Thin Man on a cross.'

wigwam. Add: **d.** A pyramidal frame-work of bamboo and similar poles used to support beans, sweet peas, etc.

1971 H. Evans *How to cheat at Gardening* viii. 120 If you must have sticks, tie them in threes, wigwam fashion. *Ibid.* 121 (*caption*) Easiest way of arranging bean-poles—the wigwam. **1978** A. Huxley *Illustr. Hist. Gardening* v. 150/2 We continue to grow beans and the like..on wigwams formed of bamboo canes.

† **wilch** (wiltʃ, wilʃ). *Hist. Suffolk dial.* Also **wilsh.** [Origin unknown.] A bottle-shaped wicker strainer formerly used in brewing to strain the liquid from grains of steeped malt. Cf. Thead.

1823 E. Moor *Suffolk Words & Phrases* 484 *Wilch*, the sediment or lees of beer, home-made wine,..also a brewing utensil. **1830** R. Forby *Vocab. East Anglia* II. 375 *Wilch*,..the wicker strainer set upright in the mash-tub, to prevent the grains from running off with the wirt. **1956** G. E. Evans *Ask Fellows who cut Hay* v. 61 The utensils used in the brewing were..a *wilch* (or wilsh), a bottle-shaped appliance made of wicker. (The wilsh was a filter used when straining off the liquid or *wort* from the *mash* of steeped malt.) **1962** A. Jobson *Window in Suffolk* i. 28 The brewing tackle would be housed in a large shed or outhouse set apart for that purpose, and would include the tubs or keelers, the wilches, mash sticks,.. mallets, spigots and taps.

wilco (wi·lko), *int.* orig. *Mil. slang.* Also **willco.** Abbrev. of '*will co*mply', used to express acceptance of instructions, esp. those received by radio or telephone. Cf. *will do* s.v. *will *v.*[1] 11 c.

1946 F. Hamann *Air Words* 56 *Willco*, will comply; will do. **1948** A. M. Taylor *Lang. World War II* (ed. 2) 221 *Wilco*, radio term for 'will comply'. Used throughout the services and also taken up by civilians. **1961** H. Waugh *Road Block* i. 12 'Roger, wilco, and out,' the staticky voice sang. **1972** D. Hart-Davis *Spider in Morning* ii. 28 'If it happens again, hold your breath.' 'Wilco.' **1977** D. Beaty *Excellency* xvii. 190 'Please clear the runway quickly for the President's Starjet!'..'Wilco,' he said.

wild, *a.* and *sb.* Add: **A.** *adj.* **I. 3. a.** *wild silk*, silk produced by wild silkworms or an imitation of this made from short silk fibres. (Earlier and later examples.)

1876 [see Tusser 1 a]. **1883** [in Dict.]. **1896** [see Tusser 1 b]. **1911** *Daily Colonist* (Victoria, B.C.) 28 Apr. 14/2 The cargo was made up as follows: Raw silk, 960 bales; wild silk, 49 bales. **1963** R. Himmel *It's Murder, Maguire* vii. 46, I always suspected him of wearing wild silk underwear. **1972** J. Aiken *Butterfly Picnic* ix. 162 Her white wild-silk bikini.

II. 6. d. *to run wild*, (*c*) of an oil-well, to release uncontrollable quantities of fluid or gas. Also *to blow wild.*

1925 [see *relief well* s.v. *relief[2] 9 b]. **1931** *Times* 18 Feb. 15/6 When the wells 'blow wild' the city is enveloped in a dark spray of oil. **1975** L. Crook *Oil Terms* 35 *Blow out*, a situation where a well becomes out of control due to the fluids from the formation 'blowing wild' at the surface.

11. b. Also const. *for.*

a **1817** Jane Austen *Persuasion* (1818) III. vi. 107 The girls were wild for dancing. **1937** J. T. Farrell *Fellow Countrymen* 184 He imagined that she was his woman... She was saying she was crazy about him... She was wild for him.

c. Also † const. *after.* (Earlier and further examples.)

a **1817** Jane Austen *Persuasion* (1818) IV. vii. 134 The men are all wild after Miss Elliot. **1865** R. Henning *Let.* 21 Oct. (1966) 214 The whole family are wild after music.

d. *like wild*: with passionate eagerness, with great excitement. Cf. *like mad* s.v. Mad *a.* 1 c.

1674 C. Stewkeley *Let.* 4 May in M. M. Verney *Mem.* (1899) IV. vii. 225 Ursula..hath bin at all the Salsbury rasis, dancing like wild with Mr Clarks. **1962** *Radio Times* 17 May 43 Should he [*sc.* a jazz musician] 'blow' with feeling, or great excitement ('like wild') [etc.].

13. a. Also in phr. *in* or *beyond one's wildest dreams*, in or beyond one's most fantastic or unrestrained imaginings or expectations.

1961 C. McCullers *Clock without Hands* x. 203 In his wildest dreams he could not associate Johnny with danger. **1969** *Listener* 24 July 123/3 The programme has succeeded beyond its instigators' wildest dreams. **1984** *Tampa* (Florida) *Tribune* 5 Apr. 6c/2 You know, it's hard to believe I'm really here. It's beyond my wildest dreams that I'd be managing a team that I once played for.

14. c. *U.S. slang.* Remarkable, unusual, exciting. Used as a general term of approbation.

1955 L. Feather *Encycl. Jazz* x. 347/2 *Wild*, adj., remarkable, exciting. **1960** [see *lay *v.*[1] 55 l]. **1968** *Listener* 22 Aug. 236/3 Los Angeles is so wild they should just let it swing and see what happens. **1978** *Hot Car* June 103/5 Naugahyde..has long been the favourite amongst Stateside rodders because of its stretchy qualities, amazing range of colours (including some wild marble-like effects).

15. b. Of a playing card: having any rank chosen by the player holding it. Also *fig.* See also *wild card*, sense 16 below.

1927 *Auction Bridge Mag.* May 26/1 These are played with all the twos as jokers and usually known as 'Deuces Wild'. **1940** O. Jacoby *On Poker* x. 139 Any card or cards may be counted as wild, in which case they have the same rights as jokers. **1963** E. Linington *Death of Busybody* vi. 72 Don't tell me, a tie-up. Look, Luis, let's not call every card in the deck wild, for God's sake. **1973** M. Catto *Sam Casanova* vi. 109 Think of the amazing variations of the game [*sc.* poker]! Five-Card stud. Seven-Card Draw with Joker wild.

III. 16. wild card, (*a*) (see sense 15 b above); also *fig.*; (*b*) *Sport* (orig. *U.S.*), a player or team chosen for a tournament at the discretion of the organizers after the regular places have been taken up; freq. *attrib.*; (*c*) *Computers*, a character that will match any character or combination of characters in a file name, etc.; **wild cherry**: see Cherry *sb.* 3 a; (examples): **wild duck**, a duck belonging to any of numerous undomesticated species; **wild garden**, a group of hardy plants, exotic or native, in an informal setting, designed to look as natural as possible; hence **wild gardener, gardening; wild geranium** *S. Afr.* = Geranium 2; **wild ginger**, in North America, any of several plants of the genus *Asarum*, esp. *A. canadense*, or, in India, a wild plant of the genus *Zingiber*; **wild grape**, a wild species of *Vitis* or its fruit; **wild lime**: see Lime *sb.*[2] b; also, in Australia, = *kumquat 2; (examples); **wild orange**: see Orange *sb.*[1] 3; also, in Australia, any of several species of *Capparis* or *Canthium*; in South Africa = *Kaffir orange* s.v. *Kaffir 4; (examples); **wild parsnip**: see Parsnip 2; also, = Cow-parsnip; also, a poisonous plant of the family Umbelliferæ, esp., in North America, the water hemlock, *Cicuta maculata*, or, in Australia, *Trachymene glaucifolia*; (later examples); **wild party**, a boisterous, unchecked, or dissolute party; **wild pig** = *Captain Cooker; **wild pitch** *Baseball*, a pitch which is not hit by the batter and cannot be stopped by the catcher, enabling a base-runner to advance; hence as *v. trans.*, to enable (a runner) to advance in this way; **wild plum**: see Plum *sb.* 3; (earlier and later examples); **wild rice**, an aquatic grass, *Zizania aquatica*, native to North America, having seeds resembling rice and used as food; (earlier and later examples); **wild rye**: see Rye *sb.*[1] 2 c; a North American grass of the genus *Elymus*; (earlier and later examples); **wild talent**, any of various psychic powers such as extrasensory perception, telepathy, telekinesis, etc.; **wild track** *Cinematogr.* (see quot. 1940); **wild well**, an oil well which is out of control and blowing oil or gas from the borehole (cf. sense 6 d (*c*) above).

1940 O. Jacoby *On Poker* x. 138 The Bug, three sixes and a ten merely count as three sixes since the Bug is not strictly a wild card. **1970** *New Yorker* 3 Oct. 34/3 The other thirteen games..will be 'wild-card' encounters, to be played on alternate Monday nights. **1971** *Guardian* 17 June 12/6 Kennedy is the wild card in the 1972 Deck, as the Nixon men see it. **1976** M. Nelson *Crusoe Test* iii. 35 The joker. The wild card. The card the holder can use as he pleases. **1976** *Sunday Mail* (Brisbane) 15 Aug. 3/11 Renee was not ranked high enough to be accepted on her standard of play, but she could be nominated as the 'wild card'—a crowd pleaser. **1977** *Hongkong Standard* 14 Apr. 11/2 Fifteen-year-old Betty Newfield of the US reached the second round by defeating Marlie Buehler of Australia 4–6, 6–0, 7–5 after getting into the draw as a wild card. **1981** *Washington Post* 18 Mar. D3 The conference championship games are now played on the home field of the competitor that has the best season record, unless it's a wild-card team. **1984** *Times* 21 Sept. 19/6 The wild card in the BPCC pack is Mr Maxwell's dual role as head of both BPCC and Mirror Group Newspapers. **1984** K. Buckner et al. *Using UCSD p-System* vi. 56 The wildcard '?' should be used to remove several files from a disk. *Ibid.* xv. 156 the WILD unit makes available wild card pattern matching on string variables. **1985** *Personal Computer World* Feb. 244/1 (Advt.), Powerful wild cards permit editing of categories of file name in one instruction. **1666** *Brief Descr. Province Carolina* 4 There are many sorts of fruit Trees, as Vines, Medlars, Peach, Wild Cherries. **1784** W. Walton *Narr. Captivity B. Gilbert* 81 They were under the Necessity of eating wild Cherries. **1899** S. O. Jewett *Queen's Twin* 81 She had a sprig of wild-cherry blossom in her dress. **1972** G. Chadbund *Flowering Cherries* 11 Wild cherries occur naturally on chalky soil. **1538, 1676** Wild duck [in Dict., sense 1 a]. **1723** J. Nott *Cook's & Confectioner's Dict.* sig.M6, Draw and truss your Wild Ducks, parboil them, and half roast them. **1881** O. Wilde *Poems* 115 The water-rat.. Made for the wild-duck's nest. *a* **1916** 'Saki' *Toys of Peace* (1919) 82 By the time they had arrived at the wild duck course it was beginning to be a rather expensive lunch. **1852** C. M. Yonge *Two Guardians* iii. 29 Strangers would..think her wild garden a collection of weeds. **1925** J. Buchan *John Macnab* xiii. 268 An expert from Kew..had made a wonderful wild garden. **1980** A. Wilson *Setting World on Fire* ii. vi. 170 It's your garden parties that are ridiculous... And Rosemary's famous wild garden. **1966** 'J. Berrisford' *Wild Garden* x. 117 The wild gardener who is also a plantsman..may grow the meconopses. **1870** W. Robinson *Wild Garden* i. 19 It [*sc.* Caucasian comfrey] will soon run about, exterminate the weeds, and prove quite a lesson in wild and natural gardening. **1911** *Daily Colonist* (Victoria, B.C.) 30 Apr. (Mag. Section) 3/4 The cult of wild gardening is apt to run into the same kind of excesses as the pursuit of the simple life. **1978** A. J. Huxley *Illustr. Hist. Gardening* ix. 309 William Robinson and Gertrude Jekyll..preached a return to more naturalistic and even 'wild' gardening. **1840** Wild geranium [see *ivy-berry b]. **1966** E. Palmer *Plains of Camdeboo* xvii. 281 Here and there are Pelargoniums—wild geraniums to us. **1804** M. Lewis *Jrnl.* 1 June in *Orig. Jrnls. Lewis & Clark Exped.* (1905) VI. iv. 154 Wild ginger grows in rich bottom land. **1866** [see Ginger *sb.* 2 b]. **1964** R. Perry *World of Tiger* xi. 160 The Great Indian rhino..feeding on the succulent shoots of marsh reeds and especially the wild ginger. **1973** M. Crowell *Greener Pastures* 187 We recognize the wild ginger. **1763** G. Milligen-Johnston *Short Descr. Prov. S. Carolina* (1770) 9 Wild Grapes grow on this Land. **1843** [see *guarri]. **1929** M. de la Roche *Whiteoaks* xvi. 202 The jewelled leaves of the wild grape..scarcely dried before another dew. **1958** G. A. Petrides *Field Guide to Trees & Shrubs* 114 A number of cultivated varieties have been developed from wild grapes. **1767** P. Collinson *Let.* 31 July in W. Darlington *Mem. J. Bartram & H. Marshall* (1849) 292 The Wild Lime..is a singular plant. **1832** D. J. Browne *Sylva Amer.* 221 In Georgia this tree is known by the name of Sour Tupelo and Wild Lime. **1863** R. Henning *Let.* 26 Nov. (1966) 147 We went out to pick some wild limes for preserving. They are a little fruit about the size of a large gooseberry, but in colour, taste, smell and shape exactly like a small lemon. **1965** Wild lime [see *kumquat 2]. **1969** T. H. Everett *Living Trees of World* xxi. 209/1 The wild-lime (*Zanthoxylum fagara*) of Florida, Mexico, the West Indies..is an evergreen species. **1802** J. Drayton *View S. Carolina* 8 Small rising grounds sometimes present themselves, on which grow..wild orange. **1858** J. A. Warder *Hedges & Evergreens* 44 Our beautiful Wild Orange..is much planted about Southern residences, for hedges. **1932** [see *klapper]. **1936** F. Clune *Roaming round Darling* xvii. 165 The wild orange, ten feet high, dark green brittle leaves, large yellow-stemmed flowers, and bearing fruit as big as tennis-balls, with pomegranate seeds inside. **1969** T. H. Everett *Living Trees of World* xx. 172/1 Known as wild-orange and mock-orange, it [*sc. Prunus carolina*] has creamy white flowers and glossy black fruits. **1790** *Trans. Amer. Philos. Soc.* III. 234, I have heard this poisonous herb, called by the names of Wild-Carrot, Wild-Parsnep,..and Mock-Eel-Root. **1807** [see *musquash-root* s.v. *MUSQUASH 3]. **1889** J. H. MAIDEN *Useful Native Plants Austral.* 142 The sudden death of numbers of cattle in the vicinity of Dandenong..was attributed to their having eaten a plant known as the wild parsnip. **1932** J. W. WINSON *Weather & Wings* 51 The poison is described further as being 'wild-parsnip', 'cowbane', [etc.]. **1955** *Arctic Terms* 88/1 *Wild parsnip.* The cow parsnip. **1965** *Austral. Encycl.* VIII. 546/2 The wild parsnip of inland plains, does seem to be responsible for stock losses. **1925** F. SCOTT FITZGERALD *Lett.* (1964) 295 It is true I saved McAlmon from a beating he probably deserved and that we went on some wild parties in London with a certain Marchioness of Milford Haven. **1970** 'D. HALLIDAY' *Dolly & Cookie Bird* iii. 35 He was probably just afraid of the talk. It was rather a wild party. **1840** W. DEANS *Let.* 30 Oct. in J. Deans *Pioneers of Canterbury* (1937) i. 29, I will visit it [*sc.* Palliser Bay] in company with 50 or 60 natives who are going to hunt wild pigs. **1930** L. G. D. ACLAND *Early Canterbury Runs* 1st Ser. x. 237 Stonyhurst has always been a great place for wild pigs. **1977** C. MCCULLOUGH *Thorn Birds* iv. 75 Wild pigs frightened of nothing, savage and flesh-eating, black hairy things the size of fully grown cows. **1867** *Ball Players' Chron.* 4 July 1/2 Zeller,..getting round on a passed ball and wild pitch, came home on another passed ball. **1970** *Washington Post* 30 Sept. D1/8 In the first game, young Bob Grich led off the home 10th with a single and Coleman wild-pitched him to second base. **1979** *Arizona Daily Star* 1 Apr. c6/4 Greg Laing walked in the bottom of the eighth and scored on a wild pitch. **1709** J. LAWSON *New Voy. Carolina* 105 The wild Plums of America are of several sorts. **1838** E. FLAGG *Far West* II. 177 Endless thickets of the wild plum..were to be seen. **1863** R. HENNING *Let.* 26 Nov. (1966) 146 We sat down under the shade of a wild-plum tree. *Ibid.*, They are not bad, those wild plums; they are about the size of a medlar, quite black in colour, and when ripe they taste very like sloes. **1925** Z. A. TILGHMAN *Dugout* 56 Fan being gone after some wild plums down the creek. **1951** W. FAULKNER *Requiem for Nun* III. 213 A mere dusty widening of the trace, trail, pathway in a forest of oak and ash and..wild plum. **1748** H. ELLIS *Voy. Hudson's-Bay* 170 By the Sides of Lakes and Rivers there is abundance of wild Rice. **1778** J. CARVER *Trav. N.-Amer.* 522 Wild Rice..grows in the greatest plenty throughout the interior parts of North America. **1911** G. S. PORTER *Harvester* vi. 94 Wild rice..he had planted for the birds. **1934** H. MILLER *Tropic of Cancer* 47 They were eating too. A young chicken with wild rice. **1980** *Times Lit. Suppl.* 26 Sept. 1064/5 The paper..was full of reports of discontent around Ompah at overcropping of wildrice. **1984** *Times* 13 June 9/4 Wild rice is not really rice at all but the seeds of a grass that grows wild along the waters-edge of lakes in Minnesota, Wisconsin and southern Canada. **1751** C. GIST *Jrnl.* 27 Jan. (1893) 43 The wild Rye appeared very green and flourishing. **1968** F. W. GOULD *Grass Systematics* 181 Widespread and variable in the United States are *Elymus canadensis* L., Canada wildrye, and *E. virginicus* L., Virginia wildrye. **1944** A. HUXLEY *Let.* 28 July (1969) 510 The fact of what Charles Fort calls 'wild talents' is admitted by all open-minded people. **1960** K. AMIS *New Maps of Hell* (1961) iv. 98 A new type of human being, sometimes outré in appearance, more often gifted with the 'wild talent' which has become a science fiction catch-phrase and convention. **1940** *Chambers's Techn. Dict.* 908/2 *Wild track*, a sound-track which is recorded independently of any photographic track or mute, but is destined to be used in editing a sound-film. **1964** HALL & WHANNELL *Popular Arts* ix. 258 The..combined use of wild-track voices with counter-pointing visual images. **1980** 'P. LORAINE' *Lions' Ransom* I. iii. 51 Fox was..making a 'wild-track' of Busai's morning birdsong. **1915** REDWOOD & EASTLAKE *Petroleum Technologist's Pocket-bk.* iv. 244 '*Wild*' *well.* This term is used to denote a well which produces such quantities of oil or gas, or both, under such high pressure that it is either impossible to bring it under control or it is only controlled when a very considerable time has elapsed after the oil or gas has been met with. **1977** *Sunday Times* 24 Apr. 1/2 If the wild well..is not brought under control within the next 24 hours, the fight could last for weeks, months even.

17. a. *wild-caught* adj.; **b.** *wild-brained* (example), *-coloured, -haired* (earlier example), *-hearted, -winged* (later examples) adjs.; **d.** in nonce *poet.* uses, as *wild-worst, -worth.*

1894 'MARK TWAIN' in *Harper's Mag.* Oct. (1914) 675/2 Wild-brained martyrdom was succeeded by uprising and organization. **1949** *Amer. Speech* XXIV. 98 American mink may be either wild-caught or ranch-raised. **1970** SAUNDERS & PHELPS in H. W. Mulligan *Afr. Trypanosomiases* xiv. 329 The ovaries of wild-caught females..can be used. **1954** M. K. WILSON tr. *K. Z. Lorenz's Man meets Dog* (1964) xix. 176 The striped markings in the face of the 'wild-coloured' cat enhance the least movements of the facial skin. **1872** J. G. WHITTIER in *Atlantic Monthly* Apr. 474 The wild-haired Bacchant's yell. **1904** W. DE LA MARE *Henry Brocken* viii. 83 Beasts of a long-sharpened sagacity, wild-hearted, rebellious. **1916** JOYCE *Portrait of Artist* (1969) iv. 171 He was alone and young and wilful and wild-hearted. **1906** HARDY *Dynasts* II. I. v. 161 A straggler merely he... But they decide, At last, to post his news, wild-winged or no. **1936** L. B. LYON *Bright Feather Fading* 45 The wild-winged bliss. **1876** G. M. HOPKINS *Poems* (1967) 59 The cross to her she calls Christ to her, christens her wild-worst Best. *c* **1878** *Ibid.* 75 Only the breathing temple and fleet Life, this wildworth blown so sweet.

B. *sb.* **4.** Phr. *to play the wild*: to behave in a careless or reckless manner; to play havoc with. *U.S.*

1849 J. B. JONES *Wild Western Scenes* i. 10 But love can play the 'wild' with any young man. **1911** R. D. SAUNDERS *Col. Todhunter* ix. 143 I'm shorely glad to get home. I been playin' the wild in St. Louis.

wild cat. Add: **3. b.** (Earlier example.)

1861 'MARK TWAIN' *Lett.* (1917) I. iii. 54 'Wild cat' isn't worth ten cents.

c. An exploratory oil-well, drilled where there is only a possibility of success. Cf. *WILD *a.* 6 d, *wild well* s.v. *WILD *a.* 16.

1877 *Sci. Amer.* 22 Dec. 387/3 A large number of 'wildcats', or test wells, have gone down off the eastern edge of the defined line, but with very few exceptions they have proved to be dusters. **1943** *Jrnl. Sedimentary Petrol.* XIII. 111/2 Both deep, off-structure wildcats and and field wells are important. **1977** *Offshore Engineer* May 39/1 Esso is drilling in the deepest water off Egypt's Mediterranean coast with a second wildcat in 470m of water 100km off Alexandria.

d. Illicitly distilled whisky. Cf. *wild-cat whisky*, sense 4 b in Dict.

1887 A. A. BROWN *Lumbering on Cumberland* vii. 80 Mr. Kearney alighted and tendered us a drink from his bottle of 'wild cat'. **1945** M. LYON *Fresh from Hills* iv. 47 You can keep on a-makin' wildcat till hell freezes over.

e. *ellipt.* for *wildcat strike*, sense 4 c below.

1959 *Daily Mail* 28 Oct. 1 (*heading*) War on the wild-cats. **1969** *Guardian* 22 Aug. 9/1 The TUC made their 'solemn and binding declaration' to the Prime Minister about dealing with wildcats. **1978** J. WAINWRIGHT *Ripple of Murders* 43 They'd thought he was bluffing... So there's been wildcats and pickets, and lock-ins.

4. b. Also with reference to wildcat strikes (see sense 4 c below).

1959 *Daily Tel.* 31 Dec. 11/2 'Wildcat' risk in bank staffs. **1973** *Black Panther* 29 Sept. 3/3 A majority of the Black workers ..voted to reject the union proposal, upholding the original wildcat demand. **1976** M. MACHLIN *Pipeline* xix. 241 Some people think it was some wildcat members of 798 that set them after the company laid off about a hundred of them.

c. Special Comb.: **wildcat drilling,** the drilling of a wildcat well; **wildcat strike,** a sudden and unofficial strike; hence **wildcat striker**; similarly *wildcat stoppage, walkout*; **wildcat train** *U.S.*, an extra train running in addition to those on the timetable (see quot. 1885); occas. *ellipt.*; similarly *wildcat engine*; **wildcat well** = sense 3 c above.

1937 *Bull. Amer. Assoc. Petroleum Geologists* XXI. 1079 A study of wildcat drilling in the Gulf Coast Plains during 1935 and 1936 indicates that between 7 and 11 per cent of all such holes opened new oil or gas pools, the remaining 93-89 per cent having been dry. These figures speak eloquently of the risk involved in wildcat drilling. **1976** *Offshore Platforms & Pipelining* 60/1 The time span from hard freeze in late autumn to the melt in the late spring leaves an opportunity for no more than about 6,000 ft of wildcat drilling. **1888** *Missouri Republican* 23 Feb., The Montreal night express was thrown from the track..by a wild-cat engine that had been turned loose..by an evil-disposed person. **1891** E. S. ELLIS *Check No. 2134* xiii. 88 There was just one chance in a hundred of a wild-cat engine approaching. **1974** *Telegraph* (Brisbane) 5 Feb. 16/1 Freelance truckers entered the fifth day of their wildcat stoppage. **1937** *Sun* (Baltimore) 16 Nov. 3/1 A clause..conceding to the corporation the right to discipline persons responsible for 'wildcat' strikes. **1954** *Encounter* June 7/2 [The workers'] behaviour itself becomes a judgement... It takes the form of slow-downs, a silent war against production standards, and most spectacularly in the violent eruptions of wildcat strikes against 'speed-ups' or changes in the timing of jobs. **1978** S. BRILL *Teamsters* v. 179 Carey led a militant wildcat strike over a symbolic issue. **1945** *Chicago Daily News* 10 Dec. 1/9 (*caption*) Would fire or fine wildcat strikers. **1981** M. NABB *Death of Englishman* II. iii. 89 He wasn't going to stand by and see his country insulted, disrupted..by wildcat strikers. **1870** *Daily Territorial Enterprise* (Virginia City, Nevada) 22 Oct. 3/1 In company with four or five others, he had gone out on the road upon a hand car, when a 'wild cat train' (an extra train running on no regular time) overtook them. **1885** *Good Words* July 452/1 Every now and then the newspapers allude to 'wild-cat' trains... The 'wild-cat' is the slowest of all trains. It is only used for freight, and reaches its destination when it can, running whenever the line is clear, and shunting when a passenger train is due on the same track. **1942** *Sun* (Baltimore) 26 Sept. 9/6 Our estimated 400 were out in what both union and management termed a 'wildcat' walkout. **1977** *Time* 28 Mar. 46/2 The month-long wildcat walkout by 3,000 precision toolmakers at British Leyland. **1883** Wildcat well [in Dict., sense 4 b]. **1907** *Bull. U.S. Geol. Survey* No. 318. 25 In making maps of subsurface strata in areas that have not been productive, most of the records used for making a convergence sheet must be taken from 'wild-cat wells'. **1975** W. G. ROBERTS *Quest for Oil* (rev. ed.) iii. 35 It is nowadays extremely rare to hear of anyone sinking a true 'wildcat' well—that is, one drilled simply because someone has a hunch that his patch of ground has oil beneath.

wild-catter. Add: *spec.* (*a*) a prospector who sinks wildcat wells; (later examples); (*b*) a wildcat striker.

1925 A. B. THOMPSON *Oil-Fields Explor. & Devel.* I. vii. 314 The speculative spirit aroused by the gusher has had much to do with..inspiring the wild-catter to pursue his quest for extended areas of development. **1947** R. BEDICHEK *Adv. with Texas Naturalist* x. 116, I left the highway, following an old road which led me to the site of some wildcatter's dream and disillusionment. **1966** *Punch* 23 Mar. 404/3 That union refusing membership to a one-armed labourer may have had a point. Just as you don't hit a boy with glasses, even the wildest wildcatter might jib at intimidating this man. **1973** [see *SHOOT-'EM-UP]. **1980** A. COPPEL *Hastings Conspiracy* iv. 31 The militant wildcatters or the British air traffic controllers' union. **1981** *Sci. Digest* Aug. 118/3 Like wildcatters bringing in a gusher, a few of the students develop products with gilt-edged possibilities.

wild-catting, *vbl. sb.* Add: *spec.* (*a*) the drilling of a wildcat well; (later examples); (*b*) participation in a wildcat strike; occas. also as *ppl. a.*

1909 W. S. TOWER *Story of Oil* v. 66 Many of the most valuable oil deposits..have been revealed by the more or less random process of 'wild-catting'. **1967** *Economist* 18 Mar. 1014/2 Just like wild-catting shop stewards, they [*sc.* demonstrators] brought into disrepute the cause that they affected to support. **1969** *Guardian* 22 Sept. 15/1 The West Berlin workers decided that anything their Ruhr brothers can do in the way of wildcatting the Berliners can do better. **1972** L. M. HARRIS *Introd. Deepwater Floating Drilling Operations* xv. 159 Nearly always, a floating drilling operation is a wildcatting venture in an area previously undrilled. **1976** M. MACHLIN *Pipeline* xxxii. 370 The way things are going these days, I think I might just go back to the wildcatting in East Texas.

Wildean (wəi·ldiăn), *a.* [f. the name of Oscar *Wilde* (see below) + -AN.] Of, pertaining to, or characteristic of the Irish writer Oscar Fingal O'Flahertie Wills Wilde (1854–1900), or his works.

1924 *Nation* 26 Mar. 352/1 Epigrams are his undoing. The Wildean nineties are in his blood. **1937** *Scrutiny* V. 386 Ravel is Wildean, 'witty' in the nineteenth century salon. **1958** R. WILLIAMS *Culture & Society* II. ii. 171 A good example of the Wildean paradox. **1967** *Listener* 6 July 15/1 Social morality is turned on its head with a Wildean comment on one of the film's less violent fatalities: 'Marie's tragic death restored my faith in suicide.' **1977** *Time* 21 Feb. 28/3 They are cold, loveless creatures, incapable of responding to one another except by lobbing epigrams, Wildean in rhythm but not in wit, back and forth.

wildebeest. Add: Also **wildebees.** Generic name *Connochætes taurinus* or *C. gnou.* (Earlier and later examples.)

[**1801** J. BARROW *Acct. Trav. S. Afr.* I. iv. 259 The *gnoo* or *wild beast*, as it is called by the Dutch.] **1824** W. J. BURCHELL *Trav. S. Afr.* II. 109 Wild animals; among which were..many *wilde-beests* or *gnues*. **1929** D. REITZ *Commando* 129 Great herds of zebra, wildebeest, and sable, stood fearlessly gazing at us. **1958** *Cape Times* 13 Aug. 3/4 For the rest it was impala, wildebeest and koodoo. **1970** *Life* Jan. 50 Their faces covered with grotesque tufts of hair, the wildebeest..are the oddest and fiercest-looking antelopes.

wilderness. Add: **3. c.** *in the wilderness* (in allusion to *Numbers* xiv. 33), (*a*) of a politician, political party, etc.: out of office; (*b*) *gen.*, unrecognized, out of favour.

1930 *Economist* 2 Aug. 220/1 For Charles X represented a Restoration of the *Ancien Régime*..which had 'learnt nothing and forgotten nothing' during a quarter of a century in the wilderness. **1958** *Spectator* 6 June 719/3 Parties should liquidate their failures and frustrations in the wilderness, not in power. **1966** *Listener* 5 May 661/2 Richard Baker asked Bernard Keeffe why Mahler, so long in the wilderness as far as England was concerned, is now a box-office success. **1969** *Ibid.* 3 July 12/3 Carmichael has now accepted a junior post in the Panther hierarchy and Rap Brown and Jim Foreman have been driven into the wilderness. **1976** *Southern Even. Echo* (Southampton) 17 Nov. 22/3 If he fails to gain the title he lost to Cain on a cut eye decision, it could mean months in the wilderness and set him back even further. **1984** *Times* 1 Aug. 17/2 After months in the wilderness, which has seen the price slip from a high of 95½p to a low of 65½p shares of Marley..is [*sic*] back in favour with the institutions.

wild-fire, wildfire. Add: **4. b.** A leaf-spot disease of tobacco, caused by the bacterium *Pseudomonas tabaci.* Also *attrib.*

1918 *Jrnl. Agric. Res.* XII. 451 The disease appeared so quietly, spread so rapidly, and affected the leaves so seriously that it was commonly given the appropriate designation 'wildfire'. **1955** *Sci. News Let.* 29 Jan. 73/2 Immunity to wildfire..was first transferred..from a wild tobacco species. **1971** *Nature* 15 Jan. 174/1 Wildfire disease of tobacco is perhaps the most thoroughly studied of all toxin-mediated plant diseases.

‖ **Wildflysch** (vi·ltfliʃ). *Geol.* Also **wildflysch.** [Ger. (F. J. Kaufmann 1871, in B. Studer *Index der Petrogr.* (1872) 258): see FLYSCH.] Flysch containing large, irregularly distributed blocks and occupying beds that are distorted.

1929 P. G. H. BOSWELL tr. *Heritsch's Nappe Theory Alps* iv. 47 A great part of the sheared Flysh has the character of the Wildflysch: dark, puckered and highly micaceous marls with interbedded seams of sandstone, quartzite, limestones, breccias, conglomerates and exotic blocks. **1960** *Bull. Geol. Soc. Amer.* LXXI. 878/2 The general aspect of Wildflysch forcibly suggests submarine slumping and sliding on a large scale. **1963** [see *FAMENNIAN *a.*]. **1981** A. HALLAM *Facies Interpretation* iv. 82 A thick series of shallow-water carbonate platform deposits..are overlain by a wildflysch unit with a chaotic jumble of limestone blocks in a shaly matrix.

wild life. Also **wildlife, wild-life.** [f. WILD *a.* 1 and 2 + LIFE *sb.* 1.] **1.** The native fauna and flora of a particular region.

1879 R. JEFFERIES (*title*) Wild life in a southern county. **1912** A. R. DUGMORE (*title*) Wild life and the camera. **1958** *Times Lit. Suppl.* 21 Nov. p. xxii/2 The ıance to live among country things and indulge a native assion for wild life (for if you scratch an Englishman ou are likely to find a naturalist *manqué*). **1982** *Times* 8 Oct. 20/8 Ancient woods..are especially important for ildlife.

2. a. *attrib.*

1936 *Discovery* June 190 His description of the patient rogress of the wild-life photographer has authority ehind it. *Ibid.* 191/2 (*heading*) The wild-life film. **1943** . S. HUXLEY *TVA* 12 The total range of activities overed by the TVA..includes..wild life conservation. *bid.* 54, I spoke earlier of the wild life survey of the egion. **1958** *Times Lit. Suppl.* 10 Jan. 24/1 A well-llustrated anthology based on the B.B.C.'s wild-life and aturalist programmes. **1982** G. HAMMOND *Fair Game* . 47 The shooting man..needs a rich wildlife scene. **984** *Guardian* 22 Oct. 3/2 The Liberals estimate that nnual compensation to farmers who are preserving cenic land or important wildlife habitats ..is running at he rate of £1 million.

b. *Comb.*, as **wildlife park**, a collection of vild animals kept in conditions as close as ossible to their natural ones; **wildlife sanctuary**, an area of land in which hunting, collecting, or any other disturbance of the ıative fauna and flora is forbidden.

1965 P. WAYRE *Wind in Reeds* xvi. 234 We became fficially known as the Norfolk Wildlife Park. Britain's irst wildlife park was away to a flying start. **1976** P. R. WHITE *Planning for Public Transport* viii. 157 Coach perators' inclusive prices for visits to stately homes and wild-life parks. **1936** D. MCCOWAN *Animals Canad. Rockies* i. 12 A warning to poachers in a wild life sanctuary. **1973** V. CANNING *Flight of Wild Goose* iv. 57 The whole of that area was kept as a wild life sanctuary.

Hence **wi·ldlifer**, a person interested in the study and conservation of wild plants and animals.

1963 *Spectator* 8 Feb. 177/3 Children either drop the whole thing or become wildlifers of the intrepid, modern, TV-inspired kind. **1982** G. HAMMOND *Fair Game* v. 49, I can just picture a bunch of slightly hostile wild-lifers.. running the estate.

wildling. 2. (Earlier example.)

1841 S. BAMFORD *Passages in Life of Radical* I. xi. 72 All said he was killed... The doctor..approached along an avenue made through those wildlings.

wild man. 1. c. (Earlier examples, in *sing.* and *pl.*)

1905 D. G. PHILLIPS *Plum Tree* 266 And I wished for a 'wild man' as the candidate for governor. **1910** BELLOC *Pongo & Bull* xix. 287 The Wild Men on the Opposition side might cheer.

Wild Turkey. The proprietary name of a brand of whisky; a drink or glassful of this.

1949 *Official Gaz.* (U.S. Patent Office) 26 Apr. 1007 Austin Nichols & Co., Incorporated, Brooklyn, N.Y... Wild Turkey... For Whiskey. Claims use since May 29, 1942. **1968** *Trade Marks Jrnl.* 20 Mar. 448/1 Wild Turkey 917,193. Wines, spirits (beverages) and liqueurs. Five Mills Limited, 37 Grafton Way..London W.1; Merchants. **1975** *New Yorker* 20 Jan. 30/1, I know—it took me seven weeks to do a page and a half the last time, but I was into the Wild Turkey then, and you'd be amazed how fast I can write when my pencil can actually form legible letters. **1979** J. CROSBY *Party of Year* (1980) viii. 48 He poured Cassidy another Wild Turkey. **1980** J. KRANTZ *Princess Daisy* xvi. 258 Two bottles of Soave Bolla and one of Wild Turkey bourbon.

wild type. *Genetics.* The type of strain, gene, or characteristic that prevails among individuals in natural conditions, as opposed to an atypical mutant type. Freq. *attrib.* or as *adj.*

[**1913** C. B. BRIDGES in *Jrnl. Exper. Zool.* XV. 587 When a female [Drosophila] with white eyes is mated to a wild male with red eyes, the daughters have red, and the sons, white eyes.] **1914** —— in *Science* 17 July 107/2 Half of the wild-type daughters..when out-crossed to barred males..gave exceptions as follows:..Exceptions. 5% of both sexes. Wild type ♀; barred ♂. **1932** [see *SUPPRESSOR 2]. **1946** *Nature* 19 Oct. 558/1 These include wild-type strains [of *E. coli*] with no growth-factor deficiencies, and single mutant types requiring only thiamin or phenylalanine. **1970** *Sci. Amer.* Mar. 103/1 Most mutant genes are nonfunctional or do something very different from wild-type genes, so that they can be easily distinguished. **1970** *Nature* 22 Aug. 806/1 Albinism is monofactorial and is recessive to wild type pigmentation. **1976** *Ann. Rev. Microbiol.* XXX. 90 A number of compounds produce phenocopies of morphological mutants when added to the growth medium of wild type.

Wild West. Also **wild west, wild West. 1.** The western part of the U.S. during its lawless frontier period.

1849 C. BRONTË *Shirley* III. xiii. 272 What suggested the wild West to your mind? **1851** [see WILD *a.* 4]. **1898** H. JAMES in *Literature* 30 Apr. 512/1 Has he [*sc.* Bret Harte] continued to distil and dilute the Wild West because the public would only take him as wild and Western? **1903** CHESTERTON *Robert Browning* v. 111 A gambling hell in the Wild West. **1937** PHILLIPS & NIVEN *Colour in Canad. Rockies* ix. 61 On my first visit there were many marked qualities of the 'wild west' there. **1977** *Times* 20 Sept. 12/1 The Rio Grande..has been oversold in the legends and songs of the old Wild West.

2. *transf.* and *fig.*

1889 G. B. SHAW *London Music in 1888–89* (1937) 170 Somewhere in the wild west of the Old Brompton Road. **1944** F. CLUNE *Red Heart* 69 Australia's Wild West, as picturesque as Texas, was buzzing with rumours of raids, hold-ups. **1975** J. O'FAOLAIN *Women in Wall* 11 My setting is the Wild West of an age often called 'Dark'.

3. a. *attrib.*

1922 E. E. CUMMINGS *Let.* 26 Feb. (1969) 82 Attacks by Bedoins, wild-west style, shooting at Dos with rifles. **1922** E. M. FORSTER *Life to Come* (1972) 100 They passed through the village, on their way back past a cinema, which was giving a Wild West stunt. **1940** 'G. ORWELL' in *Horizon* Mar. 193 The Wild West story..with its cattle-rustlers. **1965** A. NICOL *Truly Married Woman* 5 She removed the Wild West novels and romance magazines. **1971** *Advocate-News* (Barbados) 17 Sept. (Guyana Suppl.) p. iv/2 There it will link up at the 'wild west' border town of Lethem with a similar road the Brazilian army engineers are building to connect with Manaus and the Pan-American Highway.

b. Special Comb.: **Wild West show,** a circus or fairground entertainment depicting cowboys and Indians with exhibitions of riding, shooting, etc.; also *fig.*; similarly *Wild West exhibition.*

1885 in B. A. Botkin *Treas. Amer. Folklore* (1944) I. 150 Buffalo Bill's 'Wild West' Prairie exhibition and Rocky Mountain show. **1895** 'MARK TWAIN' in *N. Amer. Rev.* July 8 A man who could hunt flies with a rifle and command a ducal salary in a Wild West show. **1914** A. BENNETT *Price of Love* vii. 133 Skating-rinks, Wild West exhibitons, Dutch auctions. **1937** N. MARSH *Vintage Murder* xxiv. 268 'Shut up. This isn't a Wild West show.' 'You give me the lie!' 'Oh, for God's sake don't go native.' **1976** *Billings* (Montana) *Gaz.* 20 June 8-c/2 Later, the way it worked in the 'wild west' shows of the day, the U.S. cavalry came along, rescued the passengers and drove off the Indians. **1979** J. WAINWRIGHT *Duty Elsewhere* vii. 29 'Y'mean—illegal methods? Something of a wild west show.' 'That's one way of putting it.'

Hence **wild we·stern** (also with initial capitals) *a.*, characteristic of or resembling the Wild West; as *sb.*, a film about the Wild West; = *WESTERN B. 4; **Wild We·sterner.**

1864 M. B. CHESNUT *Diary* 2 Dec. in C. W. Woodward *M. Chesnut's Civil War* (1981) 682 He had come to take Serena—alone. That is his wild western fashion. **1934** *Cinema Q.* III. iv. 198 'Wild Western' was, almost from the inception of the film, one of its most popular subjects. **1963** I. FLEMING *On Her Majesty's Secret Service* xvii. 192 A group of harlequins, Wild Westerners and pirates. **1967** D. FRANCIS *Blood Sport* viii. 95 Jackson preserved its own wild western flavour to the extent of a small authentic stage coach waiting in front of the drug store. **1981** A. LURIE *Lang. of Clothes* iv. 112 At any national convention the Wild Westerners will be the easiest to identify. **1982** W. MANKOWITZ *Mazeppa* vii. 118 The Menken enjoyed the Washoe wild western atmosphere.

Wilfridian (wilfri·diăn). *Eccl. Hist.* [f. St. *Wilfrid* (634–709) + -IAN.] A member of a religious fraternity founded by Father F. W. Faber (1814–63) for his fellow-converts to Roman Catholicism; later united with the oratory of St. Philip Neri, Birmingham.

1847 F. W. FABER *Let.* 23 Sept. in J. W. Bowden *Life & Lett. Frederick William Faber* (1869) viii. 329 The Wilfridians are allowed to work their double work, against ignorance and brutal sin. **1848** J. H. NEWMAN *Let.* 2 Jan. (1962) XII. 144 What seems to me best is..for..St John and you to go to Cotton to take charge of the Wilfridians. **1869** J. W. BOWDEN *Life & Lett. Frederick William Faber* viii. 295 From the name of the latter Saint they were commonly called Wilfridians. **1928** *St. Wilfrid* xvii. 231 Father Faber did much to make him known and loved... In his first year as a Catholic priest, he and his forty Wilfridians converted a whole parish in Staffordshire. **1981** S. CHITTY *Gwen John* ix. 134 Frederick Faber.. became a Catholic and founded the order of Wilfridians at Elton.

wilful, *a.*[1] Add: **1. c.** In nonce Comb. with *wavy.*

1877 [see *meal-drift* s.v. *MEAL *sb.*[1] 3 a].

Wilhelmine (vi·lhelmain), *a.* [f. the Ger. name *Wilhelm* William (see below) + -INE[1].] Of or pertaining to (the reign of) William II, emperor of Germany 1888–1918. Also **Wilhe·lmian, Wilhelmi·nian** [cf. G. *wilhelminisch*] *adjs.*

1931 C. R. TURNER tr. *G. Schultze-Pfaelzer's Hindenburg* xii. 279 A swaggering general of the later Wilhelminian period. **1948** A. HUXLEY *Ape & Essence* (1949) 21 Floating products of Wilhelmine wealth and culture. **1956** S. BEDFORD *Legacy* IV. v. 282 The events..shed a queer light on the Wilhelminian era. **1957** *Cassell's German & Eng. Dict.* I. 614/2 *Wilhelminisch, adj.*, of William II, Wilhelmian (*of Germany*). **1962** *Times* 14 Nov. 16/2 The Wilhelmian empire. **1973** *Times Lit. Suppl.* 5 Oct. 1183/1 Like so many intellectuals in Wilhelminian Germany. **1975** *Historical Jrnl.* XVIII. 821 It was in this situation that the role of the Centre party in Wilhelmine politics became decisive. **1979** *Observer* 18 Nov. 35 The mood of fatalism that overtook the Wilhelmine Empire of Germany before the advent of the First World War.

Wilhelmstrasse (vi·lhelm,ʃtrā:sə). [Ger.] The name of a street in Berlin, the site of the German foreign office until 1945; hence used for the pre-war German foreign office and its policies.

1914 in *Conc. Oxf. Dict.* Addenda. **1919** LD. F. HAMILTON *Vanished Pomps of Yesterday* i. 28 The Ambassador took the hint, and that was the last note in Russian that reached the Wilhelmstrasse. **1923** G. BUCHANAN *My Mission to Russia* I. iv 45 The reception, however, accorded to this tentative proposal by the Wilhelmstrasse was not encouraging. **1938** H. NICOLSON *Diary* 21 Sept. (1966) I. 363 What remains of Czechoslovakia..must subordinate her foreign policy to that of the Wilhelmstrasse. **1956** S. BEDFORD *Legacy* III. iv. 143, I can't think what they made of him at the Wilhelmstrasse. **1979** G. ST. AUBYN *Edward VII* vii. 316 Chamberlain was resolved to seek partnership with France..should discussions with the Wilhelmstrasse break down.

‖ **wili, willi** (vi·li). *Slavonic Mythol.* [Ger. or Fr. *wili, willi*, ad. Serbo-Croat *vila* nymph, fay. Cf. *VILA.] (See quot. 1949.) Chiefly used in connection with the ballet *Giselle.*

[**1841** VERNOY DE SAINT-GEORGES et al. *Giselle ou Les Wilis* 14 C'est l'heure lugubre où, selon la chronique du pays, les Wilis se rendent à leur salle de bal.] **1949** A. CHUJOY *Dance Encycl.* 511/1 *Wilis* (or *Willis*), in Western-Slavic and Eastern-German legends, the spirits of betrothed girls who have died as a result of being jilted by faithless lovers. They came out to dance at night and led the faithless ones to their death by making them dance until they fell dead of exhaustion. **1961** *Times* 2 Oct. 16/6 Miss Jill Bathurst..danced Odette and the wili Giselle. **1963** P. HANSFORD JOHNSON *Night & Silence* xx. 138 The cat continued to dance, star of the snowy ballet, with a million Wilis whirling behind him. **1977** *N.Y. Rev. Bks.* 13 Oct. 44/2 She gazes out of the fascinating portrait that Henri Lehmann painted of her in 1843 like some supernatural being, a willi, a peri, or a refined succubus.

wiliwili (wī·liwīli). [Hawaiian.] A coral tree, *Erythrina sandwicensis*, of the family Leguminosæ, native to Hawaii and Tahiti and bearing clusters of orange flowers.

1888 W. F. HILLEBRAND *Flora Hawaiian Islands* 100 'Wiliwili' ..loses its leaves in late summer. **1913** J. F. ROCK *Indigenous Trees Hawaiian Islands* 191 The very soft, white wood of the Wiliwili..is still used by the natives for outriggers on their fishing canoes. **1917** *Nature* 20 Sept. 57/2 In the arid regions is found the wiliwili .., a deciduous tree with gnarly growth. **1965** *N.Z. Listener* 17 Dec. 4/2 The Hawaiian chiefs..riding the lighter, balsa-like wili-wili boards.

wilkeite (wi·lki,ait). *Min.* [f. the name of R. M. *Wilke*, 20th-c. U.S. mineral collector + -ITE[1].] A silicate and sulphate mineral of the apatite group occurring as translucent pink or yellow hexagonal crystals (see quot. 1982).

1914 EAKLE & ROGERS in *Amer. Jrnl. Sci.* CLXXXVII. 263 The writers take pleasure in naming it wilkeite in honor of R. M. Wilke, who as a mineral collector and dealer has done much to advance the science of mineralogy. **1937** *Amer. Mineralogist* XXII. 977 It has become necessary to investigate the substitutions of the sort found in wilkeite. **1975** *Nature* 27 Feb. 722/1 Among the minerals described to have any significant degree of P(V)–Si(IV) partial substitution are viseite, nagatelite and wilkeite, an apatite with partial $SiO_4 + SO_4$ substitution for PO_4. **1982** *Amer. Mineralogist* LXVII. 90 Wilkeite is not a valid mineral species, since it is only one of many solid solutions involving the six end-members fluorapatite, hydroxyapatite, chlorapatite, fluorellestadite, hydroxyellestadite, and chlorellestadite.

Wilkism (wi·lkiz'm). [Irreg. f. the name of John *Wilkes* (1727–97), English radical politician + -ISM.] The principles or policies associated with John Wilkes.

1769 MRS. HARRIS *Let.* 24 Mar. in Earl of Malmesbury *Lett.* (1870) I. 177 The Wilkism, and obscenity of the woman proved the greatest attraction. **1778** J. WITHERSPOON *Address to Natives Scotl. residing in Amer.* 5 What effect this *Wilkism* (If I may so speak) of many Americans may be supposed to have had upon the minds of gentlemen from Scotland, it is not difficult to explain. **1930** R. POSTGATE *'That Devil Wilkes'* xiv. 248 (*heading*) The end of Wilkism.

Also **Wi·lkite**, a follower of John Wilkes or his ideas.

a **1797** J. WILKES in Lincoln & McEwen *Lord Eldon's Anecdote Bk.* (1960) 15, I have nothing to do with such a Man. He was a Wilkite, which I never was. **1917** H. BLEACKLEY *Life Wilkes* xiv. 251 The zeal of hundreds of sturdy Wilkites had oozed away. **1930** R. POSTGATE *'That Devil Wilkes'* xiv. 258 They knew only that he had shot down Wilkites.

will, *sb.*[1] Add: **II. 5. c.** Chiefly used in the names (often hyphenated) of supposed natural instincts or drives, as *will to art* [tr. G. *wille zur kunst*]; *will to be, believe, live* (earlier example; also *transf.*); *will to* (or † *unto*) *power* [tr. G. *wille zur macht*), in Nietzsche's philosophy and, later, in analytic psychology (esp. A. Adler's individual psychology): the driving force behind all human behaviour which should lead to self-mastery but when frustrated can become the will to dominate others; cf. *POWER-DRIVE *sb.* 2; (later examples).

1889 G. B. SHAW *How to become a Musical Critic* (1960) 147 Vegetarianism, the higher Buddhism..negation of the Will-to-Live..all these are but samples of what Wagnerism involves nowadays. **1891** —— *Let.* 29 July (1965) I. 301 John Robertson seeks for facts that support his will-to-believe that Materialist-Rationalists are the only honest Secularists. **1923** J. van Teslaar tr. *Stekel's Psychoanal.* II. 61 That 'will to power' means, 'Above all, I want to be loved.'.. Will to power is will to be loved. **1926** Galsworthy *Silver Spoon* I. xiv. 110 Humanity has got to save itself! To save itself—what was that, after all, but expression of 'the will to live'? **1929** H. Read *Staffordshire Pottery Figures* 21 The 'folk' spirit which makes the early salt-glaze..figures so precious as evidences of an innate 'will-to-art'. **1930** D. H. Lawrence *Virgin & Gipsy* ii. 35 Yvette suddenly saw the stony, implacable will-to-power in the old..Granny. **1931** J. S. Huxley *What dare I Think?* iv. 143 Only by banishing the driving force of emotion and the false certitude of the will-to-believe..does she [*sc.* Science] arrive at greater power. **1945** W. de la Mare *Burning-Glass* 12 And naught but his marooned precarious self For questing consciousness and will-to-be. **1948** R. Stagner *Psychol. of Personality* (ed. 2) xv. 288 Adler believed..that the will to power was a fundamental drive, and that it was thwarted by some inferiority. **1963** N. Frye *Romanticism Reconsidered* 14 The tremendous will-to-power finales of Beethoven. **1972** D. V. Tansley *Radionics* iv. 33 The ancient seers of India.. observed that the base chakra was responsible for.. providing a channel for the will-to-be to express itself. **1976** J. Goode in Mitchell & Oakley *Rights & Wrongs of Women* vii. 232 Partly this is based on a will to power, the demand for a totally submissive love. **1977** *Times* 2 Dec. 21/3 The [Crown] agents' 'remarkable will to live' pushed them into critical change in their financial operation in 1966. **1979** E. H. Gombrich *Sense of Order* vii. 193 That 'will to art', which Riegl had conceived as an alternative to the mechanistic explanations of individual motifs, developed into a vitalistic principle underlying the whole history of art. **1985** E. Gellner *Psychoanalytic Movement* i. 27 The Will to Power is a far, far more disturbing, more corrosive idea for human optimism than is the domination of the human psyche by sexuality.

V. 24. a. *will-web.* **c. will-form**, a form on which a will may be made out.

1924 D. H. Lawrence *England, my England* 150 Say I want to see Mr. Whittle as soon as he can, and will he bring a will-form. **1948** 'J. Tey' *Franchise Affair* vi. 56 An old woman..wanted to alter her will... So Robert had taken some new will-forms. **1904** Hardy *Dynasts* I. I. 6 As key-scene to the whole, I first lay bare The Will-webs of thy fearful questioning.

will, *v.*[1] Add: **B. I. 11. c.** *will do* (with omission of *I*): an expression of willingness to carry out a request. Cf. *wilco. *colloq.*

1955 W. Tucker *Wild Talent* xvi. 217 'Paul! Bring my gate pass.'..'Will do.' **1967** L. White *Crimshaw Memorandum* v. 91 'And find out where the bastard was.'..'Will do,' Jim said. **1971** J. Wainwright *Last Buccaneer* II. 220 'Make sure he comes.' 'Will do,' said the D.D.I. **1981** A. M. Stein *Body for Buddy* ix. 176 'Let me know.' 'Will do,' I said.

II. 29. (Further examples.) Also, could naturally or inevitably be expected to, esp. in the light of one's known character or tendencies. *colloq.*

1919 'C. Dane' *Legend* 43 One never knew what Madala would do next, and yet when she'd done it, one said—'Of course! Just what Madala *would* do!' **1926** C. Mackenzie *Rogues & Vagabonds* 268 'He always pushes me out.' 'He would.' **1930** E. Waugh *Vile Bodies* ix. 150 There's our Lily now. You know how she would go in for being a manicurist. **1932** M. H. Rinehart *Miss Pinkerton* xvi. 164 'We're interested in Monday night, and that's all.'.. 'You would be!' **1946** H. J. Massingham *Where Man Belongs* iii. 96 He, Ireson told me, 'is the most promising boy of the lot.' He would be. **1963** *Times* 1 July 6/6 Mr. Burge asked: Do you know Lord Astor has made a statement to the police saying that these allegations of yours are absolutely untrue? Miss Rice-Davies: He would, wouldn't he? **1980** 'T. Hinde' *Daymare* i. 8 'Well, he would, wouldn't he,' she says. 'It's what you'd expect of a born capitalist.'

III. 42. d. *I wouldn't know*: see *know *v.* 11 g.

47. b. *wouldn't it?* (ellipt. for *wouldn't it rock you?*, *wouldn't it root you?*, and similar catch-phrases): an exclamation of annoyance and disgust or (less usually) amusement. *Austral.* and *N.Z. slang.*

1940 *Telegraph* (Sydney) 13 Jan. 4/7 Favorite expression with the troops is, of course, '*Wouldn't it?*'—Short for 'Wouldn't it make you sick?' **1941** *2nd N.Z.E.F. Times* 3 Nov. 6 Well, *wouldn't* it? **1951** Cusack & James *Come in Spinner* 382 Guinea kicked a hassock across the room. 'Wouldn't it!' she muttered furiously, 'wouldn't it!' **1954** J. Cleary *Climate of Courage* xii. 185 'Asking your wife if you can write to her. Wouldn't it?'

Willesden (wi·lzdĕn). The name of a suburb of north-west London, used *attrib.* to denote forms of paper or canvas that have been toughened and waterproofed by being treated with cuprammonium solution.

1895 C. F. Cross et al. *Cellulose* I. 13 Vegetable textile fabrics passed through a bath of the cuprammonium hydroxide are 'surfaced' by the film of gelatinized cellulose... These fabrics are sold under the style or description of 'Willesden' goods; the manufacture being in the hands of a company whose works are situated at Willesden. The company's processes are based on the patents of Drs. J. Scoffern and C. R. A. Wright. **1907** *Yesterday's Shopping* (1969) 283/1 Patent Sleeping Valise... No. 3. Willesden Kharki cotton canvas throughout. No. 4. In Willesden flax canvas. **1911** *Encycl. Brit.* XXIII. 705/1 'Willesden paper'..is cardboard chemically treated to render it tough, waterproof and fire-resisting. **1912** R. A. Freeman *Singing Bone* I. ii. 30 Boscovitch continued to stare up at the little square case covered with Willesden canvas... Thorndyke good-naturedly lifted it down and unlocked it. As a matter of fact he was rather proud of his 'portable laboratory'. **1926–7** *Army & Navy Stores Catal.* 219/3 Willesden Canvas. Suitable for.. awnings, shelters, etc. **1964** J. S. Scott *Dict. Building* 358 *Willesden paper*, a building paper made of cardboard treated with cuprammonium hydroxide to rotproof it. **1982** J. Sherwood *Shot in Arm* xiv. 141 A second-hand Willesden canvas cabin trunk with leather corners.

willi, var. *wili.

William. Add: **2.** An obsolete Dutch coin (see quot. 1893).

1844 T. B. Macaulay *Let.* 9 Oct. (1977) IV. 218 While he was changing me a gold William I got away from the old villain. **1893** R. Bithell *Counting-Ho. Dict.* (rev. ed.) 317 *William*, a gold coin formerly used in Holland, and valued at 10 guilders. Its metallic value was about 16s. 2d. sterling.

3. *slang.* [With a pun on Bill *sb.*[3]] **a.** An account for payment, a bill.

1859 H. J. Byron *Maid & Magpie* ii. 18 When de farmers around are behind in their rent I does little Villiams, at sixty per shent. **1903** Farmer & Henley *Slang* VII. 353/2 *To meet sweet William*, to meet a bill on presentation.

b. A dollar note. (See also quot. 1869.) *U.S.*

Sometimes without a capital initial.

1865 *Republican Banner* (Nashville, Tenn.) 5 Oct. 3/1 Will. had to remember the Workhouse in his will to the tune of a 'ten dollar William'. **1869** *Overland Monthly* III. 128 $100 bills were there [*sc.* in Texas] called 'Williams', and $50 bills 'Blue Williams'. **1887** in Wentworth & Flexner *Dict. Amer. Slang* (1960) 580/1 [He] lost his five dollar William. **1927** C. A. Siringo *Riata & Spurs* i. 10 Mr. Myers wrote me..to buy a suit of clothes with the twenty-dollar 'william'.

4. Used *attrib.* to designate the style of architecture, furniture, etc., associated with the reign of monarchs of this name; esp. **William and Mary** (freq. hyphenated), with reference to William III and Mary, joint King and Queen of Great Britain, 1689–94; **William IV**, with reference to William IV, King of Great Britain, 1830–7.

1905 Fenn & Wyllie *Old Eng. Furnit.* vii. 74 The low-backed armchair..was..subsequently displaced by the more dignified and far more comfortable high-backed kind known to us as the 'Stuart' and the 'William and Mary' chair. **1927** *Daily Tel.* 29 Nov. 7/1 Jacobean and William and Mary chests. **1948** D. Welch *Jrnl.* 31 Aug. (1952) 266 Our chairs were William and Mary with high caned backs. **1955** 'W. Mole' *Hammersmith Maggot* iii. 41 A fine set of William IV chairs. **1977** *New Scientist* 3 Mar. 512/1 A William-and-Mary country house in the depths of Somerset. **1982** 'J. Gash' *Firefly Gadroon* i. 13 A blazing row over a William IV davenport desk.

Williamite. Add: **2. b.** Of glass: bearing portraits or emblems of William III, as an indication of anti-Jacobite feelings.

1905 P. Bate *Eng. Table Glass* xii. 105 No. 213 is a Williamite glass bearing the inscription—'*The immortal memory*'; others read, '*To the glorious memory of King William*'. **1936** *Burlington Mag.* Oct. p. xxiii/1 Many specimens of engraved glasses including Jacobite specimens..and Williamite, Volunteer and other inscribed glasses. **1973** *Country Life* 22 Mar. Suppl. 72/2 A rare Williamite glass.

William Morris. = *Morris.

1944 D. Welch *Jrnl.* 26 Oct. (1952) 135 We had tea at Pitt's Cottage, on a William Morris, mortifying sofa. **1962** I. Murdoch *Unofficial Rose* xiv. 128 The bright blue bird-woven William Morris tiles. **1969** S. Sitwell *Gothic Europe* xiii. 155 They are Brussels tapestries..too 'flowered' in the foreground and therefore too 'William Morris' in style. **1981** M. E. Atkins *Palimpsest* ii. 18 You'll splash the wallpaper, it's William Morris.

Hence **Wi·lliam Mo·rrisy** *a.*, resembling, or in the style of, William Morris.

1960 *Times* 29 July 13/5 A William Morrisy life of craftsmanship close to the soil. **1968** 'O. Mills' *Sundry Fell Designs* viii. 88 She's a William Morrisy person; and all she was after was the simple, creative life. **1977** R. Barnard *Blood Brotherhood* x. 113 A William Morrisy stained-glass window.

william-nilliam (wi·lyăm ni·lyăm), *adv.* Humorously extended form of Willy-nilly *adv.*

1907 G. S. Gordon *Let.* 9 Sept. (1943) 23, I have called you sweet girl. But I will not..retract; and so sweet girl you must remain william nilliam. **1917** A. Huxley *Let.* 8 Apr. (1969) 123, I..found myself pushed—almost william-william [*sic*]—into a very nasty and ill-paid job. **1959** P. Bull *I know Face, But...* x. 188 A splendid change from ordinary digs where the plate is plonked in front of you william-nilliam.

Williams[2] (wi·lyămz). *Computers.* [The name of F. C. *Williams* (1911–77), English electrical engineer, who with T. Kilburn described such a tube in 1948.] *Williams tube*: a cathode-ray tube used in some early computers to store and display an array of spots representing bits; so *Williams memory.*

1950 W. W. Stifler et al. *High-Speed Computing Devices* x. 202 The proposed machine will have an electrostatic storage system consisting of a bank of Williams tubes. **1970** O. Dopping *Computers & Data Processing* x. 150 The Williams memory had many weaknesses but until the middle fifties it was the only available memory in the microsecond class apart from the expensive flip-flop registers. **1982** D. P. Siewiorek et al. *Computer Structures* vii. 107/2 The Williams Tube which implemented the control register was also used to hold the present instruction..itself subsequent to its being read out of main store.

willies (wi·liz), *sb. pl.* *slang* (orig. *U.S.*) [Etym. unknown.] *the willies*: a fit of nervous apprehension. Chiefly in phrs. *to give* (someone) *the willies*, *to get the willies.*

1896 *Dialect Notes* I. 427 *To have the willies*, to be nervous. **1900** G. Bonner *Hard Pan* 99 It just gives me the willies to think of your being down on your luck. **1913** J. London *Valley of Moon* 105 Bert gives me the willies the way he's always lookin' for trouble. **1927** H. A. Vachell *Dew of Sea* 261, I sure got the willies at the thought of meeting you. **1942** G. Kersh *Nine Lives Bill Nelson* ix. 57 It *can* give you the willies when, in broad daylight, you hear a rifle go off. **1953** F. Swinnerton *Month in Gordon Square* 202 Gosh! She was getting the willies. It was awful. **1962** J. Heller *Catch-22* xii. 127 Chief White Halfoat shuddered. 'That guy gives me the willies,' he confessed. **1975** Felton & Fowler *Best, Worst* 277 You can now visit Winchester House. But we wouldn't advise it if you suffer from the willies. **1984** A Carter *Nights at Circus* III. i. 199 Not that the 'wagon salon' isn't very pleasant, if it don't give you the willies.

will-o'-the-wisp, *v.* Delete † and add later examples.

1926 J. B. Priestley *G. Meredith* v. 129 Woman..is far less likely than man to be Will-o'-the-Wisped away by sheer unreason masquerading as reason. **1954** L. MacNeice *Autumn Sequel* xxvi. 159 Words may will-o'-the-wisp him.

willow, *sb.* Add: **II. 5.** (Earlier example.) Cf. *King Willow* s.v. *king *sb.* 6 b.

1846 J. Martin in *Frederick Lillywhite's Cricket Scores & Biographies* (1863) III. 442 And now the 'willow' see them wield.

III. 6. a. *willow bottom* (later example), *walk* (earlier example), *wand* (later example). **b.** *willow-lined* adj. **c. willow gentian**, a herbaceous perennial, *Gentiana asclepiadea*, native to Europe and bearing deep blue or white flowers in axils along its curving stems; **willow grouse**, (*b*) the ruffed grouse, *Bonasa umbellus*, called thus chiefly in British Columbia; **willow leaf**, also as *adj.* = *willow-leaved* adj., sense 6 b; **willow-leaved pear(-tree)**, a tree, *Pyrus salicifolia*, that is related to the pear and is native to S.E. Europe and Asia Minor, bearing long narrow leaves and small fruit and often thorny; **willow oak** (later examples); also, the laurel oak, *Q. laurifolia*; **willow tit (mouse)**, a black-headed, buff-coloured European tit, *Parus montanus* (formerly *P. atricapillus*); **willow-ware** (*b*) articles woven from osiers; **willow-wielder** (earlier example).

1962 W. Stegner *Wolf Willow* I. i. 12, I see a black iron bridge, new, that evidently leads some new road off into the willow bottoms. **1883** W. Robinson *Eng. Flower Garden* 136/1 Willow Gentian prefers a sheltered position. **1935** C. Elliott *Rock Garden Plants* 123 The Willow Gentian of sub-alpine woods, grows two feet high, with arched wiry stems, strung along their upper half with fine blue trumpet-flowers. **1962** R. Page *Education of Gardener* xiii. 357, I may choose *Gentiana asclepiadea*, the willow gentian. **1907** J. G. Millais *Newfoundland* 274 The Newfoundland willow grouse..fly in large bodies from one district to another. **1960** *Gulf Islander* (Galiano, B.C.) 23 July 1/1 We listened to the resonant call of the willow grouse. **1961** W. P. Keller *Canada's Wild Glory* II. 93 The grouse came back, too. These were the willow grouse or as the same bird is known in the east, 'the drummer' or ruffed grouse. **1818** A. Eaton *Man. Bot.* (ed. 2) 447 Willow-leaf golden-rod. **1975** *Country Life* 20 Mar. 699/3 Willow-leaf pears..form charming leafy tapestries. [**1789** W. Aiton *Hortus Kewensis* II. 176 Willow-leav'd Crab Tree. Nat[ive] of the Levant.] **1820** *Bot. Reg.* VI. 514 (*heading*) Willow-leaved pear-tree. **1914** W. J. Bean *Trees & Shrubs Hardy in Brit. Isles* II. 292 Willow-leaved Pear... Branchlets covered with down which is quite white when young. **1980** V. Canning *Fall from Grace* ix. 155 A carpet of silvery *Cineraria maritima* spread under a group of willow-leaved pears. **1946** J. W. Day *Harvest Adventure* x. 159 Half-way between Yarmouth and Acle on that dead straight, willow-lined road. **1813** Willow oak [see *grey oak* s.v. *grey *a.* 8]. **1897** [see *peach oak* s.v. *peach *sb.*[1] 6]. **1949** *Amer. Forests* Sept. 18/3 A tall willow oak drips slender verdant fingers. **1975** *Country Life* 2 Jan. 38/3 More native trees were also planted, notably..the willow oak. **1907** *Brit. Birds* I. 44 The Willow Tit varies a good deal geographically. **1979** C. M. Perrins *Brit. Tits* vii. 60 The Willow Tit was the last British species to be recognized. **1958** *Spectator* 22 Aug. 244/1, I discovered a rare bird, then almost unknown,..at Beckenham—a willow titmouse. **1803** J. Palmer *World as it Goes* II. 14 The carriage entered a willow-walk, terminated by a small antique building. **1954** J. R. R. Tolkien *Fellowship of Ring* iii.

80, I shall be as thin as a willow-wand. **1851** C. Cist *Cincinnati* 172 Baskets, cradles, wagons and other willow-ware. **1880** *Harper's Mag.* June 30/1 We find women employed in making..willow-ware and cane chairs. **1870** *John Wisden's Cricketers' Almanack* 91 With willow wielders like these, it is no wonder Notts holds the high position it does as a batting shire.

f. Short for *willow pattern* (Willow *sb.* 6 c), as *willow cup, plate, pottery*. See also *willow ware* in Dict.

1926 R. Macaulay *Crewe Train* II. x. 179 It would look jolly with blue willow cups and plates on it. **1928** T. S. Eliot in E. Pound *Sel. Poems* p. xvii, People who like Willow pottery and Chinesische-Turms in Munich and Kew. **1961** M. Beadle *These Ruins are Inhabited* (1963) xi. 142 In contrast, the laburnums..curved earthward with willow-plate grace.

willowy, *a.* Add: Hence **wi·llowily** *adv.*; **wi·llowiness.**

1932 A. Huxley *Brave New World* xi. 192 He put his arm round the Head Mistress's waist. It yielded, willowily. **1972** *Daily Tel.* 13 Mar. 11 Virile shoulders, tapering downward to a more traditional willowiness, are the hallmark of the 1972 Cardin man.

willy, willie, *sb.*[2] Add: **2.** *slang.* An infantile name for the penis. Also *Comb.*, as *willy-warmer.*

1905 *Eng. Dial. Dict.* Suppl. 178/2 *Willy*, the male organ; a slang name for a child's penis. Cum., Wm. **1972** *Listener* 22 June 841/3 The gallant soldier-boys are afflicted with 'syph, darling' ('their willies rot away'). **1975** *Observer* 7 Dec. 27/3 Joky gifts are speechlessly embarrassing; this season's dud is a woolly willy-warmer. **1977** J. Wilson *Making Hate* ix. 113 A younger male [baboon]..fingered its crimson penis... 'It's playing with its *willie*!' Nicky squealed. **1985** P. Angadi *Governess* x. 93 We used to hold each other's willies... We didn't know about sex then.

willy (wi·li), *sb.*[3] [Prob. related to Williwaw: cf. Willy-willy.] In the South Atlantic (Tristan da Cunha): (see quots.).

1832 A. Earle *Narr. Residence N.Z.* (1966) 204 These sudden squalls are called '*Willies*', at least, such is the name given them by the sailors who frequent the island [*sc.* Tristan da Cunha]. **1941** A. B. Crawford *I went to Tristan* xi. 158 A shower is a 'light squall' and 'willies' are eddies of spray above the surface of the sea caused by small whirlwinds. *Ibid.* 268 *Willie*, whirlwind of spray over the sea.

willya (wi·lyă). Repr. colloq. pronunc. of 'will you..?', esp. as a tag after an imperative.

1941 B. Schulberg *What makes Sammy Run?* ix. 241 Willya find out who rang for a messenger boy? **1956** 'E. McBain' *Cop Hater* (1958) iv. 38 Hey, shut up, will-ya? **1968** C. Burke *Elephant across Border* i. 28 Now go away, willya? **1981** G. McDonald *Fletch & Widow Bradley* viii. 28 Write a new story... Only get the competition to print it this time, willya, Fletch?

willyamite (wili͵ă-məit). *Min.* [See quot. 1893 and -ite[1].] A sulphide and antimonide of cobalt and nickel, (Co,Ni)SbS, in which Co exceeds Ni, found as white or grey pseudo-cubic crystals having a metallic lustre.

1893 E. F. Pittman in *Jrnl. & Proc. R. Soc. New S. Wales* XXVII. 366, I propose to name the mineral Willyamite (pronounced Willy-ah'-mite) after Willyama the official name of the Broken Hill township, and the aboriginal word meaning a hill with a broken contour. **1976** *Norsk. Geol. Tidsskr.* LVI. 449 Ullmannite, cobaltian ullmannite and willyamite occur as blebs and laths in galena from Espeland mine, Aust-Agder, Norway.

willy wet-leg: see *wet-leg* s.v. *Wet *a.* 20.

Wilms (vilmz). *Path.* [The name of M. *Wilms* (1867–1918), German pathologist.] *Wilms('s)* or (erron.) *Wilm's tumour*: a malignant tumour of the kidney that occurs in infants and children.

1910 E. L. Keyes *Dis. Genito-Urinary Organs* 974/2 (Index), Wilms tumor of kidney. **1928** Eisendrath & Rolnick *Text-bk. Urol.* xlviii. 753 These tumors in their pure state have been termed mixed cell or Wilms tumors and are composed of..muscle fibres, blood vessels, cartilage, [etc.]. **1948** R. A. Willis *Path. of Tumours* lx. 925 Many names have been applied to the embryonic renal tumours—'adenosarcoma',..'Wilms's tumour'.. and 'nephroblastoma'... It is now clear that there is but one entity, embryonic renal tumour. **1961** R. D. Baker *Essent. Path.* xiii. 307 Embryonal and mixed tumors are most frequently mixed salivary gland tumors, Wilm's tumor of the kidney, and testicular and teratomatous tumors. **1971** *Brit. Med. Bull.* XXVII. 68/1 Retinoblastomata and Wilms' tumours were found to have shorter latent periods. **1980** *Jrnl. R. Soc. Arts* Jan. 99/1 In rhabdomyosarcoma, Ewing's sarcoma and Wilm's tumour considerably increased survival has been obtained.

wilsh, var. *Wilch.

Wilson[1] (wi·lsən). *Path.* [The name of S. A. Kinnier *Wilson* (1878–1937), English neurologist.] *Wilson's disease*: = *hepato-lenticular degeneration* s.v. *Hepato-.

1915 Stedman *Med. Dict.* (ed. 3) 1032/2 *Wilson's disease*, progressive degeneration of the lenticular nucleus, occurring as a familial disease associated with cirrhosis of the liver. **1919** *Arch. Internal Med.* XXIV. 497 (*heading*) Progressive lenticular degeneration associated with cirrhosis of the liver (Wilson's disease). **1978** *Brit. Med. Jrnl.* 18 Nov. 1384/2 Though originally described as a neurological disorder with associated cirrhosis, we now recognise hepatolenticular degeneration (Wilson's disease) as a copper storage disorder in which other tissues become affected as the excess copper is released from the liver.

Wilson[2] (wi·lsən). *Physics.* The name of C. T. R. *Wilson* (1869–1959), Scottish physicist, used *attrib.* and in the possessive to designate the cloud chamber (see *Cloud *sb.* 12) invented by him.

1917 *Sci. Abstr.* A. XX. 337 Wilson's condensation chamber..was still smaller than the author's small sphere. **1931** *Ann. Reg. 1930* 59 Harkins and Smith took 39,000 photographs of the tracks of 390,000 α-particles in a Wilson cloud chamber containing nitrogen. **1961** *New Scientist* 23 Feb. 474/2 The Wilson cloud chamber had done heroic work for many years in the examination of the tracks of particles, but its limitations in speed and scope were becoming increasingly apparent.

Wilsonian (wilsōᵘ·niăn), *a.* (and *sb.*) [See -ian.] Pertaining to or characteristic of Woodrow *Wilson* (1856–1924), president of the United States 1913–21, noted for his uncompromising idealism. Also as *sb.*, a follower of Woodrow Wilson.

1921 *Labour Monthly* Sept. 285 In whatever shades or purgatory await our public men after the completion of their labours, a special circle should be reserved for the Old Wilsonians. **1924** *Amer. Mercury* Jan. 53/1 It was at this precise moment in his career that the Wilsonian storming of Valhalla began. **1934** H. G. Wells *Exper. Autobiogr.* II. ix. 694 The Wilsonian notion of a League. **1962** *Listener* 22 Mar. 524/1 Mr. Tillman remains a starry-eyed Wilsonian. **1980** J. Lees-Milne *Harold Nicolson* I. vii. 116 The French bitterly opposed the very idea of the covenant as Wilsonian idealistic nonsense.

Also **Wi·lsonism,** the policies of Woodrow Wilson.

1920 *Harvey's Weekly* 16 Oct. 13/1 No more time need be lost in following the slush-fund herring trail away from the vital issue of Wilsonism. **1945** Koestler *Yogi & Commissar* III. i. 125 Movement followed Movement and withered away. Jacobinism,..Wilsonism, the League of Nations..they were all branches of the same tree rooted in the Age of Enlightenment. **1977** *N.Y. Rev. Bks.* 12 May 16/4 But they were fighting to save Wilsonism, if need be from Wilson himself.

wilt, *sb.*[2] (Later examples of *Bot.* sense.)

1918 [see *Psylla]. **1946** *Nature* 13 July 56/1, I came across what is apparently a hitherto undescribed wilt disease of the oil palm. **1961** A. Schoenfeld tr. *Stapp's Bact. Plant Pathogens* I. 103 This wilt disease [of beans] can be said with certainty not to occur in Germany. **1981** Buczacki & Harris *Collins Guide to Pests of Garden Plants* 306 Most wilts are caused by Deuteromycete fungi.

wilt, *v.* Add: **2. b.** *Agric.* To leave (mown grass, etc.) to dry partially in the open before putting it in a silo.

1971 *Power Farming* Mar. 9/1 'But,' said Mr. Whitton, 'the loader must be used as part of a system, and it is most essential that the silage be wilted and chopped.' **1974** *BSI News* May 8/3 The process of wilting the crop [of grass] from 75%–85% moisture content down to 55%–65%. **1980** *Daily Tel.* 28 Jan. 10/4 New techniques such as wilting the crop in the field before it is ensiled.

wilting, *vbl. sb.* Add: **wilting coefficient,** the moisture content of the soil (expressed as a percentage of its dry weight) when a plant begins to wilt.

1912 Briggs & Shantz in *Bull. U.S. Bureau Plant Industry* No. 230. 9 It appears advisable to use a more specific term for the moisture content of the soil corresponding to the wilting point of a plant, and we have employed the term 'wilting coefficient' in this sense in the present paper. **1980** *Communications Soil Sci. & Plant Analysis* XI. 843 Studies were performed to determine the wilting coefficient of various selected light tropical soils collected at different locations in..Venezuela.

Wilton[2] (wi·ltən). The name of a farm near Grahamstown, Cape Province, South Africa; used *attrib.* to denote a later Stone Age culture of southern Africa.

1928 A. J. H. Goodwin in *Ann. S. Afr. Mus.* (1929) XXVII. x. 251 Our first knowledge of the Wilton Industry comes from the Cape Peninsula, various crescents, thumbnail scrapers, and the like appearing from a number of kitchen middens and sand-dune sites in this district. **1936** L. S. B. Leakey *Stone Age Afr.* v. 96 In the Wilton culture the most typical tools are,..crescents and other small geometric microliths, together with small double-end and thumb-nail scrapers. **1959** J. D. Clark *Prehist. S. Afr.* ii. 41 The Wilton [culture] is named from the rock-shelter on the farm of that name west of Grahamstown. Its distribution is very wide. **1980** *Cambr. Encycl Archaeol.* 174/1 The microlithic industries (known as Wilton in eastern and southern Africa) of the early to mid-Holocene.

Wiltshire. Add: (*a*) *Wiltshire Horn(ed)*, (a sheep of) a recently revived breed, distinguished by its very light short wool; (*c*) (earlier examples; also *North Wiltshire*).

1816 Jane Austen *Emma* I. x. 188 She was come in herself for the Stilton cheese, the north Wiltshire, the butter, the cellery, [etc.]. **1863** H. Jones *Jrnl.* 20 Aug. in F. W. Lindsay *Cariboo Dream* (1971) 38, 1 case Gloucester Cheese $75.72 Wiltshire do. $97.35. **1945** J. F. H. Thomas *Sheep* ii. 34 The Wiltshire Horned..is no longer to be found in Wiltshire..; the main area of distribution is now Northamptonshire and Buckinghamshire. **1970** *Observer* 26 Apr. (Colour Suppl.) 36/1 Wiltshire Horn..has no wool but, instead, a thick matted coat. **1977** *Jrnl. R. Soc. Arts* CXXV. 708/1 Supposing, for example, that wool became a nuisance and that it was far better to keep sheep that were wool-less and just had hair. It so happens that we have got such a breed, the Wiltshire Horn, that has a rather hairy coat, and so we can use that.

wimble, *sb.* Add: **3*.** Also **wimbel.** An implement for twisting together strands (esp. of straw) to make rope for tying up hay-trusses, fleeces, etc. Cf. *Wimbrel[2].

1863 J. R. Wise *New Forest* 288/1 *Wimble*, an instrument with which to take up faggots or trusses of hay. **1874** Hardy *Far fr. Madding Crowd* I. xxii. 243 Gathering up the fleeces and twisting ropes of wool with a wimble for tying them round. **1886** —— *Mayor Casterbr.* I. i. 2 A rush basket, from which protruded at one end the crutch of a hay-knife, a wimble for hay-bonds being also visible. **1969** E. H. Pinto *Treen* 97 Wimbels are essentially cranked devices for twisting ropes out of straw, formerly required for binding corn stooks.

wimble, *v.*[1] Add: **3.** *trans.* To make (a rope) using a wimble (sense 3*).

1874 Hardy *Far fr. Madding Crowd* I. x. 131 'What have you been doing?' 'Tending thrashing-machine, and wimbling haybonds.'

wimbling *vbl. sb.* (later examples in sense *3 of vb.); **wi·mbler,** one who makes ropes with a wimble.

1964 *Courier-Mail* (Brisbane) 21 Dec., The policeman asked Godfrey Booth: 'Your occupation, sir?' Mr. Booth ..replied 'Cag handed straw wimbler.' Mr. Booth lives in Bobbington, Staffordshire. *Ibid.*, Mr. Booth said: 'When I left school I took up farming, and wimbling took second place.'

Wimbledon (wi·mb'ldən). The name of a district of South London, used *colloq.* to designate the Lawn Tennis Championships on Grass played annually at the All-England Lawn Tennis and Croquet Club there. Also *transf.* and *attrib.*

1907 F. W. Payn *Tennis Topics & Tactics* xvi. 157 The presence of nearly 30,000 spectators in all at the Wimbledon Championships. **1919** *Country Life* 5 July 29/1 Mr. Gore, the former champion, whose twenty-eighth Wimbledon this is. *Ibid.* 12 July 54/2 Whether the 'Victory' Championships will go down to history as 'The Wet Wimbledon' or 'The Wonderful Wimbledon' time alone can tell. **1930** A. P. Herbert *Water Gipsies* xxv. 381 Fay's *livid*—Says she wouldn't marry him now if he gave her free seats for Wimbledon. **1935** *Encycl. Sports* 385/2 No record of the Wimbledon championships would be complete without mention of a few of the winners of the men's and women's doubles championships. **1965** V. Canning *Whip Hand* xii. 134 He's.. Wimbledon standard tennis, Olympic standard swimming. **1971** *Guardian* 17 Nov. 10/3 Alun Owen is an old hand at the ding-dong, the ping-pong, the Wimbledon of sex. **1979** D. Anthony *Long Hard Cure* v. 42 Was that the year you won Wimbledon?

wimble-wamble (wi·mb'l͵wǫ·mb'l), *adv.* and *sb. dial.* or *arch.* [Redupl. f. Wamble *sb.* and *v.*] **a.** *adv.* (See quot.) **b.** *sb.* ? The 'general run', the ordinary crowd.

1890 J. D. Robertson *Gloss. Dial. & Archaic Wds. Glos.* 179 *Wimble-wamble, to go sort of, vb.* to roll about in walking. **1937** H. G. Wells *Star Begotten* viii. 142 They will observe how they resemble each other and how they differ from the wimble-wamble of the common world.

wimbly-wambly (wi·mbli͵wǫ·mbli), *a. dial.* Also **wimley-wamley.** [Redupl. f. Wambly *a.*] Shaky, unsteady; feeble, effeminate.

1881 *Leeds Loiners' Comic Olmenac* 24, I went all wimley-wamley e me head. **1882** F. W. P. Jago *Ancient Lang. & Dial. Cornwall* 312 I'm all wimbly-wambly. **1929** D. H. Lawrence *Pansies* 113 Flat-chested, crop-headed, chemicalised women, of indeterminate sex, And wimbly-wambly young men, of sex still more indeterminate.

wimbrel[1], var. Whimbrel.

1688 [in Dict., s.v. Whimbrel]. **1898** J. A. Gibbs *Cotswold Village* 102 There are wimbrels and curlews that have been shot here..stuffed and hung up in glass cases.

wimbrel[2], dial. var. *Wimble *sb.* 3*.

1939 D. Hartley *Made in England* ii. 76 There are other types [of implement], such as the wimbrel, rather like the spindle of a spinning wheel in principle. **1969** E. H. Pinto *Treen* 97 Other country names for them [*sc.* wimbles] include wimbrels, straw twisters, [etc.].

Wimmera (wi·məră). The name of a river and the region surrounding it in north-western Victoria, Australia, used *attrib.* in **Wimmera rye-grass** to designate a grass belonging to a drought-resistant variety of *Lolium rigidum* first identified in the area about 1900.

1920 *Proc. R. Soc. Victoria* XXXII. 199 Wimmera Rye

Grass. **1928** R. G. STAPLEDON *Tour Austral. & N.Z.* ix. 74 The so-called Wimmera rye-grass..first appeared in Victoria, presumably as a stowaway, about thirty years ago. **1934** *Bulletin* (Sydney) 4 Apr. 28/1 Next sow (in N.S.W. anyway) 5 lb. Wimmera rye grass. **1973** TOTHILL & HACKER *Grasses Southeast Queensland* 197 Wimmera ryegrass..is grown widely in southern Australia. **1977** *Weekly Times* (Melbourne) 19 Jan. 10/5 Wimmera rye grass is regarded as a curse.

wimmin (wi·min). A semi-phonetic spelling of 'women', recently adopted by some feminists as a form not containing the ending *-men*. Also, at an earlier date, occasionally used ironically in other contexts.

1910 H. G. WELLS *Hist. Mr Polly* vi. 201 'Wimmin's a toss up,' said Uncle Penstemon. 'Prize packets they are, and you can't tell what's in 'em till you took 'em 'ome and undone 'em. Never was a bachelor married yet that didn't buy a pig in a poke.' **1938** *Snow White & Seven Dwarfs* 31 'Didn't I tell you?' sniffed Grumpy. 'She's crazy. Wimmin! Pah!' **1983** *Observer* 13 Mar. 16/4 Another woman was writing the words of a song... 'We coil and spring we grow and sing we dance with the tree of life we are the serpents of healing and rebirth wimmin have reclaimed the earth'... 'Why 'wimmin'?' I asked... 'We want to spell women in a way that does not spell men.' **1983** *Sunday Times* 10 Apr. 36/3 Return to Greenham Common, view the wool webs, the papier mâché masks, the eccentric re-spelling of words like 'wimmin', the improbable cosiness of the little tents in a landscape of wire fencing and policemen. **1983** *Listener* 14 Apr. 4/1 Meanwhile, what of the Peace Women ('wimmin' in feminist placards) camped outside Greenham Common? **1983** *Private Eye* 22 Apr. 5/2 (*heading*) Wimmin. **1985** *Sunday Tel.* 11 Aug. 13/8 The Greenham women—God bless 'em! (Sorry—I should write 'wimmin', since the word 'women' contains the horrid inclusion of 'men'. Their little eccentricity!)

wimp[1] (wimp). *slang.* [Origin uncertain; perh. an abbreviated corruption of *women*.] A woman or girl.

'*Wimp* was also used as a verb at Oxford *c.* 1917, e.g. *to go wimping*' (M. Marples, *University Slang* (1950), p. 98).

1923 J. MANCHON *Le Slang* 338 *Wimp*, femme, fille, donzelle. **1937** PARTRIDGE *Dict. Slang* 959/1 *Wimp*, a (young) woman, a girl: from ca. 1920. **1940** [see *Skinny Liz* s.v. *SKINNY *a.* 6].

wimp[2] (wimp). *slang.* (orig. *U.S.*). [Origin uncertain; perh. f. WHIMPER (cf. Eng. dial. *wimp* (of a dog) to whine.] A feeble or ineffectual person; one who is spineless or 'wet'. (Used only as a term of abuse or contempt.)

1920 ADE *Hand-made Fables* 97 Next day he sought out the dejected Wimp. **1964** *Amer. Speech* XXXIX. 119 A *baff* is 'a person who does silly things deliberately'; but *wimp* is still mysterious and undefined in my notes. **1966** *Current Slang* Winter 8 *Wimp*, a backward person... He's a real *wimp* on a date. **1970** *New York* 16 Nov. 10/2 That Goodell, he's nothing but a wimp. And this Ottinger, it got so I couldn't stand the sight of him. **1976** *New Mus. Express* 31 July 8/2 Although he's best known here as a fairly muscular MOR wimp,..he has a big reputation as a prodigiously talented multi-media whizz in the States. **1979** T. GIFFORD *Hollywood Gothic* (1980) xxii. 220 Solly Roth and his wimp of a son.. what a wet bunch that family was. **1981** P. THEROUX *Mosquito Coast* vi. 48, I can afford to be robbed... But what about the poor wimps who can't afford it? **1984** *Sunday Tel.* 30 Dec. 15/6 In daily life Ronnie Lee is a wimp. Put him in a balaclava and he thinks he's a he-man. **1985** *She* July 140/2 Masseur! Huh! He sounds a right little wimp.

Wimpey, var. *WIMPY *sb.* 2.

wimpish (wi·mpiʃ), *a.* *slang.* (orig. *U.S.*). [f. *WIMP[2] + -ISH[1].] Characteristic of a 'wimp'; feeble, ineffectual; snivelling. Freq. of persons.

1925 S. LEWIS *Arrowsmith* xxvi. 288 They looked like lunching grocers: brisk featureless young men;..wimpish little men with spectacles, men whose collars did not meet. **1977** *Sounds* 9 July 30/6 The ever so slightly wimpish 'Give Me Some Time'. **1978** J. IRVING *World according to Garp* xiii. 255 You call that wimpish asshole and say good-bye. **1982** *Mail on Sunday* 2 May 13/3 The wimpish young schoolmaster. **1983** *Times* 28 May Suppl. 1/5 The only motive for reading it may be to swank about it at literary cocktail parties, which is a wet and wimpish reason. **1985** *Times* 11 Feb. 14/1 The Duke of Edinburgh had adopted a new 'limp' handshake... Expecting something flabby and wimpish, the men got royal bonecrushers.

Hence **wi·mpishness**, ineffectual character or behaviour; feebleness.

1978 *Oxford Times* 6 Jan. 13/4 *Renaissance: Novella* (Warner Bros. K 56422)—It's fashionable to sneer at the 'wimpishness' of delicate music like this but..I like it. **1983** *Times* 9 Mar. 10/1 If Michael Straight is a wimp (weakling or 'wet') as some people allege, the wimpishness is not immediately apparent. **1984** *Daily Express* 17 July 8/1 Now he has raised a coast-to-coast horselaugh by his best ever display of wimpishness. Having sacked the party's incompetent national chairman, he promptly reinstated him in the face of protests.

wimpling, *ppl. a.* Add: **2.** Also *transf.* in *poet.* use.

1877 G. M. HOPKINS *Poems* (1967) 69 How he rung upon the rein of a wimpling wing In his ecstasy.

Wimpy (wi·mpi), *sb.* [The name of the cartoon character J. Wellington *Wimpy* in the 'Popeye' cartoon strip, who was often portrayed eating a hamburger.] **1. a.** A proprietary name for a variety of hamburger. Also (*rarely*) in slang use.

1935 *Official Gaz.* (U.S. Patent Office) 21 May 557 Wimpy Grills, Inc., Chicago, Ill... *Wimpy*..For sandwiches, roasted and toasted meats... Claims use since Sept. 12, 1934. **1935** J. HARGAN *Gloss. Prison Lang.* 8 *Wimpy*, hamburger. **1943** *American Mercury* Nov. 553/2 Other chow terms in popular use..*wimpies* for hamburgers. **1954** *Trade Marks Jrnl.* 20 Jan. 63/2 Wimpy... B720, 112. Bread rolls containing cooked foods. Edward Vale Gold, 140, North Dearborn, Chicago, Illinois, United States..Manufacturer and Merchant. **1959** *Observer* 8 Nov. 3/1 The bright glossy bars where Wimpies are served are the most striking example of Britain's changing eating habits. **1967** T. HARKNETT *Two-Way Frame* x. 77, I had a sterile Wimpy and cup of insipid black coffee. **1981** C. STORR *Vicky* vii. 56, I can always go out and get a Wimpy or something.

b. Shortened form of *Wimpy bar*, sense 3 below.

1966 M. WADDELL *Otley* xix. 171 We wound up in the Wimpy by the Broadway. **1968** *Listener* 13 June 763/1 Two years of success by any standard and then a break-up. Mecca had opened a dance hall... A Wimpy came and a bowling alley.

2. Usu. in form *Wimpey*. A Wellington bomber aeroplane. *slang.*

1942 *Tee Emm* (Air Ministry) II. 81 You have the mad sort of chauffeur who tries to roll a Wimpey. **1944** 'N. SHUTE' *Pastoral* i. 1 There was a Wimpey running up one engine, somewhere away out in the middle distance of the aerodrome. **1954** [see *map reference* s.v. *MAP *sb.*[1] 4].

3. *attrib.* and *Comb.*, as *Wimpyburger*, *culture*, *-eating*; **Wimpy Bar**, an establishment where Wimpy hamburgers are sold.

1959 *Observer* 8 Nov. 3/1 At least once a week a 'Wimpy Bar' is being opened somewhere in England. **1966** 'K. A. SADDLER' *Gilt Edge* xiii. 180 That night in the Wimpy Bar..Len had summed him up at a glance. He had only agreed to take part in the job to get out of the Wimpy Bar. **1982** M. GILBERT *Final Throw* v. 35 'Let's find somewhere to eat.'.. They found a Wimpy Bar that was open. **1939** *Amer. Speech* XIV. 154/2 *Wimpyburger*, a specially large hamburger sandwich. **1971** LAVER & COLLINS *Education of Tennis Player* xvi. 209 A tea garden..is located outside of Centre Court [at Wimbledon] where the famous strawberries and cream are sold.., along with a concession to the present day: Wimpy-burgers. **1971** 'J. QUARTERMAIN' *Man who walked on Diamonds* i. 7 A London throbbing with traffic and Wimpy culture. **1959** *Observer* 8 Nov. 3/1 Behind this wave of Wimpy-eating lies a simple commercial formula.

wimpy (wi·mpi), *a.* *slang* (orig. *U.S.*). [f. *WIMP[2] + -Y[1].] = *WIMPISH *a.*

1967 *Current Slang* Spring 5, [1964] *Wimpy*, stupid or sluggish. **1969** *Publ. Amer. Dial. Soc.* LI. 16 *Wimpy*, spineless. **1977** D. LINZEE *Discretion* (1981) i. 16 'It is exquisite.' 'I think it's kind of a wimpy little picture, personally.' **1977** *Sounds* 9 July 31/1, I vaguely anticipated something wimpy and limpy prattling about San Francisco and love and peace man. **1980** *High Fidelity* June 106/2 The Seventies witnessed macho rock & rollers sneering at singer/songwriters as 'wimpy'. **1984** *Nutshell* (Gainesville ed.) Spring 52/2, I *was* this little wimpy kid in elementary school and high school. **1984** *Melody Maker* 6 Oct. 15/4 Dennis had a brilliant artist last summer, really strong drawings, but now it's gone back to being a bit wimpy.

Hence **wi·mpiness** = *WIMPISHNESS.

1982 *Chicago Sun-Times* 1 Sept. 54 (*caption*) Wanna be a political activist? Are you held back by wimpiness?

Wimshurst (wi·mzhɒɹst). *Physics.* [The name of James *Wimshurst* (1832–1903), English engineer.] *Wimshurst machine*: an electrostatic generator consisting of two or more counterrotating discs of insulating material mounted close together on a common axle and having a ring of metal sectors around their periphery; each disc has a stationary pair of brushes at diametrically opposite positions which are electrically connected, so that successive sectors become inductively charged as they come into contact with a brush and give up their charge later in the turn as they pass a fixed set of needle points connected to one or other electrode.

1886 R. WORMELL *A. von Urbanitzky's Electricity in Service of Man* I. 63 The Wimshurst machine and that of Carré..are the least subject to these defects of any that we are acquainted with. **1978** *Sci. Amer.* Apr. 159/1, I placed my candle between the oppositely charged poles of a Wimshurst machine, the ancient hand-crank generator of high-voltage static electricity.

win, *v.*[1] Add: **3. a.** Also *transf.* in catch-phr. *to win the peace*, to bring about the successful reconstruction of a country defeated in or severely damaged by a war. Hence *win-the-peace* attrib.

1942 H. A. WALLACE *Century of Common Man* (1944) 10 As part of the effort to win the peace, I am hoping that what might be called the 'ever normal granary principle' can be established for a number of commodities on a world-wide scale. **1945** *Daily Herald* 31 Aug. 2/1 The nation, girding itself for a supreme win-the-peace endeavour, will derive high encouragement from this enterprise by the mining community. **1950** A. HUXLEY *Themes & Variations* 243 That the Russians have been 'winning the peace' is due..to the fact that they profess and teach, as absolutely true, a clear-cut philosophy of man and nature. **1962** *Listener* 8 Mar. 402/2 They have also tried to agree that nobody was going to win the peace, but nobody was going to lose it either.

b. Phrs. *you can't win them all*; *you win some, you lose some*, etc.

1954 R. CHANDLER *Long Goodbye* xxiv. 122 Take it easy, Doc. You can't win them all. **1966** P. O'CONNELL *Sabre-Tooth* xiv. 189 You win a few, you lose a few, and it's no good getting sore. **1976** *Times* 23 Nov. 14/1 You look like being saddled with the uninspiring Willy... On the other hand, you seem to have got your way over Mrs. Thatcher's nominee... You win some, you lose some. **1979** K. M. PEYTON *Marion's Angels* ix. 151 'It'll be all right,' she said. 'I daresay. You can't win them all.' **1984** *Listener* 1 Nov. 24/3 Academic friends..have found just one definite factual error... Ah, well; win some, lose some.

4. b. Phrs. *you can't win*, said (often in exasperation) to emphasize that whatever one does, it will be judged wrong or insufficient; *you win*, used to concede defeat in argument, etc.

1926 J. BLACK (*title*) You can't win. **1943** N. MARSH *Colour Scheme* vi. 99 All right... You win. I apologize. **1962** *Redbook* Mar. 44/2 She says I should always be dignified in front of him. Next she hands me the garbage pail and says, 'Take this out.' You can't win, no matter which way you turn! **1976** P. LIVELY *Stitch in Time* v. 55 'You can't win,' said Martin with sudden gloom, 'when you're the eldest. Whatever you do, you shouldn't have because you're old enough to know better.' **1982** 'S. WOODS' *Enter a Gentlewoman* II. iii. 113 'It's hardly fair to judge other people by one's own principles.' 'All right, you win.'

12. d. *to win out* (as opp. to *out of*): orig. *U.S.*; cf. *to lose out* s.v. *LOSE *v.*[1] 4 d; (further examples); *to win through* (adv. and prep.) (later examples).

1868 J. C. ATKINSON *Gloss. Cleveland Dial.* 575 He's sair an' badly. But t'doctor thinks he'll *win thruff*. **1896** *Voice* 9 Apr. 4/5 McKinley will lead on the first ballot, but 'who will win out' is a different question. **1902** KIPLING *Traffics & Discoveries* (1904) 7 But on delusions—as to their winning out next Tuesday week at 9 a.m.—they are—if I may say so—quite British. **1924** GALSWORTHY *Forest* III. 78 You, Lockyer—a soldier! One spurt and we'll win out. Come! **1927** *Daily Express* 14 Dec. 13/5 It is good to know that Wodehouse's clever humour has won through. **1931** A. L. ROWSE *Politics & Younger Generation* i. 262 If the League can manage to win through the divisions of the post-war world,..it will have established itself. **1947** 'G. ORWELL' *Eng. People* 38 The American tendency is to burden every verb with a preposition that adds nothing to its meaning (*win out, lose out, face up to*, etc.). **1959** *Listener* 28 May 958/1 He made many enemies, but finally won through opposition to become one of the most controversial commanders of the last war. **1969** A. J. MEADOWS *High Firmament* vii. 160 Eventually, the uniformitarian concept won out in both astronomy and geology. **1974** 'M. INNES' *Appleby's Other Story* i. 7 Victorian bankers who won out when all the little local concerns began to be bundled up together. **1977** 'E. CRISPIN' *Glimpses of Moon* ii. 28, I won through, though... I survived. **1984** *Times Educ. Suppl.* 30 Nov. 28/1 The book has a brisk story and impeccable moral attitudes: gypsies, orphans, teachers and policemen are all good, ordinary people who win out in the end.

winability: see *WINNABILITY.

winceyette (winsi,e·t). [f. WINCEY + -ETTE; cf. FLANNELETTE.] A lightweight napped cotton fabric used for nightclothes, etc. (see quot. 1955).

1922 *Daily Mail* 14 Nov. 1 (Advt.), Ponting's offer of shirtings and winceyette. **1955** *Textile Terms & Definitions* in *Jrnl. Textile Inst.* (*Standardisation*) XLVI. 544 *Winceyette*, a light-weight fabric, originally and usually of cotton, raised on both sides, the weave usually being plain or twill. **1962** *Economist* 20 Jan. 253/2 The Nelson [cotton] factory was to begin production of denim, winceyette, cotton wool and surgical dressings in May. **1979** D. COOK *Winter Doves* II. v. 87 She applied the paste with two fingers, wiping them clean on her Winceyette nightdress.

winch, *sb.*[1] Add: **6.** *winch-machine*; **winchman:** also, a man lowered by a winch from a helicopter, esp. to rescue people from shipwrecks, etc.

1824 R. STEVENSON *Bell Rock Lighthouse* vi. 329 A winch-machine, with wheel, pinion and barrel, round which last the chain was wound. **1946** A. J. HALL *Stand. Handbk. Textiles* iv. 169 The winch machine is essentially a vat..above which is mounted a horizontal winch. **1958** *Times* 23 June 6/1 The girls..were brought up into the helicopter by winchman Sergeant Jim Gilpin. **1977** *R.A.F. News* 27 Apr.–10 May 1/4 Along with winchman FS Roger Lynn he airlifted a two-ton cabin into the garden of a Durham man so that a kidney machine could be installed. **1979** *Globe & Mail* (Toronto) 15 Aug. 1/2 (*caption*) Winchman on a rescue helicopter hangs over a crew member from yacht Ariadne.

Winchester. Add: **I. 1. a.** (*c*) In mod. use (see quots. 1959, 1972). Also *Winchester bottle*.

1862 *Chemist & Druggist* 15 Feb. (Advt. sect.) 37/1

Druggists' Bottles... Winchester, 100 oz. **1959** *Gloss. Packaging Terms* (*B.S.I.*) 28 *Winchester*, a term applied to round, narrow or wide-mouth bottles usually used for the distribution of chemicals or pharmaceutical products. **1963** *Pharm. Jrnl.* CXCI. 59 The author suggests that the Winchester bottle was thus named by the druggists who utilised it for supplying the [Winchester] hospital's drug orders. **1972** *Bottlers' Year Bk. 1972–73* 423 *Winchester*, a large bottle of variable capacity used for soluble essences, etc., usually containing from about 6 to 10 lb. of the product.

b. *Winchester quart*: (*a*) a quart (2 pints) in Winchester measure; (*b*) *Pharm.*, 4 Imperial pints, i.e. 80 fluid ounces (in quot. 1870, 100 fl. oz.); also, a bottle holding 4 pints.

See *Pharm. Jrnl.* (1963) CXCI. 59 for an argument that in sense (*b*) it is properly 85 fl. oz., a quarter of the new barn gallon of $2\frac{1}{8}$ Imperial gallons.

1742 W. Ellis *Mod. Husbandman* July x. 61 At our Country Towns, they sell a Winchester Quart of Milk.. for a Penny. **1758** *Rep. Comm. House of Commons Weights & Measures* 39 Standard weights and measures in the possession of the Hall-keeper of the Guild-Hall... 1 corn half peck marked 1601. 1 Winchester quart ditto. 1 ditto pint ditto. **1816** P. Kelly *Metrology* 89 The Coal Bushel holds one Winchester quart more than the Winchester bushel [*sc.* 2150.42 cubic inches]; it therefore contains 2217.62 cubic inches. **1870** *Pharm. Jrnl.* XI. 650 Omagh is said to take about 400 Winchester quarts (equal to 250 gallons) [of methylated ether] yearly. **1874** *Ibid.* 2nd Ser. V. 442/1 A Winchester quart (four pints) is first half filled with infusion. **1880** [in Dict., sense 1(*b*)]. **1897** *Chemist & Druggist* 5 June 891/1 The questions on which we should like information are—What is a Winchester quart the fourth of, or how it came to designate a half-gallon? and whether it and the Winchester pint were ever recognised measures? **1963** *Pharm. Jrnl.* CXCI. 60/1 The Winchester quart's success was due, one suspects, to the fact that it is the largest bottle which can conveniently be held in one hand.

2*. *Winchester school*, a southern English style of manuscript illumination of the 10th and 11th cent., originating at Winchester. Also *Winchester manner, style*.

1892 J. H. Middleton *Illuminated MSS. Classical & Mediaeval Times* vii. 101 Another very fine example of the Winchester school of illumination is the manuscript Charter which King Edgar granted to the new minster at Winchester in 966. *Ibid.*, In artistic power this tenth century Winchester school of illuminators appears, for a while at least, to have been foremost in the world. **1910** G. F. Warner in Warner & Wilson *Benedictional of Saint Æthelwold* p. xl, It is an example of Canterbury modification of Winchester style. **1928** E. G. Millar *Eng. Illuminated MSS XIVth & XVth Cent.* ii. 14 The Anglo-Saxon outline draughtsmen of the Winchester and related schools. **1954** M. Rickert *Painting in Britain: Middle Ages* ii. 42 But it is not until the second half of the tenth century that the full force of Carolingian art under Æthelwold's sponsorship of the production of manuscripts resulted in the development at Winchester of the famous Winchester style. **1970** *Oxf. Compan. Art* 559/1 *Winchester School*... Though some splendid manuscripts came from Winchester, books decorated in the 'Winchester' manner were certainly made in other southern English monasteries.

II. 3. b. *Computers.* Used *attrib.* and *absol.* with reference to a hermetically sealed storage device incorporating one or more high-capacity hard discs with heads and sometimes also a drive unit. [So called because the original device was intended to contain two 30 megabyte discs and its IBM number would have been 3030, the same as that of a famous Winchester rifle (which used a 0·30 calibre cartridge containing 0·30 grains of powder).]

1973 *Modern Data* July 60/1 The 'Winchester' Disk... The product of the so-called 'Winchester' project, the eventual nature of the 3340 has been the subject of rumors reported in the trade press. **1976** *Computer Weekly* 26 Aug. 16/6 There are also special cabinets for the Winchester type of disc module—a recording medium that is expensive in itself irrespective of the data stored on it, and that requires extremely careful handling. **1978** *IEEE Trans. Magnetics* XIV. 201/1 An example of the current state of the art in fixed head designs utilizing Winchester technology are the fixed heads used in IBM's 3340 and 3350 disc drives. **1980** *Sci. Amer.* Aug. 117/2 It is now known generically as Winchester technology, that being the code name under which the device was developed at IBM. A Winchester disk memory has one or more rigid disks, either eight or 14 inches in diameter. **1985** *Which Computer?* Apr. 61/2 One machine has twin floppies, the other has a 10MB Winchester.

winchite (wi·ntʃəit). *Min.* [f. the name of H. J. *Winch* + -ite[1].] A blue or violet monoclinic mineral of the amphibole group, approximately $NaCa(Mg,Fe^{2+})_4(Al,Fe^{3+})Si_8O_{22}(OH)_2$.

1906 L. L. Fermor in *Trans. Mining & Geol. Inst. India* I. 79 *Winchite*..is the name which has been bestowed ..upon the blue amphibole... An analysis of this mineral shows it to be closely allied to tremolite in chemical composition. **1980** *Canad. Mineralogist* XVIII. 101/1 In composition, this asbestos probably ranges from a potassian richterite to a potassian winchite.

Winco: see *Wingco.

wind, *sb.*[1] Add: **I. 2. b.** *Mah Jong.* Any of the four compass-positions about the wall of tiles taken up by a player; the player who occupies this place. Also, any of sixteen tiles (four of each sort) representing one of the four winds used in the game.

1922 M. S. Rosenblatt *Majong* 2 There are 4 'Winds'.. and there are 4 pieces of each 'Wind'. **1925** [see *pung *v.*[2], *sb.*[3], and *int.*]. **1938** V. L. Cecil *Maajh* 2 Each player took the position of one of the four Winds. **1960** R. C. Bell *Board & Table Games* vi. 152 The tiles are grouped into: Cardinal tiles... Winds... Honour tiles... Minor tiles. *Ibid.* 156 Each wind in turn becomes the wind of the round. The first round is East Wind's. **1979** M. Hammer *Learn to play Mah Jongg* ii. 35 The next step is to evaluate which tiles are more prevalent—odds, evens, winds, singles, pairs.

6. Also *to spit against* (or *into*) *the wind*.

1578 H. Wotton tr. *Yver's Courtlie Controversie* ii. 109 Thou shalte be like him that spitteth againste the winde, whose slaver fleeth in his owne face. **1612** Webster *White Divel* sig. E4, For your names, of Whoore and Murdresse they proceed from you, As if a man should spit against the wind, The filth returne's in's face. **1968** *Guardian* 1 Oct. 8/5 The decision to withdraw our forces.. was inevitable, and Mr Heath is spitting into the wind when he tells Australian audiences that a Conservative Government would go back. **1975** *Times* 10 Nov. 12/4 To adopt a vivid barrack-room expression, it is no good spitting against the wind or shouting against thunder.

II. 8. b. (*a*) (Later *fig.* examples.)

1823 J. Bric *Let.* 22 Feb. in *Corresp. D. O'Connell* (1972) II. 447 You have hit the thing between wind and water and whilst you have justly elevated your own name you have done much for your country. **1967** M. Gilbert *Dust & Heat* iii. 239 Mallinson *must* have guessed what was coming. Nevertheless, it hit him between wind and water.

10. b. *to put the wind up* (a person) (earlier example).

1918 W. Owen *Let.* 11 Oct. (1967) 584 Shells so close that they thoroughly put the wind up a Life Guardsman in the trench with me.

11. c. (Examples of *to slip one's wind*.)

1883 *Gringo & Greaser* 1 Sept. 2/2 He had entirely slipped his wind—for want of which he was buried the 11th ult. **1896** H. Lawson *While Billy Boils* 233 He laid the longest strip [of bark] by the side of the corpse... 'Come on, Brummy,..yer ain't as bad as yer might be, considerin' as it must be three good months since yer slipped yer wind. I spect it was the rum as preserved yer.'

d. *second wind* (earlier example); also *transf.* and *fig.*

1824 *Sporting Mag.* XIV. 166/2 Langan shewed a faint glimpse of second wind, and came up boldly. **1907** W. James *Mem. & Stud.* (1911) x. 229 Everybody knows what it is to 'warm up' to his job. The process of warming up gets particularly striking in the phenomenon known as 'second wind'. **1948** 'J. Tey' *Franchise Affair* i. 15 Perhaps it was the presence of an ally that had heartened her; or perhaps she had just got her second wind. **1963** Mrs. L. B. Johnson *White House Diary* 21 Dec. (1970) 18, I believe I am about to catch my second wind.

12. b. Also *pl.*, wind instruments.

1976 *Early Music* July 293/1 The author seems not to differentiate sufficiently between 'folk' and 'art' instruments of the Middle Ages, and especially when he deals with winds. **1978** P. Griffiths *Conc. Hist. Mod. Music* vii. 102 His [*sc.* Berg's] atonal chamber concerto for piano, violin and thirteen winds..is full of triple formations.

13*. The solar wind (see *solar *a.* 7), or a similar stream of particles emanating uniformly from any other star.

1966 *McGraw-Hill Encycl. Sci. & Technol.* III. 500/2 Presumably the wind is stronger when solar activity is high, but direct observations cannot be made before the next maximum. **1968** *Times* 5 Dec. 8/7 The fascinating region of space where the earth's magnetic field interacts with the 'wind' of atomic particles streaming out from the sun. **1982** *Sci. Amer.* July 83/1 Most stars, including the sun, are known to be losing mass in the form of a stellar wind.

III. 15. Also freq. in formula *wind*(*s*) *of*... **a.** (*b*) (later examples); *wind of doctrine* (later examples in allusion to *Eph.* iv. 14); also *fig.*

1907 W. Raleigh *Shakespeare* iv. 108 If once we are foolishly persuaded to go behind the authority of Heminge and Condell..we ..are afloat upon a wild and violent sea, subject to every wind of doctrine. **1913** G. Santayana *Winds of Doctrine* ii. 25 Prevalent winds of doctrine must needs penetrate at last into the cloister. **1926** R. H. Tawney *Relig. & Rise of Capitalism* iii. 179 With such a wind of doctrine in their sails men were not far from the days of complete freedom of contract. **1953** H. Weisinger *Tragedy & Paradox of Fortunate Fall* vi. 267 The winds of new doctrine swept through the streets of Athens and London and left the old and conventional modes of religious thought bare. **1953** E. Coxhead *Midlanders* vii. 158 The winds of want still blew about the world. **1962** *Listener* 26 Apr. 717/1 Ideas..become ossified if they are not exposed to the wind of criticism. **1968** *Globe & Mail* (Toronto) 3 Feb. 10/5 To protect their own lives and those of their children, they will bend with the winds of war.

b. (Further examples.)

1914 T. Dreiser *Titan* xiii. 103, I know all about this. I've seen which way the wind is blowing. **1929** 'E. Queen' *Roman Hat Mystery* xxii. 301 Ellery got his first indication of which way the wind blew during the meeting at the Ives-Pope house. **1957** N. Mitford *Voltaire in Love* x. 115 Thieriot..seeing..that the wind was now blowing in Voltaire's direction, consented..to give the required evidence. **1976** Ld. Home (*title*) The way the wind blows.

c. *spec.* in phr. *wind* (also *winds*) *of change.* Harold Macmillan (Lord Stockton) delivered his celebrated 'wind of change' address to the South African parliament in Cape Town on 3 Feb. 1960 (see quot.). Our records show a marked increase in the frequency of the phrase after this date.

1905 S. Naidu *Golden Threshold* 97 The wind of change for ever blows Across the tumult of our way. **1927** D. H. Lawrence *Mornings in Mexico* 154 The place of after-life and before-life, where house the winds of change. **1932** J. Clapham *Econ. Hist. Mod. Britain* II. iii. 107 The [gas] companies or municipal works with their comfortable monopoly areas..began to find a little wind of change blowing among their retorts and coke heaps. **1954** J. Masters *Bhowani Junction* xxxix. 345 Then the great changes swept across India and the world, and she had searched, not by deliberate plan but because the wind of change blew through her too, for ways of escape. **1960** H. Macmillan in *Times* 4 Feb. 15/3 The wind of change is blowing through the continent. **1960** *Economist* 15 Oct. 275/2 This is but one way in which the mining complex of De Beers, Anglo American and Rhodesian Anglo American is adapting itself to the winds of change in Africa. **1965** D. Francis *Odds Against* vi. 86 'Is this your own show..or whose?' 'I suppose—mine.' 'Uh-huh... The wind of change, if I read it right?' **1971** *Nature* 26 Nov. 179/1 The universities are also likely to feel some eddies from the winds of change that are swirling around the White House. **1976** 'J. Charlton' *Remington Set* xiv. 69 The winds of change are beginning to blow..and your purpose in life isn't quite as defensible..as it used to be.

16. c. *to sniff the wind*: to try the atmosphere; to examine the prevailing state of affairs before taking action (cf. sense 4).

1972 'R. Crawford' *Whip Hand* i. v. 22 Schuyler sniffed the wind and took his time about it. **1974** 'D. Kyle' *Raft of Swords* viii. 78 'I have no *reason*... I just know.' 'You sniff the wind. Very sensible. What do you smell?' **1977** *Time* 22 Aug. 5/2 Certainly the Labor government and the nation's judiciary system are sniffing the wind.

IV. 20. in the wind. a. (Earlier example.)

1818 'A. Burton' *Johnny Newcome* iii. 175, I did not think..I was so much in drink! But now by th'holy smut I find That cursedly I'm in the wind.

29. with the wind. Now esp. in *fig.* phr. *gone with the wind*: gone completely (as if blown away by the wind), disappeared without trace.

1896 E. Dowson *Verses* 17, I have forgot much, Cynara! gone with the wind. **1918** Galsworthy *First & Last* ix, in *Five Tales* 61 A man, when he drowns, remembers his past. Like the lost poet he had 'gone with the wind'. Now it was for him to be true in his fashion. **1936** M. Mitchell (*title*) Gone with the wind. **1948** W. S. Churchill *Gathering Storm* xix. 271 The services of thirty-five Czech divisions..[were] cast away,..all gone with the wind.

V. 30. a. *wind-dispersal, effect, -flaw* (Flaw *sb.*[2]), *-force, -puff* (later example), *resistance, -rush, -shift, -song, -speed, -streak, -torrent, -walk, -wave, -well; wind-shelter.*

1911 J. A. Thomson *Biology of Seasons* iii. 277 Any structural peculiarity that increases area without increasing weight will aid in wind-dispersal. **1937** Wind effect [see *air position* s.v. *air *sb.*[1] III. 1]. **1941** B. Hellström in *Ingeniörsvetenskapsakad. Handl.* No. 158. 8 A denivellation of the water surface takes place, by which the level of the lake is lowered at the windward and raised at the leeward shore. This denivellation is called the Wind Effect. **1913** J. Masefield *Daffodil Fields* 110 Flicking windflaws fill the air with brine. **1931** E. Linklater *Juan in Amer.* i. 15 A frown on that bland forehead was like the wind-flaw on a saucer of milk that some petulant child has blown across. **1935** *Geogr. Jrnl.* LXXXVI. 533 The most remarkable feature was the great variation in wind-force and direction. **1976** *Islander* (Victoria, B.C.) 14 Nov. 7/2 The seas began to look greyer—but we hadn't had anything more than windforce seven—so far. **1881** G. M. Hopkins *Poems* (1967) 89 A windpuff-bonnet of fawn-froth Turns and twindles. **1934** *Discovery* Dec. 344/2 At a high speed, wind resistance becomes an important factor. *a* **1945** E. R. Eddison *Mezentian Gate* (1958) xxxix. 218 Their pure eyes..turned..to that thunder-laced windrush of darkness which is the heat and unpicturable secret centre of light's and beauty's self. **1976** 'A. Hall' *Kobra Manifesto* xv. 201 The faint scream of the windrush [under an aeroplane at take-off] in the roaring background. **1930** E. Pound *XXX Cantos* viii. 30 With the road leading under the cliff, in the wind-shelter into Tuscany. **1968** G. Maxwell *Raven seek thy Brother* ix. 127 Windshelters..of stone or turf and furnished with artificial nesting sites, are usually colonized immediately [by eider ducks]. **1914** J. Masefield *Philip the King* 53 A sudden windshift snatched us from our graves And drove us north. **1963** *Times* 30 May 14/7 A windshift..brought the nauseating smell of the penguin rookery straight over the camp. **1946** J. W. Day *Harvest Adventure* vi. 83 Rigging drummed and whistled a raw wind-song. **1934** *Discovery* June 150/2 High wind-speeds in relation to aircraft. **1977** J. L. Harper *Population Biol. Plants* x. 323 Turbulence falls off rapidly down through a canopy but is a function of wind speed, even deep in a corn crop. **1930** E. Pound *XXX Cantos* xxvii. 127 Twig where but wind-streak had been. **1973** C. Sagan *Cosmic Connection* (1975) viii. 62 The Mariner 9 photography of the Martian volcanoes, windstreaks, moons, and polar icecaps. **1929** Blunden *Near & Far* 57 Dim stars like snowflakes are fluttering in heaven, Down the cloud-mountains by wind-torrents riven. **1877** G. M. Hopkins *Poems* (1967) 70 Summer ends now; now, barbarous in beauty, the stooks rise Around; up above, what wind-walks! **1900** G. K. Chesterton *Wild Knight* 7 Meadows where the wind-waves pass. **1946** L. D. Stamp *Britain's Struct. & Scenery* vi. 51 The waves of the sea are primarily wind-waves. **1984** A. C. & A. Duxbury *Introd. World's Oceans* viii. 249 Most waves observed at sea are progressive wind waves..generated by the wind. **1936** Dylan Thomas *25 Poems* 23 Why east wind chills and south wind cools Shall not be known till windwell dries.

b. *wind-cheating, -screening* adjs.

1963 Bird & Hutton-Stott *Veteran Motor Car* 246

Both had their engines placed..very low down so as to allow the use of flat wind-cheating bodies. **1977** *Lancashire Life* Jan. 81/1 Because of their wind cheating shape and fairly high overall gearing, the Citroen CXs are very economical on long motorway journeys. **1923** Kipling *Land & Sea Tales* 214 She hovers On the summits of wind-screening seas.

c. (Further examples, mainly poetical compounds.) *wind-aided, -beat, -beaten* (later examples), *-bit, -bitten, -borne, -broken, -buffeted, -chilled, -curled, -dappled, -driven, -flawed, -flown, -flushed, fluted, -formed, -hardened, -heeled, -laced, -laden, -laid, -lifted, -loved, -mastered, -milled, -perplexed, -pollinated, -powered, -rinsed, -ripped, -scarred, -scoured, -scourged, -shorn, -snatched, -sown, -spun, -stirred, -stormed, -sucked, -thrashed, -torn, -tossed* (earlier example), *-transported, -turned, -washed, -waved* (later example), *-wrinkled, -writhen.*

1959 *Times* 12 Mar. 3/3 Langton kicked another long wind-aided penalty goal. **1978** *Detroit Free Press* 16 Apr. E 3/2 He won the 100-yard dash with a wind-aided performance of 9.5 seconds. **1877** G. M. Hopkins *Poems* (1967) 66 Wind-beat whitebeam! airy abeles set on a flare! **1900** W. B. Yeats *Shadowy Waters* 45 These waste waters and wind-beaten sails. **1973** *Canadian Antiques Collector* Jan.-Feb. 59/1 Inland, behind wind-beaten villages and red capes. **1892** Kipling *Other Verses* 161 In the heel of the wind-bit pier. **1919** J. Masefield *Reynard the Fox* II. 61 Blown Hilcote Copse, Wind-bitten beech. **1965** F. Sargeson *Memoirs of Peon* ix. 270 The trees..had redeemed a windbitten waste from its native barbarism. **1842** Emerson *Saadi* in *Poems* (1914) 133 To northern lakes fly wind-borne ducks. **1969** Bennison & Wright *Geol. Hist. Brit. Isles* xvi. 368 The brickearths may, however, have been not solely laid down in expanses of water but be in part wind-borne. **1914** J. Masefield *Philip the King* 44 They have died, Far from wind-broken Biscay, far from home. **1901** 'L. Malet' *Hist. R. Calmady* v. i. 383 Heavily-cloaked figures tacking, wind-buffeted, across the grey-black street. **1921** D. H. Lawrence *Tortoises* 25 The autumn, wind-chilled sunshine. **1952** L. MacNeice *Ten Burnt Offerings* 51 Wind-curled fountain, tigerish weir, garrulous rain. **1883** R. Bridges *Prometheus the Firegiver* in *Poet. Works* (1912) 25 Piloting over the wind-dappled blue Of the summer-soothed Aegean. **1920** J. Masefield *Enslaved* 109 The grey sea..cloud-coloured, flat, Wind-dappled from the glen. **1882** W. D. Hay *Brighter Britain!* I. iii. 89 The sun shining on the wind-driven sand that covers them [*sc.* hilltops]. **1967** *Oceanogr. & Marine Biol.* V. 102 The Strait of Dover may accept a wind-driven residual current averaging $3\frac{1}{2}$ miles and occasionally reaching 20 miles per lunar day. **1971** G. M. Brown *Fishermen with Ploughs* 95 A huge wind-flawed mirror. **1938** C. Day Lewis *Overtures to Death* 30 The wind-flown tower. *Ibid.* 55 To reproach you we rise Wind-flushed and early. **1943** —— *Word over All* 15 Wherein the shores Foam-fringed, wind-fluted of the strange earth dwell. **1911** F. O. Bower *Plant-Life* 124 The wind-formed dune takes a very definite crescentic shape styled a Barchan. **1926** D. H. Lawrence *Sun* iv. 17 He was powerless against her rosy, wind-hardened nakedness. **1939** Dylan Thomas *Map of Love* 20 Wind-heeled foot in the hole of a fireball. **1887** G. M. Hopkins *Poems* (1967) 104 Curls Wag or cross-bridle, in a wind lifted, windlaced—See his wind lilylocks -laced. **1928** C. Day Lewis *Country Comets* 9 The unconscious dignity Of hills and wind-laden grass. **1965** G. J. Williams *Econ. Geol. N.Z.* ix. 132/2 Both water- and wind-laid blacksand sediments formed. **1924** 'L. Malet' *Dogs of Want* iv. 112 The soft green blur and flickering flames resolved themselves into gently wind-lifted leaves and distant sparkling water. **1936** Auden *Look, Stranger!* 11 Upon wind-loved Rowley. **1945** P. A. Larkin *North Ship* 27 Two tall ships, wind-mastered, wet with light. **1947** Dylan Thomas *In Country Sleep* in *Horizon* Dec. 303 The dew falls on the wind-Milled dust of the apple tree. **1864** G. M. Hopkins *Poems* (1967) 128 His body sway'd upon tiptoes Like a wind-perplexed rose. **1911** F. O. Bower *Plant-Life* 96 As for instance in the Rue (Thalictrum), which has become wind-pollinated. **1968** F. W. Gould *Grass Systematics* i. 7 Grasses..are wind-pollinated. **1976** *Jrnl. R. Soc. Arts* CXXIV. 732/1 It is very logical to feed wind-powered energy in the form of either electricity or direct heat directly into a buffer system and thence to direct use. **1948** L. MacNeice *Holes in Sky* 20 Wind-rinsed plumage of oat-field. **1960** S. Plath *Colossus* (1967) 33 The spindrift Ravelled wind-ripped from the crest of the wave. **1939** S. Spender *Still Centre* 41 Beyond the wind-scarred hill. **1896** Kipling *Seven Seas* 73 Bone-bleached my decks, wind-scoured to the graining. **1980** D. K. Cameron *Willie Gavin* vi. 54 There was hardly a year when the winter ploughs did not turn up an old hunter of that wind-scoured plain. **1898** J. G. Whittier *M. Martin* in *Poet. Works* 67/2 You wind-scourged sand-dunes, cold and bleak. **1924** 'L. Malet' *Dogs of Want* ii. 29 Bare, wind-scourged, rock-strewn slopes. **1867** J. G. Whittier *Poet. Works* (1898) 280/2 Lonely and wind-shorn, wood-forsaken..Lieth the island of Manisees. **1933** W. de la Mare *Lord Fish* 61 Gnarled, wind-shorn trees. **1980** R. Mabey *Common Ground* II. i. 70 At no more than 590 feet above sea level some of its windshorn oaks are reduced to a metre or so in height. **1925** C. Day Lewis *Beechen Vigil* 32 The wind-snatched rumour. **1902** W. Stevens *Jrnl.* 18 Aug. in *Lett.* (1967) 59, I lay under a group of dark cedars near that strange wind-sown cactus with its red blossom. **1922** Blunden *Shepherd* (ed. 2) 74 Windspun leaves burn silver-grey. **1843** J. G. Whittier *Poet. Works* (1898) 388/1 And down again through wind-stirred trees He saw the quivering sunlight play. **1946** R. Macaulay in E. Brontë *Wuthering Heights* p. vi, The lonely, wind-stormed old farmhouse that stood on the heights above Haworth's grey streets. **1946** R. S. Thomas *Stones of Field* 26 The wind-sucked bone shows blue. **1933** Somerville & 'Ross' *Smile & Tear* ix. 98 A few miserable wind-thrashed ash-trees. **1910** Kipling *Rewards & Fairies* 244 The wind-torn breaker-tops. **1957** T. Gunn *Sense of Movement* 58 Not like the fighting boys and wind-torn rooks. **1838** J. R. Lowell *Class Poem* 20 Flapping his raven pinions in the west, The thunder brooding o'er his wind-tost crest. **1946** F. E. Zeuner *Dating Past* iii. 56 Minute grains of wind-transported pollen caught on the wet surface of the bog. **1935** Dylan Thomas in *Life & Lett. To-day* Dec. 75 Doom on deniers at the wind-turned statement. **1971** *Country Life* 8 July 84/1 The raw elements of Millet's compositions, granite walls, dirty-legged cattle,..wind-turned trees. **1912** C. Mackenzie *Carnival* xvi. 186 At such an hour..even Piccadilly Circus stands..wind-washed and noble. **1919** J. Masefield *Reynard the Fox* 92 The wind-washed steeple stood serene. **1928** Blunden *Retreat* 18 The wind-waved bough betrayed the wild sylph glancing. **1925** V. Woolf *Mrs Dalloway* 242 Suddenly she shoots to the surface and sports on the wind-wrinkled waves. **1921** F. B. Young *Black Diamond* ix. 116 They crossed a zone of huge, wind-writhen hawthorns. **1954** J. R. R. Tolkien *Fellowship of Ring* 401 High ridges crowned with wind-writhen firs.

d. *wind-grey, -hard, -long, -raw, -smooth, -wild.*

c **1944** A. Power *From Old Waterford House* xi. 95, I had seen it under so many moods, from wind-grey to sun-yellow. **1954** W. Faulkner *Fable* 184 Like the wind-hard banner of the old Norman earl. *a* **1890** G. M. Hopkins *Poems* (1967) 180 Or wind-long fleeces on the flock A day off shearing day. **1922** Joyce *Ulysses* 48 About her windraw face her hair trailed. **1929** E. Sitwell *Gold Coast Customs* 38 Wind-smooth fruits. **1936** C. Day Lewis *Noah & Waters* 50 Under the wind-wild sky.

31. wind axis *Aeronaut.*, each of a set of rectangular coordinate axes having their origin in the aircraft and the *x*-axis in the opposite direction to the relative wind; usu. *pl.*; **wind-balanced** *a.*, applied to rotary gun mountings on aircraft having a device which automatically compensates for the turning moment caused by air pressure on the guns; also **wind-balancing** *vbl. sb.*; **wind-bells** *sb. pl.*, slips of glass or porcelain suspended from a frame so as to tinkle against one another in the wind; **wind-blow,** (*a*) a stretch of land eroded by wind; (*b*) (see quot. 1955); (*c*) = *windthrow* below; **windblown bob** [*Bob *sb.*[1] 5 b], a bobbed hairstyle popular among women in the 1930s (see quot. 1975); **wind-bracing,** substitute for def.: connecting members designed to stiffen a building or other structure against the wind; the provision of such members; (further examples); **windbreaker,** (*b*) *U.S.* = Wind-break 1; (*c*) *U.S.* (with capital initial) the proprietary name of a kind of shirt or leather blouse; *gen.* (chiefly *N. Amer.*) = *windcheater* (*b*) below; **windburn** [after *sunburn*, etc.], (usu. superficial) inflammation or discoloration of the skin caused by exposure to wind; hence **wind-burned, -burnt** *a.*; **windcap** *Mus.* [tr. G. *windkapsel*] = *reed cap* s.v. *Reed *sb.*[1] 13 a; freq. *attrib.*; **wind-channel** = *wind tunnel* below; **windcharger,** a small windmill which generates electricity for a farm, dwelling, etc.; **windcheater,** (*a*) *Golf*, a ball driven low into the wind, *spec.* one played with strong back-spin (see quot. 1909); (*b*) a kind of wind-resistant jacket or blouson; **wind chill,** the cooling effect of moving air on a body; also, = **wind-chill factor*; **wind-chill factor, index,** a measure or scale of the combined effect of low temperature and wind-speed on body temperature (see quot. 1939); **wind chimes** *sb. pl.* = *wind-bells* above; **wind cone** *Aeronaut.* = *wind sock* below; **windcrust** *Mountaineering*, a crust formed on the surface of soft snow by the wind (see quot. 1936); **wind energy,** evergy obtained from harnessing the wind; cf. *Solar *a.* 4 a; **wind farm,** a group of energy-producing windmills or wind turbines; **wind-firm** *a.*, of a tree: firmly rooted so as to be able to withstand strong winds; hence **wind-firmness; wind-flag,** a flag on a shooting-range designed to indicate the direction and force of the wind; **wind-gap:** *spec.* (see quot. 1939); (examples); **wind-god** (later example); **wind-jacket** = *windcheater* (*b*) above; **windjammer:** substitute for def.: *slang*, (*a*) *U.S.* a bugler, bandsman; (*b*) a sailing-vessel (*obs.* exc. *Hist.*); (*c*) *U.S.* a rumour-monger, a loquacious person; (*d*) = *windcheater* (*b*) above; (further examples); hence **windjamming,** (*a*) sailing a wind-jammer; (*b*) talking, gossiping; (*c*) playing a wind instrument; **wind-lane,** a current on the surface of a body of water, caused by the wind; **wind load** *Engin.*, the force on a structure arising from the impact of wind on it; also **wind loading; wind-lop** *Canad.* [Lop *sb.*[6]], a choppy surface on the sea, caused by wind; **wind machine,** (*a*) *spec.* one that blows out relatively warm air for protecting crops against frost (see quot. 1976[2]); (*b*) in theatrical and other productions, a machine for simulating the sound or other effects of wind; also *fig.*; (further examples); **wind noise,** the sound of the wind against a motor vehicle moving at speed, as heard within the vehicle; **windproof** *a.*, impervious or resistant to wind; used esp. of outer garments; hence *ellipt.* as *sb.*, a windproof garment; **wind-reef** *U.S.*, the semblance of a reef on the surface of a river, caused by the wind; **windrock,** damage to the roots of young plants, caused by the movement of the stem in the wind; also as *v. trans*,; so **wind-rocking; wind-scorpion** = Solpugid in Dict. and Suppl.; **wind-screen** (earlier U.S. examples in sense 'windbreak'); **windscreen washer** = *screen-washer* s.v. *Screen *sb.*[1] 7 a; **windscreen wiper,** a device (usu. one of a pair) on a motor vehicle for automatic wiping of the outside of the windscreen during rain, snow, etc., usu. consisting of a mechanically or electrically operated moving rubber blade; also one on an aircraft; **wind shadow,** (*a*) *nonce-use*, a ripple caused by the wind on water and having the appearance of a shadow running over it; (*b*) an area behind a moving object where the air is disturbed and its pressure reduced; **wind shear,** a variation in wind velocity along a direction (usu. vertical or horizontal) at right angles to the wind's direction; **windship,** a wind-powered ship; a sailing-ship; **wind-sight,** a special arrangement of the back-sight of a rifle capable of adjustment to compensate for the effect of wind on the bullet; **wind-slab** *Mountaineering*, a thick wind-crust, of a kind liable to slip and create an avalanche; cf. *slab avalanche* s.v. *Slab *sb.*[1] 6; **wind-slash,** slash resulting from windthrow; **wind sleeve** *Aeronaut.* = *wind sock* below; **wind sock,** a cloth cone flown from a mast, esp. on an airfield, to indicate the direction of the wind; = *Drogue 3 (*c*); **wind-spider** = *wind-scorpion* above; **wind-splitter** *colloq.* (chiefly *U.S.*), something so sharply drawn or so swift as to suggest the notion of splitting the wind; cf. Wind-cutter; so **wind-splitting** *a.*; **wind sprint** *Athletics* (see quot. 1948); **wind-stocking** = *wind sock* above; **wind-stream,** an air-stream, esp. the disturbed air in the wake of an aircraft; **wind stress,** stress or force due to wind; **wind-swept** *a.*, (*a*) (see sense 30 c in Dict.); (*b*) *spec.* of a hair-style, designed to give the appearance of having been blown by the wind (cf. *windblown bob* above); **windthrow,** the uprooting and blowing down of trees by the wind; also (usu. *attrib.*) of timber so uprooted; **wind tunnel,** a tunnel-like apparatus for producing an air-stream of known velocity past models of aircraft, buildings, etc., in order to investigate flow or the effect of wind on the full-size object; also *attrib.*, *transf.*, and *fig.*; **wind turbine,** a turbine driven by wind; an apparatus designed to generate electricity when a large vaned wheel is rotated by the wind; **windway,** (*b*) also in a woodwind instrument; **wind wing** *U.S.*, † an adjustable glass ventilation panel attached to the side of the windscreen of a motor vehicle (*obs.*); a small ventilation window or quarterlight on a motor vehicle.

1932 *Jrnl. R. Aeronaut. Soc.* Mar. 194 Calculations..of a complete model rotated about the wind axis..give a fair approximation to the spinning characteristics of the aeroplane. **1984** F. J. Hale *Introd. Aircraft Performance* i. 4 The wind axes are not body axes; that is, they are not fixed to the aircraft other than at the cg. A change in the direction of flight can change *x* without changing the attitude of the aircraft. **1928** *Daily Tel.* 6 Mar. 6/3 Royalties not exceeding £7,500 to Messrs. Vickers, Ltd., for wind-balanced ring mountings. **1928** G. F. S. Gamble *Story N. Sea Air Station* xiii. 219 A wind-balancing gear was provided which relieved the observer of much fatigue at high altitudes. **1901** 'L. Malet' *Hist. R. Calmady* II. ii. 105 They pressed him back and back against the base of a seven-storied pagoda, the wind-bells of which jangled far above him from the angles of its tiers of fluted roofs. **1983** *Daily Tel.* 21 Oct. 16/1 Windbells tinkled from the eaves of temples, spreading the Holy Word of Buddha, keeping demons away. **1921** H. Guthrie-Smith *Tutira* xx. 180 The sheep..are returfing the naked windblows. **1944** W. Stevens in *Q. Rev. Lit.*

spring 157 The drivers in the wind-blows cracking whips. **1955** *Britannica Bk. of Year* 489/2 *Wind-blow*, a destructive gale of wind. **1961** *New Scientist* 16 Mar. 662/2 Comparisons have been made of trees on sites where wind-blow has occurred and those where similar trees are stable. **1979** *National Trust* Spring 18/3 Marram grass.. holds the sand together and reduces the effects of wind blow. **1933** N. Waln *House of Exile* III. i. 187 She had her hair cut in a new fashion which, she told me, was called a windblown bob. **1975** *Fairchild's Dict. Fashion* 62/2 *Wind-blown bob*, popular 1930's woman's hairstyle, cut short and shingled,..so that hair fell softly about the face as if blown by the wind. **1911** Husband & Harby *Structural Engin.* ix. 278 Wind bracing in roofs is employed to counteract the overturning moment of the wind acting on the ends. **1961** *Listener* 28 Sept. 464/1 An enormous funnel of unoccupied space goes from top to bottom of it [*sc.* a skyscraper] in order to provide mere wind bracing for the rest of it. **1974** *Sci. Amer.* Feb. 98/2 The statue [of Liberty] posed a special problem in wind bracing. **1873** J. H. Beadle *Undevel. West* xxxiv. 730 If there is any wind-breaker northwest, between there and Alaska, I had no evidence of it. **1918** *Official Gaz.* (U.S. Patent Office) 5 Nov. 214/2 The Hilker-Wiechers Manufacturing Co., Racine, Wis. *Windbreaker*... Men's shirts for outer wear. **1925** *Ibid.* 13 Jan. 256/2 Gufterman Bros., Inc., St. Paul, Minn... *Windbreaker*... Leather blouses, shirts, [etc.]. **1934** *Beaver* (Winnipeg) June 6/2 The wind-breakers and coats are shown by a series of photographs. **1964** 'R. Macdonald' in H. Q. Masur *Murder most Foul* (1973) 109 A man with a bulky shoulder harness under his brown suede windbreaker. **1985** *Times* 9 Feb. 36/4 The terminal was full of muscular young men in windbreakers and running shoes. **1939** C. Morley *Kitty Foyle* xxx. 313 It was comical to see the dames.. worrying about windburn and sunsquint and brittle nails. **1977** *Birds* Spring 40 All night my skin is hot with windburn, and between my teeth..the salt-sharp flavour of the rain. **1942** J. Steinbeck *Moon is Down* vi. 137 They were windburned and strong..Will Anders and Tom Anders, the fishermen. **1954** 'Bryher' *Fourteenth of October* ii. 17 His eyes were the same blue in his windburnt face. **1981** 'E. Lathen' *Going for Gold* iv. 40 Practicing for the Swiss women's slalom team had left her with windburned cheeks. **1940** C. Sachs *Hist. Musical Instr.* (1942) xv. 320 Wind-cap instruments were first introduced to art music in the fifteenth century. The cromorne was the oldest European instrument with a wind cap. **1970** W. Apel *Harvard Dict. Music* 588/2 More important are the *crumhorns*... Their tube was nearly cylindrical,..and a pierced cap (wind cap) covered the reed so that the player could not touch it. **1980** *Early Music Gaz.* Apr. 13/3 There will be a weekend for players of the recorder, gemshorn, windcap instruments, cornetti and for renaissance dancers in Hutton Hall, near Carlisle. **1918** Cowley & Levy *Aeronautics* iv. 98 A series of experiments are conducted in the wind channel to test the lift and drag for different forms of sections. **1972** *Nature* 18 Aug. 375/1 The secrecy..was lifted in 1919 to reveal.. developments in techniques for scale model testing in wind 'channels' (tunnels). **1946** E. W. Manning *Igloo for Night* 156 We could hear the wind tearing past, and the high screaming whine as it met the wires of the radio masts and the wind-charger. **1949** *Farmer's Weekly* (S. Afr.) 13 July 69/5, I have an old car generator. Can this be converted into a windcharger? **1976** *Sci. Amer.* June 94/3 The introduction of the windcharger in the 1930's brought to remote farms and ranches enough electricity to power radios and a few light bulbs and appliances. **1909** P. A. Vaile *Mod. Golf* xii. 180 The wind-cheater, the ball that skims away over the daisies and then rises gracefully at the end of its flight, to fall sometimes almost dead. **1940** [see *crew neck* s.v. *crew *sb.*[1] 7]. **1956** L. McIntosh *Oxford Folly* 53 Incongruous in his neat suit and tidy hair among the tousled undergraduates in windcheaters or polo-necked sweaters. **1977** G. Peper *Scrambling Golf* ix. 162 One of those low, delayed-rising 'wind-cheaters'. **1982** C. Thomas *Jade Tiger* 195 The first chill of the night, seeping through his thin windcheater, alerted and refreshed him. **1939** P. A. Siple *Adaptations of Explorer to Climate of Antarctica* (Ph.D. diss., Clark University) 166, I therefore propose in this discussion to multiply temperatures in degrees Centigrade below freezing by wind velocity in meters per second, the product of which I shall call the *wind-chill index*. *Ibid.* 177 July exhibited a mean wind-chill of 462·8. **1949** *Jrnl. R. Aeronaut. Soc.* LIII. 1/2 'Wind Chill'... This is the worst form of cold weather to encounter, as not only does it cause exhaustion, low morale, pain and frustration, but in some cases the lack of the will to live when the wind chill factor is unusually high. **1959** R. E. Huschke *Gloss. Meteorol.* 629 *Wind-chill index*—(Also called *wind-chill factor*), the cooling effect of any combination of temperature and wind, expressed as the loss of body heat in kilogram calories per hour per square meter of skin surface. **1963** *New Scientist* 7 Feb. 276/1 Wind chill, which is actually another name for the dry convective cooling power of the atmosphere, is a term descriptive of the cooling effect of air movement and low temperature. **1977** J. F. Fixx *Compl. Bk. Running* xiii. 151 Because of the wind-chill factor, a given temperature feels colder than in still weather. **1985** *Times* 8 Jan. 26/4 Francis Wilson, the BBC weatherman, yesterday introduced *Breakfast Time* viewers to a new and chilly forecasting feature: the 'wind chill factor'. **1958** T. Williams *Orpheus Descending* III. iii. 85 Someone has entered the confectionery door, out of sight, and the draught of air has set the wind-chimes tinkling wildly. **1976** M. Millar *Ask for Me Tomorrow* (1977) iii. 18 Go..to the glass door and shake the wind chimes good and hard. She's in Marco's room. **1918** *Flight* 2 May 496/1 A wind cone set up in..fields.. near aerodromes, would enable cross-country fliers to know..where to land and in what direction. **1936** E. A. M. Wedderburn *Alpine Climbing* iv. 50 Wind both causes the snow to drift and forms a crust on the powder snow; this is the chief kind of crust found in winter. It is most important to distinguish between sun crust and wind crust. **1955** E. Hillary *High Adventure* 69 The surface here was most unpleasant—a thick wind-crust over deep unstable snow. **1976** *Jrnl. R. Soc. Arts* CXXIV. 731/2 At present the main bar to developing and using wind energy in this country is very high capital costs of equipment. **1980** *Sunday Times* 24 Aug. 4/4 The plan is to set up one (windmill) of medium size as soon as possible to gain experience, and then to establish a 'wind farm', of about ten windmills, each capable of generating a megawatt of electricity. **1982** *Energy Spectrum* (Shell Internat. Petroleum Co. Ltd.) 8/1 Larger systems of more than 1 MW are also envisaged either singly or in 'wind farms' for integration into utility grids. **1895** W. R. Fisher *Schlich's Man. Forestry* IV. iv. iii. 469 The westerly border-trees..have now become so wind-firm that the severance-felling might be widened. **1927** *Forestry* I. 21 To keep plantations wind-firm..initial spacings of the order of six feet..are necessary. **1981** *Southern Horticulture* (N.Z.) Spring 31/2 Containerisation of such material without this evening-out treatment produces trees that are neither wind-firm in the container, nor on the planting site. **1962** *Times* 1 Jan. 6/4 It [*sc.* a tree] was there to increase the wind-firmness of the woodland. **1923** Kipling *Land & Sea Tales* 181 He pointed towards the stiff-tailed wind-flags that stuck out at all sorts of angles as the eddy round the shoulder of the Down caught them. **1889** Wind-gap [see Gap *sb.*[1] 5 b]. **1895** *Geogr. Jrnl.* V. 144 If the land should be raised a few hundred feet, these head-waters would soon be gained by the Trent; and the divide between the successful and defeated systems would be pushed to the notch in the hard Oölite, which would then be a 'wind-gap', instead of a 'water-gap', as the Pennsylvanians say. **1939** *Bull. Geol. Soc. Amer.* L. 1343 The term 'wind gap' is now more commonly restricted to abandoned water gaps, while those gaps not believed to have been former water gaps are designated as 'cols'. **1977** Wind gap [see *river capture* s.v. *river *sb.*[1] 4 d]. **1930** Blunden *Summer's Fancy* 31 They stole away, and heard the windgod trill Winging the corn that to the bright west rolled. **1940** F. Smythe *Adventures of Mountaineer* xi. 201 It was all we could do.. to pull off our wind jackets. **1955** G. Band *Road to Rakaposhi* vii. 87 David and I, who were wearing bright red windjackets,..slipped carefully past. **1880** *United Service* Oct. 458 [The adjutant] watched the roll-call of his 'wind-jammers'. **1892** *Rudder* Sept. 217/1 The deck-hands on the liners contemptuously refer to [sailing vessels] as 'wind-jammers'. **1917** S. Lewis *Job* 209 We do our work and don't howl about like all these socialists and radicals and other wind-jammers. **1930** *Even. Standard* 20 Aug. 2 (Advt.), Thousands of golfers wear the Barker 'Windjammer' and report it to be a splendid garment. **1931** *Amer. Mercury* XXIV. 354/2 [Circus Words.] *Windjammer*, a band musician. **1932** Auden in *Rev. Eng. Stud.* (1978) Aug. 282 My hand was wrung By one bareheaded in a windjammer jacket. **1942** M. Hargrove *See here, Private Hargrove* xlii. 119 *Windjammer*, the bugler. **1976** *Milton Keynes Express* 25 June 4/4 The very popular zip-fronted cotton velour wind-jammer..is also great weekend gear with jeans. **1886** D. Kemp *Man. Yacht & Boat Sailing* (ed. 5) 658/1 Wind jamming. A new-fashioned slang term for sailing by the wind. **1893** *Columbus* (Ohio) *Dispatch* Oct. 5 Could this power of wind-jamming have been saved there would have been some good accruing from the extra session. **1894** *Nautical Mag.* Feb. 102 People would begin to understand the meaning of seamanship as apart from the so-called and much-despised 'wind-jamming'. **1919** S. Lewis *Free Air* 182 You're the worst wind-jamming liar I ever met. **1946** *Seafarers' Log* 18 Jan. 4/1 He really fooled the entire crew, and the Chief Mate was so impressed with his windjamming that he wanted to make him Bosun. **1943** T. Dudley-Gordon *Coastal Command at War* 22 He knows its direction by the 'wind-lanes' on the sea. **1979** *Fisherman's Weekly* 21 June 6/1 Thousands of tiny shucks from the freshly opened beech leaves, blown onto the surface, had collected in floating rafts, and were marking the wind lanes. **1911** Husband & Harby *Structural Engin* ii. 36 (*heading*) Wind load. **1961** *B.S.I. News* Dec. 16/2 Stability requirements for cranes (including consideration of wind loads). **1970** *New Scientist* 17 Sept. 584/2 The BRS project will improve wind-tunnel techniques, as well as increasing knowledge of windloads—which means better, safer, and perhaps more economic building. **1924** P. A. Franklin in Hool & Kinne *Movable & Long-Span Steel Bridges* I. 47 Design machinery for wind loadings as set forth in chapter of design of operating machinery. **1985** *Times* 19 July 13/4 In windy winter conditions the windloading presses the door up against the weatherstrip. **1908** N. Duncan *Every Man for Himself* i. 18 An' the sea was runnin' high—a fussy wind-lop over a swell that broke in big whitecaps. **1974** F. Mowat *Boat who wouldn't Float* xix. 234 The combination of wind-lop and heavy swell produced a motion that was indescribable. **1906** R. A. Streatfeild *Mod. Music & Musicians* xix. 338 The fantastic pieces of musical extravagance that are a special feature of 'Don Quixote', such as the wind machine and the bleating sheep, are thoroughly in keeping with..Strauss's real methods. **1928** D. H. Lawrence *Lady Chatterley's Lover* xvi. 282 So many people, like your famous wind-machine, have only got minds tacked on to their physical corpses. **1928** A. Rose *Stage Effects* 9 Fig. 4 shows a wind machine, as used in many theatres. It is built up in the form of a paddle-wheel. **1962** A. Nisbett *Technique Sound Studio* x. 181 A wind machine consists of a weighted piece of heavy canvas hung over a rotating, slatted drum... A wind machine produces just one sound: wind. And the same goes for thunder sheets. **1976** *Gramophone* Apr. 1611/2 Calling as it does for no fewer than twenty horns.., quadruple woodwind, six trumpets and trombones.., not to mention the windmachine, thunder-machine and numerous other percussion instruments, it is impractical to mount nowadays. **1976** *Upper Valley Progress* (Mission, Texas) 6 Oct. 10/1 (Advt.), With thermal inversion, created by our Tropic Breeze wind machine, crop level temperatures are raised as much as 10 degrees. **1936** Wind-noise [see *fairing *vbl. sb.*[2]]. **1984** *Buses* Aug. 346/2 Only the wind noise through the roof light..gave any indication of our speed. **1616, 1856** Wind-proof [in Dict., sense 30 b]. **1923** F. Wild *Shackleton's Last Voyage* v. 76 Each man was provided with a fur-lined leather cap, heavy pea-jacket, light windproof jacket, a stout pair of trousers. **1937** F. Smythe *Camp Six* xiv. 150 Too tired..to remove our ice-caked windproofs. **1975** E. Hillary *Nothing venture, Nothing Win* viii. 120 We..crawled out of our tents, dressed in all our warm clothing and windproofs. **1977** *Navy News* July 16/3 Availability of the windproof jacket will lead to the progressive phasing out of personal greatcoats and overcoats. **1875** 'Mark Twain' in *Atlantic Monthly* Mar. 288/1 It wasn't a bluff reef... It wasn't anything but a wind reef. The wind does that. **1969** *Gloss. for Landscape Work* (*B.S.I.*) v. 19 Wind rock. The loosening of the root ball of a tree or plant through the oscillation of the stem by wind. **1972** S. Emberton *Year in Shrub Garden* III. 151 Any plants which have..been wind-rocked..must be staked upright. *Ibid.* 181 Roses, bush types—shorten to prevent wind-rocking. **1981** Buczacki & Harris *Collins Guide to Pests of Garden Plants* 486 Windrock very commonly occurs on young trees, shrubs and herbaceous plants with a large top in relation to their root system. **1912** J. H. Comstock *Spider Bk.* 35 The solpugids are exceedingly agile; on this account they have been called wind-scorpions. **1959** *Southwest Rev.* Spring 137/1 An arachnid frequently, and naturally, confused with the true vinegarone is the solpugid—or wind-scorpion, wind-spider, or sun-spider. **1858** J. A. Warder *Hedges & Evergreens* 240 The common Cedar is..much used.. where a quick, permanent, and effective wind-screen is wanted. **1887** *Cent. Mag.* Mar. 740/2 That department.. was nearly surrounded by a wind-screen of hemlock boughs and odd pieces of canvas. **1948** *Autocar* 5 Nov. 1093/1 Trico-Folberth's windscreen washer drives home the lesson..'None so blind as those who can't see.' **1973** *Country Life* 22 Feb. 468/2 Windscreen washers and wipers are operated by a right-hand steering column stalk. **1984** B. Francis *AA Car Duffer's Guide* 18 I've been fiddling about for ages trying to get the windscreen washers to work properly. **1922** *Motor* 21 Nov. 831/3 (*heading*) An automatic windscreen wiper. **1975** *Daily Tel.* (Colour Suppl.) 4 Apr. 18/2 Peter Wallace, the Flight Engineer, began his safety check, examining everything from the windscreen wipers to the radar. **1985** *Computing* 15 Aug. 25/2 We still have to make do with dreadful windscreen wipers in cars. **1909** D. H. Lawrence in *English Rev.* No. 565, I wait for the baby to wander hither to me, Like a wind-shadow wandering over the water. **1931** *Flight* 25 Dec. 1269/2 He had found that behind the wings of an aeroplane 'wind shadows' existed covering a region of reduced pressure. **1977** J. F. Fixx *Compl. Bk. Running* xvii. 202 It also makes sense to vary your speed in order to take advantage of an opponent's wind shadow. **1951** *Gloss. Aeronaut. Terms* (*B.S.I.*) III. 36 Wind shear. **1976** *Sci. Amer.* Nov. 32 For a typical wind shear of one mile per hour per mile of height and an average wind speed of 20 miles per hour, the pattern of fallout 100 miles downwind from ground zero would be about 25 miles wide. **1977** *Time* 18 Apr. 37/3 'Wind shear', created by colliding air masses, was listed as the probable cause of an Eastern 727's crash while landing. **1934** A. J. Villiers (*title*) Last of the wind ships. **1980** *Times* 7 Nov. 21/4 Will the rising price of oil bring back the sailing ship—or windship as it is now called—to the trade routes of the world from which it was largely banished a century ago? **1985** *Tel. Sunday Mag.* 18 Aug. 9/1 At 75 he [*sc.* Jacques Cousteau] is as lean and as trim as his revolutionary new 'wind ship', Alcyone, which he has just sailed successfully—and using less fuel—across the Atlantic. **1923** Kipling *Land & Sea Tales* 182 Give your wind-sight another three degrees, Walters. **1920** Wind slab [see *slab *sb.*[1] 6]. **1936** E. A. M. Wedderburn *Alpine Climbing* iv. 51 A form of wind crust is wind slab. As this causes the worst kind of avalanche it is important to detect it. Its surface is smooth and unfortunately often little wind marked and its colour is matt white or yellowish. Wind slab is often found alternating with patches of softer wind marked snow. **1975** E. Hillary *Nothing venture, Nothing Win* xviii. 286, I had..noticed the debris of two large windslab avalanches nearby. **1978** Y. Chouinard *Climbing Ice* ii. 40 The wind will also scour ridges and deposit some snow on the lee side; this then becomes an unstable mass called wind slab. **1866** *N.Y. Times* 13 Apr., All persons having occasion to..start a fire in any old chopping, wind-slash..[etc.] shall give five days' notice. **1905** *Forestry Bureau Bull.* No. 61. 53 An area upon which the trees have been thrown by the wind... blow down, wind slash. **1971** F. C. Ford-Robertson *Terminol. Forest Science* 244/1 All such material [*sc.* slash] blown down by wind is termed wind slash. **1920** *Flight* 29 Apr. 470/1 Three wind sleeves have been installed at Lyons (Bron) aerodrome... Two of these 'sleeves' are red, and are situated on the western side of the landing-ground. **1939** *Air Ann. Brit. Empire* 371 Pilots of those days mistrusted a wind sleeve, which was difficult to see. **1929** E. W. Dickman *This Aviation Business* 139 It requires more work than to stake out a cow pasture, put up a hangar and wind sock, and announce the opening. **1958** *Woman* 9 Aug. 31/4 Briony walked..along the sands as far as the wind-sock up on the golf-course. **1979** J. Leasor *Love & Land Beyond* vi. 88 A wind sock hung limply on a mast. **1959** Wind-spider [see *wind-scorpion* above]. **1966** C. Sweeney *Scurrying Bush* vi. 88 A large solipugid, a very hairy, fast running arachnid that in Africa is often called a 'hunting spider' or sometimes a 'wind spider'. **1893** M. A. Owen *Voodoo Tales* 28, I seed dem ole win'-splitteh s [*sc.* long lean hogs]. **1900** *Daily Express* 13 July 6/6 The wind-splitter..keeps up a wonderful pace. **1941** I. L. Idriess *Great Boomerang* vii. 51 No 'wind-splitters' nearly as wide across the hips as the forehead. **1890** *Harper's Mag.* Dec. 58/2 A tall thinnish man, with..a white wind-splitting face. **1900** *Daily Express* 13 July 6/6 The 'wind-splitting train' was tested over the line between Baltimore and Washington recently. **1948** Duncan & Bone *Oxf. Pocket Bk. Athletic Training* 35 'Wind-sprints'..consist of covering one or two laps of the track, and in so doing moving up very gradually from walking or slow running into faster running and then reversing the process, which will be repeated several times. **1981** *North-east Woods & Waters* Jan. 19/1 My last ¼ of a mile was done doing wind sprints to help my lungs and heart to weather the beating of what was to come. **1932** D. Garnett *Rabbit in Air* II. 60 It seemed to me several points different if judged by the factory smoke than if judged by the wind stocking. **1983** P. Devlin *All of Us There* vii. 78 The wind-stocking fluttering to show pilots which way the wind is blowing. **1929** *Oxford Poetry* 1 Let's pick the petals of all joy apart, And launch them uncontrolled on the wind-stream. **1934** *Discovery* June

155/1 The wind-stream is so powerful that a man could not possibly stand against it. **1954** FISHER & LOCKLEY *Sea-Birds* v. 127 The oceanic travellers..spend their time making ground by..excursions (by gravitational falls) into the sheltered trough between the crests of the waves, out of the main wind-stream. **1976** A. WHITE *Long Silence* vii. 59 You don't go out at right angles to the plane or the windstream can spin you. **1884** *Engineering* 5 Sept. 225/1 The position and character of the floor between the girders also materially affect the wind stresses. **1953** *Jrnl. Marine Res.* XII. 249 (*heading*) Wind stress on an artificial pond. **1984** A. C. & A. DUXBURY *Introd. World's Oceans* viii. 272 The sea surface slopes, as happens..under wind stress. **1932** *Daily Tel.* 2 Mar. 9/5 Curls have ousted points of straight hair, and the old windswept hair is dead. **1940** GRAVES & HODGE *Long Week-End* xvi. 280 The 'windswept' coiffure came over from Paris in 1931... The hair was cut short, brushed forward with a swirling movement. **1963** WODEHOUSE *Stiff Upper Lip, Jeeves* iii. 29 She is..as loony a young shrimp as ever wore a wind-swept hair-do. **1985** *Hair* Summer 64 (*caption*) Windswept layered hair requires mousse. **1939** H. J. LUTZ in *Amer. Jrnl. Science* CCXXXVII. 392 This investigation was devoted particularly to the influence of tree windthrow on soil morphology. **1953** *Brit. Commonw. Forest Terminol.* I. 147 *Windthrow*, uprooted by wind; a tree or trees so uprooted. Syn. *Windblow*. **1966** *Brit. Columbia Logging* 3/1 They also can sell in their local areas wind-throw timber and stands threatened with destruction by disease or insects. **1981** *N.Z. Jrnl. Forestry* XXVI. 96 Line transects recording soil depth and percentage windthrow were made through single-aged stands of trees where definite patterns of windthrow occurred. **1911** *Aeronaut. Jrnl.* Oct. 53 The planes were tested in a 'wind tunnel'. *Ibid.* 62 Wind tunnel experiments. **1933** *Jrnl. R. Aeronaut. Soc.* XXXVII. 36 The aerodynamic characteristics were observed on a model of the airship in a wind tunnel. **1961** L. MUMFORD *City in History* (1966) x. 355 Not by accident did the medieval townsman, seeking protection against winter wind, avoid creating such cruel wind-tunnels as the broad, straight street. **1970** *New Scientist* 23 July 194/2 Wind-tunnel tests..establish airflow patterns over ships. **1974** *Times Lit. Suppl.* 13 Dec. 1410/5 The Weimar Republic was above all a testing time, part of that great German wind tunnel in which ideas and principles, standards and personalities were subjected to the gale of history. **1983** *Aviation News* 8 Sept. 339/1 To compare inflight data with wind tunnel data for the same aircraft. **1985** *Times* 1 Mar. 3/3 The ultimate aim was C15, in every way a family car, using a very streamlined body already being tested in a wind tunnel. **1909** *Chambers's Jrnl.* Mar. 203/1 A small petrol or oil engine as a standby to be used when there is insufficient wind to drive the wind-turbine. **1946** A. HUXLEY *Let.* 5 Nov. (1969) 557, I gather that the experimental wind turbine which has been producing fifteen hundred kilowatts in Maine has proved entirely satisfactory. **1982** *Daily Tel.* 17 Nov. 1/6 A £650,000 wind turbine machine..was switched on yesterday by Sir Walter Marshall, chairman of the Central Electricity Generating Board. **1959** Windway [see *FLÛTE-À-BEC]. **1979** *Early Music* July 365/1 It is also possible to wash the windway with water and washing-up liquid... This is recommended for very dirty or mouldy windways. [**1933** *Automobile Trade Jrnl.* Nov. 52/1 Such items as windshield wings, either as a part of or separate from front door windows [etc.].] **1934** Wind wing [see *STICKER[1] 5 a]. **1951** R. CHANDLER in Gardiner & Walker *R. Chandler Speaking* (1962) 110 It sounded like old Simpson's Chevvy... He could tell by the broken windwing.

wind, *v.*[1] Add: **II. 20*. wind down. a.** *intr.* To draw gradually to a close.

1952 DYLAN THOMAS *Coll. Poems* p. ix, This day winding down now At God speeded summer's end. **1977** *Time* 19 Sept. 22/1 Instead of winding down, investigations were being stepped up. **1985** R. BARNARD *Disposal of Living* vi. 75 The fête was beginning to wind down then. I *think* Mary was still around.

b. *intr.* for *refl.* Of a person who has been 'screwed up' to a certain pitch or is in a state of tension: to relax, to unwind.

1958 *Observer* 7 Sept. 3/5 He is slowly 'winding down' after his exhausting television shows. **1970** *New Yorker* 24 Oct. 50/1 Even the West Indian was winding down. **1979** *Homes & Gardens* June 77/2 It takes him about two days to wind down. When your husband runs his own firm his stress is very great. **1985** R. HUNTER *Fourth Angel* viii. 137 An evening at the theatre and a chance to wind down and relax.

c. *trans.* To open (the window of a vehicle) downwards by rotating a handle. Cf. *wind up*, sense 22 e (*c*) below.

1961 I. MURDOCH *Severed Head* viii. 71 The windscreen was becoming opaque... I wound down the window on my side and the cold choking air came in. **1975** D. LODGE *Changing Places* v. 165 Philip stopped at a red light and wound down his window.

d. *fig.* To reduce in scale gradually; to bring (an activity) to an end.

1969 *Washington Post* 16 Apr. A22/2 Very little else is possible before the war is wound down. **1969** *Guardian* 5 Aug. 2/7 The enemy might prefer gradually to 'wind down' the level of combat step by step. **1977** *Rolling Stone* 16 June 56/3 Natalie is pregnant and will wind down her work schedule in anticipation of a fall delivery. **1981** *Daily Tel.* 26 Nov. 21 He might be able simply to wind the business down to a size which becomes manageable again.

21*. wind on. *Photogr.* To turn (the film in a camera) to the next position in readiness for taking another photograph. Also *absol.*

1947 A. RANSOME *Great Northern?* xxiii. 289 Dick wound on the film, closed the camera and put it in its case. **1964** 'F. CLIFFORD' *Hunting-Ground* vi. 67 Thirty-six on the film and I'm supposed not to have wound on once. **1982** C. THOMAS *Jade Tiger* iii. 66 He adjusted the focus... Click, wind on, click again.

22. wind up. d. (*e*) *intr.* Of a person, etc.: to end up, to finish up (in a certain place or condition); to find oneself eventually. *colloq.*

1918 V. WOOLF *Diary* (1979) I. 115, I went to have my tooth finished, winding up for tea at the Club. **1921** E. O'NEILL *Emperor Jones* i. 155 When I gits a chance to use it I winds up Emperor in two years. **1942** W. STEVENS *Let.* 2 Oct. (1966) 421 The same reasons would prevent her from marrying as long as the war goes on, and..she may wind up as an old maid. **1952** WODEHOUSE *Barmy in Wonderland* iii. 29 Men who own hotels always wind up in the breadline with holes in their socks. **1968** *Globe & Mail* (Toronto) 17 Feb. 3/1 Canada has made no written request that military equipment sent to the United States should not wind up in Vietnam. **1976** *National Observer* (U.S.) 13 Mar. 9/2 Somebody who wants to get away from it all is likely to wind up in a chalet in a Heidilike village on a mountain. **1980** L. BIRNBACH et al. *Official Preppy Handbk.* 111/1 Many of these forays.. wind up involving mayhem or destruction of property.

e. (*c*) In reference to a motor vehicle: to close (the window) by rotating a handle. Cf. *wind down*, sense 20* c above.

1970 H. R. F. KEATING *Inspector Ghote breaks Egg* ii. 16 He slowly wound up the window of his big car. **1971** P. D. JAMES *Shroud for a Nightingale* i. 16 She wound up the car window and stepped on the accelerator.

wind, *v.*[2] Add: **II. 6.** To cause (a baby) to bring up wind after feeding; to 'burp'.

1958 *Observer* 19 Oct. 10/6 My five-month-old son, though well fed, thoroughly winded and much loved, delights in yelling loud and long. **1961** *Guardian* 28 June 6/3 Two babies..to feed and wind and change. **1978** D. MURPHY *Place Apart* x. 211 Paddy's wife handed him their six-months-old daughter, to be 'winded' while she was undressing their two-year-old son... The baby burped dutifully.

windage. 3. Delete 'also,...' and transfer quot. 1903 to sense *4.

4. The (actual or potential) air resistance of a moving object, esp. a vessel or a rotating machine part; also, the force of the wind on a stationary object.

1897, 1898 [in Dict., sense 2]. **1903** [in Dict., sense 3]. **1909** A. WILLIAMS *Engin. Wonders of World* III. 42/2 The designer has to consider how to curve the [propeller] blades so as to give a maximum thrust for a minimum windage. **1948** *Times* 24 Nov. 2/2 A new type of anchor designed to prevent warships, particularly aircraft-carriers with their large windage area, from dragging their anchors. **1953** C. S. FORESTER *Hornblower & 'Atropos'* 60 Their twelve oars hardly sufficed to control their more than forty feet of length, and the windage of the huge cabin aft was enormous. **1958** *Engineering* 31 Jan. 157/3 The radar aerial..is of parabolic section and slatted to reduce windage. **1961** E. LIGHTFOOT *Moment Distribution* v. 123 Design against windage is important in skyscraper buildings. **1971** *Sci. Amer.* Dec. 7/1 If the time cycle between storage and retrieval is long, most of the stored energy [of the flywheel] is lost in windage and friction. **1977** *Mod. Boating* (Austral.) Jan. 98/1 There is a tremendous amount o windage in that topsides and cabin.

5. Special Comb.: **windage loss**, loss of power through the air resistance of rotating parts.

1922 *Encycl. Brit.* XXX. 35/2 In determining the useful H.P. of rotary engines, 'windage loss'..had first to be determined. **1966** *McGraw-Hill Encycl. Sci. & Technol.* IV. 449/1 Windage loss is relatively large in air-cooled high-speed machines.

wind-bag, windbag. Add: **3.** *Naut. slang.* A sailing ship or 'windjammer'.

1924 R. CLEMENTS *Gipsy of Horn* 11 A sailing ship—an old wind-bag, as the young, up-to-date watchkeeper would call it. **1930** J. MASEFIELD *Wanderer of Liverpool* 47 A crowd of windbags moored fore and aft, to buoyed anchors. **1946** W. MCFEE *In First Watch* i. 15 He had been cook in a windbag and a sailor before the mast.

wind-break, *sb.* **1.** For Chiefly *U.S.* read orig. *U.S.* and add earlier and later examples. Now freq. without hyphen as one word.

1861 *Trans. Ill. Agric. Soc.* IV. 479 These trees, which are valuable as shade and wind-breaks, should be planted. **1910** W. SCHLICH *Man. Forestry* (ed. 4) II. 123 Species with a thin crown are indifferently adapted for wind breaks. **1934** *Times Educ. Suppl.* 10 Feb. p. iv/3 Whether as ornament or to secure privacy, as a windbreak or to indicate a boundary, a hedge has its place in most gardens. **1950** *N.Z. Jrnl. Agric.* July 5/3 Such a wind-break is very valuable for sheltering dipped sheep. **1962** *Coast to Coast 1961–62* 138 An old limestone place, with a slate roof, and a windbreak of pepper-trees at one side. **1968** *Southerly* XXVIII. 172 The pine trees acted as a wind-break for the solitary house set a hundred yards lower down. **1970** J. H. B. PEEL *Country Folk* ii. 38 A hedge serves as a windbreak for crops and as a nesting-place for birds. **1975** *Toronto Star* 27 Dec. D4/1 So except in balmy weather, be sure to tote a plastic or canvas wind-break. **1981** *Farmstead Mag.* Winter 49/1 Some people prefer deciduous trees in all or part of the windbreak.

wi·nd-down. *colloq.* [f. vbl. phr. *to wind down*: see *WIND *v.*[1] 20*.] The process of bringing or coming to an end; a gradual reduction in scale.

1969 *Time* 21 Feb. 29 The campaign heralds the official wind-down of the Cultural Revolution, a finale that is to climax in 'all-round victory'. **1971** *New Scientist* 8 July 95/3 The reduction in the number of students.., the cutback in..spending, the cancellation of the SST, the wind-down of space exploration, [etc.]. **1971** *Guardian Weekly* 25 Dec. 3 Even now, with the virtual completion of the wind-down begun in 1970, the military break with Indochina is not complete.

wind-drift. Add: **b.** The action of wind currents, esp. on water.

1898 *Geogr. Jrnl.* June 662 The sand so produced is rounded by wind-drift in an unmistakable manner, the grains being entirely different from those of sea-sand. **1964** *Oceanogr. & Marine Biol.* II. 257 This patch [of effluent] is subject to wind-drift and can be carried directly on to beaches. **1967** *Ibid.* V. 103 Since the cross sections of these two straits are much less than that of the throat of the Celtic Sea much surface wind drift water must return to the Atlantic some other way.

winded, *ppl. a.*[1] **3.** (Earlier example.)

1883 'MARK TWAIN' *Life on Miss.* iii. 49 They couldn't keep that up very long without getting winded.

windego, obs. var. *WINDIGO.

winder, *sb.*[2] Add: **2. b.** *fig.* † *spec.* a sentence of transportation for life (*obs. slang*).

1812 J. H. VAUX *Vocab. Flash Lang.* in *Mem.* (1964) 279 A man transported for his natural life, is said..to have *knap'd a winder.* **1836** J. F. O'CONNELL *Residence in New Holland* 37 Previous convictions and character must have affected his sentence, as it was, in flash phraseology, a winder. **1913** D. H. LAWRENCE *Sons & Lovers* ix. 243 It's a winder when you have to pour your own tea out—an' nobody to grouse if you team it in your saucer and sup it up.

winder (wi·ndəɹ), *sb.*[5] Repr. dial. or slovenly pronunc. of WINDOW *sb.*

1684 G. MERITON *Yorks. Dialogue* in *Praise of Yorks. Ale* 49 Ah Nan steek th' winderboard, & mack it dark. **1838** DICKENS *Nickleby* (1839) viii. 69 We go upon the practical mode of teaching, Nickleby;..W-i-n, win, d-e-r, der, winder, a casement. **1877** [see *window bottom* s.v. *WINDOW *sb.* 5 d]. **1901** M. FRANKLIN *My Brilliant Career* xxxii. 272 Lizer, shut the winder quick. **1976** *Trans. Yorks. Dial. Soc.* XIV. 37 Ah've just been cleeanin' t'winders.

windfall. Add: **2.** *fig.* Applied (*poet.* ⁻¹) to a flood of unexpected light.

1945 DYLAN THOMAS *Fern Hill* in *Horizon* Oct. 221 And once below a time I lordly had the trees and leaves Trail with daisies and barley Down the rivers of the windfall light.

3. *Econ.* **windfall profit**, unexpectedly large or unforeseen profit; similarly *windfall gain, loss*, etc.

1936 J. M. KEYNES *Gen. Theory Employment* II. vi. 57 The change in the value of the equipment, due to unforeseen changes in market values, exceptional obsolescence or destruction..may be called the *windfall loss.* *Ibid.* v. xx. 288 The windfall gain will wholly accrue to those entrepreneurs who happen to possess products at a relatively advanced stage of production. **1951** SLOAN & ZURCHER *Dict. Economics* 266 *Windfall profit*, a profit in excess of that which can be considered normal. **1973** *Times* 21 Dec. 6/7 A proposal for Congress to impose 'an emergency windfall profits tax' on the oil company. Although President Nixon himself told the American consumer, 'there will be no windfall profits at their expense.' **1977** *N.Y. Rev. Bks.* 26 May 31/4 The shift to free market pricing would give the oil companies windfall profits.

wind-gall[2]. (Earlier example.)

1823 J. F. COOPER *Pilot* I. ii. 19 There be streaked wind-galls in the offing, that speak..plainly..to shorten sail.

Windies (wi·ndiz), *sb. pl.* *colloq.* (orig. *Austral.*). [Contraction of *West Indies.*] West Indians, *spec.* the West Indian cricket team; also, immigrants from the West Indies.

1965 W. GROUT *My Country's Keeper* 69 The Australian public..took the Windies to their hearts from that moment. **1971** J. BRUNNER *Honky in Woodpile* ii. 15 Skinheads and others were out bashing Pakis and Windies. **1976** *Sunday Tel.* 4 Jan. 52 Windies roll with brutal pace beating. **1980** *Economist* 21 June 51/1 Would the West Indies beat England in the first Test match?.. In the cricket match, the 'Windies' scraped home in a nail-biting finish.

windigo (wi·ndigo). Also 9 **weendego(ag, wendigo; wihtigo, witiko**, etc.; and with capital initial. [Ojiwa *wintiko*, pl. *wintikok*; some spellings reflect the Cree cognate *wihtikow.*] In the folklore of the northern Algonquian Indians: a cannibalistic giant, the transformation of a person who has eaten human flesh.

1714 J. KNIGHT *Jrnl.* 7 Oct. in W. Cowan *Papers of Seventh Algonquian Conference 1975* (1976) 21 Some Indians came from Fort Nelson who says they saw a Whitego wch is an Apparition. **1830** E. JAMES *Narr. John Tanner* 316 The Muskegoes, who inhabit the low and cheerless swamps on the borders of Hudson's Bay, and are themselves reproached by the other tribes as cannibals, are said to live in constant fear of the Weendegoag. **1847** J. B. NEVINS *Two Voyages* 115 When Windego saw him, he was very angry, and said, 'What do you mean, boy, by coming out and making that noise? I am going to eat you.' **1859** P. KANE *Wanderings of Artist among Indians*

N. Amer. 60 The Weendigoes are looked upon with superstitious dread and horror by all Indians. **1924** *Chambers's Jrnl.* Mar. 170/1 At midnight they were wakened by what Jacques took to be a wendigo in the woods behind. **1933** J. M. Cooper in *Primitive Man* Jan. 20 The Cree Witiko Psychosis... This peculiar form of mental disturbance is characterized by (1) a craving for human flesh, and (2) a delusion of transformation into a Witiko who has a heart of ice or who vomits ice. **1934** *Jrnl. Abnormal & Social Psychol.* XXIX. 7 The repugnance to food is construed as positive evidence that the person is becoming a 'wihtigo', *i.e.*, a cannibal. **1960** T. Stacey *Brothers M.* ii. xxxii. 361 Daudi..was still utterly subjected, as if by some unseen windigo that was withdrawing him to its own element. **1961** O. Nash *Coll. Verse* 425 The Wendigo, The Wendigo! Its eyes are ice and indigo! **1971** *Brit. Med. Bull.* XXVII. 78/1 States of excitement or panic may be so influenced by local conditions as to give the appearance of specific psychoses. . The Windigo psychosis of the Chippewa, Ojibwa and Cree Indians illustrates the way in which such states can develop.

windiness. **1.** (Later examples.)

1922 A. Machen *Far off Things* i. 10 Holborn has a certain vastness and windiness about it as the sky grows from black to grey. **1957** G. E. Hutchinson *Treat. Limnol.* I. vii. 446 (*heading*) Windiness and area. **1971** *Nature* 10 Dec. 345/1 The classic loess deposits in China.. can probably only be explained in terms of greater windiness in the China/Gobi Desert area.

winding, *vbl. sb.*[1] Add: **I. 2. b.** (Later example.)

1917 T. S. Eliot *Prufrock & Other Observations* 18 Among the windings of the violins And the ariettes Of cracked cornets.

II. 8. b. *Electr.* An electric conductor that is wound round a magnetic material, esp. (*a*) a coil encircling part of the stator or rotor of an electric motor or generator, or an assembly of such coils connected to form one circuit; (*b*) one forming part of a transformer.

1888 S. P. Thompson *Dynamo-Electric Machinery* (ed. 2) xii. 259 If the successive sections are to be connected up consecutively, then they must be wound.. alternately with right-handed and left-handed windings. **1947** R. Lee *Electronic Transformers & Circuits* v. 141 In step-down transformers the capacitance may be regarded as existing mainly across the primary winding; in step-up transformers, across the secondary winding. **1962** *Newnes Conc. Encycl. Electr. Engin.* 894/1 The simplest type of winding is a field coil around a salient pole.., the coil comprising a number of turns (between one and several thousand) of wire or strip. **1979** Nasar & Unnewehr *Electromechanics & Electric Machines* iii. 67 Transformer windings are constructed of solid or stranded copper or aluminum conductors.

winding, *vbl. sb.*[2] (Later example.)

1940 W. de la Mare *Pleasures & Speculations* 48 The first windings of the Last Trump.

windmill, *sb.* Add: **3. c.** *Cricket.* A style of bowling with a high overarm delivery. ? *Obs.*

1867 *Australasian* 19 Jan. 76/3 A change in bowling was tried, Wardill going on with his 'windmills', *vice* Conway. **1900** W. A. Bettesworth *Walkers of Southgate* 124 Taking his run up to the wicket, swinging his arm in what has been described as 'a windmill action'. **1920** in P. F. Warner *Cricket* 86 Spofforth's windmill deliveries.

4. b. (Examples of phr. *to tilt at windmills*.)

1898 [see Tilter *sb.*[1] 1]. **1937** A. Christie *Death on Nile* xxiv. 238 Rather eccentric..inclined to tilt at windmills. **1978** P. Bryers *Cat Trapper* viii. 57 Mike was into the sort of thing I'd like to be doing... Tilting at windmills?

5*. An airscrew, esp. one of the kind designed by Cierva for the autogiro. Now *Hist.*

1931 Cierva y Cadorniu *Wings of Tomorrow* 88, I designed the blades of the windmill. **1935** *Sun* (Baltimore) 31 Jan. 3/3 This new fast auto gyro will have no propeller. It will tilt its present windmill, gear it to the engine and so get its lift and forward drive. **1949** *Gloss. Aeronaut. Terms* (*B.S.I.*) ii. 20 *Windmill*, an airscrew designed to produce power by axial transmission relative to the air.

6. a. (sense 5* above) *windmill aeroplane*, (*air*)*plane*, *rotor*, *wing*; **b. windmill brake state** *Aeronaut.* (see quot. 1969).

1931 *Statesman* (Calcutta) 5 Dec., The Autogiro or 'windmill' aeroplane has just been put on the public market in this country for the first time. **1928** *Daily Express* 10 Aug. 11/4 A 'windmill' airplane is to fly the channel. **1948** *Jrnl. R. Aeronaut. Soc.* 269/1 In the windmill brake state, the rotor is again working in a regular slipstream. **1969** *Gloss. Aeronaut. & Astronaut. Terms* (*B.S.I.*) v. 19 *Windmill-brake state*, the operating condition of a rotor when the rotor thrust and the axial flow through and outside the rotor disc area are all in the same direction. **1927** *Times* 27 Apr. 16/3 It was agreed to use the word .aerodyne to designate all heavier-than-air craft, in which category the class name for the windmill plane appears as gyro plane. **1944** H. F. Gregory *Anything Horse can Do* iv. 48 The stick [of the Autogiro] was connected to the hub of the windmill rotor by push-pull tubes and cables. **1931** Cierva y Cadorniu *Wings of Tomorrow* 82 A flying machine with a windmill wing.

windmill, *v.* Add: **b.** *trans.* and *intr.* To move (one's arms or legs) in a manner suggestive of a windmill.

1927 W. E. Collinson *Contemp. Eng.* 18 At this school we had our first taste of fighting or rather windmilling with the arms. **1928** *Daily Express* 6 Nov. 8 They..set about their efforts again, windmilling his arms and legs until he gasped with unconscious exhaustion. **1959** R. Collier *City that wouldn't Die* v. 67 Windmilling your arms to keep the blood coursing. **1979** S. Brett *Comedian Dies* v. 55 Lennie Barber..seemed to lose his balance and sank back, arms windmilling, on to the side of his chair. **1982** W. Boyd *Ice-Cream War* 4 The colonel windmilled his arms and cracked his knuckles.

c. *intr.* Aeronaut. Of the propeller or rotor of an aircraft: to spin unpowered; *to windmill down*, to descend with the rotor spinning; also *fig.*

1934 *Jrnl. R. Aeronaut. Soc.* XXXVIII. 18 Captain Barnwell said..that it could be assumed that when an engine was fully throttled the airscrew was windmilling freely. **1942** *Flight* 26 Mar. 296/2 When an airscrew is wind-milling..the effect is exactly opposite to its normal one. **1958** *Listener* 2 Jan. 10/1 The rotor windmilling freely as on an autogiro. **1963** Sobey & Suggs *Control of Aircraft & Missile Powerplants* vii. 181 The forward flight of the airframe will cause the engine to windmill and create sufficient airflow through the engine to minimize the probability of a hot start. **1976** *Shooting Times & Country Mag.* 16–22 Dec. 29/2, I shot at another goose which peeled off, flew fluttering for a hundred yards, and then windmilled down stone dead. **1978** M. Babson *Tightrope for Three* xxvi. 152 Autorotation was a standard and perfectly safe manoeuvre, the helicopter windmilling down with the pilot still in complete control.

Hence **wi·ndmilling** *ppl. a.* and *vbl. sb.*

1945 *Jrnl. R. Aeronaut. Soc.* XLIX. 716 With the windmilling propeller the changed air-flow over the aircraft does not impair the handling characteristics. **1959** C. A. Meyer in O. E. Lancaster *Jet Propulsion Engines* 149 A typical curve showing the drag of a turbo-jet engine during windmilling is shown in Fig. C, 11f. **1973** J. Wainwright *Touch of Malice* 98 The young man was obviously a nutter... His slobbing mouth. His windmilling arms. **1978** M. Farren *Feelies* 33 The other girl was spun, flat on her back with windmilling arms and legs.

Windmill Hill. The name of the site of a causeway camp near Avebury, Wilts., type site of the neolithic age in Britain, used to designate the type of culture, pottery, etc., characteristic of that period.

1930 E. C. Curwen in *Antiquity* IV. 26 The varieties of pottery..have been collectively described as the Windmill Hill type. **1947** J. & C. Hawkes *Prehist. Britain* ii. 40 The mausoleum most fashionable among the Windmill Hill people was the long barrow. **1954** S. Piggott *Neolithic Cultures* ii. 18 The Windmill Hill culture was basically that of cattle-breeders. **1963** *Field Archaeol.* (Ordnance Survey) (ed. 4) 33 While 'Windmill Hill' pottery predominates, most other forms of Neolithic pottery are represented. **1971** *World Archaeol.* III. 239 The Q1 skeleton strongly suggested that a member of the Windmill Hill Culture was cut to pieces by this type of large metal weapon. **1983** P. A. Crowl *Intell. Traveller's Guide to Historic Britain* i. 15 Those large mounds of earth thrown up by people of the Windmill Hill culture to cover their dead.

windolite (wi·ndǝlait). Also **Windolite**, **windowlite.** [f. Window *sb.* + *-lite* (alteration of Light *sb.*).] The name of a transparent material serving as a substitute for glass.

A proprietary name in Australia.

1927 *Glasgow Herald* 1 Feb. 6/4 If the pullets are to be confined..wide shelter boards and glass, or 'windolite', shutters must be fixed. **1935** *Times Educ. Suppl.* 16 Mar. p. iv/1 A sheet of glass or windolite or a small *cloche* will afford them [*sc.* plants] shelter. **1951** 'N. Shute' *Round Bend* 30 An upstairs window was broken and shut up with windowlite tacked over the frame.

wi·nd-on, *a. Photogr.* [f. vbl. phr. *to wind on*: see *Wind *v.*[1] 21*.] Designating or pertaining to (part of) the mechanism for advancing a film to the next position.

1963 *Listener* 31 Jan. 198/2 As for the camera..the wind-on mechanism jammed. **1976** J. McClure *Rogue Eagle* vi. 101 Oeloefse removed a sliver of film from behind the wind-on spool.

window, *sb.* Add: **3. d.** *Geol.* = *Fenster.

1908 H. B. C. Sollas tr. *Suess's Face of Earth* III. viii. 350 This term 'window' has been brought into use by our fellow geologists in Switzerland, and we shall adopt it in this work for those cases in which a subjacent tectonic element is brought to light by erosion. **1927** L. W. Collet *Structure of Alps* ii. i. 26 Three windows occur in the Eastern Alps. **1939, 1954** [see *Fenster]. **1980** *Sci. Amer.* Oct. 131/2 The presence of sedimentary rocks in the windows of the Blue Ridge indicates that the crystalline rocks there overlie sedimentary material.

e. A transparent panel in a package, through which the contents can be seen; *spec.* on an envelope (see *window-envelope*, sense 5 d).

1914 [see *window-envelope*, sense 5 d below]. **1938** D. E. A. Charlton *Art of Packaging* 94 The latest.. improvement..[paper] napkins visible through a cellophane window. **1952** E. J. Labarre *Dict. Paper & Paper-making* (ed. 2) 90 The use of..envelopes..with cellophane windows is prohibited by most continental postal administrations. **1977** C. McCarry *Secret Lovers* iii. 40 Wilson..flipped the plastic windows to make certain that all the papers were still in the wallet.

f. Freq. with capital initial. Mil. code name: = *Chaff *sb.*[1] 6 b.

1942 Ld. Cherwell in *Oxf. Mag.* (1963) 9 May 283/1 If you go into the meeting and try to get 'Window' used, you'll find me and Tizard united against you. **1946** J. P. Baxter *Scientists against Time* vi. 93 The British used Window for the first time over Hamburg on the night of July 24–25, 1943. **1947** [see *chaff *sb.*[1] 6 b]. **1962** A. P. Rowe *Let.* in R. V. Jones *Most Secret War* (1978) iv. 41 What I want to emphasize is that from no one at no time did I hear a breath of anything like window. **1963** D. Irving *Destruction of Dresden* iii. iii. 135 The crews of these new bomber formations had been cascading *Window* into the air in copious amounts. **1980** M. Middlebrook *Battle of Hamburg* viii. 125 It is not known which aircraft dropped the first bundle of Window.

g. *Computers.* (i) The screen of a VDU regarded as a means of displaying part of a drawing stored in a computer; the part of a drawing, program, etc., chosen for display.

1966 *Computer Jrnl.* IX. 21/1 The 10-inch square display screen..is treated as a 'window' on to a very large drawing board. *Ibid.* 22/1 The display 'window' can be moved one grid space in any of four directions. **1968** *IBM Systems Jrnl.* VII. 163 A subsequent computation can determine the point at which any line crosses the edge of the window. **1982** J. E. Scott *Introd. Interactive Computer Graphics* vii. 124 The size and location of the window are expressed in user coordinates because the window is specified in relation to the drawing... The dimensions and center point of the viewport are expressed in normalized screen coordinates.

(ii) = *Viewport 2.

1974 *AFIPS Conf. Proc.* XLIII. 251/1 The display screen is divisible into rectangular, possibly overlapping 'windows'. **1980** W. Newman in C. E. Vandoni *Eurographics 80*, 4 NAN..uses overlapping windows, in this case in colour but with contents restricted to text. **1983** *MicroComputer Printout* Sept. 57/2 A similar, but more flexible system allows you to split the screen into two windows for viewing different sections of the model at once. **1985** *Acorn User* Feb. 37/2 Windows can be created which can then be rearranged to provide any print format required.

4. b. *to go* (*be thrown*, etc.) *out of the window* (U.S. without *of*), to be abandoned, discarded, or made worthless; also (U.S.) *to be out the window.*

1939 H. L. Ickes *Secret Diary* (1954) III. 3 Steve Early ..said that the 'brain trust was out of the window'. **1945** *Sun* (Baltimore) 1 Oct. 4-0/3 Production of specialty goods—such as birthday and wedding cakes—was 'out the window'. **1946** *Ibid.* 6 July 4/1 As a guide, past experience went out the window early this year when the number of retirements suddenly increased. **1964** S. M. Miller in I. L. Horowitz *New Sociol.* 300 The concept of 'unemployables' was largely thrown out the window. **1968** F. Lundberg *Rich & Super-Rich* iv. 173 As FDR himself said, 'the New Deal is out the window.' **1969** G. Donaldson *Fifteen Men* xi. 184 'The Uncle Louis kissing babies went out of the window this afternoon', said Green. **1977** *Chicago Tribune* 2 Oct. xiii. 24/3 The old rule-of-thumb of putting insulation with a resistance rating of 19 in your attic (R-19) is 'out the window'.

c. A continuous range of electromagnetic wavelengths for which the atmosphere (or some other medium) is relatively transparent.

1949 *Bull. Amer. Meteorol. Soc.* XXX. 233/1 Dr. Buettner indicated as one problem the measurement of solar radiation near 0·21μ, where absorption due to ozone decreases and that due to oxygen increases, forming a 'window' in the solar spectrum. **1969** *Guardian* 6 Feb. 9 The earth's infra-red 'windows' are at wavelengths of 1 to 2 and 8 to 14 microns. **1970** *Nature* 10 Oct. 158/1 This particular solvent is transparent in the region of the neodymium laser wavelength (1·06 μm) and..the absorption spectrum of the resulting solution exhibits a 'window' in this region. **1974** *Sci. Amer.* Apr. 71/3 The most recently opened window on the galactic center is at X-ray wavelengths.

d. = *launch window* s.v. *Launch *sb.*[1] 7; *weather window*: see *Weather *sb.* 7. Chiefly *U.S.*

1965 [see *launch window* s.v. *launch *sb.*[1] 7]. **1967** *N.Y. Times* 18 Oct. 30/1 The Soviet and American vehicles flew to Venus close together because both were fired during one of the periodic 'windows' for such shots. **1968** *Sci. Jrnl.* Dec. 17/2 Between February and April next year the 'window' will be open for launchings to Mars. **1973** *Times* 15 May 1/5 There will be tomorrow only a 10-minute 'window'—the period in which the rocket must be launched to reach the appropriate orbit. **1977** A. Peccei *Human Quality* ix. 190 This is therefore the time to act. The seventies offer what in space exploration is called a 'window', an opportunity, and probably one of the last ones, for us to launch such an undertaking.

e. Hence used more widely in sense 'a period of time', in phrases *window of opportunity* (or *vulnerability*), esp. with reference to the arms race. orig. *U.S.*

1979 *Hearings U.S. Congr. Sen. Comm. Armed Services* i. 168 We are facing a window of ICBM vulnerability during the period of 1982 to 1986. **1980** *N.Y. Times* 22 Sept. A27/2 To intimidate the Americans with a Soviet 'window of opportunity' to knock out Minuteman missiles. **1981** *Ibid.* 3 Oct. 13/1 Mr. Reagan..enlarged upon the meaning of his oft-repeated theme about the 'window of vulnerability'... The term is generally used to mean the time period in which American land-based missiles are believed to be vulnerable to a surprise Soviet attack. Today, Mr. Reagan said it also applied to Soviet superiority at sea and in Europe. **1982** *Nature* 4 Mar. 5/1 Environmentalists and labour union groups are seizing this 'window of opportunity' between the failure of the last industry challenge and the eventual tightening up of administrative requirements to get as much information on existing pesticides..as they can. **1985** *Sunday Times* 16 June 60/8 Regional bank bosses know that..they must rush to acquire their neighbours, to make the most of their window of opportunity.

5. a. *window-bay* (cf. BAY-WINDOW), *-circle, -hole* (earlier example), *-hook, -pole, -shade* (later N. Amer. examples), *-shaft, -slit, -square, -sticker* (*STICKER 5 a), *-unit.* **b.** *window-breaker.* **c*.** Appositive, 'that is a window', consisting chiefly of glass, as *window door, wall.*

1861 ROSSETTI *Let.* June (1965) II. 406, I offered to paint figures of some kind on the blank spaces of one of the gallery window bays. **1920** D. H. LAWRENCE *Women in Love* i. 3 Ursula and Gudrun Brangwen sat..in the window-bay of their father's house..working and talking. **1903** 'O. HENRY' in *McClure's Mag.* July 333/1 We'll get that cannon..and fire some window-breakers with it. **1944** BLUNDEN *Cricket Country* i. 14 Marbles, tops of various shape and various function—the window-breaker never was so bad as his name, the peg-top always looked more sinister. **1865** G. M. HOPKINS *Poems* (1967) 34 The towers musical, the quiet-walled grove, The window-circles. **1926** D. H. LAWRENCE *Plumed Serpent* xi. 181 Ramón..closed the window-doors. **1884** 'MARK TWAIN' *Huck. Finn* xxxiv. 351 When we got to the cabin, we took a look..and on..the north side we found a square window-hole. **1659** [Harvard] *College Book* 1, in *Publ. Colonial Soc. Mass.* (1925) XV. 10 It[em] for window-hookes ..—04[d.]. **1932** BLUNDEN *Face of England* 130 One bird came to the window-hook. **1922** W. B. YEATS *Trembling of Veil* I. xix. 64 A fellow-theosophist once found him hanging from the window-pole. **1984** *New Yorker* 24 Dec. 44/2 Dusk was gathering in the tall windows that needed a window pole to close. **1921** *Daily Colonist* (Victoria, B.C.) 20 Oct. 7/4 If you want window shades for your home, we will be pleased to send our men and give you an estimate. **1978** S. BRILL *Teamsters* iv. 127 Though darkened by the drawn windowshade it was a comfortable room. **1918** D. H. LAWRENCE *New Poems* 54 Petals heaped between the window-shafts In a drift die there. **1880** 'MARK TWAIN' *Tramp Abr.* xlii. 490 It [*sc.* the Castle of Chillon] has romantic window-slits that let in generous bars of light. **1955** J. R. R. TOLKIEN *Return of King* VI. i. 184 A door on his left faced a window-slit looking out westward. **1699** J. WALLIS *Let.* 10 Oct. in *Private Corresp. Samuel Pepys* (1926) I. 189 The sun-shine does appear with the distinct figure of the window-squares upon the ground within doors. **1956** D. GASCOYNE *Night Thoughts* 24 Behind the rows of window-squares. **1963** *Daily Tel.* 3 Dec. 15/4 A new window-sticker and poster campaign. **1962** *Listener* 11 Jan. 63/2 The endlessly repeated small window-units of multi-storey buildings tend to be both boring and overpowering. **1970** *Globe & Mail* (Toronto) 25 Sept. 34/7 (Advt.), Recreation room .with 'window wall' walkout to patio and garden. **1977** *Chicago Tribune* 2 Oct. XII. 10/2 Two large terraces which can be entered through window walls provide a breathtaking lake view.

d. window bill, a poster or advertisement for display in a window; **window bottom** *dial.* = WINDOW-SILL; **window-box** (earlier example); **window-card,** a card to be displayed in a window; **window display,** a display of goods in a shop-window; **window-dress** [back-formation f. *window-dresser,* etc.], (*a*) *intr.* to arrange and display goods to the best advantage in a shop-window; (*b*) *trans.* (in quots. *fig.*: see *window-dressing* (*c*)); **window-envelope** (earlier example); **window garden,** (a display of plants in) flower pots or boxes on a window-ledge or sill; **window-gazing,** staring at the displays in shop-windows, window shopping (see *window-gazer,* sense 5 c); hence (as back-formation) **window-gaze** *v. intr.*; **window guidance,** a form of credit rationing practised by Japanese banks; **window operation** = prec.; (see quot. 1965); **window-pane,** (*c*) *slang,* a monocle; (*d*) in full, *window-pane check*: a kind of large check pattern on clothes; a single square of this; also **window-pane checked** *a.*; **window plant,** (*a*) a plant grown indoors in the light of a window; (*b*) any of several succulent plants of the genera *Mesembryanthemum, Lithops,* or closely related genera, which grow almost buried in the ground, with only a transparent section of a leaf visible above it; **window-screen,** (*b*) *U.S.,* a screen of mesh designed to be put across a window-opening to admit air whilst excluding insects, etc.; **window-seat,** also a seat by the window in a train, bus, aeroplane, etc.; **window-shop** *v. intr.,* to go from shop to shop to look at the goods displayed in shop-windows without buying; freq. as *pres. ppl.*; also in extended use and *fig.*; hence **window-shopper; window-shopping** *ppl. a.* and *vbl. sb.*; **window table,** a table (pleasantly situated) by the window in a restaurant, etc.; **window-trimmer** *U.S.* = *window-dresser*; **window-trimming** *U.S.* = *window-dressing*; also *fig.*; **window-washer** (chiefly U.S.), (*a*) = *screen-washer* s.v. *SCREEN *sb.*[1] 7 a; (*b*) one whose job is to wash windows, a window-cleaner; also **window-washing** *vbl. sb.*; **window winder:** in a motor vehicle, a mechanism for opening and shutting the (side-)windows.

1868 *Era Almanack* p. xi, Theatrical posters, window bills, show cards, portraits, &c. **1965** *Spectator* 29 Jan. 124/1 Window-bills went up in streets where they had never formerly been seen. **1877** J. HARTLEY *Halifax Clock Almanack* 43 Sam made a grab at it, an it flew to th' winder-bottom. **1914** D. H. LAWRENCE *Prussian Officer* 162 The daffodils in the white window-bottoms shone across the room. **1960** *Times* 24 Oct. 12/6 Altar and every window-bottom would be bright with rosy apples. **1895** 'MARK TWAIN' in *Harper's Mag.* Dec. 144/1 A watering-pot in her hand and window-boxes of red flowers under its spout. **1905** Window-card [see *CUT-OUT *sb.* 2 c]. **1965** F. SARGESON *Memoirs of Peon* v. 115 There was a window-card that advertised board and lodging. **1897** *Sears, Roebuck Catal.* 689/1 Store Lamp... Just the thing to throw light on a window display. **1930** *Daily Express* 6 Oct. 9/2 A blaze of warm, glowing colours, elaborate window displays .usher in..the autumn shopping season. **1962** E. SNOW *Other Side of River* (1963) lxx. 538 One corner store nearby offered a neat window display of ready-made, well-tailored children's garments. **1913** J. M. KEYNES *Indian Currency & Finance* vii. 205 It is scarcely possible..that they should 'window-dress' their balance sheets. **1928** *Britain's Industr. Future* (Liberal Industr. Inquiry) 417 The common practice of 'window-dressing' the published statements by making them refer to the figures of specially selected days instead of the daily averages should be made illegal. **1957** A. C. L. DAY *Outl. Monetary Economics* xiii. 177 Each of the four of the Big Five banks which window-dressed its balance sheet made it up on a different day of the week from the others. **1971** D. CLARK *Sick to Death* iii. 56 Nobody will let us near a shop to window dress on Saturdays... But on Sundays we get a free run because the shops are shut. **1980** *Daily Tel.* 24 Sept. 17/8 The cheque was part of an elaborate fraud designed to 'window-dress' the balance sheet of a troubled banking company. **1914** *Maclean's Mag.* Dec. 124/1 Use B-E window envelopes. **1884** G. W. CABLE *Dr. Sevier* xii. 81 The asylumed window of 'St. Anna's' could glance down into it over their poor little window-gardens. **1980** *News & Observer* (Raleigh, N. Carolina) 28 Oct. WA-2/7 Additions, solariums, greenhouses, window gardens, decks. **1959** *Spectator* 21 Aug. 218/3 As you walk the busy streets and window-gaze. **1968** *Daily Mirror* 20 Aug. 9/4 Take a look at the men's wear section in the chain stores; window-gaze in any man's shop. **1949** M. STEEN *Twilight on Floods* IV. vi. 614 Up the Haymarket to Regent Street for an orgy of window-gazing. **1961** R. GRAVES *More Poems* 42 Window-gazing, at one time or another In the course of travel. **1964** *Econ. Picture of Japan* (Keidanren) IV. 53 For several years after the War, the financial policy of the Bank of Japan was characterized more or less by a qualitative control policy or a selective loans system or a so-called 'window guidance'. **1977** *Ann. Rep. Bank Internat. Settlements* 60 In Japan the authorities kept 'window guidance' ceilings on bank credit expansion in force as a precaution. **1961** *Monthly Econ. Rev.* (Bank of Japan) Sept. 9/1 The practice of the Bank of Japan in giving guidance to client commercial banks regarding their fund position and operation..has come to be..known as 'window operation'. **1965** H. T. PATRICK in W. W. Lockwood *State & Econ. Enterprise in Japan* xii. 609 In 1954..and especially in 1957 and 1961–1962, the Bank of Japan had to resort to direct credit rationing... The term for this is *madoguchi shidō.* The Bank of Japan does not like to have this technique called credit rationing, referring to it instead as 'window operation', a more literal translation. **1923** J. MANCHON *Le Slang* 338 *Window-pane,*..un monocle. **1935** D. L. SAYERS *Gaudy Night* xvii. 372 Winderpane, we called 'im, along of the eyeglass, but meanin' no disrespect. **1966** WODEHOUSE *Plum Pie* ix. 249 Freddie no longer wore the monocle. . His father-in-law had happened to ask him one day would he please remove that damned window-pane from his eye. **1966** *Guardian* 28 Sept. 3/3 Trends towards large windowpane checks. **1969** 'O. BLEECK' *Brass Go-Between* (1970) v. 60, I had the chance to admire his fawn trousers with their burnt orange windowpanes. **1978** L. BLOCK *Burglar in Closet* i. 4 My suit was a tropical worsted, a windowpane check in light and dark gray. **1973** *Country Life* 10 May 1330/1 Window pane checked Voile shirt £10.50. **1863** MRS. GASKELL *Let.* 5 Dec. (1966) 720, I have been waiting..for my cousin Mr Holland to bring me in his list of subscriptions to Mr Parkes' 'booklet' on window-plants. **1895** C. COLLINS (*title*) Greenhouse and window plants. [**1951** *Dict. Gardening* (R. Hort. Soc.) III. 1290/2 Some species..normally grow buried in the soil with only the upper surface of the leaves exposed; this upper surface is translucent..: such plants are known as 'windowed plants'.] **1971** *Stand. Encycl. S. Afr.* III. 652/2 The amazingly adapted 'window-plant',..almost entirely embedded in the ground, only the transparent apical part of the corpusculum being exposed to the air, allowing light to enter the body of the leaf. **1892** *Vermont Agric. Rep.* XII. 135 Mills manufacturing..furniture and window screens. **1907** *St. Nicholas* May 614/1 We tried to buy wire netting—the sort we use for window screens at home. **1942** W. FAULKNER *Go down, Moses* 158 Walks out of the cell toting the door over his head like it was a gauze window-screen. **1926** KIPLING *Debits & Credits* 410 They entered the little train... 'Isn't it lucky we've got window-seats?' **1967** O. HESKY *Time for Treason* x. 77 He took a window-seat in the special bus. **1967** E. HUNT *Danger Game* viii. 142 In the plane Elaine was annoyed to find Mrs. Delf had the window seat allotted her. **1981** G. MARKSTEIN *Ultimate Issue* 289 The train came into the station, and Verago took a window seat. **1922** S. LEWIS *Babbitt* ix. 122 They ate chocolates, went to the motion-pictures, went window-shopping. **1936** B. & S. SPEWACK *Boy meets Girl* II. iii. 70 Is it true, Mrs. Seabrook, that you and Larry have been window shopping? **1945** G. ENDORE *Methinks the Lady* ii. 27 Sometimes I went window-shopping with that apartment in mind. **1951** *Landfall* V. 167 'Maybe we could window-shop then?' Wally said. 'Care for a diamond necklace like that one?' **1957** *Times* 12 Nov. (Canada Suppl.) p. xv/3 At weekends carloads of three-generation family groups visit suburban areas to 'window-shop' for somewhere to live. **1973** R. BUSBY *Pattern of Violence* vi. 96 The office girls came out..and..joined the phalanxes on the pavements to window-shop outside the big stores. **1934** WEBSTER, Window-shopper. **1951** H. MACINNES *Neither Five nor Three* xxv. 341 A pavement filled with window-shoppers. **1972** P. MARKS *Collector's Choice* I. 23 Behind a window..stood a Boudin drawing... The window-shopper smiled. **1955** D. DAVIE *Brides of Reason* 32 And at our back His eye augments our window-shopping greed. **1956** D. M. DAVIN *Sullen Bell* xi. 72 The old, innocent pleasure of window-shopping in Regent Street. **1978** *Lancashire Life* Nov. 140/2 (Advt.), Window-shopping may be fun. But instead of admiring from the outside we'd like to welcome you inside. **1936** KIPLING *Something of Myself* v. 143, I..was elected to the Athenaeum... I managed to be taken to a delightful window-table [for lunch]. **1957** M. KENNEDY *Heroes of Clone* I. v. 46 She and Roy shared a window table. Mundy sat..at the other end of the dining-room. **1979** *Tucson Mag.* Apr. 78/2 Ask for a window table or one on the patio. **1910** *Chambers's Jrnl.* Aug. 512/1 Mr. W. W. Sawyer..was originally a window-trimmer in the cites of Chicago, Milwaukee, and Portland. **1980** *Washington Post* 1 Feb. B4/3 Mr. Van Der Linden began working for Woodward & Lothrop in 1926 as a window trimmer. **1926** *Publishers' Weekly* 22 May 1676/1 Window-trimming. **1984** *N.Y. Times* 21 Mar. D21/3 They even have an Association of Legal Administrators, which is not just window trimming but evidence of the increasing importance of business managers. **1968** *Globe & Mail* (Toronto) 17 Feb. 49/9 (Advt.). 65 Austin.. new tires, window washers. **1970** *Wall St. Jrnl.* 15 June 7/1 Mr. Welk arrived at his office building early and encountered a window-washer. **1977** *New Yorker* 27 June 84/2 One of the cops..had been sent out on a window-washer's platform to talk him into coming down. **1910** W. JAMES *Mem. & Stud.* (1911) xi. 291 To coal and iron mines,..to dishwashing, clothes-washing, and window-washing..would our gilded youths be drafted off. **1950** S. F. PAGE *Body Engin.* iii. 59 Window pillars and window winders should not be permitted to obstruct the view. **1971** *Sunday Times* (Johannesburg) (Business Sect.) 28 Mar. 4/6 The faults usually consisted of..faulty window winders, loose door handles and sticky locks. **1976** *Derbyshire Times* (Peak ed.) 3 Sept. 20/6 They'll be even more irritated by low-geared window winders.

windowing. Restrict † *Obs.* to sense in Dict. add: **2.** *Computers.* The process of selecting part of a stored image for display or enlargement.

1969 S. BIRD in Parslow & Prowse *Computer Graphics* I. 20 The display file is produced from the data structure by the display program package and the transformations such as expansion..and 'windowing' are carried out in the process. **1973** NEWMAN & SPROULL *Princ. Interactive Computer Graphics* viii. 154 In the case of the windowing routine, there are various ways in which the page-to-screen transformations may be defined: one obvious way is to specify window and viewport boundaries. **1981** *Internat. Jrnl. Numerical Methods Engin.* XVII. 1110 Only a segment of the first-level window may be delegated to second-level windowing; the rest should remain permanently in operational memory. **1985** *Personal Computer World* Feb. 165/1 It includes functions to deal with the more esoteric of the QL's facilities, such as windowing and general screen-handling.

windowy, *a.* Restrict † *Obs. rare* to sense in Dict. and add: **2.** Having many or large windows.

1863 'G. HAMILTON' *Gala-Days* 353 The homes of the students, which seem to have been built..solely to furnish shelter,—angular, formal, stiff, windowy. **1888** *Harper's Mag.* June 130/2 Several large, ugly, windowy wooden bulks grew up for shoe shops.

windrow, *sb.* Add: **c.** (Further examples.) Also *fig.* Used of similar rows of various things not exposed to or caused by the wind.

1948 *Times* 13 Feb. 5/6 Bulldozers then level off the soil and uprooted bush, packing it aside to form banks known as 'windrows' between each contour. **1957** L. EISELEY *Immense Journey* 49 The slowly contracting circle of the water left little windrows of minnows. **1974** *Sci. Amer.* Aug. 21/1 The water soon turned cold again and the fish departed, leaving windrows of dead *Pleuroncodes* along the beaches. **1980** *Ibid.* Oct. 156/2 The soft rock is gathered into long windrows and transferred mechanically to conveyor belts that carry it away to the processing plant.

windrow, *v.* Add: **windrowed** *ppl. a.*: for 1893 citation read '**1851** H. MELVILLE *Moby Dick* I. xli. 311' and add later examples; **wi·ndrower,** a machine for cutting and raking crops into windrows; **wi·ndrowing** *vbl. sb.*

1946 R. CAMPBELL *Talking Bronco* 24 All round the snarled and windrowed sands Expressed the scandal of the waves. **1948** TURNER & JOHNSON *Machines for Farm, Ranch & Plantation* x. 316 Select side-delivery windrowers when cutting grass-seed crops such as alfalfa. **1955** 'P. JANVIER' in *Astounding Sci. Fiction* Nov. 68/1 Straggled clumps and windrowed hay..were all that remained of the shrubbery and the lawn. **1970** K. C. WILLETT in H. W. Mulligan *African Trypanosomiases* xxx. 583 If 'windrowing' (clearing of the felled vegetation into wind-rows) is necessary the cost is greatly increased. **1976** *Columbus* (Montana) *News* 17 June 5 (Advt.), Hay Equipment... Windrowers... Balers.

wind-shake, *sb.* Add: **b.** A shaking (of something) in or by the wind. *poet. nonce-use.*

1939 DYLAN THOMAS *Map of Love* 12 After the funeral, mule praises, brays, Windshake of sailshaped ears.

windshield (wi·ndʃīld). [f. WIND *sb.*[1] + SHIELD *sb.*] **a.** Any of various devices for shielding a person or thing from wind; *spec.*

(chiefly *U.S.*) on a motor vehicle = *windscreen* s.v. WIND *sb.*[1] 31.

1902, [in Dict. s.v. WIND *sb.*[1] 30 a]. **1907** *Yesterday's Shopping* (1969) 320D/1 [Coat] Fitted with wind shield and storm cuffs, for driving or motoring. **1911** *N.Y. Times* 16 Oct. 12/7 (Advt.), Speedwell 1911 four-passenger, semi-racer..extraordinary equipment includes top, windshield, shock absorbers, [etc.]. **1924** P. C. MACFARLANE *Tongues of Flame* ii. 12 She steadied herself with one hand upon the wind-shield while the other waved to the enthusiastic group of welcomers. **1941** F. H. JOSEPH *Lett. Home from Britain at War* (1942) 6 We circled the airport three times to allow the captain to clear his windshield of ice by hand. **1946** B. MACDONALD *Egg & I* 110 A blast went off almost under the truck and the rocks broke my windshield. **1962** A. NISBETT *Technique Sound Studio* 277 *Windshield*.., shield which fits over microphone and protects diaphragm from 'rattling' by wind, and also contours the microphone for smoother airflow round it. **1978** W. F. BUCKLEY *Stained Glass* 230 Fifty cars, with special passes on their windshields, squatted around the tall, leafless elm trees.

b. *attrib.* and *Comb.* *windshield cleaner, scraper, squirter*; **windshield wiper** = *windscreen wiper* s.v. *WIND *sb.*[1] 31.

1921 *Daily Colonist* (Victoria, B.C.) 13 Mar. 10/6 The Folberth automatic windshield cleaner. **1927** *Sat. Even. Post* 24 Dec. 56/2 Each has extra wide windshield..and windshield wiper. **1955** W. TUCKER *Wild Talent* v. 62 Paul could see the rain falling, could see the madly swinging windshield wipers on the waiting cars. **1975** B. GARFIELD *Hopscotch* xxvi. 275 A combination windshield-scraper and brush. **1976** M. MACHLIN *Pipeline* ii. 31 The misty, sentimental look on Steele's face disappeared as though a giant windshield wiper had cleared its teary ambience. **1978** *Time* 10 Apr. 22/1 Johnson.. once had to halt his automobile to solve the problem of turning on the windshield squirter.

Windsor. Add: **1. Windsor blue** = *phthalocyanine blue* s.v. *PHTHALOCYANINE b; **Windsor knot**, a large, loose knot in a (neck)-tie; so **Windsor-knotted** *a.*; **Windsor pear** (see quots.); **Windsor Red**, the name of a recently introduced type of English cheese containing red wine; **Windsor soap** (earlier example); **Windsor tie** *U.S.*, a broad bias-cut necktie or scarf; **Windsor uniform** (earlier example).

1912 R. RIDGWAY *Color Standards & Color Nomenclature* 40/1 Windsor blue. **1938** H. NICOLSON *Let.* 17 Apr. (1966) 336 His Windsor blue eyes were wistful. **1970** Windsor blue [see *MONASTRAL]. **1953** *Man about Town* Spring 117 (*caption*) How to tie the 'Windsor' knot. **1959** T. WILLIAMS *Sweet Bird of Youth* III. 111 He nods slightly, loosening the Windsor-knot of his knitted black silk tie. **1976** J. H. SPENCER *Surgenor Campaign* i. 18 The tie was a crisp silver, the sort normally worn only with morning dress and tied in a Windsor knot. **1953** K. AMIS *Lucky Jim* ix. 98 His Windsor-knotted silk tie. **1664** J. EVELYN *Kalendarium Hortense* 72 August..Pears. Windsor, Soveraign, Orange, [etc.]. **1860** R. HOGG *Fruit Man.* 221 Windsor... A fine old pear for orchard culture. Ripe in August. It should be gathered before it becomes yellow. **1940** J. BETJEMAN *Old Lights for New Chancels* 17 Remaining orchards ripening Windsor pears. [**1969** *Vogue* 15 Mar. 65/2 *Red Windsor*, a new British cheese.. basically an English cheddar, gets its pink tinge from an English wine.] **1969–70** *Wine & Food* Dec.–Jan. 11/2 More ideas for cheese gifts. . Windsor Red in plain jar, each 10/6. **1982** P. RANCE *Gt. British Cheese Bk.* I. ii. 50 These cheeses are made by breaking up Cheddar or Double Gloucester..and..in the case of Windsor Red, pouring wine over the re-milled curd. **1822** B. HAYDON *Jrnl.* 16–17 Sept. in *Mem.* (1926) I. 321 A barber who shaved me..so praised his Windsor soap, that I..took six cakes. **1895** *Montgomery Ward Catal.* 95/2 Windsor Ties... Japanese Silk Windsors... Size $4\frac{1}{2}$ × 34 inches. **1912** J. LONDON *Smoke Bellew* 147 He went on dressing,.. tying a Windsor tie in a bow-knot at the throat of his soft cotton shirt. **1968** J. IRONSIDE *Fashion Alphabet* 114 A bias-cut wide tie, usually black, tied in a loose bow in front of the neck—known in America as a Windsor tie. **1781** *Gentl. Mag.* LI. 391/2 The birth-day of the Prince of Wales..was celebrated with extraordinary magnificence... The King, the Prince, the Duke of Cumberland, the great officers of state, and nobility, appeared in the Windsor uniform on this occasion—blue and scarlet.

2. (Further examples.)

1836 T. POWER *Impressions of America* I. 440 A bit of old brown Windsor to shave withal. **1840** THACKERAY in *Comic Almanack* Nov. 45, I never..knew Naples from brown Windsor. **1895** [see *Windsor tie*, sense 1 above]. **1901** [see *comb-back* s.v. *COMB *sb.*[1] 9]. **1939** F. THOMPSON *Lark Rise* vi. 102 If the father had a special chair..it would be but a rather larger replica of the hard windsors with wooden arms added. **1969** 'J. MORRIS' *Fever Grass* ii. 21 A small electric fan..and two more Windsors, were the room's only furnishings. **1976** J. PHILIPS *Backlash* (1977) I. ii. 27 Two armchairs, Windsors, for visitors.

windsurf (wi·ndsɒːf), *v.* orig. *U.S.* [Back-formation f. *WINDSURFER: see next.] *intr.* To ride a sailboard; to sailboard. Also **wi·ndsurfing** *vbl. sb.*

1969 *Chr. Sci. Monitor* 17 Nov. 17/1 Depending on the wind and water conditions, older as well as young people can windsurf. *Ibid.*, Windsurfing is new, so new that it's been on the market only within the past month. **1972** *Islander* (Victoria, B.C.) 16 Jan. 3/1 Spreading up and down the west coast is a brand new water sport—windsurfing. **1976** *Southern Even. Echo* (Southampton) 11 Nov. 23/1 Windsurfing, a cross between sailing, surf-riding and high-wire walking, has one big attraction: your boat can be small enough to carry under your arm. **1977** *Austral. Sailing* Jan. 69/2 Young or old, guy or girl, thick or thin, we'll teach you to windsurf in a few short hours. **1980** C. MATTHEWS *Loosely Engaged* 9 Swam, sunbathed and wind-surfed the whole day. **1984** *U.S.A. Today* 6 Apr. 2C/1 But windsurfing—on the Windsurfer—is merely a demonstration sport in the 1984 Olympic Games. **1984** *Times* 25 Aug. 11/3 Earlier this year..an Oxford graduate, aged 25, spent 10 weeks windsurfing clockwise around the coast of Britain.

Windsurfer (wi·ndsɒːfəɹ). orig. *U.S.* Also **windsurfer.** [f. WIND *sb.*[1] + *SURFER.] **1.** The proprietary name in the U.S. of a kind of sailboard.

1969 *Chr. Sci. Monitor* 17 Nov. 17/2 The board segment of the Windsurfer is shaped, with 'slight changes', like a surfboard, though it is heavier, at 37 pounds and longer, at 12 feet. **1974** *Official Gaz.* (U.S. Patent Office) 20 Aug. TM 166/1 Windsurfer, Windsurfing International Inc., Santa Monica, Calif... For sailboats comprising a surf board type hull and a sail. **1981** *Daily Mail* 9 Apr. 39/3 He [*sc.* Hoyle Schweitzer] kept production of his Windsurfer down in order to monitor quality. **1983** *Reader's Dig.* Apr. 132 More Windsurfers have been sold than any class of sailing boat ever. **1984** *Sunday Times* (Colour Suppl.) 28 Oct. 25/2, I wanted to learn more and get myself back on a windsurfer as soon as I could.

2. One who engages in the sport of windsurfing, a sailboarder.

1969 *Chr. Sci. Monitor* 17 Nov. 17/3 The lone windsurfer (one per board) stands near the middle, left foot just ahead of the mast and hands holding tightly to the 'wishbone'. **1977** *Austral. Sailing* Jan. 27/3 Clive Colonso is one of Britain's few expert windsurfers. **1982** *Times* 3 May 5/1 Twenty windsurfers were rescued from the North Sea yesterday. **1984** *Times* 25 Aug. 11/7 Windsurfers tend to be individualists, happy to sail alone.

wind-up, *sb.*[1] and *a.* Add: **A.** *sb.*[1] **2.** *Baseball.* The motions of a pitcher preparing to pitch the ball. Also *fig.* and in other sports.

1931 D. RUNYON in *Collier's* 25 Apr. 38/2, I take a good wind-up..but..the ball does not break as I expect. **1936** *Philadelphia Rec.* 30 July 19/1 Blanton is the sort of orator who cannot shorten his pitching motion... He is unable to make a simple motion without taking a full windup. **1951** [see *STRETCH *sb.* 1 i]. **1974** MILLS & BUTLER *Tackle Badminton* v. 45 The great temptations to be avoided with drop shots are..making an exaggerated wind-up with over-emphasized power, [etc.]. **1976** *Webster's Sports Dict.* 483/2 The windup, which is usually accompanied by a rocking of the body, sets a rhythm which the pitcher follows until the ball is released.

3. a. Material that has become wound round something. **b.** The action of winding or coiling something round something else. **c.** The action of becoming twisted or stressed by the application of torque.

1964 *Gloss. Letterpress Rotary Printing Terms* (B.S.I.) 21 *Wind up*, paper accidentally wrapped round the impression cylinder, plate cylinder, or inking rollers. **1966** J. S. COX *Illustr. Dict. Hairdressing & Wigmaking* 165/2 *Wind-up*,..the winding of the hair on curlers. **1969** W. R. R. PARK *Plastics Film Technol.* ii. 15 This technique..generates a greater percentage of scrap or recycle material than the use of a stationary windup. **1972** *Sci. Amer.* Dec. 51/1 The carriage was pushed back and forth by the spinner, one way during the drawing-twisting operation and the other way during windup. **1975** *Drilling Technol. & Collet Chuck* (Bristol Erikson Ltd.) 4 Since the forces created in any cutting action are never constant, it follows that the amount of torsional 'wind-up' will be continually varying. **1976** G. ROBSON *Land-Rover* vii. 117 To take care of transmission wind-up..the new car was to have a third, central differential, with a limited-slip mechanism inside it. **1978** *Hot Car* July 89/4 Traction bars..are..bolted by way of U-bolts and brackets to the rear leaf springs of a car such that they prevent wind-up of the rear axle on full-power starts.

B. *adj.* **1.** (Later examples, now used esp. of toys and gramophones.) Also of a window: made to be moved up (to shut) and down (to open) by means of a handle wound with a rotary motion.

1951 *Festival of Britain Catal.* 149/1 Wind-up plate glass window, weatherproof and draughtproof. **1962** E. O'BRIEN *Lonely Girl* v. 64 The last record lay on the green baize of the wind-up gramophone. **1968** 'E. MCBAIN' *Fuzz* ix. 155 The police in this city are like wind-up toys with keys sticking out of their backs. **1970** *Motoring Which?* July 98/1 A few of these modifications—wind-up windows..also appeared on the ordinary Mini. **1982** N. PAINTING *Reluctant Archer* vii. 105 There were other gramophones, too. Wind-up ones.

wind-up (wi·nd,ʌp), *sb.*[2] *colloq.* [f. phr. *to get the wind up* s.v. WIND *sb.*[1] 10 b.] A state of nervous anxiety or fear; an occurrence of this.

1917 G. S. GORDON *Let.* 13 Feb. (1943) 69 By that time my runner was showing signs of 'wind-up'... He thought I was very unfeeling, not to go down to a cellar till the shower [of shelling] was over. **1922** *Encycl. Brit.* XXX. 64/1 Many other pilots..have been through the same stages of 'wind-up'. **1931** J. HILTON *Murder at School* x. 204 We were having a smoke... We got an awful wind-up, thinking somebody..might have smelt something. **1952** *Chambers's Jrnl.* Feb. 82/2 Putting on a bold face, but with a fair amount of wind-up, I walked..in the direction the hand pointed to. **1980** A. PRICE *Hour of Donkey* xiv. 220 Bit of nerves..the old wind-up.

windy, *a.* Add: **II. 8. a.** (Later examples.)

1918 C. J. BIDDLE *Fighting Airman* (1968) 147 He thought what made the men more 'windy' than anything else..was the thought of..having to lie there all day before being able to get to a doctor. *a* **1948** D. WELCH *Voice through Cloud* (1950) iv. 39 He [*sc.* a patient facing an operation] laughed so much that the man with the bandaged ear became exasperated and said, 'Why do you make so much noise? That shows you're windy. If you didn't care, you wouldn't say anything.' **1960** J. R. ACKERLEY *We think World of You* 123 'E was windy, but I swore it was safe and that nothing could 'appen. **1985** D. CLARK *Performance* ii. 40 'Are you feeling windy?' 'Do I look as if I am?'

b. Applied to a frightening or nerve-wracking place or situation. *Services'.*

1919 *Narrative Battery A, 101st Field Artillery* (U.S. Artillery) 118 It was a 'windy' place to be.., as the enemy raked it with machine gun and trench mortar fire all day and night. **1925** FRASER & GIBBONS *Soldier & Sailor Words* 305 *Windy Corner*, any place specially dangerous or trying to the nerves on account of enemy fire. **1927** A. M. SULLIVAN *Old Ireland* xi. 226 All the 'windy corners' of his front. **1928** T. E. LAWRENCE *Let.* 1 May (1938) 599 Such performances require a manner to carry them off... A windy business.

9. *Windy City* (U.S.), a nickname for Chicago.

1887 *Courier-Jrnl.* (Louisville, Kentucky) 31 Jan. 5/1 An alleged anarchist dynamite plot from the Windy City. **1908** K. MCGAFFEY *Show Girl* 58 Chicago is surely rightly named when they call it the Windy City. **1948** *News-Dispatch* (Michigan) 3 Apr. 9/3 The handsome Windy City youngster has an enormous following. **1979** K. BONFIGLIOLI *After you with Pistol* xvi. 120 The scent of the Chicago River as it slides greasily under the nine bridges in the centre of the Windy City.

windy (wi·ndi), *sb.*[1] Repr. colloq. and dial. pronunc. of WINDOW *sb.* Cf. *WINDER *sb.*[5]

1830 W. CARLETON *Traits & Stories Irish Peasantry* I. 193 Will you hand me over that other clew out of the windy-stool [= window-sill] there? *c* **1883** D. BOUCICAULT *Shaughraun* II. i. 11 He got sight of my face agin the windy. **1921** V. JACOB *Bonnie Joann* 37 Lowse ye the windy-sneck a wheen. **1977** *Hot Car* Oct. 15/2 Another problem with fitting 'lectric windys to English cars is their narrow door design.

windy (wi·ndi), *sb.*[2] *N. Amer. local slang.* [f. WINDY *a.* 6 a.] A tall story; a piece of boasting or exaggeration.

1933 *Amer. Speech* VIII. I. 53/2 *Windy*,..a tall tale, a wildly unreasonable story. **1933** J. V. ALLEN *Cowboy Lore* III. 60/2 *Telling a windy*, telling a boastful story. **1935** H. L. DAVIS *Honey in Horn* iii. 24 He could invent windies about his stand-in with the girls.

wine, *sb.*[1] Add: **1. g.** *wine and cheese* (*party*, etc.).

1961 *Daily Tel.* 5 Dec. 9/2 To my mind, the ideal wine and cheese party is given around midday. **1969** *Times* 25 Sept. 27/2 All 550 members of the staff have been invited to a wine and cheese party on that day. **1976** M. DUKE *Death at Wedding* xiii. 148 He's gone to the local Labour Party wine-and-cheese do. **1977** B. PYM *Quartet in Autumn* xvii. 155 She did not feel capable of guessing what kind of an evening party, for she could only think of 'wine and cheese' which seemed altogether unworthy of Mr Strong.

2. (Earlier *lit.* examples of *the wine of the country*.)

1817 H. MATTHEWS *Diary of an Invalid* (1820) ii. 39 As much of the wine of the country as you like. **1865** A. TROLLOPE *Can you forgive Her?* II. xxxvi. 287 He had ordered a bottle of Sauterne; but the landlord had thought..that a bottle of ordinary wine of the country would do as well.

4. (Earlier example.)

1857 'C. BEDE' *Mr Verdant Green Married* xii. 101 Mr Bouncer..gave his last wine (wherein he produced some 'very old port').

6. (Further example.) Also in *sing.*

1935 W. A. THORPE *Eng. Glass* iv. 129 Mansell had three grades of 'wines' which in 1639 he described as follows.. 'Ordinary Drinking-Glasses—for Wine.' **1947** *Glass Notes* Dec. 16 *Problem for 1948*, to discover the following:..a facet stem wine with a domed foot. **1974** *Habitat Catal.* 72/2 *Bistro.* Really good value for drinking anything from sherry to sweet stout. $3\frac{1}{2}$ oz sherry 14p, 5 oz wine 15p 8 oz goblet 16p.

6*. Passing into *adj.* A dark red colour.

1895 *Montgomery Ward Catal.* 3/1 Royal Serge, 22 inches wide, in plain, solid colors..Colors: Cardinal, wine, brown. **1923** [see *LAUREL *sb.*[1] 2 e]. **1950** B. PYM *Some Tame Gazelle* xv. 166 She had visions of herself..in her brown velvet or wine crêpe de Chine. **1981** *Country Life* 22 Jan. 226/3 Feather-stitch grey and wine pullover.

7. a. (*a*) *wine-breath, -sap.*

1922 W. B. YEATS *Seven Poems* 1 Being sharpened by his death To drink from the wine-breath While our gross palates drink from the whole wine. **1917** D. H. LAWRENCE *Look! We have come Through!* 158, I want the fine, kindling wine-sap of spring.

(*b*) *wine basket, box, cistern, -cup* (*lit.* examples), *-district, funnel, -gourd, industry, jug, -kitchen, -land* (later examples), *table, -trade* (later examples).

1835 DICKENS *Sk. Boz.* (1836) 1st Ser. I. 291 Waiters with wine-baskets in their hands are placing decanters of Sherry down the tables. **1974** *Habitat Catal.* 81/2 Wicker wine basket. For serving fine delicate wines, without disturbing the sediment. **1982** *Daily Tel.* 8 Dec. 17/1 Wine boxes have made buying easier... Wine boxes are generally about £7.50 for three litres. **1984** *Which?* May 195/1 *Which? Wine Monthly* has been testing wine boxes again. A few this time were rather nice..but many were still disappointing, particularly when they'd been opened for a week or so. **1881** W. J. CRIPPS *College & Corporation*

Plate v. 132 (*caption*) *Wine Cistern*, circa 1701. **1971** *Country Life* 1 Apr. 766/1 His [*sc.* Thomas Heming's] earlier shallow sauce tureens..were echoed in his own 1,457-ounce massive wine cistern for Belton House. **1819** W. Scott *Ivanhoe* I. xiv. 294 He raised..the wine-cup to his lips. **1910** S. W. Bushell *Chinese Art* II. 17 The poets of the time liken their wine cups to 'disks of thinnest ice'. **1980** *Catal. Fine Chinese Ceramics* (Sotheby, Hong Kong) 75 An incised white dragon Winecup of thinly potted bell shape. **1835** J. E. Alexander *Sk. in Portugal* xi. 260 A considerable reach of the river was also seen to the east and west, and the wine-district in the far distance of Alto Douro. **1976** *National Observer* (U.S.) 4 Dec. 8/3 A bureau spokesman says it could be the first step toward establishment of a national wine-district system similar to that of France. **1838** J. G. Flügel *Compl. Dict. Ger. & Eng. Languages* II. 833/2 *Wein,..-trichter, m.* wine-funnel. **1981** *Times* 17 Oct. 12/7 A Dundee wine funnel of about 1820 by William Law sold for £680. **1952** L. MacNeice *Ten Burnt Offerings* 56 Did not these whitewashed rooms among wine-gourds, goat-skins, ikons, Include a letter or two with a foreign postmark. **1966** P. V. Price *France* 132 More than three million Frenchmen are engaged in the wine industry and there are about a million and a half wine growers. **1976** R. M. Stern *Will* iv. 24 Prohibition stifled the California wine industry. **1922** Joyce *Ulysses* 142 'Tis the hour, methinks, when the winejug, metaphorically speaking, is most grateful in Ye ancient hostelry. **1981** R. Manheim tr. *G. Grass's Meeting at Telgte* xv. 88 His busy treasure hunting seemed to leave him no free hand for the wine jug. **1924** D. H. Lawrence in M. Magnus *Mem. Foreign Legion* 45 So we went into a little cave of a wine-kitchen to drink a glass of wine. **1963** *Punch* 21 Aug. 280/2 The most northerly German winelands. **1971** *Sunday Times* (Johannesburg) 28 Mar. 25/1, (Advt.), On a southern mountain slope, in the heart of the Stellenbosch winelands, the skills of man and the secrets of nature combine to create five distinctive wines. **1839** Poe in *Burton's Gentleman's Mag.* Oct. 212, I had indulged more freely than usual in the excesses of the wine-table. **1935** *Burlington Mag.* May p. xli/2 A superb wine-table, also tripod, a pair of torchères, *circa* 1760. **1976** *Derbyshire Times* (Peak ed.) 3 Sept. 15/5 (Advt.), Two Walnut pie crust wine tables. **1966** P. V. Price *France* 133 The wine trade in Great Britain consider that the British wine drinker is protected..by the laws of the country. **1977** *Times* 14 May 13/3 Accommodation will be heavily booked at vintage time by the wine trade.

b. *wine-drinker, -importer, -shipper; wine-loving, -making, -producing* (earlier example), vbl. sbs. and ppl. adjs.

1935 A. G. Macdonell *Visit to Amer.* x. 183 California could produce a vin ordinaire to sell at thirty or forty [cents]. If she did, she would gradually build up a great community of wine drinkers. **1983** *Listener* 14 July 18/3 Burgundy and Bordeaux are still the British wine-drinker's dream lands. **1959** E. H. Clements *High Tension* ii. 21 My family were wine-importers with offices in London, Edinburgh and Bordeaux. **1981** W. J. Burley *House of Care* i. 6 His job with a firm of London wine importers. **1921** 'L. H. Davison' *Movements in European Hist.* iv. 43 The Romans of Latium were short, dark men of the wine-loving lands. **1980** *Times* 27 Nov. 21/1 A wine-loving traveller. **1814** P. P. Carnell (*title*) A treatise on family winemaking. **1881** V. Lush *Jrnl.* 27 Aug. (1975) 245 If life and health be spared to us, wine-making will become henceforth like jam making and fruit tinning, one of the fixed employments of the Autumn. **1979** A. Maling *Koberg Link* (1980) xxv. 135 'We have vineyards.'..'Tough business, winemaking.' **1846** R. Ford *Gatherings from Spain* xiv. 150 The wine-producing districts. **1949** C. Graves *Ireland Revisited* x. 151 The traditional story about James Lynch Fitzstephen is that he was a leading wine-shipper in Galway. **1972** *Times* (Wines & Spirits Suppl.) 27 Nov. p. viii/5 With their large number of outlets they could go direct to wine growers on the Continent, by-passing the wine shippers.

c. *winebig, -drenched, -ensanguined, -fizzling, -flushed, -heavy, -stained, -warm* adjs.

1922 Joyce *Ulysses* 249 John Henry Menton..stared from winebig oyster eyes. **1914** W. B. Yeats *Responsibilities* 2 Those wine-drenched eyes. **1925** H. Acton in *Oxf. Poetry* 4 And we had thought to fashion of our joy Round crackling pearls to pelt our wine-drenched loves. **1928** W. B. Yeats tr. *Sophocles' King Oedipus* 6 And Bacchus' wine-ensanguined face that all the Maenads sing. **1922** Joyce *Ulysses* 420 Come on, you winefizzling..existences! **1912** E. Pound *Ripostes* 26 Wealthy and wine-flushed. **1964** J. Michie tr. *Horace's Odes* i. vii. 33 Set on his wine-flushed brow brave garlands of poplar. **1897** W. B. Yeats *Secret Rose* 2 The old and foolish king..snored fitfully in a wine-heavy sleep. **1899** —— *Wind among Reeds* 49 Dwelt among wine-stained wanderers in deep woods. **1983** J. Masters *Man of War* xxiii. 299 A Michelin map spread out on the wine-stained..table. **1953** C. Day Lewis *Italian Visit* vi. 65 When cypresses jetted like fountains of wine-warm air.

8. **wine bar,** (*a*) a bar or counter in a club, shop, etc., where wine is kept or sold; (*b*) a licensed establishment specializing in the serving of wine (and food); **wine book,** (*a*) a book for keeping records of wines bought and consumed; (*b*) a book about wines; **wine-buff,** a wine enthusiast; **wine butler,** a servant who has charge of the wine-cellar and serves the wine (cf. Butler *sb.* 1 a); **wine coaster** = Coaster 6; **wine-cooler** (later examples); **wine-dance,** a dance performed in celebration of wine; **wine-dark:** occas. (*poet.*) as *sb.*; **wine-dot** [joc. f. Wyandotte] *Austral. slang*, an addict of cheap wine; **wine farm** *S. Afr.*, a farm on which grapes are grown for wine-making and on which wine is frequently made; so **wine farmer; wine fountain,** a large vessel for holding and dispensing wine; **wine-grower** (earlier example); **wine gum** [*Gum *sb.*^{2} 1 g], a fruit-flavoured sweetmeat made with gelatine; **wine label,** (*b*) the paper label affixed to a bottle of wine, stating its name and provenance; **wine lake,** a stockpile or surplus of wine; **wine list** (now the usual term) = *wine-card*; **wine lodge,** (*a*) = Lodge *sb.* 12 c; (*b*) a licensed establishment selling wine, beer, and soft drinks; **winemanship,** the display of real or pretended knowledge about wine; **wine rack,** a frame with compartments for holding bottles of wine; **wine room,** a bar-room where wine is served; **wine-skin:** also *transf.*; **wine snob** (see quot. 1951); hence **wine-snobbery; wine steward,** a servant responsible for serving wine; **wine-tasting,** testing the quality of wine by tasting; an occasion when this is done; **wine-vault,** (*a*) (earlier example); (*b*) (earlier example); **wine waiter,** a waiter responsible for serving wine; similarly **wine waitress; wine writer,** a person who writes about wine for publication.

1938 R. Graves *Count Belisarius* iii. 65, I was busy at some task behind the wine-bar. **1940** M. Sadleir *Fanny by Gaslight* i. 270 He offered her a job as barmaid... Her new place of business was a girlery as well as a wine-bar. **1976** *Amer. Speech 1974* XLIX. 117 *Wine bar*, counter in a liquor store, stocked with wines. **1981** B. Knox *Killing in Antiques* iv. 87 Dunbar stopped the car in a side street..just a stone's throw from the wine bar. **1983** *Which?* Dec. (Publications Suppl.), For an accurate description of over 200 wine bars across the country, this section of the book is unbeatable, with critical comments on the range of wines, and an assessment of the food and perceptive summing-up of the atmosphere. **1947** L. G. Green *Tavern of Seas* vii. 59 Documents, wine-books, casks and iron chests..all make a picture of careful work and gay entertainment. **1975/76** *Listener* 25 Dec. & 1 Jan. 891/1 It is easy to mock the pretensions of wine writers... Writing a new wine book is as difficult as building a better mouse-trap. **1976** *Ibid.* 5 Aug. 158/2 One area which beer connoisseurs will have to cultivate in order to approach the influence of wine-buffs—the language of appreciation. **1880** E. W. Hamilton *Diary* 9 May (1972) I. 10, I have been offered and have undertaken the post of Chief Wine Butler to Mr. G., which I hope will secure something rather less nasty in his cellars. **1973** *Times* 25 Aug. 12/6 Wine service is of such skill that it should make the average English wine butler blush. **1956** G. Taylor *Silver* ix. 201 *Wine Coasters*, circular wooden base on baize, with silver sides. **1971** *Country Life* 15 July 183/1 The platform [of a cruet] was encircled with a deep gallery of wood..in the manner of a giant wine coaster. **1848** Wine-cooler [see *en permanence s.v.* *en *prep.*]. **1977** W. M. Spackman *Armful of Warm Girl* 29 The waiter had swooped in rolling a second wine-cooler to set beside the first. **1920** D. H. Lawrence *Touch & Go* i. ii. 29 They begin to sing, dancing meanwhile, in a free little ballet-manner, a wine-dance, dancing separate and then together. **1934** W. B. Yeats tr. *Sophocles' Oedipus at Colonus* in *Coll. Plays* 543 Come praise The wine-dark of the wood's intricacies. **1953** T. A. G. Hungerford *Riverslake* 35 'Is he a wine-dot?' 'Is he hell!.. He's never off it.' **1976** D. Hewett *This Old Man comes rolling Home* 11 Gawd, you smell like an old wine-dot, Laurie. **1923** O. Schreiner in *Cape Times* 18 Aug. 3/1 The sinking valley with its sprinkling of wine-farms. **1970** *Cape Times* 28 Oct. 21/1 (Advt.), Choice Wine Farm in extent 40 morgen. **1984** *Times* 1 Nov. 27/7 He had invited Miss Budd to stay on his wine farm. **1915** G. McC. Theal *Hist. S. Afr. 1795–1872* ii. 36 The British government held out great inducements to South African winefarmers to increase the quantity of their produce. **1889** *Cent. Dict.*, Wine-fountain. **1931** E. Wenham *Domestic Silver* ii. 17 Wine-fountains nearly 4 feet long and 3 feet wide. **1969** E. H. Pinto *Treen* 53/1 The lignum vitae wine fountain..is part of the Burrell Bequest to Glasgow Museum and Art Gallery. **1844** Mill *Ess. Pol. Econ.* i. 45 The wine-growers of France..imagine that free trade would relieve their distress by raising the price of their wine. **1953** Winegum [see *hundred *sb.* and *a.* 7]. **1981** *Times* 1 May 19/3 Energy is stored in plastic pellets, like wine gums. **1954** 'M. Cost' *Invitation from Minerva* 209 On the wine label, above the sycamore..is a coat of arms. **1980** N. Freeling *Castang's City* xxi. 139 People belonged to a multiplicity of little gatherings..Wine-label collectors, neighbourhood betterment leagues. **1974** Wine lake [see *lake *sb.*^{4} 1 b]. **1979** *Guardian* 14 Mar. 14/1 Wine-lakes and butter-mountains may be jokes, but they are sick ones. **1984** *Times* 4 Oct. 1/4 The table wines..have..fared reasonably well, to the distress no doubt of the European community, whose wine lake is already overflowing. **1898** G. B. Shaw *You never can Tell* ii. 251 Crampton snatches the wine list rudely from him and irresolutely pretends to read it. **1935** A. G. Macdonell *Visit to America* x. 182, I waved the wine list..and shouted for the wine waiter. **1972** P. V. Price *Eating & Drinking in France* 248 The Nicolas establishments are reliable and the wine lists especially attractive. **1880** Wine lodge [see Lodge *sb.* 12 c]. **1922** Joyce *Ulysses* 392 *Mort aux vaches*, says Frank then in the French language that had been indentured to a brandy shipper that has a winelodge in Bordeaux. **1962** *Guardian* 24 Dec. 4/3 There's the Wine Lodge. You can get a glass of small white Australian for ninepence. **1977** *Punch* 31 Aug.–6 Sept. 345/1 Huge and dingy, the saloon bar looked like a cross between the main hall in the old Euston railway station and one of Yates's less-glamorous Wine Lodges. **1958** *Observer* 11 May 16/4 (*heading*) Winemanship. **1977** T. Heald *Just Desserts* v. 87 A passable imitation of genuine winemanship. **1974** *Habitat Catal.* 82/1 Wine rack. Wood and metal frame. **1981** 'J. Sturrock' *Suicide Most Foul* vii. 129 Wine racks, but..not many bottles. **1865** *Leaves from Diary Celebrated Burglar & Pickpocket* xxxv. 116/1 Several ladies..made their way to where we were sitting, and in the usual wine-room style flung themselves into our lap! **1898** A. Bennett *Man from North* xxvi. 224 Seated in a wine-room or lager-beer hall. **1965** O. Arundell *Sadler's Wells* viii. 102 [In 1825] they made Rosoman's old private house at the New River Head end of the theatre into box-offices, wine-rooms and saloon. **1923** D. H. Lawrence *Birds, Beasts & Flowers* 15 What is it, in the grape turning raisin, In the medlar, in the sorb-apple, Wineskins of brown morbidity. **1928** E. Waugh *Decline & Fall* x. 113 Hullo, Prendy, old wine-skin! How are things with you? **1951** R. Postgate *Plain Man's Guide to Wine* i. 17 A Wine Snob is a man..who uses a knowledge of wine, often imperfect, to impress others with a sense of his superiority. **1977** Wine snob [see *snob *sb.*^{1} 3 d]. **1982** 'W. Haggard' *Mischief-Makers* i. 17 He bought it [*sc.* wine] at a multiple grocer but his excellency was not a wine snob. **1966** H. W. Yoxall *Fashion of Life* xxv. 241 There's been much talk recently about wine snobbery, most of it rather stupid. **1898** A. M. Binstead *Pink 'Un & Pelican* iii. 65 'Aha!' cried Swears..'here's a bit o' luck—the wine-steward! Half a dollar is never thrown away on a wine-steward.' **1978** *Chicago* June 237/1 Freddy's the least intimidating and probably most knowledgeable wine steward in town. **1936** 'R. West' *Thinking Reed* vii. 216 He paused..to say in his thick, wine-tasting voice: 'Your wife's looking very pretty!' **1945** E. Waugh *Brideshead Revisited* i. iv. 75 Sebastian had found a book on wine-tasting, and we followed its instructions. **1958** [see *put *v.*^{1} 38 f (*a*)]. **1980** *Sunday Times Mag.* 14 Sept. 96 He or she might take a dozen trips abroad each year, attend five or six wine tastings in a week, sample 30 or so bottles of wine a day. **1791** J. Woodforde *Diary* 27 Sept. (1927) III. 301 Mr. J^{no} Priest having the keys of his Father's Wine Vaults, I went and tested some Port Wine. **1837** Dickens *Sk. Boz.* 2nd Ser. 73 The old tottering public-house is converted into a spacious and lofty 'wine-vaults'. **1927** C. Connolly *Let.* 11 Feb. in *Romantic Friendship* (1975) 251, I met the Spanish wine waiter. **1969** I. Drummond *Man with Tiny Head* i. 24 The wine-waitress brought the wine-list. **1974** *Times* 9 Oct. 18/7 A race by wine waiters and waitresses..each carrying a tray bearing four glasses and an open bottle of wine. **1975** Wine writer [see *wine book* above].

wine, *v.* Add: **2.** Freq. in collocation with *dine*: cf. sense 3 in Dict. (Later examples, not in a university context.)

1937 L. Hart in R. Rogers *Rodgers & Hart Songbk.* (1951) 166 I've wined and dined on mulligan stew, and never wished for turkey. **1961** *Guardian* 10 Nov. 7/1 Mr Delmer dined and wined with the enemies of democracy in Germany. **1981** *N.Z. Listener* 4 July 80/1 Impressive consultants (with many of whom I have wined and dined).

wineberry. Add: **2.** *N.Z.* = *makomako^2.

1889 T. Kirk *Forest Flora N.Z.* 223 The makomako or 'wine-berry' of the settlers was discovered by Banks and Solander. **1910** L. Cockayne *N.Z. Plants & their Story* iii. 37 The wineberry..has distinctly pleasing rosy-coloured flowers. **1966** [see *makomako^2]. **1971** *N.Z. Listener* 6 Sept. 17/1 There were wineberry trees in the bit of bush.

Winebrennarian (wəinbrĕnēᵊ·riăn), *sb.* (and *a.*) *U.S.* Also **Winebrennerian.** [f. the name of John *Winebrenner* (1797–1860), founder member of the sect + *-arian.] A name given to a member of the Church of God, an evangelical sect founded in 1830 in Pennsylvania. Occas. also as *adj.*

1867 W. H. Dixon *New Amer.* II. xxix. 309 No sect escaped this rage for separation..[neither] River Brethren, nor Winebrennarians. **1889** *Cent. Dict.*, Winebrennarian..*a.* and *n.* **1903** *Christian Advocate* 8 Jan. 7 Christian Scientists..Church of God (Winebrennarian). **1925** T. Dreiser *Amer. Tragedy* (1926) II. ii. xlvii. 65 It was the summer seat and gathering place of some small religious organization or group—the Winebrennarians of Pennsylvania. **1974** R. Kern *John Winebrenner* p. vii, It would be regrettable if only 'Winebrennerians' of all sorts read the book.

wine-cellar. Add: **b.** The wine stored in a wine-cellar, esp. with reference to its quality.

1861 Mrs Beeton *Bk. Househ. Managem.* 963 Nothing spreads more rapidly in society than the reputation of a good wine-cellar. **1976** J. Archer *Not a Penny More* viii. 87 James arrived carrying a bottle of Beaune Montée Rouge 1971—even his wine cellar was fast disappearing. **1976** P. G. Winslow *Witch Hill Murder* (1977) ii. 30 Her cook, her wine cellar and the service at her table were not to be matched.

wined, *ppl. a.* Add: **2.** Also const. *up*.

1973 C. Bonington *Next Horizon* ii. 41 'We'll get them well wined up tonight, and persuade them that there's a good route round the back of the Tower,' said Barrie. **1982** *Newsweek* 11 Jan. 26/2, I think they were wined up and looking for a joy ride.

wine-glass. Add: **a.** (Earlier examples = *wineglassful*.)

1786 J. Woodforde *Diary* 18 Aug. (1926) II. 264 She is to take a Wine Glass of the Mixture..every six Hours. **1846** *Jewish Man., or Pract. Information Jewish & Mod. Cookery* i. 2 Pour in a wine-glass of port-wine.

wine-grape. **2.** For *U.S.* read orig. *U.S.* and add later examples.

1922 Joyce *Ulysses* 468 Mammoth roses murmur of scarlet winegrapes. **1981** *Times* 7 Feb. 13/4 They do not want any modification of traditional Dao style by the introduction of other European wine grapes.

winey, var. Winy *a.*

wing, *sb.* Add: **II. 5. d.** (*a*) (Earlier example of the plane of an aeroplane); (*b*) (earlier and later examples of a pilot's badge: also *transf.* and *fig.*); (*c*) *slang*, an arm (examples); also *transf.*

1883 W. Aitken *Lays of Line* 65 Cam' an auld sodger yince wha was short o' a wing. **1904** O. & W. Wright *Brit. Pat.* 6732 1 The superposed horizontal surfaces.. formed by stretching cloth upon frames of wood and wire, constitute the 'wings', or supporting part of the apparatus. **1917** 'Contact' *Airman's Outings* i. 5 The pilots have passed their tests and been decorated with wings. **1947** *Sun* (Baltimore) 3 Apr. 20/1 He came up with a bad arm during the season, and had been troubled before with it. If the big man's wing behaves this year he should be of considerable value. **1964** J. Cheever *Wapshot Scandal* ii. xxvii. 259 He..began to pitch the eggs... He had a good wing and by heaving the eggs far away.. he was able to divert the..crowd. **1967** *Boston Globe* 22 Mar. 11/1 Wins wings as stewardess for American Airlines. **1976** *Publishers Weekly* 19 Apr. 78/3 Mike Hagen earns his wings as a crop duster in rural Florida.

6. b. Also *spec.* of jumps for horse-riding: see quot. 1953[1].

1953 G. Brooke *Introd. Riding & Stablecraft* 12 *Wings to a fence*, something in the nature of hurdles placed on either side and at an angle to a fence to prevent a horse from running out to either hand. *Ibid.* iv. 39 It is advisable to start over a small fence with wings. **1960** *Times* 23 July 9/4 The moment to hit the pony is when it is well into the wings and about half a stride from the jump. **1977** J. Kidd *Horse & Pony Man.* iv. 56 When the fence is introduced always place wings or sloping poles on either side to discourage the horse from running out.

e. (Examples of a motor vehicle.)

1928 *Daily Mail* 25 July 9/3 The force of the impact threw the car temporarily out of control, but with its front wings crumpled it continued its dash towards London. **1955** *Times* 10 May 7/7 The visibility forward would be better if it took in the near side front wing, but the rearward view through the 3ft. 9in. wide window is excellent.

9. a. Also in extended use, any more or less separate section of a building, esp. of a hospital or prison.

1908 J. M. Sullivan *Criminal Slang* 27 *Wing*, a section of a prison. **1959** L. Lee *Cider with Rosie* 132 Hannah Brown was put to bed in the Woman's Wing, and Joseph lay in the Men's. **1967** *Listener* 1 June 718/3 Three weeks later he was back in C wing. **1981** C. Priest *Affirmation* iii. 19, I found a letter from the Governor of Durham Prison, saying that Uncle William had been admitted to the hospital wing.

c. Also in *fig.* phr. *waiting in the wings* and varr., ready to act or make an appearance; (for the moment) taking no part in the action.

1876 H. James in *Atlantic Monthly* Dec. 691/1 The author has given him a mother who..has been kept waiting in the wing, as it were, for many acts. **1946** P. Bottome *Lifeline* iii. 39 We've Churchill waiting in the wings, to take the helm when the storm breaks. **1963** V. Nabokov *Gift* iv. 237 Already famous, he remained as it were in the wings of his busy, talkative thought. **1977** *Sat. Rev.* 3 Sept. 44/1 Despite vast expenditures on research and development..the videodisc is still hovering diffidently in the wings. **1985** *Times* 19 Jan. 21/1 Yesterday's huge jump in the share price suggests there is a buyer in the wings.

11*. *Physics.* A part of a spectral line where the intensity tails off to nothing at either side of it.

1959 *Canad. Jrnl. Physics* XXXVII. 1252 (*caption*) Graph illustrating the dispersion line form for the high-frequency wing of the S(1) line of normal hydrogen at 85° K. **1982** *Sci. Amer.* July 77/3 At positions in the cloud other than the position of the infrared source the broad velocity wings disappeared and the lines had the narrow widths we had originally expected.

III. 18*. *to spread* (*stretch, try*) *one's wings*: to test or develop one's powers; to lead a life of wider scope than hitherto.

1864 G. Meredith *Let.* 1 June (1970) I. 260 One thought my Marie merely trying her wings. **1872** Geo. Eliot *Middlem* II. iv. xxxiv. 192 He is trying his wings. He is just the sort of young fellow to rise. **1876** Trollope *Prime Minister* III. xx. 332 When I found myself the son-in-law of a very rich man I thought I might spread my wings a bit. **1926** R. H. Tawney *Relig. & Rise of Capitalism* ii. 67 It was in an age of political anarchy that the forces destined to dominate the future tried their wings. **1953** 'W. Cooper' *Ever-Interesting Topic* v. ii. 252 He decided to compose music as well as to play it: he began to try his wings as a creative artist, and he found they held him up. **1973** 'P. Malloch' *Kickback* xi. 69 'Hagan's stretching his wings a bit.' 'Beginning to feel his weight, is he?' **1978** S. Radley *Death & Maiden* xv. 145 She wanted to spread her wings a bit, meet new people.

19. *wing-and-wing* (earlier examples).

1781 J. Greenwood in *Maryland Hist. Mag.* (1910) V. 129 We were now wing and wing, that is right before the wind. **1828** J. F. Cooper *Red Rover* I. iii. 84 That.. schooner would make more way going wing-and-wing than jammed up on a wind.

19*. *a wing and a prayer*, a joc. form of reference (after quot. 1943) to an emergency landing by an aircraft. Also *fig.* and as *attrib. phr.* in allusion to reliance on hope in desperate situations.

1943 H. Adamson *Comin' in on a Wing & a Prayer* (song), Tho' there's one motor gone, we can still carry on, Comin' In On A Wing And A Pray'r. **1967** *Economist* 3 June 998/2 The ITA's problem is to decide which applicants give most promise of maintaining an improvement over six years... This is largely a wing and a prayer decision. **1971** P. O'Donnell *Impossible Virgin* xii. 250, I reckoned it was better to get kitted up for a proper job rather than come charging down 'ere on a wing and a prayer. **1977** W. Marshall *Thin Air* xii. 150 The co-pilot brought it in... Wing and a prayer! **1980** T. Barling *Goodbye Piccadilly* xvi. 334 The pilot spoke to him... 'This is real wing and a prayer weather.'

IV. 20. a. (In reference to parts, structure, or function) (*a*) *wing-beat, -bone, -length, -shoulder* (later example), *-span, -spread*; (*b*) (of aeroplanes) *wing-length, -skid, -span, -spread, -stay*; (*d*) (in sense 7) *wing-back, commander* (examples); (in sense 7 b) *wing-man* (examples); (*e*) *wing-nut* (later examples).

(*a*) **1826** Wing-bone [in Dict.]. **1897** 'N. Blanchan' *Bird Neighbors* 143 Bank Swallow... About an inch shorter than the English sparrow, but apparently much larger because of its wide wing-spread. **1909** *Westm. Gaz.* 2 Nov. 2/3 For wing-beats of great angels we would hear the herdsman's call. **1922** Joyce *Ulysses* 505 Head askew, arches his back and hunched wingshoulders. **1927** *Daily Express* 31 Aug. 8/3 It..is shaped like the wing-bone of a chicken. **1943** A. Clarke *Coll. Plays* (1963) 173 This big wind that filled My wingbones blew me into the trees. **1946** *Nature* 21 Dec. 904/1 The accompanying table shows..the weight in kgm. and wing-length in cm. of the female. **1949** *Brit. Birds* XLII. 187 The wing-span was found to measure nearly four feet, and the length was 21 inches. **1957** *New Yorker* 13 July 22/2 We got over six hundred bats, from insectivorous ones with an eight-inch wingspread to fruit eaters with a five-foot wingspread. **1971** *Sci. Amer.* Dec. 79/3 For aerodynamic reasons large birds have a slow wingbeat. **1977** P. Way *Super-Celeste* 123 The skull and upper bones of the [eagle's] wingspan had..driven like a cannon ball into the pilot's belly.

(*b*) **1908** H. G. Wells *War in Air* x. 317 It had taken only an hour or so to substitute wing stays from the second flying-machine and to replace the nuts he had himself removed. **1910** R. Ferris *How it Flies* xx. 474 *Wing skid*, a small skid, or runner, placed under the tip of the wings of an aeroplane. **1912** *Q. Rev.* July 231 If the 1000 lb. aeroplane is to travel slower, it must have a larger wing-spread. **1918** Pagé & Montariol *Gloss. Aviation Terms* 33/1 Wing span. **1920** *Flight* XII. 864/1 The Loughead S1 model, as it is called, is a single-seater biplane with a wing span of 28ft. **1975** *Farnborough 76* (Soc. Brit. Aerospace Companies) 30/2 The world's smallest jet aircraft, the Bede BD-5J..with a wing span of only 17ft. **1978** R. Jansson *News Caper* 9 There was the fighter again, flying parallel half a winglength away. **1978** *Sci. Amer.* Nov. 135/1 In 1899 the Wrights built a biplane kite with a five-foot wingspread that embodied their wing-twisting roll control.

(*d*) **1914** *Times* 22 Dec. 4/3 Royal Flying Corps..Wing Commander.—Brev. Maj. H. R. M. Brooke-Popham, Oxf. and Bucks. L.I. **1933** *Time* 13 Nov. 57/1 A wing-back is..a halfback who takes position about a yard and a half behind the line of scrimmage and about the same distance outside his own end. **1942** *Sun* (Baltimore) 26 Jan. 4/1 Baltimore scored first on a pass from Charley Ernst, center forward, to Harry McAdams, newly acquired wingman. **1943** J. B. Priestley *Daylight on Saturday* xxviii. 217 And a real wing-commander came in yesterday and talked to me. **1974** Wingback [see *rush *v.*[2] 6 g]. **1976** *Derbyshire Times* (Peak ed.) 3 Sept. 26/1 Matlock, in contrast, always looked dangerous with Peter Scott, the Fenoughty brothers, Mick and Nick, and wing-man Colin Oxley constantly troubling the Runcorn defence with their speedy breaks.

(*e*) **1910** *Chambers's Jrnl.* May 349/1 The wing-nut on its shaft is released, the detachable rim-wheel placed on the shaft, and the nut replaced. **1971** *Flying* Apr. 26/2 The control and gust locks..are adjustable to fit virtually any light aircraft by means of easy-to-operate wing nuts.

b. *wing-borne, -flapping, -like* (earlier example), *-shadowed, -shattered, -stiff, -weary* adjs.

1934 Webster, Wing-borne. **1942** S. Smith *Mother, what is Man?* 67 Than earth-born engine-borne, heaven-born wing-borne is better? **1977** *Guardian Weekly* 5 June 3/2 About half the crashes happened when the aircraft was hovering, or in transition from normal wingborne flight. **1915** E. Pound *Cathay* 10 He goes out to Hori, to look at the wing-flapping storks. **1953** N. Tinbergen *Herring Gull's World* xxi. 183 A screaming, wing-flapping tangle. **1795–1804** W. Blake *Vala* vi, in *Compl. Writings* (1972) 318 And the wing-like tent of the Universe, beautiful, surrounding all. **1938** D. Gascoyne *Hölderlin's Madness* 28 The bewildered words which try to tell The tale of his bright night And his wing-shadowed day. **1928** Blunden *Retreat* 60 But now the grey age passes by my faint senses And charm lies wing-shattered or dead. **1945** P. A. Larkin *North Ship* 33 It was your severed image that grew sweeter, That floated, wing-stiff, focussed in the sun. **1868** J. G. Whittier in *Atlantic Monthly* Jan. 1 The sky is hot and hazy, and the wind, Wing-weary with its long flight from the south. **1946** J. W. Day *Harvest Adventure* x. 154 The woodcock come in wing-weary from their North Sea voyagings.

21. wing-back chair = *wing chair*, sense 20 a (*e*) in Dict; also *ellipt.*; **wing-bud,** in insect larvæ, a histoblast from which the wings develop; **wing-clapping,** the production of a noise by a bird slapping its wings against its body; hence **wing-clap** *sb.* and *v. intr.*; **wing collar,** a high stiff shirt collar with the upper corners turned down; **wing-dam** *sb.* (earlier examples); **wing-flap:** see *flap *sb.* 5 e; **wing flutter** *Aeronaut.*, flutter (*flutter *sb.* 1 d) of an aircraft wing; **wing-footed** *a.*, also *fig.*; **wing formula** (see quot. 1964); **wing loading** *Aeronaut.*, the gross weight of an aircraft divided by the total wing area; (in quot. 1912 perh. used differently); cf. *power loading *vbl. sb.* 1; **wing-man,** the pilot of an aircraft which is positioned behind and to one side of the leading aircraft, as in formation for combat; the aircraft itself; **wing mirror,** (*a*) a side mirror (freq. adjustable) on a dressing table; (*b*) a rear-view mirror projecting from the side of a motor vehicle; **wing-over,** of an aircraft or hang-glider (see quot. 1959); **wing-poke (collar)** = *wing collar* above; **wing root** *Aeronaut.*, the part of a wing where it is attached to the fuselage; **wing-shot** *sb.* and *a.* (earlier examples); **wing-tag** *v. trans.*, to attach a distinguishing marker to the wing of a bird; **wing-tip,** (*c*) chiefly *U.S.*, applied *attrib.* to shoes with a toecap having a backward extending point and curving sides, suggestive of the shape of a wing; also *absol.*; **wing-walking,** acrobatic stunts performed on the wings of an aircraft which is airborne, as a public entertainment; **wing-warping,** in early powered flight, the bending or twisting of a wing by means of an attached wire as a method of stabilizing the aeroplane or turning it.

1933 J. Steinbeck *To God Unknown* i. 1 The wing-back chair by the fireplace. **1977** *Chicago Tribune Mag.* 2 Oct. 9/1 (Advt.), The chair that stands still in time—the Classic Wingback with Chippendale legs. **1973** 'D. Jordan' *Nile Green* xlvi. 247 She sat in her wingback chair flicking through one of the coffee table books. **1917** R. J. Tillyard *Biol. of Dragonflies* iii. 47 The wing-bud is simply an ectodermal evagination, in the form of a small bag lined internally with hydoderm cells, and externally with the cuticle. **1969** R. F. Chapman *Insects* xxi. 407 A progressive development of the wing buds occurs at each moult. **1941** H. F. Witherby et al. *Handbk. Brit. Birds* IV. 142 Performance [of display-flight by turtle-dove] may be accompanied by wing-clapping. **1964** A. L. Thomson *New Dict. Birds* 631/2 More rattling or clattering wing-claps may be made by pigeons suddenly taking wing when alarmed. **1976** *Country Life* 18 Mar. 672/2 The mechanical production of snaps from the beak may be compared with wing-clapping by birds... The long-eared owl will wing-clap during its spring nuptial flight. **1915** H. L. Wilson *Ruggles of Red Gap* (1917) ii. 33, I chose a shirt of white piqué, a wing collar with small, square-cornered tabs, and a pearl ascot. **1975** *Times* 19 May 12/7 Saturday's guide was Charles E. Lee, a transport historian whose wing collar..enhanced the building's period atmosphere. **1809** T. G. Fessenden *Pills Poetical* 36 All his rhetorick was directed toward election districts, and wingdam bills, and seconding motions. **1863** Wing dam [see *paddock *v.* 2]. **1927** *Daily Tel.* 21 Jan. 10/7 The new theory..suggests that wing-flutter may be more common than has been supposed. **1982** C. L. Ruhlin et al. *Transonic Flutter Study of Wind-Tunnel Model* (NASA Rep. 82-23239) viii. 5/2 Most of the winglet effect on the wing flutter speed was due to the winglet mass, not aerodynamics. **1977** *Time* 22 Aug. 13/1 Wing-footed United Nations Ambassador Andrew Young has been exploring the politically and economically troubled waters of the Caribbean, and soon will attend an anti-apartheid conference in Lagos, Nigeria. **1936** *Brit. Birds* XXX. 226 This specimen..has..a wing formula as follows. **1964** A. L. Thomson *New Dict. Birds* 892/2 Wing formula: a statement of, mainly, the relative lengths of the primary feathers. **1912** *Q. Rev.* July 246 A range of this amount is obtained entirely by proportioning the position of masses, the wing-curve and the wing-loading. **1916** A. W. Judge *Design of Aeroplanes* iii. 29 In current practice the wing loading expressed in pounds per square foot for biplanes is about 0.005V², ..where V is the maximum designed speed in feet per second. **1972** *Times* 19 May 17/4 It cannot be a glider, as it has far too high a wing-loading. **1946** *Sat. Even. Post* 6 Nov. 86/2, I looked to both sides of us. Our two wing men were gone. **1981** S. Dunmore *Ace* i. i. 15 We will fly together... You will be my wingman..to protect my rear end. **1982** *Daily Tel.* 25 May 1/4 He hit two Mirages with Sidewinder missiles while his wingman hit the third in the formation. **1925–6** *T. Eaton & Co. Catal.* Fall & Winter 311/2 Dressing table..triple mirrors, centre one beveled.. two plain wing mirrors. **1948** *Motor* 3 Nov. 396/3 An assortment of wing mirrors. **1959** C. Williams *Man in Motion* vi. 62 The dressing-table with its wing mirrors. **1959** *Motor Manual* (ed. 36) viii. 217 Additional wing mirrors are..very useful, particularly on the off-side as traffic on the point of overtaking is then clearly visible. **1981** M. Nabb *Death of Englishman* iii. i. 143 He..had banged his head on a Carabiniere car wing-mirror. **1928** *Morning Post* 20 Oct. 9/3 One of the passengers got panicky when the pilot executed a 'wing-over'. **1959** F. D. Adams *Aeronaut. Dict.* 183/2 *Wing-over, noun*, an airplane maneuver in which the airplane makes a steep zooming climb then banks and turns in the vertical plane into a dive or glide from which the recovery is made at approximately the original altitude and in a direction opposite to the original direction. **1978** A. Welch *Bk. Airsports* i. 9/2 They indulge in 'show-off' flying—fast dives and steep wing-overs—that the simple hang glider was never designed to take. **1905** H. G. Wells *Kipps* iii. i. 351 Kipps wears a grey suit, with a wing poke collar. **1910** —— *Hist. Mr. Polly* i. 13 His collar was chosen from stock, and with projecting corners, technically a 'wing-poke'. **1906** A. Samuelson *Flight-Velocity* i. 12 Near the wing root an outrigger or boom..is fastened. **1966** M. Woodhouse *Tree Frog* xxvi. 195, I jumped down off the wing root..and started to think about search parties. **1875** *Fur, Fin & Feather* 118 Bogardus, champion wing-shot of America, uses Orange Lightning [powder] for trap-shooting. **1878** C. Hallock *Hallock's Amer. Club List & Sportsman's Gloss.* p. xii, *Wing-shot*, a., hit in the wing. *Wing-shot*, n., a shot at birds on the wing;

one who shoots at birds while flying. **1953** Scott & Fisher *Thousand Geese* 215 Five of the young were wing-tagged. **1981** *Animal Behaviour* XXIX. 302/1 Three females and one male were wing-tagged. **1928** *World* (N.Y.) 23 May 4/6 (Advt.), Wing tip oxfords by Horsheim have unusually good style. **1971** *Weekend World* (Johannesburg) 9 May 14/5 (Advt.), Walk tall in the elegant clean lines of a Bostonian wing-tip or genuine handsewn moccasin. **1976** 'B. Shelby' *Great Pebble Affair* 45 Get a pair of black wingtip shoes. **1980** M. Gordon *Company of Women* I. ii. 38 The hard, expensive shoes of John F. Kennedy, the shoe with pinholes in the leather, wing tips they were called. **1927** C. A. Lindbergh *We* i. 11 Exhibitions..in which I usually made a jump and did a little wing-walking. **1979** *Sunset* Apr. 3/3 Also awesome is a wing-walking act in which specially trained gymnasts do headstands and other maneuvers on the wings of a W.W.II Stearman biplane as it loops, rolls, and lands. **1910** R. M. Neilson *Aeroplane Patents* 27, 6732 of March 19, 1904.—O. and W. Wright. This is the famous wing-warping patent. **1969** K. Munson *Pioneer Aircraft 1903–14* 7 Wing-warping was not, in itself, an invention of the Wrights; what was significant was their improvement of linking the warp-control cables with a single, hinged rudder.

wing, *v.* Add: **I. 2.** Also (chiefly *U.S.*) with an aircraft as subject, or *transf.* of a passenger, to travel by aircraft. No longer restricted to *poet.* or *rhetorical* use.

1938 *Sun* (Baltimore) 21 July 1/8 (*heading*) English plane wings swiftly over Atlantic. **1973** C. Sagan *Cosmic Connection* (1974) xxviii. 197 A single bit of radio information, sent winging across space to the Earth, would cost far less than a penny. **1977** *Time* 30 May 25/2 As Air Force One winged toward Washington, one Californian was clearly relieved that Carter's visit had been so brief. **1983** *Fortune* 18 Apr. 137/1 Winging into New Hampshire from Los Angeles headquarters aboard an Arco jet one Sunday, Cooper began the next three days at 7:30. **1984** *Times* 4 Aug. 32 The Prince of Wales flies back from Monaco, only to wing off within hours for Papua New Guinea.

5. (Later example with aircraft as subj.)

1976 C. Egleton *State Visit* xiv. 123 The VC 10 winged him back to Heathrow.

II. 10. b. *intr.* *to wing out*: to set a sail on a boom projecting sideways. Hence *winged out* or *wung out*, = *wing-and-wing* s.v. Wing *sb.* 19.

1867 G. E. Clark *Seven Yrs. Sailor's Life* i. 14 Here was I, deep-loaded, winged out, and oft-times flying before the winter blast. **1890** Webster, wung out. **1907** *Rudder* Nov. 827/2 On rounding, the schooners winged out; but..the wind came out of East of South, and they jibed their foresails and trimmed sheets a little. **1956** A. F. Loomis *Hotspur Story* 109 Thither we sailed, mainsail to starboard and staysail wung out. *Ibid.* 214 The wung-out schooner which we had noticed earlier in the afternoon lost the race. **1969** H. Horwood *Newfoundland* x. 71 Tearing down the outside passages with sails 'wung out' before a roaring nor'-wester.

11. (Earlier *intr.* example.) Hence in phr. *to wing it*; now usu. in *slang* use (orig. and chiefly *U.S.*), to improvise; to speak or act without preparation, to make statements on unstudied matters (see also quot. 1950).

1885 *Stage* 21 Aug. 12/2 'To wing'..indicates the capacity to play a *rôle* without knowing the text, and the word itself came into use from the fact that the artiste frequently received the assistance of a special prompter, who..stood..screened..by a piece of the scenery or a wing. **1933** P. Godfrey *Back-Stage* iii. 39 He must give a performance by 'winging it'—that is, by refreshing his memory for each scene in the wings before he goes on to play it. **1950** *Amer. Speech* XXV. 238/1 *Wing it, vb.*, to lay off an approximate 90° angle by eye. **1959** *Esquire* Nov. 70 *Wing*, to do something without preparation. **1970** *Time* 26 Jan. 12 *Cox*: The resistance put up against us dictates [our] strategy. *Bernstein*:..You mean you've got to wing it. **1971** *Publishers' Weekly* 6 Dec. 20/2 They can talk about the book, kind of winging it based on the ads, just like other people do with reviews. **1979** *Globe & Mail* (Toronto) 22 Jan. 8/2 Mr. Trudeau came without notes, choosing to wing it, and struggled..unsuccessfully to establish Mr. Leger's resemblance to an owl.

Wingco (wi·ŋko). *R.A.F. slang.* Also **Winco, Winko,** and with small initial. Abbrev. of *Wing Commander*: see Wing *sb.* 20 a (*d*).

1941 Michie & Graebner *Lights of Freedom* iii. 45 A cockney member of the ground crew piped: 'Sir, I think the 'Winko' [wing commander] is after the Hun.' **1942** *R.A.F. Jrnl.* 3 Oct. 12 One of them was a Winco and the other two were Army officers. **1943** 'T. Dudley-Gordon' *Coastal Command at War* ix. 88 On another raid... The wingco, was leading. **1944** 'N. Shute' *Pastoral* iii. 54 Don't let Winco hear him, or he'll get us into trouble. **1957** J. Braine *Room at Top* xii. 120 I've sung that.. with Wingcos and Group Captains joining in. **1974** T. Allbeury *Snowball* xxii. 135 Wing Commander Pallin from the Ministry of Defence... I'd like to ask the Wingco to keep himself free to check..on the state of the game in Moscow. **1982** F. Parrish *Snare in Dark* ii. 25 There was a pub..taken over by a retired Wing Commander... The Winco, as he liked to be called, was a ready market.

wing-ding, wingding (wi·ŋ,diŋ). Also **whingding.** [Redupl. of Wing *sb.*] **1.** *U.S. slang.* A fit or spasm, esp. as simulated by a drug addict; freq. in phr. *to throw a wing-ding*. Also in weakened sense, a furious outburst.

1927 *Amer. Speech* II. 281/1 *Wingding*, a false illness or fit. **1933** *Ibid.* VIII. ii. 28/1 When an addict who.. cannot obtain dope..becomes desperate, he may throw a wing-ding (feign a highly realistic fit in public) in the hope that the doctor..will administer narcotics to quiet him; professional wing-dingers are addicts who make a practice of obtaining their narcotics in this manner. **1939** R. Chandler *Big Sleep* xxxii. 292 She threw a wingding. Looked like a mild epileptic fit. **1944** *Amer. Speech* XIX. 107 A wing-ding is a particularly explosive fit of rage or frustration (I'm telling you the mate will throw a wing-ding!). **1946** 'J. Evans' *Halo in Blood* xiv. 166, I.. watched her take deep unsteady breaths... Her hands were locked together in her lap but that didn't keep them from trembling. 'About a minute,' I said mildly, 'You're going to throw a wing-ding they'll hear in Detroit. You're wound up tighter than a dollar watch.' **1957** V. Packard *Hidden Persuaders* ix. 102 This venture back to the womb touched off a little wingding in advertising circles. **1965** P. Tamony *Americanisms* (typescript) No. 11. 3 It assigned..Winifred Sweet..to throw a wing-ding..in Market Street.

2. *slang* (orig. and chiefly *U.S.*). A wild party; a celebration or social gathering.

1949 *Sat. Even. Post* 5 Mar. 10/3 We are not sure just what the Festival is to be, but some sort of native whingding no doubt. **1955** R. Bradbury *October Country* 18 We would have to arrive when the local Rotary's having its whingding. **1964** *Punch* 15 July 79/3 My invitation to a White House schnapps wingding. **1972** *Sunday Sun* (Brisbane) 6 Aug. 3/4 Last Tuesday was Pat's birthday, so there was a big wing-ding at Maroochydore's posh Surfair pub. **1975** *Listener* 18 Dec. 832/3 The funeral bak'd meats will serve the triple economy of a divorce wing-ding as well. **1979** A. Hailey *Overload* iii. xi. 243 How are you, Nim? Don't see you often at these Jewish wingdings.

Hence **wing-di·nger,** (*a*) (see quot. 1933); (*b*) a pretended fit; a wild outburst.

1933 [see sense 1 above]. **1949** V. J. Monteleone *Criminal Slang* (new ed.) 253 *Wing-dinger* (*n.*), a pretended fit or spasm; a forced faint. **1976** *Telegraph* (Brisbane) 5 Aug. 39/3 This leads to a wing-dinger of a brawl, when Bobbie's brother..sights the louts who have busted up his father and their truck on the bridge.

winge, var. Whinge *v.* in Dict. and Suppl.

winged, *a.* Add: **3. c. winged bean,** a tropical legume, *Psophocarpus tetragonolobus,* native to south-eastern Asia and cultivated for its edible leaves, winged pods, and tubers; cf. *Goa bean* s.v. Goa[1]; **winged thistle** *N.Z.,* either of two thistles of the genus *Carduus, C. tenuiflorus* or *C. pycnocephalus,* which have winged stems.

1910 H. F. Macmillan *Handbk. Trop. Gardening & Planting* 189 *Psophocarpus tetragonolobus.* Winged bean; Goa bean; Manilla bean. **1915** *N.Z. Jrnl. Agric.* 21 June 550 Winged thistle [seed]. About the same size as spear-thistle seed. **1966** *Encycl. N.Z.* III. 599/1 Noxious weeds . are here listed... Winged thistle. **1975** *Times* 30 Aug. 12/7 An international panel. [is] recommending a major development effort to turn..the winged bean into a main crop.

winged, *ppl. a.* **1.** (Earlier example.)

1789 *Ess. on Shooting* xiv. 223 He [*sc.* the dog] should be held in a string, ready to be slipped in case of need, after a winged partridge, or a wounded hare.

wingedness. (In Dict. s.v. Winged *a.*) (Later example.)

1909 W. Bateson *Mendel's Princ. Heredity* i. x. 172 Here we see that the one 'dose' of wingedness—as we may call it—sufficed only to bring the wings to half the full size, and two 'doses' are needed to develop them properly.

wingeing, var. Whinging *vbl. sb.* and *ppl. a.* in Dict. and Suppl.

winger. Add: **2.** Also in *Hockey* and *Lacrosse*, a wing player.

1922 *Daily Mail* 15 Dec. 13 No right winger has more visibly impressed me than Sutcliffe this season. **1969** *West Australian* 5 July 32/3 Allowing winger Kaye Olsen to gain position and put Wembley into attack.

3. *Naut. slang.* **a.** A steward.

1929 F. C. Bowen *Sea Slang* 152 *Winger*, a steward waiting at table, with the class prefixed. **1962** *Times* 26 Apr. 15/2 A winger is a steward on a passenger liner. **1962** [see *blood *sb.* 15 d].

b. A comrade or friend (see also quot. 1977).

1943 *Penguin New Writing* XVII. 46 He had seen his 'winger', his best friend, decapitated. **1948** Partridge *Dict. Forces' Slang* 208 *Winger*, an assistant or 'stooge'. The term has displaced 'raggie' as a name for a pal. (Navy.) **1957** R. Watson-Watt *Three Steps to Victory* xl. 233 Bickell,..Max's *fidus Achates* and 'winger' in M.A.P. and in the wide circles which rippled..out from that most explosive of Ministries. **1977** G. Melly *Rum, Bum & Concertina* v. 57 The expression 'winger' means, at its most innocent, a young seaman who is taken under the wing of a rating or Petty Officer older and more experienced than himself to be shown the ropes.

4. *left-winger, right-winger*: see *left wing, *right wing.

wingy (wi·ŋi), *sb. colloq.* [f. Wing *sb.* + -y[6].] A one-armed man; also (with capital initial) used as a nickname. Cf. *wing *sb.* 5 d (*c*).

1880 D. W. Barrett *Navvies* (ed. 2) ii. iii. 49 If a poor fellow..is short of a leg or an arm, 'Peggy' or 'Wingy' is at once affixed to him. **1910** H. Lawson *Stories* (1964) 2nd Ser. 296 Wingy..is a ratty little one-armed man whose case is usually described in the head-line as 'A 'Armless Case' by one of our great dailies. **1931** 'D. Stiff' *Milk & Honey Route* v. 58 Missions are very anxious to recruit the 'wingies' and 'armies', or the one-armed hobos. **1964** T. Ronan *Packhorse & Pearling Boat* 129 As Dad later referred to him as 'Wingy' Collins I presume that he had one arm amputated, or some similar disability.

wink, *sb.*[1] Add: **3. c.** In *Work Study*, a unit of time equivalent to one two-thousandth of a minute. Also *Comb.*, as *wink-counter*. orig. *U.S.*

1937 R. M. Barnes *Motion & Time Study* ix. 72 There are 100 equal divisions on the dial of the clock; therefore, time is indicated directly in 1/2000 of a minute by the large hand. This time interval of 1/2000 of a minute was called a 'wink' by Gilbreth. **1946** R. L. Morrow *Time Study & Motion Economy* ix. 90 The wink-counter..is a small motor driven device, originated by Professor David B. Porter..to be used for both motion and time studies. In appearance it resembles a 'speedometer'. **1961** *Engineering* 15 Sept. 352/1 A very early type of micromotion filming was used by the Gilbreths in the early days of motion study, and the unit of time which they employed, a two thousandth of a minute or a 'wink', is still often used for detailed motion analysis.

wink, *sb.*[4] Shortening of *tiddlywink 2 c. orig. *U.S.*

1890 *Game of Tiddledy Winks* (McLoughlin Bros., New York) 1 Its great interest and success lies in the novel feature of jumping the Winks into the Wink-pot. **1957** *Times* 17 Dec. 9/4 Tiddlywinks does not yet qualify for a 'blue', or even half a one, but it is nice to know that the club has a tie, dark blue with a blue cup and a wink rampant. **1979** F. R. Shapiro *Encycl. Tiddlywinks* 8 The Silver Wink, donated by Prince Philip, is awarded to the winner of an annual elimination tournament for universities.

wink, *v.*[1] Add: **2. c.** Also with advbs.: to go *out* or *off* suddenly; to come *on* suddenly.

1848 Wink out [in Dict.]. **1930** W. Faulkner *As I lay Dying* 244 He locks the door. Dewey Dell is inside. Then the light winks out. **1972** *Sci. Amer.* Jan. 108/3 An observer who is a few miles away but within the shadow sees the star wink off and five minutes later reappear slightly west of the moon. **1979** *Tucson* (Arizona) *Citizen* 20 Sept. 7B/6 (*heading*) 'Buck Rogers' no supernova, but it won't wink out, either. **1982** *Washington Post* 21 Mar. 3/2 Bleuzinski perched on the pool table, leaned forward, and looked directly into the camera. The red light winked on.

wink, *v.*[3] orig. *U.S.* [f. *wink *sb.*[4]] *intr.* To play tiddlywinks. Freq. as *vbl. sb.* Occas. *trans.* (in quot. *fig.*).

1955 V. Nabokov *Lolita* i. v. 26 This is all very interesting, and I daresay you see me already frothing at the mouth in a fit; but no, I am not; I am just winking happy thoughts into a little tiddle cup. **1958** *Sunday Times* 2 Mar. 16/3 While practising secretly, I pulled an important muscle in the second or tiddly joint of my winking finger. **1962** *Boston Globe* 14 Oct. 81 The Crimson tiddlers winked their way to a 23 to 12 victory over a green Purple team. **1979** *Harvard Mag.* May–June 38 They went to many carpet stores to find the perfect surface for winking.

winked, *ppl. a.* Add: *winked-at* (later examples).

1971 J. Brunner *Honky in Woodpile* iii. 24 Some winked-at gambling and smuggling. **1979** *Dædalus* Summer 107 Such genre paintings represent not a random clutter of whimsically winked-at transgressions but an array of symbols encoding quite specific moral instructions.

winkel. (Earlier example.)

1827 G. Thompson *Trav. & Adv. S. Afr.* i. iii. 35 The village contains a couple of small retail shops, or *winkels*, as they are called.

winker[1]**.** Add: **4.** A direction indicator on a motor vehicle in the form of a flashing light; = *indicator 3 g.

1951 *Autocar* 2 Nov. 1411/1 Another advantage of the 'winkers' is the fact that no mechanical fault can develop. **1960** *News Chron.* 21 July 6/4 On the M1..there are no curves to cancel the winkers. **1967** *Autocar* 28 Dec. 2/2 The main-beam and winker lights have little, pull-down 'eyelids'. **1970** A. Sillitoe *Start in Life* v. 255, I put on the winkers, swung out, and swept forward.

Hence (in sense 3) **wi·nkered** *a.*

1804 M. Wilmot *Let.* 5 July in *Russ. Jrnls.* (1934) i. 110 Women..dress'd in a sort of winker'd cap of *pearls* which showes the face very becomingly. **1907** J. M. Synge *Playboy of Western World* iii. 61 That's the playboy on the winkered mule.

winker[2]**.** Short for *tiddlywinker* (b) s.v. *tiddlywink. orig. *U.S.*

1958 *N.Y. Times* 9 May 28 Tomorrow..the Cantab Winkers play the Oxonian Tiddlers in Oxford. **1965** *Times* 5 Jan. 116 The nation's 'winkers' have two ambitions for 1965. **1979** *Harvard Mag.* May–June 39 Winkers lost interest in recruiting new winkers.

winkle, *sb.* Add: **2.** *slang* (chiefly *juveniles'*). The penis (of a young boy).

1951 Partridge *Dict. Slang* Add. 1223/2 *Winkle, n.*, penis: children's, (young) schoolboys': late C. 19–20. **1970** *Guardian* 3 Feb. 8, I was mildly troubled by the insistence, especially of one headmaster, on the 'proper names for things'. Penis is right and winkle is wrong. **1970** T. HUGHES *Crow* 63 O do not chop his winkle off His Mammy cried. **1973** M. AMIS *Rachel Papers* 78 'Thanks,' he said to his (new) witch-like girlfriend as she handed him a joint so ill-made that it resembled a baby's winkle.

3. *Comb.*, as **winkle-picker** *slang*, a shoe with a long pointed toe; **winkle-pin** *Mil. slang* = BAYONET 2.

1960 *Spectator* 15 Apr. 553 The incredibly pointed custom-built shoes in which teenagers keep other teenagers at arm's length... The shoes, called winklepickers, look like something out of Grimm's fairy tales. **1960** *News Chron.* 13 Sept. 5/3 The 'winkle picker' high heels and the high spirits have gone. **1978** C. SYKES in R. Buckle *U & Non-U Revisited* 57 The mass-produced variety, popularly known as 'winkle-pickers', were very ugly. **1980** *Bulletin* (Sydney) 6 May 5/3, I had the hairdo, the lairy shirt, the winkle-picker shoes. **1924** KIPLING *Debits & Credits* (1926) 314 As his sergeant I had to check him for misusin' his winkle-pin on dirt. **1950** PARTRIDGE *Here, There & Everywhere* 62 The bayonet..has many names..[e.g.] *winkle-pin.*

winkle, *v.*[2] *colloq.* (orig. *Mil. slang*). [f. WINKLE *sb.*] trans. *to winkle out*: to extract or eject (as a winkle from its shell with a pin); to draw forth, find out or elicit.

[**1925** FRASER & GIBBONS *Soldier & Sailor Words* 306 *Winkle, to,* to capture individual prisoners by stealth... Also,..to steal.] **1942** 'M. HOME' *House of Shade* ii. 20 What's winkled you out at this goddam hour? **1943** *People* 31 Oct. 1/7 Methodically winkling the Germans out of their strongpoints. **1951** 'M. INNES' *Operation Pax* v. vi. 220 Until we winkle out this young man..you and I make not a bad team. **1958** J. PRESS *Chequer'd Shade* 4 It is illegitimate to compare the far-fetched conjectures of Eliot's commentators with the inside information which we might have winkled out of Donne. **1966** *Listener* 20 Jan. 111/3 It's the cunning of the interviewer that counts most of all, and certainly Mr Muggeridge manages to winkle out some interesting bits and pieces. **1970** *Sunday Mail Mag.* (Brisbane) 17 May 14/1 He could winkle out sin where no other man dreamed it existed. **1976** A. EDEN *Another World* vii. 79 Hart's skills were in a sense wasted upon us, and he was at length winkled out to the advantage of a base hospital.

winkler. (In Dict. s.v. WINKLE *sb.*) Add: **2.** *slang.* One who assists in the eviction of tenants (see quot. 1970). Cf. *WINKLE *v.*[2]

1970 *Sunday Times* 15 Nov. 3/5 Plausible, highly-paid 'winklers' who are hired by property companies and landlords to persuade families to leave their rent-controlled tenancies so the homes can be sold at high prices. **1977** *Whig-Standard* (Kingston, Ontario) 29 Sept. 26/3 The tenants said the agents aided by middlemen called 'winklers', had bribed and harassed them to get them to move.

winkling (wi·ŋkliŋ), *vbl. sb.* [f. *WINKLE *v.*[2] + -ING[1].] The action of the vb., esp. with reference to the removal of tenants from rented accommodation. Also *winkling-out.* Cf. *WINKLER 2.

1970 *Guardian* 20 Nov. 7/1 'Winkling'—persuading private tenants to quit. **1973** *Daily Tel.* 24 May 11/2 He described the 'winkling' processes followed by certain developers to rid themselves of unwanted but protected tenants. **1974** E. AMBLER *Dr Frigo* III. 195 An army assault team had been called in. In their winkling-out of the defenders they had..made rather a mess of the Palace. **1975** *Listener* 18 Nov. 826/1 Mr Skeaping had been accused of 'winkling'; bribing his tenants to leave so that he could sell the property with vacant possession.

winks (wiŋks). Shortening of *tiddlywinks*: see TIDDLYWINK 2 b. *U.S.*

1942 R. & L. FREEMAN *Cavalcade of Toys* xvi. 366 Back in 1903 'Battle Winks' was a popular game. **1962** *Harvard Crimson* 6 Nov. 3/2 (*heading*) Crimson winks squad downs two opponents. **1979** *Technology Rev.* Mar./Apr. B23 Unlike chess, which has limited predictable moves, winks is a game of chance as well as skill, says Mr. Lockwood.

winky. Add: Also **winkie.** (Further examples.)

1846 W. CROSS *Disruption* vii. 61 Jimes and mee are going On with owre studdys already like winkie. **1901** M. FRANKLIN *My Brilliant Career* xix. 163 Every one has to obey him like winkie or they can take their beds up and trot off quick and lively. **1923** KIPLING *Land & Sea Tales* 115 This Baxter-man..SOS'ed like winkie.

winless (wi·nlės), *a. N. Amer.* [f. WIN *sb.*[1] + -LESS.] Characterized by an absence of victories in a series of sporting contests; also, designating a period of time during which no victory was won.

1966 *Daily Progress* (Charlottesville, Va.) 8 June 30/1 People keep telling VMI's Gary McPherson he has the very best winless basketball team in the country. **1970** *Globe & Mail* (Toronto) 25 Sept. 32/3 Winless in 14 previous starts this season, Miss Ella Cinders had little trouble with Sandy Hawley up last Saturday as she galloped to a 12-length win. **1972** J. MOSEDALE *Football* iii. 36 They..went through another winless season. **1977** *Arab Times* 3 Dec. 9/3 Bechtel now go into their final game against AG & P with both teams winless in what should be quite a battle to see which team makes it out of the cellar.

winnability (wi:năbi·liti). Also **winability.** [f. WINNABLE *a.*: see -ITY.] Capacity for winning or being won.

1972 *New Society* 16 Nov. 400/2 The penal cases committee seems to be heavily influenced by two considerations... The other is the 'winability' of the case; the penal cases committee refers chiefly open-and-shut cases to the disciplinary committee. **1975** W. SAFIRE *Before the Fall* I. iv. 43 'My biggest problem,' Nixon concluded, 'is "Nixon can't win".'.. We discussed ways to build 'winability'. **1979** *Guardian* 2 Nov. 13/6 Kennedy..has that overriding quality—winnability. **1983** *Times* 16 Apr. 2/5 The most detailed work on the winnability of the new seats has been done by a few academics.

Winnebago (winəbē[i]·go), *sb.* (*a.*) [ad. Fox *wi·nepye·ko·ha*, lit. 'person of dirty water', an allusion to the muddy waters of the Fox River below Lake Winnebago, which became clogged with dead fish in the heat of the summer.] **1. a.** (A member of) a Siouan people of eastern Wisconsin. **b.** The language of this people. Also *attrib.* or as *adj.*

1766 J. CARVER *Jrnl.* 25 Sept. in J. Parker *Jrnls. J. Carver & Related Documents, 1766–70* (1976) I. 78 Arrivd at the great town of the Winebaygoes. *Ibid.* 79 The town of the Winebagoes is situate on the south east end of an island at the east end of the Winebago Lake. **1827** *Spirit of Seventy-Six* (Frankfort, Kentucky) 2 Aug. 2/1 An express reached here this moment from Galena.. with information of hostilities having been commenced by the Winnebago Indians, on the settlers. **1835** C. F. HOFFMAN *Winter in West* I. 257 The Winnebago chief.. [had] just left the establishment. **1839** H. R. SCHOOLCRAFT *Algic Researches* I. 13 The Winnebagoes are clearly of the Abanic stock. **1860** *Harper's Mag.* Sept. 568/2 As he could not speak Winnebago, the first thing to be done was to find an interpreter. **1881** *Encycl. Brit.* XII. 832/1 The Winnebagoes are a branch of the Dakota family. **1907** L. H. MORGAN *Anc. Society* III. iii. 440 In Winnebago and Achaotina she is 'my sister'. **1910** F. W. HODGE *Handbk. Amer. Indians* II. 958/1 The Winnebago have been known to the whites since 1634, when the Frenchman Nicollet found them in Wisconsin, on Green Bay. **1933** [see *MANDAN *a.* and *sb.*]. **1966** A. C. HARDY *Divine Flame* iii. 65 Those tribes belonging to the great Sioux family such as the Omaha, Ponka, Kansas, Dakota, Iowa, Winnebago, etc. **1973** A. H. WHITEFORD *N. Amer. Indian Arts* 81 Winnebago women's mocassins have a flap over the toe. **1975** *Language* LI. 317 Ferguson..suggests that Hockett's analysis of Winnebago is unusual.

2. Special Comb.: **Winnebago camper,** a motor vehicle with insulated panels used as living accommodation by campers (a proprietary term in the U.S.); also *ellipt.*

1966 *Mobile Home Jrnl.* Oct. (Advt., rear cover), Your most enjoyable travel companion is a Winnebago Pickup Camper Coach. **1970** *Official Gaz.* (U.S. Patent Office) 17 Nov. TM 132 Winnebago Industries, Inc., Forest City, Iowa. Filed Aug. 6, 1969. Winnebago... For Vehicles and Components..—Namely Motor Homes, Travel Trailers, House Trailers, Camper Coaches, [etc.]..First use April 1959. **1975** I. K. MARTIN *Regan & Manhattan File* 104 Regan..noted..a Winnibago camper parked to the rear. ..The back door of the Winnibago opened.

winner. Add: **2.** (Later examples of 'a thing that scores a success': now *colloq.*) Also, a potentially successful project, enterprise, etc.

1934 *Punch* 14 Nov. 552/1 The growing function of the outlying theatres is to spot winners for the West-End. **1948** M. LASKI *Tory Heaven* v. 66 'I'd like to be a land-agent... I do really think I could have made a success of it.' 'I'm sure you would... It sounds like a winner to me.' **1958** *Times* 12 Sept. 13/1 The last crop of new ballets commissioned for the Edinburgh International Ballet company includes one winner, a near miss, and a very honourable mention. **1972** *Sunday Express* 9 Jan. 5/3 The warmth of wool plus good, classic styling, makes this coat a winner this winter. **1976** *Southern Even. Echo* (Southampton) 18 Nov. 4/3 Cyril Berry..must be on a winner with his latest book. **1985** *Woman's Own* 22 June 36/2 The actor believes that combining the strong with the sensitive is exactly what makes a man a winner—on screen and off.

3. *winner-take(s)-all*, attrib. phr. used to denote contests or conflicts in which victory is outright or the successful competitor alone is rewarded; occas. (without hyphens) in non-attrib. use as an idiomatic sentence.

1969 *Listener* 10 Apr. 496/1 When you say war, I think that's what you mean: nations and empires clashing, and there will be one winner and one loser on clear-cut lines. I won, you lost. But here there's not supposed to be, the way I understand it, a winner-take-all-type thing. **1972** *National Observer* (U.S.) 27 May 5/1 Should McGovern win the June 6 California primary with its winner-take-all bag of 271 votes,..he then would be within easy range of a first-ballot nomination at the convention opening on July 10. **1972** *Guardian* 8 June 12/1 In California winner takes all. It will be almost impossible now to deny McGovern the nomination. **1973** *Times* 16 Nov. 1/1 The Government has accepted that there is no way out of a grim, winner-takes-all clash with the National Union of Mineworkers. **1976** 'H. CARMICHAEL' *False Evidence* iv. 63 There must've been a worthwhile rakeoff... The outcome was that winner took all. **1978** A. PRICE *'44 Vintage* xxiii. 264 A winner-takes-all lottery.

winning, *vbl. sb.*[1] Add: **9. winning-chair** (earlier example); **winning-post** (earlier example); also *fig.*; **winning streak** orig. *N. Amer.*, a sequence of successes, esp. in sporting contests.

1835 W. DYOTT *Diary* Oct. (1907) II. 212 A platform was erected in front of the winning chair [on Lichfield Race Course] to accommodate the ladies who were to deliver the standards [to a regiment]. **1759** A. MURPHY *Let.* 22 July in D. Garrick *Private Corr.* (1831) I. 101 You must judge whether they [*sc.* horses] are *marketable*, or likely to tire before they come to the winning-post. **1790** T. WILKINSON *Mem.* II. 194 Miss Notable and Miss Prue from the archness and excellent acting of Mrs Abington, seemed to have the decision at the winning post for fame. **1951** *Times* (Weekly Ed.) 30 May 3 Meals are landmarks, milestones which must be passed before the winning-post of bed-time is finally and thankfully reached. **1968** Winning streak [see *goal-tending* vbl. sb. s.v. *GOAL *sb.* 6]. **1976** *New Yorker* 15 Nov. 162/1 'We're on a winning streak. We're on a hot roll,' one city official said happily last summer, during the triumphal series of events that began with Operation Sail and extended through other local Bicentennial celebrations. **1976** *Cumberland News* 3 Dec., Gilsland's Station Hotel team, playing in the Irthing Valley Sunday League, are still in a winning streak.

winning, *ppl. a.* Add: **2.** In U.S. colloq. use also in superlative.

1974 *State* (Columbia, S. Carolina) 5 Mar. 6-A/7 John Bates, coach of Maryland-Eastern Shore, at 26–1 the winningest college basketball team in the nation. **1979** *Tucson* (Arizona) *Citizen* 20 Sept. 5D/1 Slota defeated Sarah Cap, the winningest active greyhound with 113 career victories. **1985** *Dirt Bike* Mar. 23/2 (Advt.), That's the moment you know what the winningest racers and most satisfied riders know.

winningly, *adv.* (Later examples.)

1934 G. B. SHAW *On Rocks* I. 208 *Sir Arthur* [*winningly*] And do you, Miss Brollikins, feel that you have got nothing? **1980** *Times Lit. Suppl.* 20 June 702/2 Clothes and hair styles [of petty criminals in the 1870s] repay scrutiny: no one ever dressed up or posed winningly for these pictures.

Winnipeg (wi·nĭpeg). The name of the capital of Manitoba, Canada, used *attrib.* in *Winnipeg couch*, a couch convertible into a double bed.

1954 S. M. RUSSELL *Living Earth* 233 He sat on the Winnipeg couch that stood at one end of the room. **1962** J. ONSLOW *Bowler-Hatted Cowboy* viii. 74 Beneath an old army blanket I drowsed to sleep on my Winnipeg couch. **1973** B. BROADFOOT *Ten Lost Years* xiii. 153 A couch, one of those Winnipeg couch things in the living room.

Hence **Wi·nnipegger,** a native or inhabitant of Winnipeg.

1882 G. M. GRANT *Picturesque Canada* I. 288 Winnipeggers..never make comparisons with any city smaller than Chicago. **1936** MENCKEN *Amer. Lang.* (ed. 4) x. 549 Richmonder, Winnipegger, Montrealer, Lynner. **1971** J. GRAY *Red Lights* ii. 27 They watched Winnipeggers frantically planting trees all over the place.

winny (wi·ni). *U.S. slang.* Var. *WIENIE. Also *Comb.*, as *winny-wurst*. Cf. *WEENY *sb.*[2]

1867 J. CHRISTISON *Crime & Criminals* 37 For a week longer he served at his usual business, which was that of peddling 'winnies', mostly among the saloons. **1914** B. TARKINGTON *Penrod* xix. 199 Winnies! *Here's* your hot winnies! Hot winny-*wurst!* **1929** T. WOLFE *Look Homeward, Angel* xx. 272 Fortune out of winnies. They're hot, they're hot.

wino (wəi·no). *slang* (orig. *U.S.*). [f. WIN(E *sb.*[1] + *-O[2].] An habitual drinker of cheap wine; an alcoholic or drunkard, esp. one who is destitute.

1915 *World* (N.Y.) *Mag.* 9 May 14/3 *Wineoe*, a wine bum; known on the Pacific Coast, especially in California. **1926** J. BLACK *You can't Win* xii. 153 The wine dumps, where wine bums or 'winos' hung out. **1946** [see *JUICED *a.* 2]. **1957** J. KEROUAC *On Road* I. i. 9 Working..without pause eight hours a night..in greasy wino pants with a frayed fur-lined jacket and beat shoes that flap. **1958** *Times* 24 Nov. p. viii/5 In fact, Canadians have reserved the term 'wino' for the most reprehensible of their drinkers. **1961** *Guardian* 28 Feb. 8/7 A conglomeration of hop-heads, winos, overworked policemen. **1967** *Sunday Truth* (Austral.) 16 July 28/4 To save gas she washes in public toilets, and if she feels like a drink she has a swig from a wino's bottle at South Brisbane. **1973** 'J. MARKS' *Mick Jagger* (1974) 106 That sonuvabitch Dean Martin..that lousy wino wop! **1979** *Evening Standard* 2 Mar. 19/4, I am in sympathy with the plea by Mrs A. L. Hughes for the survival of buskers, but feel her attack on 'winos' is both misdirected and lacking in human understanding. **1981** M. LEITCH *Silver's City* xii. 103 He saw the winos watching him out of bleary eyes as they huddled on their benches passing their brown bottles to and fro.

Winstonian (winstō[u]·niăn), *a.* [f. the name of Sir *Winston* Leonard Spencer Churchill, British prime minister 1940–5 and 1951–5: see -IAN.] Of, pertaining to, or characteristic of Sir Winston Churchill. Cf. *CHURCHILLIAN *a.*

1905 W. S. CHURCHILL *Let.* 9 May in R. S. Churchill *Winston S. Churchill* (1969) II. Compan. I. 391 It is vy kind of you to write me such a long letter. It will be carefully preserved among the Winstonian archives. **1945** S. SASSOON *Siegfried's Journey* viii. 79 The Winstonian exposition continued until Eddie reappeared with an apologetic intimation that Lord Fisher was growing restive. **1967** *Guardian* 16 May 8/6 Winstonian echoes to match the countless plaster busts in shop windows.

wint, var. WENT.

winter, *sb.*[1] Add: **3. a.** (*b*) Of clothing (further examples).

1628 F. DRAKE *World Encompassed* 64 Notwithstanding

it was in the height of Summer..we could..haue beene contented to haue kept about vs still our Winter clothes. **1759** G. Clough *Let.* 30 Sept. in *Essex Inst. Hist. Coll.* (1861) III. 104/1 Cold weather..will make us..put on our Winter Clothing. **1838** *Workwoman's Guide* in Walkley & Foster *Crinolines & Crimping Irons* (1978) xi. 165 Care should be taken to separate..winter clothing from that worn in summer. **1870** E. G. E. Ward *Jrnl.* 9 Nov. in D. P. Carew *Many Years, Many Girls* (1967) i. 33, I have been able to-day to send my children in England some winter clothes. **1874** Geo. Eliot *Let.* 16 June (1956) VI. 57 The cold winds..have forced us to put on winter clothing. **1876** C. M. Yonge *Three Brides* I. iii. 35 Her hair and pretty Parisian winter dress arranged to perfection. **1892** *Daily News* 12 Dec. 1/2 (Advt.), Gentlemen's undervests. Winter weight, 32 in. to 48 in. chests. **1934** G. B. Shaw *On Rocks* II. 226 There is a generous fire in the grate; and the visitors wear winter clothes. **1940** L. I. Wilder *Long Winter* ix. 73 They dressed carefully in their woolen winter dresses. **1979** T. Barling *Olympic Sleeper* xi. 138 He was warm in his winterweight pin-striped suit. **1984** W. Beechey *Rich Mrs. Robinson* xii. 89 He needs some winter vests badly.

(*c*) *winter-while* (poet.).

a **1889** G. M. Hopkins in *Dublin Rev.* (1920) July-Sept. 46 They came from the south, Where winter-while is all forgot.

(*d*) *winter cruise*.

1934 Winter cruise [see *front-pager* s.v. *front *sb.* (and *a.*) 14]. **1976** *Liverpool Echo* 6 Dec. 7/1 Aznar Line are having a record breaking season with their winter cruises out of Liverpool.

c. (Further example.)

1939 *WPA Guide to Florida* (Federal Writers' Project) I. 7 The traveler..may detour inland to discover the hidden winter-vegetable kingdom on the muck lands.

4. (instrumental) *winter-heavy, -left, -locked, -wearied, -weary, -weighed*; (similative) *winter-blue, -cold, -white*; ('in or during winter') *winter-felled* (earlier example), *-flowering* (earlier example), *-hardy, -sown* (later example); appositive, as *winter-spring*.

1936 R. Frost *Let.* 6 Feb. (1964) 270 And Sirius is a winterbluegreen star. **1958** J. W. Day *Lady Houston* xv. 225 Never had..the winter-blue woods of Kimbolton or the generous warmth of Brampton Park..beckoned more seductively. **1944** E. Sitwell *Green Song* 7 Henry thought me winter-cold When to keep his love I turned from him as the world Turns from the sun. **1742** Ellis *Timber-Tree* II. 13 From whence they infer, that the worm can't breed so soon in a Summer-fell'd Tree, as in a Winter-fell'd one. **1794** Winter-flowering [see Aconite 3]. **1960** *Farmer & Stockbreeder* 5 Jan. 43/1 We may..be given a more winter-hardy, leafier kale. **1975** *Daily Colonist* (Victoria, B.C.) 20 July 22/7 As it is not winter-hardy here, it is commonly grown as an annual. **1920** D. H. Lawrence *Women in Love* xxix. 435 This was an old world she was still journeying through, winter-heavy and dreary. **1955** S. Spender *Coll. Poems 1928–53* ix. 173 Its vermilion seems A Red Admiral's wing, with veins Of lichen and rust, an underwing Of winter-left leaves. **1926** S. Leslie *Cantab* xv. 183 He sobbed like a winter-locked river hastening over the weir at the first warmth of spring. **1946** Dylan Thomas *Deaths & Entrances* 34 Two proud, blacked brothers cry, Winter-locked side by side. **1960** *Farmer & Stockbreeder* 15 Mar. 141/3 Tri-Farmon 41 effectively controls the widest possible range of weeds in winter and spring-sown wheat. **1888** W. D. Hay *Blood* vii. 29 Although it was so late in the winter-spring season, the weather was wild and wintry. **1967** *Oceanogr. & Marine Biol.* XVI. 409 The 'Atlanto-Scandian' winter-spring spawning stocks. **1892** J. G. Whittier *At Sundown* 58 This stormy interlude Gives to our winter-wearied hearts a reason For trustful gratitude. **1917** D. H. Lawrence *Look! we have come Through!* 160 We who are winter-weary in the winter of the world. **1866** J. G. Whittier *Snow-Bound* 46 And woodland paths that wound between Snow drooping pine-boughs winter-weighed. **1915** E. Sitwell *Mother* 16 Her ice-cold breast was winter-white.

5. a. winter annual (see quot. 1900); **winter carnival** *Canad.*, 'an organized winter social activity featuring winter sports, beauty contests, ice-sculpture, etc.' (*Dict. Canadianisms*); **winter coat,** (*a*) the coat of an animal in winter, where this differs from that in summer; (*b*) a (woman's) coat suitable for winter weather; **winter country** *N.Z.*, land where livestock can be wintered; **winter garden,** (*b*) (earlier and later examples); (*c*) a building used for concerts, plays, dances, etc., at a seaside resort; **winter-killed** *pa. pple.* and *a.*, **-killing** (earlier examples); also **winter-kill** *v. intr.*, to become winter-killed; *trans.*, to make winter-killed; also *absol.*; **winter-kill** *sb.*; **winter oil,** edible oil that remains clea. at low temperatures owing to the removal of constituents that would have caused congelation or precipitation; **Winter Olympic Games, Winter Olympics,** international competitive winter sports held under the auspices of the International Olympic Committee, usually every four years; **winter packet** *Canad.* (*Obs.* exc. *Hist.*), a boat or land party carrying mail in winter-time between trading posts; the mail itself; **winter road** *Canad.*, a road or a route used in winter when the ground is frozen or there is snow; **Winter War** (also with small initials), the war between the U.S.S.R. and Finland in 1939–40; **winter woollies**: see *woolly *sb.* 1.

1900 B. D. Jackson *Gloss. Bot. Terms* 290/2 *Winter-annual*, a plant which germinates in autumn, and living through the winter, fruits and dies. **1977** J. L. Harper *Population Biol. Plants* xviii. 547 A single population [of *Papaver dubium*] includes winter annuals and spring annuals. **1884** *Outing* (U.S.) Feb. 400/2 The winter carnival at Montreal, which was so successfully inaugurated last year, will open on February 4. **1973** *Globe & Mail* (Toronto) 13 Jan. 33/1 Most winter carnivals in Ontario rely less heavily on the snowmobile for their fun week-ends. **1894** Winter coat [in Dict., sense 3 a (*b*)]. **1920** [see *bear fur* s.v. *bear *sb.*[1] 9]. **1956** R. Macaulay *Towers of Trebizond* viii. 78 The camel..was very smooth, having just shed its winter coat. **1982** C. Fremlin *Parasite Person* xix. 128 Helen felt the warmth of the sun..through her thick winter coat. **1898** Morris *Austral English* 513/1 *Winter country*, in New Zealand (South Island), land so far unaffected by snow that stock is wintered on it. **1912** A. Wall *Century N.Z.'s Praise* 80 Good winter-country, where sweet grasses grow. **1949** P. Newton *High Country Days* 197 Safe country which is saved for the winter is 'winter country'. **1783** T. Blaikie *Diary of Scotch Gardener* (1931) 179 The winter Garden adjoining to the Hott houses, was more Beautifull than Elegant. **1951** *Dict. Gardening* (R. Hort. Soc.) IV. 2282/2 The Winter Garden is usually of sufficient size to allow the central part of the interior being laid out in walks and large beds. **1977** *Lancs. Life* Nov. 81/1 The Palace incorporated a winter garden from which the stage could be seen without spectators needing to go through into the auditorium. **1817** S. Brown *Western Gaz.* 49 That wheat ..never gets winter-killed or smutty. **1845** *Farmers' Cabinet* 15 Jan. 195/1 This blight is not to be confounded with winter-killing. *Ibid.* 15 Feb. 202/2 It is not so hardy as some varieties: it is more subject to winter-kill. **1846** E. Emmons *Agric. N.Y.* I. 281 The grain very rarely winter-kills. **1849** *Ex. Doc. 31st U.S. Congress 1 Sess. House* No. 5. II. 653 The..snow which lies upon the ground nearly six months in the year would be likely to 'winter-kill' it. **1918** S. S. Visher *Geogr. S. Dakota* 56 Red clover is not a success..largely because it winter-kills. **1945** *Ecol. Monogr.* XV. 343 (*heading*) Limnological conditions in ice-covered lakes, especially as related to winter-kill of fish. **1977** *Chicago Tribune* 2 Oct. XI. 1/4 High nitrogen fertilizer..would only promote late growth that would winterkill. **1980** *Northeast Woods & Waters* Dec. 18/1 Last year's rate of winterkill was lower than usual because of the relatively mild weather conditions. **1894** C. R. A. Wright *Animal & Veg. Oils* xi. 257 Oils that have been thus treated are sometimes termed 'winter oils'. **1920, 1939** Winter oil [see *demargarinated *a.*]. **1970** T. J. Weiss *Food Oils* iii. 59 The solid portion of the oil which had set up in storage tanks in the winter at 40°–42° F..was settled out and removed, leaving an oil which would remain clear when chilled. Cottonseed oils were thus divided into *summer* and *winter* oils. [**1928** *Times* 17 Feb. 6/4 The usual clean crisp snow has given place to an earthy slush, and as a result the second celebration of a Winter Olympiad has come to an abrupt standstill.] **1932** *Times* 1 Feb. 7/4 A thaw which has set in threatens to destroy..the third winter Olympic Games. **1936** *Times* 27 Jan. 5/1 The Lake Placid bob-run..provided some of the most exciting spectacles at the 1932 Winter Olympics. **1956** *Times* 6 Jan. 9/5 In 1948..I won a bronze medal in the Winter Olympic Games. **1981** 'E. Lathen' *Going for Gold* i. 11 It took the Winter Olympics to keep him in the continental United States in February. **1831** E. Smith *Let.* 25 Nov. in *Champlain Soc. Publ.* (1938) XXIV. 79 Our Winter Packet being now preparing to Travell on to your Quarter, I will not let it go without acknowleging the receipt of your friendly epistle. **1971** J. McDougall *Parsons on Plains* xi. 92 We saw the flicker of a campfire. We found that it was the one winter packet from the east on its way to Edmonton. **1801** A. Mackenzie *Voy. from Montreal* vi. 84 One of the natives who followed us, called it the Winter Road River. **1808** H. Gray *Lett. from Canada* (1809) 254 The country people who first form the winter roads on the snow, direct their *Carioles* by the nearest course where the snow is most level; and they go in as straight a line as possible, to the place where they are destined. **1916** *Yukon Territory* 194 In the summer of 1902 the government built a winter road between Dawson and Whitehorse, a distance of approximately 333 miles. **1971** *Country Life* 24 June 1572/1 We had been told to follow a path until it joined a 'winter road' which would in turn lead us to the marsh. **1973** *Kingston* (Ontario) *Whig-Standard* 26 Jan. 7/2 The winter road over the ice is about four lanes wide and is 'brushed' with evergreens at the sides as a guide during swirling snow storms. **1979** A. M. Tizzard *On Sloping Ground* ix. 130 The bay would be frozen over and there was always a good winter road across Twillingate Island. **1942** F. Owen in W. P. & Z. Coates *Soviet–Finnish Campaign* p. i, What about the Finns? In the Winter War they gained a deserved fame for valour and military skill. **1957** *Times Lit. Suppl.* 11 Oct. 603/2 The so-called 'Winter War', resulting from the Soviet attack on Finland in November, 1939, and ending with the Finnish surrender of March, 1940. **1971** W. H. McNeill in A. Bullock *20th Century* 49/2 The Finns' success in holding the Russians at bay for the long weeks of the so-called 'winter war' (1939–40). **1973** J. Fleming *You won't let me Finish* x. 82 The cook came here during the Winter War.

b. winter-crack (see quot. 1898); **winter duck,** (*a*) (later examples); **winter flounder** (earlier example); **winter gnat** = *winter midge* in Dict.; **winter grape** (earlier and later examples); **winter peach,** the fruit of a peach-tree cultivated in a greenhouse and fruiting during autumn or winter; **winter sleeper,** an animal that hibernates; **winter squash** (earlier and later examples); **winter-sweet** (*b*) a shrub, *Chimonanthus præcox*, of the family Calycanthaceæ, native to China and bearing pale yellow fragrant flowers in winter before the leaves appear.

1877 E. Peacock *Gloss. Words Manley & Corringham, Lincs.* 276/2 *Wintercrack*, a small green plum, the fruit of which ripens very late. **1898** *N. & Q.* 13 Aug. 235/2 A fair-sized round, yellowish plum, only fully ripe in November, is known in Derbyshire as the 'winter-crack'. They are called 'cracks' because with the first frosts the fruit cracks on one side, being then fully ripe. **1914** D. H. Lawrence *Prussian Officer* 282 There were some..winter-crack trees. **1885, 1917** Winter duck [see *lady-bird 3]. **1814** S. L. Mitchill *Fishes N.Y.* 387 New-York Flatfish..is called the winter flounder. **1899** D. Sharp in Harmer & Shipley *Cambr. Nat. Hist.* VI. vii. 473 The winter gnats of the genus *Trichocera* are a fair sample of this sub-family. **1926** A. H. Hamm in J. J. Walker *Nat. Hist. Oxf. District* 257 Four species of 'Winter-gnats' are always common from autumn to spring. **1968** *Oxf. Bk. Insects* 122/1 There are ten British Winter Gnats, which belong to the family Trichoceridae and look like small crane-flies. They get their English name from their way of 'dancing' in large swarms on winter afternoons. **1771** G. Washington *Diary* 20 Nov. (1925) II. 43 Began to Plant Cuttings of the Winter Grape. **1789** [see *frost-grape* s.v. *frost *sb.* 7 c]. **1949** *Amer. Photogr.* Apr. 244/2 Winter grape is one of our commonest species from northern New York to Michigan. **1787** J. Woodforde *Diary* 31 Oct. (1926) II. 354 Mr. Custances Garden brought us this Morning a Basket of Winter Peaches. **1960** I. Wallach *Absence of Cello* (1961) 199 Marian wanted a winter peach. **1709** Winter-sleeper [in Dict., sense 3 a (*e*)]. **1911** J. A. Thomson *Biol. Seasons* IV. 333 A survey of the Winter-sleepers seems to show that the life-saving reaction must have arisen by..natural selection. **1775** *Boston Transcript* 26 Apr. III. 12/7, I have a fine prospect of a Crop of..winter Squashes this fall. **1969** *Oxf. Bk. Food Plants* 122/2 Winter squashes are cut in the autumn and can be kept for 3 or 4 months or longer. **1893** W. Robinson *Eng. Flower Garden* (ed. 3) 325/2 Winter Sweet is a lovely shrub which in our country requires a wall. It flowers in December and January; beautiful, and of delicious fragrance. **1934** Ld. Berners *First Childhood* ii. 20 Just outside the windows there grew a shrub of the early-blossoming chimonanthus. (Winter-sweet it was called in the days before gardeners grew so refined.) **1955** [see *chimonanthus]. **1980** *Gardener's Dozen* 12 My winter-sweet.. sometimes gets knocked about by the frost and snow.

winter, *v.* Add: **1.** Also (*Canad.*) with *out*.

1870 in C. Wilson *Campbell of Yukon* (1970) 165, I..had long consultations with most of the Freemen, wintering out in this quarter. **1968** E. Russenholt *Heart of Continent* viii. 132 When November [comes]..the population of Assiniboia is 'at home'—excepting only, those hundreds who elect to 'winter out' on the plains and along the waterways. **1970** R. Symons *Broken Snare* xvi. 112 He [*sc.* a steer] had found a bunch of wild horses...So he had wintered out quite happily with his kind hosts.

2. c. With *over*. = *over-winter *v.* 4. Also *intr.*

1979 C. Kilian *Icequake* iv. 42 How are we supposed to winter over on a goddam iceberg? **1982** 'E. Lathen' *Green grow Dollars* i. 12 A tomato that could be planted, wintered over, then harvested.

winterer. Add: **1. c.** A hibernating animal.

1930 *Observer* 6 Apr. 24/2 Sudden warmth..may awake a winterer too precociously.

Winterhalter (vi·ntəɹhaltəɹ). The name of Franz Xavier *Winterhalter* (1806–73), German portrait painter of royalty, used *attrib.* to designate things characteristic of his pictures, esp. court settings and a style of women's formal dress.

1923 *Daily Mail* 11 Sept. 11/2 The 'period' dress, Winterhalter or Velasquez, is almost entirely restricted to dinner, or formal afternoon, wear. **1937** H. Nicolson *Helen's Tower* vii. 146 How did she cope with the Winterhalter atmosphere of that decaying court? **1944** 'Brahms' & 'Simon' *No Nightingales* xxvii. 155 An..old lady tottering but aristocratic, at grips with a son-in-law too mean to buy a Winterhalter ball-gown for dining *en famille*. **1957** M. B. Picken *Fashion Dict.* 376/2 *Winterhalter*, name applied to costumes characterized by off-shoulder necklines, corseleted waistlines, crinoline skirts with flounces. **1970** R. T. Wilcox *Dict. Costume* 398/2 *Winter-halter*, another term for the crinoline period.

winterim (wi·ntərim), *a.* and *sb.* *U.S.* [Blend of Winter *sb.*[1] and Interim *adv.*, *sb.*, and *adj.*] (Of or pertaining to) a short winter term in some private schools in the U.S., part of which is spent by some pupils on projects away from the school.

1972 *Handbk. Private Schools* (ed. 53) 1079 A four-week 'Winterim' in which juniors and seniors may go off campus and a special program is run for freshmen and sophomores. **1976** *National Observer* (U.S.) 22 May 15/1 (Advt.), Winterim on-and-off campus work/study program—Thorough college preparation. **1979** *N.Y. Times Mag.* 30 Sept. 91/2 (Advt.), Interscholastic and recreational sports—On and off campus Winterim. **1980** L. Birnbach et al. *Official Preppy Handbk.* 52/2 Winterim session spent skiing.

wintering, *vbl. sb.* Add: **II. 5*.** Land where livestock may be wintered.

1937 A. Fraser *Sheep Farming* iv. 46 The ewes can be helped if the hill is cleared as much and as early as possible..by getting the ewe hoggs to their wintering at the earliest possible date. **1978** *Dumfries & Galloway Standard* 21 Oct. 21/3 (Advt.), Wintering wanted for 45 Blackface Ewe Lambs from November till 1st March 1979.

III. 6. *wintering ground* (examples).
1805 Z. M. Pike *Jrnl.* 15 Oct. in *Acct. Expeditions Sources Mississippi* (1810) I. 33 This day's march made me think seriously of our wintering ground. *c* **1890** R. Campbell in C. Wilson *Campbell of Yukon* (1970) xi. 104 Do away with a wintering ground which, from the starvation so frequently experienced there, our men hold in actual dread and abhorrence. **1977** *Monitor* (McAllen, Texas) 9 Jan. B 8/4 The request for Texas biologists to investigate the whitewing wintering grounds came from the International Whitewinged Dove Council.

wi·nterishly, *adv.* [f. Winterish *a.* + -ly[2].] In a manner suggestive of winter.
1905 *Smart Set* Oct. 26/1 Though by good rights the day might have been winterishly cold it was of a balmy mildness.

winterize (wi·ntəraiz), *v.* orig. and chiefly *U.S.* [f. Winter *sb.*[1] + -ize.] *trans.* To adapt or prepare (something) for operation or use in cold weather.
1938 *Amer. Speech* XIII. 160/1 A radio announcer... urged his listeners to have their cars winterized. **1949** A. Hayes *Girl on Flaminia* iv. 90 She sat on the hard canvas cushion of the jeep, and she must have felt exposed. The jeep had not been winterized. **1950** *Jane's Fighting Ships 1950–1* 454 *Arneb* has been refitted for Arctic Service... Other vessels are also to be 'winterized'. **1954** E. W. Eckey *Veg. Fats & Oils* iii. 124 The temperature below which no portion of the oil should be chilled is a little above the cloud point of the oil to be winterized. **1964** S. Bellow *Herzog* 96 This is a fine house you have... Summer only, isn't it? You could winterize it easily. **1973** B. Wright *Four Seasons North* 42 Sam winterized the rifles, wiping away all the lubrication, which would freeze if left in the guns. **1980** L. Auchincloss *House of Prophet* vii. 101 We agreed to take over my parents' summer house in Seal Cove and winterize it.
Hence **wi·nterized** *ppl. a.*, **wi·nterizing** *vbl. sb.*; **winteriza·tion.**
1926 *Jrnl. Oil & Fat Industries* III. 421/1 Some of the cottonseed stearine made by the winterizing process and the hydrogenated oil are used in margarine. **1927** *Oil & Fat Industries* IV. 301/2 Depending upon the length of time winterized oil will stand clear, brilliant and limpid when exposed to the so-called Winter Oil Test, an oil is more or less suitable for..salad oil and mayonnaise manufacturers. **1940** *PM* 29 Nov. 14/3 Instead of having an entire company of trainees, even one 'winterized tent' of trainees, all together,..there will be throughout the 44th Division scads of veterans surrounding each new man. **1940** *Capital* (Topeka) 8 Dec. 2A (Advt.), Buy any car... Plus complete winterization. **1943** *Oil & Soap* July 131/2 The present slow and inefficient winterization process for cottonseed oil. **1955** Smalley & Klohr in F. S. Mallette *Probl. & Control of Air Pollution* xvii. 199 *(caption)* Winterized sulfur recovery plant. **1957** *Encycl. Brit.* VI. 584/2 Winterization is a process by which a portion of the refined and bleached oil is solidified by chilling and filtered off. **1966** *Economist* 22 Jan. 341/3 Builders..are showing considerable interest in 'winterisation'... Over a third now have some degree of lighting on site. **1970** *Toronto Daily Star* 24 Sept. 39/7 (Advt.), Winterized jackets have the accent on fashion with bright colours. **1971** C. Bonington *Annapurna South Face* 286 All the cameras functioned well, and although only the Nikons were winterized, there was no trouble from freezing up. **1978** *N.Y. Times* 30 Mar. B15/2 (Advt.), Two 5 rm winterized cottages. **1979** *Farmington* (New Mexico) *Daily Times* 27 May 6c/3 (Advt.), Experiments on winterizing and solar energy retrofits.

winter quarters. Add: **1.** Also, such a place occupied by any travelling company or by private individuals. (Further examples.)
1714 W. Vickers *Let.* 21 Sept. in M. M. Verney *Verney Lett.* (1930) II. xxi. 16 Miss Pen comes to our winter quarters in the middle of next week. **1897** A. Beardsley *Let.* 29 July (1970) 353 At the end of this week I shall move to Paris, and then into winter quarters as soon as possible. **1939** *Florida* (Federal Writers' Project) III. 395 Bailey circus winter quarters.

winters (wi·ntəɹz), *adv. U.S.* [Pl. of Winter *sb.*[1]] During the winter.
1907 'Mark Twain' *Christian Sci.* II. 235 It can appoint its own furnace-stoker, winters. **1978** *Chicago* June 158/1 Winters, William is the tennis director at the Genesee Valley Tennis Club in Flint.

wi·ntersome, *a. rare*[−1]. [f. Winter *sb.*[1] + -some[1].] = Wintry *a.*
1864 Trollope *Small Ho. Allington* II. xv. 148 The fourteenth of February in London was quite as black, and cold, and as wintersome as it was at Allington.

winter sport. a. A sport enjoyed in the winter; *spec.* an outdoor sport on snow or ice, such as skiing or skating. Usu. *pl.*
1828 *Ladies' Mag.* Mar. 141 (*heading*) Children at their winter sports. **1847** C. M. Yonge *Scenes & Characters* xiii. 163 Intent upon the various winter sports in which William and Lord Rotherwood allowed him to share [at an English country house]. **1879** H. Chadwick (*title*) Handbook of winter sports. Embracing: skating (on ice and on rollers,) rink-ball, curling, ice-boating, and American football. **1906** *Dress* Dec. 18/1 Tobogganing, another favorite winter sport introduced from Canada, has many devotees. **1934** F. Scott Fitzgerald *Tender is Night* I. iii. 17 Vivid advertising cards of the railroad companies..winter sports at Chamonix. **1956** A. H. Compton *Atomic Quest* 213 Winter sports, especially skiing, were popular. **1975** *Oxf. Compan. Sports* 950/2 Skibobbing is a new winter sport, combining the virtues of the ski, the bobsleigh, and the velocipede in a downhill run.

b. *attrib.* (in *sing.* and *pl.*).
1908 E. & M. Syers *Bk. Winter Sports* 323 Some notes on winter-sport resorts. **1922** *Cook's Continental Timetable* Jan. 377 (Advt.), Central position. Close to all Winter Sports places. **1950** E. Hemingway *Across River* xxxiii. 207 It would be just like any winter-sports hotel. **1966** N. Freeling *King of Rainy Country* 38 She had gone..on a wintersport holiday. **1975** *Country Life* 30 Oct. 1192/2 A really beautiful collection of winter sports clothes.
Hence **winter-sport** *v. intr.*, to engage in winter sports; **winter-sporting** *vbl. sb.*
1948 M. Laski *Tory Heaven* ix. 128 I'd like to go winter-sporting in January. **1955** T. H. Pear *Eng. Social Differences* xi. 265 Few who 'winter-sport'..feel that their social rating is thereby raised. **1961** *Times* 13 May 11/2 The famous winter-sporting centres. **1974** *Guardian* 23 Mar. 14/2 If you've fished in Scotland, if you've winter sported in Switzerland, you can do it all in Sweden.

wipe, *sb.* Add: **1. c.** *Cinemat.* and *Television.* An effect in which an existing picture seems to be wiped out by a new one as the boundary between them moves across the screen (the pictures themselves remaining stationary). orig. *wipe-dissolve.*
1933 *Cinema Q.* II. I. 43, I..deplored the constant use of wipe-dissolves to cover the weak continuity. **1934** C. Lambert *Music Ho!* IV. 263 There is no real equivalent in music even of the 'wipe-dissolve' which leads the eye gently but quickly from one scene to another. **1936** A. Brunel *Film Production* 43 It may be argued that wipes are not easily achieved. **1960** *Guardian* 8 June 7/3 A special effects generator..enables 20,000 different shades of 'wipe' to be deployed... It makes a fascinating variety of shapes and devices upon the screen. **1979** *Broadcast* 1 Oct. 54/2 Within the SqueeZoomed sequence of archive TV shots..Tony Rayner inserted two wipes to blue..which allow live 'headline' shots from that day's programme to be chromakeyed in.

2. a. *a wipe in the eye*: a disappointment or rebuff; = *smack in the eye* s.v. *smack *sb.*[2] 3 a. Cf. Wipe *v.* 9 d in Dict. and Suppl.
[**1644**: in Dict.] **1926** T. E. Lawrence *Let.* 6 Apr. (1938) 495 Your statement that the hospital passage would be a wipe in the eye for 19 readers out of 20 puts it out of court. **1949** D. M. Davin *Roads from Home* III. iii. 236 It was a wipe in the eye for John the way he was getting out.

4. a. (Earlier example.)
1708 *Memoirs of John Hall* 23 *Wipe*, a Handkerchief.
b. A disposable piece of soft absorbent cloth or tissue, sometimes impregnated with a cleansing agent, for wiping clean one's hands or anything small.
1971 *Textile Industries* Dec. 50/1 Towels, Covers, Pads, and Wipes. **1974** Hawkey & Bingham *Wild Card* ix. 87 Half-empty boxes of medical wipes lying on the ultra-centrifuge. **1978** 'M. Yorke' *Point of Murder* ii. 19 Kate's hands had got oily..but she kept some tissue wipes in the car. **1980** *Chem. in Brit.* XVI. 449/4 For situations where protective gloves are inconvenient, Chicopee has brought out Dermawipe impregnated hand wipes.

wipe, *v.* Add: **1. c.** *absol.* = *dry *v.* 1 c. Also with *up*. Cf. *wash *v.* 1 i.
1943, 1962 [see *wash *v.* 1 i]. **1968** R. V. Beste *Repeat the Instructions* ii. 19 He wiped while Huskion..scrubbed away in the sink. **1974** M. Birmingham *You can help Me* vii. 169, I was helping Mrs Hope wipe up in the kitchen. **1981** A. Wilson in T. Thompson *Edwardian Childhoods* iii. 78 One'd wipe and one'd wash—we didn't make hard work of it.

d. To demagnetize (a ship) by passing a horizontal current-carrying cable up and down the hull; also, to remove a recording from (magnetic tape).
1946 'L. Luard' *Changing Horizons* 145 'No complaints, except she's steel.' 'And not wiped or degaussed,' the Skipper commented. **1947** Crowther & Whiddington *Science at War* 171 He arranged that ships should be 'wiped' with temporary horizontal coils. **1962** R. W. Clark *Rise of Boffins* iv. 95 Demagnetizing the ships..by 'wiping' the sides..with a horizontal cable carrying a strong current. **1962** E. Salter *Voice of Peacock* xx. 203 In the case of auditions, the tape was sometimes wiped so's it could be used again. **1965** D. Francis *Odds Against* x. 137, I wiped the tape clean. **1980** *Listener* 8 May 594/2, I presume the BBC wiped, as they say, the original tape.

2. d. To erase (a magnetic recording, or data stored on a magnetic medium). Freq. with *off, out.*
1900 *Engin. Mag.* XIX. 758/1 When it is desired to wipe out a record, the electromagnet..is attached to a constant battery and run over the wire, thus magnetising it uniformly once more and preparing it to receive a new message. **1934** *Wireless World* 5 Jan. 8/3 When a record is no longer required, the programme recorded on the strip can be 'wiped out'. **1976** *Broadcast* 23 Aug. 10/3 He was staggered at the quantity of programmes in which James MacTaggart had been involved. Most of it has been wiped. **1981** *Times* 4 July 10/3 This is a three-hour reusable tape with an hour's quite sophisticated cabaret already recorded, which you can keep or wipe off. **1984** *Computerworld* 26 Mar. 14/2 If one formats an IBM Personal Computer XT and does not indicate which drive to format, the machine formats the hard disk and wipes out all data on it.

e. (Without *prep.*) To dismiss, reject, repudiate (esp. a person). *Austral.* and *N.Z. slang.*
1941 K. Tennant *Battlers* 196 Giving her money..in the casual manner that wiped her from all consideration as a human being. **1946** *Coast to Coast 1945* 123 Listen pal—your girl wiped you, didn't she? **1948** *Landfall* June 111 Hands in pockets, shoulders hunched, he strode bitterly up the street from the pub. He'd wipe them, have nothing to do with the morons. **1954** T. A. G. Hungerford *Sowers of Wind* 162 She dumped me, wiped me like a dirty nose. **1967** F. Sargeson *Hangover* xiv. 124 If it came to that one of his reasons for wiping university was a senior lecturer who had failed to avoid the same gross error. **1975** R. Beilby *Brown Land Crying* 295 You can wipe that idea, if that's what you're thinking.

6. e. Also, to kill (a person); also with *out. slang.*
1968 J. Philips *Hot Summer Killing* III. i. 129 Is he the one who was wiped earlier tonight in the Molyneaux Hotel? **1969** C. Burke *God is Beautiful, Man* (1970) 47 They decided to find a way to get rid of him, to wipe him out. **1977** *Time* 12 Sept. 40/2 You could be wiped out if you moved a single inch. **1980** J. McClure *Blood of Englishman* ii. 18 Someone tried to wipe Bradshaw... The shot caught him here in the collar-bone.

h. *to wipe* (an expression, esp. a smile) *off a person's* or *one's face*: (to cause him) to cease showing it. *slang.*
[**1567**: cf. sense 6 d in Dict.] **1895** Conrad *Almayer's Folly* xii. 256 A face from which all feelings and all expression are suddenly wiped off by the hand of unexpected death. [**1898**: cf. sense 6 c in Dict.] **1935** *Time* 24 June 28/1 Wipe dat smile offen his face! **1936** D. Carnegie *How to win Friends & influence People* II. ii. 99 Bill, you are going to wipe the scowl off that sour puss of yours today. **1972** D. S. Viscott *Making of Psychiatrist* ii. 37 Terry O'Conner seemed to think it was funny but wiped the smile off her face every time her eye caught Larry's. **1977** *Observer* 14 Aug. 3/7 Only one sentence would have wiped the smile off Mason's face. **1978** G. Greene *Human Factor* VI. i. 305 She realised she was smiling at the telephone—thank God, they hadn't yet invented a visual telephone, but all the same she wiped the smile off her face.

i. *pass.* or *intr. Surfing.* To be knocked from one's surfboard. With *out. slang.*
1962 T. Masters *Surfing made Easy* 66 *Wiped out*, getting knocked off of a surfboard, usually by a wave. **1965** [see *locked *ppl. a.* g]. **1966** *Weekly News* (N.Z.) 19 Jan. 6/3 When 'wiping-out' a surfer should try to hold his board. **1968** *Surfer Mag.* Jan. 48/2 Frye misjudged one of his turns high in the curl and wiped-out in the white water.

8*. *Cinemat.* and *Television.* To pass from or *from* one scene to another by means of a wipe; to employ a wipe.
1951 Halas & Privett *How to cartoon for Amateur Films* 118 We now wish to wipe from one scene to another. **1952** *Cinema* 7 Jan. 97/1 [The Director] can cut, fade, wipe or mix at will.

9. d. (Later examples.)
1928 D. L. Sayers *Unpleasantness at Bellona Club* xiv. 168 'I'm glad somebody appreciates me. Anyhow,' he added viciously, 'I bet that's wiped old Pritchard's eye.' **1929** F. M. Ford *Let.* 11 Sept. (1965) 187 He had only got me away from Duckworth in order to wipe Gerald's eye. **1949** N. Mitford *Love in Cold Climate* I. vi. 60 At teatime the village policeman reappeared.., having wiped the eye of all the grand detectives who had come from London in their shiny cars. He produced a perfect jumble-sale heap of objects which had been discarded by the burglars. **1956** 'A. Gilbert' *And Death came Too* xiv. 146 Eventually he agreed to take the case (his heel of Achilles being an inability to pass up a chance of wiping the official eye).

e. *to wipe the floor with*: (earlier examples); also *to wipe up the floor* or *ground with.*
1887 *Courier-Jrnl.* (Louisville, Kentucky) 4 Jan. 2/6 Two brothers wipe up the floor with a Missouri newspaper man. **1888** in Farmer & Henley *Slang* (1903) VII. 359 The Scroggin boy was as tough as a dog-wood knot. He'd wipe up the ground with him; he'd walk all over him. **1896** *Dialect Notes* I. 427 *Wipe the floor with*, to defeat. **1897** *Nat. Police Gaz.* 26 May 7/4 Green fairly wiped the floor with Roberts in the first two rounds. **1908** *Magnet* I. I. 3/1 I've wiped up the ground with bigger fellows than you, for far less cheek than you've given me.

10. The vb.-stem in combination, as **wipe-clean** *attrib.* or as *adj.*, designating fabrics or furnishings that may be cleaned simply by wiping.
1962 *N.Y. Times Mag.* 9 Sept. 102 In new wipe-clean Boltaflex Vinyl Suede. **1965** *Economist* 13 Feb. 700/2 The [synthetic] shoes, although theoretically 'wipe-clean', tend to look grubby when unpolished. **1970** *Vogue* Jan. 25/1 Lovely cookers with plain glass tops—put the pan down..and you are on the hob, yet this is a wipe-clean glass surface. **1977** *Austral. House & Garden* Jan. 114 (Advt.), Interiors are wipe clean, white melamine laminate, edged in white P.V.C. **1983** *Which?* Dec. (Publications Suppl.), Both binders are hardwearing and have wipe-clean covers.

wi·peable, *a.* Also **wipable.** [f. Wipe *v.* + -able.] Capable of being wiped.
1926 *Pocket Oxf. Dict.* s.v. *Wipe*, Wipable. **1979** *Personal Computer World* July 23/2 The single unit..has a wipeable light brown plastic housing with a robust typewriter style keyboard and separate numerical keypad. **1981** *Washington Post* 26 Aug. B5/2 For the latest in lunch carriers this fall, go with this wipeable tote decorated with elephants, sailboats or pigs. **1982** *Times* 20 Feb. 11/5 The tape..will be wipeable, leaving a tape..pristine for one's own recording.

wipe-out (wəi·paut). [f. vbl. phr. *to wipe out*: see Wipe *v.* 6.] **1.** *Radio.* The condition in which a strong received signal renders impossible the reception of other signals (either wanted ones or interference).

1921 *Wireless World* IX. 13/1 With radiotelephony the case is worse, as the wipe out is continuous if it occurs at all. **1929** *Encycl. Brit.* IV. 218/2 Within a 'wipe-out' area uninterrupted service can be guaranteed, unless the interference is produced by listeners themselves. **1940** *Amateur Radio Handbk.* (ed. 2) x. 160/1 There are three types of interference that may be caused in neighbouring receivers working on broadcast waves, by an amateur telegraphy transmitter. First, the 'wipe-out' effect, where the signal from the transmitter 'blocks' the receiver due to either the excessive field strength of the transmitter, or the inselectivity of the receiver, or both.

2. *Surfing.* A fall from one's surfboard as a result of a collision with another surfer or a wave. Cf. *WIPE *v.* 6 i. *slang.*

1962 *Austral. Women's Weekly* 24 Oct. Suppl. 3/4 *Wipeout*, a dramatic fall off a board when a rider is trying to catch a wave. **1963** [see *SURFIE]. **1969** *Observer* 3 Aug. 33/1 The biggest danger always lies in a 'wipe-out', with a loose board which may hit the rider or other surfers. **1970** *People* (Austral.) 26 Aug. 20/1 One bad wipeout—at Sunset Beach, Hawaii—earned him broken ribs.

3. Destruction, annihilation; a killing; a crushing defeat; an overwhelming experience. *slang* (orig. *U.S.*).

1968 *Sun* (Baltimore) 7 July 5/2 Charlie is 1810. We had a wipeout... *Translation.* Girl: Charlie is old news. We broke up. **1971** J. HENDERSON *Copperhead* vi. 71 Less than thirty-six hours to incapacitate 85 percent of the population. The remaining 15 percent would take a little more than a week. Strategically it would be a wipe-out. **1972** *Jazz & Blues* Sept. 8/1 When I heard Art it was a wipeout. He just wiped me out man. **1977** *Daily Mirror* 12 Apr. 27/7 A record 140,000 [motor-cycling] fans have watched the embarrassing wipe-out by 410 points to 379. **1979** L. MEYER *False Front* iii. 24 This is something like the wipeout of a personal fortune. **1984** 'M. HEBDEN' *Pel & Pirates* xviii. 143 Think it was a gang wipe-out, Patron?

wiper. Add: **2. b.** (Earlier examples.)

1826 *Price List* in *Austin Papers* (1924) 1369 To wiper claw for rifle . .50. **1827** J. KERR *Let.* 27 Feb. in *Ibid.* 1607 Thimble rod and socket end of wipers lost... 50.

c. = *windscreen wiper* s.v. *WIND *sb.* 31. Also *attrib.*, as *wiper blade, switch.*

1929 *Times* 2 Nov. 4/7 The driver has an all-enclosed cab, with..a sloped adjustable screen, with a wiper, in front. **1942** W. FAULKNER *Go down, Moses* 337 It was the youngest face of them all,..staring sombrely through the streaming windshield across which the twin wipers flicked and flicked. **1953** L. DURRELL *Balthazar* iv. 67 The windscreen became gradually snowed-up and he switched on the wipers to keep it clear. **1959** *Times* 25 Sept. 8/2 Wiper blades dry the screen and then park automatically. **1970** *Motoring Which?* July 93/1 On the 1800s and 1800Ss the lights or wiper switches collapsed in about one in four cars. **1976** H. KEMELMAN *Wednesday the Rabbi got Wet* xiii. 80 It was coming down so fast that my wipers couldn't handle it.

6. A pivoted arm that automatically rotates through an arc to make electrical contact with any of a curved row of terminals in a telephone exchange; also, the rotary or sliding contact of a potentiometer.

1906 J. POOLE *Pract. Telephone Handbk.* (ed. 3) xxx. 483 Opposite the lower part of each 'bank' a short arm is fitted, on the ends of which are 2 springs, which, when the rod is rotated, sweep over and under the strips of contacts, and are, therefore, called 'wipers'... The circular ratchet teeth..enable the vertical rod with the wipers to be raised. **1926** [see *BANK *sb.*³ 10 b]. **1969** [see *slide-wire* s.v. *SLIDE- a]. **1975** C. D. TODD *Potentiometer Handbk.* vii. 166/2 Many different variations of the mechanical means which moves the wiper across the resistive element are possible. **1976** T. H. FLOWERS *Introd. Exchange Systems* iii. 82 In the L. M. Ericsson five-hundred-line switch, a stick carrying a set of wipers is rotated..to point in one of twenty-five angular directions,..then the stick is slid linearly outwards for the wipers to engage with one of twenty sets of fixed contacts.

7. *Comb.*: **wiper arm** = sense 6 above.

1933 K. B. MILLER *Telephone Theory & Practice* i. 2 The subscriber,..by sending the proper number of impulses over one of his line wires, could cause the wiper arm of his switch to step *up* to the row containing the contact of the line desired and then..to step *around* to engage the particular one. **1967** D. EADIE *Introd. Basic Computer* xv. 348 A full-fledged analog multiplier..can be constructed if we take the pot just described and drive the wiper arm with a servomotor.

wiping, *vbl. sb.* Add: **3. wiping head,** a head (*HEAD *sb.* 11 g) for removing any recording from a magnetic tape or wire; an erase head.

1938 *Jrnl. Inst. Electr. Engineers* LXXXII. 266/2 The wiping head carries a direct current adequate to saturate the tape completely, so that it leaves the head fully magnetized. **1950** [see *record button* s.v. *RECORD *v.* 12 a].

wirble, *sb.* (Later example.)

1932 J. JOYCE *Let.* 1 Aug. (1966) III. 251 But what about me in my present wirbel of worries.

wire, *sb.* Add: **II. 2. d.** *U.S.* A wire stretched across and above the track at the start and finish of a racecourse. Freq. in phrases: *down to the wire*, up to, or all the way to, the finishing-line; freq. *transf.* and *fig.*; (*from*) *wire to wire*, from start to finish of a race; also *transf.* and *attrib.*; *under the wire*, at the finishing-line; *fig.*, (to fall) within the limits or scope of something.

1887 *Courier-Journal* (Louisville, Ky.) 5 May 1/1 Eva K., Little Munch..were first under the wire. **1901** 'H. MCHUGH' *Down the Line* 93 Swift often told himself that he could give Marshall P. Wilder six sure-fires and beat him down to the wire. **1920** C. SANDBURG *Smoke & Steel* 138 He flashed his heels to other ponies..and hardly ever came under the wire behind the other runners. **1929** M. C. WORK *Compl. Contract Bridge* v. 75 There are some hands which may just 'get under the wire' of the above definitions. **1950** *Keowee Courier* (Walhalla, S.C.) 31 Aug. 2/2 Baseball season is coming down to the wire, and the leading teams are about as close as two Scotchmen on bargain day. **1974** *State* (Columbia, S. C.) 15 Feb. 4-B/5 Nicklaus..led from wire to wire in the Hawaiian Open [Golf Tournament]. **1975** *New Yorker* 10 Nov. 137/2 Bertram Firestone's Honest Pleasure wound up his racing for the year with a wire-to-wire victory in the Laurel Futurity last weekend. **1982** 'E. LATHEN' *Green grow Dollars* xviii. 151 We're going to force Vandam's into court as fast as we can. I think we'll just make it under the wire. **1984** *Miami Herald* 6 Apr. 22A/1 Odds remain good that the Democrats' race will go down to the wire.

† **e.** *the straight wire*: the honest truth; also used without article as a phrase emphasizing the truth of an assertion. *Austral. slang. Obs.*

1892 'J. MILLER' *Workingman's Paradise* 203 When it's all over you'll remember what I say and know it's the straight wire. **1909** A. WRIGHT *Rogue's Luck* 70 'Now, no kid, Harry,' said Ned anxiously. 'Straight wire, did you beat him?' **1936** M. FRANKLIN *All that Swagger* xlii. 394 'Will you?' said Humphrey... 'Straight wire, I will.'

f. *to pull one's wire*: see *PULL *v.* 19 j.

3. a. *live wire* (fig.): see *LIVE *a.* 8.

b. (Earlier example.) *crossed wires*: see *CROSS *v.* 5 c.

1846 *Punch* 5 Dec. 238/2 If this plan of Electric Telegraphs for the million should be carried out, the Post Office..might be turned into a central terminus for all the wires.

d. The telephone system; an individual telephone connection. Freq. in phrases *over the wire* (or † *wires*), *on the wire.*

Now somewhat old-fashioned.

1902 *Chambers's Jrnl.* Feb. 128/2 A Parisian dentist had discovered a process of 'seeing by wire', which.. means that he can while speaking through the telephone *see* his correspondent at the other end of the line of communication. **1925** H. CRANE *Let.* 4 June (1965) 207, I did enjoy that talk with you over the wires to Cleveland! Your voice is so much better than ink and paper. **1925** F. SCOTT FITZGERALD *Great Gatsby* viii. 186, I tried [Gatsby's house] four times; finally an exasperated central told me the wire was being kept open for long distance from Detroit. **1929** 'E. QUEEN' *Roman Hat Mystery* xiv. 211 I'll get the newspaper boys on the wire and ask them to ballyhoo the opening. **1932** [see *NUMBER *sb.* 4 f]. **1935** W. CATHER *Lucy Gayheart* I. vii. 51 Every day his concert agent ..called him up as soon as his wire was open. **1947** S. BELLOW *Victim* xxiii. 280 He ought to have spoken to Nunez about the broken chain while he was on the wire. **1974** WODEHOUSE *Aunts aren't Gentlemen* iii. 24 And now for heaven's sake get off the wire, I'm busy.

e. A private warning or message. Chiefly in phr. *to give the wire. slang.*

1925 FRASER & GIBBONS *Soldier & Sailor Words* 307 *Wire, to give the*, to give a secret warning. **1930** E. H. LAVINE *Third Degree* xvi. 210 The real thieves get 'a wire', and play poker. **1936** J. CURTIS *Gilt Kid* vi. 60 He'd been straight with her and had given her the wire right in the beginning. **1972** R. BUSBY *Reasonable Man* xviii. 161 He gave me the wire that there was a big one coming off.

8. (Earlier example of *to pull the wires.*)

1813 *Deb. & Proc. Congr. U.S.* 5 Jan. (1853) 12th Congr. 2nd Sess. 562 When those who pulled the wires saw fit, they passed away.

IV. 14. b. Also, a wire-haired dachshund.

1938 *Times* 1 Jan. 1/6 (Advt.), Beautiful Corgis,.. Wires, Dachshunds, [etc.]. **1975** *Country Life* 6 Feb. (Advt. Suppl.) 27/1 Puppies for sale..Long Haired Wires.

V. 15. a. *wire basket, mesh* (also *attrib.*), *netting* (earlier example), *trolley.* **b.** *wire-framed, -rimmed.* **c.** *wire-clipper, -milker* (see MILK *v.* 4 d), *-nippers*; *wire-like* (later example).

1845 E. ACTON *Mod. Cookery* vii. 196 A wire basket..is convenient for frying parsley and other herbs. **1961** J. STROUD *Touch & Go* vii. 69 The people..carry the same wire baskets round the same Supermarket. **1964** D. FRANCIS *Nerve* ii. 16 There were a few letters..in the wire basket on the inner side of the door. **1977** C. MCCULLOUGH *Thorn Birds* ii. 31 A piece of boned fish.. fried in the smoking well of liquid fat along with the chips, only in a separate wire basket. **1916** H. L. WILSON *Somewhere in Red Gap* iii. 109 That fresh bunch of campers had a pair of wire clippers in the whip socket. **1971** S. HILL *Strange Meeting* i. 28 The sound of the man sleeping above him in the wire-framed bunk. **1979** B. MALAMUD *Dubin's Lives* i. 6 She wore wire-framed blue-tinted glasses. **1952** E. POUND *Personae* 180 The wire-like bands of colour involute mount from my fingers. **1932** J. DOS PASSOS *1919* 271 There were knots of police in blue standing about..outside and inside the wiremesh gates huskylooking young men in khaki. **1944** *Living off Land* v. 109 Tanks..are best dealt with by screening all openings with a protective wire mesh. **1974** T. HUGHES in *Listener* 4 Apr. 438/2 The sheep..in her wire-mesh compound. **1899** C. HYNE *Further Adv. Capt. Kettle* vi. 131 The wire-milkers. **1801** in *Deb. & Proc. Congr. U.S.* 21 Dec. (1851) 7th Congr. 2nd Sess. 1292 The books shall be..set up in portable cases ..with wire-netting doors and locks. **1914** B. M. BOWER *Flying U Ranch* 168 Want me to go back and get the wire nippers? **1974** A. LURIE *War between Tates* (1977) ix. 185 Slouched down on the sofa.. is a skinny adolescent boy with thick wire-rimmed spectacles. **1976** *Southern Even. Echo* (Southampton) 17 Nov. 13/3 She had separated the meat and cold goods into a bag to stop them contaminating sugar in the wire trolley.

16. wire act, an acrobatic act performed on a tightrope; **wire bed,** (*a*) a bed fitted with a wire spring base or mattress; (*b*) in paper-making, a moving bed of wire over which the pulp is passed, its fibres at this stage beginning to form a web; **wire birch** *Canad.*, a small birch, *Betula populifolia*, which has light-coloured bark and is found in eastern North America; **wire brush,** (*a*) *Jazz* = *BRUSH *sb.*² 1 b; (*b*) a brush with stiff wire bristles used in cleaning, esp. for removing rust; hence **wire-brush** *v. trans.*, to clean with a wire brush; so **wire-brushed** *ppl. a.*, **-brushing** *vbl. sb.*; **wire-cartridge** (earlier example); **wire-cutter,** (*a*) (earlier example of term applied to a person); **wire-dancing** (earlier example); **wire edge** (earlier example); **wire-frame** *a.*, (*a*) applied to a picture (usu. computer-generated) in which every edge of an object is depicted, regardless of its visibility on the object itself, and nothing else; also *ellipt.*; (*b*) (of spectacles) having a frame made of wire; **wire ground** (earlier example); **wire-guided** *ppl. a.*, directed (in quot. 1922, carried out) by means of electric signals transmitted along a wire; *spec.* applied to a missile connected to a control point by a wire; **wire house** *U.S.*, a brokerage firm having branch offices connected to its main office by private telephone and telegraph wires; **wire recorder,** an apparatus for magnetically recording sounds, etc., on wire and afterwards reproducing them; so **wire recording,** a recording so made, or the process of making one; **wire-rim** *a.* = *wire-frame* adj. (*b*) above; also *ellipt.*; **wire service** *U.S.*, a news agency that supplies syndicated news by wire to its subscribers; **wire-stitcher,** an automatic stapling machine which takes continuous wire and forms the staples as an integral part of the stapling operation; so **wire-stitching** (also *attrib.*); hence (as back-formations) **wire-stitch** *v. trans.*, **wire-stitched** *ppl. a.*; **wire story** *Journalism*, a story distributed by a wire service; **wire-strainer** *Austral.* and *N.Z.* = *wire-stretcher* below; **wire-stretcher** chiefly *N. Amer.*, a tool for making taut the wire of a fence or the like; **wire-walking** (examples); **wireway,** a channel or duct for enclosing lengths of wiring, esp. one made of sheet metal; ducting of this nature; **wire wheel,** a car wheel having wire spokes (used esp. on sports models); **wire wool,** matted thin wire, used esp. for scouring kitchen utensils; **wire-wound** *a.* (further examples in *Electr.*).

1906 *Variety* 13 Jan. 7/2 The Roses..have a wire act with some good tricks. **1912** C. MACKENZIE *Carnival* xi. 136 They did not object to interminable wire-acts, and put up with divination feats of the most exhausting dullness. **1976** *National Observer* (U.S.) 24 Jan. 18/5 You always knew a wire act would open the show. **1882** W. WHITMAN *Daybks. & Notebks.* (1978) II. 296 Wire beds—829 110. 10th st. **1918** W. OWEN *Let.* 31 Oct. (1967) 591 Other officers repose on wire beds behind me. **1962** F. T. DAY *Introd. Paper* iv. 38 The wire bed is kept perfectly level while it oscillates to bring about the interlacing of fibres in the pulp. **1917** B. R. MORTON *Native Trees of Canada* 68 *Betula Populifolia*..White birch, grey birch, wire birch. **1956** [see *Indian pear* s.v. *INDIAN *a.* 4 b]. **1974** J. DOWELL *Look-Off Bear* p. viii, Beyond our grove of pines there were mixed growths of wire-birch, swamp willow, [etc.]. **1927** *Melody Maker* Apr. 389/1 In quiet passages, the wire brush on a Chinese cymbal gives a very pleasing effect. *a* **1935** T. E. LAWRENCE *Mint* (1955) I. xxii. 76 Our job was to wire-brush and repaint a lot of salvaged sheeting... A good job, it looked. Six of us and six wire brushes. **1957** MANVELL & HUNTLEY *Film Music* iii. 98 Wire-brush percussion. **1974** A. ROSS *Bradford Business* 76 Even the short heavy bolts had been rubbed up with a wire brush. **1978** J. WAINWRIGHT *Thief of Time* 210, I should ..check the trays of seed potatoes... Wire-brush the seed-trays. **1955** *Archit. Rev.* CXVII. 68 Construction: reinforced concrete frame with mainly brick walls, but certain panels of wire-brushed concrete. **1978** *Country Life* 28 Dec. 2212/1 The furniture in wire-brushed carved oak. **1980** *Yachts & Yachting* 29 Feb. 672/2 Lead is perhaps the easiest needing only one coat of undercoat and one of Metallic Primocon between wirebrushing (or rubbing down) and the new antifoul. **1978** E. GUNDREY *Simple Plumbing* 22 Rust removal involves wire-brushing. **1839** W. WATT (*title*) Remarks on shooting, in verse, comprehending..the recent and admirable invention of the patent wire cartridge. **1888** in W. P. Webb *Great Plains* (1931) 314 While a man was putting up his fence one day in a hollow a crowd of wire-cutters was cutting it behind him in another hollow. **1785** *Daily Universal Reg.* 1 Jan. 4/1 Must he [*sc.* an editor]...have writers of tumbling—wire dancing—and hurly burly description? 1807 H. H. BRACKENRIDGE *Mod. Chivalry* II. iv. 21 In the course of mixing with good company, the wire edge of art would wear off, and an ease of demeanor be attained. 1963 *AFIPS Conf. Proc.* XXIII. 348 A prototype graphical communications system capable of manipulating straight line, 'wire frame', figures in three-dimensional space is now in operation. 1977 E. LEONARD *Unknown Man No. 89* ii. 13 His tinted wire-frame glasses glistened. 1982 BALLARD & BROWN *Computer Vision* ix. 292 A set of vertices or edges can define many different solids. (It is possible, however, to determine algorithmically all possible polyhedral boundaries described by a three-dimensional wireframe.) 1982 J. E. SCOTT *Introd. Interactive Computer Graphics* viii. 135 A wire-frame drawing is less pleasing visually, but it is considerably faster for the computer to produce. 1983 *New Scientist* 24 Mar. 819/1 The more detail in a wire frame, the harder it is to understand. 1983 L. DEIGHTON *Berlin Game* viii. 83 Bret put his wire-frame glasses into their case. 1865 F. B. PALLISER *Hist. Lace* iii. 27 The honeycomb network or ground..is of various kinds; wire ground, Brussels ground, [etc.]. 1922 *Encycl. Brit.* XXXII. 1022/1 Wire-guided high frequency telegraphy and telephony. 1958 C. C. ADAMS *Space Flight* 52 The latter two [rockets].. are wire-guided. 1972 [see TOW s.v. *T 6 a]. 1982 *Sci. Amer.* May 103 (Advt.), The wire enables the Hughes TOW to have one of the highest velocities and longest ranges (2·3 miles) of any wire-guided missile in the world. 1982 *Daily Tel.* 10 May 4/3 Two wire-guided torpedoes of the Tigerfish type. 1904 *N.Y. Evening Post* 18 June (Financial Sect.) 1/7 The so-called 'wire house'..is a product of the boom times. 1966 *Economist* 25 June 1436/1 It [*sc.* the New York Stock Exchange] has been firing salvos..about possibly setting up an auxiliary trading floor somewhere in New Jersey... Several larger nation-wide 'wire' houses have already said that they are considering some such plans to relocate. 1982 *Times* 27 July 15/4 United States banks..in the past have left financial futures very much to the brokers and major 'wire houses' such as Bache or Hutton. 1942 *Frontier* Sept. 3/1 (*caption*) The wire sound recorder developed by Armour Research Foundation differs from previous types in the type of recording head. 1957 *Encycl. Brit.* XI. 29/2 Three types of recording systems are in common use: (1) mechanical, as in the disk phonograph; (2) optical, as in the sound film; and (3) magnetic, as in the tape or wire recorder. 1978 'D. KYLE' *Black Camelot* ix. 130 'I think we'd better record this as we go along.'.. The wire recorder had been produced and checked. 1933 *Amer. Speech* VIII. II. 77/1 Similar information should be given for film, strip, and wire recordings. 1943 *Electronics* Oct. 236 (*caption*) A wire recording of the Army Hour is taken off the air by..engineers. 1966 *McGraw-Hill Encycl. Sci. & Technol.* XIV. 518/2 Except for minor details, the techniques and systems used for magnetic wire recording are similar to those for magnetic tape. 1982 *Sunday Tel.* (Colour Suppl.) 21 Nov. 8/2, I just read the words, they were recorded straight on to disc, then transferred on to wire recording tape and that was the end of it. 1977 *Sat. Rev.* 23 July 10/2 Slender, with a trim beard and wire-rim glasses. 1982 J. VALIN *Day of Wrath* (1983) xvii. 131 He's got long hair, wears wire rims, muttonchops. 1950 *Mag. of Fantasy & S.F.* Fall 7, I monitored a couple of newscasts; the second one carried a story by another wire service on the domes. 1962 E. LACY *Freeloaders* viii. 181, I didn't think the *Herald Tribune* used wire services for Europe. 1976 *National Observer* (U.S.) 6 Nov. 24/1 A morning newspaper in the East, using a wire service's totals, had Rockefeller ahead. 1985 *Times* 11 May 21/1 Reuters is keeping a close watch on its troubled American wire service rival, United Press International. 1902 *Census Bull.* (U.S.) No. 216. 65 A..combination folding and wire-stitching machine, which by a continuous and automatic operation takes the sheets from the feeders, and folds, gathers, collates, covers and wire-stitches copies of magazines and pamphlets. 1921 T. J. WISE *Bibliogr. Writings Joseph Conrad* (rev. ed.) I. 27 There are no signatures, the pamphlet being composed of a single halfsheet..issued wire-stitched. 1887 *Courier-Journal* (Louisville, Ky.) 20 Feb. 3/2 Printing-Office... Card Cutter, Wire Stitcher [etc.]. 1967 Wire stitcher [see *SHORT RUN *sb.* 4]. 1881 *Even. News* 26 July 4 (Advt.), Over one hundred machines in motion [in a printing and paper-making exhibition]... Wire stitching, paging, gumming, etc. 1957 *Encycl. Brit.* III. 859/2 The automatic assembling, wire-stitching and covering machine units complete the operation of pamphlet binding. 1943 Wire story [see *HOT-SHOT 1 b]. 1979 J. CROSBY *Party of Year* (1980) iii. 25 The foreign desk was behind a glass screen... Feinberg was editing a wire story. 1882 ARMSTRONG & CAMPBELL *Austral. Sheep Husbandry* xviii. 204 Novel Wire Strainer... This instrument..should be made of light iron... Three short spikes, or legs, should be fixed behind, so as to give the instrument a grip of the post as soon as the wire is tightened. 1959 A. UPFIELD *Bony & Black Virgin* xxiii. 215 The big man studied the method of joining the cut wires... 'Chain wire-strainer was used.' 1975 *N.Z. Jrnl. Agric.* Sept. 57/1 The installation of permanent wire strainers on each strand of a new fence..would overcome this difficulty. *a* 1877 KNIGHT *Dict. Mech.* III. 2797/2 *Wire-stretcher*, a tool for straining lightly telegraph or fence wires. 1954 W. FAULKNER *Fable* 187 Cowboy..exterminated from the earth by a tide of men with wire-stretchers and pockets full of staples. 1958 J. G. MACGREGOR *North-West of 16* ix. 132 Then it [*sc.* barbed wire] had to be tightened with our wire-stretchers (a simple block-and-tackle arrangement) until when you plucked it, it sang like a fiddle string. 1981 *Farmstead Mag.* Winter 43/4, I assemble my supplies for next year's battle: my fence staples, spare wire, my fencing pliers and wire stretcher. 1898 *Pearson's Mag.* Sept. 332 Wire-walking..must always retain a greater amount of fascination. 1920 *Variety* 31 Dec. 124 She learned acrobatics..wire walking and aerial work. 1932 A. L. ABBOTT *National Electr. Code Handbk.* viii. 97 (*caption*) A length of wireway with hinged cover. *Ibid.* 99 Wireways may extend transversely through dry walls. 1953 H. A. CHINN *Television Broadcasting* xv. 606 In order to provide protection for audio, video, communications, control, and a-c cables..it is customary to instal such cables in conduit, raceways, pipe shafts,..and similar wireways. 1964 R. F. FICCHI *Electrical Interference* x. 192 A bare ground wire rubbing against a chassis or wireway can cause a considerable amount of noise in a system. 1912 *Motor Manual* (ed. 14) (Advt., rear cover), Rudge-Whitworth detachable wire wheels lengthen the life of tyres 70%. 1926 *Daily Colonist* (Victoria, B.C.) 4 July 26/4 (Advt.), Sport Roadster $675 Delivered. Racy streamlines, wire wheels, [etc.]. 1963 [see *GAS *sb.*[1] 5 d]. 1976 N. THORNBURG *Cutter & Bone* i. 8 A classic 1948 MG-TC with running board and wire wheels. 1958 J. CANNAN *And be Villain* iii. 71 A cupboard where detergents, a reserve of dishcloths and the rolls of wire wool were kept. 1977 'J. LE CARRÉ' *Hon. Schoolboy* xii. 264 His hair was like wire wool crimped into small trenches. 1931 *Boys' Mag.* XLV. 125/2 The potentiometer should be a 'Colvern', wire wound. 1946 *Nature* 30 Nov. 799/2 The development of a vitreous enamel coating for fixed wire-wound resistors. 1975 D. G. FINK *Electronics Engineers' Handbk.* VII. 7 Rheostat (Power). These are variable wire-wound resistors used as speed controls.

wire, *v.* Add: **2. a.** (Example of *to wire a cork.*)

1796 M. EDGEWORTH *Parent's Assistant* (ed. 2) I. 74 Did not I order you..to carry these bottles to the cellar; and did not I charge you to wire the corks?

c. Also, to cover *over* with wire.

1774 J. WESLEY *Let.* 26 July (1931) VI. 104 You must..wire over the cupola.

e. Also, to make electrical connections to; to connect electrically *to*; to provide *with* by means of connecting wires; *spec.* to fit with a concealed listening device. Also with *up*. (Earlier and later examples.)

1891 E. I. BAX *Pop. Electr. Lighting* iv. 27 To admit of this the expense of wiring the room will have to be increased. 1923 *Wireless World* 19 May 205/2 It is preferable to wire the valve panel before fixing it to the baseboard. 1960 *Practical Wireless* XXXVI. 393/1 The heater circuit is best wired first, leads being run close against the chassis. 1970 J. EARL *Tuners & Amplifiers* vi. 140 It is not usually difficult to wire the stereo loudspeaker pair and programme sources for the correct left and right channels. 1978 S. BRILL *Teamsters* iv. 144 The prosecutor wired Henderson's phone so that there would be tapes of Faugno and Andretta threatening him. 1978 *Australian* 21 Aug. 9/2 One in every five homes with television are wired to a cable system. 1982 *Sci. Amer.* Sept. 68/2 The explosive charge is wired with electric blasting caps and detonated from a safe distance. 1983 J. FULLER *Convergence* xxx. 303 Just tell the truth... We have to wire you up.

f. To incorporate (a facility, etc.) *into* a device by electric wiring. Cf. *WIRED-IN *a.* 2.

1962 *Communications Assoc. Computing Machinery* V. 159/1 A scheme for wiring binary-to-decimal conversion into a machine at a small cost.

8. [Cf. WIRE *sb.* 13.] *intr.* To practise pick-pocketing. Also *trans.*, to pick the pocket of. *slang.*

1853 M. CARPENTER *Juvenile Delinquents* i. 40 There are ..at least ten times as many boys 'wiring' (picking pockets) as when I was young. *Ibid.* iv. 145 If he was bigger he could wire a man of his poke. 1891 'F. W. CAREW' *No. 747* xxxv. 414, I used to go wirin' in the main-thoroughfares.

wired, *ppl. a.* Add: **1.** *spec.* of glass.

1908 [in Dict.]. 1930 *Engineering* 12 Dec. 755/1 Plate glass, rolled figured glass, corrugated glass, and wired glass, all produced by rolling. 1979 P. WAY *Sunrise* xi. 116 He had pushed through the wired-glass door.

3. Also with *up*, and *fig.*

1946 *Coast to Coast 1945* 216 The gate was thoroughly wired up—three Queensland hitches of No. 8 wire. 1975 *Washington Post* 29 Sept. A-20/4 Let us..concede that point for a moment—although it shouldn't be conceded until it is properly wired up with all sort of qualifications.

6. a. Employing wires or similar physical connections to convey electric signals, *spec.* for television or radio.

1924 *Telegraph & Telephone Jrnl.* XI. 6/1 Here are some extremely interesting particulars regarding 'Wired Radio' Broadcasting. 1930 E. E. HUNT *Audit Amer.* 20 In 1913 there were only 48 wired homes per 1,000 of the non-farm population. 1937 *Wireless World* 2 Dec. 565/2 (*heading*) Wired television. 1958 *Oxford Mail* 26 Aug. 3/6 In a discussion on wired television..Coun. W. G. White asked if the present or any future council was going to bar the television aerial from its housing estates. 1960 GREGORY & VAN HORN *Automatic Data-Processing Systems* ii. 61 Computers with externally stored programs..get their operating instructions from wired plug-boards. 1960 *Electronics Weekly* 30 Nov. 2/4 A wired sound and television service may soon be provided. for Leicester. 1969 *Electr. Communications* XLIV. I. 14/1 The best compromise was sought between wired-logic control, which is very efficient but inflexible, and stored-program control. 1971 *New Scientist* 1 July 19/2 It is often argued that the provision of more radio and TV channels, particularly on the greatly expanded scale of the 'wired city', will lower standards. 1972 *Listener* 6 July 3/2 As America becomes increasingly a wired nation, with cables reaching out already into millions of homes, the channel limitations of over-the-air television are being superseded. 1976 BRZOZOWSKI & YOELI *Digital Networks* ii. 30 Wired logic refers to the capability of tying together the outputs of gates to realize either the AND..or the OR..function without additional hardware.

b. Fitted with, or wearing, an electronic listening device; more fully *wired for sound.* Also *fig. colloq.*

1957 J. D. MACDONALD *Man of Affairs* ix. 141 The joint is wired, he says... The next step is cameras and infra red and tape recorders, I guess. 1967 *Boston Sunday Globe* 23 Apr. 18/3 Several agreed with the words of one who said he knew enough 'to stay away from Karafin... He's wired for sound 24 hours a day... He can keep stories out of the paper or get them in.' 1982 G. LYALL *Conduct of Major Maxim* xiv. 129 The very idea of being 'off the record' was nonsense, since the room was almost certainly wired.

c. With *up* in either of prec senses.

1971 *New Scientist* 16 Sept. 614 (*heading*) The visual systems in their brain are wired up to match the visual world that is important to them. 1972 D. BLOODWORTH *Any Number can Play* xix. 197 That one-sided chat you had with the wired-up Goddess of Mercy. 1982 P. D. JAMES *Skull beneath Skin* xxv. 210 She was glad that she wasn't wired up to a lie machine. 1984 *Listener* 26 July 20/1 Dr Glover came to the orchestra on the strength of being well wired-up with broadcasting contacts.

wired-in (stress variable), *a.* [f. WIRED *ppl. a.* + IN *adv.*] **1.** Bounded by wire, in the form of netting or fencing. Cf. WIRE *v.* 2 c.

1855 [see WIRED *ppl. a.* 2]. 1973 J. THOMSON *Death Cap* ix. 128 She was feeding the chickens..in the wired-in run. 1975 J. MCCLURE *Snake* ix. 118 Wessels..hid behind the wired-in back of a parked truck.

2. Incorporated in or connected to a device or system by means of wiring. Also *fig.*

1957 C. E. OSGOOD et al. *Measurement of Meaning* i. 5 Certain stimulus patterns have a 'wired-in' connection with certain behaviour patterns (unconditional reflexes) and additional stimuli have acquired this capacity (conditional reflexes). 1962 *Commun. Assoc. Computing Machinery* V. 159/1 (*heading*) On a wired-in binary-to-decimal conversion scheme. 1975 P. ELBOW *Oppositions in Chaucer* v. 120 His predilection for language and thought frees him..from a single, rigid, programmed, or wired-in response to a fox. 1975 *Language for Life* (Dept. Educ. & Sci.) xv. 234 This should be fitted with sound-proof projector booth, wired-in good quality speakers, and a large permanent screen. 1982 *Data Communications* Oct. 119/2 These terminals are dedicated to specific tasks through specific wired-in instructions and have no built-in intelligence. 1984 *Science* 22 June 1304/3 The wired-in semantics of these connections substitutes for the time-consuming interpretation process needed in systems that pass symbolic information.

wire-grass. 2. (Earlier example.)

1790 W. BLIGH *Narr. Mutiny on Board H.M.S. Bounty* 48 In the hollow of the land there grew some wire grass.

wireless, *a.* (*sb.*) For **a, b** read **A, B** and add: **A.** *adj.* (Further examples.) *wireless telegraphy*: also, in British law, used to include wireless telephony; *wireless telephony*: the transmission of speech and other uncoded signals by means of radio waves; = *RADIO-TELEPHONY. Now chiefly *hist.*, having been superseded by *radio(-).*

1898 *Jrnl. Inst. Electr. Engineers* XXVII. 799 The general principles of electric space telegraphy—or wireless telegraphy, as it seems to wish to be called. 1903 C. H. SEWALL *Wireless Telegr.* I. 88 Wireless telephony. Telephoning without wires has not gained by the great developments in its sister-art. 1904 *Act 4 Edw. VII* c. 24. §78 The expression 'wireless telegraphy' means any system of communication by telegraph..without the aid of any wire connecting the points from and at which the messages or other communications are sent and received. 1906 S. R. BOTTONE tr. *Mazzotto's Wireless Telegr. & Teleph.* xi. 390 After the discovery of wireless telegraphy by means of electric waves, many attempts were made to apply the same principle to telephony. 1913 A. H. VERRILL *Harper's Wireless Bk.* xiii. 113 There is no reason to suppose that wireless telephony will not soon have the range of wireless telegraphy. 1922 JOYCE *Ulysses* 702 A private wireless telegraph which would transmit by dot and dash system the result of a national equine handicap. 1923 A. HUXLEY *On Margin* 49 If they are a little more up-to-date they adjust their wireless telephone to the right wave-length and listen-in to the fruity contralto at Marconi House, singing 'The Gleaner's Slumber Song'. 1936 G. B. SHAW *Simpleton Unexpected Isles* II. 51 (*stage-direction*) A writing table littered with papers and furnished with a wireless telephone. 1949 *Act 12 & 13 Geo. VI* c. 54. §685 The expression 'wireless telegraphy' means the emitting or receiving, over paths which are not provided by any material substance..of electromagnetic energy of a frequency not exceeding three million megacycles a second, being energy which either—*a*) serves for the conveying of messages, sound or visual images..or *b*) is used in connection with the determination of position, bearing or distance, or for the gaining of information as to the presence..of any object. 1952 [see *sound radio* s.v. *SOUND *sb.*[3] 7 b]. 1960 *Practical Wireless* XXXVI. 403/1 This station, which was built by Guglielmo Marconi, was the first to span the Atlantic with wireless telegraphy. 1981 *Daily Tel.* 12 Feb. 9/1 HMS Inskip, the Navy's wireless-telegraphy station, near Preston, Lancs.

B. *sb.* Substitute for def.: **1.** Wireless telegraphy or (esp.) telephony; sound broadcasting; = *RADIO *sb.* 2 a, b; also, a particular radio station (= *RADIO *sb.* 2 c).

Largely superseded by *radio* exc. in *hist.* contexts.

1903 *N.Y. Commercial Advertiser* 31 Jan. S 2/2 First in this great field of making the 'wireless' a handmaid of commerce is the de Forrest system, which has won the approval also of the United States government. 1904 [in Dict., sense b]. 1915 GRAHAME-WHITE & HARPER *Aircraft in Gt. War* IV. xi. 150 The application of wireless to aeroplanes has, in the British Flying Corps, been studied very carefully. 1922 [see *BROADCASTER 1]. 1924 [see *SUPRANATIONAL *a.*]. 1927 C. CONNOLLY *Let.* 27 Jan. in *Romantic Friendship* (1975) 231 Chesterton is trying to be funny over the wireless. 1932 R. A. KNOX *Broadcast*

Minds i. 13 We say 'the' wireless... For the wireless, in England, is a unique force; there is no question of two wirelesses differing, as two newspapers may differ in their outlook. **1939** *Daily Tel.* 18 Dec. 1/5 Moscow wireless claims advances in the Murmansk district. **1951** *Sport* 27 Apr.–3 May 2/1 Photos in the papers and interviews on the wireless. **1952** *Times Rev. of Year* 1 Jan. p. v/2 Sound radio (wireless declined farther towards archaism) has done much during the year. **1971** *Daily Tel.* 20 Jan. 10/3 [The Misses Waters] belong to the days when radio was 'the wireless'. **1978** E. Blishen *Sorry, Dad* II. i. 40 Wireless was still quite raw and improbable. The Dockrees next door had one... It was a crystal set. **1980** *Bookseller* 5 Jan. 23 The table shows the books recorded in December... Wireless and Television..42.

2. A radio-telegram.

1904 *Everybody's Mag.* Aug. 161/2 This is how it is taken down in those unerring short-hand notes of the recording angel and sent by special wireless to the type-writer for His Majesty of the Sulphur Trust. **1911** G. Stratton-Porter *Harvester* xvi. 351 Is Ajax [*sc.* a peacock] now sending a wireless to Ceylon asking for a mate? **1926** Galsworthy in *Scribner's Mag.* Aug. 192/1 Going home to have a look at Kit and send Fleur a wireless, he passed four musicians. **1940** N. Marsh *Surfeit of Lampreys* (1941) ii. 25 The steward gave her two [letters] and a wireless message. She opened the wireless first.

3. Short for *wireless set* (see sense 4 below); a radio.

1927 T. E. Lawrence *Let.* 4 Oct. (1938) 543 We have no wireless, and I don't look at papers. **1933** A. Thirkell *High Rising* i. 16 He could..repair the headmaster's wireless and drive his car. *a* **1944** K. Douglas *Alamein to Zem Zem* (1946) 49 The wirelesses in the new tanks had to be checked. **1954** W. Faulkner *Fable* 166 It's too bad every house he passes don't have a wireless, like ships do. **1971** *Daily Tel.* 13 May 7/1 As a child I used to stand alone in front of that big brown box that used to be called a 'wireless' and conduct symphony concerts. **1972** M. Gilbert *Petrella at Q* (1977) 37 P.C. Owers..summoned assistance on his pocket wireless. **1973** [see *radio play* s.v. *radio *sb.* 5 b].

4. *attrib.* and *Comb.*, in senses 1 and 3 above (in U.S., and increasingly in British use, replaced by the corresponding Combs. with *radio*), as *wireless aerial, announcer, battery, broadcast, broadcasting, mast, operator, set, station, transmitter, valve*; in the sense 'transmitted or broadcast by wireless', as *wireless concert, news, play, programme, talk*; **wireless cabinet**, a cabinet incorporating a radio; **wireless licence**, an official permit needed for the possession of a radio; **wireless shack** = *radio shack* s.v. *radio *sb.* 7; **wireless silence** = *radio silence* s.v. *radio *sb.* 7; **wireless wave** = *radio wave* s.v. *radio *sb.* 7.

1924 *Radio Times* 12 Dec. 527 (*caption*) Them's 'is wireless aerials. **1937** *Discovery* Feb. 37/1 The wireless aerial and its stays would become coated with an almost uniform layer of this frost. **1983** C. Dexter *Riddle of Third Mile* i. 12 The voice..of a pre-war wireless announcer... What they called an 'Oxford' accent. **1933** *Radio Times* 14 Apr. 83 (Advt.), Ever Ready wireless batteries. **1930** G. B. Shaw *Apple Cart* p. xi, Last October (1929) I was asked to address the enormous audience created by the new invention of Wireless Broadcast. **1980** J. Lees-Milne *Harold Nicolson* I. xi. 205 On the 2nd May [1923].. he..heard a wireless broadcast over the air for the first time. **1923** *Radio Times* 28 Sept. 6 Wireless broadcasting service. **1930** Kipling *Limits & Renewals* (1932) 208 [He] came back with a couple of cigarettes from the store behind the wireless cabinet. **1923** *Radio Times* 28 Sept. 18/1 Much has..been written on the subject of wireless concerts. **1920** *Radiograph* May 147 (Advt.), Applicants for wireless licence who specify them will not be required to furnish diagrams. **1928** *Melody Maker* Feb. 187 (*heading*) The over-taxed Frenchman! Wireless licences two-pence per annum. **1958** *Whitaker's Almanack 1959* 1098/1 If application is made at any other office which conducts wireless licence business, arrangements can be made for a licence to be issued at a Head Post Office. **1943** F. Thompson *Candleford Green* x. 167 Now..a wireless mast in every back garden. **1948** Wireless mast [see *rev-counter* s.v. *rev *sb.* 2]. *c* **1919** H. C. Witwer *Smile a Minute* iv. iii. 158 Joe, I have just seen the wireless news [received on board ship]. **1926** in *Listener* (1974) 25 Apr. 519 Wireless news will be broadcasted by the B.B.C. **1942** E. Waugh *Put out More Flags* ii. 139 She sat..listening to wireless news from Germany. **1978** P. G. Winslow *Coppergold* 127 Joss's death..had been on the wireless news. **1910** Wireless operator [see sense b in Dict.]. **1929** *Daily Express* 7 Nov. 1/1 Crew. Flight-Captain Rod Schinka..(first pilot)... Herr Niklas..(wireless operator). **1978** F. Maclean *Take Nine Spies* iv. 138 Their mission had been joined by a second wireless-operator. **1929** *Radio Times* 8 Nov. 406/1 *Journey's End* was written for stage representation and is, therefore, not in the more restricted sense a 'wireless play'. **1948** D. Welch *Jrnl.* 7 July (1952) 259 Last week there was a wireless programme on Marie Bashkirtseff. **1923** J. Reith *Diary* 19 Mar. (1975) ii. 131, I was standing talking to them with the wireless set at my back and I pushed the switch. *a* **1944** K. Douglas *Alamein to Zem Zem* (1946) 25 About dusk the wireless sets in all tanks were switched on. **1978** *Dumfries Courier* 13 Oct. 10/4 In the 20 years up to 1950 the radio set—or wireless set as it was affectionately called—was the focal point of home entertainment. **1937** G. H. Grant *Heels of Gale* vi. 59 The wireless shack..had been lifted on board by a crane on the day before sailing and bolted to the wooden planks. **1961** J. Bisset *Commodore* xxvii. 281 On this deck also was the Wireless Shack. **1915** Ld. Fisher 12 Apr. in M. Gilbert *Winston S. Churchill* (1972) III. Compan. i. 793 It seems to me that the positions are all well chosen for all our different activities, and Jellicoe fully alive to wireless silence. *a* **1944** K. Douglas *Alamein to Zem Zem* (1946) 49 Wireless silence was in force. **1909** *Chambers's Jrnl.* July 428/2 At Aldershot..there is a powerful wireless station. **1926** T. E. Lawrence *Seven Pillars* (1935) iii. xxix. 170 My life was spent in moving back and forth..to the town, the port, the wireless station. **1978** D. A. Stanwood *Memory of Eva Ryker* xxvi. 251 The Cape Race Wireless Station has a record of the message... It was transmitted from the *Titanic* five minutes before she struck ice. **1930** J. S. Huxley *Bird-Watching & Bird Behaviour* p. vii, Six wireless talks. **1923** *Radio Times* 28 Sept. 26/3 A small wireless transmitter will be installed at the 'Old Vic'. **1978** F. Maclean *Take Nine Spies* iv. 144 Bernhardt had established two wireless transmitters. **1923** *Radio Times* 28 Sept. 33 (Advt.), A new wireless valve. **1915** H. H. Turner *Voyage in Space* vi. 250 Suppose you pretend that a second is itself like a year; divide it into..30 million parts; one of these tiny parts will be about the time that what we may call a 'wireless' wave of electricity takes to vibrate. **1936** *Discovery* Sept. 285/1 The reason why wireless waves travel round the earth's surface instead of disappearing into space has been explained by investigations of the properties of the upper atmosphere. **1960** *Practical Wireless* XXXVI. 403/1 Marconi announced that signals from Poldhu had bridged the Atlantic. .. That news..confounded the many learned critics who had said that wireless waves would never reach beyond the horizon.

wireline (wəiᵊ·ɹləin). Also **wire line.** [f. Wire *sb.* + Line *sb.*^{2}] **1.** (In Dict. s.v. Wire *sb.* 16.)

2. *Oil Industry.* **a.** A cable for lowering and raising tools and the like in a well shaft. Freq. *attrib.*

1916 A. B. Thompson *Oil-Field Devel. & Petroleum Mining* x. 468 At each pulley a short length of chain is inserted to accommodate the change of direction, and at each well a wire line can be led over the top derrick pulley and direct on to the pump. **1948** *Petroleum Handbk.* (Shell Internat. Petroleum Co.) (ed. 3) v. 92 Where a core head can drill more than 20 feet without getting dull, a retractable or 'wire line' inner-core barrel is used. After a core has been cut, the inner barrel containing the core can be brought to the surface with a wire line lowered inside the drill pipe. **1977** *Offshore Engineer* May 11/1 To prepare the well, the 'Christmas tree'. is.. replaced with a temporary single-pipe ram preventer which allows wireline tools to be introduced.

b. An electric cable used to connect measuring devices in a well with indicating or recording instruments at the surface.

1972 L. M. Harris *Introd. Deepwater Floating Drilling Operations* ii. 6 Logging or other wireline operations. **1974** P. L. Moore et al. *Drilling Practices Manual* xi. 279 The use of wireline logs for determining pore pressures is well documented. **1977** *Offshore Engineer* May 60/3 Various methods for monitoring grouting were used, including a radio-active isotope scheme.., and more conventional wireline temperature surveys.

3. A telegraph or telephone line of wire.

1934 in Webster. **1947** *Trans. Amer. Inst. Electr. Engineers* LXVI. 492/3 The necessary frequency space for wide-band operation usually is not justified economically for wire line operation. **1983** *Mini-Micro Systems* July 240/2 The FCC is currently examining applications from wire-line and non-wire-line carriers for licenses to provide cellular mobile phone service in 30 large U.S. cities.

4. A fishing line of metal wire.

1974 *Encycl. Brit. Macropædia* VII. 374/1 Wire lines created from extruded Monel Metal or stainless steel assist in the sinking of a moving lure... But fish caught on metal or metal core lines are not eligible for International Game Fish Association records. **1984** *Miami Herald* 6 Apr. 9F/6 Boats are limited to four fishing lines... 'We allow use of the kite rig but do not permit use of wireline.'

wireman. Add: **2. b.** A wire-tapper. *colloq.*

1973 *Telegraph* (Brisbane) 24 May 12/4 Watergate conspirator James McCord was one of the best 'wiremen' in the eavesdropping game. **1977** *Time* 21 Feb. 19 He had been one of the most sought-after 'wiremen', or electronic eavesdroppers, in the East, supplying bugging and recording devices to clients on both sides of the law.

3. A journalist working for a telegraphic news agency.

1973 D. May *Laughter in Djakarta* iv. 61 An American wire-man..who lived in Djakarta. **1977** 'J. le Carré' *Hon. Schoolboy* xv. 338 Keller was..a wireman..and Jerry knew him from other wars.

wirephoto (wəiᵊ·ɹfōᵘto). orig. *U.S.* Also with hyphen and as two words. [f. Wire *sb.* + Photo.] A facsimile process for transmitting pictures over telephone lines; also (*colloq.*), a photograph transmitted by this means.

1939 Webster *Add.*, Wirephoto. **1940** *Chicago Daily Tribune* 11 May 1/3 All these pictures were sent..by radio and wirephoto. **1964** M. McLuhan *Understanding Media* ii. xx. 203 The newspaper mesh of dots that is called 'wirephoto'. **1972** T. Ardies *This Suitcase* xvii. 189 A picture of the teenaged Helmut Stern..came in last night via wirephoto. **1973** C. Sagan *Cosmic Connection* (1974) xv. 109 The television pictures from *Mariner 9* were radioed from Mars to Earth in much the same way that a newsprint wire-photo is transmitted on Earth. **1981** 'D. Shannon' *Murder Most Strange* vii. 147 The wire photo came in..and Higgins took it to show the Ortiz girl and she identified it.

So **wire-photograph.**

1962 *Listener* 12 July 57/1 Cartoonists in the United States rely for day-to-day material on newspaper morgues and wire-photographs. **1968** J. Sangster *Touchfeather* ix. 92 'Come and look at this.' The 'this' was a wire photograph... The transmission hadn't been up to much.

wire-puller. (Earlier example.)

1833 in J. R. Commons et al. *Documentary Hist. Amer. Industr. Soc.* (1910) VIII. 340 Wire-pullers..for the furtherance of..party interest.

wirescape (wəiᵊ·ɹskēᶦp). [f. Wire *sb.* + Scape *sb.*^{3}, after *landscape.*] Scenery, or a scene, dominated by overhead wires and their supports.

1951 *Archit. Rev.* CX. 377 Wire, lots of wire, lining streets, crossing fields, acting as totems in villages and skeleton umbrellas on towns, by reducing the endless variety of the human and natural scene to the common denominator—wirescape—has made a dreadful uniformity out of the world it seeks to unite. **1959** *Times Lit. Suppl.* 9 Jan. 16/1 Each year the demands of the new industrial revolution gnaw away more insistently at the countryside... How many of us realize the Wirescape that impends? **1965** *New Statesman* 5 Nov. 713/1 The visual squalor, of which a notable feature is the appalling wirescape, of New York's periphery. **1969** E. Sandon *View into Village* x. 86 In the street is also to be seen that typically modern feature—an appalling wirescape. **1978** *Gold Coast Bulletin* (Austral.) 29 Sept. 7/1, I think we should be removing these unsightly wirescapes from the central precincts of the city.

wire-tap (wəiᵊ·ɹtæp), *sb.* [Back-formation from next.] An act of tapping a telephone line, esp. as a form of surveillance; also, the device by which this is done.

1955 H. Roth *Sleeper* xiv. 113 He had..refrained from any discussion of wire taps or followers. **1963** L. Deighton *Horse under Water* xvii. 72 He has R.N. Signals Gibraltar doing a wire-tap job on me. **1976** *Billings* (Montana) *Gaz.* 11 July 7-A/1 Agents risked doing such things as roughing up antiwar radicals or placing illegal wiretaps. **1978** S. Brill *Teamsters* iii. 103 The wiretaps were to end on March 6. **1982** H. Kissinger *Years of Upheaval* iv. 103 The next morning it became apparent that Nixon had been talking about the wiretap records.

wi·re-tapper, *vbl. sb.* [f. Wire *sb.* + Tapper^1. Cf. Tap *v.*^{1} 2 c in Dict. and Suppl.] One who makes a (usually secret) connection to a telephone or telegraph circuit in order to intercept messages or eavesdrop.

1893 *Blue & Gray* Apr. 313/2 In that band of wire-tappers I had the honor to serve for four years. In 1863 I was appointed or employed as a telegraph operator in the field. **1894** [in Dict. s.v. Wire *sb.* 15 c]. **1906** *N.Y. Tribune* 1 Feb. 8/2 On the day he bet his money, the wiretappers made it appear to Felix..that such sportsmen as James R. Keene and John W. Gates were betting thousands on Old Stone, through them, and advised him to 'get in on the good thing', too. **1910** 'O. Henry' *Strictly Business* 36 Who wears the diamonds in this town? Why, Winnie, the Wiretapper's wife. **1929** *U.S. Rep.* CCLXXVII. 453 The wire tapper destroys this privacy... Does not wire tapping involve an 'unreasonable search' of the 'house' and of the 'person'? **1953** 'S. Ransome' *Drag Dark* (1954) xv. 146 A call..couched in cryptic terms calculated to fool a wire tapper. **1969** *N.Y. Rev. Books* 2 Jan. 41/2 In the process, Macdonald proves himself more reprehensible than a wiretapper, for he uses intimacy, rather than electronics, to do his dirty work. **1977** 'J. D. White' *Salzburg Affair* vi. 52 He could only drive on, find another telephone, in case the M.F.S. wire-tappers had traced the first call.

So **wire-tapping** *vbl. sb.*, the practice or activity of a wire-tapper; (as a back-formation) **wi·re-tap** *v. trans.*, to tap the telephone line of; to monitor (a call) by means of a wire-tap.

1904 *Outing* Dec. 334/1 Despite the habitual exposure in American newspapers of the..'wire-tapping' swindle, the victim continues to be parted from his thousands with painful frequency. **1929** *U.S. Rep.* CCLXXVII. 474 The progress of science in furnishing the Government with means of espionage is not likely to stop with wire-tapping. **1952** W. R. Burnett *Vanity Fair* vi. 56 Chad Bayliss did not want to discuss anything as important..over his apartment house phone... There had been a rash of wire-tapping. **1959** A. Harrington *Life in 'Crystal Palace'* (1960) iv. 75 The private citizen is..being wire-tapped while he is looking for a job. **1973** *Times* 23 May 8/4 His telephone calls had not been wiretapped. **1973** *Black Panther* 21 July 2/3 The FBI, through their wire-tapping,..was practicing electronic surveillance. **1976** *National Observer* (U.S.) 27 Mar. 2/4 The U.S. Army may not wire tap American civilians in foreign countries unless it first gets a warrant from an American judge. **1978** R. Nixon *Memoirs* 388, I authorized Hoover to take the necessary steps—including wiretapping—to investigate the leaks. **1985** *Sunday Times* 20 Jan. 9/4 The U.S. customs officials say that his allegation of illegal wiretapping has been totally disproved.

wirework. Add: **3.** Wire-walking.

1906 *Variety* 3 Mar. 21/2 For sensationalism, the Meers in their wire work make the heart beat quicker. **1928** *Daily Express* 13 June 13/3, I learned acrobatics, wire work, dancing, and juggling.

wire-worker. Add: **2. b.** (Later example.)

1883 C. F. Wilder *Sister Ridnour's Sacrifice* 130 The politician grasps the hand of his wire-worker and tool.

3. = *wire-walker* s.v. Wire *sb.* 16.

1970 M. Kelly *Spinifex* v. 91 She was one of the Flying Volantes, a bloody good wire worker.

wire-working *vbl. sb.* (*b*) (earlier example); also as *ppl. a.*; hence (as a back-formation) **wire-work** *v. trans.*, to influence by pulling wires.

1831 *American* (Harrodsburg, Ky.) 28 Jan. 3/2 One of

the *wire-working* writers in the Union, seems disposed to consider it a little less than treason. **1843** J. Q. ADAMS *Diary* 23 Mar. (1876) XI. xxii. 343 James Monroe was recalled by President Washington through Thomas Pickering, wireworked by Alexander Hamilton. **1857** B. HAYES *Diary* 11 Sept. (1929) v. 167, I have kept aloof from the wire-working as well as from the more stormy scenes of politics.

wiring, *vbl. sb.* Add: **2. a.** Esp. the electric wires in an apparatus or building. (Further examples.)

1887 *Jrnl. Soc. Telegr.-Engineers* XVI. 182 This would be supplied from central stations (but without any outlay for insulated conductors beyond the 'wiring' of the actual domiciles to the extent rendered necessary by the number and position of the lamps required). **1923** *Wireless World* 5 May 135 (*caption*) The underside of the panel, showing the arrangement of the components and the wiring. **1958** C. FREMLIN *Hours before Dawn* iii. 29 A rather cultured way of making me put a two-bar fire in her room... It's a matter of the wiring on the top floor. **1979** V. CAPEL *Burglar Alarm Systems* x. 107 This is about the worst place, as an intruder could soon silence the alarm by.. cutting the bell wiring.

3. wiring diagram, a diagram of the wiring of an electrical installation or device, showing the electrical relationship of connections and components and usu. also their physical disposition; also *fig.*

1946 G. M. CHUTE *Electronics in Industry* viii. 63 Another kind of diagram... is called the connection or wiring diagram, because it shows the wire connections between the various parts. **1967** 'A. CORDELL' *Bright Cantonese* xvii. 203 'There must be a switch assembly somewhere.'.. 'She gave me a wiring diagram.' **1969** *Times* 13 Feb. 10/3 He believes that until more is known about how the wiring diagram is modified, there can be little evidence in support of theories assuming that changes in nerve connexions are the basis of learning and memory. **1979** B. SCADDAN *Mod. Electr. Installation* II. iv. 63 A circuit diagram shows how the system *functions*... A wiring diagram shows how the system is to be *wired*, and all components of the circuit should be shown in their correct places.

wirra, *int.* Add: (Earlier example.) **wirrasthru** (earlier example).

1829 G. GRIFFIN *Collegians* I. vii. 153 O, wirra, Eily! this is the black day to your ould father. *c* **1874** D. BOUCICAULT in M. R. Booth *Eng. Plays of 19th Cent.* (1969) II. 190 Ses he, 'You won't see home for six months.' Then I set up a wierasthru. *Ibid.* 214 Oh, weir asthru! What'll I do!

wirra (wi·ră), *sb. Austral.* [Aboriginal.] **1.** A species of acacia, *Acacia salicina*, burnt by Aborigines for its ash; = *COUBA.

1906 J. H. MAIDEN *Wattles & Wattle-Barter* (ed. 3) 90 *A. salicina*, Lindl... Following are some additional aboriginal names..'Wirrha', Cooper's Creek, near Lake Eyre. **1941** I. L. IDRIESS *Great Boomerang* xiv. 102 Burned leaves of the wirra (a species of acacia, the leaves of which when burned yield a powder of potash).

2. A shallow wooden scoop used by Aborigines.

1935 H. H. FINLAYSON *Red Centre* vii. 74 A hunting party may decide suddenly to move on to another ground. Without more ado, the men reach for their spears and walk away, and their women follow, carrying no more than a yamstick, a *wirra*, and their youngest child. **1956** *Landfall* June 99 She carried two large pitchi, her four-foot-long mulga digging-stick, which she had freshly sharpened..by charring..; and her wirra, a shallow wood scoop.

wirrah (wi·ră). *Austral.* [Aboriginal.] An Australian saltwater fish, *Acanthistius serratus* (family Serranidæ) that is greenish brown with blue spots.

1882 J. E. TENISON-WOODS *Fish & Fisheries N.S.W.* 34 'Wirrah' or Plectropoma is a genus similar to that of Serranus, but armed with a row of spinous teeth on the lower jaw..besides the pair of canines above. **1933** *Bulletin* (Sydney) 11 Jan. 21 We had caught a number of more genteel fish, so we heaved the common wirrahs and leather-jackets overboard. **1978** J. M. THOMSON *Field Guide Common Sea & Estuary Fishes Non-Tropical Austral.* 100 Except for the Wirrah most of the rock cods are regarded as good eating.

‖**Wirt** (virt). In 9 **Wirth.** [Ger.] The landlord of a German inn.

1858 GEO. ELIOT *Jrnl.* July in J. W. Cross *Life* (1885) II. viii. 48 The stout, red-faced *Wirth.* **1970** *Guardian* 28 Feb. 12/4 The Swabian *Weinstube* is a cosy place... The *Wirt* will make his round to bid every one of his guests a personal good evening.

‖**Wirtschaft** (vi·rtʃaft). *rare.* In 9 **Wirth-.** [Ger.] **1.** Domestic economy, housekeeping.

1850 C. M. YONGE *Henrietta's Wish* ii. 21 The house.. was very soon pretty and cheerful, and the *wirthschaft*.. well ordered and economical. **1889** —— *Reputed Changeling* I. viii. 138 The Doctor..[asked] whether the ladies abroad were given to housewifery. 'The German dames make a great ado about their *Wirthschaft*, as they call it..but as to the result! pah!'

2. [Ger., short for *gastwirtschaft*, f. *gast* GUEST *sb.*] = *WIRTSHAUS.

1903 G. W. HARTLEY *Wild Sport* iii. 60 They had some beer at a snug little *wirtschaft*, and then they all fished. **1950** E. HEMINGWAY *Across River* xxxviii. 269 What is there to eat in this *Wirtschaft*?

Hence **Wi·rtschaftswunder,** (erron.) **-schaftwunder** (-vu:ndəɹ), the 'economic miracle' of West Germany, i.e. the substantial and lasting recovery in its economic state and standard of living following the war of 1939–45; also *transf.*

1959 *Times* 13 Mar. 16/3 Some of the pot-holes in the present age of prosperity, the *Wirtschaftswunder*, are laid bare in a manner that leaves little to the imagination. **1961** *Times* 10 Apr. 11/6 A *Wirtschaftswunder* incomparably greater than the Federal Republic's. **1965** *Punch* 22 Sept. 411/1 The peoples of both India and Pakistan are shockingly poor... There is no possibility here of miraculous recovery, the *Wirtschaftwunder*. **1980** 'D. GRANT' *Emerald Decision* i. 14 My daughters..are products of the Socialist *wirtschaftwunder*. **1983** *London Mag.* July 62/1 The Germany of the mind's eye; not..the concrete cities of the Wirtschaftswunder.

‖**Wirtshaus** (vi·rtshaus). In 9 **Wirths-.** Pl. **Wirtshäuser** (-hoizəɹ). [Ger.] In German-speaking countries: a hostelry, inn.

1829 C. WILMOT *Jrnl.* 6 Sept. (1935) 330 They..have a Wirthshaus and tables and chairs to eat and drink and be merry. **1967** *Sat. Rev.* 22 Apr. 37/2 They returned home with precious addresses of tiny bistros and *brasseries* and *osterias* and *Wirtshäuser.* **1982** G. LYALL *Conduct of Major Maxim* xx. 179, I have an unfinished beer at the *Wirtshaus.* Would you like to join me?

Wisconsin (wiskǫ·nsin). *Geol.* The name of a state of the north central U.S.A., used *attrib.* and *absol.* to designate (the time of) the fourth and final Pleistocene glaciation of North America, corresponding to the Würm glaciation of the Alps.

[**1894** T. C. CHAMBERLIN in J. Geikie *Gt. Ice Age* (ed. 3) xlii. 763 All this complex is grouped under a single term—the East-Wisconsin formation—because the grounds for a formal subdivision are not yet sufficiently clear.] **1895** *Amer. Naturalist* XXIX. 240 The second, third, and fourth glacial stages of the European Ice age..were probably also time equivalents, respectively, with the Kansan, Iowa, and Wisconsin stages in the United States and Canada. **1896**, etc. [see *ILLINOIAN *a.*]. **1967** E. B. LEOPOLD in Martin & Wright *Pleistocene Extinctions* 235 Taylor considers that the Pliocene and Quaternary climates before the late Wisconsin were much less continental than now. **1981** J. E. SANDERS *Princ. Physical Geol.* xiii. 332 The last ice mass to cover the Great Lakes basin arrived during the late Wisconsin Stage, starting 20,000 years ago.

Hence **Wisco·nsinan** *a.* (also *absol.*).

1968 [see *WEICHSEL]. **1978** *Nature* 8 June 456/2 These volcanics are thought to have been formed under ice of Wisconsinan age. **1981** F. W. SHOTTON in Neale & Flenley *Quaternary in Brit.* xiii. 142 This is the way the Wisconsinan ice invading the U.S.A. from the Canadian Shield is interpreted.

wisdom. Add: **1. f.** Phr. *in his* (or *its*, etc.) *wisdom*: now usually ironic.

1852 QUEEN VICTORIA in *Hansard* CXXIII. 20 To enable the Industry of the Country to meet successfully that unrestricted Competition to which Parliament, in its Wisdom, has decided that it should be subjected. **1863** N. HAWTHORNE *Our Old Home* 397 Possibly his Lordship thought, in his wisdom, that the good feeling which was sure to be expressed by a company of well-bred Englishmen, at his august and far-famed dinner table, might have an appreciable influence on the grand result. **1930** W. FAULKNER *As I lay Dying* 68 If you have no son, it's because the Lord has decreed otherwise in His wisdom. **1974** K. CLARK *Another Part of Wood* vi. 232 In the 1930's, when the country was at least ten times as rich as it is today, the Treasury 'in its wisdom' twice found it necessary to cut off our annual purchase grant altogether.

wise, *sb.*[1] Add: **II. 3. b.** (Further examples.) No longer *arch.*

The meaning is 'in the manner of', 'in the..manner'.

1851 H. MELVILLE *Moby Dick* II. xxviii. 192 Ahab.. took Stubb's long spade..and striking it into the lower part of the half-suspended mass, placed its other end crutch-wise under one arm. **1854** H. D. THOREAU *Walden* 21 Waiting at evening on the hill-tops for the sky to fall, that I might catch something, though I never caught much, and that, manna-wise, would dissolve again in the sun. **1885** *Cornhill Mag.* Mar. 283 Priests sitting with their legs tucked up tailor-wise, in the attitude of Buddha. **1919** R. FIRBANK *Valmouth* iv. 52 Flecked with wood shavings, Saint Joseph-wise, it [*sc.* a gown] brought with it suggestions of Eastern men. **1921** KASTNER & CHARLTON *Poetical Wks. of Sir Wm. Alexander* I. p. lvii, The style throughout, Seneca-wise, ought to be magnificent and grave. **1923** R. MACAULAY *Told by an Idiot* I. ii. 11 Her mass of chestnut hair parted Rosetti-wise in the middle. **1940** 'GUN BUSTER' *Return via Dunkirk* II. iv. 117 In a few minutes our vehicles were coiled serpent-wise round the château.

(ii) Used in the same way but with the sense: as regards, in respect of. *colloq.* (orig. *U.S.*).

1942 E. R. ALLEN in J. J. Mattiello *Protective & Decorative Coatings* II. viii. 252 It should be noted that there are two types of hydrogen atoms positionwise. **1948** *Sat. Rev.* 6 Mar. 16/3 Plotwise, it offers little more or little less of what-happens-next interest than may be found [etc.]. **1958** *Spectator* 10 Jan. 37/2 John Robert Russell, 13th Duke of Bedford..in twelve TV performances, was the greatest, successwise, among the aristocrats. **1958** *Times* 5 Sept. 11/5 An ill-disciplined, over-paid, frustrated youth, whose life chances have been vastly improved moneywise without commensurate social adjustment. **1961** *Far East Film News* (Tokyo) Apr. 5/1, 1961 so far has been UA [*sc.* United Artists] all the way prize-wise with this company taking an even dozen Oscars. **1976** J. I. M. STEWART *Memorial Service* xii. 184 These were a gentle race..desperately worried over the grim state of the market job-wise. **1981** *Gossip* (Holiday Special) 24/1 Acting-wise, I like Katharine Hepburn, Joanne Woodward, Judy Garland and, of course, Marilyn.

wise, *a.* (*sb.*[3], *adv.*) Add: **1. a.** *wise old man*; spec. = *WISE MAN 4.

1940 [see *SHADOW *sb.* 1 d]. **1956** R. F. C. HULL tr. *Jung's Symbols of Transformation* in *Coll. Wks.* V. II. vii. 332 The archetype of the wise old man first appears in the father, being a personification of meaning and spirit in its procreative sense. **1961** G. ADLER *Living Symbol* xvii. 397 The more remote and more powerful figure of the 'wise old man' represents a further step..to a higher and more comprehensive wisdom. **1968** 'A. WHITNEY' *Every Man has his Price* viii. 61 Now he was a wise old man, greatly feared, much respected. **1975** D. DANIELL *Interpreter's House* iii. 60 There is a Wise Old Man.. blind and of immense strength who..blesses John Burnet. **1977** M. GREEN *Children of Sun* i. 36 A whole movement focuses passionate values..on them [*sc.* young men]—as opposed to focusing them on the wise old man.

3. b. (*b*) For U.S. colloq. read colloq. (orig. *U.S.*). (Earlier and further examples.)

1896 ADE *Artie* ii. 14, I told him that when he wanted to get wise to what was in my hand all he had to do was to dig up his bit and come in. *Ibid.* xvii. 155 There was somethin' ailed me, but I was n't wise to it. **1913** A. BENNETT *Regent* x. 296 'Tell me,..she hasn't got herself arrested yet, has she?' 'No. And she won't!' 'Why not?' 'The police have been put wise.' **1937** G. HEYER *They found Him Dead* ii. 41 Say, sister, get wise to this! You can't put nothin' across on me! **1950** G. GREENE *Third Man* ii. 21, I met him my first term at school... He was a year older and knew the ropes. He put me wise to a lot of things. **1955** M. GILBERT *Sky High* xv. 210, I suppose Bill had just about got wise to you. **1977** F. PARRISH *Fire in Barley* v. 49 Dan wondered if the arty woman was wise to him.

c. *wise guy* (colloq., orig. *U.S.*): an experienced or knowledgeable man; usu. ironic or derog., a know-all, a wiseacre; someone who makes sarcastic or annoying remarks; also (with reversal of meaning), someone easily duped; also *attrib.*

1896 ADE *Artie* xvi. 150 He was the wise guy and I was the soft mark. **1903** H. HAPGOOD *Autobiogr. of Thief* iv. 82 When these Rufus's up the State get a Yorker or a wise guy, they'll strip him down to his socks. **1910** W. M. RAINE *Bucky O'Connor* ii. 28 You're wise guys, gents, both of yez. **1920** B. TARKINGTON in *On Plays, Playwrights & Playgoers* (1959) 42 However, they'd made the crowd aware of wise guy superiority. **1922** WODEHOUSE *Adventures of Sally* xiii. 219 Obviously one of the Wise Guys of whom her friend the sporting office-boy had spoken, he was frankly dissatisfied with the exhibition. **1929** W. T. SCANLON *God have Mercy on Us!* lvi. 331 We had positive orders not to pick up any form of documents and to leave them for the Intelligence Section—the 'Wise Guy Section', as we called it. **1932** [see *CON *v.*]. **1935** [see *EASY *a.* 13 b]. **1941** B. SCHULBERG *What makes Sammy Run?* (1943) i. 7 Listen, wise guy,..if you found something wrong..why didn't you come and tell me? **1959** C. WILLIAMS *Man in Motion* xi. 150 'What're you, a wise guy?' he snarled. **1972** *Village Voice* (N.Y.) 1 June 50/3 The cop..told Rob he didn't think it was funny, portfolio or not, declared that he was a clear-cut wise guy and placed him under arrest. **1976** *National Observer* (U.S.) 7 Aug. 17/1 Kramer and Roberts seem unable to shake off the brittle, knowing, wise-guy tone of voice.

8. b. *wise-ass* sb. and adj. (cf. *SMART-ARSE, -ASS). **c.** *wise-assed.*

1971 *Current Slang* V. iv. 21 *Wise ass*, n., a wise guy. **1972** J. POYER *Chinese Agenda* iii. 17 Listen to what I have to say, then you can make all the wise-ass remarks you want. **1978** J. IRVING *World according to Garp* iv. 66 Benny Potter from New York—a *born* wise-ass. *Ibid.* 67 It was unfortunate that wise-ass Benny Potter was the first to tell Garp the news. **1967** P. TAMONY *Americanisms* (typescript) No. 18. 2 A fantastic display of brash male and female wise-assed mediocrity. **1976** 'TREVANIAN' *Main* xii. 260 Some wiseassed note about the bad luck of getting a parking ticket the same night you get killed.

wise, *v.*[2] Add: **1.** Freq. const. *on* or *to.* Also *refl.* (Earlier and later examples.)

1905 R. BEACH *Pardners* iv. 113, I cast the bad eye on the boys to wise 'em up. **1925** F. SCOTT FITZGERALD *Great Gatsby* vii. 124, I just got wised up to something funny the last few days. **1929** *Princeton Alumni Weekly* 24 May 982/2 To stick out one's neck is to commit an unpardonable error, to lay oneself open to criticism... A persistent offender should wise up on himself. **1955** W. GADDIS *Recognitions* I. iv. 158 Yeah, you got to wise up to yourself, see? **1960** C. MACINNES *Mr Love & Justice* 26 That's..what I'm wising myself up on. **1971** *Wall St. Jrnl.* (Eastern ed.) 10 Mar. 1/4 Antique dealers are wising up to the growing demand for old radios. **1984** *Listener* 7 June 36/3 'Write a poem about it,' he suggests. 'Wise up, sir,' the new generation tells him.

2. *to wise off* (U.S. slang): to make wise-cracks *at* someone.

1943 *Yank* 2 July 10 I'd love to have one of those acting noncoms wise off at me. **1981** 'P. MALLORY' *Killing Matter* xiii. 136 He's a real meanie. I wouldn't be wising off at him if I were you.

Hence **wised-up** *ppl. a.*

1926 J. BLACK *You can't Win* xx. 301, I could make a living without taking tough chances against wised-up city police. **1952** M. MCCARTHY *Groves of Academe* (1953) x. 205 His wised-up air was as irritating..as Donna's exaggerations. **1973** R. PARKES *Guardians* ix. 172 It's nasty. Very nasty. But at least I'm wised up now.

wisecrack (wəi·zkræk). *colloq.* (orig. *U.S.*). Also **wise crack, wise-crack.** [*CRACK *sb.* 5.] A clever, pithy witticism or remark. Also as quasi-*adj.*

1924 G. ADE *Let.* 20 Dec. (1973) 101 When Geraghty came yesterday, both of us had thought of putting in another character, a young wise-crack small town loafer,..who thinks he is very sly. **1925** *Sat. Even. Post* 14 Feb. 44 The Palace, Chicago, will howl at a wise crack, a nifty, that Duluth audiences won't even flag as it flies over their heads. **1950** G. B. SHAW *Buoyant Billions* 98 The satirical humor of Aristophanes, the wisecracks of Confucius, the precepts of the Buddha. **1959** I. & P. OPIE *Lore & Lang. Schoolch.* ix. 174 He might..have seen sense in the wisecracks which..scientifically minded boys indulge in..: 'What is the matter?' 'That which occupies space.' **1977** *Rep. Comm. Future of Broadcasting* (Cmnd. 6753) ii. 15 Lord Hill..saw no reason why the BBC should have been expected to apologise for a wisecrack in a satire programme..that if you can see the Prime Minister's lips moving you know he is lying. **1979** R. JAFFE *Class Reunion* (1980) I. viii. 109 Say only nice, polite, ladylike things, no nasty wisecracks.

So **wi·secrack** *v. intr.*, to make wisecracks; also *trans.*, with quoted words as obj.; **wi·secracking** *ppl. a.* and *vbl. sb.*; also **wi·secracker**, one given to making wisecracks.

1915 *Call* (San Francisco) 30 Apr. 17 Wisecrackin' city fellers ain't got nuthin' on you. **1923** *N.Y. Times* 9 Sept. VII. 2 *Wise-cracker*, a city fellow who makes wise remarks. **1924** P. MARKS *Plastic Age* 28 The lights flashed on and the crowd filed out, 'wise-cracking' about the picture. *Ibid.* 113 Carl the flippant, the voluble, the 'wise-cracker', lost his tongue. **1927** *New Republic* 12 Oct. 218/2 He has the knack of wise-cracking, and his dialogue is of that slick and well oiled kind that you may meet in good vaudeville. **1939** JOYCE *Finnegans Wake* 33 It has been blurtingly bruited by certain wisecrackers..that he suffered from a vile disease. **1940** GRAVES & HODGE *Long Week-End* xx. 345 Everyday life could be made interesting on the screen without fictitious drama or wise-cracking comment. **1946** *Sat. Rev. Lit.* 2 Nov. 41/1 Both authors wisecrack their way through adverse circumstances. **1949** H. ROBBINS *Dream Merchants* (1950) 144 Jane saw him come into the office. 'If it ain't the vice-president himself!' she wisecracked. 'How's the picture business?' **1949** G. B. SHAW *Sixteen Self Sketches* xiv. 82 Without him I might have been a mere literary wise-cracker, like Carlyle and Ruskin. **1977** *Rolling Stone* 21 Apr. 58/1 Jim Rockford is a worldly wisecracker. **1979** *Fortune* 21 May 71/1 Fraser wisecracks that the Carter Administration's voluntary wage guidelines have 'self-destructed'. **1982** *Daily Tel.* 11 May 14 He has defended rioters..with such vigour as to alarm his fellow lawyers, one of whom wisecracked to me: 'Who will rid us of this turbulent pest?' **1982** E. NORTH *Ancient Enemies* viii. 105 Liz reminds me..of Tammy, who was tough and wise-cracking.

wise man. 2. c. Delete '† *Obs.* as a specific sense'. *colloq.* in mod. use.

1959 J. BALOGH in H. Thomas *Establishment* 98 In the negotiations on the finance of NATO rearmament in Lisbon the British representative 'wise man' accepted a contribution wholly out of line with the relative capacities to bear the burden. **1969** D. ACHESON *Present at Creation* xxxi. 277 Lester Pearson has continually urged the council to set up committees of 'wise men' to find a use for it [*sc.* Article 2 of the North Atlantic Treaty]. **1973** *Times* 5 May 4/4 The appointment of two independent 'wise men' by the United States and the European Community to prepare the ground for the forthcoming round of international trade talks, was suggested. **1983** *Times* 24 Feb. 6/8 A socialist leader..has been nominated to the elite body of nine 'wise men' who form France's Constitutional Council. **1984** *Times* 29 Oct. 1/3 The Gaddafi affair..is unlikely to go away as quickly as the TUC's 'four wise men' monitoring the dispute would wish.

4. (*old*) *wise man*: an archetypal figure appearing in myths, folklore, etc., representing wisdom or meaning, esp., in the theory of C. G. Jung, one of the archetypes of the collective unconscious; cf. *wise old man* s.v. *WISE *a.* (*sb.*³, *adv.*) 1 a.

1692 W. SALMON tr. 'Hermes Trismegistus' in *Practical Physick* v. 203/1 But if thou shalt say, that Wisdom or the Wise Man does Rule or Command among all Mankind. **1940** S. DELL tr. *Jung's Integration of Personality* iii. 87 The magician is the archetype of the old wise man. *Ibid.* 88, I have been content to call it the archetype of the old wise man or of meaning. **1973** J. SINGER *Boundaries of Soul* x. 262 The archetype of the mana-personality, an Old Wise Man whose power is born of understanding the timeless life processes.

wisenheimer (wəi·zənhəimər). *U.S. slang.* Also **weisen-, wise-.** [f. WISE *a.* + *-enheimer*, as in German names such as *Oppenheimer*.] A wiseacre, a 'clever dick'. Also *attrib.* or as *adj.*

1904 R. L. McCARDELL *Show Girl & her Friends* 51 He wants to know some good way to reduce his weight... You don't know any such a way? No? Why, I thought you was a wiseheimer. **1919** MENCKEN *Amer. Lang.* v. 151 Several years ago *-heimer* had a great vogue in slang, and was rapidly done to death. But *wiseheimer* remains in colloquial use as a facetious synonym for *smart-aleck*, and after awhile it may gradually acquire dignity. **1919** *National Police Gaz.* (U.S.) 4 Jan. 3/1 Cawkins..like a true Wisenheimer, considered the gentle, goosey kind of a beautiful girl the most appetizing. **1922** S. LEWIS *Babbitt* xxiv. 287 The wisenheimers grab a look at a fellow's nails when they want to tell if he's a tinhorn or a real gent! **1937** *Amer. Speech* XII. 9/2 Some wiseheimer American newspaper man has picked this up and tagged it onto President Hoover. **1957** J. D. SALINGER *Franny & Zooey* (1964) 65 We were nervous..at the statistics on child pedants and academic weisenheimers who grow up into faculty-recreation-room savants. **1959** *Washington Post* 26 Dec. A19/2 Then some wisenheimer from the agency decided we needed a trailer. **1975** *Times Lit. Suppl.* 21 Feb. 185/1 The wisenheimer who gets his ornate come-uppance. **1977** M. BABSON *Murder, Murder, Little Star* vii. 50, I shoulda listened to her. But..I was too wisenheimer.

wish, *sb.*¹ Add: **4. wish book** *N. Amer. slang*, a mail-order catalogue; **wish card** *rare*, in fortune-telling, a card which predicts the attainment of a desired end; **wish-dream** [cf. G. *Wunschtraum*], a dream or fantasy that reflects some hidden wish; also *attrib.*; **wish list**, a list of desired objects or occurrences; **wish-thinking** = *wishful thinking* s.v. *WISHFUL *a.* 2 a.

1933 *Amer. Speech* VIII. 32/1 *Wishbook*, a mail-order catalogue. **1971** *Alberta Hist. Rev.* Summer 25/1 That was when we would look at our 'Wish Book', the mail order catalogue, until it was out of date, and then tear the pages out in the 'House of Parliament'. **1922** JOYCE *Ulysses* 761 I'll throw them the 1st thing in the morning till I see if the wishcard comes out. **1934** R. CAMPBELL *Broken Record* i. 9 Wish-dreams might account for this desire to 'headlong-hall' me into the next world. **1945** KOESTLER *Yogi & Commissar* I. iii. 31 She is not necessarily the wishdream-girl of suburban circulating libraries. **1953** *Encounter* Nov. 25/2 The wish-dream world of the Stockholm peace campaigner. **1966** *New Scientist* 28 July 222/1 Black gold in the back lot must be the standard rags-to-riches wishdream in the United States. **1972** *Times* 30 May 19/2 It had a presently confidential 'wish list' of programmes it would like to see abandoned. **1976** *National Observer* (U.S.) 10 July 9/3 Wholesale replacement of the nation's taxi fleet is hardly at the top of operators' wish lists. **1930** J. JASTROW *Piloting your Life* 170 It would take not a chapter but a volume to describe all the varieties of impediments of thought. If reduced to a schedule they might read like this:..*Wish Thinking*, believing what you hope or want to be true; [etc.]. **1945** R. KNOX *God & Atom* viii. 115 Most people who are capable of thinking, and are not deceived by wish-thinking, agree that the world is in ferment. **1958** J. LODWICK *Bid Soldiers Shoot* viii. 268 In matters of wish-thinking..the Victor of the Pacific, MacArthur, had met his match.

wish, *v.* Add: **1. a.** (*c*) *to wish to God*: to wish intensely.

c **1385,** *a* **1562** [in Dict.]. **1932** 'N. SHUTE' *Lonely Road* vii. 178, I wish to God we'd gone back to the boat. **1941** L. A. G. STRONG *Bay* 7, I wish to God I knew how to begin. **1976** *Daily Mirror* 11 Mar. 7/2 Christopher..has been sent to Borstal... His mother said: 'I wish to God we had checked up on him.'

8. To foist or impose (something or someone) *on* (*to*) someone; to endow with at another's wish.

1915 N. L. McCLUNG *In Times like These* x. 164 Women have never chosen the liquor business... It has been wished on them. **1926** *Publishers' Weekly* 22 May 1725/1 Mr. Remington..has not been able to be with us... That is why we are able to wish that good job on him. **1934** E. WAUGH *Handful of Dust* i. 20 Who was the old girl you wished on me at that party last night? **1954** 'N. SHUTE' *Slide Rule* 1 An unwanted kitten that they had wished on to my children. **1962** *Listener* 5 July 14/2 The plan was to build a much larger school than was needed, at the same time 'wishing' additional housing on the village to justify it. **1971** *Guardian* 9 Jan. 13/2 We owed money everywhere... I wouldn't wish that on any of today's young housewives. **1983** M. BABSON *Fool for Murder* xviii. 166 It really was most unfair of Uncle Wilmer to wish it on Wanda-Lu... He wasn't the one who'd have to keep the place tidy.

wisha (wi·ʃə), *int. Anglo-Ir. colloq.* [ad. Ir. *mhuise* indeed (the unlenited form *muise* gives anglicized *musha* MUSHA).] An exclamation indicating dismay, emphasis, or surprise.

1826 M. WILMOT *Let.* 29 Feb. (1935) 234 O 'wisha' 'wisha', shall I ever arrive at the ball I promised you! **1842** S. LOVER *Handy Andy* vi. 70 I'm afeard o' my life to go to bed!..Wisha! but I'd give the world it was mornin'. **1898** J. D. BRAYSHAW *Slum Silhouettes* 49 Oh, wisha! didn't he break the leg of me wid his stick? **1914** JOYCE *Dubliners* 157 'Wisha! wisha,' says I. 'A pound of chops..coming into the Mansion House.' **1936** 'F. O'CONNOR' *Bones of Contention* 8 Wisha, for goodness' sake will you come down and leave the girl sleep? **1978** 'M. M. KAYE' *Far Pavilions* lviii. 812 Wisha, but it's a gloomy devil you are an' all. **1965** *N. Munster Antiquarian Jrnl.* IX. iv. 186 Wisha, I don't know what to say.

wish-bone. (In Dict. s.v. WISH *sb.*¹) Add: Also **wishbone. 2.** *Naut.* A boom composed of two halves that curve outward from the mast, on either side of the sail, and in again, the clew of the sail that lies between them being attached to the point where they meet aft. Freq. *attrib.*, designating a sail or a boat with such a boom.

1934 U. FOX *Sailing, Seamanship & Yacht Construction* I. 54 (*caption*) Wishbone gaff. **1935** *Yachting Monthly* Feb. 306/1 The working sail area of the 'wishbone' ketch rig shown totals 2,794 sq. ft. **1954** D. H. C. PHILLIPS-BIRT *Rigs & Rigging of Yachts* ii. 60 The wishbone ketch is the result of combining an unusual form of staysail ketch rig devised by Mr. F. Fenger..with the wishbone spar invented by Nathaniel Herreshoff. **1958** *Times* 27 Oct. 10/6 The fishermen..were already launching their dug-out canoes, some under the traditional wish-bone sprit-sail. **1981** B. WEBB *Schult's Sailing Dict.* 327/1 Sailboards have wishbone booms. **1984** *Times* 25 Aug. 11 The next stop was to pick a point to steer for, ease the rig (the mast, sail and wishbone) towards me until I was looking through the transparent panel in the sail.

3. A wishbone-shaped element in the independent suspension of a motor vehicle, the two arms of which are hinged to the chassis and their join hinged to the wheel; freq. *attrib.*

1934 *Automobile Engineer* XXIV. 289/3 The American types..do not use the longitudinal radius links, and thus the wheel position depends entirely on the 'wishbone' link bearings. **1959** *Times* 27 Apr. (Rubber Industry Suppl.) p. vi/1 Such bushes are now almost universally used for springs, torque arms, and in some forms of wishbone suspension. **1983** 'D. RUTHERFORD' *Stop at Nothing* ix. 165 It took me an hour and a half to put the Saab to rights. The front wishbone had been seriously distorted.

4. *U.S. Football.* Used *attrib.* and *absol.* to designate an offensive formation in which the full back lines up ahead of the half-backs in an alignment that resembles the shape of a wishbone.

1972 *N.Y. Times* 3 Nov. 48/2 Dartmouth's best hope lies in shutting off Yale's wishbone offense as engineered by Dick Jauron. **1974** *Spartanburg* (S. Carolina) *Herald-Jrnl.* 21 Apr. 134/3 The white team ran the wishbone that UCLA used last year. **1979** *Tucson* (Arizona) *Citizen* 20 Sept. 10D/3 The fullback in the Santa Rita Wishbone has averaged nearly 30 carries per game in the first two contests.

wishful, *a.* **2. a.** Delete *Obs.* or *dial.* In mod. use in weaker sense: expressing or indicative of a wish; chiefly in *wishful thinking*, thinking, esp. belief or expectation, that is influenced by one's wishes to the extent that relevant (consciously) known facts are (subconsciously) ignored or distorted; also as *adj.*; so *wishful thinker*.

1932 *Sat. Rev. Lit.* 2 July 817/4 At two vitally important points Glenn Frank's incisive analysis fades away in a vague realm of hope or even of wishful thinking. **1940** *Illustr. London News* CXCVI. 498/2 The possibility of any relief in that direction can only exist in the minds of wishful-thinkers. **1940** L. D. WEATHERHEAD *This is Victory* ii. 58, I do not mean that that which is believed has no other support than man's wishful thinking. **1941** AUDEN *New Year Letter* I. 17 Twelve months ago in Brussels I heard the same wishful-thinking sigh. **1942** C. S. LEWIS *Screwtape Lett.* ix. 50 It all depends on whether your man is..of the wishful-thinking type who can be assured that all is well. **1951** 'A. GARVE' *Murder in Moscow* i. 20 He was a woolly wishful-thinker who happened to be inordinately vain as well. **1958** *Spectator* 6 June 724/1 He [*sc.* a prisoner] hoarded these glimpses of past happiness, rationing his wishful reminiscing to half an hour a day. **1958** *Listener* 25 Sept. 478/1 There are some embarrassingly wishful statements... 'The day when Joyce embarked in Dublin..they were burning his first book... He could see the smoke of the bonfire.'.. *Dubliners* was not burned: it was pulped. **1970** *Guardian* 10 Dec. 4/4 It is hard to reconcile this sort of picture with the one presented by the wishful-thinkers in Saigon. **1974** E. AMBLER *Dr Frigo* II. 117 I'm not a wishful-thinking idiot. **1980** *Sunday Times* (Colour Suppl.) 30 Mar. 55/2 An evocation of youth's transitoriness and innocent wishful-thinking.

wi·sh-fulfilment. [tr. G. *wunscherfüllung* (S. Freud *Die Traumdeutung* (1900) i. 64).] The imaginary fulfilment of acknowledged or unconscious wishes in dreams and fantasies; a dream or other event or object in which the fulfilment of a wish is given (usu. imaginary or symbolic) expression.

[**1901** H. ELLIS in *Jrnl. Mental Sci.* XLVII. 370 The author [*sc.* Freud] points out that..we may with much more reason regard them [*sc.* dreams] as the protectors of sleep, willing us to repose with an imagined fulfilment of our wishes.] **1908** *Jrnl. Abnormal Psychol.* III. 237 This is a hyperbolic realization of his reveries, corresponding to the wish-fulfilment of the normal dream. **1916** A. A. BRILL tr. *Freud's Wit & its Relation to Unconscious* vi. 250 Wider reading circles have contented themselves to reduce the contents [of *The Interpretation of Dreams*]..to a catchword, 'Wish fulfillment'—a term easily remembered and easily abused. **1928** C. H. DODD *Authority of Bible* iii. 66 Behind the song lies..a longing for the downfall of an implacable enemy, which finds in the picture of disaster a 'wish-fulfilment'. **1939** D. CECIL *Young Melbourne* iv. 106 Living wholly in a wish-fulfilment world of her own creation, she insisted it was the real one. **1953** A. HUXLEY *Let.* 31 Oct. (1969) 687 The jewelled palaces are partly, no doubt, wish fulfilments—the opposite of everyday experience. **1956** E. L. MASCALL *Christian Theol. & Natural Science* vi. 217 More careful examination would enable us to sift out those beliefs which had a rational justification for those which were mere wish-fulfilments. **1958** E. A. ARMSTRONG *Folklore of Birds* iii. 55 It is a man's wish-fulfilment story, as Cinderella is a woman's. **1958** *Punch* 25 June 852/2 She is gentle, charming, childlike, submissive, a young man's wish-fulfilment. **1978** M. LEVEY *Case of Walter Pater* xiv. 198 All Pater's dreams, nightmares as well as wish-fulfilments, find expression here.

So **wi·sh-fulfilling** *a.*

1922 R. S. WOODWORTH *Psychol.* xix. 501 They [*sc.* dreams] are 'wish-fulfilling'. **1945** D. L. MOORE *Vulgar Heart* i. 14 The wish-fulfilling assumption that such honours will be deserved. **1976** *Listener* 8 Apr. 447/3 A serenity that accepts as self-evident truth what we reject as wish-fulfilling illusion.

wishing, *vbl. sb.* **d.** *wishing-stone* (earlier example).

1859 G. W. DASENT *Pop. Tales from Norse* (ed. 2) p. xcii, Thus, we have *oska-steinn*, wishing-stone, *i.e.* a stone which plays the part of a divining rod.

Wishram (wi·ʃræm). Also 9 **Wish-ham.** [ad. Sahaptin *Wišxam.*] **a.** (A member of) an American Indian people living in the southern part of the state of Washington. **b.** The language spoken by this people, a dialect of Upper Chinook.

[**1836** W. IRVING *Astoria* I. 109 We would make special mention of the village of Wish-ram.] **1855** *Rep. Commissioner Indian Affairs 1857* 351 They are divided into three principal bands, namely: the Wish-hams, Click-a-hut, and Skien bands. **1907** *Amer. Anthropologist* IX. 533 The Indians formerly living on the northern shore of Columbia river..are known by their Yakima and Klikitat neighbours..as *Wúcxam*, which, in its anglicized form of Wishram, or Wishham, is their common appellation today. *Ibid.* 535 The Wishram is prevailingly sonant in its use of stops. **1930** SPIER & SAPIR *Wishram Ethnography* 153 The Wishram were one of the earliest groups known to explorers of the Columbia River Basin... Only a few Wishram still remain. **1962** *Anthropol. & Human Behavior* (Anthropological Soc. Washington) 25 'Cussing out', a Wishram Chinook's English label for a class of aboriginal speech events. **1972** *Language* XLVIII. 378, I have drawn extensively upon my field research on the Wishram–Wasco dialect of Chinook.

Wiskinkie (wiski·ŋki). *U.S.* Also **Wiskinky, Wiskinski.** [Etym. unknown.] The official of the Tammany Society of New York charged with the office of door-keeper.

1800 *Commercial Advertiser* (N.Y.) 3 Jan. 2/3 Tammany Society, in the following order: 1st, The Wiskinkie, supporting the Cap of Liberty veiled in crape. **1843** *New Mirror* 15 Apr. 18/2 They were placed in charge of the Wiskinski of the wigwam. **1864** C. G. HALPINE *Life & Adventures of Private Miles O'Reilly* 191 He had been a brave when the present Grand Sachems, Wiskinkies and Sagamores were no more than little papooses. **1905** W. L. RIORDON *Plunkitt* 99 Dan Donegan, who used to be the Wiskinskie of the Tammany Society, and received contributions from grateful office holders. **1938** J. W. NORWOOD *Tammany Legend* xi. 145 The chief of a 'Tribe' was its Sachem; the master of ceremonies, the Sagamore; the Sergeant at Arms, the Wiskinskie. **1967** CONNABLE & SILBERFARB *Tigers of Tammany* i. 28 The Wiskinkie (sergeant-at-arms) swore an oath to preserve the Society from 'intruders and eavesdroppers'.

wisp, *v.* Add: **5.** *intr.* Of hair, etc.: to hang or twine in wisps. Hence **wisped** (wispt) *ppl. a.*

1913 W. DE LA MARE *Peacock Pie* 31 Topknot to love-curl The hair wisps down. **1922** A. S. M. HUTCHINSON *This Freedom* II. ix. 164 Her face flushed; her hat awry; her hair escaped and wisped about her eyes. **1976** 'A. YORK' *Dark Passage* iv. 56 Long, straight hair which wisped on her shoulders.

wispy, *a.* Add: Hence **wi·spily** *adv.*

1923 A. HUXLEY *Antic Hay* 30 His long grey hair floated wispily about his head. **1985** M. WESLEY *Harnessing Peacocks* ix. 76 His hair hung wispily round his collar.

‖ **Wissenschaft** (vi·sənʃaft). [Ger.] (The systematic pursuit of) knowledge; learning, scholarship; science. Hence ‖ **Wi·ssenschaftslehre** (-lērə), a theory or philosophy of knowledge (used with reference to the work of J. G. Fichte, author of *Grundlage der gesammten Wissenschaftslehre* (1794)).

1834 F. D. MAURICE *Let.* 24 July in F. Maurice *Life* (1884) I. xi. 168 My friend adds, '..They all seem to think *Wissenschaft*..more important than soundness of creed.' **1846** J. D. MOREAU *Hist. & Crit. View Speculative Philos.* II. v. 72 Fichte's object was..to erect a system..of rigid scientific knowledge... Hence it was that, in place of 'Philosophy' he assumed the term 'Wissenschaftslehre', as most designative of his great purpose. **1896** W. CALDWELL *Schopenhauer's System* ix. 503 That most vicious aspect of German philosophy, so prominent in the Hegelian dialectic and Fichte's *Wissenschaftslehre*, whereby it always seems to be telling us what a fact *must be* before we know what it *is*. **1961** D. G. JAMES *Matt. Arnold* iv. 93 By 'science' he does not, of course, mean 'science' as we now ordinarily understand it; he means *Wissenschaft*, that is, as he says elsewhere, 'knowledge systematically pursued and prized in and for itself'. **1976** B. WILLIAMS *Making of Manchester Jewry* iv. 108 The emergence of Theodores as..a major English representative of the German *Wissenschaft*. **1982** C. CLEMEAU *Ariadne Clue* (1983) xi. 120 These fragments are painstakingly collected published..and roundly applauded as the choicest fruits of philological *Wissenschaft*.

Wistar (wi·stǎɪ, -āɪ). *Med.* and *Biol.* The name of the *Wistar* Institute of Anatomy and Biology, Philadelphia (founded by I. J. Wistar (1827–1905), grandnephew of Caspar Wistar (see WISTARIA)), used *attrib.* to designate rats bred from a strain developed at the Institute for laboratory purposes.

1938 *Amer. Jrnl. Cancer* XXXIV. 353 The Wistar rats used in this series were from the Experimental Colony strain of the Wistar Institute. **1956** *Nature* 10 Mar. 453/2 One series of irradiated mice was injected with a suspension of bone-marrow cells of the Wistar rat. **1970** *Jrnl. Gen. Psychol.* LXXXII. 28 This kind of preference is the same as has been found by Wagner..and Rowntree with Long-Evans and Wistar albino rats.

wistaria. Add: **b.** A light blue-purple shade, the colour of wistaria blossom.

1911 *Daily Colonist* (Victoria, B.C.) 5 Apr. 24/1 (Advt.), Important Silk Purchase..in colors of rose, Persian blue.., wisteria. **1927** *Observer* 3 Apr. 25/5 (Advt.), Sunrise, geranium, wisteria, russet. **1974** *Country Life* 25 Apr. 1025/2 Her best colours..are wistaria, ice blue..and lemon yellow.

wit, *sb.* Add: **IV. 14. b.** *wit-writing* (later example); **e. wit-wanton** *v.* (later *arch.* examples); **wit-worm:** for † read 'now *rare*'; (later example).

1922 JOYCE *Ulysses* 388 And Master Lynch bade him have a care to flout and witwanton. **1922** E. R. EDDISON *Worm* xv. 209, I will not suffer mine indignation so to witwanton with fair justice as persuade me to put the wite on Witchland. **1932** F. SCOTT FITZGERALD *Let.* 2 Aug. (1964) 498, I did not destinate to signify that you were a wiseacre..but..that you were..a longhead,..as are so many epigrammatists, wit-worms, [etc.]. **1947** C. DAY LEWIS *Poetic Image* ii. 50 The conceits of the Metaphysicals are in a way wit-writing too.

‖ **witblits** (vi·tblits). *S. Afr.* Also **witblitz** and as two words. [Afrikaans, irreg. f. Du. *wit* WHITE + G. *blitz* lightning.] Home-brewed brandy, a strong and colourless raw spirit.

1934 *Sunday Times* (Johannesburg) 8 Apr., 'Wit blits' (white lightning) was the name given to peach brandy in the Johannesburg Magistrate's Court yesterday. **1948** *Cape Times* 21 July 16/3 In cases of snakebite people on the platteland have always run for the witblitz. **1955** L. G. GREEN *Karoo* ix. 105 Farmers are allowed to distill small quantities of witblits for their own use. *Ibid.*, *Witblits*, of course, is home-distilled dop brandy with a high alcoholic content. **1966** *Economist* 12 Mar. 1044/3 Coloured people are drinking less [in South Africa], particularly the favoured types of plonk known affectionately as *witblitz*..and *skokiaan*.

witch, *sb.*[2] Add: **5. a.** *witch-act* (earlier examples); *witch-burner* (earlier example), *-master*; *witch-burning*, *witch-roasting*. **b. witch-ball,** (*b*), a hollow ball of (usu. coloured or silvered) glass, formerly displayed in a house as a charm against witchcraft and now for decorative purposes; **witch bottle,** a stone or glass bottle, filled with urine, nails, hair, etc., which was either burned or heated for the purpose of repelling or breaking a witch's power over her victim; **witch-bowl,** a decorative circular glass bowl; **witch dance,** a ritual dance performed by witches; **witch-hopple** *U.S.* = HOBBLE-BUSH; **witch-post,** in Yorkshire, a wooden post, usually of mountain ash, marked with a cross and built into a house as a protection against witches; **witch-smelling,** the smelling out of witches; also *fig.*, witch-hunting; **witch-stone** (earlier example).

1758 M. W. MONTAGUE *Let.* 14 Nov. (1967) III. 188, I..am convinced of the necessity of the repeal of the Witch-act (as it is commonly called). **1916** J. H. YOXALL *Collecting Old Glass* v. 38 Witch-balls seem to have been made at Bristol,..at Nailsea..and at Wrockwardine... These balls, it is said, were hung at each door and window, 'to keep the witches out'. **1927** *Daily Express* 22 June 9/4 There is a fashion just now to collect the deep blue or silver glass balls which our forefathers hung about the house to keep witches away. 'Witch balls' they were called. **1952** L. MACNEICE *Autumn Leaves* 19 The witch-ball on the stairs. **1978** E. ELLENBOGEN tr. *Simenon's Maigret & Toy Village* ii. 34 Its houses..its tiny carefully-tended gardens, its clay animals and glass witchballs. **1893** *Jrnl. Brit. Archaeol. Assoc.* XLIX. 267 Nails were formerly placed in an earthen vessel, and buried beneath the floor, near the hearth, to keep away the witches, and to afford protection from the 'evil eye'; hence such vessels were called 'witch-jugs' or 'witch-bottles'. **1908** E. SMITH in A. C. Kelway *Memorials Old Essex* 252 An old witch-bottle..found 'below the floor and very near the fireplace' ..contained some water, about fourteen horse-nails, and twenty thorns! **1966** G. E. EVANS *Pattern under Plough* vi. 74 Under the hearthstone was the spot most frequently chosen to bury the witch-bottle. **1980** *Rescue News* Sept. 2/3 Both pots must have been buried on purpose, perhaps as charms but the bellarmine is thought to be rather too early to be a witch-bottle. **1955** *Times* 13 May 12/5 Along with salt-cellars, ash-trays, witch-bowls, and the curious jam dishes. **1964** G. SIMS *Terrible Door* xiv. 75 What looked like a fish-bowl was a 'witch bowl' with glass fishes suspended from floating glass bubbles in stagnant water. **1892** *Review of Reviews* Feb. 170/1 (*heading*) A plea for the witch-burners. **1909** *Strand Mag.* XXXVIII. 692/1 They had taken to witch-burning. **1928** G. ADE *Let.* 10 July (1973) 135 Sooner or later we should elect a Catholic to the Presidency just to prove that we are living in the 20th century instead of the 18th and that witch-burning and religious persecutions are no longer the pastimes of a free and intelligent people. **1921** M. MURRAY *Witch-Cult in Western Europe* v. 132 The round dance was..essentially a witch dance. **1971** *Country Life* 9 Sept. 633/3 The round reel survives from the prehistoric witch-dance. **1840** C. F. HOFFMAN *Greyslaer* II. 44 Tangled thickets of moss wood and wytch-hopple gave now the springy footing the tired hunter loves. **1943** R. PEATTIE *Great Smokies* 283 This is the hobblebush or witch hobble [*sic*], an abundant high-mountain shrub whose large rounding leaves reach their color peak in September. **1910** KIPLING *Rewards & Fairies* 96 'What's a Witch-master?'..'A master of witches, of course.' **1931** V. RANDOLPH in B. A. Botkin *Folk-Say* 86 My pappy follered gunsmithin' mostly, but he was a witch-master too. *a* **1944** J. FORD *Some Reminiscences of Danby Parish* (1953) 96 It was the custom of the Priest to cut the Roman X on the upright oak post which went up to the low ceiling... They came to be called 'Witch Posts'. **1957** E. E. EVANS *Irish Folk Ways* v. 64 In north Yorkshire the jamb post, called the witch post, is occasionally found to be covered with designs intended to protect the hearth from evil spirits. **1971** K. THOMAS *Religion & Decline Magic* xvii. 543 Other preservatives included 'witch-posts' built into the structure of the house. **1922** JOYCE *Ulysses* 202 A Scotch philosophaster with a turn for witchroasting. **1937** H. G. WELLS *Star Begotten* vii. 130 Some sort of world-wide witch-smelling for Martians everywhere... You could tell them because *instinctively* you dislike them. **1940** 'G. ORWELL' *Inside Whale* 157 Frenzied witch-smellings after 'Bolshevism'. **1953** J. S. HUXLEY *Evolution in Action* vi. 141 The witch-smelling ordeals of Africa. **1855** G. BORROW *Jrnl.* 23 Aug. in *Exped. to Isle of Man* (1915) 8 What could those witch-stones be?

c. witch's tit: in fanciful proverbial phr. (*as*) *cold as a witch's tit*, extremely cold.

1932 VAN WYCK MASON *Spider House* xviii. 210 It's cold as a witch's tit outside. **1974** *Times* 17 Aug. 7/3 It was cold as a witch's tit, so I sat there and shivered. **1980** R. L. DUNCAN *Brimstone* viii. 200 Just listening to a weather report...Albuquerque's clear but cold as a witch's tit.

witch (witʃ), *v.*[2] *U.S.* [f. WITCH *sb.*[2]] *intr.* and *trans.* To dowse for water with a divining rod. Hence **wi·tcher,** a dowser.

1963 G. THOMSON *Crocus Country* xi. 74 The term to 'witch for water' is said to come from the fact that it was usually done with a witch-hazel wand. *Ibid.*, The witcher would walk up and down in the general area where a well was needed, with the ends of a forked hazel twig held firmly in his hands. **1970** J. BLACKBURN *Land of Promise* ii. 32 The witcher came to a place where the stem of the willow could no longer be held upright. **1978** *Country Life* 7 Dec. 1953/3 He got a well-digger to survey the site... The first driller and others consulted all 'witched' the situation.

witch-doctor. Add: **2.** *Mil. slang.* A psychiatrist.

1966 *Listener* 29 Dec. 960/3, I did not again rub shoulders with..the fraternity until I entered the army.., where they were known..as 'trick-cyclists', 'head-shrinkers', or 'witch-doctors'. **1979** D. ANTHONY *Long Hard Cure* vi. 58 That sounds like one of your witch doctors at the Retreat.

Hence **witch-doctoring** *vbl. sb.*, **-doctory** (also *fig.*).

1924 KIPLING *Debits & Credits* (1926) 182 All the cars I met were 'protected' [with a label] as mine was—till I reached..the limit of the witch-doctoring. **1927** G. B. SHAW in *Sunday Express* 7 Aug. 7/7 The dismal survivals of augury and witch-doctoring. **1944** J. S. HUXLEY *On Living in Revolution* iv. 45 As irreconcilable as is.. witch-doctoring with preventive medicine, or number-mysticism with higher mathematics. **1962** *Observer* 13 May 6/5 'Organisation and management' was for a long time regarded—as one Treasury man put it—as 'third-rate witchdoctory'. **1972** H. A. WILLIAMS *True Resurrection* ii. 22 And this was called scientific medicine as opposed to all forms of witch-doctory. **1977** P. JOHNSON *Enemies of Society* xv. 197 Those who practise psychiatric medicine are in the position of early-nineteenth-century doctors, trying to get round as yet unsolved difficulties by witch-doctoring.

witchert, var. *WICHERT.

witchetty. Add: Also (*rare*) **wichetty, widgety.** Substitute for def.: In full *witchetty grub.* A large white grub (the larva of certain moths and other insects) which infests the roots and stem of the *witchetty bush* (= MULGA 1 a in Dict. and Suppl.), from which it is extracted for use as food by Aboriginals and as bait by fisherman. (Further examples.)

1899 *Contemp. Rev.* Mar. 407 In the witchetty grub totem this sacred painting tallies with..a stone kist at Tillicoutry. **1935** H. H. FINLAYSON *Red Centre* iii. 30 The broad-leafed mulga or witchetty bush, the roots of which harbour a grub beloved by the blacks. **1944** F. CLUNE *Red Heart* 37 The sun gleamed on a motor-bike beneath a clump of witchetty bushes. **1954** B. MILES *Stars my Blanket* viii. 50 The widgetty grub tree at the roots of which the natives dig for the grubs which are like fat white slugs. **1960** *Times* 5 July 11/7 'Witchetty' bushes, a kind of wattle with bright yellow blossom. **1961** P. WHITE *Riders in Chariot* xi. 373 You look to me..like you was made out of old wichetty grubs. **1962** *Oxf. Univ. Gaz.* 19 Mar. 849/1 It is a pointed, oval, red-ochre-coloured, wooden bullroarer with designs of witchetty-grubs. **1968** M. PYKE *Food & Society* iv. 42 Witchetty grubs are famous as an article of diet eaten by aborigines. **1977** C. MCCULLOUGH *Thorn Birds* viii. 178 There were witchetty grubs, fat and white and loathsome.

wi·tch-hunt, *sb.* Also **witch hunt, witchhunt.** [WITCH *sb.*[2]] **1.** A search for witches, or for someone suspected or accused of witchcraft.

1885 R. HAGGARD *K. Solomon's Mines* x. 151 To-night ye will see. It is the great witch-hunt, and many will be smelt out as wizards and slain. **1927** J. Buchan *Witch Wood* xvi. 272 David had..seen a witch hunt..as a boy—and then there had been a furious and noisy crowd. **1960** D. Hudson *Forgotten King* 17 Elizabethan inns and beards and witch hunts give place to the coffee house and the Restoration theatre. **1975** A. Fraser *Whistler's Lane* 9 Her mind had been..on the witch hunts of the early seventeenth century.

fig. **1915** 'I. Hay' *First Hundred Thousand* xiii. 178 Platoon commanders were bidden to hold a witch hunt, and smell out a chiropodist.

2. a. A single-minded and uncompromising campaign against a group of people with unacceptable views or behaviour, *spec.* communists; *esp.* one regarded as unfair or malicious persecution.

1938 'G. Orwell' *Homage to Catalonia* xi. 241 Rank-and-file Communists everywhere are led away on a senseless witch-hunt after 'Trotskyists'. **1947** *Partisan Rev.* XIV. 344, I don't like Stalin's methods, but I shall never, never join in that witch-hunt. **1950** *Here & Now* (N.Z.) Dec. 8/1 Inside the Labour Party there was a witch-hunt of unbelievable viciousness against the Government's critics. **1958** *Times Lit. Suppl.* 21 Nov. 669/4 The story of a security officer in America in the days when McCarthy witch-hunts were frequent and when communists lurked ..under every bed. **1972** *Guardian* 31 Aug. 6/7 Delegates to the annual Conference at the TUC at Brighton next week are urged .not to indulge in a witch hunt..when discussing the 34 affiliated unions which have remained on the register of trade unions. **1976** *Survey* Spring 179 Literary zealots..then took part in the anti-zionist and anti-revisionist witch-hunt. **1977** *Gay News* 24 Mar. 3/1 During the operation—labelled a 'witch-hunt' by the local gay community—28 men were arrested. **1977** *Times* 28 Apr. 2/1 Mr Orme, Minister for Social Security,. said he was not prepared to countenance a witch-hunt against claimants. **1979** A. Price *Tomorrow's Ghost* vii. 120 We must be absolutely fair... This isn't a witch-hunt. **1983** P. Ustinov *My Russia* i. 8 It is fashionable today to conduct a moderate witchhunt for that pro-Soviet bunch of Cambridge undergraduates..who spied for Russia.

b. A campaign *against* an individual.

1960 *Daily Tel.* 29 Jan. 1/2 The Opposition Front Bench do not intend to conduct a 'witch-hunt' against Mr Marples over his business connections. **1973** C. Bonington *Next Horizon* i. 20 The argument had developed into a witch-hunt against Barrie with, I suspect, very little justice. **1977** *Daily Mirror* 30 Mar. 31/1 After the Germans had strolled home 5-1, the controversial Neale accused non-playing captain Peter Simpson of leading a 'witch-hunt' against him.

wi·tch-hu:nter. 1. = Witch-finder a.

1867 Harland & Wilkinson *Lancs. Folk-Lore* i. 184 Dr. John Webster (who detected Robinson, the Lancashire witch-hunter).

2. One who takes part in or publicly advocates a witch-hunt (sense *2).

1935 *New Republic* 19 June 158 (*heading*) Witch-hunters at work. **1940** H. L. Ickes *Diary* 22 Feb. (1954) III. 139 Probably the witch-hunters are largely responsible for this. No one likes to be called a Communist and yet that is what every liberal has to submit to. **1960** *Encounter* Mar. 78/2 It is .necessary to that public to learn that its witch-hunters are corrupt. **1980** J. O'Faolain *No Country for Young Men* xvi. 347 Obsessed as a pair of witch-hunters, minds zipping along their single track, they challenged him.

wi·tch-hu:nting, *vbl. sb.* **1.** The activity of seeking out witches and obtaining evidence against them.

1640 B. Jonson *Sad Shepherd* ii. vii, in *Workes* II. 149 You speake, Alken, as if you knew the sport of Witch-hunting, Or starting of a Hag. **1885** Rider Haggard *King Solomon's Mines* xv. 249 Ignosi..reaffirmed the promises..that witch-hunting should cease. **1935** B. Russell *Relig. & Sci.* iv. 99 In New England, a fierce outbreak of witch-hunting occurred at the end of the seventeenth century. **1950** Auden *Enchafèd Flood* (1951) ii. 51 The actual horrors of persecution, witch-hunting, and provincial superstition from which they were trying to deliver mankind. **1981** M. Warner *Joan of Arc* v. 114 Double-think is..endemic to the business of witch-hunting, for..the witch-hunter is the alleged witch's most committed believer.

2. Participation in or advocacy of a witch-hunt (sense *2).

1932 J. F. Carter *What we are about to Receive* xviii. 204 Once the election is over..we shall quietly lay aside our witch hunting. **1943** G. Greene *Ministry of Fear* ii. i. 125 You can't avoid witch-hunting in war-time. **1968** *Daily Tel.* 16 Nov 16/3 We have been treated to a plethora of half-truths, innuendo, witch-hunting and ignorance. **1977** *Socialist Press* 2 Mar. 5/5 Despite this combination of administrative hysteria, right wing witch hunting and Stalinist betrayal, the fees issue is still alive at Essex.

Also as *ppl. a.* Hence (as a back-formation) **wi·tch-hunt** *v.*, (*a*) *trans.*, to subject to a witch-hunt (sense *2); (*b*) *intr.*, to take part in a witch-hunt.

1889 W. H. D. Adams *Witch, Warlock & Magician* ii. v. 402 Our witch-hunting King offers an explanation of a peculiarity which..our readers have already noted. **1946** *Sun* (Baltimore) 19 July 20/1 The War Department hasn't gone off half-cocked to 'witch hunt, red bait or to bust' unions. **1948** 'J. Tey' *Franchise Affair* v. 49 Give those Midland morons a good excuse and they'll witch-hunt with the best. **1960** *Twentieth Century* Apr. 380 Assorted political personages (including a witch-hunting Senator). **1960** *News Chron.* 29 June 6/7 That uncouth, witch-hunting and paederastic gowk [*sc.* James I]. **1975** *Listener* 4 Dec. 754/2 David Niven..has severe words for it [*sc.* Hollywood]..for letting itself be..libelled and witch-hunted by..gossip columnists. **1980** *Jrnl. R. Soc. Arts* Mar. 180/1 There is..a tendency to witch-hunt when any disaster happens. **1983** W. McIlvanney *Papers of Tony Veitch* x. 59 'When did you join the vigilantes, Jack?' 'Never. I'm not witch-hunting whoever did it.'

witchit, var. *Wichert.

witch knot. Add: **1. b.** A knot tied for the purpose of making or averting a spell.

1884 A. Lang in M. Hunt *Grimm's Household Tales* I. p. xlvi, All over the world savages..tie 'witch-knots'. **1947** A. Runeberg tr. E. H. Meyer in *Witches & Demons in West-European Folk Belief* vii. 95 Witches..twist twigs into witchknots, and leave the fairy rings in the grass after their dances. **1957** E. E. Evans *Irish Folk Ways* xxi. 304 The cow-doctor uses sympathetic magic.. by drawing apart over the animal's back the loose ends of a string tied in a complicated witch-knot or 'bat',.. which comes undone when pulled.

witchy, *a.* Delete *rare* and add later examples. Also, characteristic or suggestive of a witch.

1968 S. Plath in *Atlantic Monthly* Sept. 54/2 Over the trees at the far side of the Common the..torch flare flattens and recovers under some witchy invisible push. **1975** M. Drabble *Realms of Gold* iii. 241 It [*sc.* a figurine] had a witchy, androgynous, yet friendly look. **1976** *Listener* 4 Nov. 590/2 The witchy black of the Grimm forests.

witful. Restrict *rare* to sense 1 and add: **2.** (Later examples.)

1924 *Countries of World* I. 639/2 The women deck these stands with witful skill. **1935** W. de la Mare *Early One Morning* 321 A willing and witful child. **1980** *N.Y. Times* 26 Aug. c-8/5 Ravel's Sonato for Violin and Cello... For pinpoint gestural precision and witful repartee, this sophisticated instrumental dialogue is an unending source of fascination.

witgat (vi·tχat). *S. Afr.* [Afrikaans, f. *wit* white + *gat* hole.] Any of several trees of the genus *Boscia*, which have pale bark and are found in dry areas of southern Africa, esp. the evergreen *B. albitrunca*. Also *witgatboom* [Afrikaans *boom* tree].

1824 W. J. Burchell *Trav. Int. S. Afr.* II. 18 Their trunks..appeared at a little distance as if they had been whitewashed. From this singular character, they have gained the name of *Wit-gat boom.* **1860** Harvey & Sonder *Flora Capensis* I. 362 A tall tree called *Witgat* by the colonists. **1932** C. Fuller *Louis Trigardt's Trek* 47 We were standing under a *witgatboom.* **1966** E. Palmer *Plains of Camdeboo* iv. 54 Close to this grew a witgat tree not fifteen feet tall but with a thick, seamed, milk-white trunk and a dense grey-green crown of tough little leaves. *Ibid.* xvii. 271 They..made coffee from the roots of the witgat. **1972** Palmer & Pitman *Trees S. Afr.* I. 620 Witgat wood is heavy and tough. **1973** Y. Burgess *Life to Live* 25 Coffee made from the roots of the witgat tree.

with, *prep.*, (*adv.*, *conj.*). Add: **II. 9. e.** *what's with——?* what about, what are the circumstances of?; how are things with, what's the matter with? *colloq.* (orig. *U.S.*).

1940 J. O'Hara *Pal Joey* 125 What's with the free food? Explain. **1962** E. Linington *Extra Kill* viii. 122 He says.. 'What's with Whalen?' When he hears Whalen's out, he gets mad. **1969** 'V. Packer' *Don't rely on Gemini* (1970) viii. 62 'What's with you and these long baths?' Archie asked. **1978** K. Amis *Jake's Thing* xv. 158 What's with Jake is that he can't get it up any more, and what's with Brenda is she thinks it's her fault for having gotten middle-aged and fat.

22. a. Also in phr. *with us, them,* alive, still living.

1611 Bible *Acts* ix. 39 All the widowes stood by him weeping, and shewing the coats and garments which Dorcas made, while shee was with them. **1961** E. Williams *George* xxiii. 391 That Mr Bellis, he's gone dead, not that he had that much life in him when he was with us, poor fellow. **1966** *Listener* 3 Feb. 166/2 The English church at Shiraz..was built entirely thanks to the enthusiasm of the then incumbent, who was a very learned man (is indeed still with us).

e. *to be with* (a person), to follow his line of reasoning, to keep up with and understand his explanation, instructions, etc. *colloq.*

1900 F. P. Dunne *Mr. Dooley's Philos.* 248 We keep our thoughts fixed upon th' inanity iv th' finite in comparison with th' onthinkable truth with th' ondivided an' onimaginable reality. Boys ar-re ye with me? **1933** *Punch* 8 Feb. 150/3 'Does it look to you as if the Boss keeps his skeletons in any ice-boxes around here?' 'Huh?' she said, not quite with me yet. **1955** N. Fitzgerald *House is Falling* xi. 190 'I'm with you so far,' said Hugh who for the first time was really giving his mind to the problem. **1977** T. Heald *Just Desserts* viii. 188 'She will have to be taken in hand. Which..has been the point of the exercise all along.' 'I'm not with you.'

f. *to be with it,* to be within a particular fashionable or exclusive group or set, to be up-to-date or *au fait* with the latest news, ideas, etc.; to be mentally alert. Also *to get with it,* to become informed or up-to-date, etc. *slang* (orig. *U.S.*). Cf. *With-it *a.*

1931 *Amer. Mercury* Nov. 353/2 *Not with it,* said of an outsider. 'He's not with it.' **1959** R. Condon *Manchurian Cand.* (1960) vii. 108 They are with it, Raymond. Believe me, they are even away ahead of me. **1960** *Guardian* 9 Dec. 13 The new *Time and Tide,* to borrow the language of the teen-ager, is 'with it'. **1961** J. O'Hara in *Assembly* 159 Bud come to see you, especially when you had a chance of winning? Get *with* it, boy. **1971** *Daily Mail* 6 May 24/4 Horne made a strong attempt to get with it. Result: the stronger emphasis on fashionwear. **1976** *Jrnl. R. Soc. Arts* CXXV. 17/1 The need to be in fashion—in the swim—up to date—'with it'—might not have been the least of our driving forces for general progress. **1981** M. Doody in Martin & Mullen *No Alternative* iv. 37 What is 'with it' for one or two generations can seem palpable folly a hundred years later. **1985** W. J. Burley *Wycliffe & Four Jacks* vii. 149 There's an old man, living in a home... He's quite with it—I mean he's mentally alert.

24. d. *with-profit(s)* adj., of a life assurance policy: allowing the insured to receive a share of the profits of the insurance company, usu. in the form of a bonus. Also applied to holders of such policies, the associated payments, etc. Cf. *without-profit(s)* adj. s.v. *Without *prep.* 7 c.

1924 Tayler & Tyler *Life Assurance* ii. 19 Nearly all the offices transacting life assurance business issue two great classes of policy—(*a*) Those which share in the profits, known as 'with-profit' or 'participating' policies; and (*b*) Those which do not share in the profits, known as 'without-profit' or 'non-participating' policies. **1944** S. d'E. Colam *Life Assurance for Agents* 16 Premiums for with profit policies are larger than for without profit policies. **1950** *Economist* 18 Nov. 840/2 In trying to assess the relative merits of with-profit contracts, the only firm basis of comparison is the actual amount paid. **1961** *Observer* 10 Dec. 4/3 A modest writing-up of book values would add to the good times which with-profit-holders can expect in the future in the form of bumper bonuses. **1965** *Economist* 24 July p. xxii/2 These profits go to the with-profits policyholders, as well as the profits on the with-profits business itself. **1979** *Financial Times* 20 Jan. 7/6 If you are shopping around for a with-profits policy, take a look at how insurance brokers work out projections of maturity value. **1982** *Equity & Law Life Assurance Co. Ann. Rep. 1981* 16 The rate of terminal bonus depends on the year of entry as a with-profit benefit and is applied to the with-profit sum (or annuity) and attaching bonus.

withdrawal. Add: **4. b.** *Psychol.* The state or process of psychic retreat from objective reality or social involvement; also *transf.*

1916 C. E. Long tr. *Jung's Coll. Papers on Anal. Psychol.* vi. 203 Autistic withdrawal into one's own phantasies is what I formerly designated as the obvious overgrowth of the phantasies of the complex. **1937** K. Horney *Neurotic Personality of our Time* v. 98 The fourth means of protection [*sc.* against the basic anxiety] is withdrawal. **1957** P. Lafitte *Person in Psychol.* xii. 181 Withdrawal and regression..are general classes of behaviour as compared to the social specificity of striving for advancement or mendacity. **1970** Touraine & Pécaut in I. L. Horowitz *Masses in Lat. Amer.* iii. 90 At the lowest level, we find *withdrawal,* characterized by a rejection of the industrial world. **1973** *Jrnl. Genetic Psychol.* June 315 One type of children's fantasy is 'withdrawal'.

5. Cessation of use or provision of a drug; *spec.* the interruption of doses of an addictive drug, with resulting craving and physical reactions.

The 1897 example is an isolated one.

1897 [see Injector 2]. **1929** D. Hammett *Dain Curse* xxi. 237 Tears were one of the symptoms of morphine withdrawal. **1965** Wilner & Kassebaum *Narcotics* vi. 96 Withdrawal of morphine by substitution and subsequent withdrawal of methadon. **1972** *Nature* 22 Dec. 443/1 Dr R. Ericsson..suggested that the criteria for a successful antispermatogenic drug were..return of fertility on withdrawal, and normal libido. **1977** *Lancet* 29 Jan. 255/1 Any doctor prescribing or patient receiving this potent drug should consider carefully the effect of withdrawal which has not, to my knowledge, been researched.

6. = *coitus interruptus* s.v. *Coitus.

1889 W. T. Stead *Diary* 20 Jan. in J. W. R. Scott *Life & Death of Newspaper* (1952) xix. 244, I have from the birth of Willie practised simple syringing with water. Of late always withdrawal. **1923** M. C. Stopes *Contraception* iv. 48 Vaginal stimulation consummating the ejaculation after withdrawal, commonly called '*coitus interruptus*'. **1963** M. McCarthy *Group* iii. 66 What method of contraception had been used..?' 'Withdrawal,' murmured the doctor. **1978** G. Cunningham *New Woman & Victorian Novel* 6 Such methods as the safe period, the sheath, the sponge..and withdrawal.

7. *attrib.* and *Comb.*, as (sense *5) *withdrawal pain, period, syndrome,* etc.; **withdrawal slip,** a form which must be filled in when withdrawing money from a bank or other place of deposit; **withdrawal symptom,** an unpleasant physiological reaction resulting from the process of ceasing to taken an addictive drug; usu. *pl.*; also *fig.*

1924 *Brit. Jrnl. Inebriety* XXI. 88 The *withdrawal symptoms* of addiction disease. **1929** Light & Torrance in *Arch. Internal Med.* XLIV. 11 The general behavior and symptomatology of these addicts were uniform during the forty-eight hour withdrawal period. *Ibid.* 14 Addicts will admit that when they are unable to obtain drugs and when withdrawal symptoms..become severe, the assurance of an available supply at a considerable distance will cause them to travel..with remarkable speed and efficiency. **1961** *Lancet* 23 Sept. 677/1 A steroid withdrawal syndrome occurs in patients who have stopped corticosteroid therapy. **1962** *Ibid.* 6 Jan. 54/2 Lobeline sulphate closely resembles nicotine in many of its pharmacological actions. Using it as a substitute for tobacco during the withdrawal phase, Dorsey found the results 'encouraging'. **1962** 'K. Orvis' *Damned & Destroyed* xvi. 113, I had seen that stare and twitching frequently enough now..to be able to tag it as an indication of the degree of withdrawal sickness. **1965** *New Statesman* 7 May 716/1 Often these women directly sabotaged the programme. One flushed her son's withdrawal medication down the lavatory. *Ibid.* 3 Dec. 866/2, I asked him how long it was since the withdrawal pains had stopped. **1966** C. E. ISRAEL *Hostages* 94 She wouldn't have had the dreg end of her withdrawal agonies yet. **1967** *Guardian* 7 Dec. 1/6 Methedrine has been used in heroin withdrawal treatment. **1970** G. F. NEWMAN *Sir, You Bastard* v. 140 Morgan was entering the withdrawal stage and would soon be requiring another intravenous dose. **1970** G. GREER *Female Eunuch* 276 Mrs J.S. used up two supplies of pills in all innocence, and then discovered that she had withdrawal symptoms. **1973** 'E. MCBAIN' *Let's hear It* xv. 226 On the withdrawal slip before him, he wrote the date, and the number of his account, and then he filled in the amount. **1976** *Times* 18 Oct. 3/7 Sir Harold Wilson..the former Prime Minister..says he has suffered no 'withdrawal symptoms' since resigning. **1979** F. OLBRICH *Sweet & Deadly* ix. 110 The bank manager..showed Ramesh the withdrawal slip for four thousand rupees.

withdrawn, *ppl. a.* Add: Also *spec.* in *Psychol.*, characterized by isolation and loss of contact with objective reality. Cf. *WITHDRAWAL 4 b.

1932 *Smith. Coll. Stud. Social Work* III. 145 Only four of the patients..were of the..type often thought to be common among the pre-schizophrenic... Perhaps children of the withdrawn, timid type are only rarely referred to a child guidance clinic. **1950** *Times* 12 May 7/7 The emotional re-education of the severely withdrawn type was at best a tricky business, for which frequent consultation between the school staff and the psychologist was advisable. **1971** H. KOHUT *Analysis of Self* ix. 243 He not only would tend to become generally withdrawn..and diffusely depressed, but..also manifested a striking change in his dream pattern.

withdraw·nness. [f. prec. + -NESS.] Withdrawn or retired character.

1927 *Public Opinion* Feb. 102/1 He has the curiosity and interest of a young man and has none of the settled habits and introspection and withdrawnness of an old man. **1976** *Classical Q.* XXVI. 161 A more general characteristic of the Homeric style, the restrained objectivity and aristocratic withdrawnness.

withe, with, *sb.* Add: **5.** *withe axe*; **withe-rod,** a deciduous shrub, *Virburnum nudum*, native to North America and bearing clusters of small white flowers; also, a thin flexible twig from this or a similar shrub; (earlier and later examples).

1819 KEATS *Let.* 5 Sept. (1958) II. 156 At the days end his thoughts will run upon a withe axe if he ever had handled one. **1776** G CARTWRIGHT *Jrnl.* 19 Oct. (1792) II. 215 The people came down from the lodge, and brought..a bundle of white-rods [*sic*]. **1846** G. B. EMERSON *Rep. Trees & Shrubs growing in Forests Mass.* 364 The Naked Viburnum. Withe Rod... A slender, erect shrub. **1943** R. PEATTIE *Great Smokies* 265 We recognize the..withe rod..and wintergreen.

wither, *v.*[2] Add: **3. b.** *spec.* in phr. *to wither away*, used with reference to the belief held in Marxist philosophy that when the dictatorship of the proletariat has effected the necessary changes in society, the state will eventually cease to be necessary and will therefore disappear; also used allusively or generally. So *withering away*.

1919 tr. *Lenin's State & Revol.* i. 21 Engels speaks here of the *destruction* of the capitalist State by the proletarian revolution, while the words about its withering away refer to the remains of a *proletarian* State *after* the Socialist revolution. *Ibid.* 22 Only the proletarian State or semi-State withers away after the revolution. **1935** E. BURNS tr. *Engels' Anti-Dühring* III. ii. 315 The government of persons is replaced by the administration of things and the direction of the process of production. The state is not 'abolished', it withers away. **1937** *Times* 7 July 17/6 The Marxist theory of the 'withering away' of the State. **1948** M. LASKI *Tory Heaven* v. 81 Reynolds is an M.I.5 nark... Eventually, they say, all that sort of thing will just wither away. **1971** *Guardian* 9 Sept. 13/1 Stormont was designed to wither away. It was invented in the hope that the two parts of Ireland would become united within the British Empire. **1980** D. FERNBACH tr. *Buci-Glucksmann's Gramsci & State* xii. 285 The transition from an inevitable 'productivist' phase to an integral state thus takes place by way of hegemony and the distant tendential perspective of a withering away of the state. *Ibid.* 289 A state that withers away to the extent that its function withers away.

witherling[1]. For † *Obs.* read *Obs.* exc. *arch.* and add later example.

1922 W. STEVENS *Let.* 21 Dec. (1967) 232, I have omitted many things, exercising the most fastidious choice, so far as that was possible among my witherlings.

withers, *sb.* Add: **c.** *wither pad.*

1963 E. H. EDWARDS *Saddlery* xv. 112 Numnahs and wither pads are used in conjunction with saddles. **1976** *Horse & Hound* 3 Dec. 52 (Advt.), The John Ayres New Zealand Rug... Featuring a sheepskin wither pad.

withershin(s), widdershin(s), *a.* [f. the adv.] Moving in an anticlockwise direction, contrary to the apparent course of the sun (considered as unlucky or sinister); unlucky, ill-fated, relating to the occult.

1926 D. H. LAWRENCE *Plumed Serpent* vi. 112 She made up her mind, to be alone, and to cut herself off from all the mechanical widdershin contacts. *Ibid.*, He, too, was widdershins, unwinding the sensations of disintegration and anti-life. **1936** DYLAN THOMAS *Twenty-Five Poems* 16 Shall I still be love's house on the widdershin earth, Woe to the windy mansions at my shelter? **1973** G. M. BROWN *Magnus* vi. 112 There is a black joy abroad, a dance of the deadly sins, a withershin rout. **1976** *Early Music* Oct. 399/1 The sentiments and rituals of the court can be grotesquely guyed by the spirits (widdershins dances, sick-caricature mimes to accompany the Sorceress's prophecies and provoke those ho-ho outbursts, etc.).

withholding, *vbl. sb.* Add: **2.** Special Comb.: **withholding rate** *U.S.*, the rate for a withholding tax; **withholding table** *U.S.*, a table showing amounts of tax to be deducted from a dividend payment, salary, etc.; **withholding tax** orig. *U.S.*, a tax deducted at source, *spec.* one levied by some countries on interest or dividends paid to a person resident outside that country.

1972 *Time* 17 Apr. 43/3 Spending has been held back in part because of a colossal blooper by the House Ways and Means Committee in setting the new withholding rates. **1976** *Billings* (Montana) *Gaz.* 30 June 6-A/1 The House unanimously passed and sent to President Ford Tuesday a two-month extension of current lower income tax withholding rates. **1947** *Sun* (Baltimore) 15 May 2/8 The Finance Committee halved the House bill for the current year and made the new withholding tables effective as of July 1. **1940** *U.S. Federal Rep.* 2nd Ser. CXII. 1000/2 Intra-company payments designated as 'interest' would not be so regarded..for the purpose of the withholding tax. *Ibid.*, The principal amount..was due complainant on account of withholding taxes. **1950** *Tax Cases* XXXIII. 346 The Appellant received her arrears of interest as follows: In June, 1943... $18,000 *Less*: U.S. withholding tax at 30 per cent... 5,400. **1960** I. WALLACH *Absence of Cello* (1961) 7 Will you tell me why the hell you never paid the withholding taxes for your employees? **1971** *Financial Mail* (Johannesburg) 26 Feb. 717/1 Interest accruing to non-residents of the Republic is subject to deduction of a withholding tax at the rate of 10 per cent, exemption from the tax having been granted in respect of accruals of interest amounting to R20 or less in any one year. **1979** *Daily Tel.* 27 Oct. 27/1 Many foreign countries have tax laws, which, in principle, require the foreign payer of the dividends or interest to deduct a withholding tax when making the payment to a non-resident. **1984** *Times* 5 Oct. 25/1 The German withholding tax was introduced in 1965 to prevent an overvaluation of the Deutschemark injurious to exports.

within, *prep.* Add: **6. d.** *a story within a story* and varr., a story, performance, etc., complete in itself but occurring within another. Cf. *play within a play* s.v. *PLAY *sb.* 14 a.

1961 WEBSTER s.v. *Within*, A musical within a musical. **1971** J. GORES in 'E. Queen' *Magicians of Mystery* (1976) 162 A new kind of procedural detective story..it uses the dream 'story-within-a-story' which antedates even.. The Vision of Pierce Plowman. **1976** C. BERMANT *Coming Home* II. ii. 125 A plump, bespectacled woman..grasped him in a tearful embrace. Was this a drama within a drama, a man who had thought he'd lost his wife and would rather that she had stayed lost? **1978** *Listener* 19 Jan. 86/3 Fitzgerald was featured creating one of his.. short stories... This device allowed for a film within a film. **1984** B. PAUL *Renewable Virgin* ii. 38 There was some sort of a crime-within-a-crime just waiting to be discovered.

within (wiðiˑn), *sb.* [f. the adv.] That which is within or inside (esp. *fig.*).

1912 J. STEPHENS *Crock of Gold* xiii. 166 It [*sc.* anger] is not the beneficent blindness which prevents one from seeing without, but it is that desperate darkness which cloaks the within, and hides the heart and the brain from each other's husbandly and wifely recognition. **1938** L. MACNEICE *Mod. Poetry* 28 Wyndham Lewis maintains that it is the artist's or writer's business to depict the Without of people and not their Within. **1973** *Times* 26 Nov. 15/8 Having every intention of looking again and again before the exhibition finally departs for its permanent home in the 'Great Within', or wherever—I feel I must compliment the compilers of the excellent catalogue.

within-door, *adv. phr.* (*a.*) For † *Obs.* read Now *rare* and add later examples.

1884 TENNYSON *Becket* I. i. 35 They [*sc.* moths] burn themselves *within*-door. **1954** M. SHARP *Gipsy in Parlour* xxi. 200 All female within-door work had been properly done.

with-it (wiˑðit), *a. slang.* [f. vbl. phr. *to be with it*: see *WITH *prep.* 22 f.] Fashionable, up-to-date.

1962 *Listener* 29 Nov. 909/2 Curtain designs for the really with-it 'contemporary home'. **1963** [see *FAR-OUT *a.* b]. **1970** J. G. VERMANDEL *Dine with Devil* ix. 52 The with-it Mr. Angel enjoyed a more subtle turn of mind. **1977** J. I. M. STEWART *Madonna of Astrolabe* v. 94 The silly woman just thought it a with-it thing to say to a celebrated dramatist.

Hence **wi·th-it-ness.**

1963 *Punch* 22 May 752/1 The headlong rush of..social notabilities to win themselves the TW badge of with-itness. *a* **1974** R. CROSSMAN *Diaries* (1976) II. 445 This has all paid off in terms of the audience ratings where the B.B.C. has been doing well in the last six months, winning the battle for the audience by its with-itness.

withness. (Earlier and later examples.)

1904 W. JAMES *Ess. Rad. Empiricism* (1912) ii. 47 This imperfect intimacy, this bare relation of *withness* between some parts of the sum total of experience and other parts. **1929** A. N. WHITEHEAD *Process & Reality* II. ii. 88 The account..traces back these secondary qualities to their root in physical prehensions expressed by the 'withness of the body'. **1946** *Sci. & Society* X. 244 Conversely union and withness, the *ta-tong* of Chinese thought, has been the aim of democracies. **1962** *Times* 11 Dec. 11/4 The 'withness' is all.

without, *adv., prep., conj.* Add: **B.** *prep.* **III. 7. c.** *without profit(s)* adj., of a life assurance policy: providing normal cover but not allowing the insured to receive a share of the profits of the insurance company. Also applied to the associated funds, business, etc. Cf. *with profit(s)* adj. s.v. *WITH *prep.* 24 d.

1924, 1944 [see *WITH *prep.* (*adv., conj.*) 24 d]. **1960** *Times* 24 Oct. (Financial Rev.) p. xiii/4 For without-profits contracts are tending to come down. **1965** *Economist* 24 July p. xxii, When interest rates are high and there is significant inflation, profits on the without-profits businesses are high, since the premiums were originally fixed on the basis of lower money returns than are now being earned. **1982** *London Life Association Ann. Rep.*, Total without profit funds.

C. *conj.* **2.** Also, chiefly in U.S. dial. use: unless, without its being the case that.

1867 J. R. LOWELL *Biglow Papers* 2nd Ser. p. lvii, I don't git much done 'thout I bogue right in along 'th my men. **1903** 'T. COLLINS' *Such is Life* (1937) i. 51 A man shouldn't make a dog of his self without he's well paid for it. That's my religion. **1955** F. O'CONNOR *Wise Blood* iii. 52 Everything she looked at was that child... She couldn't lie with that man without she saw it. **1962** E. ALBEE *Who's Afraid of V. Woolf?* (1964) I. 51 Man can put up with only so much without he descends a rung or two on the old evolutionary ladder. **1984** A. CARTER *Nights at Circus* ii. 46 No two deaths without a third follows.

D. *sb.* For *nonce-use* read *rare*. (Further example.)

1938 [see *WITHIN *sb.*].

witless, *a.* Add: **7.** Alluding to a state of extreme fear. Esp. in *colloq.* phr. *to be scared witless*.

1975 D. BAGLEY *Snow Tiger* 19 It's the last job he'll ever have and he's scared witless that he'll lose it. **1982** S. BRETT *Murder Unprompted* ii. 19 'How are you feeling?'.. 'Scared witless, darling.'

witness, *sb.* Add: **I. 8. b.** = *Jehovah's Witness* s.v. *JEHOVAH 2. orig. *U.S.*

1931 *Watchtower* 15 Oct. 316/2 If any one does become fearful and ceases to be a witness, he ceases to be of the remnant and of God's anointed or Christ. **1935** *Time* 18 Nov. 59/1 By last week 28 Witnesses of Jehovah had popped up in the U.S. public schools. Cora Foster.. faced dismissal after confessing that she, too, was a Witness. **1974** *Watchtower* 15 Jan. 56/1 Suddenly, under religious animosity, the young man whipped out a knife and stabbed the Witness to death. **1980** R. HILL *Spy's Wife* ii. 8 Charity collectors went away happy, and..even Mormons and Witnesses had got enough courtesy to bring them back.

III. 15. witness-stand (earlier example).

1853 THOREAU *Let.* 10 Apr. (1958) 304 Expect no trivial truth from me, unless I am in the witness-stand.

witogie (vitūᵊˑχi). *S. Afr.* Also **witoogie, witteoogje.** [Afrikaans, f. Du. *wit* white + *oog* eye + *-ie* diminutive suffix.] Any of several birds of the genus *Zosterops* found in southern Africa, esp. *Z. pallidus* (formerly *Z. capensis*).

1867 E. L. LAYARD *Birds S. Afr.* 116 *Zosterops Capensis*..Witteoogje, lit. white eye. **1936** E. L. GILL *First Guide S. Afr. Birds* 37 Witogie... The Cape White-eye sings all through the summer. **1949** *Cape Argus* 15 Oct. (Mag. Sect.) 2/7 Those pretty little birds known as white-eyes or witogies..are well-known in most parts of the country as small green or yellowish birds with a characteristic circle of white feathers round each eye. **1957** *Cape Times* 11 Dec. 11/2 This burly bird has had a couple of twittering *witoogies* in close attendance. **1963** M. KAVANAGH *We Merry Peasants* x. 110 The tiny *witogies* have for their own use a fruit-laden pomegranate tree.

witteboom. (Earlier and later examples.)

1799 A. BARNARD *Let.* 4 Apr. in *Lett. Lady Anne Barnard to Henry Dundas* (1973) 185 Her Ladyship..is soon to present the Regiment with their colors [*sic*], in which the Whittebomb [*sic*]..is Happily blended and united with the Royal oak. **1926** C. G. BOTHA *Our S. Afr.* (1938) 85 *Witteboomen*..is the name of the well known silver trees found in the Cape Peninsula. **1972** PALMER & PITMAN *Trees S. Afr.* I. 493 Witteboom..is believed to grow naturally only in the Cape Peninsula.

witter, *v.*: see *WHITTER *v.* 3.

Wittgensteinian (viˑtgənstəiˑniăn), *a.* and *sb.* [f. the name of the Austrian-born philosopher Ludwig *Wittgenstein* (1889–1951) +

-IAN.] **A.** *adj.* Of, pertaining to, or characteristic of Wittgenstein, or his theories or methods. **B.** *sb.* An adherent of Wittgenstein's ideas.

1946 *Mind* LV. 25 Unfortunately, for the outsider there exists no official and adequate statement of the Wittgensteinian technique. *Ibid.*, 'W—ns' will be used for 'Wittgensteinians'. **1954** [see *RUSSELLIAN *a.* and *sb.*]. **1966** D. JENKINS *Educated Soc.* iii. 140 The Wittgensteinian line of concluding that when one cannot profitably speak one must perforce be silent. **1969** T. F. TORRANCE *Theol. Sci.* i. 19 To use Wittgensteinian language, are these 'images' 'pictures' or 'tools'? **1973** *Listener* 4 Jan. 21/2 A hard-line defence, by a leading Wittgensteinian, of the Pope's pronouncement on contraception. **1980** *Times Lit. Suppl.* 20 June 714/2 Professor Wright..picks up some Wittgensteinian themes and explores how they might be developed. *Ibid.* 714/4 The question of whether ..a Wittgensteinian can defend the distinction between necessary and contingent propositions.

Wittig (vi·tiχʸ, -ig). *Chem.* The name of Georg Friedrich Karl *Wittig* (b. 1897), German chemist, used *attrib.* to designate various synthetic techniques introduced by him, as **Wittig reaction,** a method for the preparation of substituted alkenes utilizing the action of an alkyl phosphorus ylide on a carbonyl compound (aldehyde or ketone); **Wittig rearrangement,** the conversion of benzyl or allyl ethers in the presence of a strong base to the corresponding secondary or tertiary alcohol.

1951 *Jrnl Amer. Chem. Soc.* LXXIII. 1437 The Wittig rearrangement of benzyl ethers by lithium phenyl. **1956** *Chem. Abstr.* L. 6443 The previous attempt to prep. a model vitamin D triene by the Wittig reaction..has been continued. **1974** GILL & WILLIS *Pericyclic Reactions* vi. 195 This elegant experiment proved that the migration involves a *supra-supra* interaction in Wittig rearrangements. **1979** *Sci. Amer.* Dec. 74/1 Vitamin A is synthesized industrially using the Wittig reaction. **1980** *Chem. in Brit.* XVI. 466/3 Vitamin A acetate is produced industrially *via* the Wittig synthesis.

wittite (vi·təit). *Min.* [ad. Sw. *wittit* (K. Johansson 1924, in *Ark. f. Kemi, Mineral. och Geol.* IX. IX. 2), f. the name of Th. *Witt*, Swedish mining engineer: see -ITE¹.] A mineral containing lead, bismuth, selenium, and sulphur and occurring as grey monoclinic crystals.

1924 *Mineral. Abstr.* II. 340 Wittite resembles molybdenite in appearance. **1980** [see *WEIBULLITE].

wiv (wiv). Representation of a vulg. pronunc. (esp. Cockney) of WITH *prep.* (*adv.*, *conj.*).

1898 J. D. BRAYSHAW *Slum Silhouettes* 1 Tall an' thin, yer say? Wot, wiv long white 'ands, an' black 'air—Yus! **1933** D. L. SAYERS *Murder must Advertise* xix. 332 You'll 'ave 'im steppin' aht ter meet me wiv' a crimson carpet and a bokay. **1981** 'J. GASH' *Vatican Rip* iv. 44 Want me to come wiv yer, Lovejoy?

wiwi¹. (Earlier and later examples.)

1840 J. S. POLACK *Manners & Customs New Zealanders* II. 285 *Wi-wi*, kind of wiry grass that is pulled up in tufts, it also is the produce of the marsh. **1970** MOORE & EDGAR *Flora N.Z.* II. 59 The Maori name for rushes and rush-like plants is *Wiwi*.

wi-wi². For *Austral.* read *Austral.* & *N.Z.* and add earlier example.

1841 E. J. WAKEFIELD in *N.Z. Jrnl.* II. XLV. 243/1 Should the *Wiwis*, or French, kill any of our Chiefs.

Wiyot (wī·yǫt). [Wiyot *wiyat* (people of) the Eel River delta.] An American Indian people formerly living on the coast of northern California; the Macro-Algonquian language of this people. Also *attrib.* or as *adj.*

1851 G. GIBBS *Jrnl.* 9 Sept. in H. R. Schoolcraft *Information respecting Indian Tribes* (1853) III. iv(3). 127 The name given to this people by their neighbors is Wee-yot. **1911** A. L. KROEBER *Lang. Coast Calif.* 384 The Wiyot occupied the Coast from the Bear River mountains north as far as to Little river. *Ibid.*, Wiyot is spoken indistinctly and lacks .phonetic clarity. **1918** *Univ. Calif. Publ. in Amer. Archaeol. & Ethnol.* XIV. III. 232 Cedar though present on Wiyot territory, is not abundant enough for the purposes for which a soft wood is needed. **1925** *Ibid.* XXII. I. 5 There are also some Wiyot living among the Athapascans at Blue Lake. *Ibid.* 6 The individual differences of Wiyot speech will be discussed. **1946** L. BLOOMFIELD in C. Osgood *Linguistic Structures Native Amer.* 201 Two languages of California, Wiyot and Yurok, have been suspected of kinship with Algonquian. **1961** H. DRIVER *Indians N. Amer.* xiv. 251 From the Wiyot to the Bella Coola, such usufruct was patricentered. **1964** R. H. ROBINS *Gen. Linguistics* 308 Isolated languages in the western states, Blackfoot..and Wiyot and Yurok (California). **1974** *Encycl. Brit. Micropædia* X. 720/1 Wiyot settlements were located on streams of bays, rather than on the ocean itself. **1977** *Language* LIII. 501/1 Pentland expands on Karl Teeter's suggestion ..that the rule affricating dental stops which is operative in diminutives in Wiyot..as well as in Algonquian, should be ascribed to Proto-Algic.

wiz, var. *WHIZZ, WHIZ *sb.*²

wizard, *a.* and *sb.* Add: **A.** *sb.* **2. b.** *Wizard of the North* (examples). Also freq. as *financial wizard*, a person skilled in making money, or in organizing financial affairs.

1869 R. WALTON *Random Recoll. Midl. Circuit* 134 Fortunately the 'Wizard of the North' came upon the spot [*sc.* Kenilworth], and 'Henceforth' (as a modern historian has it) 'the ruined place was to be sanctified [etc.]'. **1893** *Ladies' Home Jrnl.* May 27/2 Sir Walter Scott was called 'The Wizard of the North'. **1952** G. SARTON *Hist. Sci.* I. xix. 471 The eunuch, Hermeias, who began his career as a money-changer, was a kind of financial wizard and became very wealthy and powerful. **1967** G. F. FIENNES *I tried to run a Railway* v. 58, I had energy..to be the financial wizard on the parochial church council. **1975** *Times* 24 May 4/7 Judge Kennet..noted that Mr Tzour had been noted as a financial wizard.

†**d.** A professional conjuror. *U.S. Obs.*

1859 L. WRAXALL tr. *J. E. Robert-Houdin's Mem.* II. iv. 108 On my arrival in England, a conjuror of the name of Anderson, who assumed the title of *Great Wizard of The North*, had been performing for a long period at the little Strand Theatre. **1895** *N.Y. Dramatic News* 14 Dec. 6/1 The wonderful record established at the California theatre by Hermann the Great..has finally been broken.. [by] the wonderful wizard [himself].

B. *adj.* **2. b.** *slang.* Excellent, marvellous, very good.

1922 S. LEWIS *Babbitt* xvii. 216 The Rev. Dr. John Jennison Drew .is a wizard soul-winner. **1932** E. WAUGH *Black Mischief* vii. 277 They. righted themselves and stopped dead within a few feet of danger. 'Wizard show that,' remarked the pilot. **1943** J. B. PRIESTLEY *Daylight on Saturday* i. 1 The roofs are nicely camouflaged, and the stiff coloured netting..is a wizard show. **1954** [see *SUPER *a.* 3]. **1958** 'R. CROMPTON' *William's Television Show* vii. 189 Gosh, that party of Ginger's last Christmas was *wizard*. *a* **1966** 'M. NA GOPALEEN' *Best of Myles* (1968) 25 How awfully wizard being at the theatre with you! **1974** *Times* 17 Aug. 7/3 'How wizard!' they said... 'How absolutely super!'

wizardry. Add: **2.** Also more *loosely*, skill, expertise, or the result of this.

1951 *Sport* 27 Jan.–2 Feb. 3/3 Rounding off the wing wizardry of Finney and Morrison are inside men Horton, Wayman and Bobby Beattie. **1974** W. J. BURLEY *Death in Stanley Street* viii. 142 Bits of electrical wizardry which must have come from a record player or a television set. **1979** *Arizona Daily Star* 5 Aug. (Comic Suppl.), Peter Parker uses his scientific wizardry.

wizen, *a.* (Earlier example of *Comb.*)

1819 M. EDGEWORTH *Let.* 17 Apr. (1971) 201 An old thin stupid wizzen looking Mr. Evelyn received us.

wobbegong (wǫ·bĭgǫŋ). Also **wobbygong, wobegong.** [Aboriginal name.] A brown carpet shark with buff markings, *Orectolobus maculatus*, found off the coast of Australia.

1852 G. C. MUNDY *Our Antipodes* I. xii. 392 The most hideous to behold of the shark tribe is the wobegong, or woe-begone, as the fishermen call it... His broad back is spotted over with leopard-like marks. **1882** J. E. TENISON-WOODS *Fish & Fisheries N.S.W.* iv. 94 The wobbegong. is chiefly nocturnal. **1917** *Chambers's Jrnl.* Sept. 588/1 There is also the well-known wobbygong, a creature of extraordinary and beautiful colouring. **1937** Z. GREY *Amer. Angler in Austral.* vi. 53 The most remarkable feature of the wobbegong is his teeth. **1956** S. HOPE *Diggers' Paradise* xx. 183 The worst types are the white pointer,..hammerhead and carpet shark, also called the wobbegong. **1981** B. STONEHOUSE *Sharks* iv. 46 Woggegongs..add to their camouflage by growing fronds that look like seaweed on their faces.

wobble, wabble, *sb.* Add: (The spelling *wabble* is now obsolete.) **2.** *Biochem.* The variable pairing that is possible between a base in a transfer RNA anticodon and the corresponding base in a messenger RNA codon. Freq. *attrib.*

1966 F. H. C. CRICK in *Jrnl. Molecular Biol.* XIX. 548 (*heading*) Codon–anticodon pairing: the wobble hypothesis. *Ibid.* 551, I now postulate that in the base-pairing of the third base of the codon there is a certain amount of play, or wobble, such that more than one position of pairing is possible. **1974** *Nature* 22 Feb. 517/2 tRNAf^{met} of *E. coli*, yeast and mouse ascites tumour cells has the ability to recognise both the codons ApUpG and GpUpG and to thus exhibit code degeneracy or 'wobble' at the third base (3′ end) of the anticodon. **1982** K. H. MUENCH in T. M. Devlin *Textbk. Biochem.* xix. 921 According to the wobble rules 31 different tRNAs would suffice to read the 64 codons.

wobble, wabble, *v.* Add: (The spelling *wabble* is now obsolete.) **5. wobble plate** = *swash-plate* s.v. *SWASH *sb.*¹ 9; freq. *attrib.*

1929 V. W. PAGÉ *Mod. Aviation Engines* II. xlvi. 1897 A peculiar 'wobble' plate mechanism replaces the usual crankshaft arrangement. *Ibid.* (*caption*) Wobble plate. *Ibid.* (*caption*) A typical example of a 'wobble' plate or barrel type engine. **1943** Wobble-platemeter [see *NUTATE *v.*].

wobbler. Add: **2.** *Mech.* **a.** A projection on a roll in a rolling-mill, by means of which it may be turned.

1904 J. W. HALL in F. W. Harbord *Metallurgy of Steel* xvi. 294 At the outer end of each neck forming part of the casting is a 'wobbler', provided with either three or four prongs or corners, by means of which the roll is driven. **1919** *Jrnl. Inst. Metals* XXII. 383 Rolls.—These are usually of chilled cast iron or hardened steel. For wobbler ends, the four-horn design is the most general in use... A rule is suggested regarding length of spindles and clearancee between wobbler and box. **1930** *Engineering* 25 Apr. 539/1 A driving bar socket for the wobbler drive is bolted to the face-plate. **1978** W. L. ROBERTS *Cold Rolling of Steel* iii. 64 Wobblers are shown in Figure 3-3, and flat roll ends in Figure 3-4.

b. = *wobble plate* s.v. *WOBBLE, WABBLE *v.* 5.

1950 W. E. WILSON *Positive-Displacement Pumps & Fluid Motors* iii. 42 Oil pressure forces the pistons against the nonrotating wobbler. The resultant force is transmitted through ball and roller bearings to the wobbler plate on the shaft and imparts a rotating action to it.

3. *Angling.* A lure that wobbles and does not spin.

1928 E. F. SPENCE *Pike Fisher* v. 55 The 'shining streak of silver' does not resemble any inhabitant of river or lake, but the 'wobbler' does look something like an injured fish. **1945** [see *LEERVIS]. **1960** M. SHARCOTT *Place of Many Winds* vii. 120 'I bought a dozen new wobblers,' he says as he lifts the lid to reveal the shiny brass cohcespoons. **1977** *Best of Austral. Angler* 49/1 The wobbler and spoon type lure, however, whilst also being highly attractive to trout, are more suited to the physical requirements.

wo·bbly, *sb.* orig. *U.S.* [Origin uncertain.] A member of the Industrial Workers of the World (see *INDUSTRIAL *a.* e).

[**1913** *Miners Mag.* 24 Apr. 5 Joe Elton, Sabotist, Syndicalist and fearless I.W.W. with a red, flowing tie, with fire in his eye and fight in his backbone, the I Wobbily-Wobbily organizer..is traveling the country delivering his message. **1914** *Rep. Calif. District Courts of Appeal* (1915) 402 He telegraphed... Send all speakers and wobbles [*sic*] possible... It appeared at the trial that the term 'wobbles' meant members of the I.W.W.] **1914** *Voice of People* (Portland, Oregon) 1 Oct. 2/4 The workers are..asking why the wobblies are not holding meetings. **1921** *Outing* (U.S.) Nov. 94/3, I saw an angel and the devil standing side by side. The devil wore a 'Wobbly' (I.W.W.) button. **1923** *Nation* 5 Sept. 242/2 In Vancouver, in 1911, we had a number of Chinese members and one restaurant keeper would trust any member for meals. He could not pronounce the letter *w*, but called it *wobble*, and would ask: 'You *I. Wobble Wobble?*' and when the card was shown, credit was unlimited. Thereafter the laughing term among us was *I. Wobbly Wobbly*. **1932** E. WILSON *Devil take Hindmost* xxi. 218 The Wobbly leaders..called the men out of the tunnels. **1948** V. PALMER *Golconda* xxx. 251 And sometimes he [*sc.* the Labour Party candidate] was bothered by young fellows, usually advocates of One Big Union, who tried to lure him into deep water... He came to recognize them in the end and to stop them with light thrusts before they had lured him too far. 'What're you fellows? Wobblies, aren't you? I.W.W.—I Won't Work, but listen to me talk, eh?' **1957** [see I.W.W. s.v. I III]. **1967** A. L. LLOYD *Folk Song in Eng.* v. 387 'The celebrated working man', a song of American origin.. was brought to Durham by a Wobbly collier from Kentucky. **1980** *Times* 21 June 6/1 A poor white American, probably a Wobbly—a member of the Industrial Workers of the World, a group of radical labour unions largely made up of itinerant workers.

wobbulator (wǫ·biŭlatəɹ). *Electronics.* Also **wobulator.** [f. WOBB(LE *sb.* or *v.* + MOD)ULATOR.] A device for producing a signal whose frequency varies rapidly and repeatedly between two limits.

1945 COOKE & MARKUS *Electronics Dict.* 428/1 Wobbulator. **1958** *Electronic Engin.* XXX. 541 A wobulator for amplitude testing often gives errors because of unwanted signal amplitude variations. **1977** S. W. AMOS *Radio, T.V. & Audio Technical Reference Bk.* xxxii. 9 Alignment should not be attempted on any u.h.f. tuner without the use of a u.h.f. wobbulator.

So **wo·bbulated** *ppl. a.*, varied or produced by means of a wobbulator; **wobbula·tion,** repeated variation of a frequency by a wobbulator.

1944 *Electronic Engin.* XVI. 327/3 A powerful high-frequency sound with a wobbulated effect might give the birds a disagreeable sensation. **1957** *Practical Wireless* XXXIII. 569/1 Apply a 10·7 Mc/s signal, wobbulated 300 kc/s, to a test point. **1965** *New Scientist* 15 Apr. 156/1 'Wobbulation' or the sweeping of the modulation frequency through 15 per cent either way of its mean value. **1982** *IEEE Jrnl. Solid-State Circuits* XVII. 671/1 The initial and final frequencies, the wobbulation rate, the ramp amplitude and frequency, and the wobbulation mode are all controlled from the input data.

Wodehousian (wudhau·siăn), *sb.* and *a.* [f. the name of Sir Pelham Greville *Wodehouse* (1881–1975), British author + -IAN.] **A.** *sb.* **a.** A typical character in one of the comic novels of P. G. Wodehouse. **b.** An admirer or an habitual reader of Wodehouse's novels. **B.** *adj.* Pertaining to or characteristic of Wodehouse or of his works.

1931 *Times Lit. Suppl.* 21 May 409/4 Berry Conway and Lord Biskerton, the lads who are after Big Money, are true Wodehousians, stamped with the authentic stamp. **1938** *Ibid.* 12 Feb. 107/3 One may wince at Wodehousian baronets taking lodgers. **1943** *Scrutiny* XI. 288 About every seven pages some Wodehousian character receives a severe and almost mortal shock. **1958** *Times Lit. Suppl.* 14 Feb. 85/4 An up-to-date version of gaily irresponsible Wodehousian farce. **1973** M. MUGGERIDGE *Infernal Grove* iv. 229 The broadcasts, in point of fact, are neither anti- nor pro-German, but just Wodehousian. **1979** *Daily Tel.* 2 Aug. 11/3 With some minor reservations.., this addition to Wodehousian lore can safely be admitted. **1980** *Times* 2 Feb. 7/2 The experienced Wodehousian's heart leaps.

wodge. Substitute for entry:
wodge (wǫdʒ). *colloq.* (orig. *dial.*). Also **wadge.** [Perh. phonæsthetic alteration of *wedge*: cf. WEDGE *sb.* 4 and *Eng. Dial. Dict.*] A bulky mass; a chunk or lump; a wad (of paper).

1860, 1862 [see WADGE]. **1913** E. POUND *Let.* 7 Nov. (1971) 25, I don't want a great wadge of prose, but about double what we have at present. **1922** [in Dict.]. **1949** D. SMITH *I capture Castle* II. viii. 112 You must take only one kind of food on the fork at a time; never a nice comfortable wodge of meat and vegetables together. **1958** HAYWARD & HARARI tr. *Pasternak's Dr. Zhivago* I. vii. 195 He held out a wadge of papers across the handrail. **1963** A. SMITH *Throw out Two Hands* iii. 39 We strode out into the rain with a wodge of well-stamped supplications. **1977** *Private Eye* 4 Mar. 7/3 True, there's a wadge of self-opinionated dolts who drive around in head scarves and Range Rovers. **1981** *Brit. Med. Jrnl.* 21 Mar. 968/1 A posterior pack is made from a wadge of gauze as large as the end of the patient's thumb, which is rammed tightly into the posterior choana. **1984** *Listener* 6 Dec. 35/1 These tomes are usually given a lively, busy design, with screaming wodges of colour. *Ibid.* 20–27 Dec. 7/2 Cross-headings, the lay reader should know, are those devices used to break a grey wodge of type and encourage you to keep reading.

wodgy, *a.* Add: (Later examples.) Also *fig.*

1928 *Daily Express* 8 June 5/5 Wedding cakes ..are fattening and indigestible; they are 'wodgy' to the palate. **1978** *Daily Tel.* 30 Aug. 13 (*caption*) Swirl a piece of totally straight hair high, pin a little wodgy bun of bright crepe paper on over the kerby grips: that's Patrick Ales [*sic*] way. **1979** *Hi-Fi News* Dec. 169/2, I only wish I could be as totally enthusiastic about the recording. At average levels it is fine but sudden fortes come with a wodgy quality that is not at all pleasing; there are too many individual resonances for the ear to cope.

wodginite (wǫ·dʒinəit). *Min.* [f. *Wodgina*, name of a locality in Western Australia + -ITE[1].] A rare oxide of tantalum, niobium, and manganese (usu. also containing tin and iron) which occurs as brown or black monoclinic crystals or grains.

1963 E. H. NICKEL et al. in *Canad. Mineralogist* VII. 390 The name wodginite is proposed for a mineral found at two widely separated localities—Wodgina, Australia and Bernic Lake, Manitoba. **1978** *Mineral. Rec.* IX. 18/2 (*caption*) Unusual twin crystal of wodginite/cassiterite. The size is about 6 × 4·5 × 3·5 cm.

woe, *sb.* Add: **1. a.** Freq. in phr. *tale of woe*, a narrative of (one's) misfortunes. Now usu. *joc.*

1790 [in Dict.]. **1882** E. FIELD *Compl. Tribune Primer* 111 (*heading*) A tale of woe. **1951** *Sport* 16–22 Mar. 4/2 Listen to the tale of woe from Swindon Town, who.. suffered their 16th away league defeat... Swindon..lost goalkeeper Norman Uprichard at a goalless stage of the game. **1967** BAKER & JONES *Coffee, Tea or Me?* xvi. 199 Kelman savored a crisp piece of sausage pizza as he thought about our tale of woe. **1973** *Times* 11 June 18/8 Yet it is not all a tale of woe. An entirely new management structure has been brought into force, and Liverpool was the first port in the world to link a computer service to its cargo handling.

woffle, var. *WAFFLE *v.*, *sb.*[2]

wog[2] (wǫg). *slang.* [Origin uncertain: often said to be an acronym, but none of the many suggested etymologies is satisfactorily supported by the evidence.] **1.** A vulgarly offensive name for a foreigner, esp. one of Arab extraction.

1929 F. BOWEN *Sea Slang* 153 *Wogs*, lower class Babu shipping clerks on the Indian coast. **1932** R. J. P. HEWISON *Essay on Oxford* 5 And here the *Ethiop* ranks, the wogs, we spy. **1937** F. STARK *Baghdad Sketches* 90 When I return, Nasir fixed me with real malignity in his little placid eyes. 'I knew she wanted me to go,' he said. 'I could see what she was thinking. They call us wogs.' **1942** C. HOLLINGWORTH *German Just behind Me* xiii. 258 King Zog Was always considered a bit of a Wog, Until Mussolini quite recently Behaved so indecently. **1944** [see *COME *v.* 38 e]. **1955** E. WAUGH *Officers & Gentlemen* II. 323 He turned up in western Abyssinia leading a group of wogs. **1958** *Times Lit. Suppl.* 11 Apr. p. vi/3 We have travelled some distance from the days when Wogs began at Calais. **1965** [see *COMMIE]. **1982** J. SAVARIN *Water Hole* I. iv. 42 He hated Arabs... They were all wogs to him.

2. The Arabic language.

1977 P. RAYMOND *Matter of Assassination* vi. 63, I can't speak Wog and don't seems to be getting anywhere. **1982** 'W. HAGGARD' *Mischief-Makers* xiv. 157 'I've picked up a few words of wog, sir.'.. The driver spoke terrible barrack-room Arabic.

3. a. *attrib.* passing into *adj.*

a **1963** J. LUSBY in B. James *Austral. Short Stories* (1963) 236 Wog chappie scuttling around seeking safe side of the beast. **1970** G. F. NEWMAN *Sir, You Bastard* viii. 234 We were hawking, and getting treated like bleeding wog brush salesmen. **1973** *Daily Tel.* 31 May 3/2 Judge Sheldon heard that trouble started..when white girlfriends of coloured soldiers..were taunted by members of the Royal Scots as 'wog lovers'. **1977** *Drive* Sept.–Oct. 112/2 Any foreign car, even a Ferrari or a Mercedes, is a *wog motor*, unless it's a *Yank*.

b. *Comb.* **wogland** *derog.*, a foreign country.

1961 [see *NIG, NIG *sb.*[3]]. **1967** 'J. MUNRO' *Money that Money can't Buy* ii. 24, I don't live in Wogland [*sc.* Spain] because I like it.

Hence also **wo·gger; wo·ggy** *a.*

1922 JOYCE *Ulysses* 740 She called him wogger. *Ibid.* 741 She may have noticed her wogger people were always going away. **1973** M. CATTO *Sam Casanova* iv. 75, I met some kid in a night-club here, does some sort of Woggy belly-dance. **1979** REESE & FLINT *Trick 13* 100 That woggy fellow..was cleaning up.

wog[3]. *Austral. slang.* [Origin uncertain.] A germ or parasite; an insect; an illness or disease. Cf. *BUG *sb.*[2] 4 d.

1934 *Bulletin* (Sydney) 31 Oct. 20/4 Buckley's fluke.. is a wog that enters the nostrils of these snakes during hibernation. **1941** C. BARRETT *Coast of Adventure* iii. 51 Jolly little people..popping into old jam tins a miscellany of wogs—from bull-ants to scorpions and centipedes. **1953** A. UPFIELD *Murder must Wait* xxi. 191 The wogs flying about the light. **1964** R. BRADDON *Year Angry Rabbit* i. 9 But find the wog, find the super-myxomatosis, the whatever-it-may-be that kills today's rabbits. **1976** D. FRANCIS *In Frame* viii. 126 A beastly stomach wog, so he couldn't come.

Wogdon (wǫ·gdən). Also erron. **Wogden.** The name of Robert *Wogdon* (fl. 1776–1800), a noted gunsmith, used *absol.* to designate a duelling pistol made by him.

c **1810** W. HICKEY *Mem.* (1923) III. 150 By God, Bill, you shall shoot the dirty little rascal through the head. I have a delicate pair of Wogdens that will do his business effectually. **1969** G. LYALL *Venus with Pistol* xxv. 161 Give it a little time for the word to go round that Bert Kemp had matched a pair of fancy Wogdons. **1981** 'J. STURROCK' *Suicide Most Foul* vi. 127 Had I been armed with only one of my Wogdons the end would have been different, but a gentleman does not take pistols to a ball.

wo·ggle, *sb.* [Origin unknown: cf. TOGGLE *sb.*] A loop or ring of leather, cord, etc., through which the ends of a Scout's neckerchief are threaded.

1930 *Daily News* 10 May 4/4 Woggles have now become an established part of Scout uniform, and I have seen some very good examples made by Scouts. **1977** *Grimsby Even. Tel.* 27 May 2/7 The woggle—the ring holding the neckerchief in place on the Scout uniform. **1983** J. DEFT *Beaver Leader's Handbk.* 32 You must decide yourself whether each new Beaver should be asked to pay for his scarf and woggle, or whether these should be provided by the Colony.

Wogul, vogul. Add: The usual form is now **Vogul. a.** (Earlier and later examples of this form.)

1880 A. H. SAYCE *Introd. Sci. Lang.* II. x. 325 The Hungarians were once the neighbours of the savage Voguls of the Ural. **1948** D. DIRINGER *Alphabet* 483 The Voguls in the Ural mountains. **1975** [see *OSTYAK].

b. The language of this people, belonging to the *OB-UGRIAN group.

1908 T. G. TUCKER *Introd. Nat. Hist. Lang.* 133 Ugric, which comprises..Vogul and Ostiak, dialects of a few thousands scattered over a wide region eastward from the Northern Ural and about the Obi River. **1933**, etc. [see *OB-UGRIAN]. **1951** W. K. MATTHEWS *Languages U.S.S.R.* iii. 21 The 'primitive' or East Ugrian languages, Ostyak and Vogul. **1980** *Amer. N. & Q.* Oct. 29/1 Marianne Sz. Bakró-Nagy..has pulled together some 500 terms..on the bear as a tabu animal in the Urals among the Ostyak (Khanty) and Vogul (Mansi) speaking peoples.

Wogulian: delete † and add later example.

1925 P. RADIN tr. *Vendryès's Language* II. iii. 118 In Wogulian *mini* 'he goes'..[is] formed like *puri* 'taking'.

Wöhler (vǿ·ləɹ). *Mech.* [The name of August *Wöhler* (1819–1914), German railway engineer.] *Wöhler test*: a fatigue test in which a horizontal bar is rotated axially while supported at one end and loaded at the other.

[**1888** *Rep. Brit. Assoc. Adv. Sci. 1887* 434 (*caption*) Limits of stress from Wöhler's endurance tests.] **1911** *Jrnl. Iron & Steel Inst.* LXXXIV. 655 The testing machines include..a rotary fatigue (Wöhler test) machine **1948** P. F. FOSTER *Mech. Testing of Metals & Alloys* x. 203 One objection urged against the Wöhler test is that it is merely a skin test, since the major part of the section is but comparatively lightly stressed. **1980** *Proc. European Offshore Steels Res. Seminar 1978* (Welding Inst.) p. III/P7–2 The test programme included Wöhler tests (fatigue tests) with an alternating load.

wok (wǫk). Also **wock.** [a. Chinese (Cantonese).] A bowl-shaped pan used in Chinese cookery.

1952 D. Y. H. FENG *Joy of Chinese Cooking* i. 37 A well-stocked Chinese kitchen usually has..several convex-bottomed circular pans hammered out of thin iron or copper called *wock.* **1962** E.-M. WONG *Chinese Cookery* i. 4 For versatility and easy handling the wock is indispensable. **1969** *Britannica Bk. of Year* (U.S.) 801/1 *Wok*, a bowl-shaped cooking utensil used especially in the preparation of Chinese food. **1972** *Maclean's Mag.* Mar. 46/3 The Chinese wok technique is my mainstay of cooking, although I do it in a plain frypan. **1973** J. GORES *Final Notice* (1974) x. 61 The pixie-like waitress came in with a boardful of fresh vegetables for the *wok.* **1977** *Sunday Times* (Colour Suppl.) 4 Dec. 20/2 Wok cooking is about to sweep the Western world. **1983** *Listener* 30 June 17/1 By 1972 I needed a small pantechnicon to convey all my books on macrobiotic cookery, my plants, wall-hangings and floor cushions, my astrological tables, women's-lib posters and my wok.

wolchonskoite, wolk-, obs. varr. *VOLKONSKOITE.

wolf, *sb.* Add: **1. c.** The skin or fur of the animal. (Chiefly *attrib.*: see sense 10 a below.)

1805 LEWIS & CLARK *Orig. Jrnls. Lewis & Clark Expedition* (1904) II. 377, I have also observed some robes among them of beaver, moonox, and small wolves. **1876** *Smithsonian Misc. Coll.* XIII. vi. 69 Furs... Wolf, (*Canis lupus*)—linings, rugs, and robes. **1940** *Chambers's Techn. Dict.* 911/1 *Wolf*, the dressed skin of one of the varieties of wolf. **1974**, etc. [see *wolf hat*, etc., sense 10 a below].

3. a. (*b*) Freq. as *Tasmanian wolf*; = THYLACINE.

1941 E. TROUGHTON *Furred Animals Austral.* 50 (*heading*) Tasmanian wolf or tiger. **1966** G. DURRELL *Two in Bush* vi. 178 The predators are represented by such things as the Tasmanian Wolf—not a true wolf, of course, but a marsupial, looking remarkably like its counterpart.

3*. = *wolf tree*, sense 10 e below.

1949 *Q. Jrnl. Forestry* XLIII. 127 Most props containing large knots have been prepared from quick-grown heavily branched trees such as wolves. **1966** *Times* 21 Apr. 16/7 Douglas fir plantations nearly always have some undesirable wolves which have to be cut out.

4. c. *slang.* (*a*) A sexually aggressive male; a would-be seducer of women; (*b*) orig. *U.S.*, a male homosexual seducer or one who adopts an active role with a partner.

Occas. applied to a woman: see quot. 1968 s.v. *WOLFESS 2.

(*a*) **1847** THACKERAY *Van. F.* (1848) xxxvii. 335 'Rawdon,' said Becky, .'I must have a sheep-dog... I mean a *moral* shepherd's dog..to keep the wolves off me.' **1862** MRS. H. WOOD *Mrs. Haliburton's Troubles* II. ii. 23, I vowed I'd tell Mark what I had seen and heard, and what sort of a wolf she allowed to make her presents of fine clothes. **1945** S. LEWIS *Cass Timberlane* xix. 113 She was innocent, but this Roskinen was a wolf. **1968** [see *KARATE *v.*]. **1973** 'E. PETERS' *City of Gold & Shadows* ii. 25 He did not look like a wolf, but he did look like a young man with an eye for a girl.

(*b*) **1917** *New Republic* 13 Jan. 293/2 The sodomist, the degenerate, the homosexual wolf. **1931**, etc. [see *JOCKER]. **1950** PATTERSON & CONRAD *Scottsboro Boy* II. ii. 91, I learned men were having men. Old guys, they called them wolves, they saw me looking at this stuff and thought I might be a gal-boy. **1978** K. J. DOVER *Greek Homosexuality* II. 87 In prisons the 'wolf' is the active homosexual, and does not reverse roles with his partners.

9. k. *to throw to the wolves*: to sacrifice (a subordinate, friend, ally, etc.) to one's enemies in order to save oneself.

1927 F. HARRIS *My Life & Loves* III. x. 146 But if Gladstone had had his letter back, I think the G.O.M. would have thrown Dilke to the wolves. **1958** *Listener* 6 Nov. 743/2 This able and agreeable doctor [*sc.* Lord Addison] was thrown to the wolves by a Prime Minister who had good reason to know that his own position was desperate. **1980** P. KINSLEY *Vatchman Switch* xli. 236 If anyone..showed disloyalty he would throw him to the wolves.

l. *lone wolf*: see *LONE *a.* 3 c.

10. a. *wolf chase* (earlier example), *eye, pelt, snow*; also with reference to the skin or fur of the animal, as *wolf coat, collar, hat, jacket*; **b.** *wolf-breeding* adj.; **d.** *wolf-coloured* (later example).

1889 W. B. YEATS *Wanderings of Oisin* 77 Wolf-breeding mountains. **1824** in *Coll. Missouri Hist. Soc.* (1928) VI. 75 Had a wolfe chase. **1977** P. WAY *Super-Celeste* II. 117 She put on her Siberian wolf coat. **1974** *Selfridge Christmas Catal.* 14 Leather coat with wolf collar and hamster lining. **1926** Wolf-coloured [see *KEESHOND]. **1922** JOYCE *Ulysses* 434 Her wolfeyes shining. **1974** *Country Life* 3 Oct. 980/2 Natural wolf three-quarter length jacket worn with a wolf hat. **1976** *Jrnl.* (Newcastle) 26 Nov. (Advt.), Mink coat..also modern wolf jacket with matching fox hat, both coats new. **1923** D. H. LAWRENCE *Birds, Beasts & Flowers* 200 On to the fur of the wolf-pelt that strews the plain. *c* **1878** G. M. HOPKINS *Poems* (1967) 73 There did storms not mingle?.. wolfsnow, worlds of it, wind there?

e. wolf call *colloq.* (orig. *U.S.*) = *WOLF-WHISTLE; **wolf-cry** [f. vbl. phr. *to cry 'wolf'*: see WOLF *sb.* 9 a] = *false alarm* s.v. *FALSE *a.* 14 c; **wolf cub,** (*a*) (see sense 10 a in Dict.); (*b*) = *CUB *sb.*[1] 2 c; also *fig.*; **wolf pack,** a number of wolves naturally associating as a group, esp. for hunting; also *fig.*, esp. denoting an attacking group of German submarines in the war of 1939–45; **wolf pen** *U.S.*, a strong box made of logs used for trapping wolves; **wolf tree,** a tree that is occupying more space than has been allowed for it, so restricting the growth of its neighbours (cf. sense 3* above;) **wolf-willow** *Canada*, any of several shrubs, esp. *Elæagnus commutata*, which has silver-grey foliage.

1948 *Time* 27 Sept. 12/1 Grins, whistles, wolf-calls.. followed her in this exclusively male territory. **1958** *Spectator* 6 June 726/3 The streets are lined by groups of lounging youths watching the girls go by (but no whistles or wolf-calls). **1915** W. J. LOCKE *Jaffery* xxii. 315, I have a habit of losing things and setting the household in frantic search,..only to discover that I have had the wretched object in my pocket all the time. So accustomed is Barbara to this wolf-cry that if I came up to her without my head and informed her that I had lost it, she would be profoundly sceptical. **1980** *Listener* 9 Oct. 462/3 The news that the Met season might have to be cancelled..is an annual threat, a wolf-cry. **1916** R. BADEN-POWELL in *Wolf Cub* Dec. 2/1 Hullo, Wolf Cubs! What swells you are to have a newspaper all to yourselves! and hamster lining. **1963** H. WILSON in *Times* 8 May 6/3 If we had to face a really dedicated and trained spy, not an overgrown wolf cub who had gone wrong, then the system would have been wide open in respect of security. **1981** E. LONGFORD *Queen Mother* ii. 35 (*caption*) Wellington: the Duchess of York inspects a pack of wolf cubs. **1895** Wolf pack [in Dict.]. **1941** *Hutchinson's Pict. Hist. War* 9 July–30 Sept. 270/1 The U-boat is now being used as a unit in a flotilla... We had a hint of it a year ago when the Berlin bulletins talked about 'wolf pack' attacks on convoys. **1951** W. STEVENS *Let.* 2 Oct. (1967) 731 There is probably a sort of wolf-pack that follows him [*sc.* Hermann Hesse] round. His idea of throwing out a poem or two to slow them up and invite them to devour each other sounds almost like folklore. **1977** *Time* 26 Sept. 9/2 What Andreas Baader and Ulrike Meinhof spawned as a small wolf pack of urban guerrillas has now become a scattered army of vicious malcontents, bent on destroying the society around them. **1980** 'D. GRANT' *Emerald Decision* vi. 129 They were headed for the perilous North Channel..if they survived the wolfpacks. **1647** in *Watertown* (Mass.) *Rec.* (1894) I. i. 12 The Towne gaue: to John Witherll: there Right in the palisado that inclosed the woulfe pen. **1876** J. S. INGRAM *Centennial Expedition* 106 The places of interest are..the Aviary, the Fox Pens, the Wolf-Pens. **1928** R. S. TROUP *Silvicultural Systems* xix. 187 The stands..were kept fairly dense in order to promote clean stems, congested thickets being thinned and wolf-trees removed. **1966** D. WATERS *Forestry* xviii. 94 Wolf trees are large mis-shapen trees which do not provide good timber. **1889** J. G. DONKIN *Trooper & Redskin* 86 The luscious perfume of wolf-willow and wild rose ..come scampering on the western breeze. **1948** A. L. RAND *Mammals Eastern Rockies* 90 Wolf-willow clumps, gopher holes, odd stones, aspen bluffs. **1974** M. LAURENCE *Diviners* 357 There were these thin prairie maples and the wolf willow.

Hence **wo·lflessness** *nonce-wd.* [cf. WOLF *sb.* 5 a], the state of 'not having the wolf at the door', i.e. being free of poverty.

1928 D. H. LAWRENCE *Rawdon's Roof* 26 The perfect wolflessness of Rawdon's door, the perfect windlessness of Rawdon's roof.

wolf, *v.* Add: **2.** Also without *const.*: cf. *WOLF *sb.* 4 c. Occas. *trans.*

1929 *World's Work* Nov. 40 The college boy (in 1929) knows a smoothie who wolfed on a friend and creamed his lady. **1934** G. & S. LORIMER *Stag Line* vii. 232 No matter how I feel, I wouldn't wolf a brother's girl. **1940** J. O'HARA *Pal Joey* 186, I give with the vocals and wolf around in a nite club.

4. *trans. U.S. Blacks.* (See quots. and cf. *WOOFING *vbl. sb.*) Occas. *intr.* with *at.*

1966 *Urban Education* II. ii. 108 *Wolf*, to make fun of someone. **1969** *Sports Illustr.* 3 Nov. 36/2, I turned round and started wolfing at the guy, and he just strolled off. **1971** E. E. LANDY *Underground Dict.* 199 *Wolf v.*, criticize; chop down. **1974** H. L. FOSTER *Ribbin', Jivin', & Playin' Dozens* iv. 172 *Wolf, wolf'n, woof, woofin, wolf ticket*, can mean anything from making fun of someone to challenging someone to a fight, a powerful person. **1978** *Detroit Free Press* 2 Apr. (Detroit Suppl.) 8/3 'C'mon, man,' they tell Balls, backing down, 'we was just wolfin' ya. We gotta be careful who we sell to.'

wolf-dog. **2.** Delete second part of def. and add further (*N. Amer.*) examples.

1896 M. MCNAUGHTON *Overland to Cariboo* 47 A large number of wolf-dogs were prowling about. **1953** B. J. BANFILL *Labrador Nurse* 19 The mossy grass knolls were dotted with tethered wolf dogs.

wolfeite (wu·lfəit). *Min.* [f. the name of Caleb W. *Wolfe* (1908–80), U.S. crystallographer + -ITE[1].] A basic phosphate of ferrous iron and bivalent manganese, $(Fe^{2+},Mn^{2+})_2(PO_4)(OH)$, that occurs as transparent or translucent monoclinic crystals and forms a series with triploidite.

1949 C. FRONDEL in *Amer. Mineralogist* XXXIV. 694 The name wolfeite is proposed for the mineral and is particularly appropriate in view of Professor Wolfe's studies of iron and managanese phosphates from Palermo and other localities. **1951** C. PALACHE et al. *Dana's Syst. Min.* (ed. 7) II. 853 The names triploidite and wolfeite are applied to those parts of the series with Mn > Fe and Fe > Mn, respectively. **1979** *Mineral. Mag.* XLIII. 507/1 Unlike wolfeite from the Palermo pegmatite, the wolfeite at Thackaringa [Australia] does not appear to be an alteration phase of a pre-existing phosphate and is a late stage phase in the core of the pegmatite.

wolfer. Restrict *rare* to sense 2 and add earlier and later examples of sense 1.

1872 *Rep. Indian Affairs 1871* 410 A regular stampede took place out of that section of the country of 'Wolfers' and whiskey traders. **1930** C. M. MACINNES *In Shadow of Rockies* 66 Even more disreputable than the whiskey traders were the wolfers. **1976** *Times* 8 July 16/4 The ghoulish wolfers poisoned the plains with strychnine. **1973** R. WIEBE *Temptations of Big Bear* II. iii. 101 Settlers ripping up land and knocking down trees and wolfers dashing about scattering poison and killing wolves and buffalo.

wolfess. Add: **2.** A woman who is sexually aggressive; a woman who seeks to seduce men.

1945 *Bulletin* (Philadelphia) 27 Nov. 42/1 A nice girl hasn't got a chance with a wolfess around. **1968** *Word Study* Dec. 4/2 *Wolf* suggests the sexually aggressive female as well as the sexually agressive male, though it is often expanded to *wolfess* when applied to a woman.

Wolffian, *a.* Add: *Wolffian ridge*, each of two longitudinal ridges on either side of the embryo on which the limb buds arise.

1874 FOSTER & BALFOUR *Elements Embryol.* I. vi. 143 The somatopleure..is raised up..into a low rounded ridge which runs along nearly the whole length of the embryo from the neck to the tail... This ridge..is known as the Wolffian ridge. **1931** A. ROBINSON *Cunningham's Text-bk. Anat.* (ed. 6) 76 By the end of the first month.. the Wolffian ridges have appeared. **1976** N. J. BERRILL *Development* xiv. 309 In amniotes the combined epidermal-mesenchymal thickening extends as a horizontal ridge along each side of the body (the Wolffian ridges). The intermediate part of the ridge later disappears, leaving anterior and posterior regions as the definitive limb areas.

Wolfian, *a.*[2] (Earlier example.)

1824 DE QUINCEY in *London Mag.* Jan. 5/1 Was the Iliad the work of one mind, or (on the Wolfian hypothesis) of many?

wolfish, *a.* Add: **2. b.** In sense 8 b of WOLF *sb. rare.*

1889 *Grove's Dict. Mus.* IV. 89/1 Bad Tenors [*sc.* tenor violins] are worse than bad violins; they are unequal and 'wolfish'.

4. *wolfish-looking* (earlier example).

1820 SCOTT *Ivanhoe* I. i. 14 A rugged wolfish-looking dog..half mastiff, half greyhound.

Wolf–Rayet (vǫ·lf,rẹ·yẹ, wulf-). *Astr.* The names of C. J. É. *Wolf* (1827–1918) and G. A. P. *Rayet* (1839–1906), French astronomers, used *attrib.* to denote any of a class of hot white-to-blue stars (first described by them in 1867) which are characterized by bright, broad spectral lines due to hydrogen, helium, carbon, or nitrogen and are believed to be short-lived and unstable.

1890 A. M. CLERKE *Syst. of Stars* v. 71 Accurate measurements of the three original Wolf-Rayet stars.. were made. **1930** R. H. BAKER *Astron.* ix. 356 The Wolf-Rayet stars are distinguished from the other Class O stars by the great width of the bright lines in their spectra. **1978** PASACHOFF & KUTNER *University Astron.* ii. 40 Astronomers think that the emission in Wolf-Rayet stars comes from shells of material that the star has ejected into the space surrounding it.

wo·lf-whistle. *colloq.* Also **wolf whistle.** [f. *WOLF *sb.* 4 c + WHISTLE *sb.* 3.] A distinctive whistle from a man expressing sexual admiration for a woman; also *transf.*

1952 *Time* 21 Jan. 29/3 No one took exception to U.S.N. wolf-whistles at the señoritas. **1953** N. BALCHIN *Sundry Creditors* 46 Some vulgar female person let out a low wolf-whistle as she passed him. **1958** *Daily Express* 13 Mar. 8/5 She heard one kid give a wolf whistle, and his chum exclaim: 'Coo, what a smashing car!' **1960** A. KIMMINS *Lugs O'Leary* i. 11 They passed the pretty probationer. Lugs gave her a low wolf whistle. **1971** *New Scientist* 29 Apr. 246/1 A young housewife..recently asked for a reduction in the rates of her residence because of nuisance from wolf-whistles. **1980** 'T. HINDE' *Daymare* vi. 61 Bob Smiles whistles at him..a hideous wolf-whistle.

Hence as *v.*, to utter a wolf-whistle (at); **wo·lf-whistling** *vbl. sb.* and *ppl. a.*

1955 *Sun* (Baltimore) 2 Sept. 1/5 The Governor of Mississippi today called for a complete investigation of the kidnap-killing of a Negro youth who allegedly wolf-whistled at a white woman. **1958** L. LITTLE *Dear Boys* 222 They had their heads and shoulders hanging dangerously out of the windows [of a coach], wolf-whistling the odd bints on the pavements. **1958** *Times* 2 Sept. 11/7 Surrounded as I am by thousands of barking dogs, wailing cats, and wolf-whistling budgerigars. **1961** WODEHOUSE *Ice in Bedroom* 41 Dolly Molloy unquestionably took the eye... Wolf-whistling is of course prohibited in the lobby of Barribault's Hotel so none of those present attempted this form of homage. **1976** J. GRENFELL *Joyce Grenfell requests the Pleasure* i. 17 An American sailor wolf-whistled at her. **1981** G. PETRIE *Tondeau of Chartres* i. 19 Julie and Elaine took their bows to a cacophony of wolf-whistling.

wolfy (wu·lfi), *a. U.S.* [f. WOLF *sb.* + -Y[1].] Wolf-like; characterized by, or suggestive of the presence of, wolves; ferocious, uncivilized.

1828 *Western Souvenir 1829* 314 'Couldn't you take a pack or two of wolves along?' said Pete, sneeringly. 'We can spare you a small gang. It's mighty wolfy about here.' **1831** J. K. PAULDING *Lion of West* (1954) ii. 54 Well, I hadn't had a fight for as much as ten days—felt as though I must kiver myself up in a salt bin to keep—'so wolfy' about the head and shoulders. **1838** B. DRAKE *Tales & Sk., from Queen City* 36, I say, Mr. Jack-of-knaves, it looks rather wolfy in these parts. **1927** C. M. RUSSELL *Trails plowed Under* 114 This talk makes the whole bunch wolfy.

Wollaston (wu·lăstən). *Physics.* [The name of W. H. *Wollaston* (1766–1828), English physicist.] *Wollaston('s) prism*: a prism made by cementing together two prisms of calcite or quartz with their optic axes perpendicular to each other and to the incident light, which is thereby separated into two diverging beams of polarized light.

1890 T. PRESTON *Theory of Light* xi. 258 Wollaston's Prism.—This prism differs from that of Rochon only in that the optic axis of the first prism ABD is parallel to the face AB, so that it is merely Rochon's prism turned through a right angle. **1970** *Nature* 18 July 264/2 The Wollaston prism, which splits the incident starlight into two beams, polarized in mutually perpendicular planes, was placed in an adjustable mounting above the spectrograph slit.

wolly (wǫ·li). *slang.* Also **wally.** [Origin unknown: cf. *WALLY *sb.*[2]] A uniformed policeman, esp. a constable. Cf. *WOOLLY *sb.* 3.

1970 G. F. NEWMAN *Sir, you Bastard* 8 The wollies were out in their cars, patrolling for drunks and discontents. **1977** 'D. CORY' *Bennett* ii. 69 The doorman.. mentioned it to one of our wollies on the beat. **1983** J. B. HILTON *Asking Price* v. 33 These traffic Wollies make sure it all goes down, once they've licked their pencils.

Wolof (wōu·lǫf), *sb.* and *a.* Also **Jolof** (yōu·lǫf), **Woloff**, etc. [Native name.] **A.** *sb.* **a.** (A member of) an African people of Senegal and the Gambia. **b.** The language of this people, belonging to the Niger-Congo family.

1745 F. MOORE in *New Gen. Coll. Voy.* II. 227/2 The Natives, who were Jolloifs, had taken his chief Mate and Surgeon Prisoners. **1823** MRS. H. KILHAM (*title*) African lessons. Wolof and English. **1848** *Rep. Brit. Assoc. Adv. Sci.* 162 Here the Woloff has not only no particular affinities, but fewer miscellaneous ones than any other language. **1883**, etc. [see *PEULH *sb.* and *a.*]. **1908** T. G. TUCKER *Introd. Nat. Hist. Lang.* 147 This process is common in Wolof. **1930** C. G. SELIGMAN *Races of Afr.* iii. 58 The lower and middle portions of the Senegal River form the ethnic divide between Hamites and Negroes. Immediately south of the river the latter are represented by the Wolof (or Jolof). **1961** *Guardian* 25 Nov. 7 Senegal combines at least six different tribes... The largest is the Wolof numbering about 800,000. **1972** J. L. DILLARD *Black Eng.* iii. 74 The widespread use of Wolof, which seems to have a special *lingua franca* status among West African languages, in the thirteen colonies. **1976** *Times* 20 Nov. 11/4 The third largest group are the Wollofs, whose women..are..among the most beautiful in Africa.

B. *adj.* **a.** *gen.*

1828 MRS. H. KILHAM *Specimens African Languages Sierra Leone* p. vii, In the Jolof Language there are two sounds of the guttural kind. **1865** R. F. BURTON *Wit & Wisdom in W. Afr.* i. 2 (*heading*) Proverbs in the Wolof tongue. **1879** J. A. FARRER *Primitive Manners & Customs* iii. 92 The Wolof proverb, that 'lies, though many, will be caught by Truth as soon as she rises up'. **1918** *Harvard Afr. Studies* II. 98 De Rochebrune distinguishes the gluteal accumulation of fat commonly found in Wolof women and girls from true steatopygia. **1961** F. G. CASSIDY *Jamaica Talk* vii. 146 The word *juke*, as in the American *juke box*..has been traced by Turner to Wolof *jug*, to misconduct oneself. **1977** J. WYLLIE *To catch a Viper* (1979) vii. 45 The original African ethnic groupings such as those represented by the Yoruba, the old nations of Ashanti, Dahomey and Goshi and the Mossi, Mende, Mandinka and Wolof peoples.

b. Special collocation: **jollof rice** (see quot. 1982).

1959 [see *FUFU]. **1966** C. ACHEBE *Man of People* ii. 25 Whenever you allowed him a say in this matter he invariably came up with Jollof rice—his favourite dish. **1982** G. M. DALGISH *Dict. Africanisms* 76/1 *Jollof rice*, a West African dish, a stew of fish, chicken or beef, tomatoes, onions, rice, and chili peppers; said to be ultimately of Sierra Leone origin.

wölsendorfite (vö·lzĕndǭɹfəit). *Min.* [a. F. *wölsendorfite* (J. Protas 1957, in *Compt. Rend.* CCXLIV. 2942), f. *Wölsendorf*, name of a locality in Bavaria: see -ITE[1].] A hydrated oxide of lead, calcium, and uranium, (Pb,Ca)-$U_2O_7.2H_2O$, found as orange or red orthorhombic crystals.

1957 *Chem. Abstr.* LI. 13659 (*heading*) Wölsendorfite, a new uranium mineral. **1975** *Mineral Abstr.* XXVI. 321/1 Red and orange aggregates of wölsendorfite are described from the oxidation zone of a U-Mo ore deposit [in the U.S.S.R.].

Wolstonian (wulstōu·niăn), *a. Geol.* [f. *Wolston*, name of the village in Warwickshire where the type site is situated: see -IAN.] Epithet of the penultimate Pleistocene glaciation in Britain (identified with the Saale of continental Europe), and of a stratigraphic stage of the Pleistocene lying above the Hoxnian and below the Ipswichian; of or belonging to this stage or glacial. Also *absol.*

1969 *Proc. Geol. Soc.* Aug. 152 It is recommended that for the Pleistocene and Holocene of the British Isles the following ages/stages be adopted as a regional scale... Pleistocene: Devensian, Ipswichian, Wolstonian [etc.]. **1975** *Nature* 9 Oct. 478/2 The Sugworth deposit lies topographically well above the Hanborough Terrace which has been ascribed both to the Hoxnian Interglacial and, more recently, to an early part of the Wolstonian. **1981** F. W. SHOTTON in Neale & Flenley *Quaternary in Brit.* xiii. 143 This makes the gravels post-Hoxnian or at least late-Hoxnian, and the overlying Wetton Till even later. So if the latter is pre-Devensian, it can only be Wolstonian.

Wolves (wulvz). [pl. of WOLF *sb.*] Colloq. name for Wolverhampton Wanderers Football Club.

1908 O. SEAMAN *Salvage* 140, I hardly care at all Whether the Wolves break up the Throstles' wings. **1923** *Racing Record* 10 Feb. 3/2 Bradford City I take to defeat the Wolves. **1960** [see *SLATE *sb.*[1] 2 b]. **1978** P. BAILEY *Leisure & Class in Victorian Eng.* vi. 139 A Church of England school team in Wolverhampton, later the Wolves.

wolvish, *a.* Delete † *Obs.* and add: **1.** (Later examples.)

1911 D. H. LAWRENCE *White Peacock* I. vi. 97 There was a report of two grey wolvish dogs. *a* **1945** E. R. EDDISON *Mezentian Gate* (1958) i. 16 'Nay, read it if you please: I had it but five minutes since.' And with a wolvish look he tossed the letter upon the table. **1978** J. UPDIKE *Coup* (1979) vii. 267 She tugged at his hand with that fretful, proprietorial impatience of her wolvish race.

2. Also *Comb.*, as *wolvish-looking* adj.

1954 J. R. R. TOLKIEN *Fellowship of Ring* iv. 101 Two wolvish-looking dogs sniffed at him suspiciously, and snarled.

wolvishness. Delete † and add later example.

a **1945** E. R. EDDISON *Mezentian Gate* (1958) xxxvii. 191 God shield us from women on our councils of war... Besides, I mistrust Parry wolvishness. And bitch-wolf was ever more fell than dog-wolf.

woman, *sb.* Add: **I. 1. i.** *new woman* (earlier example).

1893 G. GISSING *Odd Women* I. viii. 235 A strong character, of course. More decidedly one of the new women than you yourself—isn't she?

j. *woman about town*: see *TOWN *sb.* 8 b; *woman in the street*: see *STREET *sb.* 3 g; *woman of letters* (earlier example); *woman of the people*. Also *woman-to-woman*: cf. MAN *sb.*[1] 4 h in Dict. and Suppl.

1818 'T. BROWN' *Brighton; or The Steyne* I. i. 20 She passes for a woman of letters. [**1859** LYTTON *What will he do with It?* III. VI. ix. 302 Talking thus, Arabella forgot the relationship of pupil and teacher; it was a woman to woman—girl to girl—friend to friend.] **1907** G. B. SHAW *Major Barbara* III. 274, I thought she was a woman of the people, and that a marriage with a professor of Greek would be far beyond the wildest social ambitions of her rank. **1929** J. B. PRIESTLEY *Good Companions* III. v. 586 'I should think you have news,' said Susie, smiling and being tremendously woman-to-woman. **1933** KIPLING *Souvenirs of France* ii. 44 A woman of the people led her away. **1935** E. BOWEN *House in Paris* II. iii. 114 Her round slate-blue eyes rolled in a woman-to-woman way. **1962** 'L. GREX' *Terror wears Smile* iv. 58 'There's not going to be any nonsense. You know what I mean.' Those words had been uttered in a quiet woman-to-woman chat some weeks before. **1982** H. INNES *Black Tide* v. iii. 272 If I told her, woman-to-woman, the sort of person Karen was... Perhaps she'd understand then.

l. Also *hell hath no fury like a woman scorned* and var. (see SCORN *v.* 3 a, quot. 1697). Hence *woman scorned*, used allusively; also as *attrib. phr.*

1868 J. G. SAXE *Poems* 291 In classic authors we are often warned, There's naught so savage as a 'woman scorned'. [**1886** M. H. E. BATES *Chamber over Gate* xxvi. 363 You know 'Hell hath no fury', etc. If your wife should ever wake up to the true state of the case..I'm afraid she'd be an ugly customer.] **1927** W. JOHNSTON *Affair in Duplex 9B* 60 The old idea of 'the woman scorned' on which Chilton had been relying this time failed utterly. **1932** W. MCFEE *Harbourmaster* xxi. 333 They say hell hath no fury like a woman scorned. **1940** G. H. COXE *Glass Triangle* x. 126 If you really want to know who could have wanted to kill him, you might as well start with me... You've heard that one about hell having no fury like a woman scorned? Well, that was me. **1942** N. MARSH *Death & Dancing Footman* iii. 49 He broke out into..merriment calculated..to arouse in Chloris the pangs proper to a woman scorned. **1967** —— *Death at Dolphin* viii. 222 She really does bear out the Woman Scorned crack. She is..not all that charitably disposed at any time. **1971** 'J. RIPLEY' *Davis doesn't live here any More* 124 The discarded mistress—the 'woman scorned'—motive. **1973** I. MURDOCH *Black Prince* 330 'Hell hath no fury like a woman scorned.' In a way I might have been flattered.

II. 6. a. *woman-city, -eye, -flesh, -godhead, -haunt, -luck.*

1880 G. MEREDITH *Trag. Comedians* II. v. 83 Exactly what his appreciation, in womanflesh, would lead him to fix on. **1915** D. H. LAWRENCE *Rainbow* iii. 81 He must get out of this oppressive, shut-down, woman-haunt. **1922** JOYCE *Ulysses* 468 Under it lies the womancity. *Ibid.* 155 Mrs Breen's womaneyes said melancholily. **1923** D. H. LAWRENCE *Ladybird* 53 She could not finally believe in her own woman-godhead. **1946** DYLAN THOMAS *Deaths & Entrances* 40 The next-door sea dispelled Frogs and satans and woman-luck. **1971** V. CANNING *Firecrest* vi. 83 He put his arm round her shoulder..and felt through silk the warmth and firmness of woman flesh.

b. (*a*) *woman doctor, driver, -help, journalist, officer, p.c., police officer, -savage, teacher.*

1853 DICKENS *Child's Hist. Eng.* xxix, in *Househ. Words* 12 Mar. 48/2 Edward was now sinking in a rapid decline... They handed him over to a woman-doctor who pretended to be able to cure it. **1899** W. JAMES *Talks to Teachers on Psychol.* II. i. 227 What our girl-students and woman-teachers most need..is..the toning-down of their moral tensions. **1902** A. BENNETT in *Academy* 21 June 635/1 The average woman-journalist is the most loyal, earnest and teachable person under the sun. **1911** D. H. LAWRENCE *White Peacock* I. ix. 158 At any rate the extra woman-help came. **1921** R. MACAULAY *Dangerous Ages* iii. 65 Pamela bright and cool and firm, like a woman doctor. **1930** D. H. LAWRENCE *A Propos of Lady Chatterley's Lover* 25 We read of the woman-savage who wore three overcoats on top of one another to excite her man. **1968** R. L. FISH *Bridge that went Nowhere* iv. 44, I might have known it would be a woman driver! **1972** L. LAMB *Picture Frame* xviii. 154 A woman p.c. was clearing an outside drain. **1973** 'B. MATHER' *Snowline* x. 121 I'll send a couple of woman officers along. **1976** R. LEWIS *Witness my Death* i. 36 You've shown all the worst traits that can be expected in a woman doctor. **1976** *Southern Even. Echo* (Southampton) 11 Nov. 32/5 A chase through rush-hour crowds ended with a suspected shoplifter escaping into the darkness..as he was pursued by a woman police officer. **1982** D. MACKENZIE *Raven's Revenge* xi. 104 A small car stopped... The woman driver was already crossing the pavement, house-keys in hand. **1982** A. BROOKNER *Providence* ix. 108, I wonder why they didn't send a woman teacher.

c. objective, *woman-scorner* (example); *woman-worshipping* adj.; *woman-hating* adj. and sb.; similative, *woman-breasted* adj.

1928 W. B. YEATS tr. *Sophocles' King Oedipus* 42 Oedipus overcame the woman-breasted Fate. **1946** DYLAN THOMAS *Deaths & Entrances* 30 The woman breasted and the heaven headed Bird. **1939** W. FORTESCUE *There's Rosemary* xii. 87, I even got personal praise from a woman-hating Don who acted as dramatic critic for the 'Varsity magazine. **1973** E. TAYLOR *Serpent under It* xi. 172 He was really an old dear—all that woman-hating stuff was just a pose. **1935** AUDEN & ISHERWOOD *Dog beneath Skin* I. v. 57 But perhaps you're a woman-scorner. **1921** D. H. LAWRENCE *Sea & Sardinia* iii. 114 Woman-worshipping Don Juans.

7. woman-hour, an hour's work done by a woman; **woman-movement** (earlier example); **woman-power,** (*a*) the exercise of authority by women; (*b*) the number of women available for work; the power of women in work; **woman question,** a controversy over the rights of women, esp. that in the nineteenth century; **woman trouble** *colloq.*, (*a*) *U.S.*, gynæcological problems (cf. TROUBLE *sb.* 4); (*b*) difficulties caused to a man by a relationship with a woman or women; **woman-year,** a year of a woman's life; esp. used as a cumulative measure in medical tests carried out on a number of different women.

1961 *Guardian* 23 Mar. 24/6, I shudder to think how many man-hours and woman-hours are spent..typing, 'Dear So-and-So'. **1979** M. MCCARTHY *Cannibals & Missionaries* i. 4 I'm doing a serious study of the woman-hours expended in this family. **1883** *Harper's Mag.* Aug. 468/2 Whether the great progress of the 'woman movement'..is due to the agitation of 'woman's rights', or proceeds in spite of it. **1927** *Amer. Jrnl. Philol.* XLVIII. 201 In the kingdoms established by the Successors in Egypt and in Syria women appear as co-rulers with their husbands and as regents during the minority of a son or the exile of a husband. This woman-power is sometimes regarded as a Macedonian tradition. **1938** *Lancet* 5 Nov. 1071/2 If the aim is to use the woman-power of the countryside to the best advantage it will often be best for the women themselves to organise their work collectively. **1941** *New Yorker* 29 Mar. 46/3 The long-threatened drive to bring womanpower into the war effort. **1968** *Ramparts* May 8 If you had a cover on Black Power like your cover on Woman Power, it would be a picture of a sharecropper with a harmonica in one hand and a piece of watermelon in the other. **1973** *Black World* June 32 Woman power Is Black power Is Human power Is Always feeling. **1976** H. WILSON *Governance of Britain* 7 Ernest Bevin..was in charge of the industrial and military mobilization of Britain's manpower and woman-power. **1977** *Spare Rib* July 23 We're desperately short of woman-power on all areas of the magazine. **1984** *Sunday Times* (Colour Suppl.) 28 Oct. 80/2 The more progressive industries are beginning to realise that they can't afford to waste Britain's womanpower. **1857** GEO. ELIOT *Let.* 21 Sept. (1954) II. 383 Quite delivered from any necessity of giving a judgment on the Woman Question or of reading newspapers about the Indian Mutinies. **1884** T. STANTON (*title*) The woman question in Europe. **1930** J. COLLIER *His Monkey Wife* ix. 119 A belated essayist on the Woman Question. **1981** R. TREMAIN *Cupboard* ii. 31 The attitude of men to the Woman Question. **1959** N. MAILER *Advts. for Myself* (1961) 95 She comes to see him about something or other, woman trouble maybe, and he seduces her in his medical chambers. **1967** J. IRWIN *Murderous Welcome* vi. 51 She repudiated strongly any suggestion of discord between husband and wife and poured scorn on the mere idea of woman-trouble. **1977** L. MEYNELL *Hooky gets Wooden Spoon* xi. 127 'What's happening to Len Carron these days?'..'Woman trouble.' **1959** *Science* 10 July 81/2 Sixteen certain and one probable pregnancy occurred in women taking the medication; this represented a rate of 2·7 pregnancies per 100 woman-years.

8. woman's magazine, a magazine designed primarily for women; also (*colloq.*) *woman's mag*; freq. *attrib.*, esp. alluding to superficiality or stereotypical attitudes regarded as associated with such productions; **woman's movement** = *woman-movement*, sense 7 above; **woman's page,** a page of a newspaper devoted to topics intended to be of special interest to women; **woman's woman,** a woman whose qualities are appreciated by other women, a woman who is popular with other women (cf. *man's man* s.v. *MAN *sb.*[1] 21); **woman's work,** work traditionally undertaken by women.

1912 *Magazine Maker* Sept. 7 (*title*) Making a woman's magazine. **1944** U. ORANGE *Company in Evening* ii. 34 The woman's magazine short story market may be a footling one. **1958** *Observer* 23 Feb. 14/2 The play..fools about at woman's-mag-whimsy level of moral convention. *Ibid.* 25 May 16/7 A Miss Lonelyhearts on a foundering woman's mag. **1958** *Spectator* 13 June 768/2 Ophelia's infatuated woman's magazine royalism rings with a specially hollow tinkle in Glen Byam Shaw's production of *Hamlet*. **1959** J. BRAINE *Vodi* xxi. 231 Honestly, that woman's magazine stuff, just the sort of advice these damned aunties give. **1974** *Times Lit. Suppl.* 3 May 483/2 Without these pages of imaginative grace, the novel would be dangerously close to the woman's magazine level of romantic fiction with which it persistently flirts. [**1881** E. C. STANTON et al. *Hist. Woman Suffrage* I. xiv. 577 The 'Woman's Rights' Movement is a practical one.] **1894** J. E. SCHMAHL in *Englishwoman's Rev.* 16 Apr. 90 For many years Maria Deraismes was looked upon as the sole and undisputed head of the woman's movement in France. **1906** C. P. GILMAN *Women & Economics* (ed. 5) iii. 49 So utterly has the status of woman been accepted as a sexual one that it has remained for the woman's movement of the nineteenth century to devote much contention to the claim that women are persons! **1933** E. WAUGH *Scoop* I. i. 15 Those carefree days when he had edited the Woman's Page. **1952** M. STEEN *Phoenix Rising* iv. 87 An editor or a publisher or a woman's page-writer. **1971** Woman's page [see *SEXISM]. **1886** KIPLING *Plain Tales* (1888) 47 Mrs. Hauksbee was honest..and, but for her love of mischief, would have been a woman's woman. **1923** G. ATHERTON *Black Oxen* xl. 246 She had never been a 'woman's woman', and it was patent that, as ever, she was far more animated in the company of men. **1976** 'M. NELSON' *Crusoe Test* i. 12 Elegant was the word for Carla Bayer... She was not a woman's woman. [**1670** Woman's work: see WOMAN *sb.* 1 l.] **1890** A. J. ARMSTRONG *Ingleside Musings* 139 Thae bairns are just a woman's wark To keep them clean an' tidy. **1971** K. MILLETT *Sexual Politics* (1972) I. ii. 39 The 'woman's work' in which some two thirds of female population..are engaged is work that is not paid for.

9. a. *women doctors* (later example), *drivers, friends, journalists, ministers, priests, professors, students.*

1878 *Harper's Mag.* Mar. 602/2 The established physicians shook their heads. They never believed in 'women doctors'. **1896** C. L. DODGSON (*title*) Resident women-students. **1930** A. BENNETT *Imperial Palace* xi. 63 A strong sex-bias which had persuaded him that women-drivers were capable of any enormity. **1935** D. L. SAYERS *Gaudy Night* vii. 147 There are much better ways of enjoying Oxford than fooling round..with the women students. **1941** J. D. CARR *Case of Constant Suicides* xi. 142 What kind of a professor are you, anyway? Running around with women professors from other colleges. **1956** A. S. C. ROSS in M. Black *Importance of Lang.* (1962) 97 The custom is now obsolescent, save perhaps between close women-friends. **1967** L. MEYNELL *Mauve Front Door* xi. 138, I switched off the engine and climbed out of the cab; bloody women drivers, I thought. **1971** *Guardian* 15 Apr. 11/1 The diocese of Hong Kong, the only diocese out of 300 to have stated openly its support for the ordination of women priests. *Ibid.* 11/2 In the Congregationalist church..it can no longer be considered particularly unusual to have women ministers. **1975** *Ibid.* 21 Jan. 6/2 Creches should be provided at places where women journalists work. **1981** 'J. ROSS' *Dark Blue & Dangerous* iv. 22 Did he have friends? Women friends? **1981** 'A. CROSS' *Death in Faculty* ix. 106 Most women students..don't really believe women professors actually exist.

c. women liberators, women's liberationists (see sense 10 below); **womenpower** = *women-power*, sense 7 above; **women-wise** *adv.*, in the fashion or way of women; **women-years,** *pl.* of *woman-year*, sense 7 above.

1969 *Time* 21 Nov. 53 Women Liberators at Atlantic City. **1968** *Ramparts* Feb. 28 Her concept of women power, then, is assimilation to achieve a grey-flannel equality for the purpose of bettering women's estate in society by having them beat the hell out of..the men at the Establishment game. **1978** *Daily Tel.* 3 May 17/2 Consultants to advise businesses on..how to improve their use of manpower (or womenpower for that matter). **1930** Women-wise [see *man-wise* s.v. *MAN *sb.* 20 a]. **1977** *Lancet* 29 Oct. 922/1 The latest report is based on 206 689 women-years of observation.

10. women's college, a university college that admits only women as students; **women's group,** a group formed for the discussion or furtherance of the interests of women; **Women's Institute,** an organization of women in rural areas who meet regularly and engage in various social and cultural activities; **women's liberation,** the liberation of women from subservient social status and all forms of sexism; also (usu. with cap. initial) a militant movement with these aims; also abbrev. as **women's lib** (cf. *LIB); hence **women's libber** [*LIBBER], **liberationist; women's magazine** = *woman's magazine*, sense 8 above; similarly *women's mag*; **women's movement,** (*a*) = *woman-movement* s.v. WOMAN *sb.* 7; (*b*) the women's liberation movement (see above);

women's page = *woman's page*, sense 8 above; **women's room** *U.S.* = *ladies* s.v. *LADY *sb.* 4 f; **Women's Rural Institute**: see *RURAL *a.* 7; **women's studies** orig. *U.S.*, academic studies concerning women, their role in society, etc.; **women's wear**, clothing for women; **women's work** = *woman's work*, sense 8 above.

1867 GEO. ELIOT *Let.* 22 Nov. (1956) IV. 401 There is a scheme on foot for a women's college, or rather university..to be in connection with the Cambridge university. **1920** A. N. WHITEHEAD *Concept Nature* i. 7 Suppose that the expositor is in London, say in Regent's Park and in Bedford College, the great women's college which is situated in that park. **1948** M. LASKI *Tory Heaven* vii. 92 The women's colleges at Oxford..became reserved for B's. **1984** 'A. CROSS' *Sweet Death* xi. 129 Can you offer me one reason for women's colleges these days? **1968** *Ramparts* May 8 Your attitude was condescending throughout, and your analysis of radical women's groups..amounted to a movement fashion report. **1977** *Evening Post* (Nottingham) 27 Jan. 4/4 He is a solicitor..and while in Paris he was invited to talk to an American women's group. **1906** *Rep. Women's Institutes Province of Ontario* 69 After placing before them the aims and objects of the Women's Institute..the warden kindly assured us that he was..in sympathy with our work. **1909** *Jrnl. Home Econ.* I. 161 The usual practice has been to hold the Women's Institute on the same day..as the institute for men. **1912** *Rep. Farm & Agricultural Schools & Colleges in France, Germany, & Belgium* (Board of Educ.) 20 The success which has followed the formation of Women's Institutes in Poland, the United States, and Canada incited some social and agricultural reformers in Belgium to organise similar means of education. *Ibid.* 20 The Women's Institute is an association of farmers' wives, daughters, and sisters who meet periodically..to hear lectures, read papers, and study books on professional subjects. **1921** *Daily Colonist* (Victoria, B.C.) 20 Mar. 32/2 The first general meeting of the Victoria Women's Institute..was held Friday afternoon. **1924** [see *SCOUT *sb.*[4] 2 c (*a*)]. **1935** *N. & Q.* 2 Feb. 87/2 The Women's Institute of the old village of Cambo. **1982** *Daily Tel.* 25 Nov. 14/6 With reference to the letter from a Women's Institute member in Yorkshire regarding the splitting up of the Yorkshire federation [etc.]. **1969** *Time* 21 Nov. 15 'My twelve-year-old son has been hearing a lot about Women's Lib lately,' says Ruth. **1971** *Times* 17 July 5/8 Ecology..one Texas paper said recently, has replaced women's lib as the people's favourite cause. **1976** P. & W. PROCTOR *Women in Pulpit* i. 10 The earring criticism soon subsided as they got used to her and saw that she wasn't interested in staging women's lib demonstrations. **1971** Women's libber [see *LIBBER]. **1973** *Lancet* 24 Feb. 419/1 We have heard a lot lately from unhappy ones of one kind and another—the women's libbers, the occasional bleat from the male side, [etc.]. **1978** J. GALWAY *Autobiogr.* ii. 16 It sounds now like a good case for the women's libbers but my mother was essentially a happy woman. **1985** *Observer* (Colour Suppl.) 14 Apr. 23/2 What the women's libbers don't realise is that what they denigrate as domestic drudgery is exactly the right sort of thing to be doing when you are mucking around with the under-twos. **1966** *New Left Rev.* Nov./Dec. 12 Fourier was the most ardent and voluminous advocate of women's liberation and of sexual freedom among the early socialists. **1967** *New Left Notes* 10 July 4/1 The SDS National Convention adopts the following statement and program as written by the Women's Liberation Workshop. **1974** L. DEIGHTON *Spy Story* v. 55 Women's Liberation..planned to march to Westminster. **1978** S. SHELDON *Bloodline* iv. 64 There were rumors that Hélène Roffe was an advocate of the women's liberation movement. **1969** *Leviathan* (Berkeley, Calif.) June 43/1 The radical women's liberationists believe that the true extent of women's oppression can be revealed and fought only if the women's liberation movement is dominated by working class women. **1979** R. RENDELL *Means of Evil* 147 Sheila singing lustily, Sylvia, the Women's Liberationist, with less assurance as if she doubted the ethics of lending her support to so..sexist a ceremony. **1959** *Observer* 18 Jan. 19/2 The daydream world of women's mags. **1942** D. POWELL *Time to be Born* ii. 42 All Vicky could do was to read the women's magazines and discover how other heroines had solved this problem. **1960** K. AMIS *New Maps of Hell* iii. 81 Art is mentioned..with a frequency not even paralleled in women's-magazine stories. **1981** J. B. HILTON *Playground of Death* vi. 72 There were shopping notes, memos..a pile of women's magazines. **1902** H. BLACKBURN *Women's Suffrage* vi. 107 The Married Women's Property Bill occupied the main attention of those engaged in the women's movement. **1944** G. MYRDAL *American Dilemma* App. 5 The women's movement got much of its public support by reason of its affiliation with the Abolitionist movement. **1968** *Ramparts* Feb. 31 The most active of the new radical women's movements is in Berkeley—which should surprise no one. **1985** *Observer* (Colour Suppl.) 14 Apr. 18/3 She champions women who simply want to stay at home with their babies without a lot of pressure from the women's movement. **1929** E. LINKLATER *Poet's Pub* xiii. 154 She had had two or three articles accepted for the women's page of the *Daily Day*. **1980** M. BABSON *Dangerous to Know* i. 8 There weren't all that many openings for Women's Page Editors around the Street these days. **1961** WEBSTER, Women's room. **1977** M. FRENCH (*title*) The women's room. **1981** 'A. CROSS' *Death in Tenured Position* i. 5 The women's room on the ground floor. **1972** *Newsweek* 10 Dec. 124/3 In the classroom, many women think less of competing with men than of learning about themselves. 'Women's studies' was nearly unknown before 1970; now 78 institutions have complete women's studies programs. **1976** *Spare Rib* Nov. 14/2 Last year there was one women's studies course here. This year four are planned. **1919** MENCKEN *Amer. Lang.* iv. 121 Women's wear, in English shops, is always ladies' wear. **1980** *Times* 22 Jan. 9/6 Austin Reed is planning to open a womenswear area in the Regent Street branch. **1974** R. ADAMS *Shardik* xxv. 209, I can't help wondering why he trims lamps at noon. Or why he trims lamps at all, if it comes to that, seeing it's women's work and he has that girl to help him. **1977** *Undercurrents* June–July 41/3 Spinning, weaving, knitting, crocheting, sewing are women's work and are called crafts.

womanfully, *adv.* (Earlier example.)

1821 M. EDGEWORTH *Let.* 29 Jan. (1971) 236, I will trample..upon all the prickles of the impossibilities and flatten them womanfully.

woman-hater. (Further examples.)

1847 [see *woman-spiter* s.v. WOMAN *sb.* 6 c]. **1951** M. MCLUHAN *Mech. Bride* (1967) 99/1 The glamour business..is crammed with both women-haters and men-haters of dubious sex polarity. **1982** J. FOX *White Mischief* xxi. 247 Colvile was a great woman hater.

womanly, *a.* Add: **1.** Freq. in phr. *womanly woman.*

1387–8 [in Dict.]. **1872** (*title*) Woman's rights and the wife at home. By a womanly woman. **1891** G. B. SHAW *Quintessence of Ibsenism* iii. 34 In real life a self-sacrificing woman, or, as Mr. Stead would put it, a womanly woman, is not only taken advantage of, but disliked as well for her pains. **1926** WODEHOUSE *Heart of Goof* iii. 96 The least you can do, as a good womanly woman, is to have a capable lawyer watching your interests. **1958** M. KENNEDY *Outlaws on Parnassus* xii. 196 Telemachus..upbraids his mother for not behaving like a womanly woman. **1978** J. PORTER *Dead Easy for Dover* vii. 78 The Brigadier..only exists to make Madame more credible as a womanly woman.

womanness. Add: Also, the quality of being a woman. (Later examples.)

1926 D. H. LAWRENCE *Plumed Serpent* ii. 29 They hated her mechanically for the very fact that she was a woman. They hated her womanness. **1971** *Guardian* 2 Dec. 11/4 There may be something about 'woman-ness' which has to be defined in its own terms, not by reference to maleness.

woman's rights, women's rights. Add: (Further examples.)

1632 (*title*) The lawes resolutions of womens rights, or the lawes provision for woemen. **1842** E. PEASE *Let.* 29 Mar. [MS. in Library of Society of Friends, London], I believe that the Chartists generally hold the doctrine of the equality of woman's rights. **1859** A. J. MUNBY *Diary* 28 Jan. (1972) 18 Those who prate of women's rights, if they knew their own meaning, would honour such mighty daughters of the plough. **1876** H. JAMES *Roderick Hudson* xi. 378 Five unmarried sisters, one of whom gave lyceum-lectures on woman's rights. **1897** E. BELLAMY *Equality* xx. 119 There was a great stir about women's rights, but the programme then announced was by no means revolutionary. **1902** G. B. SHAW *Let.* 20 June (1972) II. 276 The Woman's Rights young lady. **1963** B. FRIEDAN *Feminine Mystique* i. 28 The fact is that no one today is muttering angrily about 'women's rights', even though more and more women have gone to college. **1977** *Socialist Press* 2 Mar. 4/1 The latest in a series of non-political jamborees organised around the question of women's rights took place at Alexandra Palace last Saturday. **1982** *N.Y. Times Mag.* 1 Aug. 6 Campaigning by the women's-rights movement to purge the English language of sexism.

woman's righter (earlier U.S. example).

1858 J. J. BOYER *Let.* 9 July in *Lawrence* (Kansas) *Republican* 15 July 1/4 Capt. Holmes and lady joined us. She is a regular woman's righter, wears the Bloomer, and was quite indignant when informed that she was not allowed to stand on guard.

womanthrope (wu·mănþrōᵘp). [Joc. formation f. WOMAN *sb.* + *-thrope* as in MISANTHROPE.] A hater of women.

1891 O. WILDE *Intentions* 126 They would become confirmed misanthropes, or if I may borrow a phrase from one of the pretty Newnham graduates, confirmed womanthropes for the rest of their lives. **1902** 'COLDSTREAMER' *Ballads of Boer War* iv. 35 I'm quite willing for to be Wot scholards calls a 'womanthrope'.

womb, *sb.* Add: **2.** Also in phr. *womb-to-tomb*, esp. used *attrib.* to denote procedures, etc., which span a lifetime. Cf. *cradle-to-grave* s.v. *CRADLE *sb.* 2.

1964 A. WYKES *Gambling* i. 8 During our womb-to-tomb progress we never stop gambling, for we cannot know the outcome of each of the many decisions we have to make every day. **1967** MCLUHAN & FIORE *Medium is Massage* 12 Electrical information devices for universal, tyrannical womb-to-tomb surveillance are causing a very serious dilemma between our claim to privacy and the community's need to know. **1968** G. JACKSON *Let.* 29 June in *Soledad Brother* (1971) 163 From the womb to the tomb this plays in our minds. We are not worth more than the amount of capital we can raise. **1979** *Bookseller* 23 June 2830/3 *Kane and Abel*..is a womb-to-tomb tale.

5. (Mostly *poet.*) *womb-element, -fruit, -land, -life; womb-fibrilled, -like* adjs.; *womb-ward* adv.

1923 D. H. LAWRENCE *Birds, Beasts & Flowers* 94 Who lies with the waters of his silent passion, womb-element?—Fish in the waters. **1923** Womb-fibrilled [see *INTURNED *ppl. a.*]. **1922** Wombfruit [see *QUICKENING *vbl. sb.*]. **1930** A. HUXLEY *Vulgarity in Literature* iv. 16 Those yearning popular songs which are the national anthems of Wombland. **1876** G. M. HOPKINS *Wr. Deutschland* vii, in *Poems* (1967) 53 Warm-laid grave of a womb-life grey. *a* **1930** D. H. LAWRENCE *Last Poems* (1932) 308 The shell-like, womb-like, convoluted shadow. **1981** J. WAINWRIGHT *All on a Summer's Day* 24 An Interview Room..is womb-like in its complete isolation. **1923** D. H. LAWRENCE *Birds, Beasts & Flowers* 19 There was a flower that flowered inward, womb-ward.

Womble (wǫ·mb'l). [Shortening of *Wombledon*, fanciful alteration of *WIMBLEDON.] An imaginary animal depicted as inhabiting Wimbledon Common (see quot. 1968). Also, a soft toy representing this creature. Also *transf.*

1968 E. BERESFORD *Wombles* (1974) (*dust-jacket*), The Wombles are a bit like teddy bears to look at but they have real claws and live underneath Wimbledon Common and devote their lives to 'tidying up' all the things those untidy Human Beings leave behind. **1975** *Sunday Express* 15 June 6/3 In addition to the Wombles pop group and the TV series, there are Womble jigsaws, Womble dolls, Womble T-shirts, Womble pillow cases... Now..there are Womble-approved crisps. **1977** *Lancashire Life* Dec. 77/2 Now she had locked herself in the ladies' with five rubber frogs and a selection of plastic Wombles and was refusing to come out. **1978** *Times* 26 Aug. 3 (*caption*) Members of the Outset youth service group felling and clearing dead trees on Wimbledon Common. These 'Wombles' have also assisted in pond clearing. **1982** *Buses* Sept. 393/2 The customers being predominantly senior citizens or 'wombles' in the London Transport vernacular.

womby, *a.* Delete *rare* and add later examples. Also *fig.*

1934 DYLAN THOMAS *Let.* 2 May (1966) 117 I've a good mind to ferret an Old Boys' Society, & read them the waxiest and wombiest efforts that I've got. **1951** W. SANSOM *Face of Innocence* xi. 150 The sense of round shapes about—the rounder mouldings of stone, the curves of boats..roundness, if you like, that is womby. **1977** *Time* 5 Sept. 44/1 It [*sc.* a van] is self-contained and self-containing, and its womby little room is packed with the motherly comforts of home.

womenfolk. (Earlier U.S. example of *womenfolks.*)

1851 J. J. HOOPER *Widow Rugby's Husband* 50 Such wimmen folks.

wo·menish, *a.* [f. *women*, pl. of WOMAN *sb.* + -ISH[1].] Of, pertaining to, or characteristic of, women. Also in phr. *wine and womenish*: cf. WINE *sb.*[1] f (*b*).

1892 S. HALE *Let.* 28 Apr. (1919) 273 The day was so hot that it smelled perspiration of emigrant women-ish. **1920** D. H. LAWRENCE *Let.* 4 Jan. (1962) I. 606 At midnight the Monty crowd ordered champagne and tried to look wine and womenish.

womens (wi·minz). *U.S. dial.* Non-standard pl. of WOMAN *sb.*

1928 [see *SPADE *sb.*[2] 3 a]. **1945** L. SAXON et al. *Gumbo Ya-Ya* i. 8 'It's damn funny' Fisher sniffed, 'how womens is.' **1967** *Boston Sunday Herald* 26 Apr. (Comic Section), Sometime I think wimmens is the strongest gender. **1970** R. D. ABRAHAMS *Positively Black* iv. 84, I got so many womens I cannot call they name.

womerah, womerar, varr. WOOMERA.

womoonless (wumū·nlės), *a.* *nonce-word.* [See def.] Joc. combination of WOMANLESS *a.* and MOONLESS *a.*

1922 JOYCE *Ulysses* 278 Croak of vast manless moonless womoonless marsh.

won (wǫn, wǭn), *sb.* [ad. Korean *wŏn* in same sense.] The basic monetary unit of (North and South) Korea.

1950 *Times* 16 Nov. 7/7 Between June 25 and October 1 expenditure totalled 28,000m. *won*,..while revenue amounted to about 1,000m. *won*. **1952** R. CUTFORTH *Korean Reporter* x. 85, I gave him 20,000 won, patted him on the back and said goodbye. **1981** 'A. HALL' *Pekin Target* vii. 62, I declared 100,000 *won* and asked where I could change pounds sterling. **1984** *Times* 25 Jan. 6/8 Twelve South Korean herb medicine dealers were arrested for selling 1bn won (£850,000) worth of false cures.

wonder, *sb.* Add: **I. 1. a.** *seven wonders of the world*: so *eighth wonder of the world* (used hyperbolically of any impressive object, etc.).

1831 M. EDGEWORTH *Let.* 20 Jan. (1971) 473 A..spoiled child of 30 whose mother and father having not been able to conceal from him that they think him the 8th wonder of the world have at last brought him to acquiesce in their opinion. **1930** *Amer. Speech* VI. *Eighth wonder of the world*... Ford runabout. **1977** H. FAST *Immigrants* IV. 267, I rode the first cable car on California Street... The Eighth Wonder of the World.

d. (Later examples.) *boneless wonder*, a gymnast; *fig.*, someone or something lacking 'backbone'; *chinless wonder*: see *CHINLESS *a.* b.

1931 W. S. CHURCHILL in *Hansard Commons* 28 Jan. 1022, I remember, when I was a child, being taken to the celebrated Barnum's Circus... The exhibit on the programme which I most desired to see was the one described as 'The Boneless Wonder'. My parents judged that that spectacle would be too revolting and demoralising for my youthful eyes, and I have waited 50 years to see the boneless wonder sitting on the Treasury Bench. **1946** Boy wonder [see *CHATTERTONIAN *a.* and *sb.*]. **1951** 'J. TEY' *Daughter of Time* xiv. 186 The spectacle of Dr. Gairdner trying to make his facts fit his theory was the most entertaining thing in gymnastics that Grant had witnessed... As a contortionist Dr. Gairdner was the original boneless wonder. **1963** *Guardian* 15 Feb. 20/6 One of those boneless wonders that go by the name of 'Observer' editorials. **1967** M. SHULMAN *Kill 3* IV. ii. 168 Reconciling more contradictory positions than could be brought up by a boneless wonder on a trapeze.

6. g. (Earlier examples.)

1782 BOSWELL *Jrnl.* 16 July in *Boswell, Laird of Auchinleck* (1977) 456 While she was out, my father and Lady Auchinleck called, for a wonder. **1811** PRINCESS CHARLOTTE *Let.* 13 Nov. (1949) 12 Soon for a wonder I plucked up courage & went in.

i. *wonders will never cease*: that is indeed surprising; now freq. *ironic.*

1828 T. CREEVEY *Let.* 11 Feb. in *Creevey's Life & Times* (1934) xii. 258 Off he went with, 'Well, Creevey, wonders will never cease!' I met Lord Bathurst at the Duke of Buccleuch's [etc.]. **1837** DICKENS *Pickwick Papers* xlv. 489 Vonders vill never cease... I'm wery much mistaken if that 'ere Jingle worn't a doin' somethin' in the vater-cart vay! **1902** CONRAD *Typhoon* xxiv. 191 'Solomon says wonders will never cease,' cried Mrs. Rout joyously. **1962** M. SUMMERTON *Nightingale at Noon* (1963) viii. 105, I offered: 'I'll help you...' She..gave me a cheeky grin. 'Hear that! Wonders will never cease!' **1974** A. PRICE *Other Paths to Glory* I. vii. 88 Wonders will never cease... Early Tudor—practically untouched.

III. 9. a. Further examples: *wonder-beauty, boy, -child, drug, -gleam, goal, -horse, -look, -woman.*

1921 D. H. LAWRENCE *Sea & Sardinia* v. 210 Real fresh wonder-beauty all around. **1922** —— *Aaron's Rod* xviii. 269 The glimmer of the open flower, the wonder-look, still lasted. **1927** E. O'NEILL *Marco Millions* III. i. 167 Worth while your waiting, eh?.. Yes, my wonder boy! **1927** A. CONAN DOYLE *Case-Bk. Sherlock Holmes* 15 A wonder-woman in every way. **1929** R. BRIDGES *Test. Beauty* IV. 188 The shifting hues that sanctify the silent dawn with wonder-gleams. **1938** *Encycl. Brit. Bk. of Year* 38/2 The one signed work in the series..was the wonder-child of the project. **1939** *Time* 14 Aug. 50/2 Sulfanilamide, the 'wonder drug', introduced into the U.S. in 1936, is credited with remarkable cures. **1939** Wonder horse [see *SECOND-GUESSER]. **1939** JOYCE *Finnegans Wake* 395 You know her, our angel being, one of romance's fadeless wonderwomen. **1948** Wonder drug [see *SUBTILIN]. **1958** P. SCOTT *Mark of Warrior* I. 82 Old Ramsay's something of a wonder boy. He'll be top cadet of the course. **1975** *Daily Tel.* 18 June 2/8 Experts..began work on the vaccines following the failure of the post-war 'wonder drugs' such as sulphonamides and penicillin to wipe out these two diseases. **1976** *West Lancs. Evening Gaz.* 15 Dec. I. 4/7 He scored a superb hat trick with a wonder goal to round it off. **1976** *Liverpool Echo* 23 Nov. 7/1 Southport's golden sands, world famous as the training track of wonderhorse Red Rum. **1980** 'R. B. DOMINIC' *Attending Physician* xiv. 117 Senator Gerald Ewell was a Democrat... 'What's Wonder Boy done this time?' demanded Tony. **1980** I. HUNTER *Malcom Muggeridge* iv. 59 Various bizarre proposals to sort out and rearrange our genes so that everyone will become superman and wonderwoman. **1985** *Times* 2 Jan. 15/2 The word from the market is that a replacement 'wonder drug' is now in clinical trials.

b. Further examples: *wonder-life, song.*

1895 KIPLING *Seven Seas* (1896) 84 The everlasting Wonder Song of Youth! **1929** R. BRIDGES *Test. Beauty* III. 105 With what other numberless wonder-lives of the Saints they wrote.

10. a. (instrumental) *wonder-ridden, -stricken* (earlier example), *-wide* adjs.

1916 D. H. LAWRENCE *Amores* 76, I see each shadow start with recognition, and I Am wonder-ridden. **1818** SHELLEY *Laon & Cythna* v. xliii. 114 The morning's golden mist, Which now the wonder-stricken breezes kist With their cold lips, fled. **1922** JOYCE *Ulysses* 530 Milly Bloom..calls, her young eyes wonderwide.

b. *wonder-fine.*

1929 R. BRIDGES *Test. Beauty* I. 29 Not to these look we with grateful pleasur or satisfaction of soul, wonder-fine tho' they be.

11. wonder-man: also in weakened sense, a man whose achievements are admired; **wonder rabbi**, in the Chasidic movement, a *TSADDIK; **Wonder State** *U.S.*, a nickname for the state of Arkansas.

1933 *Amer. Speech* VIII. III. 39/2 *Wonderman.* Foreign fighters are often thus described [by sports writers]. **1935** WODEHOUSE *Luck of Bodkins* xv. 173 They get the idea that they are sort of wonder-men who can just look around and find talent where nobody else would suspect it. **1961** *Catholic Herald* 23 June 3/1 (*heading*) De Gaulle, hero and wonderman. **1962** A. SAMPSON *Anat. of Britain* xxvii. 450 In Whitehall he had the reputation of a wonderman, and had even been tipped by some as an eventual head of the Treasury. **1907** I. ZANGWILL *Ghetto Comedies* 409 We Chassidim have no fear. Our wonder-rabbi has power over all the spheres. **1970** C. KERSH *Aggravations of Minnie Ashe* i. 11 [Her] father had been a wonder rabbi in some obscure Jewish village in Galicia—a worker of miracles. **1923** *Gen. Acts Arkansas* 804 Be It Resolved by the Senate of the State of Arkansas... That hereafter Arkansas shall be known and styled 'The Wonder State'.

wo·nderlandish, *a.* [f. WONDERLAND + -ISH[1].] Seemingly enchanted.

1929 J. B. PRIESTLEY *Good Companions* III. v. 590 He was beginning to feel wonderlandish again, what with Mr. Memsworth and the champagne.

wonderling. For † *Obs.* read *rare* and add later example.

1913 A. O'CONNOR *Poems* 8 Sweet wonderlings Of passing fancy, slight, too slight for birth, Yet dazzlingly alive with sudden mirth.

wonderstone (wʌ·ndəɹstōᵘn). [f. WONDER *sb.* + STONE *sb.*] **1.** (See quots.)

1824 *Trans. Geol. Soc.* I. 295 In the neighbourhood of Wells, and at Bleydon near the Bristol Channel, it [*sc.* the conglomerate] forms a beautiful breccia, called wonder-stone, consisting of yellow transparent crystals of carbonate of lime, disseminated equably through a dark-red earthy dolomite. **1887** H. B. WOODWARD *Geol. England & Wales* (ed. 2) II. 232 The road to Wookey Hole..and that leading to Dulcot..show in places in the Red Marl a bed termed the 'Wonder Stone'.

2. A soft bluish-grey rock of volcanic origin in South Africa that takes a high polish.

1936 *Mineral Resources Union S. Afr.* (Geol. Survey, Union S. Afr.) (ed. 2) 299 Wonderstone appears to be one of the most indestructible of building stones. **1952** *Archit. Rev.* CXI. 329/1 Some of the work in 1936 by Henry Moore in African wonderstone and by Barbara Hepworth was very derivative, in the best sense, of the shapes assumed by..the stone and pebble plants of the African Karoo. **1952** L. MACNEICE *Ten Burnt Offerings* 84 He was..Firm as a Rameses in African wonderstone. **1975** *Stand. Encycl. S. Afr.* XI. 490/1 Large quantities of high quality wonderstone are available in the Dominion Reef System, 10 km north of Ottosdal in the Western Transvaal.

wonder-working, *ppl. a.* Add: Also as *vbl. sb.*

1900 F. T. ELWORTHY *Horns of Honour* iii. 180 There is some confusion about the several stories told of its [*sc.* the hand of glory's] wonder-working.

wongai (wǫ·ŋgai). *Austral.* [Aboriginal name.] A name used in the islands off the north coast of Australia for the jujube, *Zizyphus jujuba.* Also *wongai tree.*

1947 I. L. IDRIESS *Isles of Despair* xxii. 146 All the yams and berries and wongais will soon ripen. **1959** K. TENNANT *All Proud Tribesmen* vii. 84 Wongai trees.. have big dark berries like dates. **1968** *Courier-Mail* (Brisbane) 10 July 2/8 Thursday Island..has an informal charm and friendliness which easily tempts one to bite into the sticky fruit of the wongai tree. If you eat this fruit, legend says, you are bound to return.

wonga-wonga. Add: **1.** For *picata* substitute *melanoleuca.* (Earlier example.)

1821 L. MACQUARIE *Jrnl. of Tours* (1956) 223 Major Morisett has most kindly sent his young friend Lachlan the following very handsome presents of pets; vizt. four black swans..and one wanga-wanga pigeon.

2. In full *wonga(-wonga) vine.* An evergreen climber, *Pandorea pandorana,* of the family Bignoniaceæ, native to Australia and bearing panicles of pale yellow or pink flowers.

1895 J. H. MAIDEN *Flowering Plants & Ferns N.S.W.* 33 The Wonga Wonga Vine... A tall, woody, glabrous climber with more or less twining branches. **1936** F. CLUNE *Roaming round Darling* xvii. 162 Another shrub was the wonga-wonga vine. It has white flowers, and the blacks used to hollow the stems and make whistles from them. **1946** K. TENNANT *Lost Haven* (1947) xvii. 278 The bells of the Wonga vine, milky with plum velvet in their throats.

wongi (wǫ·ŋgi). *Austral. local.* [Aboriginal.] A talk or chat; a speech.

1929 K. S. PRICHARD *Coonardoo* xxv. 243 He..had seen smoke..and come in for a bit of sugar and a wongie. **1939** X. HERBERT *Capricornia* xxiv. 354 'Give's a drink Joe—— I've rasped me old throat raw.'.. 'By cripes, Andy, that was a great wongi.' **1969** L. HADOW *Full Cycle* 178 If he asks you to have one..well, he's out for a wongi.

wonk[1] (wǫŋk). Also **wunk.** [Said to repr. pronunc. of Chin. *huāng gǒu* yellow dog.] In China, a dog. Also *wonk dog.*

1900 H. A. GILES *Gloss. Subjects Far East* (ed. 3) 318 *Wunk,*..yellow dog. A term commonly applied by foreigners to the ordinary Chinese dog. From the Ningpo pronunciation *wou̅ kyi,* of the above two characters. **1909** J. O. P. BLAND *Houseboat Days in China* vii. 78 Particularly around the great cities you find him of the modern type, sporting a muzzle-loader..and a half-trained wonk. **1939** 'A. BRIDGE' *Four-Part Setting* i. 4 Away in the Chinese village a wonk dog bayed at the moon. *Ibid.* 5 There are all these Chinks and wonks about—you oughtn't to go alone. **1967** 'A. CORDELL' *Bright Cantonese* vi. 67 Starving wonk dogs, the scavengers of China.

wonk[2] (wǫŋk). *slang.* [In sense 1 related to *WONKY *a.* The other senses may represent different words.] **†1.** In phr. *all of a wonk,* nervous, upset. *Obs. rare.*

1918 [see *DOODAH 1].

2. *Naut.* (See quots.)

1929 F. C. BOWEN *Sea Slang* 153 *Wonk,* a useless hand, or a young naval cadet who has not yet learnt the elements of his job. **1962** W. GRANVILLE *Dict. Sailors' Slang* 134/1 *Wonk,* midshipman.

3. *Austral.* **a.** A white person.

1938 X. HERBERT *Capricornia* 252 He went to the Dagoes and Roughs of second-class and won their friendship by..telling them how he had been cast out by the Wonks of the saloon. **1959** BAKER *Drum* 157 *Wonk,* a white man or white woman. Aborigines (esp. half-castes) use this pejorative much as whites use the word *boong* to denote an aboriginal.

b. An effeminate or homosexual man.

1945 BAKER *Austral. Lang.* vi. 123 An effeminate male is a..gussie, spurge and wonk. **1970** P. WHITE *Vivisector* 213 I'd have to have a chauffeur to drive me about—with a good body—just for show, though. I wouldn't mind if the chauffeur was a wonk.

4. *U.S.* A disparaging term for a studious or hard-working person.

1962 *Sports Illustrated* 17 Dec. 21 A wonk, sometimes called a 'turkey' or a 'lunch', roughly corresponds to the 'meatball' of a decade ago. **1970** E. SEGAL *Love Story* 32 Who could Jenny be talking to that was worth appropriating moments set aside for a date with me? Some musical wonk? **1980** *N.Y. Times Mag.* 20 July 8 At Harvard the excessively studious student is derided as a 'wonk', which Amy Berman, Harvard '79, fancifully suggests may be 'know' spelled backward. (In British slang, 'wonky' means 'unsteady'.)

wonky (wǫ·ŋki), *a. slang.* [Obscure: the G. element *wankel-* has similar force.] Of a person: shaky, groggy; unstable. Of a thing: faulty, unsound; unreliable.

1919 LD. NORTHCLIFFE *Let.* in *Hist. The Times* (1952) IV. I. xi. 507 Am weak, and wonky, as the telephone girls say, after a bad morning with the subscribers. **1923** H. C. BAILEY *Mr Fortune's Practice* iii. 81 'Who runs the "Daily Watchman?".. It's the wonkiest print on the market.'.. 'You said "on the market"... Corrupt?' 'Well, naturally.' **1925** E. WALLACE *Strange Countess* ix. 83 Financial adviser to some heads of departments, whose accounts went a little wonky. **1929** P. GIBBS *Hidden City* xvi. 79 It had made his heart jump in a wonky sort of way. **1932** KIPLING *Limits & Renewals* 127 Haman's head-light's wonky. Something *must* have happened. **1957** *Listener* 11 July 67 Despite the perfection of isolated lines and phrases..most of the poems seem slightly out of shape, wonky, as if the kiln had not been hot enough. **1958** *Observer* 23 Feb. 15/5 Would they really have sent her on a dangerous mission with an ankle still wonky from an old parachute fall? **1981** *Times Lit. Suppl.* 5 June 633/3 The vast majority of murderers are *ipso facto* acutely wonky, and most frequently wonky in dispiriting and unimaginative ways. **1983** D. BOGGIS *Woman they sent to Fight* ii. 17 The window fitted badly, and her chair was..wonky with one short leg. **1984** A. CARTER *Nights at Circus* II. vii. 156 'How's the wonky arm?' she enquired. He showed his sling.

Hence **wo·nkiness.**

1982 *Times* 29 Apr. 10/8 Do not be disconcerted by its [*sc.* a book's] wonkiness of style.

wonst: see *ONCE *adv.* A. δ.

wontedly, *adv.* Delete 'Now *rare* or *Obs.*' and add later examples.

1913 W. OWEN *Let.* 4 Jan. (1967) 175 The Vicar's presence (taciturn instead of wontedly gay)..sat heavy on my soul the night. **1980** *N.Y. Times* 12 Dec. C-30/3 On Sunday at 7.30 P.M., South Street's 19th-century surroundings will be wontedly hushed, except at Bowne. **1981** *Guardian* 4 Oct. 21 Dexter was wontedly tough on some of the actors.

won ton (wǫn tǫn). Also **wan tan, wun tun,** and as one word. [Chinese (Cantonese), Pinyin *húntun.*] A small round roll or pocket of dough containing a savoury filling, eaten alone (after being deep-fried) or boiled in soup (*won ton soup*).

1948 R. W. DANA *Where to eat in New York* 66 The theater and night-club performers drop in late for chicken egg foo yong, a won ton soup, squab, or Chinese steak. **1952** W. Y. HONG *Chinese Cook Bk.* 37 Pick up about ½ teaspoon of meat (or fish) mixture and place on one corner of the won-ton skin. Roll almost to the opposite corner... The usual serving is 12 to 15 won-tons per person. *Ibid.* 38 Chicken Won-Ton Soup... 8 cups super soup stock... 2 cups chicken meat... 90 pieces of won-ton. **1956** 'E. MCBAIN' *Cop Hater* (1958) xx. 172 The wonton soup was crisp with Chinese vegetables... The wontons were brown and crisp. **1972** K. LO *Chinese Food* I. 54 Well made *wuntuns* floating in clear soups resemble clouds. **1976** *Times* 20 Aug. 12/8 Two spring rolls for 25p, skins for Wan Tan dumpling at 6op a lb. **1976** *Time* 27 Sept. 63/2 The Chinese deep-fry everything from shrimp toast and *wontons* to beef and chicken.

woo (wū), *v.*[2] [Origin unknown.] = *MAH JONG *v.*

1922 H. STERLING *Standard Rules & Instr. Chinese Game Mah Chang* (ed. 4) 6 Experienced players invariably prefer to 'Woo' quickly with a small score rather than fail to 'Woo' at all. *Ibid.* 12 The Woo hand adds 2 points if he Woo with only one possible piece..or if he hold one of his last pair and Woo with the other. **1943** K. S. WHITEHEAD *Mah Jong Chinese Way* § 59 A player whose hand contains a false set has a 'foul hand', and cannot woo. **1973** J. SCARNE *Scarne's Encycl. Games* xxiii. 451 When he completes his hand, four sets and a pair, a player may *woo* or *mah-jongg* by showing his whole hand. He wins the deal, ending play.

woo (wū), *sb.* [f. WOO *v.*[1]] (A spell of) caressing or love-making; esp. in phr. *to pitch a woo*: see *PITCH *v.*[1] 17 d.

1937, etc. [see *PITCH *v.*[1] 17 d]. **1938** N. MARSH *Artists in Crime* ix. 120 Hello, you two, what are you up to? Having a woo or something? **1959** —— *Singing in Shrouds* vi. 111 A pair of tango dancers..strutted and stalked..and frowned ineffably at each other. 'What an angry woo,' Tim said. **1968** *Guardian* 27 Nov. 9/6 Couples making woo in motor-cars should be careful not to rock them too much.

wood, *sb.*[1] Add: **I. 5. i.** *to have the wood on* (a person) and varr.: to have the upper hand, to have a hold on. *Austral.* and *N.Z. colloq.* Cf. *to have the goods on* s.v. *GOODS *sb. pl.* 2 b.

c **1926** 'MIXER' *Transport Workers' Song Bk.* 7, I hold the 'wood' on those who work. **1944** J. H. FULLARTON *Troop Target* VI. xxii. 168 Then we've taken another hiding. And I thought we had the wood on Jerry today. **1954** T. A. G. HUNGERFORD *Sowers of Wind* xxi. 264 Can't you realize I've got the wood on you? You've got two minutes. **1965** L. HAYLEN *Big Red* i. 55 It was another of her occasions of fear: she liked having the wood on you. **1974** D. STUART *Prince of My Country* ix. 66 Father stands up. 'Look, Marney... Get down and be civil or shut up and get to hell out of it'! Mr Marney dismounts. . Mr Molloy pours tea and makes room on the bench. It looks as if Father has the wood on this sour old man right from the start.

II. 7. c. (Earlier example.)

1822 *Sunday Times* 20 Oct. 1/2 (Advt.), The long established system of serving wine from the wood, in full measures.

g. A golf club with a wooden head; a shot made with such a club (more commonly *wood shot*).

1915 A. W. TILLINGHAST *Cobble Valley Golf Yarns* 75 Hodge couldn't quite get there with two from his wood. **1927** JONES & KEELER *Down Fairway* xv. 203 For the drive with the wood, and for all normal wood shots, I play the ball opposite the arch of the left foot. **1928** *Evening News* 5 May 8/3, I do not think another professional golfer in America is hitting such terrific tee shots and full woods off the fairway as Gene. **1952** W. J. COX *Play Better Golf* xi. 54 The normal flight of the ball from a No. 4 wood is high. **1971** 'D. HALLIDAY' *Dolly & Doctor Bird* viii. 104 Lady Edgecombe. .hit her first ball. .a good third of the distance, nicely placed for a wood shot fairly close to the green. **1977** *Times* 17 June 28/1 (Advt.), Uxbridge Golf Centre... 4 woods, Nos 1, 3, 4, 5 and Irons 3–9.

h. The wooden frame or handle of a racquet, with reference to a shot in which these parts are accidentally used instead of the strings.

1955 *Times* 30 June 4/1 Could Nielsen save the set? He did after a lucky one off the wood had been a help. **1961** [see *double-fault* vb. s.v. *DOUBLE *a.* C. 3]. **1974** MILLS & BUTLER *Tackle Badminton* ii. 27 A fault can occur even when the shuttle is struck by the wood.

8. f. *dead wood*: see DEAD WOOD in Dict. and Suppl.

g. *to touch wood*: see TOUCH *v.* 29.

III. 9. b. (*a*) *wood-end* (later example), *-ride* (later examples), *-riding, shadow, -song* (later example), *-wonder*; *wood-child, -rhapsodist, -woman*; (*b*) *wood smoke* (earlier example); *wood box* (earlier example). **c.** (*b*) *wood-carrier* (later example), *-chopper* (earlier example), *-sculptor*; *wood-chopping* (earlier and later examples; cf. *wood-chop*, sense 10 a below); *wood sculpture*. **d.** (*a*) *wood-retreat, -well*; (*b*) in sense 7 c, as *wood port*. **e.** (*a*) *wood-grown, -lost* adjs.; (*b*) *wood-cased* (earlier example), *-feeding, -fired, -tongued* adjs. **h.** similative, as *wood-green, -wild* adjs.

1850 S. JUDD *R. Edney* ix. 135 The Old Man romanced with the fire, making it seem how he could graduate it exactly to the necessities of the room, and the state of the wood-box. **1921** *Daily Colonist* (Victoria, B.C.) 8 Oct. 9/1 (Advt.), Before you put on your slippers fill up one of our strong, attractive, useful, tidy Wood Carriers. It holds about six pieces of stove wood. **1892** W. B. YEATS *Countess Kathleen* 71 Between the pepper-pot And wood-cased hour glass. **1925** BLUNDEN *Eng. Poems* 86 The wood-child with man's torture racked Dares seek him out, if he'll retract. **1779** *Mass. Hist. Soc. Coll.* (1814) II. 458 The Century discov[er]ed a man creeping towards the wood choppers. **1845** THOREAU *Jrnl.* 14 July in *Writings* (1906) VII. 367 He was going to do his woodchopping. **1933** *Bulletin* (Sydney) 23 Aug. 35/3 Woodchopping. .is a fine, healthy and manly sport. **1919** J. MASEFIELD *Reynard* 69 The wood-end rang with the clear voice crying. **1946** *Nature* 9 Nov. 644/2 Protozoa and bacteria are essential for digestion in the wood-feeding termites. **1974** W. TRAGER in K. Elliott et al. *Trypanosomiasis & Leishmaniasis* 247 Hypermastigote flagellates of the wood-feeding roach *Cryptocercus* .have a whole variety of sexual phenomena. **1956** *Railway Mag.* Mar. 163/1 The wood-fired locomotives were never very efficient. **1978** M. DUFFY *Housespy* vi. 157 I've built a wood-fired kiln. **1807** J. BARLOW *Columbiad* v. 169 The sandy stream-bank and the woodgreen plain Raise into sight the new made seats of man. **1925** E. SITWELL et al. *Poor Young People* 10 His wood-green laughter. **1922** W. B. YEATS *Trembling of Veil* 135 Little wood-grown islands. **1956** R. MACAULAY *Towers of Trebizond* xiii. 142 The white-walled, red-roofed town and the wood-grown height beyond it. **1916** BLUNDEN *Pastorals* 15 Voices of wood-lost winds. **1972** *House & Garden* Feb. 109/4 Each shipment of wood ports will have a continuity of quality. . Ruby, tawny and white ports are all matured in wood. **1909** T. S. ELIOT in *Harvard Advocate* 26 Jan. 135 As if one should meet A pensive lamia in some wood-retreat. **1885** W. B. YEATS in *Dublin Univ. Rev.* May 82/1 The birds that nestle in the leaves are sad, Poor sad wood-rhapsodists. **1928** BLUNDEN *Retreat* 36 And wood-rides never reach the glittering gate. **1972** R. ADAMS *Watership Down* vii. 24 The head moved slowly, taking in the dusky lengths of the wood-ride in both directions. **1934** BLUNDEN *Mind's Eye* 154 An abundant round of skilful practical doings, from the wagon-shed to the wood-riding. **1943** *N. & Q.* 9 Oct. 234 *Wood-riding*, green way across a wood. Northants. **1968** *Canad. Antiques Collector* Aug. 13/3 Quevillon, one of the leading wood-sculptors of the early 19th century, worked at Longueil from 1818 to 1821. **1977** *Belfast Tel.* 27 Jan. 10/7 It's a new oak prie-dieu. . and it has taken wood sculptor Billy Graham and joiner Tommy Simons 120 man-hours to turn it out. **1974** *Saturday* (Charleston, S. Carolina) 20 Apr. 5-A/2 (Advt.), Children up to 15 are encouraged to come and participate free in learning to paint, make jewelery, wood sculpture and other crafts with all materials free. **1922** JOYCE *Ulysses* 11 Woodshadows floated silently by through the morning peace. **1747** H. GLASSE *Art of Cookery* ii. 42 Hang it up in a Chimney where Wood-Smoke is. **1930** T. S. ELIOT *Marina*, Those who suffer the ecstasy of the animals, meaning Death Are become unsubstantial, reduced by a wind, A breath of pine, and the woodsong fog By this grace dissolved in place. **1938** DYLAN THOMAS *Map of Love* (1939) 13 But I, Ann's bard on a raised hearth, call all The seas to service that her wood-tongued virtue Babble like a bellbuoy over the hymning heads. **1920** E. SITWELL *Wooden Pegasus* 106 Dark wood-wells. **1953** —— *Gardeners & Astronomers* 37 And is blown by the bright air Upon your wood-wild April-soft long hair. **1903** W. B. YEATS *In Seven Woods* 21 And the wood-woman whose lover was changed to a blue-eyed hawk. **1925** BLUNDEN *Eng. Poems* 92 Oh could it but be held by these wood-wonders.

10. a. wood-and-water joey *Austral. slang*, an odd job man; **wood-block,** (*b*) *Mus.*, a hollow wooden block used as a percussion instrument; cf. *Chinese block* s.v. *CHINESE *a.* 2 and *temple block* s.v. *TEMPLE *sb.*[1] 6 c; **wood-burner,** (*a*) a locomotive that is fuelled with wood; (*b*) a wood-burning stove or fire; **wood-burning** *a.*, using wood as fuel; **wood-butcher** (earlier example); **woodchip,** a chip of wood; also (in full *woodchip paper*), wallpaper with woodchips, etc., embedded in it to give an uneven appearance; *woodchip board* = *chipboard* s.v. *CHIP *sb.*[1] 9; **wood-chop** *Austral.* and *N.Z.*, a wood-chopping contest; † **wood-corder** *U.S.*, a town official responsible for stacking cut wood for sale into standard 'cords' or piles; **wood-flat** *U.S.*, a raft or flat-bottomed boat used for transporting wood by water; **wood-free** *a. Paper-making*, made free from mechanical wood, though not necessarily from chemical wood; also as *sb.*, a wood-free paper; **wood-heap** *Austral.* = *wood-pile* in Dict.; **wood-lot:** for *U.S.* read orig. *U.S.* and add earlier and later examples; **wood-mote** (later examples); **wood-pile,** (*b*) phr. *a nigger in the woodpile*: see *NIGGER *sb.* 1 d; also in allusive and euphemistic varr.; (*c*) *Mus. slang*, a xylophone; **wood-ranger:** for *U.S.* read orig. and chiefly *U.S.*; (earlier and later examples); **wood ray** *Bot.* (see quot. 1933); **wood-road,** a track or rough road through woods; **wood rot,** a fungal disease that causes wood to rot; so **wood-rotting** *a.*; **wood-saw** (examples); **wood-sawyer,** (*a*) (earlier and later examples); **wood-skin** (later examples); in full *woodskin canoe*; **wood-wind:** also, an individual instrument of this kind (now often made of some other material); **wood-wing** *Theatr.*, a wing which is shaped and decorated so as to represent a tree or trees.

1887 *All Year Round* 30 July 67/2 A 'wood-and-water Joey' is a hanger about hotels, and a doer of odd jobs. **1930** V. PALMER *Passage* I. v. 42, I wanted you to be something different from a wood-and-water joey, earning a few pounds here and there. **1966** *Woman's Day* (Sydney) 31 Oct., He is a 'wood and water joey'—the lad who does the odd jobs around the homestead. **1930** *Étude* Sept. 620 (*caption*) The drummer in a modern theater orchestra uses the assortment of instruments here shown. There are .Trap Console, Italian Tam Tam, and Wood Block. **1969** *Listener* 23 Jan. 121/2 The viola player also plays woodblock, and the viola and cello bow a suspended cymbal. **1972** *Jazz & Blues* Oct. 28/2 The drummer accompanies on the drums, with woodblocks used to give tonal contrast. **1901** *World's Work* (N.Y.) Dec. 1518/2, I began when there was nothing but wood-burners, big flaming smokestacks, and all that. **1965** G. MCINNES *Road to Gundagai* v. 81 A gas stove and an old fashioned woodburner. **1980** *Sunday Times* (Colour Suppl.) 30 Mar. 69/3 Finland's last wood-burner steams through an Arctic Circle blizzard. **1951** W. FAULKNER *Requiem for Nun* III. 225 The light-wheeled bulb-stacked wood-burning engines shrieking among the swamps. *Ibid.* 251 The intractable and obsolescent of the town who still insisted on wood-burning ranges. **1960** *Times* 20 Oct. 15/2 A wood-burning river steamer. **1980** A. E. FISHER *Midnight Men* xv. 187 Sarah's studio. .was warm. .with a big wood-burning stove. **1883** *Sporting Life* 27 May 4/3 What has he done to the New York *Clipper*'s wood butcher that he should be thus caricatured? **1958** *Times Rev. Industry* Dec. 61/3 Information service, covering all aspects of the production of wood-chip board. **1973** *Nation Rev.* (Melbourne) 31 Aug. (Suppl.) 1/1 The impending threat to Australia's native forests from intensive forestry, and particularly from woodchip projects. **1976** *Dumfries & Galloway Standard* 25 Dec. 4 (Advt.), Top quality woodchip reduced from 49p to only 39p roll. **1976** *Milton Keynes Express* 18 June 14/1 (Advt.), Woodchip paper—ideal for overpainting. Sale price 37p. **1977** *Abingdon Herald* 2 June 9/2 (Advt.), Fine quality woodchip (ideal for overpainting) only 39p per roll. **1918** *Bulletin* (Sydney) 16 May 48/2 Bill Lucas will chop against a local champion... After the wood-chop five rounds between. **1934** T. WOOD *Cobbers* xvi. 191, I saw a good wood-chop and some tumultuous steer-riding. **1964** *Courier-Mail* (Brisbane) 27 July 8/5 It will be dearer at this year's Show if you want to just drop in to see one or two woodchops. **1681** *Rep. Record Commissioners City of Boston* (1881) VII. 143 Chosen Overseers of Wood Corders. **1781** *First Records Baltimore Town* (1905) 43 The Commissers had it [*sc.* an oath] administred to him and afterwards appointed him Wood-corder. **1850** *Knickerbocker* XXXVI. 105 When he has a long wand, he is a wood-corder. **1785** in *Maryland Hist. Mag.* (1925) XX. 42 He hath gone up and down frequently in battans, scows and wood-flats. **1838** *Jrnl. & Register* (Columbus, Ohio) 27 Apr. 2/5 There were no boats at hand except a few large and unmanageable wood flats which were carried to the relief of the sufferers. .by the few persons on the shore. **1883** 'MARK TWAIN' *Life on Mississippi* 237 The Pennsylvania was creeping along, . . towing a wood-flat which was fast being emptied. **1904** *Jrnl. Soc. Chem. Industry* 15 Jan. 34/2 (*heading*) Manufacture of wood-free cardboard for printing. **1966** *Economist* 24 Sept. 1269/1 The mill will make. .good quality 'wood-frees'. **1979** *Morning News* (Karachi) 24 May 5/2 This variation is applied for woodfree and mechanical pulp. **1943** K. TENNANT *Ride on Stranger* (1968) iii. 21 Get back to the wood-heap. **1966** 'J. HACKSTON' *Father clears Out* 77 Father was out at the woodheap chopping Mother's wood for her. **1658** *Suffolk* (Mass.) *Deeds* (1885) III. No. 174, I heeretofore purchased. .all the rights to any wood Lott. **1706** *Town Records* (Manchester, Mass.) (1889) I. 115 It is Voted and agreed to lay out 50 or 60 Acors of land at the west end of our common for a wood lot. **1975** *N.Z. Jrnl. Agric.* Sept. 25/2 Burning requires fuel, but. .piles of branches from the woodlots .are soon used up. **1976** *Shooting Times & Country Mag.* 18–24 Nov. 28/2 Not that Jim wouldn't shoot a woodcock that got up in front of him, or a pheasant from the plough between a couple of woodlots. **1900** J. NISBET *Our Forests & Woodlands* i. 29 In the Charter of 1217 provision was made for a Court of Attachment or 'Woodmote' being held every forty days... Like the Woodmote, the Swainmote was originally held at irregular times. **1978** *Lancashire Life* Apr. 27/2 One named Ughtred Hodgkinson attended a woodmote at Whitewell in Bowland in 1570. **1936** *Metronome* Feb. 61/2 *Wood pile*, xylophone. **1936** W. STEVENS *Let.* 13 May (1967) 311, I agree that there is something wrong in the woodpile. **1951** *Time* 22 Oct. 69 Red Norvo kept salting his half-hour stands with such tunes as .he used to rap out on his 'woodpile' (xylophone) with Paul Whiteman's band 20 years ago. **1977** 'J. D. WHITE' *Salzburg Affair* xvi. 139 He was the odd man out, the African in the woodpile. **1734** in *Acct. Progress Colony Georgia* (1741) App. v. 51 [The French] have Five hundred Men in Pay, constantly employed as Wood-Rangers, to keep their neighbouring *Indians* in Subjection. **1915** W. B. YEATS *Reveries* (1916) 137, I could not sleep from my fear of the wood-ranger. **1933** *Trop. Woods* XXXVI. 3 *Wood ray* or *xylem ray*, the part of a ray internal to the cambium. **1975** *Sci. Amer.* July 102/2 Among the components of the cambium are what are called ray initials; the continuation of a ray initial down into the sapwood of a stem, a branch or a trunk is known as a wood ray. **1821** J. F. COOPER *Spy* (1831) vii. 81 The English captain took the advice of this mysterious being and finding a wood-road. .turned down its direction. **1891** *Century Mag.* Apr. 921, I moved camp, following the wood-road to the summit. **1954** C. BRUCE *Channel Shore* 89 In early winters he and James had cut firewood there and hauled it out over the wood road he had swamped, and up the main road, home. **1926** *Rev. Appl. Mycol.* V. 521 The winter draws attention to the misleading impression created by the use of the term 'branch canker' for two totally distinct types of injury: one caused by the attacks of such organisms as *Macrophoma theicola*, and the other resulting from a wood rot. **1931** E. E. HUBERT *Outline of Forest Path.* xi. 449 The classification of wood rots is largely based upon the colour changes produced in wood by fungi. The discolorations produced by wood-rot and sap-stain fungi. are responsible for a large part of the loss due to degrade in lumber. **1973** C. BONINGTON *Next Horizon* viii. 128 The garden bounded by a high hedge with an old wooden seat, softened with age and wood-rot. **1918** Wood-rotting [see *sap-rot* s.v. *SAP *sb.*[1] 7 a]. **1971** P. H. B. TALBOT *Princ. Fungal Taxonomy* i. 17 One can only conjecture how different the course of history might have been if the British fleet had not been laid low at times by the action of wood-rotting fungi. **1816** *Austin Papers* (1924) I. 264, 1 Wood Saw. **1884** 'MARK TWAIN' *Huck. Finn* vi. 39, I found an old rusty wood-saw without any handle. **1815** *North Amer. Rev.* II. 143 Deaths by Violence... In New York Mr. John Wood, killed in the street by Patrick Hart, a wood-sawyer, with a stick of wood. **1891** M. E. WILKINS *New Eng. Nun* 43 Matilda's antecedents had come of wood-sawyers and garden-laborers. **1904** W. H. HUDSON *Green Mansions* xxi. 289 Some compassionate voyager would let me share his wood-skin. **1934** E. WAUGH *Handful of Dust* v. 287 The canoes were made of woodskin. . They worked patiently but clumsily; one woodskin was split in getting it off the trunk. **1958** J. CAREW *Wild Coast* iii. 44 He had to fetch his woodskins from Honey Reef. **1966** P. SHERLOCK *West Indian Folk-Tales* 37 Each morning the men of the tribe went out in their woodskin canoes. **1922** JOYCE *Ulysses* 280 Double-basses, helpless, gashes in their sides. Woodwinds mooing cows. **1926** WHITEMAN & MCBRIDE *Jazz* ix. 195 Musicians recognize four general classes of instruments in speaking of the orchestra—strings, wood winds, brasses, and the battery of traps. **1967** T. STOPPARD *Rosencrantz & Guildenstern are Dead* III. 83 One of the sailors has pursed his lips against a woodwind. **1978** *Early Music* July 333/2 Vivaldi had to rely on Austrian and German makers for the newer woodwinds. **1933** P. GODFREY *Back-Stage* i. 19 Wood-wings are lugged into position. **1974** D. SMITH *Look back with Love* xvi. 164 One of these quick-changes occurred during my first scene, and to cover it, I had. .a short soliloquy, halfway through which a glance into the wood-wings showed me that our leading man was still three-quarters Lesurques when he should have been seven-eighths Dubosc.

b. *wood bee* (later examples), *moth* (later example); **wood buffalo** (later examples);

wood-cat, (*b*) (earlier example); **wood-duck** (earlier and later examples); **wood-grouse,** (*b*) (examples); **wood grub,** the larva of any of several wood-boring insects; † **wood hog** *U.S.*, a variety of pig which feeds in woods; **wood hoopoe,** any of several birds of the genus *Phœniculus* (or the family Phœniculidæ), native to Africa and distinguished by blue and green plumage and a long tail; **wood-leopard (moth):** = *leopard-moth* s.v. LEOPARD 6 b; (earlier example); **wood(s)-pussy** *N. Amer. colloq.*, a skunk.

1836 *Southern Lit. Messenger* II. 96 The wood-bee levels on their sweets. **1953** A. CLARKE *Coll. Plays* (1963) 44 The wood-bees court tangles of dew. **1897** E. COVES *New Light on Early Hist. Greater Northwest* II. xviii. 622 They are the wood buffalo, more shy and wild than those on the plains. **1961** W. P. KELLER *Canada's Wild Glory* 274 One small pocket of pure wood buffalo persist in a remote corner of the area, and plans are afoot to establish new sanctuaries for these. **1972** Wood buffalo [see *plain(s) buffalo* s.v. *PLAIN *sb.*[1] 10]. **1791** J. LONG *Voyages* 1 The country every where abounds with wild animals, particularly..otters, martins, minx, wood cats, racoons, etc.]. **1777** Wood duck [see *NARRAGANSETT 2]. **1911** C. E. W. BEAN '*Dreadnought' of Darling* vi. 57 Wood duck ..are really not duck at all, but Queensland goose. **1980** *Outdoor Life* (U.S.) (Northeast ed.) Oct. 80/1 Grain-fed mallards or pintails are superb table fare, as are wood ducks fattened on acorns. **1838** T. NEED *Six Years in Bush* iv. 30 And the woods with partridges, wood-grouse, black squirrels and occasionally a turkey. *a* **1861** T. WINTHROP *John Brent* (1862) xxii. 245 The brace of wood grouse he had shot that morning. **1917** T. G. PEARSON *Birds Amer.* II. 14 Hudsonian Spruce Partridge. *Canachites canadensis canadensis*... Wood Grouse; Wood Partridge. **1956** *Numbers* (Wellington, N.Z.) May 8 The rotten wood..split lengthwise and fell apart, baring the wet sawdust tunnels of woodgrubs. **1964** R. BRADDON *Year Angry Rabbit* (1967) xx. 158 Her husband fed their child with a wriggling wood grub. **1805** R. PARKINSON *Tour in Amer.* 290 The real American hog is what is termed a wood-hog: they are long in the leg, narrow on the back, [etc.]. **1840** *Cultivator* VII. 81 The next fall, *mast* was plenty, and 'wood hogs' were fat. **1908** HAAGNER & IVY *Sk. S. Afr. Bird-Life* 26 The Wood Hoopoes..are represented in South Africa by two well-marked species. **1953** R. CAMPBELL *Mamba's Precipice* xi. 115 A whole flock of wood-hoopoes with scarlet beaks and silk-shot, glossy, green and purple feathers were raising the most amazing din in the tree. **1964** A. L. THOMSON *New Dict. Birds* 894/2 The wood-hoopoes..are very unlike the true hoopoes in general appearance. **1819** Wood leopard-moth [see LEOPARD 6 b]. **1916** A. HUXLEY *Burning Wheel* 24 Mottled and grey and brown they pass, The wood-moths, wheeling, fluttering. **1899** F. D. BERGEN *Anim & Plant Lore* 61 Wood pussy, skunk. **1950** *Chicago Daily News* 16 Feb. 5/1 Miss Bennett paid $35 for the deodorized house-broken wood pussy. **1972** *Islander* (Victoria, B.C.) 18 June 9/2 You would never have known that said woods pussy had met its doom and left so many 'scents' behind in its will.

c. wood betony, (*b*) *N. Amer.*, a kind of lousewort, *Pedicularis canadensis*; **wood sanicle:** see SANICLE 1.

1886 *Harper's Mag.* Dec. 99/1 The wood-betony, it is called—to select its worthier title—a common early flower of our woods. **1976** *Hortus Third* (L. H. Bailey Hortorium) 832/1 Wood betony. Pubescent per., to $1\frac{1}{2}$ ft.. Spring. Que. to Fla., W. to Tex. and n. Mex. **1793** J. SOWERBY *Eng. Bot.* II. 98 (*table*) Sanicula europæa Wood Sanicle... Common enough in woods, growing among dead leaves of trees. **1857** A. PRATT *Flowering Plants & Ferns* III. 12 S[anicula] *Europæa* (Wood Sanicle). **1961** R. W. BUTCHER *New Illustr. Brit. Flora* I. 816 The Wood Sanicle is a perennial plant with erect, ribbed stems.

d. *pl.* used *attrib.* in senses 2 or 3, as **woods boss** *N. Amer. Lumbering*, a foreman in charge of lumberjacks; **woods colt** *U.S. colloq.*, a horse of unknown paternity; also, a foundling; an illegitimate child.

1928 C. PERRY *Two Reds of Travoy* 44 'He's a scrapper from way back. Sort of a bully in the village, I guess.' 'Derosier's woods boss,' breathed Gwen. **1946** K. TENNANT *Lost Haven* (1947) xiv. 231 Alec strolled ashore to talk with the 'woods boss'. **1970** *Islander* (Victoria B.C.) 17 May 6/3 Pete Haramboure became manager and his son, John, woods boss. **1895** *Dial. Notes* I. 395 *Woods colt*, foundling. Winchester, Ky. **1903** *Ibid.* II. 337 *Woods colt*, a horse of unknown paternity. Also applied to a person of illegitimate birtn. **1913** [see *OUTSIDER 1 c]. **1959** W. FAULKNER *Mansion* i. 4 Will Varner was going to have to marry her off..quick, if he didn't want a woods colt in his back yard next grass.

Wood (wud), *sb.*[3] The name of B. *Wood* (see quot. 1860[1]) used in the possessive to designate an easily melted alloy consisting of bismuth, lead, tin, and cadmium in decreasing proportions and used esp. for soldering.

Patented by Wood in *U.S. Patent* 27,590 (1860).

1860 *Amer. Jrnl. Sci.* LXXX. 271 [New 'fusible metal'. —Dr. B. Wood of Nashville, Tenn., has secured a patent (Weekly Scientific Artizan, Cincinnati, May 5th, 1860,) for an alloy composed of cadmium, tin, lead and bismuth, which fuses at a temperature between 150° and 160° F.] *Ibid.* 272 We have had time only to repeat a few of Dr. Wood's interesting experiments. . The alloy made by fusing together two parts of cadmium, two parts tin, four parts lead and eight parts bismuth melts at a temperature varying not far from 70° C. (158° F.) It may appropriately be called 'Wood's fusible metal'.—Eds. **1876** *Jrnl. Chem. Soc.* XXX. 592 The author then describes the method adopted by himself to measure the volumes of the four following fusible alloys at temperatures between 0° and 120°:—... III. Wood's alloy, the composition of which is represented by the formula $Bi_4\ Pb\ Cd_2\ Sn_2$. **1947** J. C. RICH *Materials & Methods of Sculpture* vi. 192 Wood's metal is rarely employed sculpturally although the material could be used as a casting medium because of its low melting point. **1974** *Nature* 11 Oct. 506/2 One eye was centred on a projection perimeter..and the visuotectal representation for that eye on the right tectum mapped with a Woodsmetal microelectrode.

Wood (wud), *sb.*[4] *Med.* The name of Robert W. *Wood* (1868–1955), U.S. physicist, used in the possessive to designate (*a*) a special glass that is opaque to visible light but transmits ultraviolet, and (*b*) ultraviolet light obtained by using this glass as a filter to remove visible components.

1925 *Index Medicus* X. 988/1 Experimental tumours studied by Wood's light. **1927** *Brit. Jrnl. Actinotherapy* Jan. 24/2 The healthy scalp under Wood's light gives only a feeble fluorescence of a dark violet colour. **1927** *Brit. Jrnl. Dermatol. & Syphilis* XXXIX. 352 Wood's glass costs about 1*s.* 6*d.* per square inch, but only a small piece is required. **1951** WHITBY & HYNES *Med. Bacteriol.* (ed. 5) xiv. 261 The microscope is illuminated by a mercury-vapour lamp with a Wood's glass filter which transmits ultraviolet but not visible light. **1958** *New Biol.* XXVII. 56 In 1925 two French workers discovered that *Microsporum*-infected hairs showed a very characteristic greenish fluorescence in ultra-violet light which had been filtered through glass containing nickel oxide, the so-called Wood's Light. **1961** R. D. BAKER *Essent. Path.* ix. 223 (*caption*) A Negro child developed papular white scaly oval lesions. . The involved regions fluoresced with Wood's light. **1983** *Oxf. Textbk. Med.* I. v. 371/1 When large numbers of children are involved, screening of scalp infections with a filtered ultra-violet (Wood's light) lamp is useful.

woodbine. Add: **2*. a.** (Normally **Woodbine.**) A proprietary name for a brand of cheap cigarettes; a cigarette of this brand.

[**1886** *Trade Marks Jrnl.* 6 Jan. 8 *Wild Woodbine Cigarettes.* W. D. & H. O. Wills, Bristol & London.] **1907** *Ibid.* 11 Sept. 1602 *Woodbine*... Tobacco whether manufactured or unmanufactured. The Imperial Tobacco Company.., Bedminster, Bristol. **1910** *Sessions Paper of Central Criminal Court* 16 Nov. 18 Prisoner asked for a packet of Woodbine cigarettes (1 d). **1914** *Autocar* 21 Nov. 736/1 'Woodbine! This is a bit of luck,' he exclaimed, taking a cigarette. **1924** H. DE SÉLINCOURT *Cricket Match* ii. 21 He picked a woodbine out of its paper on the mantelpiece. **1939** JOYCE *Finnegans Wake* 587 First a couple of Mountjoys and nutty woodbines..in the snug at the Cambridge Arms. **1970** B. CARTLAND *We danced All Night* vii. 198 It was only during the war [of 1914–18] that Tommies had got used to the cheaper type, especially Woodbines. **1979** 'P. O'CONNOR' *Into Strong City* x. 29 A Woodbine cigarette found in my pocket. **1983** J. CROALL *Neill* viii. 148 As long as..he had enough for a packet of Woodbines, he was fine.

b. An Englishman, esp. a soldier, considered as a habitual smoker of Woodbine cigarettes. *Austral. slang.*

1919 W. H. DOWNING *Digger Dial.* 54 *Woodbine*, an English soldier, so called from the name of a cheap brand of cigarette favored by Englishmen. **1937** E. HILL *Water into Gold* 192 Bagtown became 'Woodbine Ave'..so-called for the number of English settlers in residence. [**1978** R. BEILBY *Gunner* 43 'Inglesi,' he grinned. 'Pommies. Chooms. 'Bines. That's what we call them.']

woodchuck. Add: **a.** For *Arctomys* substitute *Marmota.* (Earlier example.)

1674 *Cal. State Papers, Amer. & W. Indies* (1889) VII. 581 The natural inhabitants of the woods, hills, and swamps, are..rabbits, hares, and woodchucks.

b. *woodchuck hole.*

1853 H. D. THOREAU *Jrnl.* 29 Mar. (1949) V. 62 Looking at the mouth of a woodchuck-hole..[I see] that those places are sprinkled with..salt-shaped masses of frost. **1974** P. GZOWSKI *Bk. about this Country* 43/2 The hay wagon had dropped into a woodchuck hole.

woodcock, *sb.* **3. d.** (Earlier example.)

1861 MRS. BEETON *Bk. Househ. Managem.* xxxiii. 822 (*heading*) Scotch woodcock.

Wood Cree. Also **Woods Cree.** [f. WOOD *sb.*[1] + *CREE *sb.* and *a.*: a shortening of earlier *Strong* (also *Thick*) *Woods Cree*, tr. a Wood Cree name.] **1. a.** One of the major divisions of the Cree Indians, inhabiting woodland areas of Saskatchewan and Manitoba in Canada. **b.** A member of this people. Cf. *PLAINS CREE.

1885 *Boston Jrnl.* 23 June 1/8 The Wood Crees have gone back to get a cache of provisions. **1910** F. W. HODGE *Handbk. Amer. Indians* II. 414/1 *Sakawithiniwuk* ('people of the woods'). The Wood Cree, one of the several divisions of the Cree. **1947** *Beaver* June 15/1 The Wood Crees, who were in the minority, were, in general, less troublesome. **1972** [see *PLAINS CREE].

2. The language spoken by the Wood Cree.

1958 R. A. LOGAN *Cree Lang.* 4 One dialect (Moose Cree) uses the sound of L where another dialect (Northern or Woods Cree) uses the sound of TH... Only Northern Cree uses TH. **1978** D. H. PENTLAND in Cook & Kaye *Ling. Stud. Native Canada* 190 Woods Cree is now spoken by about five per cent of the total number of Cree Speakers.

wooden, *a.* Add: **I. 3. b.** *U.S.* = WOODED *ppl. a.* ? *Obs.*

1816 U. BROWN *Jrnl.* 15 Aug. in *Maryland Hist. Mag.* (1910) X. 358 To Smith field a Wooden Town in a Wooden Country & a wooden bred set of Tavern-keepers. **1843** [see sense 3 in Dict.]. **1891** M. E. RYAN *Pagan of Alleghanies* i. 12 And then there are others more seldom seen, the women from the 'wooden' country of the interior.

II. 7. wooden spoon. Hence **wooden-spooner, -spoonist,** a competitor who is awarded the 'wooden spoon'; a loser.

1927 *Daily Express* 23 Mar. 13/3 Champions and wooden spoonists of the Isthmian League last season were opposed on the Civil Service ground at Chiswick. **1954** J. FINGLETON *Ashes crown Year* 275 Somerset were wooden-spooners last summer and will be so again. **1973** *Nation Rev.* (Melbourne) 31 Aug. 1442/3 4BH slips to fourth place in the five station market, with perennial wooden spooners, 4BK, only 2000 listeners behind. **1975** *Globe & Mail* (Toronto) 26 May S5/1 England won the British soccer championship..with Wales, once again the wooden spoonists. **1981** *Daily Mail* 25 Nov. 30 (*heading*) A flat rate from the wooden spoonists.

9. wooden cross *Mil. slang*, a wooden cross on a serviceman's grave; hence, death in action regarded ironically as an award of merit; **wooden kimono** *U.S. slang*, a coffin; **wooden nickel** (or **money**) *U.S. slang*, a worthless or counterfeit coin; chiefly in *fig.* phr. *to take a wooden nickel* and varr., to be swindled or fooled; **wooden nutmeg:** see NUTMEG 1 b; **wooden overcoat:** see *OVERCOAT; **wooden pear** (earlier example); **wooden suit** *slang*, a coffin; **wooden wedding:** for *U.S.* read orig. *U.S.* and add earlier and later examples.

1917 A. G. EMPEY *Over Top* 314 *Wooden Cross*, two pieces of wood in the form of a cross placed at the head of a Tommy's grave. **1919** in *Amer. Speech* 1972 (1975) XLVII. 117 Seven of the 'Blue Tails' went down to get their Wooden Crosses. **1949** A. MURPHY *To Hell & Back* xvi. 195 There is no other branch of the army that offers so many chances for the Purple Heart, the Distinguished Wooden Cross, the Royal Order of the Mattress Covers. **1926** MAINES & GRANT *Wise-Crack Dict.* 15 *Wooden kimona*, case for cold storage. **1946** MEZZROW & WOLFE *Really Blues* ii. 19, I expected the man to turn up..with his tape measure to outfit me with a wooden kimono. **1915** C. MATHEWSON *Catcher Craig* ii. 25 He was instructed . not to take any wooden money. **1922** S. LEWIS *Babbitt* v. 67 S'long! Don't take any wooden money. **1971** F. P. GROVE *Tales from Margin* 27 'Well,' said Walt, 'be good, fellah! Don't take any wooden money!' Even this cheap vulgarity irritated her now. **1927** *Amer. Speech* III. 132 [College slang.] Not to 'take any wooden nickels', in other words, to be alert. **1937** L. HELLMAN *Diary* 23 Oct. in *Unfinished Woman* (1969) viii. 100 Luis and I got to Madrid. He said I was not to take any wooden nickels. **1964** in Hamblett & Deverson *Generation X* 90 Then one night I met Johnny, one of the biggest sharks in the Mayfair aquarium, and that was the end of that. Nobody ever sold Johnny a wooden nickel. **1971** M. TORRIE *Bismarck Herrings* ii. 29 Having advised her..not to accept any wooden nickels, [he] drove back. **1971** R. DENTRY *Encounter at Kharmel* iii. 58 There hadn't been a tribal rising worth a wooden nickel since the Partition troubles died down. **1860** G. BENNETT *Gatherings of Naturalist* 322 The Wooden Pear-tree of the colonists..is peculiar to Australia. **1968** W. GARNER *Deep, Deep Freeze* xx. 188 Any mistake on his part could win him the prize of the wooden suit. **1972** J. S. HALL *Sayings from Old Smoky* 42 When a guy comes and steals my stuff, he better be ready for a wooden suit or Boot Hill. **1870** D. MACRAE *Americans at Home* II. 293 The fifth anniversary is called the wooden wedding... The presents suitable to this anniversary are of wood. **1918** H. BARNETT *Canon Barnett* I. xiv. 162 In 1893 we decided to commemorate our wooden wedding by a congregational party.

III. 10. woodentop *slang*, (*a*) a uniformed policeman; (*b*) a dim-wit.

1981 J. WAINWRIGHT *All on Summer's Day* 96 I'm a copper. An ordinary flatfoot... A real old woodentop. That's me. **1983** A. BEEVOR *Faustian Pact* v. 33 They've even got the bleeding Army out... Bunch of woodentops from Chelsea barracks. **1984** *Listener* 16 Feb. 24/3 A policeman who is called a 'butter boy' or a 'wolly' must be something like a 'woodentop'.

wooden *v.*, (*b*) *Austral.* and *N.Z. slang*, to render insensible; to knock unconscious; also const. *out*; **woodenness** (earlier examples).

1904 'G. B. LANCASTER' *Sons o' Men* 252 He'll wooden more of you out if you scare him. *c* **1926** 'MIXER' *Transport Workers' Song Bk.* 126 It [*sc.* a block of ice] 'woodened' him out, and he lay there quite flat. **1952** M. ALLINGHAM *Tiger in Smoke* xi. 184 If you 'ad only woodened 'er, we'd have 'ad all the time in the world. **1974** *Southerly* XXXIV. 145 If you can't wooden 'em [*sc.* kangaroos] at a 'undred yards with one I.C.I. bullet, you're not tryin'! **1854** H. D. THOREAU *Walden* 356 Many concentric layers of woodenness in the dead dry leaf of society. **1860** F. W. FABER *Precious Blood* ii. 66 Considerable dryness, stiffness, woodenness,..would characterize this philanthropic city.

woodhenge (wudhe·ndʒ). *Archæol.* [f. WOOD *sb.*[1], after STONEHENGE.] A henge (a prehistoric circular bank enclosing a circular ditch) believed to have contained a circular timber structure, as represented by a ring of post holes; *spec.* (with capital initial) and orig., the proper name of the first example of this kind to be discovered, near Stonehenge.

1927 M. E. CUNNINGTON in *Antiquity* Mar. (*caption to plate between pp.* 92 *and* 93) 'Woodhenge': oblique view from the south. **1927** *Times* 28 Nov. 17/5 Woodhenge is assigned to the Early Iron Age, say, 500 B.C., with a claim that the close correspondence in lay-out proves it to be a prototype in wood of Stonehenge. **1933** W. A. DUTT *Norfolk* (ed. 8) 60 One of the remarkable prehistoric circles known as 'Woodhenges'. **1935** *Nature* 7 Sept. 365/1 The generic term 'Woodhenge' was first used by Mrs. M. E. Cunnington to describe the circle near Amesbury with wooden uprights in place of stone, which she excavated in 1926 and 1928. The Norfolk Woodhenge, which was discovered from the air in 1929, was known from air photographs to be a striking example of the type. **1939** JOYCE *Finnegans Wake* 596 The Diggins, Woodhenge, as to hang out at. **1951** [see *HENGE[2]]. **1970** *Sci. Amer.* May 58 The four largest henge monuments in England, each surrounded by earthworks measuring more than 1,000 feet in diameter, are Avebury and three woodhenges. **1977** *Griffith Observer* (Griffith Observatory, Los Angeles) May 14/2 The Cahotian circles bore a superficial resemblance to neolithic timber structures like Woodhenge, near Stonehenge... Wittry therefore dubbed Circle 2 as an 'American Woodhenge'.

woodhouseite (wu·dhausəit). *Min.* [f. the name of C. D. *Woodhouse*, 20th-c. U.S. mineral collector + -ITE[1].] A hydrated sulphate and phosphate of calcium and aluminium, $CaAl_3(PO_4)(SO_4)(OH)_6$, found as colourless rhombohedral crystals and belonging to the beudantite group.

1937 D. M. LEMMON in *Amer. Mineralogist* XXII. 943 Woodhouseite is a late hydrothermal mineral lining vugs in quartz veins that cross the andalusite zones [in a Californian deposit]. **1980** *Mineral. Mag.* XXXI. 318/2 Heating such minerals as apatite..and woodhouseite to 600°–800° followed by quenching destabilizes these phosphates and allows more complete extraction of their uranium content.

woodie (wu·di) [-IE], *colloq.* abbrev. of WOOD-PIGEON.

1947 *Contemp. Rev.* June 368 Their habits were not so regular as the woodies. **1960** *Farmer & Stockbreeder* 23 Feb. 57/3 These birds eat wood pigeons' eggs... Some keen observers estimate that something like 80 per cent of the 'woodies' ' eggs that are laid are so destroyed. **1972** *Shooting Times & Country Mag.* 4 Mar. 17/3 There shouldn't be many woodies remaining in the area. **1980** G. HAMMOND *Reward Game* ix. 129 Do you want sixty-odd woodies for the freezer?

woodie, var. *WOODY *sb.*

woodland. Add: **1. b. woodland caribou,** a northern caribou, *Rangifer tarandus*, found in forested areas of Canada.

1854 MAYNE REID *Young Voyageurs* 154 He had killed three caribou, of the large variety known as 'woodland caribou'. **1879** [in Dict.]. **1921** *Daily Colonist* (Victoria, B.C.) 30 Oct. 21/1 The only caribou I've ever hunted were in the Kootenays, woodland caribou. **1965** F. SYMINGTON *Tuktu* 44 The woodland caribou eats about the same forage as the barren-ground caribou.

2. *Archæol.* (With capital initial.) The name of a culture that existed in eastern North America between approximately 1000 B.C. and A.D. 1000, characterized by agriculture, hunting, burial mounds, and a distinctive style of pottery.

1917 C. WISSLER *Amer. Indian* xiv. 219 We now come to the so-called Eastern Woodland area, the characterization of which is difficult. **1946** *Nature* 2 Nov. 615/2 A single mound-group belongs to a later phase, the Middle Mississippi, and the village site and one mound are ascribed to the Woodland-culture pattern, probably still later. **1967** *Listener* 2 Mar. 290/2 Most of the characteristic traits of the late, *i.e.*, the Woodland, period are found in incipient form in the late Archaic, and it is a period about which it is difficult to generalize. **1977** G. CLARK *World Prehistory* (ed. 3) ix. 408 Hunting and fishing continued to play significant roles..even during the terminal phase of the Woodland culture (A.D. 900–1300).

Hence **woo·dlanded** *ppl. a.*, covered with woodland; **woodlander**: also, a plant whose natural habitat is in woodland.

1945 J. BETJEMAN *New Bats in Old Belfries* 6 By roads 'not adopted', by woodlanded ways She drove to the club in the late summer haze. **1948** W. ARNOLD-FORSTER *Shrubs for Milder Counties* iv. 113 D[*aphne*] *Blagayana*. A dwarf woodlander, evergreen. **1974** *Country Life* 12 Dec. 1896/1 American woodlanders, such as shortias and erythroniums revel in it [*sc* beech leaf-mould]. **1982** *Garden* CVII. 487/2 All [clintonias] are woodlanders or shade plants.

woodpecker. Add: **3.** *U.S.* and *Austral. Mil. slang.* A machine-gun.

1898 J. H. PARKER *Hist. Gatling Gun Detachment* vii. 127 Goin' to let the woodpeckers go off? **1932** J. DOS PASSOS *1919* 410 The shrill bullets combing the air and the sorehead woodpeckers the machineguns mud cooties gasmasks and the itch. **1945** BAKER *Austral. Lang.* viii. 157 *Woodpecker*, a Japanese .77 machine-gun. **1945** *Yank* 27 July 7 The Japs opened up with what sounded like dual-purpose 75s, 20-mm pompoms and woodpeckers. **1976** G. MARKHAM *Japanese Infantry Weapons World War Two* 41 The popular Taishō 3rd year type machine-gun.. was introduced in 1914. Its peculiar stuttering fire earned the gun the Australian nickname of 'woodpecker' (or 'woodchopper').

Woodruff[2] (wu·drɒf). *Mech.* [See quot. 1892.] *Woodruff key*: a key whose cross-section is part circular (to fit into a curved keyway in a shaft) and part rectangular.

1892 P. BENJAMIN *Mod. Mechanism* 455 [The Woodruff System of Keying.—The Woodruff Manufacturing Co., of Hartford, Conn., has brought out a novel system of keying.] *Ibid.* 924 (Index), Woodruff keys. **1923** C. D. ALBERT *Machine Design Drawing Room Probl.* i. 63 Woodruff keys are quite extensively used in machine tools and in machine construction generally. **1976** *New Motorcycling Monthly* Oct. 34/1 Remove Woodruff key from its slot in magneto shaft.

woodruffite (wu·drɒfəit). *Min.* [See quot. 1953 and -ITE[1].] A hydrated oxide of zinc and manganese, $(Zn,Mn_3^{4+})Mn^{4+}O_7.1\text{–}2H_2O$, found as black or grey monoclinic crystals.

1953 C. FRONDEL in *Amer. Mineralogist* XXXVIII. 769 The name woodruffite is proposed for this species after Samuel Woodruff (deceased), for many years employed as a miner by the New Jersey Zinc Company. **1979** *Ibid.* LXIV. 1214/1 The spectrum of woodruffite shows it to be a structural analog of todorokite, as has been assumed from the similarity of their X-ray powder patterns.

woodshed (wu·dʃed), *sb.* Also **wood shed, wood-shed.** [f. WOOD *sb.*[1] + SHED *sb.*[2]] **1.** A shed for storing wood, esp. for fuel. Also *euphem.*, a lavatory.

1844 [in Dict. s.v. WOOD *sb.*[1] 9 b]. **1854** H. D. THOREAU *Walden* 54, I have also a small wood-shed adjoining, made chiefly of the stuff which was left after building the house. **1868** N. HAWTHORNE *Passages from Amer. Notebks.* II. 9 We have been employed partly in an augean labor of clearing out a wood-shed. **1921** W. DE LA MARE *Mem. Midget* ii. 10 Pollie had gone to the woodshed to fetch kindling. **1940** W. FAULKNER *Hamlet* II. ii. 129 Serve you right for keeping a mare like that in a woodshed. **1974** M. HOYT *Thirty Miles* i. 1 The plumbing wasn't. Its place was taken by a small building known by the somewhat less-than-frank title of 'woodshed'.

2. *fig.* **a.** Phr. *to take into the woodshed* and varr.: to reprimand or punish. *N. Amer. colloq.*

From the old tradition of giving a child a spanking in the woodshed, i.e. not in the presence of others.

1907 *St. Nicholas* July 826/2 He could save himself and most of his companions from unpleasant reckonings in various and sundry woodsheds. **1949** *Time* 18 Apr. 22/2 If you don't do what we tell you to do we are going to take you out into the woodshed. **1966** *Toronto Daily Star* 21 Dec. 14 (*heading*) Taking the Senator to the woodshed. **1983** *Chicago Sun-Times* 16 July 34 Assuming the Fed is traditionally pliant, why does not Reagan simply take Volcker to the woodshed and tell him to ease up?

b. Phr. *something nasty in the woodshed*: see *NASTY *a.* 7. Also in allusive varr.

1940 AUDEN *Another Time* 111 What was it, Ernst, that your shadow unwittingly said? O did the child see something horrid in the woodshed Long ago? **1958** *Times Lit. Suppl.* 17 Jan. 30/1 Mr Amis does not, however, present Garnet Bowen as a case-history, whose dislike of foreign parts could be explained on a woodshed basis. **1959** *Listener* 8 Jan. 78/3 As the leading Torquemada, Miss Margaret Lane clearly felt some obligation to strive to uncover something—well—interesting in the woodshed.

c. *Mus. slang.* As a place where a musician may, or should, practise in private (see also quot. 1937).

1937 *Printers' Ink Monthly* May 45/3 *Wood shed*, a severe rehearsal. **1946** *Hollywood Note* June 4 T.D. [*sc.* Tommy Dorsey] goes back to the woodshed. **1977** *Rolling Stone* 16 June 66/2 Leavell's playing won't scare many jazz pianists into the woodshed.

woodshed (wu·dʃed), *v. Mus. slang.* [f. the sb.] *trans.* and *intr.* To practise or rehearse, esp. privately (see also quot. 1978).

1936 L. ARMSTRONG *Swing that Music* 71 We used to practice together, 'wood-shed' as we say (from the old-time way of going out into the wood-shed to practice a new song). **1946** MEZZROW & WOLFE *Really the Blues* viii. 108 I'll have to woodshed this thing awhile so I can get straight with you all. **1950** BLESH & JANIS *They all played Ragtime* (1958) x. 203, I would hear the tunes and, to make sure, go home and 'woodshed' them in every key, put them in major and minor and all the ninth chords. **1968** A. YOUNG in A. Chapman *New Black Voices* (1972) Drew's got an alto [horn]... Drew dont hardly touch it, he too busy woodsheddin his drums. **1978** *Amer. Speech 1975* L. 302 [Jargon of barber-shop singing.] *Woodshed*, work out the harmony parts (to a known melody) by ear; sing as a group for the first time..; improvise (an interpretation).

Hence **woo·dshedding** *vbl. sb.*, (*a*) the dispensing of punishment; (*b*) the practice or rehearsal of music; (*c*) spontaneous or improvised barber-shop singing.

1940 *Amer. Speech* XV. 205 *Woodshedding*, disciplinary action. **1946** MEZZROW & WOLFE *Really the Blues* ix. 151 Instead of woodshedding, he went out after the big money with the primitive equipment he had when he started. **1955** SHAPIRO & HENTOFF *Hear me talkin' to Ya* xi. 190 It was here that the term 'woodshedding' originated. When one of the gang wanted to rehearse his part, he would go off into the woods and practice. **1956** S. LONGSTREET *Real Jazz* xiii. 101 Bix [Beiderbecke] did plenty of woodshedding, playing alone, to some recording on the family Victrola. **1973** T. PYNCHON *Gravity's Rainbow* I. 129 No head falsetto here but complete, out of the honest breast, a baritone voice brought over years of woodshedding up to this range. **1974** *Harmonizer* Jan.-Feb. 18/2 Woodshedding is not a 'spectator sport'—only participants can fully enjoy it. **1976** *Times* 27 Sept. 12/4 Spontaneous barbershopping is known as woodshedding, because a woodshed is as good a place as any to burst into sudden song.

Woodsia (wu·dziă). *Bot.* Also **woodsia** [mod.L., f. the name of Joseph *Woods* (1776–1864), architect and botanist + -IA[1].] A fern of the genus of this name (family Polypodiaceæ), comprising small, rock-loving tufted plants found in mountainous parts of Britain and other temperate regions and in the Arctic.

1815 R. BROWN in *Trans. Linnean Soc.* XI. 171 This genus I have named in honour of my friend Mr. Joseph Woods... The character distinguishing *Woodsia*..consists in its involucrum being inserted under the group of capsules..the *sorus*, which it completely surrounds at the base; while it is in every stage open at top. **1848** T. MOORE *Handbk. Brit. Ferns* iii. 37 The Woodsias have no especial claim to be esteemed for their elegance. *a* **189**[illegible] W. FALCONER *Let.* in W. Robinson *Wild Garden* (ed. 4) viii. 83 Woodsias, tiny Aspleniums, and other Ferns. **190**[illegible] E. STEP *Wayside & Woodland Ferns* 55 Oblong Woodsia (*Woodsia ilvensis*). This species differs but slightly from the Alpine Woodsia, and some botanists deny its distinctness. **1961** R. W. BUTCHER *New Illustrated Brit. Flora* I. 176 *Woodsia alpina*... This Northern Woodsia occurs very rarely on mountain cliffs and rocks in a few places in Scotland and N. Wales.

woodsy, *a.* For *U.S.* read orig. and chiefly *U.S.* and add later examples.

1973 *Times Lit. Suppl.* 27 Apr. 472/5 The merely woodsy setting of the keeper's activities and of his meetings with Connie. **1977** *Daily Tel.* 9 Apr. 7/3 Scatter them on woodsy bits of the garden. **1981** 'D. JORDAN' *Double Red* xxi. 92 The same perfume, a cool tinge of something woodsy. **1985** *Dirt Bike* Mar. 44/2 Duane Summers powers the XC up a woodsy trail.

Woodward–Hoffmann (wu·dwǫɹd hǫ·fmæ̆n). *Chem.* The names of Robert Burns *Woodward* (1917–79), U.S. chemist, and Roald *Hoffmann* (b. 1937), Polish-born U.S. chemist, used *attrib.* with reference to a series of generalized symmetry selection rules first proposed by them in 1965 which predict whether a particular pericyclic reaction will be allowed under the given conditions.

1968 *Jrnl. Amer. Chem. Soc.* XC. 1920/2 A considerable amount of research has been directed toward exploring the validity and extent of applicability of the 'Woodward-Hoffmann rules'. **1974** GILL & WILLIS *Pericyclic Reactions* iv. 100 (*heading*) The general Woodward-Hoffmann rule for pericyclic reactions. **1980** M. ORCHIN et al. *Vocab. Org. Chem.* x. 330 Sigmatropic shifts. Here the 'migrating bond' is treated as though it were heterolytically cleaved, then the Woodward-Hoffmann rules are applied.

woodwaxen. (Later example of spelling *woadwaxen*.)

1946 G. STIMPSON *Thousand Things* 50 It is supposed that the original green cloth made at Kendal by the Flemish weavers was colored with a dye obtained from the plant known as woadwaxen.

woodwork, wood-work. Add: **1. c.** *Assoc. Football slang.* The frame of the goalposts.

1960 *Times* 21 Nov. 4/2 Three more times they hit Bonetti's woodwork. **1977** *Grimsby Even. Tel.* 5 May 18/6 Twice in the first half, Scunthorpe hit the Bradford woodwork.

d. Phr. *to come* or *crawl out of the woodwork* and varr., to come out of hiding; to emerge from obscurity. So *to crawl* (*back*) *into the woodwork* and varr., to disappear into obscurity.

1964 'E. LATHEN' *Accounting for Murder* (1965) vii. 59 These nutboys start crawling out of the woodwork. **1973** *Times Lit. Suppl.* 9 Feb. 154/4 The Nazi elite faded into the woodwork without waiting to be removed, making it tempting to say that denazification should have been left to the Germans. **1973** *Current Affairs Bull.* (Sydney) Aug. 31/1 They are the new Australian playwrights and they are coming out of the woodwork everywhere. **1974** 'M. INNES' *Appleby's Other Story* iv. 30 At least we can tell this bloody wog to crawl back into the woodwork. **1977** C. MCCULLOUGH *Thorn Birds* xii. 289 Funny how the men in my life all scuttle off into the woodwork, isn't it? **1979** 'J. LE CARRÉ' *Smiley's People* (1980) iii. 39 George Smiley, sometime Chief of the Secret Service..had one night come out of the woodwork to peer at some dead foreigner. **1984** *Broadcast* 7 Dec. 27/1 The imminence of a BBC licence increase application brings the advertising agencies out of the woodwork.

3. c. Forestry, work done in woods.

1738 W. ELLIS *Timber-Tree Improved* I. 24 There is in my Neighbourhood a Man that is..often imployed in Wood-Work. **1904** G. A. B. DEWAR *Glamour of Earth* x. 243 Making a good and sure living..and filling an honourable post in wood work, to our surprise he took one day a strange step: flung up his work and migrated.. to the town.

4. *attrib.*

1959 I. & P. OPIE *Lore & Lang. Schoolch.* xvii. 362 The gardening master is commonly 'Spuds', the woodwork teacher is 'Chips'. **1980** E. BLISHEN *Nest of Teachers* I. iv. 22 The woodwork master..insisted that I come with him to his woodwork centre.

woodworking: also, forestry.

1950 *New Yorker* 26 Aug. 71/1 Woodworking firms are making a candid twelve-per-cent profit. **1951** R. FIRTH *Elem. Social Organization* ii. 51 Their introduced steel tools must have materially lightened the labour of woodworking and clearing of brush-wood in agriculture.

woody (wu·di), *sb.* *slang* (orig. *Surfing*). Chiefly *U.S.* Also **woodie.** [f. Wood *sb.*[1] + -y[6].] An estate car with timber-framed sides.
1961 *Surfer Q.* Winter 34 (*caption*) A 'woodie' piled high. Photographer Larry Stephens..challenges anyone to produce a picture of a surf car with more boards than his. **1969** *Surf Internat.* (Austral.) I. xi. 13 Nat and Paul push the woodie, it's stoked too, an' finally blows its gasket. **1973** J. Marks *Mick Jagger* 87 Ramada Inn, the Yucca Hotel, Holiday Inn and the Seven Seas Hyatt Lodge—all in a row—saluting Dominique and the horde of military foundlings who plunge along Hotel Circle in borrowed *woodies*—those immaculate 1954 jobs by Ford: sturdy station wagons, armoured in wood. **1980** L. Birnbach et al. *Official Preppy Handbk.* 18/1 The other children were quite happy with their little red wagons; she would accept nothing but a woody.

woof, *int.* and *sb.*[2] Add: **2.** Var. Whoof *int.* (*sb.*) in Dict. and Suppl.

3. Low-frequency sound of poor quality from a loudspeaker.
1961 in Webster. **1962** *Listener* 22 Nov. 882/1 It isn't only technicians who can justifiably complain about too much tweet and woof. **1978** *Gramophone* Jan. 1298/3 They..are every bit the equal of the LPs, a beautifully warm and detailed orchestral tapestry, with..a richly resonant bass (without too much 'woof').

woof, *v.*[2] (In Dict. with Woof *int.* and *sb.*[2]) **1.** (Later examples.)
1932 E. M. Brent-Dyer *Chalet Girls in Camp* vi. 97 Rufus..crossed the meadow at his best pace, woofing indignantly at intervals. **1955** V. Nabokov *Lolita* II. xxviii. 171 A nondescript cur came out from behind the house, stopped in surprise, and started good-naturedly woof-woofing at me, his eyes slit, his shaggy belly all muddy, and then walked about a little and woofed once more. **1974** *Publishers Weekly* 5 Aug. 53/3 His attempt suggests a puppy woofing at a caterpillar—but keeping a safe distance.

2. *U.S. Blacks' slang.* **a.** *intr.* To talk (or, *trans.*, to say) in an ostentatious or aggressive manner.
1934 *Amer. Speech* IX. 290/1 [Negro slang.] *Woof*, to talk much and loudly and yet say little of consequence. **1935** Z. N. Hurston *Mules & Men* I. iv. 86 The men would crowd in and buy soft drinks and woof at me, the stranger, but I knew I wasn't getting on. **1941** *Life* 27 Jan. 78 To reinforce a statement, a sub-deb says, *I ain't woofin'*..which means 'I'm not fooling'. **1941** *Direction* Summer 15/2 Stack got all big at the nose and woofed: 'All right, boss, you either fixes me up with that gin, or I pulls down this bar!. **1972** J. Wambaugh *Blue Knight* vi. 86 He was woofing me, because he winked at the blond kid. **1974** H. L. Foster *Ribbin', Jivin', & Playin' Dozens* iv. 140 A student might say, 'Mr. Foster, he's woofin' on me.' This may have meant anything from he is challenging me to a fight, to he is making fun of my clothing or my mother.

Hence **woo·fing** *vbl. sb.* and *ppl. a.*
1942 *Amer. Mercury* July 96/2 *Woofing*, aimless talk, as a dog barks on a moonlight night. **1969** H. R. Brown in H. L. Foster *Ribbin', Jivin', & Playin' Dozens* (1974) v. 179 Those young brothers came out of this woofing, diddy-bopping and raising hell period. **1973** B. G. Cooke in T. Kochman *Rappin' & Stylin' Out* 45 'Woofing' is a style of bragging and boasting about how 'bad' one is and is sometimes used by males and females when rapping to each other. **1975** *Today's Education* Sept./Oct. 54 Some of the woofin' has been precipitated by Whites trying to hustle Blacks out of goods and materials which have been promised or which are rightfully theirs. **1977** *Time* 14 Nov. 90/3 Cosby, who has one of the great faces of the Western world, is the best thing in this woofin', shuckin' film.

woofer (wū·fəɹ, wu·fəɹ). [f. prec. + -er[1].]
1. *U.S. Blacks' slang.* (See quot. 1934.)
1934 *Amer. Speech* IX. 289/1 *Woofer*, applied to one who talks constantly, loudly, and in a convincing manner, but who says very little. **1935** Z. N. Hurston *Mules & Men* I. iv. 88, I want outside to join the woofers, since I seemed to have no standing among the dancers. **1974** H. L. Foster *Ribbin', Jivin', & Playin' Dozens* v. 202 The woofer may also move his body in a menacing way to make his woof more threatening and intimidating.

2. A loudspeaker designed to reproduce accurately low-frequency sounds whilst being relatively unresponsive to those of higher frequency. Cf. *squawker 3, *tweeter.
1935 K. Henney *Radio Engin. Handbk.* (ed. 2) xxiv. 830 Wide range of frequency response is sometimes secured by using as many as three groups of speakers: low ('woofers'), medium, and high ('tweeters'). **1959** *Consumer Rep.* Sept. 453/1 The Best Buy..is much the better value of the two tweeters when coupled to a check-rated woofer. **1964** M. McLuhan *Understanding Media* (1967) xxxi. 348 It is like a badly wired woofer in a hi-fi circuit that produces a tremendous flutter in the bottom. **1979** *Arizona Daily Star* 5 Aug. I. 10/1 (Advt.), Big savings on a great sounding speaker. 8″ woofer for deep bass and 2½″ tweeter for clear highs.

woofits (wū·fits). *slang.* [Origin unknown.] An unwell feeling, esp. in the head; moody depression.
1918 J. M. Grider *War Birds* (1927) 96 Curtis says he is suffering from the Woofits, that dread disease that comes from overeating and underdrinking. *Ibid.* 207, I drank too much coffee before getting up and I'm as nervous as a kitten now. Must be getting the Woofits. **1932** *Amer. Speech* VII. 338 [Johns Hopkins jargon.] *Woofits*, ailment that comes with 'the morning after the night before'. **1958** 'N. Shute' *Rainbow & Rose* 100 Getting the woofits now, because I don't sleep so good.

woofter (wu·ftəɹ, wū·ftəɹ). *slang.* Also **wooftah.** [Fanciful alteration of *poofter.] = *poofter.
1977 *Private Eye* 8 July 5/1 The headshrinker had been reduced to a nervous wreck, and was prepared to dismiss the rabidly heterosexual Tynan as a wooftah. **1980** A. N. Wilson *Healing Art* iv. 47 The two young woofters in the pub.

woofy (wu·fi), *a.*[2] [f. Woof *int.*, *sb.*[2], and *v.*[2] + -y[1].] Of reproduced sound: having too much bass, or bass that is indistinct.
1932 J. H. Reyner *Mod. Radio Communication* (ed. 4) xx. 204 We shall experience a loss of the upper frequencies, the reproduction lacking brilliance and sounding 'woofy'. **1975** *Gramophone* Nov. 819/2, I prefer the sound of the horns..on the Decca Ace of Diamonds record, a much cleaner sound than the rather 'woofy' quality on the new record.

woofy, *a.*[3] [Relationship to Woof *sb.*[1] and *sb.*[2] not clear.] Gruff; densely-textured.
1960 C. P. Snow *Affair* xl. 371 The hairline which, when he was drunk, separated the diffuse and woofy benevolence from a suspicion of all mankind. **1976–7** *Art N.Z.* Dec./Jan. 15/1 She would have none of the delirious woofy mango-swamp muck of the then Auckland School. **1983** R. Sutcliff *Blue Remembered Hills* xvi. 124 A moustache..not of the woofy RAF variety but more akin to the kind worn by sergeant-majors.

wool, *sb.* Add: **1. g.** (*b*) (Earlier examples.) Also † *to spread* (etc.). For *U.S.* read orig. *U.S.* (*g*) *all wool and a yard wide* and varr., of excellent quality; thoroughly sound or honourable. (*h*) *wool away!* (Austral. and N.Z.) (see quot. 1965). (*i*) *to lose one's wool* (slang), to lose one's temper; similarly *to keep one's wool.*
(*b*) **1839** *Jamestown* (N.Y.) *Jrnl.* 24 Apr. 1/6 That lawyer has been trying to spread the wool over your eyes. **1842** *Spirit of Times* (Phila.) 29 Sept. (Th.), Look sharp, or they'll pull wool over your eyes.
(*g*) **1882** G. W. Peck *Peck's Sunshine* 85 You want to pick out (as the 'boss combination girl' of Rock Co.) a thoroughbred, that is, all wool, a yard wide. **1909** [see *lallapaloosa]. **1913** J. London *Valley of Moon* 60 You're a live one, all wool, a yard long and a yard wide. **1963** L. Meynell *Virgin Luck* v. 114 It didn't seem to matter so much with people as decent as that about. She was all wool and a yard wide, that one. **1974** 'A. Gilbert' *Nice Little Killing* iii. 40 No one will ever catch her..with an alibi all wool and a yard wide.
(*h*) *c* **1897** D. McK. Wright in A. E. Woodhouse *N.Z. Farm & Station Verse* (1950) 33 Wool away! Wool away is the cry And the merry game of busting is begun. **1949** P. Newton *High Country Days* v. 53 The call of 'wool away' had lagging fleecies dashing to rescue fleeces before the shearer would be out with his next sheep. **1965** J. S. Gunn *Terminol. Shearing Industry* II. 38 *Wool away*, the call of a shearer who wants the picker-up to carry away a fleece. This has to be done after each sheep, and fleeces are not left lying around on the floor while another sheep is being shorn.
(*i*) **1926** 'A. Berkeley' *Wychford Poisoning Case* v. 48 'All right,' Alec said soothingly. 'Keep your wool on.' **1944** D. Welch *In Youth is Pleasure* v. 87 Dennis said a lot more, growing increasingly vicious with each new sentence... 'My dear, don't lose your wool,' she said, mimicking old-fashioned schoolboy slang. **1959** [see *rag *sb.*[1] 3 c]. **1967** O. Norton *Now lying Dead* vi. 108, I lost my wool then.

3. a. Also, a woollen garment.
1933 H. Allen *Anthony Adverse* II. iv. xxv. 354 'I *am* a little cold after all,' said Father Xavier, looking at the fire regretfully. 'A second till I change into my wool' **1952** M. Laski *Village* v. 94 The beige silk frock could at last be discarded for a really not-too-bad navy blue wool. **1975** Byfield & Tedeschi *Solemn High Murder* (1976) i. 10 Mueller had taken away his rumpled suit, leaving his heavier wools hanging in the open closet. **1978** S. Brill *Teamsters* ix. 340 The custom-tailored wools that might.. have made him look like a well-heeled Wall Street lawyer.

5. a. *wool basket, bin, -hat* (see sense 5 d below), *shop.* **b.** *wool-classer, -grower* (later examples). **c.** *wool-lined* (earlier example), *-woven* adjs.
c **1878** J. Albery *Dram. Wks.* (1939) II. 300 Fawley places a note in Haidee's wool-basket. **1965** J. S. Gunn *Terminol. Shearing Industry* II. 38 *Wool basket.* There are several of these containers into which various locks and bellies are thrown to be baled up separately. **1933** *Press* (Christchurch, N.Z.) 30 Dec. 13/7 *Wool bins*, open compartments like stalls in a stable, where wool is stacked by classes until it is pressed. **1974** D. Stuart *Prince of My Country* i. 3 The woolbins loom broad and tall, the press towers above them, there are bales in squat heaps. **1892** W. E. Swanton *Notes on N.Z.* ii. 96 There is the wool classer with his assistant rollers. **1911** W. H. Koebel *In Maoriland Bush* viii. 122 The wool-classer takes his stand before the sorting table. **1968** *Guardian* 29 Feb. 14/3 Ian Redpath (Victoria), 26. Wool classer. Opening bat. **1921** *Daily Colonist* (Victoria, B.C.) 11 Oct. 6/3 Mr. Vernon, a wool-grower of Albert Head. **1962** *Economist* 31 Mar. 1275/1 Australian woolgrowers stand to earn £24 million more this season. **1971** *Sunday Australian* 8 Aug. 1/5 Half of Australia's 93,000 woolgrowers will get less than $600 each from the Federal Government's new wool subsidy. **1824** E. Weeton *Let.* 22 May (1969) II. 270 My wool-lined beaver gloves. **1923** *Harmsworth's 'Best Way' Series No. 95* 15/1 Ask at any wool shop for 'Beehive' Recipe Card No. 50 (price 2d.). **1943** A. Christie *Moving Finger* xiii. 147 She was knitting—ever so vexed she'd run out of wool... So I ran her in, dropped her at the wool shop. **1983** C. Bowder *Birth Rites* I. 38 The colour's a bit unusual. It was a discontinued line in my local wool-shop. **1888** G. M. Hopkins *Poems* (1967) 198 No more: off with—down he dings His bleachèd both and woolwoven wear.

d. wool alien, a plant introduced into a country by means of imported wool containing its seed; **wool-blind** *Austral.* and *N.Z.*, (of a sheep) having its sight obscured by its growth of wool; also *ellipt.*; hence **wool-blindness; wool church**, one of the English churches built or modified out of the wealth produced by the Tudor wool trade; **wool clip** = Clip *sb.*[2] 2 b; **wool-clipper,** a clipper for carrying wool; **wool-dyed** *a.* (earlier and *fig.* examples); **wool-fat** (earlier example); **wool-grease** (earlier example); **wool hat,** (*a*) a hat made of coarse wool; † (*b*) *U.S.*, a supporter of the Democratic Party (*obs.*); (*c*) *U.S.*, a small farmer, or an unsophisticated or conservative countryman, from the South; also (senses (*b*) and (*c*)) *wool hat boy*; **wool king** *Austral.* and *N.Z. colloq.*, a wealthy or large-scale sheep farmer; **Woolmark,** an international quality symbol for wool instituted by the International Wool Secretariat; also *transf.*; **wool-press** (earlier example); **wool presser,** one who operates a wool press; **wool-pulling** *vbl. sb.*, (*a*) the removal of wool from a sheepskin; (*b*) the act of pulling the wool over a person's eyes; deception; **wool-shed:** also *N.Z.* (earlier and later examples); **wool table** *Austral.* and *N.Z.* (see quot. 1965); **wool team** *Austral.* and *N.Z.*, a team of draught animals for transporting wool; **wool-track** *Austral.*, a track along which wool was conveyed to a port; **wool-wax,** (*a*) = Suint; (*b*) = Lanolin.
1919 Hayward & Druce *Adventive Flora Tweedside* p. xxi, It must not..be assumed that all the wool aliens will disappear. **1961** *Proc. Bot. Soc. Brit. Isles* IV. 221 The party visited a railway siding in the same county, and further wool aliens were found... On enquiry he found that wool waste ('shoddy') was unloaded at the sidings and delivered to local farmers for use as a manure, and when this was followed up foreign weeds were found to be plentiful in their fields. **1976** *B.S.B.I. News* Sept. 22 J. R. Palmer searched hop fields near Wateringbury (Kent) and also found wool aliens present although no 'shoddy' has been used here for at least four years. **1933,** **1953** Wool-blind [see *eye-clip* vb. s.v. *eye *sb.*[1] 28]. **1955** J. Morrison in B. James *Austral. Short Stories* (1963) 158 Worse than pushing a mob of wool-blinds up the ramp of a shearing shed. **1965** J. S. Gunn *Terminol. Shearing Industry* II. 37 The wig is removed with all the wool during shearing..because, if it is not done, the sheep may become 'wool-blind' before shearing time. **1950** *N.Z. Jrnl. Agric.* Oct. 349/3 Through eye clipping, wool blindness is avoided. **1936** M. Allis *Eng. Prelude* xxxiii. 252 Long Melford..with the stately 'wool' church, a miracle of lace in stone and flint. **1950** H. J. Massingham *Curious Traveller* ix. 175 Wild nature is the architect in Pembrokeshire and the massive castles..bear the same architectural relation to cliff and mountain as..the wool-churches of the Cotswolds. **1976** *Cambridge Independent Press* 16 Dec. I. 3/5 An interesting talk, illustrated with coloured slides, on the wool churches of East Anglia was given. **1862** *Rep. Comm. Patents 1861: Agric.* 131 The wool-clip of New England commands a ready cash market in Boston. **1893** [in Dict., sense 5 a]. **1977** *Weekly Times* (Melbourne) 19 Jan. 3/4 The Corporation had put proposals to the Minister for Primary Industry..to acquire the export portion of the Australian wool clip. **1984** *N.Z. Farmer* 12 Apr. 12/1 The wool clip never strayed far from about 5kg per sheep wintered. **1984** *Oxf. Illustr. Hist. Brit.* iii. 160 Their reserves of liquid capital enabled Italian companies to offer attractive terms. They could not only buy an abbey's entire wool clip for the current year; they could also buy it for years in advance. **1903** C. Protheroe *Life in Mercantile Marine* 4 The *Chatto* was a full-rigged ship of a thousand odd tons, in reality a wool-clipper, but being winter time, she was now loaded with tallow and grain. **1924** J. Masefield *Sard Harker* 37 The wool-clippers and big four-masters were being squeezed out. **1832** *Niles' Weekly Reg.* XLIII. 65/2 Messrs. Randolf and Ritchie who are chiefs of the 'wool-dyed democrats' of the present day. **1904** *Charlotte* (N. Carolina) *Observer* 19 June 2 Higginson is one of the old abolition gang, is wool-dyed and blind. **1875** *Chem. News* 15 Jan. 26/2 The question as to the composition of the wool-fat could not be fully solved. *Ibid.*, We have examined two fresh kinds of wool-grease. **1794** T. Coxe *View U.S.* 314 Wool hats, of Winchester make, are in much repute. **1828** *Western Intelligencer* (Hamilton, Ohio) 3 Oct. 3/1 Thus has Mr. Woods endeavored to gain the votes of the wool hats as he terms his Jackson friends in Washington. **1836** *Western Hemisphere* (Columbus, Ohio) 3 Aug. 1/7 The very men whom a few years ago they called the 'ragged wool hat boys' and 'Tories', they are now seeking to attach to their [Whig] party!! **1856** [in Dict., sense 5 a]. **1880** *Harper's Mag.* Dec. 159 An old 'wool-hat' came along with a cart drawn by a single ox. **1898** B. H. Young *Hist. Jessamine County, Kentucky* 163 They made wool hats. **1927** K. Eubank *Horse & Buggy Days* 170, I was a smart boy from town, and this particular guy thought I was a wool-hat boy. **1942** J. A. Rice *I came out of Eighteenth Cent.* ii. 95 South Carolinians liked their hatred to be personal, and the 'Wool Hat Boys' whooped with delight when Tillman ripped the hide off the 'Columbia Ring' and the Charlestonian gentlemen. **1942** *Time* 21 Sept. 19/3 Georgia's 'wool-hat' boys (small farmers). **1960** *Spectator* 2 Sept. 332 The 'wool-hats' (i.e. dyed-in-the-wool segregationists) of the rural Tobacco Roads who fear negro competition. **1980** *Washington Star* 29 Sept. A13/5 Carter knows that when..Eugene Talmadge

shouted about 'state's rights', the 'woolhats' of Georgia knew what he was saying. **1889** G. R. HART *Stray Leaves from Early Hist. Canterbury* iii. 19 Founders of the present race of wool kings in many parts of Canterbury. *a* **1922** H. LAWSON in *Penguin Bk. Austral. Ballads* (1964) 156 These are men who died to make the Wool-Kings rich. **1964** *Wool Future* Sept. 1/1 Woolmark, the international quality symbol for pure new wool, will be seen in British and Irish shops for the first time this month. **1980** *Times* 8 July 10/5 To get the Woolmark seal of approval you can only have a minute percentage of gorse..or whatever still stuck on the yarn. **1983** D. DUNNETT *Dolly & Bird of Paradise* xi. 141 One or two sheep..with no barbed wire in sight to ruffle their gorgeous Woolmark. **1846** C. J. PHARAZYN *Jrnl.* 21 Dec. (MS., Turnbull Libr., Wellington, N.Z.) 67 Employed all day at Watarangi assisting in packing fleeces. George making wool press. **1892** W. E. SWANTON *Notes on N.Z.* ii. 96 There is . the wool presser and his mate to bale up the wool. **1847** J. S. ROBB *Squatter Life* 16 In short I'm up to the whole 'wool pulling' system. **1885** Wool-pulling [in Dict., sense 5 b]. **1971** D. BAGLEY *Freedom Trap* iii. 59, I was given permission to start correspondence courses. . It was all a bit of wool-pulling to make them think Rearden was reconciled to his fate. **1846** C. J. PHARAZYN *Jrnl.* 11 Dec. (MS., Turnbull Libr., Wellington, N.Z.) 67 Counted rams after breakfast. George finished washing penn at river with Robin and Teddy and self to wool shed at Watarangi and finished the same. **1977** *N.Z. Herald* 8 Jan. 4-7/7 (Advt.), Four-brm home, 3-stand woolshed, barn, yards, airstrip. **1865** M. A. BARKER *Let.* 1 Dec. in *Station Life N.Z.* (1870) 32 We next inspected the wool tables, to which two boys were incessantly bringing armfuls of rolled-up fleeces. **1950** *N.Z. Jrnl. Agric.* Oct. 310/2 The scrubbing of the shearing board and the wool table is an essential practice. **1965** J. S. GUNN *Terminol. Shearing Industry* II. 40 *Wool table*, a table of spaced ridged lateral slats on which the fleece is rolled and skirted and the pieces picked. Any loose locks fall through to be picked up. **1865** R. HENNING *Let.* 18 Feb. (1952) 82/3 Biddulph..has sent both the bullock-drivers to the Port with the wool-teams. **1959** H. P. TRITTON *Time means Tucker* v. 41/2 Yarragrin..was also famous as a camp for the wool-teams, coming in from the north-west. **1903** 'T. COLLINS' *Such is Life* (1937) vi. 317 These wool-tracks, that knew him so well, will know him no more again for ever. **1959** J. WRIGHT *Generations of Men* (1960) xvii. 217 They followed a line through the trees that led southward across the road, once an important wool-track to the coastal ports. **1911** *Encycl. Brit.* XX. 51/2 An exceptional position [among animal waxes] is occupied by wool wax, the main constituent of the natural wool fat which covers the hair of sheep. . Wool fat is now being purified on a large scale and brought into commerce, under the name of lanolin, as an ointment. **1943** *Thorpe's Dict. Appl. Chem.* (ed. 4) VI. 135/2 Wool grease (wool fat..) is the crude mixture of wool wax and fatty acids recovered from the soapy liquor used for the scouring of raw wool. *Ibid.*, Crude wool grease is used as a lubricant..; some is refined for use as 'lanolin' (pure wool wax) in..cosmetics,..rust preventives, etc. **1954** [see *DEGRAS, DÉGRAS b]. **1956** *Nature* 10 Mar. 470/1 Further work was carried out..on the formation of polyacrylonitrile in wool and on suint and wool wax. **1964** N. G. CLARK *Mod. Organic Chem.* xvii. 340 Wool wax occurs to the extent of 20 to 30 per cent in raw sheep's wool. **1966** GETTENS & STOUT *Painting Materials* 81 Wool Wax..is the natural grease from the fleece of sheep.

wool, *v.* **2.** (Earlier example.)

c **1831** A. LINCOLN in H. Binns *Life Lincoln* (1927) 34, I never use tussle and scuffle. I don't like this wooling and pulling.

wool-carding, *vbl. sb.* and *ppl. a.* (Earlier example.)

1806 *Balance* (Hudson, N.Y.) V. 288/2, I was, lately, much pleased with seeing a wool-carding machine in operation.

Woolfian (wu·lfiăn), *a.* and *sb.* [f. the name *Woolf* + -IAN.] **A.** *adj.* Of, pertaining to, or characteristic of Virginia Woolf (1882–1941), English writer, or her work. **B.** *sb.* An admirer or devotee of Virginia Woolf. *rare.*

1936 *Scrutiny* V. 183 The more discerning might have noticed that it [sc. *A Note in Music*] was drawn not from life but from *Jacob's Room* and *Mrs. Dalloway*, a solemn exercise in Woolfian style and structure. **1944** E. H. W. MEYERSTEIN *Let.* 24 Nov. (1959) 296, I read the proofs of *Mrs. Dalloway* years ago which a Woolfian gave a friend of mine. **1977** W. HILDICK *Loop* viii. 40, I don't think I'd ever used the word 'lark' like that..before. It was..something I'd picked up in my Woolfian researches.

woo·lgathersome, *a. nonce-wd.* [-SOME[1].] Suggestive of wool-gathering.

1922 C. E. MONTAGUE *Disenchantment* vii. 91 The average German soldier, the docile blond with yellow hair, long skull, and blue, woolgathersome eyes.

woollenize (wu·lĕnəiz), *v.* [f. WOOLLEN *a.* and *sb.* + -IZE.] *trans.* To impart to (vegetable fibres) the appearance and texture of wool. Hence **woo·llenizing** *vbl. sb.*

1890 *Times* 19 Aug. 10/4 The various processes to be carried out at the model fibre factory..comprise.. cottonizing and woollenizing fibres to imitate fine cotton or wool. **1927** *Daily Tel.* 21 June 8 (Advt.), Successful fancy cloth effects have been attained by the application of mercerising and woollenising processes to these yarns.

woolleny (wu·lĕni), *a. rare.* [f. WOOLLEN *a.* and *sb.* + -Y[1].] Made of or resembling woollen cloth.

1863 'G. HAMILTON' *Gala-Days* 41 I have a veil—none of your woolleny gruff fabrics.

Woollies (wu·liz). Also **Wooleys, Woolies, Woollys.** *colloq.* name for a shop bearing the name of F. W. *Woolworth* PLC (cf. *WOOLWORTH); occas. used for the company itself.

1939 *Airman's Gaz.* Dec., At Woollies store they congregate For powders, creams and lotions. **1957** R. HOGGART *Uses of Literacy* v. 120 Popular shops (with 'Wooley's'—Woolworth's—a clear favourite with working-class people). **1962** *Guardian* 24 Dec. 4/2 Some of them are shoplifting: not Woollies combs, but watches and rings. **1971** *Daily Tel.* 16 July 17 'Woolies' says that profits for the first half included a surplus of £261,000 on property sales. **1980** J. DITTON *Copley's Hunch* I. ii. 33 It's a good one. Not one of your Woollie's specials at a tanner a throw.

woollily (wu·lili), *adv.* Also **woolily.** [f. WOOLLY *a.* (*sb.*) + -LY[2].] In a way lacking in clarity or incisiveness.

1937 *Daily Express* 5 Feb. 13/2 Since nothing reads more woolily than descriptions of colours..I'll skip a list of new shades. **1979** *Guardian* 26 Oct. 2/8 Mr Atkins [was] saying a thing woollily not once..but twice.

woolly, *a.* (*sb.*) Add: **3. c. woolly bear**, (*a*) (further examples); also *spec.* the larva of the carpet beetle; freq. *attrib.*; (*b*) *Mil. slang* (see quots.); **woolly mammoth** = MAMMOTH *sb.* 1; **woolly worm** *U.S.*, a hairy caterpillar.

1909 WEBSTER, *Wooly worm*, the larva of any sawfly that covers itself with a white woolly secretion. **1911** E. FERBER *Dawn O'Hara* ii. 19 I'd eat wooly worms if I thought they might benefit me. **1915** *War Illustr.* 31 July 546/2 The German high-explosive shell, known to our men by the nickname of the 'Woolly Bear',..detonates with a cloud of thick white smoke. **1918** H. W. MCBRIDE *Emma Gees* 135 'Woolly Bear' is the name given to a large, high explosive shell, with a time fuse, which bursts overhead, giving out a dense black smoke. **1923** KIPLING *Irish Guards in Gt. War* II. 82 They were drenched with a five hours' bombardment of 4.2's and 'woolly bears'. **1933** A. S. ROMER *Vertebr. Paleontol.* xix. 376 The woolly mammoth was a form adapted to cold climates. **1940** R. G. RUSSELL *101st Field Artillery 1917–19* 94 A German 150-millimetre battery fired 'woolly bears', time-fuse shells, which burst too high to do any harm. **1950** *N.Z. Jrnl. Agric.* Nov. 478/3 The most common enemy of cinerarias in New Zealand is the 'woolly-bear' caterpillar, the larva of the magpie moth. **1951** *Good Housek. Home Encycl.* 324/2 *Woolly bear.* This is the grub of a small beetle which..congregates in hot airing cupboards. **1961** Woolly bear [see *carpet beetle* s.v. *CARPET *sb.* 5]. **1969** BENNISON & WRIGHT *Geol. Hist. Brit. Isles* xvi. 359 The presence of either the woolly mammoth or the reindeer does not necessarily indicate an arctic climate. **1972** E. WIGGINTON *Foxfire Bk.* 209 The woolly worm tells of a bad winter if: there are a lot of them crawling about. **1974** A. DILLARD *Pilgrim at Tinker Creek* xiv. 247 Woolly bears, those orange-and-black-banded furry caterpillars of the Isabella moth, were on the move. **1976** *Islander* (Victoria, B.C.) 16 May 6/1 The woolly mammoth..roamed the tundra areas. **1980** *Blair & Ketchum's Country Jrnl.* Oct. 28/2 October is the month when the woolly bear caterpillar, sometimes called a fuzzy-wuzzy or woolly worm, can be seen crossing country roads. **1983** *Listener* 27 Oct. 16/3 Our wall-to wall carpets attract the 'woolly bear' grubs of the carpet beetle.

d. (Earlier example.) Also *transf.*, and as *woolly* simply.

1884 A. J. SOWELL *Rangers & Pioneers of Texas* xi. 330 Occasionally, in some Western village, you will hear a voice ring out on the night air..'Wild and woolly',.. and then you may expect a few shots from a revolver. It is a cowboy out on a little spree. **1891** M. E. RYAN *Told in Hills* III. iv. 191 Let us 'move our freight', 'hit the breeze', or any other term of the woolly West that means action. **1907** S. E. WHITE *Arizona Nights* viii. 130 'Who's your woolly friend', the shiny Jew asks of the girls. **1940** R. S. LAMBERT *Ariel & All his Quality* viii. 197 [They] looked with scepticism upon a plan which they regarded as wild and woolly.

7. *woolly-witted* adj.

1927 *Observer* 6 Nov. 15/1 The managerial attitude towards producers is at present woolly-witted. **1949** ST. J. ERVINE *Craigavon* II. lvii. 273 That woolly-witted insurrectionist.

B. *sb.* **1.** *winter woollies*, warm underwear (not necessarily of wool); freq. *joc.* Also *fig.*

1926 WODEHOUSE *Heart of Goof* vi. 194 His mother had bought him a new set of winter woollies which felt like horsehair. **1933** DYLAN THOMAS *Sel. Lett.* (1966) 24 Catch him [*sc.* Wordsworth]..walking the hills with a daffodil pressed to his lips, and his winter woollies tickling his chest. **1964** *Observer* 13 Sept. 11/3 If we wear the winter woollies of traditional trade unionism against the hot sun of automation, we may sweat it out instead of thinking it out. **1974** *Nature* 18 Oct. 569/1 The dinosaurs' unsatisfied need was not so much for laxatives as for winter woollies!

2. A sheep; esp. (*Austral.* and *N.Z.*) one before shearing. *U.S.*, *Austral.*, and *N.Z. colloq.*

1910 J. G. NEIHARDT *River & I* iii. 92 In Scotland when a feller sees a sheepman coming down the road with his sheep, he says: 'Behold the gentle shepherd with his fleecy flock!'.. In Montana, that same feller says..'Look at that crazy blankety-blank with his woolies!' **1930** *Bulletin* (Sydney) 2 Apr. 23/1 We curse the stubborn woollies..as the sweating shearers tussle. **1935** H. DAVIS *Honey in Horn* xi. 162 She had a little short-bodied guitar of the kind that Mexican sheep herders used to carry around behind their saddles to entertain the woolies with. **1949** F. SARGESON *I saw It in my Dream* II. xiii. 111 White dots that you could tell were both sheep and lambs; and they were so white it was easy to tell that they weren't woollies any more. **1972** P. NEWTON *Sheep Thief* vi. 48 The biggest proportion proved to be Totara sheep of mixed ages, three of them woollies.

3. [Cf. *WOLLY.] A uniformed policeman. *slang.*

1965 R. E. RIDGWAY in B. Wannan *Fair Go, Spinner* II. 66 Later on, as the station expanded and more 'woollies' were added, the shed grew accordingly. **1975** *Listener* 6 Feb. 163/2 Sir Robert Mark...saw its [*sc.* the CID's] members behaving as if they could walk on water, and looking down on the 'woollies' who had to plod the beat in uniform. **1978** 'B. GRAEME' *Double Trouble* xv. 191 One of the woollies blew his whistle. **1984** *Private Eye* 20 Apr. 6/2 A small army of 'Woollies'—CID slang for uniformed officers—were summoned.

Woolpit (wu·lpit). The name of a village in Suffolk, used *attrib.* in *Woolpit brick*, a pale-coloured brick made from earth there.

1887 J. E. TAYLOR *Tourist's Guide Suffolk* 103 One of its chief industries is brickmaking, for the bed of brick-earth here makes a beautiful stone known everywhere as 'Woolpit Brick'. **1966** G. E. EVANS *Pattern under Plough* ii. 36 The Tudor front of the house was given a severe façade of Woolpit brick.

Woolton (wu·ltən). The title of F. J. Marquis (1883–1964), 1st Earl of *Woolton*, used in (*Lord*) *Woolton pie*, a vegetable pie publicized when he was wartime Minister of Food.

1941 *Food Facts for Kitchen Front* 44 *Lord Woolton Pie.* The ingredients of this pie can be varied according to the vegetables in season. Potato, swede, cauliflower and carrot make a good mixture. **1955** E. WAUGH *Officers & Gentlemen* II. vi. 291 The London crowd shuffled past, surfeited with tea and Woolton pies. *a* **1969** O. SITWELL *Queen Mary* (1974) 47 At luncheon . we found a new and rather horrible war-time dish had been prepared for us, called Lord Woolton Pie. **1981** *Times* 16 Mar. 12/7 A wartime diet of Woolton Pie and whalemeat.

wool-winder. Add: **2.** A frame on which wool is wound.

1969 *Canad. Antiques Collector* Aug. 20/2 An old wool-winder, still in its original state, stands to the left. **1976** *Evening Post* (Nottingham) 15 Dec. 20/6 (Advt.), Knitmaster 321 Punchcard Knitting machine, with worktable, woolwinder, punch etc.

Woolworth (wu·lwəɹþ). The name of the retailing company (orig. sixpenny store) F. W. *Woolworth* PLC, used *attrib.* to designate low-priced goods regarded as typical of its merchandise.

1931 *Times Lit. Suppl.* 5 Nov. 862/3 Miss Helen Simpson is refreshingly modern with her 'Woolworth craze' at Oxford as the real villain. **1932** AUDEN in *Rev. Eng. Stud.* (1978) XXIX. 292 Moving woodenly like a woolworth doll, A lady came in clothes so ugly..that the eye was cruel. **1939** T. S. ELIOT *Old Possum's Bk. Pract. Cats* 22 One of the girls Suddenly missed her Woolworth pearls. **1948** 'J. TEY' *Franchise Affair* vii. 69 Some Woolworth plants in the gardens. **1974** *Guardian* 21 Mar. 10, I am never likely to be involved in a study of..Lehar and can only look on all of it as real Woolworth stuff (in contrast to, say, Mozart, who is vintage Fortnum and Mason). **1980** I. ST. JAMES *Money Stones* III. iii. 106 You couldn't swing a Woolworth watch on diamonds found here.

Hence **Woolwo·rthian** *a.*

1933 R. W. CHAMBERS *Whatever Love Is* xx. 286 A strange, stark, snowless, dingy Christmastide with a Woolworthian cheapness about it. **1937** P. THORNTON *Dead Puppets Dance* II. vii. 144 There were hundreds of people at Kućevište, and many of them wore..high-heeled shoes and Woolworthian stockings if their husbands could afford..them. **1978** *Washington Post* 27 Aug. c-38/2 Nowadays the plates are chipped and the tables lit by Woolworthian gilded pierced tin lamps flickering with candles.

woomph (wūmf, wumf), *int.* (*sb.*, *adv.*) *slang.* Also **woomf.** [Imitative.] (Expressing) a sound similar to a 'whoof' (*WHOOF *int.* (*sb.*) 2) but with a deeper or more resonant component. Cf. the synonymous *WHOOMPF *int.* (*sb.*).

1955 LD. WINTERTON *Fifty Tumultuous Years* 82 Two old gentlemen were dozing in their chairs when the 'Woomph', 'Boomph' of a bomb simultaneously woke them up. **1979** R. FIENNES *Hell on Ice* ix. 144 There was a sudden *woomf* as the fumes and the liquid ignited. **1982** S. BRETT *Murder Unprompted* xiv. 133 He threw a cushion, which went woomph into the side of Charles's head.

woon. Add: Also **wun.**

1898 H. F. HALL *Soul of People* vii. 92 Outside Mandalay the country was governed by *wuns* or governors. **1972** A. T. Q. STEWART *Pagoda War* ix. 112 (*caption*) Thibaw's envoy, the *wun* with his golden umbrella, stands beside him.

woop woop (wu·p,wup). *Austral.* and *N.Z.* Also **woop-woop(s, wop-wop.** [Sham Aboriginal (but see below).] **a.** A jocular name for a remote rural town or district; also (without *the* and with capital initials) as the name of an imaginary place in a remote area.

One suggestion is that the term is derived from the 'geelorious town o' Whoop-Up' in E. L. Wheeler's *Deadwood Dick on Deck* (1878), where 'Whoop-Up' is the name of a back-country American goldmining town.

1926 'J. Doone' *Timely Tips for New Australians* 23 *Woop Woop*, a humorous method of alluding to the country districts used most frequently in New South Wales. **1928** A. Wright *Good Recovery* 34 They're chasin' Murraba out along the Woop Woop Road, or somewhere. **1930** *Bulletin* (Sydney) 1 Jan. 28/2 'Who on earth is she?' gasped the visitor from Woop-Woop. **1958** J. Lindsay *Life Rarely Tells* 213 Next morning he'd rush away. 'Off to the Woop-woop!' Somewhere in the backblocks that meant. **1960** N. Hilliard *Maori Girl* III. i. 174 'Where do you come from?' 'Up in the wilds—the woop-woops, Taranaki.' **1963** *Truth* (Wellington, N.Z.) 8 Oct., A job was found right out in the wop-wops. **1970** *N.Z. Listener* 21 Dec. 51/2 While you're out in the woop-woops next time, spare a thought for the local farmer. **1975** *Courier-Mail* (Brisbane) 26 Mar. 12/6 Police feared they would be transferred to 'Woop Woop'.

b. An inhabitant of such a place; a country bumpkin. *rare.*

1936 M. Franklin *All that Swagger* 472 Adrienne was no blob or woop-woop. **1950** *Coast to Coast 1949–50* 201 I'll make a fair dinkum woop-woop out of you in no time.

woosh, var. Whoosh *v.*, *sb.* in Dict. and Suppl.

Wooster (wū·stəɹ). The name of Bertie *Wooster*, an amiable, vacuous, young man about town in the novels of P. G. Wodehouse, used allusively. Also *attrib.*

1939 Auden & Isherwood *Journey to a War* i. 44 He was so much more subtle, more intelligent than his cultivated Bertie Wooster drawl. **1960** *New Statesman* 24 Sept. 424/2 Very young men about town..quite amiable in a Bertie Wooster sort of way. **1963** R. H. Morrieson *Scarecrow* (1964) xii. 135 Her husband, the aged Wooster type whom Angela and I had encountered.

Also as *v. intr.*, to behave in the manner of Bertie Wooster; **Woo·sterish** *a.*; **Woo·sterism,** a remark or action characteristic of Wooster.

1959 *Observer* 26 Apr. 23/5 Harold ..lives in a pretty Woosterish way. **1964** *Punch* 17 June 906/3 Frolicsome nitwits woostering in well-heeled suburbia. **1969** *Times* 5 May 23/3 Dapper, cheerful young men without the disdain of the real Jeeves when provoked by inane Woosterisms. **1978** *Country Life* 14 Dec. 2103/1 A ridiculous pink velvet dog with inane Woosterish eyes. **1979** K. Bonfiglioli *After you with Pistol* xvii. 130 We Woostered away for a while, giggling slightly. *Ibid.*, While we idly bandied these Woosterisms ..he slid a scribbling-pad across the desk. **1983** *Times* 17 Oct. 15/4 This show..reducing Olivia to a charm-school hostess, Andrew to a Woosterian silly ass and..Toby to a bar-fly.

woozy, *a.* Add: Also **whoosy, whoozy, woozey.** For *U.S. slang* read *colloq.* (orig. *U.S.*). **1.** Further examples.)

1915 Wodehouse *Psmith, Journalist* xvi. 114 'He's still woozy,' said the Kid. 'Still—what exactly, Comrade Brady?' 'In the air,' explained the Kid. 'Bats in the belfry. Dizzy.' **1929** Kipling *Limits & Renewals* (1932) 356 He had kept himself going on rum sometimes, and was woozy when the pinch came. **1937** *Black Mask* Jan. 24/2, I got hit. It made me woozey for a minute. **1952** B. Malamud *Natural* 17 He got up whoozy and walked, finding it hard to believe his eyes. **1961** J. B. Priestley *Saturn over Water* iii. 29 The woozy state I was in. **1977** M. Hinxman *One-Way Cemetery* xix. 139 He'd have phrased it more delicately if he hadn't felt quite so whoosy. **1978** *Daily Tel.* 17 Jan. 17/2 Liquid lunches can leave a man weak and woozy late in the afternoon, drinkers were told.

2. Representing or marked by muddled thinking or unclear expression; lacking rigour or discipline; sloppy.

1941 Auden *New Year Let.* II. 37 All vague idealistic art..Is up his alley, and his pigeon The woozier species of religion. **1961** *Catholic Gaz.* May 129/2 To Dickens, Christmas meant a debauch of vague and woozy sentiment. **1970** Auden in *New Yorker* 21 Feb. 118/1 Like Ruskin, he can at times write sentences which I would call 'woozy'; that is to say, too dependent upon some private symbolism of his own to be altogether comprehensible to others. **1971** *Daily Tel.* 15 Mar. 13/4 One wonders if it is not simply the drink that has made so many Irish writers bury their poetic insights beneath so much that is garrulous, maudlin and whoozy. **1975** *New Yorker* 3 Feb. 84/2 There are gaps in the plot and woozy lapses in time. **1977** *Rolling Stone* 24 Mar. 41/2 She supports the old male stereotype of woman as overwhelmingly physical, instinctual, and her writing is too woozy for me. **1977** *N.Y. Rev. Bks.* 9 June 16/3 The other poem of 1939 [by Auden], with its 'affirming flame', is woozy too. **1980** *Times Lit. Suppl.* 25 Apr. 470/5 A level of woozy tautology.

Hence **woo·zily** *adv.*, **woo·ziness.**

a **1911** D. G. Phillips *Susan Lenox* (1917) I. xxi. 395 'Shut up!' cried the drunken man... He caught them each by an arm, stared woozily at Etla. **1924** *Black Mask* Nov. 48/2 This thing had fallen on me while my nerves were ragged from three days of boozing... [Now] my wooziness had passed. **1937** *Ibid.* Jan. 23/2, I shook my head woozily. **1937** Auden *Let.* in Auden & MacNeice *Lett. from Iceland* 221 Landscape's so dull if you haven't Lawrence's wonderful wooziness. **1967** *Listener* 9 Feb. 193/2 Staring woozily at a wine flask. **1977** C. Isherwood *Christopher & his Kind* xii. 181 Much of what Christopher called Wystan's wooziness was essentially religious in context. **1984** *Observer* 19 Feb. 25/5 Later in life she more stubbornly shut herself off from the world's demands behind the defences of deafness, bad English and Benedictine-fuelled wooziness.

wop (wɒp), *sb.*[1] and *a.* *slang* (orig. *U.S.*). Also **Wop.** [Origin uncertain; perh. ad. It. dial. *guappo* bold, showy, ruffian, f. Sp. *guapo* bold, dandy, f. L. *vappa* sour wine, worthless fellow.] **A.** *sb.* **a.** An Italian or other southern European, esp. as an immigrant or foreign visitor (see also quot. 1914). Now considered *offensive.*

[**1912** A. Train *Courts, Criminals & Camorra* ix. 232 There is a society of criminal young men in New York City... They are known by the euphonious name of 'Waps' or 'Jacks'. These are young Italian-Americans who allow themselves to be supported by one or two women... They form one variety of the many gangs that infest the city.] **1914** Jackson & Hellyer *Vocab. Criminal Slang* 88 *Wop*, noun. Used principally in the east. An ignorant person; a foreigner; an impossible character. .. Example: 'You couldn't find a jitney with a search warrant in this bunch of wops.' **1915** Wodehouse *Psmith, Journalist* xix. 138 He's a wop, kid... A wop. A dago... An Italian. **1924** E. Hemingway *In our Time* 17 Wops, said Boyle, I can tell wops a mile off. **1930** G. B. Shaw *Apple Cart* II. 78 *Lysistrata.* What they call an American is only a wop pretending to be a Pilgrim Father. He is no more Uncle Jonathan than you are John Bull. *Magnus.* Yes: we live in a world of wops, all melting into one another. **1940** N. Mitford *Pigeon Pie* i. 7 Luke's Italian was far more affected than that of any native wop. **1942** *R.A.F. Jrnl.* 13 June 26 The pilots.. suggested that the 'Wops were yellow' or that they could not 'take it through cloud'. **1952** E. F. Davies *Illyrian Venture* ii. 26 We had breakfast in the mess tent, waited on by a cheerful wop. **1973** 'I. Drummond' *Jaws of Watchdog* ii. 26 Sandro dived into the pool... 'You great fat clumsy Wop,' said Jenny, 'you've put my cigarette out.'

b. The Italian language.

1937 [see *for all I know* s.v. *know *v.* 11 g]. **1938** E. Pound *Let.* 6 May (1971) 313 'Sardinia is Barbagia' don't seem either English or Wop. **1982** A. Melville-Ross *Trigger* xx.225 There's a lot of chat in Wop which I doesn't understand.

B. *adj.* Italian.

1938 E. Pound *Let.* 8 Jan. (1971) 303 'Praedis': I don't care how you spell your wop painters. **1940** [see *kike]. **1941** C. E. Milburn *Diary* 15 Feb. (1979) 83 We have dropped parachutists in Italy... A very nice surprise for our 'Wop' enemy! **1955** E. Waugh *Officers & Gentlemen* 326 You'll find her full of wop prisoners. **1983** S. F. X. Dean *It can't be my Grave* iv. 64 Are you telling me, you Wop son of a bitch, that I can't get into my father's lift?

wop (wɒp), *sb.*[2] *R.A.F. slang.* [Acronym from *w*(*ireless op*(*erator* (cf. *op[3] 2 b).] A radio operator.

1939 *Airman's Gaz.* Dec., You have a choice of three.. trades—..W.O.M.,..W.E.M.,..and the W/Op. which rude people twist into Wop (most unfairly). **1957** R. Barker *Ship-Busters* iv. 70 Wireless operator/air gunners ..most of the wop/A.G.s..came straight from gunnery school.

wops, dial. and joc. var. Wasp *sb.* in Dict. and Suppl.

Worcester. Add: **1.** Also *ellipt.* for *Worcester sauce.*

1889 J. K. Jerome *Three Men in Boat* ii. 22 If Harris's eyes fill with tears,..it is because Harris has been eating raw onions, or has put too much Worcester over his chop. **1981** T. Heald *Murder at Moose Jaw* ix. 103 A straight tomato juice with a liberal splashing of Worcester.

2. Used *attrib.* (with *Pearmain* or *apple*) and *absol.* to designate an early, slightly conical red-skinned eating apple belonging to a variety introduced to cultivation about 1875 by Richard Smith, a Worcester nurseryman.

1877 *Garden* 13 Oct. 344/1 Worcester Pearmain Apple. —Of this beautifully coloured, fully flavoured new Apple, Mr. Richard Smith, of Worcester, has sent us samples. **1929** E. A. Bunyard *Anat. Dessert* 6 The really ripe Worcester has character..and the Raspberry flavour distinctive. **1958** *Listener* 27 Nov. 903/1 Four medium-sized Worcester Pearmain apples. **1936** H. V. Taylor *Apples of England* iii. 43 Worcester Pearmain..became the most important of the commercial early dessert apples. **1982** R. Holles *Sun Blight* i. 6 She walked along ..inspecting the piles of Worcester apples. *Ibid.* ix. 98 In the Portobello Road ..mounds of apples grinned at him, Worcesters, Granny Smiths, Golden Delicious.

Worcesterberry (wu·stəɹberi). Also **worcester-.** [f. prec. + Berry *sb.*[1]] A small black gooseberry of the North American species *Ribes divaricatum*, once believed to be a hybrid of the blackcurrant and the gooseberry and sold as such by a Worcester nurseryman.

1923 *Amat. Gardening* 27 Oct. p. ix/3 (Advt.), Worcesterberry. Cross between gooseberry and black currant. Fruiting trees. 3/- each. Richard Smith & Co... Worcester. **1926** *Observer* 5 Sept. 9/2 New fruits, such as the logan and most excellent worcesterberry, multiply almost yearly. **1969** *Oxf. Bk. Food Plants* 80/2 The so-called 'Worcesterberry'..seems first to have been sold by a nurseryman in Worcester who thought it was a black currant gooseberry hybrid. **1980** *Amat. Gardening* 25 Oct. 20/2 If spraying fails, or if you do not like doing it, why not try growing the Worcesterberry instead?

Worcestershire. (Earlier example of *Worcestershire sauce.*)

1843 *Naval & Military Gaz.* 1 Apr. 208/2 (Advt.), Lea and Perrin's 'Worcestershire Sauce', prepared from a recipe of a nobleman in the county.

word, *sb.* Add: **I. 1. d.** *too —— for words:* —— to an extent that cannot adequately be described. *colloq.*

1913 *Vanity Fair* Nov. 65 New York is beginning to look too smart and clean for words. **1928** E. O'Neill *Strange Interlude* VIII. 289 But for Gordon to..propose marriage — it's too idiotic for words! **1937** J. Mercer *Too Marvellous for Words* (song), You're just too marvellous, too marvellous for words.

2. c. Also *a word in your ear* (colloq.): a brief message for you in confidence.

1599 Shaks. *Much Ado* IV. ii. 27 Come you hither, sirrah; a word in your ear, sir. **1838** Dickens *Let.* 25 Jan. (1965) I. 360 A word in your ear. Macready *objected* to Talfourd's play. **1980** *Daily Tel.* 9 May 18 Salome and Kumba [*sc.* two gorillas] would like a word in your ear.

5. *to have words* (examples); also *to have a word.*

1777 W. Mawhood *Diary* 24 Aug. in *Publ. Cath. Rec. Soc.* (1956) L. 117 Came to Town to breakfast had words with Mrs. Mawhood. **1839** Dickens *Nicholas Nickleby* xlviii. 480 'We were a very happy little company, Johnson,' said poor Crummles. 'You and I never had a word.' **1901** 'Zack' *White Cottage* 37 Have you and Mark had wuds? **1910** King George V in H. Nicolson *George V* (1952) vii. 105, I have lost my best friend & the best of fathers. I never had a word with him in his life. **1935** Z. N. Hurston *Mules & Men* II. vi. 287 Celestine is not mad any more about the word we had last week.

6. a. (Further examples in *sing.* without article.)

1948 'H. Green' *Concluding* 205 Word had gone round that at last they were engaged. **1958** M. L. King *Stride toward Freedom* iii. 45 The arrest..was becoming public knowledge. Word of it spread around the community like uncontrolled fire. **1983** *Times* 16 Sept. 16/2 Word is the Government is offering a fixed price for small investors. **1984** *Times* 14 June 22/2 Word in the market suggests Mr Holmes a'Court may be prepared to sell on his stake.

b. Delete Now *rare* or *Obs.* and substitute: Now usu. in phr. *the word is that* (..). Chiefly *U.S.*

1963 R. Jessup *Cincinnati Kid* iv. 55 Money is beginning to show for you against The Man, Kid... The word is..that you're good enough to take Lancey, if anybody can. **1965** P. O'Donnell *Modesty Blaise* vii. 82, I know of him. The word is that he's good. **1982** P. Lovesey *False Inspector Dew* IV. 153 The word is that the captain will be speaking to us.

II. 12. a. Also *four-letter word*: see *four-letter* adj. s.v. *four C. 2.

f. *Telegr.* Any of the sequences of a prescribed fixed number of characters (including a space) in a telegraphic message that has been coded or redivided for transmission.

1897 J. Nicolson *Telegraphic Signals* ii. 20 Artificial letter-grouping, mathematically called 'words', or permutations,..is referred to in a pamphlet by the French cryptographist, M. le Marquis de Viaris..as a substitute for telegraphic codes composed of dictionary words. **1911** *Encycl. Brit.* XXVI. 521/2 An experimental printer constructed about 1908 by the British Post Office, operated ..at the rate of 210 words (1260 letters) per minute. **1976** R. N. Renton *Telegraphy* i. 14/2 The 'telegraph word' is taken as an arbitrary 5-letter word with one letter-space, making six characters in all.

g. *Math.* An ordered sequence of generators of a group.

1952 S. C. Kleene *Introd. Metamath.* xiii. 382 A finite sequence of zero or more (occurrences of) the letters, we call a word. **1971** G. Higman in Powell & Higman *Finite Simple Groups* vi. 212 Any word in the n_i and their inverses determines a partial map of the set of equivalence classes into itself. **1972** M. Kline *Math. Thought* xlix. 1141 There may be relations among the generators, and these would be of the form $F_i(A_i) = 1$; that is, a word or combination of words equals the identity element of the group. **1981** *Sci. Amer.* Mar. 26/1 A lovely 'pretty pattern' called the 6-*U* state..can be reached from the start position by way of the word $L'R^2F'L'B'UBLFRU'RLR_8F_8U_8R_8$.

h. *Computers.* A consecutive string of bits that can be transferred and stored as a unit (see quot. 1969); *machine word*, a word of the length appropriate for a particular fixed word-length computer.

1946 [see *write *v.* 3 h]. **1948** *Proc. R. Soc.* A. CXCV. 272 Certain of these numbers or 'words' are read, one after another, as orders. **1954** *Computers & Automation* Dec. 16/1 *Machine word*, a unit of information of a standard number of characters, which a machine regularly handles in each register. **1964** F. L. Westwater *Electronic Computers* ix. 140 The basic unit of internal storage is called a 'word', which may contain either instructions or data. **1969** P. B. Jordain *Condensed Computer Encycl.* 566 Computers with words less than 9 bits long call the words bytes, characters, or digits (decimal). **1970** A. Cameron et al. *Computers & O.E. Concordances* 58 It is heavily dependent upon fitting *x* number of characters into each machine word, a problem we cannot get around easily. **1980** C. S. French *Computer Sci.* vi. 24 The number of bits in each location (word), known as the word length will depend on the make and model of computer.

III. 15. b. (Earlier example.)

1841 Mrs. Gaskell *Lett.* (1966) 44 My word! authorship brings them in a pretty penny.

19. Also *word of mouth* sb. phr., oral communication, oral publicity.

1934 in Webster. **1951** B. Schulberg *Disenchanted* vi. 67 He tells everyone..that you're one of his favorite American authors and..that kind of word of mouth ain't bad. **1967** B. WHITAKER *Of Mice & Murder* xiii. 147, 'I wonder how he heard it was for sale.' 'Word of mouth, I suppose.' **1980** 'D. KAVANAGH' *Duffy* iii. 43 The only way to get successful..was to work at being really efficient and then hope for word-of-mouth to back you up. **1984** A. BROOKNER *Hotel du Lac* i. 14 The only publicity from which the hotel could not distance itself was the word of mouth recommendations of patrons of long standing.

20. b. *word by word*: also *spec.*, in alphabetization; opp. *letter by letter* (see *LETTER *sb.* 1 c).

1938 L. M. HARROD *Librarians' Gloss.* 12 There are two methods [of alphabetization] in use: 1, 'letter by letter'; 2, 'word by word', or 'nothing before something'. In the former method 'Newton' *precedes*, in the latter it *follows*, 'New York'. **1951** *British Standard Alphabetical Arrangement* (B.S.I.) 6 Items having the same first word shall be arranged in the alphabetical order of the second word, those with no second word standing first. Similarly those having two words in common are arranged in the alphabetical order of their third word and so on. The whole group thus arranged shall precede any word alphabetically qualified to follow the first word of the group. (This is known as the 'word-by-word' or 'nothing-before-something' principle.) **1979** *Amer. Speech 1976* LI. 149 This dictionary uses word-by-word rather than letter-by-letter alphabetizing.

IV. 29. a. Simple attrib., as *word-boundary, -break, -combination, -division, -element, -end, -ending, -family, -form, -function, -game* (also *fig.*), *-idea, -memory* (earlier example), *-music* (examples), *-order* (earlier and later examples), *-pattern, -patterning, -position, -sound, -status, -stem, -store, -stress, -structure, -study, -taboo, -tone, -usage, -value*; (with agent-n. or the like), as *word-artist, -merchant, -musician, -smith* (later examples); *word-smithing*; also *word-based, -like* adjs. **b.** Instrumental, as *word-drunk* adj. **c.** Objective, as *word-coiner*; *word-finding, -hunting* (later example), *-making* (earlier examples; see also sense d below), *-setting* (SET *v.* 73), *-twisting* sbs.; *word-choice, -creation, -formation* (earlier example); also *word-formational, -formative* adjs. **d. word association** *Psychol.*, a psychodiagnostic technique based on analysis of a person's reactions to the presentation of stimulus words, esp. with regard to the (subconscious) contents and type of the immediate associations formed, reaction time, etc.; more generally, the associations connected with certain words; freq. *attrib.*; **word-base** *Philol.*, the simple word from which its derivatives and inflected forms arise; a root morpheme, etc.; **word-blind** *a.* (earlier example); **word-category** *Linguistics* = **word-class*; **word-class** *Linguistics* [cf. G. *wortklasse*], a category of words of similar form or function; esp. applied to parts of speech; **word-count,** a statistical study of *word frequency* (see below); **word-field** *Linguistics*, a group of lexical items seen as associated in meaning because occurring in similar contexts; **word-final** *a.*, occurring at the end of a word; also as *sb.*, a letter or sound occurring in this position; hence **word-finally** *adv.*; cf. *word-initial* adj. below; **word frequency,** the relative frequency with which a word is used in a given text or corpus; **word geography,** the study of the regional distribution of words and phrases, or a book treating of this; hence **word-geographical** *a.*; **word-hoard** (earlier example as a conscious Anglo-Saxonism); recently in general use, the words used by a person or group of people, vocabulary; also, a source or store of words; **word-index,** a list of the words used by a given author or in a given work (or corpus) with reference to the passages in which they occur, but without quotations (cf. CONCORDANCE *sb.* 6 b); **word-initial** *a.*, occurring at the beginning of a word; also as *sb.*, a letter or sound occurring in this position; hence **word-initially** *adv.*; **word-internally** *adv.*, = *word-medially* below; **word-ladder,** a puzzle in which a word has to be converted into another of equal length by being taken through a series of word-changes, each word differing by one letter from the last; also called *doublets*; **word length** *Computers*, the number of bits, digits, etc., in a word (sense 12 g above); **word-magic** *Anthropol.*, magic thought to be exerted by the knowledge or use of the proper name or term for something, or the supposed magical property residing in such a name; also *transf.*; **word-making and word-taking,** a game played with lettered cards, app. a forerunner of the modern Lexicon or Scrabble; **word mark,** (*a*) a real or invented word used as a trade mark; (*b*) *Computers*, a bit that takes a different value according as the character containing it does or does not begin (or end) a word; a character containing such a bit; **word-medial** *a.*, occurring in the middle of a word; hence **word-medially** *adv.*; **word method** *Educ.*, a method of teaching pupils to read in which they are taught to recognize words as complete units before learning the letters or syllables which compose them; the 'look-and-say' method (see *LOOK *v.* 47); **word-painted** *a.*, (*a*) decorated or adorned with words; (*b*) 'painted' or described vividly in words; **word-pair,** a pair of words resembling each other in sound or form; **word-palatogram** (see quot. 1948); **word-picture** (earlier example); **word-play** (earlier and later examples); **word problem** *Math.*, the problem of determining whether two different products are equal, or two sequences of operations are equivalent; **word processing** [cf. G. *textverarbeitung* text processing], the storing and organizing of texts by electronic means, *spec.* by a word processor; hence (as a back-formation) **word-process** *v. trans.*, to edit, produce, etc., using a word processor; **word-processed** *ppl. a.*; **word processor,** a keyboard device incorporating a computer programmed to store, amend, and format text that is keyed in, a printer to print it automatically, and often also a screen to display it; **word recognition** *Educ.*, the process or faculty of perceiving words in reading and identifying them with the ideas they represent; **word-salad,** a type of speech indicative of advanced schizophrenia in which random words and phrases are mixed together unintelligibly; also *fig.*; **word-sign,** something used to represent a word; *spec.* a graphic character representing a complete word; esp., in Egyptian hieroglyphics, etc. = *LOGOGRAM 2 b; **word-stock,** (in Dict., sense 29 a) the sum of words available to a language, dialect, etc.; vocabulary; also *fig.*; (later examples); **word-symbol,** a word used as a sign or symbol; *spec.* = *LOGOGRAM 2 b; **word time** *Computers*, the time between the reading of the first bits of successive words; **word-type,** (*a*) a word used to symbolize or represent an idea; (*b*) *Philos.* (see quot. 1936); (*c*) a word forming a distinct item in a vocabulary; **word-watch** *v. intr.*, to observe linguistic usage, esp. with regard to changes and innovations; also **word-watcher; word-watching** *vbl. sb.*; **word-wrap** [cf. *WRAP-AROUND *sb.* 3] (see quot. 1982); so **word-wrapping** *vbl. sb.*; **word-writing,** Bloomfield's term for ideographic writing.

1933 DYLAN THOMAS *Let.* Sept. (1966) 20 Mr. Neuburg has payed you a..compliment. 'One of the most exquisite word-artists of our day.' **1945** C. BAX *Vintage Verse* III. 95 This faultless word-artist [*sc.* Milton]..was buried in St. Giles's, Cripplegate. **1910** *Rev. Neurol. & Psychiatry* VIII. 641 (*title*) The practical value of the word-association method in the treatment of the psychoneuroses. **1918** M. D. EDER *Jung's Stud. in Word-Association* p. v, We owe to Dr. Jung..the application of the association method to *unconscious* mental processes... These studies in word association have now acquired a permanent place in the historical development of this [*sc.* psychoanalytical] theory. **1946** A. CHRISTIE *Hollow* xxvi. 221 'What is there about that that interests you so, M. Poirot?..' 'Association—a point of the psychology.' 'Word association? Horse and cart. Rocking horse?' **1952** C. P. BLACKER *Eugenics: Galton & After* 52 Galton also tried out on himself an elaborate system of word-association tests. His method was different..from that later popularized by C. G. Jung, but the underlying idea was the same. **1971** J. ELSOM *Theatre outside London* vii. 126 These discussions were linked with word-association games. **1977** *Canad. Jrnl. Linguistics 1976* XXI. II. 200 'Navaho word associations', which examines the role of grammatical form-classes in word association tests, has no subject under the age of seventeen. **1931** C. L'E. EWEN *Hist. Surnames* xiv. 360 The root of Skr. and Pers. *yuvan* 'young' may well be one of the word-bases of Ewan, Owen [etc.]. **1956** *Essays & Studies* IX. 98 The appearance of the same word-base in various forms (polyptoton): (al) ar knitt & onyd in this onyng, & made holy in this holyhede. **1964** J. VACHEK in D. Abercrombie et al. *Daniel Jones* 195 Some ModE affixes (especially the word-formative ones) are..more easily separable from their word-bases than others. **1963** J. LYONS *Structural Semantics* ii. 11 A word-based grammar seems to be more satisfactory than a morpheme-based grammar for the description of languages of the 'inflecting' type. **1890** W. JAMES *Princ. Psychol.* I. ii. 55 If this order of association be ingrained and habitual in that individual, injury to his *visual* centres will make him not only word-blind, but aphasic as well. **1933** L. BLOOMFIELD *Language* xxiii. 419 At the time of the loss of *-n*, the language did not distinguish word-boundaries in the manner of present-day English. **1978** *Language* LIV. 21 The well-known word-boundary phenomena of French, such as liaison, elision, and *h*-aspiré. **1968** J. R. BIGGS *Basic Typogr.* 41/1 Spacing is consistent but the right-hand margin is left irregular. This does not always reduce word breaks very much. **1980** B. CRUTCHLEY *To be a Printer* 55 Bad word-breaks at the end of lines and similar shoddiness. **1938** B. L. WHORF in *Language* XIV. 275 *Word Category*; a category (overt or covert or mixed) which delimits one of a primary hierarchy of word classes each of limited membership (not coterminous with entire vocabulary), e.g. the familiar 'parts of speech' of Indo-European and many other languages, vs. *Modulus Category*; one which modifies, either any word of the vocabulary, or any word already allocated to a delimited class, e.g. voices, aspects, cases. **1964** J. VACHEK in D. Abercrombie et al. *Daniel Jones* 195 The comparative suffix *-er* does not imply the change of the word-category of the basic word, while the agentive *-er* necessarily does so. **1941** E. BLUNDEN *Thomas Hardy* xi. 236 An innovation of word-choice. **1914** L. BLOOMFIELD *Introd. Study Lang.* iv. 108 (*title*) Word-classes. *Ibid.* iv. 109 Other word classes which are not expressed by formational similarity. **1924** O. JESPERSEN *Philos. Gram.* iv. 61 We have a great many words which can belong to one word-class only: *admiration, society, life* can only be substantives [etc.]. **1953** C. E. BAZELL *Linguistic Form* vi. 76 The so-called parts of speech (still more inappropriately word-classes) are classes of stem-morpheme. **1973** *Computers & Humanities* VII. 159 Lyne's resolution of word class problems (is *y* an adverb or a pronoun?) uses a rather complex algorithm. **1935** *Vanity Fair* Nov. 38/1 There appears to be little leakage of their vernacular into even so ambitious a word-coiner as *Variety*. **1981** *Verbatim* Spring 14/2 Since I started publishing *Verbatim*, these and other word-coiners have been sending their creations to me, pressing for recognition. **1864** W. D. WHITNEY in *Ann. Rep. Bd. Regents Smithsonian Inst. 1863* 108 The conditions of that ancient period, and the degree in which they could quicken the now sluggish processes of word-combination and formation are beyond our ken. **1932** A. GARDINER *Theory of Speech & Lang.* iii. 158 Syntax..may be defined as the study of the forms both of the sentence itself and of all free word-combinations which enter into it. **1930** *Proc. Brit. Acad.* XVI. 147 There are prejudices, preferences, analyses, comparisons, statistics, verse-tests, word-counts, sense of style, poetical feelings, intuitions—but we must not call all this evidence. **1937** PALMER & HORNBY *Thousand-Word Eng.* 11 The compiler has recourse to statistics of word-frequency; he organizes a 'word-count'. **1957** *Eng. Lang. Teaching* (British Council) XII. 1.10 There are valuable word-counts which give a clear picture of the relative importance of specific words in our total lexicon. **1980** *Amer. Speech 1977* LII. 7 A computerized word count. **1884** *Amer. Jrnl. Philol.* July 187 That species of word-creation commonly designated as parasynthetic. **1952** W. D. JACOBS *William Barnes, Linguist* 7 Are there means of word-creation and actual words themselves in the writings of Barnes by which English might well profit? **1914** L. BLOOMFIELD in *Trans. Amer. Philol. Assoc.* XLV. 66 We have many instances of the writing of uneducated people..in which the word-division is entirely wrong. **1929** K. SISAM in *S.P.E. Tract* XXXIII. 441 A respectably printed American book..is not noticeably different in [typographical] word-division from a contemporary English book. **1976** *Classical Q.* XXVI. 95 His word-divisions are probably his own and without any authority. **1912** KIPLING *Diversity of Creatures* (1917) 23 Word-drunk people. **1964** *Punch* 15 Apr. 575/1 The word-drunk Don Adriano. **1928** O. JESPERSEN *Internat. Lang.* II. 121 In Novial the elements are separate words, in Esp[eranto]—Ido inseparable word-elements. **1964** C. BARBER *Ling. Change Present-Day Eng.* iv. 78 These [new learned words] are usually formed from Latin or Greek word-elements. **1965** W. S. ALLEN *Vox Latina* i. 35 It [s] is not voiced between vowels or at word-end as in English *roses*. **1878** W. BARNES *Outl. Eng. Speechcraft* 83 (*heading*) The power of the word-endings [*sc.* suffixes]. **1966** J. DERRICK *Teaching English to Immigrants* vi. 210 Meaning is conveyed.. with a reduced form of grammar—word-endings are left off, structural words omitted, etc. **1926** FOWLER *Mod. Eng. Usage* 553/2 A phonetically consistent method is in English peculiarly hard to reconcile with the keeping together of word families. **1978** *Language* LIV. 237/1 Finding translation equivalents and association of morphological word-families. **1952** H. BASILIUS in *Word* VIII. 103 Jost Trier's study of the German word-fields relating to the concept reason, its powers and qualities. **1965** *Amer. Speech* XL. 62 *Job* is not identical with *Arbeit*; it stands at the lowest level of this word-field. **1918** A. W. ARON in C. Hockett *Leonard Bloomfield Anthol.* (1970) 58 These variations in word-initial [in Irish] do depend on the phonetic character of the original preceding word-final. **1949** E. A. NIDA *Morphology* (ed. 2) ii. 24 Only the word-final tones are indicated. **1977** G. P. DELAHUNTY in D. Ó Muirithe *Eng. Lang. in Ireland* 132 Devoicing of word-final voiced consonants. **1983** *Word* XXXIV. 149 We find that in modern Swabian they all occur in word-final position. **1965** *Canad. Jrnl. Linguistics* Fall 64 Those [vowel segments] which occur both before consonants and word-finally. **1978** *Language* LIV. 443 High vowels are dropped after heavy stems word-finally. **1955** R. JAKOBSON in Saporta & Bastian *Psycholinguistics* (1961) 423/2 The more difficulties he has with word-finding in the proper sense of this neuropsychiatric term; that is, difficulties with spontaneous selection of words. **1874** H. BENDALL tr. *A. Schleicher's Compar. Gram.* 3 The Semitic, which is not akin to the Indo-European, has more word-forms. **1952** *Mind* LXI. 239 As society discovers.. that judgments imputing responsibility..are never justified, the word-form 'responsibility' comes to change its meaning. **1967** D. G. HAYS *Introd. Computational Linguistics* ii. 21 The plan is to record, before each word form, the number of cells it occupies. **1856** W. D. WHITNEY in *Jrnl. Amer. Oriental Soc.* V. 197 The work..exhibits.. the phenomena of the agreement and disagreement of the Greek and Sanskrit accentuation, throughout the departments of declension, conjugation and word-formation. **1948** L. SPITZER *Linguistics & Lit. Hist.* ii. 81 Thus Cervantes has expressed his perspectivistic vision in a word-formational pattern of the Renaissance reserved for hybrids. **1979** *Dictionaries* I. 18 Lexicographers very often assume a kind of word-formational capacity or knowledge when they list derivatives as run-on entries. **1964** Word-formative [see *word-base* above]. **1928** B. Q. MORGAN *German Frequency Word Bk.* p. ix, It was our original intention to publish the figures for word frequency, group frequency, and basic frequency. **1951** *Archivum Linguisticum* III. II. 123 (*heading*) Word-frequency in Norwegian. **1974** BEDFORD & DILLIGAN *Concordance Poems Alexander Pope* II. 669/1 A six-page analytic table showing word-frequency distribution and the ratio between each word and the number of its occurrences. **1912** L. BLOOMFIELD in C. Hockett *Leonard Bloomfield Anthol.* (1970) 35 The relation of word-form to word-function. **1910** R. B. STERN *Neighborhood Entertainments* vi. 263 (*heading*) Some word games [describes anagrams, logomachy, etc.]. **1922** S. LEWIS *Babbitt* xviii. 227 Word-games in which you were an Adjective or a Quality. **1929** A. C. S. ASHMORE (*title*) Word games and word puzzles. **1934** *Mind* XLIII. 117 Those who are reluctant to regard philosophy as mere mystery-mongering or as an academic word-game. **1953** E. COXHEAD *Midlanders* vi. 143, I never could do word-games or cross-words. **1975** R. LEWIS *Double Take* iv. 124 We aren't here to play word games... If this is the way you want to conduct the discussion we might as well call it off. **1974** PASSMORE & ROBSON *Compan. Med. Stud.* III. xxxiv. 8/1 Wittgenstein described speech as a 'word game', implying that language follows defined rules similar to those which govern sports. **1962** A. MCINTOSH in Davis & Wrenn *Eng. & Medieval Stud.* 240 Word-geographical criteria..may well therefore turn out to provide the only practicable line of attack. **1921** E. C. ROEDDER in *Jrnl. Eng. & Ger. Philol.* XX. 183 The finding and fixing of the isolectic lines is a task of word geography. **1949** H. KURATH (*title*) A word geography of the Eastern United States. **1980** *Amer. Speech* LV. 195 Its lexicology is sketched here as a development of conventional word geography. **1869** W. BARNES *Early England & Saxon-English* 130 A Hoard, as herd, is a kind of gathering of any kind of things, as..Word-hoard—Vocabulary. **1961** WEBSTER *Pref.* 6a/1 Books consulted in the Springfield City Library whose librarians have..given the editorial staff..access to its large and valuable word-hoard. **1966** *Listener* 24 Nov. 779/2 Thomas was immensely proud of his bulging word-hoard. **1975** P. FUSSELL *Great War & Mod. Memory* (1977) ii. 49 *Lousy with*, meaning *full of*,..entered the colloquial word-hoard around 1915. **1935** A. HUXLEY *Let.* 13 Jan. (1969) 389 Nothing is more inclined to keep me awake than word-hunting. **1902** E. W. SCRIPTURE *Elem. Exper. Phonetics* x. 150 A word-idea should be learned as parts of various courses of thought in order to form the necessary language associations. **1922** D. H. LAWRENCE *Aaron's Rod* xiii. 175 Even his deepest ideas were not word-ideas, his very thoughts were not composed of words and ideal concepts. **1937** M. L. HANLEY (*title*) Word index to James Joyce's *Ulysses*. *Ibid.* p. iii, In 1931..I had made a word index and partial concordance to the B-Text of *Piers Plowman*. **1960** *Amer. Speech* XXXV. 215 A lamentable deficiency is the lack of a full word index. **1918** Word-initial [see *word-final* above]. **1926** L. BLOOMFIELD in Saporta & Bastian *Psycholinguistics* (1961) 29/2 English word-initial [st-]. **1949** E. A. NIDA *Morphology* (ed. 2) ii. 16 Word-initial prevowel glottal stops. **1981** *N. & Q.* Oct. 398/1 A large number of unexplained intersubstitutions of *c* and *g* in word-initial position. **1973** A. H. SOMMERSTEIN *Sound Pattern Anc. Gr.* iii. 103 Not all rules with left-hand environments can apply word-initially. **1964** D. WARD in D. Abercrombie et al. *Daniel Jones* 385 The substitution of corresponding voiceless phonemes for all voiced phonemes except sonants in word-final position and word-internally before voiceless consonants. **1945** *N. & Q.* 6 Oct. 151/1 In the amusement sections of newspapers it [*sc.* the game or puzzle called 'Doublets'] is usually referred to as 'Word-Ladder'. **1958** *Birmingham Mail* 27 Jan. 6/7 Today's puzzle is for your shortest Word Ladder from *Head* to *Body*. It can be done in five easy steps without using any unusual words. **1982** D. PARLETT *Penguin Bk. Word Games* 98 Word Ladders. **1951** *Proc. IRE* XXXIX. 277/2 Digital computers commonly use a fixed word length (that is, a fixed number of characters) which is a characteristic of each computer. **1970** O. DOPPING *Computers & Data Processing* vi. 98 The word length is usually chosen in such a way that a numeric operand or result in general can be stored in one memory cell with 'normal' precision. **1960** J. B. CARROLL in Saporta & Bastian *Psycholinguistics* (1961) 338/2 A single word or word-like utterance. **1923** OGDEN & RICHARDS *Meaning of Meaning* ii. 42 The earlier writers are full of the relics of primitive word-magic. To classify things is to name them..to know their names is to have power over their souls. **1938** S. CHASE *Tyranny of Words* iv. 37 Here, to follow Malinowski, we note the seeds of word magic, in which *the name gives power over the person or thing it signifies*. **1960** H. READ *Forms of Things Unknown* vii. 121 The name he chooses is magically apt, and in word-magic we must acknowledge the primordial intensive aspect of poetry. *a* **1856** J. STODDART *Glossology* (1858) x. 231 *Onomatopoeia*. The literal signification of the term..is nothing more than 'word-making'. **1867** W. D. WHITNEY *Lang. & Study of Lang.* 116 All word-making by combination..is closely analogous with phrase-making. **1935** *Encycl. Sports, Games & Pastimes* 396/1 The games played with these [cardboard] letters are very numerous. Word making and word taking may be mentioned first. **1952** G. RAVERAT *Period Piece* xii. 243 Our chief intellectual exercise [*c.* 1900] was the Letter Game; Word-making and word-taking. **1980** L. LEWIS *Private Life of Country House* ii. 20 My mother.. scattered on the floor the cardboard letter squares from a game called 'Wordmaking and Wordtaking'. **1902** *Encycl. Brit.* XXXIII. 387/1 The registration of 'word marks' was first provided for by the Trade Marks Act, 1883. In that statute, however, clause (d) read 'a fancy word or words not in common use'. **1964** T. W. MCRAE *Impact of Computers on Accounting* i. 11 The programmer then looks at the data..and divides up the storage locations as required by setting a 'wordmark' in the far right-hand position of each variable-length storage word. **1969** P. B. JORDAIN *Condensed Computer Encycl.* 567 Each instruction must begin with a word mark [in a variable word-length computer]. **1976** *Century of Trade Marks* (Patent Office) i. 1/2 These were early instances of word marks, though usually in conventional form—for example, CATIM (Cati manu: from the hand of Cato), and OFALBIN (officina Albini: the workshop of Albinus)—whereas earlier marks had been almost invariably devices or ideographic symbols. **1980** J. FRATES *Introd. Computer* vi. 165 The storage location of the last piece of data will store a word mark in addition to the character to indicate to the computer that it has reached the end of that particular item of data. **1949** E. A. NIDA *Morphology* (ed. 2) 293 (*heading*) Reduction of word-medial consonant clusters. **1963** J. LYONS *Structural Semantics* iv. 68 There is an opposition.., in word-initial and word-medial position, between the voiced and the voiceless plosives. **1968** *Language* XLIV. 532 A variety of further clusters occurred word-medially. **1890** W. JAMES *Princ. Psychol.* I. xvi. 684 'Ataxic' and 'amnesic' aphasia, 'word-deafness', and 'associative aphasia' are all practical losses of word-memory. **1920** *Punch* 7 Jan. 9/2 The word-merchant [*sc.* a journalist] was laughing at us all the time. **1977** *Grimsby Even. Tel.* 14 May 7/4 He [*sc.* Malcolm Muggeridge] is the best word merchant of our time. [**1879** *First Infant Reader* in *Mod. School Reader Series* p. 2 The experience of many years has convinced us that a judicious combination of the Word and Phonic methods of teaching Children to read is the best.] **1932** in E. Blyton *Mod. Teaching in Infant School* v. 62 The Word Method, or the Look-and-say Method. **1981** D. ROWNTREE *Dict. Educ.* 350 *Word method*, teaching a pupil to read by getting him to recognize whole words right from the start. **1855** GEO. ELIOT in *Westm. Rev.* Oct. 596 As long as the English language is spoken, the word-music of Tennyson must charm the ear. **1895** G. B. SHAW *Our Theatres in Nineties* (1932) I. 77 M. Maeterlinck's fragile word-music. **1962** *Observer* 22 Apr. 23/4 The ailing cause of Shakespeare-designed-to-be-read-as-word-music. **1895** 'MARK TWAIN' in *N. Amer. Rev.* July 11 This is [James Fenimore] Cooper. He was not a word-musician. His ear was satisfied with the *approximate* word. **1892** H. SWEET *New Eng. Gram.* I. §113. 42 We find the same grammatical relation expressed..sometimes by word-order. **1958** *Aspects of Translation* 35 Inflexions and grammar impose a more rigorous word-order on the French language than on English. **1965** O. FUNKE in *English Studies* Feb. 58 The transition from paradigmatic to syntagmatic (prepositional or word-order) expression. **1973** *Archivum Linguisticum* IV. 28 The comparative fixity of word-order relative to grammatical function is the conditional par excellence for the supposed superfluity of gender distinctions. **1870** J. G. WHITTIER in *Atlantic* Apr. 467 Not by the page word-painted Let life be banned or sainted. **1937** 'C. CAUDWELL' *Illusion & Reality* v. 100 The word-painted lands of the nightingale, of the Grecian urn, of Baiae's isle. **1936** G. K. ZIPF *Psycho-Biol. of Lang.* iv. 134 Word-pairs like *submit* and *remit*, or *accuse* and *excuse*. **1964** J. VACHEK in D. Abercrombie et al. *Daniel Jones* 194 The ModE word-pair *longer* [lɔŋgə] (comparative of *long*): *longer* [lɔŋə] (the noun of agent derived from the verb *to long*). **1948** J. R. FIRTH *Papers in Linguistics 1934–51* (1957) xi. 150 Palatograms here presented..are *word-palatograms*. That is to say, they are used for the abstraction of articulatory contact and possibly also of movement from suitably selected words taken as whole utterances. **1957** Word-palatogram [see *KYMOGRAPHY]. **1912** M. BEERBOHM *Christmas Garland* 66 Intensive vision has this Mr. Hardy, With a dark skill in weaving word-patterns. **1938** L. MACNEICE *Mod. Poetry* ii. 40 The normal business of poetry is the conveying of information through certain kinds of word-patterns. **1957** C. E. BAZELL in *Miscelanea Homenaje a André Martinet* I. 27 Some languages confer word-status by integrating a unit into the particular word-pattern. **1951** R. FIRTH *Elem. Social Organiz.* vii. 221 It does this..by response to the aesthetic qualities of the word-patterning and imagery used. **1851** J. BROWN *Let.* 23 June (1912) 119, I wish you would paint some word pictures, some studies from Nature as you take your drives. **1855** H. MARTINEAU *Autobiogr.* (1877) I. 397 An opportunity..for paradox, and word-play. **1962** W. NOWOTTNY *Lang. Poets Use* v. 99 The next [chapter] will discuss some aspects of conspicuous word-play—or, to use a more convenient term—of 'verbal schemes'. **1967** *Sci. Amer.* Sept 268/1 The double acrostic..was..the most popular form of word-play in English-speaking countries throughout the last quarter of the 19th century and until the end of World War I. **1967** C. L. WRENN *Word & Symbol* 13 The medieval love of riddling and word-play was occasionally displayed by Anglo-Saxon versifiers. **1982** I. HAMILTON *Robert Lowell* (1983) ii. 18 Argument pursued for the sake of wit and wordplay rather than for any just or true solution. **1894** O. JESPERSEN *Progress in Lang.* iv. 99 Is it beneficial to a language to have a free word-position? **1961** *Brno Studies* III. 46 The number of word-positions in which the correlation could be utilized. **1947** *Jrnl. Symbolic Logic* XII. 90 The word problem for semigroups. **1972** M. KLINE *Math. Thought* xlix. 1143 For one defining relation Wilhelm Magnus (1907–) showed that the word problem is solvable. But the general problem is not. **1984** *Which Micro* Dec. 73 (Advt.), For word processing letters in professional type. **1985** *Daily Tel.* 10 June 11/1 To a newspaper reporter, the ability to wordprocess stories on aircraft and in hotel bedrooms must truly be a boon. **1984** *N. & Q.* Dec. 552/1 This text (excepting the chapter-notes and bibliographies) reproduces a word-processed typescript. **1970** *Administrative Management* Nov. 36/3 'Word processing', a concept that combines the dictating and typing functions into a centralized system. **1977** *Times* 12 Sept. 5 Word processing can already be seen to be at the forefront of the next revolution in the office... The keyboard of the word-processing typewriter..is standard but typing on it produces not only a paper copy but also a magnetic recording which can be automatically searched and edited. **1970** *Administrative Management* Nov. 37/1 In 1970..ITEL..introduced its 'Word Processor'. **1974** *Ibid.* Mar. 48/2 The multi-functional word processor can handle a whole range of text manipulations. **1977** *N.Y. Times* 1 Jan. 22 Word processors call up documents, page by page and line by line, on cathode ray screens for editing. They print out finished versions automatically or send them via telephone lines to distant points. **1979** *Daily Tel.* 24 Dec. 16/3 Word-processors show their greatest strengths when they are used to produce long reports which need to be constantly altered and with any typing which must be word perfect. **1981** *Times Lit. Suppl.* 22 May 588 (Advt.), Manuscripts typed, edited, corrected and indexed by word processor. **1984** D. LODGE *Small World* II. ii. 121 A roomful of secretaries..would wait patiently beside their word-processors, ready to type..his latest reflections. **1928** *Funk's New Stand. Dict.*, Word recognition. **1956** T. W. CLYMER in R. H. Beck *Three R's Plus* 139 Word-recognition skills have been mentioned... Context clues are the quickest and easiest of the word-recognition techniques. **1978** J. BARON in W. K. Estes *Handbk. Learning & Cognitive Processes* VI. iv. 159 Let us assume that one mechanism of word recognition in reading involves activation of a semantic code directly from a letter or spelling-pattern code. **1915** *Stedman's Med. Dict.* (ed. 3) 1034/2 *Word-salad*, a term applied by Forel to the jumble of meaningless words uttered by a patient suffering from catatonia. **1930** L. E. HINSIE *Schizophrenia* ii. 28 The symptomatology is ordinarily not at all bizarre; there is not the scattering of thought, nor the 'word-salad'. **1960** R. D. LAING *Divided Self* xi. 215 Her 'word-salad' seemed to be the result of a number of quasi-autonomous partial systems striving to give expression to themselves out of the same mouth at the same time. **1976** N. POSTMAN *Crazy Talk* 228 The exorbitant fee one must pay..is made to seem plausible by a word salad of imposing proportions. **1960** *Times* 18 Jan. 3/1 And so many composers have turned gratefully to word-setting. **1985** *Times* 13 June 13/8 Why is word-setting generally so difficult for English composers? **1900** *Jrnl. Anthrop. Inst.* XXX. 156 As regards word-signs, in general the connection of the meaning of the word with the picture is obvious enough once it is pointed out. *Ibid.*, The connecting link between the picture and its word-sign value. **1908** G. K. CHESTERTON *Man who was Thursday* ix. 165 It did not take him long to learn how he might convey simple messages by what would seem to be idle taps upon a table or knee... 'We must have several word-signs,..words that we are likely to want.' **1941** *Language* XVII. 149 In my opinion, *ideogram* and *word-sign* are not interchangeable terms, either in Egyptian or English. **1964** P. A. D. MACCARTHY in D. Abercrombie et al. *Daniel Jones* 162 Four uniliteral 'word-signs' for *the, of, and, to*, are standard. **1961** *Observer* 23 July 19/3 Gunther has lost none of his old skill as a wordsmith: the adjectives come pouring out in a torrent of enthusiasm, bristling with brackets, dashes, afterthoughts, and statistics. **1968** *Daily Tel.* 7 Nov. 23/1 We already know John Updike as a resourceful wordsmith, a fine writer. **1976** *Bookseller* 4 Sept. 1645/1 That ubiquitous wordsmith A. J. P. Taylor. **1958** Wordsmithing [see *copy-writing* vbl. sb. s.v. *COPY *sb.* C]. **1981** *Maledicta* V. 346 Enjoys word-smithing, learning languages, and the study of names. **1925** I. A. RICHARDS *Princ. Lit. Criticism* xvi. 119 Many people are able to imagine word-sounds with greater delicacy..than they can utter them. **1951** N. M. GUNN *Well at World's End* xxx. 295 She was making word-sounds, lapping him about. **1937** A. H. GARDINER in *Mélanges Ling. et Phil. offerts à J. van Ginneken* 310 It seems necessary, as between the different classes [of proper names], to assign independent word-status further only to classes II and V. **1982** *Papers Dict. Soc. N. Amer. 1977* 67 In such cases the problem of word-status is involved. **1948** L. SPITZER *Linguistics & Lit. Hist.* i. 7 This French word-family..was a blend of at least two word-stems. **1962** W. NOWOTTNY *Lang. Poets Use* v. 100 Syntactical patterns and individual words (or word-stems). **1911** L. BLOOMFIELD in C. Hockett *Bloomfield Anthol.* (1970) 29 The farther back we look into the history of any IE. language, the more diversified and concrete a word stock do we find. **1940** J. H. JAGGER *Eng. in Future* i. 25 About two per cent. of the word-stock consists of words of this sort [*sc.* slang words that have entered Standard English] made since the Norman conquest. **1973** *Computers & Humanities* VII. 195 Normal discourse draws upon a word-stock which in any theorizing must be treated as infinite. **1863** W. BARNES *Gram. & Gloss. Dorset Dial.* 9 In searching the word-stores of the provincial speech-forms of English, we cannot but behold what a wealth of stems we have overlooked at home. **1971** J. Z. YOUNG *Introd. Study Man* xxxv. 489 [The region behind the superior temporal gyrus] has also been called 'the area of ideational speech' or indeed 'word store'. **1924** H. E. PALMER *Gram. Spoken Eng.* I. 6 *Word-stress*. (In the opinion of the author the term *syllable-stress* would be more appropriate.) This term is used with reference to a syllable (in a word of more than one syllable) which is susceptible of receiving one of the four nucleus-tones. **1953** C. E. BAZELL *Linguistic Form* viii. 100 Word-stress is therefore highly marginal in language. **1966** J. DERRICK *Teaching Eng. to Immigrants* iii. 111 This distribution of stress in the individual word, 'word stress' as it is called, is a basic difficulty for the foreign learner. **1951** *Essays & Studies* IV. 123 Alliteration, assonance.. can be considered as markers or signals of word-structure or of the word-process in the sentence. **1975** *Language for Life* (Dept. Educ. & Sci.) xi. 183 Their attention should constantly be drawn to details of word structure. **1940** *Amer. Speech* XV. 183 Mrs. Ernst presents for her pupils ..the essentials of word-study. **1979** *N. & Q.* June 245/2 The author of a word-study. **1904** Word-symbol [see *ideogenetic* a. s.v. *IDEO-]. **1933** L. BLOOMFIELD *Language* xvii. 287 In the writings of other languages, where words are of various lengths, we find word-symbols used for phonetically similar parts of longer words. **1955** G. A. KELLY *Psychol. Personal Constructs* 459 A preverbal construct is one which continues to be used even though it has no consistent word symbol. **1923** OGDEN & RICHARDS *Meaning of Meaning* ii. 37 In Fraser's *Golden Bough* numerous examples of word taboos are collected. **1978** *Language* LIV. 217 The importance of word taboo on the basis of more recent linguistic-anthropological work. **1954** *Computers & Automation* May 22/1 Word time. **1969** P. B. JORDAIN *Condensed Computer Encycl.* 567 All activities must be calculated in multiples or submultiples of word time or cycle time. **1894** O. JESPERSEN *Progress in Lang.* ix. 340 So much for word-tones; now for the sentence melody. **1928** *Proc. Brit. Acad.* XIV. 354 The four word-tones used in the Mandarin language of Peking to keep otherwise identical words apart. **1964** *Archivum Linguisticum* XVI. 81 He gives some interesting examples of how word-tones and sentence intonation may combine. **1920** D. H. Lawrence *Women in Love* xxiii. 339, I know your dodges. I am not taken in by your word-twisting. **1959** I. & P. Opie *Lore & Lang. Schoolch.* xiv. 320 By using slang, local dialect,..word-twistings, codes and sign language, children communicate with each other in ways which outsiders are unable to understand. **1911** S. S. Colvin *Learning Process* (1931) vii. 108 The word-types of images, as can be readily seen, are symbolic; they stand for concrete realities, which, however, generally are not revived in connection with the symbol. **1936** *Jrnl. Philos.* 17 Dec. 702 Let us call a 'word-type' a class or kind of defining character of a class of tokens which are similar to one another in certain essential aspects. **1961** *Brno Studies* III. 33 Mathesius laid special stress on the part played in English complex condensation cases by three types of nominal forms derived from verbal bases... The word-types will be referred to as..condensers. **1976** *Biometrika* LXIII. 435 How many word types did Shakespeare actually know? **1924** R. M. Ogden tr. *K. Koffka's Growth of Mind* v. 270 A difference in the serial order of the correct word-usage must then depend ..upon a difference in the colour-phenomenon itself. **1971** *Jrnl. Gen. Psychol.* Apr. 188 Creativity and originality were not measured by any of the three types of word-usage. **1932** Faucett & Maki (*title*) Study of English word-values. *Ibid.* 8 This book will ..be useful to those interested..in fixing a graded vocabulary scale for supplementary readers,..in helping teachers and students to develop a sense of word-values [etc.]. **1938** I. Goldberg *Wonder of Words* xx. 438 For *&* has the phonetic value of *et*, but it has the word-value of *and*. **1968** *Listener* 25 Apr. 525/1 What happens if in turn we word-watch on Mr. Davie? Could it be that to use the word 'histrionic' ten times in one short article is itself somewhat histrionic? **1973** *N.Y. Times* 7 May 39/1 Word watchers introduce a note of good sense..to the action and passion of their times. **1980** *Amer. Speech* LV. 77, *-gate* has undergone some developments that should interest word-watchers. **1981** *Verbatim* VII. iii. 20/2 Collectors are needed to find quotations for a new dictionary of American slang... The chief motivation for volunteering should be interest in specialized word-watching. **1977** *IEEE Trans. Professional Communication* June 14/2 One very useful feature ..is called word wrap. **1982** A. J. Meadows et al. *Dict. New Information Technol.* 193/1 *Word-wrap*, a word processing term. It refers to the way in which a partially typed word is moved to a new line if its length proves too much to fit into the existing line. **1983** *Austral. Personal Computer* Sept. 124/2 Automatic wordwrap operates at the end of a screen line (40 chars). **1984** *Computing Today* May 93 (*heading*) Word-wrapping. **1985** *Listener* 25 Apr. 38/1 Word-wrapping, that puts in the ends of lines automatically on reaching the right-hand side of the screen, was another counter-creative feature. **1933** L. Bloomfield *Language* xvii. 285 A better name [for ideographic writing]..would be word-writing or logographic writing. **1942** —— in C. Hockett *Bloomfield Anthol.* (1970) 385 In word writing each word is represented by a conventional sign... Chinese writing is the most perfect system of this kind.

word, *v.* Add: **4. d.** *intr.* for *pass.* To admit translation into words. *poet.*$^{-1}$ (after Wear *v.*[1] 15).

1935 L. MacNeice *Poems* 26 My dream will word well — But will not wear well.

5. To speak to, accost; to tell, pass word to. Also, to rebuke or tell off. *Austral. slang.*

1906 E. Dyson *Fact'ry 'Ands* i. 2 I'll word 'em [girls] when they pass again. **1916** C. J. Dennis *Songs Sentimental Bloke* 50 I met 'im on the quite, An' worded 'im about a small affair. **1936** N. Marsh *Death in Ecstasy* vi. 79 He looks more like a regular dick. An' yet if I worded him maybe he'd talk back like a bud's guide to society stuff. **1945** Baker *Austral. Lang.* vi. 121 He..*words* him, rebukes him. **1967** K. S. Pritchard *Subtle Flame* 234 Ted worded a mate of his on the *Western Star*.

wordage. Delete *rare* and add later examples. In recent use also, an amount of words written or spoken; the number of words in a document.

1926 *Glasgow Herald* 19 May 7/2 Managers of the great news agencies ..have never placed upon the cables so large a wordage concerning any British domestic event. **1958** *Times* 26 Aug. 5/7 Telegrams will carry a fixed charge irrespective of wordage. **1966** *Punch* 21 Sept. 455/2 Obviously he took his correspondence as seriously as he took his Journals and his daily wordage of publishable prose. **1975** G. Howell *In Vogue* 64/1 [Tallulah Bankhead] spoke seventy thousand words a day—the wordage of *War and Peace* over a weekend. **1985** *Univ. Cape Town Studies in English* Feb. 61 Scientists and scholars who have published in abundance are actively solicited by editors, bookmen, and publishers for still more wordage to be put into print.

wordlore. Add: **b.** (Earlier example.) Hence **wo·rdlorist.**

1861 *Trans. Philol. Soc. 1860–1* 154 A perfect Dictionary must not only be a complete Repertory, but also an available Directory within the whole province of word-lore (*wort-lehre* as distinguished from *satz-lehre*). **1929** *N. & Q.* 15 June 419/2 No word-lorist who studies place-names.

wordly, *a.* (Later example.)

1927 M. Sadleir *Trollope* 370 This fact indicates.. two of his personal qualities..his wordly proficiency and his good manners.

wordmonger. In recent use also without contemptuous overtones.

1916 *Daily News* 8 Nov. in E. Weekley *Etymol. Dict. Mod. Eng.* (1921) 944 Professor Weekley is well known to our readers as the most entertaining of living wordmongers. **1981** V. Glendinning *Edith Sitwell* 4 She is a poet of dream and vision, a musical wordmonger.

wordmongery (earlier example).

1881 Max Müller tr. *Kant's Critique Pure Reason* II. ii. iii. 223 There remains nothing but mere wordmongery.

wordsman (wɒ̄·ɹdzmæn). = Wordman. So **wor·dsmanship.**

1959 I. & P. Opie *Lore & Lang. Schoolch.* iii. 50 Wordsmanship. It is common practice to snub a companion who makes irritating use of words such as 'Well!' 'What?' and 'Eh?' **1962** *Canadian Intelligence Service* XII. ii. 3/1 The U.S. Senate Security Subcommittee recently issued a report entitled *Wordsmanship; Semantics as a Communist Weapon.* **1981** W. Safire in *N.Y. Times Mag.* 27 Apr. 18/3 Robert Burchfield, chief editor of the Oxford Dictionaries, known to wordsmen as 'Superlex'. **1984** *N.Y. Times Mag.* 30 Dec. 6/2 The occasion was a gathering at the library of renowned scholars, including a babble of wordsmen, to mark the 200th anniversary of the death of Samuel Johnson.

wordster (wɒ̄·ɹdstəɹ). *nonce-wd.* [f. Word *sb.* + -ster.] One who deals in or handles words: (*a*) one who indulges in talk rather than action; (*b*) a skilful user of words; (*c*) a student of words and their meanings.

1917 H. A. Jones *Pacifists* [Dedication], *Dedicated* To the tribe of Wordsters, Pedants, Fanatics, and Impossibilists, who so rabidly pursued an ignoble peace, that they helped to provoke a disastrous war. **1965** *English Studies* XLVI. 465 [The suffix *-ster*] may serve the function of condensing long words such as 'philologist' and 'lexicographer' into short *wordster.* **1971** 'J. Quartermain' *Man who walked on Diamonds* ii. 14 The..brilliant wordster, always good for the *bon mot.* **1976** *Verbatim* Dec. 8/2 As an amateur wordster, my personal lexicon contains lengthy lists of various types of words.

Wordsworthian, *sb.* and *a.* Add: **b.** *adj.* (Earlier examples.)

1817 W. Whewell *Let.* in M. Moorman *William Wordsworth* (1965) II. ix. 325 His [*sc.* Coleridge's] critique on the Daffodils might serve as a model for similar strictures on all Wordsworth's Wordsworthian poems. **1845** A. de Vere *Let.* 28 Sept. in *Recoll.* (1897) x. 204 You are a greater admirer of the special Wordsworthian genius.

Wo:rdsworthia·na [*-iana suffix], things connected with Wordsworth, writings about Wordsworth; **Wordsworthy** *a. colloq.*, typical or suggestive of Wordsworth.

1889 W. Knight (*title*) Wordsworthiana: papers read to Wordsworth Society. **1938** S. Beckett *Murphy* v. 106 They [*sc.* sheep] seemed in rather better form, less Wordsworthy. **1983** *London Rev. Bks.* 7–20 July 18/4 Recent items of Wordsworthiana include *The Visionary Company.*

work, *sb.* Add: **I. 1. b.** (Later examples.)

1739 J. Wesley *Doctrine of Salvation* 5 Because all Men are Sinners against God, and Breakers of his Law, therefore can no Man by his Works be justified, and made righteous before God. **1883** W. C. Dowding *Luther & his Work* 6 We are accounted righteous before God only for the merits of our Lord Jesus Christ, by faith; and not from our own works or deservings. **1906** W. Walker *John Calvin* xv. 415 Calvin..leaves room for a conception of 'works' as strenuous..as any claimed by the Roman communion. **1963** E. P. Thompson *Making of Eng. Working Class* xi. 364 How, then, to keep grace? Not by good works, since Wesley had elevated faith above works:.. Works were the snares of pride and the best works were mingled with the dross of sin; although.. works might be a *sign* of grace. **1972** Q. Bell *Virginia Woolf* I. i. 4 The Clapham Sect was concerned with works rather than with faith.

d. (Further examples.)

1749 J. Cleland *Mem. Woman of Pleasure* II. 120 All this was not the work of the fourth part of a minute. **1871** Hardy *Desperate Remedies* II. ii. 74 To bring him out and lay him on a bank was the work of an instant. **1927** C. Asquith *Black Cap* 73 To light his candle and put on his dressing-gown and slippers was the work of a moment.

5. c. *slang.* A criminal act or activity. Cf. Job *sb.*[2] 1 b.

1812 J. H. Vaux *Vocab. Flash. Lang.* in *Mem.* (1964) 279 An offender having been detected in the very fact..is ..said to have been *grab'd at work.* **1865** in *Comments on Etym.* (1983) XIII. iii.–iv. 17 We..surrounded her from observation while at 'work'. **1926** J. Black *You can't Win* xxi. 338 Coppers located 'work' for burglars and stalled for them while they worked. *Ibid.* xxiv. 379 That kind of 'work' is unprofessional, unnatural, and disgusting. **1963** T. Tullett *Inside Interpol* xiv. 192 If he netted only about 200 guilders he would start 'work' again in a week.

8. (Earlier example.)

1832 W. Whewell *First Princ. Mech.* iv. 52 The *work done* does not depend on the pressure alone. *Ibid.* 53 The work done by a machine may be represented as certain pressures exerted through certain spaces.

II. 18. b. Phr. *in the works* = *in the pipeline* s.v. *pipe-line *sb.* b. *N. Amer.*

1973 *Globe & Mail* (Toronto) 12 July 2/3 In his statement, Mr. Cote said he had been informed during the election campaign that a 'telegraph organization was in the works in certain ridings of the South Shore'. **1976** *National Observer* (U.S.) 16 Oct. 10/3 As might be expected, a movie deal is in the works. **1979** *Tucson Mag.* Jan. 10/3 Actually there is a sequel in the works and the project was begun as a two film package. **1984** *National Times* (Austral.) 2 Nov. 41/2 There are, of course, follow-up books in the works.

20. a. (Later *colloq.* examples, also applied to persons.)

1906 E. Dyson *Fact'ry 'Ands* xv. 197 'Ceptin fer er hunexpected wail he jerked out iv 'is works now 'n 'again, that cat was just er livin' silence. **1884** 'Mark Twain' *Huck. Finn* xxxii. 333 Here we're a running on this way, and you hain't told me a word about Sis, nor any of them. Now I'll rest my works a little, and you start up yourn. **1885** —— in *Century Mag.* Dec. 196/1 Then it would bray—..spreading its jaws till you could see down to its works. It was a disagreeable animal.

b. *slang* (orig. *U.S.*). *the* (*whole*) *works*, the whole lot, everything; *esp.* in phrases, *to give* (or *tell*) *the works*: to tell the whole story; *to shoot the works*: see *shoot *v.* 23 j; *to give* (someone) *the works*: to give (him) a rough time, *spec.* to murder; also, to give (someone) the full treatment (not necessarily unpleasant); *to get the works*: to receive severe punishment, reprimand, adverse criticism, etc.

1899 J. London *Let.* 18 May (1966) 38, I..quite enjoyed the thought of saying good-bye to the whole works. **1920** *Collier's* 5 June 36/3 'I ain't trying to jimmy into your most intimate affairs, but is they—*is* they a girl?'.. He ..sat down..and gimme the works. **1927** *Vanity Fair* XXIX. 134/2 'Giving a guy the works' is handing someone a raw deal. **1928** *Amer. Mercury* Apr. 429/2 One-Lung here squealed, an' I got the works for two years —poundin' rocks wit' a sledge. **1929** C. F. Coe *Hooch* vii. 156 This man never was bumped here at all. They gave him the works some place a long way off. **1930** *Daily Express* 23 May 11/3 Threatening that unless the money was produced somebody would 'get the works'. **1934** Wodehouse *Right Ho, Jeeves* ix. 111 Heave a couple of sighs. Grab her hand. And give her the works. Right. **1936** J. Steinbeck *In Dubious Battle* iii. 35 Tell him the works. **1969** E. Bagnold *Autobiogr.* xii. 236 *The Chinese Prime Minister* is a better play than *The Chalk Garden* but it didn't get the works. **1979** L. Kallen *Introducing C. B. Greenfield* xiv. 193, I have uncovered a sensational story that is crying to be written... Bestseller list, movie, the works.

c. *pl.* A drug addict's equipment for taking drugs. *U.S. slang.*

1934 L. Berg *Revelations of Prison Doctor* iv. 42 All became adept in the use of 'the works'; this was a syringe and needle. **1951** *N. Y. Times* 15 June 14/3 Do they ask you if you want the 'works' when you're buying needles? **1953** W. Burroughs *Junkie* xiv. 140, I went into the bathroom to get my works. Needle, dropper, and a piece of cotton.

III. 27. out of work: (earlier modern example and earlier and later *attrib.* and *sb.* examples); hence *out-of-worker*; *out-of-workness.*

1864 J. O'Neil *Diary* 10 Apr. in J. Burnett *Useful Toil* (1974) i. 85 One half of the time I was out of work and the other I had to work as hard as ever I wrought in my life. **1885** *Marine Engineer* 1 Sept. 157/2 'Out-of-work benefit' came to £57,000. **1888** [see Out of III.]. **1894** A. Morrison *Tales of Mean Streets* 48 The advent of a flush sailor .., disposed to treat out-o'-workers. **1903** A. McNeill *Egregious Engl.* v. 49 Out-of-workness is.. the most fearful thing in life that can happen to an Englishman. **1913** A. Spender in H. Barnett *Canon S. A. Barnett* (1918) II. xlvi. 273 How to tide over the winter for the out-of-work docker. **1939** 'G. Orwell' *Coming Up for Air* ii. ix. 153 We'd suddenly changed from gentlemen ..into miserable out-of-works whom nobody wanted. **1955** M. Gilbert *Sky High* viii. 105 He was an out-of-work actor. **1974** R. Butler *Buffalo Hook* v. 45 I'm just an out-of-work who wants to stay that way.

30. Also with *for* in colloq. phr. and var. (Further examples.)

1843 Dickens *Christmas Carol* ii. 61 Old Fezziwig stood out to dance with Mrs. Fezziwig. Top couple too; with a good stiff piece of work cut out for them. **1862** Trollope *Orley Farm* II. xxxi. 247 Then Mr. Chaffanbrass rose ..and every one knew that his work was cut out for him. **1874** Hardy *Far from Madding Crowd* II. xxii. 276 What with one thing and another, I see that my work is well cut out for me. **1893** R. L. Stevenson *Catriona* vii. 71 'Ye'll find your work cut out for ye to establish that,' quoth she. **1899** E. W. Hornung *Amateur Cracksman* 43 'We shall have our work cut out,' was all I said. **1927** R. Austin Freeman *Magic Casket* vii. 222 'You will have your work cut out,' I remarked, 'to trace that man. The potter's description was pretty vague.' **1951** *Sport* 27 Jan.–2 Feb. 9/3 The Quakers will have their work cut out to keep the bigger clubs away.

32. b. In trivial sense, esp. in phrases *carry on with, get on with, keep up*, etc. *the good work.*

1920 'Sapper' *Bull-Dog Drummond* xii. 309 Vallance Nestor carried the good work on. **1938** G. Greene *Brighton Rock* vii. ix. 347 Drink up. We better get on with the good work. *a* **1953** E. O'Neill *Long Day's Journey* (1956) i. 17 So keep up the good work, Mary.

IV. 34. a. Simple *attrib.*, as *work-boat, -chant, -life, light, -load* (*load *sb.* 4 c), *-norm* (*norm 1 c), *-plan, -site, -song, -tool* (later example), *-week*; (of persons), *work-gang, -lass, -person*; (of animals), *work-stock* (earlier examples); (of clothes) worn for work, as *work boot, -clothes, pants, -shirt, -shoe, -wear.* **c.** *work-gnarled, -hard, -soiled, -thickened, -weary* adjs. **d. work-and-back** *Printing* = *sheet-work* s.v. Sheet *sb.*[1] 12 b; **work and tumble, work and turn, work and twist,** methods of printing the second side of a sheet of paper from the same forme as the first (see quots.); **work book,** (*a*) in a business firm etc., a book containing a record of daily duties, work (to be) done, etc.; (*b*) (chiefly *U.S.*), a book in which are set out problems to be worked out, questions to be answered, etc.; **work-box** (earlier examples); **work camp** orig. *U.S.*, (*a*) a camp organized for a work project, esp. by volunteers serving the community; (*b*) = *labour camp* s.v. *LABOUR, LABOR *sb.* 8; **work card,** (*a*) a card issued by one's employer and serving as a kind of identity document; (*b*) a pupil's card on which are set out questions to be answered, problems to be worked, etc. (cf. *work-book* (*b*) above); **work ethic,** work seen as virtuous in itself, a term usu. connected with Protestant attitudes and deriving from Max Weber's thesis on the origins of modern capitalism (cf. *Protestant ethic* s.v. *PROTESTANT *a.* 1 b); **work experience,** work projects arranged for the purpose of providing experience of employment, esp. for school-leavers; **work-fellow** (later examples); **work flow,** in an office or industrial organization, the sequence of processes through which a piece of work passes from initiation to completion; **work-force,** the workers or employees collectively, usu. of a particular firm or industry; **work furlough** *U.S.*, leave of absence from prison by day in order to continue in one's daily work; **work group,** (*a*) a group of people in a factory or the like who customarily work together; (*b*) = *work party* (*a*) below; **work-hand** (earlier example); **work-harden** *v. trans. Metallurgy*, to toughen (a metal) by cold-working; also *intr.*, to become tough as a result of cold-working; so **work-hardened** *ppl. a.*, **work-hardening** *vbl. sb.*; **work head,** (*a*) = HEADSTOCK 1 b; (*b*) an interchangeable working attachment for a powered implement or tool; **work-horse,** (*a*) a horse used for work on a farm (later example); (*b*) *fig.*, a machine, person, etc., that dependably performs arduous labour; **work-in-progress,** work undertaken but not completed, esp. (*a*) in commerce (see quot. 1978); (*b*) in the arts; **work measurement** (see quot. 1979); **work-minded** *a.*, eager to work hard; eager to go out to work; hence **work-mindedness; work name,** an alias used by someone engaged in secret intelligence work; **work party,** (*a*) a group of people who come together to carry out a piece of work of mutual or social benefit; (*b*) = *working party* s.v. *WORKING *ppl. a.* 2 c (*d*); **work permit,** a document representing official permission to take a job in a foreign country; **workpiece,** the object which is worked on with a machine or tool; **work point,** in the People's Republic of China, a unit used in calculating wages due, based on the quality and quantity of work done; **work rate** *Football*, the extent to which a player contributes towards the fatiguing running and chasing in a game; **work release** *U.S.* = *work furlough* above; **work-rule** *U.S.*, one of a set of regulations governing working procedures, conditions, etc., in a business or industry; **work-sharing,** short-time working by all employees within an industry intended to prevent redundancies when there is an excess of available man-power; **work-sheet,** (*a*) = *work-book* (*a*) above; also *fig.*; (*b*) *U.S.*, a questionnaire; (*c*) a paper on which are recorded notes, calculations, etc., relating to work in progress; (*d*) a list of exercises, problems, etc., to be worked by a student (cf. *work-book* (*b*) above); **work-shy** *a.*; also *absol.* as *sb.*; **work-space,** (*a*) *Computers* = *working storage* s.v. *WORKING *vbl. sb.* 16 b; (*b*) space (for people) to work in; **work study,** (*a*) investigation of the methods of working in a business, etc., with the aim of increasing output and efficiency; (*b*) used *attrib.* with reference to schemes of combining work and study established in Communist China; **work surface** = *work-top* below; cf. *working surface* s.v. *WORKING *vbl. sb.* 16 b; **work-table** (earlier example); **work-team,** (*a*) a team of draught-horses, oxen, etc.; (*b*) a team of people who work together, a work group, *spec.* in Communist China any of the working units making up a commune; **work-top,** a table or other flat surface suitable for working on, *esp.* in a kitchen.

1959 L. M. HARROD *Librarians' Gloss.* (ed. 2) 249 *Sheet work*, printing one side of a sheet of paper from an 'inner forme' and the other from an 'outer forme'. Also called 'work and back'. **1967** E. CHAMBERS *Photo-litho-Offset* ii. 18 Sheet work is the term used to indicate that two formes are used to print the sheet, sometimes called 'work and back'. **1931** H. JAHN *Hand Composition* xvi. 251 The work-and-tumble method..in a broad sense is also a work-and-turn method. *Ibid.* 254 In the work-and-tumble form the pages are so imposed that the sheet must be 'tumbled' or turned on the 'long cross'. **1959** L. M. HARROD *Librarians' Gloss.* (ed. 2) 296 *Work and tumble*, the method of printing the second side of a sheet of paper by turning it over in its narrow direction and feeding it into a printing machine to print the reverse side. **1888** Work and turn [see *sheet-work* s.v. SHEET *sb.* 12 b]. **1919** V. POSSNETT *Stonework* 49/3 The sheet may be turned over after the first side has been printed, and the same edge of the sheet fed to the grippers for a second impression. This is termed 'work-and-turn'. **1931** H. JAHN *Hand Composition* xvi. 263 The Dexter standard jobbing folder..makes thirteen different folds adapted to work-and-turn and sheetwise forms. **1964** Work-and-turn [see *half-sheet* (*b*) s.v. *HALF- II. n]. **1930** *20th Cent. Encycl. Printing* viii. 253 The work and twist form is used for the printing of ruled work where the vertical and horizontal rules of a sheet are printed with one impression. **1968** *Gloss. Terms Offset Lithogr. Printing* (B.S.I.) 25 *Work and twist*, printing one side of the sheet, then reversing the sidelay edges and front and back edges of the sheet, and printing the same side again with the same printing plate. **1941** H. I. CHAPELLE *Boatbuilding* v. 339 Lines of a 45-foot workboat. **1977** *Washington Post* 4 Sept. A12/3 A fleet of workboats is continually dredging a passable channel. **1910** A. BENNETT *Clayhanger* III. vi. 371 Edwin was familiar with every detail of the printer's work-book. **1932** W. D. LEWIS et al. (*title*) Practical workbook in English. **1959** HALAS & MANVELL *Technique Film Animation* xix. 171 The Work Book is derived directly from the final storyboard, and is an analysis of each shot and sequence on a frame-by-frame basis. **1960** G. E. EVANS *Horse in Furrow* ix. 115 Work Books offer us a great deal of information about farming methods at this time [*sc.* early nineteenth century]. **1975** *Publishers Weekly* 17 Nov. 98/1 With its workbook approach of charts, graphs, questionnaires and the like, this book will put some women off. **1976** *National Observer* (U.S.) 22 May 16/1 At first wearing a suit, then gradually assuming work boots and old clothes. **1605** P. ERONDELL *French Garden* sig. E7 verso, I haue not my siluer thimble, it is within my worke-boxe. **1790** F. BURNEY *Diary* Jan. (1940) 263 Everything..was spread about, as in any common day—work-boxes, netting-cases, etc. etc! **1933** NICHOLS & GLASER *Work Camps for America* 13 The types of participants in work camps vary according to the purpose of the camps and the organizations which control them. **1943** F. L. WRIGHT *Autobiogr.* (rev. ed.) IV. 309 Now by way of an architect's work-camp comes fresh adventures in the desert. **1964** M. BANTON *Policeman in Community* iii. 56 They stopped to talk with a youth they knew who was serving a sentence in a work camp. **1970** *Honey* June 106/3 International Work Camps are held in most countries. Some camps offer paid work in forestry or farming. Others have specific projects that are usually related to social service. **1981** 'W. HAGGARD' *Money Men* i. 18 The Gestapo..had sent him back to Germany to a work camp where he'd been starved to death. **1984** *Listener* 11 Oct. 26/1 An elaborate process of deception was instituted, by which the evacuation of Jews to the death-camps was disguised as a 'resettlement' into 'work-camps'. **1959** M. LEVIN *Eva* 4, I managed to get a blank German work card. **1966** J. DERRICK *Teaching Eng. to Immigrants* 239 The work cards, picture-cards, wall pictures and flashcards which accompany the course, are also recommended. **1975** A. WATSON *Living in China* iv. 99 The work card issued by the place of employment is an important means of social identification. **1980** *Daily Tel.* 12 Feb. 6/8 Instead of text books the scheme uses a series of work-cards... These..are distributed to the pupils according to their ability. **1946** R. BLESH *Shining Trumpets* I. iii. 57 Perhaps the most familiar form of work-chant is the vendor's street cry. **1967** A. L. LLOYD *Folk Song in Eng.* i. 54 The work-chants of Portland quarrymen. **1901** 'MARK TWAIN' in *Century Mag.* Nov. 26/2 Tommy was..in his dreadful work-clothes. **1978** F. WELDON *Praxis* xx. 170 She changed out of her work clothes. **1959** *Past & Present* xv. 44 Weber also asserted that Calvinistic Protestantism was an indispensable precondition of the development of a capitalistic work ethic. **1973** P. A. WHITNEY *Snowfire* vi. 112 The work ethic, you mean?..my little Puritan. **1980** *Jrnl. R. Soc. Arts* July 468/1 *They* are showing the way which we should follow—if only we were not 'locked on to' some puritanical work ethic. **1975** *Whitaker's Almanack 1976* 1041/2 In recent years there has been a marked growth in the provision of 'work-experience' schemes which involve the participation of pupils in the work of industrial, commercial and other firms. **1983** *Fortune* 16 May 112/3 CETA's primary approach, providing 'work experience' in temporary public service jobs, does no good at all, presumably because the jobs don't lead anywhere. Work experience has big payoffs, however, when it comes in the form of on-the-job training for a permanent position in the private sector. *a* **1890** J. H. NEWMAN *Meditations* (1893) II. 289 We thus pray..for our associates and work-fellows. **1903** C. COLERIDGE *Charlotte M. Yonge* x. 276 She was the most delightful comrade, workfellow, or playfellow. **1950** I. A. HERRMAN *Office Methods, Systems, & Procedures* vii. 131 Work flow diagrams are effective in solving various kinds of problems. **1976** *National Observer* (U.S.) 19 June 2/4 Byrd is a master of legislative detail with a reputation as a fair-minded manager who accelerates the work flow. **1961** *Times* 30 May 13/7 Books come off no assembly line. The raw material is provided by a notoriously undisciplined work-force. **1982** *Daily Tel.* 18 Nov. 2/1 They were non-unionised because 'that is the wish of the majority of the work force'. **1957** *Statutes of California 1956 & 1957* II. MDLXXX. 2933 If the court so directs that the prisoner be permitted to continue in his regular employment, the work furlough administrator shall arrange for a continuation of such employment so far as possible without interruption. *Ibid.* 2934 This section shall be known..as the 'Work Furlough Rehabilitation Law.' **1970** *Criminology* May 63 Work furlough has been used..for felons as well as misdemeanants. **1980** *New Age* (U.S.) Oct. 15/2 Both men received suspended jail sentences and three years probation; each will serve about a month in a work-furlough program or community service and must undergo psychiatric counselling. **1948** *Common Ground* Summer 41/2 Their pianos sound the work-gang chorus. **1981** W. EBERSOHN *Divide Night* xii. 157 A work gang..cleaning up the litter along the road. **1913** D. H. LAWRENCE *Sons & Lovers* x. 256 She began to spare her hands. They, too, were work-gnarled now. **1957** J. KEROUAC *On Road* vi. 216 A wiry..man..with work-gnarled hands. **1954** J. A. C. BROWN *Social Psychol. of Industry* iv. 114 A factory or a society is not ordinarily a mass of isolated individuals..; it is an integrated pattern of primary work-groups. **1960** *Ann. Reg. 1959* 381 All of them [*sc.* sects] laid emphasis on activity: dancing, propagation of the faith, and free labour with work-groups building and cleaning temples. **1972** M. ARGYLE *Social Psychol. of Work* ix. 233 Many studies have shown that job satisfaction is affected by relationships in the work group. **1834** W. SEWALL *Diary* (1930) 154 He was an excellent work hand. **1932** W. FAULKNER *Light in August* i. 14 The gray woman not plump and not thin, manhard, workhard, in a serviceable gray garment. **1924** *Engineer* 7 Mar. 249/1 Metal rolled cold or drawn through dies may be work-hardened to an extent rendering it quite unsuitable for further working. *Ibid.* 251/2 It may be that its [*sc.* 'browning''s] real function is to reduce the tendency of the steel to work-harden. **1961** *New Scientist* 16 Mar. 672/1 The ability of the material to work-harden by deformation more than compensates for the thermal weakening of the interatomic bonds. **1972** *Mineral. Mag.* XXIII. 265/2 Naturally deformed galena has been 'work-hardened' by tectonic movement. **1984** E. P. DEGARMO et al. *Materials & Processes in Manuf.* (ed. 6) ii. 41 When most materials are plastically deformed, they work-harden; that is, they become harder and the yield-point stress is raised. **1924** *Jrnl. Iron & Steel Inst.* CX. 431 The abnormally low value of the limit of proportionality..is found in both quench-hardened and work-hardened steels. **1973** J. G. TWEEDDALE *Materials Technol.* II. iv. 102 Cold drawing can impart a good surface finish and accurate size to a product and leaves the material in a work-hardened condition which is often desirable. **1924** *Engineer* 7 Mar. 248/2 (*heading*) Work-hardening of metals and the Herbert tester. **1973** J. G. TWEEDDALE *Materials Technol.* II. iv. 87 The work-hardening can be used to give enhanced strength. **1930** *Engineering* 25 Apr. 538/3 A pair of flat ways for the work-head, tailstock and journal supports. **1960** *Farmer & Stockbreeder* 12 Jan. 121/1 (Advt.), Other workheads, quickly interchangeable without tools, include—12 and 17in. hedge-cutters, pruning saw,..etc. **1964** S. CRAWFORD *Basic Engin. Processes* vii. 194 The workhead is..a self-contained unit carried at the opposite end of the table to the tailstock. **1949** *Sun* (Baltimore) 3 Oct. 2/6 This caliber howitzer has gained the reputation of being the 'work horse' of the Army. **1966** *Electronics* 3 Oct. 54 The satellites will be launched on improved versions of the workhorse Delta vehicle. **1973** *Listener* 20 Dec. 841/2 Gerald Ford..has been known..as the most dependable of Republican work-horses. **1981** H. ENGEL *Ransom Game* (1982) xxii. 133 The big barn doors. The entrance is on the lower floor, where the cows and work horses used to be. **1982** *Habitat Catal. 1982/83* 56/2 A real workhorse of a table, with maple block top. **1985** A. BLOND *Book Book* iii. 42 An admirable workhorse of a publisher. **1930** *Times* 25 Mar. 24/5 'Work in progress, less instalments thereon,' is £141,069, against £47,351 in the previous year. **1952** R. GIROUX *Let.* 10 Mar. in Breit & Lowry *Sel. Lett. M. Lowry* (1967) 450 It is clear that the place of the finished book will be important in your long work-in-progress. **1976** P. ISRAEL *French Kiss* (1977) ii. 24 The work-in-progress on one of the easels. **1978** J. KELLOCK *Elements of Accounting* x. 176 *Work-in-progress*, is the value of incomplete work in the factory and is usually computed on the following basis: the cost of materials and production labour plus the proportion of indirect expenses chargeable to the work up to its present stage of manufacture. **1920** D. H. LAWRENCE *Lost Girl* vi. 98 Yet it was always packed with colliers and work-lasses. **1946** J. W. DAY *Harvest Adventure* vii. 112 The pond..is tenanted by tame decoy ducks, pinioned, whose work-life is to lure the wild birds down. **1977** *National Observer* (U.S.) 1 Jan. 1/2 Men..committed to serious and demanding work lives. **1947** J. STEINBECK *Wayward Bus* 13 Get the work-light on the long cord connected. **1977** *Chicago Tribune* 2 Oct. I. 53 (Advt.), Self-cleaning oven. Fluorescent worklight. **1946** Work-load [see *LOAD *sb.* 4 c]. **1962** *Listener* 4 Jan. 4/1 The application of time study to speed and tighten up the work load. **1962** J. GLENN in *Into Orbit* 195, I pushed and pulled thirty times at the bungee cord which permitted me to exercise with a known workload. **1978** G. A. SHEEHAN *Running & Being* xv. 210, I shift to shorter steps..to maintain the same workload. **1985** *Times* 18 Jan. 5/1 He is one of more than 1,000 teachers whose workload is being analysed by the National Union of Teachers in a survey to be published next week. **1948** (*title*) Manual of procedures: work measurement in public works offices (U.S. Bureau of Yards & Docks). **1969** J. ARGENTI *Managem. Techniques* 271 The procedure used in Work Measurement to determine the amount of labour required to do a job is to time how long it takes the average man to perform each element of the job. **1979** *Gloss. Terms Work Study* (*B.S.I.*) 2 *Work measurement*, the application of techniques designed to establish the time for a qualified worker to carry out a task at a defined rate of working. **1954** *Encounter* Sept. 33/1 The Army requires..work-minded people who try to do a good job of whatever they're told to do. **1968** *Economist* 11 May 46/1 The more 'work-minded' a mum in her later years, the less available she is to look after her daughter's kids. **1960** *Encounter* Nov.

27/1 William H. Whyte, Jr.,..points out that some large corporations, worried about the decline in 'work-mindedness', are seeking to substitute an ideology of corporate loyalty. **1977** 'J. LE CARRÉ' *Hon. Schoolboy* iii. 54 Karla ..was the workname of the Soviet case officer who had recruited Bill Haydon..and had the running of him. **1959** *Encounter* Feb. 14/2 At the local level, there must always be potential disputes between workers and management over redundancy, work-norms, wage-differentials..and so on. **1980** *Times* 24 May 14/7 You can poke fun at life under Communism how to fiddle your work-norms. **1927** *Amer. Speech* II. 366/2 The man had on his work pants this morning. **1978** H. C. RAE *Sullivan* I. ii. 19 Denim workpants slung low on his thick hips. **1957** R. FRANKENBERG *Village on Border* 20 They [*sc.* women] also work together in sewing groups and work-parties preparing material for sales-of-work. **1957** V. W. TURNER *Schism & Continuity in an African Society* i. 22 The cutting and clearing of bush .may involve a collective work-party..of kin and neighbours. **1981** I. BOLAND tr. *Ginzburg's Within Whirlwind* I. iii. 22 Many considered the shock of being drafted to a work party every bit as bad as being arrested. **1965** *Globe & Mail* (Toronto) 26 June 13/3 The Union des Artistes will give endless work permits, he points out, but is most cautious about applications for membership. **1971** *Times* 25 Feb. 4/1 A Commonwealth citizen wishing to work here in future will need a work permit issued for a specific job in a specific place for a fixed initial period. **1983** *Daily Tel.* 12 May 4/8 Work permit clamp. The Singapore Government has tightened up on employment permits for foreigners. **1807** *Monthly Mag.* I Feb. 67/1 The return of the carriage without any assistance from the work-person. **1980** S. BRETT *Dead Side of Mike* ii. 17 Even the most brilliant workperson in the world needs some sort of tools. **1934** WEBSTER, Workpiece. **1949** *Tool Engineers Handbk.* (Amer. Soc. Tool Engineers) xcviii. 1544 Improper workpiece locating can readily result in excessive troubles and spoilage. **1952** *Economist* 6 Dec. 721 The guiding wheel is charged negatively and the workpiece positively. **1978** *Sci. Amer.* Nov. 110/2 The surface of the workpiece undergoes much more heating in abrasive machining than in conventional machining. **1957** J. KEROUAC *On Road* II. ix. 170 A paper for the want ads and workplans. **1976** *Columbus* (Montana) *News* 10 June 1/1 A district program and a work plan was written outlining the conditions and situations relating to soil and water conservation within the district. [**1959** C. K. YANG *Chinese Village in Early Communist Tradition* xvii. 246 For most co-operatives the distribution of income was based neither on equal sharing nor on individual needs but on the quantity and quality of labor performed under the system of labor units or points.] **1964** *Current Scene* 15 Apr. 2/2 The use of work points rather than absolute money terms to express wages..preserves Peking's control over the allocation of the harvest. **1969** [see *TACHAI]. **1979** *China Now* Jan.–Feb. 14/1 She cultivates vegetables..and earns nine workpoints a day. **1969** Work-rate [see *through ball* s.v. *THROUGH- 2]. **1976** *South Notts. Echo* 16 Dec. 7/5 In midfield J. Uren read the game well and with a higher work rate could be destined for higher things. **1957** *Session Laws & Resolutions State of N. Carolina* 489 The governing body of the State Prison System is authorized and directed to establish a work release plan for those serving sentences for misdemeanors. **1981** C. BARTOLLAS *Introd. Corrections* viii. 168 Objectives of work release. **1963** *Economist* 16 Mar. 997/2 A committee made a two-year study of the railway dispute and recommended far-reaching changes in the work-rules on the trains [in the U.S.], to try to eliminate the 'feather-bedding' which keeps unnecessary men on the job. **1979** *Wall Street Jrnl.* 20 Dec. 18/5 Mr. Church will be under considerable pressure to implement the [U.S. mineworkers'] convention's..work-rule demands. **1934** *Planning* II. xxxiv. 12 Another group of proposals look to work-sharing as a method of adjusting labour to labour requirements. *a* **1974** R. CROSSMAN *Diaries* (1976) II. 56 They were entirely concerned about the problem of redundancy and in particular the impression created by Gunter's public statements that in principle the Government is opposed to work-sharing in the motor-car industry. **1925** S. LEWIS *Arrowsmith* xxxix. 427 'I'll find out from my wife what dates we have already and telephone you tomorrow evening'. 'So you let the Old Woman keep the work-sheet for you, huh?' **1930** *Dialect Notes* VI. 73 Professor Jud made a number of specific suggestions regarding mechanical features of the work-sheets. **1958** *Listener* 31 July 155/1 Sorted away in the stacks are some 5,000 sets of poets' worksheets, the notes, drafts, revisions. **1966** J. DERRICK *Teaching Eng. to Immigrants* 238 A new type of course, designed for eight-year-old foreign learners, consisting of gramophone records, teacher's notes, and pupils' 'working scripts' which are work-sheets and meant to be expendable. **1967** R. BREGZIS in Cox & Grose *Organization & Handling Bibl. Rec. by Computer* v. 118 NUC catalogues and other files or catalogues are checked as necessary, and all information [is] recorded on a catalogue worksheet. **1975** *Language for Life* (Dept. Educ. & Sci.) x. 145 It is even less likely to happen where children work individually through assignment cards or work sheets. **1976** P. ALEXANDER *Death of Thin-Skinned Animal* xx. 206 Look, if you haven't done any maintenance there, boyo, how come I've got a work-sheet for renewing thirty foot of ogee guttering and repointing the bloody gable end? **1981** *Amer. Speech* 1977 LII. 167 He employed a variable questionnaire based upon the New England short worksheets. **1923** *Dialect Notes* V. 235 A work shirt made of crossbarred cotton cloth. **1980** *Daily Tel.* 19 Nov. 15/8 (Advt.), Fisherman's smock. Original workshirt of local fishermen. **1965** H. I. ANSOFF *Corporate Strategy* (1968) vi. 96 Royal Little has built the successful Textron Corp. composed of consumer electronics, textiles, helicopters, work shoes, and satellite motors. **1980** D. E. WESTLAKE *Castle in Air* vi. 63 Manuel was dressed in rough corduroy trousers,.. heavy workshoes, and a coarse cotton shirt. **1928** *Daily Express* 2 Apr. 7/4 To make the lot of the work-shy as favourable as that of the worker. **1983** *Times* 12 Oct. 14/5 The Gravediggers' Union, understandably affronted by having their members portrayed as drunken workshies. **1975** *BP Shield Internat.* May 5/4 Up to three teams of divers may be maintained under these conditions to permit a 24-hour per day diving operation at the work-site. **1980** *Daily Tel.* 20 Mar. 28 (Advt.), He must be an engineer, between 30 and 50, perfectly fluent in French and English, with overseas experience in work-site construction. **1932** W. FAULKNER *Light in August* ii. 28 The men in faded and work-soiled overalls. **1911** *Jrnl. Amer. Folk-lore* XXIV. 379 Like the other songs, the work-songs give a keen insight into the negro's real self. **1933** E. CALDWELL *God's Little Acre* xiv. 205 The sound of the picks..rose and fell in their ears to the rhythm of Uncle Felix's work-song. **1977** *Listener* 25 Aug. 244/3 The persistent play with three for four notes suggests incantation or work-songs. **1959** *New Scientist* 25 June 1375/2 Such a code would mean building an automatic translating system into existing designs of computers, thereby reducing their 'work-space'. **1979** KRAFT & TOY *Mini/Microcomputer Hardware Design* viii. 413 Its general register set is placed in main storage and realized as a 16-word area of memory that is considered a workspace. **1979** *Tucson* (Arizona) *Citizen* 20 Sept. 1c/1 Several high-rise government office buildings with a combined work space of perhaps 100,000 to 150,000 square feet. **1985** *Which Computer?* Apr. 53/2 Even on a fully configured IBM PC..you can find yourself running out of workspace. **1877** *Rep. Indian Affairs* 22 Unprecedented storms and heavy roads had..broken down our light Indian work-stock. **1883** 'MARK TWAIN' *Life on Miss.* 603 The people cared first for their work stock,..horses and mules were housed in a place of safety. *c* **1951** (*title*) The implications of work study (Imperial Chemical Industries Ltd.). **1962** E. SNOW *Other Side of River* (1963) xxx. 227 Part-time and work-study middle schools are discussed in the next chapter. **1965** J. CH'ÊN *Mao & Chinese Revolution* (1967) I. iii. 72 In August 1920 Mao and others founded a small Russian affairs study group as well as sponsoring a Work-study Scheme for students to go to Russia. *Ibid.* v. 95 Work-study students who had just returned from France or Russia. **1978** *Cornish Guardian* 27 Apr 6/7 (Advt.), Applicants would be expected to have at least two years' practical experience in the Work Study and O & M field. **1971** *House & Garden* Dec. 76/2 Spotlights illuminating work surfaces and dining-area. **1979** J. BARNETT *Backfire is Hostile!* xii. 117 They were inside a kitchen, work surfaces, refrigerator, an electric cooker gleamed. **1790** F. BURNEY *Diary* Jan. (1905) IV. 348 Dr. Fisher says he hopes it was not a card-table, and rather believes it was only a Pembroke work-table. **1885** *Ann. Rep. U.S. Office Indian Affairs* 41 There is a growing desire among these Indians to obtain and care for stock and work cattle... The desire to obtain work-teams has been great. **1933** L. I. WILDER *Farmer Boy* xi. 75 He was old enough to..drive the old, gentle work-team... They were wise, sober mares. **1951** R. FIRTH *Elem. Social Organization* ii. 47 The clash between the values of.. work-team and church which so often occurs in a highly differentiated larger community. **1965** *New Statesman* 3 Sept. 321/1 The giant communes were divided into smaller units. The basic unit is a work-team, generally about the size of an average village. **1972** M. ARGYLE *Social Psychol. of Work* x. 252 The construction of work-teams, introducing democratic supervision, participation in management, and arousal of intrinsic motivation all increase cooperation. **1978** *China Now* Mar./Apr. 18/2 Each family belongs to a work team,..a group of teams makes up a brigade, and..the brigades together make up the commune as a whole. **1931** W. FAULKNER *Sanctuary* xvi. 146 Along the fence a row of heads hatted and bare above work-thickened shoulders. **1970** L. JEFFERS *My Blackness is the Beauty of this Land* 8 Work-thickened hand thoughtful and gentle on grandson's head. **1955** E. POUND *Classic Anthol.* I. 78 We have blunted our axes, We lack work-tools. **1953** *Archit. Rev.* CXIV. 127/1 Though not as highly resistant to abrasion as Formica it is considerably cheaper, and suitable for anything but worktops where there is much cutting and sliding. **1967** *Observer* 21 May 30/5 A work-top bridging two drawer units makes a perfectly good dressing-table. **1978** *Lancashire Life* Oct. 125/1 (Advt.), Now in our upstairs showroom shown in three displays of door and worktop colour—the kitchen of rounded edges—doors and worktops in a host of colours and textures. **1984** *Which?* Oct. 458/3 If you are going to use tilesf or a worktop, check that they have good scratch resistance. **1967** *St. Andrews Citizen* 25 Feb. 5/4 Men's workwear. Full range mens overalls..trousers, jackets, coats and boilersuits. **1981** *Daily Tel.* 22 Sept. 9 (Advt.), The workwear rental company. **1853** C. BRONTË *Villette* I. v. 82 A brief holiday, permitted for once to work-weary faculties. **1935** *Economist* 26 Oct. 802/1 Hourly wage rates are a little higher;..the work-week is a little longer. **1980** *News & Observer* (Raleigh, N. Carolina) 28 Oct. 21/3 Layoffs in a local furniture plant and shortened workweeks at county textile mills.

35. *attrib.* and *Comb.* with *works* (sense 18), as *works bus, canteen, club, kitchen, manager, outing*; **works committee, council**, a committee of workers or their representatives, formed for joint discussions with employers.

1969 R. BLYTHE *Akenfield* iv. 80 Works-bus waiting to carry him from door to site. **1980** A. TOWNSIN *Blue Triangle* iii. 48/1 A second works bus. **1963** A. HOWARD in Sissons & French *Age of Austerity* i. 17 The Naafi and the works-canteen. **1978** J. B. HILTON *Some run Crooked* iii. 19 He ate his midday meal in a works canteen. **1908** *Mod. Business* Aug. 69/1 Any surplus is devoted to some charity or to some of the works clubs. **1917** *Interim Rep. on Joint Standing Industr. Councils* 4 in *Parl. Papers* 1917–18 (Cd. 8606) XVIII. 415 We are of opinion that.. Works Committees, representative of the management and of the workers employed, should be instituted..to act in close co-operation with the district and national machinery. **1966** T. LUPTON *Managem. & Social Sci.* iii. 63 In a small firm, Joint Consultation might take place in a Works Committee. **1925** *Glasgow Herald* 31 July 5 The most important is the Works Council Law of 1920, which requires a works council to be set up in each establishment employing 20 persons or more. **1977** *Times* 22 Sept. 2/8 The need to develop industrial democracy on the shop floor through works councils. **1908** *Mod. Business* Aug. 69/1 Another valuable outlet for its energies is the management of a Works Kitchen. **1918** A. BENNETT *Pretty Lady* xxvii. 177, I used to take their part against the works-manager. **1976** *Derbyshire Times* (Peak ed.) 3 Sept. 3/7 Mr..Marshall (26), works manager, ..escaped unhurt. **1943** J. B. PRIESTLEY *Daylight on Saturday* viii. 47 His bus ride to the factory..took on the air of a works outing. **1974** *Listener* 23 May 664/2 A works outing to Blackpool.

work, *v.* **B. I. 1. c.** For † *Obs.* read *Obs.* exc. in *Freemasonry*, and add later examples.

1884 W. J. HUGHAN *Origin Eng. Rite Freemasonry* i. 5 It seems difficult to understand how any one conversant with their noble Histories can cherish the fancy that the Craft..and other degrees were worked by our ancient brethren during the seventeenth century. **1903** J. T. LAWRENCE *Masonic Jurisprudence & Symbolism* viii. 74 What generally takes place in a lodge of instruction is that the lectures, or sections of them, are worked, officers to conduct the same being appointed at a previous meeting. **1954** W. HANNAH *Christian by Degrees* iv. 65 The 26th degree known as Prince of Mercy (not worked in England) also regards Hiram as a type of Christ in His death and resurrection. **1978** *Lochaber News* 31 Mar. 2/7 An EA Degree was worked and was well received by the Brethren present.

10. Esp. in phr. *to work havoc*, where the pa. t. *wrought* is common (though it is often interpreted as the pa. t. of *wreak*: cf. *WREAK *v.* 8 b).

1900, 1908 [see *HAVOC *sb.* 2]. **1978** *Washington Post* 30 Nov. A-14/2 Settlers who are prone to California dreaming,..and on whom..the anything-goes atmosphere and the wide-open spaces work havoc. **1983** *National Law Jrnl.* (U.S.) 4 July 14/2 With hard disk technology.. power failures can often work havoc. **1984** *Financial Times* 4 June III. p. vii, A decade of inflation had wrought havoc with its portfolio of fixed interest mortgages.

11. b. *colloq.* To arrange, engineer, or bring about. Usu. const. *it*.

1889 E. DOWSON *Let.* 1 Mar. (1967) 42 If you can *possibly* work it meet me somewhere to-morrow. **1911** G. B. SHAW *Doctor's Dilemma* III. 57 The way to work it is this. I'll postdate the cheque next October. **1953** K. TENNANT *Joyful Condemned* xxxi. 305 I'll get young Rene... I guess I can work it. **1962** WODEHOUSE *Service with Smile* xi. 177 Uncle Fred, did you work this? **1975** D. LODGE *Changing Places* i. 17 Masters (who was Chairman) was prepared to work it for Philip if he was interested.

12. h. (Earlier examples.) Also *fig.*

1727 'E. DORRINGTON' *Hermit* II. 121 He sees.. Hay-makers, going to work,..and resolves to make one of their Number, and work his passage up to London. **1743** [see PASSAGE *sb.* 4 b]. **1803** D. WORDSWORTH *Jrnl.* 25 Aug. (1941) I. 257 He was just come from America... I do not think that he had brought much [money] back with him, for he had worked his passage over. **1934** G. B. SHAW *Village Wooing* 113, I have no time for talk. I have to work my passage. **1958** *Oxf. Mag.* 15 May 448/2 Italy, liberated piecemeal and 'working her passage' to the improved status of the Hyde Park Declaration and the New Deal for Italy. **1973** *Times* 20 Mar. 13/2 One of the greatest bores in packing is choosing which shoes to take... They are heavy..and do not really work their passage.

i. (*e*) of a thief, esp. a pickpocket.

1865 *Leaves from Diary Celebrated Burglar & Pickpocket* xvi. 55/2 They agreed, upon their discharge, to 'work' together. *Ibid.* xvi. 53/1 Joe edged himself into the Scotch Boy's 'mob'..and 'worked' with them. **1882** J. D. MCCABE *New York* 520 Even vessels lying at anchor in the harbor, are busily worked by [thieves]. **1905** E. WALLACE *Four Just Men* viii. 153 The night being comparatively young, Billy decided to work the trams. **1930** —— *Lady of Ascot* i. 19 It's the same crowd that has been working country houses for weeks. **1938** F. D. SHARPE *Sharpe of Flying Squad* xvi. 181 They [*sc.* pick-pockets] used to go off in busloads..to 'work' various districts of London. **1951** W. C. WILLIAMS *Autobiogr.* xlv. 299 He had been a fur thief working the big department stores. **1963** T. TULLETT *Inside Interpol* xii. 171 A Pole.. last caught in August, 1957, working a crowd in Geneva.

14. d. (Earlier example.)

1884 'MARK TWAIN' *Huck. Finn* xix. 183 Preachin's my line, too; and workin' camp-meetin's.

16. a. Also of a locomotive engine, to pull (a train).

1912 [in Dict.]. **1982** *Railway Mag.* Nov. 508/1 A replacement..powered the train as far as Carnforth where another '47' was later provided to work it forward.

b. To herd (sheep, cattle, etc.). Also *intr.* for *pass.* Chiefly *Austral.* and *N.Z.*

1930 L. G. D. ACLAND *Early Canterbury Runs* 1st Ser. i. 5 The practice was for a shepherd to go round the boundary once or twice a day, and at night work the sheep below one of the river terraces to camp. **1946** F. DAVISON *Dusty* (Foreword), Sheep dogs..working lost flocks in the mountain gullies. **1950** *N.Z. Jrnl. Agric.* July 5/2 Sheep work and draft best on a slight up-grade. **1961** B. CRUMP *Hang on a Minute* 87 With Jack working along the top of the ridge and Sam half-way down the side they worked all the sheep off that side of the valley. **1976** *Evening Post* (Bristol) 23 Apr. 24/9 (Advt.), Border collie bitch starting to work cattle.

19. a. *spec.* in *N.Z.*, to use (a dog) for the purpose of herding sheep or cattle.

1878 E. S. ELWELL *Boy Colonists* 48 Fricker..[was] delighted to shew the 'new chum' how to work a cattle dog. **1928** P. T. KENWAY *Pioneering in Poverty Bay* viii. 56 It was said of the Highland shepherd in New Zealand, that he would..work his dogs, getting in stray sheep, every day for a month.

II. 23. d. *to work like a charm*: see *CHARM *sb.*[1] 1 c.

24. a. *to work like a beaver, horse, nigger*: see these words. Similarly *to work like a dog, to work one's tail off*.

1926 [see *PERISH *v.* 1 e]. **1969**, etc. [see *TAIL *sb.*[1] 5 a]. **1976–7** *Sea Spray* (N.Z.) Dec./Jan. 95/2 These lads have worked like dogs all winter.

26. a. Also *out of* (a place), to use it as a base, office, etc., for work; *to* (a person), to be responsible to as one's immediate superior or supervisor.

1941 B. SCHULBERG *What makes Sammy Run?* xii. 300 She's turned pro... She's working out of Gladys'. **1961** B. FERGUSSON *Watery Maze* xiv. 360 The Forward Officer (Bombardment) working to H.M.S. *Roberts* was killed with his signaller. **1972** *Where* Sept. 263/1 Registration officers work to the Registrar General. **1975** I. MURDOCH *Word Child* 6, I worked to a man called Duncan, now briefly seconded to the Home Office. **1976** M. DELVING *China Expert* i. 12 He had no shop but worked out of the small, comfortable house he had bought. **1979** P. COSGRAVE *Three Colonels* viii. 174 They had all worked either to Davies..or Morgan... None had come in contact with the head of the department.

27. a. For '*Obs.* exc. as in b' read '*Obs.* exc. as in b, c, and d'.

c. *slang.* (See quot. 1839.) Cf. sense 12 i (*e*) above.

1839 H. BRANDON in W. A. Miles *Poverty, Mendicity & Crime* 166/1 *Work*, to rob, or act in any way according to the divers occupations of thieves, &c. **1882** *Sydney Slang Dict.* 10/2 We went to the gaff that night and tried to work. **1955** *Publ. Amer. Dial. Soc.* xxiv. 70 Some Americans [*sc.* pickpockets]..are front workers..; that is, they can and do work facing the victim. **1963** T. TULLETT *Inside Interpol* x. 150 Huffman 'worked' for a short time in Rome, where he defrauded several shop-keepers.

d. *to work to rule*: to follow the rules of one's occupational duties punctiliously in order to reduce efficiency, usu. as a form of protest in an industrial dispute. So *work-to-rule* attrib. phr.; also as *sb.* Similarly, in the professions, *work-to-contract*.

[**1940** *Ann. Reg. 1939* 310 A 'ca' canny' movement—called 'work to rules'—among the [railway] employees.] **1950** *Ann. Reg. 1949* 40 The delegates replied by ordering a general work-to-rule 44-hour week..unless claims were settled. **1952** *News Chron.* 13 Mar. 5/7 That conductor was working to rule... All passengers must be seated before moving off; no overtaking of other buses; and no efforts to make up lost time. **1958** *Times* 4 Aug. 6/4 A report that prison officers..were working to rule in protest against the report .that prisoners there had been assaulted. **1959** *Daily Tel.* 21 Nov. 1/5 The work-to-rule and shut-down were expected to be carried out in Manchester, Birmingham, Liverpool and other provincial cities. **1960** *Guardian* 13 June 1/6 A 'work-to-rule' plan instituted by members of the Amalgamated Engineering Union after pay negotiations..had broken down. **1962** *Spectator* 26 Jan. 96 What about lesser sanctions—go-slows, work-to-rules and overtime bans? **1967** R. WHITEHEAD in Wills & Yearsley *Handbk. Managem. Technol.* 69 The system would fail even more often if the staff stuck rigidly to the rules. We see the results when they 'work to rule', as it is. **1969** *Daily Tel.* 19 Apr. 23/3 Members of the London Schoolmasters' Association will 'work to contract' next term because of the two weeks' suspension without pay earlier in the year of 22 teachers. **1972** 'M. SINCLAIR' *Norslag* x. 82 A work-to-rule among ground staff had led to some flights being delayed. **1975** *Times* 13 Jan. 15/1 Instead of wholesale industrial action by most of the [medical] profession, we are left with the consultants and their 'work-to-contract'.

III. 36. work in. c. To co-operate or get along *with*.

1915 E. FENWICK *Diary* 14 Oct. in *Elsie Fenwick in Flanders* (1981) 89, I had tried so hard to work in with her. **1960** M. SPARK *Ballad Peckham Rye* viii. 181 If Mr. Druce thought I was working in with you, he'd kill me. **1974** O. MANNING *Rain Forest* I. ix. 101, I am a very fast learner, and I work in well with Mr. Axelrod.

37. work off. c. Also, to get rid of, palm off, pass off. Occas. *refl.*

1813 M. L. WEEMS *Wks. & Ways* (1929) III. 92 The Maps..may be work[ed] off and in time to give you bank interest. **1884** KIPLING *Let.* 21 Nov. in C. Carrington *Rudyard Kipling* (1955) iv. 58 I've been writing a story... I'm trying to work it off on some alien paper to get myself pice thereby. **1897** 'O. THANET' *Missionary Sheriff* 7 The lightning-rods ain't in it with this last scheme—working his self off as a Methodist parson. **1900** 'MARK TWAIN' *Speeches* (1910) 164 He has not written as many plays as I have, but he has had that God-given talent, which I lack, of working them off on the manager. **1948** V. PALMER *Golconda* viii. 58 Corney had been skiting about his claim for months, and everyone knew it was a duffer, but he hung on in the hope of working it off on someone.

38. work out. a. Also *refl.*

1906 *Jrnl. Abnormal Psychol.* I. 37 We might properly say that the 'uncompleted emotion'..could be given an opportunity to work itself out.

l. Also *gen.* to practise, take exercise, rehearse.

1929 *Cosmopolitan* Aug. 72/2 Feet's feet take up so much room when he is on the floor that only two other dancers can work out at the same time. **1948** G. VIDAL *City & Pillar* II. ix. 264 Jim worked out in the YMCA. **1965** C. BROWN *Manchild in Promised Land* viii. 221 I'd go up to the gym and work out for a little while, and I wasn't tired any more. **1973** R. L. SIMON *Big Fix* (1974) xv. 110, I sat..watching the members of the *Teatro Comunal* work out. **1980** J. BALL *Then came Violence* xiv. 117 He belonged to a health club where he worked out regularly. **1984** *Daily Tel.* 30 Apr. 15/7 He does not look his 59 years. Perhaps it helps that he had his face lifted twice, works out with weights and had synthetic implants in his jaw.

38*. work over. *slang.* To beat up, thrash (a person).

1927 *Dialect Notes* V. 467 *Work one over*, to resort to violence in the third degree inquisition of the police. **1934** D. HAMMETT *Thin Man* viii. 37 Morelli's face was a mess: the coppers had worked him over a little just for the fun of it. **1947** *Partisan Rev.* XIV. 329 The crooked cop can't look at Marlowe without a self-revealing yen to 'work him over'. **1970** *Daily Tel.* 11 Dec. 1/1 An engineer was followed into a sub-station by two men who threatened to 'work him over'. **1978** R. PERRY *Dutch Courage* ii. 23 Alan held me and Bernard worked me over.

39. work up. n. *U.S. Med.* (See quot.) Cf. *WORK-UP 2.

1961 *Amer. Speech* XXXVI. 145 *Work up*, to perform a series of diagnostic procedures (X-rays, laboratory blood tests, electro-cardiograms, and so forth).

workably (wɒ̄·ɹkăbli), *adv.* [f. WORK *v.* + -ABLY.] In a workable way; so as to be workable.

1943 NISSEN & BERGMANN *Cineplastic Operations on Stumps of Upper Extremity* iii. 36 Three sutures are placed, one in each of the free corners..and one in the centre edge of the pediculated flap for the purpose of holding it workably tense. **1971** *Nature* 12 Mar. 69/2 Should there not..be some kind of rebate for bulk delivery or, more workably, a charge for single delivery which is mitigated by bulk delivery?

workaholic (wɒ̄ɹkăhǫ·lik). *colloq.* (orig. *U.S.*). [f. WORK *sb.*, after *alcoholic*.] One who is addicted to work, or who voluntarily works excessively hard and unusually long hours. Also *attrib.* or as *adj.*

1968 W. E. OATES in *Pastoral Psychology* Oct. 16 (*heading*) On being a 'workaholic'. **1971** —— (*title*) Confessions of a workaholic. **1973** *Bulletin* (Sydney) 25 Aug. 45/2 The workaholic, as an addict is called, neglects his family, withdraws from social life, and loses interest in sex. **1974** *Daily Colonist* (Victoria, B.C.) 17 July 18/8 Often the workaholic boss threatens the health and welfare of those unfortunate enough to work for him. **1976** *S. Wales Echo* 27 Nov. 6/9 At all costs you should avoid becoming a 'Workaholic'... You should leave your work behind with the office. **1981** *Time* 13 May 67/3 Unlike their workaholic American cousins Europeans tend to see lengthy vacations as somehow part of the natural order of things. **1984** *Guardian* 22 Oct. 11/4 They're concerned about the pressures of their jobs, which demand that they become workaholics.

Hence **wo·rkaholism**, the condition of being a workaholic.

1968 W. E. OATES in *Pastoral Psychol.* Oct. 16/2, I have dubbed this addiction of myself and my fellow ministers as 'workaholism'. **1971** —— *Confessions of a Workaholic* i. 1 Workaholism is a word which I have invented... It means addiction to work, the compulsion or the uncontrollable need to work incessantly. **1981** *Farmstead Mag.* Winter 23/2 For them it requires no effort of will to go off energy-saving appliances,..leave off gluttony on home-grown foods or security schemes, give up workaholism. **1983** *Sunday Tel.* (Colour Suppl.) 20 Feb. 14/4 We talked about..workaholism, autobiography and Isaac Asimov.

workalike (wɒ̄·ɹkălaik), *a.* and *sb.* Also **work-alike.** [f. WORK *v.* + ALIKE *adv.*] **A.** *adj.* Of a computer: able to use the software of another machine and behaving in the same way when the software is used. **B.** *sb.* A workalike computer.

1981 *Infoworld* 13 Apr. 54 (*heading*) PMC-80: TRS-80 'workalike' computer. *Ibid.* 54/1 Personal Micro Computers has renamed the Video Genie PMC-80, and uses the phrase 'TRS-80 workalike' in some of its advertising. **1983** *Austral. Personal Computer* Aug. 90/2 Most software writers recognise the existence of IBM workalike machines and therefore attempt to avoid nucleus calls to direct device I/O. **1983** *Popular Computing* Dec. 83/2 The Ace is an Apple II workalike that accepts Apple II software, disk drives, and..add-on cards. **1985** *Daily Tel.* 9 Sept. 2 (Advt.), A true, 16-bit, μPD8086 chip. (Not the humble 8088 of so many IBM work-alikes.)

workaway (wɒ̄·ɹkăwē[i]). *U.S.* [f. WORK *v.* + *-a-* + WAY *sb.*[1]] One who works his passage on a ship.

1906 *Federal Reporter* CXXXIX. 92 He authorized the mate to take four men as workaways to earn their passage from Nome to Tocoma. **1933** M. PELL *S.S. Utah* 58 The workaway, a quiet young Swede, also went. **1945** *Seafarers' Log* 20 July 3/3 From there [*sc.* from Honolulu] they were sent as workaways back to San Francisco. **1973** *Art Internat.* Mar. 100/2 If one didn't have the price, one could present one's self to a ship's purser and ask for a job as a workaway.

worked, *ppl. a.* **5.** (Earlier examples of *worked-out, -up.*)

1831 P. EGAN *Show Folks* 41 Like a well-worked up scene on the stage. **1864** 'MARK TWAIN' in *Californian* Nov. 5 We admire his mature judgment in selling out of a worked-out mine.

worker. Add: **2. e.** (Earlier example.)

1873 'MARK TWAIN' *Gilded Age* xliv. 399 In Washington he was..clerk of two house committees, a 'worker' in politics.

5. worker-director, a worker who is also on the board of directors of a firm; **worker participation** [*PARTICIPATION 2 b], participation of workers in the management of the firms or industries for which they work; **worker-peasant,** used *attrib.* with reference to co-operation between urban and rural communities in Communist China; similarly **worker-peasant-soldier; worker-priest,** orig. a Roman Catholic priest in post-war France who earned his living as a factory-worker or the like; now more widely, a priest who engages in secular work for part of his time.

1968 *Economist* 3 Aug. 53 The proposal—that worker-directors should be put on the boards of a number of nationalised industries..—is a waste of time. **1980** *Whitaker's Almanack 1981* 583/2 Sir Keith Joseph announced the ending of the Post Office worker-director experiment. **1973** *Guardian* 19 June 17/4 Mr Heath's..flourish of the worker participation banner. **1978** *Jrnl. R. Soc. Arts* CXXVI. 326/2 'Industrial democracy', probably better called 'worker participation'. [**1937** E. SNOW *Red Star over China* IV. vi. 173 The Chinese Workers' and Peasants' Revolutionary Committee was organized about this time.] **1962** —— *Other Side of River* (1963) xviii. 135 This he managed to do by means of postulating the existence of a 'rural proletariat' and a worker-peasant army under the leadership of the Communist party itself acting as the vanguard of the true (urban) proletariat. **1968** in Gray & Cavendish *Chinese Communism in Crisis* 210 All enterprises with suitable conditions should introduce in a big way the worker-peasant labour system. **1976** tr. Tuan Jui-hsia in *Yenan Seeds & Other Stories* 19 Spring was very much in the air in the Worker-Peasant-Soldier Theatre. **1949** *Commonweal* 29 July 385/2 We must bow our heads in deep humility before the heroism of the worker priest. **1959** *Manch. Guardian* 4 Aug. 3/3 Five worker-priests..believed to be the only ones in the Church of England..do manual work, live on their factory earnings and receive no ecclesiastical stipends. **1970** *Daily Tel.* 29 Dec. 11/3 The Anglican church makes a distinction between worker-priests, who exercise a priestly function at their workplace, and priest-workers, who do an ordinary job, then return to parish work, usually as curate, in their 'spare time'. **1984** *Times* 28 May 10/8, I could not help wondering how it would be received by the congregations of, say, a worker priest in Nicaragua.

6. *Comb.* with *workers'*, as (sense 2 c) *workers' committee, control, flat*; **Workers' Educational Association,** the name of an organization founded in 1903 to provide evening classes and tutorials in economic, political, and liberal studies, originally for working people.

1965 J. KOLAJA *Workers' Councils* II. 28 The highly skilled workers' committee, and the apartments committee were considered temporary. **1972** M. ARGYLE *Social Psychol. of Work* viii. 217 The workers' committees have worked well, and members have acted responsibly on them. **1928** *Britain's Industrial Future* (Liberal Party) III. xviii. 228 Consultation with a body of workers will improve and strengthen it [*sc.* a business]; anything that can accurately be described as 'workers' control' will destroy it. **1974** *Times* 5 Apr. 16/5 As a trades unionist, I am in favour of workers' control. **1903** Workers' Educational Association [in Dict., sense 2 c]. **1936** *N. & Q.* 11 July 19/2 What is gained from the University Extension, the Workers' Educational Association, or a year of study at Ruskin College? **1980** J. L. THOMPSON *Adult Education for Change* 22 The Workers' Educational Association provision has in many respects become barely distinguishable from that promoted by the universities, despite its roots in workers' education and political and economic studies. **1932** S. JAMESON *Single Heart* v. 127 She was able..to buy a slum estate in Evan's constituency and build on it blocks of workers' flats. **1982** S. GRANT DUFF *Parting of Ways* vi. 54 The shelling of the workers' flats in Vienna in February 1934.

workerist (wɒ̄·ɹkərist), *a.* and *sb.* [f. WORKER + -IST.] **A.** *adj.* Of, pertaining to, or characteristic of a worker-oriented view of society; (too) sympathetic to the role of labour in the class struggle. **B.** *sb.* One who adopts workerist values; *spec.* applied (somewhat *derog.*) to a member of the middle or upper classes who espouses the cause of the working class.

1959 W. BIRMINGHAM tr. J. Daniélou in *Cross Currents* Fall 381/2 The workerist conception locates poverty on the level of the standard of living. The 'collectivist' locates poverty on the level of private property. **1981** *Filmnews* (Austral.) May 6/2 The practice of Cinema Action was criticised as workerist for assuming that there was a unified working class. **1984** *Sunday Tel.* 2 Dec. 21/2 Oxford, long the home of what is now known as the 'workerist' (public school student turning very Left-wing). **1985** *Daily Tel.* 11 Feb. 12/2 The genuine proletarians of the hard Left who regard him [*sc.* Mr. Benn] as 'workerist'.

workfare (wɒ̄·ɹkfeᵊɹ). orig. and chiefly *U.S.* [f. WORK *sb.*, after *welfare*.] A policy of requiring recipients of welfare money to do some work in exchange for this benefit.

1968 *Harper's* July 71 One of Evers' programs is what he calls workfare; he has said that everybody ought to work for what he gets. **1969** R. NIXON in *Washington Post* 9 Aug. 1/2 What America needs now is not more welfare but more 'workfare'. **1978** *Globe & Mail* (Toronto) 28 Nov. 5/3 Mr. Walker, one of the most conservative politicians in the Legislature..thinks they would support a pilot project in an interested municipality, although he is not claiming Government support for workfare. **1981** *Daily Tel.* 26 May 5 Two California towns..are at the forefront of a movement to implement 'workfare'—projects aimed at forcing welfare recipients to do some labour in exchange for taxpayers' money. **1985** *Times* 12 Feb. 14/5 There must be a real inducement to work. In the US a number of states have introduced 'Workfare' to complement welfare.

work function. *Physics.* [f. WORK *sb.* + FUNCTION *sb.*] **1.** The minimum quantity of energy, characteristic of the material concerned, which is required to remove an electron to infinity from the surface of a solid (usu. a metal). Symbol: ϕ.

1923 *Proc. R. Soc.* A. CIV. 637 The estimations of the photo-electric work function..are in all cases a good deal greater than the corresponding values of the thermionic work function. **1950** A. KOLIN *Physics* xxxv. 715 The work function can be determined by finding the threshold frequency ν_0 below which no photoelectrons are emitted. **1972** *Sci. Amer.* Mar. 53/1 When two metals are placed in contact, electrons pass from one to the other because of the difference in the metals' quantum-mechanical work functions. This process continues until an equilibrium is reached.

2. A thermodynamic property of a system: its internal energy minus the product of its temperature and entropy. Symbol: A.

1929 R. H. FOWLER *Statistical Mech.* iv. 96, $k\log K(T)$ for the crystal is the thermodynamic function known as Planck's characteristic function, and $-kT \log K(T)$ is the more usual work function..A. **1937** P. S. EPSTEIN *Textbk. Thermodynamics* v. 92 When the temperature and the volume of a system are kept constant, its work function has a tendency to decrease. **1978** P. W. ATKINS *Physical Chem.* v. 139 If we know the value of ΔA for a change we can also state the maximum amount of work the system can do. This relation is the reason why A is sometimes called the maximum work function, or the work function.

workhouse. Add: **3.** (Examples.)

1653 *Boston Rec.* (1886) X. 26 The setting up of a Bridewell or Workehouse for Prisoners Malefactors &..poore people. **1772** A. G. WINSLOW *Diary* 25 Feb. (1895) 36 She..soon got into the workhouse for new misdemeanours. **1870** 'MARK TWAIN' *Curious Dream* (1872) 83 Eggs..so unwholesome that the city physician seldom or never orders them for the workhouse. **1964** *Federal Probation* Dec. 8/2 The Workhouse receives and releases the work-release prisoner any time during the day or night, depending on his working hours.

4. b. workhouse sheeting (examples).

1875 L. TROUBRIDGE *Life amongst Troubridges* (1966) 116 A Workhouse sheeting jacket, body and *tablier*..to wear with dark blue frilled petticoat and sleeves. **1880** [see *BOLTON].

work-in (wɜ̄·ɹkin). [f. WORK *v.* + *-IN³.] A form of protest, usu. against threatened closure of a factory, etc., in which workers occupy the work-place and continue working. Also *transf.*

1968 *Punch* 6 Mar. 327/1 Student protest reached an all-time high with Leicester University's plan to stage a '24-hour work-in'. **1973** *Times Lit. Suppl.* 30 Nov. 1469/1 The series of work-ins or sit-ins in the past two or three years in which workers have occupied factories in pursuit of wage claims or as a refusal to accept redundancy notices. **1976** [see *SIT-IN *sb.* 1]. **1983** *Daily Tel.* 23 June 19/3 A judge strongly attacked the police for staging a dawn raid to break up the work-in.

working, *vbl. sb.* Add: **I. 1. b.** *working to rule,* the action of strictly observing the limits of one's occupational duties; also = *work-to-rule* sb. (see *WORK *v.* 27 d).

1927 W. E. COLLINSON *Contemp. Eng.* 84 The inconveniences of lightning-strikes, ca' canny policy (deliberate restriction of output) and working-to-rule. **1951** *Engineering* 2 Nov. 568/3 The overtime ban and working to rule have remained in force. *Ibid.*, Similar working-to-rule methods..were put into operation by lightermen at the Port of London. **1958** *Times* 19 Aug. 8/3 To what extent the 'working to rule' will apply will depend on the attitude of individual busmen. **1964** M. ARGYLE *Psychol. & Social Probl.* xiv. 172 Anti-organization practices such as restriction of output, unofficial strikes and working to rule. *a* **1974** R. CROSSMAN *Diaries* (1976) II. 686, I tried to make them realize..what I meant by quietism. I suggested that it meant a 'non-enthusiastic execution'—working to rule, shall we say?

2. b. *spec.* in *Freemasonry,* (the performance of) a rite, a system of ritual.

1884 W. J. HUGHAN *Orig. Eng. Rite Freemasonry* p. iii, Although under various Grand Lodges the details of the working differ, the landmarks remain practically identical. **1903** J. T. LAWRENCE *Masonic Jurisprudence & Symbolism* viii. 75 The more important one [*sc.* duty] is to see that ceremonies are conducted in accordance with working sanctioned by the Grand Lodge of England. **1932** S. M. HILLS *Freemason's Craft* viii. 64 The Articles of the Union..stipulated that there should henceforth be perfect unity of working, and the Lodge of Reconciliation was formed..to agree upon a working.

5. f. Of a bus, train, etc.

1978 M. KEELEY et al. *Birmingham City Transport* 181 City—Bull Ring—Coventry Road—Lyndon End. Short working of 94. **1982** *Railway Mag.* Nov. 508/1 A reader who visited Scarborough..noted a wide variety of locomotive classes in use on summer-holiday workings.

III. 15. *working-out*: spec. in *Mus.* = DEVELOPMENT 10; *working-over* (*slang*) = *GOING OVER, GOING-OVER 2 b and c.

1889 GROVE *Dict. Mus.* IV. 486/2 *Working-out* (also called Free Fantasia; and Development; Durchführung), the central division of a movement in Binary form, such as commonly occupies the first place in a modern sonata or symphony. **1936** *Discovery* Apr. 124/1 The music of Bach, with its perfect counterpoint and logical working-out. **1948** *Penguin Music Mag.* VII. 43 The..sleight-of-hand that Grieg saw fit to employ in a 'working-out'. **1960** C. HAMBLETT in J. Pudney *Pick of Today's Short Stories* XI. 143 The cops frisked him..hoping he would put up a fight, so they could give him a working-over first. **1964** L. DEIGHTON *Funeral in Berlin* viii. 55 A girl with too much make-up..gave her eyebrows a working over.

IV. 16. a. *working arrangement, bee, model.* **b. working-box** (earlier example); **working card** *U.S. obs.* = *union-card* s.v. *UNION *sb.*¹ 11 c; **working copy,** a copy of a book or other document used or annotated by someone working on its contents; **working dinner, lunch,** a dinner or lunch at which those present discuss business; **working order** (earlier example); **working plan,** a plan serving as the basis for the construction of a building, management of a project, etc.; *spec.* in *Forestry* (see quots. 1895, 1926); **working space** = *working storage*; cf. *work-space* (*b*) s.v. *WORK *sb.* 34 d; **working storage,** part of a computer's memory that is used by a program for the storage of intermediate results or other temporary items; **working surface** = *work-top* s.v. *WORK *sb.* 34 d; **working title,** a provisional title given to a book, film, or other work before the final title is settled; **working top** = *work top* s.v. *WORK *sb.* 34 d.

1854 *Household Narrative* Apr. 80/2 He stated..that the more complete fusion of capital into one company ought not to be sanctioned, but that sort of combination known as working arrangements should be encouraged. **1904** *Windsor Mag.* June 16/1 A simple working arrangement is usual based on a percentage division of the gross receipts between the two. **1970** *New Yorker* 29 Aug. 45/1 Jews and pagans would never get to Heaven, with the exception of..Moses, who had a close working arrangement with Allah. **1883** 'A LADY' *Facts: or, Exper. Recent Colonist in N.Z.* viii. 68 The ladies of the community..meet for a common cause..Working bees are then got up. **1956** W. R. BIRD *Off-Trail in Nova Scotia* i. 23 We were told much of working bees, barn raisings, the making of maple sugar. **1778** J. WOODFORDE *Diary* 9 Sept. (1924) I. 235 It..looks when covered like a working Box for Ladies. **1872** *Pacific States Enterprise* (San Francisco) 16 Mar. 3/1 They have adopted the 'working card' system. **1874** *Internat. Typogr. Union Proc.* 34 Subordinate Unions are recommended to..enforce the 'working-card' system. **1896** *Ibid.* 35/2 It was agreed to issue him a working card. **1923** *Proc. 43rd Convention Amer. Fed. of Labor* 324/2 This resolution..affects such other organizations as they seek to affect with an exchange of working cards and other courtesies. **1897** W. C. HAZLITT *Confessions of Collector* vi. 100, I would gladly pay him a guinea for it, and find him a working copy into the bargain. **1967** E. R. LANNON in Cox & Grose *Organization & Handling Bibl. Rec. by Computer* IV. 95 We can..print the dictionary in two forms; one form is referred to as the 'Working Copy' edition, intended for the use of our own editorial staff. **1970** *Daily Tel.* 22 Sept. 1/8 Union chiefs and chairmen of five nationalised industries had a 'working dinner'..last night. **1964** *Guardian* 27 Oct. 18/6 After these meetings there was a 'working' lunch at the British Embassy. **1966** H. MOORE *On Sculpture* 247 The first maquette for the wood Interior Exterior Forms was produced in 1951, later the same year I made the working model (24½ in. high), which was cast into bronze. **1982** *Sunday Tel.* (Colour Suppl.) 14 Nov. 33/1 Carvings were plastercast, moulds were taken and durable metal-alloy working models were made. **1845** *Knickerbocker* XXVI. 410 The use of steam-pumps is requisite night and day, to keep them [*sc.* mines] in working order. **1880** 'MARK TWAIN' *Tramp Abroad* xxxiv. 370 The ghastly desolation of the place was as tremendously complete as if Doré had furnished the working-plans for it. **1895** W. SCHLICH *Man. Forestry* III. III. 173 Forest working plans regulate, according to time and locality, the management of forests in such a manner, that the objects of the industry are as fully as possible realized. **1926** TANSLEY & CHIPP *Study of Vegetation* xi. 255 The Working Plan forms..a scheme for exploiting the forest whereby regeneration will keep pace with exploitation. **1983** *National Trust* Spring 10/1 Constructive, planned woodland management..only became possible after the war, and our oldest working plans are now barely thirty years old. **1954** Working space [see *surface sterilization* s.v. *SURFACE *sb.* 6 c]. **1973** M. WOODHOUSE *Blue Bone* vii. 63 The converted hold..had contained a full-sized billiards table. There was, at least, plenty of working space. **1954** *Computers & Automation* Dec. 23/1 Working storage. . Like a worksheet in pencil and paper calculation. **1971** N. CHAPIN *Computers* xv. 445 In the operand data structures, programers commonly distinguish between constants that are not part of the program, working storage (for intermediate results and status or progress indicators), and input-output buffer areas. **1983** D. H. SANDARS *Computers Today* v. 113 This total earnings figure is copied (instruction, 08) in address 15, which is the working storage area. **1962** A. WISE *Death's-Head* iii. 23 The electric percolator standing on the formica working-surface. **1970** *Which?* Sept. 279/1 Three of the small freezers..had laminated tops you could use as a working surface. **1940** R. CHANDLER *Let.* 27 June in Gardiner & Walker *Raymond Chandler Speaking* (1962) 211 The title of my book is not *The Second Murderer.* I used that for a while as a working title, but I didn't like it. **1977** G. FISHER *Villain of Piece* iii. 32, I was now busy turning the whole caboodle into a series of four articles... I gave it a working title: 'My Life with Britain's Top Villain'. **1959** *Housewife* June 70/2 Table-top refrigerators are popular because they give an additional working top. **1980** D. CLARK *Golden Rain* v. 115 'Which cupboard please?' 'The last one under the working-top on the left.'

working, *ppl. a.* Add: **2. a.** Also *spec.* of a girl or woman: that goes out to earn a living rather than remain at home; *working girl*: also *euphem.*, a prostitute (*U.S. slang*).

1865 DICKENS *Mut. Fr.* II. IV. vi. 209, I am removed from you and your family by being a working girl. **1889** [see *SISTER *sb.* 2]. **1913** J. VAIZEY *College Girl* ix. 119 'I shall have to earn money myself, so I want to pass all the exams. I can.' The Percivals stared... They had never met a prospective *working* girl before! **1933** D. C. PEEL *Life's Enchanted Cup* xv. 183 It was, perhaps, because she had known what it was to study in the intervals of tending children..that she could sympathise with working mothers. **1963** *Times* 2 Jan. 10/3 Many Australians had to take two jobs to make ends meet, and 'there were any number of working wives'. **1970** O. NORTON *Dead on Prediction* i. 7 I'm going to be a working girl again now. Doing some articles for *Mercia*, for a start. **1978** F. WELDON *Praxis* xx. 174 Praxis gave up her job: Ivor did not want a working wife. **1979** *Arizona Daily Star* 5 Aug. J 3/2 There were studies showing juvenile delinquents springing from single-parent or working-mother homes.

1968 *Current Slang* (Univ. S. Dakota) Fall 52 *Working girl*, n., a prostitute. **1971** *N.Y. Times* 9 Aug. 33/5 They call themselves 'working girls'... Their work is a 'business', or even..a 'social service'... By the prostitute's code, prostitution is moral. **1984** *Chicago Sun-Times* 26 Mar. 12 U.S. Prostitutes has estimated that thousands of 'working girls' will travel to San Francisco for business generated by the convention.

c. Restrict Mil. to sense in Dict. and add: (*b*) a group of women, meeting to do work, esp. sewing, for a good cause; (*c*) a committee appointed to examine and report on a particular subject and to make recommendations based on its findings; (*d*) a group of prisoners engaged on outdoor work, freq. outside the perimeter of the prison.

1876 C. M. YONGE *Three Brides* I. viii. 127 Cecil had offered to take Anne to see the working party, and let her assist thereat. **1900** —— *Modern Broods* vii. 72 The parish room, where the ladies were to hold a working party for the missions. **1946** *Times* 10 Jan. 2/3 The 'working party' is a device for securing the best possible guidance on the policies that should be adopted to bring an industry to the highest pitch of efficiency under private enterprise. **1948** *Hansard Commons: Written Answers* 8 Mar. 112 The Working Party on the Turn-Round of Shipping was set up to examine the causes of delay... Teams from the Working Party have visited the major ports. **1963** T. PARKER *Unknown Citizen* v. 136 Charlie was out of the prison that day, on a working party at a farm some miles away. **1976** L. KENNEDY *Presumption of Innocence* I. 46 One day at Parkhurst he walked away from an outside working-party... Although he was wearing prison overalls, no one paid any attention. **1981** E. LONGFORD *Queen Mother* v. 82 The Queen and her working party met twice a week to make surgical dressings and comforters for the troops. **1982** *Church Times* 12 Nov. 1/3 The General Synod's Board of Education has set up a working party on independent schools which will look at the Independent sector in education 'from a Christian perspective'.

d. Also of dogs used for hunting, herding, guard duties, etc. Also *fig.*

1897 *Blackw. Mag.* June 744/1 Notwithstanding the care most people take to buy pups of 'good working parents', it is the blood that tells. **1936** *Times Lit. Suppl.* 25 Jan. 73/2 The American husband (in fiction) is losing his working-dog quality, his ambition to toil. **1947** C. L. B. HUBBARD (*title*) Working dogs of the world. **1982** G. HAMMOND *Fair Game* xi. 99 [The dog] went for the pigeon..and fetched it back... Miss Wyper was overwhelmed. This was her first introduction to the truly fulfilled dog, the working dog doing the job for which it was bred.

4. (Later example.)

1934 DYLAN THOMAS in *New Verse* No. 9. 12 The dry Sargossa of the tomb Gives up its dust to such a working sea.

7. (Earlier examples of *working model.*)

1770 J. FERGUSON *Introd. Electricity* 134 A working model of the great crane at *Bristol.* **1822** C. F. PARTINGTON *Hist. & Descr. Account Steam Engine* i. 13 In the following year a working model of the above engine was submitted to the Royal Society.

working class. Add: **a.** (Earlier examples.)

1789 J. GRAY in G. Dempster *Discourse containing a Summary of Proceedings of Soc. for extending Fisheries & improving Sea Coasts of Gt. Britain* 50 More spacious plots of ground..may be allowed to the clergyman and schoolmaster, and to other persons superior to the working class. **1795** J. AIKIN *Descr. Country 30–40 Miles round Manchester* 262 Houses for the working class are not procured without difficulty.

b. (Earlier examples.)

1839 J. S. MILL in *Westm. Rev.* Apr. 497 The Working Men's Association..who represent the best and most enlightened aspect of working-class Radicalism. **1849** F. D. MAURICE *Let.* 3 Mar. in J. F. Maurice *Life F. D. Maurice* (1884) I. xxv. 513 Thank you very much for entering so heartily into my working class meetings.

working-day. **2.** (Earlier example.)

1853 *Hogg's Instructor* X. 282/2 To grant the Saturday afternoon holiday, and to limit the duration of every other working day within a certain definite period of time, not exceeding twelve hours, including the proper interval for meals.

working-man. Add: **b.** *Comb.* in the possessive, denoting institutions established for working men, as *working man's* (or *men's*) *association, club, college, institute.*

1839 Working men's association [see *WORKING CLASS b]. **1844** *Lexington* (Ky.) *Observer* 2 Oct. 3/1 The Working Men's Clay Club of this city will hold an adjourned meeting. **1861** MRS. GASKELL *Let.* 16 Apr. (1966) 650 He has..established a small working man's Club, with the help of a *low* Church curate. **1961** *Economist* 30 Dec. 1270/1 The Working Men's Club and Institute Union achieves its centenary next year. **1976** *National Observer* (U.S.) 18 Dec. 18/3 It opens in a Manchester secondary-school classroom, where a sextet of aspiring stand-up comics has assembled for their Big Chance, an audition before a real..agent at a local working-man's club. **1856** C. FOX *Let.* 27 June in *Jrnls.* (1972) 223 Oxford... I was delighted to hear of their successful experiment to unite Town and Gown by a Working Man's College. **1921** G. B. SHAW *Back to Methuselah* II. 61, I was asked to deliver an address to the students at the Working Men's College. **1971** G. STEINER *Bluebeard's Castle* iii. 61 The categories of schooling and public enlightenment—the lyceum, the public library, the working men's college. **1882** F. A. KEMBLE *Records of Later Life* III. 293 A reading that I gave for the Working Men's Institute in Brighton. **1980** E. BLISHEN *Nest of Teachers* I. i. 4 A Working Men's Institute..established in the last century.

workman. Add: **6.** *Comb.* in the possessive, denoting things (esp. transport) provided for workmen (sense 1), as *workman's* (or *workmen's*) *bus, club, compensation, train, tram.*

1965 A. PRIOR *Interrogators* xi. 198 An early morning workman's bus roared and rumbled. **1980** 'D. GRANT' *Emerald Decision* i. 20 Workmen's bus, heading for the harbour. **1911** G. B. SHAW *Doctor's Dilemma* I. 22 Except for the workmen's clubs, my patients are all clerks and shopmen. **1921** *Daily Colonist* (Victoria, B.C.) 12 Mar. 6/4 Compensation was paid to him by the Workmen's Compensation Board and he was later discharged as having recovered. **1940** *Economist* 3 Feb. 198/2 An all-round increase in the rates payable for workmen's compensation. **1872** JERROLD *London* p. ix, The workman's train and the crowds pressing over London Bridge. **1975** P. MCCUTCHAN *Very Big Bang* xi. 105 'They'll call back when the current's off.' 'No more workmen's trains?'..'Not on this section.' **1906** *Jackson's Oxford Jrnl.* 8 Sept. 6/6 At 5.10 the workmen's tram joined in the procession. **1970** S. ALEXANDER *St. Giles's Fair* 19 The workman's tram passed through St. Giles at five ten a.m.

work-out. Add: **a.** Also more widely, an exercise session, practice, or test. (Earlier and later examples.)

1909 R. A. WASON *Happy Hawkins* 161, I expect to give it a fair good work-out before I'm through with it. **1923** H. C. WITWER *Fighting Blood* iii. 96 I ain't going to get no gym workout. **1938** M. K. RAWLINGS *Yearling* ix. 98 'Will we take both dogs?' 'Nobody but old Julia. She ain't had a work-out since she was hurt. A slow hunt'll do her good.' **1952** *Sun* (Baltimore) 3 Mar. 28/3 The United States Air Force Filter Center here had its first surprise workout yesterday. **1960** *Sunday Express* 27 Nov. 14/3 Work-out gymnasia with..general slimming equipment. **1963** A. ROSS *Australia 63* vii. 128 Both teams had work-outs at the Oval, over-watered pitches making net practice impracticable. **1972** *Daily Tel.* 6 Sept. 6/8, I am not suggesting that old people should do strenuous physical work-outs, but stiff joints and muscles may be helped by properly supervised exercises. **1979** *Tucson Mag.* Apr. 56/1 (Advt.), A multitude of weight training systems designed to accommodate your kind of workout room. **1981** J. FONDA *Jane Fonda's Workout Bk.* (1982) 22 She took me to an exercise class that put me through the most vigorous and thorough workout I had ever had.

b. *fig.*

1934 J. O'HARA *Appointment in Samarra* i. 17 Four of the young men had had work-outs with her off the dance floor, and as a result Constance was not a virgin. **1941** *Punch* 10 Sept. 222 This passage of rich prose is designed as a sort of test or work-out for the new alphabet. **1958** B. HAMILTON *Too Much of Water* viii. 161 A public work-out would test audience reaction. **1967** *Melody Maker* 29 Apr. 10 (Advt.), The totally new snare drum. This one you must see! Get round to your dealer and give it a workout. **1977** *New Yorker* 24 Oct. 173/1 The Villa-Lobos provides a thorough workout for the bassoon.

wo·rkover. [f. WORK *v.* + OVER *adv.*] The repair or maintenance of an oil well.

1976 *Offshore Platforms & Pipelining* 232/3 A conventional wellhead is installed, and the wells are completed by a workover rig. **1977** *Financial Times* 1 Apr. 11/5 Some have suggested a well work-over every three years; others say once every 15 years will be sufficient. **1977** *Offshore Engineer* Aug. 12/3 The workover programme on B-14 well is now complete. **1980** *Daily Tel.* 11 Sept. 29 (Advt.), Jack Up Rig in the Southern North Sea on Viking workovers and new developments. **1985** *New Yorker* 22 Apr. 51/1 The auction business thrived: deep rigs, workover rigs.

workshop. Add: **2. a.** A meeting for discussion, study, experiment, etc., orig. in education or the arts, but now in any field; an organization or group established for this purpose.

1937 *N.Y. Times* 1 Aug. VI. 5/3 The major requirement for admission to this Summer workshop is an approved project for which the applicant seeks aid and advice. **1938** L. MACNEICE *Mod. Poetry* xi. 200 The communist poet, Maiakovski, established a 'word workshop'..to supply all revolutionaries with 'any quantity of poetry desired'. **1952** L. ROSS *Picture* (1953) 21 The elder Reinhardt..came to Hollywood in 1934... For the next five years, he ran a Hollywood school known as Max Reinhardt's Workshop. **1959** *Ottawa Citizen* 14 Sept. 6/1 At a conference or 'workshop' on road safety sponsored by the Ontario Department of Transport recently, there was general agreement that much more must be done to improve driving standards. **1961** in *B.B.C. Handbk.* (1962) 36, I want to see a Television Workshop—a regular period in which everyone feels he can have a go without having to mind too much whether he is successful straight off. **1967** P. MCGIRR *Murder is Absurd* ii. 33 In college Kenny joined the..drama workshop and began work on a play. **1972** *Computers & Humanities* VII. 96 The participants then divided into four workshops and, after five intensive meetings, reconvened to present their findings at the fourth and final plenary session. **1984** *Times* 17 Mar. 15/8 Priority bookings for their tastings, wine workshops and special dinners.

b. *attrib.*

1937 *N.Y. Times* 1 Aug. VI. 5/4 The importance of the workshop idea to American education. **1968** *Globe & Mail* (Toronto) 3 Feb. B 2/3 Local residents considered.. 17 consumer protection items suggested by workshop groups conducted on Thursday. **1976** S. BRETT *So much Blood* ii. 25 The Masonic Hall was not free for Charles to rehearse in... Michael Vanderzee had just started a workshop session... Charles..had no objection to.. workshop techniques. They were useful exercises for actors. **1983** *National Trust* Spring 24/1 In the morning, group discussions were led by the Company's seven actor/teachers in a 'workshop' atmosphere concentrating on the social history of the early eighteenth century.

work station. Also **wo·rkstation.** [f. WORK *sb.* + STATION *sb.*] **1.** A location at which one stage in the manufacture or assembly of a product is carried out before it is moved on for the next stage.

1950 T. M. LANDY *Production Planning & Control* vii. 161 The assigning of work stations by the planners is largely influenced by these considerations: costs, centralization of work within a section..and existing labor load. **1980** M. P. GROOVER *Automation, Production Systems & Computer-Aided Manufacturing* iv. 66 An automated flow line consists of several machines or workstations which are linked together by work handling devices that transfer parts between the stations.

2. A desk with a computer terminal and keyboard; the terminal itself.

1977 *Which Computer?* Sept. 25 Another cavil on the workstation is the absence of a 'home' key to return the cursor to the head of a new page. **1981** *Office* June 23/1 Wordcom 70 can be used as a shared facility system with up to eight work-stations using the cartridge disk. In this way a number of departments can have access to a single database. **1983** *What's New in Computing* Jan. 53 (Advt.), Featured above in teak: printer stand, linking quadrant and 3′ by 2′ workstation with monitor shelf. **1985** *Which Computer?* Apr. 122/3 It can then be viewed by users at any workstation attached to the system.

work-to-contract, work-to-rule: see *WORK *v.* 27 d.

wo·rk-up. [f. vbl. phr. to *work up*: see WORK *v.* 39.] **1.** *Printing.* A piece of spacing material that works loose in the forme and prints a smudge, or the mark so printed. Also, an instance of this.

1948 R. R. KARCH *Graphic Arts Procedures* x. 270 The pressfeeder watches the sheets carefully so that if *work-ups* appear he will not spoil the run. A work-up is spacing material that has risen in the form so that it prints on the sheet. **1950** D. G. HYMES *Production in Advertising* vii. 279 Alert pressmen can..stop the press, and hammer down the workups after only a few sheets have been spoiled. **1967** KARCH & BUBER *Offset Processes* ii. 24 The letterpress printer may be plagued by 'work-up'.

2. *Med.* A diagnostic examination of a patient. orig. *U.S.*

1961 in WEBSTER. **1966** *Current Diagnosis* 206/2 (*heading*) Diagnostic work-up for patients with diastolic hypertension. **1972** *Sci. Amer.* Aug. 71/3 A mother who was told that her child would be 'admitted for a work-up' did not realise that he was to be hospitalized. **1977** *New Yorker* 12 Sept. 103/1 We gave him the usual workup, including neurological and ear-nose-and-throat evaluations. **1978** PARSONS & SOMMERS *Gynecol.* (ed. 2) xx. 313/2 A few cases where the borderline between virilism and hirsutism is hazy will benefit from an extensive work-up.

3. *Chem.* The experimental procedures followed to separate and purify substances for analysis or the products of a chemical reaction.

1967 *Chem. Abstr.* LXVII. 10187/2 (*heading*) Workup of chlorohydrin process waste products. **1971** *Canad. Jrnl. Chem.* XLIX. 2467/1 The resulting mixture was then heated to reflux for 1 h to complete the acetylation and gave after usual work-up a quantitative yield of [compound] 12. **1978** *Jrnl. Amer. Chem. Soc.* C. 3548 Water added during work-up serving as the proton source at C-1.

4. The process of bringing a ship into seaworthy condition.

1971 *Daily Colonist* (Victoria, B.C.) 27 May 35/4 Canadian forces ships work on a 20-month cycle basis containing four parts: refit, trials, workups, and operational. **1978** *Navy News* Oct. 2/6 After trials and work-up the Achilles will return to Chatham for Christmas.

workwise (wɒ̄·ɹkwəiz), *adv.* [f. WORK *sb.* + -WISE.] As far as work is concerned.

1962 *Punch* 6 June 864/1 Workwise, your future is clear. **1979** *Yale Alumni Mag.* Apr. (Suppl.) cn32/1 Although Carol has kept herself busy (workwise) she managed to spend Thanksgiving in Portugal. **1981** S. JACKMAN *Game of Soldiers* I. ii. 33 The unit ticks over well enough work-wise... Trouble is, there's not enough work.

world, *sb.* Add: **II. 7. g.** *broke to the world*: see *BROKE *ppl. a.* 3; (*it's a*) *small world*: see *SMALL *a.* 3 b; (*on*) *top of the world*: see *TOP *sb.*[1] 16.

17. b. *to get up in the world, to go down in the world*: (earlier examples).

1791 J. WOODFORDE *Diary* 20 Mar. (1927) III. 257 John Greaves, my Carpenter..married about 2 Years or more ago, to a Servant Maid of Mrs. Lombe's..and lived very happy together and daily getting up in the World. **1837** J. S. MILL *Let.* 6 Aug. in *Works* (1963) XII. 346 To alter their style of living and go (as the vulgar phrase is) down in the world.

IV. 19. a world. a. *a world of good* (earlier example).

1791 F. BURNEY *Jrnl.* Sept. (1972) I. 57 The Water has done me a World of good—I drink it at morning & Noon regularly.

20. the world. e. *to think the world of* (earlier U.S. example).

[**1852** H. B. STOWE *Uncle Tom's Cabin* II. xxxiv. 206 He had a cousin come to New Orleans, who was his particular friend,—he thought all the world of him.] **1892** 'MARK TWAIN' *Amer. Claimant* iii. 24 They..think the world of Mulberry.

f. *woman of the world* (earlier examples).

1780 F. BURNEY *Diary* Apr. (1904) I. VII. 328 She is an easy, chatty, sensible woman of the world. **1822** M. EDGEWORTH *Let.* 10 Apr. (1971) 393 Lady Clare is a painted—made up—vulgar thorough going woman of the world.

22*. this world. a. *out of this world*: (i) superlatively good, fine beyond description; beautiful, delightful, wonderful. Also as adv. and attrib. phrases. *colloq.* and *slang* (orig. *U.S. Jazz*).

1928 R. FISHER *Walls of Jericho* 303 *Out* (*of*) *this world*, beyond mortal experience or belief. **1931** *Inter-State Tattler* 17 Dec. 12 Alberta Hunter..warbles out of this world. **1935** *Swing Music* July 114/2 Benny's clarinet playing here is out-of-this-world for beauty of tone. **1946** *Sat. Rev. Lit.* (U.S.) 19 Oct. 25/3 Petarded on his own cliché And violently hurled, Should be the Joe whose one bon mot Is 'It's out of this world!' **1952** G. WILSON *Julien Ware* 36 A slender, graceful, out-of-this-world bridge Claud...had been. **1957** J. BRAINE *Room at Top* vi. 51 You've got a lovely part. Out of this world. **1972** J. ROSSITER *Rope for General Dietz* v. 61 She gave me the skinned fruit... With Cointreau poured on, mine tasted out of this world.

(ii) In neutral or derogatory contexts: unworldly; quite remarkable; also, incredibly bad or repulsive.

1941 B. SCHULBERG *What makes Sammy Run?* vii. 149 The gallery was in a funny little bungalow with an easy-going, out-of-this-world atmosphere. **1951** 'A. GARVE' *Murder in Moscow* ii. 32 They hate our guts, and the way they behave is out of this world. **1958** *Oxford Mail* 27 Aug. 6/1 The worst part of a woman's magazine..is the fiction. Stories about quite impossible people in out-of-this-world situations. **1963** P. WILLMOTT *Evolution of Community* viii. 92 The L.C.C.'s wallpapers..are very antiquated, out of this world.

b. *the* (personal or other proper name, pl.) *of this world*: people (countries, etc.) considered to represent the type specified; people, etc., like (sb. sing.). *colloq.* Freq. somewhat *derog.*

1960 J. STROUD *Shorn Lamb* iv. 44 He's settling... We're quite used to the Egberts of this world. **1969** M. PUGH *Last Place Left* xiv. 106 The Pardoes of this world would always brownnose to the landed gentry. **1972** *Observer* 20 Feb. 11/3 There is a limit on how far the Libyas of this world can bid up the price of oil.

23. a. *world-construction, cruise, -end* (attrib.), *events, -formula, government, -image, -model, -outlook, première, principle* (earlier example), *record, sorrow* (earlier example), *-structure, -system, -theory, tour, -will.* (Not clearly distinguishable from some of the examples in sense 24 b in Dict. and Suppl.)

1906 W. R. INGE *Truth & Falsehood in Relig.* 115 Science has no commission to produce an ideal world-construction on a materialistic basis. **1933** World cruise [see *CRUISE *sb.* 1 a]. **1977** A. C. H. SMITH *Jericho Gun* iv. 54 Let's take a world cruise. **1896** KIPLING *Seven Seas* p. vii, I was born in her gate... Where the world-end steamers wait. **1940** J. PEDERSEN *Israel* II. IV. 559 Like Isaiah he [*sc.* Jeremiah]..undertakes to interpret world-events. **1888** J. ROYCE *Let.* 21 May in R. B. Perry *Thought & Char. W. James* (1935) I. 800, I have largely straightened out the big metaphysical tangle about continuity, freedom, and the world-formula. **1907** W. JAMES *Pragmatism* ii. 50 The whole function of philosophy ought to be to find out what definite difference it will make to you and me, at definite instants of our life, if this world-formula or that world-formula be the true one. **1915** N. L. MCCLUNG *In Times like These* ix. 153 The problems of discovery have been solved; the problems of colonization are being solved. and when the war is over the problem of world government will be solved. **1958** B. W. ALDISS *Non-Stop* IV. v. 241 The ship is in an orbit round Earth and there it must stay. That was the edict of the World Government. **1981** *Washington Post* 18 Mar. 1 He would never be part of an organization that advocated world government. **1936** *Discovery* May 162/1 The Determinists have created for themselves an intellectual structure which represents a world-image or rather a physical world-image. **1949** G. J. WHITROW *Structure of Universe* v. 75 In order to obtain some picture of the universe as a whole, we must construct a world-model which will reproduce satisfactorily the properties of this observable (limited region of space and time). **1915** (*serial title*) World outlook. **1929** *New Statesman* 31 Aug. 628/1 All poetic genius has always fumbled instinctively for a world-outlook in which everything has significance at all times. **1976** tr. Shih Min in *Yenan Seeds & Other Stories* 75 Remould your world-outlook and steel yourself into a self-aware revolutionary. **1934** WEBSTER, World première. **1948** *Daily Ardmoreite* (Ardmore, Okla.) 7 July 1/5 'Return of the Bad Man' will open a three day engagement in Ardmore just one day after its world premier. **1981** LD. HAREWOOD *Tongs & Bones* ix. 150 He..put on several important world premières of British operas. **1854** GEO. ELIOT tr. *L. Feuerbach's Essence of Christianity* x. 101 Individual subjectivity..is regarded as the highest essence—the omnipotent world-principle. **1909** G. B. SHAW *Pen Portraits & Reviews* (1931) 236 In his stories of mystery and imagination Poe created a world-record for the English language. **1976** *Daily Tel.* 20 July 1/5 Cornelia Ender won 100m women's freestyle gold model in world record 55.65 secs. **1868** GEO. ELIOT *Spanish Gypsy* II. 173 Silva had thought To melt hard bitter grief by fellowship With the world-sorrow trembling in his ear In Pablo's voice. **1920** A. S. EDDINGTON *Space, Time & Gravit.* ix. 150 The world-structure is not of a kind which can be traced in an exact way by mesh-systems, and in any large region the mesh-system drawn must be considered arbitrary. **1874** G. H. LEWES *Problems* I. 85 Our parochial system will sometimes be favourably contrasted with the results of their world-system. **1977** P. JOHNSON *Enemies of Society* ii. 12 We have characterized its [*sc.* Freedom's] development into the Roman world-system as essentially a liberal economic process, presided over by a night-watchman state. **1834** J. S. MILL in *Monthly Repos.* VIII. 657 They are probably as sincere as they are capable of being, in any creed, or world-theory, or abstract principle. **1960** W. V. O. QUINE *Word & Object* i. 24 The saving consideration is that we continue to take seriously our own..aggregate science, our own particular world-theory or loose total fabric of quasi-theories, whatever it may be. **1958** J. POPE-HENNESSY in P. Quennell *Lonely Business* (1981) III. 210 Maps of his world-tours on the walls. **1971** 'G. BLACK' *Tome for Pirates* v. 84 A very slow world tour from which he returned with reluctance. **1891** G. B. SHAW *Quintessence of Ibsenism* iv. 70 The world-will shall answer for Julian's soul. **1892** J. ROYCE *Spirit Mod. Philos.* 239 We ourselves are embodiments of the world-will.

b. Objective, as *world-changer, -girdler, -saver, -wielder*; *world-building, -making* (earlier example); *world-beating, -creating, -destroying, -devouring* (later example), *-embracing* (earlier U.S. example), *-enfolding, -girdling, -lifting* (example), *-mothering, -renouncing* (examples), *-shattering, -surrounding* (earlier example), *-transforming, -troubling, -wielding* adjs. **c.** Instrumental, as *world-besotted, -forgotten, -read* adjs. **d.** In other adverbial uses: (*a*) *world-lost, -minded* (so *-mindedness*) adjs.; (*b*) *world-famed* (earlier example), *-renowned* (earlier example) adjs.

1928 *Sunday Express* 24 June 20/4 The way he flashed the passing shot wide of Higgs..was world-beating stuff. **1977** *Daily Mail* 24 Sept. 15/1 The BBC..never became the really 'world-beating station that I would like it to have been'. **1932** W. B. YEATS *Words for Music* 15 Imitate him if you dare, World-besotted traveller; he Served human liberty. **1920** A. S. EDDINGTON *Space, Time & Gravit.* x. 160 It might seem that this kind of fantastic world-building can have little to do with practical problems. **1891** W. JAMES *Let.* 30 Jan. (1920) I. 305 Verily you are the stuff of which world-changers are made! **1854** GEO. ELIOT tr. *Feuerbach's Essence Chr.* xxii. 218 The world-creating activity in itself negatives every determinate activity. **1909** G. K. CHESTERTON *Orthodoxy* (ed. 2) iv. 92 We count on the ordinary course of things... We risk the remote possibility of a miracle as we do that of a poisoned pancake or a world-destroying comet. **1938** DYLAN THOMAS *Let.* 1 June (1966) 199 A world-devouring ghost creature bit out the horror of tomorrow from a gentleman's loins. **1807** J. BARLOW *Columbiad* IV. 155 The world-embracing scope That prompts his genius and expands his hope. **1928** W. B. YEATS tr. *Sophocles' King Oedipus* 6 For all is world-enfolding sea. **1858** World-famed [see *seven-cubit* s.v. *SEVEN *a.* and *sb.* C. 2]. **1861** *Westm. Rev.* LXXVI. 281 Such a world-forgotten village as Raveloe. **1941** I. L. IDRIESS *Great Boomerang* iv. 29 This man's dream was to become a peaceful and world-forgotten patriarch. **1892** *Outing* (U.S.) Mar. 447/1 They probably learned enough about it to make them treat the next world-girdler with high respect. **1934** A. WOOLCOTT *While Rome Burns* 93 Twenty such world-girdling tales. **1978** H. WOUK *War & Remembrance* xxi. 209 All the members of a world-girdling alliance were attacking us. **1894** KIPLING *Seven Seas* (1896) 45 O' that warld-liftin' joy no after-fall could vex. **1854** J. G. WHITTIER in *Nat. Era* 17 Aug. 130/4 New-born, the world-lost anchorite A man became! **1941** T. WOLFE *Hills Beyond* iii. 235 He abandoned finally the world-lost fastnesses of Zebulon for the more urban settlement of Libya Hill. *a* **1776** HUME *Dialogues conc. Nat. Relig.* (1779) v. 61 A slow, but continued improvement carried on during infinite ages in the art of world-making. **1945** G. MURPHY *Human Nature & Enduring Peace* xvi. 241 What we mean by world-minded education. We mean education for intelligent world citizenship. **1979** *Amer. Speech* 1976 LI. 79 Germans have traditionally been world-minded, receptive to foreign influences. **1926** *Religious Education* Apr. 190 Character is not a cause of world-mindedness, it is a result of world-mindedness and many other attributes. **1960** A. BJERSTEDT in *Jrnl. Conflict Resolution* IV. 185 (*title*) Ego-involved world-mindedness. **1883** G. M. HOPKINS *Poems* (1967) 93 Wild air, world-mothering air, Nestling me everywhere. **1912** HARDY *Jude the Obscure* p. x, An influential article..printed in a world-read journal. **1910** W. MONTGOMERY tr. *A. Schweitzer's Quest Hist. Jesus* xvi. 247 Inexhaustible reserves of world-renouncing, world-contemning sayings. **1964** C. S. LEWIS *Discarded Image* iii. 47 A world-renouncing, ascetic, and mystical character then marked the most eminent Pagans. **1831** CARLYLE in *Foreign Q. Rev.* Oct. 372 The wild, deep, and now world-renowned, *Legend of Faust*, belongs to a somewhat later date. **1952** B. WOLFE *Limbo* IV. 214 A 'messianic complex', an urge to be a 'world-saver'. **1974** M. TIPPETT *Moving into Aquarius* II. 155 During those years there have been huge and world-shattering events in which I have been inevitably caught up. **1817** SHELLEY *To Constantia Singing* in *Posthumous Poems* (1824) 144 Whilst, like the world-surrounding air, thy song Flows on. **1935** W. B. YEATS *Full Moon in March* 68 What sacred drama through her body heaved When world-transforming Charlemagne was conceived? **1895** —— *Poems* 259 And shook at Invar Amargin The hearts of the world-troubling seamen. **1881** G. M. HOPKINS in *Note-Bks. & Papers* (1937) 346 Satan..is the κοσμοκράτωρ, the worldwielder. **1887** —— *Poems* (1967) 70 And the azurous hung hills are his world-wielding shoulder.

24. Passing into adj. **b.** (Further examples.) (Not clearly distinguishable from some of the examples in sense 23 a in Dict. and Suppl.)

1833 J. S. MILL in *Monthly Repos.* VII. 510 The most stirring scenes of that mighty world-drama, under his pen turn flat, cold, and spiritless. **1879** G. H. LEWES *Stud. Psychol.* ix. 162 The World-process has been assigned to a Soul of the World. **1890** W. MORRIS *News from Nowhere* xv. 129 They had gradually created..a most elaborate system of buying and selling, which has been called The world-market. **1898** G. B. SHAW *Perfect Wagnerite* 14 He is trusting to another great world-force, the Lie. **1904** W. JAMES *Ess. Radical Empiricism* (1912) i. 8 Experience, at this rate, would be much like a paint of which the world pictures were made. **1910** A. G. SPINK *National Game* 309 (*heading*) World champions. **1914** G. FRANKAU *Poet. Wks.* (1923) I. 185 Battlers for world-peace, slaves of Honour's lamp. **1920** B. RUSSELL *Pract. & Theory Bolshevism* IX. 109 The following passages [from article by Lenin] seemed to me illuminating:—The present world-situation in politics places on the order of the day the dictatorship of the proletariat. **1921** J. C. MAXWELL GARNETT (*title*) Education and world citizenship. **1921** D. H. LAWRENCE *Sea & Sardinia* v. 163 Will the last waves of enlightenment and world-unity break over them [*sc.* the Sardinians] and wash away the stocking-caps? **1923** —— *Fantasia of Unconscious* 15 No more little Excelsiors crying world-brotherhood. **1927** A. CECIL *Brit. Foreign Secretaries* vii. 353 Aberdeen would have felt all the talk about German world-domination too journalistically sensational to be politically probable. **1929** J. BUCHAN *Courts of Morning* 14 America... could not take a big hand in world affairs... She had too much to do at home. **1930** J. H. RANDALL (*title*) A world community. **1932** A. G. HERBERT tr. *Nygren's Agape & Eros* I. vi. 146 For Plotinus the whole world process is summed up in the double conception of the out-going of all things from the One..and the return of all things to the One. **1936** *Mind* XLV. 460 It was left to the Stoics to elaborate the conception of the world-state and of the world-citizen. **1936** World-culture [see *CULTURE *sb.* 5 d]. **1937** 'G. ORWELL' *Road to Wigan Pier* xii. 247 It is quite easy to imagine a world-society, economically collectivist. **1940** World opinion [see *APPEASE *v.* 2 c]. **1943** E. M. W. TILLYARD (*title*) The Elizabethan world picture. **1945** AUDEN *For Time Being* 89 Instead of Country Fair, there is World Market. **1946** J. S. HUXLEY *Unesco* i. 17 The task of unifying the world mind. **1948** L. SPITZER *Linguistics & Literary History* 220 This is also the main idea of Claudel's Spanish Catholic world-drama *Le soulier de satin*. **1954** 'M. COST' *Invitation from Minerva* 218 The world-press..was hourly dominated by bulletins of their plight. **1959** *New Yorker* 24 Oct. 185/1 Joyce..gave her..world rights to publish and sell 'Ulysses'. **1962** *Listener* 22 Mar. 498/1 Goethe, it will be remembered, spoke of *Weltkultur*... The great Russian component of world culture is as individual as our own or the French. **1966** S. BEER *Decision & Control* xv. 391 As usual, the study begins with a..world situation. **1967** P. D. JAMES *Unnatural Causes* I. xv. 116 He was completely unconcerned with world affairs. **1974** I. WALLERSTEIN (*title*) The modern world system..and the origins of the European world-economy in the 16th century. **1977** P. JOHNSON *Enemies of Society* v. 61 Britain expanded this initial overseas foothold by the Navigation Acts..which ..constituted the beginning of an English-controlled world market. **1981** *Listener* 2 July 3/1 American columnists..are querying whether Reagan is not hazarding world peace. **1981** N. TUCKER *Child & Book* iv. 108 In Enid Blyton's work, this excessively simple world picture is carried to extremes. **1983** *Times* 14 May 8/3 The power of world opinion is a vital adjunct to non-violence.

25. world-all [tr. G. *weltall*], the world considered as a unit; the universe; **world-auxiliary,** a language (esp. an invented one) which may be used as a standard means of communication between speakers from different language communities throughout the world; cf. *auxiliary language* s.v. *AUXILIARY *a.* 2 a; **World Bank,** an international banking organization established to control the distribution of economic aid between member nations, *spec.*: † (*a*) the Bank for International Settlements, established through the League of Nations at Basle in 1930 (*obs.*); (*b*) the International Bank for Reconstruction and Development, affiliated to the United Nations and operational since 1946; **world-class** *a.*, applied to persons or things regarded as outstanding throughout the world; **World Court,** the International Court of Justice (formerly, the Permanent Court of International Justice, 1921–45), established in 1946 as the principal judicial arm of the United Nations; **World Cup,** in Assoc. Football, a quadrennial competition amongst national teams for the Jules Rimet trophy, first contested in 1930; also *transf.* in other sports; **world English** = *Standard English* s.v. *STANDARD *a.* 3 e; **world fair** = *world's fair*, sense 26 a below; **world ground,** the reality, or principle, that underlies the world; **World Health Organization,** an international body established in 1948 to promote co-operation between nations to improve health conditions (abbrev. *W.H.O.*: see *W 3); **world-historical** *a.* (earlier example); **world-language,** (*b*) (earlier example); **world-line** *Physics* and *Philos.* [tr. G. *weltlinie* (H. Minkowski, as for *world-point*)], the succession of points in space-time that are occupied by a particle; **world literature** [cf. G. *weltliteratur*], (*a*) a body of work drawn from many nations and recognized as literature throughout the world; (*b*) (the sum of) the literature of the world; **world-point** *Physics* and *Philos.* [tr. G. *weltpunkt* (H. Minkowski in H. A. Lorentz et al. *Das Relativitätsprinzip* (1913) 57)], a point in space-time; a particular point in space at a particular instant of time; **world-policy, -politics** [cf. G. *weltpolitik*]: also **world-political** *a.*; **world-ranking** *a.*, that ranks among the best in the world; **World Series,** a series of games contested annually as a play-off between the champions of the two major baseball leagues in the U.S.; also *transf.*; **World Service,** a B.B.C. radio service with a strong content of news and current affairs, broadcast principally for English-speaking listeners overseas (formerly called the *Overseas Service*); **world-spirit,** (*b*) (earlier example).

1847 J. D. MORELL *Hist. Philos.* (ed. 2) I. II. 369 Fichte founded a subjective idealism in which the me was the *world-all*. **1925** R. M. OGDEN tr. *Koffka's Growth of Mind* 347 For a child there is as yet no single world-all. **1927** E. S. PANKHURST *Delphos* v. 49 The world-auxiliary, used by everyone as a second language, will obviate the need for any other language save the native one. **1930** *Business Week* 28 May 9/2 French shares for the World Bank were offered publicly this week. **1943** *N.Y. Times* 5 Apr. 6/3 Senator Elmer Thomas said..that the establishment of a world bank founded on a standard international coin was inevitable. **1944** *St. Louis* (Missouri) *Post-Dispatch* 23 July 6A/3 (*heading*) Russia agrees to boost quota in World Bank. **1973** 'D. JORDAN' *Nile Green* xi. 47 The statistical boys..had worked out all the flaws in the World Bank report. **1950** *Sport* 22–28 Sept. 14/2 Such is the magnetism of world class heavyweight boxers! **1973** *Daily Express* 11 May 22/1 Keegan, looking every inch a world-class player..scored with a spectacular header. **1973** *Guardian* 22 Oct. 21/4 The timescale of astronomers is human and to those in world class research ..too short to waste much time on bumbledom. **1979** *Beautiful British Columbia* Winter 40 A total of more than $100 million is expected to be spent at Whistler..to make the area competitive with world-class resorts in the United States and Europe. **1927** *New Republic* 21 Sept. 110/2 Our reservations to the resolution adhering to the World Court were received with an apathy which was next door to hostility. **1946** *N.Y. Times* 7 Feb. 8/2 (*heading*) 15 Judges elected for World Court. **1984** *Times* 10 Apr. 1/6 The Reagan Administration said yesterday it believed the World Court in The Hague did not have jurisdiction. **1950** B. WRIGHT *Captain of England* xvii. 154 For the first time in my experience the words 'World Cup' began to come into the discussions footballers have when they meet, and as the four British home associations had re-entered F.I.F.A., it was only to be expected that they would..enter this competition. **1954** *Times* 8 Nov. 10/1 (*heading*) Rugby League results..World Cup. **1967** *Times* 9 Nov. 16/4 (*heading*) World Cup golf. **1978** R. WESTALL *Devil on Road* xx. 185 An action-replay of a World Cup goal on telly. **1927** K. MALONE in *Amer. Speech* II. 323/2 He..warns against a slavish conformity to the dictionary, i.e., to the prescriptions of standard English, or world-English, as some people call it. **1980** *English World-Wide* I. 1. 80 The categories or types of AVE..can be seen as existing across a scale having 'World English' ('book English', 'standard English', 'teachers' preferred English', &c.), at one end, and a national variety most distinct from it at the other. **1899** C. STUMPF *Let.* 8 Sept. in R. B. Perry *Thought & Char. W. James* (1935) II. 193 The tumult of a world fair—even the thought of it makes me nervous! **1978** P. BOARDMAN *Worlds of Patrick Geddes* vi. 179 A brief..account of the city [*sc.* Paris]..from pre-Roman times up to the greatest of world fairs. **1898** W. JAMES in *Psychol. Rev.* July 424 The world is evidently more complex than we are accustomed to think it, the 'absolute world-ground', in particular, being farther off (as Mr. F. C. S. Schiller has well pointed out) than it is the wont either of the usual empiricisms or of the usual idealisms to think it. **1948** *Scot. Jrnl. Theol.* I. 121 The most that science, working with its concepts of causation on a different level, can offer is a world-ground, or mind-energy at work in the world. **1946** *N.Y. Times* 28 June 9/1 The vanquished nations..with their large health problems, have acute need of the World Health Organization that the United Nations is creating. **1977** *New Scientist* 7 Apr. 3/2 All the more horrendous, then, are the statistics which the World Health Organisation has published to publicise World Health Day, which falls today (7 April). **1854** C. C. J. BUNSEN *Outl. Philos. Universal Hist.* I. 64 Both these researches, the philosophical and the world-historical, will be reserved for the second volume of our sketch. **1867** W. D. WHITNEY *Lang. & Study Lang.* xii. 469 If we expect..that our tongue become one day a world-language, understood and employed on every continent.., then it is our bounden duty [etc.]. **1916** *Monthly Notices R. Astron. Soc.* LXXVI. 700 The points of space occupied by a given material point at successive times form in the four-dimensional time-space a continuity of one dimension, which is called the world-line of the point. **1946** *Mind* LV. 146 The intersection of the world-lines AM and TM. **1962** *Listener* 27 Dec. 1095/3 According to Einstein's General Theory of Relativity it seems that objects which appear to be responding to the pull of gravity..are simply following the shortest available world-line through the space-time continuum. **1976** *Nature* 1–8 Jan. 30/2 The collapsing star is represented by some of its (time-like) worldlines including the worldline of its centre. **1831** CARLYLE in *Edin. Rev.* CV. 179 Instead of isolated, mutually repulsive National Literatures, a World Literature may one day be looked for? **1908** P. E. MORE *Shelburne Essays* V. 140 Longfellow brought from Germany the ideal of a world literature which should absorb the best of all lands. **1949** WELLEK & WARREN *Theory of Lit.* v. 41 The term 'world literature', a translation of Goethe's Weltliteratur, is perhaps needlessly grandiose. **1963** *English Studies* XLIV. 148 He has noted the widespread occurrence of the bond-story of *The Merchant of Venice* in world-literature. **1923** PERRET & JEFFERY tr. H. Minkowski in *Lorentz's Princ. Relativity* v. 76 A point of space at a point of time, that is, a system of values *x*, *y*, *z*, *t*, I will call a world-point. The multiplicity of all thinkable *x*, *y*, *z*, *t* systems of values we will christen the world. **1930** L. SILBERSTEIN *Size of Universe* I. 1 The event thus localized in space..and in time is called a worldpoint. **1967** R. A. GEORGE tr. *Carnap's Logical Structure of World* iv. 194 The points of n-dimensional, real-number space, we call *world points.* **1975** R. ADLER et al. *Introd. Gen. Relativity* (ed. 2) iv. 122 An event is a point in four-space: a world-point. **1936** World-political [see *anti-Comintern* s.v. *ANTI-[1] 3 a]. **1958** S. SPENDER *Engaged in Writing* vii. 133 He was the first world-political, international, intellectual man. **1970** *Daily Tel.* 19 Aug. 10/4 Here in Britain we have two world-ranking centres of radio astronomy. **1913** *Collier's* 4 Oct. 5/1 In this next impending world-series carnival between Giants and Athletics we have had the hunch [etc.]. **1951** *Time* 12 Mar. 59 For Norwegians..the Holmenkollen is the World Series, and stars such as Hoel and Björnstad are Norway's Di Maggios and Musials. **1973** M. WOODHOUSE *Blue Bone* iii. 20 'We could have played half the World Series by now.'.. 'Yes, we take three days to play a game of cricket.' **1966** *B.B.C. Handbk.* 83 The *World Service* addresses itself to those who understand English, wherever they happen to be—listeners throughout the Commonwealth and English-speaking people in other countries. **1981** *Times* 22 Jan. 8/7 The embassy press officer..was waiting for news from the World Service of the BBC. **1846** G. H. LEWES *Biogr. Hist. Philos.* IV. 212 The World-Spirit (*Weltgeist*) has at last succeeded in freeing himself from all incumbrances.

26. In the possessive. **a.** In senses corresponding to those at 24 and 25, as *world's championship, record, Series*; **world's fair** orig. *U.S.*, an international exposition of arts, science, industry, and agriculture.

1888 *Spaulding's Base-Ball Guide* 47 In 1887 the world's championship series had become an established supplementary series of contests. **1910** A. G. SPINK *National Game* 312 The world's championship. **1850** *New-England Farmer* II. 413 The State Board of Agriculture are making up a collection of samples of Indian corn for the World's Fair. **1908** E. TERRY *Story of my Life* xii. 280, I had loved the Chicago of the Lake with the white buildings of the World's Fair shining on it. **1982** J. S. BORTHWICK *Case of Hook-Billed Kites* iv. 193 Like those rides at world's fairs..where you sit in a little car that draws you through different habitats. **1893** *Outing* (U.S.) XXII. 154/2 He has..held the world's record in the pole vault for distance. **1905** *Sporting Life* 7 Oct. 3/1 Jack Sheridan and Hank O'Day have been appointed to umpire the world's series. **1925** F. SCOTT FITZGERALD *Great Gatsby* iv. 88 He's the man who fixed the World's Series back in 1919. **1965** F. O. DU PRE *U.S. Air Force Biogr. Dict.* 58/1 He won the Schneider Cup Race—the World's Series of seaplane racing—in 1925, with an average speed of 232 mph.

b. In hyperbolical phr. *the world's worst* (..), the very worst or most incompetent. *colloq.*

1921 T. WOLFE *Let.* 13 Nov. (1956) 22 'The Woman of Bronze', the world's worst play. **1929** J. B. PRIESTLEY *Good Companions* II. i. 248 She was easily the world's worst as a pianist. **1933** L. EINSTEIN in O. W. Holmes *Holmes-Einstein Lett.* (1964) 352, I hasten to add that they are the world's most famous bridge players and she the world's worst! **1954** R. BISSELL *High Water* i. 11 He shaved every other day and of all the Second Mates in the company they could have dumped on me he was the world's worst. **1962** C. DRAPER *Mad Major* iv. 88, I am probably the world's worst dancer.

c. In colloq. phr. *one of the world's workers*, an industrious person. Freq. in neg. contexts.

1933 [see *PULL *v.* 24 f]. **1964** D. GRAY *Devil wore Scarlet* x. 91 'Mr. Weston isn't one of the world's workers, exactly,' said Mary. **1976** G. MOFFAT *Short Time to Live* ii. 20 Jackson..is *not* one of the world's workers, as you must have noticed.

wo·rlded, (*ppl.*) *a.* *rare* (chiefly *poet.*). [f. WORLD *sb.* or *v.* + -ED.] Containing worlds. Also with qualifying word.

1885 TENNYSON *Tiresias* 167 The fires that arch this dusky dot—Yon myriad-worlded way. **1907** 'MARK TWAIN' in *Harper's Mag.* Dec. 44/2, I think there is such a planet..in one of the thinly worlded corners of the universe. **1934** DYLAN THOMAS *18 Poems* 31 How light the sleeping on this soily star, How deep the waking in the worlded clouds.

world-power. Add: **2.** (Earlier example.) Also *transf.* of a person.

1860 [see WORLD *sb.* 23 a]. **1900** *Congress Rec.* 29 Jan. 1259/1 We have become a 'world power'.

World War, world war. [f. WORLD *sb.* + WAR *sb.*[1]; cf. G. *weltkrieg.*] **1.** A war involving many important nations; *spec.* that of 1914–18 or of 1939–45.

1909 [see WORLD *sb.* 24 b]. **1914** B. VAUGHAN *What of To-Day?* xii. 103 What the South African War failed to teach I really believe this world-war will bring home to us. **1921** A. HUXLEY *Crome Yellow* ix. 82 Armageddon, that world war with which the Second Coming is to be so closely associated. **1949** G. A. BIRMINGHAM *Laura's Bishop* 171 To call this, when it comes, a world war is to minimize its importance. It will be worse than a world war. **1978** I. B. SINGER *Shosha* v. 90 Let's snatch a little peace before another world war breaks out.

2. In the designation of a particular (real or hypothetical) war, as *First World War*, *World War* (*No.*) *I* (or *One*): see *FIRST *a.* C. 2 a; *Second World War, World War* (*No.*) *II* (or *Two*): a subsequent world war, *spec.* that of 1939–45: see *SECOND *a.* 7 a; *Third World War, World War* (*No.*) *III* (or *Three*): see *THIRD *a.* 5. Also *transf.*

1919 *Manch. Guardian* 18 Feb. 10/2 (*heading*) World War No 2. **1939** *Time* 11 Sept. 38/1 Some of the diplomatic juggling which last week ended in World War II was old-fashioned international jockeying for power. *Ibid.* 18 Sept. 10/2 Exports of arms, munitions and related materials in World War I amounted..to only 25% of total exports to the Allies. **1945** DUKE OF BEDFORD *Let.* 16 Apr. in B. Russell *Autobiogr.* (1969) III. i. 44 You will have to postpone your visit until the brief interlude between this war & world-war no 3. **1947** *Time & Tide* 29 Nov. 1269/2 The despair and cynicism that followed what it has now become fashionable to call World War One. **1948** N. WIENER *Cybernetics* 7 When I came to the Institute after World War No. 1 [etc.]. **1959** *N.Z. Listener* 17 Apr. 6/1 Clearly the meaning of the treaties in case of wars which can be limited is somewhat different from the meaning they have in the event of World War III. **1963** D. BROUN *Egypt's Choice* i. 12 'During World War Deuce, sir,' the Colonel said. **1968** K. BIRD *Smash Glass Image* viii. 102 Rattling their rifles as if they were fighting World War Three. **1968** *Listener* 12 Dec. 787/3 When World War Two broke out on 3 September 1939, Monnet remembered his World War One experiences. **1976** P. R. WHITE *Planning for Public Transport* iv. 72 As early as World War One some minor stations and routes were closed.

world-wide, *a.* Add: Now freq. **worldwide.** **b.** as *adv.* (Later examples.)

1953 *Reader's Digest* July 27 World-wide, three million dogs have already safely got this..vaccine. **1972** *Nature* 24 Mar. 184/3 Workers in the field number no more than about fifty, worldwide. **1980** *Bookseller* 14 June 2528/1 (Advt.), Subscriptions manager required for expanding publishing business trading worldwide.

worm, *sb.* Add: **I. 3. e.** transf. and fig. phr. *worm's-eye view* [after *bird's-eye view* (BIRD's-EYE *a.* 3); see also *EYE VIEW], a view taken as from the standpoint of a worm, i.e. from ground-level; a revealing or detailed perspective of a subject. Also *worm's-eye map* (Geol.) (see quot. 1972).

1908 [see *EYE VIEW, EYE-VIEW]. **1933** *Archit. Rev.* LXXIII. 67/2 The illustration is a worm's-eye view of a corner of the building. **1945** A. HUXLEY *Time must have Stop* xiv. 145 He..looked..up at the statue above him. What a curious worm's-eye view of a goddess! **1951** KRUMBEIN & SLOSS *Stratigr. & Sedimentation* xiii. 421 Such paleogeologic maps, in which the observer looks upward at the base of a higher unit, have been called worm's eye maps. **1960** *John o' London's* 14 Apr. 428/3 His 'worm's eye view' of Dublin was beginning to give way to the great vision of a major artist. **1964** *Bull. Amer. Assoc. Petroleum Geologists* XLVIII. 1187/2 A lap-out map, commonly known as a 'worm's eye' map, is a special method of paleogeologic expression where post-unconformity geologic relations are portrayed. **1972** *Gloss. Geol.* (Amer. Geol. Inst.) 797/1 *Worm's-eye map*, (a) a term applied..in reference to the pattern of formations that would be visible to an observer looking upward at the bottom of the rocks overlying a given surface. (b) A map showing overlap of sediments. **1982** A. PRICE *Old Vengeful* ix. 147 This is the worm's-eye view of what you seek. If you wish for the eagle's-eye view, you must go to Paris.

8. c. In colloq. phr. (*to open*) *a can of worms*, (to address) a complex and largely unexamined problem or state of affairs the investigation of which is likely to cause much trouble or scandal.

1962 *Times* 21 Feb. 12/4 He..knew that he had opened the bidding on what is sometimes called 'a can of worms'. **1969** *N. Dakota Law Rev.* XLV. 215 Counsel can..better comprehend..the domestic can-of-worms that appears in so many delinquency and neglect cases. **1973** *Times* 22 May 16/5 Mr Berger has opened, in the old American phrase, a fine can of worms. He is suggesting that an impeached President, should he be found guilty, could appeal to the Supreme Court. **1976** L. BERNSTEIN *Unanswered Question* vi. 418 There are so many of those 'underlying strings'..waiting to be tied up; so many cans of worms have been opened, and a lot of those slippery little beasts are still wriggling around. **1984** A. PRICE *Sion Crossing* vii. 137 Oliver isn't up to this sort of thing. And this is my can of worms.

IV. 17. a. *wormfinger*; instrumental, as *worm-chewed, -laid* adjs.; parasynthetic, as *worm-faced* adj.

1927 D. H. LAWRENCE *Mornings in Mexico* 28 Rattling the worm-chewed window-frames. **1934** DYLAN THOMAS *Let.* 12 Apr. (1966) 105 Avaunt, you worm-faced fellows of the night. **1922** JOYCE *Ulysses* 550 Jogging, mocks them with thumb and wriggling wormfingers. **1933** C. S. LEWIS *Pilgrim's Regress* 248 Once the worm-laid egg broke the wood.

b. *worm-tackle* (earlier example).

1835 *Chambers's Edin. Jrnl.* Jan. 390/3 First of all, the worm-tackle. For this, sizeable hooks..are generally preferred.

c. *worm-syrup* (later examples).

1897 *Sears, Roebuck Catal.* 27/2 *Worm syrup*..for expelling worms from children. **1972** E. WIGGINTON *Foxfire Bk.* 247 Take 'worm syrup' which is made by boiling Jerusalem oak and pine root together.

d. *worm-geared* adj.

1936 *Discovery* Aug. 238/2 It [*sc.* the camera] is loaded into position on the plane with a worm-geared winch and pulley system. **1973** *Gloss. Terms Materials Handling* (*B.S.I.*) VI. 16 *Worm geared chain pulley block*,..mechanical advantage is obtained chiefly by..use of a worm wheel and worm.

f. *worm-killer*, a preparation for destroying garden worms.

1915 H. H. THOMAS *Gardening for Amateurs* I. 22/1 Proprietary worm-killers can also be obtained, and these must always be employed as directed. **1959** *Times* 7 Mar. 9/1 There are always the lead arsenate wormkillers.

worm, *v.* Add: **II. 4. b.** To treat (an animal) with a preparation designed to free it of parasitic worms.

1932 N. MITFORD *Christmas Pudding* xi. 179 Lady Bobbin spoke to those about her of horses, hounds, and such obscure eventualities as going to ground..and being thoroughly well wormed. **1940** W. FAULKNER *Hamlet* IV. i. 276 He drenched and wormed and..drew the teeth of horses and mules. **1961** C. H. D. TODD *Pop. Whippet* 69 Having decided upon your puppy..ask if it has been wormed. **1978** *Detroit Free Press* 5 Mar. c 20/3 (Advt.), Collie Pups..wormed, pet or show.

IV. 13. b. To wind packing strips between (the cores of a multicore electric cable) so as to give a more nearly circular cross-section; also, to wind (conductors) together to form such a cable.

1909 COYLE & HOWE *Electric Cables* ii. 112 Prior to impregnating, the paper-insulated cores are laid up together and wormed with jute. **1953** C. C. BARNES *Power Cables* i. 6 The laid-up cores are wormed into circular formation and are armoured overall. **1982** KING & HALFTER *Underground Power Cables* ii. 31 These solid-type multicore cables are of belted construction, in which the conductors are separately paper-insulated, 'wormed' together and the interstices filled with a packing or filling of fibrous material in order to obtain a circular section.

wormer. Add: **4.** A preparation used to rid animals of worm infestations.

1934 in WEBSTER. **1971** *Farmer & Stockbreeder* 23 Feb. 45 (Advt.), An ideal wormer. It is highly effective against all roundworms in the gut. **1980** *Kenya Veterinarian* June p.v (Advt.), There's only one total spectrum wormer for sheep and cattle.

wormery (wɒ̄·ɹməri). [f. WORM *sb.* + *-ERY 2 b.] A place or container in which worms are kept.

1952 *Britannica Bk. Year* 667/1 *Wormery*, a place for breeding worms. **1972** *Daily Tel.* 10 July 14 We kept a wormery and during our observations we found the worms had pulled leaves down under the soil. **1980** M. DRABBLE *Middle Ground* 129 She complained about the smell of the hamster and rabbits, and thought the wormery disgusting.

worm-hole. Add: Also **wormhole.** **2.** *Physics.* A hypothetical interconnection between widely separated regions of space-time.

1957 MISNER & WHEELER in *Ann. Physics* II. 532 This analysis forces one to consider situations..where there is a net flux of lines of force through what topologists would call a handle of the multiply-connected space and what physicists might perhaps be excused for more vividly terming a 'wormhole'. **1978** PASACHOFF & KUTNER *University Astron.* xii. 326 Thus, in principle, mass that disappears in a black hole may emerge somewhere else. If the somewhere else is a distinct region in our universe, the connection is called a wormhole. **1981** P. DAVIES *Edge of Infinity* ix. 179 The quantum disturbance will be so severe that even the topology of spacetime will alter. Instead of a 'bumpy sheet', it will display a foam-like structure, full of worm-holes and bridges.

wormhood. (Later *fig.* example.)

1917 LD. BRAYE *Lines in Verse & Fable* 63 Extinction of all influence and fame, And abject knowledge of my wormhood.

worming, *vbl. sb.* Add: **2. b.** Treatment administered to rid an animal of parasitic worms.

1936 J. Z. Rine *Dog Owner's Man.* vi. 99 All worming may prove more effective if preceded by a twenty-four-hour diet of buttermilk. **1947** *New Biol.* III. 69 The cost and labour of rounding them [*sc.* sheep] up for this periodical 'worming' may be..great. **1981** *Times* 22 May 3/2 Worker cats needed neutering, vaccinating, worming, regular feeding.

6. b. The action of worming electric cables; also *concr.*, material used for this.

1909 Coyle & Howe *Electric Cables* ii. 112 The specific gravity of the worming jute. **1949** *Proc. Inst. Electr. Engineers* XCVI. ii. 633/1 Would the author indicate.. in what sizes additional worming or padding is required to allow the inclusion of the 0.0225-in² conductor and yet produce a good cable design? **1962** P. Dunsheath *Hist. Elect. Engin.* xvi. 259 Much attention was given to such refinements as..construction of wormings.

wormish, *a.* For † *Obs.* read *rare* and add: (Later *fig.* example.) Also **wo·rmishness,** wormish or craven behaviour.

1923 V. Woolf *Let.* 1 Apr. (1977) III. 26 Murry wrote me a wormish letter, by the way, about the differences between us, and our memories and so on. **1925** H. Nicolson *Let.* 23 July in J. Lees-Milne *Harold Nicolson* (1980) I. xi. 239 My wormishness to Elizabeth.

worn, *ppl. a.* Add: **2. a.** Also *Comb.*, as *worn-looking* adj.

1918 Mrs. B. Lowndes *Out of War?* 48 Stern worn-looking man. **1978** D. Murphy *Place Apart* vi. 120 They seem so watchful and worn-looking.

worried, *ppl. a.* Add: Also *Comb.*, as *worried-looking* adj.

1942 'N. Shute' *Pied Piper* 26 Howard saw him the first Saturday that he was there, a sandy-haired, worried-looking man of forty-five or so. **1982** T. Holme *Devil & Dolce Vita* vii. 49 She's been a bit worried-looking... Distracted.

Hence **wo·rriedly** *adv.*, in a worried or distressed manner, concernedly.

1924 'L. Malet' *Dogs of Want* v. 125 She worriedly wondered whether green isn't a more trying colour than blue when you get hot. **1952** S. Kauffmann *Philanderer* (1953) xii. 195 'That's wonderful.' He looked at her worriedly. 'Only it's got to be your decision. Your responsibility.' **1976** 'R. Gordon' *Doctor on Job* iii. 18 'It won't take long, will it?' he asked worriedly.

worriment. (Earlier example.)

1833 S. Smith *Life & Writings Major J. Downing* 161 I've had a good many head-flaws and worriments in my life time.

worrisome, *a.* Add: (Earlier example.)

1845 W. G. Simms *Wigwam & Cabin* 1st Ser. viii. 107, I..followed the old man into the house, with my feelings getting more and more strange and worrisome at every moment.

worrisomely *adv.* (later examples).

1973 *Newsweek* 23 Apr. 22/1 Three simultaneous crises..that seemed worrisomely different from those of the past. **1981** G. McDonald *Fletch & Widow Bradley* xiii. 51 Charley is a worrisomely tight man... Anything out of the ordinary rattles him.

worry, *sb.* Add: **4.** Special Combs. **worry beads,** a string of beads manipulated by the fingers as a means of occupying one's hands and calming the nerves; **worry lines,** lines or wrinkles on the forehead supposedly formed by a habitual expression of worry.

1964 in M. McLuhan *Understanding Media* viii. 78 You will notice that many Greek men..spend a lot of time counting the beads of what appear to be amber rosaries... They are *komboloia* or 'worry beads'. **1978** G. Greene *Human Factor* v. i. 233 The man had a rosary in his lap and seemed to be using it like a chain of worry beads. **1985** *Observer* 3 Feb. 19/3 Sheikh Yamani, worry beads to hand, sums up the general feeling of unease as OPEC last week managed to preserve its fragile unity. **1972** 'J. Quartermain' *Rock of Diamond* xvi. 99 Worry lines creased his forehead. **1982** L. Cody *Bad Company* xiv. 102 There was grey in her hair and worry lines between her brows.

worry, *v.* Add: **5. c.** (Earlier example with *down.*) Also without *adv.* (*phr.*), to worry about (a problem, etc.) (*U.S. colloq.*).

1811 Jane Austen *Sense & S.* II. x. 186 She was sometimes worried down by officious condolence to rate good-breeding as more indispensable to comfort than good-nature. **1959** N. Mailer *Advts. for Myself* (1961) 119 He had always asked too many questions, he had worried the task too severely. **1963** *N. & Q.* Dec. 443/1, I shall not worry the distinction between *alba* and *aube*. **1978** T. L. Smith *Money War* i. 17 He had worried the chance meeting on the flight home.

7. c. Also in colloq. phrases, as *I should worry*: see *shall *v.* 18 d; *not to worry*: see *not *adv.* 4.

8. b. *to worry along* (earlier example).

1871 'Mark Twain' *Screamers* xxix. 146 My friend, you seem to know pretty much all the tunes there are, and you worry along first rate.

9. worryguts *dial.* and *colloq.* = next; freq. as a term of address; **worry wart** *colloq.* (chiefly *U.S.*), an inveterate worrier, one who frets unnecessarily.

1932 *Somerset Year Bk.* 83 The missis, who be a prapper worryguts. **1966** O. Norton *School of Liars* iv. 72 He laughed. 'Worryguts!' 'I wasn't worried. I was just trying to be efficient.' **1982** D. Phillips *Coconut Kiss* ix. 94 It's all right..isn't it?' I asked. ''Course it is, Worryguts,' said Vera. **1956** I. Belknap *Human Problems of State Mental Hospitals* x. 177 The persevering, nagging delusional group—who were termed 'worry warts', 'nuisances', 'bird dogs', in the attendants' slang. **1974** J. Heller *Something Happened* 445 'Don't be such a worry wart.' 'Don't use that phrase. It makes my skin prickle.'

worse, *sb.* **3. c.** (Later examples.)

1739–40 Richardson *Pamela* (1740) I. xxvii. 85 How easy it is to go from bad to worse, when once People give way to Vice. **1894** Somerville & 'Ross' *Real Charlotte* I. vii. 87 The land went from bad to worse. [**1930** F. A. Pottle *Stretchers* 64 The weather was warm, and if worse came to worst, we could encamp in our pup tents where we were.] **1961** New Eng. Bible *2 Tim.* iii. 13 Wicked men and charlatans will make progress from bad to worse.

worship, *sb.* Add: **III. 10.** *worship service.*

1954 *Grove's Dict. Mus.* (ed. 5) VIII. 10/2 In the worship services of those groups among which the urban urge has been less evident, they [*sc.* gospel songs] have been immensely useful now for nearly a century. **1978** R. M. Nixon *Mem.* 538 On our first Sunday in the White House we held the first White House worship service in the East Room.

worship, *v.* Add: **1. b.** (Earlier examples of phr. *to worship the ground* (one) *walks* or *treads on.*)

1848 A. Brontë *Tenant of Wildfell Hall* II. viii. 147 As to looking askance to another woman—he's safe enough for that..he worships the very ground I tread on. **1854** Dickens *Hard Times* iii. iii. 287 There are ladies—born ladies ..who next to worship the ground I walk on.

wo:rsification. *rare.* [Humorous corruption of *versification*, as if f. Worse *a.* and -fication.] The composition of bad verses; poor versification.

1849 J. R. Lowell in *Mass. Q. Rev.* Dec. 51 Since we have found fault with some of what we may be allowed to call the worsification, we should say that the prose work is done conscientiously and neatly. **1908** *Let. to F. J. Furnivall* 27 Nov., The worsification of the poetry written in younger days is far more complete and thorough in the Italian and French poets [*sc.* Tasso and Ronsard] than in the English one [*sc.* Langland].

worst, *a.* Add: **2. c.** (Later example.) Also, *the worst way.*

1904 *N.Y. Tribune* 26 June (Illustr. Suppl.) 4/4 'So you want to go to Cuba, do you?' asked Colonel Roosevelt. 'I do, worst kind,' replied McShane. **1914** G. Atherton *Perch of Devil* i. 55, I need new duds the worst way.

d. *worst-case* adj. phr.: that is or pertains to the worst of a number of possibilities.

1964 R. F. Ficchi *Electrical Interference* ii. 18 It is first assumed, using a worst-case analysis technique, that the mean beam of the receiver and transmitter antenna are in direct line of sight. **1979** R. Littell *Debriefing* v. 88 Worst-case contingency planning is still the basis of scenario construction. **1980** *Times* 18 Jan. 14/1 Analysts believe that the Kremlin drew up a 'worst-case' scenario which took into account both an embargo on American grain and a threat to the Moscow Olympics. **1985** *Harper's Mag.* Jan. 68/2 Pickens could spin off a royalty trust, perhaps sell the downstream operations. . Such a move had been possible all along, but it was obviously the worst-case method of going about the task.

worst, *adv.* Add: **c. worst-seller,** a book distinguished commercially by its low sales (opp. *best seller* s.v. *best *adv.* 3 b); the writer of such a book; also **worst-selling** *a.*

1924 O. Sitwell *Triple Fugue* 73 Could a written testimonial be obtained from the shades of..Dryden,.. Gray, Keats ..and from their heirs, the worst-sellers of to-day, it is probable that the purport..would be found..to be remarkably alike in every case. **1925** V. Woolf *Common Reader* 262 There is..the best-seller public and the worst-seller public. **1933** T. E. Lawrence *Let.* 17 Dec. (1938) 783, I confess to a lively apprehension of that potential worst-seller of yours. **1956** A. Huxley *Adonis & Alphabet* 120 If there were no 'angels', there would be no worst-selling literature to leaven the enormous lump of intellectual and artistic conformity. **1980** 'J. Gash' *Spend Game* vi. 65 A tatty copy of the world's worst-seller like Dr Chase's book.

worsted, *sb.* Add: **2. c.** *ellipt.* for a garment made of worsted cloth; a worsted jacket or suit.

1962 L. Deighton *Ipcress File* i. 9, I struggled into the dark worsted and my only establishment tie. **1972** K. Bonfiglioli *Don't point that Thing at Me* iii. 20, I put on a dashing little tropical-weight worsted, curly-brimmed coker and a pair of buckskins. **1975** *Times* 8 Jan. 12/7 Behaving in a manner more suited to the canvas jacket than the charcoal-grey worsted.

5. worsted work, embroidery done with worsted yarn on canvas; an example of this; hence **worsted-worked** *a.*

c **1702** C. Fiennes *Journeys* (1947) 277 One with a half bedstead as the new mode, dimity with fine shades of worsted works well made up. **1826** M. Wilmot *Let.* 25 Sept. (1935) 250, I do *worsted work*..but..my eyes are too weak to count the threads of any but coarse canvas... What do you make of yours? Foot stools! cushions! bell pulls! **1888** Mrs. H. Ward *Robert Elsmere* I. i. x. 280 His wife, whose head was bent close over her worsted work. **1853** Mrs. Gaskell *Cranford* viii. 116 Carlo lay on the worsted-worked rug.

wort, *sb.*[1] Add: **4.** *wort-blue* adj.

1933 Auden in *Rev. Eng. Stud.* (1978) Aug. 304 Wound round neck the wort-blue tie.

‖ **Wörter und Sachen** (vö·ɹtəɹ unt za·χĕn). [Ger., words and things (R. Meringer *Indogermanische Forschung* (1904) XVI. 101).] (See quot. 1964.) Freq. *attrib.*

1937 J. Orr tr. *Iordan's Introd. Romance Linguistics* i. 73 Their researches imply the investigation of a variety of cultural influences and exchanges which entitles them to be associated..with the Wörter and Sachen movement. **1957** *Language* XXXIII. 54 The twin methods of 'Wörter-und-Sachen' and 'Sachen-und-Wörter', devised half a century ago by..Meringer and Schuchardt.. require no formal introduction at this late date. **1964** R. H. Robins *Gen. Linguistics* 79 A special aspect of dialect study is known as *Wörter und Sachen*... This involves the detailed study in different dialects of the forms of words relating to material objects and processes. **1976** *Amer. Speech 1973* XLVIII. 164 The Wörter-und-Sachen technique has been used for five decades by Swiss and German dialectologists to probe the relationship between words and the objects and processes they describe.

worth, *a.* Add: **I. 3. c.** (Earlier example.)

1875 'Mark Twain' *Sk. New & Old* 310 We shall fly our comet for all it is worth.

3. d. *for what it is worth,* a dismissive phr. intimating that something (esp. an accompanying statement) is of uncertain or little value. Often *parenthetically.*

1888 J. Ross *Three Generations* 228 There is my opinion; I give it for what it is worth. **1922** F. Harris *My Life & Loves* I. xv. 327 However, the fact is so peculiar that I insert it here for what it may be worth. **1952** M. Norton *Borrowers* xx. 157 'Well,' she conceded at last. 'I'll tell you. For what it's worth.' **1962** A. Huxley *Let.* 19 Jan. (1969) 928 Laura brought up the idea suddenly and it fired my imagination. So here, for what it is worth, it is. **1979** J. Johnston *Old Jest* 152 You're going to have to decide which side you're on. Nancy, for what it's worth, seems to have made her decision.

worthy, *sb.* **1. c.** (Later *transf.* example.)

1906 G. B. Shaw *Let.* 29 Sept. (1972) II. 657 The points we cannot accept. These are ..2. The triumvirates, on the ground that the nine worthies cannot be found to take the responsibility.

wot (wǫt), non-standard written form of What *pron.*, *a.*[1], etc.

1829 [see Slap-Up *a.* b]. **1865** [see Water *sb.* 6 f]. **1898** [see *chivvy *sb.*]. **1925** [see *garden *sb.* 1 f]. **1949** E. Pound *Pisan Cantos* lxxvii. 50 I'll tell you wot izza comin'. **1972** 'H. Carmichael' *Naked to Grave* v. 60 He's going to have a tough job convincing the police he wasn't the one wot done it.

b. In phr. *wot, no* —— *?*: orig. (in the war of 1939–45) a catchphrase protesting against shortages, written as the caption accompanying a Chad (see *Chad); now also in extended humorous use.

1945 *Sunday Express* 2 Dec. 2/3 Chad is the Watcher... He peers over walls and asks, 'Wot, no...?' **1946, 1950** [see *Chad, chad]. **1958** J. Townsend *Young Devils* ii. 16 A rusty drawing-pin supported an old Teachers' Union notice. It had scribbled across it 'Wot, no money?' **1979** K. Conlon *Move in Game* i. v. 64 Joanna sent a postcard which said, 'Wot no tulle and confetti?'

wotcher (wǫ·tʃəɹ), *int.* Colloq. corruption of 'what cheer?' (Cheer *sb.* 3 b), a familiar greeting.

1894 A. Chevalier *Humorous Songs* 4 'Wot cher!' all the neighbours cried, 'Who're yer goin' to meet, Bill?' **1899** *North-China Herald* 13 Nov. 962/3 (Advt.), 'Wot Cher, Mate?' may be a rough form of salutation. **1928** *Granta* 2 Nov. 71 (*caption*) Wotcher! **1954** J. Masters *Bhowani Junction* xxxii. 279 Howland waved violently to Victoria..and shouted, 'Wotcher, Vicky!' **1980** 'J. Gash' *Spend Game* xvi. 162 'Hello, Lovejoy.' 'Wotcher, love.'

would, pa. t. of Will *v.*[1]

woulda (wu·dă), repr. U.S. dial. pronunc. of 'would have'.

1913 *Dialect Notes* IV. 6 *Would a went,* would have gone. **1925** T. Dreiser *Amer. Trag.* (1926) I. i. xii. 83, I coulda chucked my job, and I woulda. **1952** B. Malamud *Natural* 103 If it was something serious you woulda been caught long ago. **1978** G. Vaughan *Belgrade Drop* x. 63 Security woulda got her. She'd never have the chance to tell DI.

would-be, *a.* Add: **c.** (Earlier example.)

1813 Jane Austen *Let.* 11 Oct. (1952) 343 A large, ungenteel Woman, with self-satisfied & would-be elegant manners.

e. Used *predicatively*: mannered, pretentious. (App. restricted to the works of D. H. Lawrence.)

1922 D. H. Lawrence *Lett.* (1932) 556 These drawings are so completely without irony, so crass, so strained and so would-be. **1928** *Ibid.* 751 James Joyce bores me stiff—too terribly would-be and done-on-purpose, utterly without spontaneity or real life. **1932** A. Huxley in *Lett. D. H. Lawrence* p. xvii, The symphony oppressed him; it was too big, too elaborate, too carefully and consciously worked out, too 'would-be'—to use a characteristic Lawrencian expression. He was quite determined that none of his writings should be 'would-be'. He allowed them to flower as they liked from the depths of his being.

wound, *sb.* Add: **8. a.** *wound-fever* (earlier example); *wound-dressing* (concr.: cf. 8 b in Dict.). **b.** *wound-healing.*

1887 T. LONGMORE in J. B. Hamilton *Trans. Internat. Med. Congress, 9th Session* II. III. 117 Primary wound dressings shall be available at all times and in all places. **1959** *First-Aid Boxes in Factories Order* 21 May in *Stat. Instruments 1959* (1960) I. 1266 A sufficient number (not less than twelve) of adhesive wound dressings of an approved type and of assorted sizes. **1976** D. FRANCIS *In Frame* xi. 159 The outer bandages proved to be large strong pieces of linen..just below my shoulder blade, a large padded wound dressing. **1863** L. M. ALCOTT *Hospital Sk.* iv. 51, I..recognized a certain Pennsylvania gentleman, whose wound-fever had taken a turn for the worse. **1949** M. MEAD *Male & Female* x. 216 The resistance against certain diseases, the wound-healing capacities of a whole people, may depend upon the meticulousness with which they use learned, not specific inherent, capacities. **1964** *Oceanogr. & Marine Biol.* II. 409 Under conditions of wound-healing and repair the normal inhibitor of melanogenesis present in the rest of the animal is overcome or absent.

9. **wound-herb** = WOUNDWORT; **wound hormone** [tr. G. *wundhormon* (G. Haberlandt 1921, in *Sitzungsber. d. Preuss. Akad. d. Wissensch.* 222)], a substance that is produced in a plant in response to a wound and stimulates healing; cf. *traumatic acid* s.v. *TRAUMATIC *a.* 3; **wound stump** = CICATRIX 2; **wound-tumour disease,** a plant disease marked by tumours on roots, stems, or leaves and enlargement of veins and caused by the *wound-tumour virus, Aureogenus magnivena,* which is transmitted by leaf-hoppers.

1597, etc. Wound-herb [in Dict., sense 8 a]. **1955** A. L. ROWSE *Expansion of Elizabethan England* i. 6 Scottish practitioners flocked..to gather simples and wound-herbs. **1977** *Irish Press* 29 Sept. 10/1 The Yarrow was principally used by herbalists as a wound-herb. **1921** *Chem. Abstr.* XV. 2914 Exptl. evidence exists that the action of a wound as a stimulus in exciting cell division is due to decompn. products of the mechanically injured or dead cells. These products function as wound hormones. **1966** R. M. DEVLIN *Plant Physiol.* xvii. 427 Most plant tissues do not respond to traumatic acid, suggesting that it may be a specific wound hormone for bean-pod tissue. **1923** D. H. LAWRENCE *Birds, Beasts & Flowers* 52 Yet see him fling himself abroad in fresh abandon From the small wound-stump. **1945** L. M. BLACK in *Amer. Jrnl. Bot.* XXXII. 408/1 It now seems that the terms 'wound-tumor virus' and 'wound-tumor disease' may be more appropriate and distinctive. **1967** K. M. SMITH *Insect Virol.* xi. 219 A quick method of detecting the wound-tumor virus in the leafhopper is by staining the hemolymph smears of the insect with the D (dialysis) conjugates.

woundable. (Later examples.)

1975 *Times Lit. Suppl.* 21 Mar. 293/1 When trauma appears on the scene.. Scully shows that he is as woundable as the next boy. **1976** *Sunday Times* (Colour Suppl.) 22 Feb. 39/1 He is also shy, loyal and surprisingly woundable.

wou·nd-down, *a.* [f. *wound,* pa. pple. of WIND *v.*[1] + DOWN *adv.*] That has undergone winding down (see *WIND *v.*[1] 20*); that has been lowered by winding.

1939 DYLAN THOMAS *Map of Love* 20 The wound-down cough of the blood-counting clock. **1974** P. MCCUTCHAN *Call for Simon Shard* xii. 110 He sniffed through the wound-down window. **1984** W. GARNER *Rats' Alley* xi. 218 He could hear its [*sc.* the helicopter's] racket through the wound-down window of the car.

wound-up, *a.* Add: (Earlier example.) Also in sense 22 a of WIND *v.*[1]

1788 J. WOODFORDE *Diary* 27 Nov. (1927) III. 68 Ben returned about 4 o'clock this Aft. completely wound up, eat no Dinner but went directly to sleep in a Chair. **1973** A. GREY *Some put their Trust in Chariots* v. 22 The wound-up windows of the car.

woundward (wū·ndwǫɹd), *a. nonce-wd.* [f. WOUND *sb.*: see -WARD.] Towards wounds or wounding.

1946 DYLAN THOMAS *Deaths & Entrances* 48 The woundward flight of the ancient Young from the canyons of oblivion!

wourali, var. WOORALI.

wove, *ppl. a.* and *sb.* **1. b.** (Earlier example.)

1806 H. FOURDRINIER *Brit. Patent 2951* 4 A number of moulds of the description called laid or wove, any number of which..are capable of forming one long mould.

woven, *ppl. a.* **2.** (Later example of Comb.)

1904 HARDY *Dynasts* I. 5 O woven-winged squadrons of Toulon..draw westward Ere Nelson be near!

wow, *sb.*[1] Add: **2.** Fluctuations in pitch in reproduced sound that are sufficiently slow to be heard as such in long notes; a property in a reproducer that gives rise to this, esp. uneven speed.

1932 *Wireless World* 16 Mar. 277/2 Wobble or 'wow'—to use the expressive American term..is not so troublesome nowadays, most modern sound cameras having anti-wow mechanism. **1942** *Electronic Engin.* XIV. 640/1 The principal snag of sub-standard projectors, that of speed variations, is well cared for in so far as relates to low-frequency variations, which are known as 'wow' and not, as stated, warble. **1960** K. AMIS *Take Girl like You* xxiii. 271 Every couple of weeks Graham found out some new way of reducing distortion or filtering off surface noise or eliminating wow. **1968** *New Scientist* 20 June 615/1 The Lick Observatory conclusion was entirely spurious, the result of undetected 'wow' in the tape recorder used. **1971** *Wireless World* Oct. 478/1 Wow can be caused by a badly eccentric or warped record. **1982** *Listener* 16 Dec. 34/2 Insist on listening to some music, preferably piano music that shows up wow and flutter especially well.

wow (wau), *sb.*[2] and *a. slang* (orig. *U.S.*). [f. Wow *int.*] **A.** *sb.* A sensational success. Freq. const. *of.*

1920 *Collier's* 11 Dec. 21/1 In Round Five they stalled some more... The sixth innin' was a wow! **1926** [see *STOP *v.* 21 c]. **1927** WODEHOUSE *Small Bachelor* vi. 94 'A friend of mine tipped me off that this company was a wow'. 'A what?' 'A winner. He said it was going to be big and advised me to come in on the ground floor.' **1944** S. BELLOW *Dangling Man* 54 What a wow of a finish. **1954** C. CHURCHILL *Let.* 1 Sept. in M. Soames *Clementine Churchill* (1979) xxvi. 445 Mr Graham Sutherland is a 'Wow'. He really is a most attractive man. **1962** V. CONNAUGHT *Secret Heart of Princess Alexandra* vii. 73 From that moment forward, she was a wow with every Australian in the land. **1983** D. FRANCIS *Danger* xvii. 236 Chattering guests all having a wow of a time.

B. *adj.* Exciting or expressing admiration and delight.

1921 *Variety* 9 Dec. 31 The *wow* comedy song... *'Say It With Liquor'*. **1962** *John o' London's* 1 Mar. 211/2 A chorus of wow reviews from international critics. **1972** *Daily Colonist* (Victoria, B.C.) 13 Feb. 27/4 Two-foot-high letters inviting you to buy Vitamin E capsules, often at wow potencies, plaster the fronts of drug stores.

wow (wau), *v.*[2] *slang* (orig. *U.S.*). [f. Wow *int.*, **sb.*[3].] *trans.* To make enthusiastic, to impress or excite greatly (esp. an audience).

1924 *Variety* 24 Dec. 14/5 He doesn't wow 'em at any time and seems misplaced in the show. **1938** E. B. WHITE *Let.* 20 Dec. (1976) 191 Your Hollywood visit piece (which I had never read) wowed me. **1949** *Time* 19 Sept. 45/3 She wowed them with a dramatic reading of the death scene from *Romeo and Juliet.* **1950** BLESH & JANIS *They all played Ragtime* ii. 44 The ragtime pianists were already 'wowing' their audiences with syncopated renderings of the classics. **1961** *Sunday Express* 12 Mar. 14/5 Yet *another* new look..wowed London last week. **1980** *Times* 17 June 13/3 They are unlikely to wow anybody who does not already respond to Burne-Jones's rather wan charms. **1984** *Daily Tel.* 25 Sept. 11/4 Mr Macdonald, who supplied the off-screen commentary for this year's Channel 4 coverage of the SDP conference, had the bright notion of training up a novice speaker who would wow them at Buxton.

wow, *int.* Restrict 'Chiefly *Sc.*' to sense 1 and add: **2.** (Later examples.) Now chiefly expressing astonishment or admiration.

1896 ADE *Artie* 8 'The girls—wow!' 'Beauties, eh?' 'Lollypaloozers!' **1931** R. CAMPBELL *Georgiad* i. 11 Bang on your nose my spectacles appear And (Wow!) an earring slits my tender ear. **1941** J. D. CARR *Case of Constant Suicides* i. 17 A brown-haired girl..straightened up to stare at him. 'Wow!' said Alan inaudibly. **1962** E. CLEAVER in A. Dundes *Mother Wit* (1973) 20/1 Wow, what a sight that would be! **1980** 'R. B. DOMINIC' *Attending Physician* xxiv. 217 'Wow!' Mike Isham whistled reverently. 'No wonder she was willing to murder.'

Also **wowee·** († **wowey**) *int.*, in the same sense.

1921 S. FORD *Inez & Trilby May* xvi. 279 Think of the row that will start when it comes out that this is an inside job, with a princess playing the star part. Wowey! **1963** *Mad Mag.* July 23/2 Boy! Wow-wee! That's quite an exciting evening line-up! **1975** R. H. RIMMER *Premar Experiments* (1976) iii. 216 Bren was jubilant. 'My big sister is pregnant. Wow-ee! Unbelievable! Fantastic!' **1981** R. BARNARD *Sheer Torture* iii. 29 He had served on the Arts Council Music Panel, 1958–60. Wowee!

wowser. For *Australia* read 'orig. *Austral.* (now chiefly *Austral.* and *N.Z.*)' and add: Also **wowzer.** Perhaps most commonly in sense 'a fanatical or determined opponent of intoxicating drink'. (Earlier and later examples.)

1899 *Truth* 8 Oct. 5 Willoughby 'Wowsers' Worried. The 'Talent' get a 'Turn'... Ten young men were fined.. for having behaved in a riotous manner on the Military Rd. **1918** *Chrons. N.Z.E.F.* 79/2 The Wowzers look with disdain upon the 'Come and have a spot, old boy' kind of welcome. **1937** R. A. KNOX *Double Cross Purposes* ii. 40, I hope to God the old wowzer didn't see we'd been at it. He's as sharp as a weasel. **1939** R. CAMPBELL *Flowering Rifle* I. 18 Where wowsers may discharge their wondrous lore Who'll 'fight for peace', and yet disarm for war. **1939** X. HERBERT *Capricornia* xviii. 233 Only ones't got a victory outer that flamin' war was the blasted wowsers! **1941** C. BARRETT *Coast of Adventure* iii. 56 Men without vision or liberal views. We might call them 'wowsers' today. **1949** D. M. DAVIN *Roads from Home* I. v. 72 The good old days were gone. And it wasn't only the wowsers that had spoilt everything. **1961** *N.Y. Times* 12 Feb. 36/1 A relentless wowser (prohibitionist)..banned saloons. **1963** *Economist* 3 Aug. 422/2 Some alien wowser such as Senator Goldwater. **1970** *N.Z. Listener* 12 Oct. 13/2 A bit late to find that out, you snobbish ratbag wowser. **1975** D. STUART *Walk, Trot, Canter & Die* xxiii. 137 But now in me old age I'm a wowser an' I don't have to worry about anything. I'd have a bottle of whisky in the packs... but most trips it wouldn't even get opened, so you can't say I was a drunkard. **1977** *Times* 18 Mar. 18/7 This country's pattern of..licensing hours..is the work of wowzers of every description. **1981** M. GEE *Meg* xiv. 142 You won't drink with me, will you? Didn't think so. I'm stuck in a family of wowsers. **1982** *Times* 7 Dec. 12/6 These authoritarian wowsers would like to see a law forbidding anybody to watch any programme they disapprove of.

b. *attrib.* and *Comb.*

1934 *Bulletin* (Sydney) 12 Sept. 11/4 That morbid sex curiosity which is the curse of wowser-ridden communities. **1936** R. CAMPBELL *Mithraic Emblems* 125 Let Spender over wowser-problems fret. **1966** G. W. TURNER *Eng. Lang. Austral. & N.Z.* i. 22 The wowser tradition is stronger in New Zealand, where there is less of the bush tradition; it usually takes the form of a cautious anxiety about life rather than open Puritanism. **1969** *Age* (Melbourne) 24 May 2/5 Sir Henry, while making his attack on NSW and its poker machines, maintained that Victoria was not a 'wowser' State. **1978** P. H. JOHNSON *Good Husband* xxii. 190 There were 'no smoking' notices, at which Maisie demurred... 'I find this wowser activity uncomfortable.'

Hence **wow·serish** *a.*, of the nature of a wowser; puritanical; **wow·serism,** the practice or beliefs of a wowser or wowsers.

1909 Wowserism [in Dict.]. **1933** F. CLUNE *Try Anything Once* 122 They had lost their dash and grown wowserish. **1936** M. FRANKLIN *All that Swagger* l. 377 Novels which.. provoked attention by their unreticent details of bodily functionings and provided capital sport when flung in the face of *fin de siècle* wowserism. **1966** *New Statesman* 4 Mar. 289/2 After a time, I warmed even to Stennis and Morse; though the first was narrow and wowserish. **1966** G. W. TURNER *Eng. Lang. Austral. & N.Z.* i. 21 Wowserism is prohibition elevated into a philosophy. **1971** *Observer* 14 Mar. 15/2 Australia's peculiar 'wowserism', the often unpredictable censorship of films, books and shows by the authorities, is largely a function of older Australia. **1983** *Age* (Melbourne) 3 Dec. 11/2 Coming hard on the heels of the casino inquiry, which also recommended in the negative, the Government's decision on poker machines may give it a puritanical or wowserish image. **1984** *Daily Tel.* 24 Aug. 10/4 When Pierre Trudeau visited Australia in 1970 he told the natives: 'You have wowserism; we have Toronto.'

wow-wow, var. *WAH-WAH[2].

W particle: see *W 4 b.

W.R.A.C. Also **WRAC** and (*colloq.*) **Wrac** (ræk). [f. initial letters of its name.] The Women's Royal Army Corps, formed as the women's corps of the British Army in 1949 to replace the A.T.S.; also, a member of this corps.

1949 *Times* 1 Feb. 2/3 (*heading*) Inauguration of W.R.A.C. and W.R.A.F. *Ibid.*, The King has given orders for the following appointments in the W.R.A.C.:—The Queen to be Commandant-in-Chief the Women's Royal Army Corps. **1950** *R.A.F. Rev.* Sept. 7/2 They have defeated the W.R.A.C. in every championship shoot since the women's inter-Services championships were started in 1947. **1956** R. MACAULAY *Towers of Trebizond* xv. 179 Now the women who go with armies are not encouraged to be so useful to them, they are called Ats and Wrens and Waafs and Wracs and are kept behind the battle lines and are only a small consolation to the troops. **1982** *Whitaker's Almanack 1983* 482 Retirement Benefits... The annual rates for W.R.A.C. were given; these apply to equivalent ranks in all Services. **1984** *Daily Tel.* 7 Apr. 8/1 'You are following in the footsteps of great men,' said the Duchess, Controller-Commandant of the WRAC.

wracked, erron. var. RACKED *ppl. a.*[3] (Later examples.)

1974 *Times Lit. Suppl.* 19 Apr. 417/4 Lowry could be sodden, sullen, wracked with shame and remorse: a figure of total anguish. **1974** A. DAVIS *Autobiography* IV. 279 During the few months of our friendship, I don't think I realized how wracked he must have been by that decade of accumulated frustrations, by that terrible sense of impotence.

W.R.A.F. Also **WRAF** and (*colloq.*) **Wraf** (ræf). [f. initial letters of its name.] The Women's Royal Air Force (1918–20, re-formed 1949), the women's corps of the Royal Air Force; also, a member of this.

1918 *Times* 3 Apr. 4/4 No women for the 'mobile' branch will be enrolled at present. Candidates for posts as officers should apply to the W.R.A.F. Inquiry Office,.. Strand. **1921** *Spectator* 4 June 719/2 Sketches with pen and pencil of the duties of the 'Wrafs'. **1955** *Times* 23 May 6/6 Five women holding W.R.A.F. commissions, all with university degrees, are serving as technical officers in the R.A.F. **1977** *R.A.F. News* 11–24 May 2/5 A charity disco at Newton enabled the WRAF girls there to raise £58. **1983** *Daily Tel.* 22 Aug. 8/5 Dame Felicity Peake was director of the WRAF from its inception in 1949.

wraggle-taggle, var. *RAGGLE-TAGGLE *a.* and *sb.*

wraith, *sb.* Add: **4.** *wraith-ship.*

1924 V. F. BOYSON *Falkland Islands* viii. 181 Dimly as she came, so she passed away, as though in very truth the wraithship said to appear at every British naval fight.

wraithly (rēⁱ·þli), *a. rare.* [f. WRAITH *sb.* + -LY[1].] Resembling a wraith, wraith-like.
1909 M. B. SAUNDERS *Litany Lane* I. iv. 41 The tinkle-tinkle of a wraithly Tom Moore singing flowery love-songs at fluted-silked pianos.

wrangle, *sb.* Add: **1.** Also *fig.*
1931 BLUNDEN *To Themis* 22 Rumour multiplies the wrangle of wheels and clash of hoofs abroad.

wrangle, *v.* **4.** Delete † *Obs. rare* and add: To obtain by wrangling. (Later example.)
1934 in WEBSTER. **1976** *National Observer* (U.S.) 31 Jan. 1/3 The pall of snowdrifts and ice would have impeded reinforcements' marching even if Arnold had been able to wrangle help from American Brig. Gen. David Wooster, a procrastinator who then occupied Montreal.
7. (Earlier and later examples.)
1899 F. REMINGTON *Sundown Leflare* 11 De herd, which was more horses..dan ten men kin wrangle. **1952** H. INNES *Campbell's Kingdom* I. ii. 38 He wrangles a bunch of horses and acts as packer for the visitors in the summer

wrangled, *ppl. a.*[1] Add: Cf. *RANGLED.

wrangler. Add: **3.** Also **Wrangler.** A proprietary name for jeans. Freq. *pl.* orig. *U.S.*
1947 *Official Gaz.* (U.S. Patent Office) 16 Dec. 395/2 Blue Bell, Inc., Greensboro, N.C... *Wrangler.* For Western style dungarees and pants. Claims use since Jan. 19, 1929. **1963** *Trade Marks Jrnl.* 16 Oct. 1478/1 *Wrangler*... Articles of protective clothing..and articles of sports clothing... Kilgour & Walker Limited.., Aberdeen; manufacturers. **1966** *Ibid.* 7 Sept. 1313/2 *Wrangler*... Articles of protective clothing..; trousers, jeans [etc.]. Blue Bell, Inc.., Greensboro, State of North Carolina. **1972** *New Society* 13 Apr. 68/2, I suggested.. that the girls ..might like to travel in jeans and change into their best gear when we stopped for lunch. My idea.. produced..a unanimous decision..that they were going in their wranglers anyway. **1978** D. BLOODWORTH *Cross-talk* xxvii. 211 A tall blond youth in wranglers and ringlets. **1981** C. WATSON *Bishop in Back Seat* xxi. 131 He was in his regulation costume: Wrangler jeans, soiled Stetson.

wrap, *sb.* Add: **1. c.** Material used for wrapping, esp. very thin plastic film.
1930 *Food Industries* Jan. 13/1 [Cellophane] was first introduced into this country from France as a wrap for candy. *Ibid.*, The transparent type of wrap proved decidedly popular. **1958** *Chain Store Age* Apr. 168/3 The Aluminum Company of America is now packaging Alcoa wrap in a 'flat pak'. **1976** 'O. JACKS' *Assassination Day* v. 81 He bundled the notes up into foil wrap, put two in..his refrigerator. **1977** *Time* 14 Mar. 39/3 The thin sail (ordinary plastic kitchen wrap is five times thicker) would be coated with an aluminum reflecting layer on the side that will face the sun. **1979** *Sci. Amer.* Jan. 131/1 You could also build up layers of stretched plastic food wrap. **1980** *Outdoor Life* (U.S.) (Northeast ed.) Oct. 126/2 Cover an exposed drain valve with plastic wrap to prevent road slush from accumulating.
4. *pl.* In *fig.* phrases referring to concealment or disuse, as *under* or *in wraps*, concealed; in abeyance; *to take* or *pull the wraps off*, to disclose; to bring back into use.
1939 *Sun* (Baltimore) 18 Dec. 3/6 The fact that the belligerents have kept their air power under wraps almost from the beginning reveals more than meets the eye. **1950** 'S. RANSOME' *Deadly Miss Ashley* xv. 178 You grabbed his notebooks and tried..to keep them under wraps. **1956** A. H. COMPTON *Atomic Quest* 49 Some members of the committee were insistent that the entire uranium project should be put in wraps for the duration. **1964** *New Society* 15 Feb. 21/2 The Government took the wraps off its plan for regenerating the Northeast. **1965** MRS. L. B. JOHNSON *White House Diary* 20 Jan. (1970) 226 Next Hubert [Humphrey] stepped forward—for once his exuberance was under wraps. **1973** *Times* 4 Oct. 4/3 Only now was the truth about battered wives being revealed 'because the wraps have just been pulled off a taboo subject'. **1978** *Dumfries Courier* 20 Oct. 11/1 Show visitors will see numerous others which are still under wraps until nearer the Show. **1984** *Times* 14 May 7/2 This week will see the wraps coming off another popular project, where Britain wants to be seen leading the way.
5. *Cinemat.* and *Television.* The end of a session of filming or recording.
1974 M. AYRTON *Midas Consequence* I. 63 Other cars are heard starting up out of shot and the lights on the pergola go off so I assume it's a wrap and the crew is listening to the director saying something consequential and busy about tomorrow's call. **1980** J. KRANTZ *Princess Daisy* xii. 191 'Right, it's a wrap.'.. The large lights, cameras, sound equipment and other tools of the trade were quickly stowed away. **1983** *Listener* 23 June 18/2 The director says: 'Cut! Thank you, Ben, that's a wrap—there is no more filming.'
6. Special Combs. (see also WRAP- in Dict. and Suppl.): **wrap party** *Cinemat.*, a party held to celebrate the completion of filming; **wrap reel, wheel,** a large revolving framework on which yarn can be wound and measured.
1978 J. KRANTZ *Scruples* xiii. 388 Work on *Mirrors* finished on schedule, on Friday, August 23rd, and the wrap party was scheduled for the next night. **1978** *Morning Bulletin* (Rockhampton, Queensland) 3 Apr. 6/4 At the wrap party..Syl played host in a three-piece white suit. **1889** G. E. DAVIS *Sizing & Mildew in Cotton Goods* ii. 20 In order to test the fineness of yarn a wrap reel is used, measuring 54 inches in circumference, which is so arranged that by a single turn of a handle two complete revolutions are given to the reel itself. **1928** W. L. BALLS *Studies of Quality in Cotton* xii. 235 The lea was wound upon wrap-reels of varying diameter. **1956** S. E. ELLACOTT *Spinning & Weaving* 36/2 Arkwright's wrap reel for measuring hanks of yarn (840 yards) was a six-armed revolving star with a winch handle. **1953** Wrap wheel [see *RICE *sb.*[1] 4]. **1969** E. H. PINTO *Treen* 318 After yarn had been spun on a spindle or spinning wheel, it was transferred on to a wrap or clock wheel, a rotary instrument which skeined and measured it. The original wrap wheel is always said to have been invented by Richard Arkwright.

wrap, *v.* Add: **I. 6*.** *to wrap up* (fig.) **a.** *trans.* To put an end to, bring to completion; also, to defeat; *to wrap it up*, to stop doing something. *slang.*
1926 T. E. LAWRENCE *Seven Pillars* (1935) III. xxxvi. 213 The British were wrapping up the Arabs on all sides—at Aden, at Gaza, at Bagdad. **1937** *Amer. Legion Monthly* May 9/1 Only one shot to finish before midnight and we'd wrap it up in thirteen days. **1949** A. MILLER *Death of Salesman* II. 128 To hell with whose fault it is... Let's just wrap it up, heh? **1957** J. OSBORNE *Look back in Anger* I. 25 Wrap it up, will you? Stop ringing those bells! **1957** P. FRANK *Seven Days to Never* II. vii. 80, I guess that wraps it up for tonight... I don't know of anything else we can do. **1960** G. SANDERS *Mem. Professional Cad* II. iii. 127 'Wrap it up,' he would shout. **1976** *Billings* (Montana) *Gaz.* 2 July 1-c/1 Nastase wrapped up Ramirez, 6-2, 9-7, 6-3. **1984** *Times* 14 Mar. 2/1 (*heading*) Labour MPs advised to wrap up their muck raking.
b. *intr.* To stop talking. Freq. as imp. *slang.*
1943 HUNT & PRINGLE *Service Slang* 70 *Wrap up*, stop talking. Or, get ready to go home. **1945** C. H. WARD-JACKSON *Piece of Cake* (ed. 2) 63 *Wrap up!*, Be quiet! Pipe down! **1958** F. NORMAN *Bang to Rights* I. 49 Why dont you rap up. **1959** 'O. MILLS' *Stairway to Murder* iv. 44 'Geoff, wrap up about the jigsaws,' Charles entreated him.
6.** *intr. Cinemat.* and *Television.* To finish filming or recording.
1976 in B. Armstrong *Gloss. TV Terms* 94. **1983** *London Mag.* Aug./Sept. 30 We wrapped on schedule, three days later... The movie got terrible reviews.
II. 10. *to wrap* oneself *(a)round* (an item of food or drink): to eat or drink it. Occas. with non-*refl.* direct obj., to make (another) eat or drink. *colloq.*
1880 J. C. HARRIS *Uncle Remus* xv. 219 She cut me off er slishe..an' I sot down on de steps an' wrop myse'f roun' de whole blessid chunk. **1927** D. L. SAYERS *Unnatural Death* xii. 136 Lord Peter, having wrapped himself affectionately round an abnormal quantity of bacon and eggs, strolled out. **1946** K. TENNANT *Lost Haven* (1947) xviii. 305, I bet they had to wrap Alec round a few beers before they got him up to the mark. **1959** G. ENDORE *Detour through Devon* 3 Wrap yourself around a cup of coffee. **1962** A. LEJEUNE *Duel in Shadows* ii. 25, I shall be glad to get indoors and wrap myself round a large drink.
11. To crash (a vehicle) into a stationary object. Const. *around, round. slang.*
1950 J. D. MACDONALD *Brass Cupcake* (1955) x. 105, I took a car off the street and wrapped it around an oak tree. **1958** 'J. BROGAN' *Cummings Report* xvii. 183 Steady, or you'll have us both wrapped round a telegraph pole if you're not careful. **1969** L. G. ARTHUR in A. E. Wilkerson *Rights of Children* (1973) 132 If a child wraps a stolen car around a telephone pole, is $2,000.00 restitution..an excessive fine? **1984** *Times* 19 May 8/1 The men towing the boat from one training venue to another wrapped it round a traffic light.

wrap-. Add: **2.** *spec.* Designating a garment to be wrapped about the body for warmth, or a wraparound garment (see *WRAPAROUND *a.* 1 a).
1845 *Ainsworth's Mag.* VII. 499 A wrap-cloak, or sheet, being thrown penance-ways over the head and shoulders. **1887** Wrap shawl [in Dict. s.v. WRAP *sb.* 2 a]. **1928** *Daily Mail* 9 Aug. 3/4 A. bathing dress worn under a well cut wrap-coat of crêpe de Chine. **1976** *New Yorker* 8 Mar. 1 (Advt.), Reversible wrap skirt lined in red and white. **1980** L. BIRNBACH et al. *Official Preppy Handbk.* 131/1 Diane von Furstenburg wrap dress. **1982** BARR & YORK *Official Sloane Ranger Handbk.* 30/1 A belted wool wrap coat: this can be tweedy, checked or camel. **1984** *Chicago Sun-Times* 25 Jan. 33/1 By 1976 she had designed the wrap dress, which became an overnight success.

wraparound (ræ·părɑund), *sb.* and *a.* Also **wrap-around, wrapround, wrap-round.** [f. WRAP *v.* + AROUND *adv.* and *prep.*] **A.** *sb.*
1. A garment that is thrown or wrapped round the body; a wraparound garment (see sense B. 1 a below).
1877 [see WRAP-]. **1959** *Vogue Pattern Bk.* June-July 25 A wrap-around that buttons into place... The sort of comfort-with-elegance dress. **1973** *Harrods Christmas Catal.* 27 Casual wrap-around in figured polyester.
2. A fastening or label that wraps round a bottle.
1953 *Federal Suppl.* CXVIII. 182/2 The Guardian Seal, made of aluminum, attached to the bottle and requiring no secondary closure;..wrap arounds, a laminated foil attached to a paper with an adhesive on the inside giving the same decorative features as a cellulose band; [etc.]. **1966** J. AIKEN *Trouble with Product X* iii. 43, I switched over to copy for a counter-card, window bill and wrap-around for Bom, the Meat'n Milk Drink. **1970** K. PLATT *Pushbutton Butterfly* (1971) xiii. 149 He..came back with a bottle. He unfurled the plastic wraparound and broke it open.
3. *Computers.* The procedure or facility by which a linear sequence of memory locations or positions on a screen is treated cyclically, so that when the last has been counted or occupied the first is returned to automatically (on the line below in the case of screen displays). Also *transf.*
1965 E. A. WEISS *Programming the IBM 1620* ii. 21 This wrap-around feature does not apply to addresses used in commands. **1970** O. DOPPING *Computers & Data Processing* vi. 101 Even when the index register has no room for sign, subtraction can be done by utilizing the cyclic character of the addressing system ('wraparound'). **1979** J. E. ROWLEY *Mechanised In-House Information Syst.* I. 76 Display can be improved by..contextual wrap-around, or bringing the end of the title to the left hand side of a keyword and then marking the end of the title with a display device.
B. *adj.* **1.** *Fashion.* **a.** Of a garment: that is open all the way down, wraps around the body, and is fastened usu. by tying. Also, of a belt.
1937 M. LEVIN *Old Bunch* 13 She dressed spiffy with wrap-around sport skirts. **1938** 'E. QUEEN' *Four of Hearts* (1939) x. 143 A silver lamé hostess-gown with a trailing wrap-around skirt over Turkish trousers. **1945** [see *POP-OVER 2]. **1951** *Rep. Patent, Design & Trade Mark Cases* (U.S.) LXVIII. 256 Mr. Percival contended that the Applicants' skirt was a novel 'wrap round' skirt. **1957** *U.S. Supreme Court Rep.* 2nd Ser. I. 880/1, 1 Purple wool imitation lambskin wrap around short coat. **1972** J. GODEY *Three Worlds* ii. 19 The man was wearing a wraparound coat of some synthetic fur. **1976** *Scotsman* 20 Nov. (Weekend Suppl.) 4/3 (Advt.), Right: The unlined, hooded style of winter coat with wrap-around belt. **1976** T. STOPPARD *Dirty Linen* 9 Maddie is..wearing..a wrap-round skirt, quite short. **1982** BARR & YORK *Official Sloane Ranger Handbk.* 42/1 There are a few basic lines that continue practically for ever, like the pre-war wraparound double-breasted and the basic City three-piece.
b. Of sunglasses, goggles, etc.: that have lenses which extend around the side of the head.
1966 T. PYNCHON *Crying of Lot 49* iii. 57 There stood Di Presso, in a skin-diving suit and wraparound shades. **1968** A. WILLIAMS *Brotherhood* I. iv. 50 He was no longer wearing his wrap-around dark glasses. **1976** *National Observer* (U.S.) 27 Mar. 15 (Advt.), Space-age wraparound sunglasses make all others obsolete!
2. a. That extends round a corner, esp. of parts of a building or parts of a motor vehicle.
1954 *Archit. Rev.* CXVI. 92/1 The wrap-round cornices are used to tie it back to the side façade. **1957** H. ROTH *Shadow of Lady* xiv. 103 A sturdy little car..even if without American flourishes, like 'wrap-around' windscreens. **1959** *Motor* 21 Jan. 951/1 Protective wrap-around bumpers. **1966** *Daily Tel.* 9 Nov. 12/5 Recent years' flirtation with vestigial fins, wrap-round rear windows and other gimmicks. **1972** [see *wet-suited* adj. s.v. *WET *a.* 20]. **1972** *Village Voice* (N.Y.) 1 June 87/4 (Advt.), Huge liv rm & wraparound sundeck. **1976** *Glasgow Herald* 26 Nov. 19/5 Visibility from the reclining driver's seat is outstanding, with a very wide and deep 'wrap around' rear window. **1980** J. STROUSE *Alice James* (1981) xiii. 221 The buildings..are..ornamented with scrollwork, wraparound porches, archways.
b. Of a cinema screen: having a greater sideways extent than normal; subtending a large angle at the audience. Similarly of a view. Also *fig.*
1950 *Pop. Sci. Monthly* Aug. 75 You're not just looking *at* this 'wrap-around' movie show—you're in it! **1968** *Globe & Mail* (Toronto) 17 Feb. 25 (Advt.), Look down on the world from Stop. 33. The room with the wrap-around view. **1968** *Tel.* (Brisbane) 18 Sept. 34/5 His book is entitled *The Invasion*... Hay contents himself with a brief, wraparound picture of the real invasion. **1972** J. MCCLURE *Caterpillar Cop* i. 7 The Big Romance soon to be filmed in fabulous Technicolor on a wrap-round screen.
3. *gen.* That surrounds or encompasses.
1957 *Times Survey Brit. Aviation* Sept. 2/4 The missile has a two-stage propulsion system, consisting of wrap-around boosts and a sustainer rocket motor. **1964** M. MCLUHAN *Understanding Media* (1967) xxviii. 300 Stereo sound..is 'all-around' or 'wrap-around' sound. **1967** *Maclean's Mag.* Sept. 14 The Volkswagen is the German's ideal image of space: it's a wraparound, secure little thing. **1970** *Gloss. Aeronaut. & Astronaut. Terms (B.S.I.)* VI. 3 *Wrap-round boost*, a number of boost rocket motor assemblies located externally along the sides of the missile body. **1978** *Detroit Free Press* 5 Mar. A10 (Advt.), Wrap-around heat encircles the sides of the crockware. **1979** *Jrnl. R. Soc. Arts* CXXVII. 655/2 The 21 new rooms and the lower gallery..provide a more than adequate wrap-around environment for the works on display. **1981** *Times* 27 Jan. 1/8 His wrap-around bodyguards leapt from the flower-beds.., shouldering reporters and Saudi policemen from his path so that..it was simply not possible to see more than his eyebrows and hair.
4. *Printing.* Designating a flexible relief printing plate which is wrapped round the cylinder of a rotary press, and machines or methods which employ one.
1959 *Brit. Printer* Dec. 116/3 (Index), Wrap-around, Harris letterpress rotary. **1962** [see *ROTARY *a.* 2 b]. **1963** *Publishers' Weekly* 5 Aug. 87/1 Wrap-around relief printing—direct and indirect—is..being used increasingly... Most of the printing is for labels and packaging materials.

1972 A. TYRRELL *Basics of Reprography* xiv. 216 In this way curved or wrap-around printing formes can be prepared by reprographic methods, from relief surfaces in the flat. **1983** A. CAMPBELL *Designer's Handbk.* viii. 128 A modern development of letterpress printing is the wrap-around rotary press, which prints from a one-piece shallow relief plate fastened around a press cylinder.

5. *Publishing.* Designating (*a*) a book cover made from a single sheet of material; (*b*) a jacket whose design extends from front to back without being divided by the spine.

1968 G. A. STEVENSON *Graphic Arts Encycl.* 418 *Wrap-around cover,* soft cover used to bind or hold a booklet, brochure, etc. It consists of one sheet of stock that forms both front and back covers. Any type of mechanical binding may be used. **1972** *N.Y. Law Jrnl.* 24 Oct. 4/2 It must have a wrap-around cover page containing the usual information. **1979** *Bookseller* 23 June 2829/2 Mr. Paton thought that designers did not give nearly enough consideration to the potential of the spine. In this respect he was suspicious of the wrapround jacket.

6. *U.S. Finance.* Used with reference to (*a*) a mortgage which continues when the mortgaged property is sold, the repayments to the original lender being made by a new lender who also provides the additional funds needed for the purchase; (*b*) a tax-deferral scheme in which the interest on certain investments goes into paying the premiums for an annuity.

1968 *Federal Suppl.* CCXCII. 594 Midwestern would exchange a $2·2 million wrap around note, secured by certain hotel properties. **1971** *Legal Bull.* (U.S.) Sept. 185 Wrap-around mortgage financing. **1977** *National Observer* (U.S.) 22 Jan. 8/2 The days may be numbered for a popular tax shelter known as the investment, or 'wrap-around', annuity. **1979** *Arizona Daily Star* 5 Aug. (Advt. Section) 17/8 Priced below appraisal. Will consider a wrap-around deed or trust. **1981** *U.S. Federal Reg.* 7 Apr. 20875/1 Official Staff Interpretation FC-0146.. treats 'wrap-around' loans as the equivalent of refinancings.

wrap-over (ræ·pōᵘvəɹ), *sb.* and *a.* Also **wrap over, wrapover.** [f. WRAP *v.* + OVER *adv.*]

A. *sb.* Part of something, usu. a garment, that overlaps another part of itself.

1935 *Times* 21 Oct. 11/3 There is a good wrapover on the skirt of the coat. **1960** *Vogue Pattern Bk.* Early Autumn 37 Divided skirt..concealed by a wrap-over at front and back.

B. *adj.* **a.** Of a garment: having a wrap-over. **b.** Overlapping.

1960 *Guardian* 19 Feb. 8/7 A wrap-over petal skirt. **1973** *Harrods Christmas Catal.* 24/1 Wrap-over coat from Italy. **1979** *Nature* 19 Apr. p. xvii/3 The simple laboratory stirrer..has a wrapover top to provide spillage protection. **1979** *Homes & Gardens* June 103/1 The wrapover skirt, very fashionable this summer, is made of four flared panels, lightly gathered at the waist.

wrapped, *ppl. a.* Add: **I. 2. b.** (Earlier example.)

1793 F. BURNEY *Let.* 24 Feb. (1972) II. 26, I live a Wrapt up Invalide, close to the Fire side.

3*. Enclosed in a wrapping; *spec.* pre-packaged.

1957 M. SUMMERTON *Sunset Hour* xiii. 186 The loaf of wrapped bread. **1963** L. DEIGHTON *Horse under Water* vi. 31 Plastic spoons and large wrapped sugar segments. **1976** *Times* 13 Aug. 2/6 The familiar wrapped and sliced white loaf still accounts for more than half of bread sales. **1984** C. CURZON *Masks & Faces* viii. 90 He fetched the wrapped loaf and filled the toaster.

wrapper, *sb.* Add: **I. 1. d.** (Earlier example.)

1853 *Heal & Son Catal.: Illustr. Catal. Bedsteads* 5 The plain Quilts..are applicable wherever extra warmth is required, either as a wrapper in the carriage, or as an extra covering on the bed.

4. a. Also *wrapper leaf.*

1944 [see *RUN *sb.*[1] 20 e]. **1978** D. WILLIAMS *Treasure up in Smoke* v. 50 All hand-made cigars consist of a thick core of compressed tobacco leaf, a binder.., and finally a wrapper leaf.

wrapper, *v.* Add: **2.** Also *absol.* or *intr.*

1934 H. G. WELLS *Exper. Autobiogr.* I. iv. 151 Half an hour before closing time we began to put away for the last time and 'wrapper up'.

wrapping, *vbl. sb.* Add: **3. wrapping-paper** (earlier examples).

?**1715** POPE *Let.* in *Corr.* (1956) I. 317 If the Fruit is not so good as I wish, let the Gallantry of this Wrapping-paper make up for it. **1768** J. LYNDON *Let.* 17 June in *Rec. Colony of Rhode Island* (1861) VI. 548 One paper mill, at which is manufactured wrapping, package and other coarse paper. **1789** *Deb. Congr. U.S.* (1834) 1st Congress 1 Sess. App. 2130 The several duties shall be aid on the following goods... On all writing, printing and wrapping paper.

wrap-round: see *WRAPAROUND *sb.* and *a.*

wrap-up (ræ·pʌp), *sb.* and *a.* [f. vbl. phr. *to wrap up*: see *WRAP *v.* 6* a.] **A.** *sb.* **1. a.** An easily satisfied customer; an easy sale. **b.** Any easy task.

1938 *Amer. Speech* XIII. 150/2 *Wrap-up,* an easy sale. Also a customer easily satisfied. **1940** 'E QUEEN' *New. Adventures* 284 Not too tough. A wrap-up. **1952** *N.Y. Times Mag.* 21 Sept. 58/3 The ideal customer is known as a 'wrap-up', which is self-explanatory.

2. A summary or résumé, esp. of news; a conclusion.

1960 WENTWORTH & FLEXNER *Dict. Amer. Slang* 588/2 *Wrap-up,*..a conclusion, an ending; a summary and conclusion. **1961** *Times Lit. Suppl.* 13 Oct. 677/4 Finally, Mr. Kalb gives us what he calls the wrap-up [of a book]. **1969** *New Yorker* 30 Aug. 20 (*caption*) Suddenly..a wrap-up of the highlights of my life flashed before my eyes. **1973** H. GRUPPE *Truxton Cipher* xv. 155 'I have no further questions for you.'.. This was the wrap-up. Harry knew ..he would be handed over for court-martial. **1975** *New Yorker* 5 May 128/2 NBC presented a thirty-minute 'special report' on Cambodia, which consisted mainly of a wrapup of NBC's regular news footage of the previous week. **1980** U. CURTISS *Poisoned Orchard* ix. 97 The wrap-up of a job I've been working on will have to be done tonight. **1981** *Daily Mail* 18 May 19/4 Last night's wrap-up saw the old soldier with the black eye-patch welcomed by desert Bedouins. **1985** *Village Voice* (N.Y.) 8 Jan. 39/2 Only in his final wrap-up does he concede that power can also take the form of creative 'attention, or love'.

B. *adj.* That concludes or sums up.

1968 MRS. L. B. JOHNSON *White House Diary* 9 Apr. (1970) 658 Here on the courthouse square at Gonzales was the wrap-up scene, an official good-by for our five-day adventure. **1976** *Publishers Weekly* 27 Sept. 82/2 A long wrap-up section amplifies this practical aspect of their book. **1977** *Church Times* 7 Apr. 2/4 A two-day centennial programme... The Archbishop will..address the wrap-up banquet. **1980** *Jewish Chron.* 21 Mar. 23/3 This is what is described as a 'wrap-up' volume, summarising, in non-technical language, what has been learned. **1980** *Quilt World* Sept./Oct. 16/3 The group session wound down with a light monologue..on 'Fifty Ways to Lose Business', and then small group discussions were held, followed by a wrap-up session.

wrassle, U.S. dial. var. WRESTLE *v.* in Dict. and Suppl.

wrath, *sb.* Add: Now usu. with pronunc. (rɒþ). **1. d.** Also *fig.* in phr. *like the wrath of God,* dreadful, terrible; dreadfully, terribly.

1936 J. BUCHAN *Island of Sheep* xii. 224 The winds..in the Norlands can blow like the wrath of God. **1955** M. ALLINGHAM *Beckoning Lady* xiii. 178 Fancy coming home like the wrath of God and starting a fight. **1967** 'R. FOLEY' *Fear of Stranger* (1968) v. 56 You look like the wrath of God, Kay... No flesh on you to speak of. **1982** 'W. R. DUNCAN' *Queen's Messenger* ii. 19 Are you ill? You look like the wrath of God.

6. *wrath-bearing.*

1920 T. S. ELIOT *Ara Vos Prec* 12 These tears are shaken from the wrath-bearing tree.

wreak, *v.* Add: **III. 8. b.** Esp. in phr. *to wreak havoc.* (For *wrought havoc* see *WORK *v.* 10.)

1926 A. CHRISTIE *Murder of R. Ackroyd* xx. 239 Annie is not allowed to wreak havoc with a dustpan and brush. **1976** B. FELL *America B.C.* viii. 101 The storm waves could surely wreak more havoc upon the timbered hulls of Phoenician galleys than on the steel plates of modern ships. **1978** C. RAYNER *Long Acre* vii. 70 Fenton, well aware of the havoc he was wreaking in poor Miss Emma's heart, wickedly fed her passion for him. **1983** *Times* 21 Nov. 7/7 Moko, the banana disease, has already wreaked havoc on the trade. **1984** *Daily Tel.* 5 Nov. 20/2 The feared shake-out in microcomputer manufacturing..will wreak havoc in the industry.

wreck, *sb.*[1] Add: **II. 9. c.** *N. Amer.* A road or railway accident.

1912 J. SANDILANDS *Western Canad. Dict. & Phrase-Bk., Wreck,* the word to apply to a railway accident; or, more correctly, train wreck. **1974** *Evening Herald* (Rock Hill, S. Carolina) 19 Apr. 11/4 In spite of the reduction in accidents, the sergeant said, 'We still have too many wrecks.' **1979** N. MAILER *Executioner's Song* (1980) I. xviii. 304 On the drive back to Springville, she was dreaming away and got in a wreck. Nobody was hurt but the car.

d. The death of a large number of pelagic birds, usually as the result of a storm.

1936 *Brit. Birds* XXIX. 327 In January, 1915, there was a great oil 'wreck' of Scoters. **1971** *New Scientist* 8 Apr. 69/1 There have been similar wrecks in the past, and the report mentions 11 for guillemots and the auks in the last century.

wrecked, *ppl. a.* Add: **2. c.** Intoxicated; under the influence of drugs. *U.S. slang.*

1968–70 *Current Slang* (Univ. S. Dakota) III-IV. 139 *Wrecked,* intoxicated. **1973** D. LANG *Freaks* 63, I could not get it on, could not get it *on,* not unless I was, one: totally wrecked; and, two: had to have a gun in my hand.

wrecker[1]**.** Add: **3.** A demolition worker.

1958 J. THURBER in *Atlantic Monthly* Feb. 52/1 Jacob Volk, a building wrecker..who tore down two hundred and fifty big structures in Manhattan. **1968** *Globe & Mail* (Toronto) 17 Feb. 6/3, I was saddened to discover wreckers' hoardings surrounding the Royal Bank building at 10-12 King Street East. **1977** H. FAST *Immigrants* vi. 352 He stood on the corner of California Street on Nob Hill watching the wreckers take the Seldon mansion apart, stone by stone.

wrecker[2]**.** Add: **2. a.** (Earlier example.)

1789 O. EQUIANO *Life* II. viii. 57 They met with this little sloop, called a wrecker; their employment in those seas being to look after wrecks

b. A railway vehicle with a crane or hoist for removing crashed trains or similar obstructions; also, a breakdown truck. Also *attrib.*

1904 *Booklovers' Mag.* May 663 This special train has been dubbed the 'Wrecker'. Really it is a relief train, ready to respond to any call for aid in case of accident. **1955** V. NABOKOV *Lolita* II. xxx. 188 Around midnight, a wrecker dragged my car out. **1970** *Globe & Mail* (Toronto) 28 Sept. 31/6 (*caption*) Ward has picked Maggie up..in a wrecker! **1973** *Amer. Speech 1969* XLIV. 257 The wrecker train..has a flatcar with a crane. **1978** *Detroit Free Press* 16 Apr. F8/10 (Advt.), Business offered... Car wash, wrecker service and..service station. **1980** R. L. DUNCAN *Brimstone* vi. 126 A couple of police cars and a wrecker pulling apart three cars that had tailgated.

wrecking, *vbl. sb.*[1] Add: **1.** (Further examples.)

1940 *Construction Methods* Apr. 110/2 Wrecking is, in reality, construction in reverse gear... At the Louisville, Ky. East End slum clearance project..there were approximately 480 buildings to wreck... The Cleveland Wrecking Co. has had many large contracts of this type. **1972** *Times* 10 Mar. (Suppl.) p. ii/1 (Advt.), The most experienced firm in the U.K. in the wrecking of blast furnaces.

3. *attrib.,* as *wrecking company*; **wrecking ball,** a large, heavy metal ball which, hung from a crane, may be swung into a building to demolish it; **wrecking bar,** an iron bar with one end chisel-shaped for prising and the other bent and split to form a claw.

1952 *Business Week* 19 July 33/2 Instead of using a one-ton wrecking ball at the end of a 60-ft. beam, the building must be knocked down..with a 16-lb. sledge hammer. **1977** *Rolling Stone* 21 Apr. 34/4 It's the laugh of a man who just watched a wrecking ball smash his house to splinters so a new freeway could go through. **1984** *New Yorker* 20 Feb. 50/2 The wrecking ball bursts through the wall with the bookshelves, scattering the works of famous authors. **1924** *Sears, Roebuck Catal.* No. 148. 866/3 Wrecking Bars. Forged steel 24-inch, 30c. **1947** *Construction Methods* Mar. 88/2 To minimize damage to material during removal, the contractor developed his own tools as supplements to the standard wrecking bar and claw hammer. **1940** Wrecking company [see sense 1 above]. **1976** *National Observer* (U.S.) 3 Apr. 7/1 A wrecking company recently signed a contract to level all 30 of the remaining 11-story buildings.

wrecking, *vbl. sb.*[2] Add: **1.** (Further example.)

1969 *Sydney Morning Herald* 24 May 63/2 (Advt.), Jaguars, wrecking now. Continually dismantling 2·4, 3·4 and 3·8.

2. b. (Examples relating to motor vehicles.)

1939 [see *OUT-CITY *a.*]. **1968** *Globe & Mail* (Toronto) 13 Feb. 32/2 (Advt.), Well established wrecking business with living quarters on large lot fronting on Napanee River.

wrecking, *ppl. a.* Add: **1.** *wrecking amendment* (Pol.), one designed to defeat the purpose of the bill concerned.

1967 M. PINTO-DUSCHINSKY *Polit. Thought of Lord Salisbury* vii. 145 Its very moderation led directly to the passing of a wrecking amendment by Lord John Russell, who favoured a different and much more far-reaching measure. **1979** H. WILSON *Final Term* ix. 189 Again the Conservatives, with considerable Labour support, moved 'wrecking' or near-wrecking amendments.

wrecky (re·ki), *a.* [f. WRECK *sb.*[1] + -Y[1].] Broken-down; debilitated.

1925 *Brit. Weekly* 17 Sept. 541/1 After which you are left a wreck and probably remain wrecky next day. **1973** M. AMIS *Rachel Papers* 15, I had a well-earned-half at the pub and chatted with the landlord and his wrecky wife.

wren. Add: **2*.** A woman, esp. a young woman. *U.S. slang.*

1920 S. LEWIS *Main Street* 388 Some tank, that wren! Ha, ha, ha! **1927** *Amer. Speech* III. 167/1 *Dame, frail, skirt, Jane, wren, broad,* girl. **1929** A. CONAN DOYLE *Maracot Deep* 198 Scanlan has..married his wren in Philadelphia. **1946** B. TREADWELL *Big. Bk. Swing* 125/2 *Wren,* small, fickle young girl. **1982** M. MCMULLEN *Until Death do us Part* (1983) 9 Midge was, in her quiet unobtrusive way, a perfect marvel of efficiency, 'My dear wren,' Jane sometimes called her.

3. *wren-king*; *wren-nested* adj.; **wren-warbler,** any of several warblers of the genus *Primia,* found in tropical Africa or Asia; also, a brightly coloured wren of the subfamily Malurinæ, found in Australasia.

1965 AUDEN *About House* (1966) 13 From gallery-grave and the hunt of a wren-king to Low Mass and trailer camp is hardly a tick by the carbon clock. **1925** BLUNDEN *Eng. Poems* 104 Wren-nested hedges. **1924** E. C. S. BAKER *Fauna Brit. India: Birds* (ed. 2) II. 530 The Ashy Wren-Warbler breeds from March to September. **1931** *Discovery* May 141/2 The tiny new wren warbler..a wee mite of a bird with a tail almost as long as its body. **1955** MACKWORTH-PRAED & GRANT *Birds E. & N.E. Afr.* 392 Wren-warblers..occur in both woodland and thorn-scrub. **1974** I. ROWLEY *Bird Life* vi. 68 Most *Malurus* have distinctive and attractive songs so that the name 'wren-warbler' is an apt one.

Wren[2] (ren). Also **wren.** [f. three of the initial letters of the name of the Service, made into a singular noun.] A member of the Women's Royal Naval Service, formed in 1917; also (*pl.*), the Service itself.

1918 [see *PENGUIN 2 b]. **1927** *Glasgow Herald* 15 Apr. 7 The war years with all their Waacs and Wrens and Wrafs, seem now to be immeasurably far off. **1940** *War Illustr.* 5 Jan. 558 At all Naval depots 'Wrens' are now doing work as clerks, cooks and in many other capacities, thus relieving men for more active work. **1946** 'TACKLINE' (*title*) You met such nice girls in the Wrens. **1956** [see *W.R.A.C.]. **1979** D. GURR *Troika* xi. 75, I..reported to the Admiralty... 'Captain Jackson's office, please?' 'Second floor, sir.' A good bust and a smile on the duty wren cheered me up.

Hence **Wre·nnery** *joc.*, a building used to accommodate Wrens.

1943 HUNT & PRINGLE *Service Slang* 70 *Wrennery*, billets of the 'Jenny Wrens'. **1945** 'N. SHUTE' *Most Secret* 124, I shall be living in the Wrennery and coming out to Dittisham every day. **1959** P. MCCUTCHAN *Storm South* ii. 41 Where did you pick up all this insight into human nature—in the Navy? Serve in a Wrennery or something, did you? **1964** *Navy News* July 5/4 The work included.. the building of a Wrennery to accommodate 200 Wrens.

Wrenaissance (renē^{i}·sǎns, -ans). *Archit.* [f. the name of Sir Christopher *Wren* (see WRENEAN *a.*) after RENAISSANCE.] An architectural style modelled on or influenced by that of Wren, esp. as represented by some of the work of Sir Edwin Lutyens.

1942 R. LUTYENS *Sir Edwin Lutyens* iii. 40 Gothic and Renaissance ('Wrenaissance'! as father has punned..) are both architectures of meaning. **1944** *Archit. Rev.* XCV. p. xlvi/1 We cannot..allow ourselves, out of affection for a great man [*sc.* Lutyens] and out of admiration for his highly personal style, to be saddled with a Wrenaissance London as a monument to a period which the first world war brought to a murderous close. **1967** *Time* (Atlantic ed.) 26 May 45/1 Frederick Gibberd... extended a piazza to roof over an English Wrenaissance crypt built in the 1930s. **1980** M. LUTYENS *Edwin Lutyens* iv. 62 In 1906, with the building of Heathcote at Ilkley, Yorkshire, for Mr Ernest Hemingway..he reached what he called his 'Wrenaissance'; Wren thereafter became his lodestar. **1981** *Times* 12 Feb. 17/4 That heavy, florid..brick and stone style christened 'Wrenaissance'.

wrench, *sb.*^{2} Add: **6. wrench fault** *Geol.* = *strike-slip fault* s.v. *STRIKE *sb.* 20.

1951 E. M. ANDERSON *Dynamics of Faulting* (ed. 2) i. 2 The term 'Blatt' will be translated as wrench fault. **1977** A. HALLAM *Planet Earth* 61/1 Major wrench faults (e.g., the Great Glen Fault of Scotland) exhibit displacements of 100km..or more.

wrenching, *vb. sb.* Add: **1. c.** *N.Z.* = *root-pruning* s.v. ROOT *sb.*^{1} 22.

1950 *N.Z. Jrnl. Agric.* July 55/1 Toward the end of August root crops..tend to run to seed. This growth can be retarded considerably by wrenching..pushing a fork or spade into the soil..and..levering the roots up slightly. This breaks the extreme end of the taproot.

Wrenean, *a.* Add: Also **Wrenian.**

1944 *Burlington Mag.* Oct. 260/1 The complete reinstatement of a destroyed Wrenian interior. **1973** *Country Life* 13 Dec. 2017/3 The style is about half correct Classical or Wrenian and half Victorian Italianate.

wrenlet (re·nlėt). [f. WREN + -LET.] A young wren.

1858 *Chambers's Jrnl.* Aug. 82/2 It affords a cradle to near a score of wrenlets. **1927** *Observer* 22 May 23/2 In a knot in the rope was a wren's nest, with two or three wrenlets visible inside.

wrestle, *v.* Add: Also, in *U.S. dial.*, with pronunc. (ræ·s'l). For 8 **rassle** read 8– (latterly *U.S. dial.*) **rassle**; also *β* (chiefly *U.S. dial.*) **rastle, wrassle. I. 1. a.** (Further example.)

1974 *Black World* Jan. 56/2 He might be stronger'n me and he might wrassle the best, but I got his waters on, all right.

b. (Further examples.)

1940 L. I. WILDER *Long Winter* xvi. 150 I've spent this whole morning rasseling with that dumb horse. **1941** *Harper's* Feb. 329/2 Leaving..us to rassle with the bear. **1962** W. FAULKNER *Reivers* v. 101 'What you been doing? wrassling with hogs?' 'We got in a mudhole.'

c. (Further example.)

1936 in P. Oliver *Screening Blues* (1968) vi. 189 If you keep on rasslin' you gonna make me break my needle off.

II. 6. a. (Further examples.)

1940 *Sat. Even. Post* 22 June 39/2 He could rassle any three men. **1968** *Listener* 30 May 702/3 In this picture he rides horses, climbs mountains and wrassles Indian chiefs. **1976** *Ibid.* 24 June 817/1 Thrown to the ground and wrastled by the brutally handsome Provo.

b. (Further example.)

1893 N. K. GRIGGS *Lyrics of Lariat* 46 A Maverick daisy he saw—..And so He rastled it low And gave it a touch of his brand.

7. Delete *rare*$^{-1}$ and add: More widely, to move (something inanimate or inert) with physical force. Const. various preps. and advbs.

1970 J. DICKEY *Deliverance* 186, I..dropped down on one knee and wrestled him across my shoulders in the fireman's carry from boy scout days. **1973** M. AMIS *Rachel Papers* 38 Eventually he wrestled all the string and paper into an armful-sized bundle and forced it down the Aga. **1973** M. WOODHOUSE *Blue Bone* vii. 63 We wrestled the crates down through the forward hatch. **1975** *Globe & Mail* (Toronto) 11 Sept. 2/7 Agents wrestled a ·45 calibre automatic pistol out of her hands. **1976** A. PRICE *War Game* I. viii. 142 The same hand, strong and supple.., had once wrestled a bomb-laden Lancaster into the air. **1976** SCOTT & KOSKI *Walk-In* x. 53 He wrestled one of the line of overhead doors up. **1981** J. D. MACDONALD *Free Fall in Crimson* xiv. 159 A truck pulled up... Two men hopped out and started to wrestle the wicker basket out of the back.

wrestler. Add: Also *U.S.* **rassler, wrassler. 1.** (Further examples.)

1900 F. P. DUNNE *Mr. Dooley's Philos.* 207 He was a gr-reat rassler an' whin he had a full Nelson on th' foolish man that wint again him, he used to say, 'Dear me, am I breakin' ye'er neck, I hope so.' **1941** J. THURBER in *Sat. Even. Post* 5 Apr. 10/3 'Wrasslers,' says Magrew, cold-like, 'that's what I've got for a ball club, Mr. Du Monville, wrasslers—and not very good wrasslers at that.'

2. (Further example.)

1964 N. MAILER in *Esquire* Nov. 170/4 He was just another hog-wrassler of rhetoric.

wrestling, *vbl. sb.* (Examples of *U.S. dial.* forms: cf. *WRESTLE *v.*)

1901 W. CHURCHILL *Crisis* II. vi. 162 He an' de Colonel done commence wrastlin' 'bout a man name o' Linkum [*sc.* Lincoln]. **1930** *Amer. Speech* V. 494 Did any boy of the latter part of the last century ever *wrestle*? Ozarkers are not peculiar in their *rasseling*. **1974** *Plain Dealer* (Cleveland, Ohio) 27 Oct. 2-c/1 Even the second Ali-Frazier fight became a financial success for the promoters after Ali put on his rassling match with Frazier during that TV interview. **1975** *New Yorker* 1 Sept. 21/3 Mr. Hayes betrayed this when he mispronounced 'wrestling'; he called it 'wrestling'. Most self-respecting promoters, like Sid Morse, of Saginaw, Michigan, know that the correct pronunciation is 'rasslin''. **1976** L. DEIGHTON *Twinkle, twinkle, Little Spy* xiii. 133 Crude Yankee wrassling, was it? Not the kind of cricket you play at Lord's?

wretched, *a.* Add: **1. b.** Phr. *wretched of the earth* [tr. F. *damnés de la terre* (F. Fanon 1961, as book title)].

1965 C. FARRINGTON tr. F. Fanon (*title*) The wretched of the earth. **1970** *Guardian* 21 Aug. 11/3 Are the refugees, the most wretched of the earth, fertile ground for revolutionary activity on a mass scale? **1979** *Country Life* 11 Oct. 1236/3 Our own native 'wretched of the earth', the alcoholics, the inadequates, the very poor. **1983** C. DRIVER *British at Table* viii. 140 Protein alone cannot rescue the wretched of the earth.

wriggle, *v.* Add: **1. c.** Also with quasi-obj. *to wriggle it*, to move with a wriggling motion.

1922 JOYCE *Ulysses* 477 Come on, boys! Wriggle it, girls!

wriggle-. Add: **wriggle-work** (see quot. 1960); cf. *wriggled work* (next entry).

1960 *Connoisseur's Handbk. Antique Collecting* 312/2 *Wrigglework*, a form of engraved decoration on pewter and silver, employing a zig-zag line cut by rocking a gouge from side to side in its progress. Used in conjunction with line engraving at certain periods, principally late in 17th cent. **1975** *Oxf. Compan. Decorative Arts* 616/2 The flat-lid tankard shows the pewterer's craft at its best. The plain drum..was sometimes decorated with 'wriggle-work' designs of symbolic or commemorative significance. **1982** 'J. GASH' *Firefly Gadroon* v. 62 The plate..was wriggle-work... This was a William III plate, with..a rim decorated by engraved wriggles.

wriggled, *ppl. a.* (In Dict. s.v. WRIGGLE v.) Add: *wriggled work* = *wriggle-work* s.v. *WRIGGLE-.

1906 N. H. MOORE *Old Pewter* i. 22 The tool which makes the wriggled work is of the nature of a chisel. **1955** R. F. MICHAELIS *Antique Pewter* ix. 86 English pewter from the best period, i.e. the 17th century,..displays remarkably fine applied decoration..in the form of 'wriggled-work' engraving.

wring, *sb.*^{2} Add: **4.** Comb.: *wring-world*.

1885 G. M. HOPKINS *Poems* (1967) 99 But ah, but O thou terrible, why wouldst thou rude on me Thy wring-world right foot rock?

wring, *v.* Add: **IV. 22.** Comb.: † **wring-jaw** *U.S. slang*, rough cider.

a **1775** [see *'SIMMON *sb.*^{3}]. **1845** J. F. COOPER *Chainbearer* I. iii. 46 'To get a sup of cider for old Jaap.'.. His weakness in favour of wring-jaw being a well-established failing.

wringer. Add: **6. b.** Fig. phr. *to put through the wringer* and varr.: to try or test (a person or, *rarely*, a thing); *esp.* to subject to severe questioning. *slang* (orig. *U.S.*).

1942 *Sun* (Baltimore) 20 June 15/1 With its capitalization put through the wringer through reorganization..the Erie board voted a payment of 550 cents a share. **1950** T. STERLING *House without Door* (1951) xviii. 196 Every one of them was being blackmailed..except one woman, and she was put through the wringer another way. **1965** J. PHILIPS *Twisted People* iv. 56 We felt..that there had been sabotage... Everybody..was put through a wringer by the CIA. **1972** L. LAMB *Picture Frame* xv. 133 Do you think we had better pick him up and put him through the wringer? **1977** D. FRANCIS *Risk* xiv. 184 If I hadn't recently been through so many wringers..I wouldn't have given it another thought. **1984** *Times* 3 July 12/6 Not since the controversial Bishop of Durham..has an episcopal appointee been put through the wringer in this fashion.

wrinkle, *sb.*^{1} Add: **I. 3. b.** *spec.* A minor difficulty or irregularity; a snag; freq. in phr. *to iron out the wrinkles*.

1966 D. F. JONES *Colossus* i. 15 As a project it's practically finished, we can't find any more wrinkles to iron out we've checked and checked again. **1975** *Economist* 22 Feb. 92 The way for the east Europeans to reach western markets without accumulating further huge trade deficits is to import skills which can be exported in hardware. This also enables them to iron out wrinkles in their own system without having to embark on risky economic reforms. **1979** *Guardian* 30 Aug. 3/6 The BBC wanted to make certain advances in technical practices... Wrinkles still remained. **1984** *New Yorker* 14 May 43 Willa had sold her story to Universal Pictures and was in California ironing out some wrinkles in the deal.

II. 8. a. Esp. (*U.S.*) in phr. *a new wrinkle*.

1941 W. C. HANDY *Father of Blues* iv. 35 In addition to twirling their batons, they added the new wrinkle of tossing them back and forth to each other as they marched. **1969** *Wall St. Jrnl.* 12 Aug. 3/3 The idea for the briefings, a new wrinkle in selling Presidential policy, came from White House communications director Herbert Klein. **1978** *New York* 3 Apr. 37/3 In his budget proposals, the president came up with an investment tax credit with a new wrinkle: If passed by Congress, it will apply to structures as well as to capital equipment. **1984** *Gainesville* (Florida) *Sun* 29 Mar. 4A (*cartoon*) This guy Chernenko should put a new wrinkle in Russian politics.

III. 10. *winkle-free, -proof, -resistant* adjs.; **wrinkle ridge** *Astr.*, one of the long, irregular ridges that can be seen on the maria of the moon and Mars.

1963 *New Yorker* 8 June 74 (Advt.), Stay neat and wrinkle-free all day. **1978** *Detroit Free Press* 16 Apr. 9A (Advt.), Sheets in wrinkle-free and easy-care cotton/polyester percale. **1957** *Economist* 31 Aug. 685/2 The steady introduction of new fibres..new chemicals..to render cloth..wrinkle-proof. **1957** M. B. PICKEN *Fashion Dict.* 382/2 Wrinkle-resistant. **1969** *Sears Catal.* Spring/Summer 20 Perma Prest for great no-iron, wrinkle-resistant performance. **1944** J. E. SPURR *Geol. applied to Selenology* I. viii. 60 The wrinkle-ridges are distinct from faults in appearance... The ridges on the surface of the mare are not straight; they are curving, branching, imbricating, plaited. **1971** I. G. GASS et al. *Understanding Earth* vii. 106 (*caption*) The wrinkle ridges on the surface of Mare Tranquilitatis. **1978** *Sci. Amer.* Mar. 81/1 The Viking orbiter photographs show that much of the surface of Mars retains crisp topographic detail: lava flows, wrinkle ridges and crater ejecta stand out in sharp relief.

wrinkly, *a.* Add: **B.** *sb.* Also **wrinklie.** An old or middle-aged person. *slang.*

1972 A. BIRCHALL *Living in Landscape* 51 (*heading*) What do we do with the Wrinklies? **1976** *Times* 31 Aug. 10/8 A Henley reader..says that her teenage daughter reserves 'wrinklie' for the 60-year-old generation. The reader and her husband..are known as 'oldies'. **1980** *Times* 28 Oct. 12/6 It's pointless to go on a CND march. They're all wrinklies. **1982** BARR & YORK *Official Sloane Ranger Handbk.* 159/3 *Wrinkly* n., middle-aged Sloane—between 40 and 50. **1983** *Church Times* 11 Mar. 13/2, I am a wrinkly whose monthly cheque from the Church Commissioners is labelled 'Diocesan Dignitary'.

wrist. Add: **1. c.** (Earlier example.)

1803 D. WORDSWORTH *Jrnl.* 10 Jan. (1941) I. 188 Worked all day—petticoats—Mrs. C.'s wrists.

5. a. *wrist-bangle*; in the names of devices worn on the wrist, as *wrist compass, radio*, etc.

1922 JOYCE *Ulysses* 432 Fiercely she slaps his haunch, her goldcurb wristbangles angriling. **1983** D. HART-DAVIS *Fire Falcon* xxiii. 272 His only means of steering was his wrist compass. **1972** *Times* 3 Nov. 33/3 It is a world first, it enables the memorable 'wrist radio' label of the Dick Tracy strip cartoons to become reality. **1984** *Listener* 17 May 36/3 You have the Snoop-Mobile, a wrist-radio, a list of suspects and information about each of them. **1984** *Tampa* (Florida) *Tribune* 5 Apr. 6B/4 Cellular mobile radio telephone service..could be the forerunner of Dick Tracy-like wrist telephones. **1972** D. BLOODWORTH *Any Number can Play* x. 81 I'm going to grow up into a millionaire cowboy with a two-way wrist-television and a formula car.

c. *wrist-play* (earlier example), *-stroke* (earlier example).

1851 J. PYCROFT *Cricket Field* vii. 141 All that is required is, straight play and a free wrist... Without wrist play there can be no good style of batting. **1888** R. H. LYTTELTON in Steel & Lyttelton *Cricket* ii. 61 The cut..requires a very strong use of the wrist, and, like all wrist strokes, charms the spectator by accomplishing great results at the expense of apparently little effort.

d. wrist-length *a.*, (*a*) (of a glove) reaching as far as the wrist; (*b*) (see quot. 1957); **wrist-slap** *slang*, a mild rebuke; so **wrist-slapping; wrist-spin** *Cricket*, spin imparted to a ball by the wrist; cf. *finger-spin* s.v. *FINGER *sb.* 15; so **wrist-spinner, wrist-spinning** *vbl. sb.*; **wrist-wrestling**, a contest of strength between two people, each trying to force the arm of the other person backwards (strictly by interlocking thumbs instead of gripping hands); arm-wrestling; so **wrist-wrestler.**

1935 E. FARJEON *Nursery in Nineties* IV. iii. 172 Long evening gloves and wrist-length, kid and suède gloves! **1957** M. B. PICKEN *Fashion Dict.* 382/2 *Wrist length*, length of coat or other garment, taken with arms hanging at sides, which reaches to wrist. **1963** *Guardian* 1 Feb. 9/7 Jackets are either straight and short to the hips or straight to wrist-length. **1977** M. EDELMAN *Political Lang.* viii. 148 Antitrust laws similarly sanction mergers and pricing agreements, with occasional token wrist slaps to keep the symbolism pure. **1979** *Time* 13 Aug. 36/3 Critical as the investigators may have been of the utility, the NRC itself got a wrist slap from Congress. **1958** *Times* 24 May 4/2 This unusual example of mass wrist-slapping has been going on for a week. **1979** N. SLATER *Falcon* viii. 141 There was no sherry decanter in evidence, no coffee... This was turning out to be a right old wrist-slapping session. **1960** E. W. SWANTON *West Indies Revisited* iii. 49 He is reputedly unhappy against wrist-spin. **1977** *New Society* 3 Feb. 246/2 Raffles was a leg-break bowler: can wrist-spin ever be *really* kosher? **1957** T. BAILEY *Cricket Bk.* vi. 66/1 Bruce Dooland..clearly showed what destruction a top-class wrist-spinner can achieve in Championship cricket. **1977** *Listener* 5 May 588/1 Garfield Sobers—finger-spinner, wrist-spinner, seam-bowler. **1963** T. E. BAILEY *Improve your Cricket* i. 31 Slow bowlers [from overseas] are more frequently of the wrist-spinning variety. **1978** *Detroit Free Press* 16 Apr. 1A/1 My uncle Gerald is a pretty good wrist wrestler. **1973** *N.Y. Times* 29 July x. 4/5 Wrist wrestling, also known as arm wrestling, has its real roots in Petaluma, Calif., where the world championship matches have been televised on ABC's Wide World of Sports for the past four years. **1978** *Maclean's Mag.* 12 June 62 It seems perfectly natural for a wristwrestling championship to be held in Timmins.

wristband. Add: **4.** In sport, a strip of material worn round the wrist to absorb perspiration.

1969 *New Yorker* 14 June 68/3 Ashe wipes his forehead with his wristband. **1984** *Oxford Times* 29 Feb. 3/7 (Advt.), Headband and wristband pack—£1.79.

wristy, *a.* Delete *Cricket* and add earlier and later examples.

1867 *Australasian* 9 Mar. 300/2 Fowler, pretty wristy style, but not a very safe one. **1936** WODEHOUSE *Laughing Gas* xxii. 242, I remember..wondering how the dickens a female of her slight build and apparently fragile physique could possibly get that wristy follow-through into her shots. **1955** *Times* 18 July 12/3 With the deftest turn to leg and wristy punches through the covers he seemed set for an imposing score. **1959** *Times* 26 June 4/2 Krishnan's forte lay in his lovely wristy stop volleys. **1977** *World of Cricket Monthly* June 41/2 There was no prodding or pushing but a free swing on wristy cut. **1980** R HILL *Spy's Wife* xix. 148 He downed his pale spirit in one quick wristy movement.

Hence **wri·stily** *adv.*

1963 A. ROSS *Australia 63* iii. 82 Barrington cut wristily to beat third man. **1972** P. BRENT *Godmen of India* ii. 33 Women polish the earthen floors, bending straight-legged as they work wristily away with a flat stone.

writable, *a.* Add: Also **writeable**. **1.** (Later examples.)

1913 G. B. SHAW *Let.* 26 Mar. (1952) 104, I have written everything that is writeable: The rest must be viva voce. **1926** B. KARLGREN *Philol. & Anc. China* vii. 159 If the literary language is based on the modern colloquial language, it should..also be writable phonetically. **1970** *IEEE Trans. Computers* XIX. 710/2 The control memory of LX-1 is read-only with respect to the microprogram, but is externally writeable. **1983** *Sci. Amer.* Mar. 43/2 Endowing a computer with a writable control store is a way of removing the hardware barrier from user microprogramming.

write, *v.* Add: **I. 1. d.** Freq. in phr. *to be* (or *have*) *written all over* a person.

a **1899** [in Dict.]. **1914** 'I. HAY' *Knight on Wheels* (ed. 2) xxix. 292 It must be written all over me if you can spot it... Yes, you are right... I'm in love. **1967** G. F. FIENNES *I tried to run Railway* iii. 28 He had horse written all over him. **1979** J. GARDNER *Nostradamus Traitor* vi. 20 One was with her... Had DDR written all over him.

3. d. Also in analogous *fig.* phrases, as *writ double, small*, etc.

1951 E. BARKER *Princ. Social & Political Theory* I. 39 Corporativism may be defined as syndicalism writ double. **1959** *Times* 25 Feb. 11/2 This year's Defence White Paper..is last year's writ quietly. **1961** *Observer* 23 Apr. 5/2 In a curious way he's [*sc.* Sir Isaac Hayward's] an amalgam, writ small, of Attlee, Morrison and Bevin. **1967** *Listener* 8 June 762/1 J. P. Donleavy's *The Saddest Summer of Samuel S.* is just *The Ginger Man* writ smaller and smaller.

h. *Computers.* To enter (an item of data) *in, into, on,* or *to* a storage medium (esp. a disc or tape) or a location in store; to enter data in or on (a storage medium). Also *absol.* Cf. *to read in* s.v. *READ *v.* 6 f.

1946 GOLDSTINE & VON NEUMANN in J. von Neumann *Coll. Wks.* (1963) V. 28 In 'writing' a word into the memory, it is similarly not only the time effectively consumed in 'writing' which matters, but also the time needed to 'find' the specified location in the memory. *Ibid.*, A number that is to be written, i.e. stored, has to be placed at a definite, possibly inconvenient place in the memory. **1948** *Math. Tables & Other Aids to Computation* III. 123 The machines will be able to read from, or write on, the tapes. **1953** B. V. BOWDEN *Faster than Thought* iv. 95 He proposed to make it impossible to write into a store unless it contained zero. **1966** *McGraw-Hill Encycl. Sci. & Technol.* IV. 188/1 The store instruction selects an address through the selection circuit for writing the contents of the accumulator in the memory location specified. **1970** [see *READ *v.* 5 h]. **1973** C. W. GEAR *Introd. Computer Sci.* iv. 161 A typical large computer system has many readers and printers... Usually several different jobs are being read and several different outputs are being written at the same time. **1980** *Sci. Amer.* Aug. 114/1 The head that writes the data can also be used to read it. **1980** S. HOCKEY *Guide Computer Applications in Humanities* ii. 28 Information can only be written to the tape when this ring is in place.

i. Of a recording device: to produce (a graphical record).

1949 [see *MAREOGRAM]. **1975** *Nature* 6 Feb. 423/1 Our predicted signals do not resemble those of typical creep events as written by creepmeters.

j. To sit or take (a written examination). Chiefly *S. Afr.*

1958 *Cape Argus* 7 Nov. 3/3 Several women attended the course but Miss — was the only one to write the course examinations. **1971** *Sunday Express* (Johannesburg) 28 Mar. (Home Jrnl.) 14/2 My daughter is writing Matric this year. **1974** *Advocate-News* (Barbados) 19 Feb. 1/1 Students from Government primary schools will now write the Common Entrance Examination at their respective schools.

7. a. Also, to insert (provisions, etc.) *into* a law, agreement, etc.

1962 *Listener* 25 Jan. 155/1 All sorts of safeguards have been written into the agreements. **1962** *Rep. Comm. Broadcasting 1960* 138 in *Parl. Papers 1961-2* (Cmnd. 1753) IX. 259 A suitable form of words to this effect should be written into the new Charter. **1967** *N.Y. Herald Tribune* (International ed.) 11-12 Feb. 3 The 25th Amendment to the Constitution, spelling out procedure for the vice-president to serve as acting president when the president is disabled, was written into law to-day.

12*. = UNDERWRITE *v.*[1] 2 b.

1882 'F. ANSTEY' *Vice Versâ* xvi. 298 They talked of 'risks', of someone who had only been 'writing' a year and was doing seven thousand a week,..and of the uselessness of 'writing five hundred on everything'. **1931** *Times* 14 Mar. 12/6 Not all insurance companies have felt justified in writing the risks. **1967** *Listener* 6 July 14/3 The company was still writing insurance in eleven American states. **1976** *Daily Tel.* 1 Nov. 16/2 Settlement of any claims will cost up to 50 p.c. more than had been expected when the risk was written.

13. write down. f. To write (a literary work) in a style adapted to the level of readers of supposedly inferior intelligence or taste. Cf. sense 21 c below.

1876 C. M. YONGE *Womankind* xxviii. 243 Books.. which do not dwarf the mind as a series of books written *down* are apt to do.

14. write in. b. To send (suggestions, etc.) in written form to an organization. Cf. sense 22 c below.

1928 *Publishers' Weekly* 14 July 183 The customers.. were not slow about writing in their suggestions. *a* **1961** J. BRITTON in WEBSTER, Teachers are encouraged to write in their requests.

c. To insert (the name of an unlisted person) on a ballot-paper or the like, as the candidate of one's choice. *U.S.*

1932 *Sun* (Baltimore) 23 Aug. 2/2 He knew nothing of the circulation of cards in the Middle West urging voters to write in Smith's name on the Presidential ballot. **1944** *Greeley* (Colorado) *Daily Tribune* 16 Sept. 2/2, I greatly appreciate the good will expressed and effort expended by the friends who wrote in my name as candidate for County Judge on the Republican primary ballot. **1957** *Ann. Reg. 1956* 174 Democratic voters 'wrote in' their preference for Mr. Stevenson over Senator Kefauver in the proportions of 8 to 5. **1968** *New Yorker* 9 Mar. 32 You know who I wrote in? You, Earl.

15. a. write off. Now freq. *fig.*, to dismiss from consideration as insignificant or irrelevant.

1957 P. LAFITTE *Person in Psychol.* 44 The psychologist..can write off the difficulty as not falling within the scope of scientific method. **1963** L. MACNEICE *Var Parable* (1965) i. 21 A suspension of antipathy towards its author's attitude will give weight to what otherwise might be written off as whimsical. **1973** *Times* 20 Oct. 18/6 He is part of me and I of him. I find that painful. Perhaps he does too. But we cannot write each other off. **1984** A. SMITH *Mind* v. xv. 297 To cover all possibilities so that the seemingly dead are not written off medically and therefore legally, before their time. **1985** *Times* 11 Jan. 12/6 All this is part of an exercise..to help girls be more assertive and self-confident about their educational potential: to stop writing themselves off as mere future wives and mothers.

c. *slang* (orig. *Air Force*). To damage beyond repair, wreck (an aeroplane, motor vehicle, etc.).

[**1922** *Flight* 27 July 423/1 In another way, it may be stated that, should the work of the Committee lead to a reduction by one of the aeroplanes written off per year as a result of crashes, [etc.].] **1931** *Ibid.* 23 Jan. 80/1 The D.H.37..got down without much damage. The D.H.9.C..was less fortunate, and was written off in a forced landing. **1942** N. BALCHIN *Darkness falls from Air* ii. 44 They seemed to be dropping a hell of a lot of stuff... I saw next morning that they'd written off a pub in Notting Hill. **1973** C. BONINGTON *Next Horizon* xi. 166 She had crashed the car twice, writing it off completely on the second occasion. **1982** *Daily Tel.* 27 Oct. 3/6 He.. wrecked his lorry and two cars; pulled out in front of a van and wrote that off too.

16. b. write out. (Earlier example.)

1817 *Blackw. Mag.* L. 519/2 We have heard fears expressed, that Miss Edgeworth might have written herself out.

c. To eliminate or contrive the temporary absence of (a character, etc., in a long-running radio or television serial), with the story-line written so as to account for it.

1967 *Listener* 13 Apr. 503/2 That [*sc.* the *Forsyte*] *Saga* is now more than half way through (Saturdays, BBC-2)... Some of the old characters have been written out. **1969** *Photoplay* Jan. 64/2 Being 'written out' of 'Peyton Place' is no disgrace. It has happened to other fine players. **1971** O. NORTON *Corpse-Bird Cries* i. 2 You got them to write you out for a bit. **1982** A. ROAD *Dr. Who: Making of TV Series* 16/1 Eric Saward was asked..in the course of his story..to 'write out' the Doctor's sonic screwdriver. **1984** 'M. INNES' *Carson's Conspiracy* xiv. 149 Appleby took a searching look at her and—as it might be expressed —wrote her out of the story.

18. e. write up. (Earlier example.)

1726 [see sense 13 c in Dict.].

III. 21. c. Esp. as *to write down*, to adapt one's literary style to the level of readers of supposedly inferior intelligence or taste; freq. const. *to*. Cf. sense 13 f above.

1809 [in Dict.]. **1851** *Househ. Words* 11 Jan. 372/2 Mr. Blackbrook and his disciples are hapless materialists, verse-makers without a sense of the beautiful. They are patronised by those to whom they write down. **1861** [in Dict.]. **1903** A. BENNETT *Truth about Author* xii. 150, I had entered into a compact with myself that I would never 'write down' to the public in a long fiction. **1921** *Sci. Amer.* Nov. 20/1 The Editor both 'writes down' and 'writes up'... He may translate the Einstein theories into the nontechnical phrases of everyday life. **1944** L. MACNEICE *Christopher Columbus* 9 The inference that to hold the attention..a writer has got to 'write down'. (By writing down I mean pandering—writing by standards which the writer considers low.) **1960** *Guardian* 25 Feb. 6/4 English writers seem to write down to their readers and American writers write as if addressing their equals.

22. b. (*b*) (Further examples.)

The use is more widespread than is indicated in Dict.

1864 NEWMAN *Apologia* vi. 346 When friends wrote me on the subject, I either did not deny or I confessed it. **1892** G. & W. GROSSMITH *Diary of Nobody* iii. 41, I wrote Merton to that effect. **1900** [see PHONE *sb.*[2] and *v.*]. **1905** HAVELOCK ELLIS *Stud. Psychol. Sex* IV. 239 She wrote me saying that she could not see me any more. **1922** C. MACKENZIE *Altar Steps* xxiii. 263, I will write you again when I have seen Father Burrowes. **1924**—— *Old Men of Sea* xi. 175, I shall write Mr. Hibben about that little joke. **1928** D. L. SAYERS *Ld. Peter views Body* iv. 74 He wrote me yesterday and said he'd accidentally left a bag in the cloakroom. **1953** WOODHOUSE *Performing Flea* 69 She is going to find out about quarantine and then write me. **1955** J. P. DONLEAVY *Ginger Man* xi. 104, I haven't. You can't blame me. I'm sorry I wrote your father. I'm sorry for it. **1968** *Globe & Mail* (Toronto) 17 Feb. B3 (Advt.), For free literature describing the..accommodation..write [*address given*]. **1973** *Black Panther* 17 Nov 10/2 It is circulating an impeachment petition nationwide while encouraging all citizens to write their congressmen. **1974** I. MURDOCH *Sacred & Profane Love Machine* 35, I wrote you all about California—quite long letters—about the animals and so on. **1977** I. SHAW *Beggarman, Thief* I. i. 2 He lives in Chicago now and writes me often.

c. write in (earlier *Theatr.* example). Also in gen. use, to send a written comment, request, etc., to an organization. Cf. sense 14 b above.

1849 *Theatrical Programme & Entr'Acte* 23 July 59/2 The time that elapsed between his last application to Drury-lane and his appearance was many months, for he 'wrote in', as it is termed from Exeter about the early part of the summer of 1813, acted first in London, January 26th 1814. **1931** *Publishers' Weekly* 5 Dec. 2471/2 The 'Brooklyn Eagle', however, complains bitterly about distribution: 'About seven hundred readers have written in—ever since that squib of ours appeared..asking where they can put their hands on one.' **1949** N. MARSH *Swing, Brother, Swing* ix. 209 It's a mystery, that paper... The types that write in are amazing. **1957** M. MCCARTHY in *New Yorker* 23 Mar. 76/2, I wrote in for a Vogue pattern to make a tennis dress. **1972** *Listener* 28 Dec. 904/3 If anyone else doesn't know... write in and I'll explain. **1977** *Broadcast* 13 June 10/1 The chap who writes in about a programme.

d. *to write home about*: see *HOME *adv.* 7 d.

V. 27. *Computers.* The infin. used *attrib.* and in *Comb.* with the sense 'writing': **write-permit ring** (pə̄·mit), a ring which has to be inserted in the hub of a tape reel before the tape can be written to or erased; **write-protect** *v. trans.*, to protect (a disc) from accidental writing or erasure, as by removing the cover from a notch in its envelope; also as *sb. attrib.*, designating such a notch, etc.

1951 *Proc. Inst. Electr. Engineers* XCVIII. II. 15/2 A number can be..written in via the 'write' terminal. **1958** *Communications Assoc. Computing Machinery* Feb. 30 In each track, and separated by ·005" from the associated read head, is the 'write head'. **1961** L. W. HEIN *Electronic Data Processing for Business* v. 77 The reflective spot activates the switch only if the tape unit is in write status, that is, information is being written on the tape. **1964** F. L. WESTWATER *Electronic Computers* iv. 78 In the early applications valves were used to supply the relatively large read and write currents. **1965**, etc. [see *READ *v.* 22]. **1970** A. CHANDOR *Dict. Computers* 402 Write permit ring. **1980** C. S. FRENCH *Computer Sci.* xii. 62 Each record is written onto tape in response to a 'write instruction'. **1980** S. HOCKEY *Guide Computer Applications in Humanities* ii. 27 One way of ensuring that this does not happen is to use..a write permit ring, a plastic ring which can be inserted in the back of a tape reel. **1981** *Your Computer* May–June 100/3 *Write protect*, to remove the cover from the notch in a floppy disk so that it cannot be written on. **1983** *Austral. Personal Computer* Aug.

104/2 The only other hole in the disk envelope of importance to the user is the write protect notch... This notch must be covered up by an opaque material to write protect the disk.

writeable, var. WRITABLE *a.* in Dict. and Suppl.

wri·te-back. [f. the vbl. phr. *to write back.*] The process of restoring to profit a provision for bad or doubtful debts previously made against profits and no longer required.

1979 *Financial Times* 24 Jan. 21/5 In future the clearers..will only make provision for the taxes actually expected to become payable in the forseeable future. This will result in the write-back into shareholders' funds of substantial amounts. **1980** *Times* 5 Aug. 17/7 Only then will it emerge whether there are any writebacks to profits arising from the results of the first six months of this year. **1983** *Times* 14 Mar. 14/6 Large write-backs of provisions made in earlier years and no longer needed kept the total [of provisions for bad and doubtful debts] to only £42m in 1981.

wri·te-down. [f. the vbl. phr. *to write down*: see WRITE *v.* 13 e.] A reduction in the estimated or book value of assets.

1932 *Daily Express* 28 Jan. 10/7 This has involved a write-down of securities. **1955** *Times* 10 May 19/2 Consequent write-downs which, with the higher prices now ruling for footwear, are necessarily more severe than in the past. **1972** *Accountant* 23 Mar. 383/2 A large part of AEI's profit shortfall was attributable to stock and work-in-progress write-downs. **1978** S. BRILL *Teamsters* vi. 253 Executive Director Shannon, while only conceding 'possible write-downs', said it would take $10,000,000 just to appraise all the properties involved in the loans. **1979** *N.Y. Times* 13 Sept. D1/2 The Polaroid Corporation.. would take a $68 million write-down in the third quarter.

wri·te-in. [f. the vbl. phr. *to write in*: see *WRITE *v.* 14 c, 22 c. For sense 2 (first part of def.), cf. also *-IN^3.] **1.** The name of an unlisted candidate inserted by a voter on a ballot-paper, etc., as the candidate of his choice; a vote cast for such a candidate, or the act of voting in this way. Freq. *attrib.* orig. and chiefly *U.S.*

1932 *Sun* (Baltimore) 23 Aug. 2/2 (*heading*) Smith's office denies all knowledge of write-in cards being circulated. **1933** *Ibid.* 4 May 2/2 In that election McKee, although not even a candidate, received a 'write-in' vote of nearly a quarter of a million. **1937** *Ibid.* 18 Sept. 10/3 The really significant item in the returns from New York..is the extraordinary number of 'write-ins' for Mayor La Guardia on Democratic ballots. **1950** *Chicago Tribune* 2 Apr. 40/1 Such an attempted write-in for any candidate might result in many spoiled ballots. **1959** *Listener* 10 Dec. 1022/1 Stevenson got a tremendous write-in vote in one famous primary. **1964** MRS. L. B. JOHNSON *White House Diary* 10 Mar. (1970) 84 There was a creditable number of write-in votes for Attorney General Kennedy for Vice President. **1971** *Daily Colonist* (Victoria, B.C.) 2 Nov. 1/8 Another man who was out of town when filing closed says he'll gladly be a write-in candidate for councilman. **1982** *Daily Tel.* 13 Aug. 2/1 Three other spaces will be left for 'write-ins'.

2. A protest in the form of mass letters of complaint; also, an invitation from a radio broadcast to its listeners to write in and express their views. Cf. *PHONE-IN.

1972 *Listener* 15 June 780/3 I'm proposing a mass write-in to request reassessment of most of the rates. **1981** MARSH & CHAMBERS *Abortion Politics* i. 27 Both organizations lobbied in Parliament and both organized meetings and write-in campaigns in the constituencies. **1981** *Church Times* 7 Aug. 16/5 In 1978, when the BBC's *Sunday* programme ran a write-in on the subject of a Graham mission, 15,000 listeners replied. **1984** *Times* 10 Nov. 1/4 There has been a 'strong response' to a direct-mail campaign asking pitmen to complete a write-in slip.

wri·te-off. [f. the vbl. phr. *to write off*: see WRITE *v.* 15 a in Dict. and Suppl., *WRITE *v.* 15 c.] **1.** (In Dict. s.v. WRITE *sb.*^{2} 1 a.)

2. (In Dict. s.v. WRITE *sb.*^{2} 1 b).) Substitute for def.: The cancellation from an account of a bad debt, worthless asset, etc.; an asset so treated; an amount cancelled or lost. (Later examples.)

1957 *Times Lit. Suppl.* 20 Dec. 766/5 It is the point made earlier about the need for resources wherewith to make and replace the automation machines, the need for more rapid write-offs of those machines once installed, and the parallel need to 'pay' the machines more than normal machines have hitherto been 'paid'. **1970** K. PLATT *Pushbutton Butterfly* vii. 72, I understand you are behind a movement called World Peace... A foundation.. Good tax write-off. **1971** *Daily Tel.* 26 Apr. 15/4 Above all, can share-holders..be given an analysis of write-offs and a pre-tax comparison for the two halves? **1978** S. SHELDON *Bloodline* xxi. 243 The write-offs in our experimental laboratory. **1982** S. BELLOW *Dean's December* iv. 96 'Have you ever gotten a penny out of it?' 'I got tax write-offs.' **1984** *Times* 23 May 20/8 In competitor countries the comparison varies between one sort of asset and another but, in general, our write-off periods will be comparable with those overseas.

3. a. An aeroplane, motor vehicle, etc., so badly damaged as to be not worth repair; a wreck; an act of irreparably damaging. orig. *Air Force.*

1918 J. M. GRIDER *War Birds* (1927) 89 He wasn't hurt but the Spad [*sc.* an aeroplane] was a write-off. **1927** E. W. SPRINGS *Nocturne Militaire* 250 Both machines were complete write-offs and the only things they salvaged were the magnetos. **1944** [see *OVERSHOOT *sb.*]. **1953** J. TRENCH *Docken Dead* xiii. 199 'What have you done to my car?' 'I'm afraid it's rather a write-off, sir, as far as immediate use goes, anyway.' **1963** N. MARSH *Dead Water* (1964) ix. 249 The hotel launch was still jammed... A complete write-off, it was thought. **1971** *E. Afr. Standard* (Nairobi) 10 Apr. 8/3 The car I tried was well run in and had in fact been rebuilt from a write-off condition. **1977** *Offshore Engineer* June 13/1 The Ekofisk incident has served to sharpen the risk potential of something more serious—like a major explosion, causing a platform write-off, and pollution seepage.

b. Something or someone dismissed as worthless or ineffectual; a failure.

1960 *Guardian* 26 Sept. 7/5 On English televison this [film] would have been a write-off. **1966** *Listener* 17 Feb. 257/3, I find the new record of Rossini's *Stabat Mater*..an almost complete write-off, because this New York performance ..is..vulgarly and insensitively sung **1974** J. COOPER *Women & Super Women* 20 In fact she's [*sc.* the pregnant woman's] a write-off from the sex appeal point of view after the fourth month. **1982** M. RUSSELL *All Part of Service* ii. 15 If it involves such an effort, I think it might well prove to be a write-off from the start. **1984** A. BROOKNER *Hotel du Lac* v. 65 The day would be a write-off.

writer. Add: **3. e.** *writer's block* [*BLOCK *sb.* 19 e], a periodic lack of inspiration afflicting creative writers; *writer's writer*: a writer whose appeal is primarily to his fellow writers (cf. *poet's poet* s.v. *POET 1 c).

1950 E. BERGLER *Writer & Psychoanal.* vi. 113 Writer's block sets in the moment the inner conscience rejects the alibi and substitute alibi. **1966** G. BAXT *Queer Kind of Death* xi. 150 Seth has had a *serious* writer's block for almost two *years* now. **1975** M. BRADBURY *History Man* x. 169 This book..has decidedly not gone well. I've had what they call writer's block. The words won't come. **1983** *Listener* 13 Jan. 12/3 Graham Greene relies heavily on the unconscious to get round 'writer's block' as he revealed in an interview with Nigel Lewis.

1941 'G. ORWELL' in *Listener* 12 June 841/1 Hopkins is what people call a writer's writer. He..appeals to people who are professionally interested in points of technique. **1951** *Sunday Times* 15 Apr. 3/2 She [*sc.* Ivy Compton-Burnett] is in the first place 'a writers' writer', because she is fascinated by words and phrases as such. **1980** *Times Lit. Suppl.* 12 Sept. 992/1 Nigel Williams is a writer's writer.

f. *writer-in-residence*: a writer given a residential post in a university, etc., in order to share his professional insights. Cf. *poet-in-residence* s.v. *POET 1 e; *RESIDENCE *sb.*^{1} 2 b.

1957 J. D. SALINGER *Zooey* in *New Yorker* 4 May 33/3 The second-eldest child, Buddy, was what is known in campus-catalog parlance as 'writer-in-residence' at a girls' junior college in upper New York State. **1972** [see *RESIDENCE 2 b]. **1980** *Times Lit. Suppl.* 2 May 496/3 The initiative to hold a poetry festival to celebrate..his [*sc.* Basil Bunting's] birthday came from Tom Pickard, writer-in-residence for this year at the University of Warwick.

writerly (rəi·təɹli), *a.* [f. WRITER + -LY^1, after *painterly*.] Appropriate to, characteristic or worthy of a professional writer or literary man; consciously literary.

1957 *Times Lit. Suppl.* 16 Aug. p. xxxvii/2 Serious Canadian writers at present are firmly resolved to concentrate upon the writerly virtues. **1958** *Spectator* 24 Jan. 114/1 A clever and writerly book. **1977** M. COHEN *Sensible Words* i. 25 Dryden..sees his writerly obligations in new terms. **1982** *Listener* 23/30 Dec. 56/3 James Saunders dissecting writerly old age and the onset of what appears to be terminal cynicism.

wri·te-up. (In Dict. s.v. WRITE *sb.*^{2} 2.) For Orig. (and chiefly) *U.S.* read orig. *U.S.* and add: Now more loosely, any journalistic account or review, whether favourable or not. (Earlier and later examples.)

1885 *Weekly New Mexican Rev.* 19 Feb. 4/1, I have prepared quite an extensive 'write-up' of the resources of this country. **1910** *Chambers's Jrnl.* July 431/1 The 'write-up' and the interviews are prominent features. **1919** WODEHOUSE *Damsel in Distress* ii. 28 My missus says she ain't seen a livelier show for a long time... *The Morning Leader* gave it a fine write-up. **1933** P. GODFREY *Back-Stage* viii. 102 In so far as a play is sensitively conceived..the newspaper write-ups of its story may be..extremely misleading. **1948** *Penguin Music Mag.* Oct. 29 He (or rather she) studies music with an eye sooner or later to engagement, a photograph in the 'press', and a 'write-up', as they call all criticism appearing in print. **1951** *Sport* 30 Mar.-5 Apr. 15/1 The critics.. dismissed him in pre-fight write-ups as 'another Phil Scott'. **1965** *New Statesman* 14 May 753/2 The *Stern* reporter..gave [Prince] Philip one of the worst write-ups of his career. **1973** P. EVANS *Bodyguard Man* xviii. 117 He..never give me a good write-up unless I've played really well. **1985** *Contact* (Pre-School Playgroups Assoc.) Feb. 14/2 They prepared a paper summarising their findings... This was circulated to the press, who gave a good write-up.

writhen, *ppl. a.* Add: **1. c.** *spec.* Of antique glass or silver: having spirally twisted ornamentation.

1919 M. PERCIVAL *Glass Collector* viii. 115 The..writhen glasses of funnel shapes are survivors of the old Venetian tradition. **1935** *Burlington Mag.* Oct. 150/1 Light vertical flutings, matching the bowl and wrythen in delivery. **1960** *Times* 9 Feb. 20/7 A Henry VIII spoon with writhen finial. **1970** *Canad. Antiques Collector* Oct. 17 The jugs and bowls are decorated with writhen ornament. **1981** *Times* 31 Oct. 8/6 An Edward IV wrythen-knop spoon made in London about 1463.

Hence **wry·thening** *vbl. sb.* (see quot. 1960.)

1960 H. HAYWARD *Antique Coll.* 313/2 *Wrythening*, diagonally twisted or swirled ribbing or fluting on the bowl or stem of a glass vessel. **1967** S. CROMPTON *Eng. Glass* II. 209 (*caption*) Jug in bottle-green glass with white wrythening.

writhing, *vbl. sb.* Add: **1.** Also *spec.*, in old glass: cf. *WRITHEN *ppl. a.*

1926 G. R. FRANCIS *Old Eng. Drinking Glasses* p. xxxi, Wrythen, external decoration of the bowl by twisting or wrything while still hot. **1929** W. A. THORPE *Hist. Eng. & Irish Glass* v. 166 The wrything was done by twisting the paraison while it was being blown.

writing, *vbl. sb.* Add: **I. 1. d.** *Computers.* The process of causing an item of data to be entered into a store or recorded in or on a storage medium.

1946 [see *WRITE *v.* 3 h]. **1970** O. DOPPING *Computers & Data Processing* xv. 244 Most writing errors on tape, like most reading errors, are caused by small particles of dust between tape and magnetic head, and in most cases the dust particle is removed..if the writing is repeated. **1973** C. W. GEAR *Introd. Computer Sci.* iv. 164 A computer input/output controller..sequences the reading and writing of characters.

3. d. (Later examples with *down*: cf. *WRITE *v.* 21 c.) Also with *up*.

1951 E. E. EVANS-PRITCHARD *Social Anthropol.* v. 88 In this writing-up side of his work the social anthropologist faces a serious difficulty. **1960** *Guardian* 24 June 10/7 Simplification without 'writing down' can serve a good purpose. **1972** *Listener* 9 Nov. 644 The slick writing-down that many professional children's writers indulge in.

II. 6. Phr. *the writing on the wall* (with allusion to *Daniel* v. 5 and 25–28): warning signs of impending disaster, misfortune, etc.

? **1720** SWIFT *Poet. Wks.* (1736) 93 A baited Banker thus desponds, From his own Hand foresees his Fall; They have his Soul who have his Bonds; 'Tis like the Writing on the Wall. [**1837**: in Dict.]. **1884** [in Dict.]. **1906** (*title*) The writing on the wall. **1949** E. COXHEAD *Wind in West* viii. 211 Just try to see the thing with..your famous detachment, and you'll soon recognise the writing on the wall. You've had your fling. **1965** *Listener* 2 Dec. 925/3 The 'eighties and 'nineties were the Golden Age [of music hall]; and in 1905 the writing was on the wall... Musical comedy, the cinema, television all hastened the decline. **1978** *Lancashire Life* Mar. 50/1, I was a fool not to see the writing on the wall when textile machinery manufacturers were rushing all over the world erecting spinning and weaving machinery.

7. b. Also *spec.* = HAGIOGRAPHA *sb. pl.*

1909 [Dict., in note s.v. PROPHET *sb.* 3]. **1941** R. H. PFEIFFER *Introd. to O.T.* (ed. 5) iv. 61 The third division of the Hebrew Bible, following the Law and the Prophets, is simply called the 'Writings' (Hebrew, *Ketûbîm*) or 'Hagiographa' (sacred writings), because it consists of a miscellany of independent books. **1976** *Church Times* 30 Jan. 6/1 He begins with Ecclesiastes and some of the other books from the Writings—namely, Proverbs, Job and the Psalms.

III. 12. a. *writing-chair* (later examples), *-speed*, *-system.*

1906 P. MACQUOID *Hist. Eng. Furnit.* III. iv. 139 (*caption*) Mahogany writing-chair. **1946** H. P. MAYNARD in W. S. Knickerbocker *20th-Cent. Eng.* 188 One of the most important skills is that of writing-speed. **1953** C. F. HOCKETT in Saporta & Bastian *Psycholinguistics* (1961) 58/1 In devising a writing-system one can..eliminate a symbol needed earlier. **1979** *Country Life* 14 June 1910/3 Corner chair appears to be the usual description nowadays: they used to be known as writing chairs. **1980** *English World-Wide* I. 1. 20 Almost all Native American writing systems developed..for bilingual education purposes utilize writing systems similar to English.

b. *writing-brush, implement* (earlier example).

1854 DICKENS *Hard Times* II. i. 134 Mrs. Sparsit was conscious that by coming in the evening-tide among the desks and writing implements, she shed a feminine.. grace. **1921** H. E. PALMER *Princ. Language-Study* vii. 85 Suppose we wish to make Chinese characters with a native writing-brush. **1978** *China Now* Mar./Apr. 34/3 The following suggested items can be obtained from shops which cater for local Chinese communities: wok (a deep frying pan), abacus, Chinese writing brush.

f. *writing clerk* (earlier example).

1772 J. WEDGWOOD *Let.* 28 Sept. (1965) 136 What were all the rest of the Writing Clerks doing not to observe this.

13. writing bed, a board or level surface for writing on; **writing block,** (*a*) [*BLOCK *sb.* 10 c] a pad of writing-paper; (*b*) [*BLOCK *sb.* 19 e] = *writer's block* s.v. *WRITER 3; **writing-case** (earlier example); **writing-pad,** (*a*) a blotter serving as a surface for writing on, sometimes (quot. 1895) furnished with writing materials, etc.; (*b*) a pad (PAD *sb.*^{3} 4) of note-paper; **writing slider** (see quot. 1969); **writing speed,** (*a*) *Electronics*, the maximum speed at which the electron beam can scan the screen of a cathode-ray tube and its path still be recorded by the excitation of phosphors or on photographic film; (*b*) the effective speed of videotape past a head when the rotation of the head is taken into account.

1911 *Daily Colonist* (Victoria, B.C.) 14 Apr. 3/5 (Advt.), Writing Desks. Just the thing for the home, nicely finished in Imperial Golden Oak, large writing bed with enclosed pigeon holes for papers. **1971** *New Yorker* 8 May 3 Open, it's a sewing table. Closed, it's a writing bed..a fine mahogany Sheraton. **1913** 'S. ROHMER' *Mystery of Dr Fu-Manchu* xxix. 294 For this dreary vigil I had come prepared with a bunch of rough notes, a writing-block, and a fountain pen. **1950** E. BERGLER *Writer & Psychoanal.* p. ix, They came with only one purpose in mind—to be cured of their 'writing block' (a euphemism for sterility of productivity). **1977** *N.Y. Rev. Bks.* 15 Sept. 36/3 This connection would also help to explain Darwin's long delay in publishing his theory (certainly he had no 'writing block'). **1983** T. ALLBEURY *Pay Any Price* xvii. 179 As Randall sat down the consultant took out a pen and reached for a writing block. **1813** M. EDGEWORTH *Let.* 19 Apr. (1971) 25 Mrs. Sneyd and Emma have given me a most convenient red morocco writing case. **1865** Writing-pad [in Dict. s.v. PAD *sb.*[3] 4]. **1895** *Army & Navy Co-op Soc. Price List* 598 The 'York' Knee Writing pad. Contains Safety Ink, Scissors, Paper Knife,..pockets filled with Note Paper and Envelopes [etc.]. **1906** E. JOHNSTON *Writing & Illuminating* ii. 50 Under the writing-paper there should be a '*writing-pad*', consisting of one or two sheets of blotting-paper. **1917** *Harrods General Catal.* 297/2 Harrods Writing Pads. 100 Sheets. No. 1. Large 8vo., Thick Cream Wove, Plain, 8 × 5. 0/6. **1972** 'W. HAGGARD' *Protectors* i. 3 Scobell had risen behind his desk. There was a writing-pad on it, a pen—nothing more. **1803** T. SHERATON *Cabinet Dict.* 261 The top drawer [of a lobby chest] is usually divided into two; and sometimes there is a writing slider which draws out under the top. **1969** J. GLOAG *Short Dict. Furnit.* (rev. ed.) 731 *Writing slider*, a sliding shelf, made to draw out beneath the top of a chest of drawers. **1933** R. A. W. WATT et al. *Applic. Cathode Ray Oscillograph* II. 37 This statement should not..be read as indicating the limiting 'writing speed' of the oscillograph used. **1954** LEWIS & WELLS *Millimicrosecond Pulse Techniques* vi. 196 A small spot size is required in order that the deflection sensitivity [of the cathode ray tube] may be high, but if the size is reduced too much there will not be sufficient brightness to give the necessary writing speed. **1981** I. HICKMAN *Oscilloscopes* vii. 95 Writing speed is defined as the maximum speed at which a spot, passing once across the tube face, can be photographed under specified conditions. **1983** E. TRUNDLE *Beginner's Guide Videocassette Recorders* i. 3 This was simply the idea of moving the record or replay heads rapidly over the surface of a slowly-moving tape to achieve the necessary high 'writing' speed. **1984** *What Video?* Aug. 24/1 The soundtrack was being recorded at a writing speed of 580 cm per second—that's over 15 times the speed of professional studio recordings.

writing-box. Add: Also, a small portable writing-desk. Cf. WRITING-DESK 2.

1960 H. HAYWARD *Antique Coll.* 312/2 *Writing-box stands*: the post-Restoration writing-box might be placed on a stand instead of a table. This had gate-legs and the fall-down flap of the box opened on to them for writing. **1971** *Country Life* 1 July 22/1 Portable table-desks or writing-boxes were recorded in the 15th century.

writing-desk. 1. (Earlier *attrib.* example.)

1807 JANE AUSTEN *Let.* 8 Feb. (1952) 178 She is now talking away..& examining the Treasures of my Writing-desk drawer.

writing tablet. Also, a pad (PAD *sb.*[3] 4) of paper for making notes, etc.; = *TABLET *sb.* 1 e.

1895 *Army & Navy Co-op. Soc. Price List* 619 Writing Tablets. 'The Remember.' Bound in long-grained, polished French Morocco. The Refills are made to slip in and out of case. **1917** *Harrods General Catal.* 296/2 Writing tablets. For Scribbling Memoranda and for School Purposes.

written, *ppl. a.* Add: **1. c.** Expressed in due literary form.

1909 J. R. WARE *Passing Eng.* 183/2 *Not enough written* (Authors', 1870), not sufficiently corrected for style. **1922** F. M. FORD *Let.* 14 Aug. (1965) 141 *Felicity Chimney* is a much more ambitious matter. The only thing that is wrong with it is that it is too written. **1963** *Times Lit. Suppl.* 1 Mar. 154/1 The writing is slipshod and frequently repetitive; in fact, as Henry James would say, it is not 'written' at all.

2. b. Also with *on*.

1948 A. N. KEITH *Three came Home* vii. 124 They were constantly looking for my papers, written-on or otherwise. **1955** E. BOWEN *World of Love* iv. 77 The written-on blue envelope.

5. b. (Earlier and later examples with *up*.) Also with *off*.

1890 G. B. SHAW in *Star* 7 Mar. 2/3 The imagination of the public has undoubtedly been strongly seized by the spectacle of the much-written-up Tosca at the height of its prosperity. **1961** *Sunday Express* 12 Feb. 9/2 He accuses them of..selling 'written off' car wrecks. **1964** *Times Rev. Industry & Technol.* Feb. 9/1 The old British Lion Corporation..was..wound up in 1954 with a written-off loss of £2,969,000. **1972** *Listener* 6 July 3/2 *Catch 44*..is becoming one of the most written-up television projects in America.

c. *written out*: *spec.* of a writer, that has exhausted his creative capacity. Cf. WRITE *v.* 16 b.

a **1911** D. G. PHILLIPS *Susan Lenox* (1917) II. xii. 355 He's had several failures... They say he's written out. **1959** C. WILLIAMS *Man in Motion* ii. 21 Suzy Patton, the has-been. The written-out writer. **1978** A. POWELL *Messengers of Day* vii. 108 After a lifetime of work a novelist can possibly be 'written out'.

wrong, *a.* and *adv.* Add: **A.** *adj.* **II. 4. c.** *Criminals' slang.* Untrustworthy, unreliable; not sympathetic to or co-operative with criminals. Cf. *RIGHT *a.* 8 e.

1908 J. M. SULLIVAN *Criminal Slang* 27 *Wrong*, man too familiar with police; not to be trusted. **1928** E. BOOTH in *Amer. Mercury* May 81/2 Aw, don't rap [i.e. speak indiscreetly] to that guy; he's wrong. **1953** W. BURROUGHS *Junkie* (1972) vi. 58 By and large, the reason a man can't score is because he is known to be 'wrong'. **1955** D. W. MAURER *Whiz Mob* ix. 130 He [*sc.* a pick-pocket] tries to avoid those cities or those districts which are known to be *wrong*, or where the police will not have any part of protecting him. *Ibid.* 140 He was what thieves call a *wrong copper*; that is, he did not take the *fix*.

5. d. Of a painting: having an erroneous attribution.

1969 C. IRVING *Fake!* (1970) xiv. 173 It's an ugly thing ..when you have to tell a client he's bought a fake. Of all things in this business..the thing I dislike most is being called in to tell if a painting is right or wrong... Fernand..brazenly offered Juviler a genuine Roualt in exchange for the 'wrong' Dufy. **1979** *Daily Tel.* 28 Feb. 10/2 There are huge numbers of 'wrong' paintings and other works on the market, not strictly fakes, although they often become fakes when resold with the intention to deceive. 'Forty per cent. of the pictures we see are wrong,' said Mr Peter Nahum, the Victorian paintings expert at Sotheby's Belgravia. 'They are wrongly attributed, have a false signature or are genuine contemporary copies.' **1983** *Sunday Times* 10 July 2/3 They invited Ronald Alley, deputy director of the Tate to inspect the pictures. He pronounced them 'wrong'—in art world parlance, fakes.

7. b. *to catch* (a person) *on the wrong foot*, *to get off*, etc., *on the wrong foot*: see *FOOT *sb.* 29.

f. Mus. *wrong note*: a note such as one would not expect in a given key, a discordant note. Freq. *attrib.*

1934 C. LAMBERT *Music Ho!* II. 127 The spicing up of a simple harmonic basis by the addition of what are popularly—and rightly—known as 'wrong notes', such as we find in Auric. **1946** C. MASON in A. L. Bacharach *Brit. Music* x. 139 The 'wrong-note lyricism' of Prokofiev's Third Piano Concerto is as vulgar as the street tunes it distorts. **1958** *Listener* 16 Oct. 623/3 The fierce new musical idioms that had been developed by those whom he [*sc.* Vaughan Williams] called 'wrong-note' composers. **1979** *Oxf. Jun. Compan. Mus.* (ed. 2) 269/2 His [*sc.* Poulenc's] style was neo-classical, full of unexpected twists and delightful 'wrong-note' harmonies.

10. a. *spec.* Of the side (of a highway) reserved for oncoming traffic (in Great Britain the right-hand side, in most other countries the left). Also *joc.* with reference to roads in countries having the opposite system to one's own.

1838 [in Dict.]. **1914** M. BEERBOHM in *Eng. Rev.* Dec. 19 Our car..*was*, for an instant, full on the wrong side of the road. **1933** A. G. MACDONNELL *England, their England* xv. 264 A motor-bicycle..had been taking the natural advantage of its speed..to pass the limousine at fifty-five miles an hour on the wrong side at a blind corner. **1965** L. SANDS *Something to Hide* ii. 31 'We..usually winter abroad.' 'Very nice too! If you can get used to driving on the wrong side.' **1972** *Guardian* 27 Nov. 12/7, 750,000 British drivers took their cars abroad last year... Many.. accidents..[were] possibly caused by confusion over driving on the 'wrong' side of the road.

B. *adv.* **4. b.** *to get* (someone) *wrong*: to misunderstand a person's meaning or intentions, to misinterpret someone. *slang* (orig. *U.S.*).

1927 DUNNING & ABBOTT *Broadway* (1928) xix. 196 'Ever been accused of murder?'..'Don't get me wrong—that stuff ain't in my line.' **1934** T. WILDER *Heaven's my Destination* ii. 39 Don't get her wrong. **1942** WODEHOUSE *Money in Bank* (1946) xii. 91 We got Soapy all wrong, Chimp. He's explained everything. **1966** *Listener* 20 Oct. 561/1 Old L.B.J. is riddled with anxiety over the thought that we shall go to our graves having got him all wrong. **1968** *Ibid.* 5 Sept. 308/2 Stuart Hood's review of Harold Nicolson's last volume of *Diaries*..ends sympathetically, but begins with a devastating attack on my father's 'snobbishness'... I think, not merely as his son and editor, that they have got him wrong, and are a little uncertain what snobbishness really means. **1974** N. FREELING *Dressing of Diamond* 200 Don't get me wrong; there's no offence meant.

6. c. wrong-reading *a.*, such as can only be read after being first reversed by a mirror.

1955, 1967 [see *right-reading* s.v. *RIGHT *adv.* 16 b].

wrong-foot, *v. trans.* (Stress variable.) [f. WRONG *a.* + FOOT *sb.*] **1.** In tennis, football, etc.: (by deceptive play) to cause (an opponent) to have his balance on the wrong foot.

1928 [implied at the vbl. sb. below]. **1959** *Times* 7 Sept. 15/5 Viney and Hasty caught the defence wrong-footed. **1960** E. S. & W. J. HIGHAM *High Speed Rugby* xi. 136 You could pick up the ball as though to go one side, and then, having picked up the ball, swing to the other side... It will wrong-foot the attackers, thereby giving you more time for your kick. **1960** *Times* 29 Nov. 17/4 Truman found himself being wrong-footed by masked drop-shots [in squash rackets]. **1967** J. POTTER *Foul Play* (1968) ii. 28 The younger Fitch was holding forth about his patent method of wrong-footing full backs. **1976** DEXTER & MAKINS *Testkill* 21 Abbott, playing back instinctively, was wrong-footed, bat adrift in his hands.

2. *fig.* To disconcert by an unexpected move; to catch unprepared.

1957 F. HOYLE *Black Cloud* iv. 79 'Let me tell you.. that the Government has made enquiries and we are not at all satisfied with the accuracy of your report.' Kingsley was wrong-footed. **1963** 'W. HAGGARD' *High Wire* xii. 130 The tall man's technique was precisely calculated to put him at a disadvantage... Somehow they could always wrong-foot you. **1971** A. HUNTER *Gently at Gallop* xii. 128 They sensed he was close, and they were trying to wrong-foot him. **1983** *Listener* 6 Jan. 5/1 What happens in Washington, Moscow and Geneva will leave British political leaders moving quickly in order not to be wrong-footed. **1984** *Daily Tel.* 5 July 1/2 A walk-out would wrong-foot the union in its endeavour to appear ready for negotiations at all times.

Hence **wrong-footing** *vbl. sb.* and *ppl. a.*

1928 *Daily Tel.* 7 Aug. 12/3 His ground strokes had not the same speed and polish as Austin's, nor could he steer all his volleys into the same wrong-footing area. **1971** LAVER & COLLINS *Educ. of Tennis Player* xvi. 216 Wrong-footing is hitting to the place your opponent has just vacated. **1980** *Sunday Times* 17 Apr. 42/5 They emerge as wry, reflective, deliberately wrong-footing to outsiders.

wrongo (rǫ·ŋo, rǫ·ŋgo). *slang* (chiefly *U.S.*). Also **wronggo.** [f. WRONG *a.* + *-O[2].] A bad, dishonest, or untrustworthy person; a 'wrong 'un'. Also, a counterfeit coin.

1937 'J. CURTIS' *You're in Racket Too* xxvi. 264 'Sure it ain't duff?' 'Never brought you nothing that was a wrongo yet, did I?' **1938** J. H. O'HARA *Hope of Heaven* x. 139 If I ever saw a wronggo, that Henderson is it. **1953** T. RUNYON *In for Life* v. 87 Tailoring skill was never called on more than in the case of wrongos. A well-known and disliked phony was likely to get a specially made suit not designed to please. **1968** L. W. ROBINSON *Assassin* vii. 78 Phyllis Carr was a wrongo from the beginning. **1985** 'D. RAYMOND' *Devil's Home* xxxiv. 163 I've had my eye on both of you..and you look like a couple of wrongos to me.

wrongousness. For †*Obs. rare* read '*Obs.* exc. as *nonce-wd.* (in form *wrongeousness*, after *righteousness*)' and add later example.

1923 D. H. LAWRENCE *Kangaroo* xvi. 333 The heroic effort to carry out the old righteousness becomes at last sheer wrongeousness.

wrong-slot (stress variable), *v.* [WRONG *adv.* + SLOT *v.*[2]] In rally driving: to take the wrong road.

1961 *Motoring News* 23 Nov. 10/3 This was a special stage and..Walter had, in effect, only wrong-slotted. **1963** P. DRACKETT *Motor Rallying* iii. 36 We wrong-slotted just before the Gavia and dropped three. **1968** [see *ROLL *v.*[2] 18 a].

Hence **wrong-slotting** *vbl. sb.*

1963 P. DRACKETT *Motor Rallying* iii. 45 Amazing the number of competitors who lose marks because they fail to take into account the extra miles they accrued after wrong-slotting.

wrong 'un (rǫ·ŋ'n). *slang.* Also occas. in standard form **wrong one.** [f. WRONG *a.* + UN, 'UN[2].] **1.** *Horseracing.* (In Dict. s.v. WRONG *a.* 6 b, c.) Also *fig.*

1889, 1895 [see WRONG *a.* 6 b, c]. **1935** H. SPRING *Rachel Rosing* xxv. 301 Hansford had never been known to tip a wrong 'un.

2. A bad, dishonest, or untrustworthy person, a rogue or crook; one who has gone wrong (see WRONG *adv.* 2 b).

1892 I. ZANGWILL *Childr. Ghetto* I. xi. 243 'What! aren't you *froom*?' she said... 'No, I'm a regular wrong 'un,' he replied. 'As for phylacteries, I almost forget how to lay them.' **1896** [in Dict. s.v. WRONG *a.* 4 a]. **1902** *Daily Tel.* 11 Feb. 10/7 A welsher can be had up for fraud, and anyone who is known as a wrong one is excluded from the racecourse. **1908** A. BENNETT *Old Wives' Tale* III. ii. 295 She was a tremendous—er—wrong 'un here in the forties. Made a lot of money. **1920** D. H. LAWRENCE *Lost Girl* vi. 107 The policeman was now convinced the man was a wrong-'un. **1925** E. WALLACE *King by Night* xiii. 63, I don't suppose there's a 'wrong one' in London that you don't know. **1951** L. P. HARTLEY *My Fellow Devils* 194 She could not..expect him to confess in so many words that he was a wrong 'un. **1978** J. B. HILTON *Some run Crooked* ii. 15 It seemed quite a hobby with her —Teds, and drop-outs and wrong 'uns.

3. *Cricket.* **a.** A ball that calls for defensive play on the part of the batsman. **b.** *spec.* = *GOOGLY *sb.*

1897 K. S. RANJITSINHJI *Jubilee Bk. Cricket* iii. 118 Stockwell steadies himself after this, and will not pick another 'wrong 'un'. **1911** E. W. BALLANTINE in *Even. News* 18 Dec. 1/3, I see Hordern got Woolley with a 'wrong 'un'. For the benefit of those who may not grasp what a 'wrong 'un' is, it may here be stated that the 'wrong 'un' is the ball which breaks the opposite way to that indicated by the bowler's action. **1931** *Daily Tel.* 31 July 17/2 Weir deserved better of fate than to be bowled by Peebles' wrong 'un in the last over of the day. **1956** N. CARDUS *Close of Play* 142 These devices were of no use against the mysterious and seemingly illogical spin of the 'wrong 'un'. **1977** *World of Cricket Monthly* June 42/2 Neil showed who was the boss by repeatedly stepping out and driving Gupte's wrong 'uns to the fence.

4. A counterfeit coin.

1899 C. ROOK *Hooligan Nights* iv. 58 Billy the Snide produced a wrong 'un, and bade young Alf plant it at a big house near the Walk.

wrongways (rǫ·ŋwēⁱz), *adv. nonce-wd.* [f. WRONG *sb.*² + -WAYS.] In the direction of wrong-doing.

1922 JOYCE *Ulysses* 389 She beguiled him wrongways from the true path by her flatteries.

wrong-wise, *adv.* (Later example.)

1903 A. H. LEWIS *Boss* i. 6, I found such stimulus [*sc.* beatings with hickory] to go much against the grain and to grievously rub wrong-wise the fur of my fancy.

wrought, *ppl. a.* **II. 9.** (Later example.)

1962 AUDEN *Dyer's Hand* (1963) 508 Whereupon we are shown Antony talking to his friends in a wrought-up state of self-dramatization and self-pity.

wrung, *ppl. a.* Add: **1.** Also with *out.*

1976 *Times* 26 Jan. 12/4 Feeling like 60 wrung-out dishrags we stumbled out. **1979** P. WALLAGE *Restoration Post-War Cars* ii. 26/2 Wiping it off with a wrung-out cloth.

3. c. *wrung out*: completely exhausted.

1962 A. LURIE *Love & Friendship* iv. 68 Say, you do look kinda peaked... Not real bad, just kinda wrung out. **1975** *New Yorker* 29 Dec. 15/2 Although she caromed around her office there at enormous speed, she claimed to be 'wrung out'.

wry, *a.* and *adv.* Add: **C.** *wry-angled, -formed.*

1906 HARDY *Dynasts* II. v. vi. 781 What lewdness lip those wry-formed phantoms there? **1937** Wry-angled [see *mountain-roofed* a. s.v. *MOUNTAIN 7 e].

wrying, *vbl. sb.*² **3.** (Later example.)

1879 G. M. HOPKINS *Let.* 9 Apr. (1935) 78 It seems to me to hit the mark it aims at without any wrying.

Wu (wu). [Chinese *wú.*] Used *attrib.* of a group of Chinese dialects spoken in Shanghai, the south of Jiangsu province, and most parts of Zhejiang province, China. Also *absol.*

1908 M. KENNELLY tr. *Richard's Comprehensive Geogr. Chinese Empire* v. 348 The Ngeu..or Wu Dialects, comprising: 1—The Wênchow dialect. 2—The Ningpo dialect. 3—The Sungkiang or Shanghai dialect. **1943** *China Handbk.* i. 30 The Wu group is spoken south of the Yangtze in Kiangsu... It is characterized by the preservation of the ancient voiced stops as aspirated voiced consonants. **1948** R. A. D. FORREST *Chinese Lang.* xi. 224 The Wu language has in modern times a greater than average hostility to final consonants... Where palatalisation occurs in Wu before a..we regularly find the occlusive beside the fricative. **1964** [see *MIN *a.* and *sb.*⁴]. **1977** 'S. LEYS' *Chinese Shadows* (1978) ii. 95 The gracious Wu dialect used in south Kiansu and north Chekiang. **1978** *Whitaker's Almanack 1979* 838/1 The Chinese language has many dialects, Cantonese, Hakka,.. Wu (Shanghai) and the northern dialect.

‖ **Wufan** (wu·fan). Also **wu-fan.** [Chinese *wŭfăn*, f. *wŭ* five + *făn* anti-, against.] Used *attrib.* to designate an official campaign launched in China in 1952 against bribery, tax evasion, theft of state property, skimping on work and cheating on materials, and theft of state economic information.

1956 *Contemporary China 1955* I. 63 The *wu-fan* movement against the 'five vices' in the private sector: bribing, tax evasion, theft of government property, cheating on government contracts, and stealing economic information from government sources for private speculation. **1966** D. WILSON *Quarter of Mankind* iii. 35 Within a few months the second campaign followed, this time the *wufan* or 'five-antis' movement to root out bribery, tax evasion, theft of state property, theft of state economic secrets and embezzlement in carrying out state contracts. **1966, 1971** [see *SANFAN].

wuff, *v.* (Later examples.)

1928 D. H. LAWRENCE *Lady Chatterley's Lover* xii. 197 The dog wuffed softly, slowly wagging her tail. **1932** E. M. BRENT-DYER *Chalet Girls in Camp* vi. 84 'That dog just worships you, Jo.'.. Rufus 'wuffed' joyfully.

wuffer (wɒ·fəɹ). *rare*⁻¹. [f. WUFF *v.* + -ER¹.] A dog with a loud, deep bark.

1923 D. H. LAWRENCE *Ladybird* 245 The white cool monster was a Siberian steppe-dog. Alexander wondered what the steppes made of such a wuffer.

Wulfilian (wulfi·liăn), *a.* [f. Gothic *Wulfila* Ulfilas (see below) + -IAN.] Of or pertaining to Ulfilas (311–382), missionary, translator of the Bible into Gothic, and inventor of the Gothic alphabet.

1926 G. W. S. FRIEDRICHSEN *Gothic Version Gospels* 144 It is quite clear, however, that this is no Wulfilian text. **1968** *Language* XLIV. 731 Thus there was no confusion between the two graphemes in Wulfilian orthography.

Wulfrunian (wulfru·niăn). [f. the name of *Wulfrun*, the 10th-century lady of the manor from whose name *Wolverhampton* is derived + -IAN.] An inhabitant of Wolverhampton (see also quot. 1959).

1959 J. W. GODSELL *I was no Lady* iii. 50 My English husband had attended the ancient and exclusive Gothic-arched Wolverhampton Grammar School, thereby becoming a Wulfrunian. **1974** *Times* 12 Nov. 15/7 There are 'self-made' Wulfrunians of many centuries on our roll. **1979** *Times* 26 Nov. 4/6 'Are you proud to live in Wolverhampton? Or do you, when asked where you come from, ..try to change the subject?' Those are the searching questions that Wulfrunians are being asked by their borough council.

wump (wɒmp). *slang* (somewhat *rare*). [Origin unknown.] A foolish or feeble person.

1908 [see *motor-bicyclist* s.v. *MOTOR A. *sb.* 6]. **1934** R. NICHOLS *Fisbo* 31 Hail to thee, thou much sniffed at by superior Persons and all wowsers, wumps and knock-knees.

wump, var. *WHUMP *v.*, *WHUMP *sb.* (and *int.*).

wumph (wɒmf). [Echoic; cf. *WHUMP *sb.* (and *int.*).] A sudden deep sound, as of the impact of a soft, heavy object.

1913 *Daily News & Leader* 15 Aug. 5, I was ashamed of the heavy 'wumph' with which I landed on the other side amid the nettles. **1924** *Glasgow Herald* 20 Dec. 4/2 The female [bittern]..sometimes answers back with a subdued but exciting 'wumph'. **1967** *Punch* 3 May 640/1 The whiplash crack from the shock wave of the small fighters we were flying is no guide to the wumph of an airliner weighing up to 300 tons. **1971** 'A. DIMENT' *Think Inc.* viii. 141 A deep wumph as the fuel oil..caught fire.

wun, var. WOON in Dict. and Suppl.

‖ **Wunderkind** (vu·ndəɹkint). Also **wunderkind.** Pl. **Wunderkinder, wunderkinds.** [Ger., lit. = wonder child.] **a.** A highly talented child, a child prodigy, esp. in music.

1891 G. B. SHAW in *World* 23 Dec. 15/2 Every generation produces its infant Raphaels and infant Rosciuses, and *Wunderkinder* who can perform all the childish feats of Mozart. **1913** W. J. LOCKE *Stella Maris* iii. 28 You call her Ariel, or Syrinx, or a Sprite of the Sea, or a Wunderkind whose original trail of glory-cloud has not faded into the light of common day. **1923** D. H. LAWRENCE *Stud. Classic Amer. Lit.* (1924) 102 The absolute duplicity of that blue-eyed *Wunderkind* of a Nathaniel. **1931** *N. & Q.* 3 Jan. 16/1 A great many instances of *Wunderkinder* were brought together by the late Dr. Leonard George Guthrie, in his Fitzpatrick Lectures to the Royal College of Physicians (1907), entitled 'Contributions to the study of Precocity in Children', privately printed, 1921. **1947** A. EINSTEIN *Music in Romantic Era* xv. 213 Chopin was a *wunderkind*, both as virtuoso and composer. **1973** L. HEREN *Growing up Poor in London* iii. 65 Again I suppose that the [school] orchestra was better than most of its kind because of the Jews. Some took private lessons, and were regarded as *Wunderkinder* by their parents. **1984** P. ROSE *Parallel Lives* (1985) 81 His career at the Royal Academy school was impressive; indeed he was something of a *wunderkind* in the art world.

b. A talented or successful young man, a 'whizz-kid'. Also *transf.*

1930 E. CULBERTSON *Contract Bridge Blue Bk.* xvii. 227 He [*sc.* a bridge player] may belong to a proud class of *wunderkinder* who 'never need a book' or who 'have no system'. **1940** H. G. WELLS *Babes in Darkling Wood* I. i. 31 He was in the habit of calling his host and hostess 'The ultimate generation, the last and so far the best'. They were, he said, his '*Wunderkinds*'. **1972** [see *KAPUT *a.*]. **1975** *New Yorker* 25 Aug. 50/3 Zen, the colt by Damascus that horsemen say will be the *Wunderkind* of the season, ran a temperature before the Sanford Stakes and was scratched. **1982** R. LUDLUM *Parsifal Mosaic* xx. 320 He's received a fair amount of media exposure—the thirty-year old *wunderkind*.

Wundtian (vu·ntiăn), *a.* and *sb. Psychol.* [f. the name of the German psychologist Wilhelm *Wundt* (1832–1920), + -IAN.] **A.** *adj.* Of or pertaining to the school of experimental and physiological psychology founded in Leipzig by Wundt or to his ideas or methods. **B.** *sb.* A follower of Wundt, one who adopts his ideas or methods.

1890 W. JAMES *Princ. Psychol.* I. iii. 93 The facts, however, do not seem to me to warrant even this amount of fidelity to the original Wundtian position. **1932,** etc. [see *HERBARTIAN *a.* and *sb.*]. **1945** *Mind* LIV. 215 The later Wundtians, particularly and most ingeniously E. B. Titchener, tried to save sensationism. **1972** H. J. EYSENCK *Encycl. Psychol.* II. 61/1 Külpe..and his students ..used a more molar type of introspection, believing that the Wundtian approach was too atomistic.

wunnerful (wɒ·nəɹful). Also **wonnerful, wunnaful.** Repr. *dial.* or *U.S.* pronunc. of WONDERFUL *a.*, (*sb.*), and *adv.*

1924 H. DE SELINCOURT *Cricket Match* vi. 190 Wonnerful wholesome stuff celery, they say. **1930** M. ALLINGHAM *Mystery Mile* xiii. 122, I be a wunnerful smart old man. **1945** A. KOBER *Parm Me* 16 Certainly sounds like a wunnaful pickcha, Jen. **1977** *Sounds* 9 July 8/1 Mink's main claim for the credibility stakes is that he's been produced by Jack Nitzche, who scores pretty high in the living legend section of this wunnerful business.

wunst: see *ONCE *adv.* A. δ.

wun tun, var. *WON TON.

wurley. Add: Also **whirlie**; in *pl.* **wurlies.**

1934 A. RUSSELL *Tramp Royal in Wild Austral.* x. 78 The camp was made up of a cluster of spinifex-covered wurlies. **1936** I. L. IDRIESS *Cattle King* vi. 51 A hundred warriors were lazing about their wurlies, sleeping the midday peace away. **1954** B. MILES *Stars my Blanket* xi. 76 A huddle of wurlies and a yapping throng of lean kangaroo dogs..told us the blacks were camped. **1959** A. UPFIELD *Bony & Black Virgin* x. 80 Several whirlies of bark and odd sheets of corrugated iron and hessian bags, inhabited by aborigines. **1961** *Times* 19 July 12/6 We found them [*sc.* aborigines]..sitting outside their whirlies.

Wurlitzer (wɒ̄ɹ·litsəɹ). The proprietary name of various musical instruments made by the Rudolf Wurlitzer Company, *spec.* a type of large electric organ, or a player-piano. Freq. *attrib.*

1925 T. DREISER *Amer. Trag.* I. I. xvii. 124 A Victrola and Wurlitzer player-piano furnished the necessary music. **1926** *Official Gaz.* (U.S. Patent Office) 23 Mar. 840/2 *Wurlitzer.* Particular description of goods.—pianos, player pianos, ..organs,..banjos,..bassoons..and parts of such musical instruments. Claims use since Jan. 1, 1857. **1926** *Trade Marks Jrnl.* 12 May 1108 *Wurlitzer*... Musical instruments. The Rudolf Wurlitzer Company.., Cincinnati, State of Ohio, United States of America; manufacturers. **1930** C. BEATON *Diary* Dec. in *Wandering Years* (1961) IX. 200 Religious jazz played through a Wurlitzer. **1956** A. HUXLEY *Adonis & Alphabet* 231 The tail-coated organist at the console of his Wurlitzer. **1975** *Guardian* 20 Jan. 9/6 They play Wurlitzer music not inspiring to skate to. **1980** *Times* 1 Oct. 12/6 The daily organ recital on what must be the world's best known Mighty Wurlitzer.

Würm (vüɹm). *Geol.* The former name of a lake (the Starnberger See) in Bavaria, adopted by A. Penck (in Penck & Brückner *Die Alpen im Eiszeitalter* (1909) I. I. 110) and used *attrib.* to designate the fourth and final Pleistocene glaciation in the Alps; also *absol.* Cf. *RISS.

1910, etc. [see *RISS]. **1968** [see *WEICHSEL]. **1972** *Sci. Amer.* Mar. 60/2 The very numerous remains found in the Dragon's Lair were evidently deposited there during the final Pleistocene ice advance, the 60,000-year Würm glaciation that ended some 12,000 years ago. **1977** G. CLARK *World Prehistory* (ed. 3) xi. 455 Access was easier during the last glaciation, but only noticably so during its colder phases, that is during the Early and Main Würm, to use designations taken from the Swiss Alpine sequence.

Hence **Wü·rmian** *a.* (also *absol.*).

1927 PEAKE & FLEURE *Hunters & Artists* iv. 40 It is.. possible that the Capsian industry had passed from Tunis through Sicily to Italy during, or even before, the Würmian glaciation. **1967** *Oceanogr. & Marine Biol.* V. 453 One may conclude that the cooling of the water during the Würmian was very slight in the Eastern Basin [of the Mediterranean]. *Ibid.*, The shallow-water Würmian beds.

wurra (wɒ·rə), *int. Anglo-Ir.* [Ir. (*a*) *Mhuire* (O) Mary.] An exclamation of grief or despair.

1898 J. D. BRAYSHAW *Slum Silhouettes* 21 Oh! wurra, wurra, that I should live to see him stiff and cowld. **1936** M. MITCHELL *Gone with Wind* x. 206 He groaned. 'Wurra the day!' **1952** E. O'NEILL *Moon for Misbegotten* II. 91 I'm not like you, owning up I'm beaten and crying wurra wurra like a coward.

wurst (wɒ̄ɹst, v-). Also **worsht, wourst.** [a. Ger.] Sausage, esp. of the German type; a German sausage. Also *transf.*

1855 [see *KRAUT 1]. **1868** *Amer. Odd Fellow* VII. 403/1 Sausages, or 'wourst', as they call them, are made in links. **1892** I. ZANGWILL *Childr. Ghetto* I. xvii. 59 Mrs. Hyams fried a piece of *Worsht* for Miriam's supper and put it into the oven to keep hot. **1939** C. ISHERWOOD *Goodbye to Berlin* 221 There were plates of ham and cold cut wurst. **1955** T. H. PEAR *Eng. Social Differences* 181 Liver-sausage and similar 'wursts'. **1966** L. DAVIDSON *Long Way to Shiloh* x. 142 We finished the *wurst* sandwiches. **1967** *New Scientist* 10 Aug. 281/2 The name given to the dam was apparently chosen because of the obliging way in which this huge water-filled wurst.. returns to its original unostentatious shape when deflated. **1977** *Drive* May–June 124/2 In the South, one shop had invented its own delicacy: Satan's Sizzlers, 'the great curry wurst'.

Württemberger (vü·ɹtĕmbɒ̄ɹgəɹ). Also **Würtemberger, -burger, Wur-.** [a. Ger., f. *Württemberg*, the name of a former state in S.W. Germany (now part of the *Land* of Baden-Württemberg) + -ER¹.] A native or inhabitant of Württemberg.

1896 G. A. HENTY *Through Russian Snows* x. 190 The seven battalions of Spaniards, Wurtembergers, and men from the Duchy of Baden. **1926** F. M. FORD *Man could stand Up* II. i. 78 Those blessed Wurtembergers would never that day get out of their trenches. **1934** W. S. CHURCHILL *Marlborough* II. xxiv. 539 The Würtembergers and Westphalians were only now approaching. **1938** C. V. WEDGWOOD *Thirty Years War* viii. 384 Of two thousand Württembergers who joined Horn in 1632 at least half deserted in less than a month. *a* **1974** J. POPE-HENNESSY in *Lonely Business* (1981) III. 267 To meet young Württembergers. **1977** N. FREELING *Gadget* IV. 182 'You're a Wurtemberger aren't you?' 'Badener, from Karlsruhe.' **1978** L. DEIGHTON *SS-GB* xxxviii. 333 We should have polished off all you bloody Württembergers in 1918.

wurtzilite (vɒ̄·ɹtsiləit). *Min.* [f. the name of Henry *Wurtz* (1828–1910), U.S. mineralogist + *-i-* + -LITE.] A black, massive, sectile, asphaltic pyrobitumen produced by the metamorphosis of petroleum.

1889 W. P. BLAKE in *Engin. & Mining Jrnl.* XLVIII. 542/2 In now proposing for it the name *Wurtzilite* I desire to compliment my friend, Dr. Henry Wurtz, of New York who in 1865 described the mineral to which he gave the name grahamite. **1918** [see *pyrobituminous* adj. s.v. *PYRO- 2]. **1965** [see *IMPSONITE]. **1979** J. M. HUNT *Petroleum Geochem. & Geol.* viii. 403 Wurtzilite appears to be a more indurated polymer with an origin similar to elaterite.

‖ **wushu** (wū·ʃū·). Also **wu shu** and with capital initial. [Chinese *wǔshù*, f. *wǔ* military + *shù* technique, art.] The Chinese martial arts.

1973 P. J. SEYBOLT *Revolutionary Educ. in China* xxii. 252 In the gymnasium,..others, wielding swords and spears, were practicing the traditional Chinese *wushu*. **1975** *Times* 27 June 5/5 Some energetic youngsters are practising *wushu* (military art). **1977** O. SCHELL *China* (1978) III. 241 He has just come from *wu shu* practice (martial arts). **1978** CHOW & SPANGLER *Kung Fu* p. xii, Today Wu Shu remains the official term for martial arts in the People's Republic of China, although the emphasis is on its use as a national sport 'to serve the people' in the promotion of health. **1979** *Tel.* (Brisbane) 31 May 2/3 A few lessons in Wushu.

wuss (wɒs). Repr. *colloq.* or *dial.* pronunc. of WORSE *a.* and *sb.*, or *adv.*

1862 A. J. MUNBY *Diary* 22 Mar. in D. Hudson *Munby* (1972) 117 That's wuss than a day's work, that is. **1869** J. GREENWOOD *Seven Curses of London* vi. 91 She'll tell you that, wuss luck, I've got in co. with some bad uns. **1894** [see *STRAIGHT *adv.* 6]. **1896** A. MORRISON *Child of Jago* vi. 61 Nobody's none the wuss for me knowin' about 'em. **1936** M. MITCHELL *Gone with Wind* lix. 994 It been awful! An' it's gwine be wuss. **1945** J. RHYS-WILLIAMS *Stern Daughter* xv. 97 Lucky if it aint no wuss, Sister.

wüstite (vü·stəit). *Chem.* Also **wustite.** [ad. G. *wüstit* (R. Schenck et al. 1927, in *Zeitschr. f. anorg. Chemie* CLXVI. 141), f. the name of F. *Wüst*, German metallurgist: see -ITE[1].] An isometric solid solution of magnetite (Fe_3O_4) in iron oxide (FeO).

1928 *Chem. Abstr.* XXII. 566 The existence of 2 solid solns. is shown: (1) a soln. of small quantities of Fe_3O_4 in FeO for which the name '*Wüstite*' is coined, [etc.]. **1957** *Jrnl. Iron & Steel Inst.* CLXXXVII. 78/1 The gradient of the iron content of these layers was determined, and the wüstite composition at the iron–wüstite and wüstite–magnetite phase boundaries was used to define the wüstite area. **1977** *Nature* 6 Oct. 500/1 There are few reports on the direct reduction of wustite by carbon according to an autocatalytic mechanism. **1980** *Ibid.* 30 Oct. 778/1 The extraterrestrial nature of a specific spherule can be confirmed if it contains wüstite—a metastable iron oxide formed at high temperatures and low oxygen partial pressures. Wüstite slowly decomposes into α-iron and magnetite..and is thus almost unknown in nature.

wuther, *sb.* and *v.* Add: Hence **wu·thering** *vbl. sb. rare.*

1879 G. M. HOPKINS *Poems* (1967) 80 If a wuthering of his palmy snow-pinions scatter a colossal smile Off him, but meaning motion fans fresh our wits with wonder. **1951** J. STRACHEY *Man on Pier* 20 The routine hours that are without inspiration in a day—those spent in buying stamps for letters, in filing receipts, in the dreary wuthering of machineries, in the changings from place to place.

‖ **wu ts'ai** (wū· tsai·). Also **wucai, Wu ts'ai.** [Chinese *wǔcǎi*, f. *wǔ* five + *cǎi* colour.] Polychrome; polychrome decoration in enamels applied to porcelain; porcelain with polychrome decoration esp. of the Ming and Qing dynasties.

1904 E. DILLON *Porcelain* vii. 101 We come again to a pentad of colour—not, however, quite the same as the *wu-tsai* of Wan-li times. **1906** S. W. BUSHELL *Chinese Art* II. viii. 32 The ordinary class of polychrome (*wu ts'ai*) decoration of the Ming period. **1915** R. L. HOBSON *Chinese Pott. & Porc.* II. ii. 8 There are the beautiful barrel-shaped seats, some with openwork ground, the designs filled in with colours (*wu ts'ai*). **1964** M. MEDLEY *Handbk. Chinese Art* 88/1 *Wu-ts'ai*.., a term applied to porcelains of the Ming and Ch'ing Dynasties decorated in overglaze enamel colours, and often with coarsely-handled under-glaze blue. **1971** L. A. BOGER *Dict. World Pott. & Porc.* 115/1 Wu ts'ai, which is practically a Chinese way of saying polychrome, is most commonly applied to a decoration comprising designs painted in enamel colors. **1980** *Catal. Fine Chinese Ceramics* (Sotheby, Hong Kong) 62 A fine pair of wucai (wu ts'ai) square Dishes of shallow flared form with brown-edged rims.

‖ **wu-wei** (wu·wē^i·). Also **Woo-wei, wu wei.** [Chinese *wúwéi*, f. *wú* no, without + *wei* doing, action.] **a.** The Taoist doctrine of letting things follow their own course. **b.** *Hist.* In China, the name of a minor sect.

1859 J. EDKINS *Relig. Condition of Chinese* xiv. 260 One of the most interesting among the minor sects in China is that called the Woo-wei-keaon. It is an off-shoot from Buddhism. The words Woo-wei, mean non-action. These words are, in China, a favourite philosophical phrase, used by all schools of a contemplative or mystic tendency. The Taouists, who spoke of the Eternal Reason which underlies all existences, held that it could be understood, and the perfection of our nature reached only by rest, by stillness physical and mental, by abstaining from external methods of improvement, and by disbelief in their efficacy. This they called Woo-wei, 'to do nothing'. **1917** *Encycl. Sinica* 545/1 Confucius believed in the power of human nature to remain upright *if properly taught*; Lao Tzû believed it would keep straight *if left to itself*. This is his famous doctrine of *Wu-wei*, (Inaction or Non-assertion). *Ibid.* 609/2 *Wu Wei* or Non-Action Society. A secret sect, variously stated as having been founded by disciples of Lao Tzû towards the end of the Chou dynasty, by Lo Huai, the originator of the Lung Hua and Hsien T'ien sects, who lived in the 15th and 16th centuries, and to have been begun three hundred years ago... Its members are described by Edkins as 'a kind of reformed Buddhists'. **1934** A. D. WALEY *Way & its Power* iii. 145 He slips in..*wu-wei*, 'non-activity', *i.e.* rule through *tê* ('virtue', 'power') acquired in trance. **1965** C. & W. CHAI *Humanist Way in Ancient China* 56 To govern by *Wu-wei* (inaction or noninterference), Shun was the one! **1970** H. G. CREEL *What is Taoism?* i. 9 The mere idea of all this toiling for immortality is repugnant to that of *wu wei*, not striving. **1975** C.-Y. CHANG *Tao* lxxiii. 194 *Wu-wei* does not mean that one does not act. It means that one acts but is free from ulterior motives.

wuz (wɒz). Also **wus.** Repr. *colloq.*, *dial.*, or *vulg.* pronunc. of *was*.

1886 F. H. BURNETT *Little Lord Fauntleroy* xi. 222 The rooms wus locked up 'n' empty. **1901** M. FRANKLIN *My Brilliant Career* iii. 16 Some of us wuz always good fer a toon on the concertina. **1945** J. RHYS-WILLIAMS *Stern Daughter* xv. 97 Sister wuz wunnerful good to me back at Wipers in 1917. **1966** *Listener* 15 Sept. 397/2 We were promised a discussion about the programme on BBC-2's *Late Night Line-Up*; we wuz robbed, the discussion hardly mentioned the programme at all. **1973** C. HIMES *Black on Black* 168 Mah belly feels lak mah throat wus cut. **1976** *Observer* 22 Aug. 5 (Advt.), Wor lad wuz in a reet steeut.

Wuzeerá, var. *WAZIR[2].

wuzzy (wɒ·zi), *a.* *colloq.* Confused, fuddled, vague. Cf. WOOZY, MUZZY, *adjs.*

1896 *Dialect Notes* I. 427 *Wuzzy*,..confused. **1921** E. A. J. B. LYTTON *Let.* 10 Mar. in Ld. Lytton *Antony* (1935) iii. 74, I am very nearly mad, I am quite slowly turning wuzzy. **1937** J. B. PRIESTLEY *Two Time Plays* 79, I can't remember... I'm—a bit—wuzzy.

Wyandotte. Substitute for entry.

Wyandot (wəi·ăndǫt). Also † **Wayandott, Wyandot(t)e.** [ad. F. *Ouendat*, ad. Huron *Wendat*.] **1.** (A member of) a North American Indian people belonging to the Huron nation and originally living in Ontario; the language of this people. Also *attrib.* or as *adj.*

1749 J. HAMILTON *Let.* 2 Oct. in *Documents Colonial Hist. New-York* (1855) VI. 531 The Twitchwees & Wayandotts..for two or three years past have dealt largely with our Traders. **1785** T. JEFFERSON *Notes Virginia* xi. 187 Tribes..Wyandots..Near Fort St. Joseph's and Detroit. **1786** [see *HURON]. **1789** [see *SAUK]. **1804** *Maryland Hist. Mag.* IV. 6 The Indian chief, Tarhie, a Wyandote..[was] hunting bears. **1826** J. F. COOPER *Last of Mohicans* III. ii. 46 What will our fathers think the tribes of the Wyandots have become? **1837** [see *SHAWNEE *sb.* 1]. **1913** A. S. PALMER *Samson-Saga* xiv. 167 The Wyandot Indians have a like myth. **1965** *Canad. Jrnl. Linguistics* Spring 105 He [*sc.* Sapir] knew something about Wyandotte. **1979** B. A. LEITCH *Conc. Dict. Indian Tribes N. Amer.* 189 By the 1970s Wyandot were among the leading citizens of Ottawa County, Oklahoma, numbering about 1,000.

2. (Usu. with spelling **Wyandotte.**) One of a breed of medium-sized domestic fowls, of American origin.

1884, etc. [in Dict.].

Wyatt (wəi·ăt). The name of the architect and designer James *Wyatt* (1746–1813), used *attrib.* to designate buildings or architectural features designed by him or characteristic of his Gothic Revival style.

1819 M. EDGEWORTH *Let.* 4 May (1971) 206 A most comfortable sitting room (scarlet cloth and black furniture —Large Wyatt window plate glass—tables most comfortable). **1936** A. DALE *James Wyatt* vi. 32 The Wyatt window, a tripartite aperture similar to the Venetian window. **1962** *House & Garden* Dec. 63/2 Sienna marble columns (..from a Wyatt house in Somerset). **1973** *Country Life* 18 Jan. 152/3 It is unusual for a Philadelphia house... There is a vaguely Wyatt feeling about the whole concept.

Hence **Wyatte·sque, Wy·attish** adjs.

1942 J. LEES-MILNE *Jrnl.* 18 Jan. in *Ancestral Voices* (1975) 10 A terrible house.., with only a vestige of the eighteenth century in the central stairwell, where there is a trace of Wyattesque or Adamesque treatment, a frieze with ram's skulls. **1946** —— *Diary* 23 Nov. (1983) 108, I found the stairwell actually more Wyattish than Adamatic. **1973** *Country Life* 20 Sept. 776/3 Wyattesque decoration.

wye[2]. Add: *spec.* (*a*) *Plumbing.* A short pipe with a branch joining it at an acute angle. (*b*) *Electr. Engin.* = *STAR *sb.*[1] 12 i.

a **1877** KNIGHT *Dict. Mech.* III. 2823 *Wye*... A name applied to a stem or pipe with branches. **1916** C. E. MAGNUSSON *Alternating Currents* ix. 97 If the three circuits be connected as shown..it is called a Star or Wye connection. **1964** R. F. FICCHI *Electr. Interference* x. 200 With a source that is wye-connected, the system neutral is readily available. **1978** K. W. SESSIONS *Homeowner's Handbk. Plumbing & Repair* iv. 145 (*caption*) Some cast-iron soil-pipe 90° wye branches. **1980** SLEMON & STRAUGHEN *Electric Machines* ii. 143 Three similar single-phase transformers may be connected to give 3-phase transformation, and since the primary and secondary windings may be connected either in delta or in wye, there are four possible combinations of connections.

Wykhamite (wi·kăməit). [f. the name William of *Wykeham* (see WYKEHAMIST *sb.* and *a.*] = WYKEHAMIST *sb.*

1828 M. R. MITFORD *Our Village* III. 203 Two or three more of our young Etonians and Wykhamites. **1972** *Daily Tel.* 1 June 21/3 He is a Wykhamite and Balliol man who was originally destined for the Civil Service.

wyn, wynn[2] (win). Now the usual forms of WEN[2].

[**1892** S. A. BROOKE *Hist. Early Eng. Lit.* II. xxiii. 201 W. was sometimes taken to mean *Wyn, joy*, and sometimes *Wen, hope.* **1910** F. TUPPER *Riddles of Exeter Bk.* 234 W always demands the interpretation *Wyn*, a rendering of the rune sustained by the Anglo Saxon alphabet in the Salzburg MS.] **1912** A. J. WYATT *Old Eng. Riddles* p. xxxix, The commoner Anglian runes.. ƿ w wynn (joy). **1955** *Jrnl. Eng. & Gmc. Philol.* LIV. 6 In later Old English *fuþorcs*, *wyn* and *wen* are generally confused, owing to some extent..to the semantic link existing between the two words, although the name of the W-rune was unquestionably *wyn*. **1965** C. BARBER *Flux of Lang.* vii. 129 The runic symbol 'wynn' was used for the Old English *w* sound. **1978** *Norfolk Archaeol.* XXXVII. 56, G offers one or two forms hardly explicable except as corruptions of original spellings with *wynn* for *w*.

wynd. Add: **1. d.** *transf.*

1952 DYLAN THOMAS *Coll. Poems* 170 Small fishes glide Through wynds and shells of drowned Ship towns to pastures of otters.

wysiwyg (wi·ziwig). Also **WYSIWYG.** [Acronym (see quots. 1984).] (See quots.)

1982 *Byte* Apr. 264/2 'What you see is what you get' (or WYSIWYG) refers to the situation in which the display screen portrays an accurate rendition of the printed page. **1982** *Economist* 1 May 8 If he wishes to converse with computer buffs, he will have to cope with neologisms such as 'wysiwyg' (what you see is what you get), pronounced 'whizziwig'. **1984** *Sci. Amer.* Sept. 54/3 Perhaps the most important principle is WYSIWYG ('What you see is what you get'): the image on the screen is always a faithful representation of the user's illusion. *Ibid.* 135/1 The resulting interface between the computer and the user would then fall into the class of interfaces known as WYSIWYG, which stands for 'What you see is what you get'.

X

X. Add: **I. 1. a.** *x-* (rarely *X-*)*height* (Typogr.), the height of a printed lower-case *x*, esp. as representative of the size of the fount to which it belongs.

1945 J. C. Tarr *Printing To-day* 177 *x-height*, the height of lower-case letters (excluding descenders and ascenders), i.e. the height of a lower-case x. **1959** T. Harrod *Librar. Gloss.* (ed. 2), 99 *Descender*,..that part which extends below the 'X' height. **1964** P. A. D. MacCarthy in D. Abercrombie et al. *Daniel Jones* 160 Any attempt to preserve traditional usage by having only x-height letters for vowels. **1978** J. Lewis *Typography* ii. 79 Typefaces with a large x-height are more suitable for an age accustomed to reading sans serif signs... VIP Palatino is another large x-height typeface.

b. *X chair*, a chair in which the underframe resembles the letter X in shape; so *X-frame* (usu. *attrib.*).

1904 P. Macquoid *Hist. Eng. Furnit.* iii. 52 It is a very common error to assign all these 'X' chairs to foreign importation. **1918** [see *Savonarola 2]. **1945** *Burlington Mag.* May 110/2 These X chairs throughout the sixteenth century, when made for the homes of the wealthy, were covered with rich cloths of gold, velvets, and silks. **1955** R. Fastnedge *Eng. Furnit. Styles* i. 33 (*caption*) Arm chair of X-frame construction... Early seventeenth century. **1961** L. G. G. Ramsey *Connoisseur New Guide to Antique Eng. Furnit.* 20 Another form of chair, of different origin from the boxchair, was the X chair... Both chairs are assigned to about the same period—that is the middle of the sixteenth century. **1976** X-frame [see *saddle seat 3 b].

d. Used to mark a location on a map or the like; esp. in phr. *X marks the spot* and varr.

1813 M. Edgeworth *Let.* 16 May (1971) 59 The three crosses X mark the three places where we were let in. **1918** J. M. Barrie *Echoes of War* 5 In the rough sketch drawn for to-morrow's press, 'Street in which the criminal resided'..you will find Mrs. Dowey's home therein marked with a X. **1928** R. Knox *Footsteps at Lock* iv. 36, I wish I could be there, to see you diving in the mud on the spot marked with an X. **1968** B. Norman *Hounds of Sparta* ix. 64 A message from our alcoholic friend. X seems to mark the spot where he lives.

II. 3. a. *axis of x* (example); now always *x-axis*; also *transf.*; *X-cut* adj. (Electronics), of, pertaining to, or designating a quartz crystal cut in a plane normal to its X-axis; *X-plate* (Electronics), each of a pair of electrodes in an oscilloscope that control the horizontal movement of the spot across the screen.

1885 J. Casey *Treat. Analytical Geom.* ii. 22 If the equation of the line contains no *x*, it is parallel to the axis of *x*; and if it contains no *y*, it is parallel to the axis of *y*. **1886** W. B. Smith *Elem. Co-Ordinate Geom.* i. i. 10 *OX*, *OY*, are called Co-ordinate Axes, or axes of *X* and *Y*, or *X*- and *Y*-axes. **1929** *Internat. Critical Tables* (U.S. Nat. Res. Council) VI. 211/1 The *z*-axis coincides with the crystallographic *c*-axis of 3-fold symmetry, the *y*-axis is ⊥ to a face of the hexagonal first order prism, and, in dextro crystals, the + direction of the *x*-axis is outward through one of the faces .of the trigonal pyramid. **1930** W. G. Cady in *Proc. IRE* XVIII. 2139 We consider first the manner of indicating the orientation of the more common 'cuts' [in quartz crystals]... In the first case, we have the cut variously referred to in the literature as 'Curie cut'..or 'normal cut'... However, a still more concise term would be the 'X-cut', denoting a plate the normal to whose face, and hence for which the applied electric field, is parallel to an X-axis. Similarly, the term 'Y-cut' would apply to the second type of quartz plate, which has hitherto been referred to as the '30-deg. cut' or 'parallel cut'. **1933** J. H. Morecroft *Electron Tubes* xii. 337 The velocity of [compression] wave travel is different in the Y axis direction from that along the X axis. *Ibid.* 338 An X-cut plate has a negative temperature coefficient, i.e. the frequency of oscillation decreases as the temperature rises... The Y-cut plates have a positive coefficient. **1934** J. H. Reyner *Television* vii. 71 We then apply a suitable periodic voltage across the X plates which spreads the trace-out at right angles and produces a pattern on the screen. **1945** *Electronic Engin.* XVII. 723 These two equations define the components of the velocity of the spot along the X and Y axes. **1946** *Ibid.* XVIII. 23/1 A D.C. connexion must be made between the output of the time base and the X plates of the tube. **1969** *Funk & Wagnalls Dict. Electronics* 170/1 *X-axis*, in a quartz crystal, a reference axis chosen so as to connect two opposite vertices of its hexagonal cross section; one of the axes showing the greatest electrical activity. **1973** S. K. Stein *Calculus & Analytic Geom.* ii. 26 Far to the right and to the left the graph gets closer and closer to the *x* axis without ever touching it. **1978** D. T. Rees *Cathode Ray Oscilloscope* 9 A voltage applied to the X-plates will deflect the beam sideways. **1982** *IEEE Trans. Industr. Electronics* XXIX. 158/1 The rotated *X*-cut orientation has been found to be optimum from the viewpoint of its frequency versus temperature and pressure characteristics. **1983** V. M. Ristic *Princ. Acoustic Devices* vi. 180 The relationship between the natural axes *a*, *b*, *c* and the crystallographic axes *X*, *Y*, *Z* must be known in order to use the proper constants. These relationships, for each crystal system, have been adopted by convention. Various piezoelectric, elastic, and other constants of a particular crystal specimen are evaluated in terms of *X*, *Y*, *Z* axes.

e. *Genetics.* (Now always as a capital.) [First used in German by H. Henking 1891, in *Zeitschr. f. wissensch. Zool.* LI. 706.] The symbol of the *X chromosome. So **X-linked** (stress variable) *a.*, being or determined by a gene that is carried on the X chromosome.

1902 T. H. Montgomery in *Trans. Amer. Philos. Soc.* XX. 177 One of these three [chromosomes of *Protenor belfragei*], that designated *x* in Figs. 119–123, imposes by its relatively very large volume... We shall call this the 'chromosome *x*'. **1902** *Biol. Bull.* Dec. 29 (*caption*) All the chromosomes including the accessory (x), show indications of a longitudinal split. **1909** E. B. Wilson in *Science* 8 Jan. 57/1 In all the species half the spermatozoa are characterized by the presence of a special nuclear element which I shall call the 'X-element', while the other half fail to receive this element. **1910** [see *heterogametic *a.*]. **1911** *Biol. Bull.* Jan. 118 The case of the aphids and phylloxerans has been the strongest argument for the hypothesis that two *X* chromosomes [in mosquitoes] give a female and..*XY* a male. **1949** Darlington & Mather *Elem. Genetics* ii. 49 The tortoiseshell cat is heterozygous for the X-linked gene, one allelomorph of which gives black, the other yellow, when homozygous. **1968** M. W. Strickberger *Genetics* xii. 216 In some instances, both compound X's and compound Y's may be found together in the same species. An extreme example of compound sex chromosomes occurs in the beetle *Blaps polychresta*, where the male has 12 X's and 6 Y's in addition to 18 autosomes. **1977** N. V. Rothwell *Human Genetics* iv. 83 One important point to note is that a male never passes an X-linked gene to his sons. **1983** *Oxf. Textbk. Med.* I. iv. 16/2 The triple X female with 47 chromosomes shows very little physical abnormality... It is possible that only one X is working in any cell at a given time. **1983** [see *Y chromosome].

f. *x-chaser*, etc.: a naval officer proficient in examinations or good at his work (see also quots. 1946, 1962). *slang.*

1904 'Vanderdecken' *Mod. Officer of Watch* vi. 64 To get on at sea it is not necessary to be an X hunter, a man may be a smart officer without ever having been near enough to an X to drop salt on its tail. **1912** 'Aurora' *Jock Scott, Midshipman* i. 4 He was what we called an *x* catcher; in fact, he passed out of the *Britannia* a midshipman and was wearing his patches the day he left. **1916** 'Taffrail' *Pincher Martin* v. 71 He was an *x*-chaser, in that he had done remarkably well in all his different examinations. **1946** J. Irving *Royal Navalese* 190 *X chaser*, a mathematically minded man; a theoretician. Also, a navigating officer who has qualified..as the navigator of a First Class ship. **1962** A. G. Course *Dict. Naut. Terms* 215 *X chaser*, a meticulous navigator in the Royal Navy.

g. In the analysis of games of Bridge x represents a card between 2 and 9, inclusive.

1920 A. G. L. Owen *Mod. Bridge* ii. 56 A similar position is this:—Z xxx A King xx B J 10 xx YAQ. If A leads his King, Y makes Ace and Queen. **1933** C. Vandyck *Contract Contracted* i. 10 x = any small card... An easy way of remembering the Kx and Qx in different suits is to think of it as the *Grand Marriage*. **1959** Reese & Dormer *Bridge Player's Dict.* 14 East holds..Kxxxx. **1972** *Country Life* 4 May 1119/3 The trump finesse could not gain, even if East held Q xx.

h. *x-question* (Linguistics) (see quots.)

1924 Jespersen *Philos. Gram.* xxii. 303 In the other kind of questions we have an unknown 'quantity'... We may therefore use the well-known symbol x for the unknown and the term *x-question* for a question aiming at finding out what x stands for. **1957** S. Potter *Mod. Linguistics* iii. 71 Tune 1 falls after the turn. It is used in completed statements, in direct commands, and in special or x-questions which cannot be answered by 'yes' or 'no' and which are generally introduced by an interrogative pronoun or adverb. **1964** M. Chapallaz in D. Abercrombie et al. *Daniel Jones* 306 X-questions, that is, questions beginning with a specific interrogative word.

i. *Genetics.* (Now written as lower case.) A symbol representing the lowest number of chromosomes which make up a genome; freq. with preceding number, designating the number of sets of these in a cell, or in each cell of an organism.

1924 *Hereditas* V. 144 Summarizing our results on the chromosome set in *C*[*arex*] *pilulifera*, we may now state that this species has 9 chromosomes (X) of which there are 3 long, 4 medium and 2 short ones. *Ibid.* 161 In *Triticum* Sakamura..and Sax..found one species with 14 chromosomes (2X), four species with 28 and three with 42 chromosomes. **1932** C. D. Darlington *Recent Adv. Cytol.* iii. 61 Since a zygote usually receives two similar sets of chromosomes from its two parental gametes, their number is conventionally referred to as *2n*; where the chromosomes pair regularly at meiosis they therefore form n pairs. Now in a particular individual these *2n* chromosomes may consist of three sets or four sets of chromosomes relative to its own parents or ancestors. In the present work, therefore, the 'basic number' of this ancestral set is distinguished by the sign *x*. Thus in *Triticum vulgaer* $2n = 42$ and $x = 7$, the somatic chromosome number is therefore hexaploid (6*x*). **1979** A. F. Dyer *Investigating Chromosomes* ii. 47/2 *Rosa canina* ($2n = 5x = 35$ = AABCD). **1980** J. Schulz-Schaeffer *Cytogenetics* vii. 122 Very often, ploidy levels are erroneously reported for n-numbers. But the number reserved for ploidy levels is the x-number or basic genome number (x, 2x, 4x, 6x, etc.).

j. *X factor* (Mil. colloq.), the aspects of a serviceman's life that have no civilian equivalent; pay made in recognition of these.

1969 *Second Rep. Pay Armed Forces* (Nat. Board for Prices & Incomes) vi. 21 in *Parl. Papers* (Cmnd. 4079) 517 There are special conditions of employment..common to all servicemen and which..make it more uncertain and on occasions more hazardous than the normal..employment in civilian life... The elements..constitute, what we have termed the X factor. **1979** *Navy News* May 48/3 The Ministry of Defence have proposed a substantial increase in the X factor across the board on the grounds that the elements that make up the justification for it have shifted to the disadvantage of the Services.

5*. Used to represent a kiss, esp. in the subscription to a letter.

1763 G. White *Lett.* (1901) I. vii. 132, I am with many a xxxxxxx and many a Pater noster and Ave Maria, Gil. White. **1894** W. S. Churchill *Let.* 14 Mar. in R. S. Churchill *Winston S. Churchill* I. Compan. i. (1967) vii. 456 Please excuse bad writing as I am in an awful hurry. (Many kisses.) xxx WSC. **1951** S. Plath *Let.* 7 July (1975) i. 72 Some gal by the name of Sylvia Plath sure has something—but who is she anyhow?..x x Sivvy. **1953** Dylan Thomas *Under Milk Wood* (1954) 41 Yours for ever. Then twenty-one X's. **1982** C. Fremlin *Parasite Person* vi. 40 A row of 'X's', hurried kisses, all he had time to scribble.

5.** *X-band*: the range of microwave frequencies around 10,000 megahertz, used in radar transmission.

1946 *Radar: Summary Rep. & Harp Project* (U.S. Nat. Defense Res. Comm., Div. 14) 144/2 *X-band*, refers to wavelengths around 3 cm. **1952** [see *S-band* s.v. *S. 12]. **1976** *Sci. Amer.* June 72/1 Most spacecraft now transmit to the earth a second radio signal at an X-band frequency (8·5 gigahertz).

5*.** *Cinemat.* X is used to denote films classified as suitable for adults only, or to which only those older than a certain age are to be admitted; so *X-rated* adj. (hence *X-rate* vb. trans.), *X-rating* vbl. sb. Also *fig.*

In Britain replaced by *15* and *18* in 1983.

1950 *Rep. Departm. Comm. on Children & Cinema* 64 in *Parl. Papers* (Cmd. 7945) VII. 238 We recommend that a new category of films be established (which might be called 'X') from which children under 16 should be entirely excluded. **1950** *Times* 14 July 8/4 The X certificates..will cover films other than those of a 'horrific' character, which are 'wholly adult in conception and treatment'. **1956** 'M. Innes' *Appleby plays Chicken* i. xvii. 139 'I'm going up.' 'You're doing nothing of the sort. It's X Certificate stuff, my boy, and not for general exhibition. There's a high-up copper who says so.' **1958** *Times* 9 July 6/3 Mr. Davie..has his 'X' certificate pictures..in which his obsessional imagery has taken on an existence, outside the vague allusiveness of the paint, which is too specific for comfort. **1970** *N.Y. Times Index* 1248/2 Panel of 3 Fed judges rules Penna's new law forbidding showing of previews of x-rated movies. **1972** *Daily Colonist* (Victoria, B.C.) 6 Feb. 2/3 There was only one explicit scene—the incest sequence—which caused the film to get an X (no one under 17 admitted). **1973** M. Amis *Rachel Papers* 136 Sebastian had gone into Oxford to see an X film ('any X film' he said) and to moon around looking for girls with his spotty mates. **1974** *Florida FL Reporter* XIII. 35/3 'Community standards' should determine whether X-rated movies should be allowed to be shown or not. **1974** *Newsweek* 20 May 23 His communicators..kept insisting that the transcripts actually clear the President of any crime more grievous than using X-rated language and thinking unsavory thoughts. **1976** *Publishers Weekly* 24 May 54/3 Most readers will surely X-rate the author's dicta; only the far-out minority will accept them. **1981** *TV Picture Life* Mar. 6/1 For it was daytime TV shows, or 'soaps' as they are affectionately called, that first explored the 'X'-rated areas of life. **1983** *Guardian* 15 Oct. 10/7 In America..X-rating is used only for out-and-out porn.

5**.** *X-C* (or *XC*) *skiing* (N. Amer.) with pronunc. (krɒs)), cross-country skiing.

1972 [see *ski-touring* s.v. *ski *sb.* 2 b]. **1976** *National Observer* (U.S.) 13 Mar. 11/1 Alpine and XC skiing. **1977** *N.Y. Rev. Books* 14 Apr. 42/4 (Advt.), Midwest Photographer, 33, likes bike rides, hikes, x-c skiing, concerts, theater,..seeks woman friend.

III. 6. (Later examples of *Xtian*, *-ity*.)

1811 Xtianity [see *inerasable *a.*]. **1845** M. Arnold *Let.* Mar. (1932) 55 When Tait had well observed that strict Calvinism devoted 1000s of mankind to be eternally,—and paused—I, with, I trust the true Xtian Simplicity suggested '—'. **1915** A. Huxley *Let.* Oct. (1969) 79 The ethics are identical with Xtian ethics. **1940** E. Pound *Cantos* lviii. 74 They drove the Xtians out of Japan. **1966** D. Jones *Let.* 8–16 June in R. Hague *Dai Greatcoat* (1980) iv. 223 All chaps should be awfully good ..is..more or less what the present notion of Xtianity boils down to.

7. b. In commercial (esp. *U.S.*) use put for the final *-cks* (or *-cs*) of (esp. monosyllabic) words, as *clox, *pix², *snax, *sox.

x (eks), *v.* Pa. t. **x-ed, x'd.** **1.** (In Dict. s.v. X.) *rare*$^{-1}$.

2. *trans.* To obliterate (a typewritten character) by typing 'x' over it; to cross *out* in this way; = *EX *v.* Also *fig.*

1942 W. STEVENS *Let.* 28 Jan. (1967) 400, I felt that.. you had x-ed me out. *c* **1945** U. TROUBRIDGE *Life & Death Radclyffe Hall* (1961) 71 As she dictated she continued to polish and the typist had always to be prepared to 'X' out at demand any word or sentence. **1958** C. BAKER *Friend in Power* vi. 163 He set the capital key and X'd the sentence through. **1969** J. N. CHANCE *Abel Coincidence* iii. 54 You should x it off your card. **1977** J. AIKEN *Last Movement* ii. 39 She crossed out that line, x-ing it vigorously to ensure its illegibility. **1978** H. KEMELMAN *Thursday the Rabbi walked Out* xxi. 89 You want me to make the correction on my typewriter? I can x it out.

Hence **x-ed** (*out*) *ppl. a.*, **x-·ing** (*out*) *vbl. sb.*

1966 *Punch* 31 Aug. 310/1 There shall be no 'X-ing out' of rival goods with black crosses. **1969** M. LAND *Quicksand* 59 He knew the uneven lines of his portable and the X'd-out words would annoy Dave Winters. **1982** M. McMULLEN *Until Death do us Part* (1983) v. 29 A sheet of manila paper... A good deal of X-ing out to be seen.

Xanadu (zæ·nădū). [Poetic ad. *Xandu*, i.e. Shang-tu, the Mongol city founded by Kublai Khan.] A place suggestive of the Xanadu portrayed in Coleridge's poem *Kubla Khan*, with its dream-like magnificence and luxury.

[**1625** *Purchas his Pilgrimes* III. I. iv. 80 Xandu, which the great Chan Cublay..built; erecting..a maruellous.. palace of marble. **1816** S. T. COLERIDGE *Kubla Khan* 55 In Xanadu did Kubla Khan A stately pleasure-dome decree.] **1948** 'J. TEY' *Franchise Affair* i. 7 To that douce country lawyer..Scotland Yard was as exotic as Xanadu, Hollywood, or parachuting. **1958** M. KENNEDY *Outlaws on Parnassus* xi. 165 Desirable readers..do not expect Xanadu to put them in mind of Yarmouth. **1962** *Holiday* Aug. 70/1 It was only about half an hour's drive to the Xanadu of *le facteur* Cheval. **1969** *Guardian* 12 Nov. 5/7 Bob's double-tiered hideaway..overlooking the fairy-lit battlements of his Xanadu in Mayfair. **1972** K. BONFIGLIOLI *Don't point that Thing at Me* viii. 76 The Ambassador was at some Xanadu-like golf-links far away. **1977** *Time* 25 July 2/1 We have lived in Southern California for twelve years and watched nearly everything encapsulate itself within a plastic bubble; not only giant 'pop Xanadus' like Sea World and Universal Studios, but also miniature golf courses, shopping centers and finally the American home.

Xanga, var. *SHANG.

xanthan (zæ·nþæn). *Chem.* Also **xantham.** [f. XANTH(O- + -AN; *-am* is unexplained.] A powdery polysaccharide composed of glucose, mannose, and glucuronic acid, produced by the bacterium *Xanthomonas campestris* and used in drilling muds and the food industry. Usu. as *xanthan gum.*

1964 *Australasian Jrnl. Pharmacy* XLV. Suppl. No. 19. S80/1 The material is known variously as Polysaccharide B-1459, Xantham Gum, Corn Sugar Gum [etc.]. **1970** *Biotechnol. & Bioengin.* XII. 75 Previous publications from this Laboratory have reported batch fermentations to produce a biopolymer, xanthan, using *Xanthomonas campestris.* **1972** *Materials & Technol.* V. 44 Xanthan gum is used in oil well drilling muds, because of its heat stability and tolerance of salts. **1982** *S. Afr. Food Rev.* IX. 515/1 Since Xanthan gum solutions have a high viscosity at rest..xanthan gum is widely used in food systems as a stabiliser for emulsions.

xanthate. Add: **a.** More widely, a salt or ester of any acid of the form RO·CS·SH, where R is an alkyl or similar radical. (Further examples.)

1895 CROSS & BEVAN *Cellulose* III. 248 The precipitated xanthate may be treated with solutions of suitable salts of the heavy metals, and the cellulose xanthate of the metals prepared. **1945** *Jrnl. Chem. Soc.* 666 Debus.. showed that *O*-ethyl *S*-ethyl xanthate, EtO·CS·SEt, could be readily prepared by the interaction of potassium xanthate and ethyl iodide. **1951** C. R. NOLLER *Chem. Org. Compounds* xvi. 311 The sodium alkyl xanthates are used as collecting agents in the flotation process for the concentration of ores. **1974** *Encycl. Brit. Micropædia* X. 777/1 The most important group of xanthates are the sodium salts produced from cellulose.

xanthation (zænþēⁱ·ʃən). *Chem.* [f. XANTHATE + -TION.] A stage in the viscose process for making rayon, in which alkali-cellulose is treated with carbon disulphide to form cellulose xanthate.

1927 T. WOODHOUSE *Artificial Silk* iv. 30 The larger quantity of Viscose silk is made from wood-pulp... This process is termed Xanthation. **1962** J. T. MARSH *Self-Smoothing Fabrics* iv. 30 When xanthation is complete, the solid is dissolved in dilute caustic soda. **1978** *Nature* 12 Oct. 530/1 Mechanically pulped wood or papers are not generally useful, as the structure resists solution after xanthation.

So **xa·nthate** *v. trans.*, to cause to undergo xanthation; also *absol.*; **xantha·ted** *ppl. a.*, **xantha·ting** *vbl. sb.*

1938 *Thorpe's Dict. Appl. Chem.* (ed. 4) II. 465/2 Surplus carbon disulphide is removed..and the xanthated crumbs are then dispersed by churning with NaOH solution. **1952** *U.S. Patent* 2,592,355 1 In manufacturing viscose-rayon fiber, a low cellulose, high alkali and low viscosity is prepared..by xanthating and dissolving same in usual way. *Ibid.* 4 Without subjecting to aging, it is xanthated in a xanthating apparatus. **1962** J. T. MARSH *Self-Smoothing Fabrics* iv. 30 The crumbs of alkali-cellulose are then xanthated by treatment with carbon disulphide in a rotating churn for about 3 to 4 hr. **1964** V. E. YARSLEY et al. *Cellulosic Plastics* x. 149 The xanthated cellulose. *Ibid.*, The aged alkali-cellulose is charged to the xanthating churns, which rotate slowly. **1978** *Jrnl. Appl. Polymer Sci.* XXII. 897 Starch polyampholytes (xanthated starch amines)..were prepared, characterized, and evaluated as wet- and dry-strength agents in paper handsheets. **1983** *Jrnl. Macromolecular Sci.: Chem.* A. XX. 218 Partially xanthated cellulose.

xanthene (zæ·nþīn). *Chem.* Also **-en.** [f. XANTHO- + -ENE.] A tricyclic crystalline compound, $O(C_6H_4)_2CH_2$, derivatives of which are used as brilliant, often fluorescent, dyes. Usu. *attrib.*

1898 *Jrnl. Chem. Soc.* LXXIV. I. 643 Xanthen gives a *dichloro*-derivative, $C_{13}H_8Cl_2O$. **1902** *Chem. News* 17 Jan. 36/1 The mono-halogenated derivatives of the xanthene series possess basic properties. **1947** L. S. PRATT *Chem. & Physics Org. Pigments* viii. 189 The rhodamines are representative of the basic-type xanthene colors, and the fluoresceins, eosins, phloxins, erythrosins, and rose bengals are representative of the acid type. **1959** [see *EUXANTHIC *a.*]. **1971** R. L. M. ALLEN *Colour Chem.* viii. 120 Xanthene dyes containing salicylic acid or other metallisable structures are manufactured as mordant dyes.

xanthic, *a.* Add: **1. b.** More widely, any acid of the general formula RO·CS·SH or RO·CS·SR'. (Further examples.)

1945 *Jrnl. Chem. Soc.* 666 To interpret results obtained in other aspects of the chemistry of xanthic acid derivatives.., we found it necessary..to systematise current knowledge concerning the isomeric compounds RO·CS·SR', R'O·CS·SR, RS·CO·SR', the first two being esters of xanthic acids and the last an ester of *sym.* dithiocarbonic acid. **1956** KIRK & OTHMER *Encycl. Chem. Technol.* XV. 150 The relatively unimportant xanthic acids are unstable, colorless or yellow oils, and have been known, on occasion, to decompose with explosive violence.

xanthine. Add: **1. b.** Any of several substituted derivatives of xanthine.

1956 I. FINAR *Org. Chem.* II. xvi. 613 Three important methylated xanthines that occur naturally are caffeine, theobromine and theophylline. **1974** M. C. GERALD *Pharmacol.* xv. 280 The xanthines..have proved to be valuable drugs for the treatment of such respiratory diseases as asthma, bronchitis, and emphysema.

2. xanthine oxidase, an enzyme catalysing the oxidation of hypoxanthine to xanthine and of xanthine to uric acid.

1905 *Jrnl. Chem. Soc.* LXXXVIII. II. 271 The presence of oxygen is necessary to obtain in liver extract uric acid from the purine bases it contains, or that are added to it. The uric acid found comes almost exclusively from xanthine, and is due to a ferment, xanthine-oxydase. **1983** *Oxf. Textbk. Med.* I. IX. 79/1 Not all patients with xanthine stones have xanthine oxidase deficiency.

xantho-. Add: **2. xanthochro·mia** *Med.* [Gr. χρῶμα colour], (*a*) (see quot. 1894); = XANTHOCHROIA; (*b*) a yellowish discoloration of the cerebrospinal fluid as a result of haemorrhage in the spinal cord or brain; hence **xanthochroma·tic, -chro·mic** *adjs.*; **xa·ntho-derm** (also **Xa·ntho-**) [Gr. δέρμ-α skin], a person of a yellow-skinned (mongoloid) race; **xa·nthophore** *Zool.* [a. G. *xanthophor* (R. Keller 1895, in *Arch. f. Physiol.* LXI. 148): see -PHORE], a cell (as in an animal's skin) containing a yellow pigment; **xantho·pterin** *Chem.* [a. G. *xanthopterin* (Wieland & Schopf 1925, in *Ber. d. Deut. Chem. Ges.* LVIII. 2179): see *PTERIN], a yellow pterin present in the wings of some butterflies and moths and in the urine of mammals and forming leucopterin upon oxidation; 2-amino-4,6-dihydroxypterine, $H_2NC_6HN_4(OH)_2$.

1922 *Arch. Neurol. & Psychiatry* VIII. 24 Elsberg and Rochfort in a study of ninety-two cases of chronic diseases of the spinal cord found xanthochromatic cerebrospinal fluid in fourteen instances. **1969** EDINGTON & GILLES *Path. in Tropics* ii. 79 [In congenital toxoplasmosis] the protein in the cerebrospinal fluid is increased and may be xanthochromatic. **1894** G. M. GOULD *Dict. Med.* 1622/2 *Xanthochromia*, a persistent condition of yellow skin, resembling but not identical with jaundice. **1905** —— *Dict. of New Med. Terms* 568/1 *Xanthochromia*, Tuffier and Miliau's [*read* Milian's] name (1902) for the yellow hemorrhagic discoloration of the cephalorachidian fluid, diagnostic of hemorrhage of the neuraxis. **1912** *Lancet* 7 Sept. 685/2 On the value of a quantitative albumin estimation of the cerebro-spinal fluid (with special reference to the syndrome of massive coagulation and xanthochromia). **1977** *Ibid.* 24–31 Dec. 1352/1 There were no cells in the C.S.F. and no xanthochromia. **1952** F. A. ELLIOTT et al. *Clin. Neurol.* ix. 184 Xanthochromic fluid bleaches on exposure to daylight. **1979** *Jrnl. Neurosurg.* LI. 352/1 The presence of subarachnoid hemorrhage (SAH) is diagnostically confirmed by the detection of bloody and/or xanthochromic cerebrospinal fluid. **1924**, **1935** Xanthoderm [see *melanoderm* sb. and adj. s.v. *MELANO-]. **1935** [see *leucoderm* s.v. *LEUCO-]. **1977** *Scripta Medica* L. 35 By and large, Melanoderms and Xanthoderms have either black or brown hair and there is not enough variation to be of practical interest. **1903** *Proc. Amer. Acad. Arts & Sci.* XXXIX. 261 The two remaining types of pigment bodies in the chameleon, erythrophores and xanthophores, were not identified in Anolis. **1948** [see *NEUROHUMOUR]. **1965** LEE & KNOWLES *Animal Hormones* x. 127 The hormone MSH [*sc.* melanocyte stimulating hormone] not only acts on the melanophores, but also on the xanthophores and erythrophores. **1974** D. & M. WEBSTER *Compar. Vertebr. Morphol.* viii. 173 Other chromatophores, called xanthophores, contain carotenoid and pteridine pigments and cause much of the yellow-to-red coloration. **1926** *Chem. Abstr.* XX. 902 The residue was rubbed up 4 times with H_2O and centrifuged and the crude dirty yellow pasty pigment (xanthopterin (I)) extd. with 20% HCl and pptd. with NaOAc. **1974** *Encycl. Brit. Macropædia* IV. 922/2 Xanthopterin occurs in human urine.

xanthoma. Add: Pl. **xanthomas, xanthomata.** Also, esp. in mod. use, such a patch or tubercle. Freq. with mod.L. adjs. (Earlier and further examples.)

1869 *Jrnl. Cutaneous Med.* III. 241 (*heading*) On xanthoma, or vitiligoidea. *Ibid.* 317 After entry into hospital, patches of xanthoma developed in both eyelids. **1874** W. TAY tr. *Hebra & Kaposi's Dis. Skin* III. 345 There are two forms of the disease—1st, it occurs in the form of yellow patches—Xanthoma planum..; 2nd, in the form of tubercles—Xanthoma tuberosum. **1896** N. WALKER tr. *Unna's Histopath. Dis. Skin* 945 The xanthoma of the eyelid may gradually develop protuberances, without giving up its own peculiar histological character. **1949** R. L. & R. L. SUTTON *Handbk. Dis. Skin* 385 Tuberous xanthomas are occasionally solitary. **1961** *Lancet* 12 Aug. 341/2 All her plasma-lipids tended to return to normal values..and her xanthomata completely disappeared. **1968** A. ROOK et al. *Textbk. Dermatol.* II. xxxviii. 1229/1 Xanthoma disseminatum is a rare histiocytic proliferative disorder characterized by widespread cutaneous xanthomata..but usually without evidence of systemic disturbance of lipid metabolism. **1974** S. L. ROBBINS *Pathologic Basis Dis.* xxx. 1410/1 These xanthomas may be widespread and occur in varied forms, such as xanthoma tuberosum.

Hence **xanthomato·sis**, a metabolic disorder marked by the accumulation of excess lipid and by the presence of multiple and widespread xanthoma.

1900 DORLAND *Med. Dict.* 764/1 Xanthomatosis. **1923** *Brit. Jrnl. Dermatol.* XXXV. 90 Xanthomatosis is probably a process of infiltration dependent primarily upon hypercholesterolæmia. **1961** [see *hypercholesterolæmic* adj. s.v. *HYPER- IV]. **1983** *Oxf. Textbk. Med.* I. IX. 113/1 The relationship between cerebrotendinous xanthomatosis and spinal cholesterosis..is uncertain.

xanthophyll. Add: **a.** Now recognized as an oxygenated carotenoid identical with LUTEIN. (Further examples.)

1934 *Science* 25 May 488/2 Xanthophyll (lutein) appears to be structurally related to α-carotene and zeaxanthin to β-carotene. **1945** *Biol. Rev.* XX. 115/1 Following a convention which is being more widely adopted the specific pigment which has been termed 'xanthophyll' is here called 'lutein'. **1964** E. J. H. CORNER *Life of Plants* i. 5 The orange-yellow carotin and the yellow xanthophyll..cause the yellow colour of those parts of variegated leaves unable through some deficiency to make chlorophyll.

b. [After R. Kuhn et al. 1931, in *Zeitschr. f. physiol. Chem.* CXCVII. 141.] Any of a group of yellow pigments (as lutein and violaxanthin) that are oxygenated carotenoids.

1931 *Chem. Abstr.* XXV. 3659 The term xanthophyll should be used to designate the entire group of OH-contg. carotenoids with 40 C atoms. The individuals thus far known are: lutein and zeaxanthin.., violaxanthin.., and fucoxanthin. **1952** *Chem. & Engin. News* 7 Jan. 104/2 Two of the rules on carotenoids adopted at the London Conference of 1947 were revised to give the following text:.. The name 'xanthophyll' is a group name..for carotene derivatives of natural origin which are soluble in alcohol and are not saponifiable. **1955** G. M. SMITH *Cryptogamic Bot.* (ed. 2) I. ii. 12 There are several xanthophylls [in the Chlorophyta] not found in other algae, and of these lutein is the most abundant. **1976** *Monitor* (McAllen, Texas) 27 Sept. 4A/2 Brown tannin pigments blend with xanthophylls to produce yellow-gold and gold-brown leaves.

Hence **xanthophy·llic** *a.*, of or containing xanthophyll.

1941 *Biol. Bull.* LXXX. 451 In the herbivores, the echinoids too contained some xanthophyllic pigments without exception. **1982** *Monitor* (McAllen, Texas) 2 Apr. 6-c/2 Miss Arden claims she now has a substance, extracted from a xanthophyllic-carotin mixture, which will drain the last vestige of visibility from succeeding generations of frogs but she feels it would serve no useful purpose.

xanthoxenite (zænþozī·nəit). *Min.* [ad. G. *xanthoxen* (Laubmann & Steinmetz 1920, in *Zeitschr. f. Krist.* LV. 580), f. Gr. ξανθο- XANTHO-, after G. *cacoxen* CACOXENITE: see -ITE[1].] A hydrated basic phosphate of calcium and ferric iron, $Ca_4Fe^{3+}{}_2(PO_4)_4(OH)_2 \cdot 3H_2O$, occurring as yellow translucent triclinic crystals that are soft and have a waxy appearance.

1920 *Jrnl. Chem. Soc.* CXVIII. II. 698 Xanthoxenite, a new species from Rabenstein, occurring as small, wax-yellow, monoclinic crystals,..intimately associated with dufrenite and cacoxenite. **1949** *Amer. Mineralogist* XXXIV. 698 Xanthoxenite occurs abundantly although inconspicuously at the Palermo mine as one of the last formed of the hydrothermal reworked products of triphylite. **1978** *Mineral. Mag.* XLII. 309/1 Xanthoxenite of Laubmann and Steinmetz (1920) is probably stewartite (in part)... The xanthoxenite of Frondel (1949) is proposed as the species type. It is triclinic.

xanthoxin (zænþǫ·ksin). *Biochem.* [f. *VIOLA)XANTH(IN + OX- + -IN[1].] A photo-oxidation product, $C_{15}H_{22}O_3$, of violaxanthin that occurs in certain plant tissues as a growth inhibitor.

1970 TAYLOR & BURDEN in *Nature* 18 July 302/2 We have extracted a neutral growth inhibitor from the seedlings of dwarf bean..and wheat... The name xanthoxin is now proposed for the inhibitor, the activity of which in the *cis,trans* configuration is comparable with the known naturally occurring inhibitor abscisic acid (ABA). **1980** *Physiologia Plantarum* XLIX. 309/1 The inhibitory effect of both ABA and xanthoxin on total lateral root length was mainly due to their suppression of primordia emergence and their strong inhibition of elongation.

Xavante (ʃava·nti). Also **Chavante, Shavante.** [a. Port., of uncertain origin.] **a.** (A member of) any of several groups of semi-nomadic Indians of the interior savanna of central and east-central Brazil, esp. the Akwẽ-Xavante. **b.** The Ge language of the Akwẽ-Xavante, or the language of any group called Xavante. Also *attrib.* as *adj.*

1904 H. VON IHERING *Anthropol. State S. Paulo, Brazil* 10 Of all the Indians of S. Paulo, the Chavantes are the darkest, and the most backward. **1927** K. G. GRUBB *Lowland Indians Amazonia* vii. 121 The Chavante, irreconcilably hostile, occupy the River Manso or das Mortes. **1950** J. B. D'AVILA in J. H. Steward *Handbk. S. Amer. Indians* VI. 76 To the same [*sc.* Ge] group belong the Shavante, between the Araguaya and Tocantins Rivers;.. the Sherente and Craho. **1950** J. A. MASON in *Ibid.* 299 Four groups of Southern Brazil of very different linguistic affinities are known to the Brazilian natives by the name *Chavanté*... Three of them..form small independent (provisionally) families; the fourth is a *Ge* language. **1971** J. S. WEINER *Man's Natural Hist.* v. 221 'Micro-evolution' comparable to that found in the Xavante villages obtains in other South American aboriginal tribes. Ibid. 222 The extraordinary contrast between the high standard of physical fitness and stamina of the young Xavante and his later health and life expectation. **1978** *Sunday Times* (Colour Suppl.) 18 June 33 (*caption*) Xavante Indians in their village close to the River of the Dead..held the white off until recently. **1983** *Word* XXXIV. 61 A number of Brazilian Amazon languages (e.g., Apuriña, Urubú, Xavante, and Nadeb) also rely on both pragmatic and syntactic considerations in determining linear order.

Xaverian (zē[1]vi[ə]·riăn), *a.* and *sb.* [f. the name *Xav(i)er* + -IAN.] **A.** *adj.* **a.** Of, pertaining to, or designating a teaching order of Roman Catholic monks founded in 1839 and named in honour of St. Francis Xavier. **b.** Of or pertaining to St. Francis Xavier (1506–56), Spanish missionary. **B.** *sb.* A Brother of the Xaverian order.

1882 PABISCH & BYRNE tr. *Alzog's Man. Univ. Church Hist.* IV. 333 The Xaverian Brothers, founded at Bruges.. in 1839, and introduced into the United States..in 1854, have under their charge, Mt. St. Joseph's College, Carrollton, Md. **1912** *Catholic Encycl.* XIII. 284/2 After holding the office of Superior General of the Xaverians for twenty-seven years. **1915** C. C. MARTINDALE *In God's Army* I. 118 The whole Xaverian history had been one of deliberate ambition. **1931** M. YEO *St. Francis Xavier* vi. 69 One sentence seems to have the true Xaverian ring. **1967** *New Catholic Encycl.* XIV. 1058/1 The Xaverian Brothers played an important role in the development of Catholic education. *Ibid.* 1058/2 In the U.S. the Xaverians staffed most of the parish schools of Louisville.

X chromosome. *Genetics.* Also †**x chromosome.** [*X 3 e.] A chromosome with different morphology and properties from others in the complement, now recognized as a sex chromosome occurring in both sexes of a species, man and other mammals having one in the somatic cells of the male and two in those of the female.

[**1902**], **1911** [see *X 3 e]. **1933** R. H. WOLCOTT *Animal Biol.* lxxiii. 537 In fowls and in moths females have either one *x*-chromosome or both an *x*-chromosome and a *y*-chromosome, while the males have the two *x*-chromosomes. **1961** P. GRAY *Encycl. Biol. Sci.* 232/1 In most species of Spiders there are two different kinds of X-chromosomes but no Y, so that the males have X_1X_2 and the female $X_1X_1X_2X_2$. **1966** *Lancet* 24 Dec. 1397/1 The small size of the Y chromosome relative to the X chromosome has been attributed to the gradual loss of genetic material not concerned with sex determination. **1983** M. B. ZALESKI et al. *Immunogenetics* ii. 36 The X chromosome carries a set of genes that determines a wide variety of traits that do not necessarily affect the sex of the organism.

X disease. [X 3.] **1.** *Path.* (chiefly *Austral.*) A disease now identified as Murray Valley encephalitis (see *MURRAY VALLEY).

1918 *Med. Jrnl. Australia* 6 Apr. 278/2 On 25th August, 1917, I published in the *Journal* an account of an epidemic at Broken Hill of what is now called the 'X' disease. **1951** *Ibid.* 2 June 800/1 Our case differs from the classical picture of X disease..in the lack of cellular infiltration in the brain. **1964** [see *Q FEVER]. **1983** *Oxf. Textbk. Med.* I. v. 101/1 Murray Valley (formerly) Australia encephalitis. This disease was originally called Australian X disease.

2. *Vet. Sci.* = *blue comb* (*disease*) s.v. *BLUE *a.* 13. (Now known to be caused by a mycotoxin.)

1950 [see *blue comb* (*disease*) s.v. *BLUE *a.* 13]. **1961** *New Scientist* 17 Aug. 403/3 A consignment of groundnut meal from Brazil contained an agent toxic to young turkeys, which proved responsible for the death of some 100,000 birds from the hitherto mysterious X disease... The exact nature of the toxic principle has still not been found.

xeno-. Add: **xenoa·ntibody** *Immunol.*, an antibody produced in response to a xenoantigen; **xenoa·ntigen** *Immunol.*, a xenogeneic antigen; so **xe:noantige·nic** *a.*; **xenoa·ntiserum** *Immunol.*, an antiserum rich in xenoantibodies; **xenobio·tic** *sb.* and *a.* [BIOTIC *a.*], (designating) a substance foreign to the body; **xe·noblast** *Geol.* [a. G. *xenoblast* (F. Becke 1903, in *Compt. Rend. IX. Congr. Géol. Internat.* (1904) II. 564): see -BLAST] (see quot. 1920); hence **xenobla·stic** *a.*; **xeno·cracy** [-CRACY], a ruling body of foreigners; **xe·nocryst** *Geol.*, a crystal not derived from the magma that gave rise to the igneous rock containing it; hence **xenocry·stal, -cry·stic** *adjs.*; **xe:nodiagno·sis** *Med.* [ad. F. *xénodiagnostic* (E. Brumpt 1914, in *Bull. de la Soc. de Path. Exotique* VII. 706)], a diagnostic procedure in which clean, laboratory-bred vectors of a disease are allowed to feed on the individual or material that may be infected and are then examined for the pathogen; hence **xe:nodiagno·stic** *a.*; **xenoglo·ssia, xe·noglossy** (Gr. γλῶσσα tongue], the practice or faculty of using intelligibly a language one has not learnt; **xe·nograft** *Med.*, a graft of tissue between individuals of different species; = *HETEROGRAFT; **xenola·lia** [Gr. -λαλία speaking, after GLOSSOLALIA] = *xenoglossia* above; **xe·nolith** *Geol.* [-LITH], a piece of rock in an igneous mass which differs from its surroundings and is considered to have been picked up by and incorporated into the mass when the latter was in the form of magma; hence **xenoli·thic** *a.*, containing xenoliths; also, occurring as a xenolith; **xe·nophil(e** *a.* [-PHIL, -PHILE], fond of or attracted by foreign things or people; also as *sb.*, such a person; hence **xenophi·lia**, the state of being xenophile; **xenophi·liac** *a.* [-AC] = *xenophil(e* adj. above; **xenophi·lic, xeno·philous** *adjs.* = *xenophil(e* adj.; **xenothe·rmal** *a. Petrol.*, applied to mineral deposits formed by hydrothermal action at high temperatures but at a shallow depth; **xenotro·pic** *a. Microbiology* [*-TROPIC], (of a virus) present in a host species in an inactive form and only able to infect and replicate in organisms of other species; hence **xenotro·pism.**

1974 *Brit. Jrnl. Cancer* XXX. 304/1 Gel filtration was used to show that the tumour specific xenoantibody responsible for protection was not IgM but was in the IgG fraction. **1984** *Human Immunol.* X. 57 Xenoantibodies to idiotypes of the anti-HLA-A2, A28 MoAb CR11-351 were isolated from an antiserum raised in rabbit #81. **1975** *Nature* 24 Apr. 716/2 An important characteristic of the immune system is the ability to discriminate between antigens expressed on normal tissues within the individual and the many foreign antigens expressed on normal tissues of other species (xenoantigens) and even on normal tissues of members of the same species (alloantigens). **1984** *Jrnl. Immunol.* CXXXII. 2522/1 An increase in specific antigenic activity for the *Rana*-specific xenoantigen. **1973** *Tissue Antigens* III. 5/1 Some of the eluted fractions possessed both alloantigenic and xenoantigenic activity. *Ibid.* 18/2 Strain-discriminating effects of xenoantisera were reported..over thirty years ago. **1978** *Nature* 26 Oct. 711/1 Experiments with xenoantiserum to murine tissues provided the first, fortuitous indication that Thy-1 included an hitherto unrecognised specificity. **1965** H. S. MASON et al. in *Federation Proc.* XXIV. 1172 (*heading*) Microsomal mixed-function oxidations: the metabolism of xenobiotics. *Ibid.*, We would like to call the components of this chemical environment which are foreign to the metabolic network of an organism 'xenobiotic' compounds. **1975** WILLIAMS & WILSON *Biologist's Guide to Princ. & Techniques Pract. Biochem.* i. 13 In order to study the metabolism of a xenobiotic, it is advantageous to administer it in an isotopically-labelled form. **1981** *Internat. Jrnl. Environ. Stud.* XVII. 11/2 Many xenobiotic substances reduce blood concentrations of one or more vitamins. **1920** A. HOLMES *Nomencl. Petrol.* 241 *Xenoblast*, a term applied to crystals which have grown during metamorphism without the development of their characteristic faces. **1962** Xenoblast [see *IDIOBLAST 3]. **1931** A. JOHANNSEN *Descr. Petrogr. Igneous Rocks* I. 232 *Xenoblastic*, a texture in metamorphic rocks corresponding to the xenomorphic in igneous rocks. The crystals lack proper crystal faces. **1980** *Mineral. Mag.* XLIII. 781/1 In thin-section all the felsic grains are seen to be xenoblastic. **1965** E. WEBER in Rogger & Weber *European Right* 507 Everywhere Eminescu looked..he saw foreigners and cryptoforeigners; the intelligentsia, recruited from men who had inherited their character and ideas from Greek or Bulgarian forebears; the ruling Liberals, who drew their manners and policies from the Seine, the Spree, and the Bosphorus... Altogether one vast xenocracy. **1975** H. LUKE in K. M. Setton *Hist. Crusades* III. xi. 394 While it is unlikely that the Cypriote peasantry under the Lusignan kingdom were politically worse off..than the peasantry of other Near Eastern countries.., it is not surprising that by the end of the Venetian occupation they had come to conceive..a profound hatred of the Latin xenocracy. **1894** W. J. SOLLAS in *Trans. R. Irish Acad.* XXX. 493 As a distinctive appelation appropriate to the crystals, both of pyroxene and of plagioclase felspar, which have found their way from the gabbro into the granophyre, the term 'xenocrysts' may be employed. Correspondingly included fragments of the whole rock may be called 'xenoliths'. **1964** G. A. JOPLIN *Petrogr. Austral. Igneous Rocks* ii. 26 Xenocrysts commonly show some resorption or corona indicating that they have reacted with the magma. **1983** *Jrnl. Geol.* XCI. 277 Xenocrysts and xenoliths from three Ithaca kimberlite localities are consistent with derivation from mantle depths of less than 150 km. **1963** *Amer. Mineralogist* XLVIII. 172 Classification of Kerguelen rocks is to a large extent dependent on the amount of xenocrystal material present. **1981** *Jrnl. Geophysical Res.* LXXXVI. 10515 This particular granite cannot be a primary magma... It is a possible product of partial fusion of pelitic rocks between about 20 km and 40 km depth..and xenocrystal muscovite or sillimanite from the source rocks. **1978** *Nature* 19 Oct. 640/1 The phlogopite is derived from the parental magma or its derivatives and is not a xenocrystic phase. **1947** *Anales del Instituto de Medicina Regional* (Tucuman) II. 60 The authors describe..artificial xenodiagnosis for cases in which it is not possible to perform it directly upon patients. **1976** *Nature* 15 July 215/2 Using only male bugs of a susceptible stock for xenodiagnosis should enhance the sensitivity of this diagnostic test. **1955** *O Hospital* (Rio de Janeiro) XLVII. 187 The authors make a comparison between the positivity of xeno-diagnostic tests performed in two ways. **1974** R. ZELEDÓN in K. Elliott et al. *Trypanosomiasis & Leishmaniasis* 58 New xenodiagnostic tests in an endemic area of Chagas' disease in Costa Rica. **1978** *Amer. Speech* LIII. 67 Samarin would call the event of persons speaking in a language unknown to them xenoglossia, something different from glossolalia. **1981** *Times Lit. Suppl.* 3 July 765/3 The traditional view was that, while at Corinth glossolalia had occurred, meaning that there were lexically non-communicative utterances, at Pentecost what occurred was xenoglossia, utterance in an actual foreign language. **1914** A. TEIXEIRA DE MATTOS tr. *Maeterlinck's Unknown Guest* III. 101 Xenoglossy is well known not to be unusual in automatic writing; sometimes even the 'automatist' speaks or writes languages of which he is completely ignorant. **1932** I. EMERSON tr. E. Bozzano (*title*) Polyglot mediumship (xenoglossy). **1980** *Brit. Med. Jrnl.* 9 Aug. 432/2 The investigators are reported to regard her xeno-glossy (ability to speak a foreign language without having learnt it) as a truly paranormal experience. **1961** *Nature* 25 Mar. 1024/2 Grafts between species..of less general interest..have been called xenografts or heterografts. **1974** R. M. KIRK et al. *Surgery* ii. 35 A xenograft..is poorly tolerated by the recipient. **1977** *Proc. R. Soc. Med.* LXX. 480/2 A xenograft in one patient was unsuccessful. **1984** *Times* 21 Aug. 4/1 Surgeons have a choice of artificial valves, or those made from human or animal tissue. The latter, xenografts, are silent and rendered rejection-proof. **1978** D. CHRISTIE-MURRAY *Voices from Gods* xii. 167 There appears to be no evidence of genuine, responsive xenolalia (that is, intelligent conversation carried on in a recognized language completely unknown to the speaker) in any native culture studied by anthropologists. **1981** *Times* 8 Oct. 15/5 There is a distinction between glossolalia (paranormal speaking in tongues) and xenolalia (paranormal speaking in allegedly foreign languages). **1894** Xenolith [see *xenocryst* above]. **1942** [see *METASOMATIZE *v.*]. **1956** 'H. MACDIARMID' *Stony Limits & Scots Unbound* 41 Ultra-basic xenoliths that make men look midges. **1975** *Nature* 10 Apr. 489/1 Xenoliths thought to represent material from the deeper parts of the upper mantle are brought to the surface in kimberlite magmas. **1900** *Q. Jrnl. Geol. Soc.* LVI. 665 The whole of the cliffs around Annestown Bay are composed of the widespread pink and greenish xenolithic felsites. **1930** PEACH & HORNE *Geol. Scotl.* ii. 67 Grey igneous gneiss is interposed..and is xenolithic. One of the pale xenoliths was found to consist of malacolite..and green hornblende. **1980** *Sci. Amer.* May 97/1 With the exception of xenolithic..fragments of mantle that are occasionally brought to the surface by kimberlite pipes and some basalt formations, direct sampling of the upper mantle is impossible. **1934** WEBSTER, Xenophile, -phil *adjs.* **1945** W. PLOMER *Dorking Thigh* 10 And in fancy dress she lingers With a locket in her fingers Containing a curl from That xenophil Greek. **1948** *Penguin New Writing* XXXIV. 128 New York and Los Angeles seem to be replacing Paris as the goal of Colombian xenophiles. **1968** P. B. AUSTIN *On being Swedish* xx. 149 Almost in spite of herself, she becomes a xenophile. **1959** *Times* 3 Dec. 15/7 Among the subjects covered by books in our stock are X-rays, xenophilia, [etc.]. **1964** *New Statesman* 1 May 694/1 The uniters are..more prone to xenophilia. Literature being the least internationsl of the arts, those who wish to infuse it with music and colour tend to be internationalists. **1982** *Times* 7 Aug. 8/5 When will Americans realise how xenophiliac their short order cuisine is—hamburgers ..which Hamburg would not understand, French fries incomprehensible to the French. **1974** *Encycl. Brit. Macropædia* X. 309/2 Tension between the xenophobic (fear of strangers) and xenophilic (love of strangers) in postexilic Judaism was finally resolved some two centuries later. **1984** *New Yorker* 16 Jan. 32/2 Even the most xenophilous among us may feel a twinge of alarm. **1935** A. F. BUDDINGTON in *Econ. Geol.* XXX. 209 The writer therefore proposes the term *xenothermal* for these deposits, ..suggestive of the peculiar textures for the normal high-temperature mineral assemblages involved, of the abnormal association of high temperature with shallow depth, and of the 'telescoped' character of many of the deposits. **1976** *Nature* 10 June 482/2 The tin mineralisation of Missouri bears a resemblance to the subvolcanic (xenothermal) deposits of Japan. **1973** J. A. LEVY in *Science* 14 Dec. 1151/2 The results show that this NZB type virus is endogenous in other strains of mice and is xenotropic; that is, it grows only in cells foreign to the host. **1978** *Nature* 30 Mar. 456/2 Defective type C RNA tumour viruses which are genetic recombinants between ecotropic and xenotropic viruses have been described and suggested to be the real transforming agents during the course of viral-induced lymphatic leukaemia. **1974** *Ibid.* 22 Mar. 279/3 Another example of xenotropism is the endogenous feline virus which when activated replicates in human cells. **1982** *Jrnl. Virology* XLIII. 472 (*heading*) Monoclonal antibody to spleen focus-forming virus-encoded gp52 provides a probe for the amino-terminal region of retroviral envelope proteins that confers dual tropism and xenotropism.

xenogeneic (zenodʒenī·ik, -ē¹·ik), *a. Immunol.* [f. XENO- + Gr. γενε-ά race, stock + -IC.] Derived from an individual of a different species.

1961 P. A. GORER et al. in *Nature* 25 Mar. 1025/1 'Hetero-specific' has been used before and cannot be said to be illogical; but it is a Greco-Latin hybrid and we feel that 'xenogeneic' goes well with the other two terms we have suggested and is perhaps preferable. **1969** *Ibid.* 27 Sept. 1376/1 Until recently all procedures that were effective in prolonging the lives of allografts..were usually ineffective for sustaining xenogeneic grafts. **1977** *Lancet* 21 May 1105/2 Patients with widespread metastatic melanoma were treated with..xenogeneic anti-melanoma immunoglobulin. **1981** *Jrnl. Immunol.* CXXVI. 2397/1 Xenogeneic anti-Id antibodies.

xenon. Add: (Further examples.) Also *attrib.* and *Comb.*

1938 *Ann. Reg. 1937* 358 Laporte..showed that white light could be obtained from a xenon tube through which brief but very intense currents were passed. **1957** T. L. J. BENTLEY *Man. Miniat. Camera* (ed. 5) v. 74 The practical uses of electronic flash sets are governed by the characteristics of the modern xenon-filled flash tube. **1959** *New Scientist* 1 Jan. 12/1 The main lighting was provided by a pulsed xenon compact source lamp, and its intensity was of the order of 50,000 foot candles. **1962** *Newnes Conc. Encycl. Nucl. Energy* 877/1 Xenon is of importance in nuclear technology because several radioactive isotopes of the element are found among the fission products. One of these, Xe^{135},..gives rise to fission-product poisoning of the reactor. **1963** [see *REACT *v.*¹ 1 c]. **1971** Xenon arc [see *SPECTRALLY *adv.* 2]. **1971** *Sci. Amer.* Oct. 92/3 The compounds they studied were two chlorides of xenon, $XeCl_2$ and $XeCl_4$, which they produced indirectly by synthesizing analogous compounds where radioactive iodine 129 took the place of xenon... It will be recalled that xenon used to be called an inert, or 'noble', gas because it was thought to be chemically completely unreactive. **1976** *Daily Times* (Lagos) 8 July 17/1 Most film theatres in this country operating in 35mm have such poor and antiquated projection equipment that a good 16mm heavy duty projector equipped with a xenon lamp will certainly aehieve better picture and sound quality.

xenophobia (zenǒfōᵘ·biă). Also **xe·nophoby, zenophobia** (both *rare*). [f. XENO- + Gr. φόβ-ος fear + -IA¹, -Y³.] A deep antipathy to foreigners.

1909 Xenophoby [in Dict. s.v. XENO-]. **1919** *Nation* 20 Dec. 800/1 We are often told in criticism of the Nationalist movements in Egypt, Turkey, Persia, and China that legitimate agitation for self-government and democratic institutions is marred by xenophobia. **1934** R. MACAULAY *Going Abroad* xxix. 249 Violent and inhospitable outbursts of xenophoby have..characterised them [*sc.* the Basques] from their first appearance in history. **1936** E. WAUGH *Waugh in Abyssinia* i. 34 The zenophobia of the people was an insuperable barrier to all free co-operation. **1940** E. POUND *Cantos* lvi. 67 Showed no zenophobia. **1963** *Economist* 1 June 908/1 The mild xenophobia..which informed such *Punch* lines as "e's a stranger: 'eave 'arf a brick at 'im'. **1971** H. MACMILLAN *Riding Storm* ii. 49 This kind of isolationism or economic nationalism, amounting to xenophobia, seized all nations, great and small, from time to time. **1976** N. ROBERTS *Face of France* iv. 49 Eight per cent of France's total working population is immigrant... Here were all the conditions needed for the release of latent xenophobia.

Hence **xenopho·bic** *a.*, pertaining to or exhibiting xenophobia; **xenopho·bically** *adv.*; also **xe·nophobe**, a xenophobic person; also as *adj.*

1912 Xenophobic [in Dict. s.v. XENO-]. **1922** *Mail* 24 May 327/1 The Afghans are said to be suspicious of foreigners, even to be xenophobes. **1937** D. B. WYNDHAM-LEWIS in L. Russell *Press Gang!* 245 Grey, scrawny, xenophobe, oinophil NY chilled-steel tycoon. **1951** H. ARENDT *Burden of our Time* I. i. 3 The identification of antisemitism with rampant nationalism and its xenophobic outbursts. **1956** P. JENNINGS *Model Oddlies* 34 The kind of London pub which..has a more closely-knit, xenophobe clientèle than the remotest village hostelry. **1977** T. HEALD *Just Desserts* vii. 146 It wasn't that he was ..a xenophobe..but the foreignness was obtrusive. **1978** *Listener* 8 June 724/2 Xenophobically named after the old Roman province, the Dacia is, in fact, a licence-built French Renault. **1980** *Times Lit. Suppl.* 22 Aug. 937/5 At that moment [*sc.* the start of a major war], for discreditable xenophobic reasons, Haldane's reputation as a War Minister sank to its nadir, but from 1918 onwards it has always been high. **1983** P. LIVELY *Perfect Happiness* vi. 72 A stubborn and unfashionably xenophobic refusal to attempt foreign languages. **1983** N. FREELING *Back of North Wind* 77 'Another bloody foreigner! I hate a lot of foreigners,' said Castang xenophobically.

Xenopus (ze·nǒpǒs). [mod.L. (coined in Ger. by J. G. Wagler 1827, in *Isis von Oken* XX. 726/2), f. XENO- + Gr. πους, ποδ- foot.) A toad of the African genus *Xenopus*, which has claws on its digits and which was formerly used in pregnancy testing as it produces eggs when injected with the urine of a pregnant woman; a clawed toad.

1890 *Proc. Sci. Meetings Zool. Soc.* 70 *Xenopus* is a most admirable swimmer, and remarkable for the manner in which it remains poised for a long time immediately under the surface of the water. **1955** [see *ŒSTRADIOL]. **1974** *Encycl. Brit. Macropædia* XI. 803/2 In the toad *Xenopus*, each group of hair cells in a neuromast connects to its own nerve fibre.

xerarch (ze·rāɹk), *a. Ecol.* [f. XER(O- + Gr. ἀρχ-ή beginning.] Of a plant succession: having its origin in a dry habitat.

1913, 1960 [see *HYDRARCH *a.*]. **1973** P. A. COLINVAUX *Introd. Ecol.* vi. 75 Later American work..sought to explain the existence of beech-maple forests on old sand dunes near the southern shore of Lake Michigan as resulting from a particularly dramatic xerarch succession.

xeric (zīᵊ·rik), *a. Ecol.* [f. XER(O- + -IC.] Having or characterized by a scanty amount of moisture.

1926, etc. [see *HYDRIC *a.*²]. **1932** FULLER & CONARD tr. *Braun-Blanquet's Plant Sociol.* v. 115 In spite of this temporary excess of precipitation, the vegetation of the southern Cévennes has many xeric features. **1967** M. E. HALE *Biol. Lichens* vii. 94 Xeric savannas and mesic maple woods. **1979** *Jrnl. Arid Environments* II. 255 This soil represents an edaphically xeric condition.

xero-. Add: **xeroderma pigmentosum** *Path.* [L. *pigmentōsus* pigmented], a rare, hereditary disorder in which skin exposed to the ultraviolet light of the sun becomes discoloured and swollen, chronic injury leading in childhood to cancer and often death; **xe·romorphy** *Bot.* [Gr. μορφή shape, form], the possession by a plant of features characteristic of a xerophilous plant; hence **xeromo·rphic** *a.*; also **xe·romorph**, a xeromorphic plant; **xerophil(e** *sb.*: also as *adj.*; [ad. F. *xérophile sb.* (J. Thurmann in *Essai de phytostatique* (1849) I. xiii. 268)]; (earlier and later examples); **xerophi·lic** *a.* = *xerophilous* adj. in Dict. and Suppl.; **xerophilous** *a.*: also *Zool.*; **xe·rosere** *Ecol.* [*SERE *sb.*²], a plant succession having its origin in a dry habitat.

1884 *Medico-Chir. Trans.* LXVII. 169 (*heading*) Three cases of xeroderma pigmentosum, Kaposi or atrophoderma pigmentosum. **1952** C. P. BLACKER *Eugenics* 248 Among these genes are those believed to determine retinitis pigmentosa, a severe disease of the eye leading to blindness; epidermolysis bullosa and xeroderma pigmentosum, both diseases of the skin. **1975** *Sci. Amer.* Nov. 68/2 An inherited defect in the enzymes that repair DNA damaged by ultraviolet light, called *xeroderma pigmentosum*, leads to multiple skin cancers. **1934** WEBSTER, Xeromorph. **1953** *Sci. News* XXVII. 10 The term 'xerophyte' is now limited to those plants able to endure conditions of drought, while salt-marsh plants are known as 'xeromorphs'. **1981** *Austral. Jrnl. Bot.* XXIX. 518 *G*[*revillea*] *annulifera* has the nutritional characteristics common to xeromorphs plus strategies to channel nutrients very efficiently to its seeds. **1909** E. WARMING *Œcol. of Plants* xvi. 445 Xeromorphic structures such as thick cuticle, soil and the xeromorphic structure which has been described. **1938** WEAVER & CLEMENTS *Plant Ecol.* (ed. 2) xvi. 445 Xeromorphic structures such as thick cuticle, waxy covering, or abundant development of hairs have little value in directly reducing the rate of transpiration of xerophytes so long as the stomata are open. **1974** *Nature* 26 Apr. 807/2 The *Hybanthus* shrubs conspicuous by their apparent lack of xeromorphic adaptation to a climate which becomes increasingly arid towards the continental interior. **1909** E. WARMING *Œcol. of Plants* xlvi. 194 This xeromorphy of plants growing on wet moor-soil occurs all the world over. **1963** *Nature* 30 Nov. 909/2 It is well known that xeromorphy is of physiological importance to the aquatic plants which exhibit it and certain tissues become altered in relation to environment. **1980** *Bot. Jrnl. Linnean Soc.* LXXX. 319 Most of the variable characters are related to xeromorphy and are taxonomically useful within the framework of the present classification. **1878** Xerophile [see *HYGROPHILOUS *a.*]. **1921** H. PRINTZ *Vegetation of Siberian-Mongolian Frontiers* 14 At a short distance from the river..the xerophile typical steppe vegetation predominates. **1936** *Hereditas* XXI. 290 *Viola crassa* is xerophile and alpine. **1985** *Times* 4 Jan. 12/2 The site was then abandoned, a conclusion that Dr Evans bases on the high diversity of snail species and the general paucity of xerophile species. **1961** WEBSTER, Xerophilic. **1965** B. E. FREEMAN tr. *Vandel's Biospeleology* xiii. 213 The Tenebrionidae are mainly xerophilic insects. **1972** *Science* 19 May 788/1 He is equally good when describing various kinds of vegetation, from the aquatic to the xerophilic. **1968** *Jrnl. Zool.* CLV. 365 Many xerophilous species occupying desert or semi-arid areas have adapted their breeding physiology to take advantage of the unpredictable and sporadic rainfall that may occur at any time. **1926** Xerosere [see *hydrosere* s.v. *HYDRO-]. **1952** P. W. RICHARDS *Tropical Rain Forest* xii. 287 Opportunities for observing xeroseres in the tropics are..not infrequent, particularly in regions of volcanic activity.

xerocopy (zīᵊ·ro-, ze·rokǫpi). [f. next + COPY *sb.* (*a.*).] A xerographic copy; a photocopy. Hence **xe·rocopying** *vbl. sb.*

1963 *Fortune* Sept. 225/2 (Advt.), Which is the 5c xerocopy? **1964** *Economist* 22 Aug. 695/1 (Advt.), Xerocopying is an essential part of modern business communication. **1966** *English Studies* XLVII. 152 Most of the items are also available as paperbound xerocopies. **1971** *Fremdsprachen* XV. 278 Dry permanent xerocopies at a ratio of 14·5× are automatically reproduced on single cut sheets of ordinary unsensitised paper.

xerography (zīᵊr-, zěrǫ·grăfi). [f. XERO- + -GRAPHY, after *photography*.] A dry copying process in which an electrically charged surface retains both the charge and a pigmented powder on areas not illuminated by light from bright parts of the document, so that a permanent copy may be immediately obtained by placing paper on the surface and applying heat to fuse the powder to it; photocopying.

1948 *N.Y. Times* 23 Oct. 17/8 A revolutionary process of inkless printing..was announced yesterday... Invented by Chester F. Carlson, a New York lawyer, and known as 'Xerography', this basic addition to the graphic arts reproduces pictures and text at a speed of 1,200 a minute. **1957** *Technology* July 164/2 A new copying process, Xerography, attracted constant attention. **1962** *Daily Tel.* 30 Oct. 20 (Advt.), Xerography is capturing a growing share of a market in office copying. **1967** MCLUHAN & FIORE *Medium is Massage* 123 Xerography ..heralds the times of instant publishing. **1970** A. TOFFLER *Future Shock* (1971) xii. 280 Advances in offset printing and xerography have radically lowered the costs of short-run publishing. **1976** *Globe & Mail* (Toronto) 1 Nov. 17/4 Asked whether xerography might become the next big movement in art, Bidner insisted on caution.

Hence **xerogra·phic** *a.*, **xerogra·phically** *adv.*

1948 *N.Y. Times* 23 Oct. 17/8 Even an unskilled person can make good Xerographic prints easily. **1958** *Times Lit. Suppl.* 5 Dec. 712/3 The enormous possibilities of applying the xerographic process to microfilms of books. **1968** *U.S. Patent 3,413,716* 1 A xerographically formed pattern of chemical resist is placed on the conductive material. **1976** *Nature* 22 Jan. 204/2 We sampled the air in an unventilated room..housing a xerographic machine. **1979** *Lore & Lang.* Jan. 14 This recitation has been printed many times and is common in the xerographically transmitted broadsheets. **1982** *Trans. Yorks. Dialect Soc.* LXXXII. 49 (Advt.), Available in microform and xerographic form.

xeroradiography (zīᵊ:ro-, ze:rorē¹diǫ·grăfi). [f. prec. + *RADIOGRAPHY.] A xerographic process for obtaining an X-ray picture, the X-rays impinging on an electrically charged surface like light in conventional xerography. Hence **xerora·diograph**; **xe:roradiogra·phic** *a.*

1950 *Non-Destructive Testing* IX. 1. 11/1 Xeroradiography is a rapid, low-cost, all-electric method of obtaining permanent X-Ray images. *Ibid.*, The xeroradiographic plate..may be made flexible, and placed in intimate contact with the curved surface of the test object. **1955** *Amer. Jrnl. Roentgenol.* LXXIII. 7/1 The xeroradiographic plate consists of a sheet of metal..on which has been deposited ..a thin layer of selenium. *Ibid.* 8/1 (*caption*) Aluminum step-wedge xeroradiographs. **1960** *Aeroplane* XCIX. 722/2 The inspection of light-alloy castings, hidden structures and assemblies, is stated to be among the applications of xeroradiographic equipment. **1972** *Lancet* 2 Dec. 1186/1 A feature of the xeroradiograph is the remarkably sharp, clearcut 'edge effect' of the powder pattern. **1975** *Nature* 25 Sept. 276/2 The discharging of a selenium plate by X rays was embodied in the original Xerox patents but, despite some investigation in the 1950s, 'xeroradiography' has not been widely used.

Xerox (zīᵊ·rǫks, ze·rǫks). Also **xerox.** [Invented word f. *XERO(GRAPHY.] A proprietary name for photocopiers (see quots. 1952, 1953); also used *loosely* (*attrib.* and *absol.*) to denote any photocopy.

1952 *Trade Marks Jrnl.* 19 Aug. 748/2 *Xerox*... Electrophotographic copying machines and apparatus for fusing powder images onto paper in connection with electrophotographic copying machines. The Haloid Company. **1953** *Official Gaz.* (U.S. Patent Office) 12 May 327/2 The Haloid Company, Rochester, N.Y... *Xerox* for electrophotographic copying machines, cameras, plates... Claims, use since June 22, 1949 **1966** *Economist* 15 Oct. 299/3 In most American offices executives instruct subordinates to 'make me a Xerox of this report' rather than 'make me a copy of it'. **1972** M. WILLIAMS *Inside Number 10* xi. 289 The Rank Organization in Brighton installed a xerox copying machine in the office and we also had an electric duplicating machine. **1975** D. LODGE *Changing Places* iii. 128, I enclose a Xerox of the anonymous letter. **1976** M. MACHLIN *Pipeline* xxvii. 317 It had appeared in Xerox form on bulletin boards in most of the administrative offices of Denali. **1977** M. FRENCH *Women's Room* (1978) iii. 272 They had a terrible fight one evening in the Xerox room of the library. **1979** *Author* XC. 157 Reprography..—xerox photocopying. **1980** *London Rev. Bks.* 15 May 8/3 How will the industry cope with new technologies, like tele-ordering, new EEC copyright complications and piracy both in the Middle East and (as we all guiltily know) in every xerox room in the British Isles? **1981** P. ROTH *Zuckerman Unbound* 52 Virtually all they had left in common was the rented Xerox machine.

fig. **1979** *Nature* 15 Mar. 209/3 The set is often referred to as 'the first generation of elementary particles'... Nature seems to have made xerox copies: a second generation (μ^- ν' and cs) and possibly a third.

xerox (zīᵊ·rǫks, ze·rǫks), *v.* Also **Xerox.** [f.

prec.] *trans.* To reproduce by xerography; to photocopy.

1966 'E. V. CUNNINGHAM' *Helen* iv. 40 Anything you want copies of, why we'll Xerox it out. **1967** MCLUHAN & FIORE *Medium is Massage* 123 Custom-make your own book by simply Xeroxing a chapter from this one, a chapter from that one—instant steal! **1978** *Globe & Mail* (Toronto) *Weekend Mag.* 21 Oct. 14/3 He xeroxes the menu himself and stamps out to post it on the notice-board. **1979** N. MAILER *Executioner's Song* II. iv. 555 Tamera had gone to work at 5 A.M. and spent six hours Xeroxing Gary's letters. **1982** P. M. MARGOLIN *Last Innocent Man* II. iii. 115 He had Xeroxed the clippings for David.

Hence **xe·roxed** *ppl. a.*, **xe·roxing** *vbl. sb.* (both also with capital initial).

1965 *New Society* 14 Oct. 28/2 Inadequate library provision..has forced university teachers to..prepare.. roneoed or xeroxed material. **1973** *Jrnl. Social Psychol.* LX. 32 The Xeroxing, which made each sheet look less as though it had been individually prepared, was done to prevent distortion of the ratings. **1976** S. LLOYD *Mr Speaker, Sir* vii. 154 During July 1974, we frequently had to rely on Xeroxed copies of the order paper, amendments, and the Official Report. **1978** K. AMIS *Jake's Thing* xiv. 139 He..reached for the xeroxed sheet on the bedside table. **1978** *Early Music* Oct. 605/3, I wonder how publishers who want to remain in business will react to Mr Rooley's complaint about xeroxing rules. **1980** E. BEHR *Getting Even* ii. 21 The xeroxing propensities of.. one of the top confidential secretaries. **1982** *Amer. Speech* LVII. 268 The dry duplicating process known as Xeroxing has gained great popularity. **1984** *Monitor* (McAllen, Texas) 15 Jan. 16A/6 Conference participants are also urged to bring xeroxed copies of their utility bills. **1985** A. S. BYATT *Still Life* 4 Schoolgirls were dutifully filling in xeroxed, hand-written, one-word-answerable questionnaires.

Xhosa (kǭᵘ·ză, kǭ·ză, -să), *sb.* and *a.* Also 9 Koossa, etc.: 9- **Xosa.** [Their own name for themselves.] **A.** *sb.* **a.** A member of any of several related tribes in Cape Province, South Africa, that form part of the Nguni branch of the Bantu; such people collectively.

1801 J. BARROW *Trav. Interior S. Afr.* I. iii. 219 The Kaffers call themselves *Koussie*, which word is pronounced by the Hottentots with a strong palatal stroke of the tongue on the first syllable. **1812** A. PLUMPTRE tr. *Lichtenstein's Trav. Southern Afr.* I. xviii. 250 The tribe of which I mean more particularly to speak call themselves Koossas, or Kaussas. **1827** G. THOMPSON *Trav. Southern Afr.* App. No. I. 439 The national appellation of the Southern Caffers is *Amakosa*, the singular of which is *Kosa.* **1881** *Encycl. Brit.* XIII. 818/2 The Ama-Fengus are regarded both by the Ama-Zulus and Ama-Xosas as slaves or out-castes, without any right to the freedom and privilege of true-born Kaffres. **1948** B. G. M. SUNDKLER *Bantu Prophets in S. Afr.* iv. 96 The Zionist prophets, operating in Zululand, are in many cases not Zulus, but Sotho, Xhosa, or sometimes men from..Nyasaland. **1981** A. PATON *Towards Mountain* xxii. 189 The suggestion was made at a white staff meeting that we should try allotting separate dormitories to Xhosas, Zulu, Basotho, and so on.

b. The Nguni language of the Xhosas, a tonal language of the Bantu family very similar to Zulu.

1872 W. J. DAVIS *Dict. Kaffir Lang.* p. vi, The author of this, the first Dictionary of Xosa Kaffir. **1928** *Africa* I. 479 Xosa is established as the literary language of Kaffraria and the Transkei. **1970** *Cape Times* 28 Oct. 2/6 Four hundred people of all races attended prayers for racial harmony, held at St. George's Cathedral, Cape Town last night. The service—conducted alternately in English, Afrikaans and Xhosa—formed part of 24 hours of continuous prayer. **1977** *N.Y. Rev. Bks.* 4 Aug. 41/2 After testifying for four days in his native Xhosa, he asked if he could address the court in English. **1983** M. KENYON *Free-Range Wife* i. 17 His English was so weird..he might well, as compensation, have flawless French, German, Finnish, Xhosa too.

B. *adj.* Pertaining to or designating the Xhosas or their language.

1812 A. PLUMPTRE tr. *Lichtenstein's Trav. Southern Afr.* I. App. sig. a2ʳ In the Koossa dialect *u* is the vowel that occurs the most frequently. **1872** W. J. DAVIS *Dict. Kaffir Lang.* p. v, When a word is both Xosa and Zulu in form and signification, both these letters are prefixed to its meaning. **1935** *Critic* (Cape Town) Oct. 1 From the Xhosa verb *bonga* is derived the noun *isibongo*. **1948** B. G. SUNDKLER *Bantu Prophets S. Afr.* ii. 42 The Order of Ethiopia can hardly be said to have succeeded in attracting the broad masses of Ethiopians... It has remained exclusively Xhosa. **1963** *Times Lit. Suppl.* 17 May 354 A successful Xhosa cattle breeder. **1975** *Cricketer* May 15/2 A running commentary in the Xhosa language kept Bantu spectators in the picture.

xi (sɔi, zɔi, ksɔi, gzɔi). *Particle Physics.* [Gr. ξεῖ, ξῖ, name of the fourteenth letter (Ξ, ξ) of the Greek alphabet.] Either of a pair of hyperons (and their antiparticles) having a mass of approximately 1320 MeV, spin of ½, hypercharge −1, isospin ½, and even parity, which on decaying usually produce a lambda particle and a pion. Freq. represented by Ξ. Usu. *attrib.*

1954 GELL-MANN & PAIS in *Proc. Glasgow Conf. Nucl. & Meson Physics* (1955) 344 It is interesting to consider the 'cascade particle', which we shall call Ξ^- and which has the decay scheme $\Xi^- \to \Lambda^0 + \pi^- + (\sim 65\text{ MeV})$. **1964** *New Scientist* 20 Feb. 460/3 According to the conservation of baryons and hypercharge, the omega-minus should be produced in collisions between K-minus mesons and protons and should decay (weakly, with a change of hypercharge) to a xi-particle and pion, or to a lambda-particle and K-minus. **1974** *Nature* 13 Dec. 524/1 The elementary particles nearly obey a number of simple and elegant symmetry rules. Many useful approximate calculations can be made assuming that the symmetries are perfect—for instance..by assuming that the proton and neutron have the same interactions as the lambda, sigma and xi hyperons. **1980** J. S. TREFIL *From Atoms to Quarks* vii. 109 There are two xi particles, one neutral and one with a negative charge.

X-irradia·tion. [f. X (RAYS + IRRADIATION.] **a.** Irradiation with X-rays. **b.** X-rays, X-radiation.

1956 *Nature* 11 Feb. 287/1 A visible coloration is produced upon X-irradiation of the above silver-free base glass. **1962** O. HOCKWIN in A. Pirie *Lens Metabolism Rel. Cataract* 422 The application of a high dose of X-irradiation causes changes of lens metabolism immediately after the end of irradiation. **1964** G. H. HAGGIS et al. *Introd. Molecular Biol.* vii. 196 Chromosome breaks induced during leptotene by X-irradiation should..show up later as injuries to both daughter chromatids. **1976** *Internat. Jrnl. Radiation Biol.* XXIX. 367 X-irradiation..was delivered on four abdominal fields over 15 days.

Hence **X-irra·diate** *v. trans.*, to irradiate with X-rays; **X-irra·diated** *ppl. a.*

1958 *Jrnl. Compar. & Physiol. Psychol.* LI. 178 (*heading*) Maze learning in pre- and neonatally X-irradiated rats. **1971** *Nature* 9 Apr. 367/1 The solution was to X-irradiate the haploid sperms of one species. **1978** *Jrnl. Exper. Med.* CXLVIII. 15 Labeling studies in animals X-irradiated with hind-limb shielding gave a Kupffer cell labeling index of 5–10% of the normal values. **1980** *Photochem. & Photobiol.* XXXII. 183 With both treatment regimens, tumor susceptibility could be transferred to X-irradiated recipients with lymphoid cells.

xography (zǫ·grăfi). [f. X (of unknown significance) + -OGRAPHY.] A photographic process producing images with a three-dimensional effect (see quots.). So **xo·graph,** an image of this kind.

1965 R. R. KARCH *Graphic Arts Procedures* (ed. 3) xiii. 336 Xography provides three-dimensional printing which can be seen without benefit of special reading glasses. **1974** *Encycl. Brit. Macropædia* XIV. 1059/1 In the 1960s a three-dimensional print was developed, essentially an illustration bearing two views, superimposed, of the same image taken from slightly different angles, on a transparent mount striped with a multitude of imperceptible parallel strips (Xograph process). **1977** J. HEDGECOE *Photographer's Handbk.* 301 The basis of the xography process is a cylindrical 'lenticular' screen..which is built into the back of the camera just in front of the film plane.

X organ. *Zool.* Also **x organ** and with hyphen. [After G. *organ X*, *X-organ* (B. Hanström 1931, in *Zeitschr. f. Morphol. u. Ökol. d. Tiere* XXIII. 200, 202), so called because indicated by the letter X in a diagram published by G. Bellonci 1882, in *Mem. dell' Accad. Sci. dell' Ist. di Bologna* III. 419 ff.] A group of neurosecretory cells in the eye-stalk of some crustaceans, one of the secretions of which inhibits the production of moulting hormone by the Y organ.

1938 [see *sinus gland* s.v. *SINUS 6]. **1959** W. ANDREW *Textbk. Compar. Histol.* xiii. 513 There is a definite pathway..by which the axons of the nerve cells of the x-organ travel to the sinus gland. **1975** *Sci. Amer.* Feb. 74/1 The eyes of crabs are mounted on movable stalks. The stalks also house a neuroendocrine unit called the X-organ sinus-gland complex, which secretes a hormone that causes the pigments to disperse within the chromatophores.

Xosa, var. *XHOSA *sb.* and *a.*

X-radiation. (In Dict. s.v. X RAYS.) (Earlier and later examples.)

1896 *Strand* July 108/1 If a solid object is placed in the path of this stream..it may become the seat of the production of that which is..variously known as Röntgen radiation or X-radiation. **1974** *Physics Bull.* Dec. 581/2 The developing use of synchrotrons as an intense source of x radiation.

X-ra·diograph. [After X RAYS.] A radiograph made using X-rays. So **X-radio·graphy.**

1899 G. B. SHAW *Let.* 12 Apr. in *B. Shaw & Mrs. Campbell* (1952) 11, I have just had an Xradiograph [*sic*] taken; and lo! perfectly mended solid bone. **1948** *Endeavour* VII. 110/2 An X-radiograph [of the picture] made after cleaning revealed the density in the region near the proper right hand. **1961** M. LEVY *Studio Dict. Art Terms* 121 X-radiography. **1963** B. FOZARD *Instrumentation Nucl. Reactors* i. 7 The effect of radiation upon the crystals of silver bromide in a photographic emulsion is well known and the process is used in X- and gamma-radiography. **1975** *Nature* 26 June 697/1 Skeletal X radiography is a powerful tool for studying both modern and fossil corals. **1983** *National Gallery News* Oct. 4/1 This is a long and delicate process which involves.. taking X-radiographs of the painting to ascertain its original state.

X rays, *sb. pl.* Add: Also **x-rays. I. 1. a.** Now known to be a form of electromagnetic radiation of wavelength less than that of short-wave ultraviolet light (i.e. less than about 4 to 40 nm). (Later examples.)

X-rays are often defined as being produced by deceleration of charged particles (esp. electrons) or by electron transitions in atoms, in contrast to the otherwise similar *gamma rays* which arise from radioactive decay of nuclei. Since gamma rays tend to be of shorter wavelength than most X-rays, they have been classified variously either as very short X-rays, or as constituting a separate class of very short wavelengths beyond X-rays. Cf. *gamma rays* s.v. *GAMMA 1 c (ii).

1930 [see *gamma rays* s.v. *GAMMA 1 c (ii)]. **1948** *Sci. News* VII. 35 Procedure for the generation of x-rays..is to accelerate a beam of electrons to the required energy, and then stop it by allowing the electrons to hit a metal target. **1958** CONDON & ODISHAW *Handbk. Physics* VII. viii. 118/2 Although there is no precise definition of the high-energy limit of the energy of quanta called X rays, this term is usually restricted to radiations of fewer than several million electron volts of energy, above which the radiation is referred to as γ radiation. **1971** D. W. SCIAMA *Mod. Cosmol.* ii. 31 The distinction between X- and γ-rays is a somewhat arbitrary one, but.. we may take the dividing line to be an energy of 100 keV. **1983** *Oxf. Textbk. Med.* I. VI. 86/1 Gamma-rays. These are identical in properties to X-rays but are produced by the spontaneous disintegration of radioactive atoms.

b. (Earlier example.)

1896 *Boston Med. & Surg. Jrnl.* CXXXV. 610/2, I am.. nursing an X-ray finger.

c. (*X-ray.*) Used *attrib.* with reference to primitive pictures in which some representation is given of the insides of people and animals.

1940 L. ADAM *Primitive Art* xiv. 119 Characteristic of the northern territory are the so-called 'X-ray' drawings —a special variety of naturalistic art..whereby the artist, when drawing human beings and animals, represents the inner parts of the body. **1956** C. P. MOUNTFORD *Rec. Amer.-Austral. Scientific Exped. Arnhem Land* I. iii. 112 Nor do the subjects of the X-ray artists show any movement. It is essentially a static art. **1959** E. A. FISHER *Anglo-Saxon Archit. & Sculpture* 88 Still earlier in really primitive art, and among some primitive races today, the same idea of showing the inside, the backbone, ribs and internal organs..is found, e.g. in the so-called X-ray drawings of some of the natives of the Melanesian area of the Pacific. **1977** G. CLARK *World Prehist.* (ed. 3) XI. 479 The X-ray figures of Arnhem Land..may well reflect exotic influences.

II. The sing. form, *X-ray*.

2. (An) examination of a person in which an X-ray picture is taken.

1933 V. BRITTAIN *Testament of Youth* viii. 409 Ten patients..were for immediate operation; a dozen more were for X-ray; several were likely to hæmorrhage at any moment. **1960** 'R. GORDON' *Doctor in Clover* vi. 47, I popped her in a taxi and drove her round to the casualty entrance at St Swithin's, where Miles organised X-rays. **1983** *Daily Tel.* 13 Oct. 18, I injured my back..and after a great deal of pain and misery I had an X-ray.

3. = *X-RADIOGRAPH.

1934 in WEBSTER. **1942** M. DICKENS *One Pair of Feet* viii. 164 Siddons was subjected to all the indignities and discomforts of gastric investigation... X-ray after X-ray was taken and various different diets tried. **1957** 'R. GORDON' *Doctor in Love* xii. 107, I had a difficult x-ray which I thought she could help me interpret. **1969** *Ithaca Jrnl.* 27 Nov. 30 Some doctors try to head off possible litigation by ordering unnecessary and expensive x-rays. **1977** *Daily Tel.* 2 Mar. 19/5 It was not known when Miss Doris Hunt..swallowed the spoon, first seen on an X-ray last year.

4. (Without article.) An X-ray department in a hospital.

1955 'R. GORDON' *Doctor at Large* xiv. 143 Apart from the nurses, there were the buxom dieticians, the cheerful girls in X-ray, the neat secretaries, [etc.]. **1974** 'H. CARMICHAEL' *Motive* x. 116 Dr Egan had gone to X-ray but would be back soon. **1978** J. IRVING *World according to Garp* ii. 28 Her books..outgrew the shelf space and slid into the main infirmary..and into X-ray.

III. 5. a. Applied to instruments and techniques using or producing X-rays, as *X-ray analysis, microscope, microscopy, spectrograph, spectrometer, spectroscopy* (hence *X-ray spectroscopic*), *telescope*; **X-ray astronomy,** the branch of astronomy concerned with the X-ray emissions of heavenly bodies; so **X-ray astronomer.**

1924 *Econ. Geol.* XIX. 1 Physicists have developed X-ray analysis in recent years to such a point that the internal structure of any opaque crystalline substance can be determined. **1980** P. LUGER *Mod. X-Ray Analysis* vi. 288 The method which has been used from the earliest days of X-ray analysis is the drawing of contours obtained from the electron density map. **1969** *Times* 13 May 14/1 X-ray astronomers have to use rockets or balloons to carry their instruments above as much of the atmosphere as possible. **1982** *Jrnl. Brit. Interplanetary Soc.* XXXV. 291 Coded aperture techniques have been employed to great advantage by X-ray astronomers. **1963** *Daily Tel.* 6 June 21 The first news was given today by the United States at the International Space Research meeting in Warsaw of a new kind of astonomy, X-ray astronomy. **1964** *Space Res.* IV. 966 (*heading*) X-ray astronomy. **1970** *Sci. Jrnl.* May 17/4 It is some years since the accidental discovery of the X-ray source Sco X-1 ushered in the new field of X-ray astronomy. **1979** *Jrnl. R. Soc. Arts* CXXVII. 580/2 X-ray astronomy took its first real spurt forward in 1970 with the launch of NASA's small 'Uhuru' X-ray satellite. **1948** *Jrnl. Optical Soc. Amer.* XXXVIII. 774/1 It is clear that an x-ray microscope is now a definite possibility. *Ibid.* 766/1 A satisfactory x-ray microscopy would open up fields of investigation closed to the optical microscope because of its limited resolution. **1966** *McGraw-Hill Encycl. Sci. & Technol.* VIII. 368*b*/1 The x-ray microscopes used in microradiography utilize x-radiation to form images of resolution in the 0·2–2·0 micron..range. *Ibid.*, With this method, x-ray microscopy has not only become competitive with direct light microscopy in resolving power but has gained important advantages. **1981** *Rev. Sci. Instruments* LII. 211/2 The construction of a photoelectron x-ray microscope appears to be feasible and, moreover, this instrument should fairly fulfill the requirements demanded for the extension of x-ray microscopy. **1925** G. A. Lindsay tr. *M. Siegbahn's Spectrosc. X-Rays* iv. 92 The evidence essential for a better answer to these questions was afforded by X-ray spectrographs and Röntgen tubes with hot cathodes. **1983** *IEEE Trans. Nucl. Sci.* XXX. 491 (*heading*) High throughput non-dispersive hard X-ray spectrograph. [*Note*] 'Spectrograph' and 'spectrometer' are used interchangeably in this paper. **1915** W. H. & W. L. Bragg *X Rays & Crystal Structure* iii. 22 The X-ray spectrometer has already determined both the absolute wave lengths of various types of X-radiation and the arrangement of the atoms in several crystals. **1955** *Sci. News Let.* 23 July 1 The electronic assayer is known as an X-ray spectrometer, and the technique, which can be applied to most minerals, is called fluorescent X-ray analysis. **1977** A. Hallam *Planet Earth* 18/1 The X-ray spectrometer mapped aluminium:silicon ratios and delineated the extent of the aluminous highlands. **1925** G. A. Lindsay tr. *M. Siegbahn's Spectrosc. X-Rays* iii. 33 In order to meet such demands of X-ray spectroscopic work, the firm of Emil Gundelach..has constructed tubes embodying a slight modification. *Ibid.* 52 This rotating crystal method was first employed in X-ray spectroscopy by de Broglie. **1966** J. G. Brown *X-Rays & their Applic.* vii. 124 The methods of X-ray spectroscopy which depend on crystal diffraction are essentially methods of measuring the Bragg angle. **1983** *Jrnl. Physics B* XVI. L77 (*heading*) The determination of parameters of recombining laser-producing plasmas by means of x-ray spectroscopy. *Ibid.*, Among the various methods of plasma diagnostics the most preferable in this case are the x-ray spectroscopic methods. **1963** *Daily Tel.* 6 June 21/4 The X-ray telescope has to be raised above the earth's atmosphere and a technique found for focusing X-rays. **1978** Pasachoff & Kutner *University Astron.* xii. 333 It still looks as though Cygnus X-1 represents the first observational detection of a black hole. The new generation of x-ray telescopes should tell us more.

b. Applied to astronomical bodies that emit X-rays in detectable or significant quantities, as *X-ray nova, pulsar, star*; **X-ray burster**, a cosmic source of intermittent, short-lived, powerful bursts of X-rays, typically lasting about a second.

1976 *Nature* 17 June 542/1 This object..is perhaps the most enigmatic 'X-ray burster' found to date. **1978** Pasachoff & Kutner *University Astron.* xxv. 632 (*caption*) Half a dozen of the strong x-ray sources in the galactic bulge region have been possibly identified with x-ray bursters. **1970** *Sci. Jrnl.* Apr. 64 The second example of an 'X-ray nova' was reported during the summer of 1969, based on observations from two US Vela satellites built to monitor man-made nuclear explosions in space. **1977** *Dædalus* Fall 53 One particular kind of variable X-ray stars are the *transient sources*, sometimes called X-ray novae. **1969** G. Fritz et al. in *Science* 9 May 709/1 We wish to report the discovery of an x-ray pulsar in the general direction of the Crab Nebula. The data were obtained during an Aerobee rocket flight on 13 March 1969. **1978** Pasachoff & Kutner *University Astron.* xi. 315 (*caption*) The x-ray pulsar SMC X-1 in the Small Magellanic Cloud has a period of 0·716 sec. **1964** *Daily Tel.* 31 Mar. 17/1 Evidence of the existence of a previously unknown kind of star has been collected by American astronomers. Using an Aerobee rocket..they found two distinct 'X-ray stars'. **1977** *Sci. Amer.* Oct. 42/2 One can say with considerable certainty that X-ray stars are dense remnants of stars that have exhausted their supply of nuclear energy and have collapsed under the attractive force of their own gravity.

6. Special Combs. (of sing. form *X-ray*): **X-ray crystallography,** the study of crystals and their structure by means of X-ray diffraction techniques; hence **X-ray crystallographer; X-ray dermatitis,** dermatitis caused by X-rays; **X-ray diffraction,** the diffraction of X-rays by the regularly spaced atoms of a crystalline material, esp. as a technique of X-ray crystallography; **X-ray eyes,** the apparent ability to see beyond an outward form or through opaque material; very perceptive discernment; also, *X-ray scrutiny*; **X-ray spectrum,** a graph of intensity against wavelength or frequency for the X-rays absorbed or emitted by a material; **X-ray tube,** an electron tube for generating X-rays by accelerating the electrons to high energies and causing them to strike a target that is also the anode, producing the X-rays.

1962 *Listener* 10 May 809/1 Botanists or X-ray crystallographers. **1971** J. W. Jeffery *Methods X-Ray Crystallogr.* p. v, When one is generation 3..of X-ray crystallographers, one cannot expect to do much direct quarrying in that famous paper whose product, the Bernal chart, is known to every crystallographer. **1930** R. W. James *X-Ray Crystallogr.* i. 2 X-ray crystallography is descended from, and constantly uses, the results of the older crystallography. **1968** M. Pyke *Food & Society* vii. 101 A few milligrams of vitamin B_{12} had been isolated and the nature of its complex molecule established by a combination of advanced organic chemistry and X-ray crystallography. **1977** R. S. Drago *Physical Methods in Chem.* xvii. 589 Using X-ray crystallography, one can generally determine the precise composition and atomic arrangement of almost any molecule. **1900** *Philadelphia Med. Jrnl.* V. 187 The believers in the electrical cause of x-ray dermatitis are found to be exclusively physicians. **1908** [in Dict., sense b]. **1959** *Med. Jrnl. Australia* I. 290/1 In November, 1897, Sylvanus Thompson described X-ray dermatitis, and in the following year the Röntgen Society set up a committee to investigate possible hazards. **1977** *Acta Dermato-Venereologica* LVII. 487/1 The fluid from spontaneous blisters in 15 patients with various bullous dermatoses, such as..X-ray dermatitis, all contained measurable amounts of activity. **1924** *Econ. Geol.* XIX. 15 A complete description of X-ray diffraction has been given by the Braggs. **1950** *Sci. News* XV. 139 The techniques of X-ray diffraction, which have contributed so much to the understanding of the inner structure of metals and alloys. **1969** *Times* 28 Jan. 6/6 X-ray diffraction techniques..show that the orientation of the graphite crystals in the fibre depends on the degree to which it is stretched during the heat treatment. **1982** R. M. Schultz in T. M. Devlin *Textbk. Biochem.* ii. 73 The most important of the techniques for the study of a protein's secondary, tertiary, and quaternary structure is x-ray diffraction. **1939** M. Allingham *Mr. Campion & Others* ii. 36 The conviction that he had actually encountered a man with X-ray eyes at last. **1971** 'R. Macdonald' *Underground Man* xxvi. 186 I've been feeling watched, tonight. Drawing the curtains doesn't really help. Whatever it is out there has X-ray eyes. Call it God, or call it the Devil, it hardly matters. **1976** J. Wainwright *Who goes Next?* 205 He didn't have X-ray eyes. He couldn't see through the sides of a parked van. **1982** M. Millar *Mermaid* vi. 68, I got X-ray eyes when it comes to people's weaknesses. **1899** G. Allen *Miss Cayley's Adventures* ii. 45 She looked me through and through again with her X-ray scrutiny. **1925** G. A. Lindsay tr. *M. Siegbahn's Spectrosc. X-Rays* vi. 150 The X-ray spectrum is an atomic property... The frequencies involved in X-ray spectra are very great. **1983** *Jrnl. Physics B* XVI. L79 The large dimension of the spectrograph slit..allowed us to observe the x-ray spectra of H- and He-like F viii and F ix ions. **1896** *Nature* 12 Nov. 31/2 Unexplained variations in the behaviour of the X-ray tubes. **1974** *Encycl. Brit. Macropædia* XIV. 345/1 Small gamma-ray sources are placed in areas inaccessible to X-ray tubes such as inside pipelines.

X-ray *v.* (earlier example); also *fig.*; hence **X-rayed** (e·ks-) *ppl. a.*, **X-raying** (e·ks-) *vbl. sb.*

1899 *Bristol Med.-Chir. Jrnl.* XVII. 234 Cases that have to be X-rayed in their bedrooms. **1920** *Glasgow Herald* 5 Oct. 7/2 Advantage is claimed for 'X-raying' over sterilization. **1941** *Cold Spring Harbor Symp. Quantitative Biol.* IX. 156/1 X-rayed Bar-M2 males (4000r) were crossed to females with the genes scute vermilion forked and carnation. **1973** *Sci. Amer.* Apr. 30/3 The only way to 'X ray' the earth for such fine structure is to use short-period seismic waves that interact with the boundary of the core. **1977** W. Marshall *Thin Air* i. 6 It took two hours for the poor old Japs to even clear body search... Let alone the X-raying of freight and luggage. **1977** *Time* 22 Aug. 30/3 The treaty will have to be X-rayed by the university. **1977** *New Yorker* 26 Sept. 43/3 She..could feel the plaster armoring his X-rayed ribs. **1980** J. O'Faolain *No Country for Young Men* v. 102 The men were terrifying. She remembered their eyes X-raying her clothes.

Xtal, xtal (kri·stăl). [Cf. X 6.] Abbrev. of Crystal *sb.* and *a.*

1957 *Practical Wireless* XXXIII. 454/1 Remove Xtal unit by cutting off all leads at the source. **1971** *Gramophone* July 257/2 The crystal pickup button is labelled 'xtal' which is engineer's shorthand.

xylary (zəi·lări), *a. Bot.* [f. Xyl(em + -ary[2].] Of, pertaining to, or constituting xylem.

1953 K. Esau *Plant Anat.* xv. 367 The terms phloic procambium and xylary procambium..may be used to stress the early differentiation of the meristem into the two parts. **1973** *Nature* 13 Apr. 479/2 Between 2000 h and 2400 h the developing xylary tissues will rapidly withdraw water from the immediately adjacent developing phloem tissues.

xylitol (zəi·litǫl). *Chem.* [ad. G. *xylit* (Fischer & Stahel 1891, in *Ber. d. Deut. Chem. Ges.* XXIV. 538), f. *xyl-ose* Xylose + *-it*, -ite[1]: see -ol.] A sweet, crystalline, pentahydric alcohol, $CH_2OH(CHOH)_3CH_2OH$, derived from xylose and present in some plant tissues.

1891 *Jrnl. Chem. Soc.* LX. i. 668 Xylose yields a new compound, xylitol, which forms a non-crystallisable syrup. **1962** R. van Heyningen in A. Pirie *Lens Metabolism Rel. Cataract* 402 The lens is the only mammalian tissue in which xylitol has been found. **1977** *Daily Colonist* (Victoria, B.C.) 1 Dec. 11/1 A storm of adverse publicity over the natural sweetener xylitol isn't going to deter major chewing gum manufacturers from marketing products containing the substance.

xylo (zəi·lo). Colloq. abbrev. of Xylonite.

1926 *Ironmonger* 16 Jan. (Suppl.) 50 (Advt.), This knife is made of stainless steel in four qualities with wood, xylo and ebonite handles. **1962** L. S. Sasieni *Optical Dispensing* ix. 218 Run the thumb-nail round between the xylo and the metal.

xylo-. Add: **xy·lulose** *Chem.* [*-ulose[2]], a keto pentose that corresponds to the aldo pentose xylose and occurs in the urine of pentosurics.

1936 Levene & Tipson in *Jrnl. Biol. Chem.* CXV. 731 For simplicity it would seem desirable to term the ketose '*d*-xylulose', in conformity with the nomenclature accepted for other keto sugars. **1964, 1968** [see *pentosuric *a.* and *sb.*]. **1974** B. S. Hartley in Carlile & Skehel *Evolution in Microbial World* 170 A mutant of this organism constitutive for ribitol dehydrogenase grows on xylitol by utilising a side specificity of this enzyme to produce xylulose.

xylographica (zəilogræ·fikă), *sb. pl.* [mod.L., f. Xylographic *a.* after *typographica *sb. pl.*] Block-books, woodcuts, and the like; xylographic matter.

1931 M. B. Stillwell *Incunabula & Americana* iii. i. 177 Blockbooks, although produced during the same period [as incunabula], are those printed *a full page at a time*, each page being printed from a wooden block... Such books are sometimes called 'xylographic books', or 'xylographica', meaning that they are wood-engraved throughout. **1952** J. Carter *ABC for Bk.-Collectors* 37 Block books, or xylographica, as produced in Europe are presumed..to have preceded the invention of printing from movable metal types. **1982** *Times Lit. Suppl.* 6 Aug. 866/1 Volume I will carry descriptions of block-books and other xylographica.

xylocaine (zəi·lokēin). *Pharm.* [f. Xylo- + *-caine*, after Cocaine.] = *lignocaine.

1946 Löfgren & Lundqvist in *Svensk Kemisk. Tidskrift* LVIII. 208 The compound ω-diethylamino-2,6-dimethylacetanilide is called xylocaine (LL 30) and is an ideal local anaesthetic, which seems to be superior to procaine in every respect. **1954** [see *lignocaine]. **1961** *Times* 4 Feb. 12/2, I injected a total of 30 c.c. of xylocaine. **1978** *Jrnl. R. Soc. Med.* LXXI. 320/1 Shortening the duration of the convulsive activity in the brain by administering xylocaine before the inducing shock does reduce the therapeutic effects.

xylophonist (zəilǫ·fŏnist). [f. Xylophone + -ist.] One who plays a xylophone.

1927 *Daily Tel.* 10 May 12/1 Teddy Brown the xylophonist. **1952** B. Ulanov *Hist. Jazz in Amer.* (1958) xvii. 207 He became a xylophonist. **1976** *Gramophone* Aug. 345/1 There is a really brilliant xylophonist in 'Fossils'.

xylorimba (zəi·lŏrimbă). [f. Xylo(phone + *ma)rimba.] (See quots. 1938, 1980.)

1938 *Oxf. Compan. Mus.* 1026/2 *Xylorimba*, an American form of lightweight marimba. **1961** *Times* 10 Nov. 18/7 The icy, scientific precision of xylorimba. **1978** P. Griffiths *Conc. Hist. Mod. Music* ix. 137 Xylorimba and percussion suggest the influence of black African music. **1980** *New Grove Dict. Music* XX. 564/2 *Xylorimba*... An instrument of the xylophone family with a compass sufficiently large to embrace the low-sounding bars of the Marimba and the highest-sounding bars of the xylophone.

Y

Y. Add: **3. a. Y cross,** (*a*) (example); hence **Y-crossed** *ppl. a.*; **Y-front,** a proprietary term for men's underwear, used esp. to denote close-fitting briefs with Y-shaped seaming at the front; freq. as *sb. pl.*, briefs of this kind; **Y gun** *U.S.*, an anti-submarine gun with two firing arms for discharging depth charges; **Y junction,** a junction at which a road forks into two branches, or one road joins another at an angle different from 90 degrees.

1881 G. G. Scott *Ess. Hist. Eng. Church Archit.* 114 St. Regnobert's chasuble at Bayeux, and St. Thomas's at Sens, are examples of the use of the Y cross in France. *Ibid.*, The Y-crossed vestment of Ruben's picture. **1953** *Trade Marks Jrnl.* 17 June 526/1 *Y-front*... Pants and vests, all for men. Lyle and Scott Limited,..Hawick, Scotland; manufacturers. **1959** H. Hobson *Mission House Murder* xxix. 188 Here I was, in my athlete's vest and Y-front briefs. **1961** *Harper's Bazaar* May 103/1 The demand for a T-shirt and a Y-front in Act II. **1976** T. Stoppard *Dirty Linen* 23 He produces..a large pair of Y-front pants. **1978** M. Page *Pilate Plot* (1979) xii. 183 He stripped to his Y-fronts and plunged into the pool. **1918** *Ann. Rep. Secretary U.S. Navy Dept.* 56 A new gun known as the 'Y' gun has been designed and built especially for firing depth charges. **1937** *Jane's Fighting Ships* 471 Y-gun or Depth Charge Projector. **1961** *Guardian* 18 Sept. 3/4 Local Y junctions where drivers.. expect others prophetically to divine the route they are about to take. **1982** M. Duke *Flashpoint* xxv. 182 When he came to a Y-junction he made a sharp turn right.

4. a. *axis of y* (example); now always *y-axis*; also *transf.*; *Y-cut* adj. (Electronics), of, pertaining to, or designating a quartz crystal cut in a plane normal to its Y-axis; *Y-plate* (Electronics), each of a pair of electrodes in an oscilloscope that control the vertical movement of the spot on the screen.

1885, etc. [see *X 3 a]. **1930**, etc. Y-cut [see *X-cut* adj. s.v. *X 3 a]. **1934** J. H. Reyner *Television* vii. 71 In the ordinary applications of the tube we apply the voltage to be examined across one pair of plates (usually termed the Y plates) which causes the spot to be elongated into a line. **1945** *Electronic Engin.* XVII. 723 These two equations define the components of the velocity of the spot along the X and Y axes. **1946** *Ibid.* XVIII. 23/2 The signal [may be] fed to one Y plate and a pulse derived from the anode of V_4 fed to the other Y plate. **1965** J. R. Frederick *Ultrasonic Engin.* iv. 65 If the second digit is 4, 5, or 6 this refers to a shear strain around the *x*, *y*, or *z* axes, respectively. **1969** Maddox & Davies *Elem. Functions* i. 12 The graph is a straight line parallel to the *y*-axis and situated 2 units to the right of the *y*-axis. **1976** *Appl. Physics Lett.* XXIX. 76/1 Our measurements were made on a polished *Y*-cut single-crystal quartz substrate with a pair of aluminum thin-film interdigital transducers ..with orientation for wave propagation along the *X* axis. **1978** D. T. Rees *Cathode Ray Oscilloscope* 9 A voltage applied to the Y-plates will move the beam and the spot in a vertical direction. **1979** Faux & Pratt *Computational Geom.* i. 18 The most familiar equation of a straight line is $y = mx + c$, in which m is the slope, and c the intercept on the *y*-axis.

b. *Genetics.* (Now always as a capital.) [After *X 3 e.] The symbol of the *Y chromosome. So **Y-linked** (stress variable) *a.*, being or determined by a gene that is carried on the Y chromosome.

1909 E. B. Wilson in *Science* 8 Jan. 57/2 The X-element..appears as a 'large idiochromosome' which has a synaptic mate... The latter chromosome, or its homologue, I shall designate as the 'Y-element'. **1910** *Amer. Naturalist* XLIV. 491 We should..imagine that when a sperm bearing a Y enters an egg a male results. **1911**, etc. [see *X 3 e]. **1917** *Amer. Naturalist* LI. 534 Y or W linked or plastid inheritance. **1949** Darlington & Mather *Elem. Genetics* ii. 51 In *Drosophila* and in man, there are completely Y-linked genes without any allelomorph in the X. **1981** *Heredity* XLVII. 238 A majority of male secondary sexual colour patterns are Y-linked [in the guppy]. **1983** M. B. Zaleski et al. *Immunogenetics* ii. 36 For essentially all mammalian species discussed in this book, females are *X/X* and males are *X/Y*... Other types of sex determination are also known to exist in various species and are called *Protenor* (females are *X/X* and males are *X/O*), *Abraxas* (females are *X/Y* and males are *X/X*) and haploidy-diploidy (males are haploid and sterile, whereas females are diploid and fertile).

7. Y (*colloq.*, chiefly *U.S.*), short for YMCA or YWCA; Y, yuan; YA (*U.S.*), young adult; YAG: see *yag; Y.E., Your Excellency; Y.F.C., Young Farmers Club (formerly Clubs); YHA, Youth Hostels Association; YIG, yttrium iron garnet; Y.M. (*colloq.*), short for YMCA; also, a YMCA hostel; Y.M.C.A.: also, a hostel run by the YMCA; YOP, Youth Opportunities Programme; also, a young person taking part in this scheme; Y.P., young prisoner; yr, year; yr., yr, your; yrs, yours; YTS, Youth Training Scheme; Y.W. (*colloq.*), short for YWCA; also, a YWCA hostel; Y.W.C.A.: also, a hostel run by the YWCA.

1915 *Dialect Notes* IV. 236 [College slang.] *Y*, abbreviation for the college Y.M.C.A. **1945** N. L. McClung *Stream runs Fast* xxvii. 259 Mary would have to have her bath at the 'Y'. **1956** H. Kurnitz *Invasion of Privacy* ii. 22 She's married to this English G.I. she met at the Y, where they have the service dances. **1977** *New Yorker* 27 June 35/3 Rose..did not yet have a place to live; she was staying at the Y. **1962** in E. Snow *Other Side of River* (1963) lxv. 495 The State invested Y. 37,000,000 in the livelihood needs and productive capital construction. **1973** *Times* 21 Mar. (China Trade Suppl.) p. iii/6 The basic unit of renminbi..is the yuan, represented by the symbol Y. **1974** *Publishers Weekly* 7 Oct. 63/1 A powerful and tragic book, 'Betrayed' is as much for adults as YAs. **1870** *Weekly Standard* (Buenos Aires) 9 Mar. 14/2, I beg to communicate to Y.E. the following despatch of Gen. Camara. **1945** G. Cunningham *Let.* 27 Nov. in N. Mitchell *Sir George Cunningham* (1968) v. 117, I feel terribly for Y.E. and for Claude A. in this. **1931** *Young Farmer* Mar. 77/1 The speakers..had motored many miles to come to this..third Y.F.C. meeting. **1960** *Farmer & Stockbreeder* 8 Mar. 65/1 This competition..is also of special interest to Y.F.C.s. **1982** *Financial Times* 30 Apr. 25/6 The YFC movement. **1931** *Ruc-Sac* July 18/1 The Y.H.A. (the Youth Hostels Association of Great Britain) have sent us an advance copy of their handbook. **1982** R. Hill *Who guards Prince* iv. vi. 228 The best British equivalent [hotel] in terms of remoteness and height would be a YHA hut. **1959** *Physical Rev. Lett.* II. 499/1 (*caption*) The specific heat per unit volume of polycrystalline YIG analyzed into its two components. **1975** D. G. Fink *Electronics Engineers' Handbk.* xiii. 113 In addition to mechanical tuning, both YIG and varactor tuning techniques are applicable. **1913** Y.M. [see *lowbrow, low-brow *a.*]. **1916** W. Owen *Let.* 1 Feb. (1967) 377 We are refused admission to the Y.M. or Canteen. **1931** R. Campbell *Georgiad* i. 25 Androgyno..Well on the road... Half way to Georgiana's Y.M. hostel. **1920** S. Lewis *Main St.* xxi. 257, I wish there were a Y.M.C.A. here, so I could take up regular exercise. **1931** R. Campbell *Georgiad* i. 17 Like some Y.M. or W.C.A. It welcomes waifs whom love has cast away. **1956** R. Macaulay *Towers of Trebizond* xiv. 157 There would be a Y.M.C.A and a Y.W.C.A., where billiards and boxing would be played. **1978** *Times Higher Educ. Suppl.* 5 May 28/5 Young people..eligible for the YOP in Cardiff..will be asked for their views. **1983** *Financial Times* 12 Apr. 19/3 One can employ a school leaver on the Youth Opportunities Scheme (YOP), the cost of whom is reimbursed by the MSC. All I had to do was take on a YOP as a personal assistant. **1952** *Chambers's Jrnl.* 1 June 356 They go all sentimental over the Y.P.s. **1976** H. Ferguson *Confessions of Long Distance Acid Head* 56 Ashford..is also used as a place where young offenders who have done Borstal, and a Borstall [*sic*] re-call, serve their sentence. These are known as Y.P.'s (young prisoners). **1880** W. Whitman *Daybks. & Notebks.* (1978) I. 172 Robert Norris..28 yrs old. **1942** W. Faulkner *Go down, Moses* 264 Percavil Brownly 26 yr Old. cleark. **1968** E. Knight in S. Henderson *Understanding New Black Poetry* (1973) iii. 326 Last yr Like a salmon quitting The cold ocean..I hitchhiked. **1772** J. Knyveton *Jrnl.* 12 June in E. Gray *Man Midwife* (1946) i. 59 The two rooms and the closet will furnish yr. obdt. with lecture rooms and office. **1811** Shelley *Let.* 3 Jan. (1964) I. 35 Not that I like yr. heroine. **1876** Ld. Beaconsfield *Let.* 13 Sept. in R. S. Churchill *Winston S. Churchill* (1967) I. Compan. i. 54, I earnestly hope that these arrangements may be consistent with Yr Grace's decision to accept the high office of the Queen's Representative in Ireland. **1973** *Black World* Sept. 84 Ever get tired of people playing with yr life? PBS. **1811** Shelley *Let.* 11 Jan. (1964) I. 38 Yr's with affection. **1922** Joyce *Ulysses* 740 Yrs affly xxxxx. **1932** W. Faulkner *Light in August* xviii. 412 Given it toe barer yrs truly. **1984** *Times* 17 Nov. 2/7 The YTS is not available for many 17-year-olds. **1985** *Times Educ. Suppl.* 9 Aug. 4/1 Thus, all one's instincts and reflexes impel one to support YTS. **1937** Partridge *Dict. Slang* 968/1 *Y.W.*...The Young Women's Christian Association. **1979** M. Soames *Clementine Churchill* xxvi. 424 Clementine never severed her links with the 'Y.W.'. **1931, 1956** Y.W.C.A. [see Y.M.C.A. above]. **1961** *Times* 10 Oct. 16/1 A jolie-laide innocent looking for the Y.W.C.A.

8. In *Particle Physics*, *Y* denotes the hypercharge quantum number of sub-atomic particles.

1956 [see *hypercharge]. **1974** S. Gasiorowicz *Quantum Physics* xxvi. 443 The missing $I = 0$, $Y = 0$ pseudoscalar meson was found in the examination of $\pi^+\pi^-\pi^0$ masses in bubble-chamber pictures.

Y' (y). **a.** Abbrev. of Ye *pers. pron.*, q.v., sense A. b.

b. Repr. a spoken abbrev. of You *pers. pron.* as subject, esp. in phrases of the type *you know, you see.*

1859 Geo. Eliot *Adam Bede* I. i. i. 7 Ye might get religion, and that 'ud be the best day's earnings y'ever made. **1889** Kipling *From Sea to Sea* (1899) I. 341 As a bell, y' know, it's rather a failure... They don't ring it properly. **1932** J. B. Priestley *Faraway* i. 49 Y'see, you know about the island. **1953** E. Coxhead *Midlanders* vii. 168 Y'know..I just wanted a spot of land to farm. **1981** J. Wainwright *All on Summer's Day* 14 But y'know ... Sopworth money also meant Sopworth bobbying.

-y⁶, -ie. Add: Also appended to surnames to form a familiar name.

1941 J. Hilton *Random Harvest* v. 352 She ran into his arms calling out: 'Oh, Smithy—Smithy—it may not be too late.' **1958** A. Hackney *Private Life* ix. 84 'Who's Old Kitey?' 'A Mr. Kite. He's our shop steward.' *Ibid.* xvii. 171 'Mr. Cox arranged it.' .. 'You've got to be careful with old Coxy.'

ya² (yā, yă) repr. *U.S.* and *dial.* pronunc. of (*a*) You *pers. pron.*; (*b*) Your *poss. adj.*

(*a*) **1941** B. Schulberg *What makes Sammy Run?* xi. 193 Sunset Club... They've got a new dinge band there that'll kill ya. **1959** N. Mailer *Advts. for Myself* (1961) 46 Stay off the railroads, they bleed ya dry. **1973** E. Bullins *Theme is Blackness* 64 Won't ya please move out of the way, honey? **1980** *Dirt Bike* Oct. 8/1 All of you mini riders can start drooling now, because as soon as we can get our gloves on one, we'll test it for ya.

(*b*) **1946** K. Tennant *Lost Haven* (1947) iii. 50 What ya done with ya collar? **1970** K. Platt *Pushbutton Butterfly* xi. 138 He waved the Luger. 'On ya feet.' I got up. **1973** *Black World* Oct. 56/2 Put ya hands on 'a table.

yaa-boo, var. *yah boo *int.* (and *sb.*).

yaas (yæs, yās), repr. a drawled pronunc. of Yes *adv.*, esp. in U.S. speech.

1893 H. A. Shands *Some Peculiarities of Speech in Mississippi* 68 *Yaas*, the almost universal pronunciation of *yes.* **1895** A. W. Pinero *Second Mrs. Tanqueray* iii. 104 *Paula.* Your wife? *Sir George.* Yaas—Birdie. **1913** Kipling *Diversity of Creatures* (1917) 285 I've become an Episcopalian since I married. Ya-as. **1931** W. Faulkner in *Harper's Mag.* Sept. 401/2 'Yaas,' the man in overalls said in a dry, drawling tone. 'Yaas. It got caught.'

ya bass (yæ bæs), repr. Sc. rendering of 'You bastard.'

1968 *Daily Tel.* (Colour Suppl.) 4 Oct. 21/2 We saw a film, *The Terror of the Tongs*... When we came out, we just started shouting: 'Tongs! Tongs, ya bass!' **1973** Boyd & Parkes *Dark Number* vii. 72 There was a crate of dead wine bottles... *Vino Fino* from Argentina, ya bass. **1974** *Punch* 6 Mar. p. v/1 That archetypal graffito, the Glaswegian *Ya bass.*

yabba (yæ·bă). *Jamaica.* Also **yabah.** [Jamaican.] A large wooden or earthenware vessel used for cookery or storage.

1889 *Victoria Q.* (Kingston, Jamaica) May 50 The familiar 'Yabba' or earthen vessel. **1929** M. W. Beckwith *Black Roadways* 27 Earthen bowls, hand turned and covered with a rude glaze, are always to be had in the Kingston market, but they are more rare in the hills where the old-time 'yabba' is being supplanted by tinware. **1953** *Caribbean Anthol. Short Stories* 103 She took a handful of cornmeal out of the wooden yabba. **1953** R. Mais *Hills were Joyful Together* i. i. 11 Ras..spat in an earthenware yabba set beside him for the purpose. **1959** A. Salkey *Quality of Violence* iv. 56 He picked up an empty *yabah* which was resting on a Bible... He..let it slip from his hands. It..splintered in jagged pieces.

yabber, *sb.* (Earlier example.)

1855 R. Carboni *Eureka Stockade* iv. 5 There was further a great waste of yabber-yabber about the diggers not being represented in the Legislative Council.

yabby (yæ·bi). *Austral.* Also **yabbie, yappy.** [Aborginal.] **a.** A small, edible freshwater crayfish found in the eastern part of Australia, esp. one of the genus *Charax.* **b.** A burrowing, prawn-like, littoral crustacean of the order Thalassinidea.

1886 F. A. Hagenauer in E. M. Curr *Austral. Race* III. 554/1 Crayfish—yappy. **1894** *Argus* (Melbourne) 6 Oct. 11/2 Small crayfish, called 'yabbies'..may be found all over Australia, both in large and small lagoons. **1897** *Australasian* 30 Jan. 224/4 The bait used is 'yabby', a small crayfish found in the sand on the beach at low tide. **1930** V. Palmer *Men are Human* vi. 49 The yabbies they had cooked in a treacle-tin down by the lagoon. **1944** *Living off Land* iii. 49 Digging out these burrows will secure yabbies... The yabbie can be toasted. **1963** A. Upfield *Madman's Bend* xvi. 130 Been in the water days, by the look of him. Yabbies been at him too. No blood, but hole's here. **1966** *Courier-Mail* (Brisbane) 1 Oct. 2/6 This tasty fresh water crustacean is more frequently called the Yabby, which immediately brings about a confusion with the much-used marine Yabby. **1973** P. White *Eye of Storm* x. 490 Used to come here after yabbies. I'd like to poke around a bit. **1977** *Caravan World* (Austral.) Jan. 105/1 A restaurant serving fresh, succulent yabbies has opened near the Murray Mouth.

ya·bby, *v.* *Austral.* [f. prec. sb.] *intr.* To hunt for yabbies. So **ya·bbying** *vbl. sb.*

1934 *Bulletin* (Sydney) 24 Oct. 21/2 Here's a sport for those who..forget their bait when yabbying. **1941** K. Tennant *Battlers* v. 53 He..asked about the boys. 'They've gone yabbying.' **1964** *Sunday Mail* (Brisbane) 5 Apr., He participated personally in yabbying forays.

ya boo, var. *yah boo *int.* (and *sb.*).

yacca, var. *YAKKA.

yacht, *sb.* Add: **b.** *yacht-club* (earlier and later examples), *marina*; **yacht basin,** a dock constructed for the mooring of yachts; a marina; **yacht broker,** a dealer in yachts; so **yacht brokerage; yacht-yard,** a yard where yachts are built or repaired.

1929 *Motorboat* 10 Mar. 20/1 For many years there has been much talk of public yacht basins. **1952** P. ATKEY *Juniper Rock* i. 2 An engine breakdown..had compelled Roy to take the *Marsouin* limping into the yacht basin at Marseilles. **1981** L. DEIGHTON *XPD* xii. 102 One of the parking places near the yacht basin. **1882** *Yachting Q.* July (Advt.), Cox and King, Yacht brokers & Yachting auctioneers. **1982** N. J. CRISP *Brink* ix. 187 The yacht brokers were still in business... The pubs were still full of yachting types. **1974** J. DIMONA *Last Man at Arlington* I. 51 In Nassau..he had managed to set up a profitable yacht brokerage. **1834** G. CRABBE JR. in *Poet. Wks. G. Crabbe* I. 13 A party of amateur sailors was formed—the yacht club of Aldborough. **1981** L. DEIGHTON *XPD* xii. 101 The Marina del Rey..has the swanky yacht club as a centre-piece. **1973** 'A. YORK' *Captivator* ii. 32 The ah, sloop put into Cuxhaven... It entered the yacht marina there, secured a berth. **1983** P. FERRIS *Distant Country* ii. 15 The yacht marina..would reopen with brand-new quays and pontoons. **1933** 'L. LUARD' *All Hands* 236 The proprietor of a yacht-yard. **1980** P. MOYES *Angel Death* xx. 248 We have to get down there..to the yacht yard. There's something wrong.

yachtie (yǫ·ti), *sb. colloq.* (chiefly *Austral.* and *N.Z.*). Also **yachty.** [f. YACHT *sb.* + -IE.] A yachtsman.

1943 *Amer. Speech* XVIII. 88 [New Zealand English.] Yachty. **1965** G. MCINNES *Road to Gundagai* x. 184 One should never..leave them [*sc.* bottles] bobbing about the bay the way the careless 'yachties' did. **1972** *Sat. Rev.* 21 Oct. 62 Dunnie's a yachtie, he lives up on the cliff, and he's a rich guy. **1976–7** *Sea Spray* (N.Z.) Dec./Jan. 35/2 (Advt.), Laid polyester rope. The yachties' workhorse. **1977** *Herald* (Melbourne) 17 Jan. 19/2 They are really to cater for the spillover from Port Phillip Bay as more and more yachties realise that they can be much nearer to the blue water both inside and outside. **1977** *Pacific Islands Monthly* Feb. 25 (*heading*) Slugged yachtie.

yachting, *vbl. sb.* Add: In *attrib.* use applied *esp.* to garments designed for use on yachts.

1873 *Young Englishwoman* June 280/2, I always wear yachting shoes without heels, made of the white canvas, and with leather toes and straps, as now worn by boating and yachting gentlemen. **1894** *Country Gentlemen's Catal.* 155/1 Blue cloth yachting caps, from 8/6. **1931** E. F. BENSON *Mapp & Lucia* vii. 200 Contempt for Georgie..had been intensified by the sight of his yachting cap. **1976** 'A. GARVE' *Home to Roost* iii. 37 He was wearing..a battered old yachting cap. **1983** G. THOMPSON *Nobody cared for Kate* iv. 26 Maggie..had dressed for the barge trip... She wore a yachting suit.

yachty (yǫ·ti), *a. colloq.* [f. YACHT *sb.* + -Y[1].] Of or pertaining to yachts.

1950 E. ALLCARD *Single-Handed Passage* 177 Don't use 'yachty' fittings. They are only good for the Solent. **1983** *Times* 19 Aug. 24/1 The yachts displace a lot of money which slops into the town to support..galleries selling yachty prints.

yack, *sb.* Add: **2.** *slang.* Also **yak. a.** Incessant talk of a trivial or boring nature. Freq. reduplicated and as *int.*

1958 J. CANNAN *And be Villain* i. 5 That blasted Primrose will have arrived by now—yak yak yak, talking Eve into God knows what. **1965** W. KING in *Black Short Story Anthol.* (1972) 306 Then, through the yak-yak, Mac began to tell us the 'unusual something' that he had just recently done. **1972** C. WESTON *Poor, Poor Ophelia* (1973) xxxii. 205 A lot of yak in the news about the missing boot. **1983** N. FREELING *Back of North Wind* 99 The sudden head-down butt jabbed into someone's face, is a highly effective way of putting a stop to his yack.

b. An accent or tone of voice.

1957 M. SPARK *Comforters* vi. 138 He fiddled with the tape machine... The voice came with an exaggerated soppy yak: 'Caroline, darling.' **1975** *Camping & Trailering Guide* Oct. 33/1 You will hear French Canadian patois mixed with Ontario English, down-Maine tones and New York yak.

yack (yæk), *v. slang.* Also **yak.** [Echoic, or f. prec. sb.] *intr.* To engage in trivial or unduly persistent conversation; to chatter.

1950 'P. QUENTIN' *Follower* v. 38 Yakked a lot. Know how she is. Talk your ear off... She yakked on about you being in South America. **1955** 'H. ROBBINS' *Stone for Danny Fisher* I. ix. 65, I was busy yakking with a broad. **1956** W. H. WHYTE *Organization Man* (1957) xxvi. 359 Four or five of the girls and their kids will be yakking away. **1958** T. ROETHKE *Let.* 16 Aug. (1970) 220 I've spent nearly the whole of three sessions with my doctor yacking about you. **1958** L. WHISHAW *As far as You'll take Me* iv. 47 Didn't have any breakfast, too busy yacking about women. **1977** J. PORTER *Who the Heck is Sylvia?* vi. 57 She should have acted first and yacked about it afterwards. **1981** J. TRENHAILE *Kyril* xix. 142 Those two will yak all day.

Hence **ya·cking, yakking** *vbl. sb.* and *ppl. a.*

1959 'S. RANSOME' *I'll die for You* ii. 29 She could sit at any bar.., with an ear out for all the yakking that goes on, and pick up any amount of gossip. **1971** *Time* 7 June 31/1 [The ability] to switch away from yakking actresses and the necessity of having yakking starlets for the ratings. **1976** N. FREELING *Lake Isle* xxvii. 192 Shopkeepers..yelling in the street at yacking housewives. **1977** *N.Y. Rev. Bks.* 12 May 6/4 The sound which emerges from the pages is that of the yakking of debutantes.

yacker (yæ·kəɹ), *sb. slang.* Also **yakker.** [Echoic.] **1.** Talk, conversation, chatter. *Austral.*

1882 *Sydney Slang Dict.* 9/1 Yacker, talk. **1973** P. WHITE *Eye of Storm* vii. 306 She wished it had been a hospital, when she could have produced a chart, handed over.., and swept off without further yakker. *Ibid.* ix. 441 Couldn't get on with me work—not with all the yakker that was goin' on in 'ere.

2. [f. *YACK *v.* + -ER[1].] **a.** A chatterbox or gossip. **b.** = *YACK *sb.* 2 b.

1959 G. MITCHELL *Man who grew Tomatoes* vi. 87 Now that will be enough ammunition for the yakkers, if there are any present. **1960** 'R. SIMONS' *Frame for Murder* viii. 99 'What sort of a bloke?' 'Tall. Flashy dressed. Got a slight American yakker.' **1973** *Tel.* (Brisbane) 13 Sept. 30/1 Last, but hardly least, is the yakker, who talks continually to his passengers. **1984** *N.Y. Times* 28 Aug. B-2/5 She just brought the parrot along for the ride... He was quite a yakker.

yacker (yæ·kəɹ), *v. slang.* [f. *YACK *v.* + -ER[5].] = *YACK *v.*

1961 S. PRICE *Just for Record* x. 109 They're yackering away in the kitchen. **1982** *Financial Times* 20 Aug. 11/4 'Yellow Polka-Dot Bikini'—one of the scratchy 78s..—yackers melodiously while the characters gallivant through daytime Calcutta.

yacket (yæ·kėt), *v. slang.* [f. *YACKET(Y *int.*] *intr.* = *YACK *v.* So **ya·cketing** *ppl. a.*

[**1953**: see *YACKETY-YACK(ET)ING *vbl. sb.* and *ppl. a.*] **1958** P. DE VRIES *Mackerel Plaza* 153 All this yacketing oratory. **1969** *New Yorker* 29 Nov. 51/3 We warn them, we yacket away night and day..but they never learn.

yackety (yæ·kėti), *int. slang.* Also **yackity, yaketty, yakkety, yakkity.** [Echoic.] Expressing the sound of incessant chatter. Usu. reduplicated or with *ya(c)k*.

1953 BERREY & VAN DEN BARK *Amer. Thes. Slang* (1954) § 189/2 Idle talk; chatter... Yackety-yack,.. yackety-yackety. **1955** M. MILLAR *Beast in View* vi. 93 She..parks herself in the phone booth, and there she sits, yackity, yackity, yackity. **1959** S. GIBBONS *Pink Front Door* iii. 36 She went yaketty-yak to Katy. **1959** L. SMITH *One Hour* (1960) xviii. 231 The TV going yakkety yak. **1959** 'J. WELCOME' *Stop at Nothing* vii. 113 Mildred..has been going yackety yack-yack about you to some purpose. **1976** *Billings* (Montana) *Gaz.* 26 June 5-B/5 I'm talking away, yakkity yak, and he started gasping for breath. **1982** D. BAGLEY *Windfall* xxix. 288 The Sergeant ..only talks when he has something to say. Everybody else goes yacketty-yack all the time.

Also **ya:ckety-ya·ck(ety** *sb.* = *YACK *sb.* 2 a; *v. intr.* = *YACK *v.*; **ya:ckety-ya·ck(et)ing** *vbl. sb.* and *ppl. a.*

1953 M. DICKENS *No More Meadows* iv. 185 Our laundry's full of yackety-yacketing women this morning. **1958** *Observer* 15 June 15/7 A muddle-headed momma.. who knows no better than to drive away her husband..by constant yackety-yack and pleas to stay at home. **1959** *Woman* 6 June 10/1 For once the place will be free of giggles and girlish yakitty-yak. **1960** *N.Y. Times Bk. Rev.* 3 July 1 (*heading*) How to dig the hips' yackety-yak. **1976** *Billings* (Montana) *Gaz.* 26 June B-14/8 A man working alone could never have enjoyed 'chewing the fat and the yakety yaking and drinking coffee'.

yaffle, *sb.*[2] Add: **2.** The call of the green woodpecker.

1955 D. A. BANNERMAN *Birds Brit. Isles* IV. 77 It [*sc.* the green woodpecker] is a bird which attracts attention by its loud cry or 'yaffle'. **1976** *Southern Even. Echo* (Southampton) 12 Nov. 18/4 The yaffle of a green woodpecker and needle-like sounds from the tits and goldcrests.

yaffle (yæ·f'l, yǫ·f'l), *v.*[2] *dial.* Also **yoffle.** [Echoic.] *intr.* To eat or drink, esp. noisily or greedily.

1788 GROSE *Dict. Vulgar T.*, *Yaffling*, eating. *a* **1821** J. W. MASTERS *Dick & Sal at Canterbury Fair* in Parish & Shaw *Dict. Kentish Dialect.* (1887) p. xx, Sa when we lickt de platters out, An yoffled down de beer. *a* **1935** T. E. LAWRENCE *Mint* (1955) viii. 30 You bloody swaddies can't half yaffle.

yag (yæg). Also **YAG.** [f. the initial letters of *yttrium aluminium garnet*.] A synthetic crystal of yttrium aluminium garnet, used in certain lasers and as a simulated diamond in jewellery.

1964 *Q. Rep. Bell Telephone Lab.* No. 2 (AD 439–628). 3 The splitting of the ^7F_J..manifolds of the trivalent Europium and Terbium ions..has been used to calculate crystal field parameters for Eu and Tb in YAG. **1964** *Appl. Physics Lett.* V. 201/2 Predictions of the laser behavior were tested on singly and doubly doped YAG crystals. **1971** *Daily Tel.* 22 Nov. 13 Have you got a yag yet? They are the latest form of simulated diamonds. Almost as hard as a sapphire, which is almost as hard as a diamond, they are 'grown' in America, brought over here to be faceted, set in 18-carat gold in Hatton Garden and sold as Diamonairs. **1977** *Jrnl. R. Soc. Arts* CXXV. 779/2 The YAG laser..is used routinely..for trimming resistors. **1979** [see *SIMULANT *sb.*]. **1984** *National Geographic* Mar. 341/2 A flash lamp can excite atoms of neodymium, a rare earth, in a rod of YAG.

‖**yagé** (yā·ʒe, yāhē·). Also **yage, yajé.** [Amer. Sp.] **a.** A South American liana of the genus *Banisteriopsis* used by the Indians to make a hallucinogenic infusion. **b.** The drink made from this.

1924 C. W. DOMVILLE-FIFE *Among Wild Tribes of Amazons* xvi. 229 A curious potion is made from a plant called *yagé*. **1931** *Jrnl. Washington Acad. Sci.* XXI. 487 One of the most interesting plants found in the region of the upper courses of the Putumayo and Caquetá Rivers [in Colombia] is the *yagé*. The Indians make a beverage from either the wild or cultivated *yagé*, boiling it in a large earthenware vessel an entire day... They add to the *yagé* the leaves and the young shoots of the *oco yagé* or *chagro panga*.., and it is the addition of this plant which produces the 'bluish aureole' of their visions. **1945** F. R. FOSBERG in F. Verdoorn *Plants & Plant Sci. Lat. Amer.* 28/1 Two other plants..are used by the Amazonian Indians for their narcotic effect. *Maikoa* (*Brugmansia arborea*) and *yagé* or *caapi* (*Banisteriopsis caapi*) both produce hallucinations. **1953** W. BURROUGHS *Junkie* xv. 149 Maybe I will find in yage what I was looking for in junk and weed and coke. **1960** *Spectator* 29 July 176 Yage, a vine-bark stew..supposedly invests the user with telepathic powers. **1969** *Science* 17 Jan. 253/2 The Siona of today frequently mix *Datura* leaves with *Banisteriopsis* in preparing yajé. **1975** *High Times* Dec. 80/1 You trek 900 miles overland into the Amazon jungle to sample yagé in its natural habitat. **1977** LEWIS & ELVIN-LEWIS *Med. Bot.* xviii. 413/1 No more interesting or complex narcotic drink can be found than ayahuasca, caapi, or yaje.

yager. b. Substitute for def.: An obsolete kind of rifle. Also *yager rifle*. (Earlier and later examples.)

1817 E. P. FORDHAM *Narr. Trav.* (1906) 141 Sent the two P—s..for the yager rifle, and the Wallet. **1826** T. FLINT *Francis Berrian* I. 60 Their trade with the Americans supplied them with rifles and yagers. *a* **1918** G. STUART *40 Yrs. on Frontier* (1925) I. 187 Nine Pipes.. came to get a nipple to put on his Yager rifle.

Yaghan, var. *YAHGAN.

Yaghnobi (yɑgnǭ·bi). Also **Yagnobi.** A modern Iranian language spoken by the Yaghnobs in parts of Tadzhikistan.

1932 W. L. GRAFF *Lang. & Languages* x. 372 Many.. Iranian dialects..are spoken over large areas of Asia. The chief among them are the Caspian, the Kurdish,..the Yagnobi, and the Ossetic dialect. **1960** *Language* XLIV. 281 The alternative is to assume the more traditional view that Sogdian is a descendant of Avestan, and Yaghnobi of Sogdian. **1974** *Encycl. Brit. Macropædia* IX. 451/2 Yaghnobi is still spoken by a small number of people southeast of Samarkand. It has two main dialects.

Yagi (yā·gi). *Broadcasting.* The name of Hidetsugu *Yagi* (b. 1886), Japanese scholar and electrical engineer, used *attrib.* and *absol.* to designate a highly directional aerial that he invented (*Proc. IRE* (1928) XVI. 715) for receiving or transmitting VHF or UHF waves within a narrow frequency band, consisting of a number of short rods mounted transversely on an insulating support that points towards the signal source.

1943 *Gloss. Terms Telecomm.* (*B.S.I.*) 66 The term *Yagi aerial*, which relates to a particular form of end-fire array, should not be used as a generic term for all end-fire arrays. **1950** *Austral. Jrnl. Sci. Res.* A. III. 20 The array of nine Yagis in three groups of three, one wavelength apart, is fixed on an equatorial mounting. **1951** A. C. CLARKE *Sands of Mars* iv. 42 He produced a rough sketch of a simple Yagi aerial. **1960** *Practical Wireless* XXXVI. 362/2 (Advt.), 2 Metre beam 5 element W.S. Yagi. **1975** L. DEIGHTON *Yesterday's Spy* xi. 88 Did he think we needed the eight Yagi aerials for TV?

Yagnobi, var. *YAGHNOBI.

yagona: see *YANGGONA.

yah, *adv.* (Earlier example, representing Lancashire speech.)

1863 A. J. MUNBY *Diary* 20 Aug. in D. Hudson *Munby* (1972) 170 'Dus Jaan Brahn work here?' 'Yah!' said some of the maidens: 'Aye!' said others.

yah boo (yā bū), *int.* (and *sb.*). *slang* (orig. *children's*). Also **ya(a) boo** and with hyphen. [f. YAH *int.*[1] + BOO *int.*] An exclamation of scorn or derision. Also *attrib.* and *transf.*

1921 H. WILLIAMSON *Beautiful Years* 83 Willie and Jack, scorning to reply to the yaa-boos of the retreating urchins, were licking their hurts. **1926** 'R. CROMPTON' *William the Conqueror* i. 16 'Yah—boo, softie!' he called over the wall. **1961** *Times* 7 Apr. 20/7 It [*sc.* a boo] is far from a pretty sound—rather moronic, in fact—and smacks too much of the 'yah boo' which used to be the height of brilliant preparatory school repartee. **1968** [see *SUCK *sb.*[1] 11]. **1973** *Times* 28 Dec. 8/6 People..who are tired of the 'Yah-boo' school of debate. *a* **1976** A. CHRISTIE *Autobiogr.* (1977) II. ii. 76 Two small boys arrived..preparing as usual to say, 'Yah. Boo. Shan't go.' **1981** *London Rev. Bks.* 19 Nov.–2 Dec. 12/2 The impatient rejection of 'Ya! Boo!' politics.

Hence **yah boo sucks** [*SUCK *sb.*[1] 11], used similarly.

1980 'A. SKINNER' *Mind's Eye* xiii. 181 Ya boo sucks to anyone who was interested. **1983** *Listener* 22 Dec. 62/2 This is neither a tranche of free advertising, nor a yah-boo-sucks to temperance advocates.

Yahgan (yā·găn). Also **Yaghan, -ane.** [App. a native name.] (A member of) one of the three indigenous peoples of Tierra del Fuego, found in the most southerly part of the slands. Also *attrib.* or as *adj.*

1884 *Proc. R. Geogr. Soc.* VI. 348 The natives, who inhabit Tierra del Fuego and this archipelago of Cape Horn, belong to three principal tribes:..(iii.) the Yaghanes, inhabiting both banks of the Beagle Passage and all the islands in the south of the archipelago. *Ibid.* 349 The Yaghane..passes his time squatting in his hut. **1961** G. CLARK *World Prehistory* ix. 238 (*heading*) Yahgan, Ona and Alacu peoples of Tierra del Fuego. *Ibid.*, The Yahgan and their neighbours the Ona and Alacu maintained down to modern times the most southerly settlements of mankind. **1972** *Bk. of Thousand Tongues* (rev. ed.) 459/1 The Yahgan language, which once comprised five mutually intelligible dialects, is related to no other known tongue. **1974** *Encycl. Brit. Macropædia* VIII. 1159/2 The Yahgan are canoe-using fishermen and shellfish gatherers. **1983** *Times* 9 July (Saturday Suppl.) 2/8 Of the poor, ill-clad and wretched Yahganes there is only one left.

yahoo, *sb.* Add: **1.** (Further examples.) In mod. use, a person lacking cultivation or sensibility, a philistine; a lout, a hooligan.

1912 J. SANDILANDS *Western Canad. Dict. & Phrase-Bk.*, *Yahoo*, a lout from the back-country, an ignoramus, a know-nothing. **1914** 'I. HAY' *Lighter Side School Life* iii. 83 You must not behave like a yahoo in my mathematical set. **1943** J. LEES-MILNE *Ancestral Voices* (1975) 200, I took the young yahoo..to the station. **1968** *Courier-Mail* (Brisbane) 21 May 6/4 A Brisbane boat owner has complained that 'young yahoos' are stripping cars left at bayside boat ramps. **1977** *New Yorker* 20 June 56/2 Sarge Waller—who is, among other things, a professional riverman—later commented on Cook and Ulvi's journey and described them as 'yahoos'.

2. = WILD MAN 2.

c **1810–20** *Handbill*, During the Fair... Two surprising large Yohoes; or, Wild Men of the Woods, being the most Wonderful of the kind ever Exhibited. **1814** *Lincoln, Rutland & Stamford Mercury* 22 Apr. 3/5 Just arrived, and to be seen in a commodious booth, in the Crown and Anchor Yard, Lincoln... The Great Yahoo, or Wild Man of the Woods.

3. *Austral.* [Perh. a different word.] A probably mythical creature resembling a big hairy man, said to haunt eastern Australia. Cf. *YOWIE².

1842 in G. C. JOYNER *Hairy Man South Eastern Austral.* 1977) 5 A contested point has long existed among Australian naturalists whether or not such an animal as the Yahoo existed. **1844** L. A. MEREDITH *Notes & Sketches N.S.W.* x. 95 They have an *evil* spirit, which causes them great terror, whom they call 'Yahoo', or 'Devil-devil.' **1876** *Austral. Town & Country Jrnl.* 4 Nov. 729 For many years past it had been believed by the settlers of that wild part of the country, that the Walla Walla scrub was inhabited by a monster called 'the hairy man of the wood', or what all the blacks stand so much in dread of—the Yahoo. **1937** *Mankind* II. iv. 91 [J.N., a Kumtangerai, told me that big hairy men lived in the scrub at Nana Glen (North Coast, N.S.W.), and were called by the native Jarrā-wahu.] *Ibid.*, In the Mudgee district..a scrubby place was reputed to be the abode of a 'Yahu', and a resident in the Maitland district told me a 'Yahu' was reputed to live in thick scrub there. Each said he was a big hairy man.

yahoodom: also, behaviour characteristic of a yahoo; (earlier example).

1890 KIPLING *Let.* in C. Carrington *Rudyard Kipling* (1955) vii. 162 The grotesque Yahoodom of nipping pieces off a half-presented foetus and slamming it into the market.

yahrzeit (yā·ɹtsəit). Also **jahr-; yore-, yort-** (yǫ·ɹ-); and with capital initial. [Yiddish, f. MHG *jarzît* anniversary, f. OHG. *jâr* YEAR + *zît* time.] Among Jews, the anniversary of the death of someone, esp. a parent.

1852 *Asmonean* 10 Dec. 91/1 Men, who..when they have Yahrzeit, will go to congregational meetings, and oppose most violently every reform measure. **1876** GEO. ELIOT *Dan. Deronda* II. iv. xxxiv. 359 'Your mother has been a widow a long while, perhaps.'..'Ay, ay, it's a good many *yore-zeit* since I had to manage for her and myself,' said Cohen. **1881** *Fraser's Mag.* Apr. 496 On the *Jahrzeit* Maier takes the boy to the synagogue. **1917** E. FERBER *Fanny Herself* 200 There would be no *Yahrzeit* light burning for twenty-four hours. **1964** W. MARKFIELD *To an Early Grave* (1965) x. 177 They buried my brother-in-law... In two and a half weeks, God spare us, he'll have his *yahrzeit*. **1971** I. B. SINGER *Isaac Bashevis Singer Reader* 300 Their 'questions' inevitably concerned the observance of a *yortzeit*.

Yahtzee (yā·tsi). Chiefly *U.S.* [f. YACHT *sb.*] The proprietary name of a game (orig. 'the yacht game') played with dice and a score sheet.

1957 *Official Gaz.* (U.S. Patent Office) 1 Jan. TM 12/2 E. S. Lowe Company, Inc., New York... *Yahtzee*. For poker dice games. **1970** *Trade Marks Jrnl.* 8 Apr. 563/1 *Yahtzee*... Boxed games; dice, boards, counters and cards (other than ordinary playing cards), all for games. E. S. Lowe Company, Inc... New York. **1973** M. KAYE *Toy is Born* 56 Initially popular as a men's game—probably because of the gambling mystique of dice—Yahtzee went on to fascinate women's clubs. **1974** *N.Y. Times* 10 Nov. II. 37 We sat with a few friends and played Yahtzee all night long. **1977** *Monitor* (McAllen, Texas) 19 June 5c/1 Following the dinner, members met..and spent the evening listening to music and playing Yahtzee.

Yahudi (yăhū·di). *slang* (orig. and chiefly *U.S.*). Also 9 **Yahooda, -ee, Yehoodi; Yehudi.** [Arab. *yahūdī*, Heb. *yehudi* JEW sb.] **a.** A Jew; Jews. **b.** *attrib.* as *adj.* Jewish.

1823 C. M. DOUGHTY *Trav. Arabia Deserta* II. 382 When I was trafficking in Irâk, I had dealings with a certain Yahûdi. **1858** *Asmonean* 19 Mar. 180/3 We are credibly informed that not less than eight hundred families of Yehoodim..are utterly destitute. **1862** J. A. GRANT *Jrnl.* 14 Aug. in *Walk across Africa* (1864) xi. 264 Frij and all Seedees believe that the Jews, or Yahoodee, living in Calcutta, seize people, and tie them up by the heels till blood falls from them into a dish. **1900** G. ADE *More Fables* 117 The flip Yahooda, with the City Education and Thirty Centuries of Commercial Training.., saw that here was a Chance to work off some Old Stock. **1930** R. L. STRAUSS *Amer. Remnant* 117 Dot *mensch* certainly knew his bissness..and look at all the *Yehudim* here too! **1932** [see *HUBSHEE *sb.* and *a.*]. **1959** I. JEFFERIES *Thirteen Days* i. 16 As far as the Yehudis were concerned I knew the dirt that was being done. *Ibid.* vi. 83 We ate well, and drank a good Yehudi wine. **1977** *Washington Post* 17 June c-5/3, I see the hate in your eyes, you Yahudi (Jewish) whore, and when we go to work on you, you'll be sorry.

Yahweh. Add: Now the usual form of the word among scholars.

1885 *Studia Biblica* I. 3 Delitzsch..propounds the following theory. The forms *Yahu*, *Yah*,..are of foreign origin. The form *Yahweh*, on the other hand, is distinctively Hebrew. **1913** H. W. ROBINSON *Relig. Ideas of Old Test.* iii. 53 No certain evidence for the pre-Mosaic use of the form Yahweh..seems yet to have been brought forward. **1936** W. L. WARDLE *Hist. & Relig. Israel* viii. 147 God reveals to Moses as something previously unknown that his name is Yahweh. **1958** S. GODMAN tr. *Noth's Hist. Israel* I. ii. 99 In Jos. xxiv, there is no mention at all of sacrifices, but rather of a profession of faith in Yahweh. **1973** D. J. WISEMAN *Peoples Old Testament Times* p. xxi, The Sinai covenant was the seal of Yahweh's choice of the people. **1984** *Church Times* 23 Nov. 7/2 He is a New Testament scholar concerned to expound..the growth of the biblical idea of Yahweh as the God who cares for the poor.

yair (yēᵊɹ), Austral. var. of *YEAH *adv.*

1953 A. UPFIELD *Venom House* i. 3 'You manage all right without brakes?' 'Yair. Nothing wrong with the ruddy engine to ease her up.' **1959** S. H. COURTIER *Death in Dream Time* xii. 164 'My coat still there?' 'Yair.' **1964** R. BRADDON *Year Angry Rabbit* (1967) i. 8 'You can virtually rig the ballot in two of our most important rural divisions?' 'Yair,' said Alfill. **1977** C. MCCULLOUGH *Thorn Birds* xv. 344 Yair, but in the glasshouse youse don't keep getting shot at. **1980** *Herald* (Melbourne) (City ed.) 14 Apr. 2/2 Yair, but it was only in Melbourne.

yajé, var. *YAGÉ.

yak. a. For *Poephagus* read *Bos* and add earlier example.

1795 *Asiatick Res.* IV. 351 The Yak of Tartary..is about the heighth of an English bull.

b. *yak-herd*; **yak butter**, butter made from the milk of the yak; **yak lace** (earlier example).

1962 L. DAVIDSON *Rose of Tibet* v. 87 He had bought tea bricks..and a large cake of yak butter. **1980** *Times* 12 Aug. 10/1 Crowds file through the little shrine rooms lit by flickering lamps of yak butter. **1958** *Illustr. London* (City ed.) 14 Apr. 2/2 Yair, but it was only in Melbourne. *News* 13 Dec. 1041/1 Greatest of all the village-festivals was the *Dumje*, celebrated in early July, before the villagers dispersed with their yak-herds to the high pastures. **1872** *Young Englishwoman* Nov. 606/1 The trimming consists of a narrow passementrie border and black yak lace.

yak, var. *YACK *sb.*, *v.*

‖**yakdan** (yæ·kdān). Also 9 **yakhdan.** [Pers. *yakhdān* ice-house, (also) portmanteau, f. *yakh* ice + *dān*, (affix denoting) what holds or contains anything.] In Iran, a trunk or portmanteau.

1824 J. J. MORIER *Adv. Hajji Baba* II. vii. 112, I was in want of a pair of *yakhdans*, or trunks. **1922** *Blackw. Mag.* June 761/1 The bachelor's rule should be never to possess anything which he cannot squeeze into a yakdan. **1954** J. MASTERS *Bhowani Junction* xxxvii. 320 Then he delved in a yakdan and brought out some food I'd had cooked. **1978** 'M. M. KAYE' *Far Pavilions* i. 13 Four locked *yakdans* containing botanical specimens

yaketty, var. *YACKETY *int.* **yakhdan,** var. *YAKDAN.

Yakima (yæ·kimă), *sb.* and *a.* Also 9 **Yacama; Iakima.** [Native name.] **A.** *sb.* **a.** (A member of) a group of American Indians who lived in the area of the Columbia and Yakima Rivers in south central Washington before their confinement, with other tribes, on the Yakima Reservation in 1858; since then, (a member of) the Indians of this reservation. **b.** The language of the Yakima, a member of the Sahaptin group. **B.** *adj.* Pertaining to or designating the Yakima.

1852 S. EASTMAN in H. R. Schoolcraft *Indian Tribes U.S.* (1853) III. *facing* p. 96 Yackimas. **1855** *N.Y. Herald* 15 Nov. 2/3 All the Yacama Indians are in the field, and the war has fairly begun. **1857** *Spirit of Times* 4 July 277/3, I have..become a sub in one of Uncle Sam's regular regiments engaged in the late campaigns against the Yakima. **1940** M. W. SMITH *Puyallup-Nisqually* 20 The two Sahaptin dialects, Kittitas and Iakima. **1946** J. T. ADAMS *Album Amer. Hist.* III. 84 In 1855 The Yakimas attacked parties of prospectors. **1973** A. H. WHITEFORD *N. Amer. Indian Arts* 39 The..Yakima..make baskets with thick, hard coils of cedar root strips. **1976** *Billings* (Montana) *Gaz.* 1 July 3-B/2 Indians..led by Sid Mills, a Yakima Indian from Washington. **1978** [see *RANKLE *v.* 5 b].

‖**yakitori** (yækitōᵊ·ri). Also **yaki-tori.** [Jap., f. *yaki* toasting, grilling + *tori* bird.] A Japanese dish consisting of pieces of chicken grilled on a skewer.

1962 M. DOI *Art of Jap. Cookery* 69 Yaki-tori... Chicken Meat..cut into mouthfuls..and soak ten minutes in *tare*... Place skewered chicken directly over fire and broil. **1970** J. KIRKUP *Japan behind Fan* 4 *Yakitori* stands selling bamboo skewers of roasted bits of chicken and liver. **1983** *Daily Tel.* 10 Nov. 17/2 We have planned a modest meal..making the main course one of two Japanese skewered specialities: one called Yakitori.

yakka (yæ·kă). *Austral. slang.* Also **yacca, yacka, yacker, yakker.** [Aboriginal.] Work, toil; esp. in phr. *hard yakka.*

1888 *Boomerang* 14 Jan. 13 The Brisbane wharf labourers..are so accustomed to hard yacker that they can't be happy for a single day without it. **1898** *Bulletin* (Sydney) 8 Oct. 31/2 Some [swagmen] ask for 'yacker', some's lookin' for 'graft', and some's 'after a job'. **1906** [see *AFTER *colloq. abbrev.*]. **1909** H. THOMPSON *Ballads about Business* 91 You'll be sure to get some yacker and more country you will see. **1939** X. HERBERT in E. M. Fry *Tales by Australians* 133 It'd be a richer country if everyone..did real hard honest yakker. **1944** *Coast to Coast 1943* 121 They'd been shoved in the background, told they weren't wanted, all the hard yacca put upon them in the home. **1946** K. TENNANT *Lost Haven* (1947) 139, I vote we leave the Methodist part alone, and go and clear up where somebody's going to get some *benefit* out of our yacka. **1948** V. PALMER *Golconda* iv. 28 If there's a cove on this field making money at anything but hard yakker it isn't Macy Donovan. **1968** *Courier-Mail* (Brisbane) 13 Nov. 6/7 Australian scholarships have always been hard yakka. **1981** *National Times* (Austral.) 2 Aug. 29/1 He imposes some hard yakka on his readers.

yakker, var. *YACKER *sb.*, *YAKKA. **yakkety,** var. *YACKETY *int.* **yakking** var. *YACKING *vbl. sb.* **yakkity,** var. *YACKETY *int.*

‖**yaksha** (ya·kʃă). *Indian Mythol.* Also **yaksa,** and with capital initial. Fem. **yakshī, yakshi·ṇī.** [Skr. *yakṣa*, fem. *yakṣī*, *yakṣiṇī*.] **a.** Any of a class of demi-gods or nature spirits, often inoffensive tutelary guardians of a place; *esp.* one attendant upon Kubera, the god of wealth. **b.** A statue or carving representing one of these.

1785 C. WILKINS tr. *Bhăgvăt-Gēētā* xi. 92 The *Găndhărvs* and the *Yăkshăs*, with the holy tribes of *Soors*, all stand gazing on thee, and all alike amazed! **1810** E. MOOR *Hindu Pantheon* 276 His servants and companions are the *Yakshas* and *Guhyakas*, into whose forms transmigrate the souls of those men who in this life are addicted to sordid and base passions, or absorbed in worldly prosperity. **1882** A. BARTH *Religions of India* v. 164 Civa.. sits enthroned on Kailâsa, the fabulous mountain of the North..surrounded and waited on by the Yakshas. **1928** A. K. COOMARASWAMY *Yaksas* I. 17 The essential element of a Yakṣa holystead is a stone table or altar..placed beneath the tree sacred to the Yakṣa. **1931** *Times Lit. Suppl.* 24 Dec. 1042/1 The important part played by *yakshas* in Buddhist religion and art is incontestable. **1963** *Times* 12 Feb. 12/4 The highest price of the afternoon was..paid..for a fifth century..carving of a Yakshi or tree nymph, probably part of a pillar. **1971** *Illustr. Weekly India* 11 Apr. 9/1 (*caption*) Each Tirthankara is identified by the tree under which the vows of asceticism were taken and the attendant yakshas and yakshinis. **1977** *Jrnl. R. Soc. Arts* CXXV. 570/2 This seated *yakṣa*, perhaps Kubera, from Nagpur District..has only recently come to light.

Yakut (yæku·t), *sb.* and *a.* Also 8 **Yakouti, Yakuty,** 9 **Yakute.** [Russ.] **A.** *sb.* **a.** (A member of) a Mongoloid people of northeastern Siberia who now form most of the population of the Yakutsk Republic of the Soviet Union.

1763 J. BELL *Travels* I. 240 The Yakuty differ little from the Tongusians. **1797** *Encycl. Brit.* XVI. 570/2 Besides these, there are in the Russian dominions the Nagay Tartars;..the Yakouti; and the white Kalmuks. **1890** J. G. FRAZER *Golden Bough* I. i. 26 When the day is hot and a Yakut has a long way to go. **1974** T. P. WHITNEY tr. *Solzhenitsyn's Gulag Archipelago* I. I. ii. 51 The Yakuts were imprisoned after the revolt of 1928. **1981** M. C. SMITH *Gorky Park* I. viii. 107 Some twenty-odd Russians and Yakuts surrounding a small group of Westerners and Japanese.

b. The language of the Yakuts, an Altaic one usually placed in the Turkic group.

1908 T. G. TUCKER *Introd. Nat. Hist. of Lang.* viii. 134 The linguistic connection within this group is very close, the languages of the extremes, Turkish and Yakut, for instance, being at least as distinctly related as English and German. **1951** W. K. MATTHEWS *Languages U.S.S.R.* ii. 8 Before the Revolution Yukagir was proscribed in favour of Yakut and Russian. **1976** 'S. HARVESTER'

Siberian Road xiv. 165 The middle-aged woman translated what he said into a language he took to be Yakut.

B. *adj.* Pertaining to or designating the Yakuts.

1854 Max Müller in C. Bunsen *Outl. Philos. Universal Hist.* I. 279 The Yakute dialect became separated at a very early time from the still undivided Turko-Tataric speech. **1887** *Encycl. Brit.* XXII. 9/1 The Tunguses.. occupy as their hunting-grounds an immense region on the high plateau and its slopes to the Amur, but their limits are yearly becoming more and more circumscribed both by Russian gold-diggers and by Yakut settlers. **1963** V. Nabokov *Gift* iv. 267 Making clumsy paper boats for Yakut children. **1981** I. Boland tr. *Ginzburg's Within Whirlwind* II. iv. 218 He was a Yakut boy—or at least his mother was Yakut.

‖**yakuza** (yăkū·ză). Also **yakusa.** [Jap., f. *ya* eight + *ku* nine + *za, sa* three (see below).] A Japanese gangster or racketeer; usu. in *pl.* sense, such people collectively.

8–9–3 is the worst set of cards in a player's hand at a gambling game: hence, the worst sort (K. Koike).

1964 *Newsweek* 14 Sept. 42/2 The youngsters had to listen to boss Sakamoto expound on the noble traditions of the *yakuza*, as gangsters are called in Japan. **1971** *Ibid.* 22 Mar. 42/1 The yakuza, or gangster, is an enduring feature of Japanese life. **1975** *New Yorker* 24 Mar. 98/2 The yakuza are the Japanese gangsters who in recent years have moved from gambling, drugs and prostitution into shakedown rackets. **1977** J. van de Wetering *Japanese Corpse* v. 53 Amsterdam is full of Japanese... Even their gangsters seem to be here, the yakusa. **1979** *Honolulu Advertiser* 8 Jan. A-6/1 Yakuza—the Japanese Mafia—are thriving in Hawaii as members of a crime syndicate.

Yale[2] (yē[i]l). [f. the name of the company founded by Yale (see def.).] A proprietary name for locks and keys, used esp. to denote a lock with a cylindrical barrel that can be turned only when a key with a specially serrated edge is inserted so as to displace a number of pins by the correct distances (invented by Linus Yale, Jr. (1821–68), U.S. locksmith).

1869 *Price List of Yale Lock Manfg. Co.* 3 The manufacturers of the Yale Locks desire to say a few words in relation to the recent changes in their organization, location and prices. **1875** *Iron Age* 1 July 10/1 (Advt.), Yale locks for all uses. **1885** *Trade Marks Jrnl.* 15 Apr. 346 *Yale.* The Yale and Towne Manufacturing Company (Incorporated), Stamford, Connecticut... Locks. Bronze hardware. **1895** *Montgomery Ward Catal.* Spring & Summer 375/2 Yale pattern night lock. *Ibid.* 382/1 Yale padlocks. **1907** *Official Gaz.* (U.S. Patent Office) 7 May 437/1 The Yale & Towne Mfg. Co., Stamford, Conn.... *Yale...* Locks and keys. **1920** W. J. Locke *House of Baltazar* xxv. 306 The little brass Yale latchkey. **1930** W. de la Mare *On the Edge* 11 The Yale gear-key which usually lay in the little recess to the left of the dash-board was missing. **1949** M. Mead *Male & Female* v. 114 Each small family is so isolated from others that no one knows how peculiar or how usual are..the behaviours that are shut behind each Yale lock. **1974** *Encycl. Brit. Macropædia* XI. 12/1 Magnetic forces can be used in locks working on the Yale principle. **1974** S. B. Hough *Fear Fortune, Father* vi. 45 It was a Yale key and the back door had a Yale lock. **1976** C. G. Smith *Let.* in *Daily Mail* 28 May 35/2 Yale is a registered trade-mark and in no way refers to one particular lock. Since 1949 we have specialised in marketing automatic, semi-automatic and double-locking night-latches, engineered to foil the glass-breaking and bolt-forcing intruder.

b. *ellipt.*

1918 G. Frankau *One of Them* xxx. 235 Where each man's latchkey fits his neighbours' Yales. **1954** R. Macaulay *Let.* 14 Mar. in *Last Lett. to Friend* (1962) 148, I have changed my lock, but they can pick 'Yales'. **1983** *Oxford Consumer* Autumn 11/2 Your cylinder-lock (what people are apt to call a 'Yale', whether it is actually made by the Yale Co. Ltd. or not).

‖**yali** (yăli·). [ad. Turk. *yalı* shore, waterside residence, f. Gk αἰγιαλός sea-shore.] A house of a type found on the shore of the Bosporus.

1962 J. Fleming *When I grow Rich* i. 9 Most large wooden houses on the Bosphorus are called either *yalis* or palaces. **1976** *Times* 28 Feb. (Turkish Suppl.) p. i/3 Ahead..flows the deep blue Bosporus. From its either shore rise green hills..dotted with..those lovely old wooden houses called *yalis.* **1978** S. Sheldon *Bloodline* i. 15 Not the tourist Istanbul..but the out-of-the-way places.., the *yalis*, and the small markets beyond the *souks.*

Yalie (yē[i]·li). *U.S. colloq.* [f. *Yale* + -IE.] A student or graduate of Yale University.

1969 *Newsweek* 12 May 71/1 One new Yalie..attended Harvard summer school and found time to visit New Haven to look Yale over. **1970** E. Segal *Love Story* xviii. 114 He's a Yalie, Ol... A total Yalie. College *and* Med School. **1972** *Nature* 4 Feb. 290/2 The availability of feminine companionship during the Monday-to-Friday period during which Yalies have traditionally gone without. **1983** *Washington Post* 21 Nov. B15/3 FDR, as editor of the Crimson, is said to have once gotten out a special post-victory edition, sticking it to the Yalies just as the fans were leaving the stadium.

y'all (yǭl). *U.S. dial.* Also **yall.** Abbrev. *YOU-ALL *pers. pron.*

1909 *Dialect Notes* III. 390 Where are yall goin'? **1928** *Amer. Speech* IV. 103, I heard a young lady, in greeting a group of her friends, say, 'How're y'all this morning?' **1935** *Scribner's Mag.* Feb. 120/2 Ah ain' gwi' be wid yall long. **1944** C. Himes *Black on Black* (1973) 199 'Bout how much ken y'all pick, shawty? **1968** E. J. Gaines *Bloodline* 134 Unc' Toby won't feel right if y'all don't eat his lovely food. **1971** *Black World* Apr. 55 Yall woulda held a stop watch on God-all-mighty. **1982** J. S. Borthwick *Case of Hook-Billed Kites* xxxiv. 114 Yes, Doctor. You'll be in the breakfast room. Y'all have a nice day.

yaller, var. YELLOW *a.* and *sb.* in Dict. and Suppl.

yam[1]. Add: **3. yam house,** a building in which to store yams.

1910 C. G. Seligmann *Melanesians Brit. New Guinea* xlix. 672 The number of yam houses makes each hamlet look larger than it really is. **1949** M. Mead *Male & Female* ix. 190 Among the Trobriand Islanders, each man fills the yam-house of his sister, not that of his wife.

yam (yæm), *v. dial.* Also **nyam.** [Derived through W. Indian from W. African words such as Hausa *nama* flesh, meat, Swahili *nyama* meat, Fulah *nyama* to eat; ult. the same word as YAM[1].] *trans.* To eat, esp. with relish.

1725 *New Canting Dict., Yam*, to eat heartily, to stuff lustily. **1801** T. Dancer *Medical Assistant* 174 [Dirt-eaters] display as much curiosity and nicety in their choice of the earth they yam, as snuff-takers or smokers in the kind of tobacco they make use of. **1816** M. G. Lewis *Jrnl.* (1834) 256 There's rice in the pot, take it, and yam-yamme. **1841** Jamieson *Scottish Dict., Nyam*, to chew. **1846** *Swell's Night Guide* 136/1 *Yam*, to eat hearty. **1862** W. G. Hamley *Captain Clutterbuck's Champagne* iv. 68 They purchased the congenial [sugar-cane] plant, and *nyaming* greedily its fibre, were entranced. **1864** Hotten *Slang Dict.* 273 *Yam*, to eat. This word is used by the lowest class all over the world; by the Wapping sailor, West India negro, or Chinese coolie. **1905** *Eng. Dialect Dict.* VI. 563/2 *Yam*, to eat greedily and with noise; to chew. **1970** C. Major *Dict. Afro-Amer. Slang* 125 *Yam*, to eat.

Also as *sb.*[3], food.

1788 P. Marsden *Acct. Island Jamaica* 49 The negroes say, the black parroquets are good for *yam*, i.e. good to eat. **1828** *Marly; or Life of Planter in Jamaica* (ed. 2) 13 Eh! Mosquitoes hab grandy nyamn on dat new buckra! **1835** R. R. Madden *Twelvemonths Residence W. Indies* I. 188 Him want no nyam, no clothes, no sleep. **1903** Farmer & Henley *Slang* VII. 368/2 *Yam* (nautical), food. **1953** *Caribbean Q.* III. iii. 176 That was a wicked Jamaican lizard 'mash up him common-law wife for mout'ful of nyam'.

‖**Yamato** (yamā·to). [Jap., = 'Japan'.] **1.** The style or school of art in Japan which culminated in the 12th and 13th centuries and dealt with Japanese subjects in a distinctively Japanese (rather than Chinese) way. Usu. as **Yamato-e** († **-we**)[*e* picture]; also **-ryū** [*-ryū* style, orig. stream, school].

1879 *Trans. Asiatic Soc. Japan* VII. 345 Motomitsu is spoken of as the originator of the *Yamato-we. Ibid.* 346 Takanobu was a pupil of the Yamato riu. **1880** T. W. Cutler *Gram. Jap. Ornament* 5 In the thirteenth [century] was founded the Yamato, or Japanese school. **1911** *Encycl. Brit.* XV. 174/1 It did not take shape as a school until the beginning of the 11th century..; it then became known as *Yamato-ryū*, a title which two centuries later was changed to that of *Tosa*, on the occasion of one of its masters..assuming that appellation as a family name. **1935** K. Toda *Jap. Scroll Painting* ii. 19 Another important example of early *Yamato-e* is a series of wall paintings at Hōryūji. **1970** *Oxf. Compan. Art* 607/2 The demand for a more refined art from the aristocratic society of Kyoto, combined with the decline of the T'ang dynasty in China, encouraged the Japanese to incorporate more native elements in their art, especially in the picture scrolls..of the *yamato-e* style. **1980** R. Illing *Art Jap. Prints* vi. 87 In the 1720s Okumura Masanobu and Shigenaga produced prints of landscape views, rather in the style of the older *yamato-e* album paintings, showing the *Omi hakkei.*

2. *Yamato-damashii*: the Japanese spirit.

1942 *R.A.F. Jrnl.* 13 June 6/2 He will be filled with what is called *yamato damashi* [sic] or the pure spirit of Japan. **1957** *Encycl. Brit.* XII. 954O/1 The Japanese.. have been profoundly influenced by a specific type of ideology—sometimes known as *Yamato Damashii* (the soul of Japan), which was partly embodied in..the code of the warrior knight. **1974** in A. Murakami *Romanized Japanese* (1979) 23 And there was no doubt then that the warrior code..*Bushido*..and the Japanese spirit.. *Yamato-damashii*..steeled the Japanese soldier.

yammer, *sb.* Restrict *Sc.* and *dial.* to 'a cry [etc].' and add examples of sense 'a loud noise, a din'.

1932 'L. G. Gibbon' *Sunset Song* 16 There the din of the gulls is a yammer night and day. **1978** *Poetry* Mar. 328 They huddle, and their tabled ground rejoices To the flat yammer of their American voices. **1984** *Washington Post* 11 June B4/3 Diamanda Gala's score, consisting of shrieks, yammers, gasps and vocal but incoherent hysterics.

yammer, *v.* Restrict *Obs.* exc. *Sc.* and *dial.* to senses 1 and 3 and add: **2.** (Further examples.)

1932 'L. G. Gibbon' *Sunset Song* 38 Her five bairns were all yammering blue murder at the same minute. **1952** W. R. Burnett *Vanity Row* viii. 73 Joe Sert yammering and getting purple in the face. **1958** 'W. Henry' *Seven Men at Mimbres Springs* xi. 125 Somewhere off in the eastern hills a coyote yammered with the crazed wildness which never fails to startle the oldest listener. **1959** W. H. Canaway *Seal* i. 16 His guts clanked and yammered like air-locked water-pipes. **1970** C. Sandburg *Compl. Poems* 372 They banged their spoons and bowls on the table And went on yammering for more to eat. **1980** F. Weldon *Puffball* 202 In the kitchen..Mabs' children yammered and cowered and snivelled and were slapped and shouted at. **1984** *Times* 5 Nov. 13/6 Just when women are yammering to be the hand that holds the briefcase..here's this little upstart letting the side down.

yammering *vbl. sb.* and *ppl. a.* (further examples in sense 2 of the vb.).

1937 [see *SKRIKING *vbl. sb.*]. **1940** L. MacNeice *Poems 1925–40* 249 The city's Yammering fire alarms. **1969** M. Braithwaite *Never sleep Three in Bed* ix. 105 There was always so much yammering from us kids that no adult had a chance to say anything. **1977** *Time* 31 Jan. 43/3 Visitors..shepherded round the Acropolis by yammering guides.

yamun, yamen. (Earlier example.)

1747 *Astley's New Gen. Coll. Voy.* IV. I. vi. 275 Each Magistrate, great or small, has his Tribunal, or *Ya-men.*

Yana (yā·nă). [a. Central and Northern Yana (men's speech) *ya·na* person, people.] **a.** The language of the Yana Indians, a member of the Hokan group.

[**1888** *6th Ann. Rep. Bur. Amer. Ethnol.* p. xxxvii, Work was begun on the Nosa language (Yanan family) at Redding, Cal.] **1891** J. W. Powell in *7th Ann. Rep. Bureau Amer. Ethnol.* 135 Yanan Family. Derivation: Yana means 'people' in the Yanan language. **1903** *Amer. Anthropologist* V. 18 Yana shows so few similarities to other languages that it cannot be included in any group. **1913** [see *Hokan]. **1933** Bloomfield *Language* iii. 46 The differences between the two sets of Yana forms can be stated by means of a fairly complex set of rules. **1956** J. Lotz in Saporta & Bastian *Psycholinguistics* (1961) 12/1 In Yana, an Indian language of California, men and women use an entirely different vocabulary. **1971** *Language* XLVII. 831 Although most shifts move only one degree up the scale, Yana and Luiseño advance two degrees in shifting $l > n$ and $r > ð$ respectively.

b. (A member of) an American Indian people formerly living in northern California. Also *attrib.*

1910 *Univ. Calif. Publ. Amer. Archeol. & Ethnol.* IX. 3 These boundaries are somewhat uncertain, it remaining doubtful whether the Yanas reached the Sacramento. **1933** Bloomfield *Language* iii. 46 The classical instance is that of the Carib Indians; a recently authenticated one is the language of the Yana Indians in northern California. **1962** *Guardian* 23 Feb. 7/3 In 1911..in California..a man..was identified as a survivor of a subtribe of Yana Indians thought to be extinct. **1974** *Encycl. Brit. Micropædia* X. 796/1 The last known Yahi survivor..died in 1916. Other Yana, if they survive, are intermixed with other northern Californian Indians.

yandy (yæ·ndi), *v. Austral.* [Aboriginal.] *trans.* To separate (grass seed) *from* refuse by shaking the mixture in a special way; to separate (ore) similarly or by winnowing. Hence **ya·ndying** *vbl. sb.*

1933 C. Fenner *Bunyips & Billabongs* vi. 158 When a gin has collected a coolamon..full of seed she has also a good deal of sand, dust, grass and leaves. But by shaking and twisting the coolamon in a particularly skilful way an almost perfect separation is made. This art of separation is called 'yandying'. **1937** E. Hill *Great Austral. Loneliness* vi. 50 The black woman... can yandy infinitesimal grass-seeds from their husks for the camp breakfast. **1944** M. J. O'Reilly *Bowyangs & Boomerangs* 48 Yandying, in blackfellow language, means shake-about. It is the natives' method of separating the grass seeds from the husks. **1962** D. Stuart *Yaralie* i. 9 While her mother had sat resting from her work of yandying and specking..she had wandered about. **1975** *National Geographic* Feb. 166 [Native Australian] women often earn money by 'yandying'—winnowing by tossing panfuls of ore into the wind to separate dirt from tin or gold. **1978** O. White *Silent Reach* xi. 113 The only tin that comes out of that country is what the gins yandi—dry blow by hand out of a coolamon.

yandy (yæ·ndi), *sb. Austral.* [from prec.] (See quot. 1959.)

1959 D. Stuart *Yandy* 158 *Yandy, tjardoo*: long shallow oval dish, of wood sometimes, but now almost always of sheet-iron, in which mineral is separated from the alluvial rubbish by means of a complicated racking action. **1962** —— *Yaralie* i. 12 Her mother and father had worked mightily, with the pick and shovel, and the yandy, and the loaming dish for days.

‖**yang** (yæŋ). Also **Yang.** [Chinese *yáng* yang, sun, positive, male genitals.] In Chinese philosophy, the masculine or positive principle (characterized by light, warmth, dryness, activity, etc.) of the two opposing cosmic forces into which creative energy divides and whose fusion in physical matter brings the phenomenal world into being. Also *attrib.* or as *adj.* Cf. *YIN.

1671 J. Ogilby tr. *Montanus' Atlas Chinensis* II. 549 The Chineses by these Strokes..declare..how much each Form or Sign receives from the two fore-mention'd Beginnings of Yn or Yang. **1736** R. Brookes tr. *Du*

Halde's Gen. Hist. China III. 357 The Chinese lay down two natural Principles of Life, vital Heat and radical Moisture..: They give the Name of Yang to the vital Heat, and that of Yn to the radical moisture. **1836** J. F. Davis *Chinese* II. xii. 65 The *Tae-keih* is said to have produced the *Yâng* and *Yin*, the active and passive, or male and female principle, and these last to have produced all things. **1845**, etc. [see *T'ai Chi 1]. **1871** A. B. Mitford *Tales of Old Japan* I. 150 The Chinese doctrine of the Yang and Yin, the male and female influences pervading all creation. **1934** R. Fry *Let.* 12 Apr. (1972) II. 690 Later on they discovered that the god of the furnace being male..to throw the wife in..alone sufficed to provide the Yang and the Yin. **1958** W. Willetts *Chinese Art* I. iv. 271 Light is the essence of *yang*. **1963** 'R. Erskine' *Passion Flowers in Italy* ix. 125 Giorgio looked even taller than usual..and (to all seeming) quite adequately Yang, whatever Consolata might say. **1969** *New Scientist* 10 July 53/1 For balance, the rational needs the irrational, the intellect must mesh with the emotions, the *yang* needs the *yin*. **1971** F. Mann *Acupuncture* (ed. 2) v. 63 In the treatment of disease, if Yang is hot and over-abundant, thus injuring the Yin fluid..the surplus Yang can be decreased by a method called 'cooling what is hot'. **1971** *Guardian* 18 Dec. 9/2 A macrobiotic diet .was the way Zen monks cooked... Foods were divided into Yin things and Yang things.. . Yang is meat for instance. **1980** *Holistic Health News* (Berkeley, Calif., Holistic Health Center) Sept./Oct. 1/3 In the past 300 years with the rise of empirical science, modern technology, property orientation, and the decline of the sacred, we have seen the creation of an extremely yang, overmasculine world-view.

b. Comb.: **yang-yin** = *yin-yang* s.v. *yin b. **1959** R. F. C. Hull tr. *Jung's Aion* in *Coll. Wks.* IX. ii. v. 58 This vision..might easily be a description of a genuine yang-yin relationship. **1968** E. B. Irving *Reading of Beowulf* iv. 179 The poem does seem to have something of a Yang-Yin structure to it..: as the kind of heroic achievement that Beowulf represents nears its end..self-destructiveness..—the negative side of the heroic ideal—comes into clearer and clearer focus. **1975** *New Yorker* 26 May 32/3 When I was a kid, the Technocrats used to drive these gray cars with the yang/yin symbol on the door.

‖**yangban** (yæ·ŋbæn). Also **yang-ban, yang ban; yangpan;** and with capital initial. [ad. Korean *ˈyāngpan*, f. *ˈyāng* both, a pair + *pan* social class.] **a.** The former ruling class in Korea. **b.** A member of this; an aristocrat or gentleman; (see also quot. 1972).

1898 I. L. Bird *Korea & her Neighbours* I. iv. 60 The youths who swing and lounge on sunny afternoons along the broad streets, aping the gait of *yang-bans*, are aspirants for official position. **1904** W. E. Griffis *Corea* (ed. 7) xlix. 443 In the Land of Morning Radiance there is a governing minority consisting of about one-tenth of the whole population. These, the Yangban..living on ancient privilege and prerogative and virtually paying no taxes or tolls, prey upon the common people. **1906** H. B. Hulbert *Passing of Korea* ii. 47 The common people constantly went down in the scale and the so-called *yangban* went up, until a condition of things was reached which formed the limit of the people's endurance. **1908** G. T. Ladd *In Korea with Marquis Ito* xii. 292 As for the Yang-ban, on no account will he do manual work. **1952** C. Osgood *Koreans* viii. 147 The taking of concubines by rich husbands was a commonplace and, in the event that a son was not born to the legal wife..it became an almost inevitable procedure on the part of a Yangpan of distinguished family. **1972** P. M. Bartz *South Korea* iv. 46/2 The civil service was known as *Tongban* (eastern class) and the military as *Soban* (western class), and the two together as *Yangban*, a word later used generally to refer to the nobility, and today used by women of the middle class in polite reference to their husbands or other men. **1977** *Korea Jrnl.* Dec. 21/2 All the citizens had to read the intentions of the ruling *yangban* class and Confucian scholars.

‖**yang ch'in** (yæŋ tʃin). Also — **ching, jin, kin,** and as one word. [Chinese *yángqín*, f. *yáng* high-sounding or *yáng* foreign + *qín* musical instrument, zither.] A Chinese musical instrument similar to the dulcimer.

1876 Stainer & Barrett *Dict. Mus. Terms* 455/1 *Yang Kin*, a Chinese instrument furnished with brass strings, which are struck with two small hammers, like a dulcimer. **1934** *Jrnl. R. Asiatic Soc.* Apr. 334 This would appear to have been similar to the dulcimer which is known to-day in China as the *yang-ch'in*. **1962** E. Snow *Other Side of River* (1963) lxxiii. 566 They may specialize in piano, violin, cello, flute, or one of the standard Chinese strings: *p'i-p'a, yang-ch'in, yueh-ch'in*, and others. **1970** R. D. Taring *Daughter of Tibet* i. 2 His favourite instrument was the Chinese *yangjin*, which has strings like a harp and is beaten with two bamboo sticks. **1974** *Early Music* Oct. 250/2 One recent Chinese recording has the Yang Ching as an obbligato instrument backed by the classical orchestra. **1980** *New Grove Dict. Music* IV. 275/2 The *yang-ch'in* is used in many types of popular music, including various styles of regional opera, sung narratives and solos.

‖**Yang Dipertuan** (yæŋ dipəˈɹtū·ăn). Also 9 **Iang de Pertuan; Yang di-Pertuan,** etc. [Malay, lit. 'he who is tuan': see *tuan.] In Malaysia, a king, an acknowledged ruler. Also with adjs., as *Yang Dipertuan Agung* [Malay *agung* principal], *besar* [Malay *besar* important].

1834 P. J. Begbie *Malayan Peninsula* iv. 140 Rajah Alli..could not view the appointment of Rajah Laboo to the office of the Iang de Pertuan *Besar*, with any other feelings than those of great distrust. **1907** F. Swettenham *Brit. Malaya* vi. 131 These places..were placed under the general control of a Raja from Mĕnangkâbau, in Sumatra, with the title Yang di Pertuan. **1947** R. Winstedt *Malays* 51 In Negri Sembilan, custom prescribed that only the Yang di-pertuan (or Ruler) could have four wives. **1972** *Straits Times* 23 Nov. 13/3 The hotel doormen should stop using the doormen's costume. ..The head-dress..is like the one worn by the Yang Dipertuan Agung.

‖**yanggona** (yæŋgōᵘ·nă). Also (in Fiji) **yaqona** (with the same pronunc.). (Other spellings recorded below are 'South Sea solecisms' (G. B. Milner).) [Fijian.] The Fijian name for Kava.

1858 T. Williams *Fiji* I. ii. 24 The leading men drink *yaqona* with the king elect. **1879** *Encycl. Brit.* IX. 156/2 The use of the kava root, here called yanggona.., was introduced, it is said, from Tonga. **1913** R. Brooke *Let.* 15 Dec. (1968) 545 *Yagona* (pron. Yangona) is the drink: same as Samoan Kava. It is made by pounding up a root, and is non-intoxicant, though *slightly* narcotic. **1922** A. B. Brewster *Hill Tribes of Fiji* xviii. 179 Christening now takes the place of the old custom of sprinkling the children with water from the *yangona* bowls. **1953** G. K. Roth *Fijian Way of Life* iii. 114 The vessel from which *yanggona* is regularly drunk nowadays is a cup made from the distal half of a coconut shell cut laterally. **1977** *Times* 17 Feb. 16/5 The Queen was..presented with . the potent locally-brewed drink called Yaqona. **1983** *Guardian Weekly* 25 Sept. 12/4 The great council of chiefs—the supreme body for Fijian affairs—met over a bowl of *yakona*.

yang jin, yang kin, varr. *yang ch'in.

‖**yang-ko** (yæŋko·, ‖yaŋgə). Also **yangko** and as two words. [Chinese *yānggē*, f. *yāng* seedling, sprout + *gē* song.] A type of folk-dance popular in northern China.

1954 *Folk Arts of New China* 30 Well-known forms of folk art like the *yangko* dances of the Shansi peasants or the Yangtse River boatmen's songs. **1967** J. R. Levenson in A. Feuerwerker et al. *Approaches to Mod. Chinese Hist.* 278 Communists might trip the Shensi light fantastic, the *yang-ko*, partly to get themselves into Shensi—and partly to get Shensi into China. **1973** R. F. S. Yang in Yuan-li Wu *China* 750 Since its Yenan days, the Communist party has utilized the *yang ko* (songs in sprouting time), an improvised version of folksinging and folkdancing, as a very useful propaganda weapon. **1975** C. P. Mackerras *Chinese Theatre in Mod. Times* x. 165 The first [phase]..was characterized by an emphasis on the local peasant drama of the Communist base area in northern Shensi (in particular, the small-scale song-and-dance form called *yang-ko*).

Yang–Mills (yæŋˌmilz). *Physics.* The names of C. N. *Yang* (b. 1922), Chinese-born physicist, and R. L. *Mills* (b. 1927), U.S. physicist, used *attrib.* with reference to a class of gauge theories with non-Abelian gauge invariance.

1961 *Bull. Amer. Physical Soc.* VI. 59/1 The Yang-Mills field has been quantized in the gauge $b_3 = 0$ (a similar analysis also holding in the gauges $b_1 = 0$ and $b_2 = 0$). **1977** *Nature* 21 July 207/2 There is wide agreement as to the ingredients in a propsective theory of hadrons: quarks, colour, gluons and the Yang–Mills interaction, to name the most obvious. **1979** *Sci. Amer.* Feb. 88/3 A Yang–Mills field is the essential element in a theory that seems to unify two of the four fundamental forces of nature, the weak force and the electromagnetic one. **1981** M. Gell-Mann in J. H. Mulvey *Nature of Matter* viii. 180 The theory of QCD and the theory of QFD..belong to the same class of theories. They are called Yang–Mills theories.

yangona: see *yanggona. **yangpan,** var. *yangban.

Yang-shao (yæŋ ʃau). *Archæol.* Also **Yang Shao, Yang shao.** The name of a village in the Henan province of China, used *attrib.* and *absol.* to designate a Neolithic Chinese culture (*c.* 5000–3000 B.C.), and its artefacts, evidence of which was first discovered there in 1921.

1923 J. G. Andersson *Early Chinese Culture* 31, I propose that we coin a local term and name it from the type locality *The Yang Shao culture*. **1948** A. L. Kroeber *Anthropol.* (rev. ed.) xvii. 735 Various early polychrome wares of the West have been spoken of as 'similar' to Yang-shao. **1965** T. R. Tregear *Geogr. of China* ii. 47 Yang Shao pottery has several unique shapes. *Ibid.*, Yang Shao Man lived on the loess plateau at a time when the water-table must have been much higher than it is today. **1973** *Genius of China* 48/2 The pigment used in decorating Yang-shao bowls..was generally applied directly on the burnished clay surface. **1978** *Nagel's Encycl.-Guide: China* 106 Proof of cultivation of cereals.. exists from the Yang shao period onwards.

yank, *sb.*¹ Add: **1. b.** For *dial.* and *U.S.* read *colloq.* (orig. *dial.* and *U.S.*). Also *fig.*

1906 *N.Y. Globe* 20 Aug. 6 Here is a fantastic proposition from Germany, which takes one back with an unpleasant yank into the middle ages.

Yank, *sb.*² Add: **2.** An American car.

1959 *Listener* 4 June 982/1 The young labourer..will invest his cash in buying a car 'on the 'ire'—not a modest second-hand British product but a 'big Yank'. **1977** *Hot Car* Oct. 11/3 It's not raunchy like a yank but it sure is clean and ripe for customising.

yank, *v.* For *dial.* and *U.S.* read orig. *dial.* and *U.S.* and add: **1. a.** (Further examples.)

1950 R. Macaulay *World My Wilderness* xii. 102 His companion, a younger man with less of the Gael in his aspect and speech, jumped down into the copse,..and yanked her to her feet. **1964** F. Chichester *Lonely Sea & Sky* xii. 129, I kept the seaplane on the surface, planing until I thought it was going as fast as it could, when I yanked the stick back hard, to pull her off suddenly. **1966** *Listener* 14 Apr. 534/1 Any incident, from three youths yanking a cigarette machine off a wall to the mods' and rockers' riots, qualifies as 'gang delinquency'. **1968** B. Hines *Kestrel for Knave* 57 Crossley grabbed a boy by the arm and began to yank him into the open. **1977** C. McCullough *Thorn Birds* i. ii. 35 Fee's muscular arm yanked the brush ruthlessly through knots and tangles until Meggie's eyes watered. **1983** *Austral. Personal Computer* Aug. 62/1 If you want the disks back..you cannot just yank them out.

b. (Further examples.)

1896 G. B. Shaw *Let.* 7 Dec. in *Ellen Terry & Shaw* (1931) 139 Hearing that Janet..had no refuge but the Solferino, she promptly went to that haunt, yanked Janet ..out of it,..and delivered her punctually..for the performance. **1922** Joyce *Ulysses* 421 Alexander J. Christ Dowie, that's yanked to glory most half this planet from 'Frisco Beach to Vladivostok. **1948** *Sunday Pictorial* 18 July 16/6 In the end attendants had to dive in and yank them out. **1977** J. I. M. Stewart *Madonna of Astrolabe* xiv. 197, I had to yank him out of Oxford—a shocking place, if Cambridge is anything to go by.

c. To withdraw (a theatrical show, an advertisement, etc.); to cancel. *U.S. colloq.*

1940 *Amer. Speech* XV. 205/1 *Yank*, to withdraw, usually because of poor attendance. **1976** *Time* 27 Sept. 65/1 The paper..ticked off 24 local real estate advertisers with a dispiriting account of development along a local lake; they have since yanked their ads. **1978** *Chicago* June 12/1 The *Tribune* flung up more flak for Greene in ads on TV and at the top of page one (it yanked an Arts & Fun ad that repeated the 'prostitute' column).

2. (Further examples.) Usu. const. *at.*

1906 'O. Henry' in *Munsey's Mag.* Aug. 556/2 (1961) ix. 131 The drawer stuck, and he yanked at it savagely. **1957** J. Kerouac *On Road* i. ix. 55, I yanked at the window; it was nailed. **1977** C. McCullough *Thorn Birds* i. 8 She..bagan to comb Agnes's hair... She was yanking inexpertly at a large knot. **1981** *Sunday Express* (Colour Suppl.) 19 July/2 Suddenly Sally/Julie yanks at the neckline of her dress.

Yankee, *sb.* and *a.* Add: **A.** *sb.* **6.** = *Yankee jib* in sense C. b. below.

1912 Heckstall-Smith & Du Boulay *Compl. Yachtsman* vi. 152 The 'Yankee' is a strong pulling sail. **1953** *Yachting* June 48 We handed the yankee in favor of the working jib and forestops'l. **1967** J. Anderson *Vinland Voyage* 211 Peter decided to use the No. 2 yankee, leaving the big No. 1 to its proper job of pulling forward. **1974** *Islander* (Victoria, B.C.) 11 Aug. 11/1 We were lost without the mizzen. With motor and yankee we inched our way..forward.

7. *Horse-racing.* A composite bet on four or more horses, composed of doubles, trebles, and one or more accumulators.

1967 C. Cockburn *I, Claud* xxxiii. 404, I stepped into the betting-shop and placed the type of bet known as a 'Yankee' on four of the races... I was able to collect.. over £72 for the twenty-two shillings I had bet. **1970** *Guardian* 17 Apr. 12/3, I have..won in 4-, 5- and 6-horse yankees sums of up to £200. **1981** B. Hines *Looks & Smiles* 184, I won it on the horses. Me and Phil had a Yankee up.

C. b. Yankee bet *Horse-racing* = sense A. 7 above; **Yankee jib (topsail),** a large jib topsail used in light winds, set on the topmast stay.

1964 A. Wykes *Gambling* viii. 194 (*caption*) The 'Yankee bet' (a permutation bet covering four horses) that can be made with off-course bookmakers in Britain. **1976** *Daily Record* (Glasgow) 29 Nov. 23/5 Yankee bet: Six doubles, four trebles and an accumulator—Pikey (12.0 Windsor), Escapologist (1.45 Wolverhampton), Corrieghoil (2.15 Wolverhampton), Heidelberg (3.0 Windsor). [**1904** B. Heckstall-Smith *Dixon Kemp's Man. of Yacht & Boat Sailing* (ed. 10) v. 94 The sheeting of a modern large jackyard topsail requires a master hand's attention, especially when it is fitted 'Yankee fashion', having three sheets, as very many now are—namely, the main topsail sheet, the outer and inner sheets on the ends of the jack-yard.] **1912** Heckstall-Smith & Du Boulay *Compl. Yachtsman* vi. 152 A useful sail is the Yankee jib-topsail. This is the largest or balloon jib-topsail, and the modern and most efficient form of balloon jib-topsail is cut, like all modern head-sails should be, very high in the clew. **1928** *Daily Mail* 9 Aug. 19/6 There is a Yankee jib which, as one sail, covers more than the combined area of jib and foresail. **1939** U. Fox *Crest of Wave* 145 We had settled down with the large Yankee jib topsail set in the place of the double clewed jib. **1976** *Yachts & Yachting* 20 Aug. 339/3 At 30 knots across the deck she dropped her yankee jib and kept going under staysail and heavily reefed main.

Hence **Yankeeish** *a.* (examples); **Ya·nkeeness,** Yankee character.

1818 H. C. Robinson *Diary* 30 Apr. (1967) 58 Allston has a mild manner, a soft voice, and a sentimental air with him, not at all Yankyish. **1830** *Collegian* (Cambridge, Mass.) Apr. 117 Comparisons are generally 'odorous', particularly Yankeeish, and decidedly condemned by Captain Basil Hall. **1909** 'O. Henry' *Roads of Destiny* xxi. 352 Any Yankeeness I may have is geographical.

Yankee Doodle. Add: **2.** (Earlier example.)

1787 J. F. Bryant *Verses* 15 And we'll give the Yankee-doodles a dowse in the jaws.

Hence **Yankeedoodledo·dom** *nonce-wd.* = YANKEEDOM; **Yankeedoodledom** (earlier example).

1843 T. CARLYLE *Let.* 3 July in *Lett. Charles Dickens* (1974) III. 542/1 The last *Chuzzlewit* on Yankeedoodle-dodom is capital. We read it with loud assent. **1845** P. HONE *Diary* 20 May (1889) II. 248 The ladies of this family (natives though they be of Yankee-doodle-dom) seem to possess, in a high degree, the power of capturing the aristocracy of England.

Yanqui (yæ·ŋki), *a.* and *sb.* [a. Sp. *Yanqui* YANKEE *sb.* and *a.*] = YANKEE *sb.* and *a.*: used esp. in Latin American contexts.

1929 [see *PARROT-HOUSE]. **1937** [see *PANAMAN *sb.* and *a.*]. **1952** *Caribbean Q.* II. IV. 9 Latin America replied with denunciations of what is called 'Yanqui Imperialism'. **1969** *Guardian* 6 Oct. 11/2 The Mexicans..naturally were loath to prosecute their own kind..on evidence collected by the Yanquis. **1975** *New Yorker* 30 June 23/3 Pelé, the King of Soccer, the Black Pearl, lured from Brazil by four million seventeen hundred thousand Yanqui dollars and his own sense of duty, was here to play his first game for Warner Communications' New York Cosmos. **1976** *Times Lit. Suppl.* 6 Aug. 989/4 Roosevelt's seizure of Panama led him to publish his archetypal anti-Yanqui diatribe. **1982** J. D. MACDONALD *Cinnamon Skin* xxiv. 257 It was a childish game with them, to effortlessly outdistance the heaving sweating Yanquis.

yantra (ya·ntrǎ). [a. Skr. *yantra* device or mechanism for holding or fastening, f. *yam* to hold, support.] A geometrical diagram used as an aid to meditation in tantric worship; any object used similarly.

1877 M. WILLIAMS *Hinduism* ix. 129 As to the *Yantras* these are mystical diagrams—generally combinations of triangular figures. **1928** E. B. HAVELL *Indian Sculptures & Painting* (ed. 2) ii. 16 To this day *yantras*, or geometric symbols, are used in higher Brahmanical ritual in preference to images of the Hindu pantheon. **1946** H. ZIMMER in J. Campbell *Myths & Symbols in Indian Art* iv. 141 In Hindu devotional tradition, 'yantra' is the general term for instruments of worship, namely, idols, pictures, or geometrical diagrams. **1980** *Dædalus* Spring 123 The mouse child uses the image as a yantra to meditate on nothing and infinity. **1982** *N.Y. Times* 7 Nov. XXI. 35/2 An ecstatic state..would be achieved..by contemplation of the mandalas and yantras, abstract diagrams of cosmic forces.

Yao (yau), *a.*[1] and *sb.*[1] Also 9 **Yaou.** [Native name.] **A.** *adj.* Of, pertaining to, or designating a mountain-dwelling people of the Guangxi, Hunan, Yunnan, Guangdong, and Guizhou provinces of China and northern parts of Vietnam.

1834 C. GUTZLAFF *Sketch of Chinese Hist.* I. i. 30 In the mountains of Kwang-tung and Kwang-se live great numbers of the Meaou and Yaou tribes, who appear to be the aborigines of the country. **1897** *Fortn. Rev.* July 104, I will now close the subject by saying a few words touching the language of the Kakhyens. Like the Chinese, Annamese, Shan, Miao-tsze, Yao, and Burmese languages, it is monosyllabic and tonal. **1976** R. CONDON *Whisper of Axe* I. xv. 90 The KMT troops..took Shan or Yao or Lahu wives. **1977** YIN MING *United & Equal* 3 In the 1930s the reactionary warlords perpetrated massacres of the Hui people in Kansu and the Miao and Yao peoples in Kwangsi.

B. *sb.* **a.** The Yao people. **b.** The language of the Yao.

1883 *Encycl. Brit.* XVI. 224/1 The Yaou-jin, or Goblin clan, are said to have books, which, though they are now unable to read, they still regard with reverent awe. **1901** E. H. PARKER *China* i. 7 In the southern portion of the eastern half there are still a few independent..tribes, known as Yao or Miao. **1939** [see *MIAO *sb.* and *a.*]. **1948** R. A. D. FORREST *Chinese Lang.* v. 89 In Indo-China the Yao (akin to the Miao) are also known as Man. *Ibid.* 91 Miao and Yao were assigned by..Schmidt, along with Khamti, Shan, and Ahom, to the northern group of T'ai languages. **1982** B. HOOK *Cambridge Encycl. China* 102/1 Because of culture-contact they were..familiar with the notion of writing, and consequently came to employ a neighbouring language, using its script as their own written language. This happened with the Yao, who wrote their poems and hymns in a..modified form of Han Chinese.

Yao (yau), *sb.*[2] and *a.*[2] [Native name.] **A.** *sb.* **a.** (A member of) a Bantu people found east and south of Lake Nyasa in East Africa. **b.** The language of the Yao.

1894 *Rep. Admin. Brit. Central Africa* 23 in *Parl. Papers* (C. 7504) LVII. 771 As the coast people and Arabs began to penetrate East Central Africa they came in contact with the Yao, who, from his predatory nature, took to the idea of slave-raiding with real appreciation. **1916** *Blackw. Mag.* Apr. 551/1 The Africans were Yaos, little men, affectionately termed 'Golliwogs' by their British officers. **1924** [see *NYANJA *sb.* and *a.*]. **1957** LD. HAILEY *African Survey 1956* iii. 97 Nyanja is the lingua franca throughout Nyasaland..though Tumbuka has also been recently recognized as the medium in the Northern Province, and Yao in the Yao-speaking areas. **1974** *Encycl. Brit. Micropædia* X. 799/3 Through Arab contact most Yao are Muslims.

B. *adj.* Pertaining to or designating a Yao or the Yao.

1910 *Encycl. Brit.* III. 360/1 The extensive *Yao* genus of languages stretches from just behind the coast of the Lindi settlements..to the north-east shores of Lake Nyasa. **1955** M. GLUCKMAN *Custom & Conflict in Afr.* iv. 96 When a Yao headman in Nyasaland is installed his taste for human meat is tested in the installation ceremony: because Yao witches eat the corpses of those they kill. **1974** *Encycl. Brit. Micropædia* X. 799/3 Yao social life features annual initiation ceremonies involving circumcisions for boys.

yap, *sb.*[1] Add: **1. b.** A fool, someone easily taken in; also, an uncultured or unsophisticated person. *dial.* and *U.S. slang.*

c **1894** C. H. HOYT *Texas Steer* (1899) III. 6 Instead of his being the only 'yap', as he calls it, in Congress there were about two hundred other members. **1895** W. STEVENS *Let.* 4 Aug. (1967) 6 Paul and Several other Yaps are up with them. **1898** B. KIRKBY *Lakeland Words* 157 *Yap*, a chap 'at's a bit ov o gomeril. **1901** 'FLYNT' & 'WALTON' *Powers that Prey* I. iii. 21 This yap from the country. *Ibid.* III. i. 60 I've seen those yaps come to town an' throw up their hands at sights that a Bowery kid wouldn't drop a cigarette snipe to see. **1915** W. CHURCHILL *Far Country* xxiv. 452 The yaps that listen to him don't understand him, but somehow he gets under their skins. **1926** J. BLACK *You can't Win* iv. 36 You are just the kind of a yap that gets up in the middle of the night and hides his money so carefully that he has to have a policeman find it for him in the morning. **1977** *New Musical Express* 12 Feb. 12/2 Then this yap starts yowling about anarchy, ..and eventually the record seems to end in the middle.

2. b. The mouth. *U.S. slang.*

1900 *Dialect Notes* II. 70 *Yap*, the mouth. **1937** J. WEIDMAN *I can get it for you Wholesale* i. 8 Every time you open your yap to say something. **1959** N. MAILER *Advts. for Myself* (1961) 43 There was a guy screaming his yap off next to him,..holding his face. **1977** H. FAST *Immigrants* IV. 243 They know that if they open their yaps, we'll close them down.

c. Idle or loquacious talk; chatter; = YAWP, YAUP *sb.* b. *slang.*

1907 *Dialect Notes* III. 204 *Yap*, offensive or superfluous talk. 'Shut up your yap.' **1926** KIPLING *Debits & Credits* 314 He'd preserved it in his head through all those weeks..o' Bert's yap. **1928** A. P. HERBERT *Trials of Topsy* 133 All this *pragmatical* yap about *tea* being a necessity and *beer* being a vice. **1945** *Coast to Coast 1944* 1 It wasn't much fun listening to all that yap when it really didn't mean a thing. **1968** K. WEATHERLY *Roo Shooter* 21 Never mind that yap. Where's the tucker?

d. A chat. *slang.*

1930 SAYERS & 'EUSTACE' *Documents in Case* 145 I'd like to have a yap with somebody who talks my language. **1957** R. LAWLER *Summer of Seventeenth Doll* II. i. 66 Real ear-basher he is, always on for a yap.

Yap (yæp), *sb.*[2] (See quots.)

1984 *Chicago Sun-Times* 25 Mar. (Views) 7/1 Yumpies, young upwardly mobile professionals, a.k.a. Yaps (young aspiring professionals). **1984** *Sunday Times* (Colour Suppl.) 28 Oct. 12/3 Phillips' Yaps believe in vigorous self-advancement, jogging and BMWs. **1985** *Times* 9 Feb. 11/1 (*heading*) Yaps, or Young Aspiring Professionals are brash, bright and bound for the top.

yap, *v.* Add: **2. b.** To talk idly or loquaciously; to chatter. Also *trans.*, with quoted words as obj. *slang* (orig. *dial.*).

1886 F. T. ELWORTHY *W. Somerset Word-Bk.* 844 *Yappy*,..to chatter. The use of the word is distinctly depreciatory. Mind yer work, and neet bide there yappin. **1893** DARTNELL & GODDARD *Gloss. Words Wilts.* 185 *Yap, Yop*, to talk noisily. 'What be a yopping there for?' **1898** R. BLAKEBOROUGH *Wit, Character, Folklore, & Customs N. Riding Yorks.* 473 *Yap*, to talk foolishly. **1899** S. CRANE *Monster* xviii. 76, I told him to keep his trap shut. But then you know how he'll go all over town yapping about the thing. **1922** S. LEWIS *Babbitt* x. 141 He hands me the cold-boiled stare and yaps, 'I dunno, friend, I'll see.' **1937** J. WEIDMAN *I can get it for you Wholesale* iii. 28 You've been yapping away. **1946** K. TENNANT *Lost Haven* (1947) xix. 315 Len wished Alec wouldn't yap so much. **1963** *Australasian Post* 14 Mar. 51/2 If you want to yap on like a drongo in the DTs..go ahead: be a gig! **1975** *Daily Tel.* 30 June 13/7 A lot of women who are happy to yap away normally, became tongue-tied when they had to talk and drive. **1985** A. T. ELLIS *Unexplained Laughter* 49 They end up writing books about it and yapping away on the television.

Hence **ya·ppingly** *adv.*

1924 *Chambers's Jrnl.* Feb. 128/1 Bob danced yappingly around him.

yappy (yæ·pi), *a.* [f. YAP *sb.* or *v.* + -Y[1].] **a.** Given to yapping. **b.** Suggestive of a dog's yap.

1909 in *Cent. Dict.* Suppl. **1937** H. T. MILLER *Let me die Tuesday* i. 12 You're a yappy kid with no bringing up whatever. **1977** P. CARTER *Under Goliath* vi. 31 He had a wee tight face like one of those little dogs that snap at your heels, and he had a voice like one, thin and yappy. **1977** R. PERRY *Dead End* ii. 21 One yappy white poodle.

Hence **ya·ppiness.**

1928 *Daily Express* 28 Aug. 4/4 Pekingese..are not addicted to 'yappiness', and thus differ from many toys.

yaqona, var. *YANGGONA.

Yaqui (yæ·ki), *sb.* and *a.* [a. Sp., earlier *Hiaquis* pl., ad. Yaqui *hiaki.*]

A. *sb.* **a.** (A member of) an Indian people of north-western Mexico.

1861 *Hist. Mag.* V. 164/2 The Indian population is large, and, properly regulated, would be exceedingly useful... The most numerous tribe is that of the Yaquis. **1875** H. H. BANCROFT *Native Races of Pacific States* I. v. 575 The Chinipas, Yaquis, Opatas and Conchos build.. more substantial dwellings of timber and adobes. **1946** *Nature* 13 July 69/2 The Cáhita Indians of western Mexico consist of two surviving groups, the Yaqui and the Mayo. **1953** E. HAUGEN *Norwegian Lang. in Amer.* II. xiv. 367 An interesting description is available of conditions among the Yaqui, a tribe in Arizona, whose villages were hispanicized by missionaries and political functionaries by the end of the 17th century. **1977** C. SCHAEFFER tr. *Simenon's Bottom of Bottle* vi. 95 He was a Yaqui, bigger and stronger than I am.

b. The Uto-Aztecan language of the Yaqui.

1911 *Bull. U.S. Bureau Amer. Ethnol.* No. 44. 12 Three dialects—Yaqui, Mayo, and Tehueco—are usually mentioned. **1943** *Amer. Anthropologist* XLV. 428 Yaqui and Mayo stand in the relation of mutually intelligible dialects. **1957** *Publ. Amer. Dial. Soc. 1956* XXVI. 55 In Yaqui the Spanish word *díos* 'God' appears both as *díos* and *líos*.

B. *adj.* Of, pertaining to, or designating the Yaqui.

1861 *Hist. Mag.* V. 165/1 From that day [*sc.* 1609] to this, the Yaqui Indians have retained their pueblos, or towns, along their river, governed by chiefs of their own tribe, appointed by the Spanish and Mexican governments. **1884** H. H. BANCROFT *Hist. N. Amer. States* ix. 216 A party of Tehuecos were..sent with two converted Yaqui women. **1943** *Amer. Anthropologist* XLV. 428 A fuller consideration..of Yaqui history. **1964** F. O'ROURKE *Mule for Marquesa* (1967) ii. 24 From Nogales he peddled arms and ammunition.., his most valued customers the Yaqui Indians. **1978** *Tucson Mag.* Dec. 104/3 They perform a Yaqui Deer Dance in addition to Aztec dances and a variety of regional folk dances.

yar(r, *v.* (Later examples.)

1866 J. E. BROGDEN *Provincial Words & Expressions Lincs.* 227 *Yar*, to snarl. **1953** G. M. DURRELL *Overloaded Ark* x. 181 A young and foolish bitch..had yapped and yarred herself into a fit of hysterical bravery.

yard, *sb.*[1] Add: **1. f.** *U.S.* A college campus or the area enclosed by its main buildings; *spec.* at Harvard: *the Yard*, the quadrangle formed by the original college buildings.

1637–9 *Harvard Coll. Rec.* in *Publ. Colonial Soc. Mass.* (1925) I. 172 Mr Nathaniel Eatons Account... The frame in the Colledge Yard & digging the cellar. **1841** *Harvard Faculty Orders & Regul.* 6 Collecting in groups round the doors of the College buildings or in the yard [shall be considered a violation of decorum]. **1871** L. H. BAGG *Four Years at Yale* 27 Besides the fourteen buildings already described, the only others within the yard..were the two wooden dwelling-houses. **1902** *Boston Even. Record* 18 Mar. 8/4 (*heading*) Out of the 'Yard'—how the Harvard students have gone to the 'Gold Coast'. **1942** BERREY & VAN DEN BARK *Amer. Thes. Slang* §829.12 *Campus*, camp, orchard,..yard. **1947** *Harvard Alumni Bull.* 12 Apr. 586/2 Few people have likely ever thought of the Yard as a bird sanctuary... What of the Yard? There must be bird records. **1970** 'E. QUEEN' *Last Women in his Life* III. 163, I found out the truth about myself in my freshman year at Harvard... There was an episode in a bar, well away from the Yard. **1981** 'D. JORDAN' *Double Red* xv. 71 Stumbling across the Yard..after too much Harvard Provision Co. gin.

3. For Now *dial.* read Now chiefly *N. Amer.* and *dial.* and add further examples.

1835 J. H. INGRAHAM *South-West* II. 88 Striped grass, cultivated in yards at the north. **1877** H. G. MURRAY *Tom Kittle's Wake* 21 My daughter, Molly tief pass, maam, den go da him yard. **1907** W. JEKYLL *Jamaican Song & Story* 163 The immediate surroundings of the house are called the yard. They seldom speak of going to a friend's house. They say they are going to his yard. **1932** 'L. G. GIBBON' *Sunset Song* 97 The berries hung ripe in the yard of the gardener Galt. **1947** J. A. LOMAX *Adventures Ballad Hunter* vii. 185 She says, 'Can you cut yards?' an' I says, 'Yes ma'am.' She says, 'Go roun,..to de back ..., you'll find a lawn-mower there, and then begin cuttin'.' **1956** G. E. EVANS *Ask Fellows who cut Hay* iv. 55 The village was almost entirely self-supporting, most families living on what they grew or reared on their yards or allotments. **1980** W. MAXWELL *So Long, see you Tomorrow* (1981) ii. 22 The rented house had no yard to speak of.

4. c. *The Yards*, the stockyards where cattle are collected for slaughter, esp. in Chicago. *U.S.*

1865 *Atlantic Monthly* Jan. 83/2 The average weekly expenditure by butchers at the New York yards during the year 1863 was $328,865. **1906** U. SINCLAIR *Jungle* xv. 170 Already the yards were full of activity. **1935** A. G. MACDONELL *Visit to America* vii. 114 As in Chicago, the pride of Omaha is the Stock-yards... I was looking straight down into the Yards. **1974** 'M. ALLEN' *Super Tour* ii. 57 I've been called all kinds of things ever since I was a kid back of the Yards.

6. (*a*) *yard-broom*; (*b*) *yard-dung* (earlier example); (*c*) **yard-boy** a general labourer; a gardener or gardener's boy (*obs.* exc. *Caribbean*); **yard sale** *U.S.*, a sale of miscellaneous second-hand items held in the garden of a private house; (*d*) *yard-master* (earlier example).

(*a*) **1921** *Blackw. Mag.* Feb. 195/1 Dip an old yard-broom in a bucket of water. **1982** J. SCOTT *Local Lads* iii. 32 Billy took up an aged, patchily moulted yardbroom.

(*b*) **1744** W. ELLIS *Mod. Husb.* Jan. xi. 73 He may now carry out his Stable or Yard Dung.

(*c*) **1788** J. WOODFORDE *Diary* 7 Jan. (1927) III. 2 To my Yard Boy, Charles Crossley, for 3 Quarters of a Years Wages pd o. 15. 9. **1831** C. FARQUHARSON *Jrnl.* 2 Dec. in *Relic of Slavery* (1957) 47 Employed all hands weeding.. along with the yard boys. **1958** S. SELVON *Turn again Tiger* viii. 185, I take the worst job that was going—as a kind of yard-boy by the white people house. **1975** *New Rev.* May 10/2 In and around Port of Spain cooks, ironers and yardboys in attendance. **1976** *Flint* (Michigan)

Jrnl. 12 July c-5 *Yard sale*—1508 Webber canning jars, screen tent, patterns, books, [etc.]. **1982** M. McMullen *Until Death do us Part* (1983) vii. 46 There was a yard sale down our street.

(*d*) **1864** *Rep. Children's Employment Comm.* 139/1 in *Parl. Papers* XXII. 487/1 Mr Thomas Wheat, yard-master... My duty is to give orders..and manage the work.

yard, *sb.*[2] Add: **9. b.** *by the yard* (earlier example); also, of books or paintings: bought by quantity or size rather than for quality.

1845 J. W. Turner *Razor Strop Man* 3 He was spinning poetical rhyme by the yard; Had Shakespear been living 'twould astonish'd the bard. **1933** J. Betjeman *Ghastly Good Taste* i. 12 The old books..can be sold..by the yard to America as wall decoration. **1976** 'O. Bleeck' *No Questions Asked* ii. 29 He bought fine paintings by the yard and rare books by the case.

11*. *U.S. slang.* One hundred dollars; one thousand dollars; a bill for this amount.

1926 *Amer. Mercury* Dec. 465/2 One hundred dollars is a *century* or a *yard*. **1929** C. F. Coe *Hooch* vi. 130 He slips him $300 an' promises him $700 more if they'll spring him... Baldy..promises to come right to me for the seven yards that make the grand. **1932** *Amer. Speech* VII. 118 *Yard*,..a thousand-dollar bill. **1942** Berrey & Van den Bark *Amer. Thes. Slang* § 18.5 (*One*) *G, -gee* or *grand, thou,* (*one*) *yard*, one thousand. *Ibid.* § 467.2 *One C, yard*, a hundred dollars. **1979** V. Patrick *Pope of Greenwich Village* vii. 70 You throw a hundred to the guy who makes the loan... He writes the loan for thirteen hundred, you take twelve, and a yard goes south to him.

12. yard goods, fabric sold by the yard; **yard-stick** (earlier example); also *fig.*, a standard of comparison (later examples).

1941 L. I. Wilder *Little Town on Prairie* v. 33 He'll get most of the trade in yard goods, with somebody there in the store making them up into shirts. **1964** M. Laurence *Stone Angel* iv. 113 At the back was the section where yard-goods were sold, and ladies' and children's ready-to-wear garments hanging dejectedly on racks. **1982** S. T. Haymon *Ritual Murder* xix. 134 Patter of the travelling men who sold crockery and yard goods. **1822** in W. R. Alger *Life Edwin Forrest* (1877) I. 100 Furnish me with every particular, especially how our Tid is, and whether she reads with the yard-stick. **1929** *Morning Post* 4 June 15/6 This is considered more effective than a rough comparison by means of tonnage or range... It is hoped that this new American 'yardstick' will be ready for General Dawes when he leaves for London. **1949** *Here & Now* (N.Z.) Oct. 33/2 What yardstick should we use in assessing success or failure in farming? **1960** A. S. Neill *Summerhill* (1962) vi. 334 We all have our standards of values and we measure others by our personal yardstick. **1984** A. Smith *Mind* iv. xiv. 262 Whatever yardstick is used, it is probable that at least a million people on this planet kill themselves each year.

yard, *v.*[1] **1. a.** (Earlier examples.)

1758 in *Essex Inst. Hist. Coll.* (1874) XII. 140 The Dutch here have a nasty practice of yarding their cows in ye Street before their doors. **1826** J. Atkinson *Agric. & Grazing N.S.W.* 66 When they seem pretty well reconciled to the place, they are *bedded* out one night, and *yarded* the next.

yardage[1]**.** (Earlier example.)

1867 *Trans. Illinois Agric. Soc.* VI. 322 Net cash receipt for yardage, and profit on feed.

yardang (yā·ɹdæŋ). *Physical Geogr.* Also **jardang.** [a. Turk., abl. of *yar* steep bank, precipice.] A sharp, irregular ridge of sand or the like, lying in the direction of the prevailing wind in exposed desert regions and formed by erosion by the wind of adjacent less resistant material.

1904 S. Hedin *Sci. Results Journey in Central Asia* I. xxvii. 439 At intervals furrows or trenches in the clay subsoil, called *jardangs*, traced between long elevations or ridges, crop up amongst the dunes. **1934** *Bull. Geol. Soc. Amer.* XLV. (*caption facing* p. 160) Looking down one of the narrower wind-scoured troughs, with a sharp yardang (seven feet high) on the left and a higher one on the right. **1970** R. J. Small *Study of Landforms* ix. 301 Probably the only landforms of deserts that can be confidently ascribed to wind abrasion alone are the comparatively unimportant 'yardangs' and allied 'ridge-and-furrow' features. **1979** *Nature* 5 Apr. 535/1 In other regions [of Mars], the surface has been stripped, yardangs have formed, and in general the topography seems to have been largely configured by aeolian activity.

yard-arm, *sb.* Add: **e.** Phr. *when the sun is over the yard-arm* and varr., the time of day when it is permissible to begin drinking.

1899 Kipling *From Sea to Sea* I. xxiv. 454 The American does not drink at meals as a sensible man should... Also he has no decent notions about the sun being over the yard-arm or below the horizon. **1945** J. C. Colcord *Sea Lang. comes Ashore* 211 An officers' quip..is 'When the sun is over the yardarm..it's time to take a drink'. **1964** *Amer. N. & Q.* III. 23/2 Frequent reference is made to the undesirability of drinking before 'the sun has crossed the yardarm'. **1968** 'J. le Carré' *Small Town in Germany* ii. 20 Just one hour till the sun was over the yardarm.. He'd have a beer first. **1979** A. Morice *Murder in Outline* iii. 26, I had promised to take a jugful of dry martini with him and Vera..as soon as the sun went over the yardarm.

yard-arm *v.*, (*a*) also *to yard-arm it*: *transf.* of persons, to fight at close quarters.

1829 P. Egan *Boxiana* 2nd Ser. II. 358 'Long bowls,' said Curtis to Savage, 'will not answer: you must *yard-arm* it with your adversary.'

ya·rdbird. *U.S. slang.* Also **yard bird.** [f. Yard *sb.*[1] + Bird *sb.* (see sense *1 e), perh. after *jail-bird.*] **a.** *Mil.* A recruit, a newly-enlisted serviceman; also, a serviceman under discipline for a misdemeanour; one assigned to menial tasks. Also *transf.*

1941 *Amer. Speech* XVI. 169/2 *Yard bird*, a raw recruit. **1942** [see *red-line *v.*]. **1943** J. Goodell *They sent me to Iceland* 102 With this wealth of jargon we were able to produce a quiz on army slang..for the benefit of the newly arrived men—better known as 'yardbirds'. **1943** *American Mercury* Nov. 552/1 If he's in the Army he's referred to as a *yardbird*..an old Army term for camp-confined newcomers. **1947** *Amer. Speech* XXII. 111 A soldier, sailor, or marine who frequently receives punishments for offenses against the regulations is designated as a *Y.B.* or 'yard bird'. **1965** C. Brown *Manchild in Promised Land* iii. 80 For the next two weeks, K. B. was Claiborne's yardbird. He had to go everywhere Claiborne went from morning till night. He even had to ask Claiborne when he wanted to go to the bathroom.

b. A convict.

1956 S. Longstreet *Real Jazz, Old & New* 148 A yardbird is a low mug. **1980** A. Pearl *Dict. Popular Slang* 189/1 *Yardbird*, a convict..an ex-convict.

c. A worker in a yard (Yard *sb.*[1] 4) (see quots.). *U.S.*

1963 T. Pynchon *V.* xvi. 427 'Yardbirds are the same all over,' Pappy said... The dock workers fled by, jostling them. **1968** *Amer. Speech* XLIII. 290 *Yard bird*, a disabled engineer, fireman ,or switchman who may work only within the yard limits. **1971** M. Tak *Truck Talk* 190 *Yard bird*, a driver who spots trailers and moves vehicles around a terminal yard.

yarder (yā·ɹdəɹ). *N. Amer.* [f. Yard *v.*[1] + -er.] A kind of donkey-engine used in logging.

1911 *Pacific Monthly* Apr. 376/2 The hook-tender gives the signal to the engineer of the 'yarder' as the donkey-engine is termed. **1919** *Camp Worker* 2 June 3/3 [There were] two Ledgerwood skidders, one yarder, one swing and one roader. **1942** Berrey & Van den Bark *Amer. Thes. Slang* § 512.10 *Yarder*, a donkey engine which hauls logs from where they are felled to the landing or skid road. **1955** *Bush News* (Port Arthur, Ont.) Feb. 7/1 About 1,100 men are involved on the haul plus 450 horses, 125 trucks, ..and 4 yarders. **1979** *Beautiful Brit. Columbia* Fall 37 In some logging areas, mechanical grapple yarders, machines that resemble construction cranes, settle into the forest floor.

ya·rdful. (f. Yard *sb.*[1] + -ful 2.] As much or as many as a yard will hold. Also *fig.*

1860 in Webster. **1960** *Farmer & Stockbreeder* 15 Mar. 95 A yardful of well-finished Hereford-cross beef. **1978** J. L. Hensley *Killing in Gold* xii. 165 I'm surprised you haven't a yardful of law around here.

yardland. Add: **3.** *Comb.*, as *yardland-holder.*

1890 E. W. Watson *Ashmore* 31 The two plough-oxen, the universal outfit of the English yardland-holder.

Hence **ya·rdlander**, a yardland-holder.

1891 *Athenæum* 16 May 632/3 The notes he gives as to the families of the yardlanders are most interesting. **1906** N. J. Hone *Manor* i. ii. 11 In 1279 a yard-lander at Newington, Oxon, was bound to plough an acre of winter tillage. **1964** H. P. R. Finberg *Lucerna* ii. 32 It would obviously make for convenience to group the strips of each yardlander.

yark: see also *york *sb.*[2]

Yarkand (yā·ɹkænd, yāɹkæ·nd). [The name of a river, district, and city in Sinkiang Uighur (formerly Chinese Turkestan), an autonomous region of western China.] **1.** A language or dialect of the central Turkic or Turco-Tatar group of Altaic languages, spoken in the district of Yarkand. Also *attrib.*

1875 [see *Kashgar 1]. **1954** M. A. Pei *Dict. Linguistics* 236 *Yarkand*, an Asiatic language, member of the Central Turkish group of the Altaic sub-family of the Ural-Altaic family of languages.

2. Used *attrib.* and *absol.* to designate a type of Turkoman carpet.

1880 G. C. M. Birdwood *Industrial Arts of India* II. 168 The tree of life represented on modern Yarkand rugs is always a pomegranate tree. **1913** W. A. Hawley *Oriental Rugs* xii. 251 In Plate L..are two of the most typical and interesting stripes of Samarkands and Yarkands... A stripe with simple archaic pattern peculiar to Yarkands is seen in Plate L. **1931** [see *Kashgar 2]. **1967** U. Schürmann *Oriental Carpets* 72 The eastern Turkestan rugs commonly known..as 'Samarkand' come..from the three oasis-cities of Kashgar, Yarkand and Khotan... A small number of silk Yarkands also exist. **1970** J. Franses *European & Oriental Rugs* 146 (*caption*) Eastern Turkestan Yarkand runner in the form of a saph. *Circa* 1800.

3. *Zool.* Used *attrib.* to designate a heavily built kind of red deer with short antlers that is found in Sinkiang Uighur.

1892 *Proc. Zool. Soc.* 116 Mr. W. T. Blanford exhibited two heads..and a skin of the Yarkand Stag. *Ibid.* 117 The name *C*[*ervus*] *yarkandensis* may be applied to the Yarkand and Tarim Deer. **1918** R. Lydekker *Wild Life of World* II. 231 Very distinct from the wapiti type is the Yarkand deer..of the forests of the Tarim Valley. **1982** G. K. Whitehead *Hunting & stalking Deer* iv. 111 Among the most endangered are the Yarkand deer..of Chinese Turkestan.

Yarkandi (yāɹkæ·ndi), *sb.* and *a.* Also 9– **Yarkundi.** [f. prec.] **A.** *sb.* A native or inhabitant of the city or district of Yarkand.

1841 H. H. Wilson *Trav. Moorcroft & Trebeck* I. ii. iii. 351 A Yarkandi asserted that an infusion of poppy-heads was employed to render the leaves of the tea adhesive. **1875** in T. D. Forsyth *Report Mission to Yarkund* iii. (*facing page*) 118 (*caption*) Yarkundis. **1901** P. W. Church *Chinese Turkestan* iii. 33 The guileless Yarkandis. **1926** C. P. Skrine *Chinese Central Asia* viii. 106 A charming..and well educated Yarkandi called Murad Qari.. partook of tea. **1981** A. Ali in *Himalayan Jrnl.* XXXVII. 115 The Yarkandis used this route [*sc.* Saser La in the Karakorams] for trade and for going on haj to Mecca.

B. *adj.* Of or pertaining to Yarkand or its people.

1854 A. Cunningham *Ladák* iii. 49 My informants, who were also Yarkandi merchants, stated exactly the reverse. **1893** H. Lansdell *Chinese Central Asia* II. xxxiv. 108 Turdi Akhoon, a Yarkandi merchant..had arrived from India. **1928** 'Ganpat' *Magic Ladakh* xiv. 255 It is a hard life on the Central Asian trade route if you happen to be a hired ponyman travelling with a callous Yarkandi merchant. **1973** M. Bence-Jones *Palaces of Raj* viii. 144 A portly General endeavoured to stop his Yarkundi pony from jumping over the railings.

yarling (yā·ɹliŋ), *ppl. a.* *Midl.* (and *north.*) *dial.* [f. dial. *yarl* vb. to utter a loud discordant sound: see *Eng. Dial. Dict.*] Howling, wailing.

1911 D. H. Lawrence *White Peacock* i. vii. 119, I heard more plainly..the peevish, wailing, yarling cry of some beast in the wood. **1972** Ld. Robens *Ten Year Stint* ii. 32 They were a 'yarling mob'—crude, vulgar and unfit to lead the decent men I know in the pits.

yarmulke (yā·ɹmŏlkə). Also **yarmulka;** (more rarely) **jarmulka, yarmolka,** etc. [ad. Yiddish *yarmolke*, ad. Polish *jarmulka* cap.] A skull-cap worn by male Orthodox Jews at all times, and by other male Jews on religious occasions: = *koppel.

1903 *Jewish Encycl.* IV. 301/2 The so-called Jewish garb of Poland, including even the 'jarmulka' (under-cap), is simply the old Polish costume which the Jews retained. **1929** *Menorah Jrnl.* XVI. 37 Jacob..saw and did not revere the squat figure clumsy in its..*yarmelke*. **1930** M. Gold *Jews without Money* 95 My father took me to the tailor and had made a handsome velvet *yamalka*. **1941** B. Schulberg *What makes Sammy Run?* ix. 232 There in the synagogue,..with his impressive shawl, his *yarmolka* and his great beard, there life was rich. **1957** L. Stern *Midas Touch* i. v. 45 He wore his *yamulka* (skull cap) when it was ritually required. **1962** 'E. McBain' *Empty Hours* 111, I was collecting the prayers shawls and the *yarmelkas*. **1963** T. Pynchon *V.* iv. 97 He went out of his way to cultivate the Tagliacozzi look:..wearing a bushy mustache, pointed beard, sometimes even a skull-cap, his old schoolboy yarmulke. **1966** L. Davidson *Long Way to Shiloh* xv. 221 You have the yarmulkah? Remember to put it on. **1966** H. Kemelman *Saturday Rabbi went Hungry* (1969) i. 14 He wondered if the cantor had put on his robes and tall white yarmulka. **1971** B. Malamud *Tenants* 90 Sam Clemence, a Mephistophelean type in yarmulke and yellow dashiki. **1975** *Church Times* 7 Nov. 5/1 A lively man in a business suit and embroidered *yarmulka*—the little skull-cap worn by orthodox Jews. **1979** 'A. Hailey' *Overload* iii. xi. 244 Hardly any of us took a yarmulke. I didn't. Had to borrow one when I went to the Wall in Jerusalem. **1984** *Times* 24 Sept. 4/6 The captain, who wore Israeli army uniform with a red yarmulka fringed with gold on his head.

yarn, *sb.* Add: **2. b.** A chat, a talk. *colloq.* (chiefly *Austral.* and *N.Z.*).

1857 H. W. Harper *Lett. from N.Z.* (1914) iii. 49 This has been a long yarn. **1883** Stevenson *Treasure I.* x. 80 'Come away, Hawkins,' he would say; 'come and have a yarn with John.' **1888** 'R. Boldrewood' *Robbery under Arms* I. xii. 156 After tea father and I and Jim had a long yarn. **1929** K. S. Prichard *Coonardoo* xv. 147 Meenie and Bandogera had taken advantage of her absence to have a smoke and a yarn together at the wood-heap. **1937** D. Cowie *N.Z. from Within* vii. 109 The word is used in its oldest sense. The New Zealander's 'yarn' is the Scotsman's 'news'. **1966** G. W. Turner *Eng. Lang. Austral. & N.Z.* vi. 124 Other counts have been based on written material and the Australian one on spoken. This accounts for the inclusion of *kid* ('child').., *yarn* ('talk').., [etc.]. **1979** B. Moore *Mangan Inheritance* ii. 295 We can take it easy for a while and have a real yarn together. **1984** *Times* 11 Sept. 32/8, I still see some of the Roman Catholics in the street..and we have a yarn.

3. *yarn-carrier*; **yarn count** = *count *sb.*[1] 2 b.

1927 T. Woodhouse *Artificial Silk* 100 The yarns now pass to their respective yarn carriers, the function of which is to place the yarn in the path of the single set of sinkers. **1957** *Textile Terms & Definitions* (Textile Inst.) (ed. 3) 109 *Yarn carrier*,..the final element which guides the yarn to the knitting instruments. **1923** Yarn count [see *number *sb.* 6 g]. **1963** Jerrard & McNeill *Dict. Sci. Units* 154 In the textile industry the yarn count or yarn number gives either the mass per unit length or the length per unit mass of a yarn fibre.

yarn, *v.* Add: **1.** Also, to chat or talk. (Further examples.)

1857 *St Leonard's Station Diary* 14 May, in L. R. C MacFarlane *Amuri* (1946) iii. 125 Hanging round the station, yarning and sleeping. **1901** M. Franklin *My Brilliant Career* (1966) iii. 3 Too friendly to pay a short call, they came and sat for hours yarning about nothing in particular. **1939** A. Powell *What's become of Waring* vii. 206 If I..start yarning with him..we shall be late for dinner. **1941** I. L. Idriess *Great Boomerang* xvii. 122 In the whitewashed Birdsville Hotel, low-roofed but with dim, cool rooms, the blokes yarn the time away. **1944** *R.A.F. Jrnl.* Aug. 256 There is practically nothing to do but..yarn with your friends. **1958** L. Durrell *Balthazar* ii. 37 We were sitting at a café yarning. *a* **1966** 'M. Na Gopaleen' *Best of Myles* (1977) 55 He does be yarnin with the brother above in the digs of a Sunday. **1972** M. Shadbolt *Strangers & Journeys* xi. 195 In the town, where men gathered to yarn on street corners. **1977** C. McCullough *Thorn Birds* vi. 120 Their parents yarned over cups of tea, swapped tall stories and books.

† **b.** *trans.* To recount or narrate. *Obs. rare.*

1840 A. Russell *Tour Austral. Colonies* 40 One who can yarn the dangers of the deep so well.

yarooh (yarū·), *int.* Also **yaroo.** A humorous stylized representation of a cry of pain. (One of Billy Bunter's characteristic exclamations: see quots.)

1909 *Magnet* 20 Nov. 4/2 'Oh!' roared Bunter, as Bulstrode's heavy boot biffed on him. 'Ow! Yah! Yarooh!' **1918** *Ibid.* 8 June 12/2 'Don't keep me waiting, or I shall help you on—like that!' 'Yaroooh!' **1940** 'G. Orwell' in *Horizon* Mar. 178 'Oooogh!', 'Grooo!' and 'Yaroo!' (stylized cries of pain). **1953** *Manch. Guardian Weekly* 23 July 11/2 With a 'Yarooh!' on nearly every page William G. Bunter is on the war-path again. **1972** *Guardian* 21 Jan. 1/5 'Yarooh!' they yelled... 'Get out, you cad!' **1977** M. Amis in A. Thwaite *My Oxford* 205 A sign reading 'Yaroo—College Squit!' suspended from my neck.

† **yarraman** (yæ·rămăn). *Obs.* Pl. **yarramen, -mans.** An Australian Aboriginal word for a horse.

1848 H. W. Haygarth *Bush Life in Austral.* x. 108 A stockman..meets some of the blacks, to whom his first question is 'You make a light yarraman belonging to me' (*i.e.* Have you seen my horses?). **1882** A. J. Boyd *Old Colonials* 69 There's seventeen yarramen—call 'em thirty pounds a head. **1905–6** 'T. Collins' *Rigby's Romance* (1971) v. 21 He needn't be frightened o' these yarramans. I got them like lambs. **1930** A. W. Groom *Merry Christmas* xx. 156 'We tie yarraman here,' he suggested. They fastened their horses to low snags on the dead tree. **1959** Baker *Drum* 158 *Yarraman*, an outlaw horse or wildly behaved station hack. **1964** W. S. Ramson in *Southerly* I. 58 Other aboriginal words, *bora*, *coolamon*, *goondie*, *humpy*, and *yarraman*, came from tribes in the Sydney and Moreton Bay districts.

yary (yēᵊ·ri), *a. dial.* (chiefly *Newfoundland*). Also **yarry.** [var. of Yare *a.*] Quick, sharp; alert, energetic; wary, wide awake; rising early.

1855 *Trans. Philol. Soc.* 38 [Norfolk] *Yary*, brisk. **1863** J. Moreton *Life & Work in Newfoundland* iii. 35 *Yary*, wary. **1868** in *Dict. Newfoundland Eng.* (1982) 622/2 Here we saw a great number of wild geese in the lagoon.. but it was impossible to get within shooting distance of them, these birds are so wild and extremely yarry. **1881** *Even. Telegram* (St. John's, Newfoundland) 20 Sept. 1 We don't find the cruising war-ships of our yarry neighbours the French and the Americans, lying in port for weeks at a time. **1906** N. Duncan *Adventures Billy Topsail* 256 'Hi, b'y! Get yarry (wide awake)!' cried the captain in the morning. **1925** *Dialect Notes* V. 346 *Yary*,..1. energetic; smart. 2. early. 3. wary. **1966** A. R. Scammell *My Newfoundland* 90 That would be Skipper John Elliott, yary as ever, hi-tailing it for Jacob's ground before the Eastern Tickle crowd got the choice berths for the day.

yas (yæs), repr. colloq. and U.S. Blacks' pronunc. of Yes *adv.* See *yassuh *int.*

1887 H. Baumann *Londinismen* 238 *Yas*,..yes. **1909** L. M. Montgomery *Anne of Avonlea* xxiv. 279 'Was Ginger hurt?'..'Yas'm. He was hurt pretty bad. He was killed.' **1927** *N.Y. Times Mag.* 24 Apr. 4/2 Yas, sir. Dat right, sir. **1936** M. Mitchell *Gone with Wind* xxxii. 546 'I suppose you heard Jonas Wilkerson and that Emmie—' 'Yas'm,' said Mammy. **1966** *Keystone Folklore Q.* XI. 85 Caddy always taught the children not to say 'Yas suh, No suh and Yas 'um'..to white folks.

‖ **yashiki** (ya·ʃiki). Also 9 **yaski.** Pl. **yashiki,** (anglicized) **-s.** [Jap., f. *ya* house + *shiki* a space, site.] The residence of a Japanese feudal nobleman, including the palace or mansion and grounds, and the quarters for his retainers.

1727 J. G. Scheuchzer tr. *Kæmpfer's Hist. Japan* II. ix. 486 *Sokkokf Dai Mio Jassiki*, that is, Palaces and houses of the princes and Lords of the Empire.] **1863** R. Alcock *Capital of Tycoon* II. xiii. 280 The Daimios' *Yaskis* are merely a low line of barracks of the same construction, rather higher in the roofs. **1871** A. B. Mitford *Tales of Old Japan* II. 206 The principal yashikis (palaces) of the nobles are for the most part immediately round the Shogun's castle. **1906** R. A. Cram *Impressions Jap. Archit.* iii. 57 The arrangement of these 'yashiki' varied but little: a hollow square..was formed by the barracks for the daimyo's retainers; these barracks were usually two stories in height. **1959** R. Kirkbride *Tamiko* ix. 65 It was at once obvious to him that it was part of the ruins of a magnificent yashiki, destroyed by fire during the war. **1970** J. W. Hall *Japan* x. 170 All daimyo were obliged to build residences (*yashiki*) in Edo where they kept their wives and children.

yassuh (yæ·sʊ), *int.* Chiefly *U.S.* Repr. Black colloq. pronunc. of 'yes, sir' (often somewhat obsequious). Cf. *yas *adv.* + *suh.

1936 M. Mitchell *Gone with Wind* xxiii. 391 'She's not dead? Is she breathing?' 'Yassuh, she breathin.' **1944** C. Himes *Black on Black* (1973) 199 'Take good care of me, Chops,' I said... 'Yassuh.' **1963** Prange & Vitols in A. Dundes *Mother Wit* (1973) 631/2 Yassuh, I sees all dat. **1973** J. Pattinson *Search Warrant* ii. 33 'You live alone here?' 'Yassuh. Jus' me an' my mem'ries.'

Yates (yēᶦts). *Statistics.* [The name of Frank *Yates* (b. 1902), English statistician, who published the correction in 1934 (*Suppl. Jrnl. R. Statistical Soc.* I. 217).] *Yates'(s) correction*: a correction for the discreteness of the data that is made in the chi-square test when the number of cases in any class is small and there is one degree of freedom, consisting in the subtraction of ½ from each difference when evaluating chi square.

1934 R. A. Fisher *Statistical Methods for Research Workers* (ed. 5) iv. 96 (*heading*) Yates' correction for continuity. **1968** P. A. P. Moran *Introd. Probability Theory* ii. 76 The use of the correction ½ results in a closer numerical approximation and is known as Yates's correction. **1972** *Jrnl. Social Psychol.* LXXXVII. 53 As the expected frequency in some cells was less than 10, Yate's [*sic*] correction for continuity was applied. **1977** R. Holland *Self & Social Context* vi. 211 Cooper..shows with the help of chi-squared and Yates' correction the effectiveness of conjoint family and milieu therapy.

yatter (yæ·təɹ), *v. colloq.* (orig. *Sc. dial.*). [Imitative, perh. after Yammer *v.* + Chatter *v.*; cf. also Natter *v.*] *intr.* To talk idly and incessantly; to chatter, or gossip; to gabble; to complain peevishly. Freq. const. (*on*) (*about* something or *at* someone). Occas. *trans.*

1825 Jamieson (Suppl.) II. 703/2 She's ay yatter-yatterin, and never devaulds. **1831** *Gasometer* 457 She yattered about an ugly man that cam' in a fiddle case. **1896** P. A. Graham *Red Scaur* viii. 121 Grace likes to yatter about the days when she bondaged for him. **1919** J. Buchan *Mr. Standfast* I. vi. 122 No company but a wheen ignorant Hielanders that yatter Gawlic. **1942** N. Streatfeild *I ordered Table for Six* 203, I don't like to yatter about flying much. **1950** 'P. Woodruff' *Island of Chamba* 124 As long as the British yatter on about going and don't go, things are bound to get worse in India. **1963** J. N. Harris *Weird World of Wes Beattie* (1964) v. 62 This dear old Betty was yattering at me on Sunday morning when I was hung over to the eyeballs. **1977** J. I. M. Stewart *Madonna of Astrolabe* ii. 48 The confounded thing might tumble around our ears while we yattered.

Hence **ya·ttering** *vbl. sb.* and *ppl. a.*

1859 J. Watson *Living Bards of Border* 193, I winna get up, sae yer yatterin's vain. **1878** R. Ford *Hamespun Days* 105 A thrawart, yatterin', blatterin' mither. **1935** D. Rorie *Lum Hat* 58 Ta'en in By a yatterin' lump o' original sin. **1972** *Hawick News* 7 Jan. 7/4 Their yatterin', like the stream, goes on for ever.

ya·tter, *sb. colloq.* (orig. *Sc. dial.*). [See prec.] Idle talk; incessant chatter or gossip.

1827 J. Watt *Poems* 72 Gin ane hae walth to keep him lievin', Nae cravin' body's yater deevin'. **1898** J. Buchan *John Burnet of Barns* II. ix. 188 The shrill yatter of the fishwives. **1935** F. Niven *Flying Years* i. 10 Any yatter of human follies and failings. **1955** E. Pound *Section: Rock-Drill* xciv. 95 To the Odes to escape abstract yatter. **1978** *Sunday Mail* (Brisbane) 28 May 3/4 No one in the Brisbane Valley any longer believes the tourist yatter given out by Government..circles.

yautia (yaʊtī·ă). [Amer. Sp.] In the West Indies, any of various herbaceous perennials of the genus *Xanthosoma*, esp. *X. sagittifolia*, which belong to the arum family and are widely cultivated for their edible tubers; = Tania, tanier, tannier.

1899 W. Dinwiddie *Puerto Rico* xii. 141 The other root,..known commonly as 'yautia', is much cultivated by the peasantry and held in high esteem, being always on sale in the markets. *Ibid.*, From the 'yautia' roots considerable starch is made..and is sold principally for laundry purposes. **1917** L. H. Bailey *Stand. Cycl. Hort.* VI. 3523/1 The corms and cormels (offsets) of some taros, and the cormels of some varieties of yautia, are free from acridity even in the raw state as cultivated in southern United States. **1975** E. L. Ortiz *Best of Caribbean Cooking* 135 Add the yautía, yams, pumpkin, cassava, plantains, salt and Tabasco to taste. **1981** P. Theroux *Mosquito Coast* xvii. 223 Seeing me with some yautia plants..I told them they were yautias and that their roots were as tasty as carrots.

yava. (Earlier example.)

1774 W. Wales *Jrnl.* 26 June in J. Cook *Jrnls.* (1961) II. 846 They [*sc.* the Tongans] brought off with them the Yauva, or pepper-Root.

yaw, *sb.*¹ Add: Angular motion or displacement about a yawing axis. Also *Aeronaut.* and *Astronaut.*

1916 G. C. Loening *Military Aeroplanes* xii. 166 Struts of large fineness ratio..present considerable side surface and affect the directional center, at different angles of yaw. **1935** [see *pitch *sb.*² 2 b]. **1950** *Engineering* 3 Mar. 255/2 The Desynn type of transmitter and indicator..is used to transmit to the recording apparatus such variables as control forces, angle of yaw, pressures, etc. [in a prototype aircraft]. **1974** *Physics Bull.* Jan. 11/1 The six component wind tunnel balance..will be able to measure three forces (lift, drag and side force) and three moments (pitch, yaw and roll) on any aircraft model it supports. **1977** *Offshore Engineer* May 44/3 During these tests, the data acquisition system recorded..pitch, roll, heave, surge, sway and yaw of the lay barge, pull and length of mooring cables, and anchor positions. **1978** R. Jansson *News Caper* 7 The Captain manoeuvred the big jet back to stability, damping out yaw and roll.

c. yaw axis = *yawing axis* s.v. *yawing *vbl. sb.*

1959 F. D. Adams *Aeronaut. Dict.* 184/1 Yaw axis. **1962** F. I. Ordway et al. *Basic Astronaut.* ix. 368 Any vehicle motion will take place about three axes... These axes are the yaw axis, the pitch axis, and the roll axis. **1978** *Sci. Amer.* Nov. 137/1 For the first time the machine included a pair of fixed vertical surfaces behind the wings to stabilize motion about the yaw axis.

yaw, *v.*¹ Add: **1. b.** *Aeronaut.* and *Astronaut.* Of an aircraft or spacecraft: to rotate about a vertical axis, to undergo yawing.

1912 *Q. Rev.* July 243 This disposition tends to offer an ever-increasing amount of surface sideways to the air when a turn is begun, thus accentuating the turn initiated by the rudder and causing the craft to yaw. **1935** C. G. Burge *Compl. Bk. Aviation* 108 The forces on the two wing tips are neither steady nor equal, so that the aeroplane tends to roll and yaw. **1964** [see *pitch *v.*¹ 19 f]. **1979** *Daily Tel.* 7 Apr. 3/2 It then yawed to the right, did a barrel roll like a light aircraft starting at an aerial show, and went into a nose-dive.

3. (Examples in *Aeronaut.*)

1920 *Engineering* 8 Oct. 462/2 It was found that the control was not reversed at large angles of incidence up to 20 deg. unless the model was yawed. **1960** Welch & Denes *Go Gliding* i. 20 Moving the left foot forward yaws the glider's nose to the left. **1975** L. J. Clancy *Aerodynamics* xvi. 525 The aircraft is yawed to starboard.

yawing, *vbl. sb.* Add: (Examples in *Aeronaut.* and *Astronaut.*) **yawing axis,** a vertical axis through a ship or aircraft; an axis through a spacecraft normal to both the longitudinal and lateral axes.

1915 A. Fage *Aeroplane* vi. 86 An indifference [on the part of pilots] to yawing, and possibly to rolling, is regarded favourably in many aeronautical circles. **1935** C. G. Burge *Compl. Bk. Aviation* 238/1 This causes a 'yawing' effect in the opposite direction to the turning effect of the rudder [of the plane]. **1953** Yawing axis [see *rolling axis* s.v. *rolling *vbl. sb.*² 9 a]. **1975** L. J. Clancy *Aerodynamics* xvi. 525 If the aircraft has a yawing velocity, *r*, this affects the fin incidence in the same way that pitching velocity affects the tail incidence. **1978** *Jrnl. Fluid Mech.* LXXXVII. 533 These passive yawing motions are studied to find their amplitude, the yawing axis and any associated energy dissipation.

yawl (yǭl, yāl), repr. (Southern) U.S. pronunc. of *y'all *pers. pron.*

1919 *Dialect Notes* V. 40 *Yawl*,..you-all. **1938** C. Himes in *Black on Black* (1973) 167 Why doesn't yuh git happy an' praise de Lawd? Doesn' yawl know who Ah is? **1978** J. R. Gaskin in *Sewanee Rev.* LXXXVI. 426 Dillard accounts for *y'awl*, or *you all*, not as the simple concatenation of two English forms.

yawmeter (yǭ·mitəɹ). [f. Yaw *sb.*¹ + -meter.] An instrument used to detect changes in the direction of flow round an aircraft or other body.

1921 *Flight* 28 July 511/1 A new direction and velocity meter (yawmeter) has recently been constructed. **1947** *Jrnl. R. Aeronaut. Soc.* LI. 15/2 We imagine aerofoil and observer to be stationary and the aerofoil to be immersed in a stream of air of speed *V* normal to the span..the direction of the stream being made known to the observer by, for example, a yawmeter. **1969** *Jrnl. Physics E* II. 989/1 Calibration of the instrument as a yawmeter. Most of the tests on the instrument have been made near the outlet end of an open water channel. **1983** *Ibid.* XVI. 231/1 (*heading*) A yawmeter for steady and low-frequency unsteady flows.

yawn, *sb.* Add: **2. c.** *transf.* and in *transf.* contexts, denoting something that induces boredom; a tedious activity. *colloq.*

1889 E. C. Dowson *Let.* 3 Feb. (1967) 32 My dear Moore. Here goes for my accustomed Sunday yawn to you! Thanks for your note. **1974** D. Gray *Dead Give Away* ii. 24 To you it may be one big yawn, or the laugh of a life-time... But to me it's important. **1978** G. A. Sheehan *Running & Being* viii. 102 For them the Super Bowl is three hours of yawns. **1979** *Broadcast* 4 June 8/3, 7 June will be a major event for psephologists..if..a yawn a minute for British voters. **1984** *Times* 3 Oct. 13/1 So much proscription may sound like a recipe for a great gastronomic yawn.

yaw·nfully *adv.*

1914 W. De Morgan *When Ghost meets Ghost* I. xviii. 691 'On my way to Poynders,' said the Countess yawnfully.

yawner. Add: **1. b.** *transf.* Something dreary or boring. *colloq.* (orig. *U.S.*).

1942 Berrey & Van den Bark *Amer. Thes. Slang* § 276/2 *Something uninteresting*,..washout, yawner. **1969** A. Glyn *Dragon Variation* ii. 42 The game between him and Wheaton, still to be played, should be a real yawner. **1980** *Globe & Mail* (Toronto) 5 Nov. 17 (*heading*) The Awakening is a real yawner. **1983** *Chicago Sun-Times* 6 Aug. 76 (*heading*) Opener likely to be yawner.

yawp, yaup, *sb.* Add: **b.** Chiefly *U.S.*, sometimes in allusion to Whitman's use. (Earlier and further examples.)

1835 J. H. INGRAHAM *South-West* I. 29 'Hold your yaup, you youngster you,' roared the old man in reply. **1855** W. WHITMAN *Leaves of Grass* 55, I sound my barbaric yawp over the roofs of the world. **1870** 'MARK TWAIN' in *Galaxy* Oct. 571/1 He..ordered me to 'hold my yop'. **1904** *Buffalo* (N.Y.) *Commercial* 25 Aug. 6 When this contest is ended, the insincere and ridiculous yawp about the fierce belligerency of Theodore Roosevelt will be laid away with the other feeble fakes. **1973** *Publishers' Weekly* 26 Mar. 61/3 American readers may miss the experimentation and 'barbaric yawp' of avant-garde American poetry.

yawp, yaup, *v.* Add: **1. b.** To speak foolishly or noisily. *U.S. colloq.*

1872 S. HALE *Let.* 28 Oct. (1919) 90 Perhaps it is just as well, however, not to yawp much about our going *alone*, as it may be considered loose in America. **1926** T. BEER *Mauve Decade* vi. 233 Where the boys who badgered Richard Harding Davis for autographs in 1890 will be yawping over 'Billy Baxter's Letters' in 1900.

yay (yēⁱ), *adv.* Also **yea.** *U.S. slang.* [Prob. f. YEA *adv.*] In phrases *yay big* (or *high*), 'this big', 'this high': freq. accompanied by a gesture indicating the size intended.

1960 WENTWORTH & FLEXNER *Dict. Amer. Slang* 591 *Yea big, yea high*, 1. This big, or this high, accompanied with the spreading of the hands to indicate the size; very large, or high, overwhelmingly large or tall. 2. Not very big or high. **1972** T. KOCHMAN *Rappin' & Stylin' Out* 242 Jeff fired on him. He came back and all this was swelled up bout yay big, you know. **1978** P. THEROUX *Picture Palace* 259 Why does a daughter of mine, whom I've loved and respected ever since she was yay high, go out of her way to made a jackass of me?

‖**yayla** (yēⁱ·lă). Also 9 **yaila; yaylak.** [Turk.] A summer camping-ground in the mountains or Turkestan used by Kurdish and other semi-nomadic peoples; the encampment pitched there.

1864 A. VAMBERY *Trav. Central Asia* xvi. 308 A Yaylak (summer abode), near to the hill on the sea-shore. **1896** D. G. HOGARTH *Wandering Scholar in Levant* iii. 53 Others come and go, and the place of the summer *yaila* is fixed hard by the village itself. **1953** O. CAROE *Soviet Empire* xi. 181 In the same country in winter the *yaylaks* will be deep under snow. **1975** J. RATHBONE *Kill Cure* III. ii. 85 At last they had come to the yayla or summer pasture.

Yayoi (yā·yoi). The name of a quarter in Tokyo, used *attrib.* and *absol.* to designate a type of early Japanese (wheel-thrown) pottery first discovered at this site in 1884, and hence applied to the mainly neolithic culture characterized by this ware. Cf. *JOMON.

1906 N. G. MUNRO in *Trans. Asiatic Soc. Japan* XXXIV. 24 The pottery..is called *Yayoishiki*, 'Yayoi sort', because it was first encountered in breaking ground at Yoyoi [*sic*] Street in Tokyo. **1931** G. B. SANSOM *Japan* I. i. 3 This latter type is known as the Yayoi type, because of certain characteristic earthenware first found in a neolithic site at a place of that name. **1955** *Far Eastern Q.* XIV. 329 It is not entirely clear why so few workers paid any serious attention until extremely recent years to the archaeology of the Yayoi period. **1960** B. LEACH *Potter in Japan* vi. 136 Jomon pottery 3,000 B.C. on to Yayoi from A.D.o. **1968** *Encycl. Brit.* XVIII. 523/2 The prehistoric period in Japan is characterized by two principal cultures known as Jōmon and Yayoi... Yayoi pottery seems to have its beginnings in the 3rd century B.C. and is mostly wheel-thrown. **1970** J. W. HALL *Japan* iii. 19 The Yayoi people brought with them the horse and the cow, though not in abundance.

Y chromosome. *Genetics.* Also †**y chromosome.** [*Y 4 b.] A sex chromosome which occurs in only one of the sexes (in man and other mammals, the male) or in some species is absent altogether, its presence or absence in the zygote determining in man and many other species the sex of the organism.

1911 *Biol. Bull.* Jan. 119 We have associated the *X* and *Y* chromosomes of the male with sex-determination, but possibly they have some other meaning. **1933**, etc. [see *X CHROMOSOME]. **1965** R. P. MOREHEAD *Human Path.* vi. 170/1 Proved cases of mutation involving the Y chromosome are extremely rare... As Y chromosomes occur only in males, the characteristic pedigree of such mutations should contain only affected males, never affected females, and all affected males should transmit the defect to all their sons. **1974** P. CAVE *Dirtiest Picture Postcard* x. 57 You've buttonholed me to give me long and boring lectures upon Germaine Greer, the faulty Y chromosome and the drudgeries of housework and child-bearing. **1982** *Nature* 2 Dec. 404/2 When a Y chromosome is present the foetal gonad, which has the potential to become either ovary or testis, differentiates into a testis and, when absent, into an ovary... Recent genetic analysis shows that this first step is not as simple as first thought and appears to be controlled by an interaction between autosomal genes and a gene(s) on the Y chromosome, for normal male differentiation. **1983** J. R. S. FINCHAM *Genetics* ii. 72 In grasshoppers and other insects of the order Orthoptera..there is usually no Y-chromosome. The females are XX and the males just X.

yea, *adv.* (*sb.*) Add: **C. yea-and-nay** *a.*, (*a*) (later examples referring to the phr. *Richard Yea-and-Nay*, a nickname for King Richard I); **yea-say** *v.*: hence **yea-saying** *vbl. sb.* (later examples) and *ppl. a.*; **yea-sayer,** one who says 'yea' or who agrees; a person inclined by nature to assent, or to act in a positive manner.

1911 FLETCHER & KIPLING *School Hist. Eng.* 70 'Richard Yea and Nay', so called because he spoke the truth. **1957** A. DUGGAN *Devil's Brood* xii. 165 Because he [*sc.* Bertrand de Born] could not persuade Richard to make war at his bidding he gave him the opprobrious nickname Yea-and-Nay. **1934** WEBSTER, Yea-sayer. **1940** 'G. ORWELL' *Inside Whale* 176 There are the 'progressives', the yea-sayers, the Shaw-Wells type, always leaping forward to embrace the ego-projections which they mistake for the future. **1972** A. FRIEDMAN in Cox & Dyson *20th-Cent. Mind* I. xii. 434 The Wilcoxes..are businessmen, robust, conservative, organized, practical yea-sayers who lead lives of 'telegrams and anger'. **1960** *Partisan Rev.* Fall 609 In literary criticism..artless enthusiasm..has modulated into..more restrained yea-saying. **1960** *Times* 14 Oct. 18/3 Matthew Smith's art, so much..in tune with the traditional, yea-saying materialism of French painting. **1972** *Jrnl. Social Psychol.* LXXXVI. 220 Subjects who obtained scores of 0, 1, and 11, 12 were dropped from the analysis as representing extremes of yeasaying or naysaying.

yeah (yēᵊ), *adv. colloq.* (orig. *U.S.*). Repr. a casual pronunc. of YES *adv.* Cf. *OH YEAH.

1905 *Dialect Notes* III. 67 *Yeah, yep*,..variants of *yes.* **1925** F. S. FITZGERALD *Great Gatsby* iv. 87 'That's a very interesting idea.' 'Yeah.' He flipped his sleeves up under his coat. **1936** M. KENNEDY *Together & Apart* IV. 293 'You were in Sweden with him last year, weren't you?' 'Yeah.' **1940** *Music Makers* May 17/3 *Yeah, man*, exclamation of assent. **1949** E. BIRNEY *Turvey* 153 'Yeah, yeah, Hayes was pretty hot but the ref—'. **1950** 'D. DIVINE' *King of Fassarai* xx. 166 'I take it the natives are friendly?'..'Yeah... We had us a party last night.' **1961** J. HELLER *Catch-22* (1962) xix. 194 'Will that be all, sir?' asked the chaplain. 'Yeah,' said Colonel Cathcart. 'Unless you've got something else to suggest.' **1977** B. LANGLEY *Death Stalk* xx. 104 'The shooting. That was Tony.' 'Tony?' 'Yeah, he done that.'

year[1]. Add: **3. a.** Also with cardinal number following, denoting a period of a political regime as a means of calendar reckoning.

1933 E. WAUGH *Scoop* II. iv. 226 New Calendar. Year One of the Soviet State of Ishmaelia. **1971** *Times Lit. Suppl.* 27 Aug. 1015/2 When he refers to 'the language of the Year III', he means that of the Year II [of the 1870 Commune]. **1972** R. COBB *Reactions to French Revolution* i. 38 The *coup d'état* of Fructidor year V (Sept. 1797). **1980** P. VAN GREENAWAY *Dissident* vii. 147 The Seventeen Revolution is Year One to our country.

b. (*a*) Freq. with qualifying word, as *financial, fiscal, sabbatical, school, tax year*: see under the first elements. *academic year*: in a school, college, etc., in the Northern hemisphere usu. reckoned from the beginning of the autumn term until the end of the summer term.

1932 *Handbk. Univ. Oxford* 103 An overseas application made..a few weeks before the beginning of the academic year has little or no prospect of success. **1957** *Encycl. Brit.* XXII. 876/2 The master's degree is usually obtained for one academic year of graduate work. **1971** *Morning Star* 28 Dec. 4 Every September boys and girls..return to school..to begin a new academic year. **1983** *Oxf. Univ. Gaz.* 10 Nov. 218/2 The college proposes to elect a distinguished visitor to a Visiting Senior Research Fellowship during the academic year 1984–5.

(*b*) Used *attrib.* or *absol.* with preceding ordinal numeral to denote a student at a particular stage of education. Also *collect.*

1851 B. H. HALL *Coll. College Words & Customs* 266 In the University of Cambridge, Eng., the title of *Second-Year Men*..is given to students during the second year of their residence at the University. **1894** A. MORRISON *Tales of Mean Streets* iii. 50 A fourth-year London Hospital student. **1913** J. VAIZEY *College Girl* II. xix. 268 One word in your ear! Don't ask a third-year girl to dance with you. **1927** R. LEHMANN *Dusty Answer* III. i. 124 I've done six hours every day this vac... Sibyl Jones has done ten hours every day... Third years ought to be more sensible. **1935** D. L. SAYERS *Gaudy Night* vii. 139 There are some oddities in the First Year... I expect the Third Year said the same about us..but..I should call the whole of our year pretty sound. **1966** E. H. JONES *Margery Fry* v. 44 Margery..was the obvious choice from the First Year when a committee was formed to arrange a garden-party in May 1895. **1979** D. BRIERLEY *Cold War* iii. 26 Sociology second years from Nanterre. **1982** D. CLARK *Doone Walk* viii. 179 He's a Bristol University third-year bloke.

d. Such a period officially designated for special celebration or to focus public attention on a particular object of concern; esp. *Holy Year*, a year so designated by the Pope, now usu. once every 25 years, during which special Indulgences are granted and ceremonies held.

1699 J. JACKSON *Let.* 25 Dec. in *Lett. & Second Diary of Samuel Pepys* (1932) 291 Wee made our entry here on Tuesday last, about 23 a clock, and were soon after deafned with the jangling of all the bells of the town, which for severall days, morning and evening, had proclaimed the approach of the Holy Year. **1776** PIUS VI (*title*) Instructions & Directions for Gaining the Grand Jubilee of the Holy Year, celebrated at Rome anno 1775, and extended to the universal Church anno 1776, by his Holiness Pius VI. **1858** H. E. WISEMAN *Recoll. Last Four Popes* II. iv. 270 The practice has been, that on Ascension Day of the preceding year, the Pope promulgates the Holy Year, or Jubilee. **1900** H. THURSTON *Holy Year of Jubilee* ix. 358 During the Holy Year, and also during the time of the extension of the Jubilee to the rest of Christendom, the Holy Father grants extraordinary powers to confessors. **1957** J. S. HUXLEY *Relig. without Revelation* (rev. ed.) ix. 205 Mass celebrations, like those of the Holy Year or the rallies and parades of Nazism and Communism. **1960** *Stamp Mag.* May 454/1 Commemorative. For World Refugee Year (Overprint on the rest of the 1958 World Exhibition stamps, with surcharge in aid of World Refugee Year 1960). **1965** *Ibid.* Apr. 244/1 The Australian Post Office will issue a stamp this year to commemorate International Co-operation Year. **1971** M. LEE *Dying for Fun* xliv. 212 He..decided to organize and launch Compassion Year. **1974** *Times* 7 Feb. 15/8 In the year 2073..many of the trees planted in Tree Planting Year 1973 will still be with us. **1983** *Out of Town* Dec. 52/4 Those of us who go to church already know that 1984 is Christian Heritage Year.

4. a. (Later example.) Also *spec.* with reference to the vintage of wine.

1864 'J. WARD' *Diary* 22 May in J. Burnett *Useful Toil* (1974) I. 85 Everything looks well in fields and gardens, with every prospect of a good fruit year. **1941** B. SCHULBERG *What makes Sammy Run?* xi. 206 Laurette.. told the waiter to send it back. 'If you haven't *1927*, don't bother. That's the only good year left.' **1967** 'L. BLACK' *Two Ladies in Verona* x. 161 A bottle of Mumm Cordon Rouge. I leave the year to you, but it'd better be good. **1984** *Sunday Tel.* 20 May 12/8, I bought the wine. 1964 was quite a good year.

7. a. of the year: denoting things or persons considered to be outstanding examples of their kind in a particular year; **the year dot:** see *DOT *sb.*[1] 4 c; **the year one:** see ONE *numeral* 4; **year in (and) year out** (earlier example); **year-on-year** *adj. phr.*: in *Economics*, used with reference to a comparison of figures with corresponding ones for a date twelve months earlier; **year-to-year** *adj. phr* (later examples).

1883 H. JAMES in *Atlantic Monthly* Sept. 316/1 Wherever the traveler goes, in France, he is reminded of this very honorable practice—the purchase by the government of a certain number of 'pictures of the year'. **1936** L. P. SMITH *S.P.E. Tract* XLVI. 220 The market-place where the books of the year are sold in large editions. **1968** 'E. LATHEN' *Stitch in Time* vi. 46, I hope they haven't confused Wendell Martin with the GP of the year. **1983** *Daily Tel.* 18 Aug. 8/4 A 35-year-old mother..beat 523 competitors to win the London Chamber of Commerce and Industry's award as top secretary of the year.

1830 *Massachusetts Spy* 28 July 4/1 I've been to.. school *year in and year out*.

1976 *Daily Tel.* 20 July 1/5 It is hoped this will show a year on year rise in average earnings of between 14 and 15 per cent. **1982** *Listener* 16 Dec. 27/3 Over a ten-week period from September to November, the year-on-year decline recorded is equivalent to 12 per cent of individuals, or 7 per cent of households.

1962 *Lebende Sprachen* VII. 113/3 Year-to-year growth ratio. **1977** J. L. HARPER *Population Biol. Plants* 203 The relative constancy of mean seed weight over a density range in this experiment is particularly interesting because the year to year variation in seed weight is quite large.

c. *to see the New* (*Old*) *Year in* (*out*) and varr.: to stay up until after midnight on 31 December, to celebrate the start of a new year.

1840 DICKENS *Let.* ? 18 Dec. (1969) II. 169 Will you dine with us on the last day of the old year—just to see it jollily out. **1875** L. TROUBRIDGE *Life Amongst Troubridges* (1966) 134 It's eleven o' clock now, and shall I tell you what we three are doing? Watching the Old Year out and the New Year in. **1916** M. DIVER *Desmond's Daughter* III. x. 227 Accepting an invitation to..'see the New Year in' with Thea. **1921** W. DE LA MARE *Mem. of Midget* xv. 99, I had written..an invitation to herself and Fanny to sit with me and 'see in' the New Year. **1939** H. NICOLSON *Diary* 31 Dec. (1967) II. 52, I do not stay to watch the New Year in or the Old Year out. I write this diary at 11.45 and shall not wait.

8. *year-hedged* adj.; **year class,** the individuals of a particular kind of animal (usu. a fish) that were born in any one year.

1936 DYLAN THOMAS *25 Poems* 41 The year-hedged row is lame with flint, Blunt scythe and water blade. **1910** J. HJORT in *Publications de Circonstance* No. 53. 18 Very characteristic in this respect are the analyses of samples of the typical Norse spring-herring, where the year-class which formed its first winter-ring in 1904 preponderates largely over all the other year-classes. **1958** *Jrnl. Marine Res.* XVII. 505 The population [of sea-urchins] probably consists of four year-classes. **1967** [see *RECRUIT *v.* 3 e]. **1981** *Trans. Amer. Fisheries Soc.* CX. 185/1 By optimizing the yield from dominant year classes, greater yields from the fishery can be realized for all groups involved.

year[2] (yīᵊɪ, yɒ̄ɪ). Repr. dial. (chiefly U.S.) pronunc. of EAR *sb.*[1]

1863 *Southern Confederacy* (Atlanta, Georgia) 9 May 1/2 You should git the strait of it from one who seed it with his eyes, and hearn it with his years. **1886** *West Somerset Word-Bk.* 845 *Year*,.. the ear. **1891** *Dial. Hartland, Devonshire* 122 *Year* (yur), the ear. **1929** W. FAULKNER *Sound & Fury* 72, I wish I was young like I use to be, I'd tear them years right off your head. **1935** Z. N. HURSTON *Mules & Men* (1970) I. viii. 173 He took and galloped out in de middle of de road right in front of John's horse and laid his years back.

year-book. Add: Now freq. as one word. **2. b.** *U.S.* An album published annually by the graduating class of a high school or college.

1926 B. MANBERT (*title*) Inter-Scholastic Year Book Manual. **1928** A. H. ANDERSON *School-Built Annual* 21 Don't think you can get out an annual in a week. A yearbook is a year's job. **1939** D. E. MITCHELL *Journalism & Life* xxx. 413 The yearbook is a more formal and permanent production than a newspaper. **1972** M. MEAD *Blackberry Winter* vii. 83, I did not see Luther again, but he sent me his yearbook... Luther was four years older than I and a senior in college. **1978** S. BRILL *Teamsters* vi. 233 The mob looks at high-school yearbooks and picks a hundred guys who look smart and clean.

yearling, *sb.* and *a.* Add: **A.** *sb.* **3.** *U.S. colloq.* A student in his first year or beginning his second year at college.

1900 *Dialect Notes* II. 70 *Yearling*, a second year man. **1940** BERREY & VAN DEN BARK *Amer. Thes. Slang* § 825/6 *Freshman*...yearling. **1944** *Collier's* 23 Sept. 69/1 His femme fell for a [West Point] yearling.

4. *Econ.* A yearling bond (see sense 3 of the adj. below).

1966 *This is Bill-Broking* (Allen, Harvey & Ross Ltd.) 38/1 *Yearlings*, stocks issued by local authorities for a period of a year and quoted either on the stock exchange or in the discount market. **1970** *Daily Tel.* 29 Sept. 17/5 (*heading*) Local authority yearlings at 8p.c. **1977** *Guardian* 19 Apr. 17/2 At the moment the yearlings give a return of 10 per cent which may be lower than what is available on the ordinary bonds, but are flexible. **1981** *Observer* 18 Oct. 20/1 An interesting alternative [to Government stocks] is the local authority negotiable bond—or the 'yearling', so-called because of its one-year term.

B. *adj.* **3.** *Econ.* Applied to bonds issued by a local authority usu. for one year.

1964 *Times* 2 Apr. 18/1 Under present conditions a quotation for a yearling bond would mean additional expense. **1969** *Daily Tel.* 12 Apr. 5/7 Most yearling bonds mature in..a year, sometimes two to five years. **1975** *Economist* 19 July 95 The explosion in the yearling bond market. **1977** *Guardian* 19 Apr. 17/2 Yearling bonds.. which come in units of £1,000, are much more flexible—and like the local authority bonds disgorge interest twice a year. They last for 12 months only and then investors have to start again.

yearly, *a.* (*sb.*) Add: **2. d.** *Yearly Meeting*, in the Society of Friends (Quakers), a national assembly held annually to deal with legislation and questions of policy (see *esp.* quot. 1869). Cf. *quarterly-meeting* (*a*) s.v. *QUARTERLY *a.* 3.

1688 *Testimony for the Lord, & His Truth* (Women Friends, York) 1 Given forth by the Women Friends at their Yearly Meeting at York, being a Tender Salutation of Love to their Friends and Sisters in their several Monthly Meetings. **1714** in *Jrnl. Friends Hist. Soc.* (1918) 28 Thence into Maryland to friends yearly-meeting at Tradaven-Creek..wherein Truth was plentifully afforded to ye bowing of many souls here. **1831** in S. B. Weeks *Southern Quakers & Slavery* (1896) xi. 300 There is not a school in the limits of the [North Carolina] Yearly Meeting that is under the care of a committee of either monthly or preparative meeting. **1869** BECK & BALL *London Friends' Meetings* v. 53 The Yearly Meeting was from its commencement..first and chiefly, a gathering of public Friends (i.e. ministers), to confer together on matters of faith and doctrine... The ministers alone formed the Annual Assembly in London; but in 1677 the invitation for deputies from the Quarterly Meetings was renewed... The representative element has been formally recognised, and thereby the Yearly Meeting has come to its position of legislative importance in the Church. **1923** E. B. EMMOTT *Short Hist. Quakerism* xi. 171 The proposal for a General Meeting for the whole country (which we now call the Yearly Meeting) came in the first instance from Durham Friends..in 1659. **1949** *Friend* 17 June 497/1 When the Clerk, in Yearly Meeting, announces the Report of the Committee on Accounts, it is quite astonishing to note how many Friends..get up and walk out. **1974** G. HUBBARD *Quaker by Convincement* I. iii. 41 Through the queries answered in writing four times a year by Monthly Meetings, the Yearly Meeting kept a watchful eye on departures from the norm.

yearning, *ppl. a.* Add: Hence (*nonce-wd.*) **yea·rningness.**

a **1916** H. JAMES *Sense of Past* (1917) 304 The ideal thing for dramatic interest..would be that there is just one matter in which..he betrays himself, gives himself away..it should..affect her..with but a finer yearningness of interest.

year-round, *a.* and *adv.* [f. the phr. *all the year round* s.v. ROUND *adv.* 1 e in Dict. and Suppl.] **A.** *adj.* That exists, occurs, is used, etc., all the year round. Also of persons: residing in a place for the whole year.

1939 *Florida* (Federal Writers' Project) II. 177 The western district..contains..many homes of year-round residents. **1939** R. CAMPBELL *Flowering Rifle* II. 38 And thaws numbed strikers from their year-round frost. **1945** NELSON & WRIGHT *Tomorrow's House* x. 111/1 One advantage of the inside bathroom..is that it has year-round ventilation. **1960** *House & Garden* Aug. 40/1 A skilfully-planned year-round family house. **1961** *Guardian* 8 May 8/6 A moment, known increasingly to year-round Londoners. **1976** *Sci. Amer.* July 118/1 Where the diversion of local streams would not provide a year-round supply of water it was necessary to build a reservoir. **1980** P. MOYES *Angel Death* i 7 Year-round sunshine.

B. *adv.* = *all the year round.*

1968 *Globe & Mail* (Toronto) 17 Feb. 47/8 Enjoy swimming year-round in the outdoor and indoor pools. **1979** *Wall Street Jrnl.* 20 Dec. 18/1 The yuletide bulge chiefly reflects the greater number of people in the stores at that time. However, the crime is rising year-round. **1981** C. MILLER *Childhood in Scotland* 58 Rabbits..were shot year-round.

yeast, *sb.* Add: **1. b.** (Earlier example of *German yeast.*)

1845 E. ACTON *Mod. Cookery* xxviii. 650 German yeast, imported in a solid state, is now much sold in London.

d. Delete *Path.* and substitute for def.: A fungus that exists predominantly as single cells rather than a mycelium and in which vegetative reproduction takes place by budding or fission. (Further examples.)

Now not usu. regarded as constituting any particular taxon.

1906 G. MASSEE *Text-bk. Fungi* III. 275 Symbiotic relationship between yeasts and bacteria is not uncommon. **1922** H. GWYNNE-VAUGHAN *Fungi* i. 7 Yeasts and filamentous fungi are abundant in woodland soils. **1930** H. M. FITZPATRICK *Lower Fungi* i. 16 In the lower Ascomycetes the asci are formed without order throughout a mould-like mycelium, or exist as isolated cells as in the yeasts. **1977** R. C. COOKE *Fungi, Man & his Environment* i. 14 Yeasts appear in the Ascomycetes, Basidiomycetes, and Fungi Imperfecti. This is because the term 'yeast' refers to a special mode of growth and does not describe a particular, special assemblage of fungi. **1983** *Oxf. Textbk. Med.* I. v. 372/2 *Candida albicans*... It is a saprophytic yeast often found as a commensal in the mouth and gastrointestinal tract and commonly present in the vagina.

4. yeast bread, bread made with yeast (i.e. ordinary bread); **yeast-cake,** (*a*) (later examples); (*b*) a cake made light with yeast; **yeast-powder** (later examples).

1853 *Southern Ladies Bk.* (New Orleans) I. 130 The chicks in the free states live on yeast bread. **1945** *A B C of Cookery* (Ministry of Food) xviii. 67 Nowadays yeast bread is seldom made in the home. **1855** E. ACTON *Mod. Cookery* (rev. ed.) xxxi. 604 To test bread that has been cut (or yeast-cakes), press down the crumb..with the thumb. **1897** R. M. STUART *Simpkinsville* 136 Here, too, had passed pantalet patterns, bits of yeast-cake and preserving-kettles. **1908** *McClure's Mag.* Feb. 421/2 We are to be the yeast-cake for democracy's dough. **1973** *Listener* 20 Sept. 377/2 Tea was served by Auntie Golda.. thick slices of cinnamon-veined yeast-cake. **1857** W. CHANDLESS *Visit Salt Lake* I. vi. 95 Three boxes of yeast-powder (at thirty cents each) to improve our bread. **1876** *Amer. Cycl.* XVI. 777 Yeast powders, or baking powders, substitutes for yeast, used in making bread.

yeast, *v.* Add: Also (*fig.*) with *up.*

1921 A. HUXLEY *Crome Yellow* ix. 88 It must inevitably take a long time for Armageddon to ripen, to yeast itself up.

Yeatsian (yēⁱ·tsiăn), *a.* (*sb.*) Also **Yeatsean.** [f. the name of the Irish poet and playwright William Butler *Yeats* (1865–1939) + -IAN.] Of, pertaining to, or characteristic of Yeats or his writing. Also as *sb.*, an admirer of Yeats.

1928 S. O'CASEY *Let.* 5 June (1975) I. 261 Since Mr. Yeats has..shouted a lot of things in at O'Casey's window, he shouldn't be surprised,..when he finds O'Casey hammering at the Yeatsian door. **1941** *Scrutiny* IX. 381 Mr. MacNeice does attempt to define the essence of the Yeatsian idiom. **1954** *N. & Q.* CXCIX. 535/2 Yeatsians are doubtless all familiar with Dr. Jeffares' story of the composition of 'The Wheel' at Euston on 17 September 1921. **1959** *Encounter* Nov. 78/2 The misguided Neo-Platonism of some Yeatsians. **1969** *Listener* 13 Mar. 361/2 Though Reisz can give us a Yeatsian despair ('Ah dancer, ah, sweet dancer'), he fails to evoke a Yeatsian gaiety. **1978** *Studies in Eng. Lit.: Eng. Number* (Tokyo) 157 Through his long poetic career, he changed from his early Yeatsean stance to his later self-assurance. **1982** J. GROSS in A. Thwaite *Larkin at Sixty* 86 Larkinesque irony..and high Yeatsian romance.

yech (yek, yək), *int. U.S. slang.* Also **yecch, yeck;** (*rare*) **yee(c)ch.** [Imitative. Cf. *YUCK *int.*, *sb.*², and *a.*] = *YUCK *int.*

1969 C. BURKE *God is Beautiful, Man* (1970) 76 Well, Jesus did the craziest thing you ever heard. He took some clay from the road and he spit on it...yeck! **1972** *Even. Telegram* (St. John's, Newfoundland) 23 June 3/1 Yeecchhhh! How messy. A St. John's pigeon just passed his opinion of a Bayman. **1973** *Daily Tel.* (Sydney) 17 May 36/1 She (yecch) pins a plastic gardenia into her hair. **1975** *Hi-Fi Answers* Feb. 41/1 Colouration introduced by the cartridge will be carried right through the system and emerge at the other end added to the inevitable individual speaker character, result...yeech! **1979** 'A. HAILEY' *Overload* IV. xviii. 389 As for the food there—yech! **1984** *N.Y. Times* 30 Mar. A. 6/2 We come up with new information and we tell them and they go 'Yecch—what a mess.'

yechy (yə·ki), *a. U.S. slang.* Also **yecchy.** [f. prec. + -Y¹. Cf. *YUCKY *a.*] = *YUCKY *a.*

1969 *Current Slang* (Univ. S. Dakota) Summer 17 *Yecchy*, adj. Extremely unpalatable (of food or drink). **1975** *New Yorker* 16 June 25/1 They thought the green peppers and onions were 'yechy'. **1983** *Washington Post* 23 Dec. 15/1 She goes on and on about him in yecchy voice-overs: He was like 'a licorice billygoat sniffing the wind for sexual sweat'.

yedda (ye·dă). Also **yeddo.** [Origin unknown.] A type of grass used for making straw hats (see quot. 1925). Freq. *attrib.* as *yedda braid, plait, straw.*

1918 C. R. AIKEN *Millinery Dept.* 28 Yedda braid was first produced in Italy, but the Japanese have made an imitation... Yedda is a tall grass grown in Italy, Japan, and the Philippines. **1922** F. ANSLOW *Pract. Millinery* viii. 93 The Yedda plaits, made of Japanese and Chinese grass, are soft and pliable, and can be dyed in most beautiful shades, of which, perhaps, the mole, grey and blue are the most attractive. **1923** *Sketch* 9 May 300 Dove-grey yedda straw makes this attractive shady hat. **1925** N. KNEELAND *Millinery* ii. 17 Yeddo is a tall grass grown in Italy, Japan, and the Philippines. The hats made from this fiber are loosely woven, light, and delicate. **1927** *Daily News* 20 June 2/4 A smart little hat of varnished black yedda straw. **1929** *Millinery Trade Rev.* May 46 A diversity of summer fabrics is being featured..as well as the ever popular straw items, Bakou, balibuntal, yedda, [etc.]. **1957** E. R. E. LANGRIDGE *Textbk. Mod. Millinery* vi. 62 Yeddo is a knotted straw made entirely by hand and worked up by the Swiss peasants in their houses.

Yeddo (ye·do). The former name of Tokyo, used *attrib.* to designate materials, etc., originating there (before 1868, in which year the name was changed), as † *Yeddo crepe, poplin*; **Yeddo spruce,** the Japanese spruce, *Picea jezoensis.*

1866 in A. Adburgham *Shops & Shopping* (1964) xii. 126 Costumes at reduced prices in Yeddo Poplin. [**1906** ELWES & HENRY *Trees Gr. Brit. & Ireland* 87 Mayr informed me last year that the Yezo spruce was not introduced into Europe until 1891.] **1932** W. DALLIMORE in F. J. Chittenden *Conifers in Cultivation* 26 Picea... jezoensis Carr... Yeddo Spruce--N.E. Asia to N. Japan. **1952** A. G. L. HELLYER *Sanders' Encycl. Gardening* (ed. 22) 378 *Picea..jezoensis*, 'Yeddo Spruce', not so hardy as var. *hondoensis*, 80 to 100 ft., Japan. **1960** C. W. CUNNINGTON et al. *Dict. Eng. Costume* 280/2 *Yeddo crepe*, 1880, a cotton fabric thick as linen but soft... *Yeddo poplin*, 1865, of pure llama wool, resembling French merino. **1981** F B. HORA in *Oxf. Encycl. Trees of World* 70/2 *P. jezoensis* Yeddo Spruce. NE Asia, Japan.

yeep (yīp), *v. rare.* [Imitative.] *intr.* To cheep. Hence **yee·ping** *ppl. a.* and *vbl. sb.*

1834 T. KEIGHTLEY *Tales & Popular Fictions* I. 11 His feathered charge, who go along *yeeping* and leisurely picking their steps. **1945** B. MACDONALD *Egg & I* (1946) iii. 44 Seven hundred and fifty yeeping chicks. *Ibid.* vii. 91 The yelping of a puppy and the stronger, louder yeeping of the chicks.

yeh (ye), *colloq.* or *dial.* var. of YES or YEA. Cf. *YEAH *adv.*

1920 GALSWORTHY *Skin Game* I. 13 *Hillcrist.* Did you meet the Jackmans? *Dawker.* Yeh. **1934** J. FRANKLYN *This Gutter Life* xx. 160 'I hope your son will be happy'. 'Yeh!—I 'opes so lidy.' **1955** W. GADDIS *Recognitions* I. vi. 206 Yeh, I could write a book. **1962** G. E. EVANS *Ask Fellows who cut Hay* (ed. 2) xxv. 235 The affirmative in the East Anglian dialect is 'yeh', which is undoubtedly not a corruption of yes, but a true survival of the early 'ye' ('Let youre ye be ye, and youre naye naye' of Tindal's Bible). **1963** LENNON & MCCARTNEY in *Golden Beatles Bk.* (1966) 37 She loves you yeh yeh yeh. **1973** *Black World* Nov. 91 Can you imagine the R&B band funky as they want to be, using a bass figure that kind of remind you of sweetback, yeh sweetback.

Yehudi, var. *YAHUDI.

yell, *sb.* Add: **e.** *slang.* Something or someone extremely amusing; a joke, a 'scream'.

1926 E. HEMINGWAY *Sun also Rises* xvi. 179 'Bill's a yell of laughter,' Mike said. **1938** N. MARSH *Artists in Crime* xv. 238 'Well, of course!' exclaimed Miss O'Dawne, greatly diverted. 'Aren't you a yell!' **1949** E. COXHEAD *Wind in West* ii. 32 All these doctors and their ecologists —what a yell. **1970** [see *LOOK *v.* 10 a].

yellow, *a.* and *sb.* Add: **A.** *adj.* **1. d.** (Earlier and further examples.) In U.S. use freq. as *yaller* when applied to light-skinned Blacks.

1787 *Asiatick Researches* (1790) II. 2 That the Turks have any just reason for holding the coast of Yemen to be a part of India, and calling its inhabitants Yellow Indians. **1834** *Sun* (N.Y.) 20 Mar. 2/2 A huge looking 'yaller gall' was hammering away at the eyes of a small white man.., because he called her a *snow* ball. **1888** L. A. SMITH *Music of Waters* 37 Oh, sigh her up, my yaller gals. **1913** *Punch* 19 Feb. 138/3 Believers in the Yellow Peril who wish everyone else to realise the importance of that menace are proposing to bring it home by means of All Yellow Suppers. **1927** [see *monkey-man* s.v. *MONKEY *sb.* 17 a]. **1937** C. HIMES *Black on Black* (1973) 141 The nervous profile of the driver bent low over the wheel. A yellow nigger. **1942** Z. N. HURSTON in A. Dundes *Mother Wit* (1973) 28/2, I done slept with yaller women. **1956** J. BARTH *Floating Opera* xxviii. 268 Ah fails to unnerstan' How a wuthless, shif'less dahkie such as you, sah, Kin conglomerate de money fo' a Caddylac sedan, Jest to keep yo' yaller gal fren' sweet and true, sah. **1966** *Listener* 17 Mar. 401/1 The setting is..England now, with a cold war and a yellow peril. **1977** C. MCCULLOUGH *Thorn Birds* xv. 348 But Japan was Asia, part of the Yellow Peril poised like a descending pendulum above Australia's rich, empty, underpopulated pit.

2. b. Craven, cowardly. *colloq.* (orig. *U.S.*).

1856 in P. T. Barnum *Struggles & Triumphs* (1869) 400 We never thought your heart was yellow. **1918** J. M. GRIDER *War Birds* (1927) 264 One of our noblest he-men, a regular fire-eater to hear him tell it, has turned yellow at the front. **1932** E. WALLACE *When Gangs came to London* xv. 121 The yellow jury..acquitted 'em on a murder charge. **1950** J. AGEE in *Botteghe Oscure* VI. 392 Then something happened that made me know I was scared of them and I admitted to myself: I'm yellow. **1974** *Guardian* 30 Jan. 24/3 It frightens me when moderate voices are taken to be from weak and yellow men. **1977** 'O. JACKS' *Autumn Heroes* xiv. 203 You're yellow scum. You'll fight when the odds are with you.

c. Of or pertaining to an organization, a policy, or to persons opposed to militant action by a trade union or trade unions. See also *yellow union*, sense C. 1 e below.

1913 J. A. ESTEY *Revolutionary Syndicalism* ii. 47 The so-called *syndicats jaunes*, or yellow syndicats, formed in the interest of employers for the purpose of strike-breaking. **1920** *Glasgow Herald* 12 Sept. 7 The railwaymen.. will be content to follow the lead of the General Confederation of labour and stick to the Amsterdam International, which the dictators of Russia have labelled 'yellow'—that is to say 'blackleg'. *Ibid.* 24 Nov. 8/3 The Russian Soviet Republic has insolently rejected it as 'a Congress of yellow leaders who continually betray the fundamental interests of the Labour movement'. **1922** B. G. DE MONTGOMERY *Brit. & Continental Labour Policy* vi. 58 The bus-traffic and road-transport were organized by the members of the 'yellow' or anti-strike syndicates, and by the *bourgeois* class. **1939** A. PHILIP in H. A. Marquand *Organized Labour in Four Continents* 51 The Confederation of Professional Unions, a 'yellow' organization benefiting from employer support. **1972** G. L. MOSSE in *Jrnl. Contemp. Hist.* VII. 206 France was regarded as the classical land of yellow trade unionism.

4. Of or pertaining to a political party whose colour is yellow. Cf. sense 4 of the *sb.*

1834 F. WITTS *Diary* 12 Aug. (1978) 97 The respective parties mustered when the poll was over at their headquarters, the Bell Hotel being the Blue house and the King's Head the yellow. **1874** TROLLOPE *Phineas Redux* I. ii. 14 He remained there for three or four days..staying at the 'Yellow' inn.

B. *sb.* **1. d.** Cowardice. Cf. sense 2 b of the adj. above.

1896 G. ADE *Artie* vi. 57 This is how I found that streak of yellow in him. **1914** B. M. BOWER *Flying U Ranch* 146, I was just b'ginnin' to think this bunch was gitting all streaked up with yeller.

2. a. Also *U.S.*, gold. *Obs.*

1858 *Pike's Peak Guide Bk.* 329 We commenced sending prospecting parties into the mountains, but they returned every night with 'nary yellow'. **1901** M. E. RYAN *That Girl Montana* xviii. 227 She would watch some strange miner dig and wash the soil in his search for the precious yellow.

c. A yellow ball used in the game of snooker.

1910 *Encycl. Brit.* III. 938/2 If it is pocketed, the player scores one and is at liberty to play on any of the coloured balls; though in some clubs he is compelled to play on the yellow. **1950** L. H. DAWSON *Hoyle's Games Modernized* III. 346 At the beginning of the game [of snooker] Yellow is placed on the right-hand corner of the D. **1977** *Cleethorpes News* 6 May 29/4 After potting the yellow he more or less forced Barnes to take green, brown and blue.

d. A golden Labrador.

1945 C. L. B. HUBBARD *Observer's Bk. Dogs* 97 As long as we have bred Labradors we have had yellows. **1973** *Country Life* 8 Feb. (Suppl.) 325/1 Some of the yellows were a light creamy colour.

3. See also *high yellow* s.v. *HIGH *a.* 21.

6. *ellipt.* for *yellow alert*, sense C. 1 e below.

1940 *Mass-Observation Archive* 1 Aug. in Calder & Sheridan *Speak for Yourself* (1984) iii. 78 Soon after eleven we were remarking that it was time we got the yellow, when the telephone went. **1943** [see *RED *sb.*[1] 8]. **1949** [see *ALERT *sb.* 1 b]. **1978** 'G. VAUGHAN' *Belgrade Drop* xiii. 84 President Turner had been in touch with the other Nato head of state and their forces had gone on yellow.

C. 1. a. *yellow Labrador*; **yellow-bob**, a shrike-robin, *Eopsaltria australis*, found in forested areas of south-eastern Australia; **yellow snake,** one of several yellowish snakes, esp. a boa, *Epicrates subflavus*, found in the West Indies; **yellow warbler,** one of several North American warblers of the genus *Dendroica*. **b. yellow bean,** the yellow seeds of one of several varieties of soya bean; **yellow birch,** a North American tree, *Betula lutea*, which has yellow or grey bark; **yellow box,** an Australian gum-tree, *Eucalyptus melliodora*, which has yellowish inner bark; **yellow cedar** = *Nootka cypress* s.v. *NOOTKA *a.* 2; **yellow poplar,** one of several North American softwood trees or their wood, esp. the tulip-tree, *Liriodendron tulipifera*; **yellow yam,** one of several species of *Dioscorea* producing yellow-fleshed tubers; also, the tubers themselves. **c. yellow ground,** kimberlite that is exposed at the surface and has become yellow as a result of atmospheric oxidation; **yellow jack** = *yellow jacket* (*b*), sense C. 2 c in Dict.; **yellow phosphorus** = *white phosphorus* s.v. *WHITE *a.* 11 c; **yellow ware** (earlier and later examples). **e. yellow alert,** an instruction to be prepared for or an initial state of readiness to cope with an emergency (cf. *red alert* s.v. *RED *a.* 19 a); **yellow badge,** a badge of identification that Jews have sometimes been required to wear, esp. by the Nazis in Germany (cf. *yellow star* below); **yellow band,** a mark on a lamp-post to indicate that motor vehicles are not permitted to wait in the vicinity; freq. *attrib.*; also = *yellow line* below; **yellow belt,** the belt worn by one who has attained a certain standard of proficiency in judo (see quots.); **yellow book,** (*a*) an official report of government affairs in various European countries; (*b*) a report issued by the Liberal Party in 1928 on the industrial future of Britain; **yellow card,** in Association Football, a card shown by the referee to a player when he is cautioned; † **yellow jacket,** a military decoration in imperial China (*obs.* exc. *Hist.*); **yellow jersey** [tr. F. *maillot jaune*], a jersey awarded to the winner of (a stage of) a cycle race, *esp.* the *Tour de France*; **yellow leaf,** used (in allusion to quot. 1605) to refer to the process of ageing; **yellow light** *U.S.* a yellow-coloured cautionary light in traffic signals (cf. *AMBER *a.* b); also *fig.*; **yellow line,** a yellow road-marking, usu. parallel to the kerb, indicating that parking of motor vehicles is restricted (though local regulations vary); also **double yellow line** indicating that parking is forbidden; **yellow pages** *sb. pl.* orig. *U.S.*, an index printed on yellow paper; *spec.* the classified section of or supplement to a telephone directory, listing firms, products, and services; **Yellow Pressman,** a journalist or reporter working for the yellow press (cf. sense 3 of the adj.); **yellow rain,** a yellow powder reported as falling through the air in S.E. Asia and causing severe blistering and sometimes death; **yellow rust,** a disease of wheat caused by the fungus *Puccinia glumarum*; **yellow spot** (earlier example); = *macula lutea* s.v. *MACULA 2; **yellow star,** a piece of yellow cloth bearing the Magen David, which the Nazis required Jews to wear; **yellow streak,** a trait of cowardice; **yellow union** [tr. F. *syndicat jaune*: cf. sense 2 c of the *adj.* above] a union of workers favouring free enterprise and usually opposed to strike action; **yellow warning** = *yellow alert* above.

1968 *Punch* 28 Aug. 279/1 NATO forces had quickly been placed on 'Yellow Alert'. **1969** *Times* 17 Sept. 1/8 A yellow alert..on hospital beds..means that all cases not in need of immediate attention will not be admitted to hospitals. **1978** 'G. VAUGHAN' *Belgrade Drop* iii. 23 The United States president..put his missile submarines throughout the world on yellow alert. **1876** GEO. ELIOT *Daniel Deronda* III. v. xxxvii. 127 To Deronda just now the name Cohen was equal to the ugliest of yellow badges. **1892** I. ZANGWILL *Childr. Ghetto* I. 2 People who have been living in a ghetto for a couple of centuries are not able..to efface the brands on their souls by putting off the yellow badges. **1942** I. COHEN *Jews in War* iii. 31 *The Yellow Badge* The crowning device for humiliating the Jews was the revival of a mediæval practice. In October 1941, a decree was issued requiring them to wear a yellow armlet marked with the 'Shield of David', which the Jews of Poland had been wearing for the past two years. **1962** BRIDGER & WOLK *New Jewish Encycl.* 38/1 (*caption*) The yellow badge the Nazis required Jews to wear in Germany and Nazi-occupied countries. **1948** *Times* 13 May 2/3 When the no-waiting order was first introduced in the West End it was announced that permanent signs would be erected as soon as the materials were available, the yellow bands being temporary. **1959** *Times* 8 Dec. 5/6 Vast numbers of cars..are left at the kerbside all day in all parts of central London except the yellow-band streets. **1962** R. JEFFRIES *Exhibit No. Thirteen* iv. 36 Parked my car in a yellow-band area. **1967** R. RENDELL *Wolf to Slaughter* ii. 17 The car drew up... 'Not on the yellow band, Drayton,' Burden said sharply. **1965** H. BURKE *Chinese Cooking for Pleasure* 150 In small cans are bamboo shoots,..red bean curd, black bean, yellow soy bean, [etc.]. **1972** CLAIBORNE & LEE *Chinese Cookbk.* (1973) xi. 422 *Bean Sauce*... Also called 'Whole Bean Sauce' or 'Yellow Bean Sauce', this thick sauce is made from yellow beans, flour, and water and is sold in.. tins. **1983** *Observer* 16 Jan. (Colour Suppl.: Living Extra) 7/4 Black beans..and yellow beans are both products of the versatile soya bean. **1941** M. FELDENKRAIS *Judo* 166 A white belt is worn by beginners, corresponding to the sixth Kyu. The next grade, the fifth, is indicated by a yellow belt. **1979** *Observer Mag.* 17 June 39/1 For several years he went to judo classes, reached yellow-belt standard (three below black belt). **1787** W. SARGENT in *Mem. Amer. Acad.* IX. 158 Black and Yellow Birch... The bark of the latter is used by the Indians for making canoes. **1851** J. S. SPRINGER *Forest Life* 23 The general outlines of the Yellow Birch often resemble the Elm. **1943** R. PEATTIE *Great Smokies* 156 A yellow birch on Whitetop Mountain was found to be seven feet three inches thick. **1974** M. BRAITHWAITE *Ontario* xi. 169 Hemlock, oak, maple, and yellow birch, they were all there, just waiting to be cut down and sawed up into lumber. **1909** A. E. MACK *Bush Calendar* 68 Then a yellow-bob came to visit us. **1965** *Austral. Encycl.* VII. 470/1 Another common and familiar bird is the yellow robin ('yellowbob') of eastern Australia, a species with a breast of bright yellow. **1883** *Pall Mall Gaz.* 5 Dec. 8/1 Paris, Dec. 5.—The first volume of the new Yellow-book on Tonkin affairs. **1897** *Times* 23 Nov. 5/1 The *Berliner Neueste Nachrichten* reminds the French Republic that..in former Yellow-books there is plenty of evidence to show how generous was the help afforded by Germany to France. **1929** D. LLOYD GEORGE *We can conquer Unemployment* 3 In the 'Yellow Book', published a year ago, the Liberal Industrial Enquiry presented exhaustive proposals for dealing with the grave unemployment situation with which Britain was, and is still, faced. **1949** *Time* (Atlantic ed.) 14 Feb. 18/1 The Communists issued a 'Yellow Book' containing what they called Mindszenty's written confession. **1983** *Daily Tel.* 24 Nov. 18/4 Had the Liberal Yellow Book been published in 1920 our history might have been different. **1877** F. VON MUELLER *Introd. to Bot. Teaching at Schools of Victoria* 15 This tree passes by the very unapt vernacular name Yellow Box-tree. **1934** *Bulletin* (Sydney) 31 Jan. 21/2 We lop mainly yellow box. **1977** *Meanjin* (Austral.) XXXVI. 1. 71 I'll..split off kindling wood From the yellow-box log. **1976** *Times* 11 Nov. 12/4 Two Villa men were shown the yellow card for fairly innocuous offences. **1884** *N.Y. Times* 5 Oct. 5/2 Red and yellow cedar..are the other trees most frequently met with. **1910** [see *ALASKA]. **1957** *Handbk. of Softwoods* (Forest Prod. Res. Lab.) 61 'Yellow cedar'..is confined to the Pacific Coast area from Alaska south to southern Oregon. **1886** Yellow ground [see *blue ground* s.v. *BLUE *a.* 13]. **1947** *E. African Ann. 1946–7* 122/1 The portion of a pipe at the surface which has been altered or weathered and is usually of a yellowish colour is known as 'yellow ground', in contrast to the blue-green colour of the unaltered kimberlite or blue ground. **1978** *Sci. Amer.* Apr. 120/3 Most kimberlite exposed at the surface, called 'yellow ground' by miners and prospectors, is severely weathered. **1927** M. M. BENNETT *Christison of Lammermoor* iv. 49 These trees called yellowjacks are soft wood, so white ants enclose them with earth walls and eat the wood out. **1943** A. MARSHALL in *Coast to Coast 1942* 14, I tied the horse to a yellowjack and crept towards the river. **1864** *North-China Herald* 18 June 99/2 [They] being each and all pre-eminent for bravery, contempt for death, and a generous emulation, are invested with the yellow jacket as a reward for their merits. **1878** H. A. GILES *Gloss. Ref. Far East* 84 A yellow *ma-kwa* is a distinction conferred by the Emperor on high officials; sometimes called the *Yellow Jacket*. **1918** H. B. MORSE *International Relations Chinese Empire* II. v. 104 On Li Hung-chung was conferred the military distinction of the Yellow Jacket and the civil distinction of Junior Guardian to the heir apparent. **1964** *Guardian* 16 June 6/6 Metcalfe (England) won his seventh yellow jersey with another aggressively defensive ride. **1983** *Times* 1 July 12/5 It's hard enough even to get a ride in the Tour [de France]... To be the raceleader, to wear the yellow jersey, that's almost worth dying for. **1948** C. L. B. HUBBARD *Dogs in Britain* xix. 232 The Yellow Labrador sometimes called the Golden Labrador..differs in several respects from the black Labrador. **1974** *Times* 4 May 23/8 (Advt.), Country home urgently wanted for two purebred Yellow Labrador bitches. [**1605**: see SERE, SEAR *a.*[1] 1 b]. **1913** L. STRACHEY in *Edin. Rev.* Jan. 68 The radiant creatures of Sceaux had fallen into the yellow leaf. **1935** C. ISHERWOOD *Mr. Norris changes Trains* vii. 107 Yes, I shall be fifty-three... I find it difficult to become accustomed to the thought that the yellow leaf is upon me. **1974** A. A. THOMPSON *Swiss Legacy* xvi. 157 He guided the Mercedes through the traffic..taking chances.. He ran a yellow light and then a red one. **1977** *N.Y. Rev. Bks.* 27 Oct. 16/4 They only ask a 'yellow' light—the right to proceed with caution. **1965** *Autocar* 24 Sept. 609/1 The leaflet recently published by RoSPA in conjunction with the Ministry of Transport..states that a yellow line by the kerb means no waiting *except* for loading and unloading. **1968** J. FLEMING *Kill or Cure* iv. 56 The local police.. allow me to park on the double yellow line with impunity, when absolutely necessary. **1975** J. SYMONS *Three Pipe Problem* xviii. 180 Traffic wardens can start booking cars on yellow lines after eight o'clock. **1983** *Church Times* 23 Dec. 11/1 Christmas shoppers who had taken the risk of parking on the single yellow line. **1908** *Sears, Roebuck Catal.* (*verso rear cover*), See the yellow pages in back of this book. **1956** R. A. HEINLEIN in *Mag. of Fantasy & Sci. Fiction* Oct. 51/2 Get me the yellow-pages phone book... I want to check the exact phrasing of a firm name. **1966** D. G. HAYS in *Automatic Transl. of Lang.* (NATO Summer School, Venice, 1962) 152 In a telephone book.. in the..'Yellow Pages', the major variable is name of product or service. **1969** *Times* 5 May 26/2 Yellow Pages are the classified guide that will be part of everyone's GPO telephone directory soon. **1982** S. BRETT *Murder Unprompted* i. 10 The random selection method of sticking a pin in the 'Theatrical and Variety Agents' section of the Yellow Pages. **1985** *Punch* 23 Jan. 24/2 I started by ringing a few cowboys through the *Yellow Pages*, just to check on prices. **1866** H. E. ROSCOE *Less. Elem. Chem.* xv. 133 The weight of red substance produced is exactly equal to that of yellow phosphorus used. **1944** J. A. TIMM *Gen. Chem.* xli. 443 Yellow phosphorus is formed when the liquid solidifies. **1774** J. R. PEYTON *Let.* 21 July in J. L. Peyton *Adv. My Grandfather* (1867) 127 The forest of Kentucky consists of yellow and white poplar, walnut, red bud. **1876** W. WHITMAN *Specimen Days* (1882–3) 89 Here is one of my favorites now before me, a fine yellow poplar, quite straight, perhaps 90 feet high. **1955** *Sci. News Let.* 7 May 302/2 The tulip tree is also variously known as tulip poplar, yellow poplar, whitewood and fiddle-tree. **1909** G. K. CHESTERTON *Tremendous Trifles* 131 The Yellow Pressman seems to have no power of catching the first fresh fact about a man. **1918** S. SASSOON *Counter-Attack* 29 The boys came back... And Yellow-Pressmen thronged the sunlit street To cheer the soldiers who'd refrained from dying. **1979** W. SAFIRE in *N.Y. Times* 13 Dec. A31/5 The Laotians call it 'the yellow rain'. **1981** *N.Y. Times* 24 Nov. C-1/5 The United States has been trying since 1976 to verify reports that chemical weapons, known popularly as 'the yellow rain', are being used against remote villages in Laos, Cambodia and, more recently, Afghanistan. **1982** *Sci. News* 20 Feb. 122/1 Blood samples were drawn from nine individuals supposedly exposed to a 'yellow rain' gas attack in the fall of 1981... Mirocha 'was able to tentatively identify'..a metabolite of the trichothecene mycotoxin T_2, in samples from only two. **1907** *Jrnl. Agri. Sci.* II. 129 He [*sc.* Mr. Biffen] has discovered and grown several wheats which show to a greater or lesser degree immunity to the attacks of *Puccinia glumarum*, Yellow Rust. **1973** *Scotsman* 7 Aug. 4/6 Mr Blakebell was speaking of yellow rust in wheats. **1725** H. SLOANE *Voy. Jamaica* II. 325 Serpens major subflavus..The yellow Snake. **1851** P. H. GOSSE *Naturalist's Sojourn in Jamaica* 314 A serpent of the Boa kind..is distinguished by the appellation of Yellow Snake. **1860** MAYNE REID *Odd People* 22 The 'Yellow Snake', or South African Cobra. **1868** J. G. WOOD *Homes without Hands* iii. 85 A Yellow Snake..is very plentiful in Jamaica and is perfectly harmless to man. **1819** *Phil. Trans. R. Soc.* CIX. 302 The yellow spot of Soemmerring .. is never seen to advantage until this membrane be removed. **1967** *Guardian* 21 Oct. 8/3 'Private Eye' recently labelled me 'D. A. N. Jew'. Now it happens that I haven't the right to claim the yellow star. **1981** *Times Lit. Suppl.* 6 Nov. 1296/5 Germans like Captain Ernst Janger..who declared himself 'ashamed'..when he saw Jews in Paris wearing their yellow stars. **1911** H. S. HARRISON *Queed* v. 55 'A yellow streak in him, and we didn't know it!' bellowed the Major. **1977** 'D. MACNEIL' *Wolf in Fold* xi. 116 I'm not showing a yellow streak! But we're going to have casualties. **1947** H. W. EHRMANN *French Labor* vii. 126 The CGT could not properly identify the Catholic trade unions with the various movements, in French usage commonly referred to as 'yellow' unions, which were organized under the auspices of the employers. **1957** M. P. FOGARTY *Christian Democracy* xv. 192 Widespread support was given to the yellow unions, notably by the clergy. **1970** R. A. H. ROBINSON *Origins of Franco's Spain* 331 Socialists were also determined that no 'yellow' unions should flourish, eg a strike-threat by the UGT procured the dismissal of 20 members of the *Federación Española de Trabajadores*. **1783** J. LATHAM *Gen. Synopsis Birds* II. 482 Spotted Yellow Warbler. **1845** S. JUDD *Margaret* I. 160 The leafless Butternut, whereon..the yellow warbler made its nest, sprawls its naked arms. **1938** M. THOMPSON *High Trails* 153 The yellow warbler..and many other birds fill the air with their songs. **1971** *Islander* (Victoria, B.C.) 13 June 13/2 Overhead a pair of yellow warblers trilled out their song. **1785** J. WOODFORDE *Diary* 7 Nov. (1926) II. 213 To Nancy for 2 new yellow Ware Chamber Pots 1. 0. **1887** *Harper's Mag.* Dec. 31/1 Sometimes a cherry would fall upon her dark braids, and drop thence in among the verdant contents of the yellow-ware bowl. **1967** *Canadian Antiques Collector* Apr. 9/2 During the next ten years the Bells extended their pottery production to include Rockingham and yellow wares. **1963** *Times* 22 Jan. 10/3 The service have issued a 'yellow warning'. This is intended to warn hospitals to cut down on routine admissions so as to make room for emergencies. **1973** *Times* 13 Nov. 1/2 In electricity supply terms a national 'yellow warning'..means possible voltage reductions. **1913** W. HARRIS *Notes Fruit & Veg. Jamaica* 42 Yellow yam and its varieties belong to *Dioscorea cayennensis*. **1971** [see *negro yam* s.v. *NEGRO 7]. **1973** N. FARKI *Countryman Karl Black* iv. 38 Rice and two pieces of yellow yam in one plate.

2. a. *yellow-blue, -golden*; also *yellow-fluffy, -gleamy, -pale*.

1940 W. FAULKNER *Hamlet* IV. ii. 328 There were three buzzards soaring against the high yellow-blue. **1916** D. H. LAWRENCE *Amores* 50 Flutter for a moment, oh the beast is quick and keen,—Extinct one yellow-fluffy spark. *a* **1930** —— *Phoenix* (1936) I. 3 In the yellow-gleamy sunset, wild birds began to whistle faintly. **1946** S. SPENDER *European Witness* i. 15 In the foreground yellow-golden fields, with above a flat wall of greyish sky. *a* **1963** L. MACNEICE *Astrol.* (1964) iii. 96 Leo the yellow-golden fire of organized mentality. *a* **1930** D. H. LAWRENCE *Last Poems* (1932) 315 Black lamps .Giving off darkness, blue darkness, upon Demeter's yellow-pale day.

b. *yellow-beaked* (later example), *-belled, -browed* (later examples), *-covered* (examples), *-crowned* (later examples), *-eyed, -fanged, -finned* (later examples), *-flecked, -headed* (later examples), *-livered, -mottled, -necked, -robed* (earlier example), *-slashed, -slobbered*, adjs.

1966 E. PALMER *Plains of Camdeboo* xvi. 262 By far the showiest is the yellow-beaked Stapelia, *Stapelia flavirostris*, with dark flowers marked with yellow and ornamented with silver hairs. **1881** O. WILDE *Poems* 122 On this side and on that a rocky cave, Hung with the yellow-belled laburnum stands. **1913** H. K. SWANN *Dict. Names Brit. Birds* 264 Yellow-browed Warbler... A Siberian species of Willow Warbler. **1971** *Country Life* 25 Mar. 705/3 Almost any rarity can turn up, such as..yellow-browed warbler. **1849** *Merchants' Mag.* XX. 118 The yellow-covered literature of the day—translations from the French. **1915** H. YOUNG *Hard Knocks* 23 The little yellow covered novels were the cause of it. **1925** J. FERGUSON in *Oxf. Poetry* 18 Like stately flowers, yellow-crowned. **1950** *Caribbean Q.* II. III. 41 Nor were the larger and stronger Yellow crowned Night Herons, to be outdone. **1881** O. WILDE *Poems* 180 The hot jungle where the yellow-eyed huge lions sleep. **1957** T. HUGHES *Hawk in Rain* 39 A square-pupilled yellow-eyed look. **1954** J. R. R. TOLKIEN *Two Towers* III. iii. 50 It was the yellow-fanged guard. **1908** C. F. HOLDER *Big Game at Sea* xxiii. 342 The boatmen..called it the 'yellow-finned tuna'... This was in 1904, and ever since the new tuna, with its vivid lemon finlets, has appeared every August or September. **1936** *Zoologica* XXI. 190 The various nominal forms of the yellow-finned tuna belong to the same species. **1920** D. H. LAWRENCE *Lost Girl* iv. 55 The seam of yellow-flecked coal. **1846** *Ex. Doc. 30th U.S. Congress I Sess. House* No. 41. 436 [We saw] large flocks of the yellow headed black bird. **1972** R. & R. WRIGHT *Cariboo Mileposts* 50 Stands of tules or reeds will hold the woven nests of red-wing and yellow-headed blackbirds. **1935** S. LEWIS *It can't happen Here* 156 The meanest, lowest, cowardliest gang of yellow-livered, back-slapping, hypocritical guntoters. **1979** *PN Rev.* No. 9. 27/1 O green, green eating out my eyes, A yellow-livered green in a wet light. **1916** BLUNDEN *Harbingers* 64 Toadstools..Yellow, and yellow-mottled red, and black. **1889** *Cent. Dict.* 7016/3 The yellow-necked caterpillar..feeds in communities on the foliage of apple, hickory, and walnut in the United States. **1908** E. J. BANFIELD *Confessions of Beachcomber* I. iii. 98 Yellow-necked Mangrove Bittern. **1921** G. E. H. BARRETT-HAMILTON *Hist. Brit. Mammals* II. 547 The Yellow-necked Field Mouse is distinguished from *A. sylvaticus* by its larger size. **1979** *Essex Countryside* XXVII. 72/2 The hoarding habits of yellow-necked mice are well known. **1819** *Methodist Mag.* Oct. 723 We took leave of our yellow-robed acquaintances. **1928** V. WOOLF *Orlando* v. 225 The yellow-slashed sky of dawn. **1922** JOYCE *Ulysses* 222 Two barefoot urchins, sucking long liquorice laces, halted near him, gaping..with their yellowslobbered mouths.

c. yellow-back, (*b*) more widely, any cheaply issued or reprinted novel; (earlier and later examples); (*c*) a U.S. currency note having the back coloured yellow; **yellow-fin,** esp. **yellow-fin tuna,** one of several species of *Thunnus*, esp. *T. albacares*, a large fish found in warmer parts of both the Atlantic and Pacific oceans; **Yellow Hat,** *colloq.*, used *attrib.* or *absol.* in *pl.* to denote a Tibetan Buddhist sect (Gelugpa) founded in the fourteenth century by Tsong-kha-pa; **yellow-head,** (*d*) a warbler, *Mohoua ochrocephala*, found in the South Island of New Zealand; **yellow jacket,** (*c*) *slang* (orig. *U.S.*), a pentobarbitone capsule; **yellow-leg,** (*b*) *N. Amer. colloq.* [from the yellow stripe down the side of the breeches], a U.S. cavalryman or a member of the Royal Canadian Mounted Police; **yellow-throat** (later examples); **yellow underwing,** one of several noctuid moths.

1877 *Living Age* 14 Apr. 128/1 Four days ago Ley and I started down the river on an exploring expedition, and he took it into his head to rope ('lasso', as the yellow-backs have it) a buffalo. **1902** H. L. WILSON *Spenders* xiv. 150 She was dead in love with the nice long yellow-backs that I've piled up. **1928** M. SADLEIR *Trollope: a Bibliogr.* 68 In 1868 *The Belton Estate* was issued at two shillings as a 'yellow back'. **1943** *Copper Camp* (Writers' Program, Montana) 37 They occasionally found yellowbacks tucked in their shoes. **1976** T. EAGLETON *Crit. & Ideology* ii. 47 The 'yellowback' railway novel is available to a mass public. **1922** *Pacific Fisherman* Feb. 12/1 Each of these new species—bluefin tuna, yellowfin tuna and striped tuna—proved itself well adapted to the same canning method as the albacore. **1975** *Islander* (Victoria, B.C.) 7 Sept. 4/2 They [*sc.* whales] travel in schools in the eastern Pacific, followed by yellow-fin tuna which feed on their leavings. **1747** *Astley's New Gen. Coll. Voy.* IV. II. iv. 450/2 They being of the yellow Hat, or Chinese party. **1931** C. BELL *Relig. Tibet* viii. 129 With the enthronement of the fifth Dalai Lama as sovereign over the whole country, the power of the Yellow Hats was greatly increased. **1962** H. E. RICHARDSON *Tibet & its Hist.* ii. 40 The Dalai Lamas..owed their appearance to the great religious teacher known as Tsong Khapa (1357–1417), the founder of a new sect, the Gelugpa, popularly called the Yellow Hats. **1978** C. HUMPHREYS *Both Sides Circle* xx. 212 The famous monastery at Ghoom..belongs to the Gelug-pa or Yellow Hat sect of Tibetan Buddhism. **1873** *Trans. N.Z. Inst.* VI. 144 Yellow-head. Average weight of specimens, 1½ ounce. **1966** *Encycl. N.Z.* I. 206/2 Still widely distributed in the deeper forests are..whitehead ..and yellowhead. **1953, 1969** Yellow jacket [see *NEMBIE]. **1974** M. C. GERALD *Pharmacol.* xi. 205 Short-acting barbiturates such as pentobarbital ('yellow jackets'). **1894** J. A. FRYE *Fables of Field & Staff* 109 The 'Yellow-Legs' are always great on dismounted duty. **1943** W. CHASE *Sourdough Pot* xix. 120 Numbers of these prisoners were marched down the main street in charge of a Mountie, or 'Yellow-leg', as they were called on account of the yellow strip running down the outside of their trouser leg. **1957** G. SHIRREFFS *Rio Bravo* (1972) i. 6 He glanced back at the rough country through which they had come, almost as though looking for the beefy figure of Francis Xavier Feeley, one of the best yellowlegs who had ever forked a McClellan. **1974** W. HUNT *North of 53* xix. 139 The 'yellow legs'—the Mounties—were not permissive in law enforcement. **1865** *Atlantic Monthly* XV. 521, I miss in the woods..the Yellow Throat. **1949** V. S. REID *New Day* I. xxviii. 143 A..yellowthroat warbler whistles back. **1977** *Blair & Ketchum's Country Jrnl.* May 43/1 The yellow-throats will reemerge on other days. **1749,** etc. Yellow underwing [see UNDERWING 2]. *a* **1941** V. WOOLF *Death of Moth* (1942) 9 The commonest yellow-underwing asleep in the shadow of the curtain. **1968** *Oxf. Bk. Insects* 72/1 Like the other Yellow Underwings..this species baffles its enemies by the way it shows its colours.

ye·llow-be:llied, *a.* **1.** Applied to birds or animals having yellow underparts. Also in extended use (in quot. 1909 of an airship).

1709, 1783 [in Dict. s.v. YELLOW *a.* and *sb.* C. 2 c]. **1827** J. L. WILLIAMS *View W. Florida* 30 Black-head fly catcher... Yellow-bellied do. **1869** [see *SCRUNCHING *vbl. sb.*]. **1908** E. J. BANFIELD *Confessions of Beachcomber* I. iii. 95 Yellow-bellied Fig-bird. **1909** KIPLING *Actions & Reactions* 140 Yellow-bellied ore-flats..punted down leisurely out of the north. **1936** *Discovery* Oct. 307/2 There are many varieties of flying phalanger, the yellow-bellied 25 inches in length with a bushy tail an inch longer than the body. **1942** R. PEATTIE *Friendly Mts.* 210 A sweet or black birch tree..had been tapped by a yellow-bellied sapsucker. **1971** *Islander* (Victoria, B.C.) 25 July 16/2 Most members of his species (the yellow-bellied marmot) weigh about 13 pounds at maturity.

2. *fig.* Cowardly, craven. Cf. *YELLOW *a.* 2 b, *YELLOW-BELLY 5. *slang* (orig. *U.S.*).

1924 P. MARKS *Plastic Age* ix. 75 Yellow-bellied quitters. **1930** [see *potato-mouthed a.* s.v. *POTATO *sb.* 7]. **1943** J. MITCHELL *McSorley's Wonderful Saloon* (1946) I. 24 You yellow-bellied jerk. **1965** J. PORTER *Dover Two* xiv. 185 Anything to save his own skin, the yellow-bellied rat! **1971** [see *MALT *sb.*[2]]. **1979** 'M. HEBDEN' *Pel & Faceless Corpse* vi. 58 I'm..a yellow-bellied, lily-livered coward.

yellow-belly. Add: **1. b.** (Earlier and later examples.)

1787 GROSE *Provincial Gloss.* s.v. *Lincolnshire*, Yellow bellies. This is an appellation given to persons born in the Fens, who, it is jocularly said, have yellow bellies, like their eels. **1982** *Times* 5 Oct. 4/5 The Lincolnshire 'yellowbellies' of south Humberside .for generations have entertained a healthy disregard for Yorkshire 'tykes' on the north bank of the Humber.

3. (Earlier and later examples.) *derog.*

1842 *New Orleans Crescent* 16 Mar. (Extra) 1 God send that they bayonet every 'yellow belly' in the Mexican army. **1845** [see *COPPERHEAD 3]. **1934** 'G. ORWELL' *Burmese Days* x. 155 They're Eurasians—sons of white fathers and native mothers. Yellow-bellies is our friendly nickname for them. **1966** [see *slant-eye(s)* s.v. *SLANT *a.* 3].

5. A coward. Cf. *YELLOW *a.* 2 b, *YELLOW-BELLIED *a.* 2. *slang* (orig. *U.S.*).

1930 J. LAIT *Put on Spot* 215 Yellow-belly. Coward. **1942** BERREY & VAN DEN BARK *Amer. Thes. Slang* § 404/3 *Coward*..yellow-back, -belly or guts. **1952** H. INNES *Campbell's Kingdom* III. ii. 271 What are you?.. A bunch of yellow-bellies to be fooled into hiding away. **1952** J. STEINBECK *East of Eden* 517 I'm a cowardly yellow-belly. **1965** *Austral. Women's Weekly* 20 Jan. 50/5 'Yellowbelly baby... Spoiled-cat crybaby,' Steve yelled at him. **1969** K. M. WELLS *Owl Pen Reader* II. 209 Grandad's knees shook, and he wasn't no yellow-belly either. **1972** 'H. HOWARD' *Nice Day for Funeral* ix. 128 She'd call me every kind of yellow belly if I suggested throwing in my hand.

yellow-boy. For ? *Obs.* read *Obs.* exc. *Hist.* and add later examples.

1883 'MARK TWAIN' *Life on Miss.* xxxvi. 389 A round ten thousand dollars in yellow-boys. **1898** A. M. BINSTEAD *Pink 'Un & Pelican* x. 219 Gazing contemptuously at the yellow-boy, and then at its donor, she cried: 'An' since when has a "new hat" ceased to be a guinea?' **1957** A. BRYANT in J. B. Booth *Palmy Days* p. xi, He reconstructs a vanished world: the last age of horses and 'yellow boys'

ye·llowcake. Also **yellow cake.** [f. YELLOW *a.* + CAKE *sb.*] An oxide of uranium (and other elements) obtained as a yellow precipitate in the processing of uranium ores.

1950 *Mining Congr. Jrnl.* Oct. 30/2 Through pH adjustment by regulated additions of sulphuric acid virtually all of the uranium is precipitated as 'yellowcake', an artificial carnotite. **1955** KIRK & OTHMER *Encycl. Chem. Technol.* XIV. 439 If the uranium and vanadium are present in the carbonate leach liquors in the proper stoichiometric ratio, then neutralization by acid leads to the very complete precipitation of sodium uranyl vanadate, the 'yellow cake' of Colorado Plateau extractive metallurgy. **1971** *Daily Colonist* (Victoria, B.C.) 11 June 7/7 A West German..group has undertaken to find a market for 4 million pounds of uranium oxide (yellow cake) annually. **1977** *Telegraph* (Brisbane) 5 Sept. 5/1 Police and 200 anti-uranium demonstrators traded kicks and punches, when a fresh consignment of yellowcake reached the White Bay container terminal today. **1981** T. BARLING *Bikini Red North* i. 34 Will anything positive be done to stop the French selling yellowcake or hardware on the open market?

yellow dog. *U.S.* **1.** A mongrel dog of a yellowish colour.

c **1770,** etc. [in Dict. s.v. YELLOW C. 1 a]. **1873** M. HOLLEY *My Opinions* 237 If I was a yeller dog, she couldn't seem to look down on me any more, and treat me any worse.

2. *fig.* **a.** A person or thing of no account or of a low type.

1881 E. W. NYE *Bill Nye & Boomerang* 166 The presiding officer had lost control, and a surging crowd of yellow dogs had the floor. **1903** *Everybody's Mag.* Oct. 562 In a cut-rate combination you are lucky if you get what you pay for. If there are five magazines in the combination, two of them are good. The rest are 'yellow-dogs'. **1924** A. J. SMALL *Frozen Gold* i. 44 Understand, I won't allow no yellow dog of a Siwash to step over me. **1975** *New Yorker* 8 Dec. 126/2 Calling someone a yellow dog would not imply that the person so called was actually yellow and wagged his tail. It is just the sort of cultural misunderstanding that student-exchange programs were once expected to clear up.

b. *attrib.*; applied *spec.* to organizations, etc., opposed to trade unionism.

1894 KIPLING *Day's Work* (1898) 71 America's paved with the kind er horse you are—jist plain yaller-dog horse—waitin' ter be whipped inter shape. **1902** —— *Just So Stories* 92 Old Man Kangaroo is being rude to Yellow-Dog Dingo. Yellow-Dog Dingo has been trying to catch Kangaroo all across Australia. **1902** *Mine Workers' Jrnl.* July 1 A yellow dog lease. **1903** *Outlook* 15 Aug. 931/2 In preference to a Tammany 'yellow dog' ticket his organization would support the Fusion candidate. **1920** *Motorman & Conductor* Oct. 34 A yellow dog contract. **1930** *Sun* (Baltimore) 6 May 12/2 The 'yellow dog' contract, requiring men to barter away their right to organize as the price of a job. **1956** *Mag. of Fantasy & Sci. Fiction* Oct. 32/2 It was the latest form of the yellow-dog clause, one in which the employee agrees to refrain from engaging in a competing occupation for five years by letting his former employers pay him cash to option his services on a first-refusal basis. **1976** *Amer. N. & Q.* XIV. 136/1 The committee scrutinized the records and books of the four major New York companies uncovering the existence of the so-called 'yellow dog funds'.

yellow-fish. Add: **b.** In South Africa, one of several freshwater fishes of the genus *Barbus*.
1834 A. Smith *Diary* 9 Dec. (1939) I. 168 Fish in the pools of this river of two kinds, the flat head and the bearded yellow fish. **1896** H. A. Bryden *Tales S. Afr.* i. 18 The pouch contained..a 'yellow fish', a barbel-like fish of a pound and a half. **1912** J. Stevenson-Hamilton *Animal Life Afr.* xix. 334 The yellow fish..is the commonest fish of South Africa. **1952** [see *kurper]. **1975** *Stand. Encycl. S. Afr.* XI. 563/1 The yellow-fishes..are popular angling fishes, ranging from one kg to over 14 kg in weight.

yellow-haired, *a.* Add: Also *fig.*
1917 D. H. Lawrence *Look! We have come Through!* 155 Scyllas and yellow-haired hellebore, jonquils, dim anemones.

yellowing, *ppl. a.* Add: Turning yellow, becoming yellow (quots. in Dict.). Also *fig.*
1961 E. Williams *George* xxi. 339 Divvers—..a routine side-exam based on the yellowing idea that an Oxford graduate must have a solid religious training. **1977** *Guardian Weekly* 10 July 17/4 All that is left is a batch of yellowing declarations of good intentions.

yellowishness. (Later example.)
1941 E. R. Eddison *Fish Dinner* xi. 184 The cloudbank was indigo against that yellowishness of the sky.

yellowly, *adv.* Delete *rare* and add later examples.
1932 W. Faulkner *Light in August* xiv. 314 He saw before daylight a lamp come yellowly alive in the kitchen. **1958** I. Fleming *Dr. No* vi. 78 The centipede was whipping from side to side in its agony... Bond hit it again. It burst open, yellowly. **1968** P. Dickinson *Skin Deep* ix. 165 The home-made candles burnt yellowly. **1978** H. Wouk *War & Remembrance* x. 100 The lights flickered yellowly on.

yellows. Add: **I. 3. b.** (Earlier examples.) **c.** A similar virus or deficiency disease in other plants.
1808 [see *peach yellows* s.v *peach *sb.*[1] 6]. **1822** S. Deane *New-England Farmer* (ed. 3) 318/2 Peach trees are subject to a disease called the 'Yellows', of which we have seen no particular description. **1926** *Amer. Jrnl. Bot.* XIII. 647 Asters affected with yellows never show mottling. **1933** *Times Lit. Suppl.* 16 Mar. 187/2 A disease of the tea-bush known as 'yellows' is due to a deficiency of sulphur in the soil. **1957** *New Scientist* 8 Aug. 31/3 At least 2,800 tons of beet were lost from yellows infection.. in the Shotley peninsula.

yellow-wood. Add: (Earlier S. Afr. examples.) Also *attrib.*
1767 in *Country Life* (1973) 7 June 1607/1 A mahogany Commode, with yellow wood ornaments, and Drawers for medals. **1790, 1801** [see *geelhout]. **1871** H. H. Dugmore *Reminisc. Albany Settler* 27 Plain dinners and hearty suppers,..served up in tin dishes on yellow wood benches. **1915** Rider Haggard *Holy Flower* iv. 63 It.. rolled under a great yellow-wood chest. **1952** G. M. Mills *First Ladies of Cape* 42 Cupboards..were usually framed by stinkwood and yellow-wood doors. **1981** *N. & Q.* June 193/2 The most important furnishings of the *groote kamer* were a yellow-wood cupboard and a stinkwood four-poster bed. **1985** *New Yorker* 18 Mar. 65/2 Old yellowwood and stinkwood chests.

Yemeni (ye·měni); *sb.* and *a.* [ad. Arab. *yamanī*, f. *Yemen* name of two States in the south-west of the Arabian peninsula.] **A.** *sb.* A native or inhabitant of North Yemen or South Yemen. **B.** *adj.* Of or pertaining to North Yemen, South Yemen, or the inhabitants of either.
[**1888** C. M. Doughty *Trav. Arabia Deserta* II. 688 *Yémeny*, a man of el-Yémen.] **1916** *Handbk. Arabia* I. vi. 151 The Yemeni is not regarded as particularly fanatical. **1955** *Times* 1 July 11/6 Britain was obliged to deliver a strong Note protesting about border raiding. This pointed out..that in June there had been a serious attack on Mukeiras by a mixed force of Yemeni troops and tribesmen. **1959** W. Thesiger *Arabian Sands* xiii. 247, I had ridden..with two Arab companions and three.. Yemeni pilgrims. *Ibid.*, One of the Yemenis fetched us food from the market. **1959** *Listener* 27 Aug. 308/2 The southern Yemeni provinces. **1968** *Ibid.* 4 Jan. 7/1 A guerrilla attack on the outskirts of Sanaa for a few Yemini riyals. **1973** 'D. Jordan' *Nile Green* xxv. 105 Mara was wearing..a silver medallion... I decided it must be Yemini. **1982** P. Way *Belshazzar's Feast* xix. 208 Would these people have been Arabs, Yemeni Arabs? *Ibid.* xx. 223 The Soviets..have used their East German puppets, the Yemenis, to create trouble. **1982** M. A. Zabarah *Yemen* 53 Through the Yemeni emigrant and the Yemeni commercial entrepreneur, modern ideas were reaching not only city dwellers but also the tribes.

Yemenite (ye·měnəit), *sb.* and *a.* [Senses b, c. f. prec. + -ite[1].] **A.** *sb.* †**a.** [f. an earlier form of the personal name.] A member of a family belonging to the tribe of Benjamin. *Obs.* **b.** = *Yemeni *sb.* **c.** A Jew who was, or whose ancestors were, formerly resident in the Yemen.
1566 Bible I. *Sam.* ix. 21 Am not I the sonne of a Jaminite of the smallest tribe of Israel: and my kyured is the leest of all the kyuredes of the trybe of Ben Jamin. **1568** *Ibid.*, Am not I the sonne of a Jeminite. **1862** J. T. Thomson *Some Glimpses Life Far East* lviii. 323 By race he was a Yemenite. **1902** *Encycl. Brit.* XXV. 518/2 The Yemenites rashly invited Turkish intervention. **1926** tr. *Granovsky's Land Prob. Palestine* I. 18 The history of Jewish colonization in Palestine shows many attempts to create a class of Jewish farm laborers..by establishing small settlements for Yemenites (Jewish immigrants from Southern Arabia). **1935** A. Revusky *Jews in Palestine* xii. 206 The Sephardim and Yemenites, the two main groups of Oriental Jews. **1965** M. Spark *Mandelbaum Gate* iv. 91 Those Arab girls, those Yemenites, Syrians, those Israelites, Samaritans. **1976** C. Bermant *Coming Home* II. iii. 154 One of those private schools..basically.. for the sons of Arab oil sheiks, but it also housed..tall, lean Persians, tiny, dusky Yemenites, a few bombastic Greeks.

B. *adj.* Of, pertaining to, or designating a Yemeni Arab or a Yemeni Jew.
1876 R. D. Osborn *Islam under Arabs* III. i. 296 The Yemenite Arabs of Syria were known as the Kelbites. **1902** *Encycl. Brit.* XXXI. 329/2 The present Sultan, a descendant of those Yemenite Imams who consolidated Arab power in Zanzibar. **1926** *Sunday at Home* July 636/1 Another industry which has been revived in Jerusalem is the silver filigree work of the Yemenite Jews. **1949** [see *gun moll* s.v. *gun *sb.* 15]. **1955** S. N. Eisenstadt in *Public Opinion Q.* XIX. 156 (*heading*) Communication in a traditional Yemenite community. **1978** *Church Times* 16 June 11/2 In the Flea Market [of Tel Aviv].. the Guide did not want us to miss the sight of Arabs buying from Yemenite salesmen. **1982** D. Wiltse *Wedding Guest* ix. 113 He was an Arab, but he could have been anything from Moroccan to Yemenite.

yen[2] (yen). *slang* (orig. *U.S.*). Also **yin, ying.** [Prob. of Chinese origin. The most likely etymon is Chinese (Cantonese) *yăn* craving; the forms *yin* and *ying* may reflect the Mandarin pronunciation *yĭn* of the same character. Reinforcement from *yen[3] is possible. See also *yen-yen.
See E. C. Knowlton in *Amer. Speech* (1961) XXXVI. 175–80 for further discussion and documentation of this word, *yen[3], and *yen-yen.]

1. The craving of a drug-addict for his drug (orig. for opium). (See also quots. 1929, 1937, 1974.)
1876 H. A. Giles *Chinese Sketches* 115 Chinamen ask if an opium-smoker has the *yin* or not; meaning thereby, has he gradually increased his doses of opium until he has established a craving for the drug. **1891** A. W. Douthwaite *Opium Habit* 5 The frequent and regular repetition of this process of stimulation and depression induces the '*ying*', or carving, which is simply a demand by the nervous system for its accustomed stimulant, without which it is unable to properly perform its functions. **1912** D. Lowrie *My Life in Prison* vii. 79, I even saw two or three guys eat chloride o' lime to stop their yen. **1922** E. Murphy *Black Candle* II. i. 113 When 'the black candle' is ready for lighting and the smoker has the *ying* upon him—that is to say the mad longing for indulgence —the procedure is like this [etc.]. **1929** Light & Torrance in *Arch. Internal Med.* XLIII. 210 If he falls asleep, which is often the case, he falls into a deep slumber well known as the 'yen'. **1933** [see *muggle[2]]. **1937** A. R. Lindesmith *Nature of Opiate Addiction* iv. 107 The drug user does not ordinarily find that his efforts to explain what he means by 'yen' (which signifies both withdrawal symptoms and desire for opiates) are very successful. *Ibid.*, The drug user says, 'he wakes up some morning with a yen.' **1948** F. Brown *Murder can be Fun* v. 78 He hadn't thought Wilkins would know a biological urge from an opium yen. **1974** M. C. Gerald *Pharmacol.* xiii. 251 Symptoms begin within 8 to 12 hours after the last dose... The addict experiences tearing, a running nose, sweating, yawning, and difficulty in sleeping. This restless sleep is commonly referred to as the 'yen'.

2. *gen.* A craving, a yearning or longing.
1906 H. Green *Actors' Boarding House* 248 He had a yen to gamble and bet high. **1928** J. O'Connor *Broadway Racketeers* ix. 107 The kid..had a burning yen for champagne and poker. **1932** S. Gibbons *Cold Comfort Farm* xx. 267 Ezra, who had a secret yen for horticulture. **1952** *Here & Now* (N.Z.) Jan. 19 This yen for a dog that will do everything has had a lot to do with the waning of pointers, setters and retrievers. **1961** *Time* 6 Jan. 4/2 The yen of Christian churchmen for achieving church unity is more pathetic then peculiar to behold. **1967** A. Christie *Endless Night* ii. 21 He'd got such a yen for a picture that he managed to get the money together. **1983** *Listener* 7 July 17/3 You write your music because you have a real yen to write it.

Hence **yen** *v. intr.*, to crave for a drug; to yearn, desire strongly; **ye·nny** *a.*, affected by a craving for drugs.
1919 Mencken *Amer. Lang.* iii. 93 A great many of them [*sc.* Chinese words] have remained California localisms, among them such verbs as *to yen* (to desire strongly, as a Chinaman desires opium). **1935** N. Ersine *Underworld & Prison Slang* 80 He's yenning for morph. **1936** F. M. Ford *Let.* 6 Sept. (1965) 261 Not that I particularly yen to mention the Deity, but that I believe that publishers should be as sadistically punished as possible. **1936** E. Pound *Let.* Sept. (1971) 282 Am afraid I got 'em stuck with some bad grub, but it was the only place I cd. count on being open... The violin player yenned toward another place, where I thought they wd. git stuck a price. **1953** W. Burroughs *Junkie* (1972) vi. 63 Nick is followed all the time now. You know yourself when a guy is yenning, he doesn't look behind him. He's running. **1975** H. White *Raincoast Chron.* (1976) 147/1 'We brought a bit of shit in with us to taper off on... Too bad she's all gone.' 'Yeah,' said Pat longingly, 'I sure get yenny sometimes.' **1977** *Times* 11 Feb. 12/2 The need for new educational certainties..cannot be met by yenning for the relative simplicities of the old 'elementary' education.

yen[3] (yen). *U.S. slang* and *techn.* [Prob. a. Chinese (Cantonese) *yīn* opium, or (Mandarin) *yān* opium: cf. *yen[2] and *yen-yen.] **1.** Opium.
1926 J. Colton *Shanghai Gesture* III. 188 [Servant enters with..opium...] Here's the yen! **1935** A. J. Pollock *Underworld Speaks* 135/1 *Yen in the cheek*, gum opium or yen shee placed and sucked in back of lower teeth which produces comfort to the addict (this is frequently used when traveling in public conveyances). **1942** Berrey & Van den Bark *Amer. Thes. Slang* § 509/2 Opium..yen.

2. *attrib.* and *Comb.*, as (sense 1, with varying degrees of naturalization) **yen hock, hok** and varr., a needle used in the preparation of opium in the form of pills; **yen hop,** an opium pipe; **yen pock, pox,** and varr. (see quots. 1935 and 1959); **yen she(e)** and varr., the deposit of opium ashes formed in the bowl of an opium pipe; also *loosely*, opium; **yen siang, tsiang,** an opium pipe.
1882 H. H. Kane *Opium-Smoking in Amer. & China* iii. 35 The other articles..for a smoker's outfit are..a needle (*yen hauck*) on the end of which the opium is taken up, 'cooked', and placed over the small opening in the upper surface of the bowl. **1886** T. Byrnes *Professional Criminals Amer.* 385 Among the frequenters of his place could be seen..such noted characters as..'Yen Hock' Harry, who earned his title by stabbing a man with a 'yen hock'. **1909** I. L. Nascher *Wretches of Povertyville* II. v. 176 The needle or yen hok is merely a short knitting needle, sometimes with a handle. **1926** *Variety* 29 Dec. 7/4 The dopes and hop heads, with their 'stem', 'yen hok', [etc.]. **1955** *U.S. Senate Hearings* (1956) VIII. 4162 *Yen hock*, a long needle-shaped instrument, flat on one end and used to roll the 'pill' and hold same for cooking. **1968–70** *Current Slang* (Univ. S. Dakota) III–IV. 140 *Yen hok, n.*, a slender needle used in preparing opium for smoking. (Drug users' jargon). **1901** C. R. Wooldridge *Hands Up!* 215 It consists of the 'yen hop', or pipe, usually made of a section and a half of heavy bamboo. **1918** F. Hunt *Blown in by Draft* iii. 60 In the rare old fiction days 'corking a pill' had to do with yen hop, today it tells of naught but rolling a cigarette. **1934** *Detective Fiction Weekly* 21 Apr. 114/1 Yen pok, pill of opium after being prepared for smoking. **1935** A. J. Pollock *Underworld Speaks* 135/1 *Yen pock*, a cooked opium pill often eaten by addicts to produce normalcy and temporary relief. **1946** Mezzrow & Wolfe *Really Blues* xiv. 249 We'd..pack along some yen pox (opium pills that you eat). **1955** [see *mud *sb.*[1] 2 d]. **1959** W. Burroughs *Naked Lunch* 12 Yen pox is the ash of smoked opium. **1882** H. H. Kane *Opium-Smoking in Amer. & China* iii. 35 A straight and curved knife for cleaning the bowl of the ash (*yen tshi*) that rapidly collects and renders the pipe foul. **1892** H. Campbell *Darkness & Daylight* xxviii. 565 And a little box of tin held the *yen she* or bits of refuse opium. **1901** C. R. Wooldridge *Hands Up!* 215 The 'yen she gow', or small chisel, for cleaning out the bowl of the pipe. **1912** A. H. Lewis *Apaches of New York* xi. 229 Number-one hop is $87.50 a can, an' yen-chee..not less'n $32. **1918** *Policeman's Monthly* Oct. 16/3 In answer to this, it was learned that fifty-eight began by smoking opium..eight ate morphine, three ate 'yen shee', the ashes of opium, and the remaining cases started by using cocaine and laudanum, or eating opium. **1947** A. Meyers in J. H. Jackson *San Francisco Murders* 291 Liu uttered..a pathetic plea that he be allowed his daily pipe of 'yen-shee' or opium. **1952** J. Steinbeck *East of Eden* xix. 219 Odors from Chinatown, roasting pork and punk and black tobacco and yen shi. **1882** H. H. Kane *Opium-Smoking in Amer. & China* iii. 35 The whole pipe is called the *Yen Tsiang*, or opium pistol. **1909** J. S. Thompson *Chinese* viii. 336 At last its consistency suits. He places the gummy head on the large flute-like pipe, or *yen siang* (smoking pistol).

Yenan (yenæ·n). [Chinese (Pinyin) *Yan'an.*] The name of a town in northern Shaanxi province, China, which was the headquarters of the Chinese Communist Party in the years 1936–49, used *attrib.* to designate this period in the history of the Party, or to describe the principles and policies evolved by it at that time.
1949 F. C. Jones *Manchuria since 1931* xii. 231 The Yenan régime had no hold upon the country in general before August 1945. **1957** P. S. H. Tang *Communist China Today: Domestic & Foreign Policies* v. 197 Thoroughness of rural regimentation characterized.. administration of the Shensi–Kansu–Ninghsia border region during the Yenan period. **1966** F. Schurmann *Ideology & Organization in Communist China* i. 59 The scattered guerrilla forces of the Yenan period had to report back to headquarters in systematic ways. **1970** E. Snow *Red China Today* (1971) xxxii. 257 After 1966 foreign ballets were seen no more in China; traditional Chinese opera was also overhauled to make it conform to Yenan principles. Mao Tse-tung's dicta, *Talks at the Yenan Forum on Art and Literature*, became the guidelines for stage and screen performances. **1975** I. C. Y. Hsü *Rise of Mod. China* (ed. 2) xxiv. 714 The heart of the Yenan Way was the perfection of the mass line and the sharpening of revolutionary nationalism in the countryside, which became the twin pillars of Maoism. **1979** *Encounter* Feb. 74/1 The 'Great Leap Forward' led to a re-evaluation of the significance of the Yenan period of the late 1930s and early 1940s.

Yenisei (ye·nĭsēⁱ, yenĭsēⁱ·). [a. the name of the river *Yenisei* in Siberia.] One of a group of Palæo-Siberian languages belonging to the Finno-Ugric group. Usu. in *Comb.*, esp. as 'enisei- Ostiak, the designation of this linuistic group.

1888 *Encycl. Brit.* XXIV. 1/1 *Samoyedic. Yurak* and 'enisei, White-Sea to the Yenisei. **1908** T. G. TUCKER *ntrod. Nat. Hist. Lang.* viii. 149 The Hyberborean peeches of Asia, some of which may or may not form a amily, include..Yenissei-Ostiak (a tongue to be disnguished from the Ural-Altaic Ostiak, with which it grees neither in its roots nor in the principle of vowelarmony). **1932** W. L. GRAFF *Lang. & Languages* 406 he Yenisei-Ostiak variety is believed to be related to ibeto-Chinese. **1939** L. H. GRAY *Foundations of Lang.* 69 The languages of the Uralic family are as follows:.. amoyede group: Yurak, Yenisei-Samoyede, [etc.]. 948 R. A. D. FORREST *Chinese Lang.* 22 A remarkable utlier of the Sinitic family, and more specifically of the ibeto-Burman group, is..a group of dialects known as 'enisei-Ostiak and Kottish. They are now spoken by a w villagers far in the north of Siberia, on the river 'enisei, northwards of Yeniseisk. **1951** W. K. MATTHEWS *anguages U.S.S.R.* iii. 17 Yurak (Nenets)..is spoken om the Kanin peninsula to the estuary of the Yenisei ver, Yenisei (Enets) along its lower course. **1958** .. S. C. ROSS *Etymology* i. 27 In the language called 'enisei-Ostyak..a variation of a kind very similar to M[oder]n E[nglish]..is found. **1967** [see *NENETS].

'enny, *a.*: see *YEN².

'enta (ye·ntă). *U.S.* Also **yente,** (*rare*) **'enteh.** [Yiddish, orig. a personal name.] A gossip or busybody; a noisy, vulgar person; a colding woman or shrew.

1923 A. YEZIERSKA *Salome of Tenements* 12 The attern *yentehs* lounging on the stoops..were transgured. **1931** B. HECHT *Jew in Love* 122 Jesus God, you alk like a typical *yenta*. **1948** *Commentary* V. 500/1 'ente has become synonymous with noisiness and ulgarity, plus implications of rough good-heartedness. 968 *Encounter* Sept. 27/1 *Yenta*, I am told, was a perfecty acceptably name for a lady, derived from the Italian *entile*—until some ungracious *yenta* gave it a bad name. 970 S. ELLIN *Bind* xxiii. 114 A couple of *yentas* got othing better to do, they'll take a sunbath right by my window. **1975** *New Yorker* 24 Nov. 167/3 It is to the irector's credit that she manages to hold down Doris Roberts' performance as the *yente*. **1978** I. B. SINGER *Shosha* ii. 38 You were always ready to trade me for the rst available yenta.

'entz (yents), *v.* *U.S. slang.* [Yiddish, f. *yentzen* to copulate.] *trans.* To cheat, to swindle (see also quot. 1939). Also *fig.* Cf. *SCREW *v.* 6 d, 12*.

1930 *Amer. Mercury* Dec. 458/2 *Yentz*, to cheat. They try to yentz me out of me end.' **1939** *Amer. Speech* XIV. 240/2 *To yentz*, to cheat; to fornicate. **1969** S. J. PERELMAN in *Holiday* Mar. 104/4 The faintness one characteristically experiences on discovering that he as been yentzed. **1978** J. KRANTZ *Scruples* x. 276 'I lon't *yentz* them,' Maggie explained, Coca-Cola-colored eyes all innocence, 'they just yentz themselves and I try not to run out of tape.'

yen-yen (ye·nyen). *U.S. slang.* Also † *inyun* [Prob. ad. Chinese (Cantonese) *yīnyǎn* craving for opium, f. *yīn* opium + *yǎn* craving: cf. *YEN² and *YEN³.] A craving for opium, the 'opium-habit'.

1886 T. BYRNES *Professional Criminals Amer.* 385 A fiend suffering with the *inyun* is a man to be avoided. *Ibid.* 384, I was a victim to the opium habit, or, as the Chinese have it, *inyun fun*. **1892** H. CAMPBELL *Darkness & Daylight* xxviii. 569 'I've got the *yen-yen* (opium habit) the worst way', said one woman, 'and must have my pipe every night.' **1904** H. HAPGOOD *Autobiogr. of Thief* x. 207 Perhaps it was the sight or smell of the hop, but anyway I got the yen-yen and shook as in the ague. **1926** J. BLACK *You can't Win* xvii. 238 He [*sc.* the old Chinaman] was shaking with the 'yen yen', the hop habit. **1961** *Amer. Speech* XXXVI. 178 If Cantonese *yen yen* be regarded as the probable source of English *yen-yen* we may assume that the syllables represent the individual etymons for *yen* 'opium' and *yen* 'craving'.

ye olde (yī ōᵘld, ōᵘ·ldi), *a.* [f. *ye* graphic var. of THE *dem. adj.* (see Y (3)) + *OLDE *a.*] Employed to suggest (spurious) antiquity in collocations the other words of which are often also archaistically spelt. Also *absol.* as *sb.*, a building characterized by (spurious) antique furnishings.

1896 W. WROTH *London Pleasure Gardens* I. 56 A modern public-house. 'Ye olde Bagnigge Wells.' **1900** *Confectioners' Union Hand-bk.* 167 Ye olde English toffee. **1919** WODEHOUSE *Damsel in Distress* xxvi. 298 In London, when a gentlewoman becomes distressed..she collects about her two or three other distressed gentlewomen..and starts a tea-shop in the West-End, which she calls Ye Oak Leaf, Ye Olde Willow-Pattern, Ye Linden-Tree, or Ye Snug Harbour, according to personal taste. **1933** [see *OLDE *a.*]. **1951** 'M. INNES' *Operation Pax* v. ii. 197 Not a tourist centre. Nothing ye olde. **1972** P. CLEIFE *Slick & Dead* iv. 36 The Inn was the complete trendy-contemporary Ye Olde—all ship's lanterns, copper pans, chintz and candelabra. **1977** *New Yorker* 16 May 107/1 Quincy Market..basically a suburban shopping mall done up in the instant charm of ye olde exposed brick.

yeoman. Add: **2. c.** *yeoman of signals* (earlier example). Also *ellipt.*

1898 KIPLING *Fleet in Being* 82 The Yeoman of Signals came to the captain's cabin at the regulation pace... 'Signal from the flagship, sir.' **1918** T. S. ELIOT *Let.* 13 Nov. in *Waste Land Drafts* (1971) p. xv, I was *sent for* by the Navy Intelligence, who said..that..they would make me a Chief Yeoman and raise me to a commission in a few months. **1978** H. WOUK *War & Remembrance* i. 6 My chief yeoman's got the logs and other records all lined up.

3. *yeoman warder* (later examples).

1947 *Tower of London* (Min. of Works) 13/2 The interior is shown to the public..on application to the Yeoman-Warder on duty. **1979** J. GARDNER *Nostradamus Traitor* i. 2 'You are a Beefeater, yes?' 'Yeoman Warder, Ma'am. Beefeater's a kind of nickname.'

yep, repr. a dial. (esp. U.S.) or vulgar pronunc. of YES. (Earlier and later examples.)

1891 *Harper's Mag.* Nov. 970 He gently and peacefully murmured, 'Yep'. **1907** J. W. SCHULTZ *My Life as an Indian* xxv. 284 'You must cut your hair.' 'Yep.'.. 'An' quit gamblin.' 'Yep.' **1926** J. GALSWORTHY in *Scribner's Mag.* Dec. 581/1 Their 'Yeahs!' and their 'Yeps!' Americans no longer said 'Yes' it seemed! **1962** E. BIRNEY *Sel. Poems* (1966) IV. 99 Yep ain't nothin we kin do. **1967** *Listener* 19 Jan. 96/3 'Would you like a cigarette?' I got a typically aggressive 'Yep'. **1977** *Time* 16 May 39/2 Yep, I let the American people down. **1979** R. JAFFE *Class Reunion* (1980) I. vi. 74 'Oh? You got a new car?'.. 'Yes... Look out the window.'

yer¹ (yɜ̄ɹ), repr. a dial. or vulgar pronunc. of YOU. (Examples.)

1848 [see YOU *pers. pron.* 4 a]. **1856** *Punch* 2 Feb. 41/1 (*caption*) That's how it was, yer see. **1867** [see *YERE]. **1880** A. E. HOUSMAN *Let.* 10 May (1971) 20 Yah! yer aint got no votes! **1916** G. B. SHAW *Pygmalion* I. 106 Theres manners f' yer! Te-oo banches o voylets trod into the mad. **1946** K. TENNANT *Lost Haven* (1947) iii. 50 Hey! Wait a minute... I want to see yer. **1978** *Hot Car* June 93/1 Brian *would* like to get in a plug for Micky Mees who helped with the heavy stuff. Good on yer, Mick.

yer² (yɜ̄ɹ), repr. a dial. or vulgar pronunc. of YOUR. (Examples.)

1814 [see YOUR *poss. pron.* and *a.* 2 a]. **1894** *Jrnl. Amer. Folk-Lore* VII. 148 She is gwine ter keep de house straight and yer britches mended. **1922** JOYCE *Ulysses* 419 Aweel, ye maun e'en gang yer gates. **1954** W. FAULKNER *Fable* 85 'Use yer boot,' the sergeant muttered. **1973** J. SPEIGHT *Thoughts of Chairman Alf* 26 Yer Queen should have a veto to..overrule Parliament... 'Cos she's born to rule. Not like yer Labour rubbish. **1980** *Herald* (Melbourne) 3 Apr. (City ed.) 2 Wouldn't it rot yer footy socks! Someone's about to contest Cazaly's musical mark.

yerba. (Earlier example of *yerba-maté*.)

1839 [see *PARAGUAY 1].

yerba buena (yɜ̄·ɹbă buˌe·nă). [Sp., lit. 'good herb': cf. YERBA.] A trailing perennial herb, *Satureja douglasii* (formerly *Micromeria chamissonis*) of the family Labiatæ, native to western North America and bearing aromatic leaves and white or purplish flowers.

1847 *Calif. Star* (San Francisco) 30 Jan. 2/3 The town [*sc.* San Francisco] takes its name from an herb to be found all around it which is said to make good tea; and possessing medicinal qualities; it is called good herb or Yerba Buena. **1882** B. HARTE *Flip, & Found at Blazing Star* 15 He seized a few of the young tender green leaves of the yerba buena vine..and ate them. **1915** ARMSTRONG & THORNBER *Western Wild Flowers* 436 Yerba Buena, Tea-vine..was used medicinally by California Indians, so it was called 'good herb' by the Mission Fathers, and is still used as a tea. **1935** J. STEINBECK *Tortilla Flat* xv. 261 Tea made from yerba buena will be good. **1975** *Islander* (Victoria, B.C.) 3 Aug. 3/3 Beside the pond speedwell..yerba buena [etc.].

yere, repr. a dial. (esp. U.S.) or vulgar pronunc. of HERE.

1867 *Harper's Mag.* Feb. 274/2 This yere is Colonel N— who wants ter know yer. **1907** J. W. SCHULTZ *My Life as an Indian* xxv. 284 You must..help me run this yere boardin' house. **1929** W. FAULKNER *Sartoris* IV. i. 270 Yere dey is, Cunnel. **1956** [see *JONG¹]. **1973** J. PATTINSON *Search Warrant* ii. 34 Like young folks is these yere days—long hair, beards.

yeri (ye·ri). [Russ.] The name of the Russian vowel ы, the twenty-eighth letter of the Russian alphabet.

1921 E. SAPIR *Language* ix. 212 Both nasalized vowels and the Slavic 'yeri' are demonstrably of secondary origin in Indo-European. **1977** *Word 1972* XXVIII. 249 The /i/ is a back unrounded vowel, similar to the Russian yeri.

yerk, yark, *sb.* Add: See also *YORK *sb.*²

Yerkish (yɜ̄·ɹkiʃ), *sb.* (and *a.*). [f. the name of R. M. *Yerkes* (1876–1956), U.S. primatologist + -ISH¹.] A sign language for chimpanzees based on geometric symbols, chiefly devised by E. C. von Glasersfeld for experimental purposes and first published in 1973. Also *attrib.* or as *adj.*

1973 D. M. RUMBAUGH et al. in *Behavior Research Methods & Instrumentation* Sept. 385/2 The study program..included the design of the language system (Yerkish). *Ibid.* 387/2 Each correlator links two items that are expressed in the Yerkish phrase or sentence. **1973** *Science* 16 Nov. 731 Each Yerkish word, or 'lexigram', is a distinctive geometric white symbol on a colored background. **1974** E. C. VON GLASERSFELD in *Amer. Jrnl. Computational Linguistics* (microfiche 12), The Yerkish language for nonhuman primates. **1974** *N.Y. Times* 29 May 52/3 Lana's [*sc.* a chimpanzee's] computerized language, called *Yerkish* in honor of the primate center's founder, Dr. Robert M. Yerkes. **1977** E. C. VON GLASERSFELD in D. M. Rumbaugh *Language Learning by Chimpanzee* v. 114 The grammar of Yerkish had to be kept as simple as possible for several reasons. **1980** *Times* 3 July 16/3 'Yerkish', an artificial language especially developed by Professor D. M. Rumbaugh at the Yerkes Primate Research Centre, Emory University, near Atlanta, United States, for a chimpanzee called Lana.

yerra (ye·ră), *int. Anglo-Ir.* Also **yerrah.** [Ir.] An asseverative oath or exclamation.

1892 E. LAWLESS *Grania* II. iii. 32 Yerra! give him his bit and his sup and his bed,..and 'tis all he wants. **1898** M. MACDONAGH *Irish Life & Character* ix. 156 'What's the matter with the old gentleman?' he was asked. 'What's the matter with him! Yerrah, look at the walk of him... Begor, he only touches the ground in an odd place.' **1914** JOYCE *Dubliners* 155 Yerra, sure the little hop-o'-my-thumb has forgotten all about it. **1939** —— *Finnegans Wake* 95 Yerra, why would he heed that old gasometer. **1958** B. BEHAN *Borstal Boy* III. 218 'Yerra, 'tis nothing,' said I, jovial and Irish, but making every move to work on a bit more. **1965** *N. Munster Antiquarian Jrnl.* IX. IV. 186 Yerra there's no good in talking to you. **1977** J. HODGINS *Invention of World* iii. 83 This is no ordinary boy... Yerra, this is a boy apart.

yerse (yɜ̄ɹs), repr. a non-Standard pronunc. of YES. Also **yers.**

1937 PARTRIDGE *Dict. Slang* 970/2 *Yers; yerse*, yes: sol.: C. 19–20. **1965** J. PORTER *Dover Two* vi. 69 Yerse, we was. Only they nabbed us first. **1969** J. GARDNER *Founder Member* ii. 16 'All three of us going to New York..' parried Boysie. 'Yerse,' said Griffin. **1980** P. G. WINSLOW *Counsellor Heart* v. 80 'A plant?'.. 'Yerse.' She described the plant. **1985** M. GILBERT *Long Journey Home* xii. 125 'Was it as obvious as that?' 'Yers. Well, you can always tell.'

yersinia (yɜ̄ɹsi·niă). *Bacteriol.* Also **Yersinia.** Pl. **-ae.** [mod.L. (J. J. Van Loghem 1944, in *Antonie van Leeuwenhoek* X. 15), f. the name of A. E. J. *Yersin* (1863–1943), Swiss-born French bacteriologist + -IA¹.] A bacterium of the genus *Yersinia* (formerly included in *Pasteurella*), which includes Gram-negative rods that are facultative anærobes present in many animals and causing plague and yersiniosis in man.

1967 *Acta Path. & Microbiol. Scand.* LXXI. 384 Morphologically, they were fairly easy to distinguish from Yersinia. **1982** E. A. GORZYNSKI in Milgrom & Flanagan *Med. Microbiol.* xxi. 316/1 Yersiniae are facultative intracellular parasites. **1983** *McGraw-Hill Yearbk. Sci. & Technol.* 482/1 Once isolation of a suspect yersinia has been accomplished, the biochemical identification ensues more logically.

Hence **yersinio·sis** [-OSIS], infection with or a disease caused by yersiniæ (other than *Y. pestis*, the cause of plague), which in man is self-limiting and usu. marked by lymphadenitis of the mesentery and ileitis or by enteritis and occurs chiefly in children and young adults.

1971 *Country Life* 2 Dec. 1530/1 In older leverets, parasitism may be the main problem, and in adults yersiniosis, formerly called pseudotuberculosis, a bacterial disease occurring in either the acute or chronic form, appears to be a common cause of death. **1983** *Brit. Med. Jrnl.* 27 Aug. 593/1 A large outbreak of yersiniosis in 1980 in a boys' school in Dorset was attributed to contact with a pig kept on the school farm.

yes, *adv.* (*sb.*²) Add: **1. c.** *yes and no*, in answer to a question to which it is difficult to reply: partly, perhaps, to a certain degree.

1873 C. M. YONGE *Pillars of House* I. vii. 154 'Do you come from his father?' 'Well—yes and no. His father is still in Oregon; but he and I have always been one.' **1896** 'M. RUTHERFORD' *Clara Hopgood* xxii. 212, I said 'yes and no' and there is another side. **1933** W. S. MAUGHAM *Sheppey* III. 75 *Bessie*:..Expecting somebody? *Florrie*: Yes and no. **1964** R. PETRIE *Murder by Precedent* v. 78 'That's why you gave him a home?' he asked. 'Well yes and no.' **1981** B. MURPHY *Enigma Variations* xiii. 137 'Do you believe that if you continue seeing me you'll be damned?' 'Yes and no.'

d. *yes or no*: used *attrib.* (freq. hyphenated) to denote a question, etc., answerable by, or definable in terms of, *yes* or *no*; *spec.* in *Linguistics*. Also *ellipt.* as *yes-no*.

1924 [see *PRONOMINAL *a.* 2]. **1935** [see *OKEY-DOKE *a.*]. **1952** *Mind* LXI. 52 The yes-or-no question is the one we like to ask. **1957** D. L. BOLINGER in *Publ. Amer. Dialect Soc.* XXVIII. 24 Yes-no Qs are essentially true-false Qs. **1961** F. W. HOUSEHOLDER in Saporta & Bastian *Psycholinguistics* 17/1 Beside this graded kind of 'grammaticalness'..there is also an absolute yes-or-no type. **1963, 1964** [see *MORE C. *adv.* 2]. **1966** A. BATTERSBY *Math. in Management* vii. 180 This type of work [*sc.* simulation] lends itself very readily to electronic computation, because it comprises a number of repetitive 'loops' of instructions, controlled by simple 'yes-no' decisions. **1976** H. KEMELMAN *Wednesday Rabbi got Wet* xlvi. 257 The law is not a yes-or-no thing. **1977** *Times* 8 Feb. 17/1 The Government is proposing to put a single yes-no question to the voters of Scotland and Wales.

1979 *Economist* 16 June 98/2 Whitehall's traditional passion for compromise only makes for trouble in a crisis which needs yes-or-no decisions, fast. **1984** *Word* XXXV. 188 Sentences other than declaratives are broken up into a speech act operator (a wh-question operator, a yes-no question operator, a command operator, etc.) and a propositional kernel.

yes, *v.* Add: **2.** *trans.* To say 'yes' to or agree with (someone); to flatter by habitual assent. *U.S.*

1921 R. W. LARDNER in Mencken *Amer. Lang.* (rev. ed.) 393 He..crossed me up. I ast him for a hook and he yessed me and then throwed a fast one. **1928** J. P. MCEVOY *Show Girl* ix. 134 They yes you to death. **1933** *Times Lit. Suppl.* 23 Nov. 844/2 For Mr. Leonard..there is no fun in life as lived in the United States. Too much work..yessing the boss and dud liquor. **1935** [see *RAVE *sb.*[2] 2 b]. **1945** S. LEWIS *Cass Timberlane* xvi. 89 A lot of bums are always yessing you..but me and Boone are good-enough friends to tell you the truth. **1983** *N.Y. Times* 23 Oct. 19/6 Mr. Reagan..is unable to get his proposal off the ground..; his aids yes him to death with plans.

yeshiva (yəʃī·vă). Also **yeshiba(h, yeshivah,** and with capital initial. Pl. **yeshivoth, yeshiva(h)s;** also **yeshibot.** [a. Heb. *yĕšīḇāh*, f. *yashav* to sit.] An Orthodox Jewish college or seminary; a Talmudic academy.

1851 *Living Age* XXIX. 154/2 The hope of seeing him one day decorated with the dignity of rabbi..will impel them cheerfully to make all the sacrifices which his outfit and partial support at the yeshibah (*academy*) entail. **1881** *Encycl. Brit.* XIII. 681/2 The rabbis received their education at the Yeshiboth ('sessions' of academies devoted to the Talmud, the *Shulchan Aruch*, and their commentators). **1904** *Sat. Rev.* 24 Sept. 404/1 The Jewish orphan..is brought up..at a yeshiva, or seminary, where the Talmud is almost the sole object of study. **1916** H. SACHER *Zionism & Jewish Future* 38 They had passed by so swift and drastic a revolution from the *Cheder* and the *Yeshiba* to the Gymnasium and the University, that the only culture they were interested in was German culture. **1926** S. ASH *Kiddush Ha-Shem* x. 88 Famed far and wide were the yeshivahs of Poland. **1949** KOESTLER *Promise & Fulfulment* III. i. 295 Israel's first Prime Minister..and many of the other political leaders, started their education in the *Yeshivot*, the religious schools of Russian Jewry. **1957** *Encycl. Brit.* XIII. 63D/1 Orthodox Judaism created the Rabbi Isaac Elchanan Theological seminary in New York (1896), which developed into the Yeshiva university, a liberal arts college. **1960** L. P. GARTNER *Jewish Immigrant in England, 1870–1914* ii. 39 Yekuthiel Sussmann Schlosser.. arrived in 1852 as an itinerant solicitor for a projected yeshibah in Kalish. **1965** J. A. MICHENER *Source* 461 Sometimes the yeshiva students contrived ingenious answers. *Ibid.* 705 He..tries always to attend one of the yeshivot. **1976** C. BERMANT *Coming Home* I. i. 17 Yeshivah students..had been equipped for a life of prayer, contemplation and study. **1981** *Amer. Speech* LVI. 3 Orthodox Jews are typically strict Sabbath observers who maintain their own religious day schools and yeshivas. **1985** *Listener* 3 Jan. 27/3 He overcomes this obstacle by making a donation to a yeshiva, or religious seminar.

ye·s-man. *colloq.* (orig. *U.S.*). Also **yes man.** [f. YES *adv.* + MAN *sb.*[1]] A man who agrees from self-interest or fear with everything put to him by a superior; an obsequious subordinate.

1912 *Century Mag.* July 339/2 We're both yes-men, Edward. We've got to take orders now. **1924** H. C. WITWER in *Cosmopolitan* Apr. 69/2, I thoroughly enjoy.. the yes-men who hang about the executives and hold their jobs by simply being constantly affirmative. **1928** *Sunday Express* 15 July 3/6 Heeney is paying the strictest attention to his instructors, and in this respect is very different from Tunney, who directs his own training, and whose camp associates are all 'Yes' men. **1933** C. DAY LEWIS *Magnetic Mountain* 51 What do they believe in, these yellow yes-men. **1949** [see *closed shop* s.v. *CLOSED *ppl.a.* 3]. **1954** D. UNWIN *Governor's Wife* v. 119 Your administration..favours the boot-lickers, the sycophants, the yes-men who do as they're told and don't make trouble. **1959** [see *BAND-WAGON]. **1973** *Times* 31 Jan. 14/3 This is not a demand for 'yes men' but for common standards. **1979** J. WAINWRIGHT *Duty Elsewhere* i. 8 The heavies and the molls—the pimps and the yes-men.

Hence **ye·s-girl, -woman,** an obsequiously subordinate woman.

1930 K. BRUSH *Young Man of Manhattan* v. 56 Her attitude.., so respectful, so impressed, hardened his heart. 'Just a yes-girl!' he thought bitterly. **1933** S. LEWIS *Ann Vickers* xxxviii. 454 They want to boss a gang of meek yes-women or they want to be received socially, like princesses. **1937** H. G. WELLS *Star Begotten* vii. 128 All his most trusted henchmen, tools, stooges, subordinates, intimates, Watsons, yes-girls. **1942** E. WAUGH *Put out More Flags* i. 17 'That's right,' said the yes-woman. **1950** D. CUSACK *Morning Sacrifice* in *3 Austral. Three-Act Plays* I. 188 It..Prepares them to accept all, question nothing, and grow into nice well-behaved yes-girls. **1979** M. SOAMES *Clementine Churchill* xvi. 235 Devoted and fiercely loyal, she never became a 'yes-woman'.

yessir (ye·səɪ, yes͵sɜ̄·ɪ). *colloq.* [Repr. an informal pronunc. of *yes, sir*: see *SIR *sb.* 8 c.] **a.** = *yes, sir* s.v. *SIR *sb.* 8 c. **b.** A formula of assent to a superior. Occas. as *sb.*, a quick utterance of 'yes, sir'. Cf. *NOSSIR.

There is much variation in the placing of the main stress in both the ordinary use and in the verbal forms.

1913 R. BROOKE *Let.* 17 Sept. (1968) 511 That notebook.. I lost it in British Columbia—yessir, isn't it *too* bloody. **1930** [see *NOSSIR]. **1931** M. ALLINGHAM *Look to Lady* xxi. 215 The girl vanished with a startled 'yessir'. **1933** D. L. SAYERS *Murder must Advertise* vi. 102 'Yessir.' Ginger grinned confidentially. **1936** WODEHOUSE *Laughing Gas* xxiv. 262 'And,' said George, 'it's yessir sure enough the picture of the dead wife he loved.' **1962** L. DEIGHTON *Ipcress File* xviii. 118 A couple of 'yessirs' when you know that 'not on your life' is the thing to say. **1968** *Globe & Mail* (Toronto) (Mag.) 17 Feb. 1 A perfect specimen, yessir, the Canadian Hercules. **1973** A. BROINOWSKI *Take One Ambassador* ix. 125 The commanding officer went past, giving you marks for..the crispness of your Yessir. **1982** M. NABB *Death of Dutchman* vii. 143 'Do you understand me?' 'Yessir!'

Hence **yes(-)si·r, yessi·r** *v.*, (*a*) *trans.*, to defer to (someone) as a superior; (*b*) *intr.*, to say 'yes, sir', esp. obsequiously; **yes-si·rring** *vbl. sb.*

1966 *Punch* 21 Sept. 454/2 Yessiring in the office is insufficient, he offers his clammy devotion to the whole family as well. **1968** L. DEIGHTON *Only when I Larf* i. 16 Imagine..yes sirring the boss until superannuation... Not me, man. I'm for the open road. **1977** 'J. D. WHITE' *Salzburg Affair* xii. 104 He came in bowing and yessirring, although no one..was there to overhear. **1980** H. R. F. KEATING *Murder of Maharajah* xv. 182 You're used to people yessirring you left and right.

yes, siree (yes sərī·). *U.S. colloq.* Also **yes sir-ee, yes sirree.** [f. YES *adv.* + SIRREE.] Yes indeed; certainly. Cf. *NO SIREE.

1846 *Dollar Newspaper* (Philadelphia) 1 July 3/4 'Will you take this man to be your lawful husband?' said the Justice; to which she responded with breathless haste, '*Yes, sir-ee*'. **1898** J. C. HARRIS *Tales of Home Folks* 225 Cassy Tatum! Yes, siree! The very gal! **1900** [see SIRREE]. **1924** H. J. LASKI *Let.* 29 July (1953) I. 638 For local colour he added that when you emphatically approve of an opinion you write 'yes, sirree' on it. **1927** J. N. MCILWRAITH *Kinsmen at War* xxvii. 277 Yes, siree, our army's been going ashore plundering and destroying helpless villages all along the sea-coast of the United States. **1956** B. HOLIDAY *Lady sings Blues* (1973) xxiv. 203 Yes siree bob, life is just a bowl of cherries.

yessum (yes'm). *U.S. dial.* contraction of *yes, ma'am* [cf. MA'AM], a polite form of assent addressed to a woman.

1913 *Dialect Notes* IV. 1 *Yessum*, adv., yes, ma'am. **1929** W. FAULKNER *Sound & Fury* 6 'Take his overcoat and overshoes off.'.. 'Yessum.' Versh said. **1938** M. K. RAWLINGS *Yearling* x. 88 'You feel all right?' she asked. 'Yessum. Sort o' weakified.' **1942** W. FAULKNER *Go down, Moses* 11 Miss Sophonsiba said..neighbors just a half day's ride apart ought not to go so long as Uncle Buck, and Uncle Buck said Yessum.

yest, also, an epistolary abbrev. of YESTERDAY.

1894 DUCHESS OF MARLBOROUGH *Let.* 21 May in R. S. Churchill *Winston S. Churchill* (1967) I. Compan. I. vii. 486 Your father returned yest morn and went to Harrow.

yester-. Add: *yester-tempest.*

1888 G. M. HOPKINS *Poems* (1967) 105 Delightfully the bright wind boisterous ropes, wrestles, beats earth bare Of yestertempest's creases.

yesterday, *adv.*, *sb.*, and *a.* Add: **A.** *adv.* **2.** *I was not born yesterday* (earlier examples).

1757 R. DEMERE *Let.* 10 Aug. in W. L. McDowell *Docs. relating to Indian Affairs* (1970) II. 398, I was not born Yesterday. **1837** MARRYAT *Snarleyyow* xii. 62, I was not born yesterday, as the saying is.

3. *fig.*, *colloq.* Used to suggest extreme urgency or impatience, esp. in phr. *to want* (or *need*) *something yesterday*.

1974 *Times* 7 Feb. 14/7 Attacks by Miss Brigid Brophy and her group, whose case was, roughly, that they wanted everything, and wanted it yesterday. **1978** D. A. STANWOOD *Memory of Eva Ryker* xxi. 196, I need the information yesterday. **1980** T. BARLING *Goodbye Piccadilly* xv. 309 Don't ask me... Just get us down there yesterday.

B. *sb.* **3. b.** In the possessive, as *yesterday's man*, a man, esp. a politician, whose career is finished or past its peak.

1966 'G. BLACK' *You want to die, Johnny?* ii. 27 John saw himself as one of yesterday's men, a survivor. **1972** *Guardian* 14 Jan. 13/8 Support for Nkrumuh still remains limited to his fellow tribesmen in the remote South-west and to those who fell off the high-living Fascist bandwagon when he was overthrown. These people are 'yesterday's men' in the eyes of most Ghanaians. **1979** *Jrnl. R. Soc. Arts* CXXVII. 349/2 The politicians..do not know if they will walk out as ministers..or as yesterday's men.

yet, *adv.* Add: **1. f.** Used as an ironic intensive at the end of a sentence, clause, etc. (imitating the use of Yiddish *noch*). *colloq.* (orig. *U.S.*).

1936 *Sat. Even. Post* 19 Dec. 11/3 'The only kinda men I want are ones who wouldn't be afraid to try out for Whiteman.' 'Whiteman yet!' scoffed one. **1943** M. SHULMAN *Barefoot Boy with Cheek* vii. 68 'Not just a little story, but a big story, and on the front page and with pictures.' There were admiring whistles and cries of 'Pictures, yet!' from the audience. **1957** *N.Y. Times Times Book Rev.* 17 Mar. 8 The counter-claim was dismissed (with costs yet). **1962** T. MEEHAN in *Sunday Times* 5 Aug. 20/3 And that spooky organ music they got piped in all over the place—E. Power Biggs instead of Muzak, yet. **1972** D. S. VISCOTT *Making of a Psychiatri*[st] ii. 32 You can bet your Phi Beta Kappa pin, junior yea[r] yet, that D. J. Marley knows exactly what to put dow[n] **1975** *Times Lit. Suppl.* 7 Mar. 250/2 If you own a Bea[u]mont and Fletcher folio, don't lend it. At least not [to] someone who will return it with extensive annotatio[ns] (in ink yet!). **1980** *Oxford Times* 22 Aug. 13/3 The track[s] include..'To Know Him is to Love Him' (with Davi[d] Bowie on saxophone, yet!).

yeti (ye·ti). Also **Yeti.** [ad. Tibetan *yeh-te* little manlike animal.] Native (Sherpa) nam[e] for a hypothetical ape-like animal whos[e] tracks have supposedly been found in snov[w] on the Himalayan mountains; = *Abominabl[e] Snowman* s.v. *ABOMINABLE *a.* 1 c.

1937 *Times* 13 Nov. 13/5 The Sherpas had no hesitatio[n] in pronouncing them [*sc.* tracks] to be those of a Snowma[n] or 'Yeti'. **1951** *Times* 6 Dec. 5/7 Sen Tensing immediatel[y] pronounced them to be tracks of yetis or Abominabl[e] Snowmen... He describes it as half man half beast, abou[t] five feet six inches tall, covered with reddish-brown hai[r] but with a hairless face. **1955** [see *Abominable Snowma[n]* s.v. *ABOMINABLE *a.* 1 c]. **1956** C. EVANS *On Climbin[g]* xiii. 185, I had heard that there was a *yeti* scalp there, an[d] I wanted to see it. **1972** J. NAPIER (*title*) Bigfoot: th[e] yeti and sasquatch in myth and reality. **1975** E. HILLAR[Y] *Nothing venture Nothing Win* xv. 238 Even in the Thyang[-]boche Monastery—traditionally the source of muc[h] Yeti lore and Yeti sightings—we were unable to fin[d] anyone who had seen a Yeti.

yew, *sb.* Add: **3.** *yew-frond.*

1922 JOYCE *Ulysses* 491 The walls are tapestried with paper of yewfronds.

yew (yü), repr. a vulgar pronunc. of You Also **yewall** = *YOU-ALL *pers. pron.*

1890 KIPLING *Abaft Funnel* (1909) 272 'Do *yew* know, as the Private Secretary said at Simla,..'it's remarkabl hard for an Anglo-Indian to get along in England.' **192** H. WILLIAMSON *Beautiful Years* 204 'Yew wait... Common as dirt, are we?.. Yew wait, young cocky-boy. 'Yes, yew wait, yew slug-face, bag o' bones.' **1968** A DIMENT *Great Spy Race* i. 8 How can I help yew? **197** *Custom Car* Nov. 14/1 Thank yewall. **1981** P. MACDONAL *One Way Street* xix. 189 Yew just scoot, yew an' young John.

yé-yé (yeye), *a.* (*sb.*) Also **Ye-Ye.** [a. Fr., tr. of *yeah-yeah*, redupl. of *YEAH *adv.*] Designating or pertaining to the modern style of music, dress, etc., associated with France in the 1960s. Also applied to persons. Occas. as *sb.*

The redupl. form *yeah-yeah* freq. occurred in Eng. popular songs of the 1960s.

1960 *Daily Tel.* 24 Oct. 9/3, I found one dramatically *yé-yé* shop in old Lyons..which sells only British goods of a somewhat bizarre kind. **1966** *Guardian* 1 Apr. 10/7 In Paris, clothes are still a lot more class-divisive with Ye-Ye girls and debutantes thoroughly opposed. *Ibid.* 7 Apr. 8 Paris once had twenty music halls; now it has two—the Olympia, which caters more for *yé-yé* singers, and Bobino. *Ibid.*, The Bobino. is no place for *yé-yés*. **1967** *Sat. Rev.* 4 Mar. 49 Amplified like yé-yé music. **1968** *N.Y. Times* 3 July 30 The orchestra Chez Régine will play anything 'from yé-yé to regular music'. *Ibid.* 23 July 42 The name of a high-priced haute couture boutique here, run by Arlette Nastat, a forever yé-yé designer. **1972** M. GOLDBERG *Karamanov Equations* xvii. 161 He sipped a coffee and a Cinzano..watching the mini-skirted yé-yé girls and their hairy escorts parading by. **1979** J. WYLLIE *To catch Viper* viii. 49 Coca-Cola signs and bars, fashionable young women in miniskirts and teen-age *yé-yé* boys.

yez. For *Anglo-Irish* read *dial.* (esp. *Anglo-Ir.*) and add: Also **yeez.** (Later examples.)

1842 S. LOVER *Handy Andy* xxxiv. 280 Who are yiz at all, gintlemin? **1884** D. BOUCICAULT *Shaughraun* I. iv. 10/2 Away with yeez—hide! **1901** M. FRANKLIN *My Brilliant Career* xvii. 147, I have the table laid out for both of yez. **1908** J. JOYCE *Let.* 8 Dec. (1966) II. 226, I will send him very gladly if that will make yiz all happy and loving. **1939** —— *Finnegans Wake* 8 Now yiz are in the Willingdone Museyroom. **1962** D. PHILLIPS *Lichty Nichts* 30 Yez ur gitn a rare day. **1966** [see *JACK *sb.*[1] 1 d]. **1969** in Halpert & Story *Christmas Mumming in Newfoundland* 211 Some people will say, 'How many of yez?' and the janneys will shout back, 'Two or three.' **1977** *Transatlantic Rev.* LX. 147 'Aye, OK,' I says. 'How but? Did yiz arrange that afore?' **1977** *Sounds* 9 July 8/5 It's not going to be on general release and yez can't buy it at general outlets.

Yi (ī). [Chinese.] The name of a minority nationality in China, distributed over Yunnan, Sichuan, and Guizhou; = *LOLO. Also, the language of this people. Also *attrib.* or as *adj.*

1960 CHANG-TU HU et al. *China* v. 66 The Yi (Lolo) are located principally in the Liang Shan area on the borders of Szechwan and Yunnan. **1962** E. SNOW *Other Side of River* (1963) lxxviii. 596 Some of the Yi people in Yunnan planted grain as the American Indians did. **1968** [see *LOLO]. **1974** *Encycl. Brit. Micropædia* X. 818/3 The traditional Yi culture includes a primitive hoe-using agriculture, livestock herding, and hunting. **1978** *Nagel's Encycl.-Guide: China* 65 The Tibeto-Burmese group includes Tibetan, Yi (or Lolo), Hani and Tujia. **1979** *China Now* Mar./Apr. 16/1 The Yi people, like many peasant societies, still want lots of children. **1984** *National Geographic* Mar. 290/2 These people number about 750,000 and belong to the larger group of five million Yi scattered over a wider area.

‖ **yichus** (yi·kəs, yi·χəs). Also **yiches.** [Yiddish f. Heb. *yīḥūs* pedigree.] Honour, prestige, status.

1907 tr. *Frank's Simon Eichelkatz* 431/2 *Yichus*, aristocracy; good family connection. **1927** *Amer. Mercury* X. 172/2 There was a steady demand from wealthy prospective fathers-in-law for professional men whose titles would add *yiches* (prestige) to their wealth. **1946** *Commentary* May 63/1 On the other hand our butcher's daughters..had even less *yichus*. **1964** S. BELLOW *Herzog* 86, I know you Herzogs and your *Yiches*. Don't give me that hoity-toity. *Ibid.* 141 All branches of the family had the caste madness of *yichus*. No life so barren ..that it didn't have imaginary dignities, honors to come. **1976** C. BERMANT *Coming Home* I. vii. 99 If I could become a doctor he might recover something of his former grace. A doctor meant *yichus*, social status, prestige.

yicker, var. *YIKKER *v.*

Yid. Add: Also † **Yit(t).** Substitute for def.: A (usu. offensive) name for a Jew. (Later examples.)

1874 HOTTEN *Slang Dict.* 344 *Yid*, or *Yit*, a Jew. *Yidden*, the Jewish people. The Jews use these terms very frequently. **1898** [see *SCHLEMIEL]. **1912** G. FRANKAU *One of Us* vi. 53 As the Yid Knows well the slump-signs ere the slump convulses. **1935** [see *CRAP *sb.*¹ 7 b]. **1940** E. POUND *Cantos* lii. 11 Sin drawing vengeance, poor yitts paying for—. **1946** KOESTLER *Thieves in Night* 279, I became a socialist because I hated the poor; and I became a Hebrew because I hated the Yid. **1963** V. NABOKOV *Gift* iii. 180 Then she went and married a yid. **1971** B. MALAMUD *Tenants* 203 Then they go to a synagogue late at night,..and make Yid noises, praying.

Yiddish, *sb.* (*a.*) (Earlier and later examples.)

1875 *New Era* 5 May 285 In fact, this corrupt German is known as Yiddish or Jewish German. **1917** *Edin. Rev.* Apr. 310 In 1903..Yiddish was solemnly proclaimed the Jewish national language. **1938** *Better English* Feb. 50 As a rule, Yiddish-speaking people do not move in higher society. **1939** [see *JUDÆO-, JUDEO-]. **1970** *Language* XLVI. 939 Standard Yiddish is the only variety taught in the schools. **1977** *Rolling Stone* 16 June 43/2 'Never point your gun at someone,' Prince clucked in a Yiddish accent. **1979** *Guardian* 28 May 11/8 The Jewish community of eastern Europe, the Yiddish-speaking, Ashkenazi quasi-state. **1981** G. CLARE *Last Waltz in Vienna* (1982) I. 11 He must also have spoken Yiddish, the language of the ghetto.

Yiddisher. Substitute for entry: **Yi·ddisher,** *sb.* and *a.* Also **yiddisher.** [ad. G. *Jüdischer* Jew.] † **Yidısher. A.** *sb.* A Jew. Also *transf.* (cf. JEW *sb.* 2).

1859 MATSELL *Vocabulum* 97 *Yidisher*, a Jew. **1890** [in Dict.]. **1896** E. TURNER *Little Larrikin* xxiv. 292 But why..that agent..refused to take the premium.. beats me..for he's more than a bit of a yiddisher. **1931** R. CAMPBELL *Georgiad* iii. 62 Doctors much to praise in it can see And with the ancient Yiddishers agree. **1933** L. GOLDING *Magnolia Street* I. iii. 59 Can't he mind his own business, now..he's got hold of a stinking Yiddisher? **1976** *Publishers Weekly* 19 Apr. 81/3 With yiddishers, reasonableness and gentle satire, Vorspan.. sets out to convince you that a bit of suffering is good for you.

B. *adj.* Also **Yiddische,** etc. [ad. G. *jüdische* (inflectional form of *jüdisch*).]

1892 I. ZANGWILL *Childr. of Ghetto* I. iii. 94 At least, she would have starved in a Yiddishe country, not in a land of heathens. **1898** A. M. BINSTEAD *Pink 'Un & Pelican* xii. 276 One very enquiring Yiddisher youth stood munching a shoot of celery. **1925** J. YELLEN (*song-title*) My Yiddishe Momma. **1961** P. DE VRIES *Through Fields of Clover* i. 27 Jokes about hot pastrami... To say nothing of Yiddisher Mamas. **1965** D. S. DAVIS *Pale Betrayer* iv. 52 I'm a real *Yiddishe* mama. **1971** C. FICK *Danziger Transcript* 177, I laughed like a Yiddische baby. **1973** *Jewish Chron.* 18 May 15/3 A Clever Yiddisher boy working next door, heard strange noises. **1976** R. SANDERS in D. Villiers *Next Year in Jerusalem* 198 The young Irving Berlin composed both Italian and Yiddisha pastiche. **1979** *Guardian* 22 Mar. 9/1 In Israel..plangent Yiddischer mammas are passé.

Yi·ddishism. orig. *U.S.* [f. YIDDISH *sb.* (*a.*) + -ISM.] **a.** A linguistic feature influenced by or derived from Yiddish. **b.** Advocacy of Yiddish culture and language.

1926 *Amer. Mercury* VII. 207/1 Most Yidgin writers qualify their Yiddishisms with parenthetical English explanations. **1933** in A. A. Roback *Curiosities of Jewish Lit.* viii. 124 Doeblin sees his model in something on the lines of Yiddishism on a world scale. **1938** *Better Eng.* Feb. 50 No one has yet made an attempt to collect all these Yiddishisms into a single collection. **1962** *Amer. Speech* XXXVII. 202 The use of *better* with *should* here is another Yiddishism..repeated in the announcer's next sentence: 'Better we should stop the clock.' **1966** *New Society* 12 May 9/2 The idiom of the New Yorker—Gentile or Jew—is..full of translated Yiddishisms ('I should live so long', 'Who needs it?' 'You should pardon the expression' and 'Now he tells me'.) **1978** *Soviet Jewish Affairs* VIII. 73 Since Tsinberg's claim, there has been debate as to whether the sixteenth, seventeenth and eighteenth century 'Yiddishists' can properly be viewed as forerunners of modern Yiddishism. **1981** *Amer. Speech* LVI. 17 The noun *glitsh* is a Yiddishism..from the verb *glitshn* 'to slide'.

Yi·ddishist, *sb.* (*a.*) [f. YIDDISH *sb.* (*a.*) + -IST.] An adherent or supporter of Yiddishism (sense a); *spec.*, an advocate of the exclusive use of Yiddish by Jews. Also, a student of Yiddish language or literature. Also *attrib.* or as *adj.*

1917 *Edin. Rev.* Apr. 310 Russian Jewry rang for a time with the bitter controversy of the so-called Hebraists and Yiddishists. The Yiddishists..won... In 1903.. Yiddish was solemnly proclaimed the Jewish national language. **1933** *B'nai B'rith Mag.* XLVIII. 32/3 What will the Yiddishists..say to this? **1964** S. BELLOW *Herzog* 108 Her father had been..a member of the Arbeiter-Ring, a Yiddishist. **1970** *Language* XLVI. 938 The title of this book [sc. *The Field of Yiddish*] suggests that it is primarily of interest to Yiddishists. **1971** *Encycl. Judaica* X. 62/2 The Yiddish movement which came at the beginning of the 20th century, laid the accent on Yiddish as the spoken and living language of the vast majority of world Jewry. **1972** H. KEMELMAN *Monday Rabbi took Off* xlvii. 276 'My husband was a Yiddishist,' said Gittel stiffly, 'He did not speak the language out of principle.' **1976** I. B. SINGER in D. Villiers *Next Year in Jerusalem* 62 The leftist Yiddishists tried to identify Yiddish with the social revolution... Russia had promised its Jews a Yiddishist cultural autonomy. **1982** *Lang. Problems & Lang. Planning* VI. II. 208 Yiddishists apply the term [Yiddish] retroactively to all earlier stages of the language, until its very beginnings about a thousand years ago.

‖ **Yiddishkeit** (yi·diʃkəit). Also **yiddishkeit.** [ad. Yiddish *yidishkeyt.*] = JEWISHNESS, JUDAISM 1; Yiddishness.

1892 I. ZANGWILL *Childr. of Ghetto* I. iii. 87 All they teach them in the school is English nonsense... The good Yiddishkeit goes to the wall. **1901** M. WOLFENSTEIN *Idylls of Gass* 25 They do say she reads German books with not a word of *Yiddishkeit* (Judaism) in them. **1956** 'H. MACDIARMID' *Stony Limits & Scots Unbound* 28 A *Yiddishkeit* crutch. **1966** *New Statesman* 6 May 648/2 The most sophisticated Israelis are those who are often most attached to *yiddishkeit* and many accept the rabbinical regime as part of Jewish culture without which Israel would have no identity. **1976** B. WILLIAMS *Making of Manchester Jewry* xi. 271 A..strictly observant Jewish society based upon the exclusive *Yiddishkeit* of the Eastern European ghetto. **1984** *Listener* 20 Sept. 14/2 With them the immigrants brought their richest possessions: Yiddish and Yiddishkeit—their language and their way of life.

yield, *sb.* Add: **6.** Esp. under a stress greater than the yield stress; also, the stage in the progressive stressing and deformation of a body when the yield stress is reached.

1913 *Proc. R. Soc.* A. LXXXVIII. 464 Yield occurred.. while there was still a large margin of elasticity left in the side bars. **1925** J. CASE *Strength of Materials* xxxiv. 538 The drop of stress which occurs at yield with materials like wrought-iron and mild steel. **1967** J. G. RAMSAY *Folding & Fracturing of Rocks* vi. 314 The stress conditions which initiate plastic yield. **1981** C. HALL *Polymer Materials* iii. 73 The search for improved impact performance has more recently stimulated a similar systematic study of yield and fracture processes in polymers.

7. Special Comb.: **yield table** *Forestry*, a table giving (usu. with other information) the average value or volume of a species of timber that can be expected from unit area of woodland each successive year.

1888 W. WEISE (*title*) Yield tables for the Scotch pine. **1953** H. L. EDLIN *Forester's Handbk.* xiv. 222 Yield tables..show the likely rate of growth and timber yield of tree crops of a certain kind of tree, grown in a certain country. **1980** *Forestry* LIII. 23 These regressions were solved for the appropriate values of volume or volume increment from published yield tables for this species.

yield, *v.* Add: **III. 20.** *spec.* To deform inelastically; to undergo a large increase in strain without a corresponding increase in stress.

1900 *Phil. Mag.* L. 77 The assumption..that the material yields when one of the principal stresses reaches a certain amount. **1927** F. V. WARNOCK *Strength of Materials* iii. 46 At the point *C* the material has yielded a large amount, and the corresponding stress is known as the 'Yield Stress'. **1968** A. H. COTTRELL *Introd. Metallurgy* xxi. 395 Suppose that the central grain..has in fact so yielded (e.g. because of the stress-concentrating effect of a foreign inclusion in it), but its neighbours are still elastic.

IV. 22. yield gap, the excess rate of return of long-dated or undated Government stocks over that of ordinary shares; **yield-point,** substitute for def.: (the stress corresponding to) the point on a stress–strain diagram at which the strain begins to increase substantially without a corresponding increase in stress: in some metals differentiated as *upper yield point*, a point at which the stress ceases to increase as the strain increases, prior to a fall to the *lower yield point*, from which the strain increases while the stress remains almost constant at the lower value; also, esp. in *Geol.*, the elastic limit or the yield strength; **yield sign** *U.S.* = *GIVE-WAY SIGN; **yield strength,** in materials that do not exhibit a well-defined yield point, the stress at which (in addition to the elastic deformation) a definite amount of plastic deformation is produced (usu. taken as 0·2 per cent of the unstressed length); **yield stress,** the value of stress at a yield point or at the yield strength.

1959 *Economist* 25 Apr. 353/1 Investors today keep a careful eye on the 'yield gap'—the margin between dividend yields on ordinary shares and long term rates of interest set by the yield on irredeemable Consols. **1981** *Observer* 4 Oct. 19/2 It would also draw attention to the widening yield gap between gilts and shares. [**1870** G. BERKELEY in *Exper. Mech. & Other Properties Steel* 4 Within the 'yielding point' of Steel the amount of lengthening from tension, or shortening from compression, produced by equal forces per unit of area is nearly the same.] **1886** K. PEARSON in I. Todhunter *Hist. Theory Elasticity & Strength of Materials* I. 887 When a bar is subjected to increasing traction, a certain stretch is reached after which there is a sudden and rapid increase of stretch... The point at which this change takes place is very marked, and various names have been suggested for it, as the limit of fatigue, the limit of stability, and the break-down point. The latter name brings out the character of the phenomenon, but at the same time suggests a point related to absolute strength or cohesion; I have therefore spoken of this point in the present work as the yield-point. **1919** FULLER & JOHNSTON *Appl. Mech.* II. x. 378 If the material is very ductile a yield point in torsion will appear at a torque somewhat higher than the elastic limit, similar to the yield point in tension. **1967** J. G. RAMSAY *Folding & Fracturing of Rocks* vi. 258 The specimen has..been permanently strained because the elastic limit has been exceeded. The point where this limit is first exceeded is known as the yield point. **1968** A. H. COTTRELL *Introd. Metallurgy* xxi. 390 In some materials..general yielding can begin in a very striking manner with a yield drop in which the applied stress falls, during yielding, from an upper yield point to a lower yield point. **1971** B. SCHARF *Engin. & its Lang.* iv. 23 Many metals such as aluminium, copper and brass have high ductility but no definite yield point (yield stress). **1981** *Pop. Hot Rodding* Feb. 66/1 To delve into this whole subject more deeply, we discussed it with SPS engineer Jack Schmidt, who spoke to us of tensile strength, yield points, and clamping loads. **1951** C. E. RIGGS in *Amer. City* June 133/1 On one street of each open intersection the sign reading *slow yield right of way* is erected... The new 'yield' signs are..of distinctive shape. **1977** J. CHEEVER *Falconer* 48 Putting up traffic signs, speeding signs, yield signs, stop signs. **1935** *Proc. Amer. Soc. Testing Materials* XXXVIII. 1315 *Yield strength*, the stress at which a material exhibits a specified limiting permanent set. **1967** *Times Rev. Industry* Feb. 45/2 Some British orders went overseas because of the inability..to cope with the more difficult combinations of pipe diameter, wall thickness and yield strength. **1982** *Materials Sci. & Engin.* LVI. 10/1 The yield strength of tempered lath martensitic 0·4% C steels is generally independent of packet size. **1913** *Proc. R. Soc.* A. LXXXVIII. 465 The observed stress at yield might..be below the true yield stress. **1954** C. W. MACGREGOR in W. R. Osgood *Residual Stresses in Metals* 110 Local yielding occurred with an applied uniform tensile stress considerably less than the yield stress. **1971** [see *yield-point* above]. **1973** C. R. BARRETT et al. *Princ. Engin. Materials* vi. 208 The applied tensile stress required to induce plastic behavior is known as the elastic limit or yield stress. **1973** J. G. TWEEDDALE *Materials Technol.* I. iv. 81 The yield stress is slightly above the elastic limit since it clearly represents the incidence of gross plastic strain.

yielding, *vbl. sb.* Add: **4.** (Later example.)

1922 W. SCHLICH *Man. Forestry* (ed. 4) I. 97 Timber fit for sawing would begin to be cut about 10 to 15 years later, and by the eightieth year the forests should be in full yielding.

6. (Further examples. Cf. *YIELD *v.* 20.)

1899 J. A. EWING *Strength of Materials* iii. 31 There is.. a well-marked yield point..at which extension goes on for a time through a considerable distance without increase of load. After this the extension becomes less rapid until the final yielding occurs just before rupture. **1961** LUBAHN & FELGAR *Plasticity & Creep in Metals* v. 104 When a piece of metal is loaded in such a way that the elastic stress is non-uniform,..yielding begins at the most highly stressed point. **1973** C. R. BARRETT et al. *Princ. Engin. Materials* viii. 257 The yielding usually starts at a small notch or irregularity in the sample and subsequently propagates throughout the sample.

yielding, *ppl. a.* **2.** (Later example.)

1849 C. LANMAN *Lett. Alleghany Mts.* xx. 159 The yielding wells are somewhat over two hundred feet deep.

yieldless, *a.* Delete † *Obs.* and add later example of sense 'not productive'.

1974 R. ADAMS *Shardik* xxxiv. 285 There was..something sinister about this place, unhusbanded and yieldless in the midst of the abundant land all about.

yieldy, *a.* **a.** Delete *Obs.* and add later U.S. local example.

1933 *Amer. Speech* VIII. I. 53/2 That 'ar west bottom never was much yieldy, nohow.

‖ **Yigdal** (yi·gdăl). *Judaism.* Also 9 **Yigdol.** [Heb., = 'may he be magnified', the opening word of the hymn.] A Hebrew hymn, thought to have been composed by Daniel ben Judah (fl. *c* 1300), embodying the thirteen articles of the Jewish faith, and recited at morning prayer and on Sabbath and festival eves.

1845 *Jewish Chron.* 19 Sept. 244/1 The children sang in a beautiful manner the hymn Yigdol (Sabbath Hymn). **1892** I. ZANGWILL *Childr. Ghetto* I. xii. 269 You confound the air of the Passover *Yigdal* with the New Year ditto. **1907** J. JULIAN *Dict. Hymnol.* (ed. 2) II. 1149/2 The hymn [sc. *The God of Abraham Praise*] is a free rendering, with, as Olivers puts it, as decided 'a Christian character' as he could give to it, of the Hebrew *Yigdal* or Doxology, which rehearses in metrical form the thirteen articles of the Hebrew Creed.

Yi Hsing (ī ʃiŋ). Also **I-hsing, Yi-hsing.** [f. the name *Yi Xing* of a town in Jiangsu prov., China.] In full *Yi Hsing yao, Yi Hsing ware.* A type of unglazed stoneware (esp. for tea-pots) first produced at Yi Xing in the Song dynasty and reaching its height in the later part of the Ming dynasty.

1904 E. Dillon *Porcelain* x. 165 The Yi-hsing yao, made at a place of that name..includes the red unglazed ware. **1910** *Encycl. Brit.* V. 744/2 The manufacture of red teapots, mugs, bowls, cups, &c., in imitation of the Yi-Hsing-Yao was widespread during the late 17th and early 18th centuries under the name of red porcelain. **1915** R. L. Hobson *Chinese Pott. & Porc.* xv. 178 The Yi-hsing wares in the celebrated Chinese ceramic collection formed by Augustus the Strong at Dresden supplied designs for the fine red stoneware made in the first years of the eighteenth century by Böttger. **1945** (see *Boccaro). **1970** *Ashmolean Mus.: Rep. Visitors 1969* 47 Tea-pot, I-hsing brown stoneware, Chinese, 18th century. **1971** L. A. Boger *Dict. World Pott. & Porc.* 378/2 Yi Hsing Yao..an unglazed stoneware produced at Yi-hsing-hsien in Kiang-su province... Its greatest productive period was during the latter part of the Ming dynasty and during the Ch'ing period.

yike (yəik), *sb.*[2] *Austral. slang.* [Origin unknown.] An argument, a dispute; a fight, a brawl. Occas. as *v. intr.*

1940 *Mod. Standard Eng. Dict.* (rev. ed.) 697/2 *Yike*, v. to fight. **1945** R. Rene *Mo's Memoirs* 186 There's that tram connie having a yike with a drunk. **1951** D. Stivens *Jimmy Brockett* 86 It was a pretty good yike while it lasted. **1952** T. A. G. Hungerford *Ridge & River* 213 Don't let's yike about it. **1964** G. Johnston *My Brother Jack* 244 Sorry your party ended up in a yike. **1976** *Sunday Sun* (Brisbane) 11 Apr. 6/2 ALP circles have scoffed at suggestions of a political 'yike' between State Opposition Leader Tom Burns and TLC chief Egerton. **1984** *Business Rev. Weekly* (Australia) 7–13 Jan. 18/1 We have had a couple of small yikes, mainly on things like contract prices.

yikes (yəiks), *int. colloq.* [Origin unknown, but cf. Yoicks *int.*] An exclamation of astonishment.

1971 *TV Comic* 5 June 8 Yikes! He's blown out the candles all right..blown them out of the cake! **1973** G. Sims *Hunters Point* xiii. 115 Holding her nose..and exclaiming: 'Yikes! It seems that a cat has been shut up there.' **1978** *Detroit Free Press* 5 Mar. B 5/1 Yikes! Even Paul Newman loses the woman in this new breed of movies.

yikker (yi·kəɹ), *v.* Also **yicker.** [Echoic, f. *yik* + -er[5].] *intr.* Of a bird or other animal: to make repeated short, sharp cries.

1951 *Chambers's Jrnl.* Sept. 528/2 As we pushed through the bilberry bushes, rowan, and stunted Scots fir, a lemming yikkered angrily at the disturbance. **1959** W. K. Richmond *Brit. Birds of Prey* ix. 113 Sometimes he yikkers to himself as he goes,..a low, emphatic chatter. **1960** 'L. Lamplugh' *Sixpenny Runner* xiii. 137 Good track dogs wait..yickering eagerly and ready to fly out. **1964** T. H. White *Goshawk* III. 154 A pair of young badgers..greedily fought for warm milk and sugar out of a champagne bottle, and nipped my ankles yikkering when they were not nipping the rubber teat.

‖**yimkin** (yi·mkin), *adv. slang.* Also **yimpkin.** [a. Iraqi Arabic *yimkin.*] Perhaps (see also quot. 1966).

1925 Fraser & Gibbons *Soldier & Sailor Words* 311 *Yimkin*, perhaps. An Arabic word used colloquially among troops on the Eastern Fronts. **1966** 'L. Lane' *ABZ of Scouse* 120 *Yimkin*, nonsense; I don't believe it. **1967** *Sunday Times* (Colour Suppl.) 10 Sept. 46/4 Yimpkin, perhaps. Expressive of extreme scepticism. 'When Tunis falls we're all going home, yimpkin!' (Ar.)

‖**yin** (yin). Also **Yin, Yn.** [Chinese *yīn* shade, feminine; the moon.] **a.** In Chinese philosophy, the feminine or negative principle (characterized by dark, wetness, cold, passivity, disintegration, etc.) of the two opposing cosmic forces into which creative energy divides and whose fusion in physical matter brings the phenomenal world into being. Also *attrib.* or as *adj.*, and *transf.* Cf. *Yang.

1671, etc. [see *Yang]. **1845**, etc. [see *T'ai Chi 1]. **1850** [see *Qi]. **1911** *Encycl. Brit.* XXIII. 68/1 The altar to the Earth is dark and square, on the north side of the city, the region of *yin*, the principle of cold and gloom. **1931** A. U. Dilley *Oriental Rugs & Carpets* ix. 210 Other primitive motives are..male and female forms called Yin and Yang. **1963** 'R. Erskine' *Passion Flowers in Italy* xi. 144 The things that woman was doing to us.. More truly Yin than you could believe. **1976** H. Ferguson *Confessions of Long Distance Acid Head* 17 Lucy was so yin, receptive and feminine, that the passions, slumbering in my bosom, were consciously aroused.

b. *Comb.*, as **yin-yang,** the combination or fusion of the two cosmic forces; freq. *attrib.*, esp. as *yin-yang symbol*, a circle divided by an S-shaped line into a dark and a light segment, representing respectively *yin* and *yang*, each containing a 'seed' of the other.

1850 *Chinese Repository* XIX. 375 The Great Extreme ..is not exterior to or separate from the Yin-yáng. **1934** A. D. Waley *Way & its Power* App. II. 112 The aim of the *yin-yang* philosophers was not the triumph of Light, but the attainment in human life of perfect balance between the two principles. **1958** W. Willetts *Chinese Art* I. iv. 273 The observed behaviour of this stellar couple accorded perfectly with the *yin yang* theory. **1972** Manaka & Urquhart *Layman's Guide Acupuncture* (1977) I. 32 Their relativity and inseparability are symbolized by the inclusion, in the Chinese yin-yang symbol, of a small portion of each within the other. **1976** C. Soo *Chinese Art of T'ai Chi Ch'uan* iii. 19 When these [outlines] are put together, 'the Yin-Yang symbol is obtained. **1977** Miller & Swift *Words & Women* iv. 69 The ancient belief that contrasting male and female forces are at work in everything—the yin-yang of dark and light..too easily becomes an adversary concept.

yin, ying, varr. *Yen[2].

‖**ying ch'ing** (yiŋ tʃiŋ). Also **Ying Ch'ing, Ying ch'ing,** etc. [Chinese, lit. 'shadowy blue'.] A type of glazed porcelain produced in Jiangxi and other provinces, chiefly during the Song dynasty. Freq. *attrib.*

1922 A. L. Hetherington *Early Ceramic Wares China* xix. 139 The ware..with a very translucent, white sugary body and a bluish-white glaze tending to a more pronounced blue..is known as *ying ch'ing yao* .: *ying ching*.. may be translated 'shadowy blue'. **1934** *Burlington Mag.* May 214/1 The *ying ch'ing* species of white porcelain. **1936** *Ibid.* Jan. 10/1 With pale bluish glaze currently known as Ying Ch'ing (misty blue). **1943** [see *Sung *sb.* b]. **1949** [see *Ju]. **1954** H. Garner *Oriental Blue & White* ii. 9 *Ying ch'ing* (shadow blue) is a thin translucent white porcelain covered with a clear glaze of bluish tint. The term is a modern one, invented by Chinese dealers, which has unfortunately become established in the West. **1977** O. Impey *Chinoiserie* II. vii. 89/2 The famous 'Fonthill vase', a Yüan dynasty *ying ch'ing* bottle fitted with a gothic silver-gilt and enamel mount.

Yinglish (yi·ngliʃ), *sb.* (*a.*) orig. *U.S.* [f. Yi(ddish *sb.* (*a.*) + E)nglish *sb.*] A jocular name for a blend of English and Yiddish spoken in the United States; a form of English containing many Yiddishisms. Also *attrib.* or as *adj.*

1951 W. & S. Schack in *Commentary* Dec. 586/2 A Jewish American theater in which..the material is of mixed nature, and the language neither the King's English nor the *rebbetzin's* Yiddish but a crossbreed that we might call 'Yinglish'. **1953** H. J. Gans in *Amer. Q.* V. 213 (*title*) The 'Yinglish' music of Mickey Katz. *Ibid.* 215 Katz's life is as Yinglish as the concept of a Bar Mitzvah ranch. **1967** *N.Y. Times* 6 Apr. 44 This show.. is a mixture of Yinglish (English with Yiddish) and Yidlish (Yiddish with English). **1968** [see *O.K. *adj.* a]. **1970** L. M. Feinsilver *Taste of Yiddish* iii. 372 *Yinglish.* This coined term describes English that contains Yiddish idiom, pronunciation and/or intonation. **1974** *Observer* 31 Mar. 39/4 The text, written in Yinglish and American, abounds in euphemisms. **1983** *Listener* 7 July 20/3 One of the joys of the *Oxford American Dictionary* is searching out the progress of Yinglish.

yip (yip), *sb.* orig. *U.S.* [Echoic.] A short high-pitched cry, as from a dog; a shout, an exclamation; a complaint, an expostulation.

1911 H. Quick *Yellowstone Nights* xii. 303 They chase 'em, with wild whoops an' yips over the undulatin' reservation. **1928** Wodehouse *Money for Nothing* ix. 208 If I'd been a life-insurance company I'd have paid up on him without a yip. **1945** B. MacDonald *Egg & I* xii. 179 The dog began to bark and, guided by his excited yips, I was able to follow the progress of the hunt around the ranch. **1946** E. Hodgins *Mr. Blandings* iii. 48 This is the first faint yip of pain he's drawn. **1962** J. Steinbeck *Travels with Charley* 221 He [*sc.* a dog] ran..and laughed and gave little yips of pure joy. **1971** *Shankar's Weekly* (Delhi) 4 Apr. 5/1 In the old days, there would have been a spate of..discussions... But today? Not a yip.

yip, *v.* Restrict. *Obs.* or *dial.* to sense in Dict. and add: **2.** *intr.* To utter a sharp cry or yelp (with a dog or human being as subj.); to shout; to complain. orig. *U.S.*

1907 K. D. Wiggin *New Chron. Rebecca* vii. 177 He would walk right up close and cuff 'em if they dared to yip. **1922** S. Lewis *Babbitt* vii. 99 There's a swell bunch of Lizzie boys and lemon-suckers..that love to fire off their filthy mouths and yip that Mike Monday is vulgar and full of mush. **1927** P. Marks *Lord of Himself* 15, I love to hear you yip at him. **1945** B. MacDonald *Egg & I* ii. 176 Sport and the puppy..yapping and yipping at each other. **1963** *New Statesman* 11 Jan. 38/3 Yet how does the victim react? He yips with delight. **1978** S. Radley *Death & Maiden* i. 6 [The] Jack Russell terrier had yipped itself to the edge of hysteria.

3. *trans.* To cry or exclaim (with the words spoken as direct obj.). *U.S.*

1927 *Sat. Even. Post* 24 Dec. 84/2 'Hey!' Jim yipped,.. 'Get away from there!' **1974** Wodehouse *Aunts aren't Gentlemen* x. 81 'Has he brought it yet?' she yipped.

Hence **yi·pping** *vbl. sb.* and *ppl. a.*; also **yip-yipping.**

1910 *N.Y. Even. Post* 14 Oct. 4 The applause was really deafening..; not yip-yipping..but steady volume of vocal uproar. **1951** J. Masters *Nightrunners of Bengal* xv. 195 Women's voices rang clear..on the verandah, and a child's excited yipping. **1956** H. Gold *Man who was not with It* (1965) xi. 85 The inner yipping of a man who had assaulted the Pittsburgh of his babyhood may have given them obscure desires to kick me. **1960** Cross *Backward Sex* ii. 60, I could not help making slight yipping noise as I tried to clear my throat. **197**[illegible] *New Yorker* 26 Sept. 42/1, I have spoken to those peop[le] about that yipping dog. **1980** A. Desai *Clear Light [of] Day* i. 3 He [*sc.* a dog] has such a beautiful voice, it's pleasure to hear him. Not like the yipping and yapping [of] other people's little lap dogs.

yip (yip), colloq. pronunc. of Yes. Cf. Yep.

1934 'R. Crompton' *William—the Gangster* iii. 49 '[illegible] that a fair down there?' 'Yip,' answered Willian[m] **1954** —— *William & Moon Rocket* i. 13 'That's fixed it said the youth. 'Yip,' said the man.

yippee (yipī, stress variable), *sb.* and *in[t.]* orig. *U.S.* Also **yip-ee.** [Perh. connecte[d] with Hip *int.* (*sb.*[4]).] An exclamation o[f] delight or excitement.

1920 S. Lewis *Main St.* 86 She galloped down a block and as she jumped from a curb across a welter of slush she gave a student 'Yippee!' **1939** R. Chandler *Bi[g] Sleep* xii. 80, I was being brought into camp. I was goin[g] to yell 'Yippee!' **1947** N. Marsh *Final Curtain* xvi. 24[illegible] She said 'Yip-ee' like a cow-girl. **1951** J. Fleming *Ma[n] who looked Back* xvi. 212 He permitted himself a lou[d] 'Yippee!' **1961** *Guardian* 19 Apr. 5/1 Yippee. I've bee[n] blooded. It's lovely. **1976** Botham & Donnelly *Valentino* vii. 51 Rodolpho let rip a great cowboy yippee. **198**[illegible] A. Cornelisen *Strangers & Pilgrims* viii. 162 It's a boy *A boy!* Yippee!

Hence as *v. intr.*, to make this exclamation **yippee·ing** *vbl. sb.*

1938 M. K. Rawlings *Yearling* xxvi. 351 They caperec together and shouted and yippeed until their throats were hoarse. **1963** A. Lubbock *Austral. Roundabout* 18[illegible] There was bush ballads, and a whistling and yippee-ing! **1977** 'E. Crispin' *Glimpses of Moon* v. 69 Clarence Tully hilloed. His sons yippeed.

yippie, Yippie (yi·pi). orig. *U.S.* Also **yippy.** [f. the initials of *Y*outh *I*nternational *P*arty + -ie, influenced by *hippie, hippy *sb.* and *a.*] A member of a group of politically active hippies, orig. in the United States.

1968 *Time* 5 Apr. 55/1 The Yippies—1968's version of the hippies... The term Yippie comes from Youth International Party. **1968** *Listener* 3 Oct. 428/2 One student outlines his own theories to me. 'This whole scene began with Dylan, the Beatles, and of course pot.' Another complains that the militants need a sense of humour and hopes the Yippies move in with their 'politics of ecstasy'. **1968** *Time* 11 Oct. 28 Pierson had infiltrated a yippie group known as the Headhunters, and soon rose to the dizzying position of personal bodyguard to the yippie leader. **1971** *Bulletin* (Sydney) 19 June 15/3 The news that Sydney's Yippies ('Yippie is a fun Revolution') were preparing to play an energetic part in the strenuously humorless Vietnam Moratorium came as a surprise. **1976** *Times* 18 Aug. 4/7 If we're going to save democracy, we've got to put an end to all this yippy filth, these abortions, [etc.]. **1981** J. Dunning *Deadline* (1982) xiv. 138 Bill Neal was one of those yippie types... One of those bearded nonconformists.

yips (yips), *sb. pl. colloq.* [Origin obscure.] In *Golf*, a state of nervousness which causes a player to miss an easy putt in a competition. Usu. with the def. article.

1963 *Times* 10 June 4/2 His left-below-right putting stroke designed to prevent the 'yips', is most effective once it begins to flow. **1972** *Tel.* (Brisbane) 1 Jan. 5/7 Nevertheless, Jones got a dose of what golfers call 'the yips'. **1984** *Times* 21 Sept. 9/4 Golfers suffer from the 'yips', which means that their muscles seize up and freeze when they are faced with a short putt and they cannot play the stroke.

Yishuv (yiʃū·v, yi·ʃuv). Also **Yishub.** [ad. Heb. *yiššūḇ* settlement.] The Jewish community or settlement in Palestine during the nineteenth century and until the formation of the State of Israel in 1948.

1918 *Round Table* VIII. 321 The Jewish *Yishub*, or settlement in Palestine. **1922** *Encycl. Brit.* XXXII. 1130/1 This new Palestinian *Yishub* (settlement), strengthened in the early years of the present century by a number of young men and women who went to Palestine with the ideal of working as labourers on its soil, became the basis of the political success which Zionism achieved during the World War. **1940** *Contemp. Jewish Rec.* III. 599 The Yishub has made available over £P200,000 for emergency purposes. **1940** A. Ulitzur *Two Decades of Keren Hayesod* ii. 40 From the beginning of the Third *Aliyah* until the end of September, 1940..the Yishuv grew by about 432,000 persons. **1949** Koestler *Promise & Fulfilment* I. xii. 130 Let the Yishuv, the Diaspora and the whole world know what Bevin, Attlee and their henchmen are preparing for us. **1962** *Observer* 20 May 25/5 The British Zionists with whom I worked—infected, no doubt, by the free life of the Yishuv in Palestine—did not give me an inkling of what goes on in the mind of an orthodox Jew. **1970** I. Sieff *Memoirs* vi. 107 These Jews of the old *Yishuv* (meaning settlement) were usually advanced in years before they left their country of origin. **1980** *Times Lit. Suppl.* 14 Nov. 1288/5 The extent and scale of the massacres tended to be under-estimated for a while by Jews in the West.., by the *Yishuv* in Palestine, and even by Jews in Europe themselves.

yit, obs. form of Yet. Add: Still current in *dial.* use. (Examples.)

c **1460** [see Yet *adv.* 1]. **1857** H. S. Riddell *Book of Psalms in Lowland Scotch* lxviii. 61 Thouch ye hae læyne mang the pats, yit sall ye be as the wings o' ane dow. 380 [see *SHOOT *v.* 23 g]. **1908** KIPLING *Lett. of Travel* 920) 146 There's them that can't see *yit.* **1939** JOYCE *'innegans Wake* 138 An yit he wanna git all his flesch uemaid. **1977** *Transatlantic Rev.* LX. 147 'Naw', he says. east, no yit.'

'it(t), varr. YID in Dict. and Suppl. **yiz,** ar. YEZ in Dict. and Suppl.

'izkor (yi·zkǫɹ). Also **Yiskor, Yizcor.** [Heb., t. 'may he [*sc.* God] remember'.] A memorial ervice, formally known as *Hazkarat Nesha-iot,* held by Jews on certain holy days for eceased relatives, martyrs, etc.

1934 *Encycl. Jewish Knowl.* 644/1 *Yizkor,* popular ame for Memorial Service, the full title being Haz-arath Neshoma. **1946** *Commentary* Aug. 173/1 They may still be on time to say *Yizcor.* **1956** S. BELLOW *Seize Day* . 86 He asked him whether he had reserved his seat in he synagogue for Yom Kippur... 'Well, you better urry up if you expect to say Yiskor for your parents.' 966 H. KEMELMAN *Saturday Rabbi went Hungry* viii. 46 he Memorial Service for the Dead..the Yizkor service. 976 C. BERMANT *Coming Home* II. v. 189 Four times a ear special remembrance prayers, known as *yizkor,* are ead in synagogue... The word means memorial.

-yl. Add: Also with pronunc. (əil). For 'F. *yle* (also *-ule*)' read 'G. *-yl*'; for '(*Ann. de Chimie,* 1832, LI. 286)' read '(*Ann. der Pharm.* (1832) III. 262)'; and for *benzoyle* ead *benzoyl.* Now in more formal use in *Organic Chem.* (see quots.).

1952 *Jrnl. Chem. Soc.* 5075 Rule 58.5. Radicals derived rom amino-acids which have trivial names in *ine* by emoval of OH from all —CH(NH_2)·CO_2H and related groups will be named by replacing the ending *ine* with *yl.* **1965** *Recommended Names for Chemicals used in Industry (B.S.I.)* 11 Univalent radicals derived from cycloalkanes with no side chain are named by replacing the ending -ane' of the hydrocarbon name by '-yl'. **1966** [see *FURYL]. **1971** *Nomencl. Org. Chem.* (I.U.P.A.C.) (ed. 3) A. 5 Univalent radicals derived from saturated unbranched acyclic hydrocarbons by removal of hydrogen from a terminal carbon atom are named by replacing the ending '-ane' of the name of the hydrocarbon by '-yl'. *Ibid.* B. 70 Univalent heterocyclic radicals whose names end in '-yl'. *Ibid.* C. 128 Radicals derived from unsubstituted ring assemblies are named by adding '-yl',..*etc.,* to the name of the assembly.

ylem (ī·lem). *Astr.* [f. med.L. *hўlem,* acc. of *hўlē* HYLE.] In the big-bang theory, the primordial matter of the universe, orig. conceived as composed of neutrons at high temperature and density.

[**1390**: see HYLE.]. **1948** R. A. ALPHER in *Physical Rev.* LXXIV. 1581/1 Very shortly after the beginning of the universal expansion, the ylem was a gas of neutrons only. [*Note*] According to Webster's New International Dictionary..the word 'ylem' is an obsolete noun meaning 'The primordial substance from which the elements were formed.' It seems highly desirable that a word of so appropriate a meaning be resurrected. **1954** *Sci. Amer.* Mar. 61/2 As the Universe went on expanding and the temperature of ylem dropped, protons and neutrons began to stick together, forming deuterons..and heavier elements. **1959** J. BLISH *Clash of Cymbals* vii. 171 The ylem was the primordial flux of neutrons out of which all else emerged. **1974** FRAUENFELDER & HENLEY *Subatomic Physics* xviii. 475 It is interpreted as the radiation that is left over from the primordial fireball and thus provides some information about the conditions in the ylem.

ylid (i·lid). *Chem.* Also **ylide** (-əid). [a. G. *ylid* (Wittig & Felletschin 1944, in *Ann. d. Chem.* DLV. 133): see -YL, -ID[4].] Any neutral compound containing a negatively charged carbon atom directly bonded to a positively charged atom of another element (commonly sulphur, phosphorus, or nitrogen). Hence **yli·dic** *a.*

1951 *Chem. Abstr.* XLV. 6166 The reaction of PhLi upon suitable quaternary ammonium salts results in compds. with a semipolar bond between N and adjacent C. These compds. are called ylides. **1970** *Nature* 25 July 335/2 Silylated ylides of phosphorus, arsenic and sulphur, in which the silyl group is both a stabilizing and an efficient leaving group, transferring the ylidic moiety in very mild conditions. **1972** S. J. WEININGER *Contemporary Org. Chem.* xviii. 491 Ylids are extremely useful reactive intermediates for syntheses and are the subject of a good deal of research effort at the present time. **1979** *Nature* 15 Nov. 231/3 The zwitterionic ylides were obtained from the reaction of phenyl-lithium with quaternary ammonium halides. **1982** *Heterocycles* XIX. 1849 Cycloimmonium ylides..possessing two electron-withdrawing groups covalently bonded to the ylidic carbon..can be isolated.

-ylidene (-i·l-, -əi·lidīn), *suffix. Chem.* [f. as *-IDENE.] Used in place of *-IDINE when the name of the parent compound does not end in *-yl.*

1971 *Nomencl. Org. Chem.* (I.U.P.A.C.) (ed. 3) A. 17 Names of bivalent radicals derived from saturated or unsaturated monocyclic hydrocarbons by removal of two atoms of hydrogen from the same carbon atom of the ring are obtained by replacing the endings '-ane', '-ene', '-yne', by '-ylidene', '-enylidene' and '-ynylidene', respectively.

Yn: see *YIN.

-yne (-əin), orig. var. -INE[5], now used in its own right to denote a triple bond between carbon atoms, as in *BUTYNE, *PROPYNE.

1931 *Jrnl. Chem. Soc.* 1610 Definitive Report of the Committee [of the International Union of Chemistry] for the Reform of Nomenclature in Organic Chemistry... The name of hydrocarbons containing the triple linkage will end in *yne, diyne,* etc.

yo, obs. form of YOU: In mod. use, repr. dial. pronunc. of *you, your,* esp. in Black English.

1848 MRS. GASKELL *Mary Barton* I. vi. 90 Yo stop here, and I'll be back in half-an-hour. **1897** [see *SHOOT *v.* 2 d]. **1931** W. FAULKNER *Sanctuary* xxiv. 271 Minnie tapped at the door. 'Here yo dinner.' **1937** C. HIMES *Black on Black* (1973) 139 Niggah, ef'n yo is talkin' tuh me, Ah ain' liss'nin'. **1969** R. FAIR in A. Chapman *New Black Voices* (1972) 114 Oh, shut yo mouf up man. **1973** *Black World* June 61 Saturday nite take yo shoes off at the door.

yo (yōᵘ), also **yoe,** repr. dial. (esp. U.S.) pronunc. of EWE *sb.*[1] Cf. YOW(E in Dict. and Suppl.

1891 *Dialect Notes* I. 71 *Yo,* ewe. **1899** B. W. GREEN *Word-bk. Virginia Folk-Speech* 434 *Yoe, n.*: yow, yeo; eow; yowe; a female sheep. 'Breeding yoes & a Ramm.' **1922** BLUNDEN *Shepherd* 12 While each one came from the poor frightened yoes. **1946** *Amer. Speech* XXI. 98 S. Illinois] *Yo,* ewe.

yob (yǫb). *slang.* [Backslang for BOY *sb.*[1]] Orig., a boy, a youth; in mod. use, a lout, a hooligan; (see also quot. 1918).

1859 HOTTEN *Dict. Slang* 131 *Yob,* a boy. **1886–96** in Farmer & Henley *Slang* (1903) VII. 375/1 And you bet that each gal, not to mention each yob, Didn't care how much ooftish it cost 'em per nob. **1908** A. N. LYONS *Arthur's* II. i. 108 It'd take more'n a yob in a squash 'at to call *me* a blighted sooper. **1918** FARROW *Dict. Milit. Terms* 673 *Yob,* a slang term used by soldiers meaning an officer or one who is easily fooled. **1927** J. C. GOODWIN *Crook Pie* iii. 71 A yob shouted: 'Now for yer belts, boys!' and my friend was thrashed. **1930** P. MACDONALD *Link* 130 Well, sir, I sez to meself, what does A do? Then I thinks, keep the mob off. So I jest backs into the door of the public, and doesn't let any of the yobs get out. **1957** J. OSBORNE *Look Back in Anger* I. 15 'Let's go to the pictures.'.. 'And have my enjoyment ruined by the Sunday night yobs in the front row?' **1962** J. WAIN *Strike Father Dead* VII. 303 If you're expecting a description of what those yobs did to us, please forget it. **1977** *Western Morning News* 30 Aug. 1/3 One police officer sheltering from a bombardment of missiles behind a plastic shield said: 'It's just a bunch of yobs.' **1984** *Times* 16 Feb. 3/1, I would not want anybody looking at me to think this man is a thick, stupid, illiterate yob.

Hence **yo·bbery,** hooliganism; **yo·bbish** *a.* characteristic of a yob; **yo·bby** *a.,* loutish.

1955 E. BLISHEN *Roaring Boys* iv. 210 Though I don't hold with Grimes' yobby way of dressing, I think the Edwardian style's a good thing in itself. **1972** *Guardian* 16 Feb. 12/1 The 16-year-old boy..was.. adopting a yobbish air which drove his mother into nerve-twanging tantrums. **1974** *Times Lit. Suppl.* 1 Mar. 215/2 A comparative study of urban adolescent vandalism and upper-class yobbery. **1980** *Observer* 9 Nov. 12/4 It is one thing to deplore the collective yobbery of Mr. Benn's supporters. **1982** E. NORTH *Ancient Enemies* ii. 19 The boys, although none of them as individuals are that dim or yobby, jeered. **1984** *Listener* 27 Sept. 22/1 A club with one of the worst records for drunken yobbery, Tottenham Hotspur,..brazenly makes a deal with the makers of Holstein lager. **1984** *Sunday Tel.* 2 Dec. 20/6 The loony Left should not be confused with that other Left which has been described as the Left of the yobbish tendency.

yobbo (yǫ·bo). *slang.* Also **yobo.** Pl. **yobbos,** occas. **yobboes.** [An extended form of prec.] A lout, a hooligan.

1922 *Contemp. Rev.* CXXII. 368 To him the boys are always the 'yobos'. **1938** *Evening News* 7 Mar. 11/5 A few inverted words have found common acceptance; slop (policeman), yob or yobbo (street rough, an inverted form of boy). **1940** R. POSTGATE *Verdict of Twelve* I. v. 74 Hardly any one about except a few yobos who had got nothing to do, and hung around in irritated idleness, spitting manfully in the gutter and telling dirty stories. **1955** E. BLISHEN *Roaring Boys* III. 147 'Yoboes!' said my colleague. 'My God, I wouldn't teach again in a senior school... Their insolence and rowdiness.' **1959** J. BRAINE *Vodi* xii. 165 Some yobbos in 1916 broke Nisbauer's shop window. **1960** *News Chron.* 9 Feb. 6/6 The local Teddies and yobbos swing their dubious weight behind the strike. **1964** in Hamblett & Deverson *Generation X* 56 Ever since that Profumo lark I've come to the conclusion that we working class yobos, as they like to call us, have less to be ashamed of than those establishment geezers. **1972** T. STOPPARD *Jumpers* II. 80 That astronaut yobbo is good for twenty years hard. **1978** [see *street-corner* s.v. *STREET *sb.* 4 b]. **1982** *Age* (Melbourne) 4 Feb. 9/4 We get the odd guarded comment from the yobbo on the street about our dress.

yock (yǫk), *sb.* (and *v.*) *Theatr. slang* (chiefly *U.S.*). Also **yok.** (Cf. Eng. dial. *yocha* to laugh.] A laugh. Also as *v. intr.* (and quasi-*trans.*).

1938 H. M. ALEXANDER *Strip Tease* 83 'Listen to 'em yock out there,' says the comic...'Yock' is a belly laugh. **1949** *N.Y. Times* 4 Sept. 7/6 It makes me furious when I have a corny line and it gets a yock. **1951** *New Yorker* 12 May 32/3 There'd be Don, yockin' it up like crazy,..he's so hysterical with loyalty laughter. **1957** S. J. PERELMAN *Road to Miltown* 73 Brother, I've heard some dillies in my day, but that's the payoff... What a yock this'll give the mob at Sardi's! **1957** WODEHOUSE *Over Seventy* xiii. 134 A few gay observations on the weather and he is ready for the big yoks. **1961** *Daily Mail* 4 Mar. 8 'I'm right in saying that you wouldn't do this to me, madam?' asked the colonel... The producer said, 'You'd have got a helpful yok from the audience there, colonel.' **1965** *New Yorker* 31 July 56/3 A chuckle or even a short, muted yock is acceptable from time to time. **1973** *Publishers Weekly* 26 Feb. 50/1 (Advt.), An hilarious collection of jokes, rhymes, riddles, tongue twisters, teasers and other assorted high-flying nonsense. The riddles and illustrations sprinkled throughout this page give just a brief taste of this yok-filled book. **1975** *New Yorker* 2 June 36/3 'Maybe you were a king in Babylon and I was a Christian slave,' I chaffed him. 'But enough with the yocks.'

yod. Add: Also **yodh. 1.** (Further examples.)

1861 *Grammatography* 10 Yodh. **1958** D. DIRINGER *Story of Aleph Beth* I. iii. 36 Several letters in the Aḥiram sarcophagus (*aleph, waw,..yodh,..*and *resh*) indicate a cursive rather than a monumental development. **1982** *Canad. Jrnl. Linguistics* XXVII. 76 Part II also has several appendices, dealing with Middle High German and Old Yiddish transcription, with the source of double waw and double yodh.

2. *Phonetics.* Also **jod.** The semi-vowel (y).

1934 M. K. POPE *From Lat. to Mod. Fr.* II. i. 55 The voiced fricative sound *j* (*jod*), heard in *bien* bjẽ. **1954** PEI *Dict. Linguistics* 237 *Yodization,* the changing of a pure-vowel (usually *e* or *i*) in hiatus into the semivowel which in English orthography is usually written *y,* and called *yod* after a letter of the Hebrew alphabet. **1971** *Canad. Jrnl. Linguistics* XVII. 19 Discussion is limited to two aspects of palatization in French: velars followed by front vowels, and clusters of single consonant plus yod. **1982** J. C. WELLS *Accents of English* I. ii. 163 The *cure* vowel is frequently preceded by a yod, /j/... GenAm reflects more widespread Yod Dropping than RP and most other British accents. *Ibid.* II. v. 435 Yod Coalescence in stressed syllables is common in Dublin..; *dew* = *due* = *Jew.* **1984** *Word* XXXV. 70 The consequence of this for yod assibilation in Irish English is that it is not found in instances where it might be expected.

yodel, *v.* Add: **yodel(l)ing** *vbl. sb.,* **yodel(l)er** (earlier example of each).

1827 M. WILMOT *Jrnl.* 18 Aug. in *More Lett.* (1935) 288 The wild yodling of two young girls, who suddenly begun [*sic*] to sing their mountain melody. **1880** 'MARK TWAIN' *Tramp Abroad* xxviii. 289 Now the jodeler appeared.. and..we gave him a franc to jodel some more.

yodization (yǫdəizēⁱ·ʃən). *Phonetics.* [f. *YOD 2 + -IZATION.] = *YOTIZATION.

1954 [see *YOD 2]. **1966** [see *PROSODY 2*]. **1982** *Times Lit. Suppl.* 3 Sept. 953/5 Such phonological phenomena as yodization and consonantal dissimilation.

yoe: see *YO, repr. EWE *sb.*[1]

yoga. Delete ‖ and add: Now a widespread cult in many countries outside India. (Further examples.)

1934 A. HUXLEY *Let.* 22 July (1969) 382 Some modification of this yoga technique may provide what's needed.. since it is as..independent of religion..as Freudism—many Indian yogis being in fact atheists. **1937** 'G. ORWELL' *Road to Wigan Pier* xiii. 254 If only..every.. creeping Jesus [could be] sent home..to do his yoga exercises quietly! **1967** *Daily Tel.* 1 Feb. 13/1 All kinds of yoga (*the word means 'union' or 'joining'*) are practised, including yoga of action, wisdom, knowledge, devotion, sounds and higher faculties, but far the most common in Britain is hatha yoga, the philosophy of physical well-being. **1977** 'M. YORKE' *Cost of Silence* iv. 31 She had managed..to enrol..in a weekly yoga class. **1977** J. A. KOTARBA in Douglas & Johnson *Existential Sociol.* ix. 266 Osteopaths, naturopaths, yoga instructors, acupuncturists, and anyone else who offers hope. **1979** R. JAFFE *Class Reunion* (1980) III. i. 308 She took all sorts of lessons: gourmet cooking,. macramé, origami, yoga. **1982** 'A. J. QUINNELL' *Snap Shot* i. 27 She had immersed herself in the expatriate social routine... Ikebana classes on Tuesdays and Yoga on Thursdays. **1984** *Times* 17 Mar. 15/3 Yoga postures..are demonstrated by a small group.

Yogacara (yōᵘgătʃā·ră). [ad. Skr. *yogācāra* (also used), f. *yoga* YOGA + *ā-cāra* conduct, practice.] **a.** A school of Mahayana Buddhism which teaches that only consciousness is real.

1889 M. MONIER-WILLIAMS *Buddhism* x. 225 Our present concern is..with the growth and development of mystical Buddhism in India.., through its connexion with the system of philosophy called Yoga and Yogācāra. **1932** M. HIRIYANNA *Outl. Indian Philos.* ix. 219 Objects according to the Yogācāra are not..encountered by the mind, but are created by it. **1951** E. CONZE *Buddhism* vii. 165 The tradition of Yogacara logic is still active in Tibet. *Ibid.,* Together with Buddhism, the Yogacara school disappeared from India about 1,100 A.D. **1960** J. HEWITT *Teach Yourself Yoga* 11 Buddhist meditation utilizes Yoga, especially the Yogacara school which lays emphasis on the trance. **1978** *Pacific Affairs* LI. 513 The author's equation of Yogacara philosophy with 'mind-only doctrine'..is, on the basis of Tibetan writings, open to doubt.

b. An adherent of the Yogacara school.

1915 R. W. FRAZER *Indian Thought* ix. 181 This sect was known as Yogācāras; the only thing they would admit the reality of was a series of thoughts or consciousnesses... As Yogācāras, teachers of Yoga, they adhered to a Yoga system of philosophy. **1922** S. DASGUPTA *Hist. Indian Philos.* I. x. 411 The Yogācāras or idealistic Buddhists..say that since we can come into touch with knowledge and knowledge alone, what is the use of admitting an external world of objects as the data of sensation determining our knowledge? **1933** E. J. THOMAS *Hist. Buddhist Thought* xvii. 246 It was among the Yogāchāras that Tantrism developed.

Hence **Yogaca·rin** = sense b above.

1951 E. CONZE *Buddhism* vii. 161 It was the function and purpose of the Yogacarins to give due emphasis to the outlook on the world revealed by withdrawal into trance. **1974** *Encycl. Brit. Micropædia* X. 822/3 Yogācārins were not unique among Buddhists in practicing meditation.

yoghurt, var. YOGURT in Dict. and Suppl.

yogi. Add: **2.** = YOGA.

1925 A. HUXLEY *Let.* 25 Feb. (1969) 242 His little book..is a sort of explanation of the ethics of Christianity ..Lose one's life in order to gain it. . It is the same idea as lies at the bottom of the Yogi system. **1943** D. POWELL *Time to be Born* i. 22 He had no pot at all due to his Yogi exercises. **1952** 'R. GORDON' *Doctor in House* iv. 43 There was another medical student there, a man from St. Mary's who kept tropical fish in a tank in his bedroom and practised Yogi. **1960** R. CROFT-COOKE *Thief* i. 9 One day he was in a shop with her when she put her bag down on a chair while she looked at something. I don't know how he got out with it, but then . I'm not a thief. It seemed like Yogi to me, or at least conjuring.

Hence **yo·gified** *a. nonce-wd.*, treated in a yogic manner; **yogi-man** *poet.*, a devotee of yoga.

1938 L. MACNEICE *Mod. Poetry* v. 78 In T. S. Eliot Hyde is the yogi-man. **1938** —— *Earth Compels* 58 It's no go the Yogi-Man, it's no go Blavatsky. *a* **1960** E. M. FORSTER *Maurice* (1971) 235 Carpenter's yogified mysticism.

Yogi Bear (yōᵘ·gi bēᵊɹ). The name of a popular U.S. cartoon character, used *attrib.* of toys, garments, etc., featuring the bear.

1960 *Newsweek* 18 July 84/2 Yogi Bear, who lives with a small bear-buddy, Boo-Boo, in a national preserve called Jellystone Park, spends a good deal of his time trying to cadge food. **1962** *Punch* 19 Dec. p. xviii, Marshall & Snelgrove's Toy Shop features..Yogi bear hobby sticks. **1963** *Sunday Express* 3 Mar. 15/4 Another baby bit a chunk out of a yogi bear hat. **1974** P. DICKINSON *Poison Oracle* 188 The Shaikhah had easily found jeans and a Yogi-Bear tee-shirt to fit her.

yogibo·geybox. *nonce-wd.* [f. YOGI + BOGY, BOGEY + BOX *sb.*²] The paraphernalia of a spiritualist.

1922 JOYCE *Ulysses* 189 Yogibogeybox in Dawson Chambers. *Isis Unveiled.* Their Pali-book we tried to pawn... He thrones an Aztec logos, functioning on astral levels, their oversoul mahamahatma. **1965** *Spectator* 15 Jan. 73/1 Yeats, like AE..stood for the whirlpool, Madame Blavatsky and the yogibogeybox.

yogic (yōᵘ·gik), *a.* Also **Yogic.** [f. YOG(A + -IC.] Of or pertaining to yoga.

1921 STREETER & APPASAMY *Sadhu* v. 136 The object of the Yogic trance is not the heart but the head. **1946** A. HUXLEY *Let.* 26 Oct. (1969) 551 In yogic practices there is a form of intense concentration which induces 'false samadhi', or self-hypnosis. **1960** J. HEWITT *Teach Yourself Yoga* 17 The Yogic internal cleansing method of swallowing a long strip of cloth, retaining it for a while in the stomach to absorb bile, etc. **1960** R. P. JHABVALA *Householder* i. 58 Yogic exercises, you know. He's getting quite good at them. **1967** *Listener* 7 Sept. 298/1 A few serious young people squatting in Yogic postures, spines straight, hands receptively cupped. **1980** *Dædalus* Spring 103 Repressed Hindus rejoice in myths of extreme forms of ascetic yogic mortification.

yogin. (In Dict. s.v. YOGI.) (Further examples.)

1959 *Times Lit. Suppl.* 27 Mar. 181/5 It is not to divide Time and Eternity that the yogin undertakes his arduous task of re-creation, but to restore to them their true relation. **1962** A. HUXLEY *Island* v. 39 The Yogin and the Stoic—two righteous egos who achieve their very considerable results by pretending, systematically, to be somebody else. **1965** P. WYLIE *They both were Naked* I. iii. 131 Sitting opposite me on my divan cross-legged as a yogin etc. **1973** J. BLOFELD *Secret & Sublime* i. 19 To yogins steeped in the arts of rejuvenation, prolonging life and achieving one of several kinds of immortality, it meant both of these. **1979** R. CASSILIS *Arrow of God* IV. vii. 121 A little rent in the seamless garment of self-mastery. On, yogin, heal thyself!

yogini (yōᵘginī·). [a. Skr. *yoginī* (also used), fem. of *yogī*, f. *yoga* YOGA.] **a.** In India, a female demon or sorceress, esp. one of a group attendant on Durga or Siva. **b.** A female yogi.

1883 M. WILLIAMS *Relig. Thought & Life in India* vii. 188 Another class of manifestation is that of the Yoginīs. These are sometimes represented as eight fairies or sorceresses..sometimes as mere forms of that goddess [*sc.* Durgā], sixty or sixty-five in number. **1910** *Encycl. Brit.* XIII. 512/1 The different classes of sorceresses and ogresses, called *Yoginis, Dakinis* and *Sakinis.* **1928** A. K. COOMARASWAMY *Yakṣas* I. 9 The Seven Mothers.., the Sixty-four Joginīs,..and some forms of Devī..must have been Yakṣinīs. **1969** 'R. FARRE' *Beckoning Land* xvi. 196 She wore an unbleached off-white sari and her black hair hung loose denoting that she had freed herself from worldly ties and that she was a yogini (a female yogi). **1972** B. N. SHARMA *Social & Cultural Hist. N. India* iv. 76 There was a *Yoginī Saimpradāya* among the *Sāktas* and many persons received the highest knowledge from the female ascetics. **1979** *Telegraph* (Brisbane) 15 Aug. 7/4 Meditation can cure many illnesses caused by mental and physical tension, according to a yogini (female yogi) visiting Brisbane.

yogurt. Delete ‖ and add: Now in the U.K. usu. with pronunc. (yǫ·gət). Also **yoghurt.** Now common in many English-speaking countries as a commercial semi-solid, often flavoured, foodstuff. (Further examples.)

1925 C. H. BROWNING *Bacteriol.* vii. 154 'Yoghurt', which contains very little alcohol, is prepared by the Bulgarians, Greeks and Turks from cow's milk. **1934** E. WAUGH *Handful of Dust* i. 13 Mrs. Beaver stood with her back to the fire, eating her morning yoghourt. She held the carton close under her chin and gobbled with a spoon. **1955** G. FREEMAN *Liberty Man* I. ii. 32 Miss Parrot, who ate only yoghourt for lunch, would dip a teaspoon into the bottle. **1970** R. LOWELL *Notebook* 185 Open books, yogurt cups in the unmade bed. **1980** *Sunday Times* (Colour Suppl.) 14 Sept. 85/4 Stokowski..was concerned with retaining his youth—and Garbo, always a food faddist, was into the 'yoga and yoghourt' experience.

Hence **yo·g(h)urty** *a.* (and varr.), fed on or smeared with yoghurt; containing or being yoghurt.

1981 *Times* 20 June 12/3 The dull and dispirited expressions that lie on their yoghurty faces. **1983** *N.Y. Mag.* 18 July 15 Not everything yogurty, performs magically—certainly, frozen yogurt hasn't in the last few years.

yohimbine. (Later examples.)

1977 E. J. TRIMMER et al. *Visual Dict. Sex* (1978) vi. 65 Yohimbine is incorporated in a preparation that many doctors prescribe for patients with loss of sexual desire and ability. **1979** *Nature* 29 Feb. 600/1 (*caption*) Inhibition by yohimbine and indoramin of the response of human platelets to adrenaline. **1983** *Guardian* 11 Aug. 18/4 Curare blocks acetylcholine receptors, another alkaloid, yohimbine, does the same for noradrenaline. **1984** *Observer* 9 Dec. 14/4 The detailed promotional material claims that the drug—containing..yohimbine and strychnone—will improve both erections and sperm.

yok (yɔk). *slang.* [Yiddish, *GOY reversed with unvoicing of final consonant.] A pejorative Jewish term for a non-Jew, a Gentile.

1923 A. YEZIERSKA *Children of Loneliness* 75 She stands there like a *yok* with her eyes in the air! **1960** *Times* 17 May 17/4 Mr. Faulks..said that on February 10, 1958, Mr. Daniels had said to Mr. Lincoln: 'Unless you join me and Mr. Jackson against that bloody Yok I will crush you, smash you and drag you into the gutter.' His Lordship asked the meaning of 'Yok' and was told that it was a Yiddish word meaning a Gentile, a rude way of saying a 'Goy'. A woman member of the jury.—It is not rude. **1969** R. ESSER *Hot Potato* 34 My God, this could all be a Nasser plot. And you let this yok into our Intelligence camp! **1970** *Guardian* 21 July 8 Jews..in the arts area *are* pretty smashing but then some of the yoks are fabulous. **1981** R. SAMUEL *East End Underworld* vii. 76 There were five Jewish boys in the gang—I was the only 'Yok'.

yok, var. *YOCK *sb.* (and *v.*).

yoke, *sb.*¹ Add: **I. 3. b.** (Earlier example.)

1880 *Girl's Own Paper* 20 Mar. 191/3 Make a new yoke and sleeves, and add a scarf to tie round the neck.

4. c. *Electr. Engin.* The part of a magnet or electromagnet that joins the poles or pole-pieces.

1884 S. P. THOMPSON *Dynamo-Electric Machinery* vii. 145 One such iron mass..is attached solidly to each pole-piece, and the two are united at the top by a still heavier yoke of iron. **1924** A. L. COOK *Elements Electr. Engin.* xi. 88 On the ring-shaped portion or yoke are inwardly projecting cores, which carry the exciting windings and have pole pieces, curved to fit the armature. **1951** R. B. DOME *Television Princ.* ix. 230 Another problem, that of high-voltage surges across the yoke and tube during flyback, must be taken into account in designing the components. **1975** D. G. FINK *Electronics Engineers' Handbk.* XI. 42 For PPI deflection one common arrangement is to have the single-axis yoke rotated physically by an external motor..driven by the radar antenna.

d. *Aeronaut.* = *control column* s.v. *CONTROL *sb.* 5.

1934 in WEBSTER. **1956** W. A. HEFLIN *U.S. Air Force Dict.* 576/2 *Yoke*,..a control column, esp. a dual control column. **1971** R. DENTRY *Encounter at Kharmel* ix. 151 Ed eased back on the yoke and made a slow, climbing turn. **1984** *Miami Herald* 27 Mar. 2D/5 A co-pilot immediately pulled back on the yoke.

9. (sense 1) *yoke-weary* adj.; (sense 3 b) *yoke-back*; **yoke-skey**: see also *JUKSKEI; (earlier and later examples).

1895 *Montgomery Ward Catal.* Spring & Summer 278/3 Men's Overshirts..Gathered yoke back. **1981** *Country Life* 22 Jan. 226/2 Mr. Tommy Nutter wears..a jacket of honey-toned Donegal tweed, yoke back, single-breasted. **1817** G. BARKER *Diary* 29 May (MS.), Made yoke schegen. **1835** A. SMITH *Diary* 31 Mar. (1939) I. 338 The woman looked at her for a moment and then took up a yokeskey. **1934** B. BUCHANAN *Pioneer Days in Natal* 31 The straight yoke was placed across their necks and secured by the throat strap attached to the wooden yokeskeys. **1948** W. S. CHADWICK *Mother Africa hits Back* i. 21 When transport riding in Barotseland I had two good but rather cheeky Zulu drivers. One night after an argument they threatened me with yoke-skeys and I got in the first blow. **1910** KIPLING *Rewards & Fairies* 219 And a wet yoke-weary bullock Pushed in through the open door.

yoke (yōᵘk), *sb.*² *Anglo-Irish.* [Origin unknown.] A thing; a thingummy.

1910 P. W. JOYCE *English as we speak it in Ireland* xiii. 352 Yoke; any article, contrivance, or apparatus for use in some work. 'That's a *quare* yoke Bill,' says countryman when he first saw a motor car. **1958** N. FITZGERALD *Student Body* v. 69 Don stooped to pick u the gun... 'Where's the safety-catch on these yokes? **1979** K. DOWLING *Interface: Ireland* I. iii. 26 This feckin yoke is maggots up to here!

yoke, *v.* **8. b.** (Later examples.)

1765 BOSWELL *Let.* 11 May in *Corr. Boswell & Johnson* (1966) 167 At any trade I shall be in no hurry to *yoke* a my Father calls it. **1920** R. MACAULAY *Potterism* II. i. 6 She is yoking together with an unbeliever.

yokel. Add: (Earlier *attrib.* example.) Also quasi-*adv.*, as *yokel-stubborn.*

1829 P. EGAN *Boxiana* 2nd Ser. II. 665 If he stood still in his *yokel* attitude, he was laughed at by the spectators. **1935** L. MACNEICE *Poems* 15 The moon's glare, Goggling yokel-stubborn.

yokeless (yōᵘk'le·s), *sb. nonce-wd.* [f. YOKEL + -ESS.] A female yokel.

1925 D. H. LAWRENCE *Refl. on Death of Porcupine* 18 As for the yokel, his little stream may have flowed out o commonplace little hills, and been ready to mingle with the streams of any easy, puddly little yokeless.

yoke-mate. Delete Now *rare* and add later, chiefly *fig.*, examples. So **yoke-mated** *a.* (*rare*).

1882 G. M. HOPKINS *Let.* 1 Jan. (1956) 162 One of our Fathers, who was..my yokemate on that laborious mission, died there yesterday night. **1911** FLETCHER & KIPLING *School Hist. England* 223 The very marrow of Youth's dream, and still, Yoke-mate of wisest Age that worked her will! **1914** *Nineteenth Cent.* July 111 In water, Oxygen is still further subjugated by its yoke-mate, Hydrogen. **1917** *Q. Rev.* Apr. 276 The Austrians.. to the disgust of their German allies, did nothing to endear themselves to their unequal yoke-mates, the Italians. **1929** R. BRIDGES *Test. Beauty* IV. 145 Where lay the harness'd bones of the yoke-mated oxen. **1973** L. RUSSELL *Colonial Canada* iv. 46 If one ox of a pair were lost or killed, the other was usually unfit to work, because it would not function in unison with a new yoke-mate.

yoker. (Later example.)

1913 R. HARRIS *Boanerges* xxxvii. 341 Since Jason is alone, another pair of twin yokers will come to his assistance.

‖**yokozuna** (yōᵘkŏ,zū·nă). [Jap., f. *yoko* across + *zuna*, f. *tsuna* rope, festoon, orig. a sacred straw festoon presented to a champion wrestler.] A grand champion sumo wrestler.

1966 *Manch. Guardian Weekly* 9 June 7 The last six bouts were the most important with two yokozuna (grand champions) and several ozeki (champions) fighting. **1972** *Times* 19 July 6/7 The only *Yokozuna* or grand champion at present active, Kitanofuji, was unable to take part in the Nagoya tournament because of injury. **1974** *Daily Tel.* (Colour Suppl.) 22 Feb. 40/3 The *yokozuna* is the embodiment of all the highest virtues of Sumo and no slightly less than brilliant *sumotori* will ever be allowed to degrade the status of the Grand Champion.

·Yokuts (yōᵘ·kɒts), *sb.* and *a.* [Yawelmani Yokuts *yokʰoč* person, people.]

A. *sb.* **a.** (A member of) any of about 40 closely related Indian peoples of central California; these peoples collectively.

1877 *Contrib. N. Amer. Ethnol.* III. 370 At the time of the American advent..the Yokuts occupied the south bank of the Fresno. **1929** A. H. GAYTON *Yokuts & Western Mono Pottery-Making* 249 These sherds are related stylistically to southern California ware rather than to that of the Yokuts. **1973** A. H. WHITEFORD *N. Amer. Indian Arts* 39 In southern California the baskets of the Yokuts and Mono have thin grass coils.

b. The language family of the Yokuts, or the language of any Yokuts group.

1912 [see *PENUTIAN *sb.* and *a.*]. **1921** E. SAPIR *Lang.* iv. 77 In another Indian language, Yokuts, vocalic modifications affect both noun and verb forms. **1965** *Canad. Jrnl. Linguistics* X. 139 Yokuts is a language family that is centered in the San Joaquin Valley and is flanked by languages of the Uto-Aztecan family.

B. *adj.* Of, pertaining to, or designating the Yokuts.

1877 *Contrib. N. Amer. Ethnol.* III. 370 In the Yokuts nation there appears to be more political solidarity.. than is common in the State. **1944** S. S. NEWMAN (*title*) Yokuts language of California. **1974** *Encycl. Brit. Micropædia* X. 824/2 Yokuts ceremonies included puberty rite for boys, involving use of the hallucinogen *tolguache*, made from jimsonweed.

yolk, *sb.*¹ Add: **5.** Also *yolk-coloured* adj.; **yolk plug**, a mass of yolk cells partly filling the blastopore in the development of certain fish, amphibians, and insects.

1869 G. M. HOPKINS *Jrnls. & Papers* (1959) 189 The other evening..there was a slash of glowing yolk-coloured sunset. [**1881** F. M. BALFOUR *Treat. Compar. Embryol.* II. vii. 102 Shortly after the stage represented in fig. 71 B, the plug of yolk, which fills up the opening of the blastopore, disappears, and the mesenteron communicates freely with the exterior by a small circular blastopore.] **1892** E. L. MARK tr. *O. Hertwig's Text-bk.*

mbryol. of Man & Mammals vi. 117 The inner lamella f the Triton embryo]..is connected with the mass of olk-cells.., which lies like a wall in front of the blasto- ore and even projects into it as the Rusconian yolk-plug. 928 [see *INDUCTION 9 b]. **1959** SOUTHWOOD & LESTON and & Water Bugs 299 Fertile eggs [of the bug Capsus ter] commence to develop at once and the grey band of he yolk plug forms just below the operculum about 2 eeks after laying. **1980** Jrnl. Exper. Zool. CCXIV. 323 'SL [sc. yolk syncytial layer] cytoplasm which reaches he yolk plug during epiboly is not a part of the syncy- ium when gastrulation begins.

olky, *a.*[1] (Later example of the form *yelky.*)
1918 W. J. LOCKE *Rough Road* ix. 104 With a hazardous lunge of his spoon he had made a yellow yelky horror of the egg-shell.

Yom Kippur (yǫm ki·pəɹ). Also 9 **Jaum-kipur.** [a. Heb. *Yōm Kippūr*, f. *yōm* day + *kippūr* atonement.] The Day of Atonement, the annual Jewish fast day of repentance and expiation that ends the Ten Days of Penitence; *Yom Kippur War*, an Arab-Israeli war that began on Yom Kippur on 6 October 1973 and ended in the same month.
1854 *Asmonean* 6 Oct. 198/3, I will tell thee now why the Jews in Gneson do not wear the *kittel* at *Jaumkipur.* **1878** *Harper's* Oct. 768/2 This..is a *Shophar*, such as is blown in the synagogues on the Jewish New Year..and the Day of Atonement (*Yom Kippur*). **1907** I. ZANGWILL *Ghetto Comedies* 20 With a woman *Yom Kippur* is a wonder-working day. **1922** JOYCE *Ulysses* 149 Their butteries and larders. I'd like to see them do the black fast Yom Kippur. **1941** *Contemp. Jewish Record* IV. 429/2 Last Yom Kippur..Nazi elite guards..evicted Jews from a synagogue in Szczucin. **1973** *Guardian* 29 Oct. 3/5 The Yom Kippur war had given them [*sc.* the superpowers] a greater hold over their respective clients. **1974** *Ann. Reg. 1973* 200 Yom Kippur (the Day of Atonement), when there is no public transport [in Israel] or private or public business and even non-observant Jews stay at home, fell on 6 October. **1980** 'E. ANTHONY' *Defector* v. 101 We [Russians] made very good use of the opportunities given to us by the Yom Kippur war. **1981** C. MACLEOD *Palace Guard* xii. 89 'Have you ever in your life seen anybody eat the way he does?' 'Yes, my Uncle Hymie on the night after Yom Kippur.'

yomp (yǫmp), *v.* orig. *Mil.* [Origin unknown.
The word came into prominence when used by the Royal Marines during the Falklands conflict of 1982. It was subsequently identified with *YUMP *v.* by correspondents familiar with the terminology of rally driving, but whether correctly or not has not been confirmed.]
a. *intr.* To march with heavy equipment over difficult terrain. Also *fig.* **b.** *trans.* To cover (a certain distance) in this way.
1982 *Daily Tel.* 3 June 36/6 And always in the cold light of the Falklands dawn, the..Marines..have been ready to 'yomp on' for the next stage of the journey. **1982** *Observer* 20 June 3/2 Yomping round the sodden and trackless wastes of the constituency, I found the voters in less martial mood. **1983** *Listener* 20 Jan. 31/2 Mrs. Thatcher may begin yomping..around the hustings considerably sooner. **1983** *Guardian* 15 Apr. 10/1 Our boys..who yomped all those miles in the Falklands. **1984** *Sunday Times* 14 Oct. 9/3 So the sweaty soldier yomping to battle ends up with blisters and a pool of water inside the boot.
So **yo·mping** *vbl. sb.* and *ppl. a.*; also **yo·mper.**
1982 *Daily Tel.* 3 June 1/1 (*heading*) Yompers surprise the enemy. *Ibid.*, Yomping they call it in the Royal Marine Commandos. It means marching, humping up to 120 lb. of equipment and all the arms needed for attack at the far end of the trek. **1982** *Standard* 6 Aug. 8/1 (Advt.), Yompers wanted..in teams of 3 for 40 mile mountain express 24-hour walk. **1983** *Financial Times* 28 Jan. 16/6 Will robots replace the 'yomping' soldier in the army of the future?

yom tov (yǫ·m,tǫv). Also **yomtov,** 9 **yontef,** and with capital initial(s). [Yiddish, f. Heb. *yōm* day + *ṭōḇ* good.] A Jewish holiday or holy day.
1854 *Asmonean* 7 July 96/2 Now, Shlome's grandfather was a kind of careless man who preferred making 'yontef' throughout the year. **1892** I. ZANGWILL *Childr. Ghetto* II. 166 He had been so proud of having earned enough money to make a good *Yomtov.* **1933** A. VAN SON tr. C. van Bruggen in J. Leftwich *Ysräel* 1012 A Jewish woman cannot be too ill to hear the Seder... That's right, it's Yomtov now. **1962** B. ABRAHAMS tr. *Life Glückel of Hameln* iii. 51 Before we eat I must first take my child..some food. It is *Yom Tov.* **1976** M. HOROVITZ in D. Villiers *Next Year in Jerusalem* 113 Quite often, in the midst of supra-national poetry events, I find myself involuntarily imagining *yom tov.*

Yomud (yōᵘ·mʊd, yǫmū·d). Also 9 **Yimoot; Yomut.** [Native name.] **a.** (A member of) an ethnic group of Turkmen people (once a nomadic tribe) inhabiting the Turkmen Soviet Socialist Republic of the U.S.S.R. Also *attrib.*
1834 A. CONOLLY *Journey India Overland* I. iv. 35 The large tribe of Yimoot occupy the banks of the Goorgaun river. **1864** A. VÁMBÉRY *Trav. Central Asia* xvi. 307 The Yomuts inhabit the East shore of the Caspian Sea and some of its islands. **1889** G. N. CURZON *Russia in Central Asia* viii. 275 The Turkomans under Khivan rule are Yomuds, Chadars, Emrali, Ata and Alili. **1938** E. O. LORIMER tr. *Krist's Alone through Forbidden Land* ii. 38 We had reached Qala-Qaya, the standing camp or village of the Yomut. **1963** L. KRADER *Peoples Central Asia* iii. 58 Yomud had an alternative division, based on subsistence type rather than genealogy. **1974** *Even. Stand.* 12 Feb. 48/5 (Advt.), Superb oriental carpets & rugs. Including:.. A special collection of unique Persian Nomadic rugs from the Yomut..and Quashgai tribes.
b. *attrib.* Designating rugs made by this people, often distinguished by a diamond-shaped motif.
1900 J. K. MUMFORD *Oriental Rugs* xii. 234 One might reasonably say, looking at some of the Yomud rugs, that they had come from the Shirvan or Dagestan looms. **1940** A. B. THACHER *Turkoman Rugs* 24 This type of juval is the aristocrat of Yomud rugs in respect to density of knotting. **1974** *Encycl. Brit. Micropædia* X. 825/2 The large Yomud carpets are entirely of wool or of goat hair.

yon, *dem. adv.* Restrict *Obs.* exc. *dial.* to sense a and add: **b.** *hither and yon*: (non-*dial.* examples).
1903 H. JAMES *Ambassadors* II. v. 53 What carried him hither and yon was an admirable theory that nothing he could do would not be in some manner related to what he fundamentally had on hand. **1939** W. S. MAUGHAM *Christmas Holiday* iv. 94 The wan characters of Chekov's stories drifted hither and yon at the breath of circumstance like dead leaves before the wind. **1963** BIRD & HUTTON-STOTT *Veteran Motor-Car* 52 Untidy chain or belt drives running hither and yon. **1978** *Nature* 27 Apr. 768/2 It is inaccurate, full of fanciful and unilluminating analogies, infuriatingly unsystematic, and skims hither and yon over the surface of the subject.

yonder, *sb.* Restrict (*nonce-use*) to sense in Dict. and add: **2.** [After quot. 1939.] The far and trackless distance; usu. with preceding adj.
1939 R. CRAWFORD *Army Air Corps* (song), Off we go in to the wild blue yonder, Climbing high into the sun. **1948** *N.Y. World Telegram* 30 Dec. 11/6 A pilot..took wing into that wonderful yonder on a training flight. **1967** C. COCKBURN *I, Claud* xxxiii. 410 The ex-editor of *The Week* had suddenly appeared out of the deep green yonder of Ireland. **1974** *Times* 26 Feb. 12/3 Mr. Wilson's ..policy for controlling inflation, which consists of holding down prices by law while letting wages go up, up, up into the wide blue yonder. **1979** 'D. KYLE' *Green River High* viii. 103 My father had vanished into the great green yonder of a million square miles of jungle. **1985** W. GOLDING *Egyptian Journal* iv. 57 Minya is a centre for scarpering, for fading away, for disappearing into the blue yonder.

yonks (yǫŋks). *slang.* [Origin unknown.] A long time, 'ages'; chiefly in phr. *for yonks.*
1968 *Daily Mirror* 27 Aug. 7/1, I rang singer Julie Driscoll... She said: 'I haven't heard from you for yonks.' **1977** 'J. GASH' *Judas Pair* iv. 54 Any man that says he can remain celibate for yonks on end is not quite telling the truth. **1980** *Oxford Times* 20 June 18 Even though Gabriel left Genesis yonks ago, his music and particularly his vocals remind one of Genesis. **1984** *Listener* 10 May 32/2 The English have been writing poetry for yonks, and have become damned good at it too. **1985** A. BLOND *Book Book* ix. 142 Nicholas Bagnall and David Holloway have run the *Telegraph*'s book pages for yonks.

yonnie (yǫ·ni). *Austral. slang.* [Origin unknown.] A small stone; a pebble.
1941 BAKER *Dict. Austral. Slang* 84 *Yonnie*, a small stone, a pebble. **1979** *Sun-Herald* (Sydney) 18 Mar. 79 There were two lamp posts..each equipped with one electric bulb... Young couples courting would smash each of them with a well-aimed 'yonnie' on pay night.

yoo-hoo (yū·hū), *int.* (*sb.*) [Cf. YOHO *int.*] A call made to attract attention, esp. to one's arrival or presence; also as *sb.*
1924 *Dialect Notes* V. 280 *Yoo-hoo* (call). **1926** *New Yorker* 2 Jan. 18/3 Yoo-hoo! When did your school let out? **1937** M. ALLINGHAM *Case of Late Pig* vii. 49 He opened the breakfast-room door. 'Yoo-hoo!' said someone inside. **1946** A. MARSHALL in Murdoch & Drake-Brockman *Austral. Short Stories* (1951) 316 There was a faint 'yoo-hoo!' from behind us. We all turned. **1959** L. LEE *Cider with Rosie* 150 I'm coming—yoo-hoo! Just mislaid my gloves. **1959** A. WESKER *Roots* I. 16 Girl's Voice (off): Yoo-hoo! Any one home? **1970** J. UPDIKE *Bech* 182 Mildred..waved an alabaster, muscular arm: 'Yoo-hoo, Henry, over here.' **1973** E. BULLINS *Theme is Blackness* 62 Yoo Hoo up there! Someone will be up to give you a hand with the rest of those things. **1983** 'J. GASH' *Sleepers of Erin* viii. 61 Patrick..trilled a roguish yoo-hoo.
Hence **yoo·hoo, yoo-·hoo** *v. intr.* and *trans.*, to call 'yoo-hoo!' (to); **yoohoo·ing** *vbl. sb.*
1948 D. BALLANTYNE *Cunninghams* 14 He..yoohooed for a chair. **1954** *Partisan Rev.* Nov.–Dec. 599 Life, despite their frantic yoohooing, had passed them by. **1957** J. KEROUAC *On Road* I. xiii. 88 Then they yoohooed us. **1969** 'E. LATHEN' *When in Greece* xxii. 231 Leaving the ladies to their yoohooing, the three men followed the officer's directions. **1978** 'J. GASH' *Gold from Gemini* iii. 24 Patrick yoo-hooed me over to his place. **1982** —— *Firefly Gadroon* xiii. 122 Margaret blew a kiss... Patrick yoohooed.

yop, var. YAWP, YAUP *sb.*

yore, *adv.* Add: **5.** *Yore-flood* (nonce-use), the biblical Flood.
1876 G. M. HOPKINS *Wreck of Deutschland* xxxii, in *Poems* (1967) 62, I admire thee, master of the tides, Of the Yore-flood.

yorezeit, var. *YAHRZEIT.

‖**yorgan** (yǫɹgɒ·n). Also **yorghan.** [Turk.] A quilt.
1914 *Blackw. Mag.* Dec. 759/2 He..brought a heavy quilted *yorghan*, a warm covering for the coldest night. **1962** *Times* 6 June 16/7 Blankets and silk *yorgans*—Turkish eiderdowns.

Y organ. *Zool.* Also **y organ** and with hyphen. [tr. F. *organe Y* (M. Gabe 1953, in *Compt. Rend.* CCXXXVII. 111), after *X ORGAN.] An endocrine gland in certain crustaceans which secretes a hormone that causes moulting.
1959 E. SCHARRER in E. Gorbman *Compar. Endocrinol.* 239 The final common path for the resulting decision to molt is represented by the neurosecretory cell which presumably activates the Y-organ. **1965** LEE & KNOWLES *Animal Hormones* xi. 137 The Y organ is located in the antennary segment of those species which have a maxillary excretory organ, and in the second maxillary segment of those which have an antennary excretory organ. **1973** *Nature* 9 Mar. 133/2 An insect does not enter premoult if its thoracic glands have been removed, nor a crustacean if its y-organs have been removed.

York, *sb.*[1] Add: **1. a.** *York ham* (later examples); **York-Antwerp rules** [adopted at *York* in 1864 and modified at *Antwerp* in 1877], an international set of rules governing the application of general average in marine insurance.
[**1877** TWISS & JENCKEN in H. D. Jencken *York & Antwerp Rules* 20 The Rules which your committee now bring before you as the basis for a uniform system of General Average for all maritime countries, and to which the title might be given of the 'York and Antwerp Rules', are appended.] **1881** R. LOWNDES *Pract. Treat. Law Marine Insurance* vii. 203 The York–Antwerp Rules constitute a sort of international code of general average, not as yet obligatory. **1970** York ham [see *Cambridge sausage* s.v. *CAMBRIDGE]. **1974** E. R. H. IVAMY *Marine Insurance* (ed. 2) xiv. 191 The policy almost invariably provides that either a foreign law or the York–Antwerp Rules 1974 shall apply. **1983** *Harrods Mag.* Xmas. 44/1 At Christmas the whole York ham, costing £35. **1984** J. GRIGSON *Brit. Cookery* 122 Today, York ham has become a generalised term, meaning no more than a mild cured ham.
5. The name of *York Factory*, a trading settlement in northeastern Manitoba, used *attrib.* in **York boat,** a type of inland cargo boat used in Canada between *c* 1790 and 1930.
1864 *Nor' Wester* (Red River Settlement) 26 Apr. 2/5 Gentlemen of practical experience gave their opinion that the present York boats (bateaux) could be used for the transportation of goods from Lake of the Woods to Lake Superior with as little difficulty as is encountered between this place and York Factory. **1909** G. BRYCE *Romantic Settlement Lord Selkirk's Colonists* 71 The birch-bark canoe is a mere trifle on the portage, but the heavy York boat capable of carrying three or four tons is a clumsy lugger. **1971** R. RUSSELL *Carlton Trail* 10 The company hired Scotsmen, Metis, and Indians to man brigades of York Boats.

york (yǭɹk), *sb.*[2] *dial.* Also **yark, yerk.** [Perh. the same word as YERK, YARK *sb.*] Something used to tie a trouser leg beneath the knee. Usu. *pl.*
1905 *Eng. Dialect Dict.* V, *Yark*, a strap or piece of string to fasten the trousers to keep them free from mud. [*Cites a quot. with 'yerks'.*] **1958** K. ETHERIDGE *Welsh Costume* 66 When kneeling at the coal-face, dirt and small coal are apt to get inside the trouser-leg... Tying of the trouser leg just below the knee prevents this. A piece of string, or a leather strap..may be used for this. The strap..is called a 'york'. **1967** *Listener* 19 Oct. 504/3 The 'tyings' or straps worn below the knees..are, or were, used by the South Wales colliers, whose term for them is 'yorks'. **1977** SCOLLINS & TITFORD *Ey up, mi Duck!* III. 12 Mr. Flint, who played the Fool, wore moleskin trousers tied with 'yorks'. **1984** *Guardian Weekly* 22 Jan. 4/2 They wore corduroy trousers fastened below the knee with leather straps ('yarks' is the technical name).

york, *v.*[1] (Earlier example.)
1882 *Australians in Engl.* 42 Butler was 'yorked' the second ball he received.

york (yǭɹk), *v.*[2] [f. *YORK *sb.*[2] Cf. YERK, YARK *v.*] *trans.* To keep *up* trouser legs by tying them with 'yorks'.
1960 R. WILLIAMS *Border Country* 258 The thongs which yorked the trouser legs just below the knees. **1969** M. HARRIS *Kind of Magic* 178 He always wore thick brown cord trousers yorked up below the knee with leather straps, and his face was the colour of a bit of old leather.

yorker[2]. (Earlier example.)
1861 *Bell's Life* 25 Aug. (Suppl.) 2/1 Buchanan stopped sometime, and bothered the bowlers much, as he would not hit even a 'Yorker'.

yorker[3] (yǭ·ɹkəɹ). [f. *YORK *sb.*[2] + -ER[1].] = *YORK *sb.*[2]
1940 H. SPRING *Fame is Spur* xiii. 362 Checked mufflers..were at the throats of most [miners], and their trousers were hitched up with yorkers below the knee. **1972** [see *NICKY TAM].

York gum. [Named after *York*, a town in Western Australia east of Perth.] A gum-tree, *Eucalyptus loxophleba*, of Western Australia, or its timber.

1846 [see *GUM *sb.*[2] 5]. **1889** J. H. MAIDEN *Useful Native Plants Austral.* ix. 449 Samples of this timber were sent to the Colonial and Indian Exhibition under the name 'York gum' (*E. loxophleba*). **1934** T. WOOD *Cobbers* viii. 101 In addition to seeds for me—yates gum and york gum and mallee wattle—a cold turkey sat in the back seat. **1944** *Coast to Coast 1943* 60 The slope..rose towards his own home, a thin tracery of york-gums screening the house. **1965** *Austral. Encycl.* III. 407/1 York gum..and wandoo..are pale-coloured Western Australian timbers.

Yorkie (yǭ·ɹki). Also 9 **Yorky.** [f. YORK(SHIRE + -IE, -Y[6].] **1.** A Yorkshireman; † a nickname for a Yorkshireman. *colloq.*

1818 P. EGAN *Boxiana* (ed. 2) II. 301 Yorky did not appear wholly without judgment. **1938** 'J. CURTIS' *They drive by Night* xiii. 144 You're in Yorkshire now... Them Yorkies never was any good. **1950** W. BIRD *This is Nova Scotia* 14 The gallant young Yorkie hushed up her every attempt to talk. **1980** 'J. GASH' *Spend Game* x. 107 Joseph Bramah was a Yorkie, and a genius... His legendary lock patent is dated 1784.

2. A Yorkshire terrier. *colloq.*

1950 A. C. SMITH *Dogs since 1900* xiii. 321 A bigger Yorkie..is as satisfactory a companion as could be desired. **1967** 'A. GILBERT' *Visitor* vi. 95 'Mrs. Warren is telling me poodles are out!..'And Yorkies are in?' I suggested. **1977** *S. Wales Echo* 18 Jan. 12/3 (Advt.), Wanted, Toy Poodles..and Yorkies. **1984** *Hampstead & Highgate Express* 14 Dec. 27/5 Yorkie and Westie pups, inoculated, guaranteed.

Yorkshire. Add: **1. b. Yorkshire chair,** a type of 17th-century upright chair, usu. distinguished by an open backrest and arched cross-rails; **Yorkshire fog,** a perennial greyish-green grass, *Holcus lanatus,* bearing pale green or purplish panicles; **Yorkshire pudding:** now usu. cooked and served as a separate item to accompany roast beef; hence **Yorkshire pud** *colloq.*; **Yorkshire Relish,** the proprietary name of a kind of savoury sauce; **Yorkshire teacake,** a kind of baked yeast teacake occas. made with currants or sultanas; **Yorkshire terrier,** a small, long-coated, tan and blue-grey terrier belonging to a breed developed in the West Riding of Yorkshire about 1870.

[**1900** E. SINGLETON *Furnit. of Our Forefathers* I. i. 46 There were not so many kinds of single chairs in the seventeenth century... There were two very favourite patterns, the Derbyshire and the Yorkshire... The Yorkshire model .is rather more ornamental.] **1906** W. E. MALLETT *Introd. Old Eng. Furnit.* 20 A solid oak chair of the Stuart period. These are often called Yorkshire chairs. **1976** *Southern Even. Echo* (Southampton) 12 Nov. (Advt. Suppl.) 19/3, 4 Yorkshire chairs and 1 carver, £300. **1874** C. C. BABINGTON *Man. Brit. Bot.* (ed. 7) 419 *H. lanatus*... Meadows and pastures... Yorkshire Fog. **1954** C. E. HUBBARD *Grasses* 237 'Yorkshire Fog' is generally regarded as a weed, but when young it has some value for grazing. **1977** *New Yorker* 8 Aug. 58/3 The fairways were edged by the wispiest kind of rough—a thin, random collection of fescue, buttercups, plantain shoreweed, Yorkshire fog, dandelions, and assorted other weeds, grasses and wild flowers. **1975** *New Society* 21 Aug. 411/2 The roast beef and Yorkshire pud dinners provided on Sundays. **1976** C. BERMANT *Coming Home* II. iv. 169, I was given roast beef and Yorkshire pud. **1877** *Trade Marks Jrnl.* 13 Jan. 78 *Yorkshire Relish*... William Powell, of..the firm of Goodall Backhouse and Co., Leeds..; drysalters and general merchants. **1881** *Cassell's Family Mag.* Dec. 46/1 And two table-spoonfuls of Yorkshire Relish. **1926** *Daily Colonist* (Victoria, B.C.) 17 Jan. 7/7 (Advt.), Genuine Yorkshire Relish. **1877** *Cassell's Dict. Cookery* 1157/2 *Yorkshire tea-cakes*... Two pounds of good flour;..an ounce of German yeast..two well-beaten eggs and six ounces of butter... Leave it in a warm place to rise... Divide it into ten portions. **1945** 'R. CROMPTON' *William & Brains Trust* v. 84 One of his happiest memories was the Yorkshire tea cakes that his mother used to make. **1977** E. DAVID *Eng. Bread & Yeast Cookery* 488 The following nineteenth-century recipe for plain Yorkshire tea cakes comes from..Marcus Woodward. [**1871** R. PEARSON in *Field* 13 May 386/2 Some friends of mine in Yorkshire wish me to put a matter right in connection with dog shows, namely, the classification of a breed of dogs they claim as of Yorkshire origin—those beautiful blue and tan long-haired terriers, now sometimes entered in the Scotch and broken-haired, also rough-haired terrier classes. They with myself think it would much simplify the matter by calling them the 'Yorkshire blue and tan long-haired terrier'.] **1872** 'STONEHENGE' *Dogs of Brit. Islands* (ed. 2) v. 108 The silver-grey Yorkshire terrier is not a distinct breed, being merely a paler variety of the blue-tan. **1922** D. MATHESON *Terriers* I. 188 Yorkshire Terriers are hardy, game little dogs. **1959** *Observer* 1 Feb. 12 Yorkshire Terrier. Coat should hang straight and evenly down each side. **1971** *Country Life* 6 May 1098/3 Mrs. Huxham makes it clear..how much pleasure and entertainment she gets from her gay little Yorkshire terriers.

c. The name of a breed of white pig, now widely bred for bacon.

1770 Yorkshire hog [in Dict., sense 1 b]. **1845** *Encycl. Metrop.* XXV. 310/1 The Old Yorkshire Pig is by some considered as the very worst of the large varieties, very long legged, weak loined, not of strong constitution, nor good stye pigs, but yet quicker feeders. **1856** J. C. MORTON *Cycl. Agric.* II. 942/1 The Old Lincolnshire, or Yorkshire Pig, was one of largest breeds in the kingdom, and probably the worst... The large breed, or *improved* wold pig, has probably undergone as great a change as any, and has become..the most profitable kind we have. **1914** 'SAKI' *Beasts & Super-beasts* 24 Tarquin, the huge white Yorkshire boar-pig, had exchanged the narrow limits of his stye for the wider range of the grass paddock. **1974** *Encycl. Brit. Macropædia* X. 1281/2 The Yorkshire pig, which originated early in the 19th century in England, where it was considered a bacon type, is long, lean, and trim with white hair and skin. Found in most countries, this breed is probably the most widely-distributed in the world.

3. (Earlier and later examples of sense 'Yorkshire dialect'.) Also, Yorkshire pudding; a Yorkshire pig; a Yorkshire terrier.

1717 M. W. MONTAGU *Let.* 1 Apr. (1965) I. 333 'Tis as ridiculous to make use of the expressions commonly us'd, in speaking to a Great Man or a Lady, as it would be to talk broad Yorkshire or Somersetshire in the drawing room. **1898** J. D. BRAYSHAW *Slum Silhouettes* 235 Now's yer time, gents, fer a nice 'ot dinner, cut off the jint.., an' two wedgetables; plum-tart or Yorkshire—a shilling. **1902** *Encycl. Brit.* XXV. 194/2 The latter [*sc.* recognized breeds] include the Large White, Middle White, and Small White, which were all formerly embraced under the general term of Yorkshires, and are still so called in other countries. **1922** D. MATHESON *Terriers* I. 181 Originally designed as a sporting dog, the Yorkshire has gradually passed into a lap-dog. **1956** A. WILSON *Anglo-Saxon Attitudes* I. ii. 41 Theo..said, 'Shame!' in his broadest Yorkshire. **1967** M. KENYON *Whole Hog* viii. 93 They're Large Whites. You [*sc.* Americans] call them Yorkshire. **1971** R. J. WHITE *Second-Hand Tomb* ix. 95 Rammel. That's Yorkshire for rubbish. **1977** J. WAMBAUGH *Black Marble* (1978) viii. 105 The handler two stations down had a Yorkshire with a touch-up. **1977** *S. Wales Guardian* 27 Oct. 5/3 Oh the joy of digging into tender roast beef and Yorkshire!

Yorkshireism: also **Yorkshirism.**

1962 P. BENTLEY *'O Dreams, O Destinations'* iv. 56 Her voice was pleasant, quite devoid of Yorkshirisms. **1971** J. WAINWRIGHT *Dig Grave & let him Lie* 128 'Aye.' The open-vowelled Yorkshirism was heavy with self-disgust.

yortzeit, var. *YAHRZEIT.

Yoruba (yǫ·rubă), *sb.* and *a.* Also 9 **Yarriba.** [Native name.] **A.** *sb.* **a.** The language of the Yorubas, a tonal language of the Kwa group.

1841 *Outl. Vocab. Lang Western & Central Africa* 2 (*heading*) Ako, Eyo, Yabú, or Yarriba. **1843** S. CROWTHER (*title*) Vocabulary of the Yoruba language. Part I.—English and Yoruba, Part II.—Yoruba and English. **1888** *Encycl. Brit.* XXIV. 755/1 The Bible and several religious treatises have been translated into Yoruba. **1927** E. S. PANKHURST *Delphos* v. 51 Yoruba, one of the African languages, conjugates its verbs as in English, though its vocabulary is entirely different. **1964** *New Statesman* 1 May 681/1 In Accra recently a Nigerian company, under the direction of the brilliant young artist Demas Nwoko, presented a dramatised version, in Yoruba, of Amos Tutuola's *The Palm-Wine Drinkard.* **1972** B. EMECHETA *In Ditch* i. 6 The landlady started scolding her husband in Yoruba.

b. (A member of) a Black people of western Nigeria and neighbouring parts.

1843 S. CROWTHER *Vocab. Yoruba Lang.* p. iii, The Yorubas, like other nations, have always considered themselves the first people in the world. **1897** M. H. KINGSLEY *Trav. W. Afr.* xiii. 526, I had a set of porters composed of four Bassa boys, two Wei Weis, one Dualla, and two Yorubas. **1937** *Discovery* July 225/1 The Yoruba have only the vaguest tradition of their own past. **1960** *Guardian* 15 July 14/3 The Yorubas live in the largest urban agglomerations to be found in traditional Africa. **1970** P. OLIVER *Savannah Syncopators* 32 Between the lands of the Ibo and those of the Ashanti (Akan) of the old Gold Coast (Ghana) lie the domains of the Yoruba of Nigeria and Dahomey.

B. *adj.* Of, pertaining to, or characteristic of this people.

1843 [see sense A. b above]. **1883** *Encycl. Brit.* XVI. 517/1 In the Yoruba lands the Church Missionary Society has 11 stations. **1938** J. CARY *Castle Corner* 357 Four big Yoruba soldiers. **1957** M. BANTON *W. Afr. City* viii. 153 A Yoruba secret society called *Engugun.* **1978** *Jrnl. R. Soc. Arts* CXXVI. 366/2 In Nigeria, Yoruba woodcarvers have adapted their techniques to work in concrete.

Hence **Yo·ruban** *sb.* and *a.*

1853 S. TUCKER *Abbeokuta* (ed. 2) ii. 15 There were few or no Yorubans brought to Sierra Leone till the year 1822. *Ibid.* viii. 100 It afforded Mr. Townsend the opportunity of becoming in some degree acquainted with the Yoruban language. **1879** J. A. FARRER *Primitive Manners* iii. 89 Captain Burton justly calls attention to the possibility of many Yoruban proverbs being relics of the Moslems. **1936** V. A. DEMANT *Christian Polity* xi. 193 The thunder-god of the Yorubans is decidedly an earthly king who became a god. **1957** M. STEARNS *Story of Jazz* iii. 27 The musical instruments for such occasions consist of Yoruban drums, shaped like hour glasses, and the drumming and singing are in the Yoruban style.

Yoshiwara (yǫʃiwā·ră). Also **yoshiwara.** In Japan, an area (esp. one in Tokyo) where brothels were officially recognized. Freq. *attrib.*

Official recognition was withdrawn in May 1958.

1870 *Fortn. Rev.* Aug. 154 At Yokohama, indeed, and at the other open ports, the women of the Yoshiwara are loud in their invitations to visitors. **1877** A. C. MACLAY *Let.* 25 Nov. in *Budget of Lett. from Japan* (1886) xix. 342 That strange institution of the feudal Government of Japan known as the *Yoshiwara* system.. This was a system of legalized prostitution..under government patronage. **1896** KIPLING *Seven Seas* 70 And tell the Yoshiwara girls to burn a stick for him. **1911** *Daily Colonist* (Victoria, B.C.) 27 Apr. 3/4 The fire..destroyed the new yoshiwara at Tokyo, sweeping away 6555 houses. **1944** H. G. WELLS *'42 to '44* 102 The child may be apprenticed to Fagin's academy, it may be sold into the Yoshiwara. **1966** *New Statesman* 2 Dec. 840/1 A short look at *A Harlot's Progress,* and then—if not at a yoshiwara house by a Japanese master of the Floating World—at Botticelli's *Venus.* **1978** *Country Life* 24 Aug. 500/ The brothels in the red light district of Edo, the Yoshiwara.

yotization (yǫtəizē^i^·ʃən). *Phonetics.* [f. *yot-* repr. IOTA + -IZATION.] The prefixing of the semivowel (y) to another sound or syllable; the change of a sound into (y). So **yo·tized** *ppl. a.*

1936 *Bull. School Oriental Stud.* VIII. 525 Peanius.. presents various types of syllable such as those 'quibus copulatur *ja,* seu *jota*', which we may describe as 'yotized'. *Ibid.* 532 Basic type of articulation..yotization..labio-velarization..nasalization. **1951** [see *PROSODY 2*].

you, *pers. pron.*, etc. Add: **II. 5. c.** Phr. *you and your—*: a contemptuous, impatient, or good-natured dismissal of the thing or person mentioned. *colloq.*

1607 SHAKS. *Coriolanus* IV. vi. 97 You haue made good worke, You and your Apron men. **1837** H. MARTINEAU *Society in America* III. III. i. 80 An old acquintance of Noah's..said.., 'Go, get along, you and your old ark! I don't believe we are going to have much of a shower.' **1899** KIPLING *Stalky & Co.* 177 'I was born there... It was called after my uncle.' 'Shut up—you and your uncle!' **1943** J. B. PRIESTLEY *Daylight on Saturday* xxii. 172 I've told 'im... 'You an' your Teds!' I told 'im. **1955** E. BLISHEN *Roaring Boys* I. 27 'Progressing!' He relished it. 'You and your long words!' **1980** P. G. WINSLOW *Counsellor Heart* xiv. 171 Ah, you and your Colonel. Worms' meat, he is now.

d. *you and who else?*: see *WHO *pron.* 4 a; *you and yours*: see YOURS *poss. pron.* 2 b.

III. 10. b. (Further examples.)

1964 'E. LATHEN' *Accounting for Murder* xv. 142 We run tests... Then, once we had really found the real you, we..would try to find a place that provided a challenge to your best creative talents. **1974** *Spartanburg* (S. Carolina) *Herald* 25 Apr. A-5 (Advt.), Vicaltein can be your ticket to a newer, slimmer you. **1978** J. GRENFELL *Stately as Galleon* 38 Learn..to dance the natural nature way. Let the music through, find the inner you. **1981** *Sci. Amer.* July 14/3 For every quantum-mechanical branch point in your life..you have split into two or more you's riding along parallel but disconnected branches of one gigantic universal wave function.

10*. As *adj.*: expressive of or suited to your taste, personality, etc.

1918 R. FRY *Let.* 12 Mar. (1972) II. 425 I've read your *Lucretius*... I feel sure it's both immensely him and also very much you. **1936** U. ORANGE *Begin Again* xi. 247 'I think it's lovely,' said Jane unkindly, 'So *you,* somehow.' **1960** N. MARSH *False Scent* viii. 232 The boudoir.. had been created by Bertie... 'Almost indecently *you,* darling!' Bertie had told Miss Bellamy. **1981** M. SPARK *Loitering with Intent* ii. 44, I thought your piece was very much you.

11. you-know-what (later examples); **you-know-who, -whom,** a deliberately unnamed person whose identity is apparent to the hearer.

1766 O. GOLDSMITH *Vicar of Wakefield* II. ix. 143, I danced last night with Lady G—, and could I forget you know whom, I might be perhaps successful. **1796** M. EDGEWORTH *Parent's Assistant* (ed. 2) I. 174 Do nothing in this till we have consulted *you know who* about whether it's right or wrong. **1912** C. MACKENZIE *Carnival* xiii. 167, I don't think I'm jealous of you know who. **1936** O. NASH *Primrose Path* 198 Be my gazelle, my wishing well..But never my you-know-what. **1937** M. ALLINGHAM *Dancers in Mourning* xiii. 179 Not a word to Mrs. You Know Who. **1956** L. MCINTOSH *Oxford Folly* 37 She's madly gay, but hard as nails when it comes to you know what. **1975** *Verbatim* Dec. 1/2 John O'Donnell expressed his delight that 'we're going to arm German panzer divisions for you-know-what'. **1976** *New Yorker* 26 Apr. 99/1 She gives me a pain in my you-know-what. **1978** J. IRVING *World according to Garp* xviii. 390 Old You-Know-Who—the Under Toad, that's who, Helen thought. **1981** Q. CRISP *How to become Virgin* vi. 81 Since neither I nor Mr. Hurt .flashed you-know-what before the cameras..we might both by modern standards be considered old-fashioned.

you-all (yū·ǭl, yū,ǭ·l), *pers. pron.* *U.S. dial.* Also **you all.** [f. YOU *pers. pron.* + ALL *a.*] Used in place of YOU *pers. pron.*

Used, with no clear pattern, both as *sing.* and as *pl.*

1824 'A. SINGLETON' *Lett. South & West* 82 Children learn from the slaves some odd phrases;..as ..will you *all* do this? for, will *one* of you do this? **1871** R. M. JOHNSTON *Dukesborough Tales* vii. 95 You all little fellows was.. skeered. **1875** [see *WE-ALL *pron.*]. **1901** A. H. RICE *Mrs. Wiggs of Cabbage Patch* vi. 81 Some of you all shake down the stove an' pull the door to fer me. **1919** R. FROST *Let.* 24 Mar. (1972) 56 The second thing is to ask you what you-all are thinking of to want me to judge in a lyric contest. **1924** W. M. RAINE *Troubled Water* xix. 201 You-all are losing a better man than Missie ever had. **1926** E. FERBER *Show Boat* 299 You-all one of them Suhveys? **1926** *Amer. Speech* II. 476/1, I was born in South Carolina..and have worked on a New Orleans paper for two years, and I have not once in my life heard the expression 'you-all' used except in plural address. **1927** *Ibid.* III. 5 *You-all* certainly is used as singular in the Ozarks—I have heard it daily for weeks at a time. *You-uns*, however, . . is nearly always plural in the Ozark country. **1928** *Ibid.* IV. 54 Here in Missouri . . I have again and again heard 'you all' used in speaking to one person. **1942** M. K. RAWLINGS *Cross Creek* xxii. 344, I ain't never been as far as you-all aim to go. **1944** *Amer. Speech* XIX. 147/2 In almost a score of years of residence in North Carolina I have never heard anyone say 'you all', unless the plural was definitely and distinctly intended. **1954** G. DURRELL *Three Singles to Adventure* 15 Is youall to catch the Parika train? **1981** *TV Picture Life* Mar. 46/3 Then I walked into this audition, put my feet up on the desk, finished my beer, and drawled, 'What kind of character you-all looking for?'

So **you-all's** and varr., your.

1869 *Overland Monthly* Aug. 131 During the war we all heard enough of 'we-uns' and 'you-uns', but 'you-alls' was to me something fresh. **1887** *Scribner's Mag.* Oct. 478/1 How are you all's little trick? **1929** W. FAULKNER *Sound & Fury* 347, I try to obey his wishes for you alls' sakes. **1934** C. CARMER *Stars fell on Alabama* 190 We are honored to have you-all's company.

young, *a.* (*sb.*[1]) Add: **A.** *adj.* **1. b.** *young master*: see MASTER *sb.*[1] 22 in Dict. and Suppl.; *young 'un* (earlier and later examples); also *youngun.*

c **1810** W. HICKEY *Mem.* (1960) iv. 64 So the young'un there wanted to be off, but I said as I how I knew a trick worth two of that. **1922** JOYCE *Ulysses* 418 Collar the leather, Youngun. **1940** C. MCCULLERS *Heart is Lonely Hunter* I. iv. 56 A youngun was sitting on the banisters. . . He had seen her somewhere before. **1981** J. D. MACDONALD *Free Fall in Crimson* xix. 219 Here and there are little groups of younguns who know what an original idea tastes like.

(*b*) *young-girlish* adj., *-girlishly* adv.

1928 A. HUXLEY *Point Counter Point* xi. 174 She flushed with a young-girlishly timid pleasure. **1975** *New Yorker* 28 Apr. 66/3 Her young-girlish way of lowering her eyes with an air of anguish when I asked her what had happened to her affair with the man she said she had loved.

C. 1. a. Also with names of political parties and movements, denoting a young member or (*pl.*) a section organized by and for young members, as *Young Communist, Conservative, Farmers,* etc.; **young** (or **Young**) **America,** (*a*) a slogan used in connection with an expansionist movement within the Democratic Party in the 1840s and 1850s (*obs.* exc. *Hist.*); (*b*) American youth collectively; **Young Turk:** see also TURK[1] 2 e in Dict. and Suppl.

1844 *St. Louis Reveille* 30 Nov. 2/2 No mammoth bank . . can form any part of the creed of the *Young America!* **1852** *U.S. Mag. & Democratic Rev.* Feb. 185/2 We are not for all the young men before the country, but only for the bold, active honor and talent of Young America. **1880** 'MARK TWAIN' *Tramp Abr.* xxxviii. 444 He and the innocent chatterbox whom I met on the Swiss lake are the most unique and interesting specimens of Young America I came across during my foreign tramping. **1924** *Outlook* 10 Sept. 45/1 Young America could with profit leave such affairs alone. **1962** E. WILSON *Patriotic Gore* p. xxii, Douglas . . had been the leader of the 'Young America' movement in the Democratic Party, which had favored . . the annexation of Mexico, Cuba and . . Central America. **1936** J. BELL *Let.* 4 Jan. in *Ess., Poems & Lett.* (1938) II. 294 While I have been writing these last pages, I have been acutely aware of 'the adversary'. He takes the form of an enthusiastic member of the Young Communist League and he bellows incessantly. **1966** 'H. MACDIARMID' *Company I've Kept* viii. 188 Some of the Edinburgh University students, members of the Young Communist League, . . came to the rescue. **1982** *Manch. Guardian Weekly* 21 Nov. 10/3 He had a good secondary education and joined the Young Communists in 1923 while he was at a metallurgical school. **1924** *Times* 17 Mar. 13/5 (*heading*) The 'Young Conservatives Union'. *Ibid.*, This union has been formed by Young Conservatives who desire to prove by attaching themselves to constituencies for social service that their Conservative ideal is one which they are prepared to maintain by action. **1938** B. R. BRAINE in *Torchbearer* Apr. 41/3 The prefix 'Junior' we dislike, and the word 'Imps' infers an extreme and irresponsible youthfulness that is certainly not in accordance with reality . . I suggest . . that we take steps to become the 'Young Conservative League'. **1944** *Times* 11 July 2/2 The Conservative Party has decided to establish a new Young Conservative movement which will take the place of the Junior Imperial League. **1959** E. H. CLEMENTS *High Tension* x. 165 Fiona isn't a Young Conservative! She's a Communist. **1977** J. WAINWRIGHT *Do Nothin' till You hear from Me* iv. 52 It is a Young Conservative hop, in a neighbouring town. **1968** P. JENNINGS *Living Village* 71 The flourishing Young Farmers Club movement. **1981** J. WAINWRIGHT *Urge for Justice* I. v. 35 The lads from the local Young Farmers branch put on a New Year's Ball. **1983** *Economist* 21 May 37/1 As usual, the Young Liberals attacked it from a neo-Trotskyite stand. **1980** *Christian Science Monitor* 28 Jan. 12/3, 80,000 pounds—none of which, say the editors, came from abroad. Much of it probably came through the Labour youth movement, Young Socialists, where the tendency reportedly has strong support.

b. young grammarians *sb. pl. Philol.* [tr. Ger.] = *JUNGGRAMMATIKER *sb. pl.*; cf. *NEO-GRAMMARIAN; so **young-grammarian** *a.*; **young lion,** a young and vigorous man.

1922 Young-grammarian [see *JUNGGRAMMATIKER *sb. pl.*]. **1947** *Essays & Studies* XXXII. 89 This was bound to shake the young-grammarian theory of the inviolability of the sound laws. **1856** C. M. YONGE *Daisy Chain* ix. 92 Take care of my arm! . . I was . . a little in dread of such a young lion! **1917** H. JAMES *Middle Years* iii. 36 Frederic Harrison . . one of his [*sc.* Matthew Arnold's] too confidently roaring 'young lions' of the periodical press. **1937** K. BLIXEN *Out of Africa* v. v. 407 It was curious to hear the young Kikuyu lions speak with reverence and awe of . . the old dancers. **1977** *Listener* 17 Feb. 216/2 An orchestra comprising most of the 'young lions' from the home front.

2. a. *young-born* adj.: also *absol.*; *young-seeming* adj. **b.** *young-minded* adj. **young-blood:** delete † and add: revived in *U.S.* as a hyphenated or one-word form of *young blood* (see BLOOD *sb.* 15).

1946 MEZZROW & WOLFE *Really the Blues* viii. 106 He was a tall blond good-looking youngblood. **1979** *N.Y. Times Mag.* 30 Sept. 28/4 The fault always lay with . . veterans rather than the youngbloods that Willis himself had drafted. **1915** D. H. LAWRENCE *Rainbow* i. 2 Every year throws forward the seed to begetting, and . . leaves the young-born on the earth. **1930** *Daily Express* 23 May 10/4 The Italians and the Russians are young-minded. **1951** S. SPENDER *World within World* 113 An old man. . . With young-seeming nervous fingers he touched the rim of his glass.

Young (yʌŋ), *sb.*[2] *Physics* and *Mech.* [The name of Thomas *Young* (1773–1829), English physician and physicist.] *Young's modulus*: = *modulus of elasticity* s.v. MODULUS 3.

1865 *Proc. R. Soc.* XIV. 293 Young's 'modulus', which has generally been called simply *the* modulus of elasticity of a solid, is the longitudinal traction of a stretched rod or wire of the substance, divided by the extension produced by it. *Ibid.*, Several accurate determinations of Young's modulus have been made upon wires of different substances hung in the College Tower of the University of Glasgow. **1930** *Engineering* 11 Apr. 465/1 The modern theory of the elasticity of isotropic materials makes use of a number of physical constants, all of which are definitely related to Young's Modulus E. **1967** M. CHANDLER *Ceramics in Mod. World* iv. 118 The harder it is to stretch a material, the higher is its Young's modulus. **1978** *Jrnl. R. Soc. Arts* CXXVI. 683/1 The stresses built up in a structure due to these temperature differences are proportional to E (Young's Modulus), α (the linear coefficient of expansion) and ΔT (the temperature difference).

young (yʌŋ), *v. Geol.* [f. YOUNG *a.*] *intr.* Of a structure or formation: to present the apparently younger side (in a specified direction). Hence **you·nging** *vbl. sb.*

1934 E. B. BAILEY in *Q. Jrnl. Geol. Soc.* XC. 469, I have . . been forced to coin the barbaric verb 'to young', in the sense 'to present the younger aspect'. **1969** BENNISON & WRIGHT *Geol. Hist. Brit. Isles* viii. 164 It seems probable that beds 'young' both southwards and northwards from the St. Austell Granite. **1972** *Nature* 28 Apr. 431/2 The eastward younging of plutons was taken to indicate an eastward migration of the downwelling plate margin. **1975** TINDALL & THORNHILL *Blandford Rock & Mineral Guide* I. 30 The direction of younging in a single layer of rock can sometimes be established if there is clear evidence of erosion. **1982** COLLINSON & THOMPSON *Sedimentary Structures* ii. 9/2 A sequence [of beds] could therefore be reported as 'younging to the east' for example.

youngberry (yʌ·ŋbĕri). Also **Young-**. [f. the name of B. M. *Young* (fl. 1905), U.S. horticulturist, who first produced it + BERRY *sb.*[1]] A dewberry derived from a cross made in Louisiana in 1905 between a blackberry and a dewberry; also, a fruit of this plant, similar to a loganberry.

1927 *Calif. Cultivator* 30 July 104 (*heading*) The Youngberry. *Ibid.* 20 Aug. 178/4 As to the Youngberry plant it does not produce a dewberry fruit and if the name dewberry cheapens a most excellent fruit and is misleading as well we can see no reason why, in California, dewberry should not be dropped and Youngberry . . adopted. **1935** *Ann. Rep. Oregon State Hort. Soc.* XXVII. 74 Our oldest Youngberries were set in the spring of 1931. **1971** *Post* (Cape ed.) 9 May (Suppl.) 10/4 Ingredients: . . Apple Jelly, . . 2 cups boiling water, 2 cups milk, 1 tin youngberries or loganberries. **1980** *Times* 9 June 6/4 A few untended youngberry bushes are all that remain of the thriving farming community that once lived here [in Zimbabwe].

younger, *a.* (*sb.*) Add: **1. a.** *younger generation*, the next or rising generation, seen in contrast to the current one or one's own.

1896 G. B. SHAW *Our Theatres in Nineties* (1932) II. 289 A fine young woman in rational dress who . . treads the boards with no little authority and assurance as one of the younger generation knocking vigorously at the door. **1914** L. WOOLF *Wise Virgins* iv. 93 'Most lakes . . are repulsive,' ejaculated Harry. 'Ah,' said Mr. Macausland tolerantly, 'there spoke the younger generation.' **1931** R. CAMPBELL *Georgiad* i. 25 Writers of the younger generation. **1939** T. S. ELIOT *Family Reunion* I. i. 14 The younger generation Are undoubtedly decadent. **1976** 'J. FRASER' *Who steals my Name?* ii. 22 Mr. Cedric was a member of the younger generation.

b. (Earlier and later examples of its use in the titles of Scottish heirs.)

1567 in R. Pitcairn *Criminal Trials in Scotland* (1833) I. II. 496 (*heading*) Deposition by John Hay, ȝounger of Tallo. **1982** *Who's Who* 1425/2 Hugh Magnus Macleod, younger of Macleod.

young fogey. Also **young fogy** and with capital initials. [f. YOUNG *a.* + FOGY, FOGEY 2.] A young person of noticeably conservative tastes or outlook. Cf. *old fogey* s.v. FOGY, FOGEY 2.

Though occasionally used at an earlier date in contrast with *old fogey*, the expression did not become common until the 1980s.

c **1909** C. S. PEIRCE *Coll. Papers* (1935) VI. I. xii. 218, I expect the day will come when another generation of old and young fogies will be equally indisposed to admit that there is any corner of the whole field that I have not turned up. **1929** 'D. YATES' *Maiden Stakes* 11 Fashions, outlook, the spirit and manners of the age—I found the lot beyond me. . . I was a young fogey. **1980** *Business Week* 6 Oct. 95 Noting a split in the profession between 'old Turks and young fogies', Aaron says: 'The older generation of economists was stimulated by external problems.' **1981** *N.Y. Times* 18 Mar. A27/1 At their worst, conservatives were old fogeys. There were some young conservatives, of course, but they were unbrilliant young fogeys. **1983** *Listener* 27 Jan. 21/3 He implies that this is a consequence of the decline in educational standards of the past decades. Mr. Wilson, though he has many admirable qualities, is a bit of a professional young fogey. **1985** *Times* 16 July 30 Mr. Gorbachov is something of a young fogy, though with an inquiring mind. **1985** S. LOWRY *Young Fogey Handbk.* i. 8 The present resurgence of the Young Fogey ties up neatly with the reinvention of the class system that has been going on at least in the South of England ever since Tina Brown revamped *Tatler*.

Young-Helmholtz (yʌŋ he·lmhǫlts). The names of Thomas *YOUNG and von *HELMHOLTZ used *attrib.* to designate the theory that in the eye there are receptors sensitive to one or other of three colours (red, green, violet) and every colour sensation is due to the stimulation of these in different proportions.

1889 in *Cent. Dict.* **1896** [see TRICHROMATIC *a.*]. **1935** *Discovery* July 187/2 In 1801, Dr. Thomas Young (1773–1829), . . propounded the theory which now, as the result of the latter work of Helmholtz, commonly bears the name of the Young-Helmholtz theory of colour vision. **1974** *Encycl. Brit. Macropædia* VII. 108/2 All the evidence points to the correctness of the Young-Helmholtz hypothesis with respect to the three colour basis.

young lady. Add: **young ladyship** (earlier example).

1871 [see *GROWN-UP-DOM].

youngly, *adv.* **2.** (Later example.)

1922 JOYCE *Ulysses* 192 Yes, Mr. Best said youngly, I feel Hamlet quite young.

young man, † youngman. Delete † and add later examples of *youngman.*

Not in standard use.—Ed.

1961 *Evergreen Rev.* July–Aug. 15 There was a youngman I had seen often around Times Square. Like me, he was . . hustling. **1963** J. RECHY *City of Night* I. 43 Part of Pete's technique as a hustler was to tell the men he'd been with that he knew other youngmen like himself. **1967** R. MCGOUGH in A. Henri et al. *Mersey Sound* 91 Let me die a youngman's death not a clean & inbetween the sheets holywater death. **1977** *Sunday Times* (Lagos) 6 Feb. 3/3 A police dog also bit a youngman who was rushed to the hospital for treatment.

young-mannish *a.* (earlier example).

1854 C. M. YONGE *Heartsease* I. II. xii. 310 He looked more young-mannish and sentimental than he does now.

youngstock (yʌ·ŋstǫk). [f. YOUNG *a.* + STOCK *sb.*[1]] Young (domestic) animals.

[**1888** W. DAY *Horse* xviii. 250 To put them [*sc.* yearlings] into small paddocks totally unfitted for rearing young stock in is a sad blunder.] **1963** *Times*, 9 May 17/6 Some excellent hunter youngstock classes came before Major Stoddart at the Oxfordshire Show today. **1971** *Pony* Oct. 6/3 There were 325 entries in the classes for pony youngstock. **1979** *Proc. 11th Ann. Convention Amer. Assoc. Bovine Practitioners* 72/2 Cold housing is generally preferred for youngstock. **1982** *Proc. Internat. Conf. Goat Production & Disease* III. 499/1 Perinatal and youngstock mortality data of a 5 year period . . of 8 goat breeding farms.

your, *poss. pron.* and *a.* Add: The first pronunc. given in Dict. has been largely superseded by (yǭɹ).

Similarly with YOURS *poss. pron.* and related words.

youraballi, var. *JURIBALLI.

yours, *poss. pron.* Add: **1. c.** *yours truly* (earlier *joc.* example).

1833 DICKENS *Let.* Oct. (1965) I. 31 Pray give my love to Letitia; 'accept the same from yours truly' as schoolboys say.

2. e. Phr. *what's yours?* (colloq.): what would you like to drink?

1930 AUDEN *Poems* 12 There's time for a quick one before changing. What's yours? **1982** P. LOVESEY *False Inspector Dead* v. 177 What's yours, Inspector?

yourself, *pron.* Add: **II. 3. b.** Added as a retort after repeating something just said to oneself. *colloq.*

1897 H. G. WELLS *Plattner Story, & Others* 214 William came up beside her and said, 'Hello!' 'Hello yourself!' she said. **1944** S. BELLOW *Dangling Man* 39 'Minna,' I said, 'Minna yourself!' *a* **1945** C. Williams *Seed of Adam* (1948) 77 *Hell* (*to Grace*) Stop that noise! *Grace* Noise yourself!

4. b. Now esp. in Anglo-Irish.

1805 G. Colman *John Bull* iv. i. 65 Och! and is it yourself I see, at last? **1896** C. M. Yonge *Release* ii. ix. 160 And is it yourself, Miss Caroline, as would honour me by sailing under my flag.' **1907** J. M. Synge *Tinker's Wedding* ii. 32 And it's yourself is wedding her, Michael Byrne? **1970** N. Marsh *When in Rome* iv. 92 The monk.. spoke with a superb brogue... 'Ah, it's yourself again,' he said.

yourt. Add: (Examples of *yurt*, *yurta*: now the usual forms.) Also, a circular skin- or felt-covered tent, with collapsible frame, used by the nomadic peoples of Siberia and Central Asia. Also *transf.*

1883 S. W. Williams *Middle Kingdom* (rev. ed.) I. iv. 206 A first-class *yurt* is by no means an uncomfortable dwelling, with its furniture, lining, shrine, and hot kettle in the centre. **1904** H. G. C. Swayne *Through Highlands Siberia* vi. 98 Occasional groups of true Kalmak huts, extinguisher-shaped,..felt 'yurtas', which are used by the richer Kalmuks, through I believe they are properly the Kirghiz type of dwelling. **1911** P. T. Etherton *Across Roof of World* iv. 60 The habitations of the Kirghiz are the 'yurts', or 'khirgas', constructed of felt on a wooden framework, with an opening at the top to let out smoke from the fire lighted in the centre. **1924** *Blackw. Mag.* Aug. 255/2 We had seen little camps of their Yurtas, large black tents. **1940** *Antiquity* XIV. 410 Dwelling of the semi-dugout type. This was probably a conical structure similar to a yurt. **1953** J. Masters *Lotus & Wind* xx. 247 Groups of the round black felt tents called yurts dotted the grass. **1974** *Publishers Weekly* 4 Mar. 5/2 (Advt.), Build a yurt. The round house you can make... It's a portable dwelling for people and pets... Inspired by the ancient Mongolian felt-and-hide structures, the yurt is the newest thing in housing. **1978** A. Grey *Chinese Assassin* ii. 38 The yurt camps..were now quickly dispersing..across the steppes. **1979** J. Halifax *Shamanic Voices* (1980) ii. 49 Kyzlasov lived a distance from his village..in an isolated and impoverished yurta constructed of logs and surrounded by birch trees. **1981** *Nordic Skiing* Jan. 51/2 Skiing the system of five yurts set five miles apart in the Sawtooth Mountains is what Leonard Expeditions is all about.

yous (yūz), also **youse**, dial. varr. You *pers. pron.* (with pl. inflection, though used in sing. sense also). Cf. Yez.

1893 S. Crane *Maggie* i. 8 Youse kids makes me tired. *Ibid.* ii. 13 Ah, Jimmie, youse bin fightin' agin. **1901** M. Franklin *My Brilliant Career* xxx. 256 Ye and Lizer can have a little fly round. It'll do yous good. **1907** J. M. Synge *Playboy of Western World* iii. 63 Is it mad yous are? **1929** Wodehouse *Gentleman of Leisure* xiv. 110 Say, youse won't want me any more, boss. **1930** J. Dos Passos *42nd Parallel* i. 102 Say, yous guys, this is fellowworker McCreary. **1939** X. Herbert *Capricornia* xiii. 183, I want yous two back here at Black Adder. **1968** S. L. Elliott in E. Hanger *Three Austral. Plays* ii. i. 74 Good luck to youse. **1975** [see *store *sb.* 12 a]. **1981** S. Rena *Painless Death* xx. 132 We've a telephone installed in the lounge since yesterday and none of yous even noticed it!

youth. Add: **7.** *youth cult, culture, -day, -group, movement, organization*; *youth-bereft, -charmed, -oriented* ppl. adjs; **Youth Aliyah** [Heb. *ăliyah* ascent], a movement, begun in 1933 for the emigration of young Jews to Palestine; **youth and old age** = Zinnia; **youth camp,** one of the camps of various kinds that were established for young people in Germany under the Nazis; **youth centre,** a building providing social and recreational facilities for young people; **youth club,** a social club provided for the spare-time activities of young people; the premises of such a club; **Youth Employment Service,** an advisory service for school leavers set up in 1948 and superseded by the Careers Advisory Service; also *ellipt.*; so *Youth Employment office, officer*; **youth hostel** [tr. G. *jugendherberge*], a hostel providing cheap overnight accommodation for young travellers and holiday-makers; hence **youth-hostel** *v. intr.*, **-hostelling** *vbl. sb.*; **youth hosteller; youth leader,** a person having charge of young people in a youth club or other youth organization; **Youth Opportunities Programme,** a Government-sponsored service introduced in 1978 to provide temporary work experience for unemployed young people and replaced in 1983 by the *Youth Training Scheme* (see below); **youth orchestra,** an orchestra open only to young musicians; **youth service,** a service, esp. of local government, providing social and recreational facilities for young people; **Youth Training Scheme,** a Government-sponsored scheme introduced in 1983 to replace the *Youth Opportunities Programme* (see above) and offering job experience and training for unemployed school leavers; **youth work,** social work among young people; hence **youth worker.**

1936 H. Szold *Let.* 4 Sept. in M. Lowenthal *Henrietta Szold: Life & Lett.* (1942) xvi. 312 We build homes, we work our heads off over Youth Aliyah and social service. **1968** P. Durst *Badge of Infamy* i. 3 A Youth Aliyah village in a kibbutz south of Tel Aviv. **1975** E. Avriel *Open the Gates!* vi. 62 We had a number of special immigration certificates for youngsters from the separately functioning body of Youth Aliyah. **1889** G. Nicholson *Illustr. Dict. Gardening* IV. 241/2 Zinnia... Youth and Old Age. **1971** *Farmer & Stockbreeder* 16 Feb. 80/1 Zinnias—common name 'youth-and-old-age'—have normally bloomed in late summer. **1911** M. Beerbohm *Zuleika Dobson* xix. 292 As on the towing-path, so on the youth-bereft rafts of the barges, yonder, stood many stupefied elders, staring at the river. [**1936** *Liverpool Echo* 5 Sept. 4/1 (*heading*) A visit to a Hitler youth camp.] **1942** E. Waugh *Put out More Flags* iii. 217 Those absurd instructors who harangued the youth camps. **1975** H. W. Koch *Hitler Youth* ix. 196 Officials of the party and the Hitler Youth participated. Final selection of candidates was made early each year in what was described as 'Youth Camp'. **1942** H. C. Warner *Christian Youth Leadership* ii. 26 We have seen the sudden outcrop of Youth Centres, Youth Service Corps, Juvenile Civil Defence Units, etc. **1958** I. Murdoch *Bell* xx. 251 The opening of a new youth centre. **1976** 'W. Trevor' *Children of Dynmouth* i. 21 The Youth Centre curtains are apparently unavailable for the Easter Fête, dear. **1943** C. Day Lewis *Word over All* 16 Oh youth-charmed hours. **1940** *Times* 19 Sept. 7/3 Youth clubs may be found in all districts of the city. **1955** E. Blishen *Roaring Boys* iv. 249 Some of the blocks..had community centres and youth clubs. **1957** J. Osborne *Entertainer* 28, I was teaching Art to a bunch of Youth Club kids. **1980** P. Lively *Judgement Day* i. 7 He was no good at Youth Clubs and disturbed black teenagers. **1968** *Harper's* Oct. 8/3 That temptation to jump on the youthcult bandwagon is hard to resist. **1976** B. Bova *Multiple Man* vii. 73 Aspen was once a center of the youth cult... Kids from all over the country flocked there. **1980** J. O'Faolain *No Country for Young Men* x. 209 Typical Ireland! They got the youth cult ten years late. **1958** *Listener* 28 Aug. 308/2 We know little or nothing about the motivation of the new youth culture, whose emergence is one of the key phenomena of the 'fifties. **1977** M. Dickstein *Gates of Eden* 289 The best ongoing rock criticism, some of it quite sharp, appeared in periodicals associated with the youth culture of the sixties, such as *Rolling Stone, Creem, Crawdaddy* and the *Village Voice.* **1985** *Isis* 3 May 4/2 Youth culture implies the new, the non-conformist, the intractable, yet these still form themselves into cults with rules to keep you right. **1953** C. Day Lewis *Italian Visit* v. 55 I too gave tongue in my piping youth-days. **1948** *Youth Employment Service* (Min. Labour) 1 Local Education Authorities in England and Wales..may be authorised by means of a scheme approved by the Minister of Labour and National Service to operate a Youth Employment Service. **1966** P. Willmott *Adolescent Boys* vi. 105 In theory, the youth employment service is available to help school leavers find suitable work. In fact, although more of the boys in the sample had got their first job through the Youth Employment Officer than any other single source, they were not a majority. **1976** L. Thomas *Dangerous Davies* iv. 30 She had gone to the youth employment office..to inquire about..becoming a nurse. **1946** Koestler *Thieves in Night* 155 The youth-group for a while looked on critically at us rapturous elders. **1929** *Liverpool Post & Mercury* 13 Dec. 7/5 (*heading*) Youth hostels. *Ibid.*, A meeting..held last evening in Liverpool, passed a resolution in favour of proceeding with the formation of a local Youth Hostel Association for the purpose of providing hostels in North Wales for holiday sojourns on the lines of those already existing on the Continent, in Scotland, and Northumberland. **1948** 'N. Shute' *No Highway* ix. 185 'Are you fond of hiking?' 'We used to do a lot,' he said. 'Staying in Youth Hostels?' she inquired. **1972** D. Devine *Three Green Bottles* i. iv. 39, I was youth-hostelling on a hired bicycle. **1977** *Daily Colonist* (Victoria, B.C.) 5 June 24/4 When the original—and still operating—youth hostel opened its doors in the West German town of Altena 68 years ago, its purpose was to provide inexpensive accommodations for young students on walking trips. **1977** C. McCullough *Thorn Birds* xvii. 441 The typical fate of Australians in England, youth-hosteling on a shoestring, working for a pittance. **1933** *Y.H.A. Rucksack* Summer 42/1 This is written as a challenge to Youth Hostellers everywhere to send us word whether they want such a hostel. **1977** M. Drabble *Ice Age* ii. 152 Whenever he went to any of the three pubs..he had to spend his time listening to complaints about the behaviour of delinquent youth hostellers. **1947** (*title*) Youth hostelling abroad. **1959** *Woman* 2 May 3/4 Youth Hostelling *is* great fun, for those who enjoy an outdoor holiday, with a sufficiency of male escorts. **1936** *Liverpool Echo* 5 Sept. 4/1 In the streets [of Germany] we met policemen, storm-troopers, youth-leaders, soldiers,..all in their various uniforms. **1958** *Listener* 21 Aug. 256/1 Youth leaders trained in Spain by Franco's Falange. **1973** 'B. Mather' *Snowline* i. 10 A youth leader at a church club in London. **1921** *Survey* 31 Dec. 487 (*heading*) Youth movement of Germany. **1941** 'G. Orwell' *Lion & Unicorn* i. 16 No party rallies, no Youth Movements. **1982** *Listener* 11 Feb. 3/1 The youth movements and their clashes with the police in the 1960s. **1977** *Dept. of Employment Press Notice* 29 June 1 Up to 230,000 unemployed youngsters each year will have a chance of work experience or training under a new £160 million Youth Opportunities Programme announced today by Mr. Albert Booth, Secretary of State for Employment. **1983** *Sunday Tel.* 16 Oct. 11/4 A Midlands businessman who has successfully employed Jamaican youngsters under the Youth Opportunities Programme. **1948** *Times* 22 Apr. 7/4 The Bath Assembly..opened this afternoon in the Pavilion with a concert given by the National Youth Orchestra. **1972** *Daily Tel.* 18 Jan. 9/5 Leicestershire Schools Symphony Orchestra, a 100-strong unit which has a considerable reputation as a youth orchestra. **1959** *Listener* 2 July 17/2 Local institutions: for example, water boards, youth organizations and universities. **1977** *Gay News* 7–20 Apr. 8/3 It's always been known as a youth-oriented action spot. **1982** S. Brett *Murder Unprompted* v. 51 The new youth-oriented culture. **1943** *Ann. Reg. 1942* 68 The Council..advocated ..adequate youth services. **1962** *Guardian* 25 Sept. 6/4 A great impact would be felt if this country had a fully developed..youth service staffed by trained social workers and youth leaders. **1975** *Times* 2 Jan. 3/1 Libraries and the youth services will be among the main victims of cuts..in 1975. **1981** *Hansard Commons* 15 Dec. 153 We are able to ask the Manpower Services Commission to ensure that this new youth training scheme is in full operation by the autumn of 1983. **1983** *Times* 18 Jan. 1/4 The Government is putting a £100-a-head value on the work and training opportunities created by new jobs 'brokers' under the £1000m Youth Training Scheme, which starts in Sept. **1944** *Ann. Reg. 1943* 306 Trust funds..for the development of youth work. **1964** 'J. H. Roberts' '*Q*' *Document* (1965) iv. 84 She..had pangs of conscience and decided to go into youth work. **1976** *Equals* Dec. 6/1 A youth worker is to be appointed to escort young people to interviews,..and generally support those making an uncertain start in work or training.

youthful, *a.* Add: **4.** Comb. *youthful-looking* adj.

1846 Poe in *Godey's Mag.* July 15/1 The likeness conveys a good general idea of the man, but it is far too stout and youthful-looking for his appearance at present. **1954** W. Faulkner *Fable* 8 A man not so young actually, but rather simply youthful-looking. **1977** *New Yorker* 19 Sept. 66/3 Mrs. McCabe is a youthful-looking woman.

youthify (yū·pifəi), *v.* [f. Youth + -ify.] *trans.* To make (a person) appear more youthful. Hence **you·thifying** *ppl. a.*

1945 H. L. Mencken *Amer. Lang.* Suppl. I. 573 *Beauty-parlor*..was displaced by *beauty-shop*... The girls have produced a considerable vocabulary of elegant terms to designate their operations, *e.g. to youthify.* **1960** *Housewife* May 24/3 She..has both to 'youthify' and age actors. **1976** U. Holden *String Horses* iii. 41 He wasn't such a bad looker.., his summer tan was youthifying.

youthly, *a.* Add: **1.** (Later examples.)

1922 E. R. Eddison *Worm Ouroboros* xxvi. 323 Yet is Corinius..a valiant and puissant soldier,..and this one in his youthly age. **1923** H. J. Laski *Let.* 23 Oct. in *Holmes-Laski Lett.* (1953) I. 553, I have read a new *Early Life of Burke* which is full of good things, especially in its recovery of some youthly essays of his which have not appeared before.

2. (Later example.)

1925 T. Dreiser *Amer. Tragedy* (1926) II. ii. xxviii. 347 All seeking a glimpse of the astonishingly youthly slayer.

youthquake (yū·þkwēɪk). *colloq.* [f. Youth after Earthquake.] The series of radical political and cultural upheavals occurring among students and young people in the 1960s.

1967 *Punch* 8 Nov. 708/2 Mary Quant opened her first Bazaar shop..simultaneously with the first tremors of the youthquake. **1970** R. Neville *Play Power* 18 A unique feature of today's Youthquake—as *Vogue* once dubbed it—is its intense, spontaneous internationalism. **1976** *Sunday Mail* (Brisbane) 5 Sept. 19/3 He's built an empire based on the youthquake.

you-uns (yū·ʌnz), *pron. U.S. dial.* Also 9 **youns;** 20– **you uns.** [f. You *pers. pron.* + *uns*, dial. var. *ones* (One *pron.*).] Used in place of You *pers. pron.*

1810 M. V. H. Dwight *Jrnl.* 10 Nov. in *Journey to Ohio* (1912) 37 Youns is a word I have heard used several times, but what it means I don't know. **1869** [see *you-all's* s.v. *you-all *pers. pron.*]. **1885** 'C. E. Craddock' *Prophet Great Smokey Mountains* 7, I hev no call ter spen' words 'bout sech ez that, with a free-spoken man like you-uns. **1927** *Amer. Speech* II. 345 The paterfamilias questioned solicitously: Did you uns sleep good last night? **1934** W. Faulkner *Dr. Martino* 341 Why did you uns have to stop here? **1941** *Amer. Mercury* June 660/2 'Proud to know ye!' Sam will beam. 'Why, you-uns be a-comin' in ter th' fire an' set a spell.'

yow, *int.* Add: **a.** In mod. Austral. and N.Z. use = Wow *int.* 2 in Dict. and Suppl. (Later examples.)

a **1943** L. Esson in *Penguin Bk. Austral. Ballads* (1964) 232 Not er shutter lifted Since they jugged 'im. Yow! **1978** P. Grace *Mutuwhenua* vi. 35, I know. Matter of fact, some of those girls you went round with. Yow! **1983** 'F. Parrish' *Bait on Hook* viii. 111 The rain came... 'Yow,' said Cedric, and shot back into the pub.

yow (yau), *sb. Austral. slang.* [Origin unknown.] In phr. *to keep yow*, to keep a look-out, esp. in order to protect some criminal activity.

1942 E. Langley *Pea Pickers* xix. 283 You keep yow, and whistle..if anyone comes along. **1965** G. McInnes *Road to Gundagai* xii. 206 Molly kept a look out ('kept yow', as we used to say).

yow(e, obs. ff. Ewe *sb.*[1]: for 'obs.' read 'obs. (exc. dial)' and add examples.

1903 'T. Collins' *Such is Life* (1937) v. 249 He went out back, Cooper's Creek way, with three thousand Gunbar yowes. **1925** 'H. McDiarmid' *Sangschaw* 2 Ae weet forenicht i' the yow-trummle I saw yon antrin thing. **1978** *Jrnl. Lakeland Dial. Soc.* xl. 14 I' a field wid sum yows in ther was a crab apple tree. **1979** L. Derwent *Border Bairn* i. 15 Her brother, the shepherd..accepted me more or less as one of his flock. A yowe or a gimmer, a stirk or a stot.

yowie[2] (yau·i). *Austral.* [Origin unknown.] A large, hairy, man-like creature supposedly inhabiting south-eastern Australia.

1976 *Australasian Express* 17 Sept. 10/4 Since 1795 there have been over 3,000 reported sightings of the Snowy Mountains version of the abominable Snowman nick-named the Yowie. **1980** *Courier-Mail* (Brisbane) 4 Jan. 1/8 The 'yowie', a large hairy animal similar to the Himalayan yeti and American Big Foot, has existed in Aboriginal folklore for thousands of years. **1984** *Truckin' Life* (Austral.) Feb. 80/1 'In search of a Yowie.' That was how Theiss Toyota promoted its media function for the release of its new HiLux [*sc.* type of van]..last year.

yowl, *v.* Hence **yow·ler,** one who or that which yowls (in quot. 1935 applied to a crooner).

1935 Wodehouse *Blandings Castle* v. 120 He's a yowler, and girls always fall for yowlers. They have a glamour. **1966** 'L. Lane' *ABZ of Scouse* 120 *Yowler*, a cat. **1979** *Tucson* (Arizona) *Citizen* 20 Sept. 10A/3 In every airport I stand, sip, sleep, weep, wail and yowl in, I find an equal number of other standers, sippers, sleepers, weepers, wailers and yowlers.

yo-yo (yōᵘ·yōᵘ), *sb.* [Origin uncertain, but prob. from one of the Philippines languages.] **1.** Also **Yo-Yo.** A proprietary name for a toy in the form of two conjoined cones or discs with a deep groove between them in which a string is attached and wound, its free end being held so that the toy can be made to fall under its own weight and rise again by its momentum.

1915 *Philippine Craftsman* Dec. 363 Sumpit (blowgun), pana (arrow), and yo-yo, however, are names very generally used throughout the islands. *Ibid.* 364 There is evidently some commercial possibility in Filipino toys, for a patent was recently secured upon the yo-yo by a firm in the United States. **1932** *Trade Marks Jrnl.* 2 Mar. 279/2 *Yo Yo*... All good included in Class 49 [*i.e.* toys and games equipment]. Henry Clement Conlin,.. Vancouver, British Columbia, Canada; merchant. **1932** *Evening Standard* 1 June 17/4 He asked me to hold his hand until he became proficient, and I experienced a queer thrill as I brought his hand slowly up and down to make the Yo-Yo respond to the twitch of the string. **1932** Auden in *Rev. Eng. Stud.* (1978) Aug. 281 In the year of my youth when yoyos came in The carriage was sunny and the Clyde was bright. **1933** D. L. Sayers *Murder must Advertise* vi. 99 Ginger brought a Yo-Yo to the office with him and broke the window in the boys' room practising 'Round the World' in his lunch-hour. **1958** *Observer* 12 Oct. 15/7 The yo-yo craze of the thirties. **1972** *Daily Tel.* 20 Dec. 14 Overall trading was at a low ebb and bored dealers spent a very quiet afternoon in yo-yo competitions and other pre-Christmas pastimes. **1984** *New Yorker* 23 July 76/2 They've got the right string but the wrong yo-yo.

b. The pastime of playing with a Yo-Yo.

1932 *Daily Express* 2 July 3/3 Some boys playing yo-yo attracted the Queen's attention. **1932** *Morning Post* 15 July 10/5 Games similar to Yo-Yo have been played in almost every age.

2. *fig.* or in fig. context. **a.** Something or someone going continually up and down, or to and fro; also, such a motion or fluctuation. Freq. used in comparative phrases referring to emotions or spirits rising and falling like a Yo-Yo.

1958 *Listener* 16 Oct. 623/2 What is it like to be a human yo-yo, driving all day on a ten-minute bus route. **1963** L. Deighton *Horse under Water* xi. 47 Singleton was jumping in and out of the water like a yo-yo. **1973** C. Bonington *Next Horizon* xii. 168 With a bit of luck the constant yo-yo between Scheidegg and the snow cave would be over. **1975** *Times Lit. Suppl.* 12 Dec. 1496/4 Confronted by these dramatic developments, transport policy ceased to be the political yo-yo it had previously been. **1976** J. Grenfell *Joyce Grenfell requests Pleasure* xvi. 230 Our spirits went up and down like yo-yos. **1980** *Times* 13 Sept. 10/5 Alarming yo-yos in the quality of food and service. **1981** *Daily Tel.* 19 Oct. 25/4 (*heading*) Interest rates all a big yo-yo. **1984** S. Townsend *Growing Pains A. Mole* 23 Your emotions are up and down like a yo-yo.

b. A stupid person, a fool. *U.S. slang.*

1970 *New Yorker* 28 Nov. 40 He would leer, and categorize them in a loud, mocking voice. ('Weirdo' was one of his favourite appellations; also 'Freak', 'Yo-Yo', and creep.) **1975** *Ibid.* 20 Jan. 29/1 Some yo-yo of a technician there pulls the control rods out of the core to polish them with Rally wax. **1978** V. Bugliosi *Till Death us do Part* xi. 325 I've got enough problems without some punk yo-yo threatening me.

3. *attrib.* Marked by a continual up-and-down or to-and-fro motion; continually passing from and into a condition. Also *fig.*

1932 *Amer. Speech* VII. 272 *Yo-yo driller*, a cable-tool driller. **1960** *Spectator* 30 Sept. 501 It isn't the industry's fault that we have a yo-yo economy. **1963** T. Pynchon *V.* i. 29 Though they only thought about one another at random, though her yo-yo hand was usually busy at other things, now and then would come the invisible, umbilical tug. **1977** *Lancet* 15 Oct. 792/1 There was no improvement in patients with severe on-off disabilities with freezing and rapid oscillations ('yo-yo' effect). **1979** *Globe & Mail* (Toronto) 22 Jan. 4/3, I want this job because all the jobs I've had have been yo-yo jobs, I've been laid off my job four times in the last six years.

yo-·yo, *v.* [f. prec. sb.] **1.** *intr.* To play with a Yo-Yo.

1932 *Daily Express* 30 June 12/6 (*heading*) Do you yo-yo? **1973** *N.Y. Times* 14 Apr. 18/2 The idea is to go where the kids are and to teach them how to yo-yo.

2. *fig.* To move up and down, or between one point and another; to fluctuate.

1967 *Punch* 12 Apr. 514 The hard facts underlying our economic health—as opposed to the headlines and Treasury press releases—just don't yo-yo about like this. **1973** C. Bonington *Next Horizon* xi. 166 In those early stages of the climb we yo-yo'd back and forth between Kleine Scheidegg and the Rock Band. **1976** *Time* 20 Dec. 23/2 He has yo-yoed between 210 and 296 lbs., now carries a bulky 263. **1978** *Sunday Times* 21 May 53/1 City rates of interest have yo-yoed.

Hence **yo·-yoing** *vbl. sb.* and *ppl. a.*; also **yo·-yoer, yo·-yoist,** one who plays or performs with Yo-Yos.

1933 *Spectator* 6 Jan. 23/2 Surely the unkind girl of figure fifty-eight is the precursor of the modern yoyoist. **1947** *Sat. Even. Post* 10 May 12 His Caspar Milquetoast model for timid yo-yoists was lighter, and, he added, prettier. **1963** T. Pynchon *V.* i 30 As it turned out, the New Year's party was to end all yo-yoing. **1967** F. Conroy *Stop-Time* viii. 114 The greatest pleasure in yo-yoing was an abstract pleasure—watching the dramatization of simple physical laws. **1973** *N.Y. Times* 14 Apr. 18/2 When you're a professional yo-yoer, how can you take anything very seriously? **1976** *Alyn & Deeside Observer* 10 Dec. 34/5 It is more volatile than the yo-yoing pound. **1980** *Illustr. London News* Mar. 56/1 The uncomfortable and costly yo-yoing of temperature experienced in light-weight buildings with large areas of window.

yperite (ī·pərəit). [ad. F. *ypérite*, f. *Ypres*, name of the town in Belgium where the gas was first used, in 1917: see -ITE[1].] = *mustard gas* s.v. *MUSTARD *sb.* 3 c.

1919 *Chem. Abstracts* XIII. 3063 (*heading*) Yperite and poisonous gases. **1940** *Times* 17 Aug. 4/4 Dr. Gerard C. Savoy, of Lausanne, has produced a preparation which is the most efficient known antidoe to yperite (mustard gas). *Ibid.*, Fifty per cent. of the yperite present in the wound is destroyed after one hour. **1979** *Microbiology* XLVIII. 246 Nitrous yperite and other alkylating substances with a radiomimetic effect can inhibit cell division in *Escherichia coli* B.

Ypresian (ipre·siăn), *a. Geol.* [ad. F. *ypresien* (A. H. Dumont 1850, in *Bull. de l'Acad. des Sci.*, etc., *de Bruxelles* XVI. II. 368), f. as prec.: see -IAN.] Of, pertaining to, or designating the lowest stage of the Eocene in western Europe, lying above the Landenian. Also *absol.*

[**1852** *Q. Jrnl. Geol. Soc.* VIII. 323 The group of tertiary strata which we meet with next in the descending order in Belgium (comprising the 'Systèmes Laekenien, Bruxellien et Ypresien' of M. Dumont) corresponds most nearly..in age with the Barton, Bagshot, and Bracklesham beds.] **1880** J. D. Dana *Man. Geol.* (ed. 3) III. 512 London Clay; Lower Ypresian of Belgium. **1969** Bennison & Wright *Geol. Hist. Brit. Isles* xv. 339 The Ypresian cycle commenced with the basement bed of the London clay. **1977** A. Hallam *Planet Earth* 227 The most commonly accepted stages [of the Eocene] include (from oldest to youngest) the Ypresian, Lutetian and Bartonian.

Yquem (ike·m). The name of Château d'*Yquem*, a vineyard in the Gironde, France, used *absol.* and (*rarely*) *attrib.* to denote a variety of fine, rich Sauternes wine produced and bottled there.

1869 A. Trollope *Phineas Finn* I. viii. 29 They give you a capital little dinner at Moroni's, and they've the best Chateau Yquem in London. **1902** Belloc *Path to Rome* 396 He had..Yquem with his fish, the best Chambertin during the dinner. **1927** C. Connolly *Let.* 11 Feb. in *Romantic Friendship* (1975) 252, I drank..Yquem at 300 francs the bottle. **1959** *Sunday Times* 1 Nov. 32/5, I find Yquem too sweet. **1982** D. Peppercorn *Bordeaux* xi. 315 A good vintage of Yquem is the quintessence of Sauternes.

yrast (i·ræst), *a. Nucl. Physics.* [See quot. 1967.] Pertaining to or designating any nuclear energy level that is the lowest for some value of the spin; *yrast line*, a line on a graph of spin against nuclear rotational energy (or some function of each of these), connecting points representing the various yrast states of a nuclide.

1967 J. B. Grover in *Physical Rev.* CLVII. 832 It has been proposed that the lowest-energy excited state at a given angular momentum be called 'yrast' level for that angular momentum. *Ibid.* 832/1 The yrast levels play a crucial role in deciding the course and outcome of many nuclear reactions. [*Note*] By 'yrast' level of a given nucleus, at a given angular momentum, is meant the level with least energy at that angular momentum. The English language seems not to have a graceful superlative form for adjectives expressing rotation. Professor F. Ruplin (of the Germanic Languages Department of the State University of New York, Stony Brook) suggested the use of the Swedish adjective *yr* for designating these special levels. This word derives from the same Old Norse verb *hvirfla* (to whirl) as the English verb *whirl*, and forms the natural superlative, *yrast*. It can thus be understood to mean 'whirlingest', although literally translated from Swedish it means 'dizziest' or 'most bewildered'. **1971** *Physics Lett.* XXXIVB. 575 Non-axially symmetric deformation of a nucleus is introduced to account for the admixture of the collective rotational bands and the distribution of the yrast levels. **1974** Frauenfelder & Henley *Subatomic Physics* xvi. 435 The yrast line of a nucleus gives *E* as a function of *J*. **1983** *Nucl. Physics* A. CDIII. 421 Precession of the yrast 2_1^+, and 4_1^+, and the second 2_2^+ states in ^{24}Mg have been measured.

yttro-. Add: **yttrotu·ngstite,** a basic oxide of yttrium and tungsten, $YW_2O_6(OH)_3$, occurring as yellow monoclinic crystals.

1950 E. H. Beard in *Colonial Geol. & Mineral Resources* I. 51 The results show conclusively that the term 'thorotungstite' is inapplicable as a true description of the mineral... It is suggested that the mineral in future be called yttrotungstite. **1971** *Mineral. Mag.* XXXVIII. 262 All the specimens studied consisted mainly of a fine-grained aggregate of pale-yellow earthy yttrotungstite, with rare druses lined by yttrotungstite crystals.

yu (yū). *Archæol.* [Chinese.] An ancient Chinese wine vessel in the form of a small metal pail with a swing handle and a decorative cover, popular in the Shang and Early Zhou periods.

1904 S. W. Bushell *Chinese Art* I. iv. 90 The sacrificial wine vessels illustrated..have been selected as the most ancient pieces in the collection... The first is an ovoid jar (*yu*), of the shape used by the old kings for presents of wine to deserving subjects, with a cover surmounted by a knob, and a loop handle ending in dragons' heads. **1945** P. Ackerman *Ritual Bronzes of Anc. China* iv. 99/1 *Yu* range from six to nine inches high... They often come in pairs. **1973** W. Watson in *Genius of China* (R. Acad.) II. 74/2 The *yu* with its high handle is an invention of late Shang.

Yuan[1] (yu,ā·n, ‖ yue·n). Also 7 **Ivena,** 8 **Ywen,** 8–9 **Yuen; Yüan.** [a. Chinese *yuán*, lit. 'first'.] **a.** The name of the Mongol dynasty established as rulers of all China by Kublai Khan in 1279 and in power until 1368.

Kublai Khan named his kingdom Yuan in 1271, and the Yuan dynasty is often described as beginning in that year.

1673 [see *Sung *sb.* a]. **1738** tr. *J. B. Du Halde's Descr. of Empire of China & Chinese Tartary* I. 214 (*heading*) The twentieth dynasty, call'd Ywen, which contains nine emperors in the space of eighty nine years. **1788** Gibbon *Decl. & Fall* VI. lxiv. 298 The annals of the Moguls or Yuen. **1836** J. F. Davis *Chinese* I. v. 182 On the accession of Koblai Khan, the first of the *Yuen* dynasty,..an order was promulgated to burn all the books of the Taou sect. **1948** D. Diringer *Alphabet* 355 This character.. was only sparsely used but it lingered on at the imperial Chancery under the Yüan dynasty. **1966** F. Schurmann *Ideology & Organization in Communist China* i. 53 The Yüan Mongols relied heavily on a traditional bureaucratic elite to rule the country. Many of these bureaucrats remained loyal to the Yüan after 1368. **1977** *N.Y. Rev. Bks.* 26 May 22/1 The wreckers had found, during their work, the foundations of a gate of the Yuan era.

b. Used *attrib.* and *absol.* of the art and porcelain of the Yuan period.

1888 F. Hirth *Ancient Porc.* 50 Pieces of a surface which bears no resemblance to any of the classical Sung or Yüan monochrome vessels..are very common. **1933** [see *Sung *sb.* b]. **1969** R. Quest *Cerberus Murders* iv. 30 Whistler and his circle went in for blue-and-white.. but it was all late stuff... This is all Hsüan-tê or Yüan. **1978** *Nagel's Encycl.-Guide: China* 199 In old Yuan opera, one actor alone, the hero of the play, had the privilege of singing certain parts of his role.

yuan[2] (yu,ā·n). Also **yüan.** Pl. **yuan.** [a. Chinese *yuán* round.] **1.** A Chinese unit of currency introduced in 1914, equal to 10 *jiao*; a coin of this value.

1921 J. V. A. MacMurray *Treaties & Agreements with China 1894–1919* I. 853 The Law for the National Currency.—January 1914... Article 2.—The unit of the national coins shall be called *yuan*, and the *yuan* shall contain..23·97795048 grammes of pure silver. **1927** *Glasgow Herald* 14 Jan. 8 The surtax imposition will yield ..an advantage of 12,000,000 yuan of revenue. **1949**, etc. [see *jiao]. **1962** E. Snow *Other Side of River* (1963) ii. 23 At the Hsin Ch'iao a small suite consisting of a sitting room, bedroom and bath cost me 24 yuan..a day. **1976** W. H. Canaway *Willow-Pattern War* xvii. 173 Yang Ma-wei gave me a fistful of yüan and told me to.. find Thupten at the tea-house, and pay him. **1982** C. Thomas *Jade Tiger* ii. 51 He offered the stallkeeper one of his own grubby ten yuan notes.

2. *Chinese Archæol.* A flat ring or perforated disc made of jade, widely circulated from the Shang period to the Hang dynasty.

1912 *Field Museum Nat. Hist.* X. v. 154 There are three kinds of annular jade objects, called *pi*..*yüan*..and *huan*... The former is a disk with a round perforation in the centre, the two latter are rings. **1958** W. Willetts *Chinese Art* I. ii. 89 The *yüan* has a perforation twice the width of the body substance, so that its diameter is half that of the whole ring. **1963** K. Chang *Archaeol. Anc. China* ix. 276 A ceremonial pit was uncovered which contained over twenty stone discs of various sizes and a number of jade and stone ceremonial objects (circular *yüan*, square *tsung* tubes, *wuan-kui*, etc.).

yuan[3] (yu,ā·n). Also **Yuan.** Pl. **yuan.** [a. Chinese *yuàn* courtyard, yard.] Each of several government institutions (e.g. *guo wu yuan* the State Council, *waiyuxueyuan* a foreign languages institute) in China.

1928 *China Year Bk.* xxvi. 1234 Administrative Court (*P'ing Cheng Yuan*)... The principal officials of the Administrative Court are the President (Yuan Chang).. and 15 judges. **1938** E. TEICHMAN *Affairs of China* xiv. 205 On the governmental side the Central Executive Committee of the Kuomintang gives birth to the National Government of the Republic of China, composed of a President..and five *Yuan*, or governing committees: the Legislative *Yuan*, charged with the making of laws; the Judicial *Yuan*, charged with the administration of justice..the Examination *Yuan* charged with selection of officials of the public service; the Control *Yuan*, charged with the supervision of the national administration..and the Executive *Yuan*, charged with the actual administration of the government. **1947** *Sun* (Baltimore) 22 Aug. 6/3 They..will be asked to participate in the selection of the National Assembly and the legislative Yuan. **1967** *Sunday Times* 14 May 6/1 Chiang's executive Yuan (Cabinet) has discussed measures. **1979** *China Yearbk.* ix. 98/2 In the event of a dispute among the various Yuan, the President may call a meeting of the Presidents of the Yuan concerned for consultation on a solution.

‖ **yuan hsiao** (yüä·n χʸiau). Also **yüan hsiao** and with hyphen. [Chinese *yuánxiāo* (in Wade-Giles *yüanhsiao*), f. *yuán* first + *xiāo* night.] A sweet rice-flour dumpling made for the Chinese Lantern Festival (15 January in the lunar calendar).

1956 B. Y. CHAO *How to cook & eat in Chinese* II. xvii. 210 Orange soup with *yüan-hsiao*... Knead the glutinous rice flour with ½ cup hot..water. Then make into globules of about ⅜ inch in diameter. These are the *yüan-hsiao*. **1972** K. LO *Chinese Food* I. 56 *Yuan hsiao* is a form of Chinese festival sweet, served in a rather bland rice soup. *Ibid.* 57 We Chinese love these *yuan hsiaos*, partly, I think, because of happy childhood memories of being allowed to do the rolling

Yucatec (yū·kătek). Also **Yucate·co** and with small initial. [ad. Sp. *yucateco*, f. *Yucatán*, earlier *Yocotán*, adapted from a Maya name for the language of the Mayan Chontal Indians.] **a.** An American Indian of the Yucatán Peninsula in eastern Mexico; such Indians collectively. **b.** *colloq.* Any present-day inhabitant of the Peninsula or of the Mexican state of Yucatán in its northern part.

1843 J. L. STEPHENS *Incidents of Travel in Yucatan* I. vi. 139 No native ever calls himself a Yucateco, but always a Macegual or native of the land of Maya. **1845** *Trans. Amer. Ethnol. Soc.* I. 107 The Yucatecs differed materially from the Mexicans with regard to the time of the solar year. **1875** H. H. BANCROFT *Native Races Pacific States* II. xxi. 675 So great was the horror in which the Yucatecs held this crime that they did not always wait for conviction,..but sometimes punished a suspected person. **1912** *Contemp. Rev.* Feb. 257 The better Yucatecos do not lean to this profession [of clergyman], which is unendowed. **1966** T. PYNCHON *Crying of Lot 49* v. 119 He was part-owner here with a yucateco who still believed in the Revolution. **1974** *Encycl. Brit. Micropædia* X. 841 The Yucatec were the Classical Maya who were conquered by the Spanish and whose calendar, architecture, and hieroglyphic writing marked them as a highly civilized people. **1983** *Word Ways* Aug. 152 Originate in Yucatan and you are a Yucatec.

c. The language of the Yucatán Indians, a Mayan language.

1940 F. JOHNSON in *Maya & their Neighbors* vi. 107 The divisions of the Yucatec-speaking Maya are relatively indistinct. **1954** J. E. S. THOMPSON *Rise & Fall Maya Civilization* i. 28 Yucatec is spoken by many whites and mestizos of Yucatán as a second language and is said to be easy to learn. **1977** *Language* LIII. 296 Tall people can be reclassified by one of the long classifiers in Bantu.., Japanese, and Yucatec.

d. *attrib.* or as *adj.*

1875 H. H. BANCROFT *Native Races of Pacific States* II. xxi. 665 A Yucatec noble who wedded a woman of inferior degree, descended to her social level. **1934** A. TOYNBEE *Study of Hist.* I. 123 The Yucatec Society was apparently incorporated into the Mexic Society by conquest at about the turn of the twelfth and thirteenth centuries of the Christian Era. **1956** *Publ. Amer. Dial. Soc.* XXVI. 25 It is their speech which Vasquez..describes as 'yucateco Spanish', characterized by Mayan phonemes and Mayan phrases. **1975** *Sci. Amer.* Oct. 74/3 They spoke a dialect unlike the Yucatec Maya dialect heard generally throughout Yucatán; it was Chontal Maya, one of the dialects of the Cholan Maya group. **1983** *Washington Post* 13 July E-3/1 You can be sure that Yucatec farmers don't waste maize on their cows. **1983** *Times Lit. Suppl.* 7 Oct. 1090/5 The Yucatec city of Chichen Itza.

Hence **Yucate·can** *a.* and *sb.*

1869 *Proc. Amer. Philos. Soc.* XI. 5 The most important dialects of the Maya are the Yucatecan, the Quiche, the Cakcquichel, [etc.]. **1886** *U.S. Cons. Rep.* LXVII. 495 A fair sample of Yucatecan agriculture. **1909** *Athenæum* 4 Dec. 688/1 Of the Yucatecans themselves the authors have nothing good to say. **1931** E. H. MORRIS *Temple of Warriors* xix. 228 Gold and copper were the only metals known to pre-Columbian Yucatecans. **1950** *Caribbean Q.* II. II. 30 Actual settlement was limited at first to the Belize district, and even that was made precarious by the attack of the Spaniards and Yucatecan Indians.

Yuchi (yū·tʃi). Also 8–9 **Euchee, Euchi(e, Uchee.** [a. Creek, of uncertain origin.] **a.** (A member of) an Indian people formerly inhabiting the region of the Savannah river in Georgia and South Carolina, and now incorporated into the Creek nation in Oklahoma.

1738 W. STEPHENS *Jrnl.* in *Colonial Rec. Georgia* (1906) IV. 75 He understood they were a Party of the Euchies. **1741** in *South Carolina Hist. Soc. Coll.* (1887) IV. 40 Thomas Jones..was Employed..as a Linguist to the Creeks and Euchees. **1744** in *Georgia Hist. Soc. Coll.* (1840) I. 145 Their cattle..had strayed away and eat the Uckee's corn. **1818** *Lynchburg* (Va.) *Press* 25 Dec. 3/1 The captain..reports to have taken three warriors, a Creek, a Choctaw, and a Uchee. **1893** *Amer. Anthropologist* VI. 280 The Yuchi believe themselves to be the offspring of the sun. **1965** [see *CREEK *sb.*³]. **1975** W. L. BALLARD in J. M. Crawford *Stud. Southeastern Indian Lang.* 163, I spent approximately six weeks in Sapulpa, Oklahoma, interviewing Yuchis.

b. The language of this people.

1836 *Trans. & Coll. Amer. Antiq. Soc.* II. 96 These five languages, the Muskhogee and the Hitchittee, the Uchee, the Natches, and the Alibamon or Coosada are, it is believed, the only ones spoken by the different tribes of the Creek confederacy. **1909** F. S. SPECK *Ethnol. Yuchi Indians* 15 It is quite certain now that Yuchi is spoken in only one dialect. **1975** W. L. BALLARD in J. M. Crawford *Stud. Southeastern Indian Lang.* 163 A number of tapes of conversations in Yuchi were made.

yuck (yɒk), *sb.*¹ *slang* (orig. *U.S.*). Also **yuk.** [Origin unknown.] A fool; a boor; anyone disliked or despised.

1943 H. A. SMITH *Life in Putty Knife Factory* xiv. 239 *Yuck* is a word introduced into the language by Fred Allen. A yuck is a dope who makes a practice of going around appearing on quiz programs. That was its original definition; it now means a dope of any description. **1948** R. CHANDLER *Let.* 27 Jan. (1981) 105 The public's capacity and adaptability to a quality of entertainment which the yucks seem to be afraid to give them. **1957** M. SHULMAN *Rally round Flag, Boys!* (1958) vi. 67 The yucks who look at television don't know the difference between Ernest Hemingway and Huntz Hall. **1972** P. ROWLANDS *Fugitive Mind* xi. 132 'Is your brother a yuk?' Clare asked Sally. 'Oh yes! He's a *terrible* yuk! He shouts a lot, he breaks my toys, he pushes me over.' **1979** J. WAINWRIGHT *Duty Elsewhere* xx. 56 Three no-good yucks had felt like playing footsie with the law.

yuck (yɒk), *int.*, *sb.*², and *a.* *slang.* Also **yuk.** [Imitative. Cf. *YECH *int.*, *YUCK *v.*¹] **A.** *int.* An expression of strong distaste or disgust.

1966 R. H. RIMMER *Harrad Experiment* (1967) 25 Across the table; Dorothy Stapleton and Valerie Something-or-other belong (yucks, is that the right word?) to Herber Snyder and Peter Longini. **1970** *It* 12–25 Feb. 16/4 The whole tenor of the epistle is that of one elite talking to another without reference to..those who have paid...Yuk. **1976** G. MOFFAT *Short Time to Live* vii. 58 'Fish pie perhaps, and parsley sauce.' 'Yuk,' said Arabella. **1981** P. DICKINSON *Seventh Raven* x. 130 You took a harmless animal and chopped it up..to please your God—yuck, they thought. **1983** D. SIMPSON *Puppet for Corpse* xx. 172 It was the way he talked about her... 'You know what older women are, wink, wink.'.. Yuk!

B. *sb.*² Messy, unpleasant, or distasteful material. *lit.* and *fig.*

1966 *New Statesman* 19 Aug. 258/1 Rotting wodges of chilly yuck which once were apples and pears. **1971** P. PURSER *Holy Father's Navy* xxxviii. 187 There was a lot of yuk which I didn't investigate too closely, and a bit of ear definitely in the wrong place. **1977** *Times* 17 Oct. 12/6, I asked Nancy Grimes, a freelance who arranges plants for people... 'The offices now are so ugly and so standard, such standardized urban yuk... They want to see something that can actually survive and grow here. It gives them reassurance.' **1981** M. E. ATKINS *Palimpsest* xii. 118 One of those syndicated advice columns... All noble sentiments and romantic yuk.

C. *adj.* **1.** = *YUCKY *a.* a.

1971 *TV Times* (Austral.) 24 Feb. 39/2 Business was a bit yuk and I was bugged by this lack of confidence. **1973** P. DICKINSON *Green Gene* ii. 28 She's got a really yuck family, even worse than mine.

2. Comb. **yuck-making** *ppl. a.* = *sick-making* ppl. adj. s.v. *SICK *a.* 11.

1972 *Courier-Mail* (Brisbane) 30 Mar. 1/10 The BBC yesterday described a song about the former Australian Prime Minister..as the biggest 'yuk-making' piece of propaganda in politics. **1975** *Listener* 7 Aug. 168/3 Nasty, yuk-making remarks.

yuck (yɒk), *v.*¹ *Canad. dial.* [Imitative.] *intr.* To vomit.

1963 *Amer. Speech* XXXVIII. 301 [Newfoundland.] *Yuck*, to vomit. **1981** *Publ. Amer. Dial. Soc.* LXVIII. 54 [Newfoundland.] *To vomit*, yuck.

yuck (yɒk), *v.*² *slang.* (chiefly *N. Amer.*). Also **yuk.** [Origin unknown. Cf. *YOCK *sb.* (and *v.*).] *intr.* **a.** To fool around; to act so as to cause laughter. **b.** To laugh. Also *to yuck it up.*

1964 S. BELLOW *Herzog* 119 And Gersbach, boisterous, yucking it up, poured whisky, wine, pounded the table. **1967** *Boston Sunday Herald* 2 Apr. (T.V. Mag.) 9/2 Russ Tamblyn and Sidney Poitier yuk it up as the lightly clad barbarians; Rosanna Schiaffino and Beba Loncar play it cool as the lightly clad camp followers. **1969** *Listener* 23 Jan. 98/3 An American watches British television..for visions of America. Stray ones move us: Wally Schirra yukking it up in space. **1974** *Publishers Weekly* 12 Aug. 55/3 Laurel and Hardy fans..should enjoy this semi-biography... Old-timers who yukked when they saw the movies way-back-when should swell the market. **1975** *Time Out* 11 Apr. 36/4 Pryor has them yukking at whitey one moment and at themselves the next.

Hence **yuck** *sb.*³, a laugh.

1971 *Daily Colonist* (Victoria, B.C.) 10 Feb. 5/2 The biggest yuks, as might be expected, are to be found right here in Canada. **1976** *National Observer* (U.S.) 16 Oct. 10/3 The biggest yuck of the night was when Mr. T. called Mrs. Llewelyn 'Mrs. Rreweryn'. **1977** *Canadian* 2 Apr. 20/1 Humor is his forte. Looking for yuks? Phone Sammy. **1984** *Sun-Times* (Chicago) 17 Feb. 49/2 The movie gets its yuks with slapstick scenes where one guy goes out the window when the other guy comes in the door.

yucky (yɒ·ki), *a.* *slang.* Also **yukky.** [f. *YUCK *a.*] **a.** Nasty, unpleasant; sickly sentimental.

1970 D. UHNAK *Ledger* v. 79 She wanted to go to a lousy, yukky secretarial college. **1977** *Oxford Times* 1 July 15 The sweetness is fused with enough real feeling to avoid being sugary, except for the rather yucky spoken introduction to 'Meadows of Springtime'. **1980** *Sunday Times* 13 Jan. 61/1 To develop an improved instrument for doctors dealing with emergency cases of perforated lungs, the research boys set to work with butchers' skewers and a lot of belly of pork. It may sound yukky to the squeamish. **1981** M. GORDON *Company of Women* III. 240 It's only bats, I say... 'They're weird,' says Linda. 'Yucky.'

b. Messy, 'gooey'.

1975 *Times Lit. Suppl.* 13 June 661/3 Peanut butter, that yucky staple standby of the American snack-eater. **1977** J. WILSON *Making Hate* v. 62 Let's get these yucky things off and get you washed.

Hence **yu·ckiness.**

1982 E. NORTH *Ancient Enemies* ix. 120 The ringing in my ears and general lassitude and yuckiness. **1984** *InfoWorld* 14 May 18/1 So you go for 100 shares... Let's say that by November it soars back up to 68 5/8, where it peaked before all this market yuckiness began.

yud (yud), dial. var. HEAD *sb.* *rare.*

1874 [see *INNARDS *sb. pl.*]. **1882** E. L. CHAMBERLAIN *Gloss. W. Worcestershire Words* 35 *Yud*,..head. **1974** W. FOLEY *Child in Forest* I. 100 I'll 'old her yud still, and ..you get a good dose down 'er gullet.

Yüeh¹ (yü·ə). Also **Yueh.** [f. the name *Yüeh* Chou of a town (now called Shaoxing) in Zhejiang Province, China.] A type of stoneware distinguished by a celadon glaze, first produced in the Six Dynasties period and perfected during the Tang dynasty. Freq. *attrib.*, esp. as *Yüeh ware.*

[**1887** *Jrnl. R. Asiatic Soc. N. China Branch* XXII. 134 The author of the *T'ao-Shuo* begins his treatise on ancient porcelains with the Yüeh-chou potteries of the T'ang dynasty.] **1910** S. W. BUSHELL *Descr. Chinese Pott. & Porc.* II. ii. 35 The Hsing-chou porcelain resembles silver, while the Yueh-chou porcelain resembles jade... Hsing is inferior to Yueh. **1915** R. L. HOBSON *Chinese Pott. & Porc.* v. 59 Surely this cannot be far removed from the 'secret colour' of the Yueh ware. **1933** *Burlington Mag.* Sept. 122/2 When Yüeh Chou was capital of a principality, Yüeh ware was made exclusively for the princely court and was known as *pi sê yao* or ware of forbidden colour. **1958** W. WILLETTS *Chinese Art* II. vi. 439 In 1930 a Yüeh Kiln was found by Yonayama at Tê-ch'ing near Hangchow. *Ibid.* vi. 442 A number of whole bowls in the shape of lotus flowers are illustrated, all reputedly being Yüeh *yao.* **1972** *Trans. Oriental Ceramic Soc.* XXXVIII. 23 The fully evolved ware which T'ang poets praised is generally termed *Yüeh ware*..the earlier product being called *Old Yüeh* by the Japanese.

Yüeh² (yü·ə). Also **Yueh.** [Chinese.] (A member of) a group of peoples originally living in the coastal provinces of southern China, who expanded into south-east Asia during the third century B.C.

1901 E. A. PARKER *China* ii. 23 The..Yüeh tribes.. seem to have very soon lost their separate identity, and to have either permanently retired into Annam proper or to have been merged into the Chinese. **1934** K. S. LATOURETTE *Chinese* I. ii 51 Both Wu and Yüeh seem to have depended in part upon boats for their victories, navigating these craft on the sea and on the rivers and lakes in which their possessions abounded. **1966** W. G. GODDARD *Formosa* i. 16 The Yueh in coastal China. **1972** M. SHEPPARD *Taman Indera* 5 At the beginning of the Christian era well-established trade links existed between South China, India and the Red Sea. Many different traders and sailors joined in operating this route,..leaving the Yuehs to control the final sector. **1974** *Encycl. Brit. Macropædia* XIX. 120/1 A long-held notion that identified the Vietnamese with one tribe of the Viets of southern China (Yüeh in Chinese) has been abandoned.

Yüeh³ (yü·ə). Also **Yue.** [ad. Chinese *Yuè*, a former name for Guangdong province.] A Chinese dialect spoken in parts of the provinces of Guangdong and Guangxi. Freq. *attrib.*

1954 M. A. PEI *Dict. Ling.* 34 *Cantonese*..spoken in Kwang-tung... The indigenous name of this vernacular is *Yüeh.* **1961** CHANG-TU HU et al. *China* v. 101 Yüeh or Cantonese is spoken by some forty million people in China and abroad. **1974** *Encycl. Brit. Macropædia* XVI. 801/2 The most important representative of the Yüeh languages is Standard Cantonese of Canton, Hong Kong, and Macao. **1978** *Nagel's Encycl.-Guide: China* 70 *Yue* dialect: most of Guang dong and south eastern Guang xi. **1982** C. THOMAS *Jade Tiger* ii. 43 The man spoke in northern Min dialect as opposed to his own expatriate Yue dialect.

‖ **yüeh**[4] (yü·ə). *Archæol.* Also **yueh.** [Chinese *yuè*.] A bronze battle-axe or halberd, esp. one of the Shang period.

1956 W. C. WHITE *Bronze Culture Ancient China* 4 *Axes* (Yüeh), the most common type of axe is found in a variety of shapes. *Ibid.* 58 (*caption*) Axe-head (Yüeh), with socket for hafting. **1960** CHENG TE-K'UN *Archaeol. in China* II. iv. 69 Larger, and consequently richer, tombs would be provided with bronze vessels as well as weapons, such as *ko* dagger axes..*yueh* broad-axes. **1964** M. MEDLEY *Handbk. Chinese Art* 14/2 Axes, called *yüeh, ch'i* or *fu*, are either tanged or socketed. **1978** *New Archaeol. Finds in China* II. 29 Also found was a bronze weapon *yueh*.

‖ **yüeh ch'in** (yü·ə tʃin, kin). Also **yueh-ch'in, yu-kin, yukin,** 9 **yuĕ kin.** [Chinese (Pinyin *yuè qín*), lit. 'moon guitar'.] A Chinese lute with four strings and a flat, circular body.

1839 *Chinese Repository* VIII. 44 The *pepa* and *yuĕ kin* are of easy purchase. **1909** *Cent. Dict.* Suppl. *Yu-kin*,..a Chinese lute or guitar with a large circular body, a short neck, and four strings. **1954** *Grove's Dict. Mus.* (ed. 5) II. 239/2 *Yüeh ch'in*.., flat lute of four strings. Used..to accompany ballads. Now rare. **1962** E. SNOW *Other Side of River* (1963) lxxiii. 566 They may specialize in piano, violin, cello, flute, or one of the standard Chinese strings: *p'i-p'a, yang-ch'in, yueh-ch'in*, and others. **1971** J. R. BERNASCONI *Collectors' Gloss.* 396 *Yukin*, a Chinese instrument with four strings played by plucking. **1975** [see *SAN HSIEN].

yugawaralite (yugæ·wărāləit). *Min.* [f. *Yugawara*, name of a town in Japan near where it was first found + *-l-* + -ITE[1].] A hydrated aluminosilicate of calcium, $CaAl_2Si_6O_{16}.4H_2O$, that is a member of the zeolite group and occurs as colourless or white monoclinic crystals having a vitreous lustre.

1952 SAKURAI & HAYASHI in *Sci. Rep. Yokohama Nat. Univ.* Section II. I. 77 We can not identify this mineral with the other zeolites, and we may consider this to be a new zeolite. We wish to [call] it 'Yugawaralite' after its locality. **1969** *Acta Cryst.* B. XXV. 1190/1 It is difficult to place yugawaralite in any of the seven recognized groups of zeolites, although it shows certain similarities to both mordenite and heulandite. **1978** *Mineral. Rec.* IX. 296/1 Yugawaralite, a relatively rare calcium zeolite,..has been found in specimens mined from the Khandivali quarry near Bombay, India.

‖ **yugen** (yū·gən). Also **yūgen** and with capital initial. [Jap., f. *yū* dark + *gen* the unfathomable.] In traditional Japanese Court culture, esp. poetry and, later, the No play, a hidden quality of graceful beauty or mystery; profound aestheticism.

1921 A. WALEY *Nō Plays of Japan* 21 The difficult term yūgen which occurs constantly..is derived from Zen literature. It means 'what lies beneath the surface'; the subtle, as opposed to the obvious; the hint as opposed to the statement. **1932** *Times Lit. Suppl.* 6 Oct. 715/1 Such a couplet..can hardly be said to capture the spirit of *yugen*. **1959** *Ibid.* 15 May 291/2 This brief basking in the Shōgun's favour led Zeami to stress the importance in performance of Yūgen, or elegant beauty and gentleness. **1970** *Daily Tel.* 16 May 9/4 His smooth curving movements of a fan, together with circling movements across the stage..gave a poetic suggestion of flight, illustrating the *Yugen*—indirection, allusiveness, mystery—which lies at the heart of No.

Yugo (yū·go), colloq. abbrev. of *YUGOSLAVIAN *a.* and *sb.*

1941 *Daily News* (N.Y.) 20 Mar. 19/1 (*heading*) Yugos and Axis in compromise. *Ibid.* 24 Mar. 3/3 (*heading*) Yugo disorders, Greek warning stay Axis pact. **1963** I. FLEMING *On H.M. Secret Service* xi. 117 'Which one was it, anyway?' 'One of the Yugos. Bertil.' **1982** 'I. I. MAGDALEN' *Search for Anderson* I. x. 47 There was someing wrong about that Yugo shoot-out. It stank.

Yugoslav (yū·goslāv, yūgoslā·v), *sb.* and *a.* Also **Jugo-;** 9 **Iugo-Slav, Yougo-Slave, Yugo-Slave.** [ad. G. *Jugoslawe* (F. *Yougoslave*), f. Serbo-Croat *jugo-*, comb. form of *jug* south + G. *Slawe* SLAV *sb.*] **A.** *sb.* **a.** (A member of) various groups of southern Slavs, comprising the Serbs, Croats, and Slovenes; also, since 30 Oct. 1918, a native or inhabitant of the State of Yugoslavia. **b.** *rare.* The Slavonic language dominant in Yugoslavia; = *Serbo-Croat* s.v. *SERBO-.

1853 L. H. KERR tr. *Robert's Slave Prov. Turkey* in *Ranke's Hist. Servia* (ed. 2) 382 Toasts were drunk to..the New Servian Kingdom, which will reunite all the Yugo-Slaves under the eternal patronage of the house of Romanoff. **1867** MACKENZIE & IRBY *Trav. Slavonic Provinces of Turkey-in-Europe* xxv. 369 The situation was reversed when the Russians had shaken off the Tartar, and the Iugo-Slav fell under the Turk. **1881** MRS. A. O. BRODIE tr. *Tissot's Unknown Hungary* I. 111 The Yougo-Slaves, or Slaves of the south of Austria. **1917** F. S. COPELAND tr. *Vosnjak's Bulwark against Germany* xv. 250 The unification of the Jugoslavs. **1922** *Encycl. Brit.* XXX. 372/1 The Yugoslavs..are the most numerous people in the [Balkan] peninsula. **1943** J. B. PRIESTLEY *Daylight on Saturday* xxv. 194 If you've got the morale—and even if you've got hardly anything else, like the Jugo-Slavs—you stand up and fight. **1948** R. A. D. FORREST *Chinese Lang.* i. 28 The feature *sc.* distinctive tone]..survives to this day in one Lithuanian dialect, with traces in Scandinavian and in a variety of Yugoslav. **1973** *Times* 29 Oct. 12/7 The new Electra is Danica Mastilovic, a Yugoslav, making her debut in the house.

B. *adj.* Of, pertaining to, or designating the people or state of Yugoslavia.

1853 L. H. KERR tr. *Robert's Slave Prov. Turkey* in *Ranke's Hist. Servia* (ed. 2) 378 Gaï's 'Illyrian Journal', the organ of the Serb and Yugo-Slave interests. **1916** B. VOSNJAK *Jugoslav Nationalism* 11 There have been..three Jugoslav state creations. **1920** *Edin. Rev.* July 42 Whatever else may be said of the Yugoslav movement..it is at any rate a national movement having its origins within..the peoples whose destiny it affects. **1967** *Listener* 29 June 843/3 Italian, Yugoslav, or Spanish workers have migrated to West Germany..or Switzerland. **1981** L. DEIGHTON *XPD* xxviii. 226 The duty officers could be sure of a bottle of Yugoslav riesling.

Yugoslavian (yūgoslā·viăn), *a.* and *sb.* Also **Jugo-.** [f. prec. + -IAN.] **A.** *adj.* = *YUGOSLAV *a.* **B.** *sb.* **a.** A native or inhabitant of Yugoslavia. **b.** *rare.* The Serbo-Croat language.

1923 W. J. LOCKE *Moordius & Co.* xiii. 180, I must be back to give dinner to the Jugo-Slavian minister. **1924** *Contemp. Rev.* Apr. 448 They cannot effectively crush the revolutionaries on Yugoslavian soil. **1949** E. POUND *Pisan Cantos* lxxx. 96 White boy says: do you speak Jugoslavian? **1953** A. SMITH *Blind White Fish in Persia* x. 204 Firstly, our Yugoslavian visas had not come through. **1962** A. LURIE *Love & Friendship* ii. 31 They didn't have them [*sc.* Boy Scouts] in Yugoslavia. Anyway, only for Yugoslavians. **1977** *New Yorker* 19 Sept. 49/2 There was a Yugoslavian boy who had brought along a portable silent keyboard with a weight attached to each key, to regulate the action. **1983** *Times* 3 Oct. 1/4 The Greek and the Yugoslavian were accustomed to the heat.

yuh (yə), repr. a colloq. (esp. Black English) pronunc. of YOU.

1906 [see *OUTA]. **1922** [see *tough nut* s.v. *TOUGH *a.* 10 a]. **1933** *Publ. Texas Folklore Soc.* XI. 101 She tol' me to ax yuh. **1952** [see *MACOUMÈRE]. **1967** E. BRATHWAITE in Ramchand & Gray *West Indian Poetry* (1972) 25 Yuh does get up, walk 'bout. **1969** [see *SECKO]. **1977** *Rolling Stone* 30 June 80/3 So get back to me as soon as you can, will yuh.

yuk, var. *YUCK *int.*, *sb.*[2], and *a.*

Yukaghir (yū·kăgiᵊɹ, yukăgīᵊ·ɹ), *sb.* (*a.*) Also **Yukaghire, Yukagir(e).** **a.** (A member of) a Mongoloid people of Arctic Siberia. **b.** The Palæo-Siberian language (of unknown affiliation) of this people. Also *attrib.* or as *adj.*

1842 C. H. COTTRELL *Recoll. Siberia* iv. 104 The Yukaghires, settled on the banks of the river Anuiy, maintain themselves the whole year on the reindeer they kill in spring and autumn. **1879** C. H. EDEN *Frozen Asia* ix. 208 The head-quarters of the Yukagires is on the River Anyui. **1898** [see *KORYAK]. **1906** *Daily Chron.* 4 Apr. 7/5 The sole survivors of a group of ten Yukagirs, are charged with having eaten the man's nephew... After that the Yukagir, although he had caught a swan, continued to eat human flesh. **1908** T. G. TUCKER *Introd. Natural Hist. Lang.* 149 The Hyperborean speeches of Asia, some of which may or may not form a family, include..*Yukaghir*. **1932** [see *CHUKCHEE, CHUKCHI *sb.* and *a.*]. **1948** D. DIRINGER *Alphabet* 35 Sad love-story of a Yukaghir girl. **1951** W. K. MATTHEWS *Languages U.S.S.R.* ii. 3 Yukagir (Odul), the mother-tongue of fewer than 500 persons in Northern Yakutia. **1964** tr. *Levin & Potapov's Peoples of Siberia* 789 The name 'Yukagir' was borrowed by the Russians from the Yakuts, but its origin is probably Tungusic. **1972** W. B. LOCKWOOD *Panorama Indo-Europ. Lang.* 154 There are isolated languages spoken by diminutive populations. These are Gilyak..and, with a thousand speakers..or less..Yukagir (Yukagir National Area). **1981** M. C. SMITH *Gorky Park* I. xiv. 213 He was more Siberian than any of us... The Borodins..lived with the Yukagir, the reindeer herders. **1983** *Word* XXXIV. 217 The focus system of Yukagir, and case and negation in Uralic are treated in syntax sections.

‖ **yukata** (yuka·ta). Also **Yukata, yukatta;** 9 **ukata.** [Jap., f. *yu* hot water, bath + *kata* short for *katabira* a light kimono.] A light cotton kimono, freq. with stencil designs, orig. intended to be worn after a bath, but now also used as a housecoat.

1822 F. SHOBERL tr. *Titsingh's Illustr. Japan* II. 254 The *ukata.*, a robe of fine linen; it is put on in coming out of the bath to dry the body. **1881** SATOW & HAWES *Handbk. Japan* p. xvi, Japanese loose cotton gowns (*yukata*). **1886** J. LA FARGE *Let.* 3 Sept. in *Artist's Lett. from Japan* 229 A—..rode along with only a partial covering of *yukatta*, and attracted no attention. **1936** K. NOHARA *True Face of Japan* v. 130 Dons the *yukata*, the light, informal, Japanese house-jacket of coloured cotton. **1960** B. LEACH *Potter in Japan* vi. 133 My Yukata (provided cotton kimono) reached to my knees. *Ibid.* ix. 195 Visitors were strolling the streets in 'yukatta' (cotton kimono provided by hotels). **1970** *Guardian* 12 Dec. 6/6 The donning of the cool cotton *yukata* robe and slippers is the first sloughing of Western identity. **1981** J. MELVILLE *Sort of Samurai* ix. 75 All four of them were now wearing cotton *yukatas*.

Yukawa (yukā·wă). *Nucl. Physics.* The name of H. *Yukawa* (b. 1907), Japanese physicist, used *attrib.* with reference to the theory of the strong interaction between nucleons put forward by him, in which it is mediated by the exchange of particles (*Yukawa particles*) subsequently identified with pions; **Yukawa potential,** a potential function of the form $V = V_0(r/r_0)^{-1}$ exp-$(-r/r_0)$, occurring in Yukawa's theory of the nuclear force.

1938 *Nature* 1 Oct. 592/2 The discovery of a new particle, the Yukawa particle or 'heavy electron', has given a new orientation to many of our ideas. **1948** *Proc. Cambr. Philos. Soc.* XLIV. 90 As an illustration of the treatment developed above the nuclear field as described by the Yukawa potential $U(r) = -b\lambda r^{-1}e^{-\lambda r}$ will be treated. **1964** *Listener* 29 Oct. 661/1 Immediately after the war, many physicists..became deeply involved in these problems, especially the nature of protons, neutrons, and the Yukawa mesons. **1968** C. G. KUPER *Introd. Theory Superconductivity* xv. 258 The Yukawa force between nucleons has a pairing part, and the methods of the BCS theory are applicable. **1973** R. J. BLIN-STOYLE *Fund. Interactions & Nucleus* i. 3 The earlier Lagrangian formulation of strong interactions based on Yukawa type interactions has continued to play an important role. **1974** FRAUENFELDER & HENLEY *Subatomic Physics* viii. 187 If virtual pions are exchanged between nucleons, the basic Yukawa reaction $N \to N' + \pi$ should conserve isospin. **1977** P. D. B. COLLINS *Introd. Regge Theory & High Energy Physics* i. 42 The simplest form of potential which has the short-range character appropriate to strong interactions is the Yukawa potential $U(r) = g^2 e^{-\mu r}/r$, where g^2 is the coupling strength and μ^{-1} is the range.

Yuki (yū·ki), *sb.* (*a.*) Also 9 **Yuka, Yukeh,** etc. [a. Wintu *yu·keh*, lit. 'stranger, enemy'.] **a.** (A member of) a group of linguistically related American Indian peoples, comprising the Yuki, Huchnom, and Wappo tribes, inhabiting the coast of north-western California. **b.** The language spoken by this people. Also *attrib.* or as *adj.*

1858 S. P. STORMS *Let.* 14 Aug. in *Ann. Rep. Commissioner of Indian Affairs for 1858* CIX. 307 About three thousand Nome Cults or Yukas make this valley [*sc.* Round Valley in northern California] their headquarters. **1863** *Hist. Mag.* VII. 123/1 The Yukeh, or as the name is variously spelt, Yuka, Yuques, and Uca, are the original inhabitants of the..Round Valley in Tehama County, California. **1875** H. H. BANCROFT *Native Races Pacific States* III. II. iii. 648 In Round Valley, northern California, there is the..Yuka language. *Ibid.* 643 At Humboldt Bay a language called Patawat is mentioned, and in Round Valley the Yuka. **1877** S. POWERS *Tribes Calif.* xiv. 129 If a Yuki stumbles and falls on the march..it is a bad omen. *Ibid.*, He has seen Yuki dead left on the field. **1900** J. FRAZER *Golden Bough* (ed. 2) I. i. 34 When the men of the Yuki tribe of Indians in California were away fighting, the women at home..danced..in a circle, chanting and waving leafy wands. **1923** A. L. KROEBER *Anthropol.* iii. 90 In the native Californian language known as Yuki, *ko* means go. **1939** H. M. WORMINGTON *Ancient Man in North Amer.* vi. 256 Among living Indians in North America the Cahuilla tribes of inland southern California and the Pomo and Yuki of northern coastal California, are thought to show the greatest number of Amurian traits. **1965** *Canad. Jrnl. Linguistics* X. 99 Hokan-Siouan in Sapir's arrangement includes six major constituent units..Hokan-Coahuiltecan, Yuki, [etc.]. **1974** *Encycl. Brit. Micropædia* X. 844/1 Warfare was apparently frequent—between certain communities, between the different Yuki groups, and with other Californian Indians. *Ibid.* 844/2 The Yuki..were organized into communities composed of several scattered settlements. **1981** A. B. KEHOE *North Amer. Indians* vii. 376/2 Yuki and its sister language Wappo, both spoken north of San Francisco Bay.

yukky, var. *YUCKY *a.*

Yukon (yū·kɒn). [The name of the *Yukon* Territory in north-west Canada.] *Yukon stove*, a lightweight portable stove consisting of a small metal box divided into firebox and oven.

1898 W. B. HASKELL *Two Years in Klondyke* 75 The 'Yukon stove'..is a small sheet iron box with an oven at the back and a telescope pipe. **1943** W. CHASE *Sourdough Pot* xvi. 97 The stove, a sheet-iron affair, known as a Yukon stove, had a limited capacity. **1974** W. HUNT *North of 53* iv. 15 A wood-fired 'Yukon' stove, either square or round bottomed, and containing a small oven at the back end, provided cooking facilities and kept the cabin warm in the winter.

Also **Yu·koner,** an inhabitant of the Yukon Territory; **Yu·konesque** *a.*

c **1898** Yukoner [see *HOOCHINOO 2]. **1924** M. H. MASON *Arctic Forests* 84 These things have made the Yukoners the finest, most generous, and most virile population to be found on the whole continent of America. **1934** A. HUXLEY *Beyond Mexique Bay* 128 Our Yukonesque stampedes into any business that seems, at any given moment, to be doing well **1977** Yukoner [see *OUTSIDER I].

yulo (yū·loᵘ). Also **yuloh, yulow,** etc. [Prob. ad. Chinese (Cantonese) *iū-lŏ* to scull a boat, f. *iū* to shake + *lŏ* oar.] A Chinese sculling oar (see quot. 1899). So also as *v. intr.* to scull a boat with such an oar. Hence **yu·lohing** *vbl. sb.*

1878 H. A. GILES *Gloss. Reference* 170 *Yuloh, to,* to

scull a boat with an oar at the stern. From the Shanghai pronunciation of..*yao* to work..*lu* an oar. **1888** A. J. LITTLE *Through Yang-tse Gorges* 320 In addition to these, two lateral yuloes (sculls worked by a screw motion),..were attached to the sides. **1899** I. L. BISHOP *Yangtze Valley & Beyond* xiii. 145 Others are toiling at *yu-lows*, big broad-bladed sculls, worked over the stern or parallel to the junk's side. **1905** *N. & Q.* 22 Apr. 305/1 The *yuloh* is the single oar used over the stern for the propulsion of sampans and barges, after the manner sometimes called sculling in England. To *yuloh* is to row a boat in that fashion. The meaning is literally 'push and pull wood'. **1911** J. D. BALL *Chinese at Home* xvi. 203 Ferryboats slowly cross the river... The loads of the coolies are put in the bows of the boat, where also occasionally is to be seen a leper, who is not allowed amongst the other passengers. The ferryman *yeeoo-loes* at the stern. **1921** *Outward Bound* June 36/1 The junk is propelled when possible by great oars, called by the Chinese 'yulos', projecting out from either side. **1927** *Chambers's Jrnl.* Mar. 163/1 We pass a fishing boat; a woman with a willowy figure bending to the yulow at one end. **1941** J. HOMER *Dawn Watch in China* iv. 93 Junks bound downstream were manned on the foredeck with six or eight or a dozen oarsmen, who stood, each to his oar poling forward into the fast water and singing in unison the minor wordless river chant of the sacred Yangtze. Now and then, the helmsman would *yuloh* in a high-pitched scream were he called forth the wind. **1966** G. R. G. WORCESTER *Sail & Sweep in China* ii. 11 In rowing, as in so many other arts, the Chinese show their great independence of thought; and in the yuloh or sculling oar, they demonstrate a perfect example of applied mechanics which can, confidently, be dated back to the Later Han Dynasty AD25–220. *Ibid.* 12 When operated by a Chinese, even by a child, yulohing appears to be supremely simple. **1981** *Jrnl. R. Naval Med. Service* LXVII. 46/2 Navigable by one man using a large yulo at the stern.

yum (yʌm), *int.* [Echoic.] An exclamation of pleasurable anticipation, with implication of sensual or gustatory satisfaction; freq. reduplicated as *yum-yum*, etc.

Some of the reduplicated examples are not clearly distinguishable from those given s.v. *YUM-YUM *sb.* and *a.* below.

1878 *Burlington Hawkeye* in *Irish Monthly* VI. 688 How we would like to get hold of the man... Alone. In the woods, with a revolver in our hip-pocket. Revenge is sweet; yum, yum, yum. **1899** KIPLING *Stalky & Co.* 239 Pretty lips..Seem to say—Come away. Kissy! come, come!..Yummy-yum-yum! **1922** JOYCE *Ulysses* 173 Kissed her mouth. Yum. **1942** O. NASH *Good Intentions* 143 And fish are only something about which some people say, 'Yum yum, right out of the water and fried to a delicate golden brown.' **1959** 'J. CHRISTOPHER' *Scent of White Poppies* iii. 40 When she had gone, Bella said: 'Yum-yum. Really luscious.' **1962** A. LURIE *Love & Friendship* iii. 45 Miranda cut a piece of warm coffee cake, handed it to Emmy... 'Oh, yum. Thank you.' **1982** S. PARETSKY *Indemnity Only* xii. 155 'Lotty talked her into..making homemade enchiladas, yum-yum.' 'Yum-yum,' the two little girls chorused.

Hence **yu·mmy** *a. colloq.*, delicious, delectable; also as *int.*

1899 [see *YUM *int.*]. **1934** WEBSTER, Yummy *adj.* **1950** 'S. RANSOME' *Deadly Miss Ashley* xii. 147 Lora's attractive face or Dorothea's yummy figure. **1955** J. P. DONLEAVY *Ginger Man* xix. 213 Sitting, facing one another across the white table. Bacon and eggs, tea, bread and butter. Yummy. **1955** H. KURNITZ *Invasion of Privacy* (1956) vi 47, I adore movie stars. Gregory Peck! Yummy! **1970** P. ZELVER *Honey Bunch* xx. 96 Thanks a lot for the lemonade. It was yummy. **1979** *Evening Standard* 18 Sept 23/2 Mr. Zamoyski is a handsome devil himself—such a yummy photograph on the back of the jacket.

Yuma[1] (yū·mă), *sb.* and *a.* Also 9 **Umea.** [a. Sp., ad. Pima-Papago *yu·mi*.] **A.** *sb.* **a.** (A member of) an Indian people inhabiting south-west Arizona and the adjoining areas of Mexico and California, now officially referred to as the Quechan. **b.** The language of this people. **B.** *adj.* Of, pertaining to, or designating this people or their language.

1831 J. O. PATTIE in R. G. Thwaite *Early Western Trav.* (1905) XVIII. 188 Here we found the tribe of Umeas. **1849** A. W. WHIPPLE *Jrnl.* 1 Dec. in H. R. Schodcraft *Hist. & Stat. Information Indian Tribes* (1852) II. IV. 118 To this day among the Yumas I have never seen anger expressed. *Ibid.*, I will add a vocabulary of the Yuma (or rather Cuchan) language. **1877** H. S. GATSCHET *Indian Lang. Pacific States* 156 The term *opa*, composing several of these tribal names, is taken from the Yuma, and means man. **1891** D. G. BRINTON *Amer. Race* II. ii. 109 It has also been called..the Apache, that being the Yuma word for 'fighting men'. **1892** *Amer. Anthropologist* Oct. 326 This pamphlet..is the fourth of the author's Yuma series. **1907** [see *G STRING 2 a]. **1942** *Amer. Anthropologist* July–Sept. 425 Certain structural features of the Yuma language should be outlined... Yuma has three 'parts of speech'. **1965** *Language* XLI. 305 Yuma has /a/. **1973** A. H. WHITEFORD *North Amer. Indian Arts* 13 Modeling and paddling is a technique..still used by the Papago and Yuma of Arizona. **1979** *Tucson Mag.* Apr. 27/3 In 1780 Teodoro de Croix..ordered that two new settlements of Spaniards be established among the Yuma Indians on the Lower Colorado River.

Yuma[2] (yū·mă). The name of *Yuma* county in north-eastern Colorado, used chiefly *attrib.* to designate the remains of a prehistoric culture discovered there, and applied esp. to a type of projectile point. Cf. *FOLSOM.

1932 E. B. RENAUD in *Proc. Colorado Museum Nat. Hist.* 19 Nov. 5 Yuma and Folsom artifacts. *Ibid.*, The number and variety of artifacts of this splendid collection from the Yuma district contributed greatly to our better knowledge of the points which, in recognition, we named 'Yuma points' to distinguish them from the true Folsom type. **1948** A. L. KROEBER *Anthropol.* (rev. ed.) xvi. 684 Points called Yumas have now and then been found in Folsom association, as at Clovis. **1949** *Time* 12 Sept. 69/1 Not much is known about Yuma Man, for no Yuma skeleton has yet been found. **1960** C. WINICK *Dict. Anthropol.* 277/2 Yuma implements are unfluted.

Yuman (yū·măn), *a.* and *sb.* [f. *YUMA[1]: cf. -AN.] **A.** *adj.* Of, pertaining to, or designating various related Indian peoples of Arizona, Mexico and California, or the languages spoken by them. **B.** *sb.* **a.** A member of this group of peoples. **b.** A language family of Hokan stock to which the languages of these people belong.

1891 J. W. POWELL in *7th Ann. Rep. Bureau Amer. Ethnol.* 13 With the exception of certain small areas possessed by Shoshonean tribes, Indians of the Yuman stock occupied the Colorado River from its mouth as far up as Cataract Creek. **1901** G. W. JAMES *Indian Basketry* x. 161 The carrying frame and net of the Mohave Indians, of the Yuman stock, dwelling about the mouth of the Colorado River. **1920** *Univ. Calif. Publ. Amer. Archaeol. & Ethnol.* XVI. 478 The Yuma, who call themselves Kwichyana..are known to other Yumans by dialect variants of the same name. **1933** L. SPIER *Yuman Tribes of Gila River* 151 The Maricopa have transposed the normal Yuman word from south to west. **1950** *Nat. Hist.* Feb. 76/3 They speak essentially the same language —a dialect of the Yuman tongue. **1952** *Amer. Anthropologist* Jan.–Mar. 80 The cultivated plants and the agricultural methods of the Yumans. **1963** [see *SHASTAN *a.* and *sb.*]. **1965** [see *MOHAVE]. **1970** *Language* XLVI. 533 The Yuman languages..were early recognized as constituting a linguistic family. **1974** *Encycl. Brit. Micropædia* X. 845/3 The total number of Yuman peoples remaining in the 1970s..was uncertain. **1978** *Language* LIV. 219 It crops up again in Southern California, in one subgroup of the Yuman family. *Ibid.* 505 The present collection indicates that such a tradition has now also been established for Yuman, a Hokan family of Arizona, California.

yump (yʌmp), *v. slang.* [Alteration of JUMP *v.*, repr. the supposed pronunciation of it by Swedish speakers or the Norw. *jump* jump (sb.), *jumpe* jump (vb.).] *intr.* Of a rally car or its driver: to leave the ground while taking a crest at speed. So **yu·mping** *vbl. sb.*

1962 *Motoring News* 22 Nov. 7 (*caption*) 'Yumping', a pastime dear to Scandinavian rallyists, was seen practised to the full for the first time in this country during the R.A.C. Rally. **1968** [see *ROLL *v.*[2] 18 a]. **1968** *Sun* 12 Nov. 8/5 Yumping happens..when cars literally jump into the air. They take off when taking crests at speed.

Also as *sb.*, an instance of 'yumping' (see also quot. 1980).

1975 *Country Life* 4 Dec. 1529/2 Clark had an enormous 'yump' (Swedish rally parlance for a car leaving the ground and hurtling for some distance before landing heavily). **1980** *Sunday Express* 24 Aug. 23 (Advt.), Yump: Rally jargon for a sharp crest in the road, which causes a car to take off at speed.

yumpie (yʌ·mpi). *colloq.* (orig. *U.S.*). Also **yump, Yumpie.** [f. the initial letters of *y*oung *u*pwardly *m*obile *p*eople: see -IE.] = *YUPPIE.

1984 *Economist* 17 Mar. 40 Mr. Hart seems to have drawn much of his support from young upwardly mobile people and young urban professionals—yumps and yuppies, as they are called. **1984** *Times* 21 Mar. 14/2 Sometimes 'Yuppies' are referred to as 'Yumpies', meaning Young, upwardly-mobile people. **1984** *N.Y. Times Rev. Bks.* 25 Mar. 20 The yumpies climbing the ladder of success with great agility can be described as upscaling. **1984** *Chicago Sun-Times* 25 Mar. 7 The ultimate Yumpie status symbol is to have a child suffering flash-card burn-out.

yum-yum: see *YUM int.

yum-yum (yʌm,yʌm), *sb. slang.* [Redupl. of *YUM *int.*] **a.** An action providing a pleasurable or delicious sensation; love-making; also (*Naval slang*), love-letters. Also *yum-yum girl* (euphem.), prostitute.

1885 *Punch* 3 Jan. 4/1 You and me's got our notions of yum-yum, as isn't fur wide o' the mark. **1939** A. HUXLEY *After Many a Summer* I. iv. 45 Enjoying what she called 'a bit of yum-yum'. **1943** HUNT & PRINGLE *Service Slang* 71 *Yum yum*, love letters. **1960** 'S. HARVESTER' *Chinese Hammer* xxv. 202 Yum-yum tarts from Hong Kong or ex-temple dancers from Java. **1962** A. BUCHWALD *How Much is that in Dollars?* 124 One of the chiefs said, 'Don't let her kid you. All her girls are really yum-yum girls from the dance halls'. **1962** *Times* 12 July 13/5 Would the sin bosun (chaplain) frown, one wonders, at hearing a love-letter described as a 'yum-yum'? **1967** S. BECKETT *Texts for Nothing* III. 86 Come, ducky, it's time for yum-yum.

b. *spec.* Tasty food (of various kinds).

1889 *'Aunt Babette's' Cook Book* 330 *Yum-Yums.* Grate one cocoanut, reserving the milk; one pound and a half of pulverized sugar, whites of three eggs. **1932** O. O. MCINTYRE *Another 'Odd' Book* 5 Whenever I mention a longing for such old-fashioned yum-yums as gingersnaps..the response is immediate. **1941** J. SMILEY *Hash House Lingo* 58 *Yum-yum*, sugar.

yum-yum, *a. slang.* [f. as prec.] Excellent, first-class; delectable.

1890 BARRÈRE & LELAND *Dict. Slang* II. 428/2 *Yum-yum* (London), first-rate, elegant. **1922** JOYCE *Ulysses* 372 Howth settled for slumber tired of long days, of yumyum rhododendrons. **1962** R. PRAWER JHABVALA *Get Ready for Battle* iii. 135, I wish my cook could learn..how to make cheese pakoras like these, they are absolutely yum-yum.

Yunani (yunā·ni), *a.* Also **Unani.** [a. Arab. *yūnānī*, lit. 'Greek'.] Designating a Western system of medicine (opp. *AYURVEDIC *a.*). Occas. also applied to other disciplines (see quot. 1958).

1922 [see *AYURVEDIC *a.*]. **1958** O. CAROE *Pathans* iii. 45 The Yunani or Greek lore which so largely influenced Islamic *literae humaniores.* **1977** *Times Lit. Suppl.* 3 June 684/2 The traditional Hindu (Ayurvedic), Muslim (Unani) and Chinese medicine... Unani is Arabic for 'Ionian' and thus declares its descent from Greek medical thought. **1979** *Social Sci. & Med.* XIII.B. 339 Yūnāni medicine which lasted for a few centuries in the court of medieval Baghdad. **1979** V. MEHTA *Mamaji* iii. 39 The Unani system, which is based on ancient Greek medicine and relies on metallic compounds.

Yunca (yu·ŋkă). Also **Yunga, Yunka.** [Amer. Sp., a. Quechua *yunca* plain, valley.] **a.** The Chipayan language formerly spoken by a group of Indian peoples inhabiting the coast of Peru; = *MOCHICA *sb.* b. **b.** A member of such a people. Also *attrib.* or as *adj.*

1853 F. L. HAWKS tr. *Von Tschudi's Peruv. Antiquities* v. 117 The Quichua language has various dialects strongly marked..the *Yunca*, in the bishopric of Truxillo. **1871**, etc. [see *MOCHICA *a.* and *sb.*]. **1908** *Athenæum* 11 Apr. 447/1 Customary with the Natchez, Muizcas, Pokomames, Yuncas, and Incas of the American continent. **1950** J. A. MASON in J. H. Steward *Handbk. S. Amer. Indians* VI. 194 The *Yunca, Mochica*, or *Chimu* language..is practically extinct. **1954** *Internat. Jrnl. Amer. Ling.* Jan. 24 (*heading*) Yunka, language of the Peruvian coastal culture. *Ibid.*, A comparison of the Yunka language with Quechua has been made.

Yung Chêng (yuŋ tʃeŋ). Also **Yung Cheng, Yung-ching,** etc. The name of the reign of the third Chinese Emperor of the Ching dynasty (1723–35), used *attrib.* and *absol.* to denote a kind of porcelain produced during his reign, characterized by its delicate colouring.

1902 W. G. GULLAND *Chinese Porcelain* II. 384 It [is]..impossible to tell whether many of these rose pieces were made during this reign or early in the following, but they are all spoken of as Yung-ching pieces. **1906** R. L. HOBSON *Porcelain* iv. 34 The Yung-chêng porcelain has a character of its own and includes many innovations worthy of separate notice. **1908** J. F. BLACKER *Chats on Oriental China* ix. 115 The contrast between the delicacy of the detail is striking when compared with the broad treatment of the Kang-he period. On the one hand there is fine stipple work. This is Yung-ching. On the other hand there is a broad wash of colour. **1925** R. L. HOBSON *Later Ceramic Wares of China* vii. 62 (*heading*) Yung Chêng Porcelain (1723–35). **1949** G. SAVAGE *Ceramics for Collector* ii. 83 Celadons take on a bluish tinge, and obviously have some cobalt mixed with the glaze colour. Colour is applied in washes and fine, detailed drawing usually indicates Yung Chêng. **1971** R. QUEST *Death of Sinner* v. 42 'You mean it's not K'ang Hsi?' 'It's later—Yung Cheng.' **1976** SCOTT & KOSKI *Walk-In* x. 55 A wealthy importer of usually genuine Chinese *objets d'art*, mostly Yung-chêng porcelain.

Yunnanese (yunănī·z), *sb.* and *a.* Also 9 **Yun-Nese.** [Chinese *Yúnnán* (see below) + -ESE.] **A.** *sb.* **a.** A native or inhabitant of Yunnan, a province in S.W. China; also *collect.*, the people of Yunnan. **b.** The dialect of Yunnan. **B.** *adj.* Of or pertaining to Yunnan.

1849 *Ann. Propagation Faith* Mar. 109 A young physician from the province of Yun-nan evinced more generosity... This young Yun-Nese had led so strange a life. **1909** *N. China Herald* 18 Sept. 671/3 With their catch crops the Yunnanese in the eastern part of the province seemed as satisfied as they were at the time before wheat took the place of the now-departed opium. **1927** *Blackw. Mag.* Mar. 308/1 He had a full knowledge of Yunnanese, but these men were Lolos from Szechuan, and understood not a word. **1933** N. WALN *House of Exile* III. ii. 200 These Yunnanese soldiers were hired henchmen that Sun Yat-sen had brought to Canton to police the city. **1948** G. H. JOHNSTON *Death takes Small Bites* iv. 85 'It's usually thronged with people,' Coates continued boredly. 'Kachins and Shans, Yunnanese, Lisus, Burmese, Miaos.' **1959** C. OGBURN *Maurauders* (1960) iii. 92 Cantonese and Yunnanese..slammed their vehicles from one gear to another with a grinding scream. **1959** *Times* 19 Mar. 14/7 It was found expedient not to have Yunnanese mules in Lucifer's section. **1964** M. A. K. HALLIDAY et al. in J. A. Fishman *Readings Sociol. of Lang.* (1968) 145 In China, you speak Cantonese if you come from Canton, Pekinese if you come from Peking and Yunnanese if you come from Yunnan. **1981** P. BARR *Chinese Alice* iv. 94 Golden Persimmon sang..and the Yunnanese watched her.

yup (yʌp), colloq. (orig. U.S.) var. of YES. Cf. YEP, dial. pron. of YES.

1906 *Cent. Mag.* Jan. 410/2 'Will you go—if I swear?' 'Yup,' said Pinchas, airing his American. **1919** G. MURRAY *Aristophanes & War Party* 36 *Demos.* You see those rows and rows of people? *Offal-monger.* Yup. **1923** E. F. WYATT *Invisible Gods* II. iv. 78 'Paul as mean as ever?' 'Yup,' replied Hancock..'and a little meaner.' **1947** [see *supercolossal* adj. s.v. *SUPER- 9 a]. **1959** E. H. CLEMENTS *High Tension* iv. 63 'You're staying here, then?' 'Yup.' **1968** S. CHALLIS *Death on Quiet Beach* v. 75 'Will you pay the fine?'..'Yup.' **1978** J. IRVING *World according to Garp* xii. 232 'Is that you, Roger?' 'Yup.'

Yupik (yū·pik), *a.* and *sb.* [See quot. 1951¹.] **A.** *adj.* Of, pertaining to, or designating an Eskimo-Aleut language spoken in Siberia and Alaska, or the speakers of it. **B.** *sb.* This language.

1951 M. SWADESH *Internat. Jrnl. Amer. Ling.* Apr. 69/1 The phonologic material shows an unmistakable cleavage between two groups of dialects which may be conveniently called the Yupic and Inupik divisions by reference to their treatment of the root for *human being* (juk versus inuk; these are the words for *real person* in Kuskokwim and Barrow respectively). *Ibid.* 70/2 The dichotomy between Yupik and Inupik is clear and geographically abrupt. *Ibid.*, We find nothing in the [Wales] dialect which minimizes the depth of its separation from Yupik Eskimo. **1967** W. H. OSWALT *Alaskan Eskimos* p. xiv, In Alaska two languages, Inupik and Yupik are spoken. *Ibid.* iv. 115 The Yupik speakers..would be expected to have had a greater long-term stability than the Inuit. **1974** *Encycl. Brit. Macropædia* VI. 963/2 In 1961 a program was started..with the active participation of Yupik Eskimos, for working out a systematic Eskimo orthography in the Roman alphabet. *Ibid.*, Greenlandic *ũvoq*..is related to the Asian Yupik form *ugu-*. **1977** *New Yorker* 20 June 55/2 The big river delivers the wood to the Yupik Esimos of the western coast. **1980** M. E. KRAUSS *Alaska Native Languages* App. II. 91 There is.. the well known sharp division between Yupik and what we in Alaska usually call Inupiaq. *Ibid.* 103 With a dense and increasing population, almost entirely Yupik, the Yupik language remained..strong.

yuppie (yʌ·pi). *colloq.* (orig. U.S.). Also **Yuppie.** [f. the initial letters of *y*oung *u*rban *p*rofessional: see -IE.] A jocular term for a member of a socio-economic group comprising young professional people working in cities. Also *attrib.* Cf. *YUMPIE.

1984 PIESMAN & HARTLEY (*title*) The yuppie handbook. **1984** [see *YUMPIE]. **1984** *Times* 21 Mar. 14/2 A new term has been introduced into the American political lexicon... It is 'Yuppie', which stands for Young, urban professional people. **1984** *Observer* 8 Apr. 12/1 We have got to break this yuppie image. **1984** *Guardian* 22 Oct. 6/6 The yuppies themselves, in the 25–34 age group, supported Senator Gary Hart in the primaries.

Yurak (yiūᵊ·ræk). [Native name.] = *NENETS (see quot. 1972). Also *Comb.*, as *Yurak-Samoyed(e)*.

1882 H. LANSDELL *Through Siberia* I. viii. 103 Reclus ..speaks of the Yurak-Samoyedes as still practising their bloody rites. **1911** *Daily News* 3 Nov. 1 Great praise is due to the Russian Red Cross Society for the noble way in which the women of this corps work among the revolting and diseased Yuraks. **1939** L. H. GRAY *Foundations of Lang.* 369 The languages of the Uralic family are as follows..*Samoyede* group: Yurak, Yenisei-Samoyede, [etc.]. **1952** *Trans. Philol. Soc.* 118 Yurak-Samoyede *paju, pal'* 'close, thick'. **1954**, etc. [see *NENETS]. **1964** tr. *Levin & Potapov's Peoples of Siberia* 547 Before the Revolution the Russians called the Nentsy Samoyeds or Yuraks. **1972** *Language* XLVIII. 208 Calling the language and people 'Yurak' is an anachronism. Since 1917 a native self-designation has come into use in the Soviet Union, which I render as 'Nenets'. 'Yurak' arose from a term applied to the eastern Nenets by their Enets and Nganasan neighbours. **1975** G. F. CUSHING tr. *Hajdu's Finno-Ugrian Languages & Peoples* iii. 216 The Nenets are generally termed Yurak-Samoyeds

Yurok (yiūᵊ·rǫk), *sb.* and *a.* Also 9 **Euroc, Youruk.** [a. Karok *yúruk* (a considerable distance downriver; cf. *yurúkva·rara* Yurok Indian, lit. 'downriver person'.] **A.** *sb.* **a.** (A member of) an Indian people of northern California. **b.** The language of this people, distantly related to Algonquian and Wiyot. **B.** *adj.* Of, pertaining to, or designating this people or their language.

1851 [see *KAROK]. **1872** *Overland Monthly* Apr. 326/2, I have seen a half-dozen tatterdemalion Eurocs.. come rushing down through the *chaparral.* **1875** H. H. BANCROFT *Native Races Pacific States* III. 641 On the lower Klamath, the Euroc language prevails. **1904** *Univ. Calif. Publ. Amer. Anthrop. & Ethnol.* II. III. 95 The belief in a previous world..is not uncommon. The Torint of the Eskimo ..the Waghe of the Yurok. **1913** *Amer. Anthropologist* XV. 621 Our knowledge of Wiyot and Yurok is still very incomplete. **1921** [see *CULTURALLY *adv.*]. **1946** L. BLOOMFIELD in H. Hoijer et al. *Ling. Structures Native America* 85 Two languages of California, Wiyot and Yurok, have been suspected of kinship with Algonquian. **1954** E. A. HOEBEL *Law of Primitive Man* ii. 25 An aggrieved Yoruk who felt he had a legitimate claim engaged the legal services of two nonrelatives from a community other than his own. **1962** [see *KAROK]. **1973** A. H. WHITEFORD *N. Amer. Indian Arts* 47 Half-twist overlay was used by the Yurok ..for fine flexible mats. **1977** R. HOLLAND *Self & Social Context* ii. 40 Witness the astonishingly beautiful analogy between the oral anxiety of the Yurok people and the uncertainty of the salmon run on which they depend as a culture. **1981** A. B. KEHOE *N. Amer. Indians* vii. 376/2 Macro-Algonkian is represented by two language isolates, Yurok..and Wiyot.

Yurrup (yʌ·rəp). Repr. a supposed U.S. pronunc. of *Europe*.

1883 *National Police Gaz.* 17 Mar. 3/1 The entire court of shyster lawyers, wives and contractors' daughters who have been to Yurrup. **1960** N. MITFORD *Don't tell Alfred* iii. 34 There are the [American] business men trying to make a better position for themselves at home as experts on Yurrup. **1980** R. MCCRUM *In Secret State* xiii. 123 American students enthusing about Yurrup.

Yuruk (yiūᵊ·ruk), *sb.* (*a.*). [a. Turk. *yürük* (also used) = nomad.] (A member of) a nomadic people inhabiting Anatolia. Also *attrib.* or as *adj.*

1869 H. F. TOZER *Researches Highlands of Turkey* I. i. 13 In one of these glades we found a tribe of Yuruk with their flocks. **1896** D. G. HOGARTH *Wandering Scholar in Levant* iii. 53 The 'Turk', most rightly so called, is the despised *Yuruk*, the 'wanderer', a name applied to the half-settled population, roaming in summer.., collected in the winter into villages. **1907** G. BELL *Let.* 1 May (1927) I. xi. 233 So we rode back along the beautiful grassy shores of the lake, where the Yuruks were watching their flocks and herds. **1959** *Listener* 6 Aug. 221/1 Three weeks among the Yuruks. **1963** *Times* 9 May 14/6 The Yürüks are a tribe of nomads who spend their winter in the equable south of Anatolia and move up to the plateaux and highlands for the summer. **1974** *Encycl. Brit. Micropædia* X. 848/2 *Yürük rugs*, handwoven by nomadic people in various parts of Anatolia... Rugs from Eastern Anatolia, many of them Kurdish rugs..but classed as Yürük, show a wide range of rich and unusual colour shades. **1983** J. THOMPSON *Carpet Magic* 19/2 (*caption*) One member of a Turkish nomad, or Yuruk, family on migration.

yus, obs. form of YES. Add: Still current in *dial.* and non-Standard use. Also **yhus** (*once*), **yuss.** (Examples.)

a **1300** [see YES *adv.* 2 a, 3 a]. **1828** W. CARR *Dial. Craven* (ed. 2) II. 279 *Yus*, Yes. **1888** S. O. ADDY *Gloss. Words Sheffield* 292 *Yus, adv.*, yes. **1890** KIPLING *Many Inventions* (1893) 284 Ho yuss! 'Taint much though, is it? **1898** J. D. BRAYSHAW *Slum Silhouettes* 15 'Yus!' responded his wife. **1934** J. FRANKLYN *This Gutter Life* xx. 159 Yhus, movin' aht, are yer? Norra bad flet. **1968** C. M. VINES *Little Nut-Brown Man* i. 32 'Please, may I ask you something?' 'Yus!' said he [*sc.* Lord Beaverbrook], employing, in good humour, this cheerful Canadianism.

yusho (yū·ʃōᵘ). *Path.* [Jap., f. *yu* oil + *sho* disease.] A disease characterized by the development of brown staining of the skin and severe acne, caused by the ingestion of polychlorinated biphenyls.

1969 GOTO & HIGUCHI in *Fukuoka Acta Med.* LX. 409 (*heading*) The symptomatology of yusho (chlorobiphenyls poisoning) in dermatology. *Ibid.*, We thought its cause might be rice oil... The case has been called Yusho. **1973** G. L. WALDBOTT *Health Effects of Environmental Pollutants* xviii. 226/1 In 1968 about 1000 persons in southern Japan developed darkened skin..and severe acne... The illness was named 'Yusho', or rice oil disease, because the patients had eaten food cooked with contaminated rice oil. **1977** *Lancet* 22 Jan. 176/1 Chisato Hirayama provides a chapter on the clinical aspects of *yusho* (oil disease), the important skin symptoms being reviewed separately.

Yusufzai (yū·sufzai), *sb.* and *a.* Also **Yusafzai**; 9 **Eusofzye, Eusafzai,** etc. [Pers. *yūsuf* Joseph + *-zāī* bringing forth.] **A.** *sb.* (A member of) a Pathan tribal group inhabiting the North-West Frontier Province of India. **B.** *adj.* Of, pertaining to, or designating this people.

1815 M. ELPHINSTONE *Caubul* III. i. 328 The Eusofzyes are a very numerous tribe. **1838** in *Parl. Papers 1839* XL. 29 Shah Shooja-ool-Moolk disclaims all title ..to.. Peshaur, with the Eusefzye territory. **1857** S. COTTON *Nine Years on North-West Frontier* (1868) ix. 220 The column placed under his orders on the Euzofzaie Border. **1886** [see *-OLOGY, OLOGY 2]. **1887** KIPLING *Plain Tales from Hills* (1888) 24 A Eusufzai horse-thief. **1899** *Dict. Pathan Tribes* 234/1 *Yusufzai* (73,000), a great group of Pathan tribes which includes those of the Black Mountain, the Bunerwals, the Swatis, the people of Dir and the Panjkora valley, and the inhabitants of the Yusufzai plain in British territory. **1900** R. WARBURTON *Eighteen Years in Khyber* v. 52 Mukarrub Khan of Panjtar..was another pleasing character connected with Yusufzai politics. **1940** P. SYKES *Hist. Afghanistan* I. xix. 290 In the autumn of that same year Babur..decdied on an expedition against the Yusufzais. **1953** O. CAROE *Soviet Empire* v. 86 Another Yusufzai *maira.* **1958**—— *Pathans* i. 14 A Yusufzai or a Khalil..if he is asked who he is, will always reply, 'I am an Afghan.' **1978** 'M. M. KAYE' *Far Pavilions* xi. 170 The men of his own troop were drawn largely from the Border tribes: Yusafzai, Orakzai and Khattak. **1983** J. C. GRIFFITHS *Queen of Spades* ii. 26 Hussein Rahman, a Yusufzai Pathan.

Yuvaraja (yuvărā·dʒā). Also **Jubaraj, Yuvaraj, Yuveraj, Yuvraj.** [a. Hindi, f. Skr. *yuva-* young + *rājā*: see RAJA, RAJAH.] The male heir to an Indian state or principality; the crown prince.

1893 R. LETHBRIDGE *Golden Bk. India* p. xv, In some of the Orissa Tributary Mahâls ..the heir-apparent is styled *Jubaraj* or *Yuvaraj.* **1916** N. SINGH *King's Indian Allies* I. xii. 150 To distinguish the heir-apparent from the other sons, it is customary to call the former by some distinctive title, *Yuvaraja* in the case of Hindus. **1931** *Times of India* 6 Nov. 5/4 On May 28, 1930, he was received, with the Yuvraj, at Court at Buckingham Palace. **1937** W. H. SAUMAREZ SMITH *Let.* 3 Jan. in *Young Man's Country* (1977) ii. 50 On the 30th, I saw Prince Jaya's father, the Yuvaraja. **1953** E. M. FORSTER *Hill of Devi* 161 Vikky, henceforward to be referred to as the Yuvraj (Crown Prince), had now developed into a charming and intelligent youth. **1978** 'M. M. KAYE' *Far Pavilions* iii. 54 The young crown-prince, Lalji, Yuveraj of Gulkote. **1982** K. SINGH *Heir Apparent* i. 1 The birth of a Yuvaraj (heir apparent) was always a matter for rejoicing.

yuzbashi (yuzbɑ·ʃi). Also **Yuzbachi, Yuz-bashi, Yuzbashi.** [Turk. *yüzbaşı*, lit. 'one who is head of a hundred', f. *yüz* hundred + *baş* head.] A captain in the Turkish army; in the Turkish navy, a first lieutenant. Cf. *BIMBASHI.

1876 [see *BIMBASHI]. **1907** *Blackw. Mag.* June 806/2 Our procession was headed by a Yuz-bashi. **1908** M. PICKTHALL *Children of Nile* xxxiii. 268 Word of his coolness during the bombardment having reached the ear of power, he found himself raised to the rank of yuzbashi and honoured with a small command. **1920** *Glasgow Herald* 21 Jan. 4 The author..is an umquile Yuzbashi of the Imperial Ottoman Naval College. **1969** R. MILLAR *Kut* v. 87 The Turkish *yuzbashi* (equivalent to a captain, literally means the commander of 100 troops) was ushered into the office still blindfolded.

‖ **yūzen** (yū·zen). Also **yuzen** and with capital initial. The name of Miyazaki *Yūzen*-sai (fl. mid-18th cent.), Japanese inventor of a technique of dyeing silk fabric in which rice-paste is applied to areas which are not to be dyed, used *attrib.* and *absol.* with reference to this process and the designs produced. Also **yūzen-zome** (see quot. 1983).

1902 [see *HABUTAI]. **1911** *Encycl. Brit.* XV. 183 The difference between the results of the ordinary and the yūzen process of dyeing is, in fact, the difference between a stencilled sketch and a finished picture. **1958** K. NOMACHI *Jap. Textiles* 21 Yuzen pattern is the design printed by the Yuzen process, with beautiful and graceful flowers and birds..as the motifs. The Yuzen process is of three kinds: Yuzen proper, hand painting, and stencil printing. **1964** NEWMAN & RYERSON *Jap. Art* x. 77 *Yūzen zome*, a method of producing elaborate multi-colour designs by starch dyeing. Came into vogue in the Edo period. **1968** G. T. WEBB tr. *Seiroku's Arts Japan* II. 214/2 The design of this *furisode*..a garment traditionally worn only by young girls, is executed in a variety of techniques, including *yūzen* and *shibori* dyeing and gold appliqué. In *yūzen-zome*, a hand-painted dyeing method, the patterns are first outlined with a color-resist of rice paste applied with a paper funnel or a chopstick-like wooden implement, and later filled in with dyes of any color desired. **1980** *Textile Designs Japan* (rev. ed.) I. 21 The invention of a new starch-resist dyeing technique, known as *yūzen*, during this period..led to undreamed of achievements in the dyeing of free-style graphic designs. **1983** Y. TAZAWA *Biogr. Dict. Jap. Art* 652 During and after the Genroku era..stencil dyeing was developed and became popular, for a large number of *yūzen* designs are mentioned... From amongst these dyes, the term *yūzen-zome* came to be used thereafter to refer to *all* such pattern dyeing and it is still used thus to the present day.

Yvorne (ivǭ·ɹn). The name of a village in the Vaud canton of S.W. Switzerland, used *absol.* to designate a white wine produced in the region.

1871 J. MURRAY *Handbk. for Travellers in Switzerland* (ed. 14) p. xxxii, *Yvorne* is considered the best Swiss white wine. **1888** [see *CORTAILLOD]. **1935** A. L. SIMON *Wines & Liqueurs* 61 *Yvorne*, one of the best Swiss white wines from Aigle, in the Upper Rhône Valley. **1962** *Economist* 29 Dec. 1283/1 The best whites are perhaps Yvorne and Dézaley. **1980** G. GREENE *Doctor Fischer of Geneva* ix. 54 Beside every plate was a bottle of good Yvorne.

Z

Z. Add: In the U.S. pronounced (zī). **I. 2. Z-bend,** a series of bends in a road forming a shape like a letter Z; **Z-fold** *a.* (of print-out paper) in a continuous strip that comes folded in alternate directions in a stacked pile; **Z-plan** *Archit.*, the ground-plan of a type of Scottish castle having a central block with a tower placed at each of two diagonally opposite corners; **Z-plastic** *a. Surg.*, involving the use of Z-shaped incisions; also as *sb.*, Z-plastic surgery; so **Z-plasty,** a technique in which one or more Z-shaped incisions is made (the diagonals forming one straight line) and the two triangular flaps of skin so formed are rotated and drawn across the diagonal before being stitched, so as to give a less obvious Z-shaped scar and minimize the effect of contraction; an operation in which this technique is used; also *Comb.*, as **Z-shaped** *a.*, in the shape of a Z; *spec.* in *Archæol.*, designating a rod motif found on Pictish stones.

1887 MACGIBBON & ROSS *Castellated & Domestic Architect. Scotl.* II. 6 As one form of plan is designated the L plan, it has occurred to us that the form we are now considering might..be called the Z plan. We have accordingly adopted this nomenclature. **1901** *Proc. Soc. Antiquaries Scotl.* XI. 91 The double-disc and crescent symbols of the Pictish stones may be connected with the worship of the Blessed Virgin, the Z and V-shaped rods being her floriated sceptre. **1908** F. R. FRAPRIE *Castles & Keeps of Scotl.* i. 22 A new and entirely Scotch plan is very common. This has been called the zigzag or Z plan. **1913** S. L. MCCURDY in *Surg., Gynecol. & Obstetr.* XVI. 209 (*heading*) Z-plastic surgery. *Ibid.* 212/2 (*caption*) Z-plastic operation of the neck for burn scar. **1927** *Sc. N & Q.* 3rd Ser. V. 2/1 Two plates of silver engraved with the double disc and Z-shaped rod symbol. **1934** *Surg., Gynecol. & Obstetr.* LVIII. 178/1 Davis has been interested in tracing the history of the use of Z plastic. **1940** *Ibid.* LXX. 942/1, 2 patients returned for further work after a Z plasty with skin graft. **1958** *New Statesman* 1 Nov. 590/2 The shops were grouped round the angles of a Z-bend in the road. **1964** R. BATTLE *Plastic Surg.* xii. 316 A Z-plasty should be done only on one aspect of the finger at a time, thereby avoiding complete disruption of the circulation. **1967** *Electronics* 6 Mar. 282/2 The smudge is gone from Z-fold paper. **1967** I. HENDERSON *Picts* v. 104 A selection of the commoner symbols is illustrated here, the most common of all being the crescent with an applied V-shaped rod, the double disc with an applied Z-shaped rod. **1973** J. LEASOR *Host of Extras* v. 69 About twelve miles of diabolical Z-bends. **1977** *Proc. R. Soc. Med.* LXX. 256/2 The Achilles tendon is lengthened by Z-plasty and then the posterior capsules of the ankle and subtalar joints are incised transversely. **1977** *Clinics in Plastic Surg.* IV. 207/1 Z-shaped techniques other than Z-plasties, which are referred to as 'Z-plastics', differ in the movement or lack of movement of the flaps formed by the zigzag incision. **1978** A. & G. RITCHIE *Anc. Monuments Orkney* 79 Began 1560, it is an excellent example of a Z-plan castle, comprising towers at diagonally opposite corners of a main block. **1982** *Computerworld* (U.S.) 15 Mar. 66 It [*sc.* a digital plotter] also uses Z-fold paper and disposable fiber-tip pens.

4. a. (Further examples.) Also conventionally representing the sound of snoring. Also as *v. intr.* to make such a noise or noises.

1909 H. G. WELLS *Tono-Bungay* I. ii. 67 He had a way of drawing air in at times through his teeth that gave a whispering zest to his speech. It's a sound I can only represent as a soft Zzzz. *Ibid.* III. ii. 326 He meditated for a time and Zzzzed softly. **1924** *Dialect Notes* V. 259 *Z-z-z* (buzzing, or snoring). **1951** *Blue Book Magazine* Jan. 25/1 A spark danced between two terminals, a filament snake spat an irate, 'Zzzt!' **1966** L. COHEN *Beautiful Losers* I. 16 Hiccup, jerk, zzzzzz, snort. **1967** V. C. WELBURN *Johnny so Long* II. i. 46 Lola: (*makes buzzing noise*) Zzzzzzz. **1975** *New Yorker* 21 Apr. 36/3 David sits in the chair, puts his arms on the armrests, presses his neck against the back of the chair, and moves his feet together. 'Zzzz,' he says, and his head falls forward. **1976** *Cambridge Independent Press* 16 Dec. 11. 3/2 The zzzzz-noise of the electric hare gliding past the opening traps grabs everyone's attention. **1983** *Private Eye* 4 Nov. 6/2 Once you have hit on a commercial product you just go on producing more of the same, over and..zzzz..over and..zzzz..over and..zzzzzzzzzzzzzzzz zzzzzzzzzzzzzzzzzzzzzzzzzzz. **1984** *Wall Street Jrnl.* 9 Oct. 28/2 We suspect public interest..more nearly resembles a cartoonist's depiction of a man sawing wood—ZZZZZZZZZ. **1984** *Oxford Star* 29/30 Nov. 19/3 Zzzzing off for forty winks on a regular basis may not sound much like Action Man stuff, but for Alex Gardner it's the most exciting part of the day.

b. In *colloq.* phr. *to catch some z's* and varr., to get some sleep (where z represents the sound of snoring). *U.S.*

Pronounced (ziz) in the U.S.

1963 *Amer. Speech* XXXVIII. 174 An onomatopoetic construction reported four times is *get some Z's*... Variants occurring once were: *bagging Z's, copping some Z's, cutting Z's,* and *knocking out Z's.* **1973** A. DUNDES *Mother Wit* 238 Got to go..cop me some z's. **1977** C. MCFADDEN *Serial* (1978) xxxii. 71/1 All Harvey wanted..was to pop his Sominex and catch a few z's.

II. 5. *axis of z*: now always *z-axis*; also *transf.*

1929, etc. [see *X 3 a]. **1967** *Electronics* 6 Mar. 2 (Advt.), Plug-in markers offer not only variable bandwidth, but also Z-axis or pulse-type marking.

8. Genetics. *Z* is used to designate the male-determining sex chromosome in species in which the female rather than the male is the heterogametic sex.

1917 T. H. MORGAN in *Amer. Naturalist* LI. 534 Since the female here [*sc.* in pigeons] is the heterozygotic sex (ZW) the results are such as would follow a direct influence on the sex chromosomes when the polar body is eliminated. **1925** *Ibid.* LIX. 133 The locus of the male tendency gene (M) is in the 'Z-chromosome' of which two are present in the male and one in the female. **1966** *Lancet* 24 Dec. 1397/2 The phenotypic expression of plumage factors on the Z chromosome of birds seems to be a function, principally, of gene dosage. **1971** [see *HETEROGAMETIC *a.*]. **1976** *Nature* 17 June 598/2 In avian species, the heterogametic (Z W) female sex possesses W-linked histocompatibility antigen.

9. Physics. *Z* is the symbol for the atomic number of an element.

1931 *Proc. R. Soc.* A. CXXXIII. 234 We have taken Z=8 (oxygen). **1962** F. I. ORDWAY et al. *Basic Astronautics* xii. 502 Electrons such as those in the outer Van Allen radiation belt are easily stopped by a few millimeters of a low-*Z* material such as aluminum or magnesium. **1978** P. W. ATKINS *Physical Chem.* xiv. 438 The next atom to build is lithium, $Z = 3$.

10. *Z* is used to denote one of the two directions of twist in spinning (see quot. 1935); hence *z-spun* adj.

1935 [see *S II. 8]. **1964** H. HODGES *Artifacts* ix. 128 In thigh spinning, for example, a right-handed person will almost always produce Z-spun yarn. **1980** A. FRITZ *Fibre of Clothing* iii. 40 There are two types of twist possible in a yarn. One is an S twist, the other a Z twist.

11. *Particle Physics.* *Z* is the symbol of a heavy, uncharged vector boson that forms a triplet with the two Ws.

1967 S. WEINBERG in *Physical Rev. Lett.* XIX. 1265/2 The only unequivocal new predictions made by this model have to do with the couplings of the neutral intermediate meson Z_μ. *Ibid.* 1266/1 Our Z_μ and W_μ mesons get their mass from the spontaneous breaking of the symmetry. **1971** —— in *Ibid.* XXVII. 1688 This procedure..resulted in a model involving electrons, electron-type neutrinos, charged intermediate bosons (W_μ), neutral intermediate bosons (Z_μ), [etc.]. **1977** *Dædalus* Fall 32 The family of intermediate vector bosons, of which the photon is a member, is believed to contain one heavy charged particle and its antiparticle, called the W^+ and W^-, and one even heavier neutral particle, called the Z°. **1982** [see *W 4b]. **1983** *New Scientist* 12 May 355 (*heading*) CERN physicists find the Z particle. **1983** *Nature* 25 Aug. 686/2 This resulted in a total of six examples of the Z particle (four decaying into e^+e^- and two into $\mu^+\mu^-$) and 52 W± particles.

III. Abbreviations. **12. a.** ZANU, Zanu, Zimbabwe African National Union; ZAPU, Zapu, Zimbabwe African People's Union; ZBB (*U.S.*), zero-base(d) budgeting; Z-DNA (*Biochem.*), DNA in which the double helix has a left-handed rather than the usual right-handed twist and the sugar phosphate backbone follows a zigzagged course; ZPG, zero population growth. See also *Z band* (s.v. *Z LINE), *Z LINE.

1963 *Times* 10 Aug. 5/2 The split in the Southern Rhodesian African nationalist movement has come to a head. A breakaway group..has formed..the Zimbabwe African National Union. The president is the Rev. Ndabaningi Sithole, formerly one of Mr. Nkomo's staunchest lieutenants, as are all the members of the new Zanu executive. **1964** *Ann. Reg. 1963* II. v. 105 On 8 August a new organization, the Zimbabwe African National Union (Z.A.N.U.), was formed with the Rev. Sithole as leader. **1977** *Times* 17 Sept. 15/3 Nobody wants to clear an arena for a final fight between Zapu and Zanu armies for supremacy. **1961** *Guardian* 18 Dec. 1/3 A new African political party, to be known as the Zimbabwe African People's Union, has been launched in Southern Rhodesia..by Mr. J. M. N. Nkomo... Mr. Nkomo said..ZAPU would press for immediate negotiations for a fresh constitutional arrangement. **1972** J. BIGGS-DAVISON *Africa—Hope Deferred* xi. 100 The rival parties Z.A.P.U. and Z.A.N.U. **1977** *Daily Times* (Lagos) 27 Jan. 3/2 Mr. Moyo..was with Nkomo in ZAPU before the revolt which Nkomo faced prior to 1963. **1976** *N.Y. Times* 27 Aug. DI Z.B.B., as it is widely known, calls for the justification of all spending in relation to priorities. **1978** *National Civic Review* LXVII. 132 ZBB was formally delineated and put into practice for the first time by Texas Instruments, Inc., 15 years ago. **1979** A. H.-J. WANG et al. in *Nature* 13 Dec. 681/2 In looking at this left-handed helix..it is apparent that the ribose-phosphate backbone follows a zig-zag course resulting from alternating residue conformations. Accordingly, we propose to call this Z-DNA. **1983** *Sci. Amer.* Dec. 92/1 In Z DNA..the repeating un[it] of the helix is not a single base pair, as it is in *A* and [B] DNA, but rather two successive base pairs: *G–C* follow[ed] by *C–G*. **1970** *N.Y. Times* 3 June 61/6 Of all the cries th[at] have arisen, perhaps none is quite so superficially appea[l]ing, or so profound in its long-range social and econom[ic] implications, as zero population growth—'ZPG' in th[e] slogans of the day. **1978** *Nature* 6 Apr. 491/3 This ma[y] have reduced the maximum possible number of childre[n] per female to around five, and it does not then requi[re] harsh assumptions about mortality rates to end up wi[th] ZPG.

b. In combinations containing the abbrevia[tion] Z followed by a word, as **Z-car,** a polic[e] patrol car (after the title of a popular U.K. television series, from the radio call-sig[n] 'zulu' allotted therein to a group of such cars); also used allusively; **Z-day** *Mil.* = *zero da[y]* s.v. *ZERO *sb.* 7 a.

1961 *Radio Times* 28 Dec. 29/2 The call-sign is ZULU—they call them Z-cars. There are two young constables i[n] each, ready to deal with trouble. **1963** *Daily Mail* 23 Ap[r.] 1/6 (*heading*) Z-car crashes. **1965** *Sunday Mail* (Brisbane) 19 Dec. 32/5 Two black Z-cars—powerful Humbers—keep driving around the half-mile circle every fiv[e] minutes watching for strangers. **1976** 'D. CRAIG' *Fai[r] Hope & Death* xviii. 127 It's not like Barlow and Z Car[s] all that shouting stuff and strong jaws. These boys, the[y] was slimy. **1925** FRASER & GIBBONS *Soldier & Sailo[r] Words & Phrases* 312 The opening of the main attack [of] the battle of the Somme was fixed for June 29th, an[d] notified beforehand as 'Z Day'. **1930** S. SASSOON *Mem[oirs of an] Infantry Officer* IV. 61 Operation Orders..notified us tha[t] Thursday was 'Z' (or zero) day. **1938** BLUNDEN *O[n] Several Occasions* In the sour concrete hole the corpor[al] shows his muddy map, his Z Day zone of fire.

za (zā). Also **'za.** U.S. slang abbrev. of *PIZZA.

1968–70 *Current Slang* (Univ. S. Dakota) III–IV. 1[4] *Za*.., pizza. **1980** L. BIRNBACH et al. *Official Prepp[y] Handbk.* 44/2 You can go for 'za, burgers, and ice crea[m] without signing out. **1983** *Verbatim* IX. IV. 1/1 One of th[e] boys called up and asked the parlor to *bag the za* (meanin[g] 'cancel the pizza'). **1984** *Amer. Speech* LIX. 89 I[n] surveying my classes for campus slang I learned tha[t] pizza is referred to as *za* and to get or eat a pizza is t[o] *do a za.*

zabaglione (zabalʸo·ne). Also **sambaglione, zabaione,** etc. [a. It., perh. ult. ad. late Lat. *sabaia* an Illyrian drink.) A dessert con[-]sisting of egg yolks, sugar, and (usu. Marsala) wine, whipped to a frothy texture over a gentle heat and served either hot or cold. Cf. *SABAYON.

1899 M. NINET *Dainty Meals for Small Households* xiv. 223 *Sambaglione.*—Put into a saucepan about si[x] new-laid eggs, and two sherry-glassfuls of Madeira. **1901** W. G. WATERS *Cook's Decameron* 175/1 Zabajone i[s] a kind of syllabub. *Ibid.* 175/2 (*heading*) Iced zabajone. **1914** C. E. EDWARDS *Bohemian in San Francisco* 10 This was followed by a glass of zabaione for dessert. **1917** *Blackw. Mag.* Jan. 111/1 We dined off onion pilaff and sponge-cake of maize flour with zabayone. **192[.]** M. KENNEDY *Constant Nymph* xvi. 222 She had in[-]structed Roberto to beat up some eggs..that she migh[t] make zabaglione. **1932** *Times Lit. Suppl.* 10 Nov. 836/[.] At a single opening of the book we find..zabaglion[e] (the reviewer would prefer to omit the lemon-juice but t[o] add a pinch of yeast). **1958** *Times* 2 Oct. 11/4 A natio[n] that is content at midday with shepherd's pie..mus[t] dine out off kebabs and zabagliones. **1960** *House & Garden* May 94/3 A copper zabaglione pan. **1974** *Countr[y] Life* 25 Apr. 1006/1 The best-known Italian sweet *zabaglione.* **1981** R. AIRTH *Once a Spy* ix. 100 Zac ordere[d] blackberry, peach, pineapple [ices] and *zabaione.* **198[.]** *Listener* 1 Nov. 42/2 Whatever food is mentioned, from aubergines to zabaglione, they are ready to garnish i[t] with some unsavoury gobbet of introductory junk music.

† **zabernism** (zæ·bəɹniz'm). *Obs.* [f. *Zabern*, German name of the village of Saverne in Alsace + -ISM.] The misuse of military power or authority; bullying, aggression (see quot. 1921). Also **za·bernize** *v. intr.*

1914 *Daily News & Leader* 6 Apr. 1/7 A quaint illustra[-]tion of an attempt to 'zabernise' in business life..i[s] published..to-night. **1916** [see *ROUNDING *vbl. sb.*[1] 1a]. **1918** *Nineteenth Cent.* Dec. 992 The acquisitive commerc[-]ialists and financiers of Germany—the Zabernism c[-] industry and *l.s.d.*—were up to the eyes in it [*sc.* the war]. **1918** H. G. WELLS *In Fourth Year* iii. 36 Both countrie[s] have been slaves to Kruppism and Zabernism. **192[.]** *Glasgow Herald* 7 Apr. 8 The advance of the Governmen[t] troops into the Ruhr district, coupled with a marke[d] exhibition of 'Zabernism', has stiffened the Spartacis[t] resistance. **1921** E. WEEKLEY *Etym. Dict. Mod. Eng.* 1658/2 *Zabernism* (*hist.*), military jackbootery. From a[n] incident at *Saverne* (Ger. *Zabern*) in Alsace (1912), whe[n] an excited Ger. subaltern cut down a lame cobbler wh[o] smiled at him.

‖ **zabuton** (zabu·tǫn). [Jap., f. *za* sitting, a seat + *buton* f. *futon* cushion, padded mat tress.] A flat floor cushion on which one sits or kneels.

1889 M. B. HUISH *Japan & its Art* vii. 85 The Japanese ..is only comfortable when resting on his knees and heels on a cushion (*zabuton*). **1928** J. I. BRYAN *Jap. All* vi. 76 In a Japanese house the guest does not sit, but kneels down and rests on the heels with toes out behind. A cushion, called *zabuton*, is given to rest the knees on. **1960** *Sunset* Mar. 137/1 The word *zabuton* applies to a Japanese floor cushion designed for sitting. It comes from the Japanese words *za* meaning to sit, and *futon* meaning bedding. **1973** A. BROINOWSKI *Take One Ambassador* v. 57 There were *shoji* screens and *zabuton* cushions on the *tatami* round the table. *Ibid.* xii. 193 She brought a *zabuton* and sat on the floor on that.

zac (zæk). *Austral. slang.* Also **zack, zak.** [Origin unknown.] A sixpence.

1898 *Bulletin* (Sydney) 1 Oct. 14 6d., a 'zack'. **1924** *Truth* (Sydney) 27 Apr. 6 *Zack*, sixpence. **1941** *Coast to Coast 1941* 213 'Only one, then,' I said. 'We'll only have one more, so we'll make it a sixpence in.' 'Don't worry about the zac,' said Tom. **1952** M. TRIPP *Faith is Windsock* ii. 29 Arthur spent the break losing bobs and tanners while the tall Australian reckoned his profits in dieners and zaks. **1962** *John o' London's* 8 Mar. 229/2 And all you get for it is a zack. **1966** *Tel.* (Brisbane) 13 Oct. 13/2 The zack, now the 5c piece, is in such demand that very often its scarcity makes one wonder if it is gradually going out of circulation. **1966** P. MATHERS *Trap* ii. 31 Two taps with an improvised hammer and anvil, a two bob and a zac. **1977** *Sunday Sun* (Brisbane) 1 May 16 When it comes to unique competitions the people of outback Winton reckon they're the full quid—and you can bet your last zac or traybit on it.

zacate: see *SACATE, ZACATE; **zacaton:** see *SACATON, ZACATON.

'zackly, 'zactly (zæ·kli, zæ·ktli). Repr. a dial. or colloq. pronunc. of EXACTLY *adv.*

1886 BAUMANN *Londinismen* 239/1 '*Zactly*..., exactly. **1893** H. A. SHANDS *Some Peculiarities of Speech in Mississippi* 69 *Zackly*.., negro for *exactly*. **1929** W. FAULKNER *Sartoris* III. vi. 232 'Yessuh,' Simon agreed readily. 'Hit struck me jes' 'zackly dat way.' **1929** H. WILLIAMSON *Beautiful Years* (rev. ed.) vi. 63 'Isn't the sunshine lovely, Mr. Lewis?' 'Eh, ooh? 'Zactly!' **1973** *Amer. Speech* 1970 XLV. 77 Her dress was 'zactly like mine. **1983** R. SUTCLIFF *Blue Remembered Hills* xii. 91 Some people believed that Mr. Snow was, in West Country parlance 'not quite zackly'... I think he was just simple in the true sense of the word.

zaddik, zadik, varr. *TSADDIK.

Zadokite (zē^{i}·dǒkəit), *sb.* and *a.* [f. the name of *Zadok*, a high priest of Israel in the time of King David + -ITE[1].] **A.** *sb.* A member of a Jewish sect which seceded from orthodox Judaism in the second century B.C., and traced its authority back to Zadok.

1910 S. SCHECHTER *Fragments of Zadokite Work* p. xxi, It is the Zadokites from which the Sect derived its spiritual pedigree. **1920** *Encycl. Relig. & Ethics* XI. 43/2 The Sadducees were thus not a religious party at all, but simply a body of people bound together by a common interest to maintain the existing *régime*. The name is explained as meaning 'Zadokites', and was given to them by their opponents, the Pharisees, who borrowed it from an earlier age..when the descendants of Zadok, who then filled the high-priestly office, identified themselves with Hellenism in its most dangerous forms. **1960** tr. *Noth's Hist. Israel* III. ii. 316 It may also be that..some deported Zadokites returned to Jerusalem. **1974** *Encycl. Brit. Macropædia* XIV. 190/1 The Zadokites may have constituted the survival of an ancient Jebusite (Canaanite) royal priesthood.

B. *adj.* Of, pertaining to, or designating the members of this sect; *spec.* applied to fragments of sectarian texts discovered in Cairo in 1896–7 and later traced back to the Dead Sea Scrolls.

1910 S. SCHECHTER (*title*) Fragments of a Zadokite work. **1912** R. H. CHARLES *Fragments of Zadokite Work* p. vii, There is no question as to the genuineness of the orders of the Zadokite Priests and Levites. *Ibid.* p. x, The Zadokite Party represents an attempt at reform beginning within the ranks of the priesthood and extending outwards so as to embrace a strong lay element. **1921** J. MOFFATT *Approach to New Testament* i. 60 In the so called Zadokite document of Jewish piety, just before the days of Jesus, the idea of a new covenant, a covenant of repentance, began to be linked to the expectation of a messiah. **1954** [see *QUMRAN]. **1974** *Encycl. Brit. Macropædia* II. 938/2 Another sectarian book of ordinances is the Damascus Document (the Zadokite Fragments). The work was already known from two medieval copies before the discovery of the Dead Sea Scrolls, but fragments of it also were found in Qumrān.

‖ **zadruga** (zadrū·ga). Pl. **zadrugas, zadruge.** Also with capital initial. [Serbo-Croat, = patriarchal commune, association.] A type of patriarchal social unit traditional to (agricultural) Serbians and other southern Slavic peoples, orig. comprising an extended family group which worked the land and lived communally round the main house; the customs and rules associated with this type of unit.

1887 *Encycl. Brit.* XXII. 146/2 The Slavs know nothing of private property,—the land being held in common under the care of the *vladika* or *stareshina*, as in the Servian *xadrugas* at the present day. **1900** 'ODYSSEUS' *Turkey in Europe* viii. 375 The old system of Zadruga, or communal village based upon the family. **1911** PRINCE LAZAROVICH-HREBELIANOVICH *Servian People* i. 39 The basis of the Serb organisation is the family, either in its narrowest sense of blood-relationship, in communistic organisation, or other individuals grouped together for common work and with common possessions. These forms are called 'Zadruga'. **1934** *N.Y. Times* 24 June IV. 3/4 Zadruga in Serbia means a big family where brothers and sisters..lead a community life, under the leadership usually of the eldest member of the family. **1943** L. ADAMIC *My Native Land* 214 From their Russian homeland the Slavs brought a democratic institution called *zadruga*, a clan or family cooperative, which some of the tribes tried to extend and adjust to the wider forms of government necessary in their new homelands. *Ibid.* 216 They lived in their primitive villages and held onto their Old-Slavic *zadrugé* and 'heart culture'—decency, friendliness, hospitality. **1963** *Times Lit. Suppl.* 25 Jan. 49/3 The *dvor* or peasant household..is the same elastic unit which was familiar in medieval Europe, and survives today in the *zadruge* of the Balkans. **1979** *Internat. Jrnl. Sociol. of Law* VII. 270 The old customary Slavonic 'family' law, the zadruga. **1980** A. TOFFLER *Third Wave* ii. 44 People tended to live in large, multi-generational households,..from the 'joint family' in India to the 'zadruga' in the Balkans.

‖ **zaftig** (zæ·ftig), *a. U.S. colloq.* Also **zoftig, zofti(c)k.** [Yiddish, a. G. *saftig* juicy.] Of a woman: plump, curvaceous, 'sexy'.

1937 M. LEVIN *Old Bunch* II. 394 He could see himself on the road, whizzing by a flaming poster—a beautiful . girl, snappy, modern, *zaftig*. **1950** *Commentary* IX. 460/2 The owner of the local barber shop..installed a *zoftig* blond manicurist. **1960** 'E. MCBAIN' *Heckler* x. 91 A *zaftig* redhead..in her early thirties. **1967** P. WELLES *Babyhip* (1969) xxiv. 139 'And see how *zoftik* she is.' Mrs. Green felt pleased she had spotted someone over-weight. **1970** S. J. PERELMAN *Baby, it's Cold Inside* 188 This demure but *zoftick* freshman, with a brain rivalling Spinoza's encased in the body of a Lollobrigida. **1973** R. HAYES *Hungarian Game* xxx. 179 That *zoftig* colonel wasn't a colonel at all. I checked her out in Budapest. **1981** *Gossip* (Holiday Special) 11/2 Zaftig Dolly Parton..once described herself as looking like a 'hooker with a heart of gold'.

Zaghlulist (zaglū·list), *sb.* and *a.* Also **Zaghloulist.** [f. the name of the Egyptian politician *Zaghlūl Sa'd* (1857–1927) + -IST.] **A.** *sb.* An adherent or supporter of the nationalist and separatist principles and policies of Zaghlūl Sa'd. **B.** *adj.* Of, pertaining to, or designating members of this political group.

1921 *Times* 29 Dec. 9/3 The Zaghlulists have raised the familiar Indian cry of non-cooperation. **1924** *Times* 14 Jan. 11/5 The comparative nonentity who was his Zaghlulist opponent. **1924** [see *OMDAH, OMDEH]. **1927** *Daily Express* 9 Sept. 1/1 A congress of Zaghlulist parliamentarians to decide on a policy consequent on the death of their leader will open on September 15 or immediately after, when the Wafdists (champions of Home Rule)..arrive. **1943** LD. WAVELL *Allenby in Egypt* vii. 102 The completeness of the Zaghlulist victory surprised every one..even Zaghlulists themselves. **1955** H. W. JARVIS *Pharaoh to Farouk* xxxii. 267 The Zaghloulists, however, were determined that a 'Tantah' incident *should* be repeated in some part of Egypt. **1971** P. MANSFIELD *British in Egypt* xxii. 252 Allenby.. departed to genuine expressions of regret from the Egyptian public including the Zaghlulists.

‖ **zaguan** (zagwā·n, sa-). Also 9 **saguan.** [Sp., = vestibule, hallway.] The passage running from the front door to the central patio in houses in South and Central America and in the south-western U.S.

1851 *Harper's Mag.* Sept. 465/2 Don Pedro was heard within, moving toward the 'Saguan'. **1863** *Rio Abajo Press* 28 Apr. 1/2 She had just seen Juanito's ghost in the saguan door. **1880** G. W. CABLE *Grandissimes* 131 It was a long, narrowing perspective of arcades, lattices, balconies, *zaguans*, dormer windows, and blue sky. **1921** *Chambers's Jrnl.* Mar. 258/1 There is the *zaguan* or vestibule at the outside, then the *cancel* or grating, and next the *patio* within. *Ibid.* Nov. 821/1 A couple of Moors —in the vestibule or *zaguan*—conduct a peculiar performance. **1927** D. H. LAWRENCE *Mornings in Mexico* 12 Some stranger comes into the *zaguan*.

Zahal (tsaha·l). [Heb., f. *Ṣĕḇā' Hăgānāh Lĕ-Yiśrā'ēl* Israel Defence Force.] The name applied by the Israelis to their defence forces, formed originally in 1948 by the fusion of pre-independence military organizations.

1959 A. M. HELLER *Israel's Odyssey* 61 The Haganah disbanded, the Irgunist and the Sternist forces and their members were fused into the Zahal, made up of the initial Hebrew letters of Zva Haganah L'Israel—Israel's National Army. **1969** A. PERLMUTTER *Mil. & Politics in Israel* v. 55 Zahal's chief of staff was delegated the operational function of maintaining and training the army. **1971** *Scope* (S. Afr.) 19 Mar. 17/3 Very few top-ranking Israeli officers gave their Zahal (Defence Force) more than one chance in three of pulling it off. **1975** C. A. HADDAD *Moroccan* i. 7 The twins did not have to lose two years to the Zahal, as the [Israeli] army does not draft religious girls. **1982** MURRAY & VIOTTI *Defense Policies of Nations* ix. 378 The leadership opted for a unified command for *Zahal* in which there would be one general headquarters and a chief of staff.

‖ **zaibatsu** (zaibæ·tsu). Also **Zaibatsu.** [Jap., f. *zai* wealth + *batzu* clique.] In Japan, a large capitalist organization, usu. based on a single family having controlling interests in a variety of companies, of a type that existed before the war of 1939–45; since 1947, a cartel or conglomerate. Also, the members of such an enterprise.

1937 *Econ. Jrnl.* June 272 These concerns are popularly known in Japan as the *Zaibatsu* or money-cliques. **1947** R. BENEDICT *Chrysanthemum & Sword* iv. 93 A chosen financial oligarchy, the famous Zaibatsu. **1957** *Pacific Affairs* XXX. 219 The *zaibatsu* and the landlords. **1959** R. KIRKBRIDE *Tamiko* (1960) vi. 41 By getting the right people to sit for you. The zaibatsu. The Royal Family. **1964** *Asia Mag.* 26 July 15/2 While the companies being merged presently are old Zaibatsu connected firms, and the groups are sponsoring the moves, the economics of the mergers themselves have little to do with such connections. **1965** *Economist* 11 Dec. 1219/2 The *Zaibatsu* are becoming concerned about the problems of seniority and management. **1970** [see *CONGLOMERATE *sb.* 3]. **1974** P. GORE-BOOTH *With Great Truth & Respect* 45 When a community, historically prone to become the victim of unreason, finds itself in a position of success amid failure, its only recourse is probably to go to ground. The Japanese *Zaibatsu* understood this; a really successful Japanese business man was and is rarely obtrusive. **1982** K. OHMAE *Mind of Strategist* (1983) ix. 109 Japan's prewar *zaibatsu* holding companies.

‖ **zaikai** (zai·kai). [Jap., f. *zai* wealth + *kai* community.] In Japan: financial circles; the business world or power élite who control it.

1968 C. YANAGA *Big Business in Jap. Politics* ii. 32 A new postwar term, zaikai,..practically supersedes zaibatsu... It is frequently interpreted .as a synonym for 'business circles', 'financial circles', and even 'business community'. More inclusive than zaibatu, it is nevertheless restricted to big business... Zaikai also denotes the place where the craving for political power is openly expressed and gratified. **1970** *Times* 19 Aug. 5/2 A Japanese economic magazine recently conducted a survey of opinion among leading representatives of the *zaikai*, the world of business and high finance. **1975** G. L. CURTIS in E. F. Vogel *Mod. Jap. Organization & Decision-Making* 38 The men who make up this elite in Japan spend an extraordinary amount of time in so-called *zaikai* activities..that are not directly related to their own companies, but which seek to represent the interests of the business community as a whole. **1981** J. B. KIDD in P. G. O'Neill *Tradition & Mod. Japan* 50 The process of *nemawashi* operating in the senior levels of the *zaikai* world enable the companies to secure long-term goals.

zaire (zai,i^{ə}·ɹ). [f. *Zaïre*, local name of the Congo River in Central Africa.] The basic monetary unit of the Republic of Zaïre; a coin of this value, equal to 100 makuta (see *LIKUTA).

1967 *Times* 9 Nov. 6 They tried to recruit former Katangese gendarmes... They offered seven zaires (£5) to every man who enlisted. **1971, 1972** [see *LIKUTA]. **1976** L. SANDERS *Hamlet Warning* (1977) xvi. 133 A bribe... Five thousand zaire—ten thousand dollars.

Zairean (zai,i^{ə}·riăn), *sb.* and *a.* Also **Zairian.** [f. the name of the Republic of *Zaïre* (cf. prec.) + -AN, -IAN.] **A.** *sb.* A native or inhabitant of the Republic of Zaïre, formerly the Democratic Republic of the Congo. **B.** *adj.* Of or pertaining to Zaïre.

1972 *Observer* 19 Nov. 2/1 Dead victims..have been found dumped close to the frontier with Zaire... They were taken there by contract drivers, many of them Zaireans. **1973** *Black World* May 80 The dollar value of this manpower is considerable and most of it is defrayed by the Zairian Government. **1973** *Daily Tel.* 1 Oct. 19 Two British geologists yesterday described their fortnight's ordeal under armed Zairean Gendarme guards. **1973** *Times* 11 Dec. (Zaire Suppl.) p. vii/2 None of the young Zairians danced. **1977** *Times* 12 Apr. 13/1 Both the Moroccans and Zaireans are using their own planes to transport the troops. **1977** *Daily Tel.* 14 Apr. 1/8 The spokesman said that on Saturday two Zairean jets violated Zambian airspace. **1982** S. JOHNSON *Marburg Virus* x. 121 The logistic support of the Zairian army.

Zairese (zai,i^{ə}rī·z), *a.* and *sb.* [f. as prec. + -ESE.] = *ZAIREAN *sb.* and *a.* Cf. next.

1974 *N.Y. Times* 10 Feb. 11/1 A 700-page, 30,000 word Swahili dictionary..is the work of a Zairese priest. **1975** *Business Week* (Industrial ed.) 27 Oct. 94H On the other side of the lake, the Zairese would like to build a new recovery unit. **1977** *Bangladesh Times* 19 Jan. 11/6 A lack of co-ordination between Belgian and Zairese security officials at Brussels airport, where the Belgian monarch was greeting President Mobutu. **1978** *Washington Post* 18 June A18/4 In the name of 'authenticity', he declared that in French revolution fashion Zairese should call each other 'citizen'.

Zairois (zai,i^{ə}rwa·), *sb.* and *a.* Also **Zaïrois.** [a. Fr.] = *ZAIREAN *sb.* and *a.*

1973 J. J. MACKELVEY *Man against Tsetse* iv. 228 The state of war against tsetse as the Zairois assess it will dictate the role that this institution may play in further research. **1974** *Observer* 22 Sept. 20/3 The Zairois people are warm, helpful and charming. **1975** R. BARCLAY *Ernest Bevin & Foreign Office* viii. 159 It is in any case an offence for a Zaïrois to wear such an 'un-authentic' item of dress as a tie. **1977** *New Day* Summer 10 (*caption*) A Zairois student learns how to take a skin smear. **1982**

Financial Times 26 Jan. 22/1 The Government intends the industry to employ an eventual 700 Zairois.

‖**zakat** (zăkā·t). Also **zakah, zakkat,** † **zecchat.** [Pers. *zakāt*, Turk. *zekât*, etc., ad. Arab. *zakāh*.] An obligatory tax payable annually under Islamic law on certain kinds of property in order to raise money for charitable and religious objects.

1802 J. Pinkerton *Mod. Geogr.* I. 452 [Turkey.] This revenue is partly derived from..the *zecchat*. **1875** Bellew & Chapman in T. D. Forsyth *Rep. Mission to Yarkund* ii. 103 The *zakât* is a Mahommedan tax... It is one part in forty of all live-stock, and of merchandise entering the country. **1957** Ld. Hailey *African Survey 1956* x. 671 In Mauretania those who are not liable to *zakkat* pay the personal tax and in addition a capitation fee on every animal. **1960** C. Geertz *Religion of Java* x. 123 The fifth pillar [of Islam] is the *zakah*, the religious tax. **1979** *Observer* 4 Mar. 12/3 Their principal objection was to 'zakat', a partly-compulsory Islamic welfare tax which General Zia proposes to introduce in July. According to Shi-ism zakat has to be an individual act of conscience and can never be levied compulsorily by the State, he said.

‖**zakuska** (zăku·skă). Also **zakouska.** Pl. **zakuskas, zakuski.** [a. Russ. *zakúska* (usu. as pl. *zakúski*).] An hors d'œuvre. Freq. pl.

The sing. form is occas. erron. const. as pl.

1885 A. J. C. Hare *Stud. in Russia* v. 203 The refreshment-room is enormous,..with a great buffet at one end, whither the Russians resort before dinner for the customary *zakuska* of pickles, sardines, vodki, &c. **1919** H. Walpole *Secret City* I. xii. 79 The 'Zakuska' were on a side-table near the door—herrings and ham and smoked fish and radishes and mushrooms and tongue and caviare. **1920** E. & P. Sykes *Through Deserts & Oases Central Asia* iv. 73 It began with many *zakuskas*, consisting principally of dubious-looking tinned fish. **1922** W. S. Maugham *On Chinese Screen* vi. 27 The emotion..was diverted by the appearance of two Chinese servants in long silk robes and four-sided hats with cocktails and zakouski. **1933** H. Nicolson *Let.* 7 Nov. (1966) 156 There were also little snippets of lobster in tomato cocktails, which were among the least successful of *zakouska* that I have ever known. **1951** V. Nabokov *Speak, Memory* xiv. 213, I detest crowds, harried waiters, Bohemians, vermouth concoctions, coffee, *zakuski*, floor shows and so forth. **1981** T. Keene *Skyshroud* i. 18 The *Zakouski*, the *borshch* and the *blini* of his homeland.

‖**zamacueca** (zamakwē̆ⁱ·kă, sa-) Also 9 **-cuca.** [Amer. Sp.] A South American, esp. Chilean, dance in which a couple move around one another, accompanied by chords on the guitar and rhythmical handclapping. Shortened as *cueca.

1855 E. R. Smith *Araucanians* vi. 65 The fashionable dances soon gave way to the more national *Zamacúca*. The Zamacúca has been very much reviled by foreigners, who have seen it only in sea-port towns. **1895** L. Grove et al. *Dancing* xii. 375 The 'Zamacueca' is an inimitable dance, in which the handkerchief plays a prominent part. **1917** [see *cueca]. **1974** *Encycl. Brit. Macropædia* I. 669/1 The Creole people of the coast and plains [of South America] have been replacing the indigenous music of the mountains with their own music, especially with the ubiquitous *cueca*, or *zamacueca*.

zamarra. Add: Also 9 **semara.** (Earlier examples.)

1839 E. E. Napier *Jrnl.* 4 May in *Excursions along Shores of Mediterranean* (1842) II. vi. 81, I observed a tall, gentlemanly-looking man, dressed in a semara. **1841** G. Borrow *Zincali* I. ii. i. 231 Another Gypsy.. dressed in a zamarra of sheep-skin.

Zambian (zæ·mbiăn), *sb.* and *a.* [f. *Zambia* (see def.) + -an.] **A.** *sb.* A native, citizen, or inhabitant of Zambia (formerly Northern Rhodesia), a country in south central Africa.

1964 *Economist* 15 Feb. 607/2 With only 180 'Zambians' (Northern Rhodesia's name when independent) taking school certificate this year. **1976** *Drum* (E. Afr. ed.) Aug. 8/1 Another reason for the shortage here is that the township council has turned down licence applications from non-black Zambians and foreigners. **1977** 'O. Jacks' *Autumn Heroes* xiv. 207 *Everyone* had learned to freeze into silence the moment the Zambian made pronouncements.

B. *adj.* Of, pertaining to, or characteristic of Zambia or its people.

1964 *Times* 13 Nov. 11/3 A European in Zambia whose father was born in Britain might decide after a year to acquire Zambian citizenship. **1966** *Listener* 15 Dec. 879/2 The whole Rhodesian situation has driven Zambian politicians into a kind of neurosis. **1970** *Cape Times* 28 Oct. 2/5, I was furious when we found ourselves on the Zambian side of the lake. **1977** *Whitaker's Almanack 1978* 588/1 The Zambian Minister of Home Affairs signed deportation orders for 55 aliens who it was said had entered the country illegally.

Hence **Za·mbianize** *v. trans.*, to make Zambian in character, by replacing foreign personnel by native Zambians; **Zambianiza·tion.**

1968 *Times* 18 Nov. (Zambia Suppl.) p. v/2 The Zambian government wants to see the whole industry Zambianized, with no whites and indeed no foreign Africans in any jobs. **1968** *Economist* 14 Dec. 26/2 ANC claims simply that it could have done better, picking out the soaring cost of living, wasteful public expenditure and falling standards in the police force—the last two linked with too-rapid Zambianisation. **1969** *Listener* 14 Aug. 221/3 That may have led to the proposal to 'Zambianise' the judiciary. **1976** G. C. Bond *Politics of Change in Zambian Community* x. 166 Its policy of rapid Zambianization siphoned off the more educated and progressive elements. **1984** *Mining Jrnl.* 26 Oct. 287/2 Zambianization of the mining industry was a natural consequence of independence.

Zamboni (zæmbōᵘ·ni). Chiefly *N. Amer.* Also **zamboni.** [See quot. 1965.] A proprietary name for a machine used to resurface ice rinks.

1965 *Official Gaz.* (U.S. Patent Office) 16 Feb. TM 93 Frank J. Zamboni & Co., Paramount, Calif...*Zamboni* for ice resurfacing machines and dump attachments therefor. First use July 1962. **1968** *Trade Marks Jrnl.* 3 Apr. 517/2 *Zamboni*... Machines for resurfacing ice rinks and parts and fittings therefor. **1974** *Kingston* (Ontario) *Whig-Standard* 11 July 14/2 With 12 scrapers, I could do that ice in nine minutes. With the Zamboni, it took a little longer..but I will have to admit it does do a better job. **1978** *Winnipeg Free Press* 25 Sept. 53/4 A crack in the boards near the door used by the zamboni helped Guindon open the scoring. **1984** *N.Y. Times* 11 Feb. I. 22/6 Then the ice was glazed by a smooth-nosed French cousin of the Zamboni before another Soviet skater..glided to gold medals.

zambuk (zæ·mbʊk). *Austral.* and *N.Z. colloq.* Also **zambuc, -buck,** and with capital initial. [A proprietary name of a type of antiseptic ointment.] A first-aider, a St. John's ambulance man or woman, esp. at a sporting occasion. Also *attrib.* and *transf.*

[**1904** *Trade Marks Jrnl.* 23 Nov. 1406 *Zam-buk*... Chemical substances prepared for use in medicine and pharmacy, but not including gelatine capsules... The Bile Bean Manufacturing Company,..Leeds; vendors of proprietary medicines.] **1918** [see *gutser]. **1943** *Amer. Speech* XVIII. 95 A few trade names have caught the public fancy, and become generalised. Thus *Zambuk*, a brand of ointment, is regularly used for a 'first-aid man' (usually a member of the St. John's Ambulance Corps), or even as an appeal for first aid. **1950** B. Sutton-Smith *Our Street* iv. 50 Everybody would shout, 'Zambuk! Zambuk!' until the first-aid man came to the rescue. **1965** *N.Z. Listener* 5 Nov. 4/5 Perhaps he might have concussion... A zambuck came with sal volatile. **1968** *Wanganui Photo News* 31 Aug. 13 (*caption*) No injuries to attend to so these 'Zambuk' ladies get on with their knitting at the basketball recently. **1969** *N.Z. Listener* 23 May 12/3 The driver was dead... There was a girl in a bad way mixed up with him. 'Better leave it for the zambucs,' Payne said. **1972** P. Mathers *Wort Papers* 95 They even supplied the zambuck, a priest with brown attaché case containing oils and waters for extreme unction.

zamindari, -y, varr. Zemindary in Dict. and Suppl.

‖**zampogna** (zæmpǫ·nʸă). *Mus.* [It.:–LL. *sumpōnia, symphōnia* (see Symphony). Cf. Sp. *zampoña*, Pg. *sanfon(h)a*.] A traditional wind-blown bagpipe of southern Italy having two chanters and two drones; also, any wood-wind instrument.

1740 Grassineau *Mus. Dict.* 343 *Zampogna*, sometimes written *Sampogna*..is..any instrument that sounds like a Flute and particularly a Bag-pipe, being an assemblage of divers pipes of different sizes. **1801** T. Busby *Dict. Mus.*, *Zampogna*, or *Sampogna*, the flute-à-bec, or common flute. **1826** M. Kelly *Reminisc* (1975) ii. 30 The peasantry and shepherds from Abruzzo, Calabria, and Apulia,..come from the mountains in their sheepskin dresses, playing on their various instruments, some on the Zampogna, (a kind of bagpipe), others on the Colascione. **1876** Stainer & Barrett *Dict. Mus. Terms* 455/1 A rough-toned reed instrument without a bag is also called Zampogna or Zampugna. **1954** *Grove's Dict. Mus.* (ed. 5) I. 351/1 Italian pipers..make a practice of coming into the towns at the Christmas season to serenade the images of the Infant Christ, which are set up at the roadside. They also formerly visited Britain as strolling musicians, but they appear to have abandoned this habit many years ago; they were all players of the *zampogna*. **1977** *Early Mus.* Oct. 555/2 It was..good to see no less than two sets of zampognas, from the early 19th century. **1983** *N.Y. Times* 26 June XI. (Westchester Weekly) 13/1 Vocalists will be accompanied on such classic Old World instruments as the zampogna.

Zande (zæ·ndi). Also 9 **Zandey**; 9–**Zandeh.** Pl. **Zandes, Azande** († **A-Zande**). [Native name.] **a.** (A member of) a people of mixed ethnic origin inhabiting central Africa. **b.** The language of this people. Also *attrib.* as *adj.*

1873 E. E. Frewer tr. *Schweinfurth's Heart of Afr.* II. xiii. 6 As marks of nationality, all the 'Zandey' score themselves with three or four tattooed squares. **1884** *Encycl. Brit.* XVII. 474/1 The A-Zandey are to be regarded as rather of mixed Negroid than of pure Negro stock. *Ibid.* The Zandey language..appears to be everywhere spoken with considerable uniformity. **1891** A. H. Keane tr. *W. Junker's Trav. in Africa* II. iv. 102 The hair, arranged Zandeh-fashion, though somewhat carelessly, in tresses, projected under a tarbush round the occiput. **1902** *Encycl. Brit.* XXXI. 230/1 The Zandehs proper..are now found to stretch, with interruptions, from the White Nile above the Sobat confluence to the Shari affluent of Lake Chad. **1918** R. G. C. Brock in *Sudan Notes & Records* Oct. 249 The Zande tribe. *Ibid.*, The true Azande live in the Belgian Congo. *Ibid.* 253 The Azande are divided into different clans and most of these believe that they return to the earth in the form of some animal. *Ibid.* 257 The ordinary Zande dance is a very dull affair. **1938** E. M. North *Bk. of Thousand Tongues* 353/2 Zande... Spoken by perhaps 300,000 people in northeastern Belgian Congo, eastern French Equatorial Africa and southern Anglo-Egyptian Sudan. **1955** M. Gluckman *Custom & Conflict in Afr.* iv. 85 If a Zande murdered a fellow-tribesman with his spear he was tried in court by his chief. *Ibid.* 90, I find it difficult to see exactly how the Azande witchcraft charges work. **1978** J. Skorupski in Hookway & Pettit *Action & Interpretation* 85 Winch's account of the meaning of Zande magic is ultimately not at all unlike that which some symbolist writers might give.

zanella. Add: Also 9 **zenilla.** (Earlier example.)

1876 F. Kilvert *Diary* 28 Apr. (1940) III. 272, I found she had taken my umbrella and left me a much better one, a fine silk umbrella in place of my zenilla.

zany, *sb.* Restrict *arch.* and *dial.* to senses in Dict. and add: **2. c, e.** (Further examples.)

1925 *Sunday at Home* Nov. 91/2 He went capering about all his tasks with a zany-like glee. **1929** C. Day Lewis *Transitional Poem* I. 11 A burly wind playing the zany In fields of barleycorn. **1976** G. Langford (*title*) Death of the early morning hero. Episodes of a zany in love.

3. Now apprehended as a simple adj., and the dominant use of the word, with the sense: comically idiotic, crazily ridiculous.

In quot. 1938, 'simple-minded' (cf. sense 2e in Dict.).

1918 G. B. Shaw in *Nation* 22 June 308/2 Before Shakespear touched Hamlet there was a zany Hamlet who mopped and mowed. **1938** L. MacNeice *I crossed Minch* viii. 117 The gardener who was apparently zany, used to level his stick at an obelisk. **1957** Manvell & Huntley *Technique Film Music* v. 204 *Sloppy Jalopy* (UPA), a zany cartoon. **1959** *House & Garden* June 76 Luncheon-mats of the subtlest as well as the zaniest designs. **1978** J. Krantz *Scruples* xii. 349 Television shows that lean heavily on the brand of humor known as 'zany', consisting largely of sight gags and the stupid fun of appealing people making cheerful fools of themselves. **1983** D. Cecil *Portrait of Lamb* ii. ii. 143 A sympathetic spirit able to appreciate his more characteristic and zany vein of humour.

Hence **za·nily** *adv.*; **za·niness.**

1958 S. Ellin *Eighth Circle* (1959) I. i. 11 In Central Park sea lions barked zanily at the sky. **1960** *Sat. Rev.* 6 Feb. 13/2 Ginsberg, for all his carefully cultivated (and natural) zaniness, is a writer far above Kerouac. **1966** M. Laurence *Jest of God* ix. 170 I've..emptied the crucial and precious capsules out of my window, zanily. **1976** *Times Lit. Suppl.* 21 May 602/2 His wider appeal owes much more to his modern zaniness and irreverence. **1980** L. Birnbach et al. *Official Preppy Handbk.* 111/1 Many of these forays into zaniness actually wind up involving mayhem or destruction of property. **1984** *Financial Times* 25 July 13/6 The play is a staple of the repertory and amateur theatre diet, and while it may not inspire to the zanily surreal heights of *See How They Run* or *Madame Louise*, Dighton is certainly a name worth conjuring with. **1985** *Listener* 21 Mar. 28/3 How could anything with Jerry Lewis not fall into a comic range somewhere between surrealistic zaniness and childish destructiveness?

zanza, zanze, varr. *sansa.

Zanzibari (zæ:nzibā·ri), *sb.* and *a.* [f. *Zanzibar*, name of an island off the east coast of Africa, now part of Tanzania + *-i.] **A.** *sb.* A native or inhabitant of Zanzibar. **B.** *adj.* Of, pertaining to, or characteristic of Zanzibar or its people.

1888 G. W. Brooke *Let.* 18 July in M. E. Herbert *Afr. Slave Trade* (1890) 12 The Zanzibaris express horror and disgust at the bare idea of associating with them. *Ibid.* 13 The women and children are hurried off to the Zanzibari camps. **1890** W. Booth *In Darkest Eng.* I. i. 12 Mr. Stanley's Zanzibaris lost faith. **1917** G. B. Shaw in *Daily Express* 28 Nov. 3/2 When the Sultan of Zanzibar ordered the admiral of his second-hand penny steamboat to go out and sink the British fleet, and the poor devil actually went, we laughed... No doubt Ireland, north and south, teems with Zanzibari courage. **1959** *Daily Tel.* 1 Dec. 8/6 It is uphill work to persuade the Zanzibaris to make a partial switch to other products, which they could fairly easily do in their fertile island. **1966** D. Wilson *Quarter of Mankind* xvi. 205, I have sat on a train in Manchuria and heard Zanzibari visitors ask their guides why colonialism had not yet been expelled from Hongkong. **1975** *Nat. Geographic* Apr. 501/1 Towering above all a tree bearing tiny reddish buds—the famous cloves, basis of the Zanzibari economy. **1985** *Daily Tel.* 20 Aug. 4/7 Zanzibaris with foreign exchange were allowed to import essential goods.

zaouia, var. *zawiya.

zap (zæp), *int. slang* (orig. *U.S.*). [Echoic.] **1.** Used to represent the sound of a ray gun, laser, bullet, etc.; also *fig.*, expressing any sudden or dramatic event.

1929 P. F. Nowlan in *Washington Post* 7 May 16/3 Ahead of me was one of those golden dragon Mongols, with a deadly disintegrator ray... Br-r-rr-r-z-zzz-zap. **1962** *Amer. Speech* XXXVII. 288 The jokester, pretending to be a creature from outer space, pointed his cosmic ray gun (finger) at his friend's genitals and exclaimed, 'Zap! You're sterile.' **1967** L. Deighton *Only when I Larf* (1968) xii. 160 Shouting idiotic things and going, 'Whoop,' 'Zap,' and 'Yap,' all the time. **1968** *Maclean's Mag.* Mar. 77 Bang! Zap! Pow! With laser beams and cracking doomsday machines, the deadly-serious superheroes. **1970** *Daily Tel.* (Colour Suppl.) 15 May 34/4 I'm against the war in Vietnam. But I'm not among the people who say let's stop Vietnam, zap. **1971** *Frendz* 21 May 17/1 Getting down to a blow job, she suddenly produces a razor and zap—the man bleeding and gushing blood, is screaming on the floor. **1974** *Globe & Mail* (Toronto) 12 Sept. 7/2 We have been told..we needn't worry, the sections are not being enforced. Then zap, another homosexual is denied entry for being honest. **1978** *Fortune* 18 Dec. 101 (Advt.), The solution receives a positive charge, the truck a negative charge. Zap! The primer and the GMC are joined with a magnetic-like bond. **1985** *Parade Mag.* 31 Mar. 9 A staff meeting will be Wick just shooting out those things one after another—zap, zap, zap.

2. zap gun, a ray gun or the like.

1969 K. VONNEGUT *Slaughterhouse-Five* iv. 65 Billy's will was paralyzed by a zap gun aimed at him from one of the portholes. **1976** *Publishers Weekly* 15 Mar. 59/1 Plot is subordinated to character exploration, but there's more adventure in that than in many a zap-gun epic. **1977** *Sunday Sun* (Brisbane) 30 Jan. 7/1 New York police have confiscated two space-age 'zap' guns from blind singer Stevie Wonder... The guns look like flashlights and fire two darts attached to 20 ft. thin copper wires.

zap (zæp), *v. slang* (orig. *U.S.*). Also (*rare*) **zapp** [Echoic.] **I.** *trans.* **1. a.** To kill, esp. with a gun; to deal a sudden blow to.

1942 BERRY & VAN DEN BARK *Amer. Thes. Slang* §118/3 *Kill; murder,*..wipe out, work off, zap. **1965** *Time* 10 Dec. 34 *Zap*..means to clobber. **1966** *Current Slang* (Univ. S. Dakota) Fall 6 *Zap*, v., to slap... I got *zapped* when I tried that. **1969** I. BROWN *Rhapsody of Words* 143 In Vietnam a man knocked out was said to be zapped. **1970** *Courier-Mail* (Brisbane) 14 Dec. 3/3 A council workman on-duty during the week zapped any rat foolish enough to wiggle a whisker within a hundred yards of the place. **1971** *Sunday Times* 28 Mar. 9/1 He wants to prove a Hanoi man can zapp a Saigon man. **1971** *Radio Times* 18 Nov. 15/4 This year the system has zapped the counter-culture member in the sneakiest way of all, by robbing him of a decent way of making a living after graduation. **1977** *Time* 6 June 55/2 Proto..fires a beam of electrons at the pellet, zapping it with a jolt equal to 8 trillion watts. **1979** *Mod. Photogr.* Oct. 64 You can't run a darkroom without plug-in power, so you'd better make it electrically safe or you might get zapped! **1981** *Observer* 2 Aug. 10 God is not going to zap women for coming forth. **1982** N. FREELING *Wolfnight* 161 Unbureaucratically, any bugger who shoots, you zap. **1984** *Weekly World News* (U.S.) 25 Dec. 29/1 Teenager Vickie Parker was zapped to death by 640 volts of electricity when she wandered onto the tracks of an elevated train and accidentally touched the 'live' third rail. **1985** *N.Y. Rev. Bks.* 9 May 23/3 (Advt.), In a New York restaurant, a young man celebrating with friends was zapped in the face by a man with an aerosol spray can.

b. To put an end to, do away with.

1976 *Courier-Mail* (Brisbane) 22 Apr. 21/4 We can zap a headache almost immediately. **1982** *Sunday Sun-Times* (Chicago) 17 Oct. 62 (*heading*) Atari seeks to zap X-rated video games.

2. To fail (someone) in a test, course, etc.; to punish (see also quot. 1969).

1961 *Amer. Speech* XXXVI. 149 The cadet who is *zapped* is the recipient of a large number of demerits or other cadet punishments. The term was probably taken from a favorite cadet newspaper comic strip, 'B.C.', where *zapp* is used as the sound of any blow. **1969** *Current Slang* (Univ. S. Dakota) Winter 12 *Zap*, v., to 'put down'; to put someone in his place. **1976** *National Observer* (U.S.) 17 Jan. 8/5 A graduate student whose 'scholarly potential' is not overwhelmingly lauded 'is going to get zapped'.

3. To overwhelm emotionally.

1967 *Punch* 26 July 123/1 I'll be zapped with love, blow the mind of straight people. **1970** *New Yorker* 22 July 4/3 If the music doesn't zap you..you can contemplate..movies on the wall. **1971** *Daily Colonist* (Victoria, B.C.) 30 May 47/1 Our politicians turn to the architects, presuming them to be the theatrical stage managers of the city to zap the masses with compelling masques and follies. **1974** A. LURIE *War between Tates* (1977) vi. 134 If The Book is published in time, and the right people in Washington read it, it's going to really zap them. **1977** *It* May 31/3 (Advt.), Bring you own sounds!!, and get zapped. **1983** *Theology* Jan. 15 A well-known evangelist invited the undergraduates of Oxford to allow themselves to be 'zapped by the Holy Spirit'.

4. To send, put, or hit in a forceful way.

1967 *Time* 22 Dec. 56 For quick acceleration..the nickel-cadmium batteries would cut in briefly, could zap the car from a standstill to 50 m.p.h. in 20 seconds. **1972** D. DELMAN *Week to Kill* 139, I nosed the car out of town and on to 118, where I zapped it into high. **1974** *Farm & Country* 9 Apr. 11 (*heading*) Computers zap farmers through space-age door. **1976** *National Observer* (U.S.) 29 May 12/4 Won't they be surprised when Ms. Klutz limberly zaps the ball over the net.

5. To demonstrate against or at.

1972 *Sat. Rev.* 12 Feb. 24/1 Homosexuals..'zap' (confront) politicians until they express themselves..on equal housing..for homosexuals. **1980** *Observer* 3 Aug. 8/5 Columbia and Warner Bros. were 'zapped' last week; this Tuesday it's the turn of 20th Century Fox. An itinerant army of 1,000 striking actors..will parade at the old studio's grimy portals.

6. *Computers.* To erase or change (an item in a program).

1982 *Times* 14 Jan. (Information Technol. Suppl.) p. v/5 When the program is erased, the PROM is said to be 'zapped'. **1983** 80 *Microcomputing* Jan. 29/3 On DRS 304, RB 2C you will find the byte to be 20H. Zap this to 18H. **1983** *Your Computer* Sept. 86/1 Since I keep a hard copy listing of the assembly of MODEM7, the easiest thing to do was to zap the offending byte.

II. *intr.* **7.** To move quickly and with vigour.

1968 *Maclean's* Sept. 55 Nothing is quite as sad as watching Lynn watching Lightfoot zap off out of a parking lot. **1972** *Observer* 27 Feb. 33/5 The well-known routine of zapping from studio to studio. **1977** *Mod. Boating* (Austral.) Jan. 30/3 We're zapping over Kogarah Bay with 45 miles an hour on the clock. **1981** *Times* 22 July 12/4 When those self-satisfied pop singers and dizzy girls from Hollywood zap in and out they are not drinking themselves silly at our expense. **1985** *Times* 6 Apr. 11/1 Several smaller craft zap past.

8. To use a fast-forward facility on a video recorder to go quickly *through* the advertisements in a recorded television programme; to switch *through* other channels for the duration of the advertisements when watching programmes off-air.

1983 [implied in *ZAPPING *vbl. sb.*]. **1984** *Broadcast* 7 Dec. 27/2 People are beginning to record the best commercial programmes on their VCRs so they can zap through the commercials. **1985** *Marxism Today* May 34/1 People with the technology use it to avoid commercial breaks, either by zapping through other channels or by fast-forwarding material recorded off-air.

Hence **zapped** *ppl. a.* and *pa. pple.*

1962 *Amer. Speech* XXXVII. 71 'Zapped.'..I first heard it in 1952 while I was an undergraduate at Brown University. The term was in vogue..to designate precisely the process by which a student..had his 'comeuppance' in class or on an examination. **1966** *Punch* 21 Dec. 911/3 Maybe truce negotiations won't be possible until the Viet Cong are zapped to the point of accepting the impossibility of military victory. **1976** *National Observer* (U.S.) 22 May 12/4 Despite his allure, could she really endure him? But the chap's got her zapped. **1980** R. ADAMS *Girl in Swing* xix. 254 She was pale and sweating; clearly what Mr. Steinberg would call 'zapped'.

zap (zæp), *sb. slang* (orig. *U.S.*). [f. *ZAP *v.*, *int.*] **1.** Liveliness, energy, power, drive; also, a strong emotional effect.

1968 *N.Y. Times* 2 Aug. 3 When the heat's too much and the gin's lost its zap.., tranquilize your jangled nerves with the Swinging Wonder. **1972** *Publishers' Weekly* 6 Mar. 62/2 As for those lyrics—probably only the over-30s will dig them. Anyone older or younger won't grasp the 'organic' zap of rock's years of innocence. **1975** *Harpers & Queen* May 128/3 The zap of his language drawn from every dialect of the underground. **1979** *Chatelaine* (Canada) Jan. 50 She loves sports, especially skiing, but found she had lost some of her old zap. **1979** *Mod. Photogr.* Oct. 68 Electricity arrives at your neighborhood at a level of 2400 [*read* 240] volts... If the transformers were perfect you would get precisely the 110 volts you wanted and could care less about the big zap lurking outside. **1984** *New Yorker* 16 Apr. 141/1 He gives the film a manic zap.

2. A demonstration (by a group against something).

1972 *Sat. Rev.* 12 Feb. 26 Despite six zaps, New York's Mayor Lindsay has consistently refused to meet with any homosexual delegation. **1974** *Times* 7 Oct. 12/3 A demonstration, alternatively described as a community action or a zap, had been planned..in Brixton's Tesco supermarket.

3. *Computers.* A change in a program.

1983 80 *Microcomputing* Jan. 29/1, I would like to provide the following zaps to TRSDOS 1·3 for the Model III. To provide a 30ms track stepping rate you must change the nine bytes listed below.

4. A short, varying sound of the kind expressed by 'zap!'

1984 *Verbatim* X. III. 17/2 The whir of the flippers—pin-ball machines—the zaps of the video games.

Zapata (zăpā·tă). The name of Emilio *Zapata* (1879–1919), Mexican revolutionary, used *attrib.* to designate a type of moustache in which the two ends extend downwards to the chin.

Zapata was portrayed with a moustache of this kind by Marlon Brando in the film *Viva Zapata!* in 1952.

1968 *Punch* 25 Dec. 903/1 He stood now, in the centre of the enormous white vault of the school's auditorium, a willowy figure in a green velveteen frock-coat, Zapata moustache and a Donovan cap. **1972** A. ROSS *London Assignment* 84 One of the younger men, wearing nothing now but his Zapata moustache.., came up for a fresh joint. **1977** *N.Y. Rev. Bks.* 4 Aug. 11/1 He is a heavy, buccaneering figure with a Zapata mustache. **1983** *Manch. Guardian Weekly* 22 May 20/1, I was delighted to see a few shots of Karajan as stage actor—hiding behind a Zapata moustache as a bit-part cardsharper in the Carmen film he made in 1967.

‖**zapateado** (þapateā·ðo). Also **Zapateado.** [Sp., f. *zapato* shoe.] **a.** A flamenco dance which involves complex rhythmic syncopated stamping of the heels and toes in imitation of castanets.

1845 R. FORD *Handbk. Spain* I. 190 The chief dances are the *Jota* of Arragon..the *Zapateado* and *Seguidilla* of La Mancha..and the *Zortico* of Biscay. **1902** *Encycl. Brit.* XXVII. 374/2 Other provincial dances now in existence are the *Jaleo de Jerez*,..the *Zapateado*, the *Zorongo*.. and the *Tripola Trapola*. **1952** *Ballet Ann.* VI. 30 Antonio is in certain details of the Spanish dance the greatest exponent I have seen... Both his Bolero and his Zapateado must be seen to be believed. **1958** *Times* 23 Sept. 3/4 There is a good selection of flamenco dances, including solo and *à deux* Zapateados. **1973** *Daily Tel.* 19 Nov. 12/1 They danced without music and—like flamenco dancers performing a Zapateado—they used a very wide variety of sounds produced with their heels and toes so that music was superfluous. **1985** *Listener* 28 Feb. 18/3 Soon the girls are dancing with sensuous frenzy and a young man leaps on a table to execute a fine *zapateado*.

b. Dancing or footwork of this kind.

1959 *Sunday Times* 17 May 20/8 José's imprisonment, his rage expressed in zapateado, and the drama of Carmen's death, are adroitly planned. **1980** 'M. FONTEYN' *Magic of Dance* 56 Antonio, an electrifying dancer of flamenco and particularly of the language of foot and heel beats called zapateado. **1981** *Daily Tel.* 26 Aug. 9/8 Maya..has a superb grasp of subtle and varied zapateado.

zapote (zăpōᵘ·te). [Sp.: see SAPOTA.] = SAPOTE.

1842 S. MAVERICK *Jrnl.* 16 Dec. (1953) ix. 185 Fruit—oranges, Zapotes, etc. **1909** *Chambers's Jrnl.* Aug. 557/2 The Zapote..should secure the appreciation of the English fruitarian. **1926** D. H. LAWRENCE *Plumed Serpent* xiv. 229 A big basket piled with mangoes, papayas, zapotes—all the tropical fruits one did not want, in hot weather. **1948** G. M. FOSTER *Empire's Children* 27/2 Fruit trees include the fig,..white and black *zapotes*.

Zapotec (zæ·potek), *sb.* and *a.* Also 8- **Zapoteca, -o,** 9 **Zapoteque.** [ad. Sp. *zapoteco, zapoteca*, ad. Nahuatl *tzapoteca*, pl. of *tzapotecatl*, lit. 'person of the place of the sapodilla'.]

A. *sb.* A member of an American Indian people of southern Mexico.

1797 *Encycl. Brit.* XI. 668/1 To the south-east..were the great provinces of the Mixtecas, the Zapotecas, and the Chiapanecas. **1875** *Ibid.* I. 694/2 In Chiapa were the Zapotecs, in Yucatan the Mayas. **1877** L. H. MORGAN *Anc. Soc.* II. vii. 195 The confederacy was confronted by hostile..tribes..: the tribes of Chiapas, and the Zapotecs. **1953** S. BEDFORD *Sudden View* III. v. 231 The ancient Zapotecs..who may have come from Asia across the Behring Straits, and who are believed to have built.. these temples at Mitla and Monte Albàn. **1979** P. THEROUX *Old Patagonian Express* v. 75 These Indians—the Zapotecs—were a matrilineal people.

b. Any of several dialects or languages of the Zapotecs.

1881 *Encycl. Brit.* XII. 828/1 The other chief stock or at least not yet classified Mexican tongues are the Miztec and Zapotec of Oajaca, [etc.]. **1936** E. C. PARSONS *Mitla* i. 16 These ladies understand Zapoteco..but they do not speak it. **1965** *Language* XLI. 73 In Trique, Isthmus Zapotec, and certain other languages of Mexico, certain clause types have the preferred ordering predicate, subject, object. **1973** *Times* 24 Mar. 11/8 The student of architecture we met in the square of Oaxaca was talking Zapotec to his girl-friend.

B. *adj.* Of or pertaining to the Zapotecs.

1861 [see *EXPECTANT *ppl. a.* 1 b]. **1927** D. H. LAWRENCE *Mornings in Mexico* 45 Four words in the *idioma*, the Zapotec language..'You understand them?' **1934** A. HUXLEY *Beyond Mexique Bay* 46 A bas-relief of an ithyphallic man—the work..of the pre-Zapotec occupants of the site. **1972** *Bk. Thousand Tongues* (rev. ed.) 464/2 The Zapoteco language is spoken in a number of regional dialects. **1980** *Sci. Amer.* Feb. 46/3 Its hieroglyphs, mostly carved from 500 B.C. to A.D. 700, record the rise and decline of the Zapotec state.

Hence **Zapote·can** *a.* and *sb.*

1922 K. AL-SHIMAS *Mexican Southland* vii. 122 The Zapotecan tongue is spoken by at least 500,000 souls. *Ibid.* 126 Those accosted made answer in Zapotecan. **1962** E. BIRNEY *Ice Cod Bell or Stone* 54 Rhythmic and Zapotecan-proud the classic women dance. **1978** *Language* 506/2 In the Zapotecan family of Oaxaca, 'Choapan Zapotec phonology', by Larry and Rosemary Lyman.. employs 'a hierarchically oriented framework' of five levels, from phoneme to 'phonological sentence'.

zapper (zæ·pəɹ). [f. *ZAP *v.* + -ER¹.] **a.** A person, technique, etc., that kills or does away with something. **b.** *spec.* Any of various devices for destroying or warding off pests; also (properly with capital initial), a proprietary name in the U.S. for an agricultural machine of this kind.

1969 *Guardian* 27 May 8/5 The United States colonel who formerly commanded them..is now busy evolving a 'zapper' technique for scything down nippa palm groves where Vietcong are reported to be hiding with direct fire artillery. **1970** *Courier-Mail* (Brisbane) 14 Dec. 3/3 The rat zapper does not work on Saturdays or Sundays, but there were still no rats to be seen there yesterday. **1973** *Sci. Amer.* Sept. 74/2 One particularly promising application, making use of small portable zappers, is for greenhouses and other horticultural enterprises where the cost of soil preparation per acre is not an important consideration. For row crops..the self-propelled Zapper is presently economic only when chemical weed-control costs are higher than $15 per acre. **1975** *Official Gaz.* (U.S. Patent Office) 25 Mar. TM 271/2 *Zapper.* For agricultural machine which employs microwaves to control vegetation and vegetation damaging pests. **1976** *Nature* 12 Feb. 441/1 The general message is that although various alternatives are promising, there is no magic 'insect zapper', as Kennedy put it, to replace chemical poisons in the near future. **1977** *Globe & Mail* (Toronto) 30 July 4/1 How many bugs do zappers zap? **1983** *Monitor* (McAllen, Texas) 23 June 10c (Advt.), 1 acre bug zapper. $59·97. 35 watt ultraviolet fluorescent bulb has an effective range up to 1 acre for outdoor comfort.

zapping (zæ·piŋ), *vbl. sb. slang.* [f. *ZAP *v.* + -ING¹.] The action of *ZAP *v.*; *spec.* the practice of skipping advertisements when watching television programmes.

1972 *Daily Colonist* (Victoria, B.C.) 8 Jan. 17/7, I wouldn't take the zapping he has taken, to use the contemporary word, for a million dollars. **1983** *Times* 27 Oct. 8/3 The practice is known in the US as 'zapping'. Apparently people who have remote control devices are substantially more likely..to switch over to another channel when ads come on. **1983** *Austral. Personal Computer* Nov. 32/2 You could add suitable sound-effects to an applications program—zapping noises as a word processor deletes characters, maybe? **1984** *Listener* 9 Feb. 14/2 For the ITV companies there is the additional problem of 'zapping' to contend with—the habitual use of the fast-forward button to bypass the commercial breaks in recorded material.

zappy (zæ·pi), *a. slang.* [f. *ZAP *sb.* + -Y[1].] Lively, amusing, energetic; striking.

1969 *Guardian* 1 Mar. 5/2 The Minister wore in his lapel..a zappy coloured badge of the 'Cocoa makes you sterile' type. **1971** 'J. MAYO' *Asking for It* xxiv. 155 They were both giving each other big zappy grins. **1972** *Observer* 16 July 30/2 We badly need some zappy young editor who will start making his more garrulous authors prune their books. **1983** *Times Lit. Suppl.* 30 Dec. 1448/3 The best of contemporary American prose sometimes has a zappy elegance. **1984** *Listener* 3 May 30/4 The company felt the need for a zappier profile.

zarf, zurf. For etym. read [ad. Arab. *ẓarf* vessel.] and add later examples.

1854 R. CURZON *Armenia* 80 One brought coffee on a tray..and then came a man bringing to each of us a cup, well frothed up, and in a zarf, or outer cup. **1978** *Times* 2 May 13/3 (*caption*) A diamond and emerald zarf, mounted in gold and silver, 19th century, 6·5 cm high.

zariba, *sb.* Add: **c.** (Further examples.) In these uses usu. as **zareba.**

1916 'TAFFRAIL' *Pincher Martin* iii. 42 The orchestra..took their places behind a zareba of bunting-covered biscuit-boxes and hired palms erected in front of the stage. **1940** G. GREENE *Power & Glory* II. ii. 128 The shadows of the palms pointed at him like a zareba of sabres. **1961** WODEHOUSE *Ice in Bedroom* vii. 52 Owing to his *obiter dicta* having to be filtered through a zareba of white hair, it was not always easy to catch exactly what Mr. Cornelius said. **1965** G. MAXWELL *House of Elrig* x. 139 The final approach to any birds' nest was an affair of struggle and achievement. My hand reaches through the twigged zareba of basket and basket handle, touches the soft lining, touches the firm intimacy of the eggs. **1974** *Author* Spring 33 A novelist..has direct access to his readers, with no thorny zariba of a cast of actors to battle through. **1984** *Listener* 3 May 24/2 The two previous ones faced the reader in their opening chapters with an almost impenetrable zareba of thickset descriptions of the committee structure.

‖**zarzuela** (þaɪþuē·la). [Sp.] A traditional form of popular musical comedy in Spain.

In its theatrical sense the word is said to be derived from the name *Real Sitio de la Zarzuela* in Madrid, where these works were first performed in the early 17th century.

1888 *Lippincott's Mag.* July 51 It had all transpired in a flash, like some of the absurd things he had seen in pantomimes by the *zarzuela* companies at the theatres. **1922** J. HERGESHEIMER *Bright Shawl* (1923) 54 The zarzuelas, the operettas of one act, largely improvised with local allusions. **1947** A. EINSTEIN *Music in Romantic Era* xvii. 328 The way was being prepared for the Italianization of Spanish music as early as Calderón's period, which brought forth the old *zarzuela*, a mixture of song and dance with spoken dramatic dialogue. **1973** *Oxford Times* 30 Mar. 14/5 The modern zarzuelas are really operettas or lyric dramas, which are a kind of Spanish equivalent of Gilbert and Sullivan and the Viennese operetta, full of tunes which have become part of Spain's popular culture. **1973** R. A. CRAMPSEY *Puerto Rico* viii. 130 Less common are the old *zarzuelas*, the traditional musical dramas. **1983** *Listener* 21 Apr. 31/2 A Catalan born in 1871,..he [*sc.* Amadeo Vives] was evidently best known as a *zarzuela* composer.

zastruga, var. *SASTRUGA.

1982 B. ALDISS *Helliconia Spring* ii. 89 Only Yuli had experience of the tundras and zastrugi, which stretched away to the north of the Quzint.

zat (zæt), repr. a colloq. pronunc. of the cricket appeal 'How's that?' (see How *adv.* 2 b in Dict. and Suppl.).

1934 *Humorist* 27 Jan. 38/3 Not a bad record..for a game that consists chiefly of standing about..and shouting 'Zat?' at intervals. **1966** M. WOODHOUSE *Tree Frog* xxiii. 167 Outside the window a sharp yelp of 'Zat?' sounded.

zatch (zætʃ). *vulg.* [Perh. corruption of SATCHEL in similar slang sense.] The buttocks; the female genitals; an act of copulation.

1950 E. B. WHITE *Let.* 6 June (1976) 321 You are just sticking out your zatch, and many a tosspan and strutfart will run you through. **1971** R. DENTRY *Encounter at Kharmel* v. 88 Scotsmen playing the bagpipes give me a pain in the prick... Pathan tribesmen playing them is enough to make the harlot of Jerusalem snatch her zatch! **1980** J. KRANTZ *Princess Daisy* xii. 191 You're going to take her home and give her a zatch.

‖**zawiya** (zā·wiă). Also **zawia, zawiyah, zawya; zaouia.** [Arab. *zāwiya* (hence F. *zaouia*) corner, prayer room.] In North Africa, a Muslim religious community or its mosque, usually containing the shrine of a holy person.

1836 E. W. LANE *Acct. Manners & Customs Mod. Egyptians* II. xi. 190 These lights were not hung merely in honour of the Prophet: they were near a *zawiyeh* (or small mosque) in which is buried the sheykh Durweesh El-Ashmawee; and this night was his Moolid. **1874** R. L. PLAYFAIR *Handbk. Trav. Algeria* II. 70/2 The *Djamâa*, or rather *Zaouia* of *Abd-er-Rahman eth-Thalebi*..contains the tomb of that saint, who died in 1471. **1911** *Encycl. Brit.* XXVII. 289/1 Kufra..is a centre of the Senūssite brotherhood, whose *zawya* (convent) at Jof, in Kebabo, ranks in importance with that of Jarabub. **1911** D. S. MARGOLIOUTH *Mohammedanism* v. 184 A *zawiyah*, or 'hermitage' was offered him by the Pasha. **1924** W. M. SLOANE *Greater France in Afr.* viii. 166 The sacred colleges of the Moslem fraternities, zaouias, are the scenes of wild, maniacal, religious orgies. **1958** N. EPTON *Saints & Sorcerers* ii. 28 The sheikh (this word signifies either the head of a *zaouia* or of a tribe..) lives close to the *zaouia* with his family and the devotees. **1968** T. BLUNSUM *Libya* x. 105 The *zawias*, or houses of learning and worship, were documentation centres where copies of the Koran were prepared for distribution. **1977** *Times* 30 Apr. 11/3 Nefta..a village..whose roof lines are broken by the cupolas of mosques and zaouias. **1978** J. UPDIKE *Coup* (1979) iii. 122 Who was it used to tell reporters I was a *zawiya* Berber too pious to be seen?

‖**zazen** (zāze·n). Also 8 **Sasen; Zazen.** [Jap., f. *za* sitting, a seat + *zen* *ZEN.] Zen meditation.

1727 J. G. SCHEUCHZER tr. *Kæmpfer's Hist. Japan* I. III. i. 242 A posture, which is thought to engage one's mind in so profound a meditation, and to wrap it up so entirely within itself, that the body lies for a while as it were sens less... This profound Enthusiasm is by them call'd *Safen* [sic: read *Sasen*]. **1897** *Princ., Pract. & Enlightenment Soto Sect* 22 How can you think of not-thinking? That is thinking of nothing. This is the most important art of Zazen. **1907** *Jrnl. Pali Text Soc. 1906–7* 36 Zazen is not meant to induce a trance or a state of self-hypnotization. **1960** KOESTLER *Lotus & Robot* II. xi. 257 Zazen meditation, unlike Yoga, holds no promise of supernatural rewards. **1973** A. BROINOWSKI *Take One Ambassador* viii. 108 Three hours of daily *zazen* meditation. **1983** M. FURLONG *Cousins* xxi. 167 He had taken to practising what he hoped was *zazen* in the yard.

Z band: see *Z LINE (as a main entry).

Zealander. Add: **b.** A native or inhabitant of New Zealand; orig. and esp. a Maori.

1773 W. BAYLY *Jrnl.* 12 Apr. in R. McNab *Hist. Rec. N.Z.* (1914) II. 207 The Zeelanders never eat greens of any kind. **1821** M. EDGEWORTH *Let.* 7 Dec. (1971) 288 Captain Thompson..went some years ago to New Zealand and when he was taking leave of the Zealanders one of their chiefs consented to accompany him to England. **1949** E. POUND *Pisan Cantos* lxxx. 92 And persuaded an Aussie or Zealander or S. African To kneel with him in prayer.

zearalenone (zɪ͵ăræ·lĕnōᵘn). *Biochem.* [f. ZEA + *-ralenone*, f. *r*esorcylic *a*cid *l*act*one* + -ENE, repr. a double bond + -ONE.] A white crystalline bicyclic latone, $C_{18}H_{22}O_5$, that is a metabolic product of certain cereal fungi and causes disorders of the reproductive system in pigs.

1966 W. H. URRY et al. in *Tetrahedron Lett.* XXVII. 3109 Study of the substance of striking physiological activity isolated from the mycelia of the fungus Gibberella zeae..has shown that it is one of the enantiomorphs of 6-(10-hydroxy-6-oxo-*trans*-1-undecenyl)-*β*-resorcylic acid lactone I... Zearalenone I..gives reactions that indicate it has one olefinic and one ketonic group, and two phenolic hydroxyls and an ester group in a *β*-resorcylate structure. **1977** *Lancet* 26 Mar. 671/2 Analytical tests failed to show the presence of aflatoxin,..although zearalenone was found in maize samples. **1978** [see *TRICHOTHECENE]. **1981** M. L. CLARKE et al. *Veterinary Toxicol.* (ed. 2) VIII. 277/1 The phenolic macrolide zearalenone (F-2 toxin) produced by *Fusarium graminearum*..and other *Fusarium* species growing on maize, barley and wheat destined for incorporation into animal feeds, is probably one of the most widespread and economically important mycotoxins.

zearat, var. *ZIARAT.

zeatin (zī·ătin). *Biochem.* [f. ZEA + *-t-* + -IN[1].] A purine derivative occurring as a cytokinin in maize kernels and other plants; 6-(4-hydroxy-3-methylbut-2-enyl)-aminopurine, $C_{10}H_{13}N_5O$.

1963 D. S. LETHAM in *Life Sciences* No. 8. 572 For this factor the name zeatin is proposed since it was first isolated in crystalline form from *Zea mays.* **1973** D. W. KROGMANN *Biochem. Green Plants* xi. 196 Coconut milk..contains a high concentration of zeatin. **1980** *Physiologia Plantarum* XLIX. 304/1 All the cytokinins, at $10^{-6}M$ and above, inhibited both the initiation and the emergence of lateral roots, zeatin being the most powerful inhibitor.

zeaxanthin (zɪ͵ăzæ·nþin). *Biochem.* [a. G. *zeaxanthin* (P. Karrer et al. 1929, in *Helvetica Chim. Acta* XII. 791): see ZEA and XANTHIN.] A xanthophyll, $C_{40}H_{56}O_4$, originally isolated from Indian corn, *Zea mays.*

1929 *Chem. Abstr.* XXIII. 4480 (*heading*) Zeaxanthin, a new carotinoid pigment in maize. **1934** [see *XANTHOPHYLL a]. **1978** [see *VIOLAXANTHIN].

zebra, *sb.* Add: **2. c.** Also, a striped prison uniform.

1895 *Harper's Weekly* 10 Aug. 753/3 At present I understand that he is in limbo, wearing the famous 'zebra'—the penitentiary dress. **1935** A. J. POLLOCK *Underworld Speaks* 136/1 *Zebra*, striped prison clothing.

d. A zebra crossing. *colloq.*

1951 O. LANCASTER in *Daily Express* 15 Dec. 1/5 If we can only find a Zebra, we can sit down and relax. **1959** *Woman* 24 Jan. 4/3, I often wait ten minutes or more, even at a zebra, while super new cars speed past. **1968** *Listener* 15 Aug. 201/3 Outside, on the road, trucks wait for me to cross a zebra. **1976** *S. Wales Echo* 27 Nov. 9/2 [He] pleaded guilty to stopping a car in a zebra-controlled area.

3. *zebra marking, skin*; *zebra-marked, -striped* (examples) adjs.; **zebra crossing,** a pedestrian crossing marked by broad black and white stripes on the road and Belisha beacons on the kerb; **zebra danio** (dē[i]·nio), a small Indian freshwater fish with horizontal dark and light stripes, *Brachydanio rerio* (family Cyprinidæ), which is popular as an aquarium fish; **zebra fish:** also, any of several striped tropical fishes, esp. the zebra danio; (further examples); **zebra spider,** any of several striped spiders of the family Salticidæ; **zebra-wood** (further examples).

[**1949** *Surveyor* 8 July 407/1 Investigations by the Road Research Laboratory..have led to the full-scale trials of the striped (zebra) markings for pedestrian crossings. **1950** *Times* 18 Feb. 2/5 Experiments are now being carried out..to test the efficacy of the zebra striped pedestrian crossing when illuminated at night.] **1950** *Surveyor* 23 June 365/2 The initial values of the percentage of drivers giving way are higher on the 'zebra' crossings than on the plain. **1977** B. PYM *Quartet in Autumn* ii. 23 He..called out angrily after a car which had failed to stop at a zebra crossing. **1917** W. T. INNES *Goldfish Varieties & Tropical Aquarium Fishes* (ed. 2) vii. 86 *Danio rerio*, Zebra Danio. **1962** D. W. TUCKER tr. *Sterba's Freshw. Fishes of World* 265 Some species, such as the Zebra Danio, will spawn over gravelly bottoms even when there are no plants present. **1980** *Sci. Amer.* Feb. 127/2 McCutchen has employed his rig to study the motion of a small fish, a zebra danio (*Brachydanio rerio*), which is about three centimeters long. **1895** *Aquarium* Apr. 172/1 (*heading*) Brazilian Zebra Fish (*Heros facetus*). **1925** *Aquatic Life* June 18/1 Danio rerio, those swift, graceful, blue and white and sometimes golden striped zebra fish, have many admirers. **1934** C. W. COATES *Tropical Fishes as Pets* v. 49 The Zebra Fish (*Pterois volitans*), a marine beast from the Indian Ocean, erects all his fins, faces his future meal, and appears to drift toward it. **1962** *Listener* 22 Nov. 852/2 The three black-and-white-striped zebra fish were speed-merchants [in the tank]. **1979** H. F. AXELROD et al. *Exotic Marine Fishes* 121 The scorpion fishes..often called butterfly cod or zebra fishes..are mostly hardy, attractive predators. **1924** J. A. THOMSON *Science Old & New* v. 30 Butterflies like the unpalatable zebra-marked Heliconius, which insectivorous birds leave unmolested. **1949** Zebra marking [see *zebra crossing* above]. **1973** G. BEARE *Snake on Grave* xiii. 68 Walls, floor, and ceiling were all done in a zebra-skin motif. Everything..was covered in zebra skin. **1978** S. NAIPAUL *North of South* II. vi. 230 Copies of *Playboy* were scattered on a zebra-skin rug. **1866** *Hours at Home* III. 331/1 Next to the garden-spider, the hunting or zebra spider is the most common. **1966** C. SWEENEY *Scurrying Bush* vi. 87 The commonest of these [jumping spiders] was banded black and white like a zebra... Zebra spiders are able to leap..in an eighteen-inch arc. **1852** Zebra-striped [see *dove orchis* s.v. *DOVE *sb.* 5 b]. **1950** [see *zebra crossing* above]. **1976** *National Observer* (U.S.) 21 Aug. 1/3 There was Clarabell in his green-and-white zebra-striped clown suit. **1934**, etc. Zebrawood [see *ZINGANA 2].

zebrano (zĕ-, zèbrā·no). [Irreg. f. ZEBRA *sb.*] Striped wood furnished by various species of African trees, esp. ones of the genus *Microberlinia.*

1928 *Sunday Express* 29 July 15/4 We take the most handsome pieces of..sapele mahogany, or of lesser known woods like macassar, ebony, zebrano, amboyna. **1934** *Archit. Rev.* LXXV. 144 (*caption*) The furniture is in Indian rosewood and Japanese chestnut and the panelling in zebrano. **1965** *Wireless World* Sept. 37 (Advt.), Finish zebrano, mahogany, walnut or teak veneers. **1980** E. SCOTT *Illustr. Encycl. Working in Wood* 248 *Microberlinia brazzavillensis* Zebrano. Normally coarse texture; interlocked grain.

zebrina (zĕbrəi·nă). *Bot.* Also **Zebrina.** [mod.L. (A. Schnitzlein 1849, in *Bot. Zeitung* VII. 870/2), f. ZEBR(A, in allusion to the striped leaves of some species + -INA[2].] A creeping recumbent herb of the genus of this name (family Commelinaceæ) that is native to central America, bears ovate, often striped, leaves and clusters of small flowers, and is grown as a greenhouse and indoor plant.

1946 M. FREE *All about House Plants* iii. 15 English Ivy, Tradescantia, and Zebrina (to trail over edge [of a window-box]). **1960** *Times* 30 Jan. 11/2 The green or white and green striped zebrinas. **1963** [see *PERICLINAL *a.* (*sb.*) 2 b]. **1978** *Homes & Gardens* Oct. 42/2 Among these summer sun-lovers are beloperone..and zebrina.

zebroid (zī·-, ze·broid), *a.* and *sb.* [f. ZEBR(A + -OID.] **A.** *adj.* (In Dict. s.v. ZEBRA *sb.* Further example.)

1974 *Nature* 22 Mar. 296/2 G. Nobis's study of the horse teeth recognised three groups: two larger species with primitive 'zebroid' features.

B. *sb.* The offspring of a horse and a zebra.
1899 *Tablet* 25 Nov. 848/2 The zebroid, or hybrid between the horse and the zebra, 'will be the mule of the 20th century'. **1926** *Daily Colonist* (Victoria, B.C.) 18 July 24/1 The first man to have any practical success in crossbreeding the zebra and the horse is Dr. W. E. Hastings of Mt. Vernon, Ind. The result is a new mule, the zebroid. **1973** *Daily Tel.* (Colour Suppl.) 5 Oct. 31/4 Another Kenya 'character'..crossed ponies with zebras, and used the resulting 'zebroids' as pack animals for safaris. **1983** *Listener* 20 Jan. 25/1 Christina Dodwell, in *Travels with Fortune*, paddled a dug-out canoe, and rode a camel and a zebroid, in her journey through Africa.

zebrule (zī·brūl, ze·brūl). [f. ZEBR(A + M)ULE¹.] = next.
1903 in P. Fleming *Bayonets to Lhasa* (1961) viii. 102 In my Section are two Zebrules, half zebra and half donkey. **1978** J. MORRIS *Farewell the Trumpets* vii. 132 By December 13, 1903 every last yak and zebrule had crossed the frontier of Tibet.

zedonk (zī·dǫŋk, ze·dǫŋk). Also **zeedonk.** [f. ZE(BRA + DONK(EY.] The offspring of a male zebra and a female donkey. Cf. *ZONKEY.
1971 *Daily Tel.* 17 Apr. 8/5 The staff at Colchester Zoo have described their newcomer as a 'Zedonk'. **1976** *Observer* (Colour Suppl.) 5 Sept. 42/3 Donkeys crossed with zebras, sometimes called zeedonks, have been used like mules..as pack animals. **1978** *Panorama* (Austral.) Aug. 13/2 Zareeba the zedonk (half zebra, half donkey) is one of only five of his kind known in the world.

Zeeman (zēⁱ·măn). *Physics.* The name of P. *Zeeman* (1865–1943), Dutch physicist, used *attrib.* with reference to the splitting of a spectral line into three or more closely spaced components when the light source is in a magnetic field not strong enough to produce the Paschen–Back effect.
Observed by Zeeman in 1897.
[**1897** *Phil. Mag.* XLIV. 503 A theoretical analysis.. can be developed in connexion with Zeeman's phenomenon, which may help to throw light on the nature of the electric vibrations in the molecule.] **1899** *Rep. Brit. Assoc. Adv. Sci. 1898* 789 An effect converse to the Zeeman effect occurs in those cases where the body is absorbing instead of emitting light. **1904** [see *MAGNETO-GYRIC *a.* 1]. **1926** [see *LARMOR]. **1962** W. B. THOMPSON *Introd. Plasma Physics* i. 3 There are several ways of inferring the existence of magnetic fields, of which the most direct is from a measurement of the Zeeman splitting of spectral lines. **1971** *New Scientist* 18 Feb. 381/1 When a nucleus is placed in a high magnetic field, each energy level splits into several sublevels known as magnetic sublevels or Zeeman levels. **1978** PASACHOFF & KUTNER *University Astron.* viii. 219 (*caption*) From studies of the splitting of lines that are sensitive to the Zeeman effect, the magnetic field on the sun can be mapped.

zeep (zīp), *v. rare*⁻¹. [? var. ZIP *v.*] *trans.* To elicit a zipping sound from.
1935 S. BECKETT *Echo's Bones*, Tires bleeding voiding zeep the highway.

Zeiss (zəis). The name of Carl *Zeiss* (1816–88), German optical instrument maker, used *attrib.* to designate binoculars manufactured by the firm he founded.
1905 W. JAMES *Let.* 3 Apr. (1920) II. 224 Now I will stop, and use my Zeiss glass on the land, which is getting nearer. **1912** A. CONAN DOYLE *Lost World* viii. 126 He had his Zeiss glasses in his hand. **1938** S. BECKETT *Murphy* iv. 60, I have worshipped her from afar... All last June, through Zeiss glasses. **1971** R. DENTRY *Encounter at Kharmel* vii. 127 There were..Zeiss binoculars..at the back of the glove compartment. **1983** T. POCOCK *1945* vii. 217 The luckiest found Leica cameras and Zeiss binoculars.

‖**zeitgeber** (tsəi·tgēbəɹ). *Physiol.* Pl. same or (anglicized) **zeitgebers.** [Ger. (J. Aschoff 1954, in *Naturwissenschaften* XLI. 49), f. *zeit* time + *geber* giver.] A rhythmically occurring event, esp. in the environment, which acts as a cue in the regulation of certain biological rhythms in an organism.
1964 E. BÜNNING *Physiological Clock* ii. 9 The change of light and dark or alternations of high and low temperatures have a synchronizing effect on the endodiurnal rhythm; they function as 'Zeitgeber' (cues, synchronizers). **1969** *New Scientist* 21 Aug. 369/2 Light is known to be the *zeitgeber* for the ant-lion's solar-day rhythm. **1975** D. VINCE-PRUE *Photoperiodism in Plants* v. 169 The signals responsible for entrainment have been called *zeitgebers.* **1975** *Nature* 27 Nov. 291/2 The various rhythms respond to changes in the phase or period of the entraining cycle (the Zeitgeber). **1983** *Brit. Med. Jrnl.* 6 Aug. 426/2 Melatonin is secreted by the pineal gland during the night... In rats it will act as a 'zeitgeber' or synchroniser of the rest-activity cycle under conditions of zero environmental input.

Zeitgeist. Add: Also **Zeit Geist, Zeit-Geist** (both *rare*), and with small initial. (Earlier and later examples.)
For **1893** M. ARNOLD in Dict. read **1873** M. ARNOLD. **1848** M. ARNOLD *Let.* Nov. (1932) 95, I..took up Obermann, and refuged myself with him..against your Zeit Geist. **1876** *Mind* I. 369 There is a *Zeitgeist*, he says. **1884** *Macmillan's Mag.* Aug. 254 For realism in one form or another is the zeitgeist which will master us all. **1889** G. B. SHAW *Let.* Aug. (1965) I. 222 My business is to incarnate the Zeitgeist. **1933** A. HUXLEY *Let.* 9 Oct. (1969) 374 The Zeitgeist is a most dismal animal and I wish to heaven one cd escape from its clutches. **1946** AUDEN *Litany & Anthem for S. Matthew's Day*, May we worship neither the flux of chance, nor the wheel of fortune, nor the spiral of the zeit-geist. **1972** *Science* 2 June 991/3 A clear mark of the Zeitgeist of the late 1960's and the 1970's is the increased demand for participation in decision-making by those affected by it. **1982** D. PIPER *Image of Poet* i. 13 Shakespeare becomes in a sense an ever-changing embodiment of the *Zeitgeist.*

zek (zek). [Russ., prob. repr. pronunc. of *z/k*, abbrev. of *zaklyuchënnyĭ* prisoner.] In the U.S.S.R., a person confined in a prison or forced labour camp.
1968 T. P. WHITNEY tr. *Solzhenitsyn's First Circle* p. x, All the zeks at the Mavrino sharashka belonged, though they were not at the time in hard-labor camps, to the realm of GULAG. **1977** *Guardian Weekly* 26 June 22/2 And didn't his author work gratefully too in the same *sharashka*, or Island of Paradise, as the zeks called these 'soft' research camps? **1982** T. BINYON *Swan Song* viii. 58 They got him for parasitism and a few other offences. Now he was presumably..east of the Urals and taking the zeks for their bread ration.

Zeldovich (ze·ldǒvitʃ). *Chem.* The name of Y. B. *Zeldovich* (b. 1914), U.S.S.R. physicist, used *attrib.* to designate a mechanism proposed by him for the oxidation of nitrogen to nitric oxide in flames via a two-stage free-radical reaction.
1973 S. J. WILLIAMSON *Fund. Air Pollution* x. 298 The formation of NO occurs primarily through two simultaneous reactions known as the Zeldovich mechanism: $N + O_2 = NO + O$; $O + N_2 = NO + N$. **1982** *Sci. Amer.* Feb. 94/1 At temperatures low enough to suppress the Zeldovich reactions other reactions still generate nitric oxide.

zelkova (zelko·vă). Also **Zelkova.** [mod.L. (E. Spach 1841, in *Ann. des Sci. Nat.: Bot.* 2nd Ser. XV. 352), f. *zelkoua, tselkwa*, cited by Spach as local names for *Z. carpinifolia* in the Caucasus: cf. mod.Russ. *dzel'kova grabolistnaya.*] A deciduous tree of the genus of this name (family Ulmaceæ), which is native to China, Japan, and the Caucasus, and bears toothed leaves and small green flowers. Also *zelkova tree.*
1893 A. D. WEBSTER *Hardy Oranamental Flowering Trees & Shrubs* 134 Zelkova Tree..is a handsome, large growing tree, with oblong deeply-crenated leaves, and small inconspicuous flowers. **1957** M. HADFIELD *Brit. Trees* 226 The zelkova..deserves more extensive planting. **1976** *Daily Tel.* 5 July 8/6 Three thousand Zelkova trees imported from Germany are being planted in Peterborough to replace elms killed by Dutch Elm disease. **1978** *Vole* Dec. 27/1 Zelkovas are a rather special group of trees. They belong to the Elm family and have delicate, toothed leaves.

zemindary. Add: Also **zamindary.** (Examples of this form and **zamindari.**)
1914 W. G. LAWRENCE *Let.* 30 July in *Home Lett. T. E. Lawrence* (1954) 563 We all ate together of food one could stick one's teeth in, thick Zamindari bread. **1917** *Chambers's Jrnl.* Dec. 781/1 There is no such man within my zamindary as can catch the living snake. **1932** *Ann. Reg. 1931* I. 155 Movements against the payment of rents and land revenue, particularly in the United Provinces, where the *zamindari* (landlord) system is prevalent. **1968** *Times* 6 Apr. (Pakistan Suppl.) p. v/4 After independence, many Hindu zamindars fled, the zamindary system was abolished and the land divided into tiny portions and sold to the Muslims. **1976** M. S. HOQUE *Hunger* II. vi. 41 Parents now think that their son is a Zamindari estate on auction sale.

‖**zemirah** (zəmīᵊ·ra). *Judaism.* Pl. **zemirot(h** (zəmīᵊ·rōᵘt, s-). [Heb.] A religious song sung in Hebrew at Sabbath meals.
1831 [see *MITZVAH]. **1892** I. ZANGWILL *Childr. Ghetto* II. xviii. 82 When supper was over grace was chanted, and then the *Zemiroth* were sung—songs summing up, in light and jingling metre, the very essence of holy joyousness. **1973** *Jewish Chron.* 9 Feb. 21/5 The service was followed by supper and zemirot in the communal hall.

zemstvo. Add: Pl. **zemstvos,** ‖ **zemstva.**
1958 *Times Lit. Suppl.* 10 Jan. 14/3 The history of the pressure for political freedom was closely interwoven with the development of the organs of local self-government, the *Zemstva.* **1967** *Listener* 2 Nov. 559/1 At any time in those final decades of the last century even a central assembly of representatives of the *zemstvos* would have constituted an important safety-valve. **1980** *Times. Lit. Suppl.* 14 Nov. 1306/3 Linked closely to the work of the *zemstva*, new local units of administration, medicine became the first true profession in Russia. **1983** P. USTINOV *My Russia* xi. 122 Members of local *zemstvos* might soon enjoy a voice in the internal government of the country.

Zen (zen). Also 8 **Sen.** [a. Jap. *zen*, ad. Chin. *chán* quietude, ad. Skr. *dhyāna* meditation.] A school of Mahayana Buddhism that emphasizes meditation and personal awareness and became influential in Japanese life from the 13th century after being introduced from China.
1727 J. G. SCHEUCHZER tr. *Kæmpfer's Hist. Jap.* I. II. v. 199 In the 1850 streets of this city, there were 1050 [families] of the *Ten Dai's* Religion,..11 016 of *Sen.* **1834** [see *SHINGON]. **1911** *Encycl. Relig. & Ethics* IV. 704/1 Meditation came to have more weight than the other two factors, until in China and Japan there arose a sect, the Zen..in which it is the most essential part of the entire teaching. **1921** *Eastern Buddhist* (Japan) I. 13 Zen in its essence is the art of seeing into the nature of one's own being. **1960** *Spectator* 15 July 101 *What* do they know about Zen—the programme-writer, the film-makers, the beatniks, the lot? **1967** D. & E. T. RIESMAN *Conversations in Japan* 123 Another boy, who..was their top judo athlete, said that he got his values from Zen. **1976** A. DAVIS *Television* 122 By the late sixties, religious programmes were beginning to reflect the interest of young people in Eastern religions such as Buddhism, Hinduism, Zen and the cult of the Maharishi. **1977** J. F. FIXX *Compl. Bk. Running* ii. 14 Our society puts considerable emphasis on personal development and the maximizing of one's potential. Zen, transcendental meditation, assertiveness training..and similar movements are all directed at making us fulfilled human beings.

2. *attrib.* and *Comb.*, esp. in *Zen Buddhism, Buddhist.*
1881 *Trans. Asiatic Soc. Japan* IX. 179 (*heading*) Zen sect. **1894**, etc. [see *SOTO]. **1902** *Encycl. Brit.* XXIX. 681/1 The Zen doctrines of Buddhism, which contributed so much to the development of the heroic and the sentimental,..were therefore favourable to the stability of military feudalism. **1921** *Eastern Buddhist* (Japan) I. 13 (*heading*) Zen Buddhism as purifier and liberator of life. *Ibid.* 26 Whether an enlightened Zen master or an ignoramus of the first degree, neither can escape the so-called laws of nature. **1923** *Ibid.* II. 341 It remained for the Chinese Zen Buddhists to invent their own methods according to their own needs and insight. **1947** *Archit. Rev.* CII. 32/2 Taoism and nature mysticism, transmitted through the vehicle of Zen Buddhism. **1950** A. HUXLEY *Themes & Variations* 98 As the Zen Masters like paradoxically to put it, 'Buddha never taught the saving truth.' **1960** KOESTLER *Lotus & Robot* II. x. 234 The monk's rudeness..was in the right tradition of Zen-teasing. **1965** W. SWAAN *Jap. Lantern* v. 58 The canons of Japanese aesthetic appreciations were formulated to a very large degree under the influence of Zen Buddhist philosophy. **1971** 'G. BLACK' *Time for Pirates* iii. 45 Mr. Akamoro..contrived..to leak the thought.. that it is time for Japanese initiative to take over with Zen Buddhism for the moral trimmings. **1979** B. MALAMUD *Dubin's Lives* viii. 280 She said she had been talking to a Zen Master in South San Francisco... 'I'm thinking of entering a Zen commune... I expect to become a Zen disciple.'

zendo (ze·ndo). [a. Jap. *zendō*, f. *zen* *ZEN + *dō* hall.] A place for Zen Buddhist meditation and study.
1959 *Encounter* XII. I. 20 The *Zendo* or meditation-hall. **1968** *Time* 18 Oct. 62/3 Students must report to the *zendo* (meditation hall) by 5. **1974** *Country Life* 14 Feb. 326/1, I was taken to the Zendo, the special hall for contemplation, by a young monk. **1981** 'E. V. CUNNINGHAM' *Case of Sliding Pool* vii. 77, I thought I would drive down to the Zendo... I feel a need to talk to the Roshi.

Zener (zī·nəɹ). Also **zener. 1.** The name of K. E. *Zener* (1903–61), U.S. psychologist, used *attrib.* to designate a pack of 25 cards that he designed for use in parapsychology experiments, containing five each of five different cards, each showing a simple symbol.
1934 J. B. RHINE *Extra-Sensory Perception* iv. 50 We have once since substituted a 'heart' for the 'waves' figure but later returned to the latter. I shall hereinafter call these cards the 'Zener cards'. **1940** *Proc. Soc. Psychical Res.* XLVI. 153 The guesser at Zener cards all unwittingly was guessing correctly..a card which was one or two places earlier or later in the sequence. **1949** *Mind* LVIII. 390 Extra-sensory perception (ESP) is investigated by means of the card-guessing technique. Zener cards are generally used. **1969** *Listener* 6 Mar. Mar. 301/2 Rhine devised a new kind of test for ESP. He made packs of 25 cards called Zenercards, with geometrical designs: cross, square, circle, waves and star. **1978** D. BLOODWORTH *Crosstalk* xiv. 119 There are a dozen ways of beating the odds with the Zener packs they use for card-guessing tests.

2. *Electronics.* The name of C. M. *Zener* (b. 1905), U.S. physicist. **a.** Used *attrib.* to denote various concepts, etc., connected with or arising from his researches, as **Zener breakdown** = *Zener effect* below; **Zener diode,** a junction diode in which the forward characteristic is like that of an ordinary diode but there is a sudden large increase in reverse current at a certain constant reverse voltage owing to the Zener effect or the avalanche effect, making it useful as a voltage regulator and in switching circuits; **Zener effect,** the increase in reverse current of a Zener diode when attributed to the tunnelling of current-carriers through the transition region rather than to the avalanche effect; **Zener voltage,** the voltage at which Zener breakdown occurs; the reverse breakdown voltage of a Zener diode.

1956 L. P. Hunter *Handbk. Semiconductor Electronics* III. 17 The two mechanisms which have been observed for semiconductor contacts in the absence of thermal breakdown are Zener breakdown..and avalanche breakdown. **1962** [see *Zener effect* below]. **1981** Nashelsky & Boylestad *Devices: Discrete & Integrated* ii. 29 As V_z [*sc.* the Zener voltage] decreases to very low levels, such as −5V, another mechanism, called Zener breakdown, will contribute to the sharp change in the characteristic. **1957** R. F. Shea *Transistor Circuit Engineering* iii. 62 One of the simplest methods of obtaining such a [stable collector-voltage] supply is with the aid of a diode biased into breakdown in the reverse direction (so-called Zener diode). **1975** *Gramophone* Aug. 384/3 Stabilisation of the feedback input stages is achieved with a zener diode. **1981** J. C. Sprott *Introd. Mod. Electronics* vi. 136 In the forward direction a Zener diode behaves like any other diode. **1957** W. C. Dunlap *Introd. Semiconductors* viii. 168 Internal field emission, often called Zener effect because of the early theoretical contributions made to the subject by C. Zener,..is analogous to field emission from metals. **1962** Simpson & Richards *Physical Princ. Junction Transistors* iv. 69 Lower voltage units usually have negative temperature coefficients indicating the existence of Zener effect. In such devices the transition region is apparently too thin to allow appreciable carrier multiplication to take place and Zener breakdown occurs before the critical avalanche condition has been reached. **1952** *Proc. IRE* XL. 1349/2 The Zener voltage for this junction was 21·5 volts. **1969** J. J. Sparkes *Transistor Switching* i. 13 At Zener voltages of about 6V the slope resistance of the diode characteristic is minimal. **1980** C. F. G. Delaney *Electronics for Physicist* ix. 215 The Zener voltage..is a function of the resistivity (that is, of the doping) of the materials from which the diode is constructed.

b. *ellipt.* A Zener diode.

1965 *Wireless World* July 14 (Advt.), Ask for details of zeners from 400 mW to 50W, and 3·6V to 200V. **1976** *Pract. Electronics* Oct. 791/1 To provide any given voltage, it is only necessary to select a Zener having a voltage exceeding the required voltage by 0·7 volts.

Zengakuren (zengăkū·rĕn). [Jap., acronym f. *Zen* Nihon *Gaku*sei Jichikai *Ren*go, = All-Japan Federation of Student Self-Government Associations (formed in 1948).] In Japan, an extreme left-wing student movement, noted for its violent interventions in national politics. Also *attrib.* or as *adj.*

1952 E. S. Colbert *Left Wing in Japanese Politics* v. 299 The Communist-dominated student organization, the *Zengakuren. Ibid.* 300 On May 23, [1950] at a *Zengakuren* convention. **1960** *Times* 21 Sept. 16/6 He is rather naturally unloved by the members of Zengakuren, the radical student movement. **1967** D. & E. T. Riesman *Conversations in Japan* 121 The large Zengakuren ideas and practical accomplishments. **1970** *Guardian* 1 Apr. 11/1 The students, armed with quarter-staves,..with the colours and battle-cry of the Zengakuren sect to which they belonged. **1975** *New Yorker* 18 Aug. 50/2 Five student groups, including two main ones called Kakumaruha (the Revolutionary Marxists) and Chukakuha (the Middle Core), both composed of self-styled Trotskyites, are offshoots of the original Zengakuren, a radical association that led demonstrations against the security treaty and instigated campus riots that succeeded in closing down a number of universities over a period of months in 1969.

zenick. In def. for *zenik* read *suricatta*. Add: = Meerkat 2 b, Suricate. (Earlier example.)

1801 J. Barrow *Acct. Trav. S. Afr.* I. iii. 231 Others of this genus [*sc.* Viverra] are the muskiliatte cat, or zenik,.. the tigrina [etc.].

zenilla, obs. var. Zanella in Dict. and Suppl.

zenithal, *a.* (In Dict. s.v. Zenith.) Add: *zenithal projection*, any of a class of map projections in which a portion of the globe is projected on to a plane tangential to a point on that portion, usu. made the centre of the map.

1882 T. Craig *Treat. on Projections* v. 89 The name zenithal projections is..derived from the fact that they can always be considered as the representation of the hemisphere situated above the horizon of the given point, and having the zenith for pole. **1910,** etc. [see *projection *sb.* 7b]. **1961** L. F. Brosnahan *Sounds of Language* iii. 74 A continuous distribution of the O blood-group gene frequencies in Europe was..redrawn on a map of zenithal equal-area projection. **1974** *Encycl. Brit. Micropædia* IV. 587/3 *Gnomic map*, type of zenithal projection in which the Earth's grid is projected by radials from a point at the centre of the sphere into a tangent plane so that all great circles are represented by straight lines.

zenithward, *adv.* (In Dict. s.v. Zenith.) (Earlier example.)

1868 Carlyle *Jrnl.* 8 June in J. A. Froude *T. Carlyle* (1884) II. xxxi. 371 It was as a ray of everlasting light and insight this, that had shot itself *zenithward* from the soul of a man.

Zenker (ze·ŋkəɹ). **1.** The name of F. A. Zenker (1825–98), German pathologist, used in the possessive and occas. *attrib.* to designate (*a*) a hyaline degeneration of striated muscle occurring chiefly in cases of acute infectious disease, esp. typhoid and cholera (described by Zenker in 1864); (*b*) a pathological diverticulum at the junction of the pharynx and œsophagus (described by Zenker & von Ziemssen in *Cycl. Practice of Med.* (1878) VIII. 1–214).

1890 Billings *Med. Dict.* II. 789/2 *Zenker's degeneration*, waxy degeneration as seen in muscles after acute attacks of fever. **1898** W. S. Lazarus-Barlow *Man. Gen. Path.* xii. 521 In Zenker's degeneration the muscular fibres themselves look dull and semi-opaque, and microscopically are found to have lost their striation. **1910** *Lippincott's New Med. Dict.* 1103/2 Zenker's pulsion diverticulum. **1932** *Jrnl. Amer. Med. Assoc.* XCVIII. 965/2 The symptoms of a Zenker pulsion diverticulum depend on the size of the pouch. **1970** Passmore & Robson *Compan. Med. Stud.* II. xxiv. 25/1 In typhoid fever, patches of necrosis develop in striated muscles. Here, the fibres lose all structure and become glassy and eosinophilic (Zenker's hyaline degeneration). **1975** *Year Bk. Ear, Nose & Throat* 279 A variety of neuromuscular disorders, with or without Zenker's diverticulum.

2. *Histology.* [The name of Konrad *Zenker*, German histologist, who described the fluid in 1894 (*Arch. f. path. Anat. und Physiol.* CXXXV. 147).] *Zenker's fluid*: a fixative (see quot. 1902).

1902 E. A. Schäfer *Essentials of Histol.* (ed. 6) 397 General methods of preserving and hardening tissues and organs.—The fluids which are more commonly used are.. Müller's fluid (bichromate of potash 2½ parts, sulphate of soda 1 part, water 100 parts); Zenker's fluid (which is Müller's fluid containing 5 parts per cent. of mercuric chloride, to which 5 c.c. of acetic acid is added at the time of use); [etc.]. **1941** [see *fixer 2]. **1976** *Path. Ann.* XI. 130 Tumors that have been fixed in Zenker's fluid almost invariably show affinity for chrome salts, so that brown granules are easily discerned.

zeno- (zī·no), f. Gr. Ζηνο-, comb. form of Ζεύς, used as a word-forming element with the sense 'the planet Jupiter', as **zenoce·ntric** *a.*, measured or expressed with reference to the centre of Jupiter; **zenogra·phic** *a.*, measured or expressed with reference to the surface of Jupiter.

1968 *Dissertation Abstr.* B. XXIX. 858/1 For each year the study has reconfirmed that there are two zenocentric intervals of Io's position in which we observe this influence. **1978** *Nature* 14 Sept. 111/1 The ±3·3° variation of the zenocentric declination of the Earth is sufficient to lead to a 15° variation of the..sub- Io longitude of the emission. **1971** *Icarus* XIV. 343 A bright spot at zenographic latitude 23°.8 N displayed the shortest rotation period ever recorded on Jupiter. **1979** *Nature* 5 July 42/2 Values..synthesised on a 10° by 10° zenographic θ (co-latitude) and λ (longitude) grid.

zenophobia: see *xenophobia.

zeolite. Add: Hence **zeoli·tically** *adv.*, as in a zeolite.

1951 C. Palache et al. *Dana's Syst. Min.* (ed. 7) II. 993 The water content can vary zeolitically over a range from $8H_2O$ to $5H_2O$. **1969** H. T. Evans tr. *G. Hägg's Gen. & Inorg. Chem.* xxi. 510 Water in a solid phase may.. be zeolitically bound.., so that the proportion of water can vary without breaking down the crystal structure. **1980** *Nuclear Technol.* LI. 143/2 This study shows that similar enrichment of ^{234}U occurs in zeolitically altered volcanic ash and tuff.

Zep, also **Zepp** and with small initial, colloq. abbrev. of Zeppelin *sb., v.*

1915, etc. [in Dict. s.v. Zeppelin]. **1915** W. Owen *Let.* 12 June (1967) 338 The spot where a Zep. Bomb fell in a cross-roads. **1915** A. Huxley *Let.* Oct. (1969) 79 The dear old Boches and their Zepps, which always get back bomb for bomb. **1916** *Morning Post* 15 Mar. 1 (Advt.), Anti-Zep blinds. **1919** C. Orr *Glorious Thing* ii. 20 We're exceedingly preoccupied with the war—Zepp. raids and things. **1931** *Flight* 28 Aug. 855/1 The most interesting feature of our trip was a personally escorted tour of the entire Zep whilst crossing over France. *a* **1935** T. E. Lawrence *Mint* (1955) II. xxii. 159 There were Zepps in a cloud (sausages and mashed) and Adam and Eve on a raft (Hoxtonian for fried eggs on toast). **1974** *Listener* 7 Feb. 177/3 This aeroplane..flew towards the zepp, and he started firing.

Zephiran (ze·fĭrăn). *Pharm.* A proprietary name for an antiseptic preparation of benzalkonium chloride.

1935 *Trade Marks Jrnl.* 17 July 887/1 *Zephiran*... Chemical substances prepared for use in medicine and pharmacy. Bayer Products Limited,.. London, E.C.2; merchants and manufacturers. **1936** *Official Gaz.* (U.S. Patent Office) 28 Jan. 687/2 I. G. Farbenindustrie Aktiengesellschaft, Frankfort-on-the-Main... *Zephiran* for antiseptic and disinfectant. **1951** A. Grollman *Pharmacol. & Therapeutics* xxv. 503 Benzalkonium chloride (Zephiran ®) is of comparatively low toxicity. **1974** M. C. Gerald *Pharmacology* xxvi. 448 Iodine tincture.., Zephiran, and hexachlorophene are representative examples of local anti-infective agents.

Zéphirine Drouhin (ze·firīn dru,æ̃n). A thornless shrub or climbing Bourbon rose of the variety of this name, which bears fragrant pink flowers and was first introduced in France in 1868.

1931 H. H. Thomas *Rose Bk.* viii. 72 The old thornless Rose (Zéphirine Drouhin) makes an excellent bush, and its lovely, fragrant blooms of soft rose-colour..are freely produced for weeks together. **1940** A. Christie *Sad Cypress* II. xii. 193 Do you know the name of this rose? It is Zephyrine Droughin [*sic*]. **1983** *Woman's Jrnl.* Jan. 85/2 Zephirine Drouhin is a fragrant climber with cerise-pink semi-double flowers and is thornless.

zephyr (ze·fəɹ), *v.* [f. the sb.] *intr.* To blow like a zephyr. Hence **ze·phyring** *ppl. a.*

1922 Hardy *Late Lyrics & Earlier* 111 An aura zephyring round, That care infected not. **1939** Joyce *Finnegans Wake* 418 Since longsephyring sighs sought heartseast for their orience? **1973** J. Jones *Touch of Danger* xxiii. 131 A light little breeze zephyred in..from the open water.

Zepp: see *Zep.

Zeppelin, *sb.* Add: Hence also (both *rare*⁻¹) **Ze·ppelinist**, a member of the crew of a Zeppelin; **Zeppelini·stic** *a.*, resembling a Zeppelin in shape.

1930 Kipling *Limits & Renewals* (1932) 328 He called Saint Jukamus a militarist and an impostor—this defaitist of a Zeppelinistic belly! **1937** F. Morison *War on Great Cities* iv. 127 The demons who drove and dealt death cared as little for us as the earlier Zeppelinists cared.

zeppole (ze·pole). *U.S.* Pl. **zeppoli.** [It.] A kind of doughnut.

1976 *Monitor* (McAllen, Texas) 14 Oct. c 2/6 The mingled smells of salsiccia, bracciola, zeppole and calzone wafted from the stalls of food vendors around Father Zemo Square. **1979** *New Yorker* 8 Oct. 32/1 There aren't a lot of food venders. We wanted to differentiate this from other street fairs. Also, I didn't want people dropping zeppoli all over our books.

zero, *sb.* **1. a.** Delete 'Now *rare*' and add further examples.

1940 E. T. Bell *Devel. Math.* iii. 48 The introduction of zero as a symbol denoting the absence of units or of certain powers of ten..has been rated as one of the greatest practical inventions of all time. **1959** Koestler *Sleepwalkers* II. iii. 105 The Indian system of numerals based on the symbol zero. **1969** P. B. Jordain *Condensed Computer Encycl.* 572 Users can be confused and misled by leading zeros: they may hide the true size of the numeral and make it harder to grasp at a glance.

4. c. *Linguistics.* In grammar, the absence of an overt mark, written or spoken, as against its presence in corresponding positions elsewhere (e.g. *cut* pa.t. as against *putted*).

1891 S. C. Vasu *Ashṭádhyáyí of Pánini* 56 In Sanskrit Grammar, this 'lopa' is considered as a substitute or âdeṣa, and as such this grammatical *zero* has all the rights and liabilities of the thing it replaces. **1914** Bloomfield *Introd. Study Lang.* v. 154 If..we take into view..*amo* 'I love', *amāvit* 'he loved', *amētur* 'he may be loved', it is possible to call them all related by affixation, the kernel being *am-*... In this instance the group does not contain a word that equals the kernel, or, as we might say, has 'affix zero'. **1933**—— *Language* xiii. 209 In *sheep : sheep* the plural-suffix is replaced by zero. **1946** *Jrnl. Amer. Oriental Soc.* LXVI. 98/1 Zero counts as an ending if it has the same function as an overt ending in another paradigm. **1957** *Eng. Lang. Teaching* (British Council) Oct.–Dec. 11 If the pronoun is object, zero should be used if the subject is a personal pronoun. **1972** R. Quirk et al. *Gram. Contemporary Eng.* xiii. 866 With time adjuncts, omission of the preposition is usual whether the pronoun is *that* or zero..: That is the time (that) he arrives (at). **1979** *Amer. Speech* LIV. 31 Fifteen items take zero as the plural suffix.

6. a. Also, an absence or lack of anything; nothing. (Further examples.)

1883 *Proc. Inst. Mech. Engineers* Jan. 74 We have again a zero of current. **1915** J. Huneker *Ivory, Apes & Peacocks* iii. 35 We should soon reach a zero if we only registered the absence of 'necessary' traits in our poet. **1967** *Boston Globe* 21 May (Confidential Chat) 8/3 True, there is a certain amount of 'freedom' in their use but the wearing of them adds up to absolutely zero! **1977** C. McCarry *Secret Lovers* xii. 159 'What about the airlines, the hotel, car rentals.' 'Zero, I'd have used phony paper, wouldn't you?'

b. *spec. Mil.*, the time or the day when an attack or operation is due to begin.

hour of zero: now *obs.* (superseded by *zero hour* or *zero*).

1916 *King's R. Rifle Corps Chron. 1915* 104 Zero, the time the gas and smoke was to start, was 5.50 a.m. **1918** E. A. Mackintosh *War, the Liberator* IV. 124 We've got to be at Battalion Headquarters at 5, although I don't suppose zero'll be for a good time after that. **1924** Kipling *Debits & Credits* (1926) 314 The men's teeth chatterin' behind their masks between rum-issue an' zero. **1942** W. S. Churchill in *Second World War* (1950) IV. I. xiii. 225 It should be assumed..that zero [for an attack on Madagascar] should be about April 30. **1954** W. Faulkner *Fable* 10 At zero, nobody left the trench except the officers and a few N.C.O.'s. **1983** L. Macdonald *Somme* v. 41 The main body was ordered to Thiepval..timing their arrival for Zero plus two hours.. to stride on to consolidate the third objective.

7. a. zero-base, -based *adjs.*, applied to a budget and to budgeting in which each item is costed anew, rather than in relation to its size or status in the previous budget; cf. ZBB s.v. *Z 12 a; **zero-crossing**, the crossing of the horizontal axis by a function as it passes through zero and changes sign; a point where this occurs; also *attrib.* with reference to the analysis of complex waveforms through the study of such points; **zero day** *Mil.*, the day on which an attack or operation is scheduled to begin; also *transf.*; **zero hour:** also *transf.*; (*b*) the hour when something is at its lowest ebb (*nonce-use*); (*c*) the hour from which the time of day is measured; **zero-point** (later examples); *spec.* in *Physics*, used *attrib.* with reference to properties and phenomena in quantized systems at absolute zero; esp. *zero-point energy* (see quot. 1935).

1970 P. A. Pyhrr in *Harvard Business Rev.* Nov.–Dec. 111 In this speech [Arthur F.] Burns identified the basic need for what we at Texas Instruments have come to call zero-base budgeting... Burns was advocating that government agencies start from ground zero, as it were, with each year's budget and present their requests for appropriations in such a fashion that all funds can be allocated on the basis of cost/benefit or some similar kind of evaluative analysis. **1977** *Wisconsin State Jrnl.* 1 Feb. 1 Zero-base budgeting was used by President Carter when he was governor of Georgia. He asked state agencies to justify their existence and the programs they administer from zero up, rather than merely bringing in requests for more programs, money and staff. **1976** *National Observer* (U.S.) 27 Mar. 3/3 To curb inflation, he advocates a 'zero based' Federal budget, in which each program must be justified every year. **1983** *Financial Times* 10 Nov. 9/1 Sir Douglas Wass..proposed two specific changes... The first would be to introduce 'zero-based budgetting' to make spending departments consider their action if the money available to them were drastically cut. **1950** *Jrnl. Acoustical Soc. Amer.* XXII. 821/2 Vowel sounds were the first to become intelligible, presumably because for them the density of zero crossings in the input to the time quantizer is lower than it is for consonants. **1969** *New Scientist* 1 May 225/1 Equipment capable of analysing and recognizing speech..has achieved considerable success using the so-called zero crossing technique. **1982** *Electronics Today Internat.* Oct. 78/2 Switching the zero-crossing point of the mains cycle eliminates the need for RFI suppression. **1929** *Papers Mich. Acad. Sci., Arts & Lett.* X. 335/2 *Zero day*, the day for an attack. **1938** *Brit. Jrnl. Psychol.* XXVIII. 325 On zero-day (the day preceding the beginning of training with the aid of the electric shock) each rat was immersed six times in the tank. **1947** L. Hastings *Dragons are Extra* iv. 80, I..fixed a zero-day three months ahead. **1978** R. V. Jones *Most Secret War* xxxix. 350, 20th October had been fixed as Zero Day for rocket attacks on London to begin. **1930** *Daily Express* 23 May 1/6 Psychologists have fixed 11 a.m. as the zero hour of the worker. **1939** Wodehouse *Uncle Fred in Springtime* xviii. 269 Your duties will not begin till after dinner. Zero hour is at nine-thirty sharp. **1939** Joyce *Finnegans Wake* 403 Methought..I heard at zero hour as 'twere the peal of vixen's laughter among midnight's chimes. **1946** K. Tennant *Lost Haven* (1947) vii. 98 Desperate over the nearness of zero hour for the punt service, he seized her by the hand and snatched her along. **1953** A. Huxley *Let.* 2 Feb. (1969) 664 Incidentally, zero hour for tax-payments is approaching. **1978** A. Price *'44 Vintage* viii. 86 He had..the..impression.. that they had been travelling at breakneck speed,..as though the Americans were determined to deliver them on time for some impossible pre-arranged zero hour. **1826** *Mem. Astron. Soc.* II. 469 Every star observed in the course of the sweep which can be identified with a star in any catalogue, and whose place is determined with certainty, is taken as a zero point. **1895** *Physical Rev.* II. 326 The balls were placed horizontally in their neutral position, and the reading of the zero-point of the scale taken. **1935** J. Dougall tr. *Born's Atomic Physics* 339 According to the classical theory, the state of least energy of an oscillator is that of zero energy. According to wave mechanics, however, the ground state has a finite energy $E = \frac{1}{2}h\nu_0$...This zero-point energy can be explained by Heisenberg's uncertainty principle. **1938** R. W. Lawson tr. *Hevesy & Paneth's Man. Radioactivity* (ed. 2) xx. 194 If account be taken of zero-point energy, it is found that at low temperatures the lighter isotope must have the higher vapour pressure, whereas if there is no zero-point energy it will have the lesser vapour pressure. **1955** H. B. G. Casimir in W. Pauli *Niels Bohr* 130 The interaction with the zero point vibrations of the crystal lattice leads to an interaction between electrons. **1969** P. Anderson in Cockburn & Blackburn *Student Power* 263 When neither society nor man are anywhere put in question, culture stops. In England, it has gradually slowed towards zero point. **1970** G. K. Woodgate *Elem. Atomic Struct.* iv. 67 A quantized radiation field has a zero-point energy equivalent to a mean-square electric field so that even in a vacuum there are fluctuations in this zero-point radiation field. *Ibid.*, Zero-point fluctuations. **1973** *Sci. Amer.* Jan. 91/1 In quantum physics the ground state is not a state of absolute rest or motionlessness but only a singular 'zero point' form of motion in which there are no quasiparticles.

c. (Further examples.) Also more widely as adj. in the sense 'no, not any'.

1938 *Brit. Jrnl. Psychol.* XXVIII. 329 If each such contact [*sc.* a mild electric shock received by rats] had been counted as an error, the number of cases of zero-error would have been considerably reduced. **1960** [see *social distance* s.v. *SOCIAL *a.* 12]. **1962** *Times* 30 Oct. 4/6 Good design points include 'zero torque'. **1972** *Listener* 22 June 820/3 Why is the notion of zero economic growth so seductive for those who embrace environmental causes? **1976** *New Yorker* 24 May 28/1 Because he had zero toads, Howard had to content himself with the tub of thin green gruel. **1978** *Peace News* 6 Oct. 2/1 We can't call together the group at zero notice. **1981** *TV Picture Life* Mar. 39/3 Jackie claims they now have 'zero communication'.

d. *Linguistics.* In sense *4 c: denoting an absence of a feature (as an inflection, or a phonetic or syntactic element) that is present in other cases, and is often indicated by the following word; **zero-derivation** *Linguistics*, derivation in which the parent word is not altered; the use of a word with a different grammatical function or in a different (though related) sense; hence **zero-derivative** *a.* and *sb.*, **-derived** *a.*; **zero grade** *Philol.*, the absence or extreme reduction of an ablaut vowel from a syllable.

1905 *Amer. Jrnl. Philol.* XXVI. 179 The intrusion of the *é* grade on the zero grade..is..attested for the nasal verbs of the Indo-Iranian group. **1926** Bloomfield in *Language* II. 160 *Alternation*... Absence of sound may be a phonetic or formal alternant... Such an alternant is a zero element. The postulation of zero elements is necessary for Sanskrit..for Primitive Indo-European..and probably economical for English (singular *book* with affix zero, as opposed to *book-s*, cf *f-oo-t*; *f-ee-t*). **1933** —— *Language* xiii. 215 Another extreme case is that of zero-alternants.., in which a constituent is entirely lacking, as in the plurals *sheep, deer, moose, fish.* *Ibid.* xiv. 236 In English, the nouns *longlegs, bright-eyes, butterfingers* are exocentric, because they occur both as singulars, and, with a zero-affix, as plurals (*that longlegs, those longlegs*). *Ibid.* xv. 252 We have zero-anaphora for participles after forms of *be* and *have*, as in *You were running faster than I was.* **1942** *Language* XVIII. 170 In *He cut it* there is a zero morpheme meaning 'past time' after *cut.* **1947** *Ibid.* XXIII. 340 We may set up the tentative portmanteau.. as an alternant of that constituent morpheme which it resembles phonemically, and set up a zero morph as an alternant of the other constituent morpheme. **1954** M. Pei *Dict. Linguistics* 238 *Zero ending*, in morphology, the bare stem of a word when used as such in discourse is said to have zero ending. **1959** *Brno Studies in English* I. 43 The indefinite article and its zero plural variant. **1960** H. Marchand *Categories & Types of Present-Day English Word-Formation* v. 295 (*heading*) Zero-derivation as a 'specifically English' process. *Ibid.* 297 There are quite a few vbs with French roots for which no French verbs are recorded and which may accordingly be treated as zero derivatives: *feeble* vb.., *master* vb, [etc.]. **1963** F. T. Visser *Hist. Syntax Eng. Lang.* I. iv. 538 The Authorised Version of the Bible clearly fights shy of it: in those places where the Hebrew has a zero-clause, it uses a relative pronoun printed in italics (e.g. Ps. 7, 5, 'he is fallen into the ditch *which* he made'). **1964** *English Studies* XLV. (Suppl.) 63 The *be going + infinitive* group has had a partially independent development. Its opposite in this case is the *will + zero infinitive* group. **1965** *Language* XLI. 519 The unfortunate myth that there is some essential connection between aorist aspect and stems consisting of zero-grade root plus accented thematic vowel in Indo-European. **1971** *Canad. Jrnl. Linguistics* Fall 31 The use of zero morphs would have greatly facilitated the description..of several problems in Japanese. **1976** *Archivum Linguisticum* VII. 129 Zero-derivation..must be regarded an extremely productive word-formative process both in English and German, but also in other languages. *Ibid.* 132 The Direct Object-type based on (17b) has two different surface realizations in English: payment and also the zero-derived noun *payØ*. *Ibid.* 133, I believe..that *act* (noun) must be regarded as zero-derivative (*actØ*) from the corresponding verb. **1979** *Dictionaries* I. 19 The last point concerns zero-derivatives or homographs. **1981** *Amer. Speech* LVI. 229 Other details on which there have been ethnic speculations are the zero genitive of nouns..and the zero subject of a relative clause.

e. Special Combs. (see also senses 7 a in Dict. and Suppl., *7 d): **zero-balance** *a.*, applied to a bank account operated with no continuing balance, funds being transferred into it when necessary to just the extent required to meet drawings made on it; **zero beat,** a condition existing between two equal frequencies, in which no beats are produced; *spec.* in *Radio*, applied *attrib.* to a method of reception in which the incoming signal is mixed with a receiver-generated oscillation of the same frequency as the carrier wave (see *homodyne* s.v. *HOMO-); **zero-coupon** *a.*, applied to a bond carrying no interest but issued below its redemption price; **zero-energy** *a.* (Nucl. Physics), applied to a small reactor, usu. built for research purposes, that develops so little power that no cooling and little shielding are required; **zero g** or **G** = *zero gravity* below; **zero gravity,** the state or condition in which there is no apparent force of gravity acting on a body, either because the force is locally weak, or because both the body and its surroundings are freely and equally accelerating under the force; = *WEIGHTLESSNESS; **zero grazing** *vbl. sb.* (Agric.) = Soiling *vbl. sb.*^{4} 1; so **zero-graze** *v. trans.* = Soil *v.*^{4} 1; **zero-grazed** *ppl. a.* = Soiled *ppl. a.*^{2}; **zero growth,** an absence of increase (in population, production, etc.); **zero-length** *a.* (of a rocket launcher) no longer than the rocket it supports; **zero norm,** in a period of pay restraint, a recommended value of zero for the percentage increase in pay; **zero option,** a disarmament proposal that if the Soviet Union would withdraw its SS-20 missiles from Europe the U.S.A. would abandon its plans to deploy Pershing and cruise missiles there; **zero population growth,** an absence of any increase (or decrease) in a population over a period of time; abbrev. ZPG s.v. *Z12 a; **zero-power** *a.* (Nucl. Physics) = *zero-energy* adj. above; **zero rating,** a rating of zero for the purposes of value added tax; also as *vbl. sb.*, the practice of assessing the VAT at zero for a particular item; so **zero-rate** *v. trans.*, to assess at a VAT rate of zero; **zero-rated** *a.*; **zero sound:** see *sound *sb.*^{3} 1 d; **zero-sum** *a.*, in the theory of games, applied to a game in which the sum of the winnings of all the players is always zero; also *transf.*, denoting any situation in which advantage to one participant necessarily leads to disadvantage to one or more of the others; **zero tillage** (Agric.) = *sod planting* s.v. *sod *sb.*^{1} 5 b; **zero-zero** (Aeronaut.), (*a*) a situation in which both the (horizontal) visibility and the cloud ceiling are technically zero; (*b*) used *attrib.* to designate an ejection seat that works even at rest and at zero altitude.

1974 *U.S. Investor/Eastern Banker* 26 Aug. 42/2 With a Zero Balance account, a customer will pay a small charge for actual activity. **1983** *Fortune* 18 Apr. 76/2 A controlled disbursement account is a type that bankers call a 'zero balance account'—it contains no cash at the end of the day after all checks have been paid. There are no funds left idle. **1927** *Mod. Wireless* Mar. 334/2 The results of fading on an ordinary set using high-frequency amplification were large compared with these effects in zero-beat reception. **1957** *Practical Wireless* XXXIII. 370/1 Tune a signal to zero-beat at the high-wavelength end of the scale. **1982** *Amer. Jrnl. Physics* L. 137/1 With this arrangement, one can explore the zero-beat situation (when frequencies are matched) as well as a variety of non-zero-beat situations. **1979** *Jrnl. Finance* XXXIV. 189 The relationship between yield curves for zero coupon bonds and coupon-bearing bonds is important. **1983** *Chicago Sun-Times* 29 May 5 Following the birth of their first child, the couple purchased $7,000 worth of zero coupon bonds in their daughter's name. **1951** *Canad. Chem. & Process Industries* Jan. 42 (*heading*) Zero Energy Experimental Pile. **1954** R. Stephenson *Introd. Nucl. Engin.* iii. 82 The smaller one is known as ZEEP (zero energy experimental pile) and is very similar..except that its power level is limited to a few watts. **1981** *Nucl. Energy* XX. 467 Fast neutron fluence measurements in the core of a zero-energy research reactor. **1952** A. C. Clarke *Islands in Sky* v. 80 She was escorted by an elderly woman who seemed to be quite at home under zero 'g' and gave Linda a helpful push when she showed signs of being stuck. **1962** F. I. Ordway et al. *Basic Astronautics* xii. 477 Walking will be impossible in zero G. **1970** N. Armstrong et al. *First on Moon* vi. 127 Deke Slayton ate the same food we did... In our zero-G situation we were always full. **1978** *Radio Times* 28 Jan. 59/2 *Horizon* explores all these aspects, with footage from Skylab and reminiscences from ex-inhabitants—the astronauts who call this world zero gravity—zero G for short. **1951** A. C. Clarke *Sands of Mars* i. 5 I'll take you into the zero-gravity section and see how you manage there. **1968** *New Scientist* 12 Sept. 545/1 Astronauts of the future will probably have to build vehicles in space. This will entail joining different metals together under zero-gravity conditions. **1978** [see *zero g* above]. **1979** *United States 1980/81* (Penguin Travel Guides) 553 You'll be offered the opportunity to.. experience weightlessness in a zero-gravity machine. **1984** *News* (Mexico City) 12 Mar. 22/4 Two of the first drugs that will be produced in zero gravity in mass quantities are beta cells..and interferon. **1956** *Britannica Bk. of Year* 316/1 Studies indicated that green-chopping, sometimes called zero-grazing or soiling (bringing the pasture to the livestock), resulted in forage yields about double those from grazing. **1958** *Agriculture* LXV. 129 Zero grazed animals also put on greater weight during the summer months than those out grazing. *Ibid.* 131 The cattle have been zero grazed since May 1956. **1970** R. Jeffries *Dead Man's Bluff* vi. 56 Cows were zero-grazed and never stepped off concrete. **1978** *Exper. Husbandry* No. 33, 18 (*heading*) Beef from spring-born zero-grazed Friesians—comparison of bulls, steers and late castrates. **1984** 'D. Archer' *Ambridge Yrs.* 19 There are other herds that never go out into pasture... They have their grass cut and carted to them, a method called 'zero-grazing'. **1973** *Science* 15 June 1143 The possibility of zero growth in the population of the United States. **1976** *Atlantic Monthly* Jan. 4 Can economies have simultaneously zero growth, rapid inflation, substantial unemployment, and a balance of payments deficit? **1976** *N.Y. Times Mag.* 4 July 73 Power to stop new construction is wielded through the..water board.., a majority of which is dedicated to zero growth. **1954** K. W. Gatland *Developm. Guided Missile* (ed. 2) iii. 79 (*caption*) A later G.A.P.A. rocket being adjusted on a 'zero-length' launcher. **1966** *Economist* 17 Dec. 1214/1 There is no bogy-man so dismal to those who run Britain's economy as the dreaded Zero Norm, the spectre who is supposed to rule over pay negotiations in the six-month period of 'severe restraint' that replaces the total pay freeze from New Year's Day. **1976** F. Zweig *New Acquisitive Society* II. i. 80 A zero norm which equalizes everybody is easier to endure. **1981** *Washington Post* 5 July A20/1 By reviving controversy about a moratorium and the 'zero option', Brandt's trip appears to have realized some of the fears of those in the West German government and opposition party. **1983** *Financial Times* 10 Feb. 11/6 Mr. George Bush, the U.S. Vice-President, last night confirmed Washington's willingness to consider alternatives to its zero option proposals for banning intermediate range nuclear missiles from Europe. **1967** *Science* 10 Nov. 732/2 Most discussions of the population crisis lead logically to zero population growth as the ultimate goal. **1974** *Environmental Conservation* I. 15/1 It is my estimate that zero population growth will be reached..some time during the next decade. **1950** *Nucleonics* Sept. 104/2 *Zero-power reactor*, an experimental nuclear reactor operated at low neutron flux and at a power level so low that not only is no forced cooling required but also fission-product activity in the fuel is sufficiently low to allow the fuel to be handled after use without serious hazard. **1983** *Trans. Amer. Nucl. Soc.* XLIV. 528/2 Plate versus pin geometry continues to be an issue for Zero-Power Plutonium Reactor (ZPPR) analysis. **1972** *Daily Tel.* 22 Mar. 19/3 Zero-rating a transaction, rather than exempting it, is advantageous, because a trader is allowed credit for any VAT paid on his inputs. **1975** *Times* 11 Feb. 6/4 The first thing the Government could do would be to zero-rate the theatre for VAT. **1972** *Daily Tel.* 22 Mar. 17/4 A firm which supplies zero-rated goods or services gets complete relief from Value Added Tax both on its purchases and on its sales. **1976** *Horse & Hound* 3 Dec. 28 (Advt.), Rubber riding boots. Best quality, shiny leather-look finish. Price £3·45 (zero rated). **1971** *Nature* 3 Dec. 310/3 The recently reported claim of the salvage industries to be given zero rating for value-added tax.. can also be extended. **1972** *Daily Tel.* 22 Mar. 17 Mr Barber explained the difference between exemption from VAT and 'zero rating'. **1984** *Bookseller* 3 Nov. 1857/1 Books are the essential tools of society and zero-rating is a very efficient way of encouraging their wide availability. **1944** von Neumann & Morgenstern *Theory of Games* ii. 47 An important viewpoint in classifying games is this: Is the sum of all payments received by all players (at the end of the game) always zero; or is this not the case?.. We shall call games of the first mentioned type zero-sum games. **1966** S. Beer *Decision & Control* x. 210 Perhaps the contestants in most important games nowadays (from labour disputes..to international diplomacy) too readily regard their games as zero-sum. **1967** L. B. Archer in Wills & Yearsley *Handbk. Management Technol.* vii. 121 Everybody *can* win. Manufacturing is not a zero-sum game. **1971** *Times Lit. Suppl.* 22 Oct. 1335/3 C. Wright Mills..used a zero-sum conception of power (i.e., the more one person had the less was available to others). **1980** *Ibid.* 26 Sept. 1072/2 In Europe [in the 1930s] class conflict was seen as a zero-sum game in which one group could only benefit at the expense of another. **1983** *Listener* 15 Dec. 31/1 We live in a zero-sum world, and it was inconceivable that the strains of setting up a completely new operation within an essentially fixed budget would not eventually begin to tell. **1971** *New Scientist* 25 Mar. 663/1 Even fairly low levels of pesticide destroyed these bacteria... The situation is made even worse by the growing popularity of 'zero-tillage'. **1979** *Austral. Financial Rev.* 16 Aug., Farmers using zero tillage leave straw and stubble on the field and this trash cover helps to eliminate erosion, conserve moisture,.. and reduce salinity problems. **1939** Hixson & Colodny *Word Ways* xvi. 141 *Zero-zero* (no visibility in any direction). **1947** *Shell Aviation News* No. 113. 7/2 There are few greater nervous strains than that experienced by a pilot of a transport in deciding to switch over from instruments and manually bring the ship in these last few hundred feet when visibility is 'zero-zero'. **1961** *Aeroplane* C. 593/2 The most interesting item in the Martin-Baker Aircraft Co., Ltd., display..is the prototype rocket-assisted 'zero-zero' ejection seat for VTOL aircraft. **1967** *Times Rev. Industry* June 53/1 Category 3C represents visibility of less than 50 metres and includes 'zero-zero' conditions under which safety experts believe operations will not be possible for a very long time. **1977** P. Way *Super-Celeste* 215 They had explained to him the controls of his zero-zero ejection seat.

zero (zɪ³·ro), *v.* [f. the sb.] **I. 1.** *trans.* To set the sights of (a rifle) using targets at known distances.

1913 A. G. Fulton *Notes on Rifle Shooting* 30 (Advt.), A Zero Target, by means of which any novice may correctly zero his own rifle. **1918** H. McBride *Emma Gees* ix. 119 'Zeroing' a rifle is the process of testing it out on a range of known distances and setting the sights to suit one's individual peculiarities of aiming. **1958** L. van der Post *Lost World Kalahari* vii. 142, I had not yet fired at a live target, though..I had zeroed it on a marked one. **1979** D. Lowden *Boudapesti 3* xxxii. 176 The rifle had been zeroed..at an elevation of 200.

2. zero in. a. *trans.* To range guns or missiles on (a target). Usu. *pass.*

1944 *Newsweek* 8 Jan. 45 Don't you know the Jerries have that road zeroed in?—a phrase meaning the Germans had sighted their guns on the road and needed only to pull their triggers. **1945** *Finito! Po Valley Campaign* (15th Army Group) 41 Road junction 711 was not only mined, but zeroed in. **1965** H. Kahn *On Escalation* iv. 74 American bases overseas and American targets on the mainland are at all times zeroed in by Soviet missiles, and vice versa. **1971** *Scope* (S. Afr.) 19 Mar. 20/4 These roads were well covered by strongpoints, and zeroed-in by artillery.

b. *trans.* To aim (a weapon) at a target. Const. *on.*

1944 *Life* 14 Aug. 57/1 Germans who had retreated out of town 'zeroed in' mortar shells among troops and light tanks which tried to follow. **1950** *N.Y. Herald* 26 Aug. 2/1 Guns are 'zeroed in' on the junction. **1961** *Time* (Atlantic ed.) 17 Feb. 16 The Russians now have some 50 ICBMs ready to go, presumably zeroed in on U.S. targets.

c. *intr.* To focus attention *on*, to concentrate *on.* Also *transf.* (const. *on*), to get a closer view of a subject with a camera.

1959 *Guardian* 1 Dec. 15/4 So far..Governor Rockefeller has spoken out on space research, the housing of Puerto Ricans, crop subsidies... Now he is zeroing-in on the social drinkers. **1961** D. Huff *Score* (1962) p. ix, This book..will narrow the subject down to the specific material you are likely to encounter in a variety of fields... Finally this book will zero-in on the increasingly important psychological tests. **1971** *Daily Tel.* 18 Oct. 14 An excited Taiwanese photographer zeroed in on the frail figure..with a long-range lens. **1972** *Screw* 12 June 21/2 The storyline, such as it is, zeros in on a classy whorehouse in a banana republic. **1974** A. Dillard *Pilgrim at Tinker Creek* viii. 143 Zero in on a well-watered shore. **1976** *Word 1971* XXVII. 142 Wittgenstein zeroes in upon linguistic constraints and logical conditions as they are made manifest in common, ordinary speech. **1983** *Listener* 14 Apr. 33/1 Its staff were slowly but surely zeroing in on the essential secret of successful breakfast broadcasting in this country. **1985** *Weekly World News* (U.S.) 1 Jan. 11/1 Security cameras were installed to stop vandalism, but they zeroed in on the athletes as they traipsed back and forth across a corridor from the shower to their locker room.

d. *intr.* To move towards, as if to a target. Also *fig.* Const. *on.*

1959 *Guardian* 26 Sept. 5/2 The squadrons of flies that zeroed in on his shiny pate. **1961** J. Steinbeck *Winter of our Discontent* xxi. 300 For twenty years that check has zeroed in on the first of every month. **1965** J. A. Michener *Source* (1966) 797 A series of bullets was beginning to zero-in on her, and in a few more steps she was sure to be hit. **1968** K. Amis *I want it Now* i. 27 By the time he got back to the girl two other men had zeroed in on her. **1972** W. Garner *Ditto, Brother Rat!* iv. 30, I zeroed in on the downstairs bar. **1974** *Newsweek* 8 Apr. 51/1 In recent months, instrumented spacecraft have zeroed in on Venus, Mars and Jupiter to provide astronomers with a wealth of significant new data on those planets. **1978** G. A. Sheehan *Running & Being* xii. 174 A pacemaker..had zeroed in on the perfect pace.

II. 3. To fix the zero hour for (a military operation).

1926 *Blackw. Mag.* Dec. 774/1 Plan no. 7 will be put in operation to-night. It will be zeroed as from 23.00 hours.

4. = *zeroize *v.*

1949 W. F. Goodell in J. F. Blackburn *Components Handbk.* x. 331 This zero convention makes it possible to 'zero' the dial of a synchro motor on one unit of a system. **1951** C. W. Kennedy *Inspection & Gaging* ix. 293 An error would result if the air gage were zeroed against a 5-microinch surface and then used to compare the diameter of a bore with a 200-microinch surface roughness. **1969** [see *odometer]. **1974** *Physics Bull.* Mar. 108/2 An offset control allows the pen to be zeroed at any point on the chart. **1982** *Homes & Gardens* Jan. 17/3 One button..can zero the read-out at any point, allowing you to add ingredients without emptying the bowl.

III. 5. zero out. *trans.* To eliminate.

1967 *Word* XXIII. 316 We 'zero out' the voicing of /b/, which is not at all to deny that /b/ is voiced. **1972** W. Labov *Language in Inner City* ii. 52 The deletion of *are* has reached such a high point that it is effectively zeroed out for many speakers. **1982** *Daily Tel.* 25 Jan. 12/7 Watch..for word of new budget cuts, including Federal programmes that are to be 'zeroed out'.

zeroable (zɪ³·roˌăb'l), *a.* [f. Zero *sb.* + -able.] **1.** *Linguistics.* That may be omitted from a sentence without loss of meaning.

1965 *Language* XLI. 395 Metaphorical and idiomatic objects are not pronounable or zeroable. **1975** *Rev. des Lang. Vivantes* XLI. 239 The relation between 'They described Vesuvius' and its metalinguistic, zeroable, expansion into 'They described Vesuvius *which is a volcano*'.

2. Capable of being set to read zero.

1974 *Physics Bull.* Aug. 349/1 A zeroable offset counter system is provided which makes it easy for the operator to measure the angular error between the ground reference face and the crystallographic planes.

ze·roing, *vbl. sb.* [f. *zero *v.* + -ing[1].] **1. a.** The adjustment of an instrument to give a reading of zero.

1949 W. F. Goodell in J. F. Blackburn *Components Handbk.* x. 331 It is to facilitate the zeroing of synchros that they are provided with standardized flanges that are accurately concentric with the shafts. **1954** *Electronic Engin.* XXVI. 118/1 The connexion of Dekatrons in cascade presents difficulties in that a carry makes necessary a cumbersome circuit for resetting or zeroing. **1975** *Chem. Engin.* 10 Nov. 223/1 A process-control computer..has been extended to control zeroing of selected instrument transmitters to improve the accuracy of the input.

b. The adjustment or setting of the sights of a gun.

1975 V. Canning *Kingsford Mark* v. 83 On the rifle were telescopic sights... He would..fire a few rounds and check the zeroing. **1979** D. Lowden *Boudapesti 3* xxxii. 176 The proper zeroing target had been used.

2. *Linguistics.* The deletion or omission of part of a linguistic form or structure.

1956 *Language* XXXII. 645 In all or nearly all dialects the first of two contiguous unstressed vowels may or may not be modified by shortening and/or raising or zeroing. **1965** *Ibid.* XLI. 393 In *I prefer that I should go first* there is no zeroing, but in the transform of this *I prefer for me to go first*→*I prefer to go first*. **1970** J. W. Gair *Colloquial Sinhalese Clause Structures* iv. 54 It is convenient to treat such clauses as derived by context-governed deletion from full clauses like them in every respect save the presence of such constituents. The term 'zeroing' will be reserved for such discourse deletion.

zeroize (zɪ³·roˌəiz), *v.* [f. Zero *sb.* + -ize.] *trans.* To adjust (an instrument or device) to give a zero reading, esp. in order to calibrate it; to assign a value of zero to. So **ze·roizing** *vbl. sb.*

1908 *Brit. Patent 23,895* 3 Such clutches have already been employed for the simultaneous zeroizing of two indicating mechanisms. **1914** E. M. Horsburgh *Mod. Instruments & Methods Calculation* 87 Mr. Trinks has invented a device which disengages the pawls from the number wheels when the latter are being zeroised. *Ibid.*, The zeroising crank is fixed on the right-hand side of the carriage, and the zeroising is effected by a half revolution of this crank. **1928** [see *register *sb.*[1] 10 c]. **1945** *Chambers's Jrnl.* Dec. 671/1 It is said to enable operational errors to be rectified in a matter of moments, and the calculations to be continued without the waste of time involved by 'zeroising' the machine and restarting the calculations from the beginning. **1956** G. A. Montgomerie *Digital Calculating Machines* ii. 28 The other major control is the zeroizing or clearance key or handle at the right-hand side of the keyboard. **1974** *Software World* V. v. 12 Integer Function JCV12C converts a positive integer L (L < 256) to a character in A1 format, zeroizing bits 24 to 1.

zeroth (zɪ³·rōᵘþ). *Math.* and *Sci.* Also (*rare*) **zero'th.** [f. Zero *sb.* + -th[2].] Coming next in a series before the one conventionally regarded as the first.

1896 *Electrician* 10 Jan. 350/2 In order to have the zeroth Bessel normal function, we need only let the conductance and permittance per unit length of cable both vary directly as the distance from $x = 0$. **1932** *Physical Rev.* XL. 56 The zeroth order wave functions which they use do indeed indicate that tetrahedral symmetry should give high stability. **1956** E. H. Hutten *Lang. Mod. Physics* iv. 143 From this the theorem is derived that one body in contact with another may be used as a thermometer, or that one body 'reads' the temperature of another. This theorem is sometimes referred to..as the zeroth law of thermodynamics. **1969** *Nature* 15 Nov. 642/1 The energy of transition between the zeroth and the first energy levels. **1976** J. H. Conway *On Numbers & Games* o. 3 In this zeroth part, our topic is the notion of number. **1984** *QL User* Dec. 33 LET input. vector = VEC 5 declares a vector of 6 words (BCPL vectors start at their zero'th element) pointed to by input.vector.

zerovalent (zɪ³rovēⁱ·lĕnt). *Chem.* [f. Zero *sb.* + *-valent.] Having an actual or formal valency of zero. Hence **zerova·lency.**

1940 *Chambers's Techn. Dict.* 919/2 Zero-valent. **1953** Barnett & Wilson *Inorg. Chem.* xxii. 282 Since the electrons forming these covalencies are supplied solely by the molecules of carbon monoxide, the metal atom is said to have zero-valency. **1965** *Jrnl. Chem. Soc.* 847 The analogous reaction..of the naphthalene complex in its zerovalent formulation..cannot be distinguished from the possible consecutive reactions. **1977** *Inorg. Chem.* XVI. 1313 (*heading*) Reactions of the zerovalent complex $Ni[HP(C_6H_5)_2]_4$. **1984** *Science* 22 June 1330/2 A greater proportion of nickel in the catalytically active zero-valent state.

zest, *sb.*[1] **1.** Delete 'Now *rare* or *Obs.*' and add later examples. Also in Fr. form *zeste* (see etym. in Dict.).

1958 L. Durrell *Mountolive* viii. 162 How good the taste of Dubonnet with a *zeste de citron*. **1967** *Guardian* 3 Feb. 8/5 The thin outer skin of oranges, known as the zest. **1974** *Homes & Gardens* Jan. 68/2 Add candied peel, lemon zeste, salt and nutmeg and mix. **1979** N. Gordimer *Burger's Daughter* ii. 269 He had fished the slice of lemon out of the bottom of his glass and was gobbling the skin with a mouth drawn by the zest. **1981** *Family Weekly* (U.S.) 12 July 10/3 Grated zest of 1 lemon. **1982** J. Grigson *Fruit Bk.* 256 Orange juice and a little zest can also be added to tomato and carrot soups.

ze·sty (ze·sti), *a.* [f. Zest *sb.*[1] + -y[1].] **1.** Of a taste or a food: piquant, agreeably sharp.

1934 in Webster. **1936** [see *pick-up *sb.* f]. **1953** 'A. Bridge' *Place to Stand* v. 67 The meal was plain and good, with the zesty taste of country cooking. **1969** *Daily Tel.* 5 Feb. 15/5 The food is spicy and zesty enough to make you nearly spring out of your seat. **1971** A. G. Seaberg *Menu-Design–Merchandising* 214 The zesty garlic butter brings out the best in this epicurean treat from the sea.

2. *fig.* Energetic, lively, stimulating.

1952 *Time* 15 Dec. 33/1 Zesty as a two-year-old rounding into the stretch, Britain's aged Prime Minister Winston Churchill last week entered his 79th year enthusiastically agallop on all his old hobbies. **1958** *Oxf. Mag.* 22 May 459/1 The little farrago ends with a bound of zesty life-assertion and merriment. **1959** *News Chron.* 23 July 5/5 To provide its zesty performance, Rootes' engineers have developed an aluminium cylinder head. **1972** *Time* 17 Apr. 43/2 Housing starts remain zesty, at an annual rate of 2,500,000 units in recent months. **1981** *N.Y. Times Mag.* 27 Apr. 18/3 The zesty lexicographer from New Zealand neither equivocates nor jazzes around. **1982** *Observer* 10 Oct. 40/8 This column's Third Rule of Television—'If it works, change it'—was given another zesty outing last week.

zeta[2]. Add: **2. zeta potential** *Physical Chem.*, the potential difference that exists across the electrical double layer at the interface of a solid and a liquid.

1939 E. A. Hauser *Colloidal Phenomena* ix. 91 In simple cases, this double layer can be regarded as an electric condenser, the potential of which is generally termed electrokinetic, or ζ (zeta), potential. **1982** *Nature* 21 Jan. 267/2 They [*sc.* electrokinetic phenomena] arise whenever there is relative motion between a charged interface and a liquid and are usually interpreted in terms of the zeta potential.

zetetic, *a.* and *sb.* Add: Hence **zete·tical** *a.*, only in *Zetetical Society*, a nineteenth-century society with mystical beliefs; also *ellipt.*

1881 (*programme*) The Zetetical Society... Committee. .. J. M. Fells... G. B. Shaw... Sidney Webb. **1882** G. B. SHAW *Let.* 30 Jan. (1965) I. 47, I have overtaxed the patience of the Almighty, and he has smitten me; and, through me, the Zetetical Society. **1905**——*Let.* 3 Jan. (1972) II. 486 After about a year of the Zetetical I joined the Dialectical. **1921**——*Immaturity* (1930) p. xl, Not until..1879, did I for the first time rise to my feet in a little debating club called the Zetetical Society. **1962** D. H. LAURENCE *Bernard Shaw's Platform & Pulpit* p. x, A meeting of the Zetetical Society.

zetetically *adv.* (later example).

1872 *Zetetic* July 8/2 (Advt.), The life and teachings of Jesus Christ zetetically considered.

zeugmatography (ziūgmătǫ·grăfi). *Med.* [f. Gr. ζεῦγμα, ζεῦγματ- a yoking (in allusion to the coupling of the electromagnetic and magnetic fields) + -O + -GRAPHY.] A form of imaging using the principles of nuclear magnetic resonance to obtain and display the structural details of soft tissue. Hence **zeugma·togram,** a picture produced by zeugmatography; **zeugmatogra·phic** *a.*, involving or produced by zeugmatography.

1973 P. C. LAUTERBUR in *Nature* 16 Mar. 190/1 Because the interaction may be regarded as a coupling of the two fields by the object, I propose that image formation by this technique be known as zeugmatography. *Ibid.* 191/1 At low radio-frequency power..the two capillaries gave nearly identical images in the zeugmatogram. *Ibid.* 191/2 Zeugmatographic techniques should find many useful applications in studies of the internal structures, states, and composition of microscopic objects. **1981** *Brit. Med. Jrnl.* 7 Nov. 1212/1 Nuclear magnetic resonance (or zeugmatography) is looming on the horizon.

zeze (zē̆·zē̆). [a. Swahili *zeze.*] A zither-like string instrument of eastern and central Africa.

1860 R. F. BURTON *Lake Region Central Africa* II. xviii. 291 The zeze, or banjo, resembles in sound the monochord Arabian rubabah, the rude ancestor of the Spanish guitar. **1978** *Times* 19 Aug. 3/3 (*caption*) A member of the Tanzania National Dance Troupe playing a 13-string zeze.

Zhdanovism (ʒdā·nǒviz'm, -fiz'm). [f. the name *Zhdanov* (see below) + -ISM.] The policy of rigorous ideological control of literature and cultural life generally that was developed in the post-war period by A. A. Zhdanov (1896–1948), Russian politician. So **Zhda·novist, -ite** *adjs.*, of, pertaining to, or resembling Zhdanov or Zhdanovism.

1957 C. HUNT *Guide to Communist Jargon* xi. 37 The Zhdanovite decrees on literature and the arts of 1946–7. **1958** *Encounter* Nov. 35/1 The ideal of Zhdanovism was, precisely, the reduction of literature to 'a small cog and a small screw' in the mechanism of the totalitarian state. **1962** H. SWAYZE *Polit. Control Lit. in U.S.S.R., 1946–59* ii. 26 (*heading*) The heyday of Zhdanovism, 1946–1952. **1966** *Listener* 3 Nov. 659/3 The decree..contained the Zhdanovist indictment of the works of Shostakovich and Khachaturian. **1975** *Times Lit. Suppl.* 31 Oct. 1280/5 Its account of Gramsci's career and the early history of the Communist Party can only be described as Zhdanovite. **1977** *Ibid.* 21 Jan. 76/4 Socialist realism he gives deservedly short shift. But the practice of Zhdanovism does not exhaust the subject.

‖**zhuyin zimu** (dʒūyin dzimū). Also with accents and (in Wade-Giles transliteration) as **chu-yin tzu-mu.** [Chinese, f. *zhùyīn* phonetic notation (f. *zhù* notes + *yīn* sound) + *zìmǔ* letters of the alphabet (f. *zì* word, character + *mǔ* mother).] The national phonetic alphabet of China made up of symbols based on Chinese characters, first adopted in 1918. Also *ellipt.* as **zhuyin.**

1938 E. M. NORTH *Bk. Thousand Tongues* 89/1 North Mandarin colloquial, Peking dialect, or Kuoyü... Chu Yin phonetics... Wang Chao phonetics... Roman characters. **1960** CHANG-TU HU et al. *China* v. 107 A set of thirty-nine phonetic symbols, *chu-yin tzu-mu*, officially promulgated in 1918 by the government. **1968** P. KRATOCHVÍL *Chinese Lang. Today* v. 168 The purpose of the first official Chinese phonemic transcription called *zhùyin zìmǔ* 'Pronunciation Alphabet'..was to serve as a stepping stone towards learning the characters, and also as a tool for promulgating the National Language. **1978** *Nagel's Encycl.-Guide: China* 95 The thirty-nine letters of the *zhuyin zimu* alphabet were taken from old, very simple Chinese characters.

‖**ziarat** (zi,ā·rat). Also 8 **zeearut; zearat, ziarath, ziarut.** [ad. Hindi f. Urdu, f. Arab. *ziyārat* pilgrimage.] A Muslim place of pilgrimage, a shrine; a pilgrimage to such a place.

1776 N. B. HALHED tr. *Code Gentoo Laws* xii. 187 Places of *zeeărut* (or religious Walks). **1913** *19th Cent.* May 993 This is said to occur frequently in the large shrines or Ziarats, such as Mashad. **1916** M. DIVER *Desmond's Daughter* II. ix. 121 A graphic tale of the manner in which his tribe had come by their first *ziarut*. **1925** *Blackw. Mag.* Dec. 796/2 That is where my brothre lives, Sahib; he likes to be next to his Ziarat. **1934** *N.-W. Frontier Province Gazetteer Peshawar Dist.* (ed. 3) I. i. 153 For the mass of the people the local *ziarats* have to suffice. **1967** F. RASUL *Bengal to Birmingham* vi. 61 At the appointed time, led by our group leader, we went for the *ziarath* (meeting the respected one). **1976** [see *ZIKR].

zibib (zi·bib, ‖zəbī·b). Also **zibeeb.** [ad. Arab. *zabīb* dried grapes, (in Egypt) zibib.] A colourless, strongly alcoholic Egyptian drink made from raisins and drunk with added water, which turns it white.

Pronounced (zi·bib) by N.Z. servicemen in Egypt in the 1939–45 war.—Ed.

1836 E. W. LANE *Acct. Manners & Customs Mod. Egyptians* II. i. 19 In the same manner, many *shurbetlees* (or sellers or sherbet) carry about for sale *zebeeb* (or infusion of raisins). **1958** L. DURRELL *Mountolive* ix. 181 He drank quite a lot of *zibib* according to the proprietor. **1977** J. HUTCHISON *Danger has No Face* (1978) iv. 41 Would I have a glass of zibeeb? He asked me. **1980** J. HOVE *Flowers of Forest* I. 8, I wandered..sherry glass in hand, imagining it zibib or some other sharp foreign drink.

Ziegfeld (zī·gfeld). The name of Florenz *Ziegfeld* (1869–1932), American theatre manager and producer, used *attrib.* with reference to the follies that he staged annually from 1907 to 1931; so *Ziegfeld girl*, an actress taking part in such a revue.

1913 *Green Bk.* Jan. 72 Never before was so much beauty shown so much as in this latest of the Ziegfeld nonsensicalities. **1915** *New Republic* 31 July 336/1 Ziegfeld Follies 1915, a musical comedy produced by F. Ziegfeld Jr. **1917** *Ibid.* 7 July 278/1 If the Ziegfeld chorus were clothed in brown jaegers.., the paucity of the entertainment..would be shockingly revealed. **1923** G. ADE *Let.* 9 Jan. (1973) 87 Do not permit encores unless actually demanded. This is most important and is the secret of the success of a good Ziegfeld show. **1929** etc. [see *FOLLY *sb.*[1] 5 b]. **1932** G. GREENE *Stamboul Train* II. i. 70 A baronet had married a Ziegfeld girl. **1976** BOTHAM & DONNELLY *Valentino* iv. 35 He chatted to the Ziegfeld Follies girls.

Ziegler (zī·glər). *Chem.* The name of Karl *Ziegler* (1898–1973), German chemist, used *attrib.* to designate a trialkyl aluminium–titanium tetrachloride catalyst discovered by him for the synthesis of stereoregular isotactic polymers of high density and crystallinity from an ethylene or propylene monomer; also, *loosely*, = next.

1957 [see *ISOPRENE]. **1961** [see *STEREOREGULAR *a.*]. **1966** PHILLIPS & WILLIAMS *Inorg. Chem.* II. xxxiii. 560 This reaction is of interest in connexion with the polymerization of olefins by Ziegler catalysts. **1980** *Nature* 20 Mar. 213/3 [They] produced thin films by exposing acetylene gas to concentrated solutions of Ziegler catalysts.

Ziegler–Natta (zī·glər næ·tă). *Chem.* The names of K. *Ziegler* (see prec.) and Giulio *Natta* (1903–79), Italian chemist, used *attrib.* to designate any catalyst of the class including the Ziegler catalyst, consisting in general of a transition metal halide and a non-transition metal organic derivative, and used with any olefin monomer. So *Ziegler–Natta catalysis.*

1965 PHILLIPS & WILLIAMS *Inorg. Chem.* I. x. 382 Whereas the ionic catalysts appear to be capable of general use with any unsaturated molecule,..Ziegler–Natta catalysts are usually employed in the polymerization of olefinic hydrocarbons—notably, ethylene and proplyene. **1974** *Encycl. Brit. Micropædia* X. 880/3 The Ziegler–Natta catalysts include many mixtures of halides of transition metals, especially titanium, chromium, vanadium, and zirconium, with organic derivatives of nontransition metals, particularly alkyl aluminium compounds. **1980** M. ORCHIN et al. *Vocab. Org. Chem.* xiv. 535 It has been suggested that Ziegler–Natta catalysis may involve metal–carbene formation.

Ziehl (tsīl). *Bacteriol.* The name of F. *Ziehl* (1857–1926), German neurologist, used *attrib.* and in the possessive to designate a red stain consisting of an alcoholic solution of fuchsine in an aqueous solution of phenol; so **Ziehl–Neelsen** [F. K. A. *Neelsen* (1854–94), German bacteriologist], applied to a method for identifying acid-fast organisms such as tubercle bacilli by staining with Ziehl's stain, decolorizing with sulphuric acid (and sometimes also alcohol), and counterstaining with methylene blue: acid-fast organisms retain the original red colour.

1892 G. M. STERNBERG *Man. Bacteriol.* I. iv. 29 (*heading*) Carbol-fuschsin (Ziehl's solution) *Ibid.* 30 (*heading*) The Ziehl-Neelson [*sic*] method. **1967** K. M. SMITH *Insect Virol.* x. 189 Immature polyhedra in the nuclei of the hemolymph cells are easily differentiated by staining the smears with Ziehl fuchsin. **1974** R. M. KIRK et al. *Surgery* ii. 21 *Mycobacterium..tuberculosis*..stained by the Ziehl-Neelsen method is acid-fast and alcohol-fast.

ziff (zif). *Austral.* (and *N.Z.*) *slang.* [Origin unknown.] A beard.

1919 W. H. DOWNING *Digger Dialects* 54 *Ziff*, a beard. **1924** C. J. DENNIS *Rose of Spadgers* 137 'E lobbed in on us sudden, ziff an' all. **1934** *Bulletin* (Sydney) 2 May 25/4 All the Druids in that show wore long, white nightgowns and ziffs down to where the tops of their trousers should have been. **1947** J. MORRISON *Sailors belong Ships* 97 We all called him The Prophet. He had a long ziff. **1971** *N.Z. Listener* 19 Apr. 56/5 So up he goes and finds he knows one of them, the one with the ziff. **1981** G. KELLY *Always Afternoon* xii. 211 'Better get rid of that ziff,' she said pointing to his embryonic beard.

zig, the first syllable of *zigzag*: (Examples of *zig* sb. and vb. used without *zag*.) Hence **zi·gging** *vbl. sb.* and *ppl. a.*

1969 *Southern Rev.* July 760 After that We drove back, zigging, cautious. **1971** G. EWART *Gavin Ewart Show* I. 11 An ant zigs quietly over the windowsill. **1977** *Time* 17 Oct. 24/3 The Carter Administration's push for Geneva will surely require much more shoving, not to mention zigging and zagging, in the weeks ahead if it is to succeed. **1978** H. WOUK *War & Remembrance* vii. 72 The transports were on a zig away. **1982** A. MELVILLE-ROSS *Trigger* v. 45 What's his course?..Go deep if it zigs towards us. *Ibid.* 53 'They've turned ninety degrees to starboard.'.. 'A zig, sir?' 'Afraid not. They've altered course.' **1983** *Sci. Amer.* July 14/2 Subtler to see is the line just below, whose zigging and zagging is 180 degrees out of phase with the top line. **1985** S. VANAUKEN *Under the Mercy* x. 246 One word more on change and development,.. the zigs and zags and the farings forward on one's pilgrimage to God.

zigabo, zigaboo, varr. *JIGABOO.

‖**Zigeuner** (tsigoi·nər). fem. **-erin,** pl. **-erinnen.** [Ger., cogn. with ZINGANO, ZINGARO.] A gypsy. **Zigeu:nerbaro·n,** a gypsy baron (in allusion to the operetta *Der Zigeunerbaron* (1885) by Johann Strauss).

[**1841** G. BORROW *Zincali* I. I. 2 They are styled in Russia, Zigáni; in Turkey and Persia, Zingarri; and in Germany, Zigeuner.] **1845** THACKERAY *Legend of Rhine* x, in *G. Cruikshank's Table-Bk.* I. 198 Here should come the gleemen and jongleurs,..the dark-eyed nut-brown Zigeunerinnen. **1963** *Times* 12 Jan. 9/7 He was a violinist, a travelling musician. His coat had a black fur collar; he looked somewhat like a refined *Zigeunerbaron*. **1964** *Listener* 25 June 1043/3 His [*sc.* Bartók's] passion for the true Hungary and its folk-music as opposed to the *Zigeunerbaron* travesties. **1970** N. FREELING *Kitchen Bk.* xix. 184 There were no musicians, though I recognized Philippa's zigeuner guitarist.

ziggety (zi·geti), *int.*, *adj.*, and *adv.* *slang* (orig. and chiefly *U.S.*). Also **ziggedy, ziggetty, ziggity.** [App. var. of (*hot*) *diggety* s.v. *HOT *a.* 12 c.] **1.** *int.* Usu. preceded by *hot* and followed by *dog* or another monosyllable: = *hot diggety* (*dog*) s.v. *HOT *a.* 12 c.

1924 *Dialect Notes* V. 265 I'll be damned, hot ziggety damn. **1926** MAINES & GRANT *Wise-Crack Dict.* 9/2 *Hot ziggetty dog*, expressing unlimited admiration. **1933** R. JAMES *Worth Remembering* iii. 62 Hot ziggity zig! **1942** BERREY & VAN DEN BARK *Amer. Thes. Slang* §277/7 Hot ziggety! hot ziggety damn! *or* darn! hot ziggety dog! **1944** M. SHULMAN *Feather Merchants* xiii. 78 'Ziggetty!' he said. **1950** A. BUCKERIDGE *Jennings goes to School* viii. 155 Oh, hefty ziggety door knobs! **1961** R. LONGRIGG *Daughters of Mulberry* viii. 97 'Hot ziggety,' said an old American. 'That's six grand I made.' **1984** *New Yorker* 21 May 46/1 Mr. Deforest entered with his face bright, his hands folded behind him. 'Well, hot ziggetty, a holiday for me. What have we got going here?'

2. *adj.* and *adv.* = ZIGZAG *a.* and *adv.* Also redupl., as *ziggety-zaggety.*

1935 J. T. FARRELL *Judgment Day* ii. 25 He pursued a ziggedy course along the sidewalk. **1956** H. GOLD *Man who was not with It* (1965) xi. 86, I had gone backwards to walk sideways, ziggety-zaggety.

zigsaw, zigzaw, obs. varr. *JIG-SAW *sb.* b.

1912 H. MAXWELL *Early Chron. Rel. Scotl.* I. 16 One of those zigzaw puzzles which had a fleeting vogue two or three years ago. **1919** D. WYLLARDE *Holiday Husb.* xiii. 167 As neatly as if she had found the right pieces of a zigsaw puzzle.

zigzag, *sb.*, *a.*, *adv.* Add: **A.** *sb.* **5.** (**Zig(-) Zag.**) A proprietary name for cigarette paper.

1909 *Official Gaz.* (U.S. Patent Office) 14 Dec. 594/1 Braunstein & Cie, Paris... *Zig Zag*... Cigarette-paper. **1927** *Trade Marks Jrnl.* 13 Apr. 675 Zig-zag No. 114... Cigarette papers. Société anonyme des anciens Établissements Braunstein Frères.., Paris. **1968** *Current Slang* (Univ. S. Dakota) Fall 52 *Zig-zag*, paper of high quality which is commonly used in rolling marijuana. **1977** C. MCFADDEN *Serial* (1978) xxx. 67/1 She stuffed her..Zig Zags back into her purse.

6. *attrib.*, as **zigzag machine,** a sewing machine with a swing needle that may be used to produce a zigzag stitch and decorative stitches derived from it.

[**1950** *Vogue Pattern Book* Apr.–May 81/2 It was Pfaff that developed the famous Zig-Zag Model 130.] **1952** *Consumers' Res. Bull.* Sept. 11/1 All the zig-zag machines but one..were heavy. **1963** *Which?* June 165/2 For plain zig zag machines, the *width* of the stitch limits the range of patterns they can make. **1978** *Detroit Free Press* 5 Mar. D14 (Advt.), Fashionmate zig zag machine featuring our front drop-in bobbin.

B. *adj.* **2*.** *Mil. slang* (chiefly *U.S.*). Drunk.
1918 Hamilton & Corbin *Echoes from over There* (1919) 125 He got a trifle zig-zag. **1919** W. H. Downing *Digger Dialects* 54 *Zig-zag*, drunk. **1923** E. Paul *Impromptu* 149 He groped and floundered..not completely 'zigzag'. **1930** Brophy & Partridge *Songs & Slang Brit. Soldier* 181 *Zig-zag*, drunk. **1961** *Times* 27 Apr. 17/2 What is that to a nation which uses some 400 synonyms for 'drunk'—from 'all geezed up' to 'zig-zag'?

3. zigzag connection *Electr. Engin.*, a form of star connection of three-phase circuits, each branch of which is interconnected and contains portions of two consecutive phases.
1922 P. Kemp *Alternating Current Electr. Engin.* (ed. 2) xiii. 188 This affects the magnetising current and may result in an appreciable increase in iron loss owing to flux distortion, and to minimize this effect zig-zag connections are sometimes adopted. **1947** R. Lee *Electronic Transformers & Circuits* iii. 47 Unbalanced direct current in the half-wave rectifiers requires larger transformers than in the full-wave rectifiers. This is partly overcome in three-phase transformers by the use of zigzag connections.

zigzag, *v.* Add: **1. b.** Of a sewing-machine: to make zigzag stitches.
1950 *Consumer Rep.* May 212/1 The Necchis [*sc.* sewing-machines] which zigzagged were inferior to the.. *Necchis* which didn't. **1956** *Sears, Roebuck Catal.* Fall-Winter 1068/1 Whether you want to embroider..zig-zag or sew a straight seam, you'll find the '84' unsurpassed. **1976** *Woman's Weekly* 6 Nov. 68/2 (Advt.), It's a pocket-size sewing machine which you hold in one hand—that sews, bastes, hems, zig-zags, sews on buttons and even zippers.
2. b. To traverse in a zigzag manner.
1930 Bird & Ryan *Recall Public Officers* 42 He literally zigzagged the whole tremendous territory, visiting almost every hamlet. **1978** J. Wainwright *Ripple of Murders* 78 The vans..zig-zagged the near-deserted streets.

zigzagged, *a.* Add: Hence **zi·gzaggedly** *adv.*
1921 W. de la Mare *Mem. Midget* xxxiii. 230 How zigzaggedly you talk. What has poetry to do with Mr Crimble? **1977** R. Katz *Ziggurat* vi. 55 It [*sc.* a ball] rolled zigzaggedly for a while.

zig-zig, U.S. Mil. slang var. *jig-a-jig.
1918 H. V. O'Brien *Diary* 30 Jan. in *Wine, Women & War* (1926) 18 Zig-zig—nothing else but. **1930** in S. Longstreet *Canvas Falcons* (1970) 271 Zig-zig wif me? **1962** W. Robinson *Barbara* (1964) 135 'Allo, baybee! Comment alley vooz—zigzig?

zikkurat, ziggurat. Add: The latter is now the usual spelling. **b.** *transf.* and *fig.*
1959 *Times* 21 Oct. 11/3 The burnished ziggurats of copper saucepans. **1970** *Daily Tel.* (Colour Suppl.) 30 Oct. 26/3 The bags are abandoned, of course, and join the rest of the overkill of trash imagery, now heaped into ziggurats, festooning vegetation, scrawled in livid drifts on the downs. **1979** *Jrnl. R. Soc. Arts* Nov. 761/1 His Dallas Chapel in the form of a spiral ziggurat..borrows quite directly from the ninth-century minaret at Samarra. **1980** *Bee Culture* July 376 The photograph will give an idea of the real engineering performed to make this temple a 'ziggurat' of comb—upward from the base above the regular [honey]combs.

‖**zikr** (zik'r). Also **zikir.** [ad. Arab *ḏikr* remembrance.] A Muslim ritual prayer in which an expression of praise is continually repeated.
1836 E. W. Lane *Acct. Manners & Customs Mod. Egyptians* II. xi. 170 They had not yet begun their performances or *zikrs*, in concert; but one old durweesh, standing between the two rows, was performing a zikr alone; repeating the name of God (Alláh), and bowing his head each time that he uttered the word, alternately to the right and left. **1877** *Encycl. Brit.* VII. 114/1 The Zikr consists mainly in a chant, always becoming louder and more violent, of the first attribute [of God]. **1900** 'Odysseus' *Turkey in Europe* v. 193 Dervishes..have also their own characteristic form of worship called Zikr, consisting of the repetition, sometimes continued during several hours, of some religious formula, such as 'There is no God but God', or the ninety and nine names of the Deity. **1923** *Blackw. Mag.* Aug. 251/1 Dervishes shouting themselves into ecstasy at their zikr. **1954** M. Murray in G. B. Gardner *Witchcraft Today* 16 The solemn *zikr* of the Egyptian peasant. **1976** *Bangladesh Times* (Dacca) 12 Jan. 2/5 Monday, January 26: after Esha prayer Khatme Holy Quran, Khatme Gousia and Khatme Khajegan at 2 a.m. Zikir, Zearat and Munazat.

Zilavka (zila·fkă). The name of a white wine of Yugoslavia.
1926 P. M. Shand *Bk. Wine* x. 255 *Bosnia-Herzegovina*..The principal wines are the red growth of Blatina..and the white Zilavka, a potent, greenish-yellow wine with a Muscatelle bouquet. **1954** M. Krippner *Yugoslavia Invites* 199 Zilavka, a yellow wine, and Blatina, a heavy claret, both come from Herzegovina. **1965** *Sun* 23 Jan. 6/6, I tried Zilavka—a wine..from the Macedonian vineyards near the Greek frontier. **1978** *Chicago* June 220/2 We recommend Zilavka from Mostar vineyard, white but with enough richness and strength for meats.

zilch (zıltʃ), *sb.* (and *a.*) *slang* (orig. and chiefly *U.S.*). [Origin uncertain.] Nothing, nil; also as *adj.*, no; non-existent.
1931 *Ballyhoo* I. i. 1 (*heading*) President Henry P. Zilch. Chairman of the Board Charles D. Zilch. Treasurer Otto Zilch. *Ibid.* ii. 10 (*caption*) 'Mr. Zilch, you don't often stay in so long.' 'No I don't often lose my bathing trunks.' **1940** Berrey & Van den Bark *Amer. Thes. Slang* §184/1 *Dinglegoofer, Mr. Zilch*, indefinite nick-names.] **1966** *Current Slang* (Univ. S. Dakota) Winter 8 *Zilch*, adj. Nothing, zero... What a day—*zilch* from everybody. **1967** P. Welles *Babyhip* ii. 25 Half-starved, no doubt. The old whore probably fed him zilch. **1973** *Daily Colonist* (Victoria, B.C.) 14 Jan. 13/7, I feel that since I was elected to the board of directors last year I have accomplished zilch. **1976** *New Musical Express* 17 Apr. 6/6 My knowledge of classical music is zilch **1976** *Billings* (Montana) *Gaz.* 27 June 2-E/2 In the light of data developed from the city's own 1975 studies, the 17th Street project rates zilch in priorities. **1977** *Tel.* (Brisbane) 3 Feb. 14/3 Georgeous faces but zilch talent. **1977** *Playgirl* May 12/2 Our sex life is practically zilch, and he almost never pays any attention to me. **1984** *Daily Tel.* 8 Mar. 36/5 The power of the legislature over the executive being slightly better than zilch, any MP..who bounces the Home Office deserves a small roll of drums. **1984** *Sounds* 1 Dec. 38/3 Three further 45s ensued in 1979 and '80, plus an album which didn't sell. After that, zilch.

zillah. Add: *zillah parishad*: see *parishad.

zillion (zi·lyən). *slang* (chiefly *U.S.*). [f. Z + M)illion.] A very large but indefinite number.
1944 D. Runyon *Runyon à la Carte* (1946) 165, I love him a zillion dollars' worth. **1947** *Esquire* May 40/2 Faithful to their zillions of fans. **1976** *National Observer* (U.S.) 10 Jan. 10/4 A zillion or so years ago, while I was a student nurse. **1976** J. Crosby *Snake* (1977) xvii. 93 She was going to break the story to her zillion readers. **1983** *Sunday Tel.* 9 Oct. 20/2 Broken Hill Proprietary..is Australia's biggest company and a zillion times bigger than his own. **1984** *Guardian* 29 Oct. 9/2 The whiff of news managers at work, rather than an urge to hear about British Telecom's zillion-pound share sale from the horse's mouth, took me to BT's big press conference on Friday.
Hence **zillionai·re**, a very rich person; **zi·llionth** *a.*, following very many others; 'umpteenth'; *sb.*, a tiny fraction *of* anything.
1946 D. Runyon *Runyon à la Carte* ix. 143 She plays the frost for all who are not well established as practically zillionaires. **1959** I. Fleming *Goldfinger* iv. 50 He's a zillionaire himself. . He's crawling with money. **1969** *Daily Tel.* (Colour Suppl.) 15 Aug. 21/3 A sprinkling of.. Texas zillionaires, film stars, socialites and international playboys. **1972** *Good Housekeeping* Apr. 69/1 'We have strict controls on television,' said Mrs. Hamon [an American]. 'We don't hear a zillionth of what you hear.' **1975** *Listener* 24 Apr. 554/3 Anchorman Peter Snow..said, for the zillionth time, 'Well, there it is.' **1983** 'J. Gash' *Sleepers of Erin* xviii. 141 The Heindricks' scam was so big that even zillionaires were keen on its successful execution. **1984** *Listener* 6 Dec. 26/3 For the zillionth time, the hardback edition only is credited in reviews.

Zimba (zi·mbă). (A member of) an African people that was active in the vicinity of the Zambezi in the sixteenth century.
1901 G. M. Theal tr. J. dos Santos in *Rec. South-Eastern Africa* VII. xvii. 291 Facing Tete on the other side of the river..there are two tribes of Kaffirs who eat human flesh, one called the Mumbos and the other the Zimbas or Muzimbas. **1913** C. A. Stigand *Land of Zinj* i. 17 The Zimba, a powerful tribe of barbarians who lived N.E. of Tete on the Zambezi, are now first heard of in these parts. In 1588 they invaded Kilwa, and the next year passed up the coast and invaded Mombasa. **1968** R. Oliver in J. Biggs-Davison *Africa—Hope Deferred* (1972) iii. 26 The Zimbas who swept up the east coast of Africa in the late sixteenth century. **1972** *Stand. Encycl. S. Afr.* VI. 341/1 Mirale occupied Mombasa in 1589, but the Portuguese received unexpected help from the interior when the mysterious cannibal Zimba tribe arrived from the south, destroying Mombasa and most of its occupants. **1974** *Encycl. Brit. Macropædia* XVII. 277/2 The Zimba.. were followers of a Manganja chief living to the south of the Shire River.

Zimbabwe (zimbā·bwe). Also **zimbabwe.** [The name in Bantu of the first such ruin to be discovered, in what is now the State of Zimbabwe.] One of the numerous ruined stone-walled settlements scattered across Zimbabwe and neighbouring countries and dating from medieval times.
1902 Hall & Neal *Anc. Ruins Rhodesia* iii. 36 They introduced fresh features in building, as shown..by new Zimbabwes, which they erected. **1929** J. Buchan *Courts of Morning* ii. 288 The subsidiary towers..recalled in their shape pictures she had seen of the Rhodesian Zimbabwes. **1931** G. Caton-Thompson (*title*) The Zimbabwe culture. **1963** R. Summers in E. Bacon *Vanished Civilisations* iii. 36/2 Other 'Zimbabwes'—over 200 of them..—lie scattered all over Southern Rhodesia. **1976** *Times* 17 July 14/6 Another, early, stone-walled *zimbabwe* of the type best known from the Great Zimbabwe ruins in Rhodesia has been discovered..in Mozambique. **1980** *Nature* 1 May 5/3 In 1975..after independence in Mozambique one of the Zimbabwes—Manyikeni, 50 km west of Vilanculos was excavated.

Zimbabwean (zimbā·bweăn, -bæb-), *sb.* and *a.* [f. *Zimbabwe* (see below) + -an.] **A.** *sb.* **a.** Before 1980, when Rhodesia became Zimbabwe, (*a*) an African nationalist name for a black Rhodesian; (*b*) an inhabitant of a future state of Zimbabwe. **b.** Since 1980, a native or inhabitant of Zimbabwe. **B.** *adj.* Of or pertaining to Zimbabweans or Zimbabwe.
1967 *Times* 30 Dec. 4 Let us work untiringly for the total mobilization of the four million Zimbabweans for Chimurenga (war of liberation). **1973** *Black Panther* 28 Apr. 9/1 (*caption*) Brother Kumbirai Kangai, freedom fighter in the Zimbabwean people's struggle. **1975** *Times* 11 Feb. 12/2 Whatever the future holds in store for an independent Zimbabwe, the white Zimbabwean will continue to play his part alongside his black counterpart. **1976** *Daily Tel.* 19 Aug. 14 Zimbabwean Nationalists who patiently tried a negotiated settlement cannot now be expected to lay down arms. **1979** *African Affairs* LXXVIII. 253 (*heading*) Zimbabwean economic and social historiography since 1970. **1984** *News* (Mexico City) 12 Mar. 7/2 Nkomo..suggested Zimbabweans were no freer than they were under the white-minority colonial government.

zimbalom, -n, var. *cimbalom, cimbelom.
1910 F. W. Galpin *Old Eng. Instrum. Music* iv. 66 The large Dulcimer, used in Hungarian Bands at the present time, is known by the Magyar musicians as the *zimbalom*. **1925** *Glasgow Herald* 17 Oct. 6/2 The zimbalon, which is an improved type of dulcimer, has been honoured with a d.-s. record made by Nitza Godolban. **1975** *New Yorker* 19 May 90/1, I spent two weeks in Shiraz and Persepolis, listening for hours every day to percussion from all over the world:..to varieties of dulcimer (zither, santir, zimbalon).

‖**zimbel** (tsi·mbəl). *Mus.* [Ger., ad. L. *cymbalum* (see Cymbal).] = Cymbal 3.
1910 F. W. Galpin *Old Eng. Instrum. Music* xiv. 264 We also find an organ-stop called the *Zimbel*..and this.. was a compound stop or mixture intended to represent the sound of bells. **1976** *Gramophone* Oct. 628/3 An exuberant finale contrasts the zimbel with the cornet. **1980** *New Grove Dict. Mus.* XIII. 791/1 'Mixture' was normally used to denote the Principal-scaled chorus Mixture as distinct from the high Zimbeln or the solo Cornets.

zimes, var. *tzimmes. **Zimmenthal,** var. *Simmental.

Zimmer (zi·məɹ). Also **zimmer.** [Maker's name.] A proprietary name for orthopædic appliances, used esp. *attrib.* to designate a kind of walking frame.
1951 *Trade Marks Jrnl.* 11 Apr. 358/1 *Zimmer*... Orthopaedic appliances and instruments. Zimmer Orthopaedic Limited,..London, W.1..; manufacturers. **1957** *Official Gaz.* (U.S. Patent Office) 16 Apr. tm 116/2 *Zimmer*. For orthopedic appliances and fracture equipment. First use in May of 1927. **1974** Passmore & Robson *Compan. Med. Stud.* III. ii. xxxiv. 103/1 For patients with unsteadiness and ataxia, a simple walking frame of 'Zimmer' pattern is valuable. **1981** *Church Times* 10 Apr. 14/4, I had felt too ill to try and use my zimmer-frame and calipers. **1982** E. Dewhurst *Whoever I Am* iii. 44 Incapable of walking without a Zimmer frame.

zinc, *sb.* Add: **1. c.** Galvanized iron. Chiefly *S. Afr.* and *W. Indies*. Cf. *zinc roof* in sense 2 c below.
1873 F. Boyle *To Cape for Diamonds* xix. 252 These hoppers are made of perforated zinc, or wire, the latter being preferable. **1953** R. Mais *Hills were Joyful Together* i. vi. 57 Surjue went through a zinc fence—through a hinged zinc sheet in a zinc fence that looked like a solid stretch of iron sheeting down one side of a lane. **1973** *Eastern Province Herald* (Port Elizabeth) 23 Jan., The brazier, zink bath and cooking utensils. were obtained from Coloureds in the area. **1977** *Daily Express* 29 Jan. 7/3 All six members of the cast take turns to strip off and bathe in a zinc bath.
d. The zinc-covered bar of a café or public house; by metonymy, a café. (A gallicism.)
1914 *19th Cent.* Feb. 286 Elections are made or marred *chez le marchand de vin*, or, as the Parisians familiarly call him, le *mastroquet*... The 'organised democracy marching towards the good of progress and liberty, etc.'..is in reality nothing else than the disorganised and demoralised *plebs* marching towards the *zinc* of the *mastroquet*. *a* **1936** Kipling *Something of Myself* (1937) iv. 81 My barmaid..had watched it [*sc.* evil] across the zinc she was always swabbing off. **1948** W. Fortescue *Beauty for Ashes* xx. 148 We even supplied a little bar with a *zinc* and a motherly Frenchwoman to look after it. **1965** V. Canning *Whip Hand* xii. 138, I..tottered to the nearest zinc, and called for a triple cognac. **1979** A. M. Stein *Rolling Heads* vi. 103 The last of the cafés shut down—it was a laborers' zinc down a back street.
2. a. *zinc-lining*. **b.** *zinc-coated, -covered, -plated, -topped*. **c. zinc-air** *a.*, applied to a type of primary cell employing a zinc anode, a porous carbon cathode able to utilize atmospheric oxygen, and an alkaline electrolyte; **zinc chloride,** a white, crystalline, deliquescent solid, $ZnCl_2$, used as a preservative, a flux, and in Leclanché cells; **zinc chromate,** a toxic, yellow, water-insoluble powder, $ZnCrO_4$, used as a pigment; **zinc chrome** = *zinc yellow* below; **zinc green,** a mixture of zinc and cobalt oxides used as a pigment; **zinc roof** *S. Afr.* and *W. Indies*, a corrugated roof of galvanized iron; **zinc sulphide,** (*U.S.*) **sulfide,** a yellow, water-insoluble powder, ZnS, used as a pigment and as a phosphor; **zinc white** (earlier example);

zinc yellow, a greenish-yellow pigment consisting principally of zinc chromate.

1970 C. L. MANTELL *Batteries & Energy Systems* vi. 63 These portable zinc-air batteries are being used in man-pack transceivers, night vision devices, and space satellite communications. **1978** *Jrnl. Electrochem. Soc.* CXXV. 333c/2 The Gould zinc-air button cell is..used in hearing aids and other devices which require a moderately high current. **1851** H. WATTS tr. *Gmelin's Hand-bk. Chem.* V. xxviii. 32 ZnCl, 9ZnO..[is prepared] by precipitating aqueous zinc-chloride with an insufficient quantity of ammonia and filtering immediately. **1911** *Encycl. Brit.* XXVIII. 984/1 Zinc chloride, $ZnCl_2$, is produced by heating the metal in dry chlorine gas, when it distils over as a white translucent mass. **1981** BRADY & HOLUM *Fund. Chem.* xx. 700 Zinc chloride, which is exceptionally soluble in water.., has a range of uses that extend from embalming, to fireproofing lumber, to the refining of petroleum. **1851** H. WATTS tr. *Gmelin's Hand-bk. Chem.* V. xxviii. 48 The crystals..really consisted of ordinary zinc-sulphate containing small quantities of zinc-chromate intimately bound up with them. **1974** *Encycl. Brit. Macropædia* IV. 571/2 Zinc yellow, a basic zinc chromate, is used as a corrosion-inhibiting primer on aircraft parts fabricated from aluminum or magnesium. **1892** G. H. HURST *Painters' Colours, Oils, & Varnishes* iv. 132 Zinc chrome is a yellow pigment of good colour and body. **1963** *Times* 22 Apr. 6/5 Zinc chromes, with zinc chromate as the major constituent, form an important class of pigments. **1930** *Jrnl. Iron & Steel Inst.* CXXI. 749 An investigation of the corrosion fatigue of zinc-coated steel specimens. **1981** M. C. SMITH *Gorky Park* III. iv. 361 The sables..climbed zinc-coated mesh walls. **1890** A. CONAN DOYLE *Firm of Girdlestone* xxx. 238 A very seedy-looking individual..was leaning with his elbows upon the zinc-covered counter. **1847** *Brit. Pat. 11,616* 5 Processes for manufacturing on a large scale zinc yellow..and zinc green. **1973** E. LALOR in T. C. Patton *Pigment Handbk.* I. 850/1 Much of the zinc yellow manufactured was mixed with Prussian blue to make various shades of a permanent zinc green. **1912** C. N. MOODY *Saints of Formosa* vi. 132 Boxes had to be made or furnished with zinc-lining. **1859** G. A. SALA *Twice round Clock* 117 There is the rotunda of the Bank of England, with its many-slamming, zinc-plated doors. **1966** *McGraw-Hill Encycl. Sci. & Technol.* IV. 531/1 Zinc-plated coatings are usually purer than hot-dipped coatings. **1883** 'R. IRON' *Story Afr. Farm* I. I. ii. 11 The zinc roofs of the out-buildings, the stone walls of the 'kraals', all reflected the fierce sunlight. **1946** U. KRIGE *Way Out* vi. 82 There was a mass of dry maize leaves under a zinc roof jutting out from the wall. **1851** H. WATTS tr. *Gmelin's Hand-bk. Chem.* V. xxviii. 19 Nöggerath and Bischof..found in an old mine a quantity of zinc-sulphide mixed with washings of the ore. **1937** *Discovery* Feb. 44/2 The [television] screen is coated with a powder consisting of zinc sulphide and other chemicals. **1974** *Encycl. Brit. Micropædia* X. 883/3 Zinc sulfide is insoluble in water but dissolves in mineral acids. **1938** E. AMBLER *Cause for Alarm* (1940) xiii. 203 A zinc-topped bar and four marble-topped tables. **1847** *Brit. Pat. 11,616* 9 The dryer is added to the color prepared with the zinc white. **1847** Zinc yellow [see *zinc green* above]. **1901** A. C. WRIGHT tr. *Bersch's Manuf. Mineral & Lake Pigments* xiv. 152 Zinc yellow may be prepared by the immediate precipitation of a solution of zinc sulphate by a solution of potassium chromate. **1974** *Encycl. Brit. Macropædia* XIII. 889/1 Zinc yellow has a greenish cast because of a high content of chromic oxide.

d. As *adj.*: Having a basically greyish colour.

1922 'K. MANSFIELD' *Let.* 11 Aug. (1977) 271 A zinc greengage or two. **1960** *New Yorker* 1 Oct. 44/2 Faultless eyes gone blank beneath the immense Zinc-and-gunmetal northern sky.

zincian (zi·ŋkiăn), *a. Min.* [f. ZINC *sb.* + *-IAN 2.] Of a mineral: having a (small) proportion of a constituent element replaced by zinc.

1930 W. T. SCHALLER in *Amer. Mineralogist* XV. 571 Zinc—zincian. **1968** I. KOSTOV *Mineralogy* ix. 498 Pisanite is a cuprian variety..; sommairite zincian melanterite. **1977** *Amer. Mineralogist* LXII. 463/2 The proportion of zinc is probably insufficient to justify a new name... It might, therefore, be called a zincian takovite.

zinckenite. Add: Now the usu. spelling of ZINKENITE.

‖**zindan** (zindā·n). [Pers. *zindān*, Turk. *zindan*.] A prison in Persia or neighbouring parts.

1889 G. N. CURZON *Russia in Central Asia* vii. 217 In another part of the citadel was the Zindan, or prison. **1924** *Glasgow Herald* 29 May 9/7 In Persia..I saw for the first time a Central Asian underground prison called Zindan... Prisoners..cannot possibly escape out of a deep pit with only a circular opening at the top. **1959** *Listener* 21 May 883/1 The Zindan or prison where Stoddart and Conolly spent so many miserable months [in Bokhara].

zine (zīn). *U.S. colloq.* Shortened form of *FANZINE.

1965 *New Yorker* 21 Aug. 24 The fanzines, or fan magazines, which are also known as amazines, or amateur magazines, do a great deal of research on the Golden Age, and some of the faneds, or fan-magazine editors, do a remarkably good job. Some zines specialize—like *ERB-dom*, which caters to the fans of Edgar Rice Burroughs—but most of them concentrate on the fantasy adventure or superhero comics, on which most fanac, or fan activity, centers. **1975** *Piece of Action* (Houston) Jan. 6 The above zine should not be confused with another proposed zine called *The Atavachron*. **1982** *Amer. Speech* LVII. 20 A publisher of a fanzine would send copies of his zine to a central location for collation with other zines and subsequent distribution. **1985** *Times* 25 Jan. 12/2 A zine is what its addicts call a postal games magazine, of which there are about 50 in the country.

zineb (zi·neb). [f. *zinc ethylene bisdithiocarbamate*, the systematic name: see ETHYLENE, BIS-².] A white powder used as a fungicide on vegetables and fruit; Zn-$(\cdot S\cdot CS\cdot NH\cdot CH_2\cdot)_2$.

1950 *Phytopathology* XL. 118 The Subcommittee on Fungicide Nomenclature of The American Phytopathological Society, cooperating with the Interdepartmental Committee on Pest Control, has selected common names for five commercially-available fungicidal chemicals... *Zineb* for the fungicidal chemical, zinc ethylene bisdithiocarbamate... *Ziram* for the fungicidal chemical, zinc dimethyl dithiocarbamate. **1966** *McGraw-Hill Encycl. Sci. & Technol.* V. 563/2 Organic fungicides have become increasingly important since 1934... Examples are..nabam, zineb, and maneb, the sodium, zinc, and manganese salts, respectively, of ethylenebis(dithiocarbamic acid). **1981** [see *ZIRAM]. **1981** *Bull. Environmental Contamination & Toxicol.* XXVII. 418 Zineb is an important fungicide widely used in agriculture.

Zinfandel. Add: **b.** The grape from which this wine is made. In full, *Zinfandel grape*.

1880 *Californian* II. 219/1 The favorite wine grapes are the Zinfandel, Riesling and Chasselas. **1977** H. FAST *Immigrants* IV. 254 'What kind of grapes do you grow for the market?' 'Zinfandels mostly. We have some Thompsons—' 'Ah, well the color of zinfandels is excellent, but we want a sweeter grape.' **1980** *Times* 23 Sept. 10/1 We were..in California. My companion..grows Chardonnay, Cabernet and Zinfandel grapes.

zing (ziŋ), *sb. colloq.* (orig. *U.S.*). [Echoic.] **1.** A sharp, high-pitched ringing sound; a twang.

1911 D. RUNYON *Tents of Trouble* 22, I felt him fall and I sensed the 'zing' of a boob-face Arab's knife. **1922** C. SANDBURG *Slabs of Sunburnt West* 63 Then the axmen came and the chips flew to the zing of steel and handle. **1930** E. FERBER *Cimarron* xx. 331 He seized the typewriter by its steel bar and plumped it to the floor with a force that wrung a protesting whine and zing from its startled insides. **1961** E. WILLIAMS *George* xxv. 403 There was the confident zing of tennis-rackets in the Parks. **1970** *Washington Post* 30 Sept. B-1/1 The butterfly chair, that zing-zong-zang of tubular metal.

2. Energy, vigour, liveliness; zest; a quality that induces alertness or vitality.

1918 *Independent* 14 Dec. 369/1 They were the picked athletes of the whole English Army and were doing their calisthenics with a precision and spirit I have never seen equaled anywhere. The 'pep', 'zing' and 'vim' were thrilling. **1931** [see *BELT *v.* 4 b (*b*)]. **1941** G. KERSH *They die with their Boots Clean* II. 83 I'll soon get that paleness off your faces and put some zing into those limbs. **1955** 'S. RANSOME' *Deadly Bedfellows* i. 7 Lake Haven's air..was full of zing and bounce. **1964** *Punch* 27 May 796/3 The show had zing. **1979** *Brit. Jrnl. Photogr.* 21 Sept. 917/1 In the old days a photographer used to go to work with a holdall and could be on the other side of the world. That doesn't happen very often nowadays in Fleet Street. It's lost its zing. **1983** *Daily Tel.* 21 Dec. 9/2 Freshly-squeezed lemon or lime has a unique impact, adding a zing to almost any combination in flavours. **1985** *Spectator* 28 Sept. 9 While death has not lost its sting, sex has undoubtedly lost its zing.

zing (ziŋ), *int.* Chiefly *U.S.* [Echoic. Cf. *ZINGO *int.*] Representing the sudden advent of a new situation or emotion.

1919 WODEHOUSE *Damsel in Distress* vi. 75 The generous blood of the Belphers boiled over, and then—*zing*. They jerked him off to Vine Street. **1948** *Sun* (Baltimore) 3 Dec. 14/2 A method of freezing concentrated orange juice was developed, and zing! the first thing they knew they had a new and depression-beating industry on their hands. **1955** W. GADDIS *Recognitions* I. iv. 161 String a good piece of piano wire across the road..and take a couple of shots at them. They go after you..and zing zing zing there go their heads just like that. **1977** M. FRENCH *Women's Room* (1978) iv. 248 So one day you meet this guy, right? And, ZING! He is gorgeous!

zing (ziŋ), *v. colloq.* (orig. *U.S.*). [f. the sb. or int.] **1.** *intr.* **a.** To make a sharp, high-pitched ringing or whining sound; to travel rapidly producing such a sound.

1920 S. LEWIS *Main Street* ii. 18 Go zinging along on a fast ice-boat. **1949** N. MARSH *Swing, Brother, Swing* v. 88 Lord Pastern banged, and rattled, and zinged... 'Oh,' she thought, 'how vulnerable he is among his tympani!' **1960** I. CROSS *Backward Sex* i. 12 It would be better if this old chap did not..hear the bullet zing past. **1962** S. PLATH *Johnny Panic & Bible of Dreams* (1977) III. 247 The bees, now Charlie had lifted the top off the hive, were zinging out and dancing round. **1963** T. PYNCHON *V.* xi. 345 Had his coincidence, the accident to shatter the surface of this stagnant pool and send all the mosquitoes of hope zinging away to the exterior night; had it happened? **1977** G. DURRELL *Golden Bats & Pink Pigeons* ii. 38 A group of zosterops,..zinging and twittering to each other.

b. *fig.* To move energetically and with ease; to abound *with* energy.

1961 *John o' London's* 29 June 724/2 She zings along the tight-rope which passes for plot. **1969** N. FREELING *Tsing-Boum* xx. 145 They had been busy enough already in Holland! In Marseilles they had been zinging with ambitious energy. **1973** *Playboy* May 44 As pure escapist entertainment..the movie zings right along. **1973** *Daily Tel.* 7 Nov. 15/2 When..she denounces him to her husband for the imaginary seduction..of a 16-year-old girl pupil, matters zing into focus.

2. *trans.* With *up*. To enliven, invigorate. *U.S.*

1970 *New Yorker* 14 Nov. 154 Charles Revson is the philosopher-king of the cosmetic world... He claims to know by instinct how to 'zing up' a face. **1978** *Chicago* June 234/3 Delicious, spicy pickled-pepper relish..which you can use to zing up the otherwise mild dishes.

3. To abuse; to criticize. *U.S.*

1974 *Evening Herald* (Rock Hill, S. Carolina) 18 Apr. 7/4 In the eighth, Mitterwald doubled and..the rest of the Cubs zinged him for not hitting a fourth homer. **1975** *New Yorker* 21 Apr. 61/3 Brodie told me..of another investigator who, in his haste, 'zinged a dead man' and delivered an investigative report concerning his insurability.

4. To deliver (a witticism, question, etc.) with speed and force. *U.S.*

1975 W. SAFIRE *Before Fall* III. vi. 179 [Nixon] read what they wrote and surprised them later by remembering it and occasionally zinging it back at them. *Ibid.* VII. i. 474, I zinged out a couple of one-liners. **1977** *Time* 10 Jan. 26/2 Her usual practice of zinging brash, hostile questions at world leaders.

Hence **zi·nging** *ppl. a.*

1954 G. DURRELL *Three Singles to Adventure* vi. 144 A group of sandflies discovered us with zinging cries of joy. **1963** *Times* 16 Jan. 6/5 Mr. Richard Daley, the last of the big city political bosses, has promised him a rough ride in a 'swinging, zinging, campaign, the roughest, toughest ever seen in Chicago'. **1970** 'D. HALLIDAY' *Dolly & Cookie Bird* xi. 170 There was a sharp pop, a clang, and the zinging noise of a ricocheting bullet. **1972** *Daily Tel.* (Colour Suppl.) 4 Feb. 8/3 She beat me like a rug, pounded me like dough, using karate chops, zinging finger stabs, incredible flicks. **1978** G. DURRELL *Garden of Gods* iii. 59 The air was..full of the zinging cries of cicadas.

zingana. [See ZINGANO.] **1.** Fem. of ZINGANO.

2. = *ZEBRANO.

1934 A. L. HOWARD *Man. Timbers of World* (ed. 2) 582 *Zebrano* or *Zingana*. ? *Cynometra* aff. *C. Lujai* Willd... West Coast of Africa... Known as 'zebra' wood in the United Kingdom and America. **1947** J. C. RICH *Materials & Methods of Sculpture* x. 297 Zebrawood, also known as Zingana and Zebrano, is a tropical wood imported from Africa. **1957** N. CLIFFORD *Timber Identification* IV. 134 (*table*) Common name..Zebrano... Alternative names..Zingana; Zebrawood... Botanical name..*Brachystegia fleuryana* Chev... Habitat: West Africa. **1973** *Observer* (Colour Suppl.) 8 Apr. 13/1 (Advt.), The grapefruit knife's got a stainless steel blade, zingana wood handle. **1974** F. N. HOWES *Dict. Useful & Everyday Plants* 286 Zingana, *Microberlinia brazzavillensis*, W. Afr., a commercial timber.

Zingaro. Add: **2.** pl. *I* (or *The*) *Zingari*: the name of an amateur cricket club founded in 1845.

1846 W. DENISON *Cricketer's Compan. 1845* p. xiii, Everybody knows that the 'Zingari' are a tribe of wanderers... Just such a race of individuals is the Club which bears the name and title of 'I Zingari'. As a Club, they have neither habitation nor home. **1867** 'OUIDA' *Under Two Flags* I. v. 106 The Household [Cavalry] played the Zingari. **1905** H. A. VACHELL *Hill* x. 222 After the Zingari Match, Desmond got his Flannels. **1922** JOYCE *Ulysses* 731 A new raincoat on him with the muffler in the Zingari colours. **1948** E. WAUGH *Loved One* i. 5 Sir Ambrose wore dark grey flannels, an Eton Rambler tie, an I Zingari ribbon in his boater hat. **1978** *Times* 17 June 13/6 The Household Brigade might turn out in jack-boots, gauntlets, [etc.]..to contend with the Zingari.

zinger (zi·ŋəɹ). *U.S. slang.* [f. *ZING *sb.* + -ER¹.] **1.** Something outstandingly good of its kind.

1955 M. ALLINGHAM *Beckoning Lady* vi. 99, I don't know why it was such a zinger, unless it was that it was very big and very cheap. **1968** *Times* 30 May 10, I think every actress needs one zinger of a part early in her career. **1973** *N.Y. Times Bk. Rev.* 4 Nov. 79 (*caption*) A zinger of a novel. **1976** *New Yorker* 9 Feb. 84/2 It's a zinger of a scene: an educated, socially conscious woman dating a lumpen lost soul. **1980** R. ADAMS *Girl in Swing* v. 63 My private collection was becoming what an American friend..described as a 'zinger'.

2. a. A wisecrack; a punch line.

1970 *Time* 12 Oct. 7 Ann-Margret is giving him a hard time on the home front, too, tossing out little zingers about his advancing age like 'Flab is reality'. **1970** *Life* 30 Oct. 40 In casual chatter the zingers [of Dick Cavett] are just as fast and frequent as they are on the show. **1975** *Homemaker's Mag.* Oct. 28/2 The Vancouver Status of Women group is planning to put out a booklet of useful zingers... Sometimes you just need one sharp line to show you mean business. **1979** *Courier-Mail* (Brisbane) 31 Mar. 76 (*caption*) One more zinger about my height, and I shall be compelled to thrash you mercilessly about the feet and ankles. **1980** *Maledicta* III. 254 Sorry. After having exhibited immense self-control not to quip,..I just had to shoot off this little zinger.

b. A surprise question; an unexpected turn of events, e.g. in a plot.

1973 R. THOMAS *If you can't be Good* (1974) vii. 51, I would drone along..asking tired questions... Then I would throw in the zinger and watch what happened. **1976** *Publishers Weekly* 2 Feb. 91/1 There's a zinger toward the end, in which the nominal hit man gets hit, but it doesn't really compensate for the tedium the reader's gone through. **1983** *Fortune* 11 July 134/2 The supervisor should also encourage discussion..of what may seem like personal issues... In the process, though, be wary of 'zingers', heart-to-heart matters brought up at an awkward time, often near the end of a meeting.

Zingg (ziŋ, tsiŋ). *Petrol.* The name of Theodor *Zingg* (b. 1905), Swiss meteorologist and engineer, used *attrib.* with reference to his system of classification of pebble shapes, in which two ratios formed from three mutually perpendicular diameters are used to assign a pebble to one or other of certain basic shape classes.

1941 *Jrnl. Sedimentary Petrol.* XI. 67/1 (*heading*) Relation between sphericity and Zingg shape classes. **1949** F. J. Pettijohn *Sedimentary Rocks* ii. 49 (*caption*) Chart showing relationship between sphericity and Zingg shape indices. **1979** *Nature* 8 Feb. 496/3 Very simple probabilistic methods were used to estimate the formation of the four basic Zingg shapes (disks, spheres, blades and rods).

zingiber (zi·ndʒibəɹ). [See Ginger.] = Ginger *sb.* 1, 2.

1902 L. H. Bailey *Cycl. Amer. Hort.* IV. 2010/1 Zingibers are occasionally cultivated as stove decorative plants. **1970** *Guardian* 2 June 12/5 Bottles..of everything from Advocaat to Zingiber wine. **1971** *Country Life* 20 May 1252/2 But the particular forte of most [herbs] is as permanent foliage foils for other, brighter things as well as in their own right, from angelica to zingiber.

zingo (zi·ŋgo), *int.* Chiefly *U.S.* [Echoic. Cf. *zing *int.*] = *zing *int.*

1914 *Sat. Even. Post* 17 Jan. 7/1 Just when he was bursting with happiness because he was going to be a real big leaguer and one of us—zingo! he was back where he started. **1941** B. Schulberg *What makes Sammy Run?* ii. 32 It didn't take nearly this long to think. It went zingo, just a look. **1968** *Sunday Times* 25 Aug. 29/5 The stock is 24 asked and I reach for it and I get 200 shares and it moves up 28, zingo. **1970** *New Yorker* 17 Oct. 40/3 Zingo, another pair of jokers..bust in.

zingy (zi·ŋi), *a.* [f. *zing *sb.* + -y[1].] Energetic, exciting, lively. Also *ellipt.*

1948 [see *mambo 1]. **1962** *Guardian* 7 Feb 9/1 A zingy collection..that every with-it girl is going to adore. **1966** *Daily Tel.* 17 Aug. 11/5 With her own fashion taste, a delicate blend of the elegant and the zingy, a model like Fiona Campbell-Walter looks set for a great comeback career. **1968** *Globe & Mail* (Toronto) 3 Feb. 11/1 With some zingy comedy, they're an act that the regular club-haunters around town wait for. **1975** *Observer* 9 Nov. 22/6 A zingy Moselle, from a world famous estate. **1976** *Publishers Weekly* 16 Aug. 116/1 Some zingy, down-to-earth comments... She doesn't mince words.

Zinjanthropus (zindʒæ·nþrǒpǒs). *Palæont.* [mod.L. (L. S. B. Leakey 1959, in *Nature* 15 Aug. 491/2), f. *Zinj*, ancient name for East Africa + Gr. ἄνθρωπος man.] = *Nutcracker Man* s.v. *nut-cracker 5.

1959 *Nature* 15 Aug. 493/2 *Zinjanthropus* comes from Olduvai Gorge. **1961**, **1962** [see *Nutcracker Man* s.v. *nut-cracker 5]. **1973** B. J. Williams *Evolution & Human Origins* ix. 143/1 The species *Australopithecus robustus* includes..'*Zinjanthropus*' from East Africa. **1977** A. Hallam *Planet Earth* 286 From the early beds.. are recognized two kinds of hominids. One is *A. boisei* (sometimes called Zinjanthropus).

zinnober (zi·nobəɹ). Also **zinnobar.** [a. G. *zinnober* Cinnabar, vermilion.] *zinnober green*: = *chrome green* (*b*) s.v. Chrome 3.

1895 *Montgomery Ward Catal.* Spring & Summer 252/3 Zinnobar Green, Light. Zinnobar Green, medium. Zinnobar Green, deep. **1897** *Sears, Roebuck Catal.* 360/3 Colors for Artists... Zinnober Green, light. **1942** Gettens & Stout *Painting Materials* 178 Zinnober Green is a term ordinarily synonymous with chrome green..which is a processed mixture of chrome yellow and Prussian blue. More specifically, it is given to mixtures that are olive in hue. **1973** F. Taubes *Painter's Dict. Materials & Methods* 253 Zinnober green is a mixture of Prussian blue and cadmium yellow.

Zinoviev (zinǫ·vief). Also **Zinovieff.** [The assumed name of Y. A. Radomyslsky (1883–1936).] *Zinoviev letter*: a letter published in the press in 1924 as having been sent by Zinoviev, a Russian statesman, to British Communists and urging them to commit subversive acts; it was later discovered to be a forgery.

1924 *Times* 28 Oct. 8/1 (*heading*) The Zinovieff letter. *Ibid.*, If the Zinovieff letter is a forgery, it shows the amount of scoundrelliness with which we are surrounded. **1925** (*title*) The 'Zinoviev' letter: report of investigation by British delegation to Russia. **1957** *Encycl. Brit.* XIII. 554/2 In the general election of 1924 the Labour party met with a serious reverse, largely because of the confusion attending the publication of the 'Zinoviev' letter. **1958** C. Cockburn *Crossing Line* iv. 64 The timely forgery by the Intelligence Service of the 'Zinoviev letter'. **1972** 'M. Sinclair' *Norslag* xi. 101 The stories in the 'twenties about the Zinovieff letter. **1979** *Guardian* 28 Apr. 32/8 Mr Benn told a Bristol audience that the Tories..were dragging out the old Zinoviev Letter technique.

Hence **Zino·vievite**, in Russia, a supporter of Zinoviev and his anti-Stalin faction in the 1920s and 1930s; also *attrib.* or as *adj.*

1937 *Foreign Affairs* XVI. 50 The Trotskyites and Zinovievites. *Ibid.* 64 Designated by the government of the U.S.S.R. as members of a 'Trotskyite–Zinovievite Center'. **1970** S. Talbott tr. *Khrushchev Remembers* (1971) i. 28 The Fifteenth Party Congress, at which Stalin and his supporters squared off against the Zinovievites, or 'Leningrad opposition', as they were then called. **1974** T. P. Whitney tr. *Solzhenitsyn's Gulag Archipelago* I. i. viii. 329 Centers keep creeping in all the time... Trotskyite–Zinovievite Centers, Rightist–Bukharinite Centers, but all of them are crushed.

Zionism. Add: (Later examples.) Now concerned chiefly with the development of the State of Israel (see *Israel 3).

1948 *Sunday Pictorial* 18 July 7/6 The Government took office solemnly pledged to support Zionism. **1949** [see *revisionism 2]. **1955** *Ann. Reg. 1954* 241 Social democracy..and Zionism were..repeatedly condemned. **1955** *Times* 9 May 9/3 It happened that Jewish workers in considerable numbers were the first to come to Palestine in answer to the appeal of Zionism. **1975** *Globe & Mail* (Toronto) 14 Nov. 7/6 To [Jews], Zionism is and remains a precious term of honor, tied to the heart of their religious and national dreams.

Zionist. (In Dict. s.v. Zionism.) Add: **1.** (Later examples.)

1906 *Times* 29 Oct. 10/5 The Zionist Congress, which is the nearest approach to a Jewish Parliament, permitting women deputies equally with men. **1923** *Jewish Chron.* 19 Jan. 5/1 It will be seen from this how far right the Zionist leaders, Dr. Weizmann and Mr. Sokolow in particular, were in the estimate they put upon that Statement. **1940** E. Gill *Autobiogr.* vii. 252 The agricultural, arboricultural and horticultural work of the young Zionist colonies..superb in itself and of great educational benefit to the Arabs. **1955** *Times* 9 May 9/3 The private sector—politically represented in the main by the General Zionists. **1966** C. Potok *Chosen* (1967) xiii. 213 He had become involved in Zionist activities and was always attending meetings where he spoke about the importance of Palestine as a Jewish homeland. **1977** *Time* 30 May 10/2 Begin..joined the youth organization of the Zionist-Revisionists, a group of right wing militants who condemned the regular Zionist leadership as misguided and soft.

2. A member of any of a group of independent churches in southern Africa similar to pentecostal churches but containing distinctive African elements of worship and belief. [Named after the first such church, the Christian Catholic Apostolic Church in *Zion*, brought from Chicago to S. Africa in 1904.]

1948 B. G. M. Sundkler *Bantu Prophets in S. Africa* ii. 55 Theologically the Zionists are now a syncretistic Bantu movement with healing, speaking with tongues, purification rites, and taboos as the main expressions of their faith. **1956** H. Bloom *Episode* xvii. 318 Among the crowd were a number of Sunday pilgrims, location Zionists of various sects. **1970** *Standard Encycl. Southern Afr.* II. 55/1 Most 'Zionists' have a characteristic form of dress, worn to all services by all members: long dresses and capes, mostly white, decorated with coloured figures (stars, crosses, rings, angels, etc.), veils for women and special forms of headdress for men. *Ibid.*, The 'Zionist' phase has led to extensive proliferation of small groups. **1977** *Time* 27 June 18/3 Some aspects of the old Soweto still exist: the neatly kept gardens of middle-class black homes;..the Zionists, an Africanized Christian sect, famous for their daylong religious dances that begin at prayer services in backyard tents on Saturday nights.

Zionward(s, *adv.* (Earlier example.)

1705 R. Smyth *Let.* 17 Feb. in *Lett. J. Pinney* (1939) 117, I am sure there are too few y[t] sett their faces Zionward, here in this Town.

zip, *sb.*[1] Add: **3.** Nothing, nought, zero. Cf. *zilch *sb.* (and *a.*). *colloq.* (orig. and chiefly *U.S.*).

1900 *Dialect Notes* II. 70 *Zip, n.*, a zero in marks. **1904** *N.Y. World Mag.* 1 May 6/5 'Zip' is the same as 'zero'. **1927** *Amer. Speech* III. 455 *Swabo, zip,* zero. **1972** D. E. Westlake *Cops & Robbers* (1973) viii. 111 Before this, neither one of us had known zip about stocks and bonds. **1976** *Times* 27 Apr. 10/8 The successful team are said to have won one-nothing, one-zero or, more fashionably now, one-zip. **1977** J. Cheever *Falconer* 65 Armed robbery. Zip to ten. Second offense. **1980** J. Krantz *Princess Daisy* xxv. 443 No launch, no commercials, no nothing. Zip! Finished! Over!

4. Also **zipp.** A form of fastener for clothes, luggage, etc., consisting of two flexible strips with interlocking projections closed or opened by a sliding clip pulled along them. In full, *zip-fastener, -fastening* (see sense 5 below). Cf. *zipper.

1928 E. M. Forster *Arthur Snatchfold* in *Life to Come* (1972) 102 He felt the shirt..and he gave the zip at the throat a downward pull. **1940** *Punch* 5 June 612/2 Miss Fisher used to wear some lovely plum-coloured trousers with a zip to match. **1957** J. Braine *Room at Top* ix. 90 There was too much messing about with buttons and zips and straps. **1969** *Homes & Gardens* Nov. 190/1, I lost marks in a dressmaking competition because the zipp was machine-stitched in. **1972** *Lancet* 10 June 1271/1 The plain apron front has an off-centre..fastening by a heavy-duty metal 'Zipp', 30 in. long. **1985** *Vogue* July 77 Over this go..flared shorts..some with zips placed to show not pockets but a sliver of flesh.

5. *attrib.* and *Comb.*, as (sense *4), *zip bag, -bedding, -case, -fastener, -fastening, -front, jacket, pocket, shirt, side, suit, top*; *zip-fastened, -topped* adjs.; also with advbs. forming adjs., as *zip-down, -in, -off, -on, -out, -over, -up*; **zip gun** *U.S. colloq.*, a cheap home-made or makeshift gun; **zip lock** *U.S.*, used *attrib.* to denote plastic bags with an airtight fastening of two interlocking strips; also (a proprietary name) **Ziploc**; **zip-top** *a.* = *ring-pull* adj. s.v. *ring *sb.*[1] 18 a.

1937 L. MacNeice in Auden & MacNeice *Lett. from Iceland* 133 The permutations..of zip bags, Of compacts ..and coiffures. **1948** W. Fortescue *Beauty for Ashes* xxx. 235 Only at Croydon did I discover that my small zip bags had been stowed away in a locker directly under my legs. **1933** T. E. Lawrence *Home Lett.* (1954) 384 The new zipp-bedding is a great success. **1960** N. Kneale *Quatermass & Pit* i. 22 The Minister's Private Secretary enters quickly, clutching a zip-case. **1971** C. Bonington *Annapurna South Face* 241 [Breeches with] zip-down side to allow putting on over boots and crampons. **1950** J. Cannan *Murder Included* vii. 158 A brown zip-fastened handbag. **1927** *Daily Express* 22 Nov. 3/5 Many of the new sports suits have zip-fasteners. **1973** A. Price *October Men* vii. 95 He stumbled down the nearest alleyway.. fumbling as he went for the zip-fastener on his fly. **1927** *Daily Express* 6 Sept. 3/4 The airwoman's costume of tango suède, complete from the zip fastening to the little hat..is attracting many admirers. **1942** 'M. Innes' *Daffodil Affair* i. 24 The pomps of death: dissolution had once been a comfortably solid affair. Now it was papier-mâché coffins and zipp-fastening shrouds. **1965** *N.Y. Herald-Tribune* 11 Apr. 8 Zip-front seersucker 'skimma'. **1974** *Harrods Xmas Catal.* 9/1 Hostess gown with zip-front. **1950** *N.Y. Post* 29 Sept. 2 Three Bronx schoolboys were held by police today after admitting shooting off a home-made 'zip' gun... It was fashioned of a 6-inch stainless steel tube taped to a wooden block with an ordinary closet bolt for a 'trigger'. By means of a rubber band, a long ·22 caliber bullet could be shot from it. **1971** B. Malamud *Tenants* 103, I..had thoughts to kill him off with my zip gun but was afraid to. **1984** *Listener* 7 June 7/2 With the decline of the chicano movement and the increase in sophisticated weapons—zip-guns were replaced with sawn-off shotguns and sometimes automatic weapons—violence rocketed in the Seventies. **1974** *Amer. Speech 1970* XLV. 179 *Chil-dodger*.., zip-in garment to be worn under jackets, coats, or over lounge clothes for extra warmth. **1958** *Spectator* 6 June 729/1 A blue zip jacket and slacks. **1970** *Official Gaz.* (U.S. Patent Office) 17 Feb. tm134 *Ziploc.* The Dow Chemical Company... Filed 9–9–68. **1977** C. McFadden *Serial* (1978) l. 107/1 Spenser rummaged among the Ziploc bags in his briefcase. **1982** *Town Crier* (McAllen, Texas) 31 Mar. 1–a/4 Wrapped in foil in a clear zip lock bag. **1957** *Housewife* Sept. 26 Zip-off covers for easy cleaning. **1974** *Harper's & Queen* Sept. 36/2 Zip-off mink £925, extra maxi piece £300. **1959** *Housewife* June 57 Silk cushions ..with zip-on covers. **1963** *New Yorker* 26 Oct. 6 Enter the Chesterfield in Black Tweed..with warm acrylic pile zip-out liner. **1962** 'A. Gilbert' *No Dust in Attic* v. 63 He'd left his luggage..one of the zip-over bags. **1979** *Daily Tel.* 20 Nov. 3/1 When Mrs Robabeh Moheby..was strip-searched, a bundle of banknotes was found in a zip pocket in her knickers. **1976** *Morecambe Guardian* 7 Dec. 32/4 (Advt.), Boys short-sleeved, zip shirts. **1940** *Punch* 4 Dec. p. xvii (Advt.), A Dunlopillo sleeping bag. It has..soft upper lining, zip side,..and makes an ideal holdall. **1978** F. Mullally *Deadly Payoff* ii. 25 He handed Fernandez a zip-suit of grubby white fatigues. **1970** *Times* 16 Feb. p. iii, Ring-pull and zip-top cans are already available. **1974** *Harrods Xmas Catal.* 18/1 Bag..with side pocket, zip top. **1976** *Globe & Mail* (Toronto) 30 Dec. 27/6 Here plastic fish surface and bob for zip-top rings from beer and pop cans. **1979** *This England* Winter 19/3 She folded her cap inside her apron and pushed both into her zip-topped bag. **1959** M. Shadbolt *New Zealanders* 26 He wore an open-neck check shirt and a zip-up jacket. **1973** 'D. Rutherford' *Kick Start* i. 12 The zip-up calf-length boots. **1985** *Times* 24 Jan. 3/2 He was described as aged between 18 and 20, of West Indian appearance..wearing a beige zip-up jacket.

zip (zip), *sb.*[2] *U.S.* Also **Z.I.P., ZIP, Zip.** [f. the initials of *Z*oning *I*mprovement *P*lan.] Used esp. *attrib.* in *zip code*: a series of digits representing a particular area in a city, etc., used in addressing mail (see quots.).

1963 *N.Y. Times* 5 May 86/3 Z.I.P. codes, for the present at least, are for big business, and more particularly big users of the mails such as publishers, banks, insurance companies and mail-order houses. **1964** *N.Y. Times Book Rev.* 5 Apr. 3/2 Among his petty peeves are . Zip codes and automatic telephone dialling. **1969** *Computers & Humanities* IV. 69 The zip code has been another, but less successful, step towards using computer recognition to improve our lives. *Ibid.*, Once a person has miswritten the zip, the computer just misdirects the mail. **1973** *Black Panther* 21 July 16/2 (Please print) Name Address..City..State/Zip. **1975** *New Yorker* 5 May 2 (Advt.), In ordering a change of address, subscribers should give four weeks' notice, providing both old and new addresses, with Zip Codes. **1977** *Chicago Tribune* 2 Oct. vi. 26/4 A 13-cent U.S. commemorative honoring 50 years of talking pictures will go on sale Thursday in Hollywood, Cal., where the postmaster Zip is 90028. **1980** *Christian Sci. Monitor* (Midwestern ed.) 4 Dec. 2/2 The Postal Board of Governors.. withheld final approval of a controversial plan to expand ZIP codes to nine digits.

zip, *v.* (In Dict. s.v. Zip *sb.*) Add: **1.** Also, to move briskly or with speed.

1852 *Knickerbocker* XL. 182 How we did '*z-i-p!*' Seven miles, at one time, in less than seven minutes. **1897** Kipling *Day's Work* (1898) 234, I heard my flanges zippin' along the ties. **1907** A. Bennett *Grim Smile of Five Towns* 222 'Let her zip,' said Mr. Colclough. **1922** S. Lewis *Babbitt* xviii. 221 Everything zips at the Chatham Road Church. **1929** *Evening News* 3 Jan. 4/2 He..hardly saw it [*sc.* the ball] after it pitched, as it zipped off the ground and whipped round his bat to take the off stump. **1958** *Daily Mail* 24 Feb. 12/2, I found the man..zipping round the garden..on a toy trike. **1967** *Electronics* 6 Mar. 46/2 Rail travelers will be able to make telephone calls while zipping along at speeds of up to 160 miles an hour from New York City to Washington, D.C. **1976** *Guardian Weekly* 26 Sept. 9/3 The millions of Orange County commuters, who zip past on the Santa Ana Freeway each morning. **1984** *Times* 30 Nov. 11/2 Even though she is likely to spend as much time immersed to the elbows in washing up as zipping down the slopes, there is no stigma of 'service' attached to the job.

2. *trans.* To close with a zip-fastener. Freq. const. *up* and with a person being or getting dressed as obj. Also *intr.* for *pass.* and *refl.* Also *fig.*

1932 A. Huxley *Brave New World* iii. 50 He zipped up his trousers. **1936** *Sears Catal.* 163/4 Easy to 'Zip' baby in and out! **1939** *Punch* 11 Oct. 412/2 The most marvellous outfits..that you step into and zip up. **1942** *Time* 23 Feb. 78 (Advt.), Zips flawlessly. **1942** in *Amer. Speech* (1943) XVIII. 305/2 Zip your lip. **1944** *Penguin New Writing* xx. 60 Zipping on her enchanted house-coat over her night-dress. **1948** *Chicago Tribune* 28 Mar. (Comics) 4 Stand still, now, while I zip you up! **1956** G. N. Patterson *God's Fool* i. 14 Shivering in the icy atmosphere, [I] zipped myself into my double-layer sleeping bag. **1968** B. Hines *Kestrel for Knave* 23 His mother pulled her skirt on and tried to zip it on the hip. **1973** J. Drummond *Bang! Bang! You're Dead!* viii. 13 Authority, including the B.B.C., did not speculate about guilt. Mouths were carefully zipped. **1980** T. Barling *Goodbye Piccadilly* ii. 36 The cistern flushed and Cave emerged, zipping up.

3. *trans.* To beat (an opposing team) comprehensively by not allowing it to score. Cf. *ZIP *sb.*[1] 3.

1976 *Daily News* (N.Y.) 16 Jan. 82 The Adams Division leaders zipped Los Angeles, 4–0. **1978** *Time* 16 Jan. 66 The Broncos went out and beat the hell out of them, then the next week, went and zipped Cleveland.

Hence **zipped** *ppl. a.*, fastened or provided with a zip. Also *zipped-in, -up* adjs. Also *fig.*

1944 [see *slide fastener* s.v. *SLIDE- a]. **1946** 'S. Russell' *To Bed with Grand Music* i. 13 She picked up her mother's zipped travelling bag. **1959** *Listener* 2 Apr. 593/2 The chemical configuration of starch..is a long zipped-up chain of glucose molecules. **1959** *Times* 5 Oct. 6/2 A zipped-in detachable lining. **1966** T. Pynchon *Crying of Lot 49* vi. 158 Blobb inquired around about the Trystero organization, running into zipped mouths nearly every way he turned. **1972** D. Haston *In High Places* xi. 117 Down suit and fully zipped windproofs. **1982** M. Kenyon *God Squad Bod* ii. 22 Zipped-up moneybags, satchels and briefcases.

Zipf (zipf). The name of George Kingsley *Zipf* (1902–50), American linguist, used in the possessive in *Zipf's law*, a principle in *Psycholinguistics* (see quots.).

1960 É. Delavenay *Introd. Machine Transl.* v. 68 To lend support to arguments based on Zipf's law, Yngve produced evidence likely to convince unbelievers. **1967** M. Schlauch *Language & Study of Languages Today* vii. 143 Some three decades ago, G. K. Zipf undertook to investigate what relation, if any, exists between the length of words and their frequency of occurrence in sample languages chosen for investigation. He came to the conclusion that the length of a word tends to decrease as its relative frequency of use increases... The formula..has come to be known as 'Zipf's Law', often quoted if also sometimes questioned. **1971** *Jrnl. General Psychol.* Oct. 297 Zipf's law predicts an inverse ratio in the rank order distribution of varieties such that a minimal number of varieties covers a maximal number of responses and a maximal number of varieties covers a minimal number of responses. **1980** *Verbatim* Spring 9/2 A psycholinguist will say that this phenomenon is working proof of Zipf's Law, which states loosely that one can generally determine the relative age of a particular word or phrase by how short it has become.

Ziph (zif). [Origin unknown.] An invented language used at Winchester College.

1853 De Quincey *Autobiogr. Sketches* I. vii. 209 Lord Westport and I communicated our thoughts occasionally by means of a language..which bore the name of *Ziph*. The language and the name were both derived..from Winchester. **1922** O. Jespersen *Lang.* viii. 150 'Ziph' or 'Hypernese' (at Winchester) substitutes *wa* for the first of two initial consonants and inserts *p* or *g*, making 'breeches' into *wareechepes*. **1942** E. Partridge *Usage & Abusage* 160/2 *Gibberish* is applied mostly to Ziph (*shagall wege gogo* = shall we go).

zi·pless, *a.* *coarse slang.* [f. *ZIP *sb.*[1] 4 + -LESS.] Denoting a brief and passionate sexual encounter.

1973 E. Jong *Fear of Flying* i. 11 My response.. was..to evolve my fantasy of the Zipless Fuck... Zipless because when you came together zippers fell away like petals. **1978** G. Vidal *Kalki* iii. 79 Girls who feared flying tended to race blindly through zipless fucks. **1984** *Times* 2 Nov. 11/1 This small hand I'm shaking..launched a thousand zipless erotic encounters for her heroine.

zipper (zi·pəɹ), *sb.* orig. *U.S.* [f. Zip *sb.* + -ER[1].]

1. = *ZIP *sb.* 4. Also *transf.* and *fig.*

Zipper was registered in the U.S. as a trade mark in April 1925 (with use of the term claimed since June 1923), but in the sense 'boots made of rubber and fabric'. It is no longer a proprietary term in any of its uses. Quot. 1925, which appeared in the first Supplement to the *O.E.D.* (1933), and in the *Dictionary of Americanisms*, does not appear in surviving copies of *Scribner's Mag.*

1925 *Scribner's Mag.* Oct. 22/2 (Advt.), No fastening is so quick, secure, or popular as the 'zipper'. **1928** *Daily Express* 11 Oct. 5/5 Bootees..fastening with 'zippers', press studs, or inset clips. **1933** A. G. Macdonell *England, their England* viii. 130 Brown leather jerkins fastened up the front with that singular arrangement which is called a zipper. **1957** *New Yorker* 29 June 24/2 He hated fiddling with things like zippers caught on tiny strips of cloth. **1959** *Listener* 2 Apr. 593/2 We possess a biological zipper—an enzyme—which enables us to undo the chain [of the glucose molecules of starch]. **1966** F. Shaw et al. *Lern Yerself Scouse* 21 *Purra zipper on it*, please be silent. **1979** R. Jaffe *Class Reunion* I. xi. 105 She reached for the zipper of her skirt.

2. *attrib.* and *Comb.*, as *zipper bag, fastener, fastening*, etc.

1925 *Harper's Bazaar* June 108/3 (Advt.), A 'zipper' closing bag sometimes used to carry champagne. **1925** *Scribner's Mag.* June 31/1 (Advt.), The most convenient and attractive form of the pocket purse is this one of lizard calf, leather lined, with a zipper fastening. **1928** *Daily Express* 15 Aug. 4/3 One 12-inch zipper fastener. *Ibid.* 11 Oct. 5/5 Zipper-fastened. **1937** D. Aldis *Time at her Heels* ix. 196 He was wearing his dark blue zipper jacket. **1939** A. Keith *Land below Wind* xx. 311 There were two zipper bags with dutiable goods. **1941** [see *FLY *sb.*[2] 4 a]. **1959** C. Williams *Man in Motion* vii. 81 The briefcase..was a slender one, of the type with no handles, zipper-closed. **1960** M. Spark *Ballad Peckham Rye* ii. 22 He sat down among his belongings, which were partly in and partly out of his zipper bag. **1969** *Sears Catal.* Spring/Summer 6 Center zipper pocket divides bag into two handy sections. **1978** *Lancashire Life* Mar. 70 (Advt.), Ladies zipper coats £11.50. **1982** R. Rendell *Master of Moor* xvi. 175 He put on the zipper jacket and went out.

zi·pper, *v.* orig. *U.S.* [f. the sb.] *trans.* To fasten with a zipper. Also *transf.* and *fig.* Freq. const. *up*.

1930 J. Lait *Put on Spot* 215 Zipper. To shut something up, principally the mouth. **1935** N. Ersine *Underworld & Prison Slang* 80 *Zipper, v.*, to cease talking. (Almost invariably the term is a command.) '*Zipper* that mug!' **1961** *John o' London's* 5 Oct. 398/2 Jean Renoir himself capering about zippered up..in a bear-suit. **1966** D. F. Galouye *Lost Perception* vi. 60 Driving wind.. tunnelled through the TUT's open cab and Forsythe zippered up his jacket. **1971** *Nature* 3 Sept. 48/2 It seems to act by zippering together chromosomes which have their homologous telomeres attached next to each other at the nuclear membrane. **1974** H. L. Foster *Ribbin', Jivin', & playin' Dozens* vi. 284 After he tucked in his shirt, he closed his pants, zippered them up, put his belt back, and then left. **1984** *Sunday Tel.* (Colour Suppl.) 19 Feb. 12/3 Much was made of the 'keep it zippered' dressing-down he gave to his fellow-astronauts.

zi·ppered, *ppl. a.* orig. *U.S.* [f. *ZIPPER *sb.* + -ED[2].] Fastened with a zipper; having a zipper.

1939 *Times* 31 Mar. 19/7 A charming wool frock with sun-ray decoration round the neck and neatly zippered might be chosen. **1941** *Time* 25 Aug. 2/3 His zippered ankle-high shoes. **1959** *Harrods News* Summer 15 Pigskin clothes brush with zippered top. **1971** B. Malamud *Tenants* 35 A bulky zippered briefcase was squeezed under his left arm. **1982** S. Radley *Talent for Destruction* vi. 36 A thin man in a zippered fawn cardigan.

Zippo (zi·po). Also **zippo.** The proprietary name of a make of cigarette lighter.

1934 *Official Gaz.* (U.S. Patent Office) 10 July 270 Zippo Manufacturing Company, Bradford, Pa... *Zippo* for pocket lighter of the pyrophoric type. **1938** *Trade Marks Jrnl.* 16 Mar. 320/1 *Zippo*..Pyrophoric lighters. Miriam Barcroft Blaisdell..trading as Zippo Manufacturing Company,..Bradford, State of Pennsylvania, United States of America; manufacturers. **1964** G. McDonald *Running Scared* iii. 35 The Zippo lighter he had given Casey. **1966** G. Lyall *Shooting Script* xxii. 174 Luiz flicked a Zippo under my nose. **1977** McKnight & Tobler *Bob Marley* ix. 108 A novel sleeve made to look like a zippo lighter. *Ibid.* 112 Gone was the zippo, replaced by a picture of Marley smoking a kingsize splif. **1982** R. Ludlum *Parsifal Mosaic* viii. 111 He extracted one [cigarette] and lit it with an old, tarnished Zippo purchased a quarter of a century ago.

zippy (zi·pi), *a.* *colloq.* (orig. *U.S.*). [f. Zip *sb.* 2 + -Y[1].] Bright, lively, energetic; fresh, invigorating; fast, speedy.

1904 G. Ade *True Bills* 108 Vivian, our bright-eyed little Daughter..is the zippiest High-Flyer that speeds the Boulevard. **1917** *National Police Gazette* 25 Aug. 2/4 It bubbles o'er with song and jest, Its fun is keen and 'zippy'. **1926** *Bulletin* (Glasgow) 26 Oct. 18/2 A zippy show is 'Cheerio' at the Glasgow Empire this week. **1939** *Better English* Jan. 29 (*heading*) Your words—are they zippy? **1953** *Amer. Mercury* Jan. 67/2 The March evening was zippy outside but cupped in it the breath of spring. **1959** I. Jefferies *Thirteen Days* xii. 202 My idea..was to get a zippy load into Richon and then move on to T.A. **1966** R. H. Rimmer *Harrad Experiment* (1967) 161 All we have to do now is to put together a zippy script. **1971** *Daily Tel.* 23 June 11/6 The engine warms up rapidly and provides zippy acceleration. **1980** M. Broadbent *Great Vintage Wine Bk.* 134 Ch. Potensac. Zippy little wine. **1984** *Guardian* 5 Nov. 12/1 One advantage to being on Castleton social services committee is that they do have zippy meetings.

Hence **zi·ppily** *adv.*; **zi·ppiness.**

1924 Wodehouse *Bill the Conqueror* viii. 152 This series on Bookmakers' Swindling Methods..had always reached a fair level of zippiness; but never..had it so outzipped itself as in the present instalment. **1983** *Times* 10 June 17/6 The piece is zippily staged..and sung with immense liveliness.

ziram (zəi·ræm). [f. *zi*nc dimethyl dithiocar*bam*ate, the systematic name: see Carbamate.] A white powder used as a fungicide, esp. on vegetables and some fruit crops; $Zn(\cdot S{\cdot}CS{\cdot}N(CH_3)_2)_2$.

1950 [see *ZINEB]. **1960** [see *FERBAM]. **1969** *New Scientist* 8 May 299/2 The two main breakdown products of the fungicide, ziram (zinc dimethyldithiocarbamate) were carbon disulphide and dimethylamine. **1981** *Jrnl. Agric. & Food Chem.* XXIX. 729 The limit of detection in water solutions for zineb, ziram, and thiram was 0·05, 0·01, and 0·01 ppm, respectively.

Ziranian, var. *Siryenian *sb.* and *a.*

zircaloy (zə̄·ɹkăloi). Also **zircalloy.** [f. Zirc(onium + Alloy *sb.*] Any of several alloys of zirconium, tin, and other metals that are used chiefly as cladding for nuclear reactor fuel.

1956 Thomas & Forscher in *Jrnl. Metals* VIII. 640/1 Zircaloy-2, a low alloy of zirconium, was developed by the Westinghouse Atomic Power Div. during 1952. **1963** H. R. Clauser *Encycl. Engin. Materials & Processes* 769/1 Zircaloy resists corrosion very well in high-temperature water and steam. **1973** *Nature* 2 Feb. 318/1 The rods are zirconium alloy (zircalloy) tubes filled with pellets of uranium dioxide (UO_2) ceramic. **1977** J. H. Schemel *ASTM Manual on Zirconium & Hafnium* (ASTM Special Technical Publ. No. 639) i. 6 Zircaloy is used to designate a series of zirconium, tin, iron, chromium, nickel alloys developed by the U. S. Navy Nuclear Propulsion Program for nuclear service in water-cooled reactors. Zircaloy-1 and Zircaloy-3 are obsolete. Zircaloy-2 and Zircaloy-4 are the most commonly used alloys in nuclear service.

zircon. Add: **b. zircon blue,** a light blue colour.

1949 *Brit. Colour Council Dict. Colours* III. 28/2 *Zircon blue*... Matched to specimens of the precious stone at the B.M. **1972** 'E. Peters' *Death to Landlords!* i. 30 Withdrawing her zircon-blue eyes from the heavens. **1976** *Evening Post* (Nottingham) 13 Dec. 12/3 (Advt.), Rover 2000 1969. H. Zircon blue with black trim.

zirconian, *a.* Add: *spec.* in *Min.*, applied to a mineral in which zirconium replaces a (small) proportion of some constituent element (cf. *-IAN 2).

1930 W. T. Schaller in *Amer. Mineralogist* XV. 572. **1963** *Doklady Acad. Sci. USSR: Earth Sci. Sect.* CXLI. 1301/1 Apatite, nepheline, and perovskite were observed, frequently forming intergrowths with the zirconian schorlomite. **1972** *Nature* 31 Mar. 197/2 The appearance of zirconian SiO_2-free minerals in the granitic fraction is rather strange.

zirconolite (zə̄ɹkǫ·nŏləit). *Min.* [ad. Russ. *tsirkonolit* (L. S. Borodin et al. 1956, in *Dokladȳ Akad. Nauk SSSR* CX. 845): see Zircon and -lite.] A mixed oxide of (essentially) calcium, zirconium, and titanium, now regarded as identical with zirkelite.

1957 *Chem. Abstr.* LI. 6440 (*heading*) The new mineral zirconolite, a complex oxide of the type AB_3O_7. **1975** *Amer. Mineralogist* LX. 341/1 Zirconolite, $CaZrTi_2O_7$, was described in 1956..as a new mineral and the zirkelite of Blake and Smith was considered to be zirconolite... New analyses and X-ray studies of type material show that all these are a single mineral species of composition $(Ca,Th,RE)Zr(Ti,Nb,Fe)_2O_7$. The name zirkelite has priority. **1980** *Nature* 17 Jan. 282/1 Synthetic zirconolite, $CaZrTi_2O_7$, has attracted interest recently, as it has been proposed as a constituent phase of an artificial rock (SYNROC) which may immobilise, in solid solution, the elements occurring in high-level nuclear reactor wastes. **1981** [see *ZIRKELITE].

zirkelite (zə̄·ɹkĕləit). *Min.* [f. the name of Ferdinand *Zirkel* (1838–1912), German mineralogist + -ITE[1].] A black monoclinic (pseudocubic) oxide of zirconium, calcium, thorium, titanium, rare earths, and other elements, $(Ca,Th,Ce)Zr(Ti,Nb)_2O_7$.

1895 Hussak & Prior in *Mineral. Mag.* XI. 86 Zirkelite. A new calcium zirconate and titanate. **1962** *Mineral. Abstr.* XV. 538/1 Zirkelite is widely distributed in the Palaeozoic ultrabasic and alkaline complexes of the Kola Peninsula where it occurs as an accessory mineral in calcite-amphibole rocks; [etc.]. **1972** *Nature* 31 Mar. 215/1 We find that terrestrial zirkelite bears the closest comparison with the tranquillityite group, and yet contains sufficient CaO..to provide a possible link with any calcic lunar zirconian phases yet to be established. **1975** [see *ZIRCONOLITE]. **1977** *Amer. Mineralogist* LXII. 408 Zirconolite and niobozirconolite..are synonymous with zirkelite. **1981** K. Frye *Encycl. Mineral.* 220/1 There is considerable controversy over the exact formulas of zirkelite and zirconolite. Some evidence suggests that there is no difference.

zit (zit). *slang* (chiefly *N. Amer.*). [Origin unknown.] A pimple. Also in extended and *fig.* use. Occas. in *Comb.*

1966 G. C. Sauer *Man. Skin Dis.* (ed. 2) 284 *Zits*, term in teen-agers' vernacular for 'pimples' of acne. **1966** *Current Slang* (Univ. S. Dakota) Summer 5 *Zit*, something bad or unpleasant; crude... What's that *zit* on your coat? **1972** B. Rodgers *Queens' Vernacular* 45 *Vit* (late '60s, fr. sl. *zit* = a pimple: boy with Pepsi consciousness, *i.e.*

nothing going on between the ears). **1975** *Atlantic Monthly* Mar. 51 One splendid effort in 1971 featured . districts with remarkable pimples in their boundary lines, zits that popped up to include the home of one liberal incumbent in the district of another liberal incumbent. **1975** *Maclean's Mag.* June 59/1 When did you last have a zit on your face? **1977** *Amer. Speech 1975* L. 69 *Zit n*, reddish mark caused by kissing. 'She has a big zit on her neck.' **1977** J. Wambaugh *Black Marble* (1978) vi. 77 How old is the little zit-faced, coke-snorting, hash-smoking son of a bitch? **1980** *Courier-Mail* (Brisbane) 30 Apr. 46/3 (*caption*) You know playing with teenagers will give you zits. **1984** S. Townsend *Growing Pains A Mole* 105 Forgot to send you an invite, zit face, but come anyway, dress as a warlock or you won't get in.

zita (zi·ta). Pl. **zite, ziti.** [It.] A tubular variety of pasta resembling large macaroni.

1845 E. Acton *Mod. Cookery* (ed. 4) p. xxx, *Zita*, Naples maccaroni. **1943** A. L. Simon *Conc. Encycl. Gastron.* iv. 141/1 *Zita*, pl. *zite*, one of the fancy Italian pastes... It is made of the gluten of hard wheat and eggs, like Macaroni, in hollow, straight tubes of larger diameter than Macaroni. **1964** *Guardian* 22 May 8/6 *Ziti*, cut macaroni tubes slightly curved. **1978** R. F. Capon *Food for Thought* vii. 106 Why not sauces for ziti, for occhi di lupo, [etc.]? **1979** *Tucson Mag.* Sept. 68/2 Bargain specialties—like gnocchi, zita, linguine, and so-so meat dishes. **1983** *Fortune* 21 Feb. 78/1 For the one-time shopper, goods from auto-parts to ziti.

zither. Add: **b.** *zither-playing, -tinkling* adjs.

1982 C. McIntosh *Swan King* viii. 83 A fun-loving, zither-playing, somewhat bohemian character. **1925** E. Sitwell et al. *Poor Young People* 2 Among the zither-tinkling round green leaves.

zi·ther, *v.* [f. the sb.] *intr.* To play the zither. Also *fig.* (occas. also *trans.*). Hence **zi·thering** *ppl. a.*

Some of the examples could equally well be interpreted as being of echoic origin, with the sense 'to make a sibilant humming sound, buzz lightly'.

1906 W. J. Locke *Beloved Vagabond* (1907) ix. 120 We wandered and fiddled and zithered and tambourined through France. **1930** R. Campbell *Adamastor* 71 The sunlight, zithering their flanks with fire, Flashes between the shadows as they pass. **1958** J. Townsend *Young Devils* iv. 35 His squeaky voice zithered through morning or afternoon. **1973** *Art Internat.* Mar. 57/1 Balla's zithering *Rhythm of the Violinist* is considerably more effective. **1979** H. McLeave *Double Exposure* i. 1 The helicopter..trailing a zithering shadow. **1981** B. Carter *Black Fox Running* xxvii. 176 Insects zithered and chirred.

ziti: see *zita.

zitkamer, zit-kamer, varr. *sitkamer.

zizith, var. *tsitsith.

zizz, *sb.* Add: **1. a.** (Later examples.) Also extended to other whizzing or buzzing noises (see quots.).

1904 G. A. B. Dewar *Glamour of Earth* vi. 131 The zizz of the cricket, or the shrill of the bat. **1955** D. Barton *Glorious Life* xxv. 232 The sustained, high-pitched zizz of a party was audible. **1965** *Listener* 17 June 900/3 The zizz of a trishaw's wheels passing on the road. **1976** *Drive* May–June 53/2 Gear lever zizz is irritating.

b. Gaiety, liveliness, 'sparkle'. *colloq.*

1942 Berrey & Van den Bark *Amer. Thes. Slang* § 240/2 *Animation; spirit; vim;*..zing, zip,..zizz. **1970** *Gourmet* Jan. 18/2 No party got into full swing until Tallulah arrived to put her particular type of zizz into it. **1983** *Times* 22 Feb. 12/6 The Queensgate centre lacks, perhaps, finesse and a touch of zizz.

2. Also **ziz.** A short sleep, a nap. Cf. *Z 4 b. *slang.*

1941 *Tee Emm* Aug. 17 He could not have caught our Pilot Officer Prune at three o'clock one afternoon having a zizz full-length on a mess settee. **1960** 'N. Shute' *Trustee from Toolroom* v. 105 'Captain's having a ziz now,' said the navigator. 'Supper's at eleven o'clock, Greenwich. He's getting up for that.' **1970** P. Dickinson tr. *Aristophanes' Wasps* in *Plays* I. 169 Just what I aim to forget by having A quiet ziz. **1979** M. Tabor *Baker's Daughter* i. 31 Philip's having a zizz He can't stay awake. **1985** *Guardian* 24 Jan. 1/3 They would not film any lord who had drifted off in the warmth of the lights for a refreshing zizz.

zizz, *v.* [f. the sb.] **1.** *intr.* To make a whizzing or buzzing sound. Occas. *trans.* (causally). Also const. *up*, to liven up.

a **1934** in Webster s.v., Trolleys went zizzing along. **1961** E. Williams *George* ix. 112 The pince-nez zizzed back to her lapel. **1963** *Punch* 1 May 621/3 Then she [*sc.* a bee] saw the carpet and zizzed. **1965** *Harper's Bazaar* Feb. 21/2 An adventurous buyer deciding that model 127 is just the thing to zizz up his mid-season collection. **1970** T. Lewis *Jack's Return Home* 89 The banger'd started zizzing furiously. **1970** *Daily Tel.* 16 Dec. 11 Darts and circles about on the floor after its wheels are zizzed smartly. **1978** *Ibid.* 19 July 12/5 The gearchange.. is light but slightly notchy, and tended to 'zizz' on the overrun.

2. *slang.* To doze or sleep. Occas. *trans* with *away*.

1942 [see below]. **1961** D. Moore *Highway of Fear* xxxvi. 240 Reckon this sector's safe. Might as well zizz. **1972** K. Bonfiglioli *Don't point that Thing at Me* xii. 94, I zizzed away the worst of the afternoon, awaking some three hours later. **1978** *Sunday Mail Color Mag.* (Brisbane) 30 Apr. 20/6 When everyone inside the building had zizzed off he had sneaked inside.

Hence **zi·zzing** *vbl. sb.* and *ppl. a.*

1942 *Gen* 1 Sept. 13/1 Sleeping is 'zizzing' whether it's on the job or in the hammock. **1951** J. Strachey *Man on Pier* 37 The flies on the window-pane woke up and started to rage together with a venomous zizzing. *Ibid.* 88 Confusion continued, it seemed to Ned, to the old background of zizzing flies, bellowing cows, walks, and hot, cloudy weather. **1961** E. Williams *George* ix. 111 There was a terrified zizzing noise from an obedient coil-spring.

zi·zzy, *a.* *colloq.* [f. Zizz *sb.* + -y[1].] Showy, spectacular; lively, uninhibited.

1966 *Guardian* 5 Feb. 7/6 And who's going to pay for 'Danger Man' with that zizzy Patrick McGoohan, then? **1975** *New Yorker* 21 Apr. 24/3 If you accept the silly, zizzy obviousness, it can make you laugh helplessly. **1976** *Times* 4 Oct. 7 My wife said I should wear a dark suit but I did risk a particularly zizzy tie. **1983** *Guardian Weekly* 6 Feb. 1/2 Zizzy little TV charts.

Z line (zed, *U.S.* zī, ləin). *Histology.* [Partial tr. G. *schicht z* z layer (T. W. Engelmann 1873, in *Arch. f. die ges. Physiol.* VII. 37), f. initial letter of *zwischenscheibe* intervening disc.] A transverse dark line in a fibril of striated muscle formed by Krause's membrane (see *Krause b); the membrane itself.

1916 Jordan & Ferguson *Text-bk. Histol.* iv. 105 This stripe or accessory disk..bisects the portion of the J disk between the Z line and the succeeding Q disk. **1954** *Nature* 22 May 976/1 The series elastic component is provided either by the actin filaments themselves, or, more probably, by their mode of attachment to the Z-line. **1979** *Sci. Amer.* May 94/2 In muscle fibers the actin filaments are anchored to flat protein structures called *Z* lines, which are emplaced between every two contractile units.

Also **Z band.**

1950 A. W. Ham *Histology* xix. 283/1 When a substantial degree of contraction has occurred, an appearance, often referred to as a 'reversal of striations', becomes apparent. This is due to the substance of the myofibril on each side of the Z band, which was formerly light, becoming dark, and the dark material of the Q band becoming light. **1964** G. H. Haggis et al. *Introd. Molecular Biol.* iv. 101 The segment from one Z-band to the next, along a fibril, is termed a sarcomere. **1970** [see *Krause b].

zloty (zlǫ·ti, ‖ zwǫ·ti). Pl. **zloty, zlotys.** [a. Polish *złoty*, f. *złoto* gold, cogn. w. Russ. *zóloto*: see Gold.] **a.** A gold or silver coin of monarchic Poland. **b.** The monetary unit of the Polish republic; a note or coin of the republican currency.

1915 *Publ. Scottish Hist. Soc.* lix. 63 The fourth witness . hath borne witness in the following words:—'I..have seen how Jan Furman, a Scot, hath taken..40 Polish zloty, from that Kilian.' **1923** *Times* 3 Mar. 16/6 The Polish Minister of Finance has decided that State loans . shall..be effected in Polish zlotys (a zloty is equivalent to a Swiss franc), at the current market rate. **1923** *Times* 13 Aug. 14/5 The zloty, or gold franc, the nominal unit of Poland. **1944** V. G. Garvin tr. *R. Gary's Forest of Anger* xxiii. 90 They've imposed a fine of 100,000 zlotys on Pinski! **1960** S. Becker tr. *Schwarz-Bart's Last of Just* ii. 40 When you have a few zlotys in hand, you can come back here and reimburse me. **1970** *New Yorker* 6 June 33/1 He promised me a room, food, and a small salary in Polish marks. The zloty wasn't yet established as a currency. **1983** *Nature* 28 July 299/2 The Polish Government has raised the price of edible salt to between 11 zloty and 17 zloty per kilo.

Zoar, obs. var. *Zohar.

zob (zǫb). *U.S. slang. rare.* [Origin unknown.] A weak or contemptible person; a fool.

1911 W. F. Kirk *Right off Bat* 13 He came here in the early Spring with all the try-out mob Striving to bat like Wagner and to slide (spikes first) like Cobb. Some of the vets cried, 'Bonehead!' Others remarked, 'Poor zob!' **1920** S. Lewis *Main Street* xxxv. 416 And the same thing goes for that crowd of crabs and snobs Down East, and next time you hear some zob from Yahooville-on-the-Hudson chewing the rag..you tell him that no..Westerner would have New York for a gift! **1922**—— *Babbitt* x. 140, I don't know how you fellows feel about prohibition, but the way it strikes me is that it's a mighty beneficial thing for the poor zob that hasn't got any will-power but for fellows like us, it's an infringement of personal liberty. **1942** Berrey & Van den Bark *Amer. Thes. Slang* § 396 Terms of disparagement..yaphead, yazzihamper, zob.

zocalo (zǫ·kălo). Also **zócalo** and with capital initial. [a. Sp.] In Mexico, a public square, a plaza.

1884 J. W. Steele *To Mexico by Palace Car* v. 75 The square in front of the Cathedral, called the Zócalo, is the place of universal resort. **1884** F. H. Ober *Trav. in Mexico* xii. 232 Beneath us is the great square, with the smaller one, the zocalo, or pleasure garden, in its center. **1912** E. H. Blickfeld *Mexican Journey* x. 119 The Zocalo, as it is called, is the real center of Mexico City. **1927** D. H. Lawrence *Mornings in Mexico* 39 And a *plaza* is a *zocalo*, a hub. **1957** M. Lowry *Let.* 17 Mar. (1967) 398, I read of revolutions, counterrevolutions..in the zócalo. **1975** *Times* 24 May 10/3 Oaxaca..its zocalo, with its trees and its arcades.

‖ **zoco** (zǫ·ko). Also **Soko.** [Sp., ad. Arab.: see *souk.] = *souk; also *transf.*

1892 M. Thomas *Scamper through Spain & Tangier* xii. 232 The Soko is an unpaved square surrounded with booths, outside the walls, where on Thursdays and Sundays, as in Spain, the market is held. **1903** A. F. Calvert *Impressions of Spain* 96 Toledo—? She is at least faithful to the dead past. . So she retains her old *Soko*, and will have naught to do with the correct *Plaza de la Constitucion.* **1921** *Chambers's Jrnl.* Dec. 817/2 Tangier..cosmopolitan enough as it seems to be to any one who ambles through the little *zoco*, has been administratively mismanaged. **1924** *Ibid.* Sept. 689/2 The minaret of the new mosque overlooking the big zoco cuts through the blue. **1965** C. D. Eby *Siege of Alcázar* (1966) i. 34 The Gobierno resembled the *zoco* of a North African town except that the jewellery boxes, bundles of clothing, ..and whimpering children were not for sale.

zodico, var. *Zydeco.

zoetekoekie, var. *soetkoekie.

zoetrope. (Earlier example.)

1867 'Aunt Carrie' *Popular Pastimes for Field & Fireside* 229 The Zoetrope is a newly invented toy. It presents a series of striking optical delusions.

zoftick, zoftig, zoftik, varr. *zaftig *a.*

zograscope (zǫ·grăskōᵘp). *Obs.* exc. *Hist.* [Etym. uncertain, perh. f. Zogra(pher, Zogra(phy + -scope.] An optical instrument, consisting of a vertically suspended convex lens in front of a pivotally adjustable mirror mounted on a stand, designed for the viewing of prints in magnified form and with stereoscopic effect.

1753 in G. Adams *Descr. & Use Universal Trigonometrical Octant* 3 (Advt.), Zograscopes for viewing perspective Prints. **1953** *Ann. Sci.* IX. 315 (*heading*) The zograscope or optical diagonal machine. *Ibid.*, No reference to the zograscope has so far been found in the literature of the eighteenth or nineteenth centuries, save in certain..advertisements listing instruments made..by [George Adams]. **1969** E. H. Pinto *Treen* 284 Usually described and sold as Georgian shaving mirrors; this, they are not; they are zograscopes,..probably invented about 1750... Also known, during its long life, as an optical machine..intended for viewing prints, etc., in a magnified form.

zohar (zōᵘ·haɹ). Also 7 **zoar.** [Heb., lit. 'light, splendour'.] The major text of Jewish Cabbalism, in the form of an allegorical interpretation of the Pentateuch.

1682 W. Payne *Learning & Knowl.* 12 A studying Judiciary Schemes, and fancifull Cabalas, and mysterious zoars. **1837** *British & Foreign Rev.* V. 419 The work called Zohar is written in Chaldaic, and develops the mysterious science called *Cabala.* **1843** G. Borrow *Bible in Spain* III. xv. 295 He knew more Zohar and more secrets than the wisest of them. **1888** J. C. Murray tr. *Maimon's Autobiogr.* xiv. 95 The principal work for the study of the Cabbalah is the *Zohar*, which is written in a very lofty style in the Syrian language. **1932** A. Benson *Zohar* i. 11 Although they derived their inspiration from the same source—Zohar and Kabbala—Ashkenazi and Sepharadi mysticism inevitably took different directions. **1941** [see *Tel Avivian *sb.* and *a.*]. **1965** J. A. Michener *Source* (1966) 662 Ximeno had given Dr. Abulafia a manuscript of the Zohar, the arcane book of Kabbalism. **1978** I. B. Singer *Shosha* i. 8 There stood on our shelves volumes of the Zohar.., and other cabalistic works.

zoid *sb.* Delete '(Disused)' and add further examples.

1960 *Bot. Gaz.* CXXII. 33/1 Most algae, excluding the Cyanophyta, reproduce sexually by gametes and asexually by spores of various kinds (collectively called 'zoids', except for aplanospores). **1981** *Austral. Jrnl. Zool.* XXIX. 365 Subterminal ovicell complexes bud distally from part of the complex and are generally composed of female zoid with ovicell, lateral zoid, and ovicell zoid with apical chamber.

zoite (zōᵘ·əit). *Zool.* [The suffix used as an independent word.] (See quots.).

1963 E. N. Kozloff in J. Ludvík et al. *Progr. Protozool.* (Proc. First Internat. Congr. Protozool., Prague, 1961) 78 It appears advisable to reconsider the terminology applied to stages in the life-histories of gregarines and coccidians... *Zoite*, an infective stage, produced by division of a zygote, and usually surrounded by an envelope which is either a zoitocyst or zygocyst. **1969** *New Scientist* 29 May 465/1 Another stage in the development of *Toxoplasma* is the cystic form or zoite. **1977** *Jrnl. Protozool.* XXIV. 36/1 Electronmicroscopic studies revealed that the structure of *T. gondii* zoites (trophozoites, merozoites, 'spores', etc.) is similar to that of the zoites of the coccidia *Eimeria* and *Isospora*. **1979** *Ibid.* XXVI. 437/1 Uninucleate, dinucleate, and multinucleate zoites. **1980** *Jrnl. Parasitol.* LXVI. 67/1 Ultrastructurally, cysts of *T*[*oxoplasma*] *gondii* and *H*[*ammondia*] *hammondi* cannot be distinguished with certainty in skeletal muscle. Classification is based on the typical distribution of cysts and their zoites in the intermediate host.

-zoite (zōᵘ·əit), *suffix.* [f. Gr. ζῷ-ον animal + -ite[1].] A word-forming element used in zoological terms in the sense 'spore', as in *merozoite* s.v. *mero-[1], *tachyzoite* s.v. *tachy-.

Zollinger–Ellison syndrome (zǫ·lindʒəɹ e·lisɒn). *Path.* [Named after M. *Zollinger* (b. 1903) and E. H. *Ellison* (1918–70), American physicians, who described the syndrome in

955 (*Ann. Surg.* CXLII. 709).] A syndrome haracterized by excessive gastric acid secre-on (producing recurrent peptic ulcers) asso-iated with a gastrin-secreting tumour or yperplasia of the islet cells of the pancreas.
1956 EISEMAN & MAYNARD in *Gastroenterology* XXXI. 02 For the sake of simplicity we propose this clinical ntity be called the Zollinger-Ellison syndrome. **1960** *rnl. R. Coll. of Surgeons of Edin.* V. 191 Since that time *c.* 1955] over 100 instances of co-existent peptic ulcer nd islet cell tumours have been described and the ssociation appears to constitute a clinical entity called, y general consent, the 'Zollinger-Ellison syndrome'. **962** [see *ISLET 3]. **1974** R. M. KIRK et al. *Surgery* vi. 5/1 In the Zollinger-Ellison syndrome, ulcers may occur t the duodenojejunal junction.

Zöllner (tsö·lnəɪ, z-). *Psychol.* Also **Zoellner.** The name of the German astro-nomer and physicist, Johann Karl Friedrich *Zöllner* (1834–82), used *attrib.* and in the ossessive to designate the optical illusion noted by him of parallel lines which, when marked with short diagonal lines, appear to converge. Now usu. as *Zöllner illusion.*
1890 W. JAMES *Princ. Psychol.* II. xx. 232 In what is nown as Zöllner's pattern.., the long parallels tip owards each other the moment we draw the short lanting lines over them. **1911** *Encycl. Brit.* XXVIII. 42/1 (*caption*) Zoellner's Figure showing an illusion of direction. **1922** K. DUNLAP *Elem. Sci. Psychol.* xiii. 295 n the Zöllner figure, the long lines, really parallel, seem o converge. **1955** H. E. GARRETT *Gen. Psychol.* v. 179 *caption*) Zoellner illusion. The four horizontal lines are parallel. **1971** [see *HERING]. **1980** *Sci. Amer.* Jan. 91/1 The Zöllner illusion, which exhibits assimilation at extremely small angles and contrast at larger angles.

zolo go, var. *ZYDECO.

zombie (zǫ·mbi). Also **zombi** and with capital initial. [Of W. Afr. origin; cf. Kongo *nzambi* god, *zumbi* fetish.] **1.** In the West Indies and southern states of America, a soulless corpse said to have been revived by witchcraft; formerly, the name of a snake-deity in voodoo cults of or deriving from West Africa and Haiti.
1819 R. SOUTHEY *Hist. Brazil* III. xxxi. 24 Zombi, the title whereby he [chief of Brazilian natives] was called, is the name for the Deity, in the Angolan tongue... NZambi is the word for Deity. **1872** SCHELE DE VERE *Americanisms* 138 *Zombi*, a phantom or a ghost, not unfrequently heard in the Southern States in nurseries and among the servants. **1886** *Century Mag.* Apr. 815/2 This spiritual influence or potentate is the recognized antagonist and opposite of Obi, the great African manitou or deity, or him whom the Congoes vaguely generalize as Zombi. **1929** W. B. SEABROOK *Magic Island* II. ii. 94 At this very moment, in the moonlight, there are *zombies* working on this island. **1943** R. OTTLEY *New World* 46 Adding the zombies, jumbies, and obeah men to the gallery of voodoo characters. **1966** G. GREENE *Comedians* iv. 104 Luckily no one dared move on the roads at night; it was the hour when only zombies worked or else the Tontons Macoute. **1979** J. RHYS *Smile Please* 30 Zombies were black shapeless things. They could get through a locked door and you heard them walking up to your bed. You didn't see them, you felt their hairy hands round your throat. **1984** *Times* 26 Jan. 12/6 A zombie, as every schoolboy knows, is a person who has been killed and raised from the dead by sinister voodoo priests called bocors.

2. *fig.* A dull, apathetic, or slow-witted person. Also as a general term of disparagement. *colloq.*
1936 H. L. MENCKEN *Amer. Language* (ed. 4) xi. 587 Any performer [in a film] not a Caucasian is a *zombie.* **1941** H. MACINNES *Above Suspicion* ix. 80 He nodded..in the direction of those concentrating on the mastication of specially chosen vitamins to build a specially chosen race. 'Zombies is, I believe, the technical term,' suggested Richard. **1946** J. B. PRIESTLEY *Bright Day* xi. 329 They've spent their lives starving their imagination, just starving it to death. And now they're zombies. **1957** J. BRAINE *Room at Top* i. 17 To Charles and me it was always Dead Dufton and the councillors and chief officials and anyone we didn't approve of were called zombies. **1961** [see *LOVE *sb.*[1] 4]. **1974** S. MIDDLETON *Holiday* xiii. 233 He had no time for her as a zombie, preferring her moody volatility to this flabby acquiescence. **1981** P. CAREY *Bliss* iv. 156 They'll give us electric shocks... They'll give us pills and make us zombies. **1984** *Guardian* 22 Oct. 3/1 Mr. Dawson describes the committee as a parliament of zombies.

3. *Canad. Mil. slang.* In the war of 1939–45, an opprobious nickname applied to men conscripted for home defence.
1943 *Daily Express* 16 Sept. 4/1 The Canadian Government is reducing its 'Home Guard' army. . These troops were jocularly dubbed 'Zombies', after the Voodoo cult which insists that dead men can be made to walk and act as if they were alive. **1946** [see *OLD MAN 1 a]. **1953** D. M. LE BOURDAIS *Nation of North* 245 The first men were drafted for service... Contemptuously referred to as 'zombies', they were never taken seriously by the military authorities. **1963** A. S. MORTON *Kingdom of Canada* 481 A nasty distinction arose between the volunteers for service overseas and the conscripts for home defence, who were given the pungent nickname of 'zombie', a West Indian word for impotent spirits. **1978** *Daily Colonist Mag.* (Victoria, B.C.) 1 July 12/1 When the Canadian Army was struggling on the Western Front in the early winter of 1944 and there was an urgent call for reinforcements, yet, in the military camps in Vernon and Terrace the Zombies mutinied when orders came for their movement overseas.

4. A long mixed drink consisting of several kinds of rum, liqueur, and fruit juice (see quot. 1958).
1942 M. K. RAWLINGS *Cross Creek* xvii. 221 There is a passion fruit liqueur that is the primary ingredient..of that marvelous..drink, the Zombie. **1958** A. L. SIMON *Dict. Wines, Spirits & Liqueurs* 167/1 *Zombie,*..lime juice;..pineapple juice;..Falernum, or simple syrup;.. White Label Rum;..Gold Label Rum;..Jamaica Rum; ..Demerara Rum;..apricot liqueur. Shake well and strain... Garnish with..orange and..mint. **1968** J. M. ULLMAN *Lady on Fire* vi. 80 The bartender..went off to prepare a zombie. Forbes hated zombies, but it was the longest drink that came to mind. **1977** *Zigzag* Apr. 10/1 It's a Polynesian drink, a rum drink..a killer drink. There was a restaurant I found very close to The Cage that I went to every day... Like I would wake up, go there at noon, have a Zombie, go back and start writing.

5. a. *attrib.*
1956 M. STEARNS *Story of Jazz* (1957) xviii. 222 Thelonius Monk, whose weird..and pioneering modulations were referred to as 'Zombie music' by the musicians themselves, more in awe than anger. **1958** A. WILSON *Middle Age of Mrs. Eliot* I. 77 The breathing zombie orchestra around her. **1966** *New Statesman* 14 Jan. 58/3 A dream-sequence in a cemetery with zombie-hands sprouting like crocuses. **1968** P. ABLEMAN *Vac* xxiv. 113 Stop clashing those zombie lips and glide to the bar. **1973** [see *one-nighter* s.v. *ONE B. 33]. **1976** D. LODGE *Changing Places* v. 162 He could send home, when the time came, some zombie replica of himself.

b. *Comb.*, as **zombie-like** *a.*, characteristic of or resembling a zombie; lifeless, unfeeling.
1957 J. KEROUAC *On Road* (1958) 302 His arms hanging zombie-like at his sides. **1962** *Times* 25 July 13/1 Future ..where everybody lives a zombie-like existence. **1975** *Publishers Weekly* 10 Feb. 57/3 White Brian is a zombie-like boy who wanders unseeing and unseen through life. **1983** *Times* 4 Oct. 10/6 On state occasions, a few old men shuffle on to the balcony of the Kremlin and raise their hands in zombie-like salutation.

Hence **zombie·sque, zo·mboid** [-OID] *adjs.*; **zo·mbi,ism.**
1956 M. STEARNS *Story of Jazz* (1957) v. 51 The Calinda dance is connected with zombiism in Haiti. **1972** *Vogue* Jan. 7/3 Ponderax. sidetracks the appetite but leaves the character..muted, zombiesque. **1974** *Observer* 3 Feb. 31/5 Zombiesque Security Guard charged with shooting. **1974** *Radio Times* 18 Mar. 22/4 We're not putting up with 'Zombyism'. The aim of our programme is to give hope. **1975** *Sunday Times* (Colour Suppl.) 20 July 11/3 'I'm David Bowie,' he intones with a zomboid air. **1979** *Guardian* 18 Oct. 11/6 Some of the most zomboid heroines in recent fiction. **1983** *Daily Tel.* 15 Oct. 17/1 Zombi-ism exists and is a social phenomenon that can be explored logically.

zona. Add **b. zona fasciculata, glomerulosa, reticularis** [mod.L. (see FASCICULATE *a.*, etc.), coined in Ger. by J. Arnold 1866, in *Arch. f. path. Anat. & Physiol.* XXXV. 66], the middle, outer, and inner layers respectively of the cortex of the adrenal gland; **zona radiata,** a radially striated form of the zona pellucida surrounding the ova of certain vertebrates as seen in the light microscope.
1874 R. J. DUNGLISON *Dict. Med. Sci.* (new ed.) 1130/1 Zona reticularis... Zona glomerulosa... Zona fasciculata. **1881** F. M. BALFOUR *Treat. Compar. Embryol.* II. iv. 55 The ovum [of Teleosei] when laid is usually invested in the zona radiata only. **1883** E. KLEIN *Elem. Histol.* xliii. 340 The cortex of the [suprarenal] gland consists of an outer, middle, and inner zone... The outer one is the *zona glomerulosa. Ibid.* 341 Next follows the middle zone, or *zona fasciculata. Ibid.*, Next follows the inner zone, or *zona reticularis.* **1925** E. B. WILSON *Cell* (ed. 3) iv. 272 The zona radiata of the vertebrate ovum, conspicuously shown in the fishes, is a thick and often double membrane traversed by fine radial canals. **1964** PARKER & HASWELL *Text-bk. Zool.* (ed. 7) II. 319 The ovum [of *Salmo trutta*, the brown trout] is covered by a thick membrane, the zona radiata. **1965** LEE & KNOWLES *Animal Hormones* iv. 70 The cells in the innermost layer are in the form of a reticulum—the zona reticularis. *Ibid.*, The zona glomerulosa secretes mineralocorticoid. *Ibid.* 71 Hypophysectomy results in shrinkage mainly of the zona fasciculata and reticularis, and the blood glucose falls.

zonal, *a.* Add: **4.** *Soil Sci.* [a. F. *zonal* (N. Sibirtsev 1897, in *Compt. Rend. de la VII*[e]. *Session, Congr. géol. internat.* (1899) II. III. v. 80).] Of a soil: regarded as characteristic of a particular climatic or geographic zone and as reflecting the predominant influence of the climate in its formation.
1908 *Jrnl. Agric. Sci.* III. 84 The seven fundamental groups of 'zonal' soils just enumerated are spread over the surface of large continents in zones which coincide with the physico-geographical zones of those continents. **1927**, etc. [see *INTRAZONAL *a.*]. **1952** [see *AZONAL *a.*]. **1972** J. G. CRUICKSHANK *Soil Geogr.* iv. 110 Apart from being an over-simplification of reality, the zonal system had the unfortunate effect of restricting, in the mind of the student, the distribution of each zonal soil within the limits of its climatic zone.

zonation. a. Delete '(see ZONE *sb.* 7)' and add examples. Also *spec.* in *Ecol.*, the distribution of plants into specific zones which are characterized by their dominant species.
1898 *Rep. Brit. Assoc. Adv. Sci. 1897* 863 (*heading*) The zonal constitution and disposition of plant formations. By Frederic E. Clements. *Ibid.*, The author has here reviewed the phytogeographical contributions bearing upon the subject in hand, with especial reference to the part they have played in the elaboration of the conception of zonation. In addition, he has endeavoured to demonstrate the fundamental universality of zonation in all divisions of the floral covering. **1904** [see *ECOTONE]. **1926** TANSLEY & CHIPP *Study of Veg.* iv. 53 Adjacent plant communities are often arranged in more or less definite zones, following one another in constant order. This is specially noticeable in ascending a mountain (where it is called altitudinal zonation). **1936** J. MUIR *Geol. Tampico Region, Mexico* 121 Reliable local zonation of both the Eocene and the Oligocene has been worked out in the Tampico area. **1969** *Nature* 15 Mar. 1005/2 Marine work during the first eight months concentrated on community structure and zonation on cliffs, reef flats and in mangrove woodland. **1971** *Scot. Jrnl. Geol.* VII. 306 It is first necessary therefore to establish a regional metamorphic zonation. **1981** *Birds* Autumn 63/3, I would have preferred to have seen an accompanying annotated sketch so that the plant zonations could be easily recognised.

b. Substitute for def: Formation of zones in the oocytes of certain plants and animals. (Earlier and later examples.)
1899 *Bot. Gaz.* XXVIII. 237 There is a stage called zonation in which the nuclei, usually in metaphase, are lined up around the ooplasm. **1975** *Acta Anat.* XCIII. 512 The zonation of the ooplasm reveals that a majority of the oocytes [of the teleost *Schizothorax richardsonii*] have a darkly stained inner and a lightly stained outer zone.

zone, *sb.* Add: **2. c.** (*Town-*)*Planning.* A district or an area of land subject to particular restrictions concerning use and development.
1909 H. I. TRIGGS *Town Planning* iv. 177 The usual method in formulating town building plans on a large scale is to divide the urban area into building zones. **1910** F. HOWKINS *Housing Acts 1890–1909, & Town Planning* ix. 125 Certain portions of the area would be reserved for the erection of better class residences... This would be similar to the 'zone' system which has been adopted in certain towns on the Continent. **1939** H. M. LEWIS *City Planning* xvi. 166 A single map will show the subdivision of the area into zones, which in a typical case might be defined as follows: One family zones. Two family zones. [etc.]. **1953** [see *SMOKELESS *a.* 2]. **1964** J. S. SCOTT *Dict. Building* 364 Certain areas can be kept for light industry, others for heavy industry, dwellings, offices..and so on, each area being called a zone.

d. *N. Amer. Football* and *Basketball.* A specific area of the court to be defended by a particular player; also, a mode of defensive play employing this system (cf. *zone defence,* sense 9 a below).
1927 G. S. WARNER *Football Coaches & Players* 191 In the zone defense the players playing back of the line of scrimmage..are so stationed that they can knock down or intercept any pass that comes into their territory or zone. **1942** C. BEE *Zone Defense & Attack* i. 1 Certain coaches believe only the 'zone' can be called a team defense. **1964** ANDERSON & ALBECK *Coaching Better Basketball* ix. 209 You cannot win consistently..utilizing the zone. **1971** L. KOPPETT *N.Y. Times Guide to Spectator Sports* iii. 83 Each player is given a specific portion of the floor as 'his territory', and he guards, in turn, any offensive player who enters his 'zone'. **1979** *Farmington* (New Mexico) *Daily Times* 27 May 8A/7 The defense must be a man-to-man with no presses or zones allowed.

e. One of those areas of Germany and Austria occupied by British, American, French, or Russian forces after the war of 1939–45 until 1955. Subsequently occas. applied to East German territory; also *transf.*
1945 *Times* 13 Feb. 4/1 The conference of Mr. Churchill, President Roosevelt, and Marshal Stalin, held at Yalta, in the Crimea, has drawn up military plans for the final defeat of Germany... The forces of the three Powers will each occupy a separate zone of Germany, and a central control commission will have headquarters in Berlin. France will be invited to take a zone of occupation. **1947** *Daily Tel.* 25 Sept. 5/8 German machinery..will be delivered to Hungary in the next three months under a trade agreement signed between Hungary and the Soviet zone of Germany. **1954** W. FAULKNER *Fable* 128 Frenchmen had been spending their leaves..among the combat-troop rest-billets not only throughout the entire French Army zone, but the American and the British ones too. **1956** *Ann. Reg. 1955* III. v. 223 Some political leaders expressed the view that German interests would be furthered by direct negotiations with the Soviet Union, and that it would ease conditions for the people of the Soviet Zone if there was limited collaboration with the East German authorities. **1963** 'J. LE CARRÉ' *Spy who came in from Cold* xiii. 127 The GDR... The Zone if you prefer. **1964** L. DEIGHTON *Funeral in Berlin* vii. 50 Not too near the Sektor boundary and within a mile of the Soviet Zone... Sometimes we prefer to put our cargo on ice in the zone... Anywhere from Lübeck to Leipzig. **1976** W. D. GRAF *German Left since 1945* iii. 77 This movement aimed at the restoration of German unity... It was founded on the basis of proposals put forward by the communist leadership in the Soviet Zone.

8*. A hole in certain punched cards that is punched above the column of holes representing non-zero digits and is used in conjunction with these latter holes to represent non-numerical characters. Usu. *attrib.*

1950 W. W. STIFLER *High-Speed Computing Devices* 149 For alphabetical representations, two perforations in a single column are used for each letter; one of these is a zone punch (0, 11, or 12) while the other perforation is made in the position identifying one of the digits 1 to 9. **1959** M. H. WRUBEL *Primer of Programming for Digital Computers* ii. 33 Alphabetic information is recorded by using two punches in the same column: the upper punch (sometimes called the 'zone') is always a 12, 11, or 0. **1970** O. DOPPING *Computers & Data Processing* ii. 44 A letter in the English alphabet is coded with one zone punch (12, 11, or 0) together with one underpunch. **1972** W. R. PRICE *Introd. Data Processing* vii. 179 The correspondence between the Hollerith zones and the 1401 zones. **1979** DAVIS & MCCORMACK *Information Age* vi. 98 Later, when the need for alphabetic data arose, the zone positions, rows 12 and 11, were added.

9. a. *zone-mind*; **zone centre**, *spec. in Teleph.*, an exchange which acts as a main switching centre in an area containing a number of exchange groups; **zone defence,** (*U.S.* **defense**), *N. Amer. Football* and *Basketball*, a system of defensive play whereby each player guards an allotted portion of the field of play; **zone electrophoresis**, electrophoresis in which a solid but porous medium such as paper is used to ensure that the components remain separated in zones or bands according to their differing electrophoretic mobilities; **zone fossil** *Geol.*, a fossil characteristic of a particular zone or belt of strata; **zone levelling**, a process similar to zone refining in which the molten zone is passed repeatedly to and fro to produce a more homogeneous material; so **zone-level** *v. trans.*, **-levelled** *ppl. a.*; **zone leveller**, an apparatus used for zone levelling; **zone melting** = *zone refining* below; so **zone-melt** *v. trans.*; **zone plate** (examples); **zone refining**, a method of refining used to produce semiconductors and metals of very high purity by causing narrow zones of molten material to travel slowly along an otherwise solid rod or bar, so that impurities become concentrated at one end or the other if their solubilities in the liquid and the solid phases differ; so **zone-refine** *v. trans.*, **-refined** *ppl. a.*; **zone refiner**, an apparatus used for zone refining; **zone therapy**, a technique in which different parts of the feet (or palms) are massaged to relieve conditions in different parts of the body with which they are held to be associated; **zone time**, mean solar time at the standard meridian on which the local time zone is based, taken as the standard time throughout the zone (cf. *Zulu time* s.v. *ZULU *sb.* and *a.* 6).

1934 G. S. BERKELEY *Traffic & Trunking Princ. in Automatic Telephony* i. 12 Level 94 is used for trunk calls instead of level 0 in the case of exchanges in Trunk Zone Centres. **1948** [see *ROUTE *v.* c]. **1960** R. SYSKI *Congestion Theory in Telephone Systems* ii. 53 A suitable exchange (zone centre) is established within each zone to handle the long-distance calls to and from that zone. **1971** *Gloss. Electrotechnical, Power Terms (B.S.I.)* III. ii. 8 *Zone centre*, exchange acting as the main switching centre. **1927** Zone defense [see sense 2d above]. **1929** H. C. CARLSON *You & Basket Ball* vi. 128 Zone defense, in which each individual is responsible for a certain zone. **1937** C. ALLEN *Better Basketball* xviii. 291 It is to be noticed in charting these penetrating offensive plays against a zone defense that the setup of the offense is identical with that used in penetrating the man-for-man defense. **1970** G. SULLIVAN *Pro Football A to Z* 341 *Zone defense*, a type of pass defense in which each of the three linebackers and four deep backs is assigned to cover a specific area of the field. Zone defense contrasts with man-to-man defense. **1952** *Proc. Soc. Exper. Biol. & Med.* LXXX. 42 (*heading*) Zone electrophoresis in a starch supporting medium. **1964** G. H. HAGGIS et al. *Introd. Molecular Biol.* ii. 23 (*caption*) The separation of some of the human plasma proteins by zone electrophoresis. **1975** DAVIS & SIMPKINS in Williams & Wilson *Biologist's Guide to Princ. & Techniques Pract. Biochem.* iv. 100 A common feature of the use of all supporting media is that the substances migrate as distinct zones which at the end of the analysis can be readily detected by suitable analytical techniques... The term zone electrophoresis has been applied to this method. **1904** Zone-fossil [see ZONAL *a.* 3]. **1969** BENNISON & WRIGHT *Geol. Hist. Brit. Isles* ii. 23 It may be possible to recognize a zone without actually finding a specimen of the zone fossil itself if other highly characteristic species are found. **1975** J. G. EVANS *Environment Early Man Brit. Isles* iii. 69 Evolution needed the temporal and biological continuum which Lyell's theory made possible. And from this came the concept of the 'zone fossil'. **1953** W. G. PFANN in *Trans. Amer. Inst. Mining & Metall. Engineers* CXCIV. 752/1 The discussion of zone-melting has been confined to the categories of zone-leveling and zone-refining. **1956** *Bell Syst. Technical Jrnl.* XXXV. 657, *p* fluctuations in zone leveled material are generally coarse. *Ibid.* 660 A zone leveler has been developed to provide growth conditions suitable for the production of quality germanium single crystals. **1974** *Jrnl. Physics* D. VII. 33 The mixed alloy was then placed in a porcelain boat and zone-levelled by passing through 10–15 zones. **1978** P. W. ATKINS *Physical Chem.* x. 301 A modification of the technique, zone levelling, is used to introduce controlled amounts of impurity (for example, indium into germanium). **1952** W. G. PFANN in *Jrnl. Metals* IV. 747/1 A number of procedures will be indicated which have in common the traversal of a relatively long charge of solid alloy by a small molten zone. Such methods will be denoted by the general term *zone-melting*. **1965** PHILLIPS & WILLIAMS *Inorg. Chem.* I. viii. 305 All such techniques as precipitation, partition, distillation, crystallization, chromatography, and zone-melting are based on phase equilibria. **1982** *Materials Lett.* I. 33/2 Dielectrically isolated single crystals of large extent may be fabricated by zone melting a thin silicon sheet that is encapsulated between SiO_2 layers. **1983** *Rev. Sci. Instruments* LIV. 385/2 The use of the heater assembly in the specific case of zone melting of mercury cadmium telluride compounds is described. **1932** BLUNDEN *Halfway House* 55 When gong-like struck The violent crisis of zone-minds That chilled us with clouds turned winds. **1890** T. PRESTON *Theory of Light* ix. 178 A zone plate has therefore the power of a condensing lens. **1937** G. S. MONK *Light* xii. 167 The intensity of the image produced with a zone plate will be greater if alternate zones are not blocked out but are left transmitting, with a phase difference of one half period introduced between them and adjacent zones. **1978** *Sci. Amer.* Nov. 65/1 When the zone plate is illuminated with an X-ray plane wave, a converging spherical wave will come out. **1952** W. G. PFANN in *Jrnl. Metals* IV. 750/2 The particular merit of zone-refining becomes evident when repeated crystallizations are desired. **1956** —— in *Chem. & Engin. News* XXXIV. 1443/3 F. Montariol and coworkers..found that zone-refined aluminum cannot be hardened by cold-working. **1962** *New Scientist* 5 Apr. 813/2 To zone-refine and produce single crystals from such [refractory] materials, N. V. Philips's Gloeilampenfabrieken, Eindhoven,..has developed a carbon-arc image furnace. **1973** J. G. TWEEDDALE *Materials Technol.* I. vi. 152 Probably the most effective and generally used method of refining to this kind of standard is zone refining. **1978** P. W. ATKINS *Physical Chem.* x. 301 Bismuth is normally regarded as a hard, brittle metal, yet when it has been zone refined it forms rods which can be bent without fracture. **1983** *Metallurgical Trans.* A. XIV. 223/2 Straining electrode experiments were performed in zone refined and vacuum melted nickel alloys. **1959** *Times* 24 Nov. 19/7 It will be possible to obtain high quality single-crystal rods after a few passes in the zone-refiner. **1980** *Analytical Chem.* LII. 1738/1 A novel zone refiner is described, in which a single helical heater rotates in an annular sample space. **1917** W. H. FITZGERALD *Zone Therapy* xvi. 157 Dr. Roemer..examined him in a characteristic zone therapy way. He searched the patient's fingers with a metal comb to find out what was the matter with his teeth. **1971** N. SAUNDERS *Alternative London* xv. 123 Zone Therapy is based on the premise that one zone of the body acts as a microcosm of the whole. **1979** D. E. BAYLY in A. Hill *Visual Encycl. of Unconventional Med.* 61 The origin of the reflex method is obscure. It is said that it came from China to the West... It is known to have been used by the natives of Kenya, and also by some American Indian tribes. At the beginning of this century it was called zone therapy by one Dr Fitzgerald [*sic*] in America who used it as a form of anaesthesia to render the patient insensible to pain when performing small operations, and to ease childbirth. **1908** H. B. MORSE *Trade & Admin. Chinese Empire* viii. 203 The Eighteen Provinces roughly extend from longitude 98° to 122° E., comprising the seventh and eighth hours of the Zone time east of Greenwich. **1930** *Daily Express* 16 Aug. 1/3 The passengers wonder whether they should retire by Greenwich or zone time. **1981** G. WATKINS *Exercises in Astro-Navigation* ii. 22 A vessel's chronometer or watch is not generally adjusted or altered at any time while the vessel is at sea, but her clock is altered as she moves through each zone in such a way that it should always be indicating the correct Zone Time for the vessel's position.

zone, *v.* Add: **4.** (*Town-*)*Planning*. To divide (a city, land, etc.) into areas subject to particular planning restrictions; to designate (a specific area) for use or development in this manner. Occas. *intr.* Also (*U.S.*) const. *out*, to forbid (the siting of an enterprise) in a given area. orig. *U.S.*

1916 *N.Y. Times* 4 Feb. 17/2 The plan to zone the city and regulate the height of buildings. **1919** *Melbourne Argus* 28 Aug. 6 The question of 'zoning' the metropolitan area, or separating the city into districts, in order that regulations may be applied to control the erection of shops and factories near residential sites, has recently been occupying the attention of the Melbourne City Council. **1934** W. H. HEATH in E. Betham *House Building 1934–36* xviii. 180 There is practically no area around London that is zoned in a reasonable manner. **1939** H. M. LEWIS *City Planning* xvi. 169 All the frontage of main streets was placed in business zones although.. only a small fraction of areas so zoned can ever be used for that purpose. **1967** *Boston Sunday Herald* 26 Mar. I. 9/4 Planners..are concerned that a community will be thoughtfully zoned overall. **1971** P. GRESSWELL *Environment* 267 There is no guarantee that land zoned for housing will be released by the landowners. **1975** *N.Y. Times* 16 Oct. 29/1 A law that would 'zone out' massage parlors from the Times Square area on the principle that their proliferation is not sound community planning. **1976** *National Observer* (U.S.) 14 Aug. 7/2 When a municipality zones for industry and commerce for local tax benefits it..must zone to permit adequate housing within the means of the employes involved in such uses. **1977** *Chicago Tribune Mag.* 2 Oct. 8/2 At that time, which was before horse racing was zoned out of the city, the track was on Stony Island Avenue near 63rd Street. **1978** J. UPDIKE *Coup* (1979) vii. 274 The land, they say, is zoned for agribusiness.

5. To restrict the distribution of (a commodity) to a designated area; used *spec.* concerning the allocation of foodstuffs in the war of 1939–45.

1942 *Hansard Lords* 3 June 103 We have arranged that the deliveries of bread shall be zoned. **1945** *Dail Herald* 31 Aug. 2/1 (Advt.), Cyder, like many other things is now zoned to save transport and labour. **1952** *Ann Reg. 1951* 394 The Group scheme of the National Filr Finance Corporation has been announced. This 'zoned' considerable proportion of British production.

Hence **zo·ner,** one employed in the applica tion of planning restrictions to particula areas.

1962 *Punch* 6 June 848/2 Planners and zoners won' apparently make up their minds. **1976** *Daily Tel.* 4 Apr 3/6 This district contains about 1,000 homes approved by town zoners..after they were assured restrictive dee clauses would make the district a 'permanent adul community'.

zoned, *ppl. a.* Add: **4. b.** Distributed according to zones. Cf. *ZONE *v.* 5.

1943 *Daily Express* 16 Sept. 3/3 Compelling some grocers to buy their zoned cake through the co-ops.

5. (*Town-*)*Planning*. Designated for a particular type of use or development. orig. *U.S.*

1920 *Michigan Rep.* (Michigan Supreme Court) May 210 A penalty is provided for violation of said ordinance with a mandate prohibiting departments of the city from issuing permits for erection of the forbidden buildings within such zoned district. **1939** *Florida* (Fed. Writers' Project) III. 396 Zoned residential, business, and industrial districts. **1970** *Cape Times* 28 Oct. 20/3 (Advt.), Paarl shopping centre. On 11000 sq. ft., zoned special business with free car park..in fast developing area.

Zonian (zōᵘ·niăn), *sb.* (*a.*) [f. Panama Canal *Zone* (see below) + -IAN.] An American inhabitant of the Panama Canal Zone, a ten mile wide strip of land crossing the Isthmus of Panama on both sides of the Panama Canal, which was granted to the United States as a territory in 1904 and became independent in 1978. Also *attrib.* or as *adj.*

1910 *Everybody's Mag.* Mar. 322/1 Whatever your job, digging a canal, or driving a taxi-cab, or writing stock quotations, don't wear a uniform... The Zonian has a uniform, though, in spite of himself. It is the umbrella. **1950** *Social Forces* Dec. 161/1 The man marrying a girl of mixed blood may be unaware of the general Zonian prejudice that classes all Panamanians as 'colored'. **1951** *Panama Canal Rev.* 3 Aug. 9/3 Zonians..need no longer do without—just because the commissaries are closed. **1964** *Observer* 12 Jan. 1/5 'Zonians', American inhabitants of the [Panama Canal] Zone. **1979** P. THEROUX *Old Patagonian Express* xii. 170 Within a very few months the treaty would be ratified. I told this to a Zonian lady... The Zonians, 3,000 workers for the Panama Canal Company..saw the treaty as a sell-out.

zoning, *vbl. sb.* (In Dict. s.v. ZONE *v.*) Add: **1.** (Later examples.)

1942 *Times* 5 June 2/3 Further steps, including the zoning of the distribution of manufactured goods..are being investigated by the Ministry. **1945** *Daily Tel.* 17 May 5/7 In the zoning of Germany the United States Navy has been allotted the ports of Bremen and Bremerhaven. **1946** *How Britain was fed in War Time* (H.M.S.O.) iii. 22 The transport of food from production or import points to wholesalers' stores was effected by 'zoning' schemes... The country was divided into..zones, and movement between different zones..was allowed only by permit. **1968** *New York City* (Michelin) 16 After the First World War... A new zoning law regulated the height of buildings in relation to the width of the streets.

2. *spec.* in (*Town-*)*Planning*, the regulation of land use by particular planning restrictions in designated areas. orig. *U.S.*

1912 *Proc. 4th Nat. Conference City Planning* 190 In view of..existing indirect zoning laws, why not add some of the building laws in force in Frankfurt-on-the-Main? **1914** *Proc. 6th Nat. Conference City Planning* 92 The well-established principle of zoning that has been in operation for a generation or more in that country [*sc.* Germany]. **1921** *Glasgow Herald* 25 Mar. 8/3 'Zoning' means the locating of industries in the areas which are best suited for them and the reserving for housing of districts best adapted for this purpose. **1940** GRAVES & HODGE *Long Week-End* xi. 175 The Town-Planning Act of 1932 perpetuated this cleavage... Now there was 'zoning'..segregating families according to their incomes. **1943** J. S. HUXLEY *TVA* 31 Some States have introduced compulsory 'agricultural zoning' by which certain types of farming are prohibited in certain areas. **1966** R. F. BABCOCK (*title*) The zoning game: municipal practices and policies. **1978** J. A. MICHENER *Chesapeake* xiii. 830 Crossing over to the rivers south of Annapolis,.. Chris had a chance to see how lack of zoning and policing had encouraged this shoreline to become a marine slum.

zonk (zɒŋk), *int.* (*sb.*) *slang*. [Echoic.] Representing the sound of a blow or heavy impact, used to indicate finality. Occas. as *sb.* (see quots.).

1949 T. RATTIGAN *Harlequinade* 38 Just sit there and relax and I'll dash and get you an enormous zonk of whisky. **1958** *Spectator* 15 Aug. 218/2, I..hurl it with a great zonk into the waste-paper basket. **1961** *Radio Times* 16 Nov. 47/2, I never took a note when I was interrogating. The moment you got hold of a piece of paper they'd think 'ah-hah..' and zonk! they'd button up. **1968** L. DEIGHTON *Only when I Larf* i. 12 Silas.. closed the safe door a few times. Zonk. It closed with a clang. **1979** R. BLYTHE *View in Winter* i. 64 He was a man with a catapult. He'd knock a pheasant down—*zonk!*

zonk, *v. slang*. [f. prec.]. **1.** *trans*. To hit, strike, or knock. Also *fig.*

1950 A. MELVILLE *Castle in Air* I. in *Plays of Year* III. 38 If the Third Earl found that his wife had nipped off ith another man while he was away at the Crusades, he'd ave zonked her over the head with his kitbag. **1959** P. ULL *I know Face* xi. 201 We found ourselves back in my at..zonking down the drink. **1960** I. CROSS *Backward ex* 188 She zonked me again on the head with this airbrush. **1975** *New Yorker* 21 July 67/1 William Green ied to assure them that care had been taken to put rovisions in the bill to see to it that New England loesn't get zonked'. **1979** G. WATSON *Black Jack* xxii. 78, I felt zonked by this idea. It had never occurred to e. **1982** *Observer* 14 Nov. 15 ICI has invented a new daptation to ethylene crackers that will zonk the ompetition and make feedstock costs less critical.

2. *intr.* To fail; to lose consciousness, to die.

1968 *Listener* 14 Mar. 352/3 If Johnny zonked, it would e bad for my book. **1977** *N.Y. Times Mag.* 4 Dec. 142 n a burst of determination, she'd been sitting in the athtub doing her breathing for five hours straight—in ne nostril, out the other—until she zonked and went igid.

3. const. *out.* **a.** *intr.* To fall heavily asleep. **.** *trans.* To overcome or knock out (in *fig.* enses).

1970 J. SANGSTER *Touchfeather, Too* iii. 75 He left me t seven a.m. and I zonked out until after mid-day. 973 *Austral. Women's Weekly* 26 Dec. 32/5, I sank into ny bed.., zonked myself out with sleeping pills, and woke p Friday. **1980** *Telegraph* (Brisbane) 21 Mar. 6/3 It's .R.'s power that zonks women out. **1984** *N.Y. News Mag.* 18 Mar. 18/2 If mothers zonk out at three in the fternoon every day, they may continue that pattern fter it's no longer necessary. **1985** *Sunday Times* 24 'eb. 36/6 No Junoesque oarswomen though... 'I think row because it zonks me out, then I don't row with nyone.'

Hence **zo·nking** *ppl. a.* (freq. as quasi-*adv.* n *zonking great*).

1958 *Spectator* 25 July 130/2 He would give one a onking great clip on the ear. **1959** P. BULL *I know Face* i. 100 She was now technically a 'star' owing to her onking success as Claudia. *Ibid.* vii. 126 She..is a onking great film star. **1973** *Daily Tel.* (Colour Suppl.) 9 'eb. 36/4 *Long Day's Journey*..was the first big, zonking art he played after his cancer. **1976** *Times* 21 May 4/7 Rather than play these zonking great parts..I will try o find some dazzling little cameo roles.

onked (zǫŋkt), *ppl. a.* (chiefly *pred.*). *slang.* f. *ZONK *v.* + -ED[1].] **1.** Intoxicated by drugs or alcohol; 'stoned'. Freq. const. *out.* Also *ransf.* and *fig.*

1959 *Esquire* Nov. 70J, *Zonked*, one who is stoned, high, drunk. **1967** *New Scientist* 19 Oct. 185/1 Most of the drivers one meets should not be allowed to take charge of a car when sober—let alone when three parts zonked. **1967** P. WELLES *Babyhip* iv. 53 If only Mr Green weren't Jewish, he could swing around the world on the magic carpet completely zonked out. **1968** T. WOLFE *Electric Kool-Aid Acid Test* vi. 70 Everybody..had taken acid and they were zonked. **1972** J. WAMBAUGH *Blue Knight* (1973) xiv. 246 We sat..drinking *arak* and wine, and then beer, and we all got pretty zonked. **1973** H. NIELSEN *Severed Key* x. 107 I'm serious. Zonked about her. Way out. **1975** *Publishers Weekly* 20 Jan. 78/1 Susan begins an affair with a zonked-out type who calls himself Commander Cloud. **1977** *Rolling Stone* 24 Mar. 84/1 Thousands of young people squeezed themselves into Radio City Music Hall to enjoy, scream at, get zonked to Jethro Tull. **1979** *Daily Tel.* 25 Apr. 21/5 A..Caucasian woman obviously zonked out..and a tracery of leaves resembling cannabis.

2. Exhausted, tired *out.*

1972 *Maclean's Mag.* Oct. 40/1 This portrait of his wife..zonked out on a floating sofa. **1976** J. FARRIS *Fury* i. 10 You just collapsed and..pulled the covers up around your head... You were completely zonked. **1978** *Washington Post Mag.* 19 Mar. 42/2 Patricia Wells, three hours after providing the high point of 2,300 people's evenings, was 'zonked' and went back to her hotel to bed. **1980** *Daily Tel.* 28 July 8/6 'Fairly zonked' by his non-stop 17 weeks of filming, he is recharging himself for the next stage.

zonkey (zǫ·ŋki). [f. Z(EBRA + D)ONKEY.] The offspring of a zebra and a donkey. Cf. *ZEDONK.

1953 *N.Y. Herald Tribune* 2 Sept. 1/7 Mr. [Gene] Holter explained that a zonkey was half zebra and half donkey, a combination the zoomen had never seen. *Ibid.*, 'Zonkey is not exactly a scientific name and I'm no scientist' Mr. Holter said, 'But I don't know what else you would call it.' **1973** *Indian Express* 29 Oct. 6/8 A zebra and a donkey are expecting an offspring next March, Brooklyn's Prospect Park Zoo authorities say. It will be New York's first zonkey, though. The others were born in western zoos. **1983** *N.Y. Times* 6 Mar. x. 53/4 Melancholy exemplars abound: a male camel who recently injured a foreleg;..and a morose-looking zonkey—the mother a zebra, the father a donkey.

zonky (zǫ·ŋki), *a.* (*sb.*) *slang.* Also **zonkey**, [f. *ZONK(ED *ppl. a.* + -Y[6].] Odd, weird, 'freaky'. Hence as *sb.*, a person in this state.

1972 *Daily Colonist* (Victoria, B.C.) 26 Apr. 22/5 'Wow, is this zonky?' breathed an admiring observer softly, as she gazed incredulously at the newly opened, all-cardboard room. **1975** *Globe & Mail* (Toronto) 25 Oct. 34/1 Unlike the honkey-tonk zonkies who used to hang out at his..workshop, shooting up or having sex in public view..Warhol has rarely, personally, done anything scandalous. **1977** *N.Y. Rev. Bks.* 28 Apr. 12/3 That combination of the new and old seems to have escaped most journalists except—in one of his zonky moments of insight—Hunter Thompson. **1979** B. MALAMUD *Dubin's Lives* i. 22 All the guy there does is..shakes his head. Makes you feel zonky..twittery. **1980** *Times* 6 Nov. 12/6 His book is really a study in ideas—or to coin an appropriately zonkey term—*weirdology.*

zonule. Add: **2.** *Geol.* (See quot. 1928.)

1928 C. L. & M. A. FENTON in *Amer. Naturalist* XI. 21 We have discussed the need for some term to designate the rocks bearing a faunule with several stratigraphers. In the course of one conversation Dr. Weller suggested 'zonule', and it has been approved by others... We propose the term, therefore, with the following definition: A zonule is the stratum or strata which contain a faunule, its thickness and area being limited by the vertical and horizontal range of that faunule. **1958** *Bull. Geol. Soc. Amer.* LXIX. 113/1 A zonule is a biostratigraphic unit that is recognizable in a sedimentary basin or similar restricted area of sedimentation. **1976** *BMR Jrnl. Austral. Geol. & Geophysics* I. 109 The assemblage can be referred to the middle Eocene *Proteacidites confragosus* Zonule on the basis of the presence of the nominate species.

zoo. Add: **2.** *transf.* A (diverse) collection, esp. of people; the place where they are assembled. (Freq. mildly contemptuous.)

1924 GALSWORTHY *White Monkey* I. ii. 11 You won't keep me in your Zoo, my dear. I shan't hang around and feed on crumbs. **1935** E. BLUNDEN *Edward Gibbon & his Age* 14 He [*sc.* Gibbon] passed through Oxford, gathering little but materials for his future monody on a moribund zoo of dons. **1964** in *Current Slang* (Univ. S. Dakota) (1967) Spring 5 *Zoo*, place where students congregate. **1975** J. I. M. STEWART *Young Pattullo* i. 9 The Glencorrys were..the principal figures of fun in Ninian's and my own family zoo.

3. Comb. *zoo-crazy* adj.; **zoo-keeper,** an animal attendant employed in a zoological garden; also, a zoo owner or director; **zooman** *U.S. colloq.* = prec.; similarly **zoowoman** (*rare*).

1938 L. MACNEICE *Zoo* iv. 71 A curate who was Anglo-Catholic..and..zoo-crazy. **1936** L. R. BRIGHTWELL *Zoo you Knew?* viii. 163 Zoo keepers gave up whistling 'Ta-ra-ra-boom-dehay'. **1960** D. H. S. RISDON *Zoo Keeper* vi. 53 Minor ailments should be curable by the Zoo keeper if he knows his job properly. **1977** *Monitor* (McAllen, Texas) 17 July 2F/4 Zookeepers caring for a two-week-old orphaned hippopotamus have taken to..wading into a pool..to nurse the hippo from a bottle. **1930** *Time* 13 Oct. 32/3 U.S. zoomen, animal catchers and park directors attended the annual meeting of the American Association of Zoological Parks and Aquariums... One zooman had too many elephants. *Ibid.* 33/2 Conspicuous among the zoomen was the only zoowoman in the world. **1942** BERREY & VAN DEN BARK *Amer. Thes. Slang* § 458/17 *Zooman*, a zoo director or caretaker. *Ibid.* § 624/16 Animal man, zooman. **1973** *Times Lit. Suppl.* 9 Mar. 262/4 The increasing value of the *Yearbook* to zoomen and biologists.

zoo-. Add: **zo:o,archæo·logy,** the study of the animal remains of archæological sites; hence **zo:o,archæo·logist; zooce·ntric** *a.*, centred upon the animal world; regarding or treating the animal kingdom as a central fact; **zo·ochore** (-kōᵊɹ) [Gr. χωρεῖν to spread], a plant whose seeds are dispersed by animals; hence **zoocho·rous** *a.*; **zoo·chory,** the dissemination of plant seeds by animals; **zoomagnetism** (earlier example); **zoonose**: read **zoono·sis** (pl. **-noses** (-nōᵘ·sīz)); usu. restricted to diseases transmitted naturally to man from animals; (further examples); hence **zoono·tic** *a.*; **zoopla·nkter** [*PLANKTER], an individual organism of the zooplankton; **zooplankto·nic** *a.*, of, pertaining to, or consisting of zooplankton; **zoopraxo·graphy** [Gr. πρᾶξις], the study of animal locomotion; **zo:osemio·tics** *sb. pl.* (const. *sing.*), the study of animal communication through the investigation of signalling behaviour in and between species; **zootheism** (earlier example).

1984 *Nature* 1 Mar. 88/2 John Speth's *Bison Kills and Bone Counts* extends such an invitation to zooarchaeologists and to everyone who uses faunal evidence from archaeological sites to reconstruct past human diet. **1972** *Science* 20 Oct. 297/2 Recently the *Atlas of Animal Bones* by Elisabeth Schmid has become available for research workers in zooarcheology. **1985** *Times Lit. Suppl.* 7 June 646/1 Taphonomy..has..only recently become an integral part of zoo-archaeology (or, as the subject of faunal analysis is more usually called in Europe, archaeozoology). **1882** *Trans. Anthropol. Soc. Washington* I. 93 In later times a few of this school have expanded their scheme to embrace the animal world in general, rendering it zoöcentric instead of anthropocentric. **1977** J. L. HARPER *Population Biol. Plants* 433 Virtually all of the work reported is that of zoologists and the research is zoocentric. **1905** F. E. CLEMENTS *Res. Methods Ecol.* 216 Migration results when spores, seeds, fruits, offshoots, or plants are moved out of their home by water, wind, animals, man, gravity,..or mechanical propulsion. Corresponding to these agents there may be recognized the following groups:..Animals, zoochores. *Ibid.* 218 Species which grow in exposed grassy or barren habitats are for the most part anemochores, while those that are found in the shelter of forests and thickets are usually zoochorous. **1960** *McGraw-Hill Encycl. Sci. & Technol.* X. 499/2 Animal dispersal, zoochory, is divided into epizoochory (barbed or sticky disseminules, desmochores..) and endozoochory (disseminules eaten and egested by animals). **1969** L. VAN DER PIJL *Princ. Dispersal in Higher Plants* v. 24 We enter here the more general field of zoochory. *Ibid.*, All following zoochorous classes can be subdivided by crosswise partitions as follows. **1974** *Nature* 8 Feb. 407/1 Modes of dispersal, namely aerial (both active and passive), hydrochorous, zoochorous and anthropochorous, are discussed at some length. **1980** *Botanisk Tidsskrift* LXXV. 159 Dispersal is probably mostly by means of water flowing through pores and channels in the soil, but zoochory also plays a role. *a* **1834** S. T. COLERIDGE *Table Talk* (1884) 73 Nine years has the subject of Zoo-magnetism been before me. **1894** G. M. GOULD *Med. Dict.* 1631/1 *Zoonosis*, any disease communicated or communicable from one of the lower animals to man. **1956** *Nature* 3 Mar. 407/2 When a zoonosis gets under way, man-to-man contact may be sufficient to keep the infection spreading. **1972** N. D. LEVINE in T.-T. Chen *Res. Protozool.* IV. 340 This was the first proof that simian malaria is a true natural zoonosis. **1974** R. ZELEDÓN in K. Elliott et al. *Trypanosomiasis & Leishmaniasis* 51 Chagas' disease..became a zoonosis when the reduviid insect vectors adapted to human dwellings. **1900** DORLAND *Med. Dict.* 769/2 Zoonotic. **1956** *Nature* 3 Mar. 407/2 In searching for explanations of..zoonotic outbreaks, there are limitations in the taxonomic approach which should be borne in mind. **1980** *Brit. Med. Jrnl.* 29 Mar. 928/2 Zoonotic pathogens, such as salmonellas.., may be present in any type of slurry. **1963** *Spec. Sci. Rep. U.S. Fish & Wildlife Service* No. 452 (*title*) A towed pump and shipboard filtering system for sampling small zooplankters. **1979** *Nature* 1 Feb. 353/2 Zooplankters must also cope with the consequences of living in a transparent medium. **1911** *Rep. Brit. Assoc.* 422 In the high Alpine lakes there exists an outstanding production of zooplanktonic organisms. **1964** *Oceanogr. & Marine Biol.* II. 152 This technique..is well suited to analysis of zooplanktonic extracts. **1978** *Nature* 20 July 246/1 Determinations of element concentrations in the fecal pellets from a common zooplanktonic species, the euphausiid *Meganyctiphanes norvegica*, are now available for 18 elements. **1891** E. MUYBRIDGE (*title*) The science of animal locomotion (zoöpraxography). **1893** —— *Descriptive Zoöpraxography* 2 In the presentation of a lecture on Zoöpraxography the course usually adopted is to project..a series of the most important phases of some act of animal motion. **1947** L. EDWARDS *Reminisc. Sporting Artist* xv. 151 The science of animal motion (Zoöpraxography) cannot be entirely ignored by artists, more especially since the advent of instantaneous photography has familiarised the public with the camera's version of animal movement. **1974** *Country Life* 2 May 1059/1 His [*sc.* Lionel Edwards'] preoccupation with zoopraxography is a desire to capture a precise impression of the rhythm of venery and racing. **1963** T. A. SEBEOK in *Language* XXXIX. 465 The term *zoosemiotics*—constructed in an exchange between Rulon Wells and me—is proposed for the discipline, within which the science of signs intersects with ethology, devoted to the scientific study of signaling behavior in and across animal species. **1968** *Language* XLIV. 211 The Section of Semiotics and Linguistics of the Laboratoire d'Anthropologie Sociale is assembling a library of offprints on the areas within its purview (viz., linguistics, oral and written literature,..theory of languages, scientific languages, zoösemiotics, and the like). **1978** *New Yorker* 17 Apr. 78 In a collection of papers written by various experts in the field of..'zoosemiotics'—in other words, animal communication—each writer tries valiantly to define what he means by the term. **1881** *Abstr. Trans. Anthropol. Soc. Washington* 128 Let us hope that American students will not fall into this line of error by assuming that zoötheism is the lowest stage, because this is the status of mythology most widely spread on the continent.

zoochlorella (zōᵘ:oklore·lă). *Bot.* Also **Zoo-.** Pl. **-æ.** [mod.L. (coined in Ger. by K. Brandt 1881, in *Arch. für. Anat. & Physiol.: Physiol. Abt.* 571), f. ZOO- + CHLOR-[1] + L. *-ella* (see -EL[2]).] One of the numerous green unicellular organisms, believed to be algæ, that are present as symbionts in the cytoplasm of many freshwater invertebrates.

1889 in *Cent. Dict.* **1899** F. S. LEE tr. *M. Verworn's Gen. Physiol.* ii. 84 Among such symbiotic organisms are especially many algæ, the *Zooxanthellæ* and the *Zoochlorellæ*, the nature of which as independent organisms has been for a long time in dispute. They occur abundantly in the cells of lower animals. **1924** J. A. THOMSON *Sci. Old & New* xxvii. 150 The same kind of co-operation is illustrated by a number of green Protozoa, in cases where the green colour has been shown to be due..to a partnership with minute algae (Zoochlorellae and Zooxanthellae). **1972** M. S. GARDINER *Biol. of Invertebrates* i. 34/1 Zooxanthellae are limited to marine species, and zoochlorellae almost entirely to freshwater species. **1979** *Nature* 5 July 58/2 Traces of chlorophyll *b* in extracts of pigments from intact animals suggested that *Amphistegina* spp. and *Amphisorus hemprichii* also contained symbiotic zoochlorellae.

zoogeographic, *a.* (Examples.)

1907 *Jrnl. Geol.* XV. 296 Zoögeographic works in all points confirm the conclusions. **1971** *Nature* 9 July 88/1 The largest zoogeographic group so far recovered..is found in the southern shallow waters of the Florida–Halteras slope.

zooglœa. Add: Hence **zooglœ·al** *a.*

1934 A. T. HENRICI *Biol. of Bacteria* xviii. 289 *Nitrosomonas* species may appear in cultures in two forms—as zoögloeal masses which rest at the bottom of liquid cultures, in which the cells are non-motile; and as motile 'swarmers'. **1976** *Ann. Rev. Microbiol.* XXX. 265 Protozoa crawl about the zoogloeal mass and occur in the liquor; most are free-swimming or stalked ciliates.

zoological, *a.* Add: **a.** (Earlier example.)

1807 J. PINKERTON *Mod. Geogr.* (ed. 2) I. p. xxvii, Conceiving that the zoological part might admit of some improvements..the author applied to Dr. Shaw of the British Museum.

b. Also *zoological park.*

1899 *N.Y. Times* 9 Nov. 14/3 A splendid stretch of 261 acres of country, that is destined to accommodate one of the finest collections of wild animals in the world, and will be known as the New York Zoological Park, was formally opened..yesterday. **1935** *Chambers's Encycl.* X. 811/1 The Zoological Park of Edinburgh,..one of the most beautiful. **1978** JORDAN & ORMROD *Last Great Wild Beast Show* i. 48 Stellingen itself remains the finest example of the use of moated enclosures in zoological parks.

zoologizing, *vbl. sb.* (Earlier example.)
1815 [see ENTOMOLOGIZE *v.*].

zoology. Add: Also popularly with pronunc. (zū,ǫ·lǒdʒi). (Earlier example.)
Similarly with the derivatives.

zoom, *v.* Add: **1.** Also, to travel or move (as if) with a 'zooming' sound; to move at speed, to hurry. Also *loosely*, to go hastily. Freq. with advbs. *colloq.*

1924 *Brit. Weekly* 18 Dec. 270/1 Trams zoom along and buses rattle past. **1946** WODEHOUSE *Joy in Morning* xxix. 280 How would it be..to zoom off immediately, without waiting to pack. **1960** T. MCLEAN *Kings of Rugby* 118 Hewitt soon zoomed away on the right. **1976** *National Observer* (U.S.) 14 Aug. 16/1 Every night..a speedboat zooms into the Jones Beach Marine Theater. **1977** G. DURRELL *Golden Bats & Pink Pigeons* v. 121 Three cleaner fish..worked assiduously on their three customers, zooming in to suck the parasites off their skin.

2. a. (Later examples.) Also *transf.* In recent use, often not distinguished from sense 1.

1920 *Blackw. Mag.* July 71/2 The bird checked, swerved and dived and zoomed back into level flight again. **1934** [see *DOG-FIGHT *v.*]. **1940** *War Illustr.* 19 Jan. 620/3 The mother-ship would be guarded by 350 m.p.h. fighters that would zoom up into the skies about her on the first hint of danger. **1962** S. CARPENTER in *Into Orbit* 75 At 28,000 feet, diving at 900 mph..we suddenly pulled through and started to zoom up again..This manœuvre converted some of our speed into zoom energy. **1980** J. DITTON *Copley's Hunch* II. i. 115 He zoomed up and over to gain height.

b. *trans.* To cause (an aircraft) to zoom; also, to fly over (an obstacle) in this manner.

1918 *Independent* 16 Nov. 208/2, I 'gave 'er all the gun' and 'zoomed' the château—that is, I almost went up the front of the place. **1928** V. PAGÉ *Mod. Aircraft* 521 A machine should never be 'zoomed' or made to jump into the air by a too-rapid movement of the elevator flaps.

c. *intr.* fig. Of prices, costs, etc.: to rise sharply; to soar or rocket. *colloq.*

1970 *Daily Tel.* (Colour Suppl.) 6 Feb. 17/3 They must double labour and work overtime. Costs zoom. **1976** *National Observer* (U.S.) 17 July 3/1 By March 1978..the dropout total would zoom to 498,300—50 times the total as of March 1972. **1981** *Times* 12 Sept. 2/1 He did not think that the Prime Minister had ever said the economy was going to zoom.

3. *Cinematogr.* and *Photogr.* **a.** *intr.* Of a camera, lens, etc.: to close up on a subject (esp. rapidly) without losing focus; more generally, to alter range by variation of focal length. Freq. const. *in* (*on*). Also *fig.*

1948 *Jrnl. Soc. Motion Picture Engin.* LI. 296 Does the speed change while zooming?..The speed is independent of the zoom. **1959** HALAS & MANVELL *Technique Film Animation* xix. 237 The scene opens with a full screen live-action back-projection shot which zooms to a miniature. **1962** *Daily Tel.* 8 June 23/7 The lens is capable of 'zooming-in' on a set target up to a mile distant. **1970** *Amateur Photographer* 11 Mar. 13 (Advt.), Needle-sharp f1.8 lens—zooms from telephoto to wide angle. **1973** H. J. EYSENCK *Inequality of Man* ii. 84 The computer will continue to select items in such a way as to 'zoom in' on the crucial set of items which will really test the subject's IQ, avoiding all the useless items which are below or above his true level. **1978** *N.Y. Times* 30 Mar. D18/2 The TV camera zoomed in on a triumphant Holmes.

b. *trans.* To cause (a lens fitment, camera, etc.) to alter range in this manner.

1952 *Applied Electronics Ann.* 1951 57/1 The construction makes it possible for the operator to 'zoom' the lenses after the ball or player. **1975** *Physics Bull.* Nov. 481/2 The image magnification, AEI claims, can be zoomed continuously up to × 15 000 000 with no change in image focus or brightness. **1979** *SLR Camera* Mar. 5/3 Have you tried focusing and zooming a lens that operates in the opposite direction to others in your gadget bag?

Hence **zoo·ming** *vbl. sb.* and *ppl. a.*

1917 [see ZOOM *v.* 2]. **1923** *Blackw. Mag.* July 7/1 We settled into steady, zooming flight. **1961** G. MILLERSON *Telev. Production* iii. 34 (*caption*) The zoom angle can be adjusted anywhere in the zooming range. **1982** L. COOK *Under Etna* I. i. 11 'I hate this zooming-in bit.' She gazed hypnotically at the strip of runway coming up to meet them.

zoom, *sb.* (In Dict. s.v. ZOOM *v.*) Add: **1.** *Aeronaut.* (Further examples.) Also *attrib.*

1918 *Blackw. Mag.* June 762/1 The Hun's third repetition of the manœuvre was varied by a straight zoom instead of a climbing turn. **1932** [see *BLACKING *vbl. sb.* 1 c]. **1960** *Aeroplane* 2 Dec. 741/1 At the zoom altitudes which the Mirage is capable of reaching, there is insufficient airflow through the engine to maintain afterburner combustion.

2. *Cinematogr.* and *Photogr.* **a.** A camera shot in which the range is (usu. rapidly) shortened to close-up without loss of focus; this process.

1934 [see *FADE-OUT 1]. **1948** [see *ZOOM *v.* 3 a]. **1962** *Movie* Dec. 6/3 The film ends on a zoom into a close up of Tolly's clenched fist. **1967** MCLUHAN & FIORE *Medium is Massage* 128 The audience had..been preconditioned by television commercials to abrupt zooms.., no story lines, flash cuts. **1977** J. HEDGECOE *Photographer's Handbk.* 125 (*heading*) Zoom and tilt.

b. = *zoom lens*, sense 4 below.

1974 *Some Technical Terms & Slang* (Granada Television), *Zoom*, lens allowing a change of view from long-shot to close-up. **1978** *Amateur Photographer* 29 Nov. 120 He uses a Nikon with 24mm, 43–86mm and 80–200mm zooms, and uses Kodachrome exclusively. **1982** 'A. J. QUINNELL' *Snap Shot* vi. 99 [He] had taken the telephoto lens off the camera and replaced it with an all-purpose zoom.

3. *fig.* Zest, energy; sparkle, zip. Cf. *ZOOM *int. colloq.*

1964 in Hamblett & Deverson *Generation X* 97 Perhaps also a man has to have a bit of an inferiority complex.. to give him that extra zoom as a lover. A smug, inbred type like Roger doesn't care if he's a dead loss to a woman between the sheets. *a* **1974** R. CROSSMAN *Diaries* (1977) III. 297, I am definitely losing political zest, looking and feeling more detached, with less zoom, watching, not believing in things, not as enthusiastic or inspired.

4. Comb. **zoom lens** *Cinematogr.* and *Photogr.*, a camera lens whose focal length (and hence the magnification and the field of view) can be smoothly varied while the image remains in focus; cf.* VARIFOCAL *a.*; **zoom shot**, a camera shot taken with a zoom lens.

1936 *World Film News* Apr. 12 No British manufacturer makes a nice, cheap zoom-lens. **1949** R. H. ALDER *Movie Making for Everyone* vi. 67 Most amazing of all is the 'Zoom' lens, in which the angle of view can be changed while the picture is actually being taken. **1962** L. DEIGHTON *Ipcress File* xxiv. 154 A zoom lens, one that would change its focal length. **1978** J. GARDNER *Dancing Dodo* xix. 146 The drifting began. Like a huge, long pull-back on a zoom lens so that everything diminished. **1984** A. C. & A. DUXBURY *Introd. World's Oceans* iii. 104 The Alvin was equipped with a new color television camera that had a special zoom lens for inspecting the vent animals. **1966** *Listener* 24 Feb. 286/1 A pre-credit titles vertical zoom-shot is served as *hors d'œuvre* for those with appetites for impudently expert camera work. **1977** T. ALLBEURY *Man with President's Mind* x. 108 A zoom shot on the representatives of OPEC.

zoom (zūm), *int.* [See the vb.] Representing a 'zooming' sound, such as that made by something travelling at speed. Freq. used *fig.* to denote a sudden rise (to success, etc.) or equivalent fall.

1942 D. POWELL *Time to be Born* vi. 130 Men..just lucky enough to hold a job a few years and then—zoom! **1942** BERREY & VAN DEN BARK *Amer. Thes. Slang* § 2/11 All of a sudden..socko..whang, zoom. **1976** *National Observer* (U.S.) 25 Dec. 4/2 People began to talk about him. An article appeared in Advertising Age, a trade magazine. Then he wrote a guest column for the Hollywood Reporter. Zoom.

Zoomar (zū·mar). Also **zoomar.** A proprietary name in the U.S. for a make of zoom lens.

1946 *Jrnl. Soc. Motion Picture Engineers* XLVII. 465 (*caption*) Optical principle of Zoomar lens. **1947** *Official Gaz.* (U.S. Patent Office) 10 June 177/2 'Zoomar' for varifocal camera lenses. **1961** A. L. M. SOWERBY *Dict. Photogr.* (ed. 19) 712 The first zoom lens for a miniature camera, the Voigtländer Zoomar, gave focal lengths from 36 mm to 82 mm. **1971** D. E. WESTLAKE *I gave at Office* (1972) 68 Rudy had a zoomar lens and got as close as he could for greater clarity. **1973** D. OSMOND-SMITH tr. *Bettetini's Lang. & Technique of Film* ii. 94 By making use of a complicated system of lenses, called 'pancinor' or 'zoomar', it is in fact possible to vary in a continuous progression the focal length of the shot and, therefore, to move the lens with apparent continuity towards or away from an object or person.

zoomorph. (Earlier example.)
1889 [see *SKEUOMORPH 1].

zoomorphism. **1.** (Earlier example.)
1822 tr. *Malte-Brun's Universal Geogr.* I. xxiii. 576 The most gross is the religion of the Egyptians, in which the attributes of the divinity were represented under the figures of animals... This may be termed *zoomorphism.*

zo,omorpho·sed, *ppl. a. rare.* [f. ZOOMORPH, after METAMORPHOSED *ppl. a.*] Of a decorative or symbolic design: formed into an animal-like shape; rendered zoomorphic (sense 1).

1955 *Proc. Prehist. Soc.* XXI. 234 The famous sheath with zoomorphosed wave-tendril,..which forms part of his Third La Tène style. **1967** *Antiquaries Jrnl.* XLVII. 211 In two recent papers de Navarro has discussed the most common and indeed interesting occurrence of the horse in Celtic art—as part of a zoomorphosed lyre.

zoon (zūn), *v.* (and *int.*) *U.S. colloq.* [Echoic; cf. ZOOM *v.*] **a.** *intr.* To make a humming or buzzing sound; to move quickly. **b.** *trans.* To (cause to) travel with such a sound; to propel. Also as *int.* Hence **zoo·ning** *vbl. sb.* (also applied *spec.* in *Black English* to a style of preaching and response characterized by the repetition of words and phrases with tonal variation).

1883 J. C. HARRIS *Nights with Uncle Remus* xxxvii. 22 Bimeby Brer Rabbit year de skeeters come zoonin' 'roun', en claimin' kin wid 'im. **1909** *Dialect Notes* III. 391 *Zoon, v.i.* and *tr.*, to make a humming or buzzing sound, to cause to make such a sound. 'That rock came *zoonin'* by my head.' 'Watch me *zoon* this rock.' **1911** M. JOHNSTON *Long Roll* xv. 197 *Zoon—Zoon—Zoon!* O Lord! listen to that shell. **1922** *Outward Bound* Nov. 137/1 The zoonings and ploppings of blundering winged intruders. **1950** W. L. JAMES in *Phylon* XVI. I. 19 The prayer maker is too full for any utterance which is not colored tonally by his emotions. This is called 'Zooning'. **1977** J. L. DILLARD *Lexicon Black Eng.* iii. 55 The 'cries'.. may come relatively early in the [church] service and show the importance of tonal phenomena in the Black sermon. There is even a term for one such practice: *zooning*, 'crying (a word or phrase) over and over with variations'.

‖**zoon politikon** (zōᵘ·ǫn poli·tikǫn). [Gr.] = *political animal* s.v. *POLITICAL *a.* 6 (q.v.).

1958 W. STARK *Sociology of Knowledge* 238 Anybody who regards man as necessarily..a *zoon politikon.* **1971** A. GIDDENS *Capitalism & Mod. Social Theory* 5 In the Greek *polis* every free man—that is, every free citizen—was a *zoon politikon*: the social and political were inextricably fused.

zoophagan, *sb.* (Earlier example.)
1840 [see *entomophagan* s.v. *ENTOMO-].

zoophilia (zōᵘofi·liă). *Psychol.* Also **zoö-philia.** [f. Gr. ζῷον animal + φιλία affection.] Attraction to animals that acts as an outlet for some form of sexual energy, formerly not implying sexual intercourse or bestiality.

[**1899** REBMAN tr. *Krafft-Ebing's Psychopathia Sexualis* iii. 267 In close relation to stuff-fetichism, certain cases must be considered in which beasts exercise an aphrodisical influence over human beings. One feels tempted to call it *Zoophilia Erotica.* This perversion seems to be rooted in a fetichism the object of which is the skin of the beast.] **1906** H. ELLIS *Stud. Psychol. Sex* V. 71 There is..the more or less sexual pleasure sometimes experienced..in the sight of copulating animals. This I would propose to call Mixoscopic Zoophilia; it falls within the range of normal variations. **1908** M. E. PAUL tr. *Bloch's Sexual Life of our Time* xxiii. 641 We will first describe zoophilia, a sexual inclination towards animals without actual sexual intercourse. **1940** HINSIE & SHATZKY *Psychiatric Dict.* 558/2 Zoöphilia..is a term coined by Krafft-Ebing to denote sexual excitement caused by the stroking and fondling of animals. It does not refer to sexual intercourse with animals. **1960** *Arch. Gen. Psychiatry* III. 442/1 Zoophilia was known in antiquity. **1966** R. & D. MORRIS *Men & Apes* iii. 65 The extent to which zoophilia involving monkeys was actually practised is difficult to assess. **1978** *Daily Tel.* 2 Dec. 16 One of your contemporaries referred in its review to the 'zoophilia' in this film. A simpler word is animalism or bestiality.

zo,o·philic, *a.* [f. as ZOOPHILE + -IC.] **a.** Characterized by zoophilism; animal-loving. **b.** *Psychol.* Characterized by zoophilia.

1947 *New Biol.* 152 Our chief concern, however, is with the dog as a beast of burden. In England, presumably owing to the prevalence of zoophilic organisations such as the R.S.P.C.A. such practices are illegalised. **1951** J. STEINBECK *Log* p. xxiv, A sexual, a religious, a zoophilic or a gustatory impulse. **1965** *Movie* Spring 23/2 Although some spectators may derive a premature zoophilic *frisson* from Marnie's words to her horse, 'Oh, Forio, if you want to bite anyone, bite me,' we don't learn that there is anything psychologically wrong with Marnie until the sequence in which we meet Mother.

zoot (zūt). *U.S. slang.* [See next.] **1.** A zoot suit.

1965 'MALCOLM X' *Autobiogr.* iv. 59, I saw some of the real Roxbury hipsters eyeing my zoot. **1973** C. HIMES *Cotton gonna kill me Yet* in *Black on Black* 196 This George Brown was strictly an icky, drape-shaped in a fine brown zoot with a pancho conk slicker'n mine. **1973** T. PYNCHON *Gravity's Rainbow* II. 246 Where'd you get that zoot you're wearing, there?

2. *Comb.* **zoot-shirt**, a (brightly coloured) shirt designed to be worn with a zoot suit.

1959 A. FULLERTON *Yellow Ford* viii. 95 He wore a multi-coloured zoot shirt. **1961** *Times* 8 Mar. 14/7 For men students zoot shirts..are banned.

Hence **zoo·ty** *a.*, in the style of a zoot suit; (strikingly) fashionable, 'sharp'.

1946 MEZZROW & WOLFE *Really the Blues* IV. xvi. 313 Colored kids..work on their dungarees, pegging the legs till they're real sharp and zooty. **1952** *Amer. Speech* XXVII. 20 What the zootie character and the dude have in common is an overfastidious regard for clothing. **1964** S. BELLOW *Herzog* 240 Her lover, too, with long jaws and zooty sideburns. **1974** *Listener* 8 Aug. 166/1 The suits were..the zooty type—that's the American style of suiting with a straw hat.

zoot suit (zū·t sⁱūt). orig. *U.S. slang.* [Redupl. rhyming formation on SUIT *sb.*] **1.** A type of man's suit of exaggerated style popular in the 1940s (orig. worn by U.S. Blacks), characterized by a long, draped jacket with padded shoulders, and high-waisted tapering trousers.

1942 GILBERT & O'BRIEN *Zoot Suit* (song) 3, I want a ›ot Suit with a reat pleat, with a drape shape. **1942** [see ɾEET *a*.]. **1949** R. CHANDLER *Little Sister* xxix. 218 aking knives away from grease-balls in zoot suits. **1951** . PAUL *Springtime in Paris* xv. 269, I saw a few Zoot iits, please believe me, on Negroes headed for the bar : No. 12. **1969** *Time* 14 July 16/2 Chavez became a ıchuco, affecting a zoot suit with pegged pants. **1982** . FANTONI *Stickman* xxix. 206 Two coloured tap dancers ı dazzling yellow zoot suits. **1984** *Guardian* 5 Oct. 3/1 aggy zoot suits and skinhead styles have revived the dult market.

2. *transf.* in various *Mil.* uses. Chiefly *U.S.*

1943 *Yank* 15 Oct. 3 Some of the Japs even wore our ıngle 'zoot suits'. **1945** BAKER *Austral. Lang.* 158 *Zoot uit* (which, of course, came originally from U.S. jive ang) for the crude civilian clothes given to discharged ɛrvicemen. **1952** D. CLARKE *Eleventh at War* xvii. 416 he warm 'tank suits'..were soon known to the troops s 'zoot suits', and were aptly described as a 'mass of zip-ısteners joined together by windproof and waterproof ıaterial'. An ingenious manipulation of the zips could ›nvert the zoot suit into a sleeping-bag. **1975** H. WHITE *Raincoast Chronicles* (1976) 144/1 Bernie Grimes, older eteran of the first, wartime zootsuit gangs.

Hence **zoot-suited** *a.*, dressed in a zoot suit; **oot-suiter**, a zoot-suited person; *spec.* one of group or gang of young men wearing zoot uits.

1969 Zoot-suited [see *crash-helmeted* adj. s.v. *CRASH *b.*¹ 7 a]. **1971** A. PRICE *Alamut Ambush* ix. 105 We met t poor old David's nuptials—you were one of the zoot-uited ushers, weren't you? **1943** *Chicago Daily News* 12 une 6/2 A new human variety has excited the populace n California]—the 'zoot suiters'. **1952** Zoot-suiter [see DADDY-O]. **1972** J. WAMBAUGH *Blue Knight* (1973) i. 18 t was almost twenty years [ago]... It was real bad then. Ve had B-girls and zoot-suiters and lots of crooks.

zooxanthella (zōᵘ:ozænþe·lă). *Bot.* Also **Zoo-**. Pl. **-æ.** [mod.L. (coined in Ger. by K. Brandt 1881, in *Arch. für Anat. & Physiol.: Physiol Abt.* 572), f. ZOO- + XANTH(O- + L. *ella* (see -EL²).] One of the numerous yellow-brown unicellular organisms present in the cytoplasm of many radiolarians, corals, and other marine invertebrates, probably symbionts.

1889 in *Cent. Dict.* **1899, 1924** [see *ZOOCHLORELLA]. **1967** NOLAND & GOJDICS in T.-T. Chen *Res. Protozool.* II. 38 The zooxanthellae found in Radiolaria and Foramini-era (as well as in some lower invertebrates) are probably pecialized dinoflagellates or cryptomonads. Presumably hey play the same role that zoochlorellae do in fresh-water forms, but a mutually beneficial relationship has not been experimentally proved. **1972** [see *ZOOCHLOREL-LA]. **1975** *Nature* 6 Nov. 37/1 The only chlorophyll in corals is contained in the brown zooxanthellae. **1983** *McGraw-Hill Yearbk. Sci. & Technol.* 150/1 All the available evidence suggests that the nudibranchs have evolved mechanisms to maintain healthy populations of zoo-xanthellae in their tissues and are able to extract photo-synthetic products from the dinoflagellate partner.

‖**zoppa** (tsǫ·pă), *a. Mus.* [It., fem. of *zoppo* limping (formerly also used).] (See quots.) Freq. in phr. *alla zoppa*.

1740 GRASSINEAU *Mus. Dict.*, *Zoppo*, lame..hopping; ..Hence..they call those counter-points.. *Contrapunti alla Zoppa*... One is obliged to place in each bar to the subject given one note between two others ..which, when it comes to be played..,by the frequent syncopes, seems to proceed..in a jumping manner. **1889** GROVE *Dict. Music* IV. 514/1 *Zoppa, alla*, a term applied to a rhythm in which the second quaver in a bar of 2–4 time is accentuated. **1959** WESTRUP & HARRISON *Collins Mus. Encycl.* 17/1 *Alla zoppa*,..in a limping manner, syncopated. **1963** *Times* 25 Feb. 5/1 Once heard, in closing gavotte, with the crisp, jaunty, and insinuating appoggiaturas of the kind called *zoppa*, hangs in the mind for ever after.

Zoque (sōᵘ·ke), *sb.* (and *a.*) [a. Sp., of uncertain origin.] Any of a group of Central-American Indian languages of the Mixe-Zoquean family; this group of languages collectively. Also *attrib.* or as *adj.*

1891 D. BRINTON *Amer. Race* III. vi. 144 (*heading*) Zoque linguistic stock. **1911** THOMAS & SWANTON *Indian Lang. Mex. & Central Amer.* 60 (*heading*) Zoque. **1940** F. JOHNSON in *Maya & Neighbors* VI. 109 The territory in which the Zoque language was spoken has scarcely been changed on any map since Thomas. **1953** [see *non-phonemic* s.v. *NON- 3]. **1964** E. A. NIDA *Toward Sci. Transl.* vi. 134 As in Zoque, spoken in Mexico, the Biblical expression 'Perfect love casts out fear' becomes 'we do not fear when we truly love'. **1972** [see *MIXTEC].

zores, -us, varr. *TSORES.

‖**zori** (zǫ·ri), *sb. pl.* Also 9 **sori.** [Jap., f. *sō* grass, (rice) straw + *ri* footwear, sole.] Japanese thonged sandals with straw (or leather, wood, etc.) soles.

1823 F. SCHOBERL *Japan* V. 131 The shoes of the Japanese consist of straw soles or slips of wood. Those in common use are called *sori*. **1884** [see *GETA]. **1939** A. KEITH *Land below Wind* xviii. 298 Even her *zori* were blue, with sapphire soles and bright blue straps which came between the toes. **1962** *Amer. Speech* XXXVII. 288 Japanese *zori* or the American adaptation, thong sandals. **1970** J. KIRKUP *Japan behind Fan* 180 On summer days, *zori* of a specially fine quality, made of bamboo sheaths, may be used for strolling in the garden. **1984** *Coaching Award Scheme* (Brit. Judo Assoc.) 9/1 Zori (flip-flops) are compulsory wear at BJA events and should be worn off the mat in Clubs, Schools, etc.

zorrino: see ZORRO.

zos-grass (zǫ·sgrɑs). [Abbrev. of ZOS(TERA + GRASS *sb.*¹] = ZOSTERA.

1937 J. W. DAY *Sporting Adventure* 129 Five ducks come out of the sunset and swing low above me out to the muds and bared *zos* grass. **1974** *Times* 9 Mar. 14/1 They [*sc.* brent geese] cleared the mud-flats of the zos-grass, their natural feed.

Zotzil, var. *TZOTZIL.

Zouave. 1. c. (Earlier examples.)

1860 *Chicago Tribune* 23 Feb. 1/4 The gallant Zouaves.. attracted much attention and admiration by their fine appearance and exact drills. **1861** J. CHESNUT *Let.* 12 June in M. B. Chesnut *Diary* (1949) 67 Reinforcements were sent from here last night, the New Orleans Zouaves.

†**Zou-Zou** (zū·zū). *Obs.* exc. *Hist.* Also (*rare*) **Zu-Zu.** [a. Fr.] Colloq. diminutive of ZOUAVE.

1860 *Leisure Hour* 15 Mar. 190/2 The *gamins* of Paris, we believe, first applied to the world-renowned Zouaves the pet name of *Zous-Zous*; and France has confirmed the pleasant diminutive. **1863** *Harper's Mag.* Mar. 569/2 A zou-zou..found himself arrested by the guard. **1866** L. P. BROCKETT *Camp, Battlefield, & Hospital* III. 458 He soon after moved off, followed by the Zou-zous. **1894** [see *NOUNOU]. **1944** J. S. PENNELL *Hist. Rome Hanks* 70 Tom thought it was the boy who sang the Zu-Zu song at the creek.

zowie (zau·i, zau,ī·), *int. U.S. colloq.* An exclamation of astonishment (generally, or as a reaction to a sudden or surprising act), and freq. of admiration.

c **1913** S. FORD *On with Torchy* 302 'Zowie! A plush one!' says I. **1922** S. LEWIS *Babbitt* xiii. 169 You're a natural-born orator and a good mixer and—Zowie! **1931** [see *POW *int.*]. **1958** E. BIRNEY *Turvey* iv. 32 Visitors.. they slap me where it's sore yet and zowie they're off! **1962** [see *BAM *int.*]. **1972** WODEHOUSE *Pearls, Girls, & Monty Bodkin* xi. 171 He gets out and *zowie* a gang of thugs come jumping out of the bushes, and next thing you know they're off with your jewel case. **1978** G. McDONALD *Fletch's Fortune* (1979) ix. 60 She was totally unconscious... Gently, he put her head on the floor. 'Zowie.'

zoysia (zoi·ziă). [mod.L (C. L. Wildenow 1801, in *Neue Schriften Gesellsch. Naturfreunde Berlin* III. 440), f. the name of Carl von *Zoys* zu Laubach (1756–*c* 1800), Austrian botanist + -IA¹.] A perennial grass of the genus of this name, native to eastern Asia, and sometimes used for lawns in subtropical regions. Also *zoysia grass*.

1965 M. C. NEAL *In Gardens of Hawaii* 67 Zoysia, a turf-forming grass from the Mascarene Islands has proved excellent for lawns in Hawaii. **1968** F. W. GOULD *Grass Systematics* i. 6 Southern lawns and other turfs are mainly..zoysia grasses. **1969** 'J. MORRIS' *Fever Grass* viii. 69 It was fronted by a rectangle of zoysia grass. **1974** *Marlboro Herald-Advocate* (Bennettsville, S. Carolina) 18 Apr. 11/2 For bermuda or zoysia type lawns, [cut] one-half to three-quarters of an inch. **1982** *Birmingham* (Alabama) *Post-Herald* 22 June A3/1 Zoysia lawns along curving and curbed streets.

zubr. Add: Also 8 **zuber.** (Earlier example.)

1763 J. BELL *Trav.* I. 294 The stags are of two kinds; one called zuber, the same with the German crownhirsh, but somewhat larger.

‖**zucca** (zu·kă). *rare.* Pl. **zucche.** [It.: see next.] A gourd, esp. a pumpkin.

Shelley's (plural) form is erroneous.

1818 SHELLEY *Let.* 6 Nov. (1964) II. 45 Vast heaps of many coloured zucki or pumkins..piled as winter food for the hogs. **1946** BLUNDEN *Shelley* xxii. 272 Perhaps ..it was Mary who placed a zucca in a vase on the window-sill.

zucchini (zukī·ni), *sb. pl.* [a. It., pl. of *zucchino* (small) marrow, dim. of *zucca* gourd.] **a.** Courgettes. Also const. as *sing.*

The usual word for the vegetable in N. America and Australia.

1929 *Sunset* Feb. 58/2 Wash the succini and slice thinly into a baking pan. **1945** B. MACDONALD *Egg & I* IV. xiii. 183 Succulent summer squash and zucchini where it seemed only a matter of an hour ago there were blossoms. **1960** *Guardian* 15 July 8/7 The miniature vegetable marrows called courgettes in France and zucchini in Italy. **1966** T. PYNCHON *Crying of Lot 49* iv. 82 Around them all, Negroes carried gunboats of mashed potatoes, spinach, shrimp, zucchini, pot roast, to the long, glittering steam tables. **1975** *Telegraph* (Brisbane) 11 Sept. 30/2 Zucchini, although a relatively new vegetable, is rapidly becoming an alternative to the old standards. **1982** L. KALLEN *C. B. Greenfield* xiii. 125, I kept on to the market..to replenish our store of onions, zucchini, and Bartlett pears.

b. *attrib.*

1960 *House & Garden* Aug. 72/3 We..will grow..those exquisite little Zucchini marrows. **1967** *Courier-Mail* (Brisbane) 4 Nov. 8 They were all charged with having stolen four cases of zucchini melons. **1979** E. NEWMAN *Sunday Punch* XV. 127 The waiters had wheeled in zucchini quiche.

Zuckerkandl (zu·kəɹkænd'l). *Anat.* The name of E. *Zuckerkandl* (1849–1910), Austrian anatomist, used *attrib.*, in the possessive, and with *of* to designate the para-aortic bodies. [Described by Zuckerkandl in *Verhandl. d. Anat. Ges.* (1901) XIX. 95.]

1910 *Lippincott's New Med. Dict.* 1107/2 Zuckerkandl's body *or* organ. **1927** *Jrnl. Anat.* LXI. 317 Under the high power of magnification the cells of the Zuckerkandl bodies at full time resemble the larger cells described in the suprarenal medulla. **1930** [see *PARAGANGLION]. **1983** *Oxf. Textbk. Med.* II. XIII. 286/1 The commonest extra-adrenal site [of phaeochromocytomas] appears to be the organ of Zuckerkandl, adjacent to the bifurcation of the aorta.

zufolo (tsu·fŏlo, z-). *Mus.* Also **zuffolo.** [a. It. *zuf(f)olo.*] A flageolet, a small flute or whistle (see quots.).

1724 *Short Explic. Foreign Words in Mus. Bks.*, *Zufolo*, a Bird Pipe or Small Flagelet. **1740** GRASSINEAU *Mus. Dict.*, *Zuffolo*, a little Flute or Flageolet. *c* **1801** T. BUSBY *Dict. Music*, *Zuffolo*, any little flute or flageolet: but more especially that which is used to teach birds. **1876** STAINER & BARRETT *Dict. Mus. Terms* 456/1 *Zufolo*.., a flageolet or whistle. **1954** *Grove's Dict. Mus.* (ed. 5) IX. 427/2 There..is no reason for concluding ..that Keiser's *zuffolo* was a small shawm. **1960** [see *PICCO PIPE]. **1976** D. MUNROW *Instruments Middle Ages & Renaissance* vi. 58/1 Leonardo clearly envisaged the possibility of a keyed trumpet and a keyed *zufolo* or pipe.

zug (tsūg). Also **Zug.** The name (formerly proprietary) for a variety of waterproofed leather used esp. for the uppers of climbing boots.

1899 *Trade Marks Jrnl.* 6 Sept. 1092 *Zug*...222,699. Leather. W. & J. Martin, 63, Brunswick Street, Glasgow; Leather Merchants and Manufacturers. **1899** *Shoe & Leather Trader* (Glasgow) 7 Dec. p. ii (Advt.), W. & J. Martin, tanners, curriers, and leather factors, Albion Leather Works... Sole makers of Zug leather. 63 Brunswick Street, Glasgow. **1900** *Ibid.* 12 Apr. 819/1 The firm made a speciality of 'zug' leather, a new production... The manufacture of 'zug' is an entirely new process. The leather ..will not burn like ordinary leather, and the fibre cannot be destroyed even by boiling... In the process of manufacture, the gelatine of the hide becomes oxidised, and is rendered insoluble and repellant [*sic*] to water. **1907** [see *CHROME *sb.* 2 c]. **1929** *Footwear Organiser* July 37/2 Sports shoes, of pigskin, calf, crocodile, and zug. **1933** G. D. ABRAHAM *Mod. Mountaineering* x. 179, I would have soft, almost glove-like, zug or beaver leather for the uppers.

‖**zugtrompete** (tsū·ktrǫmpē·tə). *Mus.* [Ger., f. *zug* pulling, tugging + *trompete* TRUMPET.] A slide trumpet.

[**1938** *Oxf. Compan. Music* 962/2 *Slide trumpet*... Zugtrompete (Ger.). **1959** WESTRUP & HARRISON *Collins Mus. Encycl.* 681/2 The slide trumpet.., G. Zugtrompete, ..was used in Germany in the early 18th cent. (e.g. in Bach's cantatas).] **1978** *Early Music* Oct. 539/1 The zugtrompete illustrated at the foot of the page is from Naumburg not Nuremberg.

‖**Zugunruhe** (tsū·ku:nrū,ə). *Ornith.* [Ger.] Migratory restlessness; the migratory drive in birds.

1950 *Condor* May 108 *Zugunruhe*..is the restlessness displayed by caged migratory birds during the migratory period. **1971** *Sci. Amer.* Apr. 76 The behavior of the four groups was studied in terms of signs of *Zugunruhe*, or migratory urge, as shown by night activity and by the molt of feathers. **1978** *Nature* 13 July 154/1 The birds were housed under natural photoperiod in an outdoor aviary, and tested only after they showed migratory restlessness (*Zugunruhe*) in activity cages and exhibited subcutaneous fat deposits.

‖**Zugzwang** (tsū·ktsvaŋ). *Chess.* [Ger., f. *zug* move + *zwang* compulsion, obligation.] A position in which a player is obliged to move but cannot do so without disadvantage; the disagreeable obligation to make such a move. Freq. *in Zugzwang*. Also *transf.*

1904 *Lasker's Chess Mag.* I. IV. 166 White has struggled bravely and only loses by 'Zugzwang'. **1930** *British Chess Mag.* I. 196 The move..puts Black into a Zugswang [*sic*] position that speedily loses. **1935** SMITH & BONE tr. *Tarrasch's Game of Chess* I. 5 White has constrained his opponent to move, has placed him, as we say in Germany, in *Zugzwang*. **1942** H. GOLOMBEK *Fifty Great Games Mod. Chess* 53/2 Black now has only a few pawn moves left after which he is in complete 'Zugzwang'. **1963** [see *GRAB *sb.*² 5 b]. **1973** *Country Life* 13 Sept. 744/2 She is, to use a chess term, in complete *Zugzwang*. She could only make six tricks for a penalty of 200.

Zulu, *sb.* and *a.* Add: **1.** (*sb.* or *adj.*) **c.** A derogatory term for a Black person. *U.S.*

1931 *Amer. Mercury* Nov. 354/2 *Zulus*, negroes who participate in spec. **1967** 'D. SHANNON' *Chance to Kill* vii. 91, I just didn't care to have any damn zulu saying I didn't do the work right. **1970** J. BROWN *Un-Melting Pot* xi. 169 Expressions of colour antagonism can at times be bizarre—witness the New York West Indian boy who was heard to call a Barbadian girl a 'bloody Zulu bastard'.

2. (Earlier examples.)

1839 W. C. HARRIS *Wild Sports Southern Africa* 150 Andries..possessed a smattering of zooloo, and we thus hoped to be able to proceed without the aid of a sworn interpreter. **1849** *Jrnl. Amer. Oriental Soc.* I. 50 The Zulu alphabet..contains the same letters as the English... The English language abounds with short words, but in the Zulu such words are very few.

4. *Zulu hat*, a kind of straw hat with a wide brim. *Obs.* exc. *Hist.*

1880 *Girl's Own Paper* 27 Nov. 144/1 Wreaths of grapes and a few poppies serve best as trimming for a Zulu hat. **1893** YONGE & COLERIDGE *Strolling Players* viii. 54 She had managed, while seizing a Zulu hat, to divest herself of the apron. **1895** M. BEERBOHM in *Yellow Bk.* Jan. 280 Zulu hats shaded their faces. **1941** F. THOMPSON *Over to Candleford* x. 144 Both [children] wore what were then known as Zulu hats, plaited of rushes and very wide brimmed.

5. A kind of fishing-boat formerly used in Scotland. *Obs.* exc. *Hist.*

1884 *Trans. Highland Soc.* 122 Ten or twelve boats of the carvel-zulu shape have been built. **1905,** etc. [see *FIFIE, FIFIE]. **1952** G. MAXWELL *Harpoon at Venture* (1955) ii. 37 She was a seventy-foot 'zulu', lugsail-rigged, and with two Kelvin paraffin engines. **1963** P. MACTYRE *Fish on Hook* iii. 43 MacAra's window looked on to the jibs of disused cranes and the carcasses of two rotting 'Zulu' boats. **1976** *Oxf. Compan. Ships & Sea* 964/2 *Zulu*, a type of fishing vessel peculiar to the north-east coastal ports of Scotland... They were..first produced during the Zulu War (1878–9), hence their name.

6. The radio code word for the letter 'z'; *spec.* (in full *Zulu time*) (Aeronaut. colloq.) = *zone time* s.v. *ZONE *sb.* 9 a.

1960 'N. SHUTE' *Trustee from Toolroom* 104 We'll have a meal..at twenty-three zulu—at eleven o'clock English time. **1976** B. JACKSON *Flameout* (1977) v. 90 'Check Zulu 10.50.28,' he said, using airmen's and Air Traffic Control jargon for time... 'Okay. The line after Zulu 10.50.30.' **1978** PASACHOFF & KUTNER *University Astron.* v. 125 Astronomers often keep track of events according to the standard solar time that corresponds to the Greenwich time zone. This is called G.M.T. (Greenwich Mean Time), U.T. (Universal Time), or Z (which is colloquially called Zulu Time). **1981** T. BARLING *Bikini Red North* zii. 260 Projected detonation deadline at fourteen-hundred hours, Zulu Time.

zumbi, var. *JUMBY.

Zuñi. Delete ‖ and add: Also **Zuni**. Pl. usu. **Zuñi**. **a.** (Earlier and later examples.) Also *Zuni Indian*.

1834 A. PIKE *Prose Sk. & Poems* 200 The Moqui (pronounced *Mokee*,) and the Suni (Sunee) live near the Nabajo. **1853** L. SITGREAVES *Exped. Zuñi & Colorado Rivers* 5 The cornfields of the Zuni Indians extend..for several miles. **1910** F. W. HODGE *Hand. Amer. Indians North of Mexico* II. 1017/1 Fray Martin de Arvide..was killed by 5 Zuñi. **1929** *Amer. Speech* V. 115 Among these Pueblo tribes we find..the *Zuñi*, who called themselves *Ashiwi*, Zuñi being a Spanish adaptation of *Sunyitsi*, the Keresan name for this tribe. **1937** A. HUXLEY *Ends & Means* iii. 20 Among the Zuñi Indians..individuals are not led into the kind of temptation which invites the men of our civilization to work for fame, wealth, social position or power. **1960** R. C. BELL *Board & Table Games* I. ii. 49 The Zuni Indians played another game on the roof-tops called Kolowis Awithlaknannai. **1969** *Vogue* Nov. 30/2 Marvellous chokers, from the Zuni of the southwest.

b. The language of this people.

1882 *Atlantic Monthly* Sept. 367/2 Then I spoke in Zuñi. **1932** [see *ATHAPASCAN *sb.* 2]. **1956** J. LOTZ in Saporta & Bastian *Psycholinguistics* (1961) 12/2 Color-recognition tests were given to both Zuni and English speakers. **1972** *Language* XLVIII. 847 His list can be supplemented from..Yuma, Zuni.

‖ **zuppa** (tsu·pa). [It.] Soup. *Comb.*, esp. as *zuppa di pesce* (pe·ʃʃe), fish soup. Also *transf.* and *fig.* in phr. *zuppa inglese* (iŋglē·ze) [lit. 'English soup'], a rich trifle.

[**1935** M. MORPHY *Recipes of all Nations* 124 (*heading*) Zuppa di fagioli alla fiorentina (Haricot Bean Soup à la Florentine).] **1961** W. VAUGHAN-THOMAS *Anzio* xi. 231 The tourists eat their *zuppa di pesce* in the restaurants on the quayside. **1962** L. DEIGHTON *Ipcress File* xvi. 95 We ordered the Zuppa di Lenticchie. **1975** F. BRESLER *You & Law* 77 My favourite culinary term, '*zuppa inglese*', the Italian's idea of a sickly English trifle. **1976** *Times* 10 July 10/8 A true Italian zuppa di pesce. **1977** *Listener* 10 Feb. 189/2 One way and another, [the book is] a *zuppa inglese*, heavy with leftovers and alcoholic seasonings. **1981** 'J. GASH' *Vatican Rip* xii. 101 We'd decided on *Zuppa inglese* for pud... Who can resist trifle in hooch?

zur. For 'southern dial.' read 'dial. (chiefly south-western)' and add: Also **zurr**. (Earlier and later examples.)

1803 G. COLMAN *John Bull* I. i. 16 *Dan.* I be ready, zur. **1921** H. WILLIAMSON *Beautiful Years* 117 Beg pardon, zur, but can't abide here while they be a-reapin'. **1977** F. PARRISH *Fire in Barley* iii. 30 A-ben sleepen in m'bed, zurr, 'tel cock d'crow for dawnen.

Zurich (zūᵊ·rik, ‖ tsū·riχʸ). Also **Zürich**. The name of a city on Lake Zurich in Switzerland, used *attrib.* to designate porcelain manufactured there in the eighteenth century.

1870 C. SCHREIBER *Jrnl.* 18 Feb. (1911) I. 71 Crispin still possessed the Zurich cups we saw there two years ago. **1875** *Ibid.* 26 Feb. 360 Some very pretty Zurich écuelles. **1897** F. LITCHFIELD *Chaffers's Marks Pott. & Porc.* (ed. 8) 530 Mr. H. Angst..has the most important collection of Zurich porcelain known. **1949** W. B. HONEY *European Ceramic Art* 42 Zurich porcelain at its best shows a belated Rococo and a rare beauty of colour. **1981** *Times* 25 May 10/5 Among features in the sale..were.. Zurich porcelains. *Ibid.*, £3,721, for an attractive Zurich hunting group of about 1770.

b. *Zurich gnome*: see *GNOME¹ 1 c.

1970 K. GILES *Death in Church* vii. 168, I arranged to 'buy' it from our Swiss agent, a nice Zurich gnome. **1972** D. LEES *Zodiac* 11, I certainly wasn't going to break up the Zurich gnome's marriage—not even for money. **1981** 'D. JORDAN' *Double Red* ii. 14 Those who really believe in Zürich gnomes and see in each day's gold fixing the action of some giant hidden hand.

‖ **zurla** (zūᵊ·ɹlă). *Mus.* Also **surla**. [Serbo-Croatian, f. next.] A kind of oriental shawm introduced into Yugoslavia by gypsies.

1940 C. SACHS *Hist. Musical Instr.* (1942) xiii. 249 When the drums join in, the two larger oboes accompany the sibs in the lower octave. This must be an old custom, for the same is true for the Turkish oboes *surle* played by Croatian gypsies. **1953** Y. ARBATSKY *Beating Tupan in Central Balkans* 4 We may assume that the Persian word zurnā is the root from which zurna, zurne, zurla and surla were derived. **1957** A. BAINES *Woodwind Instruments & their Hist.* ix. 229 We have only the notion, based on general historical grounds, that the parent instrument of the staple-bearing kind is the Middle Eastern shawm *surna*, a variety of which, frequently heard at our folk-dance festival, is the Macedonian *zurla*. **1962** *Jrnl. Gypsy Lore Soc.* XLI. 43 The Gypsies in Balkan countries used, at the beginning of the nineteenth century, the following musical instruments: tambourine, cymbalum, drum and zurla (a wind-instrument of Oriental origin). **1975** L. PICKEN *Folk Mus. Instr. of Turkey* IV. 499 The facts suggest that the modern Turkish shawm represents a development independent of the shawms of Western Europe. The two types co-exist today in Yugoslavia, where the *zurla* has a 'head' comparable with that of Anatolian and Thracian *zurna*. *Ibid.* 500 To group (b) belong the shawms-with-finger-holes of Macedonia, both those of Yugoslavia—*zurla*..and those of Greece—*zourná*.

‖ **zurna** (zūᵊ·ɹna). *Mus.* Also 9 **zourna**; 20– **surna**. [Turk.; cf. Pers. *surnā*.] A Turkish pipe resembling a bagpipe or shawm.

1870 C. ENGEL *Descr. Catal. Mus. Instr. S. Kensington Museum* 17 *Zourna*, a kind of hautboy... The *zourna* has usually a mouthpiece consisting of a brass tube. *Hindustan. Ibid.* 28 Zourna Vezirli [from Turkey]. **1876** STAINER & BARRETT *Dict. Mus. Terms* 456/1 *Zurna*, a Turkish wind instrument similar in character to the oboe. **1941** N. BESSARABOV *Anc. European Mus. Instr.* 20 Nine musicians playing the *zurna* (a kind of oboe), including their chief..the bandmaster. **1953,** etc. [see prec.]. **1965** *Listener* 24 June 940/3 Speaking of the mouth-blown cylindrical pipes which she inclines to regard as ancestors of the modern clarinet, would she be referring to the *zurna*, sometimes known as *duduk*? **1976** *Southern Even. Echo* (Southampton) 11 Nov. 20/2 If you are genuinely interested in the derivation, history and characteristics of musical instruments,..you will find everything from the accordion to the zurna in 'Musical Instruments of the World'.

zussmanite (zɒ·smănəit). *Min.* [f. the name of J. *Zussman* (b. 1924), English mineralogist + -ITE¹.] A rhombohedral aluminosilicate of potassium, ferrous iron, and other metals, $K(Fe^{2+},Mg,Mn)_{13}(Si,Al)_{18}O_{42}(OH)_{14}$, found as pale green tabular crystals.

1965 S. O. AGRELL et al. in *Amer. Mineralogist* L. 278 (*heading*) Deerite, howieite and zussmanite, three new minerals from the Franciscan of the Laytonville district, Mendocino Co., California. **1980** *Mineral. Mag.* XLIII. 611/2 Zussmanite compositions at their most aluminium-rich become quasi-isochemical with stilpnomelane and in many rocks a back-reaction can be seen with a fine-grained stilpnomelane fuzz (brown in colour) developing along cracks in the zussmanite.

‖ **zut** (züt), *int.* [Fr.] An exclamation expressing annoyance, contempt, impatience, etc.

1915 W. OWEN *Let.* 25 July (1967) 350 For Gautier... Zut! I never read him. **1923** W. J. LOCKE *Moordius & Co.* ix. 129 'Well, what if I am?' she said, rebelliously. '*Zut!*..Why shouldn't I?' **1967** R. PETRIE *Foreign Bodies* ii. 23 If his own wife read such trash as the Professor's, he reflected, *zut!* he'd have something to say. **1980** A. HUNTER *Honfleur Decision* x. 136 *Zut!* Come without your gun, or do not come at all.

zuur-veldt. (Earlier examples.)

1785 G. FORSTER tr. *Sparrman's Voy. to Cape Good Hope* I vi. 249 What are termed by the colonists *Zuurvelden* or *Sour-fields*, are such as lie somewhat higher and cooler than the shore, and thus are better supplied with rain than the other plains. **1827** T. PHILIPPS *Scenes in Albany & Caffer-Land* 119 The pasture is all *Zureveldt*.

Zu-zu, var. *ZOU-ZOU. **zwart wit pens,** var. *SWARTWITPENS.

zwieback (tsvī·bak). Also **zwei-**. Pl. -(s). [a. Ger., f. *zwie* (*zwei*) twice + *backen* BAKE.] A (sweet) rusk or biscuit made by baking a small loaf, and then toasting slices until they are dry and crisp.

1894 *N.Y. Weekly Tribune* 14 Mar. 5/3 These Zweiback will keep for a long time if put in a dry place. **1907** *Practitioner* Apr. 552 On the seventh day, some well-cooked rice and a few softened Zwieback are allowed. **1925** [see *BISCUITY *a.*]. **1949** M. MEAD *Male & Female* xiii. 273 The game of 'I give you something and you give me something' s not necessarily cross-sexe when it is based on bottles and zwieback. **1957** V NABOKOV *Pnin* v. 132 The various biscuits, wafers pretzels, zwiebacks. **1978** J. IRVING *World according t Garp* xv. 287 Hope gave Nicky a zwieback and he stoppe crying.

‖ **zwischenzug** (tsvi·ʃəntsūk). *Chess.* [Ger. f. *zwischen* intermediate + *zug* move.] A interim or temporizing move.

1941 F. REINFELD *Keres' Best Games of Chess* 108/ This masterly *Zwischenzug* is the finest move in the whol game. **1969** A. GLYN *Dragon Variation* ix. 292 Car thought about the move for thirty-five minutes, and ther made a temporising move, a zwischenzug, checking with his Bishop. **1978** *Spectator* 26 Aug. 27/3, 50 P-K6ch Black resigns. 50... K × P now fails to the *zwischenzug* 51 B-N3!

zwitterion (tsvi·təɪˌəi:ǫn). *Chem.* Formerly also **zwitter-ion** and with capital initial. [a. G. *zwitter-ion* (F. W. Küster 1897, in *Zeitschr. f. anorg. Chem.* XIII. 136), f. *zwitter* hermaphrodite, hybrid (OHG. *zwitar(a)n*, f. *zwi-* TWI-, TWY-) + *ion* ION.] A molecule or ion having separate positively and negatively charged atoms or groups.

1906 G. MANN *Chem. Proteids* vi. 210 Ions which are simultaneously electro-positive and electro-negative (Bredig), and which Küster calls 'Zwitter-ions', *i.e.* hermaphrodite-ions. Thus the 'Zwitter-ion' of glycocoll is the group $H_3N—CH_2—COO$. **1925** *Jrnl. Chem. Soc.* CXXVII. I. 1381 The 'isomeric change' now takes the form of a fission of the molecule by the rupture of a bond, the final ionisation of which provides the electric charges which are needed to neutralise those already present in the 'Zwitterion'. **1937** *Nature* 18 Sept. 492/1 One of the greatest advances in the understanding of the physico-chemical behaviour of amino-acids and proteins is due to the zwitterion theory introduced by Bjerrum in 1923. **1948** *Endeavour* VII. 85/2 The products of [penicillin] inactivation are *zwitter-ions*. **1949** E. CHAIN in H. W. Florey et al. *Antibiotics* II. xxii. 847 The penicilloic acids are zwitterions with two acid groups and one basic group. **1968** D. W. WOOD *Princ. Animal Physiol.* iii. 35 At the pH of living cells, lecithin forms a balanced zwitterion. **1982** R. M. SCHULTZ in T. M. Devlin *Textbk. Biochem.* ii. 41 It is useful to calculate the exact pH at which an amino acid is electrically neutral and in its zwitterion form.

Hence **zwi:tterio·nic** *a.*

1946 *Nature* 16 Nov. 703/1 A hybrid structure derived from a number of ionic states of which there are..eight zwitterionic forms. **1949** ABRAHAM & HEATLEY in H. W. Florey et al. *Antibiotics* I. ii. 94 These [substances]..may be neutral, acidic, basic, or zwitterionic. **1981** *Biochimica & Biophysica Acta* DCLXVIII. 117 Vesicles of zwitterionic phosphatidylcholine.

Zydeco (zəi·dĕkō). *U.S. Blacks.* Also **zodico, zolo go.** [? Creole pronunc. of Fr. *les haricots* from dance-tune title 'Les haricots sont pas salés'.] A kind of Afro-American dance music of southern Louisiana; the dance itself. Also *attrib.*

1949 in Leadbitter & Slaven *Blues Records 1943–66* (1968) 136 Zologo (Organ Blues)—1. Gold Star 669. **1960** M. MCCORMICK notes to LP record *Treasury of Field Recordings I* 31 Two local groups..have achieved nation-wide record sales with their interpretations of Zydeco music. **1964** *Amer. Folk Music Occasional* I. 28 'Zydeco' is a mixture of the blues and the music of the early Acadian settlers and is very popular in Southern Louisiana and along the Southeast Texas Gulf Coast especially in Houston, Texas. **1964** [see *rub-board* s.v. *RUB *v.*¹ 18]. **1979** *Guardian* 13 June 10/7 [The Twisters] have two records currently available here: Doin' The Zydeco..and Zy-De-Blue. **1979** N. SPITZER notes to LP record *Zodico: Louisiana Creole Music* 3/1 *Zodico* refers to the fast, syncopated dance numbers in a Creole band's repertoire as well as to the dance event itself. **1984** *New Yorker* 1 Oct. 29/3 Clifton Chenier strapped on his accordion to play some loud, rollicking Creole music known as *zydeco*.

zygnomic (zəi·gnǫmik), *a. Law.* [f. ZYG(O- + Gr. νόμ-ος law + -IC.] In the terminology of A. Kocourek: 'a jural relation which involves an act the evolution of which directly abridges..the freedom of the servus in the enjoyment..of the substance of a legal advantage'. Opp. *MESONOMIC *a.*

1926 A. KOCOUREK in *California Law Rev.* XV. 19 Zygnomic relation is a legal relation which (i) directly constrains the *servus* of the relation in his physical freedom *and* (ii) with the support of the law. **1927,** etc. [see *MESONOMIC *a.*]. **1927** [see *REGENERABLE *a.*]. **1930** A. KOCOUREK *Introd. to Science of Law* iv. 294 A zygnomic relation is one which works an immediate and direct constraint on human freedom at a given moment with the support of the law.

zygo-. Add: **zygoge·nesis** [-GENESIS], reproduction involving the formation of a zygote; so **zygogene·tic** *a.*; **zy·gomere** *Cytology* [*-MERE], a site on a chromosome thought to be responsible for the initiation of pairing between homologous chromosomes during zygotene in eukaryotes; **zygone·ma** *Cytology* [a. F. *zygonema* (V. Grégoire 1907, in *La Cellule* XXIV. 371), f. Gr. νῆμα thread], † (*a*) a chromosome at zygotene; (*b*) = *ZYGOTENE; now *rare*; **zy·gophore** *Bot.* [-PHORE], a differentiated hypha in Zygomycetes that takes part in conjugation; hence **zygopho·ric** *a.*; **zy·gosome** *Cytology* [ad. G. *zygosom* (E. Strasburger 1904, in *Sitzungsber. d. k. Preuss. Akad. d. Wissensch.* 606): see *-SOME[4]] = *BIVALENT *sb.*

1950 *Adv. Genetics* III. 194 The most common mode of animal reproduction is, however, sexual reproduction or gamogony or zygogenesis. *Ibid.* 198 In other parthenogenetic animals both parthenogenetic and zygogenetic reproduction are present. **1973** B. J. WILLIAMS *Evolution & Human Origins* iii. 37/2 It [*sc.* random genetic drift] includes all events that lead to sampling error in random zygogenesis. **1978** *Biol. Bull* CLV. 273 (*heading*) *Artemia* hemoglobins: genetic variation in parthenogenetic and zygogenetic populations. **1966** J. SYBENGA in *Genetica* XXXVII. 188 General occurrence of localization of the function of initiation of chromosome pairing (long-distance attraction) in discrete units on specific loci is considered a useful working hypothesis. In analogy to 'centromere', 'chromomere' and 'telomere' the term '*zygomere*' is proposed for such units. **1981** *Cytologia* XLVI. 527 Since the bivalent formation has not been disturbed, at least one of two zygomeres seems to be able to have a complete activity. **1911** *Q. Jrnl. Microsc. Sci.* LVII. 32 The debatable stages of the meiotic prophases in which parasyndesis and its associated phenomena occur—leptonema, zygonema..—have been dealt with by many experienced cytologists. *Ibid.* 33 By the time the zygonema is fairly far advanced we do get appearances not unlike what may occasionally..be found in the condensation of a somatic chromosome. **1976** *Nature* 8 Apr. 534/2 It is generally known that during zygonema (stages XII–XIV in rat spermatogenesis) the homologous sets of sister chromatid pairs begin to come together and associate with one another. **1904** A. F. BLAKESLEE in *Science* 3 June 866/1 In all species of both homo- and heterothallic groups..the swollen portions (progametes) from which the gametes are cut off do not grow toward each other..but arise as a result of the stimulus of contact between more or less differentiated hyphæ (zygophores). **1970** J. WEBSTER *Introd. Fungi* II. ii. 116 When two compatible strains approach each other aerial club-shaped branches or zygophores develop which show directional growth towards zygophores of the opposite strain. Zygophores of the same strain repel each other. **1904** Zygophoric [see *HETEROGAMIC *a.*]. **1978** *Canad. Jrnl. Bot.* LVI. 1061 One or more slender, lateral zygophoric filaments proliferate from the subterminal portion of a septate, erect hypha. **1905** *Ann. Bot.* XIX. 249 A similar operation of the law of chance has been suggested by Strasburger ('04) in the separation of the chromatin granules as a result of the division of the 'zygosome'. **1910** [see *parasynaptic* adj. s.v. *PARA-[1] 1]. **1974** *Jrnl. Heredity* LXV. 257/1 The varying amounts of the *q* segments present in the zygosome may account in large measure for the physical and mental deviation of these mongoloid patients from the usual spectrum of characteristics typical of mongoloids bearing three independent chromosomes 21.

zygocactus (zəi·gokæktŏs). *Bot.* Also **Zygo-.** [mod.L. (K. Schumann 1890, in C. F. Martius *Flora Braziliensis* IV. II. 223): see ZYGO- and CACTUS.] Any cactus of the Brazilian genus *Zygocactus* (sometimes included in *Schlumbergera*), the members of which have branched and jointed stems bearing zygomorphic flowers in various shades of red, and are freq. grown as houseplants.

1950 V. HIGGINS *Cactus Grower's Guide* iv. 54 Two other Epiphyllums which have been much cultivated are now placed in Schlumbergera—*Schlumbergera Gaertneri* and *S. Russelliana*; both are similar in habit to Zygocactus but the flowers are regular. **1962** *Amateur Gardening* 24 Mar. 29/1 Zygocactus should be watered throughout the year. **1980** *Daily Tel.* 24 Sept. 14/5 Among the new plants on show are..zygocactus in pastel colours with a future as room plants, from Rochford.

zygology (zəigǫ·lŏdʒi). [f. ZYGO- + -OLOGY: coined by Mr. C. G. Hardie, Magdalen College, Oxford.] The branch of technology concerned with joining and fastening. Hence **zygolo·gical** *a.*, **zygo·logist.**

1970 *Assembly & Fastener Engin.* Oct. 48/3 We at Oxford Polytechnic are now offering courses in Zygology. *Ibid.*, I do not wish to suggest that all your readers should be considered as practising zygologists. **1971** *New Electronics* May 56 (Advt.), We are zygologists—experts in fastening techniques. We have specialised in riveting for years. **1973** *Oxford Times* 14 Dec. 40 (Advt.), Oxford Polytechnic... Postgraduate diploma in zygology. **1976** W. C. WAKE *Adhesion* i. 4 Adhesion science should thus include adhesives and joints under its wing and is, if the reader likes classification, a branch of zygology. **1978** *Engin. Materials & Design* Apr. 37/2 Not that adhesion is the only zygological process available for joining one piece of plastics material to another.

Zygomycetes (zəigomәisī·tīz), *sb. pl. Bot.* Also (*rare*) **zygo-.** [mod.L., ad. G. *Zygomyceten* (O. Brefeld *Bot. Untersuchungen über Schimmelpilze* (1872) I. 53): see ZYGO-, MYCETES *sb. pl.*] A class of saprophytic and parasitic fungi in which sexual reproduction is by fusion of usu. similar gametangia to produce a zygospore and asexual reproduction is by means of non-motile spores; fungi of this class. Occas. in *sing.* **Zygomycete** (-məi·sīt). Hence **zygomyce·tous** *a.*

[**1874** *Q. Jrnl. Microsc. Sci.* XIV. 56 Brefeld does not admit that *Chætocladium* and *Piptocephalis* possess sporangia, but only conidia. According to his views, therefore, the term *Zygomycetes* is more expressive than *Mucorini*, which he restricts to the sporangiferous *Zygomycetes*. This, however, appears to us founded on an error.] **1887** H. E. F. GARNSEY tr. *A. de Bary's Compar. Morphol. & Biol. of Fungi* vi. 345 This coincidence with a fixed period of the year is at least not a general rule in the zygospores of the Zygomycetes. **1928** C. W. DODGE tr. *Gäumann's Compar. Morphol. Fungi* xxxvi. 621 A convergent development has apparently occurred in the Zygomycetous sporangia which have become gonotoconts. **1930** H. M. FITZPATRICK *Lower Fungi. Phycomycetes* ii. 34 The origin of the Zygomycete line is somewhat more obscure, though forms possessing one or more undoubted zygomycetous characters exist among the Ancylistales and Chytridiales. **1937** GWYNNE-VAUGHAN & BARNES *Struct. & Developm. Fungi* (ed. 2) 16 The Zygomycetes..are the first fungi to colonise dung. **1952** C. J. ALEXOPOULOS *Introd. Mycol.* vii. 180 Such a theory is based almost entirely on the asexual cycle, the zygomycetous reproduction having no counterpart in the present-day Saprolegniaceae which might give us a clue to its origin. **1978** *Bio Sysems* X. 97/2 There are several eukaryote groups where there is, so far, no solidly based evidence for a flagellate ancestry: ..(4) zygomycete fungi. **1979** I. K. ROSS *Biol. of Fungi* xiii. 378 There are three main methods by which spores are actively released: the bursting of a turgid cell (ascomycetes and some zygomycetes), the rounding off of a surface under tension (some zygomycetes, some basidiomycetes) and the so-called ballistospore discharge. **1982** *Phytopathology* LXXII. 1102 (*heading*) Synoptic keys to the genera and species of zygomycetous mycorrhizal fungi.

zygosity (zəigǫ·siti). *Genetics.* [f. ZYGOS(IS + -ITY.] **a.** The genetic relationship of twins, triplets, etc., in respect of their being either monozygotic or dizygotic.

1952 *New Biol.* XII. 42 Instead of exchanging skin between the twin animals whose zygosity it is desired to establish, grafts are being transplanted from both of them to a third, unrelated recipient. **1971** *Nature* 23 July 277/1 Before recent developments with marker genes, it was not possible to assign with certainty the zygosity of a substantial proportion of twin pairs. **1978** *Jrnl. R. Soc. Med.* LXXI. 311/2 The type of twinning and determination of zygosity are given attention.

b. The degree of genetic similarity between alleles which determines whether an individual is homozygotic or heterozygotic for the characteristic expressed.

1967 *Jrnl. Clin. Investigation* XLVI. 681 (*heading*) Relationship between Rh_0(D) zygosity and red cell Rh_0(D) antigen content in family members. *Ibid.*, The members of two families showed a poor correspondence between antibody binding and zygosity. **1972** *Transplantation* XIV. 793/1 Efforts have been made to determine HL-A zygosity of unrelated subjects by use of the gene-dose effect.

zygospore. Add: Hence **zygospo·ric** *a.*, of the nature of or producing zygospores.

1906 *Science* 27 July 122/2 Zygosporic cultures of the 'Harvest Strain' have..been kept running for nearly ten years. **1970** J. WEBSTER *Introd. Fungi* II. ii. 141 In some species [of the genus *Endogone*]..the fruit-body is entirely zygosporic.

zygote. Add: **zygotic** *a.* (examples); **zygo·tically** *adv.*, in the zygote; in terms of the zygote.

1909 W. E. CASTLE *Inheritance in Rabbits* (Carnegie Inst. Publ. No. 114) 58 The enumeration of the conceivable different varieties of gray rabbit, all alike in appearance but all different in breeding capacity, *i.e.*, of different zygotic formula. **1915** *Jrnl. Genetics* V. 45 Zygotically therefore the three forms [of rabbit] may be represented thus: Self-coloured..CCSS, Himalayan..CCss, Albino..ccss. **1931** *Ibid.* XXIV. 448 It is probable that the new combinations will be less successful than the old, both zygotically and gametically. **1977** J. COHEN *Reproduction* ix. 163 The second phase of embryology begins, controlled by zygotic genes. **1980** *Genetics* XCVI. 187 The possibility that essential loci in the zeste-white region of the *Drosophila melanogaster X* chromosome are expressed both maternally and zygotically has been tested.

zygotene (zəi·gotīn). *Cytology.* [a. F. *zygotène* (V. Grégoire 1907, in *La Cellule* XXIV. 371): see ZYGO- and *-TENE.] The second stage of the prophase of meiosis, following leptotene, during which homologous chromosomes begin to pair.

1911 *Jrnl. Morphol.* XXII. 752 This view..goes on to show that after the last spermatogonial mitosis the chromosomes become very delicate slender threads, the leptotene condition..; these then approximate themselves parallel into pairs making the zygotene condition. **1939** [see *DIAKINESIS]. **1974** *Nature* 9 Aug. 469/2 At leptotene of meiotic prophase in many organisms, all the telomeres become gathered together and attached to a small area of the nuclear envelope, presumably so as to facilitate pairing during zygotene.

Zyklon (zəi·klǫn). Also **Cyclon.** [a. G. *Zyklon*, of unknown etym.] Hydrogen cyanide adsorbed on, or released from, a carrier in the form of small tablets, used as a fumigant and formerly as a poison gas. Usu. as *Zyklon B.*

[**1926** *Official Gaz.* (U.S. Patent Office) 9 Nov. 298/1 Deutsche Gesellschaft für Schädlingsbekämpfung, m.b.H., Frankfort-on-the-Main... *Zyklon*... Apparatus for measuring the quantities of substances which generate poisonous gases—for instance, hydrocyanic acid.] **1939** METCALF & FLINT *Destructive & Useful Insects* (ed. 2) ix. 281 The other type of dry cyanides, such as the zyklon products, undergo no chemical change when exposed. **1944** *Chem. Abstr.* XXXVIII. 3416 The application of Cyclon B (0.4 g./cc.) for 24 hrs. destroyed all insects but imparted a peculiar taste to the tobaccos. **1964** L. DEIGHTON *Funeral in Berlin* xxxi. 169 With Cyclon B they killed two and a half million at Auschwitz. **1975** W. CRAIG *Strasbourg Legacy* (1976) i. 9 Former SS soldiers.. had functioned so anonymously in the camps that hardly anyone lived who could identify them as guards once manning machine guns or dropping Zyklon B tablets into gas chambers. **1977** *Times* 8 June 9/7 [He] was tried and acquitted at Nürnberg in 1948 for supplying the SS with Zykon-B gas. **1978** H. WOUK *War & Remembrance* xi. 111 Zyklon B, the powerful insecticide they have been using right along at the camp to fumigate the barracks, may be the surprisingly simple solution.

zymo-. Add: **zy·mogram** *Biochem.* and *Genetics*, a strip of electrophoretic medium showing enzymes separated by a technique such as zone electrophoresis.

1957 HUNTER & MARKERT in *Science* 28 June 1295/2 We propose the term *zymogram* to refer to strips in which the location of enzymes is demonstrated by histochemical methods. **1978** *Nature* 2 Mar. 77/2 The high degree of gene duplication in these species often confounds the genetic interpretation of zymograms. For example, how many loci code for an enzyme represented by a single electrophoretic band? **1981** *Histochemistry* LXXIII. 311 Electrofocused zymograms display species and organ differences.

zymosan (zəi·mosæn). *Biochem.* [f. ZYMO-, after *glucosan, hexosan.*] An insoluble polysaccharide of the cell wall of yeast, used in the assay of properdin.

1943 E. E. ECKER et al. in *Jrnl. Immunol.* XLVII. 185 The preparation of human complement lacking in third component. The third component is specifically removed from or inactivated in human serum by the insoluble carbohydrate prepared from fresh yeast... The insoluble carbohydrate is hereafter referred to as 'zymosan'. **1973** *Sci. Amer.* Nov. 60/3 The incubation of normal blood serum..with certain polysaccharides derived from microbial cells (such as zymosan, a carbohydrate of the yeast cell membrane) gives rise to enzymes that activate the complement factors C3 and C5.

Zyrenian, var. *SIRYENIAN *sb.* and *a.*

Zyrian (zi·riăn), *sb.* and *a.* Also **Syrian, Syryane, Syryen,** (and esp.) **Zyryan.** [ad. Russ. *Zÿryánin*: see -IAN.] **A.** *sb.* A member of the Komi people of northern central U.S.S.R. **b.** The language of this people; = *KOMI b. **B.** *adj.* Of or pertaining to this people or their language.

1886 *Encycl. Brit.* XXI. 79/2 The Permians,..including ..the Zyrians in Vologda, Archangel, Vyatka, and Perm. **1926** *Chambers's Encycl.* VIII. 101/1 The Syriăn is spoken by a large population in the districts of Perm, Viatka, Archangel, and Vologda. **1932, 1933** [see *PERMIAN *a.* (*sb.*) 2]. **1942** [see *KOMI]. **1948** D. DIRINGER *Alphabet* II. viii. 482 Other peoples..such as the Zyryans or Syryans (now called Komi). **1951** W. K. MATTHEWS *Languages U.S.S.R.* iii. 20 The Yuraks have loans from Zyryan (Komi), a Finnic language. *Ibid.* 25 Zyryan resistance to the Russians was less dogged and implacable than Ugrian. **1955** *Trans. Philol. Soc. 1954* 99 The forms are: Norwegian Lappish *miettā*..Syryane *ma* [etc.]. **1972** *Language* XLVIII. 848, 7b is given by Hockett for 'German,..French.., Zyryan'. **1978** K. RÉDEI (*title*) Zyrian folklore texts.

BIBLIOGRAPHY

This is a list of the works most frequently quoted in the four volumes of this *Supplement to the O.E.D.*, other than those already listed in the bibliography (1933) to the *O.E.D.* itself.

No revision of the bibliography to the *O.E.D.* has been attempted.

The information presented in this new bibliography reflects the work of many people. Since it was begun in 1963 those primarily involved have been (in chronological order) N. C. Sainsbury (1963–6), Miss J. M. Hawkins (1966–7), A. J. Augarde (1967–9), M. W. Grose (1969–72), G. D. Hargreaves (1973–5), and J. Paterson (since 1975), as well as members of the Department's permanent library-research team. The bibliography was assembled in its final form during 1982.

Publications of learned institutions are listed here under the name of the institution; translations under the name of the translator. The country or city of publication has not usually been given except for newspapers published outside London, and U.K. editions of books published in an earlier year abroad. Authors' dates of birth and death are usually given when any posthumous works are listed.

November 1982

J. Paterson
Bibliographical Editor

A

'Aarons, E. S.' (Paul Ayres & Edward Ronns) *Assignment treason* 1956
Abbott, David *Inorganic chemistry* 1965
Abbott, John Henry Macartney *Tommy Cornstalk* 1902
Abbs, Akosua *Ashanti boy* 1959
Abercrombie, David *English phonetic texts* 1964
Problems and principles: studies in the teaching of English as a second language 1956
—— et al. eds. *In honour of Daniel Jones: papers contributed on the occasion of his eightieth birthday* 1964
Aberdeen Press and Journal 1922–39 (continued as *Press and Journal*)
Abraham, George Dixon *Modern mountaineering* 1933
Abraham, Louis Arnold & Hawtrey, Stephen Charles eds. *A parliamentary dictionary* 1956
— (ed. 2) 1964
Abrahams, Beth-Zion tr. *The life of Glückel* [Segal] *of Hameln 1646–1724, written by herself* 1962
Abrahams, Peter Henry *Dark testament* 1942
The path of thunder 1952
Return to Goli 1953
Wild conquest 1951
Abrahams, Roger D. ed. *Jump-rope rhymes: a dictionary* 1969
Positively black 1970
Académie des Sciences (Paris) *Compte rendu hebdomadaire des séances* 1835–
Academy of Natural Sciences of Philadelphia *Proceedings* 1841–
Academy of Sciences of the U.S.S.R. *Doklady* [French ed.] 1935–47
Doklady: earth science sections 1959–
Soviet physics: Doklady [Eng. trans.] 1956–
Accountant, The 1874–
Achebe, Chinua *Girls at war, and other stories* 1972
A man of the people 1966
Things fall apart 1958
Ackerley, Joe Randolph (1896–1967) *My father and myself* 1968
Acland, Leopold George Dyke (1876–1948) *The early Canterbury runs* (ser. 1) 1930
— (complete ed.) 1951
Acronyms dictionary (Gale Research Co.) 1960 (also later editions used, and supplements with title *New acronyms and initialisms*)
Acta crystallographica 1948–
Acta radiologica 1920–
Acton, Harold Mario Mitchell *Memoirs of an aesthete* 1948
Actors by daylight; or, Pencillings in the pit 2 vols. 1838–9
Adami, John George *The principles of pathology* 2 vols. 1909–10
Adams, Andy *The outlet* 1905
Adams, Bertram Martin ('Bill') *Ships and women: an autobiography* 1936
Adams, Briggs Kilburn *The American spirit: letters* 1918
Adams, Carsbie Clifton, et al. *Space flight* 1958
Adams, Edwin Plimpton tr. *A. Einstein's The meaning of relativity* 1922
Adams, Frank Davis *Aeronautical dictionary* 1959
Adams, Ramon Frederick *Western words: a dictionary of the range, cow camp and trail* 1944
— (rev. ed.) 1968
Adams, Richard George *Shardik* 1974
Watership Down 1972
Adamson, Arthur Wilson *A textbook of physical chemistry* 1973
Adburgham, Alison *Shops and shopping, 1800–1914* 1964
Adby, Paul Raymond & Dempster, Michael Alan Howarth *Introduction to optimization methods* 1974
Addyman, Frank T. tr. *A. M. Villon's Practical treatise on the leather industry* 1901
Ade, George (1866–1944) *Artie* 1896
Doc' Horne 1899
Fables in slang 1900 (UK 1902)
Forty modern fables 1901
Hand-made fables 1920
In Babel 1903
Knocking the neighbors 1912
Letters ed. T. Tobin 1973
More fables 1900 (UK 1902)
People you know 1903
True bills 1904
Adelphi, The 1923–7; 1930–
Admiralty *See* United Kingdom. Admiralty
Advances in chemistry series 1950–
Advances in genetics 1947–
Adventure (New York) 1910–
Advisory Committee for Aeronautics *See* United Kingdom. Advisory ——
Advocate-News (Barbados) 1895–
Aeronautical journal 1897–1923; 1968–
Aeronautical Research Committee (*later* Council) *See* United Kingdom. Advisory Committee for Aeronautics
Aëronautical Society of Great Britain *Annual report* 1866–95
Aeronautics 1939–
Aeroplane, The 1911–68 (with title *The Aeroplane and astronautics* 1959–62, and *The Aeroplane and commercial aviation news* 1962–8)
Aeroplane spotter, The 1941–8
Aflalo, Frederick George *A sketch of the natural history of Australia* 1896
Africa. Journal of the International Institute of African Languages and Culture 1928–40; 1943–
African encyclopedia 1974
Agar, Wilfred Eade *Cytology, with special reference to the Metazoan nucleus* 1920
Agate, James Evershed *More first nights* 1937
Red letter nights 1944
Age, The (Melbourne) 1859–
Agger, Leo Thomas *Introduction to electricity* 1971
Agricultural and biological chemistry 1955–
Agriculture 1939–
Aharoni, Joseph *The special theory of relativity* 1959
Aiken, Joan Delano *The butterfly picnic* 1972
Last movement 1977
Aiken, John *Nightly deadshade* 1971
Ainsworth, Leopold *Confessions of a planter in Malaya* 1933
'Ainsworth, Milo' (Peter Fison) *Murder is catching* 1959
Ainsworth's magazine 1842–54
Air Conference [London], 1920 *Proceedings* 1920
Air News (Chicago) 1941–6
Aircraft engineering 1929–
'Aird, Catherine' (Kinn Hamilton McIntosh) *Henrietta who?* 1968
Airth, Rennie *Snatch!* 1969
Aitken, Adam Jack, McIntosh, A., & Pálsson, H. eds. *Edinburgh studies in English and Scots* 1971
Aitken, William *Automatic telephone systems* 3 vols., 1921–4
Aiton, William *Hortus Kewensis; or, A catalogue of plants cultivated in the Royal Botanic Garden at Kew* 3 vols. 1789
— (ed. 2, ed. by W. T. Aiton) 5 vols. 1810–13
Albanesi, Effie Maria *For love of Anne Lambert* 1910
Albee, Edward *Who's afraid of Virginia Woolf?* 1962
Albert, Abraham Adrian *Modern higher algebra* 1937 (UK 1938)
Albert, Arthur Lemuel *Fundamentals of telephony* 1943
Radio fundamentals 1948
Alberta historical review 1957–
Albery, James (1838–89) *Dramatic works* ed. W. Albery 2 vols. 1939
Albright, William Foxwell *The archaeology of Palestine* 1949
Alcock, Leslie *By South Cadbury* 1972
Alcott, Louisa May *Little men* 1871
An old-fashioned girl 1870
Alden, William Livingston *The adventures of Jimmy Brown* 1885
Aldington Richard *All men are enemies* 1933
The colonel's daughter 1931
Death of a hero 1929
The strange life of Charles Waterton 1782–1865 1949
Aldiss, Brian Wilson *The airs of earth* 1963
The moment of eclipse 1970
A soldier erect 1971
—— & Harrison, Harry Max eds. *Decade: the 1950's* 1976
Decade: the 1940's 1975
'Alexander, Mrs.' (Mrs. Annie French Hector) *A choice of evils* 3 vols. 1894
Alexander, James Edward *An expedition of discovery into the interior of Africa* 2 vols. 1838
Sketches in Portugal during the Civil War of 1834 1835
Alexander, Jerome *Colloid chemistry, theoretical and applied* 6 vols. 1926–46
Alexander, Samuel *Space, time and deity* 2 vols. 1920
Alexander, William *Sketches of life among my ain folk* 1875
Alexopoulos, Constantine John *Introductory mycology* 1952
— (ed. 2) 1962
Algren, Nelson *The man with the golden arm* 1949
A walk on the wild side 1956 (UK 1957)
Allbeury, Theo Edward Le Bouthillier ('Ted') *A choice of enemies* 1973
The lantern network 1978
The only good German 1976
Snowball 1974
The special collection 1975
Allee, Warder Clyde *Animal aggregations: a study in general sociology* 1931

Allen, Arthur Charles *The skin: a clinicopathological treatise* 1954
— (ed. 2) 1967
Allen, Clifford *A textbook of psychosexual disorders* 1962
— (ed. 2) 1969
Allen, David Elliston *British tastes: an enquiry into the likes and dislikes of the regional consumer* 1968
Allen, Frederick Lewis *Only yesterday: an informal history of the nineteen-twenties* 1931
Allen, Geoffrey Freeman *British Rail after Beeching* 1966
Allen, Herbert Stanley *Photo-electricity: the liberation of electrons by light* 1913
— (ed. 2) 1925
Allen, James Lane *The choir invisible* 1897
Allen, Jules Verne *Cowboy lore* 1933
Allen, Percy Stafford (1869–1933) *Letters* ed. H. M. Allen 1939
Allen, Ralph *Home made banners* 1946
Allen, Reginald Lancelot Mountford *Colour chemistry* 1971
Allen, William Hervey *Anthony Adverse* 1933
Allen, William Sidney *Vox Graeca: a guide to the pronunciation of classical Greek* 1968
Vox Latina: a guide to the pronunciation of classical Latin 1965
Allinger, Norman Louis, et al. *Organic chemistry* 1971
Allingham, Margery Louise (1904–66) *The beckoning lady* 1955
Cargo of eagles 1968
Coroner's pidgin 1945
Dancers in mourning 1937
Death of a ghost 1934
The fashion in shrouds 1938
Flowers for the judge 1936
Hide my eyes 1958
Look to the lady 1931
Mr. Campion and others 1939
— (another ed.) 1950
More work for the undertaker 1948 (UK 1949)
Mystery mile 1930
The tiger in the smoke 1952
Traitor's purse 1941
Allingham, Philip *Cheapjack* 1934
Allis, Marguerite *English prelude* 1936
Allport, Gordon Willard *The nature of prejudice* 1954
Personality: a psychological interpretation 1937 (UK 1938)
Allum, Peter Antony *Politics and society in post-war Naples 1945–1970* 1971 (UK 1973)
Almedingen, Edith Martha *Frossia* 1943
Alston, Arthur Reginald *Test commentary* 1956
Alta California (San Francisco) 1849–91
Amateur gardening 1884–
Amateur photographer, The 1884–
Amateur radio handbook, The (Radio Society of Great Britain) 1939
— (ed. 2) 1940
— (ed. 3) 1961
— (ed. 4, with title *The radio communication handbook*) 1968
Ambler, Eric *Cause for alarm* 1938
The dark frontier 1936
Doctor Frigo 1974
The light of day 1962
The mask of Dimitrios 1939
The night-comers 1956
Uncommon danger 1937
Ambrose, Edmund Jack & Easty, Dorothy M. *Cell biology* 1970
Ambrose, Kay *The ballet-lover's pocket-book* 1943
American, The: a national journal 1880–1900
American Academy of Arts and Sciences *Bulletin* 1948–
Memoirs 1785–1818, new ser. 1826–
Proceedings 1846–1958 (continued as *Dædalus*)
American Academy of Political and Social Science *Annals* 1890–
American Association for the Advancement of Science *Proceedings* 1848–
American Association of Petroleum Geologists *Bulletin* 1918–
Memoirs 1962–
American ballads and folk songs ed. J. A. & A. Lomax 1934
American chemical journal 1879–1913
American Chemical Society *Journal* 1879–
American city, The 1909–
American Dialect Society *Publications* 1944–
American dictionary of printing and bookmaking ed. W. W. Pasko 1894
American documentation 1950–69
American dyestuff reporter 1917–
American folk music occasional 1964–
American Geological Institute *Glossary of geology and related sciences* 1957
— (ed. 2), with Supplement, 1960
— (ed. 3) 1972
American heart journal 1925–
American Institute of Electrical Engineers *Transactions* 1884–
American journal of anatomy 1901–
American journal of diseases of children 1911–
American journal of mathematics 1878–
American journal of obstetrics and diseases of women and children 1868– (from 1920 with title *American journal of obstetrics and gynecology*)
American journal of ophthalmology 1884–
American journal of pathology 1925–
American journal of philology 1880–
American journal of physical anthropology 1918–
American journal of physics 1940–
American journal of physiology 1898–
American journal of psychiatry 1921–
American journal of psychology 1887–
American journal of public health 1912–
American journal of roentgenology 1913–
American journal of sociology 1895–
American journal of the medical sciences 1827–
American machinist, The 1877–
American magazine 1906–
American mail order fashions, 1880–1900: pictures and copy reproduced from original catalogs and magazines of the times (Americana Review) 1961
American Mathematical Society *Bulletin* 1894–
Transactions 1900–
American Medical Association *Journal* 1883–
American Mercury, The 1924–
American mineralogist, The 1916–
American museum, The 1787–92; 1798
American Museum of Natural History *Bulletin* 1881–
Memoirs 1893–
American notes and queries 1857; 1888–92; 1941–50; 1962–
American Oriental Society *Journal* 1843–
American Pediatric Society *Transactions* 1888–
American Philological Association *Transactions* 1869–
American philosophical quarterly 1964–
American Philosophical Society *Proceedings* 1838–
Transactions 1769–
American pioneer, The 1842–3
American poetry review 1972–
American political science review 1906–
American railroad journal 1832–86
American review of reviews 1907–28
American Society for Metals *Metals handbook* 1936–
American Society for Testing Materials *Proceedings* 1898–
American speech 1925–
American Veterinary Medical Association *Journal* 1915–
American Water Works Association *Journal* 1914–
Americana annual, The: an encyclopedia of current events 1923–
Ames, Delano L. *Murder, maestro, please* 1952
Amin, Adibah tr. *S. Ahmad's No harvest but a thorn* 1972
Amis, Kingsley William *The anti-death league* 1966
Girl, 20 1971
I like it here 1958
Jake's thing 1978
Lucky Jim 1954 [dated 1953]
New maps of hell: a survey of science fiction 1960 (UK 1961)
Take a girl like you 1960
Amis, Martin Louis *The Rachel papers* 1973
Success 1978
Amos, Stanley William & Birkinshaw, Douglas Crosbie *Television engineering* 4 vols. 1953–8
— Vol. I, 2nd impr., rev. 1957
— Vol. II, 2nd impr., rev. 1958
Amrita Bazar Patrika (Calcutta) 1868–
Analog science fact—science fiction (title varies) 1960–
Analysis 1933–
Analyst, The: a journal of pure and applied mathematics 1874–
Anatomical record 1906–
Anderson, Gene *Coring and core analysis handbook* 1975
Anderson, J. W. *Fur trader's story* 1961
Anderson, James M. *Structural aspects of language change* 1973
Anderson, John Neil *Applied dental materials* 1956
— (ed. 2) 1961
Anderson, John Richard Lane *Death on the rocks* 1973
Anderson, Lewis Flint *The Anglo-Saxon scop* 1903
Anderson, Maxwell & Stallings, Laurence *What price glory?* in *Three American plays* 1926
Anderson, Nels *The hobo* 1923
Anderson, Robert Henry *The trees of New South Wales* 1932
— (ed. 2) 1947
Anderson, William Arnold D. ed. *Pathology* 1948
Anderson (South Carolina) *Independent* 1924– (1925–49 with title *Anderson Independent-Tribune*)
Andersson, Carl Johan *Lake Ngami; or, Explorations and discoveries, during four years' wanderings in the wilds of South Western Africa* 1856
'Andom, R.' (Alfred Walter Barrett) *We three and Troddles* 1894
Andrade, Edward Neville da Costa *The structure of the atom* 1923
— (ed. 3) 1927
Andree, Richard Vernon *Selections from modern abstract algebra* 1958
Andrew, Warren tr. *E.D.P. de Robertis's General cytology* 1948
Textbook of comparative histology 1959
Andrews, Tom Gaylord ed. *Methods of psychology* 1948
Anglo-American cataloguing rules: British text 1967
Annals of internal medicine 1927–
Annals of mathematics 1884–9; 1900–
Annals of surgery 1885–
Annals of the Congress of the U.S. See: United States. Congress. Debates *Debates and proceedings* 1789–1824
Annals of tropical medicine and parasitology 1907–
Annals See also under the names of particular institutions
Annan, Noel Gilroy *Leslie Stephen* 1951
Annual reports on the progress of chemistry (Chemical Society of London) 1904–
Annual review of microbiology 1947–
Annual review of nuclear science 1952–
Anscombe, Gertrude Elizabeth Margaret tr. *L. J. J. Wittgenstein's philosophical investigations* 1953
Ansoff, Harry Igor *Corporate strategy: an analytic approach to business policy for growth and expansion* 1965 (UK 1968)
Anson, Peter Frederick *Bishops at large* 1964
Scots fisherfolk 1950
'Anthony, Evelyn' (Eve Stephens) *The Malaspiga exit* 1974
Anthropological linguistics 1959–
Antibiotic medicine 1955–61 (from 1956 with title *Antibiotic medicine and clinical therapy*)
Antibiotics and chemotherapy 1951–62
Antiquaries' journal 1921–
Antiquity: a quarterly review of archæology 1927–
Anzac book, The: written and illustrated in Gallipoli by the men of Anzac 1916
Apel, Willi ed. *The Harvard dictionary of music* 1944
— (ed. 2) 1970
Approved names See: United Kingdom. General Medical Council
Arable farmer and vegetable grower 1966–
Arber, Agnes *The Gramineae: a study of cereal, bamboo, and grass* 1934
Water plants: a study of aquatic angiosperms 1920
Archer, William *The theatrical 'world'* 5 vols. 1894–8
Architect, The (title varies) 1869–
Architectural review 1896–
Archives internationales de pharmacodynamie et de thérapie 1898–
Archives of biochemistry 1924– (from 1951 with title *Archives of biochemistry and biophysics*)
Archives of dermatology and syphilology (title varies) 1920–
Archives of general psychiatry 1959–
Archives of internal medicine 1908–
Archives of Maryland 1883–
Archives of neurology (London) 1899–1907
Archives of neurology and psychiatry (London) 1909–50
Archives of neurology and psychiatry (Chicago) 1919–59
Archives of ophthalmology 1879–
Archives of pathology 1928–
Archives of surgery 1920–
Archivum linguisticum 1949–80 (vols. 1970–80 are new series)
Arctic terms 1955 *See* United States. Arctic, Desert and Tropic Information Centre
Ardagh, John *The new France* 1970
Ardrey, Robert *The territorial imperative* 1966 (UK 1967)
Arendt, Hannah *Origins of totalitarianism* 1951
— (new ed.) 1967
Arey, Leslie Brainerd *Developmental anatomy: a textbook and laboratory manual of embryology* 1924 (7 later editions to 1974)
Argenti, John *Management techniques: a practical guide* 1969
Argus (Melbourne) 1846–1957 (title varies)
Argyle, John Michael *Psychology and social problems* 1964
The psychology of interpersonal behaviour 1967
Religious behaviour 1958
The social psychology of work 1972

Aristotelian Society for the Systematic Study of Philosophy *Proceedings* 1888–96; 1900– *Supplementary volumes* 1918–
Arizona Daily Star (Tucson, Arizona) 1879–
ARKELL, William Joscelyn *The Jurassic system in Great Britain* 1933
ARLEN, Michael *Man's mortality* 1933
'Piracy' 1922
The romantic lady 1921
'ARMSTRONG, Anthony' (George Anthony Armstrong Willis) *Taxi!* 1930
ARMSTRONG, Charlotte *The black-eyed stranger* 1951 (UK 1952)
Seven seats to the moon 1969
ARMSTRONG, Louis *Satchmo: my life in New Orleans* 1954 (UK 1955)
ARMSTRONG, Neil, et al. *First on the moon* 1970
ARMSTRONG, Terence, ROBERTS, Brian, & SWITHINBANK, Charles *Illustrated glossary of snow and ice* 1966
ARMSTRONG, William *Stocks and stock-jobbing in Wall Street* 1848
Army and Navy Co-operative Society, Ltd. (later Army and Navy Stores, Ltd.) *Price lists* and *Catalogues* 1878–
ARNOLD, James *The Shell book of country crafts* 1968
ARNOLD, Thomas (1823–1900) *New Zealand letters of Thomas Arnold the younger, with further letters from Van Diemen's Land and letters of Arthur Hugh Clough; 1847–1851* ed. J. Bertram 1966
ARONSON, Joseph *The encyclopedia of furniture* 1965 (UK 1966)
ASBURY, Herbert *Sucker's progress: an informal history of gambling in America from the colonies to Canfield* 1938
ASH, Edward Cecil *The practical dog book* 1930
ASHFORD, Daisy *The young visiters; or, Mr. Salteena's plan* 1919
'ASHFORD, Jeffrey' (Roderic Graeme Jeffries) *The double run* 1973
Prisoner at the Bar 1969
Ashmolean Museum *See* Oxford University. Ashmolean Museum
ASHTON-WARNER, Sylvia *Spinster* 1958
Asiatic Society of Bengal (later Royal ——) *Journal* (title varies) 1832–
Asiatic Society of Japan *Transactions* 1874–
ASIMOV, Isaac *Earth is room enough* 1957 (UK 1960)
Fantastic voyage: a novel based on the screenplay by H. Kleiner 1966
Inside the atom 1956
The naked sun 1957 (UK 1958)
Aspects of translation (The Communication Research Centre, University College, London) 1958
Association football ('Know the game' series) 1948
— (rev. ed.) 1953
Association for Computing Machinery *Communications* 1958–
Journal 1954–
Association of American Geographers *Annals* 1911–
ASTON, William George *A history of Japanese literature* 1899
Astounding science fiction 1933–60
Astrophysical journal 1895–
ATHERTON, Gertrude Franklin *Perch of the devil* 1914
ATKINS, William ed. *The art and practice of printing* 6 vols. 1932–3
ATKINSON, James *Herbert & Procter's Telephony* *See* HERBERT, Thomas Ernest
ATKINSON, Richard John Copland *Field archaeology* 1946
— (ed. 2) 1953
ATTENBOROUGH, David Frederick *Life on earth: a natural history* 1979
ATTWATER, Donald ed. *The Catholic encyclopædic dictionary* 1931
— (ed. 2) 1949
The Christian churches of the East 2 vols. 1961
ATWATER, Mary (Meigs) *Crime in corn-weather* (UK ed. with title *Murder in midsummer*) 1935
AUDEN, Wystan Hugh *About the house* 1965 (UK 1966)
The age of anxiety: a baroque eclogue 1947 (UK 1948)
Another time 1940
City without walls, and other poems 1969
Collected poetry 1945
The dance of death 1933
The dyer's hand and other essays 1962 (UK 1963)
The enchafèd flood; or, The romantic iconography of the sea 1950 (UK 1951)
For the time being 1944 (UK 1945)
Homage to Clio 1960
Look, stranger! 1936
New year letter (UK title of US *The double man*) 1941
Nones 1951 (UK 1952)
The orators: an English study 1932
Poems 1930
— (ed. 2) 1933
The shield of Achilles 1955
—— & ISHERWOOD, Christopher William Bradshaw *The ascent of F6* 1936 (US 1937)
The dog beneath the skin; or, Where is Francis? 1935
Journey to a war 1939
On the frontier 1938
—— & KALLMAN, Chester tr. *E. J. Schikaneder & K. L. Giesecke's libretto to Mozart's The magic flute* 1956 (UK 1957)
—— & MACNEICE, Frederick Louis *Letters from Iceland* 1937
—— et al. *I believe* 1939: see *I believe*
AUERBACH, Charlotte *Genetics in the atomic age* 1956
Auk, The 1884–
Aurora (Philadelphia) 1790–1830; 1834–5 (title varies)
AUSTEN, Jane (1775–1817) *Letters* ed. R. W. Chapman 2 vols. or 1 vol. 1923
— (ed. 2) 1952
Minor works ed. R. W. Chapman 1954
AUSTIN, John Langshaw *How to do things with words* (lectures, 1955) 1962
Sense and sensibilia (lectures, last delivered 1959) 1962
AUSTIN, Oliver Luther *Birds of the world* 1961 (UK 1962)
Australasian, The (Melbourne) 1864–1946
Australasian post (Melbourne) 1946–52
Australia. Commonwealth Scientific and Industrial Research Organization. Division of Entomology *The insects of Australia* 1970
Australian, The 1964–
Australian encyclopaedia, The ed. A. H. Chisholm 10 vols. 1965
Australian house and garden 1948–
Australian short stories 1951 *See* MURDOCH, Walter & DRAKE-BROCKMAN, H. F. Y.
— (2nd ser.) 1963 *See* 'JAMES, Brian'
Australian women's weekly 1933–
Australians in England: a complete record of the cricket tour of 1882 1882
Autocar, The 1895–
Autocar handbook, The 1906–
Automobile engineer, The 1910– (with title *Internal combustion engineering* 1912–14)
AVEBURY, John (Lubbock), 1st Baron *The scenery of England and the causes to which it is due* 1902
AVERY, Gillian *The greatest Gresham* 1962
Aviation age 1950–8
Aviation week 1947–
AVIS, Frederick Compton *Boxing reference dictionary* 1954
The sportsman's glossary 1961
AVIS, Walter Spencer, et al. eds. *A dictionary of Canadianisms on historical principles* 1967
Awake! (Watchtower Bible and Tract Soc.) 1919–
AYCKBOURN, Alan *Relatively speaking* 1968
AYER, Alfred Jules *The central questions of philosophy* 1973
The foundations of empirical knowledge 1940
Language, truth and logic 1936
— (ed. 2) 1946
Philosophical essays 1954
The problem of knowledge 1956
AYERST, David *'Guardian': biography of a newspaper* 1971

B

B., W. *See* BAUCKE, William
B.B.C. *See* British Broadcasting Corporation
BP shield international 1961–
B.S.I. *See* British Standards Institution
BABCOCK, Ernest Brown & CLAUSEN, Roy Elwood *Genetics in relation to agriculture* 1918
BABSON, Marian *Cover-up story* 1971
The stalking lamb 1974
BACH, Emmon *An introduction to transformational grammars* 1964
BACHARACH, Alfred Louis ed. *British music of our time* 1946
ed. *The musical companion* 1934
BACHMANN, Lawrence Paul *The ultimate act* 1972
BACON, Alice Mabel *Japanese girls and women* 1891
A Japanese interior. 1893
BACON, Gertrude *Balloons, airships and flying machines* 1905
BACON, Thomas *First impressions and studies from nature in Hindostan* 1837
Bacteriological reviews 1937–
BADDELEY, V. C. C. *See* CLINTON-BADDELEY, Victor Clinton
BADEN-POWELL, Robert Stevenson Smyth *Scouting for boys* 1908
BAGBY, George William (1828–83) *The old Virginia gentleman, and other sketches* ed. T. N. Page 1910
BAGEHOT, Walter (1826–77) *Collected works* ed. N. St. John-Stevas 1965–
BAGG, Lyman Hotchkiss *Four years at Yale* 1871
BAGGS, Thomas Alexander *Back from the front: an eye-witness's narrative of the beginnings of the Great War, 1914* 1914
BAGLEY, Desmond *The enemy* 1977
The freedom trap 1971
The snow tiger 1975
The spoilers 1969
The tightrope men 1973
Bahamian review 1952–
BAILAR, John Christian, et al. *Comprehensive inorganic chemistry* 5 vols. 1973
BAILEY, Alan Robert *A text-book of metallurgy* 1954
— (ed. 2) 1960
BAILEY, Hamilton & LOVE, Robert John McNeill *A short practice of surgery* 2 vols. 1932 (and many later editions used)
BAILEY, Henry Christopher *Dead man's shoes* 1942
Mr. Fortune's practice 1923
BAILEY, John (1864–1931) *Letters and diaries* ed. S. Bailey 1935
BAILEY, Liberty Hyde ed. *Cyclopedia of American agriculture* 4 vols. 1907–9
ed. *Cyclopedia of American horticulture* 4 vols. 1900–2
Manual of cultivated plants 1924
— (rev. ed.) 1949
ed. *The standard cyclopedia of horticulture* 6 vols. 1914–17
BAILLIE, Granville Hugh *Watches* 1929
BAILLIE-SCOTT, M. H. *Houses and gardens* 1906
BAINBRIDGE, Beryl *Sweet William* 1975
Young Adolf 1978
BAINES, Anthony ed. *Musical instruments through the ages* 1961
BAINES, John Thomas *Explorations in South-West Africa* 1864
BAINES, Thomas *Greenhouse and stove plants* 1885
BAINES, William Mortimer *The narrative of Edward Crewe; or, Life in New Zealand* 1874
BAIRD, Irene *Waste heritage* 1939
BAIRD, Robert *A view of the valley of the Mississippi; or, The emigrant's and traveller's guide to the West* 1832
BAKER, Cyril Clarence Thomas *Dictionary of mathematics* 1961
BAKER, Dorothy *Young man with a horn* 1938
BAKER, John Randal *Principles of biological microtechnique: a study of fixation and dyeing* 1958
Race 1974
BAKER, Robert Horace *Astronomy* 1930
— (ed. 8) 1964
BAKER, Roger Denio *Essential pathology* 1961
BAKER, Sidney John *Australia speaks: a supplement to 'The Australian language'* 1953
The Australian language 1945
— (ed. 2) 1966
The drum: Australian character and slang 1959 (UK 1960)
New Zealand slang 1941
A popular dictionary of Australian slang 1941
— (ed. 3) 1943
Balance and Columbian Repository (Hudson, NY) 1801–8
BALCHIN, Nigel Marlin *Darkness falls from the air* 1942
Lord, I was afraid 1947
The small back room 1943
A way through the wood 1951
BALDWIN, Faith *Innocent bystander* 1933 (UK 1935)
BALDWIN, James Arthur *Another country* 1962 (UK 1963)
Go tell it on the mountain 1953 (UK 1954)
BALDWIN, James Mark ed. *Dictionary of philosophy and psychology* 3 vols. 1901–5
BALFOUR, Isaac Bayley tr. *C. E. von Goebel's Organography of plants* 2 vols. 1900–5
BALINSKY, Boris Ivan *An introduction to embryology* 1960
BALL, John Dudley *The cool cottontail* 1966 (UK 1967)
Five pieces of jade 1972
BALL, Kenneth *Fiat 600, 600D autobook* 1970
BALLANTYNE, David Watt *The Cunninghams* 1948 (UK 1963)
Ballet annual, The 1947–
BANCROFT, Hubert Howe *The native races of the Pacific states of North America* 5 vols. 1875–6
BAND, George C. *Road to Rakaposhi* 1955
BANFIELD, Edmund James *The confessions of a beachcomber* 1908
Bangladesh Times (Dacca) 1974–
BANIM, John *The smuggler* 3 vols. 1831
BANKS, Michael Edward Borg *Commando climber* 1955
BANNERMAN, David Armitage *The birds of the British Isles* 12 vols. 1953–63
BANNISTER, Roger Gilbert *First four minutes* 1955

BANTON, Michael Parker *The policeman in the community* 1964
West African city: a study of tribal life in Freetown 1957
Baptist magazine 1809–1904
'BARBELLION, W. N. P.' (Bruce Frederick Cummings) *The journal of a disappointed man* 1919
BARBER, Charles Laurence *Linguistic change in present-day English* 1964
BARBER, Horatio *The aeroplane speaks* 1916
'BARBICAN, James' *The confessions of a rum-runner* 1927
BARCLAY, Florence Louisa *The broken halo* 1913
The rosary 1909
BARCLAY, Rachel Mary tr. *E. Kraepelin's Dementia praecox and paraphrenia* ed. G. M. Robertson 1919
BARFORD, John Edward Quintus *Climbing in Britain* 1946
BARING, Maurice *Landmarks in Russian literature* 1910
BARKER, George Granville *News of the world* 1950
Two plays 1958
BARKER, Lewellys Franklin *Monographic medicine* See under title
The nervous system and its constituent neurones 1899
——, HOSKINS, R. G., & MOSENTHAL, H. O. eds. *Endocrinology and metabolism* 5 vols. 1922
BARLOW, James *Term of trial* 1961
BARLOW, Peter *A new mathematical and philosophical dictionary* 1814
BARLOW, Walter Sydney Lazarus *A manual of general pathology* 1898
BARNARD, Howard Clive & LAUWERYS, Joseph Albert *A handbook of British educational terms* 1963
BARNARD, Keppel Harcourt *A pictorial guide to South African fishes* 1947
BARNARD, Robert *Death on the high C's* 1977
BARNES, Dallas *See the woman* 1973 (UK 1974)
BARNES, Harold *Oceanography and marine biology* 1959
BARNETT, Denis Oliver *Denis Oliver Barnett: in happy memory . . . His letters from France and Flanders, October 1914–August 1915* 1915
BARNETT, Edward de Barry *Mechanism of organic chemical reactions* 1956
BARNETT, Henrietta Octavia Weston *Canon Barnett: his life, work and friends* 1918
BARNHAM, Denis *One man's window: an account of 10 weeks of war, Malta, 1942* 1956
BARNHART, Clarence Lewis, STEINMETZ, S., & BARNHART, R. K. *The Barnhart dictionary of new English since 1963* (UK ed. with title *A dictionary of new English 1963–1972*) 1973
The second Barnhart dictionary of new English 1980
BARNUM, Phineas Taylor *Life, written by himself* 1855
Struggles and triumphs; or, Forty years' recollections 1869
— (another ed.) 1871
BARON, Joseph Alexander *From the city, from the plough* 1948
The human kind 1953
Rosie Hogarth 1951
There's no home 1950
With hope, farewell 1952
BARR, Ann & YORK, Peter *The official Sloane Ranger handbook: the first guide to what really matters in life* 1982
BARRETT, Charles Leslie *On the wallaby: quest and adventure in many lands* 1942
BARRIE, Sir James Matthew *The admirable Crichton* 1914
Plays (Uniform ed.) 12 vols. 1918–38
'BARRINGTON, Pamela' (Muriel Vere Barling) *Accessory to murder* 1968
BARRON, Harry *Modern plastics* 1945
BARRON, John N. *The language of painting: an informal dictionary* 1967
BARROW, John *An account of travels into the interior of southern Africa, in the years 1797 and 1798* 2 vols. 1801–4
— (ed. 2) 2 vols. 1806
BARROWMAN, James *A glossary of Scotch mining terms* 1886
'BARRY, C.' (Charles Bryson) *The detective's holiday* 1926
BARSTOW, Stan *A kind of loving* 1960
BARTH, John Simmons *The floating opera* 1956
— (rev. ed.) 1967
'BARTIMEUS' (Lewis Anselm da Costa Ricci) *Naval occasions* 1914
A tall ship and other naval occasions 1915
BARTLETT, Adeline Courtney *The larger rhetorical patterns in Anglo-Saxon poetry* 1935
BARTLETT, Ellis Ashmead *The battlefields of Thessaly* 1897
BARTLETT, Vernon Oldfield *This is my life* 1937
BARTLEY, Samuel Howard *Vision* 1941
BARTON, Frank Townend *The kennel encyclopædia* 1928
BARTON, R. tr. *C. Blasis's The code of Terpsichore: the art of dancing* 1830
BARTZ, Patricia McBride *South Korea* 1972
BASHFORTH, George Reginald *The manufacture of iron and steel* 2 vols. 1948–51
— (ed. 2) 4 vols. 1957–62
BASKIN, Wade tr. *F. de Saussure's Course in general linguistics* 1959 (UK 1960)
BATES, Herbert Ernest *The day of the tortoise* 1961
The jacaranda tree 1949
Love for Lydia 1952
BATESON, William *Mendel's principles of heredity* 1909
Mendel's principles of heredity: a defence 1902
Problems of genetics 1913
BATHGATE, Alexander *Colonial experiences; or, Sketches of people and places in the province of Otago, New Zealand* 1874
BATTERSBY, Albert *A guide to stock control* 1962
Mathematics in management 1966
Network analysis for planning and scheduling 1964
— (ed. 2) 1967
BATTEY, Maurice Hugh *Mineralogy for students* 1972
BAUCKE, William *Where the white man treads* 1905
— (ed. 2) 1928
BAUMANN, Heinrich *Londinismen: Slang und Cant* 1886 [dated 1887]
BAXT, George *A queer kind of death* 1966 (UK 1967)
BAYLEY, Roger Child *The complete photographer* 1906
BAYLISS, William Maddock *Principles of general physiology* 1915
BAYLY, Brian *Introduction to petrology* 1968
BAYNES, Helton Godwin tr. *C. G. Jung's Psychological types; or, The psychology of individuation* 1923
BAZELL, Charles Ernest *Linguistic form* 1953
—— et al. eds. *In memory of J. R. Firth* 1966
BEACH, Rex Ellingwood *Pardners* 1905 (UK 1912)
BEADLE, John Hanson *The undeveloped West; or, Five years in the Territories* 1873
Western wilds, and the men who redeem them 1878
— (another ed.) *c* 1882
BEADLE, Muriel *These ruins are inhabited* 1961 (UK 1963)
BEAN, Charles Edwin Woodrow *The 'Dreadnought' of the Darling* 1911
BEAN, William Jackson *Trees and shrubs hardy in the British Isles* vols. I–II, 1914; vol. III, 1933
BEARDSLEY, Aubrey (1872–98) *Letters* ed. H. Maas, J. L. Duncan, & W. G. Good 1971
BEATON, Cecil Walter Hardy *The wandering years: diaries 1922–39* 1961
BEATTIE, William *Life and letters of Thomas Campbell* 3 vols. 1849
BEATY, Arthur David *Cone of silence* 1959
Excellency 1977
BEAUMONT, Cyril William & IDZIKOWSKY, Stanislas *A manual of the theory and practice of classical theatrical dancing (méthode Cecchetti)* 1922
BEAUMONT, Reginald Arthur ed. *Aeronautical engineering* 1942
Beautiful British Columbia, land of new horizons 1959–
Beaver (Winnipeg) 1920–
BECKER, Stephen D. tr. *A. Schwarz-Bart's The last of the just* 1960 (UK 1961)
BECKETT, Samuel Barclay *Eh Joe, and other writings* 1967
More pricks than kicks 1934
Murphy 1938
No's knife: collected shorter prose 1967
Proust 1931
Stories and texts for nothing (tr. by Beckett of his *Nouvelles et textes pour rien* 1955) 1967
Waiting for Godot (tr. by Beckett of his *En attendant Godot* 1953) 1954 (UK 1956)
Whoroscope 1930
BECKSON, Karl & GANZ, Arthur *A reader's guide to literary terms* 1960 (UK 1961)
BEDFORD, Randolph *True Eyes and the whirlwind* 1903
BEDOUKIAN, Paul Z. *Perfumery synthetics and isolates* 1951
BEEBE, Charles William *Jungle peace* 1918 (UK 1919)
BEECHENO, Henry Oliver *An introduction to business studies* 1962
BEER, Max *A history of British socialism* 2 vols. 1919–20
BEER, Stafford *Cybernetics and management* 1959
Decision and control 1966
BEER, Thomas *The mauve decade: American life at the end of the nineteenth century* 1926
BEERBOHM, Henry Maximilian *And even now* 1920
Around theatres 2 vols. 1924 (in *Collected works* Vols. VIII & IX)
— (another ed.) 1 vol. 1953
A Christmas garland 1912
Letters to Reggie Turner ed. R. Hart-Davis 1964
More 1899
Observations 1925
Seven men 1919
A variety of things 1928 (in *Collected works* Vol. X)
Zuleika Dobson; or, An Oxford love story 1911
BEEVOR, Antony *The violent brink* 1975
BEGBIE, Edward Harold *Life of William Booth, the founder of the Salvation Army* 2 vols. 1920
BEHAN, Brendan Francis *Borstal boy* 1958
BEHRE, Frank ed. *Contributions to English syntax and philology* 1962
BEHREND, Arthur *The Samarai affair* 1973
Belfast Telegraph 1870–
BELL, Alexander Melville *Visible speech: the science of universal alphabetics* 1867
BELL, Eric Temple *The development of mathematics* 1940
— (ed. 2) 1945
BELL, Gertrude Margaret Lowthian (1868–1926) *Letters* sel. and ed. F. Bell 2 vols. 1927
BELL, Harold Sill *American petroleum refining* 1923
— (ed. 3) 1945
'BELL, Josephine' (Doris Bell Ball) *Crime in our time* 1962
Murder in hospital 1937
The Port of London murders 1938
The seeing eye 1958
BELL, Louis *The telescope* 1922
BELL, Peter & COOMBE, David tr. *Strasburger's textbook of botany* (tr. from 28th German ed., rewritten by R. Harder et al.) 1965
— (rev. ed. tr. from 30th German ed., rewritten by D. von Denffer et al.) 1976
BELL, Robert Charles *Board and table games from many civilizations* 2 vols. 1960–9
Bell system technical journal 1922–
Bell's life in London and sporting chronicle 1822–86
BELLAIRS, Angus d'Albini *The life of reptiles* 2 vols. 1969
BELLAIRS, George *Death in High Provence* 1957
BELLANTI, Joseph Alphonso *Immunology* 1971
BELLOC, Joseph Hilaire Pierre René *Cautionary tales for children* 1907
Charles the First, King of England 1933
Essays of a Catholic layman in England 1931
A history of England 4 vols. 1925–31
Pongo and the bull 1910
Verses and sonnets 1896
BELLOW, Saul *The adventures of Augie March* 1953
Dangling man 1944
Herzog 1964 (UK 1965)
Seize the day 1956 (UK 1957)
The victim 1947 (UK 1948)
BENCHLEY, Nathaniel Goddard *Welcome to Xanadu* 1968
BENDER, Arnold Eric *Dictionary of nutrition and food technology* 1960
BENEDICT, Ruth (Fulton) *The chrysanthemum and the sword: patterns of Japanese culture* 1946 (UK 1947)
Patterns of culture 1934 (UK 1935)
BENÉT, Stephen Vincent *John Brown's body* 1928
Thirteen o'clock 1937 (UK 1938)
BENNETT, Arnold *See* BENNETT, Enoch Arnold
BENNETT, Colin Noël *The guide to kinematography* 1917
—— et al. *The handbook of kinematography: the history, theory and practice of motion photography and projection* 1911
BENNETT, Enoch Arnold (1867–1931) *Anna of the Five Towns* 1902
The card 1911
Clayhanger 1910
The Grand Babylon Hotel 1902
A great man 1904
The grim smile of the Five Towns 1907
Hilda Lessways 1911
Imperial Palace 1930
Journals, 1896–1928 ed. N. Flower 3 vols. 1932–3
Leonora 1903
Letters ed. J. Hepburn 3 vols. 1966–70
Lilian 1922
The lion's share 1916
Lord Raingo 1926
A man from the North 1898
The matador of the Five Towns, and other stories 1912
The old wives' tale 1908
The pretty lady 1918
The Regent 1913
Riceyman Steps 1923
The roll-call 1918
Tales of the Five Towns 1905
These twain 1915 (UK 1916)
The truth about an author 1903
BENNETT, Ivy V. P. *Delinquent and neurotic children* 1960
BENNETT, John Godolphin *Witness* 1962
BENNETT, Louise *Jamaican humour in dialect* 1943

BENNETT, Mary Montgomerie *Christison of Lammermoor* 1927
BENNISON, George Mills & WRIGHT, Alan Edward *The geological history of the British Isles* 1969
BENSON, Edward Frederic *David Blaize* 1916
The image in the sand 1905
Mapp and Lucia 1931
Thorley Weir 1913
BENSON, Eugene Patrick *The bulls of Ronda* 1976
BENTLEY, Edmund Clerihew *Trent's last case* 1913
Trent's own case 1936
BENTLEY, Robert & TRIMEN, Henry *Medicinal plants* 4 vols. 1880
BENTLEY, William (1759–1819) *Diary* 4 vols. 1905–14
Bentley's miscellany 1837–68
BENTON, Kenneth Carter *The red hen conspiracy* 1977
Spy in Chancery 1972
BENTON, Thomas Hart *Thirty years' view; or, A history of the working of the American Government for thirty years, from 1820 to 1850* 2 vols. 1854–6
BERCKMAN, Evelyn *The Victorian album* 1973
BEREITER, Carl & ENGELMANN, Siegfried *Teaching disadvantaged children in the preschool* 1966
BERESFORD, Maurice *The lost villages of England* 1954
BERG, George Charles *The unconscious significance of hair* 1951
BERG, Leila *Risinghill: death of a comprehensive school* 1968
BERG, Paul C. *A dictionary of new words in English* 1953
BERGET, Alphonse *The conquest of the air: aeronautics, aviation; history, theory, practice* 1909
BERGMAN, Andrew *Hollywood and Le Vine* 1975 (UK 1976)
BERKELEY, Edmund Callis *Giant brains, or machines that think* 1949
—— & WAINWRIGHT, Lawrence *Computers: their operation and applications* 1956
BERKELEY, George Fitz-Hardinge & BERKELEY, J. *Italy in the making* 3 vols. 1932–40
BERKMAN, Al *Singers' glossary of show business jargon* 1961
BERLIN, Isaiah *Karl Marx, his life and environment* 1939
BERMANT, Chaim Icyk *Coming home* 1976
BERNARD, John (1756–1828) *Retrospections of the stage* ed. W. B. Bernard 2 vols. 1830
BERREY, Lester V. & VAN DEN BARK, Melvin *The American thesaurus of slang* 1942
— (ed. 2) US 1953, UK 1954
BERRY, Frederic Aroyce, BOLLAY, E., & BEERS, Norman R. eds. *Handbook of meteorology* 1945
BERRY, William Turner & POOLE, Herbert Edmund *Annals of printing* 1966
BERTON, Pierre *Klondike fever* 1958
BERTRAM, James Munro *The shadow of a war: a New Zealander in the Far East, 1939–1946* 1947
BESSEY, Ernst Athearn *Morphology and taxonomy of fungi* 1950
BESSINGER, Jess B. & CREED, Robert P. eds. *Medieval and linguistic studies in honor of F. P. Magoun* 1965 (US ed. has title *Franciplegius*)
Best one-act plays 1932–
BESTE, Raymond Vernon *Repeat the instructions* 1968
BETHELL, Nicholas & BURG, David tr. *A. I. Solzhenitsyn's Cancer ward* 2 vols. 1968–9
BETJEMAN, John *Collected poems* 1958
Continual dew 1937
A few late chrysanthemums 1954
High and low 1966
Mount Zion; or, In touch with the infinite 1931
New bats in old belfries 1945
Selected poems 1948
Summoned by bells 1960
BETTELHEIM, Frederick A. *Experimental physical chemistry* 1971
BEVAN, John Acton ed. *Essentials of pharmacology* 1969
BEWS, John William *The world's grasses* 1929
BHAVNANI, Enakshi *The dance in India* 1965
BIBLE *New English Bible* 3 vols. 1961–70
Bibliographical Society *Transactions* 1892–1919 (then merged with *The Library*)
BICKEL, Walter tr. *R. Hering's Dictionary of classical and modern cookery* 1958
BIDEN, C. Leo *Sea-angling fishes of the Cape* 1930
BIGELOW, Jacob *Florula Bostoniensis: a collection of plants of Boston and its environs* 1814
BILLINGS, John Davis *Hardtack and coffee* 1887
BILLINGS, Marland Pratt *Structural geology* 1942
— (ed. 2) 1954
— (ed. 3) 1972
Billings Gazette (Billings, Montana) 1901–
BINGHAM, John Michael Ward, 7th Baron Clanmorris *God's defector* 1976
The marriage bureau murders 1977
BINYON, Robert Laurence *Collected poems* 2 vols. 1931
Biochemical and biophysical research communications 1959–
Biochemical journal 1906–
Biochemistry (Easton, Pennsylvania) 1962–
Biochimica et biophysica acta 1947–
Biological abstracts 1926–
Biological bulletin 1898–
Biological reviews and biological proceedings 1926– (from 1936 with title *Biological reviews*)
BIRD, Anthony & HUTTON-STOTT, Francis *The veteran motor car pocketbook* 1963
BIRD, Kenneth *Smash a glass image* 1968
BIRD, Robert Montgomery *The Hawks of Hawk-Hollow* 2 vols. 1835
BIRD, William Richard *Off-trail in Nova Scotia* 1956
These are the Maritimes 1959
BIRKBECK, Morris *Notes on a journey through France* 1814 (Appendix, 1815)
BIRKHOFF, Garrett & MACLANE, Saunders *A survey of modern algebra* 1941
BIRMINGHAM, Maisie Poynter *The heat of the sun* 1976
Birmingham News (Birmingham, Alabama) 1888–
Birmingham Post (title varies) 1857–
BIRNBACH, Lisa, et al. *The official Preppy handbook* 1980
BIRNBAUM, Henrik & PUHVEL, Jaan eds. *Ancient Indo-European dialects: proceedings of the Conference on Indo-European Linguistics at U.C.L.A. in 1963* 1966
BISSELL, Richard Pike *High water* 1954 (UK 1955)
BITHELL, Richard *A counting-house dictionary* 1882
'BLACK, Gavin' (Oswald Wynd) *The bitter tea* 1972 (UK 1973)
The golden cockatrice 1974
A time for pirates 1971
You want to die, Johnny? 1966
BLACK, Jack *You can't win* 1926
'BLACK, Lionel' (Dudley Raymond Barker) *Death has green fingers* 1971
A healthy way to die 1976
Outbreak 1968
BLACK, Max ed. *The importance of language* 1962
The labyrinth of language 1968
The nature of mathematics 1933
ed. *Philosophy in America* 1965
BLACK, Peter *The biggest aspidistra in the world: a personal celebration of fifty years of the B.B.C.* 1972
BLACK, Rhona M. *The elements of palaeontology* 1970
Black mask, The 1920–
Black panther 1969–
Black scholar 1969–
Black world 1970–
BLACKER, Carlos Paton *Eugenics: Galton and after* 1952
BLACKSHAW, Alan *Mountaineering. From hill walking to Alpine climbing* 1965
— (rev. ed.) 1970
BLACKSHAW, Harold & BRIGHTMAN, Rainald *Dictionary of dyeing and textile printing* 1961
BLACKWELDER, Richard Eliot *Taxonomy: a text and reference book* 1967
BLAIKIE, Thomas *Diary of a Scotch gardener at the French court at the end of the 18th century* ed. F. Birrell 1931
Blair & Ketchum's country journal (Brattleboro, Vermont) 1974–
'BLAISDELL, Anne' (Barbara Elizabeth Linington) *Practice to deceive* 1971
BLAKE, Geoffrey Charles & TROTT, John Richard *Periodontology* 1962
'BLAKE, Nicholas' (Cecil Day Lewis) *The case of the abominable snowman* 1941
The deadly joker 1963
The dreadful hollow 1953
Malice in wonderland 1940
A question of proof 1935
The smiler with the knife 1939
There's trouble brewing 1937
Thou shell of death 1936
The whisper in the gloom 1954
See also: LEWIS, Cecil Day
BLAKE, William (1757–1827) *Complete writings* ed. G. Keynes 1966 (Oxford Standard Authors ed.; reprinted with corrections 1972)
BLAND, David *The illustration of books* 1951
Blast: review of the great English vortex ed. P. Wyndham Lewis 1914–15
BLEANEY, Betty Isabelle & BLEANEY, Brebis *Electricity and magnetism* 1957
'BLEECK, Oliver' (Ross Thomas) *The Procane chronicle* 1971 (UK ed. 1972 with title *The thief who painted sunlight*)
BLESH, Rudolph Pickett *Shining trumpets: a history of jazz* 1946 (UK 1949)
They all played ragtime: the true story of an American music 1950 (UK 1958)
BLISH, James *A case of conscience* 1958 (UK 1959)
A clash of cymbals 1959
Fallen star 1957
BLISHEN, Edward *Roaring boys* 1955
BLOCH, Bernard & TRAGER, George Leonard *Outline of linguistic analysis* 1942
BLOM, Eric Walter *Music in England* 1942
Blood: the journal of hematology 1946–
BLOODGOOD, Lida & SANTINI, Piero eds. *The horseman's dictionary* 1963
BLOODWORTH, Dennis *Any number can play* 1972
The clients of Omega 1975
Crosstalk 1978
BLOOMFIELD, Leonard *An introduction to the study of language* 1914
Language 1933
BLOW, Claude Montague *Rubber technology and manufacture* 1971
Blues unlimited 1963–
BLUNDEN, Edmund Charles *After the bombing, and other short poems* 1949
Choice or chance: new poems 1934
Cricket country 1944
De bello Germanico: a fragment of trench history 1930
An elegy, and other poems 1937
The face of England 1932
The harbingers 1916
The mind's eye 1934
Near and far: new poems 1929
Poems 1930
Poems, 1930–1940 1940
Retreat 1928
Romantic poetry and the fine arts 1942
Shells by a stream 1944
The shepherd, and other poems 1922
A summer's fancy 1930
Undertones of war 1928
BLUNT, Wilfrid Jasper W. *Of flowers and a village* 1963
BODKIN, Maud *Archetypal patterns in poetry: psychological studies of imagination* 1934
Bodleian Library record 1938–
BOGER, Louise Ade *The dictionary of world pottery and porcelain* 1971
BOLTZ, Cecil Leonard *Basic radio* 1943
BOND, James *Birds of the West Indies* 1936
— (another ed.) 1960
BONE, John Herbert A. *Petroleum and petroleum wells* 1865
BONFIGLIOLI, Kyril *Don't point that thing at me* 1972
Something nasty in the woodshed 1976
BONINGTON, Christian *Annapurna South Face* 1971
The next horizon: autobiography II 1973
BONNER, James Frederick *Plant biochemistry* 1950
BOOKER, Christopher *The neophiliacs: a study of the revolution in English life in the Fifties and Sixties* 1969
Bookman, The 1891–1934
Bookseller, The (title varies) 1858–
BOOTH, Andrew Donald & BOOTH, Kathleen H. V. *Automatic digital calculators* 1953
BOOTH, Michael R. ed. *English plays of the nineteenth century* 4 vols. 1969–73
BOOTH, William *In darkest England and the way out* 1890
BORN, Max & WOLF, Emil *Principles of optics* 1959
BORRADAILE, Lancelot Alexander & POTTS, Frank Armitage *The Invertebrata* 1932
BORROR, Donald Joyce & DELONG, Dwight Moore *An introduction to the study of insects* 1954
— (rev. ed.) 1964
Boston, Massachusetts. Registry Dept. *Records relating to the early history of Boston* 39 vols. 1876–1909
Boston Daily Globe (Boston, Mass.) morning ed. 1872–
— evening ed. 1878–
— Sunday ed., as *Boston Sunday Globe* 1877–
Boston Evening Transcript (title varies) 1830–1941
Boston Herald 1846–
Boston medical and surgical journal 1828–1928
Boston News-Letter (title varies) 1704–76
Boston Sunday Globe See *Boston Daily Globe*
Boston Sunday Herald (title varies) 1861–
BOSWELL, James *London journal 1762–63* ed. F. A. Pottle 1950
Botanical gazette 1876–
BOTKIN, Benjamin Albert ed. *Lay my burden down: a folk history of slavery* 1945
ed. *A treasury of American folklore* 1944
ed. *A treasury of Southern folklore* 1949
BOTTOME, Phyllis *Under the skin* 1950
BOULENGER, Edward George *Apes and monkeys* 1936

BOULGER, George Simonds *The uses of plants: a manual of economic botany* 1889
Wood: a manual of the natural history and industrial applications of the timber of commerce 1902
BOURNE, Geoffrey Howard ed. *Cytology and cell physiology* 1942
— (ed. 2) 1951; corrected impression 1952
BOVA, Benjamin *Multiple man* 1976 (UK 1977)
BOWEN, Elizabeth Dorothea Cole *Ann Lee's, and other stories* 1926
The cat jumps, and other stories 1934
Collected impressions 1950
The death of the heart 1938
The demon lover, and other stories 1945
Encounters 1923
The heat of the day 1949
The hotel 1927
The house in Paris 1935
The last September 1929
The little girls 1964
Look at all those roses 1941
Seven winters 1942
A time in Rome 1960
To the north 1932
A world of love 1955
BOWEN, Frank Charles *Sea slang: a dictionary of the old-timers' expressions and epithets* 1929
BOWEN, Godfrey *Wool away! The technique and art of shearing* 1955
— (ed. 2) 1956
'BOWER, Bertha Muzzy' (Bertha Muzzy Sinclair) *The Parowan bonanza* 1923
The phantom herd 1916
BOWER, Frederic Orpen *Botany of the living plant* 1919
Plant-life on land considered in some of its biological aspects 1911
BOWERS, Fredson Thayer *Bibliography and textual criticism* 1964
Principles of bibliographical description 1949
Textual and literary criticism 1959
BOWLES, Samuel *Our new West. Records of travel between the Mississippi River and the Pacific Ocean* 1869
BOWLEY, Arthur Lyon & STAMP, Josiah Charles *The national income, 1924: a comparative study of the income of the United Kingdom in 1911 and 1924* 1927
Bowls ('Know the game' series) 1962
BOWMAN, Walter Parker & BALL, Robert Hamilton *Theatre language: a dictionary of terms in English from medieval to modern times* 1961
BOWMAN, William Cameron, RAND, M. J., & WEST, G. B. *Textbook of pharmacology* 1968
BOWRA, Cecil Maurice *The Romantic imagination* 1950
BOX, Charles *The English game of cricket* 1877
BOYD, Edward & PARKES, Roger *The dark number* 1973
BOYLSTON, Herbert Melville *An introduction to the metallurgy of iron and steel* 1928
Boys' magazine 1922–
BRACE, Charles Loring *The new West; or, California in 1867–1868* 1869
BRACE, Gerald Warner *The spire* 1952 (UK 1953)
BRADBURY, Malcolm Stanley *Eating people is wrong* 1959
The history man 1975
Stepping westward 1965
BRADBURY, Ray Douglas *Fahrenheit 451* 1953 (UK 1954)
The illustrated man 1951 (UK 1952)
BRADBY, Mary Katharine *Psycho-analysis and its place in life* 1919
BRADDON, Russell Reading *Nancy Wake: the story of a very brave woman* 1956
The year of the angry rabbit 1964
BRADFORD, Gershom *A glossary of sea terms* 1927
— (new ed.) 1954
BRADLEY, Francis Herbert *The principles of logic* 1883
Bradshaw's railway guide (title varies) 1841–1961
Bradshaw's railway manual, shareholders' guide, and official directory for 1869 (Vol. XXI) 1869
Bradstreet's: a journal of trade, finance and public economy 1879–1933
BRAGG, Melvyn *The hired man* 1969
Without a city wall 1968
BRAHMACHARINI USHA *A Ramakrishna-Vedanta wordbook* 1962
'BRAHMS, Caryl' (Doris Caroline Abrahams) & 'SIMON, S. J.' (Simon Jasha Skidelsky) *Titania has a mother* 1944
Trottie True 1946
BRAIN, Walter Russell *Diseases of the nervous system* 1933
Speech disorders 1961
Brain: a journal of neurology 1878–
BRAINE, John *Life at the top* 1962
Room at the top 1957
The Vodi 1959
BRAITHWAITE, David *Fairground architecture* 1968
BRAM, Gary & DOWNS, C. *Manufacturing technology* 1975
'BRAMAH, Ernest' (Ernest Bramah Smith) *A little flutter* 1930
BRAMBLE, Albert York *Air-plane flight* 1952
BRANDON, David Godfrey *Modern techniques in metallography* 1966
BRANDON, H. ed. *Poverty, mendicity and crime ... To which is added a dictionary of the flash or cant language* 1839
BRANDON, John Gordon *The pawnshop murder* 1936
BRANDT, David Julius O. *The manufacture of iron and steel* 1953
— (ed. 2) 1960
BRANFORD, Jean *A dictionary of South African English* 1978
— (new ed.) 1980
BRANSTON, Frank *An up and coming man* 1977
BRAUN, Hugh *Parish churches: their architectural development in England* 1970
BRAUN, Lilian Jackson *The cat who ate Danish Modern* 1967
BRAWLEY, Ernest *The rap* 1974
— (paperback ed.) 1975
BRAY, Warwick M. & TRUMP, David Hilary *A dictionary of archaeology* 1970
BRAYSHAW, J. Dodsworth *Slum silhouettes: stories of London life* 1898
BRAZIL, Angela *The new girl at St. Chad's: a story of school life* 1912
BRECK, Samuel (1771–1862) *Recollections, with passages from his note-books* ed. H. E. Scudder 1877
BRELAND, Osmond Philip *Animal friends and foes* 1957
BRENAN, Edward Fitz-Gerald (Gerald Brenan) *The face of Spain* 1950
BRENNAN, Paul, HESSELYN, Ray, & BATESON, Henry *Spitfires over Malta* 1943
'BRENT OF BIN BIN' (Stella Maria Sarah Miles Franklin) *Up the country: a tale of the early Australian squattocracy* 1928
BRERETON, Cloudesley Shovell Henry & ROTHWELL, Frederick tr. *H. L. Bergson's Laughter* 1911
BREWSTER, Ben R. tr. *L. Althusser & E. Balibar's Reading Capital* 1970
— (paperback ed.) 1975
BRICKHILL, Paul & NORTON, Conrad *Escape to danger* 1946
'BRIDGE, Ann' (Mary Dolling, Lady O'Malley) *Four-part setting* 1939
Frontier passage 1942
Peking picnic 1932
The Portuguese escape 1958
BRIDGES, Robert Seymour *The testament of beauty* 1929
BRIGGS, Charles Frederick *The adventures of Harry Franco* 2 vols. 1839
BRIGGS, Fred N. & KNOWLES, Paulden Ford *Introduction to plant breeding* 1967
BRILL, Abraham Arden tr. *S. Freud's The interpretation of dreams* 1913
tr. *S. Freud's Selected papers on hysteria and other psychoneuroses* 1909
tr. *S. Freud's Three contributions to sexual theory* 1910
tr. *S. Freud's Totem and taboo: resemblances between the psychic lives of savages and neurotics* 1918
BRINKLEY, Frank *Oriental series* 12 vols. 1901–2
Britain's industrial future (Liberal Industrial Inquiry) 1928
Britannica book of the year 1938– (UK eds. 1938–41 with title *Encyclopædia Britannica book of the year*)
British Academy *Proceedings* 1905–
British birds 1907–
British Broadcasting Corporation *B.B.C. handbook* (title varies: also *B.B.C. year-book* and *B.B.C. annual*) 1928–
The B.B.C. quarterly 1946–54
B.B.C. war report ed. D. Hawkins et al. 1946
Glossary of broadcasting terms See: FARQUHARSON, M. G., et al.
British chess magazine 1881–
British commonwealth forest terminology (Empire Forestry Association) 2 parts 1953–7
British dental journal 1903–
British Dominions year book, The (British Dominions Insurance Co.) 1916–24
British Engineering Standards Association *British standard glossary of terms used in electrical engineering* 1926 *See* British Standards Institution. Glossaries. *Electrical engineering*
British Interplanetary Society *Journal* 1934–9; 1946–
British journal of dermatology 1888–
British journal of medical psychology 1923–
British journal of ophthalmology 1917–
British journal of psychology 1904–
British journal of radiology 1924–
British journal of sociology 1950–
British manufacturer Nov.–Dec. 1919
British medical bulletin 1943–
British medical dictionary, The ed. A. S. MacNalty 1961
British pharmaceutical codex 1907 (and several later editions used)
British pharmacopœia 1864 (and many later editions used)
British Pharmacopœia Commission *Approved names* See: United Kingdom. General Medical Council
British printer, The 1888–
British School (of Archaeology) at Athens *Annual* 1895–
British Standards Institution *B.S.I. News* 1956
Nomenclature of commercial timbers, including sources of supply 1946
— (rev. ed.) 1955
Glossaries:
Aeronautical terms (BS 185) 1949, 1950, 1951, and other eds.
Automatic data processing (BS 3527) 1962, and several later parts
Caravan terms (BS AU129) 1967, 1975
Concrete and reinforced concrete (BS 2787) 1956
Dentistry (BS 4492) 1969
Documentation terms (BS 5408) 1976
Electrical engineering (BS 205) 1926, 1936, 1943
Electrotechnical, power, telecommunication, electronics, lighting and colour terms (BS 4727) 1971–
General building terms (BS 3589) 1963
Glass industry (BS 3447) 1962
Highway engineering terms (BS 892) 1940, 1954, 1967
Landscape work (BS 3975) 1966–9
Letterpress rotary printing terms (BS 3814) 1964
Mining terms (BS 3618) 1963–74
Nuclear science (BS 3455) 1962
Offset lithographic printing (BS 4277) 1968
Plastics industry (BS 1755) 1951, 1967–74
Radiology (BS 2957) 1955
Railway signalling (BS 719) 1936
Refrigeration (BS 1584) 1949
Sanitation terms (BS 4118) 1967
Telegraphs and telephones (BS 204) 1924, 1930, 1943 (*Telecommunication*), 1960
Timber preservation (BS 4261) 1968
British weekly, The: a journal of social and Christian progress 1886–
BRITTAIN, Vera Mary *Testament of youth* 1933
BRITTEN, Frederick James *Old clocks and watches* 1899
BRITTON, Karl *John Stuart Mill* 1953
BRITTON, Nathaniel Lord *North American trees* 1908
Brno studies in English 1959–
BROAD, Charlie Dunbar *The mind and its place in nature* 1925
Perception, physics, and reality 1914
Scientific thought 1923
BRODAL, Alf *Neurological anatomy in relation to clinical medicine* 1948
BROINOWSKI, Alison *Take one ambassador* 1973
BROMFIELD, Louis *The rains came* 1937
BROMIGE, Iris Amy Edna *The enchanted garden* 1956
BROMLEY, Gordon *In the absence of the body* 1972
BRONOWSKI, Jacob *The ascent of man* 1973
BRONSON-HOWARD, George *Enemy to society* 1911
God's man 1915
BRONTË, Anne *Agnes Grey* 1847
The tenant of Wildfell Hall 3 vols. 1848
BROOKE, Rupert Chawner (1887–1915) *Collected poems* 1918
Letters ed. G. Keynes 1968
BROOKE-ROSE, Christine Frances E. *The languages of love* 1957
BROOKS, Frederick Tom *Plant diseases* 1928
BROOKS, Henry *Natal: a history and description of the colony* 1876
BROPHY, John & PARTRIDGE, Eric Honeywood eds. *The long trail: what the British soldier sang and said in the Great War of 1914–18* 1965
Songs and slang of the British soldier, 1914–18 1930
— (ed. 3) 1931
BROSE, Henry Herman L. A. tr. *A. J. W. Sommerfeld's Atomic structure and spectral lines* 1923
— (ed. 3) 1934
BROSNAHAN, Leonard Francis *Some Old English sound changes: an analysis in the light of modern phonetics* 1953
The sounds of language 1961
BROWN, Bernard *Talking pictures* 1931
BROWN, George Mackay *An Orkney tapestry* 1969
BROWN, Ivor John Carnegie *Say the word* 1947
Words in our time 1958
BROWN, James Alexander Campbell *The social psychology of industry* 1954
BROWN, John (M.D., of Edinburgh; 1810–82) *Letters; with letters from Ruskin, Thackeray, and others* ed. J. Brown & D. W. Forrest 1907
— (ed. 3) 1912

ROWN, John *The chancer* 1972
ROWN, Michael Barratt *The economics of imperialism* 1974
ROWN, Samuel R. *The western gazetteer; or, Emigrant's directory* 1817
ROWN, Walter Varian & BERTKE, Eldridge Melvin *Textbook of cytology* 1969
ROWNE, Daniel Jay *The sylva americana; or, A description of the forest trees indigenous to the United States* 1832
ROWNING, Carl Hamilton *Bacteriology* 1925
RUNER, Jerome Seymour *Beyond the information given: studies in the psychology of knowing* ed. J. M. Anglin 1973 (UK 1974)
RUNT, David *Meteorology* 1928
RUTON, Eric Moore *Dictionary of clocks and watches* 1962
RYAN, William Alanson *Natural history of Hawaii* 1915
RYANT, Edwin *What I saw in California* 1848
— (ed. 5) 1849
BRYANT, Peter' (Peter Bryan George) *Two hours to doom* 1958
RYDEN, Henry Anderson *Animals of Africa* 1900
Kloof and karroo: sport, legend, and natural history in Cape Colony 1889
Tales of South Africa 1896
RYSON, Herbert Courtney *The gramophone record* 1935
UCHAN, John *The blanket of the dark* 1931
Castle Gay 1930
The courts of the morning 1929
The dancing floor 1926
The gap in the curtain 1932
Greenmantle 1916
The house of the four winds 1935
Huntingtower 1922
The island of sheep 1936
John Macnab 1925
Memory hold-the-door 1940
Mr. Standfast 1919
Nelson's history of the war 24 vols. 1915–19
Prester John 1910
A prince of the captivity 1933
The thirty-nine steps 1915
The three hostages 1924
BUCHANAN, Robert James McLean *The blood in health and disease* 1909
BUCK, Carl Darling *Comparative grammar of Greek and Latin* 1933
BUCK, Franklin Augustus (1826–1909) *A Yankee trader in the gold rush* ed. K. A. White 1930
BUCK, Peter Henry *The coming of the Maori* 1925
— (rev. ed.) 1949 (corrected impression, 1950)
BUCKLER, Ernest Redmond *Ox bells and fireflies* 1968
BUCKMASTER, Henrietta' (Henrietta Stephens) *The walking trip* 1972
Buenos Aires Herald 1876–
BULL, Peter *I know the face, but . . .* 1959
BULL-US, Hector' (James Kirke Paulding) *The diverting history of John Bull and Brother Jonathan* 1812
— (ed. 2) 1813
— (new ed.) 1835
BULLENS, Denison Kingsley *Steel and its heat treatment* 1916
BULLER, Walter Lawry *A history of the birds of New Zealand* 1873
Manual of the birds of New Zealand 1882
Bulletin (Glasgow) 1915–60 (1924–60 with title *Bulletin and Scots pictorial*)
Bulletin (Sydney) 1880–
Bulletin of entomological research 1910–
Bulletin of the atomic scientists 1945–
Bulletin See also under the names of particular institutions
BULLINS, Ed *The theme is blackness: 'The corner' and other plays* 1973
BULLOCK, Alan Louis Charles ed. *The twentieth century: a promethean age* 1971
BULWER, Henry Earle *A glossary of technical terms employed in connection with church bells* 1901
BUNN, Alfred *The stage: both before and behind the curtain* 3 vols. 1840
BUNTING, Brian Talbot *The geography of soil* 1965
BURBRIDGE, William Frank *From balloon to bomber* 1946
BURCHELL, William John *Travels in the interior of Southern Africa* 2 vols. 1822–4
BURDETT, Geoffrey Arnold T. ed. *Automatic control handbook* 1962
Bureau of American Ethnology *See* United States. Bureau of American Ethnology
Bureau of Standards *See* United States. National Bureau of Standards
BURGE, Cyril Gordon ed. *Complete book of aviation* 1935
'BURGESS, Anthony' (John Anthony Burgess Wilson) *Beds in the east* 1959
A clockwork orange 1962
The doctor is sick 1960
The enemy in the blanket 1958
MF 1971
The right to an answer 1960
Time for a tiger 1956
BURGESS, Francis Henry *A dictionary of sailing* 1961
BURKE, Carl F. *God is beautiful, man: interpretations of Bible passages and stories* 1969 (UK 1970)
BURKE, Jackson Frederick *Death trick* 1975 (UK 1976)
BURKE, John *Till death us do part* (adapted from the television series by J. Speight) 1967
BURKE, Thomas *Nights in town* 1915
BURKE, Thomas A. ed. *Polly Peablossom's wedding, and other tales* 1851
BURKITT, Miles Crawford *Prehistory: a study of early cultures in Europe and the Mediterranean basin* 1921
BURLEY, Dan *Original handbook of Harlem Jive* 1944
BURLEY, William John *Death in a salubrious place* 1973
Guilt edged 1971
To kill a cat 1970
Burlington magazine 1903–
BURN, Joshua Harold *Drugs, medicines and man* 1962
Lecture notes on pharmacology 1948
— (ed. 9) 1968
BURNETT, Frances Eliza Hodgson *Little Lord Fauntleroy* 1886
A little princess 1905
The making of a marchioness 1901
The secret garden 1911
The shuttle 1907
T. Tembarom 1913
BURNETT, John ed. *Useful toil: autobiographies of working people from the 1820s to the 1920s* 1974
BURNETT, William Riley *Little Caesar* 1929
Vanity Row 1952 (UK 1953)
BURNEY, Frances (Mme D'Arblay) (1752–1840) *Journals and letters* ed. J. Hemlow et al. 1972–
BURNHAM, George P. *Memoirs of the United States Secret Service* 1872
BURNSIDE, William *Theory of groups of finite order* 1897
BURRARD, Gerald, et al. *Big game hunting in the Himalayas and Tibet* 1925
BURROUGHS, William, *Jr.* *Speed* 1970
BURROUGHS, William Seward *Junkie* 1953
The naked lunch 1959
BURROW, Thomas *The Sanskrit language* 1955
BURROWS, E. Julie *Like an evening gone* 1973
'BURTON, Alfred' (John Mitford) *The adventures of Johnny Newcome in the navy* 1818
BURTON, Maurice *Wild animals of the British Isles* 1960
BURTON, Richard Francis *A plain and literal translation of the Arabian nights' entertainments* 10 vols. 1885–6 (unexpurgated Kamashastra Soc. ed.)
BURTON-BROWN, Theodore *Early mediterranean migrations. An essay in archaeological interpretation* 1960
BURY, John Bagnell *A history of Greece to the death of Alexander the Great* 1900
BUSBY, Roger *Deadlock* 1971
Pattern of violence 1973
BUSH, Harry Derrick *Atomic and nuclear physics: theoretical principles* 1962
BUSHELL, Stephen Wootton *Chinese art* 2 vols. 1904–6
— (ed. 2) 1909
Business week 1929–
Busy man's magazine (Toronto) 1896–1911 (continued as *Maclean's magazine*)
BUTCHER, A. Judith *Copy-editing: the Cambridge handbook* 1975
BUTCHER, Roger William *A new illustrated British flora* 2 parts 1961
BUTLER, Gwendoline *Coffin following* 1968
A coffin for Pandora 1973
Coffin in Oxford 1962
BUTLER, Richard *Where all the girls are sweeter* 1975
BUTLER, Samuel (1835–1902) *Erewhon; or, Over the range* 1872
Erewhon revisited twenty years later 1901
A first year in Canterbury settlement 1863
Note-books ed. H. F. Jones 1912
The way of all flesh ed. R. A. Streatfeild 1903
BUTTERWORTH, Hezekiah *Zigzag journeys in the Western States of America* 1884
BUTTERWORTH, Michael *Remains to be seen* 1976
BYATT, Antonia Susan *The virgin in the garden* 1978
BYNG, John (5th Viscount Torrington) *The Torrington diaries: containing the tours through England and Wales 1781–94* ed. C. B. Andrews 4 vols. 1934–8
BYRNE, Brian Oswald Donn *Destiny Bay* 1928

C

CB magazine (Communications Publication Corporation, Oklahoma City) 1964–
CERN *See* European Organization for Nuclear Research
CRC journal (Community Relations Commission) 1972–
C.S.I.R.O. *See* Australia. Commonwealth Scientific and Industrial Research Organization
Cabinet maker and retail furnisher (title varies) 1880–
'CABLE, Boyd' (Ernest Andrew Ewart) *Action Front* 1916
Doing their bit: war work at home 1916
The Old Contemptibles 1919
'CADE, Alexander' (Kenneth Methold) *Turn up a stone* 1969
CAIN, James Mallahan *The postman always rings twice* 1934
CAIRD, Janet *Perturbing spirit* 1966
CALDER, Nigel David Ritchie *The restless earth* 1972
CALDWELL, Erskine Preston *God's little acre* 1933
CALDWELL, William *Schopenhauer's system in its philosophical significance* 1896
Calgary Herald (Calgary, Alberta) 1883–
California. University *Publications in geography* 1913–
California Academy of Natural Sciences *Proceedings* 1854–
California Historical Society *Quarterly* 1922–
CALKINS, Gary Nathan *The biology of the protozoa* 1926
—— & SUMMERS, Francis Marion *Protozoa in biological research* 1941
Call-Bulletin (San Francisco) 1856– (title varies)
CALLOW, Clive *Power from the sea: the search for North Sea oil and gas* 1973
'CALVIN, Henry' (Clifford Leonard Clark Hanley) *It's different abroad* 1963
A nice friendly town 1967
The poison chasers 1971
Cambridge ancient history, The ed. J. B. Bury et al. 12 vols. 1923–39
— (ed. 3 of Vols. I & II) ed. I. E. S. Edwards et al. 1970–7
Cambridge and Dublin mathematical journal 1846–55
Cambridge review: a journal of university life and thought 1879–
CAMERON, Agnes Deans *The new North: being some account of a woman's journey through Canada to the Arctic* 1909
CAMERON, Alexander Thomas & GILMOUR, Clifford R. *The biochemistry of medicine* 1933
CAMERON, Angus, FRANK, R., & LEYERLE, J. eds. *Computers and Old English concordances* 1970
CAMERON, David Kerr *Willie Gavin, crofter man: portrait of a vanished lifestyle* 1980
CAMP, Walter Chauncey *Football without a coach* 1920
CAMPBELL, Alistair *Old English grammar* 1959
CAMPBELL, Allan McCulloch *Episomes* 1969
CAMPBELL, Helen Stuart *Darkness and daylight; or, Lights and shadows of New York life* 1891
CAMPBELL, Ignatius Roy Dunnachie (1901–57) *Adamastor* 1930
Broken record 1934
Collected poems 3 vols. 1949–60
The flaming terrapin 1924
Flowering rifle 1939
The Georgiad 1931
Light on a dark horse 1951
Lorca: an appreciation of his poetry 1952
Mithraic emblems 1936
Poems 1930
tr. *Poems of Baudelaire* 1952
Portugal 1957
Talking Bronco 1946
The wayzgoose 1928
CAMPBELL, Mrs. Patrick *See* SHAW, George Bernard
CAMPBELL, R. W. *Private Spud Tamson* 1915
CAMPBELL, Roy *See* CAMPBELL, Ignatius Roy Dunnachie
CAMPBELL, Thomas (1733–95) *Diary of a visit to England in 1775* ed. J. L. Clifford 1947
CAMPION, Charles Thomas tr. *A. Schweitzer's On the edge of the primeval forest* 1922
Canada. Department of the Environment. Fisheries and Marine Service *Fisheries fact sheet* 1973–
Canada. Geological Survey *Reports of progress* (later *Annual reports*) 1857–1906
Canada. Senate *Official report of debates* 1870–
Canadian annual review of public affairs 1903–
Canadian antiques collector (title varies) 1966–
Canadian geographical journal 1930–
Canadian historical review 1920–
Canadian journal of linguistics 1961–
Canadian journal of physics 1951–
Canadian journal of research 1929–50 (from 1935 divided into subject series)

Canadian Medical Association *Journal* 1911–
Canadian mineralogist 1957–
Cancer (American Cancer Society) 1948–
Cancer research 1941–
'CANDY, Edward' (Alison Neville) *Words for murder perhaps* 1971
CANFIELD, Dorothea Frances *Fables for parents* 1937 (U.K. 1938)
Understood Betsy 1917 (UK 1922)
CANFIELD, Henry Spofford *A maid of the frontier* 1898
CANNAN, Joanna Maxwell *All is discovered* 1962
And all I learned 1951
And be a villain 1958
High table 1931
Little I understood 1948
Long shadows 1955
Murder included 1950
No walls of jasper 1930
CANNING, Victor *Flight of the grey goose* 1973
The great affair 1970
The melting man 1968
The python project 1967
Queen's pawn 1969
The rainbird pattern 1972
The whip hand 1965
CANTAROW, Abraham & SCHEPARTZ, Bernard *Biochemistry* 1954
— (ed. 4) 1967
Cape Argus (Cape Town) 1888– (title varies)
Cape monthly magazine 1857–81
Cape Times (Cape Town) 1876–
CAPELL, Richard *Simiomata: a Greek note book, 1944–1945* 1946
CAPOTE, Truman *The grass harp* 1951 (UK 1952)
In cold blood: a true account of a multiple murder and its consequences 1965 (UK 1966)
Captain, The: a magazine for boys 1899–1924
CARDUS, Neville *Autobiography* 1947
Close of play 1956
Days in the sun: a cricketer's journal 1924
CAREW, Dorothea Petrie *Many years, many girls* 1967
'CAREW, Francis Wylde' (Arthur E. G. Way) *No. 747: being the autobiography of a gipsy* 1891
CAREW, Jan Alwin Rynveld *Black Midas* 1958
The wild coast 1958
Caribbean quarterly 1949–
CARLILE, M. J. & SKEHEL, J. J. *Evolution in the microbial world* 1974 (24th Symposium of the Society for General Microbiology)
CARLQUIST, Sherwin John *Hawaii: a natural history* 1970
CARLSON, Elof Axel *The gene: a critical history* 1966
CARMAN, Philip Crosbie *Chemical constitution and properties of engineering materials* 1949
'CARMICHAEL, Harry' (Leopold Horace Ognall) *Naked to the grave* 1972
The seeds of hate 1960
Too late for tears 1973
CARMICHAEL, Robert Daniel *Introduction to the theory of groups of finite order* 1937
CARNAP, Rudolf *Meaning and necessity: a study in semantics and modal logic* 1947
Carnegie Institution of Washington *Publications* 1902–
Year-book 1902–
CARPENTER, George Herbert *The biology of insects* 1928
CARPENTER, John Richard *An ecological glossary* 1938
CARPENTER, Kathleen E. *Life in inland waters* 1928
CARPENTER, Rhys *Greek sculpture: a critical review* 1960
CARPENTER, Spencer Cecil *Christianity according to S. Luke* 1919
CARR, Edward Hallett *A history of Soviet Russia: The Bolshevik revolution, 1917–1923* 3 vols. 1950–3
The interregnum, 1923–1924 1954
Socialism in one country, 1924–1926 3 vols. 1958–64
Foundations of a planned economy, 1926–1929 by E. H. Carr & R. W. Davies 3 vols. 1969–71
CARR, George Shoobridge *A synopsis of elementary results in pure and applied mathematics* 2 parts 1880–6
CARR, John Dickson *Below suspicion* 1949 (UK 1950)
CARR-SAUNDERS, Alexander Morris & JONES, David Caradog *A survey of the social structure of England and Wales, as illustrated by statistics* 1927
CARRIER, Robert *Great dishes of the world* 1963
CARRINGTON, Charles Edmund *Rudyard Kipling* 1955
CARROLL, James *Mortal friends* 1978
CARROLL, John Bissell *The study of language* 1953
——, DAVIES, P., & RICHMAN, B. *The American Heritage word frequency book* 1971
CARRUTHERS, William Alexander *See* CARUTHERS
CARSON, Gerald *Cornflake crusade* 1957 (UK 1959)
CARSON, Rachel Louise *Silent spring* 1962 (UK 1963)
CARSON, Robert Andrew Glendinning *Coins: ancient, mediaeval & modern* 1962
CARSTAIRS, John Paddy *The concrete kimono* 1965
CARTER, John Waynflete *ABC for book-collectors* 1952
— (ed. 3) 1961
CARTER, Philip Youngman *Mr. Campion's falcon* 1970
Mr. Campion's farthing 1969
CARTWRIGHT, George *A journal of transactions and events, during a residence of nearly sixteen years on the coast of Labrador* 3 vols. 1792
CARUTHERS, William Alexander *The Kentuckian in New York; or, The adventures of three Southerns* 2 vols. 1834
CARVIC, Heron *Miss Seeton sings* 1973 (UK 1974)
CARY, Arthur Joyce Lunel (1888–1957) *The African witch* 1936
Aissa saved 1932
An American visitor 1933
The captive and the free 1959
Castle Corner 1938
Except the Lord 1953
Herself surprised 1941
Mister Johnson 1939
CASAMASSA, Jack V. ed. *Jet aircraft power systems: principles and maintenance* 1950
CASEY, James P. *Pulp and paper* 2 vols. 1952
Cassell's cyclopædia of photography ed. B. E. Jones 1911
Cassell's dictionary of abbreviations 1966 *See* GURNETT, John William & KYTE, Colin Henry John
Cassell's family magazine 1874–97
CASSIDY, Frederic Gomes *S. Robertson's The development of modern English* (ed. 2) 1954 *See* ROBERTSON, Stuart
Jamaica talk: three hundred years of the English language in Jamaica 1961
—— & LE PAGE, Robert Brock eds. *Dictionary of Jamaican English* 1967
— (ed. 2) 1980
CASTLE, Don *Do your own time* 1938
'CASTLE, John' & 'HAILEY, Arthur' *Flight into danger* 1958
CATHER, Willa Sibert *Death comes for the Archbishop* 1927
Catholic dictionary of theology, A ed. H. F. Davis et al. 1962–
Catholic encyclopedia, The 17 vols. 1907–17
Catholic Herald 1884–
CATTO, Maxwell Joseph *Bird on the wing* 1966
'CAUDWELL, Christopher' (Christopher St. John Sprigg) *Illusion and reality* 1937
CAVELL, Stanley Louis *The world viewed: reflections on the ontology of film* 1971
CAWS, Peter *The philosophy of science* 1965
CECIL, Edward Christian David *Two quiet lives: Dorothy Osborne, Thomas Gray* 1948
CECIL, Mirabel *Heroines in love 1750–1974* 1974
Cercle Linguistique de Prague *Travaux* 1929–
Ceylon Daily News (Colombo) 1918–
Ceylon Observer (Colombo) 1834–
CHADWICK, Hector Munro *The origin of the English nation* 1907
CHADWICK, Henry *The art of pitching and fielding* 1886
CHADWICK, Leigh E. tr. *W. Linsenmaier's Insects of the world* 1972
CHAFFERS, William *Marks and monograms on pottery and porcelain* 1863
— (ed. 2) 1866
CHALLINOR, John *A dictionary of geology* 1961
CHALLIS, Simon *Death on a quiet beach* 1968
CHAMBERLAIN, Basil Hall *Things Japanese* 1890
CHAMBERLAIN, E. *The Indiana gazetteer; or, Topographical dictionary of the State of Indiana* (ed. 3) 1849
CHAMBERLAIN, John (1554?–1628) *Letters* ed. N. E. McClure 2 vols. 1939
CHAMBERLAIN, John *Hosiery, yarns and fabrics* 1926
CHAMBERLIN, Thomas Chrowder & SALISBURY, Rollin Dean *Geology* 3 vols. 1904–6 (UK 1905–6)
CHAMBERS, Edmund Kerchever *The English folk-play* 1933
The mediæval stage 2 vols. 1903
CHAMBERS, Eric *Photolitho-offset* 1967
CHAMBERS, Robert William *The common law* 1911
The firing line 1908
Chambers's technical dictionary ed. C. F. Tweney & L. E. C. Hughes 1940 (and several later editions used)
CHANDLER, Maurice Henry *Ceramics in the modern world: man's first technology comes of age* 1967
CHANDLER, Raymond Thornton (1888–1959) *The big sleep* 1939
Farewell, my lovely 1940
The high window 1942 (UK 1943)
The lady in the lake 1943 (UK 1944)
The long good-bye 1953
Raymond Chandler speaking [letters and an unfinished novel] 1962 (paperback ed. 1966)
Trouble is my business, and other stories 1950
CHANG, Kwang-chih *See* KWANG-CHIH CHANG
CHANNING, George G. *Early recollections of Newport, R.I., from the year 1793 to 1811* 1868
CHAPLIN, Charles Spencer *My autobiography* 1964
CHAPMAN, Abraham ed. *New Black voices: an anthology of contemporary Afro-American literature* 1972
CHAPMAN, James *Travels in the interior of South Africa* 2 vols. 1868
CHAPMAN, Reginald Frederick *The insects structure and function* 1969
CHAPMAN, Robert McDonald & BENNETT, Jonathan eds. *An anthology of New Zealand verse* 1956
CHAPMAN, Ronald George *Father Faber* 1961
CHAPMAN, Royal Norton *Animal ecology: with especial reference to insects* 1931
CHAPMAN, Valentine Jackson *Coastal vegetation* 1964
CHARLES-EDWARDS, Thomas Charles & RICHARDSON, Brian *They saw it happen* Vol. III (1689–1897) 1958
CHARLESWORTH, John Kaye *The quaternary era* 2 vols. 1957
CHARLTON, Lionel Evelyn Oswald *Britain at war: the Royal Air Force from September 1939 to September 1945* 5 vols. 1941–7
CHASE, John Centlivres *The Cape of Good Hope and the Eastern Province of Algoa Bay* ed. J. S. Christophers 1843
Chatelaine (Toronto) 1928–
CHATFIELD, Charles Hugh & TAYLOR, Charles Fayette *The airplane and its engine* 1928
— (ed. 2) 1932
CHATTERTON, Edward Keble *The auxiliary patrol* 1923
CHEADLE, Walter Butler *Journal of a trip across Canada, 1862–1863* 1931
CHEESEMAN, Thomas Frederick *Manual of the New Zealand flora* 1906
Chemical abstracts 1906–
Chemical and engineering news 1942–
Chemical gazette 1842–59
Chemical news and journal of physical science (title varies) 1859–1932
Chemical Society of London *Annual reports on the progress of chemistry* See under title
Journal 1862–
Proceedings 1890–1914
Quarterly reviews 1947–71
Chemistry and industry 1932–
Chemistry in Britain 1965–
CHENG, Thomas Clement *The biology of animal parasites* 1964
CHESHIRE, Geoffrey Leonard *Bomber pilot* 1943
CHESTERFIELD, 4th Earl of (Philip Dormer Stanhope) (1694–1773) *Letters* ed. B. Dobrée 6 vols. 1932
CHESTERTON, Gilbert Keith *Autobiography* 1936
The club of queer trades 1905
The flying inn 1914
Four faultless felons 1930
George Bernard Shaw 1910
The incredulity of Father Brown 1926
The innocence of Father Brown 1911
The man who was Thursday: a nightmare 1908
The Napoleon of Notting Hill 1904
Orthodoxy 1909
The thing 1929
The wisdom of Father Brown 1914
CHEYNEY, Reginald Evelyn Peter S. *I'll say she does!* 1945
You can always duck 1943
Chicago (title varies) 1952–
Chicago Daily News 1876–1960
Chicago Record 1881–1901
Chicago Tribune 1847–
CHILDE, Vere Gordon *The Danube in prehistory* 1929
The dawn of European civilization 1925
— (ed. 3) 1939
— (ed. 6) 1957
The most ancient East 1928
— (rewritten with title *New light on the most ancient East*) 1934
— (rewritten) 1952
China now 1970–
CHOMSKY, Avram Noam *Aspects of the theory of syntax* 1965
The logical structure of linguistic theory 1975
Syntactic structures 1957
—— & HALLE, Morris *The sound pattern of English* 1968
CHOPPIN, Gregory Robert *Experimental nuclear chemistry* 1961
Christian 1973–
Christian Century, The 1900–
Christian Science Monitor (Boston, Mass.) 1908–
Christian World, The 1857–

CHRISTIE, Agatha Mary Clarissa (1890–1976) *The ABC murders* 1936
An autobiography 1977
The body in the library 1942
Come, tell me how you live 1946
Curtain: Poirot's last case 1975
Elephants can remember 1972
Evil under the sun 1941
Lord Edgware dies 1933
The mirror crack'd from side to side 1962
The moving finger 1943
Murder in the mews 1937
The murder of Roger Ackroyd 1926
Murder on the Orient Express 1934
The mysterious affair at Styles 1921
The pale horse 1961
Peril at End House 1932
Poirot investigates 1924
Postern of fate 1973
Third girl 1966

'CHRISTOPHER, John' (Christopher Samuel Youd) *The twenty-second century* 1954

CHRISTOPHERSEN, Paul *The articles: a study of their theory and use in English* 1939

CHRYSLER, Charles Byron *White slavery* 1911

CHUJOY, Anatole *The dance encyclopedia* 1949
— (rev. ed. by A. Chujoy & P. W. Manchester) 1967

CHURCH, Richard Thomas *The voyage home* 1964

Church Missionary Society *A grammar and vocabulary of the language of New Zealand* ed. S. Lee from materials supplied by T. Kendall 1820

Church quarterly review 1875–1968

CHURCHILL, Randolph Spencer & GILBERT, Martin *Winston S. Churchill* 1966–

CHURCHILL, Winston (1871–1947) *Coniston* 1906
The crisis 1901

CHURCHILL, Winston Leonard Spencer *The end of the beginning: war speeches, 1942* compiled by C. Eade 1943
Into battle: speeches compiled by R. S. Churchill 1941
My early life: a roving commission 1930
The Second World War 6 vols. 1948–53 (UK 1948–54)
Secret session speeches compiled by C. Eade 1946
Victory: war speeches, 1945 compiled by C. Eade 1946
The world crisis 6 vols. 1923–31

'CHURTON, Henry' (Albion Winegar Tourgée) *Toinette* 1874

CIST, Charles *Cincinnati in 1841: early annals and future prospects* 1841
ed. *The Cincinnati miscellany* 2 vols. 1845–6
Sketches and statistics of Cincinnati in 1851 1851

CLABBURN, Pamela *The needleworker's dictionary* 1976

CLACY, Ellen *A lady's visit to the gold diggings of Australia in 1852–53* 1853

CLAIBORNE, John Francis Hamtramck *Life and correspondence of John A. Quitman* 2 vols. 1860

CLANCEY, Phillip Alexander *The birds of Natal and Zululand* 1964

CLAPHAM, Alfred William *Romanesque architecture in western Europe* 1936

CLAPPERTON, Richard *No news on Monday* 1968

Clarendonian, The 1919–

CLARK, Alfred Joseph *Applied pharmacology* 1923
— (ed. 6) 1937

CLARK, David *Plane and geodetic surveying for engineers* 2 vols. 1923

CLARK, Donald Thomas & GOTTFRIED, Bert A. *Dictionary of business and finance* 1957
— (Apollo ed., with title *University dictionary of* ——) 1967

CLARK, Douglas *Death after evensong* 1969
Dread and water 1976
The gimmel flask 1977
Premedicated murder 1975
Sick to death 1971

CLARK, George Thomas *Leland Stanford, war governor of California* 1931

CLARK, Grahame *See* CLARK, John Grahame Douglas

CLARK, John Desmond *The prehistory of southern Africa* 1959

CLARK, John Grahame Douglas *Archaeology and society* 1939
— (ed. 3) 1957
World prehistory 1961
— (ed. 3) 1977

CLARK, Kenneth McKenzie *Another part of the wood: a self-portrait* 1974
Civilisation: a personal view 1969
The nude: a study of ideal art 1956

CLARK, Matthew *Home trade* 1930

CLARK, Nigel George *Modern organic chemistry: an introduction* 1964

CLARK, Percy Missen *The autobiography of an old drifter* 1936

CLARK, Ronald William & PYATT, Edward Charles *Mountaineering in Britain* 1957

CLARK, Walter John *International language, past, present & future* 1907

CLARK, Wilfrid Edward Le Gros *The tissues of the body* 1939

CLARKE, Arthur Charles *The deep range* 1957
The exploration of space 1951
The sands of Mars 1951

CLARKE, Austin *Later poems* 1961

CLARKE, George Sydenham *Fortification: its past achievements, recent development and future progress* 1890

CLARKE, John Henrik ed. *Harlem, U.S.A.* 1964

CLARKE, Marcus Andrew Hislop *His natural life* 1874 (UK 3 vols. 1875)

CLARKE, William *Every night book; or, Life after dark* 1827

CLARKE, William Eagle *Studies in bird migration* 2 vols. 1912

Clarke County Democrat (Grove Hill, Alabama) 1856– (title varies)

Classical Association *Proceedings* 1904–

Classical quarterly 1907–

Classification of occupations 1960 *See* United Kingdom. General Register Office

Classification of occupations and directory of occupational titles 1972 *See* United Kingdom. Department of Employment

CLAUSER, Henry Ray ed. *The encyclopedia of engineering materials and processes* 1963

CLEARY, Jon *High Commissioner* 1966
The long pursuit 1967
Peter's Pence 1974
The safe house 1975
The sundowners 1952

CLEGG, John *The freshwater life of the British Isles* 1952

CLEGG, John Trafford *Works: stories, sketches and rhymes in the Rochdale dialect* 2 vols. 1895–8

CLEIFE, Kenneth Philip H. *The slick and the dead* 1972

CLELAND, John *Memoirs of a woman of pleasure* 2 vols. 1749

CLEMENTS, Eileen Helen *High tension* 1959
Honey for the Marshal 1960

CLEMENTS, Frederic Edward *Plant indicators: the relation of plant communities to process and practice* 1920
Plant succession: an analysis of the development of vegetation 1916
Research methods in ecology 1905

CLEMENTS, Rex *A gipsy of the Horn* 1924

CLERK, Dugald *The gas engine* 1886

CLERKE, Agnes Mary *The system of the stars* 1890

CLEUGH, James tr. *R. Jungk's Brighter than a thousand suns* 1958

Cleveland Plain Dealer (Cleveland, Ohio) 1845–

CLEVELY, Hugh Desmond *Public enemy* 1953

Clinical pharmacology and therapeutics 1960–

CLINTON-BADDELEY, Victor Clinton *No case for the police* 1970
Only a matter of time 1969
To study a long silence 1972

CLOWES, Evelyn Mary *On the wallaby through Victoria* 1911

CLUNE, Francis Patrick (Frank) *The red heart: sagas of Centralia* 1944
Roaming round the Darling 1936

CLUTE, Willard Nelson *The common names of plants and their meanings* 1931

Coast to coast: Australian stories 1941–

COBB, Richard Charles *Reactions to the French Revolution* 1972

COBINE, James Dillon *Gaseous conductors* 1941

COCKAYNE, Leonard *New Zealand plants and their story* 1910

COCKBURN, Alexander & BLACKBURN, Robin eds. *Student power* 1969

COCKERELL, Douglas *Bookbinding, and the care of books* 1901

COCKETT, Sydney Russell & HILTON, Kenneth Arthur *Dyeing of cellulosic fibres and related processes* 1961

COCKLE, G. R. ed. *Car and locomotive cyclopedia of American practice* 1966
— (ed. 3) 1974

COCKTON, Henry *The life and adventures of Valentine Vox, the ventriloquist* 1840

COE, Malcolm James *The ecology of the Alpine zone of Mount Kenya* 1967

'COE, Tucker' (Donald Edwin Westlake) *Wax apple* 1970 (UK 1973)

COHEN, Antoine *The phonemes of English: a phonemic study of the vowels and consonants of Standard English* 1952

COHEN, Gerda Lesley *What's wrong with hospitals?* 1964

COHEN, Julius Berend *Organic chemistry for advanced students* 2 vols. 1907–13

COHEN, Laurence Jonathan *The diversity of meaning* 1962
— (ed. 2) 1966

COHEN, Leonard *Beautiful losers* 1966 (UK 1970)

COHEN, Morris Raphael & NAGEL, Ernest *An introduction to logic and scientific method* 1934

COHEN, Murray *Sensible words: linguistic practice in England 1640–1785* 1977

COHN, Nik *Pop from the beginning* 1969
— (reissued with title *Awopbopaloobopalopbamboom: pop from the beginning*) 1970

COKE, Desmond Francis Talbot *The bending of a twig* 1906
Sandford of Merton: a story of Oxford life 1903

Cold Spring Harbor symposia on quantitative biology 1933–

COLE, George Douglas Howard *Workshop organization* 1923
—— & COLE, Margaret Isabel *Murder at the munition works* 1940

COLEMAN, James Smoot *Nigeria* 1958

COLENSO, John William *Ten Weeks in Natal* 1855

COLERIDGE, Christabel Rose *Charlotte Mary Yonge: her life and letters* 1903

COLERIDGE, Samuel Taylor (1772–1834) *Philosophical lectures* ed. K. Coburn 1949

COLINVAUX, Paul Alfred *Introduction to ecology* 1973

Collector's guide 1942–

College English: an official organ of the National Council of Teachers of English (US) 1939–

College humor 1921–

COLLIER, John Henry Noyes *His monkey wife; or, Married to a chimp* 1930

COLLIER, Richard Hugheson *The city that wouldn't die: London, May 10–11, 1941* 1959
A house called Memory 1960

Collier's: the national weekly (US) 1905–57

COLLINGWOOD, Robin George (1889–1943) *An autobiography* 1939
The idea of history 1946
The idea of nature 1945
The new Leviathan; or, Man, society, civilization and barbarism 1942
The principles of art 1938
Roman Britain 1923

COLLINGWOOD, William Gershom *Scandinavian Britain* 1908

COLLINS, Archie Frederick *Manual of wireless telegraphy* 1906

COLLINS, Gilbert *The valley of eyes unseen* 1923

'COLLINS, Tom' (Joseph Furphy) *Such is life: being extracts from the diary of Tom Collins* 1903

Collins music encyclopaedia by J. A. Westrup & F. L. Harrison 1959

COLLINSON, William Edward *Contemporary English: a personal speech record* 1927

COLLOCOTT, Thomas Charles ed. *Dictionary of science and technology* 1971

COLMAN, George ('the younger', 1762–1836) *John Bull; or, The Englishman's fireside* 1803 (pirated ed.)
— (authorized ed.) 1805

COLMAN, Henry *Report on the agriculture of Massachusetts* See: Massachusetts. Agricultural Survey

Colonial and Indian Exhibition, 1886 *Reports on the colonial sections of the exhibition* ed. H. T. Wood 1887

Colorado magazine 1923–

COLT, Miriam Davis *We went to Kansas* 1862

Columbus Evening Dispatch (Columbus, Ohio) 1871–

Columbus News (Columbus, Montana) 1901–

COLYER, Charles Norman & HAMMOND, Cyril Oswald *Flies of the British Isles* 1951

Commentary, incorporating Contemporary Jewish record (American Jewish Committee) 1945–

Commission Géologique de la Finlande *Bulletin* 1895–

Committee of Inquiry on Decimal Currency *Report* 1963 *See* United Kingdom. Parliamentary papers

Committee on Broadcasting *Report* 1960 *See* United Kingdom. Parliamentary papers

Committee on the Future of Broadcasting (Chairman: Lord Annan) *Report* 1977 (Cmnd. 6753)

Commonwealth Scientific and Industrial Research Organization *See* Australia. Commonwealth Scientific ——

Compte rendu (Académie des Sciences) *See* Académie des Sciences

COMPTON, Arthur Holly *Atomic quest* 1956

COMPTON-BURNETT, Ivy *Darkness and day* 1951
A house and its head 1935
More women than men 1933

Computer journal 1958–

Computers and automation 1953–

Computers and the humanities: a newsletter 1966–

COMSTOCK, John Henry & COMSTOCK, Anna *A manual for the study of insects* 1895

CONAN DOYLE, Arthur *See* DOYLE, Arthur Conan

Concise Oxford dictionary of opera by H. Rosenthal & J. Warrack 1964

CONDON, Edward Uhler & ODISHAW, Hugh *Handbook of physics* 1958
— (ed. 2) 1967
—— & SHORTLEY, G. H. *The theory of atomic spectra* 1935

CONDON, Richard *The Manchurian candidate* 1959 (UK 1960)
The whisper of the axe 1976
Congressional globe See: United States. Congress. Debates
Congressional record See: United States. Congress. Debates
Connecticut *Public records of the Colony of Connecticut* 1850–90
Connecticut Academy of Arts and Sciences *Transactions* 1866–
Connecticut Agricultural Experiment Station *Annual report* 1877–
Bulletin 1877–
Connecticut probate records See: MANWARING, Charles William
CONNERS, Bernard F. *Don't embarrass the Bureau* 1972 (UK 1973)
Connoisseur, The: an illustrated magazine for collectors 1901–
CONNOLLY, Cyril Vernon *A romantic friendship: the letters of Cyril Connolly to Noel Blakiston* 1975
Conquest: a magazine of modern endeavour 1919–26
CONRAD, Joseph (Teodor Józef Konrad Korzeniowski) *Almayer's folly: a story of an eastern river* 1895
Lord Jim 1900
Nostromo: a tale of the seaboard 1904
The rover 1923
The shadow-line: a confession 1917
Suspense: a Napoleonic novel 1925
Victory: an island tale 1915
—— & HUEFFER, Ford Madox *Romance* 1903
CONSTABLE, John (1776–1837) *Correspondence* ed. R. B. Beckett 6 vols. 1962–8
Constellation, The 1829–32
Consumer reports 1942–
'CONTACT' (Alan John Bott) *An airman's outings* 1917
CONWAY, Robert Seymour, et al. *The præ-Italic dialects of Italy* 3 vols. 1933
COOK, James Henry *Fifty years on the old frontier, as cowboy, hunter, guide, scout, and ranchman* 1923
COOK, Robin *The crust on its uppers* 1962
COOKE, Deryck *The language of music* 1959
COOKE, John Esten *The Virginia comedians; or, Old days in the Old Dominion* 2 vols. 1854
COOKE, Nelson Magor & MARKUS, John *Electronics and nucleonics dictionary* 1960
COOKE, Rose Terry *Steadfast: the story of a saint and a sinner* 1889
'COOLIDGE, Susan' (Sarah Chauncey Woolsey) *What Katy did* 1873
What Katy did at school 1873 (UK 1874)
COON, Carleton Stevens *The races of Europe* 1939
COOPER, Courtney Ryley *Here's to crime* 1937
COOPER, David Graham *Psychiatry and anti-psychiatry* 1967
COOPER, Evelyn Barbara *Drown him deep* 1966
COOPER, James Fenimore *The deerslayer* 2 vols. 1841 (UK eds. 1 & 2, both 3 vols., both also 1841)
Home as found 2 vols. 1838 (UK ed. as *Eve Effingham; or, Home* 3 vols. 1838)
Homeward bound; or, The chase 2 vols. 1838 (UK ed. 3 vols. 1838)
Ned Myers; or, A life before the mast 1843 (UK ed. 2 vols. 1843)
The oak-openings 2 vols. 1848 (UK ed. as *The bee-hunter* 3 vols. 1848)
The red rover 3 vols. 1827
COOPER, John Butler *Coo-oo-ee! A tale of bushmen from Australia to Anzac* 1916
COOPER, Leonard *The accomplices* 1960
COOPER, Lettice Ulpha *Tea on Sunday* 1973
COOPER, Susan Augusta Fenimore *Rural hours* 1850
'COOPER, William' (Harry Summerfield Hoff) *Memoirs of a new man* 1966
The struggles of Albert Woods 1952
COPI, Irving Marmer *Symbolic logic* 1954
COPLESTON, Frederick Charles *A history of philosophy* 9 vols. 1946–75
COPSON, Edward Thomas *Metric spaces* 1968
CORCORAN, Dennis *Pickings from the portfolio of the reporter of the New Orleans 'Picayune'* 1846
'CORDELL, Alexander' (George Alexander Graber) *The bright Cantonese* 1967
CORELLI, Marie *The secret power* 1921
Thelma 3 vols. 1887
CORIAT, Isador H. *Abnormal psychology* 1911
Cork Examiner 1841–
CORKHILL, Thomas W. ed. *A concise building encyclopaedia* 1932
CORLETT, Peter Norman & TINSLEY, John David *Practical programming* 1968
CORMACK, William Epps *Narrative of a journey across the island of Newfoundland* 1856
CORNELL, Frederick Carruthers *The glamour of prospecting* 1920
Cornell University Agricultural Experiment Station *Bulletin* 1888–
Memoirs 1913–
CORNER, Edred John Henry *The life of plants* 1964
The natural history of palms 1966
Wayside trees of Malaya 2 vols. 1940
CORNISH, John *The provincials* 1951
CORRI, Eugene *Thirty years a boxing referee* 1915
'CORRIGAN, Mark' (Norman Lee) *Why do women —?* 1963
CORSON, Dale R. & LORRAIN, Paul *Introduction to electromagnetic fields and waves* 1962
'CORVO, Baron' *See* ROLFE, Frederick William
'CORY, Desmond' (John Lloyd McCarthy) *Bennett* 1977
Sunburst 1971
COSGRAVE, Patrick *Cheyney's law* 1977
Cosmopolitan, The 1886–1925
COTTON, Charles A. *Landscape, as developed by processes of normal erosion* 1941
Volcanoes as landscape forms 1944
COTTON, Frank & WILKINSON, Geoffrey *Advanced inorganic chemistry* 1962
— (ed. 2) 1966
— (ed. 3) 1972
COTTON, Harry *Advanced electrical technology* 1967
COTTRELL, Alan Howard *An introduction to metallurgy* 1967
COUES, Elliott ed. *New light on the early history of the Greater Northwest: the manuscript journals of Alexander Henry .. and of David Thompson* 3 vols. 1897
COULTER, John Merle, BARNES, C. R., & COWLES, H. C. *A textbook of botany for colleges and universities* 2 vols. 1910–11
COULTER, Stephen *The château* 1974
Embassy 1969
The Soyuz affair 1977
Country gentleman, The 1853–65; 1898–
Country gentlemen's catalogue 1894–
Country gentlemen's magazine 1900–
Country life 1897–
Countryman, The 1927–
COURANT, Richard & ROBBINS, Herbert Ellis *What is mathematics?* 1941
Courier and Advertiser (Dundee) 1926–
Courier-Journal (Louisville, Kentucky) 1868–
Courier-Mail (Brisbane) 1953–
COURSE, Alfred George *A dictionary of nautical terms* 1962
Coursing calendar and review of the season 1857–1918
COURTENAY, Florence *Physical beauty: how to develop and preserve it* 1922
COURTIER, Sidney Hobson *Death in dream time* 1959
COUSTEAU, Jacques Yves & DUMAS, Frédéric *The silent world* 1953
COVARRUBIAS, Miguel *Island of Bali* 1937
— (another ed.) 1972
COWAN, James *The Maoris of New Zealand* 1910
COWAN, Lester ed. *Recording sound for motion pictures* 1931
COWARD, Noël Pierce *Australia visited, 1940* 1941
Blithe spirit: an improbable farce 1941 (UK 1942)
Design for living: a comedy 1933
Future indefinite 1954
Middle East diary 1944
Play parade 6 vols. 1934–62
Present indicative 1937
Private lives 1930
To-night at 8.30: plays 3 vols. 1936
COWELL, Colin Robert, et al. *Inlays, crowns, and bridges* ed. G. F. Kantorowicz 1963
COWELL, Emilie Marguerite *The Cowells in America: the diary of Mrs. S. Cowell, 1860–1861* ed. M. W. Disher 1934
COWELL, Joseph *Thirty years passed among the players in England and America* 1844
COWPER, William (1731–1800) *Correspondence* ed. T. Wright 4 vols. 1904
COX, Charles Brian & DYSON, Anthony Edward *The twentieth-century mind: history, ideas and literature in Britain* 3 vols. 1972
COX, James Stevens *An illustrated dictionary of hairdressing and wigmaking* 1966
COX, Nigel Shaun Maturin & GROSE, Michael William eds. *The organization and handling of bibliographic records by computer* 1967
COX, Ross *Adventures on the Columbia River* 2 vols. 1831 (US 1 vol. 1832)
COXE, William *A view of the cultivation of fruit trees, and the management of orchards and cider* 1817
COXHEAD, Eileen Elizabeth *The figure in the mist* 1955
One green bottle 1951
The thankless muse 1967
A wind in the west 1949
'CRADDOCK, Charles Egbert' (Mary Noailles Murfree) *In the Tennessee mountains* 1884
CRADDOCK, Harry *The Savoy cocktail book* 1930
'CRAIG, David' (Allan James Tucker) *A dead liberty* 1974
Young men may die 1970
CRAIG, Elizabeth *Collins family cookery* 1957
CRAIGIE, William Alexander & HULBERT, James R. eds. *A dictionary of American English on historical principles* See under title
Cramer's Pittsburgh almanac 1812–14; 1816–17
CRANDALL, Irving Bardshar *Theory of vibrating systems and sound* 1927
CRANDALL, Lee Saunders *The management of wild mammals in captivity* 1964
CRANE, Harold Hart *Letters 1916–32* ed. B. Weber 1952
— (paperback ed.) 1965
CRANE, Stephen *Maggie, a girl of the streets* 1893
The red badge of courage. An episode of the American Civil War 1895
CRAPSEY, Edward *The nether side of New York or, The vice, crime, and poverty of the great metropolis* 1872
CRASKE, Margaret & BEAUMONT, Cyril William *The theory and practice of the allegro in classical ballet* 1930
CRAWFORD, James Coutts *Recollections of travel in New Zealand and Australia* 1880
'CRAWFORD, Robert' (Hugh Crauford Rae) *Whip hand* 1972
CRAWFORD, Samuel *Basic engineering processes* 1964
CRAWFURD, John *History of the Indian archipelago* 3 vols. 1820
CREED, David *The trial of Lobo Icheka* 1971
Crescendo 1962–
'CRÈVECŒUR, J. H. ST. JOHN DE' (Michel Guillaume St. Jean de Crèvecœur) *Letters from an American farmer* 1782
CREW, Peter *Encyclopædic dictionary of mountaineering* 1968
Cricket 1882–1913
Cricketer, The 1921–
'CRISPIN, Edmund' (Robert Bruce Montgomery) *Buried for pleasure* 1948
Frequent hearses 1950
Glimpses of the moon 1977
The long divorce 1951
CRITCHLEY, Macdonald *Developmental dyslexia* 1964
The parietal lobes 1953
Critic, The (New York) 1881–1906
Critical review; or, Annals of literature 1756–1817
CROCKETT, David *Colonel Crockett's exploits and adventures in Texas .. written by himself* 1836 (attributed to Richard Penn Smith)
Narrative of the life of David Crockett 1834
Sketches and eccentricities of Colonel David Crockett See under title
CROCKETT, Samuel Rutherford *The dew of their youth* 1910
CROFT, John Michael *Spare the rod* 1954
CROFTS, Freeman Willis *Inspector French and the Cheyne mystery* 1926
CROKER, Bithia Mary *The Company's servant: a romance of Southern India* 1907
CROKER, Temple Henry, et al. *The complete dictionary of the arts and sciences* 3 vols. 1764–6
'CROMPTON, Richmal' (Richmal Crompton Lamburn) *Just — William* 1922
Still — William 1925
William again 1923
William and the evacuees 1940
William and the moon rocket 1954
William carries on 1942
William does his bit 1941
William — the detective 1935
CRONIN, Archibald Joseph *The citadel* 1937
Hatter's Castle 1931
The stars look down 1935
CRONIN, Bernard *Timber wolves* 1920
'CRONIN, Michael' (Brendan Leo Cronin) *Dead . . . and done with* 1959
CRONIN, Vincent *The wise man from the west* 1955
CROOKE, William *The tribes and castes of the North-Western Provinces and Oudh* 4 vols. 1896
CROOME, Honoria Renée Minturn *The faithless mirror* 1946
The forgotten place 1957
You've gone astray 1944
CROSBY, Elizabeth Caroline, et al. *Correlative anatomy of the nervous system* 1962
CROSBY, John Campbell *Nightfall* 1976 (UK 1977 with title *Snake*)
CROSS, Charles Frederick & BEVAN, Edward John *A text-book of paper-making* 1888
CROSS, Ian Robert *The backward sex* 1960
The God boy 1957 (UK 1958)
'CROSS, James' (Hugh Jones Parry) *To hell for half-a-crown* 1967
CROSSMAN, Richard Howard Stafford (1907–74) *The diaries of a Cabinet Minister* 3 vols. 1975–7
CROUDACE, Glynn *The scarlet bikini* 1970
CROWEST, Frederick James *Beethoven* 1899
CROWTHER, Sir Geoffrey *Outline of money* 1940
— (rev. ed.) 1948
CROWTHER, James Gerald & WHIDDINGTON, Richard *Science at war* 1947

CROY, Homer *How motion pictures are made* 1918 *R.F.D. No. 3* 1924
CRUICKSHANK, James G. *Soil geography* 1972
CRUMP, Barry John *A good keen man* 1960 *Hang on a minute, mate* 1961 (UK 1963)
CRUMP, James Irving & MAUL, Norman *Our airliners* 1940
CRYSTAL, David *Linguistics* 1971
—— & QUIRK, Charles Randolph *Systems of prosodic and paralinguistic features in English* 1964
CULBERTSON, Ely *Contract bridge blue book* 1930 *Contract bridge complete* 1936
CULLEY, Richard Spelman *A hand-book of practical telegraphy* 1863
'CULOTTA, Nino' (John Patrick O'Grady) *They're a weird mob* 1957 (UK 1958)
Cultivator, The: a monthly journal for the farm and the garden 1834–65
Cultural news from India 1960–
CULVER, Charles Mortimer tr. *E. Landolt's The refraction and accommodation of the eye and their anomalies* 1886
CUMBERLAND, Marten *Murmurs in the Rue Morgue* 1959
Cumberland News 1910–
CUMING, Fortescue *Sketches of a tour to the western country* 1810
CUMMINGS, Edward Estlin *eimi* 1933 *The enormous room* 1922 *Selected letters* ed. F. W. Dupee & G. Stade 1969
CUNNINGHAM, Daniel John *Text-book of anatomy* 1902
— (ed. 4) ed. A. Robinson 1913
CUNNINGTON, Cecil Willett *English women's clothing in the present century* 1952
——, CUNNINGTON, P. E., & BEARD, C. *A dictionary of English costume* 1960
Curme volume of linguistic studies 1930 See HATFIELD, James Taft, et al.
Current researches in anesthesia and analgesia 1922–56
Current slang (University of South Dakota) 1966–71
Current trends in linguistics 1963–
'CURTIS, James' *The gilt kid* 1936 *They drive by night* 1938
CUSACK, Norman Edward *The electrical and magnetic properties of solids* 1958
CUSHING, George Frederick tr. *P. Hajdú's Finno-Ugrian languages and peoples* 1975
CUSHING, Harvey Williams *The pituitary body and its disorders* 1912
Custom car 1970–
CUTHILL, Ronald tr. *J. Schober's Silk and the silk industry* 1930
Cyclopedia of American government ed. A. C. McLaughlin & A. B. Hart 3 vols. 1914

D

Dædalus 1955– (continuation of *Proceedings* of the American Academy of Arts and Sciences)
DAGLISH, Eric Fitch tr. *E. Schneider-Leyer's Dogs of the world* 1964
Daily Ardmoreite (Ardmore, Oklahoma) 1893–
Daily Colonist (Victoria, British Columbia) 1886–
Daily Evening Bulletin (San Francisco) 1855–95
Daily Graphic 1890–1926
Daily Herald 1912–64
Daily Mirror 1903–
Daily Nation (Nairobi, Kenya) 1960–
Daily News (New York) 1919–
Daily News (Perth, Western Australia) 1882–
Daily Oklahoman (Oklahoma City) 1894–
Daily Picayune (New Orleans) 1836–1914
Daily Progress (Charlottesville, Virginia) 1892–
Daily Record (Glasgow) 1895–
Daily Report 1904–9
Daily Sketch 1909–71
Daily Universal Register 1785–7 (continued as *The Times*)
DAKIN, Douglas *The unification of Greece, 1770–1923* 1972
DALE, Celia *Other people* 1964 *A spring of love* 1960
DALES, Rodney Phillips *Annelids* 1963
DALLAS, Eneas Sweetland *Kettner's book of the table: a manual of cookery* 1877
DALLIMORE, William & JACKSON, Albert Bruce *A handbook of coniferæ, including ginkgoaceæ* 1923
DALTON, Edward Tuite *Descriptive ethnology of Bengal* 1872
'DALY, Rann' (Edward Vance Palmer) *The outpost* 1924
DALY, Reginald Aldworth *The changing world of the Ice Age* 1934 *Igneous rocks and the depths of the earth* 1933
DANA, Edmund *Geographical sketches on the western country* 1819
Dancing times 1894–
DANGERFIELD, Stanley & HOWELL, Elsworth eds. *The international encyclopaedia of dogs* 1971
DANIEL, Glyn Edmund *A hundred years of archaeology* 1950
DARBISHIRE, Otto Bernhard tr. *A. von Buzágh's Colloid systems* 1937
D'ARBLAY, Mme Frances See BURNEY, Frances
DARLING, Malcolm Lyall *At freedom's door* 1949 *Wisdom and waste in the Punjab village* 1934
DARLINGTON, Cyril Dean *Cytology* 1965 *Recent advances in cytology* 1932
—— & MATHER, Kenneth *The elements of genetics* 1949
DARLINGTON, Philip Jackson *Zoogeography: the geographical distribution of animals* 1957
DAUBENMIRE, Rexford F. *Plants and environment* 1947
DAVEY, Wheeler Pedlar *A study of crystal structure and its applications* 1934
DAVID, Elizabeth *A book of Mediterranean food* 1950
— (another ed.) 1955
French country cooking 1951
French provincial cooking 1960
Italian food 1954
DAVIDS, Thomas William Rhys *Buddhism: being a sketch of the life and teachings of Gautama the Buddha* 1877
DAVIDSON, Lionel *A long way to Shiloh* 1966 *The night of Wenceslas* 1960 *The Rose of Tibet* 1962
DAVIES, Benjamin Lionel *Technology of plastics: manufacture: structure: design* 1949
DAVIES, David Pettit *Handling the big jets* 1967
DAVIES, Edmund Frank *Illyrian venture: the story of the British military mission to enemy-occupied Albania, 1943–44* 1952
DAVIES, Leslie Purnell *The shadow before* 1971 *What did I do tomorrow?* 1972
DAVIES, Rodney Deane & PALMER, Henry Procter *Radio studies of the universe* 1959
DAVIN, Daniel Marcus *For the rest of our lives* 1947
The gorse blooms pale 1947
ed. *New Zealand short stories* 1953
For 2nd ser. *see* STEAD, Christian Karlson
Not here, not now 1970
Roads from home 1949
The sullen bell 1956
'DAVIOT, Gordon' (Elizabeth Mackintosh) *The man in the queue* 1929
See also: 'TEY, Josephine'
DAVIS, Alec Edward *Package and print: the development of container and label design* 1967
DAVIS, Arthur Hoey *See* 'RUDD, Steele'
DAVIS, Charles Carroll *The marine and fresh-water plankton* 1955
DAVIS, Frederick Clyde *See* 'RANSOME, Stephen'
DAVIS, John Gilbert *A dictionary of dairying* 1950
— (ed. 2) 1955
DAVIS, Kingsley *Human society* 1949 (1948 = 'preliminary ed.')
DAVIS, Norman & WRENN, Charles Leslie eds. *English and medieval studies presented to J. R. R. Tolkien on the occasion of his 70th birthday* 1962
DAVIS, Peter Hadland & HEYWOOD, Vernon Hilton *Principles of angiosperm taxonomy* 1963
DAVISON, Frank Dalby *Children of the dark people: an Australian folk tale* 1936 *Dusty: the story of a sheep dog* 1946
DAVSON, Hugh *Textbook of general physiology* 1951
DAWE, Edward Arthur *Paper and its uses: a treatise for printers, stationers and others* 1914
DAWKINS, Richard *The selfish gene* 1976
DAWSON, Henry Christopher *The age of the gods: a study in the origins of culture in prehistoric Europe and the ancient East* 1928
DAY, Charles Russell *The music and musical instruments of Southern India and the Deccan* 1891
DAY, Frederick T. *An introduction to paper: its manufacture and use* 1962
DAY, Michael Herbert *Guide to fossil man* 1965
DAY LEWIS, Cecil *See* LEWIS, Cecil Day
DEAN, Francis Medcalf *Naturally occurring oxygen ring compounds* 1963
DEANS, John ed. *Pioneers of Canterbury: Deans letters, 1840–1854* 1937
DEARMER, Percy *The parson's handbook* 1899
— (ed. 13, by C. E. Pocknee) 1965
Debates and proceedings in the Congress of the United States See: United States. Congress. Debates
DE BEER, Gavin Rylands *Embryology and evolution* 1930
Vertebrate zoology 1928
— (ed. 2) 1951
DE BRES, Joris tr. *E. Mandel's Late capitalism* 1975
Dedham, Massachusetts *The early records of the town of Dedham, Massachusetts* ed. D. G. Hill 5 vols. 1886–99
DEE, Liang-lao tr. *Hsia Chih-yen's The coldest winter in Peking* 1978
DEEPING, George Warwick *Kitty* 1927
Roper's Row 1929
Second youth 1919
The secret sanctuary; or, The saving of John Stretton 1923
Sincerity 1912
Sorrell and son 1925
Three rooms 1924
DEER, William Alexander, et al. *An introduction to the rock-forming minerals* 1966 *Rock-forming minerals* 5 vols. 1962–3
DEFENDORF, Allen Ross tr. *E. Kraepelin's Clinical psychiatry: a text-book for students and physicians* 1902
DE FERRANTI, Basil ed. *Living with the computer* 1971
DEIGHTON, Len *Billion-dollar brain* 1966
An expensive place to die 1967
Funeral in Berlin 1964
Horse under water 1963
The Ipcress file 1962
Len Deighton's London dossier with contributions by A. Bailey et al. 1967
Only when I larf 1968
SS–GB 1978
Spy story 1974
Twinkle, twinkle, little spy 1976
XPD 1981
Yesterday's spy 1975
DE KERCHOVE, René *International maritime dictionary* 1948
'DELAFIELD, E. M.' (Edmée Elizabeth Monica Dashwood) *Thank Heaven fasting* 1932
DE LA MARE, Walter John *The burning-glass, and other poems* 1945
Collected stories for children 1947
The connoisseur, and other stories 1926
Crossings: a fairy play 1921
ed. *Early one morning, in the spring: chapters on children and on childhood* 1935
The fleeting, and other poems 1933
The listeners, and other poems 1912
The Lord Fish 1933
Memoirs of a midget 1921
Memory, and other poems 1938
Private view 1953
The riddle, and other stories 1923
Songs of childhood 1902
This year, next year 1937
The three mulla-mulgars 1910
The traveller 1946
The veil, and other poems 1921
The wind blows over 1936
Winged chariot 1951
DELAND, Margaret Wade *Old Chester tales* 1898
DE LA ROCHE, Mazo *Finch's fortune* 1931
Jalna 1927
The master of Jalna 1933
Whiteoak harvest 1936
Whiteoaks (US ed. with title *Whiteoaks of Jalna*) 1929
Young Renny 1935
DELAVENAY, Émile *An introduction to machine translation* tr. by K. M. Delavenay and the author 1960
Delineator 1873–1937
DE LISSER, Herbert George *The cup and the lip* 1956
DELL, Jeffrey *Nobody ordered wolves* 1935
DELMAN, David *Sudden death* 1972 (UK 1973)
DEMANT, Vigo Auguste *Christian polity* 1936 *Religion and the decline of capitalism* 1952
DE MAUNY, Erik *The huntsman in his career* 1949
Democrat See *Clarke County Democrat*
Democratic State Journal (Sacramento, California) 1852–8
DE MORGAN, William Frend (1839–1917) *Alice-for-short* 1907
Joseph Vance 1906
The old madhouse (completed by M. E. De Morgan) 1919
The old man's youth and the young man's old age (completed by M. E. De Morgan) 1920 (UK 1921)
When ghost meets ghost 1914
DEMPSEY, Jack (William Harrison Dempsey) *Championship fighting* 1950
DENISON, William *Cricket: sketches of the players* 1846
DENLINGER, William Watson *The complete Boston [terrier]* 1955
DENNIS, Clarence James *The moods of Ginger Mick* 1916
The songs of a sentimental bloke 1915 (1916 impression used)
DENNY, Grace Goldena *Fabrics and how to know them* 1923
DENNYS, Nicholas Belfield *A descriptive dictionary of British Malaya* 1894
DENT, Colin *Quantity surveying by computer* 1964
DENTRY, Robert *Encounter at Kharmel* 1971

Department of Education and Science *See* United Kingdom
DEPUY, Charles H. & CHAPMAN, Orville L. *Molecular reactions and photochemistry* 1972
DERBY, George Horatio *See* 'PHOENIX, John'
Derbyshire Times 1854–
DERRICK, June *Teaching English to immigrants* 1966
DESCH, Cecil Henry *Metallography* 1910
DE SÉLINCOURT, Hugh *The cricket match* 1924
DESHA, Lucius Junius *Organic chemistry: the chemistry of the compounds of carbon* 1936
Design: a monthly journal for manufacturers and designers 1949–
Design and work 1876–81
Design engineering 1971–
DE SITTER, Lamoraal Ulbo *Structural geology* 1956
DE SOLA, Ralph & DE SOLA, Dorothy *A dictionary of cooking* 1969
DE TOLEDANO, Ralph ed. *Frontiers of jazz* 1947
Detroit Free Press (title varies) 1835–
DEUEL, Harry James *The lipids: their chemistry and biochemistry* 3 vols. 1951–7
DEUTSCH, Sid *Theory and design of television receivers* 1951
DEUTSCHER, Isaac *Marxism in our time* ed. T. Deutscher 1971 (UK 1972)
Stalin: a political biography 1949
DEVANNY, Jean *Bushman Burke* 1930
The butcher shop 1926
Dawn beloved 1928
Old savage, and other stories 1927
Developmental biology 1959–
DE VOTO, Bernard Augustine *Across the wide Missouri* 1947
DE VRIES, Leonard *Victorian advertisements* 1968
DE VRIES, Peter *The glory of the hummingbird* 1974 (UK 1975)
The Mackerel plaza 1958
DEWEES, William B. *Letters from an early settler of Texas* ed. 'C. Cordelle' (E. C. Kimball) 1852
DEXTER, Colin *Last seen wearing* 1976
Dial, The (Chicago) 1880–1929
DICK, Everett Newfon *The Dixie frontier* 1948
DICK, William Brisbane *The American Hoyle; or, Gentleman's hand-book of games* 1864 (and several later editions used)
DICKENS, Charles (1812–70) *Letters* ed. M. House et al. 1965–
Pictures from Italy 1846
DICKENS, Monica Enid *The happy prisoner* 1946
The heart of London 1961
Man overboard 1958
No more meadows 1953
One pair of feet 1942
One pair of hands 1939
DICKINSON, Emily Elizabeth (1830–86) *Poems* ed. T. H. Johnson 3 vols. 1955
DICKINSON, Gordon Cawood *Maps and air photographs* 1969
DICKINSON, Peter Malcolm de B. *The lizard in the cup* 1972
The poison oracle 1974
A pride of heroes 1969
Sleep and his brother 1971
DICKINSON, Reginald Ernest *Electric trains* 1927
DICKINSON, Thomas Albert *The aeronautical dictionary* 1945
DICKSON, Mora *A world elsewhere* 1964
DICKSON, William Puride tr. *T. Mommsen's The history of Rome* 4 vols. 1862–6
Dictionary of American English on historical principles, A ed. W. A. Craigie & J. R. Hulbert 4 vols. 1938–44
Dictionary of Americanisms on historical principles, A ed. M. M. Mathews 2 vols. 1951
Dictionary of Canadianisms on historical principles, A See: AVIS, Walter Spencer, et al.
Dictionary of Jamaican English See: CASSIDY, Frederic Gomes & LE PAGE, R. B.
Dictionary of national biography ed. L. Stephen et al. 63 vols. & Supplements 1885–
Dictionary of occupational terms 1921 *See* United Kingdom. Ministry of Labour
Dictionary of South African English, A See: BRANFORD, Jean
DIEHL, Edith *Bookbinding: its background and technique* 2 vols. 1946
DILLARD, Joey Lee *Black English: its history and usage in the United States* 1972
DILLEY, Arthur Urbane *Oriental rugs and carpets* 1931
DILLS, Lanie *The 'official' CB slanguage language dictionary and cross-reference* ed. D. Gilbertson 1975
— (rev. ed.) 1976
DIMENT, Adam *The bang bang birds* 1968
The dolly dolly spy 1967
The great spy race 1968
Think Inc. 1971
DI MONA, Joseph *Last man at Arlington* 1973 (UK 1974)
DINGWALL, William Orr ed. *A survey of linguistic science* 1971
DIRAC, Paul Adrien Maurice *The principles of quantum mechanics* 1930
— (ed. 3) 1947
DIRINGER, David *The alphabet: a key to the history of mankind* 1948
Discovery: a monthly popular journal of knowledge 1920–66
Diseases of the nervous system 1940–
DISRAELI, Benjamin *The voyage of Captain Popanilla* 1828
Dissertation abstracts 1952–
DITCHBURN, Robert William *Light* 1952
— (ed. 2) 1963
DITMARS, Raymond Lee *The reptile book* 1907
Snakes of the world 1931
DIVER, Katherine Helen Maud *Candles in the wind* 1909
'DIVINE, David' (Arthur Durham Divine) *The King of Fassarai* 1950
'DIX, Dorothy' (Elizabeth Meriwether Gilmer) *Fables of the elite* 1902
DOBIE, James Frank ed. *Rainbow in the morning* 1965 ('reprint ed.' of Vol. V of *Publications of the Texas Folklore Society* 1926)
DOBSON, Gordon Miller Bourne *Exploring the atmosphere* 1963
— (ed. 2) 1968
Documentary history of American industrial society, A ed. J. R. Commons et al. 11 vols. 1910–11
Documents relative to the colonial history of the State of New-York, procured in Holland, England and France collected by J. R. Brodhead; ed. E. B. O'Callaghan & B. Fernow 15 vols. 1853–87
DODD, Robert Edward *Chemical spectroscopy* 1962
'DOESTICKS, Q. K. Philander' (Mortimer Neal Thomson) *Doesticks, what he says* 1855
Doklady See: Academy of Sciences of the U.S.S.R.
DOLINSKY, Meyer *There is no silence* 1959
'DOMINIC, R. B.' (Mary Jane Latsis & Martha Henissart) *Epitaph for a lobbyist* 1974
See also: 'LATHEN, Emma'
DOMINY, Eric Norman *Teach yourself judo* 1954
DOMMETT, William Erskine *A dictionary of aircraft* 1918
DONCASTER, Leonard *An introduction to the study of cytology* 1920
DONLEAVY, James Patrick *The ginger man* 1955
DONOVAN, Charles Henry Wynne *With Wilson in Matabeleland; or, Sport and war in Zambesia* 1894
DOOGUE, Raymond Brian & MORELAND, John Munn *New Zealand sea anglers' guide* 1960
'DOONE, Jice' (Vance Marshall) *Timely tips for new Australians* 1926
DOPPING, Olle *Computers and data processing* 1970
DORSON, Richard M. ed. *Peasant customs and savage myths: selections from the British folklorists* 2 vols. 1968
DOS PASSOS, John Roderigo *The best times: an informal memoir* 1966 (UK 1968)
The big money 1936
The 42nd parallel 1930
1919 1932
Streets of night 1923
Three soldiers 1921 (UK 1922)
DOUGALL, John tr. *M. Born's Atomic physics* 1935
DOUGHERTY, George S. *The criminal as a human being* 1924
DOUGLAS, George Norman *London street games* 1916
South wind 1917
DOUGLAS, Jack D. & JOHNSON, John M. eds. *Existential sociology* 1977
DOUGLAS, Keith Castellain (1920–44) *Alamein to Zem Zem* 1946
DOUGLAS, Lloyd Cassel *Forgive us our trespasses* 1932 (UK 1937)
White banners 1936
DOUGLAS, Norman *See* DOUGLAS, George Norman
'DOUGLAS, O.' (Anna Buchan) *Penny plain* 1920
DOUGLAS-TODD, Charles Henry *The popular whippet* 1961
DOUGLASS, Frederick *Narrative of the life of Frederick Douglass, an American slave* 1845
Down beat 1934–
DOWNEY, Hal ed. *Handbook of hematology* 4 vols. 1938
DOWNING, W. H. *Digger dialects* 1919
Downside review 1880–
DOWSON, Ernest Christopher (1867–1900) *Letters* ed. D. Flower & H. Maas 1967
DOXIADIS, Constantinos Apostolou *Between dystopia and utopia* 1966 (UK 1968)
DOYLE, Arthur Conan *The green flag, and other stories of war and sport* 1900
His last bow 1917
The history of spiritualism 2 vols. 1926
The lost world 1912
The Maracot Deep, and other stories 1929
The valley of fear 1915
DRABBLE, Margaret *The Garrick year* 1964
Jerusalem the golden 1967
The millstone 1965
A summer bird-cage 1962
The waterfall 1969
DRACKETT, Philip Arthur *Motor rallying* 1963
DRAKE, Daniel *Natural and statistical view; or, Picture of Cincinnati and the Miami country* 1815
DRAPER, Alfred *The death penalty* 1972
Swansong for a rare bird 1970
DRAYTON, John *A view of South-Carolina, as respects her natural and civil concerns* 1802
DREISER, Theodore *An American tragedy* 2 vols. 1925 (UK 1926)
The financier 1912
DRISCOLL, Peter *The white lie assignment* 1971
The Wilby conspiracy 1972 (UK 1973)
Drive 1967–
DRIVER, Christopher *The disarmers* 1964
Drum (East African ed.) 1965–
DRUMMOND, Charles *Death and the leaping ladies* 1968
A death at the bar 1972
Death at the furlong post 1967
The odds on death 1969
'DRUMMOND, Ivor' (Roger Erskine Longrigg) *The jaws of the watchdog* 1973
The man with the tiny head 1969
The power of the bug 1974
DRUMMOND, June *Bang! Bang! You're dead!* 1973
The black unicorn 1959
The Gantry episode 1968
DRUMMOND, Montagu tr. *G. Haberlandt's Physiological plant anatomy* 1914
DRURY, William D. ed. *The book of gardening: a handbook of horticulture* 1900
DUANE, Alexander tr. *E. Fuchs's Text-book of ophthalmology* 1892
Dublin University review 1885–7
Duckett's register 1946–
'DUDLEY-GORDON, Tom' (Dudley Barker et al.) *Coastal Command at war* 1943
DUFF, David Skene *Victoria in the Highlands* 1968
DUFFY, Maureen *That's how it was* 1962
DUGGAR, Benjamin Minge *Fungous diseases of plants* 1909
DUKE-ELDER, William Stewart *Parsons' Diseases of the eye* See: PARSONS, John Herbert
Text-book of ophthalmology 7 vols. 1932–54
—— et al. *System of ophthalmology* 1958–
DU MAURIER, Daphne *The breaking point: eight stories* 1959
Rebecca 1938
DU MAURIER, George Louis Palmella Busson *The Martian* 1897
The young George du Maurier: a selection of his letters, 1860–67 ed. D. du Maurier 1951
Dumfries and Galloway Standard 1843–
DUNBAR, Carl Owen & RODGERS, John *Principles of stratigraphy* 1957
DUNBAR, Janet *Mrs. G. B. S.: a biographical portrait of Charlotte Shaw* 1963
DUNCAN, Lee *Over the wall* 1936
DUNCAN, Lew Wallace & SCOTT, Charles F. *History of Allan and Woodson Counties, Kansas* 1901
DUNCAN, William Murdoch *The big timer* 1973
DUNDES, Alan ed. *Mother wit from the laughing barrel: readings in the interpretation of Afro-American folklore* 1973
DUNDY, Elaine *The dud avocado* 1958
DUNLAP, William *Memoirs of George Fred. Cooke, Esq., late of the Theatre Royal, Covent Garden* 2 vols. 1813
Thirty years ago; or, The memoirs of a water drinker 2 vols. 1836
DUNLOP, Derrick Melville ed. *Textbook of medical treatment* 1939
— (ed. 10) ed. D. M. Dunlop & S. Alstead 1966
DUNN, Robert *The shameless diary of an explorer* 1907
DUNNE, Finley Peter *Mr. Dooley in peace and in war* 1898
DUNPHY, Eamon *Only a game? The diary of a professional footballer* ed. P. Ball 1976
DURANTE, James Francis ('Jimmy') & KEFOED, Jack C. *Night clubs* 1931
DURRANT, Philip John & DURRANT, Beryl *Introduction to advanced inorganic chemistry* 1962
DURRELL, Gerald Malcolm *The Bafut beagles* 1954
Catch me a Colobus 1972
The drunken forest 1956
Encounters with animals 1958
Menagerie Manor 1964
My family and other animals 1956
The overloaded ark 1953
Three singles to adventure 1954
Two in the bush 1966
The whispering land 1961
A zoo in my luggage 1960

Durrell, Lawrence George *Balthazar* 1958
Bitter lemons 1957
Clea 1960
Justine 1957
Mountolive 1958
Nunquam 1970
Spirit of place: letters and essays on travel ed. A. G. Thomas 1969
Tunc 1968
Durst, Paul *Badge of infamy* 1968
Dury, George Harry ed. *Essays in geomorphology* 1966
Du Toit, Alexander Logie *Our wandering continents* 1937
Dwight, Margaret van Horn *A journey to Ohio in 1810* ed. M. Farrand 1912
Dyer, Robert *Nine years of an actor's life* 1833
Dyott, William *Diary 1781–1845* ed. R. W. Jeffery 2 vols. 1907
Dyson, Edward George *Fact'ry 'ands* 1906

E

Eaddy, Percy Allen *Hull down* 1933
Eagleson, Robert D. & McKie, Ian *The terminology of Australian national football* 3 parts 1968–9 (Sydney University: Australian Language Research Centre: Occasional Papers Nos. 12–14)
Eagleton, Terence Francis *Criticism and ideology: a study in Marxist literary theory* 1976
Earl, John *How to choose and use tuners and amplifiers* 1970
Earle, Augustus *A narrative of a nine months' residence in New Zealand, in 1827; together with a journal of a residence in Tristan D'Acunha* 1832
— (new ed.) ed. E. H. McCormick 1966
Early music 1973–
Earth-science reviews 1966–
East Africa journal 1964–
East African annual 1936–
East African Standard (Nairobi, Kenya) 1902–
East Hampton, New York *Records* 5 vols. 1887–1905
East London (Daily) Dispatch (East London, Cape Province) 1872–1925
Eastern Evening News (Norwich) 1882–
Eastern Province Herald (Port Elizabeth, S. Africa) 1845–
Eastlake, Charles Lock *Hints on household taste in furniture, upholstery and other details* 1868
Eastman, Charles Rochester, et al. tr. *K. A. von Zittel's Text-book of palæontology* 3 vols. 1900–25
Eastman, Max Forrester tr. *L. Trotsky's The history of the Russian Revolution* 3 vols. 1932–3
Eaton, Amos *A manual of botany for the northern states* 1817
— (ed. 2 with title —— *for the northern and middle states*) 1818
Eaton, Timothy, & Co. Ltd. *A shopper's view of Canada's past: pages from Eaton's catalogues 1886–1930* 1969
Eberhart, Mignon Good *Danger money* 1974 (UK 1975)
Ebers, John *Seven years of the King's Theatre* 1828
Eby, Cecil DeGrotte *The siege of the Alcázar* 1965 (UK 1966)
Eccles, William Henry *Wireless telegraphy and telephony: a handbook of formulae, data and information* 1915
Ecclestone, Alan *A staircase for silence* 1977
Ecological monographs 1931–
Ecology 1920–
Economic geology and Bulletin of the Society of Economic Geologists 1905–
Economic journal 1891–
Economist, The 1843–
Eddington, Arthur Stanley *The internal constitution of the stars* 1926
The nature of the physical world 1928
New pathways in science 1935
Report on the relativity theory of gravitation 1918
Space, time and gravitation: an outline of the general relativity theory 1920
Eddison, Eric Rücker (1888–1945) *A fish dinner in Memison* 1941
— (new ed.) 1968
The Mezentian Gate 1958
— (new ed.) 1972
Mistress of mistresses 1935
The worm Ouroboros 1922
Eddy, Arthur Jerome *Cubists and Post-Impressionism* 1914 (UK 1915)
Eddy, Mary Baker *Science and health* 1875
Edelman, Jacob Murray *Political language* 1977
Edgcumbe, Kenelm *Industrial electrical measuring instruments* 1908
Edgeworth, Maria *Letters from England 1813–1844* ed. C. Colvin 1971
Maria Edgeworth in France and Switzerland: selections from the Edgeworth family letters ed. C. Colvin 1979
Edib, Halidé *The clown and his daughter* 1935
Edinburgh Evening News 1873– (title varies)
Edinburgh medical and surgical journal 1805–55
Edinburgh new philosophical journal 1826–64
Edinburgh Obstetrical Society *Transactions* 1868–1921
Edington, George Miller & Gilles, Herbert Michael *Pathology in the tropics* 1969
— (ed. 2) 1976
Edlin, Herbert Leeson *Collins guide to tree planting and cultivation* 1970
The forester's handbook 1953
Edmonton Journal (Edmonton, Alberta) 1903–
Edward, David B. *The history of Texas* 1836
Edwardes, Annie *A Girton girl* 3 vols. 1885
Edwards, Anthony William Fairbank *Likelihood: an account of the statistical concept of likelihood and its application to scientific inference* 1972
Edwards, Elwyn Hartley *Saddlery* 1963
Edwards, John Newman *Shelby and his men; or, The war in the west* 1867
Edwards's botanical register 1829–47
'Egan, Lesley' (Barbara Elizabeth Linington) *Blind search* 1977
Paper chase 1972 (UK 1973)
Egan, Pierce *Anecdotes of the turf, the chase, the ring and the stage* 1827
Boxiana; or, Sketches of ancient and modern pugilism 3 vols. 1812–21 (Vol. IV, 1824, by J. Badcock)
— (new ser.) 2 vols. 1828–9
The life of an actor 1825
Eggleston, Edward *The circuit rider: a tale of the heroic age* 1874
The end of the world: a love story 1872
The Hoosier school-master 1871 (UK 1872)
Egleton, Clive *Seven days to a killing* 1973
Ehrenberg, Victor L. *From Solon to Socrates: Greek history and civilization during the sixth and fifth centuries B.C.* 1968
Einstein, Albert *See* Adams, Edwin Plimpton
Einstein, Alfred *Music in the Romantic era* 1947
Eiseley, Loren Carey *The immense journey* 1957
Ekwall, Bror Oscar Eilert *The place-names of Lancashire* 1922
Electrical communication 1922–
Electrical world (title varies) 1899–
Electrician, The 1861–1952
Electrochemical industry 1902–9 (1905–9 with title *Electrochemical and metallurgical industry*)
Electronic engineering 1941–
Electronics (New York) 1930–
Eliason, Norman E. *Tarheel talk: an historical study of the English language in North Carolina to 1860* 1956
Eliot, Charles Norton Edgcumbe *A Finnish grammar* 1890
See also: 'Odysseus'
'Eliot, George' (Marian Evans) (1819–80) tr. *L. Feuerbach's The essence of Christianity* 1854
The George Eliot letters ed. G. S. Haight 7 vols. 1954–6
tr. *D. F. Strauss's The life of Jesus, critically examined* 3 vols. 1846
Eliot, Thomas Stearns (1888–1965) tr. *Anabasis* by 'St.-J. Perse' (A. St. Léger Léger) 1930
Ara vos prec 1920
Burnt Norton 1941
The cocktail party: a comedy 1950
Collected poems, 1909–1935 1936
Collected poems, 1909–1962 1963
The confidential clerk 1954
The dry salvages 1941
East Coker 1940
The elder statesman 1959
Elizabethan essays 1934
The family reunion 1939
Little Gidding 1942
Murder in the cathedral 1935
Notes towards the definition of culture 1948
Old Possum's book of practical cats 1939
On poetry and poets 1957
Poems 1919
Prufrock, and other observations 1917
The rock: a pageant play 1934
Selected essays 1917–1932 1932
— (ed. 3) 1951; new impression 1953
Sweeney agonistes 1932
The waste land 1922 (UK 1923)
The waste land: a facsimile and transcript of the original drafts including the annotations of Ezra Pound ed. V. Eliot 1971
'Ellan, B. J.' *Spitfire!: the experiences of a fighter pilot* 1942
Ellery Queen's mystery magazine 1941–
Ellin, Stanley *The bind* 1970 (UK ed. with title *The man from nowhere* 1971)
The eighth circle 1958 (UK 1959)
Elliot, John Herbert *Duel* 1969
Ellis, Carleton *The chemistry of synthetic resins* 2 vols. 1935
Ellis, Henry Havelock *Studies in the psychology of sex* 7 vols. 1897–1928
Ellis, William *A journal of a tour around Hawaii* 1825
Emblen, Donald Lewis *Peter Mark Roget, the word and the man* 1970
Emerson, Ralph Waldo (1803–82) *Journals* ed. E. W. Emerson & W. E. Forbes 10 vols. 1909–14
Emory, William Hemsley *Notes of a military reconnaissance, from Fort Leavenworth, in Missouri, to San Diego, in California* 1848
Empey, Arthur Guy *'Over the top' by an American soldier who went, together with Tommy's dictionary of the trenches* 1917 (UK also 1917 with title *From the fire step*)
Empson, William *The gathering storm* 1940
Poems 1935
Seven types of ambiguity 1930
Some versions of pastoral 1935
The structure of complex words 1951
Encounter 1953–
Encyclopædia Britannica book of the year See *Britannica book of the year*
Encyclopedia Canadiana ed. J. E. Robbins 10 vols. 1957–8
Encyclopaedia Judaica ed. C. Roth & G. Wigoder 16 vols. 1971–2
Encyclopædia medica ed. C. Watson 15 vols. 1899–1910
Encyclopedia of chemical technology See: Kirk, Raymond E. & Othmer, Donald F.
Encyclopaedia of New Zealand, An ed. A. H. McLintock 3 vols. 1966
Encyclopedia of philosophy, The ed. P. Edwards et al. 8 vols. 1967
Encyclopedia of polymer science and technology ed. H. Mark et al. 1964–
Encyclopaedia of psychology ed. H. J. Eysenck et al. 3 vols. 1972
Encyclopædia of religion and ethics ed. J. Hastings 13 vols. 1908–26
Encyclopedia of sports, games and pastimes 1935
Encyclopædia of the social sciences ed. E. R. A. Seligman et al. 15 vols. 1930–5
Encyclopædic dictionary, The by R. Hunter et al. 7 vols. 1879–88
— (reissue with Suppl. 1902–4)
Encyclopaedic dictionary of physics ed. J. Thewlis et al. 9 vols. 1961–4; Suppl. 2 vols. 1966–7
Endeavour 1942–
Endocrinology 1917–
Engel, Carl *A descriptive catalogue of the musical instruments in the South Kensington Museum* 1870
— (ed. 2) 1874
Engineering 1866–
Engineering news-record 1874–
English journal (US National Council of Teachers of English) 1912–
English language teaching 1946– (from 1973 with title *English language teaching journal*)
English mechanic, The (title varies) 1865–1923
English studies: a journal of English letters and philology 1919–
Englishwoman, The 1909–21
Ennes, Harold Eugene *Television broadcasting: equipment, systems and operating fundamentals* 1971
Ensor, Robert Charles Kirkwood *England, 1870–1914* 1936
Entomological Society of London (later Royal ——) *Proceedings* 1926–76 (from 1936 divided into separate series)
Transactions 1834–
Entwistle, William James *Aspects of language* 1953
Environmental conservation 1974–
Erdman, Paul *The silver bears* 1974
Ersine, Noel *Underworld and prison slang* 1935
Erskine-Murray, James *A handbook of wireless telegraphy* 1907
Esau, Katherine *Plant anatomy* 1953
Esquire 1933–
Essays and studies by members of the English Association 1910–
Essays in criticism: a quarterly journal of literary criticism 1951–
Essex Institute [Salem, Massachusetts] historical collections 1859–
Essig, Edward Oliver *College entomology* 1942
Etc.: a review of general semantics 1943–
Etherington, Harold ed. *Nuclear engineering handbook* 1958
Eugene Register-Guard (Eugene, Oregon) 1955–
European Organization for Nuclear Research (Conseil Européen pour la Recherche Nucléaire) *Proceedings of CERN symposium* 2 vols. 1956
Evans, Arthur John *The Palace of Minos* 7 vols. 1921–36
Evans, Bergen & Evans, Cornelia *A dictionary of contemporary American usage* 1957

Evans, Charles See Evans, Robert Charles
Evans, Emyr Estyn *Irish folk ways* 1957
Evans, George Ewart *Ask the fellows who cut the hay* 1956
The horse in the furrow 1960
The pattern under the plough 1966
Where beards wag all 1970
Evans, Howard T. tr. *G. Hägg's General and inorganic chemistry* 1969
Evans, John G. *The environment of early man in the British Isles* 1975
Evans, Philip *The bodyguard man* 1973
Evans, Robert Charles *On climbing* 1956
Evans, Robley Dunglison *The atomic nucleus* 1955
Evans-Pritchard, Edward Evan *Social anthropology* 1951
—— et al. *The institutions of primitive society* 1954
Evelyn, John (1620–1706) *Diary* ed. E. S. de Beer 6 vols. 1955
Evening News (Edinburgh): see *Edinburgh Evening News*
Evening News (London) 1881–1980
Evening Post (Nottingham) 1878–
Evening Post (Wellington, New Zealand) 1865–
Evening Standard 1860–1980 (continued as *New Standard*)
Evening Sun (Baltimore, Maryland) 1910–
Evening Telegram (St. John's, Newfoundland) 1879–
Everett, Thomas H. *Living trees of the world* 1969
Everybody's magazine (US) 1899–1929
Ewart, Alfred James tr. *W. Pfeffer's The physiology of plants* 3 vols. 1900–6
Ewart, Gavin *The Gavin Ewart show: poems* 1971
Experiment station record (United States Department of Agriculture) 1889–1946
Experimental wireless and the wireless engineer 1923–31
Eye opener 1902–22
Eyre, Mary *A lady's walks in the south of France in 1863* 1865

F

Fabian News 1891–
Fairbanks Daily News-Miner (Fairbanks, Alaska) 1903–
Fairbridge, Rhodes Whitmore ed. *The encyclopedia of atmospheric sciences and astrogeology* 1967
ed. *The encyclopedia of geomorphology* 1968
Fairchild, Henry Pratt ed. *Dictionary of sociology* 1944
Falla, Robert Alexander, Sibson, R. B., & Turbott, E. G. *A field guide to the birds of New Zealand and outlying islands* 1966
Famous plays 12 vols. 1931–9
Faraday, Wilfred Barnard ed. *A glossary of aeronautical terms* 1919
Faraday Society *Transactions* 1905–
Farber, Marvin *The foundation of phenomenology; Edmund Husserl and the quest for a rigorous science of philosophy* 1943
Farmer, Fannie Merritt *The Boston Cooking-School cook book* 1896 (and several later editions used)
Farmer and stockbreeder, The 1889–
Farmers weekly 1934–
Farnie, Henry Brougham *The golfer's manual* 1857
Farnol, John Jeffery *The broad highway* 1910
The definite object 1917
Farquharson, M. G., et al. *Glossary of broadcasting terms* 1941
Farrell, James Thomas *Studs Lonigan: a trilogy* (Young Lonigan; The young manhood of Studs Lonigan; Judgment day) 1935 (UK 1936)
Young Lonigan: a boyhood in Chicago streets 1932
The young manhood of Studs Lonigan 1934
Farrer, Reginald John *My rock-garden* 1907
Farrow, Edward Samuel *A dictionary of military terms* 1918
Fast, Howard Melvin *The immigrants* 1977
Fastnedge, Ralph *English furniture styles, from 1500 to 1830* 1955
Faulkner, William *Absalom, Absalom!* 1936
As I lay dying 1930 (UK 1935)
A fable 1954 (UK 1955)
Go down, Moses, and other stories 1942
The hamlet 1940
Light in August 1932 (UK 1933)
Sanctuary 1931
Sartoris 1929 (UK 1932)
The sound and the fury 1929
The wild palms 1939
Fay, Albert Hill *A glossary of the mining and mineral industry* 1920
Fearon, Diana *Murder-on-Thames* 1960
Fearon, William Robert *An introduction to biochemistry* 1934
Feather, Leonard Geoffrey *The encyclopedia of jazz* 1955 (UK 1956)
Inside be-bop 1949
Federation proceedings (Federation of American Societies for Experimental Biology) 1942–
Feinsilver, Lillian Mermin *The taste of Yiddish* 1970
Feldenkrais, Moshé *Judo: the art of defence and attack* 1941
Femina (Bombay) 1959–
Fennessy, J. C. *The sonnet in the bottle* 1951
'Fenwick, Elizabeth' (Elizabeth Fenwick Way) *Impeccable people* 1971
A long way down 1959
Ferber, Edna *Dawn O'Hara, the girl who laughed* 1911
Ferguson, Charles D. *The experiences of a forty-niner during thirty-four years' residence in California and Australia* ed. F. T. Wallace 1888
Fergusson, Bernard Edward *The watery maze: the story of combined operations* 1961
Fergusson, Erna *Our Southwest* 1940
'Fern, Fanny' (Sara Payson Parton) *Ginger-snaps* 1870
'Ferrars, Elizabeth' (Morna Doris Brown) *Breath of suspicion* 1972
Murder in time 1953
Ferris, Paul *The detective* 1976
Ferris, Richard *How it flies; or, The conquest of the air* 1910
Fessenden, Thomas G. *Pills, poetical, political, and philosophical* 1809
Festival of Britain, 1951. South Bank Exhibition *Catalogue of exhibits* 1951
Ficchi, Rocco F. *Electrical interference* 1964
Fick, Carl *The Danziger transcript* 1971 (UK 1973)
Field, Edward Salisbury *A six-cylinder courtship* 1907
Field, George *Chromatography; or, A treatise on colours and pigments* 1835
Field, Samuel & Weill, A. Dudley *Electroplating: a survey of modern practice* 1930
Field archaeology (Ordnance Survey Professional Papers) 1932
— (ed. 4) 1963
Fielding, Alexander Wallace ('Xan') *The stronghold: the four seasons in the White Mountains of Crete* 1953
Fiennes, Celia (1662–1741) *Journeys* ed. C. Morris 1947
Fiennes, Gerard F. G. Twisleton-Wykeham- *I tried to run a railway* 1967
Fieser, Louis Frederick & Fieser, Mary A. *Advanced organic chemistry* 1961
Organic chemistry 1944
Filippini, Alessandro *The international cook book* 1906
Filson, John *The discovery, settlement, and present state of Kentucke* 1784
Financial Times 1888–
Finar, Ivor Lionel *Organic chemistry* 2 vols. 1951–6
Findlay, Alexander tr. *W. Ostwald's The principles of inorganic chemistry* 1902
Findlay, John Niemayer *Values and intentions: a study in value-theory and philosophy of mind* 1961
Finer, Samuel Edward *The man on horseback: the role of the military in politics* 1962
Fingleton, John Henry Webb *The Ashes crown the year: a Coronation cricket diary* 1954
Four chukkas to Australia: the 1958–59 M.C.C. tour of Australia 1960
Finito! The Po Valley Campaign 1945 (15th Army Group) 1945
Fink, Donald Glen ed. *Electronics engineers' handbook* 1975
Principles of television engineering 1940
Finlayson, Hedley Herbert *The red centre: man and beast in the heart of Australia* 1935
Finlayson, Roderick David *Brown man's burden* 1938
The schooner came to Atia 1952
Firth, Anthony *Tall, balding, thirty-five* 1966
Firth, John Rupert *Papers in linguistics, 1934–1951* 1957
Speech 1930
The tongues of men 1937
Firth, Raymond William *Elements of social organization* 1951
Fischer, Martin Henry tr. *W. Ostwald's Handbook of colloid-chemistry* 1915
Fisher, Ernest Arthur *An introduction to Anglo-Saxon architecture and sculpture* 1959
Fisher, James Maxwell McConnell & Lockley, Ronald Mathias *Sea-birds: an introduction to the natural history of the sea-birds of the North-Atlantic* 1954
Fisher, Joseph William & Hartree, Douglas Raynor tr. *M. Born's The mechanics of the atom* 1927
Fisher, Ronald Aylmer *The genetical theory of natural selection* 1930
Statistical methods for research workers 1925
Fisher, Seymour *The female orgasm: psycholog physiology, fantasy* 1972 (UK 1973)
Fisher, William Rogers tr. *A. F. W. Schimper' Plant-geography upon a physiological basis* 190
See also: Schlich, William *A manual of forestr*
Fishman, Joshua Aaron ed. *Readings in th sociology of language* 1968
Fithian, Philip Vickers *Journal and letters 1767–1774* ed. J. R. Williams 1900
Journal, 1775–1776 ed. R. G. Albion & L Dobson 1934
Fitzgerald, Francis Scott Key (1896–1940 *The beautiful and damned* 1922
The great Gatsby 1925 (UK 1926)
The last tycoon 1941 (UK 1949)
Letters ed. A. Turnbull 1963 (UK 1964)
Tender is the night 1934
This side of Paradise 1920 (UK 1921)
Fitzgibbon, Theodora *The art of British cookin* 1965
Fitzsimons, Frederick William *The snakes o South Africa* 1910
— (new ed.) 1912
Fixx, James F. *The complete book of runnin* 1977
Flagg, Edmund *The far west; or, A tour beyond the mountains* 2 vols. 1838
Flattely, Frederick William & Walton, Charles Livesey *The biology of the sea-shore* 1922
Flavell, John Hurley *The developmental psychology of Jean Piaget* 1963
Fleming, Ian Lancaster (1908–64) *For your eyes only* 1960
Goldfinger 1959
The man with the golden gun 1965
Moonraker 1955
On Her Majesty's Secret Service 1963
Thunderball 1961
You only live twice 1964
Fleming, Joan Margaret *Kill or cure* 1968
Miss Bones 1959
Nothing is the number when you die 1965
You won't let me finish 1973
Young man, I think you're dying 1970
Fleming, John Ambrose *The principles of electric wave telegraphy* 1906
Short lectures to electrical artisans 1886
Fleming, Robert Peter *Brazilian adventure* 1933
News from Tartary: a journey from Peking to Kashmir 1936
Flemming, Louis Andrew *Practical tanning* 1903
Fletcher, Charles Robert Leslie & Kipling, Rudyard *A school history of England* 1911
'Fletcher, David' (Dulan Friar Barber) *Don't whistle 'Macbeth'* 1976
Flexner, Stuart Berg *Listening to America* 1982
Flight 1908– (title varies; from 1962 with title *Flight international*)
Flitch, John Ernest Crawford *Modern dancing and dancers* 1911
Florey, Howard Walter, et al. *Antibiotics: a survey of penicillin, streptomycin and other antimicrobial substances from fungi, actinomycetes, bacteria, and plants* 2 vols. 1949
Florey, Mary Ethel *The clinical application of antibiotics* 4 vols. 1952–61
Florida FL Reporter 1962–
Florida plantation records See: Jones, George Noble
Florkin, Marcel & Stotz, Elmer Henry eds. *Comprehensive biochemistry* 1962–
Flügel, John Carl *A hundred years of psychology, 1833–1933* 1933
Flying 1917–19
Flying (New York) 1927–
Flynn's (title varies) 1924–8
'Flynt, Josiah' (Josiah Flynt Willard) *The rise of Ruderick Clowd* 1903 (UK 1904)
Tramping with tramps 1899 (UK 1900)
The world of graft 1901
—— & 'Walton, Francis' (Alfred Hodder) *The powers that prey* 1900
Focal dictionary of photographic technologies, The See: Spencer, Douglas Arthur
Focal encyclopedia of film and television techniques 1969
Focal encyclopedia of photography, The 1956
— (rev. Desk ed.) 1969
Focus 1945–
Foley, Winifred *A child in the forest* 1974
Folk-lore 1890–
Foot, Michael Richard Daniell *SOE in France: an account of the work of the British Special Operations Executive in France 1940–1944* 1966
Foote, Henry Stuart *Texas and the Texans; or, Advance of the Anglo-Americans to the south-west* 2 vols. 1841
Foote, Horace *A companion to the theatres, and manual of the British drama* 1829
Forbes, Duncan *The heart of Malaya* 1966
Forbes, Henry Ogg *A hand-book to the primates* 2 vols. 1894

FORD, Edmund Brisco *Mendelism and evolution* 1931
Moths 1955
FORD, Ford Madox (until 1919 had name Joseph L. Ford H. Madox Hueffer) *The good soldier: a tale of passion* 1915
Letters ed. R. M. Ludwig 1965
A man could stand up 1926
No more parades 1925
The panel: a sheer comedy 1912
FORD, Kenneth William *The world of elementary particles* 1963
FORD, Paul Leicester *The Honorable Peter Stirling and what people thought of him* 1894 (UK 1898)
FORD, Sewell *Inez and Trilby May* 1921
Shorty McCabe 1906 (UK 1908)
Side-stepping with Shorty 1908
FORD-ROBERTSON, F. C. ed. *Terminology of forest science, technology, practice and products* 1971
Foreign review and continental miscellany 1828–30
FORESTER, Cecil Scott *The commodore* 1945
The good shepherd 1955
Hornblower and the Atropos 1953
Mr. Midshipman Hornblower 1950
The ship 1943
A ship of the line 1938
Forestry 1927–
Forestry bureau bulletin See: United States. Department of Agriculture. Bureau of Forestry
FORGAN, Robert *The golfer's handbook* 1881
FORRESTER, Larry *A girl called Fathom* 1967
FORSTER, Edward Morgan (1879–1970) *Abinger harvest: a miscellany* 1936
Aspects of the novel 1927
The hill of Devi: being letters from Dewas State Senior 1953
Howards End 1910
The longest journey 1907
Maurice 1971 (written 1913–14, revised 1959–60)
A passage to India 1924
A room with a view 1908
Two cheers for democracy 1951
Where angels fear to tread 1905
FORSTER, Harold *Flowering lotus: a view of Java* 1958
FORSYTH, Frederick *The day of the jackal* 1971
The dogs of war 1974
FORTES, Meyer ed. *Social structure: studies presented to A. R. Radcliffe-Brown* 1949
Fortnum & Mason Ltd. *Price list* c 1938
Fortune 1930–
Forum, The (New York) 1886–1930
Forum, The (Johannesburg) 1938–
FOSDICK, Harry Emerson *A pilgrimage to Palestine* 1927 (UK 1928)
FOSTER, Adriance Sherwood & GIFFORD, Ernest Milton *Comparative morphology of vascular plants* 1959
FOSTER, Brian *The changing English language* 1968
FOSTER, Frank Pierce ed. *An illustrated encyclopædic medical dictionary* 4 vols. 1888–92
FOSTER, Harry La Tourette *The adventures of a tropical tramp* 1922
A beachcomber in the Orient 1923
A tropical tramp with the tourists 1925
FOSTER, Herbert L. *Ribbin', jivin', and playin' the dozens: the unrecognized dilemma of inner city schools* 1974
FOSTER, Idris Llewellyn & ALCOCK, Leslie eds. *Culture and environment: essays in honour of Sir Cyril Fox* 1963
FOSTER, Robert Frederick *Foster's complete Hoyle* 1897
FOSTER-HARRIS, William *The look of the old West* 1955
FOWLER, Henry Watson *A dictionary of modern English usage* 1926
— (ed. 2, rev. by E. A. Gowers) 1965
FOWLER, Jacob (1765–1850) *Journal* ed. E. Coues 1898
FOWLES, Anthony *Dupe negative* 1970
Pastime 1974
FOWLES, John *The collector* 1963
The French lieutenant's woman 1969
The magus 1966
FOX, Caroline (1819–71) *Journals* ed. W. Monk 1972
FOX, Charles *Educational psychology: its problems and methods* 1925
FOX, Cyril Fred *The archaeology of the Cambridge region* 1923
FOX, Lawrence Webster *Diseases of the eye* 1904
FOX, Leslie *The numerical solution of two-point boundary problems in ordinary differential equations* 1957
—— & MAYERS, D. F. *Computing methods for scientists and engineers* 1968
FOX, Richard Middleton & FOX, Jean Walker *Introduction to comparative entomology* 1964

FOYE, William Owen ed. *Principles of medicinal chemistry* 1974
FOZARD, Basil *Instrumentation and control of nuclear reactors* 1963
FRAAS, Arthur Paul *Aircraft power plants* 1943
FRAENKEL, Gottfried S. & GUNN, D. L. *The orientation of animals* 1940
FRAENKEL-CONRAT, Heinz Ludwig & WAGNER, R. R. ed. *Comprehensive virology* 1974–
FRAME, Janet *The edge of the alphabet* 1962
The lagoon: stories 1951
Owls do cry 1957 (UK 1961)
FRANCIS, Dick (Richard Stanley Francis) *Blood sport* 1967
Bonecrack 1971
Dead cert 1962
Enquiry 1969
Flying finish 1966
For kicks 1965
Forfeit 1968
In the frame 1976
Knock down 1974
Nerve 1964
Odds against 1965
Rat race 1970
Risk 1977
Slay-ride 1973
FRANCIS, Peter W. *Volcanoes* 1976
FRANK, Andre Gunder *Latin America: underdevelopment or revolution* 1969
FRANK, Pat Harry Hart *Seven days to never* 1957
FRANKAU, Gilbert *More of us, being the present-day adventures of 'One of us': a novel in verse* 1937
'Tid'apa': what does it matter? 1914 (UK 1915)
FRANKAU, Pamela *The winged horse* 1953
FRANKLIN, Benjamin (1706–90) *Writings* ed. A. H. Smyth 10 vols. 1905–7
FRANKLIN, John *Narrative of a journey to the shores of the Polar Sea, 1819–22* 1823
FRANKLIN, Stella Maria Sarah Miles *All that swagger* 1936 (UK 1947)
My brilliant career 1901
See also: 'BRENT OF BIN BIN'
FRANKLYN, Julian E. *A dictionary of nicknames* 1962
A dictionary of rhyming slang 1960
FRASER, Edward & GIBBONS, John *Soldier and sailor words and phrases* 1925
'FRASER, James' (Alan White) *A cock-pit of roses* 1969
Heart's ease in death 1977
Who steals my name? 1976
FRAYN, Michael *The Russian interpreter* 1966
The tin men 1965
FRAYNE, John George & WOLFE, H. *Elements of sound recording* 1949
FRAZEE, Irving Augustus & BEDELL, Earl L. *Automotive fundamentals* 1949
FREE, Montague *All about house plants* 1946
FREEBODY, John William Henry *Telegraphy* 1959
Freedomways 1961–
FREELING, Nicolas *Because of the cats* 1963
Criminal conversation 1965
Double-barrel 1964
The Dresden Green 1966
Dressing of diamond 1974
The king of the rainy country 1966
Lake isle 1976
A long silence 1972
Love in Amsterdam 1962
Strike out where not applicable 1967
Tsing-boum 1969
What are the bugles blowing for? 1975
FREEMAN, B. E. tr. *A. Vandel's Biospeleology: the biology of cavernicolous animals* 1965
FREEMAN, Gillian *Jack would be a gentleman* 1959
The liberty man 1955
FREEMAN, Mary Eleanor (Wilkins) *See* WILKINS, Mary Eleanor
FREEMANTLE, Brian *The November man* 1976
Fremdsprachen 1957–
FREMLIN, Celia Margaret *Appointment with yesterday* 1972
By horror haunted: stories 1974
The jealous one 1965
FRÉMONT, John Charles *Report of the exploring expedition to the Rocky Mountains in . . 1842, and to Oregon and North California in . . 1843–'44* 1845
Frendz 1971–2
FREUD, Sigmund *See* BRILL, Abraham Arden; RIVIERE, Joan; STRACHEY, James
FRIEDLÄNDER, Michael *The Jewish religion* 1891
FRIEND, John Albert Newton *A text-book of physical chemistry* 2 vols. 1932–5
Friend, The 1843–
FRIES, Charles Carpenter *American English grammar: the grammatical structure of present-day American English with especial reference to social differences or class dialects* 1940
FRISCH, Otto Robert ed. *The nuclear handbook* 1958

FRITSCH, Felix Eugen *The structure and reproduction of the algae* 2 vols. 1935–45
FROST, Robert Lee (1874–1963) *Collected poems* 1930
— (new ed.) 1939
Letters to Louis Untermeyer ed. L. Untermeyer 1964
—— & FROST, Elinor *Family letters* ed. A. Grade 1972
FROUD, Nina, et al. tr. *P. Montagné's Larousse Gastronomique* 1961
FRUTON, Joseph Stewart & SIMMONDS, Sofia *General biochemistry* 1953
— (ed. 2) 1958
FRY, Christopher *The lady's not for burning: a comedy* 1949
Venus observed 1950
FRY, Roger Eliot (1866–1934) *Cézanne: a study of his development* 1927
Letters ed. D. Sutton 2 vols. 1972
Transformations: essays on art 1926
FRYE, Northrop *Anatomy of criticism* 1957
ed. *Romanticism reconsidered* 1963
ed. *Sound and poetry* 1957
FULFORD, Roger Thomas Baldwin ed. *Dearest child: letters between Queen Victoria and the Princess Royal, 1858–1861* 1964
ed. *Dearest Mama: letters between Queen Victoria and the Crown Princess of Prussia, 1861–1864* 1968
ed. *Your dear letter: private correspondence of Queen Victoria and the Crown Princess of Prussia, 1865–1871* 1971
FULLARTON, John H. *Troop target* 1944
FULLER, George D. & CONARD, H. S. tr. *J. Braun-Blanquet's Plant sociology: the study of plant communities* 1932
FULLER, Jane G. *Uncle John's flower-gatherers* 1869
FULLER, Richard Buckminster *Operating manual for Spaceship Earth* 1969
Untitled epic poem on the history of industrialization 1962
FULLER, Roy Broadbent *The ruined boys* 1959
The second curtain 1953
Funk & Wagnalls Co. *A standard dictionary of the English language* ed. I. K. Funk et al. 2 vols. 1893–5
— (new ed.) 2 vols. 1928
Standard dictionary of folklore, mythology, and legend ed. M. Leach 2 vols. 1949–50

G

GADDIS, William *The recognitions* 1955
GAIGER, Sydney Herbert & DAVIES, Gwilym Owen *Veterinary pathology and bacteriology* 1932
Galaxy, The 1866–78
GALBRAITH, John Kenneth *The affluent society* 1958
GALE, Frederick *Echoes from old cricket fields; or, Sketches of cricket and cricketers from the earliest history of the game to the present time* 1871
The game of cricket 1887
The life of the Hon. Robert Grimston 1885
The public school matches, and those we meet there 1853
GALLAHER, David & STEAD, W. J. *The complete rugby footballer on the New Zealand system* 1906
GALLICO, Paul William *The foolish immortals* 1953
The snow goose 1941
GALOUYE, Daniel Francis *The lost perception* 1966
GALSWORTHY, John *Captures* 1923
The country house 1907
Five tales 1918
The fugitive 1913
In Chancery 1920
The Inn of Tranquility: studies and essays 1912
Maid in waiting 1931
The man of property 1906
The roof 1929
A sheaf [essays] 1916
The silver spoon 1926
Swan song 1928
To let 1921
The white monkey 1924
GALTON, Francis *Natural inheritance* 1889
GALWEY, Geoffrey Valentine *The lift and the drop* 1948
GAMBLE, Charles Frederick Snowden *The story of a North Sea air station* 1928
GAMBLE, James Sykes *A manual of Indian timbers* 1881
GAMMOND, Peter ed. *The Decca book of jazz* 1958
ed. *Duke Ellington: his life and music* 1958
Gandalf's garden 1968–9

GARDINER, Alan Henderson *Egypt of the Pharaohs: an introduction* 1961
The theory of proper names 1940
The theory of speech and language 1932
GARDNER, Erle Stanley *The case of the blonde bonanza* 1962 (UK 1967)
The case of the queenly contestant 1967 (UK 1973)
The case of the stuttering bishop 1936 (UK 1937)
The D.A. draws a circle 1939 (UK 1940)
GARDNER, G. B. *Keris and other Malay weapons* 1936
GARDNER, Helen Louise *The business of criticism* 1959
GARDNER, Hy *So what else is new?* 1959
GARDNER, John Edmund *A complete state of death* 1969
The corner men 1969
Founder member 1969
Madrigal 1967
GARFIELD, Brian Wynne *Hopscotch* 1975
GARNER, Harry Mason *Oriental blue and white* 1954
GARNER, William *A big enough wreath* 1974
The deep, deep freeze 1968
Ditto, Brother Rat! 1972
The us or them war 1969
GARNETT, David *War in the air: September 1939 to May 1941* 1941
GARRARD, Lewis Hector *Wah-to-Yah, and the Taos trail* 1850
GARRATT, George Alfred *The mechanical properties of wood* 1931
GARRETT, Robert *Run down: the world of Alan Brett* 1970
GARROD, Dorothy A. E. & BATE, D. M. A. *The Stone Age of Mount Carmel* Vol. I 1937
GARTNER, Lloyd P. *The Jewish immigrant in England, 1870–1914* 1960
'GARVE, Andrew' (Paul Winterton) *Boomerang* 1969
The golden deed 1960
The late Bill Smith 1971
Murder in Moscow 1951
GARVIN, James Louis *The economic foundations of peace; or, World-partnership as the truer basis of the League of Nations* 1919
GASCOYNE, David Emery *Night thoughts* 1956
Opening day 1933
Poems 1937–1942 1943
A short survey of surrealism 1935
A vagrant, and other poems 1950
'GASKELL, A. P.' (Alexander Gaskell Pickard) *The big game, and other stories* 1947
GASKELL, Elizabeth Cleghorn (1810–65) *A dark night's work* 1863
Letters ed. J. A. V. Chapple & A. Pollard 1966
GASKELL, Philip *A new introduction to bibliography* 1972
GASS, Ian Graham, SMITH, P. J., & WILSON, R. C. L. eds. *Understanding the earth: a reader in the earth sciences* 1971
GASTON, William James ('Bill') *Drifting death* 1964
GATES, Reginald Ruggles *A botanist in the Amazon Valley* 1927
Heredity in man 1929
Human genetics 2 vols. 1946
GATLAND, Kenneth William *Development of the guided missile* 1952
— (ed. 2) 1954
GATSCHET, Albert Samuel *The Klamath Indians of southwestern Oregon* 1890
Gay News 1972–
GAYNOR, Frank ed. *Pocket encyclopedia of atomic energy* 1950
GEAR, Charles William *Introduction to computer science* 1973
GÉBLER, Ernest *Shall I eat you now?* 1969
GEDDES, Patrick *Cities in evolution: an introduction to the town planning movement and to the study of civics* 1915
—— & THOMSON, John Arthur *Sex* 1914
GEDDES, Paul *The Ottawa allegation* 1973
GELL, Philip George H. & COOMBS, Robin Royston A. eds. *Clinical aspects of immunology* 1963
Gen: the Services' fortnightly 1942–5
General linguistics 1955–
General systems 1956–
Genetics 1916–
Geo abstracts 1972–
Geochimica et cosmochimica acta 1950–
Geofysiske publikationer (title varies) 1919–
Geographical review 1916–
Geological Society of America *Bulletin* 1890–
Memoirs 1934–
Special papers 1934–
Geological Society of London *Proceedings* 1826–45; 1952–
Quarterly journal 1845–
Transactions 1811–56
Geologiska Föreningens i Stockholm *Förhandlingar* 1872–
Geologists' Association *Proceedings* 1859–
Geomorphological abstracts 1960–5
GEORGE, Charles B. *Forty years on the rail* 1887 (UK 1888)
GEORGE, David Lloyd *Family letters 1885–1936* ed. K. O. Morgan 1973
GEORGE, Russell D. *Minerals and rocks: their nature, occurrence and uses* 1943
Georgia *The colonial records of the State of Georgia* ed. A. D. Candler et al. 1904–
Georgia Historical Society *Collections* 9 vols. 1840–1916
GERALD, Michael C. *Pharmacology: an introduction to drugs* 1974
GÉRIN, Winifred *Charlotte Brontë: the evolution of a genius* 1967
Elizabeth Gaskell: a biography 1976
Germanic review 1926–
GERTH, Hans Heinrich & MARTINDALE, Don Albert tr. *M. Weber's Ancient Judaism* 1952
GIBB, Jocelyn ed. *Light on C. S. Lewis* 1965
'GIBBON, Lewis Grassic' (James Leslie Mitchell) *Sunset song* 1932
GIBBONS, Floyd Phillips *The red Napoleon* 1929 (UK 1930)
GIBBONS, Stella Dorothea *Cold Comfort Farm* 1932
The matchmaker 1949
A pink front door 1959
GIBBS, Philip Hamilton *The battles of the Somme* 1917
Unchanging quest 1925
GIBBS-SMITH, Charles Harvard *The aeroplane: an historical survey of its origins and development* 1960
GIBSON, Guy Penrose *Enemy coast ahead* 1946
GIBSON, William Ralph Boyce tr. *E. Husserl's Ideas: general introduction to pure phenomenology* 1931
GIDDENS, Anthony *Studies in social and political theory* 1977
GIELGUD, Val Henry *The candle-holders* 1970
Conduct of a member 1967
In such a night 1974
A necessary end 1969
GIFFEN, George *With bat and ball: twenty-five years' reminiscences of Australian and Anglo-Australian cricket* 1898
GIFFORD, Thomas *The Cavanaugh quest* 1976 (UK 1977)
'GILBERT, Anthony' (Lucy Beatrice Malleson) *And death came too* 1956
Death against the clock 1958
Death takes a wife 1959
Don't open the door 1945
Knock, knock, who's there? 1964
Missing from her home 1969
No dust in the attic 1962
Ring for a noose 1963
Tenant for the tomb 1971
GILBERT, Martin *Winston S. Churchill* See: CHURCHILL, Randolph Spencer & GILBERT, Martin
GILBERT, Michael Francis *Blood and judgement* 1959
The body of a girl 1972
Close quarters 1947
The dust and the heat 1967
Flash point 1974
Sky high 1955
GILBERT-CARTER, Humphrey tr. *C. Raunkiaer's The life forms of plants* 1934
GILES, Henry Earl *Harbin's Ridge* 1951
GILES, Herbert Allen *A glossary of reference on subjects connected with the Far East* 1878
GILES, Howard ed. *Language, ethnicity and intergroup relations* 1977
GILES, Kenneth *Death and Mr. Prettyman* 1967
Death cracks a bottle 1969
Death in diamonds 1967
A death in the church 1970
A file on death 1973
Some beasts no more 1965
'GILES, Norman' (N. R. McKeown) *The ridge of white waters* 1934
GILES, Peter *A short manual of comparative philology for classical students* 1895
GILL, Edwin Leonard *First guide to South African birds* 1936
GILL, Gerald Byron & WILLIS, Martin Richard *Pericyclic reactions* 1974
GILL, Merle Avery *Underworld slang* 1929
GILLEN, Lucy *Return to Deepwater* 1975
GILLESPIE, Alexander Douglas *Letters from Flanders* 1916
GILLIARD, Ernest Thomas *Living birds of the world* 1958
GILMAN, Caroline *Recollections of a southern matron* 1838
GILMAN, Henry *Organic chemistry: an advanced treatise* 3 vols. 1938–53
— (ed. 2) 2 vols. 1943
GILMOUR, Samuel Carter *Paper: its making, merchanting and usage* 1955
GILPIN, Alan *Dictionary of economic terms* 1966
GIMSON, Alfred Charles *An introduction to th pronunciation of English* 1962
GISH, Lillian & PINCHOT, A. *Lillian Gish: th movies, Mr. Griffith and me* 1969
GISSING, George Robert *New Grub Street* 3 vols 1891
The odd women 3 vols. 1893
The private papers of Henry Ryecroft 1903
—— & WELLS, Herbert George *George Gissin and H. G. Wells: their friendship and cor respondence* ed. R. A. Gettman 1961
GIVEN, Meta H. *Modern encyclopedia of cookin* 2 vols. 1947
GLAISTER, Geoffrey Ashall *Glossary of the boo* 1960
GLASCOCK, William Nugent *The naval sketch book; or, The Service afloat and ashore* 2 vols 1826
— (ed. 2) 2 vols. 1826
— (2nd ser.) 2 vols. 1834
GLASGOW, Ellen Anderson Gholson (1874–1945 *The deliverance: a romance of the Virgini tobacco fields* 1904
Letters ed. B. Rouse 1958
GLASGOW, Roy Stanley *Principles of radi engineering* 1936
Glasgow Herald 1805–
GLASS, David Victor & EVERSLEY, D. E. C. eds *Population in history* 1965
GLASSER, Otto ed. *The science of radiology* 193 (UK 1934)
GLASSOP, Lawson *We were the rats* 1944
GLASSTONE, Samuel *An introduction to electro chemistry* 1942
Principles of nuclear reactor engineering 1956
Sourcebook on atomic energy 1950
Text-book of physical chemistry 1940 (UK 1941
— (ed. 2) 1946 (UK 1948)
GLATT, Max Meier, et al. *The drug scene in Grea Britain* 1967
GLAZEBROOK, Richard Tetley ed. *A dictionary of applied physics* 5 vols. 1922–3
GLAZIER, Richard *A manual of historic ornamen* 1899
GLEASON, Henry Allan (b. 1882) & CRONQUIST, Arthur *The natural geography of plants* 1964
GLEASON, Henry Allan (b. 1917) *An introduction to descriptive linguistics* 1955
— (ed. 2) 1961
Linguistics and English grammar 1965
GLEMSER, Bernard *A dear Hungarian friend* 1966
GLISAN, Rodney *Journal of army life* 1874
GLOAG, John Edwards *A short dictionary of furniture, containing 1764 terms used in Britain and America* 1952
Globe and Mail (Toronto) 1844– (1844–1936 with title *Globe*)
GLUCKMAN, Herman Max *Custom and conflict in Africa* 1955
GLUECK, Bernard & LIND, John Edward tr. *A. Adler's The neurotic constitution: outlines of a comparative individualistic psychology and psychotherapy* 1917 (UK 1921)
GLYN, Anthony Geoffrey L. S. *The dragon variation* 1969
GLYN, Elinor *'It', and other stories* 1927
GODDEN, Jon & GODDEN, Margaret Rumer *Two under the Indian sun* 1966
GODDEN, Margaret Rumer *Black narcissus* 1939
The greengage summer 1958
In this house of Brede 1969
Kingfishers catch fire 1953
GODFREY, Eve *Retail selling and organization* 1962
GODFREY, James William & AMOS, Stanley William *Sound recording and reproduction* 1952
GODFREY, Philip *Back-stage: a survey of the contemporary English theatre from behind the scenes* 1933
GOLD, Herbert *The man who was not with it* 1956 (UK 1965)
GOLD, Robert S. *A jazz lexicon* 1964
Jazz talk 1975
GOLDBERG, Isaac *The wonder of words* 1938
GOLDIN, Hyman Elias ed. *Dictionary of American underworld lingo* 1950
GOLDING, Louis *Magnolia Street* 1932
GOLDING, William Gerald *Free fall* 1959
Lord of the flies 1954
Pincher Martin 1956
The spire 1964
GOLLANCZ, Victor *My dear Timothy: an autobiographical letter* 1952
GOMBRICH, Ernst Hans Josef *Art and illusion* 1960
The story of art 1950
GOOD, Carter Victor ed. *Dictionary of education* 1945
— (ed. 2) 1959
Good food guide, The 1951–
Good housekeeping (London) 1922–
Good housekeeping (New York) 1885–

Good housekeeping's cookery book: compiled by The Good Housekeeping Institute 1948
— (rev. ed.) 1954
— (rev. ed.) 1960
Good housekeeping's home encyclopaedia 1951
— (ed. 4) 1956
Good motoring 1935–
Goodchild, George Frederick & Tweney, C. F. *A technological and scientific dictionary* 1904–6
Goodfield, June *Courier to Peking* 1973
Goodge, William T. *Hits! skits! and jingles!* 1899
Goodier, James Hillis *Dictionary of painting and decorating trade terms* 1961
Goodman, Clark ed. *The science and engineering of nuclear power* 2 vols. 1947–9
Goodman, Richard Merle ed. *Genetic disorders of man* 1970
Goodman, William Louis *The history of woodworking tools* 1964
Goodwin, Derek *Pigeons and doves of the world* 1967
Goolden, Barbara *At the foot of the hills* 1956
For richer, for poorer 1959
Gordimer, Nadine *Burger's daughter* 1979
The lying days 1953
Six feet of the country: 15 short stories 1956
A world of strangers 1958
Gordon, Eric Valentine *An introduction to Old Norse* 1927
Gordon, Mildred & Gordon, Gordon *The informant* 1973
Ordeal 1976 (UK 1977)
'Gordon, Richard' (Gordon Stanley Ostlere) *Doctor at sea* 1953
Doctor in the house 1952
Gordon, Rupert Montgomery & Lavoipierre, Michel M. J. *Entomology for students of medicine* 1962
Gordon, Taylor *Born to be* 1929
Gorer, Geoffrey Edgar Solomon *Africa dances* 1935
Gores, Joseph N. *Dead skip* 1972 (UK 1973)
Hammett 1975 (UK 1976)
Gorman, James Thomas *Modern weapons of war* 1942
Gortner, Ross Aiken *Outlines of biochemistry* 1929
Gosse, Edmund William *Father and son: a study of two temperaments* 1907
Gosvami, O. *The story of Indian music* 1957
Gotlieb, Calvin Carl & Hume, J. N. P. *High-speed data processing* 1958
Gott, John (1830–1906) *Letters of Bishop Gott, arranged by members of his family* 1918
Gould, George Milbry *A dictionary of new medical terms* 1905
Gould, Joseph *The letter-press printer* 1876
— (ed. 3) 1884
Gould, Julius & Kolb, William L. eds. *A dictionary of the social sciences* 1964
Gowers, Ernest Arthur *A dictionary of modern English usage* (ed. 2) 1965 *See* Fowler, Henry Watson
Gowing, Margaret Mary *Britain and atomic energy, 1939–1945* 1964
Grabau, Amadeus William *Principles of stratigraphy* 1913
A textbook of geology 2 vols. 1921
Grabbe, Eugene Munter, Ramo, S., & Wooldridge, D. E. eds. *Handbook of automation, computation and control* 3 vols. 1958–61
Grace, Alfred Augustus *The tale of a timber town* 1914
Grace, William Gilbert *Cricket* 1891
'Graeme, Bruce' (Graham Montague Jeffries) *Tomorrow's yesterday* 1972
Two and two make five 1973
Graff, Willem Laurens *Language and languages* 1932
'Graham, James' (Henry Patterson) *Bloody passage* 1974
Graham, Neill *Murder in a dark room: a Solo Malcolm thriller* 1973
Graham, Stephen *Europe — whither bound?: being letters of travel from the capitals of Europe* 1921
Grahame, Kenneth *The wind in the willows* 1908
Grahame-White, Claude & Harper, Harry *The aeroplane: past, present and future* 1911
Aircraft in the Great War: a record and study 1915
Gramophone, The 1923–
Granada Television *Some technical terms and slang* 1974
Grant, George Monro *Ocean to ocean: Sandford Fleming's expedition through Canada in 1872* 1873
Grant, James A. *A walk across Africa* 1864
Granta, The (Cambridge) 1889–
Granville, Wilfred *A dictionary of sailors' slang* 1962
A dictionary of theatrical terms 1952
Grattan, John Henry Grafton & Gurrey, Percival *Our living language: a new guide to English grammar* 1925
Grau, Robert *The theatre of science: a volume of progress and achievement in the motion picture industry* 1914
Graves, Charles Patrick Ranke *Life line* 1941
Graves, Robert von Ranke *Claudius the god and his wife Messalina* 1934
Collected poems 1938
The feather bed 1923
Good-bye to all that: an autobiography 1929
I, Claudius 1934
Mock Beggar Hall 1924
The pier-glass 1921
Poems, 1926–1930 1931
Poems, 1938–1945 1946
Poems, 1953 1953
Seven days in new Crete 1949
Welchman's hose 1925
Whipperginny 1923
—— & Hodge, Alan Searle *The long week-end: a social history of Great Britain, 1918–1939* 1940
Gray, Alexander tr. *R. Grelling's The crime* 3 vols. 1917–18
Gray, Cecil William Turpie *Contingencies, and other essays* 1947
Gray, Dulcie Winifred C. *Dead give away* 1974
Gray, James Henry *The boy from Winnipeg* 1970
Gray, John *Archaeology and the Old Testament world* 1962
Gray, Laurence F. & Graham, Richard *Radio transmitters* 1961
Gray, Louis Herbert *Foundations of language* 1939
Graymore, Clive N. ed. *Biochemistry of the eye* 1970
Great Exhibition *Official descriptive and illustrated catalogue of the Great Exhibition of the Works of Industry of all Nations* 5 parts 1851
Greatorex, Wilfred *Crossover* 1976
Green, Abel & Laurie, Joe *Show biz, from vaude. to video* 1951
Green, Bennett Wood *Word-book of Virginia folk-speech* 1899
Green, Helen *At the actors' boarding house* 1906
The Maison de Shine: more stories of the actors' boarding house 1908
'Green, Henry' (Henry Vincent Yorke) *Living* 1929
Green, John Herbert *Basic clinical physiology* 1969
Green, Lawrence George *Great African mysteries* 1935
In the land of afternoon 1949
Tavern of the seas 1947
To the river's end 1948
Green, Martin Burgess *Children of the sun: a narrative of 'decadence' in England after 1918* 1976
Green, Peter tr. *R. Escarpit's The novel computer* 1966
Greene, Henry Graham *The basement room, and other stories* 1935
Brighton rock 1938
A burnt-out case 1961
The comedians 1966
The confidential agent 1939
The end of the affair 1951
England made me 1935
A gun for sale 1936
The heart of the matter 1948
The honorary consul 1973
The human factor 1978
It's a battlefield 1934
Journey without maps 1936
The lawless roads: a Mexican journey 1939
The Ministry of Fear: an entertainment 1943
Nineteen stories 1947
Our man in Havana 1958
The power and the glory 1940
The quiet American 1955
The third man, and The fallen idol 1950
Travels with my aunt 1969
Greener, Michael *The Penguin dictionary of commerce* 1970
Greenlee, Sam *The spook who sat by the door* 1969
Greenough, James Bradstreet & Kittredge, George Lyman *Words and their ways in English speech* 1901 (UK 1902)
Greenwood, Frederick & Greenwood, James *Under a cloud* 3 vols. 1860
Greenwood, Peter Humphrey *J. R. Norman's A history of fishes* (ed. 2) 1963 *See* Norman, John Roxborough
Greer, Germaine *The female eunuch* 1970
Gregg, Josiah *Commerce of the prairies; or, The journal of a Santa Fé trader* 2 vols. 1844
Gregory, Edwin *Metallurgy* 1932
Gregory, Jackson *The maid of the mountain: a romance of the California wilderness* (UK ed. with title *Bab of the backwoods*) 1925
Man to man 1920 (UK 1921)
Gregory, John Walter & Barrett, Benjamin Hilton *General stratigraphy* 1931
Grenfell, Wilfred Thomason *A Labrador doctor* 1919 (UK 1920)
Gresswell, Peter *Environment: an alphabetical handbook* 1971
Greville, Robert Fulke (1751–1824) *Diaries* ed. F. M. Bladon 1930
Grew, Sydney *The art of the player-piano: a text-book for student and teacher* 1922
'Grey Owl' (George Stansfield Belaney) *The men of the last frontier* 1931
Grider, John McGavock *War birds: diary of an unknown aviator* 1926 (UK 1927)
Grierson, Edward *A crime of one's own* 1967
Reputation for a song 1952
Grierson, George Abraham *Linguistic survey of India* 12 vols. 1903–22
Grierson, John *High failure* 1936
Grieve, Maud *A modern herbal* 2 vols. 1931
Griffin, Gerald *The collegians* 3 vols. 1829
Griffith, Thomas *The waist-high culture* 1959 (UK 1960)
Grigson, Geoffrey Edward Harvey *The Englishman's flora* 1955
Grimble, Arthur Francis *A pattern of islands* 1952
Return to the islands 1957
Grollman, Arthur *Pharmacology and therapeutics* 1951 (and several later editions used)
Groom, Percy & Balfour, Isaac Bayley tr. *J. E. B. Warming's Oecology of plants* 1909
Grossinger, Jennie *The art of Jewish cooking* 1958
Grossmith, George & Grossmith, Walter Weedon *The diary of a nobody* 1892
Grout, Frank Fitch *Petrography and petrology* 1932
Growth (Menasha, Wisconsin) 1937–
Gruber, Jeffrey S. *Lexical structures in syntax and semantics* 1976
Grundy, George Beardoe *Fifty-five years at Oxford* 1945
Guardian, The (continuation of *The Manchester Guardian*) 1959–
Guardian Weekly, The (continuation of *Manchester Guardian Weekly*) 1968–
Guenther, Ernest *The essential oils* 6 vols. 1949–52
Guggisberg, Charles Albert Walter *S.O.S. Rhino* 1966
Guilfoyle, William Robert *Australian plants suitable for gardens, parks, timber reserves, etc.* 1911
Gulbenkian, Nubar *Pantaraxia* 1965
Gulland, William Giuseppi *Chinese porcelain* 1898
Gullick, John Michael *Malaysia* 1969
Gulliver, Sam *The Vulcan bulletins* 1974
'Gun Buster' (John Austin) *Return via Dunkirk* 1940
Gunn, Mrs. Aeneas (Jeannie) *We of the Never-Never* 1908
Gunn, J. S. *An opal terminology* 1971 (Sydney University: Australian Language Research Centre, Occasional Paper No. 15)
The terminology of the shearing industry 1965 (as above, Occasional Papers Nos. 5 & 6)
Gungwu, Wang *See* Wang Gungwu
Gunn, Thom *Fighting terms: poems* 1954
The sense of movement 1957
Gunter, Archibald Clavering *Mr. Potter of Texas* 1888
Günther, Alfred *Microphotography in the library* 1962 (Unesco; reprinted from *Unesco bulletin for libraries* Vol. XVI, No. 1, Jan.–Feb. 1962)
Gurnett, John William & Kyte, Colin Henry John *Cassell's dictionary of abbreviations* 1966
Gurney, Oliver Robert *The Hittites* 1952
Gurr, Edward *The rational use of dyes in biology, and general staining methods* 1965
Synthetic dyes in biology, medicine and chemistry 1971
'Guthrie, John' (John Brodie) *The little country* 1935
Guthrie, Virgil B. *Petroleum products handbook* 1960
Guthrie-Smith, William Herbert *Tutira: the story of a New Zealand sheep station* 1921
Guy, Albert Glasgow *Physical metallurgy for engineers* 1962
Guy's Hospital reports 1836–
Guyton, Arthur Clifton *Textbook of medical physiology* 1956
Gwynne-Vaughan, Helen Charlotte I. & Barnes, Bertie Frank *The structure and development of the fungi* 1927
Gzowski, Peter *Peter Gzowski's book about this country in the morning* 1974

H

Haagner, Alwin Karl & Ivy, Robert Henry *Sketches of South African bird life* 1908

HAAS, Paul & HILL, Thomas George *An introduction to the chemistry of plant products* 1913
HABBERTON, John *The Jericho road: a story of western life* 1877
HABER, Heinz *Man in space* 1953
HACKFORTH-JONES, Frank Gilbert *One-one-one: stories of the Navy* 1942
Sixteen bells: stories 1946
'HACKSTON, James' (Harold Frederick N. Gye) *Father clears out* 1966
HADDON, Alfred Cort *The races of man and their distribution* 1909
HADDON, Archibald *Green room gossip* 1922
HADEN, Ernest Faber, HAN, M. S. & HAN, Y. W. *A resonance-theory for linguists* 1962
HADFIELD, Miles *British trees* 1957
HAGGAR, Reginald George *The concise encyclopedia of continental pottery and porcelain* 1960
A dictionary of art terms 1962
See also: MANKOWITZ, C. W. & HAGGAR, R. G.
HAGGARD, Henry Rider *Benita: an African romance* 1906
'HAGGARD, William' (Richard Henry Michael Clayton) *The arena* 1961
Closed circuit 1960
The hard sell 1965
The hardliners 1970
The high wire 1963
The power house 1966
The protectors 1972
HAGGIS, Geoffrey Harvey ed. *Introduction to molecular biology* 1964
HAGUE, Douglas Chalmers *Managerial economics: analysis for business decisions* 1969
'HAIG, Alec' *Peruvian printout* 1974
HAILEY, William Malcolm (Baron Hailey) *An African survey* 1938
— (rev. ed.) 1957
HALAS, John & MANVELL, Arnold Roger *The technique of film animation* 1959
HALBERSTAM, David *The powers that be* 1979
HALDANE, John Burdon Sanderson & HUXLEY, Julian Sorell *Animal biology* 1927
HALE, Edward Everett *If, yes, and perhaps* 1868
HALE, John *The grudge fight* 1964
HALE, Mason Ellsworth *The biology of lichens* 1967
HALE, Susan (1833–1910) *Letters* ed. C. P. Atkinson 1919
HALIBURTON, Thomas Chandler *The attaché; or, Sam Slick in England* 2 vols. 1843
— (2nd ser.) 2 vols. 1844
Sam Slick's wise saws and modern instances; or, what he said, did, or invented 2 vols. 1853
HALL, Abraham Oakley *The Manhattaner in New Orleans; or, Phases of 'Crescent City' life* 1851
'HALL, Adam' (Trevor Dudley-Smith) *The Kobra manifesto* 1976
The 9th directive 1966
The Striker portfolio 1969
The Tango briefing 1973
See also: 'TREVOR, Elleston'
HALL, Archibald John *The standard handbook of textiles* 1946 — (ed. 7) 1969
A student's textbook of textile science 1963
HALL, Bert & NILES, John Jacob *One man's war: the story of the Lafayette escadrille* 1929
HALL, Frederick Michael *An introduction to abstract algebra* 2 vols. 1966–9
HALL, James *Letters from the West* 1828
Statistics of the West, at the close of the year 1836 1836
HALL, James Norman *Kitchener's mob: the adventures of an American in the British Army* 1916
HALL, John Scoville ed. *Radar aids to navigation* 1947
HALL, John Whitney *Japan from prehistory to modern times* 1970
HALL, Mildred Lillington ed. *Newnes complete amateur photography* See under title
HALL, Richard Pinkham *Protozoology* 1953
HALL, Robert Anderson *External history of the Romance languages* 1974
Introductory linguistics 1964
HALL, Thomas Winthrop *Tales* 1899
HALL, William Thomas *Textbook of quantitative analysis* 1930
HALLAM, Anthony ed. *Planet earth: an encyclopedia of geology* 1977
HALLIDAY, David *Introductory nuclear physics* 1950
'HALLIDAY, Dorothy' (Dorothy Dunnett) *Dolly and the cookie bird* 1970
Dolly and the doctor bird 1971
Dolly and the nanny bird 1976
Dolly and the starry bird 1973
HALLIDAY, Michael Alexander Kirkwood, McINTOSH, A., & STREVENS, P. *The linguistic sciences and language teaching* 1964
HALLOCK, Charles *American club list and sportsman's glossary* 1878
HALPERT, Herbert & STORY, G. M. eds. *Christmas mumming in Newfoundland: essays in anthropology, folklore and history* 1969
HAM, Arthur Worth *Histology* 1950
HAMILTON, Alexander (1712–56) *Hamilton's itinerarium: being a narrative of a journey from Annapolis, Maryland, through Delaware [etc.]..1744* ed. A. B. Hart 1907
HAMILTON, Augustus *Maori art* 1901 (first published in 5 parts 1896–1900)
HAMILTON, Bruce *Too much of water* 1958
HAMILTON, Cosmo *Prisoners of hope* 1924
HAMILTON, Edward Walter *Diary 1880–1885* ed. D. W. R. Bahlman 2 vols. 1972
HAMILTON, Elizabeth Vidal *The Mordaunts: an eighteenth-century family* 1965
HAMILTON, Ferelith ed. *The world encyclopedia of dogs* 1971
HAMILTON, Francis *An account of the kingdom of Nepal* 1819
HAMILTON, Frederic Spencer *P.J.: the Secret Service boy* 1922
'HAMILTON, Gail' (Mary Abigail Dodge) *Gala-days* 1863
HAMILTON, Henrietta *Answer in the negative* 1959
HAMILTON, Ian *The man with the brown paper face* 1967
The thrill machine 1972
HAMILTON, Stanislaus Murray ed. *Letters to Washington, and accompanying papers* 5 vols. 1898–1902
HAMILTON, Walter *The Æsthetic Movement in England* 1882
HAMMERTON, John Alexander ed. *ABC of the RAF* 1941
ed. *Countries of the world* 6 vols. (originally published in 40 parts) 1924–5
HAMMETT, Samuel Dashiell *The Dain curse* 1929 (UK 1930)
The Maltese falcon 1930
Red harvest 1929
HAMMOND, Rolt *Mobile and movable cranes* 1963
HAMP, Eric P., HOUSEHOLDER, F. W., & AUSTERLITZ, R. eds. *Readings in linguistics II* 1966
HAMPTON, Christopher James *The philanthropist: a bourgeois comedy* 1970
Savages 1974
HAMSHER, Donald Henze ed. *Communication system engineering handbook* 1967
HAMSON, Denys Otto Harry *We fell among Greeks* 1946
'HAN SUYIN' (Elizabeth Comber) *A mortal flower, China: autobiography, history* 1966
HANCOCK, Lyn *There's a seal in my sleeping bag* 1972
HANCOCK, William Keith *Australia* 1930
Handbook of hardwoods, A 1956 *See* United Kingdom. Department of Scientific and Industrial Research. Forest Products Research Laboratory
— (ed. 2) 1972 *See* United Kingdom. Department of the Environment. Building Research Establishment
Handbook of softwoods, A 1957 *See* United Kingdom. Department of Scientific and Industrial Research. Forest Products Research Laboratory
HANDY, William Christopher ed. *Blues: an anthology* 1926
Father of the blues: an autobiography ed. A. Bontemps 1941 (UK 1957)
HANLEY, William *Blue dreams; or, The end of romance and the continued pursuit of happiness* 1971
HANNETT, John *Bibliopegia* 1835
HANSEN, Joseph *Fadeout* 1970 (UK 1972)
HANSON, John Lloyd *A dictionary of economics and commerce* 1965
HAPPÉ, Louis Bernard *Basic motion picture technology* 1971
Happy landings (Air Ministry) 1946–8
HARBEN, William Nathaniel *Abner Daniel* 1902
The Georgians 1904
Westerfelt 1901
HARBORD, Frank William & HALL, John William *The metallurgy of steel* 1904
— (ed. 7) 1923
HARCOURT, Palma *At high risk* 1977
A fair exchange 1975
HARDEN, Donald Benjamin *The Phoenicians* 1962
HARDY, Alister Clavering *The open sea, its natural history* Part I *The world of plankton* 1956
— Part II *Fish and fisheries* 1959
HARDY, Arthur Cobb & PERRIN, Fred Hiram *The principles of optics* 1932
HARDY, Thomas (1840–1928) *Collected letters* ed. R. L. Purdy & M. Millgate 1978–
A group of noble dames 1891
Late lyrics and earlier, with many other verses 1922
One rare fair woman: letters to Florence Henniker 1893–1922 ed. E. Hardy & F. B. Pinion 1972
HARDY, William George *Unfulfilled* 1952
HARE, Richard Mervyn *Freedom and reason* 1963
The language of morals 1952
HARGAN, James *Glossary of prison language* 1935 (typescript, referred to on p. 361 of *Journal of abnormal and social psychology*, December 1935)
HARGREAVES, Elisabeth *Fair green weed* 1972
HARGREAVES, Reginald *The enemy at the gate: famous sieges* 1945
HARKER, Alfred *The natural history of igneous rocks* 1909
Petrology for students: an introduction to the study of rocks under the microscope 1895
HARLEY, John Brian *Ordnance Survey maps: a descriptive manual* 1975
HARMAN, Richard Alexander, MILNER, A., & MELLERS, W. *Man and his music* 1962
HARMAR, Hilary *Pet Library's chihuahua guide* 1968
HARMON, Daniel Williams *A journal of voyages and travels in the interiour of North America* 1820
HARMSWORTH, Alfred Charles William, et al. *Motors and motor-driving* 1902
Harmsworth encyclopædia, The ed. G. Sandeman 8 vols. (originally published in 40 parts) 1905–6
Harmsworth's wireless encyclopedia ed. O. J. Lodge 3 vols. (originally published in 24 parts) 1923–4
HARNEY, William Edward *Taboo* 1943
— (ed. 3) 1944
HARNWELL, Gaylord Probasco *Principles of electricity and electromagnetism* 1938
HARPER, Henry William *Letters from New Zealand, 1857–1911, being some account of life and work in the province of Canterbury, South Island* 1914
HARPER, John L. *Population biology of plants* 1977
Harpers and Queen 1970–
Harper's bazaar (New York) 1867–
— (UK ed.) 1929–70
Harper's weekly 1857–1916
HARRINGTON, Robert Edward *Quintain* 1977
HARRIS, Corra May *Eve's second husband* 1911
HARRIS, Frank *See* HARRIS, James Thomas Frank
HARRIS, Fred Henry ed. *Dartmouth out o' doors* 1913
HARRIS, Henry *Nucleus and cytoplasm* 1968
HARRIS, James Thomas Frank *My life and loves* 4 vols. 1922–7
HARRIS, Joel Chandler *Mingo, and other sketches in black and white* 1884
Nights with Uncle Remus 1883
Sister Jane, her friends and acquaintances 1896
Uncle Remus and his friends 1892
HARRIS, John Norman *The weird world of Wes Beattie* 1963 (UK 1964)
HARRIS, Leldon M. *An introduction to deepwater floating drilling operations* 1972
HARRIS, Miriam Coles *The tents of wickedness* 1907
HARRIS, Rosemary *The double snare* 1974
The nice girl's story 1968
HARRIS, Stanley *Fundamental principles of contract bridge* 1947
HARRIS, Walter Kilroy *Outback in Australia; or, Three Australian overlanders* 1913
HARRIS, William Cornwallis *The wild sports of southern Africa: being the narrative of an expedition from the Cape of Good Hope..to the Tropic of Capricorn* 1839
HARRIS, Zellig Sabbettai *Methods in structural linguistics* 1951
HARRISON, A. W. C. *The manufacture of lakes and precipitated pigments* 1930
HARRISON, Constance Cary *Woman's handiwork in modern homes* 1881
HARRISON, Harry Max *The Technicolor time machine* 1967 (UK 1968)
HARRISON, Henry Sydnor *Queed* 1911
HARRISON, Michael *Reported safe arrival* 1943
Harrison Mayer. A complete service to the craft potter [Catalogue of Harrison Mayer Ltd., Meir, Stoke-on-Trent] *a* 1977
HARRISSON, Barbara *Orang-utan* 1962
HARRISSON, Thomas Harnett & MADGE, Charles Henry eds. *War begins at home* 1940
HARROD, Leonard Montague *The librarians' glossary* 1938
— (ed. 2) 1959
— (ed. 3) 1971
HARROW, Benjamin & SHERWIN, Carl P. eds. *Textbook of biochemistry* 1935
HART, Basil Henry Liddell *Europe in arms* 1937
HART, Frances Noyes *The Bellamy trial* 1927 [play], 1928 [novel]
HART, Fred H. *The Sazerac lying club: a Nevada book* 1878
HART, Horace *Notes on a century of typography at the University Press, Oxford, 1693–1794* 1900
HART, Jerome *A vigilante girl* 1910

HART, Norman de Villiers *The bridge players' bedside book* 1939
HARTE, Francis Bret *Gabriel Conroy* 1876 (US 1 vol., UK 3 vols.)
The story of a mine 1877
—— & 'TWAIN, Mark' (S. L. Clemens) *Sketches of the sixties: being forgotten material now collected..from The Californian* ed. J. Howell 1926
HARTLEY, Leslie Poles *Eustace and Hilda* 1947
The go-between 1953
The hireling 1957
A perfect woman 1955
Two for the river, and other stories 1961
HARTMANN, Reinhard Rudolf K. & STORK, Francis C. *Dictionary of language and linguistics* 1972
HARTREE, Douglas Rayner *Calculating instruments and machines* 1949 (UK 1950)
HARTSHORNE, Albert *Old English glasses* 1897
HARTSHORNE, Charles Henry *English medieval embroidery* 1848
Harvard studies in classical philology 1890–
Harvard University. Computation Laboratory *Annals* 1946–
'HARVESTER, Simon' (Henry Gibbs) *The Chinese hammer* 1960
A corner of the playground 1973
Treacherous road 1966
HARVEY, Peter & BOHLMAN, Kenneth John *Stereo F.M. radio handbook* 1974
HARVEY, Ruth *Curtain time* 1949
HASELGROVE, Maurice Lawrence *Photographers' dictionary* 1962
HASTINGS, James ed. *Encyclopædia of religion and ethics* See under title
HASTINGS, Lewis *Dragons are extra* 1947
HASTINGS, Macdonald *Cork and the serpent* 1955
HASTON, Dougal *In high places* 1972
HATCH, Frederick Henry & RASTALL, Robert Heron *The petrology of the sedimentary rocks* 1913
— (ed. 4, revised by J. T. Greensmith) 1965
HATFIELD, James Taft, LEOPOLD, W., & ZIEGLSCHMID, A. J. F. eds. *Curme volume of linguistic studies* 1930
HAURWITZ, Bernhard *Dynamic meteorology* 1941
HAUSMAN, Louis *Clinical neuroanatomy, neurophysiology and neurology* 1958
HAWKES, Jessie Jacquetta & HAWKES, Charles Francis Christopher *Prehistoric Britain* 1943
— (rev. ed.) 1947
HAWKEY, Raymond & BINGHAM, Roger *Wild card* 1974
HAWKINS, Benjamin (1754–1816) *A sketch of the Creek country, in 1798 and 1799* (Georgia Historical Society) 1848
HAWKINS, Charles Caesar & WALLIS, F. *The dynamo: its theory, design and manufacture* 1893
HAWKINS, John & HAWKINS, Ward *Death watch, and The missing witness* 1958 (UK 1959)
HAWKINS, Nehemiah, et al. *Hawkins' electrical dictionary* 1910
'HAY, Ian' (John Hay Beith) *The first hundred thousand: being the unofficial history of a unit of 'K(1)'* [*Kitchener's First Army*] 1915
Housemaster 1936
A knight on wheels 1914
The last million 1919
The lighter side of school life 1914
The poor gentleman 1928
'The right stuff': some episodes in the career of a North Briton 1908
A safety match 1911
—— & 'ARMSTRONG, Anthony' (A. A. Willis) *Orders are orders* 1933
HAY, John Milton *The bread-winners: a social study* 1884
HAY, Malcolm Vivian *Foot of pride: the pressure of Christendom on the people of Israel for 1900 years* 1950
HAY, Roy & SYNGE, P. M. *The dictionary of garden plants* 1969
HAY, William Delisle *Brighter Britain! or, Settler and Maori in northern New Zealand* 2 vols. 1882
Three hundred years hence; or, A voice from posterity 1881
HAYASHI, Takashi ed. *Olfaction and taste II* 1967 (Proceedings of the 2nd International Symposium on Olfaction and Taste, Tokyo, 1965)
HAYCRAFT, Howard *Murder for pleasure: the life and times of the detective story* 1942
HAYDEN, Arthur *Chats on old furniture: a practical guide for collectors* 1905
HAYDON, Benjamin Robert (1786–1846) *The life of Haydon, from his autobiography and journals* ed. T. Taylor 3 vols. 1853
HAYES, Arnold Richard W. *Revision physics for sixth forms* 1962
HAYES, Augustus Allen *New Colorado and the Sante Fé trail* 1880 (UK 1881)
HAYES, Roy *The Hungarian game* 1973
HAYES, William *The genetics of bacteria and their viruses* 1964
HAYGARTH, Henry William *Recollections of bush life in Australia during a residence of eight years in the interior* 1848
HAYMAKER, Webb Edward tr. *R. Bing's Text-book of nervous diseases* 1939
HAYS, David G. *Introduction to computational linguistics* 1967
HAYWARD, Charles Brian *Practical aeronautics* 1912
HAYWARD, Harry Maxwell & HARARI, Manya tr. *B. Pasternak's Dr. Zhivago* 1958
HAYWARD, Helena ed. *The Connoisseur's handbook of antique collecting: a dictionary of furniture, silver, ceramics, glass, fine art, etc.* 1960
HAYWARD, John Davey *Prose literature since 1939* 1947
HAZARD, Thomas Benjamin (1756–1845) *Nailer Tom's diary* ed. C. Hazard 1930
Heal and Son *Heal's catalogue 1853–1934* 1972 [facsimile reproductions from catalogues]
HEALD, Frederick Deforest *Introduction to plant pathology* 1937
Manual of plant diseases 1926
HEALD, Timothy Villiers *Deadline* 1975
Just desserts 1977
Let sleeping dogs die 1976
HEALEY, Edna May *Lady unknown: the life of Angela Burdett-Coutts* 1978
HEARN, Patricio Lafcadio T. C. *In ghostly Japan* 1899
Japan: an attempt at interpretation 1904
Kokoro: hints and echoes of Japanese inner life 1896
Kottō: being Japanese curios, with sundry cobwebs 1902
HEARNE, John *Stranger at the gate* 1956
Hearst's international 1925–
Heart: a journal for the study of the circulation 1909–33
HEATH, Peter tr. *G. A. Wetter's Soviet ideology today* 1966
HEAVISIDE, Oliver *Electromagnetic theory* 3 vols. 1893–9
HECHT, Ben & MACARTHUR, Charles *The front page* 1928
HEDGECOE, John *The photographer's handbook* 1977
HEFFNER, Roe-Merrill S. *General phonetics* 1949
HEFFRON, Dorris *Crusty crossed* 1976
A nice fire and some moonpennies 1971
HEFLIN, Woodford Agee ed. *Aerospace glossary* 1959
ed. *The United States Air Force dictionary* 1956
HEILBRON, Ian Morris ed. *Dictionary of organic compounds* 3 vols. 1934–7
HEIN, Leonard William *An introduction to electronic data processing for business* 1961
HEINLEIN, Robert Anson *The door into summer* 1957 (UK 1960)
HEINRICH, Eberhardt William *Microscopic petrography* 1956
HEITLER, Walter *The quantum theory of radiation* 1936
HELLER, Joseph *Catch-22* 1961 (UK 1962)
Something happened 1974
HELLMAN, Lilian *The little foxes* 1939
Pentimento: a book of portraits 1973 (UK 1974)
An unfinished woman: a memoir 1969
HELLYER, Arthur George Lee *T. W. Sanders' Encyclopaedia of gardening* (ed. 22) 1952
The encyclopaedia of garden work and terms 1954
Practical gardening for amateurs 1935
HELME, Elizabeth tr. *F. Le Vaillant's Travels from the Cape of Good-Hope, into the interior parts of Africa* 2 vols. 1790
HELMER, Olaf tr. *A. Tarski's Introduction to logic and to the methodology of deductive sciences* 1941
HEMINGWAY, Ernest *Across the river and into the trees* 1950
Death in the afternoon 1932
A farewell to arms 1929
The fifth column [a play], *and The first forty-nine stories* 1938 (UK 1939)
For whom the bell tolls 1940
Green hills of Africa 1935 (UK 1936)
In our time 1924
— (enlarged ed.) 1925 (UK 1926)
Men without women 1927 (UK 1928)
The old man and the sea 1952
The sun also rises 1926 (UK ed. with title *Fiesta* 1927)
To have and have not 1937
The torrents of spring: a romantic novel in honour of the passing of a great race 1926 (UK 1933)
HEMPSTEAD, Joshua *Diary, 1711–1758* 1901
HENDERSON, A. G. tr. *V. Cousin's The philosophy of Kant: lectures* 1854
HENDERSON, Alexander Morell & PARSONS, Talcott tr. *M. Weber's Theory of social and economic organization* 1947
HENDERSON, David Kennedy & GILLESPIE, Robert Dick *A text-book of psychiatry for students and practitioners* 1927
— (ed. 9) 1962
HENDERSON, George C. *Keys to crookdom* 1924
HENDERSON, Stephen *Understanding the new Black poetry: Black speech and Black music as poetic references* 1973
HENDRICK, Burton Jesse *The life and letters of Walter H. Page* 3 vols. 1922–5
HENISSART, Paul *Winter quarry* 1976
HENNEY, Julian Keith *Principles of radio* 1929
ed. *The radio engineering handbook* 1933
— (ed. 5) 1959
—— & DUDLEY, Beverley eds. *Handbook of photography* 1939
HENNING, Rachel (1826–1914) *Letters* ed. D. Adams 1966
HENROT, Thérèse *Belgium* (English version by R. E. Wolf and the author) 1961
HENRY, Frank Souder *Printing for school and shop* 1917
'HENRY, Joan' (Constance Ann Standage) *Who lie in gaol* 1952
'HENRY, O.' (William Sydney Porter, 1862–1910) *Cabbages and kings* 1904
The four million 1906 (UK 1916)
The gentle grafter 1908 (UK 1928)
Heart of the west 1907 (UK 1912)
Options 1909 (UK 1916)
Roads of destiny 1909
Rolling stones 1912 (UK 1916)
Strictly business 1910 (UK 1917)
The trimmed lamp 1907 (UK 1915)
Whirligigs 1910
HENRY, Thomas Anderson *The plant alkaloids* 1913
HENTY, George Alfred *Through Russian snows: a story of Napoleon's retreat from Moscow* 1896
HEPWORTH, Cecil Milton *Animated photography: the ABC of the cinematograph* 1897
HERAK, Milan & STRINGFIELD, V. T. eds. *Karst: important karst regions of the northern hemisphere* 1972
HERBERT, Alan Patrick *Holy deadlock* 1934
Independent Member 1950
Laughing Ann, and other poems 1925
Plain Jane 1927
The water gipsies 1930
What a word! 1935
HERBERT, Alfred Xavier *Capricornia* 1938 (UK 1939)
HERBERT, Thomas Ernest *Telegraphy: a detailed exposition of the telegraph system of the British Post Office* 1906
Telephony: an elementary exposition of the telephone system of the British Post Office 1923
— (new ed., by T. E. Herbert & W. S. Procter) 2 vols. & Suppl. 1932–40
— (new ed., by J. Atkinson) 2 vols. 1948–50
HERBERT, Xavier *See* HERBERT, Alfred Xavier
Here and now: an independent monthly review 1949–
HEREN, Louis *Growing up on 'The Times'* 1978
HERGESHEIMER, Joseph *The bright shawl* 1922 (UK 1923)
HERON, Alastair ed. *Towards a Quaker view of sex: an essay by a group of Friends* 1963
HERON, James *The Celtic Church in Ireland* 1898
HERON, Patrick *The changing forms of art* 1955
'HERRIOT, James' (J. A. Wight) *It shouldn't happen to a vet* 1972
HERSKOWITZ, Irwin Herman *Genetics* 1962
HERVEY, George F. *A handbook of card games* 1963
HESS, Fr. Cuthbert (Lawrence Anthony Hess) ed. *God and the supernatural: a Catholic statement of the Christian faith* 1920
HEWER, Evelyn Everard *Text-book of histology for medical students* 1937
HEWITT, James *Yoga* 1960
HEWLETT, Richard Tanner *A manual of bacteriology, clinical and applied* 1898
— (ed. 2) 1902
HEYER, Georgette *A blunt instrument* 1938
Death in the stocks 1935
False colours 1963
They found him dead 1937
HEYERDAHL, Thor *Fatu-Hiva: back to nature* 1974
The Kon-Tiki expedition See: LYON, Francis Hamilton
HICK, John Harwood ed. *The myth of God incarnate* 1977
HICKEY, William (1749?–1830) *Memoirs* ed. A. Spencer 4 vols. 1913–25
— ed. P. Quennell 1960
Hi-fi answers 1972–
Hi-fi sound 1967–77
HIGGIN, Louis *Handbook of embroidery* ed. M. Alford 1880
HIGGINS, George Vincent *A city on a hill* 1975
Dreamland 1977
The friends of Eddie Coyle 1972
The judgement of Deke Hunter 1976

'High Jinks, Junior' (Harold Poe Swartwood) *Choice slang* 1914
High times (New York) 1974–
Higham, Edward Spencer & Higham, William Richard Joseph *High speed rugby* 1960
Higham, Robert Robin Alger *A handbook of papermaking* 1963
Higher education: report See: United Kingdom. Parliamentary papers. Committee on Higher Education
Highsmith, Patricia *The tremor of forgery* 1969
Hildick, Edmund Wallace *The boy at the window* 1960
The loop 1977
Hildreth, James *Dragoon campaigns to the Rocky Mountains* 1836
Hiler, Hilaire *Notes on the technique of painting* 1934
Hilgard, Ernest Ropiequet *Theories of learning* 1948
— (ed. 2) 1956 (UK 1958)
Hilgard, Eugene Waldemar *Soils: their formation, properties, composition, and relations to climate and plant growth in the humid and arid regions* 1906
Hilgendorf, Frederick William *Weeds of New Zealand, and how to eradicate them* 1926
Hill, Albert Frederick *Economic botany* 1937
Hill, Archibald Anderson *Introduction to linguistic structures* 1958
Hill, Archie *Summer's end* 1976
Hill, Beth & Hill, Ray *Spirit in stone: petroglyphs of the Northwest Coast Indians* 1974
Hill, Peter *The hunters* 1976
Hill, Reginald *A fairly dangerous thing* 1972
Ruling passion 1973
Hill, Susan *Gentleman and ladies* 1976
Strange meeting 1971
Hillary, Edmund *High adventure* 1955
Hillary, Richard Hope *The last enemy* 1942
Hillebrand, William *Flora of the Hawaiian Islands* 1888
Hilliard, Noel Harvey *Maori girl* 1960
A piece of land 1963
Hillis, Marjorie (Marjorie Hillis Roulston) *Orchids on your budget; or, Live smartly on what have you* 1937 (UK 1938)
Hillyard, George Whiteside *Forty years of first-class lawn tennis* 1924
Hilton, James *Lost horizon* 1933
See also: 'Trevor, Glen'
Hilton, John Buxton *Gamekeeper's gallows* 1976
Hilton, Timothy *The Pre-Raphaelites* 1970
Himes, Chester *Black on black: Baby sister, and selected writings* 1973
Blind man with a pistol 1969
The heat's on 1966
Hind, Herbert Lloyd *Brewing* 2 vols. 1938–40
Hindmarsh, William Russell ed. *Atomic spectra* 1967
Hindu, The (Madras) 1878–
Hindustan Times (New Delhi) 1924–
Hine, Gerald John & Brownell, G. L. eds. *Radiation dosimetry* 1956
Hinsie, Leland Earl & Shatzky, Jacob *Psychiatric dictionary, with encyclopedic treatment of modern terms* 1940
— (ed. 3, by L. E. Hinsie & R. J. Campbell) 1960
Hinxman, Margaret *End of a good woman* 1976
Hiscock, Eric Charles *Around the world in Wanderer III* 1956
Hobart, George Vere *Jim Hickey: a story of the one-night stands* 1904
See also: 'McHugh, Hugh'
Hobson, Hank *Mission house murder* 1959
Hobson, John Atkinson *The problem of the unemployed* 1896
Hobson, Laura Keane (Zametkin) *The celebrity* 1951 (UK 1953)
'Hobson, Polly' (Julia Evans) *Titty's dead* 1968
Hobson, Richmond Pearson *Nothing too good for a cowboy* 1955
Hockett, Charles Francis *A course in modern linguistics* 1958
ed. *A Leonard Bloomfield anthology* 1970
A manual of phonology 1955
Hodge, Frederick Webb ed. *Handbook of American Indians north of Mexico* 2 vols. 1907–10
Hodge, Herbert *Cab, sir?* 1939
Hodge, Hiram C. *Arizona as it is* 1877
Hodges, Henry *Artifacts: an introduction to early materials and technology* 1964
Hodgins, Eric *Mr. Blandings builds his dream house* 1946 (UK 1947)
Hodgkinson, Harry *Doubletalk: the language of Communism* 1955
Hodkin, Frederick William & Cousen, Arnold *A textbook of glass technology* 1925
Hodson, James Lansdale *Our two Englands* 1936
Hodza, Aaron C. & Fortune, George *Shona praise poetry* 1979
Hoffman, Charles Fenno *A winter in the west* 2 vols. 1835 (UK ed., also 2 vols. 1835, with title —— *in the far west*)
Hogan, Jeremiah Joseph *The English language in Ireland* 1927
An outline of English philology 1934
Hogarth, David George *The Nearer East* 1902
Hogg, Alfred George *Redemption from this world; or, The supernatural in Christianity* 1922
Hoggart, Herbert Richard *Auden: an introductory essay* 1951
The uses of literacy: aspects of working-class life, with special reference to publications and entertainments 1957
Holbrook, David Kenneth *Flesh wounds* 1966
Holden, Anne *The girl on the beach* 1973
Holiday, Billie *Lady sings the blues* 1956 (UK 1958; new impr. 1973)
Holiday 1946–
Holland, John Henry *The useful plants of Nigeria* 4 vols. 1908–22
Holland, Ray *Self and social context* 1977
Hollander, Zander ed. *The modern encyclopedia of basketball* 1969
Holley, Marietta E. *My opinions and Betsey Bobbet's* 1873
Hollinshead, William Henry *Textbook of anatomy* 1962
Holloway, Christopher John *Language and intelligence* 1951
Holman-Hunt, Diana *My grandmothers and I* 1960
Holmes, Arthur *The nomenclature of petrology, with references to selected literature* 1920
Principles of physical geology 1944
— (ed. 2) 1965
Holmes, Harry Nicholls *Introductory colloid chemistry* 1934
Holmes, John Clellon *Nothing more to declare* 1968
Holmes, Mary Jane *Tempest and sunshine; or, Life in Kentucky* 1854
Holmes, Oliver Wendell (the younger) *The Pollock–Holmes letters* See: Pollock, Frederick
—— & Laski, Harold Joseph *Holmes–Laski letters: the correspondence of Mr. Justice Holmes and Harold J. Laski, 1916–1935* ed. M. DeW. Howe 2 vols. 1953
Holmes, Sarah Katherine (Stone) *Brokenburn: the journal of Kate Stone, 1861–1868* ed. J. Q. Anderson 1955
Holmes, Thomas K. *The man from Tall Timber* 1919
Holroyde, Peggy *Indian music* 1972
Holt, Edwin Bissell *The Freudian wish and its place in ethics* 1915
Holtby, Winifred *Poor Caroline* 1931
South Riding 1936
Home, Lord (Alexander Frederick Douglas-Home) *The way the wind blows* 1976
'Home, Michael' (Charlie Christopher Bush) *The house of shade* 1942
Home chat 1895–
Homes and gardens 1923–
Hone, Joseph *The flowers of the forest* 1980
The sixth directorate 1975
Hooker, Joseph Dalton *Handbook of the New Zealand flora* 2 parts 1864–7
See also: Huxley, Leonard
Hool, George Albert & Johnson, Nathan Clarke *Concrete engineers' handbook* 1918
Hooper, Johnson Jones *Some adventures of Captain Simon Suggs* 1845
— (another ed.) 1846
Hooper, Robert *Lexicon medicum; a new medical dictionary* 1802
— (ed. 7, rev. by K. Grant) 1839
'Hope, Anthony' (Anthony Hope Hawkins) *The prisoner of Zenda* 1894
Tristram of Blent 1901
Hope, William Edward Stanton *Diggers' paradise* 1956
Hopkins, Gerard Manley (1844–89) *Further letters* ed. C. C. Abbott 1938
— (ed. 2, by C. C. Abbott) 1956
Journals and papers ed. G. Storey 1959
Letters to Robert Bridges ed. C. C. Abbott 1935
— (2nd rev. impr.) 1955
Note-books and papers ed. H. House 1937
Poems ed. R. Bridges 1918
— (ed. 3, by W. H. Gardner) 1948
— (ed. 4, by W. H. Gardner & N. H. MacKenzie) 1967
Sermons and devotional writings ed. C. Devlin 1959
A vision of the mermaids (facsimile ed. of manuscript text dated 1862) 1929
Hopkins, Keith ed. *Hong Kong, the industrial colony: a political, social and economic survey* 1971
Hopkinson, Diana *The incense-tree* 1968
Horizon: a review of literature and art 1940–50
Hornsby, Henry *Lonesome valley* 1949
Hornung, Ernest William *The amateur cracksman* 1899
The black mask 1901
Horowitz, Irving Lewis ed. *Masses in Latin America* 1970
ed. *The new sociology* 1964
Horrobin, David Frederick *Science is God* 196[illegible]
Horse and hound 1884–
Horsley, Terence *Find, fix and strike: the wor[illegible] of the Fleet Air Arm* 1943
Hortus third: a concise dictionary of plants cultivated in the United States and Canad[illegible] (Liberty Hyde Bailey Hortorium) 1976
Horwill, Herbert William *A dictionary of modern American usage* 1935
— (ed. 2) 1944
Horwood, Harold Andrew *Newfoundland* 1969
Hostetter, Gordon L. & Beesley, Thomas Q[illegible] *It's a racket!* 1929
Hostettler, Rudolf, et al. *Technical terms of th[illegible] printing industry* 1949
— (ed. 3) 1959
Hot car 1968–
Hotel world, The 1875–
House and garden (New York) 1901–
UK ed. 1920–4
— (new series) 1946–
Household, Geoffrey Edward West *Doom'[illegible] caravan* 1971
Rogue male 1939
Householder, Fred Walter *Linguistic speculations* 1971
—— & Saporta, Sol eds. *Problems in lexicography* [report of the Conference on Lexicography, Indiana University, 1960] 1962
Housewife 1939–
Housman, Alfred Edward (1859–1936) *Collected poems* 1939
Letters ed. H. Maas 1971
More poems 1936
Housman, Laurence *The unexpected years* 1937
Houston, Margaret Bell *The witch man* 1922
Houston Chronicle (Houston, Texas) 1901–
Hovering craft and hydrofoil 1961–
Hovland, Carl I., Lumsdaine, A. A., & Sheffield, F. D. *Experiments on mass communication* 1949
Howard, Alexander Liddon *A manual of th[illegible] timbers of the world* 1920
— (rev. ed.) 1934
Howard, Elizabeth Jane *After Julius* 1965
'Howard, Hartley' (Leopold Horace Ognall[illegible] *Highway to murder* 1973
Nice day for a funeral 1972
Howard, John A. *Aerial photo-ecology* 1970
Howard, Richard tr. *S. de Beauvoir's Force o[illegible] circumstance* 1965
Howard journal 1921–
Howarth, Thomas Graham *South's British butterflies, based extensively on the classic by Richard South* 1973
Howat, Gerald Malcolm D. & Taylor, A. J. P[illegible] eds. *Dictionary of world history* 1973
Howe, Ellic ed. *The London compositor: documents relating to wages, working conditions and customs of the London printing trade 1785–1900* 1947
Howe, Henry *Historical collections of Ohio* 184[illegible]
Howells, William Dean *Literature and life. studies* 1902
Howitt, William *The rural and domestic life o[illegible] Germany* 1842
Howitt's journal of literature and popular progress 1847–8
Howson, Albert Geoffrey *A handbook of terms used in algebra and analysis* 1972
Hoyle, Edmond *Hoyle's games modernized* (new ed., rev. by L. H. Dawson) 1923
— (ed. 20, rev. by L. H. Dawson) 1950
Hoyle, Fred *The black cloud* 1957
Frontiers of astronomy 1955
Galaxies, nuclei and quasars 1965 (UK 1966)
Ice 1981
The nature of the universe: a series of broadcast lectures 1950
Hubbard, Clifford Lionel Barry *Dogs in Britain* 1948
The observer's book of dogs 1945
Hubbard, Philip Maitland *The custom of the country* 1967 (UK 1969)
High tide 1970 (UK 1971)
Picture of Millie 1964
Hubble, Edwin Powell *The realm of the nebulæ* 1936
Hudson, Charles Thomas & Gosse, P. H. *The rotifera* 2 vols. & Suppl. 1886–9
Hudson, Derek Rommel *Munby: man of two worlds. The life and diaries of Arthur J. Munby 1828–1910* 1972
Hudson, Kenneth *The jargon of the professions* 1978
Hudson, William Henry *Far away and long ago: a history of my early life* 1918
Green mansions: a romance of the tropical forest 1904

:udson's Bay Record Society *Publications* 1938–
:UEFFER, Ford Madox *See* FORD, Ford Madox
:UGHES, Arthur Frederick William *The mitotic cycle: the cytoplasm and nucleus during interphase and mitosis* 1952
IUGHES, Dorothy Belle *The expendable man* 1963 (UK 1964)
IUGHES, George Edward & LONDEY, David George *The elements of formal logic* 1965
IUGHES, Mary Vivian *A London child of the seventies* 1934
IUGHES, Richard Arthur Warren *A high wind in Jamaica* 1929
In hazard 1938
IUGHES, Ted *Crow: from the life and songs of the crow* 1970
The hawk in the rain 1957
Lupercal 1960
IUGHES, Thomas Patrick *A dictionary of Islam* 1885
IUKE, Douglas Wynne *Introduction to natural and synthetic rubbers* 1961
IULL, Clark Leonard *Principles of behavior: an introduction to behavior theory* 1943
IULL, Richard Francis Carrington, et al. tr. *C. G. Jung's Collected works* 20 vols. 1953–79
IULME, Alfred Cresswell *The biochemistry of fruits and their products* 2 vols. 1970–1
IULME, Kathryn Cavarly *The nun's story* 1956
Iuman world: a quarterly review of English letters 1970–
IUMPHREY, George *Thinking* 1951
IUMPHREY, John Herbert & WHITE, R. G. *Immunology for students of medicine* 1963
IUMPHREYS, David *The Yankey in England* 1815
IUMPHRIES, Derek W. & HUMPHRIES, Evelyn E. tr. *H. & G. Termier's Erosion and sedimentation* 1963
IUNT, John Leslie & PRINGLE, Alan George *Service slang* 1943
IUNT, Robert Nigel Carew *A guide to Communist jargon* 1957
IUNT, Robert William Gainer *The reproduction of colour* 1957
Iunt's merchants' magazine and commercial review See *Merchants' magazine and commercial review*
IUNTER, Alan James Herbert *Gently at a gallop* 1971
Gently coloured 1969
Gently continental 1967
Gently French 1973
IUNTER, John Marvin ed. *The trail drivers of Texas* 1920
HUNTER, Matthew' *The Cambridgeshire disaster* 1967
IUNTER, Robert, et al. *The encyclopædic dictionary* See under title
IUNTING, Henry Gardner *The vicarion* 1926
IURREN, Bernard John *Eastern Med.* 1943
IURST, Fannie *Humoresque: a laugh on life with a tear behind it* 1919
IURSTON, Zora Neale *Mules and men* 1935
— (another ed.) 1970
IUSCHKE, Ralph E. ed. *Glossary of meteorology* 1959
IUSKEY, Harry Douglas & KORN, G. A. *Computer handbook* 1962
Iutching's illustrated California magazine 1856–61
HUTCHINGS, Ernest A. D. *A survey of printing processes* 1970
HUTCHINSON, Arthur Stuart Menteth *If winter comes* 1921
Once aboard the lugger: the history of George and his Mary 1908
One increasing purpose 1925
This freedom 1922
HUTCHINSON, George Evelyn *A treatise on limnology* 1957–
HUTCHINSON, Horace Gordon *Golfing* 1893
HUTCHINSON, Robert William *A first course in wireless* 1926
Hutchinson's pictorial history of the war ed. W. V. Hutchinson 1939–45
HUTCHISON, Isobel Wylie *North to the rime-ringed sun: being the record of an Alaskan-Canadian journey made in 1933–34* 1934
HUTTEN, Ernest Hirschlaff *The language of modern physics* 1956
HUTTON, John Henry *Caste in India: its nature, function and origins* 1946
HUXLEY, Aldous Leonard (1894–1963) *Adonis and the alphabet* 1956
After many a summer 1939
Along the road: notes and essays 1925
Antic hay 1923
Ape and essence 1948 (UK 1949)
Beyond the Mexique Bay 1934
Brave new world 1932
Brave new world revisited 1958 (UK 1959)
Brief candles 1930
Crome yellow 1921
Do what you will: essays 1929
Ends and means: an enquiry into the nature of ideals and into the methods employed for their realization 1937
Essays new and old 1926
Eyeless in Gaza 1936
The genius and the goddess 1955
Grey eminence: a study in religion and politics 1941
Island 1962
Jesting Pilate: the diary of a journey 1926
Leda 1920
Letters ed. Grover Smith 1969
Music at night, and other essays 1931
The olive tree, and other essays 1936
The perennial philosophy 1945 (UK 1946)
Point counter point 1928
Proper studies 1927
Themes and variations 1950
Those barren leaves 1925
Time must have a stop 1944 (UK 1945)
Vulgarity in literature 1930
HUXLEY, Anthony Julian *An illustrated history of gardening* 1978
Plant and planet 1974
HUXLEY, Elspeth Josceline *Back street new worlds* 1964
HUXLEY, Julian Sorell *Bird-watching and bird behaviour* 1930
Essays in popular science 1926
Essays of a biologist 1923
Evolution in action 1953
Evolution: the modern synthesis 1942
Evolutionary ethics 1943
The individual in the animal kingdom 1912
On living in a revolution 1944
Problems of relative growth 1932
Religion without revelation 1927
— (rev. ed.) 1957
TVA: adventure in planning 1943
Unesco: its purpose and philosophy 1946
The uniqueness of man 1941
What dare I think? 1931
—— & HADDON, Alfred Cort *We Europeans* 1935
See also: HALDANE, John Burdon Sanderson
HUXLEY, Leonard *Life and letters of Sir Joseph Dalton Hooker* (based on materials collected and arranged by Lady Hooker) 2 vols. 1918
HVISTENDAHL, Herbert Selwyn *Engineering units and physical quantities* 1964
HYAMS, Edward Solomon *Gentian violet* 1953
Into the dream 1957
Soil and civilization 1952
Taking it easy 1958
HYAMS, Joseph *The pool* 1978
'HYDE, Robin' (Iris Guiver Wilkinson) *Check to your king: the life history of Charles, Baron de Thierry, King of Nukahiva, Sovereign Chief of New Zealand* 1936
Nor the years condemn 1938
Passport to hell: the story of John Douglas Stark, Bomber, Fifth Regiment, New Zealand Expeditionary Forces 1936
HYLAND, Henry Stanley *Top bloody secret* 1969
Who goes hang? 1958
HYLANDER, Clarence John *The Macmillan wild flower book* 1954
HYMAN, Libbie Henrietta *Comparative vertebrate anatomy* 1922
— (ed. 2) 1942
The invertebrates 5 vols. 1940–59
HYNE, Charles John C. W. *Mr. Horrocks, purser* 1902
HYNES, Martin *Medical bacteriology* (ed. 7) 1961
— (ed. 8) 1964
For earlier eds. see WHITBY, Sir Lionel E. H.
HYNES, Samuel Lynn *The Auden generation: literature and politics in England in the 1930's* 1976

I

IBM journal of research and development 1957–
IEEE *See* Institute of Electrical and Electronics Engineers
IRE *See* Institute of Radio Engineers
I.U.P.A.C. *See* International Union of Pure and Applied Chemistry
I believe: the personal philosophies of certain eminent men and women of our time [by W. H. Auden et al.] 1939 (UK 1940)
ICKES, Harold LeClair (1874–1952) *Secret diary* 3 vols. 1953–4 (UK 1955)
IDDINGS, Joseph Paxson *Igneous rocks: composition, texture and classification, description and occurrence* 2 vols. 1909–13
Rock minerals 1906
Idler magazine (title varies) 1894–1911
IDRIESS, Ion Llewellyn *The cattle king* 1936
The great boomerang 1941
In crocodile land: wandering in Northern Australia 1946
Isles of despair 1947
Lasseter's last ride: an epic of Central Australian gold discovery 1931
Ilkeston Advertiser and Erewash Valley Weekly News 1881–
Illinois. Department of Agriculture *Transactions* 1855–1921 (1855–71 with title *Transactions of the Illinois State Agricultural Society*)
Illinois State Historical Society *Journal* 1908–
Transactions 1899–
Illuminating Engineering Society (U.S.) *Transactions* 1906–40
Illustrated weekly of India (Bombay) 1879–
IMMS, Augustus Daniel *A general textbook of entomology* 1925
— (ed. 9) 1957 *See* RICHARDS, Owain Westmacott & DAVIES, R. G.
Immunology 1958–
Incorporated linguist 1962–
Independent, The (New York; later Boston, Mass.) 1848–1928
Index-Journal (Greenwood, South Carolina) 1897–
Indian journal of medical research 1913–
Indian music journal 1964–
Indiana. House of Representatives *Journal* 1816–46
Indiana Historical Society *Publications* 1895–
Indiana magazine of history 1905– (1905–13 with title *Indiana quarterly magazine of history*)
Industrial and engineering chemistry 1923–46
Industrial chemist and chemical manufacturer, The 1925–
INGE, William Ralph *Lay thoughts of a dean* 1926
INGRAHAM, Joseph Holt *The South-West, by a Yankee* 2 vols. 1835
INGRAM, George *Cockney cavalcade* 1935
'Stir' 1933
'Stir' train 1935
INGRAM, J. S. *The Centennial Exposition, described and illustrated* 1876
Ink 1971–2
Inland printer 1883–
Inlander, The (University of Michigan) 1891–1931 (title varies)
Inner life, The: essays in liberal evangelicalism 2nd ser. 1925
INNES, Hammond *The big footprints* 1977
The blue ice 1948
Campbell's kingdom 1952
'INNES, Michael' (John Innes Mackintosh Stewart) *Appleby plays chicken* 1956
Appleby's answer 1973
Appleby's other story 1974
An awkward lie 1971
Christmas at Candleshoe 1953
The daffodil affair 1942
Death at the President's lodging 1936
Hamlet, revenge! 1937
The journeying boy 1949
Old Hall, New Hall 1956
The open house 1972
Operation Pax 1951
See also under real name
Inside Kenya today 1953–
Institut Pasteur *Annales* 1887–
Institute of Cost and Management Accountants *Terminology of management and financial accountancy* 1974
Institute of Electrical and Electronics Engineers *IEEE transactions on computers* 1968–
IEEE transactions on electronic computers 1963–7
Proceedings 1963–
Institute of Radio Engineers *Proceedings* 1913–62
Transactions on electronic computers 1952–63
Institution of Civil Engineers *Minutes of proceedings* 1837–1937
Institution of Electrical Engineers *Journal* 1889–
Proceedings 1949–
Institution of Mechanical Engineers *Proceedings* 1847–
Institution (later Royal —) of Naval Architects *Transactions* 1860–
International and comparative law quarterly 1952–
International Congress of Genetics, 6th, 1932 *Proceedings* 2 vols. 1932
International Congress of Linguists, 8th, 1957 *Proceedings* 1958
International Congress of Medicine, 17th, 1913 23 sections 1913–14
International Congress of Phonetic Sciences, 2nd, 1935 *Proceedings* 1936
——, 3rd, 1938 *Proceedings* 1939
International Congress of Soil Science, 1st, 1927 *Proceedings and papers* 5 vols. 1928
——, 2nd, 1930 *Proceedings and papers* 7 vols. 1932–5
——, 7th, 1960 *Transactions* 4 vols. 1960
International encyclopaedia of the social sciences 17 vols. 1968
International Herald Tribune See *New York Herald Tribune International*

International journal of American linguistics 1917–
International journal of psycho-analysis 1920–
International Union of Pure and Applied Chemistry *Information bulletin* 1956–77
Nomenclature of inorganic chemistry 1959
— (ed. 2) 1971
Nomenclature of organic chemistry 3 parts 1958–65
— (ed. 2) 3 parts 1966–71
Inter-Ocean (Chicago) 1872–1914
Into orbit, by the seven astronauts of Project Mercury (US ed. with title *We seven*) 1962
Inverness Courier 1817–
IONESCU, Ghiţa & GELLNER, E. *Populism, its meaning and national characteristics* 1969
Iowa State Agricultural Society *Report* 1854–99
Irish Times 1859–
Iron and Steel Institute *Journal* 1871–
IRONSIDE, Janey *A fashion alphabet* 1968
IRVING, John *The 158-pound marriage* 1974
The world according to Garp 1978
IRVING, John James Cawdell *Royal navalese: a glossary* 1946
IRWIN, Godfrey *American tramp and underworld slang* 1931
ISHERWOOD, Christopher William Bradshaw *Goodbye to Berlin* 1939
Mr. Norris changes trains 1935
Prater violet 1945 (UK 1946)
A single man 1964
See also: AUDEN, Wystan Hugh
Isis, The (Oxford) 1892–1914; 1919–36; 1945–
Islander, The (Victoria, British Columbia) 1953–
It 1966–75 (1966–7 with title *International Times*)

J

JACKSON, Emily *A history of hand-made lace* 1900
JACKSON, George *Soledad Brother: the prison letters of George Jackson* 1970 (UK 1971)
JACKSON, Kenneth Hurlstone *Language and history in early Britain* 1953
JACKSON, Louis E. & HELLYER, C. R. *A vocabulary of criminal slang, with some examples of common usages* 1914
JACKSON, Richard A. *Mechanism: an introduction to the study of organic reactions* 1972
JACOB, Gordon Percival Septimus *Orchestral technique* 1931
JACOB, Henry ed. *On the choice of a common language* 1946
A planned auxiliary language 1947
JACOBS, Arthur *A new dictionary of music* 1958
JACOBS, Roderick A. & ROSENBAUM, Peter S. eds. *Readings in English transformational grammar* 1970
JACOBSEN, Charles W. *Oriental rugs: a complete guide* 1962
JACOBSON, Dan *The confessions of Joseph Baisz* 1977
A dance in the sun 1956
The trap 1955
JAFFE, Rona *Class reunion* 1979
— (Dell paperback ed.) 1980
The fame game 1969 (UK 1970)
JAKOBSON, Roman & HALLE, Morris *Fundamentals of language* 1956
JAMES, Brian *England v Scotland* 1969
'JAMES, Brian' (John Lawrence Tierney) ed. *Australian short stories* (2nd ser.) 1963
For 1st ser. *see* MURDOCH, Walter & DRAKE-BROCKMAN, H. F. Y.
JAMES, Edwin *Account of an expedition from Pittsburgh to the Rocky Mountains, performed in the years 1819, 1820. Compiled from the notes of Major Long, Mr. T. Say, and other gentlemen of the party* 3 vols. 1823
JAMES, Glenn & JAMES, Robert Clarke eds. *Mathematics dictionary* (multilingual ed.) 1959
JAMES, Henry (1843–1916) *The ambassadors* 1903
The awkward age 1899
The golden bowl 2 vols. 1904
The ivory tower 1917
The middle years 1917
Notebooks ed. F. O. Matthiessen & K. B. Murdock 1947
The reverberator 2 vols. 1888
The sense of the past 1917
The spoils of Poynton 1897
The wings of the dove 2 vols. 1902 (UK ed. in 1 vol.)
JAMES, Leigh *The chameleon file* 1967 (UK 1968)
JAMES, Phyllis Dorothy *Death of an expert witness* 1977
Shroud for a nightingale 1971
An unsuitable job for a woman 1972
JAMES, Walter *A word-book of wine* 1959
JAMES, William (1842–1910) *Collected essays and reviews* ed. R. B. Perry 1920
Essays in radical empiricism ed. R. B. Perry 1912
Letters ed. H. James 2 vols. 1920
The meaning of truth: a sequel to Pragmatism 1909
Memories and studies ed. H. James 1911
A pluralistic universe 1909
Pragmatism: a new name for some old ways of thinking 1907
Some problems of philosophy: a beginning of an introduction to philosophy 1911
Talks to teachers on psychology, and to students on some of life's ideals 1899
A text-book of psychology 1892
The will to believe, and other essays in popular philosophy 1897
See also: PERRY, Ralph Barton
JAMESON, Margaret Ethel Storm *A richer dust* 1931
Jane's all the world's aircraft (title varies) 1909–
Jane's fighting ships (title varies) 1898–
Jane's freight containers 1968–
Jane's surface skimmer systems (title varies) 1967–
JARVIS, Derek tr. *D. Hess's Plant physiology* 1975
Jazz and blues 1971–3
JEFFERIES, Ian *Dignity and purity* 1960
House-surgeon 1966
It wasn't me! 1961
Thirteen days 1959
JEFFRIES, Roderic Graeme *Dead man's bluff* 1970
Evidence of the accused 1961
Exhibit no. thirteen 1962
A traitor's crime 1968
JEKYLL, Gertrude *Colour in the flower garden* 1908
— (ed. 3, with title *Colour schemes for the flower garden*) 1914
Wood and garden 1899
JENKINS, Daniel Thomas *The educated society* 1966
JENKINS, Elizabeth *The tortoise and the hare* 1954
JENKINS, Geoffrey *A bridge of magpies* 1974
A twist of sand 1959
JENKINS, Herbert George *John Dene of Toronto: a comedy of Whitehall* 1919
JENKINS, James Travis *The fishes of the British Isles* 1925
— (ed. 2) 1936
JENKINS, Vivian Gordon J. *Lions down under: the British Isles Rugby tour of Australia and New Zealand, 1959* 1960
JENKINS, Warren *The Ohio gazetteer, and traveler's guide* 1837
JENNESS, Diamond *The Indians of Canada* 1932
— (ed. 2) 1934
JENNETT, Seán *The making of books* 1951
JENNINGS, Paul *The living village* 1968
JERRARD, Harold George & MCNEILL, Donald Burgess *A dictionary of scientific units, including dimensionless numbers and scales* 1963
JERROLD, William Blanchard *London* (illustr. G. Doré) 1872
Jersey Evening Post (St. Helier, Jersey) 1890–
JESPERSEN, Jens Otto Harry *Essentials of English grammar* 1933
Growth and structure of the English language 1905
An international language 1928
Language: its nature, development and origin 1922
Mankind, nation and individual from a linguistic point of view 1925
A modern English grammar on historical principles 7 parts 1909–49 (parts 6 & 7 by Jespersen & N. Haislund)
The philosophy of grammar 1924
The system of grammar 1933
Jewish Chronicle 1841–
Jewish encyclopedia, The ed. I. Singer 12 vols. 1901–6
Jewish manual, the; or, Practical information in Jewish and modern cookery, with a collection of valuable recipes & hints relating to the toilette, edited by a Lady 1846
JHABVALA, Ruth Prawer *Get ready for battle* 1962
The householder 1960
A new dominion 1972
To whom she will 1955
JOESTEN, Joachim *They call it intelligence* 1963
JOHANNSEN, Albert *A descriptive petrography of the igneous rocks* 4 vols. 1931–8
— (ed. 2) Vol. I 1939
JOHANNSEN, Hano & ROBERTSON, Andrew *Management glossary* ed. E. F. L. Brech 1968
John Edwards Memorial Foundation *Quarterly* (title varies) 1965–
John o' London's weekly 1919–54; revived as *John o' London's* 1959–
Johns Hopkins Hospital *Bulletin* 1889–1966
JOHNSON, Bryan Stanley *Travelling people* 1963
JOHNSON, Lady Bird (Mrs. Lyndon Baines Johnson) *A White House diary* 1970
JOHNSON, Myron ed. *American advertising 1800–1900* 1960
JOHNSON, Pamela Hansford *The humbler creation* 1959
Night and silence, who is here? 1963
The unspeakable Skipton 1959
JOHNSON, Paul Bede *Enemies of society* 1977
JOHNSON, William Ernest *Logic* 3 parts 1921–4
JOHNSTON, Edward *Writing and illuminating, and lettering* 1906
JOHNSTON, George Henry *Death takes small bites* 1948
JOHNSTON, Harry Hamilton *A comparative study of the Bantu and semi-Bantu languages* 2 vols. 1919–22
JOHNSTON, James Finlay Weir *Notes on North America; agricultural, economical and social* 2 vols. 1851
JOHNSTON, Ronald *The black camels of Qashran* 1970
JOLY, John *The surface-history of the earth* 1925
JONES, Bernard Edward ed. *Cassell's cyclopædia of photography* See *Cassell's* ——
The cinematograph book 1915
JONES, Cheslyn Peter M., WAINWRIGHT, G., & YARNOLD, E. eds. *The study of liturgy* 1978
JONES, Daniel *An outline of English phonetics* 1918 (and several later editions used)
The phoneme: its nature and use 1950
JONES, Eli Stanley *The Christ of the Indian road* 1925
JONES, Enid Huws *Margery Fry, the essential amateur* 1966
JONES, Ernest tr. *S. Ferenczi's Contributions to psycho-analysis* 1916
Papers on psycho-analysis 1913
— (rev. ed.) 1918
JONES, Ernest Beachcroft *Instrument technology* 3 vols. 1953–7
JONES, George Noble *Florida plantation records* ed. V. B. Phillips & J. D. Glunt 1927
JONES, Gwyn *A history of the Vikings* 1968
JONES, Henry Festing *Samuel Butler, author of Erewhon, 1835–1902: a memoir* 2 vols. 1919
JONES, John Morris *A Welsh grammar, historical and comparative* 1913
JONES, Mervyn *Potbank* 1961
JONES, Owen *The grammar of ornament* 1856
JONES, Philip Mitchell *The fifth defector* 1967
JONES, Reginald Victor *Most secret war* 1978
JONES, Robert Walter *Dictionary of banking* (ed. 10) 1951 *See* THOMSON, William
JONG, Erica Mann *Fanny: being the true history of the adventures of Fanny Hackabout-Jones* 1980
JORDAIN, Philip Bernard ed. *Condensed computer encyclopedia* 1969
'JORDAN, David' *Black account* 1975
Nile green 1973
JORDAN, David Starr *A guide to the study of fishes* 2 vols. 1905
JOSEPH, Horace William Brindley *An introduction to logic* 1906
— (ed. 2) 1916
JOSEPH, Michael Kennedy *I'll soldier no more* 1958
Journal of abnormal psychology 1906– (1921–64 with title *Journal of abnormal and social psychology*)
Journal of agricultural research 1913–49
Journal of anatomy and physiology 1866– (from 1916 with title *Journal of anatomy*)
Journal of applied physics 1937–
Journal of applied physiology 1948–
Journal of bacteriology 1916–
Journal of biological chemistry 1905–
Journal of biophysical and biochemical cytology 1955–61
Journal of cellular and comparative physiology 1932– (from 1966 with title *Journal of cellular physiology*)
Journal of chemical education 1924–
Journal of chemical physics 1933–
Journal of chromatography 1958–
Journal of clinical endocrinology and metabolism 1941–
Journal of clinical investigation 1924–
Journal of comparative neurology 1891– (1904–10 with title *Journal of comparative neurology and psychology*)
Journal of comparative psychology 1921–46
Journal of ecology 1913–
Journal of economic entomology 1908–
Journal of education 1879–
Journal of endocrinology 1939–
Journal of English and Germanic philology 1903–
Journal of experimental psychology 1916–
Journal of experimental zoology 1904–
Journal of general physiology 1918–
Journal of general psychology 1928–
Journal of genetic psychology 1954–
Journal of genetics 1910–
Journal of geophysical research 1949–
Journal of glaciology 1947–
Journal of heredity 1914–
Journal of hygiene 1901–

Journal of immunology 1916–
Journal of industrial and engineering chemistry 1909–22
Journal of infectious diseases 1904–
Journal of investigative dermatology 1938–
Journal of laboratory and clinical medicine 1915–
Journal of linguistics 1965–
Journal of medical research 1901–24
Journal of mental science 1855–1962
Journal of molecular biology 1959–
Journal of morphology (title varies) 1887–
Journal of natural philosophy, chemistry and the arts 1797–1813
Journal of neurology and psychopathology 1920–37
Journal of neurology, neurosurgery and psychiatry 1944–
Journal of nutrition 1928–
Journal of obstetrics and gynaecology of the British Empire (later —— *Commonwealth*) 1902–
Journal of organic chemistry 1936–
Journal of paleontology 1927–
Journal of pathology and bacteriology 1892–
Journal of pediatrics 1932–
Journal of pharmaceutical sciences 1911–
Journal of pharmacology and experimental therapeutics 1909–
Journal of philosophy 1904– (1904–20 with title *Journal of philosophy, psychology and scientific methods*)
Journal of physiology 1878–
Journal of political economy 1892–
Journal of polymer science 1946–
Journal of protozoology 1954–
Journal of scientific instruments 1922–
Journal of sedimentary petrology 1931–
Journal of social psychology 1930–
Journal of soil science 1949–
Journal of speech and hearing disorders 1936–
Journal of symbolic logic 1936–
Journal of theological studies 1899–
Journal of tropical medicine and hygiene 1898– (1898–1906 with title *Journal of tropical medicine*)
Journal See also under the names of particular institutions
Jowitt, William Allen & Walsh, Clifford eds. *Dictionary of English law* 2 vols. 1959
Joyce, James Augustine Aloysius (1882–1941) *Chamber music* 1907
Dubliners 1914
Exiles 1918
Finnegans wake 1939 (quotations are mostly taken from ed. 3, 1964, but dated simply 1939)
Giacomo Joyce ed. R. Ellmann 1968
Letters ed. S. Gilbert & R. Ellmann 3 vols. 1957–66
Pomes penyeach 1927
A portrait of the artist as a young man 1916 (quotations are mostly taken from the 1964 Viking Press ed., 15th printing, 1969)
Stephen hero: part of the first draft of 'A portrait of the artist as a young man' ed. T. Spencer 1944
— (ed. J. J. Slocum & H. Cahoon) 1955
Ulysses 1922 (quotations are mostly taken from the Random House ed., 1946, but dated simply 1922)
Joyce, Thomas Athol *Mexican archaeology* 1914
Jubb, Kenneth Victor F. & Kennedy, Peter C. *Pathology of domestic animals* 2 vols. 1963
— (ed. 2) 1970
Judd, Charles Hubbard tr. *W. Wundt's Outlines of psychology* 1897
Judge, Arthur William ed. *Modern motor cars* 3 vols. 1924
Modern petrol engines 1946
Stereoscopic photography: its application to science, industry and education 1926
Judge, The 1881–1939
Jukes-Browne, Alfred Joseph *The student's handbook of stratigraphical geology* 1902
Jung, Carl Gustav *See* Baynes, Helton Godwin; also Hull, Richard F. C., et al.

K

Kahn, David *The codebreakers: the story of secret writing* 1967 (UK 1968)
Kahn, Herman *On escalation: metaphors and scenarios* 1965
Kaleidoscope, The; or, Literary and scientific mirror 1818–31
Kane, Harry Hubbell *Opium-smoking in America and China* 1882
Kansas City Star (Kansas City, Missouri) 1880–
Kansas City Times (Kansas City, Missouri) 1868–
Kantor, Jacob Robert *An objective psychology of grammar* 1936
Kantorowicz, G. F. ed. *Inlays, crowns, and bridges* See: Cowell, Colin Robert, et al.
Kapp, Gilbert *Dynamos, alternators, and transformers* 1893
Karch, Robert Randolph & Buber, Edward J. *Graphic arts procedures: the offset processes* 1967
Karp, David *All honorable men* 1956
Leave me alone 1957
Karsner, Howard Thomas *Human pathology* 1927
Katz, Jerrold Jacob *The philosophy of language* 1966
Kauffman, Donald T. *Dictionary of religious terms* 1967
Kauffmann, Stanley Jules *If it be love* 1960
The tightrope 1952 (UK ed. 1953 with title *The philanderer*)
Kay, Stephen *Travels and researches in Caffraria* 1833
Kaye, Marvin *A lively game of death* 1972
'Kaye, Mary Margaret' (Mary Margaret Kaye Hamilton) *The far pavilions* 1978
House of shade 1959
Kaye-Smith, Sheila *Mrs. Gailey* 1951
Kazmann, Raphael G. *Modern hydrology* 1965
Keane, Augustus Henry *The Boer states: land and people* 1900
Man, past and present 1899
tr. *A. Hovelacque's The science of language* 1877
Keane, Charles Alexander *Modern organic chemistry* 1909
Keating, Henry Reymond Fitzwalter *Bats fly up for Inspector Ghote* 1974
Filmi, filmi, Inspector Ghote 1976
Inspector Ghote hunts the peacock 1968
Inspector Ghote plays a joker 1969
Keaton, Buster (Joseph Francis Keaton) *My wonderful world of slapstick* 1960 (UK 1967)
Keats, John (1795–1821) *Letters* ed. M. B. Forman 2 vols. 1931
Letters, 1814–1821 ed. H. E. Rollins 2 vols. 1958
Keeney, Arthur Hail *Ocular examination: basis and technique* 1970
Keepnews, Orrin & Grauer, William *A pictorial history of jazz: people and places from New Orleans to modern jazz* 1955
Keesing, Felix Maxwell *Cultural anthropology, the science of custom* 1958
Kefauver, Estes *Crime in America* ed. S. Shalett 1951 (UK 1952)
Kehoe, Vincent J. R. *Aficionado! The pictorial encyclopedia of the Fiesta de Toros of Spain* 1959
The technique of film and television make-up 1957
Keim, De Benneville Randolph *Sheridan's troopers on the borders: a winter campaign on the plains* 1870
Keith, Agnes Newton *Land below the wind* 1939
Keith, Arthur *The antiquity of man* 1915
Human embryology and morphology 1902
Keller, Helen Adams *The story of my life* ed. J. A. Macy 1903
Kelly, Mary Theresa *The Christmas egg* 1958
The spoilt kill 1961
Kelly, Michael *Spinifex* 1970
Kemble, Frances Anne *Records of later life* 3 vols. 1882
Kemelman, Harry Gregory *Monday the rabbi took off* 1972
Saturday the rabbi went hungry 1966 (UK 1967)
Wednesday the rabbi got wet 1976
Kemp, Ian *British G.I. in Vietnam* 1969
Kemp, James Furman *A handbook of rocks, for use without the microscope* 1896
Kemp, Peter Kemp *Fleet Air Arm* 1954
Kemp, Peter Mant MacIntyre *Alms for oblivion* 1961
Mine were of trouble 1957
No colours or crest 1958
Kendall, George Wilkins *Narrative of the Texan Santa Fé expedition* 2 vols. 1844
Kendall, Maurice George & Buckland, William R. *A dictionary of statistical terms* 1957
Kendrew, Wilfrid George *The climates of the continents* 1922
Kennedy, Ludovic Henry Coverley *Very lovely people* 1969
Kennedy, Margaret *The constant nymph* 1924
The heroes of Clone 1957
Lucy Carmichael 1951
Kenneison, William C. & Spilman, Alan J. B. *Dictionary of printing, papermaking and bookbinding* 1963
Kent, Ruth Kimball *The language of journalism: a glossary of print-communications terms* 1970
Kenyon, John Samuel *American pronunciation: a text-book of phonetics for students of English* 1924
— (ed. 6) 1935
Kenyon, Kathleen Mary *Archaeology in the Holy Land* 1960
Digging up Jericho 1957
Kenyon, Michael Forbes *Deep pocket* 1978
The 100,000 welcomes 1970
Mr Big 1975
The whole hog 1967
Kenyon review 1939–70
Kephart, Horace *Camping and woodcraft* 2 vols. 1916–17
— (new ed.) 1921 (2 vols. in 1)
Our southern highlanders 1913
Ker, William Paton *The Dark Ages* 1904
Kerouac, Jack *On the road* 1957 (UK 1958)
Kersh, Cyril *The aggravations of Minnie Ashe* 1970
Kersh, Gerald *They die with their boots clean* 1941
Kersley, Leo & Sinclair, Janet *A dictionary of ballet terms* 1952
Kettle, Edgar Hartley *The pathology of tumours* 1916
Kew bulletin (title varies) 1887–
Keynes, John Maynard *The economic consequences of the peace* 1919
The general theory of employment, interest and money 1936
A treatise on money 2 vols. 1930
Keynes, John Neville *Studies and exercises in formal logic* 1884 (and several later editions used)
Kichenside, Geoffrey Michael & Williams, Alan Reginald *British railway signalling* 1963
Kilvert, Robert Francis (1840–79) *Diary* ed. W. Plomer 3 vols. 1938–40
— (selections, ed. W. Plomer) 1944
Kimenye, Barbara *Kalasanda revisited* 1966
Kincaid, Dennis *British social life in India, 1608–1937* 1938
King, Francis Henry *The widow* 1957
King, Gordon John *The audio handbook* 1975
King, John Edward & Cookson, Christopher *The principles of sound and inflexion as illustrated in the Greek and Latin languages* 1888
King, Martin Luther *The trumpet of conscience* 1968
King, Woodie ed. *Black short story anthology* 1972
Kingsley, John Sterling *Comparative anatomy of vertebrates* 1912
Kingsley, Nelson *Diary* (1849–51) ed. F. J. Teggart 1914
Kingston Whig-Standard (Kingston, Ontario) 1926–
Kinloch, Alexander Angus Airlie *Large game shooting in Thibet and the Northwest* 2 vols. 1869–76
Kinsey, Alfred Charles, et al. *Sexual behavior in the human female* 1953
Sexual behavior in the human male 1948
Kipling, Rudyard (1865–1936) *Actions and reactions* 1909
A book of words 1928
Debits and credits 1926
A diversity of creatures 1917
From sea to sea 2 vols. 1899 (UK 1900)
Independence 1923
ed. *The Irish Guards in the Great War* 2 vols. 1923
Just so stories 1902
Land and sea tales 1923
Letters of travel 1920
Limits and renewals 1932
The phantom 'rickshaw, and other tales 1888 (UK 1890, revised)
Puck of Pook's Hill 1906
Rewards and fairies 1910
Something of myself for my friends known and unknown 1937
Songs from books 1912 (UK 1913)
Wee Willie Winkie, and other child stories 1888 (UK 1890)
The years between 1919
See also: Fletcher, Charles Robert Leslie
Kirby, Thomas Austin & Woolf, H. B. *Philologica: the [Kemp] Malone anniversary studies* 1949
Kirk, Raymond E. & Othmer, Donald F. eds. *Encyclopedia of chemical technology* 17 vols. 1947–60
— (ed. 2) 23 vols. 1963–71
Kirk, Raymond Maurice, Maynard, J. D., & Henry, A. N. *Surgery* 1974
Kirk, Thomas *The forest flora of New Zealand* 1889
Kirkaldy, John Francis *General principles of geology* 1954
Kirkbride, Ronald *Tamiko* 1959
'Kirke, Edmund' (James Roberts Gilmore) *My southern friends* 1863
Kirkland, Caroline Matilda *Forest life: a tale* 2 vols. 1842
A new home—who'll follow? Or, Glimpses of western life 1839
Western clearings 1845
Kirkland, John *The modern baker, confectioner and caterer* 6 vols. 1907–9
Kirkup, James Harold *Japan behind the fan* 1970
The only child 1957
Tropic temper: a memoir of Malaya 1963

Kirwan, Daniel Joseph *Palace and hovel; or, Phases of London life* 1870
Kleene, Stephen Cole *Introduction to metamathematics* 1952
Mathematical logic 1967
Klibansky, Raymond ed. *Contemporary philosophy: a survey* 4 vols. 1968–71
Kneale, William Calvert *Probability and induction* 1949
—— & Kneale, Martha *The development of logic* 1962
Knecht, Edmund, Rawson, C., & Loewenthal, R. *A manual of dyeing* 2 vols. 1893
Kneebone, Geoffrey Thomas *Mathematical logic and the foundation of mathematics* 1963
Knickerbocker, William Skinkle ed. *Twentieth century English* 1946
Knight, Albert E. *The complete cricketer* 1906
'Knight, Brigid' (Kathleen Henrietta Sinclair) *The covenant* 1943 (UK 1944)
Westward the sun (UK ed. with title *The sun climbs slowly*) 1942
Knight, Damon ed. *One hundred years of science fiction* 1969
Knight, Sarah (Kemble) *The journals of Madam Knight, and Rev. Mr. Buckingham ..written in 1704 & 1710* 1825
Knight, Sophia *Window on Shanghai: letters from China 1965–67* 1967
Knott, Frank Alexander *Clinical bacteriology* 1939
Knowles, Robert Edward *The attic guest* 1909
Knox, Alexander *Glossary of geographical and topographical terms* 1904
Knox, 'Bill' *See* Knox, William
Knox, Ronald Arbuthnott *Broadcast minds* 1932
The footsteps at the lock 1928
God and the atom 1945
The hidden stream: a further collection of Oxford conferences 1952
In soft garments: a collection of Oxford conferences 1942
Still dead 1934
Knox, William ('Bill') *Blacklight* 1967
Little drops of blood 1962
The tallyman 1969
Kober, Arthur *Parm me* 1945
Koch, Sigmund ed. *Psychology: a study of a science* 6 vols. 1959–63
Kochman, Thomas ed. *Rappin' and stylin' out: communication in urban black America* 1972
Koebel, William Henry *In the Maoriland bush* 1911
The return of Joe, and other New Zealand stories 1907
Koestler, Arthur *The age of longing* 1951
Arrow in the blue: an autobiography 1952
Insight and outlook: an inquiry into the common foundations of science, art and social ethics 1949
The invisible writing [2nd vol. of *Arrow in the blue*] 1954
The lotus and the robot 1960
Promise and fulfilment: Palestine 1917–1949 1949
Scum of the earth 1941
Spanish testament 1937
Thieves in the night: chronicle of an experiment 1946
The trail of the dinosaur, and other essays 1955
Twilight bar: an escapade in four acts 1945
The yogi and the commissar, and other essays 1945
—— et al. *The god that failed: six studies in communism* ed. R. H. S. Crossman 1950
Koninklijke Akademie van Wetenschappen te Amsterdam. Section of Sciences *Proceedings* (English ed.) 1899– (1955– with title *Proceedings* of the Koninklijke Nederlandsche Akademie van Wetenschappen)
Koppett, Leonard *The New York Times guide to spectator sports* 1971
Kops, Bernard *The Hamlet of Stepney Green: a sad comedy* 1959
Körner, Stephan *The philosophy of mathematics* 1960
Kostov, Ivan *Mineralogy* tr. by the author, ed. P. G. Embrey & J. Phemister 1968
Kracke, Roy Rachford & Garver, Hortense Elton *Diseases of the blood and atlas of hematology* 1937
Kramsch, Dieter M. tr. *E. Grundmann's General cytology* 1966
Krantz, Judith *Scruples* 1978
Krapp, George Philip *The English language in America* 2 vols. 1925
Kratochvíl, Paul *The Chinese language today: features of an emerging standard* 1968
Kroeber, Alfred Louis *Anthropology* 1923
— (rev. ed.) 1948
Krogh, Schack August S. *Osmotic regulation in aquatic animals* 1939
Krohn, F. tr. *G. Glaser de Cew's Magneto- and dynamo-electric machines* ed. P. Higgs 1884
Krueger, Robert G., Gillham, N. W., & Coggin, J. H. *Introduction to microbiology* 1973
Kuhn, Irene *Assigned to adventure* 1938
Kuper, Charles Goethe *An introduction to the theory of superconductivity* 1968
Kurath, Hans *Studies in area linguistics* 1972
A word geography of the Eastern United States 1949
Kurnitz, Harry *Invasion of privacy* 1955 (UK 1956)
Kwang-chih Chang *The archaeology of ancient China* 1963
— (ed. 3) 1977
Kyle, Robert *Venus examines* (UK ed. with title *The love laboratory*) 1968

L

Labarre, Émile Joseph *A dictionary of paper and paper-making terms* 1937
La Bern, Arthur Joseph *Goodbye Piccadilly, farewell Leicester Square* 1966
Labov, William *Language in the inner city: studies in the Black English vernacular* 1972
'Lackland, Thomas' (George Canning Hill) *Homespun; or, Five-and-twenty years ago* 1867
Lacy, Ed *Double trouble* 1965
The freeloaders 1962
Ladies' field, The 1896–1928
Ladies' home journal 1883–
Ladies' repository 1841–76
Lafitte, Paul *The person in psychology: reality or abstraction* 1957
Lagler, Karl F., Bardach, J. E., & Miller, R. R. *Ichthyology* 1962
Lagowski, Joseph John *Modern inorganic chemistry* 1973
Lahee, Frederic Henry *Field geology* 1916
Laidler, F. F. ed. *A glossary in English, French, German, Spanish of terms used in home economics education* 1963
Lake, Philip & Rastall, Robert Heron *A textbook of geology* 1910
Lamb, Charles (1775–1834) & Lamb, Mary Ann (1764–1847) *Letters* ed. E. V. Lucas 3 vols. 1935
Lamb, Lynton *Man in a mist* 1974
Picture frame 1972
Lamb, Sydney M. *Outline of stratificational grammar* 1966
Lamb, Warren *Posture and gesture: an introduction to the study of physical behaviour* 1965
Lambert, Constant *Music ho!* 1934
Lambert, Richard Stanton *Ariel and all his quality* 1940
'La Meri' (Russell Meriwether Hughes) *Spanish dancing* 1948
— (ed. 2) 1967
Lancashire Dialect Society *Journal* 1951–
Lancashire life 1947–
'Lancaster, G. B.' (Edith Joan Lyttleton) *Jim of the ranges* 1910
Sons o' men 1904
Lancaster, Osbert *Homes sweet homes* 1939
Lancaster, Massachusetts *Early records 1643–1725* ed. H. S. Nourse 1884
Landau, Thomas ed. *Encyclopaedia of librarianship* 1958
— (ed. 2) 1961
Landfall: a New Zealand quarterly 1947–
Landy, Eugene E. *The underground dictionary* 1971
Lane, Arthur *Greek pottery* 1948
'Lane, Linacre' *The ABZ of Scouse: how to talk proper in Liverpool, Vol. 2* ed. F. Spiegel 1966 (For Vol. 1 *see* Shaw, Frank, et al.)
Lang, R. F. tr. *F. A. Henglein's Chemical technology* 1969
Langbridge, Rosamond *The flame and the flood* 1903
Langford, Michael John *Basic photography* 1965
Langford-Smith, Fritz *Radio designer's handbook* 1940
— (ed. 4) 1953
Langton, Mary Beach *How to know oriental rugs: a handbook* 1904
Language: journal of the Linguistic Society of America 1925–
Language learning 1948–
Lanham, Peter *Blanket boy's moon* (based on an original story by A. S. Mopeli-Paulus) 1953
Lankester, Edwin Ray *Diversions of a naturalist* 1915
Lanman, Charles *Letters from the Alleghany Mountains* 1849
A summer in the wilderness; embracing a canoe voyage up the Mississippi and around Lake Superior 1847
Lantern: politics, amusement, literature (New Orleans) 1886–9
Laqueur, Walter ed. *A dictionary of politics* 1971
Lardner, Ringgold Wilmer *Gullible's travels* 1917 (UK 1926)
Larkin, Philip Arthur *Jill* 1946
The less deceived 1955
The north ship 1945
Larsell, Olof *Anatomy of the nervous system* 1942
— (ed. 2) 1951
Laski, Audrey Louise *The keeper* 1968
Seven other years 1967
Laski, Harold Joseph *Holmes–Laski letters* See: Holmes, Oliver Wendell
Laski, Marghanita *Little boy lost* 1949
Love on the supertax 1944
Tory heaven; or, Thunder on the right 1948
The village 1952
See also: 'Russell, Sarah'
Lasky, Melvin J. *Utopia and revolution* 1976 (UK 1977)
Laslett, Thomas Peter R. ed. *Household and family in past time* 1972
'Lathen, Emma' (Mary Jane Latsis & Martha Henissart) *Accounting for murder* 1964 (UK 1965)
Banking on death 1961 (UK 1962)
By hook or by crook 1975
Come to dust 1968 (UK 1969)
The longer the thread 1971 (UK 1972)
Murder without icing 1972 (UK 1973)
Pick up sticks 1970 (UK 1971)
Sweet and low 1974
When in Greece 1969
See also: 'Dominic, R. B.'
'Lauchmonen' *Old Thom's harvest* 1965
Laurie, Peter *Scotland Yard: a personal inquiry* 1970
Laver, James *Taste and fashion, from the French Revolution until to-day* 1937
Victoriana 1966
Law, James Thomas *Law's Grocer's manual* 1896
Lawrence, David Herbert (1885–1930) *Aaron's rod* 1922
Apocalypse 1931 (UK 1932)
Birds, beasts and flowers: poems 1923
Collected letters ed. H. T. Moore 2 vols. 1962
A collier's Friday night 1934
David: a play 1926
England, my England, and other stories 1922 (UK 1924)
Etruscan places 1932
Fantasia of the unconscious 1922
Kangaroo 1923
Lady Chatterley's lover 1928
Last poems ed. R. Aldington & G. Orioli 1932
Letters ed. A. Huxley 1932 (See also *Collected letters*)
Look! We have come through! 1917
The lost girl 1920
Love among the haystacks, and other pieces 1930
Love poems and others 1913
The lovely lady 1933 (dated 1932)
A modern lover 1934
Mornings in Mexico 1927
Nettles 1930
New poems 1918
Pansies: poems 1929
Phoenix: posthumous papers ed. E. D. McDonald 1936
Phoenix II: uncollected, unpublished and other prose works ed. F. W. Roberts & H. T. Moore 1968
The plumed serpent (Quetzalcoatl) 1926
Psychoanalysis and the unconscious 1921
The rainbow 1915
Reflections on the death of a porcupine, and other essays 1925
St. Mawr, together with The princess 1925
Sea and Sardinia 1921
Sons and lovers 1913
Studies in classic American literature 1923
Touch and go: a play 1920
The virgin and the gipsy 1930
The white peacock 1911
The widowing of Mrs. Holroyd: a drama 1914
The woman who rode away, and other stories 1928
Women in love 1920 (UK 1921)
—— & Skinner, Mary Louisa *The boy in the bush* 1924
Lawrence, George H. M. *Taxonomy of vascular plants* 1951
Lawrence, Thomas Edward (1888–1935) *The home letters of T. E. Lawrence and his brothers* ed. M. R. Lawrence 1954
Letters ed. D. Garnett 1938
The mint: notes made in the R.A.F. Depot between August and December 1922, and at Cadet College in 1925 by 352087 A/c Ross 1936 (UK, rev. 1955)
Seven pillars of wisdom: a triumph 1926
— (trade ed.) 1935
Lawrence, William Witherle *Beowulf and epic tradition* 1928
Lawson, Henry Archibald Hertzberg (1867–1922) *Stories* ed. C. Mann 3 ser. 1964
Verses, popular and humorous 1900

LAWSON, Robert William tr. *G. von Hevesy & F. A. Paneth's A manual of radioactivity* 1926
— (ed. 2) 1938
tr. *A. Einstein's Relativity: the special and the general theory: a popular exposition* 1920
LAYARD, Edgar Leopold *The birds of South Africa: a descriptive catalogue* 1867
LEACH, Bernard *A potter in Japan 1952–1954* 1960
LEACH, Edmund Ronald *Lévi-Strauss* 1970
LEACH, John Albert *An Australian bird book* 1911
LEACOCK, Stephen Butler *Over the footlights, and other fancies* 1923
LEAKEY, Louis Seymour Bazett *The Stone Age cultures of Kenya Colony* 1931
LEAR, Edward (1812–88) *Indian journal* ed. R. Murphy 1953
Laughable lyrics 1877
LEASOR, Thomas James *A host of extras* 1973
They don't make them like that any more 1969
LEAVIS, Frank Raymond *The great tradition: George Eliot, Henry James, Joseph Conrad* 1948
—— & THOMPSON, Arthur Denys H. *Culture and environment: the training of critical awareness* 1933
LEAVIS, Queenie Dorothy *Fiction and the reading public* 1932
Lebende Sprachen 1956–
'LE CARRÉ, John' (David John M. Cornwell) *The honourable schoolboy* 1977
The looking-glass war 1965
A murder of quality 1962
A small town in Germany 1968
Smiley's people 1979 (UK 1980)
The spy who came in from the cold 1963
Tinker tailor soldier spy 1974
LEE, Harper *To kill a mockingbird* 1960
LEE, John D. *The ninth man* 1976
LEE, John Alexander *Children of the poor* 1934
Civilian into soldier 1937
LEE, Julius & KNOWLES, Francis *Animal hormones* 1965
LEE, Laurie *Cider with Rosie* 1959
LEE, Rawdon B. *A history and description of the modern dogs of Great Britain and Ireland* 3 parts 1893–4
LEE, Reuben *Electronic transformers and circuits* 1947
LEECH, Geoffrey N. *English in advertising* 1966
LEEDS, Herbert Daniel & WEINBERG, Gerald Marvin *Computer programming fundamentals* 1961
LEES, Dan *The rainbow conspiracy* 1971
Rape of a quiet town 1973
Zodiac 1972
LEES-MILNE, James *Ancestral voices* 1975
LEESON, Charles Roland & LEESON, Thomas Sydney *Histology* 1966
— (ed. 2) 1970
LEFF, Gordon A. *History and social theory* 1969
LEFSCHETZ, Solomon *Introduction to topology* 1949
LEGMAN, Gershon *The fake revolt* 1967
LEHMANN, Rosamond Nina *The ballad and the source* 1944
Dusty answer 1927
The echoing grove 1953
The gipsy's baby, and other stories 1946
Invitation to the waltz 1932
A letter to a sister 1931
A note in music 1930
The weather in the streets 1936
LEIGHTON, Robert *The complete book of the dog* 1922
The new book of the dog: a comprehensive natural history of British dogs and their foreign relatives 1907
LEINSTER, Mary *Dew on the leaf* 1926
Leisure hour, The 1852–1905
LEJEUNE, Anthony *Duel in the shadows* 1962
LEMARCHAND, Elizabeth *Death of an old girl* 1967
Death on Doomsday 1971
Let or hindrance 1973
LEONARD, Elmore *Unknown man, no. 89* 1977
LEONARD, Zenas *Narrative of the adventures of Zenas Leonard* 1839
— (ed. W. F. Wagner) 1904
LEPSCHY, Guilio Ciro *A survey of structural linguistics* 1970
LESLIE, John Randolph Shane *The Anglo-Catholic* 1929
The Oppidan 1922
LESSING, Doris May *Five: short novels* 1953
The golden notebook 1962
In pursuit of the English 1960
Shikasta 1979
This was the old chief's country: stories 1951
Letters of Miss Riversdale [anon. novel] 3 vols. 1803
LEVI, Herbert W. & LEVI, Lorna R. tr. *A. Kaestner's Invertebrate zoology* 3 vols. 1967–70
LEVY, Mervyn Montague *The Studio dictionary of art terms* 1961

LEWES, Vivian Byam *Oil fuel* 1913
LEWIS, Alfred Henry *The apaches of New York* 1912
The boss, and how he came to rule New York 1903
Confessions of a detective 1906
Wolfville days 1902
LEWIS, Arthur William *A glossary of woodworking terms* 1966
LEWIS, Cecil Day tr. *Virgil's Aeneid* 1952
Beechen vigil, and other poems 1925
The buried day 1960
Child of misfortune 1939
The friendly tree 1936
tr. *Virgil's Georgics* 1940
A hope for poetry 1934
An Italian visit 1953
The Otterbury incident 1948
Overtures to death, and other poems 1938
Poems, 1943–1947 1948
A time to dance, and other poems 1935
Transitional poem 1929
Word over all 1943
See also: 'BLAKE, Nicholas'
LEWIS, Clarence Irving *A survey of symbolic logic* 1918
Symbolic logic 1932
LEWIS, Clive Staples (1898–1963) *The allegory of love: a study in medieval tradition* 1936
Letters ed. W. H. Lewis 1966
Perelandra 1943
Poems ed. W. Hooper 1964
The problem of pain 1940
The Screwtape letters 1942
Studies in words 1960
Surprised by joy 1955
That hideous strength: a modern fairy-tale for grown-ups 1945
LEWIS, Dominic Bevan Wyndham *On straw, and other conceits* 1927
LEWIS, Ethelreda *Mantis* 1926
LEWIS, Griselda ed. *Handbook of crafts* 1960
LEWIS, Meriwether & CLARK, William *Original journals of the Lewis and Clark expedition, 1804–1806* ed. R. G. Thwaites 8 vols. 1904–5
—— & ORDWAY, John *The journals of Captain Meriwether Lewis and Sergeant John Ordway, kept on the expedition of western exploration, 1803–1806* ed. M. M. Quaife 1916
LEWIS, Percy Wyndham (1882–1957) *The apes of God* 1930
Blasting and bombardiering 1937
Letters ed. W. K. Rose 1963
LEWIS, Roy (John Royston Lewis) *Blood money* 1973
Witness my death 1976
LEWIS, Sinclair (Harry Sinclair Lewis) *Arrowsmith* (UK ed. with title *Martin Arrowsmith*) 1925
Babbitt 1922
Bethel Merriday 1940
Cass Timberlane 1945 (UK 1946)
Free air 1919 (UK 1924)
It can't happen here 1935
Main Street: the story of Carol Kennicott 1920
The man who knew Coolidge 1928
Mantrap 1926
Our Mr. Wrenn: the romantic adventures of a gentle man 1914
LEWIS, Wilfrid James *The language of cricket* 1934
LEWIS, Wyndham *See* LEWIS, Percy Wyndham
LEY, Willy *The conquest of space* 1949 (UK 1950)
LEYDEN, John tr. *Malay annals* 1821
—— & ERSKINE, William tr. *Memoirs of Zehir-Ed-Din Muhammed Baber, Emperor of Hindustan, written by himself in the Jaghatai Turki* 1826
Liberty 1924–30
Library, The 1889–
Library Association record 1899–
Library journal: journal of the American Library Association 1876–
LICHINE, Alexis *Encyclopædia of wines and spirits* 1967
Wines of France 1952
LIDDELL, Billy (William Beveridge Liddell) *My soccer story* 1960
LIDDELL, Robert *The Morea* 1958
LIEBERMAN, Jethro K. & RHODES, Neil S. *The complete CB handbook* (new ed.) 1976
LIEF, Max *Hangover* 1929
Life 1936–72
Life and work (Church of Scotland) 1879–
LILICO, James Ewart *Sheep dog memoirs* 1934
LILLEY, Arthur Augustus *Twenty-four years of cricket* 1912
LILLYWHITE, Frederick ed. *The guide to cricketers* 1853–66
LILLYWHITE, James *James Lillywhite's cricketers' annual* 1872–7; 1879–93
LILLYWHITE, John *John Lillywhite's cricketers' companion* (title varies) 1865–85
LINCOLN, Abraham (1809–65) *Collected works* ed. R. P. Basler 9 vols. 1953

LINCOLN, Joseph Crosby *Cap'n Warren's wards* 1911
Partners of the tide 1905
LINDGREN, Ernest *The art of the film* 1948
LINDOP, Audrey Erskine *Sight unseen* 1969
LINDSAY, Jack *Life rarely tells* 1958
LINDZEY, Gardner ed. *Handbook of social psychology* 2 vols. 1954
— (ed. 2, by Lindzey & E. Aronson) 5 vols. 1968–9
LINGEMAN, Richard R. *Drugs from A to Z: a dictionary* 1969
Lingua: international review of general linguistics 1947–
LININGTON, Barbara Elizabeth *See* 'BLAISDELL, Anne'; 'EGAN, Lesley'; & 'SHANNON, Dell'
LINKLATER, Eric Robert Russell *Juan in America* 1931
Magnus Merriman 1934
Poet's pub 1929
Private Angelo 1946
Linnean Society of London *Proceedings* 1838–
Linnean Society of New South Wales *Proceedings* 1876–
LINNETT, John Wilfred *The electronic structure of molecules: a new approach* 1964
LINSSEN, Eugene F. *Beetles of the British Isles* 2 ser. 1959
LINTON, David Leslie ed. *Sheffield and its region* 1956
Lippincott's medical dictionary by R. W. Greene et al. 1897
Lippincott's monthly magazine (title varies) 1868–1915
Lippincott's new medical dictionary ed. H. W. Cattell 1910
Listener, The 1929–
LISTER, Raymond George *Decorative cast ironwork in Great Britain* 1960
Decorative wrought ironwork in Great Britain 1957
LITCHFIELD, Frederick *Pottery and porcelain: a guide to collectors* 1900
Literary digest 1890–1938
Literary guide 1894–1954
Little folks: a magazine for children 1871–1933
Liverpool Echo 1879–
Living off the land: a manual of bushcraft, compiled from articles contributed to 'Salt', the army education journal (Australia) 1944
LIVINGSTON, Milton Stanley *Particle physics: the high energy frontier* 1968
LLOYD, Albert Lancaster *Folk song in England* 1967
LLOYD, Christopher *The well-tempered garden* 1970
LLOYD, Hannibal Evans tr. *J. B. von Spix & C. F. P. von Martius's Travels in Brazil, 1817–20* 2 vols. 1824
LLOYD GEORGE, David *See* GEORGE, David Lloyd
LOBECK, Armin Kohl *Geomorphology* 1939
LOCK, Joan *Lady policeman* 1968
LOCKE, William John *Ancestor Jorico* 1929
At the gate of Samaria 1894
The beloved vagabond 1906
The coming of Amos 1924
Derelicts 1897
The glory of Clementina Wing 1911
The house of Baltazar 1920
Idols 1898
Jaffery 1915
Moordius and Co. 1923
The morals of Marcus Ordeyne 1905
The mountebank 1921
The old bridge 1926
The red planet 1917
The rough road 1918
Septimus 1909
Simon the jester 1910
Stella maris 1913
Stories near and far 1926
The tale of Triona 1922
The wonderful year 1916
LOCKET, George Hazlewood & MILLIDGE, Alfred Frank *British spiders* 2 vols. 1951–3
LOCKHART, Laurence William Maxwell *Fair to see* 3 vols. 1871
LOCKRIDGE, Frances Louise & LOCKRIDGE, Richard *Murder has its points* 1961 (UK 1962)
Practise to deceive: a Captain Heimrich mystery 1957 (UK 1959, as by 'Francis Richards')
LOCKWOOD, William Burley *Panorama of Indo-European languages* 1972
LOCKYER, Keith Gerald *An introduction to critical path analysis* 1964
LODGE, David John *The British Museum is falling down* 1965
Changing places 1975
LOGAN, Olive *Before the footlights and behind the scenes* 1870
LOMAX, Alan *Mister Jelly Roll: the fortunes of Jelly Roll Morton, New Orleans Creole and inventor of jazz* 1950 (UK 1952)

LONDON, Jack (John Griffith London) (1876–1916) *The call of the wild* 1903
The iron heel 1907 (UK 1908)
The jacket (US ed. with title *The star rover*) 1915
Letters ed. K. Hendricks & I. Shepard 1965 (UK 1966)
The road 1907 (UK 1914)
A son of the sun 1912 (UK 1913)
The valley of the moon 1913
White Fang 1906 (UK 1907)
London & Globe Telephone & Maintenance Company, Ltd. *List of subscribers* 1884 [reproduced in facsimile in *Three Victorian telephone directories* 1970]
London at table; or, How, when, and where to dine and order a dinner; and where to avoid dining 1851
London magazine: a monthly review of literature 1954–
London Mathematical Society *Proceedings* 1865–
London medical gazette 1827–51
London medical record 1873–87
London mercury 1919–39
London review 1835–6
London review of books 1979–
London society 1862–98
LONG, Constance Ellen tr. *C. G. Jung's Collected papers on analytical psychology* 1916
LONG, Joseph W. *American wild-fowl shooting* 1874
LONG, Ralph Bernard *The sentence and its parts: a grammar of contemporary English* 1961
LONGSTREET, Stephen *The real jazz, old and new* 1956
LONGWELL, Chester Ray, KNOPF, A., & FLINT, R. R. *Outlines of physical geology* 1934
'LORAC, E. C. R.' (Edith Caroline Rivett) *Ask a policeman* 1955
Murder in the mill-race 1952
LORAND, Sándor ed. *Psycho-analysis today: its scope and function* 1933
LORIMER, George Horace *Jack Spurlock—prodigal* 1908
Letters from a self-made merchant to his son 1902
Old Gorgon Graham: more letters from a self-made merchant to his son 1904
LORIMER, Hilda Lockhart *Homer and the monuments* 1950
Los Angeles Times 1881–
LOUNSBURY, Warren C. *Backstage from A to Z: a glossary of technical stage terms* 1959
LOVELOCK, Ian ('Yann') *The vegetable book: an unnatural history* 1972
LOVESEY, Peter Harmer *Invitation to a dynamite party* 1974
LOWELL, Robert Traill Spence *Near the ocean* 1967
Notebook 1970
LOWIE, Robert Heinrich *The history of ethnological theory* 1937 (UK 1938)
LOWNDES, Marie Adelaide Belloc *Diaries and letters 1911–1947* ed. S. Lowndes 1971
The Terriford mystery 1924
LOWRY, Clarence Malcolm (1909–57) *Selected letters* ed. H. Breit & M. B. Lowry 1965 (UK 1967)
Ultramarine 1933
Under the volcano 1947
LOYN, Henry Royston *Anglo-Saxon England and the Norman Conquest* 1962
'LUARD, L.' (William Blaine Luard) *All hands* 1933
Conquering seas 1935
LUARD, Nicholas *The Robespierre serial* 1975
Travelling horseman 1975
LUBBOCK, Adelaide *Australian roundabout* 1963
LUBBOCK, Alfred Basil *Round the Horn before the mast* 1902
LUBBOCK, John *See* AVEBURY, John (Lubbock), 1st Baron
LUCAS, Dione & HUME, Rosemary *'Au petit cordon bleu': an array of recipes* 1936
LUCAS, Edward Verrall *Over Bemerton's: an easy-going chronicle* 1908
Reading, writing and remembering: a literary record 1932
The vermilion box 1916
LUCAS, Norman *The C.I.D.* 1967
LUCIA, Ellis *Klondike Kate: the life and legend of Kitty Rockwell* 1962
LUDLUM, Robert *The Holcroft covenant* 1978
The Matlock paper 1973
LUGARD, Frederick John Dealtry (1858–1945) *Diaries* ed. M. Perham 4 vols. 1959–63
LULL, Richard Swann *Organic evolution* 1917
LUNN, Arnold Henry Moore *Harrovians* 1913
LUPTON, Thomas *Management and the social sciences* 1966
— (ed. 2) 1970
LURIE, Alison *Love and friendship* 1962
The nowhere city 1965
Real people 1969
The war between the Tates 1974
LUSH, Vicesimus *Auckland journals, 1850–63* ed. A. Drummond 1971
Thames journals, 1868–82 ed. A. Drummond 1975
LUTYENS, Mary ed. *Effie in Venice: unpublished letters of Mrs. John Ruskin written from Venice between 1849–1852* 1965
Millais and the Ruskins 1967
The Ruskins and the Grays 1972
LYALL, Gavin Tudor *Blame the dead* 1972
Judas country 1975
The most dangerous game 1964
Shooting script 1966
LYDEKKER, Richard *The deer of all lands* 1898
LYELL, Thomas Reginald G. *Slang, phrase and idiom in colloquial English and their use* 1931
LYLES, Sanders Truman *Biology of microorganisms* 1969
LYNDE, Francis *The grafters* 1904
The quickening 1906
LYON, Francis Hamilton tr. *T. Heyerdahl's The Kon-Tiki Expedition: by raft across the South Seas* (US ed. with title *Kon-Tiki: across the Pacific by raft*) 1950
LYON, Lilian Helen Bowes *Bright feather fading* 1936
The white hare, and other poems 1934
LYONS, Albert Michael Neil *Clara: some scattered chapters in the life of a hussey* 1912
LYONS, John *Introduction to theoretical linguistics* 1968
Semantics 2 vols. 1977
Structural semantics: an analysis of part of the vocabulary of Plato 1963
LYTTLETON, Raymond Arthur *Mysteries of the solar system* 1968
LYTTON, David *The goddam white man* 1960

M

McADOO, William Gibbs *Crowded years* 1931
MACALISTER, Robert Alexander Steward *A text-book of European archaeology* 1921 (only Vol. I published)
MACARDLE, Dorothy *Children of Europe: a study of the children of liberated countries* 1949
MACAULAY, Emilie Rose (1887–1958) *Crewe train* 1926
Dangerous ages 1921
Going abroad 1934
I would be private 1937
Keeping up appearances 1928
Last letters to a friend, 1952–58 ed. C. B. Smith 1962
Letters to a friend, 1950–52 ed. C. B. Smith 1961
Letters to a sister ed. C. B. Smith 1964
Orphan Island 1924
Personal pleasures 1935
Potterism: a tragi-farcical tract 1920
Staying with relations 1930
Told by an idiot 1923
The towers of Trebizond 1956
'McBAIN, Ed' (Evan Hunter) *Ax* [UK: *Axe*] 1964
Cop hater 1956 (UK 1958)
Doll 1965 (UK 1966)
Guns 1976 (UK 1977)
Give the boys a great big hand 1960 (UK 1962)
Hail, hail, the gang's all here! 1971
Hail to the chief 1973
Let's hear it for the deaf man 1973
Long time no see 1977
The pusher 1959
Ten plus one 1963 (UK 1964)
McBAIN, James William *Colloid science* 1950
MACBETH, George Mann *A war quartet* 1969
McCABE, John *Mr. Laurel and Mr. Hardy* 1961 (UK 1962)
McCABE, Joseph tr. *E. Haeckel's The wonders of life* 1904
McCall's sewing, in colour 1964
McCARDELL, Roy Larcom *Conversations of a chorus girl* 1903
McCARTHY, Ian Ellery *Nuclear reactions* 1970
McCARTHY, Mary Therese *Birds of America* [a novel] 1971
A charmed life 1955 (UK 1956)
The company she keeps 1942 (UK 1943)
The group 1963
The groves of Academe 1952 (UK 1953)
Memories of a Catholic girlhood 1957
On the contrary 1961 (UK 1962)
McCARTHY, Wilson *The detail* 1973
McCARTNEY, William *Olfaction and odours: an osphrésiological essay* 1968
McCLANE, Albert Jules ed. *McClane's Standard fishing encyclopedia* 1965
McCLOY, Helen *A change of heart* 1973
Panic 1944 (UK 1972)
The sleepwalker 1974
Through a glass, darkly 1950 (UK 1951)
McCLUNG, Clarence Erwin ed. *Handbook of microscopical technique* 1929
McCLUNG, Nellie Letitia *Clearing in the west* 1935
The stream runs fast 1945
McCLURE, David (1748–1820) *Diary* with notes by F. B. Dexter 1899
McCLURE, James Howe *The caterpillar cop* 1972
Rogue eagle 1976
Snake 1975
McCORMICK, John & MASCAREÑAS, Mario Sevilla *The complete aficionado* 1967
McCOWAN, Daniel *Animals of the Canadian Rockies* 1936
McCRACKEN, Daniel Delbert *Digital computer programming* 1957
McCRUM, Robert *In the secret state* 1980
McCULLERS, Carson *Clock without hands* 1961
The heart is a lonely hunter 1940 (UK 1943)
The member of the wedding 1946
McCULLOCH, Walter Fraser *Woods words: a comprehensive dictionary of loggers' terms* 1958
McCULLOUGH, Colleen *The thorn birds* 1977
McCUTCHAN, Philip Donald *Call for Simon Shard* 1974
Storm south 1959
McCUTCHEON, George Barr *The rose in the ring* 1910
McDAVID, Raven I. *See* MENCKEN, Henry Louis
'MACDIARMID, Hugh' (Christopher Murray Grieve) *The company I've kept* 1966
To circumjack Cencrastus; or, The curly snake 1930
MACDONALD, Betty Heskett *The egg and I* 1945 (UK 1946)
McDONALD, Gregory *Confess, Fletch* 1976 (UK 1977)
MACDONALD, John Dann *The brass cupcake* 1950 (UK 1955)
The executioners 1958 (UK 1959)
The girl, the gold watch, and everything 1962
ed. *The lethal sex: the 1959 anthology of the Mystery Writers of America* 1959 (UK 1962)
Pale gray for guilt 1968 (UK 1969)
'MACDONALD, John Ross' *The Galton case* See: 'MACDONALD, Ross'
MACDONALD, Philip *Mystery of the dead police* 1933
'MACDONALD, Ross' (Kenneth Millar) *The Galton case* 1959 (UK 1960)
The instant enemy 1968
MACDONELL, Archibald Gordon *Autobiography of a cad* 1938
England, their England 1933
McDOUGALL, William *An outline of abnormal psychology* 1926
MACE, Cecil Alec ed. *British philosophy in the mid-century* 1957
McEVOY, Joseph Patrick *Hollywood girl* 1929 (UK 1930)
Show girl 1928
McEWAN, Ian *The comfort of strangers* 1981
McFADDEN, Cyra *The serial: a year in the life of Marin County* 1977 (UK 1978)
McGAFFEY, Kenneth *The sorrows of a show girl* 1908
MACGILL, Patrick *The brown brethren* 1917
McGILVERY, Robert Warren *Biochemistry: a functional approach* 1970
McGIRR, Edmund *Bardel's murder* 1973
Death pays the wages 1970
An entry of death 1969
The lead-lined coffin 1968
A murderous journey 1974
McGIVERN, William Peter *The big heat* 1953
Caprifoil 1972 (UK 1973)
M'GOWAN, George tr. *A. Bernthsen's A text-book of organic chemistry* 1889
McGraw-Hill dictionary of modern economics, The 1965
McGraw-Hill encyclopedia of science and technology 15 vols. 1960
— (new ed.) 15 vols. 1966
McGraw-Hill yearbook of science and technology 1963–
MACHLIN, Milton *Pipeline* 1976
'McHUGH, Hugh' (George Vere Hobart) *Back to the woods: the story of a fall from grace* 1903
Skidoo! 1906
You can search me 1905
McILVANNEY, William *Laidlaw* 1977
MACINNES, Colin *Absolute beginners* 1959
City of spades 1957
Mr. Love and Justice 1960
McINNES, Graham *The road to Gundagai* 1965
MACINNES, Hamish *Climb to the lost world* 1974
MACINNES, Helen *Agent in place* 1976
Message from Malaga 1972
The Salzburg connection 1969
McINTOSH, Louis *Oxford folly* 1956
MACKAIL, Denis George *How amusing! And a lot of other fables* 1929
MACKAY, Kenneth *Out back* 1893
— (ed. 2) 1893
McKELLAR, Thomas Peter Huntly *Experience and behaviour* 1968
McKENNEY, Thomas Loraine *Memoirs, official and personal; with sketches of travels among the northern and southern Indians* 2 vols. 1846

MACKENZIE, Donald *Postscript to a dead letter* 1973
Raven and the kamikaze 1977
MACKENZIE, Edward Montague Compton *April fools* 1930
Carnival 1912 (some quotations taken from 1912 US ed.)
The early life and adventures of Sylvia Scarlett 1918
Gallipoli memories 1929
Guy and Pauline 1915
The heavenly ladder 1924
My life and times 10 vols. 1963–71
The old men of the sea 1924
Sinister Street 2 vols. 1913–14
Sylvia and Michael: the later adventures of Sylvia Scarlett 1919
Whisky galore 1947
MACKENZIE, John *Ten years north of the Orange River: a story of every-day life and work among the South African tribes, from 1859 to 1869* 1871
MACKENZIE, Norman Ian *Conviction* 1958
MCKERROW, Ronald Brunlees *An introduction to bibliography for literary students* 1927
MCKIE, Ronald Cecil H. *The company of animals* 1965
MACKINNON, Doris Livingston & HAWES, R. S. J. *An introduction to the study of protozoa* 1961
MACKINTOSH, Ewart Alan (1893–1917) *War, the liberator, and other pieces* 1918
MCKNIGHT, Cathy & TOBLER, John *Bob Marley: the roots of reggae* 1977
MCKNIGHT, George Harley *English words and their background* 1923
MACLAREN-ROSS, Julian *The doomsday book* 1961
Until the day she dies 1960
MACLEAN, Fitzroy Hew *Eastern approaches* 1949
MACLEAN, Magnus ed. *Modern electric practice* 6 vols. 1904–5
MCLEAN, Sarah Pratt *Cape Cod folks* 1881
MCLEAN, Terence Power *Kings of Rugby: the British Lions' 1959 tour of New Zealand* 1960
Maclean's magazine 1912–
MCLEAVE, Hugh *A question of negligence* 1970 (UK 1973)
MACLEOD, Iain *Bridge is an easy game* 1952
'MACLEOD, Robert' (William Knox) *Burial in Portugal* 1973
MCLINTOCK, Alexander Hare ed. *A descriptive atlas of New Zealand* 1959
MCLUHAN, Herbert Marshall *The Gutenberg galaxy* 1962
The mechanical bride: folklore of industrial man 1951 (UK 1967)
Understanding media: the extensions of man 1964
—— & FIORE, Quentin *The medium is the massage* 1967
MCMAHON, Patrick Joseph *Aircraft propulsion* 1971
MCMULLEN, Edwin Wallace *English topographic terms in Florida, 1563–1874* 1953
MACNAB, Angus *The bulls of Iberia: an account of the bullfight* 1957
MACNEICE, Frederick Louis (1907–63) tr. *Aeschylus' Agamemnon* 1936
Astrology ed. D. Hill 1964
Autumn journal: a poem 1939
Autumn sequel: a poem 1954
Christopher Columbus: a radio play 1944
The dark tower, and other radio scripts 1947
The earth compels: poems 1938
tr. *Goethe's Faust* 1951
Holes in the sky: poems 1944–1947 1948
I crossed the Minch 1938
The last ditch 1940
Modern poetry: a personal essay 1938
Poems 1935
The poetry of W. B. Yeats 1941
See also: AUDEN, Wystan Hugh
MCNEILE, Alan Hugh *An introduction to the study of the New Testament* 1927
MACQUARRIE, John ed. *A dictionary of Christian ethics* 1967
MACQUOID, Percy *A history of English furniture* 1904
MCRAE, Archibald Graham *The hill called Grazing: the story of a Transvaal farm* 1956
MCRAE, Thomas Watson *The impact of computers on accounting* 1964
MACREADY, William Charles (1793–1873) *Diaries* ed. W. Toynbee 2 vols. 1912
MACVICAR, Angus *The painted doll affair* 1973
MADDOX, Harry Alfred *A dictionary of stationery* 1923
Mademoiselle 1935–
Madras. Music Academy *Journal* 1930–
MAERZ, Aloys John & PAUL, Morris Rea *A dictionary of color* 1930
MAGUIRE, Michael *Scratchproof* 1976
MAIDEN, Joseph Henry *The forest flora of New South Wales* 8 vols. 1904–25
MAIER, Richard Ali & MAIER, Barbara M. *Comparative animal behavior* 1970
MAILER, Norman *Advertisements for myself* 1959 (UK 1961)
Cannibals and Christians 1966 (UK 1967)
The naked and the dead 1948 (UK 1949)
MAINES, George H. & GRANT, Bruce *Wise-crack dictionary* 1926
Mainichi Daily News (Tokyo) 1922– (title varies)
MAJOR, Clarence *Dictionary of Afro-American slang* 1970
MALAMUD, Bernard *The assistant* 1957
Dubin's lives 1979
The fixer 1966 (UK 1967)
The natural 1952 (UK 1963)
A new life 1961 (UK 1962)
The tenants 1971
Malay Mail (Kuala Lumpur) 1896–
'MALCOLM X' (Malcolm Little) *Autobiography* 1965
Maledicta: the international journal of verbal aggression (Waukesha, Wisconsin) 1977–
'MALET, Lucas' (Mary St. Leger Harrison) *The dogs of want: a modern comedy of errors* 1924
The wages of sin 3 vols. 1891
MALINOWSKI, Bronislaw Kasper (1884–1942) *Coral gardens and their magic* 2 vols. 1935
A scientific theory of culture, and other essays 1944
Sex and repression in savage society 1927
MALLETT, Edward *Telegraphy and telephony, including wireless* 1929
'MALLOCH, Peter' (William Murdoch Duncan) *Kickback* 1973
MALTHUS, Thomas Robert (1766–1834) *Travel diaries* ed. P. James 1966
Man: a monthly record of anthropological science 1901–
Management engineering 1921–3
Manchester Guardian Weekly 1919–68
MANCHON, Joseph *Le slang: lexique de l'anglais familier et vulgaire, précédé d'une étude sur la prononciation et la grammaire populaires* 1923
MANDER, John *Static society: the paradox of Latin America* 1969
MANING, Frederick Edward *Old New Zealand* 1863
MANKOWITZ, Cyril Wolf & HAGGAR, Reginald George *The concise encyclopedia of English pottery and porcelain* 1957
MANN, Anthony *Tiara* 1973
MANN, Charles Riborg & MILLIKAN, Robert Andrews tr. *P. Drude's The theory of optics* 1902
MANN, Jessica *Mrs. Knox's profession* 1972
The sticking place 1974
MANN, Mary E. *In summer shade* 3 vols. 1893
MANNING, Frederic *The middle parts of fortune* 2 vols. 1929
MANNING, Olivia *The great fortune* 1960
The rain forest 1974
'MANSFIELD, Katherine' (Kathleen Middleton Murry) (1888–1923) *Bliss, and other stories* 1920
Collected stories 1945
The doves' nest, and other stories 1923
Journal ed. J. M. Murry 1954
Letters to John Middleton Murry, 1913–1922 ed. J. M. Murry 1951
Something childish, and other stories 1924
MANSFIELD, Walter Kenneth *Elementary nuclear physics* 1958
MANVELL, Arnold Roger & HUNTLEY, John *The technique of film music* 1957
MANWARING, Charles William ed. *A digest of the early Connecticut probate records* 3 vols. 1904–6
MARAIS, Eugène Nielen *My friends the baboons* [anon. tr.] 1939
MARBUT, C. F. tr. *K. D. Glinka's The great soil groups of the world and their development* 1927
MARCHANT, Edgar Walford *Radio telegraphy and telephony* 1923
MARCUS, Stanley *Minding the store: a memoir* 1974 (UK 1975)
MARCUS, Steven *The other Victorians* 1966
MARDER, Irving *The Paris bit* 1967
MARETT, Robert Ranulph ed. *Anthropology and the classics: six lectures* 1908
MARGERISON, Donald & EAST, George C. *An introduction to polymer chemistry* 1967
MARIN, Alfred C. *The clash of distant thunder* 1968 (UK 1969)
Rise with the wind 1969
Marine engineer (title varies) 1879–1972
Mariner's mirror 1911–
MARION, Fulgence *Wonderful balloon ascents* [anon. tr.] 1870
'MARJORIBANKS' *The fluff-hunters* 1903
MARKFIELD, Wallace *To an early grave* 1964 (UK 1965)
MARKS, Percy *Collector's choice* 1972
The plastic age 1924
MARKS, Robert W. *The dymaxion world of Buckminster Fuller* 1960
MARLOTH, Hermann Wilhelm Rudolf (1855–1931) *The flora of South Africa* 4 vols. 1913–32
MARPLES, Morris *Public school slang* 1940
University slang 1950
MARQUAND, Allan *Greek architecture* 1909
MARQUAND, John Phillips *H.M. Pulham, Esquire* 1941 (UK 1942)
Wickford Point 1939
MARQUARD, Leopold *The peoples and policies of South Africa* 1952
MARRIOTT, Harry *Cariboo cowboy* 1966
MARRIOTT, William *Hints to meteorological observers* 1881
— (ed. 6) 1906
MARSH, Edward Howard *Rupert Brooke: a memoir* 1918
MARSH, John Thompson *Self-smoothing fabrics* 1962
MARSH, Ngaio Edith *Artists in crime* 1938
Black as he's painted 1974
Colour scheme 1943
Dead water 1963 (UK 1964)
Death and the dancing footman 1941 (UK 1942)
Death in a white tie 1938
Death in ecstasy 1936
Death of a fool 1956 (UK ed. 1957 with title *Off with his head*)
Death of a peer 1940 (UK ed. 1941 with title *Surfeit of Lampreys*)
False scent 1959 (UK 1960)
Final curtain 1947
Grave mistake 1978
Hand in glove 1962
A man lay dead 1934
Off with his head See above: *Death of a fool*
Opening night 1951
Overture to death 1939
Singing in the shrouds 1958 (UK 1959)
Surfeit of Lampreys See above: *Death of a peer*
Swing, brother, swing 1949
Tied up in tinsel 1972
Vintage murder 1937
MARSHAK, Robert Eugene *Meson physics* 1952 (UK 1953)
MARSHALL, Agnes B. *Mrs. A. B. Marshall's cookery book* 1888
— ('tenth thousand') 1889
Mrs. A. B. Marshall's larger cookery book of extra recipes 1892
MARSHALL, Bruce *George Brown's schooldays* 1946
MARSHALL, Humphry *Arbustrum Americanum: the American grove; or, An alphabetical catalogue of forest trees and shrubs, natives of the American United States* 1785
MARSHALL, Sybil *An experiment in education* 1963
MARSHALL, Thomas Humphrey *Citizenship and social class, and other essays* 1950
MARTIN, Basil Kingsley *Editor: a second volume of autobiography, 1931–45* 1968
Father figures: a first volume of autobiography, 1897–1931 1966
MARTIN, Helen *Tillie, a Mennonite maid* 1904 (UK 1905)
MARTIN, Joseph ed. *A new and comprehensive gazetteer of Virginia, and the District of Columbia* 1835
MARTIN, Laurence Cleveland & HYNES, Martin *Clinical endocrinology for practitioners and students* 1948
— (ed. 3, by L. C. Martin alone) 1961
MARTIN, Mary Ann *Our Maoris* 1884
MARTIN, Robert Denis tr. *W. Wickler's Mimicry in plants and animals* 1968
MARTIN, William *The New Zealand nature book* 1929 (UK 1930)
MARX, Groucho (Julius Henry Marx) (1895–1977) *The Groucho letters: letters from and to Groucho Marx* 1967
MARX, Heinrich Karl *See* MOORE, Samuel & AVELING, E. B.
Maryland historical magazine 1906–28
MASCALL, Eric Lionel *Christian theology and natural science: some questions on their relations* 1956
The recovery of unity: a theological approach 1958
MASEFIELD, John Edward *Ballads* 1903
Ballads and poems 1910
The bird of dawning 1933
Captain Margaret: a romance 1908
The Conway, from her foundation to the present day 1933
Dead Ned: the autobiography of a corpse 1938
The everlasting mercy 1911
Gautama the enlightened, and other verse 1941
The hawbucks 1929
Live and kicking Ned 1939
Lollingdon Downs and other poems, with sonnets 1917
Odtaa 1926
Reynard the fox; or, The ghost heath run 1919
Sard Harker 1924
A tarpaulin muster 1907
The tragedy of Nan, and other plays 1909

Mason, Alfred Edward Woodley *The house of the arrow* 1924
Miranda of the balcony 1899
The truants 1904
Mason, Frederick A. tr. *G. von Georgievics's A text-book of dye chemistry* 1920
Mason, Monck *Aeronautica; or, Sketches illustrative of the theory and practice of aerostation* 1838
Mason, Richard Lakin *The world of Suzie Wong* 1957
Massachusetts. Agricultural Survey *First report on the agriculture of Massachusetts* by H. Colman 1838
Second report 1839
Massachusetts (Colony). House of Representatives *Journals* 1919–
Massingham, Harold John *The curious traveller* 1950
World without end 1932
Masson, Madeleine *Birds of passage* 1950
Masterman, John Cecil *Fate cannot harm me* 1935
Masters, John *Bhowani Junction* 1954
Bugles and a tiger: a personal adventure 1956
Coromandel! 1955
The deceivers 1952
Far, far the mountain peak 1957
The lotus and the wind 1953
Nightrunners of Bengal 1951
Trial at Monomoy 1964
Masters, Ted *Surfing made easy* 1962
Masur, Harold Q. ed. *Murder most foul* 1973
Materials and technology: a systematic encyclopedia of the technology of materials used in industry and commerce 8 vols. 1968–75
Mates, Benson *Elementary logic* 1965
Mathematical reviews 1940–
Mathematical tables and other aids to computation 1943–59
'Mather, Berkeley' (John Evan W. Davies) *The break in the line* 1970
Snowline 1973
The springers 1968
Mathews, Albert Prescott *Physiological chemistry* 1916
Mathews, Anne *Memoirs of Charles Mathews, comedian* 4 vols. 1838–9
Mathews, Catharine Van Cortlandt *Andrew Ellicott: his life and letters* 1908
Mathews, Mitford M. ed. *A dictionary of Americanisms on historical principles* See under title
Mathewson, Christopher *Pitching in a pinch; or, Baseball from the inside* 1912
Second base Sloan 1917
Matsell, George Washington *Vocabulum; or, The rogue's lexicon, compiled from the most authentic sources* 1859
Matthews, Leonard Harrison *The life of mammals* 2 vols. 1969–71
Maugham, Robin (Robert Cecil Romer Maugham) *The servant* 1972
Maugham, William Somerset *The bishop's apron: a study in the origins of a great family* 1906
The bread-winner 1930
Cakes and ale; or, The skeleton in the cupboard 1930
The circle 1921
The constant wife 1926
Liza of Lambeth 1897
The moon and sixpence 1919
Of human bondage 1915
On a Chinese screen 1922
Our betters 1923
The painted veil 1925
The razor's edge 1944
Sheppey 1933
The summing up 1938
Theatre 1937
Then and now 1946
A writer's notebook 1949
Mawer, Allen & Stenton, Frank Merry *Introduction to the survey of English place-names* 1924
Maxwell, Nicole *Witch-doctor's apprentice* 1962
May, Derwent James *Laughter in Djakarta* 1973
Maycock, William Perren *Electric lighting and power distribution* 3 parts 1892–3
Electric wiring, fittings, switches, and lamps 1899
Mayer, Edgar *Clinical application of sunlight and artificial radiation* 1926
Mayer, Ralph *The artist's handbook of materials and techniques* 1940
— (UK ed.) 1951
A dictionary of art terms and techniques 1969
Mayer-Gross, Willy, Slater, Eliot T. O., & Roth, Martin *Clinical psychiatry* 1954
— (ed. 3) 1969
Maylard, Alfred Ernest *A treatise on the surgery of the alimentary canal* 1896
Mayr, Ernst *Animal species and evolution* 1963
Principles of systematic zoology 1969
——, Linsley, E. G., & Usinger, R. L. *Methods and principles of systematic zoology* 1953

Mead, Margaret *Growing up in New Guinea: a comparative study of primitive education* 1930
Male and female: a study of the sexes in a changing world 1949
Meade, Elizabeth ('Lillie') Thomasina *A sweet girl graduate* 1891
Meccano magazine 1916–
Medawar, Peter Brian & Medawar, Jean Shinglewood *The life science: current ideas of biology* 1977
Medbery, James Knowles *Men and mysteries of Wall Street* 1870
Meddelelser om Grønland (Copenhagen) 1879–
Medical annual, The 1883–
Medical journal of Australia 1914–
Medical news (Philadelphia) 1843–1905
Medical record (New York) 1866–1922
Medical Research Council *Mathematics and computer science in biology and medicine* 1965
A system of bacteriology in relation to medicine 9 vols. 1929–31
Medium ævum 1932–
Medway, Gathorne (Gathorne-Hardy), Baron *The wild mammals of Malaya and offshore islands including Singapore* 1969
Meglitsch, Paul Allen *Invertebrate zoology* 1967
Melbourne Truth (title varies) 1902–
Melchior, Ib *Sleeper agent* [anon. tr.] 1975 (UK 1976)
Mellor, Joseph William *A comprehensive treatise on inorganic and theoretical chemistry* 1922–
Modern inorganic chemistry 1912
Melly, Alan George Heywood *Owning-up* 1965
Melody maker, The 1926–
Melville, Herman *Pierre; or, The ambiguities* 1852
Redburn: his first voyage (UK ed. in 2 vols.) 1849
Typee: a peep at Polynesian life 1846
'Melville, Jennie' (Gwendoline Butler) *Ironwood* 1972
Nun's castle 1974
Mencken, Henry Louis *The American language: a preliminary inquiry into the development of English in the United States* 1919
— (rev. ed.) 1921
— (ed. 3) 1923
— (ed. 4) 1936
— Supplement 2 vols. 1945–8
— (abridged ed. with new material by R. I. McDavid) 1963
Mendelsohn, Oscar Adolf *The dictionary of drink and drinking* 1965
Men's hockey ('Know the game' series) 1950
— (rev. ed.) 1965
Merchants' magazine and commercial review 1839–70 (1851–60 with title *Hunt's merchants' magazine and commercial review)*
'Mercury' dictionary of textile terms, The 1950
Meredith, George (1828–1909) *Letters* ed. C. L. Cline 3 vols. 1970
Mereness, Newton Dennison ed. *Travels in the American colonies 1690–1783* 1916
Merriman, Arthur Douglas *A dictionary of metallurgy* 1958
Merton, Robert King *Social theory and social structure* 1949
— (rev. ed.) 1957
— (rev. ed.) 1968
Merwin, Samuel & Webster, Henry Kitchell *Calumet 'K'* 1901
Metabolism: clinical and experimental 1952–
Metals handbook See: American Society for Metals
Metcalf, Clell Lee & Flint, Wesley Pillsbury *Fundamentals of insect life* 1932
Destructive and useful insects 1928
— (ed. 4) 1962
Meteorological Office *See* United Kingdom
Metronome 1885–
Meyer, Jerome Sydney & Hanlon, Stuart *Fun with the new math* 1966
Meynell, Laurence Walter *Double fault* 1965
Hooky gets the wooden spoon 1977
The thirteen trumpeters: a Hooky Hefferman story 1973
Virgin luck 1963
Mezzrow, Milton & Wolfe, Bernard *Really the blues* 1946 (UK 1957)
Miall, Arthur Bernard tr. *C. Guenther's A naturalist in Brazil* 1931
Miall, Stephen ed. *A new dictionary of chemistry* 1940
— (ed. 2, by S. Miall & L. M. Miall) 1949
Michaux, François André *Histoire des arbres forestiers de l'Amérique Septentrionale* 3 vols. 1810–13
Michelin Tire Corporation *New York City* 1968
Michelin Tyre Company *Michelin guide to Great Britain* (ed. 7) 1923
Michell, John Henry & Belz, Maurice Henry *The elements of mathematical analysis* 2 vols. 1937

Michener, James Albert *Chesapeake* 1978
The source 1965
Michigan Academy of Science, Arts and Letters *Papers* Vol. X (for 1928) 1929
Michigan State Agricultural Society *Transactions* 1849–61
Mikes, H. George *Down with everybody!* 1951
Milk and honey: Israel explored 1950
Milburn, Clara Emily *Mrs. Milburn's diaries: an Englishwoman's day-to-day reflections, 1939–45* ed. P. Donnelly 1979
Miles, Beryl *The stars my blanket* 1954
Mill, John Stuart (1806–73) *Earlier letters* ed. F. E. Mineka 2 vols. 1963 (Vols. XII & XIII of *Collected works)*
The early draft of J. S. Mill's autobiography ed. J. Stillinger 1961
Letters ed. H. S. R. Elliot 2 vols. 1910
Millar, George Reid *Horned pigeon* 1946
Maquis 1945
Millar, Margaret *Ask for me tomorrow* 1976 (UK 1977)
The soft talkers 1957
Miller, Arthur *All my sons* 1947
Collected plays 1957 (UK 1958)
The crucible 1953 (UK 1956)
Death of a salesman 1949
The misfits 1961
Miller, Denis *The Chinese jade affair* 1973
Miller, Edwin Cyrus *Plant physiology, with reference to the green plant* 1931
Miller, Henry Valentine *Black spring* 1936
Nexus 1960 (UK 1964)
Plexus 1953 (UK 1963)
Sexus 2 vols. 1949 (UK 1969)
Tropic of Cancer 1934
Tropic of Capricorn 1939
Miller, Hugh *The open city* 1973
Miller, Joaquin *First fam'lies in the Sierras* 1875 (US 1876)
Life amonst the Modocs 1873
Millerson, Gerald *The technique of television production* 1961
Millett, Kate *Flying* 1974 (UK 1975)
Sexual politics 1970 (UK 1971)
Milliken, E. J. *'Arry ballads* 1892
Millin, Sarah Gertrude *The South Africans* 1926
Mills, Charles Wright *The power élite* 1956
White collar: the American middle classes 1951
Mills, James *Report to the Commissioner* 1972
'Mills, Osmington' (Vivian Collin Brooks) *Enemies of the bride* 1966
Headlines make murder 1962
Stairway to murder 1959
Mills, P. W. F. *The elements of practical flying* 1935
Milne, Alan Alexander *First plays* 1919
Winnie-the-Pooh 1926
Milne, Christopher Robin *The enchanted places* 1974
Milner, Christina Andrea & Milner, Richard *Black players: the secret world of black pimps* 1973
Milton, William Fitzwilliam, Viscount & Cheadle, Walter Butler *The North-West Passage by land* 1865
Milton Keynes Express 1973–
Minchin, Edward Alfred *An introduction to the study of the protozoa, with special reference to the parasitic forms* 1912
Mineralogical abstracts 1920–
Ministry of . . . *See* United Kingdom. Ministry of . . .
Minter, Davide Caroline ed. *Modern needlecraft* 1932
Missingham, Hal *A student's guide in commercial art* 1948
Mitchell, Geoffrey Duncan *Sociology: the study of social systems* 1959
Mitchell, Gladys Maude W. *Laurels are poison* 1942
The murder of Busy Lizzie 1973
The mystery of a butcher's shop 1929
Spotted hemlock 1958
Mitchell, James *Smear job* 1975
Mitchell, Margaret *Gone with the wind* 1936
Mitchison, Naomi Margaret *We have been warned* 1935
Mitford, Jessica Lucy Freeman *The American way of death* 1963
Mitford, Nancy Freeman *The blessing* 1951
Christmas pudding 1932
Don't tell Alfred 1960
Love in a cold climate 1949
Pigeon pie 1940
The pursuit of love 1945
Mittelholzer, Edgar Austin *Shadows move among them* 1951
'Mixer, The' (Henry Kirk) *The transport workers' song book* c 1926
A modern junior dictionary, specially adapted for use in Australia and New Zealand 1944
Modern Language Association of America *Publications* 1889–

Modern language notes 1886–
Modern language review 1905–
Modern law review 1937–
Modern philology 1903–
MOFFAT, Gwen *The Corpse road* 1974
Deviant death 1973
Miss Pink at the edge of the world 1975
MOGEY, John McFarlane *Family and neighbourhood: two studies in Oxford* 1956
MOHR, Charles Theodore *Plant life of Alabama* 1901
MOLLOY, Edward ed. *Radio and television engineers' reference book* 1954
MOLONEY, Peter *A plea for Mersey; or, The gentle art of insinuendo* 1966
MONCRIEFF, Robert Wighton *The chemical senses* 1944
MONEY, Charles L. *Knocking about in New Zealand* 1871
MONIER-WILLIAMS, Monier *See* WILLIAMS, Monier
Monist, The: a quarterly magazine devoted to the philosophy of science 1890–
Monographic medicine 7 vols. 1916 (by various authors)
MONSARRAT, Nicholas John Turney *The cruel sea* 1951
This is the schoolroom 1939
MONTAGU, Mary Wortley (1689–1762) *Complete letters* ed. R. Halsband 3 vols. 1965–7
MONTAGUE, Charles Edward *Disenchantment* 1922
A hind let loose 1910
MONTGOMERY, Lucy Maud *Anne of Avonlea* 1909
Anne of Green Gables 1908
Anne of Ingleside 1939
Montgomery Ward & Co. *Catalogue and buyers' guide* No. 57, Spring & Summer 1895
Monthly repository of theology (title varies) 1806–38
MONYPENNY, William Flavelle & BUCKLE, George Earle *The life of Disraeli* 6 vols. 1910–20
MOORE, Brian *Catholics* 1972
MOORE, Doris Langley *E. Nesbit: a biography* 1933
MOORE, Francis Cruger *How to build a home* 1897
MOORE, John S. ed. *The goods and chattels of our forefathers: Frampton Cotterell and district probate inventories 1539–1804* 1976
MOORE, Preston L., et al. *Drilling practices manual* 1974
MOORE, Raymond Cecil *Introduction to historical geology* 1949
ed. *Treatise on invertebrate paleontology* 1953–
——, LALICKER, C. G., & FISCHER, A. G. *Invertebrate fossils* 1952
MOORE, Ruth *Candlemas Bay* 1950
MOORE, Samuel & AVELING, Edward Bibbins tr. *K. Marx's Capital: a critical analysis of capitalist production* 1887
MOORE, Walter John *Physical chemistry* 1950
MOORE, Wilfred George *A dictionary of geography* 1949
MOOREHEAD, Alan McCrae *No room in the ark* 1959
Rum jungle 1953
MOORHOUSE, Walter Wilson *The study of rocks in thin section* 1959
MORAN, James *The composition of reading matter* 1965
MORAN, Patrick Alfred P. *An introduction to probability theory* 1968
MORE, Hannah (1745–1833) *Letters* ed. R. B. Johnson 1925
Morecambe Guardian 1920–
MOREHEAD, Robert Page *Human pathology* 1965
MORGAN, Charles Langbridge *The flashing stream* 1938
The fountain 1932
The judge's story 1947
Portrait in a mirror 1929
The voyage 1940
MORGAN, John Glanfil *Involved* 1967
MORGAN, Mary Ella *How to dress a doll* 1908
MORGAN, Thomas Hunt, et al. *The mechanism of Mendelian heredity* 1915
MORGAN, William Alphonse ed. *The 'House' on sport, by members of the London stock exchange* 1898
— (suppl. vol.) 1899
MORICE, Anne *Killing with kindness* 1974
The men in her death 1981
Murder in mimicry 1977
MORISON, Samuel Eliot *The European discovery of America: the northern voyages* 1971
The European discovery of America: the southern voyages 1974
MORLEY, Christopher Darlington *Thorofare* 1942 (UK 1943)
Kitty Foyle 1939
Morning Herald and Daily Advertiser 1780–1869
Morning Star 1966–
'MORPHY, Marcelle, Countess' (Marcelle Azra Forbes) ed. *Recipes of all nations* 1935
MORRELL, Robert Selby, et al. eds. *Synthetic resins and allied plastics* 1937
MORRIS, Charles William *Signs, language and behavior* 1946
MORRIS, Clara (Clara Morris Harriott) *Life on the stage: my personal experiences and recollections* 1901
MORRIS, Desmond John *The mammals: a guide to the living species* 1965
Manwatching: a field guide to human behaviour 1977
The naked ape 1967
See also: MORRIS, Ramona
'MORRIS, John' (John Hearne & Morris Cargill) *Fever grass* 1969
MORRIS, Ramona & MORRIS, Desmond John *Men and apes* 1966
Men and pandas 1966
Men and snakes 1965
MORRIS, Terence & MORRIS, Pauline *Pentonville: a sociological study of an English prison* 1963
MORRIS, William *News from nowhere; or, An epoch of rest* 1890 (UK 1891)
Morris owner's manual 1925
MORSE, Eric Wilton *Fur trade canoe routes of Canada: then and now* 1969
MORSE, Mary *The unattached: a report of the project carried out by the National Association of Youth Clubs* 1965
MORSE, Philip McCord *Vibration and sound* 1936
'MORTIMER, Geoffrey' (Walter M. Gallichan) *Like stars that fall* 1895
MORTIMER, John Clifford *A voyage round my father* 1971
MORTIMER, Penelope *Daddy's gone a-hunting* 1958
MORTON, Henry Canova Vollam *In search of England* 1927
In search of South Africa 1948
MOSEDALE, John *Football* 1972
MOSS, Stirling Craufurd *In the track of speed* 1957
Motor, The 1903–
Motor boat 1904–
Motor-car world 1899–1905
Motor cycle, The 1903–
Motor manual, The 1903–59
MOTTRAM, Ralph Hale *The Spanish farm* 1924
Movie 1962–
MOYER, James Ambrose & WOSTREL, J. F. *Radio handbook: including television and sound motion pictures* 1931
MOYES, Patricia *The curious affair of the third dog* 1973
Dead men don't ski 1959
Murder à la mode 1963
Who saw her die? 1970
MUHLENBERG, Gotthilf Henry Ernest *Catalogus plantarum Americæ Septentrionalis..; or, A catalogue of the..plants of North America, arranged according to the sexual system of Linnæus* 1813
MUIR, Edwin (1887–1959) *Collected poems, 1921–1958* ed. W. Muir & J. C. Hall 1960
MUIR, Robert *Text-book of pathology* 1924
—— & RITCHIE, James *Manual of bacteriology* 1897 (and several later editions used)
MUIR, Ward *Observations of an orderly: some glimpses of life and work in an English war hospital* 1917
MULFORD, Clarence Edward *Bar-20* 1907 (UK 1914)
The Bar-20 three 1921
Black Buttes 1923
The coming of Cassidy—and the others 1913
Cottonwood Gulch 1925
Hopalong Cassidy 1910
Hopalong Cassidy's protégé 1926
Johnny Nelson 1920 (UK 1921)
The man from Bar-20: a story of the cow-country 1918
The orphan 1908
Rustlers' valley 1924
—— & CLAY, John Wood *Buck Peters, ranchman* 1912 (UK 1921)
MULGAN, John Alan Edward *Man alone* 1939
MULLALLY, Frederic *The Munich involvement* 1968
MULLARD, Chris *Black Britain; with an account of recent events at the Institute of Race Relations by A. Kirby* 1973
MULLIN, Glen Hawthorne *Adventures of a scholar tramp* 1925
MUMFORD, John Kimberley *Oriental rugs* 1900 (UK 1901)
MUMFORD, Lewis *City development: studies in disintegration and renewal* 1945 (UK 1946)
The city in history: its origins, its transformations, and its prospects 1961
MUNBY, Arthur Joseph *See* HUDSON, Derek Rommel
MUNRO, George Campbell *Birds of Hawaii* 1944
MUNRO, Neil *The daft days* 1907
MUNROE, Kirk *The golden days of '49: a tale of the California diggings* 1889
MUNROE, Ruth Learned *Schools of psychoanalytic thought* 1955 (UK 1957)
MUNROW, David *Instruments of the Middle Ages and Renaissance* 1976
MUNSON, Kenneth *Pioneer aircraft 1903–1914* 1969
MURDOCH, Jean Iris *The bell* 1958
Flight from the enchanter 1956
Henry and Cato 1976
Nuns and soldiers 1980
The sacred and profane love machine 1974
The sandcastle 1957
The sea, the sea 1978
A severed head 1961
The time of the angels 1966
Under the net 1954
An unofficial rose 1962
A word child 1975
MURDOCH, Walter & DRAKE-BROCKMAN, Henrietta F. Y. eds. *Australian short stories* 1951
For 2nd ser. *see* 'JAMES, Brian'
MURPHY, Gardner *Personality* 1947
MURRAY, Amelia Matilda *Letters from the United States, Cuba, and Canada* 2 vols. 1856
MURRAY, Henry Alexander *Explorations in personality* 1938
MURRAY, Katharine Maud Elisabeth *Caught in the web of words: James A. H. Murray and the Oxford English Dictionary* 1977
MURRAY, Peter John & MURRAY, Linda *A dictionary of art and artists* 1959
MURRAY, William Buckley *The sweet ride* 1967
MURRY, John Middleton *The necessity of pacifism* 1937
Pencillings: little essays on literature 1923
The voyage 1924
Museum of Comparative Zoology, Harvard University *Bulletin* 1863–
Musical Association, The *Proceedings* 1875–
Musical quarterly 1915–
Musical times 1844–
Mycologia 1909–
MYERS, Arthur Wallis *Twenty years of lawn tennis* 1921
MYERS, Leonard Morris *Electron optics: theoretical and practical* 1939

N

NATO *Automatic translation of languages: papers presented at NATO Summer School held in Venice, July 1962* 1966
N.Z.E.F. *See* New Zealand Expeditionary Force
NABOKOV, Vladimir Vladimirovich *Bend sinister* 1947
The defence tr. by M. Scammell in collaboration with the author 1964
The gift tr. by M. Scammell and the author 1963
Invitation to a beheading tr. by D. Nabokov and the author 1960
Lolita 2 vols. 1955 (US 1 vol. 1958)
Look at the harlequins! 1974 (UK 1975)
Nabokov's dozen: a collection of thirteen stories 1958 (UK 1959)
Pale fire 1962
Pnin 1957
The real life of Sebastian Knight 1941
Speak, memory (US ed. with title *Conclusive evidence*) 1951
— (UK ed. 2) 1967
NADELL, Aaron *Projecting sound pictures: a practical textbook for projectionists and managers* 1931
NAGEL, Ernest *The structure of science: problems in the logic of scientific explanation* 1961
'NA GOPALEEN, Myles' (Brian O'Nolan) (1911–66) *The best of Myles: a selection from 'Cruiskeen Lawn'* ed. K. O'Nolan 1968
See also: 'O'BRIEN, Flann'
NAIPAUL, Shivadhar Srinivasa *Black and white* 1980
NAIPAUL, Vidiadhar Surajprasad *An area of darkness* 1964
In a free state 1971
The mimic men 1967
The mystic masseur 1957
NAMIER, Lewis Bernstein *Conflicts: studies in contemporary history* 1942
NARLIKAR, Jayant *The structure of the universe* 1977
Narragansett historical register 1882–91
NASH, Frederic Ogden *The face is familiar* 1940 (UK 1942)
Family reunion 1950 (UK 1951)
Good intentions 1942 (UK 1943)
I'm a stranger here myself 1938
Versus 1949
You can't get there from here 1957
NASMITH, Joseph *The students' cotton spinning* 1892
NASON, Leonard Hastings *Chevrons* 1926 (UK 1927)
Nation, The (Barbados) 1973–

Nation review (Melbourne) 1958–
National Academy of Sciences (Washington) *Proceedings* 1863–94; 1915–
National Bureau of Standards *See* United States. National ——
National observer (US) 1962–77
National police gazette (US) (title varies) 1845–
Natural history 1919–
Navy news 1954–
Nayler, Joseph Lawrence *Dictionary of aeronautical engineering* 1959
Neale, R. E. ed. *Whittaker's electrical engineer's pocket-book* 1920 See under title
Neblette, Carroll Bernard *Photography: its principles and practice* 1927
Nehru, Jawaharlal *An autobiography* 1936
Neill, Alexander Sutherland *A dominie's log* 1915 [dated 1916]
Neill! Neill! Orange peel!: a personal view of ninety years 1972
— (rev. ed.) 1973
Summerhill: a radical approach to education 1962
Nelson, George & Wright, Henry Niccolls *Tomorrow's house* 1945
Nelson, Stanley R. *All about jazz* 1934
Nesbit, Edith *Five children and it* 1902
The phoenix and the carpet 1904
The railway children 1906
Neuphilologische Mitteilungen 1899–
Neurology 1951–
'Neville, Margot' *Ladies in the dark* 1965
Nevin, Charles Merrick *Principles of structural geology* 1931
New acronyms and initialisms See *Acronyms dictionary*
New and complete dictionary of arts and sciences, A 4 vols. 1754–5
New biology ed. M. L. Johnson et al. 31 vols. 1945–60
New Castle (Delaware) *Records of the court of New Castle on Delaware* (Colonial Society of Pennsylvania) 1904
New Catholic encyclopedia ed. W. J. McDonald 15 vols. 1967
New England journal of medicine, The 1928–
New English weekly: a review of public affairs, literature and the arts (title varies) 1932–49
New Gould medical dictionary 1949
— (ed. 2) 1956
New Hampshire (Colony) *Probate records of the province of New Hampshire* 9 vols. 1907–41
New Jersey *Archives of the State of New Jersey* 16 vols. 1880–1917
New Jewish encyclopedia, The ed. D. Bridger 1962
New left review 1960–
New musical express 1952–
New Oxford history of music, The ed. J. A. Westrup et al. 1954–
New phytologist 1902–
New republic, The 1914–
New scientist, The 1956–
New society 1962–
New sporting magazine 1831–70
New statesman, The (title varies) 1913–
New York 1968–
New York Academy of Sciences *Annals* 1877–
New York dramatic news 1894–6
New York Evening Post 1802–1919
New York Herald Tribune (title varies) 1841–
New York Herald Tribune International (title varies) 1887–
New York law journal 1949–
New York medical journal 1865–1923
New York review of books 1963–
New York State *Documents relative to the colonial history of the State of New-York* See under title
New York State. Department of Correctional Services *Guidelines to volunteer services* 1974
New York Times, The 1857–
New York Times book review 1896–
New York World 1860–1931
New York World-Telegram 1931–66 (1950–66 with title *New York World-Telegram and Sun*)
New Yorker, The 1925–
New Zealand. Parliament. House of Representatives *Appendix to the journals* 1858–
New Zealand Expeditionary Force *Chronicles* 1916–19
New Zealand Expeditionary Force Times (2nd N.Z.E.F.) 1941–?5
New Zealand illustrated magazine 1901–5
New Zealand Institute (from 1935 Royal ——) *Transactions and proceedings* 1868–
New Zealand journal 1840–52
New Zealand journal of agriculture (title varies) 1910–
New Zealander listener 1939–
New Zealand News 1927–
New Zealand short stories 1953 *See* Davin, Daniel Marcus
— (2nd ser.) 1966 *See* Stead, Christian Karlson
New Zealand timber journal 1954–
New Zealand woman's weekly 1934–
Newbold, Thomas John *Political and statistical account of the British settlements in the Straits of Malacca, viz., Pinang, Malacca and Singapore* 2 vols. 1839
Newdigate-Newdegate, Anne Emily *The Cheverels of Cheverel Manor* 1898
Newman, Edwin *Sunday punch* 1979
Newman, Gordon F. *The price* 1974
Sir, you bastard 1970
You nice bastard 1972
Newman, Maxwell Herman Alexander *Elements of the topology of plane sets of points* 1939
Newnes complete amateur photography ed. M. L. Hall 1958
Newnes concise encyclopaedia of electrical engineering ed. M. G. Say 1962
Newnes concise encyclopaedia of nuclear energy 1962
News and Courier (Charleston, South Carolina) 1873–
News and Observer (Raleigh, North Carolina) 1872–
News and Press (Darlington, South Carolina) 1903–
News Chronicle 1930–60
News review 1936–50
Newspaper and general reader's pocket companion 2 parts 1855–6
Newsweek 1933–
Newth, George S. *A text-book of inorganic chemistry* 1894
— (ed. 12) 1907
'Newton, Francis' (Eric John Ernest Hobsbawm) *The jazz scene* 1959
Newton, Joseph *Introduction to metallurgy* 1938
Newton, Kenneth & Steeds, William *The motor vehicle* 1929 (and several later editions used)
Newton, Peter *High country days* 1949
Sheep thief 1972
Wayleggo 1947
Nichols, David *Echinoderms* 1962
Nichols, John Beverley *The sweet and twenties* 1958
Nicholson, John Kenyon *The barker* 1927
'Nicholson, Kate' (Judith Fay) *Hook, line and sinker* 1966
Nicholson, Meredith *A Hoosier chronicle* 1912
Nickerson, Elinor Barkley *Kayaks to the Arctic* 1967
Nicol, Abioseh *The truly married woman, and other stories* 1965
Nicolson, Harold George *Curzon: the last phase, 1919–25; a study in post-war diplomacy* 1934
Diaries and letters, 1930–1939 ed. N. Nicolson 1966
—— *1939–1945* ed. N. Nicolson 1967
—— *1945–1962* ed. N. Nicolson 1968
King George V: his life and reign 1952
Public faces 1932
Nida, Eugene Albert *Morphology: the descriptive analysis of words* 2 vols. 1944
— (another ed.) 1946
— ('ed. 2') 1949
Toward a science of translating 1964
Nielsen, Helen *After midnight* 1966 (UK 1967)
The brink of murder 1976
The severed key 1973
Niesewand, Peter *The underground connection* 1978
Niland, D'Arcy *The big smoke* 1959
Call me when the Cross turns over 1957 (UK 1958)
The shiralee 1955
Niles' weekly register 1814–37; continued as *Niles' national register* 1837–49
Nilson, Arvid *The timber trees of New South Wales* 1884
Nisbett, Alex *The technique of the sound studio* 1962
Nitsch, F. A. *A general and introductory view of Professor Kant's Principles concerning man, the world and the Deity* 1796
Nkosi, Lewis *The rhythm of violence* 1964
Noble, Montague Alfred *Those 'Ashes': the Australian tour of 1926* 1927
Nohara, Komakichi *The true face of Japan* 1936
Nolan, Frederick *The Oshawa project* 1974
Noller, Carl Robert *Chemistry of organic compounds* 1951
Textbook of organic chemistry 1951
Nordau, Max Simon *Degeneration* [anon. tr.] 1895
Norman, Barry *The matter of mandrake* 1967
Norman, Frank *Bang to rights: an account of prison life* 1958
Norman, John Roxborough *A history of fishes* 1931
— (ed. 2, by P. H. Greenwood) 1963
Norman, Richard Oswald Chandler *Principles of organic synthesis* 1968
Norris, Henry H. *An introduction to the study of electrical engineering* 1907
Norris, William Fisher & Oliver, Charles A. eds. *System of diseases of the eye* 4 vols. 1897–9
North, Barbara & North, Robert tr. *M. Duverger's Political parties* 1954
— (ed. 2) 1959
'North, Gil' (Geoffrey Horne) *Sergeant Cluff and the day of reckoning* 1967
Sergeant Cluff rings true 1972
North, John David *The measure of the universe* 1965
North, Lockhart *The parasites* 1928
North Carolina (Colony) *Colonial records* ed. W. L. Saunders 10 vols. 1886–90
Northern Territory News (Darwin, Australia) 1952–
Norton, Edward Felix *The fight for Everest: 1924* 1925
Norton, Olive Marion *Dead on prediction* 1970
Now lying dead 1967
A school of liars 1966
Norton, Oliver Willcox *Army letters 1861–1865: being extracts from private letters to relatives and friends from a soldier in the field during the late civil war* 1903
Norwich Mercury, Norfolk News and Journal (title varies) 1714–
Nott, John *The cook's and confectioner's dictionary; or, The accomplished housewife's companion* 1723
Nourse, Henry Stedman ed. *The early records of Lancaster, Massachusetts* See: Lancaster, Massachusetts
Novak, Emil *Gynecological and obstetric pathology; with clinical and endocrine relations* 1940
Nowakowski, T. Z. & Clarke, A. J. tr. *V. L. Kretovich's Principles of plant biochemistry* 1966
Nowell-Smith, Simon Harcourt ed. *Edwardian England* 1964
Nowottny, Winifred May T. *The language poets use* 1962
Noyce, Cuthbert Wilfrid Francis *South Col: one man's adventure on the ascent of Everest, 1953* 1954
Nuclear instruments and methods 1957– (1957–8 with title *Nuclear instruments*)
Nucleonics 1947–
'Number 1500' *Life in Sing Sing* 1904
Numbers: a quarterly review 1954–
Nunn, Thomas Percy *Education: its data and first principles* 1920
Nursing times and journal of midwifery 1905–
Nuttall, Thomas *A journal of travels into the Arkansa territory, during the year 1819* 1821
Nye, Edgar Wilson *Baled hay* 1884
Bill Nye and Boomerang; or, The tale of a meek-eyed mule 1881
Nyren, John *The young cricketer's tutor* 1833

O

Oakley, Kenneth Page *Frameworks for dating fossil man* 1964
Oates, Joyce Carol *Bellefleur* 1981
O'Brien, Edna *August is a wicked month* 1965
Country girls 1971
The lonely girl 1962
'O'Brien, Flann' (Brian O'Nolan) *At Swim-Two-Birds* 1939
The hard life: an exegesis of squalor 1961
See also: 'Na Gopaleen, Myles'
O'Brien, S. E. & Stephens, A. G. *Material for a dictionary of Australian slang, 1900–1910* (typescript in Mitchell Library, Sydney)
Obstetrics and gynecology 1953–
O'Casey, Sean (1880–1964) *Letters* ed. D. Krause 1975–
The plough and the stars 1926
The star turns red 1940
Two plays [*Juno and the paycock* and *The shadow of a gunman*] 1925
Windfalls: stories, poems and plays 1934
Oceanography and marine biology: an annual review 1963–
O'Connell, Daniel (1775–1847) *Correspondence* ed. M. R. O'Connell 1972–
'O'Connor, Frank' (Michael Francis O'Donovan) *Bones of contention, and other stories* 1936
O'Connor, Jimmy *The eleventh commandment* 1976
Odell, George Clinton Densmore ed. *Annals of the New York stage* 15 vols. 1927–49
O'Donnell, Edwin P. *Great big doorstep* 1941
O'Donnell, Lilian *The face of the crime* 1968 (UK 1969)
O'Donnell, Peter *The impossible virgin* 1971
Sabre-tooth 1966
The silver mistress 1973
'Odysseus' (Charles Norton Edgcumbe Eliot) *Turkey in Europe* 1900
O'Faolain, Julia *No country for young men* 1980
O'Faolain, Sean *A nest of simple folk* 1933

Official encyclopedia of bridge ed. R. L. Frey & A. F. Truscott 1964
Offshore (US) 1954–
Offshore engineer 1975–
Offshore platforms and pipelining (The Petroleum Publishing Co.) 1976
OGDEN, Charles Kay tr. *H. Vaihinger's The philosophy of 'as if'* 1924
—— & RICHARDS, Ivor Armstrong *The meaning of meaning: a study of the influence of language upon thought and of the science of symbolism* 1923
OGDEN, Robert Morris tr. *K. Koffka's The growth of the mind: an introduction to child-psychology* 1924
OGILVY, Charles Stanley & ANDERSON, John T. *Excursions in number theory* 1966
OGILVY, David *Confessions of an advertising man* 1963 (UK 1964)
O'HARA, John Henry *Appointment in Samarra* 1934 (UK 1935)
Pal Joey 1940 (UK 1952)
O'HARA, Kenneth *The bird-cage* 1968
The ghost of Thomas Penry 1977
Ohio archaeological and historical quarterly (title varies) 1887–
OHWI, Jisaburō *Flora of Japan* 1965
Oil and gas journal 1910–
OKEY, Thomas *An introduction to the art of basket-making* 1912
OLIVER, Paul *Savannah syncopators: African retentions in the blues* 1970
Screening the blues 1968
OLIVER, Walter Reginald Brook *New Zealand birds* 1930
OLSSON, Yngve *On the syntax of the English verb* 1961
O'NEILL, Eugene Gladstone (1888–1953) *Ah, wilderness! and Days without end: two plays* 1933 (UK 1934)
Anna Christie See below: *The hairy ape*
Beyond the horizon 1920
Desire under the elms 1925
Dynamo 1929
The Emperor Jones 1921 (UK 1925)
The great god Brown, The fountain, The moon of the Caribbees, and other plays 1926
The hairy ape, and other plays 1922 (UK 1923)
Hughie 1959
The iceman cometh 1946 (UK 1947)
Lazarus laughed 1927
Long day's journey into night 1956
Marco Millions 1927
A moon for the misbegotten 1952 (UK 1953)
The moon of the Caribbees, and six other plays of the sea 1919 (UK 1923)
More stately mansions ed. D. Gallup 1964 (UK 1965)
Mourning becomes Electra: a trilogy 1931 (UK 1932)
Strange interlude 1928
A touch of the poet 1957
Ophthalmic review 1881–1916
OPIE, Iona M. B. & OPIE, Peter M. *Children's games in street and playground* 1969
The lore and language of schoolchildren 1959
See also *Oxford dictionary of nursery rhymes, The*
Optical Society of America *Journal* 1917–
Optometry today: the vision care profession (American Optometric Association) 1971
ORCZY, Emmuska, Baroness *Lady Molly of Scotland Yard* 1910
The Scarlet Pimpernel 1905
ORDWAY, Frederick Ira, GARDNER, J. P., & SHARPE, M. R. *Basic astronautics* 1962
ORGILL, Douglas William *The Jasius pursuit* 1973
Oriental Ceramics Society *Transactions* 1923–
ORIGO, Iris *Images and shadows: part of a life* 1970
ORR, John tr. *I. Iordan's An introduction to Romance linguistics* 1937
ORTON, John Kingsley ('Joe') *What the butler saw* 1969
'ORVIS, Kenneth' (Kenneth Lemieux) *The damned and the destroyed* 1962
'ORWELL, George' (Eric Arthur Blair) (1903-50) *Animal farm* 1945
Burmese days 1934
A clergyman's daughter 1935
Collected essays, journalism and letters ed. 'S. Orwell' & I. Angus 4 vols. 1968
Coming up for air 1939
Critical essays 1946
— (new ed.) 1951
Down and out in Paris and London 1933
England your England, and other essays 1953
The English people 1947
Homage to Catalonia 1938
Inside the whale, and other essays 1940
Keep the aspidistra flying 1936
The lion and the unicorn: socialism and the English genius 1941
Nineteen eighty-four 1949
The road to Wigan Pier: on industrial England and its political future 1937
Shooting an elephant, and other essays 1950

OSBORNE, John *Dental mechanics for students* 1940
OSBORNE, John James *The entertainer* 1957
Look back in anger 1957
West of Suez 1971
The world of Paul Slickey 1959
—— & CREIGHTON, Anthony *Epitaph for George Dillon* 1958
OSGOOD, Charles Egerton *Method and theory in experimental psychology* 1953
OSLER, William *The principles and practice of medicine* 1892 (also later editions used)
—— & MCCRAE, Thomas *A system of medicine* 7 vols. 1907–10
Ottawa Citizen, The (title varies) 1844–
Ottawa Journal 1885–
OTTAWAY, Andrew Kenneth Cosway *Education and society: an introduction to the sociology of education* 1953
Our towns: a close-up, 1939–42 (Women's Group on Public Welfare, Hygiene Committee) 1943
Out west 1902–23
Outlook, The 1898–1928
Outlook (New York) 1893–1935 (title varies)
Outward bound 1920–4
Overland monthly 1868–75; 1883–1935
OWEN, David Edward *English philanthropy, 1660–1960* 1964 (UK 1965)
OWEN, Francis *Diary, 1837–38* ed. G. E. Cory 1926
OWEN, Wilfred Edward Salter (1893–1918) *Collected letters* ed. H. Owen & J. Bell 1967
Collected poems ed. C. Day Lewis 1963
Oxford book of birds, The by B. Campbell 1964
Oxford book of food plants, The by S. G. Harrison, G. B. Masefield, & M. Wallis 1969
Oxford book of invertebrates, The by D. Nicholls & J. A. L. Cooke 1971
Oxford book of wild flowers, The by S. Ary & M. Gregory 1960
Oxford classical dictionary, The ed. M. Cary et al. 1949
— (ed. 2, by N. G. L. Hammond & H. H. Scullard) 1970
Oxford companion to art, The ed. H. Osborne 1970
Oxford companion to French literature, The by P. Harvey & J. E. Heseltine 1959
Oxford companion to music, The by P. A. Scholes 1938 (also later editions used)
Oxford companion to ships and the sea, The ed. P. Kemp 1976
Oxford companion to sports and games, The ed. J. Arlott 1975
Oxford companion to the decorative arts, The ed. H. Osborne 1975
Oxford companion to the theatre, The ed. P. M. Hartnoll 1951
—(ed. 2) 1957
Oxford computer explained, The: data processing at Oxford University Press 1967
Oxford dictionary of nursery rhymes, The ed. I. & P. Opie 1951
Oxford dictionary of the Christian Church, The ed. F. L. Cross 1957
— (ed. 2, by F. L. Cross & E. A. Livingstone) 1974
Oxford diocesan magazine 1902–
Oxford history of South Africa, The ed. M. Wilson & L. Thompson 2 vols. 1969–71
Oxford junior encyclopaedia ed. L. E. Salt et al. 13 vols. 1948–56
Oxford Mail 1928–
Oxford textbook of medicine ed. D. J. Weatherall, J. G. G. Ledingham, & D. A. Warrell 2 vols. 1983
Oxford University *Report of Commission of Inquiry* 2 vols. 1966
Oxford University. Ashmolean Museum *Report of the Visitors* 1889–
Oxoniensia (Oxford Architectural and Historical Society) 1936–
Oz 1967–73

P

PMLA See: Modern Language Association of America
PACKARD, Vance Oakley *The hidden persuaders* 1957
PACKER, John & VAUGHAN, James *A modern approach to organic chemistry* 1958
PACKER, Joy *Apes and ivory* 1953
'PACKER, Vin' (Marijane Meaker) *Don't rely on Gemini* 1969 (UK 1970)
PAGE, Emma *A fortnight by the sea* 1973
PAGE, Ewan Stafford & WILSON, Leslie Blackett *An introduction to computational combinatorics* 1979
PAGÉ, Victor Wilfred *Modern aircraft* 1927 (UK 1928)
PAGET, Richard Arthur Surtees *Human speech* 1930

PAINE, Ralph Delahaye *Comrades of the rolling ocean* 1923
PALMER, Charles Skeele tr. *W. Nernst's Theoretical chemistry, from the standpoint of Avogadro's Rule and thermodynamics* 1895
PALMER, Edward Vance *Golconda* 1948
Men are human 1930
The passage 1930
Separate lives 1931
See also: 'DALY, Rann'
PALMER, Elisabeth tr. *A. Martinet's Elements of general linguistics* 1964
PALMER, Eve *The plains of Camdeboo* 1966
—— & PITMAN, Norah *Trees of South Africa* 1961
Trees of southern Africa 3 vols. 1972–3
PALMER, Harold Edward *A grammar of spoken English on a strictly phonetic basis* 1924
PALMER, Lionel Stanley *Wireless principles and practice* 1928
PANKHURST, Emmeline *My own story* 1914
PAP, Arthur *Elements of analytic philosophy* 1949
PAPPE, Karl Wilhelm Ludwig *Silva Capensis; or, A description of South African forest-trees and arborescent shrubs* 1854
Synopsis of the edible fishes at the Cape of Good Hope 1853
PARK, William Robb R. ed. *Plastics film technology* 1969
PARKER, Dorothy *After such pleasures* 1933 (UK 1934)
PARKER, Philip *Electronics* 1950
PARKER, Robert Brown *God save the child* 1974 (UK 1975)
The Godwulf manuscript 1974
PARKER, Robert Lueling tr. *P. Niggli's Rocks and mineral deposits* 1954
PARKER, Tony *The twisting lane* 1969
The unknown citizen 1963
—— & ALLERTON, Robert *The courage of his convictions* 1962
PARKER, William Hosken *Health and disease in farm animals* 1970
PARKER, William Newton tr. *R. E. E. Wiedersheim's Elements of the comparative anatomy of vertebrates* 1886
PARKES, Malcolm B. *English cursive book hands 1250–1500* 1969
PARKES, Roger *The guardians* 1973
PARKMAN, Ebenezer (1703–82) *The diary of Ebenezer Parkman, of Westborough, Mass.* ed. H. M. Forbes 1899
PARLETT, David Sidney *A short dictionary of languages* 1967
Parliamentary papers *See* United Kingdom. Parliamentary papers
PARRISH, Albert *Mechanical engineer's reference book* 1973
PARRY, Dennis *Going up—going down* 1953
PARSONS, John Herbert *Diseases of the eye* 1907
— (ed. 12, by W. S. Duke-Elder) 1954
PARSONS, Nell Wilson *Upon a sagebrush harp* 1969
PARSONS, Talcott *The social system* 1952
The structure of social action 1937
—— & SHILS, Edward Albert eds. *Toward a general theory of action* 1951
PARTINGTON, James Riddick *General and inorganic chemistry for university students* 1946
A text-book of inorganic chemistry for university students 1921
Partisan review 1934–
PARTRIDGE, Eric Honeywood *A charm of words: essays and papers on language* 1960
A dictionary of abbreviations 1942
A dictionary of catch phrases British and American, from the Sixteenth Century to the present day 1977
A dictionary of clichés 1940
A dictionary of forces' slang, 1939–45 1948
A dictionary of R.A.F. slang 1945
A dictionary of slang and unconventional English 1937 (also later eds. and supplements used)
A dictionary of the underworld, British and American 1950 [dated 1949]
English gone wrong 1957
Here, there and everywhere 1950
Slang to-day and yesterday 1933
— (ed. 3) 1951 [dated 1950]
Usage and abusage: a guide to good English 1942 (UK 1947)
Words, words, words! 1933
The world of words 1938
See also: BROPHY, John; also 'VIGILANS'
PARYSKI, Edwin tr. *T. Korzybski et al., Antibiotics* 2 vols. 1967
PASACHOFF, Jay M. & KUTNER, Marc Leslie *University astronomy* 1978
PASSMORE, John Arthur *A hundred years of philosophy* 1957
PASSMORE, Reginald & ROBSON, James Scott eds. *A companion to medical studies* 3 vols. 1968–74
PASTERNAK, Boris *See* HAYWARD, Harry M. & HARARI, Manya

Patel, H. M., et al. *Say not the struggle nought availeth: essays in honour of A. D. Gorwala's seventy-fifth birthday* 1975

Patent Office *See* United Kingdom

'Paterson, Peter' (James Glass Bertram) *Glimpses of real life as seen in the theatrical world and in Bohemia* 1864

Pathological Society of London *Transactions* 1853–1907

Pathology annual 1966–

Paton, Alan *Cry, the beloved country: a story of comfort in desolation* 1948

Hope for South Africa 1958

'Patrick, James' *A Glasgow gang observed* 1973

Patten, Brian Arthur *The irrelevant song* 1971

Little Johnny's confession 1967

Patterson, Edward McWilliam *Topology* 1956

— (ed. 2) 1959

—— & Rutherford, D. E. *Elementary abstract algebra* 1965

Patterson, Raymond Murray *Finlay's river* 1968

Paul, Elliot Harold *A narrow street* 1942

Springtime in Paris 1951

Paul, Maurice Eden & Paul, Cedar tr. *J. Stalin's Leninism* 2 vols. 1928–33

Paulding, James Kirke *John Bull in America; or, The new Munchausen* 1825

Westward ho! 2 vols. 1832

See also: 'Bull-Us, Hector'

Pauli, Wolfgang ed. *Niels Bohr and the development of physics: essays dedicated to Niels Bohr* 1955

Pauling, Linus Carl *The nature of the chemical bond and the structure of molecules and crystals* 1939

'Paxton, Philip' (S. A. Hammett) *A stray Yankee in Texas* 1853

Payne, Charles Rockwell tr. *O. Pfister's The psychoanalytic method* 1917

Peace News 1936–

Peach, Benjamin Neave & Horne, John *Chapters on the geology of Scotland* 1930

Peacocke, Arthur Robert & Drysdale, Robert Brown *The molecular basis of heredity* 1965

Peake, Harold John Edward & Fleure, Herbert John *Hunters and artists* 1927

Peake, Mervyn Laurence *Gormenghast* 1950

Titus alone 1959

Titus Groan 1946

Pear, Tom Hatherley *English social differences* 1955

Voice and personality 1931

Pearce, Brian tr. *S. Amin's Accumulation on a world scale: a critique of the theory of underdevelopment* 2 vols. 1974

tr. *E. Preobrazhensky's The new economics* 1965

Pearson, T. Gilbert ed. *Birds of America* 3 vols. 1917

Pearson, William Harrison (Bill) *Coal flat* 1963

Pearson's magazine 1896–1939

Peattie, Donald Culross *The road of a naturalist* 1941 (UK 1946)

Peck, George Wilbur *Peck's bad boy and his pa* 1883

Peck's boss book 1884

Peck's sunshine 1882

Peck, John Mason *A gazetteer of Illinois* 1834

— (ed. 2) 1837

A guide for emigrants 1831

Pediatrics: the journal of the American Academy of Pediatrics 1948–

Peel, Dorothy Constance E. *Life's enchanted cup: an autobiography, 1872–1933* 1933

Peel City Guardian and Chronicle (Peel, Isle of Man) 1882–

Peele, Robert ed. *Mining engineers' handbook* 1918 — (ed. 2) 1927

Peele, Talmadge Lee *The neuroanatomical basis for clinical neurology* 1954

Pegler, Martin M. *The dictionary of interior design* 1966 (UK 1967)

Pei, Mario Andrew *Glossary of linguistic terminology* 1966

The story of language 1949 (UK 1952)

Words in sheep's clothing 1969 (UK 1970)

—— & Gaynor, Frank *A dictionary of linguistics* 1954

Peirce, Charles Santiago Sanders (1839–1914) *Collected papers* ed. C. Hartshorne, P. Weiss, & A. W. Burks 8 vols. 1931–58

Pender, Harold ed. *American handbook for electrical engineers* 1914

Penderel-Brodhurst, James & Layton, Edwin J. *A glossary of English furniture of the historic periods* 1925

Pendlebury, John Devitt Stringfellow *The archaeology of Crete: an introduction* 1939

Penfield, Wilder Graves *Cytology and cellular pathology of the nervous system* 1932

Penguin book of Australian ballads, The ed. R. B. Ward 1964

Penguin music magazine 1946–9

Penguin new writing, The ed. J. F. Lehmann 1940–50

Pennsylvania magazine of history and biography 1877–

Penny magazine 1832–45

Penrose annual (title varies) 1895–

'Pentecost, Hugh' (Judson Pentecost Philips) *Girl watcher's funeral* 1969 (UK 1970)

See also under real name

People, The 1881–1971

People's Journal (Dundee) 1858–

Pereira, Michael *Pigeon's blood* 1970

Perelman, Sidney Joseph *Baby, it's cold inside* 1970

Crazy like a fox 1944 (UK 1945)

Westward ha! or, Around the world in eighty clichés 1947

Perkin, Harold *Key profession: the history of the Association of University Teachers* 1969

Perkowski, Robert L. & Stral, Lee Philip *The joy of CB* 1976

Perry, Frank Ernest & Ryder, Frank Raymond *Dictionary of banking* (ed. 11) 1965 *See* Thomson, William

Perry, John Howard *Chemical engineers' handbook* 1934

— (ed. 3) 1950

Perry, Ralph Barton *The thought and character of William James as revealed in unpublished correspondence, together with his published writings 1842–1910* 2 vols. 1935 (UK 1936)

Perry, Richard *The world of the tiger* 1964

Perry, Ritchie John A. *One good death deserves another* 1976

Personal computer world 1978–

Pervin, William Joseph *Foundations of general topology* 1964

'Peters, Ellis' (Edith Mary Pargeter) *Black is the colour of my true-love's heart* 1967

The piper on the mountain 1966

Peterson, Harold Leslie ed. *Encyclopædia of firearms* 1964

Peterson, Roger Tory & Fisher, James *Wild America* 1956

Petrie, Rhona *Despatch of a dove* 1969

Murder by precedent 1964

Petroleum refiner 1942–61

Petroleum review 1968–

Petticoat 1966–76

Pettijohn, Francis John *Sedimentary rocks* 1949

— (ed. 2) 1957

Pettman, Charles *Africanderisms: a glossary of South African colloquial words and phrases of place and other names* 1913

Pharmacopœia of the United States of America 1820–

Phelps, Elizabeth Stuart *See* Ward, Elizabeth Stuart

Philadelphia Bulletin (title varies) 1847–

Philadelphia Inquirer (title varies) 1829–

Philip, John *Researches in South Africa* 2 vols. 1828

Philips, Judson Pentecost *A dead ending* 1962 (UK 1963)

Escape a killer 1971 (UK 1972)

The twisted people 1965

The vanishing senator 1972 (UK 1973)

See also: 'Pentecost, Hugh'

Philips technical review 1936–

Phillips, Courtenay Stanley Goss & Williams, Robert Joseph Paton *Inorganic chemistry* 2 vols. 1965–6

Phillips, David Graham (1867–1911) *The plum tree* 1905

Susan Lenox: her fall and rise 1917

Phillpotts, Eden *The portreeve* 1906

The secret woman 1905

Philosophical review 1892–

Philosophy: the journal of the British Institute of Philosophy 1931–

Philosophy of science 1934–

'Phoenix, John' (George Horatio Derby) *Phoenixiana; or, Sketches and burlesques* 1856

Photochemistry and photobiology 1962–

Photo-miniature, The 1899–1932

Physical review 1893– (from 1970 divided into subject series)

Physical review letters 1958–

Physical Society (of London) *Proceedings* 1874–

Physics bulletin 1950–

Physiological abstracts 1916–37

Physiological reviews 1921–

Phytochemistry 1961–

Phytopathology 1911–

Picart, Bernard *The ceremonies and religious customs of the various nations of the known world* [anon. tr.] 1733

Picayune (New Orleans): see *Daily Picayune*

Pick of today's short stories, The ed. J. S. Pudney 1949–63

Pickard, George Lewson *Descriptive physical oceanography: an introduction* 1963

Picken, Laurence Ernest Rowland *The organization of cells and other organisms* 1960

Picken, Mary Brooks *The fashion dictionary* 1957

The language of fashion 1939

Pickering, Robert Easton *Himself again* 1966

Pierce, Robert Morris *Dictionary of aviation* 1911

Pieris, Ralph *Sinhalese social organization: the Kandyan period* 1956

Piggott, Stuart *The neolithic cultures of the British Isles* 1954

Pigman, William Ward *Carbohydrates* 1957

Chemistry of the carbohydrates 1948

Pigou, Arthur Cecil *The economics of welfare* 1920

Pike, Albert *Prose sketches and poems, written in the western country* 1834

Pike, Kenneth Lee *Phonetics: a critical analysis of phonetic theory and a technic for the practical description of sounds* 1943

Language in relation to a unified theory of the structure of human behavior 3 parts 1954–60

— (ed. 2) 1967

Pilley, Dorothy Eleanor *Climbing days* 1935

Pillsbury, Donald Marion, Shelley, W. B., & Kligman, Albert M. *Dermatology* 1956

Pinero, Arthur Wing *The magistrate* 1892

The second Mrs. Tanqueray 1895

Pinner, David *Ritual* 1967

Pinter, Harold *The birthday party* 1959

The caretaker 1960

The dumb waiter 1960

The homecoming 1965

The room 1960

Pinto, Edward Henry *Treen and other wooden bygones: an encyclopædia and social history* 1969

Pioneer, The (Lucknow) 1865–

Pirie, Antoinette ed. *Lens metabolism in relation to cataract: proceedings of a symposium* 1962

Pirie, Norman Wingate *Food resources, conventional and novel* 1969

Pirsson, Louis Valentine & Schuchert, Charles *A text-book of geology* 2 parts 1915 (Pt. I by Pirsson, Pt. II by Schuchert)

— (ed. 2, by Pirsson alone) 2 parts 1920–4

Pitts, Denis *This city is ours* 1975 (UK ed. 1976 with title *Target Manhattan*)

Pix (Sydney) 1938– (title varies)

Planché, James Robinson *Extravaganzas* ed. T. F. D. Croker & S. Tucker 5 vols. 1879

Planning: a broadsheet (PEP: Political and Economic Planning) 1933–

Plant physiology 1926–

Plath, Sylvia (1932–63) *Ariel* 1965

The bell jar 1963

The colossus 1960

— (another ed.) 1967

Crossing the water 1971

Platt, Kim *The pushbutton butterfly* 1970 (UK 1971)

Player, Robert *Let's talk of graves, of worms, and epitaphs* 1975

Plays of the year ed. J. C. Trewin 1949–

Plomer, William Charles Franklyn *I speak of Africa* 1927

Museum pieces 1952

Plumptre, Anne tr. *H. Lichtenstein's Travels in southern Africa* 2 vols. 1812–15

Pocknee, C. E. *See* Dearmer, Percy

Poetry (Chicago) 1912–

Pohl, Frederik & Kornbluth, Cyril M. *The space merchants* 1953 (UK 1955)

Polack, Joel Samuel *Manners and customs of the New Zealanders* 2 vols. 1840

New Zealand: being a narrative of travels and adventures 2 vols. 1838

Police journal 1928–

Police review (title varies) 1893–

Political quarterly 1930–

Political science quarterly 1886–

Pollitt, John *Depression and its treatment* 1965

Pollock, Albin Jay *The underworld speaks* 1935

Pollock, Frederick & Holmes, Oliver Wendell (the younger) *The Pollock–Holmes letters: correspondence of Sir Frederick Pollock and Mr. Justice Holmes, 1874–1932* ed. M. de W. Howe 2 vols. 1942

Polunin, Nicholas Vladimir *Introduction to plant geography and some related sciences* 1960

Ponting, Herbert George *The great white south: being an account of experiences with Captain Scott's South Pole Expedition* 1921

Poole, A. L. & Adams, Nancy M. *Trees and shrubs of New Zealand* 1963

Pope-Hennessy, James *Robert Louis Stevenson* 1974

Popenoe, Wilson *Manual of tropical and subtropical fruits* 1920

Popley, Herbert Arthur *The music of India* 1921

Popper, Karl Raimund *The logic of scientific discovery* 1959

The open society and its enemies 2 vols. 1945

The poverty of historicism 1957

Porcupine, The 1860–1915; 1923

'Porte Crayon' (David Hunter Strother) *Virginia illustrated* 1857

PORTER, Mrs. G. S. See STRATTON-PORTER, Mrs. Gene
PORTER, Horace C. tr. *E. Strasburger's A text-book of botany* 1898
PORTER, Joyce *The chinks in the curtain* 1967
Dover two 1965
It's murder with Dover 1973
A meddler and her murder 1972
Rather a common sort of crime 1970
Sour cream with everything 1966
PORTER, Katherine Anne *Ship of fools* 1962
Porter's Spirit of the times 1856–9
Portola Institute *The last whole earth catalog* 1972
Portsmouth, Rhode Island *Early records* ed. A. Perry & C. S. Brigham 1901
POST, Waldron Kintzing *Harvard stories: sketches of the undergraduate* 1893
Post-Herald (Birmingham, Alabama) 1951–
Post Office electrical engineers' journal 1908–
POSTAL, Paul Martin *Aspects of phonological theory* 1968
POSTGATE, Raymond William *The plain man's guide to wine* 1951
— (ed. 2) 1965
POSTMAN, Neil *Crazy talk, stupid talk* 1976
POTOK, Chaim *The chosen* 1967
In the beginning 1975
My name is Asher Lev 1972
POTTER, David *British Elizabethan stamps: the story of the postage stamps of the United Kingdom* 1971
POTTER, Dennis Christopher G. *The glittering coffin* 1960
POTTER, Helen Beatrix *Journal, 1881–1897* transcribed from code by L. Linder 1966
POTTER, Jeremy *Foul play* 1967
POTTER, Simeon *Language in the modern world* 1960
Modern linguistics 1957
Our language 1950
POTTLE, Frederick Albert *Stretchers: the story of a hospital unit on the Western Front* 1929 (UK 1930)
POTTS, Jean *Death of a stray cat* 1955 (UK 1956)
The evil wish 1962
POTTS, Thomas Henry *Out in the open: a budget of scraps of natural history, gathered in New Zealand* 1882
Poultry chronicle 1854–5
POUND, Ezra Loomis *Cantos LII–LXXI* 1940
Canzoni 1911
Cathay: translations for the most part from the Chinese of Rihaku 1915
The classic anthology defined by Confucius 1955
A draft of XXX cantos 1930
Hugh Selwyn Mauberley: life and contacts 1920
Letters See *Selected letters*
Lustra 1916
— (another ed., with earlier poems) 1917
Pavannes and divisions 1918
Personae: the collected poems 1909
The Pisan cantos 1948 (UK 1949)
Section: rock-drill; 85–95 de los cantares 1955
— (another ed.) 1957
Selected letters, 1907–1941 ed. D. D. Paige 1971
Thrones: 96–109 de los cantares 1959
tr. *Sophocles' Women of Trachis* 1956
POUTSMA, Hendrik *A grammar of late modern English* 2 parts in 4 vols. 1904–26
— (ed. 2 of Part I) 2 vols. 1928–9
POWDRILL, Ernest Arthur *Vocabulary of land planning* 1961
POWELL, Anthony Dymoke *The acceptance world* 1955
Afternoon men 1931
A buyer's market 1952
Casanova's Chinese restaurant 1960
A question of upbringing 1951
The valley of bones 1964
Venusberg 1932
What's become of Waring? 1939
POWELL, Dawn *A time to be born* 1942 (UK 1943)
Turn, magic wheel 1936
POWELL, John Leonard & CRASEMANN, Bernd *Quantum mechanics* 1961
POWELL, Martin Beynon & HIGMAN, Graham eds. *Finite simple groups* 1971
POWER, Tyrone *Impressions of America, 1833–1835* 2 vols. 1836
POWER, William James Tyrone *Sketches in New Zealand, with pen and pencil* 1849
Power farming 1957–
POWYS, John Cowper *A Glastonbury romance* 1932 (UK 1933)
Maiden Castle 1936 (UK 1937)
Visions and revisions: a book of literary devotions 1915
POWYS, Marian *Lace and lace-making* 1953
Practical motorist 1954–
Practical wireless 1932–
Practitioner, The: a monthly journal of therapeutics and public health 1868–
Practitioners library of medicine and surgery, The ed. G. Blumer 16 vols. 1932–41

PRATT, Lyde S. *The chemistry and physics of organic pigments* 1947
Prehistoric Society (of East Anglia) *Proceedings* 1908–
Press, The (Christchurch, N.Z.) 1861–
Press and Journal (Aberdeen) 1939– (continuation of *Aberdeen Press and Journal*)
PRICE, Anthony *The Alamut ambush* 1971
Colonel Butler's wolf 1972
The '44 vintage 1978
October men 1973
Other paths to glory 1974
Our man in Camelot 1975
War game 1976
PRICE, Henry Habberley *Perception* 1932
Thinking and experience 1953
PRICE, Pamela Vandyke *France: a food and wine guide* 1966
PRICE, Stanley *Just for the record* 1961
PRICHARD, Katharine Susannah *Coonardoo: the well in the shadow* 1929
Winged seeds 1950
PRIEBSCH, Robert Charles & COLLINSON, William Edward *The German language* 1934
PRIESTLEY, John Boynton *Angel Pavement* 1930
Bright day 1946
Daylight on Saturday 1943
Delight 1949
English journey 1934
Festival at Farbridge 1951
The good companions 1929
Home is tomorrow 1949
It's an old country 1967
Let the people sing 1939
The magicians 1954
Margin released 1962
Salt is leaving 1966
Saturn over the water 1961
They walk in the city 1936
Three men in new suits 1945
—— & HAWKES, Jessie Jacquetta *Journey down a rainbow* 1955
PRIESTLEY, Ronald & WISDOM, Thomas Henry *Good driving– the B.S.M. way* 1965
PRINGLE-PATTISON, Andrew Seth *The idea of God in the light of recent philosophy* 1917
Printers' ink 1888–1967
PRIOR, Allan *The interrogators* 1965
The operators 1966
PRIOR, Arthur Norman *Formal logic* 1955
Time and modality 1957
PRITCHETT, Victor Sawdon *A cab at the door, an autobiography: early years* 1968
The gentle barbarian: the life and work of Turgenev 1977
Private eye 1962–
Proceedings See under the names of particular institutions
PROCTER, Henry Richardson *The principles of leather manufacture* 1903
PROCTER, Maurice *Exercise Hoodwink* 1967
Man in ambush 1958
PROCTOR, Michael Charles Faraday & YEO, Peter *The pollination of flowers* 1973
Product engineering 1930–
Providence, Rhode Island *Early records* 21 vols. 1892–1915
PRYCE-JONES, Alan ed. *The new outline of modern knowledge* 1956
Psyche (subtitle varies) 1921–37
Psychiatry 1938–
Psychoanalytic review 1913–
Psychological bulletin 1904–
Psychological review 1894–
Public Ledger (Philadelphia) 1836–1934
Publications See under the names of particular institutions
Publishers' circular (title varies) 1837–1959
Publishers' weekly 1873–
Puck (New York) 1877–1918
PUGH, Marshall *Last place left* 1969
A wilderness of monkeys 1958
PULGRAM, Ernst *Introduction to the spectography of speech* 1959
PUNNETT, Reginald Crundall *Mendelism* 1905 (and several later editions used)
PURSEGLOVE, John William *Tropical crops: dicotyledons* 2 vols. 1968
PURSER, Philip *The Holy Father's navy* 1971
The Twentymen 1967
PUTNAM, Donald Fulton ed. *Canadian regions* 1952
PUTNAM, Samuel Whitehall tr. *E. da Cunha's Rebellion in the backlands* 1944
PUZO, Mario *Fools die* 1978
PYCRAFT, William Plane ed. *The standard natural history* 1931
PYKE, Magnus Alfred *Food and society* 1968
PYM, Barbara Mary Crampton *No fond return of love* 1961
Quartet in autumn 1977
Some tame gazelle 1950
PYNCHON, Thomas *The crying of Lot 49* 1966
Gravity's rainbow 1973
V.: a novel 1963

Q

'Q' (Arthur Thomas Quiller-Couch) *The mayor of Troy* 1906
See also under real name
Quarterly cumulative index medicus 1927–56
Quarterly journal of medicine 1907–
Quarterly register 1886–1934
Quarterly review of biology 1926–
'QUARTERMAIN, James' (James Broom Lynne) *Rock of diamond* 1972
'QUEEN, Ellery' (Frederic Dannay & Manfred Bennington Lee) *The four of hearts* 1938 (UK 1939)
The fourth side of the triangle 1965
The French powder mystery 1930
The Roman hat mystery 1929
Queen, The: an illustrated journal and review (title varies) 1861–1970
QUENNELL, Peter Courtney *The marble foot: an autobiography, 1905–1938* 1976
'QUENTIN, Patrick' (Richard Wilson Webb & Hugh Callingham Wheeler) *The follower* 1950
Puzzle for fiends 1946 (UK 1947)
Shadow of guilt 1959
Suspicious circumstances 1957
QUICK, Herbert *Yellowstone nights* 1911
QUILLER-COUCH, Arthur Thomas *Foe-Farrell* 1918
Major Vigoureux 1907
On the art of writing 1916
Studies in literature 3 ser. 1918–29
See also: 'Q'
Quincy Whig (Quincy, Illinois) 1838–1915 (title varies)
QUINE, Willard Van Orman *From a logical point of view* 1953
Mathematical logic 1940
Methods of logic 1950 (UK 1952)
Set theory and its logic 1963
Word and object 1960
Quinland; or, Varieties in American life 2 vols. 1857
QUINN, Arthur Hobson *Pennsylvania stories* 1899
QUINTON, Anthony Meredith *The nature of things* 1973
QUIRK, Charles Randolph *The use of English* 1962
—— & SMITH, Albert Hugh eds. *The teaching of English* 1959
—— et al. *A grammar of contemporary English* 1972
See also: CRYSTAL, David

R

R.A.F. journal See *Royal Air Force journal*
R.A.F. news See *Royal Air Force news*
RABINOWITCH, Eugene Isakovich *Photosynthesis and related processes* 2 vols. (Vol. II in 2 parts) 1945–56
RACKHAM, Bernard tr. *E. Hannover's Pottery and porcelain* Vol. I 1925 (Vols. II & III, also 1925, tr. by W. W. Worster; whole work ed. by B. Rackham)
RADDALL, Thomas Head *Hangman's beach* 1966
RADIN, Paul tr. *J. Vendryès's Language* 1925
Radio communication handbook, The See *Amateur radio handbook*
Radio review: a monthly record of scientific progress in radiotelegraphy and telephony 1919–22
Radio times, The 1923–
Radiology 1923–
RAE, Hugh Crauford *A few small bones* 1968
The marksman 1971
The shooting gallery 1972
RAE, John *The custard boys* 1960
RAFFÉ, Walter George *Dictionary of the dance* 1964
Railroad and engineering journal 1887–92
Railway magazine 1897–
'RAINE, Richard' (Raymond Harold Sawkins) *Night of the hawk* 1968
RAINE, William Macleod *Bucky O'Connor: a tale of the unfenced border* 1910 (UK 1920)
Troubled waters 1924
RALEIGH, Walter Alexander R. (1861–1922) *Letters* ed. Lady Raleigh 2 vols. 1926
— (new ed.) 2 vols. 1928
Shakespeare 1907
RAMPINI, Charles J. G. *Letters from Jamaica* 1873
RAMSAY, Diana *Descent into the dark* 1975
A little murder music 1972
No cause to kill 1974
RAMSBOTTOM, John *Mushrooms and toadstools* 1953
RAMSDEN, Evelyn tr. *E. Gram & H. Weber's Plant diseases in orchard, nursery and garden crops* 1952

Ramsey, Frederic & Smith, Charles Edward *Jazzmen* 1939 (UK 1940)
Ramsey, Leonard Gerald Gwynne ed. *The Connoisseur new guide to antique English pottery, porcelain and glass* 1961
Ramson, William Stanley *Australian English: an historical study of the vocabulary, 1788–1898* 1966
Rand, Austin Loomer *Mammals of the eastern Rockies and western plains of Canada* 1948
Rand Daily Mail (Johannesburg) 1902–
Randall-Diehl, Anna *Two thousand words and their definitions; not in Webster's Dictionary* 1888
Randolph Enterprise (Elkins, West Virginia) 1874–
Ranjitsinhji, Kumar Shri *The Jubilee book of cricket* 1897
Rankine, William John Macquorn *A manual of applied mechanics* 1858
Ransome, Arthur Michell (1884–1967) *Autobiography* ed. R. Hart-Davis 1976
Great Northern? 1947
Secret water 1939
'Ransome, Stephen' (Frederick Clyde Davis) *The deadly Miss Ashley* 1950 (US ed. published under author's real name)
Without a trace 1962
Rao, G. Subba *Indian words in English: a study in Indo-British cultural and linguistic relations* 1954
Raper, John Robert *Genetics of sexuality in higher fungi* 1966
Raphael, Chaim *A feast of history: the drama of Passover through the ages* 1972
Raphael, Frederic Michael *The glittering prizes* 1976
The limits of love 1960
Raphael, John E. *Modern Rugby football* 1918
Ratcliffe, John Ashworth *The physical principles of wireless* 1929
Rathbone, Julian *Diamonds bid* 1967
Joseph 1979
Kill cure 1975
Rattigan, Terence Mervyn *The deep blue sea* 1952
Flare path 1942
French without tears: a play 1937
Ross: a dramatic portrait 1960
While the sun shines 1944
Who is Sylvia? 1951
The Winslow boy 1946
Rattray, Robert Sutherland *Ashanti* 1923
Raven, Simon Arthur Noël *The survivors* 1976
Raverat, Gwendolyn Mary *Period piece: a Cambridge childhood* 1952
Rawlings, Marjorie Kinnan *The yearling* 1938
Rawlinson, William *Modern foundry operations and equipment* 1928
Ray, Cyril ed. *The compleat imbiber* 1956–71
Merry England 1960
Rayleigh, John William (Strutt), 3rd Baron *The theory of sound* 2 vols. 1877–8
Raymond, Ernest *The jesting army* 1930
Rayner, Dorothy Helen *The stratigraphy of the British Isles* 1967
RCA review 1936–
Read, Herbert Edward *Annals of innocence and experience* 1940
Art and industry 1934
Art and society 1937
Collected poems, 1913–25 1926
A concise history of modern painting 1959
The contrary experience: autobiographies 1963
Education through art 1943
Icon and idea: the function of art in the development of human consciousness 1955
The meaning of art 1931
The tenth muse: essays in criticism 1957
Read, Herbert Harold & Watson, Janet V. *Introduction to geology* 2 vols. (Vol. II in 2 parts) 1962–75
Read, John *A text-book of organic chemistry* 1926
Read, Piers Paul *The Villa Golitsyn* 1981
Reader's digest 1922–
Reader's digest family guide to the law 1971
Real estate review 1923–
Reaney, Percy Hide *The origin of English place-names* 1960
Recent progress in hormone research 1947–
Record, Samuel James & Hess, Robert William *Timbers of the New World* 1943
—— & Mell, Clayton Dissinger *Timbers of tropical America* 1924
Recruiter's bulletin (U.S. Marine Corps) 1915–21
Red Cross magazine 1916–20
Redbook (title varies) 1903–
Rede, Leman Thomas *The road to the stage* 1827
Redfield, Robert *Peasant society and culture: an anthropological approach to civilisation* 1956
Reece, Gordon tr. *F. Hund's The history of quantum theory* 1974
Reece, Robert H. *Night bombing with the Bedouins* 1919
Reese, John Terence & Dormer, Albert *The bridge player's dictionary* 1959
Referee, The 1877–1928
Register of debates in Congress See: United States. Congress. Debates
Reichenbach, Hans *Elements of symbolic logic* 1947
Reid, John Cowie ed. *The Kiwi laughs: an anthology of New Zealand prose humour* 1961
Reid, Thomas Mayne *The headless horseman: a strange tale of Texas* 2 vols. & 1 vol. 1866
The young voyageurs 1854
Reifer, Mary *A dictionary of new words* 1955
Rein, Johann Justus *Japan: travels and researches* [anon. tr.] 1884
Reisner, Robert George *The jazz titans; including 'The parlance of hip'* 1960
Reisz, Karel *The technique of film editing* 1953
— (ed. 9) 1961
Reith, John Charles Walsham (1889–1971) *The Reith diaries* ed. C. Stuart 1975
Release and resettlement: an explanation of your position and rights Issued by H.M. Government to all serving members of H.M. Forces 1945
Rendell, Ruth *A guilty thing surprised* 1970
Make death love me 1979
A new lease of death 1967
One across, two down 1971
Some lie and some die 1973
Report..Indian affairs See: United States *Report of the Commissioner of Indian Affairs*
Report of the Committee of Inquiry on Decimal Currency See: United Kingdom. Parliamentary papers
Report of the Committee on Broadcasting 1960 See: United Kingdom. Parliamentary papers
Reporter: the magazine of facts and ideas (New York) 1949–
Republican Review (Albuquerque, New Mexico) 1870–3
Return to the attack: with the New Zealand Division in North Africa (Army Board, N.Z.) 1944
Review of English studies 1925–
Review of scientific instruments 1930–
Reynolds, John *The pioneer history of Illinois, 1673–1818* 1852
Reynolds, Mack (Dallas McCord Reynolds) *After some tomorrow* 1967
Rhode Island Historical Society *Collections* 1827–1941
Rhys, Jean *Voyage in the dark* 1934
Wide Sargasso Sea 1966
Rice, Clara Mabel *Dictionary of geological terms* 1940
Rice, David Talbot *English art, 871–1100* 1952
Rice, Elmer Leopold *A voyage to Purilia* 1930
Rich, Jack C. *The materials and methods of sculpture* 1947
Richards, Frank James *Old-soldier sahib* 1936
Richards, Ivor Armstrong *Practical criticism: a study of literary judgment* 1929
Principles of literary criticism 1925
See also: Ogden, Charles Kay
Richards, Owain Westmacott & Davies, R. G. eds. *A. D. Imms's A general textbook of entomology* (ed. 9) 1957
Richards, Paul Westmacott *The tropical rain forest: an ecological study* 1952
Richards, Richard Kohler *Arithmetic operations in digital computers* 1955
Richardson, Alan ed. *A dictionary of Christian theology* 1969
Richardson, Edward Gick *Sound: a physical text-book* 1927
'Richardson, Henry Handel' (Edith Florence Lindesay Robertson) *The fortunes of Richard Mahony* 1917
Richardson, John *A dictionary, Persian, Arabic, and English* 2 vols. 1777–80
Richler, Mordecai *Cocksure* 1968
Richmond Enquirer (Richmond, Virginia) 1804–77
Richmond News-Leader (Richmond, Virginia) 1903–
Richmond Times-Dispatch (Richmond, Virginia) 1903–
Richmond Whig (Richmond, Virginia) 1824–88 (title varies)
Richmond–Atkinson papers, The ed. G. H. Scholefield 2 vols. 1960
Richter, George Holmes *Textbook of organic chemistry* 1938
Richter, Gisela M. A. & Milne, Marjorie J. *Shapes and names of Athenian vases* 1935
Rickert, Margaret *Painting in Britain: the Middle Ages* 1954
Rickman, Eric *Come racing with me* 1951
Riddell, Charlotte Eliza Lawson (Mrs. J. H. Riddell) *The senior partner* 3 vols. 1881
Ridge, William Pett *Affectionate regards* 1929
Ridley, Cecilia Anne *Cecilia: the life and letters of Cecilia Ridley, 1819–1845* ed. Viscountess Ridley 1958
Rieger, Rigomar, Michaelis, A., & Green, M. M. *A glossary of genetics and cytogenetics, classical and molecular* 1968
Riesenberg, Felix *Golden Gate: the story of San Francisco harbour* 1940
Riesman, David *Individualism reconsidered, and other essays* 1954
——, Denney, R. N., & Glazer, N. *The lonely crowd: a study of the changing American character* 1950
Riis, Jacob August *How the other half lives: studies among the tenements of New York* 1890 (UK 1891)
Rimmer, Robert Henry *The Premar experiments* 1975 (UK 1976)
Riordan, John *Stochastic service systems* 1962
Ritchie, Anna & Ritchie, Graham *The ancient monuments of Orkney* 1978
Ritchie, Anne (Thackeray) (1837–1923) *Letters, with forty-two additional letters from W. M. Thackeray* ed. H. Ritchie 1924
Rittenhouse, Isabella Maud *Maud* ed. R. L. Strout 1939
Rivers, William Halse R. *Kinship and social organisation* 1914
Riviere, Joan tr. *S. Freud's Introductory lectures on psycho-analysis* 1922
—— et al. tr. *S. Freud's Collected papers* 5 vols. 1924–50
Robb, Frank *Sea hunters* 1953
Roberts, E. M. *A flying fighter: an American above the lines in France* 1918
Roberts, Elizabeth Madox *The time of man* 1926 (UK 1927)
Roberts, Geoffrey Keith *A dictionary of political analysis* 1971
Roberts, Hermese E. *The third ear* 1970
Roberts, John D., Stewart, R., & Caserio, M. C. *Organic chemistry* 1971
Roberts, Nesta *The face of France* 1976
Robertson, E. Arnot (Eileen Arbuthnot Robertson) *Ordinary families* 1933
Robertson, Edith Thom & Gooding, Evelyn Graham B. *Botany for the Caribbean* 1963
Robertson, Stuart *The development of modern English* 1934 (UK 1936)
— (ed. 2, rev. by F. G. Cassidy) 1954
Robins, Elizabeth *The magnetic north* 1904
Robins, Robert Henry *General linguistics: an introductory survey* 1964
Robinson, Gilbert Wooding *Soils: their origin, constitution and classification* 1932
Robinson, Henry Crabb (1775–1867) *Diary* ed. D. Hudson 1967
Robinson, Paul A. *Freudian Left* 1969
Robinson, William *The English flower garden* 1883 (and several later editions used)
The wild garden 1870 (and several later editions used)
Roche, Harriet A. *On trek in the Transvaal; or, Over berg and veldt in South Africa* 1878
Rodd, Ernest Harry ed. *Chemistry of carbon compounds* 5 vols. in 10 parts 1951–62
Rodgers, Bruce *The queens' vernacular: a gay lexicon* 1972
Roe, Thomas *The embassy of Sir Thomas Roe to the court of the Great Mogul, 1615–1619, as narrated in his journal and correspondence* ed. W. Foster 2 vols. 1899
Rogers, Walter Thomas (d. 1912) *Dictionary of abbreviations* 1913
Roget, Samuel Romilly *A dictionary of electrical terms* 1924 (and later editions used)
Rohan, Criena *The delinquents* 1962
Rolfe, Frederick William S. A. L. M. ('Baron Corvo') (1860–1913) *The desire and pursuit of the whole: a romance of modern Venice* 1934
Hadrian the Seventh 1904
Nicholas Crabbe; or, The one and the many ed. C. Woolf 1958
Rolling stone 1967–
'Rolph, C. H.' (Cecil Rolph Hewitt) ed. *The human sum* 1957
ed. *Women of the streets* 1955
Romer, Alfred Sherwood *The procession of life* 1968
The vertebrate body 1949
Vertebrate paleontology 1933
Romilly, Joseph *Romilly's Cambridge diary 1832–42* ed. J. P. T. Bury 1967
Rook, Arthur James, Wilkinson, D. S., & Ebling, F. J. G. eds. *Textbook of dermatology* 2 vols. 1968
Roosenburg, Henriette *The walls came tumbling down* 1957
Rose, Geoffrey Keith *The story of the 2/4th Oxfordshire and Buckinghamshire Light Infantry* 1920
Rose, Howard N. *A thesaurus of slang* 1934
Rose, William ed. *An outline of modern knowledge* 1931
Rosen, Ephraim & Gregory, Ian *Abnormal psychology* 1965

Ross, Alan John *Australia 55: a journal of the M.C.C. tour* 1955
Australia 63 1963
ed. *The cricketer's companion* 1960
Ross, Alan Strode Campbell *Etymology, with especial reference to English* 1958
Ross, Angus *The Bradford business* 1974
The Dunfermline affair 1973
The Manchester thing 1970
Ross, David Alexander *Introduction to oceanography* 1970
Ross, Edward Alsworth *The Russian Soviet republic* 1923
Ross, James *Handbook of the diseases of the nervous system* 1885
'Ross, Jonathan' (John Rossiter) *The burning of Billy Toober* 1974
Dead at first hand 1969
I know what it's like to die 1976
Ross, Rodger James *Television film engineering* 1966
Rossetti, Dante Gabriel (1828–82) *Letters* ed. O. Doughty & J. R. Wahl 4 vols. 1965–7
Rossiter, John *The manipulators* 1973
A rope for General Dietz 1972
Rosten, Leo Calvin *The joys of Yiddish* 1968
Roth, Cecil *A history of the Marranos* 1932
Roth, Philip *Goodbye, Columbus* 1959
Portnoy's complaint 1969
Rotman, Jonah Joseph *The theory of groups* 1965
Round, Frank Eric *Introduction to the lower plants* 1969
Rowlands, John James *Spindrift from a house by the sea* 1960
Rowley, Jennifer E. *Mechanised in-house information systems* 1979
Rowse, Alfred Leslie *A Cornish childhood* 1942
The early Churchills: an English family 1956
The England of Elizabeth 1950
The English spirit: essays 1944
The expansion of Elizabethan England 1955
Tudor Cornwall 1941
The use of history 1946
Royal Aeronautical Society *Journal* 1923–67
Handbook of aeronautics 1931
Royal Air Force journal ?1942–6
Royal Air Force news 1961–
Royal Asiatic Society: Straits Branch (later Malayan Branch) *Journal* 1878–1920; 1923–63
Royal Asiatic Society of Bengal *See* Asiatic ——
Royal Entomological Society of London *See* Entomological ——
Royal Horticultural Society *Dictionary of gardening* ed. F. J. Chittenden et al. 4 vols. 1951
Journal 1846–55; 1866–
Royal Institution of Great Britain *Proceedings* 1851– (1851–1928 with title *Notices of the proceedings*)
Royal Society of Edinburgh *Proceedings* 1832– (from 1941 divided into subject sections)
Royal Society of Medicine *Proceedings* 1907–
Royall, Anne *The black book; or, A continuation of travels in the United States* 3 vols. 1828–9
Royce, Kenneth *Spider underground* 1973
Trap Spider 1974
Royde-Smith, Naomi Gwladys *Incredible tale* 1932
Ruark, Arthur Edward & Urey, Harold Clayton *Atoms, molecules and quanta* 1930
Rubinstein, Helena *The art of feminine beauty* 1930
Ruck, Amy Roberta (Berta) *Disturbing charm* 1919
'Rudd, Steele' (Arthur Hoey Davis) *From selection to city* 1909
Our new selection 1903
Rudder, The 1890–
Rudinger, Edith ed. *The consumer's car glossary* (Consumers' Association) 1966
— (ed. 2) 1967
ed. *Wills and probate* (Consumers' Association) 1967
Ruell, Patrick *Red Christmas* 1972
Rules of the game: the complete illustrated encyclopedia of all the sports of the world (by the Diagram Group) 1974
Rumbaugh, Duane M. ed. *Language learning by a chimpanzee: the Lana project* 1977
Rumney, George R. *Climatology and the world's climates* 1968
Runes, Dagobert David ed. *The dictionary of philosophy* 1942
Runyon, Alfred Damon *Furthermore* ed. E. C. Bentley 1938
Guys and dolls 1931 (UK 1932)
More than somewhat ed. E. C. Bentley 1937
Runyon à la carte 1944 (UK 1946)
Take it easy 1938
Rushdie, Salman *Midnight's children* 1981
Ruskin, Effie *See* Lutyens, Mary
Russell, Alexander *A treatise on the theory of alternating currents* 2 vols. 1904–6
Russell, Archer *Bush ways: a Bush-lover's wanderings on plain and range in Central and Eastern Australia* 1944
Gone nomad 1936
A tramp-royal in wild Australia, 1928–1929 1934
Russell, Bertrand Arthur William *The analysis of mind* 1921
Autobiography 3 vols. 1967–9
A history of Western philosophy 1945 (UK 1946)
An inquiry into meaning and truth 1940
Marriage and morals 1929
An outline of philosophy 1927
Principia mathematica See: Whitehead, Alfred North & Russell, B. A. W.
The principles of mathematics 1903
Religion and science 1935
Russell, Charles Marion *Trails plowed under* 1927
Russell, Frederick Stratten & Yonge, Charles Maurice *The seas: our knowledge of life in the sea and how it is gained* 1928
— (rev. ed.) 1936
Russell, George Oscar *Speech and voice* 1931
Russell, Loris Shano *Everyday life in colonial Canada* 1973
Russell, Martin James *Deadline* 1971
Double hit 1973
Murder by the mile 1975
Russell, Ralph tr. *Aziz Ahmad's The shore and the wave* 1971
'Russell, Sarah' (Marghanita Laski) *To bed with grand music* 1946
Russenholt, Edgar Stanford *The heart of the continent: being the history of Assiniboia—the truly typical Canadian community* 1968
'Rutherford, Douglas' (James Douglas Rutherford McConnell) *The creeping flesh* 1963
The gilt-edged cockpit 1969
Kick start 1973
The long echo 1957
Rutherford, Ernest *Radio-activity* 1904
—— Chadwick, J., & Ellis, C. D. *Radiations from radioactive substances* 1930
Rutten, Martin Gerard *The geology of western Europe* 1969
Rycroft, Charles *A critical dictionary of psychoanalysis* 1968
Ryder, Jonathan *Trevayne* 1973 (UK 1974)
Ryle, Gilbert *The concept of mind* 1949

S

S.L.R. camera 1964
S.P.E. *See* Society for Pure English
Sachs, Albert Louis *The jail diary of Albie Sachs* 1966
Sachs, Curt *The history of musical instruments* 1940 (UK 1942)
Sackville-West, Victoria Mary *The Edwardians* 1930
Sadeek, Sheik M. *Windswept, and other stories* 1969
Sadleir, Michael *Excursions in Victorian bibliography* 1922
Trollope: a commentary 1927
Sadler, William Samuel *Theory and practice of psychiatry* 1936
Safire, William L. *The new language of politics: an anecdotal dictionary of catchwords, slogans, and political usage* 1968
Sagan, Carl *The cosmic connection: an extraterrestrial perspective* 1973 (UK 1974)
Sagarin, Edward *Cosmetics: science and technology* 1957
Sage, Rufus B. *Scenes in the Rocky Mountains, and in Oregon, California, New Mexico, Texas, and the grand prairies* 1846
St. Clair, Leonard *A fortune in death* 1976
St. John, John Henry Herbert *Pakeha rambles through Maori lands* 1873
St. Louis Globe-Democrat (St. Louis, Missouri) 1875–
Saintsbury, George Edward Bateman *Notes on a cellar-book* 1920
The peace of the Augustans 1916
A short history of French literature 1882
'Saki' (Hector Hugh Munro) *Beasts and super-beasts* 1914
The chronicles of Clovis 1912
Reginald 1904
Reginald in Russia, and other sketches 1910
Salak, John Stephen ed. *Dictionary of American sports* 1961
Salinger, Jerome David *The catcher in the rye* 1951
Franny and Zooey 1962
Salisbury, Harrison Evans *The shook-up generation* 1958 (UK 1959)
Salter, Charles tr. *G. von Georgievics's Chemistry of dye-stuffs* 1903
tr. *G. von Georgievics's The chemical technology of textile fibres* 1902
Salter, William Henry *Zoar; or, The evidence of psychical research concerning survival* 1961
Sampson, Anthony Terrell S. *Anatomy of Britain* 1962
Sampson, Edmund *Tales of the fancy* 1889
Samuels, Michael Louis *Linguistic evolution: with special reference to English* 1972
San Francisco Examiner (title varies) 1865–
Sandburg, Carl *Chicago poems* 1916
Cornhuskers 1918
Slabs of the sunburnt west 1922
Smoke and steel 1920
Sanders, George *Memoirs of a professional cad* 1960
Sanders, Lawrence *The Anderson tapes* 1970
Sanders, Leonard *The Hamlet warning* 1976 (UK 1977)
Sanderson, C. C. ed. *Pedigree dogs as recognised by the Kennel Club* 1927
Sandilands, John *Western Canadian dictionary and phrase-book* 1912
Sangster, Jimmy *Touchfeather* 1968
Your friendly neighbourhood death pedlar 1971
Sansom, George Bailey *Japan: a short cultural history* 1931
Sansom, William *The face of innocence* 1951
Santa Fé Republican (Santa Fé, New Mexico) 1847–
Sapir, Edward *Language: an introduction to the study of speech* 1921
Saporta, Sol & Bastian, Jarvis R. eds. *Psycholinguistics: a book of readings* 1961
'Sapper' (Herman Cyril McNeile) *The black gang* 1922
Bull-dog Drummond: the adventures of a demobilised officer who found peace dull 1920
The female of the species 1928
The finger of fate 1930
The third round 1924
Sargent, Charles Sprague *Manual of the trees of North America* 1905
Sargent, Epes Winthrop *The technique of the photoplay* 1912
— (ed. 2) 1913
— (ed. 3) 1916
Sargeson, Frank *I saw in my dream* 1949
A man and his wife 1940
— (new ed.) 1944
Memoirs of a peon 1965
That summer, and other stories 1946
Saroyan, William *The daring young man on the flying trapeze, and other stories* 1934 (UK 1935)
Sarton, George Alfred Leon *A history of science* 2 vols. 1952–9 (UK 1953–9)
Sasieni, Lewis Sidney *The principles and practice of optical dispensing and fitting* 1962
Sassoon, Siegfried Loraine *Collected poems, 1908–56* 1961
Memoirs of a fox-hunting man 1928
Memoirs of an infantry officer 1930
Sherston's progress 1936
Satchell, William *The land of the lost: a tale of the New Zealand gum-country* 1902
Saturday evening post: an illustrated weekly magazine (title varies) 1821–1969
Saturday night (Toronto) 1887–
Saturday review (US) 1924– (title varies: 1924–51 with title *Saturday review of literature*; 1972–3 divided into four: *Saturday review of education; society; the arts; the sciences*; 1973–5 recombined as *Saturday review world*; 1975– with title *Saturday review*)
Saturday Westminster gazette ? 1899–1922
Saucier, Walter J. *Principles of meteorological analysis* 1955
Saucy stories 1916–25
Saunders, Margaret Baillie *Litany Lane* 1909
Saunders, Ripley Dunlap *Colonel Todhunter of Missouri* 1911
Savage, George *The antique collector's handbook* 1959
Dictionary of antiques 1970
Porcelain through the ages 1954
—— & Newman, Harold *An illustrated dictionary of ceramics* 1974
Sawyer, Frederic Henry Read *The inhabitants of the Philippines* 1900
Saxon, Lyle, Dreyer, E., & Tallant, R. *Gumbo ya-ya: a collection of Louisiana folk tales* 1945
Say, Maurice George ed. *Newnes concise encyclopaedia of electrical engineering* See under title
Sayers, Dorothy Leigh *Busman's honeymoon* 1937
Clouds of witness 1926
The five red herrings 1931
Gaudy night 1935
Hangman's holiday 1933
Have his carcase 1932
Lord Peter views the body 1928
Murder must advertise 1933
The nine tailors 1934
Strong poison 1930
Unnatural death 1927
The unpleasantness at the Bellona Club 1928

SAYERS, Dorothy Leigh & 'EUSTACE, Robert' (Eustace Robert Barton) *The documents in the case* 1930
SCHALLER, George B. *The year of the gorilla* 1964 (UK 1965)
SCHAPERA, Isaac *The Bantu-speaking tribes of South Africa* 1937
The Khoisan peoples of South Africa: Bushmen and Hottentots 1930
SCHARF, Bedrich *Engineering and its language* 1971
SCHILPP, Paul Arthur ed. *The philosophy of Bertrand Russell* 1944
ed. *The philosophy of Rudolf Carnap* 1963
SCHLAUCH, Margaret *The English language in modern times, since 1400* 1959
SCHLICH, William *A manual of forestry* 5 vols. (Vols. IV & V by W. R. Fisher) 1889–96
SCHNEIDER, Frank *Qualitative organic microanalysis* 1946
Scholarly publishing 1969–
SCHOLEM, Gershom Gerhard *Major trends in Jewish mysticism* 1941
SCHOONMAKER, Frank & MARVEL, Tom *The complete wine book* 1935
SCHREIBER, Charlotte Elizabeth *Journal, 1833–1891* extracts ed. Earl of Bessborough 2 vols. 1950–2
Journals, 1869–85 ed. M. J. Guest 2 vols. 1911
SCHREINER, Olive *From man to man* 1926
SCHUCHERT, Charles *See* PIRSSON, Louis Valentine
SCHUELL, Hildred *Aphasia theory and therapy: selected lectures and papers* ed. L. F. Sies 1974
SCHULBERG, Budd Wilson *The disenchanted* 1950 (UK 1951)
What makes Sammy run? 1941
SCHUMPETER, Joseph Alois *Business cycles: a theoretical, historical, and statistical analysis of the capitalist process* 2 vols. 1939
SCHWARTZ, Robert J. *A complete dictionary of abbreviations* 1955
SCHWARZ, Urs & HADIK, Laszlo *Strategic terminology* 1966
SCIAMA, Dennis William *Modern cosmology* 1971
Science abstracts 1898–1940 (from 1903 divided into subject sections)
Science journal 1965–71
Science news 1946–60
Science news letter 1921– (from 1966 with title *Science news*)
Science progress (title varies) 1894–8; 1906–40; 1946–
Science survey 1960–
Scientific monthly 1915–57
SCLATER, Philip Lutley & THOMAS, M. R. O. *The book of antelopes* 17 parts (4 vols.) 1894–1900
SCLATER, William Lutley *See* STARK, Arthur Cowell
SCOLLINS, Richard & TITFORD, John *Ey up, mi duck!* 3 parts 1976–7
Scope 1966–
Scots observer: a weekly journal of religious and national interest 1926–34
Scotsman, The 1817– (1855–9 with title *The Daily Scotsman*)
SCOTT, Clement William & HOWARD, C. *The life and reminiscences of E. L. Blanchard* 2 vols. 1891
SCOTT, Edward *All about the latest dances* 1919
SCOTT, Gavin *Hot pursuit* 1977
SCOTT, Jack S. *A clutch of vipers* 1979
SCOTT, John Somerville *A dictionary of building* 1964
A dictionary of civil engineering 1958
SCOTT, Paul Mark *Staying on* 1977
SCOTT, Richard John Ernst ed. *Gould's medical dictionary* 1926
SCOTT, Robert Falcon (1868–1912) *Scott's last expedition* ed. L. Huxley 2 vols. 1913
The voyage of the 'Discovery' 2 vols. 1905
SCOTT, Virgil Joseph & KOSKI, Dominic *Walk-in* 1976 (UK 1977)
SCOTT, Walter (1771–1832) *Letters* ed. H. J. C. Grierson et al. 12 vols. 1932–7
SCOTT, William Berryman *An introduction to geology* 1897
Scottish field 1903–
Scottish journal of theology 1948–
Scottish national dictionary ed. W. Grant & D. D. Murison 10 vols. 1931–76
Scottish review 1975–
Screen 1959–
SCRIPTURE, Edward Wheeler *The elements of experimental phonetics* 1902
Scrutiny: a quarterly review 1932–53
SCULTHORPE, Cyril Duncan *The biology of aquatic vascular plants* 1967
SCUPHAM, Peter *The hinterland* 1977
Sea breezes 1919–39; 1946–
Seafarers' log 1939–
SEAMAN, Donald *The bomb that could lip-read* 1974
Sears, Roebuck & Co. *Catalogs* c 1876–

SEATON, Albert Edward *A manual of marine engineering* 1883
SEDGWICK, Anne Douglas *The little French girl* 1924
SEGRÈ, Emilio Gino *Experimental nuclear physics* 3 vols. 1953–9
SELA, Owen *The Bengali inheritance* 1975
SELBIE, William Boothby *The psychology of religion* 1924
SELDON, Arthur & PENNANCE, F. C. *Everyman's dictionary of economics* 1965
SELF, Margaret Cabell *The horseman's encyclopedia* 1946
SELVON, Samuel *A brighter sun* 1952
SENHOUSE, Roger tr. *Colette's Chéri, and The last of Chéri* 1951
SENN, Charles Herman *The new century cookery book: practical gastronomy and recherché cookery* 1901
SERLING, Robert J. *The president's plane is missing* 1967 (UK 1968)
SERRA, José Autures *Modern genetics* 3 vols. 1965–8
SERVICE, Robert William *Ballads of a cheechako* 1909 (UK 1910)
Ploughman of the moon: an adventure into memory 1945 (UK 1946)
Rhymes of a rolling stone 1912 (UK 1913)
Songs of a sourdough 1907 (UK 1908)
The trail of '98: a northland romance 1910 (UK 1911)
Sessions papers [series of reports of criminal cases heard in London]:
1. *The whole proceedings of the Sessions of the Peace, and Oyer and Terminer for the City of London and County of Middlesex* 1730–1824
2. *Sessions' paper . . held at the Justice Hall, in the Old Bailey* 1825–33
3. Central Criminal Court *Minutes* 1835–1913
SETON, Ernest Evan Thompson *Trail of an artist-naturalist* 1940
SETON-WATSON, Christopher *Italy from liberalism to fascism, 1870–1925* 1967
SEVERSON, John Hugh ed. *Great surfing* 1967
SEWALL, William *Diary, 1797–1846* ed. J. Goodell 1930
Sewanee review 1892–
SEWELL, Anna *Black Beauty: the autobiography of a horse* 1877
SEWELL, Edward Humphrey D. *Rugby football up to date* 1921
SEWELL, George Harold *Amateur film-making* 1938
— (ed. 2) 1951
SEYMOUR, Gerald *The glory boys* 1976
SHACKLETON, Ernest Henry *South: the story of Shackleton's last expedition, 1914–1917* 1919
SHADBOLT, Maurice Francis Richard *Among the cinders* 1965
The New Zealanders: a sequence of stories 1959
Strangers and journeys 1972
SHAND, Philip Morton *A book of wine* 1926
SHANDS, Harley Cecil *Semiotic approaches to psychiatry* 1970
SHANDS, Hubert Anthony *Some peculiarities of speech in Mississippi* 1893
'SHANNON, Dell' (Barbara Elizabeth Linington) *Murder with love* 1971 (UK 1972)
No holiday for crime 1973 (UK 1974)
Rain with violence 1967 (UK 1969)
The ringer 1971 (UK 1972)
Unexpected death 1970 (UK 1971)
With a vengeance 1966 (UK 1968)
SHAPIRO, Nat & HENTOFF, Nat eds. *Hear me talkin' to ya: the story of jazz by the men who made it* 1955
SHARCOTT, Margaret *A place of many winds* 1960
SHARP, Lester Whyland *Introduction to cytology* 1921
— (ed. 3) 1934
SHARP, Margery *Cluny Brown* 1944
The gipsy in the parlour 1954
The nutmeg tree 1937
Something light 1960
SHARPE, Frederick Dew *Sharpe of the Flying Squad* 1938
SHARPE, May Churchill *Chicago May: her story* 1928
SHARPE, Thomas Ridley *Porterhouse blue* 1974
Wilt 1976
SHARPS, Wallace Samuel *Dictionary of cinematography and sound recording* 1959
SHAW, Dennis Frederick *An introduction to electronics* 1962
— (ed. 2) 1970
SHAW, Frank, SPIEGL, Fritz, & KELLY, Stan *Lern yerself Scouse: how to talk proper in Liverpool* 1966 (For Vol. 2 *see* 'LANE, Linacre')
SHAW, George Bernard (1856–1950) *The admirable Bashville* (in *Cashel Byron's profession*, rev. ed.) 1901
Androcles and the lion: a fable play 1914
The apple cart: a political extravaganza 1930

Back to Methuselah: a metabiological Pentateuch 1921
Bernard Shaw and Mrs. Patrick Campbell: their correspondence ed. A. Dent 1952
Buoyant billions 1949
Caesar and Cleopatra See *Three plays for Puritans*
Captain Brassbound's conversion See *Three plays for Puritans*
Collected letters ed. D. H. Laurence 1965–
The common sense of municipal trading 1904
The Dark Lady of the sonnets See *Misalliance*
The devil's disciple See *Three plays for Puritans*
The doctor's dilemma, Getting married, and The shewing-up of Blanco Posnet 1911
Ellen Terry and Bernard Shaw: a correspondence See: TERRY, Ellen & SHAW, George Bernard
Everybody's political what's what? 1944
Fanny's first play See *Misalliance*
Geneva 1939
Getting married See *The doctor's dilemma*
Heartbreak House, Great Catherine, and Playlets of the War 1919
How to become a musical critic ed. D. H. Laurence 1960
In good King Charles's golden days 1939
The intelligent woman's guide to socialism and capitalism 1928
Letters See *Collected letters*
Letters to Granville Barker ed. C. B. Purdom 1956
London music in 1888–89 as heard by Corno di Bassetto 1937
The millionairess See *The simpleton of the Unexpected Isles*
Misalliance, The Dark Lady of the sonnets, and Fanny's first play. With a treatise on parents and children 1914
On the rocks See *Too true to be good*
Our theatres in the Nineties: criticisms contributed week by week to The Saturday Review 3 vols. 1932
Peace Conference hints 1919
Pen portraits and reviews 1931
— (Standard ed.) 1932
Platform and pulpit ed. D. H. Laurence 1962
Pygmalion in *Nash's magazine* Nov.–Dec. 1914
— (combined ed. with *Androcles and the lion* and *Overruled*) 1916
The quintessence of Ibsenism 1891
— now completed to the death of Ibsen 1913
The shewing-up of Blanco Posnet See *The doctor's dilemma*
The simpleton of the Unexpected Isles, The six of Calais, and The millionairess 1936
Three plays for Puritans (The devil's disciple, Caesar and Cleopatra, Captain Brassbound's conversion) 1901
To a young actress: letters to Molly Tompkins ed. P. Tompkins 1960
Too true to be good, Village wooing, and On the rocks 1934
Translations and tomfooleries 1926
What I really wrote about the War 1930
— (Standard ed.) 1931
Widowers' houses: a comedy 1893
SHAW, Herman *A text-book of aeronautics* 1919
SHAW, Irwin *Beggarman, thief* 1977
Rich man, poor man 1970
The troubled air 1951
SHAW, William Napier *Forecasting weather* 1911
— (ed. 2) 1923
— (ed. 3) 1940
—— & AUSTIN, Elaine *Manual of meteorology* 3 vols. 1926–30
She 1955–
SHEA, Timothy Edward *Transmission networks and wave filters* 1930
SHEDLOCK, John South tr. *K. W. J. H. Riemann's Dictionary of music* 1893
SHEEHAN, George A. *Running and being: the total experience* 1978
'SHELBY, Brit' (James Grady) *The great pebble affair* 1976
SHELDON, Sidney *Bloodline* 1978
Shell aviation news 1931–
Shell International Petroleum Company *Bitumen* (Shell Briefing Service) 1977
Information handbook, 1974–5 1974
Protecting the world's crops (Shell Briefing Service) 1977
SHELLEY, Percy Bysshe (1792–1822) *Letters* ed. F. L. Jones 2 vols. 1964
SHELLY, Lou ed. *Hepcats jive talk dictionary* 1945
SHELTON, Jane de Forest *The salt-box house: eighteenth century life in a New England hill town* 1900
SHEPARDSON, George Defrees *Telephone apparatus* 1917
SHEPHERD, Edwin Colston *The military aeroplane* 1941
SHEPPARD, Mubin *Taman indera: a royal pleasure ground. Malay decorative arts and pastimes* 1972
SHEPPARD, Samuel Edward *Photo-chemistry* 1914

—— & MEES, Charles Edward Kenneth *Investigations on the theory of the photographic process* 1907
SHEPPARD, Thomas Harvey *Dictionary of railway slang* 1965
— (ed. 2) 1966
SHERIDAN, Alan tr. *J. Lacan's Écrits* 1977
SHERIDAN, Elizabeth *Betsy Sheridan's journal: letters from Sheridan's sister, 1784–1786 and 1788–1790* ed. W. LeFanu 1960
SHERIF, Muzafer *The psychology of social norms* 1936
SHERRARD, Owen Aubrey *Two Victorian girls: with extracts from the Hall diaries* ed. A. R. Mills 1966
SHERRINGTON, Charles Scott *The integrative action of the nervous system* 1906
SHERWOOD, Adiel *A gazetteer of the State of Georgia* 1827
SHERWOOD, Robert Emmet *Idiot's delight* 1936
SHEVELOV, George Yury *A prehistory of Slavic: the historical phonology of common Slavic* 1965
SHILLABER, Benjamin Penhallow *The life and sayings of Mrs. Partington* 1854
SHOBERL, Frederic tr. *I. Titsingh's Illustrations of Japan* 1822
Shooting times and country magazine 1882–
SHORT, Eirian *Embroidery and fabric collage* 1967
SHRADER, Robert Louis *Electronic communication* 1959
SHULMAN, Max *Barefoot boy with cheek* 1943
SHURR, Gertrude & YOCOM, Rachael Dunaven *Modern dance: techniques and teaching* 1949
'SHUTE, Nevil' (Nevil Shute Norway) *Beyond the black stump* 1956
The chequer board 1947
The far country 1952
In the wet 1953
Landfall 1940
Lonely road 1932
No highway 1948
On the beach 1957
Pastoral 1944
Pied piper 1942
The rainbow and the rose 1958
Requiem for a Wren 1955
Round the bend 1951
Ruined city 1938
A town like Alice 1950
Trustee from the toolroom 1960
SHUTTLEWORTH, Charles *Malayan safari* 1965
SICHEL, Allan *The Penguin book of wines* 1965
SIDGWICK, Arthur & SIDGWICK, Eleanor Mildred *Henry Sidgwick: a memoir* 1906
SIDGWICK, Cecily *Sack and sugar* 1926
Victorian 1922
SIDGWICK, Nevil Vincent *The chemical elements and their compounds* 2 vols. 1950
The electronic theory of valency 1927
SIDNEY, Richard John Hamilton *In British Malaya to-day* 1927
SIEFF, Israel *Memoirs* 1970
Sierra Club bulletin (San Francisco) 1893–
SILBERRAD, Una Lucy *The letters of Jean Armiter: a novel* 1923
SILBERSTEIN, Ludwik *The theory of relativity* 1914
SILLIMAN, Benjamin *Manual on the cultivation of the sugar cane* 1833
SILLITOE, Alan *The loneliness of the long-distance runner* 1959
Saturday night and Sunday morning 1958
SIM, Thomas Robertson *The forests and forest flora of the colony of the Cape of Good Hope* 1907
SIMAK, Clifford Donald *They walked like men* 1963
SIMMS, William Gilmore *Guy Rivers: a tale of Georgia* 2 vols. 1834
The partisan: a tale of the revolution 2 vols. 1835
Southward ho! A spell of sunshine 1854
The wigwam and the cabin; or, Tales of the South 2 ser. 1845
SIMON, André Louis ed. *A concise encyclopædia of gastronomy* 9 vols. 1939–46
A dictionary of wines, spirits and liqueurs 1958
Guide to good food and wines (rev. ed.) 1963
—— & HOWE, Robin *A dictionary of gastronomy* 1970
SIMON, Edith *The past masters* 1953
SIMON, Roger Lichtenberg *The big fix* 1973 (UK 1974)
Wild turkey 1975 (UK 1976)
SIMONDS, Herbert Rumsey & ELLIS, Carleton *Handbook of plastics* 1943
'SIMONS, Roger' (Margaret & Ivor Punnett) *A frame for murder* 1960
SIMONSEN, John Lionel *The terpenes* 2 vols. 1931–2
SIMPSON, George Gaylord *Principles of animal taxonomy* 1961
SIMPSON, John Hamilton & RICHARDS, Roger Smith *Physical principles and applications of junction transistors* 1962
SIMS, George Frederick *Hunters Point* 1973
The last best friend 1967
The sand dollar 1969
SINCLAIR, Michael *A long time sleeping* 1975
Norslag 1972
SINCLAIR, Upton Beall *The brass check: a study of American journalism* 1919
The jungle 1906
Oil! 1927
The presidential agent 1944 (UK 1945)
SINGER, Isaac Bashevis *Shosha* 1978
SINGHA, Rina & MASSEY, R. *Indian dances, their history and growth* 1967
SISAM, Kenneth *Studies in the history of Old English literature* 1953
SISSONS, Thomas Michael B. & FRENCH, P. eds. *Age of austerity* 1963
SITWELL, Edith Louisa *Bath* 1932
Bucolic comedies 1923
Gardeners and astronomers 1953
I live under a black sun 1937
The sleeping beauty 1924
Troy Park 1925
Victoria of England 1936
The wooden Pegasus 1920
SITWELL, Francis Osbert S. *Miracle on Sinai* 1933
SITWELL, Sacheverell *Golden wall and mirador* 1961
6,000 words: a supplement to Webster's Third New International Dictionary 1976
SKEAT, Walter William (1866–1953) *Malay magic* 1900
SKELTON, John (? 1460–1529) tr. *Diodorus Siculus' Bibliotheca historica* ed. F. M. Salter & H. L. R. Edwards 2 vols. 1956–7
SKERL, John George Anthony tr. *A. L. Wegener's The origin of continents and oceans* 1924
Sketch, The: a journal of art and actuality 1893–1959
Sketches and eccentricities of Colonel David Crockett, of West Tennessee 1833
SKILBECK, Oswald *ABC of film and TV working terms* 1960
SKINNER, Cornelia Otis *Madame Sarah* 1967
SLATER, Mary *Caribbean cooking for pleasure* 1970
SLATTER, Gordon Cyril *A gun in my hand* 1959 (UK 1960)
SLIM, William Joseph *Defeat into victory* 1956
SLIMMING, John *Temiar jungle* 1958
SMALL, Austin J. *Frozen gold* 1924
SMALL, Ronald John *The study of landforms: a textbook of geomorphology* 1970
SMART, John Jamieson Carswell *Between science and philosophy: an introduction to the philosophy of science* 1968
Smart set, The: a magazine of cleverness 1900–30
SMEATON, Amethe tr. *R. Carnap's The logical syntax of language* 1937
SMILEY, Jack *Hash house lingo* 1941
SMITH, Alexander *Introduction to general inorganic chemistry* 1906
SMITH, Andrew *The diary of Dr. Andrew Smith, director of the 'Expedition for exploring Central Africa', 1834–1836* ed. P. R. Kirby 2 vols. 1939–40
SMITH, Annie Lorrain *A handbook of British lichens* 1921
Lichens 1921
SMITH, Anthony John Francis *Blind white fish in Persia* 1953
Throw out two hands 1963
SMITH, Ashley *The East-Enders* 1961
SMITH, Charles Alphonso *New words self-defined* 1919
SMITH, Charles Henry *Bill Arp, so called: a side show of the Southern side of the war* 1866
SMITH, Donald John *Discovering railwayana* 1971
SMITH, Dorothy Gladys ('Dodie') *Dear octopus: a comedy* 1938
I capture the castle 1949
SMITH, Edgar Fahs tr. *V. von Richter's Chemistry of the carbon compounds; or, Organic chemistry* 1886
— (ed. 2) 1892
— (ed. 3) 2 vols. 1899–1900
SMITH, Egerton *A guide to English traditions and public life* 1953
SMITH, Gilbert Morgan *Cryptogamic botany* 1938
SMITH, Godfrey *The business of loving* 1961
The flaw in the crystal 1954
SMITH, John B. *Explanation of terms used in entomology* 1906
SMITH, John Hugh *Digital logic: basic theory and practice* 1971
SMITH, Julie P. *The Widow Goldsmith's daughter* 1870
SMITH, Kenneth M. *Insect virology* 1967
SMITH, Laura Alexandrine *The music of the waters: a collection of the sailors' chanties, or working songs of the sea, of all maritime nations* 1888
SMITH, Logan Pearsall *Words and idioms: studies in the English language* 1925 (UK 1928)
SMITH, Martin Cruz *Gorky Park* 1981
SMITH, Robert Allan *Semiconductors* 1959
SMITH, Robert Kimmel *Ransom* 1971 (UK 1972)
SMITH, Seba *The select letters of Major Jack Downing* 1834
SMITH, Solomon Franklin *The theatrical apprenticeship and anecdotical recollections of Sol. Smith* 1846
SMITH, W. H. Saumarez *A young man's country: letters of a subdivisional officer of the Indian Civil Service 1936–1937* 1977
SMITH, Walter George *Allergy and tissue metabolism* 1964
SMITH, Wilbur *Gold mine* 1970
SMITH, William tr. *J. G. Fichte's The characteristics of the present age* 1847
SMITH, William Hawley *The promoters: a novel without a woman* 1904
SMYTH, Henry Dewolf *A general account of the development of methods of using atomic energy for military purposes under the auspices of the United States government, 1940–1945* 1945
SMYTH, James Desmond *An introduction to animal parasitology* 1962
SMYTH, John Ferdinand Dalziel *A tour in the United States of America* 2 vols. 1784
SMYTHIES, John Raymond & CORBETT, Lionel *Psychiatry for students of medicine* 1976
SNELL, Walter Henry & DICK, Esther Amelia *A glossary of mycology* 1957
SNIEČKUS, Antanas *Soviet Lithuania on the road of prosperity* [anon. tr.] 1974
SNOOK, Barbara Lilian *English historical embroidery* 1960
SNOW, Charles Percy *The affair* 1960
The conscience of the rich 1958
Corridors of power 1964
Homecomings 1956
The masters 1951
Strangers and brothers 1940
SNOW, Edgar *The other side of the river: Red China today* 1962 (UK 1963)
Red star over China 1937
SNOW, John Augustine *Cricket rebel: an autobiography* 1976
Social science abstracts 1929–33
Society for Experimental Biology and Medicine *Proceedings* 1903–
Society for Pure English *Tracts* Nos. 1–66, 1919–48
Society of Biblical Archaeology *Proceedings* 1878–1918
Transactions 1872–93
Society of Chemical Industry *Journal* 1882–1950 (from 1917 divided into sections)
Society of Dyers and Colourists *Journal* 1884–
Society of Telegraph Engineers (and of Electricians) *Journal* 1872–88
Soil science 1916–
SOLLAS, Hertha Beatrice Coryn & SOLLAS, William Johnson tr. *E. Suess's The face of the earth* 5 vols. 1904–24
SOLZHENITSYN, Alexander Isayevitch *See* BETHELL, Nicholas & BURG, David; WHITNEY, Thomas Porter
SOMERVILLE, Edith Œnone & 'ROSS, Martin' (Violet Florence Martin) *All on the Irish shore: Irish sketches* 1903
The real Charlotte 1894
SOMERVILLE-LARGE, Peter *Couch of earth* 1975
Eagles near the carcase 1977
SOMMERSTEIN, Alan H. *The sound pattern of ancient Greek* 1973
SOROKIN, Pitrim Aleksandrovich *Sociological theories of today* 1966
Sounds 1970–
SOUTH, Richard *The butterflies of the British Isles* 1906
The moths of the British Isles 2 ser. 1907–8
South Africa. Senate *Debates* 1911–
South African Philosophical Society *Transactions* 1877–1909
South Carolina Gazette (Charleston, S. Carolina) 1732–?1775 (title varies)
South Carolina Historical Society *Collections* 5 vols. 1857–97
South China Morning Post (Hong Kong) 1904–
South Wales Echo (Cardiff) 1884–
SOUTHALL, James Powell Cocke ed. & tr. H. L. F. von Helmholtz et al. *Treatise on physiological optics* 3 vols. 1924
Southampton, New York *Records* 6 vols. 1874–1915
Southerly: the magazine of the Australian English Association 1940–
Southern Evening Echo (Southampton) 1958–
Southern folklore quarterly 1937–
Southern literary messenger 1834–64
SOUTHWARD, John *Modern printing: a handbook of the principles and practice of typography and the auxiliary arts* 4 vols. 1898–1900 (and several later editions used)

Southwestern historical quarterly 1912–
Southwood, Thomas Richard Edmund & Leston, Dennis *Land and water bugs of the British Isles* 1959
Southworth, Louis *Felon in disguise* 1966
Soviet physics: Doklady See: Academy of Sciences of the U.S.S.R.
Soyinka, Wole (Akinwande Oluwole Soyinka) *Kongi's harvest* 1967
The lion and the jewel 1963
The road 1965
Spaceflight 1956–
Spackman, William Mode *An armful of warm girl* 1978
Spanner, Edward Frank *The naviators* 1926
Spare rib 1972–
Spark, Muriel Sarah *The bachelors* 1960
The ballad of Peckham Rye 1960
The comforters 1957
The Mandelbaum gate 1965
The prime of Miss Jean Brodie 1961
Sparkes, John J. *Transistor switching and sequential circuits* 1969
Sparks, Bruce Wilfred *Geomorphology* 1960
Spartanburg Herald (Spartanburg, S. Carolina) 1890–
Spencer, Douglas Arthur *The Focal dictionary of photographic technologies* 1973
Spencer, John ed. *The English language in West Africa* 1971
Spender, Stephen Harold *Collected poems, 1928–1953* 1955
The edge of being 1949
European witness: impressions of Germany in 1945 1946
Learning laughter 1952
The making of a poem 1955
tr. *E. H. Toller's Pastor Hall* 1939
Poems of dedication 1947
Ruins and visions 1942
The still centre 1939
World within world: autobiography 1951
—— & Gili, J. L. tr. *F. García Lorca's Poems* 1939
Sphere, The 1900–64
'Spillane, Mickey' (Frank Morrison Spillane) *The big kill* 1951
Spinks, John William Tranter tr. *G. Herzberg's Atomic spectra and atomic structure* 1937
Spirit of the times: a chronicle of the turf, agriculture, field sports, literature and the stage 1831–61
Spitzer, Leo *Linguistics and literary history* 1948
Spock, Benjamin McLane *Decent and indecent: our personal and political behavior* 1970
Spons' Mechanics' own book: a manual for handicraftsmen and amateurs 1885
Sport (title varies) 1946–?57
Spring, Robert Howard *These lovers fled away* 1955
Spring Rice, Margaret Lois *Working-class wives: their health and conditions* 1939
Springer, Clifford Harry, Herlihy, R. E., & Beggs, R. L. *Advanced methods and models* 1965
Springfield Republican (Springfield, Massachusetts) (weekly ed.) 1824–
Sprott, Walter John Herbert *Social psychology* 1952
Spruce, Richard *Notes of a botanist on the Amazon and Andes..1849–64* ed. A. R. Wallace 2 vols. 1908
Squire, Amos Osborne *Sing Sing doctor* 1935
Srb, Adrian Morris & Owen, Roy D. *General genetics* 1952
— (ed. 2, by A. M. Srb et al.) 1965
Stage year book, The 1908–28; 1949–
Stamp, Laurence Dudley *Britain's structure and scenery* 1946
— (ed. 5) 1960
ed. *A glossary of geographical terms* 1961
An introduction to stratigraphy: British Isles 1923
Standard, The 1827–1916
Standard encyclopaedia of southern Africa 12 vols. 1970–6
Stanford, Charles Villiers & Forsyth, Cecil *A history of music* 1916
Stanley, Rupert *Text-book on wireless telegraphy* 1914
— (new ed.) 2 vols. 1919
Stanton, Isabel Alice *A dictionary for medical secretaries* 1960
Stanwell-Fletcher, Theodora Morris *Driftwood Valley* 1946
Staples, Frank Alston *Water-color painting is fun* 1948 (UK ed. 1951 with title *Water-colour painting*)
Star, The (Sheffield) 1938–
Stark, Arthur Cowell & Sclater, William Lutley *The birds of South Africa* 4 vols. (I–III by Stark, IV by Sclater) 1900–6
Stark, Freya Madeline (1893–) *Baghdad sketches* 1937
Letters ed. L. Moorehead 1974–
Letters from Syria 1942
Riding to the Tigris 1959
The southern gates of Arabia: a journey in the Hadhramaut 1936
The valleys of the Assassins, and other Persian travels 1934
Stark, Werner *The sociology of knowledge* 1958
State (Columbia, S. Carolina) 1891–
Staunton, Harold *The chess-player's handbook* 1847
Stead, Christian Karlson ed. *New Zealand short stories* (2nd ser.) 1966
For 1st ser. *see* Davin, Daniel Marcus
Stead, Christina Ellen *The man who loved children* 1940
Stearns, Marshall Winslow *The story of jazz* 1956 (UK 1957)
Stedman, Thomas Lathrop *A practical medical dictionary* 1911 (and many later editions used)
Steele, John (1764–1815) *Papers* ed. H. M. Wagstaff 2 vols. 1924
Steen, Marguerite *Phoenix rising* 1952
The tower 1959
Steffens, Joseph Lincoln (1866–1936) *Autobiography* 2 vols. 1931
Stegner, Wallace Earle *Wolf Willow* 1962
Stein, Gertrude *The autobiography of Alice B. Toklas* 1933
Steinbeck, John Ernst *Cannery Row* 1945
East of Eden 1952
The grapes of wrath 1939
In dubious battle 1936
The long valley 1938
Of mice and men 1937
The pearl 1947 (UK 1948)
A Russian journal 1948
Sweet Thursday 1954
Tortilla flat 1935
The wayward bus 1947
Steiner, George *In Bluebeard's castle: some notes towards the re-definition of culture* 1971
Language and silence: essays 1958–1966 1967
Step, Edward *Bees, wasps, ants and allied insects of the British Isles* 1932
Shell life: an introduction to the British Mollusca 1901
Sterling, George E. & Kruse, R. S. *The radio manual* 1928
Sterling, Thomas L. *The evil of the day* 1955
Stern, Nils Gustav *Meaning and change of meaning, with special reference to the English language* 1931
Stevens, Stanley Smith ed. *Handbook of experimental psychology* 1951
Stevens, Wallace (1879–1955) *Collected poems* 1954
Letters ed. H. Stevens 1967
Stevenson, Robert Louis & Osbourne, Lloyd *The ebb-tide: a trio and a quartette* 1894
Stevenson-Hamilton, James *Wild life in South Africa* 1947
Steward, Julian Haynes ed. *Handbook of South American Indians* 7 vols. 1946–59
Stewart, Ian Nicholas *Concepts of modern mathematics* 1975
Stewart, John Innes Mackintosh *Eight modern writers* 1963
The gaudy 1974
The guardians 1955
The Madonna of the astrolabe 1977
The man who won the pools 1961
A memorial service 1976
A use of riches 1957
Young Pattullo 1975
See also: Innes, Michael
Stewart, Mary *Madam, will you talk?* 1954
My brother Michael 1960
Nine coaches waiting 1958
'Stiff, Dean' (Nels Anderson) *The milk and honey route* 1931
Stifler, William Warren ed. *High-speed computing devices* 1950
Stimpson, George William *A book about a thousand things* 1946
Stinton, Darrol *The anatomy of the aeroplane* 1966
Stivens, Dallas George ('Dal') *The courtship of Uncle Henry: a collection of tales and stories* 1946
Stocqueler, Joachim Hayward *The oriental interpreter and treasury of East India knowledge* 1848
Stokoe, William John *The caterpillars of the British butterflies* 1944
The caterpillars of British moths 2 ser. 1948
— (new ed.) 2 ser. 1958
Stone, Hannah M. & Stone, Abraham *A marriage manual* 1935 (UK 1936)
Stone, Kate *See* Holmes, Sarah Katherine (Stone)
Stone, Louis *Jonah* 1911
'Stone, Zachary' *The Modigliani scandal* 1976
Stopes, Marie Charlotte Carmichael *Married love: a new contribution to the solution of sex difficulties* 1918
Stoppard, Tom *Dirty linen, and New-found-land* 1976
Jumpers 1972
The real Inspector Hound 1968
Rosencrantz and Guildenstern are dead 1967
Travesties 1975
Storey, David Malcolm *Saville* 1976
This sporting life 1960
Stornoway Gazette and West Coast Advertiser 1917–
Storr, Catherine *The Chinese egg* 1975
Marianne and Mark 1960
Tales from a psychiatrist's couch 1977
Story, Jack Trevor *Dishonourable member* 1969
Something for nothing 1963
Stouffer, Samuel Andrew *Measurement and prediction* 1950
Stout, George Frederick *Analytic psychology* 1896
Stout, Rex Todhunter *Fer-de-lance* 1934
If death ever slept 1957 (UK 1958)
Over my dead body 1940
Please pass the guilt 1973 (UK 1974)
The red box 1936 (UK 1937)
Red threads 1939 (UK 1941)
Stowe, Harriet Elizabeth (Beecher) *House and home papers* 1865
We and our neighbors 1875
Strachey, Alix & Strachey, James tr. *S. Freud's Collected papers* Vol. III *See* Riviere, Joan, et al.
Strachey, Giles Lytton *Characters and commentaries* 1933
Eminent Victorians 1918
Queen Victoria 1921
Strachey, James tr. *S. Freud's Group psychology and the analysis of the ego* 1922
tr. *S. Freud's Totem and taboo* 1950
—— et al. tr. *S. Freud's Complete psychological works* 24 vols. 1953–74
See also: Strachey, Alix
Straits Times (Malaysia) 1845– (title varies)
Stranathan, James Docking *The 'particles' of modern physics* 1942
Strand, Stanley *Marketing dictionary* 1962
Strand Electrical and Engineering Company, Ltd. *Glossary of technical theatrical terms* 1947
Strang, Barbara Mary Hope *A history of English* 1970
Metaphors and models: an inaugural lecture 1965
Modern English structure 1962
Strangways, Arthur Henry Fox *The music of Hindostan* 1914
Stratton-Porter, Gene *Freckles* 1904
A girl of the Limberlost 1909
The harvester 1911
Laddie 1913
Straumann, Heinrich *Newspaper headlines: a study in linguistic method* 1935
Strauss, Victor *The printing industry* 1967
Strawson, Peter Frederick *Individuals: an essay in descriptive metaphysics* 1959
Streatfeild, Noel *Aunt Clara* 1952
Ballet shoes 1936
I ordered a table for six 1942
Streetwalker [anon.] 1959
Strevens, Peter Derek *New orientations in the teaching of English* 1977
Papers in language and language teaching 1965
Strickberger, Monroe Wolf *Genetics* 1968
Strong, Charles Augustus *Why the mind has a body* 1903
Strong, Leonard Alfred George *All fall down* 1944
The bay 1941
The director 1944
Othello's occupation 1945
Sea wall 1933
Sun on the water, and other stories 1940
Trevannion 1948
Which I never 1950
Stroud, John Anthony *The shorn lamb* 1960
Touch and go 1961
Stuart, Granville (1834–1918) *Forty years on the frontier* ed. P. C. Phillips 2 vols. 1925
Stuart, Jesse *Men of the mountains* 1941
Stuart, Ruth MacEnery *In Simpkinsville* 1897
Stubbs, Jean *The painted face* 1974
Studholme, Edgar Channon *Te Waimate: early station life in New Zealand* 1940
— (ed. 2) 1954
Studies in English (University of Cape Town) 1970– (title varies)
Studies in English literature (University of Tokyo) 1919–
Sturgis, Russell *A dictionary of architecture and building: biographical, historical and descriptive* 3 vols. 1901–2
Sturtevant, Edgar Howard *Comparative grammar of the Hittite language* 1933
Styron, William *Confessions of Nat Turner* 1967
Sophie's choice 1979

Sudworth, George Bishop *Nomenclature of the arborescent flora of the United States* 1897
Sullivan, Joseph M. *Criminal slang* 1908
Summers, Montague (Alphonsus J.-M. A. M. Summers) *The supernatural omnibus* 1931
Summerton, Margaret *A memory of darkness* 1967
A small wilderness 1959
The sunset hour 1957
Sumner, James Batcheller & Myrbäck, Karl eds. *The enzymes* 2 vols. in 4 parts 1950–2
—— & Somers, George Frederick *Chemistry and methods of enzymes* 1943
Sumner, William Graham *Folkways: a study of the sociological importance of usages, manners, customs, mores, and morals* 1907
Sun, The (Baltimore, Maryland) 1837–
Sun, The (London) 1964–
Sun (New York) 1833– (title varies)
Sun-Herald (Sydney) 1953–
Sunday Advocate-News (Barbados) 1968–
Sunday Bulletin (Philadelphia): see *Philadelphia Bulletin*
Sunday Dispatch 1928–61
Sunday Express (London) 1918–
Sunday Express and Home Journal (Johannesburg) 1937–
Sunday Mail (Glasgow) 1919–
Sunday Nation (Nairobi) 1960–
Sunday Pictorial 1915–63
Sunday Post (Glasgow) 1920–
Sunday Times (Johannesburg) 1906–
Sunday Times (Lagos) 1953–
Sunday Times (London) 1822–
Sunday Truth (Brisbane) 1960–71
Sunset (title varies) 1898–
Suppes, Patrick *Introduction to logic* 1957
Surfer: the international surfing magazine 1960–
Surgery 1937–
Surgery, gynecology and obstetrics 1905–
Survey: a journal of East and West studies 1955–
Sutcliff, Robert *Travels in some parts of North America in the years 1804, 1805, and 1806* 1811
'Sutherland, Joan' (Joan Collings) *The circle of the stars* 1924
Suttie, Jane Isabel tr. *S. Ferenczi's Further contributions to the theory and technique of psycho-analysis* 1926
Sutton, Oliver Graham *The science of flight* 1949
'Suyin, Han' *See* 'Han Suyin'
Suzuki, Daisetsu Teitarō *Zen Buddhism and its influence on Japanese culture* 1938
Svensk botanisk tidskrift 1907–
Sverdrup, Harald Ulrik, Johnson, M. W., & Fleming, R. H. *The oceans: their physics, chemistry, and general biology* 1942
Swaan, Wim *Japanese lantern* 1965
Swan, Lester A. & Papp, Charles Steven *The common insects of North America* 1972
Swan, Michael Lancelot *British Guiana* 1957
Swann, Harry Kirke *A dictionary of English and folk-names of British birds* 1913
Swanson, Carl Pontius *Cytology and cytogenetics* 1957 (UK 1958)
Swanton, Michael J. ed. *The dream of the Rood* 1970
Swayne, James Colin *A concise glossary of geographical terms* 1956
Sweeney, Charles *The scurrying bush* 1966
Sweet, Alexander Edwin & Knox, John Armoy *On a Mexican mustang through Texas, from the Gulf to the Rio Grande* 1883 (UK 1884)
Sweet-Escott, Bickham *Baker Street irregular* 1965
Swell's night guide, The 1841
— (another ed.) 1846
— (another ed.) 1847
Swettenham, Frank Athelstane *British Malaya: an account of the origin and progress of British influence in Malaya* 1907
Swinburne, Algernon Charles (1837–1909) *Letters* ed. C. Y. Lang 6 vols. 1959–62
Swing music 1935–6
Swinnerton, Frank Arthur *The doctor's wife comes to stay* 1949
Swinson, Arthur Horace *Six minutes to sunset: the story of General Dyer and the Amritsar affair* 1964
Swyer, Gerald Isaac M. *Reproduction and sex* 1954
Sydney, University of. Australian Language Research Centre *Occasional papers* 1964–
Sydney Morning Herald 1842–
Sydney slang dictionary, The ? 1882
Symonds, John Addington (1840–93) *Letters* ed. H. M. Schueller & R. L. Peters 3 vols. 1967–9
Symons, Julian Gustave *The end of Solomon Grundy* 1964
The narrowing circle 1954
A three pipe problem 1975
Symons, R. D. *Many trails* 1963
Where the wagon led 1973
Symposia in applied mathematics *Proceedings* 1947–
Synge, John Millington *Letters to Molly: J. M. Synge to Maire O'Neill 1906–1909* ed. A. Saddlemyer 1971
The playboy of the western world 1907

T

TV times 1955–
Tablet, The 1840–
'Tackline' *Holiday sailor* 1945
'Taffrail' (Henry Taprell Dorling) *Carry on!: naval sketches and stories* 1916
Pincher Martin, O.D.: a story of the inner life of the Royal Navy 1916
Tak, Montie *Truck talk: the language of the open road* 1971
Takagaki, Shinzō & Sharp, Harold E. *The techniques of judo* 1957
Talbot, Frederick Arthur Ambrose *Moving pictures: how they are made and worked* 1912
— (rewritten) 1923
Practical cinematography and its applications 1913
Talbot, Patrick Henry Brabazon *Principles of fungal taxonomy* 1971
Talbot, Percy Amaury *The peoples of southern Nigeria* 4 vols. 1926
Tamarack review 1956–
Tansley, Arthur George *The British islands and their vegetation* 1939
—— & Chipp, Thomas Ford eds. *Aims and methods in the study of vegetation* 1926
Tararua (Tararua Tramping Club, NZ) 1947–
Tarkington, Newton Booth *The gentleman from Indiana* 1899
In the arena 1905
Penrod 1914
Tassie, L. J. *The physics of elementary particles* 1973
'Tate, Richard' (Anthony Masters) *Birds of a bloodied feather* 1974
Taubes, Frederic *The painter's dictionary of materials and methods* 1973
Tawney, Richard Henry *Religion and the rise of capitalism* 1926
Taylor, Alan John Percivale *The course of German history* 1945
English history, 1914–45 1965
See also: Howat, G. M. D. & Taylor, A. J. P.
Taylor, Anne Marjorie *The language of World War II* 1944
— (rev. ed.) 1948
Taylor, Benjamin Franklin *Between the gates: summer rambles in California* 1878
January and June: being out-door thinkings and fireside musings 1854
Summer-savory, gleaned from rural nooks in pleasant weather 1879
The world on wheels, and other sketches 1874
Taylor, Charles Fayette *The internal-combustion engine in theory and practice* 2 vols. 1960–8
Taylor, Edith *The serpent under it* 1973 (UK 1974)
Taylor, Elizabeth *At Mrs Lippincote's* 1945
The sleeping beauty 1953
Taylor, Frederick *A manual of the practice of medicine* 1890
Taylor, Hugh Stott ed. *A treatise on physical chemistry* 2 vols. 1924
Taylor, John (1753–1824) *Arator: being a series of agricultural essays, practical and political* 1813
— (ed. 2) 1814
Taylor, Michael tr. *C. Metz's Film language: a semiotics of the cinema* 1974
Taylor, Nancy Margaret ed. *Early travellers in New Zealand* 1959
Taylor, Richard *Te ika a Maui; or, New Zealand and its inhabitants* 1855
— (ed. 2) 1870
Taylor, Selwyn Francis, Cotton, L. T., & Murray, J. G. *A short textbook of surgery* 1967
— (ed. 2) 1968
Taylor, Tom *The ticket-of-leave man* c 1863
Technology: the monthly review of training and education for industry 1957–
Technology week 1966–
Tee emm [training memoranda] (Air Ministry) 1941–6
Teilhet, Darwin & Teilhet, Hildegard *Feather cloak murders* 1937
Telegraph, The (Brisbane) 1872– (title varies)
Telegraph and telephone journal 1914–33
Tempest, Paul *Lag's lexicon: a comprehensive dictionary and encyclopædia of the English prison to-day* 1950
'Templar' (Arthur Bassett Hopkins) *The poker manual* 1895
Temple, William (1881–1944) *Citizen and churchman* 1941
Thoughts in war-time 1940
Tennant, Kylie *The battlers* 1941
Foveaux 1939
The joyful condemned 1953
Lost haven 1946 (UK 1947)
Ride on stranger 1943
'Tensas, Madison' (Henry Clay Lewis) *Odd leaves from the life of a Louisiana 'swamp doctor'* 1850
Terkel, Louis ('Studs') ed. *American dreams, lost and found* 1980
Terman, Frederick Emmons *Radio engineering* 1932
— (ed. 4, with title *Electronic and radio engineering*) 1955
Radio engineers' handbook 1943
Terms used in forestry and logging 1905 *See* United States. Department of Agriculture. Bureau of Forestry
Terry, Ellen (1847–1928) & Shaw, George Bernard (1856–1950) *Ellen Terry and Bernard Shaw: a correspondence* ed. C. St. John 1931
Tetrahedron letters 1959–
Textile Institute *Textile terms and definitions* 1954
— (ed. 3) 1957
'Tey, Josephine' (Elizabeth Mackintosh) *Brat Farrar* 1949
The daughter of time 1951
The Franchise affair 1948
A shilling for candles 1936
The singing sands 1952
To love and be wise 1950
See also: 'Daviot, Gordon'
Thackeray, Christopher ('Kit') *Crownbird* 1979
Theimer, Walter & Campbell, Peter *Encyclopaedia of world politics* 1950
Theodorson, George A. & Theodorson, Achilles G. *A modern dictionary of sociology* 1970
Theology: a monthly journal of historic Christianity 1920–
Theroux, Paul *The consul's file* 1977
The mosquito coast 1981
The Old Patagonian Express: by train through the Americas 1979
Thewlis, J., et al. eds. *Encyclopaedic dictionary of physics* See under title
Thicknesse, Philip *A year's journey through France and part of Spain* 2 vols. 1777
— (ed. 2) 2 vols. 1778
— (ed. 3) 2 vols. 1789
Thilly, Frank tr. *F. Paulsen's Introduction to philosophy* 1895
Thirkell, Angela Margaret *August folly* 1936
Before lunch 1939
The headmistress 1944
This week magazine 1935–
Thomas, Donald Michael *The white hotel* 1981
Thomas, David *Travels through the Western country in the summer of 1816* 1819
Thomas, Dylan Marlais (1914–53) *Collected poems, 1934–52* 1952
Deaths and entrances: poems 1946
18 poems 1934
The map of love: verse and prose 1939
Portrait of the artist as a young dog 1940
A prospect of the sea, and other stories and prose writings ed. D. Jones 1955
Quite early one morning: broadcasts ed. A. T. Davies 1954
Selected letters ed. C. Fitzgibbon 1966
Under Milk Wood: a play for voices 1954
Thomas, Graham Stuart *The old shrub roses* 1955
Thomas, Jack *No banners: the story of A. and H. Newton* 1955
Thomas, Mary *Dictionary of embroidery stitches* 1934
Thomas, Northcote Whitridge *Kinship organisations and group marriage in Australia* 1906
Thomas, Ronald Stuart *An acre of land* 1952
The minster 1953
The stones of the field 1946
Tares 1961
Thomas, Ross *The backup men* 1971
If you can't be good 1973 (UK 1974)
The porkchoppers 1972 (UK 1974)
The Singapore wink 1969
Spy in the vodka 1966 (UK 1967)
See also: 'Bleeck, Oliver'
Thomas, Samuel Evelyn *Elements of economics* 1925
Thompson, Arthur Beeby *Oil-field exploration and development* 2 vols. 1925
Thompson, C. Patrick *Cocktails* 1919
Thompson, Flora *Candleford Green* 1943
Lark Rise 1939
Over to Candleford 1941
Still glides the stream 1948
Thompson, George *Travels and adventures in southern Africa* 1827
Thompson, William Bell *An introduction to plasma physics* 1962
Thompson, William Tappan *Major Jones's sketches of travel* 1848
Thomson, Arthur Landsborough ed. *A new dictionary of birds* 1964

THOMSON, John Arthur *The biology of the seasons* 1911
Science old and new 1924
THOMSON, June *Death cap* 1973
The long revenge 1974
A question of identity 1978
THOMSON, Mortimer Neal *See* 'DOESTICKS, Q. K. Philander'
THOMSON, William *Dictionary of banking: a concise encyclopædia of banking law and practice* 1911
— (ed. 10, by R. W. Jones) 1951
— (ed. 11, by F. E. Perry & F. R. Ryder) 1965
THOREAU, Henry David (1817–62) *Correspondence* ed. W. Harding & C. Bode 1958
Writings ed. B. Torrey & F. B. Sanborn 20 vols. 1906
THORNBURG, Newton *Cutter and Bone* 1976
THORNBURY, William David *Principles of geomorphology* 1954
THORSTENSEN, Thomas Clayton *Practical leather technology* 1969
THURBER, James Grover *My life and hard times* 1933
The years with Ross 1959
THWAITES, Reuben Gold ed. *Early western travels, 1748–1846: a series of annotated reprints* 32 vols. 1904–7
TIDYMAN, Ernest *Dummy* 1974
TIEMANN, Hugh Philip *Iron and steel: a pocket encyclopedia, including allied industries and sciences* 1910
— (ed. 2) 1919
TILDEN, Josephine Elizabeth *Algae and their life relations: fundamentals of phycology* 1935
TILLYARD, Robert John *The insects of Australia and New Zealand* 1926
TILMAN, Harold William *The ascent of Nanda Devi* 1937
Nepal Himalaya 1952
Timber trades journal 1873–
Time: the weekly news-magazine 1923– (several eds. used)
Time and tide 1920–
Time out 1968–
Times educational supplement, The 1910–
Times literary supplement, The 1902–
Times of India, The 1838–
Times review of industry, The 1947–
Times-Picayune (New Orleans) 1914–
TINBERGEN, Nikolaas *The herring gull's world* 1953
TINDALE, Norman Bartlett & LINDSAY, Harold Arthur *Rangatira, the high-born: a Polynesian saga* 1959
TITCHENER, Edward Bradford tr. *W.M. Wundt's Principles of physiological psychology* 1904
TITFORD, William Jowit *Sketches towards a Hortus Botanicus Americanus* 1811
TITUS, Harold *'Timber'* 1922
To-day 1893–1905; 1916–23
TOFFLER, Alvin *Future shock* 1970
— (Bantam ed.) 1971
TOLKIEN, John Ronald Reuel (1892–1973) *The fellowship of the ring* (*The lord of the rings*, part 1) 1954
The hobbit; or, There and back again 1937
The return of the king (*The lord of the rings*, part 3) 1955
The Silmarillion ed. C. Tolkien 1977
The two towers (*The lord of the rings*, part 2) 1954
TOMLINSON, Alfred Charles *The shaft* 1978
Topeka Daily Capital (Topeka, Kansas) 1879–
TOPLEY, William Whiteman C. & WILSON, Graham Selby *The principles of bacteriology and immunity* 2 vols. 1929
Topsfield, Massachusetts *Town records* 2 vols. 1917–20
Toronto Daily Star 1892–
'TORR, Dominic' (John B. S. Pedler) *The treason line* 1968
TORREY, Bradford *The foot-path way* 1892
TOTTLE, Charles Ronald *The science of engineering materials* 1966
TOURGÉE, Albion Winegar *Button's Inn* 1887
See also: 'CHURTON, Henry'
TOWNSEND, Albert Alan *The structure of turbulent shear flow* 1956
TOWSTER, Julian *Political power in the U.S.S.R., 1917–47: the theory and structure of government in the Soviet state* 1948
TOYNBEE, Arnold Joseph *Civilization on trial* 1948
East to west: a journey round the world 1958
An historian's approach to religion 1956
A study of history 12 vols. 1934–61
Trade marks journal (Patent Office) 1876–
TRAGER, George Leonard & SMITH, Henry Lee *An outline of English structure* 1951
TRAILL, Sinclair ed. *Concerning jazz* 1957
ed. *Play that music: a guide to playing jazz* 1956
Trans-action: social science and the community (Washington Univ.) 1963–
Transactions See under the names of particular institutions
Transatlantic review 1959–77
TRAVERS, Ben *Mischief* 1925
TREADGOLD, Mary *We couldn't leave Dinah* 1941
TREADWELL, Bill ed. *Big book of swing* 1946
TREGONNING, Kennedy Gordon Phillip *A history of modern Malaya* 1964
'TREVANIAN' *The Loo sanction* 1973 (UK 1974)
The main 1976 (UK 1977)
'TREVOR, Elleston' (Trevor Dudley-Smith) *A place for the wicked* 1968
See also: 'HALL. Adam'
'TREVOR, Glen' (James Hilton) *Murder at school* 1931
'TREVOR, William' (William Trevor Cox) *The boarding-house* 1965
The children of Dynmouth 1976
TREVOR-ROPER, Hugh Redwald (Baron Dacre of Glanton) *The last days of Hitler* 1947
TREVOR-ROPER, Patrick Dacre *Ophthalmology* 1955
TREWIN, John Courtenay ed. *Plays of the year* See under title
Tribune 1937–
TRIMMER, Eric J., et al. *The visual dictionary of sex* 1977 (UK 1978)
TRIPP, Miles Barton *Faith is a windsock* 1952
Five minutes with a stranger 1971
One is one 1968
TRITTON, Harold Percy *Time means tucker* 1959
TROLLOPE, Anthony (1815–82) *The American Senator* 3 vols. 1877
The Duke's children 3 vols. 1880
Is he Popenjoy? 3 vols. 1878
John Caldigate 3 vols. 1879
The Kellys and the O'Kellys 3 vols. 1848
Letters ed. B. A. Booth 1951
The Macdermots of Ballycloran 3 vols. 1847
Phineas Finn, the Irish Member 2 vols. 1869
Phineas Redux 2 vols. 1874
The Prime Minister 4 vols. 1876
Rachel Ray 2 vols. 1863
Tales of all countries 1861 — (2nd ser.) 1863
TROUBRIDGE, Laura (1853–1929) *Life amongst the Troubridges* ed. J. Hope-Nicholson 1966
TROUP, Gordon John Fordyce *Masers* 1959
— (ed. 2, with title *Masers and lasers*) 1963
TROUP, Robert Scott *Silvicultural systems* 1928
The silviculture of Indian trees 3 vols. 1921
TRUMAN, Margaret *Harry S. Truman* 1973
Truth (Melbourne): see *Melbourne Truth*
Truth (Sydney) 1890–1958
Truth: a weekly journal (London) 1877–1957
TUCKER, Arthur Wilson *Wild talent* 1954 (UK 1955)
TUCKER, Denys William tr. *G. Sterba's Freshwater fishes of the world* 1962
TUCKER, Thomas George *Introduction to the natural history of language* 1908
TUCKER, Wilson *See* TUCKER, Arthur Wilson
TUCKETT, Mariana *Mariana's diary: a record of a holiday at Falmouth* ed. H. Fox (Royal Cornwall Polytechnic Society) *c* 1975
Tucson Daily Citizen (Tucson, Arizona) 1879–
Tucson magazine (Tucson, Arizona) 1975–
TUNIS, Edwin *Indians* 1959
TURNER, Bill *Circle of squares* 1969
Sex trap 1968
TURNER, Charles Cyril *Aerial navigation of to-day: a popular account of the evolution of aeronautics* 1910
Aircraft of to-day 1917
TURNER, Charles Godfrey *The happy wanderer* ed. E. M. R. Rice 1922
TURNER, Ernest Sackville *Taking the cure* 1967
TURNER, Ethel Sybil *The little larrikin* 1896
TURNER, Francis John & VERHOOGEN, Jean *Igneous and metamorphic petrology* 1951
— (ed. 2) 1960
TURNER, George W. *The English language in Australia and New Zealand* 1966
ed. *Good Australian English and good New Zealand English* 1972
TURNER, John Evan *A theory of direct realism, and the relation of realism to idealism* 1925
TURNER, Victor Witter *Schism and continuity in an African society: a study in Ndembu village life* 1957
TURNER, William *An introduction to human anatomy, including the anatomy of the tissues* 2 vols. 1875–7
Tuscaloosa News (Tuscaloosa, Alabama) 1910–
TUVE, Rosemund *Seasons and months: studies in a tradition of Middle English poetry* 1933
'TWAIN, Mark' (Samuel Langhorne Clemens, 1835–1910) *The American claimant* 1892
Autobiography ed. A. B. Paine 2 vols. 1924
The celebrated jumping frog of Calaveras County, and other sketches ed. J. Paul 1867
Christian Science 1907
A Connecticut Yankee in King Arthur's court 1889
Following the equator: a journey around the world 1897
Letters ed. A. B. Paine 2 vols. 1917 (UK, abridged, 1 vol. 1920)
Letters from Hawaii ed. A. G. Day 1966 (UK 1967)
Letters to his publishers, 1867–1894 ed. H. Hill 1967
The man that corrupted Hadleyburg, and other stories and essays 1900
Old times on the Mississippi 1876
The prince and the pauper 1881 [dated 1882]
Screamers: a gathering of scraps of humour, delicious bits, and short stories 1871
Sketches new and old 1875
Speeches with introd. by W. D. Howells 1910
Speeches with introd. by A. B. Paine 1923
The stolen white elephant 1882
See also: HARTE, Francis Bret & 'TWAIN', Mark
—— & WARNER, Charles Dudley *The gilded age* 1873 [dated 1874]
TWEEDDALE, James George *Materials technology* 2 vols. 1973
TWENEY, Charles Frederick *Dictionary of naval and military terms* 1914
TWENHOFEL, William Henry *Principles of sedimentation* 1939
—— & SHROCK, Robert Rakes *Invertebrate paleontology* 1935
Twentieth century, The 1951–
TWISLETON, Ellen *Letters, 1852–1862* ed. E. T. Vaughan 1928
TYRRELL, George Walter *The principles of petrology* 1926
TYRRELL, James Williams *Across the Sub-Arctics of Canada* 1897

U

UCT studies in English See *Studies in English* (University of Cape Town)
UDDEN, A. D. tr. *N. Bohr's The theory of spectra and atomic constitution* 1922
ULANOV, Barry *A history of jazz in America* 1952 (UK 1958)
ULLMAN, Stephen *The principles of semantics* 1951
Ulverston News (Ulverston, Cumbria) 1883–
Undercurrents 1972–
UNDERHILL, Evelyn *Mysticism: a study in the nature and development of man's spiritual consciousness* 1911
UNDERWOOD, Benton J. *Experimental psychology: an introduction* 1949
'UNDERWOOD, Michael' (John Michael Evelyn) *Murder with malice* 1977
A pinch of snuff 1974
Reward for a defector 1973
United Free Church of Scotland *Missionary record* (title varies) 1901–29
United Kingdom. Admiralty *Manual of seamanship* 2 vols. 1908–9
— Vol. II (rev. ed.) 1923
Manual of seamanship for boys' training ships of the Royal Navy 1883
United Kingdom. Advisory Committee for Aeronautics (*later* Aeronautical Research Committee; *later* Aeronautical Research Council) *Technical reports* 1910–
United Kingdom. Department of Education and Science *A Language for life. Report of the Committee of Inquiry..under the chairmanship of Sir Alan Bullock* 1975
United Kingdom. Department of Employment *Classification of occupations and directory of occupational titles* 3 vols. 1972
United Kingdom. Department of Scientific and Industrial Research. Forest Products Research Laboratory *A handbook of hardwoods* 1956 (for ed. 2, see below)
A handbook of softwoods 1957
United Kingdom. Department of the Environment. Building Research Establishment *Handbook of hardwoods* (ed. 2, rev. by R. H. Farmer) 1972 (for ed. 1, see above)
United Kingdom. General Medical Council (*later* British Pharmacopœia Commission) *Approved names* 1957–66; 1970–
United Kingdom. General Register Office *Classification of occupations* 1960
United Kingdom. Meteorological Office *Meteorological glossary* 1918 (and several later editions used)
United Kingdom. Ministry of Agriculture *Journal* 1919–
United Kingdom. Ministry of Information *Manpower: the story of Britain's mobilization for war* 1944
United Kingdom. Ministry of Labour *A dictionary of occupational terms, based on the classification of occupations used in the census of population, 1921* 1927

United Kingdom. Parliamentary papers [*Note* Volume numbers in citations refer mostly to the bound collections in the Bodleian Library. The second page number in citations is the starting-page of the particular report, etc., in the overall numbering within the volume.]
Committee on Broadcasting, 1960 (Chairman: H. Pilkington) *Report* 1962 in *Parl. Papers 1961–2* (Cmnd. 1753) IX. 259
Committee of Inquiry on Decimal Currency (Chairman: the Earl of Halsbury) *Report* 1963 in *Parl. Papers 1962–3* (Cmnd. 2145) XI. 195
Committee on Higher Education, 1961–3 (Chairman: Lord Robbins) *Higher education: report* 1963 in *Parl. Papers 1962–3* (Cmnd. 2154) XI. 639
United Kingdom. Patent Office *Official journal* (title varies) 1884–
See also *Trade marks journal*
United Service journal and naval and military magazine (title varies) 1829–43
United States. Arctic, Desert and Tropic Information Center *Glossary of arctic and subarctic terms* 1955
United States. Bureau of American Ethnology *Annual report* 1881–1933
Bulletin 1886–
United States. Bureau of Fisheries *Report* See: United States. Commissioner of Fisheries
United States. Bureau of Forestry *See* —— Department of Agriculture
United States. Bureau of Standards *See* —— National Bureau of Standards
United States. Commissioner of Fisheries *Report* (title varies) 1873–1941
United States. Commissioner of Patents *Annual report* 1839–
United States. Congress. Debates *Congressional globe, The: containing the debates and proceedings..of Congress* 1834–73
Congressional record, The: containing the proceedings and debates..of the Congress 1873–
Debates and proceedings in the Congress of the United States, 1789–1824 42 vols. 1834–56
Register of debates in Congress, 1824–37 14 vols. 1825–37
Senate hearings *Illicit narcotics traffic: hearings before the Subcommittee..of the Committee on the Judiciary* (84th Congress, 1st Session) 1956
United States. Department of Agriculture *Bulletin* 1913–27
Farmers' bulletin 1889–
Yearbook 1894– (1923–5 with title *Agricultural yearbook*; 1926– with title *Yearbook of agriculture*)
Bureau of Animal Industry *Annual report* 1884–1911
Bureau of Forestry *Bulletin* 1887–1913
Terms used in forestry and logging 1905 (*Bulletin* No. 61)
United States. Geological Survey *Annual report* 1880–1932
Bulletin 1883–
Monographs 1882–1929
Professional papers 1902–
Water-supply papers (title varies) 1896–
United States. Laws and statutes *The statutes at large of the United States of America* 1845–
United States. National Bureau of Standards *Journal of research* 1928–
United States. National Cancer Institute *See* United States. Public Health Service
United States. National Museum *Bulletin* 1875–
Proceedings 1878–
Reports 1884–
United States. Patent Office *Official gazette* 1872–
United States. Public Health Service. National Cancer Institute *Journal* 1940–
United States *Report of the Commissioner of Indian Affairs to the Secretary of the Interior* (title varies) 1825–
United States *Senate hearings* VIII *See* United States. Congress. Senate hearings
United States. Statutes *See* United States. Laws and statutes
United States. War Department *Reports of explorations and surveys to ascertain the most practicable and economical route for a railroad from the Mississippi River to the Pacific Ocean made in 1853–54* 12 vols. 1855–9
Short guide to Great Britain 1942
United States magazine and democratic review 1837–51
United States 1980/81 (Penguin Travel Guides) 1979
United Telephone Company, Ltd. *List of subscribers..classified into professions and trades* (ed. 6) 1885 [reproduced in facsimile in *Three Victorian telephone directories* 1970]
List of subscribers: instructions 1885 [*ibid.*]
Universe, The 1860–
Updike, Daniel Berkeley *Printing types: their history, forms and use* 2 vols. 1922
Updike, John Hoyer *The coup* 1978 (UK 1979)
Couples 1968
Rabbit, run 1960 (UK 1961)
Upfield, Arthur William *Bony and the white savage* 1961
Bushranger of the skies 1940
Murder must wait 1953
The will of the tribe 1962
Urban, Wilbur Marshall *Valuation: its nature and laws; being an introduction to the general theory of value* 1909
Urmson, James Opie ed. *The concise encyclopaedia of Western philosophy and philosophers* 1960
Philosophical analysis: its development between the two world wars 1956
Urquhart, John W. *Dynamo construction: a practical handbook for the use of engineer-constructors and electricians-in-charge* 1981
Uttley, Alison (Alice Jane Uttley) *The country child* 1931

V

Vachell, Horace Annesley *Dew of the sea, and other stories* 1927
Virgin 1929
Vaile, Pembroke Arnold *Modern golf* 1909
Vaizey, George De Horne *Tangled web* 1974
Vaizey, Jessie *A college girl* 1913
More about Pixie 1904
Vance, John Holbrook *The deadly isles* 1969 (UK 1970)
Vance, Louis Joseph *Baroque* 1923
Cynthia-of-the-minute 1911
The destroying angel 1912 (UK 1913)
Vancouver Province 1898–
Vancouver Sun (title varies) 1888–
'Vanderdecken' (William Cooper) *Yachts and yachting* 1873
Van der Post, Laurens Jan *The heart of the hunter* 1961
The lost world of the Kalahari 1958
A story like the wind 1972
Van Deventer, C. N. *An introduction to general aeronautics* 1965
Van de Wetering, Janwillem *The corpse on the dike* 1976 (UK 1977)
Tumbleweed 1976
Vanity fair (New York) 1914–36
Van Nostrand's scientific encyclopedia 1938
— (ed. 3) 1958
Van Oosten, Henrik *The Dutch gardener; or, The compleat florist* [anon. tr.] 1703
Van Sterkenburg, P. G. J., et al. eds. *Lexicologie: een bundel opstellen voor F. de Tollenaere* 1977
Van Thal, Herbert Maurice ed. *Fanfare for Ernest Newman* 1955
Van Tyne, Josselyn & Berger, Andrew John *Fundamentals of ornithology* 1959
Van Vechten, Carl *Nigger heaven* 1926
Varaday, Desmond *Gara-Yaka: the story of a cheetah* 1964
Gara-Yaka's domain 1966
Variety 1905–
Vaughan-Thomas, Wynford *Anzio* 1961
Vawter, Bruce *The conscience of Israel: pre-exile prophets and prophecy* 1961
Venkatachalam, Govindraj *Dance in India* 1948
Venkataraman, Krishnasami ed. *The chemistry of synthetic dyes* 8 vols. 1952–78
Venner, Norman *The imperfect impostor* 1925
Verbatim: the language quarterly 1974–
Vermandel, Janet Gregory *Dine with the devil* 1970
Vermont. Board of Agriculture *Annual report* (title varies) 1872–1908
Verne, Jules *The clipper of the clouds* [anon. tr.] 1887
Verney, John *Friday's tunnel* 1959
Verney, Maria Margaret ed. *Verney letters of the eighteenth century, from the manuscripts at Claydon House* 2 vols. 1930
Verschoyle, Terence Trevor Hamilton tr. *A. E. Haas's Atomic theory* 1927
Vesey-Fitzgerald, Brian Seymour ed. *The book of the dog* 1948
Veterinary journal 1875–95; 1900–48
Veterinary record 1888–
Victoria, Queen *See* Fulford, Roger T. B.
Victoria (Australia). Mining Department *Mining surveyors' reports* 1859–63
Vidal, Gore *The city and the pillar* 1948 (UK 1949)
In a yellow wood 1947
Kalki 1978
'Vigilans' (Eric Honeywood Partridge) *Chamber of horrors: a glossary of official jargon both English and American* 1952
Village voice (New York) 1955–
Villiers, Douglas ed. *Next year in Jerusalem* 1976
Vince-Prue, Daphne *Photoperiodism in plants* 1975
Vincent, E. A. tr. *A. Rittmann's Volcanoes and their activity* 1962
Vincent, William Thomas *Recollections of Fred Leslie* 2 vols. 1894
Vines, Walter Sherrard *Humours unreconciled* 1928
Virginia *Calendar of Virginia state papers and other manuscripts* ed. W. P. Palmer et al. 11 vols. 1875–93
Virology 1955–
Visser, Fredericus Theodorus *An historical syntax of the English language* 3 parts in 4 vols. 1963–73
Vitamins and hormones 1943–
Viteles, Morris Simon *Industrial psychology* 1933
Voegelin, Charles Frederick & Voegelin, Florence Marie R. *Classification and index of the world's languages* 1977
Vogue 1892–
Voice (New York) 1884–95
Vole 1977–81
Von Arnim, Mary Annette *The enchanted April* 1922
Fräulein Schmidt and Mr. Anstruther 1907
Introduction to Sally 1926
Vonnegut, Kurt *Cat's cradle* 1963
Slaughterhouse-five; or, The children's crusade 1969
Von Engeln, Oscar Diedrich *Geomorphology* 1942
Von Neumann, John (1903–57) *Collected works* ed. A. H. Taub 6 vols. 1961–3
Von Sternberg, Joseph *Fun in a Chinese laundry* 1965 (UK 1966)
Voorloper: an interim presentation of materials for a dictionary of South African English on historical principles ed. W. Branford et al. 1976

W

Waddington, Conrad Hal *Principles of embryology* 1956
Wadman, Howard Douglas *Life sentence: a New Zealand play in three acts* 1949
Wahlstrom, Ernest Eugene *Introduction to theoretical igneous petrology* 1950
Wain, John Barrington *The contenders* 1958
Hurry on down 1953
ed. *Interpretations: essays on twelve English poems* 1955
Strike the father dead 1962
A travelling woman 1959
Wainwright, John William *The big tickle* 1969
Death in a sleeping city 1965
The devil you don't 1973
Dig the grave and let him lie 1971
Do nothin' till you hear from me 1977
Edge of extinction 1968
The evidence I shall give 1974
The hard hit 1974
High-class kill 1973
The last buccaneer 1971
A nest of rats 1977
Night is a time to die 1972
A pride of pigs 1973
Requiem for a loser 1972
Square dance 1975
The take-over men 1969
Talent for murder 1967
A touch of malice 1973
Who goes next? 1976
Wakeman, Reginald Leslie *The chemistry of commercial plastics* 1947
Waldron, Ronald Alan *Sense and sense development* 1967
Walker, Andrew Jamieson & Mott, Owen E. tr. *A. F. Holleman's A text-book of organic chemistry* 2 parts 1903
— (ed. 2) 1907
Walker, Ernest Pillsbury, et al. *Mammals of the world* 3 vols. 1964–7
Walker, James *Introduction to physical chemistry* 1899
Walker, Martin *The National Front* 1977
Wall, Bernard, et al. tr. *P. Teilhard de Chardin's The phenomenon of man* 1959
Wall Street Journal 1889–
Wallace, Richard Horatio Edgar *The double* 1928
The feathered serpent 1927
The flying Fifty-Five 1922
The Flying Squad 1928
The gunner 1928
The lady of Ascot 1930
The mind of Mr. J. G. Reeder 1925
The missing million 1923

Wallace (*cont.*)
More educated Evans 1926
Room 13 1924
When the gangs came to London 1932
Wallace, Robert *The rural economy and agriculture of Australia and New Zealand* 1891
Wallis, Arthur James & Blair, Charles F. *Thunder above* 1956 (UK 1959)
Waln, Nora *The house of exile* 1933
Walpole, Horace (1717–97) *Correspondence* ed. W. S. Lewis et al. (Yale ed.) 40 vols. 1937–80
Letters ed. Mrs P. Toynbee 16 vols. 1903–5
— Suppl. ed. P. Toynbee 3 vols. 1918–25
Walpole, Hugh Seymour *The cathedral* 1922
The dark forest 1916
Fortitude 1913
The fortress 1932
Hans Frost 1929
Judith Paris 1931
Rogue Herries 1930
The secret city 1919
Vanessa 1933
The young enchanted 1921
Walsh, John James *Understanding paraplegia* 1964
Walsh, John William Tudor *Photometry* 1926
Wambaugh, Joseph *The black marble* 1978
The blue knight 1972 (UK 1973)
Wandsworth Borough News 1884–
Wang Gungwu ed. *Malaysia: a survey* 1964
Wanganui Chronicle (Wanganui, NZ) 1856–
War illustrated, The 1914–19
War illustrated, The 1939–47
War weekly 1939–41
Ward, Edmund *The hanged man* 1976
Ward, Elizabeth Stuart (Phelps) *The story of Avis* 1877
Trotty's wedding tour 1874
Ward, Emma Georgina Elizabeth *Outside Paris during the two sieges* 1871
Ward, Mrs. Humphry *See* Ward, Mary Augusta
Ward, James *The realm of ends; or, Pluralism and theism* 1911
Ward, Mary Augusta (Mrs. Humphry Ward) *Diana Mallory* 1908
The marriage of William Ashe 1905
Ward, Russel Braddock ed. *The Penguin book of Australian ballads* See under title
Ward-Jackson, Cyril Henry *It's a piece of cake; or, R.A.F. slang made easy* 1943
— (rev. ed.) 1945
Warder, John A. *Hedges and evergreens* 1858
Warming, Johannes Eugenius Bülow *Oecology of plants* 1909
Warner, Francis R. Le P. *Early poems* 1964
Killing time 1976
Lying figures 1972
Maquettes 1972
Meeting ends 1974
Warner, James Franklin *A universal dictionary of musical terms* 1842
Warner, Pelham Francis *How we recovered the Ashes* 1904
My cricketing life 1921
Warner, Sylvia Townsend *Lolly Willowes; or, The loving huntsman* 1926
Warren, Howard Crosby ed. *Dictionary of psychology* 1934
Warren, Robert Penn *Incarnations: poems 1966–68* 1968 (UK 1970)
Night rider 1939
Warwick, Wayne *Surfriding in New Zealand* 1968
Washington, George *Diaries, 1748–1799* ed. J. C. Fitzpatrick 4 vols. 1925
Washington Academy of Sciences *Journal* 1911–
Washington Post 1877–
Wason, Robert Alexander *Happy Hawkins* 1909
Waterhouse, Keith Spencer *Billy Liar* 1959
Waterman, Talbot Howe *The physiology of Crustacea* 2 vols. 1960–1
Waters, Stanley *Indentures indorsed* 1967
Watkins, Alfred *Photography: the Watkins manual of exposure and development* 1902
— (ed. 2) 1903
Watson, Alfred Edward Thomas *The turf* 1898
ed. *The young sportsman* 1900
Watson, Colin *Bump in the night* 1960
Coffin scarcely used 1958
Hopjoy was here 1962
Watson, George Marr *The Roxburghshire wordbook* 1923
Watson, Henry Clay *Camp fires of the revolution; or, The war of independence* 1850
Watson, Hewett Cottrell *Cybele Britannica; or, British plants and their geographical relations* 4 vols. 1847–59
Watson, James Dewey *The double helix: a personal account of the discovery of DNA* 1968
Watson, John Fanning *Annals of Philadelphia* 1830
Watson, William *A text-book of physics* 1899
Watson-Watt, Robert Alexander *Three steps to victory: a personal account* 1957
Watsonia: journal of the Botanical Society of the British Isles 1949–
Watt, John Mitchell & Breyer-Brandwijk, Maria Gerdina *The medicinal and poisonous plants of southern Africa* 1932
— (ed. 2, with title —— *of southern and eastern Africa*) 1962
Waugh, Alexander Raban *The last chukka* 1928
The loom of youth 1917
Waugh, Auberon Alexander *The foxglove saga* 1960
Waugh, Evelyn Arthur St. John (1903–66) *Black mischief* 1932
Brideshead revisited 1945
Decline and fall 1928
Diaries ed. M. Davie 1976
A handful of dust 1934
Labels: a Mediterranean journal 1930
Letters ed. M. Amory 1980
The loved one 1948
Men at arms 1952
Ninety-two days 1934
Officers and gentlemen 1955
Put out more flags 1942
Remote people 1931
Scoop 1938
Unconditional surrender 1961
Vile bodies 1930
Waugh, Hillary Baldwin *The con game* 1968
Finish me off 1970 (UK 1971)
Last seen wearing — 1952 (UK 1953)
Parrish for the defense 1974 (UK 1975)
Pure poison 1966 (UK 1967)
Way, Peter *Super-Celeste* 1977
Way to play, The: the illustrated encyclopedia of the games of the world 1975
Wayre, Philip *Wind in the reeds* 1965
Weale, Robert Alexander *The eye and its function* 1960
Weatherly, Keith *The roo shooter* 1968
Weaver, John Ernest & Clements, Frederic Edward *Plant ecology* 1929
— (ed. 2) 1938
Weaver, Robert ed. *Canadian short stories* (2nd ser.) 1968
Webb, Martha Beatrice *My apprenticeship* 1926
Webb, Robert F. *Motorists' dictionary* 1963
Webster, Arthur Gordon *The theory of electricity and magnetism* 1897
Webster, Douglas & Webster, Molly *Comparative vertebrate morphology* 1974
Webster, Jean (Alice Jean Chandler Webster) *Dear enemy* 1915 (UK 1916)
Webster, John *Introduction to fungi* 1970
Webster, Noah *New international dictionary of the English language* ed. W. T. Harris & F. S. Allen 1909
— (ed. 2, ed. W. A. Neilson, T. A. Knott, & P. W. Carhart) 2 vols. 1934
— (ed. 3, ed. P. B. Gove) 2 vols. 1961 (see also *6,000 words*)
Webster, Robert *Gems: their sources, description and identification* 2 vols. 1962
Webster's sports dictionary 1976
Wedgwood, Cicely Veronica *The trial of Charles I* 1964
Wedgwood, Josiah (1730–95) *Selected letters* ed. A. Finer & G. Savage 1965
Week-end review 1930–4
Weekend world (Johannesburg) 1968–
Weekley, Ernest *Something about words* 1935
Words and names 1932
Weekly dispatch 1914–28
Weekly News (Auckland) 1863–
Weekly register 1811–14
Weems, Mason Locke *The life of General F. Marion* 1809
Weeton, Ellen *Journal of a governess, 1807–1825* 2 vols. 1969 (reprint of 1936–9 ed. with new editorial matter by J. J. Bagley & E. Hall)
Weichert, Charles Kipp *Anatomy of the chordates* 1951
Weidman, Jerome *I can get it for you wholesale* 1937 (UK 1939)
Weingarten, Joseph A. *An American dictionary of slang and colloquial speech* 1954
'Welcome, John' (John Brennan) *Hell is where you find it* 1968
Stop at nothing 1959
Wellek, René & Warren, Edward Austin *Theory of literature* 1949
Wellington, John Harold *Southern Africa: a geographical study* 1955
Wells, Alfred Kingsley *Outline of historical geology* 1938
Wells, Herbert George *All aboard for Ararat* 1940
The anatomy of frustration: a modern synthesis 1936
Ann Veronica: a modern love story 1909
Apropos of Dolores 1938
The autocracy of Mr. Parham 1930
Babes in the darkling wood 1940
Brynhild; or, The show of things 1937
Experiment in autobiography 2 vols. 1934
The first men in the moon 1901
The history of Mr. Polly 1910
The holy terror 1939
The invisible man: a grotesque romance 1897
Joan and Peter: the story of an education 1918
Love and Mr. Lewisham 1900
Men like gods 1923
The new Machiavelli 1910 (UK 1911)
The new world order 1940
The shape of things to come 1933
Things to come: a film story based on 'The shape of things to come' 1935
Tono-Bungay 1909
The war of the worlds 1898
The wheels of chance 1896
The work, wealth and happiness of mankind 1931 (UK 1932)
You can't be too careful: a sample of life 1941
See also: Gissing, George Robert & Wells, H. G.
Wells, Kenneth McNeill *The Owl Pen reader* 1969
Wells, Robert *The pastrycook and confectioner's guide* 1889
'Wells, Tobias' (Deloris Florine Forbes) *Dead by the light of the moon* 1967 (UK 1968)
Welty, Eudora *The optimist's daughter* 1973
Wentworth, Harold *American dialect dictionary* 1944
—— & Flexner, Stuart Berg *Dictionary of American slang* 1960
— (new ed.) 1967
— (new ed.) 1975
'Wentworth, Patricia' (Dora Amy Turnbull) *In the balance* 1941 (UK ed. 1942 with title *Danger point*)
Wenyon, Charles Morley *Protozoology* 2 vols. 1926
Wertheim, Willem Frederik *Evolution and revolution: the rising waves of emancipation* [anon. tr.] 1974
Weseen, Maurice Harley *Crowell's dictionary of English grammar and handbook of American usage* 1928
A dictionary of American slang 1934 (UK 1935)
Wesker, Arnold *Chicken soup with barley* (in *New English dramatists* I) 1959
Chips with everything 1962
I'm talking about Jerusalem 1960
The kitchen (in *New English dramatists* II) 1960
Roots 1959
Wesley, John (1703–91) *Journal* ed. N. Curnock 8 vols. 1909–16
Wesleyan-Methodist magazine 1822–1913
West, Anthony *The trend is up* 1960 (UK 1961)
'West, Rebecca' (Cicily Isabel Andrews) *Black lamb and grey falcon: the record of a journey through Yugoslavia in 1937* 2 vols. 1941 (UK 2 vols. 1942)
The fountain overflows 1957
The harsh voice: four short novels 1935
The modern 'Rake's progress' 1934
St. Augustine 1933
The strange necessity: essays and reviews 1928
The thinking reed 1936
West, Richard Gilbert *Pleistocene geology and biology, with especial reference to the British Isles* 1968
West, Richard Leaf *Sketches from Vietnam* 1968
West Lancashire Evening Gazette (Blackpool) 1929–
Western Mail (Cardiff) 1869–
Western Morning News (Plymouth) 1860–
Westheimer, David *Going public* 1973
Westlake, Donald Edwin *Bank shot* 1972
Cops and robbers 1972 (UK 1973)
I gave at the office 1971 (UK 1972)
Up your banners 1969 (UK 1970)
See also: 'Coe, Tucker'
Weston, Carolyn *Poor, poor Ophelia* 1972 (UK 1973)
Rouse the demon 1976 (UK 1977)
Weston, Hubert Claude *Sight, light and efficiency* 1949
— (ed. 2, with title *Sight, light and work*) 1962
Weston, Richard *The universal botanist and nurseryman* 4 vols. 1770–7
Westwater, Frank Lorimer *Teach yourself electronic computers* 1962
— (rev. ed.) 1964
Weyl, Alfred Richard *Guided missiles* 1949
Weyl, Claus Hugo Hermann *The classical groups: their invariants and representations* 1939
Weyman, Stanley John *The new rector* 2 vols. 1891
Shrewsbury: a romance 1898
Wharton, Edith Newbold *The custom of the country* 1913
The fruit of the tree 1907
The greater inclination 1899
The house of mirth 1905
Human nature 1933
Summer 1917

Wireless world 1913–
WIRTH, Louis & SHILS, Edward Albert tr. *K. Mannheim's Ideology and Utopia: an introduction to the sociology of knowledge* 1936
Wisconsin. State Historical Society *Reports and collections* (title varies) 1855–
Wisden cricketers' almanack (title varies) 1864–
WISDOM, Thomas Henry *High-performance driving for you* 1966
WISTER, Owen *The Virginian: a horseman of the plains* 1902
WITTFOGEL, Karl August *Oriental despotism: a comparative study of total power* 1957
WITTGENSTEIN, Ludwig Josef Johann *Tractatus logico-philosophicus* [anon. tr.] 1922
See also: ANSCOMBE, Gertrude E. M.
WITTS, Francis Edward (1783–1854) *The diary of a Cotswold parson* ed. D. Verey 1978
WITWER, Harry Charles *Fighting blood* 1923
From baseball to Boches 1918
The leather pushers 1921
WODEHOUSE, Pelham Grenville *The adventures of Sally* 1923
Aunts aren't gentlemen: a Jeeves and Bertie story 1974
Bill the conqueror 1924
Blandings Castle and elsewhere 1935
Carry on, Jeeves! 1925
The clicking of Cuthbert 1922
The code of the Woosters 1938
The coming of Bill 1920 (US ed. 1919 with title *Their mutual child*)
Company for Henry 1967
A damsel in distress 1919
Eggs, beans and crumpets 1940
Frozen assets 1964
The heart of a goof 1926
Hot water 1932
The inimitable Jeeves 1923
Jill the reckless 1921 (US ed. 1920 with title *The little warrior*)
Laughing gas 1936
Leave it to Psmith 1924
Lord Emsworth and others 1937
Louder and funnier 1932
The luck of the Bodkins 1935
Meet Mr. Mulliner 1927
Money in the bank 1942 (UK 1946)
Mr. Mulliner speaking 1929
Much obliged, Jeeves 1971
Pearls, girls and Monty Bodkin 1972
Performing flea: a self-portrait in letters 1953
Plum pie 1966
Right ho, Jeeves 1934
Sam the sudden 1925
Service with a smile 1961 (UK 1962)
Something fresh 1915
Tales of St. Austin's 1903
Uncle Fred in the springtime 1939
Very good, Jeeves! 1930
WOLF, Frederick Adolph & WOLF, Frederick Taylor *The fungi* 2 vols. 1947
WOLFE, Bernard *Limbo* 1952 (UK ed. 1953 with title *Limbo '90*)
See also: MEZZROW, Milton
WOLFE, Thomas Clayton (1900–38) *Look homeward, angel: a story of the buried life* 1929 (UK 1930)
The web and the rock 1939
You can't go home again 1940
WOLFE, Tom *The electric kool-aid acid test* 1968
The kandy-colored tangerine-flake streamline baby 1965 (UK 1966)
Woman 1937–
Woman's day (New York) 1937–
Woman's journal 1927–
Woman's own 1932–
Women's Group on Public Welfare. Hygiene Committee *Our towns: a close-up, 1939–42* 1943
WOOD, Christopher *'Terrible hard', says Alice* 1970
WOOD, Clement & GODDARD, Gloria *Dictionary of American slang* 1926
WOOD, Eric Stuart *Collins field guide to archaeology* 1963
WOOD, Ernest Egerton *Yoga dictionary* 1956
WOOD, James Alex F. *North beat* 1973
WOOD, Thomas *Cobbers: a personal record of a journey..to Australia* 1934
WOODFORD, Gwendolyn Green tr. *M. Gignoux's Stratigraphic geology* 1955
WOODFORDE, James (1740–1803) *The diary of a country parson* ed. J. Beresford 5 vols. 1924–31
WOODGATE, Gordon Kemble *Elementary atomic structure* 1970
WOODHAM-SMITH, Cecil Blanche *Florence Nightingale, 1820–1910* 1950
WOODHOUSE, Martin C. *Blue bone* 1973
Mama doll 1972
Rock baby 1968
Tree frog 1966
WOODHOUSE, Thomas *Artificial silk* 1927
WOODRUFF, Hiram Washington *The trotting horse of America: how to train and drive him* 1868
'WOODRUFF, Philip' (Philip Mason) *The island of Chamba* 1950
Whatever dies 1948
WOODS, Katharine Seymour *Rural crafts of England* 1949
'WOODS, Sara' (Sara Bowen-Judd) *Done to death* 1974
Enter certain murderers 1966
Enter the corpse 1973
WOODWORTH, Robert Sessions *Experimental psychology* 1938
— (rev. ed., by Woodworth & H. Schlosberg) 1954
Psychology: a study of mental life 1921 (UK 1922) (Several later editions also used)
WOOLDRIDGE, Sidney William & MORGAN, Ralph Sisk *The physical basis of geography: an outline of geomorphology* 1937
— (ed. 2, with title *An outline of geomorphology*) 1959
WOOLF, Leonard Sidney *The village in the jungle* 1913
WOOLF, Virginia (1882–1941) *Between the acts* 1941
The captain's death bed, and other essays ed. L. Woolf 1950
The common reader 1925
— (2nd ser.) 1932
Jacob's room 1922
Letters ed. N. Nicolson & J. Trautmann 6 vols. 1975–80
Mrs. Dalloway 1925
Night and day 1919
Orlando: a biography 1928
Roger Fry: a biography 1940
A room of one's own 1929
To the lighthouse 1927
The voyage out 1915
The waves 1931
A writer's diary ed. L. Woolf 1953
The years 1937
WOOLLCOTT, Alexander *While Rome burns* 1934
WOOLLEY, Charles Leonard *Alalakh: an account of the excavations at Tell Atchana, in the Hatay, 1937–1949* 1955
WOOTTON, Barbara Frances *Social science and social pathology* 1959
Testament for social science 1950
Word 1945–
Word study 1925–69
Words 1934–41
WORDSWORTH, Dorothy (1771–1855) *Journals* ed. E. de Sélincourt 2 vols. 1941
WORK, Milton Cooper *Complete contract bridge* 1929
Work 1889–1924
World archaeology 1969–
World of cricket monthly 1976–
World review 1936–53
World's work (New York) 1900–32
WORRALL, Arthur James *English idioms for foreign students* 1932
WORSLEY, Peter Maurice *The trumpet shall sound: a study of 'cargo' cults in Melanesia* 1957
WORSTER, William W. tr. *E. Hannover's Pottery and porcelain* See: RACKHAM, Bernard
WORSTHORNE, Peregrine Gerard *The socialist myth* 1971
WRENN, Charles Leslie *Word and symbol* 1967
WRIGHT, Barbara tr. *R. Queneau's Between blue and blue* 1967
WRIGHT, David McKee *Station ballads and other verses* 1897
WRIGHT, Frank Lloyd *Autobiography* 1932
WRIGHT, George Payling & SYMMERS, William St. Clair eds. *Systemic pathology* 2 vols. 1966
WRIGHT, Harold Bell *The winning of Barbara Worth* 1911
WRIGHT, Peter *The language of British industry* 1974
WRIGHT, Thomas *The romance of the lace pillow* 1919
WYBURN, George McReath, WARBRICK, J. G., & TODD, M. E. *Concise anatomy* 1967
WYKES, Alan *Gambling* 1964
WYLD, Henry Cecil *A short history of English* 1914
WYLLIE, Peter J. ed. *Ultramafic and related rocks* 1967
Wymondham and Attleborough Express 1975–
WYND, Oswald *Sumatra seven zero* 1968
Walk softly, men praying 1967
'WYNDHAM, John' (John Wyndham P. L. B. Harris) *The day of the triffids* 1951
The Midwich cuckoos 1957
The seeds of time 1956
Trouble with lichen 1960
WYNNE family *The Wynne diaries, 1789–1820* ed. A. Fremantle 3 vols. 1935–40
WYNTER, Sylvia *The hills of Hebron* 1962

X

'X, MALCOLM' *See* 'MALCOLM X'
XANTHAKIS, John N. ed. *Solar physics* 1967

Y

Yachting (US) 1907–
Yachting monthly 1906–
YADIN, Yigael *Hazor* 1972
Yale alumni magazine 1937–
Yale literary magazine 1836–
Yankee: a monthly magazine for Yankees everywhere 1935–42; 1945–
YAPP, William Brunsdon *An introduction to animal physiology* 1939
Yearbook of astronomy 1961–
Year-book of wireless telegraphy and telephony, The 1913–25
Year's work in English studies, The 1921–
YEATES, Victor M. *Winged victory* 1934
YEATS, William Butler (1865–1939) *The Countess Kathleen, and various legends and lyrics* 1892
In the seven woods: being poems chiefly of the Irish heroic age 1903
The king of the great clock tower: commentaries and poems 1934
Last poems and two plays 1939
Letters ed. A. Wade 1954
October blast 1927
Per amica silentia lunae 1918
Poems 1895
Poems (variorum ed. by P. Allt & R. K. Alspach) 1957
Responsibilities: poems and a play 1914
Reveries over childhood and youth 1915 (UK 1916)
The trembling of the veil 1922
The wanderings of Oisin, and other poems 1889
The wind among the reeds 1899
Words for music perhaps, and other poems 1932
Yesterday's shopping: the Army & Navy Stores catalogue 1907: a facsimile of the Army & Navy Co-operative Society's 1907 issue of 'Rules of the Society and price list of articles sold at the Stores' introduced by A. Adburgham 1969
YONGE, Charlotte Mary *Abbeychurch; or, Self-control and self-conceit* 1844
Burnt out: a story for mothers' meetings 1879
Chantry House 2 vols. 1886
The chaplet of pearls; or, The white and black Ribaumont 1868
The Christmas mummers 1858
Heartsease; or, The brother's wife 2 vols. 1854
Lady Hester; or, Ursula's narrative 1874
Magnum bonum; or, Mother Carey's brood 3 vols. 1879
My young Alcides: a faded photograph 2 vols. 1875
Nuttie's father 1885
An old woman's outlook in a Hampshire village 1892
Our new mistress; or, Changes at Brookfield Earl 1888
The pillars of the house; or, Under wode, under rode 4 vols. 1873
Pioneers and founders; or, Recent workers in the mission field 1871
The pupils of St. John the Divine 1868 (dated 1867)
The release; or, Caroline's French kindred 1896
That stick 2 vols. 1892
The three brides 2 vols. 1876
The two guardians; or, Home in this world 1852
The two sides of the shield 2 vols. 1885
Womankind 1876
'YORK, Andrew' (Christopher Nicole) *The eliminator* 1966
The expurgator 1972
'YORKE, Margaret' (Margaret Beda Nicholson) *Grave matters* 1973
Mortal remains 1974
The silent witness 1972
Yorkshire Post 1866–
YOUNG, Alexander Bell Filson *The complete motorist: being an account of the evolution and construction of the modern motor car* 1904
YOUNG, Charles Augustus *A text-book of general astronomy for colleges and scientific schools* 1888 (UK 1889)
YOUNG, Emily Hilda *William* 1925
YOUNG, Francis Brett *Portrait of Clare* 1927
YOUNG, Geoffrey Winthrop ed. *Mountain craft* 1920
YOUNG, John Zachary *An introduction to the study of man* 1971

YOUNG (*cont.*)
The life of vertebrates 1950
A model of the brain 1964
YOUNG, Wayland Hilton *Eros denied* 1965
Young Englishwoman, The 1865–77
YOXALL, Harold Waldo *A fashion of life* 1966
YUILL, P. B.' (Gordon Maclean Williams) *The bornless keeper* 1974
YULE, George Udny *An introduction to the theory of statistics* 1911
— (ed. 11, by Yule & M. G. Kendall) 1937

Z

ZANDVOORT, Reinard Willem *A handbook of English grammar* 1957
—— et al. *Wartime English: materials for a linguistic history of World War II* 1957
ZANGWILL, Israel *Ghetto comedies* 1907
Ghetto tragedies 1893
ZEUNER, Friedrich Eberhard *Dating the past: an introduction to geochronology* 1946
— (ed. 4) 1958
ZIGROSSER, Carl & GAEHDE, Christa M. *A guide to the collecting and care of original prints* 1965
Zigzag 1969–
ZIPF, George Kingsley *The psycho-biology of language: an introduction to dynamic philology* 1935 (UK 1936)
ZUCKERMAN, Solly *The social life of monkeys and apes* 1932
ZWEIG, Ferdynand *The new acquisitive society* 1976